Mark Twain's Humor: Critical Essays

Edited by David E. E. Sloane

Further Information: p. 634

Errata: p. 635

GARLAND STUDIES IN HUMOR
Steven H. Gale, General Editor

Mark Twain's Humor
Critical Essays

David E.E. Sloane

Garland Publishing, Inc. • New York and London

1993

Library of Congress Cataloging-in-Publication Data

Mark Twain's humor : critical essays / [edited by] David E.E. Sloane.
p. cm. — (Garland studies in humor ; vol. 3) (Garland
reference library of the humanities ; vol. 1502)
Includes bibliographical references

1. Twain, Mark, 1835–1910—Humor. 2. Humorous stories,
American—History and criticism. I. Sloane, David E.E., 1943– . II.
Series. III. Series: Garland reference library of the humanties ; vol.
1502.
PS1342.H62M37 1993
818'.409—dc20   92-14927
CIP

Printed on acid-free, 250-year-life paper
Manufactured in the United States of America

CONTENTS

Contents

The Later Career of Mark Twain:
The Comedian as a Cultural Representative

GENERAL EDITOR'S NOTE

David E.E. Sloane's *Mark Twain's Humor: Critical Essays* is the third volume in Garland's "Studies in Humor" series. Each volume in the series is devoted to an assessment of the work of an individual major humorist or group of authors within a specified category and consists of collections of both previously published and original articles on subjects such as S.J. Perelman, Black Humor, Geoffrey Chaucer, Classical Greek and Roman Humorists, Woody Allen, and American Women Humorists, among others.

The intent behind this series is to supply in a single volume a representative sample of the best critical reactions by the humorist's contemporaries and from subsequent scholarly assessments. Typically, the contents of each volume will include: a chronology of the author's life and writing; the volume editor's introduction to the writer's canon; reviews (book, play, and/or film); interviews; essays focusing on specific works (this section may contain both journal articles and parts of books); general essays treating particular aspects of the humorist's canon; a selected, annotated bibliography; and an index. This structure provides access to essential scholarship (some of which may no longer be easily obtainable) on the most important and best examples of the humorist's work as well as demonstrating popular reactions to that work and allowing for comparisons to be made in critical and popular reactions over the course of the writer's career.

Mark Twain is generally considered America's preeminent literary humorist. The nature of his humor and his purpose in creating it, though, have been the subject of a critical debate that began early in his career and continues still. In this collection Sloane has displayed the elements of this critical discourse by focusing on Twain (both as a person and a persona) and his work in three chronological periods: the early writings, in which the essays included detail the growth of the comedian; the middle career from *Tom Sawyer* to *Pudd'nhead Wilson*, in which the comedian as major author is considered; and the later career, in which the comedian is discussed as a cultural representative. There are thirty-four selections included, written by preeminent scholars of the early and the late Twain. In addition, Sloane has furnished an introduction, a selected, annotated bibliography, and an index.

What Twain says at different times as his career evolves and how what he says relates to his experiences and perceptions of life and his hopes and fears for humanity are brought together in a way that makes the works clearer and more accessible as well as bringing readers a better understanding of the man who created the canon. It is especially valuable to be able to see how critical opinions and emphases have shifted over the years, as is evident when the reviews written by Twain's contemporaries are compared with the three original essays written in 1992 that are included in the collection.

David E.E. Sloane is Professor of English at the University of New Haven. The author of *Mark Twain as a Literary Comedian*, *Adventures of Huckleberry Finn: American Comic Vision*, *The Literary Humor of the Urban Northeast, 1830–1890*, *American Humor Magazines and Comic Periodicals*, and several articles on Twain, he was the first Henry Nash Smith Fellow at the Center for Mark Twain Studies at Quarry Farm. He has also been a USIA lecturer on American humor in Brazil and a frequent speaker on Twain, and he is presently president of the Mark Twain Circle and Executive Director and Past President of the American Humor Studies Association.

Steven H. Gale
Kentucky State University

ACKNOWLEDGMENTS

Grateful thanks is extended to the following for permission to reprint articles or portions of chapters to which they hold copyrights.

Walter Blair, *Modern Philology*, the University of Chicago Press for permission to reprint "On the Structure of *Tom Sawyer*."

Edgar Branch, "'My Voice Is Still for Setchell': A Background Study of 'Jim Smiley and His Jumping Frog'," is reprinted by permission of the Modern Language Association of America from *PMLA*.

Louis Budd.

"Yankee Slang" from James M. Cox, *Mark Twain: The Fate of Humor.* Copyright © 1966 by Princeton U.P. Reprinted by permission.

Pascal Covici, Jr., Department of English, S.M.U.

American Quarterly, 19 (Spring 1967), pp. 86–103. Reprinted by permission of the author and Johns Hopkins U.P.

Leslie Fiedler, "*Huckleberry Finn*: The Book We Love to Hate" originally appeared in the Fall 1984 issue of *Proteus, A Journal of Ideas*, and is reprinted here by permission.

Allan Gribben, "'I Kind of Love Small Game': Mark Twain's Library of Literary Hogwash" reprinted with permission of the editors of *American Literary Realism.*

Shelley Fisher Fishkin, U of Texas, Austin.

"*A Connecticut Yankee* Anticipated: Max Adeler's *Fortunate Island*" © *Ball State University Forum.*

Susan K. Harris and *American Literary Realism.*

Michael Kiskis.

Life Reviews *Huckleberry Finn* by Durant Da Ponte. *American Literature* Vol. 31 (1959) published by Duke University Press, Durham. Reprinted with permission of the publisher.

Franklin R. Rogers, "The Road to Reality: Burlesque Travel Literature and Mark Twain's *Roughing It*" © 1963. The New York Public Library, Astor, Lenox, and Tilden Foundations, Reprinted by permission.

Laura Skandera-Trombley.

"A Sound Heart and a Deformed Conscience" reprinted by permission of the publishers from *Mark Twain: The Development of a Writer* by Henry Nash Smith, Cambridge, Mass.: The Belknap Press of Harvard University Press, copyright © 1961 by the President and Fellows of Harvard College.

Susanne Weil.

CHRONOLOGY

1835	Samuel Langhorne Clemens born on 30 November to Jane Lampton and John Marshall Clemens in Florida, Missouri.
1839	Clemens family moves to Hannibal, Missouri.
1847	John Clemens dies; Sam Clemens begins working as a printer's apprentice.
1852	The Boston *Carpet-Bag* publishes "The Dandy Frightening the Squatter" in company with sketches by the young Charles F. Browne and Charles H. Derby.
1857	Becomes an apprentice pilot on the Mississippi River.
1861	Leaves the East to accompany brother Orion to Nevada.
1862–4	Reports for the Virginia City, Nevada *Territorial Enterprise*, taking on the pen name "Mark Twain" in 1863.
1865	"The Celebrated Jumping Frog of Calaveras County" appears in November to instant national success.
1869	*Innocents Abroad* published.
1870	Marries Olivia Langdon. Lectures actively during this period.
1871	Moves to Nook Farm, Hartford, CT.
1872	*Roughing It* published. Son Langdon dies in infancy.
1873	*The Gilded Age* published.
1874	"A True Story" brings Twain to the pages of the respected *Atlantic Monthly*.

1876	*Adventures of Tom Sawyer* published.
1880	*A Tramp Abroad* published.
1882	*The Prince and the Pauper* published.
1883	*Life on the Mississippi* published.
1885	*Adventures of Huckleberry Finn* published.
1888	Yale awards Twain an A. M. degree.
1889	*A Connecticut Yankee* published.
1892	*American Claimant* published.
1894	*Pudd'nheqd Wilson* published. Twain enters bankruptcy due to the failure of the Paige Typesetter.
1895	Twain begins around-the-world lecture tour to pay off debts.
1896	*Joan of Arc* published. Daughter Susie dies.
1897	*Following the Equator* published.
1901	"To the Person Sitting in Darkness" published as lead article in *North American Review*.
1904	Wife Livy dies.
1906	*What Is Man?* published.
1906	Oxford University awards Twain Litt. D. degree.
1909	Daughter Jean dies.
1910	Mark Twain dies on 21 April.

INTRODUCTION

David E. E. Sloane

Mark Twain was a comedian. His art and his thought both came from a humorous response to a world which *claimed* to be good and kind and humane but *acted* badly and sometimes evilly, cruelly, and inhumanely. Beyond using detailed description to protest the atrocity of individual and corporate actions—seen in whippings, beatings, and lynchings in the novels, seen in the reversal of animal traits with human traits, or through self-deluded behavior in the short stories—Twain had relatively little of a positive political program for reforming the world. He did, however, have a compelling humanity, based not on the letter of biblical or constitutional law but on its spirit, a contentious quasi-religious humanism which he advanced from his earliest writing about the Holy Land through his last final reversals of the satanic and the human in an attempt to wrestle with the meaning of grief and death. The selections reprinted in this volume are intended to provide the case history of a literary life built on these premises. The literary life is both that of the persona Mark Twain—revered as an American icon—and of his canon—that body of literature associated with him and rising to its highest visionary level in *Adventures of Huckleberry Finn*, but shadowed everywhere in even his seemingly most trivial productions.

Much of my own scholarly career has been based on an attempt to understand Twain's humor as central to his vision and also as a representative artifact of American culture. Twain's humor, irony, sarcasm, and even comic allusions advance his uncompromising pragmatism about the centrality of freedom from self-interested authority as the basis of human well-being. Critical responses to my discussion of Twain have often complained that this sort of material wasn't funny. Even more so, this has been argued in relating Twain to the secondary northeastern humorists on whose tradition, as much as that of the Southwest, he leaned for precedents in language, metaphor, and minor characterization. Those responses were, in truth, more accurate than the critics intended. American humor as a literary and as an economic production is often not very funny; it is a record of obvious and avoidable social failures, and as a result it is angry. American humor is the humor of non-acceptance of "reality," and the "real," either literally in fact or idealistically as a literary model. In Europe the absurd is existential; in America, the absurd is a counter-irritant to the observed and a protest and demand for change. In many cases, the burlesque and grotesque exaggerations of American humor—and exaggeration has been the hallmark of European descriptions of American humor for two centuries—are restatements of the triumph of imagination over harsh surroundings, as is suggested in such anthologies as Roger Welsch's collection of Great Plains folk humor *Shingling the Fog* or Walter Blair's *Horse Sense in American Humor*, or even in collections of old-time New England humor such as those by B. A. Botkin.

Twain's humor is purposive. He intended his comic protests to change hearts and minds, to clarify vision, and to improve mankind. His despair is not a product of eastern deracination any more than is Voltaire's or Swift's. Claims that it is based on a profound superficiality of viewpoint characteristic of literary critics turned psychobiographers. Serious students of the canon find it to be consistent—and pessimistic underneath its idealism—throughout. The reason for this is simple. The optimistic idealism of the comedy is based on political premises of equality. Surrounded by the love of his wife Livy (see Laura Skandera-Trombley's article here), the pragmatic Christianity of Joe Twichell (see Leah Strong's book cited in the Bibliography but not easily excerpted), the nurturing realism of William Dean Howells (see Howells's two assessments of Clemens here), the applause—and cash receipts—of the crowd (see the hunger for Twain anecdotes in *The Ladies Home Journal* and George Ade on the subscription book), this idealism could be dominant. More important, it was the external product which writer gave reader, speaker provided audience. Underneath, the despair of a man who saw death, selfishness, and a universe out of control was not a reasonable vision to put forth. First, it was not something likely to improve mankind for the better—this is the importance of Nook Farm (and Quarry Farm as well, by the way)—on Twain: they were places populated by meliorists, and with them he was one, too. Second, his philosophical mechanism was compelling to him, but as a world-view it was half-baked, not a finished product which he shared as much because it was inartistic as because it was warmed up in hell—he published plenty of hellish satire in his later years, including "To the Person Sitting in Darkness" which John Kendrick Bangs tried so unsuccessfully to dispute in *Harper's Weekly*. Thus, a book like *What Is Man?* sneaked into print; it was unfunny, but it was also an enlarged expression of the comedian's anger which had to be vented. Partly it might have hurt his economic standing, he guessed, but also he knew it to be the product of his grief and anger, broadened by his personal losses, but something that he had always carried in him, not necessarily as the stuff of great literature. He didn't publish much of his pessimistic outpouring because it was self-indulgent. The real problem with these later manuscripts is that the scholarly community and a hungry public accept their standing in his canon as higher than it should be. There were many pieces Twain chose not to reprint from his writings. Why? Because they crossed the border between serious humor and mediocre humor. We should recognize the difference; the three essays by younger Twain scholars—Skandera-Trombley, Michael Kiskis, and Susanne Weil—are helpful in analyzing the later Twain in a modern way which leads us to this recognition and do much to extend Susan Harris's study of "Hadleyburg" to the end of Twain's career.

These statements should help focus the selections offered here, divided into groups of essays indicating the nature of Twain's early background as a technician and comic social philosopher, his middle career as a writer to be differentiated from other comedians but still abrasive to many readers, and, lastly, as a world figure whose writings, even when less visionary than the major novels, represented important cultural documents to detached observers. All the analytic critics are consistent in finding in Twain's writing a comic methodology that derives from his time and his culture and eventuates in an outcome that attempts to be socially visionary. That product is intrinsically wrapped around a humane and idealistic meaning. It would have been Christian had Twain been able to reconcile himself with the institutional church, but he could not do that except in the person of Joe Twichell, neither generally nor in the overwhelming evidence of authoritarian Catholicism; Twain was always a good American Know-Nothing. Nor could he come to terms with a true God—which God seemed determined *not* to send him a clear and unequivocal sign no matter how hard he prayed on his knees beside Twichell for belief. So, Twain created work after work out of the comic materials surrounding him, which he found abundant in the failure of the world to live up to its own image of itself. His unrest with other writers—as suggested in Alan Gribben's article on literary small game and in Walter Blair's discussion of *Tom Sawyer* — reflects this impatience with goals which were too limited, accounting, I think, as well, for the oddly distant relationship between Twain and Trowbridge so admirably captured by Rufus Coleman. He semi-fictionalized himself to create the character in the travel books and in part his major heroes, as essays by Franklin Rogers, David Sloane, Henry Watterson, and Edgar Branch suggest. He borrowed the spread-eagle rhetoric and biblical hypocrisies that were the common currency of his day just as he would borrow the pseudo-economic business and world-politick jargon of ours were he alive in the 1990s. In everything he did, however, he tapped into our cultural mainstream—A. C. Ward's trenchant point as an outside observer of American culture, but consistent with discussions of Twain by *Blackwood's* a generation earlier and by Mme. Th. Bentson two generations before that as reflected in Archibald Henderson's discussion of Twain's "international fame." The continuity of his popularity and its growth is testimony to the completeness with which his comedy incorporated the underlying forces of our culture, made clear even in the essay on farce and *The American Claimant* by Clyde Grimm. It may be that American culture as a culture shares his antagonism to reality—seen benignly in the Colonel Sellers observed by Watterson or the seemingly haphazard but actually methodical lecturer Twain seen by Will Clemens—and the pragmatic humor which overcomes it, a form of whimsy far different from other humor. Twain would have missed the humor of other cultures such as the native American cultures, which he despised for the savagery which he held in a contempt that would only have been rivalled by his contempt for the street violence of today's culture. In studying the works, then, we are studying a cultural exercise as well as a literary one. The selections here were chosen because their authors seem aware of the background of culture but maintain a focus on the mechanics of the comedian. As readers move through this book, they should find an array of minute observations which suggest a mechanic at work, but a mechanic with a cultural position. Yet, none of these essays is ideologically didactic, nor do they need to be, although I hope my own assertions in this introduction give a context which raises issues beyond belletristic ones.

The order of essays here is roughly according to the subjects that the essays deal with. Thus, an essay from *Blackwood's Magazine* published in 1907 but focused on writings from the 1880s—revolving around *Life on the Mississippi*, and one by Edith Wyatt in the 1920s—which has salient observations about *Joan of Arc*—come after scholarly criticism of Twain's early work by writers of the post-1950s era—Edgar Branch on the "Jumping Frog," Louis Budd on *The Gilded Age*, and Franklin Rogers on *Roughing It*, but before other scholars treating Twain's last decade. Practically speaking, this arrangement retains the shape of Twain's overall career as well as reprinting some worthwhile treatments of Twain's humor which have never appeared together in one volume. Three works by five younger Twain scholars appear in this volume for the first time in print and are grouped at the end of the volume. Partly this reflects an increased interest in explaining Twain's later work by writers of the late-1980s and 1990s in response to the biographical and textual mix coming out of the popular thirst for "new" Twain materials and the production schedule of the Iowa-California edition (which seemed early on to favor later unpublished, more pessimistic works) and to the several debunking biographies which take strong positions on Clemens's later life. The findings of these recent essays in many ways confirm insights into Twain's work which were current in his own day, and they are thus both "fresh" and conservative—a valuable reminder that awareness of cultural context enhances critical perception.

The purpose of this volume is to lay out documents which give an estimate of Mark Twain as a humorist in both historical scope and in the analysis of modern scholars. A number of excellent essays on various Twain topics and *Adventures of Huckleberry Finn* are omitted because (1) they are easily available in other anthologies, and (2) they tend to lead away from humor to deal with the themes of *Huck Finn*. This is not a bad thing in itself, but not necessarily the only way into the vast array of Twain's humor spread over his more than fifty years as a writer—Lionel Trilling on *Huckleberry Finn* is one obvious example. The emphasis in this collection is on how Twain developed from a contemporary humorist among many others of his generation into a major comic writer and American spokesman and, in several recent essays by younger Twain scholars, the outcomes of that development late in his career. The thrust of these inquiries lies in determining how the humor takes on meaning and importance and how the humor works in a number of ways in the literary canon and even in the persona of Mark Twain.

In some but not all cases, this volume offers materials that have been difficult to locate. Such is the case with the debate over the Philippine war teaming Twain's "To a Person Sitting in Darkness" with a response by popular 1890s humorist John Kendrick Bangs in *Harper's Weekly* of 1901—a "popular" controversy showing Twain's humor as contributing to a national argument over a universal democratic premise. Such a document gives us another way of considering Twain through an interchange that is otherwise lost to us; it shows the humorist taking political responsibility in a controversial area. It is also fascinating to see Bangs, one of the most popular humorists of the 1890–1910 period, trying to stake out a pro-imperialism position, ineptly defending the "Charity Organization Society" against Twain's fiery sarcasm at the "Blessings of Civilization Trust." Even the *ad hominem* shift fails Bangs as he cites Twainian arguments (such as Twain's acrid "Taels, I win, Heads you lose" comment for John C. Ament's insistence on indemnity and the Catholic demand for 680 heads—executions—to accompany the payment of thousands of dollars in Chinese Taels as compensation for deaths in the Boxer Rebellion) which don't even appear in the shortened version of the piece published in the facing pages of the *Harper's* production. Martha McCulloch Williams's erroneous attack on the "shoot my half" story from *Pudd'nhead Wilson* is likewise important not because of her failure to recognize the story as a Yankee story derived from P. T. Barnum's *Life* but rather because it shows a Southerner's anger at Twain's intellectual position, as further drawn out in its racial consequences in Shelley Fisher Fishkin's essay on the same work.

An item from the *Ladies Home Journal* for 1898 reports a variety of anecdotes about Twain. Since the *Journal* at that time was one of the most widely read magazines in the United

States, the short pieces suggest how much Twain was a personality as well as an author. They are offered here because they put Twain in the human context in which his readers read his works. In fact, it would be fair to say that more than any other writer of modern times, Twain is read as if he were in a dialogue with the reader through the pages of his books, rather than as if he were absent and the text stood alone. Consequently, the persona of Mark Twain is of more than passing interest and more integral to his canon than is the case with other figures of his era. Aside from that, the anecdotes give family history that has some merit as part of his record. No extreme critical insight should be claimed for them, and none is. Yet taken together with the article by George Ade, and the analysis by Durant Da Ponte and Leslie Fiedler of the reception of *Huckleberry Finn*, and Edith Wyatt on *Joan of Arc*, such materials give us a broadened picture of an author whose works were bound up in a culture in ways unparalleled in twentieth-century literature.

Several of the analytic pieces in this volume provide extraordinary technical insights into the construction and background of pieces by Twain. Walter Blair on *Tom Sawyer*, Edgar Branch on "The Notorious Jumping Frog," Henry Nash Smith on *Huck Finn*, Louis Budd on the humorist's writings in the late 1860s and early 1870s, Susan Harris on "Hadleyburg," Michael Kiskis on *Mark Twain's Autobiography*, and Susanne Weil on the "Mysterious Stranger" fall into this category, as do significant parts of other essays.

Pascal Covici's study of Mark Twain's humor is particularly valuable in showing how much the southwestern and northeastern blend in Twain's canon, especially since the "Is he dead?" joke in *Innocents Abroad* discussed at the end of the selection, is from easterner Artemus Ward. "From the Old Southwest," however, is particularly useful in giving us specific citations and sources of a less theoretical nature than those in Kenneth Lynn's *Mark Twain and Southwestern Humor*. Covici is helpful in making a trenchant distinction between the real subject matter of the Southwest and Twain as a realistic comedian. James M. Cox on *A Connecticut Yankee* is correspondingly illuminating on that book specifically.

Louis J. Budd helps us understand how innately conservative Twain's comic radicalism actually is. Indeed, Twain held fast to the basic American concepts of democracy in ways that by no means accepted the ugly side of mass culture. Like John Hay and others of his class and time, Twain came to terms with mass labor movements with some difficulty, and his approval of mass action often presumes, as is presumed in the early works discussed by Budd, that humankind will have to be educated up to revolution grade before being emancipated. This is a rather covertly gloomy vision, but it is consistent with concepts expressed in Henry Nash Smith's discussion of *Huck Finn* in "A Sound Heart and a Deformed Conscience" which takes as its premise the idea that social dictates vary from innate human decency—a premise of all of Twain's work, and a necessary assumption for any reforming egalitarian. Although this essay is generally available, it fills an appropriate place between Leslie Fiedler's historical overview and the fulminations of Robert Bridges reflected in *Life*'s 1885 review of *Huck*, and so it completes a rounded view of *Huck Finn* which is a microcosm of the larger collection.

Edward F. Foster, in showing what Max Adeler did with the same materials as found in Twain's *Connecticut Yankee,* draws back from an outright charge of plagiarism against Twain because the real value of his article is in showing the intersection of interests in chivalry versus modernity in literary comedians generally. After all, Max Adeler's "The Fortunate Island" was not the only chivalric-modern satire predating Twain; one could also cite Edgar Fawcett's dreadful verse satire, *The New King Arthur* (1885) among others, including a piece by Twain published in 1871 in *Galaxy* magazine and readily available (See *Mark Twain as Literary Comedian* for further references on this subject).

George Ade shows the context into which Twain's actual printed volumes were plunged. He suggests that while his writings were in opposition to staid works of morality, they were also placed among them. All of Twain's concerns with his writing and public seem to confirm that he, like Ade, was aware of his special, privileged place in the popular libraries of middle America. Therefore, he used their language and their context directly. Oddly enough, Theodore Dreiser also used popular terminology in *Sister Carrie* (1900) but with a stunningly different effect and outcome. The comic reversals of Twain are different from the ironic reversals of Dreiser, though critics could find plenty to dislike in both writers. An astute reader could see interesting comparisons in the use of diction and metaphor by applying Arun Mukherjee's *The Gospel of Wealth in the American Novel* (Totowa, NJ: Barnes & Noble, 1987) backwards from Dreiser's novels to Twain's *A Connecticut Yankee in King Arthur's Court.* Even the late, brief dismissal of *Tom Sawyer Abroad* by the London *Academy* in 1894, ending with a line well-known to be from Artemus Ward, Twain's chief precursor in the English concept of American humor, identifies Twain's works as being regarded within the context of his writing as a humorist, irrespective of the dismal quality of that particular novel.

Blackwood's Magazine in 1907 paid tribute to *Life on the Mississippi* and in passing to Huck and Tom, but this is after the debacle in British eyes of the irreverent *A Connecticut Yankee. Blackwood's* has not forgotten that novel, and thus moves freely through a spectrum of life in Britain and finds even in it traces of similar exaggerated cheapening and debasement. In a memorable phrase, they pillory Twain the specialist in travesty as "a bull in the china-shop of ideas," and the argument is worthy of consideration, whether right or wrong, for it highlights the fact that writers such as Twain were radical precursors of modern dissent. *Blackwood's* final objection to Twain is consistent with the position staked out by them half a century before (in "Revelations of a Showman" in volume 47: 187–201 for February 1855) in lambasting P. T. Barnum for his chicanery. Actually, the essay is testimony to sheer consistency of vision for both the Barnum-Twain-

Artemus Ward sort of American exaggerated figure and for the English cultural milieu opposed to such Americanism as a social phenomenon. Hating his "imbecile lack of taste," *Blackwood's* reminds us again of the importance of Brander Matthews's comment on Twain in "The Penalty of Humor" (not reprinted here since only a page of its several pages deals with Twain in general terms) that he had suffered more for the reputation of a humorist because he was more of a humorist than any other living writer. Controversy lies at the heart of the acceptance of Twain by disputants like Brander Matthews, H. L. Mencken, James T. Farrell, and others who admired his craft for its social content put forth in the very way that increased the offence to more pretentiously classically oriented critics, along with his rejection at the hands of Edgar Lee Masters in *Mark Twain, A Portrait*. Space precludes including these essays, but they will be found in several lists in the anthologies of Twain criticism at the back of the book. The truth is that Twain appealed through humor to a subversively unorthodox element within genteel America at the same time that his directedness toward "the belly and its members" offended the more officiously mannered of that ilk.

Edith Wyatt's "An Inspired Critic" represents the cultivated appreciation of Twain that came to dominate intelligent readers' view of him through the 1900–1920 period. *Life on the Mississippi* is effectively appraised by her, but she goes on to make a strong statement for the social truth of Twain's humor to "Chicago" and the United States generally— the real places as well as the fictional settings. Her praise of *Joan of Arc* for its "pragmatic validity" is worth noting, and her concluding paragraph is a powerful statement of Twain's popularity as a democratic idealist. Clyde Grimm's study of *The American Claimant* shows that novel to contain some rather sophisticated thinking about the nature of democracy as a sham and as a reality in response to the sham of aristocracy. Since it follows so closely on the heels of *A Connecticut Yankee*, the proximity and shared subject matter of English nobility versus American democracy make *The American*

Claimant more interesting than is allowed by those who over-hastily dismiss it as a rambling farce.

The two chapters from William Dean Howells's *My Mark Twain* are arresting because they show him trying to run counter to prevailing estimates of both periods, emphasizing Twain's seriousness in the early 1880s and his regionalism in the latter period when Twain was coming to his full stature as a world writer. Thus, we see Howells emphasizing "The Recent Carnival of Crime in Connecticut" and noting the success of the play from *The Gilded Age* with a Col. Sellers who is actually drawn from real life. In 1902, he throws his net wider, finding Twain's socio-economic basis and even some nascent feminism, a theme playing through the items offered here by Henry Watterson at the turn of the century and Laura Skandera-Trombley as a recent critic. In fact, as a humorist, Twain was a rule-breaking writer, and it is to focus on this characteristic of his comic indignation and to stress its literary side as well as its social side that Alan Gribben's article "'I Kind of Love Small Game': Mark Twain's Library of Literary Hogwash" is valuable and insightful reading. Twain responded emotionally to form as well as function, and his hatred of the staged and false in literature and in life represents both an aesthetic and a philosophical underpinning of his humanity as irony, sarcasm, exaggeration, burlesque, and satire express it.

Of particular interest is a group of essays by Twain scholars which have not before seen print: those by Kiskis, Skandera-Trombley, and Weil place the literary artifact and an accurate reading of historical detail ahead of ideology in their interpretations. Kiskis's on Twain's *Autobiography* shows how the writer's humor came full circle, in his phrase, depending on narrative patterns that he had used from the very first. Weil makes the point, responding to provocative work by Hamlin Hill and William Gibson, that even supposedly unsatisfactory later works have an identifiable place in Twain's ever-changing comedy. Her discussion of the later works helps place them properly in perspective as part of his comic canon,

The Lyceum Committeeman's Dream—Some Popular Lecturers in Character

making her contribution an important one. Skandera-Trombley, in taking up the place of women in Twain's constellation of psychological traits, brings us back to insights first broached by Henry Watterson, but too long forgotten in the face of Van Wyck Brooks, that there was a strong "feminine" consciousness in Twain, an intrinsic component of his life and art and welcome in his life, not a trivializing eastern consciousness or censorship.

Finally, the selected bibliography has been developed to help readers find essays and books which deal with Mark Twain's humor as such. For this reason, the full contents of several anthologies of criticism should be a helpful finding tool not otherwise available. A special word of thanks must be extended here to Thomas Tenney's extraordinary compilation of critical abstracts in *Mark Twain: A Reference Guide*; this exhaustive collection of materials on Twain provides thousands of insights into specific publications on Twain. Tenney's work materially advanced the work here. The bibliography offers two sections. The first provides tables of contents for several valuable and easily obtainable anthologies of secondary criticism on Mark Twain, and especially on *Adventures of Huckleberry Finn*. The second offers those articles and books, listed alphabetically by author, that deal most directly with aspects of Mark Twain's humor. This section is focussed as tightly as seems possible, and it does not include many "standard" works on Twain because of their more general and comprehensive nature. For further aid in developing sources, the supplements to Tenney's work in the *Mark Twain Journal* and the annual analytic bibliographies in *American Literary Scholarship: An Annual* year by year are unfailingly informative, and were useful also in making this compilation. Bibliographies in Walter Blair's *Native American Humor* and David E. E. Sloane's *Mark Twain as a Literary Comedian* might also be consulted for further references, and a wide array of bibliographies of Twain criticism can be found in the books cited above and elsewhere. The bibliography extends through 1989.

The Early Writings of Mark Twain:
The Growth of the Comedian

"My Voice Is Still for Setchell": A Background Study of "Jim Smiley and His Jumping Frog"

Edgar M. Branch

I

For the past fifteen years scholars have examined many facets of Mark Twain's "Jumping Frog": its narrative techniques and some of its textual history, its relation to folklore, American humor, and Clemens' theory of humorous gravity, and its political, regional, and cultural bearings.[1] This article, by focussing on the personal background to the tale, tries to cast light on the imagination that created the famous yarn. It first relates some of the tale's narrative elements—episodes, characters, names—to Clemens' prior experience, especially to some activities reflected in newly discovered examples of his San Francisco journalism of 1864 and 1865. Then it relates the tale to strong emotional currents in his life during the fall of 1865. Finally the article proposes a date of composition for the "Jumping Frog" and a reading of the tale that emphasizes the level of personal meaning.

Clemens left Nevada for San Francisco 29 May 1864, almost eighteen months before the first printing of the "Jumping Frog" on 19 November 1865, and for fifteen of those months he lived in the city. Soon after arriving he became the

Reprinted from *PMLA*, LXXXII (December 1967): 591–612.

local reporter of the San Francisco *Call*. Probably he worked for the paper from 6 June to 10 October or possibly until a week later. During these four months he published hundreds of unsigned news items as well as feature articles and sketches in the *Call*. Growing dissatisfied with his job, he took an assistant in September and began working fewer hours for lower pay. Also he began to publish more ambitiously conceived sketches in C. H. Webb's *Californian*, nine in all between 1 October and 3 December. On 4 December he went to Jim Gillis' cabin at Jackass Hill. He remained there and at nearby Angel's Camp (from 22 January to 20 February) until his return to San Francisco 26 February 1865. From 18 March Through October Clemens published twelve additional sketches in the Californian and placed a few elsewhere. At least by 20 June he had begun his correspondence for Joseph T. Goodman's Virginia City *Territorial Enterprise*—a working relationship he continued into 1866—although he may not have started his daily letter to that paper until the fall. The third major professional connection he made during 1865 was with the San Francisco *Dramatic Chronicle*. He appears to have worked as a *Chronicle* staff writer for about two months, beginning 16 October. He contributed a few sketches and some squibs, and at least part of the time he compiled the column "Amusements," which included the theater notices.

II

Clemens' experience of Angel's Camp was of course basic to the "Jumping Frog." The remote, primitive community, soggy with rain for days on end, gave him the setting for the frame and for the internal narrative, and it supplied the perfect environment to motivate nonstop indoor yarning like Simon Wheeler's. Ben Coon, whom Clemens met there, is usually regarded as the pattern for Wheeler, and Coon's yarn of Coleman and his frog is well recognized as the immediate source for the contest in which Jim Smiley's trained frog is frustrated in his specialty by "a double-handful of shot." Clemens' synopsis put down the main facts: "Coleman with his jumping frog—bet stranger $50—stranger had no frog, & C got him one—in the meantime stranger filled C's frog full of shot & he couldn't jump—the stranger's frog won."[2] Very likely Coon's deadpan manner and vernacular language made a strong impression on Clemens and helped him establish Wheeler's point of view. The frame narrator of the tale, the character Mark Twain, finds Wheeler's speech "monotonous" and "interminable" yet "exquisitely absurd" in its earnest, gravely serene progression: a mixture of feelings that may approximate Clemens' original reaction to Ben Coon.[3] But this characterization of Wheeler's narration may have been suggested to Clemens by other mining camp acquaintances as well. Before he recorded his meeting with Coon and before he summarized Coon's yarn, he wrote: "Mountaineers in habit telling same old experiences over & over again in these little back settlements. Like Dan's old Ram, while [sic] he always drivels about when drunk. And like J's [Jim Gillis'?] account of the finding of the Cardinel. . . & other great pocket, & the sums they produced in a few days or weeks (50 to 100 lbs gold a day)."[4] At least one other notebook observation made at Angel's Camp seems to reflect experience that supplied a narrative detail. Clemens developed Jim Smiley as a resourceful, dedicated gambler. Simon Wheeler says of him that "if he even see a straddle-bug start to go any wheres, he would bet you how long it would take him to get wherever he was going to, and if you took him up he would foller that straddle-bug to Mexico but what he would find out where he was bound for." That passage may be compared to this notebook entry: "Louse betting by <sold> discharged soldiers coming through from Mexico to Cal in early days. The man whose louse got whipped had to get supper. Or place them on the bottom of a frying pan—draw chalk circle round them, heat the pan & the last louse over the line had to get supper."[5]

The appeal of the mining camp raconteur to Clemens' imagination is evident in "An Unbiased Criticism," his first published sketch after his return to the city. Gladys C. Bellamy (*Mark Twain as a Literary Artist*, Norman, Okla., 1950, p. 146) has correctly recognized in this sketch a rehearsal for the "Jumping Frog." Its major figure, simply called Coon, almost immediately takes over from the Mark Twain persona, as though by force of character. Coon lacks some of Simon Wheeler's "winning gentleness" and ungrudging admiration of others, and his use of the comic *non sequitur*, a device Artemus Ward liked, perhaps adds an artificial touch. But essentially his vision and speech are Simon Wheeler's. Coon, who seems to know everything about everybody for miles around, discourses on his "mighty responsible old Webster-Unabridged, what there is left of it." The miners

> started her sloshing around, and sloshing around, and sloshing around. . . , and I don't expect I'll ever see that book again; but what makes me mad, is that for all they're so handy about keeping her sashshaying around from shanty to shanty and from camp to camp, none of 'em's ever got a good word for her. Now Coddington had her a week, and she was too many for *him*—he couldn't spell the words; he tackled some of them regular busters, tow'rd the middle, you know, and they throwed him; next, Dyer, *he* tried her a jolt, but he couldn't *pronounce* worth a d—n; . . . and so, finally, Dick Stoker harnessed her, up there at his cabin, and sweated over her, and cussed over her, and rastled with her for as much as three weeks, night and day, till he got as far as R, and then passed her over to 'Lige Pickerell, and said she was the all-firedest dryest reading that ever *he* struck."[6]

Although Coon's voice is silenced before he can spin a tale, he speaks with Simon Wheeler's rambling omniscience and rhythms. His imagination like Simon's swarms with lively grotesques whom he observes with discriminating eyes. His dictionary takes on human outline too: something like an old hand-me-down prostitute who still is more than a match for her baffled and inadequate clients. The worthy book has some of the betrayed integrity of the dog Andrew Jackson, it goes through paces as frantic as those of Smiley's fifteen-minute nag, and it is "as likely a book as any in the State," just as

Dan'l Webster "can out-jump any frog in Calaveras county." Both tale and sketch project a feeling of time hanging heavy. Their people are eccentrics preoccupied with oddities and committed to trivia. To a degree the two writings share an identical vocabulary to describe analogous details: a mouth (or door) "prized" open, a dog (or dictionary) "harnessed," a frog (or man) turning a double "summerset." Coon's monologue in "An Unbiased Criticism" permitted Clemens to test the mentality through which he later dramatized the statement: "Why, it never made no difference to *him*—he would bet on *anything*—the dangdest feller." It signals Clemens' discovery of the appropriate style to express Wheeler's consciousness in the tale.

III

The available evidence indicates that Ben Coon's narrative was restricted to the episode of the shot-laden frog and that it played up the idea of human trickery and not animal idiosyncrasy.[7] Also by 1865 Clemens was adept at creating humanized animals. Almost certainly, then, he alone—with no dependence on any mining camp raconteur—conceived the full range of Smiley's love for betting and his paternalistic exploitation of talented animals. Significantly Clemens kept the memory of Coon's yarn alive in his imagination by joking about it with Jim Gillis and Dick Stoker as all three panned for gold, and before writing the published version he may have sketched the tale in a letter to Artemus Ward and may have told it to Bret Harte and other San Franciscans.[8] The imaginative enlargement of Coon's anecdote that occurred in the long gestation is in fact partly traceable. In particular, when he composed the episodes of the fifteen-minute nag and the dog Andrew Jackson, it now appears that Clemens drew upon experience he gained as a San Francisco reporter.

Among the hundreds of local news items appearing in the *Call* during the time Clemens worked on the paper are several on the horse races held in the new and lavishly equipped Bay View Park, located on the bay shore west of Hunter's Point. Two of these turf reports are reprinted below. Although they are unsigned, in my opinion they are by Clemens and form part of the background out of which Jim Smiley's mare comes "cavorting" down the track.[9]

The Hurdle-Race Yesterday.—The grand feature at the Bay View Park yesterday, was the hurdle race. There were three competitors, and the winner was Wilson's circus horse, "Sam." Sam has lain quiet through all the pacings and trottings and runnings, and consented to be counted out, but this hurdle business was just his strong suit, and he stepped forward promptly when it was proposed. There was a much faster horse (Conflict) in the list, but what is natural talent to cultivation? Sam was educated in a circus, and understood his business; Conflict would pass him under way, trip and turn a double summerset over the next hurdle, and while he was picking himself up, the accomplished Sam would sail gracefully over the hurdle and slabber past his adversary with the easy indifference of conscious superiority. Conflict made the fastest time, but he fooled away too many summersets on the hurdles. The proverb saith that he that jumpeth fences with ye circus horse will aye come to grief.[10]

Six days later the *Call* published the lengthy "Race for the Occidental Hotel Premium." The first half of this report factually describes four heats in the trotting contest subsidized by the Occidental Hotel, where Clemens boarded. The horse Kentucky Hunter ran first in each race. The reporter then continues:

Previous to the Occidental contest, a tandem race came off for a purse of one hundred and twenty-five dollars, mile heats, best 3 in 5. "Spot" and "Latham," driven by Mr. Covey, and "Rainbow" and "Sorrell Charley," driven by Mr Ferguson, ran. Before the first half mile post was reached, Ferguson's team ran away, and Covey's trotted around leisurely and won the purse. The runaways flew around the race-track three or four times, at break neck speed, and fears were entertained that some of this break-neck would finally fall to Ferguson's share, as his strength soon ebbed away, and he no longer attempted to hold his fiery untamed Menkens, but only did what he could to make them stay on the track, and keep them from climbing the fence. Every time they dashed by the excited crowd at the stand, a few frantic attempts would be made to grab them, but with indifferent success; it is no use to snatch at a cannon ball—a man must stand before it if he wants to stop it. One man seized the lead horse, and was whisked under the wheels in an instant. His head was split open a little, but Dr. Woodward stitched the wound together, and the sufferer was able to report for duty in half an hour. Mr. Ferguson's horses should be taught to economize their speed; they wasted enough of it in that one dash, yesterday, to win every race this season, if judiciously distributed among them. The only Christian way to go out to Bay View, is to travel in one of the Occidental coaches, behind four Flora Temples, and with their master-spirit, Porter, on the box, and a crowd inside and out, consisting of moral young men and cocktails. Mr. Leland should be along, to keep the portable hotel.[11]

In the "Jumping Frog" Clemens writes of the mare whom the boys called

the fifteen-minute nag, but that was only in fun, you know, because, of course, she was faster than that—and he used to win money on that horse, for all she was so slow and always had the asthma, or the distemper, or the consumption, or something of that kind. They used to give her two or three hundred yards' start, and then pass her under way; but always at the fag-end of the race she'd get excited and desperate-like, and come cavorting and spraddling up, and scattering her legs around limber, sometimes in the air, and sometimes out to one side amongst the fences, and kicking up m-o-r-e dust, and raising m-o-r-e racket with her coughing and sneezing and blowing her nose—and always fetch up at the stand just about a neck ahead, as near as you could cipher it down.

Like Kentucky Hunter, Smiley's mare is a consistent winner, capable of rousing herself and coming from behind to score. But clearly Sam's claim to be her sire is superior to Kentucky Hunter's. Competitors of both Sam and the mare "pass" each horse "under way," thus momentarily confirming to all observers the expected role of each underdog horse as an also-run and adding that much more excitement to the eventual upset victories. Although Sam takes the hurdles gracefully, his slabbering form as a runner suggests the spraddling mare scattering her legs around, and suggests, too, that when the chips were really down, the easygoing Sam, like Smiley's nag, possibly would show up as a lathering slob. To be sure, Sam is as educated as Smiley's frog, and no doubt this training explains his casual confidence and his feeling of superiority, so different from the mare's female excitability and air of desperation. Sam's victory over the speedy Conflict, in fact, is a monument to "cultivation" in contrast to what must surely be an impressive "talent"—no less than that of the dog Andrew Jackson's—in the badly handicapped, snuffling nag. Yet these very differences help us to see that both the "Jumping Frog" and the *Call* report of the hurdle race humorously utilize, with varying emphases, the twin ideas of natural endowment and acquired training (facets of Clemens' more general speculations of necessity and freedom), ideas often linked in his thinking and writing.[12] The two unorthodox race horses are close kin in Clemens' large family of exceptional, strong-minded animals.[13]

IV

Smiley's mare was a consistent winner and so was the bull-pup Andrew Jackson until he "got shucked out bad" by the dog "that didn't have no hind legs, because they'd been sawed off in a circular saw." The disfigured hero who retired Andrew Jackson for good is a significant minor character. So far as we know, he was Jim Smiley's only nemesis before the tricky stranger walked into camp. His surprise triumph over Andrew Jackson resulted from a circumstance much less usual than the duplicity shown by the stranger. Presumably his victory might have suggested to Smiley more forcibly than it did that a sure thing, even a scrupulously educated and gifted frog, can never be taken for granted. It appears that the original of this unsung conqueror of Andrew Jackson claimed Clemens' attention during the third week of October 1865.

In a revealing letter dated 19 October 1865 and addressed to Orion and Mollie Clemens, but meant primarily for Orion, Clemens wrote: "I am also in debt. But I have gone to work in dead earnest to get out. Joe Goodman pays me $100 a month for a daily letter, and the Dramatic Chronicle pays me or rather *will* begin to pay me, next week—$40 a month for dramatic criticisms. Same wages I got on the Call, & more agreeable & less laborious work."[14] It seems clear that when Clemens wrote this letter he had begun his duties of the *Dramatic Chronicle* as a recently recruited staff member and was not, as an old hand, taking on a new assignment at an increase in pay.[15] Two days before, he had published his first sketch in the *Dramatic Chronicle,* "Earthquake Almanac," which customarily noticed the daily offerings at the theaters, museums, and resorts, included the following account of James White's Museum of freaks:

White's Museum

Meigg's wharf is the favorite resort of the little ones on Sunday. No one who goes to this part of the city should leave without paying a visit to White's Museum, where a most wonderful collection of curiosities, fully equal to anything which Barnum has, are on view. The three-quartered dog, a fine handsome fellow, and as intelligent and good-natured an animal as we have ever had the pleasure of being introduced to, is a most wonderful freak of nature. Poor fellow! Richard III was—

"Cheated of feature by dissembling nature,
Deformed, unfinished,"

but this dog is actually cheated of a quarter by dissembling nature, who sent him into the world only three parts finished. However, he does not seem to mind it a bit; he is as strong and lively as any four-legged dog, and more intelligent than many two-legged puppies.[16]

This strong dog who accepts his defect is a fit model for the conqueror of a champion. Neither he nor Andrew Jackson's opponent is as vitally handicapped as Andrew Jackson, whose rigid habitual responses and tender-minded conviction that Smiley owed him a set-up prove to be a fatal combination. But Andrew Jackson is a more important character than his conqueror and in conceiving him Clemens dug more deeply into his past. Simon Wheeler says that "to look at him you'd think he warn't worth a cent, but to set around and look ornery, and lay for a chance to steal something." Here Clemens may be remembering the orneriness and thievery of Curney and Tom, two dogs he wrote up in his Keokuk *Gate City* later of 6 March 1862. But to describe Andrew Jackson's pugnacity when the "money was up on him" he reverted to sterner imagery from his piloting days: "his under-jaw'd begin to stick out like the for'castle [sic] of a steamboat, and his teeth would uncover, and shine savage like the furnaces." Andrew Jackson with his steam up was as lethal as the riverboat with its "long row of wide-open furnace doors shining like red-hot teeth" (*Writings*, XIII, 131) that smashed Huck's and Jim's raft.

Any San Franciscan writing of dogs at this time would almost automatically recall the famous friends Bummer and Lazarus, two dogs constantly publicized during the early 1860's in the San Francisco press. Clemens was aware of them and published an account of Bummer's death.[17] Andrew Jackson was not a vagrant like Bummer, but like Andrew Jackson, the valorous Bummer was a respected fighter. Clemens commented on his dignity, a quality similar to Andrew Jackson's pride that helped to undermine his will to live after "he saw in a minute how he'd been imposed on." Disillusioned, wounded to the heart, and mildly reproachful, Andrew Jackson "limped off a piece" to die alone, a defeated romantic. This comic sentimentality may be compared to the last moments of the more sociable Bummer, who "died with friends around him to smooth his pillow and wipe the death-damps from his brow, and receive his last words of love and resignation; because he died full of years, and honor, and disease, and fleas."

V

Clemens' experience as a San Francisco journalist may have influenced—consciously or not—his choice of names for some characters in the "Jumping Frog," if only by making those names available for selection because of his recent awareness of them. His 1864 editorial "It Is the Daniel Webster" praises the Daniel Webster Mining Company for daring to make its records public at a time when most companies were not disclosing how they spent assessments. As a stockholder, Clemens suffered from the drain of assessments and had fretted about their misappropriation by secretaries and managers of mining companies.[18] The Daniel Webster Mining Company he now saw as a symbol of probity, "worthy of the name of Daniel Webster." Its policy eventually would force other companies to "adopt the system of published periodical statement." On the day, he exulted, stockholders would hear from Virginia City corporations that sport "costly and beautiful green chicken-cocks on the roof, which are able to tell how the wind blows, yet are savagely ignorant concerning dividends. So will other Companies come out and say what it cost to build their duck ponds; . . . another that we have in our eye will show what they did with an expensive lot of timbers, when they haven't got enough in their mine to shingle a chicken-coop with. . . and why they levy a forty-thousand-dollar assessment every six weeks to run a drift with. Secretaries, Superintendents, and Boards of Trustees, that don't like the prospect, had better resign."[19]

During the 1860's the name Daniel Webster still had considerable currency, and Clemens had used it sparingly for many years. The physical resemblance of any frog to the famous politician is enough to have recalled the name once again to an imagination that often visualized animals as

people, although Clemens' naming of Smiley's frog no doubt
drew upon many interwoven associations, including the one
deriving from his attack on the mining companies.

Through much of 1864 and 1865 in the *Call*, the *Dramatic
Chronicle,* and the *Territorial Enterprise* Clemens repeatedly
sniped at Albert S. Evans, the city editor of the San Francisco
Alta California who was commonly known by his pen names
Fitz Smythe and Amigo. Writing in the *Alta California* in mid-
1864, Evans invented a stooge whom he named Armand
Leonidas Stiggers, surely one of the dreariest comic characters
of all time. Clemens ridiculed the labored jokes Evans
constructed around Stiggers. His fondness for the name
Leonidas is evident during late 1865 and 1866 in his
continuing bouts with Evans, whom he rechristened Armand
Leonidas Fitz Smythe Amigo Stiggers. Leonidas, an
improbable name at best, in one sense suits the mythical
friend who was not there, "the Rev. Leonidas W. Smiley" of
the tale, whom Artemus Ward asked Mark Twain to look up.
Yet to make a minister of God lion-like is almost as
incongruous as the comic ennobling of Smiley's frog and bull-
pup by naming them after great human leaders.

The name Smiley that supplanted Ben Coon's "Coleman"
was Clemens' most brilliant choice. Paired with "Leonidas" it
aptly describes the mocking phantom who lives only within
the realm of Ward's practical joke on Mark Twain. Joined with
"Jim" it admirably fits the wily gambler, adept and enduring
in a man's world. Its source may be the case of the *United
States vs. Thomas J. L. Smiley* publicized in the San Francisco
papers during the summer of 1864 when Clemens was local
reporter on the *Call.* In 1862 the ship *Golden Gate* out of San
Francisco with almost $1,500,000 in treasure had sunk off the
coast of Mexico near Manzanillo. The adventurer Smiley was
indicted in the United States Circuit Court for salvaging and
appropriating some of the treasure. But on 29 August 1864
Judge Ogden Hoffman ordered a *nolle prosequi,* and the *Call*
reported that Smiley had compromised a second suit brought
against him. The settlement left him "in the quiet possession

of a large amount of the treasure-trove." The *Call* reporter, whether Clemens or another, gratuitously insinuated in a vein not foreign to Clemens' manner on occasion, that "Mr. Smiley, during his arrest, has moved about at his pleasure, attended by a Deputy of the Marshal, which courtesy will doubtless meet its due reward at the hands of the fortunate wrecker."[20]

Clemens characterized the appropriately named Simon Wheeler as a simple, earnest soul, gentle in character but an unswerving steamroller in his storytelling. The surname may have suggested itself to Clemens as a consequence of his acquaintance with Reverend Osgood Church Wheeler. Wheeler lectured widely for the California Branch of the United States Sanitary Commission and served as its secretary. During September Clemens reported the Mechanic's Institute Industrial Fair in San Francisco. Various Fair exhibits collected money for the Sanitary Fund to aid the Civil War wounded, a cause Clemens helped to promote. In one of the Fair writeups the *Call* reporter credits Wheeler with supplying him statistics on public contributions to the Fund. But exactly one week earlier in the *Call* the local reporter had complained of a brush-off at Wheeler's office. He concluded: "We would like, in order to benefit the commission, to give publicity to the names of contributors to the Fund; but on applying for the list, recently, were all but peremptorily refused. The individual who attends to the business of receiving and recording the subscriptions is either too lazy or too disobliging for the position. He prefers his own case to the interest of the Commission."[21] Whether the offending individual was Wheeler or a clerk is not known, but by his complaint the reporter brought his man to account—following precisely the technique Clemens used more violently in "A Small Piece of Spite" (*Call*, 6 Sept. 1864, p. 1) three days later to flatten the Coroner's clerk in Atkins Massey's funeral establishment who had denied him information.

VI

Clemens' original version of his tale begins: "Mr. A. Ward, Dear Sir:—" A minor character not present in person, Ward serves to motivate the meeting between the frame narrator Mark Twain and the internal narrator Simon Wheeler. The reference to him was Clemens' indirect acknowledgment of Ward's invitation to contribute a sketch to this forthcoming book, *Artemus Ward: His Travels,* a request Clemens recorded in his 1865 note book: "26th—Home again—home again at the Occidental Hotel, San Francisco—find letters from 'Artemus Ward' asking me to write a sketch for his new book of Nevada Territory travels which is soon to come out. Too late—ought to have got the letters 3 months ago. They are dated early in November."[22] Those letters of Ward's marked his second eruption in Clemens' life, the first having come in late December 1863 when Clemens heard his "Babes in the Woods" lecture in Virginia City and became personally acquainted with him. On both occasions Ward precipitated publications that helped Clemens' career. The opportunity that Clemens on 26 February believed he had missed opened up in succeeding months as Ward continued to press for a contribution.[23] Surely Ward, the generous friend, was alive in Clemens' thoughts during the incubation of the "Jumping Frog."

The less surprising, then, that Ward, the lecturer and writer, was alive in Clemens' literary imagination when he finally wrote the tale. One notes the letter form that begins the "Jumping Frog," suggesting the way Ward began some of his sketches. Ward's "Babes in the Woods" was a series of digressions: anecdotes and pronouncements given coherence by Ward's platform presence. Similarly the main substance of Clemens' tale, the history of "thish-yer Smiley," is a kind of self-perpetuating digression that unerringly expresses Simon Wheeler's personality. In both the lecture and the tale, as Clemens in effect demonstrates in "How to Tell a Story," the humor is founded on character that is displayed in the manner of telling. What counts is the wandering, bubbling, spun-out discourse, punctuated by studied pauses and afterthoughts, that is spoken by a narrator who is simple, innocent, earnestly sincere, unselfconscious—either naturally like Ben Coon or Simon Wheeler, or by calculated pretense like the platform artists Ward, Twain, Dan Setchell, or James Whitecomb Riley. The genius of the "Jumping Frog" dwarfs Ward's talent; in style, subtlety of organization, character creation, intellectual content, and imaginative power Clemens' tale transcends Ward's influence. Yet Ward must be counted a pioneer of the broad literary approach Clemens followed in writing the tale that made such imaginative use of a personal experience including originals like Coon and Ward himself.

Beyond strictly literary influence, however, Ward probably played a crucial role in Clemens' psychology when the "Jumping Frog" was written. Years later Clemens affirmed that "Babes in the Woods" was the funniest thing he had ever listened to, and after hearing Ward lecture in 1863 he wrote: "There are perhaps fifty subjects treated in it, and there is a passable point in every one of them, and a hearty laugh also for any of God's creatures who have committed no crime, the ghastly memory of which debars him from smiling again while he lives. The man who is capable of listening to the Babes In The Woods from beginning to end without laughing, either inwardly or outwardly, must have done murder, or at least meditated it, at some time during his life."[24] Here Clemens contrasts the worthy result of Ward's humor—a life-giving laughter common to most of "God's creatures"—with murder, an act of violence and final separation. In his letter of 19 October he confides to Orion: "I *have* had a 'call' to literature, of a low order—*i.e.* humorous. It is nothing to be proud of, but it is my strongest suit" (*MDB*, p. 6). He then makes an important commitment. He asserts he will "strive for a fame— unworthy & evanescent though it must of necessity be" by turning his attention "to seriously scribbling to excite the *laughter* of God's creatures" (*MDB*, pp. 8,6). The similar phrasing in letter and review inevitably suggests an imaginative identification of his commitment with Ward's accomplishment, the writing of humorous literature, and it reveals his concept of their identical purpose, the creation of beneficial laughter.

In "How to Tell a Story" Clemens associated Ward and the popular comedian Dan Setchell, Ward's good friend, as masters of humorous technique. His early piece from the mid-1860's, "A Voice for Setchell," further defines the value he finds in laughter. There he wrote that in "a long season of sensational, snuffling dramatic bosh, and tragedy bosh, and electioneering bosh" the people were "learning to wear the habit of unhappiness like a garment" until Setchell appeared as Captain Cuttle in John Brougham's extremely popular adaptation of *Dombey and Son* "and broke the deadly charm with a wave of his enchanted hook and the spell of his talismanic words, '*Awahst! awahst! awahst!*' And since that night all the powers of dreariness combined have not been able to expel the spirit of cheerfulness he invoked. Therefore, my voice is still for Setchell. I have experienced more real pleasure, and more physical benefit, from laughing naturally and unconfinedly at his funny personations and extempore speeches than I have from all the operas and tragedies I have endured, and all the blue mass pills I have swallowed in six months."[25] Murder, Clemens seems to say, excludes laughter, but laughter buoys up the spirit and expels dreariness. As an antidote to misery, it ultimately offers escape from self-murder. His letter of 19 October closes: "I am utterly miserable. . . If I do not get out of debt in 3 months,—pistols or poison for one—exit *me*. There's a text for a sermon on Self-M[urder,]—proceed" (*MDB*, p. 9).

In 1865, then, Clemens undoubtedly valued laughter and consequently humorous writing for at least one important reason. Later he would appreciate more fully the social value of laughter and humor. On the other hand, in 1865 his implied reluctance to pursue literature "of a low order" that was "nothing to be proud of" is an early expression of later recurrent doubts about the fitness of a career in humor for a serious writer. In view of this conflict it may be supposed that the commitment expressed in his letter resulted less from a sudden dedication to literary values—after all, he had been writing and publishing since 1852—than from his need to get our of debt and keep that way, especially at a time when his mining stocks were proving worthless. In addition to its intrinsic but "low order" value, humorous writing that was more seriously pursued presumably offered him at least a chance for success—to make a name for himself if the stuff was in him.

Clemens' commitment also was supported by Orion's faith in him and, more significantly, by a favorable press in the East. Clemens continued in his letter: "*You* see in me a talent for humorous writing, & urge me to cultivate it. But I always regarded it as brotherly partiality on your part & attached no value to it. It is only now, when editors of standard literary papers in the distant east give me high praise, & who do not know me & cannot of course be blinded by the glamour of partiality, that I really begin to believe there must be something in it" (*MDB*, pp. 7–8). He was alluding to a recently published article on American humor in the New York *Round Table* ("American Humor and Humorists," 9 Sept. 1865, p. 2). The anonymous author, possibly one of the editors, H. E. Sweetser or C. H. Sweetser, broadly characterized American humor and surveyed native humorists. He placed Mark Twain "foremost among the merry gentlemen of the California press"; Twain's writing gave promise that "he may one day take rank among the brightest of our wits." On 18 October, the day before Clemens wrote to "My Dear Bro," the *Dramatic Chronicle*, whose staff he had just joined, reprinted ("Recognized," p. 3)[sic] the part of the article that praised him.

Three days later came Clemens' newspaper writeup of the three-quartered dog. If, as I believe, that dog was the model for Andrew Jackson's conqueror, thereby evoking him in Clemens' awareness of the museum freak at this precise time is a key piece fitting superbly into the puzzle of the date the "Jumping

Frog" was composed. It seems probable that Clemens wrote "Jim Smiley and His Jumping Frog" during the week of 16–23 October. He had a new job in which he covered the city's amusements and plays. He was making every effort to clear away debt. A favorable press was waiting to be used. A clear-sighted self-examination arising from his unhappiness had called forth a commitment to write laughter-provoking humor, another name for "literature of a low order"—"a villainous backwoods sketch" (*Letters,* I, 101) was what he called his laughter-provoking tale three months later. Nor is it likely that he undertook his commitment lightly. A proud man who four years earlier had come West with dreams of wealth, he still was in a subordinate position. He believed in his talent for humor, but still it was "nothing to be proud of." He had come to know already that success of any kind came hard and that a writer's life meant a continuing risk. Finally, if he made his commitment as the best immediate way to become and remain solvent, he must have seen it partly in terms of a life-risk: success or "exit *me.*"

The suggested time of writing is late, for it comes midway in the two-month period spanning the date Ward's book is said to have been published and the appearance of the tale.[26] Yet some evidence suggests that Clemens delayed excessively in writing the tale and that it arrived late in the East.[27] Also it should be observed that given Clemens' interest in freaks, he might have visited White's Museum in the summer or early fall, a supposition that supports an earlier dating of the Andrew Jackson episode assuming one grants the causal relationship between the two handicapped dogs suggested above. Yet, an earlier visit is purely speculative. So far as we know there was no specific motive for it and, if it was made, no visible consequence of it leading into the tale, other than possibly the Andrew Jackson episode itself. On the other hand, the requirement of covering the city's amusements for the *Dramatic Chronicle* was a strong motive for an October visit to White's Museum even if he had been there earlier. The newspaper writeup with its fresh impressions working actively in his imagination—the merging images of the deformed dog and Richard III—suggests both a recent visit and an available bridge to the tale.

VII

The "Jumping Frog" itself supports the date of composition proposed for it in this paper. When Clemens wrote his letter to "My Dear Bro" the uncertainties of his present and future were so troubling that he felt compelled to reexamine his past: "I never had but two *powerful* ambitions in my life. One was to be a pilot, & the other a preacher of the gospel. I accomplished the one & failed in the other, *because* I could not supply myself with the necessary stock in trade —*i.e* religion. I have given it up forever. I never had a 'call' in that direction, anyhow, & my aspirations were the very ecstasy of presumption" (*MDB*, p. 6). The ministry, for Clemens a chimera of his distant boyhood, was for Orion, he believed, a real possibility founded on a "talent" for preaching. "You are honest, pious, virtuous," he wrote; "—what would you have more? *Go forth & preach*" (*MDB*, p. 7). Orion should become "a minister of the gospel," not a "mud-cat of a *lawyer*" (*MDB*, pp. 8, 7). The general principle was simply "that to do the right you *must* multiply the one or the two or the three talents which the Almighty entrusts to your keeping" (*MDB*, p. 6). As a climax to his own sermon, he offered to strike a bargain with Orion: each would agree to develop his natural talent, "to do what his Creator intended him to do" (*MDB*, p. 7). This proposal, which links his own performance to Orion's, further qualifies the seriousness of Clemens' commitment to humorous literature. Moreover his letter was a perfect opportunity to over-dramatize his troubles before a sympathetic audience, and it is doubtful that any resolution, however seriously intended, could keep the pluralistic Clemens in a single path for very long. Yet after all allowances are made, we cannot miss the real unhappiness in the letter, or the latent bitterness: "I have a religion. . . It is that there is a God for the rich man but none for the poor" (*MDB*, p. 9). Nor can we miss the sense of loss as he touches on the old problem of natural endowment versus training ("the Almighty did His part by me—for the talent is a mighty engine when supplied with the steam of *education*— which I have not got" [*MDB*, p. 7]), the genuine uncertainty about his future, and his keen awareness of the element of risk that lay ahead in his life. The fact that these feelings were pressing for expression at that precise time—and perhaps were not so dominant a few days before or after—strengthens the probability that the tale was composed the week of 16–23 October. For those feelings fit the tale in a deeply personal way and help us to understand it in a new and intimate dimension.

Whatever else "Jim Smiley and His Jumping Frog" may be, it also is an unwittingly articulated parable of Clemens' complex state of mind, the pass he had come to, about the time he wrote his letter to Orion. The constructive imagination that built the tale seized on the conflicts and concepts, the forebodings and ambitions, that were at work within. In the tale the character Mark Twain (in life, the relatively unknown but promising humorist) is directed by the character Artemus Ward (in life, the nationally acclaimed maker of laughs) to find "a cherished companion" of Ward's boyhood, "Rev. Leonidas W. Smiley—a young minister of the gospel." The minister turns out to be a chimera, a shade, and for the character Mark Twain to have sought him was indeed a good joke, the "very ecstasy of presumption." Yet by this means Ward brings the seeker Mark Twain (who, in life, seeks to "multiply" his talent for humor) face to face with Simon Wheeler, and Mark Twain wakens the dozing humorist. With utmost seriousness, Wheeler awake seems to give over his entire being to his humorous narration. To his visitor's question about the minister Wheeler responds as though his long irrelevant answer were perfectly proper, as though, in fact, it were really relevant to another, unexpressed question in his listener's mind. His visitor sees that Wheeler accepts his own tale as "a really important matter," and Wheeler speaks with no condescension or irony or hint of trickery. As a storyteller Wheeler is a natural. Evidently of slight education, he performs, to God's own fulness, "what his Creator intended him to do," and he does it with an impressive objectivity. It is deeply appropriate that the character Mark Twain should sit silent before this man (as one might absorb a natural wonder), letting him "go on in his own way" without interrupting him once.

By means of his narrative Wheeler introduces Mark Twain, not to a pious, virtuous minister who knows the language of exhortation like Parson Walker of the tale, or like Orion, but to Jim Smiley, a resourceful adventurer who will slop around in the mud to get what he wants, a man who has done very well in a chancy world. Smiley works his talent for betting for all it is worth. He is enterprising and makes his own opportunities. He counts on the hopes of others and on the strengths of those he bets on. Although "he would bet on *anything*," "he was lucky—uncommon lucky"; and his luck is evidence that usually he knows what he is about. He knows the importance of persistent effort born of desperation (in the mare), of talent (in Andrew Jackson), and of talent combined with training (in Dan'l Webster). Knowing these things, he is equipped to win what victories he can by calculated means. From Andrew Jackson he presumably learns about the weakness of the sensitive romantic who expects too much from the world. From Dan'l's honest belch he learns once again that the unexpected can explode in his overconfident face, but when it does he responds vigorously. He has the courage to bet even when the outcome is totally unpredictable—which bird will fly first from a fence?—and he makes risk the condition of his existence. As Mrs. Wendy Stallard Flory has said, "he embraces chance itself as a way of life."[28] Jim Smiley is the hero of a fabulous world as "exquisitely absurd" as Wheeler's manner, but that world is very real too in the limitations and possibilities it holds for men.

Clemens made Wheeler and Smiley extreme individualists, as though already he were obscurely probing the implications of seriously making humor the business of his life. For Wheeler is the complete humorist. No mere trickster, he is absorbed like a true creator in the world he fashions through his patiently vivid imagination and his serene, rhythmic style. And Smiley, the mundane hero of that world, is the shrewd and determined man of action. He believes in rational effort but knows very well the full range of risk in life. His conduct implies courage and tough-minded hope. "Mr. A. Ward," Simon Wheeler and—through the lens of Wheeler's vision—Jim Smiley, his animals, and the fateful stranger are all meaningful configurations in Clemens' consciousness at a time of uncertainty and resolve, when he wanted to give a new but risky direction to his life.

Although the "Jumping Frog" was not soon equalled by Clemens, it was an important breakthrough in the long process of his development. Years of journalism still lay ahead, but by October 1865 he must have known that San Francisco journalism held little more for him. By 7 March of the next year he was more than ready to sail for the Sandwich Islands, an assignment that would offer fresh experience and the opportunity to cast off "the habit of unhappiness like a garment." But he was not yet ready to recognize fully the heights of humor he had reached in the "Jumping Frog" or to build upon them. His creation was more complex and profound than he knew. The tale is, in fact, a number of things: a blown-up frontier anecdote, a teasing fable that suggests various social and political meanings—although these, I believe, were negligible in the creative impulse behind the tale—and, as Paul Baender has convincingly shown, a thoroughgoing illustration of Clemens' theory of humorous gravity. The voice that had spoken up for Setchell spoke for itself in the "Jumping Frog," which above all else is a first-rate yarn taking extraordinary delight in humorous expression and character. As such, the tale appears to be also an intimately personal creation rising in shapely form from depths previously unsounded by Clemens, a consideration that helps to explain its compelling appeal and its poetic unity. For if the argument of this paper is correct, in writing "Jim Smiley and His Jumping Frog" Clemens utilized, consciously or not, two main areas of his personal background: past events experienced in San Francisco as well as in the mining camps, and certain tension-laden problems, closely connected with his need to find himself, that were pressing for immediate resolution.

Notes

1. See Paul Baender, "The 'Jumping Frog' as a Comedian's First Virtue," *Modern Philology*, LX (1963), 192–200;Walter Blair, "Introduction," *Selected Shorter Writings of Mark Twain* (Boston, 1962), pp. xxi–xxiv; Hennig Cohen, "Twain's Jumping Frog: Folktale to Literature to Folktale," *Western Folklore*, xxii (1963), 17–18; Rufus A. Coleman, "Mark Twain's Jumping Frog: Another Version of the Famed Story," *Montana Magazine of History*, III (Summer 1953), 29–30; Pascal Covici, Jr., *Mark Twain's Humor* (Dallas, Tex., 1962), pp. 48–52; James M. Cox, *Mark Twain: The Fate of Humor* (Princeton, N.J., 1966), pp. 24–33; Roger Penn Cuff, "Mark Twain's Use of the Comic Pose," PMLA, LXXVII (1962), 297–304; Sydney J. Krause, "The Art and Satire of Twain's 'Jumping Frog' Story," *American Quarterly*, XVI (1964), 562–576; Kenneth S. Lynn, *Mark Twain and Southwestern Humor* (Boston, 1959), pp. 145–147; Paul Schmidt, "The Deadpan on Simon Wheeler," *Southwest Review*, XLI (1956), 270–277; Henry Nash Smith, *Mark Twain: The Development of a Writer* (Cambridge, Mass., 1962), p. 11; J. Golden Taylor, introductory remarks to "The Celebrated Jumping Frog of Calaveras County," *American West*, II (Fall 1965), 73–76.

References to the "Jumping Frog" in this article are to the first printing, "Jim Smiley and His Jumping Frog," New York *Saturday Press*, 18 Nov. 1865, pp. 248–249.

2. TS of Notebook 3, p. 8, Mark Twain Papers, Berkeley, Calif.—hereafter cited as MTP; reprinted with changes in *Mark Twain's Notebook*, ed. Albert Bigelow Paine (New York, 1935), p. 7.

3. In his "Private History of the 'Jumping Frog' Story," *North American Review*, CLVIII (1894), 447, Clemens wrote of Coon and his audience of miners: "in his mouth this episode was . . . the gravest

sort of history. . . ; he was entirely serious, for he was dealing with what to him were austere facts, and . . . he saw no humor in his tale . . . none of the party was aware . . . that it was brimful of a quality whose presence they never suspected—humor."

4. TS of Notebook 3, p. 5, MTP. Copyright @ 196- by The Mark Twain Company.

5. TS of Notebook 3, p. 8, MTP. Copyright @ 196- by The Mark Twain Company.

6. *Californian*, 18 Mar. 1865, p. 8; reprinted with some changes in *Sketches of the Sixties*, ed. John Howell (San Francisco, 1927), pp. 158–165.

7. See Clemens' emended version of "Private History. . .," *How to Tell a Story and Other Essays* (Hartford, Conn., 1900), pp. 121–122; *Mark Twain's Letters* (New York, 1917), I, 170.

8. *How to Tell a Story*, p. 126; T. Edgar Pemberton, *The Life of Bret Harte* (London, 1903), pp. 73–75; "'The Jumping Frog of Calaveras' by Mark Twain With an Introductory and Explanatory Note by J. G. H.," *Overland Monthly*, XL (Sept. 1902), 20–21; *Letters*, I, 170.

9. As recently as Oct. 1863 Clemens had written up the races at the first annual fair of the Washoe Agricultural, Mining and Mechanical Society held in Carson City. See *Mark Twain of the Enterprise*, ed. Henry Nash Smith with the assistance of Frederick Anderson (Berkeley and Los Angeles, 1957), pp. 80–86. My article "Mark Twain Reports the Races in Sacramento," to appear in *Huntington Library Quarterly*, shows that Clemens undertook a week's racetrack assignment at the 1866 California State Fair for James Anthony of the Sacramento *Union*.

10. *Call*, 4 Sept. 1864, p. 1. Reports in other city papers name the winner as Strideover, nicknamed Sam. John Wilson was the proprietor of the circus at the Jackson Street Pavilion. Sam's "easy indifference of conscious superiority" is a phrase carrying almost the force of a signature. It marks the horse as one of Clemens' large class of self-assured characters who enjoy lording it over others because of superior skill or style or experience. For examples of Clemens' use of the phrase and its variants see: "San Francisco Correspondence," Napa County *Reporter*, 11 Nov. 1865, p. 2; *The Writings of Mark Twain*, Definitive Edition (New York, 1922), XII, 46, and XIV, 317. Hereafter this edition will be cited as *Writings*.

11. *Call*, 10 Sept. 1864, p. 1. I have omitted the four concluding sentences that notice races to come. George N. Ferguson and Harris R. Covey were racetrack drivers. Wadsworth Porter owned a livery stable. Dr. George F. Woodward was the surgeon and physician of the United States Pension Bureau. Clemens' friend Lewis Leland was the

proprietor of the Occidental Hotel and Clemens often joked about him in print.

Clemens' comic use of "Christian" was routine, and he echoes his earlier review of "Mazeppa" in the phrase "fiery untamed Menkens" (Smith, *Enterprise*, pp. 78–80). Typical of his comic vision is the merging of discrete modes of being and the resulting implicit puns. Quality becomes commodity, as in the use of "break neck" and "break-neck." A burst of speed necessarily indivisible in time is coolly partitioned and distributed among several races (economizing speed for economic gain). Moral young men and cocktails combine (in two ways) to constitute a crowd (animate and animated). The bold, offhand formula for stopping a cannonball and the casually aloof phrasing of "His head was split open a little" familiarly echo the magisterial dispenser of advice and remedies and the Washoe reporter of gory prize fights.

12. It is interesting that Conflict's awkward "double summerset" is a sign of a serious limitation by virtue of his lack of training in hurdle racing, whereas Dan'l Webster's graceful "one summerset, or maybe a couple," is a sign of his free mastery of conditions through training. The fated dog Curney in Clemens' letter in the Keokuk *Gate City,* 6 Mar. 1862, turns "somersets" as he races over the desert. In *Roughing It* "the rawest dog," probably modeled on the alkalied Curney, "threw double somersaults" in his frenzy (*Writings*, III, 260).

13. For examples of Clemens' later use of turf imagery and terms relating to the *Call* pieces and to the "Jumping Frog" see: *Writings*, I, 32; IV, 99, 287; XII, 372; XIII, 206; XIV, 119; XXVII, 176; Walter F. Frear, *Mark Twain and Hawaii* (Chicago, 1947), p. 294.

14. *My Dear Bro,* ed. Frederick Anderson (Berkeley, 1961), p. 8—hereafter cited as *MDB* and documented in text.

15. See "Dictation of M. H. DeYoung," Bancroft Library, Berkeley. DeYoung helped establish the *Dramatic Chronicle* in 1865. His memory of Clemens' connection with the paper is faulty in some details.

16. "Amusements," *Dramatic Chronicle*, 21 Oct. 1865, p. 3. The comparison with Richard III (whom Huck, the Duke, and the Dauphin knew all about), the punning, the easy slide from the factual into the fanciful, and above all the familiar delight in humanizing an animal suggest Clemens' comic imagination at this time.

17. Extant as "Exit 'Bummer',” *Californian*, 11 Nov. 1865, p. 12, from the Virginia City *Territorial Enterprise*, 8 Nov. 1865. In "The Art and Satire. . ." (see n. 1) Sydney J. Krause argues that the bull-pup is Clemens' satirical portrait of the historical Andrew Jackson. He feels, e.g., that the pup's appearance of not being "worth a cent but to set around and look ornery and lay for a chance to steal something" is

"an analogue of the legendary flashes of temper with which Jackson is known to have frightened opponents into submission" (p. 570). Referring to Mark Twain's sentence quoted in the text and comparing the pup's under-jaw to a steamboat's fo'castle, Krause writes: "In addition to its suggesting the fearful union of savagery with avarice, the idea that Smiley's pup has caught the gambling fever also carries a lurking reference to the stories of Jackson's fabulous exploits in gaming" (pp. 570–571). I feel that this view is overstated.

18. See, e.g., "The Evidence in the Case of Smith vs. Jones," *Golden Era*, 26 June 1864, p. 4, collected in *The Washoe Giant in San Francisco*, ed. Franklin Walker (San Francisco, 1938), p. 82.

19. *Call*, 21 Aug. 1864, p. 2. A clipping of the item is in Moffett Scrapbook 5, p. 58, MTP. In "The Art and Satire. . . ," p. 573, Krause argues that the portrait of Dan'l the frog is Clemens' political satire of Daniel Webster, showing "how completely Twain had *done* Webster in almost every characterizing detail." It should be noted that Webster died in 1852 and that Clemens' few references to him prior to 1865 are not politically hostile. See *Mark Twain's Letters in the Muscatine Journal*, ed. Edgar M. Branch (Chicago, 1942), p. 20; Franklin R. Rogers, *The Pattern for Mark Twain's Roughing It* (Berkeley and Los Angeles, 1961), p. 35. I feel that Krause is unduly hard on Dan'l's integrity and accomplishment because he reads into him unflattering characteristics attributed to Daniel Webster the politician.

20. "A Wrecking Party in Luck," *Call*, 3 Sept. 1864, p. 2.

21. "California Branch of the U.S. Sanitary Commission," *Call*, 3 Sept. 1864, p. 1. The later *Call* item is "A Philanthropic Nation," 10 Sept. 1864, p. 1.

22. TS of Notebook 3, p. 10, MTP.

23. *Mark Twain: A Biography*, ed. A. B. Paine (New York, 1912), I, 277. Paine's chronology here is vague, but his account suggests that considerable time passed before Ward renewed his invitation and that even then Clemens delayed his composition of the tale.

24. "An Inapt Illustration," Virginia Evening *Bulletin*, 28 Dec. 1863, as preserved in Notebook 4, Carton 3, Grant H. Smith Papers, Bancroft Library, Berkeley. Courtesy of the Bancroft Library.

25. "A Voice for Setchell," *Californian*, 27 May 1865, p. 9. The article is signed "X" but is unmistakably by Clemens. The editor of the *Californian* hints broadly at the authorship, and a clipping of the piece is in Clemens' *Scrapbook of Newspaper Clippings. . .* , Beinecke Library, Yale Univ. Reviewers of Setchell's acting often compared his manner and humor to Ward's. In June 1865 Setchell played the part of Ward in *Artemus Ward, Showman*, a three-act play written for him by Fred. G. Maeder and Thomas B. Macdonough.

26. Jacob Blanck, *Bibliography of American Literature* (New Haven, Conn., 1955), I, 314, No. 1527. Blanck notes that ten years after Ward's book appeared his publisher gave 23 Sept. as the publication date. The listing of Ward's book as received in the 14 Oct. issue of the New York *Saturday Press* may indicate a later publication date. West Coast periodicals noticed the book in late Nov. and early Dec. James M. Cox (*Mark Twain: The Fate of Humor*, p. 32) believes, as I do, that Clemens wrote the "Jumping Frog" and his letter of 19 Oct. 1865 about the same time. My article was accepted for publication in its present form several months before I read Cox's excellent book.

27. See n. 23. Clemens usually claimed that the tale reached George W. Carleton too late for inclusion in *Artemus Ward: His Travels*, although he contradicts this in *Mark Twain in Eruption*, ed. Bernard DeVoto (New York, 1940), p. 144. See *Letters*, I, 102; Yale *Scrap Book*, opposite clippings of the "Jumping Frog"; *Notebook*, p. 7. Henry Clapp's admiring editorial preface to the "Jumping Frog" in the *Saturday Press* of 18 Nov. barely hints that the tale was inserted at the last moment.

28. From "A Defense of 'Jim Smiley and His Jumping Frog'. . . ," an unpublished seminar paper. In my comments on Smiley I am indebted to Mrs. Flory.

Burlesque Travel Literature and Mark Twain's *Roughing It*

Franklin R. Rogers

I n July 1870, Elisha Bliss of the American Publishing Company completed a contract with Samuel L. Clemens, the latest arrival among the ranks of the American comic writers, which called for the delivery by January 1, 1871 of sufficient manuscript to make a 600-page book. Bliss, of course, expected the author to furnish something which would repeat the success of *The Innocents Abroad*, which had been published the previous year, and Clemens proposed to outdo himself, if possible, this time with a tale based upon his trip across the Plains in 1861 and his six years' sojourn in Nevada and California. The six months allotted by the contract proved entirely too short for the completion of the projected book. The protracted illness and finally the death of Clemens's father-in-law, Jervis Langdon, and the illness and death of a house-guest, Emma Nye, consumed much of the author's time, and progress on the manuscript was further retarded by a dissatisfaction with the product of his labors which led to extensive revisions. Even an additional six months did not free him from the sense of pressure. As a result, the book which he finally produced exhibits at least two major flaws. One is the awkward break in tone, structure, and point of view evident in the last eighteen chapters, the consequence of his

Reprinted from the *Bulletin of the New York Public Library* 67 (March 1963): 155–68.

hasty incorporation at the last moment of the series of letters written from Hawaii for the *Sacramento Union* in 1866. The other is the padding of the text with statistics and quotations, principally from his newspaper clippings, which characterized a number of the earlier chapters. But despite its imperfections the book proved quite acceptable to Bliss, and its subsequent success apparently stilled any misgivings Twain himself may have had on the score of his patchwork. Interested as he no doubt was in securing another comic best-seller, Bliss ignored its faults; he probably also failed to appreciate the essential importance of the manuscript which Clemens sent him in batches during the first months of 1871. For while *Roughing It* marks the culmination of a seventy-year-old tradition in burlesque travel literature, it also represents the successful transformation of burlesque travel literature conventions into the means for significant literary expression.

The tradition to which *Roughing It* owes a substantial debt begins with William Combe's *The Tour of Dr. Syntax in Search of the Picturesque* which first appeared serially in the *Poetical Magazine*, 1809–1811. Written in a pseudo-Hudibrastic verse which "may wel be rym dogerel," the tour proved a popular success. Combe exploited its popularity with an edition in book form in 1812 and two sequels, *The Second Tour of Dr. Syntax in Search of Consolation* (1820) and *The Third Tour of Dr. Syntax in Search of a Wife* (1821); during the next half-century several British publishers managed to keep the three tours before the reading public.[1] As the title of the first poem suggests, it is a burlesque of the popular late eighteenth-century literature of picturesque travel to which Wordsworth's *An Evening Walk* and *Descriptive Sketches* are closely related. In its general conception Combe's poem reflects the work of such writers of picturesque travel poetry as Anthony Champion, Thomas Maude, and George Cumberland; the central figure, Dr. Syntax, is a caricature of William Gilpin, Rector of Boldre, who has been fittingly called "the high priest of the picturesque."[2] George Crabbe reacted to this literature with a grim realism which a hundred years later won Edwin Arlington Robinson's admiration; Combe reacted with a satire conveyed primarily through his character, Dr. Syntax, whose excessive fastidiousness and sublimity of taste cause him to reject and suppress the disturbing truths which Crabbe fastened upon. Dr. Syntax is the very quintessence of the artist in search of the picturesque, the artist who, in order to achieve the picturesque, must take liberties with the actuality before him, blinding himself to that which offends his taste and freely substituting from his imagination that which will heighten his gratification, thus forcing the observed reality into a preconceived ideal pattern of the picturesque. "What man of taste," Dr Syntax asks,

> my right will doubt,
> To put things in, or leave them out?
> 'Tis more than right, it is a duty,
> If we consider landscape beauty:
> He ne'er will as an artist shine,
> Who copies Nature line by line.[3]

According to Combe, this character stems from the mock-heroic tradition; in Canto XII of the first tour, he wrote:

> You'll see, at once, in this Divine,
> Quixote and Parson Adams shine:
> An hero well combin'd you'll view
> FOR FIELDING and CERVANTES too. (p. 41)

Certainly in structure, the Dr. Syntax poems are a derivative of the knight errant tradition on which *Don Quixote* is built, but, despite the doctor's encounter with highwaymen which is in the same vein as the battle with the huntsman's hounds in *Joseph Andrews*, very little of the mock-heroic actually appears in the series. An important difference between Don Quixote and Dr. Syntax is that Cervantes' character is deranged, totally dissociated from the actuality through which he moves; the doctor perceives the actuality, but for reasons of taste ignores some aspects of it and, ignorant of worldly matters, fails to understand others. Instead, in his extreme sentimentality and his frequent soliloquies upon picturesque or melancholy scenes, he is much closer to Mr. Yorick of Sterne's *Sentimental Journey.*

The popularity of Dr. Syntax and his adventures is demonstrated not only by the frequent editions and reprints but also by the extent to which subsequent humorists resorted to them for guidance in shaping their own burlesques of travel literature. Apparently it was not so much the doctor's pretense to refined taste and sentiment which attracted the later humorists as it was the comic possibilities inherent in the coupling of this attitude with his artistic and scientific aspirations. Armed with sketchbook and notebook, the doctor traveled about England ever ready to preserve the picturesque scene which fluttered his pulse or the "curious" information which excited his mind. As a result of this combination, a third dimension, as it were, could be added to the burlesque. Not only is the reader moved to laughter by the contrast between the traveler's expectations and the actuality encountered; he is also moved to laughter by the traveler's subsequent interpretations in the form of wretched poetry, crude drawings, or fantastic scientific theories. A host of similar travelers each equipped with sketchbook or notebook or both and eager to present the results of his travels to the reading public, crowd the pages of the British comic magazines down through the first twenty years of *Punch*, that is, from the 1840s to the 1860s, and appear in such less well-known humor magazines as *Fun, Judy,* and *Punch and Judy.* But only two of Dr. Syntax's progeny, Thackeray's Michael Angelo Titmarsh and Dickens' Mr Samuel Pickwick, P.C., have won a permanent place in literature.[4]

Imitative of the British periodicals, the American humor magazines also afford several examples of the type. Generally, the American humorists appear to have modelled their work after the current British burlesques, without any direct reference to the original tours of Dr. Syntax, but in at least one instance the American by-passed the contemporary British examples and returned directly to Combe's work. In the first issue of his *Illustrated California Magazine* (1856), J. M. Hutchings began a burlesque entitled "Dr. Dotitdown in Search of the Picturesque, Arabesque, Grotesque, and Burlesque." The title contains, of course, references to Combe's *Tour of Dr. Syntax in Search of the Picturesque* and to Poe's *Tales of the Grotesque and Arabesque.*

By the 1860s Combe's conception had undergone several mutations. One was the very early abandonment of his doggerel verse in favor of prose; another was the addition of a traveling companion who bears a distant relationship to Sancho Panza, a more immediate one to Sam Weller. A vernacular character, this companion, usually a servant or a young relative or family friend, serves a function slightly different from Sancho Panza's. As far as the reader is concerned, one of Sancho's major services is to report the actuality which the Knight, because of his delusions, cannot see. The companion of the nineteenth-century burlesque constantly reminds the reader and the traveler himself of those unpicturesque elements of the actuality which the traveler has chosen to ignore and contributes a knowledge, sometimes surprisingly full for one of his years, in those fields where the traveler in his innocence, is totally uninitiated: the properties of a wide variety of strong beverages, the wiles of worldly women, the art of gambling, and the devices of a wide variety of tricksters, swindlers, and other petty criminals. With predilections for such activities as those indicated by his knowledge, the companion is the major source of conflict for the traveler. With the emergence of the companion, this type of burlesque, some fifty years after Dr. Syntax first set out on his sway-backed mare, had become fairly conventional: the traveler is a refined and sophisticated gentleman bent upon studying art, discovering sources for other ponds of Hampstead, or devising further theories of tittlebats; his companion is his antithesis in taste, sentiments, and interests; their itinerary takes the pair to scientific wonders, monuments of antiquity, or paintings of the Masters; and a series of arguments and mishaps, precipitated by the companion, disappoint or deflate the gentleman's expectations.

The conventional character of these burlesques is suggested not only by the frequent reappearance of the same elements but also by the failure of the British magazines to keep pace with developments in travel literature. Long after the focus of interest in travel books had shifted from the haunts of the Romantics in Italy, France, and Germany, to scenes of intrepid adventure in the Near East, the Orient, Africa, and the western United States, the travelers in the burlesques still studied their art in the Louvre and the Capitol and sought the picturesque in the Lake District, the Rhine Valley, the Black Forest, and the Harz Mountains. The result, in the British magazines of the 1860s, was a dissociation of the burlesques from the literature upon which they should have fed, with a consequent loss of vitality which is reflected in the mutation of the central character, who is reduced from a caricature of the sentimental traveler to a simple straightman. No longer mad, not even north-north-west, he has become to a great degree merely the center from which we measure the antics of his ebullient companion and others. The mutation is quite visible in one of the longest of such burlesques, "Our Roving Correspondent," which began in the first issue of *Punch* for 1860. In the July 27, 1861 issue, the refined traveler, Jack Easel, comments upon young female tourists at the Italian art galleries:

> The ease and rapidity with which these charming critics form acquaintance with and discuss the merits of the Old Masters is truly astonishing. I once heard a young lady. . . remark, that she had "done" the Capitol between the hours of breakfast and lunch, adding that she would be able to give me a full description of the Borghese Collection by the time we met at dinner. "*Per Bacco!* Ma'am," I exclaimed—you know we were in Italy, and I always ejaculate, if possible in the language of the country where I am residing—"*per Bacco!* What a muff is your humble servant. Here have I

been spending months in the study of a single gallery and
am half inclined to throw up my profession in despair, at my
ignorance."

Although the comment about ejaculations suggests the
exaggerated sophistication of earlier travelers who did things
"by the book," the passage in general demands that the reader
regard Jack Easel as the standard against which the charming
critics are measured and found wanting.

In the United States the type retained a great deal of its
vitality simply because, while British readers were exploring
the mysteries of the Middle East in such books as Warburton's
The Crescent and the Cross, Curzon's *Monasteries of the
Levant*, and Burton's *A Pilgrimage to Al-Medinah and Meccah*,
the Americans were re-discovering a picturesque Europe in
such books as Sara Jane Lippincott's *Haps and Mishaps of a
Tour in Europe*, Harriet Beecher Stowe's *Sunny Memories of
Foreign Lands*, and Bayard Taylor's *Views A-Foot*. As
Professor Willard Thorp has noted in his study of such
American travel books:

> The less imaginative of the professional writers soon evolved
> a sort of standard pattern for the travel book. The author
> must begin with the excitements of the ocean voyage itself
> and devote at least a portion of a chapter to the thrill, so long
> anticipated, of setting foot on foreign soil. From this point on
> he should mix architecture and scenery. . . , skillfully work
> in a little history. . . , taking care to add a touch of sentiment
> or eloquence when the occasion permitted. If the essay or
> book required a little padding, it was always possible to
> retell an old legend or slip in an account of dangers
> surmounted in crossing the Alps.[5]

That is, the travel books which American writers were
producing lent themselves well to the sort of burlesque
treatment we have been considering; it is not surprising to find
them getting such treatment from Artemus Ward, Petroleum V.
Nasby, J. Ross Browne, and, of course, Mark Twain.

In *The Innocents Abroad*, the most famous burlesque
product of this spate of American travel books, we find Mark

Twain building upon the pattern which Thorp has noted. The first paragraph contains a passage which is, with its alliterations, rhythms, hyperboles, and clichés, at once a revelation of the delusions of the passengers and a parody of the effusive statements of anticipatory thrills in the books upon which it is modelled:

> [The passengers] were to sail for months over the breezy Atlantic and the sunny Mediterranean; they were to scamper about the decks by day, filling the ship with shouts and laughter—or read novels and poetry in the shade of the smoke-stacks, or watch for the jelly-fish and the nautilus, over the side, and the shark, the whale, and other strange monsters of the deep; and at night they were to dance in the open air, on the upper deck, in the midst of a ballroom that stretched from horizon to horizon, and was domed by the bending heavens and lighted by no meaner lamps than the stars and the magnificent moon—dance, and promenade, and smoke, and sing, and make love, and search the skies for constellations that never associate with the "Big Dipper" they were so tired of: and they were to see the ships of twenty navies—the customs and costumes of twenty curious peoples—the great cities of half a world—they were to hobnob with nobility and hold friendly converse with kings and princes, Grand Moguls, and the anointed lords of mighty empires!

But although *The Innocents Abroad* is a burlesque of travel literature, the controlling fiction of the conventional Dr. Syntax type of burlesque, the conflict between a sentimental traveler and his irrepressible companion, is missing, or rather is subordinated to such an extent that it appears only in occasional episodes.

The Innocents Abroad is actually an intermediate stage in a series of experiments through which Twain gradually shaped the burlesque conventions to his own artistic purposes. The first stage in the sequence dates from 1866, when Twain built the controlling fiction of his Sandwich Islands letters directly upon the conventional traveler-companion conflict. Adopting for these letters the pose of Mr.

Twain, a traveler with all the sensibilities and most of the aspirations of Dr. Syntax, and creating a companion, Mr. Brown, as bitter an enemy to sentiment as any of his predecessors, Twain tried to fulfill the two major conditions of his contract with the *Sacramento Union*, that he write a humorous travel sketch and that he furnish factual information about the Hawaiian Islands for the *Union* readers. The attempt to fulfill these two conditions involved Twain directly in a problem inherent in this type of burlesque from its beginnings: how to convey to the reader a clear concept of the actuality which moves the sophisticated traveler to sentimental tears or his companion to snorts of derision. As long as the burlesque is written in the third person, there is no problem. The author, on his own authority, presents the actuality and then permits the two characters to give their interpretations of it. But when, as in the greater portion of the burlesques of this type, the author chooses the first person form of narration, the problem becomes central. Whether he adopts for himself the pose of the traveler or the companion, he must accept as the price a blindness to and ignorance of certain elements in the actuality before him. Of course, he may very easily work in the reactions and interpretations of his associate as, from his point of view, shocking examples of blindness or ignorance, but the reader must discern the actuality for himself somewhere between the two extremes resulting from the traveler's exaggerated sentimentality and the companion's exaggerated skepticism and unregeneracy.

Here we can perceive what may well have been the reason for the failure of the British burlesques to keep pace with the mid-century developments in travel literature. As long as the books being burlesqued dealt with countries which the anticipated audience knew with a fair degree of intimacy, the humorist could depend upon the reader's knowledge to supply the information which his chosen pose prevented him from presenting in the burlesque. But when British travelers pushed on into new and relatively unknown regions, the humorist could not follow unless he forged new tools for his art. Mark Twain faced exactly the same problem, but one cannot say he solved it; he merely ignored the demands of consistency, slipping easily out of his pose to the role of reporter as frequently as he wished, apparently without even asking himself whether such a course indicated Emersonian greatness or artistic weakness.

The letters written for the *Alta Californian* describing Twain's journey from San Francisco to New York by way of the Isthmus in 1866–67 and the *Quaker City* excursion retain the same controlling fiction and exhibit the same disregard for consistency, but in the reworking of these letters for *The Innocents Abroad* Twain took the first major step toward the achievement of *Roughing It* when he attempted to fuse the characteristics of the traveler and his companion in one narrator. The fusion involved him in further difficulties, for this new narrator must exhibit on the one hand the sophistication and sentimentality of the traveler, on the other the uncouthness and insensitivity of the companion, and as necessary the judiciousness of the reporter. Once again he ignored the demands of consistency and let the contradictions stand. For example, his narrator is disdainful of sentimental tears after weeping over the graves of Abelard and Heloise and then learning their history, but he weeps as copiously as either Dr. Syntax or Mr. Yorick when he views Adam's tomb. Then, in order to justify his denunciation of William C. Prime's sentimental tears on the shores of Galilee, Twain must cast his narrator in the role of a clear-eyed and judicious reporter of the observed reality.

In that portion of *Roughing It* which concludes with the departure for the Sandwich Islands, Twain devised a method of reconciling the opposed points of view. *Roughing It* opens with a passage which is both similar to and subtly and significantly different from the statement of anticipatory thrills in the first pages of *The Innocents Abroad*:

> I was young and ignorant, and I envied my brother. I coveted
> his distinction and his financial splendor, but particularly
> and especially the long, strange journey he was going to
> make, and the curious new world he was going to explore.
> He was going to travel! I never had been away from home,
> and that word "travel" had a seductive charm for me. Pretty
> soon he would be hundreds and hundreds of miles away on
> the great plains and deserts, and among the mountains of the
> Far West, and would see buffaloes and Indians, and prairie
> dogs, and antelopes, and have all kinds of adventures, and
> maybe get hanged or scalped, and have ever such a fine time,
> and write home and tell us all about it, and be a hero. And
> he would see the gold mines and the silver mines, and
> maybe go about of an afternoon when his work was done,
> and pick up two or three pailfuls of shining slugs, and
> nuggets of gold and silver on the hillside. And by and by he
> would become very rich, and return home by sea, and be
> able to talk as calmly about San Francisco and the ocean,
> and "the isthmus" as if it was nothing of any consequence to
> have seen those marvels face to face.

The significant difference is in the pronoun used in each
instance. The pronoun *they* in the earlier passage directs the
ridicule toward the other *Quaker City* passengers and to
travelers who write travel books. It implicitly exempts the
narrator himself. The shift in point of view to the first person
in the *Roughing It* passage focuses the ridicule upon the
narrator himself and tends to remove travelers as a class to the
background, if not out of the picture.

A change of plan during the composition of *Roughing It*
reveals Twain's struggle with the problem of the point of view.
On March 4, 1871 he wrote to his brother, Orion, that "right in
the first chapter I have got to alter the whole style of one of my
characters and re-write him clear through to where I am
now."[6] Since the narrator himself is the only character who
appears with sufficient frequency to require the sort of
extensive revision suggested by this comment, the letter
reflects some important discovery Twain had made relative to
the point of view to be used, and his determination to act
upon it.[7] The discovery was made as Twain pored over several

letters he had written to the Keokuk *Gate City* in 1861 and '62 describing his adventures in Nevada, and therefore was apparently connected with them.[8] In these letters, Twain had adopted the pose of an unsophisticated, unregenerate "bitter enemy to sentiment" whose letters home were designed primarily to shatter the illusions of a pious, genteel, and excessively sentimental mother. That is, the relationship between the fictive mother and son in these letters prefigures the Mr. Twain-Mr. Brown relationship of the Sandwich Islands letters.

No evidence exists to indicate clearly the details of Twain's first draft of *Roughing It*, but a logical deduction from the available evidence is that, after the difficulties encountered with the point of view in *The Innocents Abroad*, he had returned to the Mr. Twain-Mr. Brown conflict of the Sandwich Islands and *Alta Californian* letters, patterning his narrator after Mr. Twain and his companion, renamed Bemis, after Mr. Brown. In the finished text, the narrator's gullibility, revealed in his prevision of the journey, and his sentimentality, his predisposition to view things through the "mellow moonshine of romance," are indications of his kinship with Mr. Twain and ultimately with Dr. Syntax.[9] And certainly Bemis exhibits in his infrequent appearances most of the characteristics of Mr. Brown not only when he climaxes the "noble sport" of buffalo hunting ignobly treed by the bull but also when he launches out on his own in Salt Lake City and experiments with a local concoction known as "valley tan" with predictable results. Such traces of the burlesque conventions in the finished text strongly suggest a more fully developed traveler-companion relationship in the first draft, that is, before the revision which Twain described to his brother.

Apparently, then, the *Gate City* letters taught Twain how he could dispense with such a character as Bemis and how he could link the contradictory points of view of a Mr. Twain and a Mr. Brown in the one character. As Professor Henry Nash Smith has demonstrated (p. 212), in the prevision of the journey and in much of the subsequent text "the pronoun 'I' links two quite different personae: the tenderfoot setting out across the Plains, and the old-timer, the veteran, who has seen the elephant and now looks back upon his own callow days of inexperience." Sophisticated and sentimental at the outset, the narrator's romantic expectations are shattered by the experiences of his journey and residence in the mining districts of Nevada. Envisioned at first as a character analogous to Mr. Twain, the narrator is transformed by his experiences into a character analogous to Mr. Brown.

Such a manipulation of the point of view, in itself a relatively simple affair, has enormous consequences for the art of that fiction which strives to build the illusion of objective reality. Stendahl's contribution to the development of literary realism, according to Erich Auerbach, is the technique of placing fictive characters in an externally real historical and social continuum: "Insofar as the serious realism of modern times," he declares, "cannot represent man otherwise than as embedded in a total reality, political, social, and economic, which is concrete and constantly evolving. . . Stendahl is its founder."[10] To the sort of time-perspective exploited by Stendahl, Twain added an internal time-perspective gained by the evolution of his narrator from tenderfoot to old-timer, an evolution which is implicit in the point of view from the very beginning of the narrative when, in introducing the tenderfoot's prevision of the journey, the old-timer comments, "I was young and ignorant." A great deal of the verisimilitude in the subsequent narrative derives from this manipulation of the point of view. By presenting the tenderfoot's prevision in a burlesque tone and coupling with it the old-timer's explicit disdain of his youthful folly, Twain predisposes the reader to a willing suspension of disbelief when the reader encounters the fictive reality which has transformed the tenderfoot into old-timer and upon which the old-timer bases his judgment. As far as the reader is concerned, the technique contributes materially to the obscuring of the distinctions between the fictive world in which the narrator moves and the external reality of travel across the Plains and life in the silver-mining regions of Nevada in the early 1860s.

The internal time-perspective, the movement from youthful delusion to mature skepticism, is not the only important consequence of the change in point of view. The movement is one in space as well as in time, almost literally a journey along a road to reality, and the wisdom of the old-timer results not so much from the time elapsed since he started out on his journey as it does from his removal from one geographical region to another and his consequent initiation, as Professor Smith has noted, into a new society, the society of the mining regions (p. 214–219). The shift in the point of view has produced a shift in the nature of the conflict which now becomes an internal one based on the differences between the mores of the East and those of the West. Bearing with him on his journey not only the heritage of his youth in the eastern United States but also highly erroneous concepts gleaned from his readings about the West, the tenderfoot must learn to adjust to the mores of the new society before he can become the old-timer. The insecurity, the humiliation, and occasionally the danger attendant upon actions performed and attitudes revealed while one is ignorant of the basic rules of the "curious new world" in which he finds himself are at the heart of the first thirty-three chapters, that is, to the point where the introduction of a new tenderfoot, General Buncombe, signals the narrator's own emergence into the community of old-timers. One humorous illustration of this inner conflict is the narrator's encounter with the desperado Slade:

> The coffee ran out. At last it was reduced to one tincupful, and Slade was about to take it when he saw that my cup was empty. He politely offered to fill it, but although I wanted it, I politely declined. I was afraid he had not killed anybody that morning, and might be needing diversion. But still with firm politeness he insisted on filling my cup, and said I had traveled all night and better deserved it than he—and while he talked he placidly poured the fluid, to the last drop. I thanked him and drank it, but it gave me no comfort, for I

could not feel sure that he would not be sorry, presently,
that he had given it away, and proceed to kill me to distract
his thoughts from the loss.

As a further consequence of the shift in point of view,
Twain transformed burlesque into a remarkable effective
fictive representation of the experience of those sensitive
Americans whose adult lives spanned the Civil War years.
With basic convictions, often excessively optimistic, formed in
the pre-Civil War era, such Americans suffered a most intense
disillusionment in the post-war era while at the same time
they gained the sobered maturity of, say, the Walt Whitman of
"Out of the Cradle Endlessly Rocking." Vernon L. Parrington
was correct when, in opening his discussion of Mark Twain in
the third volume of his *Main Currents*, he identified the
narrator of *Roughing It* as the image of the post-Civil War
American. Certainly Twain's old-timer is as powerful an image
for this period as Cooper's Natty Bumppo is for the former. But
Parrington was quite wrong when he chose the tenderfoot's
brief spree in stock speculation to epitomize the American of
the Gilded Age. The American whom Twain epitomized with
the narrator of *Roughing It* is one who, nurtured in one
culture, suddenly finds himself faced with the necessity of
adjusting to another, or succumbing. One indication of the
accuracy of Twain's image appears in the parallel between the
narrator of *Roughing It* and the Henry Adams of *The
Education*. What Twain achieved with the two personae
merged in the pronoun "I," Adams achieved by writing his
autobiography in the third person: the detachment and
distance of the educated Adams from the Henry Adams who
was undergoing the painful and seemingly fruitless education.
Like Twain's old-timer, the Henry Adams of the twentieth
century looks back with disdain upon what it pleased him to
call his deluded "eighteenth-century youth," chronicles the
events which produced the maturity, and reveals what is
implicit in Twain's narrative, the loss as well as the gain of
education. Although we can perceive it in the book, Twain did
not make much of the point that the gaining of maturity

necessarily involves a loss of that freedom from reality upon which the romantic imagination is based. The point is, nevertheless, implicit in the *Weekly Occidental* episode which occupies a rather prominent place toward the end of the adventures in Nevada. In this episode, the narrator and several fellow old-timers attempt to write a "sensation" novel in installments for their literary weekly. But the narrator and his fellow novelists are totally unable to produce such flights of the imagination as those upon which the tenderfoot's preconception of the Far West had been based. Later, in *Old Times on the Mississippi*, Twain was more explicit. Commenting upon the results of the cub's education as a river pilot, he wrote,

> Now when I had mastered the language of this water and had come to know every trifling feature that bordered the great river as familiarly as I knew the letters of the alphabet, I had made a valuable acquisition. But I had lost something, too. I had lost something which could never be restored to me while I lived. All the grace, the beauty, the poetry, had gone out of the majestic river!

The hero which Twain thus developed differs somewhat from the Young Man from the Provinces, whom Professor Lionel Trilling discerned as the defining hero in "a great line of novels" running "through the nineteenth-century as . . . the very backbone of its fiction." Professor Trilling describes the Young Man as one who "need not come from the provinces in literal fact, his social class may constitute his province. But a provincial birth and rearing suggest the simplicity and the high hopes he begins with—he starts with a great demand upon life and a great wonder about its complexity and promise. He may be of good family but he must be poor. He is intelligent, or at least aware, but not at all shrewd in worldly matters. He must have acquired a certain amount of education, should have learned something about life from books, although not the truth."[11] Twain's hero differs primarily in the assurance which is his as a result of his illusions. Confident of his superiority, or at least of his equality, in ability, social station, and sophistication, he eagerly embarks upon a penetration into a strange society, only to be exposed by his very illusions in a series of experiences to the painful truth that he has been deluded, that he must discard his previous self-conception. The successful learning of this lesson, although it involves the loss of youthful ebullience, brings mature self-knowledge.

All this is to say that the conflict which Twain developed from the mutation of the burlesque conventions anticipates that of the international novel later developed by Henry James, which Professor Oscar Cargill had defined as a novel "in which a character, usually guided in his actions by the mores of one environment, is set down in another, where his learned reflexes are of no use to him, where he must employ all his individual resources to meet successive situations, and where he must intelligently accommodate himself to the new mores, or, in one way or another, be destroyed."[12] The anticipation suggests a relatively close bond between Twain and James. But the closeness is obscured by Professor Cargill's failure to stress in his definition two essential elements: the initial illusory self-conception which precipitates a course of action leading toward an anticipated conquest in the new society, and the self-discovery resulting from the disappointment of his hopes.

Twain took the comic view; James, the tragic, first in *The American*. In doing so James created a character, Christopher Newman, whose attitudes, background, and even physical appearance are close enough to those of Twain or his fictive counterparts in *The Innocents Abroad* and *Roughing It* to cause the reader to suspect a direct indebtedness. James, of course, gave to the theme perhaps its most embracing significance when almost as if he were retelling the story of Hawthorne's Miriam, he took another American innocent, Isabel Archer, along the road that led to Rome. "Rome was actual," Henry Adams discovered on the eve of the Civil War: to him Rome meant the first painful realization of the enchainment, the confinement of the romantic imagination, the anchoring of a soaring idealism to the hard and heavy facts of actuality. To Isabel, Rome finally signifies substantially the same thing. Envisioning happiness, at the outset of her European adventures, as dashing over a strange road in a coach and four on a dark night, so self-confident and assured of a special destiny that she refuses Lord Warburton with but little trepidation, she discovers herself in Rome married to Gilbert Osmond, confined to a "dark narrow alley with a blind wall at the end." Rome is indeed the actual for her when she turns away from Caspar Goodwood's impassioned embrace to follow the "very straight path" back to Osmond.

When we recall the differences between the two writers, the fact that James was impelled to express in his fiction a theme almost identical with Twain's attests to the accuracy and, one might almost say, the universality of the image of the American evoked by the mutation of the burlesque conventions in Twain's *Roughing It.*

Notes

1. At least ten English editions and reprints appeared between 1821 and 1868.

2. Christopher Hussey, *The Picturesque* (London and New York, 1927), 111.

3. *Doctor Syntax's Tree Tours* (London, 1868), 7.

4. Franklin R. Rogers, *Mark Twain's Burlesque Patterns* (Dallas, 1960) 30–35. Further information, especially on Combe's influence on *The Pickwick Papers*, appears in Wilhelm Dibelius, "Zu den Pickwick Papers," *Angliz* XXXV (1912), 101–110.

5. "Pilgrim's Return," *Literary History of the United States*, ed. Robert E. Spiller, et al. (New York, 1953), 831.

6. *Mark Twain's Letters*, ed. A.B. Paine (New York and London, 1917), I 186.

7. On this question see also Henry Nash Smith, "Mark Twain as an Interpreter of the Far West: The Structure of *Roughing It*," *The Frontier in Perspective*, ed. Walker D. Wyman and Clifton B. Kroeber (Madison, 1958), 210, and Martin B. Fried, "The Sources, Composition, and Popularity of Mark Twain's *Roughing It*," unpublished Ph.D. dissertation (Chicago, 1951), 16.

8. Franklin R. Rogers, *The Pattern for Mark Twain's Roughing It: Letters from Nevada by Samuel and Orion Clemens, 1861–1862* (Berkeley, 1961), 19–21.

9. Rogers, *Mark Twain's Burlesque Patterns*, 61–66.

10. *Mimesis: The Representation of Reality in Western Literature* (New York, 1957), 408.

11. Lionel Trilling, "The Princess Casamassima," *The Liberal Imagination* (New York, 1950), 61.

12. Oscar Cargill, "The First International Novel." *PMLA* LXXII (Sept., 1958), 419.

From the Old Southwest

Pascal Covici, Jr.

I

Mark Twain's relationship to the humor of his region is probably less direct than it is usually thought to be. That the humor of the old Southwest is indeed part of his heritage can be, and has been, demonstrated; the proposition is by now axiomatic. Mark Twain transcends this tradition. Faced with the literary problem of presenting many of the themes and moods that in various ways attracted such diverse minds as Poe, Hawthorne, Melville, Henry James, and Henry Adams, Twain, to be sure, found solutions different from theirs. But this difference is not to be measured solely by the scale of Twain's adherence to the models of his southwestern predecessors.

Nevertheless, to understand Mark Twain's use of humor is, at least partly, to put oneself in tune with the early frontier and western humor of America. Many scholars, among them Franklin Meine, Mody C. Boatright, Bernard DeVoto, and, most recently, Kenneth S. Lynn, have shown in a multitude of ways how oral humor became more than mere pastime for hunters and keelboatmen confronting violence and loneliness and for any raw westerner confronting the snickering East. Such personal uses of humor only gradually became literary,

Reprinted from *Mark Twain's Humor: The Image of a World* (Dallas: Southern Methodist U. P., 1962), pp. 3–36, 257–8.

however, for the literate tellers of tales in the pre-Civil War Southwest almost without exception were newcomers to the regions in which their stories were set. As a result, they were moved by compulsions different from those of the "natives." Lawyers, judges, and doctors, educated on the Atlantic seaboard and suddenly thrust into the continent, they looked with wonder at the "manners, customs, amusements, wit, dialect" so different from what they had left behind.

The stories that flowed from this wonderment were largely organized around two impulses: a need to belittle and a desire to report. The gentlemen from the East looked upon their presence in the West—Alabama, Georgia, Mississippi—as a blessing to the barbarous natives from whom the Gentleman must always be careful to distinguish himself, at least in print. The lawyer might slap backs all he chose, but his duty was to make sure that the barbarian knew his place, that the political and economic fortunes of the new country were safeguarded by his own kind from public ravishment. An illuminating and just emphasis is Kenneth Lynn's on the political bias revealed through the framework of countless yarns in which a "Self-controlled Gentleman"[1] presents the actions of an uncouth lout. Lout and gentleman are separated by dialect as well as by action; there is no chance that a reader might confuse the two.

This need of gentlemanly authors to establish a moral and cultural distance between themselves and the places where they earned their living was at one with, and perhaps even helped to develop, the second impulse behind the humorous tales of the Southwest, that of realistic description. A writer who views his environment from a distance is less likely to take that environment for granted than is one wrapped up in the mores of the people he is observing. The living habits of the folk—how they talk, the pranks they play, what interests them—will seem worth reporting in proportion to their variation from the "normal" life left behind. One can see now that the striving for objectivity implicit in the aim of setting down the oddities of a new sort of civilization—or lack of one—clashed with the feeling of superiority so meticulously cultivated by the writers. Brutality and coarseness were blown up out of all proportion in order to solidify the position of the detached witness; most of the events narrated could never have been enacted by mere human beings: the half-horse, half-alligator men of the Mississippi, in fact, a whole menagerie of frontier titans, were used to accommodate the Gentleman's need for low behavior from which to disassociate himself.

But beneath the violence and exaggeration of mid-nineteenth-century southwestern humor there lies an impulse toward realism, toward a faithful presentation of the life of the region. Repeatedly, the stories about Simon Suggs, Sut Lovingood, Major Jones, and their picaresque brethren are introduced as offering intimate knowledge of a particular locality and its particular citizens. William Tappan Thompson, as he says in his preface to *Major Jones's Chronicles of Pineville* (1843), "endeavored, in a small way, to catch [the Georgia "cracker's"] 'manners living as they rise'. . . I claim no higher character for my stories" than that they present "a glance at characters not often found in books, or anywhere else, indeed, except in just such places as '*Pineville*,' Georgia." The vividness with which the frontier and the backwoods live for Americans today is at least partial testimony to the realistic bent of Thompson and his fellows. Although they dealt in exaggeration, tall tales, impossible violence, satire, and other distortions of reality, their intention to be faithful to the felt quality of life in their region cannot be mistaken.

The realism in the stories of George Washington Harris, W.T. Thompson, Augustus Longstreet, Johnson J. Hooper, et al. implies more than close observation and a nice ear for the spoken word. The expressed intention "to supply. . . the manners, customs, amusement, wit, dialect, as they appear in all grades of society to an ear and eye witness of them"[2] yielded time and again to the more subtle, less often articulated, pressure to crack the local yokels, or the damn-yankees, on their presumptuous and ill-bred snouts. The content of these satiric thrusts was apt to be anything but realism, narrowly considered, yet the distance, or disengagement, from local life that provided the perspective for satire also fostered the careful reporting of minute detail. But no sense of a transcendental oversoul, infusing both squatter and sophisticate, pervades the realism of the Southwest. Although the writers described the commonplace, they did not, with Emerson, embrace it. The effect of their stories upon a reader is to insulate him from any emotional involvement or identification with events, characters, or region.

These pre-Howells realists present the externals of action and dialogue. Had they explored through their fiction interior states of being or even acknowledged through analysis the existence of human feeling in their characters, we could not laugh at the predicaments set before us. A concern limited to the realistic surface of behavior is made almost obligatory in the case of the southwestern humorists by the nature of the humor which the "school" employed. If a reader is asked to respond to victimized protagonists, or to protagonists' victims, as though they were of the same flesh and spirit as himself, he is not going to laugh as he watches their cruel and exaggerated suffering. When Sut Lovingood leaves half of his skin stuck to his shirt by some newfangled, gluelike starch, one can laugh only if Sut is nothing more than the "nat'ral born durn'fool" he represents himself to be. The quality of Sut's humanity is so removed from ours that the distance between the two is never bridged, nor was it meant to be. On the other hand, were Huck Finn to be comparably flayed, the reader would wince, not smile; no one laughs when Nigger Jim is bitten by a snake, or when Huck hides out from the Shepherdsons by climbing a tree.

The realism of the southwestern humorists consists, then, of content—a report on what life looks like in the sticks—and of an aesthetic distance, or psychological detachment, from the object of scrutiny. The juxtaposition of educated gentry and boorish locale goes far toward accounting for the content and the attitude that shaped so much of the writing which poured out of the region. But the seeds of this village realism in a still more important way came from outside, just as did the writers themselves. Behind the attitude of objective disdain lies an assumption right out of the rationalistic eighteenth century: that a man of common sense can distinguish truth from falsehood, reality from appearance, can know what is right, can see with clarity and dispassion the world around him. The unambiguous treatment of material reinforces the epistemology of realism: direct sense-impressions are to be trusted; what seems to be, is.

For the reader who aligns himself with the rational author, the world is no mystery. Sut Lovingood shatters the slumber of an unwelcome intruder by tying a nine-foot length of intestines to the man's shirttail: the terrified "snake-bit Irishman" lights out for home, convinced that "'a big copper-headed black rattil-snake is crawlin up [his] britches,'"[3] but the reader never for a moment needs to doubt the reliability of his own senses. The boorish victims, on the other hand, repeatedly suffer from an inability to distinguish between the real and the pretended, for the discrepancy between what seems to be and what actually exists forms the crux of numerous pranks perpetrated by southwestern scalawags. It is not only Simon Suggs among them whose "whole ethical system lies snugly in his favorite aphorism—'IT IS GOOD TO BE SHIFTY IN A NEW COUNTRY.'"[4] Repeatedly, characters are victimized because they fail to recognize that "reality" has been altered for their special benefit. William Tappan Thompson's "How to Kill Two Birds with One Stone"[5] ironically applauds young lawyer Jenkins' wisdom in persuading two men that each has stolen from the other when the lawyer himself has hidden Si Perkins' wagon in Absalom Harley's cellar, in turn loading Si's wagon with Harley's bacon and other articles, in order to foment a double lawsuit and pocket double fees. The ruse works perfectly, and the reader appreciates with a Whig's awareness the "democratic" acuteness of Thomas Jefferson Jenkins while condemning with a laugh the litigious pretensions of his victims. The characters are fooled; the reader is not.

The refined reader is encouraged to trust his sense of ethics as well as his sense of what is real. The behavior of the fictional characters is held up against an implicit standard accessible to all men of reason. Again, simply the surface of what happens, the mere action, speech, and setting as they impinge upon the senses of the realist, is adequate to the purpose of the writers. What really counts is "manners"; the way in which the characters act is of more import than what they do or why they do it. When Sut Lovingood works himself into that fancily-starched shirt which subsequently rips the hide off him, he isn't being unethical, but, rather, pretentious. His pretensions to city grandeur do not mesh with his backwoods ignorance, and one laughs because Sut is ridiculous.

If there is any one pattern basic to the humor of the Southwest it is precisely this: a character is pushed by the author into a situation in which he either exposes the pretensions of others or himself emerges as ridiculous because of his pretentious behavior. The eighteenth-century concept of decorum comes to mind in this connection; what is being criticized more often than not is a failure to adhere to the standards of a cultivated civilization, a failure—so annoyingly common in raw, frontier democracy—to recognize and to accept one's inferior position in society. By considering himself to be as good as the next man, the country democrat becomes pretentious, at least in the eyes of the transplanted easterners whose aloof standards shaped the Southwest humor of the nineteenth century.

The satire embedded in this humor is a satire of the ridiculous, which means that when we talk about the humor of the American Southwest we are really talking about the kind of humor described by Henry Fielding in his preface to *Joseph Andrews*, the humor of eighteenth-century England. The tales so often and so delightfully anthologized that Americans think of as so particularly their own are American in content but English in theory and in organization. Through affectation, "the only source of the true ridiculous," according to Fielding, characters are made into figures of fun. Sometimes the affectation is motivated by vanity, "which puts us on affecting false characters, in order to purchase applause," sometimes by hypocrisy, which "sets us on an endeavor to avoid censure by concealing our vices under an appearance of their opposite virtues." Hypocrisy and vanity—under which headings outsiders could lump almost all attempts to transcend the unmannerly boorishness of a frontier community—lead to affected behavior, and "from the discovery of this affectation arises the Ridiculous—which always strikes the reader with surprise and pleasure." Fielding had no need to add that the reader's pleasure depends on his identifying with the objective viewer rather than with the vain or hypocritical character, for the very attribution of vanity or hypocrisy automatically establishes the proper aesthetic distance between author and reader on the one hand, ridiculous character on the other.

A careful reading of southwestern "American" humor will give substance to the suggestion that this particularly American tradition is in fact derived explicitly from English theory and practice of the eighteenth century. Hooper, Harris, Thompson, and others show a keen sense of the ridiculous as Fielding defines it. Repeatedly, their humor embodies Fielding's contention that "from affectation only, the misfortunes and calamities of life, or the imperfections of nature, may become the objects of ridicule." The victims of Simon Suggs's camp meeting, for example, endure considerable misfortune and calamity when the worthy Captain rides off with the dollars they have donated toward his pretended efforts to establish a church. One might expect to find a reader's sympathies aroused for the swindled congregation, but, instead, one finds oneself chuckling along with wicked old Simon as he canters off at the end of the story. Simon's victims are ridiculous, not because of what they are, necessarily, but rather because the reader has been made to observe them from the point of view of a refined and rational being.

As Hooper leads his reader into the camp meeting, he first describes realistically and objectively the various kinds of religious hysteria manifested by the throng. Then he kills off any incipient identification with the masses that may have sprung up in the reader's open mind: "The great object of all seemed to be, to see who could make the greatest noise—

> 'And each—for madness ruled the hour—
> Would try his own expressive power.'"[6]

One of the ministers, under the guise of religious zeal, is "lavishing caresses" upon the prettier among the young women. The Negro woman who is most profoundly moved by religious emotion is "huge" and "greasy," adjectives which cast doubt on the delicacy of her spiritual awakening. The minister to whom Simon attributes his spectacular—though bogus—conversion is a presumptuous ass; the whole crew get what's coming to them.

> "I-I-I can bring' em!" cried the preacher. . . in a tone of exultation—"Lord thou knows ef thy servant can't stir'em, nobody else needn't try—but the glory aint mine! I'm a poor worrum of the dust," he added, with ill-managed affectation.[7]

Affectation renders the people ridiculous and permits one to laugh at them. At the very moment when Simon is cajoling them into contributing money so that he can found a church "in his own neighborhood" and "make himself useful as soon as he could prepare himself for the ministry," his smooth talk is aimed not at their religious enthusiasm but at their desire to appear wealthy and generous before their neighbors: "Simon had excited the pride of purse of the congregation, and a very handsome sum was collected in a very short time."[8]

Nineteenth-century Americans not only ridiculed the affectations of louts, but also went still farther into eighteenth-century English practice when aiming at more specific targets.

By pretending that the object of attack was simply affecting the qualities that made him dangerous—courage, intelligence, power, or whatever—Jonathan Swift, and many others, could cut their enemies down to size, denying in the process that the enemy was worth taking seriously in the first place. George Washington Harris, for one, borrows a page from Swift when he recounts Sut Lovingood's travels with "Old Abe Linkhorn"[9] in a way that "diminishes" Lincoln to the disappearing point. The leader of the antislavery faction so inimical to Harris is too stupid to be dangerous, too cowardly to be feared. Moreover, his ugliness is inhuman enough to suggest that he can be disposed of as easily as any other harmless amphibious reptile:

> I ketched a ole bullfrog once [says Sut] and drove a nail through his lips into a post, tied two rocks to his hind toes and stuck a darnin needle into his tail to let out the moisture, and left him there to dry. I seen him two weeks after'ards: and, when I seen old Abe, I thought it were an awful retribution come onto me, and that it were the same frog—. . . same shape same color same feel (cold as ice), and I'm damned if it ain't the same smell.[10]

This technique of belittling the object of attack is by no means limited to eighteenth-century England but belongs to a tradition of literary satire familiar to any classically educated American of the nineteenth century. Since *meiosis*,* whether

---

*The "technique of rendering devils flabby is a common literary device which was discussed in rhetorical handbooks under the Greek title *meiosis,* meaning, literally, 'belittling' or 'diminuation.' Diminuation may be described briefly as the use of any 'ugly or homely images' which are intended to diminish the dignity of an object. . . diminuation is any kind of speech which tends, either by the force of low or vulgar imagery, or by other suggestion, to depress an object below its usually accepted status." (John M. Bullitt, *Jonathan Swift and the Anatomy of Satire: A Study of Satiric Technique* [Cambridge: Harvard University Press, 1953], p. 45.)

applied to northern Presidents or backwoods boobs, was so frequently and deliberately and even characteristically employed, it is fair to say that no matter how firmly anchored to American experience their lives and writings might be, the pre-Civil War humorists of the Southwest had at least one eye on foreign literary sources.

II

The characteristics of southwestern humor, then, are those of realism in content and in epistemology. Even the satirical intentions behind the humor call upon the reader to agree to the existence of clearly defined standards, identically visible to all thinking men. Instead of the moral hesitancies to be found on a frontier where old codes are daily called in question by the exigencies of a new life, this humor reflects the bland assurance of eighteenth-century men of reason that the cultivated mind can measure all things.

But to Mark Twain there was little, if any, validity in the realistic assumptions behind the humor of the frontier. When, in *Mark Twain at Work,*[11] Bernard DeVoto asserts that Twain's aim in writing *Huckleberry Finn* was to record life by the banks of the Mississippi, his comment is less applicable to the complex and ambiguous novel Twain wrote than to the literary tradition from which most of Twain's work emerges. Twain uses the materials of realism—the events and objects of the daily life of the region—but in a way that Americanizes American humor and puts it more closely in touch with the metaphysical facts of life in a new land and in our modern world: his effects do not, ultimately, depend on a detached objectivity that permits the reader to look upon scoundrels and boors as nonhuman beasts of no importance, or on a sense of the ridiculous as it arises from affectation, but, instead, on a knowledge—paid for by experience—that human reason is cruelly limited, too often unable to discriminate between what is and what seems; that the shibboleths of one generation are the jests of another; and that the powers of irrationality, rather than the deliberate exercise of will, make people appear to be other than what they are.

This is, to be sure, taking humor seriously. Yet even in the simplest episodes of Twain's narrative humor lies the basis for such a contrast between what Twain does and what his predecessors did with similar raw material. In Chapter XX of *Huckleberry Finn* (1885), the king attends a camp meeting at Pokerville much like the one to which Johnson J. Hooper had sent Simon Suggs forty years earlier. Both meetings are minutely described, and both congregations are subtly robbed. The essential difference is between the frailties that in each case lead the people to allow themselves to be cheated. Simon Suggs defrauds those who are guilty of affectation: the laity are purse-proud, and the clergy are concerned either with taking up the collection or with hugging the prettiest girls. Simon's benefactors give money to create the impression of wealth; their show of pious charity is transparently hypocritical and vain, and they are made to seem ridiculous because of affectation. Mark Twain's king exploits a very different sort of meeting: his victims, not "ridiculous through affectation," neither hypocritical nor vain, are victimized because they share humanity's penchant for romantic excitement. The king, improbably representing himself as a pirate, succeeds completely in taking in the communicants because they want to believe that an Indian Ocean pirate could brush against their own dull lives. In exchange for this fatuous belief they are willing to pay their money: "The king said. . . it warn't no use talking, heathens don't amount to shucks alongside of pirates to work a camp-meeting with" (XIII,184–85).[12] This has nothing to do with vanity or hypocrisy—and, therefore, has no connection with affectation, either. The gulled ones are just as charitable and religious as their actions suggest, but they are motivated less by charity and zeal than by their desire to share in a sensation. This, however, they do not know about themselves. In contrast to the earlier tradition, the people of

Pokerville are not trying to appear to be what they are not. Rather, they are by their very nature other than they seem.

Mark Twain's fictional world is different from that of his immediate regional predecessors because it is organized around a real, and not a contrived, discrepancy between reality and appearance. The orderly and comprehensible universe presided over by the Self-controlled Gentleman is one in which author and readers can all relax together, assured that only those who stand outside their circle can be deceived by the contrived accidents that befall frontier clowns. Sut Lovingood gladly swallows Sicily Burns's "love-potion," with terrific results, but the civilized reader knew all along that it was soda. Such assurance is foreign to the nineteenth-century American fiction most cherished today. Nathaniel Hawthorne's explorations of the effects of sin on the human heart force one to reorganize one's sense of what sin itself is, and Melville's presentation of the Mount of Titans in *Pierre*, and of Moby-Dick himself, compels one to question the seeming beneficence of smiling nature. More to our immediate purpose, Mark Twain, using the materials and surroundings of his southwestern literary progenitors, throws into doubt—as they never do—a reader's complacent evaluation of common sense as applied first to daily human behavior, and finally to man's role in the universe.

Twain's preoccupation with revealing a discrepancy between seeming and reality is central, not peripheral, to his work. A striking example, built from bits of Twain's frontier heritage, is Huck's trip to the circus to counterpoint through humor one of the most somber episodes in *The Adventures of Huckleberry Finn*. In Chapter XXI, Old Boggs, a harmless drunk, is shot down in cold blood by the ruthless but gentlemanly Colonel Sherburn. Huck Finn is the one sympathetic witness of the slaying. An orphan himself, Huck is especially touched by the pathos of Boggs's daughter as she weeps over the dying man. "She was about sixteen, and very sweet and gentle looking, but awful pale and scared." The other witnesses are totally detached. In fact, "the whole town" watches callously as Boggs breathes his last in a drugstore window, a weighty Bible laid upon his chest to ease his departing soul and increase his agony. They might be watching a show, to hear the people farther back from the window talk to those hogging the front row: "'Say, now, you've looked enough, you fellows; 'tain't right and 'tain't fair for you to stay thar all the time, and never give nobody a chance; other folks has their rights as well as you'" (199; all page numbers are to *The Writings of Mark Twain*, "Definitive Ed." NY: Harper, 1922–25).

Huck subsequently (Chapter XXII) watches another drunk at a local circus whose life is endangered not by pistol-fire but by his insistence that he be permitted to attempt equestrian acrobatics. Finally the patient ringmaster acquiesces; amid howls of laughter and derision, the drunk mounts a horse, "his heels flying in the air every jump, and the whole crowd of people standing up shouting and laughing till tears rolled down." The horse breaks loose from the roustabouts, and the drunk seems headed for certain death, to the vast delight of the audience. "It warn't funny to me, though," says Huck; "I was all of a tremble to see his danger" (206). The seeming "drunk" turns out to be a seasoned performer, a member of the circus-troupe who rides like an angel, and the laugh is on naïve Huck Finn, so easily taken in by a circus act. Huck has been sentimental, the reader may feel, in separating himself from the crowd that first jeers, then laughs at the performer. His delicacy of feeling is worthless, for the crowd's callous merriment has injured no feelings. The laughers, indeed, have added to the effect of the circus routine. As for the heartlessness of their instinctive response, well, their sympathies were as unsought as they were unstirred.

But when the reader remembers the similar excitement of this same toughened crowd when it witnessed the murder of Boggs and the drama of his death, he sees that though Huck is naïve, his simple compassion is preferable to the "smart" sensation-seeking of the empty-headed mob. Not only had the people clustered around the store window in which Boggs lay dying, but they also had had the cold-blooded detachment to enjoy a re-enactment of the slaying after the event, even offering their flasks to the "long, lanky man" who "done it perfect . . . just exactly the way it all happened" (200). In each case, Huck's reaction differs from the crowd's. Moreover, Huck's sympathy for Boggs arises from the same qualities of spirit that make Huck a gull at the circus, just as the same shallow craving for excitement motivates the crowd in both instances. Thus, although Huck's attitude at the circus appears to stem from a foolish and valueless naïveté, its true source is his fineness of soul. The reader, therefore, is compelled to reinterpret the "reality" that has been set before him. What has seemed to be and what is are inexorably opposed.

We know that Twain's murder of Boggs is in itself "realistic," for it is "almost without a hairsbreadth of variation" a duplication of Judge John Clemens' account of the shooting of "Uncle Sam" Smarr by William Owsley in Hannibal, when Sam Clemens was just over nine years old.[13] Moreover, the circus incident itself was borrowed from an earlier southwestern writer. What is at issue here, though, is something more than a question of how photographic the writer's memory happens to be. The murder and the circus not only are events in themselves; they also reveal hidden duplicities in the world. The analogue of Twain's circus scene, however, concerns itself with no such opposition between what seems and what is; it never challenges the reader to revise his first impressions. William Tappan Thompson's circus in "The Great Attraction! or The Doctor Most Oudaciously Tuck In"[14] anticipates by some forty years the one Huck attends: in each case, a conventional equestrian act precedes the pseudo-drunken "head-liner"; a witty clown cracks jokes of surpassing cleverness; and then comes the rider who turns out to be sober after all and astonishes his beholders by rising to his feet on the horse's back, then stripping off assorted suits of clothes, "twenty or more" for Thompson's hero, a mere seventeen for Twain's.

The effect of Thompson's circus is considerably simpler than that of Twain's. It appears to be, and it is, a short satire on pretension. Doctor Jones, the unhappy protagonist of the piece, is insufferably impressed with his own sophistication. Denizen of Pineville though he be, he has once visited Augusta, "that Philadelphia of the South," and feels that he is "—to use one of his own polished expressions—'bully of the tan-yard.'"[15] Everything about Augusta is immeasurably superior to whatever Pineville has to offer, and Jones, because of his exposure to the metropolis, includes himself among its wonders. He has seen everything, done everything; and he knows everything, too. When he guides the untutored young ladies of Pineville to their first circus, he assures them that what they are seeing is "nothing to what he had seen in Augusta."

Thompson's attitude toward Jones is one of ironic scorn, as any reader quickly perceives. The Doctor is pretentious. Vanity leads him to affect a sophistication, a *savoir-faire*, that he doesn't really possess, and the circus proves to be his undoing. When the "drunk" tries to ride, thus interrupting the performance, Doctor Jones rushes to the ring, intent on being the hero of the hour. Despite explicit warning by two of the townsfolk that "that chap belongs to the show," he tries valiantly to prevent the ride, only to be rudely rebuked by the clown and finally jostled into the colored section. The Doctor has failed to understand the niceties of circus shenanigans, and so is made a laughingstock, "oudaciously tuck in." Needless to say, the citizens of Pineville rejoice in his downfall. "'Is that the way they does in Augusta?'. . . and a hundred other such jeers" bring both the story and the Doctor's local glory to a close.

Thompson's story is excellently organized and accomplishes the effect that one can assume Thompson meant it to have. Because his aim was not Twain's is no reason to criticize Thompson, whose consciousness of theme is embodied even in his language. Doctor Jones's refinement is called into question by a report of his own coarse epithet for himself—"bully of the tan-yard"—a bit of backwoods lingo echoed in the description of big Bill Sweeney as the rough and tough "bully of the county." Mr. Sweeney, whose place in the story is quite subordinate, shares with Jones the fault of pretentiousness. His pretensions are not to sophistication, however, but to gentility. When he refuses to remove his hat so that others can see the show, the ensuing fracas reveals that he has no right to sit among gentlefolk, just as the main action of the story annuls the Doctor's claims to intellectual supremacy. Both men, each in his different way, have striven to "purchase applause," in Fielding's words, by "affecting false characters." There are no hidden subtleties in the story, no extraneous reverberations. Its satiric impact is obvious and direct. The motives of the characters appear clearly at the start, and one never needs to revise his estimate. This is not true of the king's camp meeting victims or of Huck Finn at his circus.

The two examples of the circus and the camp meeting suggest that although Mark Twain's writing draws upon the traditions and materials utilized by earlier southwestern humorists, its humor goes beyond an exposure of deliberate affectation. In psychological awareness, Twain is closely akin to Melville and Henry James, for he presents human beings as more disposed to misunderstand themselves, as do Pierre and the first-person protagonists of *The Turn of the Screw* and *The Sacred Fount*, than to mislead others deliberately. Consequently, his technique, his literary organization of material, is more concerned with laying bare the human heart than with presenting the rogue's world as it was at a given time and place. Anyone who reads carefully the introduction to the king's camp meeting cannot help but be impressed by the meticulous acuteness of the description, even down to benches "made out of outside slabs of logs, with holes bored in the round side to drive sticks into for legs" (XIII, 181). To say that Twain is not concerned at all with the surface appearance of the life surrounding his characters is clearly to overstate the point. It is his particular use of appearances that sets him off from his humorous predecessors.

III

The most direct way to suggest the unique quality in Twain's use of surface, or reportorial, realism is to turn from specific analogues to a technique as general as the use of spoken language. That Twain cared about reproducing the exact inflections of dialect, and that he was proud of his abilities in this direction, the author's "Explanatory" to *Huckleberry Finn* makes clear. Seven distinct varieties of speech are mentioned, and, we are reminded, "The shadings have not been done in a haphazard fashion. . . but painstakingly, and with the trustworthy guidance and support of personal familiarity with these several forms of speech" (XIII, xxi). Repeatedly he tries to make his people talk as their environment and training might make them talk in real life, adopting the vocabulary and imagery that will most precisely evoke the varieties of backwoods experience.

His westerners, for example, repeatedly speak the language of the poker table, and in this respect they are not alone in nineteenth-century fiction. Poker talk was a common device of local-color characterization in the writings of the transplanted lawyers and judges who found rural Tennessee, Georgia, Alabama, and Mississippi strikingly different from the metropolitan East they had left behind. There were many stories about gamblers in the new country, and the vocabulary of gambling provided a quick metaphorical index to the habits and origins of the speaker. "No matter what sort of a hand you've got. . . take stock!'" exhorts Simon Suggs. "'Here am *I*, the wickedest and blindest of sinners—has spent my whole life in the sarvice of the devil—has now come in on *narry pair* and won a *pile!*'"[16] That Simon presents his recent "conversion" in poker language serves to place him as a backwoods con man; also, one notes the dramatic irony of his words, for Simon's sinful life prior to the camp meeting, his newly-won "pile" as a joyful allusion to God's free grace which Simon appears to be experiencing, whereas the reader is aware that Simon is planning to win a "pile" of money on the strength of his pretended conversion, his bluff "hand" with "narry pair" in it. When he urges unrepentant sinners to join him on the mourners' bench, he reassures them that "'The bluff game aint played here! No runnin' of a body off! Every body holds four aces, and when you bet, you win!'"[17] Summing up his achievement at the end of the story, Simon concludes that "'Ef them fellers aint done to a cracklin, . . . I'll never bet on two pair again!'"[18] The principal effect of this terminology is to present Simon as a cardsharper, willing to gamble on the gullibility of the average man. But this the reader knew from the opening pages of the story. The poker talk has revealed nothing new about the Captain; it is simply part of the author's impulse toward realism, toward presenting the audible surface of the time and place.

In a bit of Mark Twain's earlier writing the same limited effect appears: poker vocabulary denotes the westerner but tells nothing specific about him as a man. Describing a rising river in 1859, Sergeant Fathom "would suggest to the planters, as we say in an innocent little parlor game, commonly called 'draw,' that if they can only 'stand the raise' this time, they may enjoy the comfortable assurance that the old river's banks will never hold a 'full' again during their natural lives."[19] This is an amateur's imitation of a technique: the effort to westernize the speaker is unsupported by dialect, and the humor is heavy-handed. Fathom is a stick figure who never comes to life. But Twain was to discover the possibilities latent in simple speech: the preparations for Buck Fanshaw's funeral in *Roughing It* not only amuse one but present a fully-drawn character as well. Scotty Briggs and the minister converse for seven pages of western slang and eastern elegance where a single page of less characteristic talk might have sufficed, but one finds that Scotty emerges in the round because of the way he talks.

The first stage of the interview presents Scotty's effort to tell the minister that Buck is dead and that the "boys" would appreciate a few comforting words at the funeral."

"'Are you the duck that runs the gospel-mill next door?'" (IV,45) asks Scotty. After the minister counters that he is, rather, "'the spiritual adviser of the little company of believers whose sanctuary adjoins these premises,'" Scotty "scratched his head, reflected a moment, and then said: 'you ruther hold over me, pard. I reckon I can't call that hand. Ante and pass the buck.'"

Scotty's perplexities increase. The minister asks for simpler language, but the request is too complexly worded. "'I'll have to pass, I judge.'" "'How?'" "'You've raised me out, pard'" (46).

Eventually the two understand each other. But the minister wonders about Buck Fanshaw's religious affiliations in language that leads Scotty to complain, "'Why, you're most too many for me, you know. . . Every time you draw, you fill; but I don't seem to have any luck. Let's have a new deal.'" "'How? Begin again?'" "'That's it.'" "'Very well. Was he a good man, and—'" "'There—I see that; don't put up another chip till I look at my hand'" (50).

Apart from giving the western flavor that Twain explicitly means to impart (42–43), poker terminology here accomplishes two ends. First, the metaphoric equation of chips and cards with words ties the episode together by providing a secondary story line. The inability of Scotty and the minister to communicate becomes as much the subject of the brief scene as is the arranging of Buck Fanshaw's funeral. The two confuse each other with their language, and a reader wonders how long their differences of terminology will keep each from "seeing" the other's point. The minister, slick though sickly easterner that he is, keeps on talking, and Scotty is "raised" out of several conversational "pots" by his flow of words. Finally, however, Scotty can "call"—"'I see that'"—and the episode comes to a close with mutual comprehension.

Secondly, Scotty's poker vocabulary displays his character. Never does he try to bluff. He admits the minister's ability to "draw and fill"; he quickly acknowledges the inadequacy of his own "hand"—his comprehension of language—and forthrightly "passes," having been "raised out." When he understands the minister's words—the "bet"—he will "see that," but he wants to "look at [his] hand" before any more chips—words—fall. Scotty's discourse is scrupulously honest and manly; his terms never suggest that he thinks the minister's ignorance is presentation of him as a sympathetic Sunday-school teacher whose rendition in slang of Bible stories "was listened to by his little learners with a consuming interest" (53). The contrast between East and West is clearly presented, but the story differs from most western stories of the time in that the contest and victory are moral and are presented through language, not through violent action: the rough westerner, in the terms of his own rough game, shows himself to be a more honest man than the educated easterner. The language of poker ties Scotty's character and story together into a simple, kindly unit.

Scotty's simplicity of 1871 contrasts with the simple-minded duplicity of Saladin Foster in "The $30,000 Bequest" (1904). The anecdote of Scotty and the minister is more or less a "set piece," an exhibition of language for its own sake. The story of the Fosters, on the other hand, has a definite plot organized around a specific theme; its concern is not to demonstrate speech but to use it to reveal character. Saladin's use of poker metaphor establishes him as an unpretentious, rather commonplace man—which is important for the total effect of the story, since the reader is supposed to feel that what happens to Saladin might happen to anyone—and simultaneously reveals his understanding of himself. The effect of the device is double: it both vivifies him and foreshadows his actions.

Saladin exhibits more self-awareness than Scotty. When his wife expresses joy at the news that his rich uncle—from whom they expect to inherit $30,000—is still living, Saladin derides her for being "'immorally pious'" (XXIV, 12). Electra is tartly certain that "'there is no such thing as immoral piety,'" and Saladin is soon overwhelmed because he doesn't know when to stop talking. He multiplies his excuses, only to entangle himself still further. "Then, musingly, he apologized to himself. 'I certainly held threes—I *know* it—but I drew and didn't fill. That's where I'm so often weak in the game. If I had stood pat—but I didn't. I never do. I don't know enough'" (13).

Saladin, one sees, laments two things. Superficially, he bemoans his unavoidable failure to "fill"—and superficially the story is built upon the Fosters' expectations (doomed to disappointment) that the uncle will make the bequest that he promised. No one can control the run of the cards at poker; likewise, Saladin is not responsible for his uncle's malicious deceit. But Saladin does have a weakness and sees it clearly: he knows that he cannot bluff successfully, whether before or after the draw. Later, as the Fosters come to live more and more in their imaginations, daydreaming about their lives as millionaires once the bequest shall have been invested a few dozen times, Saladin sinks to degrading debaucheries. He gambles; he drinks; he fornicates. His transgressions are purely mental, but Electra detects the glazed eyes and the slack face as he sits lost in fantasy. He is unable to "bluff" her; he cannot deny what in imagination he has been up to, and the happiness of their marriage is blighted. The misery that results from his failure to "stand pat" is a direct outgrowth of the character revealed through the poker-talk monologue.

Finally, to choose an example near the chronological middle of Twain's career, when Hank Morgan presents himself in Arthur's dining hall near the beginning of *A Connecticut Yankee in King Arthur's Court* (1889), one finds an intensive use of American frontier, or "Yankee," poker talk not only to characterize the protagonist but also to anticipate theme and prepare for the satiric irony behind the story. Faced with the dismal fact that he is either in the sixth century or in a lunatic asylum, with no way to determine which until an eclipse occurs or fails to occur, Hank decides to dismiss the problem from his mind: "One thing at a time, is my motto—and just play that thing for all it is worth, even if it's only two pair and a jack" (XIV, 16). Ironically, Hank Morgan's career as "The Boss" will be an attempt to inculcate the masses of Great Britain with the habits of rationality and the attributes of reflective intelligence; his whole program will be one of education in the "Man-factory." But here, he shows that he is a man who will play a bluff with the best, and foreshadows his successful eclipse-bluff, his repeated "miracles," and his final saturnalia of destruction when his "bluff" is called. The conflict between reason and irrationality, between, one may say, the doctrines of the perfectibility of man and of innate human depravity, is played off against the background of Hank's poker-faced opportunism. In the great tournament between the "magic of fol-de-rol" and the "magic of science" (396), the magic of science triumphs, but "it was a 'bluff' you know. At such a time it is sound judgment to put on a bold face and play your hand for a hundred times what it is worth; forty-nine times out of fifty nobody dares to 'call,' and you rake in the chips" (395).

Such a passage is of the frontier tradition; it is the realistic speech of an uneducated man who, by speaking the way he does, convinces a reader of the existence of his environment. Yet it accomplishes a good deal more. Hank Morgan's use of poker terminology is more significant than that of Captain Simon Suggs at his camp meeting. Suggs's poker metaphors come at the end of his story, when the reader already knows all about the Captain, but Hank's "two pair and a jack" serves to introduce both his character and the essential conflicts to be presented in his story. Hooper's satire, moreover, has nothing to do with the characterization of Simon Suggs through poker talk. Simon is no outsider whose entrance into a previously stable society disrupts the status quo. He is immediately recognized as "the very 'chief of sinners' in all that region,"[20] his physiognomy as familiar as his reputation. His vocabulary adds little to the meaning of the story, because Simon's function—to victimize the affected—does not depend on his origin as signaled by his talk. Hank Morgan, however, is an unknown quantity. His very clothing seems miraculous, and his vocabulary repeatedly sets him off from his captors. His mere presence in Arthur's court will serve to contrast Yankee ingenuity and energy with Arthurian romance and sloth; the contrast between his American language and sixth-century, knightly habits of thought will be essential to the development of the book's theme.

IV

Even when Hank Morgan is roaming the streets of Old England, his Americanism is guaranteed by his poker talk. Of even broader usefulness in suggesting nationality is the poker face, more a way of saying something, or nothing, than a vocabulary. Because it embodies an attitude rather than a regional heritage, the frontiersman's poker face was more widely appropriated than his slang by writers presenting an American to the outside world; and from the very beginning, the outside world was inescapably present in the American consciousness. Distant though he was, the frontier settler was fair game for the polished easterner, the easterner himself open to wisecracks from abroad. The conflict embodied in such antitheses as country and city, West and East, became a theme common to writers as far removed from the conventional eighteenth- and nineteenth-century nature-civilization dichotomy as Twain, Henry James, and Sinclair Lewis. In many cases, what began as western humor was quickly pressed into service on behalf of the national honor.

One may think of the tall tale as a traditionally western way of cutting the pompous outsider down to size. The heaping up of exaggerations by a narrator who never cracks a smile, or in any other way indicates that he is joking, stretches to the breaking point the stranger's predisposition to assume the worst about the new region. The Texan who disdainfully put a braggart in his place by saying, "'Only after my fourth killing, gentlemen, did I consider myself worthy of becoming a citizen of Texas,'"[21] is satirizing an unthinking acceptance of malicious anti-Texas gossip; the previous speaker, with but one corpse to his credit, plays the role of straight man.

This is folk humor hot off the range, but the technique antedates the frontier. As a defense against slander, the tall tale and the poker face enabled no less a man than Benjamin Franklin to counteract falsehoods about America that were circulating in London in 1765. Rather than attack detractors in passionate rage, Franklin quietly admitted in a letter to a London newspaper that no story, however extravagant it seemed, could give a false picture of America, which was itself so grandiose. He went on to speak of the cod and whale fishing on the Great Lakes, concluding that

> Ignorant People may object that the upper Lakes are fresh, and that Cod and Whale are Salt Water Fish: But let them know, Sir, that Cod, like other Fish when attack'd by their Enemies, fly into any Water where they can be safest; that Whales, when they have a mind to eat Cod, pursue them wherever they fly; and that the grand Leap of the Whale in the Chase up the Fall of Niagara is esteemed, by all who have seen it, as one of the finest Spectacles in Nature.[22]

In fiction, however, the development of a poker-faced manner was a sophisticated refinement that occurred only after more violent techniques of presenting western antipathy toward eastern elegance had been fully explored. The rough squatter of Hannibal, in Sam Clemens' "The Dandy Frightening the Squatter" (1852), wastes no words, forthrightly punching the overarmed but unmanned Dandy into "the turbid waters of the Mississippi."[23] Sut Lovingood frightens his intrusive Irishman right back across the ocean, to the land where there are no snakes. Thompson's Doctor Jones is led to the circus for the single purpose of being "oudaciously tuck in," for Augusta, "the Philadelphia of the South," has rendered him objectionable to his fellows at Pineville. Even in real life, the young men of Hannibal, incensed at the citified airs of one of their number who had returned from Yale in all the appurtenances of eastern fashion, turned to action, not talk: they "dressed up the warped negro bell ringer in a travesty of him—which made him descend to village fashions."[24]

The country resents the city, the West resents the East, and the theme of this hostility toward what is different—and therefore threatening—is expressed in countless stories, first by those who were intent on capturing the feelings of the folk around them, regardless of where their own sympathies lay, and, later, by men who identified themselves at least partially with their adopted, or even natal, home on the frontier. This same opposition found its way into serious fiction as a contrast between America and Europe, although as early as Revolutionary times Royall Tyler's comedy—titled, of course, *The Contrast*—was elevating the manly American above the effete Englishman. By the last third of the nineteenth century, though, the contrast had become considerably more complex. For many writers, to place an American in a European context was to provide the *donnée* for infinitely suggestive adventures. This confrontation carries with it a minor, but interesting, literary problem: how shall the author establish implicitly the particular qualities of his characters' nationality without writing an essay? Mark Twain, in *The Innocents Abroad* (1869), points the way to one sort of solution through characters whose use of a poker face stamps them as Americans from a frontier rawer than a genteel reader will approve yet worthy of respect for its clear-sighted resistance to humbug.

The immediate impulse of Twain's traveling Yankee is to disguise emotion, whether fear of Europe as it threatens an American's self-image or awe of Europe as it suggests unexplored possibilities of experience. Accomplished poker-players that they are, they deceive for gain on the byways of the Continent as expertly as they might at the card table. When Twain-the-character and his friends in *The Innocents* plague a series of guides, all rechristened "Ferguson," the iron-visaged idiocy displayed leads to one very specific gain: "The guide was bewildered—nonplussed. He walked his legs off, nearly, hunting up extraordinary things, and exhausted all his ingenuity on us, but it was a failure; we never showed any interest in anything" (I, 306). By criticizing "Christopher Colombo's" poor penmanship, by asking if an Egyptian mummy is dead, the Doctor—who "asks the questions, generally, because he can keep his countenance, and look more like an inspired idiot, and throw more imbecility into the tone of his voice than any man that lives" (303)—forces the guide of the moment on to ever greater exertions.

Like any clever poker-player, the Doctor is versatile. When a guide persists in taking Twain, Dan, and the Doctor to silk stores rather than to the Louvre, the masquerade of boredom changes to one of simulated enthusiasm. As "Ferguson" foolishly persists in his commercial scheming, the Doctor's mounting anger expresses itself as aesthetic pleasure: "'Ah, the palace of the Louvre; beautiful, beautiful edifice! Does the Emperor Napoleon live here now, Ferguson?'" (115) And at the third silk store: "'At last! How imposing the Louvre is, and yet how small! how exquisitely fashioned! how charmingly situated! Venerable, venerable pile—'" (116). This reaction is, strictly speaking, irony, but, as an attitude adopted by the Doctor for slicing through a foreigner's deceit, it also belongs to the species "poker face."

When the Doctor stonily asks, "'Is, ah—is he dead?'" before every statue, he is clearly deceiving for gain. The guide, intent on drawing a conventional show of enthusiasm from the passive Doctor, works much harder than he is paid to do in the hopes of shattering his employer's calm. But there is another side to the coin. The Innocents are impressed by what they see, for if they were not, they would find no practical advantage in pretending to be bored. "We came very near expressing interest, sometimes—even admiration—it was very hard to keep from it" (306). But the pretense means more than just a desire to gain additional sights, as one sees when the group visits the vault beneath the Capuchin Convent. The walls are decorated by the dismembered skeletons of dead monks. The guide—in this case one of the monks who will some day add his mite to the communal fresco—has shown them everything, and now they stop to examine in particular one skeleton, robed and intact, whose skull has preserved "a weird laugh a full century old!" "It was the jolliest laugh, but yet the most dreadful, that one can imagine" (II,5). Terror and humor coalesce: "At this moment I saw that the old instinct was strong upon the boys, and I said we had better hurry to St. Peter's. They were trying to keep from asking, 'Is—is he dead?'" (5)

In this instance, the poker face gains a very real but immaterial advantage for its user: it allows him to inject humor into a situation that frightens him. Certainly this is a common technique all through *The Innocents Abroad*. When Twain, the American narrator, is overwhelmed by Europe, he can find relief by laughing at it, or simply by laughing, a response similar to that of Melville's Ishmael who emerges from his first violent brush with a whale to conclude that life's vicissitudes, from "small difficulties" to "extreme tribulation" and "peril of life and limb," must be taken "for a vast practical joke" if sanity is to be retained.[25] That Twain's American laughs does not mean, always, that he is happily at ease in his world.

Twain's awareness of the impact of Europe on Americans abroad is hardly the central theme of his fiction. Still, he helped to develop the terms through which American writers were to confront the Old World with representatives of the New. The fears and insecurities that Twain revealed through humor became the clichés of the future tourist class, whether from Lewis' Zenith or from James's New York City. The materials of the humorist became touchstones of allegiance for the novelists.

Like other Americans in Europe, the Innocent Abroad is troubled; the "dreadful" laugh that is "a full century old"— older than the town of Samuel Clemens' birth, or of most nineteenth-century Americans' birth—is different from anything Mark Twain has ever known. The very existence of the skeleton suggests a way of looking at life that is foreign, for the fashions of American interior decoration have never emulated the Capuchin vaults. Twain's fascination with that ancient, that noticeably "un-American," laugh suggests Lewis' Sam Dodsworth, who is at first intrigued by and attracted to the laughter of the Count von Obensdorf, his wife's future lover: "'Kind of like an American, this fellow—this count,' said Sam. 'got a sense of humor. . . .'" But Sam is wrong.

> "Oh no, it's a very different thing," Fran [Sam's wife] insisted. "He's completely European. Americans are humorous to cover up their worry about things. They think that what they do is immediately important and the world is waiting for it. The real European has a sense of a thousand years. . . behind him."[26]

Dodsworth does "worry about things." He cannot keep from himself "a deep and sturdy recognition of his own ignorance,"[27] and on many occasions we are told, more or less directly, that "he suddenly felt insecure."[28] When he successfully orders French station-attendants around, "he admitted that he was possibly being the brash Yankee of Mark Twain."[29] But Sam Dodsworth eventually chooses a European way of life, and Lewis pointedly foreshadows Sam's un-Americanism by contrasting his unexpected appreciation of art with "the Mark Twain tradition," in which "the American wife still marches her husband to galleries from which he tries to sneak away."[30] His appreciation is unexpected because Sam Dodsworth is first presented as being very much in the tradition: "He liked whiskey and poker,"[31] and his fondness for poker is referred to often enough and in the proper contexts to make it a metaphor of his desire to be with and like Americans.[32]

Now the American poker-player's approach to European art is established for all time by Mark Twain, and the establishment sanctioned by no less a pontiff than Henry James. Twain's Innocent tells us that he "could not help noticing how superior the copies were to the original. . . . Wherever you find a Raphael, a Rubens, a Michael Angelo, a

Caracci, or a Da Vinci (and we see them every day) you find artists copying them, and the copies are always the handsomest" (I, 190). Henry James gives us, in his *The American* (1877), the transitional step between the completely westernized narrator of *The Innocents Abroad* and the potential renegade of *Dodsworth*. Christopher Newman is a synthesis of American types. He looks back upon the isolated spirit of Natty Bumppo as "he laughed the laugh in which he indulged when he was most amused—a noiseless laugh, with his lips closed."[33] He shows a more sociable sort of frontier experience, too, for—like Twain—"Newman had set with Western humorists in knots, round cast-iron stoves, and seen 'tall' stories grow taller without toppling over, and his own imagination had learned the trick of piling up consistent wonders."[34] Finally, he is mythologized as an American titan in the "*légende*" of western wealth and power that the stout Duchess, Madame d'Outreville, invents for him,[35] a myth that will be echoed by Lewis in Dodsworth's determination, at the start of his travels,[36] to return to America and create such a city as is attributed to Newman.

In our first view of him, Newman is presented most simply as the "specimen of an American," as "the American type," and although his visit to the Louvre fills him, "for the first time in his life, with a vague self-mistrust,"[37] his habitual front possesses "that typical vagueness which is not vacuity, that blankness which is not simplicity."[38] He is aware of his fears, but, good American that he is, he is poker-faced. Like Sam Dodsworth, he has gambled quite literally, in business and in sport, "glad enough to play poker in St. Louis."[39] Unlike Twain's *persona*, he has come to Europe—as so many of James's people do—to learn; but his European education does not begin until after his first stroll through the Louvre, when he is most pointedly still the American: Newman looks "not only at all the pictures, but at all the copies that were going forward around them, . . . and if the truth must be told, he had often admired the copy much more than the original."

Newman's poker-faced admiration of Mlle. Nioche's copies soon gives way to an acknowledged emotional involvement with Claire de Cintré, and to Newman's efforts to register directly on his feelings a sense of Europe. Mark Twain, playing the game of the American in Europe, retains the poker face that Newman struggles to put off, that is torn from Dodsworth by fate. (Dodsworth is not trying to educate himself into an involvement with Europe; events conspire to educate and to involve him despite himself.) For Lewis and James as well as for Twain, the American approaching Europe is poker-faced, and his reactions to European culture and customs are similar, initially, for all three writers. As James's and Lewis' protagonists succumb in their respective ways to the lure of the Continent, they lose their poker-faced detachment that has served as a defense against involvement, but their point of departure is defined by Twain's Innocent.

The three authors are concerned with tracing three variations of their common theme. For James, the impact of Europe as a civilizing force on the visiting American— Christopher Newman, Isabelle Archer, Lambert Strether, et al.—is the central concern, whether the force initiates a progression that culminates in grandeur or in futility. Lewis' *Dodsworth*, as one of the many novels in which Lewis presents America as seen through the eyes of H.L. Mencken, stresses the tawdry quality of American society, touching on the world of George F. Babbitt and focusing on the insubstantial character of Fran Dodsworth's worship of all things European. The actual impact of Europe on Sam Dodsworth is great—he chooses to leave America and live in Italy—but the weight of Europe itself is felt less throughout the book than is the density of the America from which Sam turns. The behavior of Mark Twain's Innocent merely suggests the rejection of America, and even the suggestion is only occasional. Most of the time, he appears brashly complacent in his Americanism. Indeed, his fear of Europe drives him happily back to his native shores, although he captures undertones that will become more significant in Twain's later work.

Twain's protagonist is really the most subversive of the three. Happy though the traveler returned may be, his first official act is to summarize the pilgrimage for the New York *Herald*, as Twain in fact did do, and his summary is not flattering to his fellow-Americans. His sarcastic irony—"We always took care to make it understood that we were Americans—Americans!" (II, 401)—evokes such samples of nationalism as the expedition's criminal archeological activities among the pyramids and their bad manners among the French. Boorishness and ignorance are the two most conspicuous qualities of these wandering representatives of God's latter-day Chosen People, as their spokesman's newsletter paints them. There clearly is more to Twain's treatment of America than simpleminded adulation. His ambivalence is as real as James's and Lewis', although one must see it in a more finished work to appreciate it.

Twain's use of the theme—Europe and America, East and West—and the central image for embodying this theme (the poker face) both arise from his immediate background in the humor of the southwest, of the frontier. The same theme and the same image became equally part of the equipment of writers totally removed from both the frontier and the Southwest. Twain's use of this material differs from that of James and Lewis; the gap between Twain and his own tradition is equally significant. To be clear on this point one has only to remember Hank Morgan in Arthur's Court and Simon Suggs at his camp meeting: they are both slang-slinging adventurers, out for what they can get, but Hank's use of poker talk achieves effects that Simon's does not even suggest. Mark Twain's adaptation of the standard elements of frontier humor enlarged their usefulness for literary art. How radical some of his departures were we have yet to see.

Notes

1. See *Mark Twain and Southwestern Humor* (Boston: Atlantic-Little, Brown, 1959), pp. 6ff.
2. Quoted from Augustus B. Longstreet by Donald Day, "The Humorous Works of George W. Harris," *American Literature*, XIV (January, 1943), 393.
3. George Washington Harris, *Sut Lovingood: Yarns Spun by a 'Nat'ral Born Durn'd Fool'* (New York, 1867), p. 111.
4. Johnson J. Hooper, *Simon Suggs' Adventures* (1845, reprinted Philadelphia, 1881), p. 26.
5. *Major Jones's Chronicles of Pineville* (Philadelphia, 1843), pp. 99–135.
6. Hooper, *op.cit.*, p. 132.
7. *Ibid.*, p. 138.
8. *Ibid.*, pp. 142, 143–44.
9. Reprinted from the Nashville *Union and American*, February 28, March 2, and March 5, 1861, in *Sut Lovingood*, ed. Brom Weber (New York: Grove Press, 1954), pp. 219–37.
10. *Ibid.*, pp. 221–22.
11. *Mark Twain at Work* (Cambridge: Harvard University Press, 1942), p. 69.
12. All volume and page references, unless otherwise indicated, are to *The Writings of Mark Twain*, "Definitive Edition" (37 vols, New York: Harper & Bros., 1922–25).
13. Dixon Wecter, *Sam Clemens of Hannibal* (Boston: Houghton Mifflin, 1952), pp. 107–8.
14. In *Major Jones's Chronicles of Pineville*. Twain, says DeVoto, "was thoroughly familiar with Thompson's work" (*Mark Twain at Work*, p. 68n).
15. *Major Jones's Chronicles of Pineville*, p. 18.
16. Hooper, *op.cit.*, p. 141.
17. *Ibid.*, pp. 141–42.
18. *Ibid.*, 144–45.
19. In Edgar M. Branch, *The Literary Apprenticeship of Mark Twain* (Urbana: University of Illinois Press, 1950), p. 227.
20. Hooper, *op.cit.*, p. 136.
21. In Mody C. Boatright, *Folk Laughter on the American Frontier* (New York: Macmillan, 1949), p. 22.
22. Quoted in F. O. Matthiessen, *American Renaissance* (New York: Oxford University Press, 1941), p. 639.
23. Reprinted in Branch, *op.cit.*, p. 218.

24. Quoted from Mark Twain Papers by Henry Nash Smith in "Mark Twain's Images of Hannibal," *Texas Studies in English*, XXXVII (1958), 3.

25. *Moby-Dick*, chap. xlix, "The Hyena."

26. *Dodsworth* (New York: Modern Library ed., 1929), p. 231.

27. *Ibid.*, p. 121.

28. *Ibid.*, p. 76.

29. *Ibid.*, p. 112.

30. *Ibid.*, p. 119.

31. *Ibid.*, p. 11.

32. *Ibid.*, pp. 139, 140, 188, 190.

33. *The American* (Rinehart ed.; New York: Rinehart, 1949), p. 332. See Cooper's *The Prairie* for Natty's silent laugh (Rinehart ed.; New York: Rinehart, 1950), pp. 437 and *passim*.

34. *The American*, p. 98.

35. *Ibid.*, p. 212.

36. *Dodsworth*, p. 23.

37. *The American*, p. 2.

38. *Ibid.*, p. 3.

39. *Ibid.*, p. 21.

"A Curious Republican"

Louis J. Budd

I am a candidate for the legislature. I desire to tamper with the jury law. I wish to so alter it as to put a premium on intelligence and character.—Roughing It

By moving to Buffalo, in mid-August of 1869, Twain put himself well within the orbit of the Langdon family and what he described to his future father-in-law as a "high eastern civilization." There is no sign he was reluctant to raise his social level, however apologetic he may have felt about his rough edges. Though he did not court Olivia Langdon for her money, it impressed him almost as much as her breeding and posed another challenge. Instead of gloating like a prospector who had made a lucky haul, he took the proper Victorian attitude that he had to justify her father's faith in him by working harder than ever.

The respect with which he met Jervis Langdon can be seen indirectly through his "Open Letter to Commodore Vanderbilt," attacking a notorious Wall Street pirate for his personal crudities and "lawless violations of commercial honor."[1] When this drew a defense of Vanderbilt for creating more wealth and new jobs, Twain accepted it as "able bosh"—bosh because it nicked him as well as claiming too much for a ruthless profiteer but able because it persuasively stated the case for capitalists in general. His taunts had not meant to criticize solid businessmen, who in fact resented the

Chapter Three reprinted from *Mark Twain: Social Philosopher* (Bloomington: Indiana University Press, 1962), pp. 40-63, 221–223.

disruptive forays by the robber barons as much as anybody, and he felt no impulse to bait Langdon or ridicule him behind his back. Soon after pushing into the family circle Twain gladly tried to help him collect a half-million dollars from the city of Memphis for wooden pavement.[2] There must have been backslapping around the fireside when Twain's influence produced a scolding editorial in the New York *Tribune* that did some good.

Langdon's main energy went into a network of mines and retail outlets for coal. When some voices around Buffalo accused the big companies of price-fixing, Twain answered them firmly in his own newspaper with "The 'Monopoly' Speaks," which complained that the public was listening too naively to the consumers' side and argued that legitimate market pressures were driving up the price of coal as winter came on.[3] Though Langdon put up the $25,000 with which he bought into the *Express*, Twain would not have gone so far and so openly if he agreed with the other side or cared little about the economic principles involved. Even where his loyalties were not aroused, he took up serious issues as soon as he got oriented in his new job, vaguely hoping to lift the *Express* into the class of often quoted newspapers like the Springfield *Republican* or the Toledo *Blade*. This meant he could not ignore politics. Property holders, large or small, had their stake in the state and expected to be kept informed about it. Furthermore, while they looked down on the city boss and ward-heeler, most educated or well-to-do northerners already felt a proprietary concern in the future of the Republican party.

Having finally committed himself, Twain harried the Democrats with original material in the *Express*. A typical piece, "Inspired Humor," professed to see comedy in their latest call for an honest legislature in New York and derided them as hypocrites "whose religion is to war against all moral and material progress, and who never were known to divert to the erection of a school house moneys that would suffice to build a distillery."[4] His frontal attacks were reinforced by a then standard maneuver of pointing up news items the way he did with "A pig with a human head is astonishing South Carolina. Are they rare, there?" but it so happened in the fall of 1869 that baiting the Democrats was easier than praising the Republicans, at least in New York where the spoilsmen had taken over both sides and even worked together across party lines. Letting other hands keep the *Express* filled with partisan cheers, Twain used his positive moods on more basic Republican planks like the need to recall the greenbacks issued during the war—the point of his "Adventures in Hayti," another sketch that looks weightless today as it clowns about ridiculously high prices for everyday items.

After his furious debut as an editor Twain made the lecture rounds again and then put all his thoughts into getting married. When he got back to writing for the *Express* he was more impartial and relaxed but not aimless. Unfortunately, to know that "A Curious Dream"—about corpses that move their coffins to a better neighborhood—was lampooning the rundown state of a Buffalo cemetery does not make this grisly sketch any funnier. However, such insight builds alertness to worthwhile content behind the slapstick of pieces like "A Mysterious Visit," an account of his dealings with a tax assessor which finally criticized the wealthy sharpers who falsify their returns. This restless dislike of hypocrisy soon killed his dream of being an editor. After openly complaining that "Cain is branded a murderer so heartily and unanimously in America, only because he was neither a Democrat or Republican," he acted out his disgust in "Running for Governor," a parody on a state election in New York that saw two corrupt machines splatter each other with muck. Ominously, this parody attacked the press of both parties without favor.

For the rest of his life after leaving the *Express* Twain thought of most newspaper editors as noisy puppets, and in 1871 he willingly took a big loss to set himself free. Even before then be branched out in monthly "Memoranda" for the *Galaxy* but not as an escape from writing about current affairs.

Along with frothier humor he kept turning out items like "The Coming Man," a superbly witty warning against making some ward-heeler our new minister to England. Put together while the "Memoranda" were appearing, *Mark Twain's (Burlesque) Autobiography and First Romance* had about the same mixture of ingredients. It extended his campaign to project a colorful front and gave further sign of his literary instincts, but its third facet, a sequence of cartoons on the Erie Railroad scandal, showed he had not deserted from guarding the public conscience.

Though Cornelius Vanderbilt was the best-known villain in the Erie scandal it also established Jay Gould's lurid fame, and much later Twain would pick Gould as the prime corrupter of our "commercial morals." Even in 1870 there was widespread comment in this vein—especially by conservatives like brahmin Charles Francis Adams, Jr., who also protested at length that such doings sapped the health of sound business. Keyed by apt variations on the nursery jingle about the house that Jack built, the cartoons in the *Burlesque Autobiography* proved that Twain had gathered every whisper about Jim Fisk's sex life and the payoffs to judges and editors.[5] In fact he capitalized on popular reaction instead of saying anything new; cartoons like those in his book were common and the parody on the nursery rime belonged to current folksay. But he was revolted rather than amused by the Erie tragi-comedy, which attuned him to the looming furor about Tweed's burglaries and other scandals that lead to *The Gilded Age.*

In the meantime, this mounting disgust was allowed to have only a side-effect on *Roughing It* (1872). His appetite was whetted by a steady sale for *The Innocents Abroad,* and he worked hard at spinning another best-seller. More fiction than history wherever the change might please the reader, *Roughing It* is his sunniest book. If it offended Senator Stewart, he was being too touchy. If its passing sarcasms really belittled the old territorial legislature, Twain's experiences could have inspired a much more trenchant critique. Indeed, when he refreshed his mind in 1871 by going over some clippings of his feisty columns for the *Territorial Enterprise* he scribbled a comment about the resemblance between Carson City graft and the national scandals that were building up. A few years later he made promising notes for a book about a Senator Bonanza, who routinely bought off state legislatures. Much later he jotted down ideas for a social history from 1850 that would include the effects of the "California sudden-riches disease."[6] Still, though it gave edge to *The Gilded Age*, little of this insight showed up in *Roughing It*, least of all in the now ignored Appendix C—which jeered at an alkali populist who was resisting the push of the mining companies for cozier tax laws.

Roughing It also gave darker signs of misdirected bias from Twain's western years, especially when the Indians slouched across its pages. From the time he crossed the plains he felt only contempt for the red men, and loudly and often said so. In *The Innocents Abroad,* his celebrated ear failing him, he orated against Tahoe as a primitive name not good enough for the famous lake—where he had carelessly burned a stand of trees while toying with the notion of staking out a rich timber claim. In the *Galaxy* he derided the Indian with a white settler's passion as a "filthy, naked scurvy vagabond" whose extinction by the army should continue in spite of the "wail of humanitarian sympathy" from the older sections of the country.[7] There is no good reason why he reacted so violently. Dan De Quille, his crony in Nevada, took a much kinder, more relaxed attitude, and Bret Harte could burlesque James Fenimore Cooper's stagy figures without winking at mistreatment of their flesh and blood counterparts. The ugly truth is that Twain as yet had little respect for any peoples who were outside the pattern of an industrial society. Though he managed to see more humor in tropical languor than in the Digger Indians' struggle to subsist, he also came down harder on the Hawaiian natives than he had in the letters he revised to swell his book to subscription size.

The circle of his sympathy was still actually too small to include even all classes of white Americans. In spite of his eloquent if incidental tribute to the forty-niners as "stalwart, muscular, dauntless young braves," he grimaced at the heavy "scum" on the western surge and, damning politicians as their "dust-licking pimps and slaves," fumed about the absurdity of letting this scum serve on juries. With a steadier eye on his intentions than usual, he gave an exotic picture of the mining frontier; but his colors were occasionally somber or clashing. The continual references in *Roughing It* to the "flush times" suggest that he had a secondary motif in mind and, like another old Whig, meant to highlight the ludicrous yet deplorable crumbling of order before the speculative flood. Somewhat lamely he rang the same note as Joseph G. Baldwin's *The Flush Times of Alabama and Mississippi* in his final "moral": "If you are of any account, stay home and make you way by sober diligence."

Roughing It was western and democratic in the finest sense of these terms only when Twain described himself as a tenderfoot who fraternized with seedy prospectors and shared their sourdough dreams, when readers were asked to take Scotty Briggs as a man of sterling character under his roughness and profanity or were assured that though Dick Baker was "slenderly educated, slouchily dressed and clay-soiled" his heart was "finer metal than any gold his shovel ever brought to light." Scotty's slang and Dick's muscular idiom belong to the supreme achievement of Twain's personal democracy—the sinewy vernacular that controls the choicest passages of *Roughing It.* To adapt a figure he once exploited, he was better at the tune than the words in 1871—his political attitudes needed reshaping but he rose to magnificent cadences when he chanted the virtues of his motley friends. Later, in *Huckleberry Finn* and *A Connecticut Yankee,* the vernacular style would support themes greater than robust camaraderie, and the result would be even more satisfying.

Appropriately, Twain dedicated *Roughing It* to Calvin Higbie, another "Genial Comrade" of his Washoe days. But he had first planned instead on honoring Cain as a consolation for "his misfortune to live in a dark age that knew not the beneficent Insanity Plea" to excuse his murder of Abel. This uninspired idea at least proves that Twain was not lost in a haze of Washoe memories. When a trial in 1870 set the precedent for pleading mental illness as a defense, he had reacted quickly with two protests in the Buffalo *Express* and another in the *Galaxy*, opposing what he took to be merely a legal dodge that interfered with the state's main job—the punishment of thieves and murderers.[8] It is only fair to realize that he was staggered by the first impact of questions that are still troublesome to modern minds when the defense rushes to plead temporary insanity, and that many of his contemporaries were just as afraid of encouraging crime through softness. Before he started coming around to a more humane stand, he also got excited abut juries that helped to pamper the sinners against property rights and personal safety. *Roughing It* erupted with criticism for our jury system as the "most ingenious and infallible agency for *defeating* justice that human wisdom could contrive"; and, just as *The Gilded Age* was being finished, he raged openly at the stalling and soft-soaping of the defense in a highly publicized case of wanton murder.

The friends Twain was finding in New England had no reason to mistrust him as a brash westerner who undervalued law and order, even if he wore a sealskin overcoat or was likely to veer suddenly into clowning. Indeed it soon became evident that the clowning could be harnessed to their solemn purposes, as when he dashed off a long and madly punning "ballotd" in 1871 about how the Democrats had tried to steal the last election for governor of Connecticut. Somebody, perhaps in the Hartford *Courant* office, saw fit to print it as a broadside.[9] As always making himself at home had included mixing in local politics; in old age he recalled guiltily that once he even gave twenty-five dollars to buy votes after being assured the Democrats had started playing dirty first.[10] Such close partisanship demanded of course that he do his special bit in national elections too. On the day the 1872 campaign formally began he sent the Hartford *Courant* an unsigned skit titled "The Secret of Dr. Livingstone's Continued Voluntary Exile," which claimed that the missionary, recently contacted in the heart of Africa, had decided to unpack his trunks and "unlearn" his "civilization" because of disgust at the news of Horace Greeley's accepting the Democrats' support for the presidency.[11] Committed at least as much to the Republican party as to its general, Twain hailed the results of the election as a "prodigious victory for Grant—I mean, rather, for civilization and progress."

In spite of deserting his post on the Buffalo *Express*, he had obviously remained an active citizen who studied his daily newspaper, and not just any newspaper either. Around 1870 he toyed with "Interviewing the Interviewer," which would have scolded the New York *Sun* for aiming to "achieve the applause of the bone and sinew of the backstreets and the cellars."[12] He had especially come to admire the New York *Tribune*; and, when there was a fight in 1872 over its future, he showed inside knowledge of the men and issues involved.[13] After Whitelaw Reid came out on top against the odds, Twain congratulated him, "I grieved to see the old Tribune wavering & ready to tumble into the common slough of journalism & God knows I am truly glad you saved it." At this time Reid was prominent for imploring the better classes to counteract the tyrannical, gullible majority as well as the party boss.

Less than a week after he took over the top *Tribune* slot, Reid asked Twain for "something, no matter what" and soon arranged for two long letters on Hawaii, which was again in the headlines because American planters there were again pushing for a closer link with the United States. In these letters Twain deployed his humor with a politician's touch, genially approving the royal claims of the planters' choice but echoing the *Tribune*'s distaste for the expansionist clique here and making the Kanakas look undesirable as fellow Americans.[14] Feeling secure as a valuable sport player on the new *Tribune* team, he also sent in several unsolicited letters, which were published promptly, and a telegram (signed

"Public Virtue") protesting against the raise in salary that Congress had given itself. With obvious self-satisfaction he chortled to Reid: "God knows I was intended for a statesman. I can solve any political problem that ever was invented."[15] He saw no difficulty either in expecting the *Tribune* to help the advance buildup for *The Gilded Age.* Before he suddenly decided that Reid was a "contemptible cur" and the *Tribune* must not get a review copy, there was even an editorial on the forthcoming feast of humor and wisdom. Seemingly the break came because Twain expected still more and flashier free advertising. In any event, though he added broader reasons for hating Reid as time went by, the split was personal rather than political at first. Unfortunately, it ended the flow of his squibs and letters for the *Tribune.* Reacting with his usual vehemence, he stopped buying it, much less writing for it; the dignified New York *Evening Post* became his supplement to the Republican fare of the local *Courant.* However, he had read the *Tribune* carefully between 1871 and 1873, and skimming any week's run from that period will supply at least one clue to the reference in some passage of *The Gilded Age.*

Of course *The Gilded Age* also had deeper roots drawing on Twain's basic attitudes and past experience. His Nevada days had left a suspicious contempt for men like James W. Nye, tagged by several reviewers as the senator who mails seven crates of personal odds and ends as official matter; and serving as a private secretary and a reporter in Washington had broadened his insight. Without really needing it he got a quick review by going back in July, 1870 to lobby for a bill favored by "our Tennesseans."[16] This bill probably involved the famous Clemens tract of land though the tie-up was fittingly so devious that nobody had figured it out. Exploiting old friendships he bustled around the capital for several days and, whether for business or curiosity's sake, had lunch with venal Senator Samuel C. Pomeroy. More out of disgust than prophecy, he grimly wrote to his wife: "Oh, I have gathered material enough for a whole book! This is a perfect gold mine." When the chance to collaborate on a novel with Charles Dudley Warner did come along, he was fully primed.

The fact that Warner co-authored *The Gilded Age* (1874) poses no serious problem. Twain wrote almost all the political chapters, though Warner's daily routine as editor of the Hartford *Courant* led him into the latest tunnels under public affairs. Whatever the reason for this sharing of the work, they agreed easily on the line to follow; if any minor snarls did develop, Twain was mostly the one pulling to the right. In an essay published the same year as their novel, Warner darkly preached against "loose commercial and political morality," but he also showed himself stoutly hopeful about the democratic way and nettled rather than dismayed by the growing sores of corruption.[17] Anybody who sees Hartford life as a reactionary pressure on Twain should compare Warner's ideas with his: seldom will Warner be found the more conservative, even in the 1880's.

Above all, Twain and Warner could work together smoothly because neither wanted to change anything more basic than manners and public morals. Accepting the framework of their society, they flayed minor evils like steamboat racing, religious journals that took dishonest advertising, or the rudeness of clerks and railroad conductors. In spirit, this last, recurring note harmonized with the heavy satire on parvenus who ape the ways of their betters and with the key epithet of "gilded," which appeals to owners of the real thing. Righteous gentility also guided the approach to a more serious matter, the health of our system for punishing criminals. Besides raising angry eyebrows at allowing temporary insanity as a defense, the handling of Laura's trial—spotted in New York City for the purpose—sneered at the fiasco of Boss Tweed's first trip to court. Braham, Laura's crafty lawyer, openly parodied the John Graham who protected Tweed with foxy calm but broke into sobs over his own pleadings for mercy to his client.[18] Furthermore, *The Gilded Age* stressed the Irish background of the jury and judge so heavily that anybody who had heard of Tammany Hall got the point.

The references to affairs in Washington were just as obvious for the informed. Laura's career there fitted in with a buzzing about woman lobbyists of uncertain virtue; more specifically, in the description of Lincoln's statue, alert readers found a direct criticism of a sculptress who had lately inveigled a commission through her youthful charm rather than proved ability.[19] Yet in good Victorian fashion the Lauras turned out much less blamable than men, and especially congressmen, whose trading of legislative favors for everything from railroad passes to stock in shady corporations was typified in *The Gilded Age* by giving one busy lawmaker the name of Trollop. There were also plenty of damning allusions to specific solons; and Dilworthy matched his real life model, Senator Pomeroy, with daring closeness both in mannerisms and the brazenly venal dealings that an ignominious Senate committee refused to censure. For once Twain was not exaggerating: the truth about "Old Subsidy" Pomeroy or his henchmen was extreme enough and too obvious; and when even Colonel Sellers took insult at the idea of becoming a congressman, he merely capped a standard joke of the day.

Nobody had trouble seeing also that Twain and Warner's immediate lesson was, as one magazine put it, "PURIFY THE SUFFRAGE." Yet *The Gilded Age* said little to prevent future Dilworthys from refining platitudes into bullion when it called for a return to the "old-style" congressman—the founding fathers can easily be used for a smokescreen too. It was more sensible when it scolded "good and worthy" citizens for continuing to "sit comfortably at home and leave the true source of our political power (the 'primaries') in the hands of saloon-keepers, dog-fanciers and hod-carriers," though this slur on the hod-carriers, added to numerous other slurs on voters who had a brogue or whose mouths were shaped for living on potatoes, put far too much blame on Irish immigrants. In its economics *The Gilded Age* was just as clearly genteel, preaching against the hunger "to get on in the world by the omission of some of the regular processes which have been appointed from of old." This has Warner's ring and like other, often stuffier passages in *the Gilded Age* is a happy reminder that Twain was at least not given to buttering the gospel of hard work with Christianity. But his basic attitude was just as narrow. In 1867, deploring the postwar boom, he had predicted a crash and growled like a bondholder that "the sooner it comes in its might and restores the old, sure, plodding prosperity, the better."

The Gilded Age carried over this suspicion of the boom but did not ask if the profit motive was dangerous in other ways. In fact Twain's preface for the British edition hedged strongly about "speculativeness":

> It is a characteristic which is both bad and good for both the individual and the nation. Good, because it allows neither to stand still, but drives both forever on, toward some point or another which is ahead, not behind nor at one side. Bad, because the chosen point is often badly chosen.

He went on to tip the balance cleanly, "Still, it is a trait which it is of course better for a people to have and sometimes suffer from than to be without." To forestall charges of hypocrisy from critics in the 1920's, he should also have added that he still drew a sharp line between the piratical raids by Gould or the will of the wisp chases by a Sellers and the healthy, shrewd business gambles almost always backed some invention—from the adjustable vest-strap to the typesetter—that was supposed to increase human comfort or productivity.

The closing chapters of *The Gilded Age* solemnly totted up the rewards for the different kinds of enterprise. Named for his true mettle, Philip Sterling made good after toiling hard and long and enduring a penance of discouragement for his passing interest in wildcat ventures. His success was a practical reprimand to Harry Brierly and Mr. Bolton, among others, for drifting into the clutch of promoters who angled for favors from legislatures. Digging on his own, he found a coal mine while the lobbyists went bankrupt or, like Colonel

Sellers, retreated from Washington nursing a worthless old trunk. To pull off this contrast it was necessary to glide over the Union Pacific clique and play up tinhorn operators, brokers of mudflat real-estate, and the idle apprentice who sank toward the fleshpot of federal subsidies—small fry who could not have got past Gould's secretary.

Modern critics of the robber barons have found ammunition in *The Gilded Age,* and some Wall Street entrepreneurs of 1874 must have hoped it would flop. Yet Twain and Warner were only asking for a chaste retreat. As they were getting their book into shape, E. L. Godkin, who rallied the middle class with his new weekly *Nation,* argued that corruption mainly came from the power of Congress to make grants, and he concluded: "The remedy is simple. The Government must get out of the 'protective' business and the 'subsidy' business and the 'improvement' and 'development' business. It must let trade, and commerce, and manufactures, and steamboats, and railroads, and telegraphs alone." *The Gilded Age* fully backed up this demand for pure laissez faire instead of legislative planning, and its main case of boodle hit the reformer as hard as the fixer. With no harm to what was a thin part of the plot anyway, it might have used the Tennessee land for satirizing the prodigal right-of-way grants to railroads or the windfalls from the protective tariff rather than the relatively minor larceny in a bill to found a university open to any race, creed, or sex. In fact *The Gilded Age* showed no sympathy for the common man economically or otherwise. Angrily, it implied that he deserved none since he let jackals like Tweed or Pomeroy into the public larder and was too ready to share the spoils, and one British reviewer actually took it as a terrifying picture of mob rule. Though this was too strong it did sneer at the coarser varieties in the democratic garden, saying of the jury at the Hawkins trial: "Low foreheads and heavy faces they all had; some had a look of animal cunning, while the most were only stupid. The entire panel formed that boasted heritage commonly described as the 'bulwark of our liberties.'" *The Gilded Age* was the first serious outbreak of Twain's lifelong suspicion that the mass of mankind is venal, doltish, feckless, and tyrannical, that the damn fools make up a majority anywhere.

Distinctly less penetrating than John W. De Forest's *Honest John Vane* (1875), which covered similar ground, the scolding of speculators and grafters in *The Gilded Age* only pleaded for a middle-class code of doing business. Its readers had not bought a Trojan horse in a book that fleshed out the longing of its preface for a happy hunting ground "where there is no fever of speculation, no inflamed desire for sudden wealth, where the poor are all simple-minded and contented, and the rich are all honest and generous, where society is in a condition of primitive purity and politics is the occupation of only the capable and the patriotic." There was a limit to how much of this line Twain himself could swallow, and "Life As I Find It," dashed off around the same time, parodied the homily about the boy who got his big break because his elders saw him thriftily picking up stray pins. Still *The Gilded Age* did not even side with the discontented farmers in the current debate, unheretical as their "granges" were. If the conservative side can be defined as putting fear of "paternalism" above corrective federal or state action and elitism above majority rule, then Twain's alignment was clear beneath the American habit of mixing ideas loosely.

Elsewhere he expanded on two matters handled too loosely in *The Gilded Age* for firm sense. His diatribe on "The License of the Press" indicates he had meant the novel to attack the standards of American journalism—and with just cause, seeing the way most newspapers served political and corporate masters. Yet, at least partly out of character, he merely charged that the press too often made fun of religion as well as purveying cheap sensation that further confused the "stupid" majority. Ironically, this hauteur had one happy influence. As late as 1871 he had planned to amuse the lyceums with "An Appeal in Behalf of Extended Suffrage to Boys"—a satire on the "general tendency of the times," meaning especially the rise of the suffragettes—[20] but in 1873 his essay on "The Temperance Crusade and Woman's Rights" argued that it was unreasonable to keep educated ladies from voting "while every ignorant whisky-drinking foreign-born savage in the land may hold office, help to make the laws, degrade the dignity of the former and break the latter at his own sweet will"—a position still short of Nook Farm's ideas on the subject.

These two essays, it should be noted, were done for the sake of progress. For his next bread and butter work after *The Gilded Age* Twain planned a book about England and negotiated with Thomas Nast to illustrate it. They had tried to lay out a joint project several times before, as when Nast proposed to do cartoons for a pamphlet of items that would include "The Great Beef Contract." When Twain approached him in 1873, "Nasty" Nast—as his enemies called him—was the leading political cartoonist of a hard-hitting period: this was exactly his chief lure for Twain, who assured his publisher that his text would fit Nast's genius at caricature. Their dealings fell through again, but Twain's offer is a good sign of the mixed purposes that kept his book from ever getting written.

Though he could straddle as nimbly as a circus rider, in 1872–73 his feeling about England galloped off in directions too varied even for him. Like most working journalists he had now and then twisted the lion's tail since the Civil War. Yet, though he was interested in British history and literature and swayed by the Yankee intellectuals who were eager to close the widened breach, his preface for a British edition of *The Innocents Abroad* played on the "mother-country" theme with a fervor beyond the call of politeness or profit. One enduring side of Twain paid homage to tradition, the more bejewelled and escutcheoned the better. When he trod British soil in 1872 for his first visit, he lingered awestruck in famous abbeys or castles to exclaim eventually, "God knows I wish we had some of England's reverence for the old & great."[21] His awe flowed over into admiring the Victorian present and confiding to his wife that he "would rather live in England than America—

which is treason." British audiences made the affection mutual when he started to lecture.

But he was weighing more than the nobby guards at Buckingham Palace or the crowds at his lectures. A few years afterward he claimed that he had not written a breezy book on England because he had been able to think only about "deep problems of government, taxes, free trade, finance" during his visit.[22] If this was tomfoolery it even took in the Hartford *Courant*, the newspaper least likely to misunderstand Twain. If he had typically overstated, his next comments made sober sense: England was perhaps the "most real republic" in the world, with shortcomings no worse than ours and a civil service less infested by party leeches. Over-reacting against the miasma of Grantism, he admired the British blend of elitism and democracy much more than he expected to when he asked Nast to become his illustrator.

This does not mean he had been undiscriminating as he affably raked in his lecture fees and looked after his copyrights. Anyway, he could not ignore party lines if he wanted to: the Tory-Conservative element was hostile to Yankees and quick to say so. After allowing for casual socializing it becomes clear that, like most American visitors, he gravitated toward Liberal circles, especially in his contacts with newspaper men. He was taken to Parliament by a political editor who wanted him to write for a Liberal weekly; and Frank D. Finlay, owner of the Belfast *Northern Whig* (which stuck to the Gladstone banner in hostile territory), soon rated as "one of the closest friends I have."[23] The effect of such friendships probably underlay both the six hostile pages about Prince Albert in his notebook and his cautious sympathy toward the Tichborne claimant, supposedly a prime example of the freaks that fascinated him.[24] Though he had several reasons for compiling a special scrapbook about this fight over a titled inheritance, it had become a favorite subject for Radical orators, who charged that Tory prejudice and Catholic influence were swaying the courts and denied that the claimant's sloppy manners proved he could not be blue-blooded. Twain's general scrapbook for 1872 also saved other anti-Conservative clippings about a rally to oppose the state church, a non-Anglican who refused on principle to pay tithes, and the wastefully archaic game laws that the nobility kept in force.

Unknowingly, he had stored up ammunition for *A Connecticut Yankee*, but he did a little sniping even before he finally left England in 1873. The O'Shah letters chuckled over the knighting of nonentities who had well-placed friends; a speech before a London social club joked cuttingly about the new ruling that kept plebeians out of Hyde Park. No matter how humbly he looked up to the self-made prince of industry, he held on to a Yankee Doodle hostility toward social class that was based on birth, as he showed again in his parting shot. Nettled because the nobility failed to grace his lecture audiences, he had apologized—in a letter to a stiffly Tory paper—for not arranging the "attendance of some great members of the Government to give distinction to my entertainment," and then swung into a mock alibi about having hired dressy wax figures that got ruined in transit. This was reprinted in Finlay's *Northern Whig* with the comment that "Mark Twain has been audaciously poking fun at the snobbish tendencies of the great British public."[25]

For the present this letter was his most forceful statement on England though he had time and energy to spare for the book he had counted on as his next bestseller. Disgusted by Grantism he liked what he saw there but vacillated between reverence for stability under Queen Victoria and enthusiasm for middle-class reform under Gladstone. Perhaps he was also baffled by problems more complex in many ways than those at home and posed along unfamiliar lines; while attracted to the Liberals mostly, he switched erratically to Conservative or Radical ideas. To complicate matters further, if he happened to think in terms of the Old World against the New he suddenly changed his tone, as when his preface for the British edition of *The Gilded Age* ended with a hopeful forecast on American politics. The fumbling in the O'Shah letters indicates clearly that his confusions would have sapped the fiber of any book he completed.

No major indecisions silenced or lowered his voice as he turned again to the latest affairs at home, picking up where *The Gilded Age* had left off. When a Hartford crowd met a hometown businessman after he was forced out of the cabinet by the sharks around President Grant, Twain chimed in with an appropriate bit of comedy.[26] The letter he sent to a supper for the local Knights of Saint Patrick was much less genial: imploring their patron saint to drive out reptiles like a secretary of war who saved $12,000 annually from a salary of $8,000, it witheringly scolded the President and the swarming grafters of both parties. Restlessly searching for the source of the widespread "ulcers" he settled more heavily than before on universal suffrage, elaborating his diagnosis with a paper for the Monday Evening Club and summarizing it with epigrams such as one sent to a Tammany satrap, "We know there is Unrestricted Suffrage, we *think* there is a Hell: but the question is, which do we *prefer*?"[27] His family and friends must have heard Twain's own answer many times. A house guest from Boston, who kept a diary, recorded about her host:

> He has lost all faith in our government. This wicked ungodly suffrage, he said, where the vote of a man who knew nothing was as good as the vote of a man of education and industry; this endeavor to equalize what God had made unequal was a wrong and a shame. He only hoped to live long enough to see such a wrong and such a government overthrown.

After a visit filled with lively talk she concluded that this "growing man of forty" was in "dead earnest" about life.

As Howells always claimed, it seems that to know Twain well was to take him seriously. Yet his reputation in 1875 was far short of this discovery, and he had the *Atlantic Monthly* for October publish "The Curious Republic of Gondour" without his name, not to hide from rebuttals but to get a respectful hearing. This outburst charged that the "bottom layer of society"—the "ignorant and non-taxpaying classes"—had seized control through the ballot-box, raising the problem of how to reinstate the power of "money, virtue, and intelligence." Bowing to the demagogic realities Twain merely proposed a system of extra votes but allowed these votes so generously for more property or higher education that the "hod-carriers" and their cohorts from the "ginmills" and jails would become a minority on election day at least. It is cheering to note at least that women voted in his utopian Gondour and held office, that free education ran up through the colleges, that the educated served as a "wholesome check" on the rich and as "vigilant and efficient protectors of the great lower rank," and that a top quota of votes was a higher status symbol than money. Though he never said so again, some scholars gratefully emphasize the fact that Twain also suggested more votes for education than property and implied he would mostly go in for college degrees under such a system.

The best perspective, however, is to see how closely "The Curious Republic of Gondour" was connected with other warnings that natural-rights democracy had run aground. During the stock-taking for the centennial of glorious 1776, many disciples of Manchester Liberalism openly doubted that the mob could police itself or else refrain from a feckless tyranny of its own; since monarchy belonged to the outmoded past, they called for a new patrician leadership based on brains and wealth. In the context of this debate, which raged almost as hotly here as in England, Twain's scheme of plural votes was not eccentric—though simpler proposals for giving a vote only to property-owners got heavier support. The skeptics about pure democracy also found in Gondour related features that they had been talking up like permanent judgeships and a civil service system staffed by a career elite who ran the government impartially and stopped the extorting of bribes. Such reforms, it was fondly hoped, would protect business from pickpockets like Tweed and control pirates like Vanderbilt who hired politicians to sanction their raids and would clear the road for the grand march of technology.

By now Twain had an ungilded, twenty-four-carat right to class himself among the propertied and almost as much right to consider himself well informed, with more than enough leisure to think, talk, read—the house guest from Boston said "study"—and write about what interested him. To help support this leisure he could still drop back into empty vaudeville; though Howells' review found a "growing seriousness of meaning in the apparently unmoralized drolling" the items Twain chose for *Sketches, New and Old* (1875) were more often nonsense than meaningful satire. Designed to ride a rising market for stories about boys, *The Adventures of Tom Sawyer* (1876) was another offering with a shrewd eye on his expenses though it showed more concern for ideas by quietly refracting his characters through his deepening moral skepticism. Also adult in effect, but conventionally so, was its close variation on the popular success story with the climactic boon of a fortune rightly earned. All except his best novels would assuringly end with a big cash award to somebody deserving: the emphasis on the treasure in *Tom Sawyer* as against Jim's freedom in *Huckleberry Finn* typifies the gap between the two books.

The explicit touches of social doctrine in *Tom Sawyer* were not always so reassuring. While Injun Joe fitted the local color, his cold cruelty was meant to spread the alarm about misguided softness toward criminals. In February 1876 one of Twain's strangely assorted friends sent him a general petition already endorsed by Longfellow, Whittier, and men of matching stature. He jotted on the envelope, "From that inextinguishable dead beat who has infested legislatures for 20 years trying to put an end to capital punishment. No answer."[28] For Injun Joe's case a petition was signed freely, and many "tearful and eloquent" meetings produced a committee of "sappy" women to "wail around the governor, and implore him to be a merciful ass and trample his duty under foot." Such acidities kept *Tom Sawyer* from turning saccharine as they steadily played over the townspeople drifting behind its plot. When shiftless Muff Potter was framed, the town discovered he was a murderous-looking rascal and talked about a lynching; when he was cleared, the "fickle, unreasoning world took Muff Potter to its bosom and fondled him as lavishly as it had abused him before."

Intermittently, suspicions about mass man had assailed Twain almost from the start, long before he climbed up in the world—though his first fictional use of Hannibal obviously did not record memories from the bottom layer in that village. As for his broodings about the democratic process, they would have come no matter where he was living in 1875. Reasonable cause was available to anybody who read the magazines and newspapers, and Twain was making a dogged effort to think for himself. In religion he had already moved beyond the relaxed dogma of Nook Farm, and his later feeling that he had long hidden the boldest edge of his mind referred partly to these furtive probings. But he mainly used political examples to carry the point of his dark conclusion in 1905 that "free speech is the privilege of the dead."[29] If this included his ideas on government during his first years in the Hartford house, it is because he was aware of standing often to the right of his friends as a curious Republican—hot to pry into current events but badly tempted to doubt that democracy was worth saving.

At least what he said in public made good sense to some people. The Chicago *Times* for January 27, 1876, reported:

> Mark Twain was proposed as an independent candidate for the mayor of Hartford, Conn. . . Mr. Twain, himself a considerable property-owner, would, it is intimated, accept the nomination. . . . The Hartford people believe that he would give them a decent police force, and would not be the tool of any caucus or set of politicians.

But snatches of his "Punch, brothers, punch," jingle were run in between these sentences. The country liked Twain as a funnyman and, considering his frightful monthly bills, he could not afford as yet to wish otherwise.

Notes

1. *Packard's Monthly*, I (March, 1869), 89–91; Dixon Wecter, ed., *Mark Twain to Mrs. Fairbanks* (San Marino, CA, 1949), 86–7.
2. Mark Twain Papers (hereafter, MTP), autobiog. dict. of Feb. 16, 1906; Albert Bigelow Paine, *Mark Twain: An Autobiography* (NY, 1924) II: 135; New York *Tribune,* June 15, 1869, p. 4; MTP, copies of letters from Twain to Whitelaw Reid, dated [June] 15 and June 26, 1869.
3. Dixon Wecter, ed., *The Love Letters of Mark Twain* (NY, 1949), 68–69, 108–09; Buffalo *Express,* Aug. 20, 1869. There is a core of *Express* items that can be assigned clearly to Twain; I use those assembled in MTP (HNS).
4. "People and Things," Aug. 18, 31, Sept. 1, 1869; "Inspired Humor," Aug. 19; "Which?", Aug. 24; "The Democratic Varieties," Aug. 31; "The Legend of the Sharks," Sept. 11; Franklin R. Rogers, *Mark Twain's Burlesque Patterns* (Dallas, 1960), 114–16.
5. In MTP, a letter dated Dec. 31, 1870, from Isaac E. Sheldon, publisher of the *Burlesque Autobiography,* shows Twain was a moving spirit behind the cartoons.
6. Samuel C. Webster, *Mark Twain, Business Man* (Boston, 1946), 115; Henry Nash Smith, *Mark Twain of the "Enterprise"* (Berkeley, 1957), 100; MTP, DV 791—notes for Senator Bonanza story; Kenneth R. Andrews, *Nook Farm: Mark Twain's Hartford Circle* (Cambridge, Mass., 1950), 238.
7. "The Noble Red Man," X (Sept., 1870), 427–28.
8. Albert Bigelow Paine, ed., *Mark Twain's Letters* (NY, 1917), 188; "The New Crime" and "Our Precious Lunatic," *Express*, April 16, May 14, 1870; "Unburlesquable Things," Galaxy, X (July, 1870), 137–38.
9. "A Ballotd. Owed phor the Tymz; Not the Knusepaper" (copy in Yale Univ. Lib.); it was signed "Twark Main." Blanck, *Bibliography of American Literature,* II, item 3596, doubts Twain's authorship but offers no evidence. Andrews, III, notes how closely Nook Farm followed this election.
10. MTP, Nbk 36 (1903), 8.
11. July 20, 1872, p. 2, the *Courant* announced for Grant of course. As a *Tribune* contributor Twain had good reason not to sign this attack, but his authorship is established by a letter from C.D. Warner, dated July 19,1872 (MTP), as well as by obvious similarities with Twain's speech before the Whitefriars Club-reported in New York *Sun,* Aug. 7, 1872.
12. MTP, DV 306—apparently unpublished.

13. Arthur L. Vogelback has written three excellent articles that are relevant: "Mark Twain: Newspaper Contributor," *American Literature*, XX (May, 1948), 111–28; "Mark Twain and the Tammany Ring," *PMLA*, LXX (March, 1955), 69–77; "Mark Twain and the Fight for Control of the *Tribune*," *American Literature*, XXVI (Nov., 1954), 374–83.

14. Vogelback, "Twain: Newspaper Contributor," 119–24, shrewdly analyzes his position, which is confirmed in a letter to Reid on Jan. 3, 1873. Philip S. Foner, *Mark Twain: Social Critic* (NY, 1958), 242, goes too far in stating the anti-annexation tendency of Twain's *Tribune* letters.

15. Letter on March 7, 1873, copy in MTP. The "Public Virtue" original, dated March 8, is in the New York Pub. Lib. Reid wrote on it, "Letter Editor/must."

16. *Love Letters of Mark Twain*, 153–54. This volume omits Twain's earlier and more revealing letter from Washington on July, 6, 1870 (MTP).

17. "Thoughts Suggested by Mr. Froude's 'Progress,'" *The Complete Writings of Charles Dudley Warner* (Hartford, 1904), XV.

18. Invaluable for reading *The Gilded Age* is a broadside reprint of newspaper reviews—seen in MTP.

19. Twain's comments on sculptress Vinnie Ream are reprinted in Johnson, 182–83, and *Mark Twain Quarterly*, V (Sum., 1942), 10–11. Twain's scrapbook for 1872 (MTP) included a clipping on abuses in commissioning statues of Civil War heroes.

20. *Twainian*, N.S. II (May, 1943), 6; *American Publisher*, July, 1871, p. 4; MTP, letter to Frank Bliss, dated June [1871].

21. *Mark Twain to Mrs. Fairbanks*, 175; William Dean Howells, *My Mark Twain* (NY, 1910), 12, 77; *Love Letters of Mark Twain*, 177; Howard G. Baetzhold, "Mark Twain: England's Advocate," *American Literature*, XXVIII (Nov., 1956), 334–35.

22. Hartford *Courant*, May 14, 1879, p. I.

23. *Mark Twain: An Autobiography*, II, 231–32; Stephen Gwynn, *Life of Sir Charles Dilke* (London, 1918), I, 160; Lillian Whiting, *Kate Field* (Boston, 1899), 289; *Love Letters of Mark Twain*, 188; MTP, Olivia Clemens' letters to her mother, Aug. 10–11 and Aug. 31, 1873, and Twain to one Fitzgibbon in 1873–74.

24. MTP, DV 69 and Tichborne scrapbook; in *Following the Equator* Twain referred in detail to attending one of the claimant's "showy evenings." Twain kept a copy of *The Anti-Game Law Circular* for Oct. 12, 1872.

25. H.R. Fox Bourne, *English Newspapers* (London, 1887), II, 286, 308, describes as uncompromisingly Tory the London *Morning Post*,

to which Twain's letter was addressed. The letter was reprinted in the *Northern Whig* of Dec. 13, 1873.

26. Hartford *Courant*, July 25, 1876.

27. Undated AMS in Webster letters, MTP; *Mark Twain: A Biography* (NY, 1912), 541–42; M. A. D. Howe, *Memories of a Hostess* (Boston, 1922), 251–56.

28. MTP, letter from Marvin L. Bovee, dated Feb. 10.

29. MTP, Paine 249 (dated Sept. 18, 1905).

Toward the Novel

David E.E. Sloane

T wain's voice—the persona—focuses the literary comedy. The 1860s was a time for experimentation with this voice in a variety of subjects—burlesques, travel narratives, semiserious reporting—and he never really stopped developing, as his travel narratives show. Twain advanced literary comedy significantly by using the flexibility of his voice to blend plot and author, playing humor against the dramatization of events. The literary comedian thus came to occupy a place inside the novel by virtue of his characteristic attitude toward social and political events. The recording of Pap's "call this a gov'ment" speech in Huck's voice is a natural out-growth of this management of tone, the technique which originates in the burlesques of the 1860 period. Twain's letters to the *Alta California* and a series of letters for the *Missouri Democrat* in 1866 and 1867 give particularly clear revelations of Twain's experiments in such forms. The resolution which he achieved shapes his novels.

The literary interests of the San Francisco bohemians probably encouraged Twain to attempt an increasingly elevated tone in his writing, and [Artemus] Ward had attempted to refine his voice similarly in the course of his development. Twain's writing, aside from the jumping frog story which he sent east to Ward, included reviews, city news, burlesques of plays as well as of the local government, miscellaneous items on the spiritualists, fashions, and local

Reprinted from *Mark Twain as a Literary Comedian* (Baton Rouge: L.S.U.P., 1979), pp. 84–103.

amusements, and, of course, travel letters. Edgar Branch notes the entrance into the San Francisco writing of a sense of Twain's own past, enriching descriptions with a more broadly implicative consciousness, as in the case of a mural at a local establishment which is described with mock piety as being as gorgeous "as a Presbyterian picture of hell." His letters from Hawaii are in Twainian voice, but with a perspective that reverses later views; in order that San Francisco get more whaling business, he suggests that the city "cripple your facilities for 'pulling' sea captains on every pretense that sailors can trump."[1] His later egalitarian ethics solidified on his trip from San Francisco to New York.

Where Ward's national popularity was based on contemporary events, religious sects, and local events like the visit of Albert Edward, Twain's reputation was based on more literary-seeming material, the frog story and travel letters which were identified for their representation of the narrator's American egalitarian viewpoint. His pose was not burdened with any visual limitation such as the cacography that Ward, and following him Josh Billings, labored under. The transition from reportorial commentator to lyceum lecturer was consequently more natural and corresponded comfortably to the establishment of the lyceum agency, which brought such lectures to predetermined audiences. As Twain's audience became sophisticated culturally, politically, and economically, his stance as a comedian was flexible enough to permit him to speak to them. Where Ward was aware of contemporary literature and employed the burlesque freely, Twain was not only literary but also religious in his exact biblical references and cosmopolitan in his mixture of colloquial and sublime diction and attitudes to build comic statements into longer narrative formats.

Experimenting in humorous modes, Twain recast columns of reportorial comedy into dramatic pieces. His burlesques began to capture the political and moral overtones of the democracy. A series of paralleling newspaper items exist from the 1860s which show Twain presenting material in reportorial format and then reworking the same material into dramatic pieces. He touched on marriage and morality, Barnum's candidacy for Congress, and the woman's suffrage question, exploring the possibilities of comic writing in the dual formats. A vulgar persona like Barnum or Captain Ned Wakeman could sometimes demonstrate a point through burlesque; at other times Twain the semiserious reporter could speak. The moralist of the main was finding a dramatic voice.

Twain's treatment of Barnum's American Museum in conjunction with his bid for Congress is well beyond Ward's showman even though both are burlesques of the same figure as an American type. Dated March 2, 1867, Twain's report on Barnum's museum to the *Alta California* was published on April 9, 1867, under the title "How Are the Mighty Fallen!"; "Barnum's First Speech in Congress," a variant of this article, appeared in the New York *Evening Express* on March 5, 1867.[2] In "How Are the Mighty Fallen!" Mark Twain the reporter visits Barnum's museum in New York because Barnum's running for Congress imbues everything connected to him with a new interest. He notices the stairs running from floor to floor, the crowds, and the general seediness of the museum. The eight-foot-high woman merely sits, for "there was no one to stir her up and make her show her points," a phrase reminiscent of the frog story. The giant, too, merely sits, making Twain declare that if he was impresario of the "menagerie," he would "make that couple prance around some, or dock their rations." Two dwarfs, a speckled Negro, and a Circassian girl "complete the list of human curiosities." Otherwise, Twain comments that Barnum's museum is "one vast peanut stand now."

The reporter is commenting on the same things that would preoccupy him in Europe. Experiences held out to be elevating turn out to be vulgar or fraudulent; this is more obviously the case with Barnum and such exhibits as the "Happy Family." The lions and other beasts that make up the show sleep all the time, and Twain notes the spiritless bear, mangy puppies, and meek tomcats—all "bossed and bullied" by a monkey who cuffs the rabbits and raccoons and chases all the other animals away from the feed tub. Twain remarks that "the world is full of families as happy as that," but the monkey who lost his tail to the boss monkey will have to find his solace in philosophy. The reporter Twain also describes the dust-covered Venus and the leering drunken waxwork representing Queen Victoria. These displays and the moral drama called the "Christian Martyr" compose the attraction of Barnum's show, and Twain concludes that "if he has no better show to get to Congress, he ought to draw out of the canvass." This is acerbic Twain, both expository and narrative with the description of the "Happy Family" approaching burlesque.

The parallel item to "How Are the Mighty Fallen!" is a dramatized speech to Congress by Barnum, delivered to Twain out of the future by "spiritual telegraph." The introduction which frames Barnum's speech is a considerable advance over the formal style of Twain's youthful writing, for it is cast in the relatively modern reportorial style of the 1860s rather than in the formal diction of Longstreet. Twain observes that it would be a "genuine pity" if Barnum could not find a way of dovetailing business and patriotism "to the mutual benefit of himself and the Great Republic." Barnum's burlesque speech begins crassly: "Mr Speaker—What do we do with a diseased curiosity? Sell him!" This mood is developed as Barnum takes the opportunity of the speech to praise his animals, Jenny Lind, his low admission price—reminiscent of Artemus Ward's claims for his show—and the numerous peanut stands, "two peanut stands to each natural curiosity," recapturing an idea stressed in the narrative article. Stating that his numerous curiosities are no excuse for him to become complacent, Barnum describes his spotted Negro, camels, "Sacred Cattle from the sacred hills of New Jersey," and "two plaster of Paris Venuses and a varnished mud-turtle." The last line doubles the number of Venuses from Twain's account—exaggeration—and adds the mud turtle to undercut the speech through anticlimax. The narrative account is consequently expanded through comic devices when it is placed in the voice of a character. This is a chief reason why the narrators of Twain's novels embody many of his important social ironies in their own deadpan comic presentations, and it is a controlling factor in the texture of Twain's major works.

As Barnum's speech continues, the same exhibits that Twain the reporter noticed appear as part of the boast of the burlesque congressman. Twain's line that he would dock the rations of the giant is transformed into a consistent strain of materialism in Barnum. The objective irony becomes part of the dramatization of the character. Artemus Ward's only such creation, besides the showman himself, was Jim Griggins. Barnum, however, like the congressmen in *The Gilded Age*, is a self-burlesquing dramatic entity: "Shall I bask in mine own bliss and be mute in the season of my people's peril? No! Because I possess the smallest dwarfs in the world, and the Nova Scotian giantess, who weighs a ton and eats her weight every forty-eight hours; and Herr Phelim O'Flannigan the Norwegian Giant, who feeds on the dwarfs and ruins business; and the lovely Circassian girl; and the celebrated Happy Family." Ward's style of comic rhetoric is almost reversed in this passage. Instead of using moral and political sentiments as a means of describing his show, Barnum in Twain's hands is made to employ the mentality of a showman to decide the course of the nation. In similar cases, Ward's sentiments were expressed as an incongruously idealistic projection of his professional experience, not as a part of the fabric of his commercial enterprise. By connecting the showman with this sort of submerged venality, Twain is attacking a double corruption, first of Congress, and second of the real role of businessmen. Significantly, Twain's dramatization carries an implied rejection of the likelihood of a moral truth coming from a "vulgar" person.

As Barnum continues speaking, more of the facets of his museum are drawn into the texture of his supposed world view, even including the arrangement of stairs to direct attention of displays. His mind, in fact, begins to run his show and the Congress together, as he appeals to "every true heart in this august menagerie" to save the nation from demagogues who beard the starry-robed woman in her citadel while "to you the bearded woman looks for succor." The conflict between the executive and the legislative branches of government over the Fourteenth Amendment is breaking up the happy family of the Union. Barnum further complains that the poor Negro is only white in spots like his Leopard Boy and has gained universal suffering rather than universal suffrage. By the close of the speech, Twain has completely submerged Barnum's radical Republicanism in the museum curiosities dominating the burlesque rhetoric. Irony has become literary characterization as the materialistic mind is discredited through its incapacity to sever its selfishness from the concerns of government:

> The country is fallen! The boss monkey sits in the feed-tub, and the tom-cats, the raccoons and the gentle rabbits of the once happy family stand helpless and afar off, and behold him gobble the provender in the pride of his strength! Woe is me!
>
> Ah, gentlemen, our beloved Columbia, with these corroding distresses upon her, must soon succumb! The high spirit will depart from her eye, the bloom from her cheek, the majesty from her step, and she will stand before us gaunt and worn, like my beautiful giantess when my dwarfs and Circassians prey upon her rations! Soon we shall see the glory of the realm pass away as did the grandeur of the Museum amid the consuming fires, and the wonders the world admires shall give place to trivialities, even as in the proud Museum the wonders that once amazed have given place to cheap stuffed reptiles and peanut stands! Woe is me!
>
> O, spirit of Washington! forgotten in these evil times, thou art banished to the dusty corridors of memory, a staring effigy of wax, and none could recognize thee but for the label pinned upon thy legs! . . . Woe is me!
>
> Rouse ye, my people, rouse ye! rouse ye! rouse ye! Shake off the fatal stupor that is upon ye, and hurl the usurping tyrant from his Throne! Impeach! impeach! impeach!—Down with the dread boss monkey! O, snake the

seditious miscreant out of the national feed-tub and
reconstruct the Happy Family!
  Such is the speech imparted to me in advance from the
spirit land. Mark Twain.

The happy family, the inactive giantess, the museum fire
of 1865, and the wax figures that annoyed the reporter Twain
all become parts of Barnum's mental apparatus. The speaker's
attack on Andrew Johnson, made obvious by the references to
the Fourteenth Amendment and Negro suffrage, as well as to
the "Executive," is discredited by the ridiculous boss-monkey
metaphor; Barnum's rhetorical "woe is me!" suggests a
repetitious posturing that also casts doubt on his argument.
Twain's restraint in the final sentence, which frames the story
without any comment, is an ironic contrast.[3]
  "Barnum's First Speech in Congress," like Twain's other
experiments in this political idiom in 1867 and 1868, is a
partial reflection of the influence of Ward's success in the old
showman persona. Twain rejected the mind of Barnum as he
understood it at that time but employed the comic
representation of legislators and legislative jargon, much as
Ward used the showman figure and contemporary social
events. Another piece of social commentary handled similarly
was based around Captain Wakeman's marriage of two runaway lovers on the trip from San Francisco to the Isthmus,
recorded in *Mark Twain's Travels with Mr. Brown*.[4]
Conventional morality is thrown into colloquial dialect as
Wakeman advises the lovers to "splice and make the most of
it," an ironic proposal since the couple placed no value on
marriage, according to Twain. The dominant feeling imparted
by Twain is genteel skepticism, and the bride's father is given
an imaginary line—"You miserable, heartless dog, you have
stolen away my child!"—which melodramatizes the incident;
reporting is approaching fiction increasingly in such a piece.
  Twain's newspaper burlesques on the woman's suffrage
question show an even wider range of techniques in
imaginative fiction than the other items from the 1867 period.
They burlesqued the newspaper letter, reportorial prose, and

legislative debates. "Cannibalism in the Cars," which represents a finished application of political burlesque to fiction writing, belongs to the final stage of this development. Taken together, the materials indicate a unity in Twain's newspaper writing in the late 1860s and foreshadow the political sections of *The Gilded Age.*

The suffrage items are as clearly transitional as anything Twain had previously done. In the first item, Twain creates a list of pseudo-government positions, such as "State Crinoline Directress" at $10,000 salary per year, to be filled by greedy female officeseekers. Lists of offices, as in *The Gilded Age,* are mixed with echoes of the coal oil lamp era of political canvassing seen in Ward's Baldinsville. "Mr. Twain" concludes, as a "family" man, which he was not, that his wife will leave him to such chores as wet nursing. He was following Billings in this irony; Billings said he would rather a woman beat him at nursing a baby than at a stump speech or a lecture on veterinary practice. Twain's second item uses the letter convention to present burlesque attacks on him as an opponent of female suffrage. The first two letters are closely parallel diatribes by Mrs. Mark Twain and Mrs. Zeb Leavenworth.[5] Both spend a paragraph berating Twain and threatening him with violence; they conclude with pious hopes that their arguments may have benefited the cause, enabling the two to die "happy and content." The fullness of the repetition projects the suffragists as uniformly bloody-minded harridans. More importantly, Twain's characteristic diction and exaggeration flow into his characterizations; the way was being paved toward fiction.

Twain's third letter on the suffrage issue was written in response to a real letter to the *Democrat* and was written in yet another reportorial voice. In stating his serious premises before turning to burlesque, he reveals that he, like Ward, was genteel and idealistic: "I never want to see women voting, gabbling about politics, and electioneering. There is something revolting in the thought. It would shock me inexpressibly for an angel to come down from above and ask me to take a drink with him (although I should doubtless consent); but it would shock me still more to see one of our blessed earthly angels peddling election tickets among a mob of shabby scoundrels she never saw before." The reactionary sentiment—like Ward, showing a dislike for the ignorant and loathsome with the vote[6]—is blended with the parenthetical pose of the loose-moraled reporter—an almost all-inclusive pose.

Twain describes suffragette women as interested in abolishing tobacco, alcohol, late evenings out for men, and little else. He complains that women will even want to go to war. The piece is drifting, however, toward a better stance as the irony broadens: "We will let you teach school as much as you want to, and we will pay you half wages for it, too, but beware! We don't want you to crowd us too much!" Humorous devices—the comic aside, the termagant type, legislative burlesque—are being turned to the uses of social criticism. As Louis Budd points out, the mixture of attitudes is unsatisfying in its failure to coalesce into a single unified statement.[7] Yet Ward, without the variable persona, had struggled with similar topics in similar ways. The flexibility of Twain's newspaper voice is an advance that brings him near to the first-person narratives of the travel books and novels. He is ready to offer multiple viewpoints, and his sense of ethics, and justice is beginning to form his material and infuse his voice.

The next suffrage piece, "Petticoat Government," is a dramatic burlesque along the lines of Barnum's burlesque speech to Congress.[8] The women betray their personal preoccupations—with gored dresses and waterfall hair styles—to the exclusion of any legislative business other than antidrinking and antitobacco laws. The speeches and asides are recorded as formal oratory, while interspersed among the digressions on fashion are a few harried male attempts to invoke parliamentary rules; the men's chief concern—and here Twain's consciousness is again clearly at work—is the granting of five million dollars for the relief of the Great Pacific Railroad. Beginning the report he had remarked that if women entered government "there would occur almost as disgraceful scenes as have lately blurred the record of Congressional proceedings," and he continues to make a broad application of the burlesque through the overly rhetorical complaint of Mr. Slawson, of St. Genevieve, that the tirade on fashions was "a matter trivial enough at any time, God knows, but utterly insignificant in the presence of so grave a matter as the behests of the Great Pacific Railroad." Add plot continuity and setting to this sort of humor, and the texture of *The Gilded Age* or some portions of *Roughing It* is present in mature form. In *The Gilded Age*, the antirailroad populism was converted into the symbolic encounter between Philip Sterling and Conductor Slum; the rhetoric went to Senator Dilworthy and his cohorts.

The legislative burlesque, which gave Twain scope for ironic exaggerations in diction, was a seductive medium for literary comedians, and Twain was no exception. He already knew that satire could succeed as travesty, as in "The Petrified Man" and the "Bloody Massacre" story, if the travesty did not overwhelm the satire.[9] In "Cannibalism in the Cars," Twain's ability in this area reached its most sophisticated level of expression.

"Cannibalism in the Cars," published in England somewhat later than the other burlesques in this series, is based on an inversion of social and political formality. Here, Twain used political hypocrisy in a more generalized manner than local issues such as Barnum and suffrage allowed. The representatives themselves are the subjects for discussion as various candidates for a cannibal stew. "I liked Harris," or "I have conceived an affection for you. I could like you as well as I liked Harris himself, sir," become dubious compliments.[10] When the narrator of the cannibalism story remarks to his auditor, "This decision created considerable dissatisfaction among the friends of Mr. Ferguson, the defeated candidate," the ironic reversal shows how political terms mask distorted purposes—and also shows how vanity can be contradicted by reality.

The sketch is actually more generalized than earlier related pieces through its comic diction. The frame is unobtrusive, and the story begins in a sublime suspense, in which such phrases as "eternal night" and "in the shadow of death" mark the early going. As the parliamentary rhetoric increases, however, the disjunctions between language and events become more grotesque. Even nature is personified, dragging in a sort of antipastoral element: "Nature had been taxed to the limit [by hunger]—she must yield. RICHARD H. GASTON of Minnesota, tall, cadaverous, and pale, rose up. . . . Only a calm thoughtful seriousness appeared in the eyes that were lately so wild."[11] The formal "yielding" of nature is between high comedy and pun. When the narrator comments, following the nomination of prospective dinners, that "some little caucussing followed," the diction holds the deadpan pose essential to a burlesque of democratic formuli. Human nature is actually at issue, for it is the catastrophic event and the passengers' response which is the action of the story. Cannibalism establishes the importance of the events to the nominees in exaggerated form.

Twain's diction, which seems the source of his humor, is actually subordinated to plot development as Ward's was not. The frame sequence, as with the jumping frog story, has removed the anecdote from the author's own mouth. The "member of Congress" who tells the story deserves a place beside Simon Wheeler, however, for he too is using digression and the deadpan as a means of stating his "experience." Even more significant is Twain's combination of the storyteller with a burlesque based on contemporary American materials; appropriate to the milieu of the literary comedians, the story takes place in a railroad car rather than in the backwoods. Hank Morgan, Huck Finn, and a number of lesser characters grow out of similar combinations. Because the experience is a narrated story, it has only a nominal reality; as fantasy, the social irony of self versus manners underlies the humor. The story is no more a characterization of its teller, really, than is the frog story of Simon Wheeler. Corporate ethics are at issue just as vanity is at issue in the "Jumping Frog." Many episodes in Twain's longer works depend on this effect; they are applicable as philosophical experience even though the reader knows they are unreal.

Twain is creating literature out of the material of the 1860s in "Cannibalism in the Cars." Egalitarian notions of government offer a comic mode for treating situations, and Twain is able to use such notions outside the Civil War context of Kerr and Nasby. Yet Twain's irony is inescapable. When "on the sixth [ballot], Mr. Harris was elected, all voting for him but himself," the point is again made that no amount of parliamentary rhetoric obscures the practical consideration of an individual's well-being; and so it was when Artemus Ward stepped forward and offered the vicarious sacrifice of his brother-in-law and uncle if need be to win the Civil War. The frame sequence that ends the story allows this "slurred nub" to remain an abstraction, clearly untrue but still horrifying to the auditor in the car. The texture of Twain's fiction, created by his diction and irony—his persona— appears in finished form in this short story. To understand how comparable materials condition a reader's understanding of Twain's viewpoint, it is necessary to examine the open framework for humor which Twain's travel fiction provided, and which became part of his machinery for creating the novel.

The Travel Narrative

The Innocents Abroad and the material related to it provide particularly clear relationships between literary tradition, Twainian pose, and ethical intention. In these relationships, the extension of the narrative into a rudimentary story foreshadows the novels' picaresque structure, as the material just studied foreshadows their texture. Twain's intention as a writer of literary comedy was set when he undertook the *Quaker City* voyage, and the writer's problem was thus to fit actual experience into a preconceived pose—a thoroughly literary exercise. Allusions to the Ward-Barnum tradition helped establish his viewpoint, and the interplay between the persona and the foreign milieu establish the tension between Old Europe and the new American viewpoint for which the book became famous. The book's events also coalesced around this viewpoint, however, and developed an increasingly serious demonstration of humanitarian qualities.

The book *The Innocents Abroad* was preceded by travel letters that were varied in quality but maintained the flexibility of persona and voice distinguishing his other work. Phoenix had written travel burlesques, as had Ward. Mortimer Thomson, whom Twain corresponded with about the *Quaker City* voyage, had published comic and burlesque travel adventures as early as 1855 in *Doesticks, What He Says.* Twain's own intention is shown most clearly in his letter describing Bierstadt's picture of Yosemite, which was on display in New York when he was there: "It is more the atmosphere of Kingdom-come than of California. As a picture, the work must please, but as a portrait I do not think it will answer. Portraits should be accurate. We do not want feeling and intelligence smuggled into the pictured face of an idiot, and we do not want this glorified atmosphere smuggled into a portrait of the Yosemite where it surely does not belong. I may be wrong, but still I believe that this atmosphere of Mr. Bierstadt's is altogether too gorgeous."[12]

Twain's sense of the Old Masters, as shown in "The Second Advent," applied the same realistic test to sentimentalized religion. Twain's notebooks show this skepticism toward the Holy Land even before he had been there, as Dewey Ganzel has pointed out, and he had already bracketed passages in guidebooks for special treatment. The literary comedian expresses his vision by describing, in Mr. Ganzel's words, "Missouri in Venice, the commonplace surroundings of the exotic, a pattern he was to use again and again in *IA.*"[13] The vulgarian's commonplace, almost the viewpoint of the low thief, would control the responses of the

American vandal abroad and reveal the psychology of "Mark Twain."

The beginning complaint of Twain's letters is almost an unnecessary vehicle for expressing his American vision through comedy. He complained that the travel books had shamefully deceived him, in a passage that was dropped from the Turkish Bath sequence before it went into *The Innocents Abroad*: "What is a Turkish bath in Constantinople to a Russian one in New York? What are the dancing dervishes to the negro minstrels?—and Heaven help us, what is Oriental splendor to the Black Crook?" To flesh out this view with humor, Twain borrowed freely from the tradition of literary comedy. Ward complained that all the jugs in the British Museum were of uncertain age—which did not affect him until he discovered that his chicken at lunch was also "of a uncertain age." Twain captured the same experience in a "Turkish Lunch" (II, 86–87) and expanded upon it with "euchre" terms from the American frontier. "Bishop Southgate's Matinee," in the *Alta* letters, copied Ward's burlesque panorama, which featured a drunken projectionist, from his 1866 tour. Both writers drew comic relationships between religious quackery and the Constitution. P. T. Barnum, earlier, and Twain, later, tested guides for truthfulness in the same way, and both found they lied.[14] Other jokes follow the same tradition.

The circus motif, which Barnum and Ward had developed as an American literary tradition, influences Twain's pose significantly, particularly in the crucial area of religion. In the opening sequence of the book, he masquerades as a minister with claims to the "missionary business" looking for a "show," a sort of Simon Suggs-Artemus Ward compound. Perhaps due to the presence of a Barnum agent on the *Quaker City*, many of Twain's reports reflected the circus. The cathedral at Milan was "bossed" by a "gorgeous old brick" who was mummified and displayed: "It's not part of the regular circus, you know, and so you have to pay extra." Other priests run little sideshows and perform as if they were performing outside a menagerie. Recapturing his Barnum items from St. Louis, Twain said that an Italian dwarf wouldn't stand any "show" in Constantinople: "A beggar has to have exceedingly good points to make a living" there.[15] The diction serves a distinct function in such passages, reflecting the outraged humanity of the narrator. Such brief encounters, exaggerated through ironic diction, also pile up a series of episodes that establish tension between European civilization and the angry, show-conscious traveler. The traveler finally becomes an antagonist, and his travels take on some of the aspects of a plot in which corporate Europe is the enemy.

Twain's treatment of Constantinople offers another point that indicates his method of converting the materials of the comic tradition to fit his own persona. After labeling gilt script inside the dome of St. Sophia "as glaring as a circus bill," he turns his attention from the shoddy atmosphere to the "old-master worshippers from the wilds of New Jersey," combining in a phrase the ideas of art, religion, false reverence, and provincialism. Ward, treating such persons and their entertainers in "The Show Business and Popular Lectures," complained that nine out of ten people "don't have no moore idee of what the lecturer sed than my kangaroo has of the sevunth speer of hevun." Twain complains that his set of traveling American farmers "don't know any more about pictures than a kangaroo does about astronomy."[16] Ward's showman idiom has been altered in tone and generalized to express a yankee cosmopolitanism.

Not only in single lines but also in set pieces and comic vignettes does the tradition contribute to "Twain's" experience. Barnum in Liverpool was assaulted by beggars whom he took for nobility in his innocence; and after him Artemus Ward in London said, "I don't remember a instance since my 'rival in London of my gettin into a cab without a Briton comin and purlitely shuttin the door for me, and then extendin his open hand to'ards me, in the most frenly manner possible. Does he not, by this simple yit tuchin gesture, welcum me to England?" Twain, sharing the American background of Barnum and Ward, shows the same surprise at European beggars but extends his dramatization in an *Alta* letter: "A crowd of bare-footed and ragged and dirty vagabonds, of both sexes, received us on the wharf, and with one hospitable impulse held out their hands. With one grateful impulse we seized the hands and shook them. And then we saw that their hospitality was a vain delusion—they only extended their hands to beg."[17] The earlier travelers had stopped their narrative after showing their own naïveté; Twain continues to define the community—"eminently Portuguese— that is to say, it is slow, poor, shiftless, sleepy and lazy." Continuing, Twain even locates a villain: "The good Catholic Portughee crossed himself and prayed to God to shield him from all blasphemous desire to know more than his father did before him."[18] Burlesque travel narratives take on through such identifications a tension between the narrator—Twain the American—and the milieu—dominated by static religiosity, the corporate church.

Before finishing the discussion of this nascent plot structure in the travel narrative, one or two other crucial borrowings from the tradition need to be developed as sources of the "American" persona, "Mark Twain." In Ward's London letters, the stealing of spoons, as Ward's "Uncle Wilyim" does, burlesques types who try to place themselves in an elevated social context, and newspaper items in Twain's era treat the subject of spoon stealing as comedy rather than with the life-and-death seriousness of *Moll Flanders*. Ward's letters and the Jim Griggins item use the joke as a representation of the venality of the small crook and to indicate his relative harmlessness—a sort of innocence. Twain used the "spoon stealing" joke three times in *The Innocents Abroad*, making it into a *motif* underlying the meeting between the *Quaker City* pilgrims and the Russian Czar. Twain had called into question the good sense and Christian charity of his fellow travelers early (I, 130), and here turns to satire, including through his special flexibility of voice even himself in the group. In the first reference, Twain states that he wants to steal the emperor's coat, claiming, "When I meet a man like that, I want something to remember him by (II, 110)." Then he described the tour by the *Quaker City* party: "We spent half an hour idling through the palace, admiring the cozy apartments and the rich but eminently homelike appointments of the palace, and then the imperial family bade our party a kind good-by, and proceeded to count the spoons" (II, 110). The implication of the passage is that such travelers as the pious voyagers were "low" and vulgar, sharing the traits that Jim Griggins blamed on his lack of education. Twain's borrowing from Ward thus strikes at the essence of the trip, a social pretension by upwardly mobile post-Civil War Americans. And Twain thus develops a theme. Visiting the Russian grand duke, "We bade our distinguished hosts good-by, and they retired happy and contented to their apartments to count *their* spoons" (II, 114). The ship's sailors are even supposed to expand the burlesque of the Russian reception when the third cook—Twain would make it the *third* cook—of the *Quaker City* plays the Czar, damns the formal speech of the visitors and tells his first groom to "proceed to count the portable articles of value belonging to the premises" (II, 121). There is little likelihood that such events occurred as narrated, particularly since there is a literary tradition behind Twain's line. The "low" characterization is no longer attached to a low figure—it has become almost philosophical in its ironic implications about social vanity, and Twain thus reasserts the values of the American comedians even while traveling in a cosmopolitan guise and speaking in a normal colloquial voice.

A second borrowing from Artemus Ward is equally illuminating. Artemus Ward's "Is he dead?" joke shows a British landlord's skepticism about spiritualism in "The Green Lion and Oliver Cromwell." The landlord didn't want to speak to the spirit of the historical figure, he only wanted the spiritualist's room rent. This sort of aggressive practicality, intolerant of historical humbug, is the fund upon which Twain was drawing when in *The Innocents Abroad* he shows his "boys" confronting the guides with the same question. As the guides make a sideshow out of Columbus and an Egyptian mummy, Twain's characters play credulous naifs: "Christopher Columbo—pleasant name—is—is he dead?" (I, 305). The one-line joke is elaborated into a scene and into a motif, as with the spoon-stealing joke. It appears twice in the last chapter of Book I and again in the opening chapter of Book II (I,305, 307; II,5). The transference of the joke from the municipal palace of Genoa (and before that from Ward's London surroundings) through the Vatican Museum at Rome and finally to the catacombs under the Capuchin Convent gradually extends Twain's irony about historical showmanship into the area of European Catholicism. The elaboration of the joke is more sophisticated than Ward's digressions, and the turning of the joke from European fraud to the church's view of man is appropriate to Twain's moral and humanitarian concerns in his fiction. Rather than signifying merely a verbal relation cloaking disparate and antagonistic intentions, as Bernard DeVoto has written, such open borrowings of jokes like the "Is he dead?" formula reflect the unity of viewpoint underlying the various American humorists generally.[19] Twain's elaboration and expansion of such jokes in language and format is his development of the tradition into a vision beyond the level of contemporary newspaper humor.

Finally, Twain's social reflections and religious commentary are pulled together in the Holy Land in burlesque scenes such as the Tomb of Adam sequence and in genteel statements such as those on Godfrey of Bouillon. The rhetorical high point, however, comes during the race into the Holy Land before the Sabbath. Twain's outrage at this point proves the value of his flexible voice, for his statement is intended to be taken seriously and is not burdened with a comic pose or inflection. He had made sarcastic comments about the Plymouth Collection of Hymns dominating ship life and remarked that Balaam's ass was "The patron saint of all pilgrims like us" (II,173). He is beyond this sarcasm and outside of his fictional character in attacking formulaic

Christianity as he saw its immediate consequences in the Holy Land:

> They *must* press on [the "pilgrims" trying to reach a holy point before Sunday]. Men might die, horses might die, but they must enter upon holy soil next week, with no sabbath-breaking stain upon them. Thus they were willing to commit a sin against the spirit of religious law, in order that they might preserve the letter of it. It was not worth while to tell them "the letter kills." I am talking now about personal friends; men whom I like; men who are good citizens; who are honorable, upright, conscientious: but whose idea of the Savior's religion seems to me distorted.
>
> (II, 172).

Josh Billings had commented in *His Sayings* in 1865 that "Heathen are alwus kind tew hosses, it iz only among Christian people, that a hoss hez tew trot 3 mile heats, in a hot da, for $2500 kounterfit munny," and other analogues to the attitude, notably in Dickens' *Hard Times*, predated Twain.[20] Yet so directly is the ethical position stated that problems of pose and persona become largely irrelevant. Twain has shifted from the literary comedian to the "real" (equally literary, of course) persona without apology and caused the hidden plot-action to appear in a single episode. His flexibility of voice allows for the expression of his own ethical background, fixed in his childhood and in the West as well as inherited from the comic tradition of egalitarianism. Burlesque donkey-riding sequences in Fayal at the opening of the book come to have a foreshadowing thematic relationship to the rest of the travels, and the ethics which underlie the narrator's viewpoint—the viewpoint which rejects corrupt corporations and governmental bodies in the novels and dissents from a host of social and religious vanities—protest the treatment of animals in a brief moment in the travel narrative.

There are a number of comparisons between the works of Artemus Ward and Mark Twain, but the most significant comparisons are those that show Twain's growth as an independent process. He was developing a sustained vision of society and an ethical stance out of the materials and techniques available in American literary comedy. Twain's innocent faces a more sophisticated environment than Ward's showman, and Twain's techniques are more mature and more flexible. His experiments with burlesque dramatization, as in "Barnum's First Speech in Congress," show him developing fictional characterizations to express the broad social and aesthetic criticism that distinguishes the literary comedians from the Yankee correspondents and Twain from the literary comedians in turn. The continuing presence of Ward's humor in Twain's mind through the writing of *The Innocents Abroad* is an indication of how much the tradition offered Twain in the expression of his own ethics. As he developed into a writer of books, he began to sustain and elaborate these themes from the comic tradition in his own way, deepening the form of the cosmopolitan travel burlesque as we have seen. He became capable of expressing a variety of sentiments in a variety of comic and serious modes. His writings of the 1860s are thus clearly the products of the school of literary comedy in America and just as clearly foreshadow the voice of the novelist.

Notes

1. Branch, *Literary Apprenticeship of Mark Twain*, 130; Day (ed.), *Mark Twain's Letters from Hawaii*, 94–95.

2. "How Are the Mighty Fallen!" is reprinted in Franklin Walker and G. Ezra Dane (eds.), *Mark Twain's Travels with Mr. Brown* (New York: Alfred A. Knopf, 1940), 116–19, as part of Letter XI. "Barnum's First Speech in Congress" has been made available to me by Professor Louis Budd. This selection from the New York *Express* matches a portion of the letter reprinted in Brown, 286, as being from the New York *Telegram* and subsequently the *Alta*.

3. There is a paradigm for Twain's depiction of Barnum in "Artemus Ward in Washington" in which the showman employs the terminology of national politics in conjunction with his private interests: "I'm reconstructing my show. I've Bo't a collection of life-size wax figgers of our prominent Revolutionary forefathers. I bo't'em

at auction, and got'em cheap. They stand me about two dollars and fifty cents (2 dols. 50 cents) per Revolutionary forefather. Ever as always yours, A. Ward."

4. Walker and Dane (eds.), *Travels with Mr. Brown*, 13–15, 18–19, 23–25.

5. Mark Twain, "Female Suffrage/Views of Mark Twain," St. Louis *Missouri Democrat*, March 12, 13, 1866; "Female Eddikashun," *Josh Billings: His Sayings* (New York: Carleton, 1866), 26–27. As a tangential point, the use of "Mrs. Zeb Leavenworth," offers evidence of the continuity of Twain's mind in holding comic formulations. In 1864, three years earlier, he signed the name "Zeb Leavenworth," a pilot friend from his Mississippi days, to a burlesque letter in "Those Blasted Children" which also uses strong language treating Twain as an advice-giver, while mentioning loss of hair. Here, Mrs. Leavenworth threatens to "snatch hair out of his head till he is as bald as a phrenological bust." The phrase and joke were retained together with their context and later recast to suit current needs. This ability bears on the relation between Twain and previous literary comedians.

6. Mark Twain, "Female Suffrage/The Iniquitous Crusade." St. Louis *Missouri Democrat*, March 15, 1867; Ward, *Works*, 417.

7. As Ward's Betsy Jane threatened to do in "A War Meeting," Ward, *Works*, 251. Louis Budd, *Mark Twain, Social Philosopher* (Bloomington: University of Indiana Press, 1962), 23–24.

8. Mark Twain, "Female Suffrage/Petticoat Government," New York *Sunday Mercury*, April 7, 1867, p. 3.

9. "Memoranda," *Galaxy*, IX (June, 1870), 858, reprinted in *Contributions to "The Galaxy"*, 47.

10. Mark Twain, "Cannibalism in the Cars," reprinted in *Sketches, New and Old*, 339–51. It originally appeared in *Broadway*, November, 1868, a house organ for the publishing firm of Routledge, Twain's British publisher at this time. An analogue for this story, which Artemus Ward created in London in 1866, appears in "Artemus Ward and Mark Twain," by Aaron Watson, *The Savage Club* (London: T. Fisher Unwin, 1907), 120–22, and anticipates the story in many details. Twain reduced the story to a one-line joke in "Riley—Newspaper Correspondent," *Contributions to "The Galaxy"*, 90: "had a grand human barbecue in honor of [the cannibal flag], in which it was noticed that the better a man liked a friend the better he enjoyed him."

11. Twain uses names of friends Dan Slote and Charles Langdon. Ward's "The Fair Inez" supplies a precedent for this coterie device in using names of his Cleveland friends, and the practice was probably a common one.

12. "Letter 24," *Alta California* (dated New York, June 2, 1867), in Scrapbook Seven, Mark Twain Papers, University of California, Berkeley.

13. John S. Tuckey (ed.), *Mark Twain's Fables of Man* (Berkeley: University of California Press, 1972), 50–68; Dewey Ganzel, *Mark Twain Abroad* (Chicago: University of Chicago Press, 1968), 146, 221.

14. Daniel Morley McKeithan (ed.), *Traveling with the Innocents Abroad* (Norman: University of Oklahoma Press, 1958), 132; Ward, *Works,* 444; *Travels with Mr. Brown*, 95–97. Compare Ward, *Works,* 44 on the Shakers, "said world continners to revolve round on her own axletree onct in every 24 hours, subjeck to the Constitution of the United States," with Twain's more refined addition to his letter in *The Innocents Abroad*, I, 68–69; "Antiquarians . . . agree that [Hercules] was an enterprizing and energetic man, but decline to believe him a good, bona fide god, because that would be unconstitutional." Barnum, *Life*, 268.

15. Ganzel, *Mark Twain Abroad*, 54; McKeithan (ed.), *Traveling with the Innocents Abroad*, 50–51, 115–16.

16. Ward, *Works,* 83; McKeithan (ed.), *Traveling with the Innocents Abroad*, 117.

17. Barnum, *Life*, 250–51; Ward, *Works,* 437; McKeithan (ed.), *Traveling with the Innocents Abroad*, 4.

18. McKeithan (ed.), *Traveling with the Innocents Abroad*, 16, 17.

19. DeVoto, *Mark Twain's America*, 220–21. More recently, Edwin H. Cady, *The Light of Common Day* (Bloomington: Indiana University Press, 1971), 80, has said that this "seems to me one of the classic instances of American humor, especially as it peaks in Chapter XXVII of *The Innocents Abroad*." Twain later took this same "Is he dead?" formula one step further in fabricating a story to define his attitude toward John Altgeld, who was running for the Illinois governorship on the platform that he would enforce all the laws of the state fully. Twain pretended that his anecdote was an actual experience from a circus in Little Rock, Arkansas, which was displaying an Egyptian Mummy:

> As the guide was giving (his talk) to the party of ten-cents-apiece customers, pointing out the various features of interest, a solemn-looking fellow, Bert Wheeler, interrupted him.
> "Is this man dead?" he asked.
> "Oh, yes, of course. He—"
> "How did he die?" persisted Bert.
> "Don't know," returned the attendant. "He—"
> "Ever been an inquest held over him in this country?" broke in Bert.

"No, you see, he's been dead for a long time," said the attendant. "Maybe four thousand years. So you see—"

"Makes no difference," snapped Bert, "I'm the coroner of this county, and if you haven't already a certificate on this man's death, he's got to have an inquest. That's the law. Boys, bring the deceased along. The laws of this county must be upheld."

Opie Read, *Mark Twain and I* (Chicago: Reilley & Lee, 1940), 119. This story was presented as a "real" experience, even though the "Is he dead?" element identifies it as an extension of the traditional skepticism of the literary naif. So completely does Twain come to believe in the literary expression that it finally becomes a new anecdote from the "old" Southwest to express his political views. One must not underestimate the value of this insight into Twain's use of local and vernacular-seeming materials.

20. Cited in Jesse Bier, *The Rise and Fall of American Humor* (New York: Holt, Rinehart, and Winston, 1968), 84. Sleery, the showman in Dickens' novel on factory life in England, expresses his humanity in his treatment of horses, so this idea can be seen as a cosmopolitan metaphor rather than a strictly western American one. Sleery delivers the following speech while offering to apprentice the orphaned Sissy Jupe, thus providing her with a permanent home and security: "But what I thay, Thquire, ith, that good tempered or bad tempered, I never did a horthe a injury yet, no more than thwearing at him went, and that I don't expect I thall begin otherwithe at my time of life, with a rider. I never wath much of a Cackler, Thquire, and I have thed my thay." Charles Dickens, *Hard Times* (New York: Holt, Rinehart and Winston, 1963), 35. To find an analogue for Twain's statement in a "vulgar" character such as Sleery reinforces the difference between "genteel" religion and the blunter humanism of the Twain persona as expressed in *The Innocents Abroad*.

The Middle Career of Mark Twain from *Tom Sawyer* to *Pudd'nhead Wilson*: The Comedian as Major Author

Novels of the Week:
The Adventures of Tom Sawyer

T he name of Mark Twain is known throughout the length and breadth of England. Wherever there is a railway-station with a bookstall his jokes are household words. Those whose usual range in literature does not extend beyond the sporting newspapers, the *Racing Calendar*, and the 'Diseases of Dogs,' have allowed him a place with Artemus Ward alongside of the handful of books which forms their library. For ourselves, we cannot dissociate him from the railway-station, and his jokes always rise in our mind with a background of Brown & Polson's Corn Flour and Taylor's system of removing furniture. We have read 'The Adventures of Tom Sawyer' with different surroundings, and still have been made to laugh; and that ought to be taken as high praise. Indeed, the earlier part of the book is, to our thinking, the most amusing thing Mark Twain has written. The humour is not always uproarious, but it is always genuine and sometimes almost pathetic, and it is only now and then that the heartiness of a laugh is spoilt by one of those pieces of self-consciousness which are such common blots on Mark Twain's other books. 'The Adventures of Tom Sawyer' is an attempt in a new direction. It is consecutive, and much longer than the former books, and as it is not put forward as a mere collection of "Screamers," we laugh more easily, and find some relief in being able to relax the conventional grin expected from the reader of the little

Reprinted from *The Athenaeum* No. 2539 (24 June 1876): 851.

volumes of railway humour. The present book is not, and does not pretend to be a novel, in the ordinary sense of the word; it is not even a story, for that presupposes a climax and a finish; nor is it a mere boys' book of adventures. In the Preface the author says, "Although my book is intended mainly for the entertainment of boys and girls, I hope it will not be shunned by men and women on that account, for part of my plan has been to try pleasantly to remind adults of what they once were themselves, and of how they felt and thought and talked, and what queer enterprises they sometimes engaged in." Questions of intention are always difficult to decide. The book will amuse grown-up people in the way that humorous books written for children have amused before, but (perhaps fortunately) it does not seem to us calculated to carry out the intention here expressed. With regard to the style, of course there are plenty of slang words and racy expressions, which are quite in place in the conversations, but it is just a question of whether it would not have been as well if the remainder of the book had not been written more uniformly in English.

On the Structure of *Tom Sawyer*

Walter Blair

I

Since, as several critics have suggested, *The Adventures of Tom Sawyer* (1876) attacked earlier juvenile literature in something roughly like the way *Joseph Andrews* attacked *Pamela*,[1] a note on the structure of the novel may well start (though it should not, I think, terminate) with a consideration of Clemens' book in its literary contexts. Such a consideration, by indicating the nature of the writings attacked and the way Mark Twain and other American humorists assaulted them, may emphasize certain architectural peculiarities in the volume and suggest more clearly than critics have done,[2] a unifying narrative thread.

Notable in earlier juvenile fictional works had been their characters, their preachments, and their plots. The children portrayed had been, for the most part, characterized with extraordinary simplicity: they had been good or bad, and that had been an end of it.[3] Horatio Alger's street boy heroes in the sixties, to be sure, had been more inclined towards naughtiness than flawless Little Eva or even beautifully trained Little Rollo had been.[4] But Alger's Ragged Dick, though he used profanity, patronized the Old Bowery Theatre, smoked, and played jokes on country folk, was "above doing anything mean or dishonorable. . . . or imposing upon younger boys. . . . His nature was noble and had saved

Reprinted from *Modern Philology* 37 (August 1939): 75–88.

him from all mean faults."[5] And as a rule, as a critic of the
Alger books has recently remarked:

> Our hero was. . . . a good boy, honest, abstemious (in fact
> sometimes unduly disposed to preach to drinkers and
> smokers), prudent, well-mannered (except perhaps for
> preaching), and frugal. . . . Nor did any subtleties of
> character-drawing prevent one from determining who were
> the good characters and who were the bad ones. They were
> labeled plainly.[6]

The bad children—as lacking in complexity as the good—
had been distinguished, perhaps, more by their proclivities
toward sin than by their accomplishments. Their crimes had
ranged all the way from simply being lazy or playing truant to
the most horrible outrages within their infantile powers—
lying, stealing, battering the helpless and the weak, swearing,
smoking, and even drinking. In short, with few exceptions, a
bad child had been as totally depraved (in intention) as the
non-elect of Calvinistic theology.[7]

The authors of juvenile tales, employing these angelic or
villainous children, had provided sermon-like commentaries
and had fashioned lesson-teaching plots. Constantly these
writers had "extolled the precocious child, deprecated
wholesome pleasure, and delighted in didactic
sentimentality,"[8] patting good children on the back, and
scolding bad children sternly. Even when he had skipped the
sermons, the reader of a typical story had been able to get its
point by noticing that the author's dénouement observed the
strictest poetic justice. In stories following what seemingly
was the earliest pattern—the best known instance of which is
the tale of Little Eva—the pallid virtuous child had died at the
age proverbially prescribed for the Good, but had promptly
gone to Heaven. The Alger boys, somewhat better adapted to
the Gilded Age, had survived childhood to become successful
business men. But the bad boy who had played truant "and
was not really sorry for what he had done . . . went from one
bad thing to another, and grew up to be a very wicked man,

and at last committed a murder"; while naughty Thomas, who loafed all day or played with his kite, had a depressing adulthood:

> Without a shilling in his purse,
> Or cot to call his own,
> Poor Thomas went from bad to worse,
> And hardened as a stone.[9]

During the years before *Tom Sawyer* appeared, such good-bad-child tales, with their preachments and predetermined conclusions, had suggested incongruities between fiction and life useful to many American humorists. Beginning in the forties comic writers had sporadically beguiled readers with amoral portraits of unregenerate boys. Johnson J. Hooper's Simon Suggs had cheated his father at cards in 1845,[10] and in the fifties adolescent Sut Lovengood and young Ike Partington had perpetrated sundry deviltries. Ike, perhaps the most notorious of these juvenile delinquents, in the first volume in which he had appeared, had told lies, scratched letters on a newly japanned tray, broken countless windows, stolen oranges and cakes and doughnuts, hanged a cat, and imitated the hero of *The black avenger, or the pirates of the Spanish Main*.[11] In the seventies Max Adeler's Cooley boy was creating commotions in church, and kindred spirits in the writings of other humorists were behaving, in sketches, as Tom was to behave in a book. Doubtless the incongruity between these youths and those in contemporary books not only augmented their comic appeal but also molded the form of stories about them.

At least as early as the sixties, various authors had begun an even more direct onslaught upon juvenile fictional characters. Henry Ward Beecher, for example, had said in an essay written for a New York paper:

> The real lives of boys are yet to be written. The lives of pious and good boys, which enrich the catalogues of great publishing societies, resemble a real boy's life about as much as a chicken picked and larded, upon a spit, and ready for

delicious eating, resembles a free fowl in the fields. With some honorable exceptions, they are impossible boys, with incredible goodness. Their piety is monstrous. A man's experience stuffed into a little boy is simply monstrous. . . . Boys have a period of mischief as much as they have measles or chicken-pox.[12]

In 1869, Thomas Bailey Aldrich had launched his somewhat mild full-length portrait of Tom Bailey with a defiant passage calling attention to the difference between the Model Boy and the human youngster:

I call my story the story of a bad boy, partly to distinguish myself from those faultless young gentlemen who generally figure in narratives of this kind, and partly because I really was *not* a cherub. I may truthfully say I was an amiable, impulsive lad, blessed with fine digestive powers, and no hypocrite. I didn't want to be an angel. . . . and I didn't send my little pocketmoney to the natives of the Feejee Islands, but spent it royally on peppermint drops and tiffy candy. In short, I was a real human boy, such as you may meet anywhere in New England, and no more like an impossible boy in a story-book than a sound orange is like one that has been sucked dry.[13]

The story carrying this foreword could swell the circulation of *Our young folks* in 1869, and, in book form, could quickly run through eleven editions.[14]

By the middle of the seventies, the Moral Boy had become a dependable butt for humorists. During the year 1873, when *Tom Sawyer* was incubating, James M. Bailey was surmising that the nine-year-old Concord boy whose ability to repeat the multiplication table backwards had been recorded in a news item was the same hateful paragon who had lived next door to Bailey in his childhood—a youth who "always went to bed at eight o'clock. . . . brushed his hair back of his ears, and carried a store handkerchief. . . . He was the model boy, the boy our parents used to point to, and speak of. . . . while unfitting us for sitting on anything harder than a poultice."[15] The year before *Tom Sawyer* was issued, a Detroit humorist published sketches, "The good boy" and "The bad boy," satirizing some of the excesses of Sunday school fiction.[16] In the year Clemens' novel appeared, Robert Burdette humorously referred to "well-known 'good boys' who wash their faces every morning, keep their clothes clean, wear white collars, and don't say bad words."[17]

None of these attacks, it is probable, can be thought of as a direct inspiration of Mark Twain's book about boys. They are useful only to show a common conception of the humor of childhood and the nature of children of which he could take advantage. As a matter of fact, Twain himself had been rather early in the field with "The story of the good little boy who did not prosper" (1867) and "The story of the bad little boy who didn't come to grief" (1870)—both burlesques.[18] Jim, the hero of the former sketch, stole jam without the usual consequences: "all at once a terrible feeling didn't come over him. . . . He ate that jam and said it was bully." He stole apples and survived, purloined the teacher's penknife and shifted the blame to "the moral boy, the good little boy of the village, who always obeyed his mother, and never told an untruth, and was fond of his lessons, and infatuated with Sunday-school." Jim was delighted when the paragon was whipped, because he "hated moral boys. Jim said he was 'down on them milksops.'" Thus "everything turned out differently with him from the way it does to the bad Jameses in the books." In manhood, Jim "got wealthy by all manner of cheating and rascality; and now he is the infernalest wickedest scoundrel in his native village, and is universally respected, and belongs to the legislature."

Jacob Blivens in the 1870 sketch behaved so abnormally— refusing to play hookey, to lie, and to play on Sunday—that other children decided he was "afflicted," though the real trouble was simply that he "read all the Sunday-school books. . . . This was the secret of it." Again there was an attack upon the endings of stories about children. In them, the models "always had a good time, and the bad boys had the broken legs; in his case there was a screw loose somewhere, and it all happened the other way."

II

One who turns to *Tom Sawyer* with the conventional literature and the humorous attacks on that literature by various writers including Twain in mind may see some important achievements of Clemens' novel. These were suggested by a contemporary critic who said:

> This literary wag has performed some services which entitle him to the gratitude of his generation. He has run the traditional Sunday-school boy through his literary mangle and turned him out washed and ironed into a proper state of collapse. That whining, canting, early-dying, anaemic creature was held up to mischievous lads as worthy of imitation. He poured his religious hypocrisy over every honest pleasure a boy had. He whined his lachrymous warnings on every playground. He vexed their lives. So when Mark grew old enough, he went gunning for him, and lo, wherever his soul may be, the skin of the strumous young pietist is now neatly tacked up to view on the Sunday-school door of to-day as a warning.[19]

That the attack thus suggested may have been responsible in part for the organization of the narrative becomes clear if the story is restated in the way it would have been handled in the literature attacked. The opening chapter of Clemens' novel reveals a character who, in terms of moralizing juvenile literature, has the indubitable earmarks of a Bad Boy. As the story opens, Tom is stealing. Caught in the act, he avoids punishment by deceiving his aunt. He departs to play hookey, returns to stand slothfully by while a slave boy does his chores for him, then enters the house to deceive his aunt again. His trickery exposed by his half-brother Sid, he dashes out of the door shouting threats of revenge. A few minutes later, he is exchanging vainglorious boasts with a stranger whom he hates simply because the stranger is cleanly and neatly dressed. The action of the chapter concludes with Tom pounding the strange boy into submission (for no righteous reason), then chasing him home. "At last," says the author, "the enemy's mother appeared, and called Tom a bad, vicious vulgar child. . . ." If earlier moral writers had had a chance at Tom, they would have been much more eloquent, for within a few pages he has committed many of the enormities against which they had battled for years.

But as the story continues, Bad Boy Tom continues to sin (as these authors would have put it) in a fashion almost unprecedented in the fiction of the time. Up to the last page of chapter x, he piles up enough horrible deeds to spur the average Sunday school author to write pages of admonitions. His actions are of a sort to show that he is—in the language of such an author—thievish, guileful, untruthful, vengeful, vainglorious, selfish, frivolous, self-pitying, dirty, lazy, irreverent, superstitious and cowardly.

What a chance for sermonizing! But Clemens makes nothing of his opportunity: he indicates not the least concern about his hero's mendacity. In fact, his preaching (such as it is) is of a perverse sort. Instead of clucking to show his horror, he writes of Tom's sins with a gusto which earlier authors had reserved for the deeds of Good Boys, and on occasion (as when he tells about the whitewashing trick), he actually commends the youth for his chicanery. A ragged ruffian named Huckleberry Finn who smokes and swears is set up as an ideal figure because:

> . . . he did not have to go to school or to church, or call any being master or obey anybody; he could go fishing or swimming when and where he chose, and stay as long as it suited him; nobody forbade him to fight; he could sit up as late as he pleased; . . . he never had to wash, nor put on clean clothes; he could swear wonderfully. In a word, every-thing that goes to make life precious, that boy had. So thought every harassed, hampered, respectable boy in St. Petersburg [chap. vi].

On the other hand, the sort of spiteful disdain which had been used to chasten Bad Boys in other books is actually employed here to introduce an indubitable Good Boy. To church on Sunday, says Clemens,

. . . . last of all came the Model Boy, Willie Mufferson, taking
as heedful care of his mother as if she were cut glass. He
always brought his mother to church, and was the pride of
all the matrons. The boys hated him, he was so good. And
besides, he had been "thrown up to them" so much. His
white handkerchief was hanging out of his pocket behind, as
usual on Sundays—accidentally. Tom had no handkerchief,
and he looked upon boys who had, as snobs.[20]

The ending of the book departs as determinedly from the
patterns of juvenile fiction. It staggers the imagination to guess
the sort of punishment which would have been deigned fitting
for such a monster as Tom by fictionists who had felt hanging
in adulthood was an appropriate result of youthful truancy.
From their standpoint, the author of *Tom Sawyer* must have
outraged poetic justice to the point of being hideously
immoral. Here were Tom and his companions, who had run
away, played truant, and smoked to boot, actually lionized
because they returned from Jackson's Island. Here was Tom
cheered to the echo because he saved an unjustly accused
man, compared with George Washington by Judge Thatcher
because he took Becky's punishment, lionized because he
saved the girl from the cave.[21] More shocking, here was even
the unregenerate Huck dramatically saving the life of the
Widow Douglas. And to top it all, these boys were allowed at
the end to accumulate a fortune of the size exclusively
awarded to only the best of the Alger heroes.

Thus the characterization, the perverse preaching, the
unconventional ending of the book, which gave the volume in
its day a comic appeal now all but irrecoverable, also, it is
possible, did much to mold the form of the narrative. The
simplest explanation of the arrangement of happenings in
Clemens' book is that it represented a fictional working-out of
the author's antipathy to the conventional plot so broadly
developed in "The story of a bad little boy who didn't come to
grief"—a more serious handling of a reversed moralizing
narrative.

III

One effect of this method of telling a story was, of course, to give youthful readers exactly the sort of a series of happenings likely to please them.[22] Here was the story of a character who, in their opinion, was a real boy, a character who, furthermore, time after time, when he was idolized for his achievements, fulfilled the sort of daydreams which had been their own.[23]

A second effect was perhaps even more important. In attacking in other than a burlesque fashion fictional representations of boys who were unreal, Clemens was faced with the problem of depicting, through characterization and plot, boys who were real.[24] What a real boy was was suggested by the very terms of the attack: he was not simply good or bad but a mixture of virtue and mischievousness. And he could play pranks at the same time he was developing qualities which would make him a moral adult.

This concept allowed elements of incongruity which an author might develop humorously. In this view, youngsters of Tom's age were diverting combinations of ignorance and wisdom, deviltry and morality, childhood and adulthood. These incongruities, of course, were useful to Clemens again and again.[25] But the incongruities of boy nature not only had humorous possibilities; they also had potentialities—far beyond those in good-bad-boy books—for plot structures closely linked with developing characters. As a "real" boy grew up, the common sense theory implied, unlike the consistent actions of the static character in goody-goody books, the nature of his actions would change. Not only would they change from year to year but also from month to month. Less and less, he would behave like an irresponsible and ignorant savage; more and more he would act like a responsible and intelligent adult.

If *Tom Sawyer* is regarded as a working out in fictional form of this notion of a boy's maturing, the book will reveal, I believe, a structure on the whole quite well adapted to its purpose. My suggestion, in other words, is that Clemens' divergence from the older patterns of juvenile fiction and his concept of the normal history of boyhood led him to a way of characterizing and a patterning of action which showed a boy developing toward manhood.

That this was the unifying theme of the story will be indicated, perhaps, by a consideration of the units of narrative, the lines of action, in the novel. There are four of these—the story of Tom and Becky, the story of Tom and Muff Potter, the Jackson's Island episode, and the series of happenings (which might be called the Injun Joe story) leading to the discovery of the treasure. Each one of these is initiated by a characteristic and typically boyish action. The love story begins with Tom's childishly fickle desertion of his fiancée, Amy Lawrence; the Potter narrative with the superstitious trip to the graveyard; the Jackson's Island episode with the adolescent revolt of the boy against Aunt Polly, and Tom's youthful ambition to be a pirate; the Injun Joe story with the juvenile search for buried treasure. Three of these narrative strands, however, are climaxed by a characteristic and mature sort of action, a sort of action, moreover, directly opposed to the initial action. Tom chivalrously takes Becky's punishment and faithfully helps her in the cave; he defies boyish superstition and courageously testifies for Muff Potter; he forgets a childish antipathy and shows mature concern for his aunt's uneasiness about him. The Injun Joe story, though it is the least useful of the four so far as showing Tom's maturing is concerned, by showing Huck conquering fear to rescue the widow, has value as a repetition—with variations—of the motif of the book.

That these actions are regarded by the older folk of St. Petersburg as evidences of mature virtue is suggested in each instance by their reactions. Every subplot in the book eventuates in an expression of adult approval. Sometimes this is private, like Aunt Polly's discovery that Tom has come from the island to tell her of his safety, or like Judge Thatcher's enthusiastic comments upon Tom's chivalry at school. Sometimes it is public, like the adulation lavished on the hero after the trial and after the rescue of Becky, or like the widow's party honoring Huck Finn.

The book contains various episodes extraneous to these lines of action—episodes whose only value in the scheme is variation in the display of the incongruities of boy nature from which the actions arise, but it is notable how much of the novel is concerned with these four threads. Only four of the thirty-five chapters are not in some way concerned with the development of at least one of them.[26] Hence a large share of the book is concerned with actions which show the kind of development suggested.

More important is the fact that, if the novel is regarded as one narrative including the alternately treated lines of action and the episodes as well, as the story progresses, wholly boylike actions become more infrequent while adult actions increase. No such simple and melodramatic a device as a complete reformation is employed: late in the book, Tom is still capable of treasure hunts and fantasies about robber gangs. (Clemens remarked that he "didn't take the chap beyond boyhood.")[27] But actions which are credible late in the story—actions such as Tom's taking Becky's punishment (chap. xx) or testifying for Potter (chap. xxiii)—would, I think, seem improbable early in the book.[28] One of a few slips Clemens makes strengthens this point: in chapter xxiv, Tom tells Huck that when he is rich he is "going to buy a new drum, and sure 'nough sword, and a red necktie and bull pup, and get married." Mr. Edgar Lee Masters finds this jarring. "Can any boy of that age," he asks, "be imagined talking in this way. . . . ?"[29] It is jarring in chapter xxiv, to be sure, but at any point in the first five chapters of the book, say, it would be highly appropriate.[30]

There is perhaps, then, reason for believing that the theme, the main action, and the character portrayal in the novel are one—the developing of Tom's character in a series of crucial situations. Studying the progress of the novel with this in mind, the reader will see, I believe, that though the earlier chapters emphasize Tom's mischievousness, and though a

Sunday school fictionist would therefore call him a Bad Boy, there are potentialities in these chapters for his later behavior.[31] To put the matter negatively, his motives are never vicious; to put it positively, he has a good heart. In his aunt's words, he

> . . . . warn't *bad*, so to say—only mischeevous. Only just giddy, and harum-scarum, you know. He warn't any more responsible than a colt. *He* never meant any harm, and he was the best-hearted boy that ever was. . . . [chap. xv].

An appeal to his sympathy, he himself indicates in chapter ii, is more efficacious than physical punishment or scolding. "She talks awful," he says to Aunt Polly, "but talk don't hurt—anyways it don't if she don't cry." Inevitably then, when at the end of chapter x, his aunt weeps over him, "this was worse than a thousand whippings." And a chapter later, tender-hearted Tom is ministering to poor Muff Potter as he languishes in jail.

Significant, too, is Tom's acceptance, in times of stress in the early chapters, of the adult code of the particularly godly folk of idyllic St. Petersburg.[32] His feeling that it would be pleasant to die disappears when he remembers that he does not have "a clean Sunday-school record" (chap. viii), and the howling dog's prophecy of his death brings regret that he has been "playing hookey and doing everything a feller's told *not* to do." "But if I ever get off this time," he promises, "I lay I'll just *waller* in Sunday-schools!" (chap. x). Surrounded by night on Jackson's Island, he inwardly says his prayers, and a little later, his conscience gnaws as he recalls his sins (chap. xiii). He wants to be a soldier, or a plainsman, or a pirate chiefly in order that he may stroll into the drowsy little St. Petersburg church some Sunday morning and bask in the respect of the village (chap. viii). And his impelling desire for a place of honor in the community is a key to his initiating three of the four lines of action,[33] hence the plot strands are closely linked with his character.

Beginning with the final pages of chapter x, these potentialities for something more mature than inconsiderate childhood begin to develop. Tom is touched by his aunt's appeal to his sympathy; his conscience hurts because of his silence about Potter's innocence; he suffers pangs because he realized he has sinned in running away; he worries about his aunt's concern for his safety, and so on. And well in the second half of the book, in a series of chapters—xx, xxiii, xxix, xxxii—come those crucial situations in which he acts more like a grownup than like an irresponsible boy.

IV

There are some indications that Clemens was aware of the pattern I have suggested. He was aware, undoubtedly, of the divergence from the older fictional models patently burlesqued in his "Bad boy" and "Good boy" travesties. Did he perceive, however, that deliberate divergence from older patterns had led him to create a new structure of his own, nearer to the history of boyhood as he and others conceived it? It is impossible to be sure, but some facts may have a bearing on the problem.

In Clemens' "Conclusion" to *Tom Sawyer* (the italics are his) he wrote: "So endeth this chronicle. It being strictly a history of a *boy*, it must stop here; the story could not go much further without becoming the history of a *man*." When in 1875 he wrote Howells asking him to read the manuscript, Mark Twain asked him particularly to "see if you don't really decide that I am right in closing with him as a boy."[34] And writing to Howells, shortly after the critic had read the manuscript, the humorist said he had decided to discard or not to write what would have been chapter xxxvi, and to add nothing in its place. "Something told me," he said, "that the book was done when I got to that point"—presumably, from the context, the present concluding chapter (xxxv) of the book.[35]

The concluding passage in this chapter tells how Huck Finn, tired of civilization, sneaked away from the widow and started to live again a life free from adult restraints. In chapter vi, it may be recalled, this sort of life had been, in Tom's opinion, most enviable: "everything that goes to make life precious, that boy had." So Tom had thought when all adult curbs had been hateful to him, when grown folk had seemed to be natural enemies, and their ways unnatural ways. But now Tom, bent on dragging Huck back to that civilization, tells the runaway that everybody lives cleanly and according to schedule, "And besides," he urges, "if you'll try this sort of thing just awhile longer you'll come to like it." Craftily, when Huck's chance remark helps Tom "see his opportunity," Tom dangles the bait of the robber gang. But though in chapter xiii Huck in rags was eligible for piratehood and even as late as chapter xxxiii his savagery has not been mentioned as a bar to his joining the robbers, now, to lure the boy back to the Widow's, Tom insists that Huck the Red-handed will have to live with the good woman and be "respectable" if he is to be allowed to join the gang. Something has happened to Tom. He is talking more like an adult than like an unsocial child. He has, it appears, gone over to the side of the enemy.

Notes

1. Critics who have noted the departure of the novel from conventional literature about children include Carl Van Doren, *The American Novel* (New York, 1921), p. 168; Stuart P. Sherman, "Mark Twain," in *The Cambridge History of American Literature* (New York, 1921), III, 15; and Percy H. Boynton, in his "Introduction" to the Harper's Modern Classics ed., pp. xx–xxii.

2. A typical comment is that of F.L. Pattee who, in his *American Literature since 1870* (New York, 1915), pp. 59–60, says of Twain's writings (including *Tom Sawyer*): "They are not artistic books. The author had little skill in construction. He excelled in brilliant dashes, not in long continued effort." Compare Carl Van Doren, p. 169, speaking of *Tom Sawyer:* "To a delicate taste, indeed, the book seems occasionally overloaded with matters brought in at moments

when no necessity in the narrative calls for them. . . . Nor can the murder about which the story is built up be said to dominate it very thoroughly. The story moves forward in something the same manner as did the plays of the seventies, with entrances and exits not always motivated." More recently A. H. Quinn, in *American Fiction, an Historical and Critical Survey* (New York, 1936), p. 256, has asserted that Clemens' "definition of the humorous story as one that 'may be spun out at great length and wander about as much as it pleases, and arrive nowhere in particular' is illuminating in its explanation of his strength and weakness as a writer of fiction. Like Bret Harte he is best in his episodes, and it is through them that he built up the characters. . . . by which he will be remembered," including Tom Sawyer.

3. Exceptions, in some ways, to these generalizations, had been some characters in novels by Louisa M. Alcott, Elijah J. Kellogg, and J. T. Trowbridge. The exceptions, however, do not, I think invalidate the generalizations.

4. Little Rollo, created by Jacob Abbott in 1834 to survive at least twenty-four volumes of boyhood, was surrounded by wise instructors who quickly reasoned him out of impulses toward sin. The same careful nurture kept upright his brothers and sisters in four series of books. Goodrich's Peter Parley narratives, in much the same tradition, were roughly contemporaneous.

5. *Ragged Dick* (Philadelphia, [n.d]), pp.15–18. During the course of the book, however, Dick reformed, and his evil habits were replaced with good ones. It is notable that Alger indicated his departure from the tradition of the completely virtuous hero when he said, "I have mentioned Dick's faults and defects because I want it understood, to begin with, that I don't consider him a model boy."

6. Frederick Lewis Allen, "Horatio Alger, Jr.," *Saturday Review of Literature*, XVIII (September 17, 1938), 4.

7. Some exceptions included, in addition to some Alger boys, the heroes of Oliver Optic's *In School and Out* (1863) and of Francis Forrester's *Dick Duncan* (1864), who, after sinning divertingly for several chapters, were allowed to reform. See Richard Allen Foster, *The School in American Literature* (Baltimore, 1930), pp. 134–35.

8. K. K. Maxfield, "'Goody-goody' Literature and Mrs. Stowe," *American Speech*, V (February, 1920), 201.

9. The story of the truant, which appeared in a reader, and the poem about the idle boy, from *Youth's Casket* (1857), are reprinted in E. Douglas Branch, *The Sentimental Years 1836–1860* (New York, 1934), pp. 312–13. For details concerning the preachments in the McGuffey readers, see Mark Sullivan, *Our Times* (New York, 1927), II, 23–45.

10. He had so far observed the amenities as to grow up to be a rascal, but since his creator obviously delighted in his rascality, Hooper was considered a most immoral person by contemporaries.

11. B. P. Shillaber, *Life and Sayings of Mrs. Partington* (New York, 1854). Ike, for all his resemblance to the later Tom Sawyer, was a rather sketchy character because, as a rule, he committed his crimes in the final lines of a narrative chiefly devoted to his aunt.

12. *Eyes and Ears* (Boston, 1862), pp. 73–74.

13. *The Story of a Bad Boy* (Boston, 1869), pp. 8–9.

14. Feris Greenslet, *The Life of Thomas Bailey Aldrich* (Boston, 1908), p. 92.

15. *Life in Danbury* (Boston, 1873), pp. 72–73. A section on pp. 275–83 called "The Danbury youth" burlesques the old rewards-and-punishment fiction by remarking that "boys who put stones in snow balls grow up to be bad men, and finally die a miserable death in a New York custom house" and foreshadows passages in *Tom Sawyer* by recounting how a boy "whose imagination had become diseased by too much close devotion to dime novels started off yesterday to seek fame as a slayer of bears and Indians. He. . . . was gone nearly two hours."

16. M. Quad [C.B. Lewis], *Quad's Odds* (Detroit, 1875), pp.379–87. The Bad Boy, like Tom Sawyer after him, had "an ambition which nothing could check. He wanted to be a bold pirate and sail on the raging main. . . ." "Jeems," on pp. 354–55 of the same volume, tolerantly told of the difficulty a mother had getting her son started to Sunday school.

17. *The Rise and Fall of the Mustache and Other Hawk-Eyetems* (Burlington, 1877), p. 165.

18. The former first appeared in *The Celebrated Jumping Frog of Calevaras County and Other Sketches* (New York, 1867), the latter in *The Galaxy* for May, 1870. Both were frequently reprinted before their inclusion in *Sketches New and Old* (Hartford, 1875). Both therefore appeared early enough to merit consideration as germinal for Clemens' famous story of boyhood.

19. Quoted in Will M. Clemens, *Mark Twain: His Life and Work* (Chicago, 1894), p. 126. The writer is identified as "a well-known literary critic," and the passage is drawn from a review. I have been unable, however, to find the original review.

20. Chap. v. See also chap. i, in which the author says, approvingly, of Tom: "He was not the Model Boy of the village. He knew the model boy very well though—and loathed him."

21. A female critic so strongly conditioned by preachy literature that she managed to find a moral, of all places, in *Huckleberry Finn*, in 1887 called attention to outstanding examples of Tom's nobility.

"Only a noble and tender heart," she said admiringly, "could have taken the blame upon itself when Becky accidentally tore the teacher's book, and received 'without an outcry the most merciless flogging that even Mr. Dobbins had ever administered'; and 'when he stepped forward to go to his punishment the surprise, the gratitude, the adoration that shone upon him out of poor Becky's eyes seemed pay enough for a hundred floggings.' The scene in the cave, of the rough boy folding in his arms the lost and weeping little girl, is a beautiful one"—Sarah K. Bolton, *Famous American authors* (New York, 1887), p. 369.

22. "My story," said the author in his preface, "is intended mainly for boys and girls." He made changes in his manuscript with his childish audience in view. (See *Mark Twain's letters* (New York, 1917), I, 272, 273.) However, he was not always sure that the book was not for adults.

23. Booth Tarkington's shrewd suggestion is that Clemens gave his youthful character "adventures that all boys, in their longing dreams, make believe they have. He made extravagant, dramatic things happen to them; they were pitted against murderers, won their ladyloves, and discovered hidden gold. He made them so real that their very reality is the stimulus of the adult reader's laughter, but he embedded this reality in the romance of a plot as true to the conventional mid-nineteenth century romantic novel-writing as it was to the day-dreams the boy Mark Twain himself had been"—Introduction to Cyril Clemens, *My Cousin Mark Twain* (Emmaus, Pa., 1939).

24. Clemens at least wanted to do this. "Part of my plan," he said in his preface, "has been to try to pleasantly remind adults of how they thought and talked, and what queer enterprises they sometimes engaged in."

25. The famous whitewashing scene, to cite one example, played upon some of these discrepancies: Tom, vainly trying to escape his chore, was the mischievous and ignorant boy. When, later, he got other boys, less canny than he, to do the job for him, he displayed the sort of wisdom—perhaps even of morality—becoming to an adult. "He," said his approving historian, "had discovered a great law of human action, without knowing it—namely, that in order to make a man or boy covet a thing, it is only necessary to make the thing difficult to attain."

26. Chaps. i (which is expository), v, viii, and xxi. Chap. xxii, however, contains only one sentence concerning the Becky Thatcher story. This narrative occurs in twelve chapters, the Injun Joe story twelve, the Jackson's Island episode seven, and the Muff Potter subplot five. Eight chapters contain elements of two lines of action.

27. *Letters*, I, 258.

28. Two kinds of probability are, I believe, theoretically involved here—one that which represents the intelligent person's general conception of the way a boy matures, the other that which derives from a study of the character of Tom as it is displayed in the book. In this instance, I think, the two kinds of probability coincide.

29. *Mark Twain: a Portrait* (New York, 1938), p. 125. Tom's age is not specified in the book, except by his actions. The fact that the action of the book requires only a few months seems irrelevant, since fictional rather than actual time is involved.

30. It is not incongruous, for example, with the list of Tom's treasures in chap. ii.

31. If Clemens' book was to be on a level above that of travesty, such potentialities had to be indicated. A rule of literary art which Twain himself formulated in "Fenimore Cooper's Literary Offenses," in *Literary Essays* (New York, 1899), p. 81, was "that the characters in a tale shall be so clearly defined that the reader can tell beforehand what each will do in a given emergency." Thus his very divergence from the simple motivation of earlier fictional works necessitated more complex characterization than they contained.

32. Kind-hearted Muff Potter, the grave-robbing Dr. Robinson, and the Temperance Tavern keeper who bootlegs are the nearest approach to native sin. Injun Joe and his vague companion from somewhere "up the river" are not of the community. The chief hints of vice Tom picks up anywhere are in the novels he reads.

33. The Becky Thatcher story, the exception, is, as has been suggested, also a natural expression of Tom's character.

34. *Letters*, I, 259.

35. Clemens wrote: "As to that last chapter, I think of just leaving it off and adding nothing in its place. Something told me the book was done when I got to that point—and so the temptation to put Huck's life into detail, instead of generalizing it in a paragraph was resisted" (*ibid.*, I, 267).

Mark Twain

William Dean Howells

I n one form or other, Mr. Samuel L. Clemens has told the
story of his life in his books, and in sketching his career I
shall have to recur to the leading facts rather than to offer
fresh information. He was remotely of Virginian origin and
more remotely of good English stock; the name was well
known before his time in the South, where a senator, a
congressman, and other dignitaries had worn it; but his branch
of the family fled from the destitution of those vast landed
possessions in Tennessee, celebrated in *The Gilded Age*, and
went very poor to Missouri. Mr. Clemens was born on
November 30, 1835, at Florida in the latter State, but his father
removed shortly afterward to Hannibal, a small town on the
Mississippi, where most of the humorist's boyhood was spent.
Hannibal as a name is hopelessly confused and ineffective; but
if we can know nothing of Mr. Clemens from Hannibal, we can
know much of Hannibal from Mr. Clemens, who, in fact, has
studied a loafing, out-at-elbows, down-at-the-heels,
slaveholding Mississippi River town of thirty years ago, with
such strong reality in his boy's romance of *Tom Sawyer*, that
we need inquire nothing further concerning the type. The
original perhaps no longer exists anywhere; certainly not in
Hannibal, which has grown into a flourishing little city since
Mr. Clemens sketched it. In his time the two embattled forces
of civilization and barbarism were encamped at Hannibal,

Section VII reprinted from *My Mark Twain* (NY: Harper & Bros.,
1910, pp. 113–123) originally published in *Century Magazine* XXIV
(September 1882), 780–83.

as they are at all times and everywhere; the morality of the place was the morality of a slaveholding community: fierce, arrogant, one-sided—this virtue for white, and that for black folks; and the religion was Calvinism in various phases, with its predestinate aristocracy of saints and its rabble of hopeless sinners. Doubtless, young Clemens escaped neither of the opposing influences wholly. His people like the rest were slaveholders; but his father, like so many other slaveholders abhorred slavery—silently, as he must in such a time and place. If the boy's sense of justice suffered anything of that perversion which so curiously and pitiably maimed the reason of the whole South, it does not appear in his books, where there is not an ungenerous line, but always, on the contrary, a burning resentment of all manner of cruelty and wrong.

The father, an austere and singularly upright man, died bankrupt when Clemens was twelve years old, and the boy had thereafter to make what scramble he could for an education. He got very little learning in school, and like so many other Americans in whom the literary impulse is native, he turned to the local printing-office for some of the advantages from which he was otherwise cut off. Certain records of the three years spent in the Hannibal *Courier* office are to be found in Mark Twain's book of sketches; but I believe there is yet no history anywhere of the *wanderjahre*, in which he followed the life of a jour-printer, from town to town, and from city to city, penetrating even so far into the vague and fabled East as Philadelphia and New York.

He returned to his own town—his *patria*—sated, if not satisfied, with travel, and at seventeen he resolved to "learn the river" from St. Louis to New Orleans as a steamboat pilot. Of this period of his life he has given a full account in the delightful series of papers, *Piloting on the Mississippi,* which he printed seven years ago in the *Atlantic Monthly.* The growth of the railroads and the outbreak of the Civil War put an end to profitable piloting, and at twenty-four he was again open to a vocation. He listened for a moment to the loudly calling drum of that time, and he was actually in camp for

three weeks on the rebel side; but the unorganized force to
which he belonged was disbanded, and he finally did not "go
with his section" either in sentiment or in fact. His brother
having been appointed Lieutenant-Governor of Nevada
Territory, Mr. Clemens went out with him as his private
secretary; but he soon resigned his office and withdrew to the
mines. He failed as a miner, in the ordinary sense; but the life
of the mining-camp yielded him the wealth that the pockets of
the mountain denied; he had the Midas touch without
knowing it, and all these grotesque experiences have since
turned into gold under his hand. After his failure as a miner
had become evident even to himself, he was glad to take the
place of local editor on the Virginia City *Enterprise,* a
newspaper for which he had amused himself in writing from
time to time. He had written for the newspapers before this;
few Americans escape that fate; and as an apprentice in the
Hannibal *Courier* office his humor had embroiled some of the
leading citizens, and impaired the fortunes of that journal by
the alienation of several delinquent subscribers.

But it was in the *Enterprise* that he first used his
pseudonym of "Mark Twain," which he borrowed from the
vernacular of the river, where the man heaving the lead calls
out "Mark twain!" instead of "Mark two!" In 1864, he
accepted, on the San Francisco *Morning Call,* the same sort of
place which he had held on the *Enterprise,* and he soon made
his *nom de guerre* familiar "on that coast"; he not only wrote
"local items" in the *Call,* but he printed humorous sketches in
various periodicals, and, two years later, he was sent to the
Sandwich Islands as correspondent of a Sacramento paper.

When he came back he "entered the lecture-field," as it
used to be phrased. Of these facts there is, as all English-
speaking readers know, full record in *Roughing It,* though I
think Mr. Clemens has not mentioned there his association
with that extraordinary group of wits and poets, of whom Mr.
Bret Harte, Mr. Charles Warren Stoddard, Mr. Charles H.
Webb, and Mr. Prentice Mulford, were, with himself, the most
conspicuous. These ingenious young men, with the fatuity of

gifted people, had established a literary newspaper in San Francisco, and they brilliantly co-operated to its early extinction.

In 1867, Mr. Clemens made in the *Quaker City* the excursion to Europe and the East which he has commemorated in *The Innocents Abroad*. Shortly after his return he married, and placed himself at Buffalo, where he bought an interest in one of the city newspapers; later he came to Hartford, where he has since remained, except for the two years spent in a second visit to Europe. The incidents of this visit he has characteristically used in *A Tramp Abroad*; and, in fact, I believe the only book of Mr. Clemens's which is not largely autobiographical is *The Prince and the Pauper*: the scene being laid in England, in the early part of the sixteenth century, the difficulties presented to a nineteenth-century autobiographer were insurmountable.

The habit of putting his own life, not merely in its results but in its processes, into his books, is only one phase of the frankness of Mr. Clemens's humorous attitude. The transparent disguise of the pseudonym once granted him, he asks the reader to grant him nothing else. In this he differs wholly from most other American humorists, who have all found some sort of dramatization of their personality desirable if not necessary. Charles F. Browne, "delicious" as he was when he dealt with us directly, preferred the disguise of "Artemus Ward" the showman; Mr. Locke likes to figure as "Petroleum V. Nasby," the cross-roads politician; Mr. Shaw chooses to masquerade as the saturnine philosopher "Josh Billings"; and each of these humorists appeals to the grotesqueness of misspelling to help out his fun. It was for Mr. Clemens to reconcile the public to humor which contented itself with the established absurdities of English orthography; and I am inclined to attribute to the example of his immense success, the humane spirit which characterizes our recent popular humor. There is still sufficient flippancy and brutality in it; but there is no longer the stupid and monkeyish cruelty of motive and intention which once disgraced and insulted us.

Except the political humorists, like Mr. Lowell—if there were any like him—the American humorists formerly chose the wrong in public matters; they were on the side of slavery, of drunkenness, and of irreligion; the friends of civilization were their prey; their spirit was thoroughly vulgar and base. Before "John Phoenix," there was scarcely any American humorist—not of the distinctly literary sort—with whom one could smile and keep one's self-respect. The great Artemus himself was not guiltless; but the most popular humorist who ever lived has not to accuse himself, so far as I can remember, of having written anything to make one morally ashamed of liking him. One can readily make one's strictures; there is often more than a suggestion of forcing in his humor; sometimes it tends to horse-play; sometimes the extravagance over-leaps itself, and falls flat on the other side; but I cannot remember that in Mr. Clemens's books I have ever been asked to join him in laughing at any good or really fine thing. But I do not mean to leave him with this negative praise; I mean to say of him that as Shakespeare, according to Mr. Lowell's saying, was the first to make poetry all poetical, Mark Twain was the first to make humor all humorous. He has not only added more in bulk to the sum of harmless pleasures than any other humorist; but more in the spirit that is easily and wholly enjoyable. There is nothing lost in literary attitude, in labored dictionary funning, in affected quaintness, in dreary dramatization, in artificial "dialect"; Mark Twain's humor is as simple in form and as direct as the statesmanship of Lincoln or the generalship of Grant.

When I think how purely and wholly American it is, I am a little puzzled at its universal acceptance. We are doubtless the most thoroughly homogeneous people that ever existed as a great nation. There is such a parity in the experiences of Americans that Mark Twain or Artemus Ward appeals as unerringly to the consciousness of our fifty millions as Goldoni appealed to that of his hundred thousand Venetians. In our phrase, we have somehow all "been there"; in fact, generally, and in sympathy almost certainly, we have been there. In another generation or two, perhaps, it will be wholly different; but as yet the average American is the man who has risen; he has known poverty, and privation, and low conditions; he has very often known squalor; and now, in his prosperity, he regards the past with a sort of large, pitying amusement; he is not the least ashamed of it; he does not feel that it characterizes him any more than the future does. Our humor springs from this multiform American experience of life, and securely addresses itself—in reminiscence, in phrase, in its whole material—to the intelligence bred of like experience. It is not of a class for a class; it does not employ itself with the absurdities of a tailor as a tailor; its conventions, if it has any, are all new, and of American make. When it mentions hash we smile because we have each somehow known the cheap boarding-house or restaurant; when it alludes to putting up stoves in the fall, each of us feels the grime and rust of the pipes on his hands; the introduction of the lightning-rod man, or the book-agent, establishes our brotherhood with the humorist at once. But how is it with the vast English-speaking world outside of these States, to which hash, and stovepipes, and lightning-rod men and book-agents are as strange as lords and ladies, dungeon-keeps and battlements are to us? Why, in fine, should an English chief-justice keep Mark Twain's books always at hand? Why should Darwin have gone to them for rest and refreshment at midnight when spent with scientific research?

I suppose that Mark Twain transcends all other American humorists in the universal qualities. He deals very little with the pathetic, which he nevertheless knows very well how to manage, as he has shown, notably in the true story of the old slave-mother; but there is a poetic lift in his work, even when he permits you to recognize it only as something satirized. There is always the touch of nature, the presence of a sincere and frank manliness in what he says, the companionship of a spirit which is at once delightfully open and deliciously shrewd. Elsewhere I have tried to persuade the reader that his humor is at its best the foamy break of the strong tide of earnestness in him. But it would be limiting him unjustly to describe him as a satirist; and it is hardly practicable to establish him in people's minds as a moralist; he has made them laugh too long; they will not believe him serious; they think some joke is always intended. This is the penalty, as Doctor Holmes has pointed out, of making one's first success as a humorist. There was a paper of Mark Twain's printed in the *Atlantic Monthly* some years ago and called "The Facts Concerning the Late Carnival of Crime in Connecticut," which ought to have won popular recognition of the ethical intelligence underlying his humor. It was, of course, funny; but under the fun it was an impassioned study of the human conscience. Hawthorne or Bunyan might have been proud to imagine that powerful allegory, which had a grotesque force far beyond either of them. It had been read before a literary club in Hartford; a reverend gentleman had offered the author his pulpit for the next Sunday if he would give it as a homily there. Yet it quite failed of the response I had hoped for it, and I shall not insist here upon Mark Twain as a moralist; though I warn the reader that if he leaves out of the account an indignant sense of right and wrong, a scorn of all affectation and pretence, an ardent hate of meanness and injustice, he will come indefinitely short of knowing Mark Twain.

His powers as a story-teller were evident in hundreds of brief sketches before he proved them in *Tom Sawyer* and *The Prince and the Pauper*. Both of these books, aside from their strength of characterization, are fascinating as mere narratives, and I can think of no writer living who has in higher degree the art of interesting his reader from the first word. This is a far rarer gift than we imagine, and I shall not call it a subordinate charm in Mark Twain's books, rich as they otherwise are. I have already had my say about *Tom Sawyer*, whose only fault is an excess of reality in portraying the character and conditions of Southwestern boyhood as it was forty years ago, and which is full of that poetic sympathy with nature and human nature which I always find in Mark Twain. *The Prince and the Pauper* has particularly interested me for the same qualities which, in a study of the past, we call romantic, but which alone can realize the past for us. Occasionally the archaic diction gives way and lets us down hard upon the American parlance of the nineteenth century; but mainly the illusion is admirably sustained, and the tale is to be valued not only in itself but as an earnest of what Mr. Clemens might do in fiction when he has fairly done with autobiography in its various forms. His invention is of the good old sort, like De Foe's more than that of any other English writer, and like that of the Spanish picaresque novelists, Mendoza and the rest; it flows easily from incident to incident, and does not deepen into situation. In the romance it operates as lightly and unfatiguingly as his memory in the realistic story.

His books abound in passages of dramatic characterization, and he is, as the reader knows, the author of the most successful American play. I believe Mr. Clemens has never claimed the reconstruction of Colonel Sellers for the stage; but he nevertheless made the play, for whatever is good in it came bodily from his share of the novel of *The Gilded Age*. It is a play which succeeds by virtue of the main personage, and this personage, from first to last, is quite outside of the dramatic action, which sometimes serves and sometimes does not serve the purpose of presenting Colonel Sellers. Where the drama fails, Sellers rises superior and takes the floor; and we forget the rest. Mr. Raymond conceived the character wonderfully well, and he plays it with an art that ranks him to that extent with the great actors; but he has in nowise "created" it. If any one "created" Colonel Sellers, it was Mark Twain, as the curious reader may see on turning again to the novel; but I suspect that Colonel Sellers was never created, except as other men are; that he was found somewhere and transferred, living, to the book.

I prefer to speak of Mr. Clemens's artistic qualities because it is to these that his humor will owe its perpetuity. All fashions change, and nothing more wholly and quickly than the fashion of fun; as any one may see by turning back to what amused people in the last generation; that stuff is terrible. As Europe becomes more and more the playground of Americans, and every scene and association becomes insipidly familiar, the jokes about the old masters and the legends will no longer be droll to us. Neither shall we care for the huge Californian mirth, when the surprise of the picturesquely mixed civilization and barbarism of the Pacific Coast has quite died away; and Mark Twain would pass with the conditions that have made him intelligible, if he were not an artist of uncommon power as well as a humorist. He portrays and interprets real types, not only with exquisite appreciation and sympathy, but with a force and truth of drawing that makes them permanent. Artemus Ward was very funny, that can never be denied; but it must be owned that the figure of the literary showman is as wholly factitious as his spelling; the conception is one that has to be constantly humored by the reader. But the innumerable characters sketched by Mark Twain are actualities, however caricatured—and, usually, they are not so very much caricatured. He has brought back the expression of Western humor to sympathy with the sane orthography in John Phoenix; but Mark Twain is vastly more original in form. Derby was weighed upon by literary tradition; he was "academic" at times, but Mr. Clemens is never "academic." There is no drawing from casts; in his work evidently the life has everywhere been studied: and it is his apparent unconsciousness of any other way of saying a thing except the natural way that makes his books so restful and refreshing. Our little nervous literary sensibilities may suffer from his extravagance, or from other traits of his manner, but we have not to beat our breasts at the dread apparition of Dickens's or Thackeray's hand in his page. He is far too honest and sincere a soul for that; and where he is obliged to force a piece of humor to its climax—as sometimes happens—he does not call in his neighbors to help; he does it himself, and is probably sorry that he had to do it.

I suppose that even in so slight and informal a study as this, something like an "analysis" of our author's humor is expected. But I much prefer not to make it. I have observed that analyses of humor are apt to leave one rather serious, and to result in an entire volatilization of the humor. If the prevailing spirit of Mark Twain's humor is not a sort of good-natured self-satire, in which the reader may see his own absurdities reflected, I scarcely should be able to define it.

Trowbridge and Clemens

Rufus A. Coleman

E ven among those reading widely in American literature, John Townsend Trowbridge today is little more than a name to be remembered chiefly for some verses about a boy named Darius, who, with his home-made contraption buckled to his back, made an early attempt to fly by jumping from a barn loft.[1] And yet in the seventies and eighties, Trowbridge was almost as popular a poet as Longfellow (he was a favorite with the elocutionists) and was, in addition, as editor of *Our Young Folks* and a leading contributor to the *Youth's Companion* and *St. Nicholas*, exceedingly popular with the younger generation. One critic went so far as to write that with Trowbridge a new era in juvenile literature began in America.[2] In his *Autobiography*, Theodore Roosevelt bore witness to his own allegiance, in these words:

> As a small boy I had *Our Young Folks*, which I then firmly believed to be the very best magazine in the world—a belief, I may add, which I have kept to this day unchanged, for I seriously doubt if any magazine for old or young has ever surpassed it. Both my wife and I have bound volumes of *Our Young Folks* which we preserved from our youth. I have tried to read again the Mayne Reid books which I so dearly loved as a boy, only to find, alas! that it was impossible. But I really believe I enjoy going over *Our Young Folks* now nearly as much as ever.[3]

Trowbridge (1827–1916) lived through nearly all of the nineteenth century as well as the first years of the twentieth, a

Reprinted from *Modern Language Quarterly* 9 (June 1948): 216–223.

large share of this time being spent at his Arlington home, a few miles, by trolley, from Cambridge and Boston. A man of many contacts, he met writers as widely dispersed chronologically as Mordecai Noah and Booth Tarkington. He knew many of the New England group intimately, for years being a member of the Boston Authors Club. He was a lifelong friend of Walt Whitman, a "judicious" friend, however, not an out-and-out disciple of the Bucke, Traubel, and Harned variety.

In view of such rich associations, it may seem surprising that Trowbridge did not number Samuel L. Clemens[4] among his intimates, especially since Clemens was a close friend of W. D. Howells who, for a few years, also lived at Arlington not far distant from Trowbridge. But despite common literary interests, the two met infrequently and then chiefly on public or semipublic occasions. Then, too, Trowbridge was critical of Clemens both as a speaker and as a writer, considering him diverting but prolix, episodic, and at times tiresome. Trowbridge was a stickler for form, and it was the lack of this quality and the presence of repetitiousness that prompted his critical disapproval of Whitman. Whitman's ideas on oratory especially disturbed him, as they had likewise done his friend Lewis B. Monroe,[5] for many years dean of the School of Oratory of Boston University, and editor of a series of popular school readers. An enthusiastic disciple of Delsarte, Monroe had even given Trowbridge an occasional lesson in public speaking, which accounts for the latter's frequent comments upon the poor stage presence of such men as Hale or Higginson, whose voices trailed off to a whisper so that only those in the front rows could hear them.

Trowbridge's relationship to Clemens, then, though friendly, was casual, similar in nature to his acquaintanceship with Howells, except, of course, that with the latter there was in addition a business association through the medium of the *Atlantic Monthly.*[6] Yet if the conjectures of scholars are correct, Clemens in his teens wrote his first sketch for Shillaber's *Carpet-Bag*[7] at the same time that Trowbridge, masquerading as "Paul Creyton," was one of its leading contributors.[8]

Both, however, were present at the famous Whittier dinner of 1877. Indeed, Clemens was very much in evidence. Initiated by H.O. Houghton, the enterprising publisher, this dinner was intended not only to honor the poet, but also to celebrate the twentieth anniversary of the *Atlantic Monthly*. The Boston *Daily Advertiser*[9] declared that Houghton and Company had "invited the contributors of the magazine both present and past, to meet in a never before attempted meeting," and that "the company was without doubt the most notable that has ever been seen in this country within four walls." When one casts his eye over the elaborate seating chart handed to each of the guests, one is inclined to agree with this assertion.[10]

Since Whittier disliked any kind of public display, it was considered a great piece of luck when the publishers were able to announce that the guest of honor would be there in person. After the dinner at 10:15 p.m., Whittier's brief and hesitant remarks were supplemented with the reading of some of his verses by Longfellow.[11]

The most striking episode in the whole occasion, however, was "that hideous mistake of poor Clemens,"[12] a phrase coined by Howells who, as toastmaster, was really put on the spot. To understand the extent of the offense, one should keep in mind the extreme veneration with which Holmes, Whittier, Longfellow, and Emerson were looked upon sixty or more years ago, an attitude somewhat like the Englishman's regard for his king. In this instance, however, the respect was intensified threefold. The newspaper reporter (one from the *Daily Advertiser*) reflected but the common esteem[13] when he wrote, "The three, Whittier, Emerson, and Longfellow gave a reverend, almost holy, air to the place, and their gray hairs and expressive faces, formed a beautiful group." Then what did the irrepressible Clemens do but spin a yarn about three disreputable miners masquerading as three of these mighty four, a choice part of which ran as follows:

Mr. Emerson was a seedy little bit of a chap, red-headed. Mr. Holmes was as fat as a balloon, he weighed as much as three hundred, and has double chains all the way down to his stomach. Mr. Longfellow was built like a prize fighter. His head was cropped and bristly, like as if he had a wig made of hair brushes. His nose lay straight down his face, like a finger with the end-joint tilted up. They had been drinking— I could see that.

To make matters worse, the jokester did not reveal until the very close of his speech that these reprehensibles were imposters. Carefully planned and executed as it was, his hoax failed utterly to go over. There followed a dead silence which poor Howells had to bridge over as best he could. Neither he nor Clemens got over their chagrin for months.[14] In a letter to Norton written only two days later Howells likened his friend's conduct to "demoniacal possession." Clemens spent much of the next few days writing apologetic letters. The whole affair seemed to have affected the principals more devastatingly than it did the other guests, for Trowbridge, who sat across the table from Clemens, made no reference to the incident either in notebook, letter, or autobiography. But the diplomacy of the press seldom appeared to better advantage. The reader of next morning's paper, on coming across this choice piece of mendacity, could never have guessed what had happened: "The humorist of the evening was next introduced and the amusement was intense, while the subjects of his wit, Longfellow, Emerson, and Holmes enjoyed it as much as any."

When the speaking was about half over, Whittier unobtrusively slipped away, and shortly after Trowbridge also left, despite the fact that he was on the program. His contribution, a poem entitled "The Story of a Barefoot Boy," published in the *Youth's Companion*,[15] described an episode in Whittier's life, the details of which had been furnished by Matthew Franklin Whittier, the poet's younger brother.[16] Having found that they could lift each other, the two youngsters evolved the bright idea that perhaps they might raise themselves to the ceiling, and, if they went outdoors, perhaps even higher. To be safe, however, they experimented first in their bedroom, standing on their bed. Trowbridge added his own philosophy in the following stanza:

> 'Twas a shrewd notion, none the less
> And still, in spite of ill success,
> It somehow has succeeded.
> Kind nature smiled on the wise child,
> Nor could her love deny him
> The large fulfillment of his plan,
> Since he who lifts his fellow man
> In turn is lifted by him.

That Whittier appreciated the poem is shown by the following hitherto unpublished letter:[17]

Oak Knoll
Danvers
1 Mo.[Jan.] 6, 1878

Dear Friend Trowbridge:
    Thanks for thy letter, & paper; and the bright & pleasant account of F's and my experiments in levitation. I wish it had been read at the dinner, it was just suited for such an occasion.

Cordially thy friend
John G. Whittier

Remember me to Mrs. N.[18] and thy wife.

The two celebrities met again many years later at a session of the Boston Authors Club,[19] where Clemens was the principal attraction. At the turn of the century his fame was at its peak, and in consequence a large crowd filled the three rooms open for visitors. Mrs. Julia Ward Howe read an introductory poem in his honor "by the light of a candle on a table by a wall, near a doorway, where Mark was seated"—lines of which ran:

> Mark Twain, welcome guest,
> Master of heroic jest;
> He who cheers man's dull abodes
> With the laughter of the gods;

To the joyless ones of earth
Sounds the reveille of mirth.
Well we meet, to part with pain
But ne'er he and we be Twain.[20]

Clemens was placed in a central position so that his voice could reach the adjoining rooms. When Mrs. Howe had finished, he mounted a chair. Trowbridge's notebook impressions read:

> The talk was about his two-weeks experience in Mo., the point of which was that Grant, then a Col., was personally afraid of the still more frightened squad of 23 men of whom Twain was one; then various things, chiefly his undertaking to teach the art of off-hand speaking in one lesson, his example, on the chance chose subject of portrait painting, being enlivened by ludicrously irrelevant anecdotes 'sarsparilla,' & 'more chalk' stories and others. He must have rambled on nearly an hour being diffuse and almost wearisome at times, getting in good things occasionally with a drollery that convulsed his audience. He told a good story of the 'moral' effect of stealing a green watermellon in his boyhood, & to my surprise retold the anecdote of the whistling cure for stammering which Raymond as Col. Sellers, told on the stage much better, years ago. . . .[21]

Trowbridge was a perspiring spectator at the Aldrich Memorial Services (June 30, 1908) at Portsmouth, New Hampshire, on one of the hottest days of an unusually hot month. Mrs. Aldrich had arranged for two special cars to take her guests from Boston to Portsmouth. Many, who naturally thought their tickets had been paid for, were sharply disillusioned when the conductor came around to collect fares. Despite heat, cinders, and other inconveniences, Trowbridge was not too cast down to make a pun. To a group on the train discussing the question as to whether or not Clemens' popularity was holding its own, he replied that he personally hadn't noticed any "Mark (T)wain in book sales."[22]
An excellent contemporary newspaper account of the proceeding was written for the Boston *Globe*[23] by Caro-

line Ticknor, who, first comparing these services with the similar memorial to Longfellow in the Old Boston Museum in 1867, went on to inform her readers that:

> At the celebration today, however, were literary people— famous—some of them scarcely heard of 21 years ago, and many of whom have won their Laurels within a decade. All the so-called 'schools' of American literature were represented. There was Colonel Thomas Wentworth Higginson, 85 years old, of that school which has become classic in America—the school of Emerson, Whittier, Bryant, and Lowell. There was John Townsend Trowbridge, 81 years, and there was Mark Twain, William Dean Howells, and Richard Watson Gilder who may be said to typify the second era; then came Hamilton Wright Mabie, Thomas Nelson Page, Prof. Barrett Wendell, Prof. Arlo Bates, Miss Sarah O. Jewett, Frank Dempster Sherman, John Kendrick Bangs, Mrs. Deland, Nathan Haskell Dole, Prof. Edward S. Morse, Peter Finley Dunne, T. Russell Sullivan, Robert Bridges, Nixon Waterman, Charles Warren, Edward W. Bok, Charles Gibson, and several hundred other men and women writers, and altogether about 1000 admirers, who traveled from far and near to pay their tribute of respect to the memory of one of the most genial characters in American literature—Thomas Bailey Aldrich.

Here briefly was the order of the speakers. The first literary man was Mabie, who discussed Aldrich's place in literature. Higginson came next with remarks concerning Aldrich's relation to the older school of writers. Gilder related Aldrich to the younger school, ending with his poem, "The Singing River,"[24] written especially for the occasion. Page represented the Southern group. Howells spoke of personal relations with Aldrich on the *Atlantic Monthly* staff. Then followed Clemens, who saw that to offset this monotonous and deadly eulogy something radical must be done. So lugubrious was the flow that three days later he had not recovered, writing in his notebook an excoriating account of the whole ceremonial, which, deleted from his *Autobiography*, did not appear until 1940 under the careful editorship of Bernard DeVoto.[25] Always a hater of pretension, Clemens was capable of writing of his hostess; "A strange and vanity-devoured, detestable woman! I do not believe I could ever learn to like her except on a raft at sea with no other provisions in sight."

Miss Ticknor's less jaundiced report is worth extended quoting:

> Mayor Hackett in introducing Mark Twain told of the man who took an hour to introduce Mark at one time and this left Mark only half an hour to tell all he knew. This gave Mark a cue to say a few words about long introductions, which embarrass the person who is being introduced and make the audience feel uncomfortable.
>
> He said one of the briefest introductions he ever had was out west in the mining country one time at a place called Red Dog. He had been announced to lecture and the little hall was filled with rough miners, but there was nobody to introduce him. One of the miners, appreciating the situation, stepped on the platform and said, "I don't know what to say about this fellow. I only know two things about him; one is that he has never been in jail; and the other is that I don't know why."
>
> Mr. Clemens then said that his folks had warned him in the morning to be dignified and serious, "and they insisted that I must wear black clothes. So here I am in these dark clothes all day. They seemed to think this was a funeral I was coming to, when, in point of fact, it is a resurrection and an occasion of joy. I have come here dressed in black, which I hate, and it is hot here; but while I have been sitting here I have made 150 speeches waiting for the riff raff to get through.
>
> "Aldrich's life was cheerful and happy I knew him 40 years. He was one of the brightest men it has been my fortune to meet. Some 29 years ago I met him one day at a certain place in a hotel and he looked pained; looked as if somebody had died and it wasn't the right person. I asked him why he looked so troubled, and he said, 'It is all on your account! You used to be the most popular author in this country, but that popularity has all gone.' 'How do you know?' I said. 'Come with me.' He took me around the corner to a book store, and he stepped up to the man in the place and said, 'Have you any of T.B. Aldrich's works?' and the man said 'No!' Then he said: 'Have you any of Mark Twain's works?' 'Yes,' said the man, 'I've got a whole shelf

full of them there.' 'Got any more than that?' asked Aldrich. 'Yes, the cellar's full of them,' was the reply. Then Aldrich took me out and said, 'You see your popularity has all gone. I'm popular now. He's sold out all my books.'"[26]

Outside, when the speeches were over, Trowbridge greeted Clemens with outstretched hands and mutual jokes. Clemens began it with, "Trowbridge, are you still alive? You must be a thousand years old. Why I listened to your stories while I was rocked in the cradle." Not to be outdone, Trowbridge flashed back, "Mark, there's some mistake. My earliest infant smile was wakened with one of your jokes." Albert Bigelow Paine from whom I take the above anecdote went on to say that the two were photographed in the blazing sun, their backs to a fence.[27] In one of his notebook entries Trowbridge presented more confidential impressions, referring to being photographed with Clemens and ending his notation rather caustically:

Services in the Music Hall (which was crowded) were altogether & most excessively eulogistic, and so monotonous & tiresome (11-1) enlivened by Twain's rambling drolleries & stories (the best of them about Aldrich taking him into a bookstore). Howells undertook to speak some memorized remarks, broke down, then started to read again, got mixed up & broke down again, but finally got through. . . The lunch was served to them who had "breakfast tickets"—standing— and not well dispensed. Fortunately three or four young men and women volunteered to help me and I got a poor and tasteless sandwich, a spoonfull of salad (not bad), a glass of tepid "Iced tea," and best of all, ice cream. I was thirsty.[28]

In all likelihood this was the last time Clemens and Trowbridge saw each other, as Clemens died two years later. At any rate, Trowbridge's notebooks and several hundred of his letters make no reference to a later meeting.

Notes

1. "Darius Green and His Flying Machine" first appeared in *Our Young Folks*, March, 1867.
2. *Cambridge History of American Literature*, II, 402.
3. Theodore Roosevelt, *An Autobiography* (New York, 1920), pp. 15–16.
4. There is no mention of Clemens in Trowbridge's autobiography, *My Own Story* (Boston, 1903).
5. 1825–1879.
6. William Dean Howells (1837–1920) was editor of the *Atlantic Monthly* 1872–1881. Trowbridge's story, "Pendlam," appeared in the first issue of the *Atlantic*. (See I, 70–85, November, 1857.) In all, sixty-nine of Trowbridge's stories, poems or articles were published in this magazine, seventeen of them during the period in which Howells was editor. Trowbridge's last *Atlantic* contribution, "An Early Contributor's Recollections," appeared in the issue for November, 1903.
7. For discussion of "The Dandy Frightening the Squatter," see F.J. Meine, *Tall Tales of the Southwest* (New York, 1930); Walter Blair, *Native American Humor* (New York, 1937); *American Literature* (November, 1931); Bernard DeVoto, *Mark Twain's America*, IV (Boston, 1932); and F.L. Pattee, *Mark Twain* (New York, 1933), introduction p. xix.
8. During the two-year period of this magazine's existence (March 29, 1851–March 23, 1852), Trowbridge, under the name of "Paul Creyton," contributed eleven sketches.
9. December 18, 1887.
10. Each guest was provided with an elaborate seating chart. For a copy of the one given Clemens, see A.B. Paine, *Mark Twain* (New York and London, 1912), III, opposite p. 1646. In the Trowbridge collection is an identical chart, according to which 58 people were provided for. Clemens' version of the incident, as well as a reprint of the speech itself, appears in *Mark Twain's Speeches* (New York and London, 1910), pp. 1–16. For other detailed accounts see Paine, *op. cit.*, II, 603–10, and for the speech itself, III, 1643, Appendix O; W.D. Howells, *My Mark Twain* (New York, 1910), pp. 58*ff.*; and DeVoto, *op. cit.*, pp. 196*ff.*
11. See *My Own Story*, pp 425*ff.*; also Samuel T. Pickard, *Life and Letters of John Greenleaf Whittier* (Boston and New York, 1899), II, 635–36.

12. Howells' comment in a letter to Charles Eliot Norton. See Mildred Howells, ed., *Life in Letters of William Dean Howells* (Garden City, New York, 1928), I, 243.

13. For the village-mindedness exemplified in this whole episode see DeVoto, *op. cit.*, pp. 220*ff.*

14. A few thought the speech excellent, one of these being Professor Child of Harvard, who read an account of the dinner in the next morning's paper. In later years Clemens himself came to look upon this as one of his best speeches. (See Mark Twain's Speeches, pp. 15–16.) The accounts of what followed after Clemens sat down are confused. Clemens, whose memory was notoriously faulty, differed in two of his versions. In one he wrote: "The programme for the occasion was probably not more than one-third finished, but it ended there. Nobody arose. The next man hadn't strength enough to get up." (*Mark Twain's Speeches*, p. 24.) On the other hand, Paine's biography (II, 605) reported him as saying that "Bishop, the novelist, did get up and began his speech but didn't get very far with it." Paine likewise reported Howells (II, 695) to the same effect. The Boston *Daily Advertiser* reported the dinner as if it had been a great success.

15. January 10, 1876.

16. Matthew Franklin Whittier (1812–1883) was the only brother of John Greenleaf, and five years his junior.

17. In the Trowbridge collection, at present in the possession of Mrs. Albert P. Madeira, granddaughter of Trowbridge.

18. Mrs. Alonzo Newton, the mother of Trowbridge's second wife.

19. Trowbridge's notebooks are full of references to this organization, of which he was a charter member. At the death of Thomas Wentworth Higginson, he was made honorary vice-president.

20. Mrs. Julia Ward Howe (1819–1910) has this to say of the occasion: ". . . I had worked hard all morning, but had managed to put together a scrap of rhyme in welcome of Mark Twain. A candle was lit for me to read by and afterwards M.T. jumped upon a chair and made fun, some good, some middling, for some three quarters of an hour. The effect of my one candle lighting up his curly hair was good and my rhyme was well received." (Laura E. Richards and Maud Howe Elliott, *Julia Ward Howe* [Boston and New York, 1916], II, 341.)

21. Item in Trowbridge notebook, dated October 25, 1905.

22. This anecdote was told to the writer by Nixon Waterman (1936), who was one of the group.

23. July 1, 1908.

24. Gilder had this to say: "Tuesday, the 20th at Portsmouth I read the little poem on The Singing River and another to Aldrich written

long ago and not published. The night before, Mrs. Aldrich had quite a large dinner party at the hotel and in the midst of it I asked her quietly if I could offer a 'silent toast.' She said, 'I wish you would,' knowing well what it would be—so we drank in silence to 'A bright and beautiful memory.'" (Rosamond Gilder, ed., *Letters of Richard Watson Gilder* [Boston and New York, 1916], p. 463.)

25. *Mark Twain in Eruption* (New York and London, 1940), pp. 295–99.

26. For a more concise account, see Paine, *op. cit.*, III, 1456.

27. Paine, *op. cit.*, III, 1456.

28. Item in Trowbridge's notebook, dated July 3, 1908.

Musings without Method

THE HILARITY OF LONDON—MARK TWAIN'S
MESSAGE OF MIRTH—THE LIMITATIONS
OF HUMOR—AN OBVIOUS INCONGRUITY—
THE EXAMPLE OF THE EIGHTEENTH
CENTURY—COTTON AND BRIDGES—'LIFE ON
THE MISSISSIPPI'—THE TALENT OF MARK
TWAIN—THE SIN OF EXAGGERATION—
PAGEANTS AND SPORTS.

For the last month London has suffered from a violent attack of hilarity. Painfully she has held her poor sides. So fiercely has she rocked with noisy laughter that her public monuments have been in danger of destruction. For Mark Twain has been in her midst, and has transmitted, through the voices of obsequious journalists, his messages of mirth. And Mark Twain is a humourist, a simple truth which nobody is permitted to forget. He is a humourist who cannot open his mouth without provoking the wonder of the world, and, thanks to the industry of energetic reporters, we have not lost one single pearl of his speech.

It is not Mark's fault,—Mark they call him, to prove their familiarity,—not the fault of the reporters, if a word spoken by the humourist has escaped us. All the world knows that the sublime heights of fun were climbed when Mark Twain referred happily to his own funeral. The compositors who set up this brilliant sally were so keenly conscious of their

Reprinted from *Blackwood's Magazine*, 182 (August 1907), 279–86.

privilege that they filled the master's incongruity with a bold series of misprints. Mark Twain designing his own funeral! Isn't it funny? Lives there a curmudgeon who will refrain from laughter when he hears of it? Still gayer was the phantasy which accused Mark Twain of stealing the Ascot Gold Cup. There's a pretty invention! Fleet Street accepted the joke as one man, and it will be surprising if the great man's luggage is not ransacked for the lost treasure by the Customs officers of this free and independent fatherland.

At last the humourist has left these shores. The echo of his last joke has died away, though the throats of his admirers are still husky with appreciative laughter. And so well did London play her part that if he rang his bell or asked for a lucifer match, the neighbourhood of Dover Street palpitated with excitement. Unhappily, upon this enthusiasm, as upon most others, time has and will have a chastening effect. Our exhausted capital is beginning to understand that it can have too much of a good joke, and that nothing stales so rapidly as the thing called "humour."

Humour as a solid quality and a lucrative trade is of modern invention. The ancients knew well that its effect was an effect of light and shade. They were humorous in flashes, and their humour was infinitely enhanced, because it was set against a background of gravity. To be funny at all hours and in all places is a vile a sin against taste as it would be to dissolve in floods of tears before strangers. The great men who dared to laugh in an earlier age than ours laughed in moderation and with a wise purpose. Aristophanes and Lucian, Chaucer and Rabelais, Shakespeare and Fielding, are the true humourists of the world. They did not jest and jibe out of season. They held up folly to ridicule, not to amuse the groundlings, but to reveal, in a sudden blaze of light, the eternal truths of wisdom and justice. Their humour is precious on account of its parsimony. They do not at every turn slap their reader on the back and assure him that there is nothing congruous in the visible world. Of the irreverence that turns whatever is beautiful or noble into a stupid jest they knew nothing. They kept their humour in its proper place; they used it for a wise purpose; they did not degrade it to catch an easy round of applause; and, fortunately for them, they are to-day refused the august title of humourist, which sits so appositely upon the shoulders of Mark Twain.

The essence of humour is that it should be unexpected. The modern humourist is never unexpected. He beats the drum from the moment at which he appears upon the stage. He does not cease to beat it until he quits the stage for the last time. His mouth is always awry, as though he fed upon sour apples, and he demands that his auditors, also should twist their lips. From morning till night he grins through a horse-collar and is surprised if all the world does not applaud his grimaces. To the rash fellow who confesses that he does not understand his fun, the professional humourist has a ready answer. He tells the wretch, with a shrug of pity, that he has no sense of humour, and has no right to criticise wholesome ribaldry. The boot, of course, is on the other leg. The professional humourist is the one person to whom the proper exercise of humour is forbidden, and he does but add insult to injury when he dares to criticise his victim's understanding.

Yet the professional humourist to-day inherits the earth. He is the most popular of God's creatures. He has his own "organs," in which he makes a desperate attempt to look at all things from a ridiculous point of view. He assures you, with a sentimental leer, that his fun is always amiable, as though amiability were a sufficient atonement for an imbecile lack of taste. He is prepared to tickle you with his jokes from early morn to nightfall, and he has been so grossly flattered that he believes there is a positive virtue in his antics. He is perfectly convinced that he is doing good, and he needs very little persuasion to believe that he is the only regenerator of mankind. Gradually, too, he is encroaching upon all the professions which are not legitimately his own. The pulpit knows him, and the senate. Worse still, he has invaded the Courts of Law, and sits grinning upon the bench at his own ineptitude, which appears to the obsequious barristers, who hope some day to wear his cap and bells, to sparkle with the brilliance of true Attic wit.

The secret of modern humour is revealed to all. Its basis is an obvious incongruity. Not the subtle παρὰ προσδοκίαν of the ancients, not a whimsical turn of phrase or twist of idea, which surprises us in the masters, but a coarse, crass confusion of past with present or of grave with gay. Its inventors, we regret to remind our readers, were Englishmen, aided and abetted by such Frenchmen as Motteux and D'Urfey, who were driven to these shores before or at the revocation of the Edict of Nantes, and whose native gaiety was not wholly extinguished by the persecutions endured by their fathers. Tom Brown the Facetious and the Inimitable Ned Ward were characteristic innovators. Inspired by joyousness and brandy, they laughed to scorn life and all its works. They were as cheerful a pair of ruffians as ever beat the pavement of a populous city since the infamous creatures of Petronius went splendidly upon the pad. They knew London as they knew their pockets, and they hunted the taverns with a zeal and an understanding worthy of their high purpose and higher spirits. They recalled the beggar-students of an earlier age, or the poets who, in Elizabeth's time, brought their plays to the Bankside. Ned Ward, inn-keeper though he was, had still a regard for letters, and Tom Brown was a real scholar. His style was flippant; his muse was ever down at heel, and wore a dressing-gown; his prose was alive with the slang of the gutter and the quip of the street corner. But when he took up his pen his mind went back to Lucian and to Horace; he kept always in the great tradition; and though he was determined to laugh at all things, he had too quick a sense of his art to be a humourist and nothing more.

Nevertheless, he sowed the seeds of the easy incongruity which has debauched the humour of to-day. He delighted in such mock-heroic exercises as an "Oration in praise of Drunkenness," and he taught the world to believe that nothing was beyond the reach of jocularity. One of the earliest of our comic reporters, he wore the cap and bells with a light indifference, and, Ned Ward aiding him, he understood that the journal and pamphlet were a useful substitute for the generosity of patrons. Had they lived under the Tudors or early Stuarts, Brown and Ward would have been jesters at court or in a country house. They would have worn the livery of king or duke, and repaid the munificence of their masters with a licensed effrontery. The liberal age of Anne threw them upon the people, and they forced their note to suit the foolish rufflers who bought their wares. Thus they showed the way, and their descendants in the world of humour have been only too ready to follow them.

Humour, in this baser sense, is a foolish travesty of life; and before Brown split the sides of Grub Street, Charles Cotton, fisherman and Cockney, had already converted travesty into a form of literature. If the poor humourists of to-day descend in one line from Tom Brown, in another they may trace their pedigree back to the admirable Cotton. Now Cotton, as became a gentleman of this education and pursuits, founded his humour upon the classics. He treated Virgil and Lucian precisely as the modern Yankee treats the older civilisation of Europe. He translated them into his own lingo and asked you to laugh with him at them. He delighted to trick out the heroes of antiquity in his own poor fustian, and as his knowledge of slang was as great as his daring, the result is often ludicrous. A passage or two in illustration will make the purpose of the old travesties as clear as daylight. Here is Dido's address of farewell to Æneas in Cotton's version:—

> But I'll waste on thee no more Breath,
> For whom the Wind, that fumes beneath,
> Is far too sweet: Avaunt, thou Slave!
> Thou lying coney-catching Knave,
> Be moving, do as thou hast told me!
> Nobody here intends to hold thee!
> Go: seek thy Farm, I hope 'twill be
> I' th' very bottom of the Sea:
> But shd'st thou 'scape, and not in Dike
>   lie
> Drown'd like a Puppy, as 'tis likely,

> Since in the Proverb old 'tis found,
> Who's born to hang, will ne'er be
>   drowned;
> Yet shd'st thou not be much the nigher
> I'll haunt thee like a going Fire,
> As soon as I can turn to a Ghost,
> Which will be in a week at most.

That is a fair specimen of Cotton's familiar style, and Cotton had many imitators. His contempt for grandeur, which is characteristic of the Cockney spirit, was emulated by many ingenious writers. The example which he set was followed for a century and more, and the best of his pupils handled the style with an even greater effrontery than his. Perhaps none of them, in ease of manner or bold anachronism, exceeded Bridges, whose burlesque translation of Homer is still ranked among "curiosities" in the catalogues. It is thus that in Bridges' version Agamemnon rates the angry Achilles:—

> The general gave him tit for tat,
> And answer'd, cocking first his hat,
> Go, and be hang'd, you blust'ring
>   whelp,
> Pray, who the murrain wants your
>   help?
> When you are gone, I know there are
> Col'nels sufficient for the war,
> Militia bucks that know no fears,
> Brave fishmongers and auctioneers;
> Besides, great Jove will fight for us,
> What need we then this mighty fuss?
> Thou lov'st to quarrel, fratch, and
>   jangle,
> To scold and swear, and fight and
>   wrangle.
> Great strength thou hast, and pray
>   what then?
> Art thou so stupid, canst not ken,
> The gods that ev'ry thing can see
> Give strength to bears as well as thee?

There in its origin and in its purpose is the whole of modern humour. The same flippant impertinence which distresses us in the works of popular Americans is already alive and alert. The same confusion of ancient and modern is already designed to evoke a hasty chuckle. We do not mean that the imitation is conscious; we do not suppose that Mark Twain or his predecessors ever heard the name of Charles Cotton; but when once the spirit of contempt for grave and reverend things was evoked, the worst enormities of contemporary humour were obvious and natural.

The end and aim of Mark Twain, then, are the end and aim of Cotton and Bridges. For him the art of Europe and the chivalry of King Arthur serve the purpose of Virgil and Homer. He travesties them with a kind of malignant joy. He brings whatever time has honoured down to the level of a Yankee drummer. In *The Innocents Abroad* he sets a slur of commonness upon beauty and splendour. With the vanity of a crude civilisation he finds every custom ridiculous that does not conform with the standard of the United States. The restraints of honour are food for his mirth. He holds his sides when he thinks of the old masters. They are not brought down to this our date. Nor does he understand that there are certain institutions, certain manifestations of genius, which should be sacred even for the jester. Newness is not the only virtue known to the world, and he who laughs at what is old, merely because it is old, proves a lack of intelligence which no whimsicality can excuse.

In other words, Mark Twain the humourist is a bull in the china-shop of ideas. He attempts to destroy what he could never build up, and assumes that his experiment is eminently meritorious. When, as in *A Yankee at the Court of King Arthur*, he gave full rein to his fancy, he achieved such a masterpiece of vulgarity as the world has never seen. His book gives you the same sort of impression which you might receive from a beautiful picture over which a poisonous slug had crawled. The hint of magnificence is there, pitilessly deformed and defaced. That Mark Twain is in perfect sympathy with his creature is perfectly evident. He frankly prefers Hartford, Conn., to Camelot. He believes that in all respects his native land is superior to the wisest and noblest society that the eye of Arthur saw or any other eye has seen. He is sure that refinement and "gentility" were unknown before his own time. The Knights of the Round Table, he declares, used words which would have made a Comanche blush. "Indelicacy is too mild a term to convey the idea." In our own nineteenth century, he informs us, "the earliest samples of the real lady and real gentleman discoverable in English history—or in European history, for that matter—may be said to have made their appearance." That is what it is to be a humourist. But even if we permit the humour we must still question the historical accuracy of the statement, and regret that Mark Twain ever thought it necessary to comment upon the ancients, against whom he cherishes a fierce antipathy.

His verbal humour, if less reckless than his history, is far more dismally deplorable. Here is his comment upon Merlin: "He is always blethering around in my way, everywhere I go; he makes me tired. He don't amount to shucks as a magician." Who can resist this amazing humour? And again, who, save a churl, would refuse the tribute of a laugh to the following exquisite criticism of the same wonder-worker? "Merlin's stock was flat," writes Mark Twain, "the King wanted to stop his wages: he even wanted to banish him; but I interfered. I said he would be useful to work the weather, and attend to small matters like that, and I would give him a lift now and then when his poor little parlour-magic soured on him." Isn't there a snigger in every word of it? And before this brilliancy must we not confess that humour, like delicacy and all the other virtues, made its first appearance in the nineteenth century and in America?

This monstrous incongruity demands two qualities for its indulgence: a perfect self-esteem, and an exaggerated common-sense. No one who is not confident that he engrosses the graces can affect to find pleasure in thus insulting the past. No one whose sense is not common in all respects can apply all the resources of a vulgar logic to the creations of fancy and emotion. That Mark Twain is fully equipped for his purpose is only too clear. His humour and his talk alike proclaim it. And it is the more pitiful, because he has a talent which stands in need of no folly for its embellishment. Had he never cut a joke, had he refrained always from grinning at grave and beautiful things, how brilliant a fame would have been his! When you are tired of his irreverence, when you have deplored his noisy jibes, when his funeral and his theft of the cup alike pall upon your spirit, take down his *Life on the Mississippi* and see what perfect sincerity and a fine sympathy can accomplish. Mark Twain writes of the noble river as one who knows its every change and chance. Yet he writes of it with an austere restraint and without any desire to humanise it out of its proper character. And there is humour, too, in his descriptions,—not the tortured humour of a later day, but humour sufficient to play, like light upon shade, in the grave places of his history. As he says himself, he loved the pilot's profession far better than any he has followed since, and his love and understanding shine in every page of his masterpiece. As the river kept no secrets from him, so his quick memory enabled him to recover the impressions of his youth. To cite his own expressive works, "The face of the water, in time, became a wonderful book—a book which was a dead language to the uneducated passenger, but which told its mind to me without reserve, delivering its most cherished secrets as clearly as if it uttered them with a voice. And it was not a book to be read once and thrown aside, for it had a new story to tell every day. . . . There was never so wonderful a book written by man." In this passage Mark Twain strikes the real note of his life and experience. With equal truth he tells us at what cost he acquired this deep knowledge of the river and its moods. "Now, when I had mastered the language of this water," says he, "and had come to know every trifling feature that bordered the great river as familiarly as I knew the letters of the alphabet, I had made a valuable acquisition. But I had lost something, too. I had lost something which could never be restored to me while I lived. All the grace, the beauty, the poetry had gone out of the majestic river. I still keep in mind a certain wonderful sunset which I witnessed when steamboating was new to me. . . . But, as I have said, a day came when I began to cease from noting the glories and the charms which the moon and the sun and the twilight wrought upon the river's face: another day came, when I ceased altogether to note them." Yet the very fact that Mark Twain recognised the change which had come over his vision is the best proof that he submitted willingly to the marvellous spell of the river. His mental process was the reverse of Wordsworth's. Wordsworth learned:

> To look on nature, not as in the
>   hour
> Of thoughtless youth; but hearing
>   oftentimes
> The still, sad music of humanity,
> Not harsh nor grating, though of ample
>   power
> to chasten and subdue.

Mark Twain, on the other hand, heard "the still, sad music of humanity" when he but half knew the river. A profounder knowledge silenced the music, and persuaded him to own, with sincerity, that he gazed upon the sunset scene without rapture, but with the understanding of an intimate.

The author of *Life on the Mississippi* was also the creator of Tom Sawyer and Huck Finn, two boys who will survive to cast shame upon all the humour of America. And it is for the sake of a genuine talent that we deplore Mark Twain's studied antics. It should not have been for him to light the thorns which crackle under the pot. It should not have been for him to encourage the gross stupidity of his fellows. The moderation of one who has known men and rivers should have been revealed to all the world. But Mark Twain, in submitting to the common demand, shares the general love of exaggeration. "Govern a great country as you would cook a small fish," said the Chinese philosopher; "that is, do not overdo it." The tendency of to-day is to overdo all things. Humour, which should be a relief, and nothing more, is now an end in itself. No experiment is made in any art or science but it must become a custom. Some years since an ingenious stage-manager invented what he was pleased to term a pageant. It was an attempt to reconstruct the life of an ancient town, to recover from the past the parti-coloured trappings and the forgotten background of history. Then every town, every village, must enjoy the pomp of the Middle Age. Peasants grow learned in costume and babble of "colour-schemes," whatever those may be. Even an ancient and honoured university has fallen so far beneath the level of its dignity as to connive at the creation of a vast circus and to provide a book of the words for a trifling performance. And the pageant, which might have served a useful end if handled with restraint and discretion, is plainly destined to be killed by ridicule.

And above all, the folly of exaggeration may be noted in our sports. If an English eight or an English eleven suffer defeat, it is proclaimed far and wide that England is in decay. The newspapers howl inappositely and ask the groaners to explain the ruin of their country. They forget that the sports upon which we pride ourselves are worth pursuing for their own sakes, and that it is only the professional who believes that victory alone justifies his exertion. A few weeks ago a Belgian crew carried off the Grand Challenge Cup from Henley. Its most dangerous opponent was the Leander Club, whose eight was composed of oarsmen from Oxford and Cambridge. The race was as good as conflicting courage and energy could make it, and the mere fact that the better crew won after a closely contested struggle has suggested to an idle press a mournful commentary, which is a clear negation of sportsmanship. In the first place, it is a regatta which is held at Henley, not an international meeting. The honour and enterprise of nations are not there put to a final test. If England and Belgium are to try conclusions, they must not meet in a sprint at Henley; they must fight it out, after due training, between Putney and Mortlake. And if the curse at Henley is ill fitted for an international battle, so also are the conditions of the meeting. The eight men, who represented not England but the Leander Club, had so little thought of their national responsibility that they rowed for their colleges or for themselves both before and after their race with the Belgians. They went to Henley not to defend their country against all comers but to get what enjoyment they could from the sport of rowing. But a simple understanding is not enough for this age. Exaggeration rules in humour. The amateur is blamed if he do not cultivate the vices of the specialist. The American critic assures us that the sole object of a game is to win, and our journals agree with the American critic. Some day there will be a reaction, and then it will be recognised that pleasure counts in life as much as success, and that solid blocks of humour are as blatant an outrage upon good sense as a daily pageant, or as games played with no other aim than by hook or by crook to snatch a victory.

Mark Twain and the Old Time Subscription Book

George Ade

Mark Twain should be doubly blessed for saving the center table from utter dullness. Do you remember that center table of the seventies? The marble top showed glossy in the subdued light that filtered through the lace curtains, and it was clammy cold even on hot days. The heavy mahogany legs were chiseled into writhing curves from which depended stern geometrical designs or possibly bunches of grapes. The Bible had the place of honor and was flanked by subscription books. In those days the house never became cluttered with the ephemeral six best sellers. The new books came a year apart, and each was meant for the center table, and it had to be so thick and heavy and emblazoned with gold that it could keep company with the bulky and high-priced Bible.

Books were bought by the pound. Sometimes the agent was a ministerial person in black clothes and stove-pipe hat. Maiden ladies and widows, who supplemented their specious arguments with private tales of woe, moved from one small town to another feeding upon prominent citizens. Occasionally the prospectus was unfurled by an undergraduate of a freshwater college working for the money to carry him another year.

The book-agents varied, but the book was always the same,—many pages, numerous steel engravings, curly-cue

Reprinted from *Review of Reviews* 41 (June 1910), 703–704.

tail-pieces, platitudes, patriotism, poetry, sentimental mush. One of the most popular, still resting in many a dim sanctuary, was known as "Mother, Home, and Heaven." A ponderous collection of "Poetical Gems" did not involve the publishers in any royalty entanglements. Even the "Lives of the Presidents" and "Noble Deeds of the Great and Brave" gave every evidence of having been turned out as piece-work by needy persons temporarily lacking employment on newspapers. Let us not forget the "Manual of Deportment and Social Usages," from which the wife of any agriculturist could learn the meaning of R.S.V.P. and the form to be employed in acknowledging an invitation to a levee.

Nobody really wanted these books. They were purchased because the agents knew how to sell them, and they seemed large for the price, and besides, every well-furnished home had to keep something on the center table.

Subscription books were dry picking for boys. Also they were accessible only on the Sabbath after the weekly scouring. On week-days the boys favored an underground circulating library, named after Mr. Beadle, and the hay-mow was the chosen reading room. Let one glorious exception be made in the case of "Dr. Livingstone's Travels in Africa," a subscription book of forbidding size, but containing many pictures of darkies with rings in their noses.

Just when front-room literature seemed at its lowest ebb, so far as the American boy was concerned, along came Mark Twain. His books looked, at a distance, just like the other distended, diluted, and altogether tasteless volumes that had been used for several decades to balance the ends of the center table. The publisher knew his public, so he gave a pound of book for every fifty cents, and crowded in plenty of wood-cuts and stamped the outside with golden bouquets and put in a steel engraving of the author, with a tissue paper veil over it, and "sicked" his multitude of broken-down clergymen, maiden ladies, grass widows, and college students on to the great American public.

Can you see the boy a Sunday morning prisoner, approach the new book with a dull sense of foreboding, expecting a dose of Tupper's "Proverbial Philosophy"? Can you see him a few minutes later when he finds himself linked arm-in-arm with Mulberry Sellers or Buck Fanshaw or the convulsing idiot who wanted to know if Christopher Columbus was sure-enough dead? No wonder he curled up on the hair-cloth sofa and hugged the thing to his bosom and lost all interest in Sunday-school. "Innocents Abroad" was the most enthralling book ever printed until "Roughing It" appeared. Then along came "The Gilded Age," "Life on the Mississippi," and "Tom Sawyer," one cap sheaf after another. While waiting for a new one we read the old ones all over again.

The new uniform edition with the polite little pages, high-art bindings, and all the boisterous wood-cuts carefully expurgated can never take the place of those lumbering subscription books. They were our early friends and helped us to get acquainted with the most amazing story-teller that ever captivated the country boys and small-town boys all over America.

While we are honoring Mark Twain as a great literary artist, a philosopher, and a teacher, let the boys of the seventies add their tribute. They knew him for his miracle of making the subscription book something to be read and not merely looked at. He converted the Front Room from a Mausoleum into a Temple of Mirth.

Mark Twain on the Lecture Platform

Will M. Clemens

The story of an unwilling orator, with extracts and unpublished letters written by the famous humorist

On Tuesday evening, September 29, 1866, Samuel Langhorne Clemens made his first appearance in public, at the Academy of Music in Pine Street, San Francisco. He had just returned from the Sandwich Islands, from where he had been writing letters on the islands and the islanders to the Sacramento *Union*. The appearance of Artemus Ward some months previous in San Francisco had aroused an ambition in Mark Twain, to "go and do likewise," not for the fame that might come to him, not from the money to be earned, but from a spirit of pure mischievousness. Twain was one of a coterie of Bohemians which included Bret Harte, Prentice Mulford, and Charles Warren Stoddard, and I can imagine how he chuckled to himself when he concluded to "learn a new trick and surprise the boys." He secured a hall and published a sort of Artemus Ward announcement that he would deliver a lecture about his trip to the Sandwich Islands.

Commenting upon the announcement, the San Francisco correspondent of a neighboring newspaper, wrote:

"We may expect either gay or grave remarks, for, by recently published letters, he very fully exhibited the

Reprinted from *Ainslee's Magazine* VI (August 1900), 25–32.

resources of the islands to the great satisfaction of our business community. His lecture at this time will have a peculiar interest, independent of his own rapidly augmenting popularity, from the fact that the queen (Emma) of said country is now in our midst. Everybody is going, and consequently a crowded audience will greet the maiden—I believe—lecture of the sage brusher. He is not at all an eloquent orator, and I fear, as he himself announces it, 'doors open at 7, the *trouble will* commence at 8 o'clock.'"

"The 'trouble' is over," wrote this same correspondent under date of October 3, 1866, "the inimitable 'Mark Twain' delivered himself last night of his first lecture on the Sandwich Islands, or anything else. Some time before the hour appointed to open his head the Academy of Music (on Pine street) was densely crowded with one of the most fashionable audiences it was ever my privilege to witness during my long residence in this city. The *élite* of the town were there, and so was the Governor of the state—occupying one of the boxes— whose rotund face was suffused with a halo of mirth during the whole entertainment. The audience promptly notified Mark by the usual sign—stamping—that the auspicious hour had arrived, and presently the lecturer came sidling and swinging out from the left of the stage. His very manner produced a generally vociferous laugh from the assemblage. He opened with an apology, by saying that he had partly succeeded in obtaining a band, but, at the last moment the party engaged backed out. He explained that he had hired a man to play the trombone, but he, on learning that he was the only person engaged, came at the last moment and informed him that he could not play. This placed Mark in a bad predicament, and wishing to know his reasons for deserting him at that critical moment, he replied 'that he wasn't going to make a fool of himself by sitting up there on the stage and blowing his horn all by himself.' After the applause subsided, he assumed a very grave countenance and commenced his remarks proper with the following well-known sentence: 'When, in the course of human events,' etc. He lectured fully an hour and a quarter, and his humorous sayings were interspersed with geographical, agricultural and statistical remarks, sometimes branching off and reaching beyond— soaring, in the very choicest language, up to the very pinnacle of descriptive power."

Thus we are told how Mark "tried it on the dog," and from all appearances the canine survived. Then came invitations from surrounding towns and from Nevada for Mark Twain to repeat his San Francisco success. Thereupon in January, 1867, he started forth upon a lecture tour through the smaller cities of California and Nevada. In those days almost any entertainment brought out a crowd, and when it was announced one day in Carson City that Mark was to deliver a lecture for the benefit of something or other at the Episcopal Church, it was generally understood that the house would be crowded.

"Well, the night arrived," writes a friend that was present. "Mark ascended the steps into the pulpit about 8 o'clock, there being a whole lot of the boys and young women, friends of his, as well as a good many old people in front. Mark made a very polite bow, and then unfolded a gigantic roll of brown paper. People thought at first it was a map, but it turned out to be his lecture written on great sheets of grocer's brown paper, with an ordinary grocer's marking brush. After his bow he turned his back around to the audience and craned his head up to the lamp, and thus read from the big sheets, as though it would be impossible for him to see any other way.

"The lecture was on 'The Future of Nevada,' and was the funniest thing I ever heard. He prophesied the great era of prosperity that was before us, and sought to encourage us residents of the sagebrush region by foretelling what appeared to be Golconda-like tales of impossible mineral discoveries. Right on the heels of it, however, came the remarkable discoveries at Virginia City, and then we thought he was not so far off in his humorous predictions."

In March, Mr. Clemens published his first book, "The Famous Jumping Frog of Calaveras," and soon after sailed for

New York by way of Panama. From New York he went to Washington, where he endeavored to earn his living by writing letters to the San Francisco *Alta*, and delivering a lecture or two. His lecture experience in Washington was brief but interesting, and he tells all about it in his inimitable way:

"Well, now, I'll have to tell you something about that lecture. It was a little the hardest and roughest experience I ever underwent in my whole career as a lecturer. Now, I had not been in Washington more than a day or two before a friend of mine came to my room at the hotel early one morning, wakened me out of a sound sleep, and nearly stunned me by asking if I was aware of the fact that I was to deliver a lecture at Lincoln Hall that evening. I told him no, and that he must be crazy to get out of bed at such an unseemly hour to ask such a foolish question. But he soon assured me that he was perfectly sane by showing the papers, which all announced that Mark Twain was to lecture that evening, and that his subject would be 'The Sandwich Islands.' To say that I was surprised would be drawing it mildly. I was mad, for I thought some one had put up a game on me.

"Well, on careful inquiry, I learned that an old theatrical friend of mine thought he would do me a favor. So he started out by getting drunk. While in this condition he made all the necessary arrangements for me to lecture, with the exception of the slight circumstance that he neglected to inform me of any of his intentions. He rented Lincoln Hall, billed the town, and sent the newspapers advertisements and notices about the coming lecture, and the worst of it was that he had done all his work thoroughly. After learning this I was in a dilemma. I had never prepared any lecture on the Sandwich Islands. What was I to do? I could not back out by telling the people that I was unprepared, and that my friend was intoxicated when he made these arrangements. No that was out of the question, because the public wouldn't believe it anyway. The billing of the town had been too well done for that. So there was only one thing left for me to do, and that was to lock myself in my room and write that lecture between the breakfast hour and half-past seven that evening. Well, I did it, and was on hand at the advertised hour, facing one of the biggest audiences I ever addressed.

"I did not use my manuscript, but in those days I always had my lecture in writing, and kept it on a reading stand at one end of the place where I stood on the platform. I was very good at memorizing, and rarely had any trouble in speaking without notes; but the very fact that I had my manuscript near at hand where I could readily turn to it without having to undergo the mortification of pulling it from my pocket, gave me courage and kept me from making awkward pauses. But the writing of that Sandwich Islands lecture in one day was the toughest job ever put on me."

The voyage to Europe, and the trip to Palestine came soon after this, and the subsequent publication of *Innocents Abroad*, in 1869, made Mr. Clemens famous on two continents. In the Autumn, James Redpath who was the manager of a Lyceum Bureau in Boston, encouraged Mark Twain to undertake a series of lectures or talks before church societies and lyceums in the New England states and the country round about New York. One of his first engagements was before a church society in Brooklyn, and the humorist was evidently disgusted at the spirit of the entertainment, for under date of December 4th, he wrote to Redpath:

> This is no regular course. It is an infernal mite society, a pure charity speculation.

His first lecture tour in the East was brief and disastrous to his nerves and temper. Meanwhile he had accepted an editorship on the Buffalo *Express* and had married. After his marriage he was in such demand as a platform attraction that he could not find time to reply to all the letters received, and was compelled on March 1st to have a circular printed:

Office Express Printing Co.,
Buffalo, March 1, 1870.

Dear Sir:
In answer, I am obliged to say that it will not be possible for me to accept your kind invitation. I shall not be able to lecture again during the present season.
Thanking you kindly for the compliment of your invitation, I am,

Yours Truly,
Sam'l L. Clemens.
(Mark Twain.)

But he relented at length, and during April and early in May was making lecture trips to towns in New York State, under the management of Redpath and Fall. On May 2d, he wrote to Redpath:

Buffalo, May 2, 1870

Dear Redpath:
I mislaid the letter inquiring about Cambridge, N.Y., till this moment. It got mixed with my loose papers.
They told me that the society I talked for was the leading and favorite. They half burned down the hall at 7 p.m. and yet at 8 had a full house, though a mighty wet and smoky one. It was a bad night, too.

Yours,
Mark.

Joel Benton, the author, tells a story of this period of Twain's platform career. Mark was to lecture in the village in which Benton managed the lyceum. He particularly requested the young chairman not to introduce him to the audience. It was a little whim of his, he explained. They mounted the rostrum together, and Twain gazed for a few long moments at the audience. But at last he arose, and taking a semi-circular sweep to the left, and then proceeding to the front, opened something like this. "Ladies and Gentlemen: I—have—lectured—many—years—and—in—many—towns,—large—and—small. I have traveled—north—south—east—and—west.

I—have—met—many—great—men; *very*—great—men. But—I—have—never—yet—in—all—my—travels—met—the—president—of—a—*country*—lyceum—who—could—introduce—me—to—an—audience—with—that—*distinguished*—consideration—which—my—merits deserve." After this deliverance, the house, which had stared at Benton for several minutes with vexed impatience, was convulsed at his expense.

Yet no sooner had Redpath printed circulars and arranged dates for Twain's appearance then the humorist balked. Under date of May 10th, he wrote a characteristic letter.

Elmira, N.Y., May 10, 1870

Friend Redpath:

I guess I am out of the field permanently. I am sending off those circulars to all lecture applicants now. If you want some more of them I can send them to you. ****The subscriber will have to be excused from the present season at least.

Remember me to Nasby, Billings and Fall. Luck to you!

Yours always and after,
Mark.

This last decision to cease lecturing was permanent for nearly a year, and the entreaties of Redpath and others proved of no avail. Redpath meanwhile had found a new platform star, John B. Gough, and concerning him, Mr. Clemens wrote in the following January, this letter to Redpath:

Buffalo, Jan. 22, 1871.

Friend Redpath:

Are you going to lecture Gough in California?? If so, take the advice of the only lecturer that ever *did* make lecture tours in California—and that advice is—lecture him three nights in succession and so advertise it. Then talk him two successive nights in Sacramento, one night or two in Virginia City, if you can get a church—they won't go to the nasty theatre. Then return and talk him three successive nights in San Francisco. There you are. If anybody says, "Go to San Jose, Petaluma, Grass Valley, Carson City or any other camp on the coast," tell them Artemus Ward and Mark Twain both lost money in each and every one of those places. But six nights in Platt's Hall, San Francisco, are the only ones in the ten I would give my old boots for—but they are worth close on to $8,000 gold, clean profit—more than that if you charge fifty cents extra for reserved seats (which ought to be done and you will have from 500 to 1,000 $1.50 seats that way.) I've had 1,400 reserved seats—sold them all in five hours and closed the box office at 3 p.m., at a dollar a ticket.

But maybe you ain't going to take Gough there after all. Well, put this letter where you can find it again when you do take somebody there. Nasby would have a big run there.

> Yours ever,
> Mark.

After persevering persuasion on the part of Redpath, Mark Twain was preparing to talk once more to delighted audiences during 1871. On obtaining a definite promise from the humorist, Redpath began booking him for an extended Eastern tour, while the lecturer settled down to his work of preparing the lectures. On June 27, 1871, he wrote from Elmira:

Dear Red:
> Wrote another lecture—a third one—to-day. *It* is the one I am going to deliver. I think I shall call it "Reminiscences of Some Pleasant Characters Whom I Have Met," (or should the "whom" be left out?) It covers my whole acquaintance—kings, lunatics, idiots and all. Suppose you give the item a start in the Boston papers. If I write fifty lectures I shall only choose one and talk that one only.

> Yours,
> Mark

The same day, evidently in the evening, he wrote a second letter to Redpath:

Elmira, June 27, 1871.

Dear Redpath:
Don't be in any hurry about announcing the title of my
lecture. Just say: 'To be announced." Because I wrote a new
lecture to-day, called simple[sic] "D.L.H." During July I'll
decide which one I like best.

Yours,
Mark

In July, Mr. Redpath wrote to Mark, telling him that he
had booked him for a lecture in a Brooklyn church, and
incidentally mentioned that his partner, Mr. Fall, was
suffering from the effects of a carbuncle. Twain's reply was
characteristic:

Elmira, July 10, 1871.

Dear Redpath:
* * * I never made a success of a lecture delivered in a
church yet. People are afraid to laugh in a church. They can't
be made to do it in any possible way.
Success to Fall's carbuncle and many happy returns.

Yours,
Mark.

Four days later Redpath sent him news of further
bookings, and to one engagement at least Mark demurred.

Elmira, July 14, 1871

Dear Redpath:
Don't lecture me at Jamestown, N.Y., unless Providence
compels you. I suppose all lecturers hate that place.
Shall be in Hartford 3 or 4 weeks hence and then I shall
run up and bum around with you a day or two if you ain't
busy.

Yours,
Mark.

Mark Twain's uncertainty as to his lecture engagements,
the final decision as to whether he wanted to lecture or not,

and his unsettled condition of mind as to his future plans and movements were well illustrated in a very humorous letter written to Redpath, a month later. The letter reads:

Hartford, Tuesday, Aug. 8, 1871.

Dear Red:
I am different from other men! My mind changes oftener. People who have no mind can easily be steadfast and firm, but when a man is loaded down to the guards with it, as I am, every sea of foreboding or inclination, maybe of indolence, shifts the cargo. See! Therefore, if you will notice, one week I am likely to give rigid instructions to confine me to New England; the next week, send me to Arizona; the next week withdraw my name; the next week give you full untrammelled swing; and the week following modify it. You must try to keep the run of my mind, Redpath, it is your business, being the agent, and it always was too many for me. It appears to me to be one of the finest pieces of mechanism I have ever met with. Now about the West, this week, I am willing that you shall retain all the Western engagements. But what I shall want *next* week is still with God.
Let us not profane the mysteries with soiled hands and prying eyes of sin.

Yours,
Mark.

P.S.—Shall be here two weeks, will run up there when Nasby comes.

In his next letter to Redpath he tells how to get sick just before an advertised appearance to lecture.

Elmira, N.Y., Sept. 15, 1871.

Dear Redpath:
I wish you would get me released from the lecture at—
——. Otherwise I'll have no resource left but to get sick the day I am to lecture there. I can get sick easy enough, by the

simple process of saying the word—well never mind what word—I am not going to lecture there.

> Yours,
> Mark.

Among the earlier engagements of his lecture tour in 1871 was his appearance in Washington, upon which occasion he delivered for the first time a lecture on Artemus Ward. Writing to Redpath, he said:

> Washington, Tuesday, Oct. 28, 1871.

Dear Red:

I have come square out, thrown, "Reminiscences" overboard, and taken "Artemus Ward, Humorist," for my subject. Wrote it here on Friday and Saturday, and read it from MSS. last night to enormous house. It suits *me* and I'll never deliver the nasty, nauseous "Reminiscences" any more.

> Yours
> Mark.

The lecture on Artemus Ward evidently proved even less satisfactory to the lecturer than his much condemned reminiscences, for in December he telegraphed as follows:

> Buffalo Depot, Dec. 8, 1871.

Redpath & Fall, Boston:

Notify all hands that from this time I shall talk nothing but selections from my forthcoming book, *Roughing It.* Tried it last night. Suits me tiptop.

> Sam'l L. Clemens.

His reception in the Western and Central states pleased him so well that in a letter from Logansport, Indiana, he seemed thrilled with enthusiasm, and was apparently deeply in love with his platform life.

Logansport, Ind., Jan. 2, 1872.

Friend Redpath:

Had a splendid time with a splendid audience in Indianapolis last night—a perfectly jammed house just as I have all the time out here and I like the new lecture but I hate the "Artemus Ward" talk and won't talk it any more. No man ever approved that choice of subject in my hearing, I think.

Yours,
Mark.

One never knows whether Mark is afoot or on horseback. In two weeks he had changed his mind again, and was begging for fewer engagements.

Jan. 17, 1872.

Dear Red:

No, I can't lecture anywhere outside of New England in February except it be in Troy on the first. Wouldn't talk in Utica or Newburgh either for twice the money.

Was glad Bellefontaine backed. Wish some more would. The fewer engagements I have from this time forth the better I shall be pleased.

Yours,
Mark.

Matters were going from bad to worse. Redpath was using his best endeavors to keep Twain on the platform, while the humorist was pulling like an army mule in the other direction. In February he telegraphed to Redpath from Hartford:

How in the name of God does a man find his way from here to Amherst and when must he start? Give me full particulars and send a man with me. If I had another engagement I would rot before I would fill it.

S. L. Clemens.

Summer came and Mark was glad—the lecture season was over. Then he sailed for England to arrange for the European publication of his works, and successfully secured Chatto & Windus as his English representatives, and the publishing house of Tauchnitz, at Leipzig, as his continental agent. Already he was widely known and quoted in England and was a welcome guest.

Mark tells a characteristic story, and at the same time comments upon the lecture business, in a letter written to Redpath in November.

Langham Hotel, London, Nov. 3, 1872.

Dear Redpath:

* * * I was down for a speech at the Whitefriar's Club, and the chairman had done me the honor to make me his guest and appointed me a seat at his right, and as I know nearly all the Whitefriars, I expected to have a gorgeous time, but I got it into my head, that Friday was Thursday, so I stayed in the country stag-hunting a day too long and when I reached the club last night, nicely shaved and gotten up regardless of expense, I found that the dinner was the night before.

I would like to stay here about fifteen or seventy-five years, a body does have such a good time. I am re-vamping, polishing, in other words fixing up my lecture on *Roughing It* and think I will deliver it in London a couple of times, about a month from now, just for fun.

So Stanley gets $50,000 for 100 nights. That is as it should be. They charge $2 to hear Parepa sing two pieces (fifteen minutes all told) and if you charged a dollar to hear one of us fellows squeak it would become the fashion to hear us—and then the gates of hell could not prevail against us— we would always have a full house. When I yell again for less than $500 I'll be pretty hungry. But I haven't any intention of yelling at any price.

Yours ever,
Mark.

While in London he lectured not infrequently, and with striking success. The Rev. H. R. Haweis, the literary critic, who heard him, writes:

I heard him once at the Hanover Square rooms. The audience was not large nor very enthusiastic. I believe he would be an increasing success had he stayed longer. We had not time to get accustomed to his peculiar way, and there was nothing to take us by storm. He came on the platform and stood quite alone. A little table, with the traditional water-bottle and tumbler, was by his side. His appearance was not impressive, not very unlike the representation of him in the various pictures in his *Tramp Abroad*. He spoke more slowly than any other man I ever heard, and did not look at his audience quite enough. I do not think that he felt altogether at home with us, nor we with him. We never laughed loud or long. We sat throughout expectant and on the *qui vive*, very well interested and gently simmering with amusement. With the exception of one exquisite description of the Old Magdalen ivy-covered collegiate buildings at Oxford University, I do not think that there was one thing worth setting down in print. I got no information out of the lecture, and hardly a joke that would wear, or a story that would bear repeating. There was a deal about the dismal, lone silver-land, the story of the Mexican plug that bucked, and a duel which never came off and another duel in which no one was injured; and we sat patiently enough through it, fancying that by and by the introduction would be over, and the lecture would begin, when Twain suddenly made his bow, and went off! It was over. I looked at my watch, I was never more taken aback. I had been sitting there exactly an hour and twenty minutes! It seemed ten minutes at the outside. If you have ever tried to address a public meeting, you will know what this means. It means that Mark Twain is a consummate public speaker. If he ever chose to say anything, he would say it marvelously well; but in the art of saying nothing in an hour, he surpasses our most accomplished parliamentary speakers.

Upon his return to America and to Elmira, he found Mrs. Clemens ill, and consequently he telegraphed Redpath that he would not lecture again, and told his wife that there was not enough money in America to hire him to leave her for one day. He wrote Redpath that he might arrange a lecture tour later on, if Mrs. Clemens could accompany him. He appeared occasionally during the next few years in a few of the leading cities, but his decision to quit the platform was almost final.

Only once did he appear in public as a political speaker. As a conscientious Republican in his political preferences, Mr. Clemens took an active interest in the presidential campaign of 1880. While visiting in Elmira, New York, in the fall of that year, he made a short speech one Saturday night, introducing to a Republican meeting Gen. Hawley, of Connecticut. In the course of his remarks Mr. Clemens said:

"General Hawley is a member of my church at Hartford, and the author of 'Beautiful Snow.' Maybe he will deny that. But I am only here to give him a character from his last place. As a pure citizen, I respect him; as a personal friend of years, I have the warmest regard for him; as a neighbor, whose vegetable garden adjoins mine, why—why, I watch him. As the author of 'Beautiful Snow,' he has added a new pang to winter. He is a square, true man in honest politics, and I must say he occupies a mighty lonesome position. So broad, so bountiful is his character that he never turned a tramp empty-handed from his door, but always gave him a letter of introduction to me. Pure, honest incorruptible, that is Joe Hawley. Such a man in politics is like a bottle of perfumery in a glue factory—it may moderate the stench, but it doesn't destroy it. I haven't said any more of him than I would say of myself. Ladies and gentlemen, this is General Hawley."

In 1884, Mr. Clemens and George W. Cable made a tour of the country, giving readings from their own works, under the management of Major Pond. Cordial receptions and crowded houses greeted them everywhere. Strong inducements had been offered him to lecture abroad, even so far away as Australia. In 1884 he consented to lecture in America for a period not exceeding five months.

In December, Twain and Cable appeared in Cleveland. They arrived one afternoon and registered at the Forest City House. I called to pay my respects. Was Mr. Clemens in? Yes, but he had just eaten dinner, it then being 3 o'clock, and had gone to bed, not to be disturbed until 7 o'clock, excepting in case Mr. John Hay, the author of "Little Breeches," called. Mr. Clemens would see Mr. Hay, but no other human being could

Will M. Clemens

entice him from his bed. In the evening occurred the entertainment. Mr. Cable read passages from his novel, "Dr. Sevier." Mark Twain came upon the stage walking slowly, apparently in deep meditation. Those present saw a rather small man, with a big head, with bushy gray hair, heavy dark eyebrows, a receding chin, a long face, toothless gums visible between the lips, an iron-gray mustache, closely cut and stiff. The right hand involuntarily stroked the receding chin and a merry twinkle came into his eyes, as he advanced to the front of the stage and began to recite, in his peculiar, drawling and deliberate way, "King Sollerman," taken from advance sheets of *Huckleberry Finn*. When he had finished, he turned and boyishly ran off the stage, with a sort of dog trot. Then I remember that Mr. Cable came on, told us all about "Kate Riley" and "Ristofolo," and then, in imitation of Mark Twain, tried to run off the stage in the same playful manner. I remember also what a deplorable failure Mr. Cable made of the attempt, how his gentle trot reminded me of a duck going down hill, and how eventually he collided with one of the scenes, and lastly how the audience roared with laughter. Then Mark came forward again with his "Tragic Tale of the Fishwife," followed by Cable, who walked soberly now, like a Baptist deacon. Twain told us of "A Trying Situation," and finally concluded the entertainment with one of his inimitable ghost stories.

He is a good talker, and invariably prepares himself, though he skillfully hides his preparation by his method of delivery, which denotes that he is getting his ideas and phrases as he proceeds. He is an accomplished artist in his way. His peculiar mode of expression always seems contagious with an audience, and a laugh would follow the most sober remark. It is a singular fact that an audience will be in a laughing mood, when they first enter the lecture room; they are ready to burst out at anything and everything. In the town of Colchester, Connecticut, there was a good illustration of this, the Hon. Demshain Hornet having a most unpleasant experience at the expense of Mark Twain. Mr. Clemens was advertised to lecture in the town of Colchester, but for some reason failed to arrive. In the emergency the lecture committee decided to employ Mr. Hornet to deliver his celebrated lecture on temperance, but so late in the day was this arrangement made that no bills announcing it could be circulated, and the audience assembled, expecting to hear Mark Twain. No one in the town knew Mr. Clemens, or had ever heard him lecture, and they entertained the idea that he was funny, and went to the lecture prepared to laugh. Even those upon the platform, excepting the chairman, did not know Mr. Hornet from Mark Twain, and so, when he was introduced, thought nothing of the name, as they knew "Mark Twain" was a pen-name, and supposed his real name was Hornet.

Mr. Hornet bowed politely, looked about him, and remarked: "Intemperance is the curse of the country." The audience burst into a merry laugh. He knew it could not be at his remark, and thought his clothes must be awry, and he asked the chairman, in a whisper, if he was all right, and received "yes" for an answer. Then he said: "Rum slays more than disease!" Another, but louder laugh followed. He could not understand it, but proceeded: "It breaks up happy homes!" Still louder mirth. "It is carrying young men down to death and hell!" Then came a perfect roar of applause. Mr. Hornet began to get excited. He thought they were poking fun at him, but went on: "We must crush the serpent!" A tremendous howl of laughter. The men on the platform, except the chairman, squirmed as they laughed. Then Hornet got mad. "What I say is Gospel truth," he cried. The audience fairly bellowed with mirth. Hornet turned to a man on the stage, and said: "Do you see anything very ridiculous in my remarks or behavior?" "Yes, ha, ha! It's intensely funny—ha, ha, ha! Go on!" replied the roaring man. "This is an insult," cried Hornet, wildly dancing about. More laughter, and cries of, "Go on, Twain!" Then the chairman began to see through a glass darkly, and arose and quelled the merriment, and explained the situation, and the men on the stage suddenly ceased laughing, and the folks in the audience looked sheepish, and they quit laughing, too, and then the excited Mr. Hornet, being thoroughly mad, told them he had never before got into a town so entirely populated with asses and idiots, and having said that, he left the hall in disgust, followed by the audience in deep gloom.

In Montreal, upon the occasion of Mark Twain's appearance in 1884, many Frenchmen were in the audience. This caused him to introduce into his lecture the following:

> Where so many of the guests are French, the propriety will be recognized of my making a portion of my speech in that beautiful language, in order that I may be partly understood. I speak French with timidity, and not flowingly, except when excited. When using that language, I have noticed that I have hardly ever been mistaken for a Frenchman, except, perhaps, by horses; never, I believe, by people. I had hoped that mere French construction, with English words, would answer; but this is not the case. I tried it at a gentleman's house in Quebec, and it would not work. The maid servant asked, "What would monsieur?" I said, "Monsieur So-and-So, is he with himself?" She did not understand. I said, "Is it that he is still not returned to his house of merchandise?" She did not understand that, either. I said, "He will desolate himself when he learns that his friend American was arrived, and he not with himself to shake him at the hand." She did not even understand that; I don't know why, but she did not, and she lost her temper, besides. Somebody in the rear called out, "Qui est donc la?" or words to that effect, She said, "C'est un fou," and shut the door on me. Perhaps she was right; but how did she ever find that out? For she had never seen me before till that moment. But as I have already intimated, I will close this oration with a few sentiments in the French language. I have not ornamented them. I have not burdened them with flowers of rhetoric, for, to my mind, that literature is best and most enduring which is characterized by a noble simplicity: *J'ai belle bouton d'or de mon oncle, mais je n'ai pas celui du charpentier. Si vous avez le fromage du brave menuisier, c'est bon; mais si vous ne l'avez pas, ne vous desolez pas, prenez le chapeau de drap noir de son beau frère malade. Tout a l'heure! Savoir faire! Qu'est ce que vous dites! Pâté de fois gras! Revanon à nos moutons! Pardon,*

messieurs, pardonnez moi; essayant à parler la belle langue d'Ollendorf strains me more than you can possibly imagine. But I mean well, and I've done the best I could.

Once when the late Richard Malcolm Johnston had been prevailed on a give a reading in Baltimore, Thomas Nelson Page volunteered to assist him. But a death in Mr. Page's family prevented him from appearing in the entertainment. Mark Twain heard of it. The people of Baltimore had long wanted to have Twain appear there, but he had steadfastly refused to resume his lectures. But he went on that occasion, for he appreciated the genius of Richard Malcolm Johnston, and, desiring to honor him, he left New York, at a great personal sacrifice, and appeared with him on that occasion. There was never such a crowded house in a Baltimore theatre. When the entertainment was over Col. Johnston, with his accustomed fairness and courtesy, tendered Twain the bulk of the receipts.

"No," said Mark, "not one cent shall I receive. It is such a great honor to know a man like you that I am the one who owes you the debt of gratitude."

"Well," said the colonel, "at least let me defray your expenses.""

"I have a through ticket," said Twain. "Good-by and God bless you!"

His last appearance in New York was during the winter of 1894, when he appeared at Madison Square Garden, with the late Bill Nye and James Whitcomb Riley. He had aged noticeably. The failure of his publishing firm in New York had told upon him in every way. His appearance on the platform at this time is best told in the words of a well-known journalist:

And now comes dear old Mark. Those curly grayish locks, that drooping mustache, the half-closed eyes, the gentle expression of the mouth, almost melancholy, that historic dress suit, too, a relic of several decades ago. The waistcoat barely reached the trousers. Still there was a charming quaintness about him. His self-abnegatory way of speaking was more restful than the egotism of the other two.

I took my eyes off him but once, and then it was to look on the veteran historian, Parke Godwin, who was sitting a few seats in front. There was a resemblance between the two more striking than the difference in their ages. Both show the same disregard for the prevailing fashions in dress that frequently suggests genius. The paths of these two lives have been widely divergent; there is little in common between the author of Tom Sawyer and the historian of the French Revolution. But they are alike in that to either and to both one might apply the words of Homer:

> He was the friend of man,
> For he loved them all.

And now he begins his story. It is "The Jumping Frog." The sad expression begins to fade away, the half-closed eyes are opened wider and begin to twinkle; the point is reached and Twain has once more resumed the self-contemplative look and is again another Jacques.

His lecture tour of the world begun in 1895, under the management of Major Pond, was for a purpose—to earn money with which to pay the debts of his publishing firm—and all the world knows of his success in that grand endeavor.

Life Reviews *Huckleberry Finn*

Durant Da Ponte

T he fact that *Huckleberry Finn* elicited only the scantest notice among the critics of its day is a commonplace of Mark Twain scholarship. The reasons for the neglect of Clemens's masterpiece are at best suppositional.[1] Whatever these reasons might be, the fact remains that the novel did not enjoy the critical attention which it might have been expected to call forth. Among the few reviews, one, which seems to have gone undetected by investigators of Clemens's contemporaneous reputation, appeared in the comic magazine *Life* on February 26, 1885 (V, 119), and is reproduced herewith entire.

Mark Twain's Blood-Curdling Humor

Mark Twain is a humorist or nothing. He is well aware of this fact himself, for he prefaces the "Adventures of Huckleberry Finn" with a brief notice, warning persons in search of a moral, motive or plot that they are liable to be prosecuted, banished or shot. This is a nice little artifice to scare off the critics—a kind of "trespassers on these grounds will be dealt with according to law."

However, as there is no penalty attached, we organized a search expedition for the humorous qualities of this book with the following hilarious results:

A very refined and delicate piece of narration by Huck Finn, describing his venerable and dilapidated "pap" as afflicted with delirium tremens, rolling over and over, "Kicking things every which way," and "saying there was

Reprinted from *American Literature* 31 (March 1959): 78–81.

devils ahold of him." This chapter is especially suited to amuse the children on long, rainy afternoons.

An elevating and laughable description of how Huck killed a pig, smeared its blood on an axe and mixed in a little of his own hair, and then ran off, setting up a job on the old man and the community, and leading them to believe him murdered. This little joke can be repeated by any smart boy for the amusement of his fond parents.

A graphic and romantic tale of a Southern family feud, which resulted in an elopement and from six to eight choice corpses.

A polite version of the "Giascutus" story, in which a nude man, striped with the colors of the rainbow, is exhibited as "The King's Camelopard; or, The Royal Nonesuch." This is a good chapter for lenten parlor entertainments and church festivals.

A side-splitting account of a funeral, enlivened by a "sick melodeum," a "long-legged undertaker," and a rat episode in the cellar.

The article is unsigned, but it appears as part of the weekly column entitled BOOKISHNESS, which was the special province of Robert Bridges, not to be confused with the British poet of the same name, who was literary critic for *Life* from 1883 to 1900, and who regularly signed his columns with the pen name "Droch." A note two weeks later in a column bearing Bridges's pseudonym refers to the Kemble illustrations "which enliven many a page of coarse and dreary fun."[2] Another comment a month later reads: "It is a pleasure to note that the Concord Library Committee agree with LIFE's estimate of Mark Twain's 'blood-curdling humor,' and have banished 'Huckleberry Finn' to limbo. If they will again take our advice, let them banish the School of Philosophy. Concord will then rank with other well-regulated Massachusetts towns."[3]

If these two brief comments bearing Bridges's pen name do not confirm beyond doubt his authorship of the *Huckleberry Finn* review, they at least indicate his whole-hearted agreement with the views of whoever wrote the critique in question. That Bridges, who is best remembered as being assistant editor of *Scribner's* magazine from its founding in

1887 until 1914 and editor from 1914 until 1930, failed to perceive the value of such an undeniable classic of American literature as *Huckleberry Finn* may seem odd indeed.[4] The fact is, however, that, regardless of his later development, Bridges's apprenticeship as a critic found him pretty firmly entrenched in the ranks of the romanticists. His BOOKISHNESS columns fairly bristle with attacks upon the new realistic school, the members of which he found "sadly limited."[5] His position as a spokesman in defense of the genteel tradition can best be summed up in his comments on the function of the critic: "If he is an honest critic, he will have some sincere convictions to express; if he is intelligent, he will be able to clearly present the central idea of the author to the reader, and perhaps reveal a purpose that would have remained concealed; and if he has any moral stamina, he can warn the ignorant but well-disposed against those books which can only count for evil."[6]

In addition, he believed that "A novel which faithfully though ideally reflects the life and country with which the author's deepest experiences are associated is the very best form of fiction. . . ."[7] This last statement he made in a review of Charles Egbert Craddock's *The Prophet of the Great Smoky Mountains.* And here, I think, lies the answer to the riddle of Bridges's critical personality. Mark Twain did not idealize. Miss Murfree did, and in so doing perhaps even falsified. But as Huck himself tells us about the companion volume to the one of which he is hero: "That book was made by Mr. Mark Twain, and he told the truth, mainly." The truth, one might venture to suggest, was a commodity not especially congenial to readers of the time. And so it was that the comic magazine *Life* missed a good opportunity to assist in establishing the reputation of America's great humorist.

Notes

1. See Arthur L. Vogelback, "The Publication and Reception of *Huckleberry Finn* in America," *American Literature*, XI, 260–272 (Nov., 1939), in which the author reviews the pre-publication attention accorded the novel—the serialization of excerpts in the *Century*, Twain's reading of selections on a lecture tour with Cable, the lawsuit with the Boston publishing house of Estes and Lauriat over price cutting, and so forth—all of which no doubt tended to make *Huckleberry Finn* seem like "old stuff" when it appeared belatedly in February, 1885.

2. *Life* V (March 12, 1885): 146.

3. *Life* V (April 9, 1885): 202.

4. Frederick Lewis Allen has attested to the perspicacity of his mature judgment. "One likes to think," writes Allen, ". . . of Max Perkins. . . handing over to Bridges for serial publication. . . Hemingway's *A Farewell to Arms*, which aroused the disapproval of the Boston censors. . ." ("Fifty Years of Scribner's Magazine," *Scribner's* CI (Jan., 1937): 24.

5. *Life* X (Nov. 17, 1887): 274.

6. *Life* IX (Jan. 13, 1887): 20.

7. *Life* VI (Oct. 29, 1885): 243.

Huckleberry Finn:
The Book We Love to Hate

Leslie A. Fiedler

I like to think that it would have tickled Mark Twain that a
defender of "sivilization" 1984-style rose at the first major
symposium honoring the hundredth anniversary of the
publication of *Huckleberry Finn* to demand—piously and
solemnly—that it be banned from the school curriculum in
State College, Pennsylvania. "Black kids," she contended of a
book about a white boy willing to "go to hell" to insure the
freedom of a runaway black slave, "can be humiliated by it,
white kids who are sensitive feel somehow culpable and
guilty, and others have their racial biases reinforced"; and she
further urged that an English teacher who had assigned it to a
ninth grade class, "be censured for manifestations of racial
prejudice. . . ." But no one present, as far as I can gather from
newspaper accounts of the occasion, had sense enough to
laugh.

Instead, some of the other symposiasts seconded her plea,
as unaware as she of the absurdity of advocating censorship in
the name of "enlightened liberalism"; and apparently equally
unaware that some decades earlier the book they advocated
keeping out of the hands of the young lest it foster "racism"
had been quite piously and solemnly condemned by
unabashed white racists, including a now forgotten
congressman called Joseph Shannon and the still infamous
Senator Joseph McCarthy. The former, an unreconstructed

Reprinted from *Proteus* 1, no. 2 (Fall 1984): 1–8.

apologist for the Confederacy, had described Twain as "a foresaker of the interests of the South, a coward and deserter"; while the latter apparently considered him un-American, a source of aid and comfort for the Communist enemy.

To be sure, several of the academic participants in the centennial symposium rose valiantly to its defense; but they scarcely could have done otherwise, considering that they earned their living by teaching it. Besides, there was something almost as ridiculous as the attack which cued it in their humorless insistence on the moral integrity and classic status of a book to which its author had appended an ironic "Note" warning: "Persons attempting to find a motive in this narrative will be prosecuted; persons attempting to find a moral in it will be banished. . . ." In any case, academic critics, as their latter day descendants did not trouble to remind their audience, have not always been so sure about the morality and greatness of *Huckleberry Finn*. As a matter of fact, when it first appeared it was reviewed favorably in only one "serious" literary periodical.

Part of the trouble seems to have been that it was not packaged and distributed like a "serious" book at all—but published by "subscription," which is to say, peddled like the sleaziest "commodity literature" of the time. Moreover, it seems to have disappointed the kind of genteel readers who had been encouraged by Twain's previous novel, *The Prince and the Pauper*, to believe he was shedding the bad habits he had acquired as a Western journalist, contemptuous of elegance and good taste, and learning at long last to produce books suitable for family reading in the civilized East. In *Huckleberry Finn*, however, he seemed to be reverting to inadvertent vulgarity and deliberate irreverence, farce and shameless burlesque. What is more, to make matters worse he had written his new book in colloquial backcountry American, with the deliberate misspellings and grammatical lapses on which newspaper humorists depended for easy laughs.

Small wonder then that most of the few notices he did get were more in the nature of rebukes than proper reviews.

"Vulgar and coarse," the avowed enemies of the low comic called it, "trashy and vicious..no better than the dime novels. . . not elevating. . . more suited to the slums than to intelligent, respectable people. . . ." but even the polite humorists of the time found Twain offensive; a writer in *Life*, the leading comic magazine of the era, for instance, described *Huckleberry Finn* as "coarse and dreary fun"; and after detailing its many scenes of murder and mayhem, observed snidely that such fare was apparently being proffered as "especially suited to amuse children on long, rainy afternoons." But it was the humorless hardline which triumphed and persisted; so that as late as 1920, ten years after Twain's death, a certain Professor John T. Rice, is still insisting in the *Missouri Historical Review*, of that state's best-known writer, "he is often coarse, irreverent if not blasphemous. . . Mark Twain lacks the education absolutely necessary to be a great writer; he lacks the refinement which would render it impossible for him to create such coarse characters as Huckleberry Finn; furthermore, he is absolutely unconscious of all the canons of literary art. . . ."

By the time Rice had delivered himself of this blanket condemnation, however, a counter-effort to tout *Huckleberry Finn* as "the Great American Novel" had begun in earnest. Starting with the authorized and adulatory autobiography by Albert Bigelow Paine, it had even begun to penetrate the academy. But Twain's chief apologists up to the middle of our own century tended to be not objective critics, but cultural chauvinists bound and determined to find somewhere in our past a supreme American classic, or journalists with a strong populist bias, like Bernard DeVoto, bent on redeeming a homegrown novelist whom European-oriented academic critics had hitherto denigrated or ignored. When DeVoto's *Mark Twain's America* appeared in 1932, however, he was most directly responding to another freelance nonacademic, Van Wyck Brooks. In *The Ordeal of Mark Twain* (1920), Brooks had somewhat grudgingly granted that *Huckleberry Finn* attained a certain measure of greatness, but his chief

emphasis was on the fact that it might have been even greater
if Twain had not been himself the victim of the same genteel
tradition which had found his novel vulgar and unrefined.
During the Sexual Revolution of the 'twenties, that is to say—
in one more typically ironic turn of the critical screw—Twain
was blamed for expurgating his own work in response to the
pressures of his timid family and friends—for failing, in short,
to be vulgar and unrefined *enough*.

Moreover, just as he was found lacking by the "liberated"
Freudian critics of the post-World War I era, he was adjudged
inadequate by the two critical schools which dominated the
American cultural scene during the Great Depression and
immediately after World War II, the self-declared Marxists first
and then the so-called "New Critics." To a hardline Stalinist
like Granville Hicks, for instance, Twain seemed never to have
fulfilled his promise of becoming "a great social novelist."
Failing either to confront the social conflicts of his own time
or "to regard the literary life as a serious enterprise," Twain—
Hicks contends in *The Great Tradition*, published in 1933—
ended bitter and frustrated. Ironically once more, despite their
differences on almost every other score, the defenders of High
Modernism, most of whom were politically reactionary,
agreed. After all, their most admired literary ancestor, Henry
James, had dismissed Twain as reading for the immature, and
Newton Arvin echoed him in the 'fifties, writing that Twain's
appeal was "chiefly to the very young. . . he is read not
because he makes experience more intelligible, but because he
cooperates with the desire to play hooky. . . ."

It was Hawthorne and Melville whose fiction Arvin found
infinitely more sympathetic, as did most of his more serious
and sophisticated colleagues in the university and out; not
merely teaching them assiduously, but producing numerous
full-length studies of *The Scarlet Letter* and *Moby Dick*. They
did not, however, perform a similar service for *Huckleberry
Finn*. Indeed, Twain remains oddly invisible in the Age of
Criticism which climaxed in the 'fifties. He is, for instance
absent from F.O. Matthiessen's *The American Renaissance*,

the critical study which established for that time a new canon of American literature, as he was also from an earlier work which much influenced it, D.H. Lawrence's *Studies in Classic American Literature*. Clearly, in the case of Matthiessen (who, unlike Lawrence, admired *Huckleberry Finn*) Twain was excluded for purely chronological reasons; but, in any case, neither Matthiessen himself nor anyone else hastened to fill the gap. To be sure, T. S. Eliot, who was not only the favorite poet of the first generation of New Critics, but a formidable critic as well, in 1950 declared himself convinced of the greatness of *Huckleberry Finn*. Eliot, though, was speaking nostalgically and sentimentally on the occasion of his temporary return from exile to the banks of the Mississippi, where he had been born; and he is, in any event, an erratic and untrustworthy judge of fiction. But Lionel Trilling, most literate and plausible of all American critics influenced by Karl Marx (and Sigmund Freud to boot) had gone on record to the same effect just a couple of years before. Consequently, despite the fact that both of their pieces are slight and occasional, they carried the day, making *Huckleberry Finn* as standard a part of the English curriculum as *Moby Dick* or the *Scarlet Letter* ; so that even the far later critics bent on making a negative case, have felt obligated to come to terms with so odd and formidable a united front.

This, however, is precisely what William Van O'Connor, a second-generation academic New Critic and hardline "Modernist" attempted to do in 1955, in a little essay much reprinted ever since, called "Why *Huckleberry Finn* is Not the Great American Novel." In it he argues that, in spite of Trilling and Eliot, "Twain, however gifted as a raconteur, however much genius he had as an improvisor, was not, even in *Huckleberry Finn,* a great novelist"; and he suggests as examples of writers who were: Jane Austen and Henry James. It is quite evident by the standards of Modernism that O'Connor finds Twain wanting—deficient in "serious wit," controlled form and precision of language. In light of this, then it is scarcely surprising that Cyril Connolly, drawing up in

1965 a list of the "one hundred key books" of the Modern Movement, excluded *Huckleberry Finn*, which he explained, "is over-praised, too involved and sentimental despite its prophetic use of American vernacular—a false dawn. . . ."

For a long time, moreover, Twain fared as badly with his fellow-novelists as he had earlier on with the literary critics. His Continental contemporaries by and large ignored him, and even novelists who wrote in his own tongue, both American and English, though more likely to begin by granting that he possessed considerable talent, typically ended by denying his "greatness." The British, in fact, remained skeptical well into the twentieth century: Arnold Bennett, for instance, declaring that though some of Clemens' fictions were "episodically magnificent. . . as complete works of art they are of inferior quality;" and Frank Harris dismissing him even more summarily, with the observation, "I do not think *Huckleberry Finn* among the best boys' books. *Treasure Island* of Stevenson seems to me infinitely better." As late as 1941, V. S. Pritchett though urging an apparently reluctant English audience to read the book which he described somewhat condescendingly as, "granting the limits of a boy's mind in the hero and the author, a comic masterpiece," hastens to add that "It is not a book which grows spiritually, if we compare it to *Quixote*, *Dead Souls*, or even *Pickwick*; and it is lacking in that civilized quality which you are bound to lose when you throw over civilization—the quality of pity."

Considering the British inclination to identify their own culture with "civilization" itself, the response is understandable enough. But less understandably for a while at least, Twain was regarded just as suspiciously by eminent writers in his own country. Even William Dean Howells, his life-long advocate, as well as his editor and censor and close friend, though he rushed into print enthusiastically in behalf of *Innocents Abroad*, *The Prince and the Pauper*, and *A Connecticut Yankee in King Arthur's Court*, published no review of *Huckleberry Finn*. Good and sufficient reasons have been offered for this (he had no regular reviewing assignment at the moment; he was too deeply involved with editing the book *etc. etc.*); but his perhaps embarrassed silence is too much like that of most of his respectable contemporaries to be easily explained away. Certainly, he was aware of the resistance to Twain on the part of the eminent Brahmins of New England, whom he himself had wooed and won, though initially quite as much a suspect outsider as Twain, reporting a little ruefully that "I do not think Longfellow made much of him and Lowell made less."

Henry James, though more nearly of Twain's age and generation, regarded him, as we have already noted, with equal coolness; but this is scarcely surprising in light of the fact that the mass audience which spurned his work had made a rich man of his rival. What is surprising is that Walt Whitman, who one might have supposed would find Twain with his commitment to the vernacular and his populist politics profoundly sympathetic, thought him somehow not really on his side. "I think he misses fire," the Good Grey Poet told Horace Traubel of Twain, "he might have been something: he comes near to being something; but he never arrives." Similarly, the somewhat younger Theodore Dreiser, though he respected and admired Twain for his ideas, especially his religious skepticism and his hostility to American imperialism, found him inadequate as a maker of fictions; "never a novelist," was his final word on the subject, "He could not write a novel."

It seems clear, however, that Dreiser was deeply indebted to Twain in ways he could not confess even to himself. It was only with the emergence of Faulkner and Hemingway in the late 1920s that a generation of novelists appeared willing to acknowledge fully and generously what our literature in general and they in particular owe to Mark Twain. Fittingly enough, it is the judgment of the latter which has been quoted over and over ever since, till it has come to seem an article of faith. "All modern American literature comes from one book by Mark Twain called *Huckleberry Finn*." Hemingway wrote in *The Green Hills of Africa* in 1935, ". . . All American writing comes from that. There was nothing before. There has been nothing as good since."

The grandiloquent overstatement of the conclusion, dismissing as "nothing" all of Cooper and Poe, Hawthorne and Melville, is odd enough and is, therefore, generally ignored by those citing the passage in Twain's behalf. But even odder is the qualifying proviso, indicated by my three dots just before "all American writing," which most admirers of Twain and Hemingway tend to forget. "If you read it you must stop where the Nigger Jim is stolen from the boys. That is the real end. The rest is just cheating." In the first place (obviously Hemingway had not read the novel he so highly praised in a long time and had rewritten it in his memory), Jim is not stolen from "the boys" at all, only from Huck who is unaccompanied by Tom Sawyer at that climatic moment.

Moreover, as those of us who *have* read *Huckleberry Finn* recently are uncomfortably aware, the "rest" that is "just cheating"—the long passage full of cruel horseplay and tedious burlesque involving the mock stealing out of captivity of a black slave who Tom knows has long since been freed—constitutes nearly one third of the whole book. One must slog his way through it to reach what is perhaps the most famous pair of sentences in the book (the essential clue, as I hope finally to demonstrate, to why it has bugged so many self-righteous critics ever since): "But I reckon I got to light out for the Territory ahead of the rest, because Aunt Sally she's going to adopt me and sivilize me and I can't stand it. I been there before."

What Hemingway is saying, finally, is that all of American literature comes out of two thirds of a single book, the rest of which is an esthetic botch and moral failure; and almost all the critics who succeeded him have agreed. Ironically, however, Mark Twain himself did not. After completing the first sixteen or seventeen chapters, which is to say, the part of his novel which critics have found most authentic and moving, he temporarily abandoned the whole project for five or six years, vowing that he was well-nigh determined to "pigeon hole or burn the MS when it is done." But after he had completed the long anti-climax in which all that is potentially tragic in the work is dissolved into farce, he came to believe that he had produced a "rattling good" book after all, and declared that "*I* shall *like* it, whether anybody else does or not."

But that resolve was soon shaken by the treatment *Huckleberry Finn* received from the self-appointed guardians of public morality, to whom in some ways Twain attended more closely than he did to critics and fellow writers; since their opinions much influenced his wife and his daughters, whose approval was essential to his psychic well being. But Livy and Suzy turned out to be dubious about his new book, and eventually even he came like them to regard it as second best to more refined and pretentious works of his like *The Prince and the Pauper* and especially the almost unreadable *Joan of Arc.*

It was in the very heart of New England where he himself had settled that the voice of outraged moral protest against *Huckleberry Finn* was first raised; ironically enough in Concord, Massachusetts, the very cradle of American Liberty. It was there that an irate library committee banned Twain's book from their shelves as "rough, coarse, inelegant, dealing with experiences not elevating. . . the veriest trash." And a chorus of newspaper editorials—reaching eventually back into the West out of which Twain had emerged—repeated the charges: accusing him not only of a contempt for propriety and a willingness to pander to the gross tastes of the mass audience, but of fouling his own American nest, discrediting his country and culture in the eyes of the "civilized" world.

It was indeed this kind of attack on *Huckleberry Finn* which has persisted the longest. However critics may have changed their opinions and practicing writers altered their attitudes with the passage of time, the dogooders and righteous book-banners have continued to regard his masterpiece as subversive. As late as the time in which T. S. Eliot grew up, such a view prevailed in his genteel but cultured family (after all, his grandfather had brought enlightenment to the provinces by founding Washington University in Saint Louis). "I suspect," he wrote looking back from 1950, "that a fear on the part of my parents lest I should acquire a premature taste for tobacco, and perhaps other habits of the hero of the story, kept the book out of my way." It is interesting that Eliot discreetly specifies only smoking (not yet under fire from a new wave of puritan repression in his time) rather than lying and stealing and a contempt for school and church which constitute Huck's less venial faults. The truth is that, taken seriously, *Huckleberry Finn* is not merely "rough, coarse and inelegant" as charged, but also its anti-hero, convinced as he is that what parents, preachers and teachers advocate must be rejected at the behest of his own untutored heart, is a dubious sort of model for growing boys and girls.

It was therefore predictable from the start that scarcely a year would pass during the century since its publication that has not seen Twain's book forbidden somewhere in the United States. After all, the self-righteous we have always with us. What is surprising (though finally characteristic of an America, which like that novel is divided against itself) is that even as *Huckleberry Finn* has remained a banned book, it has also become a *required* one; and that this indeed, has seemed to exacerbate the resistance to it. Truly to understand the impact of Twain's most beloved and feared novel on our culture, then, we must be aware of both sides of our ambivalent response. But from a distance, what is most highly visible is the negative pole of that ambivalence—and the almost habitual scapegoating of poor Huck in which it periodically results.

It was, therefore, possible for a Soviet critic to claim in 1959, at the height of the Cold War, that the relationship of official America to "its greatest writer" is to "try to forget him," and when that fails, to forbid his books. In proof of this, that critic quoted from an English literary journal which a few months before had listed under the heading "Banned in America," *Lady Chatterley's Lover,* the novels of Henry

Miller—and *Huckleberry Finn*. The Russian spokesman, proud of the fact that up to that time eleven million copies of Twain's book had been distributed in his country, where everything not forbidden is required, did not mention that the two other authors were (and are still) under official ban there. Nor did he seem aware that, despite the occasional attempts to forbid it, *Huckleberry Finn* had sold even better in the United States. Instead, he alluded to the attacks on Twain by the long-dead Congressman Shannon and the recently discredited Senator McCarthy, citing as a clincher the fact that only two years earlier "The Board of Education of New York City crossed the book about Huck from the books permitted for reading in elementary and junior schools."

Clearly he was suggesting that Samuel Clemens had become *persona non grata* in the United States because of his satires of American capitalism and imperialism. But the final example scarcely supports this case; since the action of the New York School Board in 1957 was undertaken not at the instigation of the Chamber of Commerce or the Veterans of Foreign Wars, but the NAACP, an organization whose fight against the evils of American racism was then being supported by the American Communist Party. Moreover, in the quarter of a century since, most of the continuing efforts to ban *Huckleberry Finn* have been launched by enlightened liberals, though attacks from genteel conservatives have not utterly ceased.

Every year since 1971, for instance, the *School Library Journal* has given a mock award called the "Huck Finn Pin" to a new book adjudged by its editor to "ill serve the limited reading time of young people." It seems obvious to me that this gallant defender of "good taste" in literature for the young would in 1885 have awarded her booby prize to the book whose anti-hero she describes (explaining why she has thus used his name) as "illiterate and inclined to stay that way." But she feels obliged at least to justify and explain; while the book-banners on the Left have grown even bolder—and more shameless.

When word leaked out in 1957 that *Huckleberry Finn* had been "barred as a textbook" in New York City, school officials felt obliged to lie to the press; explaining that it had been dropped not because of political or ethical objections from anyone, but merely because "it was not really a textbook." The NAACP, however, gave away the game, insisting that they had in fact objected to its "racial slurs" and "belittling racial designations"—meaning its frequent use of the word "nigger." They could not bring themselves actually to say the six-letter word, which at that point was considered "dirtier" than any of the once taboo four-syllable Anglo-Saxon monosyllabics. By 1982, however, the self-righteous anti-racists were out of the closet, and willing, in a good cause, to call a spade a spade.

In that year, for instance, the Human Relations Committee of the Mark Twain (*sic*) Elementary School of Arlington, Virginia, recommending the removal of *Huckleberry Finn* from the curriculum, charged it with being "anti-American," a threat to the Fourteenth Amendment and the very notion that "all men are created equal" because of its "flagrant use of the word 'nigger'." Nor is there any point in denying that Twain is guilty as charged. That offensive epithet is, indeed, repeated over and over on the pages of his book like a *leitmotif* or an obsession; so that one can understand a black school boy in the midst of whites wincing as he reads.

But how could Twain have done otherwise in a book in which he boasted he had "painstakingly" recreated seven dialects spoken in the Mississippi Basin, in all of which, (including that spoken by blacks themselves) the sole name for Afro-Americans was indeed "nigger." The deeper truth told by America about *Huckleberry Finn*, whose last words are, after all, "*Yours Truly,*" depends on its faithfulness to the language we Americans actually speak; especially terms like "nigger," which serve to remind us of not just our troubled history but of attitudes and values created by that history of which most of us have learned to be ashamed, yet from which none of us can feel wholly free. We should therefore prize Twain's dangerous and equivocal novel not in spite of its use of that wicked epithet, but for the way in which it manages to ironize it; enabling us finally—without denying our horror or our guilt—to laugh therapeutically at the "peculiar institution" of slavery.

One of my own favorite passages in the book is, indeed, the little interchange between Huck and Aunt Sally in Chapter XXXII, in which, after Huck lyingly tells her that the boat he had arrived on had blown a cylinder head, she asks, "Good gracious! anybody hurt?" "No'm, he answers; "Killed a nigger;" to which she responds, "Well, it's lucky; because sometimes people do get hurt." What initially makes this passage funny is that both of these essentially good people by thus dehumanizing the Negro diminish their own humanity; and what makes it even funnier is that Huck, obtuse of all obtuse narrators, a classically humorless "straight man," does not find it funny at all. But the real cream of the jest is that in our time self-righteous anti-racists still fail to get the joke, making it also a joke on them unto the third and fourth generation.

Ridiculous or not, however, one hundred years later they continue to suppress *Huckleberry Finn*—putting its defenders more and more on the defensive; so that some have even tried to appease the book-banners by expurgating the novel. It would appear, for instance, that in New York in 1957, the publishers of the textbook version then in use have already discreetly substituted "negro" for "nigger" throughout. As always, however, appeasement did not work, the adamant objectors protesting that that anachronistic and tasteless euphemism had not been properly capitalized. And there is no end in sight; since at this point even capital-N-Negro has become suspect to those who, however pale their actual hue, prefer to call themselves "blacks." In any case, the anti-racist objection to *Huckleberry Finn* is not finally to its language, but (once more in the words of the Human Relations Committee of the Mark Twain School) to "the demeaning way in which black people are portrayed in the book."

I must confess I find this second charge harder to grant, in light of the fact that the only black character portrayed fully in it is "Miss Watson's big nigger Jim," who is by all odds the most sympathetic of its characters. A loving parent and husband, a faithful friend, resourceful, courageous, self-sacrificing (he risks his life to save Tom's), he possesses a natural dignity and authority, which in one of the novel's most moving scenes compels Huck—whom Jim has just called "trash" for his heartlessness—to apologize abjectly. "It made me feel so mean," Huck writes. "I could almost kissed *his* foot to get him to take it back. It was fifteen minutes before I could work myself up to go and humble myself to a nigger—but I done it, and I warn't ever sorry for it afterwards, neither." It is an apology for all of white America, which its ironies (triggered once more by the key word "nigger") keep on the safe side of sentimentality. Moreover, Huck finds on the raft with Jim what he can find nowhere in the "sivilized" white world, a kind of love compatible with freedom. Together they establish a community of two, temporary and foredoomed perhaps, but providing for as long as it lasts a model for the reconciliation of blacks and whites in an America otherwise ethnically divided against itself.

But off the raft (and especially in the long farcical anti-climax which follows Chapter XXXI), the books, detractors protests,[sic] Jim is portrayed as ignorant, superstitious and gullible; thus perpetuating certain degrading "stereotypes about blacks" derived from the minstrel show, which—in the words of a Professor of Afro-American Studies who testified against *Huckleberry Finn* at the centennial symposium I began by describing—consists of "white men blacking up to entertain other whites at the expense of black people's humanity." Some thirty years earlier the same charges had been made by the eminent black American novelist, Ralph Ellison, who had explained to white readers that the Negro is "made uncomfortable" by Nigger Jim, because "Twain fitted Jim into the outlines of the minstrel tradition." Ellison, however, then went on to add—finally loving Twain's great book (and, he tells us, identifying with Huck, whatever his discomfort with Jim) that "it is from behind this stereotype mask that we see Jim's dignity and human capacity—and Twain's complexity—emerge."

What he suggests, and present enemies of the book fail to recognize, is that Twain not merely reflected but redeemed the "niggershow stereotype"—converting it to an archetype of great resonance and power: a mythic grid of perception, through which for a long time the whole world, black as well as white, perceived black Americans. The only two archetypal images of the Negro which can compete with Twain's Nigger Jim are Joel Chandler Harris' Uncle Remus and Harriett Beecher Stowe's Uncle Tom, both also created by white Americans and derived, directly or indirectly, from the minstrel show. Yet neither of the books in which they appear has ever been banned from libraries or classrooms at the behest of anti-racists. *Uncle Tom*, to be sure has been the target of Southern white racists, like *Huckleberry Finn*. Only the latter, however, has the unique distinction of having been censored not only by apologists for *both* sides in what eventuated in a bloody civil war—but also by those to whom culture and taste seemed more important than the "Negro Question," or indeed any social issue.

The persistent popularity of *Huckleberry Finn* has in fact always troubled members of any elite, esthetic, moral or political, whose members feel that they know better than the unredeemed masses what is good for them. I recall William Burroughs (improbable heir to Mark Twain as literary disturber of the peace) once observing that the world would be vastly improved if a weapon could be invented which would destroy "all those who think they are right," i.e., believe that the values in which they happen to believe are valid for everyone, everywhere and will for ever[*sic*] remain so. But *Huckleberry Finn,* it occurs to me, is precisely that weapon; killing no one, to be sure, but undermining all pretensions to final wisdom with ambiguity, irony, farce and burlesque: the universal solvent of laughter.

Without seeming to preach or teach it persuades us—at a level far below full consciousness—of the essential ridiculousness not only of our society's restrictive taboos against lying and stealing, "copping out" and "dropping out," but of its highest positive values as well: duty and hard work, heroism and honor. Moreover, in addition to mocking institutions despised by all right-thinking Americans by the end of the 19th century, royalty, aristocracy, slavery, the blood-feud and lynching, it satirizes others still dearly prized, like home, school and church, which is to say, bourgeois domesticity and Christian humanism. Certainly, the teachers and preachers and parents who defend them turn out in its pages always to be hilariously wrong. But it is worse even than this; since finally *The Adventures of Huckleberry Finn* undercuts, as Huck himself tells us (and we must—without ceasing to laugh—take him quite seriously) "civilization" itself: the reign of law and order and sweet reason, without which no community can survive, but for which the price we pay is, from the individual's point of view, in some sense too high.

To be sure, Twain himself did not live by Huck's antinomian, anarchic code but contented himself with dreaming of an orphan boy who did; and in his voice told the tale which—despite all censors—the world will not let die. Not that we who read and love it dare to "light out for the Territory" either; but turning its pages and evoking its images, we release vicariously all we have repressed in the daylight world of respectability and routine; thus therapeutically giving the devil of our unconscious his due.

Such therapeutic release of the repressed is what all literature which, like *Huckleberry Finn,* pleases many and pleases long, affords us; though not all writers are aware of this. Some indeed aspire to reinforce rather than to deliver us from the "restrictions" of civilization to justify God's ways (i.e., the reigning theology and morality of their time) to man. Mark Twain, however, was of the Devil's party and knew it. He therefore despised, as he did other preachers and teachers, those Apostles of the Art Religion who did not. About Poe and Jane Austen, for instance, he wrote, "I could read his prose on salary, but not Jane's. . . It seems a great pity they allowed her to die a natural death;" and of Henry James he once observed that he would "rather be condemned to Paul Bunyan's Heaven" than to be forced to finish *The Bostonians.*

Huckleberry Finn is a travesty of High Art quite as much as of conscience and duty and "sivilization"; and this Twain himself came finally to realize; writing in 1889, with a candor clearly bred by desperation, to Andrew Lang, one of the few critics he hoped might understand:

> Indeed I have been misjudged from the very first. I have never tried in even one single instance to help cultivate the cultivated classes. I was not equipped for it, either by native gifts or training. And I never had any ambition in that direction, but always hunted for bigger game—the masses. I have seldom deliberately tried to instruct them, but have tried to entertain them. . .to amuse them. . . .
>
> Yes, you see, I have always catered for the Belly and the Members but have been. . . criticized from the culture standard—to my sorrow and pain, because, honestly, I never cared what became of the cultured classes. They could go to the theater and the opera. They had no use for me and the melodeon.

That he did in fact win the "masses" he wooed, in *Huckleberry Finn* at least, is attested to by their having taken that book to their hearts long before official critics and moralists had managed to come to terms with it. But precisely because it has thus proved from the start available to the undereducated as well as the learned, the naive as well as the sophisticated, children as well as adults, the many as well as the few, the self-appointed guardians of culture and morality have continued to regard it with suspicion. Indeed, its scapegoating on ethical grounds has, as we have been noticing, never ceased, though those grounds have changed. But, in a sense, those who still insist that Twain's novel, written from as well as to "the Belly and the Members," rather than the

"Head," is dangerous and "vulgar" speak the truth. What falsifies *Huckleberry Finn* is the begrudged and belated praise of elitist critics, who have done their best recently to persuade us that Twain's untidy masterpiece, more improvised than structured, is "a great novel" in terms of the "culture standards" by which they also find *Pride and Prejudice* or *The Wings of the Dove* great.

The desperate plea with which Clemens ended his letter to Lang, that is to say, has never been truly or fully answered. "And now at last, " he wrote, "I arrive at my object and tender my petition, making supplication to this effect: that the critics adopt a rule recognizing the Belly and the Members, and formulate a standard whereby work done for them shall be judged. Help me, Mr. Lang. . . ." Lang did at least try but in the years since, and especially this side of the Atlantic, Twain's anguished appeal has been ignored, and the defense of popular art which underlies it dismissed as "self-serving" and insubstantial." His cry for help continues, however, to ring in my head, a reproach to me and the profession I practice. I have therefore taken advantage of the centennial celebration of the American book we most love to hate to begin at long last, tentatively—and with appropriate irony—to respond.

A Sound Heart and a Deformed Conscience

Henry Nash Smith

1

Mark Twain worked on *Adventures of Huckleberry Finn* at intervals over a period of seven years, from 1876 to 1883. During this time he wrote two considerable books (*A Tramp Abroad* and *The Prince and the Pauper*), expanded "Old Times on the Mississippi" into *Life on the Mississippi*, and gathered various shorter pieces into three other volumes. But this is all essentially minor work. The main line of his development lies in the long preoccupation with the Matter of Hannibal and the Matter of the River that is recorded in "Old Times" and *The Adventures of Tom Sawyer* and reaches a climax in his book about "Tom Sawyer's Comrade. Scene: The Mississippi Valley. Time: Forty to Fifty Years Ago."

In writing *Huckleberry Finn* Mark Twain found a way to organize into a larger structure the insights that earlier humorists had recorded in their brief anecdotes. This technical accomplishment was of course inseparable from the process of discovering new meanings in his material. His development as a writer was a dialectic interplay in which the reach of his imagination imposed a constant strain on his technical resources, and innovations of method in turn opened up new vistas before his imagination.

Reprinted from *Mark Twain: The Development of a Writer*. Cambridge: Harvard U.P., 1962; pp. 113–137.

The dialectic process is particularly striking in the gestation of *Huckleberry Finn*. The use of Huck as a narrative persona, with the consequent elimination of the author as an intruding presence in the story, resolved the difficulties about point of view and style that had been so conspicuous in the earlier books. But turning the story over to Huck brought into view previously unsuspected literary potentialities in the vernacular perspective, particularly the possibility of using vernacular speech for serious purposes and of transforming the vernacular narrator from a mere persona into a character with human depth. Mark Twain's response to the challenge made *Huckleberry Finn* the greatest of his books and one of the two or three acknowledged masterpieces of American literature. Yet this triumph created a new technical problem to which there was no solution; for what had begun as a comic story developed incipiently tragic implications contradicting the premises of comedy.

Huckleberry Finn thus contains three main elements. The most conspicuous is the story of Huck's and Jim's adventures in their flight toward freedom. Jim is running away from actual slavery, Huck from the cruelty of his father, from the well-intentioned "sivilizing" efforts of Miss Watson and the Widow Douglas, from respectability and routine in general. The second element in the novel is social satire of the towns along the river. The satire is often transcendently funny, especially in episodes involving the rascally Duke and King, but it can also deal in appalling violence, as in the Grangerford-Shepherdson feud or Colonel Sherburn's murder of the helpless Boggs. The third major element in the book is the developing characterization of Huck.

All three elements must have been present to Mark Twain's mind in some sense from the beginning, for much of the book's greatness lies in its basic coherence, the complex interrelation of its parts. Nevertheless, the intensive study devoted to it in recent years, particularly Walter Blair's establishment of the chronology of its composition, has demonstrated that Mark Twain's search for a structure capable of doing justice to his conceptions of theme and character passed through several stages. He did not see clearly where he was going when he began to write, and we can observe him in the act of making discoveries both in meaning and in method as he goes along.

The narrative tends to increase in depth as it moves from the adventure story of the early chapters into the social satire of the long middle section, and thence to the ultimate psychological penetration of Huck's character in the moral crisis of Chapter 31. Since the crisis is brought on by the shock of the definitive failure of Huck's effort to help Jim, it marks the real end of the quest for freedom. The perplexing final sequence on the Phelps plantation is best regarded as a maneuver by which Mark Twain beats his way back from incipient tragedy to the comic resolution called for by the original conception of the story.

2

Huck's and Jim's flight from St. Petersburg obviously translates into action the theme of vernacular protest. The fact that they have no means of fighting back against the forces that threaten them but can only run away is accounted for in part by the conventions of backwoods humor, in which the inferior social status of the vernacular character placed him in an ostensibly weak position. But it also reflects Mark Twain's awareness of his own lack of firm ground to stand on in challenging the established system of values.

Huck's and Jim's defenselessness foreshadows the outcome of their efforts to escape. They cannot finally succeed. To be sure, in a superficial sense they do succeed; at the end of the book Jim is technically free and Huck still has the power to light out for the Territory. But Jim's freedom has been brought about by such an implausible device that we do not believe in it. Who can imagine the scene in which Miss Watson decides to liberate him? What were her motives? Mark

Twain finesses the problem by placing this crucial event far offstage and telling us nothing about it beyond the bare fact he needs to resolve his plot. And the notion that a fourteen-year-old boy could make good his escape beyond the frontier is equally unconvincing. The writer himself did not take it seriously. In an unpublished sequel to *Huckleberry Finn* called "Huck Finn and Tom Sawyer among the Indians," which he began soon after he finished the novel, Aunt Sally takes the boys and Jim back to Hannibal and then to western Missouri for a visit "with some of her relations on a hemp farm out there." Here Tom revives the plan mentioned near the end of *Huckleberry Finn*: he "was dead set on having us run off, some night, and cut for the Injun country and go for adventures." Huck says, however, that he and Jim "kind of hung fire. Plenty to eat and nothing to do. We was very well satisfied." Only after an extended debate can Tom persuade them to set out with him. Their expedition falls into the stereotyped pattern of Wild West stories of travel out the Oregon Trail, makes a few gibes at Cooper's romanticized Indians, and breaks off.

The difficulty of imagining a successful outcome for Huck's and Jim's quest had troubled Mark Twain almost from the beginning of his work on the book. After writing the first section in 1876 he laid aside his manuscript near the end of Chapter 16. The narrative plan with which he had impulsively begun had run into difficulties. When Huck and Jim shove off from Jackson's Island on their section of a lumber raft (at the end of Chapter 11) they do so in haste, to escape the immediate danger of the slave hunters Huck has learned about from Mrs. Loftus. No longer-range plan is mentioned until the beginning of Chapter 15, when Huck says that at Cairo they intended to "sell the raft and get on a steamboat and go way up the Ohio amongst the free states, and then be out of trouble." But they drift past Cairo in the fog, and a substitute plan of making their way back up to the mouth of the Ohio in their canoe is frustrated when the canoe disappears while they are sleeping: "we talked about what we better do, and found there warn't no way but just to go along down with the raft till we got a chance to buy a canoe to go back in." Drifting downstream with the current, however, could not be reconciled with the plan to free Jim by transporting him up the Ohio; hence the temporary abandonment of the story.

3

When Mark Twain took up his manuscript again in 1879, after an interval of three years, he had decided upon a different plan for the narrative. Instead of concentrating on the story of Huck's and Jim's escape, he now launched into a satiric description of the society of the prewar South. Huck was essential to this purpose, for Mark Twain meant to view his subject ironically through Huck's eyes. But Jim was more or less superfluous. During Chapters 17 and 18, devoted to the Grangerford household and the feud, Jim has disappeared from the story. Mark Twain had apparently not yet found a way to combine social satire with the narrative scheme of Huck's and Jim's journey on the raft.

While he was writing his chapter about the feud, however, he thought of a plausible device to keep Huck and Jim floating southward while he continued his panoramic survey of the towns along the river. The device was the introduction of the Duke and the King. In Chapter 19 they come aboard the raft, take charge at once, and hold Huck and Jim in virtual captivity. In this fashion the narrative can preserve the overall form of a journey down the river while providing ample opportunity for satire when Huck accompanies the two rascals on their forays ashore. But only the outward form of the journey is retained. Its meaning has changed, for Huck's and Jim's quest for freedom has in effect come to an end. Jim is physically present but he assumes an entirely passive role and is hidden with the raft for considerable periods. Huck is also essentially passive; his function now is that of an observer. Mark Twain postpones acknowledging that the quest for freedom has failed, but the issue will have to be faced eventually.

The satire of the towns along the banks insists again and again that the dominant culture is decadent and perverted. Traditional values have gone to seed. The inhabitants can hardly be said to live a conscious life of their own: their actions, their thoughts, even their emotions are controlled by an outworn and debased Calvinism, and by a residue of the eighteenth-century cult of sensibility. With few exceptions they are mere bundles of tropisms, at the mercy of scoundrels like the Duke and the King who know how to exploit their prejudices and delusions.

The falseness of the prevalent values finds expression in an almost universal tendency of the townspeople to make spurious claims to status through self-dramatization. Mark Twain has been concerned with this topic from the beginning of the book. Chapter 1 deals with Tom Sawyer's plan to start a band of robbers which Huck will be allowed to join only if he will "go back to the widow and be respectable" and we also hear about Miss Watson's mercenary conception of prayer. In Chapter 2 Jim interprets Tom's prank of hanging his hat on the limb of a tree while he is asleep as evidence that he has been bewitched. He "was most ruined for a servant, because he got stuck up on account of having seen the devil and been rode by witches." Presently we witness the ritual by which Pap Finn is to be redeemed from drunkenness. When his benefactor gives him a lecture on temperance, it will be recalled,

> the old man cried, and said he'd been a fool, and fooled away his life; but now he was a-going to turn over a new leaf and be a man nobody wouldn't be ashamed of, and he hoped the judge would help him and not look down on him. The judge said he could hug him for them words; so *he* cried, and his wife she cried again; pap said he'd been a man that had always been misunderstood before, and the judge said he believed it. The old man said that what a man wanted that was down was sympathy, and the judge said it was so; so they cried again.

As comic relief for the feud that provides a way of life for the male Grangerfords Mark Twain dwells lovingly on Emmeline Grangerford's pretensions to culture—her paintings with the fetching titles and the ambitious "Ode to Stephen Dowling Bots, Dec'd.," its pathos hopelessly flawed by the crudities showing through like the chalk beneath the enameled surface of the artificial fruit in the parlor: "His spirit was gone for to sport aloft/In the realm of the good and great."

The Duke and the King personify the theme of fraudulent role-taking. These rogues are not even given names apart from the wildly improbable identities they assume in order to dominate Huck and Jim. The Duke's poses have a literary cast, perhaps because of the scraps of bombast he remembers from his experience as an actor. The illiterate King has "done considerable in the doctoring way," but when we see him at work it is mainly at preaching, "workin' camp-meetin's, and missionaryin' around." Pretended or misguided piety and other perversions of Christianity obviously head the list of counts in Mark Twain's indictment of the prewar South. And properly: for it is of course religion that stands at the center of the system of values in the society of this fictive world and by implication in all societies. His revulsion, expressed through Huck, reaches its highest pitch in the scene where the King delivers his masterpiece of "soul-butter and hogwash" for the benefit of the late Peter Wilks's fellow townsmen.

> By and by the king he gets up and comes forward a little, and works himself up and slobbers out a speech, all full of tears and flapdoodle, about its being a sore trial for him and his poor brother to lose the diseased, and to miss seeing diseased alive after the long journey of four thousand mile, but it's a trial that's sweetened and sanctified to us by this dear sympathy and these holy tears, and so he thanks them out of his heart and out of his brother's heart, because out of their mouths they can't, words being too weak and cold, and all that kind of rot and slush, till it was just sickening; and then he blubbers out a pious goody-goody Amen, and turns himself loose and goes to crying fit to bust.

4

Huck is revolted by the King's hypocrisy: "I never see anything so disgusting." He has had a similar reaction to the brutality of the feud: "It made me so sick I most fell out of the tree." In describing such scenes he speaks as moral man viewing an immoral society, an observer who is himself free of the vices and even the weaknesses he describes. Mark Twain's satiric method required that Huck be a mask for the writer, not a fully developed character. The method has great ironic force, and is in itself a technical landmark in the history of American fiction, but it prevents Mark Twain from doing full justice to Huck as a person in his own right, capable of mistakes in perception and judgment, troubled by doubts and conflicting impulses.

Even in the chapters written during the original burst of composition in 1876 the character of Huck is shown to have depths and complexities not relevant to the immediate context. Huck's and Jim's journey down the river begins simply as a flight from physical danger; and the first episodes of the voyage have little bearing on the novelistic possibilities in the strange comradeship between outcast boy and escaped slave. But in Chapter 15, when Huck plays a prank on Jim by persuading him that the separation in the fog was only a dream, Jim's dignified and moving rebuke suddenly opens up a new dimension in the relation. Huck's humble apology is striking evidence of growth in moral insight. It leads naturally to the next chapter in which Mark Twain causes Huck to face up for the first time to the fact that he is helping a slave to escape. It is as if the writer himself were discovering unsuspected meanings in what he had thought of as a story of picaresque adventure. The incipient contradiction between narrative plan and increasing depth in Huck's character must have been as disconcerting to Mark Twain as the difficulty of finding a way to account for Huck's and Jim's continuing southward past the mouth of the Ohio. It was doubtless the convergence of the two problems that led him to put aside the manuscript near the end of Chapter 16.

The introduction of the Duke and the King not only took care of the awkwardness in the plot but also allowed Mark Twain to postpone the exploration of Huck's moral dilemma. If Huck is not a free agent he is not responsible for what happens and is spared the agonies of choice. Throughout the long middle section, while he is primarily an observer, he is free of inner conflict because he is endowed by implication with Mark Twain's own unambiguous attitude toward the fraud and folly he witnesses.

In Chapter 31, however, Huck escaped from his captors and faces once again the responsibility for deciding on a course of action. His situation is much more desperate than it had been at the time of his first struggle with his conscience. The raft has borne Jim hundreds of miles downstream from the pathway of escape and the King has turned him over to Silas Phelps as a runaway slave. The quest for freedom has "all come to nothing, everything all busted up and ruined." Huck thinks of notifying Miss Watson where Jim is, since if he must be a slave he would be better off "at home where his family was." But then Huck realizes that Miss Watson would probably sell Jim down the river as a punishment for running away. Furthermore, Huck himself would be denounced by everyone for his part in the affair. In this fashion his mind comes back once again to the unparalleled wickedness of acting as accomplice in a slave's escape.

The account of Huck's mental struggle in the next two or three pages is the emotional climax of the story. It draws together the theme of flight from bondage and the social satire of the middle section, for Huck is trying to work himself clear of the perverted value system of St. Petersburg. Both adventure story and satire, however, are now subordinate to an exploration of Huck's psyche which is the ultimate achievement of the book. The issue is identical with that of the first moral crisis, but the later passage is much more intense and richer in implication. The differences appear clearly if the two crises are compared in detail.

In Chapter 16 Huck is startled into a realization of his predicament when he hears Jim, on the lookout for Cairo at the mouth of the Ohio, declare that "he'd be a free man the minute he seen it, but if he missed it he'd be a slave country again and no more show for freedom." Huck says: "I begun to get it through my head that he *was* most free—and who was to blame for it? Why, *me*. I couldn't get that out of my conscience, no how nor no way." He dramatizes his inner debate by quoting the words in which his conscience denounces him: "What had poor Miss Watson done to you that you could see her nigger go off right under your eyes and never say one single word? What did that poor old woman do to you that you could treat her so mean? Why, she tried to learn you your book, she tried to learn you your manners, she tried to be good to you every way she knowed how. *That's* what she done." The counterargument is provided by Jim, who seems to guess what is passing through Huck's mind and does what he can to invoke the force of friendship and gratitude: "Pooty soon I'll be a-shout'n' for joy, en I'll say, it's all on accounts o' Huck; I's a free man, en I couldn't ever ben free ef it hadn' ben for Huck; Huck done it. Jim won't ever forgit you, Huck; you's de bes' fren' Jim's ever had; en you's de *only* fren' ole Jim's got now." Huck nevertheless sets out for the shore in the canoe "all in a sweat to tell on" Jim, but when he is intercepted by the two slave hunters in a skiff he suddenly contrives a cunning device to ward them off. We are given no details about how his inner conflict was resolved.

In the later crisis Huck provides a much more circumstantial account of what passes through his mind. He is now quite alone; the outcome of the debate is not affected by any stimulus from the outside. It is the memory of Jim's kindness and goodness rather than Jim's actual voice that impels Huck to defy his conscience: "I see Jim before me all the time: in the day and in the night-time, sometimes moonlight, sometimes storms, and we a-floating along, talking and singing and laughing." The most striking feature of this later crisis is the fact that Huck's conscience, which formerly had employed only secular arguments, now deals heavily in religious cant:

> At last, when it hit me all of a sudden that here was the plain hand of Providence slapping me in the face and letting me know my wickedness was being watched all the time from up there in heaven, whilst I was stealing a poor old woman's nigger that hadn't ever done me no harm, and now was showing me there's One that's always on the lookout, and ain't a-going to allow no such miserable doings to go only just so fur and no further, I most dropped in my tracks I was so scared.

In the earlier debate the voice of Huck's conscience is quoted directly, but the bulk of the later exhortation is reported in indirect discourse. This apparently simple change in method has remarkable consequences. According to the conventions of first-person narrative, the narrator functions as a neutral medium in reporting dialogue. He remembers the speeches of other characters but they pass through his mind without affecting him. When Huck's conscience speaks within quotation marks it is in effect a character in the story, and he is not responsible for what it says. But when he paraphrases the admonitions of his conscience they are incorporated into his own discourse. Thus although Huck is obviously remembering the bits of theological jargon from sermons justifying slavery, they have become a part of his vocabulary.

The device of having Huck paraphrase rather than quote the voice of conscience may have been suggested to Mark Twain by a discovery he made in revising Huck's report of the King's address to the mourners in the Wilks parlor (Chapter 25). The manuscript version of the passage shows that the King's remarks were composed as a direct quotation, but in the published text they have been put, with a minimum of verbal change, into indirect discourse. The removal of the barrier of quotation marks brings Huck into much more intimate contact with the King's "rot and slush" despite the fact that the paraphrase quivers with disapproval. The voice of conscience speaks in the precise accents of the King but Huck is now completely uncritical. He does not question its moral authority; it is morality personified. The greater subtlety of the later passage illustrates the difference between the necessarily shallow characterization of Huck while he was being used merely as a narrative persona, and the profound insight which Mark Twain eventually brought to bear on his protagonist.

The recognition of complexity in Huck's character enabled Mark Twain to do full justice to the conflict between vernacular values and the dominant culture. By situating in a single consciousness both the perverted moral code of a society built on slavery and the vernacular commitment to freedom and spontaneity, he was able to represent the opposed perspectives as alternative modes of experience for the same character. In this way he gets rid of the confusions surrounding the pronoun "I" in the earlier books, where it sometimes designates the author speaking in his own person, sometimes an entirely distinct fictional character. Furthermore, the insight that enabled him to recognize the conflict between accepted values and vernacular protest as a struggle within a single mind does justice to its moral depth, whereas the device he had used earlier—in *The Innocents Abroad*, for example—of identifying the two perspectives with separate characters had flattened the issue out into melodrama. The satire of a decadent slave-holding society gains immensely in force when Mark Twain demonstrates that even the outcast Huck has been in part perverted by it. Huck's conscience is simply the attitudes he has taken over from his environment. What is still sound in him is an impulse from the deepest level of his personality that struggles against the overlay of prejudice and false valuation imposed on all members of the society in the name of religion, morality, law, and refinement.

Finally, it should be pointed out that the conflict in Huck between generous impulse and false belief is depicted by means of a contrast between colloquial and exalted styles. In moments of crisis his conscience addresses him in the language of the dominant culture, a tawdry and faded effort at a high style that is the rhetorical equivalent of the ornaments in the Grangerford parlor. Yet speaking in dialect does not in itself imply moral authority. By every external criterion the King is as much a vernacular character as Huck. The conflict in which Huck is involved is not that of a lower against an upper class or of an alienated fringe of outcasts against a cultivated elite. It is not the issue of frontier West versus genteel East, or of backwoods versus metropolis, but of fidelity to the uncoerced self versus the blurring of attitudes caused by social conformity, by the effort to achieve status or power through exhibiting the approved forms of sensibility.

The exploration of Huck's personality carried Mark Twain beyond satire and even beyond his statement of a vernacular protest against the dominant culture into essentially novelistic modes of writing. Some of the passages he composed when he got out beyond his polemic framework challenge comparison with the greatest achievements in the world's fiction.

The most obvious of Mark Twain's discoveries on the deeper levels of Huck's psyche is the boy's capacity for love. The quality of the emotion is defined in action by his decision to sacrifice himself for Jim, just as Jim attains an impressive dignity when he refuses to escape at the cost of deserting the wounded Tom. Projected into the natural setting, the love of the protagonists for each other becomes the unforgettable beauty of the river when they are allowed to be alone together. It is always summer, and the forces of nature cherish them. From the refuge of the cave on Jackson's Island the thunderstorm is an exhilarating spectacle; Huck's description of it is only less poetic than his description of the dawn which he and Jim witness as they sit half-submerged on the sandy bottom.

Yet if Mark Twain had allowed these passages to stand without qualification as a symbolic account of Huck's emotions he would have undercut the complexity of characterization implied in his recognition of Huck's inner conflict of loyalties. Instead, he uses the natural setting to render a wide range of feelings and motives. The fog that separates the boy from Jim for a time is an externalization of his impulse to deceive Jim by a Tom Sawyerish practical joke. Similarly Jim's snake bite, the only injury suffered by either of the companions from a natural source, is the result of another prank played by Huck before he has learned what friends owe one another.

Still darker aspects of Huck's inner life are projected into the natural setting in the form of ghosts, omens, portents of disaster—the body of superstition that is so conspicuous in Huck's and Jim's world. At the end of Chapter I Huck is sitting alone at night by his open window in the Widow Douglas' house:

> I felt so lonesome I most wished I was dead. The stars was shining, and the leaves rustled in the woods ever so mournful; and I heard an owl, away off who-whooing about somebody that was dead, and a whippowill and a dog crying about somebody that was going to die; and the wind was trying to whisper something to me, and I couldn't make out what it was, and so it made the cold shivers run over me. Then away out in the woods I heard that kind of a sound that a ghost makes when it wants to tell about something that's on its mind and can't make itself understood, and so can't rest easy in its grave, and has to go about that way every night grieving. I got so downhearted and scared I did wish I had some company.

The whimpering ghost with something incommunicable on its mind and Huck's cold shivers suggest a burden of guilt and anxiety that is perhaps the punishment he inflicts on himself for defying the mores of St. Petersburg. Whatever the source of these sinister images, they develop the characterization of Huck beyond the needs of the plot. The narrator whose stream of consciousness is recorded here is much more than the innocent protagonist of the pastoral idyl of the raft, more than an ignorant boy who resists being civilized. The vernacular persona is an essentially comic figure; the character we glimpse in Huck's meditation is potentially tragic. Mark Twain's discoveries in the buried strata of Huck's mind point in the same direction as does his intuitive recognition that Huck's and Jim's quest for freedom must end in failure.

A melancholy if not exactly tragic strain in Huck is revealed also by the fictitious autobiographies with which he so often gets himself out of tight places. Like the protocols of a thematic apperception test, they are improvisations on the basis of minimal clues. Huck's inventions are necessary to account for his anomalous situation as a fourteen-year-old boy alone on the river with a Negro man, but they are often carried beyond the demands of utility for sheer love of fable-making. Their luxuriant detail, and the fact that Huck's hearers are usually (although not always) taken in, lend a comic coloring to these inventions, which are authentically in the tradition of the tall tale. But their total effect is somber. When Huck plans his escape from Pap in Chapter 7, he does so by imagining his own death and planting clues which convince everyone in St. Petersburg, including Tom Sawyer, that he has been murdered. In the crisis of Chapter 16 his heightened emotion leads him to produce for the benefit of the slave hunters a harrowing tale to the effect that his father and mother and sister are suffering smallpox on a raft adrift in mid-river, and he is unable to tow the raft ashore. The slave hunters are so touched by the story that they give him forty dollars and careful instructions about how to seek help—farther downstream. Huck tells the Grangerfords "how pap and me and all the family was living on a little farm down at the bottom of Arkansaw, and my sister Mary Ann run off and got married and never was heard of no more, and Bill went to hunt them and he warn't heard of no more, and Tom and Mort died, and then there warn't nobody but just me and pap left, and he was just trimmed down to nothing, on account of his troubles; so when he died I took what there was left, because the farm didn't belong to us, and started up the river, deck passage, and fell overboard."

5

A number of characters besides Huck are presented in greater depth than is necessary either for purposes of satire or for telling the story of his and Jim's quest for freedom. Perhaps the most striking of these is Pap Finn. Like most of the book, Pap comes straight out of Mark Twain's boyhood memories. We have had a glimpse of him as the drunkard sleeping in the shade of a pile of skids on the levee in the opening scene of "Old Times on the Mississippi." His function in the plot, although definite, is limited. He helps to characterize Huck by making vivid the conditions of Huck's childhood. He has transmitted to his son a casual attitude toward chickens and watermelons, a fund of superstitions, a picaresque ability to look out for himself, and even the gift of language. Pap takes Huck away from the comfort and elegance of the Widow's house to the squalor of the deserted cabin across the river, and then by his sadistic beatings forces the boy to escape to Jackson's Island, where the main action of the flight with Jim begins. After the three chapters which Pap dominates (5–7) we do not see him again except as a corpse in the house floating down the river, but Huck refers to him several times later, invoking Pap's testimony to authenticate the aristocratic status of the Widow Douglas, and to support the family philosophy of "borrowing."

In the sociological scheme of the novel Pap provides a matchless specimen of the lowest stratum of whites who are fiercely jealous of their superiority to all Negroes. His monologue on the "govment" in Chapter 6, provoked by the spectacle of the well-dressed free Negro professor from Ohio, seizes in a few lines the essence of Southern race prejudice. Huck shrewdly calls attention to his father's economic code. When the flooded river brings down part of a log raft, he says: "Anybody but pap would'a' waited and seen the day through, so as to catch more stuff; but that warn't pap's style. Nine logs was enough for one time; he must shove right over to town and sell," mainly in order to buy whiskey.

But the documentary data supply only a minor part of the image of Pap in _Huckleberry Finn._ He provides some of the most mordant comedy in the book. The fashion in which he gives himself away in the monologue on "govment" is worthy of Jonson or Molière:

> It was 'lection day, and I was just about to go and vote myself if I warn't too drunk to get there; but when they told me there was a state in this country where they'd let that nigger vote, I drawed out. I says I'll never vote ag'in. Them's the very words I said; they all heard me; and the country may rot for all me—I'll never vote ag'in as long as I live. And to see the cool way of the nigger—why, he wouldn't 'a' give me the road if I hadn't shoved him out o' the way.

Even when the comedy verges on slapstick it retains its function as characterization. Pap is so completely absorbed in his diatribe that he barks his shins on the pork barrel:

> He hopped around the cabin considerable, first on one leg and then on the other, holding first one shin and then the other one, and at last he let out with his left foot all of a sudden and fetched the tub a rattling kick. But it warn't good judgment, because that was the boot that had a couple of his toes leaking out of the front end of it; so now he raised a howl that fairly made a body's hair raise, and down he went in the dirt, and rolled there, and held his toes; and the cussing he done then laid over anything he had ever done previous. He said so his own self afterwards. He had heard old Sowberry Hagan is his best days, and he said it laid over him, too; but I reckon that was sort of piling it on, maybe.

Pap's detached evaluation of his own accomplishment in swearing gives to his character an almost medieval flavor. In all his degradation he conceives of himself as enacting a role which is less a personal destiny than part of an integral natural-social reality—a reality so stable that he can contemplate it as if it were external to him. On election day he was drunk as a matter of course; it was an objective question, like an effort to predict the weather, whether he might be too drunk to get to the polls. When he settles down for a domestic evening in the cabin, he "took the jug, and said he had enough whiskey there for two drunks and one delirium tremens."

But when the delirium comes, it belies the coolness of his offhand calculation. Huck's description of the drunkard's agony is a nightmare of neurotic suffering that blots out the last vestige of comedy in Pap's image and relates itself in Huck's mind to the ominous sounds he had heard from his window in the Widow's house:

> [Pap] rolled over and over wonderful fast, kicking things every which way, and striking and grabbing at the air with his hands, and screaming and saying there was devils a-hold of him. . . Then he laid stiller, and didn't make a sound. I could hear the owls and the wolves away off in the woods, and it seemed terrible still. . . By and by he raised up part way and listened, with his head to one side. He say, very low:
>
> "Tramp—tramp—tramp; that's the dead; tramp-tramp-tramp; they're coming after me; but I won't go. Oh, they're here! don't touch me—don't! hands off—they're cold; let go. Oh, let a poor devil alone!"
>
> Then he went down on all fours and crawled off, begging them to let him alone, and he rolled himself up in his blanket and wallowed in under the old pine table, still a-begging; and then he went to crying. I could hear him through the blanket.

Pap's hallucinations externalize inner suffering in images of ghosts and portents. Presently he sees in Huck the Angel of Death and chases him around the cabin with a knife "saying he would kill me, and then I couldn't come for him no more." In fact, the mystery of Pap's anguished psyche has had a supernatural aura all along. He is in a sense a ghost the first time we see him, for his faceless corpse has been found floating in the river; and immediately before his dramatic appearance in Huck's room Jim's hair-ball oracle has announced, "Dey's two angels hoverin' roun' 'bout him. One uv' em is white en shiny, en t'other one is black. De white one gits him to go right a little while, den de black one sail in en bust it all up. A body can't tell yit which one gwyne to fetch him at de las'." Coming early in the story, at a time when Mark Twain had apparently not yet worked out the details of the plot, this sounds as if he had in mind the possibility of involving Pap more elaborately in the course of events. But aside from the relatively minor incidents that have been mentioned, what the angels might have led Pap to do is never revealed.

He does, however, have an important thematic function. He serves as a forceful reminder that to be a vernacular outcast does not necessarily bring one into contact with the benign forces of nature. Physical withdrawal from society may be plain loafing, without moral significance. Huck's life with Pap in the cabin foreshadows his life with Jim on the raft, but lacks the suggestion of harmony with the natural setting:

> It was kind of lazy and jolly, laying off comfortable all day, smoking and fishing, and no books nor study. Two months or more run along, and my clothes got to be all rags and dirt, and I didn't see how I'd ever got to like it so well at the widow's, where you had to wash, and eat on a plate, and comb up, and go to bed and get up regular, and be forever bothering over a book, and have old Miss Watson pecking at you all the time. I didn't want to go back no more. . . It was pretty good times up in the woods there, take it all around.

More explicitly, Pap's denunciation of Huck for the civilized habits the Widow and Miss Watson have imposed on him is a grotesque version of vernacular hostility toward the conventions of refined society:

> Starchy clothes—very. You think you're a good deal of a big-bug, *don't* you?. . . You're educated, too, they say—can read and write. You think you're better'n your father, now, don't you, because he can't? . . . you drop that school, you hear? I'll learn people to bring up a boy to put on airs over his own father and let on to be better'n what *he* is. . . First you know you'll get religion, too. I never see such a son.

This adds another nuance to the book by suggesting that civilized values have something to be said for them after all.

The extent to which Mark Twain's imagination was released in *Huckleberry Finn* to explore multiple perspectives upon the Matter of Hannibal and the Matter of the River can be realized if one compares Pap with the sociologically similar backwoodsmen observed from the steamboat in "Old Times." These "jeans-clad, chills-racked, yellow-faced miserables" are merely comic animals. Pap is even more degraded than they are, lazier, more miserable, but he is not an object of scorn. The fullness with which his degradation and his misery are presented confers on him not so much a human dignity—although it is also that—as the impersonal dignity of art.

In relation to the whole of *Huckleberry Finn*, Pap serves to solidify the image of Huck's and Jim's vernacular paradise by demonstrating that Mark Twain is aware of the darker possibilities confronting them when they escape from the shore to the river. The mass of superstitions with which Pap is so vividly connected (we recall the cross of nails in his boot heel to ward off the devil), standing in contrast to the intimations of blissful harmony with nature in the passages devoted to Huck and Jim alone on the raft, keeps that lyrical vision from seeming mere pathetic fallacy. And the appalling glimpse of Pap's inner life beneath the stereotype of the town drunkard makes him into what might be called a note of tragic relief in a predominantly comic story.

6

It has become a commonplace of criticism that the drastic shift in tone in the last section of *Huckleberry Finn*, from Chapter 31 to the end, poses a problem of interpretation. The drifting raft has reached Arkansas, and the King and the Duke have delivered Jim back into captivity. They make their exit early in the sequence, tarred and feathered as punishment for one more effort to work the "Royal Nonesuch" trick. Tom Sawyer reappears by an implausible coincidence and takes charge of the action, which thereafter centers about his schemes to liberate Jim from confinement in a cabin on the plantation of Tom's Uncle Silas Phelps.

These events have for their prelude a vivid description of Huck's first approach to the Phelps place:

> When I got there it was all still and Sunday-like, and hot and sunshiny; the hands was gone to the fields; and there was them kind of faint dronings of bugs and flies in the air that makes it seem so lonesome and like everybody's dead and gone; and if a breeze fans along and quivers the leaves it makes you feel mournful, because you feel like it's spirits whispering—spirits that's been dead ever so many years— and you always think they're talking about *you*. As a general thing it makes a body wish *he* was dead, too, and done with it all.

And a few lines later:

> I went around and clumb over the back stile by the ash-hopper, and started for the kitchen. When I got a little ways I heard the dim hum of a spinning-wheel wailing along up and sinking along down again; and then I knowed for certain I wished I was dead—for that *is* the lonesomest sound in the whole world.

This passage has much in common with Huck's meditation before his open window in Chapter I. They are the two most vivid expressions of his belief in ghosts, and in both cases the ghosts are associated in his mind with a deep depression not fully accounted for by the context of the story.

It would be reasonable to suppose that the cause of Huck's depression is the failure of his long effort to help Jim toward freedom. The reader knows that even if Huck could manage to rescue Jim from the Phelpses, they face insuperable difficulties in trying to make their way back up the Mississippi to free territory. Yet oddly enough, Huck does not share this estimate of the situation. He is confident he can find a way out of the impasse: "I went right along, not fixing up any particular plan, but just trusting to Providence to put the right words in my mouth when the time come: for I'd noticed that Providence

always did put the right words in my mouth if I left it alone."
Somewhat later, Huck points out to Tom that they can easily
get Jim out of the log cabin by stealing the key, and "shove off
down the river on the raft with Jim, hiding daytimes and
running nights, the way me and Jim used to do before.
Wouldn't that plan work?" Tom agrees: "Why, cert'nly it
would work, like rats a-fighting. But it's too blame' simple;
there ain't nothing *to* it. What's the good of a plan that ain't no
more trouble than that?"

The tone as much as the substance of the references to the
problem of rescuing Jim makes it plain that Huck's view of his
predicament cannot account for his depression as he
approaches the Phelps plantation. The emotion is the author's
rather than Huck's, and it is derived from sources outside the
story. In order to determine what these were we must consult
Mark Twain's autobiographical reminiscences. The Phelps
place as he describes it in the novel has powerful associations
for him because it is patterned on the farm of his Uncle John
A. Quarles where he spent summers as a boy. "I can see the
farm yet, with perfect clearness," he wrote in his
Autobiography.

> I can see all its belongings, all its details; the family
> room of the house with a "trundle" bed in one corner and a
> spinning-wheel in another—a wheel whose rising and falling
> wail, heard from a distance, was the mournfulest of all
> sounds to me, and made me homesick and low spirited, and
> filled my atmosphere with the wandering spirits of the dead.

Additional associations with the Quarles farm are
recorded in Mark Twain's "The Private History of a Campaign
That Failed," written a few months after the publication of
Huckleberry Finn. This bit of fictionalized autobiography
describes his experiences as second lieutenant of the Marion
Rangers, a rather informal volunteer militia unit organized in
Hannibal in the early months of the Civil War. The Quarles
farm is here assigned to a man named Mason:

We stayed several days at Mason's; and after all these years the memory of the dullness, and stillness, and lifelessness of that slumberous farm-house still oppresses my spirit as with a sense of the presence of death and mourning. There was nothing to do, nothing to think about; there was no interest in life. The male part of the household were away in the fields all day, the women were busy and out of our sight; there was no sound but the plaintive wailing of a spinning-wheel, forever moaning out from some distant room—the most lonesome sound in nature, a sound steeped and sodden with homesickness and the emptiness of life.

The emotional overtones of the memories recorded in "The Private History" are made more explicit in a letter Mark Twain wrote in 1890:

I was a *soldier* two weeks once in the beginning of the war, and was hunted like a rat the whole time. . . My splendid Kipling himself hasn't a more burnt-in, hard-baked and unforgettable familiarity with that death-on-the-pale-horse-with-hell-following-after which is a raw soldier's first fortnight in the field—and which, without any doubt, is the most tremendous fortnight and the vividest he is ever going to see.

But while there are references to fear of the enemy in "The Private History," they are mainly comic, and the dullness and lifelessness that afflict the neophyte soldiers at the Mason farm do not suggest the feeling of being hunted like a rat. More significant, perhaps is an incident Mark Twain places a few pages later in "The Private History." Albert B. Paine says it was invented; and it does have the air of fiction. But it reveals the emotional coloring of the author's recollections. He relates that he fired in the dark at a man approaching on horseback, who was killed. Although five other shots were fired at the same moment, and he did not at bottom believe his shot had struck its mark, still his "diseased imagination" convinced him he was guilty. "The thoughts shot through me that I was a murderer; that I had killed a man—a man who had never done me any harm. That was the coldest sensation that ever went through my marrow."

Huck also experiences a strong and not easily explicable feeling of guilt a few pages after his arrival at the Phelpses'. When he sees the Duke and the King ridden out of the nearby town on a rail, surrounded by a howling mob, he says:

> It was a dreadful thing to see. Human beings *can* be awful cruel to one another. . . So we poked along back home, and I warn't feeling so brash as I was before, but kind of ornery, and humble, and to blame, somehow—though I hadn't done nothing. But that's always the way; it don't make no difference whether you do right or wrong, a person's conscience ain't got no sense, and just goes for him *anyway*. If I had a yaller dog that didn't know no more than a person's conscience does I would pison him.

The close linkage of the Phelps and Mason farms with Mark Twain's memory of the Quarles place strongly suggests that Huck's depression is caused by a sense of guilt whose sources were buried in the writer's childhood. It is well known that Mark Twain was tormented all his life by such feelings. A fable written in 1876, "The Facts Concerning the Recent Carnival of Crime in Connecticut," makes comedy of his sufferings; but they were serious and chronic. In his twenties, because of an imaginary error in administering an opiate, he had insisted he was to blame for the death of his brother from injuries received in the explosion of a steamboat. Later he accused himself of murdering his son Langdon when he neglected to keep him covered during a carriage ride in cold weather, and the child died of diphtheria.

But why was Mark Twain's latent feeling of guilt drawn up into consciousness at a specific moment in the writing of *Huckleberry Finn*? The most probable explanation is that at this point he was obliged to admit finally to himself that Huck's and Jim's journey down the river could not be imagined as leading to freedom for either of them. Because of the symbolic meaning the journey had taken on for him, the recognition was more than a perception of difficulty in contriving a plausible ending for the book. He had found a solution to the technical problem that satisfied him, if one is to judge from his evident zest in the complicated pranks of Tom Sawyer that occupy the last ten chapters. But in order to write these chapters he had to abandon the compelling image of the happiness of Huck and Jim on the raft and thus to acknowledge that the vernacular values embodied in his story were mere figments of the imagination, not capable of being reconciled with social reality. To be sure, he had been half-aware from the beginning that the quest of his protagonists was doomed. Huck had repeatedly appeared in the role of a Tiresias powerless to prevent the deceptions and brutalities he was compelled to witness. Yet Providence had always put the right words in his mouth when the time came, and by innocent guile he had extricated himself and Jim from danger after danger. Now the drifting had come to an end.

At an earlier impasse in the plot Mark Twain had shattered the raft under the paddle wheel of a steamboat. He now destroys it again, symbolically, by revealing that Huck's and Jim's journey, with all its anxieties, has been pointless. Tom Sawyer is bearer of the news that Jim has been freed in Miss Watson's will. Tom withholds the information, however, in order to trick Huck and Jim into the meaningless game of an Evasion that makes the word (borrowed from Dumas) into a devastating pun. Tom takes control and Huck becomes once again a subordinate carrying out orders. As if to signal the change of perspective and the shift in his own identification, Mark Twain gives Huck Tom's name through an improbable mistake on the part of Aunt Sally Phelps. We can hardly fail to perceive the weight of the author's feeling in Huck's statement on this occasion: "it was like being born again, I was so glad to find out who I was." Mark Twain has found out who he must be in order to end his book: he must be Tom.

In more abstract terms, he must withdraw from his imaginative participation in Huck's and Jim's quest for freedom. If the story was to be stripped of its tragic implications, Tom's perspective was the logical one to adopt because his intensely conventional sense of values made him impervious to the moral significance of the journey on the raft. Huck can hardly believe that Tom would collaborate in the crime of helping a run-away slave, and Huck is right. Tom merely devises charades involving a man who is already in a technical sense free. The consequences of the shift in point of view are strikingly evident in the treatment of Jim, who is subjected to farcical indignities. This is disturbing to the reader who has seen Jim take on moral and emotional stature, but it is necessary if everything is to be forced back into the framework of comedy. Mark Twain's portrayal of Huck and Jim as complex characters has carried him beyond the limits of his original plan: we must not forget that the literary ancestry of the book is to be found in backwoods humor. As Huck approaches the Phelps plantation the writer has on his hands a hybrid—a comic story in which the protagonists have acquired something like tragic depth.

In deciding to end the book with the description of Tom's unnecessary contrivances for rescuing Jim, Mark Twain was certain to produce an anticlimax. But he was a great comic writer, able to score local triumphs in the most unlikely circumstances. The last chapters have a number of brilliant touches—the slave who carries the witch pie to Jim, Aunt Sally's trouble in counting her spoons, Uncle Silas and the ratholes, the unforgettable Sister Hotchkiss. Even Tom's horseplay would be amusing if it were not spun out to such length and if we were not asked to accept it as the conclusion of *Huckleberry Finn*. Although Jim is reduced to the level of farce Tom is a comic figure in the classical sense of being a victim of delusion. He is not aware of being cruel to Jim because he does not perceive him as a human being. For Tom, Jim is the hero of a historical romance, a peer of the Man in the Iron Mask or the Count of Monte Cristo. Mark Twain is consciously imitating *Don Quixote*, and there are moments not unworthy of the model, as when Tom admits that "we got to dig him out with the picks, and *let on* it's case-knives."

But Tom has no tragic dimension whatever. There is not even any force of common sense in him to struggle against his perverted imagination as Huck's innate loyalty and generosity struggle against his deformed conscience. Although Mark Twain is indulgent toward Tom, he adds him to the list of characters who employ the soul-butter style of false pathos. The inscriptions Tom composes for Jim to "scrabble onto the wall" of the cabin might have been composed by the Duke:

1. Here a captive heart busted.
2. Here a poor prisoner, forsook by the world and friends, fretted his sorrowful life.
3. Here a lonely heart broke, and a worn spirit went to its rest, after thirty-seven years of solitary captivity.
4. Here, homeless and friendless, after thirty-seven years of bitter captivity, perished a noble stranger, natural son of Louis XIV.

While he was reading these noble sentiments aloud, Tom's voice trembled. . . and he most broke down.

7

Mark Twain's partial shift of identification from Huck to Tom in the final sequence was one response to his recognition that Huck's and Jim's quest for freedom was only a dream: he attempted to cover with a veil of parody and farce the harsh facts that condemned it to failure. The brief episode involving Colonel Sherburn embodies yet another response to his disillusionment. The extraordinary vividness of the scenes in which Sherburn figures—only a half-dozen pages all told—is emphasized by their air of being an intrusion into the story. Of course, in the episodic structure of *Huckleberry Finn* many characters appear for a moment and disappear. Even so, the Sherburn episode seems unusually isolated. None of the principal characters is involved in or affected by it: Jim, the Duke, and the King are offstage, and Huck is a spectator whom even the author hardly notices. We are told nothing about his reaction except that he did not want to stay around. He goes abruptly off to the circus and does not refer to Sherburn again.

Like Huck's depression as he nears the Phelps plantation, the Sherburn episode is linked with Mark Twain's own experience. The shooting of Boggs follows closely the murder of "Uncle Sam" Smarr by a merchant named Owsley in Hannibal in 1845, when Sam Clemens was nine years old. Although it is not clear that he actually witnessed it, he mentioned the incident at least four times at intervals during his later life, including one retelling as late as 1898, when he said he had often dreamed about it. Mark Twain prepares for the shooting in *Huckleberry Finn* by careful attention to the brutality of the loafers in front of the stores in Bricksville. "There couldn't anything wake them up all over, and make them happy all over, like a dog-fight—unless it might be putting turpentine on a stray dog and setting fire to him, or tying a tin pan to his tail and see him run himself to death." The prurient curiosity of the townspeople who shove and pull to catch a glimpse of Boggs as he lies dying in the drugstore with a heavy Bible on his chest, and their pleasure in the re-enactment of the shooting by the man in the big white fur stovepipe hat, also help to make Bricksville an appropriate setting for Sherburn's crime.

The shooting is in Chapter 21, and the scene in which Sherburn scatters the mob by his contemptuous speech is in the following chapter. There is evidence that Mark Twain put aside the manuscript for a time near the end of Chapter 21. If there was such an interruption in his work on the novel, it might account for a marked change in tone. In Chapter 21 Sherburn is an unsympathetic character. His killing of Boggs is motivated solely by arrogance, and the introduction of Boggs's daughter is an invitation to the reader to consider Sherburn an inhuman monster. In Chapter 22, on the other hand, the Colonel appears in an oddly favorable light. The townspeople have now become a mob; there are several touches that suggest Mark Twain was recalling the descriptions of mobs in Carlyle's *French Revolution* and other works of history and fiction. He considered mobs to be subhuman aggregates generating psychological pressures that destroyed individual freedom of choice. In a passage written for *Life on the Mississippi* but omitted from the book Mark Twain makes scathing generalizations about the cowardice of mobs, especially in the South but also in other regions, that closely parallel Sherburn's speech.

In other words, however hostile may be the depiction of Sherburn in Chapter 21, in Chapter 22 we have yet another instance of Mark Twain's identifying himself, at least partially, with a character in the novel other than Huck. The image of Sherburn standing on the roof of the porch in front of his house with the shotgun that is the only weapon in sight has an emblematic quality. He is a solitary figure, not identified with the townspeople, and because they are violently hostile to him, an outcast. But he is not weaker than they, he is stronger. He stands above the mob, looking down on it. He is "a heap the best dressed man in that town," and he is more intelligent than his neighbors. The scornful courage with which he defies the mob redeems him from the taint of cowardice implied in his shooting of an unarmed man who was trying to escape. Many members of the mob he faces are presumably armed; the shotgun he holds is not the source of his power but merely a symbol of the personal force with which he dominates the community.

The Colonel's repeated references to one Buck Harkness, the leader of the mob, whom he acknowledges to be "half-a-man," suggest that the scene represents a contest between two potential leaders in Bricksville. Harkness is the strongest man with whom the townspeople can identify themselves. In his pride Sherburn chooses isolation, but he demonstrates that he is stronger than Harkness, for the mob, including Harkness, obeys his command to "*leave*—and take your half-a-man with you."

Sherburn belongs to the series of characters in Mark Twain's later work that have been called "transcendent figures." Other examples are Hank Morgan in *A Connecticut*

Yankee; Pudd'nhead Wilson; and Satan in *The Mysterious Stranger*. They exhibit certain common traits, more fully developed with the passage of time. They are isolated by their intellectual superiority to the community; they are contemptuous of mankind in general; and they have more than ordinary power. Satan, the culmination of the series, is omnipotent. Significantly, he is without a moral sense—that is, a conscience, a sense of guilt. He is not torn by the kind of inner struggle that Huck experiences. But he is also without Huck's sound heart. The price of power is the surrender of all human warmth.

Colonel Sherburn's cold-blooded murder of Boggs, his failure to experience remorse after that act, and his withering scorn of the townspeople are disquieting portents for the future. Mark Twain, like Huck, was sickened by the brutality he had witnessed in the society along the river. But he had an adult aggressiveness foreign to Huck's character. At a certain point he could no longer endure the anguish of being a passive observer. His imagination sought refuge in the image of an alternative persona who was protected against suffering by being devoid of pity or guilt, yet could denounce the human race for its cowardice and cruelty, and perhaps even take action against it. The appearance of Sherburn in *Huckleberry Finn* is ominous because a writer who shares his attitude toward human beings is in danger of abandoning imaginative insight for moralistic invective. The slogan of "the damned human race" that later became Mark Twain's proverb spelled the sacrifice of art to ideology. Colonel Sherburn would prove to be Mark Twain's dark angel. His part in the novel, and that of Tom Sawyer, are flaws in a work that otherwise approaches perfection as an embodiment of American experience in a radically new and appropriate literary mode.

A Connecticut Yankee Anticipated: Max Adeler's *Fortunate Island*

Edward F. Foster

A ccording to Mark Twain the idea for *A Connecticut Yankee* came to him late in 1884. G. W. Cable, with whom he was on a lecture tour, gave him a copy of *Le Morte d'Arthur*, and Twain became so fascinated by Malory that he began shortly to plan a book dealing with the Middle Ages. By November, 1886, the first chapter was written; more work in 1887 and 1888 completed the tale, and it was published in 1889.[1]

Perhaps the most striking feature of the story was the imaginative power displayed in the theme—modern man in a medieval world—and readers have always been fascinated by this part of the work. Seven years before the appearance of *A Connecticut Yankee*, however, the humorist Max Adeler published a novelette, *The Fortunate Island*,[2] which contains an identical theme and numerous interesting parallels. This paper will present an analysis of the most important similarities between the two stories, for the connection has not been previously noted.

Adeler's story is shorter and employs a much simpler framework than *A Connecticut Yankee*. The hero is a sociologist, Professor E.L. Baffin, of Wingohocking University. Baffin and his daughter, Matilda, land on an uncharted, "floating" island following a shipwreck. This island, according to the natives, had broken away from England in King Arthur's

Reprinted from *Ball State University Forum* 9 (Autumn 1968): 73–6.

time and drifted to a new location. Life on the island was frozen in the past: Knighthood flourishes; there are castles, jousts, love-sick maidens, and saintly hermits.

Professor Baffin and Matilda are taken to the castle of Sir Bors, a leading noble, where the Professor satisfies his curiosity about the new land, and amazes his hosts with demonstrations of modern inventions, his scientific gear luckily having been saved from the shipwreck. Enthralled by the possibilities before him, Baffin plans numerous projects and looks forward to a vast scheme of modernization. But before any of these technical plans can be put into practice, the Professor becomes involved in aiding a pair of lovers; he takes part in a joust, joins an expedition to rescue a kidnapped maiden, stars in a thrilling rescue, sustains the mandatory blow on the head—and wakes up aboard a rescuing vessel. He had been ill and delirious, the adventure on the Fortunate Island was a dream.

So much for the main plot details. A closer examination of certain features of Adeler's story will show that he anticipated Twain in numerous other ways. First the theme. Strictly speaking, Adeler's "frame" does not involve the temporal displacement and regression of an individual, but the net dramatic effect is the same as that of *A Connecticut Yankee*. A nineteenth-century American visits a medieval society, albeit through the medium of a dream device. The visitor plans to modernize the society, but he finds the same reverence for the past, the same unwillingness to accept change that Hank Morgan scoffed at so vigorously. Father Anselm, the hermit, tells Professor Baffin "we reverence the past. It is a matter of pride among us to preserve the habits, the manners, the ideas, the social state which our forefathers had when they were sundered from their nation."[3] The hermit also takes a gloomy view of any possibility of change or progress. "Sometimes. . . I have secret doubts whether our way is the best, whether in England and the rest of the world men may not have learned while we remained ignorant; but I cannot tell. And no one would be willing to change if we could know the truth."[4]

The respective heroes of the two stories are basically different types of men, but they react to their situation in much the same fashion. Professor Baffin, unlike Hank Morgan, is an intellectual, and when he discovers the nature of life on the island is most anxious to study it from a scientific viewpoint. Yet the Professor is at the same time a comic figure; he is neither the dreamy pedagogue nor the eccentric butterfly chaser of farce, but his nineteenth-century reactions to the discomforts of medieval housing and armor, and to the forwardness of medieval maidens lead to a number of humorous situations similar to those of Hank Morgan.

Both men share one important trait with equal force: the American zeal for progress, self-improvement, and getting ahead. When Sir Bleoberis laments his lack of fortune, the Professor remonstrates with him in proper Gilded-Age language: "Can't you go to work; go into business; start a factory, speculate in stocks, or something of that kind."[5] Another knight, Sir Agravaines, mentions that he has tried enchantment and philtres in an unsuccessful search for wealth. "Nonsense!" replies the Professor, "I don't operate with such trumpery as that. You agree to help me, and we'll give this island such a stirring up as will revolutionize it."[6]

Unlike Twain, Adeler does not venture on any criticism of medieval politics and religion. We are merely told that the ruler of the island, King Brandegore, is "wise and good." There is, moreover, no recognition of the major role played by the church in medieval society. The only religious figure in the story is the hermit, Father Anselm, who is treated sympathetically.

In the same manner, the foibles of medieval society and custom come in for only mild criticism. The nobility are pictured respectfully on the whole, though their illiteracy and disdain for work are underscored. Professor Baffin exhorts Sir Bleoberis to gain a fortune by hard work, only to receive the huffy reply, "persons of my degree never work."[7] Amorous customs of the time furnish materials for some comic situations. Both Sir Dinadan and Sir Agravaines are smitten with Matilda; each knight proposes to the lady on first meeting her, only to have his ears boxed for his audacity. Professor Baffin's rescue of Bragwaine, he finds to his discomforture, automatically makes him her fiancé. The lady is so persistent in her loving attention that the properly correct Baffin flees in confusion.

Adeler's strongest criticism of medieval customs is directed at the practice of duelling, an aspect of chivalry that Twain thoroughly detested. In one case, the joust between Sir Bleoberis and Baffin, the ludicrous aspects of the conflict are stressed. Later in the story, the tome grows more serious when Baffin is challenged by Sir Sagramor for refusing to marry Bragwaine, and Sir Bors volunteers to substitute for the American. "This," said the Professor, "is probably the most asinine proceeding upon record. Because I won't marry Sagramor's daughter, Sagramor is going to fight with a man who never saw his daughter."[8]

Perhaps the most striking parallel between *The Fortunate Island* and *A Connecticut Yankee* is the use of modern inventions to awe the natives and demonstrate the superiority of nineteenth-century American achievement. Professor Baffin employs an umbrella, a watch, a revolver, matches, cigars, and spectacles as magic objects from time to time. Following a performance by the court musician, a record of a song sung by Matilda is played on a phonograph, producing consternation in the audience. A telephone is passed off as an oracle on one occasion. Professor Baffin even makes some arrangements with Sir Bleoberis to build a short railroad line and a telegraph system, though he is as vague as Hank Morgan in explaining away the technical problems involved. While visiting King Brandegore, the Professor stages a series of electrical experiments which so impress the king that he orders the court magician executed as a fraud, an incident similar to the Yankee's vanquishing of Merlin. The climactic rescue of Ysolt is effected through a modern invention, a steam launch, just as the rescue of Hank Morgan and King Arthur is made by knights that speed to the scene on bicycles. Finally, Adeler also contrives a massacre, by no means as bloody as Twain's concluding holocaust, but gory enough to satisfy modest expectations. After the rescuers of Ysolt abandon their boat, the safety valve is tied down; the boiler explodes and kills Sir Dagonet and several of his followers as they are examining the craft.

These comparisons indicate numerous similarities of detail between *The Fortunate Island* and *A Connecticut Yankee*. Both writers move their respective heroes into another age and another time for the purpose of providing humorous and satiric contrasts between nineteenth-century America and medieval England. Adeler's work, it must be granted, is but the skeleton of a novel, because he fails to exploit his dramatic situation as does Twain, and he does not have Twain's compulsion for bitter satire. Given the unusual nature of the theme, however, the time span within which both works appeared, and the various parallels which have been noted, one must grant the existence of a remarkable literary coincidence.

There is no direct evidence in the published Twain material that Twain knew of Adeler's work, or was influenced by it. One cannot rule out absolutely the possibility of a connection, conscious or subconscious, however, because Twain read widely and was familiar with the other humorists of his time. Walter Blair, in dealing with the sources of *Huckleberry Finn* notes that Twain

> read much in several areas—in history, biography, philosophy, humor, and (though he believed he disliked it) fiction. His familiarity with contemporary literature helped him write a book which became a best seller. And in portraying more characters and incidents than students heretofore have noticed, consciously or unconsciously he echoed his wide-ranging reading.[9]

I have discovered only one published comment by Adeler on the similarities between *The Fortunate Island* and *A Connecticut Yankee*. Shortly before his death in 1915, Adeler published a collection of short stories which reprinted *The Fortunate Island*. On the first page of the story the following modest footnote appears: "It is necessary to say that this tale was first published in 1881 and antedates a story with a similar theme by a noted author."[10]

Notes

1. For detailed studies which offer differing conclusions concerning the origin of *A Connecticut Yankee*, see John Hoben, "Mark Twain's *A Connecticut Yankee*: A Genetic Study," *American Literature*, XVIII (1961), 195–214. See also Henry Nash Smith, *Mark Twain's Fable of Progress: Political and Economic Ideas in 'A Connecticut Yankee'* (New Brunswick, New Jersey, 1964).
2. *The Fortunate Island and Other Stories* (Boston, 1882). Max Adeler is the pseudonym of Charles Heber Clark (1847–1915). Clark was born in Berlin, Md., educated in Georgetown, D.C., and served as a Union soldier. He was a reporter and critic for various Philadelphia newspapers, and later became editor of the *Textile Record* and the *Manufacturer*. His most popular work was a series of humorous sketches of small-town life called *Out of the Hurly-Burly* (1874). He also published four novels and three books of short stories, none achieving the success of *Out of the Hurly-Burly*. See Stanley J. Kunitz and Howard Haycraft, *American Authors 1600–1900* (New York, 1938), p. 153. Other brief biographical sketches are in *Book Buyer* XXV (1902), 124–125; and J.F. Cooke, "Mysteries of Middle-C," *The Etude*, LXVI (1948), 4, 6, 10.
3. *Ibid.*, p. 25.
4. *Ibid.*, p. 26.
5. *Ibid.*, p. 40.
6. *Ibid.*
7. *Ibid.*
8. *Ibid.*, p. 98.
9. *Mark Twain & Huck Finn* (Berkeley, 1960), p. viii.
10. *By the Bend of the River* (Philadelphia, 1914), p. 98.

Yankee Slang

James M. Cox

A *Connecticut Yankee in King Arthur's Court* holds much the same position in Mark Twain's career that *Pierre* occupies in Melville's. Before both books stand single masterpieces; after them comes work of genuine merit, work of a higher order than they themselves represent, but work more quietly desperate, as if the creative force behind it had suffered a crippling blow. Moreover each book displays its author's ambitious effort to scale heights hitherto unattempted. Finally, the books share a similarity of substance, reaching resolutions involving self-destruction for the artist-hero. Melville's Pierre is a writer so caught in the involutions of love and creativity that suicide becomes a last refuge. Mark Twain's Hank Morgan, a brash superintendent of a Hartford Machine Shop transported into a sixth-century feudal world, assumes the role of a superman inventor in an effort to revolutionize the Arthurian world by accelerating the course of history. He does revolutionize it, only to destroy his technological marvels and defeat himself. Despite a certain audacity of conception, however, both works disintegrate into extravagant failures. Each involves an excess of energy, as if the energy invested had not been fully assimilated, leaving the author to force his way toward a destructive ending which would perforce break the identification between himself and the artist-hero.

Mark Twain:The Fate of Humor. Princeton: Princeton U. P., 1966, pp. 198–221.

Such a struggle is particularly evident in *A Connecticut Yankee*. The most revealing comment on the unfulfilled effort is Mark Twain's reply to Howells' praise of the novel: "Well, my book is written—let it go. But if it were only to write over again there wouldn't be so many things left out. They burn in me; & they keep multiplying & multiplying; but now they can't ever be said. And besides, they would require a library—& a pen warmed-up in hell."[1] This humorous exaggeration rests on two central assumptions: that the book is an incomplete expression of suppressed attitudes, and that the suppressions are self-generatively threatening the writer's personality. The entire passage points to the final incompleteness of *A Connecticut Yankee*, corroborating the incompleteness of the novel; or—to put it inversely—the novel realized the sense of incompleteness which the remark suggests. In this respect it is a new kind of failure for Mark Twain. He had failed before, and failed often, but usually in the midst of successes. For example, there is the failure of *The Innocents Abroad*—a failure of concentration and economy. And there is the failure of *Roughing It*, a failure to realize the true structure of the book. And even in *Huckleberry Finn*, there is, after everything one can say about the ending, a failure of proportion. But in all these instances the failure is directly related to and defined by a discovery in form.

In *A Connecticut Yankee*, however, the failure is as central and pervasive as it is in *The Prince and the Pauper*. Moreover, it is of greater magnitude for the simple reason that *A Connecticut Yankee* pretends to be more than *The Prince and the Pauper*. The earlier book had been addressed to a juvenile audience on the one hand and to a respectable audience on the other. It was a book which could be read aloud in the parlor to all the family. If it seemed tame, Mark Twain could rest in the solace of not having claimed it was profound, and also in the knowledge of having subtly conveyed the impression that the book had been written to please the respectable world in which he found himself. *A Connecticut Yankee* was a different thing. It was not peripheral but central; it was not respectable but genuinely irreverent; it offered itself not as an exercise but as an experiment. Like *Huckleberry Finn*, it did not come quickly but slowly, five years elapsing between the time of his first notebook entry in the late fall of 1884 and the date of publication in December, 1889. That first notebook entry— "Dream of being a knight errant in armor in the Middle Ages"—was supposedly inspired by Mark Twain's reading of Sir Thomas Malory to whose work he had been introduced by George W. Cable on their lecture tour in the fall of 1884.

Not until a year later, in December, 1885, did he actually begin to write; by March, 1886 he had written "A Word of Explanation" and the first three chapters. Then, much as he had done with *Huckleberry Finn*, he simply let the manuscript gather dust for a year and a half before returning to write sixteen chapters at Quarry Farm during the summer of 1887. This summer burst of writing carried him into Chapter 20, where Sandy and the Boss visit the Ogre's Castle. But when he returned to Hartford and the business world, his writing stopped. Not until he returned to Quarry Farm in July, 1888 did he begin the sustained assault which carried through disappointments and frustrating delays to the end of the manuscript in the spring of 1889.[2] This brief history of the composition points up the similarity between the emergence of *Huckleberry Finn* and *A Connecticut Yankee*. In each instance there was a beginning, a long delay, a return, another hesitation, and a final sustained push to, or near to, a conclusion.

But similarities have a way of pointing up essential differences, the difference in this instance being that the creative enterprise of *A Connecticut Yankee*, insofar as it parallels that of *Huckleberry Finn,* is on a slighter scale. The total time of its composition is shorter, the initial burst of writing is much less decisive, and the *literary* waste required to complete the book is almost minimal compared to the failures which marked the way toward the success of *Huckleberry Finn*. Yet—and here is the issue—*A Connecticut Yankee* sounds bigger than *Huckleberry Finn*. It makes more noise; it seems more aspiring; it is much more liberal; it exposes the evil as well as the folly of man and his institutions. It thus becomes the central book for those critics who want to see Mark Twain as a robust frontier spirit at war with tradition, and also for those who wish to measure literature in terms of political liberalism and social conscience. This is why Howells—whose awareness of Mark Twain was often so perceptive—singled out *A Connecticut Yankee* as his favorite book. It is why De Voto, though he thought the book a failure, followed Howells in thinking the *conception* extraordinarily bold. It is why, much more recently, Louis Budd, exposing Mark Twain's political conservatism, finds himself granting *A Connecticut Yankee* priority for its distinctly liberal views. Finally, it is why Henry Nash Smith considers the *Yankee* as the most difficult of Mark Twain's works to evaluate, yet the most necessary to understand.[3]

Yet for all the audacity the *Yankee* seems to have, it is actually a much tamer, safer performance. This fact is immediately evident in the Preface. Whereas the Preface to *Huckleberry Finn* was defiant and nihilistic, humorously warning the reader to look for something at the cost of his life, the *Yankee* Preface begins:

> The ungentle laws and customs touched upon in this tale are historical, and the episodes which are used to illustrate them are also historical. It is not pretended that these laws and customs existed in England in the sixth century; no, it is only pretended that inasmuch as they existed in the English and other civilizations of far later times, it is safe to consider that it is no libel upon the sixth century to suppose them to have been in practice in that day also. One is quite justified in inferring that whatever one of these laws or customs was lacking in that remote time, its place was competently filled by a worse one.[4]

Already there is the fatal appeal of *The Prince and the Pauper*: the appeal to history and at the same time the apology for fiction under the assurance of exposing eternal injustices. In a word, the Preface promises satire rather than humor, seriousness rather than mere laughter. Yet the language of *A Connecticut Yankee* was apparently vernacular, not genteel as it had been in *The Prince and the Pauper.* Promising a revolutionary revision of the past it invaded, it seemed a secure armor against the sentimentality of the earlier work. Yet *A Connecticut Yankee,* for all its hardheaded irreverence, succumbed to sentimentality.

The form of *A Connecticut Yankee* is what may be called an inverted Utopian fantasy. A graphic way to see the inversion is to compare it with Edward Bellamy's *Looking Backward,* which appeared in 1887 and was a best seller by the time the *Yankee* was ready for publication. Mark Twain himself was extremely fond of Bellamy's book, though he apparently did not read it until after the *Yankee* was completed.[5] In Bellamy's dream fantasy Julian West is precipitated into the future, where, faced with the material and ideological evolution evident in the year A.D. 2000, his own nineteenth century appears meager and startlingly inadequate. Through all his experience, West remains the observer, the listener, the interrogator who assimilates the persuasive criticism which the imaginary age affords. Bellamy's central achievement is to realize the terms of the Utopian fantasy, which is to say he conveys the notion of a dream of reason. Thus his hero finds himself being constantly persuaded that truths he had believed, values he had held, and causes he had supported are nothing more than outworn attitudes and trappings of a dead age. Being reasonable in the face of the disparity, he submits to the superior argument and assents to the promise of the strange new world.

Mark Twain, however, instead of sending his hero into an imaginary future territory outside history where the terms of criticism could operate freely to create the dream of reason, plunged him into history as if to invade and reform the past. The Yankee is not the innocent interlocutor but the chief actor of his chronicle. Just as his machine-shop lingo collides with the Malory-ese of the Age of Chivalry, his democratic ideology does battle with the aristocratic and religious dogmas of the king's realm. The superintendent of a Colt Arms machine shop, he emerges into the sixth-century Arthurian world and is able to see this feudal pastoral from the presumable advantage of democratic industrialism. Unable to resist the lure of potential power residing in his technological advantage, he finds himself "inventing" labor-saving devices, instigating reforms, and organizing the people in an effort to proclaim a republic in England. For a brief moment his regime prevails; but the Church, never quite defeated, plays upon the superstition of the populace, declares an interdict, and sends an army against the Yankee; he in turn blows up his technological world, along with the assaulting forces of Church and Chivalry. Surrounded and poisoned by the vast corpse he has made of the past, the Yankee is condemned to a thirteen-century sleep by Merlin, the old-time magician whom he initially ridiculed.

The energy generated by this incongruity between chivalric past and practical present made up—as near as one can tell—the central impulse for beginning the book. Mark Twain's letters and notebook entries say as much, and the early portions of the book itself, even after all revisions were made, are essentially built upon a burlesque contrast between two styles: Morgan's roughneck, irreverent abruptness sent against the exaggerated impersonation of Malory's circumlocutive archaism.[6] There are, particularly in the early chapters and from time to time throughout the book, amusing moments when Mark Twain is able to exploit the possibilities of the contrast to genuine advantage. His mounting the knights on bicycles, for example, or forcing them to wear placards advertising such items as Persimmons Soap or Peterson's Prophylactic Toothbrushes, have the genuine force of burlesque incongruity and exceed the expectations of the situation. And his utilizing the waste power of a genuflecting ascetic in order to operate a shirt factory has about it the old reckless irreverence which still has power to shock a safe gentility.

But as Morgan gains power in the Arthurian world, the democratic assumptions on which his identity rests assert themselves, causing the burlesque contrast to assume satiric form. Such a change produces a marked transformation of Hank Morgan's character. For insofar as the burlesque contrast is the dominant impulse, Hank Morgan is essentially the showman, his characterizing compulsion being his urge to gain attention. Wherever he appears, the Yankee must shine, and more than food or women or even life itself, he loves the effect. In a rare moment of insight, he observes that the crying defect of his character is his desire to perform picturesquely. His whole style—given to overstatement from the moment he appears until he finally collapses under Merlin's spell—is in large part a manifestation of his desire to show off. Even the sad-faced Mark Twain ruefully observes of the Yankee's dying call to arms, "He was getting up his last 'effect'; but he never finished it."

But as the satiric impulse comes to the fore, the surprise, bewilderment, and amusement with which Morgan had originally beheld the Arthurian world are displaced by the indignation he feels upon discovering the atrocities at the heart of chivalry. Whereas the burlesquing Morgan had been intent upon making fun of chivalry, the satiric Morgan becomes determined to make war upon it. Yet the satiric Morgan can never really be effective, because the narrow range of his burlesque style cannot tolerate enough analytic intelligence or wit to discharge his growing indignation. Instead, his outrage tends to reduce his democratic ideology to clamorous fulmination and noisy prejudice, so that he becomes an object of curiosity rather than an effective satiric agent. Constantly advertising his ideas, his mechanical aptitude, and his stagey jokes, he becomes a grotesque caricature of the nineteenth century he advocates. Prancing through every conceivable burlesque and flaunting himself before the stunned Arthurian world into which he bursts, he begins to be the real buffoon of the show he manages.

Mark Twain recognized the Yankee's limitations, going so far as to confide to his illustrator Dan Beard, ". . . this Yankee of mine. . . is a perfect ignoramus; he is boss of a machine shop; he can build a locomotive or a Colt's revolver, he can put up and run a telegraph line, but he's an ignoramus, nevertheless."[7] Aware of Morgan's career and Twain's own statements, certain critics have maintained that Mark Twain was directing his fire upon the nineteenth century as much as upon the sixth. Thus, Parrington insisted that Twain was "trimming his sails to the chill winds blowing from the outer spaces of a mechanistic cosmos,"[8] and Gladys Carmine Bellamy has more recently observed that the book is "a fictional working out of the idea that a too-quick civilization breeds disaster."[9]

Plausible though such arguments are in the light of the Yankee's ultimate failure, the logic of the narrative and the tone which sustains it move in precisely the opposite direction. For although the Yankee finally destroys himself, Mark Twain's major investment is in the Yankee's attitudes. After all, most of those attitudes were the same ones Mark Twain himself swore by at one time or another during his public life; and the usual response to the novel has been—and inevitably will continue to be—that he was lampooning monarchy, religion, and chivalry. There is abundant evidence that Mark Twain himself intended just such criticism. As early as 1866, he was attacking feudalism in the Sandwich Islands, and his belief in the superiority of democracy to monarchy goes back to the very beginning of his career; his hatred of an established church stretches equally far back—and further forward. Ten years after the Yankee's diatribes against organized religion, Mark Twain took special pleasure in mounting a sustained, logical attack upon Mary Baker Eddy, whose Christian Science he feared would become the official religion of the Republic. There is also clear evidence, as John B. Hoben long ago observed, that some of the Yankee's attitudes have their exact counterparts in Mark Twain's hostile responses to Matthew Arnold's strictures upon American culture.[10] Finally, Howard Baetzhold has shown that Mark Twain's picture of feudal England is at times almost a direct transcript of the elder George Kennan's lectures and writings on Russia, both of which Mark Twain particularly approved.[11]

What becomes evident is that during the composition of the *Yankee*, the hostility, anger, and indignation which were permanent aspects of his personality came into much fuller play. As he had done while writing *Huckleberry Finn*, he *gave himself up to these emotions.* To read his notebooks of either period is to come across long passages in which fury and brooding animus are often indulged, much as if the writer were cultivating those emotions in order to motivate himself to write.[12] But whereas in the vernacular of *Huckleberry Finn* he had discovered a vehicle to convert the indignation which stands behind both humor and satire into the ironic observation, apparent indifference, and mock innocence which constitute them, the vernacular of Hank Morgan lacked the inverted point of view which would convert the emotions of rage and hate into humor. Instead of being the instrument which transfers the indignation from writer to reader, as in the case of satire, or converts it to pleasure, as in the case of humor, Morgan—who is conceived as a rowdy agent of burlesque—comes to be invested with the indignation of his creator. He is therefore not fully dramatized and remains part of the author, who seems to struggle more and more desperately to free him into character. It is just this struggle which makes the ending seem like a fantasy in which the author is driving the mechanism of his hero faster and faster until it flies apart. Thus in the closing chapters of the book, what began as a burlesque dream assumes the character of a nightmare in which Morgan is electrocuting knights so rapidly and so thoroughly that the dead, being merely an alloy of brass and buttons, are impossible to identify. Trapped at the center of his destruction, the Yankee is condemned by Merlin to a thirteen-century sleep from which he awakens to find himself a stranger in his once-familiar nineteenth century. Unmoored from space, adrift in time, he lies down at last to death.

This relatively "sad" ending to what had begun as a burlesque contrast is what makes the book seem a turning point in Mark Twain's career, embodying as it does the shift from joy to despair, from dream to nightmare. The whole nature of the enterprise, in which Mark Twain finds himself killing the character who had given utterance to so many of his own criticisms and opinions, makes biographical speculation well-nigh inevitable. It is possible, for example, to show that Mark Twain's increasing involvement with the Paige Typesetter during the years the novel took shape had much to do with his growing desperation in the *Yankee*. For it was during these years, in the wake of his success with General Grant, that Mark Twain invested all his available capital in the typesetter. There is a sense in which the Yankee's demise is both a foreshadowing and a rehearsal of the fall which Mark Twain must have begun to see awaiting him. There is even a correspondence between the Yankee— whom Mark Twain indulges and almost glorifies, then brings to grief—and James Paige, the inventor of the typesetter who, like the Yankee, worked in the Colt Arms factory and was at first Mark Twain's hero, later his devil. The intricate relationship between book and typesetter is nowhere better revealed than in a letter Mark Twain wrote to his wife's brother-in-law, Theodore Crane, when, racing to finish the *Yankee*, he was also awaiting the advent of the mechanical miracle which Paige kept toying with.

> I am here in Twichell's house at work, with the noise of the children and an army of carpenters to help. Of course they don't help, but neither do they hinder. It's like a boiler-factory for racket. . . but I never am conscious of the racket at all, and I move my feet into position of relief without knowing when I do it. . . I was so tired last night that I thought I would lie abed and rest, today; but I couldn't resist. . . I want to finish the day the machine finishes, and a week ago the closest calculations for that indicated Oct. 22— but experience teaches me that their calculations will miss fire, as usual.[13]

The process of composition as Mark Twain describes it—a dumbly driven effort going on almost outside himself—is perfectly explained by his wish to finish the book on the day the machine was to be completed. He was saying, in effect, that he was a machine-driven writer; but more important, he revealed that the novel had come to be identified with the machine. There is, however, the hint of fatal doubt about Paige's invention. To accommodate his writing to its schedule was to be anchored to perpetual uncertainty. The machine was not perfected on October 22; nor was the novel completed on that date. Not until eight months later, after seasons of ecstatic hope punctuated by periods of depression or anxious alarm about the mechanical marvel, did Mark Twain succeed in completing his novel. As for the machine, it was never really completed. Paige, constantly taking it apart in an effort to perfect it to the last dimension of its complexity, was overtaken by the simpler Mergenthaler linotype. As for Mark Twain, he was left in bankruptcy.

That Mark Twain could bring the book to an end and break the identification discloses how much writing was his real business. It was the act he had ultimately to rely upon to recover from the financial involvements of his business ventures. Yet the recovery was as costly as it was desperate, for it required killing the Yankee. And the Yankee in the book is not simply a businessman or a mechanic in the Arthurian world, but an *inventor* as well; his power was indivisibly a part of Mark Twain's creative impulse. Killing the Yankee was symbolically a crippling of the inventive imagination, as if Mark Twain were driven to maim himself in an effort to survive. Understandably he considered this radical redefinition of himself to be the logical end of his writing life and went so far as to say jokingly to Howells that his career was over and he wished "to pass to the cemetery unclodded."[14] Of course, his career was not over. He wrote again and again, not simply because there were financial necessities which required it, but because writing was at last his life.

The priority of writing in Mark Twain's life brings us back
to the matter of form in the *Yankee.* For it is finally the form—
which is to say the style and character of Hank Morgan—that
failed Mark Twain. Though a change in his outlook took place
during the process of composition, and though this change is
reflected in the book, it is difficult to say—as it was difficult to
say about *Huckleberry Finn*—how much the art fed into the
life and how much the life fed the art. Thus, while it can be
said that Mark Twain's investment in his publishing hours
and the Paige Typesetter "caused" him to run into writing
difficulty, it is also possible to argue that Mark Twain's
increasing tendency to invest in business rather than in art
was a result, not a cause, of a lesion in his own creative
faculties.

That there was such a lesion is evident in the slender
frame he cast round the *Yankee.* In that frame—appropriately
entitled "A Word of Explanation"—he employed the author-
meets-narrator stratagem as a device for getting into the
narrative and also for introducing his narrator. Following a
guided tour through Warwick Castle, itself a representative of
the storied past of the tourist's imagination, the author
encounters a stranger "who wove such a spell about me that I
seemed to move among the specters and shadows and dust
and mold of a gray antiquity, holding speech with a relic of
it!"[15] Here is the familiar impersonation of the cliches of
travelogue nostalgia, and throughout the introduction Mark
Twain continues to portray himself as the dreamy-eyed tourist
bent on caressing images of the past. In this moment of
sentimental retrospection—while the guide is attempting to
explain the presence of a bullet hole in an ancient piece of
armor—the stranger appears, like the fabulous genie come
from a bottle, and into Mark Twain's ear alone proclaims
himself the author of the bullet hole. The "electric surprise of
the remark" momentarily shatters the tourist's dream, and by
the time he recovers, the stranger has disappeared. That
evening, however, sitting by the fire at the Warwick Arms,
"steeped in a dream of the olden time," Mark Twain is again

abruptly confronted by the stranger, who, knocking upon the door to interrupt the dream, takes final charge of the narrative. The frame makes clear that Morgan, instead of being a companion character, is a projection, or, more accurately, an anti-mask of the tourist Mark Twain's stock nostalgia. In the same way that Morgan has put a bullet hole in the antique armor, he punctures the sentimental dream of the past. Moreover, he comes unbidden to menace the dreamer and his retrospective vision. Speaking with casual and confident authority, he proclaims himself the antithesis of sentimentality. "I am a Yankee of Yankees—and practical; yes, and nearly barren of sentiment, I suppose—or poetry, in other words." His entire narrative, appropriately preserved on a palimpsest, is the record of an attempt to overwrite as well as override the past.

The Yankee's role, as defined in the frame, is thus one of burlesquing "Mark Twain's" tourist version of the past. Taken together in the frame, Morgan and "Mark Twain" could be considered as the essential mechanism of Mark Twain's burlesque. There are the two attitudes—nostalgia and irreverence—in collision; both attitudes are at the heart of Mark Twain's creative impulse. For in order to make the irreverence work, Mark Twain had to impersonate reverence. Even as he specialized in burlesquing the piety of retrospection, he had to cultivate his longing for the past. Sentimental as that longing could be—he speaks in his *Autobiography* of "the pathetic past, the beautiful past, the dear and lamented past"—it nevertheless inspired, at the same time it drove him back upon, his memory.

Probably his chief protection against this intense longing for the past, which he indulged as necessarily as he had to indulge anger and indignation, was his capacity for burlesque. Burlesque was the means of both mocking and checking the nostalgic impulse. In *The Innocents Abroad* Mark Twain, by discovering a perspective along the borderland between pathos and ridicule, had developed a style which contained both attitudes in a new synthesis. Yet in the frame of *A*

Connecticut Yankee he reverted to the simple division of polite tourist and vulgar companion—a division he had used in his *Travels with Mr. Brown*, only to transcend it in *The Innocents Abroad*.[16] In giving over the narrative to Hank Morgan, Mark Twain attempted to transcend the essential division at the heart of the burlesque impulse; but in displacing "Mark Twain" with Morgan rather than Huck Finn, he had no way of producing the mock gravity so essential to his earlier humor. With Morgan as narrator, there was no possibility of impersonating pained seriousness or genteel piety. For Morgan is, as he proudly proclaims, a Yankee of Yankees and barren of sentiment. Instead of embodying the underside of language and experience in the manner of Huck Finn, Hank is the rowdy and irreverent genie of burlesque. Although both Hank and Huck are involved in reconstructing history, the mode of reconstruction is opposite at nearly every point. Huck is the apparently helpless figure drifting upon the current of the mighty Mississippi; Hank is both director and chief actor in his drama. Huck thinks all his heroism is wrong; Hank is sure that his revolution is right. But whereas Huck's successive evasions bring us to the awareness that a real revolution has taken place, Hank's revolutionary indignation involves him in an ever-enlarging fantasy.

All of which brings us to Hank Morgan's style, for Hank's style, like Huck's, will tell everything about the book. It is a loud and boisterous style, given to bluntness and dogmatic attitude. Unlike Huck's Southwestern vernacular, Morgan's Yankee lingo is essentially correct as far as its grammar is concerned. Though it runs toward a jaunty boastfulness and apparently reckless contempt for conventional attitudes, it does not play havoc with the proprieties of grammar. In the final analysis, Hank's vernacular is rather conventional language masquerading as burly, rough talk.

In Huck's vernacular, Mark Twain used the illusion of illiteracy to secure the impression of simplicity while at the same time retaining a complex syntactical structure. Set against the implications of conventional syntax, the illiteracies make possible a style capable of a vast range of expressive utterance. Take, for example, Huck's reflection upon Mary Jane Wilks's offer to pray for him:

> Pray for me! I reckon if she knowed me she'd take a job that was more nearer her size. But I bet she done it, just the same—she was just that kind. She had the grit to pray for Judus if she took the notion—there warn't no back-down to her, I judge. You may say what you want to, but in my opinion she had more sand in her than any girl I ever see; in my opinion she was just full of sand. It sounds like flattery, but it ain't no flattery. And when it comes to beauty—and goodness, too—she lays over them all.[17]

Here Huck's language defines perfectly the breach between his reality and her convention. Mary Jane can approve of him only sentimentally, only because she refuses to know the extent of his sin; and Huck can approve of her only in metaphors which are unwittingly abrasive. In a very real sense his praise of her "ain't no flattery." Yet neither Mary Jane's banality, Huck's self-depreciation, nor the implicit irony of his metaphors disturb the sentiment of his approval. Compare Huck's art of language to Hank's description of a girl he meets upon entering Camelot:

> Presently a fair slip of a girl, about ten years old, with a cataract of golden hair streaming down over her shoulders, came along. Around her head she wore a hoop of flame-red poppies. It was as sweet an outfit as ever I saw, what there was of it. She walked indolently along, with a mind at rest, its peace reflected in her innocent face. . . . But when she happened to notice me, *then* there was a change! Up went her hands, and she was turned to stone; her mouth dropped open, her eyes stared wide and timorously, she was a picture of astonished curiosity touched with fear. And there she stood gazing, in a sort of stupefied fascination, till we turned a corner of the wood and were lost to her view. That she should be startled at me instead of at the other man, was too many for me.[18]

This passage is as representative as it is revealing. The features which distinguish the passage as vernacular are clear—and few. First of all, there is a certain exaggeration of metaphor and figure, as illustrated by the "cataract of golden hair streaming down over her shoulders," and "hoop of flame-red poppies." This exaggeration is also present in other areas of the style. It is evident when the Yankee speaks of "astonished curiosity" and "stupefied fascination." The method here is to call into service an adjective which overlaps the meaning of the noun in an effort to intensify the description. This doubling effect, while it can produce a certain flamboyance of description, is more likely to result—as in the passage under scrutiny—in a redundancy and loss of nuance.

Aside from the exaggeration, the Yankee's style is pervaded with literary cliches. There is the "fair slip of a girl," the "golden hair," the "flame-red poppies," the "mind at rest." Then there are the elaborately stylized locutions—"Up went her hands," "her eyes stared wide and timorously," "she was a picture of astonished curiosity," and "there she stood gazing." These two tendencies—the one toward exaggeration and loud intensity, the other toward literary cliche—reach their logical end in the last sentence of the passage, where the sentence begins with the stilted noun clause as a subject and ends by veering into colloquialism. The entire passage illustrates the essential rhythm and feature of Morgan's language. Grounded in cliches and conventional syntax, its character emerges by means of exaggeration and calculated vulgarity. The exaggeration is achieved largely by relying on cliches which generalize images and impersonate Arthurian gentility; the slang is the means of dissociating from and exposing the overelaborate impersonation.

These revelations about Hank Morgan's style put us directly in touch with his action and his character, for Morgan's action bears the same relation to his style that Huck's action bore to his. Huck, it is worth remembering, was helplessly involved in doing the thing which his society disapproved—freeing a slave. It was an action which he himself disapproved but could avoid no more than he could avoid his grammatical blunders. Both morally and grammatically he "hadn't had no start." The humor in the book lay in involving Huck in a wrong action which his society might abhor yet the reader would heartily approve. Such a strategy required either setting the action in a primitive society and using space or geography as the point of reference; or setting the book in time and using history as the referent. The game lay in playing upon the reader's—and author's— instinctive belief in progress; and Mark Twain had played it admirably in *Huckleberry Finn*. Not only had he involved his protagonist in a revolution which his reader inexorably approved; the hero could not help himself. He simply found himself helplessly and ironically in revolution against a society which he kept thinking he should admire.

In *A Connecticut Yankee*, Mark Twain tried much the same strategy. His Yankee, finding himself in the Arthurian world, sets about revolting against the monarchy and the Catholic Church—institutions which were fairly safe game for a nineteenth-century Yankee. Certainly Mark Twain could count on a general audience approval of these aims almost as much as he could count on their disapproval of slavery. But the great difference between the Yankee and Huck is that the Yankee is a reformer whereas Huck is a helpless rebel. The Yankee acts upon principle and moral confidence; he is finally a Yankee, an abolitionist, an American, who never doubts that he is right. Huck, the fugitive and helpless outcast, acts out of a sense of being always wrong.

The Yankee's assurance that he is in the right contributes as much as anything else to alienating him from the reader. For a real problem arises the moment the Yankee begins to establish his republic. It is not that the reader disapproves of the Yankee's republicanism, but that he cannot approve the revolutionary zeal which goes along with it. As long as he is simply amused at the contrast between his own century and the quaint absurdities of the Arthurian world, the Yankee at least remains plausible; but when he begins to rail at the injustice of the past, his indignation becomes misplaced. The direction of the book discloses that the *intention* of the narrative can neither sustain nor account for the emotion of the central figure; for the emotion—the indignation—is a manifestation of the failure and inadequacy of the intention. The intention of the narrative is a burlesquing or *making fun* of the past. But what begins as making fun becomes making war. Insofar as the Yankee begins to make war upon the Arthurian kingdom he loses his sense of show and pleasure. His indignation is the index to his capacity, not for the destruction of the past, but for self-destruction.

Even more important, the Yankee's revolution is really as correct as his style. It *sounds* like revolution but is actually thoroughly safe and respectable gentility. Small wonder that Howells, who was himself at the threshold of a great "conversion" to political liberalism, should have congratulated his friend upon the bravery of the novel. And so, of course, did E. C. Stedman. Actually there is no courage about the novel. It marks a great turning back for Mark Twain—a turning back in technique and a betrayal of humor. Worst of all, Mark Twain seems to have been self-deceived since he apparently thought the Yankee was a rebel. Yet the reality of the situation is that there is scarcely anything rebellious about the Yankee. His language, as we have seen, is the index of his tameness. Although he sounds and thinks as if he were rebellious, he is quite clearly echoing the sentiments of a society fairly sunk in the complacent and institutionalized "liberalism" which had sponsored the Civil War in 1860–65.[19]

That is why the book, seen in a certain light, amounts to fighting the Civil War again. It is, after all, a tale of the Yankee doing battle with chivalry. Mark Twain himself had made it eminently plain in *Life on the Mississippi* that the South he could not abide was the South which had created itself in the image of Walter Scott and chivalry. Henry Nash Smith, in a fine discussion of Mark Twain's images of Hannibal, had shown decisively how the entire Arthurian kingdom is a thinly veiled picture of Southern regional culture which Mark Twain, as he grew older, came more and more to criticize. Smith points out that Arthur's Britain is "a projection of the benighted South," a "negative image of Hannibal, of Hannibal as Bricksville."[20]

Into this "backward" region the Yankee marches to free the people from religion, aristocracy, and slavery. It is here that he seeks to establish his republic. Insofar as the action of the book amounts to a fighting of the Civil War, Mark Twain assumes the role of the Yankee; he puts on—or better, indulges in—the Yankee conscience and commits aggression after aggression upon the South in himself. For Hank Morgan does, almost from the beginning, what Huck is finally driven helplessly to do—he commits himself to the Northern conscience. This commitment Mark Twain evidently believed was rebellious; actually it is nothing less—or more—than the *approved* action. Huck's rebellion lay not at all in his "All right, then, I'll *go* to hell," but in his rejection of conscience—of hell and heaven—altogether. Having committed himself to the "approved" rebellion, Hank Morgan sounds off louder and louder about it—and the more he commits himself to it, the less real rebellion there can be. This is Hank Morgan's and Mark Twain's self-deception—a self-deception which the style reveals. For Hank's supposed vernacular is not really vernacular at all but indulged colloquialism. It is, in a word, slang, which is to say that it is simply put-on vernacular. Mark Twain, in *A Connecticut Yankee*, succumbed to the lure of mere lingo, which so many writers since his time have done. He wanted to have a hero with an ideology *and* a vernacular. The vernacular was to ground the character in "reality" and give him a "realistic" and recognizable "social" quality. Such a hero really knows what ideas are and showily makes bright philosophical formulations in the rough and salty savor of colloquial speech. But what happens in *A Connecticut Yankee*, and in many another such attempt, is simply a faking and collapse in both directions. The ideas are so crudely simplified in Morgan's vernacular that they actually become pretentious evasions. And the vernacular is nothing but a *show*, an act. It is not necessary to the action, but simply decoration, a contrast. Nothing more than one of Hank Morgan's *effects*, it is in the last analysis an affectation.

To see this failure is to see the crucial difference between vernacular and slang. Slang is a patronizing indulgence of metaphor by someone consciously taking imaginative flights for purposes of mystification, in-group solidarity, or protective, secret communication. Vernacular, however, as we defined the term in *Huckleberry Finn*, is the "lower" or illiterate language whose very "incorrectness" at once indulgently implies a correct grammar and at the same time subverts the literary vision. The more a book is committed to a vernacular hero, the more it necessarily must produce a vision which displaces the genteel values it plays upon. *Huckleberry Finn* did carry such a vision—so much so that the vernacular and vision wait upon each other to produce a new reality of form and action. In the world of childhood which Huck's language reconstructed lay the central confrontations and discoveries which Mark Twain's humor could make. There lay the pleasure principle, which somehow gave the lie to the adult reality principle.

But in moving from Southwestern boy to Yankee adult, Mark Twain actually regressed. The Yankee is in many ways Tom Sawyer grown up—but Tom Sawyer grown up is, alas, somehow grown down. Mark Twain had refused to let Tom grow up on the grounds that he would "just be like all the other one-horse men in literature." And Morgan, if we look at him carefully, does do little but be like other one-horse men. That is why he comes to believe in himself, to take himself seriously. In *Tom Sawyer*, Mark Twain had kept Tom's speech contained within a frame—a frame half-indulgently patronizing, half-burlesque, which both indulges and exposes Tom's essential conformity with the imitation of adult ways. The indulgent narration of *Tom Sawyer* had greatly enriched Tom's reality by showing that it was somehow absurd yet pleasurably *real* in a lost nostalgic way.

When he dropped himself—the "Mark Twain" narrator—out of the action in *A Connecticut Yankee*, he could never compensate for the loss of perspective; instead, he was drawn inevitably to invest the fantasy Yankee with "serious" values. But the fate of the slang form inexorably produced a reduction in the intellectual content of Hank's "thought" and an attendant excess of emotion. The result is an increased amount of sound about ideas, yet a reduction of sense in expressing them.

The conclusion to be drawn from an examination of *A Connecticut Yankee* is that Mark Twain was deceived into believing that slang and vernacular were one and the same. But in vernacular humor, the *form* indulgently inverts conventional values, whereas in slang the *character* must attack them. The one inverts relationships and values; the other moves toward overt judgment and criticism. To realize the possibilities of slang form, Mark Twain would have had to reduce Hank Morgan's intelligence, thereby producing a burlesque, or increase his capacities of criticism and move toward satire. Yet he was able to do neither. It was as if the writer, having reached the top of his form in vernacular, was actually deceived by his masterpiece into believing that the sound of language was identical with its form. By failing to realize the necessities of his form, Mark Twain was never able to be fully responsible to the book he was making. Yet if he fatally confused vernacular and slang, he did no more than many of his successors have done. Believing that they are writing vernacular *Huckleberry Finns*, they produce instead slang *Connecticut Yankees*. Take Saul Bellow's *Henderson the Rain King* as a formidable example. Like the Yankee, Henderson speaks a salty colloquial idiom. Though much more intellectual than Morgan, Henderson nonetheless indulges language in a reckless, carefree way. Both the *Yankee* and *Henderson* try to be responsible by proposing themselves as fantasies, yet the consequences of slang indulgence take their revenge anyway. Whereas the burlesque Morgan turns serious and assaults the fantasy, the intellectual clown

Henderson requires excessive folds of fantasy to make his arrantly conventional sentiments seem boldly speculative. If in the process of becoming serious Morgan negates his own burlesque identity, Henderson in the act of sustaining his fantasy more and more depletes the reality of his speculations, making them seem mere tricks of thought. Both works, in trying to give serious content to the fantasy, succeed only in becoming more and more extravagantly fantastic—and tiresome.

Notes

1. *Mark Twain-Howells Letters*, II, 613.
2. For the best account of the writing of the book, see Howard G. Baetzhold, "The Course of Composition of *A Connecticut Yankee*: A Reinterpretation," *American Literature*, XXXIII (May, 1961), 195–214.
3. Howells, in *My Mark Twain* (p. 44), says, "I wish that all the work-folk. . . could know him their friend in life as he was in literature; as he was in such a glorious gospel of equality as the *Connecticut Yankee in King Arthur's Court.*" In his essay "Mark Twain: An Inquiry," which appeared in the *North American Review* in February, 1901, and was included in *My Mark Twain* (pp. 165–85), he insisted that the book was Mark Twain's highest achievement in the way of "a greatly inspired and symmetrically developed romance" (*My Mark Twain*, p. 174). DeVoto, in *Mark Twain's America* (pp. 272–79) sees the bold satiric conception thwarted by the burlesque and frontier humor. Louis Budd (*Mark Twain: Social Philosopher* [Bloomington, Ind., 1962]) concludes his chapter on the *Yankee*: "When he snatched up the banners under which the middle-class was forcing the nobility to disgorge, he was eloquently sincere; his flaming calls to revolt against self-appointed masters are great statements of that right, and his genius at phrase-making left memorable appeals for self-respecting manliness and political equality" (p. 144). Smith has dealt extensively with the novel on two separate occasions: in *Mark Twain: The Development of a Writer* (pp. 138–70) and again in *Mark Twain's Fable of Progress* (New Brunswick, 1964). In the latter book, which is devoted exclusively to the *Yankee*, Smith feels that "at some point in the composition of this fable, he had passed the great divide in his career as a writer"

(p. 107), and that understanding an event so important is to understand the writer.
4. *Writings*, XVI, vii.
5. Budd, *Mark Twain: Social Philosopher*, p. 145.
6. Baetzhold, "Composition of *A Connecticut Yankee*," pp. 196–98.
7. Paine, *A Biography*, II, 887–88.
8. Vernon Louis Parrington, *Main Currents in American Thought*, 3 vols. in one (New York, 1930), III, 98.
9. Gladys Carmine Bellamy, *Mark Twain as a Literary Artist* (Norman, Olka., 1950), p. 314.
10. John B. Hoben, "Mark Twain's *A Connecticut Yankee*: A Genetic Study," *American Literature*, XVIII (November, 1946), 197–218.
11. Baetzhold, "Composition of *A Connecticut Yankee*," pp. 207–11.
12. Paine's edition of the notebooks omits most of Mark Twain's savage attacks, but in the years 1877–80 there are, in the unpublished notebooks, voluminous assaults on Whitelaw Reid and the French nation, to name but two targets. And during the composition of the *Yankee*, abuse is heaped on a variety of subjects.
13. *Letters*, II, 500.
14. *Mark Twain-Howells Letters*, II, 611.
15. *Writings*, XVI,I.
16. Franklin Rogers has an excellent discussion of the refined tourist and his vulgar companion (*Burlesque Patterns*, pp. 36–61). Rogers defines Mark Twain's problem of development as the difficulty of getting a narrative plank which would release the narrative from the stasis of the burlesque division. In the early travels with Mr. Brown, he merely inserted factual chapters between the burlesque chapters, but in *The Innocents Abroad* he assimilated the division into a single narrator who retained burlesque characteristics yet could narrate his travels.
17. *Writings*, XIII, 265.
18. *Writings*, XVI, 10–11.
19. Budd has an excellent account of Mark Twain's opinions in relation to the middle-class Liberalism of the period (*Mark Twain: Social Philosopher*, pp. 111–44).
20. Henry Nash Smith, "Mark Twain's Images of Hannibal: From St. Petersburg to Eseldorf," *University of Texas Studies in English*, XXXVII (1958), 15.

"I Kind of Love Small Game": Mark Twain's Library of Literary Hogwash

Alan Gribben

Mark Twain once observed that "if we read without understanding, there is no gain."[1] For him, reading with the benefit of understanding meant making judgments about what he read, and he did this almost by reflex, as the margins of books from his library testify. Indeed, Mark Twain's unliterary image may flourish so persistently partly because his unfavorable remarks about books and authors very nearly outweigh his praise. But he seldom commented on anyone's writing at length; Sydney Krause has pointed out that Mark Twain left behind not a single fully rounded book review—only desultory, scattered statements.[2]

From the miscellaneous opinions about literature that Mark Twain did set down, however, commentators have attempted to establish his critical standards. DeLancey Ferguson noted in 1943 that "pretentiousness, overwriting, inaccuracy of expression he detested. . . . His interest was always in the style, rather than the story."[3] Howard G. Baetzhold added that Mark Twain generally disliked absurdly romantic situations, excessive sentimentality, dearth of "interest," and lack of believable or likable characters.[4] Yet Mark Twain's marginalia from 1894 in his copy of Sarah Grand's *The Heavenly Twins*[5] show his willingness to over-

Reprinted from *American Literary Realism, 1870–1910* 9. no. 1 (Winter 1976): 65–76.

look objectionable plot conventions and bizarre characterizations provided that the prose style was succinct, the syntax clear, the diction appropriate.

Edgar M. Branch identified criteria applied by Mark Twain in his literary criticism between 1864 and 1866 which seem to hold for his later criticism as well: "clarity, exactitude, simplicity, honesty—all implied in his hatred for literary pretension or ambiguity."[6] Often this search for precision in style came down to a matter of diction. In 1905 Mark Twain explained that in written English prose "phrasing is everything, almost. Oh, yes, phrasing is a kind of photography: out of focus, a blurred picture; in focus, a sharp one."[7]

Generally it was easier for Mark Twain to identify and comment on examples of words used ineffectively, a practice that appealed more strongly to his instincts as a humorist. So adept did he consider himself at discovering specimens of atrocious writing, in fact, that eventually he compiled a special "Library of Literary Hogwash" for particularly delectable examples. Nearly all of these volumes of prose and verse were neglected in their own day and would have been forgotten today had not Clemens' attention fallen upon them. As Clemens confided to General Bryce on 13 October 1894 in another connection (concerning Bourget's *Outre-Mer*): "Paul's book is wretchedly small game, & not much short of idiotic; but I kind of love small game."[8] This preference for easy targets involved the type of perverse pleasure-seeking that Mark Twain had related of himself on 22 August 1878: when a young woman "cleaned out" the idlers in a hotel reading room with her "lacerating" piano rendition of "The Battle of Prague," Clemens alone remained to listen. "I staid," he explained in Notebook 15, "because the exquisitely bad is as satisfying to the soul as the exquisitely good—only the mediocre is unendurable."[9]

By at least 1870 Mark Twain had contrived a name for the literary small game he sought, and the term had associations with his journalism in Nevada and California. In a piece Mark Twain wrote for the June 1870 issue of *Galaxy*, he ridiculed as "the sickliest specimen of sham sentimentality that exists" a sketch entitled "A Touching Incident." In November 1870 he similarly derided the bathos of an obituary poem, scoffing: "There is something so innocent, so guileless, so complacent, so unearthly serene and self-satisfied about this peerless 'hogwash,' that the man must be made of stone who can read it without a dulcet ecstasy creeping along his backbone and quivering in his marrow." He added by way of explanation that "in California, that land of felicitous nomenclature, the literary name of this sort of stuff is '*hogwash*.'"[10] Accordingly, in 1876 he scrawled the words "This book belongs to S. L. Clemens's Library of Literary 'Hogwash'" across the flyleaf of his copy of Edward P. Hammond's *Sketches of Palestine*.[11] Clemens marked other volumes in his personal library with similar labels.

People who knew about Mark Twain's affection for bad writing were continually sending him fresh examples. To one such correspondent, John Horner of Belfast, Ireland, Mark Twain wrote on 12 January 1906: "Hogwash is a term which was invented by the night foreman of the newspaper whereunto I was attached 40 yrs ago, in the capacity of local reporter, to describe my literary efforts. Many years ago I began to collect Hog-Wash literature & I am glad of the chance to add to it the extraordinary book [Emanda Ros's *Irene Iddesleigh*] which you have sent to me."[12] In an Autobiographical Dictation of 16 December 1908 Mark Twain recorded that a letter from Howard P. Taylor (written on 1 December 1908) reminded him how Taylor, a Southerner on the staff of the Virginia City *Territorial Enterprise* (he was foreman of the composing room), coined the "word which I have often used in my books when I was talking about poor literary stuff that had a good opinion of itself—when I . . . wanted to compress my disparagement into a single word." Taylor used to wait while Clemens finished scribbling his day's output for the newspaper: "He never had any other name for my literature"—it was always "hog-wash" (MTP).

Not all of the inferior submissions Mark Twain received from admirers met his strict criteria as "hogwash." He dismissed the poems of Lewis Elmer Trescott of Glenwood, Long Island, for falling short in crucial areas. Clemens explained to a Mr. Lang on 21 August 1907 why Trescott was not a legitimate successor to Bloodgood H. Cutter, the "Poet Lariat" whose verse Mark Twain made celebrated in *Innocents Abroad*; Trescott's broadside poems lacked "incoherency," "idiocy," "windy emptiness," and "putrid & insistent bastard godliness" (MTP).

Mark Twain never actually made a list of selections for his "Library of Literary Hogwash," but the volumes he designated as belonging to it are easily enough identified from his inscriptions and marginalia.[13] A few other novels, sketches, and books of poetry can also be included on the basis of his comments about them, even though he did not specifically label them "hogwash." Had he ever set aside a special bookcase for this collection of literary horrors, its shelves probably would have contained:

Bishop, Levi. *The Poetical Works of Levi Bishop*. 3rd ed. Detroit: E.B. Smith, 1876/ 547 pp.
  Inscription: "This book belongs to / S.L. Clemens's / Library of Hogwash. / Hartford, 1876."
  Marginalia: Clemens underlined sentences in the biographical sketch of Bishop; at its conclusion he characterized Bishop as a useful citizen whose only failing was the delusion that his "jingling twaddle" qualified as poetry. Other marginal notes include the word "Rot" scrawled at the beginning of a poem entitled "The Oyster" (p. 490). Clemens also annotated Bishop's essay on the definition of poetry.
  Location: The Newberry Library, Chicago, Illinois.

    Copy examined: I am grateful to Richard Colles Johnson, Bibliographer of the Newberry Library, for providing a photocopy of Clemens' notations for my use.

Caster, Andrew. *Pearl Island.* NY: Harper, 1903. 266 pp.

    Marginalia: Clemens penciled markings and sneering comments throughout the volume. On the front free endpaper he recorded his opinion that Caster's dialogues are "incomparably idiotic." Beside Caster's hint in the concluding paragraph (p. 267) concerning further adventures forthcoming in another volume, Clemens swore that the author should first be flayed and hanged.

    Location: Antenne-Dorrance Collection, Rice Lake, Wisconsin.[14]

    Copy examined: Clemens' copy.

Curtis, Elizabeth Alden. *One Hundred Quatrains from the Rubiyat of Omar Khyyam / A Rendering in English Verse.* Introd. by Richard Burton. Gouverneur, N.Y.: Brothers of the Book, 1899.

Clemens bristled at this attempt to supersede Edward FitzGerald's translation, writing incredulously from London to the Reverend Joseph H. Twichell of 1 January 1900 to say that Curtis had committed "sacrilege" upon "a noble poem" by endeavoring to recast it line by line. The result, he declared, was as though a Tammany Hall boss should demolish the Taj Mahal and then reconstruct it according to his own concept of what it ought to look like (MTP).

Curtis, Lillian E. *Forget-Me-Not / Poems.* Albany, N.Y.: Weed, Parsons, 1872. 112 pp.

    Inscription: Presented to Clemens by an admirer, Edwin F. Schirely, on 12 July 1889.

Marginalia: Clemens read the book thoroughly in search of humorous passages, commenting in pencil, correcting syntax and rhymes, and occasionally making outright gibes such as the one on page 56 (concerning "Letter to My Cousin, J.W.H., On His Birthday"): "Did he have to stand this every year?" On page 58, at the penultimate stanza of the same poem, Clemens urged Curtis to "hit him again next year" (copyright 1976, Mark Twain Company).

Location: Antenne-Dorrance Collection, Rice Lake, Wisconsin.

Copy examined: Clemens' copy.

Cutter, Bloodgood Haviland (1817–1906). *The Long-Island Farmer's Poems / Lines Written on the "Quaker City" Excursion to Palestine / And Other Poems.* NY: N. Tibbals, 1886. 499 pp.

Mark Twain preserved this poetaster's place in American letters by calling him the "Poet Lariat" and chuckling over his verse in *Innocents Abroad* (1869); thereafter Mark Twain took pleasure in encouraging Cutter's publication of his effusions. Notebooks 8 (1867) and 46 (1903) contain references to Cutter (MTP). Bradley, Beatty, and Long's edition of *Huckleberry Finn* reprints an example of Cutter's "lugubrious, sentimental, and semi-literate verse."[15]

Elmore, James Buchanan. *Love Among the Mistletoe / And Poems.* Alamo, Ind.: Published by the author, 1899. 164 pp.

Inscription: "Hogwash, but not atrocious enough to be first-rate," Clemens wrote in brown ink on the inner front cover, which he also signed and dated 1902 (copyright 1976, Mark Twain Company).

> *Marginalia*: Ink markings on pages 48, 69, 70, 72, 213, 214.
>
> *Location*: Antenne-Dorrance Collection, Rice Lake, Wisconsin.
>
> *Copy examined*: Clemens' copy.

Gay, Mary Ann Harris. *Prose and Poetry / By a Georgia Lady.* Nashville, Tenn.: Privately printed, 1858. 199 pp.

Hamlin Hill, in "The Composition and the Structure of Tom Sawyer," *American Literature*, 32 (Jan. 1961), 379–392, identifies Gay's book as the one from which Mark Twain extracted two essays and a poem for graduation elocutions in Chapter 21 of *Tom Sawyer* (1876). In a footnote at the end of the chapter Mark Twain acknowledges that the declamations of Tom's female classmates "are taken without alteration from a volume entitled 'Prose and Poetry, by a Western [sic] Lady'—but they are exactly and precisely after the school-girl pattern, and hence are much happier than any mere imitations could be." Eight editions of Gay's book were issued between 1858 and 1873; the title varied. Sydney J. Krause—*Mark Twain as Critic*, pp. 114–117—found the style of Gay's volume to be "Miltonic ornamentation in a country version of the prose of sensibility."

Hammond, Edward Payson. *Sketches of Palestine / Descriptive of the Visit of the Rev. Edward Payson Hammond, M. A., to the Holy Land.* Introd. by the Reverend Robert Knox. Boston: Henry Hoyt, n.d. [Introd. is dated 8 Feb. 1868.] 180 pp.

> *Inscription*: Clemens wrote in pencil on the recto of the front free endpaper: "This book belongs to S.L. Clemens's Library of Literary 'Hogwash.' Hartford 1876." The inside front cover is signed by Edward P. Judd.
>
> *Marginalia*: Prolific annotations in pencil by Clemens, uniformly derisive. Choice passages have been

scissored from many pages, leaving the volume much mutilated. On page 148 Clemens referred to Hammond as a "putrid. . . humbug."

Location: Mark Twain Papers, Berkeley, California.

Copy examined: Clemens' copy.

Hammond wrote these "sketches" in the form of poems. On 27 October 1879 Clemens notified an unnamed correspondent that he had written a review of this "admirable singer" (Newberry Library, Chicago).

Joyce, John Alexander. *Edgar Allan Poe*. NY: F. Tennyson Neely, n.d. [cop. 1901]. 218 pp.

> *Inscription*: Katy Leary signed the inside front cover.
>
> *Marginalia*: Clemens made sarcastic notes in pencil throughout the entire volume, scoffing at Joyce's grammar as well as his conclusions. Clemens fixed his view of Joyce at the top of the first page of the text: "If he *had* an idea he couldn't word it. / The most remarkable animal that ever cavorted around a poet's grave" (copyright 1976, Mark Twain Company). Similarly belittling notes, brief ejaculations ("rot!" "bow-wow!"), and underlinings abound throughout the volume. Since Clemens compares Joyce's style to that of Mary Baker Eddy before her editors revised her writings (p. xii), he may have annotated this volume during or shortly after his intensive reading of Christian Science publications in 1902 and 1903.
>
> *Location*: Antenne-Dorrance Collection, Rice Lake, Wisconsin.
>
> *Copy examined*: Clemens' copy.

Kiefer, F.J. *The Legends of the Rhine from Basle to Rotterdam*. 2nd ed. Trans. by L.W. Garnham. Mayence: David Kapp, 1870. 313 pp.

Inscription: Original title page missing; Clemens has supplied a handwritten title page on the black recto for the frontispiece.
Marginalia: Clemens' annotations in pencil occur throughout. Inside the back cover is the sticker of a Leipzig bookseller.
Location: Mark Twain Papers, Berkeley, California.
Copy examined: Clemens' copy.

Kiefer's legends were the literary source for some of the stories Mark Twain told in *A Tramp Abroad* (1880). One legend, "The Converted Sceptic," Mark Twain reworked into the legend of Dilsberg Castle, giving a Rip Van Winkle theme to the narrative of a raft captain (chapter 19). But Garnham's cumbersome translation from the German tickled Mark Twain immensely. In chapter one of *A Tramp Abroad* he introduces Garnham's "toothsome" book to his readers, describing the translator's "quaint fashion of building English sentences on the German plan," and quoting a legend called "The Knave of Bergen" as an example. In chapter 16 he quotes Garnham's sorry attempt to translate the song titled "The Lorelei" into English: "I believe this poet is wholly unknown in America and England; I take peculiar pleasure in bringing him forward because I consider that I discovered him."

MacDonald, George. *Robert Falconer* (American edition published in 1870).
Though Clemens became friends with MacDonald and generally admired his writings, he found this novel extremely disappointing. To Mrs. Fairbanks, who had recommended the book, he complained on 2 September 1870 that he found nothing praiseworthy after the middle of the book; in fact he ended up "despising him [Robert] for a self-righteous humbug, devoured with egotism." Clemens culminated this (for him) unusually long literary disquisition by blasting "that tiresome Ericson & his

dismal 'poetry'—hogwash, *I* call it." He felt that MacDonald should have omitted his moody gypsy and his thanatotic poetry.[16]

Miller, George Ernest. *Luxilla / A Romance.* [Mobile, Alabama], n.d. [cop. 1885]. 54 pp.
   According to a note book Clemens kept during the summer of 1886, he had plans to "review 'Luxilla' that hogwash novel from the South" (Notebook 26, TS p. 9a, MTP).

Mills, S.M. *Palm Branches.* Sandusky, Oh.: Register Steam Press, 1878. 128 pp.
   Marginalia: On the recto of the blank page opposite the copyright notice Clemens speculates that the writer must be about fifteen years old. He jotted derogatory remarks throughout the volume, first in black ink, then purple ink, and finally (in the latter half) in pencil. On page 65 he penciled his opinion that "puberty will do much for this authoress." Later, on page 120, he noted that when the character named Daisy remained the same "simple, beautiful maiden" despite Mr. Russell's lavishing every luxury upon her (including "pearls and precious gems that a princess might have coveted"), it was "a schoolgirl's idea of triumph" (copyright 1976, Mark Twain Company). There are numerous other sarcastic comments.
   Location: Mark Twain Papers, Berkeley, California.
   Copy examined: Clemens' copy.

Moore, Julia A. *The Sentimental Song Book.* Grand Rapids, Mich.: C.M. Loomis, 1877. 60 pp.
   The "Queen & Empress of the Hogwash Guild" is how Clemens described this poetess to a correspondent in 1906.[17] It is generally agreed that the didactic doggerel of

this farmer's wife inspired Emmeline Grangerford's lugubrious elegies in *Huckleberry Finn*.[18] In *Following the Equator* (1897) Mark Twain returned to *The Sentimental Song Book* ("Forgotten by the world in general, but not by me," he declared), and quoted from different poems in chapter 8 ("Frank Dutton"), 36 ("William Upson"), and 44 ("The Author's Early Life"). Moore, he wrote, had that ineffable and "subtle touch" necessary for genuine hogwash—"the touch that makes an intentionally humorous episode pathetic and an intentionally pathetic one funny" (ch. 36).

Ros, Emanda M'Kittrick. *Delina Delaney*. Belfast, Ireland: R. Aickin, n.d.

> *Inscription*: Signed by Clemens in ink and dated 1906.
> *Marginalia*: Notes and markings indicate Clemens' close reading of pages 51, 170, 178, 179.
> *Location*: Presently unknown; sold to a private buyer by Seven Gables Bookshop, New York City, in June 1970.
> *Copy examined*: I am indebted to Robert H. Hirst, an associate editor of the Mark Twain Papers in Berkeley, for the facts reported in this entry. Mr. Hirst inspected Clemens' copy in June 1970.

Emboldened by Clemens' delight with Ros's *Irene Iddesleigh* (see next entry), John Horner of Belfast, Ireland, mailed him a copy of her other work, *Delina Delaney*, on 21 April 1906 (ALS in MTP).

———. *Irene Iddesleigh*. Belfast, Ireland: W. & G. Baird, 1897. 189 pp.

> *Marginalia*: Numerous pencil and black ink annotations by Clemens up to page 55. John Horner of Belfast sent the volume to him on 15 December 1905; Horner's accompanying letter is pinned to the front free endpaper. In 1908 Clemens donated the volume to the Mark Twain Library

in Redding, Connecticut, and it still contains the bookstamps of that institution.

Location: Mark Twain Papers, Berkeley, California.

Copy examined: Clemens' copy.

In a letter to the book's sender on 12 January 1906, Clemens expressed his immense pleasure in the "enchanting" volume and speculated that Julia A. Moore's reign as undisputed Empress of the Hogwash Guild might finally be at an end (dictation copy of a TLS sent by Isabel V. Lyon, Clemens' secretary, MTP).

Royston, Samuel Watson. *The Enemy Conquered / Or, Love Triumphant*. New Haven, Conn.: T.H. Pease, 1845. 31 pp.

> *Marginalia*: Two copies once owned by Clemens are extant. One lacks the paper wrappers and contains numerous markings in brown ink; the other has pencil markings throughout. Clemens cut out sentences, paragraphs, and entire pages from both copies.
>
> *Location*: Mark Twain Papers, Berkeley, California.
>
> *Copies examined*: Clemens' copies.

Professor Francis Bacon of Yale purportedly lent a copy of this absurd novelette to George Washington Cable, and Cable then introduced Clemens to the tale of Indian fighter Major Elfonzo's courtship of Ambulinia Valeer, a Southern belle.[19] On 29 January 1884 Clemens requested Charles L. Webster to procure him a copy, instructing Webster to "pay two or three dollars if necessary."[20] But eventually it was Cable, who, in 1889, came through with copies of the book for which Clemens hungered; and on the blue envelope in which he kept them Clemens wrote, "Cable's precious pamphlet / Ambulinia, written by a jackass." Clemens made a note to remind himself to return "one of those old New Haven pamphlet novels" to Cable in 1889, and 1891 he again referred to "Cable's New Haven Idiot's Romance."[21] Eventually Clemens reprinted the entire novelette, with a satiric introduction, as "A Cure for the Blues" in *The £1,000,000 Bank-Note* (1893). Guy A. Cardwell has treated Mark Twain's obsession with this pathetic romance in an insightful article that accounts for his motives behind the writing of "A Cure" and his disappointing efforts to make Royston seem funny.[22]

Stedman, S. O. *Allen Bay / A Story*. Philadelphia: Lippincott, 1876. 152 pp.

On 23 November 1877 William Dean Howells asked Clemens, "Didn't you once read me some passages out of an idiot novel called Allen Bay?"[23] Clemens undoubtedly *had* singled out certain parts for Howells' amusement, but the copy of *Allen Bay* from which he had read was then no longer in existence; he had torn many pages from the volume in the course of writing a thirty-nine-page unpublished manuscript, "Burlesque Review of Allen Bay."[24] He used purple ink and Crystal Lake Mills ruled paper in writing the undated manuscript, a paper-and-ink combination that mainly occurred during 1876 and 1877. It is one of Mark Twain's fullest book reviews, inspired in this case by his abhorrence of Stedman's style. He claims to have reread the book seven times after a first reading and launches into a stylistic analysis of its mixed metaphors, marrings of tone, poor transitions, faulty diction, and other flaws. Gradually it dawns upon the reader that Mark Twain is producing a burlesque review, spoofing the vocabulary and cliches of book reviewers as well as the reprehensible tastes of the readers and writers of such sentimental trash. Moreover, in many instances Mark Twain's purple-ink revisions of the extracts he removed from the book distort the original wording and punctuation to heighten Stedman's already-woeful problems in syntax, diction, sense, and image. Mark Twain tore out pages 143–150 to demonstrate the fatuity of Stedman's highflown bathos and plundered other pages for shorter extracts. The narrative—about a misanthropic hermit who adopts a baby girl, Judith, only to watch her (as a teenager) die of grief over her boyfriend's drowning in a millpond—is undeniably atrocious, but Mark Twain's revisions emphasize its ludicrous qualities by compressing, italicizing, and isolating them.

Van Zandt, George Harrison. *Poems of George Harrison Van Zandt.* Philadelphia: Jay & Co., 1886. 256 pp.

In 1887, while Clemens was managing the business affairs of Charles L. Webster & Company, Van Zandt approached the publishing firm with a proposal to write a historical romance. In an undated letter to Charles L. Webster, Clemens recommended that Webster consult with Van Zandt about the project (ALS in Berg Collection, New York Public Library). At the top of a letter of 21 June 1887 from Van Zandt, however, Clemens advised Fred J. Hall, his representative at Charles L. Webster & Company, not to dispel Van Zandt's delusion that he could write another *Ben Hur*, but neither to encourage his proposals. "His volume of alleged 'poems,'" Clemens assured Hall, "is mere hogwash" (quoted from Philip C. Duschnes Catalog No. 49, item #125).

Warder, George Woodward. *The Cities of the Sun.* NY: G. W. Dillingham, 1901. 320 pp. [Paperback, wrappers missing, title-page defective.]

> *Marginalia*: Approximately two hundred words of marginal notations by Clemens; most comments and underlinings occur in chapter 12. Clemens connects Warder's philosophy with that of Mary Baker Eddy.

> *Location*: University of Rochester Library, Rochester, New York. (Purchased in 1940 from Goodspeed's bookshop in Boston.)

> *Copy examined*: A Xerox copy of the title page and a description of Clemens' marginalia were supplied to me by the University of Rochester Library. The fragile condition of this volume

does not permit the photocopying of its annotations.

A disparaging review—"About Cities in the Sun"— survives in the Mark Twain Papers at Berkeley (DV357) to display Mark Twain's amusement with the book. He planned to publish this piece, and even penciled notes to the editor in the margins of his manuscript, but it never appeared in print. Mainly he pokes fun at his fellow Missourian for taking literally St. John's vision of the New Jerusalem as located in the sun (Book of Revelation 21: 1–27), especially Warder's efforts to construct a precise picture of the heavenly city. Mark Twain's essay also derides Senator Chauncey M. Depew for endorsing "this turbulent philosopher."

Mark Twain entered the courtroom of critical opinion as though each of these twenty volumes were on trial and he were authorized to prosecute a vigorous case against the untalented author. In Mark Twain's marginalia and unpublished reviews he thus inverted the type of literary criticism practiced by his friend Howells; while Howells passed judgment on the upper crust of literature,[25] Clemens rummaged through the bottom shelves of the literary bookcase, finding and ridiculing the "exquisitely bad."

The satiric literary criticism Clemens yearned to write required a healthy dose of animosity, and he found it easy to work himself up to the proper pitch of indignation at the failings of these upstart writers. Why he carried so few of his abortive "reviews" into print is not clear: he may have sensed the unfairness of subjecting these pitiable publications to his mocking scorn; or his interest may have waned after an initial encounter with the book produced his marginalia or fragmentary manuscript and drained his hostility; or perhaps he sensed that he could not adequately educate the public to appreciate the sublimely poor in literature (as the relative failure of his "A Cure for the Blues"[26] seems to prove). But whatever the considerations that kept most of these sarcasms private, his travesty "reviews" of candidates for his "Library of Literary Hogwash" periodically whetted his critical implements in anticipation of the larger game he chose to carve up in print and in private correspondence—Harte, Austen, Eliot, Scott, Cooper, and Goldsmith.

Notes

1. Notebook 39 (dated 1896), TS, p. 15, Mark Twain Papers, University of California, Berkeley—hereafter cited as MTP. The Editor of that collection, Frederick Anderson, influenced the direction and content of this essay very considerably.

2. *Mark Twain as Critic* (Baltimore: Johns Hopkins Press, 1967), p. 1.

3. *Mark Twain / Man and Legend* (Indianapolis: Bobbs-Merrill, 1943), pp. 207–208.

4. *Mark Twain and John Bull / The British Connection* (Bloomington: Indiana U Press, 1970), p. 296.

5. The volume is now in the Henry W. and Albert A. Berg Collection, New York Public Library. Clemens' notations on its pages initially disparage the characters and dialogue, then reveal a grudging admiration for certain aspects of the novel, and finally become openly complimentary.

6. *The Literary Apprenticeship of Mark Twain* (Urbana: U of Illinois Press, 1950), p. 139.

7. "Three Thousand Years Among the Microbes," published in *Mark Twain's Which Was the Dream? And Other Symbolic Writings of the Later Years*, ed. John S. Tuckey (Berkeley and Los Angeles: U. of California Press, 1967), p. 460.

8. The Willard S. Morse Collection, Yale Collection of American Literature, Beinecke Library, Yale University.

9. TS p. 29, MTP. Mark Twain added a few variations in telling about this incident in chapter 32 of *A Tramp Abroad* (1880).

10. "Hogwash," *Galaxy* 9 (Jun 1870), 862, "Favors from Correspondents," *Galaxy*, 10 (Nov. 1870), 735.

11. The volume is in the Mark Twain Papers at Berkeley.

12. Quoted from a dictation copy kept by Isabel V. Lyon, Clemens' secretary (MTP).

13. The present writer has compiled an annotated catalog of Clemens' library books and marginalia in "The Library and Reading

of Samuel L. Clemens," unpublished doctoral dissertation, U of California, Berkeley, 1974. Henry Nash Smith directed this research.

14. Katy Leary, the Clemenses' maid and (later) housekeeper, selected and kept as mementos approximately ninety volumes from Clemens' personal library after he died in 1910. I have described the contents and the provenance of these books, now known as the Antenne-Dorrance Collection, in "The Dispersal of Samuel L. Clemens' Library Books," *Resources for American Literary Study*, 5 (Autumn 1975), 147–165. Robert and Katharine Antenne, co-owners of this collection along with James and Mary Dorrance, cooperated graciously with my research.

15. *Adventures of Huckleberry Finn / An Annotated Text, Backgrounds and Sources, Essays in Criticism*, ed. Sculley Bradley, Richmond Croom Beatty, and E. Hudson Long (NY: Norton, 1962), p. 252.

16. *Mark Twain to Mrs. Fairbanks*, ed. Dixon Wecter (San Marino, Calif.: Huntington Library, 1949), pp. 134–136.

17. Clemens to John Horner, 12 Jan 1906, dictation copy by Clemens' secretary, Isabel V. Lyon (MTP); quoted in Walter Blair's *Mark Twain & Huck Finn* (Berkeley and Los Angeles: U of California Press, 1960), p. 212.

18. See, for example, Walter Blair, *Mark Twain & Huck Finn*, pp. 209–213, 406 n. 13; *The Art of Huckleberry Finn / Text, Sources, Criticisms*, ed. Hamlin Hill and Walter Blair (San Francisco: Chandler, 1962), pp. 445–451; *Adventures of Huckleberry Finn*, ed. Bradley, Beatty, and Long. pp. 253–254; and *Huckleberry Finn / Text, Sources, and Criticisms*, ed. Kenneth S. Lynn (NY: Harcourt, Brace & World, 1961), pp. 156–160.

19. According to the preface in *A Cure for the Blues*, ed. Charles V. S. Borst (Rutland, Vt.: Charles E. Tuttle, 1964), pp. vii–viii, which seems mistaken in dating the incident as occurring in February 1884. Borst says that the Reverend Joseph H. Twichell subsequently obtained six copies of *The Enemy Conquered* in New Haven for Clemens' private amusement, but that Clemens somehow misplaced these and appealed to Cable for another copy in 1889. "I have searched everywhere and cannot find a vestige of that pamphlet," Clemens wrote to Cable. "I possess not a single book which I would not sooner have parted with."

20. *Mark Twain, Business Man*, ed. Samuel C. Webster (Boston: Little, Brown, 1946), p. 233.

21. Notebook 29, TS p. 6, MTP; Notebook 31, TS p. 17, MTP.

22. "Mark Twain's Failures in Comedy and The Enemy Conquered," *Georgia Review*, 13 (Winter 1959), 424–436.

23. *Mark Twain-Howells Letters*, ed. Henry Nash Smith and William M. Gibson (Cambridge: Harvard U Press, 1960), p. 209—hereafter cited as MTHL.

24. MS in MTP (Paine 59).

25. For the most part Clemens let Howells and other established critics take care of what he once—in 1887—called "high & fine literature" (MTHL, p. 587). Though he was grateful to Howells for introducing him to such arrivals of talent as William Allen White's *In Our Town* (MTHL, pp. 808, 814–815), Clemens' most fervent praise tended to be lavished on minor authors whom he had the pleasure of "discovering" himself: writers who published magazine short stories, out-of-the-way guidebooks, unnoticed novels, overlooked poems. Phoebe Brown's autobiography, for instance, never published and still in manuscript, kept him up far into the night with its quaint charm (MTHL, p. 381); and the issuance of E. W. Howe's *The Story of a Country Town* seemed to him an unheralded event that deserved congratulations (see C. E. Schorer, "Mark Twain's Criticism of *The Story of a Country Town*," *American Literature*, 27 [Mar 1955], 109–112).

26. The publication in 1893 of this mocking analysis of Samuel Watson Royston's forgotten *The Enemy Conquered* (1845) drew scarcely any public attention.

The American Claimant:
Reclamation of a Farce

Clyde Grimm

A lthough Mark Twain's *The American Claimant* (1892)
is a hastily and crudely fabricated novel, it is an
interesting and significant work for at least two
reasons. First, having been adapted by Twain from a farce
drama written in collaboration with William Dean Howells,
the novel provides an opportunity for study of Twain's
imaginative conversion of pointless humor into meaningful
satire. Second, because it reiterates with little ambiguity
political and social themes which recur throughout Twain's
work, the novel provides a clearer as well as more mature
statement on cultural issues with which Twain had been
concerned for years.

The play from which the novel grew has a curious history
of its own, certain aspects of which warrant recapitulation.[1]
Twain and Howells never intended more than to amuse
themselves and, they hoped, a large audience by creating a
ridiculously impractical schemer who would strut and fret his
hour upon the stage in a series of ludicrous antics signifying
nothing. Just as he had based his Colonel Sellers character in
The Gilded Age (1873) on his eccentric cousin James Lampton,
Twain proposed that they base the central figure of their play
on his brother, Orion Clemens, whose fantastic schemes and
inventions seemed rich material for a farce. Evidently, by the
summer of 1878 Howells had become interested enough to

American Quarterly 19 (Spring 1967): 86–103.

start on such a play, referred to in their correspondence as both *The Steam Generator* and *Orme's Motor*, but he did not finish it. Twain continued enthusiastically to urge the project and in the spring of 1880 proposed as a model for the central character still another relative, a more distant cousin, Jesse Leathers, who was not only an inventor of laughable gadgets but also the current bearer of a longstanding family claim to the English peerage. By September 1881, as indicated in the following sketch sent to Howells, Twain's imagination had fused all three relatives into one character:

> Now I think the play for you to write would be one entitled "Col. Mulberry Sellers in Age" (75)—with that fool of a Lafayette Hawkins (aged 50) still sticking to him & believing in him & calling him "my lord" (S. Being American earl of Durham)—& has cherished his delusion until he & his chuckle-headed household believe he *is* the rightful earl & that he is being shamefully treated by the house of Lords. He is a "specialist" & a "scientist" in various ways; makes collections of pebbles & brickbats & discourses garrulously & ignorantly over them & projects original "theories" &c. Has a lot of impossible inventions, which cost somebody a good deal & then blow up & cripple disinterested parties, or poison them.

The Sellers character, originally bearing the peculiarities of only James Lampton, would thus acquire those of Orion Clemens and Jesse Leathers as well. Twain's enthusiasm seems to have blinded him to the potential danger of overloading one character with so many diverse idiosyncrasies: though the character might be original and extravagantly ridiculous, the play accommodating the number and variety of his antics might prove formless.

After having shown continued but ineffectual interest for several years, Howells proposed in April 1883 that they make definite plans to write the play in October and assured Twain that their idea had "the making of a good comedy in it without doubt." However, when in November and December of that year the two authors finally put the play together in short but intense flurries of effort, they produced what Howells less than enthusiastically called "an extreme farce." The inferiority of "extreme farce" to "good comedy," though difficult to assess precisely, no doubt contributed to Howell's eventual loss of confidence in the play and his withdrawal from arrangements to stage it.

In August 1884, apparently discouraged and exasperated by faltering negotiations to produce the play, Twain declared to Charles Webster, his nephew and the manager of his publishing firm, "I'm going to elaborate it into a novel," thus revealing for the first time an intention it would take him seven years to make good.[2] At this same time, however, John T. Raymond, who had starred as Sellers in a successful stage version of *The Gilded Age* in 1876, promised to produce the play in September. Though Raymond agreed to accept it without alterations, he strongly urged excision of the claimant idea and one of Sellers' most incredible delusions, a scheme for reviving the dead called "materialization." He particularly objected to the latter because he felt it made Sellers appear a lunatic, and Raymond did not interpret the character's eccentricity that strongly. Howells at this time regarded both the claimant idea and materialization as "vital portions" of the play and opposed their excision. Twain, though granting that "Raymond's ideas are good," nevertheless rejected his advice because it would require too extensive rewriting. When Raymond peremptorily backed out of the arrangement, declining at the last minute to produce the play without revision, Twain once more heatedly vowed to "turn it into a novel."[3] There is no telling of course what shape a novel written at this time would have taken, but the unrestrained exuberance with which Twain seems to have exercised his imagination on the Sellers character and his reluctance to tone down the farce persuade one that the adaptation was fortunately postponed.

In May 1886 negotiations for production became as farcical as the play itself. Howells had reversed his judgment and now agreed with Raymond that the Sellers character seemed a lunatic and needed a good deal of modification; he believed too that the claimant idea was not sufficiently developed to be retained. And, finally, suggesting its lack of form, he lamented, "There is nothing in the play but the idea of Sellers' character, and a lot of comic situations." Though he had urged these views on Twain, he had neither absolutely refused to have the play staged nor effectively discouraged negotiations. Only after Twain had signed a contract with A.P. Burbank, who immediately leased Daniel Frohman's theater in New York, did Howells firmly decide against staging; the belated triumph of his misgivings cost each of them $500 (for the theater lease) and indefinitely committed the acting rights to Burbank. Twain persisted alone, however, and financed several performances in September 1887. Entitled *The American Claimant* or *Mulberry Sellers Ten Years Later*, with Burbank in the role of Sellers, the play was as poorly received as both Raymond and Howells had anticipated and was soon withdrawn, never to be staged again.[4]

Surprisingly, in spite of his earlier defection and the subsequent failure of the play on the stage, Howells made one final effort to reclaim it. In January 1890 he reported showing the play to James A. Herne, the prominent actor and playwright, and discussing with him a reconstruction of it. Confirming earlier opinions of the play's weaknesses, Herne recommended excision of the materialization idea, a general toning down of Sellers' eccentricity, and creation of a new plot. However, the proposal aroused neither author's enthusiasm, chiefly because of the financial complications caused by Burbank's possession of the acting rights, and their collaborative undertaking collapsed once and for all after more than a decade. Early in 1891 Twain made good his earlier vows to turn the play into a novel. Ironically, as A.B. Paine has noted, Augustin Daly, the famous producer, thought that the novel might be turned into a very good play, though nothing came of his proposal to do so.[5] Considering its history, especially each author's contribution and relative enthusiasm, it seems a final irony that the play, entitled

Colonel Sellers as a Scientist, now appears as one of *The Complete Plays of William Dean Howells*! [6]

Perusal of the play confirms Howells' objection that there is nothing to it but character and situation. The main "plot" focuses on Sellers the zany inventor, who amid impoverished surroundings displays a variety of fantastic gadgets from which he hopes to make a fortune; ironically, a modest, practical device in which he has shown little interest ultimately proves successful and redeems him. In one underplot Sellers lays claim to an English earldom but gratuitously renounces it in the end. A second underplot, the conventional romance, brings together with unusually little difficulty Sellers' daughter and the young English heir, who also gratuitously renounces his claim. The claimant idea contributes nothing essential to the action and as an addition to Sellers' eccentricity is superfluous. Another alleged weakness, the materialization idea, provides some incidental satire and also some farcical humor when Sellers twice expresses horror at the thought that a living girl is in love with what he supposes to be a "materialized" ghost. As for its contribution to Sellers' alleged lunacy, his belief in materialization does not appear any more incredible or insane than his confidence in a fire-making fire extinguisher, which none of the play's critics objected to and which Daniel Frohman even considered its only amusing element.[7] Neither materialization nor any of Sellers' other inventions or delusions seems inappropriate for "extreme farce," which after all seldom invites serious rational scrutiny. The play suffers most from the formal weaknesses sensed by Howells and Herne: its thinness of plot and the arbitrary employment of supporting elements.

When in May 1891 Howells inquired about the relation of the new novel to their collaborative work, Twain replied, "I found I couldn't use the play—I had departed too far from its lines when I came to look at it. I thought I might get a great deal of dialogue out of it, but I got only 15 loosely written pages—they saved me half a day's work. It was the cursing phonograph [another of Sellers' inventions]. There was abundance of good dialogue, but it couldn't be fitted into the new conditions of the story." Although he borrowed little verbatim, Twain nevertheless retained all of the basic elements of the farce. However in comparing the novel with the play, it is impossible to overemphasize the transforming effect of the "new conditions" Twain refers to. He had radically altered his view of the story material and its significance and had transformed it from meaningless farce into thoroughgoing political and social satire. In doing so, he showed remarkable ingenuity in adapting and integrating those elements which Howells and the others had most objected to. He revamped the claimant plot by expanding Sellers' role as a would-be English peer and also by adding for ironic contrast a fully developed complementary plot tracing the English heir's attempts to become an American democrat. Sellers' "lunacy" remains the same in terms of his devotion to fantastic projects but gains special significance in the new context. Even the materialization scheme becomes an effective vehicle for satire. Yet in spite of its ingenious thematic unity, the novel suffers from Twain's haste in putting it together in only "71 days."[8] For example, the new episodes devoted to the young Englishman's adventures, comprising roughly a third of the novel, are crudely inserted as a virtual block in the middle of the Sellers material. The satire in these episodes especially but in others as well is heavy-handed, as Twain's telling predominates over his showing.

Notwithstanding its shortcomings as art, however, *The American Claimant* is significant for the light it throws on Twain's political and social thought. Repeating themes and devices which appear in many of his earlier works, it invites comparisons which illuminate major cultural issues which preoccupied him for many years and indicates the direction in which, at the age of fifty-six, he sought or had found resolutions. Most apparent and interesting is Twain's recapitulation of the theme of disenchantment with democracy which he had employed just a few years earlier in

A Connecticut Yankee in King Arthur's Court (1889). The disillusioned figure in *The American Claimant* is not, however, like Hank Morgan, a native American raised on common-sense utilitarianism and democratic political principles; rather he is a young English nobleman, Viscount Berkeley, who has been raised as the heir to the Earldom of Rossmore. Twain assigns Berkeley the "candor, kindliness, honesty, sincerity, simplicity, [and] modesty" which suggest innate nobility of character antecedent to social status or political rank.[9] But like Prince Edward in *The Prince and the Pauper* (1882) and King Arthur in *A Connecticut Yankee*, two other characters of innate nobility, Berkeley is also naive and inexperienced, ignorant of many realities. He has been infected with the radical political theories of Lord Tanzy of Tollmache (whose Germanic name connotes insanity) and has determined to renounce his aristocratic station, emigrate to America and make his way by ability alone. The lesson taught by his subsequent adventures is two-fold: first, that in spite of its professed equalitarianism American democracy is a corrupt sham which perpetuates inequality and changes only its bases and the processes by which it is established; second, that the abstract principle of equality, no matter how sincerely adopted and earnestly pursued, will not produce the sentiment or feeling of equality, because it is contrary to human nature.

In America, though satisfied by the absence of the artificial titles peculiar to Europe, Berkeley is greatly disturbed by the misuse of two "titles" which he continues to believe valid as legitimate marks of genuine distinction: the titles "lady" and "gentleman." His landlady warns him that in America these titles are universally applied and that to deny them to anyone is a fighting matter. When the landlady's daughter asserts that "'everybody calls himself a lady or gentleman, and thinks he *is*, and don't care what anybody else thinks him, so long as he don't say it out loud,'" Berkeley's reaction is the obvious one: that calling oneself a lady or gentleman is not equivalent to being one. Another boarder, a Mr. Barrow, intrudes to explain the difference in usage between England and America:

Over there, twenty thousand people in a million elect
themselves gentlemen and ladies, and the nine hundred and
eighty thousand *accept* that decree and swallow the affront
which it puts upon them. Why, if they didn't accept it it
wouldn't *be* an election; it would be a dead letter, and have
no force at all. Over here the twenty thousand would-be
exclusives come up to the polls and vote themselves to be
ladies and gentlemen. But the thing doesn't stop there. The
nine hundred and eighty thousand come and vote
themselves to be ladies and gentlemen *too*, and that elects
the whole nation. Since the whole million vote themselves
ladies and gentlemen, there is no question about that
election. It *does* make absolute equality, and there is no
fiction about it; while over yonder the *inequality* (by decree
of the infinitely feeble, and consent of the infinitely strong)
is also absolute—as real and absolute as our equality.
(p. 93)

The irony of this ostensible glorification of America over
England is that in neither case does self-appointed gentility
appear real and absolute or valid, and the irony strikes with
greater impact against the *universality* of presumption and
self-aggrandizement in America, a sham not differing in kind
from that of England but differing colossally in extent or
degree. Democratic leveling perverts the meaning of "equality"
and by mocking the labels for superior intelligence, character,
education and conduct tends to obliterate legitimate moral
distinctions or gradations among human beings.

Berkeley finds, moreover, that the equalitarianism implied
by this specious use of language is only nominal after all, for
inequality and deference to rank or status are widespread in
America. Immediately after arriving, he is disturbed by the
deferential treatment he receives because of his English title.
Adopting a pseudonym to avoid further such treatment, he
tries to find a job. Though competent for government work, he
fails to obtain even a modest clerkship. "Competency," Twain
sneers, "was no recommendation; political backing, without
competency, was worth six of it. He was glaringly English, and
that was necessarily against him in the political center of a
nation where both parties prayed for the Irish cause [home

rule] on the housetop and blasphemed it in the cellar" (p. 85). The platitude that America is the land of unlimited opportunities is further belied by the selfish exclusivism of organized labor, which prevents Berkeley from finding employment elsewhere. He begins to realize that he is the victim of a discriminatory system just as real, just as impenetrable and, ironically, just as oppressive or tyrannous as any in Europe, "an aristocracy of the ins as opposed to the outs" (p. 108).

In the boarding-house where he resides, a microcosm of American society, Berkeley also observes travesties of rank and deference typical of democracy and records them in his diary:

> There is respect, there is deference here, but it doesn't fall to my share. It is lavished on two men. One of them is a portly man of middle age who is a retired plumber. Everybody is pleased to have that man's notice. He's full of pomp and circumstance and self-complacency and bad grammar, and at table he is Sir Oracle, and when he opens his mouth not any dog in the kennel barks. The other person is a policeman at the capitol-building. He represents the government. The deference paid to these men is not so very far short of that which is paid to an earl in England, though the method of it differs. Not so much courtliness, but the deference is all there. (p. 107)

A much more ominous example of popular deference occurs after Berkeley conquers the boarding-house bully in a fist-fight. The gang of boarders quickly transfer their fawning adulation from the bully to him, and though he had hoped for their comradeship, he senses that this sudden acceptance has been won on terms which prevent his feeling pride or satisfaction in it. He feels degraded by this deference because it seems nothing more than the instinctive acknowledgment by animals of the superior strength or brute force of another animal; as a consequence, he considers himself worse off than the prodigal son, who fed swine but "didn't have to chum with them" (p. 114).

Twain's frequent employment of zoological metaphors to describe the boarding-house and its residents (e.g., swine, barking dogs in a kennel, hive) suggests the brutishness of this microcosm of "free and open" democratic society. This image is confirmed by one incident in particular. Everyone applauds and abets the landlord's humiliation of one of the boarders, who is without work and therefore unable to pay his keep. In response to Berkeley's puzzlement at this cruel, inhumane behavior, the cynical Barrow exclaims, "'Don't you know that the wounded deer is always attacked and killed by its companions and friends?'" (p. 105). Whereas Berkeley had thought that "'equality ought to make men noble-minded'" (p.102), his experience suggests that on the contrary the "natural" society of a democracy depresses rather than elevates character and conduct by encouraging or condoning free exercise of the most bestial instincts. This dog-eat-dog, survival-of-the-fittest environment, dominated by the physically or economically strong, confirms the absolute travesty of calling everyone "lady" or "gentleman," for the moral superiority which these titles ought to denote is neither displayed, sought for, nor appreciated in this society of "common men."

Almost from the beginning of his tenure in America, Berkeley had been aware of a discrepancy between the principles he idealistically espoused and the sentiments he actually felt. "The equality of men was not yet a reality to him," Twain explains, "it was only a theory; the *mind* perceived, but the *man* failed to feel it" (p. 94). Ashamed of his continuing involuntary resistance and determined to overcome it, Berkeley struggled through the series of experiences summarized above, trying all the while to resolve not only the conflict he felt within himself but also the glaring contradiction he observed between the principles and the practice of Americans. At last, in the company of Barrow, he attends a meeting of a Mechanics' Debating Club and hears a tirade against "unearned titles, property, and privileges," which the speaker calls upon all the monarchs and nobles of the world to renounce. Though his entire experience in America has exposed the hypocrisy or delusion of such views and his own feelings continue to oppose them, he applauds the speech, dutifully struggling to persuade himself. Barrow, however, immediately and sharply condemns the mechanic's remarks as "'an idiotic damned speech'" (p. 122) which wholly ignores human nature and advocates what only a fool would do. Though opposed to the principle of inherited rank or privilege, he asserts that the speaker or any other man, including himself, would unhesitatingly accept an earldom if it were offered and that preaching renunciation is therefore hypocritical nonsense. This candid opinion from his American associate induces Berkeley to give up his unnatural struggle to become a "democrat" and to accept his heritage:

> He had been born an aristocrat, he had been a democrat for a time, he was now an aristocrat again. He marvelled to find that this final change was not merely intellectual, it had invaded his feeling; and he also marvelled to note that this feeling seemed a good deal less artificial than any he had entertained in his system for a long time. He could also have noted, if he had thought of it, that his bearing had stiffened, over night, that his chin had lifted itself a shade. (p. 128)

Berkeley thus resumes his inherited identity as an aristocrat much as Prince Edward and King Arthur do in earlier novels. It is important to note that in his case as in theirs the rank or title signifying superiority is accompanied by real distinction of character, breeding and conduct and therefore, unlike the titles and ranks adopted or conferred in America, has a legitimate moral basis.

This need not suggest that Twain sanctions the ordinary or traditional concept of hereditary aristocracy; in fact, through Barrow, he repudiates it. Yet he does dramatize a concept of natural aristocracy, in which innate nobility and superior breeding entitle one to social distinction. Not only do men naturally fail in the practice of equalitarianism, they also naturally fail to display an equal capacity for or inclination toward intelligent, moral behavior. Reminiscent of James

Fenimore Cooper's, Twain's chief criticism of democracy in America is not that men seek and society confers distinction but that the natural aristocrat is dispossessed and ignored in favor of ridiculous, corrupt and even brutal shams.

The remaining episodes of the novel, which are dominated by Colonel Sellers, develop these themes with variations peculiar to his special temperament and background. Though some pure farce remains, Twain did a remarkably thorough job of converting pointless elements from the play into meaningful and cohesive satire for the novel.

One of the most significant revisions concerns the claimant idea. As noted earlier, the idea derives from a family legend, which Twain first learned of from his mother, Jane Lampton Clemens, when he was a boy. The Lamptons believed themselves descendants of the Lambtons of England who had become Earls of Durham; Jesse Leathers, Twain's distant cousin, went so far as to proclaim himself the rightful earl, the victim of a mistaken succession several generations in the past.[10] Though Twain often made light of these claims to aristocratic lineage, the frequency of his allusions to them and his repeated employment of similar themes in his fiction suggest that he was compelled by the idea more than he preferred to admit. Further evidence of this is the curious modification which he made, over a decade, in Sellers' claimancy. In the sketch of Sellers which he sent to Howells in 1881, Twain clearly indicates that the claim is a delusion with no basis in fact and that Sellers is utterly foolish in believing himself the rightful earl. In the play itself, however, Sellers provides a vague but plausible explanation of his claim and he acknowledges that he is only third in line among the heirs to the title. Thus, in the play, neither the claim nor Sellers remains quite as absurd as in Twain's original conception. In the novel Sellers once again believes himself to be the rightful earl, having inherited his claim upon the death of his distant Arkansaw relative Simon Lathers, the former "earl." But of greatest significance is that Berkeley's father, the Earl of Rossmore, admits that a mistake in succession occurred years ago and, though he does not believe the courts would uphold it, confirms the moral right of the American claimant. What this radical change may suggest of Twain's attitude toward his own family's claims is conjectural, but its effect on the characterization of Sellers is quite plain. Sellers in the novel cannot be ridiculed for believing himself an heir or claimant to the peerage; Twain made him, in at least one sense a legitimate pretender. Thus, whatever else may remain laughable about Sellers, this particular element of his characterization invites serious consideration.

As a matter of fact, no matter how ridiculous many of his antics appear, Sellers is one of the most "sympathetic" adult characters Twain created. Mrs. Sellers describes her husband as "the same old scheming, generous, good-hearted, moonshiny, hopeful, no-account failure he always was" (p. 21). For all his absurd impracticalities, hair-brained schemes and romantic pretensions, Sellers is a moral aristocrat, whose innate nobility matches that of Berkeley. This is best illustrated by his impractical but humane patronage of two old Negroes who had been slaves of the family and who wandered back after the war "free" but decrepit and helpless. Though the Sellerses were themselves nearly destitute, his wife reports, the Colonel passionately rejected her plea for practicality:

> "Turn them out?—and they've come to me just as confidential and trusting as—as—why, Polly, I must have *bought* that confidence some time or other a long time ago, and given my note, so to speak—you don't get such things as a *gift*—and how am I going to go back on a debt like that? And you see, they're so poor, and old, and friendless. . ." (p. 23)

His innate humanity and his breeding as a southern gentleman (albeit an impecunious one) make him incapable of betraying a moral obligation, incurred in the prewar South, and of exploiting the cash nexus established by the North's victory as the prevailing basis of human relations.

Neither the crassness and cynicism of the age nor his personal disappointments alter his character, his temperament or his basic outlook. Yet he is not naive. On the contrary, he is well aware of unpleasant actualities and is capable of perfect candor. For example, he is momentarily incredulous when Hawkins denies seeking office or preferment: "Now look here, old friend, I know the human race; and I now that when a man comes to Washington, I don't care if it's from heaven, let alone Cherokee Strip, it's because he *wants* something" (p. 160). Sellers likewise candidly appraises his own failures as "an epitome of human ambition, and struggle, and the outcome: you aim for the palace and get drowned in the sewer" (p. 17). In spite of such insights, his prevailing mood, which only rarely lapses, is one of buoyant optimism, bright fancy, noble idealism and grandiose dreams. The key to this curious contradiction between his "realism" and his "romanticism" and to his unique personality is suggested by Mrs. Sellers:

> People who don't rightly know him may think he is commonplace, but to my mind he is one of the most unusual men I ever saw. As for suddenness and capacity in imagining things, his beat don't exist, I reckon. As like as not it wouldn't have occurred to anybody else to name this poor rat-trap Rossmore Towers, but it just come natural to him. Well, no doubt it's a blessed thing to have an imagination that can always make you satisfied, no matter how you are fixed. (p. 39)

Imagination is the key to Sellers' personality, as it is to the personalities of a number of other Twain characters. Like Tom Sawyer, for example, he "lets on" that his house with its impoverished furnishings is Rossmore Towers, a manor appropriate for the noble rank he "lets on" to possess. His illusions and pretensions, like these of Tom Canty in *The Prince and the Pauper* and Sandy Carteloise in *A Connecticut Yankee*, are attempts to sustain ideals and ennobling visions which transcend sordid and depressing realities. Sellers consciously chooses to indulge an image of himself and his surroundings commensurate with his own high moral ideals and aspirations. His awareness and acknowledgment of reality distinguish his imaginations from mere sentimental or naive delusions, and the repellent sordidness of that reality justifies his romanticism as a perceptual mode of adjustment which is not only satisfying but perhaps even necessary to his moral survival. Moreover, this adjustment may reflect Twain's estimate of the greatest felicity attainable in the democratic culture which emerged in America after the Civil War.

In any case, the new context demands a thoroughgoing reappraisal of Sellers' eccentricities as having a good deal more significance than they display in the farce. One peculiarity shared by both Sellers and his daughter is a culturally split personality. The Colonel's co-existent obsessions with Franklinian inventions and with dreams of an earldom suggest that he is a product of two different cultures. Likewise Sally Sellers, Twain explains, "was as practical and democratic as the Lady Gwendolen Sellers [her alter ego] was romantic and aristocratic" (p. 49). The Colonel himself defines this duality as "intensely and practically American by inhaled nationalism, and at the same time intensely and aristocratically European by inherited nobility of blood" (p. 50). The essence of this dichotomy, variants of which appear throughout Twain's work (e.g., Huck Finn and Tom Sawyer), may be reduced to the following terms: on the one hand, matter-of-fact "realism" (which usually insists upon the sordid and ugly), utilitarian practicality, and democratic political and social sentiments; on the other hand, romantic illusion and pretense, chivalric idealism and heroic aspiration, and an aristocratic sense of distinctions and gradations among men. With Sellers as with Berkeley the aristocratic identity is innate and "natural," whereas the democratic identity is "inhaled" and in a sense artificial.[11] Berkeley inhales the intoxicating abstractions of Tanzy, Sellers those of the culture in which he was raised. But the actualities of this culture conflict with their natural instincts and repel them. Most important, however, is that both Sellers and Berkeley display genuine nobility of character which distinguishes them from the common level of men who represent democratic culture and which vindicates their natural instincts, justifying both Berkeley's resumption of his aristocratic station and Sellers' aspiration to it.

The genuine or natural aristocrat must be distinguished from the sham, the legitimate from the presumptuous and false pretender. The distinction is crucial throughout Twain's work (e.g., the "King" and the "Duke" in *Huckleberry Finn*). In addition to the shams already noted in the Berkeley episodes, he satirizes in the Sellers episodes the vulgar pretensions of the *nouveaux riches* who dominate the school which Sally attends; Colonel Sellers' description recalls Twain's satiric portrayal of the Parvenus in *The Gilded Age* and his attack on the southern "she-college" in *Life on the Mississippi* (1883):

> Rowena-Ivanhoe College is the selectest and the most aristocratic seat of learning for young ladies in our country. Under no circumstances can a girl get in there unless she is either very rich and fashionable or can prove four generations of what may be called American nobility. Castellated college-buildings—towers and turrets and an imitation moat—and everything about the place named out of Sir Walter Scott's books and redolent of royalty and state and style; and all the richest girls keep phaetons, and coachmen in livery, and riding-horses, with English grooms in plug hats and tight-buttoned coats, and top-boots, and a whip-handle without any whip to it, to ride sixty-three feet behind them—(p. 37)

Sally Sellers, of course, is to be distinguished from these snobs; indeed she recognizes their corruptness and matches their disdain for her poverty with her own scorn for their moral bankruptcy.

Twain does not, however, limit his satire to the shams and pretensions of the Gilded Age alone; he enlarges the scope and significance of his criticism of American culture by broadening its historical perspective. He does so by once again transforming none-too-promising materials retained from the farce. The first of these is the "deadly chromos" which adorn the Sellers household:

> Some of these terrors were landscapes, some libelled the sea, some were ostensible portraits, all were crimes. All the portraits were recognizable as dead Americans of distinction, and yet, through labelling added by a daring hand, they were all doing duty here as "Earls of Rossmore." The newest one had left the works as Andrew Jackson, but was doing its best as "Simon Lathers Lord Rossmore, Present Earl." (p.12)

It is significant that the Lathers "pretender," a vulgar Arkansaw "blatherskite" who is killed by a falling log in the drunken chaos of a smoke house-raising on the frontier, is identified specifically with Andrew Jackson, the symbol of radical democracy and hero of the common man—but also, from a conservative point of view, the arch villain responsible for the corruption of government and the degradation of culture in America. By this symbolic identification Twain enlarges the significance of the Lathers story to national and historical proportions. The Lathers-Jackson alignment suggests the political revolution by which the common classes ascended to power during Jackson's pre-Civil War administration; the addition of Rossmore to this alignment suggests the continuing economic, social and moral revolution by which they aspire to respectability and further dominance of the culture. Once again, however, it is necessary to distinguish the legitimate pretender from the presumptuous sham. Though Berkeley's father confirms Lathers' moral right to the title, doubting only his legal claim, it would seem that in fact only his legal claim could have any validity, for the clamorous incongruity between his vulgarity and the nobility signified by the title precludes any genuine moral right. Yet Sellers' pretension not only retains the legal basis of Lathers' claim but also gains moral justification from his superior character. His dispossession of an English title, however, is less significant thematically than his dispossession of status in his native country, of which more will be said below.

Dixon Wecter has noted one of Andrew Jackson's vanities which may have been Twain's inspiration both for the chromo device discussed above and for another use of chromos in the Berkeley episodes of the novel; Wecter reports that "an artist named Earl was hired to live at the White House during the eight years of his Administration, and do nothing but paint one picture after another of the President."[12] Such a fact would have been widely publicized in Whig circles, both during and after Jackson's tenure in office, and Twain, whose family's affiliation with the Whig party is well documented, would almost certainly have known of it. The chromo of Jackson on Sellers' wall might well have been inspired by one of Earl's portraits and intended as a direct satiric allusion. The connection between his biographical item about Jackson and the other chromo episode may appear farfetched but, if not intended, is an astonishing coincidence. The only work that Berkeley can find in America is with two old hack artists, one a retired sea captain and the other a retired shoemaker, producing chromos which depict ordinary mechanics and other commoners in absurdly grandiose postures aping great historical figures like Napoleon. This portrait-making commissioned, as it were, by the common man is a travesty of the portrait-painting by great artists of the past under the commission of European royalty and nobility. Though it is a lucrative business, Berkeley's participation clearly indicates the triumph of desperation and necessity over pride and integrity, for he knows that he is no artist and that the chromos are vulgar parodies. His experience may epitomize the plight of the natural aristocrat in America: he is reduced to prostituting himself for the self-aggrandizement of his moral and intellectual inferiors. The vanity of the mechanics and the others who pose for mock-heroic portraits is like that of their hero Jackson, who commissioned endless and no doubt heroic images of himself. In producing these shams Berkeley is doing, in essence, exactly as Jackson's kept artist did, and though Berkeley has not yet succeeded to the title, he will one day be, again like Jackson's portrayer, an "Earl."

Twain further enlarges the historical perspective of the novel by adapting Sellers' materialization scheme. Although the incidental satire achieved by this device remains much the same in the novel as in the play (e.g., Sellers' intention to revive "the trained statesmen of all ages and all climes, and furnish this country with a Congress that knows enough to come in out of the rain. . ." [p. 29]), Sellers' mistaken identification of the young Englishman as a materialized ghost, while continuing to provide farcical humor, functions in the novel as satire also and contributes much to the development of primary themes. Twain expanded the function of this device by first of all complicating the confusion of identities. Early in the novel Berkeley escapes from a hotel fire dressed in the clothes of a notorious one-armed frontier bank robber, One-Armed Pete, who is burned to death in the fire. Dressed as a cowboy, Berkeley receives the deference of both ordinary citizens and government officials but mistakenly assumes that it is again due to his English rank. In fact, however, they defer to him not as a European noble but as a peculiarly American equivalent—the "noble" Westerner. The full significance of this misidentification evolves later when Colonel Sellers contrives a burlesque theory of evolution: "Every man is made up of hereditaries, long descended atoms and particles of his ancestors. This present materialization is incomplete. We have only brought it down to perhaps the beginning of this century" (p.164). By making Berkeley an ancestor of One-Armed Pete, Sellers' theory ironically suggests that an English lord is the proper historical antecedent of an American Frontier outlaw and, by extension, that European aristocracy is the origin and counterpart of the corrupt "peerage" that dominates America. Berkeley's obviously superior character and breeding, however, make ridiculous and untenable any such attempt to identify him with Pete. Even Sellers, who had planned to capture the bank robber and collect a reward, acknowledges the injustice of delivering Berkeley to the law to pay for the crimes of his alleged "posterity":

> In him there's atoms of priests, soldiers, crusaders, poets,
> and sweet and gracious women—all kinds and conditions of
> folk who trod this earth in old, old centuries, and vanished
> out of it ages ago, and now by act of ours they are summoned
> from their holy peace to answer for gutting a one-horse bank
> away out on the borders of Cherokee Strip, and it's just a
> howling outrage! (p. 165)

Properly identified—by his moral stature, not by his clothes—
Berkeley absolves not only himself but also the centuries-old
culture of which he is a product.

Though misapplied, Sellers' theory nevertheless invites us
to view Berkeley and Pete in broad perspective and to relate
them accurately. Because of his mistaken identification,
Sellers distorts the relation between them by erroneously
placing them in the same genealogical and cultural line of
descent. But Berkeley is a contemporary of Pete, not an
antecedent; neither is he blood-related to Pete through
common ancestors as he is to Sellers. In fact Berkeley and Pete
are related only as antitheses, and when they are viewed as
representatives or symbols of their respective cultures this
antithesis becomes of greatest significance. Like the contrast in
A Connecticut Yankee between the original, sixth-century
Knights of the Round Table and the "converted," nineteenth-
century knights of the Yankee's stock exchange, this contrast
in *The American Claimant* suggests that the development of
democratic culture in America represents historical
degeneration, not "progress" as Americans are accustomed to
boast. One-Armed Pete, the frontier "knight" or literal "robber
baron," symbolized democracy's inversion of the social order
and of the moral values upon which it is based; Berkeley, on
the other hand, represents the European institutions and
culture from which America revolted. Though its distribution
of rank may be imperfect, Europe nevertheless produced
Berkeley, whose moral distinction matches his social rank and
to that extent at least vindicates the culture which makes
possible such a match.

In America, however, disparity between moral stature and social rank is the rule. One-Armed Pete, the moral bankrupt, enjoys the greatest prestige and power; Colonel Sellers, the natural aristocrat, Berkeley's true blood-relation and co-inheritor of high moral standards, is dispossessed and degraded. Pete epitomizes the travesty of America's democratic culture, Sellers its tragedy. For unlike Berkeley, who may repudiate this stultifying alien culture and return to his native land, Sellers cannot escape the "inhaled" influences of his native environment nor can he satisfactorily resolve the conflict between them and his natural instincts. His only recourse is imaginative withdrawal. Attempting to satisfy these instincts, he therefore expends his moral energies by indulging in romantic gestures and illusions which are usually ineffectual and often ridiculous. His compulsion to sustain romantic ideals and to strive for some measure of satisfaction on his own terms, as opposed to those prevailing in his environment, makes him an admirable and even heroic figure.

Sellers' absurdities, like those of Don Quixote, require that a distinction be made between spirit and manner; he is ridiculous not because of his romantic temperament, noble spirit and idealistic vision but because of the elaborate, archaic and incongruous manners and forms with which he identifies proper expression of these. In contrast to her father's ingrained and irremediable quixotism, Sally Sellers toward the end of the novel "reforms" by adopting a healthier, more mature view of aristocratic distinction, which of course complements Berkeley's reformed view of equalitarianism and democracy. She renounces the family's claimancy because of its "artificiality and pretense" but retains her respect for "real" aristocracy and nobility; moreover, she reassures Berkeley that his rank and title do not prejudice her against him because her feelings toward him are evoked by his intrinsic character, not by adventitious symbols. Thus, like Miles Hendon in *The Prince and the Pauper*, she values only essential moral distinction but repudiates or scorns its symbols only when they are false or incongruous.

Twain's deep personal involvement in the conflicts which dominate *The American Claimant* is suggested by an entry in his notebook, dated 1898, in which he makes the following confession:

> There are princes which I cast in the *Echte* (genuine) princely mold, and they make me regret—again—that I am not a prince myself. It is not a new regret but a very old one. I have never been properly and humbly satisfied with my condition. I am a democrat only on principle, not by instinct—nobody is *that*.[13]

In her report of her father's reaction to an invitation to visit German nobility, Twain's daughter Clara has provided confirmation of this profound inward conflict: ". . . we could tell that a battle was going on between a largely cultivated inclination toward democratic passions and a largely inborn inclination to worship distinction of position, which supposedly includes distinction of person."[14] Twain seems, therefore, to have revealed much of himself in his characterizations of Berkeley *and* Sellers, both of whom display this same dualism. Berkeley's conversions from aristocrat to democrat and back again no doubt parallel the alternation of Twain's own sentiments over a lifetime. Colonel Sellers' debt to his creator's personality is more complex. Though Twain had by 1881 already combined in Sellers the peculiarities of three people, he did not complete the characterization for the novel until in 1891 he added what appears to be something of himself. Beyond the dualism noted above, what he added was chiefly sympathy. Without altering the basic outlines of the Sellers character or adding substantially to the particulars of his behavior, Twain nevertheless radically changed the characterization by revising the contest in which Sellers appears and with it the tone of his presentation. It is as if Twain felt a new sympathy for James Lampton, his brother Orion, and Jesse Leathers because he recognized or acknowledged finally that he shared with them many of their "peculiarities," which he had ridiculed before but had since come to understand and appreciate. Judging by *The American Claimant*, what Twain had concluded was that for a person of the innate character and temperament of a Colonel Sellers the conditions of American life create a frustrating disparity between noble motives and opportunities for their fulfillment, which he can prevent from ending in despair only by indulging in absurd pretenses and illusions. From his revised and mature perspective—perhaps already that of despair—Twain could no longer treat these absurdities as farce but was compelled to display their tragi-comic aspect instead.

Notes

1. A useful introduction summarizing much of its history precedes the play, *Colonel Sellers as a Scientist*, in *The Complete Plays of William Dean Howells*, ed. Walter J. Meserve (New York, 1960), pp. 205–8. However, the richest source of information on the play is the two-volume *Mark Twain-Howells Letters*, eds. Henry Nash Smith and William M. Gibson (Cambridge, 1960), which in addition to the correspondence itself provides many detailed notes pertaining to the collaborative project. Except where otherwise indicated, all of the quotations and facts appearing in my summary have been drawn from this source; by this blanket acknowledgment I intend only to avoid a proliferation of footnotes, not to minimize my considerable indebtedness. I would hope that the many dates included in my text make relatively easy the locating of specific sources in the chronologically-arranged correspondence.

2. Samuel C. Webster, *Mark Twain, Business Man* (Boston, 1946), p. 273.

3. Webster, p. 277.

4. Meserve, p. 207.

5. *Mark Twain's Letters*, ed. A.B. Paine (New York, 1917), II, 563.

6. The published version of the play, appearing on pages 209–41, has been put together from a number of MSS, which Meserve identifies in his introduction (p. 208).

7. *Encore* (New York, 1937), p. 108.

8. *Mark Twain's Notebook*, ed. A.B. Paine (New York, 1935), p. 213.

9. Mark Twain, *The American Claimant and Other Stories and Sketches* (New York, 1896), p. 3. Page numbers of all subsequent citations from the novel appear in parentheses in the text and refer to this edition.

10. For a concise resumé of the Lampton and Leathers stories, see *Mark Twain-Howells Letters*, II, 869–71.

11. Although because of his nativism the pull of democracy appears to be stronger in Sellers than in Berkeley, his fantastic scheme for a republic of Siberia, the high point of his liberalism in the novel, is still essentially aristocratic: he envisions a Utopia populated entirely by the political exiles of Czarist Russia, a moral and intellectual elite which he considers "the very finest and choicest material on the globe for a republic" (p. 157)—perhaps, in Twain's view, the *only* constituency capable of creating and sustaining the ideal republic!

12. *The Saga of American Society* (New York, 1937), p. 93.

13. *Mark Twain's Notebook*, p. 357.

14. Clara Clemens, *My Father Mark Twain* (New York, 1931), p. 206.

Mark Twain—An Intimate Memory

Henry Watterson

Although Mark Twain and I called each other "cousin" and claimed to be blood-relatives, the connection between us was by marriage: a great uncle of his married a great aunt of mine; his mother was named after and reared by this great aunt; and the children of the marriage were, of course, his cousins and mine; and a large, varied and picturesque assortment they were. We were lifelong and very dear friends, however; passed much time together at home and abroad; and had many common ties and memories. The last time I saw him, a little less than two years ago, he came to lunch with me at the Manhattan Club, in New York, where he greatly amused my son, a buoyant, appreciative and promising young lawyer only a few weeks later snatched suddenly and tragically away, by his intimate reminiscences of Col. Sellers, of the "Earl of Durham," and of other fantastic members of our joint family.

Just after the successful production of his one play, "The Gilded Age," and the famous hit made by the late comedian, John T. Raymond, in its leading role, I received a letter from him in which he told me he had made in Col. Mulberry Sellers a close study of a certain mutual kinsman and thought he had drawn him to the life, "but for the love of Heaven," he said, "don't whisper it, for he would never understand, or forgive me, if he did not thrash me on sight."

Reprinted from *The American Magazine* 70 (July 1910): 372–5.

The True Col. Mulberry Sellers
Not a Comic Character

The pathos of the part, and not its comic aspects, had most impressed him. He designed and wrote it for Edwin Booth. From the first and always he was disgusted by the Raymond portrayal. Except for its amazing popularity and money-making quality, he would have withdrawn it from the stage as, in a fit of pique, Raymond himself did, while it was yet packing the theatres. The original Sellers had partly brought him up and been very good to him; a second and perfect Don Quixote in appearance and not unlike the knight of La Mancha in character. It would have been safe for nobody to laugh at him—nay, by the slightest intimation, look, or gesture, to treat him with inconsideration, or any proposal of his—however preposterous—with levity. He once came to see me upon a public occasion and during a function. I knew that I must introduce him, and with all possible dignity, to my colleagues; but he was very queer: tall and stately, wearing a black, swallow-tailed suit, shiny with age, a silk hat, bound with black crepe to conceal its rustiness, not to indicate a recent death; but his linen as spotless as new-fallen snow; and I had my doubts and fears. Happily, the company, quite dazed by the apparition, proved decorous to solemnity, and the dear old gentleman, pleased with himself and proud of his "distinguished young kinsman," went away highly gratified.

Not long after this, one of his daughters—lovely girls they were, too, and in charm altogether worthy of their Cousin Sam Clemens—was to be married, and he wrote me a lengthy summons: all-embracing, though stiff and formal; such as a baron of the Middle Ages might have indited to his noble relative, the Field Marshal, bidding him bring his good lady, and all his retinue to abide within the castle until the festivities were ended, though in this instance the Castle was a little suburban cottage not big enough to accommodate the immediate bridal party. I showed this bombastic but most hospitable and sincere invitation to Mr. Raymond, who chanced to be playing in Louisville when it reached me. He read it through with care and re-read it. "Do you know," said he, "it makes me want to cry. That is not the man I am trying to impersonate at all." Be sure it was not; for there was nothing funny about the spiritual being of Mark Twain's own Mulberry Sellers; he was as brave as a lion and as upright and stern as a covenanter.

When a very young man living in a woodland cabin down in the "Penny'rile" region of Kentucky, with a wife and two, or three, babies, he was so carried away by an unexpected windfall that he lingered over long in the village, dispensing a royal hospitality; in point of fact, he "got on a spree." Two or three days passed before he regained possession of himself. When at last he reached his home, he found his wife ill in bed and the children nearly starved for want of food. He said never a word, but walked out of the cabin, tied himself to a tree, and was literally horse-whipping himself to death when the cries of the frightened family called the neighbors and he was cut loose and brought to reason. He never touched an intoxicating drop from that day to the day of his death.

When Mark Twain had worked himself into a state of mind talking to one of us about "Old Jim," his eyes would flood with tears, and I cannot myself write about him without a choking sensation. Never such a hero lived in such a fool's paradise. Yet, as done by Raymond, never an impersonation on the American stage, or in any of our comic fictions, provoked louder and longer mirth. I do not know what Edwin Booth thought of Sellers, or indeed, whether he so much as read the part which had been intended for him. That Booth and Sellers were in Mark Twain's mind conjointly tells its own and quite a different story.

The "Earl of Durham" Touches
Mark Twain for a Tenner

Another one of these mutual cousins was the "Earl of Durham." About the middle of the eighteenth century, before the War of the Revolution, there came to Virginia four brothers Lampton, younger scions of the House of Durham. From them the American Lamptons are sprung. Sam Clemens and I grew up on old wives' tales of estates and titles, which maybe it was a kindred sense of humor in both of us we treated with shocking irreverence.

It happened some forty years ago that there turned up, first upon the plains and afterward in New York and Washington, a straight descendant of the oldest of these Virginia Lamptons—he had somehow gotten hold of or had fabricated a full set of documents—who was what Theodore Roosevelt would call "a corker." He wore a sombrero, with a rattle-snake for a band, and a belt with a couple of six-shooters, and described himself and claimed to be the Earl of Durham. "He touched me for a tenner the first time I ever saw him," drawled Mark Twain, "and I coughed it up and have been coughing them up, whenever he's around, with punctuality and regularity." The "Earl" was indeed a terror especially when he had been drinking.

His belief in his peerage was as absolute as Col. Sellers' in his millions. All he wanted was money enough "to get across" and "state his case." During the Tichborne trial, Mark Twain and I were in London, and one day he said to me, "I have investigated this Durham business down at the herald's office. There's nothing to it. The Lamptons passed out of the Earldom of Durham a hundred years ago. There were never any estates. The title lapsed. The present earldom is a new creation not the same family at all. But, I tell you what, if you'll put up five hundred dollars, I'll put up five hundred more, we'll bring our chap over here and set him in as a claimant, and, my word for it, Kenealy's fat boy won't be a marker to him!"

He was so pleased with his conceit that later along he wrote a novel and called it "The Claimant." It is the only one of his books—though I never told him so—that I never could read. Many years after, I happened to see upon a hotel register in Rome these entries "The Earl of Durham," and in the same handwriting just below it, "Lady Anne Lambton" and "The Hon. Reginald Lambton." So the Lambtons—they spelled it with a b instead of a p—were yet in the peerage and earls of Durham. The next time I saw Mark Twain I tackled him on the deception. He did not defend himself—said something about its being necessary to perfect the joke. "Did you ever meet this present peer and possible usurper?" I asked. "No," he answered, "I never did, but if he had called on me, I would have seen him."

Next Door to the "Work'us"

His mind turned ever to the droll. Once in London I was living with my family at 103 Mount Street. Between 103 and 102 there was the parochial workhouse—quite a long and imposing building. One evening, upon coming in from an outing, I found a letter he had written on the sitting-room table and left with his card. He spoke of the shock he had received upon finding that next to 102—presumably 103—was the workhouse. He had loved me, but had always feared that I would end by disgracing the family—being hanged, or something—but the "work'us," that was beyond him; he had not thought it would come to that. And so on through pages of horse-play: his relief on ascertaining the truth and learning his mistake—his regret at not finding me at home—closing with a dinner invitation. Once at Geneva, in Switzerland, I received a long, overflowing letter, full of buoyant oddities, written from London. Two or three hours later came a telegram. "Burn letter. Blot it from your memory. Susie is dead."

How much of melancholy lay hidden behind the mask of the humorist it would be hard to determine. His griefs were tempered by a vein of philosophy. He was a medley of contradiction. Unconventional to the point of eccentricity, his sense of respectability was acute. Though lavish in the use of money, he had a full realization of its value and made close contracts for his work. Like Sellers, his mind soared when it sailed financial currents. He lacked sound business judgment in the larger things, while an excellent economist in lesser.

The book-publishing failure may be ascribed to lack of forecast along with an excess of optimism. So the failure of the type-setting machine. While that venture and its rival, the Mergenthaler invention, were in the experimental stage, Mr. Stillson Hutchins, who controlled the latter, made him an offer he should have accepted, and which, if it had been accepted, would indeed have ensured him "millions." They were old acquaintances and excellent friends. "Sam," said Hutchins, "let us merge these interests, you taking Europe and I this side." No, he would none of it; so, in the end, it cost him a pretty penny.

A Happy Marriage

His marriage was the most brilliant success of his life. He got the woman of all the world he most needed; a truly lovely and wise helpmeet; who kept him in bounds and headed him straight and right while she lived; the best of housewives and mothers, and the safest of counsellors and soundest of critics. She knew his worth; she understood his genius; and she clearly saw his oddities and his angles. Her death was a grievous disaster as well as a staggering blow. It was her sympathy and her love which enabled him to survive Susie's death. When the final tragedy came, it was too much for him— it broke his spirit—he could not react against it and sank beneath the load of accumulated sorrows and infirmities.

Mark Twain's place in literature, the bent of his genius and the merit of his writing, are made the subjects of varied commentation in England, in Germany and in his own country. Probably the works of no American author traveled farther, gave more pleasure, or were better known. It is not my purpose here to venture an estimate or take note of critical opinions; the rather to jot down a few intimate memories.

In the early seventies, he dropped into New York, where there was already gathered a congenial group to meet and greet him. This radiated from Franklin Square, where Joseph W. Harper—"Joe Brooklyn," we called him—reigned in place of his uncle, Fletcher Harper, the man of genius among the original four Harper Brothers, to the Lotus Club, then in Irving Place and Delmonico's, at the corner of Fifth Avenue and Fourteenth Street, with Southerland's in Liberty Street, for a downtown place of luncheon resort, not to forget Dorlon's, in Fulton Market. The Harper contingent, beside the Chief, embraced Tom Nast and Col. Seaver, whom John Russell Young named "Papa Pendennis," and described as "a man of letters among men of the world and a man of the world among men of letters," a very apt portrayal, albeit appropriated from Dr. Johnson, and Major Constable, a giant, who looked like a dragoon, and not a bookman, yet had known Sir Walter Scott and was sprung from the family of Edinburgh publishers. Bret Harte had newly arrived from California. Whitelaw Reid, though still subordinate to Greeley, was beginning to make himself felt in journalism. John Hay played high priest to the revels. Halstead and I used to make periodic pilgrimages to the delightful shrine.

Robustious Revels

Truth to say, it emulated rather the gods than the graces—though all of us had literary aspirations of one sort and another—especially late at night—and Sam Bowles would come over from Springfield to meet us. Often we had Joseph Jefferson, then in the heyday of his great career, with, once in a while, Edwin Booth, who could not quite trust himself to go our gait. The good fellows we caught from over sea were innumerable, from the elder Sothern and Sala and Yeats to Lord Dufferin and Lord Houghton. Times went very well those days, and, whilst some looked on askance—notably Curtis and, rather oddly, Stedman—and thought we were wasting time and convivializing more than was good for us, we were mostly young and hearty, ranging from thirty to five and forty years of age, with amazing capacities, both for work and play, and I cannot recall that any harm to any of us came of it. Although robustious, our frolics were harmless enough— ebullitions of gayety sometimes, perhaps unguarded—though each shade, or survivor, recurring to those Noctes Ambrosiae, might paraphrase to the other the words of Curran to Lord Avonmore:

> We passed them not in lust, or toys or wine, But in true
> poesy, wit and philosophy, Arts which I loved, for they, my
> friend, were thine.*

Mark Twain was the life of every company and of all occasions. I remember a practical joke of his suggestion played upon Halstead. A party of us were supping after the theatre at the old Brevoort House. A card was brought to me from a reporter of the *World*. I was about to deny myself, when Mark Twain said: "Give it to me, I'll fix it," and left the table.

Presently he came to the door and beckoned me to come to him. "I represented myself as your secretary and told this man," said he, "that you were not here, but that if Mr. Halstead would answer just as well, I would fetch him out. He is as innocent as a lamb and doesn't know either of you. I am going to introduce you as Halstead and we'll have some fun."

---

* I am writing from memory, without the opportunity to verify my quotation, which may not be strictly accurate.

"Fixing" a Reporter

No sooner said than done. The reporter proved to be a little bald-headed cherub newly arrived from the isle of dreams, and I lined out to him a column or more of very hot stuff, reversing Halstead in every expression of opinion. I declared him in favor of paying the national debt in greenbacks. Touching the sectional question which was then the burning issue of the time, I made the mock Halstead say: "The 'bloody shirt' is only a kind of Pickwickian battle-cry. It is convenient during political campaigns and on election day. Perhaps you do not know that I am myself of good old North Carolina stock. My father and grandfather came to Ohio from the old North State just before I was born. Naturally, I have no sectional prejudices, but I live in Cincinnati and am a Republican."

There was a good deal more of the same sort. How it passed through the *World* office I know not, but next day it appeared. On returning to table I had told the company what Mark Twain and I had done. They thought I was joking. It did seem inconceivable. Without a word to any of us, next day Halstead wrote a note to the *World* briefly repudiating the "interview," and the *World* printed his disclaimer with a line which said: "When Mr. Halstead talked with our reporter he had dined." It was too good to keep. John Hay wrote an amusing "story" for the *Tribune*, which set Halstead right and turned the laugh on me!

Now and then we did a little after-dinner speech-making all among ourselves—toward the wee sma' hours—perhaps to try our wings—certainly to try one another. Mark Twain made much the best speech. He had the gift to think clearly upon his feet. His oratory was a kind of easy dictation, and he was hard to follow, his words were so apt. Although he disliked audiences, they did not disconcert him. His method was slow, purposely halting, and the drawl, like Travers' stammer, assisted the humor.

Inherited His Drawl from His Mother

This drawl was not affected, as many supposed it. He inherited it from his mother; a bright and captivating woman, as were all the feminine Lamptons I have ever known. The men of that family were honest and courageous, but not successful on the material side. The women were immensely successful as wives and mothers. The family had the artistic temperament. Mark Twain's childhood, though passed upon the frontier, was enveloped by a certain semi-literary atmosphere. He got the hang of books in his cradle. There may not have been many of them, but they were select, incessantly read and talked about. His rude experiences on the river and in the mining camp accentuated the baby love of letters, and, when travel gave him the chance to proceed with his education, he made the most of it; a hard worker; a closer and a more intelligent student than he seemed, for, with John Hay, in the earlier time he liked to affect the rustic. Thus, after his years of foreign experience and residence, when he came to deal with other subjects than the pilot-house on the Mississippi and the "diggings" of Nevada, he applied a touch to his work which was unexpected and possessed the quality of the surprising.

I sometimes think we Americans are a little unjust to ourselves in our literary valuations. Irving, Bret Harte and Mark Twain followed the homely rescript that "the shoemaker should stick to his last." They wrote of things familiar and they wrote with both elegance and originality, and often with power; far and away in merit—even technical skill—the seniors of the chosen ones of larger fame, the "immortals" of France, and the worthies of England and Germany, whom we are wont to consider great in this world and in Valhalla cloisters to place upon pedestals.

Of the three, Mark Twain was the strongest and broadest, covering an ampler range of production, and striking a deeper note; as vivid as Harte, with none of Harte's insincerity; as conscientious and as true and simple as Irving, but with yet more potent hand and quicker and larger fancy, an American through and through in his genius, a cosmopolitan in his attainments and his art.

The Book Hunter

"Puddenhead Wilson," Mark Twain's latest story, is the work of a novelist, rather than of a "funny man." There is plenty of humour in it of the genuine Mark Twain brand, but it is as a carefully painted picture of life in a Mississippi town in the days of slavery that its chief merit lies. In point of construction it is much the best story that Mark Twain has written, and of men and women in the book at least four are undeniably creations, and not one of them is overdrawn or caricatured, as are some of the most popular of the author's lay figures. There is but one false note in the picture, and that is the introduction of the two alleged Italian noblemen. These two young men are as little like Italians as they are like Apaches. When challenged to fight a duel, one of them, having the choice of weapons, chooses revolvers instead of swords. This incident alone is sufficient to show how little Italian blood there is in Mark Twain's Italians. But this is a small blemish, and if Mark Twain, in his future novels, can maintain the proportion of only two lay figures to four living characters, he will do better than most novelists. The extracts from "Puddenhead Wilson's Almanac," which are prefixed to each chapter of the book, simply "pizon us for more," to use Huck Finn's forcible metaphor. Let us hope that a complete edition of that unrivalled almanac will be issued at no distant day.

Reprinted from *The Idler* 6 (August 1894): 222–3.

In Re "Pudd'nhead Wilson"

Martha McCulloch Williams

A better title, perhaps, would be "The Decline and Fall of Mark Twain;" for, looking at it solely as a piece of literature, there is no denying that his much-advertised serial is tremendously stupid. If it were nothing more, the reading, even the critical, world could afford to receive it in the charity of silence, remembering the merry heart it has had these twenty years past whenever it pleased Mr. Clemens to amuse it.

"Pudd'nhead Wilson" is more than stupid. So far as it has appeared—to the end of the second installment, that is—it is at once malicious and misleading. So much so, indeed, that involuntarily one recalls the gentleman who, it was said, "went to his memory for his wit, and his imagination for his facts."

It certainly seems to me that Mr. Clemens must have imagined all the local color of his tale. It has to do with Dawson's Landing, a small Missouri town on the Mississippi, populated largely with F. F. V.'s, all of whom are slaveholders, as are the rest of the inhabitants. Right here I wish to ask why it is that the Southern man who has an honest and decent pride in the fact that he comes of good stock fares so ill at the hands of certain literary gentlemen? Bret Harte gives us Colonel Starbottle as his type. Mr. Cable has won fame and fortune and the heart of the whole North by demonstrating to its entire satisfaction how heartlessly and continually all his

Reprinted from *Fetter's Southern Magazine* 4 (1894): 99–102.

well-born gentlemen overstep the color line. Last of all, Mark Twain has set himself the task of showing how impossible it is for a man to have a great-grandfather and, at the same time, any regard for the Decalogue.

Perhaps these gentlemen are bent on gleaning the full harvest of "Uncle Tom's Cabin." Perhaps, too, they are wise in so doing. In my seven years North, I have more than once been asked by people who regarded themselves as very well-informed "if there were still in the South any pure blacks at all, or any pure-blooded whites?" At first such questioning made me angry. Later, I have come to recognize it as the legitimate outcome of the deliverances of Mr. Cable and his school. Now that Mark Twain has come under their banner, the impression will doubtless become more than ever current. For he has—and has deserved—the widest public of any living American writer. And it is a melancholy fact that the sheep instinct of humanity is so strong as to make it follow *en masse* into any pasture of opinion where he may lead. A still more melancholy fact is the inability of many folk to judge a thing with eyes blinded by the glamour of a great reputation.

Otherwise, I think, some one would have risen ere this to protest against some of Mr. Clemens' gentle idiosyncrasies displayed in the first installment. For instance, the character of Pembroke Howard, introduced solely that the author might tell us that Howard, too, was an F.F.V., also that "he was popular with the people"—and that the story has no sort of concern with him. A while later he is permitted to die. At least, there is a line to that effect. What I want to know, and would like to ask Mr. Clemens, is how a man can be "popular with the people," since popular means of, by, or with the people. It does assuredly seem to me pretty queer usage for a man who was so lately toasted and feted by the Lotos Club, as the leading exponent of literary art.

That is by no means a solitary gem of its kind. Careful reading shows the like upon almost every page. It is not too much to say, in fact, that there is slovenly construction in every other paragraph. But the manner is a trifling burden compared with the matter of it. First to last, the writer seems to feel his burden of humor-with-malice-aforethought. He had chosen his place, his people. If the facts about them are not humorous, so much the worse for facts.

Witness the naming of the hero. He had come out of Western New York to practice law in the Missouri town. One day, hearing a dog bark, he indulges in the Joe-Millerism of wishing he owned half the dog so he might make an end of it. Thereupon the by-standers "fell away from him as something uncanny, and went into privacy to discuss him." One said:

"Pears to be a fool."

"Pears? said another "*Is*, I reckon. Said he wished he owned *half* the dog." "The idiot," said a third. "What did he reckon would become of the other half if he killed his half? Do you reckon he thought it would live?"

"In my opinion he ain't got any mind."

"No. 3 said: "Well, he's a lummox, anyway."

"That's what he is," said No. 4.

"He's a labrick; just a Simon pure labrick if ever there was one."

"Yes, sir, he's a damn fool, that's the way I put him up," said No. 5. "Anybody can think different that wants to, but those are my sentiments."

"I am with you gentlemen," said No. 6. "Perfect jackass—yes, and it ain't going too far to say he is a pudd'nhead. If he ain't a pudd'nhead, I ain't no judge, that all."

Mr. Wilson stood elected. The incident was told all over town and gravely discussed by everybody. Within a week he had lost his first name. Pudd'nhead took its place.

This is humor, as the great editors understand it. To one a little bit conversant with the folk who are supposed to be humorous, it seems, contrariwise, something cheap and thin. Throughout the Southwest, for at least seventy five years, "I'd like to own that dog—and kill my half" has been a cant saying so commonly current that it is laughed at only out of compliment to the user of it. The man who should now perpetrate it as original would perhaps be called something worse than "pudd'nhead," but very certainly nobody—not the most ignorant—would find in it a suggestion of uncanniness. For the thing is so common and proverbial that little children make use of it, or rather of its implication. More than one small lad has told me, rejoicing, "Ma has stopped her half of me from going to school." And one shrewd young person within my knowledge bought half of a coveted dolly, then insisted on a property-right to play with it all the time.

So, too, of Mr. Clemens' young man who went away East to college, and came back with "Eastern polish," whatever that may be—perhaps perfect fitting clothes and a habit of wearing gloves. His old friends overlooked the polish and the clothes but could not forgive the glove habit, so he was left solitary. This is some more, doubtless, of Mr. Clemens' very peculiar humor. He ought, however, to have stated the fact in a footnote. He might have been at the same pains about the reception to the Brothers Capollo. His account of the honors thrust upon them is doubtless a sly revenge upon the misguided Southern communities, which have stretched out admiring hands to Mr. Clemens when he would rather they did not.

So much for the accidentals of the tale. To deal adequately with the story itself, either in motif or atmosphere, would require more time and space than I, at present, command. It is built around the exchange of two children, born the same day, to one father. One is his wife's son; the other, his slave's. The wife dies; the slave mother, who has sixteen parts of white blood to one of black, has sole charge of both babies. After a while, her master (as is the custom of Virginia gentlemen in the hands of high literary persons), for some trifling fault, sells all the other house-servants, though as a mark of magnanimity he sells them at home instead of sending them down the river. The life-likeness of this part will be apparent to every ex-slave owner, especially to such as remember how far beyond rubies was in those days the price of a thoroughly excellent servant. Setting wholly aside the human affection that often subsisted between white and black, few men were so foolish as to inconvenience themselves by an entire change of *menage*, without the most imperative necessity for such a proceeding. All that is, however, beside the mark. This sale goes forward, and as a result, Roxy, the white slave, puts her son in his half-brother's place to save him from the possibility of such a fate.

She also puts her creator—Mark Twain—in rather a hard dilemma. To his mind the only man worth either saving or damning in all the South country is the black man. The exigencies of fiction, however, make it necessary that the slave baby, who normally would grow up a pin feathered angel, shall, as his own young master, grow up a pretty respectable devil. Similarly, the white child must be, by the change of position, endowed with all the virtues and graces of the subject race. Anybody can see that it is hard lines for the writer. One can fancy him apologizing beforehand to the little negro for the violence he is compelled to do his character. He makes the plunge and the double transformation boldly. It is more than a little amusing, though, to one who knows experimentally the autocracy of a "black mammy," to read how Roxy, after the exchange, was surprised to see how steadily and surely the awe which had kept her tongue reverent, her manner humble towards her young master, was transferring itself to her speech and manner toward the usurper. Roxy must have been a mighty exceptional character if she did not spank her charges with natural and noble impartiality, whether they were white or black.

She had christened her own child "Valet de Chambre—no surname. Slaves hadn't the privilege." That is some more news to us who owned them, and who keep lively memories of their pride in their surnames; and how tenaciously, after freedom came, they clung to the appellations whereunto they felt themselves born. In founding their families under the new conditions, it was often laughable to see the leaning to aristocracy. In more than one case within my own knowledge, negroes abandoned the names of the living masters, in favor of that of the master's grandfather from whom they were inherited and to whose family they leaned because of its greater distinction. Truly, if they had had no privilege of surnames, there must have been confusion worse confounded in the era '65.

Time and patience fail alike in bringing to book all such matters here set down. Suffice it to say that, first to last the whole recital is unveracious. If it is meant for caricature, the result is the same as would come from exaggerating the ears, nose, and coat-tails of a Bowery tough, and labelling the picture "Ward McAllister." So far as I know, all that the South, either "Old" or "New," has ever done to Mr. Clemens has been to buy his books, when it had precious little money to buy anything, and to set him upon a pedestal as the very prince of humorists. Wherefore, I quite fail to comprehend why it pleases him to villify us as he is doing in this book.

Let me add that I am no bigot in behalf of mine own people. Some have foibles, faults galore, even sins of deepest dye. There are knaves and fools among them—uncouth fellows not a few. So much I readily grant. I will go further and admit that there is that in the social constitution which, rightly handled, might give a humorist scope to add largely to the gaiety of nations. But take them by little and large, they are neither sordid nor stolid, nor lacking in the finer parts of humanity. All this Mr. Clemens makes them out to be. And because he is who he is, a large part of our common country will take his circus-posters for accurate photographs of life and people in the South. Solely for that reason, I make, here and now, my protest against this injustice. I can not comfort myself with the belief that he has sinned ignorantly against half his countrymen. His experience has been too wide, his intelligence is too keen, for that. He is, it seems to me, thus unveracious for revenue only. He has found out the sort of book that sells best. It is not that which speaks the truth as it is, but as the reader wishes to believe it to be. Beside, it is only against a background so lurid as the one he has manufactured that the action of his story could possibly take place. As an occasional dabbler in fiction, I recognize the strength of that necessity. But I can not hold that it is sufficient to justify the falsification of all historic conditions. A long time ago, I read a speech of Mr. Clemens in which he said, at the outset, that he had chosen something he knew nothing whatever about so as to be quite unhampered by facts. To judge from "Pudd'nhead Wilson," he has contracted a habit of being unhampered by facts,—a habit which seems to grow stronger with age.

"The Tales He Couldn't Tell": Mark Twain, Race and Culture at the Century's End: A Social Context for *Pudd'nhead Wilson*[1]

Shelley Fisher Fishkin

When Mark Twain began *Adventures of Huckleberry Finn* he thought he was writing another boys' book, a simple sequel to *Tom Sawyer*; but his story was soon hijacked by a black slave and a white boy on a quest for freedom. When Twain began the book that would end up as *Pudd'nhead Wilson* he thought he was writing a book about Angelo and Luigi, Italian Siamese twins with two heads, four arms and one torso; but *that* story was soon hijacked by a man who was one-thirty-second part black and a slave who had hoped to set him free. Two of the most powerful and most powerfully flawed books in American literary history were the result.

Where did these upstarts come from, the black man who "stole" his own freedom, and the man who looked white but whom society deemed black? And why did Twain let them crash their way into his plots and unleash, as he put it himself, "no end of confusion and annoyance"?[2]

Critics have focused on the composition history of both books to explain the roots of their markedly schizophrenic structures.[3] But understanding the order in which Twain put the pieces of his books together still doesn't explore the implications of the fact that both books were "taken over" by story lines that focused on black/white issues in the ante-

Reprinted from *Essays in Arts and Sciences* 19 (May 1990): 1–26.

bellum South. When Twain allowed his initial stories to be usurped by this new and troublesome theme, the result, in both books (as both Twain and the critics agree), was a certain amount of narrative chaos. That confusion, however, was not simply the result of a second story line bumping up against Twain's original plans. It was, I would argue, the subliminal subject of the second story line which helps account for the particularly thorny and unresolved contradictions and ironies that characterize the final versions of both books. That subliminal subject is American race relations, not in the time in which the books were set, but during the period in which they were written.

Sometimes a work of art can be a prism through which a historical moment becomes refracted into its constituent parts in stunning clarity and brilliant color. Elsewhere I have argued that *Adventures of Huckleberry Finn* performs this prismatic function for the period during which Twain wrote it, 1876 through the early 1880s.[4] Here I will examine the ways in which *Pudd'nhead Wilson* encodes and reflects the contradictions, tensions and ironies that characterized American race relations from the late 1880s through the turn of the century.

The social, legal, cultural and political history of American race relations immediately before, during and after Twain's publication of this book in 1894 is confusing and ironic. At the same time as black America produced writers, artists, composers, athletes, businessmen, and educators of the first rank, white America grew obsessed with asserting black inferiority, and with ensuring—legally and extralegally—the separation of the races. And as the project of ensuring the separation of the races was elaborated more and more meticulously in a byzantine code of laws, the possibility of actually delineating those sharp lines between black and white grew increasingly elusive: for despite white America's obsession with racial "purity," America was becoming an increasingly mulatto nation.

Against this backdrop, it is clearly folly to ascribe the difficulty of making sense of Twain's *Pudd'nhead Wilson* simply to botched artistry on Twain's part. Yes, the book is flawed, frustratingly so, sometimes veering in one direction, sometimes in another. But how, one might ask, could a book dealing with race and identity, written in this bizarre and contradiction-filled period, by a writer of Twain's sensitivity and moral awareness, be otherwise? An examination of the history of American race relations at the century's end can shed new light on the complexities of this puzzling novel; and, in turn, this deeply flawed book can illuminate the chapter of history that informs it in new and fruitful ways.

Part I of this essay will limn the history of American race relations in the period during and immediately preceding and following the book's publication. Part II will explore the ways in which the novel encodes and reflects that historical moment. Part III will compare Twain's treatment of these issues with that of several of his African-American contemporaries.

I

The late 1880s through the turn of the century was a period when white America made unprecedented moves to consolidate its power: it repeatedly stripped black Americans—legally and illegally—of hard-won rights, and took a myriad of steps—often violent ones—to make sure that the canvas on which black Americans could paint their lives was as constricted as possible.

Historians C. Vann Woodward, Rayford Logan, John Hope Franklin, George Frederickson, Joel Williamson, August Meier and others have laid out the details of the web of legal and illegal maneuvers through which white supremacy installed itself during this period, and have probed some of the reasons why such raw and open hostility was directed against blacks in both the South and the North, where liberals of every stripe

beat a quick retreat from the race issue.[5] "All along the line,"
C. Vann Woodward notes, "signals were going up to indicate
that the Negro was an approved object of aggression."

> These "permissions-to-hate" came from sources that had
> formerly denied such permission. They came from the
> federal courts in numerous opinions, from Northern liberals
> eager to conciliate the South, from Southern conservatives
> who had abandoned their race policy of moderation in their
> struggle against the Populists, from the Populists in their
> mood of disillusionment with their former Negro allies, and
> from a national temper suddenly expressed by imperialistic
> adventures and aggressions against colored peoples in
> distant lands.[6]

The hatred took many forms; two particularly common
ones were the rise of "Jim Crow" laws and lynching. The
1890s saw the passage of the country's first segregation
statutes, or "Jim Crow" laws. While these laws initially
applied only to public transportation, eventually they would
mandate the creation of separate water fountains, waiting
rooms, parks, residences, textbooks, telephone booths, ticket
windows, and bibles for witnesses in courtrooms.[7] As C. Vann
Woodward observed, "the segregation code. . . lent the
sanction of law to a racial ostracism that extended to churches
and schools, to housing and jobs, to eating and drinking.
Whether by law or by custom, that ostracism eventually
extended to virtually all forms of public transportation, to
sports and recreations, to hospitals, orphanages, prisons, and
asylums, and, ultimately to funeral homes, morgues and
cemeteries."[8]

The number of blacks killed by lynch mobs across the
nation increased dramatically in the 1890s.[9] The lynchings
were most often prompted by allegations of attempted rape of
white women by black men, charges about which a writer like
Ida B. Wells expressed acidic and eloquent skepticism.[10]
Before 1889, as Joel Williamson has noted, lynching "was a
Western and all-white phenomenon, often having to do with
bands of cattle rustlers."[11] Starting in 1889, however, and

continuing through the 1890s, "lynching became a special Southern occurrence in which black men were the special victims."[12]

> The recession of the late 1880s and the depression of the 1890s also produced profound psychological effects. Southern whites had been very much taken by sex and family roles prescribed in the Victorian era. Men saw themselves as the providers and protectors in their families. As the economic world constricted, men found themselves less and less able to provide for their women in the accustomed style, and there seemed to be no promise of an end to the decline. . . . It seems fully possible that the rage against the black beast rapist was a kind of psychic compensation. If white men could not provide for their women materially as they had done before, they could certainly protect them from a much more awful threat—the outrage of their purity, and hence their piety, by black men.[13]

Lynching, as George Frederickson had observed, "represented an ultimate sociological method of racial control and repression."[14] More than three times as many blacks were lynched in 1892 as had been lynched in any year during the previous decade. Throughout the 1890s an average of 110 blacks were lynched each year.[15] Despite these horrendous figures, efforts to pass anti-lynching legislation in Congress came to naught.

Even academic "scholars" of the day reflected the deterioration in race relations, producing books with titles such as *The Negro, A Menace to American Civilization*.[16] African-American novelist Charles W. Chesnutt said in 1903 that "the rights of Negroes are at a lower ebb than at any time during the thirty-five years of their freedom, and the race prejudice more intense and uncompromising."[17]

In the 1890s then, laws designed to separate white from black proliferated. And what could not be done within the law was accomplished extralegally by lynch mobs. The price one paid for the color of one's skin was higher than ever before; during the last two decades of the century it cost over twenty-five-hundred African-Americans their lives. At the same time, however, it was becoming more and more difficult to separate white from black on a practical level, for America was becoming an increasingly mulatto nation.

This increase was quite predictable, and could be explained, to a large extent, by simple arithmetic, the legacy of generations of miscegenation. That white slaveholders had fathered thousands of mulatto children who had now grown to adulthood and were producing light-skinned children of their own was a tacitly acknowledged, if distasteful, fact of life in the South; the migration patterns meant that light-skinned blacks were increasingly seen in the North, and that blacks who could pass for white were liable to appear anywhere, North or South, wreaking havoc on the bold lines of demarcation drawn by Southerners and Northerners alike to keep the races apart.

The United States, unlike many other racially mixed societies, classified anyone with a black or mulatto ancestor going back two, three or four generations as "black." Reasonable citizens had attempted to challenge this classification scheme for many years. In 1865, for example, P.T. Barnum gave a speech in the Connecticut legislature in support of the idea of striking the word "white" from the clause that defined voter qualifications in the state constitution: "The word 'white' in the Constitution cannot be strictly and literally construed," Barnum said,

> The opposition expresses great love for the white blood. Will they let a mulatto vote half the time, a quadroon three quarters, and an octoroon seven-eighths of the time? If not, why not? Will they enslave seven-eighths of a white man because one-eighth is not caucasian? Is this democracy? Shall not the majority seven control the minority one? . . ."[18]

Despite efforts like this to point up the ironies and absurdities that it engendered, the rigid "descent rule" classification scheme (mandating that "all descendants of mixed unions" get classed "with their black progenitors"[19]) remained largely intact throughout the nineteenth and much of the twentieth century. Scholars have had trouble coming up with a satisfying explanation for why this should have been so. In his book *White Supremacy: A Comparative Study in American and South African History*, George Frederickson has noted, for example, that "one of the major challenges for scholars of comparative race relations has been to explain the unique 'descent rule' that has been the principal basis of racial classification in the United States."[20]

The fiction of "racial purity"—the notion that it was, in fact, possible to divide society into "white" and "black"— remained the precious tenet which underlay the enormously cumbersome workings of the segregation laws. While white society tried to secure the dividing line between black and white through the courts and the law on the one hand, and through mob terror on the other, the population of Americans of mixed blood was increasing geometrically.

In addition to the rise of segregation laws and the increased mixing of the races, and despite the enormous obstacles in their paths, in the late 1880s and 1890s, African-Americans made impressive forays into literature, painting, music, journalism, economics, education, theater and sports. African Americans may have been forced to ride at the back of the bus and sleep on the "wrong" side of town, but that didn't stop them from writing stories for the *Atlantic Monthly*, building businesses, founding newspapers, winning boxing championships and horse-races, and publishing eloquent and accomplished books of fiction, non-fiction and poetry.

In 1886 Charles W. Chesnutt's story "The Goophered Grapevine" was published in the prestigious *Atlantic Monthly*. This was the first time a work of fiction by a black author reached a large white audience. In 1899 Houghton-Mifflin published two collections of Chesnutt's short stories, *The Conjure Woman* and *The Wife of His Youth, and Other Stories of the Color Line*, and in 1900 Chesnutt published his novel *The House Behind the Cedars*. Other literary achievements abounded as well: In 1892 Anna Julia Cooper published her eloquent book, *A Voice From The South* and in 1893 Paul

Laurence Dunbar published his first collection of poetry, *Oak and Ivy*, followed by *Majors and Minors* in 1895, which received a favorable, full-page review by William Dean Howells in *Harper's Weekly*. His *Lyrics of a Lowly Life* won national attention in 1896. With African-American literacy rising constantly, scores of African-American periodicals—newspapers, magazines, and literary and cultural journals—came into being. By 1898 there were one hundred thirty six weekly papers, three daily papers, eleven school papers, two quarterly reviews, and a monthly cultural journal.[21]

There were milestones in music, too: George W. Chadwick's Second Symphony was published in 1886, the first symphonic work using African-American folksongs; in 1892 Sisseretta Jones, an African-American singer, was invited to perform at the White House. African-Americans entered sports, as well: In 1890 George Dixon won the world bantamweight boxing championship, holding the title through 1892. In 1890 Pike Barns, an African-American jockey, won the Belmont and Alabama Stakes and Isaac Murphy, another African-American jockey, won the Kentucky Derby.[22]

In economics and business, there was progress: Thomy Lafon, a free black tycoon from New Orleans, worth half a million dollars at his death, had "contributed so much to the development of the city that in 1893 the State Legislature ordered a bust of him to be carved and set up in some public institution in New Orleans."[23] By 1891 in Virginia's sixteen major cities and towns, African-Americans owned over three million dollars worth of land, over a third of the total value of land owned. By 1900 nearly a quarter of America's African-American population owned their own homes. African-American entrepreneurs ran banks, drugstores, mining companies, and assorted other businesses. The African-American professional class had increased dramatically as well: in 1900 there were more than 21,000 teachers, more than fifteen thousand preachers, nearly two thousand doctors, three hundred journalists, and some seven hundred lawyers. There were over 2000 actors and showmen, 236 artists, sculptors and art teachers, nearly 4000 musicians and music teachers, over 200 photographers, and some fifty architects, designers, draftsmen and inventors.[24]

There were milestones in education, too: In 1894 Harvard awarded a Ph.D. to an African-American student for the first time, a young man named W.E.B. Du Bois. His dissertation, *The Suppression of the African Slave Trade*, was soon published as a book. By 1900 more than 2000 African-Americans had college degrees.[25]

One would think that even the most die-hard "Redeemer" would be stumped to justify segregating some of the culture's finest artists, writers, musicians, businessmen, educators and athletes from the general populace on the grounds of their supposed inferiority—but racism has never been known for its rationality. Any individuals willing to open their eyes and look around them could see black Americans equalling and at times surpassing their white fellow citizens at the most complex and highly skilled endeavors. Clearly they could achieve whatever white America could achieve if they were given the opportunity. To an American aware of even a small portion of these diverse and impressive achievements, the ideology of inherent racial inferiority would have begun to ring increasingly hollow. It did for Mark Twain, whose skepticism about the supposed "superiority" of the white race would erode even further as he watched white nations brutally impose their brand of "civilization" on non-white peoples around the globe. Many of Twain's short, dark later works— "To the Person Sitting in the Darkness," for example—come out of this frame of mind.

II

What do these highly discordant elements add up to—the increased degradation and persecution of blacks coupled with increased achievement, progress and success of blacks? Or the rapidly increasing presence of blacks so light-skinned they didn't look black at all at a time when legislatures and courts tried to draw more sharply than ever the lines of demarcation between black and white? They add up to a confused and bitterly divided culture at war against itself, a society ready to sacrifice its ideals, its rational self-interest, and its prospects for a nonviolent future on a shaky altar of bigotry, hatred and racial pride.

Most of Twain's white contemporaries on the literary scene during the last two decades of the nineteenth century, both Northerners and Southerners, were content to ignore or sidestep these complicated issues when they addressed the subject of race and American culture in their fiction.[26] One looks in vain for any sense of tragedy or irony in the work of Joel Chandler Harris or Thomas Nelson Page, for example. Writers of the "plantation school" like Page offered a highly distorted view of what freedom meant to African-Americans. As Sterling Brown has noted: "Slavery was to be shown as not slavery at all, but a happy state best suited for an inferior, childish but lovable race. In this normal condition, the Negro was shown thriving. Then came his emancipation, which the better class of Negroes did not want, and which few could understand or profit by. Freedom meant anarchy. Only by restoring control (euphemism for tenant farming, sharecropping, black codes, enforced labor, segregation and all other ills of the new slavery) could equilibrium in the South, so important to the nation, be achieved."[27]

Theodore Gross has observed,

> the Southern authors' characterization of the Negro proved to be immensely popular. In the 1880s and 1890s such Northern writers as Frank Stockton, Harriet Spofford, and Constance Fenimore Woolson accepted the Southern version of Reconstruction; and the admirable freedman of Reconstruction was the devoted Negro who recalled his contented existence before the war and who voluntarily remained faithful to his past masters. The favorite formula of Reconstruction authors—Northern and Southern—was one in which the Negro alleviated his ex-master's poverty.[28]

In works by white authors written in the 1880s and 1890s that were set before the Civil War, Gross notes, most often "the noble Negro. . . refused to attempt freedom under any conditions."[29] The racism of these sentimental works from the 1880s and 1890s pales before the blistering racism of the novels Thomas Dixon would produce between 1902 and 1907.[30] However, in their dogged refusal to write about race and American culture *without* addressing any of the real anguished and contradictory tensions that marked the subject, these writers helped prepare the soil in which Dixon's foul-smelling, noxious plants would later bloom and flourish.

Mark Twain was tilling a different field.

Like many of the "plantation school" writers mentioned above, Twain sets his tale in ante-bellum days. But his ante-bellum tale is shot through with the acid irony, numbing pain and crippling despair that so many African-Americans must have found themselves struggling to overcome in the 1880s and 1890s in the face of lynchings, political intimidation, and social and cultural isolation and ostracism. In place of portraits of contented slaves who wouldn't for a moment attempt freedom, Twain gives us Roxanna, a woman who decides, by the book's third chapter, that death—for herself and her child—is preferable to slavery; it is while she plans her suicide/murder that the novel's plot is set in motion.[31] Twain's is clearly a different moral universe from that inhabited by Thomas Nelson Page. (History, as it happens, would eventually recognize the limitations of Page's world view and the strengths of Twain's. Page is now largely forgotten, while Twain has earned his niche—relatively secure if sometimes slippery—in the canon.)

Twain's Roxanna is one-sixteenth black, and her son is one thirty-second black. Still, as Twain tells us, by a "fiction of law and custom," both Roxanna and her son are black. Were Twain's numbers far-fetched? Perhaps not: as Susan Gillman has pointed out, "as late as 1970, . . . in Louisiana the legal fraction defining blackness was still one-thirty-second 'Negro blood'." "Most southern states," George Frederickson tells us, "were operating in accordance with what amounted to a 'one-drop rule'[32] meaning in effect that a person with any known degree of black ancestry was legally considered a Negro and subject to the full disabilities associated with segregation and disfranchisement."[33] This is precisely the nature of this "fiction of law and custom"—and its significance for society—that Twain's novel explores so pointedly. The everwinding spiral of absurdity that this "fiction" gets us into underlies the post-modern humor produced by Pudd'nhead Wilson himself.

David Wilson's downfall, when he first comes to town, as well as the source of his nickname and the ruin of his career, is a famous remark about a dog. (The story is not original with Twain—but in the context of the novel Twain gives it a new twist.[34]) Twain writes,

> He had just made the acquaintance of a group of citizens when an invisible dog began to yelp and snarl and howl and make himself very comprehensively disagreeable, whereupon young Wilson said, much as one who is thinking aloud:
> "I wish I owned half of that dog."
> "Why?" somebody asked.
> "Because I could kill my half."
> The group searched his face with curiosity, with anxiety even, but found no light there, no expression that they could read. They fell away from him as from something uncanny, and went into privacy to discuss him. One said:
> "'Pears to be a fool."
> "'Pears?' said another. "Is, I reckon you better say."
> "Said he wished he owned half of the dog, the idiot," said a third. "What did he reckon would become of the other half if he killed his half? Do you reckon he thought it would live?"
> "Why, he must have thought it, unless he is the downrightest fool in the world; because if he hadn't thought it, he would have wanted to own the whole dog, knowing that if he killed his half and the other half died, he would be responsible for that half just the same as if he had killed that half instead of his own. Don't it look that way to you, gents?"
> "Yes, it does. If he owned one half of the general dog it would be so; if he owned one end of the dog, and another person owned the other end, it would be so, just the same;

particularly in the first case, because if you kill one half of a general dog, there ain't any man that can tell whose half it was. . ."

No. 3 said, "well, he's a lummox anyway. . ."

"I'm with you, gentlemen," said No. 6. "Perfect jackass—yes, and it ain't going too far to say he is a pudd'nhead. If he ain't a pudd'nhead, I ain't no judge, that's all."[35]

"Irony" Twain observes, "was not for these people; their mental vision was not focused for it."[36]

We know from Twain's expressed views on the subject—as in "How to Tell a Story"—that David Wilson is a fine storyteller, too fine for his own good, perhaps. Master of the deadpan style that Twain had perfected, Wilson not only fails to crack a revealing smile during his initial performance, he also fails to let his audience know they've been "taken" for some twenty years hence! His comment is, of course, patently absurd. How can you kill half a dog? The halves are connected, kill a half and you've killed a whole. Any fool can see that. Or can he? Wilson's absurd comment that he would "kill his half" of the dog makes him a marked fool in his community. But aren't his fellow citizens engaged in just such a proposition? As they systematically degrade and destroy that "half" of the people in their land whose skin is the "wrong" color, don't they destroy their own community as well? If they don't within the confines of the book—for the book ends before the Civil War—we may be confident that this sleepy, comfortable, contented slaveholding town will be violently jarred quite shortly.

What if we think of the yelping, invisible "general dog" as the body politic or the country in 1894?[37] From the standpoint of law, custom and a range of other perspectives, the population of the United States in 1894, regardless of the actual numbers in each group, is divided into two parts: white and non-white. These two parts of the general populace together comprise the citizens of the United States of America, the equal citizens of the U.S. in fact, by virtue of the Fourteenth Amendment. Yet despite the fact that they make up an identifiable whole, the law, custom and popular parlance act as if the two parts are not only clearly identifiable, but easily separable: hence the ubiquitous Jim Crow laws designed to segregate black from white. Notwithstanding the fact that "Plessy v. Ferguson" in 1896 inscribed "separate but equal" as the law of the land, any American as clear-sighted as Mark Twain could see that there was nothing "equal" about the treatment black Americans received at the hands of the law and society.[38]

"We have ground the manhood out of them," Twain wrote on Christmas eve in 1885, referring to black people, "& the shame is ours, not theirs, & we should pay for it."[39] Throughout the 1880s and 1890s Twain embraced a variety of means to "pay for it." He paid with money (supporting black students in law school and college, or funding a black painter's apprenticeship in Paris); he paid with service (performing gratis in black churches whenever asked); he paid with his influence (writing publicity blurbs for the Fisk Jubilee Singers' international tour, interceding with President Garfield when Frederick Douglass was about to be dismissed from a Federal post); and he paid with his work—with "A True Story, Repeated Word for Word as I Heard It," with *Adventures of Huckleberry Finn,* and with *Pudd'nhead Wilson.* Twain himself, intensely conscious of the personal and national shame that was the legacy of Slavery, was prompted in the 1880's and 1890's to try, through the range of means cited here, to expand opportunities for black Americans. The majority of his fellow Americans, however, were engaged in a very different effort: as white supremacists garnered greater and greater influence in the North as well as the South, they tried to constrict the horizon of expectations of black Americans every way they could.

Despite the backing they had from the legislatures, the courts, and public opinion, however, the efforts of the white supremacists were doomed to fail. They could try to kill half a dog—but the other half—they themselves, would not escape unaffected.

Just as Slavery had dehumanized slaveholders as well as slaves in the ante-bellum era, post-war racism took its moral and psychological toll on whites as well as blacks. As Twain's contemporaries passed new Jim Crow laws, revoked rights, ostracized, reviled, insulted, abused and lynched in the 1890's, they thought they were simply killing "half a dog." The project was, of course, absurd: what they were really killing off were their own illegitimate children, the fruits of their own illegitimate power, a part of themselves, their fellow citizens, their country, their country's future.

The sickness of racism—designed to denigrate one group and elevate another—would send an entire nation, not half a nation—into painful, drawn-out convulsions. The violence and destruction of the race riots in the 1890's and at the turn of the century would be followed in the 1960's by the murder of civil rights workers, the blowing up of children in church, the assassination of Martin Luther King, Jr., and the uprisings that wracked so many cities; the legacy of the black underclass shaped by Jim Crow laws at the turn of the century is, unfortunately, all too with us as the end of our own century approaches.

Twain had an abiding affection for Pudd'nheads—and Sap-heads, which is what Huck Finn is called by Tom Sawyer when Huck fails to understand why the genies always do what "whoever rubs the lamp or ring" tells them to do. "Well," says Huck, "I think they are a pack of flatheads for not keeping the palace themselves."

> And what's more—If I was one of them I would see a man in Jericho before I would drop my business and come to him for the rubbing of an old tin lamp. "How you talk, Huck Finn. Why you'd have to come when he rubbed it, whether you wanted to or not." "What, and I as high as a tree and as big as a church? Alright, then: I *would* come; but I lay I'd make that man climb the highest tree there was in the country." "Shucks, it ain't no use to talk to you, Huck Finn. You don't seem to know anything, somehow—perfect saphead."[40]

Not inculcated, as Tom Sawyer is, with genie lore from *Arabian Nights,* Huck sees no basis for the arbitrary authority the lamp-rubber exercises over a being many times his strength and size.

While Huck nay not make that leap of insight, clearly Twain does: in *Puddn'head Wilson,* so will Roxana. "What has my po' baby done, dat he couldn't have yo' luck," she moaned to her master's baby, as he sleeps not far from her own, "He hain't done noth'n. God was good to you; why warn't he good to him? Dey can't sell *you* down de river."[41] When she makes the fateful decision to switch her own baby with the baby of her master, Roxana is, in fact, to the best of her knowledge at the time, choosing to "keep the palace" herself.

"Sap-heads" and "pudd'nheads" have much in common. Both say things that are dumb or stupid in the eyes of those around them. Both of them seem to be blind to the "obvious." Both implicitly challenge the not-to-be-questioned premises of their peers. But both of them turn out to be more right than wrong: the notion of the genie keeping the palace for himself may be less absurd than Tom Sawyer thinks it is, and the question of killing half a dog holds more significance than the citizens of Dawson's Landing suspect. Twain uses both his famous "sap-head" and his famous "pudd'nhead" as vehicles to show society's assumptions—rather than the characters who question them—to be absurd.

As Twain explores various dimensions of the question of personal identity in *Pudd'nhead Wilson,* he gives heavy weight to the idea of training as the foremost shaper of character. "Training is everything," Pudd'nhead Wilson writes in his Calendar.[42] But is it? On the one hand, Twain traces numerous character traits to precisely the training one had as a child. "Tom got all the petting, Chambers got none. . . In consequence, . . . Tom was 'fractious,' as Roxy called it, and overbearing; Chambers was meek and docile."[43] "In babyhood," we learn, "Tom cuffed and banged and scratched Chambers unrebuked, and Chambers early learned that between meekly bearing it and resenting it, the advantage all lay with the former policy. . . Outside of the house the two boys were together all through their boyhood. . . Tom staked (Chambers) with marbles to play 'keeps' with, and then took all the winnings away from him. . . In the winter season Chambers was on hand, in Tom's worn-out clothes. . . to drag a sled up the hill for Tom, warmly clad, to ride down on; but he never got a ride himself. . . He was Tom's patient target when Tom wanted to do some snowballing, but the target couldn't fire back."[44]

Yet despite all his emphasis on "training" on numerous occasions in the book, at other times Twain seems to acquiesce to what seems, at bottom, a racist idea of heredity and environment. The fact that the one "natively vicious" character in the book is Tom, who is one thirty-second part black, has opened Twain, yet again, to the charge of being a racist: why is it that the child with black blood turns out completely immoral and selfish, lacking even the most basic compassion and decency, while his white counterpart is brave, kind, compassionate and generous?[45] Why make Tom such a villain? Why make the white child such a saint?

Critics have suggested several possible answers to this question. In "What Is Man?", as Judith Berzon notes, "Twain argues that man is controlled by the training which is brought to bear upon his inherited characteristics. . . While Twain's major emphasis is on the power of training, he makes it clear that temperament cannot be ignored. It is the 'disposition you were born with. You can't eradicate your disposition nor any rag of it—you can only put a pressure on it and keep it down and quiet'."[46] Thus Tom's "evil" and Chamber's "goodness." Another critic accounts for Tom's "utterly debased" behavior in terms of character and plot development: he has to be "made as diabolical as he is so that Roxy will be motivated to reveal his identity" and to overcome the force of her maternal affection.[47]

Twain's view on the nature vs. nurture argument in the book is, in fact, inconsistent and confused. But the central explanation for Tom's "native viciousness" may be that which appears in a passage included in Twain's working version of the novel, but deleted, for reasons unknown, before publication. In the Morgan manuscript of *Pudd'nhead Wilson*, Twain has Tom consider his motivation in refusing the duel. We are told that

> what was high came from either blood, & was the monopoly of neither color; but that which was base was the white blood in him debased by the brutalizing effects of a long-drawn heredity of slave-owning, with the habit of abuse which the possession of irresponsible power always created & perpetuates, by a law of human nature.[48]

In short, if heredity plays any role in creating the monster that is Tom, it is the white blood that has debased him, not the black. When a cadet who was one-sixteenth black was expelled from West Point in the 1880s for "conduct unbecoming an officer and a gentleman," William Dean Howells recalled Twain's caustic reactions to the proceedings: "The man was fifteen parts white, but 'Oh yes,' Clemens said with bitter irony, 'It was the one part black that undid him. It made him a 'nigger' and incapable of being a gentleman. It was to blame for the whole thing.'"[49] As the passage from the Morgan manuscript of *Pudd'nhead Wilson* suggests, if any blood were to blame for the cadet's ungentlemanly conduct, the white blood, and not the black, was the more likely suspect as far as Twain was concerned.

In *Pudd'nhead Wilson*, training teaches Chambers, a white child raised as a black slave, to be meek, docile, and self-effacing, to always expect less than equal treatment, to bear with equanimity being robbed, exploited, cuffed and pelted with snowballs by the boy he thinks is his master. Training teaches Tom, a black child raised as a white master, to be arrogant and overbearing, deceitful, cowardly, dishonest, and ready to rob, steal, cuff and pelt his way through life. The book doesn't make the argument that a black child raised as a white will be as good as a white: it argues that a black raised as a white will be as bad as a white. Whether one focused on heredity or on environment, then, the "master race", in Twain's view, contained ample seeds of its own undoing.

III

Twain's two great anti-racist works of fiction, *Adventures of Huckleberry Finn* and *Pudd'nhead Wilson* may be read as incisive commentaries on the time in which they were written, the 1870s, 1880s and 1890s. Why did Twain choose to set both books in the ante-bellum era? One reason, of course, was the special pull the time of his own youth had on his imagination. Another reason, however, may be the freedom this remote setting gave him to explore contemporary issues that may have been too threatening to explore directly. (When Twain did explore such issues directly—in "The United States of Lyncherdom," for example—he was likely to censor himself before publication. "I shouldn't have even half a dozen friends left, after it issued from the press," he wrote his editor only days after sending him the proposal for the book about lynchings.[50] Some topics were just too hot to handle.)

The choice Twain made when he set *Adventures of Huckleberry Finn* and *Pudd'nhead Wilson* in ante-bellum America was not unlike that made by the African-American writer Paul Laurence Dunbar in the virtuoso poem he wrote in 1896, "An Ante-Bellum Sermon." Just as Dunbar himself tells a story ostensibly set in slave times to offer truths about the 1890s, the preacher in the poem tells a story set in Biblical times to tell truths about the time in which he and his parishioners live, truths too dangerous to tell straight-out. The preacher's—and Dunbar's—strategy is highly effective, as these excerpts reveal:

> . . . 'Now ole Pher'oh, down in Egypt,
>   Was de wuss man evah bo'n,
> An' he had de Hebrew chillun
>   Down dah wukin' in his c'n;
> Well de Lawd got tiahed o' his foolin'

An' sez he: "I'll let him know—
Look hyeah, Moses, go tell Pher'oh
Fu'to let dem chillun go."
. . . But fu' feah some one mistakes me,
I will pause right hyeah to say,
Dat I'm still a-preachin' ancient,
I ain't talkin' 'about today.
. . . So you see de Lawd's intention,
Evah sence de worl' began,
Was dat His almighty freedom
Should belong to evah man,
But I think it would be bettah
Ef I'd pause agin to say,
Dat I'm talkin' 'bout ouah freedom
In a Bibleistic way. . . .[51]

Here Dunbar, like the preacher in his poem, preached "ancient" to talk about "today." In other poems, however, such as "The Haunted Oak" and "We Wear the Mask," he wrote about contemporary problems—the physical and psychic toll taken by racism in the 1890s—in all their stark, unfiltered brutality.[52]

Twain, by way of contrast, never left off "preachin' ancient" in his published work of the 1880s and 1890s. Like the preacher in Dunbar's poem, he was always free to claim, "I ain't talkin' 'bout today." His decision to talk about freedom in an "ante-bellum way," may have insulated Twain from some of the more blatant hostility of his white contemporaries. It also may have prevented him from "connecting" intellectually, emotionally, and artistically, with black readers who might have responded to his work more intensely had he been willing to train his brilliant ironic vision on the contemporary scene. Despite his intense interest in the lives of black Americans, and despite the incisiveness with which he anatomized the dynamics of racism in his work, throughout his life he remained embedded, as an artist and as a man, in a world that was essentially white. If he read the African-American writers who were working through the same sorts of questions he was, often in the same literary forms that he himself was using, Twain unfortunately left us no record of the fact. Some interesting contrasts, however, emerge when one examines how two of Twain's African-American contemporaries, W.E.B. DuBois and Pauline Hopkins, handled some familiar themes.

The relationship Twain paints between Chambers and Tom brings to mind the story of a different pair of childhood playmates, one black and one white, who come of age in the years after Reconstruction in a story by W.E.B. Du Bois called "Of the Coming of John."[53] Each of the boys leaves home to go to school. The black boy, who had worked as a field-hand, finds the world of learning that opens up to him intoxicating: He

> wandered alone over the green campus peering through and beyond the world of men into a world of thought. . . . He caught terrible colds lying on his back in the meadows of nights, trying to think about the solar system; he had grave doubts as to the ethics of the Fall of Rome, and strongly suspected the Germans of being thieves and rascals, despite his textbooks; he pondered long over every new Greek word, and wondered why this meant that and why it couldn't mean something else, and how it must have felt to think all these things in Greek.[54]
>
> As he passed from preparatory school to college, he looked now for the first time sharply about him, and wondered he had seen so little before. He grew slowly to feel almost for the first time the Veil that lay between him and the white world; he first noticed now the oppression that had not seemed oppression before, differences that erstwhile seemed natural, restraints and slights that in his boyhood days had gone unnoticed or been greeted with a laugh. He felt angry now when men did not call him "Mister," he clenched his hands at the "Jim Crow" cars, and chafed at the color-line that hemmed in him and his. . . Daily he found himself shrinking from the choked and narrow life of his native town. And yet he always planned to go back.[55]

His former playmate, a judge's son, goes to Princeton, where he learns the arrogance with which one must occupy one's rightful place in the ruling class. When he finds himself behind a black man on a ticket line for the opera, he entertains his date with the remark, "Be careful, you must not lynch the colored gentleman simply because he's in your way." He later "flushes to the roots of his hair" when the "Negro he had stumbled over in the hallway" turns out to be seated on the other side of his date in the reserved orchestra chairs. The music of the opera stirs the black man beyond anything he has known. "A deep longing swelled in all his heart," Du Bois writes, "to rise with that clear music out of the dirt and dust of that low life that held him prisoned and befouled. . . Who had called him to be the slave and butt of all? And if he had called, what right had he to call when a world like this lay open before men?" The usher soon interrupts his reverie to insist that he move to the colored seating area, much to the relief of the white man seated in his row, who didn't recognize his childhood friend.

Both young men return to their home town, each a conquering hero for his respective race. But the die is cast. The black man preaches education, sparks his people, opens a school, tries to open to others the world that was opened to him. His behavior threatens the white establishment. "This school is closed," the Judge announces to the stunned students that cram the rickety shanty where the black schoolmaster is teaching them to read. "You children can go home and get to work. The white people of Altamaha are not spending their money on black folks to have their heads crammed with impudence and lies. Clear out! I'll lock the door myself."[56]

The story races to a harrowing and tragic end: the promising young black scholar sees the Princeton n'er-do'well, the Judge's son, attempting to rape his sister. He strikes him mortally to stop the rape, and then drowns himself. The boldest visions and noblest dreams fall victim to one small battle in a large race war, devastating in its effects on white and black alike.

One wonders what Twain would have thought of this story, had he read it. Surely he would have been struck by its resonances with the story he himself had written: two childhood playmates, one black and one white, each destined for a very different fate. As he read Du Bois' lyrical and moving description of the black boy's growing intellectual excitement Twain might have wondered if these kinds of thoughts had ever passed through the mind of A.W. Jones, a black student whose education at Lincoln University Twain had funded. Twain would have found in Du Bois' description of the white boy's arrogance and ill manners support for his own increasingly cynical views about his race.

In Du Bois' story, which is set in the 1880s or 1890s, both of the childhood playmates are killed by the spiral of tragic events set off by ingrained patterns of racism. In *Pudd'nhead Wilson*, both of the childhood playmates emerge alive: damaged, no doubt, but very much alive. Du Bois' story is ultimately much darker than Twain's; tragedy, not irony, is the dominant mode.

Similar differences obtain, as well, between Twain's "A True Story, Repeated Word for Word as I Heard It," which appeared in *The Atlantic Monthly* in 1874, and Pauline Hopkins's story, "The Test of Manhood," which was published in *The Colored American* in 1902.[57] Like Twain in "A True Story," Pauline Hopkins in "The Test of Manhood" brings about the reunion of a black mother and son who have been separated for many years. In Twain's story the post-war reunion of mother and son is fortuitous and joyful: whatever pain there is in the story comes through in the mother's memories of the auction block, the terror of separation, the degradations of slavery. In Hopkins's story, however, the reunion is itself frought with searing pain and anguished decisions. The son had been "passing" as white, and acknowledging his mother means giving up his white fiancee, his job, his life, the person he has been so happy to "become." That is his "test of manhood"—and he passes. The "happy ending," for Pauline Hopkins, is thus bought with enormous psychic and emotional pain.

* * * *

As it encodes and reflects the history that shaped it, *Pudd'nhead Wilson* illuminates that history in fresh and memorable ways. The book engages our imagination both in spite of its flaws, and because of them. It challenges us to re-examine the moral underpinnings not only of Twain's society, but of our own. The book's greatest strengths—and its greatest weaknesses—stem from Twain's determination to grapple with the complex problem of American race relations. Nine years after *Pudd'nhead Wilson* appeared, Twain's insistence on the centrality and importance of this issue would be echoed by W.E.B. Du Bois.

In his preface to his magisterial 1903 book, *The Souls of Black Folk*, W.E.B. Du Bois wrote, "the problem of the Twentieth Century is the problem of the color line." On that point, Mark Twain most likely would have agreed. In his later years in such short works of nonfiction as "To the Person Sitting in the Darkness," and diatribes against racist imperialism in the Congo or the Philippines, Twain raged at the gall of a race that claimed to have a monopoly on civilization while exporting the most heinous brutality around the globe. In fragments of unfinished fiction, such as the novel "Which Was It?", Twain showed a prescient awareness of some of the forms that pent-up rage could take if the degradations of racism went unchecked.[58] Twain's disgust with his race was deep-going and well-founded, and his prognosis for America was not good. There was a long road to travel before any real change or progress could take place and Twain knew it wouldn't happen in his lifetime. "The shame," as Twain put it in 1885, "is ours."

Notes

1. An earlier version of this essay was presented as a lecture at the Mark Twain Memorial, Hartford, Ct. in 1989. I am greatly

indebted to Jeffrey Rubin-Dorsky and David E. E. Sloane for having taken the time to offer astute criticism and helpful editorial suggestions as I revised this material for publication.

2. When Tom Driscoll's story took over the story of the Siamese twins, Twain writes, he was left with "not one story, but two stories tangled together; and they obstructed and interrupted each other at every turn and created no end of confusion and annoyance." Mark Twain, *The Tragedy of 'Pudd'nhead Wilson' and the Comedy 'Those Extraordinary Twins'* (Hartford: American Publishing Company, 1894), p. 311.

3. In the hands of a talented critic like Hershel Parker, such an analysis is illuminating and compelling. See, for example, Hershel Parker, "*Pudd'nhead Wilson*: Jack-leg Author, Unreadable Text, and Sense-Making Critics," in *Flawed Texts and Verbal Icons: Literary Authority in American Fiction* (Evanston: Northwestern University Press), 1984, pp. 115–146. Other worthwhile studies of the composition history of either *Huckleberry Finn* or *Pudd'nhead Wilson* include: Walter Blair, "When Was Huckleberry Finn Written?", *American Literature*, 30 (March 1958): 1–25; Jeffrey Steinbrink, "Who Wrote *Huckleberry Finn*? Mark Twain's Control of the Early Manuscript" in *One Hundred Years of Huckleberry Finn*, ed. Robert Sattelmeyer and J. Donald Crowley (Columbia: University of Missouri Press, 1985), pp. 85–105; Victor Doyno, "*Adventures of Huckleberry Finn:* The Growth from Manuscript to Novel," in *One Hundred Years of Huckleberry Finn*, pp.106–116; Daniel Morley McKeithan, "The Morgan Manuscript of Mark Twain's *Pudd'nhead Wilson,*' *Essays and Studies on American Language and Literature*, No. 12 (Cambridge: Harvard University Press, 1961), pp. 1–64. Susan Gillman's fascinating essay "Racial Identity in *Pudd'nhead Wilson*" combines a discussion of the book's composition history with a sophisticated awareness of a number of the complex racial issues that intertwine with that history. See Susan Gillman, *Dark Twins: Imposture and Identity in Mark Twain's America* (Chicago: University of Chicago Press, 1989), pp. 53–95.

4. Shelley Fisher Fishkin, "'Smashed All to Flinders': *Huckleberry Finn* and the Breakdown of Reconstruction," in Fishkin, *The Stories He Couldn't Tell: Mark Twain and Race*, forthcoming, Oxford University Press. See also Shelley Fisher Fishkin, "Mark Twain and the Risks of Irony," in *Twain/Stowe Sourcebook: Curriculum Resource Materials for the Study of Mark Twain and Harrier Beecher Stowe*, ed. Elaine Cheesman and Earl French (Hartford: Mark Twain Memorial and Stowe-Day Foundation, 1989), pp. 49–52.

5. C. Vann Woodward, *The Strange Career of Jim Crow* (New York: Oxford University Press, 1955) and, also, *The Burden of Southern History* (New York: Vintage/Random House, 1960); Rayford W. Logan, *The Betrayal of the Negro: From Rutherford B. Hayes to Woodrow Wilson* (originally published as *The Negro in American Life and Thought: The Nadir, 1877–1901)* (London: Collier-Macmillan, 1965); John Hope Franklin, *From Slavery to Freedom: A History of Negro Americans,* third edition (New York: Alfred A. Knopf, 1967); George M. Frederickson, *The Black Image in the White Mind: The Debate on Afro-American Character and Destiny, 1817–1914* (New York: Harper & Row, 1971); Joel Williamson, *A Rage for Order: Black-White Relations in the American South Since Emancipation* (New York: Oxford University Press, 1986); August Meier, *Negro Thought in America 1880–1915: Racial Ideologies in the Age of Booker T. Washington* (Ann Arbor: University of Michigan Press, 1963).

6. Woodward, *The Strange Career of Jim Crow,* p. 64.

7. Woodward, *The Strange Career of Jim Crow,* pp. 82–83.

8. Woodward, *The Strange Career of Jim Crow,* p. 8.

9. Woodward, *The Strange Career of Jim Crow,* and Peter M. Bergman, *The Chronological History of the Negro in America* (New York: Harper & Row, 1969).

10. Ida B. Wells, *Crusade for Justice: The Autobiography of Ida B. Wells,* ed. Alfreda M. Duster (Chicago: University of Chicago Press, 1970), pp. 65–66. Ida B. Wells describes several stories like the following, which prompted her to write her famous 1892 editorial on lynchings: "I also had the sworn statement of a mother whose son had been lynched that he had left the place where he worked because of the advances made by the beautiful daughter of the house. The boy had fallen under her spell, and met her often until they were discovered and the cry of rape was raised. A handsome young mulatto, he too had been horribly lynched for 'rape.' It was with these and other stories in mind that last week in May 1892 that I wrote the following editorial: 'Eight Negroes lynched since last issue of the *Free Speech.* Three were charged with killing white men and five with raping white women. Nobody in this section believes the old threadbare lie that Negro men assault white women. If Southern white men are not careful they will over-reach themselves and a conclusion will be reached which will be very damaging to the moral reputation of their women.'" Wells' newspaper office was destroyed by some of the leading citizens of Memphis as a result of this column.

11. Williamson, *A Rage for Order,* p. 84.

12. Williamson, *A Rage for Order,* p. 84.

13. Williamson, *A Rage for Order,* p. 84.

14. Frederickson, *The Black Image in the White Mind,* p. 272.

15. These figures refer only to documented lynchings. Actual figures probably run substantially higher. Bergman, *The Chronological History of the Negro in America*, pp. 303–327.

16. Woodward, *The Strange Career of Jim Crow*, p. 78.

17. Woodward, *The Strange Career of Jim Crow*, pp. 80–81.

18. P.T. Barnum, in a speech before the Connecticut Legislature on May 26, 1865. Quoted in P.T. Barnum, *Struggles and Triumphs, or Forty Years' Record of P. T. Barnum, Written by Himself*, intro. by Roy F. Dribble (New York: Macmillan, 1930), pp. 459–460.

19. George M. Frederickson, *White Supremacy: A Comparative Study in American & South African History* (New York: Oxford University Press, 1981), p. 96; "For attempts by social scientists to explain the North American descent rule, see Marvin Harris, *Patterns of Race in the Americas* (New York, 1964), 56, 79–94; H. Hoetnik, *The Two Variants of Caribbean Race Relations: A Contribution to the Sociology of Segmented Societies* (London, 1967), 46–47; and passim; and idem, *Slavery and Race Relations in the Americas: An Inquiry into Their Nature and Nexus* (New York, 1973), 9–20 and passim," p. 305.

20. Frederickson, *White Supremacy*, p. 96.

21. Bergman, *The Chronological History of the Negro in America*, p. 323.

22. Bergman, *The Chronological History of the Negro in America*, pp. 298, 306.

23. Bergman, *The Chronological History of the Negro in America*, p. 311.

24. Bergman, *The Chronological History of the Negro in America*, pp. 306, 329.

25. Bergman, *The Chronological History of the Negro in America*, p. 329.

26. One exception to this pattern is the work of Albion W. Tourgee, who denounced ideas of white supremacy at political gatherings and in numerous novels, the most famous of which are *A Fool's Errand* (1879) and *Bricks Without Straw* (1880). Tourgee's work, however, tended to be dismissed as "purely propagandist" artistic failures. His books never achieved the widespread popularity of, say, the work of Joel Chandler Harris. (See Theodore Gross, "The Negro in the Literature of Reconstruction," p. 72 and also Brook Thomas, "Tragedies of Race, Training, Birth, and Communities of Competent Pudd'nheads." *American Literary History*, 1.4 (Winter 1989), pp. 754–785). Another exception is William Dean Howells' novel *An Imperative Duty* (1891), which addressed in subtle and sensitive ways contemporary dilemmas faced by the mulatto.

27. Sterling Brown, the American Race Problem as Reflected in American Literature," *Journal of Negro Education*, VIII (July, 1929), p. 282 (quoted in Theodore L. Gross, *op.cit.*, pp. 75–6).

28. Theodore L. Gross, "The Negro in the Literature of Reconstruction", in *Images of the Negro in American Literature*, ed. Seymour L. Gross and John Edward Hardy (Chicago: University of Chicago Press, 1966), p. 77 (reprinted from *Phylon*, 22 (1961), pp. 5–14).

29. Theodore L. Gross, "The Negro in the Literature of Reconstruction", p. 77. Gross notes that while a "condescending attitude toward the Negro is most obvious" in the fiction of Thomas Nelson Page and Thomas Dixon, it also "appears in the stories and novels of Joel Chandler Harris, Mary Murfree, Maurice Thompson, and innumerable minor writers" (p. 73).

30. Thomas Dixon, *The Leopard's Spots* (1902), *The Clansman* (1905), the *The Traitor* (1907). D.W. Griffith's 1915 film, "The Birth of a Nation" was loosely based on Dixon's novel, *The Clansman*. The film, and the three novels, chronicle and glorify the birth of the Ku Klux Klan.

31. Mark Twain, *Pudd'nhead Wilson* (New York: Bantam Books, 1959), pp. 13–18.

32. Susan Gillman, *Dark Twins*, p. 85. (For race classification in Louisiana, Gillman cites Virginia R. Dominguez, *White by Definition: Social Classification in Creole Louisiana* (New Brunswick, N.J., 1986).

33. George Frederickson, *White Supremacy: A Comparative Study in American and South African History* (New York, 1981), p. 130.

34. Twain may well have borrowed the story about H. Bailey, who, when cheated of the proceeds for exhibiting an elephant in which he owned half interest, announced "I am fully determined to shoot my half." P.T. Barnum, *The Life of P.T. Barnum, Written By Himself* (New York: Redfield, 1855) pp. 114–115. Twain kept Barnum's book on his bedside table. Another variant of the story appears in an article titled "Yankee Humor" in the *British Quarterly Review*, vol. 122, Jan.–April 1867, p. 221. In this story a minster asks blessings on "his half" of a negro slave. See David Sloane, *Mark Twain as a Literary Comedian* (Baton Rouge: Louisiana State University Press, 1979), pp. 178–179, ftnt. 12 p. 179. Sloane finds Don Marquis, in his short story "The Mulatto" published in 1916 dealing with the issue in the same terms, with seven drops of the hero's blood out of each eight being caucasian: "The eighth being African, classified him" (Sloane, 182).

35. Mark Twain, *Pudd'nhead Wilson*, pp. 23–4.

36. Mark Twain, *Pudd'nhead Wilson*, p. 28.

37. Evan Carton has explored the notion of the "general dog" as the "body politic" in an ante-bellum context. In his illuminating essay, *"Pudd'nhead Wilson* and the Fiction of Law and Custom" in *American Realism: New Essays*, ed. Eric J. Sundquist (Baltimore: Johns Hopkins University Press, 1982), pp. 82–94, he notes, "if. . . the 'general dog' implicates a body politic, half of whose members are owned by the other half, then it would follow that the possessors could not dispose of their own possessions without destroying themselves" (p. 84).

38. For an insightful and sensitive discussion of related issues see Eric Sundquist, "Mark Twain and Homer Plessy." *Representations,* 24 (Fall 1988): 102–27.

39. SLC to Francis Wayland, December 24, 1885 (in the private collection of Nancy and Richard Stiner). See Edwin McDowell, "From Twain, a Letter on Debt to the Blacks." *New York Times* (14 March 1985), pp. 1, 16.

40. Mark Twain, *Adventures of Huckleberry Finn,* ed., Leo Marx (Indianapolis: Bobbs-Merrill, 1967), p. 25.

41. Mark Twain, *Pudd'nhead Wilson,* p. 13.

42. Mark Twain, *Pudd'nhead Wilson,* p. 26.

43. Mark Twain, *Pudd'nhead Wilson,* p. 20.

44. Mark Twain, *Pudd'nhead Wilson,* p. 21.

45. Judith R. Berzon explores these questions in interesting ways in *Neither White Nor Black: The Mulatto Character in American Fiction* (New York: New York University Press, 1978). See pp. 40–48.

46. Judith Berzon, *Neither White Nor Black,* pp. 44–45.

47. Robert Rowlette, *Mark Twain's Pudd'nhead Wilson: The Development and Design* (Bowling Green, Ohio: Bowling Green University Popular Press, 1971), p. 97, quoted in Berzon, *Neither White Nor Black,* p. 45.

48. Mark Twain, *The Morgan Manuscript of Mark Twain's Pudd'nhead Wilson,* ed. Daniel Morley McKeithan (Cambridge, Mass., 1961), pp. 137–38 quoted in Judith R. Berzon, *Neither White Nor Black,* p. 46.

49. William Dean Howells quoted in James M. Cox, *"Pudd'nhead Wilson:* The End of Mark Twain's American Dream", in Seymour L. Gross and John Edward Hardy, ed., *Images of the Negro in American Literature* (Chicago: University of Chicago Press, 1966), p. 162.

50. Mark Twain, letter to Elisha Bliss, quoted in Everett Emerson, *The Authentic Mark Twain: A Literary Biography of Samuel L. Clemens* (Philadelphia: University of Pennsylvania Press, 1985), p. 238.

51. Paul Laurence Dunbar, "An Ante-Bellum Sermon," in Cleanth Brooks, R.W.B. Lewis and Robert Penn Warren, *American Literature: The Makers and the Making*, Vol. II, p. 1744.

52. Paul Laurence Dunbar, "We Wear the Mask" (1896) and "The Haunted Oak" (1903), in Brooks, Lewis and Warren, *American Literature*, pp. 1743–1744.

53. W.E.B. Du Bois, "Of The Coming of John," in *The Souls of Black Folk* (New York: New American Library, 1969), pp. 245–263.

54. W.E.B. Du Bois, *The Souls of Black Folk*, pp. 249–250.

55. W.E.B. Du Bois, *The Souls of Black Folk*, pp. 250–251.

56. W.E.B. Du Bois, *The Souls of Black Folk*, p. 261.

57. Mark Twain, "A True Story, Repeated Word for Word as I Heard It," *Atlantic Monthly* 34 (November 1874), pp. 591–594. Pauline Hopkins (Sarah A. Allen), "The Test of Manhood." *The Colored American*, 6 (December 1902), pp. 113–119.

58. See Shelley Fisher Fishkin, *The Stories He Couldn't Tell: Mark Twain and Race* (forthcoming, Oxford University Press).

The Later Career of Mark Twain:
The Comedian as a
Cultural Representative

Mark Twain: An Inquiry

William Dean Howells

T wo recent events have concurred to offer criticism a fresh excuse, if not a fresh occasion, for examining the literary work of Mr. Samuel L. Clemens, better known to the human family by his pseudonym of Mark Twain. One of these events is the publication of his writings in a uniform edition, which it is to be hoped will remain indefinitely incomplete; the other is his return to his own country after an absence so long as to form a psychological perspective in which his characteristics make a new appeal.

The uniform edition of Mr. Clemens's writings is of that dignified presence which most of us have thought their due in moments of high pleasure with their quality, and high dudgeon with their keeping in the matchlessly ugly subscription volumes of the earlier issues. Yet now that we have them in this fine shape, fit every one, in its elect binding, paper, and print, to be set on the shelf of a gentleman's library, and not taken from it without some fear of personal demerit, I will own a furtive regret for the hideous blocks and bricks of which the visible temple of the humorist's fame was first builded. It was an advantage to meet the author in a guise reflecting the accidental and provisional moods of a unique talent finding itself out; and the pictures which originally illustrated the process were helps to the imagination such as the new uniform edition does not afford. In great part it could

Reprinted from Chapter XI from *My Mark Twain* (NY: Harper & Bros., 1910: 143–62), originally published in *North American Review* CLXXII (February 1901): 836–50.

not retain them, for reasons which the recollection of their uncouth vigor will suggest, but these reasons do not hold in all cases, and especially in the case of Mr. Dan Beard's extraordinarily sympathetic and interpretative pictures for *The Connecticut Yankee in King Arthur's Court.* The illustrations of the uniform edition, in fact, are its weak side, but it can be said that they do not detract from one's delight in the literature; no illustrations could do that; and, in compensation for their defeat, the reader has the singularly intelligent and agreeable essay of Mr. Brander Matthews on Mr. Clemens's work by way of introduction to the collection. For the rest one may acquit one's self of one's whole duty to the uniform edition by reminding the reader that in the rich variety of its inclusion are those renowning books *The Innocents Abroad* and *Roughing It;* the first constructive fiction on the larger scale, *Tom Sawyer* and *Huckleberry Finn;* the later books of travel, *A Tramp Abroad* and *Following the Equator;* the multiplicity of tales, sketches, burlesques, satires, and speeches, together with the spoil of Mr. Clemens's courageous forays in the region of literary criticism; and his later romances, *The Connecticut Yankee, The American Claimant,* and *Joan of Arc.* These complete an array of volumes which the most unconventional reviewer can hardly keep from calling goodly, and which is responsive to the spirit of the literature in a certain desultory and insuccessive arrangement.

So far as I know, Mr. Clemens is the first writer to use in extended writing the fashion we all use in thinking, and to set down the thing that comes into his mind without fear or favor of the thing that went before or the thing that may be about to follow. I, for instance, in putting this paper together, am anxious to observe some sort of logical order, to discipline such impressions and notions as I have of the subject into a coherent body which shall march columnwise to a conclusion obvious if not inevitable from the start. But Mr. Clemens, if he were writing it, would not be anxious to do any such thing. He would take whatever offered itself to his hand out of that mystical chaos, that divine ragbag, which we call the mind, and leave the reader to look after relevancies and sequences for himself. These there might be, but not of that hard-and-fast sort which I am eager to lay hold of, and the result would at least be satisfactory to the author, who would have shifted the whole responsibility to the reader, with whom it belongs, at least as much as with the author. In other words, Mr. Clemens uses in work on the larger scale the method of the elder essayists, and you know no more where you are going to bring up in *The Innocents Abroad* or *Following the Equator* than in an essay of Montaigne. The end you arrive at is the end of the book, and you reach it amused but edified, and sorry for nothing but to be there. You have noted the author's thoughts, but not his order of thinking; he has not attempted to trace the threads of association between the things that have followed one another; his reason, not his logic, has convinced you, or, rather, it has persuaded you, for you have not been brought under conviction. It is not certain that this method is of design with Mr. Clemens; that might spoil it; and possibly he will be as much surprised as any one to know that it is his method. It is imaginable that he pursues it from no wish but to have pleasure of his work, and not to fatigue either himself or his reader; and his method may be the secret of his vast popularity, but it cannot be the whole secret of it. Any one may compose a scrapbook, and offer it to the public with nothing of Mark Twain's good-fortune. Everything seems to depend upon the nature of the scraps, after all; his scraps might have been consecutively arranged, in a studied order, and still have immensely pleased; but there is no doubt that people like things that have at least the appearance of not having been drilled into line. Life itself has that sort of appearance as it goes on; it is an essay with moments of drama in it rather than a drama; it is a lesson, with the precepts appearing haphazard, and not precept upon precept; it is a school, but not always a school-room; it is a temple, but the priests are not always in their sacerdotal robes; sometimes they are eating the sacrifice behind the altar and pouring the libations for the god through the channels of their dusty old throats. An instinct of something chaotic, ironic, empiric in the order of experience seems to have been the inspiration of our humorist's art, and what finally remains with the reader, after all the joking and laughing, is not merely the feeling of having had a mighty good time, but the conviction that he has got the worth of his money. He has not gone through the six hundred pages of *The Innocents Abroad*, or *Following the Equator*, without having learned more of the world as the writer saw it than any but the rarest traveller is able to show for his travel; and possibly, with his average practical American public, which was his first tribunal, and must always be his court of final appeal, Mark Twain justified himself for being so delightful by being so instructive. If this bold notion is admissible, it seems the moment to say that no writer ever imparted information more inoffensively.

But his great charm is his absolute freedom in a region where most of us are fettered and shackled by immemorial convention. He saunters out into the trim world of letters, and lounges across its neatly kept paths, and walks about on the grass at will, in spite of all the signs that have been put up from the beginning of literature, warning people of dangers and penalties for the slightest trespass.

One of the characteristics I observe in him is his singleminded use of words, which he employs as Grant did to express the plain, straight meaning their common acceptance has given them with no regard to their structural significance or their philological implications. He writes English as if it were a primitive and not a derivative language, without Gothic or Latin or Greek behind it, or German and French beside it. The result is the English in which the most vital works of English literature are cast, rather than the English of Milton and Thackeray and Mr. Henry James. I do not say that the English of the authors last named is less than vital, but only that it is not the most vital. It is scholarly and conscious; it knows who its grandfather was; it has the refinement and subtlety of an old patriciate. You will not have with it the widest suggestion, the largest human feeling, or perhaps the loftiest reach of imagination, but you will have the keen joy that exquisite artistry in words can alone impart, and that you will not have in Mark Twain. What you will have in him is a style which is as personal, as biographical as the style of any one who has written, and expresses a civilization whose courage of the chances, the preferences, the duties, is not the measure of its essential modesty. It has a thing to say, and it says it in the word that may be the first or second or third choice, but will not be the instrument of the most fastidious ear, the most delicate and exacting sense, though it will be the word that surely and strongly conveys intention from the author's mind to the reader's. It is the Abraham Lincolnian word, not the Charles Sumnerian; it is American, Western.

Now that Mark Twain has become a fame so world-wide, we should be in some danger of forgetting, but for his help, how entirely American he is, and we have already forgotten, perhaps, how truly Western he is, though his work, from first to last, is always reminding us of the fact. But here I should like to distinguish. It is not alone in its generous humor, with more honest laughter in it than humor ever had in the world till now, that his work is so Western. Any one who has really known the West (and really to know it one must have lived it) is aware of the profoundly serious, the almost tragical strain which is the fundamental tone in the movement of such music as it has. Up to a certain point, in the presence of the mystery which we call life, it trusts and hopes and laughs; beyond that it doubts and fears, but it does not cry. It is more likely to laugh again, and in the work of Mark Twain there is little of the pathos which is supposed to be the ally of humor, little suffusion of apt tears from the smiling eyes. It is too sincere for that sort of play; and if after the doubting and the fearing it laughs again, it is with a suggestion of that resentment which youth feels when the disillusion from its trust and hope comes, and which is the grim second-mind of the West in the presence of the mystery. It is not so much the race-effect as the region-effect; it is not the Anglo-American finding expression, it is the Westerner, who is not more thoroughly the creature of circumstances, of conditions, but far more dramatically their creature than any prior man. He found himself placed in them and under them, so near to a world in which the natural and primitive was obsolete, that while he could not escape them, neither could he help challenging them. The inventions, the appliances, the improvements of the modern world invaded the hoary eld of his rivers and forests and prairies, and, while he was still a pioneer, a hunter, a trapper, he found himself confronted with the financier, the scholar, the gentleman. They seemed to him, with the world they represented, at first very droll, and he laughed. Then they set him thinking, and, as he never was afraid of anything, he thought over the whole field and demanded explanations of all his prepossessions—of equality, of humanity, of representative government, and revealed religion. When they had not their answers ready, without accepting the conventions of the modern world as solutions or in any manner final, he laughed again, not mockingly, but patiently, compassionately. Such, or somewhat like this, was the genesis and evolution of Mark Twain.

Missouri was Western, but it was also Southern, not only in the institution of slavery, to the custom and acceptance of which Mark Twain was born and bred without any applied doubt of its divinity, but in the peculiar social civilization of the older South from which his native State was settled. It would be reaching too far out to claim that American humor, of the now prevailing Western type, is of Southern origin, but without staying to attempt it I will say that I think the fact could be established; and I think one of the most notably southern traits of Mark Twain's humor is its power of seeing the fun of Southern seriousness, but this vision did not come to him till after his liberation from neighborhood in the vaster Far West. He was the first, if not the only, man of his section to betray a consciousness of the grotesque absurdities in the Southern inversion of the civilized ideals in behalf of slavery, which must have them upside down in order to walk over them safely. No American of Northern birth or breeding could have imagined the spiritual struggle of Huck Finn in deciding to help the negro Jim to his freedom, even though he should be forever despised as a negro thief in his native town, and perhaps eternally lost through the blackness of his sin. No Northerner could have come so close to the heart of a Kentucky feud, and revealed it so perfectly, with the whimsicality playing through its carnage, or could have so brought us into the presence of the sardonic comi-tragedy of the squalid little river town where the store-keeping magnate shoots down his drunken tormentor in the arms of the drunkard's daughter, and then cows with bitter mockery the mob that comes to lynch him. The strict religiosity compatible in the Southwest with savage precepts of conduct is something that could make itself known in its amusing contrast only to the native Southwesterner, and the revolt against it is as constant in Mark Twain as the enmity to New England orthodoxy is in Doctor Holmes. But he does not take it with such serious resentment as Doctor Holmes is apt to take his inherited Puritanism, and it may be therefore that he is able to do it more perfect justice, and impart it more absolutely. At any rate, there are no more vital passages in his fiction than those which embody character as it is affected for good as well as evil by the severity of the local Sunday-schooling and church-going.

I find myself, in spite of the discipline I intend for this paper, speaking first of the fiction, which by no means came first in Mark Twain's literary development. It is true that his beginnings were in short sketches, more or less inventive, and studies of life in which he let his imagination play freely; but it was not till he had written *Tom Sawyer* that he could be called a novelist. Even now I think he should rather be called a romancer, though such a book as *Huckleberry Finn* takes itself out of the order of romance and places itself with the great things in picaresque fiction. Still, it is more poetic than picaresque, and of a deeper psychology. The probable and credible soul that the author divines in the son of the town-drunkard is one which we might each own brother, and the art which portrays this nature at first hand in the person and language of the hero, without pose or affectation, is fine art. In the boy's history the author's fancy works realistically to an end as high as it has reached elsewhere, if not higher; and I who like *The Connecticut Yankee in King Arthur's Court* so much have half a mind to give my whole heart to *Huckleberry Finn*.

Both *Huckleberry Finn* and *Tom Sawyer* wander in episodes loosely related to the main story, but they are of a closer and more logical advance from the beginning to the end than the fiction which preceded them, and which I had almost forgotten to name before them. We owe to *The Gilded Age* a type in Colonel Mulberry Sellers which is as likely to endure as any fictitious character of our time. It embodies the sort of Americanism which survived through the Civil War, and characterized in its boundlessly credulous, fearlessly adventurous, unconsciously burlesque excess the period of political and economic expansion which followed the war. Colonel Sellers was, in some rough sort, the American of the day, which already seems so remote, and is best imaginable through him. Yet the story itself was of the fortuitous structure of what may be called the autobiographical books, such as *The Innocents Abroad* and *Roughing it*. Its desultory and accidental character was heightened by the co-operation of Mr. Clemens's fellow-humorist, Charles Dudley Warner, and such coherence as it had was weakened by the diverse qualities of their minds and their irreconcilable ideals in literature. These never combined to a sole effect or to any variety of effects that left the reader very clear what the story was all about; and yet from the cloudy solution was precipitated at least one character which, as I have said, seems of as lasting substance and lasting significance as any which the American imagination has evolved from the American environment.

If Colonel Sellers is Mr. Clemens's supreme invention, as it seems to me, I think that his *Connecticut Yankee* is his highest achievement in the way of a greatly imagined and symmetrically developed romance. Of all the fanciful schemes in fiction it pleases me most, and I give myself with absolute delight to its notion of a keen East Hartford Yankee finding himself, by a retroactionary spell, at the court of King Arthur of Britain, and becoming part of the sixth century with all the customs and ideas of the nineteenth in him and about him. The field for humanizing satire which this scheme opens is illimitable; but the ultimate achievement, the last poignant touch, the most exquisite triumph of the book, is the return of the Yankee to his own century, with his look across the gulf of the ages at the period of which he had been a part and his vision of the sixth-century woman he had loved holding their child in her arms.

It is a great fancy, transcending in aesthetic beauty the invention in *The Prince and the Pauper,* with all the delightful and affecting implications of that charming fable, and excelling the heartrending story in which Joan of Arc lives and prophesies and triumphs and suffers. She is, indeed, realized to the modern sense as few figures of the past have been realized in fiction; and is none the less of her time and of all time because her supposititious historian is so recurrently of ours. After Sellers, and Huck Finn, and Tom Sawyer, and the Connecticut Yankee, she is the author's finest creation; and if he had succeeded in portraying no other woman-nature, he would have approved himself its fit interpreter in her. I do not think he succeeds so often with the nature as with the boy-nature or the man-nature, apparently because it does not interest him so much. He will not trouble himself to make women talk like women at all times; oftentimes they talk too much like him, though the simple, homely sort express themselves after their kind; and Mark Twain does not always write men's dialogue so well as he might. He is apt to burlesque the lighter colloquiality, and it is only in the more serious and most tragical junctures that his people utter themselves with veracious simplicity and dignity. That great, burly fancy of his is always tempting him to the exaggeration which is the condition of so much of his personal humor, but which when it invades the drama spoils the illusion. The illusion renews itself in the great moments, but I wish it could be kept intact in the small, and I blame him that he does not rule his fancy better. His imagination is always dramatic in its conceptions, but not always in its expressions; the talk of his people is often inadequate caricature in the ordinary exigencies, and his art contents itself with makeshift in the minor action. Even in *Huck Finn*, so admirably proportioned and honestly studied, you find a piece of lawless extravagance hurled in, like the episode of the two strolling actors in the flatboat; their broad burlesque is redeemed by their final tragedy—a prodigiously real and moving passage—but the friend of the book cannot help wishing the burlesque was not there. One laughs, and then despises one's self for laughing, and this is not what Mark Twain often makes you do. There are things in him that shock, and more things that we think shocking, but this may not be so much because of their nature as because of our want of naturalness; they wound our conventions rather than our convictions. As most women are more the subjects of convention than men, his humor is not for most women; but I have a theory that, when women like it, they like it far beyond men. Its very excess must satisfy that demand of their insatiate nerves for something that there is enough of; but I offer this conjecture with instant readiness to withdraw it under correction. What I feel rather surer of is that there is something finally feminine in the inconsequence of his ratiocination, and his beautiful confidence that we shall be able to follow him to his conclusion in all those turnings and twistings and leaps and bounds by which his mind carries itself to any point but that he seems aiming at. Men, in fact, are born of women, and possibly Mark Twain owes his literary method to the colloquial style of some far ancestress who was more concerned in getting there, and amusing herself on the way, than in ordering her steps.

Possibly, also, it is to this ancestress that he owes the instinct of right and wrong which keeps him clear as to the conditions that formed him, and their injustice. Slavery in a small Missouri River town could not have been the dignified and patriarchal institution which Southerners of the older

South are fond of remembering or imagining. In the second generation from Virginia ancestry of this sort, Mark Twain was born to the common necessity of looking out for himself, and, while making himself practically of another order of things, he felt whatever was fine in the old and could regard whatever was ugly and absurd more tolerantly, more humorously than those who bequeathed him their enmity to it. Fortunately for him, and for us who were to enjoy his humor, he came to his intellectual consciousness in a world so large and free and safe that he could be fair to any wrong while seeing the right so unfailingly; and nothing is finer in him than his gentleness with the error which is simply passive and negative. He gets fun out of it, of course, but he deals almost tenderly with it, and hoards his violence for the superstitions and traditions which are arrogant and active. His pictures of that old river-town, Southwestern life, with its faded and tattered aristocratic ideals and its squalid democratic realities, are pathetic, while they arc so unsparingly true and so inapologetically and unaffectedly faithful.

The West, when it began to put itself into literature, could do so without the sense, or the apparent sense, of any older or politer world outside of it; whereas the East was always looking fearfully over its shoulder at Europe, and anxious to account for itself as well as represent itself. No such anxiety as this entered Mark Twain's mind, and it is not claiming too much for the Western influence upon American literature to say that the final liberation of the East from this anxiety is due to the West, and to its ignorant courage or its indifference to its difference from the rest of the world. It would not claim to be superior, as the South did, but it could claim to be humanly equal, or, rather, it would make no claim at all, but would simply be, and what it was, show itself without holding itself responsible for not being something else.

The Western boy of forty or fifty years ago grew up so close to the primeval woods or fields that their inarticulate poetry became part of his being, and he was apt to deal simply and uncritically with literature when he turned to it, as he dealt with nature. He took what he wanted, and left what he did not like; he used it for the playground, not the workshop of his spirit. Something like this I find true of Mark Twain in peculiar and uncommon measure. I do not see any proof in his books that he wished at any time to produce literature, or that he wished to reproduce life. When filled up with an experience that deeply interested him, or when provoked by some injustice or absurdity that intensely moved him, he burst forth, and the outbreak might be altogether humorous, but it was more likely to be humorous with a groundswell of seriousness carrying it profoundly forward. In all there is something curiously, not very definably, elemental, which again seems to me Western. He behaves himself as if he were the first man who was ever up against the proposition in hand. He deals as newly, for instance, with the relations of Shelley to his wife, and with as personal and direct an indignation, as if they had never attracted critical attention before; and this is the mind or the mood which he brings to all literature. Life is another affair with him; it is not discovery, not a surprise; every one else knows how it is; but here is a new world, and he explores it with a ramping joy, and shouts for the reader to come on and see how, in spite of all the lies about it, it is the same old world of men and women, with really nothing in it but their passions and prejudices and hypocrisies. At heart he was always deeply and essentially romantic, and once must have expected life itself to be a fairy dream. When it did not turn out so he found it tremendously amusing still, and his expectation not the least amusing thing in it, but without rancor, without grudge or bitterness in his disillusion, so that his latest word is as sweet as his first. He is deeply and essentially romantic in his literary conceptions, but when it comes to working them out he is helplessly literal and real; he is the impassioned lover, the helpless slave of the concrete. For this reason, for his wish, his necessity, first to ascertain his facts, his logic is as irresistible as his laugh.

All life seems, when he began to find it out, to have the look of a vast joke, whether the joke was on him or on his fellow-beings, or if it may be expressed without irreverence, on their common creator. But it was never wholly a joke, and it was not long before his literature began to own its pathos. The sense of this is not very apparent in *The Innocents Abroad,* but in *Roughing It* we began to be distinctly aware of it, and in the successive books it is constantly imminent, not as a clutch at the heartstrings, but as a demand of common justice, common sense, the feeling of proportion. It is not sympathy with the under dog merely as under dog that moves Mark Twain; for the under dog is sometimes rightfully under. But the probability is that it is wrongfully under, and has a claim to your inquiry into the case which you cannot ignore without atrocity. Mark Twain never ignores it; I know nothing finer in him than his perception that in this curiously contrived mechanism men suffer for their sorrows rather oftener than they suffer for their sins; and when they suffer for their sorrows they have a right not only to our pity but to our help. He always gives his help, even when he seems to leave the pity to others, and it may be safely said that no writer has dealt with so many phases of life with more unfailing justice. There is no real telling how any one comes to be what he is; all speculation concerning the fact is more or less impudent or futile conjecture; but it is conceivable that Mark Twain took from his early environment the custom of clairvoyance in things in which most humorists are purblind, and that being always in the presence of the under dog, he came to feel for him as under with him. If the knowledge and vision of slavery did not tinge all life with potential tragedy, perhaps it was this which lighted in the future humorist the indignation at injustice which glows in his page. His indignation relieves itself as often as not in a laugh; injustice is the most ridiculous thing in the world, after all, and indignation with it feels its own absurdity.

It is supposable, if not more than supposable, that the ludicrous incongruity of a slaveholding democracy nurtured upon the Declaration of Independence, and the comical spectacle of white labor owning black labor, had something to do in quickening the sense of contrast which is the fountain of humor, or is said to be so. But not to drive too hard a conjecture which must remain conjecture, we may reasonably hope to find in the untrammelled, the almost unconditional life of the later and farther West, with its individualism limited by nothing but individualism, the outside causes of the first overflow of the spring. We are so fond of classification, which we think is somehow interpretation, that one cannot resist the temptation it holds out in the case of the most unclassifiable things; and I must yield so far as to note that the earliest form of Mark Twain's work is characteristic of the greater part of it. The method used in *The Innocents Abroad* and in *Roughing It* is the method used in *Life on the Mississippi*, in *A Tramp Abroad*, and in *Following the Equator*, which constitute in bulk a good half of all his writings, as they express his dominant aesthetics. If he had written the fictions alone, we should have had to recognize a rare inventive talent, a great imagination and dramatic force; but I think it must be allowed that the personal books named overshadow the fictions. They have the qualities that give character to the fictions, and they have advantages that the fictions have not and that no fiction can have. In them, under cover of his pseudonym, we come directly into the presence of the author, which is what the reader is always longing and seeking to do; but unless the novelist is a conscienceless and tasteless recreant to the terms of his art, he cannot admit the reader to his intimacy. The personal books of Mark Twain have not only the charm of the essay's inconsequent and desultory method, in which invention, fact, reflection, and philosophy wander after one another in any following that happens, but they are of an immediate and most informal hospitality which admits you at once to the author's confidence, and makes you frankly welcome not only to his thought but to his way of thinking. He takes no trouble in the matter, and he asks you to take none. All that he required is that you will have common sense, and be able to tell a joke when you see it. Otherwise the whole furnishing of his mental mansion is at your service, to make such use as you can of it, but he will not be always directing your course, or requiring you to enjoy yourself in this or that order.

In the case of the fictions, he conceives that his first affair is to tell a story, and a story when you are once launched upon it does not admit of deviation without some hurt to itself. In Mark Twain's novels, whether they are for boys or for men, the episodes are only those that illustrate the main narrative or relate to it, though he might have allowed himself somewhat larger latitude in the old-fashioned tradition which he has oftenest observed in them. When it comes to the critical writings, which again are personal, and which, whether they are criticisms of literature or of life, are always so striking, he is quite relentlessly logical and coherent. Here there is not lounging or sauntering, with entertaining or edifying digressions. The object is in view from the first, and the reasoning is straightforwardly to it throughout. This is as notable in the admirable paper on the Jews, or on the Austrian situation, as in that on Harriet Shelley, or that on Cooper's novels. The facts are first ascertained with a conscience uncommon in critical writing of any kind, and then they are handled with vigor and precision till the polemic is over. It does not so much matter whether you agree with the critic or not; what you have to own is that here is a man of strong convictions, clear ideas, and ardent sentiments, based mainly upon common sense of extraordinary depth and breadth.

In fact, what finally appeals to you in Mark Twain, and what may hereafter be his peril with his readers, is his common sense. It is well to eat humble pie when one comes to it at the table d'hôte of life, and I wish here to offer my brother literary men a piece of it that I never refuse myself. It is true that other men do not really expect much common sense of us, whether we are poets or novelists or humorists. They may enjoy our company, and they may like us or pity us, but they do not take us very seriously, and they would as soon we were fools as not if we will only divert or comfort or inspire them. Especially if we are humorists do they doubt our practical wisdom; they are apt at first sight to take our sense for a part of the joke, and the humorist who convinces them that he is a man of as much sense as any of them, and possibly more, is in the parlous case of having given them hostages for seriousness which he may not finally be able to redeem.

I should say in the haste to which every inquiry of this sort seems subject, that this was precisely the case with Mark Twain. The exceptional observer must have known from the beginning that he was a thinker of courageous originality and penetrating sagacity, even when he seemed to be joking; but in the process of time it has come to such a pass with him that the wayfaring man can hardly shirk knowledge of the fact. The fact is thrown into sudden and picturesque relief by his return to his country after the lapse of time long enough to have let a new generation grow up in knowledge of him. The projection of his reputation against a background of foreign appreciation, more or less luminous, such as no other American author has enjoyed, has little or nothing to do with his acceptance on the new terms. Those poor Germans, Austrians, Englishmen, and Frenchmen who have been, from time to time in the last ten years, trying to show their esteem for his humor as we could; we might well doubt if they could fathom all his wisdom, which begins and ends in his humor; and if ever they seemed to chance upon his full significance, we naturally felt a kind of grudge, when we could not call it their luck, and suspected him of being less significant in the given instances than they supposed. The danger which he now runs with us is neither heightened nor lessened by the spread of his fame, but is an effect from intrinsic causes. Possibly it might not have been so great if he had come back comparatively forgotten; it is certain only that in coming back more remembered than ever, he confronts a generation which began to know him not merely by his personal books and his fiction, but by those criticisms of life and literature which have more recently attested his interest in the graver and weightier things.

Graver and weightier, people call them, but whether they are really more important than the lighter things, I am by no means sure. What I am amused with, independently of the final truth, is the possibility that his newer audience will exact this serious mood of Mr. Clemens, whereas we of his older world only suffered it, and were of a high conceit with our liberality in allowing a humorist sometimes to be a philosopher. Some of us indeed, not to be invidiously specific as to whom, were always aware of potentialities in him, which he seemed to hold in check, or to trust doubtfully to his reader as if he thought they might be thought part of the joke. Looking back over his work now, the later reader would probably be able to point out to earlier readers the evidence of a constant growth in the direction of something like recognized authority in matters of public import, especially those that were subject to the action of the public conscience as well as the public interest, until now hardly any man writing upon such matters is heard so willingly by all sorts of men. All of us, for instance have read somewhat of the conditions in South Africa which have eventuated in the present effort of certain British politicians to destroy two free republics in the interest of certain British speculators; but I doubt if we have found the case anywhere so well stated as in the closing chapters of Mark Twain's *Following the Equator.* His estimate of the military character of the belligerents on either side is of the prophetic cast which can come only from the thorough assimilation of accomplished facts; and in those passages the student of the actual war can spell its anticipative history. It is by such handling of such questions, unpremeditated and almost casual as it seems, that Mark Twain has won his claim to be heard on any public matter, and achieved the odd sort of primacy which he now enjoys.

But it would be rather awful if the general recognition of his prophetic function should implicate the renunciation of the humor that has endeared him to mankind. It would be well for his younger following to beware of reversing the error of the elder, and taking everything in earnest, as these once took nothing in earnest from him. To reverse that error would not be always to find his true meaning, and perhaps we shall best

arrive at this by shunning one another's mistakes. In the light
of the more modern appreciation, we elders may be able to see
some things seriously that we once thought pure drolling, and
from our experience his younger admirers may learn to receive
as drolling some things that they might otherwise accept as
preaching. What we all should wish to do is to keep Mark
Twain what he has always been: a comic force unique in the
power of charming us out of our cares and troubles, united
with as potent an ethic sense of the duties, public and private,
which no man denies in himself without being false to other
men. I think we may hope for the best he can do to help us
deserve our self-respect, without forming Mark Twain
societies to read philanthropic meanings into his jokes, or
studying the Jumping Frog as the allegory of an imperializing
republic. I trust the time may be far distant when the
Meditation at the Tomb of Adam shall be memorized and
declaimed by ingenuous youth as a mystical appeal for human
solidarity.

The International Fame of Mark Twain

Archibald Henderson

> "Art transmitting the simplest feelings of common life, but such always as are accessible to all men in the whole world—the art of common life—the art of a people—universal art."—Tolstoy: "What is Art?"

It is a mark of the democratic independence of America that she has betrayed a singular indifference to the appraisal of her literature at the hands of foreign criticism. Upon her writers who have exhibited derivative genius—Irving, Hawthorne, Emerson, Longfellow—American criticism has lavished the most extravagant eulogiums. The three geniuses who have made permanent contributions to world literature, who have either embodied in the completest degree the spirit of American democracy or who have won the widest following of imitators and admirers in foreign countries, still await their final and just deserts at the hands of critical opinion in their own land. The genius of Edgar Allan Poe gave rise to schools of literature in France and on the continent of Europe; yet in America his name remained until now debarred from inclusion in a so-called Hall of Fame! Walt Whitman and Mark Twain, the two great interpreters and embodiments of America, represent the supreme contribution of democracy to universal literature. In so far as it is legitimate for any one to be denominated a "self-made man" in literature, these two men are justly entitled to that characterization. They owe nothing to European literature—their genius is transcendently

Reprinted from *North American Review* 192 (December 1910): 805–815.

original, native, democratic. The case of Mark Twain is a literary phenomenon which imposes upon criticism, peculiarly upon American criticism, the distinct obligation of tracing the steps in his unhalting climb to an eminence completely international in character. Mark Twain achieved that eminence by the sole power of brain and personality. In this sense his career is unprecedented and unparalleled in the history of American literature. Criticism must define those signal qualities, traits, characteristics—individual, literary, social, racial, national—which encompassed his world-wide fame. For if it be true that the judgment to foreign nations is virtually the judgment of posterity, then is Mark Twain already a classic.

Upon the continent of Europe, Mark Twain first received notable critical recognition in France at the hands of that brilliant woman, Mme. Blanc ("Th. Bentzon"), who devoted her energies in such great measure to the popularization of American literature in Europe. The essay on Mark Twain, in the series which she wrote, under the general title "The American Humorists," appeared in the *"Revue des Deux Mondes"* in 1872 (July 15th). In addition to a remarkably accurate translation of "The Jumping Frog" into faultless French, this essay contained a minute analysis of "The Innocents Abroad"' and at this time Mme. Blanc was contemplating a translation of "The Innocents Abroad" into French. There is no cause for surprise in the discovery that a scholarly Frenchwoman, reared on classic models and confined by rigid canons of art, should stand aghast at this boisterous, barbaric, irreverent jester from the Western wilds of America. When one reflects that Mark Twain began his career as one of the sage-brush writers and gave free play to his democratic disregard of the traditional and the classic as such, it is not to be wondered at that Mme. Blanc, while honoring him with elaborate interpretation in the most authoritative literary journal in the world, could not conceal an expression of amazement over his enthusiastic acceptance in English-speaking countries:

Mark Twain's "Jumping Frog" should be mentioned, in the first place, as one of his most popular little stories—almost a type of the rest. It is, nevertheless, rather difficult for us to understand, while reading the story, the "roars of laughter" that it excited in Australia and in India, in New York and in London; the numerous editions of it which appeared; the epithet of "inimitable"' that the critics of the English press have unanimously awarded to it. . . .

We may remark that a Persian of Montesquieu, a Huron of Voltaire, even a simple Peruvian woman of Madame de Graffigny, reasons much more wisely about European civilization than an American of San Francisco. The fact is that it is not sufficient to have wit or even natural taste in order to appreciate works of art.

It is the right of humorists to be extravagant; but still common sense although carefully hidden, ought _sometimes_ to make itself apparent. . . . In Mark Twain the Protestant is enraged against the pagan worship of broken marble statues—the democrat denies that there was any poetic feeling in the Middle Ages. . . .

In the course of this voyage with Mark Twain ("The Innocents Abroad"), we at length discover, under his good-fellowship and apparent ingenuousness, faults which we should never have expected. He has in the highest degree that fault of appearing astonished at nothing—common, we may say, to all savages. He confesses himself that one of his great pleasures is to horrify the guides by his indifference and stupidity. He is, too, decidedly envious. . . . We could willingly pardon him his patriotic self-love, often wounded by the ignorance of Europeans, above all, in what concerns the New World, if only that national pride were without mixture of personal vanity. . . .

Taking the "Pleasure Trip on the Continent" altogether, does it merit the success it enjoys? In spite of the indulgence that we cannot but show to the judgments of a foreigner; while recollecting that those amongst us who have visited America have fallen, doubtless, under the influence of prejudices almost as dangerous as ignorance, into errors quite as bad—in spite of the wit with which certain pages sparkle—we must say that this voyage is very far below the less celebrated excursions of the same author in his own country.

It is only too patent that the humor of Mark Twain, the very qualities which won him his immense and sudden popularity, make no appeal to Mme. Blanc. She conscientiously and painstakingly upbraids him *au grand serieux* for those features of his work most thoroughly surcharged with *vis comica.* Three years later Mme. Blanc returns to the criticism of Mark Twain, in an essay in the *Revue des Deux Mondes* (March 15th, 1875), entitled "L'Age Dore en Amerique"—an exhaustive review and analysis of "The Gilded Age." The savage charm and genuine simplicity of Mark Twain are not devoid of attraction even to her sophisticated intelligence; and she is inclined to infer that jovial irony and animal spirits are qualities sufficient for the amusement of a young nation of people such as are the Americans, since they do not pique themselves upon being *blasés.* According to her judgment, Mark Twain and Charles Dudley Warner are lacking in the requisite mental grasp for the "stupendous tasks of interpreting the great tableau of the American scene." Nor does she regard their effort at collaboration as a success from the standpoint of art:

> From this association of two very dissimilar minds arises a work very difficult to read; at every moment we see the pen pass from one hand to the other and the romancer call the humorist to order, only too often call him in vain. . . Do not expect of Mark Twain either tact or delicacy, but count upon him for honest and outspoken shrewdness. . . . .

The charm of Colonel Sellers wholly escapes her, for she cannot understand the truly loving appreciation with which this genial burlesque of the later American industrial brigand was greeted by the American people. The remarkable talents of Mark Twain as a reporter impress her most favorably; but she is repelled by "that mixture of good sense with mad folly—disorder," the wilful exaggeration of the characters, and the jests which are so elaborately constructed that "the very theme itself disappears under the mass of embroidery which overlays it." "The audacities of a Bret Harte, the temerities of a Mark

Twain still astonish us," she concludes; "but soon we shall become accustomed to an American language whose savory freshness is not to be disdained in lieu of still more delicate and refined qualities that time will doubtless bring."

In translating "The Jumping Frog" (giving Mark Twain the opportunity for re-translating it—"clawing it back"—into English which furnished amusement for thousands), in elaborately reviewing, with long citations, "The Innocents Abroad" and "The Gilded Age," Mme. Blanc rendered a genuine service to Mark Twain, introducing him to the literary world of France and Europe. In 1881 Emile Blémont still further enhanced the fame of Mark Twain in France by publishing in free French translation a number of his slighter sketches, under the title *"Esquisses Américaines de Mark Twain."* In 1884 and again in 1886 appeared editions of "Les Aventures de Tom Sawyer," translated by W. L. Hughes. In 1886 Eugéne Forgues published in the *"Revue des Deux Mondes"* (February 15th) an exhaustive review, with lengthy citations, of "Life on the Mississippi," under the title *"Les Caravanes d'un Humoriste."* His prefatory remarks in regard to Mark Twain's fame in France at this time may be accepted as authoritative. He called attention to the commendable efforts of French scholars to popularize these "transatlantic gayeties." But the result of all the efforts to import into France a new mode of comic entertainment was an almost complete check. There was one notable exception; for "The Adventures of Tom Sawyer" was really appreciated and praised as—an "exquisite idyll"! The peculiar twist of national character, the specialized conception of the *vis comica* revealed in Mark Twain's works, tended to confine them to a restricted *milieu*. To the French taste, Mark Twain's pleasantry appeared *macabre*, his wit brutal, his temperament dry to excess. By some, indeed, his exaggerations were regarded as "symptoms of mental alienation"; and the originality of his verve did not conceal from French eyes the "incoherence of his conceptions."

"It has been said," remarks M. Forgues, "that an academician slumbers in the depths of every Frenchman; and this it was which militated against the success of Mark Twain in France. Humor, with us, has its laws and its restrictions. So the French public saw in Mark Twain a gross jester, incessantly beating upon a tom-tom to attract the attention of the crowd. They were tenacious in resisting all such blandishments. . . *As a humorist* Mark Twain has never been appreciated in France. The appreciation he has ultimately secured—an appreciation by no means inconsiderable, but in no sense comparable to that won in Anglo-Saxon and Germanic countries—was due to his shrewdness and penetration as an observer, and to his marvellous faculty for evoking scenes and situations by the clever use of the novel and the *imprévu*. There was, even to the French, a certain lively appeal in an intelligence absolutely free of convention, sophistication or reverence for traditionary views *qua* traditionary."

Although at first the salt of Mark Twain's humor seemed to be lacking in the Attic flavor, the leisurely exposition of the genially naive American in time won its way with the *blasé* Parisians. It is needless to cite those works of his which were subsequently translated into the French language. It has been recorded that tourists who could find no copy of the Bible in the street book-stalls of Paris were confronted on every hand with copies of "Roughing It"! When the English edition of Mark Twain's collected works appeared (Chatto and Windus: London), that authoritative French journal, the *Mercure de France* (December, 1899), paid him this distinguished tribute:

His public is as varied as possible, because of the versatility and suppleness of his talent which addresses itself successively to all classes of readers. He has been called the greatest humorist in the world, and that is doubtless the truth; but he is also a charming and attractive storyteller, an alert romancer, a clever and penetrating observer, a philosopher without pretensions and, therefore, all the more profound, and finally a brilliant essayist.

Perhaps the present writer may be pardoned for mentioning that when an essay of his on Mark Twain appeared in "Harper's Magazine," in 1909, M. Lux, reviewing it in _L'Indépendence Belge_, says:

> In Mark Twain's writings are to be distinguished, exalted and sublimated by his genius, the typically American qualities of youth and of gayety, of force and of faith. His countrymen love his philosophy, at once practical and high-minded. They are fond of his simple style, animated with verve and spice, thanks to which his work is accessible to all classes of readers. . . He describes his contemporaries with such an art of distinguishing their essential traits, that he manages to evoke, to _create_ even, characters and types of eternal verity. The Americans profess for Mark Twain the same sort of vehement admiration that we have in France for Balzac.

In Italy, as in France, Mark Twain was regarded as a remarkable impressionist; and "The Innocents Abroad" had wide popularity in Rome. But with the peculiar _timbre_ of Mark Twain's humor his Italian audience was not wholly sympathetic; they never felt themselves thoroughly _au courant_ with the spirit of his humor.

> "Translation, however accurate and conscientious," as the Italian critic, Raffaele Simboli, has pointed out, "fails to render the special flavor of his work." And then in Italy, where humorous writing generally either rests on a political basis or depends on _risqué_ phrases, Mark Twain's "Sketches" are not appreciated because the spirit which breathes in them is not always understood. The story of the "Jumping Frog," for instance, famous as it is in America and England, has made little impression in France and Italy.

It was rather among the Germanic peoples and those most closely allied to them racially and temperamentally, the Scandinavians, that Mark Twain found most complete and ready response in Europe. At first sight, it seems almost incredible that the writings of Mark Twain, with their occasional slang, their not infrequent colloquialisms, and their local peculiarities of dialect, should have borne translation into other languages, especially into so complex a language as the German. It must, however, be borne in mind that, despite these peculiar features of his writings, they are couched in a style of most marked directness, simplicity and native English purity.

> "He writes English," says Mr. Howells, "as if it were a primitive and not a derivative language, without Gothic or Latin or Greek behind it or German and French beside it. The result is the English in which the most vital works of English literature are cast. . ."

The ease with which Mark Twain's works were translated into foreign languages, especially the German and allied tongues, and the eager delight with which they were read and comprehended by all classes, high and low, constitute perhaps the most signal conceivable tribute not only to the humanity of his spirit, but to the genuine art of his natural and forthright style. "The Jumping Frog" one would imagine to be very recalcitrant to translation. But I was amazed to discover the naturalness and accuracy of both the French and German translations; not only was the spirit of the original preserved: the universality of the anecdote appeared in yet clearer light. Take a brief passage—that in which Smiley and the stranger touch their respective frogs in order to make them jump. First read M. Blémont's translation into French:

> "Maintenant, dit-il, êtes-vous prêt? Bon! Mettex votre bê à coté de Daniel, leurs pattes de devant bien alignées. Y êtes-vous? je donne le signal.
> "Et chacun d'eux pressa au même instant sa grenouille par derriére. La nouvelle grenouille sauta. Daniel voulut sauter aussi, Daniel fit un effort, haussa les épaules, tenez? comme ca, à la francais. Mais bah! Daniel ne pouvait plus bluger! La pauvre bête semblait plantée là aussi solidement qu'une enclume. On eût dit qu'elle était ancrée sur place. Smiley n'en fut pas médiocrement écoeuré. Mais il n'eut pas la moindre idée de ce qui s'était passé en son absence. Naturellement!"

The translation is apt and clever, for M. Blémont has preserved the spirit—the *ton goguenard*—of the original—lacking in the translation of Mme. Blanc. Equally satisfactory, in catching the *tone* of the story, is the German translation of Herr Moritz Busch:

"Na, wenn Sie jetst parat sind, so setzen Sie ihn neben Daniel'n hin, seine Vorderpfoten ganz in derselben Linie wie Daniel'n seine, und ich werde das Signal geben. Dann sagte er: 'Eins—zwei—drei—hopps!' und er und der Bursche gaben den Fröschen hinten einen Tipps, und der neue Frosch hüpfte fort. Aber Daniel that einen Säufzer und hob die Schultern—so—wie'n Franzose—aber's half nichts, er konnte sich nicht rippeln noch rappeln, er sass so fast wie ein Ambos, und er war nicht mehr im Stande, sich zu regen, als wenn er mit einem Anker festgekettet wäre. Smiley war sehr überrascht davon und sehr böse darüber, aber er hatte natürlich keine Ahnung, an was es lag."

One reason—by no means an insignificant reason—why Mark Twain is regarded in Germany almost as if he were a native German writer is that no other English or American author has had so many translators and editors. *Mark Twain's Ausgewählte Humoristische Schriften*, in twelve volumes (Lutz: Stuttgart), as the Viennese philologist, Dr. Leon Kellner, has pointed out, read "precisely like a German original"—a truly remarkable circumstance. And almost more remarkable still—Mark Twain's *Jugendschriften* have already, some years gone, passed into the fixed repertory of German school literature!

As early as 1872, Mark Twain had secured Tauchnitz, of Leipzig, for his Continental agent. German translations soon appeared of "The Jumping Frog and Other Stories" (1874, "The Gilded Age" (1874), "The Innocents Abroad" (1875), "The Adventures of Tom Sawyer" (1876). Numerous translations soon followed in Germany—published by Mann (Leipzig), Freytag (Leipzig), Lutz (Stuttgart), Reclam's *Universal-bibliothek*, etc. A few years later his sketches, many of them, were translated into virtually all printed languages, notably into Russian and modern Greek. His more extended works rapidly came to be translated into German, French, Italian, Dutch and the languages of Denmark and the Scandinavian peninsula.

The elements of the colossally grotesque, the wildly primitive, in the works of Mark Twain—the underlying note of melancholy, the strain of persistent idealism, not less than the bohemianism—awake a responsive chord in the Germanic consciousness. Mark Twain's stories of the Argonauts, the miners, and the desperadoes; his narratives of the wild freedom of the life on the Mississippi, the lawless and barbaric encounters—all appealed to the Germanic passion for the grotesque. To the Europeans, this wild genius of the Pacific Slope (strange misnomer!) seemed to function in a sort of unexplored fourth-dimension of humor—vast and novel—of which they had never dreamed. In his *"Psychopathik des Humors,"* Schleich reserved for American humor, with Mark Twain as its leading exponent, a distinct and unique category which he denominated *"phantastish," "grossdimensional."* In commenting upon the works of Mark Twain and his popularity in German Europe, Carl von Thaler unhesitatingly affirms that Mark Twain was entertained with absolutely unprecedented hospitality in Vienna—an honor hitherto paid to no German author! In Berlin the young Kaiser bestowed upon him the most distinguished marks of his esteem. He praised Mark Twain's work, notably "Life on the Mississippi," with the intensest enthusiasm; the passages in "A Tramp Abroad" dealing with German student life were also singled out for commendation. After hearing the Kaiser's eulogy on "Life on the Mississippi," Mark Twain was astounded and touched to receive a similar tribute, the same evening, from the *portier* of his lodging-hours.

> That a crowned head and a *portier*, the very top of an Empire and the very bottom of it, should pass the very same criticism and deliver the very same verdict upon a book of mine—and almost in the same hour and the same breath—

this, Mark Twain confessed, was the most extraordinary coincidence of his life.

By German critics Mark Twain was hailed as the leading exponent of American humor, not only in the United States, but, in Herr Ludwig Salomon's phrase, "everywhere that culture rules." "Robinson Crusoe" was held to exhibit a limited power of imagination in comparison with the ingenuity and resourcefulness of "Tom Sawyer." At times the German critics confessed their inability to discover the dividing-line between astounding actuality and humorously fantastic exaggeration. The description of the barbaric state of western America possessed an indescribable fascination for the Europeans. At times Mark Twain's bloody jests froze the laughter on their lips; and his "revolver humor" made their hair stand on end. "Such adventures," one bold critic observes, "are possible only in America—perhaps only in the fancy of an American!"

> "Mark Twain's greatest strength," says von Thaler, "lies in his little sketches, the literary snapshots. The shorter his work, the more striking it is. He draws directly from life. No other writer has learned to know so many different varieties of men and circumstances, so many strange examples of the *Genus Homo*, as he; no other has taken so strange a course of development."

The deeper elements of Mark Twain's humor did not escape the attention of the Germans, nor fail of appreciation at their hands. In his aphorisms, embodying at once genuine wit and experience of life, they discovered the universal human being; and it is chiefly for this reason that they found these aphorisms worthy of profound and lasting admiration. Franz Sintenis saw in Mark Twain a "living symptom of the youthful joy in existence"—a genius capable at will, "despite his boyish extravagance," of the virile formulation of fertile and suggestive ideas. On the occasion of Mark Twain's seventieth birthday, German Europe united in honoring the man and writer. Able critical reviews of his life and work were published in Germany and Austria—more in German Europe than in America! From these various essays—in such authoritative publications as the *Neue Freie Presse* (Vienna), *Tägliche Rundschau* (Leipzig), *Allgemeine Zeitung* (Munich), *Gymnasium* (Paderborn), and the *Illustrirte Zeitung* (Leipzig)—I select one short passage from the pen of the able critic, Dr. Leon Kellner, of Vienna:

> A bohemian fellow, who is full of mischief without the slightest trace of malice in it, an imaginative story-teller who is always ready to make himself and others ridiculous without coming anywhere near the truth, a fantastic and Johnny-look-in-air who nevertheless never loses the solid ground from under his feet, a vagabond and adventurer, who from crown to sole remains a gentleman and with the grand manner of a Walter Scott keeps his commercial honor unsoiled—that is the writer Mark Twain and the citizen Samuel Langhorne Clemens in one person.

He hails Mark Twain as "the king of humorists"—who understood how to transmute all earthly stuff, such as the negro Jim and the street Arab, Huckleberry Finn, into "the gold of pure literature." At the time of Mark Twain's death, when so many tributes were paid him all over the world, one of his German critics wrote, with genuine insight into the deeper significance of his work:

> Although Mark Twain's humor moves us to irresistible laughter, this is not the main feature in his works; like all true humorists, *ist der Witz mit dem Weltschmerz verbunden,* he is a witness to higher thoughts and higher emotions, and his purpose is to expose bad morals and evil circumstances in order to improve and ennoble mankind.

Mark Twain is loved in Germany, the critics pointed out, more than all other humorists, English or French, because his humor "turns fundamentally upon serious and earnest conceptions of life." It is a tremendously significant fact that the works of American literature most widely read today in

Germany are the works of—striking conjunction!—Ralph
Waldo Emerson and Mark Twain.

"The Jumping Frog" fired the laugh heard round the
world; it initiated Mark Twain's international fame. "The
Innocents Abroad" won the thoughtful attention of the English
people. Since that day Mark Twain has been the adored author
of England and the colonies; in lieu of a national author, the
English chose Mark Twain for the national author of the
English-speaking world. His popularity in England was as
great as in America or Germany; all classes read his works
with unfeigned delight; critics of the highest authority praised
his works in the most glowing terms. The personal ovation to
him in 1907, which I witnessed, was the greatest ovation ever
given by the English public to a foreign visitor not a crowned
head; and Oxford University honored him with her degree.

At that time the oldest of England's periodicals, *The
Spectator*, paid Mark Twain this significant and
comprehensive tribute:

> It is all, surely, the most admirable fun and light-
> heartedness. But fun, light-heartedness and an unrivalled
> sense of humor are by no means Mark Twain's only, not
> even, perhaps, his most commanding, characteristics. He has
> a peculiar power of presenting pathetic situations without
> "slush.". . . He is, above all, the fearless upholder of all that
> is clean, noble, straightforward, innocent and manly. . . He
> has his extravagances; some of his public, indeed, would
> insist on them. But if he is a jester, he jests with the mirth of
> the happiest of Puritans; he has read much of English
> knighthood, and translated the best of it into his living
> pages; and he has assuredly already won a high degree in
> letters in having added more than any writer since Dickens
> to the gayety of the Empire of the English language.

It is gratifying to citizens of all nationalities to recall and
recapture the pleasure and delight Mark Twain's works have
given the world for decades. It is peculiarly gratifying to
Americans to rest confident in the belief that, in Mark Twain,
America has contributed to the world an international and
universal genius—sealed of the tribe of Moliére, a congener of

Defoe, of Fielding, of Le Sage—a man who will be remembered, as Mr. Howells has said, "with the great humorists of all time, with Cervantes, with Swift, or with any other worthy his company; none of them was his equal in humanity."

An Inspired Critic

Edith Wyatt

I

Among the journeys of one's dreams there is a certain experience familiar doubtless to many dream-travelers. I mean the great journey down the river. It is a green summer afternoon. The yellow water stretches away a half a mile on each side of your raft. The arrows of far silver ripples point to snags. Around you is the sight of low bluffs, cornbottoms, highland rolling prairie, up beyond the banks. You are a perfect pilot, in your dream-power; and as in other dream-countries you have always known this wonderful place, and yet it is all new and fresh to you.

It is not by the pages of *Tom Sawyer* alone, nor *Huck Finn* alone, that Mark Twain has piloted the world on that miraculous imaginary journey down the great valley, through the center of our national life; but by his whole philosophy, his tremendous propelling power as a social critic.

The Emperor of Germany once said that *Life on the Mississippi* was his favorite American book. The remark has always remained for me an instance of the German range and thoroughness in information. The Emperor could not I believe have chosen any other volume describing American life which would have expressed the virtues and vices of our nation as truly and as aptly as this work of genius.

It is only when one thinks over Mark Twain's writings in their entirety that one realizes how numerous his social

Reprinted from *North American Review* CCV (April 1917): 603-15.

criticisms were—criticisms favorable and unfavorable, and representing, taken together, one of the most far-sighted surveys of democracy that we possess.

It was as press-correspondent, from 1863–65, on the *Enterprise* in Carson City, and later in his letters to the *Enterprise* from San Francisco, that Mark Twain began that penetrating comment on the Government of the United States, and on her social injustice which he was to continue till the end of his life.

Mr. Albert Bigelow Paine tells us in his biography that

> Those who remember Mark Twain's *Enterprise* letters (they are no longer obtainable) declare them to have been the greatest series of daily philippics ever written. However this may be, it is certain they made a stir. Goodman (the editor of the *Enterprise*) permitted him to say exactly what he pleased upon any subject. San Francisco was fairly weltering in corruption, official and private. He assailed whatever came first to hand with all the fierceness of a flaming indignation long restrained.
>
> Quite naturally he attacked the police and with such ferocity and penetration that as soon as copies of the *Enterprise* came from Virginia (in Nevada) the City Hall (in San Francisco) began to boil and smoke and threaten trouble. Martin G. Burke, the chief-of-police, entered libel suit against the *Enterprise*, prodigiously advertising the paper, copies of which were snatched as soon as the stage brought them.

As a journalist he attacked at that period so many social abuses as to gain for himself the title of "The Moralist of the Main." On his return to Nevada to report the proceedings of the legislature at Carson City for the *Enterprise*, Mark Twain was the best-known figure at the capital. His power and courage as a writer, combined with Goodman's power and courage as an editor made him respected and feared in the State Government. Mr. Paine tells us that he could control more votes than any legislative member: and with two other journalists, Simmons and Claggett, could pass or defeat any bill offered.—"He was fearless, merciless and incorruptible."

Mark Twain's contempt for the rabble of our State and national legislatures was lasting. In 1868 after he had gone East and become a Washington press-correspondent he was extremely dejected in the national capital, over the "pitiful intellects" governing the country. "This is a place to get a poor opinion of everybody in" he wrote of Congress. Thirty years later he put into the mouth of Pudd'nhead Wilson the remark that "It could probably be shown by facts and figures that there is no distinctly native American criminal class except Congress." And in 1907, in *Christian Science* he lists Congress and the American voter as among the moral failures of the Christian religion.

> If there are two tickets in the field in the city, one composed of honest men, and the other of notorious blatherskites and criminals he (the American voter) will not hesitate to lay his private Christian honor aside and vote for the blatherskites, if his "party honor" shall exact it. His Christianity is of no use to him and has no influence upon him when he is acting in a public capacity. He has sound and sturdy private morals, but he has no public ones. In the last great municipal election in New York, almost a complete one-half of the votes, representing about 3,500,000 Christians, were cast for a ticket that had hardly a man on it whose earned and proper place was outside of a jail. But that vote was present at church next Sunday the same as ever, and as unconscious of its perfidy as though nothing had happened.
>
> Our Congress consists of Christians. In their private life they are true to every obligation of honor; yet in every session they violate them all; and do it without shame.

One understands the fear and respect Mark Twain inspired as a commentator when one reads in the *Express*, the paper he owned in Buffalo soon after his marriage, the explicit manner of his statement. He was speaking of some farmers of Cohocton who had mobbed a couple whom they disapproved. "The men who did this deed are capable of doing any low, sneaking, cowardly villainy that could be invented in perdition." He appended a full list of their names.

It was with the same directness that he assailed Tammany in New York City in 1901 in his famous Waldorf-Astoria speech at the Acorn Club dinner—a paraphrase of Burke's Impeachment of Warren Hastings.

> I impeach Richard Croker of high crimes and misdemeanors.
> I impeach him in the name of the people whose trust he has betrayed.
> I impeach him in the name of all the people of America whose national character he has dishonored.
> I impeach him in the name and by virtue of those eternal laws of justice which he has violated.
> I impeach him in the name of human nature itself, which he has cruelly betrayed, injured and oppressed in both sexes, in every rank, situation and condition in life.

Our greatest humorist's critical examinations of various products of our social system, his defenses of the dumb, the oppressed, the human beings enduring injustice in our civilization, both in the United States and in almost every country in the globe, are innumerable. One may mention as prominent instances: *To the Person Sitting in Darkness*, *A Dog's Tale*, *A Horse's Tale*, *Cruel Treatment of a Boy* (a defense of Chinamen), the Croker Impeachment, the account of the Queensland-Kanaka Labor Traffic in *Following the Equator*, *The Stolen White Elephant* (a satire on the methods of American Detective Bureaus), *Leopold's Soliloquy* (a denunciation of King Leopold's Congo methods), *The Czar's Soliloquy* (a satire on the imperial divinity of the Emperor of Russia).

This was composed in the same year when a hideous massacre of Jews occurred in Moscow. At about the same time the author was asked for a Christmas sentiment for the New York press; and wrote: "It is my warm and all-embracing Christmas hope that all of us that deserve it may finally be gathered together in a heaven of light and peace, and the others permitted to retire into the clutches of Satan or the Emperor of Russia, according to preference if they have a preference."

Many people will recall with especial vividness Mark Twain's opinions on our annexation of the Philippines.

We have bought some islands from a party who did not own them: with real smartness and a good counterfeit of disinterested friendliness, we coaxed a confiding, weak nation into a trap, and closed it upon them; we went back on an honored guest of the Stars and Stripes when we had no further use for him and chased him to the mountains; we are as indisputably in possession of a wide-spreading archipelago as if it were our property; we have pacified some thousands of islanders and buried them; destroyed their fields, burned their villages, and turned their widows and orphans out-of-doors; furnished heart-break by exile to some dozens of disagreeable patriots; subjugated the remaining millions by Benevolent Assimilation, which is the pious, new name of the market.

II

"There are many humorous things in the world," he says in *Following the Equator*, "among them the white man's notion that he is less savage than the other savages."

It will be seen that the United States of his chronicle is a land of savagery. Mr. Paine's just and absorbing biography seems to speak of Mark Twain's youthful experience of lawless violence, as somehow exceptional—or at least as the experience of a past, a pioneer condition in violence, a picturesque and bygone state. He points out that the author of *Life on the Mississippi* had seen in childhood a man shot down in the street, that his father Judge Clemens, as sheriff, had kept in his own house the body of a man killed in a local feud; and that he had known at close range in early boyhood of many barbarous horrors in the community of Hannibal. It is my own belief that one day in the municipal and criminal courts of Chicago would convince Mr. Paine that neither roughness nor ruffianism had abated in the Middle West since Mark Twain's boyhood.

The state of American society and government his stories and articles present is, broadly speaking, truthfully characteristic of the state of society and government we find now in Chicago—the most murderous and lawless civil community in the world. What is exceptional in our great humorist's view of our national life is not the ruffianism of the existence he describes for us on the Mississippi and elsewhere in the United States, but the fact that he writes the truth about it.

Indeed I think that it would be possible to show that if less rough, the United States of our own contemporary experience is far more ruffianly, far more violently bullied and more acquiescent in being bullied than the communities of Mark Twain's earlier novels and tales.

The United States is filled with what may be called an excessive moderation concerning the telling of truth—though the implication is not intended that Mr. Paine's candid consideration of his subject is shadowed by that fallacy in its truthfulness. She will not admit the presence of atrocity and horror in her own commonwealth. This admission would involve the inconvenient consequences of the necessity of her disapproval of these evils. Instead of acknowledging the plain, undeniable truth such as that which Mark Twain stated about our American mobs—that they are literally composed of persons who are low, sneaking, cowardly and villainous, she generally prefers to assume the timid and evasive air of what H.G. Wells calls our "vulgar refinement" and to dodge the truth by asserting that such a characterization is excessive.

Thus when Colonel Roosevelt called Judge Baldwin a liar for his conduct in the Hoxie decision (or was said to have called Judge Baldwin a liar), instead of looking to see whether an important member of the bench really had betrayed us by twisting the truth, and had behaved irresponsibly and unworthily, the American public focused its attention on the shock it had received from Colonel Roosevelt's "unmannerliness." But apparently no one was shocked by Judge Baldwin, whose decision to at least one lay-reader of its many pages seemed to assert that the American Government licensed railroads to murder their employees.

It is my own belief that if Judea had been peopled by Americans at the time of the Massacre of the Innocents, the main portion of the comment on the occurrence would have been devoted to the bad taste and persecutive sensationalism of referring to the incident as a massacre.

III

One reason doubtless why Mark Twain discriminated so clearly against our native atrocities was because he was in literal truth a great traveler. In his *weltanschauung* he shows you democracy not only absolutely as an experiment in the United States, along the river, in *Tom Sawyer* and *Huck Finn* and *Life on the Mississippi* and in *Roughing it*, but comparatively, and against the backgrounds of other countries, the pageantry of the nations of the globe.

"It does rather look," he says in *The American Claimant* "as if in a republic where all are free and equal property and position constitute rank." He fills you with indignation when he describes a white man cuffing a helpless Hindoo servant for nothing in particular, in a Bombay palace: and then he fills you with indignation again while he tells you how he has seen his own father cuff a little negro slave boy with the same offensive injustice, and in the midst of the same surrounding subservience to his detestable performance. And you wish that Mark Twain's penetration and fresh observation would show you all the kingdoms and customs of the earth, and all the United States' own social history against that background.

IV

Mark Twain considered democracy both geographically against the background of other lands, and historically against the background of other ages. His presentation of the subject historically has a brilliancy of sympathetic expression that seems to me unsurpassed. So that *The Prince and the Pauper* and *A Connecticut Yankee in King Arthur's Court* and *Joan of Arc* fire you with resentment, grief and amusement as quickly as their author's tales of today.

When he was a boy of fifteen, a compositor in a printer's office at Hannibal, as he walked to his work after dinner one afternoon, he noticed the loose page of a book blowing down the street. Picking is up, he read its fragmentary narrative. It was the account of a conversation of Joan of Arc in her prison at Rouen, with two brutal English soldiers who were taunting her. Mark Twain had never heard of Joan of Arc before. He had read no history. Thenceforth through the open door of the wind-blown page, flung to him by fate upon that warm afternoon in the little American town, he was to travel in the realms of gold for nearly sixty years—throughout the rest of his life-time. From that day he was a passionate reader of history.

"Was somebody asking to see the soul?" says Walt Whitman: and of course the reader of fiction is always asking to see the soul: and in *Personal Recollections of Joan of Arc* may look upon and know the soul of an inspired girl, of flaming genius, the soul of a great, a rich-hearted woman, as deeply as though she had been the profoundly loved and honored friend of a life-time. I think indeed she was a friend of Mark Twain's life-time: and that from the instant, when as a boy he read the words of her chronicled conversation he saw from afar the flash of the special force in her that made her what she was, and knew at once intensely and delicately the peculiar splendor of her nature. He said he had been forty years writing *Personal Recollections of Joan of Arc* and that he liked it better than any of his other books: and as you read the pity and terror of its tragedy you easily believe both these sayings. In many ways it is the most profound, the subtlest and the most searching of his novels.

In its superb story of the courage and truth of a woman's knowledge struggling forward under the puerile frivolities of the French rule of the king, and the evil trivialities, the mob stupidities and mob superstitions of the day you read a penetrating tale of patriotism for all time.

A Connecticut Yankee is filled too with patriotism—with the only kind of patriotism which will ever make a democracy successful, the sense of individual human responsibility for social justice. One of the most original works ever written, it is increasingly useful to us. For it presents a great democratic philosophy, a vast imaginative scheme of powerful rule whose humor and common-sense give it a pragmatic validity.

"My idea of our civilization," he wrote to a friend in 1900, "is that it is a shoddy, poor thing and full of cruelties, vanities, arrogancies, meannesses and hypocrisies."

Observing the truth of this saying as applied to our own country now, as well as to King Arthur's Court, American citizens are always turning to their great men to learn what to do if one intends to abide by our social agreement. On this absorbing question of what we are to do, few of our commentators of genius on democracy shed much light. Thoreau, of course, departed from the social agreement. He sheds a clear and blazing light nevertheless on the question of the honorable, individual conduct of free persons in a democracy; but unhappily, a strength almost divine, and beyond that of most mortal creatures, is required to climb the steep path the light indicates. Henry James, in another way from Thoreau, separated himself from our American social agreement; and sheds no light at all upon what we are to do in the general muddle—which he is indeed accredited with disparaging, but which in my own view, he simply ignored. Our greatest poet so beautiful to read, yet sheds no light at all, with his happy belief in "Good in all," etc. And even his outlined democracy, his fellow-roughs hanging about each other's necks, does not exactly represent a reality, and certainly not as democratic or livable a democracy as is presented by Huck's and the negro Jim's days on the raft.

Indeed it may be accepted as a proof of the magic of Mark Twain's genius of humor and the livable character of his democratic faith, that a nation periodically insane on the subject of the negro, and almost unable to recover from the shock of his having dined with a President, has selected as one of its most popular novels a work of fiction which presents the hero as dining, breakfasting, supping and sleeping for weeks with a negro on terms of complete social equality. In their different manners, William James, William Dean Howells and Mark Twain have all expressed great democratic philosophies, in whose light we can see a little distance into our own difficulties—philosophies that one can live by, and go along the road of one's existence by, at least at intervals, and according to one's worth.

To preserve and indeed to live in a sense of social responsibility and yet maintain a cheerful demeanor, this is a philosophy of the Connecticut Yankee which has never been expressed elsewhere, I think, in so convincing and thrilling a manner. On the tide of the author's humorous genius you are carried forward with an impetus which bears you on long after you have left the Connecticut Yankee and stopped laughing at Merlin.

Another carrying power of Mark Twain's philosophy, a force rather less obvious than his invincible humor, is its extraordinary sense of the beauty, the poetry and romance of personal relationship—not simply these qualities in relationships between opposite sexes, but throughout existence. His understanding of all human contacts has an exceptional keenness and delicacy. No persons in fiction are rougher than his characters; and yet no author has exhibited a quicker dislike of having anybody unfairly bullied or patronized. In a few pages of *Cashel Byron's Profession*, Alice Goff, the unfortunate, narrow-minded companion of the brilliant and generous Lydia Carew, who is presented by her creator as a person of exceptional gentleness and equity, is worse patronized and bullied by her mistress than anyone is unfairly bullied or patronized with the author's approval, in all the cursing and fighting and rowdiness of *Life on the Mississippi, The American Claimant, Tom Sawyer* and *Huck Finn* put together.

Mark Twain appreciated the injustices of civilization not only to the poverty-stricken, but to those of mediocre fortune. One of his most eloquent passages concerns the payment of a twenty years' debt of fifty dollars by a hard-working country clergyman. There are numberless instances of his sympathy not only with great wrongs, but with ordinary difficulties and struggles. Among these is the story of how one night at a club-meeting in New York, all the other members one by one slipped away, while he remained, listening patiently with respectful attention through to the end, while a young writer read aloud, a very, very long poem.

"How did you manage to sit through it?" someone asked afterwards.

"Well," he said quietly, "that young man thought he had a divine message to deliver, and I thought he was entitled to at least one auditor, so I stayed with him."

In the unusual social faith of that tale there speaks, I think the voice of the American spirit that may save us all at last.

Mark Twain was a penetrating and imaginative critic not only of the failures of democracy in the United States and in the countries of the globe and the ages of the past, but the failures of our prevailing theology.

His objections are sprinkled through all his books and his correspondence; and are crystallized in the sparkling speculative amusement of *Captain Stormfield's Visit to Heaven* and his posthumous story *The Mysterious Stranger* describing a sojourn of a nephew of Satan's upon earth. There is a power of imagination in these works of fiction on the subject of creation which is nothing less than titanic. Their fancies have a species of bulk, and one may almost say solidity, so that compared with them the gracile [sic] fancies of Poe seem made of air, and even Hawthorne's murky shadows appear to be cast by things ethereal. But the conception of Mark Twain's semi-theological tales of the cosmogony,

Captain Stormfield's race with the comet after his death, when the billions of natives of the comet run to one side, and make it careen—and the story of the dog who has a better heart than God, in *The Mysterious Stranger*, are composed of the same stuff of world-dreams as Thor with his hammer, and the Erl King, and Prometheus torn by the eagle.

Without wishing to speak with disrespect of a view of creation greatly solacing and inspiring to many, and to many noble persons, one may say that in general these fascinating works express one of the most interesting objections to the Judean religion that we know. This may be roughly summed up in the statement that what Mark Twain seems to say about both the old and the new Judean faith is simply that it is *too small*:

> When a man goes back to look at the house of his childhood [he says in a letter to Mr. Howells] it has *always shrunk*; there is no instance of such a house being as big as the picture memory and imagination call for. Shrunk how? Why, to its correct dimensions; the house hasn't altered; this is the first time it has been in focus. Well that's loss. To have house and Bible shrink so under the disillusioning corrected angle is loss—for a moment. But there are compensations. You tilt the tube skyward and bring planets and comets and corona flames a hundred and fifty thousand miles high into the field.

Before then he remarked one day to his friend the Reverend Joseph Twichell,

> Joe, I don't believe one word of your Bible was inspired by God any more than any other book. I believe it is entirely the work of man from beginning to end—Atonement and all. The problem of life and death and eternity and the true conception of God is a bigger thing than is contained in that book.

In declaring the doctrine of the Atonement an intrinsically mundane conception and in pointing out in numbers of other passages the pettishly self-referential and heartless manner of the God of the Bible, Mark Twain made a most valuable discrimination concerning the Christian theology. For him it is not simply as a physical but as a moral explanation of the universe that the Judean philosophy is too little.

It is this inherent objection to spiritual conceptions of a rather petty nature and his admiration of ideas of the universe which have greatness that make his tremendous monograph on Christian Science a suggestive and fascinating work.

If the author had never written any other book, this volume alone would have shown him to be a great social critic. Its candor, spontaneity and big, unique sense of human values place it with those creative criticisms and interpretative surveys of influential ideas which are among the world's most enlivening possessions—with *Thus Spake Zarathustra* and *Sartor Resartus* and Thoreau's *Civil Disobedience* and *The Shortest Way with Dissenters.*

At once a keenly analytic and a widely synthetic survey of the subject it has all the faculty of the close, detailed observation, and rapid, practical deduction of the river pilot. It is a masterpiece of clear consideration and powerful, natural expression from the author's candid praise of Mrs. Eddy's great contribution to human happiness, and her genius in execution to his exposition of her love of personal worship, and her taste for showy speech.

Not the least valuable and interesting part of the book, is its literary valuations. As a commentator on expression Mark Twain is always penetrating and imaginative. No more informing literary criticism is to be found than his reply to Matthew Arnold's strangely crass and ignorant remarks on General Grant's biography. His wit on the subject of the emptiness of Fenimore Cooper, his thorough-going praise of William Dean Howells' sustained power as a writer— everything he has to say concerning the art and craft of writing has conscientiousness, truth and independence.

One of Mark Twain's best attributes as a commentator on style, on men, on religious beliefs and on the ways of nations is his capacity for profound admiration. He has no poor provincial grudges against the souls and gifts of other peoples. He could praise well. He could admire greatly. He could admire with understanding. It is the obverse side of our American sin of judgment, and of condemnation in toto for a single obvious weakness or error that we are quite as likely to praise in toto for a single excellence. Public persons or foreign nations are entirely objectionable to us, or entirely commendable. Our regard is undiscriminating—a prejudice for or against its object. The reason why Mark Twain appreciated the greatnesses and the peculiar nobilities of the souls of nations was because he could also understand their smallnesses and their inferiorities. He could admire the beauties and contributive perceptions of our democracy because he could also know its stupidities and meannesses.

No one ever told the truth about us more relentlessly. No one ever laughed more uproariously, at our mussy, imbecile romanticism and our tenth-rate, ignorant feudal tastes and our mawkish imitative "refinement" or despised more completely our smug idealizing superstitions, or our sloppy subservient government, and our endless injustice.

But it is not alone because of Mark Twain's unique humorous genius, nor because he could admire well, nor because of his many-colored wide view of life as a citizen of America and a far-sighted traveler of lands and waters, of histories and of religions, that he has been so richly appreciated by his enormous and constant audiences of readers. He had besides a certain essentially masculine faculty, in which no author has equaled him in many hundreds of years—a faculty profoundly satisfactory to the human race, to everyone who has been wronged, to everyone who has done wrong. He could curse well.

Perhaps a person of another sex, and destitute of any talent in this respect may be able to exercise a more impartial discrimination among cursers than is possible for a masculine listener; and may be more readily struck by this ability in authors. In my own view, and within my own range of reading, Mark Twain is the best curser since Isaiah. To curse in a fine, forthright style and spirit seems to require at once more intensive and more extensive moral information—more knowledge of the states of Heaven and of Hell and of excellence and splendor and miserableness and meanness in mortal character than has ever been acknowledged. Mark Twain will long gratify his country as a magnificent, an immortal execrator.

He could curse the ways of the United States excellently, and could praise them excellently because he was ceaselessly interested in the success and failure of the fortunes of American democracy. He saw that tremendous undertaking I think as no other creature has seen it for us. He saw it at close range and in exact detail in his river-pilot days and as a journalist; he saw it geographically and historically against other ages and peoples and without class-consciousness; and he looked at the vast fallacies, and dangerous poverties of its prevailing religious belief, with a strangely independent, with a brave and humane vision.

> Praise is well. Compliment is well [he once said in recognition of the honor shown him by a great over-seas audience], but affection—that is the last and final and most precious reward that any man can win, whether by character or achievement, and I am very grateful to have that reward.

In the face of all our pettiness, it is, I think, something in our favor that our country was capable of instinctively giving that reward in overwhelming measure throughout his long life-time to a sincerely denunciatory and damaging critic of extraordinary genius. Down the ages somewhere I believe it will be set down to our eternal credit that one of our most popular recreations has always been the satisfaction of embarking with our magical and profane pilot and going down the river—going down the river with Mark Twain.

The Anecdotal Side of Mark Twain

Told in Stories and Anecdotes Contributed to the Journal by the Closest Friends of the Great Humorist, and Now Published for the First Time

The Funniest Man in America is Here Treated in the Fourth Article of the Series of The Ladies' Home Journal's New Form of Biography. Fully Equal in Interest is this Article to Those Published of Thomas A. Edison, in the April Issue; of Mrs. Cleveland, in June, and of President McKinley, in July.

Mark Twain's Dislike for Clothes

Mark Twain has an intense dislike for clothes, and if it were possible would remain in his pajamas day in and day out. And whenever he can do so he eats breakfast in them, receives his friends and works in them. His favorite mode of writing is to lie flat on the floor on his stomach in his pajamas, with a pipe in his mouth. When on lecture tours he never gets out of his sleeping clothes until it is time to go to hall or opera house. When the fit strikes him he likes to exercise, and then with his customary shamble will shuffle along for miles and exhaust his most athletic companion. But he feels far more at home in his pajamas than in a street suit or evening clothes, and in them he remains as great a part of the day as Mrs. Clemens will allow him.

Reprinted from *The Ladies' Home Journal* 15 (October 1898): 5–6.

He Could Shave in Church

Among the passengers who found excuses for addressing Mark one morning on board the steamer on which he was traveling on Lake Huron there was a young man who asked him if he had ever seen or used a shaving stone, at the same time handing him one. It was a small, fine-grained sandstone, the shape of a miniature grindstone and about the size of an ordinary watch, or perhaps a trifle larger. The young man explained to Mark that all one had to do was to rub the face with this stone and the rough beard would disappear, and that the shaver could, with the greatest ease, shave anywhere.

Mark looked at it doubtfully, rubbed it on his unshaven cheek and expressed great wonder at the result; then putting it in his vest pocket he remarked with a quiet, sort of reminiscent smile: "Well, the Madam (he generally spoke of Mrs. Clemens as 'the Madam') will have no cause to complain again of my never being ready for church because it takes me so long to shave. I will just put this in my vest pocket on Sunday. Then when I get in church I'll just pull the thing out and enjoy a quiet shave in my pew during the longer prayer."

His First Two Meetings With General Grant

When Mark was first introduced to General Grant the latter shook hands in a perfunctory manner and immediately relapsed into his customary attitude of reticence. There was an awkward pause; it grew longer and longer as the humorist tried to think of something bright to say. Finally, as if in sheer desperation, Twain looked up, with an assumed air of great timidity, and said, "Mr. President, I—I feel a little bit embarrassed. Do you?" The President could not help smiling, and Mark took advantage of the chance the incident presented to give place to others.

Ten years later, when statesman and humorist met again, General Grant, with a twinkle in his eye, said, before Twain

The latest portrait of Mark Twain (photograph by Alfred Ellis, London).

The house at Hannibal, Missouri, in which Mark Twain was born.

had the chance to utter a word: "Mr. Clemens, I don't feel at all embarrassed. Do you?"

His Appeal To Baby Ruth Cleveland

Some years ago Mark Twain appeared at the Consulate of the United States at Frankfort, Germany, and found Captain Mason, the Consul-General, packing up his books and papers, and all of his personal belongings. "What's up?" he asked. "My time is up," returned Mason cheerfully. "We have a Democratic President, and as I am a Republican I have to get out and give my place to a good Democrat, soon to be appointed to this post." "That's a blessed shame!" said Mr. Clemens, and he started for the hotel, where he wrote this letter to Ruth Cleveland, then only about a year old:

> *My Dear Ruth:* I belong to the Mugwumps, and one of the most sacred rules of our order prevents us from asking favors of officials or recommending men to office, but there is no harm in writing a friendly letter to you and telling you that an infernal outrage is about to be committed by your father in turning out of office the best Consul I know (and I know a great many) just because he is a Republican, and a Democrat wants his place.

And then Mr. Clemens related what he knew of Captain Mason and his official record, and continued:

> I can't send any message to the President, but the next time you have a talk with him concerning such matters I wish you would tell him about Captain Mason and what I think of a Government that so treats its efficient officials.

Three or four weeks later Mr. Clemens received a little envelope postmarked Washington in which was a note, written in President Cleveland's own hand, that read:

Mark Twain talking to reporters in bed (photograph by Major James B. Pond)

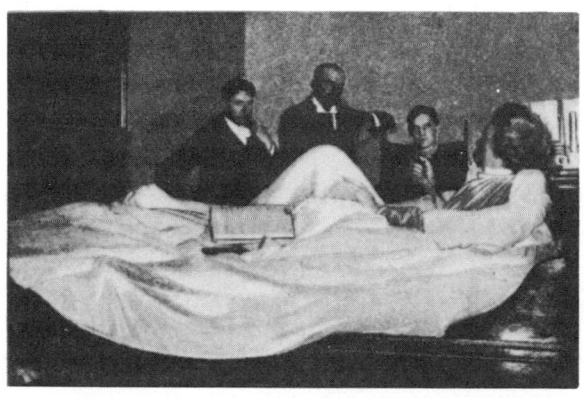

Mark Twain with his wife, and daughter, Miss Clara Clemens (photograph by Walter G. Chase)

Miss Ruth Cleveland begs to acknowledge the receipt of Mr. Twain's letter, and to say that she took the liberty of reading it to the President, who desires her to thank Mr. Twain for his information and to say to him that Captain Mason will not be disturbed in the Frankfort Consulate. The President also desires Miss Cleveland to say that if Mr. Twain knows of any other cases of this kind he will be greatly obliged if he will write him concerning them at his earliest convenience.

Compels His Manager To Keep His Contract

In order to keep a lecture engagement in the Northwest it was necessary for Mark to arrive one chilly morning in season to take the four o'clock overland train. There were five in the party, but no one grumbled. All reached the station five minutes before the time for the train, only to read on the bulletin, "Pacific Mail one hour and twenty minutes late." Mark began to grumble, saying that he had contracted to travel and give entertainments, and not to stand shivering around railroad stations. He kept this up for some time. Finally Mrs. Clemens asked him if he were not a little unreasonable. He was standing by the baggage wheelbarrow, and answered: "No, I am not. I insist on the Major's keeping his contract by keeping me traveling in this wheelbarrow." So Major Pond wheeled him up and down the platform just as the sun was coming up, when Miss Clara got the snap shot that is given above.

Mark Twain's Fondness for Cats

Mark Twain's American summer home for a number of years was at Quarry Farm, on the hill north of and overlooking Elmira, New York. Here he was invariably accompanied by a drove of cats—the cat being Mark's pet domestic animal. They followed him wherever he strolled about the place, and slept in a big chair beside the desk in his bower-study when he

went there. He had for a long time four handsome cats—
Beelzebub, Blatherskite, Apollinaris and Buffalo Bill—all
under complete control. He would call them to "come up" on
the chair, and they would all jump on the seat. He would tell
them to "go to sleep," and instantly the group were all
apparently fast asleep, remaining so until he called "Wide
awake!" when in a twinkling up would go their ears and wide
open would be their eyes.

His Way to Get Rid of Bores

Mark had an easy way, in the old days, of getting rid of
bores. He delighted to smoke a pipe that he never cleaned and
when any caller wearied him he would while seeming to be
interested in what was said, puff like a locomotive, filling the
room with such poisonous stuff as to make the unwelcome
talker glad to go.

She Would Raise Melons:
He Would Do the Rest

As everybody knows, the Secretary of Agriculture is
authorized by Congress to distribute seeds among the farmers
of the country for the ostensible purpose of introducing new
vegetables and other crops from foreign countries. While he
was Secretary of Agriculture the Hon. J. Sterling Morton
received this communication:

> *Dear Sir.* Your petitioner, Mark Twain, a poor farmer of
> Connecticut—indeed, the poorest one there in the opinion of
> envy—desires a few choice breeds of seed corn (maize), and
> in return will zealously support the Administration in all
> ways honorable and otherwise.
>   To speak by the card, I want these things to carry to Italy
> to an English lady. She is a neighbor of mine outside of
> Florence, and has a great garden and thinks she could raise

corn for her table if she had the right ammunition. I myself feel a warm interest in this enterprise, both on patriotic grounds and because I have a key to that garden, which I got made from a wax impression. It is not very good soil, still I think she can raise enough for one table, and I am in a position to select the table.

If you are willing to aid and abet a countryman (and Gilder thinks you are), please find the signature and address of your petitioner below. Respectfully and truly yours,

"Mark Twain."

P.S. A handful of choice (Southern) watermelon seeds would pleasantly add to that lady's employment and give my table a corresponding lift.

Secretary Morton sent the seeds.

Once He Was Guilty of Punning

When Mr. and Mrs. Clemens were on their wedding tour he wrote to a Buffalo friend to secure board for them. This friend met them at the station on their return, and assured them that they would find their boarding-house satisfactory. On reaching there they were welcomed by the bride's parents, who asked them to accept the house as a wedding gift. Almost overcome by the surprise, Mark took his wife's hand, and stepping up to her parents simply said "Happy twain."

One of His Dry Queries

Several years ago Mr. Clemens met an Englishman traveling through this country with the unseeing eyes of the British tourist. The humorist told him, with much zest, one of his inimitable stories, which was received with a puzzled stare and no comment. Six months later Twain was in a London hotel when an Englishman rushed up to him and burst into a

As he often strolls out (photograph by Alfred Ellis, London)

roar of laughter as he grasped both Mark's hands, exclaiming, "I see the joke now!"

He proceeded to explain that the point of the story had suddenly struck him some time before, and when he heard of Mr. Clemens' presence in London he took the fastest train up to see him. The great joker looked at him gravely a moment and then queried, "You say you took the express? Why didn't you take the freight?"

An Example of His Devices To Get a Good Story

In Berlin when one pays his fare to the conductor of a street car he receives a ticket, which is soon afterward collected by an inspector, who boards the car at a fixed point. One day, just as a joke, Mark Twain paid his fare fifteen times on one trip, each time throwing the ticket out of the window or under his seat as soon as he had deposited the regular fare with the conductor. A few minutes later the inspector would get on the car and demand tickets all around. Of course Twain had none to show and had to buy another, apparently with reluctance. The performance amused the American, dumfounded the conductor, who had never met so reckless a passenger, and tickled the native passengers, who thought the foreigner well punished for his negligence. By this modest investment material was obtained for a capital story which netted Mark Twain just five hundred dollars.

Not So Bright As He Thought He Was

It was a busy morning in the Clemens household. Mrs. Clemens had had some etchings removed from their frames in order to clean them, and they were scattered about the floor of the library; upstairs Mark was digging away on some article

Mark Twain's four favorite cats: Beelzebub, Blatherskite, Appollinaris, and Buffalo Bill (photographs by permission of Major James B. Pond)

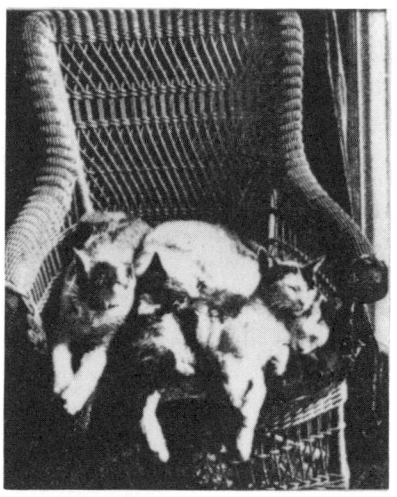

Mark insisted on traveling (photograph by Miss Clara Clemens)

that was absorbing all his attention; and just at this time an Englishman who had shown the family many courtesies and entertained them on his houseboat, rang the bell. Mrs. Clemens retreated to her chamber, and when the visitor's card was brought up told the maid to take it to Mr. Clemens and say that the gentleman was waiting and must be seen at once, as she herself was not prepared to meet him. Down came Mark, smothering the rage that was arising on account of the interruption. He had merely glanced at the card and had not recognized the name. Entering the library, and seeing the stranger bending over the array of etchings, he surmised that their caller was a dealer in pictures. "Well," he said rather brusquely, "I don't see that we need anything in your line." Then, glancing at the pictures, which he supposed had just been brought to the house, he added, "We already have this one, and this, and that one, too. At any rate, we don't need any more."

The Englishman was dumfounded. He politely offered an excuse for intruding, asked where Mr. Warner lived, and departed, while Mark returned to his writing. On the way past his wife's room he remarked triumphantly that he "got rid of that agent easily." Mrs. Clemens stared at him in horror, and then explained who the gentleman was. Mark instantly dashed across the back yard—a short cut to Warner's—with profuse apologies.

His Discovery in the New Testament

Mark Twain sat in his little library at Chelsea, London, one afternoon, when a friend who happened to be calling noticed an open Bible upon his table and inquired if he had taken to the study of the Holy Word.

"That's a good Book," Twain answered with his odd drawl. "That's about the most interesting Book I ever read. Joe Twitchell, a parson over in Connecticut recommended it to me, and I have been more interested in it than in any other book I have read for a long time. You better read it yourself. It beats any novel or history or work of science that I ever tackled. It is full of good stories and philosophy. It suggests lots of ideas, and there's news in it. I find things that I never heard of before. Did you ever know that the English people were mentioned in the Bible?"

"Why, yes, there is a theory that the lost tribes of Israel migrated over this way and settled the British Islands."

"Oh! I don't mean that. I discovered to-day that Christ spoke of the British people in the 'Sermon on the Mount.'" And, reaching over for the Book, he read:

"Blessed are the meek, for they shall inherit the earth."

Was Once a Perfumer

Probably few folk know that Mark Twain was once engaged in the perfumery business in Cleveland, Ohio, hanging out a sign: "Carl Faust, Late Perfumer to the King of Holland." He afterward told a friend that he bought all his supplies in New York, except his "pure bears' grease," which was a mixture of olive oil, wax and scent, made on the spot, and advertised by means of a bearskin hung now and then at the door. The venture was not a brilliant success, and Mark soon retired.

His Early Proclivity to Get into Trouble

One of the incidents of his boyhood in Hannibal, which does not figure in "Tom Sawyer," occurred while his sister Pamela was teaching music there. Frequently she used to entertain her pupils at her home. One night Mark was sent to bed early, while Miss Pamela and her young friends indulged in a candy-pull. At the proper moment the sweet mixture was set on the back porch to cool. Just about that time Mark was awakened by a cat fight. Here was a treat not to be missed. He crawled out of his window upon a trellis over the porch in order to get a good view, but missing his footing fell down into the pan of candy, making an alarming clatter. When the folks rushed out to see what had happened it appeared that Mark and the candy were inseparable.

Some of the Things He Likes

Mark Twain is a good billiard player and will drop almost any occupation for the sake of having a game. He likes to take long walks, and he also is fond of base-ball. Once, while at a ball game, he became so excited that he dropped his umbrella from the grandstand. Too lazy to go down under the seats for it at the time, he found, when looking for it at the end of the game, that it was missing. The next day he published this striking advertisement: "Five Dollars Reward for the umbrella, and several hundred for the body of the boy who stole it—dead or alive."

Saying a Good Word for General Hawley

Once in a while Mark has taken a hand in politics. On one occasion, being invited to speak in the interest of his fellow-townsman, Gen. Joseph Hawley, who was a candidate for reelection to the United States Senate, he said, in the course of a droll address: "General Hawley deserves your support, although he has about as much influence in purifying the Senate as a bunch of flowers would have in sweetening a glue factory. But he's all right; he never would turn any poor beggar away from his door empty-handed. He always gives them something—almost without exception a letter of introduction to me, urging me to help them."

Why Colonel Sellers Was Named "Mulberry"

One day while Mark and Charles Dudley Warner were walking together in Hartford they happened to begin a discussion of the modern novel, and one or the other suggested that it might be a good plan to burlesque it. Later, while journeying together to Boston, this suggestion took definite shape, and on their return the work was begun, one author writing a chapter, the other taking up the threads of the story the next day, and both critically examining the result each evening and asking the opinions of their wives as to the success of each stage of the undertaking. Finally they collected all the manuscript, of which there was too great a quantity, and jointly condensed it. It was owing to a suggestion by Mr. Warner that the chief character in the tale was called Colonel Eschol Sellers, and it is a fact that the man whose name was taken—a man supposed to be long dead—made a fiery demand for satisfaction, visiting Hartford for that purpose. In later editions of the story the name "Eschol" was changed to "Mulberry."

Afraid He would Run Out of "Smokes"

Mark Twain is an inveterate smoker and never lets a moment go by when possible without smoking his pipe or a cigar. When going on a long journey he has a mortal dread of running out of tobacco. When at Victoria, British Columbia, he was to sail next day for Honolulu. During a walk he espied a wholesale dealer in cheroots (small cigars) and bought three thousand of them, together with fifteen pounds of pipe tobacco. In the afternoon he went back to the store and bought three thousand more cheroots. That evening shortly after beginning his lecture he surprised his manager, who was in the audience, by beckoning him to come to the stage. The summons was obeyed with alacrity much to the curiosity of the audience. The manager mounted the platform, and when at the lecturer's side Mark Twain stopped in his talk, and turning to his manager said:

> Pond, I fear that cigar place may close before I get there. Go there now and get fifteen hundred more of those cheroots.

And turning to his audience Mark went on with his lecture as if nothing had happened. Next day he sailed with the seventy-five hundred cheroots and fifteen pounds of tobacco, perfectly happy and with his mind easy.

How He Made William II Laugh the Whole Evening

Hon. William Walter Phelps, who was the American Minister to Germany when Mark Twain first met William II, said that the incident was a striking one. "The Kaiser," said Mr. Phelps, "was then on speaking terms with but one American author, Fenimore Cooper. Now, Royal personages usually have a series of set speeches ready for emergencies. But William opened the conversation with a reference to "The Last of the Mohicans," or its author. A thoroughly well-drilled man of the world would have listened to His Majesty's remarks with the gravity becoming an apostle of wellbred boredom, and in that case the Kaiser would have done all the talking throughout the evening. Not so Mark Twain. He told His Majesty that he had come across a copy of "The Pathfinder" quite recently, and that it had struck him as the funniest thing out. And then he went on to speak of the moccasined person treading into the tracks of the moccasined enemy and thus hiding his own trail, and the master of woodcraft who had always a profusion of dry twigs ready on which somebody stepped, thereby alarming all the reds and whites for several hundred miles around. He led His Majesty "in the track of a cannon ball across the plain through a dense fog," and invited him to try and steer his yacht Hohenzollern in a gale for a particular spot on shore where he knew of an undertow that would hold her back against the gale and save her, as one of Cooper's skippers professed to have done. Then His Majesty forgot all about his fine set phrases and his desire to impress Mr. Clemens, and gave himself up to the enjoyment of American humor, its extravagance, its daring. Kaiser and humorist talked together the whole evening," concluded Mr. Phelps, "and the rest of the company received very little attention from either of them."

"3.—Mark Twain"

A.C. Ward

At one time it would have seemed an enormity equivalent to high treason to suggest that the real tragedy of Mark Twain's life might be found in the popular success of his literary gambols as a professional funny man. Now, however, it is not difficult to find those— Americans as well as Europeans—who agree that the necessities of farce, coupled with a defect of critical vision, turned some of Mark Twain's funny books into two-minded affairs, where verbal horse-play intermingles with savage satire aimed at a too-distant target. Almost certainly it would have been better for himself and for American literature if he had never discovered Europe. It is possible that his long-sighted preoccupation with the absurdities and injustices current in the Old World was in the first place determined by a well-founded conviction that America was so Europe-conscious as to put her own growth in danger of being seriously stunted; but when Mark Twain set the United States guffawing at trans-Atlantic queernesses he missed the chance of becoming his own country's most valuable satirist. There is no doubt in the minds of critics or of critical admirers that Mark Twain's work will be ruthlessly sifted by posterity, yet there is no common opinion as to what will be rejected. Since his death, a fuller portrait of the humorist's personality has revealed in him a considerable stratum of pessimism, which tended to grow in later years. This was so much at variance

Reprinted from *American Literature 1880–1930*, New York: The Dial Press, 1932, pp. 52–62.

with the common picture of him as a gay trifler (though a proper appreciation of his books could never have encouraged such a judgement) that his posthumous reputation seemed for a short time likely to rest upon such darker works as *The Mysterious Stranger* and *What Is Man?* But as the balance evens-out [sic] in a further reassessment of the various factors in his character, there will be less temptation to stress what seemed remarkable only because it had not been generally known.

In however brief an attempt to reconsider Mark Twain's contribution to the literature of his time, note must be taken of what he was qualified to do, and of how he reacted to certain contemporary influences. America from about the middle of the last century experienced the most extraordinary spate of professional funny men ever known in any country. The success of the dialect humorists depended chiefly upon the fact that their sayings and writings were a subtle if unconscious flattery of the great unlettered American public, which was tickled to death to find literary gentlemen speaking a language everybody could understand and cracking jokes comprehensible to the most unassuming intelligence. The popularity of Joe Miller, Artemus Ward and their like was not confined to the unliterary. Better-educated people found that type of humour quaint, refreshing and restful, though with this part of the audience its appeal was impermanent. Even poor jokes are always jokes to the four million, but to the four hundred a poor joke is only poor. Mark Twain grew up at a time when it was almost impossible for any ambitious popular writer to escape the spraying jet of farce, and he became at length saturated by it as a result of Artemus Ward's praise of his early journalistic writings. Though Mark Twain was then still under thirty, he had already accumulated the wide and varied experience of life which made him, at least potentially, America's most liberally informed and democratic writer. Born in the Middle West (Florida, Missouri) and owning a strain of Southern blood through his father's Virginian ancestry, Samuel Langhorne Clemens belonged to the new insurgent America which was travelling away from the puritan and intellectualist tradition. Beginning work after comparatively little schooling, the boy passed a few years in newspaper and printing offices, before he began those wanderings afield which eventually brought him to the most important of his adventures—the period (1857–61) spent on the Mississippi river-boats, upon which he became a licensed pilot and found, in a common cry of the leadsmen, his pen-name Mark Twain. With the outbreak of civil war, river-traffic was suspended and he returned, full of matter concerning men and places, to journalism, travelling, lecturing and ultimately to authorship in the full sense. Life and work on the Mississippi provided him with that swarming knowledge of humanity which populates his best books with diversified but mostly robust types. But if the pilot years taught him much, they failed to teach him some things by which he could have profited. He hated the merely anaemic virtues, and healthy readers can rejoice in his hatred; but in some respects he was disastrously insensitive, and this was in part responsible for his inability to recognize how many things he was incapable of so much as beginning to understand. As long as he could see the outsides of things he was inclined to believe that he saw and knew the whole. In an earlier generation one could have said solemnly that Mark Twain was "without reverence." The solemnity would not have injured the truth, for a man who lacks reverence (or the capacity for it) is automatically deficient in a sense of proportion and is so far unqualified to be a critic of life. Few humorists of Mark Twain's rank have had it in them to be, on occasion, so completely and finally boneheaded. To say that he was sometimes a bull in a china shop would be no more than a conventual whispered hint of the truth: at his worst he was a rhinoceros among porcelain. No doubt a rhinoceros would detect something a trifle inappropriate in such circumstances; apparently Mark Twain never did. He could barge and guffaw his way into any company without suspecting that he was the actual joke—and a bad one. If he had not been, at his best, a radiant dark angel, there would be no need to comment on his imbecilities, of which both *The Innocents Abroad* and *A Yankee at the Court of King Arthur* contain many. Nothing pleases half-baked democrats so much as demagogy, nor philistines so much as strident obtuseness. Mark Twain was in many respects a philistine, and though he was better than a half-baked democrat he did not disdain to truckle to such. It must have been with one eye steadily on this part of his audience that he wrote much of *The Innocents Abroad*, and in fairness to Mark Twain it should be remembered that he was writing the chapters (subsequently assembled to make a volume) as travel-letters for a Californian paper, and therefore for a community of average intelligences with no literary or artistic nonsense about them. In certain respects Mark Twain had something better than a *flair* for what the public wanted. Like Northcliffe in England later, he had only to consult his own taste in matters of art and politics with the assurance that popular taste would coincide. America was already horribly near becoming God's own country in Mark Twain's time; and, having only tenuous roots to its civilization, it suspected something shady at the roots of European civilization. The situation which had arisen in the American Middle and West was natural enough. The new self-consciously important nation, sickened by the Eastern States' slavish copying of European culture, was reacting with violence and, proceeding to damn or to guy what had hitherto been admired, was in danger of finding the European incubus on its shoulders in a new guise. If Mark Twain had said hail and farewell to Europe in one comprehensive Yankee cuss, no European would have begrudged him that measure of relief; but he spent several books wastefully and futilely nagging at the Old World, violently unearthing what had not been hidden, and proclaiming old abuses that a score of European writers had already laid bare. It has been remarked that *A Yankee at the Court of King Arthur* is "a sincere book, full of lifelong convictions earnestly held, a book charged with a rude iconoclastic humour, intended like the work of Cervantes to hasten the end of an obsolescent civilization." The comparison is inapposite both because the humour in *Don Quixote* is universal, whereas that in the *Yankee* is local; and because Cervantes thoroughly well understood what he tilted at, whereas there were many things in the "obsolescent civilization" of the Arthurian tradition that Mark Twain had neither the desire nor the insight to comprehend. He could not dispose of the Age of Chivalry by pointing out that it was also an age of barbarism, nor by suggesting analogies between medieval barbarism and that of the modern age. No intelligent European pretended that barbarity and a mystical apprehension of the universe were not co-existent in Arthurianism; but whereas Europe already knew about the barbarism, Mark Twain was incapable of responding to the mysticism. English people watching the Yankee's invasion of Arthurian territory feel very much as a cathedral custodian would if a boisterous holiday-maker vomited over an exquisite medieval carving. The visitor's companions might hail the disgusting exploit either as deliciously funny or as a magnificent proletarian gesture of contempt. Probably it was easier for Americans in the 'nineties than it is for English or Americans to-day to believe the book marvellously diverting and injurious to European obsolescence. America had still to learn the usefulness of a literary Munroe doctrine. What a perennially good travel-book *The Innocents Abroad* would be if the acute observations and the humor could be retained and the philistine spleen and facetiousness deleted! Yet uncontrolled by self-criticism and lacking taste or informed judgement, what a dull ass Mark Twain could be:

> We visited the Louvre. . . and looked at its miles of paintings by the old masters. Some of them were beautiful, but at the same time they carried such evidences about them of the cringing spirit of those great men that we found small pleasure in examining them. Their nauseous adulation of princely patrons was more prominent to me and chained my attention more surely than the charms of colour and expressions which are claimed to be in the pictures. Gratitude for kindness is well, but it seems to me that some

of these artists carried it so far that it ceased to be gratitude, and became worship. If there is a plausible excuse for the worship of men, then by all means let us forgive Rubens and his brethren. (*Innocents Abroad*, ch. xiv.)

The fact that in *Innocents Abroad* Mark Twain could not let even the story of Abelard and Heloise go without making a long nose does at least enable us to calculate the extent of the changes and development his mind and heart underwent before he wrote such later works as (1896) *Personal Recollections of Joan of Arc* (an historical romance based upon a careful study of the evidence concerning her) and *Eve's Diary*. Although Joan was a lifelong heroine to him, Joan's oppressors would have been rich game for his peculiar humour twenty-five years before; and Adam and Eve would have offered many opportunities for facetious quirks. While *Eve's Diary* is a minor work, Mark Twain thought *Joan of Arc* his best book. Both are characterized by insight and a comprehensive sense of pity such as were lacking in the earlier books, which, however, demanded these qualities no less. The double strain in Mark Twain's nature caused his later capacity for pity and tenderness to be counterbalanced in other writings by a pessimism so deep as to approach despair. This is best illustrated in *The Man that Corrupted Hadleyburg* (written 1898), a long short story which recounts sardonically how nineteen "honest" citizens in the town of Hadleyburg were tricked into lying by the hope of securing a sack alleged to be full of gold. By the time that story came to be written Mark Twain had no disposition to turn his eyes upon European shortcomings. His vision of humanity as a whole had become gloomy, and in *Hadleyburg* he seems to be hinting that there are few "honest" men who cannot be bought. What had darkened his outlook? Probably no other answer need be attempted to that question than the suggestion that a tendency toward depression had always been latent in him, and found its outlet early on in the spleen already mentioned as trickling through his facetiousness in the *Innocents* and other books. Shortly after he returned from the first European tour Mark

Twain married the woman upon whom he seems to be pronouncing an epitaph when he makes Adam say over Eve's grave, "Wheresoever she was, *there* was Eden." There are some who believe, despite those words, that Mark Twain chafed against the silken fetters of conventional respectability imposed upon their married life by Mrs. Clemens. Outwardly he wore the fetters with ease, but inwardly, it is clear, *something* chafed him desperately. If we do not yet know fully what it was, we can at least consider how far his two masterpieces—*Tom Sawyer* (1876) and *Huckleberry Finn* (1884)—may be used to suggest a portrait of Mark Twain himself, through their presentation of the conflict which leads nature to be at odds with custom and habit. Both Tom and Huckleberry are rebels—though (we might too readily assume) only normal boyish ones; but their rebellious instincts seem to be, in fact, more to Mark Twain than cubbish pranks. The boys are identified with their creator and he with them. Their original sin is the reflection of his mature outlook, of his impatience with conventional uses, of his firm and sweeping judgements. Tom goes unwillingly to church and Mark Twain takes the opportunity to say: "The choir always tittered and whispered all through service. There was once a church choir that was not ill-bred, but I have forgotten where it was, now. It was a great many years ago, and I can scarcely remember anything about it, but I think it was in some foreign country." (*Tom Sawyer*, ch. v.) When the public examination of the pupils attending Tom's school is held, Mark Twain comments upon the current educational system with evident contempt for its encouragement of "a nursed and petted melancholy," its insincerity and cultivation of emotional gush and stereotyped moral phraseology which infected the children's essays with an "inveterate and intolerable sermon that wagged its crippled tail at the end of each and every one of them."

> No matter what the subject might be, a brain-racking effort was made to squirm it into some aspect or other that the moral and religious mind could contemplate with edification. The glaring insincerity of these sermons was not

sufficient to compass banishment of the fashion from the schools, and it is not sufficient to-day; it will never be sufficient while the world stands, perhaps. (*Tom Sawyer*, ch. xxii.)

Over twenty years separated the writing of *Tom Sawyer* and *The Man that Corrupted Hadleyburg*, but the mood of the forty-year-old Mark Twain as displayed in the foregoing quotations is different only in degree, not in kind, from the mood of the old man whose work is bitter with disillusion. He hated the doctrine that Appearance is Everything, whether he detected it in the insincerities of the village school or in the hypocrisies of Hadleyburg; and if it is true that, in the service of domestic peace, he accommodated himself for years to a social virtue where "homely truth is unpalatable," the late outpouring of dammed-up distemper is explicable. That Mark Twain, with his actively sceptical and critical intelligence, should have filled the part of ideal husband was no doubt a triumph of domestic conquest, but its effect on Mark Twain's mind and spirit can be guessed. It is significant, too, that Tom Sawyer discovered "that to promise not to do a thing is the surest way in the world to make a body want to go and do that very thing." Did Mark Twain find, as Huck Finn found, that "whithersoever he turned, the bars and shackles of civilization shut him in and bound him hand and foot?" (*Tom Sawyer*, ch. xxiii.) From a stalactite in Injun Joe's cave, water fell slowly drop by drop every twenty minutes:

That drop was falling when the Pyramids were new; when Troy fell; when the foundations of Rome were laid; when Christ was crucified; when the Conqueror created the British Empire; when Columbus sailed; when the massacre at Lexington was "news." It is falling now; it will still be falling when all these things shall have sunk down the afternoon of history and the twilight of tradition, and been swallowed up in the thick night of oblivion. Has everything a purpose and a mission? Did this drop fall patiently during five thousand years to be ready for this flitting human insect's need, and had it another important object to accomplish ten thousand years to come? No matter. (*Tom Sawyer*, ch. xxxvi.)

The *farceur* of *Innocents Abroad*, who could vent his scepticism in splenetic references to Abelard and Heloise and other European "remains," was (by the time he came to *Tom Sawyer*) being driven inward to occasional broodings upon the follies and pretences of the human insect and upon his littleness as he faces the inescapable night of oblivion. From brooding he was to pass to disgust, perhaps to despair, and Mark Twain's pilgrimage was ended by the follower of Artemus Ward becoming not extravagantly unlike a disciple of Dean Swift. His duality could be illustrated further by reference to the rapid alternations between delicious comedy and violent tragedy in *Tom Sawyer* and *Huckleberry Finn*, but to dwell upon such points as these might be to forget the books while remembering only the evidence they offer in reference to The Case of Mark Twain. To this generation Mark Twain is interesting as a "case" because he had the misfortune to be considered in his lifetime as little more than a big-hearted and plain blunt funny man. Posthumous appreciation of his complexity and subtlety has caused some temporary overshadowing of his literary genius and his greatness as a humorist, as distinct from his quality as a verbal juggler and *farceur*. *Tom Sawyer* and *Huckleberry Finn* are among the few humorous masterpieces in world literature, altogether aside from what high merit they may also have as representations of the Eternal Boy—a creature particularly interesting to Mark Twain inasmuch as the Eternal Boy is also the Eternal Savage, the antithesis of civilized man. These two stories are honest and vigorous recreations of American life "in the raw" without trace of conscious starkness. *Huckleberry Finn* is an entirely successful continuation of the earlier book, no doubt for the very reason that it does not try to repeat a success but digresses from it into a more extensive sphere. The river adventures have the magnificent force of the realities Mark Twain knew from his Mississippi pilot days; and the two rogues—the Duke and the King—possess an almost Shakespearean amplitude with a more than Shakespearean repertory of ingenious dodges. Throughout both books hardly a sentence can be found in which humour and fun decline into facetiousness; and the tasteless insensitiveness of Mark Twain's farcical books has here become transformed into the sympathy and understanding necessary for true comedy. He was no longer living on the verbal dexterity and deliberate quaintness of approach which had served for the ramshackle structure of the *Innocents* and the *Yankee*.

No doubt it would be impossible to find three other writers with so many obvious differences as exist between Walt Whitman, Emily Dickinson and Mark Twain. Yet their fundamental qualities are not unlike, and might almost be said to be identical—for each had independent vision, and each dealt with experience in independence of the habitual attitude toward human affairs which passed for tradition and morality. Mark Twain was the most tragic figure among the three, for though each had endurances to cope with, he was the only one upon whom vital compromises were forced. By natural disposition, however (and in part in achievement also), he also confronted the universe without the chafing harness of civilization. In these three, at last, a new vision came to begin the making of a new literature for the New World.

Review of *Tom Sawyer Abroad*

It is more decent to parody Jules Verne than Sir Thomas Malory, and Mark Twain may therefore be deemed to have returned in his latest flight of humour to the limits of legitimate burlesque. We are introduced once more to Tom Sawyer, Huck Finn, and the invaluable nigger, Tim [*sic*]. These heroes obtain possession of a balloon, with a patent steering apparatus and a minimum pace of one hundred miles an hour. In this they cross the Atlantic, are driven by contrary winds to the middle of the Sahara, traverse Egypt, and finally come to anchor on "Mount Sinai, where the Ark was." On their way they fall in with oases, dust-storms, mirages, caravans, and other familiar marvels of African travel, and have a narrow escape from a somewhat improbable congregation of lions and tigers. The point of the jest appears to lie: firstly, in the shifts and expedients of the ingenious Tom Sawyer, who is certainly never at a loss for any emergency, and is able to point out to his companions the ruins of Joseph's granary, and the treasure hill of the Dervish and the Camel-driver in the *Arabian Nights*; and, secondly, in the attempt to express elementary scientific and geographical facts in terms of Yankee slang and Yankee logic. There are perpetual discussions, in which Tom Sawyer's fragments of book-learning are pitted against the ignorance and dialectic smartness of Huck Finn and the nigger, and, of course invariably get the worst of it. The chief fault of the book is that it does not strike one as particularly funny, which is perhaps a

Reprinted from *The Academy* XLVI, No. 1158 (14 July 1894): 27.

considerable defect in what is professedly a work of humour. It is a good thing, as someone once said, for a comic paper to have some jokes in it.

"Hadleyburg": Mark Twain's Dual Attack on Banal Theology and Banal Literature

Susan K. Harris

Recent criticism of Mark Twain's "The Man that Corrupted Hadleyburg" has primarily concerned itself with answering Gladys Bellamy's charge that the moralism of the story is philosophically inconsistent with its determinism. Pascal Covici, Jr., perhaps more interested in the psychological than the philosophical basis of free will, holds that "Hadleyburg" "has for its theme not the corrupting. . . but the awakening of the town to a sense of its innate depravity" and claims that the townsfolk welcome exposure and finally achieve a moral victory. In a more direct response to Bellamy, Clinton S. Burhams, Jr., feels that "Twain's determinism, . . . far from being inconsistent with his moralism, is the source of its real values. In his concern. . . with the relations between conscience and the heart, he views the moral values of conscience as determined by environment, by training; and one of his major aims is to show that such training. . . must be empirical, not merely prescriptive." Taking a slightly different tack, Henry B. Rule explicates the story in the light of R. W. B. Lewis's *The American Adam*, seeing Hadleyburg as "an ironic Eden . . . diseased by hypocrisy and money-lust" and claiming that "in Twain's treatment of the Eden myth, Satan plays the role of savior rather than corrupter," for the Stranger/Satan figure initiates the process whereby the Richardses and the town are morally reformed. Responding to Rule, Helen E.

Reprinted from *American Literary Realism, 1870–1910* XVI, No. 2 (Autumn 1983): 240–52.

Nebeker sees the original corrupter as the Calvinist God who, like the Stranger, punishes Adam and Eve by condemning their progeny to a "corrupt, moral life" of absolute depravity. Her reading of "Hadleyburg" sees the Richardses, despite their "moral bankruptcy," as "human, weak, but essentially guiltless" because they are the victims of God's vengeance. Finally, Mary E. Rucker's essay illustrates "the Richardses' freedom and their failure to attain a moral regeneration because of their not making the morally correct choices."[1]

With the exception of Covici and possibly of Rucker, the above commentators have assumed that Mary and Edward Richards, the central characters of "Hadleyburg," are intended to provide a focus for moral failings shared by the rest of the town, and that their fate is linked to the fate of the other citizens. Covici, however, notes that "Mary and Edward are overwhelmed by [the stranger's] hoax, but the rest of the town can laugh at themselves,"[2] and Rucker seems to imply that while the Richardses are damned by their failure to "act consciously and deliberately for primarily moral ends," the rest of the town is regenerated.[3] Following them, this essay will argue that, far from being representative of the town, Mary and Edward Richards are its most corrupt characters, and that their story differs both thematically and formally from the story of the town. Moreover, Mark Twain uses the elderly couple's tale not only to attack contemporary liberal notions of the power of free will but also to attack the way such ideas are embodied in current forms of short fiction.

"The Man that Corrupted Hadleyburg" actually contains two narratives, integral to each other but offering very different conclusions. The town's growth from pride in its untried virtue to humble willingness to learn how to resist temptation can be seen as an umbrella, or cover, tale for the far darker revelation of the Richardses' true nature. As William Macnaughton has pointed out, "The Man that Corrupted Hadleyburg" contains ideas from *What is Man?*, the heretical "gospel" Mark Twain was writing (but did not intend for publication in his lifetime) during the same period he was writing the short story. Because "Hadleyburg" *was* intended for publication, however, the author had to cater to popular expectations if he wanted to be read.[4] It is possible to see the apparent contradiction between moralism and determinism in the short story as evidence of Twain's ploy to make his ideas publishable: he hid his deterministic tale under a moralistic one that was both accessible and palatable to a readership accustomed to sentimental short stories which consistently implied not only that moral regeneration was possible, but that it was easy. Mark Twain uses Mary and Edward Richards to test his readers' ability to penetrate popular literary stereotypes, hoping that they will recognize that beneath the message of Christian hope implicit in the story of the town's reformation lies a message of Calvinist despair implicit in the story of the Richardses' ruin.

Because "The Man that Corrupted Hadleyburg" contains a pessimistic message disguised as an optimistic one, however, it can also be seen as an attack on the kind of short stories most often published in periodicals such as *Harper's*, *The Atlantic Monthly*, and *McClure's*, as well as in newspapers, a major market for American short fiction in the nineteenth century. Although it is a strikingly good story of its type and bears the unmistakable stamp of Twain's humor and style, the cover story, the story of Hadleyburg's reformation, nevertheless offers few surprises for readers of formulaic fiction: thematically inverting the plea from the Lord's Prayer to "lead us not into temptation" by juxtaposing to it Milton's strictures against a "blank virtue, not a pure," the cover tale formally resolves its tensions through the catharsis of the town meeting and overtly proclaims its moral through the town's revised motto. The narrative of Mary and Edward, on the other hand, dangles, neither thematically nor formally resolving its tensions. When the Richardses die they have neither recognized the magnitude of their own corruption nor exonerated the Reverend Burgess; little seems to have been learned by any of the characters concerned and there seems no "message" to the tale. Since the tensions are at best only partially resolved in the secondary tale, and since there is no neat moral to summarize the story's points, it seems inadequate and unfinished. Yet the structural raggedness of the Richardses' story is what makes it central to this work. Actively subverting the optimism projected by the cover story's design, the secondary story challenges us to re-examine our expectations of the difficulty of moral reform. It can be seen as a cautionary tale covertly seeking to awaken readers to the extent to which they have been duped by the sentimental optimism of the stories offered them in popular markets, the majority of whose careful plots, stereotyped characters, and neat resolutions convey the idea that human beings are essentially good-natured and will solve their problems once they recognize them. In fact, the subordinate story in "The Man that Corrupted Hadleyburg" can be seen as Mark Twain's rejection of the form and content of popular short stories, for in highlighting, by contrast, the facility with which moral problems are solved in formulaic fiction, it forces readers to realize that as not all stories can be resolved, so not all souls can be redeemed.

I

With the notable exception of Professor Rucker, the general tendency of readers of "Hadleyburg" has been to view Mary and Edward Richards as a rather benign elderly couple who, though sharing the moral failings of the town, are still relatively innocent and become the chief victims of the stranger's hoax only because they have been too defeated by the burdens of their lives to be able to redefine their moral universe and start a new life. They are, nevertheless, saved on their deathbeds and morally regenerated. Rucker, however, notes that "the couple's drives—fear and delirium—qualify the contention that the Richardses' death-bed confession signifies a moral regeneration."[5] Rucker's analysis of the Richardses should point us in a new—and fruitful—direction. For the

Richardses are not only driven by fear on their deathbeds, fear is one of the primary emotions of their lives. Rather than being less guilty than the rest of the town, Mary and Edward are like the boys of *The Chronicle of Young Satan* (also being composed during this period), who know that they are "not manly enough not brave enough to do a generous action when there [is] a chance that it could get [them] into trouble."[6] For instance, Mary, whose words always equate reputation and livelihood, assures Edward that he was right not to have valued his "manliness" before "public opinion" because "we couldn't afford it" (H, p. 236).

The narrator of "Hadleyburg" brings both Richardses into focus in a swift rhetorical descent from the general to the specific, a framework designed to trap the unwary reader into believing that this is a gentle old couple just like the ones he has met in stories like William Allen White's "The Home-Coming of Colonel Hucks."[7] Having introduced the town and explained its reputation for honesty, he appears to select one particular couple on whom to focus his drama, introducing them in stereotypical terms before ever naming them. The effect of their being introduced within a familiar context is to throw readers off the track instantly. For if we placidly accept the stereotype, we will never be able to see beyond it to the actual character delineated. Mary, for instance, is first heard rather than seen, "a woman's voice," which trustingly bids the stranger enter through the unlocked door. Next she is introduced as "the old lady who sat reading the *Missionary Herald* by the lamp," visual data designed to signal devoutness for readers of short stories in which simple, pious, and trusting old ladies were standard fare. In fact, the old lady is merely described in a series of cues—familiar signs directing readers to assume a particular set of characteristics—until she acts; only then does she attain a name, and only then does she begin to manifest anti-stereotypical behavior. Discovering that the man has left a sack full of gold, "Mrs. Richards" suddenly flies off to lock the door, draw the shades, and otherwise exhibit behavior ill-suited to one who believes herself surrounded by honest neighbors. Her change from passive trust to active mistrust suggests not only that she is not necessarily the gentle old soul "cued" so far, but that she expects others to respond to the money with a passion identical to her own.

Edward, too, is carefully introduced within a formulaic context before his particular character is revealed: arriving home late and tired, he moans that "it's dreadful to be poor, and to have to make these dismal journeys at my time of life," but at his wife's remonstrance ("Be comforted: we have our livelihood; we have our good name"[8]) he responds conventionally: "Yes, Mary, and that is everything. Don't mind my talk. . . Kiss me—there, it's all gone now, and I am not complaining any more" (H, p. 234). When he learns of the money, however, Edward's response is much like his wife's, though, being male, he lets her seem to bite the apple first. His proposal that they bury the sack and deny any knowledge of its existence is delivered "humorously," an emotive mask for desires he will not let himself express until she has made the first move. Yet although they are at pains to project an image of themselves which conforms to the mores of the town, both Richardses indicate their sense that they are actually spiritually alien to it. When they speculate on the identity of the good citizen whom the stranger has directed them to find, only Barclay Goodson, the local misanthrope, occurs to them as a possibility, for of all the town, he seems to have been the only citizen known to be capable of generosity. Not only do the Richardses identify him as untypically generous, they also identify him as untypically frank. Most importantly, they indicate that they share his view of Hadleyburg, thus identifying themselves as psychological outsiders rather than insiders. Although Goodson's response to Hadleyburg had been to attack it verbally, and the Richardses' has been to endorse it verbally, all three believe the town, for all its vaunted honesty, is also "narrow, self-righteous, and stingy" (H, p. 235).

Having cued readers to perceive the Richardses as decent folk, and then having hinted that their appearance may be deceptive, Twain proceeds to test his readers' ability to look behind the mask. Much of our reading of this story depends on whether we accept what the characters say or evaluate what they do. The Richardses' conscious verbal exchanges support the image they are seeking to project—for instance, they consistently counter their admissions of greed by piously acknowledging its sinfulness. Examination of their acts, however, especially their past acts, renders a very different idea of the couple's moral construction. In "The Man that Corrupted Hadleyburg" the Reverend Burgess, the town pariah, is the yardstick against which the Richardses' real moral standing is measured. For the first time, Edward confesses that he had been the instrument of Burgess's downfall years before: he had lacked the "manliness" to risk his own reputation to clear Burgess of a charge he alone knew was false. He is, then, guilty of a cowardice which, as readers of other works by Mark Twain well know, places him among the worst of the "human scum" Twain took delight in anathematizing. Moreover, Mary proves her affinities with her husband by justifying his act, despite delicately hesitating to indicate that she knows that what she is saying is "wrong." "As long as he [i.e., Burgess] doesn't know that you could have saved him, he—he—well, that makes it a great deal better," she concludes (H, p. 237).

Not only does Mark Twain undermine the stereotype the Richardses project by showing that by their acts they are consciously suspicious and cowardly, he also shows us that Edward is malicious on a subconscious level as well. If Richards's confession of cowardice does not convince us of his intrinsic corruption, his concept of a good deed should. It is significant that Mark Twain chose an incident concerning racial mixture to illustrate Richards's idea of the "favor" he might have done Goodson, because for Twain, white attitudes about blacks were always an index of moral development. When Richards convinces himself that he had been the man who had spread the word that Goodson's fiancée, "a very sweet and pretty girl," "carried a spoonful of negro blood in her veins" (H, p. 249), he shows himself a racist and a slanderer as well as a coward. The Mark Twain who had already denounced American concepts of racial "purity" in *Pudd'nhead Wilson* (1892) was not about to condone a character who saw a "spoonful" of Negro blood as defilement. For all their apparent humility and love for each other, the Richardses are—and apparently always have been—hypocritical, suspicious, cowardly, and racist.

They are, moreover, perfect exemplars of Mark Twain's concept of "the Moral Sense," the human Sense, as his spokesman defines it in *The Chronicle of Young Satan*, "whose function is to distinguish between right and wrong, with liberty to choose which of them he [i.e., man] will do. . . He is always choosing, and in nine cases out of ten he prefers the wrong" (CYS, p. 73). "The fact that man knows right from wrong proves his *intellectual* superiority to the other creatures," proclaims the Old Man in *What Is Man?* "but the fact that he can *do* wrong proves his *moral* inferiority to any creature that *cannot* " (WM?, p. 89).

As Professor Rucker points out, Mary and Edward constantly face crucial choices between right and wrong, and consistently choose the latter. Seemingly possessed of Free Will, they seem destined to make choices that will damn them. And Mark Twain clearly wants us to think of the Richardses' choices within the framework of Calvinist theology: both prate pulpit clichés which may well be intended to convey double meanings. "Ordered!" Mary cries when her husband reminds her that their age and poverty "must be for the best." "Oh, everything's *ordered,* when a person has to find some way out when he has been stupid" (H, p. 241). Just as their lives may be "ordered," so too may be their moral outlook. Suspecting that "this town's honesty is as rotten as mine is; as rotten as yours is" (H, p. 241), Mary repeatedly murmurs, as she faces temptation, "Lord, how we are made—how strangely we are made!" (H, p. 238). Made,

Twain may intend us to understand, to face temptation and to fall in full knowledge of the consequences. Furthermore, the couple's guilt is exacerbated by its secrecy: during the town meeting, even as Mary and Edward let pass the chance to confess and absolve themselves of one set of wrong choices, the townsfolk are unknowingly torturing them further by celebrating them as the only ones it *"does* like. . . ; *does* respect. . . ; more—it honors you and *loves* you—" (H, p. 263). Concealed guilt, as the Puritans well knew when they insisted that the secret places of a prospective member's soul be aired, is a sure sign of damnation, a "holding on" (in Huck Finn's words) to the worst sins of all.

Not only are the Richardses corrupt themselves, they project their spiritual worldview onto others. Like Young Goodman Brown, they see their own faults reflected in the faces of their neighbors. Burgess, grateful to Edward for having secretly warned him of the town's intent to tar and feather him during his original trouble, suppresses the Richardses' claim to the sack, and they are given the money as reward for their "honesty." But in the height of their "good fortune"—all stemming from Burgess's having lied to protect them—they suspect the minister of having learned of Edward's earlier silence and of having now turned against them, covertly exposing their claim to the money through the town. As Edward found it natural to pretend that he had spread the rumor about the racial taint of Goodson's fiancee, so now he finds it "natural and justifiable" (H, p. 277) that Burgess would "maliciously" betray him. Vicious and cowardly himself, Richards sees no barrier to suspecting others of a similar spiritual make.

Mary and Edward Richardses' acts, then, unlike their words, differ radically from those which readers of sentimental fiction had been led to expect, linking the secondary story of "Hadleyburg" closer to the naturalism of a Stephen Crane (compare, for instance, the difference between the Richardses' words and acts and the similar hypocrisy of Maggie's mother) or a Theodore Dreiser than to the more accessible—and far more prevalent—"realistic" short fiction of writers like Octave Thanet, Joseph Kirkland, or even Bret Harte. For although the general run of American short fiction published in the late nineteenth and early twentieth century often excelled at portraying American dialects or particularly American scenes, it also tended to suffer from its authors' discovery that particular formulas would get them published. Analysis of the Richardses is crucial to an understanding of Mark Twain's intention in "Hadleyburg" because without it his short story looks suspiciously like a rather sophisticated version of the optimistic—and usually sentimental—fiction with which it would have to compete for publication. While naturalistic stories were being published—Crane's "The Monster" (first published in August 1898), for instance, preceded "Hadleyburg" (December 1899) in *Harper's* by eighteen months—they were rare compared to the number of stories bearing far different underlying assumptions. In a domestic tale like Ella Higginson's "A Point of Knucklin' Down," for instance, the dramatic tensions are resolved because the young wife overcomes her pride and invites her mother-in-law back to live in her house.[9] In Rowland E. Robinson's "Out of Bondage," the protagonist, protecting an escaped slave only, at first, to win the favor of his abolitionist sweetheart, discovers the sacred pity the image of the black could inspire.[10] Similarly, stories by Ellen Olney Kirk, H.C. Bunner, Dorothy Lundt and others all involve a change of heart among their principal characters.

In 1923 Edward J. O'Brien, surveying the history of the American short story, complained that ever since Hawthorne "almost every American short story is the product of one or more of four heresies,—the heresy of types, the heresy of local color, the heresy of 'plot,' and the heresy of the surprise ending."[11] The cover story of "The Man that Corrupted Hadleyburg" reflects the prevailing tendency to overly control its plot as well as to stereotype its characters. Written by an author mindful of the perils of publication, it can be seen as a skillful piece of didactic, formulaic fiction, designed for a somewhat sophisticated audience familiar not only with the general run of writers—good and bad—of popular magazines but quite possibly also with current "theoretical" pieces concerning the aims of fiction, many of which contributed to the patterns to which O'Brien later objected. Readers of *Harper's* were of course familiar with William Dean Howells's rather moralistic essays in "The Editor's Study," but readers of the *Saturday Review* (London) and *Lippincott's Magazine* might also have read Brander Matthews's reflection on short fiction, first published in those periodicals in 1884 and 1885 respectively, then reprinted in *Pen and Ink: Essays on Subjects of More or Less Importance* in 1888, and, much later, published as *The Philosophy of the Short Story* in 1901.[12] More importantly, as the Columbia professor was Mark Twain's friend, literary correspondent, and, at times, literary antagonist (Twain had first attacked him in the *New Princeton Review* in 1888[13]) it is also probable that Twain had read the early versions of Matthews' *Philosophy*. Certainly he had Matthews on his mind during the period (May–October 1898[14]) of the composition of "Hadleyburg"; in early September 1898, Joe Twichell sent him an article by Matthews defending Goldsmith's *The Vicar of Wakefield* against Twain's attack on it in *Following The Equator*.[15]

The formal unity of the Hadleyburg tale satisfies many of the "laws" Matthews codified regarding the American short story (and which he observed himself in quaintly ethnocentric tales like "On the Steps of City Hall," where good old Judge Jerningham convinces headstrong young Van Dyne not to pollute his heritage by selling out to the political machine run by O'Donnell and McCann).[16] "Hadleyburg" has, as Matthews demanded, "The effect of 'totality,' as Poe called it, the unity of impression"—that is, a "sense of form."[17] It is "logical, adequate, harmonious," has "compression, originality, ingenuity" and "a touch of fantasy" as well.[18] It is, in fact, an extremely well-balanced story. When it opens, the town, falsely virtuous and unjustifiably proud of itself, is in a state of equilibrium. Action is precipitated when the equilibrium is disturbed (through the agency of an outsider who may be good or evil, the effect is the same); complications proliferate until the town is revealed to itself and recognizes its pretensions. The crisis is largely resolved through the cathartic effect of laughter; a new equilibrium is reached when it recognizes its errors, sheds its false pride, and vows to be wiser and better in the future. As the stranger whose machinations have brought it all about remarks to himself, the "dramatic unities" must be observed, and the story of Hadleyburg's reform is unified and therefore aesthetically satisfying as well as morally uplifting, meeting all the formal requirements its public—whether lay or professional consumers of fiction—could want.

In addition, the cover story of "The Man that Corrupted Hadleyburg" is thematically accessible, just complicated enough to flatter the intellectual ambitions of a moderately educated, upper-middle class who feel the occasional need to be reminded that they should examine their consciences, but who want assurance that if they try, they can do better. In fact, the specific audience Twain may have had in mind is signaled by the *Missionary Herald* Mary Richards is reading as the stranger enters her house. Established in 1805, the *Missionary Herald* was a congregational [*sic*] Church periodical that enjoyed immense popularity throughout the nineteenth century and well into the middle of the twentieth.[19] Largely consisting of journal reports from missionaries abroad, it provided stay-at-homes with vicarious thrills concerning the perils of the faith in alien climes. Certainly one reason for its inclusion in "Hadleyburg" was to provide a touch of local color; another was to provide ironic comment on Mrs. Richards's own lack of spiritual grace. As one of Twain's (always satiric) "practicing Christians," she feels more concern for the pagans abroad than for her own soul. But the name of the magazine also identifies Twain's target audience, people who read the *Missionary Herald* as well as literary journals— that is, literary (and usually wealthy) members of the Congregational Church. Part of the liberal Protestant Establishment, the *Missionary Herald*'s sponsors included not only congregations like Henry Ward Beecher's Plymouth Church (whose members Twain had satirized in *The Innocents Abroad* thirty years earlier) but also Hartford's Asylum Hill Congregational Church, where Twain's best friend, the Reverend Joseph Twichell, had occupied the pulpit since 1865.

The congregations from Brooklyn Heights and Asylum Hill fit the profile of the ideal readers for "Hadleyburg" exactly: grandchildren of Americans of a sterner faith, they were educated, affluent, and occasionally concerned about the effect of their money on their souls. In 1869 Twain had written Livy that he had "re-read Beecher's sermon on the love of riches being the root of evil,"[20] an indication that Beecher, at least in the early days of Twain's association with the wealthy Congregationalist crowd, was trying to instill some sense of moral conscience into his parishioners, but as Twain's portrayal of Beecher's "Pilgrims" in *Innocents* suggests, even then their consciences were of the verbal rather than the active breed. As the years passed, ministers like Beecher (in whom Twain lost faith after the minister's affair with Mrs. Tilton was exposed) and Twichell more often helped their congregations rationalize their money-lust than attacked them for it. Equally important, whatever attack they did mount was framed by the evolution of a liberal version of the doctrine of free will—or, from the opposite point of view, by the degeneration of the doctrine of predestination. Overseen by the spirit of reformers like Horace Bushnell, the Arminian strain of Congregationalist theology had come to the fore, emphasizing man's natural capacity for enlightened reform and de-emphasizing the concept of original sin.[21] Like the sentimental fiction which implied that all problems could be resolved by those willing to confront their difficulties and work hard to untangle them, the messages such ministers gave their people held that no sinner who truly wanted to change was incorrigible—a message so familiar that, in "Hadleyburg," when the Stranger claims it to have been Goodson's words to him, not one member of the community doubts that the misanthrope would have said it.

If the story of Hadleyburg's reform meets expectations of congregationalists of a later generation, however, the story of the Richardses' damnation meets the expectations of an earlier one. Offering no hope for moral redemption, its message of despair would be best grasped by the grandparents and great-grandparents of Twichell's or Beecher's flocks. For if the theme of the cover story implies that reform is possible, the theme of the subordinate story implies that it is not. In hiding his tale of Calvinist despair under a tale of latter-day Congregationalist hope, then, Mark Twain may have been aiming at the secret consciences of his affluent friends and neighbors, believing that despite the formulas taught them from the pulpit and the editor's chair they could still recognize a message that called them to a more profound examination of their spiritual state than they generally heard. Though adamantly not a professing Christian, Twain was nonetheless a man who agonized over moral questions, and by 1898, when he was writing "The Man that Corrupted Hadleyburg," *The Chronicle of Young Satan,* and *What Is Man?* he clearly felt that not enough careful consideration was being paid to the difference between the sin that was remediable, and the sin that was not.

II

One sign that the Richardses' story is not intended to provide easy answers to difficult moral problems is that it does not develop as neatly as Hadleyburg's. In fact, one of the reasons "The Man that Corrupted Hadleyburg" is so disturbing to read results from this formal dichotomy. If we insist on perceiving Mary and Edward within the scope and method of the cover story—that is, as the particular citizens whom Twain has chosen to illustrate the town's failings—we have real difficulty integrating the two conclusions, for the story of the town, on the whole, is resolved, while the story of the Richardses is not. Only if we perceive a different order operating in the sub-tale will we understand how it functions to subvert the optimism of Hadleyburg's reform. For Mary and Edward, "caressing" each other on the couch, sharing their thoughts and supporting each others' ideas, seem to be paragons of faith and faithfulness. They even dupe the town. But, as we have seen, Mary and Edward are aliens to the town rather than integral parts of it, and although they know how to make the others think well of them, they—like Mark Twain—are preying on everyone's willingness to believe that because they *look* and *talk* like sweet old people, they actually are as good as they seem.

An important difference between the Richardses and the citizens of Hadleyburg is that while the latter are initially self-satisfied, the former are not. They seem, in fact, vastly discontented with their lot: their stringent "honesty" has been rewarded with grinding poverty. According to the Puritan work ethic, especially popular in the jargon of the Gilded Age, honesty and hard labor should bring some material success, some "sign" of God's grace to the elect. The Richardses, however, have received nothing but their "good name"—not enough to render contentment in their old age. Their poverty, their complaints, and their easy fall should be the first sign that they are neither of the Calvinist elect nor even of the community which, under a liberalized theology, could hope to be saved through self-examination and reform.

In addition, as we have already noted, the Richardses have a bad record, one for which they have never tried to make amends and which they do not try to amend until pushed by paranoia. Edward "confesses" on his deathbed only, one senses, because he will not be around to face the community's disappointment in him. Neither he nor Mary understands the depth of their own corruption, however; while they confess their claim for the sack in their delirium, and Edward confesses his cowardice regarding Burgess, neither ever recognizes that their hypocrisy is rooted in their apparently total lack of sympathy for anyone other than themselves and in their unquestioned assumption of the worst of the community's prejudices. Clearly, the major difference between the cover and the subordinate stories is that the first concerns remediable error, while the second concerns irremediable sin. The Richardses, unlike most of the town, are not mistaken but evil, and their tale cannot be resolved formally because evil, unlike error, simply will not disappear when it is unmasked.

There is, furthermore, a difference between the formal movements of the town's and the Richardses' tales: a movement of the protagonists in the former case, outwards, to increased objectivity, and in the latter, inward, to increased subjectivity. In the town's case, the truth-teller is Goodson. Dead before the events of the story begin but leaving a legacy of misanthropy and oddball generosity, he originally characterized the town as stingy and self-righteous. The stranger's function is to make the townsfolk concur with Goodson's assessment, to see themselves as others see them and to experience a collective change of heart. The town meeting, where the *Mikado* tune functions as a ritualistic chant, is the means through which the collectivity purges itself as the leading citizens are mocked by the less prominent citizens whom they had dominated. This does not mean that class antagonisms are expunged, nor all the citizens "saved" through the agency of the stranger and his sack; they only learn how to *earn* salvation, they are not suddenly all saved. Some, in fact, do not even learn the lesson. Clearly Harkness, for instance, who is willing to pay $40,000 for the sack so that he can defeat his political opponent, is not changed. Rather, the sum he pays—the sum originally supposed to be in it in gold—is Mark Twain's private symbol for dirty money: avoiding the obvious symbolism of $30.00, Twain consistently employs a variant of $40.00 whenever he wishes to indicate that sums being exchanged are morally tainted.[22] Thus $40,000 signals Harkness's recalcitrance. If he is one of the few who choose not to reform, however, the majority of the citizens do, and the town's revised motto signals its collective moral readiness.

The Richardses, however, go through no such process of reassessment. In contrast to the general movement of the town's consciousness outward, to greater objectivity about and evaluation of itself, the Richardses turn inward, towards an increasingly subjective vision of the way they are perceived by others. Always as alienated as Goodson, their response has always been crucially different: whereas he tried to make the town see itself, for its own good, the Richardses have tried to make it perceive them as they wish to be perceived. Since they have no power—or rewards—other than the satisfaction they derive from the image of themselves they have projected, the threat of discovery is tantamount to a threat of complete deprivation. Consequently, even when they are saved through Burgess's intervention, they live in terror of discovery, searching the community for clues that their suspicions are justified. While the town experiences a new community through shared shame (which greatly alleviates private guilt), the Richardses develop paranoia, assuming that the others are treating them as they would treat anyone in their situation: affecting love while feeling scorn, seeking to trick them into open confession. Instead of relieving their anxieties, the town meeting and its aftermath intensifies their isolation.

Finally, while the plot complications concerning the town are resolved, the plot complications concerning the Richardses are not. Rather, each apparent resolution generates a new complication. Although Edward clears Burgess of one accusation, he leaves him with another, this one of a most unchristian act of vengeance. Certainly the couple are not "saved" by these confessions. Nor is the evil they represent extirpated by their deaths. For even if the town is disillusioned about their honesty, it never knows that they have sinned against Burgess once again. Far from being resolved, the complications generated by the tangled plot of the secondary tale, like sin itself, live on.

"The Man that Corrupted Hadleyburg," then, combines Mark Twain's attack on the debased ideology of free will with an attack on the ideological optimism inherent in current forms of the short story. As he had satirized sermons, political speeches, courtroom speeches, recitation day speeches, initiation tales, European fables, romanticized landscape descriptions and guide books throughout his career in order to show his audience how such conventions falsified their perceptions of the world, so in "Hadleyburg" he undermines his stereotyped characters and tight, conventional plot in order to force his reader to look beyond the conventional message such formulas had taught them to expect. In doing so he unites his moral intentions with his concern for literary "truth": in a two-pronged attack on banal theology and banal literature, he challenges his readers to refuse easy solutions to moral problems at the same time that they refuse easy resolutions to formal ones.

Notes

1. Gladys C. Bellamy, *Mark Twain as a Literary Artist* (Norman: Univ. of Oklahoma Press, 1950), pp. 308–309; Pascal Covici, Jr., *Mark Twain's Humor: The Image of a World* (Dallas: Southern Methodist University Press, 1962): Clinton S. Burhans, Jr., "The Sober Affirmation of Mark Twain's Hadleyburg," *American Literature*, 34 (Nov. 1962), 375–384; Henry B. Rule, "The Role of Satan in 'The Man that Corrupted Hadleyburg'," *Studies in Short Fiction*, 6 (Fall 1969), 619–626; Helen E. Nebeker, "The Great Corrupter or Satan Rehabilitated," *Studies in Short Fiction*, 8 (Fall 1971), 635–637; Mary E. Rucker, "Moralism and Determinism in 'The Man That Corrupted Hadleyburg,'" *Studies in Short Fiction*, 14 (Winter 1977), 49–54.

2. Covici, p. 203.

3. Rucker, p. 53. Rucker is not explicit on this point. However, her last line claims that "If we are to see a relation between action and the Miltonic moral embodied in the revised motto. . . we must not center attention on the individualized characters, rather, we must accept on faith what the narrator tells us about the town's achieved willingness to face temptations in an effort to attain a viable morality."

4. William R. Macnaughton, *Mark Twain's Last Years as a Writer* (Columbia: Univ. of Missouri Press, 1979), p. 100.

5. Rucker, p. 53.

6. Mark Twain, *The Chronicle of Young Satan*, in William M. Gibson, ed., *Mark Twain: The Mysterious Stranger* (Berkeley: Univ of California Press, 1970), p. 82. Hereafter abbreviated CYS and documented internally, as will be all primary works in this essay. H refers to the edition of "The Man that Corrupted Hadleyburg" in Justin Kaplan, ed., *Great Short Works of Mark Twain* (New York: Harper and Row, 1967); WM? to *What Is Man?* (New York: Harper and Brothers, 1917).

7. *McClure's*, 8 (Feb. 1897), 326–443.

8. Mary's response may be seen as a further revelation of her real values; again she equates reputation with money. Wouldn't the "real" stereotyped old woman value "good health" before "livelihood"?

9. *McClure's*, 6 (Dec. 1895), 71–75.

10. *The Atlantic Monthly*, 80 (Aug. 1897), 200–216.

11. Edward J. O'Brien, *The Advance of the American Short Story* (New York: Dodd, Mead and Co., 1923), p. 6.

12. For the publication history of Matthews's ideas see the Prefatory Note to his *Philosophy of the Short Story* (London: Longmans, Green, and Co., 1912), pp. 7–8.

13. Alan Gribben, *Mark Twain's Library: A Reconstruction* (Boston: G.K. Hall and Co., 1980), I, 458–460. Professor Gribben's work has made Mark Twain research far more coherent and accessible; it is an invaluable aid to Mark Twain scholarship.

14. See Macnaughton, pp. 100–103.

15. Albert Bigelow Paine, ed., *Mark Twain's Letters* (New York: Harper and Brothers, 1917), II, 666–667. In the same letter Twain remarks that he is receiving copies of *Harper's Century*, and *McClure's* magazines in Kaltenleutgeben.

16. *Harper's New Monthly Magazine*, 98 (Mar. 1899), 525–530.

17. Matthews, p. 17.

18. Ibid., p. 23.

19. *The Missionary Herald At Home and Abroad* ceased publication with volume 147, in 1951.

20. This letter is quoted in Gribben, (I, 55), and is available at the Mark Twain Papers. Dixon Wecter does not include it in *The Love Letters of Mark Twain* (New York: Harper and Brothers, 1949) but does include a subsequent letter (1/19/69) which makes it clear not only that Livy was sending her fiancee copies of Beecher's *Plymouth Pulpit: A Weekly Publication of Sermons Preached by Henry Ward Beecher in Plymouth Church, Brooklyn*, but that he was reading them. Clearly Twain's association of Congregationalists and wealth was laid during the sixties, when he first came into contact with Beecher's congregation, with Thomas K. Beecher (Henry Ward's half-

brother), pastor of Livy's church in Elmira; with young Joseph Twichell, and with the whole Brooklyn/Hartford "connection."

21. For a brief review of the evolution of Congregationalist theology in America, see Sydney E. Ahlstrom, *A Religious History of the American People* (New Haven: Yale Univ. Press, 1971), esp. Ch. 46, "The Golden Age of Liberal Theology." A biography of Twichell is Leah A. Strong's *Joseph Hopkins Twichell: Mark Twain's Friend and Pastor* (Athens: Univ. of Georgia Press, 1966). Recent works on Beecher are William G. McLoughlin, *The Meaning of Henry Ward Beecher* (1970), and Clifford E. Clark, Jr., *Henry Ward Beecher: Spokesman for a Middle-Class America* (Urbana: Univ. of Illinois Press, 1978).

22. This motif is consistent throughout Mark Twain's works, and has been noted by various critics. Most familiar should be the sums associated with moral inadequacies in *Adventures of Huckleberry Finn*. For instance, the slave hunters give Huck $40 instead of helping his allegedly sick family; the King trades Jim for $40; Tom gives Jim $40 for having been such a "good" prisoner.

Is The Philippine Policy of the Administration Just?

"No"
By Mark Twain

In the North American Review *for February, Mark Twain publishes an article "To the Person Sitting in Darkness," which we are permitted to reprint in part as follows:*

Extending the Blessings of Civilization to our Brother who Sits in Darkness has been a good trade and has paid well, on the whole.

There is more money in it, more territory, more sovereignty and other kinds of emolument, than there is in any other game that is played. But Christendom has been playing it badly of late years, and must certainly suffer by it, in my opinion. She has been so eager to get every stake that appeared on the green cloth, that the People who Sit in Darkness have noticed it. They have become suspicious of the Blessings of Civilization. More—they have begun to examine them. This is not well. The Blessings of Civilization are all right, and a good commercial property; there could not be a better, in a dim light. In the right kind of a light, and at a proper distance, with the goods a little out of focus, they furnish this desirable exhibit to the Gentlemen who Sit in Darkness:

LOVE,	LAW AND ORDER,
JUSTICE,	LIBERTY,

Reprinted from *Harper's Weekly* 45 (9 February 1901): 154–5.

GENTLENESS,	EQUALITY,
CHRISTIANITY,	HONORABLE DEALING,
PROTECTION TO THE WEAK,	MERCY,
TEMPERANCE,	EDUCATION,
—and so on.	

There. Is it good? Sir, it is pie. It will bring into camp any idiot that sits in darkness anywhere. But not if we adulterate it. It is proper to be emphatic upon that point. This brand is strictly for Export—apparently. *Apparently.* Privately and confidentially, it is nothing of the kind. Privately and confidentially, it is merely an outside cover, gay and pretty and attractive, displaying the special patterns of our Civilization which we reserve for Home Consumption, while *inside* the bale is the Actual Thing that the Customer Sitting in Darkness buys with his blood and tears and land and liberty.

We all know that the Business is being ruined. The reason is not far to seek. It is because our Mr. McKinley, and Mr. Chamberlain, and the Kaiser, and the Czar and the French have been exporting the Actual Thing *with the outside cover left off.*

It is a distress to look on and note the mismoves, they are so strange and so awkward. Mr. Chamberlain manufactures a war out of materials so inadequate and so fanciful that they make the boxes grieve and the gallery laugh. Next, to our heavy damage, the Kaiser went to playing the game without first mastering it. He lost a couple of missionaries in a riot at Shantung, and in his account he made an over-charge for them. And by-and-by comes America, and our Master of the Game plays it badly—plays it as Mr. Chamberlain was playing it in South Africa. It was a mistake to do that; also it was one which was quite unlooked for in a Master who was playing it so well in Cuba. In Cuba he was playing the usual and regular *American* game, and it was winning, for there is no way to beat it. The Master, contemplating Cuba, said: "Here is an oppressed and friendless little nation which is willing to fight to be free; we go partners, and put up the strength of seventy million sympathizers and the resources of the United States:

play!" Nothing but Europe combined could call that hand: and Europe cannot combine on anything. There, in Cuba, he was following our great traditions in a way which made us very proud of him, and proud of the deep dissatisfaction which his play was provoking in Continental Europe. Moved by a high inspiration, he threw out those stirring works which proclaimed that forcible annexation would be "criminal aggression"; and in that utterance fired another "shot heard round the world." The memory of that fine saying will be outlived by the remembrance of no act of his but one—that he forgot it within the twelvemonth, and its honorable gospel along with it.

****

For, presently, came the Philippine temptation. It was strong; it was too strong, and he made that bad mistake: he played the European game, the Chamberlain game. It was a pity; it was a great pity, that error; that one grievous error, that irrevocable error. For it was the very place and time to play the American game again. The game was in our hands. If it had been played according to the American rules, Dewey would have sailed away from Manila as soon as he had destroyed the Spanish fleet—after putting up a sign on shore guaranteeing foreign property and life against damage by the Filipinos, and warning the Powers that interference with the emancipated patriots would be regarded as an act unfriendly to the United States.

The more we examine the mistake, the more clearly we perceive that it is going to be bad for the Business. The Person Sitting in Darkness is almost sure to say: "There is something curious about this—curious and unaccountable. There must be two Americas: one that sets the captive free, and one that takes a once-captive's new freedom away from him, and picks a quarrel with him with nothing to found it on; then kills him to get his land."

The truth is, the Person Sitting in Darkness *is* saying things like that; and for the sake of the Business we must persuade him to look at the Philippine matter in another and healthier way. We must arrange his opinions for him. I believe it can be done; for Mr. Chamberlain has arranged England's opinion of the South-African matter, and done it most cleverly and successfully. He presented the facts—some of the facts—and showed those confiding people what the facts meant. He did it statistically, which is a good way. He used the formula: "Twice 2 are 14, and 2 from 9 leaves 35." Figures are effective; figures will convince the elect.

Now, my plan is a still bolder one than Mr. Chamberlain's, though apparently a copy of it. Let us be franker than Mr. Chamberlain; let us audaciously present the whole of the facts, shirking none, then explain them according to Mr. Chamberlain's formula. This daring truthfulness will astonish and dazzle the Person Sitting in Darkness, and he will take the Explanation down before his mental vision has had time to get back into focus. Let us say to him:

"Our case is simple. On the 1st of May Dewey destroyed the Spanish fleet. This left the Archipelago in the hands of its proper and rightful owners, the Filipino nation. Their army numbered 30,000 men, and they were competent to whip out or starve out the little Spanish garrison; then the people could set up a government of their own devising. Our traditions required that Dewey should now set up his warning sign, and go away. But the Master of the Game happened to think of another plan—the European plan. He acted upon it. This was, to send out an army—ostensibly to help the native patriots put the finishing-touch upon their long and plucky struggle for independence, but really to take their land away from them and keep it. That is, in the interest of Progress and Civilization. The plan developed, stage by stage, and quite satisfactorily. We entered into a military alliance with the trusting Filipinos, and they hemmed in Manila on the land side, and by their valuable help the place, with its garrison of 8000 or 10,000 Spaniards, was captured—a thing which we could not have accomplished unaided at that time. We got their help by—by ingenuity. We knew they were fighting for their independence, and that they had been at it for two years. We knew they supposed that we also were fighting in their worthy cause—just as we had helped the Cubans fight for Cuban independence—and we allowed them to go on thinking so *until Manila was ours and we could get along without them.* Then we showed our hand.

"We kept the positions which we had beguiled them of; and by-and-by we moved a force forward and overlapped patriot ground—a clever thought, for we needed trouble, and this would produce it. A Filipino soldier, crossing the ground, where no one had a right to forbid him, was shot by our sentry. The badgered patriots resented this with arms, without waiting to know whether Aguinaldo, who was absent, would approve or not. Aguinaldo did not approve; but that availed nothing. What we wanted, in the interest of Progress and Civilization, was the Archipelago, unencumbered by patriots struggling for independence; and War was what we needed. We clinched our opportunity. It is Mr. Chamberlain's case over again—at least in its motive and intention; and we played the game as adroitly as he played it himself.

"We and the patriots having captured Manila, Spain's ownership of the Archipelago and her sovereignty over it were at an end—obliterated—annihilated—not a rag or shred of either remaining behind. It was then that we conceived the divinely humorous idea of *buying* both of these spectres from Spain! In buying those ghosts for twenty millions, we also contracted to take care of the friars and their accumulations. I think we also agreed to propagate leprosy and small-pox, but as to this there is doubt. But it is not important; persons afflicted with the friars do not mind other diseases.

"With our Treaty ratified, Manila subdued, and our Ghosts secured, we had no further use for Aguinaldo and the owners of the Archipelago. We forced a war, and we have been hunting America's guest and ally through the woods and swamps ever since."

Having now laid all the historical facts before the Person Sitting in Darkness, we should bring him to and explain them to him. We should say to him:

"They look doubtful, but in reality they are not. There have been lies; yes, but they were told in a good cause. We have been treacherous; but that was only in order that real good might come out of apparent evil. True, we have crushed a deceived and confiding people; we have turned against the weak and the friendless who trusted us; we have stamped out a just and intelligent and well-ordered republic; we have stabbed an ally in the back and slapped the face of a guest; we have bought a Shadow from an enemy that hadn't it to sell; we have robbed a trusting friend of his land and his liberty; we have invited our clean young men to shoulder a discredited musket and do bandit's work under a flag which bandits have been accustomed to fear, not to follow; we have debauched America's honor and blackened her face before the world; but each detail was for the best. We know this. The Head of every State and Sovereignty in Christendom and ninety per cent of every legislative body in Christendom, including our Congress and our fifty State Legislatures, are members not only of the church, but also of the Blessings-of-Civilization Trust. This world-girdling accumulation of trained morals, high principles, and justice, cannot do an unright thing, an unfair thing, an ungenerous thing, an unclean thing. It knows what it is about. Give yourself no uneasiness; it is all right."

Now, then, that will convince the Person. You will see. It will restore the Business. Also, it will elect the Master of the Game to the vacant place in the Trinity of our national gods; and there on their high thrones the Three will sit, age after age, in the people's sight, each bearing the Emblem of his service: Washington, the Sword of the Liberator; Lincoln, the Slave's Broken Chains; the Master, the Chains Repaired. It will give the Business a splendid new start. You will see.

* * * *

Everything is prosperous now; everything is just as we should wish it. We have got the Archipelago, and we shall never give it up. Also, we have every reason to hope that we shall have an opportunity before very long to slip out of our Congressional contract with Cuba and give her something better in the place of it. It is a rich country, and many of us are already beginning to see that the contract was a sentimental mistake. But now—right now—is the best time to do some profitable rehabilitating work—work that will set us up and make us comfortable, and discourage gossip. We cannot conceal from ourselves that, privately, we are a little troubled about our uniform. It is one of our prides; it is acquainted with honor; it is familiar with great deeds and noble; we love it, we revere it; and so this errand it is on makes us uneasy. And our flag—another pride of ours, our chiefest! We have worshipped it so; and when we have seen it in far lands—glimpsing it unexpectedly in that strange sky, waving its welcome and benediction to us—we have caught our breath, and uncovered our heads, and couldn't speak for a moment, for the thought of what it was to us and the great ideals it stood for. Indeed, we *must* do something about these things; we must not have the flag out there, and the uniform. They are not needed there; we can manage in some other way. England manages, as regards the uniform, and so can we. We have to send soldiers—we can't get out of that—but we can disguise them. It is the way England does in South Africa. Even Mr. Chamberlain himself takes pride in England's honorable uniform, and makes the army down there wear an ugly and odious and appropriate disguise, of yellow stuff such as quarantine flags are made of, and which are hoisted to warn the healthy away from unclean disease and repulsive death. This cloth is called khaki. We could adopt it. It is light, comfortable, grotesque, and deceives the enemy, for he cannot conceive of a soldier being concealed in it.

And as for a flag for the Philippine Province, it is easily managed. We can have a special one—our States do it: we can have just our usual flag, with the white stripes painted black and the stars replaced by the skull and cross-bones.

And we do not need that Civil Commission out there. Having no powers, it has to invent them, and that kind of work cannot be effectively done by just anybody; an expert is required. Mr. Croker can be spared. We do not want the United States represented there, but only the Game.

By help of these suggested amendments, Progress and Civilization in that country can have a boom, and it will take in the Persons who are Sitting in Darkness, and we can resume Business at the old stand.

"Yes"
By John Kendrick Bangs

When, a few days ago, I took up my copy of the *North American Review* for February, it was with a great deal of pleasure that I observed, in perusing the table of contents, that Mark Twain had provided for the delectation of its readers an article entitled "To the Person Sitting in Darkness." Here, assuredly, was a treat in store, for I felt that Mr. Clemens, more than any other living writer, was entitled, because of his intrinsic sanity, to speak to those in need of light, no matter by what precise species of darkness they might be enveloped. I sat down to read and to rejoice.

I had not read far before I began to rub my eyes in astonishment, and the more I read the more did my amazement increase and my rejoicement diminish. It was incredible, and yet there it was, and the marvel grew upon me, although I was quite unable to decide at which I marvelled the more, the hardihood of the humorist in writing his article, or the temerity of the editor of the *North American Review* in printing it. But there it stood before me in plain black and white, a sort of after-dinner speech in a *Review*, in which missionary effort in heathen lands is openly and drastically discredited because of the somewhat too strenuous behavior of certain muscular Christians in the Far East; in which the extension of the blessings of civilization by the strong nations of the earth is likened to that particular kind of business in which selfishness is predominant, and in the operations of which the weak and worthy are crushed into lifelessness by the strong and vicious; and in which, for merely performing the required functions of his office, the President of the United States is held up to public contempt and classed with the land-grabbing statesmen of the Old World. I could scarce believe my eyes. I looked again at the title and the authorship.

"Surely this is not by Mark Twain," I muttered. "Perhaps Senator Pettigrew has taken to writing; or may it not be that the editor of the *Review* has got his authors mixed, and a manuscript by some member of the Atkinson Society for the Prevention of National Growth, marked for rejection, has got by mistake into the Mark Twain envelope!"

Alas! neither was the case. The article, investigation showed, was authentic, and for the first time in my life, or his, I seemed to find the great American somewhat astray in his Americanism; the great satirist wielding the bludgeon instead of the rapier; the great purveyor of sunshine to his fellow-men joining the ranks of the prophets of evil, spreading the gospel of discontent, and being governed by his disgusts rather than by his admirations.

****

As to the methods employed by the missionaries of China, I propose neither to attack nor to defend them. I prefer to take the Rev. Mr. Ament, to whom Mr. Clemens refers, exacting enormous fines from the Boxers either as an unduly muscular Christian acting with a zeal not wholly to his discredit, or as a man who in the face of a great provocation has exceeded the bounds of propriety, if indeed the newspaper stories upon which Mr. Clemens bases his attack are ever confirmed. A man may be a minister of the gospel and still remain a man of force and conviction. To be a Christian does not require that one shall be pusillanimous, and I see no more reason why a missionary should be required to sit meekly down and suffer himself and his followers to be robbed, his family to be outraged, and murder and arson committed in his own neighborhood, than that any other self-respecting man should be expected to emulate the action of the dove when the circumstances call for a tiger. To inspire respect for the Christian religion in the field to which this has been carried, the official representatives of that institution must be as strenuous in the maintenance of the principles of justice as are the representatives of the law in law-abiding communities, who are no more popular with the criminal classes than are missionaries with the Boxers. Whether the missionaries have a right to carry the gospel, as they know it, into other lands is a question which may not be discussed here. Many worthy people think that missionary work, like charity, should begin at home. Others think it should be carried far afield. It is enough to say that it is only in those lands into which the principles of Christianity have been carried by noble bands of self-sacrificing men and women that we find that enlightenment which stands for progress, for law, for order, and for a decent respect for the rights of the individual. I, for one, would rather see one acre of the pest-ridden East Side of the city of New York redeemed from vice than to have every follower of the teachings of Confucius won over to the Church; but when the Church undertakes to win over the followers of Confucius, with the consent and approbation of its greatest minds, I should regret to see its efforts fail because its missionaries were unable to inspire respect for its teachings, either for the lack of physical courage, or for yielding to a policy of non-resistance based upon pusillanimous sentimentality.

Nor do I care much when Mark Twain likens the Extension of the Blessings of Civilization to our Brother in Darkness to a business; if it has become so, so much the better for our Brother in Darkness. Organized effort in its results is far more beneficial than the well-meaning but ill-considered independent effort of the idealist. Mr. Clemens and I would have no country to be ashamed of or to be proud of respectively to-day if, in the extension of the blessings of civilization to this land, the foundations upon which our national being rests had not been laid by men who, in addition to their ideals, were gifted with practical heads and a good, hard common-sense, which goes with what men term business. That people are coming to recognize the value of organized effort is shown by the comparatively new methods of the charitably inclined. Organized charity of to-day is doing a thousandfold more and better work than could ever have been accomplished under old methods, in which there was no co-ordination of forces and under which the kindly generosity of the philanthropist was rendered of no avail in the accomplishment of permanent good. Unless we attack charity as being unmoral, then, for having become a business, we are not justified in assaulting the "Blessings-of-Civilization Trust," as Mr. Clemens calls it, for going at its work in a businesslike manner. And for the reason that one unworthy follower cannot destroy the good name of the Charity Organization Society, may we also assure ourselves that one selfish act here or one high-handed arbitrary act of aggression there is powerless to cast a blot upon the escutcheon of the nations which have undertaken to spread the principles of civilization in immediately unresponsive localities.

****

It is when Mr. Clemens flings at the President of the United States that I am inclined to find the most fault with him, because, in my judgement, his arrows are tainted with the poison of injustice. One does not like to hear him suggest a modification of the American flag for use in the Philippine Islands so that its stripes shall be black and red and its stars shall be superseded by a skull and cross-bones, because there is absolutely nothing in the Philippine situation as it exists to-day that warrants the humorist in making such a suggestion. Law is law, and it can never be superseded by mere sentimentality. The facts are so simple that it is a wonder they are at all in controversy. Our authority in the Philippine Islands is so clearly defined and our title to it so absolutely indisputable that the veriest child should be able to grasp the fact. The question that arises is as to whether or not we shall maintain that authority in the face of an armed rebellion against it. There is no other question immediately involved in the situation. It is all very well for pamphleteers, whose chief mission in life seems to be to tear down that which others are striving to build up, to try to befog the issue with all sorts of sentimental reflections upon a noble people fighting for their liberty, upon the purity of the motives of the great leader of this rebellion—a man who sold himself to the enemy, deserted his people, robbed his fellow-conspirators, and did not even keep faith with those who bought him. It invariably happens in the face of a conflict between a strong nation and a weak, the sentimentalist, right or wrong, takes the side of the weak. We had a great deal of this kind of thing at the beginning of the Transvaal trouble; indeed Mr. Clemens ladles out a lot of it to us in this latest effort of his. Mr. Kruger was the Washington of the Transvaal to these people, just as Aguinaldo is the Washington of the Pacific. Very soon some one will rise up and call Prince Tuan the Washington of China. And as time goes on we shall find the earth girdled with Washingtons, some more worthy than others, perhaps, but every man jack of them trying to stand in the way of the inexorable march of civilization, and with the inevitable result that they will be crushed to earth never to rise again. It is a wonder that Captain Herlihy has not been set down by these sentimentalists as the "Washington of the Red Light District."

I have yet to meet the man, woman, or child who is glad that we have the Philippine Islands to deal with. I think it is quite probable that ninety-nine out of every one hundred thinking men wish that Dewey might have sailed away from

Manila after having destroyed the fleet of Spain. I deem it likely that all who are not idle dreamers know that Dewey could not honorably have done so, leaving a community entitled to the protection of law of some kind to inevitable chaos. To accuse the Administration, which could not possibly have foreseen the complications that Dewey's victory entailed, of playing the game of the land-grabber, is, to my mind, a lamentable perversion of the facts. Publicly to endorse the act of a scheming adventurer in armed rebellion against the forces of the United States in other days would have been called treason, and those who ventured along similar lines during the dreadful years of 1860 to 1865 were known by the significant title of Copperhead. I should not, for one instant, think of calling Mr. Clemens either a traitor or a Copperhead, for he is neither, but I do think that upon his return last autumn after a prolonged absence from his native land, during which time he may reasonably have been expected to get out of touch with things American, he should have been inoculated against what I might call the contagion of the Atkinsonian bacillus, lately discovered in Boston, the effects of which are to promote irresponsible speech, to impair the political vision, and to stunt one's patriotic development. We have had so much destructive nonsense from the Anti-Imperialist League and so little really constructive criticism of the Philippine policy of the Administration that it is positively disheartening to find one from whom we have a right to expect so much as we expect from Mark Twain, joining the ranks of the merely captious—for Mr. Clemens indulges not at all in argument. A Philippine Philippic I should rather call this latest screed of his. I, for one, should much have preferred to hear Mark Twain's clarion voice uttering the following words at this intellectual feast of the *North American Review*: "Gentlemen,—You have asked me to speak upon the Philippine question. There is no Philippine question. When we find the situation in the Philippine Islands such that an American soldier may wear his honorable uniform without peril to his life, when we find the properly acquired authority of this great and well-meaning republic of ours respected in these islands of the far Pacific, where we find our beloved flag, the purest emblem of liberty afloat, honored in the Philippines as we honor it, then there may be a Philippine question. Until then there shall be no such thing. We do not want the Philippine Islands. We never have wanted them, but the inevitable trend of the circumstances of war, beyond our power to control, forced them upon us, and we must deal with them. I am confident that when it is possible for this nation to consider what shall be their status among the communities of the world, we shall find that the pure common-sense of the American people, the love of justice among us, our innate sympathy with the desire of all people in the world to be free, to enjoy the largest measure of self-government and liberty, have resulted in a solution of this now most difficult problem which shall prove to be of the greatest good to the greatest number of the Filipinos. Upon a great many points, which I shall not enumerate, I regret to find myself at variance with the authorities at Washington, but I must admit that the gentleman to whom we have entrusted the administration of our affairs knows more about the situation than I do. In any event, as an American citizen, I place my trust in the President. Personally, caring little for William McKinley, I care much about my President, and him I shall speak well of publicly, even though in private I may write him a letter or two which he may not care to read over a second time. Gentlemen, I give you the President of the United States, the political incarnation of ourselves, the embodiment of the power, of the conscience, of this nation. In all matters outside of our borders we and he must be one. His enemies are ours. Those who defy him, defy us, and in the face of shotten cannon, directed against the authority which he wields, let us not be found skulking at the rear, baiting our general at every move, and by our captious criticism in the face of danger distracting his mind from problems which God knows are in themselves hard enough to solve. Advice? yes, constructive— not destructive. Warnings? yes—the more the better, but whispered, and in a friendly, helpful spirit. Support? when lack of it comforts his enemies—always. Gentlemen, the President—standing."

This, it seems to me, is what Mark Twain would have said as an Innocent Abroad.

As an Oracle at home he pleases me only in the evidence which we may derive from his paper in the *North American Review* that he is, after all, merely human, and not the demigod some of us had begun to think him. There is positive comfort in the thought that even Mark Twain is not infallible.

Reconstructing the "Imagination-Mill": The Mystery of Mark Twain's Late Works

Susanne Weil

When the University of California Press began to publish Mark Twain's suppressed late works, readers expected undiscovered Hucks and *Yankees*—and found mysterious strangers. These posthumous publications seem so different from Twain's best-known writing (and from one another) that a reader might be forgiven for thinking they must have been written by a different person—perhaps by several different persons. Read as a group, the later manuscripts leave the impression that during the 1890s, Twain's familiar, wryly humorous narrative voice was radically transformed: to mix a metaphor, it is as if that voice had been projected through a prism and refracted into a broad spectrum of literary tones, even genres. Moralism, sentimentality, polemic, homely philosophy, fable, and science fantasy are all represented among his late works. Some see the extreme range and varied quality of these manuscripts as evidence that Twain's voice did not simply refract but splintered and broke; certainly the old white light of humor had disappeared. Few, if any, of the late manuscripts resemble the work of a certain wickedly funny steamboat pilot-turned-writer who became the authentic voice of the American West.

But why should they? During his life, Twain deliberately suppressed the manuscripts now emerging from the Mark Twain Papers—suppressed them despite the 1898 contract which invited him to submit whatever he wrote to Harper's and Brothers under their exclusive agreement (Hill, xxii).

Twain's refusal to publish these manuscripts should serve as a flashing neon "buyer beware" sign to new readers; instead, even critics have approached the late works hoping to sate their appetites for unread vintage Twain. They have often been disappointed, and their unrealistic expectations have obscured the different, but genuine, value of much that Twain wrote in his later years. It has become commonplace to say that Twain's late writing is inferior, an embarrassment, and to explain that writing away by citing his biography. The critics' refrain sounds something like this: poor Mark Twain was so undone by personal disasters like the death of his most talented, best-loved daughter in 1896 that he lost his sense of humor and became artistically paralyzed. Led by Hamlin Hill, who in *Mark Twain: God's Fool* (1973) branded the entire body of late writing a "literary junkyard," (273) even editors of some new volumes have denigrated them in the act of writing their introductions.

Before consigning the later Twain to this literary lunatic asylum, let us review the high points in his last fifteen years of writing. Manuscripts he opted to publish include "Fenimore Cooper's Literary Offenses" (1895); "The Man That Corrupted Hadleyburg" (1898), "To the Person Sitting in Darkness" and "To My Missionary Critics" (1901); "Eve's Diary" (1904); "The War Prayer" (1904); "The $30,000 Bequest" (1905); and the final version of "An Extract From Captain Stormfield's Visit to Heaven" (1907). Those which he withheld from publication include *The Mysterious Stranger Manuscripts* (begun in 1897 and culminating in 1905 with the finished novel *#44, The Mysterious Stranger*); the unfinished but fascinating "3,000 Years Among the Microbes" (written in 1905); *Letters from the Earth* (written during the period from 1906–1909); and the massive *Autobiography* (composed between—roughly—1904 and 1909: Twain declared these finished in December of 1909 with "The Death of Jean" [Twain 403fn]).

Even by themselves, these often-anthologized texts would represent a strong showing for any author. Add to them some of the other late writing whose value even late-Twain partisans debate (such as *What Is Man?*, the *Fables of Man* sketches, and the sentimental tales from *The Personal Recollections of Joan of Arc* on down); add the now-published "fragments"—the clusters of related, unfinished fictional pieces representing repeated attacks on ideas Twain could not get out of his head concerning the "damned human race"; and, finally, add the thousands of pages catalogued but not yet published by the Mark Twain Papers: all these comprise a body of work which, however wide its range of quality, proves that Twain's last fifteen years were hardly a creative wasteland.

It is not my intention to argue that Twain's late works are "as great as" or "greater than" his "mature" work: *The Adventures of Huckleberry Finn, Life on the Mississippi,* and the other classics of Twain's major period staked out authentic American diction and experience as the new frontier of our literature, and his late works will not have such an impact. Instead, I propose to re-evaluate Twain's late work on its own ground, leaving behind disappointed nostalgic yearnings for more *Hucks* and *Toms* to ask *why* the late works are so different. Those last fifteen years represent a major literary mystery, one which most critics have treated more like a disease in need of a cure than a question in need of an answer.

What happened? Why did Twain stop writing humorous, realistic fiction? Even recent critics who see the value of his later writing, such as John Tuckey, Sholom Kahn, and William Macnaughton, focus on rehabilitating the reputations of selected manuscripts, not on analyzing the shift in Twain's style or clarifying the relationship between the disastrous events of the 1890s and the change in Twain's view of himself as man and writer. Critics who do try to examine Twain's late years as a distinct epoch in his literary life, notably Hamlin Hill and Justin Kaplan, focus on Twain's biography rather than analyze the late works themselves in any detail: in fact, they dismiss the later manuscripts without even excerpting passages for close readings. I shall argue that through this omission—made possible by the assumption that the less one of Twain's manuscripts is like Huck, the less it is worth reading—they have lost an opportunity to look inside Twain's mind.

The unwillingness of the critical community to analyze the change in Twain's writing seems even more mysterious when we consider that Twain's shift occurred just as American realism, whose frontier Twain had helped to open, was coming into its own. No one has, as yet, offered a comprehensive, plausible analysis of why Twain's writing changed just at the moment when the American public (segments of it, at least) was beginning to sample the wares of Dreiser, Norris, Crane, et al.—just at the moment when that public was presumably ready to swallow what Twain was so sure it could not: his own social criticism unmediated by humor. What is at stake in asking why Twain's style changed is, in effect, an explanation of his refusal to join the literary movement he had helped bring to life.

If we take on the role of literary detectives, trying first to track down the time and the circumstances in which Twain's narrative style changed, we may be able to deduce the reasons why it changed. Using this approach, the crucial question becomes not which was Twain's last "great book," but which book represents Twain's last *characteristic*, completed work of fiction. I would argue that this must be *Pudd'nhead Wilson*, written in 1893 and published both serially and in book form in 1894.* *Pudd'nhead Wilson* is a tale set on the banks of the Mississippi, told with the bite of ironic humor, couched in Midwestern dialect, and expressive of the themes with which Twain was so often concerned: both the evils of slavery and

---

* One could make a case for "Fenimore Cooper's Literary Offenses" or "An Extract from Captain Stormfield's Visit to Heaven" as characteristic Twain. However, these brief works seem more like flickers within his later period, and I am concerned here with the question of why Twain did not choose to write longer works of fiction in his characteristic voice.

the conflict between conscience, social conditioning, and instinct in the decisions of individuals. Few would assert that anything Twain wrote after Pudd'nhead contains its mixture of the elements that made Twain's "mature" writing unique.

1894 was not only the year in which Twain published his last characteristic, completed work of fiction: it was the year in which his luck ran out. In the wake of the national economic panic of 1893, Twain's publishing business, Charles L. Webster and Company, like many other companies, swirled into the vortex of debt (Leary, 10–26). Twain, like other would-be captains of industry, had become accustomed to using credit in lieu of working capital, and the result was bankruptcy when the Mount Morris Bank called in Webster & Company's massive outstanding loans on April 18, 1894 (Leary, 23). 1894 also marked the failure of Twain's brainchild, the Paige typesetter, in a critical test before prospective investors (25). With that catastrophe, Twain's finances were ruined. He had invested the equivalent of modern millions in the machine, as well as an immeasurable amount of hope: not only had he intended the machine to free him of the need to write for profit, but after his bankruptcy, he had expected that its sales would make him solvent again (Kaplan, 280–81).

Finally, 1894 marked the start of Twain's financial and personal relationship with Henry Huttleston Rogers, the powerful Vice President of Standard Oil. Rogers, who became Twain's closest friend, assumed power of attorney over Twain's assets and rescued him from his financial morass by negotiating both his bankruptcy settlement and his Harpers' contract. The Twain/Rogers correspondence makes Rogers' deep respect for Twain clear; the man was ruthless in business, but he was loyal and fair to those he liked, and he liked Twain. However, their correspondence documents how, in transaction after transaction, Rogers quietly persuaded Twain to relinquish control over yet another area of his life. Although there is no evidence that Rogers ever took advantage of Twain's trust or rubbed his nose in his own poor business sense, Twain's regard for Rogers often took the form of debilitating personal comparisons: Rogers came to epitomize for him the kind of steady responsibility which he himself had never been able to maintain, and the insight was lacerating (Kaplan, 322–25; 359–60). When "the mill refused to go"— Twain's metaphor for the times when he could not write—he would go to Rogers' office and, with morbid fascination, watch his friend's "master brain and master hands" tirelessly working (Leary, 10–26).

Rogers fulfilled another of Twain's needs: reading what he wrote. Both Livy, Twain's wife, and William Dean Howells, his longtime friend and literary comrade, shrank from the corrosive bitterness of *What Is Man?* and similar works; but Rogers was willing to read them and ready to accept the views they voiced (10–26). As Twain began to bifurcate his world into realms of "sentiment" and "business," Rogers was the only close friend who would inhabit with him the regions he had come to feel were truly "real." It was precisely because Rogers was the ultimate man of business that his remark that Twain's fortune and fame had "cost no one a pang or a penny" meant so much to him. Twain might have examined the source of this comfort more closely: after all, it seems that none of Standard Oil's shenanigans—wide-reaching and brutal as Twain's never were—cost Rogers a pang, either. But in the mid-1890s, Twain desperately needed to hear those words from someone who could never be accused of sentimentality.

If we accept the proposition that *Pudd'nhead Wilson* was Twain's last characteristic work, it seems logical to conjecture that something about the bankruptcy which closely followed its publication "changed" Twain: changed him well before his daughter Susy's death and more fundamentally than the diversion of time and energy into the bankruptcy negotiations would suggest. An examination of his correspondence and notebooks from the period supports this idea (as we shall see). As Bernard DeVoto has argued, Twain's identity not simply as a success but as the real-life hero of a Horatio Alger-style romance was rocked to its basis and with it, temporarily, his power as an artist (DeVoto; Smith, 140–158).

It seems reasonable to suggest that if Twain had not been fundamentally changed by his bankruptcy, he would have been able (or would have wished) to return to his old style once his financial problems were resolved. However, it is undeniable that what came next cemented the change in him and confirmed the view of life he adopted after becoming a bankrupt. To pay off his debts, Twain realized that he would have to undertake a world lecture tour at the age of 60, depressed and in poor health. Even worse, he would have to grind out books according to the bankers' timetable. The books he would have to write would not, legally, even belong to him, but to Livy. Since Livy's inheritance had been liberally "borrowed" by Charles L. Webster & Co., Rogers was able to make her Twain's preferred creditor; thus, a large portion of the debt became "owed" to Livy and written off (Leary, 24); this also meant that until such time as all debts were completely settled, the copyrights to his books, not only present, but future—his creativity itself, in a sense—belonged to Livy. During the negotiations, he wrote to her about the mental shift this required:

> . . . It was confoundedly difficult for me to be always saying "Mrs. Clemens's books," "Mrs. Clemens's copyrights," "Mrs. Clemens's type-setter stock," and so on; but it was necessary to do this, and I got the hang of it presently. I was even able to say with gravity, "My wife has two unfinished books, but I am not able to say when they will be completed or where she will elect to publish them, when they are done." [5/4/1894] (Wecter, _LLMT_, 302)

The above letter in its entirety suggests that Twain enjoyed this role-playing, but legally, it was not a game. Twain had been determined from the moment of their engagement that he would never live on Livy's income (Kaplan, 94–102), but Rogers' arrangement made Twain financially dependent upon her. Although Livy did not want to be Twain's preferred creditor, and the record of their correspondence suggests that she did not exploit her role, it is difficult to imagine any writer feeling very good about resigning the rights to his own creativity.

In January of 1895, while planning out his lecture tour and writing *Joan of Arc*, Twain outlined the first of a series of autobiographical fantasies: tales of a phenomenally successful man who became a bankrupt and saw his life change so quickly and catastrophically that he could not be sure which, if either, was real and which was a dream—former success or current ruin. Even if the parallels between these manuscripts and Twain's life were less clear, their autobiographical nature would be evident from his notebooks, in which he set down "keys" to which characters represented which people in his life (Tuckey, 9, 151). The connection in Twain's mind between the "dream" motif and his financial disasters was so strong that he mentioned the story idea to Rogers in the same letter with which he responded to Rogers' news that the typesetter had failed (Leary, 115–16). He would never finish a single one of these "dream" tales. If unfinished, they could not be published; if not published, they could not become anyone else's property. Refusing to publish these and other highly personal, experimental manuscripts may have become Twain's way of keeping control over them, a possibility I have explored elsewhere (Weil).

The evolution of the "dream" manuscripts through a series of major changes in plot while retaining essentially the same set of autobiographical characters provides us, as DeVoto argued, with something like a road map of Twain's changing view of himself as a man and artist beginning in 1894, the year of catastrophe (140–41). DeVoto urged future critics to take that road map and explore its uncharted territory, but no one has, as yet, gone beyond his general observation that Twain became obsessed with the problem of guilt and responsibility (from the personal to the cosmic scale) to show precisely how that obsession changed Twain's characteristic voice.

In *Mr. Clemens and Mark Twain*, Justin Kaplan has convincingly shown how Twain forged that voice while writing of *The Innocents Abroad*, the watershed book that marked him as not merely a funny Western fellow but a nationally popular humorist (Kaplan, 70–72). Twain believed that he had been "forced by fate" to adopt humor "as a medium of truth" (Hill, 17), but he had adopted more than humor. Through elaborate self-fashioning, he had shaped himself to assume an ingenious comic stance, a bad-boy pose: what Leslie Fiedler, writing not of Twain as an artist but of Tom and Huck, calls "the good bad boy" (Fiedler; Smith, 130–39). The good bad boy could play pranks, swear and use slang, skip church, break rules and commit venial sins: but because he was charming, funny, and "had his heart in the right place," he would always be forgiven, even beloved.

Twain made his good-bad-boy pose a popular phenomenon. Before Mark Twain, most American literary characters, even rugged frontier scouts like Cooper's Natty Bumppo, tended to speak and act in ways that would not be out of place in the most proper parlor. Twain found his pose an attractive way to "package" his Western material for the Eastern literary establishment, as Kaplan has argued (70–72). It freed him to use then-nontraditional material—bawdy jokes, slang, and irreverence both social and religious—because the pose could be understood and rationalized by a "mature" American audience of that time: boys were allowed to tread on borderlines, as long as they did not "go too far." As Louis Budd points out in *Our Mark Twain: The Making of His Public Personality*, Twain's pose was liberating to Americans working to fit themselves into the proprieties of the increasingly corporate, post-Civil War world of business that Twain named "the Gilded Age": in his writing, he "intimated that the secret of coping was play, the spirit that burst through the workaday routine or reduced it to feckless confusion" (71). In short, Twain's audience could live vicariously through his printed escapades without outraging propriety; he could expose the "shadow" of the American middle class to light in ways acceptable to that class as a literary audience.

Twain found his bad-boy pose an invaluable asset. For example, he used it to get the license he wanted from his friends and, later, from Livy, in their role as his "literary censors." In writing, the pose intrigued and entertained them; socially, it became the Trojan Horse in which Twain was able to insinuate his remarkably unreconstructed social presence into their milieu. As we shall see, he did this less as an exercise in conscious manipulation than as a matter of habit: the role he played to tease Mary Fairbanks, one of his early literary mentors (Wecter, *MTMF*, 1–120), and played more earnestly to win well-bred Livy Langdon as his wife, became a convenience. It worked, and since it worked so well, he fell into it with ever-increasing ease.

When we examine Twain's correspondence, we can see that Twain came to use the pose in his business ventures as well, but fatally (Weil, chapters 2 and 3, *passim*). He ran his publishing company into bankruptcy with his whirlwind financial maneuvers, hopping from one scam to the next like a grown-up Tom Sawyer. When his schemes failed to pan out (their usual fate), he blamed Charley Webster and then Frederick J. Hall, his hapless business managers, even though the record of their contracts and business correspondence shows that Twain held a controlling interest in the company and that he routinely ordered his managers to "drop everything" at a moment's notice in order to attend to his financial whims and "inspirations" (Hill, *MTP* 290–99). When Twain became a bankrupt, however, he finally had to face a situation not susceptible to his persuasive charm: for once, the good-bad-boy pose could not create license. His anger and consternation at his publishers for "failing" him and at his bankers for wanting their money back turned into vehement, morbid self-blame. By the summer of 1894, he had begun to imagine life as a hellish dream: his correspondence swelled with references to this theme, and he began to consider writing something about it. Once the typesetter, too, failed him, he outlined the first of the dream manuscripts (Tuckey, 31; Leary, 115–16).

Through the metamorphoses of the fragmentary dream manuscripts, we can trace the disintegration of Twain's narrative pose. The wry narrator vanished; in the first manuscript, *Which Was the Dream?* (1897–98), there were no "good bad boys" (or men), only figures fixed at the extremes of good and evil. These figures were essentially autobiographical: as noted above, Twain's notebooks from this period list his fictional characters and the real people whom he meant them to represent; even where lists are lacking, analogies are impossible to ignore. For example, as Twain had blamed his business managers for the bankruptcy, "Tom X" blames "Jeff Sedgewick," their fictional counterpart, for his own ruin in *Which Was the Dream?* When Twain shifted from *Which Was the Dream?* to *Indiantown* (1899) and finally to *Which Was It?* (1899–1902), he made a crucial psychological shift as well: he moved his terrible sense of guilt from the purely evil Sedgewick character and invested it in a character representing himself, but with more realistically mixed motives (George Harrison in *Which Was It?*, a respectable man who discovers that he will do anything to avoid the stigma of debt). I would argue that Twain's decision to cut Sedgewick as he moved on to *Indiantown* and *Which Was It?* reflected his realization that his own Tom Sawyer-like escapades were responsible for his bankruptcy. Twain's treatment of the well-intentioned "plots" contrived by young "Tom," Harrison's son in *Which Was It?*, to surprise his father with the funds he needs, as well as Harrison's realization that those "plots" have led him into a situation in which he commits murder, lend strong support to this contention.

I have found no single letter or notebook entry that expresses any conscious realization by Twain that living his pose effectively bankrupted him, but comparisons of the plot and characters of the fragments with Twain's view of his bankruptcy (as expressed in his correspondence) make this conclusion difficult to escape. In his business ventures, he had behaved as though his actions could have no consequences: behavior typical of "good bad boys," but hard to condone in a man sixty years of age. Once illuminated by the bankruptcy, the pose became untenable. Twain rejected both the bad-boy figure and the bad-boy pose—the slyly humorous characters and narrative voice that had gotten away with so much—because, consciously or not, they had become indelibly associated with his misfortunes (Weil).

Through the process of writing the dream manuscripts, Twain not only abandoned his characteristic narrative pose but he transformed his use of his classic Midwestern setting as well. In rejecting the Eastern milieu of *Which Was the Dream?* in favor of the Midwestern locale of *Which Was It?* Twain dispensed with the setting, "family" characters, and trappings of social class that represented the life which he had built for himself as an adult: as "Mark Twain," the successful man of letters and businessman at home in the Eastern establishment. It is as if that created world and self could not coexist in Twain's mind with the cravenness that he attributed to himself not only in his letters and notebooks, but in the character representing himself in *Which Was It?* In that final fragment of the dream series, Twain placed this guilt-ridden figure in a Midwestern town closely resembling Hannibal—and infected the aspirations of every other person in that town with cravenness and guilt as well. Twain had diffused his crushing sense of self-blame throughout a world whose nature could not be "blamed" on him since he neither made nor chose it but merely found himself in it as a child and young man.

Twain's location of guilt and blame in the land of his origins poisoned the "matter of Hannibal" like a corpse in a well: everything he drew from it after the bankruptcy ("Hadleyburg," for example) tasted of the death of his faith in himself and others. To use his own metaphor for his creativity, the old "tanks" were not going to "fill up" again. He replaced them with the bitter figures and voice of *Which Was It?* He also chose other extremes: he knew that good still existed and allowed himself to embrace it blindly in the sentimental tales like *Joan of Arc*. But in his best late work, he succeeded in fusing both black and white visions in morality plays and essays written from the God's eye view of white-hot satire. This technique enabled him to handle human weakness in a more detached, analytical fashion than he did in his autobiographical writings. In his satires, he succeeded in making the question of evil less excruciatingly personal and thus more amenable to literary effort.

Twain's first self-justifying, finally self-condemnatory view of his bankruptcy, then, led him to abandon his unique, carefully forged narrative persona and voice as well as his characteristic treatment of his richest source material and locale in an attempt to contain his sense of guilt. Because this solution required a new pose and voice, Twain suddenly began to experiment with many new modes of expression. I have traced in detail the parallel disintegration of Twain's finances and his literary persona—his "imagination-mill"—as well as his work to reconstruct the "mill" in the dream manuscripts; drawing again upon (but substantially qualifying) Bernard DeVoto, I have attempted to show that Twain turned his transformed idea of himself as an artist into, in essence, the theme unifying the *Mysterious Stranger Manuscripts* (Weil). In those manuscripts, Twain set up the "stranger" characters as authorial analogues, what Henry Nash Smith has called "transcendent," powerful figures who appear mysteriously in provincial towns to play havoc with the moral assumptions of the people they find there (Smith, 135–37). Like many of Twain's later satires, the *Stranger* manuscripts are dominated not by boys (good or bad), but by these transcendent figures capable of commanding everyone around them with the sheer power of their words: Colonel Sherburn in *Huck* and Hank Morgan in *A Connecticut Yankee in King Arthur's Court* are the evolutionary forerunners of these later characters. They are isolated by their intellectual superiority to their communities, have power almost or actually supernatural, are contemptuous of mankind as a species, and are not torn by the inner conflict of "conscience and moral sense" (122–23). Because they can resist the "blurring of attitudes caused by social conformity" (118), they can be effective critics of human nature. Having lost his will to write as a "good bad boy," Twain needed to find another type of character who could perform the service which Smith, writing of Huck Finn, so aptly identifies: to "speak as moral man viewing an immoral society, an observer who is himself free of the vices and even the weaknesses he describes" (118).

The "transcendent figures" whom Smith defines served this purpose for Twain, but Smith finds in them the source of what he considers Twain's late diminution of artistic power. Writing of "The Chronicle of Young Satan," the first of the *Stranger* manuscripts, Smith alludes to the famous sequence in which the stranger figure, Young Satan, creates and then destroys a miniature village full of tiny people as

> the symbolic gesture of a writer who can no longer find any meaning in man or society. Twain's only refuge is to identify himself with a supernatural spectator for whom mankind is but a race of vermin, hardly worth even contempt. And this marks the end of his career as a writer, for there was nothing more to say. (188)

But Twain had plenty more to say in the two manuscripts with which he followed "Chronicle." In both, Twain endows #44, the new stranger figure, with the power of Young Satan, but he strikingly limits 44's willingness to abuse that power as he attempts to enlighten the people he encounters. Twain also limits 44's effectiveness in opening men's eyes to the truths he bears. Even in the scene in "Chronicle" which Smith defines as an expression of the contempt which he feels destroyed Twain's creative power, Twain emphasizes the narrator's horror and grief at Young Satan's wanton destruction—and the ease with which Satan (the creating character and authorial analogue) can manipulate people (the literary audience). When Twain shifts the function of his authorial analogues to make them less destructive, more compassionate, and more limited in their impact upon others, it seems that he is not identifying himself with contemptuous power in the simple way Smith suggests; rather, he is exploring the question of a writer's capacity to enlighten his audience.

Twain's answer to this question is the key to his decision to withhold so much of his late writing from publication in his lifetime. This analysis may, finally, reveal Twain's conception of himself as an artist: how it originally enabled him to write his best-known work, and how its metamorphosis transformed his later writing. My argument, like DeVoto's, will necessarily be speculative, but I believe that the vast evidence of Twain's manuscripts, notebooks, journals and correspondence will make it persuasive.

Before making that argument, I feel obligated to explain more fully my rather harsh view of Twain's critics. In fact, the work that Hill, Macnaughton, and Kaplan have done in their efforts to make sense of the later Twain is a provocative starting point for a detailed exploration of "what happened" to the writer in the 1890s.

Although Hamlin Hill's account of Twain's last decade in *Mark Twain: God's Fool* is detailed and painstaking biography, it becomes more descriptive than analytical when Hill discusses Twain's literary sea-change. In fact, by beginning his analysis in 1900, he avoids even touching upon Twain's transitional years. Hill writes that Twain's humor could not express the rage and indignation which became his emotional constants during the personal tragedies of 1900 onward, a time dotted with the deaths of people Twain loved. He argues that such rage and indignation must inevitably overwhelm humor and irony unless channeled with greater care than Twain could muster at that time in his life; but he also argues that Twain was actually struggling to toss off the "comic pose" that employed humor and irony and replace it with a new, "authentic" voice, primarily through writing nonfiction (to Hill, the *Autobiography* was Twain's one great late achievement [xxiii]). I agree that Twain was trying to change that pose, but what Hill argues is self-contradictory: if Twain was not even trying to use humor and irony, how could they be "overwhelmed" by rage and indignation? Hill is right to observe that Twain was trying to find a new "pose," but when he sees it he criticizes it primarily for failing to be ironic humor, Twain's old vein. In his earlier work, Twain tended to rein in his rage and indignation through the strategic use of subjective narrators like Huck, or *Connecticut Yankee*'s Hank Morgan, or the "greenhorns" of *Roughing It* and his other Western writing: this strategy for expressing "the antagonisms within him"—this use of limited or unreliable narrators to "get away with" social criticism—is not the strategy Twain used in later works like *Hadleyburg* or *Letters from the Earth*, which deliberately employ omniscient narrators. These later works are Swiftian satires, which not only can "accommodate" rage and indignation, but burn them as fuel.

A presumption that the later Twain was utterly out of control prejudices a reading of his works: it misses the possibility that in turning to acrid satire (or moral fable, or syrupy sentimentality) Twain could have made deliberate artistic choices. They may in some cases have been bad choices, but they should still be analyzed as choices—choices which may have unconscious undercurrents, even compulsions, without yet signalling the onset of senile dementia. I would argue that often they were not bad choices, and that even when they were, they opened windows onto Twain's creative processes at work.

Let us compare Hill's treatment of Twain's work in finishing *#44, the Mysterious Stranger*, with the evidence of the notebooks and manuscripts. *#44* was the final manuscript in a series of fragments concerning the incursion of a stranger with mysterious powers into a provincial village and his effect upon the people, especially the boys, who live there. Twain worked on earlier versions intermittently, beginning in 1897, before concocting the combination of narrative elements that he could bring to closure in *#44*. These manuscripts appear in holograph form in the Mark Twain Papers, and their dating has been thoroughly documented by both John Tuckey and William M. Gibson. In this excerpt from *Mark Twain: God's*

Fool, Hill analyzes the work Twain did on *#44* in 1905 through Twain's correspondence:

> On June 29th, [Twain] switched from *3000 Years Among the Microbes* to the final version of *The Mysterious Stranger.* He reported to Clara, "I have spent the day reading the book I wrote in Florence. I destroyed 125 pages and expect to go over it again tomorrow and destroy 25 more. . . ." Mark Twain continued working on the "wonderful 44 story" in July and gave the manuscript of *#44, the Mysterious Stranger* to Miss Lyon to read. . . . He told Rogers, with irresistible interest in his own productivity: "my output grows smaller daily. It has dwindled from high-water mark—32 pages a fortnight ago, one day—to 12 day before yesterday, 10 yesterday, and 8 to-day." (111)

Taking his cue from Twain's own frustration, Hill focuses on the bumpy progress of composition. Twain's "output" was dwindling—at 70, he could not "produce" at the rate he could, for example, at 50, when he finished *Huck.* Nevertheless, his notebooks clearly show that Twain did compose 155 pages in the month Hill discusses and actually finished the book (Gibson 10–11). When Hill next mentions *#44,* he calls it "a jumble of confused motives and ideas, in those parts written in 1905 as well as the segments composed earlier. The 'mysterious stranger' creates 'Duplicates' to run a printing shop, performs burlesque miracles, and in general vitiates the possibilities for effective social satire or philosophical writing with his pranks" (113). Hill's analysis of *#44* never becomes more specific than this, perhaps because his sense of the emotional context in which Twain wrote becomes his judgment of the quality of the writing itself, which he does not quote. Thus, Hill came to see Twain's late works as a "junkyard of unfinished manuscripts and ill-conceived literary ideas (which) was the most enduring testimony of the failure of Mark Twain to retain creative control over his world" (273).

Hill tends to refer to the three separate "Stranger" manuscripts collectively as *The Mysterious Stranger,* the title which Paine and Duneka used for their 1916 edition of "The

Chronicle" with the final chapter of *No. 44* improbably appended as the conclusion; this is a conjunction of materials which Twain never intended. "The Chronicle" was, as the evolutionists might say, a dead end in development: Twain never returned to it except to append its opening chapter to *No. 44*. Though related, it was very different. Its "mysterious stranger," Philip Traum, is a young, unfallen cousin of Satan out to study mankind, whereas 44 is revealed as neither an angel nor a devil but a dream emanating from the mind of August, the human narrator. 44's purpose is not to study mankind but to enlighten August concerning August's true nature, that of the world, and of God. The other major difference is that *No. 44* is a finished work: at least, Twain himself wrote in his working notes that he had finished it. To label it a "fragment" begs the question of what a literary fragment is. Whatever else may be said of *No. 44*, its narrative structure is tightly knit around the premise, revealed only in the final chapter, that 44 is one of the narrator's own recurring dreams made material, an emanation of the unconscious mind attempting to enlighten its conscious counterpart concerning its own true nature. The only instances in which August is other than shocked at 44's world-view are times when he uses it to justify his own manipulation of others (disposing of his Duplicate in order to win Marget, duping her as to his identity, etc.). These are not inconsistencies but part of a coherently conceived design which I shall elaborate below. "The Chronicle," ultimately, is a string of episodes, some surpassing *No. 44* in vividness—and necessarily, since August's straight-man tone is essential to Twain's later conception. Twain was a master in the use of the "unreliable narrator" as a satiric technique, but he always unmasks him as a fool at the close of his tale (as in his early tall tales, such as "The Notorious Jumping Frog" and "Jim Blaine and His Grandfather's Old Ram").

In his introduction to the *Mysterious Stranger Manuscripts*, William Gibson criticizes these texts for reasons which arise partly from his perspective on the significance which the stranger figure held for Twain. He writes,

> Satan, alias "No. 44," is the primary character in all three manuscripts and the most complex in his acts, in his satirical bent, the "fatal music of his voice," his Socratic way of speaking, his origins. . . In Mark Twain's theology, he is the truth-speaker momentarily banished from heaven, the preacher Koholeth, the new Prometheus who is "courteous to whores and niggers." . . . It is Satan the rebel, nonetheless, who figures most often in Twain's writings and who exhibits the richest development. (Gibson 14–15)

These remarks would work better if applied to the unfinished "Letters to Satan" and to *Letters from the Earth* than to the *Mysterious Stranger Manuscripts*. If it was Satan the rebel who most interested Twain, why is the stranger figure of all three manuscripts unfallen? Gibson says that "The Chronicle" was born out of Mark Twain's note of "Satan's boyhood—going around with other boys and surprising them with devilish miracles," and it is true that most of the "Chronicle's" action deals with this theme. The only discrepancy is that Young Satan is not Satan. Rather, he is his unfallen nephew and, far from having been cast out, has come to Earth on his own accord to study mankind. Only "Schoolhouse Hill," of the three fragments, genuinely centers on the figure of the young Satan (already at that point in Twain's progression called "44"). In that brief, unfinished tale, 44 is the son of Satan, again unfallen, and he takes up a vocation which is precisely the opposite of his father's: to rehabilitate mankind, which has been "diseased" by the fruit of the knowledge of good and evil.

Gibson assumes that Twain abandoned "Schoolhouse Hill" because

> . . . certain inherent contradictions within the character of 44 and his projected actions proved too great for Twain to resolve. Apparently he wanted to make his stranger both a boy and an angel, both a companion to Tom and Huck and a Prometheus-figure who was to enlighten the citizens of St. Petersburg concerning the damnable Moral Sense. (9)

The idea of a boy or adolescent angel is not inherently contradictory, nor is the notion that such a boy angel might, almost by definition, be Promethean in intention and effect. It seems more plausible that Twain ultimately abandoned "Schoolhouse Hill" because the figure of the mysterious stranger was ultimately more interesting to him as a foil to man than as the center of his own drama. Twain wrote "Schoolhouse Hill" in a departure from work on "The Chronicle"; after abandoning both, his next attempt to sound the stranger motif was *No. 44*, in which, again, the main figure is the naive *human* narrator, drawn to the charismatic stranger and his mysteries.

By the time Twain came to write *No. 44*, however, his emphasis had shifted. The stranger is no longer related to any figure in the Christian cosmology: he is a dream. Where previously he was utterly separate from mankind, alternately amused by and contemptuous of it ("The Chronicle") or compassionate toward it ("Schoolhouse Hill"), here, as an emanation of August's unconscious mind, he is a part of it. He tells August in the famous final chapter,

> "Nothing exists; all is a dream. God,—man,—the world,—the sun, the moon, the wilderness of stars: a dream, all a dream, they have no existence. *Nothing exists save empty space— and you!*"
>
> "I!"
>
> "And you are not you—you have no body, no bones, you are but a *thought*. I myself have no existence, I am but a dream—your dream, creature of your imagination. In a moment you will have realized this, then you will banish me from your visions and I shall dissolve into the nothingness out of which you made me . . . But I your poor servant have revealed you to yourself and set you free. Dream other dreams, and better! . . ." (404)

Like Twain himself, 44 may mock the human race for its pretensions, but he is always involved with it: the embittered tone of his mockery betrays his inescapable attachment. "On the whole," he says, "I am more sorry for the race than ashamed of it": but why should he feel ashamed of it unless he is somehow responsible for it, part of it? 44 appears whenever August is unhappy to cheer him and is hurt whenever August gets angry at him for his "blasphemies."

But Young Satan is never so solicitous of his human companions; he maintains a tone of lofty indifference throughout their Satanic dialogues. He sums up his attitude toward the human race in a speech whose tone recalls neither of the other two strangers, but Colonel Sherburn denouncing the mob which comes to lynch him for cold-blooded murder in *Huck Finn*:

> . . . Men have nothing in common with me—there is no point of contact. They have foolish little feelings, and foolish little vanities and impertinences and ambitions, their foolish little life is but a laugh, a sigh, and an extinction . . . I will show you what I mean. Here is a red spider, not so big as a pin's head; can you imagine an elephant being interested in him; caring whether he is happy or isn't; or whether he is wealthy or poor; or whether his sweetheart returns his love or not . . . Those things can never be important to the elephant, they are nothing to him, he cannot shrink his sympathies to the microscopic size of them. Man is to me as the red spider is to the elephant. The elephant has nothing against the spider, he cannot get down to that remote level— I have nothing against man . . . The elephant would not take the trouble to do the spider an ill turn; if he took the notion he might do him a good turn, if it came in his way and cost him nothing. I have done men good service, but no ill turns. (114)

It is disingenuous for the elephant to display such elaborate indifference to the red spider; it cannot be unconscious of the spider's existence and sensations if it can dilate upon them at such length nor can Young Satan. This pose of chilling severance is a convenience to him, and it is not the attitude of either 44.

These three "mysterious strangers" are not the identical beings Gibson describes, ciphers to be shuffled into whatever plot drifted across Twain's ephemeral field of attention. We may begin to sense why Twain made them different through analyzing their relationships with the boys whom they choose for companions. Early in "The Chronicle," Young Satan tells the boys that

> Man's mind clumsily and tediously and laboriously patches little trivialities together, and gets a result—such as it is. My mind *creates*! Do you get the force of that? Creates anything it desires—and in a moment. Creates without materials; creates fluids, solids, colors—anything, everything—out of the airy nothing which is called Thought. A man imagines a silk thread, imagines a machine to make it, imagines a picture, then by weeks of labor embroiders it on a canvas with the thread. I *think* the whole thing, and in a moment it is before you—created. (114)

Young Satan, creating characters and orchestrating events like a wildly imaginative author run rampant in his own text, seems at times like an authorial analogue. In the passage above, however, Twain makes him directly confront the difference between laborious physical creation and imaginative creation. An author cannot, of course, create a real silk thread with his thoughts, but he can create a representation of one; and in fact, Twain seems to play out the relationship between an author and his audience in these exchanges between Young Satan and the boys. If Young Satan is in some sense an authorial analogue, however, he represents a rather brutal author. What he creates, he feels free to destroy whenever it suits him: he concocts a miniature Creation scene to amuse the boys, only to squash between his fingers two workmen whose tiny brawl distracts him from conversation. When

> the small noise of the weeping and praying [over the dead workmen] began to annoy him, then he reached out and took the heavy board seat out of our swing and brought it down and mashed all those people into the earth just as if they had been flies, and went on talking just the same. (50)

Writers can wipe out multitudes of characters and "keep on talking," although in literature of any value such symbolic destruction will be to some purpose. To Young Satan, it is just a reflex. The boys are horrified, but Twain tells us that Young Satan "was bent on putting us at ease, and he had the right *art*" (italics mine). Before two pages have elapsed, he inspires them with "the fatal music of his voice" to dance upon the grave he has just created: "he was bent on making us feel as he did, and of course his magic accomplished his desire. It was no trouble to him, he did whatever he pleased with us."

In his San Francisco days, Twain learned the art of stand-up comedy from Artemus Ward, one of the best-known Western humorists of that day. Justin Kaplan, among others, has argued that as Twain developed his own brand of lecture-platform humor, the demands of its practice led him to see his audience as a pack of dumb, vile, pathetic sheep: the more successfully he manipulated them, the less he respected them (Kaplan, 226–27). As Kaplan says, Twain tended to think of his own humor as "something violent and painful that he did to someone else." (227) I would suggest that Twain invested in Young Satan his own contempt of his audience: the flip side of his courtship, in fact his need, of it. Young Satan's games seem to play out on a symbolic level the power Twain felt he himself could wield.

Despite the power and success of his own imagination, throughout his life Twain displayed uneasiness with the power of the imagination to wish evil on others, even though, and perhaps partially because, he could himself be so vindictive to anyone who he felt had crossed him. In *The Innocents Abroad*, Twain mused that the sea-travelers praying for a storm to pass them by were, by extension, wishing the storm on someone else; in 1905, in "The War Prayer," he drove home the point that those who pray for their country's victory in war are wishing pain and annihilation upon another country, populated by people like themselves. Twain's rigidly Presbyterian upbringing enforced upon him a sense that man is fully responsible for everything he does; although he struggled against the idea that with free will goes the guilt of human action, it was a belief too deeply ingrained to discard. After his bankruptcy and the cycle of disasters that followed it, Twain felt terrible guilt at what he called "robb[ing] my family to feed my speculations." (Leary, 351) Responsibility, a theme that runs throughout his writing, became a preoccupation after his bankruptcy, and we may see it further illustrated in *No. 44.*

When Twain turned from "The Chronicle" to *No. 44,* he chose to make the stranger figure, the authorial analogue, nonviolent. The absence of Satan's destructiveness in 44's brand of "creativity" is striking. 44 creates things, people, and considerable mischief, but destroys nothing—only himself, in two mock self-immolations. August, however, says the word that destroys his Duplicate. Further, 44 is always careful not to hurt the feelings of those around him; but August is capable of callous manipulation (again, the means by which he ensures that his Duplicate has no success with Marget) and cowardice (he never tries to help 44 when 44 is being attacked by the print-shop workers). But we must remember that August and 44 are linked: August is the conventional, prosaic-minded, waking self, and 44 is the power of his dreams, we might even say of his imagination, able to create with thought. Together, they seem to represent a polarization of the impulses which warred within Twain during his final years, with 44 representing the wild, fantastic imagination and sense of moral outrage which seeps through all of his fiction—in short, the creativity which made Twain a writer—and August representing the side of him that feared the righteous rage of public morality and desperately wanted to keep his public self from "going too far."

Early in *No. 44,* 44 absolves August of guilt for his lack of courage of his convictions, saying, "You did not make yourself. How then are you to blame?" August, it seems, is permitted his moral weakness and intellectual dullness because he is merely human, and so by definition stupid, limited, and unconscious.

But 44, having insight and creative power, is not to be permitted such weakness. I would suggest that in the progression from "The Chronicle" to *No. 44*, Twain curtailed the destructive impulses of the "authorial" figure of the mysterious stranger with whom he most strongly identified: it is as if he felt there could be no excuses for him. Thus, rather than to destroy or even to create, 44's primary mission becomes one of revelation. 44 shows August his own true nature: "But I your poor servant have revealed you to yourself and set you free. . . ." 44 is a black-comedy rendition of Dante's Virgil, treating exclusively the province of the first third of Dante's epic: he acts as a guide to the underworld of the human unconscious.

After Livy's death, Twain wrote a letter to his close friend, the Reverend Joe Twichell, of which the "nothing exists; all is a dream" close of *No. 44* is virtually a paraphrase. Quoting this letter, Gibson writes that the "almost unrelievedly dark tenor of [Twain's] letter" is only "half lightened in the 'Conclusion' [to *No. 44*] by blessed and hopeful feelings." (33) It is strange that Gibson finds anything "lightened," even by half, in such a conclusion: to end a novel with the narrator's realization that the world as we know it is only an illusion—a realization which the narrator experiences as a great relief—is surely a condemnation of that world. In justifying his view that No. 44 represents a cheerier perspective on Twain's part than does the letter to Twichell, Gibson writes, "Clemens valued the creative life above all other lives; it is a vulgar error to suppose that he did not." (33)

Certainly Twain did value "the creative life," but that does not mean that he never suffered ambivalence over its results, actual or potential. If the parallels which I have drawn between both Young Satan and 44 with Twain as an artist are plausible, we can see through Twain's use of Young Satan as an authorial surrogate his ambivalence about the moral nature of authorship: that he scrapped "The Chronicle" and went on to let 44 create, but, pointedly, not destroy, suggests that the analogy between himself and his mysterious stranger had grown too close for comfort. If the episode of the miniaturized Creation in "The Chronicle" seems more like a comment on the nature of God than of writing, I would suggest that on some level, Twain was analogizing the two: both create, and since both can, Twain felt, profit from that creation, they should bear responsibility for that creation.

In this creation sequence, Young Satan plunges the little people he has made into hellfire; Theodor, along with the other boys, feels their pain.

> [Young Satan] made us see all these things, and it was as if we were on the spot and looking at them with our own eyes. And we *felt* them, too, but there was no sign that they were anything to him, beyond being mere entertainments. Those visions of hell, those poor babes and women and girls and lads and men shrieking and supplicating in anguish—why, we could hardly bear it, but he was as bland about it as if it had been so many imitation rats in an artificial fire. (50)

The scene is eerily similar to Books XI and XII of *Paradise Lost*, in which the archangel Michael conveys to Adam the vision of the future life of the human race which God has decreed that he should see. It is ostensibly a vision of hope (at least, this was Milton's view), and yet Adam must witness Cain killing Abel, among other tragic spectacles. Having seen such a vision, how will Adam be able to take any joy in his sons when they are born? The scene is punishment masquerading as helpful information; insisting on its kind intent, as the Father does through Michael, amounts to sadism.

Twain knew *Paradise Lost* well; the similarity between the two scenes may have been intentional. After all, Twain saw the Christian God as a cosmic stand-up comic (McMichael, et al. 331–2), with Christians as the stupid, self-righteous butts of an absurd joke. In both "The Chronicle" and *Paradise Lost* XI and XII, the characters within the story suffer through the "fatal music" of the speaker's voice and the vision it gives them. Telescope the relation of speaker to listener outward to the level of author and reader, and that relation is duplicated: the reader, granted, participates in the author's effort with a consenting imagination, but the more felicitous the writer's art, the more vivid the painful impression upon the reader will be. What makes the passage above seem to serve as evidence of Twain's ambivalence about the "creative life" is that it emphasizes the boys' continuing pain and horror at the acts of their idol, Young Satan, not any ennobling (or even justifiable) purpose for those acts. Young Satan creates a race of tiny people and puts them in hell *because he can*, and Theodor says that this "made us miserable, for we loved him, and had thought him so noble and beautiful and gracious, and had honestly *believed* he was an angel; and to have him do this cruel thing—ah, it lowered him so, and we had such pride in him." (49) It "lowers" him in their eyes, but, as we have seen, they remain in thrall to him. 44 has the excuse of bearing a genuinely moral message: the visions of hell which he evokes are part of his program to lead August to an enlightened perspective on human nature, from which August may be able to "dream other dreams" (since human nature itself, at the close of *No. 44*, is a dream) "and better!" But August cannot dream a better dream: he can only relive the story he knows, grim as it is. Twain seems to suggest that the human mind is a sadomasochistic organ. Through this irony, Twain betrays his final ambivalence about the power of imaginative writing: the question of whether or not it can make any impact upon real human actions.

If we read 44 as representative of the power of the creative mind, and August, as I suggested above, as representative of the prosaic, conventional, conscious aspect which such a mind may wear, then the following description by 44—recapitulating Young Satan's view of the imagination in Twain's new context—of the radically different modes of thought possible to each one becomes especially suggestive:

> . . . But, August, I don't mean *your* kind of thought, I mean my kind, and the kind that the gods exercise. . . . A man *originates* nothing in his head, he merely observes exterior things, and *combines* them in his head—puts several observed things together, and draws a conclusion. His mind

> is merely a machine, that is all—an *automatic* one, and he
> has no control over it; it cannot conceive of a *new* thing, an
> original thing, it can only gather material from outside and
> combine it into new forms and patterns. But it always has to
> have the materials from the outside, for it can't make them
> itself. That is to say, a man's mind cannot *create*—a god's
> can, and my race can. That is the difference. *We* need no
> contributed materials, we create them—out of thought.
> (332–33)

In keeping with roles which 44 and August seem to play in
Twain's figurative drama, we may speculate that Twain
imagines the creative imagination as godlike, conjuring matter
and events out of thought with sweeping effects. Its prosaic
side is capable only of mechanical construction from pre-
existing materials: this is the merely human aspect which
seems to embody Twain's disgust with himself and is
represented by August—appropriately, a printer's apprentice.
Herr Stein, taking 44's side and promoting him to "printer's
devil," elevates publishing to the level of an "art . . . the
noblest and most puissant of all arts, and destined in the ages
to come to promote the others and preserve them." (251)

But 44's duties turn out to be the most trivial, mechanical,
and tiresome in the shop, requiring vast reserves of physical
energy. "What a devil to work he was!" says August, watching
his labors. The active, though nasty laborers of the printshop
are called "diligent and devilish spirits." "Devilish," in *No. 44*,
comes to be synonymous with "energetic"; 44's title of
"printer's devil" is the only hint of the original derivation of
the mysterious stranger figures. Twain said of Milton's Satan
that "the grandest thing in *Paradise Lost* . . . [is] [t]he Arch-
Fiend's terrible energy." (Gibson 16) In *No. 44*, Twain stressed
the tremendous effort involved in the printing process; he
knew it well, having been apprenticed to a printer at the age of
twelve (Wecter, *SCH*).

Again, 44 seems to stand in for Twain: just as in Twain's
own life the creative effort of writing supplanted the physical
drudgery of the printer's trade, 44 supplants grinding physical

labor with the ease of his own imaginative creation. When the workmen go on strike, 44 first makes invisible sprites and, later, the Duplicates to carry out the printing process. The entire episode mocks the tremendous human effort which the mechanical production of an author's imaginative work required. The result is that the creative mind of the stranger (writer) is elevated at the expense of the pathetic, mechanical efforts of men (publishers, whose conventional attitudes and rapacious business practices Twain loathed but knew necessary to the fame he craved).

Looking back from the conclusion of *No. 44* to 44's distinction between his and August's brands of thought, it seems that in making both inhabit the same being, Twain dramatized his own sense of imaginative limitation. The idea that human beings create nothing and are capable only of mechanical construction was a conviction that Twain may have held throughout his life, but it was surely reinforced by his reading of Hume: his copy of *The Origin of Ideas* has been catalogued by Alan Gribben as part of Twain's vast, heavily annotated library. Compare the following passage from Hume with 44's exposition of the distinction between "his kind of thought" and August's:

> . . . But though our thought seems to possess this unbounded liberty, we shall find, upon a nearer examination, that it is really confined within very narrow limits, and that all this creative power of the mind amounts to no more than the faculty of compounding, transposing, augmenting, or diminishing the materials afforded us by the senses and experience. When we think of a golden mountain, we only join two consistent ideas, gold and mountain, with which we were formerly acquainted. A virtuous horse we can conceive; because, from our own feeling, we can conceive virtue; and . . . a horse . . . is an animal familiar to us. In short, all the materials of thinking are derived either from our outward or inward sentiment: the mixture and composition of these belongs alone to the mind and will. Or, to express myself in philosophical language, all ideas and more feeble perceptions are copies of our impressions or more lively ones. (Hume)

The parallels are close: 44 tells August that the human mind is incapable of creating "a new thing, an original thing; it can only gather materials from the outside and combine it into new forms and patterns." Hume summarizes the problem pithily: "the most lively thought is still inferior to the dullest sensation." Could Twain have read this without wondering whether the most lively writing would not, in terms of effect on the thoughts of his human readers, be inferior to the dullest physical experience?

Given Twain's fluctuations between guilt at his actions and doubt over their effects, we may have in his view of imagination a partial answer to the question of why he published so little of the material he wrote in the last decade of his life. If he had held such a view, it could have worked in several ways. In one mood, he might focus on the inability of his prosaic audience to comprehend or even to bear the message of his growing pessimism about the "damned human race"; in another, he might doubt that his own artistic powers were sufficient to make that audience feel the force of what he wanted to say.

Certainly Twain could have felt ambivalence about his own artistic powers without Hume's encouragement, but the similarity between 44's and Hume's exposition of the same problem makes it reasonable to suggest that in Hume's philosophy, Twain found a framework in which to express his ambivalence about his own creative capacities. In venting his frustration with August's limited understanding, 44 blurts out, "one cannot pour the starred and shoreless expanses of the universe into a jug!" The title page of *No. 44* bears the legend, "An Ancient Tale found in a Jug, and freely Translated from the Jug."

In the year before his death, Twain reveled in the discovery of a new literary form: expressing his more vitriolic views in letters he never meant to send. These were letters to his closest friends, who were well acquainted with his heterodox notions. Gibson writes, "He told Howells, 'when you are on fire with theology, you'll write it to [Reverend]

Twichell because'—in imagination—'it would make him writhe and squirm and break the furniture.'" (Gibson 31) Gibson sees a "literary impulse" outweighing Twain's "private sorrow" in concocting this strategy; as Hill aptly says in *God's Fool,* Twain felt he had been "forced by fate to adopt fiction as a medium of truth," and "in his final years, he gained confidence in his autobiographical voice to express unpleasant truths." (17)

Twain may have gained some confidence but not enough to allow that autobiographical voice to be heard. If these letters had been written in the spirit of attempting to make, for example, his friend the minister understand how he felt about theology, why not send them, unless he felt that he could not make his beliefs either acceptable or comprehensible even to the people closest to him? Imagining one's friends being driven to "break the furniture" because of something you wrote to them sounds like a hostile wish or an uneasy premonition.

Since Twain's contract with Harper's obligated them to publish—literally—whatever he submitted to them, we must see Twain's failure to publish so much of his late writing as a refusal to publish. There could be no stronger testament to the sense of alienation under which Twain labored in his last years nor to the vacillations of his attitude toward his own artistic power than this refusal to make public so much of what he wrote. He knew that he could make an impact on the minds he chose to influence, but the nature and degree of that impact he could not predict. He was well aware that the sort of fiction he wanted to write, and did write, could cost him his reading public, just as sending the "imaginary" letters might have destroyed his closest relationships; he was willing to risk neither. As Ferguson has written,

> [Twain] withheld his most vitriolic comments, as he continued to withhold "The War Prayer" and his many criticisms of the God of the Old Testament. Yet it was probably not Livy's dead hand which checked him. His estimate of what would shock the public was formed before

he ever knew Livy; like his philosophy, it had its roots in the Presbyterian Sunday School of Hannibal. He never in his life wrote anything more scathing than the "Defense of General Funston," and the controversy with the missionaries; he published them, and the heavens did not fall. But it flattered him to believe that he was full of thoughts so devastating that the world could not take them. (302)

Ferguson is correct that Twain found perverse comfort in believing that the world was not ready for his work. And yet, it is striking to note that Twain was willing to publish some of his political late writing, such as "Funston" and "To the Person Sitting in Darkness," but not works treating the subject of religion in any substantive way. He knew from Hannibal, surely, that such material as *Letters from the Earth* would truly be more than that audience could "take" and that its publication could hurt the royalties from his collected works. As he wrote to Rogers during the negotiation of his Harper's contract,

> Whenever a Uniform and a Deluxe can be marketed, *that's* the time to do it; a delay of a year can be fatal, for a literary reputation is a most frail thing—any trifling accident can kill it, and its market along with it. (Leary, 348)

Any audience that could be so fickle would not, one would think, be much worth courting. And yet Twain had courted it from the 1860s onward, and, I would suggest, once his collected works began to issue, he chose to stop courting it at book length. Platform lectures, essays, and the occasional short story were sufficient to keep his memory green in the public mind, and, considering the way he spoke of his audience, calling them "sheep" and likening himself to a "trained seal barking for fish," it is not surprising that Twain felt that it could not absorb his criticisms without the teasing tenor of the good-bad-boy voice. Further, he came to see that audience more and more from a God's-eye-view. In a suggestive jotting in a notebook of 1896, Twain dilated upon the sort of God he would construct. Above all, this deity would not "trade on salvation":

> . . . He would not be a merchant, a trader. . . He would not sell, or offer to sell, temporary benefits or the joys of eternity, for the product called worship. I would have him as dignified as the better sort of men in this regard. (_MTN_, 300–301)

Twain loved worship: it exhilarated him. But perhaps, in the omniscient mood of his later works, using technically limited narrative voices that nonetheless read minds (George Harrison's tactic for telling "truth" in _Which Was It?_), creating authorial analogues who resemble deities, moods like the above as well as fears for his profits helped keep his most challenging later works out of the public eye.

At the close of _No. 44_, the fate of 44, the authorial analogue—whether he, and imagination with him, disappear altogether, or find a way to merge with August, the straight man—is left ambiguous, as the question of whether imagination could be reconciled with the demands of public life remained ambiguous for Twain until his death. If there is no way to prove that anything exists outside the mind, we are left helpless, stuck inside the joke played upon us. Twain could shake off that suspension by writing books deflecting that helplessness onto his audience, but in _No. 44_, where both satiric author and audience are symbolically contained within one mind, there is no escape, only irritation as the mind perpetually retells its own story.

Twain's last years were plagued by just such an irreducible irritation over the questions of creativity and its power, guilt, and atheism. His refusal to publish his most powerful late work was not a failure of artistic power, but a failure of will. His lack of faith—in himself as well as in God— was the agitated sort that the playwright-hero of Beckett's _Endgame_ expresses when his prayer for more characters goes unheard ("The bastard! He doesn't exist!"); and in fact, Beckett's "I can't go on—I'll go on" could serve as an epigraph to the fascinating fragments and finished works that grew out of his last fifteen years. His achievement in *No. 44* was in finding and finishing a narrative structure that could play out the questions that plagued him, even if he could not solve them.

Mark Twain came to believe that effective exercise of such power was only possible to those gigantic figures who, like Young Satan, have no compassion for the suffering of those whom their actions affect; that those who, like 44, undertake a consciously Promethean role, are doomed to suffering and failure. Only when these latter figures cloak their intent in humor does Twain concede any possibility that their Promethean mission might succeed: for, to steal the words of Young Satan, "against the assault of laughter nothing can stand." Believing this, Twain withheld the bulk of his most seriously intended later work from publication during his lifetime. In so doing, he flung down the gauntlet for later generations: if it's not a joke, can we take it?

Works Cited

Budd, Louis J. *Our Mark Twain: The Making of His Public Personality.* Philadelphia: U. of Pennsylvania P., 1983.

Clemens, Samuel Langhorne: see Twain, Mark.

DeVoto, Bernard. "The Symbols of Despair," rpt. in *Mark Twain: A Collection of Critical Essays.* Ed. Henry Nash Smith. Englewood Cliffs: Prentice-Hall, 1963. 119–29.

Ferguson, Delancey. *Mark Twain: Man and Legend.* New York: Bobbs-Merrill Co., Inc., 1943.

Fiedler, Leslie A. "As Free As Any Cretur . . ." rpt. in *Mark Twain: A Collection of Critical Essays.* Ed. Henry Nash Smith. Englewood Cliffs: Prentice-Hall, 1963. 130–39.

Gibson, William. Introduction to Mark Twain's *The Mysterious Stranger Manuscripts.* Berkeley: U. of California P., 1968. 1–34.

Gribben, Alan. *Mark Twain's Library: A Reconstruction.* Boston: G. K. Hall & Co., 1980. Volume I.

Hill, Hamlin. *Mark Twain: God's Fool.* New York: Harper and Row, 1973.

Hill, Hamlin, ed. *Mark Twain's Letters to His Publishers, 1867–1894.* Berkeley: U. of California P., 1967.

Hume, David. *An Enquiry Into Human Understanding.* Ed. Steven M. Cahn. *Classics of Western Philosophy.* Indianapolis: Hackett Publishing Co., 1977.

Kahn, Sholom J. *Mark Twain's Mysterious Stranger: A Study of the Manuscript Text.* Columbia: U. of Missouri P., 1979.

Kaplan, Justin. *Mr. Clemens and Mark Twain.* New York: Simon and Schuster, 1966.

Leary, Louis, ed. *Mark Twain's Correspondence with Henry Huttleston Rogers, 1893–1910.* Berkeley: U. of California P., 1969.

Macnaughton, William R. *Mark Twain's Last Years as a Writer.* Columbia: U. of Missouri P., 1979.

McMichael, George, Crews, Frederick, Levenson, J.C., Marx, Leo, and Smith, David E., eds. *Anthology of American Literature.* New York: Macmillan Publishing Co., 1980.

Smith, Henry Nash. *Mark Twain: The Development of a Writer.* New York: Atheneum, 1962 (rpt. 1972).

Tuckey, John S. *Mark Twain and Little Satan: The Writing of the Mysterious Stranger.* West Lafayette, Indiana: Purdue University Studies, 1963.

Twain, Mark. *The Autobiography of Mark Twain.* Ed. Charles Neider. New York: Harper and Row, 1959.

——— *The Devil's Race-Track: Mark Twain's 'Great Dark' Writings.* Ed. John S. Tuckey. Berkeley: U. of California P., 1966.

——— *Mark Twain's Notebook.* Ed. Albert Bigelow Paine. New York: Harper and Brothers, 1935.

——— *Mark Twain's Which Was the Dream? and Other Symbolic Writings of the Later Years.* Ed. John S. Tuckey. Berkeley: U. of California P., 1966.

——— *The Mysterious Stranger Manuscripts.* Ed. William M. Gibson. Berkeley: U. of California P., 1969.

Wecter, Dixon. *Sam Clemens of Hannibal.* Boston: Houghton Mifflin Co., 1952.

——— ed. *The Love Letters of Mark Twain.* New York: Harper and Brothers, 1949.

——— ed. *Mark Twain to Mrs. Fairbanks.* Los Angeles: Plantin Press, 1949.

Weil, Susanne. "Reconstructing the 'Imagination-Mill': Mark Twain's Literary Response to Bankruptcy." Diss. University of California, Berkeley, 1991.

Coming Back to Humor:
The Comic Voice in
Mark Twain's Autobiography

Michael J. Kiskis

Literary and biographical studies of the years between 1890 and 1910 focus on Mark Twain's dual tragedies—his bankruptcy in 1894 and Susy's death in 1896—as defining events: the shock, we are told, moved Twain away from humor toward a darker vision of the world, and that darker vision became the controlling theme of, as well as the impetus for, his increased output of social criticism and his preoccupations with a dream self. His life and writings succumbed to that darkness. It choked his creative process and led to his seeming inabilty to complete any lengthy fiction. He lost his counterbalance to life's pain and put aside humor, the primary ingredient in his successful storytelling. We are left with an image of a deeply troubled misanthrope who sank into bitterness and rage as he outlived his immediate family and became increasingly uncomfortable with and suspicious of his staff. We are left with a picture devoid of humor, the end of storytelling. We are left wondering what happened to Mark Twain's sense of humor.[1]

While it was certainly toned down and mixed with heavy doses of depression and anger and guilt, Mark Twain's humor remained a renewable resource.[2] It was too much a part of his public and private self to slip away unnoticed. He was much too sensitive to the call of humor and much too reliant on it as a personal and literary muse to forsake it entirely. The nature of his humor changed, however, as he worked through the range of emotions connected both with the death of his favorite daughter and with the personal sense of loss that played so heavily upon him as he witnessed the deaths of family and friends. During his final years (1906–1910), humor became less a tool for social criticism and more a hook to use to knit together the variety of his interests and memories. But Twain needed a vehicle that would allow him to revisit his muse so that he could find the raw materials he needed to build his stories. Autobiography reawakened and refocused Mark Twain's humor.[3]

This refocusing was no easy task since many of Mark Twain's writings during 1890–1910 were rooted in the difficulties of business and family tragedy. In 1890 Twain faced the growing threat from the mismanagement of the Charles Webster Company and the false optimism in the Paige typesetter. His mother, Jane Lampton Clemens, died during that year. His family faced severe financial problems. His bankruptcy in 1894 gave rise to the world lecture tour of 1895–96, which eased his debt but ended with the greater loss of Susy to spinal meningitis in 1896. His older brother Orion died in 1897. His youngest daughter Jean's condition as an epileptic became clearer during these years. Throughout this period, Twain sought solace and peace by plunging into his work; however, while that work is often dark in tone, the pattern of darkness and disappointment was not new to the 1890s. Mark Twain's adult life was haunted by rapid mood swings. If we are looking for instances of Twain's darkening vision, we are hard pressed to find images more disturbing than the violence of "A Bloody Massacre near Carson" (1863) and the tragedy of *Huckleberry Finn* (1885) or the destruction of the sand belt in *A Connecticut Yankee in King Arthur's Court* (1889). If we are looking for examples of frantic composition, we need look only to his work on *Innocents Abroad* (1869) and *Roughing It* (1872). Twain approached the precipice of darkness throughout his career as a writer. He constantly mixed the contraries of violence and depression with humor, and that mixture must be kept in mind as we examine his final decades.

Perhaps the most problematic of Twain's shifts during these years is his move away from fiction. That movement, however, did not put a stop to his writing. A quick review of Mark Twain's publication record starting as early as 1894 with *Pudd'nhead Wilson* and *Tom Sawyer Abroad* suggests that his creative drive had begun to slow or, at least, had been redirected. While he continued to publish, the nature of his work changed from the extended narratives that assured his reputation as a novelist to the essay, with only occasional forays into extended tales. After *Personal Recollections of Joan of Arc* and *Tom Sawyer, Detective* (1896), Twain completed *Following the Equator* (1897). From that point on, he devoted more attention to the essay, especially the political essay.[4] His new-found position as commentator and sage, as reformer and activist, pushed him to write more directly to the public, and the essay was best suited for direct and timely commentary. That in itself leads to an impression that he became increasingly haunted by social and political issues and less interested in humor or storytelling. We should, however, think of his explicitly designed and overtly stated social criticism as a stage of his evolution as a public figure.[5] As he tuned his satiric voice, his essays became increasingly biting and increasingly effective. And—though he would eventually stumble and then ease out of the picture—he became a leading voice in America for the Anti-imperialist movement.[6]

Though Twain completed several extended pieces after 1897—*What Is Man?* (1898; 1906), *Christian Science* (1907), *Captain Stormfield's Visit to Heaven* (1907), and *Is Shakespeare Dead?* (1909)—his work might be discussed from two perspectives: his public offerings as an essayist and satirist; his private experiments in fiction and storytelling. That split was indeed quite clear during the work that Twain completed between 1900 and 1905. Among his public offerings were the scathing essays "To The Person Sitting in Darkness," "To My Missionary Critics" (1901), "Defense of General Funston" (1902), "Tsar's Soliloquy" (1904), and "King Leopold's Soliloquy" (1905). His satires made ample use of the incongruous and burlesque as he developed his images of the imperialist powers. Their humor was severe in its tone and volume. His private writing, on the other hand, produced a variety of fragmented tales: among them "The Secret History or Eddypus, the World-Empire" (1901–02) and "The Stupendous Procession" (1901), each of which offers a blend of fiction and political essay. Other unfinished pieces are "No. 44, The Mysterious Stranger," (1902; incorporating materials from "The Chronicle of Young Satan," on which Twain worked between 1897 and 1900), "Three Thousand Years Among the Microbes" (1905), and "The Refuge of the Derelicts" (1905). While the private pieces reflect Twain's growing restiveness and interest in ontological questions, they also contain their share of humorous insights and burlesque images.

This all leads us back to Twain's work on the autobiography. With the advent of 1906 Mark Twain began to integrate the public and private as he prepared to work on his autobiography. That integration was possible because Twain used autobiography to reinvigorate himself by resurrecting humor and storytelling. We must keep in mind that humor and irony were Mark Twain's primary tools. He kept them sharp and he used them (even though he did not always publish the results). There is much to be said about the vitality of Mark Twain's humor and his use of humor as a palliative and as a recuperative tonic.

Humor was one way Twain dealt with the distractions that became especially acute with the onset of the financial storm in 1894. That blast contributed to his seeming inability to gather up the steam necessary to navigate an extended fiction. But Twain's composing process was always rather fickle: he worked until his interest fagged and then he pigeonholed the manuscript. From 1870 through 1906, manuscripts earmarked as autobiography were constantly pigeonholed. Eventually, this jackrabbit composing style worked to Twain's advantage. He went right along piling up tales and anecdotes with little concern for the overarching structure or intent. That removed the demand for consistency and logic and made it possible for a variety of tales—some tall, some poignant—to be told.

As Twain relocated himself in autobiography, he became increasingly interested in the process of the story. He was excited by the series of autobiographical dictations (at least through 1906 and 1907) because of the emphasis on talk. Twain claimed that talk was at the heart of true autobiography and the reason for his enjoyment. When he returned to dictating in 1904, he wrote William Dean Howells:

> You will never know how much enjoyment you have lost until you get to dictating your autobiography; then you will realize, with a pang, that you might have been doing it all your life if you had only had the luck to think of it. And you will be astonished (& charmed) to see how like talk it is, & how real it sounds, & how well & compactly & sequentially it constructs itself, & what a dewy & breezy & woodsy freshness it has, & what a darling worshipful absence of the signs of starch, & flatiron, & labor & fuss & other artificialities! . . . There are little slips here & there, little inexactednesses, & many desertions of a thought before the end of it has been reached, but these are not blemishes, they are merits, their removal would take away the naturalness of the flow & banish the very thing—the nameless something— which differentiates real narrative from artificial narrative & makes the one so vastly better than the other—the subtle something which makes good talk so much better than the best imitation of it that can be done with a pen (MT to WDH 1/16/04; SMTHL, 370–371).

In effect, Mark Twain found himself facing his own beginnings as a storyteller: talk was the primary currency of his youth as he sat and listened to tales around slave kitchens, of his piloting days as he sat in the wheelhouses, of his adulthood as he and Jim Gillis told and retold the story of the jumping frog and as he stood night after night on the lecture platform. Talk was the basis for much of Twain's fiction: he wove lively dialogues for any number of his characters from Simon Wheeler to Demoiselle Alisande la Carteloise, from Huck Finn to No. 44. And the potential for humor—or at least for the basic incongruities that sire that humor—is best found in his talk.

In effect, Twain's return to the autobiography in 1906 rekindled his sense of direction and revived his interest in presenting one final story to the public. But while the idea of beginning the work appealed to Twain, the dominance of the spoken word in the autobiographical dictations was not enough to keep Twain on track. He again fell prey to distractions and devoted a good deal of time to supplementing the story of his life with contemporary newspaper reports, fragments of work that he had long since pigeonholed, and long submerged but still potent affronts. The dictations became an attic, or at least a storage trunk, into which he poured memories and commentary and sentiment and vitriol.

This combination changed as Twain's conception of the project shifted—what started out as a series of interviews that Albert Bigelow Paine would use as the foundation for his biography of Twain soon developed into an intentional attempt to pile up materials for an autobiography (perhaps as a way to block Paine's work[7]). The explanation that Twain used to rationalize his private freedom from publication—"I am not interested in getting done with anything. I am only interested in talking along and wandering around as much as I want to, regardless of results to the future reader" (MTA I, 327)—would eventually succumb to the possibility of profit. While Paine's projected biography sparked Twain's interest, their work together remained private. George Harvey assured the continuation of Twain's public storytelling when he purchased and serialized chapters from Twain's autobiography.

The project changed substantially when Twain was approached by Harvey. Until that point, Twain had been using the dictations themselves as a distraction. They kept him busy. His intention was to simply present his story to his small and approving audience (at first made up of only Paine and Josephine Hobbey, a stenographer). With the arrival of Harvey, however, and with the resulting contract with the *North*

American Review, Twain adjusted his sights once more on the wider public audience. The demands of serialization, of presenting consecutive and self-contained pieces forced Twain to impose more control on his meandering commentary so that the tale would develop in a form more suitable for publication. This brought him back to the careful pruning that had always been a part of his composing process and to his tried and true formula for effective storytelling: "To string incongruities and absurdities together in a wandering and sometimes purposeless way, and seem innocently unaware that they are absurdities, is the basis of the American art. . . Another feature is the slurring of the point. A third is the dropping of a studied remark apparently without knowing it, *as if one were thinking aloud.* The fourth and last is the pause" (Essays, 158; my emphasis). Talk is basic. This talk brought Mark Twain back to humor and its variety of tools and voices. It helped him warm to the prospect of jumping back into public storytelling.

The material that Twain finally presented to his public as "Chapters from my Autobiography" during 1906 and 1907 is markedly different from the raw material that he had been accumulating in the dictations.[8] It is different in the range of topics that are covered within its twenty-five chapters, and it is different in the structure that is imposed on the materials. It is also a very different text because it is a tapestry—it weaves together his written and dictated passages. Mark Twain knew his readers, and that combination of material helped him reach his audience. He knew what would sell. And he made a conscious attempt to give the audience a self-portrait that would not vary too far from the image they already had of him—he would solidify his image as a man of letters by offering a text rich in self-effacing tales and bouts of sentiment.

Twain's success with the autobiography can be seen best if we consider the text a full and complete tale, one that has a beginning, a middle, and an end. Of course, narrative has a way of falling into that rough structure, especially autobiography because it usually grows out of the basic chronology of the life. But Twain does not rely on the cradle to grave chronology to control the tale. It is controlled by the frame that he builds: the body of the narrative exists squarely within that frame. If we unite the twenty five chapters to form a single text, the autobiography joins "The Jumping Frog," "A True Story," and *A Connecticut Yankee in King Arthur's Court* in its use of the framing device to enter and exit the tale. It is also related to several fragments of Twain's later years: "The Great Dark," "Which Was It?," "The Secret History of Eddypus" and "Three Hundred Years Among the Microbes" use the frame. With the autobiography, however, Twain returned to humor as the basic material for his frame. In this way the autobiography is more closely related to Simon Wheeler's tale than to Hank Morgan's or to Henry Edwards'.

The connection to Wheeler reverberates in the voice that dominates the frame. Throughout his career Twain made ample and successful use of one of the staples of southwestern humor—the deadpan voice: "The humorous story may be spun out to great length, and may wander around as much as it pleases, and arrive nowhere in particular. . . [it] is told gravely; the teller does his best to conceal the fact that he even dimly suspects that there is anything funny about it" (Essays, 155–156).[9] It is Wheeler's and it is Huck's. It is Sandy's. As the autobiography continues, it will be Susy's.[10] At the opening, it is Mark Twain's:

> Howells was here yesterday afternoon, and I told him the whole scheme of this autobiography and its apparently systemless system—only apparently systemless, for it is not really that. It is a deliberate system, and the law of the system is that I shall talk about the matter which for the moment interests me, and cast it aside and talk about something else the moment its interest is exhausted. It is a system which follows no charted course and is not going to follow any such course. It is a system which is a complete and purposed jumble—a course which begins nowhere, follows no specified route, and can never reach an end while I am alive, for the reason that, if I should talk to a stenographer two hours a day for a hundred years, I should

still never be able to set down a tenth part of the things which have interested me in my lifetime. I told Howells that this autobiography of mine would live a couple of thousand years, without any effort, and would then make a fresh start and live the rest of the time.

He said he believed it, and asked me if I meant to make a library of it.

I said that this was my design; but that, if I should live long enough, the set of volumes could not be contained merely in a city, it would require a State, and that there would not be any multi-billionaire alive, perhaps, at any time during its existence who would be able to buy a full set, except on the installment plan.

Howells applauded, and was full of praises and endorsement, which was wise in him and judicious. If he had manifested a different spirit, I would have thrown him out of the window. I like criticism, but it must be my way (MTOA, 3–4).

There are several points bubbling along beneath the surface of this introduction. Along with the steady and very serious voice, we also get an explanation of Twain's process, a pitch for a continual series of volumes (we might think of these as a variation on encyclopedia yearbooks), an endorsement by a major literary figure, and then a final threat which underlines the serious nature of the text ahead. And none of this is presented as remarkable or unusual. It is all very plain and clear and stable. In a compact preface, Twain has put his readers on notice that his tale will alternate between the comic and the serious. His potential attack on Howells and warning to readers sets a decidedly humorous tone (the warning functions in much the same way as does the comic disclaimer that opens _Huckleberry Finn_), and as we move into the main portion of the tale, a serious and strong personal interest supports the comedy.

The tale gets under way with a nod toward the expected family history and another backhand swipe at the reader:

Back of the Virginia Clemenses is a dim procession of ancestors stretching back to Noah's time. According to traditions, some of them were pirates and slavers in Elizabeth's time. But this is no discredit to them, for so were Drake and Hawkins and the others. It was a respectable trade then and monarchs were partners in it. In my time I have had desires to be a pirate myself. The reader—if he will look deep down in his secret heart, will find—but never mind what he will find there; I am not writing his Autobiography, but mine (MTOA, 4).

In a movement reminiscent of *Mark Twain's (Burlesque) Autobiography and First Romance* (1871), Twain pushes his ancestry back to Noah in a bid to claim deep and impressive roots.[11] It smacks of the tall tale, and of the raftman's boast. The connection to privateers ties him to the disreputable—regardless of the official stamp of approval—and reminds us of Tom Sawyer's conventional pirate band on the one hand and of Huck and Jim's rebellion on another. By calling attention to these professions, Twain draws the reader closer. He sets the stage for his own tale with hints of shady dealing and outlaw behavior. He keeps those dealings firmly for himself as he abruptly ends the ancestral line that would allow his readers that same connection. In all, then, Twain invites his readers to gather around, sit by the fire, and listen to his tale. His is the unmistakable voice of the seasoned storyteller.

The storyteller dominates the remaining chapters. While Twain's method of butting present and past together to explore the effect is prominent throughout the twenty-five chapters, it is possible to identify five general patterns of associations that unite the text: comments on Twain's early writing (chapter 2), tales of the Clemens family (chapters 1, 3, 4, and 5), famous acquaintances (chapters 6 and 7), Twain's experience in Hannibal and Nevada (chapters 8 through 14), the Clemenses in Hartford and Elmira, a loosely tied series of comments on Twain's writing, his literary acquaintances, recent experiences, and a replay of the Whittier Birthday speech (chapters 16 through 25). This is not as clean as it appears from this breakdown, since Twain weaves in and out of memories and associations as he continues his tale; however, the thematic links do help begin to refute the charge of literary chaos that has been leveled against the autobiography. The essential link, however, is Mark Twain's voice. He constantly modulates his voice to fit the explicit tales and anecdotes, but these separate pieces are stitched together much like a quilt. The essential voice—the controlling consciousness and perspective—remains consistent throughout the text: it resonates with an appreciation for the incongruities that have made up a life and cherishes the contrasts when past events are filtered through the irony that is possible only with distance. The point is that Twain uses the autobiography to reconnect with the creative formula that was at the heart of his regional, national, and international success. He mixes the tall tale with the familiar anecdote; he undercuts his tales of public acclaim with sharp blasts powered by events and details of his inept behavior in the midst of his family life. And while there are moments of supreme pathos and seemingly genuine sentiment, there are many more that focus on the comic adventures that combine to describe Twain's western and family life. All of these are interpreted by Twain as he looks back through the haze of time.

Twain's comic voice that reverberates within these sketches and anecdotes and tales is a derivative of the tenderfoot pose that he used so well in *Roughing It*.[12] This seems a very deliberate choice. Twain's version of his life offers very little of the commentary on contemporary politics that plays so prominent a role in Albert Bigelow Paine's and Bernard DeVoto's collections of dictations. Throughout the autobiography, Twain presents himself as perpetually hampered by his slow wits, his lack of social skills, his inabilty to live up to expectations. He is the quick-tempered novice editor in the west who is ultimately betrayed both by his own lack of judgement and his friends' and colleagues' joy in the preliminaries to a duel. He is the muddled husband: he places his social reputation at risk because of his decidedly low style, he fails to understand the basic workings of household items, he has temper tantrums. He is also the doting and misunderstood father: he spins yarns for his children, he keeps careful record of the children's reactions to the life around them, he wonders at the observations that Susy offers as part of her biography of him.[13]

As Twain looks into his past, his images are tempered by his at times overwhelming sense of loss. This leads him to use the autobiography as an extended eulogy for family and friends on the one hand and for an idyllic and elegiac childhood on another. Each of these movements, however, is touched by Twain's puckishness. Two well-known pieces of the autobiography help to establish this trend: Twain's shirt-throwing tantrum and his look back at the Quarrels farm.

In chapter five, Twain recalls his temper and his vain attempts to hide it and the resulting language from Livy. While dressing he was piqued at finding buttons missing from his shirts. That pique devolved into venom as he put on three shirts and just as quickly dispatched each offender out of the window. Throughout, Twain's language expanded "both in loudness and vigor of expression" until he reached for the third shirt: "I was too angry—too insane—to examine the third shirt, but put it furiously on. Again the button was absent, and that shirt followed its comrades out the window. Then I straightened up, gathered my reserves, and let myself go like a cavalry charge. In the midst of that great assault, my eye fell upon the gaping door, and I was paralyzed" (MTOA, 46–47). Livy had, of course, heard the final assault. Twain continues:

> I tried to hope that Mrs. Clemens was asleep, but I knew better. I could not escape by the window. It was narrow, and suited only to shirts. At last I made up my mind to boldly loaf through the bedroom with the air of a person who had not been doing anything. I made half the journey successfully. . . . I had to stop in the middle of the room. I hadn't the strength to go on. I believed that I was under accusing eyes—that even the carved angels were inspecting me with an unfriendly gaze. You know how it is when you are convinced that somebody behind you is looking steadily

at you. You have to turn your face—you can't help it. I turned mine. . . .

Against the white pillows I saw the black head—I saw that young and beautiful face; and I saw the gracious eyes with a something in them which I had never seen there before. They were snapping and flashing with indignation. I felt myself crumbling; I felt myself shrinking away to nothing under that accusing gaze. I stood silent under that desolating fire for as much as a minute, I should say—it seemed a very, very long time. Then my wife's lips parted and from them issued—*my latest bathroom remark*. The language perfect, but the expression velvety, unpractical, apprenticelike, ignorant, inexperienced, comically inadequate, absurdly weak and unsuited to the great language. In my lifetime I had never heard anything so out of tune, so inharmonious, so incongruous, so ill-suited to each other as were those mighty words set to that feeble music. I tried to keep from laughing, for I was a guilty person in deep need of charity and mercy. I tried to keep from bursting, and I succeeded—until she gravely said, "There, now you know how it sounds."

Then I exploded; the air was full with my fragments, and you could hear them whiz. I said, "Oh Livy, if it sounds like that I will never do it again."

Then she had to laugh herself. Both of us broke into convulsions, and went on laughing until we were physically exhausted and spiritually reconciled (MTOA, 46–48).

This long passage shows off Twain's storytelling (it can easily stand on its own as a complete tale). The contrast between Twain and Livy is, of course, at the heart of the passage. There would be no tale if that contrast were not so clear and so pronounced: he is volcanic and well acquainted with the rigors of "bathroom" remarks; she is, to say the least, inexperienced with and unappreciative of the genre. That conflict between western ruffian and eastern innocent recurs throughout the autobiography whenever Twain places himself within Livy's hearing or reach. Here it supplies the context for the humor, since the linchpin for the tale is the repeated curses.[14]

Beyond that, however, we have a scene reconstructed to offer readers a memorable image—of Livy. As a eulogist, Twain worked to present the various members of his family in an almost saintly light (like Livy, Orion survives as fundamentally innocent and honest). Here he introduces Livy not only as inexperienced with the nuances of cursing (something that is especially important to our image of her as perpetually innocent) but as unusually naive when it comes to the very sound and intention of the language. Twain drives this point home forcefully by describing Livy with an extended series of adjectives: her face is "young and beautiful"; her eyes "gracious." Her flash of anger dissipates because her version of the curse is "velvety," "unpractical," "apprenticelike," "ignorant," "inexperienced," "comically inadequate," "absurdly weak." The irony, of course, is that adjectives that normally indict—especially if they are used to describe the tenderfoot—are put together here to applaud and to praise. This twist is especially important for Twain since he is working to offer a memorial to Livy. He does that not only by placing his own increasingly disreputable self in opposition to Livy's goodness but also by turning the tenderfoot—once despised and ridiculed—into a hero. Surely part of this construction has its foundation in Twain's own perception of Livy as well as in his Victorian sensibilities. The vigor of his protection of Livy is, however, even more notable because of the combination of humor and eulogy and the conflict between civilizing (constructive in its opening new vistas to the individual) and "sivilizing" (destructive in its intention to beat naturalness and freedom out of the individual) efforts.

While Twain spent considerable time and effort composing memorials to family and friends, he also moved beyond that to offer a deeply felt tribute to youth and childhood. His tales of Nevada and Hannibal hum with good humor and well-aimed irony. He presents stories of frontier reporting, aborted duels, and a variety of games. Most importantly, however, Twain returned to Hannibal and the

Mississippi with a clear eye and a yearning for an idyllic past. His yarns of the frozen Mississippi, measles, Jim Wolf's trials with cats and wasps, and the visiting mesmerizer all bring him (and his readers) back to an Edenic childhood. To capture the idyll Twain worked back through his earlier manuscripts and resurrected a portion of the "Early Days" fragment that he had composed during 1897. The piece holds a prominent place in the structure of the autobiography: as the thirteenth of the twenty-five chapters it falls in the middle of the narrative. While that placement may actually have been somewhat fortuitous (Twain eventually came to a point where he was composing material for the serial, and that may inhibit a finding of definite intention), the content and the circumstance of composition certainly place this piece at the heart of Twain's attempt at autobiography.

Twain's move back to his childhood was one way for him to deal with the pain of Susy Clemens' death in 1896. He often retreated to autobiography during times of emotional and creative stress, and the years after Susy's unexpected death were among the most troubled of his life. His sense of loss and his sense of guilt pushed him to find solace not only in some general plan of work but in a specific and deliberate return to his boyhood. This was one way that he could transcend his pain and reconnect with his western beginnings. That return to his beginnings also reignited the basic humor that was part and parcel of those early experiences.

Twain's description of his uncle's farm is especially notable. And two sections of that description call for closer attention. The first introduces the farm itself:

> In "Huck Finn" and in "Tom Sawyer Detective" I moved [the farm] down to Arkansas. It was all of six hundred miles, but it was no trouble, it was not a very large farm: five hundred acres, perhaps, but I could have done it if it had been twice as large. And as for the morality of it, I cared nothing for that: I would move a State if the exigences of literature required it.
>
> It was a heavenly place for a boy, that farm of my uncle John's. The house was a double log one, with a spacious

floor (roofed in) connecting it with the kitchen. In the breezy floor, and the sumptuous meals—well it makes me cry to think of them. Fried chicken, roast pig, wild and tame turkeys, ducks and geese; venison just killed; squirrels, rabbits, pheasants, partridges, prairie-chickens; biscuits, hot batter cakes, hot buckwheat cakes, hot "wheat bread," hot rolls, hot corn pone; fresh corn boiled on the ear, succotash, butter-beans, string-beans, tomatoes, pease, Irish potatoes, sweet-potatoes; butter milk, sweet milk, "clabber"; watermelons, muskmelons, cantaloups—all fresh from the garden—apple pie, peach pie, pumpkin pie, apple dumplings, peach cobbler—I can't remember the rest (MTOA, 113).

Twain's comments about moving the farm set a tone for his description and, in fact, alert readers that some of what follows may in fact have been "moved"—created—by the "exigences of literature." Twain winks at his readers. He lets them know that they should be skeptical of his claim to truth telling. Anyone who would move a complete farm with so little concern would have even fewer scruples when it came to describing its fine points.

The humor is this passage is understated: it does not call attention to itself but rather builds slowly during the recitation of Twain's overloaded menu. The relentless collection of food pushes the image of home cooking and hospitality to its limit: the reader is overcome by the simple accumulation of detail. And Twain undermines his own list as be pushes back from the imagined table and gives up trying to offer a complete description: "I can't remember the rest." The passage works, too, because Twain weds it to his introductory comments tied to the Clemens family's Tennessee Land: he precedes the description of the banquet with a brief recounting of the Tennessee Land's history and an accounting of the profits he made from writing about that land; he ties the experience to the Sellers-like optimism that fed the family's dreams: "It is good to begin life poor; it is good to begin life rich—these are wholesome; but to begin it prospectively rich! The man who has not experienced it cannot imagine the curse of it" (MTOA, 111).

Twain's reference to Sellers—"Whenever things grew dark [the Tennessee Land] rose and put out its hopeful Sellers hand and cheered us up" (MTOA, 111)—establishes an important counterweight for the tales and images to come. In effect, it undercuts his position by linking the episodes with daydreams and fantasy. The combination of a Sellers boast and dream enhances Twain's characterization of the importance of his birth in Florida, Missouri: "The village contained a hundred people and I increased the population by one per cent. It is more than the best man in history ever did for any other town. It may not be modest for me to refer to this, but it is true. There is no record of a person doing as much— not even Shakespeare. But I did it for Florida, and it shows that I could have done it for any place—even London, I suppose" (MTOA, 112). It is a pretentious boast, but one made within a context ripe for hubris and inflated self images.[15]

A bit farther into the chapter, Twain comes back to his strategy of making lists. This time, however, he focuses on a series of images connected to the farm experience:

> As I have said, I spent some part of every year at the farm until I was twelve or thirteen years old. The life which I led there with my cousins was full of charm, and so is the memory of it yet. I can call back the solemn twilight and the mystery of the deep woods, the earthy smells, the faint odor of the wild flowers. . . I can call it all back and make it as real as it ever was, and as blessed. I can call back the prairie, and its loneliness and peace. . . . I can see the woods in their autumn dress. . . I can see the blue clusters of wild grapes hanging amongst the foliage of the saplings, and I remember the taste of them and the smell. I know how the wild blackberries looked, and how they tasted. . . I know the taste of maple sap, and when to gather it, and how to arrange the troughs and the delivery tubes, and how to boil down the juice, and how to hook the sugar after it is made; also how much better hooked sugar tastes than any that is honestly come by, let bigots say what they will. I know how a prize watermellon looks when it is sunning its fat rotundity

among pumpkin-vines and "siblins"; I know how to tell
when it is ripe without "plugging" it; I know how inviting it
looks when it lies on the table in the sheltered great floorspace between house and kitchen, and the children gathered
for the sacrifice and their mouths watering; I know the
crackling sound it makes when the carving-knife enters its
end, and I can see the split fly along in front of the blade as
the knife cleaves its way to the other end. . . I know how a
boy looks behind a yard-long slice of that melon, and I know
how he feels; for I have been there. . . . and I can hear Uncle
Dan'l telling the immortal tales which Uncle Remus Harris
was to gather in his books and charm the world with, by and
by; and I can feel again the creepy joy which quivered
through me when the time for the ghost story of the "Golden
Arm" was reached—and the sense of regret, too, which came
over me, for it was always the last story of the evening, and
there was nothing between it and the unwelcome bed. . . .

I remember the pigeon seasons, when the birds would
come in millions, and cover the trees, and by their weight
break down the branches. They were clubbed to death with
sticks; guns were not necessary, and were not used. I
remember the squirrel hunts, and the prairie-chicken hunts,
and the wild-turkey hunts, and all that; and how we turned
out mornings, while it was still dark, to go on these
expeditions, and how chilly and dismal it was, and how
often I regretted that I was well enough to go. A toot on a tin
horn brought twice as many dogs as were needed, and in
their happiness they raced and scampered about, and
knocked small people down, and made no end of
unnecessary noise. At the word, they vanished away toward
the woods, and we drifted silently after them in the
melancholy gloom. But presently the gray dawn stole over
the world, the birds piped up, then the sun rose and poured
light and comfort all around, everything was fresh and dewy
and fragrant, and life was a boon again. After three hours of
tramping we arrived back wholesomely tired, overladen with
game, very hungry, and just in time for breakfast (MTOA,
120–123).

The passage offers an image of calm and enjoyment. Twain
evokes the idyll using the homely images of small children
living in a prelapsarian Eden.

The domestic sphere is the focal point for the rather gentle humor that permeates this section of the autobiography. The chapter is unified by the references either to the variety of foods or to methods of gathering those foods, whether by "hooking" it or by hunting it. The idyll is given a burst of energy by memories seasoned with humor. For example, Twain turns away from his collection of sensuous images to swipe at bigots who fail to realize the improved taste of "hooked" maple sap. This move from recollection and description to a moral judgement interrupts the rhythm of the passage and calls attention to the conflict between ethical and sensual rewards—the child revels in the sensual, and so does Twain. We are also told of the watermelon that sacrificed itself for the wonder and joy of a small boy, of the creepy joy of ghost stories, and of the opening moments of the hunt when excited dogs knocked down excited—but "small"—people. There is a nod to the tall tale in the description of the multitude of birds that fell from the trees when branches broke from their weight. And all these are supplement to the variety of other comic touches: Jane Clemens' and Patsy Quarrels' aversion to bats (of his mother Twain writes, "It was remarkable the way she couldn't learn to like private bats" [MTOA, 117]), "General" Gaines' rescue from the local cave, the variety of broken bones from hickory bark swings and medical treatments, and Twain's recollection of his mother's own brand of humor:

> I was always told that I was a sickly and precarious and tiresome and uncertain child, and lived mainly on allopathic medicines during the first seven years of my life. I asked my mother about this, in her old age—she was in her 88th year—and said:
> "I suppose that during all that time you were uneasy about me?"
> "Yes, the whole time."
> "Afraid that I wouldn't live?"
> After a reflective pause—ostensibly to think out the facts—
> "No—afraid you would" (MTOA, 119).

The incongruity of the mother's reply, the direct challenge to conventional expectations, and the finish with the snapper (Jane Clemens' adept handling of the pause is a highlight) all challenge readers. In "How to Tell a Story" Twain described the humorous story as one that "bubbles gently along" (Essays, 156). His tale of the Quarrels farm presents us with the full complement of humorous devices, the most important of which is the consistency and strength of the teller's personality—his voice.

Throughout the remaining chapters, Twain continues to juxtapose his past experiences with his present position. He makes good use of his meetings with the famous (especially his experience in Germany as a dinner guest of Emperor William II [MTOA, chapter 14]); he spins yarns about George Washington Cable, Livy's "editing," games of chance, his Oxford degree. He is repeatedly caught between humor and pathos as he offers selections from Susy Clemens' biography of him and comments on her observations. But Twain most often chooses to come back to humor to control the narrative movement.

Twain approaches the end of the autobiography with a decidedly humorous emphasis. Chapter twenty-four is a mix of humor and sentiment as he recounts a series of acquaintances who have died, offers more of Susy's biography, and presents himself as representative of the race. But he also tells the tale of Jim Wolf and the wasps and recounts riotous matches of billiards and bowling. In the final chapter he comes solidly back to humor as he resurrects the text of the Whittier Birthday speech—"I have read it twice, and unless I am an idiot, it hasn't a single defect in it from the first word to the last. It is just as good as it can be" (MTOA, 237)—and recounts his days as a reporter in Washington. The autobiography ends with one of the more effective uses of comic undercutting to be found in Twain's writings. It closes the frame that was set up in the brief preface that brought Howells into the picture.

Twain sets up the punch line by introducing us to the tale of his first meeting with General Nelson A. Miles in Washington. The meeting revolves around Twain's selling Miles a dog for three dollars (MTOA, 238–242). Of course, the dog was not Twain's. The tale revolves around what happened when the animal's rightful owner eventually showed up. The final exchange between Miles and Twain is a masterful bit of comic dialogue. First, Twain:

> "I am sorry, but I have to take the dog again."
> . . . "Take him again? Why he is my dog; you sold him to me, and at your own price."
> "Yes," I said, "it is true—but I have to have him, because the man wants him again."
> "What man?"
> "The man that owns him; he wasn't my dog."
> . . . "Do you mean to tell me that you were selling another man's dog—and knew it?"
> "Yes, I knew it wasn't my dog."
> "Then why did you sell him?"
> . . . "Well, that is a curious question to ask. I sold him because you wanted him. You offered to buy the dog; you can't deny that. I was not anxious to sell him—I had not even thought of selling him, but it seemed to me that if it could be any accommodation to you—"
> He broke me off in the middle, and said,
> "Accommodation to me? It is the most extraordinary spirit of accommodation I have ever heard of—the idea of your selling a dog that didn't belong to you—"
> I broke him off there, and said, "There is no relevancy about this kind of argument; you said yourself that the dog was probably worth a hundred dollars, I only asked you three; was there anything unfair about that? You offered to pay more, you know you did. I only asked you three; you can't deny it."
> "Oh, what in the world has that to do with it? The crux of the matter is that you didn't own the dog—can't you see that? You seem to think that there is no impropriety in selling property that isn't yours provided you sell it cheap. Now, then—"
> I said, "Please don't argue about it any more. You can't get around the fact that the price was perfectly fair, perfectly

reasonable—considering that I didn't own the dog—and so arguing it is only a waste of words. I have to have him back again because the man wants him; don't you see that I haven't any choice in the matter? Put yourself in my place. Suppose you had sold a dog that didn't belong to you; suppose you—"

"Oh," he said, "don't muddle my brains any more with your idiotic reasonings! Take him along and give me a rest."

So, I paid back the three dollars and led the dog downstairs and passed him over to his owner, and collected three for my trouble.

I went away then with a good conscience, because I had acted honorably; I never could have used the three that I sold the dog for, because it was not rightly my own, but the three I got for restoring him to his rightful owner was righteously and properly mine, because I earned it. That man might never have gotten that dog back at all, if it hadn't been for me. My principles have remained to this day what they were then. I was always honest; I know I can never be otherwise. It is as I said in the beginning—I was never able to persuade myself to use money which I had acquired in questionable ways.

Now, then, that is the tale. Some of it is true (MTOA, 240–242).

There are three sections to this tale: the introduction of Miles and the opening of the Washington tale in which the dog first appears, the bickering to reclaim the dog for its owner, and Twain's reflection on the moral of the tale and on his own basic honesty. Of those three pieces, the bickering carries the most humor because of the conflict between the contrasting moral views held by Twain and Miles. That conflict—a replay of the battle between the western rough and the eastern establishment—is traced through six turns in the argument, turns that are controlled by Twain as he weaves his tale: his announcement that he did not own the dog, his point that Miles had asked to buy the dog, his statement that he sought only to accommodate the request, his asking only three dollars for the dog, his argument that the price was fair, and his asking Miles to imagine himself selling the dog. The sequence is vital to the success of the tale. Each turn sparks a stronger and more heated response from Miles and leads to the last twist—the proposed exchanging of roles. Twain's responses also become more complex and more innocent until he is finally able to use his deadpan delivery to exasperate Miles. The deadpan voice becomes stronger as Twain pronounces, "That man might never have gotten that dog back at all, if it hadn't been for me. . . . I was always honest; I know I can never be otherwise" (MTOA, 242). Honesty, of course, is the central question. Of the dog story. And of the autobiography as a whole.

The tag line illuminates the notion of honesty. It is a disclaimer not only for the modified tall tale of the general and the dog but for the the entire autobiography. It brings the autobiography full circle by suggesting the potential hoax. The introduction established the boundaries of the hoax by laying out the extremes of the autobiography's length and depth and Twain's love of criticism that is bent his way. Readers were invited to see the joke within the historical references that lampooned the conventional autobiography's reliance on family and ancestors. The final line brings us back to Twain's storytelling roots and undermines the whole tale. It performs double duty: it ends a minor tale and simultaneously brings the full autobiography to a close. The frame is complete: the tale began with Twain's deadpan voice and it ends with Twain's deadpan voice. And we are left with a vague feeling of having been conned by a comic master.

While Twain's creative output decreased during the final years of his life, he nevertheless remained true to the humor that influenced him and that he helped shape. Resurrecting the image of Mark Twain as a master storyteller—and master con man—is important to a balanced treatment of his final decades. We can begin to add shading to Twain's portrait by taking the whole of his creative output during his final decades into consideration. It is especially important to include the completed autobiography in that package. That work offers clues of just how inextricably Twain's creative self was bound to a tradition energized by strains of southwestern and northeastern humor and by a potent mix of the oral storytelling that he experienced in slave kitchens, mining camps, saloons, and boarding houses. Mark Twain's autobiography can focus an exploration of the ways in which he remained tuned to that tradition and faithful to humor even as he turned away from publishing his fiction. It can help us relocate and reaffirm Mark Twain's humor.

Notes

1. It is virtually impossible to write about Mark Twain's life without moving into the realm of literary biography. His life was so intimately tied to his literary work that the line between literary critic and biographer is often blurred. That has meant a landslide of works focusing on Mark Twain's development as a writer and on the relationship between his professional and personal life. Some of the more important studies include Clara Clemens Gabrilowitsch's *My Father Mark Twain*, William Dean Howells' *My Mark Twain*, Van Wyck Brooks' *The Ordeal of Mark Twain*, Bernard DeVoto's *Mark Twain's America* and *Mark Twain at Work*, Henry Nash Smith's *Mark Twain: The Development of a Writer*, DeLancy Ferguson's *Mark Twain: Man and Legend*, Dixon Wecter's *Sam Clemens of Hannibal*, Justin Kaplan's *Mr. Clemens and Mark Twain*, Everett Emerson's *The Authentic Mark Twain: A Literary Biography of Samuel L. Clemens*, William R. Macnaughton's *Mark Twain's Last Years as a Writer*, Hamlin Hill's *Mark Twain: God's Fool*, Louis Budd's *Our Mark Twain: The Making of His Public Personality*, Guy Cardwell's *The Man Who Was Mark Twain: Images and Ideologies*, John Lauber's *The Making of Mark Twain* and *The Inventions of Mark Twain: A Biography*, and John C. Gerbers' *Mark Twain*. Albert Bigelow Paine's *Mark Twain: A Biography* remains the central text for much of Twain's life, even though subsequent biographers have managed to deepen and broaden the image that Paine offers.
2. See James M. Cox, *Mark Twain: The Fate of Humor*.
3. Mark Twain's autobiography has been presented in a variety of forms by a variety of editors. To compare these editions, see Albert Bigelow Paine's *Mark Twain's Autobiography*, Bernard DeVoto's *Mark Twain in Eruption: Hitherto Unpublished Pages About Men and Events*, Charles Neider's *The Autobiography of Mark Twain*, and Michael J. Kiskis' *Mark Twain's Own Autobiography: The Chapters from the North American Review*.

4. See Philip S. Foner, *Mark Twain: Social Critic* and Louis J. Budd, *Mark Twain: Social Philosopher.*

5. That evolution should be neither unusual nor unappealing. It mirrors the movement that Benjamin Franklin charted as he composed his autobiographical manuscripts: the completed sections follow Franklin as he evolves a social, a community consciousness. Twain's career—while certainly not as overtly political—follows a similar course as he takes to the issues of imperialism during the final years of the nineteenth and early days of the twentieth centuries.

6. The scandal connected to Maxim Gorky's visit to America in 1906 (Gorky's "wife" was actually his mistress, Maria Andreyeva) led Twain and Howells to resign as sponsors of a major fund raising banquet. The proceeds were to aid the Russian revolt against the Czar.

7. See G. Thomas Couser, "Autobiography as Anti-biography: The Case of Twain vs. Paine."

8. "Chapters from My Autobiography," *North American Review* 183 (1906), 184, 185, 186 (1907): various issues.

9. See Franklin R. Rogers, *Mark Twain's Burlesque Patterns,* Kenneth S. Lynn, *Mark Twain and Southwestern Humor,* and David E. E. Sloane, *Mark Twain as a Literary Comedian.* Sloane's *The Literary Humor of the Urban Northeast, 1830–1890* is also helpful.

10. This opens up a series of questions related to Twain's use of the biography of him that Susy wrote during her thirteenth year. His strategy of offering bits and pieces of her writing may, in fact, foster the deadpan delivery since he juxtaposes her basic narrative with his much more energetic responses.

11. The *(Burlesque) Autobiography* is actually a list of felons presented as ancestors: an inmate of Newgate prison, a highwayman, a series of cowards, a forger, an idler and a thief, a pirate, a missionary, and a renegade. There is also a supplementary list naming more ancestors: Guy Fawkes, Sixteen-String Jack, Jack Sheppard, Baron Munchausen, Captain Kydd, George Francis Train, Tom Pepper, Nebuchadnezzar, and Baalam's Ass. The inclusion of Munchausen undercuts the list because of the Baron's reputation as the premier teller of tall tales.

12. See John C. Gerber, "Mark Twain's Use of the Comic Pose."

13. See Charles Neider's edition *Papa: An Intimate Biography of Mark Twain.*

14. The battle between East and West is basic to southwestern humor. Twain, of course, had used that conflict since 1852 in "The Dandy Frightening the Squatter."

15. The passage is reminiscent of Twain's description of his birth in the *(Burlesque) Autobiography*: "I was born without teeth—and there Richard III had the advantage of me; but I was born without a humpback, likewise, and there I had the advantage of him. My parents were neither very poor nor conspicuously honest" (24–25).

Works Cited

By Mark Twain

Adventures of Huckleberry Finn. ed. Walter Blair and Victor Fischer. Berkeley: University of California Press, 1988.

The Adventures of Tom Sawyer, Tom Sawyer Abroad, Tom Sawyer, Detective. ed. John C. Gerber, Paul Baender, and Terry Firkins. Berkeley: University of California Press, 1980.

The Autobiography of Mark Twain. ed. Charles Neider. New York: Harper & Row, 1959.

Captain Stormfield's Visit to Heaven. New York: Harper and Brothers, 1907.

"Chapters from My Autobiography," *North American Review* 183 (1906), 184, 185, 189 (1907): various issues.

Christian Science. New York: Harper and Brothers, 1907.

The Complete Essays of Mark Twain. ed. Charles Neider. Garden City: Doubleday & Company, Inc., 1963.

A Connecticut Yankee in King Arthur's Court. ed. Bernard L. Stein. Berkeley: University of California Press, 1979.

Early Tales and Sketches, vol. 1 (1851–1864). ed. Edgar M. Branch and Robert H. Hirst. Berkeley: University of California Press, 1979.

Early Tales and Sketches, vol. 2 (1864–1865). ed. Edgar M. Branch and Robert H. Hirst. Berkeley: University of California Press, 1981.

Following the Equator. The Writings of Mark Twain: Definitive Edition 20 and 21. New York: Gabriel Wells, 1923.

The Gilded Age: A Tale of Today. The Writings of Mark Twain: Definitive Edition 5 and 6. New York: Gabriel Wells, 1922.

The Innocents Abroad or the New Pilgrim's Progress. The Writings of Mark Twain: Definitive Edition 1 and 2. New York: Gabriel Wells, 1922.

Mark Twain in Eruption: Hitherto Unpublished Pages About Men and Events. ed. Bernard DeVoto. New York: Harper and Brothers, 1940.

Mark Twain's Autobiography. 2 vols. ed. Albert Bigelow Paine. New York: Harper and Brothers, 1924.

Mark Twain's (Burlesque) Autobiography. Norwood: Norwood Editions, 1975.

Mark Twain's Fables of Man. ed. John S. Tuckey. Berkeley: University of California Press, 1972.

Mark Twain's 'Mysterious Stranger' Manuscripts. ed. William M. Gibson. Berkeley: University of California Press, 1969.

Mark Twain's Own Autobiography: The Chapters from the North American Review. ed. Michael J. Kiskis. Madison: University of Wisconsin Press, 1990.

Mark Twain's 'Which was the Dream?' and Other Symbolic Writings of the Later Years. ed. John S. Tuckey. Berkeley: University of California Press, 1979.

Personal Recollections of Joan of Arc. New York: Harper & Brothers Publishers, 1896.

Pudd'nhead Wilson. The Writings of Mark Twain: Definitive Edition 16. New York: Gabriel Wells, 1923.

Roughing It. ed. Franklin R. Rogers. Berkeley: University of California Press, 1972.

Selected Mark Twain—Howells Letters, 1872–1910. ed. Frederick Anderson, William M. Gibson, and Henry Nash Smith. Cambridge: Harvard University Press, 1967.

Selected Shorter Writings of Mark Twain. ed. Walter Blair. Boston: Houghton-Mifflin Company, 1962.

'What Is Man?' and Other Essays. The Writings of Mark Twain: Definitive Edition 26. New York: Gabriel Wells, 1923.

'What Is Man?' and Other Philosophical Writings. ed. Paul Baender. Berkeley: University of California Press, 1973.

Secondary Works

Brooks, Van Wyck. *The Ordeal of Mark Twain.* New York: E. P. Dutton & Company, 1920.

Budd, Louis J. *Mark Twain: Social Philosopher.* Bloomington: Indiana University Press, 1962.

———. *Our Mark Twain: The Making of His Public Personality.* Philadelphia: University of Pennsylvania Press, 1983.

Cardwell, Guy. *The Man Who Was Mark Twain: Images and Ideologies.* New Haven: Yale University Press, 1991.

Clemens, Olivia Susan. *Papa: An Intimate Biography of Mark Twain.* ed. Charles Neider. Garden City: Doubleday & Company, Inc., 1985.

Couser, G. Thomas. "Autobiography as Anti-Biography: The Case of Twain vs. Paine." *Auto/Biography Studies* 3, no. 3 (Fall 1987): 13–20.

Cox, James M. *Mark Twain: The Fate of Humor.* Princeton: Princeton University Press, 1966.

DeVoto, Bernard. *Mark Twain's America.* Boston: Little, Brown, and Company, 1932.

———. *Mark Twain at Work.* Cambridge: Harvard University Press, 1942.

Emerson, Everett. *The Authentic Mark Twain: A Literary Biography of Samuel L. Clemens.* Philadelphia: University of Pennsylvania Press, 1984.

Ferguson, DeLancey. *Mark Twain: Man and Legend.* New York: The Bobbs-Merrill Company, 1943.

Foner, Philip S. *Mark Twain: Social Critic.* New York: International Publishers, 1958.

Gabrilowitsch, Clara Clemens. *My Father Mark Twain.* New York: Harper & Brothers Publishers, 1931.

Gerber, John C. *Mark Twain.* Boston. G. K. Hall & Co., 1988.

———. "Mark Twain's Use of the Comic Pose." *PMLA* LXXXVII (June 1962): 297–304.

Hill, Hamlin. *Mark Twain: God's Fool.* New York: Harper & Row, Publishers, 1973.

Howells, William Dean. *My Mark Twain: Reminiscences and Criticisms.* New York: Harper Brothers Publishers, 1910.

Kaplan, Justin. *Mr. Clemens and Mark Twain.* New York: Simon and Schuster, 1966.

Lauber, John. *The Inventions of Mark Twain: A Biography.* New York: Hill and Wang, 1990.

———. *The Making of Mark Twain.* New York: American Heritage Press, 1985.

Lynn, Kenneth S. *Mark Twain and Southwestern Humor.* Boston: Little, Brown, 1959.

Macnaughton, William R. *Mark Twain's Last Years as a Writer.* Columbia: University of Missouri Press, 1979.

Paine, Albert Bigelow. *Mark Twain: A Biography.* 1912; rpt. with author's note to the 1935 edition and introduction to the 1923 edition by William Lyon Phelps. New York: Chelsea House, 1980.

Rogers, Franklin R. *Mark Twain's Burlesque Patterns.* Dallas: Southern Methodist University Press, 1960.

Sloane, David E. E. *The Literary Humor of the Urban Northeast, 1830–1890.* Baton Rouge: Louisiana State University Press, 1983.

———. *Mark Twain as Literary Comedian*. Baton Rouge: Louisiana State University Press, 1979.

Smith, Henry Nash. *Mark Twain: The Development of a Writer*. Cambridge: Harvard University Press, 1962.

Wecter, Dixon. *Sam Clemens of Hannibal*. Boston: Houghton Mifflin Company, 1952.

"The Mysterious Stranger": Absence of the Female in Mark Twain Biography

Laura E. Skandera-Trombley

"**A**bsence of the Female" refers to two related issues: the absence of female Mark Twain biographers and the absence of women within Twain biography. By identifying the first and exploring the polemics of the second, a paradigm will be introduced where the women in Clemens' life are granted their importance and where the field of Twain biography may be made more accessible to interested women.

With the sheer mass of criticism that has been published concerning Mark Twain, it appears that writing about Samuel Langhorne Clemens has become a *rite de passage* for any serious scholar of American literature. Such luminaries as Van Wyck Brooks, Bernard DeVoto, Leslie Fiedler, Everett Emerson, and Hamlin Hill have all commented on Clemens; Justin Kaplan's *Mr. Clemens and Mark Twain* was awarded the Pulitzer prize. Although there is a spread of sixty years among these biographical scholars, they share two common denominators: their gender and their critical positions. The field of Twain studies has always been and continues to be one of the most heavily male-dominated areas of American scholarship; and to date only two paths of accepted biographical discourse have emerged, those of Brooks' division of self, and, in opposition, that of DeVoto's integration of the self.

With the Brooks-DeVoto battle lines drawn, so were the divergent paths that all subsequent Twain biographers would follow. In what has become a compulsory initiation ritual, biographers must choose on which side of the Brooks-DeVoto net to play. The Brooks side maintains that Clemens had a divided self and that this division became so pronounced that his capacity for fiction writing was irreparably damaged. On the DeVoto side, critics undertook to prove that Clemens' later fiction was intact—and so was his personality. This writer found both sides of the court flawed and at the same time was struck by the dearth of discussions concerning the impact female familial members and colleagues had upon Clemens. The tacit admission that Clemens was surrounded by women has been made from Brooks to Hill, but why always seen in that way—surrounded—as though no productive interaction took place?

Writing in reaction to Albert Bigelow Paine's and William Dean Howells' sympathetic biographies of Clemens, Brooks charged that there were inconsistencies in the version of Clemens portrayed by Paine and Howells and claimed that instead of perceiving Clemens as a rustic, charming storyteller, a more accurate interpretation of Clemens was as embittered, artistic failure. To examine the question of Clemens' personality, Brooks used what has been identified as one of the earliest psychoanalytic interpretations of an author (Fraiberg). Brooks asserted that there was a split in Clemens' personality and viewed the women in his life as firmly entrenched within the realm of a hostile Other. Not much has changed since Brooks first denounced then discarded Clemens' female intimates; subsequent biographers' interpretations of the role they played run the negative gamut: women were the psychological ruin of Clemens; women were the monetary ruin of Clemens; women had no effect upon Clemens; Clemens managed to survive the effect women had upon him.

A significant defect of past scholarship has been the tendency to view the women in Clemens' personal life as an indistinguishable whole. An Olivia Clemens could be substituted for a Mary Fairbanks, a Mary Ann Cord for a Katy

Leary, Susan Crane for Mary Rogers, with the three daughters interchangeable. No individual differentiation was made and simplistic conclusions were reached: women had either a debilitating effect or were nullities. What these studies all had in accord was that women were forever on the periphery, and if in particular instances they moved to the fore it would have been far better for Clemens had they not.

Cynthia Fuchs Epstein, in *Deceptive Distinctions: Sex, Gender and the Social Order*, addresses the impetus for the existence of dichotomous categorization: "It is no surprise that dichotomous models as an ideological weapon survive challenge because it is easier to propose a dichotomy than to explicate the complexities that make it invalid" (15). Clearly such a dichotomous structure currently exists in Twain scholarship. Twain biographers have identified a dichotomy in his relationships with women; but what they have failed to find is the explanation for this dichotomy—or to consider the possibility that this dichotomy may not exist outside their own constructions. With the virtual exclusion of women from studies exploring Clemens' fiction-making process (aside from the occasional articles referring to the editing by Mary Fairbanks and Olivia Clemens), these two schools and their critical offshoots have engendered and promoted this kind of dichotomous model. Why?

To date, there are no critical studies on Olivia Langdon Clemens and her first biography, by Resa Willis, is scheduled for publication in the spring of 1992. There are no published articles about Clemens' relationship with his sister-in-law Susan Crane and none discussing the Clemens family's connection with Dr. Rachael Gleason. There has been nothing published on the relationships Clemens had with suffragettes Isabella Beecher Hooker and Anna Dickinson.[1] Aside from scattered mention in biographies and select articles focused on the individual, Clemens' relationship with his contemporary female writers has been left untreated. This researcher has discovered that Clemens maintained an extremely active correspondence with over one hundred women writers from five different countries. Along with other writers of fiction, Clemens corresponded with feminists, social reformers, and women educators.

The result of this lack of scholarship on women is a distorted view of Clemens as man and as writer. A particularly odd by-product of this kind of exclusionary biography is that critics were left with the problem of Clemens' sexuality. Women were considered extraneous but Clemens' sexuality certainly was not. For the past thirty years quite an industry has been built by biographers about Clemens' supposed ambivalence toward sexual relations climaxing with Hill accusing Clemens of pedophilia. Only within the past two years, with the publication of the first volume of letters, have critics begun to reinterpret Clemens as an adult man involved with adult women.

What biographers have not recognized is that throughout his life Clemens intentionally surrounded himself with women. Clemens desired women to help define his boundaries, both personal and literary; he was a man both voluntarily controlled and influenced by women. Women shaped Clemens' life, edited his books, provided models for his fictional characters, and their correspondence and literary works heavily influenced his fiction. This absence of women is not restricted just to Twain scholarship; male writers have been historically portrayed as "immune" or "beyond" the influence of women. This gendercentric scholarship results in the male writer being interpreted as operating within an asocial context. Closeted away from the tainting influence of those "damned scribblers," male writers supposedly relied upon their one true source of inspiration—themselves. Clemens has been variously described by biographers as a King Lear, an American Adam, a fallen angel. These labels have removed Clemens, the man, into the realm of Mark Twain, the fiction. This fallacy is evident throughout Twain scholarship. The critical quorum's opinion concerning his fiction-writing ability was that outside sources and influences were unnecessary (and in fact considered potentially ruinous) as long as Clemens relied solely upon himself for inspiration. Alan Gribben's massive work, *Mark Twain's Library: A Reconstruction*, challenged the long-held misconception of Clemens as unread man. What must now be recognized is that not only was Clemens highly aware of what was being written by his female colleagues and that he utilized their work as impetus for his own fiction, but that the women in his family circle allowed Clemens access to a feminine consciousness that enabled him to create a unique brand of literature.

Departing from the Brooksian based critical position of dual selves, I contend that Clemens was indeed an integrated personality; yet, the dichotomous type of biography that has been employed has failed to recognize the major wellspring of Clemens' inspiration. Due to this exclusionary methodology, in examining Clemens' final years critics such as DeVoto and Hill have been hard-pressed to account for the waning of his fiction-writing ability and the rise of his pronounced cynicism. To examine this problem and to give a more credible reading of Clemens' final years, I have developed a paradigm consisting of the component "feminine consciousness." This feminine consciousness, provided in part by the women both in and outside Clemens' family circle, allowed Clemens entree into the female community during the latter half of the nineteenth-century.

Sydney Janet Kaplan, in her text *Feminine Consciousness in the Modern British Novel*, begins her discussion of "feminine consciousness" with a given, that "novelists have most definitely attempted to depict the consciousnesses of men and women and to show that each has a different quality" (3). According to Kaplan, feminine consciousness should be viewed as a "literary device," a method of characterization of females in fiction" (3). Kaplan is quick to qualify that the term "feminine consciousness" does not necessarily entail the "full range of any given woman's consciousness in a novel," instead just the "aspects . . . which are involved with her definition of self as a specifically feminine being" (3). Kaplan's discussion of fiction is restricted to works authored by women; I think one can open the discussion to include particular male authors such as Clemens. Clemens too was interested in depicting the variegated consciousnesses of males and females, characters such as Pudd'nhead Wilson and Roxana come immediately to mind, yet he was also interested in going beyond gendered portrayals of consciousness; in such characters as Huckleberry Finn, Judith Loftus, and Joan of Arc, Clemens questioned, satirized, and ultimately discarded the very attitudes and behaviors comprising socialized gender roles.

The valuable insights Clemens gained from his access to the feminine point-of-view were reinforced by his writing techniques and surfaced in his classic realist novels. Clemens' female half has been previously overlooked by biographers; without his feminine consciousness his ability to create extended works of fiction was eventually lost. And this is what ultimately happened. Women in effect functioned collectively as Clemens' personal and creative touchstone. Rather than envisioning Clemens as continually turning away from a harmful Other, it would be more accurate to view him as embracing and allying himself with the female. Shortly before their marriage Clemens joyfully proclaimed to Olivia: "'I' mean both of us, & 'both of us' means I of course—for are not we Twain one flesh?" (Wecter, *Mark*, 73).[2] Clemens viewed himself and his art as inseparable from Olivia. When Clemens was composing, he would retreat into his study during the day and return to his family at sundown. After the evening meal, the family would gather and he would present the day's output. Clemens did the bulk of his writing at his sister-in-law's home, Quarry Farm, in Elmira, New York, and there his audience consisted of his three daughters, his wife Olivia, his wife's adopted older sister, Susan Crane, and Mary Ann Cord, a former slave, who worked as a cook for Susan Crane. To this female audience, then, Clemens would read his work. The varied opinions Clemens received constituted his literary wellspring. Alan Gribben stresses the necessity of audience for Clemens' writing:

> Nothing else known about Clemens' reading habits seems as
> significant as his preference for oral readings before other
> people, a practice that surely helped develop the flexible
> narrative voice he strove to reproduce in his fiction. He read
> his daily output of prose to his family and friends. . . .
> ("Unsatisfactory," 55–56)

Yet this reading before a female audience resulted in more
than perfecting Clemens' narrative voice. The women became,
in a sense, the text's co-constructors. Clemens received the
insights and opinions of individuals who were as estranged
from patriarchal Victorian society as was the Southerner
Clemens from literary Brahmin New England, and as was the
young Huckleberry Finn from the slave-holding society of St.
Petersburg, Missouri.

In Olivia Louise Langdon Clemens, Clemens had a writing
partner who came from a family well known for sailing against
the tide of repressive nineteenth-century mores. When
Presbyterian church elders refused to sign an anti-slavery
pledge, the Langdons broke away and founded a
Congregationalist church that would. Rejecting allopathic
medicine's heroic practices, such as bloodletting, leechings,
and cauterization, the Langdons embraced the tenets of
hydropathic medicine (one of the irregular schools of
nineteenth-century medicine) with its emphasis on
therapeutic treatments. The Langdon's (and later the Clemens')
family physician was Dr. Rachael Gleason. Gleason is listed in
Medical Women of America as the fourth woman to receive
her medical degree in America; just two years earlier, in 1849,
Elizabeth Blackwell was granted the first such degree. The
Langdons advocated women's education and were major
supporters of Elmira Female College, founded in 1855. Elmira
College was the first to grant degrees to women which were
equal to those of men, and both Langdon daughters studied
there. At an early age, Olivia became close to such radical
suffragettes as Isabella Hooker and Anna Dickinson. In fact,
Dickinson proved so influential in Olivia's development that
at one point Olivia agonized whether she, too, should join the

public ranks of the women's movement. In a letter to Mary Fairbanks, co-written by Olivia and Clemens shortly after their marriage, Olivia defiantly proclaimed: "I am woman's rights" (Wecter, *Love*, 127).

Before their marriage, as early as their first meeting in Elmira, Olivia knew that Clemens intended to propose. From that point on, Olivia composed the movements of Clemens' suit. It was Olivia who rejected Clemens' first proposal but left the relationship intact; Olivia who insisted he write to her as a brother would a sister; Olivia who engaged in subterfuge by having Clemens address his letters to her brother; Olivia who installed Hattie Lewis as a romantic decoy so she could deliberate Clemens' overtures without public pressure; Olivia who had Clemens prove his sincerity about his intentions by writing scores of letters. It was a carefully thought-out wooing and Olivia neatly concluded it in her methodical way when she wrote on the envelope of his final letter before they married: "184th—Last letter of a 17 months' correspondence" (Wecter, *Love*, 139).

Nor did her control end at the altar. When the Clemenses decided to build a home in Hartford, it was Olivia who drew the initial sketch and was in charge of planning the construction of the house and, like her mother and older sister before her, she was the sole title holder of the land. This was the woman who married Samuel Clemens: a far cry from Hamlin Hill's characterization of her as "a delicate figurine, the Victorian ideal of a 'lady'" (xxiv). Nor does her behavior support Joyce Warren's condemnation of Clemens, that he intended "to keep [Olivia] in a state of childlike innocence—or ignorance. . . . She is Twain's ideal woman: gentle and sweet, but ignorant as a child" (167).

Following the example set by her mother, Olivia was a voracious reader who organized reading and study groups throughout her life. Judging from the contents of personal letters to friends and her Commonplace Book, Olivia was well-versed in classic and modern American and British literature. Olivia was widely read in contemporary American women's fiction and she must have been cognizant of the themes and images considered, by Susan Gubar and Sandra Gilbert, to constitute a nineteenth-century female literary tradition. Gilbert and Gubar contend that "images of enclosure and escape," are representational of Victorian women's novels (xi). These elements of entrapment, enclosure, and escape, that Gilbert and Gubar identify as evident within Victorian women's novels, also compose the primary themes and images of *Adventures of Huckleberry Finn*. I do not view this as coincidence.

Elaine Showalter urges the necessity of viewing women's writing within a historical context and regards women's literature as a kind of subculture with its own specific images and themes. Showalter emphasizes that she is uncomfortable with past attempts to develop what she terms a "female sensibility" that constitutes itself in a form specific to women's writing because of its ahistorical stance. For Showalter, this kind of interpretation runs perilously near to echoing what she calls "familiar stereotypes. . ." (12). Showalter argues that such a concept as female imagination must

> not be handled as a romantic or Freudian abstraction. It is the product of a delicate network of influences operating in time. . . including the operations of the marketplace. . . . (12)

I agree with Showalter regarding the limitations of creating a kind of female imaginary list; such an action would be dangerously inhibiting. According to Showalter the female literary tradition evidences itself not in an innate sexual attitude but in the relation women maintained with society during a particular time-span; the nature of the images Gilbert and Gubar identify reflect the sociological construct Showalter promotes. This experience of being part of, yet not a part of, patriarchal, white Victorian society was particularly valid for individuals, such as the Langdon women, who attempted to go beyond the purely domestic sphere. Clemens was granted valuable access to the feminine consciousness through Olivia's experience of estrangement from society because of her family's views concerning religion, health, and women's education, and through her awareness of what was being written by contemporary women writers.

Olivia's part in co-creating Clemens' texts was in functioning not so much as editor, although that is the role to which she has been traditionally relegated, as it was to provide an educated audience familiar with transforming and reforming social standards. Olivia was concerned with the scope and treatment of the fictive subject, not with censoring the end product. With Olivia as guide, Clemens could not overindulge in the burlesque; to elicit her approval he had to provide finesse behind the fireworks. Clemens described how necessary Olivia was in the generation of the novels in a letter to Archibald Henderson:

> I learned from her that the only right thing was to get in my serious meaning always, to treat my audience fairly, to let them really feel the underlying moral that gave body and essence to my jest. (Henderson, 183)

The connection between the expectations of the first two-thirds of Clemens' audience and *Adventures of Huckleberry Finn*, overall, is apparent. The burlesque is left intact for the amusement of the children, as in Jim's soothsaying prowess with the ox hairball, and Olivia's "serious meaning" takes precedence with this one sentence by Huck: "All right, then, I'll go to hell." In keeping with Olivia's advice to Clemens, Leland Krauth observes that the climax of the book represents "both [Huck's] greatest moment of pathos and one of the most humorous moments. . ." (382). The reason this combination can exist is that "of course we know that no one of such fine and tender feeling can be damned" (383).

Mary Ann Cord had a crucial role in the shaping of Clemens' fiction. Born a slave in Virginia, Cord claimed she had been sold twice and had all of her children taken from her before she escaped to the North (Jerome, 8). Ida Langdon, in an address she delivered at the Elmira College Convocation in

1960, remembered Cord as a "dogmatic Methodist" (Jerome, 62). Cord was very likely a member of the African Methodist Episcopal Zion Church, the first African American church founded in Elmira in 1841 (Sorin, 15). Cord's denomination is shared by Roxana in *Pudd'nhead Wilson*; in *Pudd'nhead Wilson* Clemens attributes Roxana's recent conversion to Methodism as saving her from being sold down the river by her master.

While summering at Quarry Farm Clemens composed a short story written partly in black dialect, which Sherwood Cummings first noted that he later utilized as the genesis for the main plot and theme for the first section of *Adventures of Huckleberry Finn*. This short story provided Clemens an entree into the November 1874 issue of the *Atlantic*. The piece was entitled, "A True Story Repeated Word for Word as I heard It," and related the travails of "Rachel" Cord. After reading the piece, William Dean Howells was commendatory: "I think it extremely good and touching with the best and reallest [sic] kind of black talk in it" (*Twain-Howells*, 24). The cross-over between "A True Story" and *Adventures of Huckleberry Finn* is readily apparent: in "A True Story," "Rachel" scolds a young man (who unbeknownst to her is her long-lost son) and says, "I wa'nt bawn in de mash to be fool' by trash!" (*Unabridged*, 408); in *Adventures of Huckleberry Finn* Jim utters a similar line when he rebukes Huckleberry for playing a cruel trick on him: "Dat truck dah is trash; en trash is what people is dat puts dirt on de head er dey fren's en makes 'em ashamed" (72). "A True Story Repeated Word for Word as I Heard It" is of particular importance not only because it marked the beginning of Clemens' contributions to the *Atlantic* but also because this oral history of an African American woman's road to freedom might also have served as an impetus for the composition of Clemens' greatest work.

At Quarry Farm, the wide variety in temperament, education, experience, culture, race, and age, ranging from Jean (the Clemens' youngest daughter) to Mary Ann Cord, meant that for Clemens to maintain his disparate audiences' attention he had to produce fiction that was multigenerational, multicultural, multiracial, and, most significantly, themes with which these women could identify. Viewed within the context of Clemens' female audience/feminine consciousness, the absence of overt masculine themes from *Adventures of Huckleberry Finn* should not come as entirely unexpected. Leland Krauth isolates the various episodes that traditionally comprise Southwestern humor and remarks that *Huckleberry Finn* is striking for what it is not: "[*Adventures of Huckleberry Finn*] ignores, first of all, those subjects, like courtings, frolics, dances, weddings, and honeymoons, that naturally involve adult sexuality. And secondly, it omits entirely or else skims over those activities, like hunting, fighting, gambling, gaming, horse racing, heavy drinking, and military maneuvering, that are the traditional pastimes of manly backwoods living. (Whenever such activities do appear briefly they are targets of ridicule.) In short, Twain purges from the Southwestern tradition its exuberant celebration of rough-and-tumble masculinity" (374).

What Clemens does with the character of Huck, Krauth continues, is also unprecedented within the genre of Southwestern humor; Clemens departs from the archetype of the Man of Feeling to make Huck "a comic Man of Feeling. Huck never feels good about his goodness; his altruistic emotions—with the possible exception of his aid to Mary Jane—never give him egoistic satisfaction" (381). Krauth asserts that this is one of the reasons *Adventures of Huckleberry Finn* is still so intriguing today, because the portrayal of the "Man of Feeling" still challenges conventional stereotypes of manhood. Krauth also points out, quite rightly, that while Huck is a lost boy afraid in a man's world, he is never frightened by the world of women. Clearly both Huck's and Clemens' Angst was reduced when they were with females. Krauth ends his article with this intriguing statement: "[Huck's] kind of manliness seems to elude our language for it, even today" (384). Clemens could create this sense of manliness combined with delicate sensitivity because his female collaborators, with their essential feedback into his writing process, enabled him to synthesize their feminine consciousness with his own. During his trip down the river, Huck metamorphoses into the student he was never allowed to become in St. Petersburg, and he learns about natural humanity from Jim and about the falsity of gender roles from Judith Loftus. The result of these lessons is that a radically changed conception of the traditional Southwestern character came to life in Clemens' novel.

This product by Clemens and the feminine consciousness was also clearly subject to what Showalter terms the "operations of the marketplace." Upon completion of *Tom Sawyer* and *Adventures of Huckleberry Finn* Clemens was undecided as to whether they should be considered children's or adult books. Clemens wrote to William Dean Howells to declare that he had written *Tom Sawyer* for adults: "It is not a boy's book, at all. It will only be read by adults" (*Twain-Howells*, 91). Howells replied: "I think you ought to treat it explicitly as a boy's story" (110). Clemens wrote back to Howells agreeing, "Mrs. Clemens decides with you that the book should issue as a book for boys, pure and simple—and so do I" (112). What probably proved instrumental in changing Clemens' mind was Howells' insistence that "the book consumer[s] par excellence in Victorian America" were young women (Wecter, *Sam*, 172). Howells was correct; by 1872 nearly three-quarters of all published books in America were authored by women (Coultrap, 2). Clemens ultimately took Howells' advice to heart for he finally wrote him that "the book is now professedly & confessedly a boy's & girl's book" (*Twain-Howells*, 122).[3]

The critic must not underestimate Clemens' awareness of what was successful within the literary marketplace. Clemens' knowledge about the female-authored fiction then being published came about in a few different ways: one, the novels both he and the women in the family read; two, the manuscripts submitted to him for publication within his own publishing firm; and, three, the voluminous correspondence he maintained with women writers. Clemens made it his business to know what women wanted. Clemens supported women authors by corresponding and exchanging ideas with them and by providing a commercial outlet for their work, which he did by having his company publish their writings.

What sounded the deathknell to Clemens' fiction, was the demise of Olivia on June 5, 1904. With her death, the linchpin of his connection to the feminine consciousness was gone. After 1904, Clemens produced mainly polemical writing; he attempted to write extended works of fiction a multitude of times, but the manuscripts were left incomplete. Clemens became a man bereft of his favorite audience and of the secure home life in which this feminine circle surrounded him. Without his female circle, Samuel Clemens the writer disappeared; what remained was merely the public persona. For the rest of his life, Clemens was condemned to try to recreate his source of feminine consciousness, but what he managed to construct with Isabel Lyon and the angel fish was only a poor imitation; the happiest days and most productive times of his life were over, and on a deeper level—not always consciously—Clemens knew it. Clemens became tragically morose, and his bitterness arose from his keen awareness that all of his efforts to bring back the earlier days were futile.

Samuel Langhorne Clemens' greatest achievement in writing was the novel *Adventures of Huckleberry Finn*. In Huckleberry Finn, Clemens created an androgynous character. Throughout the novel, Huckleberry (as does Jim) adopts and abandons various male and female disguises as well as rejects the world of the purely male or female. In addition, Huck enters and flees various representations of so-called "civilization" that he and Jim encounter periodically during their flight down the Mississippi. This rejection of sexual segregation is reinforced by Clemens' creating Huckleberry as a prepubescent youth, a time in his development when Huckleberry is non-sexual. At the end of the novel, Huckleberry ultimately chooses to "light out for the Territory," but what he is embarking on is a search for an integrated world where he can be freed from the confines of gender to pursue a higher realm of truth and justice. Leland Krauth states that Huckleberry Finn's kind of manliness "seems to elude our language for it, even today" (384). Huckleberry possesses the dual traits of manliness and femininity.

Contrary to Leslie Fiedler's famous argument that the novel is homo-erotic and portrays "a conventionally abhorrent doctrine of ideal love" (147), what *Adventures of Huckleberry Finn* actually concerns itself with is introducing a new kind of quest archetype, one that concentrates upon two figures both disenfranchised from the predominating white, patriarchal society. Fiedler begins his argument by automatically assuming *Adventures of Huckleberry Finn* is "precisely, [a] boy['s] book"—thus dismissing without a backward glance the female audience for whom Clemens originally wrote the novel. What Fiedler fails to perceive is that Clemens cleverly bypasses what he terms an archetypal "homo-erotic crush," thus excluding the female, by making both Huck and Jim non-sexual. Both are considered "boys": Huck by age, as prepubescent, and Jim by race, as a slave he has been symbolically castrated; equally important, by virtue of their cross-dressing, both Huck and Jim are at times identified with the female.

At the beginning of the story, both are at the mercy of their surrounding culture and are rendered powerless. Huckleberry, son of "pap" the town drunk, has been marginalized by the society of St. Petersburg. Huckleberry does not attend church, live in a conventional dwelling, or attend school until he is adopted by the Widow Douglas—and this societal rejection ultimately saves him as it is far easier for him to abandon this culture than someone who grew up within it, for instance Tom Sawyer. Jim's caste is even lower than Huckleberry's, at least that is what "pap" would like to believe, because of his slave status. Jim is objectified by Southern culture, as he is well aware, yet even before the two take raft to river Jim resists the predominating ethos: "I owns myself, en I's wuth eight hund'd dollars" (*Adventures*, 42).

As they sail down river, the world around the seemingly helpless duo becomes increasingly violent. On the river, the raft provides respite and shelter from the shore madness, yet that refuge is violated with the arrival of the Duke and the Dauphin. While on shore, the only relative safety that can be found is when females are present as with Judith Loftus and the Wilks girls. As the novel progresses, the power balance changes as both Huck and Jim repeatedly manage to outwit and escape the prevailing white, patriarchal society of the South. While Huck is perceived as an ignorant youth by the adults around him, he struggles with such issues as truth and freedom—these being beyond the grasp of his elders. Jim comes to symbolize both faith and love. To attain the goal of their quest, both Huck and Jim remain in their androgynous states, and they eventually succeed in transcending their gender-specific, racially segregated, societal confines. Huck and Jim are freed to pursue a higher quest for a kindly humanity which is more universally "feminine" in nature than the violence of the masculine format Clemens studiously avoided.

James Cox questions whether _Adventures of Huckleberry Finn_ should be considered a quest novel. Cox maintains that interpreting the text as a quest is to do so in error: "A quest is a positive journey, implying an effort, a struggle to reach a goal. But Huck is escaping. His journey is primarily a negation, a flight _from_ tyranny, not a flight toward freedom" ("Uncomfortable," 350). Cox's point is well taken. Clemens is not crafting a traditional quest tale here; there is, however, something Huck is seeking, a sense of selfhood that has been repeatedly denied to him, first by "pap," Huck has no sense of belonging to family, and second by the town of St. Petersburg, Huck constantly remains on the periphery. Huck finds these signifiers of acceptance, family, and community, on the raft with Jim. The only element missing is that Huck must discover who and what _he_ is. Throughout the novel Huck desperately seeks an identity, and by the end of the story, he has found one—that of writer.

Instead of interpreting Clemens' literary efforts, as Brooks and his subsequent critical followers do, as the result of a fragmentation of self, Clemens' genius ultimately resided in the joining of different consciousnesses to forge an androgynous whole. Within *Adventures of Huckleberry Finn*, the elements of both the traditional masculine quest novel and the sentimentalized female novel are apparent. Joseph A. Boone, in his essay "Male Independence and the American Quest Genre: Hidden Sexual Politics in the All-Male Worlds of Melville, Twain and London," recognized that "in rejecting the shore world's negative models of masculine aggression and feminine piety alike," Huck becomes a cultural misfit, like Clemens, like the Langdon women, like Mary Ann Cord. Boone identifies Huckleberry's journey as his personal response to a bifurcated sexual ethos that blocks individual wholeness or self-expression. Huckleberry, instead of attempting to gain re-entry into society, Boone concludes, "embraces an independent truth of self, rooted in an ethos of compassionate love that runs counter to all social hierarchies" (200). For it is Huckleberry's loving relationship with Jim, above all else, that becomes the measure of Huck's status as a cultural misfit and of his unretraceable deviation from a traditional standard of manhood. (199–200)

Clemens created his own genre—the androgynous quest novel, and he continued his androgynous experiments in *The Personal Recollections of Joan of Arc*.[4] Clemens' circle of female advisors underlined this self-knowledge on his part that if he was going to write fiction integrating both male and female experience and produce fiction that would appeal to both genders, he needed to have access to the feminine consciousness. To write a fully integrated novel, he required a feminine point-of-view with which he could integrate his masculine perception. When Clemens wrote to Frederick Duneka at *Harper's Magazine*, on September 15, 1902, "My wife being ill, I have been—in literary matters—helpless all these weeks. I have no editor—no censor," he was identifying a very real, and frightening situation—the loss of his most important source of female consciousness (MTP). Clemens, like Huck, had found his sense of self in his identity of writer and with the loss of his female circle, this identity, this selfhood, was threatened.

Clemens indeed, as DeVoto suggested, accepted "tuition" when he came East and he also possessed, as Edward Wagenknecht proclaimed, too much "vitality" to be averted from what he deemed important; but what Clemens realized himself and what critics have failed to perceive is that this "tuition" and "vitality" of which they speak were in effect Clemens' signaling of his openness to the world of the female.

Clemens realized early on that his fictional powers were enhanced—more than enhanced, empowered—by his interactions with women. As is evident from the time of Ann E. Taylor to the era of the "Angel Fish," Clemens relied upon his female audience for their creative inspiration. To create his greatest works of fiction, Clemens abandoned the realm of the purely male and investigated, and ultimately incorporated, the world of the female. Clemens' genius lay in his ability to synthesize these disparate forms of consciousness provided in part by his familial circle, and ultimately this ability enabled him to create his unique and masterful androgynous vision. The absence of female Twain biographers and the critical cold shoulder that the women in Twain's life have received is more than mere coincidence; it is time that both omissions be corrected so that the full multi-sexual universality of Clemens' vision may be more clearly understood.

Notes

1. For the first time, at the 1990 MLA Conference, a panel was formed to examine the issue of women in Mark Twain biography. The panel participants and paper titles are: Laura Skandera, panel organizer, "'I am Woman's Rights': Olivia Langdon Clemens and Her Feminist Circle"; Sherwood Cummings, "The Commanding Presence of Rachel Cord"; John Stahl, "Samuel Clemens and 'Mother' Fairbanks"; Michael Kiskis, "'A man's house burns down':

Father/Daughter Collaboration in Mark Twain's Autobiography." A paper on the relationship between Clemens and Susan Crane was delivered by Gretchen Sharlow, "The Cranes of Quarry Farm," September 1988, at the Center for Mark Twain Studies.

2. A line strikingly similar to the one in Clemens' letter is found in Mary Abigail Dodge's novel, *A New Atmosphere* (1865): "Neither is the man superior to the woman, nor the woman to the man, but they twain are one flesh" (284). In Alan Gribben's *Mark Twain's Library: A Reconstruction*, two works by Dodge are listed, *Skirmishes and Sketches* and *Stumbling Blocks*, as belonging to Clemens' library but not *A New Atmosphere*; however, it is likely that Clemens was aware of Dodge's *Atmosphere*.

3. Four letters in question are dated July 3, 1875; November 21, 1875; November 23, 1875; January 18, 1876.

4. Clemens often referred to androgyny in other works such as "Hellfire Hotchkiss." "Hellfire Hotchkiss [the girl] is the only genuwyne male man in this town and Thug Carpenter's [the boy] the only genuwyne female girl, if you leave out sex and just consider the business facts." Clemens was not the only nineteenth-century author to explore the novelistic possibilities of androgyny. William Dean Howells, in *The Rise of Silas Lapham*, introduced the character of Penelope, a young woman who functions as Silas' surrogate son, and who, by the end of the novel, is banished to Mexico in hopes she will find a society more accepting of her than Brahmin New England. Sarah Orne Jewett, a friend of Clemens', also introduced an androgynous narrator in *The Country of the Pointed Firs*. Jewett's narrator functions as an androgynous bridge between the opposing factions of male and female in the village of Dunnet's Landing. Clemens predated Virginia Woolf's experiments with androgyny in her novel *Orlando* by some four decades.

Works Cited

Boone, Joseph A. "Male Independence and the American Quest Genre: Hidden Sexual Politics in the All-Male Worlds of Melville, Twain and London." *Gender Studies.* Ed. Judith Spector. Bowling Green: Bowling Green State U. Popular Press, 1986.

Brooks, Van Wyck. *The Ordeal of Mark Twain.* New York: Dutton, 1933.

Coultrap-McQuin, Susan. *Doing Literary Business: American Women Writers in the Nineteenth Century.* Chapel Hill: U. North Carolina P., 1990.

Cox, James M. "The Uncomfortable Ending of *Huckleberry Finn.*" *The Adventures of Huckleberry Finn.* Ed. Sculley Bradley. New York: W. W. Norton, 1977.

DeVoto, Bernard. *Mark Twain at Work.* Cambridge: Harvard U. P., 1942.

Epstein, Cynthia Fuchs. *Deceptive Distinctions: Sex, Gender and the Social Order.* New Haven: Yale U. P., 1989.

Fiedler, Leslie. *The Collected Essays of Leslie Fiedler.* Vol 1. New York: Stein & Day, 1971.

Fraiberg, Louis. "Van Wyck Brooks versus Mark Twain versus Samuel Clemens." *Psychoanalysis and American Literary Criticism.* Detroit: Wayne State U. P., 1960.

Gilbert, Sandra, and Susan Gubar. *The Madwoman in the Attic.* New Haven: Yale U. P., 1979.

Gribben, Alan. "'It Is Unsatisfactory to Read to One's Self': Mark Twain's Informal Readings." *Quarterly Journal of Speech* 62 (1976): 49–56.

———. *Mark Twain's Library: A Reconstruction.* 2 Vols. Boston: G. K. Hall, 1980.

Henderson, Archibald. *Mark Twain.* Philadelphia: Folcroft Press, Inc. 1969 [1912].

Hill, Hamlin. *Mark Twain: God's Fool.* New York: Harper, 1973.

Jerome, Robert D., and Herbert A. Wisbey, Jr., eds. *Mark Twain in Elmira.* Elmira: Mark Twain Society, 1977.

Kaplan, Justin. *Mr. Clemens and Mark Twain.* New York: Simon and Schuster, 1966.

Kaplan, Sydney Janet. *Feminine Consciousness in the Modern British Novel.* Chicago: U. of Illinois P., 1975.

Krauth, Leland. "Mark Twain: The Victorian of Southwestern Humor." *American Literature* 54 (October 1982): 368–84.

The Mark Twain Papers (MTP). University of California, Berkeley.

Showalter, Elaine. *A Literature of Their Own.* Princeton, N.J.: Princeton U. P., 1977.

Sorin, Gretchen Sullivan. "The Black Community in Elmira." *A Heritage Uncovered: The Black Experience in Upstate New York: 1800–1925.* Ed. Cara Sutherland. Chemung County Historical Society, 1988.

Twain, Mark. *Adventures of Huckleberry Finn.* Ed. Sculley Bradley. New York: W. W. Norton, 1977.

———. *Mark Twain—Howells Letters.* Eds. Henry Nash Smith and William M. Gibson. Cambridge: Harvard U. P., 1960.

———. *The Unabridged Mark Twain*. Ed. Lawrence Teacher. Philadelphia: Running Press, 1976.

Wagenknecht, Edward. *Mark Twain: The Man and His Work*. 3rd ed. Norman: U. Oklahoma P., 1971.

Warren, Joyce W. "Old Ladies and Little Girls." *The American Narcissus: Individualism and Women in Nineteenth-Century American Fiction*. New Jersey: Rutgers U. P., 1984.

Wecter, Dixon, ed. *The Love Letters of Mark Twain*. New York: Harper, 1949.

———. *Mark Twain to Mrs. Fairbanks*. San Marino: Huntington Library, 1949.

———. *Sam Clemens of Hannibal*. Boston: Houghton Mifflin, 1952.

SELECTED BIBLIOGRAPHY

Items listed in the anthologies are usually not listed separately in the following bibliography, which is largely oriented toward materials from 1980 forward. Other listings may be found in numerous bibliographies in works cited here and in other Twain criticism.

Anthologies of Criticism

A number of collections of articles and sections of books have already appeared concerning Mark Twain. Several of the most prominent, useful, and readily accessible are listed here with their contents.

Mark Twain, the Critical Heritage. Frederick Anderson, editor. New York: Barnes & Noble, 1971. Contains

The Innocents Abroad or The New Pilgrim's Progress (1869)
    Unsigned review, *Nation*, 1869
    Unsigned review, *Packard's Monthly*, 1869
    Unsigned review, Buffalo *Express*, 1869
    William Dean Howells, review, *Atlantic*, 1869
    "Tom Folio," review, Boston *Daily Evening Transcript*, 1869
    Bret Harte, review, *Overland Monthly,* 1870
    Unsigned review, *Athenaeum*, 1870
    Unsigned review, *Saturday Review*, 1870
    William Ward, "American Humorists." Macon (Mississippi) *Beacon*, 1870

Roughing It, or The Innocents at Home (1872)
    Unsigned review, Manchester *Guardian*, 1872

William Dean Howells, review, *Atlantic*, 1872
Unsigned review, *Overland Monthly*, 1872

Sketches, New and Old (1875)
William Dean Howells, review, *Atlantic*, 1875
Matthew Freke Turner, "Artemus Ward and the Humourists of America," *New Quarterly Magazine*, 1876

The Adventures of Tom Sawyer (1876)
William Dean Howells, review, *Atlantic*, 1876
Moncure D. Conway, review, London *Examiner*, 1876
Unsigned review, *Athenaeum*, 1876
Unsigned review, London *Times*, 1876
Unsigned review, New York *Times*, 1877

A Tramp Abroad (1880)
William Ernest Henley, review, *Athenaeum*, 1880
Unsigned review, *Saturday Review*, 1880
William Dean Howells, review, *Atlantic*, 1880
H.H. Boyesen, review, *Atlantic*, 1881
E. Purcell, review, *Academy*, 1881
Unsigned review, *Athenaeum*, 1881
Unsigned review, *Century Magazine*, 1882
John Nichol on Mark Twain (1882)
William Dean Howells, "Mark Twain," *Century Magazine*, 1882
Thomas Sergeant Perry, "An American on American Humour," *St. James's Gazette*, 1883

Life on the Mississippi (1883)
Lafcadio Hearn, review, New Orleans *Times-Democrat*, 1883
Unsigned review, *Athenaeum*, 1883
Robert Brown, review, *Academy*, 1883
Unsigned review, *Graphic*, 1883

The Adventures of Huckleberry Finn (1884–5)
Unsigned review, *Athenaeum*, 1884
Brander Matthews, review, *Saturday Review*, 1885

Robert Bridges, review, *Life*, 1885
Unsigned article, "Modern Comic Literature," *Saturday Review*, 1885
Thomas Sergeant Perry, review, *Century Magazine*, 1885
Andrew Lang, "The Art of Mark Twain," *Illustrated London News*, 1891
Sir Walter Besant, "My Favourite Novelist and His Best Book," *Munsey's Magazine*, 1898
Andrew Lang, "Jubilee Ode to Mark Twain," *Longman's Magazine*, 1886

A Connecticut Yankee in King Arthur's Court (1889)
Sylvester Baxter, review, Boston Sunday *Herald*, 1889
William Dean Howells, review, *Harper's Magazine*, 1890
Desmond O'Brien, review, *Truth*, 1890
Unsigned review, *Speaker*, 1890
Unsigned review, London *Daily Telegraph*, 1890
Unsigned review, *Scots Observer*, 1890
William T. Stead: review, *Review of Reviews* (London), 1890
Unsigned review, *Athenaeum*, 1890
Unsigned review, Boston *Literary World*, 1890
Unsigned review, *Plumas National*, 1890
H. C. Vedder: article, New York *Examiner*, 1893

The Tragedy of Pudd'nhead Wilson (1894)
William Livingston Alden: review, *Idler*, 1894
Unsigned review, *Athenaeum*, 1895
Unsigned review, *Critic*, 1895

Personal Recollections of Joan of Arc (1896)
William Peterfield Trent, review, *Bookman* (New York), 1896
Brander Matthews, "Mark Twain—His Work," *Book Buyer*, 1897
Unsigned article, "Mark Twain, Benefactor," *Academy*, 1897
David Masters, "Mark Twain's Place in Literature," *Chautauquan*, 1897

D.C. Murray, article, *Canadian Magazine*, 1897

Following the Equator, or More Tramps Abroad (1897)
  Unsigned review, *Academy*, 1897
  Unsigned review, *Speaker*, 1897
  Unsigned review, *Saturday Review*, 1898
  Unsigned review, *Critic*, 1898
  Hiram M. Stanley, review, *Dial*, 1898
  Theodore De Laguna, "Mark Twain as a Prospective Classic," *Overland Monthly*, 1898
  Anne E. Keeling, "American Humour: Mark Twain," *London Quarterly Review*, 1899
  Henry Harland, "Mark Twain," London *Daily Chronicle*, 1899
  Harry Thurston Peck, "As to Mark Twain," *Bookman* (New York), 1901
  R. E. Phillips, "Mark Twain: More than Humorist," *Book Buyer*, 1901
  T. M. Parrott, "Mark Twain: Made in America," *Booklover's Magazine*, 1904
  Harry Thurston Peck, "Mark Twain at Ebb Tide," *Bookman* (New York), 1904
  Hammond Lamont, "Mark Twain at Seventy," *Nation*, 1905
  Unsigned article, "Mark Twain," *Spectator*, 1907
  William Lyon Phelps, "Mark Twain," *North American Review*, 1907
  Charles Whibley, column, *Blackwood's Magazine*, 1907
  H. L. Mencken, review, *Smart Set*, 1909
  Unsigned notice, *Saturday Review*, 1910
  Frank Jewett Mather, "Two Frontiersmen," *Nation*, 1910
  Unsigned notice, *Dial*, 1910
  Arnold Bennett, comment, *Bookman* (London), 1910
  Sydney Brooks, "England and Mark Twain," *North American Review*, 1910
  Harry Thurston Peck, article, *Bookman* (New York), 1910
  William Lyon Phelps, "Mark Twain, Artist," *Review of Reviews* (New York), 1910

Simeon Strunsky, article, *Nation*, 1910

Archibald Henderson, "The International Fame of Mark Twain," *North American Review*, 1910

John Macy on Mark Twain, 1913

H.L. Mencken, "The Burden of Humor," *Smart Set*, 1913

Critical Essays on Mark Twain, 1867–1910. Edited by Louis J. Budd. Boston: G. K. Hall, 1982. Includes

[Charles Henry Webb], "Advertisement"

[Edward H. House], "Mark Twain as a Lecturer"

Anonymous, [Review of *The Innocents Abroad*]

Henry Wheeler Shaw, "The Josh Billings Papers/Sum Biographical—Mark Twain"

[William A. Croffut], "Mark Twain Last Night"

Anonymous, [Review of a Lecture on the Sandwich Islands]

George T. Ferris, "Mark Twain"

William Dean Howells, [Review of *Mark Twain's Sketches, New and Old*]

[Robert Underwood Johnson], "A New Boy Book by Mark Twain"

Edmund H. Yates, "Mark Twain at Hartford"

Anonymous, "Not Quite an Editor/The Story about Mark Twain's Connection with the Hartford *Courant* "

Anonymous, "Mark Twain Home Again"

Anonymous, [Review of *The Stolen White Elephant*]

W. D. Howells, "Mark Twain"

John Henton Carter, "A Day with Mark Twain"

C., "Mark Twain"

Anonymous, "Mark Twain as Lecturer/How He Feels When He Gets on the Stage before an Audience"

[Frank George Carpenter], "Such Is Mark Twain"

Anonymous, "Talk with Twain. . . His Comments on Authors, Magazines and General Literature"

Edgar C. Beall, "Mark Twain's Head Analyzed"

Charles H. Clark, "Mark Twain at 'Nook Farm' (Hartford) and Elmira"

Oliver Wendell Holmes, "To Mark Twain (*On His Fiftieth Birthday*)"

Anonymous, "An Interview with the Famous Humorist/He Chats of Past and Present/His Life as a Reporter"

Andrew Lang, "The Art of Mark Twain"

Henry C. Vedder, "Mark Twain"

Frank R. Stockton, "Mark Twain and His Recent Works"

[Lute Pease], "The Famous Story-Teller Discusses Characters/Says That No Author Creates, but Merely Copies"

[Samuel E. Moffett], "Mark Twain to Pay All/On His Way Around the World Now to Raise the Money"

Anonymous, "Mark Twain in Sydney/A Further Interview"

R. C. B., "Mark Twain on the Platform"

William Peterfield Trent, "Mark Twain as an Historical Novelist"

Brander Matthews, "Mark Twain—His Work"

Anonymous, "Mark Twain Smiling through His Tears, but in Sore Straits"

Carlyle Smythe, "The Real 'Mark Twain'"

Anonymous, "Mark Twain in London/He Talks of His Visit and His Doomsday Book"

Henry Harland, "Mark Twain"

Anonymous, "Mark Twain to Spend Winter Here/Author Returns an Anti-Imperialist"

James L. Ford, "An American Humorist"

James B. Pond, [Paying Off His Debts]

Anonymous, "A Little Man and a Great Subject"

[Rollo Ogden], "Mark Twain on McKinley"

R. E. Phillips, "Mark Twain: More Than Humorist"

Anonymous, "Mrs. Astor Injures Mark Twain's Feelings"

Anonymous, "Degree for Mark Twain"

Anonymous, "Mark Twain's Farewell?"

Henry Van Dyke, "A Toast to Mark Twain!"

Anonymous, "Happy Pessimist Is Mark Twain"

William Dean Howells, "Sonnet to Mark Twain"

[Hammond Lamont], "Mark Twain at Seventy"

Anonymous, "Mark Twain's Clothes"

Anonymous, "Mark Twain"

William Lyon Phelps, "Mark Twain"

Hamilton W. Mabie, "Mark Twain the Humorist"

Archibald Henderson, "Mark Twain"

Anonymous, "Twain Pokes Fun at Union Station and Pities City"

Henry M. Alden, "Mark Twain: Personal Impressions"

Clarence H. Gaines, "Mark Twain *the* Humorist"

Anonymous, "Mark Twain"

Anonymous, "Chief of American Men of Letters"

Anonymous, "Mark Twain: An American Pioneer in Man's Oldest Art, Whose Death Is Mourned by the World at Large"

Anonymous, "Mark Twain"

Anonymous, "The Death of Mark Twain"

[Simeon Strunsky], "Serious Humorists"

George Ade, "Mark Twain as Our Emissary"

Critical Essays on Mark Twain, 1910–1980. Edited by Louis J. Budd. Boston: G. K. Hall, 1983. Contains

Archibald Henderson, "The International Fame of Mark Twain"

Anonymous, "Mark Twain's Portrait"

[Stuart P. Sherman], "A Literary American"

[William Dean Howells], [Review of A. B. Paine's *Biography*]

H. L. Mencken, "The Man Within"

Alvin Johnson, "The Tragedy of Mark Twain"

Brander Matthews, "Mark Twain and the Art of Writing"

Carl Van Doren, "Mark Twain and Bernard Shaw"

Fred Lewis Pattee, "On the Rating of Mark Twain"

Newton Arvin, "Mark Twain: 1835–1935"

Mark Van Doren, "A Century of Mark Twain"

Owen Wister, "In Homage to Mark Twain"

Robert Herrick, "Mark Twain and the American Tradition"

Robert T. Oliver, "Mark Twain's Views on Education"

Robert M. Gay, "The Two Mark Twains"

Herman Wouk, "America's Voice is Mark Twain's"

Kenneth Rexroth, "Humor in a Tough Age"

Leslie Hanscom, "Twain: A Yearning for Yesterday"

John C. Gerber, "Mark Twain's Use of the Comic Pose"

Glauco Cambon, "Mark Twain and Charlie Chaplin as Heroes of Popular Culture"

Edward Field, "Mark Twain and Sholem Aleichem"

C. Merton Babcock, "Mark Twain, Mencken and 'The Higher Goofyism'"

Richard Schickel, "Hal Holbrook Tonight!"

Maurice F. Brown, "Mark Twain as Proteus: Ironic Form and Fictive Integrity"

Stanley Brodwin, "The Theology of Mark Twain: Banished Adam and the Bible"

Janet Holmgren McKay, "'Tears and Flapdoodle': Point of View and Style in *Adventures of Huckleberry Finn* "

Arthur G. Pettit, "Mark Twain and His Times: A Bicentennial Appreciation"

Anonymous, "Mark Twain and the Pope"

Judith Fetterley, "Mark Twain and the Anxiety of Entertainment"

Leland Krauth, "Mark Twain Fights Sam Clemens' Duel"

Mark Twain: A Sumptuous Variety. Edited by Robert Giddings. London: Vision Press, 1985. Contains

Philip Melling, "Sport on the River and the Science of Play"

John S. Whitley, "Kids' Stuff: Mark Twain's Boys"

William Kaufman, "The Comedic Stance: Sam Clemens, His Masquerade"

Robert Goldman, "Mark Twain as Playwright"

A. Robert Lee, "*Huckleberry Finn*, 'Sivilization', and the Civilization of the Heart"

Lyall Powers, "Mark Twain and the Future of Picaresque"

Peter Messent, "Towards the Absurd: Mark Twain's *A Connecticut Yankee, Pudd'nhead Wilson* and *The Great Dark*"

Robert Giddings, "Mark Twain and King Leopold of the Belgians"

Eric Mottram, "A Raft Against Washington: Mark Twain's Criticism of America"

Huck Finn Among the Critics, A Centennial Selection, 1884–1894. Edited by M. Thomas Inge. Washington, D. C.: United States Information Agency, 1984.

M. Thomas Inge, "Introduction"

Arthur G. Pettit, "Mark Twain and His Times"

Hamlin Hill and Walter Blair, "The Composition of *Huckleberry Finn*"

Reviews by
William Ernest Henley,
Brander Matthews,
Thomas Sergeant Perry

Andrew Lang, "The Art of Mark Twain"

Sir Walter Besant, "My Favorite Novelist and His Best Book"

William Dean Howells, "Mark Twain: An Inquiry"

H. L. Mencken, "The Burden of Humor"

V. S. Pritchett, "America's First Truly Indigenous Masterpiece"

Lionel Trilling, "The Greatness of *Huckleberry Finn* "

Leslie Fiedler, "Come Back To The Raft Ag'in, Huck Honey"

T. S. Eliot, "Mark Twain's Masterpiece"

Leo Marx, "Mr. Eliot, Mr. Trilling and *Huckleberry Finn*"

W. H. Auden, "Huck and Oliver"

Joseph Wood Krutch, "Bad Novels and Great Books"

James M. Cox, "Remarks on the Sad Initiation of Huckleberry Finn"

Lauriat Lane, Jr., "Why *Huckleberry Finn* Is a Great World Novel"

Richard P. Adams, "The Structure of *Huckleberry Finn* "

Glauco Cambon, "Mark Twain and Charlie Chaplin as Heroes of Popular Culture"

Janet Holmgren McKay, "Tears and Flapdoodle": Point of View and Style in *Adventures of Huckleberry Finn* "

Bruce Michelson, "Huck and the Games of the World"

Hamlin Hill, "*Huckleberry Finn's* Humor Today"

Beverly R. David, "The Pictorial *Huck Finn*: Mark Twain and His Illustrator, E. W. Kemble"

Perry Frank, "*Adventures of Huckleberry Finn* on Film"

M. Thomas Inge, "A Mark Twain Chronology"

Thomas A. Tenney, "An Annotated Checklist of Criticism on *Adventures of Huckleberry Finn*, 1884–1983"

Critical Approaches to Mark Twain's Short Stories. Edited by Elizabeth McMahan. Port Washington, NY: Kennikat Press, 1981.

How Mark Twain Writes

S. L. Clemens, "Report to the Buffalo Female Academy"

S. L. Clemens, "How to Tell a Story"

George Feinstein, "Mark Twain's Idea of Story Structure"

"The Celebrated Jumping Frog of Calaveras County"

A. B. Paine, "The Jumping Frog"

Gladys Bellemy, "The Art of 'The Jumping Frog'"

Kenneth Lynn, "Upset Expectations in 'The Jumping Frog'"

Henry Nash Smith, "The Mysterious Charm of Simon Wheeler"

Sydney J. Krause, "The Art and Satire of Twain's 'Jumping Frog' Story"

James M. Cox, "The Structure of 'The Jumping Frog'"

"A True Story"
  Philip Foner, "A True Story"
  Gerald J. Fenger, "Telling it Like it Was"
  William H. Gibson, "The Artistry of 'A True Story'"

"The Facts Concerning the Recent Carnival of Crime in Connecticut"
  Maxwell Geismar, "A Curious Parable"
  William M. Gibson, "Mark Twain's 'Carnival of Crime'"

"The £1,000,000 Bank-Note"
  Philip Foner, "A Satire on the System"
  Maxwell Geismar, "Twain on the 'Get-Rich-Quick' Mania"
  Ricki Morgan, "Mark Twain's Money Imagery in 'The £1,000,000 Bank-Note' and 'The $30,000 Bequest'"

"The Man That Corrupted Hadleyburg"
  Gladys Bellemy, "Moralism Vs. Determinism in 'Hadleyburg'"
  Clinton S. Burhans, Jr., "The Sober Affirmation of Mark Twain's 'Hadleyburg'"
  Henry Nash Smith, "Twain's Mathematical Demonstration of Human Greed"
  Henry B. Rule, "The Role of Satan in 'The Man That Corrupted Hadleyburg'"
  Maxwell Geismar, "Twain's Ironic Parable on the Hypocrisy of Human Virtue"
  Stanley Brodwin, "Mark Twain's Mask of Satan in 'Hadleyburg'"

"The $30,000 Bequest"
  Maxwell Geismar, "Twain's Parody of Small Souls on the Make"
  Gerald J. Finger, "The Complete Irony of 'The $30,000 Bequest'"

"Captain Stormfield's Visit to Heaven"
  S. L. Clemens, "The Literary Evolution of Captain Ned Wakefield"

Gladys Bellemy, "The Narrative Perfection of 'Captain Stormfield's Visit to Heaven'"

Louis Budd, "Twain's Satire on Racism"

James M. Cox, "Captain Stormfield as Pure Burlesque Figure"

William M. Gibson, "The Imaginative Achievement of 'Captain Stormfield's Visit to Heaven'"

"The Mysterious Stranger"

John S. Tuckey, "'The Mysterious Stranger': Mark Twain's Texts and the Paine-Duneka Edition"

John R. May, "The Gospel According to Philip Traum: Structural Unity in 'The Mysterious Stranger'"

Raymond Verasco, "Divine Foolishness: A Critical Evaluation of 'The Mysterious Stranger'"

Edited with an Introduction by Barry A. Marks. Boston: D. C. Heath & Co., 1959. "Problems in American Civilization" Series.

Selections from

Van Wyck Brooks, *The Ordeal of Mark Twain*

Walter Blair, *Mark Twain and Native American Humor*

Bernard De Voto, *Mark Twain at Work*

Essays

Lionel Trilling, "The Greatness of *Huckleberry Finn* "

Leo Marx, "Mr. Eliot, Mr. Trilling, and *Huckleberry Finn*"

James M. Cox, "Remarks on the Sad Initiation of Huckleberry Finn"

Frank Baldanza, "The Structure of *Huckleberry Finn*"

Richard P. Adams, "The Unity and Coherence of *Huckleberry Finn*"

Lauriat Lane, Jr., "Why *Huckleberry Finn* Is a Great World Novel"

William Van O'Connor, "Why *Huckleberry Finn* Is Not the Great American Novel"

Mark Twain: A Collection of Critical Essays. Edited By Henry Nash Smith. Englewood Cliffs, NJ: Prentice-Hall, 1963.
Henry Nash Smith, "Introduction"
Van Wyck Brooks, "Mark Twain's Humor"
Maurice Le Breton, "Mark Twain: An Appreciation"
Kenneth Lynn, "*Roughing It* "
Leo Marx, "The Pilot and the Passenger"
Walter Blair, "*Tom Sawyer* "
Henry Nash Smith, "A Sound Heart and a Deformed Conscience"
Daniel G. Hoffman "From Black Magic—and White—In *Huckleberry Finn*"
W. H. Auden, "Huck and Oliver"
James M. Cox, "*A Connecticut Yankee*: The Machinery of Self-Preservation"
Leslie Fiedler, "As Free as Any Cretur"
Bernard De Voto, "The Symbols of Despair"
Tony Tanner, "The Lost America—The Despair of Henry Adams and Mark Twain"

One Hundred Years of Huckleberry Finn. Edited by Robert Sattelmeyer and J. Donald Crowley. Columbia: University of Missouri Press, 1985. All the essays deal with *Huckleberry Finn* and are new with this text.

The Critical Response to Mark Twain's Huckleberry Finn. Edited by Laurie Champion. Westport: Greenwood Press, 1991. Includes some standard essays and an ABC "Nightline" dialogue "Huckleberry Finn: Literature or Racist Trash?" of limited interest.

Articles and Books

Alden, W. L. "The Book Hunter." *Idler,* VII (May 1895): 565–76. Comments on *Personal Recollections of Joan of Arc* in the April *Harper's Magazine* as "by the Sieur Uquel Berri-Finn, and that they were originally translated into English by M. Marc Touêne. Nothing that the Sieur Uquel Berri-Finn has written is more characteristic of that charming author than are the opening chapters of this new romance," as quoted in Tenney.

Andrews, Kenneth R. *Nook Farm: Mark Twain's Hartford Circle.* Cambridge, MA: Harvard University Press, 1950; rpt. Hamden, CT: Archon Books, 1967.

Arnold, St. George, Jr. "The Twain Bestiary: Mark Twain's Critters and the Tradition of Animal Portraiture in Humor of the Old Southwest." *Southern Folklore Quarterly*, 41 (1977): 195–211.

Bacheller, Irving. "Mr. Paine's Biography of Mark Twain." *Literary Digest*, XLV (16 November 1912): 909. Tenney notes this to be less a review of Paine's biography than Bacheller's tribute to Twain: "He found the East still in the bondage of Puritanism. Lincoln freed the negro. Mark Twain freed the white man."

Ballorain, Rolande. "Mark Twain's Capers: A Chameleon in King Carnival's Court." In *American Novelists Revisited*, Fritz Fleischmann, ed. Boston: G. K. Hall, 1982. Pp. 143–70. Contends that Twain is a European writer in his sense of the "carnivalesque."

Barchilon, Jose, and Joel S. Kovel. "*Huckleberry Finn:* A Psychoanalytic Study." *Journal of the American Psychoanalytic Association*, XIV (October 1966): 775–814. A psychoanalysis of Huck Finn as a legitimate patient, excluding Twain's biography.

Bassett, John E. "*Life on the Mississippi*: Being Shifty in a New Country." *Western American Literature*, 21 (1986): 39–45. Disguise and performance as central elements in the canon and especially in *Life on the Mississippi*.

———. "*Roughing It*: Authority through Comic Performance." *Nineteenth-Century Literature*, 43 (1988): 220–34. Language is used to control audience by withholding information and creating contradictions.

Bentzon, Th. "Les Humoristes Américains, I: Mark Twain." *Revue de Deux Mondes*, 204 (15 July 1872): 313–35.

An early and thoughtful examination of Twain's humor before the establishment of his reputation as a novelist, in French.

Berkove, Lawrence I. "The Reality of the Dream: Structural and Thematic Unity in *A Connecticut Yankee*." *Mark Twain Journal*, 22, I (1984): 8–14. The novel is tightly structured around the endless repetitions of human error, as reflected by the unreliable narrator.

Blair, Walter, and Hamlin Hill. *America's Humor from Poor Richard to Doonesbury*. London: Oxford, 1978. A comprehensive study of the historical field and Twain's humor in six brief but illuminating chapters on his role as actor and storyteller within his own canon.

Blair, Walter. *Native American Humor*. San Francisco: Chandler, 1960 [1937]. The basic study of the field of American humor leading to Twain, with valuable critical and bibliographical information.

Branch, Edgar M. "'The Babes in the Wood': Artemus Ward's 'Double Health' to Mark Twain." *PMLA*, 93 (1978): 955–2. A reconstruction of the comic lecture by Ward which Twain probably heard and may have taken as inspiration for his story-telling and lecturing mode.

———. "Mark Twain: Newspaper Reading and the Writer's Creativity." *Nineteenth-Century Fiction*, 37 (1983): 576–603. Twain's extensive use of newspaper material documented and analyzed.

———. "A New Clemens Footprint: Soleather Steps Forward." *American Literature*, 54 (1982): 497–510. Finds an 1859 sketch by Twain indicating his drive to comedy even while piloting.

Brodwin, Stanley. "The Humor of the Absurd: Mark Twain's Adamic Diaries." *Criticism*, XIV (Winter 1972): 49–64. Twain's diaries of Adam, Eve and Satan highlight the grotesque irony of innocence pitted against determinism.

———. "Wandering Between Two Gods: Theological Realism in Mark Twain's *A Connecticut Yankee*." *Studies in the Literary Imagination*, 16, II (1983): 57–82. Calvinism,

Deism, and Darwinism mixed within historical experience to create the dream-ending perspective on human life.

Budd, Louis J. "Mark Twain and the Magazine World." *University of Mississippi Studies in English*, No. 2 (1982): 35–42. Shows Twain treating the magazine audience as appreciating a higher class of writing than the more generalized public he addressed.

————. *Our Mark Twain: The Making of His Public Personality*. Philadelphia: University of Pennsylvania Press, 1983. An analysis of the making of the staged persona Mark Twain as author/entertainer/entrepreneur.

————. "Who Wants to Go to Hell? An Unsigned Sketch by Mark Twain?" *Studies in American Humor*, No. 1 (1982): 6–16. Identifies a sketch by Twain subsequently verified by a set of proofs in the Mark Twain Papers.

Cheesman, Elaine, and Earl French, eds. *Twain-Stowe Sourcebook*. Hartford: Mark Twain Memorial and Stowe-Day Foundation, 1988. A teaching sourcebook including numerous lesson plans and abstracts of presentations by Louis Budd on "Humor and Ethics," Shelley Fisher Fishkin on "Mark Twain and the Risks of Irony," Hamlin Hill on "Humor and Pessimism," and David E. E. Sloane on "Mark Twain as an Urban Northeast Humorist" and "Mark Twain's Heroes: Huck and Hank," among other topics.

Cox, James M. "Humor and America: The Southwestern Bear Hunt, Mrs. Stowe and Mark Twain." *Sewanee Revue*, 83 (1975): 573–601. *Huck Finn* is a historical lie combining elements of Southwestern humor and northern consciousness into a portrait of a civilization that is a cruel joke even on readers who seek to conscientiously perfect it.

————. *"Life on the Mississippi* Revisited." In *The Mythologizing of Mark Twain*, Sara deS. Davis and Philip D. Biedler, eds. University, Alabama: University of Alabama Press, 1984. Pp. 95–115. Identifies unity in the novel in tension between Clemens the man and Twain the comic persona.

————. "Toward Vernacular Humor." *Virginia Quarterly Review*, 46 (1970): 311–30. Surveys Twain, Ring Lardner, and J. D. Salinger.

Cunliffe, Marcus. "Mark Twain and His 'English' Novels." *Times Literary Supplement*, 25 December 1981: 1503–04. Suggests *The Prince and the Pauper* was an attempt to capture the audience of the English historical novel and finds a Bulwer-Lytton analog to *Connecticut Yankee*.

Durden, Fred. "The Aesthetics of Bitterness in *Following the Equator*." *American Literary Realism, 1870–1910*, 16 (Autumn 1981): 277–85. Language, context, and landscape merge into Twain's most bitterly ironic travel narrative, completing the technique found in earlier works.

Eby, Cecil D. "Dandy Versus Squatter: An Earlier Round." *Southern Literary Journal*, 20, I (1987): 33–36. Finds Joseph Doddridge's "Dialogue of the Backwoodsman and the Dandy" as an 1821 analog.

Emerson, Everett. "A Send-Off for Joe Goodman: Mark Twain's "The Carson Fossil-Footprints." *Resources for American Literary Study*, 10 (1980): 71–78. Identifies a sketch written for Goodman in 1884 which is in the comic style of his Virginia City local newspaper writings.

Farrell, James T. "Mark Twain's *Huckleberry Finn* and *Tom Sawyer*." In *The League of Frightened Philistines*. New York: Vanguard Press, 1945. Pp. 25–30. Twain as democrat and cynic made Tom and Huck symbols of human possibilities in a spoiled world of chattel slavery.

Fischer, John Irwin. "How to Tell a Story: Mark Twain's Gloves and the Moral Example of Mr. Laurence Sterne." *Mark Twain Journal*, 21, III (1982): 17–21. Influence of Sterne's *Sentimental Journey* on Twain's glove-buying episode and the novel generally.

————. "Mark Twain, Mount Tabor, and the Triumph of Art." *Southern Review*, 14 (1978): 692–705. Close analysis of a chapter in *Innocents* suggests the conflict between art and philosophy in Twain's writing.

Fischer, Victor. "Huck Finn Reviewed: The Reception of *Huckleberry Finn* in the United States, 1885–1897." *American Literary Realism, 1870–1910*, 16, No. 1 (Spring 1983): 1–57. A complete introduction to the critical vulnerabilities of a humorist and the attempt to define American humor in the newspapers and periodicals of the 1885–1895 period, reprinting many perceptive and revelatory reviews of *Huck Finn* and of Twain.

Fisher, Marvin. "'Do Not Bring Your Dog': Mark Twain on the Manners of Mourning." In *Continuities and Ideas in American Literature*. Lanham, MD: University Press of America, 1986. Pp. 106–25. "The Tomb of Adam" sequence in *Innocents Abroad* exemplifies Twain's attack on false gentility as carried out through the funeral in *Huck Finn*.

Galligan, Edward L. "True Comedians and False: *Don Quixote* and *Huckleberry Finn.*" *Sewanee Review*, 86, I (1977): 66–83. Huck and Jim show up Tom Sawyer's humor as cruel and false even better than Twain wished.

Ganzel, Dewey. *Mark Twain Abroad*. Chicago: University of Chicago Press, 1968. Excellent background on the conscious creation of a persona and philosophy in *Innocents Abroad*.

Gibson, William M. *Theodore Roosevelt among the Humorists: W. D. Howells, Mark Twain, and Mr. Dooley*. Knoxville: University of Tennessee Press, 1980. Insights by contemporary humorists on the politician's achievements.

Goudie, Andrea. "'What Fools These Mortals Be!' A Puckish Interpretation of Mark Twain's Narrative Stance." *Kansas Quarterly*, 5, IV (1973): 19–31. Relates Twain's humorousness to Puck's role in Shakespeare's play.

Grenander, M. E. "'Five Blushes, Ten Shudders and a Vomit': Mark Twain on Ambrose Bierce's *Nuggets and Dust.*" *American Literary Realism, 1870–1910*, 17 (1984): 170–79. Studies relations between Twain and Bierce.

Gribben, Alan *Mark Twain's Library: A Reconstruction*. Boston: G. K. Hall, 1980. A massive and informative listing of volumes related to Twain with annotations on his reading of and response to them.

————. "Mark Twain Reads Longstreet's *Georgia Scenes*" in *Gyascutus: Studies in Antebellum Southern Humorous and Sporting Writing*, James. L. W. West, III, ed. Atlantic Highlands, NJ: Humanities Press, 1978. Pp. 103–11. Reading of the southwestern humorist by Twain.

Harris, Susan K. "Mark Twain's Bad Women." *Studies in American Fiction*, 13 (1985): 157–68. Treats Laura in *The Gilded Age* and Roxy in *Pudd'nhead Wilson* as showing that Twain adhered to the Victorian concept of woman's role.

Hawkins, Hunt. "Mark Twain's Involvement with the Congo Reform Movement: 'A Fury of Generous Indignation'." *New England Quarterly*, 51 (1978): 147–75. An extensive study of "King Leopold's Soliloquy."

Karnath, David. "Mark Twain's Implicit Theory of The Comic." *Mosaic*, 9 (1976): 207–18. Contends that reversing the reality of the fiction underlies Twain's sense of the comic.

Ketterer, David. "'Professor Baffin's Adventures' by Max Adeler: The Inspiration for *A Connecticut Yankee in King Arthur's Court?*" *Mark Twain Journal*, 24, I (Spring, 1986): 24–34. A valuable expansion of the work by Foster on these items reprinted in this volume.

Khouri, Nadia. "From Eden to the Dark Ages: Images of History in Mark Twain." *Canadian Review of American Studies*, 11 (1980): 151–74. Twain's methodology for handling the discontinuity between the American dream and its reality in his major works.

Kolb, Harold H. Jr. "Mark Twain, Huck Finn, and Jacob Blivens: Gilt-Edged, Tree-Calf Morality in *The Adventures of Huckleberry Finn*." *Virginia Quarterly Review*, 55 (1977): 653–69.

————. "Mere Humor and Moral Humor: The Example of Mark Twain." *American Literary Realism, 1870–1910*, 19 (1986): 52–64. A consideration of the nineteenth-century belief that humor was a low calling, shared by Twain himself, as opposed to the moral purpose which developed increasingly strongly in Twain after 1874.

Krauth, Leland. "Mark Twain: The Victorian of Southwestern Humor." *American Literature*, 54 (1982): 368–84. Twain avoided sensuality, as evident in his reworking of southwestern materials, and makes Huck genteel.

Lee, Mary K. "The Overt, Unreliable, Naive Narrator in the Tall Tale and *Huckleberry Finn*." *Mark Twain Journal*, 21, III (1983): 39.

Lenz, William. *Fast Talk & Flush Times: The Confidence Man as a Literary Convention*. Columbia, Missouri: University of Missouri Press, 1985. Sellers, Dilworthy, and the society of *Huck Finn* treated in relation to the southwestern tradition of fraud.

Lloyd, James B. "The Nature of Twain's Attack on Sentimentality in *The Adventures of Huckleberry Finn*." *University of Mississippi Studies in English*, 13 (1972): 59–63. How Twain balances head and heart through tears in *Huck Finn*.

Masters, Edgar Lee. *Mark Twain, A Portrait*. New York: Charles Scribner's Sons, 1938. Rpt. New York: Biblo & Tannen, 1966. Without historical insight or philosophical genius, Twain was a clown elevated above other comedians only by his pages about boys and the Mississippi.

Matheson, Terence J. "The Devil and Philip Traum: Twain's Satiric Purposes in *The Mysterious Stranger*." *Markham Review*, 12 (1982): 5–11. Theodor is an unreliable respondent to Young Satan's logic and the authorial voice is more ironic than has been presumed by critics.

Matthews, Brander. "The Penalty of Humor." In *Aspects of Fiction, and Other Ventures in Criticism*. New York: Charles Scribner's Sons, 1896. Pp. 43–56. Largely devoted to a historical survey of humorous writers concluding with a page or two on Twain.

Maxwell, D. E. S. "Twain as Satirist." In *American Fiction: The Intellectual Background*. New York: Columbia University Press, 1965; London: Routledge and Kegan Paul, 1965. Pp. 192–235; 292. Eighteenth-century satire related to Twain.

Mencken, H. L. "The Burden of Humor." *Smart Set,* XXXVIII (February, 1913): 151–54. Rpt. in Anderson (1971), 327–31. *Huck Finn, Life on the Mississippi, Connecticut Yankee,* and *Captain Stormfield's Visit to Heaven* "are alone worth more, as works of art and as criticisms of life, than the whole out-put of Cooper, Irving, Holmes, Mitchell, Stedman, Whittier and Bryant." Also Rpt. in *A Mencken Chrestomathy, Edited and Annotated by the Author* (New York: Alfred A. Knopf, 1967), p. 485.

Michelson, Bruce. "Ever Such a Good Time: The Structure of Mark Twain's *Roughing It.*" *Dutch Quarterly Review of Anglo-American Letters,* 17 (1987): 182–99. The work moves from fun and playfulness to disillusion to thirty chapters of less enjoyable reality.

Morris, Wright. "The Lunatic, the Lover, and the Poet." *Kenyon Review,* XXVII (Autumn 1965): 727–37; rpt. in *Twainian,* XXVI (January–February, 1967). Pudd'nhead Wilson charts Twain's personal crisis.

Nolle-Fischer, Karen. "Selling Mark Twain's *Connecticut Yankee* in America: Marketing and Illustrations." *Revue Francaise d'Etudes Americaines,* 8 (1983): 265–81. Illustrations help interpret two impulses in the novel, one toward popularity and the other toward populism.

O'Connor, Mrs. T. P. "Sir Walter Scott and the Civil War." In *My Beloved South.* New York and London: G. P. Putnam's Sons, 1913. Treats *Life on the Mississippi* as unjust to the South.

Parker, Hershel. "Pudd'nhead Wilson: Jack-leg Author, Unreadable Text, and Sense-Making Critics." *Flawed Texts and Verbal Icons: Literary Authority in American Fiction.* Evanston: Northwestern University Press, 1984. Pp. 115–45. Sees attempts to find continuity in this novel at variance with the evidence.

Pullen, John J. *Comic Relief: The Life and Laughter of Artemus Ward, 1834–1867.* Hamden: Archon, 1983. An interpretive study of one of Twain's most important predecessors as a literary comedian.

Quirk, Thomas. "'Learning a Nigger to Argue': Quitting *Huckleberry Finn.*" *American Literary Realism, 1870–1910,* 20 (Fall 1987): 18–33. Adding the King Sollermun chapter to *Huck Finn* at the end of composition shows Twain's despair over the imperfectibility of his characters, muffled because he had decided not to conclude with Jim being lynched as a final nihilistic statement.

Regan, Robert. "The Reprobate Elect in *The Innocents Abroad.*" *American Literature,* 54 (1982): 240–57. Twain's attack on the genteel pilgrims through a management of facts, intensified from the letters to the book.

Robinson, Forrest G. "'Seeing the Elephant'," Some Perspectives on Mark Twain's *Roughing It.*" *American Studies,* 21, II (1980): 43–64. A somber view finding paradoxical moral ambiguity in western experiences such as the Slade episode and the coyote description. The mining frontier was an unpleasant practical joke replayed over and over on the innocent self.

Rosen, Robert C. "Mark Twain's 'Jim Blaine and His Grandfather's Ram'." *College Literature,* 11 (1984): 191–94. The story is a logical and artistic expression of the skeptical state of mind.

Rourke, Constance. *American Humor: A Study of the National Character.* Garden City: Doubleday, 1953 [1931]. A broad history of American humor emphasizing its relation to folk-tales and myths among other elements of backwoods humor.

Rowe, Joyce A. "Mark Twain's Great Evasion: *Adventures of Huckleberry Finn.*" *Equivocal Endings of Classic American Novels: The Scarlet Letter, Adventures of Huckleberry Finn, The Ambassadors, The Great Gatsby.* London: Cambridge University Press, 1988. Pps. 46–74. The Phelps Farm episode shows the impossibility of the raft ideal being realized.

Rowlette, Robert. "Mark Ward on Artemus Twain: Twain's Literary Debt to Ward." *American Literary Realism, 1870–1910,* 6 (Winter 1973): 13–25. Substantial attention to *Roughing It* to illustrate Twain's borrowings from Ward.

Sax, Richard A. "Living in the Realm of Possibility: Beriah Sellers in *The Gilded Age*." *Mark Twain Journal*, 21, IV (1983): 38–41. Treats Sellers as a positive rather than negative figure.

Schmitz, Neil. "On American Humor." *Partisan Review*, 47 (1980): 559–77. Only touching lightly on *Huck* while surveying American literature, this article contends that Huck's language is a metaphor undercutting formal speech and metaphoric social transactions.

Seelye, John. "The Craft of Laughter: Abominable Showmanship and *Huckleberry Finn*." *Thalia*, 4, I (1981): 19–25. Practical jokes in *Huck Finn*.

Sewell, David R. *Mark Twain's Languages, Discourse, Dialogue, and Linguistic Variety*. Berkeley: University of California Press, 1987. Language, grammar, syntax, and diction are identified as central to Twain's concept of social corruption and truth and thus to the plots and meanings of his stories as well as his methods as a writer.

Sloane, David E. E. *Adventures of Huckleberry Finn: American Comic Vision*. Boston: Twayne, 1988. Analysis of the novel in relation to historical sources and reader-response criticism.

———. "A Connecticut Yankee and Industrial America: Mark Twain's Lesson." *Essays in Arts and Sciences*, 10 (1982): 197–205. Patriotic pride in industrialism, as shown in other American writers and Twain's Yankee, potentially leads to catastrophe.

———. *The Literary Humor of the Urban Northeast, 1830–1890*. Baton Rouge: Louisiana State University Press, 1982. Establishes a continuum of northeastern urban and literary humor which places Twain's short writings and burlesques in that tradition.

———. *Mark Twain as a Literary Comedian*. Baton Rouge: Louisiana State University Press, 1979. Identifies the ethical outcomes of Twain's relation to literary comedy as defined through a close study of Twain's predecessor Artemus Ward.

———. "Mark Twain's Comedy: The 1870's." *Studies in American Humor*, 2, III (January 1876): 146–56. By warping real events into comic fantasy, Twain's semifictional travel works raised him above contemporary literary comedians of the decade such as Nasby, Kerr, and Adeler.

Smith, Henry Nash. *Mark Twain's Fable of Progress: Political and Economic Ideas in a Connecticut Yankee.* New Brunswick: Rutgers University Press, 1964. A careful analysis of the novel as a political and economic fable.

Smith, Lawrence R. "Mark Twain's 'Jumping Frog': Toward an American Heroic Ideal." *Mark Twain Journal,* 20, I (1979): 15–18. Sees Twain's opposition to artificial ideals.

Sousa, Raymond J. "'Be It What It Will, I'll Go To It Laughing': Mark Twain's Humorous Sense of Life." *Thalia,* 2, I–II (1979): 17–24. Applies late Freud to *Roughing It.*

Stahl, John Daniel. "Mark Twain and Female Power." *Studies in American Fiction,* 16 (1988): 51–63. Explicates "A Memorable Midnight Experience" and *1601* in terms of women's role in society.

Steinbrink, Jeffrey. "How Mark Twain Survived Sam Clemens' Reformation." *American Literature,* 55 (1983): 299–315. Sees Twain as stabilizing as a humorist while courting Livy Langdon.

Strong, Leah A. *Joseph Hopkins Twichell: Mark Twain's Friend and Pastor.* Athens: University of Georgia Press, 1966. Twichell was "Harris" in *A Tramp Abroad,* first recipient of *1601,* and influential on Twain's philosophy particularly as expressed through Hank Morgan in *A Connecticut Yankee.*

Sumida, Steven H. "Reevaluating Mark Twain's Novel of Hawaii." *American Literature,* 61 (1989): 586–609. Explores a "lost" Twain novel on Hawaii from 1884 and suggests its views on natives and missionaries.

Tanner, Tony. "Mark Twain." In *The Reign of Wonder: Naivety and Reality in American Literature.* Cambridge: Cambridge University Press, 1965. Pp. 97–183. Discusses the implications of the vernacular from a critical but not a historical or linguistic viewpoint.

Tenney, Thomas A. "Black Writers on *Adventures of Huckleberry Finn*: One Hundred Years Later." *Mark Twain*

Journal: Special Issue, 22, II (1984). Subsequently reprinted as a book by Duke University Press, this symposium offers a wide splay of perspectives on Twain's novel in relation to Afro-Americans.

————. *Mark Twain: A Reference Guide*. Boston: G. K. Hall, 1977. An invaluable compendium of annotated abstracts of Mark Twain criticism from 1858 to 1975, subsequently updated in *American Literary Realism, 1870–1910* and the *Mark Twain Journal.*

Thoreson, Trygve. "'Virtuous According to Their Lights': Women in Mark Twain's Early Work." *Mark Twain Journal*, 21, IV (1983): 52–6. Finds evidence of kind treatment of women of dubious virtue in 1860's sketches versus humor directed at the genteel.

Tulip, James. "Huck Finn—The Picaresque Saint." *Balcony/The Sydney Review*, No. 2 (Winter, 1965): 13–18. Twain and Huck are fused in their continual escaping from the past in picaresque moments; the novel is at its best when Twain's voice supersedes Huck's.

Vallin, Marlene Boyd. "Mark Twain, Platform Artist: A Nineteenth-Century Preview of Twentieth-Century Performance Theory." *Text and Performance Quarterly*, 9 (1989): 322–33. Indicates how Twain diverged from common platform styles in his era, anticipating in his relation to the audience twentieth-century modes.

Wade, Clyde. "Twain's Psychic Farce." *Papers of the Arkansas Philological Association*, 13 (1987): 59–66. On the power of irrational humor in "The Jumping Frog," "Grandfather's Old Ram," and "Jim Baker's Blue-Jay Yarn."

Westendorp, Tjebbe A. "'He Backed Me into a Corner and Blockaded Me with a Chair': Strategies of Mark Twain's Literary Campaigns." *Dutch Quarterly Review of Anglo-American Letters*, 16 (1986): 22–36. How Twain uses narrative modes.

Wetzel-Sahm, Brigit. "Deadpan Emotionalized: American Humor in a German Translation of Mark Twain's 'Journalism in Tennessee'." *Svensak Akademiens Handlinger*, 5 (1988): 3–

16. Shows how a German translator changed the story for a German readership.

Wilson, James D. *A Reader's Guide to the Short Stories of Mark Twain.* Boston: G. K. Hall, 1987. A useful guide to plots and characters along with summaries of Twain's shorter works.

————. "In Quest of Redemptive Vision: Mark Twain's *Joan of Arc.*" *Tennessee Studies in Literature,* 20 (1978): 181–98. Sees the book as a religious-historical allegory which is hopeful rather than pessimistic.

"Yankee Humor." *Quarterly Review,* CXXII (January, April 1867): 212–37. One of the earliest and most accurate attempts to analyze American literary humor from the British perspective and thus useful background on Twain as a literary comedian.

Zall, P. M. *Mark Twain Laughing: Humorous Anecdotes by and about Samuel L. Clemens.* Knoxville: University of Tennessee Press, 1985. A usefully condensed collection of brief comic statements, stories, and jokes by Twain, most of which are available elsewhere.

INDEX

Index

Further Information: *The Mark Twain Circular* and *The Mark Twain Journal* are publications affiliated with the Mark Twain Circle, the national organization of scholars devoted to the study of Mark Twain. For information on the Mark Twain Circle contact James S. Leonard, editor, *Mark Twain Circular*, English Dept., The Citadel, Charleston SC 29409 or Secretary-Treasurer Joseph A. Alvarez, English Dept. Central Piedmont Community College PO Box 35009, Charlotte, NC 28235-5009.

Important sites for Twain Study include The Mark Twain House, 351 Farmington Ave., Hartford, CT 06105 and The Center for Mark Twain Studies at Quarry Farm, Elmira College, Elmira, NY 14901. The Mark Twain Papers are housed at the Bancroft Library of the University of California at Berkeley, CA. 94720, access is limited primarily to Twain scholars.

Further copies of this book may be ordered from Dr. David E. E. Sloane, Sloane Communications Systems, 4 Edgehill Terrace, Hamden, CT 06517.

p. vi, l. 27   page *487* should be *489*
p. xiv, l. 29   insert *are* after *it is*
p. xviii, l. 8   *five* should be *fine*
p. 68, l. 1   insert after first three words [words, for Simon's] auditors interpret "nary pair" as a reference to Simon's [sinful life...]
p. 70, l. 10   insert after first three words [minister's ignorance is] pretended--a suspicion that the reader cannot help entertaining--and he never tries to run a bluff of his own. Scotty's self-revelation prepares the reader for Twain's concluding [presentation of him...]
p. 604, l. 15   add Book title: *Mark Twain's Huckleberry Finn*, above [Edited with an Introduction by Barry A. Marks.]
p. 610. l. 15   add bibliographical entry: Fishkin, Shelley Fisher. *Was Huck Black?* New York: Oxford University Press, 1993. A significant examination of racial considerations revolving around Huck, the book, and American literature.
p. 617, l. 4   add to bibliographical entry: Leonard, James S., Thomas A. Tenney and Thadious M. Davis, *Satire or Evasion? Black Perspectives on Huckleberry Finn.* Durham, NC: Duke U P, 1992.

go [gəʊ] ... **III** v/i. *[irr.]* **10.** gehen ...

Kennzeichnung unregelmäßiger Verben durch [*irr.*] (Eine Liste der unregelmäßigen Verben befindet sich im Anhang.)

went [went] *pret. von* **go**.

gone [gɒn] **I** *p.p. von* go ...

Unregelmäßige Verbformen an alphabetischer Stelle

bet·ter[1] ['betə] **I** *comp. von* **good** *adj.* ... **III** *comp. von* **well** *adv.* ...
best [best] **I** *sup. von* **good** *adj.* ... **II** *sup. von* **well** *adv.* ...

Bei unregelmäßigen Steigerungsformen Hinweis auf die Grundform

fuse [fjuːz] **I** *s.* ... **2.** ⚡ (Schmelz)Sicherung *f* ...
... **'learn·er** [-nə] *s.* **1.** Anfänger(in); ... **3.** *mot.* *a.* ~ **driver** Fahrschüler(in) ...

Kennzeichnung des Lebens-, Arbeits- und Fachbereiches durch Symbole und Abkürzungen

cock·y ['kɒkɪ] *adj.* Ⓕ großspurig, anmaßend.
loon·y ['luːnɪ] *sl.* **I** *adj.* bekloppt ... ~ **bin** *s.* *sl.* ‚Klapsmühle‘ *f.*

Kennzeichnung der Stilebene durch Abkürzungen und einfache Anführungszeichen

... **'pave·ment** [-mənt] *s.* **1.** (Straßen)Pflaster *n*; **2.** *Brit.* Bürgersteig *m* ...
'side| ... **'~·walk** *s.* *bsd. Am.* Bürgersteig *m* ...

Kennzeichnung des britischen und amerikanischen Sprachgebrauchs

cen·ter *etc. Am.* → **centre** *etc.*

bzw. der amerikanischen Schreibung

leap [liːp] ... **2.** ... c) *a.* ~ **up** (auf)lodern *(Flammen)* d) *a.* ~ **up** hochschnellen *(Preise etc.)* ...

Erläuterungen zur Übersetzung

leap [liːp] ... **II** v/t. ... **4.** *(Pferd) etc.* springen lassen ...

Objektangabe zum Verb

lean[2] [liːn] ... **4.** lehnen *(against* gegen, an *acc.*), (auf)stützen *(on, upon* auf *acc.*) ...

Präpositionen und ihre deutschen Entsprechungen (mit Rektionsangabe)

heart [hɑːt] *s.* ... **3.** Herz *n*, (das) Innere, Kern *m*, Mitte *f*: *in the* ~ *of* inmitten *(gen.)* ... ~ *and soul* mit Leib u. Seele ...

Anwendungsbeispiele und idiomatische Ausdrücke in ***halbfetter Kursivschrift***

Mehr über den Umgang mit dem englisch-deutschen Teil dieses Wörterbuchs auf den Seiten 8–16. Die oben und im Hauptteil des Wörterbuchs verwendeten Abkürzungen finden Sie auf den Seiten 15 und 16.

Die Langenscheidt Service-Garantie:

Wenn Sie in diesem Wörterbuch ein Stichwort nicht finden, das man in einem Wörterbuch dieser Größe erwarten kann, garantieren wir Ihnen bis zum 31.12. 2007, dass Langenscheidt eine passende Übersetzung dieses Wortes für Sie sucht.

Dieser Service wird ausschließlich per E-Mail angeboten.
Bitte schreiben Sie uns an die Adresse garantie@langenscheidt.de. Geben Sie in dieser E-Mail das gesuchte Stichwort an sowie den sprachlichen Zusammenhang, in dem es steht. Das kann ein Satz sein, in dem das Wort vorkommt, oder eine Umschreibung des Begriffs. Bitte teilen Sie uns auch mit, in welchem Wörterbuch Sie das betreffende Wort vermissen.

Sie erhalten unsere Antwort so schnell wie möglich, ebenfalls per E-Mail.

Langenscheidt
Handwörterbücher

Langenscheidt

Handwörterbuch
Englisch

Teil I
Englisch–Deutsch

Herausgegeben von der
Langenscheidt-Redaktion

Langenscheidt

Berlin · München · Wien · Zürich · New York

Originalfassung bearbeitet von:
Heinz Messinger

Redaktion:
Martin Fellermayer, Helga Krüger

In der neuen deutschen Rechtschreibung

Ergänzende Hinweise, für die wir jederzeit dankbar sind, bitten wir zu richten an:
Langenscheidt Verlag, Postfach 40 11 20, 80711 München

© 2001, 2005 Langenscheidt KG, Berlin und München
Druck: La Tipografica Varese S.p.A.
Printed in Italy · ISBN 3-468-05127-1

1. 2. 3. 4. 5.   09 08 07 06 05

Vorwort

Neubearbeitung

Langenscheidt-Wörterbücher sind auf die Wünsche und Bedürfnisse ihrer Benutzer zugeschnitten. Hinter ihnen steht eine lange Tradition, die geprägt ist von der sprachlichen und fachlichen Kompetenz erfahrener Wörterbuchmacher. Sie berücksichtigen gleichermaßen die Anforderungen der modernen Lexikographie wie die Entwicklung der jeweiligen Sprache. Dies gilt auch für die vorliegende Bearbeitung des *Handwörterbuches Englisch-Deutsch*, deren wichtigste Merkmale wir hier kurz vorstellen:

Aktualität

In diese Bearbeitung wurden tausende aktuelle Neuwörter aufgenommen, sodass der Wortschatz den augenblicklichen Stand der englischen Sprache in ihrer ganzen Vielfalt widerspiegelt. Die Auswahl reicht dabei von allgemeinsprachlichen Begriffen wie *filo pastry, freebie, highlights, leaving do, quilted jacket, ruggedize, serendipitous, spin doctor, touring coach, washboard belly* und der gehobenen Schriftsprache mit Wörtern wie *non-discrimination principle, paramountcy* oder *vocational retraining* über Umgangssprachliches wie *bozo, clocking, dippy, gobsmacked, hype, mouse potato, natch, pecs, ram-raid, do a runner, schmooze, street cred, sussed, veggie, wannabe, wheelie, whunk, wobbler, zapped, zizz* bis hin zu Slangbegriffen wie *bollix, honcho, naffing, oi(c)k* oder *rozzer* und Vulgärausdrücken wie *bonk* oder *piss artist*. Alle deutschen Übersetzungen folgen den Regeln der neuen deutschen Rechtschreibung gemäß DUDEN.

Noch mehr Inhalt

Mit seinen rund 105.000 Stichwörtern und Wendungen mit rund 255.000 Übersetzungen bietet Ihnen Ihr *Handwörterbuch Englisch-Deutsch* mehr Inhalt als je zuvor.

Großes Buchformat

Zusätzliche Attraktivität, Übersichtlichkeit und Bedeutung auf dem Schreibtisch gewinnt das Werk durch das große Format.

Fachwortschatz

Hier haben wir uns besonders auf die folgende Bereiche konzentriert: Computer und Internet, z.B. *clipboard, cybermall, default, dongle, flame (mail), freeware, freeze-up, hypertext, LAN, multitasking, netiquette, page break, portal, smartphone, spamming, tagging, template, toughbook, undelete, URL, wildcard, zipping,* neue Technologien, z.B. *AVI, biotechnology, charge card, clone, cyborg, DNA fingerprint, fibre-optic cable, genetic engineering, GM foods, information scientist, keycard, keyhole surgery, leading-edge technology, MRI, speech recognition,* Gesellschaft und Politik, z.B. *age of criminal responsibility, antiabortionist, ballot rigging, body piercing, career-minded, date rape, edutainment, fanzine, glitzy, high-profile, job-creating, nuisance call, road rager, two-income family*, <u>Wirtschaft und Börse</u>, z. B. *business associate, cash cow, daytrader, downsizing, e-retailer, Footsie, globalization, intangible assets, Internet commerce, IPO, key currency, listed option, management consultancy, product liability, rat(e)able value, sort code, stock swap, venture capitalist*, <u>EU-Wortschatz</u>, z. B. *accession criteria, convergence criteria, European Monetary Union, internal market, MEP, participating country, state of convergence*, <u>Ökologie und Umwelt</u>, z. B. *animal welfare, environmental compatibility, environmentally aware, food chain, noise barrier, MCA, refill pack, renewable resources, space debris, speed ramp, sustainability, zero-emission*, und nicht zuletzt <u>Sport</u>, z. B. *carver, foosball/foozball, half-pipe, hang gliding, heliskiing, inline skates, Mexican wave, paraglider*.

Kontext

Wörter werden meist in einem typischen sprachlichen Zusammenhang verwendet. Damit die Benutzer des ***Handwörterbuches Englisch-Deutsch*** stets die treffende Übersetzung der verschiedenen Bedeutungen eines Wortes finden, bietet es eine Vielzahl von illustrierenden Beispielsätzen und typischen Wortverbindungen, z. B. *pitch-dark, talk big, freak of nature*, bzw. Redewendungen, z. B. *keep one's shirt on, throw a wobbly*.

Lautschrift und Silbentrennung

Wir verwenden die den Wörterbuchbenutzern heute vertraute Lautschrift der *International Phonetic Association* (IPA, nach Jones und Gimson, *English Pronouncing Dictionary*) und haben natürlich auch die bewährte Angabe der Trennstellen in den englischen Stichwörtern beibehalten.

Nützliche Extras in den Anhängen

In den Anhängen findet man zusätzlich britische und amerikanische Abkürzungen, Eigennamen inklusive Länder- und Städtenamen, unregelmäßige Verben, Zahlwörter, Maße und Gewichte sowie andere nützliche Extras.

Mit seinem modernen Inhalt und der bewährten Grundstruktur bietet das ***Handwörterbuch Englisch-Deutsch*** seinen Benutzern echte Langenscheidt-Qualität für alle Übersetzungen, sei es im Studium oder im Beruf.

LANGENSCHEIDT VERLAG

Inhaltsverzeichnis

Hinweise für die Benutzer

Keine Angst vor unbekannten Wörtern!

Das Wörterbuch tut alles, um Ihnen das Nachschlagen und Kennenlernen eines gesuchten Wortes so leicht wie möglich zu machen. Legen Sie diese Einführung daher bitte nicht gleich zur Seite. Folgen Sie uns Schritt für Schritt. Wir versprechen Ihnen, dass Sie mit uns am Ende sagen werden "It isn't as bad as all that, is it?"

Und damit Sie in Zukunft von Ihrem Wörterbuch den besten Gebrauch machen können, wollen wir Ihnen zeigen, wie und wo Sie all die Informationen finden können, die Sie für Ihre Übersetzungen in der Schule und privat, im Beruf, in Briefen oder zum Sprechen brauchen.

Wie und wo finden Sie ein Wort?

Sie suchen ein bestimmtes Wort. Und wir sagen Ihnen erst einmal, dass das Wörterbuch in die Buchstaben von A – Z unterteilt ist. Auch innerhalb der einzelnen Buchstaben sind die Wörter **alphabetisch geordnet**:

> hay – haze
> se·cre·tar·i·al – sec·re·tar·y

Neben den Stichwörtern mit ihren Ableitungen und Zusammensetzungen finden Sie an ihrem alphabetischen Platz auch noch
  a) die unregelmäßigen Formen des Komparativs und Superlativs (z. B. **better**, **worst**),
  b) die verschiedenen Formen der Pronomina (z. B. **her**, **them**),
  c) das Präteritum und Partizip Perfekt der unregelmäßigen Verben (z. B. **came**, **bitten**).

Eigennamen (einschließlich geographischer und Ländernamen) und Abkürzungen haben wir für Sie am Schluss des Buches in einem besonderen Verzeichnis zusammengestellt.

Wenn Sie nun ein bestimmtes englisches Wort suchen, wo fangen Sie damit an? – Sehen Sie sich einmal die fett gedruckten Wörter über den Spalten in den oberen äußeren Ecken auf jeder Seite an. Das sind die so genannten **Leitwörter**, an denen Sie sich orientieren können. Diese Leitwörter geben Ihnen jeweils (links) das *erste* fett gedruckte Stichwort auf einer Seite des Wörterbuches an bzw. (rechts) das *letzte* fett gedruckte Stichwort auf derselben Seite, z. B.

endive – engineer

Wollen Sie nun zum Beispiel das Wort *envy* suchen, so muss es in unserem Beispiel im Alphabet zwischen *enunciate* und *equable* liegen. Suchen Sie jetzt z. B. das Wort *arise*. Blättern Sie dazu schnell das Wörterbuch durch, und achten Sie dabei auf die linken und rechten Leitwörter. Welches Leitwort steht Ihrem gesuchten Wort *arise* wohl am nächsten? Dort schlagen Sie das Wörterbuch auf (in diesem Fall zwischen *architectonic* und *Armistice Day*). Sie werden so sehr bald die gewünschte Spalte mit *Ihrem Stichwort* finden.

Wie ist das aber nun, wenn Sie auch einmal ein Stichwort nachschlagen wollen, das aus zwei einzelnen Wörtern besteht? Nehmen Sie z. B. *evening classes* oder einen Begriff, bei dem die Wörter mit einem Bindestrich (hyphen) miteinander verbunden sind, wie in *baby-minder*. Diese Wörter werden wie ein einziges Wort behandelt und dementsprechend alphabetisch eingeordnet. Sollten Sie einmal ein solches zusammengesetztes Wort nicht finden, so zerlegen Sie es einfach in seine Einzelbestandteile und schlagen dann bei diesen an ihren alphabetischen Stellen nach. Sie werden sehen, dass Sie sich auf diese Weise viele Wörter selbst erschließen können.

Beim Nachschlagen werden Sie auch merken, dass viele so genannte „Wortfamilien" enstanden sind. Das sind Stichwortartikel, die von einem gemeinsamen Stamm oder Grundwort ausgehen und deshalb – aus Gründen der Platzersparnis – in einem Artikel zusammengefasst sind:

> **de·pend** – **de·pend·a·bil·i·ty** – **de·pend·a·ble**
> **– de·pend·ance** etc.
> **door** – '**~·bell** – **~ han·dle** – '**~,keep·er** etc.

Wie schreiben Sie ein Wort?

Sie können in Ihrem Wörterbuch wie in einem Rechtschreibwörterbuch nachschlagen, wenn Sie wissen wollen, wie ein Wort richtig geschrieben wird. Sind die **britische** und die **amerikanische Schreibung** eines Stichwortes verschieden, so wird von der amerikanischen Form auf die britische verwiesen:

> **a·ne·mi·a, a·ne·mic** *Am.* → *anaemia, anae-*
> *mic*
> **cen·ter** *etc. Am.* → *centre etc.*
> **col·or** *etc. Am.* → *colour etc.*

Ein eingeklammertes u oder l in einem Stichwort oder Anwendungsbeispiel kennzeichnet ebenfalls den Unterschied zwischen britischer und amerikanischer Schreibung:

> **col·o(u)red** bedeutet: britisch *coloured,*
> amerikanisch *colored*; **trav·el·(l)er** be-
> deutet: britisch *traveller*, amerikanisch *tra-*
> *veler*.

In seltenen Fällen bedeutet ein eingeklammerter Buchstabe aber auch ganz allgemein zwei Schreibweisen für ein und dasselbe Wort: **lan·o·lin(e)** wird entweder *lanolin* oder *lanoline* geschrieben.

Für die Abweichungen in der Schreibung geben wir Ihnen für das amerikanische Englisch ein paar einfache Regeln:

Die amerikanische Rechtschreibung

weicht von der britischen hauptsächlich in folgenden Punkten ab:

1. Für **...our** tritt **...or** ein, z. B. hon*or* = honour, lab*or* = labour.
2. **...re** wird zu **...er**, z. B. cent*er* = centre, meag*er* = meagre; ausgenommen sind og*re* und die Wörter auf ...*cre*, z. B. massa*cre* , a*cre*.
3. Statt **...ce** steht **...se**, z. B. defen*se* = defence, licen*se* = licence.
4. Bei den meisten Ableitungen der Verben auf **...l** und einigen wenigen auf **...p** unterbleibt die Verdoppelung des Endkonsonanten, also travel – trave*l*ed – trave*l*ing – trave*l*er, worship – worshi*p*ed – worshi*p*ing – worshi*p*er. Auch in einigen anderen Wörtern wird der Doppelkonsonant durch einen einfachen ersetzt, z. B. woo*l*en = woollen, carbure*t*or = carburettor.
5. Ein stummes **e** wird in gewissen Fällen weggelassen, z. B. ax = ax*e*, goodby = goodby*e*.
6. Bei einigen Wörtern mit der Vorsilbe **en...** gibt es auch noch die Schreibung **in...**, z. B. *in*close = enclose, *in*snare = ensnare.
7. Der Schreibung **ae** und **oe** wird oft diejenige mit **e** vorgezogen, z. B. an*e*mia = anaemia, diarrh*e*a = diarrhoea.
8. Aus dem Französischen stammende stumme Endsilben werden meist weggelassen, z. B. catalog = catalog*ue*, program = program*me*, prolog = prolog*ue*.
9. Einzelfälle sind: st*a*nch = staunch, m*o*ld = mould, m*o*lt = moult, gr*a*y = grey, p*l*ow = plough, ski*ll*ful = skilful, t*i*re = tyre etc.

Wie trennen Sie ein Wort?

Die Silbentrennung im Englischen ist für uns Deutsche ein heikles Kapitel. Aus diesem Grund haben wir Ihnen die Sache erleichtert und geben Ihnen für jedes mehrsilbige englische Wort die Aufteilung in Silben an. Bei mehrsilbigen Stichwörtern müssen Sie nur darauf achten, wo zwischen den Silben ein halbhoher Punkt oder ein Betonungsakzent steht, z. B. **ex·pect, ex'pect·ance.** Bei allein stehenden Wortbildungselementen, wie z. B. **electro-**, entfällt die Angabe der Silbentrennung, weil diese sich je nach der weiteren Zusammensetzung ändern kann.

Die Silbentrennungspunkte haben für Sie den Sinn, zu zeigen, an welcher Stelle im Wort Sie am Zeilenende trennen können. Sie sollten es aber vermeiden, nur einen Buchstaben abzutrennen, wie z. B. in **a·mend** oder **cit·y**. Hier nehmen Sie besser das ganze Wort auf die neue Zeile.

Was bedeuten die verschiedenen Schriftarten?

Sie finden **fett gedruckt** alle englischen Stichwörter, alle römischen Ziffern zur Unterscheidung der Wortarten (Substantiv, transitives und intransitives Verb, Adjektiv, Adverb etc.) und alle arabischen Ziffern zur Unterscheidung der einzelnen Bedeutungen eines Wortes:

> **feed** ... **I** *v/t.* [*irr.*] **1.** Nahrung zuführen (*dat.*)
> ...; **II** *v/i.* [*irr.*] **10.** a) fressen (*Tier*) ...; **III** *s.*
> **12.** Fütterung *f* ...

Sie finden *kursiv*

a) alle Grammatik- und Sachgebietsabkürzungen: *s., v/t., v/i., adj., adv., hist., pol.* etc.;

b) alle Genusangaben (Angaben des Geschlechtswortes): *m, f, n*;

c) alle Zusätze, die entweder als Dativ- oder Akkusativobjekt der Übersetzung vorangehen oder ihr als erläuternder Hinweis vor- oder nachgestellt sind:

> **e·lect** … **1.** *j-n in ein Amt* wählen …
>
> **cut** … **19.** … *Baum* fällen …
>
> **byte** … *Computer:* Byte *n*
>
> **bike** … ‚Maschine' *f* (*Motorrad*) …

d) alle Erläuterungen bei Wörtern, die keine genaue deutsche Entsprechung haben:

> **cor·o·ner** … ⚖ Coroner *m* (*richterlicher Beamter zur Untersuchung der Todesursache in Fällen unnatürlichen Todes*) …

Sie finden in **halbfetter kursiver Auszeichnungsschrift** alle Wendungen und Hinweise zur Konstruktion mit Präpositionen:

> **gain** … **~ experience** …
>
> **de·pend** … **it ~s on you** …
>
> **de·part** … **1.** (*for* nach) weg-, fortgehen …
>
> **glance** … **6.** flüchtiger Blick (*at* auf *acc.*) …

Sie finden in normaler Schrift

a) alle Übersetzungen;

b) alle kleinen Buchstaben zur weiteren Bedeutungsdifferenzierung eines Wortes oder einer Wendung:

> **Goth·ic** … **4.** … a) ba'rock, ro'mantisch, b) Schauer...
>
> **give in** … **2.** (**to** *dat.*) a) nachgeben (*dat.*), b) sich anschließen (*dat.*) …

Wie sprechen Sie ein Wort aus?

Hinter dem Stichwort sehen sie Zeichen in einer eckigen Klammer. Dies ist die so genannte Lautschrift. Die Lautschrift beschreibt, wie Sie ein Wort aussprechen sollen. So ist das „th" in **thin** ein ganz anderer Laut als das „th" in **these**. Da die normale Schrift für solche Unterschiede keine Hilfe bietet, ist es nötig, diese Laute mit anderen Zeichen zu beschreiben. Damit *jeder* genau weiß, welches Zeichen welchem Laut entspricht, hat man sich international auf eine Lautschrift geeinigt. Da die Zeichen von der **I**nternational **P**honetic **A**ssociation als verbindlich angesehen werden, nennt man sie auch **IPA-Lautschrift**.

Die englischen Laute in der internationalen Lautschrift

[ʌ]	much [mʌtʃ], come [kʌm]	kurzes *a* wie in *Matsch, Kamm*
[ɑː]	after ['ɑːftə], park [pɑːk]	langes *a*, etwa wie in *Bahn*
[æ]	flat [flæt], madam ['mædəm]	mehr zum *a* hin als *ä* in *Wäsche*
[ə]	after ['ɑːftə], arrival [ə'raɪvl]	wie das End-*e* in *Berge, mache, bitte*
[e]	let [let], men [men]	*ä* wie in *hätte, Mäntel*
[ɜː]	first [fɜːst], learn [lɜːn]	etwa wie *ir* in *flirten,* aber offener
[ɪ]	in [ɪn], city ['sɪtɪ]	kurzes *i* wie in *Mitte, billig*
[iː]	see [siː], evening ['iːvnɪŋ]	langes *i* wie in *nie, lieben*
[ɒ]	shop [ʃɒp], job [dʒɒb]	wie *o* in *Gott,* aber offener
[ɔː]	morning ['mɔːnɪŋ], course [kɔːs]	wie in *Lord,* aber ohne *r*
[ʊ]	good [ɡʊd], look [lʊk]	kurzes *u* wie in *Mutter*
[uː]	too [tuː], shoot [ʃuːt]	langes *u* wie in *Schuh*
[aɪ]	my [maɪ], night [naɪt]	etwa wie in *Mai, Neid*
[aʊ]	now [naʊ], about [ə'baʊt]	etwa wie in *blau, Couch*
[əʊ]	home [həʊm], know [nəʊ]	von [ə] zu [ʊ] gleiten
[eə]	air [eə], square [skweə]	wie *är* in *Bär,* aber kein *r* sprechen
[eɪ]	eight [eɪt], stay [steɪ]	klingt wie *äi*
[ɪə]	near [nɪə], here [hɪə]	von [ɪ] zu [ə] gleiten
[ɔɪ]	join [dʒɔɪn], choice [tʃɔɪs]	etwa wie *eu* in *neu*
[ʊə]	sure [ʃʊə], tour [tʊə]	wie *ur* in *Kur,* aber kein *r* sprechen
[j]	yes [jes], tube [tjuːb]	wie *j* in *jetzt*
[w]	way [weɪ], one [wʌn], quick [kwɪk]	sehr kurzes *u* – kein deutsches *w*!

11

[ŋ]	thing [θɪŋ], English ['ɪŋglɪʃ]	wie *ng* in *Ding*
[r]	room [ruːm], hurry ['hʌrɪ]	nicht rollen!
[s]	see [siː], famous ['feɪməs]	stimmloses *s* wie in *lassen, Liste*
[z]	zero ['zɪərəʊ], is [ɪz], runs [rʌnz]	stimmhaftes *s* wie in *lesen, Linsen*
[ʃ]	shop [ʃɒp], fish [fɪʃ]	wie *sch* in *Scholle, Fisch*
[tʃ]	cheap [tʃiːp], much [mʌtʃ]	wie *tsch* in *tschüs, Matsch*
[ʒ]	television ['telɪvɪʒn]	stimmhaftes *sch* wie in *Genie, Etage*
[dʒ]	just [dʒʌst], bridge [brɪdʒ]	wie in *Job, Gin*
[θ]	thanks [θæŋks], both [bəʊθ]	wie *ss* in *Fass*, aber gelispelt
[ð]	that [ðæt], with [wɪð]	wie *s* in *Sense*, aber gelispelt
[v]	very ['verɪ], over ['əʊvə]	etwa wie deutsches *w*, aber Oberzähne auf Oberkante der Unterlippe
[x]	loch [lɒx]	wie *ch* in *ach*

[ː] bedeutet, dass der vorhergehende Vokal lang zu sprechen ist.

Lautsymbole der nicht anglisierten Stichwörter

In nicht anglisierten Stichwörtern, d. h. in Fremdwörtern, die noch nicht als eingebürgert empfunden werden, werden gelegentlich einige Lautsymbole der französischen Sprache verwendet, um die nichtenglische Lautung zu kennzeichnen. Die nachstehende Liste gibt einen Überblick über diese Symbole:

[ã] ein nasaliertes, offenes a wie im französischen Wort *enfant*.

[ɛ̃] ein nasaliertes, offenes ä wie im französischen Wort *fin*.

[ɔ̃] ein nasaliertes, offenes o wie im französischen Wort *bonbon*.

[œ] ein offener ö-Laut wie im französischen Wort *jeune*.

[ø] ein geschlossener ö-Laut wie im französischen Wort *feu*.

[y] ein kurzes ü wie im französischen Wort *vu*.

[ɥ] ein kurzer Reibelaut, Zungenstellung wie beim deutschen ü („gleitendes ü"). Wie im französischen Wort *muet*.

[ɲ] ein j-haltiges n, noch zarter als in *Champagner*. Wie im französischen Wort *Allemagne*.

Kursive phonetische Zeichen und Betonungsakzente

Ein kursives phonetisches Zeichen bedeutet, dass der Buchstabe gesprochen oder nicht gesprochen werden kann. Beide Aussprachen sind dann im Englischen gleich häufig. Das kursive *ʊ* in der Umschrift von molest [məʊˈlest] bedeutet z. B., dass die Aussprache des Wortes mit [ə] oder mit [əʊ] etwa gleich häufig ist.

Die **Betonung** der englischen Wörter wird durch das Zeichen ' für den Hauptakzent bzw. ˌ für den Nebenakzent vor der zu betonenden Silbe angegeben:

on·ion ['ʌnjən] – **dis·loy·al** [ˌdɪsˈlɔɪəl]

Bei den zusammengesetzten Stichwörtern ohne Lautschriftangabe wird der Betonungsakzent im zusammengesetzten Stichwort selbst gegeben. z. B. ˌ**up'stairs**. Die Betonung erfolgt auch dann im Stichwort, wenn nur ein Teil der Lautschrift gegeben wird, z. B. **ad'min·is·tra·tor** [-treɪtə], **'dog·ma·tism** [-ətɪzəm].

Bei einem Stichwort, das aus zwei oder mehreren einzelnen Wörtern besteht, können Sie die Aussprache bei dem jeweiligen Einzelwort nachschlagen, z. B. **school leav·ing cer·tif·i·cate**.

Einige Worte noch zur **amerikanischen Aussprache**:

Amerikaner sprechen viele Wörter anders aus als die Briten. In diesem Wörterbuch geben wir Ihnen aber meistens nur die britische Aussprache, wie Sie sie auch in Ihren Lehrbüchern finden. Ein paar Regeln für die Abweichungen in der amerikanischen Aussprache wollen wir Ihnen hier aber doch geben.

Die amerikanische Aussprache weicht hauptsächlich in folgenden Punkten von der britischen ab:

1. ɑː wird zu (gedehntem) æ(ː) in Wörtern wie *ask* [æ(ː)sk = ɑːsk], *castle* ['kæ(ː)sl = 'kɑːsl], *grass* [græ(ː)s = grɑːs], *past* [pæ(ː)st = pɑːst] etc.; ebenso in *branch* [bræ(ː)ntʃ = brɑːntʃ], *can't* [kæ(ː)nt = kɑːnt], *dance* [dæ(ː)ns = dɑːns] etc.

2. ɒ wird zu ɑ in Wörtern wie *common* ['kɑmən = 'kɒmən], *not* [nɑt = nɒt], *on* [ɑn = ɒn], *rock* [rɑk = rɒk], *bond* [bɑnd = bɒnd] und vielen anderen.

3. juː wird zu uː, z. B. *due* [duː = djuː], *duke* [duːk = djuːk], *new* [nuː = njuː].

4. r zwischen vorhergehendem Vokal und folgendem Konsonanten wird stimmhaft gesprochen, indem die Zungenspitze gegen den harten Gaumen zurückgezogen wird, z.B. *clerk* [klɜːrk = klɑːk], *hard* [hɑːrd = hɑːd]; ebenso im Auslaut, z. B. *far* [fɑːr = fɑː], *her* [hɜːr = hɜː].

5. Anlautendes p, t, k in unbetonter Silbe (nach betonter Silbe) wird zu b, d, g abgeschwächt, z. B. in *property*, *water*, *second*.

6. Der Unterschied zwischen stark und schwach betonten Silben ist viel weniger ausgeprägt; längere Wörter haben einen deutlichen Nebenton, z. B. *dictionary* [ˈdɪkʃəˌnerɪ = ˈdɪkʃənrɪ], *ceremony* [ˈserəˌməʊnɪ = ˈserɪmənɪ], *inventory* [ˈɪnvənˌtɔːrɪ = ˈɪnvəntrɪ], *secretary* [ˈsekrəˌterɪ = ˈsekrətrɪ].

7. Vor, oft auch nach nasalen Konsonanten (m, n, ŋ) sind Vokale und Diphthonge nasal gefärbt, z.B. *stand*, *time*, *small*.

Was sagen Ihnen die Symbole und Abkürzungen?

Wir geben Ihnen die Symbole und Abkürzungen im Wörterbuch, um Sie davor zu bewahren, durch falsche Anwendungen einer Übersetzung in das berühmte „Fettnäpfchen" zu treten.

Die Liste mit den **Abkürzungen** zur Kennzeichnung des Grammatik- und Sachgebietsbereiches finden Sie auf den Seiten 15 und 16.

Die **Symbole** zeigen Ihnen, in welchem Lebens-, Arbeits- und Fachbereich ein Wort am häufigsten benutzt wird.

~ ♀	Tilde; siehe Seite 13.	✆	Post und Telekommunikation, *post and telecommunications*.
⚘	Botanik, *botany*.	♪	Musik, *musical term*.
⚙	Handwerk, *handicraft*; Technik, *engineering*.	⚓	Architektur, *architecture*.
⚒	Bergbau, *mining*.	⚡	Elektrotechnik, *electrical engineering*.
⚔	militärisch, *military term*.	⚖	Rechtswissenschaft, *legal term*.
⚓	Schifffahrt, *nautical term*.		Mathematik, *mathematics*.
⚕	Handel u. Wirtschaft, *commercial term*.		Landwirtschaft, *agriculture*.
⚒	Eisenbahn, *railway*, *railroad*.		Chemie, *chemistry*.
✈	Luftfahrt, *aviation*.		Medizin, *medicine*.
		→	Verweiszeichen; siehe Seite 14.

Ein weiteres Symbol ist das Kästchen: □. Steht es nach einem englischen Adjektiv, so bedeutet das, dass das Adverb regelmäßig durch Anhängung von *-ly* an das Adjektiv oder durch Umwandlung von *-le* in *-ly* oder von *-y* in *-ily* gebildet wird, z.B.

> **bald** □ = *baldly*
> **change·a·ble** □ = *changeably*
> **bus·y** □ = *busily*

Es gibt auch noch die Möglichkeit, ein Adverb durch Anhängen von *-ally* an das Stichwort zu bilden. In diesen Fällen haben wir auch das angegeben:

> **his·tor·ic** (□ ~*ally*) = *historically*

Bei Adjektiven, die auf *-ic* und *-ical* enden können, wird die Adverbbildung auf folgende Weise gekennzeichnet:

> **phil·o·soph·ic**, **phil·o·soph·i·cal** *adj.* □

d. h. *philosophically* ist das Adverb zu beiden Adjektivformen.

Wird bei der Adverbangabe auf das Adverb selbst verwiesen, so bedeutet dies, dass unter diesem Stichwort vom Adjektiv abweichende Übersetzungen zu finden sind:

> **a·ble** □ → *ably*

Was bedeutet das Zeichen ~, die Tilde?

Ein Symbol, das Ihnen in den Stichwortartikeln begegnet, ist ein Wiederholungszeichen, die Tilde (~ ♀).

Zusammengehörige oder verwandte Wörter sind häufig zum Zweck der Raumersparnis unter Verwendung der Tilde zu Gruppen vereinigt. Die Tilde vertritt dabei entweder das ganze Stichwort oder den vor dem senkrechten Strich (|) stehenden Teil des Stichworts.

> **drink·ing** ... ~ **wa·ter** = *drinking water*
> **ˈhead|·light** ... ˈ~·**line** = *headline*

13

Bei den in halbfetter kursiver Auszeichnungsschrift gesetzten Redewendungen vertritt die Tilde stets das unmittelbar vorhergehende Stichwort, das selbst schon mithilfe der Tilde gebildet worden sein kann:

,dou·ble|-'act·ing … ,~-'edged …: ~ *sword*
= *doub-le-edged sword*

Wechselt die Schreibung von klein zu groß oder umgekehrt, steht statt der einfachen die Kreistilde (♀):

mid·dle| age … ♀ A·ges = *Middle Ages*
Ren·ais·sance … 2. ♀ 'Wiedergeburt *f* …
= *renaissance*

Einige Worte zu den Übersetzungen und Wendungen

Nach dem fett gedruckten Stichwort, der Ausspracheangabe in eckigen Klammern und der Bezeichnung der Wortart kommt als nächstes das, was für Sie wahrscheinlich das Wichtigste ist: **die Übersetzung**.

Die Übersetzungen haben wir folgendermaßen untergliedert: römische Ziffern zur Unterscheidung der Wortarten (Substantiv, Verb, Adjektiv, Adverb etc.), arabische Ziffern zur Unterscheidung der einzelnen Bedeutungen, kleine Buchstaben zur weiteren Bedeutungsdifferenzierung, z. B.

face … I *s.* 1. Gesicht *n* …; *in (the) ~ of* a)
angesichts (*gen.*), gegenüber (*dat.*), b) trotz
(*gen. od. dat.*) …; II *v/t.* 11. ansehen …;
III *v/i.* …

Weist ein Stichwort grundsätzlich verschiedene Bedeutungen auf, so wird es mit einer hochgestellten Zahl, dem Exponenten, als eigenständiges Stichwort wiederholt:

chap[1] [tʃæp] *s.* F Bursche *m*, Junge *m* …
chap[2] [tʃæp] *s.* Kinnbacken *m* …
chap[3] [tʃæp] I *v/t. u. v/i* rissig machen *od.*
werden …; II *s.* Riss *m*, Sprung *m.*

Dies geschieht aber nicht in Fällen, in denen sich die zweite Bedeutung aus der Hauptbedeutung des Grundwortes entwickelt hat.
Anwendungsbeispiele in halbfetter kursiver Auszeichnungsschrift werden meist unter den zugehörigen Ziffern aufgeführt. Sind es sehr viele Beispiele, so werden sie in einem eigenen Abschnitt „*Besondere Redewendungen*" zusammengefasst (siehe Stichwort *heart*). Eine Übersetzung der Beispiele wird nicht gegeben, wenn diese sich aus der Grundübersetzung von selbst ergibt:

a·like … II *adv.* gleich, ebenso, in gleichem
Maße: *she helps enemies and friends ~.*

Bei sehr umfangreichen Stichwortartikeln werden auch die Zusammensetzungen von **Verben mit Präpositionen oder Adverbien** an das Ende der betreffenden Artikel angehängt, z. B. *come across*, *get up*.

Wie sie sicher wissen, gibt es im **britischen und amerikanischen Englisch** hier und da unterschiedliche Bezeichnungen für dieselbe Sache. Ein Engländer sagt z. B. *pavement*, wenn er den „Bürgersteig" meint, der Amerikaner spricht dagegen von *sidewalk*. Im Wörterbuch finden Sie die Wörter, die hauptsächlich im britischen Englisch gebraucht werden, mit *Brit.* gekennzeichnet. Die Wörter, die typisch für den amerikanischen Sprachgebrauch sind, werden mit *Am.* gekennzeichnet.

Sie werden bereits gemerkt haben, dass es selten vorkommt, dass nur eine Übersetzung hinter dem jeweiligen Stichwort steht. Meist ist es so, dass ein Stichwort mehrere sinnverwandte Übersetzungen hat, die durch **Komma** voneinander getrennt werden.

Die Bedeutungsunterschiede in den Übersetzungen werden gekennzeichnet:
  a) durch das **Semikolon** und die Unterteilung in **arabische Ziffern**:

bal·ance … 1. Waage *f* …; 2. Gleichgewicht
n …

  b) durch Unterteilung in **kleine Buchstaben** zur weiteren Bedeutungsdifferenzierung,
  c) durch **Erläuterungen** in kursiver Schrift,
  d) durch vorangestellte **bildliche Zeichen** und **abgekürzte Begriffbestimmungen** (siehe das Verzeichnis auf Seite 12 und die Liste mit den Abkürzungen auf den Seiten 15 und 16).

Siehe auch das Kapitel über die verschiedenen Schriftarten auf Seite 9 f.

Einfache Anführungszeichen bedeuten, dass eine Übersetzung entweder einer niederen Sprachebene angehört:

gov·er·nor … 4. F *der* ‚Alte'

oder in figurativer (bildlicher) Bedeutung gebraucht wird:

> **land·slide** … **1.** Erdrutsch *m*; **2.** … *fig.*
> ‚Erdrutsch' *m*

Häufig finden Sie auch in einem Stichwortartikel ein **Verweiszeichen** (→). Es hat folgende Bedeutungen:

a) Verweis von Stichwort zu Stichwort bei Bedeutungsgleichheit, z. B.

> **gaun·try** → *gantry*

b) Verweis innerhalb eines Stichwortartikels, z. B.

> **dice** [daɪs] **I** *s. pl. von* **die²** 1 Würfel *pl.*,
> Würfelspiel *n*: *play* (*at*) ~ → II … **II** *v/i.*
> würfeln, knobeln

c) Oft wurde anstelle eines Anwendungsbeispiels auf ein anderes Stichwort verwiesen, das ebenfalls in dem Anwendungsbeispiel enthalten ist:

> **square** … **15.** *A* a) den Flächeninhalt berech-
> nen von (*od. gen.*), b) *Zahl* quadrieren, ins
> Qua'drat erheben, c) *Figur* quadrieren; →
> *circle* 1

Das heißt, dass die Wendung *square the circle* unter dem Stichwort *circle* aufgeführt und dort übersetzt ist.

Runde Klammern werden verwendet

a) zur Vereinfachung der Übersetzung, z. B.

> **cov·er** … **4.** … (Bett-, Möbel- *etc.*)Bezug *m*

b) zur Raumersparnis bei gekoppelten Anwendungsbeispielen, z. B.

> **make** (**break**) **contact** Kontakt herstellen
> (unterbrechen) = *make contact/break contact* …

Grammatik auch im Wörterbuch?

Die **Rektion** von deutschen Präpositionen wird dann angegeben, wenn sie verschiedene Fälle regieren können, z. B. „vor", „über". Die Rektion von Verben wird nur dann angegeben, wenn sie von der des Grundwortes abweicht oder wenn das englische Verb von einer bestimmten Präposition regiert wird. Folgende Anordnungen sind möglich:

a) Wird ein Verb, das im Englischen transitiv ist, im Deutschen intransitiv übersetzt, so wird die abweichende Rektion angegeben:

> **con·tra·dict** … *v/t.* **1.** … wider'sprechen
> (*dat.*) …

b) Gelten für die deutschen Übersetzungen verschiedene Rektionen, steht die englische Präposition in Klammern vor der ersten Übersetzung, die deutschen Rektionsangaben stehen hinter jeder Einzelübersetzung:

> **de·scend** … **4.** (*to*) zufallen (*dat.*), 'überge-
> hen, sich vererben (auf *acc.*) …

c) Stimmen Präposition und Rektion für alle Übersetzungen überein, so stehen sie in Klammern hinter der letzten Übersetzung:

> **ob·serve** … **4.** Bemerkungen machen, sich
> äußern (*to*, *upon* über *acc.*) …

Außerdem finden Sie bei den Stichwörtern noch die folgenden **besonderen Grammatikpunkte** aufgeführt:

a) Unregelmäßiger Plural:

> **child** … *pl.* **chil·dren** …
> **a·nal·y·sis** … *pl.* **-ses** … (= *pl.* **analyses**)

b) Unregelmäßige Verben:

> **give** … **II** *v/t.* [*irr.*] … **III** *v/i.* [*irr.*] …
> **out·grow** … [*irr.* → *grow*] …

Der Hinweis *irr.* bedeutet: In der Liste im Anhang finden Sie die unregelmäßigen Formen.

c) Auslautendes *-c* wird zu *-ck* vor *-ed*, *-er*, *-ing* und *-y*:

> **frol·ic** … **II** *v/i. pret. u. p.p.* 'frol·icked

d) Bei unregelmäßigen Steigerungsformen Hinweis auf die Grundform:

> **bet·ter** … **I** *comp. von* **good** … **III** *comp. von*
> **well**
> **best** … **I** *sup. von* **good** … **II** *sup. von* **well** …

Im Wörterbuch verwendete Abkürzungen

a.	auch, *also.*
abbr.	*abbreviation*, Abkürzung.
acc.	*accusative (case)*, Akkusativ.
act.	*active voice*, Aktiv.
adj.	*adjective*, Adjektiv.
adv.	*adverb*, Adverb.
allg.	allgemein, *generally.*
Am.	*(originally) American English*, (ursprünglich) amerikanisches Englisch.
amer. ⎫ *amer.* ⎬	amerikanisch, *American.*
anat.	*anatomy*, Anatomie.
antiq.	*antiquity*, Antike.
Arab.	*Arabic*, arabisch.
ast.	*astronomy*, Astronomie.
art.	*article*, Artikel.
attr.	*attributive(ly)*, attributiv.
Austral.	*Australian*, australisch(es Englisch).
bibl.	*biblical*, biblisch.
biol.	*biology*, Biologie.
Brit.	*in British usage only*, nur im britischen Englisch gebräuchlich.
brit. ⎫ *brit.* ⎬	britisch, *Britisch.*
b.s.	*bad sense*, im schlechten Sinn.
bsd.	besonders, *particularly.*
bzw.	beziehungsweise, ... *and* ... *respectively.*
cj.	*conjunction*, Konjunktion.
coll.	*collectively*, als Sammelwort.
comp.	*comparative*, Komparativ.
contp.	*contemptuously*, verächtlich.
dat.	*dative (case)*, Dativ.
dem.	*demonstrative*, Demonstrativ...
dial.	*dialectal*, dialektisch.
eccl.	*ecclesiastical*, kirchlich, geistlich.
EDV	elektronische Datenverarbeitung, *electronic data processing.*
e-e, e-e	eine, *a (an).*
e-m, e-m	einem, *to a (an).*
e-n, e-n	einen, *a (an).*
engS.	im engeren Sinn, *in the narrower sense.*
e-r, e-r	einer, *of a (an), to a (an).*
e-s, e-s	eines, *of a (an).*
et., et.	etwas, *something.*
etc.	*et cetera*, usw.
EU	*Europäische Union, European Union.*
euphem.	*euphemistically*, beschönigend.
F	*familiar*, umgangssprachlich.
f	*feminine*, weiblich.
fenc.	*fencing*, Fechten.
fig.	*figuratively*, im übertragenen Sinn, bildlich.
Fr.	*French*, französisch.
gen.	*genitive (case)*, Genitiv.
geogr.	*geography*, Geographie.
geol.	*geology*, Geologie.
Ger.	*German*, deutsch.
ger.	*gerund*, Gerundium.
Ggs.	Gegensatz, *antonym.*
her.	*heraldry*, Heraldik, Wappenkunde.
hist.	*historical*, historisch; inhaltlich veraltet.
humor.	*humorously*, scherzhaft.
hunt.	*hunting*, Jagd.
ichth.	*ichthyology*, Ichthyologie, Fischkunde.
impers.	*impersonal*, unpersönlich.
ind.	*indicative (mood)*, Indikativ.
inf.	*infinitive (mood)*, Infinitiv.
int.	*interjection*, Interjektion.
interrog.	*interrogative*, Interrogativ...
Ir.	*Irish*, irisch.
iro.	*ironically*, ironisch.
irr.	*irregular*, unregelmäßig.
Ital.	*Italian*, italienisch.
j-d, j-d	jemand, *someone.*
j-m, j-m	jemandem, *to someone.*
j-n, j-n	jemanden, *someone.*
j-s, j-s	jemandes, someone's.
konkr.	konkret, *concretely.*
konstr.	konstruiert, *construed.*

Lat.	*Latin*, lateinisch.
ling.	*linguistics*, Linguistik, Sprachwissenschaft.
lit.	*literary*, literarisch.
m	*masculine*, männlich.
m-e, *m-e*	meine, *my*.
metall.	*metallurgy*, Metallurgie.
meteor.	*meteorology*, Meteorologie.
min.	*mineralogy*, Mineralogie.
m-m / *m-m*	meinem, *to my*.
m-n / *m-n*	meinen, *my*.
mot.	*motoring*, Auto, Verkehr.
mount.	*mountaineering*, Bergsteigen.
m-r, *m-r*	meiner, *of my*, *to my*.
m-s, *m-s*	meines, *of my*.
mst	meistens, *mostly*, *usually*.
myth.	*mythology*, Mythologie.
n	*neuter*, sächlich.
neg.	*negative*, verneinend.
neg.!	*negative connotation*, *offensive*, beleidigend.
nom.	*nominative* (*case*), Nominativ.
nordd.	norddeutsch, *Northern German*.
npr.	*proper name*, Eigenname.
obs.	*obsolete*, veraltet.
od., *od.*	oder, *or*.
opt.	*optics*, Optik.
orn.	*ornithology*, Ornithologie, Vogelkunde.
o.s.	*oneself*, sich.
östr.	österreichisch, *Austrian*.
paint.	*painting*, Malerei.
parl.	*parliamentary term*, parlamentarischer Ausdruck.
pass.	*passive voice*, Passiv.
ped.	*pedagogy*, Pädagogik; Schülersprache.
pers.	*personal*, Personal…
pharm.	*pharmacy*, Pharmazie.
phls.	*philosophy*, Philosophie.
phot.	*photography*, Fotografie.
phys.	*physics*, Physik.
physiol.	*physiology*, Physiologie.
pl.	*plural*, Plural.
poet.	*poetically*, dichterisch.
pol.	*politics*, Politik.
poss.	*possessive*, Possessiv…
p.p.	*past participle*, Partizip Perfekt.
pred.	*predicative*(*ly*), prädikativ.
pres.	*present*, Präsens.
pres.p.	*present participle*, Partizip Präsens.

pret.	*preterit*(*e*), Präteritum.
pron.	*pronoun*, Pronomen.
prp.	*preposition*, Präposition.
psych.	*psychology*, Psychologie.
R.C.	*Roman-Catholic*, römisch-katholisch.
Redew.	Redewendung, *phrase*.
refl.	*reflexive*, reflexiv.
rel.	*relative*, Relativ…
rhet.	*rhetoric*, Rhetorik.
Russ.	*Russian*, Russisch
s.	*substantive*, *noun*, Substantiv.
schweiz.	schweizerisch, *Swiss*
Scot.	*Scottish*, schottisch.
sculp.	*sculpture*, Bildhauerei.
s-e, *s-e*	seine, *his*, *one's*.
sg.	*singular*, Singular.
sl.	*slang*, Slang.
s-m, *s-m*	seinem, *to his*, *to one's*.
s-n, *s-n*	seinen, *his*, *one's*.
s.o., *s.o.*	*someone*, jemand(en).
sociol.	*sociology*, Soziologie.
sport	*sports*, Sport.
s-r, *s-r*	seiner, *of his*, *of one's*, *to his*, *to one's*.
s-s, *s-s*	seines, *of his*, *of one's*.
s.th., *s.th.*	*something*, etwas.
subj.	*subjunctive* (*mood*), Konjunktiv.
südd.	süddeutsch, *Southern German*.
sup.	*superlative*, Superlativ.
surv.	*surveying*, Landvermessung.
tel.	*telegraphy*, Telegrafie.
teleph.	*telephone system*, Fernsprechwesen.
thea.	*theatre*, Theater.
TM	*trademark*, Marke.
TV	*television*, Fernsehen.
typ.	*typography*, Buchdruck.
u., *u.*	und, *and*.
univ.	*university*, Hochschulwesen; Studentensprache.
V	*vulgar*, vulgär, unanständig.
v/aux.	*auxiliary verb*, Hilfsverb.
vet.	*veterinary medicine*, Tiermedizin.
v/i.	*intransitive verb*, intransitives Verb.
v/refl.	*reflexive verb*, reflexives Verb.
v/t.	*transitive verb*, transitives Verb.
weitS.	im weiteren Sinn, *more widely taken*.
z.B.	zum Beispiel, *for instance*.
zo.	*zoology*, Zoologie.
Zs.-, zs.-	zusammen, *together*.
Zssg(*n*)	Zusammensetzung(en), *compound word*(s).

A, a [eɪ] I s. **1.** A n, a n (*Buchstabe*, ♪ *Note*): *from A to Z* von A bis Z; **2.** *A ped. Am.* Eins f (*Note*); II adj. **3.** *A* erst; **4.** *A Am.* ausgezeichnet.

A 1 [ˌeɪˈwʌn] adj. **1.** ♣ erstklassig (*Schiff*); **2.** F I a, 'prima.

a [eɪ; ə], *vor vokalischem Anlaut* **an** [æn; ən] **1.** ein, eine (*unbestimmter Artikel*): *a woman*; *manchmal vor pl.*: *a barracks* eine Kaserne; *a bare five minutes* knappe fünf Minuten; **2.** der-, die-, das'selbe: *two of a kind* zwei (von jeder Art); **3.** per, pro, je: *twice a week* zweimal wöchentlich *od.* in der Woche; *fifty pence a dozen* fünfzig Pence pro *od.* das Dutzend; **4.** einzig: *at a blow* auf 'einen Schlag.

aard·vark [ˈɑːdvɑːk] s. zo. Erdferkel n.

Aar·on's rod [ˌeərənz-] s. ♀ **1.** Königskerze f; **2.** Goldrute f.

a·back [əˈbæk] adv. **1.** ♣ back, gegen den Mast; **2.** nach hinten, zurück; **3.** fig. *taken* ~ bestürzt, verblüfft, sprachlos.

ab·a·cus [ˈæbəkəs] pl. **-ci** [-saɪ] u. **-cus·es** s. 'Abakus m: a) Rechenbrett n, -gestell n, b) ⚠ Kapi'telldeckplatte f.

a·baft [əˈbɑːft] ♣ I prp. achter, hinter; II adv. achteraus.

a·ban·don [əˈbændən] I v/t. **1.** auf-, preisgeben, verzichten auf (*acc.*) (*a.* ♥), entsagen (*dat.*), *Hoffnung* fahren lassen; **2.** (*a.* ♣ *Schiff*) aufgeben, verlassen; *Aktion* einstellen; *sport* Spiel abbrechen; **3.** im Stich lassen; *Ehefrau* böswillig verlassen; *Kinder* aussetzen; **4.** (*s.th. to s.o.* j-m et.) über'lassen, ausliefern; **5.** ~ *o.s.* (*to*) sich 'hingeben, sich über'lassen (*dat.*); II s. [əˈbɑːdɔ̃] **6.** Hemmungslosigkeit f, Wildheit f; *with* ~ mit Hingabe, wie toll; **a'ban·doned** [-nd] adj. **1.** verlassen, aufgegeben; herrenlos; **2.** liederlich; **3.** hemmungslos, wild; **a'ban·don·ment** [-mənt] s. **1.** Auf-, Preisgabe f, Verzicht m; (*to* an *acc.*) Über'lassung f, Abtretung f; **2.** (⚖ böswilliges) Verlassen; (Kindes-)Aussetzung f; **3.** → *abandon* 6.

a·base [əˈbeɪs] v/t. erniedrigen, demütigen, entwürdigen; **a'base·ment** [-mənt] s. Erniedrigung f, Demütigung f, Verfall m.

a·bash [əˈbæʃ] v/t. beschämen; in Verlegenheit od. aus der Fassung bringen.

a·bate [əˈbeɪt] I v/t. **1.** vermindern, verringern; *Preis etc.* her'absetzen, ermäßigen; **2.** *Schmerz* lindern; *Stolz, Eifer* mäßigen; **3.** ⚖ *Missstand* beseitigen; *Verfügung* aufheben; *Verfahren* einstellen; II v/i. **4.** abnehmen, nachlassen; sich legen (*Wind, Schmerz*); fallen (*Preis*); **a'bate·ment** [-mənt] s. **1.** Abnehmen n, Nachlassen n, Verminderung f, Linderung f; (*Lärm- etc.*)Bekämpfung f; **2.** Abzug m, (*Preisetc.*)Nachlass m; **3.** ⚖ Beseitigung f, Aufhebung f.

ab·a·tis [ˈæbətɪs] s. sg. u. pl. [pl. -tiːz] ✕ Baumverhau m.

ab·at·toir [ˈæbətwɑː] (*Fr.*) s. Schlachthaus n.

ab·ba·cy [ˈæbəsɪ] s. Abtswürde f; **abbess** [ˈæbes] s. Äb'tissin f; **ab·bey** [ˈæbɪ] s. **1.** Ab'tei f: *the 2 Brit.* die Westminsterabtei; **2.** *Brit.* herrschaftlicher Wohnsitz (*frühere Abtei*); **ab·bot** [ˈæbət] s. Abt m.

ab·bre·vi·ate [əˈbriːvɪeɪt] v/t. (ab)kürzen; **ab·bre·vi·a·tion** [əˌbriːvɪˈeɪʃn] s. (*bsd. ling.* Ab)Kürzung f.

ABC, Abc [ˌeɪbiːˈsiː] I s. **1.** *Am. oft pl.* Abc n, Alpha'bet n; **2.** fig. Anfangsgründe pl.; **3.** alpha'betisch angeordnetes Handbuch; II adj. **4.** *the* ~ *powers* die ABC-Staaten (*Argentinien, Brasilien, Chile*); **5.** ~ *weapons* ABC-Waffen, atomare, biologische u. chemische Waffen; ~ *warfare* ABC-Kriegführung f.

ab·di·cate [ˈæbdɪkeɪt] I v/t. *Amt, Recht etc.* aufgeben, niederlegen; verzichten auf (*acc.*), entsagen (*dat.*); II v/i. abdanken; **ab·di·ca·tion** [ˌæbdɪˈkeɪʃn] s. Abdankung f, Verzicht m (*of* auf *acc.*); freiwillige Niederlegung (*e-s Amtes etc.*): ~ *of the throne* Thronverzicht m.

ab·do·men [ˈæbdəmen] s. **1.** anat. Ab'domen n, 'Unterleib m, Bauch m; **2.** zo. ('Hinter)Leib m (*von Insekten etc.*); **ab·dom·i·nal** [æbˈdɒmɪnl] adj. **1.** anat. Unterleibs..., Bauch...; **2.** zo. Hinterleibs...

ab·duct [æbˈdʌkt] v/t. gewaltsam entführen; **ab'duc·tion** [-kʃn] s. Entführung f.

a·beam [əˈbiːm] adv. u. adj. ♣, ✈ querab, dwars.

a·be·ce·dar·i·an [ˌeɪbiːsiːˈdeərɪən] I s. **1.** Abc-Schütze m; II adj. **2.** alpha'betisch (geordnet); **3.** fig. elemen'tar.

a·bed [əˈbed] adv. zu od. im Bett.

Ab·er·don·i·an [ˌæbəˈdəʊnjən] I adj. aus Aber'deen stammend; II s. Einwohner(-in) von Aberdeen.

ab·er·ra·tion [ˌæbəˈreɪʃn] s. **1.** Abweichung f; **2.** fig. a) Verirrung f, Fehltritt m, b) (geistige) Verwirrung f; **3.** phys., ast. Aberrati'on f.

a·bet [əˈbet] v/t. begünstigen, Vorschub leisten (*dat.*); aufhetzen; anstiften; ⚖ → *aid* 1; **a'bet·ment** [-mənt] s. Beihilfe f, Vorschub m; Anstiftung f; **a'bettor** [-tə] s. Anstifter m, (Helfers)Helfer m, ⚖ a. Gehilfe m.

a·bey·ance [əˈbeɪəns] s. Unentschiedenheit f, Schwebe f: *in* ~ a) bsd. ⚖ in der Schwebe, schwebend unwirksam, b) ⚖ herrenlos (*Grund u. Boden*); *fall into* ~ zeitweilig außer Kraft treten.

ab·hor [əbˈhɔː] v/t. ver'abscheuen; **ab·hor·rence** [əbˈhɒrəns] s. **1.** Abscheu m (*of* vor *dat.*); **2.** → *abomination* 2; **ab·hor·rent** [əbˈhɒrənt] adj. □ verabscheuungswürdig; abstoßend; verhasst (*to* dat.).

a·bide [əˈbaɪd] [irr.] I v/i. **1.** bleiben, fortdauern; **2.** ~ *by* treu bleiben (*dat.*), bleiben bei, festhalten an (*dat.*); sich halten an (*acc.*); sich abfinden mit; II v/t. **3.** erwarten; **4.** F (*mst neg.*) (v)ertragen, ausstehen: *I can't* ~ *him*; **a'biding** [-dɪŋ] adj. □ dauernd, beständig.

Ab·i·gail [ˈæbɪgeɪl] (*Hebrew*) I npr. **1.** bibl. Abi'gail f; **2.** weiblicher Vorname; II s. **3.** 2 (Kammer)Zofe f.

a·bil·i·ty [əˈbɪlətɪ] s. **1.** Fähigkeit f, Befähigung f; Können n; psych. A'bility f: *to the best of one's* ~ nach besten Kräften; ~ *to pay* ♥ Zahlungsfähigkeit; ~ *test* Eignungsprüfung f; **2.** mst pl. geistige Anlagen pl.

ab·ject [ˈæbdʒekt] adj. □ **1.** niedrig, gemein; elend; kriecherisch; **2.** fig. tiefst, höchst, äußerst: ~ *despair*; ~ *misery*.

ab·ju·ra·tion [ˌæbdʒʊəˈreɪʃn] s. Abschwörung f; **ab·jure** [əbˈdʒʊə] v/t. abschwören, (feierlich) entsagen (*dat.*); aufgeben; wider'rufen.

ab·lac·ta·tion [ˌæblækˈteɪʃn] s. Abstillen n e-s Säuglings.

ab·la·ti·val [ˌæbləˈtaɪvl] adj. ling. Ablativ...; **ab·la·tive** [ˈæblətɪv] I s. 'Ablativ m; II adj. Ablativ...

ab·laut [ˈæblaʊt] (*Ger.*) s. ling. Ablaut m.

a·blaze [əˈbleɪz] adv. u. adj. **1.** a. fig. in Flammen, a. fig. lodernd: *set* ~ entflammen; **2.** fig. (*with*) a) entflammt (von), b) glänzend (vor *dat.*, von): *all* ~ Feuer und Flamme.

a·ble [ˈeɪbl] adj. □ → *ably*; **1.** fähig, geschickt, tüchtig: *be* ~ *to* können, imstande sein zu; *he was not* ~ *to get up* er konnte nicht aufstehen; ~ *to work* arbeitsfähig; ~ *to pay* ♥ zahlungsfähig; ~ *seaman* → *able-bodied* 1; **2.** begabt, befähigt; **3.** (vor')trefflich: *an* ~ *speech*; **4.** ⚖ befähigt, fähig, **,able·-'bod·ied** adj. **1.** körperlich leistungsfähig, kräftig: ~ *seaman Brit.* Vollmatrose (*abbr. A.B.*); **2.** ✕ wehrfähig, (dienst)tauglich.

ab·let [ˈæblɪt] s. ichth. Weißfisch m.

a·bloom [əˈbluːm] adv. u. adj. in Blüte (stehend), blühend.

ab·lu·tion [əˈbluːʃn] s. eccl. u. humor. Waschung f.

a·bly [ˈeɪblɪ] adv. geschickt, mit Geschick, gekonnt.

A-B meth·od s. ⚡ A-B-Betrieb m.

ab·ne·gate [ˈæbnɪgeɪt] v/t. (ab-, ver-) leugnen; aufgeben, verzichten auf (*acc.*); **ab·ne·ga·tion** [ˌæbnɪˈgeɪʃn] s. **1.** Ab-, Verleugnung f; **2.** Verzicht m (*of* auf *acc.*); **3.** mst self-~ Selbstverleugnung f.

ab·nor·mal [æbˈnɔːml] adj. □ **1.** 'abnor,mal, 'anomal, ungewöhnlich; geistig behindert; missgebildet; **2.** ⊚ 'normwidrig; **ab·nor·mal·i·ty** [ˌæbnɔːˈmælətɪ] s., **ab'nor·mi·ty** [-mətɪ] s. Abnormi'tät f; Anoma'lie f.

a·board [əˈbɔːd] adv. u. prp. ♣, ✈ an Bord; in (*e-m od. e-n Bus etc.*): *go* ~ an Bord gehen, ♣ a. sich einschiffen; *all* ~! a) alle Mann od. alle Reisenden an

A

Bord!, b) 🛥 *etc.* alles einsteigen!

a·bode [ə'bəʊd] **I** *pret. u. p.p. von* **abide**; **II** *s.* Aufenthalt *m*; Wohnort *m*, -sitz *m*; Wohnung *f*: *take one's ~* s-n Wohnsitz aufschlagen; *of no fixed ~* 🛥 ohne festen Wohnsitz.

a·boil [ə'bɔɪl] *adv. u. adj.* siedend, kochend, in Wallung (*alle a. fig.*).

a·bol·ish [ə'bɒlɪʃ] *v/t.* **1.** abschaffen, aufheben; **2.** vernichten; **ab·o·li·tion** [ˌæbəʊ'lɪʃn] *s.* Abschaffung *f* (*Am. bsd. der Sklaverei*), Aufhebung *f*, Beseitigung *f*; 🛥 Niederschlagung *f* (*e-s Verfahrens*); **ab·o·li·tion·ism** [-ʃənɪzəm] *s.* Abolitio'nismus *m*: a) *hist.* (Poli'tik *f* der) Sklavenbefreiung *f*, b) Bekämpfung *f* e-r bestehenden Einrichtung; **ab·o·li·tion·ist** [-ʃənɪst] *s. hist.* Abolitio'nist(in).

'A-bomb *s.* A'tombombe *f*.

a·bom·i·na·ble [ə'bɒmɪnəbl] *adj.* ☐ abscheulich, scheußlich; **a·bom·i·nate** [-neɪt] *v/t.* ver'abscheuen; **a·bom·i·na·tion** [əˌbɒmɪ'neɪʃn] *s.* **1.** Abscheu *m* (*of* vor *dat.*); **2.** Gräuel *m*, Gegenstand *m* des Abscheus: *smoking is her pet ~* F das Rauchen ist ihr ein wahrer Gräuel.

ab·o·rig·i·nal [ˌæbə'rɪdʒənl] **I** *adj.* ☐ eingeboren, ureingesessen, ursprünglich, einheimisch; **II** *s.* Ureinwohner *m*; **ab·o·rig·i·nes** [-dʒəniːz] *s. pl.* **1.** Ureinwohner *pl.*, Urbevölkerung *f*; **2.** *die* ursprüngliche Flora und Fauna.

a·bort [ə'bɔːt] **I** *v/i.* **1.** 🦠 e-e Fehl- *od.* Frühgeburt haben; **2.** *biol.* verkümmern; **3.** fehlschlagen; **II** *v/t.* **4.** *Raumflug etc.* abbrechen; *~ a command* *Computer:* e-n Befehl abbrechen; **a·bort·ed** [-tɪd] *adj.* → **abortive** 1, 3, 4; **a·bor·ti·fa·cient** [-tɪ'feɪʃənt] *s.* Abtreibungsmittel *n*; **a·bor·tion** [ə'bɔːʃn] *s.* **1.** 🦠 a) Ab'ort *m*, Fehl- *od.* Frühgeburt *f*, b) Abtreibung *f*, 'Schwangerschaftsunter,brechung *f*: *procure an ~* e-e Abtreibung vornehmen (*on s.o.* bei j-m); **2.** 'Missgeburt *f* (*a. fig.*); Verkümmerung *f*; **3.** *fig.* Fehlschlag *m*; **a·bor·tion·ist** [ə'bɔːʃnɪst] *s.* Abtreiber(in); **a·bor·tive** [-tɪv] *adj.* ☐ **1.** zu früh geboren; **2.** vorzeitig; **3.** miss'lungen, erfolg-, fruchtlos: *prove ~* sich als Fehlschlag erweisen; **4.** *biol.* verkümmert; **5.** 🦠 Frühgeburt verursachend; abtreibend.

a·bound [ə'baʊnd] *v/i.* **1.** im 'Überfluss *od.* reichlich vor'handen sein; **2.** 'Überfluss haben (*in* an *dat.*); **3.** voll sein, wimmeln (*with* von); **a·bound·ing** [-dɪŋ] *adj.* reichlich (vor'handen); reich (*in* an *dat.*), voll (*with* von).

a·bout [ə'baʊt] **I** *prp.* **1.** um, um ... herum; **2.** umher in (*dat.*): *wander ~ the streets*; **3.** bei, auf (*dat.*), an (*dat.*), um, in (*dat.*): (*somewhere*) *~ the house* irgendwo im Haus; *have you any money ~ you?* haben Sie Geld bei sich?; *look ~ you!* sieh dich um!; *there is nothing special ~ him* an ihm ist nichts Besonderes; **4.** wegen, über (*acc.*), um (*acc.*), von: *talk ~ business* über Geschäfte sprechen; *I'll see ~ it* ich werde danach sehen *od.* mich darum kümmern; *what is it ~?* worum handelt es sich?; **5.** im Begriff, da'bei: *he was ~ to go out*; **6.** beschäftigt mit: *what is he ~?* was macht er (da)?; *he knows what he is ~* er weiß, was er tut *od.* was er will; **II** *adv.* **7.** um'her, ('rings-, 'rund)her,um: *drive ~* umher- *od.* herumfahren; *the wrong way ~* falsch herum; *three miles ~* drei Meilen im Umkreis; *all ~* überall; *a long way ~* ein großer Umweg; *~face!* *Am.*,

~ turn! *Brit.* ⚔ (ganze Abteilung) kehrt!; **8.** ungefähr, etwa, um, gegen: *three miles* etwa drei Meilen; *~ this time* ungefähr um diese Zeit; *~ noon* um die Mittagszeit, gegen Mittag; *that's just ~ enough!* das reicht (mir gerade)!; **9.** auf, in Bewegung: *be* (*up and*) *~* auf den Beinen sein; *there is no one ~* es ist niemand in der Nähe *od.* da; *smallpox is ~* die Pocken gehen um; **10.** → *bring about etc.*; **~-face**, **~-turn** *s.* Kehrtwendung *f*, *fig. a.* (völliger) 'Umschwung.

a·bove [ə'bʌv] **I** *prp.* **1.** über (*dat.*), oberhalb (*gen.*): *~ sea level* über dem Meeresspiegel; *~* (*the*) *average* über dem Durchschnitt; **2.** *fig.* über, mehr als; erhaben über (*acc.*): *~ all* vor allem; *you, ~ all others* von allen Menschen gerade du; *he is ~ that* er steht über der Sache, er ist darüber erhaben; *she was ~ taking advice* sie war zu stolz, Rat anzunehmen; *he is not ~ accepting a bribe* er scheut sich nicht, Bestechungsgelder anzunehmen; *praise ~* über alles Lob erhaben; *be ~ s.o.* j-m überlegen sein; *it is ~ me* es ist mir zu hoch, es geht über m-n Verstand; **II** *adv.* **3.** oben, oberhalb; **4.** *eccl.* droben im Himmel: *from ~* von oben, vom Himmel; *the powers ~* die himmlischen Mächte; **5.** über, dar'über (hin'aus): *over and ~* obendrein, überdies; **6.** weiter oben, oben ...: *~-mentioned*; **7.** nach oben; **III** *adj.* **8.** obig, oben erwähnt: *the ~ remarks*; **IV** *s.* **9.** *das* Obige, *das* Obenerwähnte.

a,bove-|'board *adv. u. adj.* **1.** offen, ehrlich; **2.** einwandfrei; **~-'ground** *adj.* **1.** ⚙, ⚒ über Tage, oberirdisch; **2.** *fig.* (noch) am Leben.

A-B pow·er pack *s.* ⚡ Netzteil *n* für Heiz- u. An'odenleistung.

ab·ra·ca·dab·ra [ˌæbrəkə'dæbrə] *s.* **1.** Abraka'dabra *n* (*Zauberwort*); **2.** *fig.* Kauderwelsch *n*.

ab·rade [ə'breɪd] *v/t.* abschürfen, ab-, aufscheuern; abnutzen, verschleißen (*a. fig.*); ⚙ a. abschleifen.

A·bra·ham ['eɪbrəhæm] *npr. bibl.* 'Abraham *m*: *in ~'s bosom* (sicher wie) in Abrahams Schoß.

ab·ra·sion [ə'breɪʒn] *s.* **1.** Abreiben *n*, Abschleifen *n* (*a.* ⚙); **2.** ⚙ Abrieb *m*; Abnützung *f*, Verschleiß *m*; **3.** 🦠 (Haut)Abschürfung *f*, Schramme *f*; **ab·'ra·sive** [-sɪv] **I** *adj.* ☐ abschleifend, Schleif..., Schmirgel...; *fig.* ätzend; **II** *s.* ⚙ Schleifmittel *n*.

ab·re·act [ˌæbrɪ'ækt] *v/t. psych.* abreagieren; **ab·re·ac·tion** [-kʃn] *s.* 'Abre,akti,on *f*.

a·breast [ə'brest] *adv.* Seite an Seite, nebenein'ander: *four ~*; *~ of od. with* auf der Höhe *gen. od. von*; *keep ~ of* (*od.* *with*) *fig.* Schritt halten mit.

a·bridge [ə'brɪdʒ] *v/t.* **1.** (ab-, ver)kürzen; zu'sammen-ziehen; **2.** *fig.* beschränken, beschneiden; **a·bridged** [-dʒd] *adj.* (ab-)gekürzt, Kurz...; **a·bridg(e)·ment** [-mənt] *s.* **1.** (Ab-, Ver)Kürzung *f*; **2.** Abriss *m*, Auszug *m*; gekürzte (Buch-)Ausgabe *f*; **3.** Beschränkung *f*.

a·broad [ə'brɔːd] *adv.* **1.** im *od.* ins Ausland, auswärts, draußen: *go ~* ins Ausland reisen; *from ~* aus dem Ausland; **2.** draußen, im Freien: *be ~ early* schon früh aus dem Haus sein; **3.** weit um'her, überall'hin: *spread ~* (weit) verbreiten; *the matter has got ~* die Sache ist ruchbar geworden; *a rumo(u)r is ~* es geht das Gerücht; **4.**

fig. all ~ a) ganz im Irrtum, b) völlig verwirrt.

ab·ro·gate ['æbrəʊgeɪt] *v/t.* abschaffen, *Gesetz etc.* aufheben; **ab·ro·ga·tion** [ˌæbrəʊ'geɪʃn] *s.* Abschaffung *f*, Aufhebung *f*.

ab·rupt [ə'brʌpt] *adj.* ☐ **1.** abgerissen, zs.-hanglos (*a. fig.*); **2.** jäh, steil; **3.** kurz angebunden, schroff; **4.** plötzlich, ab'rupt, jäh; **ab'rupt·ness** [-nɪs] *s.* **1.** Abgerissenheit *f*, Zs.-hanglosigkeit *f*; **2.** Steilheit *f*; **3.** Schroffheit *f*; **4.** Plötzlichkeit *f*.

ab·scess ['æbsɪs] *s.* 🦠 Abs'zess *m*, Geschwür *n*, Eiterbeule *f*.

ab·scis·sion [æb'sɪʒn] *s.* Abschneiden *n*, Abtrennung *f*.

ab·scond [əb'skɒnd] *v/i.* **1.** sich heimlich da'vonmachen, flüchten (*from* vor *dat.*); *a. ~ from justice* sich den Gesetzen *od.* der Festnahme entziehen: *~ing debtor* flüchtiger Schuldner; **2.** sich verstecken.

ab·seil ['æbseɪl, -saɪl] **I** *v/i. a. ~ down* mount. sich abseilen; **II** *s.* Abseilen *n*; *~ e·quip·ment* *s.* Abseilgeräte *pl.*; *~ ring* *s.* Abseilring *m*; *~ ropes* *pl.* Abseilgeschirr *n*.

ab·sence ['æbsəns] *s.* **1.** Abwesenheit *f* (*from* von): *~ of mind* → *absent-mindedness*; **2.** (*from*) Fernbleiben *n* (von), Nichterscheinen *n* (in *dat.*, bei, zu): *~ without leave* ⚔ unerlaubte Entfernung von der Truppe; **3.** (*of*) Fehlen *n* (*gen. od.* von), Mangel *m* (an *dat.*): *in the ~ of* in Ermangelung von (*od. gen.*).

ab·sent **I** *adj.* ☐ ['æbsənt] **1.** abwesend, fehlend, nicht vor'handen *od.* zu'gegen: *be ~* fehlen; **2.** geistesabwesend, zerstreut; **II** *v/t.* [æb'sent] **3.** *~ o.s.* (*from*) fernbleiben (*dat. od.* von), sich entfernen (von, aus); **ab·sen·tee** [ˌæbsən'tiː] *s.* **1.** Abwesende(r *m*) *f*: *~ ballot*, *~ vote pol.* Briefwahl *f*; *~ voter* Briefwähler(in); **2.** (unentschuldigt) Fehlende(r *m*) *f*; **3.** Eigentümer, der nicht auf s-m Grundstück lebt; **ab·sen·tee·ism** [ˌæbsən'tiːɪzəm] *s.* längeres (unentschuldigtes) Fehlen (am Arbeitsplatz, in der Schule); **ab·sent-'mind·ed** *adj.* ☐ geistesabwesend, zerstreut; **ab·sent-'mind·ed·ness** [-nɪs] *s.* Geistesabwesenheit *f*, Zerstreutheit *f*.

ab·sinth(e) ['æbsɪnθ] *s.* **1.** ♀ Wermut *m*; **2.** Ab'sinth *m* (*Branntwein*).

ab·so·lute ['æbsəluːt] **I** *adj.* ☐ **1.** abso-'lut (*a.* 🦠, *ling.*, *phys.*, *phls.*): *~ altitude* ✈ absolute (Flug)Höhe; *~ majority* *pol.* absolute Mehrheit; *~ temperature* absolute (*od.* Kelvin)Temperatur; *~ zero* absoluter Nullpunkt; **2.** unbedingt, unbeschränkt: *~ monarchy* absolute Monarchie; *~ ruler* unumschränkter Herrscher; *~ gift* Schenkung *f*; **3.** 🜍 rein, unvermischt: *~ alcohol* absoluter Alkohol; **4.** rein, völlig, abso-'lut, voll'kommen: *~ nonsense*; **5.** bestimmt, wirklich; 'positiv: *~ fact* Tatsache; *become ~* 🛥 rechtskräftig werden; **II** *s.* **6.** *the ~* das Absolute; **'ab·so·lute·ly** [-lɪ] *adv.* **1.** abso'lut, völlig, vollkommen, 'durchaus; **2.** F genau(!), abso'lut(!), unbedingt(!), ganz recht(!); **ab·so·lu·tion** [ˌæbsəlu:ʃn] *s.* **1.** *eccl.* Absoluti'on *f*, Sündenerlass *m*; **2.** 🛥 Freisprechung *f*; **ab·so·lu·tism** ['æbsəlu:tɪzəm] *s. pol.* Absolu'tismus *m*, unbeschränkte Regierungsform *od.* Herrschergewalt.

ab·solve [əb'zɒlv] *v/t.* **1.** frei-, lossprechen (*of* von *Sünde*, *from* von *Verpflichtung*), entbinden (*from* von *od.*

gen.); **2.** *eccl.* Absoluti'on erteilen (*dat.*)

ab·sorb [əb'sɔːb] *v/t.* **1.** absorbieren, auf-, einsaugen, (ver)schlucken; *a. fig. Wissen etc.* (in sich) aufnehmen; vereinigen (*into* mit); **2.** sich einverleiben, trinken; **3.** *fig.* aufzehren, verschlingen, schlucken; ✝ *Kaufkraft* abschöpfen; **4.** *fig.* ganz in Anspruch nehmen *od.* beschäftigen, fesseln; **5.** *phys.* absorbieren, resorbieren, in sich aufnehmen, auffangen, *Schall* schlucken, *Schall, Stoß* dämpfen; **ab'sorbed** [-bd] *adj.* □ *fig.* (*in*) gefesselt (von), vertieft *od.* versunken (in *acc.*): ~ *in thought*; **ab'sorb·ent** [-bənt] **I** *adj.* absorbierend, aufsaugend: ~ *cotton* ✠ Verbandwatte *f*; **II** *s.* Absorpti'onsmittel *n*; **ab'sorb·ing** [-bɪŋ] *adj.* □ **1.** aufsaugend; *fig.* fesselnd, packend; **2.** ◎, *biol.* Absorptions..., Aufnahme... (*a.* ✝); **ab'sorp·tion** [əb'sɔːpʃn] *s.* **1.** *a.* ✝, ✦, ◎, *biol., phys.* Auf-, Einsaugung *f*, Aufnahme *f*, Absorpti'on *f*; Vereinigung *f*; **2.** Verdrängung *f*, Verbrauch *m*; (*Schall-, Stoß*)Dämpfung *f*; **3.** *fig.* (*in*) Vertieftsein *n* (in *acc.*), gänzliche In'anspruchnahme (durch); **ab·sorp·tive** [əb'sɔːptɪv] *adj.* absorp'tiv, Absorptions..., absorbierend, (auf)saug-, aufnahmefähig.

ab·stain [əb'steɪn] *v/i.* **1.** sich enthalten (*from gen.*); **2.** *a.* ~ *from voting* sich der Stimme enthalten; **ab'stain·er** [-nə] *s. mst total* ~ Absti'nenzler *m*.

ab·ste·mi·ous [æb'stiːmjəs] *adj.* □ enthaltsam, mäßig, fru'gal (*a. Essen*).

ab·sten·tion [æb'stenʃn] *s.* **1.** Enthaltung *f* (*from* von); **2.** *a.* ~ *from voting pol.* Stimmenthaltung *f*.

ab·sti·nence ['æbstɪnəns] *s.* Absti'nenz *f*, Enthaltung *f* (*from* von), Enthaltsamkeit *f*: *total* ~ (völlige) Abstinenz, vollkommene Enthaltsamkeit; *day of* ~ *R.C.* Abstinenztag *m*; **'ab·sti·nent** [-nt] *adj.* □ enthaltsam, mäßig, absti'nent.

ab·stract¹ ['æbstrækt] **I** *adj.* □ **1.** abstrakt, theo'retisch, rein begrifflich; **2.** *ling.* ab'strakt (*Ggs. konkret*); **3.** A ab'strakt, rein (*Ggs. angewandt*): ~ *number* abstrakte Zahl; **4.** → *abstruse*; **5.** *paint.* ab'strakt; **II** *s.* **6.** *das* Ab'strakte: *in the* ~ rein theoretisch (betrachtet), an u. für sich; **7.** *ling.* Ab'straktum *n*, Begriffs(haupt)wort *n*; **8.** Auszug *m*, Abriss *m*, Inhaltsangabe *f*, 'Übersicht *f*: ~ *of account* Konto-, Rechnungsauszug; ~ *of title* ⚖ Besitztitel *m*, Eigentumsnachweis *m*.

ab·stract² [æb'strækt] *v/t.* **1.** *Geist etc.* ablenken; (ab)sondern, trennen; **2.** abstrahieren; für sich *od.* (ab)gesondert betrachten; **3.** e-n Auszug machen von, kurz zs.-fassen; **4.** ✿ destillieren; **5.** entwenden; **ab'stract·ed** [-tɪd] *adj.* □ **1.** (ab)gesondert, getrennt; **2.** zerstreut, geistesabwesend; **ab'strac·tion** [-kʃn] *s.* **1.** Abstrakti'on *f*, *a.* ✿ Absonderung *f*; **2.** *a.* ✠ Wegnahme *f*, Entwendung *f*; **3.** *phls.* Abstrakti'on *f*, abstrakter Begriff; **4.** Versunkenheit *f*, Zerstreutheit *f*; **5.** ab'straktes Kunstwerk.

ab·struse [æb'struːs] *adj.* □ dunkel, schwer verständlich, ab'strus.

ab·surd [əb'sɜːd] *adj.* □ ab'surd (*a. thea.*), unsinnig, lächerlich; **ab'surd·i·ty** [-dətɪ] *s.* Absurdi'tät *f*, Sinnlosigkeit *f*, Albernheit *f*, Unsinn *m*: *reduce to* ~ ad absurdum führen.

a·bun·dance [ə'bʌndəns] *s.* **1.** (*of*) 'Überfluss *m* (an *dat.*), Fülle *f* (von), (große) Menge (von): *in* ~ in Hülle und

Fülle; **2.** 'Überschwang *m der Gefühle*; **3.** Wohlstand *m*, Reichtum *m*; **a'bun·dant** [-nt] *adj.* □ **1.** reichlich (vor'handen); **2.** (*in od. with*) im 'Überfluss besitzend (*acc.*), reich (an *dat.*), reichlich versehen (mit); **3.** ✦ abun'dant; **a'bun·dant·ly** [-ntlɪ] *adv.* reichlich, völlig, in reichem Maße.

a·buse I *v/t.* [ə'bjuːz] **1.** miss'brauchen; 'übermäßig beanspruchen; **2.** grausam behandeln, miss'handeln; *Frau* miss'brauchen; **3.** beleidigen, beschimpfen; **II** *s.* [ə'bjuːs] **4.** 'Missbrauch *m*, -stand *m*, falscher Gebrauch; 'Übergriff *m*: ~ *of authority* ⚖ Amts-, Ermessensmissbrauch; ~ *of power* Machtmissbrauch; **5.** Miss'handlung *f*; **6.** Kränkung *f*, Beschimpfung *f*, Schimpfworte *pl.*; **a'bu·sive** [-juːsɪv] *adj.* □ **1.** 'missbräuchlich; **2.** beleidigend, ausfallend: *he became* ~; ~ *language* Schimpfworte *pl.*; **3.** falsch (angewendet).

a·but [ə'bʌt] *v/i.* angrenzen, -stoßen, (sich) anlehnen (*on*, *upon*, *against* an *acc.*); **a'but·ment** [-mənt] *s.* △ Strebepfeiler *m*, 'Widerlager *n e-r Brücke etc.*; **a'but·tals** [-tlz] *s. pl.* (Grundstücks-) Grenzen *pl*; **a'but·ter** [-tə] *s.* ⚖ Anlieger *m*, Anrainer *m*.

a·bysm [ə'bɪzəm] *s. poet.* Abgrund *m*; **a'bys·mal** [-zml] *adj.* □ abgrundtief, bodenlos, unergründlich (*a. fig.*): ~ *ignorance* grenzenlose Dummheit; **a·byss** [ə'bɪs] *s.* **1.** *a. fig.* Abgrund *m*, Schlund *m*; **2.** Hölle *f*.

Ab·ys·sin·i·an [ˌæbɪ'sɪnjən] **I** *adj.* abes'sinisch; **II** *s.* Abes'sinier(in).

a·ca·cia [ə'keɪʃə] *s.* **1.** ♀ a) A'kazie, b) *a. false* ~ Gemeine Ro'binie; **2.** A'kazien,gummi *m*, *n*.

ac·a·dem·i·a [ˌækə'diːmɪə] *s.* die akademische Welt; **ac·a·dem·ic** [ˌækə'demɪk] **I** *adj.* (□ ~*ally*) **1.** aka'demisch, Universitäts...: ~ *dress od. costume* akademische Tracht; ~ *year* Studienjahr *n*; **2.** (geistes)wissenschaftlich: ~ *achievement*; *an* ~ *course*; **3.** a) aka'demisch, (rein) theo'retisch: *an* ~ *question*, b) unpraktisch, nutzlos; **4.** konventio'nell, traditio'nell; **II** *s.* **5.** Aka'demiker(in); **6.** Universi'tätsmitglied *n* (*Dozent, Student etc.*); **ˌac·a·'dem·i·cal** [-kl] *adj.* □ → *academic* 1, 2; **II** *s. pl.* aka'demische Tracht; **a·cad·e·mi·cian** [əˌkædə'mɪʃn] *s.* Akade'miemitglied n; **a·cad·e·my** [ə'kædəmɪ] *s.* **1.** ♀ Akade'mie *f* (*Platos Philosophenschule*); **2.** a) Hochschule *f*, b) höhere Lehranstalt (*allgemeiner od. spezieller Art*): *military* ~ Militärakademie *f*, Kriegsschule *f*; *riding* ~ Reitschule *f*; **3.** Akade'mie *f der Wissenschaften etc.*, gelehrte Gesellschaft: *Academy Awards pl.* Oscar-Verleihung *f*.

ac·a·jou ['ækəʒuː] → *cashew*.

a·can·thus [ə'kænθəs] *s.* **1.** ♀ Bärenklau *m*, *f*; **2.** △ A'kanthus *m*, Laubverzierung *f*.

ac·cede [æk'siːd] *v/i.* ~ *to* **1.** e-m Vertrag, *Verein etc.* beitreten; e-m Vorschlag beipflichten, in *et.* einwilligen; **2.** zu *et.* gelangen; *Amt* antreten; *Thron* besteigen.

ac·cel·er·ant [æk'selərənt] **I** *adj.* beschleunigend; **II** *s.* ✿ 'positiver Kataly'sator; **ac·cel·er·ate** [æk'seləreɪt] **I** *v/t.* **1.** beschleunigen, die Geschwindigkeit erhöhen von (*od. gen.*); *fig. Entwicklung etc.* beschleunigen, fördern; *et.* ankurbeln; **2.** *Zeitpunkt* vorverlegen; **II** *v/i.* **3.** schneller werden; **ac'cel·er·at·ing** [-reɪtɪŋ] *adj.* Beschleunigungs...: ~

grid ⚡ Beschleunigungs-, Schirmgitter *n*; **ac·cel·er·a·tion** [ækˌselə'reɪʃn] *s.* **1.** *bsd.* ◎, *phys., ast.* Beschleunigung *f*: ~ *lane mot.* Beschleunigungsspur *f*; **2.** ✦ Akzelerati'on *f*, Entwicklungsbeschleunigung *f*; **ac·cel·er·a·tor** [-reɪtə] *s.* **1.** *bsd.* ◎ Beschleuniger *m*, *mot. a.* Gashebel *m*, 'Gaspe,dal *n*: *step on the* ~ Gas geben; **2.** *anat.* Sym'pathikus *m*.

ac·cent I *s.* ['æksənt] Ak'zent *m*: a) *ling.* Ton *m*, Betonung *f*, b) *ling.* Tonzeichen *n*, c) Tonfall *m*, Aussprache *f*, d) ♪ Ak'zent(zeichen *n*) *m*, e) *fig.* Nachdruck (*on* auf *dat.*); **II** *v/t.* [æk'sent] → **ac·cen·tu·ate** [æk'sentjʊeɪt] *v/t.* akzentuieren, betonen: a) her'vorheben (*a. fig.*), b) mit e-m Ak'zent(zeichen) versehen; **ac·cen·tu·a·tion** [ækˌsentjʊ'eɪʃn] *s. allg.* Betonung *f*.

ac·cept [ək'sept] **I** *v/t.* **1.** annehmen: a) entgegennehmen: ~ *a gift*, b) akzeptieren: ~ *a proposal*; **2.** *fig.* akzeptieren: a) *j-n od. et.* anerkennen, *bsd. et.* gelten lassen, b) *et.* 'hinnehmen, sich mit *et.* abfinden; **3.** *j-n* aufnehmen (*into* in *acc.*); **4.** auffassen, verstehen: → *accepted*; **5.** ✝ *Auftrag* annehmen; *Wechsel* akzeptieren: ~ *the tender* den Zuschlag erteilen; **II** *v/i.* **6.** annehmen, zusagen, einverstanden sein; **ac·cept·a·bil·i·ty** [əkˌseptə'bɪlətɪ] *s.* **1.** Annehmbarkeit *f*, Eignung *f*; **2.** Erwünschtheit *f*; **ac'cept·a·ble** [-təbl] *adj.* □ **1.** akzep'tabel, annehmbar, tragbar (*to* für); **2.** angenehm, will'kommen; **3.** ✝ beleihbar, lom'bardfähig; **ac'cept·ance** [-təns] *s.* **1.** Annahme *f*, Empfang *m*; **2.** Aufnahme *f* (*into* in *acc.*); **3.** Zusage *f*, Billigung *f*, Anerkennung *f*; **4.** 'Übernahme *f*; **5.** 'Hinnahme *f*; **6.** *bsd.* ✝ Abnahme *f von Waren*: ~ *test* Abnahmeprüfung *f*; **7.** ✝ a) Annahme *f od.* Anerkennung *f e-s Wechsels*, b) Ak'zept *n*, angenommener Wechsel; **ac·cep·ta·tion** [ˌæksep'teɪʃn] *s. ling.* gebräuchlicher Sinn, landläufige Bedeutung; **ac'cept·ed** [-tɪd] *adj.* allgemein anerkannt; üblich, landläufig: *in the* ~ *sense*; ~ *text* offizieller Text; **ac'cept·er, ac'cep·tor** [-tə] *s.* **1.** Annehmer *m*, Abnehmer *m etc.*; **2.** ✝ Akzep'tant *m*, Wechselnehmer *m*.

ac·cess ['ækses] *s.* **1.** Zugang *m* (*Weg*): ~ *hatch* ⚓, ✈ Einsteigluke *f*; ~ *road* *Am.* a) Zufahrtsstraße *f*, b) (Autobahn-) Zubringerstraße *f*; ~ *traffic* Anliegerverkehr *m*; **2.** *fig.* (*to*) Zugang *m* (zu), Zutritt *m* (zu, bei); Gehör *n* (bei); *Computer*: Zugriff *m* (auf *acc.*): ~ *code* Zugriffscode *m*; ~ *key* Zugriffstaste *f*, -schlüssel *m*; ~ *path* Zugriffspfad *m*; ~ *time* *Computer*: Zugriffszeit *f*; ~ *to means of education* Bildungsmöglichkeiten *pl.*; *easy of* ~ leicht zugänglich; **3.** (*Wut-, Fieber- etc.*)Anfall *m*, Ausbruch *m*; **ac'ces·sa·ry** → *accessory*; **ac·ces·si·bil·i·ty** [ækˌsesə'bɪlətɪ] *s.* Erreichbarkeit *f*, Zugänglichkeit *f* (*a. fig.*); **ac·ces·si·ble** [æk'sesəbl] *adj.* □ **1.** zugänglich, erreichbar (*to* für); *fig.* 'um-, zugänglich; **3.** zugänglich, empfänglich (*to* für); **ac·ces·sion** [æk'seʃn] *s.* **1.** (*to*) Gelangen *m* (zu *e-r Würde*): ~ *to power* Machtübernahme *f*; **2.** (*to*) Anschluss *m* (an *acc.*), Beitritt *m* (zu); Antritt *m* (*e-s Amtes*): ~ *criteria pl. EU* 'Beitrittskri,terien; ~ *to the throne* Thronbesteigung *f*; **3.** (*to*) Zuwachs *m* (an *dat.*), Vermehrung *f* (*gen.*): *recent* ~*s* Neuanschaffungen *pl.*; **4.** Wertzuwachs *m*, Vorteil *m*; **5.** (*to*) Erreichung *f e-s Alters*.

ac·ces·so·ry [æk'sesərɪ] **I** *adj.* **1.** zusätzlich, beitragend, Hilfs..., Neben..., Begleit...; **2.** nebensächlich, 'untergeordnet; **3.** teilnehmend, mitschuldig (*to* an *dat.*); **II** *s.* **4.** Zusatz *m*, Anhang *m*; **5.** *accessories pl.* ☉ Zubehör(teile *pl.*) *n, m*; **6.** oft *pl.* Hilfsmittel *n*, Beiwerk *n*; **7.** ⚖ Teilnehmer *m* an e-m *Verbrechen*: **~** *after the fact* Begünstiger *m, z. B.* Hehler *m*; **~** *before the fact* a) Anstifter *m*, b) (Tat)Gehilfe *m*.

ac·ci·dence ['æksɪdəns] *s.* ling. Formenlehre *f*.

ac·ci·dent ['æksɪdənt] *s.* **1.** Zufall *m*, zufälliges Ereignis: *by* **~** zufällig; **2.** zufällige Eigenschaft, Nebensächlichkeit *f*; **3.** Unfall *m*, Unglücksfall *m*: *in an* **~** bei e-m Unfall; **~** *benefit* Unfallentschädigung *f*; **~***-free* unfallfrei; **~***-prone* unfallgefährdet; **~** *report* Unfallbericht; **4.** Missgeschick *n*; **ac·ci·den·tal** [͵æksɪ'dentl] **I** *adj.* ☐ **1.** zufällig, unbeabsichtigt; nebensächlich; **2.** Unfall...: **~** *death* Tod *m* durch Unfall; **II** *s.* **3.** ♪ Vorzeichen *n*; **4.** *mst pl.* paint. Nebenlichter *pl.*

ac·claim [ə'kleɪm] **I** *v/t.* **1.** j-n, *fig. et.* mit (lautem) Beifall *od.* Jubel begrüßen; *j-m* zujubeln; **2.** jauchzend ausrufen: *they* **~***ed him* (*as*) *king* sie riefen ihn zum König aus; **3.** sehr loben; **II** *s.* **4.** Beifall *m*.

ac·cla·ma·tion [͵æklə'meɪʃn] *s.* **1.** lauter Beifall; **2.** hohes Lob; **3.** *pol.* Abstimmung *f* durch Zuruf: *by* **~** durch Akklamation.

ac·cli·mate [ə'klaɪmət] *bsd. Am.* → **ac·climatize**; **ac·cli·ma·tize** [ə'klaɪmətaɪz] *s.*, **ac·cli·ma·ti·za·tion** [ə͵klaɪmətaɪ'zeɪʃn] *s.* Akklimatisierung *f*, Eingewöhnung *f* (*beide a. fig.*); ⚘ zo. Einbürgerung *f*; **ac·cli·ma·tize** [ə'klaɪmətaɪz] *v/t. u. v/i.* (sich) akklimatisieren, (sich) gewöhnen (*to* an *acc.*) (*a. fig.*).

ac·cliv·i·ty [ə'klɪvətɪ] *s.* Steigung *f*.

ac·co·lade ['ækəʊleɪd] *s.* **1.** Akko'lade *f*: a) Ritterschlag *m*, b) (feierliche) Um'armung. **2.** *fig. Am.* Auszeichnung *f*. **3.** ♪ Klammer *f*.

ac·com·mo·date [ə'kɒmədeɪt] **I** *v/t.* **1.** (*to*) a) anpassen (*dat.*, an *acc.*): **~** *o.s. to circumstances*, b) in Einklang bringen (mit): **~** *facts to theory*; **2.** *j-n* versorgen, *j-m* aushelfen *od.* gefällig sein (*with* mit): **~** *s.o. with money*; **3.** *Streit* schlichten, beilegen; **4.** 'unterbringen, Platz haben für, fassen; **II** *v/i.* **5.** sich einstellen (*to* auf *acc.*); **6.** ♬ sich akkommodieren; **ac'com·mo·dat·ing** [-tɪŋ] *adj.* ☐ gefällig, entgegenkommend; anpassungsfähig; **ac·com·mo·da·tion** [ə͵kɒmə'deɪʃn] *s.* **1.** Anpassung *f* (*to* an *acc.*); Über'einstimmung *f*; **2.** Über'einkommen *n*, gütliche Einigung; **3.** Gefälligkeit *f*, Aushilfe *f*, geldliche Hilfe; **4.** Versorgung *f* (*with* mit); **5.** *a. pl.* Einrichtung(en *pl.*) *f*; Bequemlichkeit(en *pl.*) *f*; Räumlichkeit (-en *pl.*) *f*: *seating* **~** Sitzgelegenheit *f*; **6.** *Brit. sg., Am. mst pl.* (Platz *m* für) 'Unterkunft *f*, -bringung *f*, Quar'tier *n*; **7.** *a.* **~** *train Am.* Per'sonenzug *m*.

ac·com·mo·da·tion| **~ ad·dress** *s.* 'Decka,dresse *f*; **~ bill**, **~ draft** ✝ Gefälligkeitswechsel *m*; **~ lad·der** *s.* ⚓ Fallreep *n*; **~ road** *s.* Hilfs-, Zufahrtsstraße *f*.

ac·com·pa·ni·ment [ə'kʌmpənɪmənt] *s.* **1.** ♪ Begleitung *f, a. fig. iro.* Begleitmusik *f*; **2.** *fig.* Begleiterscheinung *f*; **ac'com·pa·nist** [-pənɪst] *s.* ♪ Begleiter (-in); **ac·com·pa·ny** [ə'kʌmpənɪ] *v/t.* **1.** *a.* ♪ *u. fig.* begleiten; **2.** *fig.* e-e Begleiterscheinung sein von *od. gen.*: **ac-**

companied *by od. with* begleitet von, verbunden mit; **~***ing address* (*phenomenon*) Begleitadresse *f* (-erscheinung *f*); **3.** verbinden (*with* mit): **~** *the advice with a warning*.

ac·com·plice [ə'kʌmplɪs] *s.* Kom'plize *m*, 'Mittäter(in).

ac·com·plish [ə'kʌmplɪʃ] *v/t.* **1.** *Aufgabe* voll'bringen, voll'enden, erfüllen, *Absicht* ausführen, *Zweck* erreichen, erfüllen, *Ziel* erreichen; **2.** leisten; **3.** ver'vollkommnen, schulen; **ac'complished** [-ʃt] *adj.* **1.** 'vollständig ausgeführt; **2.** kultiviert, (fein *od.* vielseitig) gebildet; **3.** voll'endet, per'fekt (*a. iro.*): *an* **~** *liar* ein Erzlügner; **ac'complish·ment** [-mənt] *s.* **1.** Ausführung *f*, Voll'endung *f*; Erfüllung *f*; **2.** Ver'vollkommnung *f*; **3.** Voll'kommenheit *f*; Könnerschaft *f*; **4.** *mst pl.* Fertigkeiten *pl.*, Ta'lente *pl.*, Künste *pl.*; **5.** Leistung *f*.

ac·cord [ə'kɔːd] **I** *v/t.* **1.** bewilligen, gewähren, *Lob* spenden; **II** *v/i.* **2.** über'einstimmen, harmonieren, passen; **III** *s.* **3.** Über'einstimmung *f*, Einklang *m*; **4.** Zustimmung *f*; **5.** Über'einkommen *n, pol.* Abkommen *n*; ⚖ Vergleich *m*: *with one* **~** einstimmig, einmütig; *of one's own* **~** aus eigenem Antrieb, freiwillig; **ac'cord·ance** [-dəns] *s.* Über'einstimmung *f*: *be in* **~** *with* übereinstimmen mit; *in* **~** *with* in Übereinstimmung mit, gemäß; **ac'cord·ing** [-dɪŋ] **I** **~** *as cj.* je nach'dem (wie *od.* ob), so wie; **II** **~** *to prp.* gemäß, nach, laut (*gen.*): **~** *to taste* (je) nach Geschmack; **~** *to directions* vorschriftsmäßig; **ac'cord·ing·ly** [-dɪŋlɪ] *adv.* demgemäß, folglich; entsprechend.

ac·cor·di·on [ə'kɔːdjən] *s.* Ak'kordeon *n*, 'Zieh-, 'Handhar,monika *f*.

ac·cost [ə'kɒst] *v/t.* her'antreten an (*acc.*), *j-n* ansprechen.

ac·couche·ment [ə'kuːʃmɑːŋ] (*Fr.*) *s.* Entbindung *f*, Niederkunft *f*; **ac·cou·cheur** [͵æku:'ʃɜː, akuʃœːr] *s.* Geburtshelfer *m*; **ac·cou·cheuse** [͵æku:-'ʃɜːz, akuʃøːz] *s.* Hebamme *f*.

ac·count [ə'kaʊnt] **I** *v/t.* **1.** ansehen als, erklären für, betrachten als: **~** *s.o.* (*to be*) *guilty*; **~** *o.s. happy* sich glücklich schätzen; **II** *v/i.* **2. ~** *for 2.* Rechenschaft ablegen über *acc.*; verantwortlich sein für; **3.** (er)klären, begründen: *how do you* **~** *for that?* wie erklären Sie das?; *Henry* **~***s for ten of them* zehn davon kommen auf H.; *there is no* **~***ing for it* das ist nicht zu begründen, das ist Ansichtssache; (*not*) **~***ed for* (un)geklärt; **4.** *hunt.* (ab)schießen; *fig. sport* ,erledigen'; **III** *s.* **5.** Rechnung *f*, Ab-, Berechnung *f*; ✝ *pl.* (Geschäfts)Bücher *pl.*, (Rechnungs-, Jahres)Abschluss *m*; 'Konto *n*: **~** *book* Konto-, Geschäftsbuch *n*; **~** *current od. current* **~** laufende Rechnung, Kontokorrent *n*; **~***s department* Buchhaltung *f*; **~** *movements* Kontobewegungen *pl*; **~***s sales* Verkaufsabrechnung; **~***s payable* Verbindlichkeiten, Kreditoren; **~***s receivable* Außenstände, Debitoren; *on* **~** auf Abschlag, a conto, als Teilzahlung; *for* **~** *only* nur zur Verrechnung; *for one's own* **~** auf eigene Rechnung; *payment on* **~** Anzahlung *f*; *on one's own* **~** auf eigene Rechnung (u. Gefahr), für sich selber; *balance an* **~** e-e Rechnung bezahlen, ein Konto ausgleichen; *carry to a new* **~** auf neue Rechnung vortragen; *charge to s.o.'s* **~** j-s Konto belasten mit, j-m in Rechnung

stellen; *keep an* **~** Buch führen; *open an* **~** ein Konto eröffnen; *place to s.o.'s* **~** j-m in Rechnung stellen; *render an* **~** (*for*) Rechnung (vor)legen (für); **~** *rendered* vorgelegte Rechnung; *settle an* **~** e-e Rechnung begleichen; *settle od. square* **~***s with*, *make up one's* **~** *with a. fig.* abrechnen mit; *square an* **~** ein Konto ausgleichen; *statement* 5; **6.** Rechenschaft(sbericht *m*) *f*: *bring to* **~** *fig.* abrechnen mit; *call to* **~** zur Rechenschaft ziehen; *give od. render an* **~** *of* Rechenschaft ablegen über (*acc.*) → 7; *give a good* **~** *of et.* gut erledigen, *Gegner* abfertigen; *give a good* **~** *of o.s.* s-e Sache gut machen, sich bewähren; **7.** Bericht *m*, Darstellung *f*, Beschreibung *f*: *by all* **~***s* nach allem, was man hört; *give od. render an* **~** *of* Bericht erstatten über (*acc.*) → 6; **8.** Liste *f*, Verzeichnis *n*; **9.** 'Umstände *pl.*, Erwägung *f*: *on* **~** *of* um ... willen, wegen; *on his* **~** seinetwegen; *on no* **~** keineswegs, unter keinen Umständen; *leave out of* **~** außer Betracht lassen; *take* **~** *of*, *take into* **~** Rechnung tragen (*dat.*), in Betracht ziehen, berücksichtigen; **10.** Wichtigkeit *f*, Wert *m*: *of no* **~** ohne Bedeutung; **11.** Vorteil *m*: *find one's* **~** *in* bei et. profitieren *od.* auf s-e Kosten kommen; *turn to* (*good*) **~** (gut) (aus)nutzen, Kapital schlagen aus; **ac·count·a·bil·i·ty** [ə͵kaʊntə'bɪlətɪ] *s.* Verantwortlichkeit *f*; **ac'count·a·ble** [-təbl] *adj.* ☐ **1.** verantwortlich, rechenschaftspflichtig (*to dat.*); **2.** erklärlich; **ac'count·an·cy** [-tənsɪ] *s.* Buchhaltung *f*; Buchführung *f*, Rechnungswesen *n*; *Brit.* Steuerberatung *f*; **ac'count·ant** [-tənt] *s.* **1.** (*a.* Bilanz)Buchhalter *m*, Rechnungsführer *m*; **2.** (*chartered od. certified* **~** amtlich zugelassener) Buchprüfer *od.* Steuerberater; *certified public* **~** *Am.* Wirtschaftsprüfer *m*; **3.** *Brit.* Steuerberater *m*; **ac'count·ing** [-tɪŋ] *s.* **1.** → *accountancy*; **2.** Abrechnung *f*: **~** *period* Abrechnungszeitraum *m*; **~** *year* Geschäftsjahr *n*.

ac·cou·tred [ə'kuːtəd] *adj.* ausgerüstet; **ac'cou·tre·ment** [-təmənt] *s. mst pl.* **1.** Kleidung *f*, Ausstattung *f*; **2.** ✗ Ausrüstung *f* (*außer Uniform u. Waffen*).

ac·cred·it [ə'kredɪt] *v/t.* **1.** *bsd. e-n Gesandten* akkreditieren, beglaubigen (*to* bei); **2.** bestätigen, als berechtigt anerkennen; **3.** **~** *s.th. to s.o. od. s.o. with s.th.* j-m et. zuschreiben.

ac·cre·tion [æ'kriːʃn] *s.* **1.** Zuwachs *m*, Zunahme *f*, Anwachsen *n*; **2.** ⚖ Anwachsung *f* (*Erbschaft*); (Land)Zuwachs *m*; **3.** ⚗ Zs.-wachsen *n*.

ac·cru·al [ə'kruːəl] *s.* ✝, ⚖ Anfall *m* (*Dividende, Erbschaft etc.*); Entstehung *f* (*Anspruch etc.*); Auflaufen *n* (*Zinsen*); Zuwachs *m*.

ac·crue [ə'kruː] *v/i.* erwachsen, entstehen, zufallen, zukommen (*to dat.*, *from, out of* aus): **~***d interest* aufgelaufene Zinsen *pl.*

ac·cu·mu·late [ə'kjuːmjʊleɪt] **I** *v/t.* ansammeln, anhäufen, aufspeichern (*a.* ☉), aufstauen; **II** *v/i.* anwachsen, sich anhäufen *od.* ansammeln *od.* akkumulieren, ☉ sich summieren; auflaufen (*Zinsen*); **ac·cu·mu·la·tion** [ə͵kjuːmjo'leɪʃn] *s.* Ansammlung *f*, Auf-, Anhäufung *f*, Akkumulation *f, a.* ☉ (Auf-)Speicherung *f, a. psych.* (Auf)Stauung *f*: **~** *of capital* ✝ Kapitalansammlung *f*; **~** *of interest* Auflaufen *n* von Zinsen; **~** *of property* Vermögensanhäufung *f*;

ac·cu·mu·la·tive [-lətɪv] *adj.* (sich) anhäufend *etc.*; Häufungs..., Zusatz..., Sammel...; **ac'cu·mu·la·tor** [-tə] *s.* Akkumu'lator *m*, 'Akku *m*, (Strom-) Sammler *m*.

ac·cu·ra·cy ['ækjurəsɪ] *s.* Genauigkeit *f*, Sorgfalt *f*, Präzisi'on *f*; Richtigkeit *f*, Ex'aktheit *f*; **'ac·cu·rate** [-rət] *adj.* □ **1.** genau; sorgfältig; pünktlich; **2.** richtig, zutreffend, ex'akt.

ac·curs·ed [ə'kɜːsɪd] *adj., a.* **ac'curst** [-st] *adj.* verflucht, verwünscht, F *a.* ‚verflixt‘.

ac·cu·sa·tion [ˌækjuːˈzeɪʃn] *s.* Anklage *f*, An-, Beschuldigung *f*: **bring an ~ against s.o.** e-e Anklage gegen j-n erheben; **ac·cu·sa·ti·val** [əˌkjuːzəˈtaɪvl] *adj.* □ ling. 'akkusativisch; **ac·cu·sa·tive** [ə'kjuːzətɪv] *s. a.* **~ case** 'Akkusativ *m*, 4. Fall.

ac·cuse [ə'kjuːz] *v/t. a.* ♱♱ anklagen, beschuldigen (**of** *gen.*; **before, to** bei); **ac'cused** [-zd] *s.* a) Angeklagte(r *m*) *f*, b) *die* Angeklagten *pl*; **ac'cus·ing** [-zɪŋ] *adj.* □ anklagend.

ac·cus·tom [ə'kʌstəm] *v/t.* gewöhnen (**to** an *acc.*): **be ~ed to do(ing) s.th.** gewohnt sein, et. zu tun, et. zu tun pflegen; **get ~ed to s.th.** sich an et. gewöhnen; **ac'cus·tomed** [-md] *adj.* **1.** gewohnt, üblich; **2.** gewöhnt (**to** an *acc.*, zu *inf.*).

ace [eɪs] I *s.* **1.** Ass *n* (*Spielkarte*): **an ~ in the hole** *Am.* F ein Trumpf in petto; **2.** Eins *f* (*Würfel*); **3.** *fig.* **he came within an ~ of losing** um ein Haar hätte er verloren; **4.** ✕ (Flieger)Ass *n*; **5.** *bsd. sport* ‚Ka'none‘ *f*, Ass *n*; **6.** *Tennis:* (Aufschlag)Ass *n*. II *adj.* **7.** her'vorragend, Spitzen..., Star...: **~ reporter**.

ac·er·bate ['æsəbeɪt] *v/t.* er-, verbittern; **a·cer·bi·ty** [ə'sɜːbətɪ] *s.* **1.** Herbheit *f*, Bitterkeit *f* (*a. fig.*); **2.** saurer Geschmack, Säure *f*; **3.** *fig.* Schärfe *f*, Heftigkeit *f*.

ac·e·tate ['æsɪteɪt] *s.* **1.** ♱ Ace'tat *n*, Aze'tat *n*; **2.** *a.* **~ rayon** Acetatseide *f*; **a·ce·tic** [ə'siːtɪk] *adj.* ♱ essigsauer: **~ acid** Essigsäure *f*; **a·cet·i·fy** [ə'setɪfaɪ] I *v/t.* in Essig verwandeln, säuern; II *v/i.* sauer werden; **a·cet·y·lene** [ə'setɪlɪn] *s.* ♱ Acety'len *n*: **~ welding** ⊕ Autogenschweißen *n*.

ache [eɪk] I *v/i.* **1.** schmerzen, wehtun; Schmerzen haben: **I am aching all over** mir tut alles weh; **2.** F sich sehnen (**for** nach), dar'auf brennen (**to do** *et.* zu tun); II *s.* **3.** (*anhaltender*) Schmerz *m*.

a·chieve [ə'tʃiːv] *v/t.* **1.** zu'stande bringen, voll'bringen, schaffen, leisten; **2.** erlangen; *Ziel* erreichen, *Erfolg* erzielen; **a'chieve·ment** [-mənt] *s.* **1.** Voll-'bringung *f*, Schaffung *f*, Zu'standebringen *n*; **2.** Erzielung *f*, Erreichen *n*; **3.** Erringung *f*; **4.** (Groß)Tat *f*, (große) Leistung, Errungenschaft *f*: **~-oriented** leistungsorientiert; **~ test** *psych.* Leistungstest *m*; **a'chiev·er** [-və] *s.* j-d, der es zu et. bringt.

A·chil·les [ə'kɪliːz] *npr.* A'chill(es) *m*: **~ heel** *fig.* Achillesferse *f*; **~ tendon** *anat.* Achillessehne *f*.

ach·ing ['eɪkɪŋ] *adj.* schmerzend.

ach·ro·ma·tic [ˌækrəʊ'mætɪk] *adj.* (□ **~ally**) **1.** *phys., biol.* achro'matisch, farblos: **~ lens**; **2.** ♪ dia'tonisch.

ac·id ['æsɪd] I *adj.* □ **1.** sauer, scharf (*Geschmack*): **~ drops** *Brit.* saure (Frucht)Bonbons, Drops; **2.** *fig.* bissig, beißend: **~ remark**; **3.** ♱, ⊕ säurehaltig, Säure...: **~ bath** Säurebad *n*; **~ rain** saurer Regen; II *s.* **4.** ♱ Säure *f*; **~-proof** ⊕ säurefest; **5.** *sl.* LS'D *n*: **~**

head LSD-Süchtiger *m*; **a·cid·i·fy** [ə'sɪdɪfaɪ] *v/t.* (an)säuern; in Säure verwandeln; **a·cid·i·ty** [ə'sɪdətɪ] *s.* **1.** Säure *f*, Schärfe *f*, Säuregehalt *m*; **2.** (‚überschüssige‘) Magensäure; **ac·id re·sist·ance** *s.* Säurefestigkeit *f*; **ac·id test** *s.* **1.** ♱, ♱ Scheide-, Säureprobe *f*; **2.** *fig.* strengste Prüfung, Feuerprobe *f*: **put to the ~** auf Herz u. Nieren prüfen.

a·cid·u·lat·ed [ə'sɪdjuleɪtɪd] *adj.* (an-) gesäuert: **~ drops** saure Bonbons; **a·cid·u·lous** [-ləs] *adj.* säuerlich; *fig.* → **acid 2.**

ack-ack [ˌæk'æk] *s.* ✕ *sl.* Flak(feuer *n*, -kanone[n *pl.*] *f*) *f*.

ack·em·ma [æk'emə] *Funkerwort für a.m. Brit. sl.* I *adv.* vormittags; II *s.* 'Flugzeug,me,chaniker *m*.

ac·knowl·edge [ək'nɒlɪdʒ] *v/t.* **1.** anerkennen; **2.** zugeben, einräumen; **3.** sich bekennen zu; **4.** (dankbar) anerkennen; sich erkenntlich zeigen für; **5.** *Empfang* bestätigen, quittieren; *Gruß* erwidern; **6.** ♱♱ *Urkunde* beglaubigen; **ac'knowl·edged** [-dʒd] *adj.* anerkannt; **ac'knowl·edg(e)·ment** [-mənt] *s.* **1.** Anerkennung *f*; **2.** Ein-, Zugeständnis *n*; **3.** Bekenntnis *n*; **4.** (lobende) Anerkennung; Erkenntlichkeit *f*, Dank *m* (**of** für); **5.** (Empfangs)Bestätigung *f*; **6.** ♱♱ Beglaubigungsklausel *f* (*Urkunde*).

ac·me ['ækmɪ] *s.* **1.** Gipfel *m*; *fig. a.* Höhepunkt *m*; **2.** ♪ 'Krisis *f*.

ac·ne ['æknɪ] *s.* ♪ 'Akne *f*.

ac·o·lyte ['ækəʊlaɪt] *s.* **1.** *eccl.* Messgehilfe *m*, Al'tardiener *m*; **2.** Gehilfe *m*; Anhänger *m*.

a·corn ['eɪkɔːn] *s.* ♀ Eichel *f*.

a·cous·tic *adj.*, **a·cous·ti·cal** [ə'kuːstɪk(l)] *adj.* □ ⊕, *phys.* a'kustisch, Schall..., *a.* Gehör..., Hör...: **~ engineering** Tontechnik *f*; **~ frequency** Hörfrequenz *f*; **~ nerve** Gehörnerv *m*; **a'cous·tics** [-ks] *s. pl. phys.* **1.** *mst sg. konstr.* A'kustik *f*, Lehre *f* vom Schall; **2.** *pl. konstr.* A'kustik *f* *e-s Raumes*.

ac·quaint [ə'kweɪnt] *v/t.* **1.** (*o.s.* sich) bekannt (*fig. a.* vertraut) machen (**with** mit); **2.** j-m mitteilen (**with a th.** et., **that** dass); **ac'quaint·ance** [-təns] *s.* **1.** (**with**) Bekanntschaft *f* (mit), Kenntnis *f* (von *od. gen.*): **make s.o.'s ~** j-n kennen lernen; **on closer ~** bei näherer Bekanntschaft; **2.** Bekanntschaft *f*: a) Bekannte(r *m*) *f*, b) Bekanntenkreis *m*: **an ~ of mine** eine(r) meiner Bekannten; **ac'quaint·ed** [-tɪd] *adj.* bekannt: **be ~ with** kennen; **become ~ with** j-n *od.* et. kennen lernen.

ac·qui·esce [ˌækwɪ'es] *v/i.* **1.** (*in*) sich fügen (in *acc.*), hinnehmen (*acc.*), dulden (*acc.*); **2.** einwilligen, ˌac·qui'es·cence [-sns] *s.* (*in*) Ergebung *f* (in *acc.*); Einwilligung *f* (in *acc.*); Nachgiebigkeit *f* (gegenüber); ˌac·qui'es·cent [-snt] *adj.* □ ergeben, fügsam.

ac·quire [ə'kwaɪə] *v/t.* (käuflich *etc.*) erwerben; erlangen, erreichen, gewinnen; *fig. a. Wissen etc.* erwerben, (er-) lernen, sich aneignen: **~d taste** anerzogener *od.* angewöhnter Geschmack; **ac'quire·ment** [-mənt] *s.* **1.** Erwerbung *f*; **2.** (erworbene) Fähig- *od.* Fertigkeit *f*; *pl.* Kenntnisse *pl.*

ac·qui·si·tion [ˌækwɪ'zɪʃn] *s.* **1.** Erwerbung *f*, Erwerb *m*; Kauf *m*, (Neu-) Anschaffung *f*; ♱ Übernahme *f* (*e-r Firma*); Errungenschaft *f*; **2.** Gewinn *m*, Bereicherung *f*: **~ cost(s** *pl.*) *s.* ♱ Anschaffungskosten *pl.*

ac·quis·i·tive [ə'kwɪzɪtɪv] *adj.* **1.** auf Erwerb gerichtet, gewinnsüchtig, Erwerbs...; **2.** (lern)begierig; **ac'quis·i·tive·ness** [-nɪs] *s.* Gewinnsucht *f*, Erwerbstrieb *m*.

ac·quit [ə'kwɪt] *v/t.* **1.** *Schuld* bezahlen, *Verbindlichkeit* erfüllen; **2.** entlasten; ♱♱ freisprechen (**of** von); **3.** (*of*) j-n e-r *Verpflichtung* entheben; **4.** **~ o.s.** (*of*) *Pflicht etc.* erfüllen; sich e-r *Aufgabe* entledigen: **~ o.s. well** s-e Sache gut machen; **ac'quit·tal** [-tl] *s.* **1.** ♱♱ Freisprechung *f*, Freispruch *m*; **2.** Erfüllung *f* *e-r Pflicht*; **ac'quit·tance** [-təns] *s.* **1.** Erfüllung *f* *e-r Verpflichtung*, Begleichung *f* *e-r Schuld*; **2.** Quittung *f*.

a·cre ['eɪkə] *s.* Acre *m* (4047 *qm*): **~s and ~s** weite Flächen; **a·cre·age** ['eɪkərɪdʒ] *s.* Fläche(ninhalt *m*) *f* (nach Acres).

ac·rid ['ækrɪd] *adj.* □ scharf, ätzend, beißend (*alle fig.*).

ac·ri·mo·ni·ous [ˌækrɪ'məʊnjəs] *adj.* □ *fig.* scharf, bitter, beißend; **ac·ri·mo·ny** ['ækrɪmənɪ] *s.* Schärfe *f*, Bitterkeit *f*.

ac·ro·bat ['ækrəbæt] *s.* Akro'bat *m*; **ac·ro·bat·ic, ac·ro·bat·i·cal** [ˌækrəʊ-'bætɪk(l)] *adj.* □ akro'batisch: **acrobatic flying** Kunstfliegen *n*; **ac·ro·batics** [ˌækrəʊ'bætɪks] *s. pl. mst sg. konstr.* Akro'batik *f*; akro'batische Kunststücke *pl.*; Kunstflug *m*.

ac·ro·nym ['ækrəʊnɪm] *s. ling.* Akro'nym *n*, Initi'alwort *n*.

a·cross [ə'krɒs] I *prp.* **1.** (quer *od.* mitten) durch; **2.** a) (quer) über (*acc.*), b) jenseits (*gen.*), auf der anderen Seite (*gen.*): **~ the street** über die Straße *od.* auf der gegenüberliegenden Straßenseite; **from ~ the lake** von jenseits des Sees; II *adv.* **3.** kreuzweise, über Kreuz; verschränkt; **4.** **ten feet ~** zehn Fuß im Durchmesser *od.* breit; **5.** (quer) hin- *od.* herüber, (quer) durch; → **come across** *etc.*; **6.** drüben, auf der anderen Seite; **a,cross-the--'board** *adj.* glo'bal, line'ar: **~ tax cut**.

a·cros·tic [ə'krɒstɪk] *s.* A'krostichon *n*.

a·cryl·ic [ə'krɪlɪk] ♱ I *s.* **1.** Ac'ryl *n*; **2.** *mst pl.* **acrylics** Ac'rylfarbe(n *pl.*) *f*; II *adj.* **3.** Ac'ryl...

act [ækt] I *s.* **1.** Tat *f*, Werk *n*, Handlung *f*, Maßnahme *f*, Akt *m*: **~ of force** Gewaltakt; **~ of God** ♱♱ höhere Gewalt; **~ of grace** Gnadenakt; **~ of state** (staatlicher) Hoheitsakt; **~ of war** kriegerische Handlung; (**sexual**) **~** Geschlechts-, Liebesakt; **catch s.o. in the ~** j-n auf frischer Tat ertappen; **get one's ~ together** F die Sache geregelt kriegen; **2.** ♱♱ a) *a.* **~ and deed** Urkunde *f*, Akte *f*, Willenserklärung *f*, b) Rechtshandlung *f*, c) Tathandlung *f*, d) (Straf)Tat *f*: → **bankruptcy 1**; **3.** *mst* ℒ Verordnung *f*, Gesetz *n*: ℒ **of Parliament** *Brit.*, ℒ **of Congress** *Am.* (verabschiedetes) Gesetz; **4.** ℒ**s** (**of the Apostles**) *pl. bibl.* Apostelgeschichte *f*; **5.** *thea.* Aufzug *m*, Akt *m*; **6.** Stück *n*, (Zirkus)Nummer *f*; **7.** F *fig.* Pose *f*, ‚Tour‘ *f*: **put on an ~** ‚Theater spielen‘; II *v/t.* **8.** aufführen, spielen; darstellen: **~ a part** e-e Rolle spielen; **~ the fool** a) sich wie ein Narr benehmen, b) sich dumm stellen; **~ one's part** s-e Pflicht tun; **~ out** F et. durchspielen; III *v/i.* **9.** (The'ater) spielen, auftreten; *fig.* ‚The'ater spielen‘; **10.** handeln, tätig sein *od.* werden, eingreifen: **~ as** fungieren *od.* amtieren *od.* dienen als; **~ in a case** in e-r Sache vorgehen; **~ for s.o.** für j-n handeln, j-n vertreten; **~ (up)on**

handeln *od.* sich richten nach; **11.** (*to-wards*) sich (*j-m* gegenüber) verhalten; **12.** *a.* 🔧, ☯ (*on*) (ein)wirken (auf *acc.*); **13.** funktionieren, gehen, arbeiten; **14.** ~ *up* F a) verrückt spielen (*Person od. Sache*), b) sich aufspielen; **'act·a·ble** [-təbl] *adj. thea.* bühnengerecht; **'act·ing** [-tɪŋ] **I** *adj.* **1.** handelnd, tätig; ~ *on your instructions* gemäß Ihren Anweisungen; **2.** stellvertretend, amtierend, geschäftsführend: *the ♌ Consul*; **3.** *thea.* spielend, Bühnen...: ~ *version* Bühnenfassung *f*; **II** *s.* **4.** Handeln *n*, A'gieren *n*; **5.** *thea.* Spiel(en) *n*, Aufführung *f*; Schauspielkunst *f*.

ac·tion ['ækʃn] *s.* **1.** Handeln *n*, Handlung *f*, Tat *f*, Akti'on *f*: *man of* ~ Mann *m* der Tat; *full of* ~ → *active* 1; *course of* ~ Handlungsweise *f*; *for further* ~ zur weiteren Veranlassung; ~ *committee pol.* Aktionskomitee *n*, (Bürger)Initiative *f*; *put into* ~ in die Tat umsetzen; *take* ~ Schritte unternehmen, handeln, et. *in e-r Angelegenheit* tun; *take* ~ *against* vorgehen gegen; → 9; **2.** *a.* ☯ a) Tätigkeit *f*, Gang *m*, Funktionieren *n*, b) Mecha'nismus *m*, Werk *n*: ~ *of the bowels* (*heart*) 🪶 Stuhlgang *m* (Herztätigkeit *f*); *put out of* ~ unfähig *od.* unbrauchbar machen, außer Betrieb setzen; → 10; ~! Film: Aufnahme!; **3.** *a.* 🔧, ☯, *phys.* (Ein)Wirkung *f*, Einfluss *m*; Vorgang *m*, Pro'zess *m*: the ~ *of acid on metal* die Einwirkung der Säure auf Metall; **4.** Handlung *f e-s Dramas*; **5.** Verhalten *n*, Benehmen *n*; **6.** Bewegung *f*, Gangart *f e-s Pferdes*; **7.** *rhet., thea.* Vortragsweise *f*, Ausdruck *m*; **8.** *Kunst u. fig.*: Action *f*, (dra'matisches) Geschehen: ~ *painting* Action-Painting *n*; *where the* ~ *is* F wo was los ist; **9.** ⚖ Klage *f*, Prozess *m*: *bring an* ~ *against j-n* verklagen; *take* ~ Klage erheben; → 1; **10.** ✕ Gefecht *n*, Kampf *m*, Einsatz *m*: *killed* (*wounded*) *in* ~ gefallen (verwundet); *go into* ~ eingreifen, in Aktion treten (*a. fig.*); *put out of* ~ außer Gefecht setzen (*a. sport etc.*; → 2); ~ *station* Gefechtsstation *f*; ~ *stations!* Alarm!; *he saw* ~ er war im Einsatz *od.* an der Front; **'ac·tion·able** [-ʃnəbl] *adj.* ⚖ (ein-, ver)klagbar; strafbar.

ac·ti·vate ['æktɪveɪt] *v/t* **1.** 🔧, ☯ aktivieren, in Betrieb setzen, (*a.* radio)ak'tiv machen; ~*d carbon* Aktivkohle *f*; **2.** ✕ *a*) *Truppen* aufstellen, b) *Zünder* scharf machen; **ac·ti·va·tion** [ˌæktɪ'veɪʃn] *s.* Aktivierung *f*.

ac·tive ['æktɪv] *adj.* □ **1.** tätig, emsig, geschäftig, rührig, lebhaft, tatkräftig, ak'tiv: *an* ~ *mind* ein reger Geist; ~ *volcano* tätiger Vulkan; *become* ~ in Aktion treten, aktiv werden; **2.** wirklich, tatsächlich: *take an* ~ *interest* reges Interesse zeigen; **3.** *a.* 🔧, 🪶, *biol., phys.* (schnell) wirkend, wirksam, ak'tiv: ~ *current* Wirkstrom *m*; **4.** ✝ produk'tiv, zinstragend (*Wertpapiere*): rege, lebhaft (*Markt*): ~ *balance* Aktivsaldo *m*; **5.** ✕ ak'tiv: *on* ~ *service*, *on the* ~ *list* im aktiven Dienst; **6.** *ling.* ak'tiv(isch): ~ *verb* aktivisch konstruiertes Verb; ~ *voice* Aktiv *n*, Tatform *f*; **'ac·tiv·ism** [-ɪzəm] *s.* Akti'vismus *m*; **'ac·tiv·ist** [-vɪst] *s. pol.* Akti'vist *m*; **ac·tiv·i·ty** [æk'tɪvətɪ] *s.* **1.** Tätigkeit *f*, Betätigung *f*; Rührigkeit *f*; *pl.* Leben *n* u. Treiben *n*, Unter'nehmungen *pl.*, Veranstaltungen *pl.*: *social activities*; *political activities* politische Betätigung(en *pl.*) *f od.* Aktivitäten *od. b.s.* Umtriebe *pl.*; *in full* ~ in vollem Gang;

~ *holiday* Aktivurlaub *m*; **2.** Lebhaftigkeit *f*, Beweglichkeit *f*; Betrieb(samkeit *f*) *m*, Aktivi'tät *f*; **3.** Wirksamkeit *f*.

ac·tor ['æktə] *s.* **1.** Schauspieler *m*; **2.** *fig.* Ak'teur *m*, Täter *m* (*a.* 🪶); '~-,**man·ag·er** *s.* The'aterdi,rektor, der selbst Rollen über'nimmt.

ac·tress ['æktrɪs] *s.* Schauspielerin *f*.

ac·tu·al ['æktʃʊəl] *adj.* □ **1.** wirklich, tatsächlich, eigentlich: *an* ~ *case* ein konkreter Fall; ~ *power* ☯ effektive Leistung; **2.** gegenwärtig, jetzig: ~ *cost* ✝ Istkosten *pl.*; ~ *inventory* (*od. stock*) Istbestand *m*; **ac·tu·al·i·ty** [ˌæktʃʊ'ælətɪ] *s.* **1.** Wirklichkeit *f*; **2.** *pl.* Tatsachen *pl.*, Gegebenheiten *pl.*; **ac·tu·a·lize** ['æktʃʊəlaɪz] **I** *v/t.* **1.** verwirklichen; **2.** rea'listisch darstellen; **II** *v/i.* **3.** sich verwirklichen; **'ac·tu·al·ly** [-lɪ] *adv.* **1.** wirklich, tatsächlich; **2.** augenblicklich, jetzt; **3.** so'gar, tatsächlich (*obwohl nicht erwartet*); **4.** F eigentlich (*unbetont*): *what time is it* ~?

ac·tu·ar·i·al [ˌæktjʊ'eərɪəl] *adj.* ver'sicherungssta,tistisch; **ac·tu·ar·y** ['æktjʊərɪ] *s.* Ver'sicherungssta,tistiker *m*, -mathe,matiker *m*.

ac·tu·ate ['æktjʊeɪt] *v/t.* **1.** in Gang bringen; **2.** antreiben, anreizen; **3.** ☯ betätigen, auslösen; **ac·tu·a·tion** [ˌæktjʊ'eɪʃn] *s.* Anstoß *m*, Antrieb *m* (*a.* ☯); ☯ Betätigung *f*.

a·cu·i·ty [ə'kjuːətɪ] *s.* Schärfe *f* (*a. fig.*); → *acuteness* 3.

a·cu·men [ə'kjuːmen] *s.* Scharfsinn *m*.

ac·u·pres·sure ['ækjʊˌpreʃə] *s.* 🪶 Akupres'sur *f*; **'ac·u·punc·ture** [-ˌpʌŋktʃə] 🪶 **I** *s.* Akupunk'tur *f*; **II** *v/t.* akupunktieren; ,**ac·u'punc·tur·ist** [-ˈpʌŋktʃərɪst] *s.* Akupunk'teur *m*.

a·cute [ə'kjuːt] *adj.* □ **1.** scharf; *bsd. A* spitz: ~ *triangle* spitzwink(e)liges Dreieck; → *angle¹* 2; **2.** scharf (*Sehvermögen*); heftig (*Schmerz, Freude etc.*); fein (*Gehör*); a'kut, brennend (*Frage*): bedenklich: ~ *shortage* 3. scharfsinnig, schlau; **4.** schrill, 'durchdringend; **5.** 🪶 a'kut, heftig; **6.** *ling.* ~ *accent* A'kut *m*; **a'cute·ness** [-nɪs] *s.* **1.** Schärfe *f*, Heftigkeit *f*, A'kutheit *f* (*a.* 🪶); **2.** Scharfsinnigkeit *f*.

ad [æd] *s. abbr. für advertisement*: *small* ~ Kleinanzeige *f*.

ad·age ['ædɪdʒ] *s.* Sprichwort *n*.

Ad·am ['ædəm] *npr.* 'Adam *m*: *I don't know him from* ~ F ich kenne ihn überhaupt nicht; *cast off the old* ~ F den alten Adam ausziehen; ~*'s ale* F ,Gänsewein' *m*; ~*'s apple* Adamsapfel *m*.

ad·a·mant ['ædəmənt] *adj.* **1.** steinhart; **2.** *fig.* unerbittlich, unnachgiebig, eisern (*to* gegenüber).

a·dapt [ə'dæpt] **I** *v/t.* **1.** anpassen, angleichen (*for, to* an *acc.*), *a.* ☯ 'umstellen (*to* auf *acc.*), zu'rechtmachen: ~ *the means to the end* die Mittel dem Zweck anpassen; **2.** anwenden (*to* auf *acc.*); **3.** *Text* bearbeiten: ~*ed from English* nach dem Englischen bearbeitet; ~*ed from* (frei) nach; **II** *v/i.* **4.** sich anpassen (*to dat. od.* an *acc.*); **a·dapt·a·bil·i·ty** [əˌdæptə'bɪlətɪ] *s.* **1.** Anpassungsfähigkeit *f* (*to* an *acc.*); **2.** (*to*) Anwendbarkeit *f* (*auf acc.*), Verwendbarkeit *f* (*für, zu*); **a'dapt·a·ble** [-təbl] *adj.* **1.** anpassungsfähig (*to* an *acc.*); **2.** anwendbar (*to* auf *acc.*); **3.** verwendbar (*to* für); **ad·ap·ta·tion** [ˌædæp'teɪʃn] *s.* **1.** *a. biol.* Anpassung *f* (*to* an *acc.*); **2.** Anwendung *f*; **3.** *thea. etc.* Bearbeitung *f* (*from* nach, *to* für); **a'dapt·er** [-tə] *s.* **1.** *thea. etc.* Bearbeiter *m*; **2.** *phys.* A'dapter *m*, Anpassungs-

vorrichtung *f*; **3.** ☯ Zwischen-, Pass-, Anschlussstück *n*, Vorsatzgerät *n*; ⚡ Zwischenstecker *m*; **a'dap·tive** [-tɪv] *adj.* → *adaptable* 1; **a'dap·tor** [-tə] → *adapter*.

add [æd] **I** *v/t.* **1.** (*to*) hin'zufügen, -rechnen (zu); 🪶 beimischen, zufügen (*dat.*): *he* ~*ed that ...* er fügte hinzu, dass ...; ~ *to this that ...* hinzu kommt, dass ...; **2.** *a.* ~ *up od. together* addieren, zs.-zählen; **3.** ✝, 🅰, ☯ aufschlagen: ~ *5% to the price* 5% auf den Preis aufschlagen; **II** *v/i.* **4.** ~ *to* hin'zukommen zu, beitragen zu, vermehren (*acc.*); **5.** ~ *up* a) 🅰 aufgehen, stimmen (*a. fig.*), b) *fig.* e-n Sinn ergeben, ,hinhauen'; ~ *up to* a) sich belaufen auf (*acc.*), b) *fig.* hinauslaufen auf (*acc.*), bedeuten; **add·ed** ['ædɪd] *adj.* vermehrt, erhöht, zusätzlich: ~ *value* ✝ Wertschöpfung *f*.

ad·den·dum [ə'dendəm] *pl.* **-da** [-də] *s.* Zusatz *m*, Nachtrag *m*.

ad·der ['ædə] *s. zo.* Natter *f*, Otter *f*, 'Viper *f*: *common* ~ Gemeine Kreuzotter.

ad·dict **I** *s.* ['ædɪkt] **1.** Süchtige(r *m*) *f*: *alcohol* (*drug*) ~; **2.** *humor.* (*Fußball-etc.*)Fan *m*; (*Film- etc.*)Narr *m*; **II** *v/t.* [ə'dɪkt] **3.** ~ *o.s.* sich hingeben (*to s.th.* e-r Sache); **4.** *j-n* süchtig machen, *j-n* gewöhnen (*to an Rauschgift etc.*); **III** *v/i.* **5.** süchtig machen; **ad'dict·ed** [-tɪd] *adj.* süchtig, abhängig (*to* von), verfallen (*to dat.*): ~ *to drugs* (*television*) drogen- *od.* rauschgift- (fernseh-)süchtig; *be* ~ *to films* (*football*) ein Filmnarr (Fußballfanatiker) sein; **ad·dic·tion** [ə'dɪkʃən] *s.* **1.** Hingabe *f* (*to an acc.*); **2.** Sucht *f*, (*Zustand*) *a.* Süchtigkeit *f*: ~ *to drugs* (*television*) Drogen- *od.* Rauschgift- (Fernseh)Sucht *f*; **ad·dic·tive** [ə'dɪktɪv] *adj.* Sucht erzeugend: *be* ~ süchtig machen; ~ *drug* Suchtmittel *n*.

add·ing ma·chine ['ædɪŋ] *s.* Ad'dier-, Additi'onsma,schine *f*.

ad·di·tion [ə'dɪʃn] *s.* **1.** Hin'zufügung *f*, Ergänzung *f*, Zusatz *m*, Beigabe *f*: *in* ~ noch dazu, außerdem; *in* ~ *to* außer (*dat.*), zusätzlich zu; **2.** Vermehrung *f* (*to gen.*), (*Familien-, Vermögens- etc.*) Zuwachs *m*: *recent* ~*s* Neuerwerbungen; **3.** 🅰 Additi'on *f*, Zs.-zählen *n*: ~ *sign* Pluszeichen *n*; **4.** ✝ Auf-, Zuschlag *m*; **5.** 🔧, ☯ Zusatz *m*, Beimischung *f*; ☯ Anbau *m*, Zusatz *m*; **6.** *Am.* neu erschlossenes Baugelände; **ad'di·tion·al** [-ʃənl] *adj.* □ **1.** zusätzlich, ergänzend, weiter(er, -e, -es); **2.** Zusatz..., Mehr..., Extra..., Über..., Nach...: ~ *charge* ✝ Auf-, Zuschlag *m*; ~ *charges* ✝ Mehrkosten; ~ *postage* Nachporto *n*; **ad'di·tion·al·ly** [-ʃnəlɪ] *adv.* zusätzlich, in verstärktem Maße, außerdem; **ad'di·tive** ['ædɪtɪv] **I** *adj.* zusätzlich; **II** *s.* Zusatz *m* (*a.* 🪶).

ad·dle ['ædl] **I** *v/i.* **1.** faul werden, verderben (*Ei*); **II** *v/t.* **2.** *Ei* verderben; **3.** *Verstand* verwirren; **III** *adj.* **4.** unfruchtbar, faul (*Ei*); **5.** verwirrt, kon'fus; '~·**brain** *s.* Hohlkopf *m*; '~-,**head·ed**, '~-,**pat·ed** *adj.* **1.** hohlköpfig; **2.** → *addle* 5.

add-on *s. Computer:* Zusatzgerät *n*: ~ *board* Erweiterungsplatine *f*.

ad·dress [ə'dres] **I** *v/t.* **1.** *Worte etc.* richten (*to* an *acc.*), *j-n* anreden (*as* als); *Brief* adressieren, richten, schreiben (*to* an *acc.*); **2.** e-e Ansprache halten an (*acc.*); **3.** *Waren* (ab)senden (*to* an *acc.*); **4.** ~ *o.s.* to sich zuwenden (*dat.*), sich an *et.* machen; sich anschicken zu; sich an *j-n* wenden; **II** *s.* **5.** Anrede *f*; Ansprache *f*, Rede *f*; **6.** A'dresse *f*, Anschrift *f*: *change one's* ~ s-e Adresse ändern, umziehen; ~ *label* Adressaufkleber *m*; ~ *tag* Kofferanhänger *m*; **7.** Eingabe *f*, Bitt-, Dankschrift *f*, Er'gebenheitsa,dresse *f*: *the ⚹ Brit. parl.* die Erwiderung des Parlaments auf die Thronrede; **8.** Lebensart *f*, Manieren *pl.*; **9.** Geschick *n*, Gewandtheit *f*; **10.** *pl.* Huldigungen *pl.*: *pay one's ~es to a lady* e-r Dame den Hof machen; **ad·dress·ee** [ˌædreˈsiː] *s.* Adres'sat *m*, Empfänger(in).

ad·duce [əˈdjuːs] *v/t. Beweis etc.* bei-, erbringen.

ad·e·noid [ˈædɪnɔɪd] *⚕* **I** *adj.* die Drüsen betreffend, Drüsen..., drüsenartig; **II** *mst pl.* Po'lypen *pl.* (*in der Nase*); (Rachenmandel)Wucherungen *pl.*

ad·ept [ˈædept] **I** *s.* **1.** Meister *m*, Ex'perte *m* (*at, in* in *dat.*); **2.** A'dept *m*, Anhänger *m* (*e-r Lehre*); **II** *adj.* **3.** erfahren, geschickt (*at, in* in *dat.*).

ad·e·qua·cy [ˈædɪkwəsɪ] *s.* Angemessenheit *f*, Zulänglichkeit *f*; **ad·e·quate** [ˈædɪkwət] *adj.* ☐ **1.** angemessen, entsprechend (*to dat.*); **2.** aus-, 'hinreichend, genügend.

ad·here [ədˈhɪə] *v/i.* (*to*) **1.** kleben, haften (an *dat.*); **2.** *fig.* festhalten (an *dat.*), *Regel etc.* einhalten, sich halten (an *e-e Regel etc.*), bleiben (bei *e-r Meinung, e-r Gewohnheit, e-m Plan*), *j-m, e-r Partei, e-r Sache etc.* treu bleiben, halten (zu *j-m*); **3.** angehören (*dat.*); **ad·her·ence** [-ərəns] *s.* (*to*) **1.** (An-, Fest)Haften *n* (an *dat.*); **2.** Anhänglichkeit *f* (an *dat.*); **3.** Festhalten *n* (an *dat.*), Befolgung *f*, Einhaltung (*e-r Regel*); **ad·her·ent** [-ərənt] **I** *adj.* **1.** (an-) haftend, (an)klebend; **2.** *fig.* festhaltend, (fest) verbunden (*to* mit), anhänglich; **II** *s.* **3.** Anhänger(in).

ad·he·sion [ədˈhiːʒn] *s.* **1.** (An-, Fest)Haften *n* (*to an dat.*); ⊛ *phys.* Haftvermögen *n*, Klebkraft *f*, Adhäsi'on *f*; **2.** *fig.* → *adherence* 2, 3; **3.** Beitritt *m*; Einwilligung *f*; **ad·he·sive** [-sɪv] **I** *adj.* ☐ **1.** (an)haftend, klebend, gummiert, Klebe...: ~ *foil* Selbstklebefolie *f*; ~ *plaster* Heftpflaster *n*; ~ *powder* Haftpulver *n*; ~ *tape* a) Heftpflaster *n*, b) Klebstreifen *m*; ~ *rubber* Klebgummi *m*, *n*; **2.** gar zu anhänglich, aufdringlich; **3.** ⊛, *phys.* haftend, Adhäsions...: ~ *power* → *adhesion* 1; **II** *s.* **4.** Bindemittel *n*, Klebstoff *m*.

ad hoc [ˌædˈhɒk] (*Lat.*) *adv. u. adj.* ad hoc, (eigens) zu diesem Zweck (gemacht), spezi'ell; Augenblicks..., Ad-hoc-...

a·dieus, a·dieux [əˈdjuːz] *pl.* Lebe'wohl *n*: *make one's* ~ Lebewohl sagen.

ad in·fi·ni·tum [ˌæd ɪnfɪˈnaɪtəm] (*Lat.*) *adv.* endlos, ad infi'nitum.

a·di·pose [ˈædɪpəʊs] **I** *adj.* fett(haltig), Fett...: ~ *tissue* Fettgewebe *n*; **II** *s.* (Körper)Fett *n*.

ad·it [ˈædɪt] *s.* **1.** *bsd.* ⚒ Zugang *m*, Stollen *m*; **2.** *fig.* Zutritt *m*.

ad·ja·cent [əˈdʒeɪsənt] *adj.* ☐ angrenzend, -liegend, -stoßend (*to* an *acc.*); benachbart (*dat.*), Nachbar..., Neben...: ~ *angle* ᴋ Nebenwinkel *m*.

ad·jec·ti·val [ˌædʒekˈtaɪvl] *adj.* ☐ 'adjektivisch; **ad·jec·tive** [ˈædʒɪktɪv] **I** *s.* **1.** 'Adjektiv *n*, Eigenschaftswort *n*; **II** *adj.* ☐ **2.** 'adjektivisch; **3.** abhängig; **4.** *Färberei:* 'adjektiv: ~ *dye* Beizfarbe *f*; **5.** ᴋ for'mell (*Recht*).

ad·join [əˈdʒɔɪn] **I** *v/t.* **1.** (an)stoßen *od.* (an)grenzen an (*acc.*); **2.** beifügen (*to*

dat.); **II** *v/i.* **3.** angrenzen; **ad·join·ing** [-nɪŋ] *adj.* angrenzend, benachbart, Nachbar..., Neben...

ad·journ [əˈdʒɜːn] **I** *v/t.* **1.** aufschieben, vertagen: ~ *sine die* ᴋ auf unbestimmte Zeit vertagen; **2.** *Sitzung etc.* schließen; **II** *v/i.* **3.** *a.* *stand* ~*ed* sich vertagen; **4.** den Sitzungsort verlegen (*to* nach): ~ *to the sitting room* F sich ins Wohnzimmer zurückziehen; **ad·'journ·ment** [-mənt] *s.* **1.** Vertagung *f*, Verschiebung *f*; **2.** Verlegung *f* des Sitzungsortes.

ad·judge [əˈdʒʌdʒ] *v/t.* **1.** ᴋ entscheiden (über *acc.*), erkennen (für), für *schuldig etc.* erklären, *ein Urteil fällen:* ~ *s.o. bankrupt* über j-s Vermögen den Konkurs eröffnen; **2.** ᴋ, *a.* *sport* zuerkennen; zusprechen; **3.** verurteilen (*to* zu).

ad·ju·di·cate [əˈdʒuːdɪkeɪt] **I** *v/t.* **1.** gerichtlich *od.* als Schiedsrichter entscheiden, ein Urteil fällen über (*acc.*): ~*d bankrupt* Gemeinschuldner *m*; **II** *v/i.* **2.** (zu Recht) erkennen, entscheiden (*upon* über *acc.*); **3.** als Schieds- *od.* Preisrichter fungieren (*at* bei); **ad·ju·di·ca·tion** [əˌdʒuːdɪˈkeɪʃn] *s.* **1.** richterliche Entscheidung, Urteil *n*; **2.** Zuerkennung *f*; **3.** Kon'kurseröffnung *f*.

ad·junct [ˈædʒʌŋkt] *s.* **1.** Zusatz *m*, Beigabe *f*, Zubehör *n*; **2.** *ling.* Attri'but *n*, Beifügung *f*; **ad·junc·tive** [əˈdʒʌŋktɪv] *adj.* ☐ beigeordnet, verbunden.

ad·ju·ra·tion [ˌædʒʊˈreɪʃn] *s.* **1.** Beschwörung *f*, inständige Bitte; **2.** Auferlegung *f* des Eides; **ad·jure** [əˈdʒʊə] *v/t.* **1.** beschwören, inständig bitten; **2.** *j-m* den Eid auferlegen.

ad·just [əˈdʒʌst] **I** *v/t.* **1.** in Ordnung bringen, ordnen, regulieren, abstimmen; berichtigen; **2.** anpassen (*a. psych.*), angleichen (*to dat., an acc.*); **3.** ~ *o.s.* (*to*) sich anpassen (*dat., an acc.*) *od.* einfügen (in *acc.*) *od.* einstellen (auf *acc.*); **4.** ✝ *Konto etc.* bereinigen; *Schaden etc.* berechnen, festsetzen; **5.** *Streit* schlichten; **6.** ⊛ an-, einpassen, (ein-, ver-, nach)stellen, richten, regulieren; *a.* *Gewehr etc.* justieren; **7.** *Maße* eichen; **II** *v/i.* **8.** sich anpassen; **9.** sich einstellen lassen; **ad·'just·a·ble** [-təbl] *adj.* ☐ *bsd.* ⊛ regulierbar, ein-, nach-, verstellbar, Lenk..., Dreh..., Stell...: ~ *speed* regelbare Drehzahl; **ad·'just·er** [-tə] *s.* **1.** j-d der *od.* et. was regelt, ausgleicht, ordnet; Schlichter *m*; **2.** *Versicherung:* Schadenssachverständige(r) *m*; **ad·'just·ing** [-tɪŋ] *adj. bsd.* ⊛ (Ein)Stell..., Richt..., Justier...: ~ *balance* Justierwaage *f*; ~ *lever* (Ein)Stellhebel *m*; ~ *screw* Stellschraube *f*; ~ *entry* Berichtigungsbuchung *f*; ~ *payment* Ausgleichszahlung *f*; **ad·'just·ment** [-tmənt] *s.* **1.** *a.* ᴋ, *psych. etc.* Anpassung *f* (*to* an *acc.*): ~ *period* Anpassungszeitraum *m*; **2.** Regelung *f*, Berichtigung *f*, Abstimmung *f*, Ausgleich *m*; **3.** Schlichtung *f*, Beilegung *f* (*e-s Streits*); **4.** ⊛ Ein-, Nach-, Verstellung *f*; Einstellvorrichtung *f*; Berichtigung *f*; Regulierung *f*; Eichung *f*; **5.** Berechnung *f* von Schadens(ersatz)ansprüchen.

ad·ju·tant [ˈædʒʊtənt] *s.* ✗ Adju'tant *m*; ~ *gen·er·al* *pl.* ~*s gen·er·al* *s.* ✗ Gene'raladju,tant *m*.

ad-lib [ˌædˈlɪb] **I** *v/i. u. v/t.* F improvisieren, aus dem Stegreif sagen; **II** *adj.* Stegreif..., improvisiert.

ad lib·i·tum [ˌæd ˈlɪbɪtəm] (*Lat.*) *adj. u. adv.* ad libitum: a) nach Belieben, b)

aus dem Stegreif.

ad·man [ˈædmæn] *s.* [*irr.*] F **1.** Anzeigen-, Werbetexter *m*; **2.** Anzeigenvertreter *m*; **3.** *typ.* Akzi'denzsetzer *m*; **ad·mass** [ˈædmæs] *s.* **1.** Kon'sumbeeinflussung *f*; **2.** werbungsmanipulierte Gesellschaft.

ad·min [ˈædmɪn] *s.* F Verwaltung *f*.

ad·min·is·ter [ədˈmɪnɪstə] *v/t.* **1.** verwalten; **2.** ausüben, handhaben: ~ *justice* (*od. the law*) Recht sprechen; ~ *punishment* Strafe(n) verhängen; **3.** verabreichen, erteilen (*to dat.*): ~ *medicine* Arznei (ein)geben; ~ *a shock* e-n Schrecken einjagen; ~ *an oath* e-n Eid abnehmen; ~ *the Blessed Sacrament* das heilige Sakrament spenden; **II** *v/i.* **4.** als Verwalter fungieren; **5.** *obs.* beitragen (*to* zu); **ad·min·is·trate** [ədˈmɪnɪstreɪt] *v/t. u. v/i.* verwalten; **ad·min·is·tra·tion** [ədˌmɪnɪˈstreɪʃn] *s.* **1.** (*Betriebs-, Vermögens-, Nachlass-, etc.*)Verwaltung *f*; **2.** Verwaltung(sbehörde) *f*, Mini'sterium *n*; Staatsverwaltung *f*, Regierung *f*; **3.** *Am.* 'Amtsperi,ode *f* (*bsd. e-s Präsidenten*); **4.** Handhabung *f*, 'Durchführung *f*: ~ *of justice* Rechtsprechung *f*; ~ *of an oath* Eidesabnahme *f*; **5.** Aus-, Erteilung *f*; Verabreichung *f* (*Arznei*); Spendung *f* (*Sakrament*); **ad·min·is·tra·tive** [-trətɪv] *adj.* ☐ verwaltend, Verwaltungs..., Regierungs...: ~ *body* Behörde *f*, Verwaltungskörper *m*; **ad·min·is·tra·tiv·i·a** [ədˌmɪnɪstrəˈtɪvɪə] *pl.* (*als sg. konstr.*) *coll.* F Verwaltungskram *m*; **ad·min·is·tra·tor** [-treɪtə] *s.* **1.** Verwalter *m*, Verwaltungsbeamte(r) *m*; **2.** ᴋ Nachlass-, Vermögensverwalter *m*; **ad·min·is·tra·trix** [-treɪtrɪks] *pl.* **-trices** [-trɪsiːz] *s.* (Nachlass)Verwalterin *f*.

ad·mi·ra·ble [ˈædmərəbl] *adj.* ☐ bewundernswert, großartig.

ad·mi·ral [ˈædmərəl] *s.* **1.** Admi'ral *m*: ⚹ *of the Fleet* Großadmiral; **2.** *zo.* Admi'ral *m* (*Schmetterling*); **ad·mi·ral·ty** [-tɪ] *s.* **1.** Admi'ralsamt *n*, -würde *f*; **2.** Admirali'tät *f*: *Lords Commissioners of ⚹* (*od. Board of ⚹*) *Brit.* Marineministerium *n*; *First Lord of the ⚹* (britischer) Marineminister; ~ *law* ᴋ Seerecht *n*; **3.** *⚹ Brit.* Admiralitätsgebäude *n* (*in London*).

ad·mi·ra·tion [ˌædməˈreɪʃn] *s.* Bewunderung *f* (*of, for* für): *she was the* ~ *of everyone* sie wurde von allen bewundert.

ad·mire [ədˈmaɪə] *v/t.* **1.** bewundern (*for* wegen); **2.** hoch schätzen, verehren; **ad·mir·er** [-ərə] *s.* Bewunderer *m*; Verehrer *m*; **ad·mir·ing** [-ərɪŋ] *adj.* ☐ bewundernd.

ad·mis·si·bil·i·ty [ədˌmɪsəˈbɪlətɪ] *s.* Zulässigkeit *f*; **ad·mis·si·ble** [ədˈmɪsəbl] *adj.* **1.** *a.* ᴋ zulässig; statthaft; **2.** würdig, zugelassen zu werden; **ad·mis·sion** [ədˈmɪʃn] *s.* **1.** Einlass *m*, Ein-, Zutritt *m*: *gain* ~ Einlass finden; ~ *free* Eintritt frei; ~ *ticket* Eintrittskarte *f*; **2.** Eintrittserlaubnis *f*; *a.* ~ *fee* Eintritt(s-geld *n*, -gebühr *f*) *m*; **3.** Zulassung *f*, Aufnahme *f* (*als Mitglied etc.*; *Am. a. e-s Staates in die Union*): *⚹ Day* Jahrestag *m* der Aufnahme in die Union; **4.** Ernennung *f*; **5.** Eingeständnis *n*, Einräumung *f*: *by* (*od. on*) *his own* ~ wie er selbst zugibt *od.* zugab; **6.** ⊛ Eintritt *m*, -lass *m*, Zufuhr *f*: ~ *stroke* Einlasshub *m*.

ad·mit [ədˈmɪt] **I** *v/t.* **1.** zu-, ein-, vorlassen: ~ *bearer* dem Inhaber *dieser Karte* ist der Eintritt gestattet; ~ *s.o. into* one's confidence j-n ins Vertrauen ziehen; **2.** Platz haben für, fassen: *the theatre ~s 800 persons*; **3.** *als Mitglied in e-e Gemeinschaft, Schule etc.* aufnehmen; *in ein Krankenhaus* einliefern, *zu e-m Amt etc.* zulassen: → *bar* 10; **4.** gelten lassen, anerkennen, zugeben: *I ~ this to be wrong* od. *that this is wrong* ich gebe zu, dass dies falsch ist; *~ a claim* e-e Reklamation anerkennen; **5.** ⚖ a) für amtsfähig erklären, b) als rechtsgültig anerkennen; **6.** ⚙ zuführen, einlassen; **7.** *~* of gestatten, *a. weitS. Zweifel etc.* zulassen: *it ~s of no excuse* es lässt sich nicht entschuldigen; **ad'mit·tance** [-təns] *s.* **1.** Zulassung *f*, Einlass *m*, Zutritt *m*: *no ~* (*except on business*) Zutritt (für Unbefugte) verboten; **2.** Aufnahme *f*; **3.** ⚡ Admit'tanz *f*, Scheinleitwert *m*; **ad'mit·ted** [-tɪd] *adj.* □ anerkannt, zugegeben: *an ~ fact; an ~ thief* anerkanntermaßen ein Dieb; **ad'mit·ted·ly** [-tɪdlɪ] *adv.* anerkanntermaßen, zugegeben(ermaßen).

ad·mix [əd'mɪks] *v/t.* beimischen (*with dat.*); **ad'mix·ture** [-tʃə] *s.* Beimischung *f*, Mischung *f*; Zusatz(stoff) *m*.

ad·mon·ish [əd'mɒnɪʃ] **1.** *v/t.* (er-)mahnen, *j-m* dringend raten (*to inf.* od. *inf., that* dass); **2.** *j-m* Vorhaltungen machen (*of* od. *about* wegen *gen.*); **3.** warnen (*not to inf.* davor, *zu inf.* od. *of* vor *dat.*): *he was ~ed not to go* er wurde davor gewarnt zu gehen; **ad·mo·ni·tion** [,ædmə'nɪʃn] *s.* **1.** Ermahnung *f*; **2.** Warnung *f*, Verweis *m*; **ad'mon·i·to·ry** [-ɪtərɪ] *adj.* ermahnend, warnend.

ad nau·se·am [,æd 'nɔːzɪæm] (*Lat.*) *adv.* (bis) zum Erbrechen.

ad·noun [ædnaʊn] *s. ling.* Attri'but *n*.

a·do [ə'duː] *s.* Getue *n*, Wirbel *m*, Mühe *f*: *much ~ about nothing* viel Lärm um nichts; *without more ~* ohne weitere Umstände.

a·do·be [ə'dəʊbɪ] *s.* Lehmstein(haus *n*) *m*, Luftziegel *m*, A'dobe *m*.

ad·o·les·cence [,ædəʊ'lesns] *s.* jugendliches Alter, Adoles'zenz *f*; **,ad·o'les·cent** [-nt] **I** *s.* Jugendliche(r *m*) *f*, Heranwachsende(r *m*) *f*; **II** *adj.* her'anwachsend, jugendlich; Jünglings...

A·do·nis [ə'dəʊnɪs] *npr. antiq. u. s. fig.* A'donis *m*.

a·dopt [ə'dɒpt] *v/t.* **1.** adoptieren, (an Kindes statt) annehmen: *~ out Am.* zur Adoption freigeben; **2.** *fig.* annehmen, über'nehmen, einführen, sich *ein Verfahren etc.* zu eigen machen; *Handlungsweise* wählen; *Maßregeln* ergreifen; **3.** *pol. e-r Gesetzesvorlage* zustimmen; **4.** *~ a town* die Patenschaft für e-e Stadt über'nehmen; **5.** *pol. e-n Kandidaten (für die nächste Wahl)* annehmen; **6.** F sti'bitzen; **a'dopt·ed** [-tɪd] *adj. an Kindes statt* angenommen, Adoptiv...: *his ~ country* s-e Wahlheimat; **a'dop·tion** [-pʃn] *s.* **1.** Adopti'on *f*, Annahme *f (an Kindes statt)*; **2.** Aufnahme *f in e-e Gemeinschaft*; **3.** *fig.* Annahme *f*, Aneignung *f*, 'Übernahme *f*, Wahl *f*; **a'dop·tive** [-tɪv] → *adopted*: *~ parents* Adoptiveltern.

a·dor·a·ble [ə'dɔːrəbl] *adj.* □ **1.** anbetungswürdig; liebenswert; **2.** allerliebst, entzückend; **ad·o·ra·tion** [,ædə'reɪʃn] *s.* **1.** *a. fig.* Anbetung *f*, Verehrung *f*; **2.** *fig.* (innige) Liebe, (tiefe) Bewunderung; **a·dore** [ə'dɔː] *v/t.* **1.** anbeten (*a. fig.*); **2.** *fig.* (innig) lieben, (heiß) verehren, (tief) bewundern; **3.** schwärmen für; **a'dor·er** [-rə] *s.* Anbeter(in); Ver-

ehrer(in); Bewunderer *m*; **a'dor·ing** [-rɪŋ] *adj.* □ anbetend, bewundernd, schmachtend.

a·dorn [ə'dɔːn] *v/t.* **1.** schmücken, zieren (*a. fig.*); **2.** *fig.* verschöne(r)n, Glanz verleihen (*dat*); **a'dorn·ment** [-mənt] *s.* Schmuck *m*, Verzierung *f*; Zierde *f*, Verschönerung *f*.

ad·re·nal [ə'driːnl] *anat.* **I** *adj.* Nebennieren...: *~ gland* → **II** *s.* Nebennierendrüse *f*; **ad·ren·al·in** [ə'drenəlɪn] *s.* Adrena'lin *n*.

A·dri·at·ic [,eɪdrɪ'ætɪk] *geogr.* **I** *adj.* adri'atisch: *~ Sea* → **II** *s. the ~* das Adriatische Meer, die 'Adria.

a·drift [ə'drɪft] *adv. u. adj.* **1.** (um'her-) treibend, Wind und Wellen preisgegeben: *cut ~* treiben lassen; **2.** *fig.* aufs Geratewohl; hilflos: *be all ~* weder aus noch ein wissen; *cut o.s. ~* sich losreißen *od.* freimachen *od.* lossagen; *turn s.o. ~* j-n auf die Straße setzen.

a·droit [ə'drɔɪt] *adj.* □ geschickt, gewandt; schlagfertig, pfiffig.

ad·u·late [ædjʊleɪt] *v/t. j-m* schmeicheln, lobhudeln; **ad·u·la·tion** [,ædjʊ'leɪʃn] *s. niedere* Schmeiche'lei, Lobhude'lei *f*; **'ad·u·la·tor** [-tə] *s.* Schmeichler *m*, Speichellecker *m*; **'ad·u·la·to·ry** [-tərɪ] *adj.* schmeichlerisch, lobhudelnd.

a·dult [ædʌlt] **I** *adj.* **1.** erwachsen; reif, *fig. a.* mündig; **2.** (nur) für Erwachsene: *~ film, ~ education* Erwachsenenbildung *f*, *engS.* Volkshochschule *f*; **3.** ausgewachsen (*Tier, Pflanze*); **II** *s.* **4.** Erwachsene(r *m*) *f*.

a·dul·ter·ant [ə'dʌltərənt] *s.* Verfälschungsmittel *n*; **a·dul·ter·ate** [ə'dʌltəreɪt] *v/t.* **1.** *Nahrungsmittel* verfälschen; **2.** *fig.* verschlechtern, verderben; **a·dul·ter·a·tion** [ə,dʌltə'reɪʃn] *s.* Verfälschung *f*, verfälschtes Pro'dukt, Fälschung *f*; **a'dul·ter·er** [-rə] *s.* Ehebrecher *m*; **a'dul·ter·ess** [-rɪs] *s.* Ehebrecherin *f*; **a'dul·ter·ous** [-tərəs] *adj.* □ ehebrecherisch; **a'dul·ter·y** [-rɪ] *s.* Ehebruch *m*.

a·dult·hood [ædʌlthʊd] *s.* Erwachsensein *n*, Erwachsenenalter *n*.

ad·um·brate [ædʌmbreɪt] *v/t.* **1.** skizzieren, um'reißen, andeuten; **2.** 'hindeuten auf (*acc.*), vor'ausahnen lassen; **ad·um·bra·tion** [,ædʌm'breɪʃn] *s.* Andeutung *f*: a) flüchtiger Entwurf, Skizze *f*, b) Vorahnung *f*.

ad va·lo·rem [,ædvə'lɔːrem] (*Lat.*) *adj. u. adv.* dem Wert entsprechend: *~ duty* Wertzoll *m*.

ad·vance [əd'vɑːns] **I** *v/t.* **1.** vorwärts bringen, vorrücken (lassen), vorschieben; **2.** a) *Uhr, Fuß* vorstellen, b) *Zeitpunkt* vorverlegen, c) hin'aus-, aufschieben; **3.** *Meinung, Grund, Anspruch* vorbringen, geltend machen; **4.** a) fördern, verbessern: *~ one's position*, b) beschleunigen: *~ growth*; **5.** *pol. Am.* als Wahlhelfer fungieren in (*dat.*); **6.** erheben (*im Amt od. Rang*), befördern (*to the rank of general* zum General); **7.** *Preis* erhöhen; **8.** *Geld* vor'ausbezahlen; vorschießen, leihen; im Voraus liefern; **II** *v/i.* **9.** vorgehen, vorwärts gehen, vordringen, vormarschieren, vorrücken (*a. fig. Zeit*); **10.** vorankommen, Fortschritte machen: *~ in knowledge*; **11.** *im Rang* aufrücken, befördert werden; **12.** a) zunehmen (*in an dat.*), steigen, b) ♦ steigen (*Preis*); teurer werden (*Ware*); **13.** *pol. Am.* a) als Wahlhelfer fungieren, b) Wahlveranstaltungen vorbereiten (*for* für); **III** *s.* **14.** Vorwärtsgehen *n*, Vor-, Anrü-

cken *n*, Vormarsch *m* (*a. fig.*); Vorrücken *n des Alters*; **15.** Aufrücken *n* (*im Amt*), Beförderung *f*; **16.** Fortschritt *m*, Verbesserung *f*; **17.** Vorsprung *m*: *in ~* a) voraus, b) vorn, c) im Voraus, vorher; *~ section* vorderer Teil; *be in ~* (e-n) Vorsprung haben (*of* vor *dat.*); *arrive in ~ of the others* vor den anderen ankommen; *order* (*od. book*) *in ~* vor(aus)bestellen; *~ booking* a) Vorbestellung *f*, Vorausbestellung *f*, b) Vorverkauf *m*; *~ censorship* Vorzensur *f*; *~ copy typ.* Vorausexemplar *n*; *~ publication typ.* Vorabdruck *m*; **18.** *a. ~ payment* Vorschuss *m*, Vor'auszahlung *f*: *in ~* in pränumerando; **19.** (Preis)Erhöhung *f*; Mehrgebot *n* (*Versteigerung*); **20.** *mst pl.* Entgegenkommen *n*, Vorschlag *m*, erster Schritt (*zur Verständigung*): *make ~s to s.o.* a) j-m entgegenkommen, b) sich an j-n heranmachen, *bsd. e-r Frau* Avancen machen; **21.** ⚔ *Am.* Vorhut *f*, Spitze *f*: *~ guard a. Brit.* Vorhut *f*; **22.** *pol. Am.* Wahlhilfe *f*: *~ man* Wahlhelfer *m*; **ad'vanced** [-st] *adj.* **1.** vorgerückt (*Alter, Stunde*), vorgeschritten: *~ in pregnancy* hochschwanger; **2.** fortgeschritten (*Stadium etc.*); fortschrittlich, modern: *~ opinions; ~ students; ~ English* Englisch für Fortgeschrittene; *highly ~* hoch entwickelt (*Kultur, Technik*); **3.** gar zu fortschrittlich, ex'trem, kühn; **4.** ⚔ vorgeschoben, Vor(aus)...; **ad'vance·ment** [-mənt] *s.* **1.** Förderung *f*; **2.** Beförderung *f*; **3.** Em'por-, Weiterkommen *n*, Aufstieg *m*, Fortschritt *m*, Wachstum *n*.

ad·van·tage [əd'vɑːntɪdʒ] **I** *s.* **1.** Vorteil *m*: a) Über'legenheit *f*, Vorsprung *m*, b) Vorzug *m*: *to ~* günstig, vorteilhaft; *have an ~ over j-m* gegenüber im Vorteil sein; *you have the ~ of me* ich kenne leider Ihren (werten) Namen nicht; **2.** Nutzen *m*, Gewinn *m*: *take ~ of s.o.* j-n übervorteilen *od.* ausnutzen; *take ~ of s.th.* et. ausnutzen; *derive od. gain ~ from s.th.* aus et. Nutzen ziehen; **3.** günstige Gelegenheit; **4.** *Tennis* etc.: Vorteil *m*; **II** *v/t.* **5.** fördern, begünstigen; **ad·van·ta·geous** [,ædvən'teɪdʒəs] *adj.* □ vorteilhaft, günstig, nützlich.

Ad·vent [ædvənt] *s.* **1.** *eccl.* Ad'vent *m*, Ad'ventszeit *f*; **2.** ⌾ Kommen *n*, Erscheinen *n*, Ankunft *f*; **'Ad·vent·ist** [-tɪst] *s.* Adven'tist *m*; **,ad·ven'ti·tious** [-'tɪʃəs] *adj.* □ **1.** (zufällig) hin'zugekommen; zufällig, nebensächlich: *~ causes* Nebenursachen; **2.** ⚘, ⚖ zufällig erworben.

ad·ven·ture [əd'ventʃə] **I** *s.* **1.** Abenteuer *n*: a) Wagnis *n*: *life of ~* Abenteurerleben *n*, b) (tolles) Erlebnis, c) ♱ Spekulati'onsgeschäft *n*; *~ playground* Abenteuerspielplatz *m*; **II** *v/t.* **2.** wagen, gefährden; **3.** *~ o.s.* sich wagen (*into* in *acc.*); **III** *v/i.* **4.** sich wagen (*on, upon* in, auf *acc.*); **ad'ven·tur·er** [-tʃərə] *s.* Abenteurer *m*: a) Wagehals *m*, b) Glücksritter *m*, Hochstapler *m*, c) Speku'lant *m*; **ad'ven·ture·some** [-tʃəsəm] *adj.* → *adventurous*; **ad'ven·tur·ess** [-tʃərɪs] *s.* Abenteu(r)erin *f (a. fig. b.s.*); **ad'ven·tur·ism** [-tʃərɪzəm] *s.* Abenteurertum *n*; **ad'ven·tur·ous** [-tʃərəs] *adj.* □ **1.** abenteuerlich: a) waghalsig, verwegen, b) gewagt, kühn (*Sache*); **2.** abenteuerlustig.

ad·verb [ædvɜːb] *s.* Ad'verb *n*, Umstandswort *n*; **ad·ver·bi·al** [əd'vɜːbjəl] *adj.* □ adverbi'al: *~ phrase* adverbiale Bestimmung.

ad·ver·sar·y ['ædvəsərɪ] s. **1.** Gegner (-in), 'Widersacher(in); **2.** ♀ eccl. Teufel m; **ad·ver·sa·tive** [əd'vɜːsətɪv] adj. □ ling. gegensätzlich, adversa'tiv: ~ word; **ad·verse** ['ædvɜːs] adj. □ **1.** entgegenwirkend, zu'wider, widrig (to dat.): ~ winds widrige Winde; **2.** gegnerisch, feindlich: ~ party Gegenpartei f; **3.** ungünstig, nachteilig (to für): ~ decision; ~ balance of trade passive Handelsbilanz; have an ~ effect (up)on, affect ~ly sich nachteilig auswirken auf (acc.); **4.** ♣ entgegenstehend: ~ claim; **ad·ver·si·ty** [əd'vɜːsətɪ] s. Missgeschick n, Not f, Unglück n.

ad·vert I v/i. [əd'vɜːt] hinweisen, sich beziehen (to auf acc.); **II** s. ['ædvɜːt] Brit. F für advertisement.

ad·ver·tise, Am. a. **ad·ver·tize** ['ædvətaɪz] **I** v/t. **1.** ankündigen, anzeigen, durch die Zeitung etc. bekannt machen: ~ a post eine Stellung öffentlich ausschreiben; **2.** fig. ausposaunen: you need not ~ the fact a. du brauchst es nicht an die große Glocke zu hängen; **2.** durch Zeitungsanzeige etc. Re'klame machen für, werben für; **II** v/i. **3.** inserieren, annoncieren, öffentlich ankündigen: ~ for durch Inserat suchen; **4.** werben, Reklame machen; **ad·vertise·ment** [əd'vɜːtɪsmənt] s. **1.** öffentliche Anzeige, Ankündigung f in e-r Zeitung, Inse'rat n, An'nonce f: put an ~ in a paper ein Inserat in e-r Zeitung aufgeben; **2.** Re'klame f, Werbung f; **'ad·ver·tis·er** [-zə] s. **1.** Inse'rent(in); **2.** Werbeträger m; **3.** Werbefachmann m; **4.** Anzeiger m, Anzeigenblatt n; **'ad·ver·tis·ing** [-zɪŋ] **I** s. **1.** Inserieren n; Ankündigung f; **2.** Reklame f, Werbung f; **II** adj. **3.** Reklame..., Werbe...: ~ agency Werbeagentur f; ~ agent a) Anzeigenvertreter m, b) Werbeagent m; ~ appeal Werbekraft f; ~ campaign Werbefeldzug m; ~ expert Werbefachmann m; ~ media Werbeträger, -medien pl.; ~ message Werbebotschaft f; ~ space Reklamefläche f; 'ad·ver·tize etc. → advertise etc.

ad·vice [əd'vaɪs] s. **1.** (a. piece of) Rat(schlag) m; Ratschläge pl.: at (od. on) s.o.'s ~ auf j-s Rat hin; take medical ~ e-n Arzt zurate ziehen; take my ~ folge meinem Rat; **2.** Nachricht f, Anzeige f, (schriftliche) Mitteilung; **3.** ♣ A'vis m, Bericht m: letter of ~ Benachrichtigungsschreiben n; as per ~ laut Aufgabe od. Bericht.

ad·vis·a·bil·i·ty [əd͵vaɪzə'bɪlətɪ] s. Ratsamkeit f; **ad·vis·a·ble** [əd'vaɪzəbl] adj. □ ratsam; **ad·vis·a·bly** [əd'vaɪzəblɪ] adv. ratsamerweise.

ad·vise [əd'vaɪz] **I** v/t. **1.** j-m raten od. empfehlen (to inf. zu inf.); et. (an)raten; j-n beraten: he was ~d to go man riet ihm zu gehen; **2.** ~ against warnen vor (dat.); j-m abraten von; **3.** ♣ benachrichtigen (of von, that dass), avisieren (s.o. of s.th.); **II.** v/i. **4.** sich beraten (with mit); **ad'vised** [-zd] adj. □ **1.** beraten: badly ~; **2.** wohl bedacht, über'legt; → ill-advised; well-advised; **ad'vis·ed·ly** [-zɪdlɪ] adv. **1.** mit Bedacht, Über'legung; **2.** vorsätzlich, absichtlich; **ad'vis·er** od. **ad-'vi·sor** [-zə] s. **1.** Berater m, Ratgeber m; **2.** ped. Am. 'Studienberater m; **ad'vi·so·ry** [-zərɪ] adj. beratend, Beratungs...: ~ board, ~ committee Beratungsausschuss m, Beirat m, Gutachterkommission f; ~ body, ~ council Beirat m; → capacity 6.

ad·vo·ca·cy ['ædvəkəsɪ] s. (of) Befürwortung f, Empfehlung f (gen.), Eintreten n (für); **ad·vo·cate I** s. ['ædvəkət] **1.** Verfechter m, Befürworter m, Verteidiger m, Fürsprecher m: an ~ of peace; **2.** Scot. u. hist. Advo'kat m, (plädierender) Rechtsanwalt: Lord ♀ Oberster Staatsanwalt; **3.** Am. Rechtsbeistand m; **II** v/t. ['ædvəkeɪt] **4.** verteidigen, befürworten, eintreten für.

adze [ædz] s. Breitbeil n.

Ae·ge·an [iː'dʒiːən] geogr. **I** adj. ä'gäisch: ~ Sea Ägäisches Meer; **II** s. the ~ die Ä'gäis.

ae·gis ['iːdʒɪs] s. myth. 'Ägis f; fig. Ä'gide f, Schirmherrschaft f: under the ~ of.

Ae·o·li·an [iː'əʊljən] adj. ä'olisch: ~ harp Äolsharfe f.

ae·on ['iːən] s. Ä'one f; Ewigkeit f.

aer·ate ['eəreɪt] v/t. **1.** (a. ♠ be- od. 'durch- od. ent)lüften; **2.** a) mit Kohlensäure sättigen, b) zum Sprudeln bringen; **3.** ✿ dem Blut Sauerstoff zuführen.

aer·i·al ['eərɪəl] **I** adj. □ **1.** Luft..., in der Luft lebend od. befindlich, fliegend, hoch: ~ advertising Luftwerbung f, Himmelsschrift f; ~ cableway Seilschwebebahn f; ~ camera Luftbildkamera f; ~ railway Hänge-, Schwebebahn f; ~ spires hochragende Kirchtürme; **2.** aus Luft bestehend, leicht, gasförmig, flüchtig; **3.** ä'therisch, zart: ~ fancies Fantastereien; **4.** ✈ Flug(zeug)..., Luft..., Flieger...: ~ attack Luft-, Fliegerangriff m; ~ barrage a) (Luft)Sperr-, Flakfeuer n, b) Ballonsperre f; ~ combat Luftkampf m; ~ map Luftbildkarte f; ~ navigation Luftschifffahrt f; ~ survey Luftbildvermessung f; ~ view (od. photography, shot) Luftaufnahme f, Luftbild n; **5.** ✿ oberirdisch, Ober..., Frei..., Luft...: ~ cable Luftkabel n; ~ wire ⚡ Ober-, Freileitung f; **6.** ⚡, Radio, TV: Antennen...: ~ wire; **II** s. **7.** ⚡, Radio, TV: An'tenne f; **'aer·i·al·ist** [-lɪst] s. Tra'pezkünstler m.

aer·ie, Am. a. **aër·ie** ['eərɪ] s. **1.** Horst m (Raubvogelnest); **2.** fig. Adlerhorst m (hoch gelegener Wohnsitz etc.).

aer·o ['eərəʊ] **I** pl. **-os** s. Flugzeug n, Luftschiff n; **II** adj. Luft(schiffahrt)..., Flug(zeug)...: ~ engine.

aero- [eərəʊ] in Zssgn: Aëro..., Luft...

aer·o·bat·ics [͵eərəʊ'bætɪks] s. pl. sg. konstr. Kunstflug m.

'aer·o·bics [eə'rəʊbɪks] pl. sg. konstr. Ae'robic n.

aer·o·drome ['eərədrəʊm] s. bsd. Brit. Flugplatz m.

aer·o|·dy·nam·ic [͵eərəʊdaɪ'næmɪk] **I** adj. □ aerody'namisch, Stromlinien...; **II** s. pl. sg. konstr. Aerody'namik f; **'~·dyne** [-daɪn] s. Luftfahrzeug n schwerer als Luft; **'~·foil** [-əʊfɔɪl] s. Brit. Tragfläche f, a. Höhen-, Kiel- od. Seitenflosse f; **'~·gram** [-əʊgræm] s. **1.** Funkspruch m; **2.** Luftpostleichtbrief m; **'~·lite** [-əʊlaɪt] s. Aero'lith m, Mete'orstein m.

aer·ol·o·gy [eə'rɒlədʒɪ] s. phys. **1.** Aerolo'gie f, Erforschung f der höheren Luftschichten; **2.** aero'nautische Wetterkunde; **aer·o·med·i·cine** [͵eərəʊ'medsn] s. 'Aero-, 'Luftfahrtmedi͵zin f; **aer·om·e·ter** [eə'rɒmɪtə] s. phys. Aero'meter m, Luftdichtemesser m.

aer·o|·naut ['eərənɔːt] s. Aero'naut m, Luftschiffer m; **~·nau·tic, ~·nau·ti·cal** [͵eərə'nɔːtɪk(l)] adj. □ aero'nautisch, Flug...; **~·nau·tics** [͵eərə'nɔːtɪks] s. pl.

sg. konstr. Aero'nautik f: a) obs. Luftfahrt f, b) Luftfahrtkunde f; **~·plane** ['eərəpleɪn] s. bsd. Brit. Flugzeug n; **~·sol** ['eərəsɒl] s. **1.** 🜂 Aero'sol n; **2.** Spraydose f; **~·space** ['eərəʊspeɪs] **I** s. Weltraum m; **II** adj. a) Raumfahrt..., b) (Welt)Raum...; **~·stat** ['eərəʊstæt] s. Luftfahrzeug n leichter als Luft; **~·stat·ic, ~·stat·i·cal** [͵eərəʊ'stætɪk(l)] adj. □ aero'statisch; **~·stat·ics** [͵eərəʊ'stætɪks] s. pl. sg. konstr. Aero'statik f.

Aes·cu·la·pi·an [͵iːskjuː'leɪpjən] adj. **1.** Äskulap...; **2.** ärztlich.

aes·thete ['iːsθiːt] s. Äs'thet m; **aes·thet·ic, aes·thet·i·cal** [iːs'θetɪk(l)] adj. □ äs'thetisch; **aes·thet·i·cism** [iːs'θetɪsɪzəm] s. **1.** Ästheti'zismus m; **2.** Schönheitssinn m; **aes·thet·ics** [iːs'θetɪks] s. pl. sg. konstr. Äs'thetik f.

aes·ti·val [iː'staɪvl] adj. sommerlich.

ae·ther etc. → ether etc.

a·far [ə'fɑː] adv. fern: ~ off in der Ferne; from ~ von fern, weither, von weit her.

af·fa·bil·i·ty [͵æfə'bɪlətɪ] s. Leutseligkeit f, Freundlichkeit f; **af·fa·ble** ['æfəbl] adj. □ leutselig, freundlich, 'umgänglich.

af·fair [ə'feə] s. **1.** Angelegenheit f, Sache f: a disgraceful ~; that is his ~ das ist seine Sache; that is not my ~ das geht mich nichts an; make an ~ of s.th. et. aufbauschen; my own ~ meine (eigene) Angelegenheit, meine Privatsache; ~ of honour Ehrensache f, -handel m; **2.** pl. Angelegenheiten pl., Verhältnisse pl.: public ~s öffentliche Angelegenheiten; state of ~s Lage f der Dinge, Sachlage f; → foreign 1; **3.** Af'färe f: a) Ereignis n, b) Skan'dal m, c) (Liebes)Verhältnis n; **4.** F Ding n, Sache f, ͵Appa'rat' m: the car was a shiny ~.

af·fect¹ [ə'fekt] v/t. **1.** lieben, e-e Vorliebe haben für, neigen zu, be'vorzugen: ~ bright colo(u)rs lebhafte Farben bevorzugen; much ~ed by sehr beliebt bei; **2.** zur Schau tragen, erkünsteln, nachahmen: he ~s an Oxford accent er redet mit gekünstelter Oxforder Aussprache; he ~s the freethinker er spielt den Freidenker; **3.** vortäuschen: ~ ignorance; ~ a limp so tun, als hinke man; **4.** bewohnen, vorkommen in (dat.) (Tiere u. Pflanzen).

af·fect² [ə'fekt] v/t. **1.** betreffen: that does not ~ me; **2.** (ein- od. sich aus-) wirken auf (acc.), beeinflussen, beeinträchtigen, in Mitleidenschaft ziehen, ✿ a. angreifen, befallen: ~ the health; **3.** bewegen, rühren, ergreifen.

af·fec·ta·tion [͵æfek'teɪʃn] s. **1.** Affektiertheit f, Gehabe n; **2.** Verstellung f; **3.** Vorliebe (of für).

af·fect·ed¹ [ə'fektɪd] adj. □ **1.** affektiert, gekünstelt, geziert; **2.** angenommen, vorgetäuscht; **3.** geneigt, gesinnt.

af·fect·ed² [ə'fektɪd] adj. **1.** ✿ befallen (with von Krankheit), angegriffen (Augen etc.); **2.** betroffen, berührt; **3.** gerührt, bewegt, ergriffen.

af·fect·ing [ə'fektɪŋ] adj. □ ergreifend; **af'fec·tion** [-kʃn] s. **1.** oft pl. Liebe f, (Zu)Neigung f (for, towards zu); **2.** Gemütsbewegung f, Stimmung f; **3.** ✿ Erkrankung f, Leiden n; **4.** Einfluss m, Einwirkung f; **af'fec·tion·ate** [-kʃnət] adj. □ gütig, liebevoll, herzlich, zärtlich; **af'fec·tion·ate·ly** [-kʃnətlɪ] adv.: yours ~ dein dich liebender (Briefschluss); ~ known as Pat unter dem Kosenamen Pat bekannt.

af·fi·ci·o·na·do → *aficionado*.

af·fi·ance [ə'faɪəns] **I** *s.* **1.** Vertrauen *n*; **2.** Eheversprechen *n*; **II** *v/t.* **3.** *j-n od. sich* verloben (**to** mit).

af·fi·ant [ə'faɪənt] *s. Am.* Aussteller (-in) e-s *affidavit*.

af·fi·da·vit [ˌæfɪ'deɪvɪt] *s.* ✠ *schriftliche beeidigte Erklärung:* ~ *of means* Offenbarungseid *m*.

af·fil·i·ate [ə'fɪlɪeɪt] **I** *v/t.* **1.** als Mitglied aufnehmen; **2.** *j-m* die Vaterschaft *e-s Kindes* zuschreiben: ~ *a child on* (*od.* **to**); **3.** (**on, upon**) zu'rückführen (auf *acc.*), zuschreiben (*dat.*); **4.** (**to**) verknüpfen, verbinden (mit); angliedern, anschließen (*dat.*, an *acc.*); **II** *v/i.* **5.** sich anschließen (**with** an *acc.*); **III** *s.* [-ɪɪt] **6.** *Am.* 'Zweigorganisati‚on *f*, Tochtergesellschaft *f*; **af'fil·i·at·ed** [-tɪd] *adj.* angeschlossen: ~ *company* Tochter-, Zweiggesellschaft *f*; **af·fil·i·a·tion** [ə‚fɪlɪ'eɪʃn] *s.* **1.** Aufnahme *f* (*als Mitglied etc.*); **2.** Zuschreibung *f* der Vaterschaft; **3.** Zu'rückführung *f* (*auf den Ursprung*); **4.** Angliederung *f*; **5.** *oft eccl.* Zugehörigkeit *f*, Mitgliedschaft *f*.

af·fin·i·ty [ə'fɪnətɪ] *s.* **1.** ✠ Schwägerschaft *f*; **2.** *fig.* a) (Wesens)Verwandtschaft *f*, Affini'tät *f*, b) (Wahl-, Seelen-)Verwandtschaft *f*, gegenseitige Anziehung; **3.** 🜪 Affini'tät *f*, stofflich-'chemische Verwandtschaft.

af·firm [ə'fɜːm] *v/t.* **1.** versichern, beteuern; **2.** bekräftigen; ✠ *Urteil* bestätigen; **3.** ✠ an Eides statt versichern; **af·fir·ma·tion** [ˌæfɜː'meɪʃn] *s.* **1.** Versicherung *f*, Beteuerung *f*; **2.** Bestätigung *f*, Bekräftigung *f*; **3.** ✠ Versicherung *f* an Eides statt; **af'firm·a·tive** [-mətɪv] **I** *adj.* □ **1.** bejahend, zustimmend, positiv; **2.** positiv, bestimmt: ~ *action Am.* Aktion *f* gegen die Diskriminierung von Minderheitsgruppen; **II** *s.* **3.** Bejahung *f*: *answer in the* ~ bejahen.

af·fix I *v/t.* [ə'fɪks] **1.** (**to**) befestigen, anbringen (an *dat.*), anheften, ankleben (an *acc.*); **2.** (**to**) beilegen, -fügen (*dat.*), hin'zufügen (zu); *Siegel* anbringen (an *dat.*); *Unterschrift* setzen (unter *acc.*); **II** *s.* ['æfɪks] **3.** *ling.* Af'fix *n*, Anhang *m*, Hin'zufügung *f*.

af·flict [ə'flɪkt] *v/t.* betrüben, quälen, plagen, heimsuchen; **af'flict·ed** [-tɪd] *adj.* **1.** niedergeschlagen, betrübt; **2.** (**with**) leidend (an *dat.*); belastet, behaftet (mit), geplagt (von); **af'flic·tion** [-kʃn] *s.* **1.** Betrübnis *f*, Kummer *m*; **2.** a) Gebrechen, b) *pl.* Beschwerden; **3.** Elend *n*, Not *f*; Heimsuchung *f*.

af·flu·ence ['æfluəns] *s.* **1.** Fülle *f*, 'Überfluss *m*; **2.** Reichtum *m*, Wohlstand *m*: *demoralization by* ~ Wohlstandsverwahrlosung *f*; **'af·flu·ent** [-nt] **I** *adj.* □ **1.** reichlich; **2.** wohlhabend, reich (*in* an *dat.*): ~ *society* Wohlstandsgesellschaft *f*; **II** *s.* **3.** Nebenfluss *m*; **af'flux** ['æflʌks] *s.* **1.** Zufluss *m*, Zustrom *m* (*a. fig.*); **2.** 🜪 (Blut-)Andrang *m*.

af·ford [ə'fɔːd] *v/t.* **1.** gewähren, bieten; *Schatten* spenden; *Freude* bereiten; **2.** *als Produkt* liefern; **3.** sich leisten, sich erlauben, die Mittel haben für; *Zeit* erübrigen: *I can't* ~ *it* ich kann es mir nicht leisten (*a. fig.*); **af'ford·a·ble** *adj.* erschwinglich.

af·for·est·a·tion [æ‚fɒrɪ'steɪʃn] *s.* Aufforstung *f*.

af·fran·chise [ə'fræntʃaɪz] *v/t.* befreien (*from* aus).

af·fray [ə'freɪ] *s.* **1.** Schläge'rei *f*, Kra'wall *m*; **2.** ✠ Raufhandel *m*.

---

af·freight [ə'freɪt] *v/t.* ⚓ chartern, befrachten.

af·fri·cate ['æfrɪkət] *s. ling.* Affri'kata *f* (*Verschlusslaut mit folgendem Reibelaut*).

af·front [ə'frʌnt] **I** *v/t.* **1.** beleidigen, beschimpfen; **2.** trotzen (*dat.*); **II** *s.* **3.** Beleidigung *f*, Af'front *m*.

Af·ghan ['æfgæn] **I** *s.* **1.** Af'ghane *m*, Af'ghanin *f*; **2.** Af'ghan *m* (*Teppich*); **II** *adj.* **3.** af'ghanisch.

a·fi·ci·o·na·do [ə‚fɪsjə'nɑːdəʊ] *s.* (*Span.*) begeisterter Anhänger *m*, ‚Fan' *m*.

a·field [ə'fiːld] *adv.* **1.** a) im *od.* auf dem Feld, b) ins *od.* aufs Feld; **2.** in der *od.* in die Ferne, draußen, hin'aus: *far* ~ weit entfernt; **3.** *bsd. fig.* in die Irre: *lead s.o.* ~; *quite* ~ a) auf dem Holzweg(e) (*Person*), b) ganz falsch (*Sache*).

a·fire [ə'faɪə] *adv. u. adj.* brennend, in Flammen: *all* ~ *fig.* Feuer und Flamme.

a·flame [ə'fleɪm] → *afire*.

a·float [ə'fləʊt] *adv. u. adj.* **1.** flott, schwimmend: *keep* ~ (sich) über Wasser halten (*a. fig.*); **2.** an Bord, auf See; **3.** in 'Umlauf; **4.** im Gange; **5.** über'schwemmt.

a·foot [ə'fʊt] *adv. u. adj.* **1.** zu Fuß, auf den Beinen; **2.** *fig.* a) im Gange, b) im Anzug, im Kommen.

a·fore [ə'fɔː] *obs.* **I** *prp.* vor; **II** *adv.* (nach) vorn; **III** *cj.* ehe, bevor; **~·men·tioned** [ə‚fɔː'menʃənd], **~·said** [ə'fɔːsed] *adj.* oben erwähnt, oben genannt; **~·thought** [ə'fɔːθɔːt] *adj.* vorbedacht; → *malice* 3.

a·fraid [ə'freɪd] *adj.*: *be* ~ Angst haben, sich fürchten (*of* vor *dat.*); *I am* ~ (*that*) *he will not come* ich fürchte, er wird nicht kommen; *I am* ~ *I must go* F leider muss ich gehen; *I'm* ~ *so* leider ja!; *I shall tell him, don't be* ~! F (nur) keine Angst, ich werde es ihm sagen!; ~ *of hard work* F arbeitsscheu; *be* ~ *to do* sich scheuen zu tun.

a·fresh [ə'freʃ] *adv.* von neuem, von vorn: *start* ~.

Af·ri·can ['æfrɪkən] **I** *s.* **1.** Afri'kaner (-in); **II** *adj.* **2.** afri'kanisch; **3.** afri'kanischer Abstammung, Neger...; ~ **A·mer·i·can** *s.* 'Afroameri‚kaner(in); **,~·'A·mer·i·can** *adj.* 'afroameri‚kanisch.

Af·ri·kaans [ˌæfrɪ'kɑːns] *s. ling.* Afri'kaans(ch) *n*, Kapholländisch *n*; **,Af·ri·'kan·(d)er** [-'kæn(d)ə] *s.* Afri'kander *m* (*Weißer mit Afrikaans als Muttersprache*).

Af·ro ['æfrəʊ] *pl.* **-ros** *s.* **1.** Afrolook *m*; **2.** *a.* ~ *hairdo* 'Afrofri‚sur *f*.

,Af·ro·A·mer·i·can [ˌæfrəʊ-] *s.* Afroameri'kaner(in); **,~·'A·sian** *adj.* 'afroasi'atisch.

aft [ɑːft] *adv.* ⚓ (nach) achtern.

af·ter ['ɑːftə] **I** *prp.* **1.** nach: ~ *lunch*; ~ *a week*; *day* ~ *day* Tag für Tag; *the day* ~ *tomorrow* übermorgen; *the month* ~ *next* der übernächste Monat; ~ *all* schließlich, im Grunde, immerhin, (also) doch; ~ *all my trouble* nach *od.* trotz all meiner Mühe; → *look after etc.*; **2.** hinter ... (*dat.*) (her): *I came* ~ *you*; *shut the door* ~ *you*; *the police are* ~ *you* die Polizei ist hinter dir her; ~ *you, sir!* nach Ihnen!; *one* ~ *another* nacheinander; **3.** nach, gemäß: *named* ~ *his father* nach s-m Vater genannt; ~ *my own heart* ganz nach m-m Herzen *od.* Wunsch; *a picture* ~ *Rubens* ein Gemälde nach (*im Stil von*) Rubens; **II** *adv.* **4.** nach'her, hinter'her, da'nach; später: *follow* ~ nachfolgen; *for months* ~ noch monatelang; *shortly* ~ kurz danach; **III** *adj.* **5.** später, künftig;

Nach...: *in* ~ *years*; **6.** ⚓ Achter...; **IV** *cj.* **7.** nach'dem: ~ *he* (*had*) *sat down*; **V** *s. pl.* **8.** *Brit.* F Nachspeise *f*: *for* ~*s* zum Nachtisch; '~·**birth** *s.* 🜪 Nachgeburt *f*; '~·**burn·er** *s.* ✈ Nachbrenner *m*; '~-‚**cab·in** *s.* ⚓ 'Heckka‚bine *f*; '~·**care** *s.* **1.** 🜪 Nachbehandlung *f*; **2.** ✠ Resozialisierungshilfe *f*; '~·**crop** *s.* Nachernte *f*; '~·**death** → *afterlife* 1; '~·**deck** *s.* ⚓ Achterdeck *n*; '~-‚**din·ner** *adj.* nach Tisch: ~ *speech* Tischrede *f*; '~-‚**ef·fect** [-ərɪ-] *s.* Nachwirkung *f* (*a.* 🜪), Folge *f*; '~-**glow** *s.* **1.** Nachglühen *n* (*a.* ☉ *u. fig.*); **2.** a) Abendrot *n*, b) Alpenglühen *n*; '~·**hold** *s.* ⚓ Achterraum *m*; '~-**hours** *s. pl.* Zeit *f* nach Dienstschluss: ~ *dealing* Nachbörse *f*; '~·**life** *s.* **1.** Leben *n* nach dem Tode; **2.** (zu)künftiges Leben; '~-**math** [-mæθ] *s.* **1.** ✓ Grummet *n*, Spätheu *n*; **2.** *fig.* Nachwirkungen *pl.*; '~·**noon** *s.* Nachmittag *m*: *in the* ~ am Nachmittag, nachmittags; *this* ~ heute Nachmittag; ~ *of life* Herbst *m* des Lebens; → *good* 1; '~-**pains** *s. pl.* 🜪 Nachwehen *pl.*; '~·**play** *s.* (sex'uelles) Nachspiel; '~-**sales serv·ice** *s.* ✠ Kundendienst *m*; '~-‚**sea·son** *s.* 'Nachsai‚son *f*; '~·**shave lo·tion** *s.* Aftershave-Lotion *f*, Rasierwasser *n*; '~·**shock** *s.* Nachbeben *n*; '~·**taste** *s.* Nachgeschmack *m* (*a. fig.*); ~ **tax** *adj.* ✠ nach Abzug der Steuern, *a.* Netto...; '~·**thought** *s.* nachträglicher Einfall: *as an* ~ nachträglich; '~‚**treat·ment** *s.* ✠, ⚙ Nachbehandlung *f*.

af·ter|ward ['ɑːftəwəd] *Am.*, '~·**wards** [-dz] *adv.* später, nach'her, hinter'her; '~·**years** *s. pl.* Folgezeit *f*.

a·gain [ə'gen] *adv.* **1.** 'wieder(um), von neuem, aber-, nochmals: *come* ~! komm wieder!; ~ *and* ~ immer wieder; *now and* ~ hin und wieder; *be o.s.* ~ wieder gesund *od.* der Alte sein; **2.** schon wieder: *that fool* ~ schon wieder dieser Narr!; *what's his name* ~? F wie heißt er doch schnell?; **3.** außerdem, ferner; **4.** noch einmal: *as much* ~ noch einmal so viel; *half as much* ~ anderthalbmal so viel; **5.** *a. then* ~ andererseits, da'gegen, aber: *these* ~ *are more expensive*.

a·gainst [ə'genst] *prp.* **1.** gegen, wider, entgegen: ~ *the law*; *run* (*up*) ~ *s.o.* j-n zufällig treffen; **2.** gegen, gegen'über: *my rights* ~ *the landlord*; *over* ~ *the town hall* gegenüber dem Rathaus; **3.** auf ... (*acc.*) zu, an (*dat. od. acc.*), vor (*dat. od. acc.*), gegen: ~ *the wall*; **4.** *a. as* ~ verglichen mit, gegenüber; **5.** in Erwartung (*gen.*), für.

a·gam·ic [‚eɪ'gæmɪk] *adj. biol.* a'gam, geschlechtslos.

a·gape [ə'geɪp] *adv. u. adj.* gaffend, mit offenem Munde (*vor Staunen*).

a·gar·ic ['ægərɪk] *s.* 🍄 Blätterpilz *m*, -schwamm *m*; → *fly agaric*.

ag·ate ['ægət] *s.* **1.** *min.* A'chat *m*; **2.** *Am.* bunte Glasmurmel; **3.** *typ. Am.* Pa'riser Schrift *f*.

a·ga·ve [ə'geɪvɪ] *s.* ♣ A'gave *f*.

age [eɪdʒ] **I** *s.* **1.** (Lebens)Alter *n*, Altersstufe *f*: *what is his* ~ *od. what* ~ *is he?* wie alt ist er?; *ten years of* ~ 10 Jahre alt; *at the* ~ *of* im Alter von; *at his* ~ in seinem Alter; *be over* ~ über der Altersgrenze liegen; *act one's* ~ sich s-m Alter entsprechend benehmen; *be your* ~! sei kein Kindskopf!; *a girl your* ~ ein Mädchen deines Alters; *he does not look his* ~ man sieht ihm sein Alter nicht an; **2.** (Zeit *f* der) Reife: *full* ~ Volljährigkeit *f*; (*come*) *of* ~ mündig *od.* volljährig (werden); *under* ~ minderjährig; **3.** *a. old* ~ Alter *n*: ~ *before beauty* Alter kommt vor Schönheit; **4.** Zeit *f*, Zeitalter *n*; Menschenalter *n*, Generati'on *f*: *Ice* ⚥ Eiszeit *f*; *the* ~ *of Queen Victoria*; *in our* ~ in unserer (*od.* der heutigen) Zeit; *down the* ~*s* durch die Jahrhunderte; **5.** *oft pl.* F lange Zeit, Ewigkeit *f*: *I haven't seen him for* ~*s* ich habe ihn seit e-r Ewigkeit nicht gesehen; **II** *v/t.* **6.** alt machen; **7.** *j-n* um Jahre älter machen; **8.** ⚙ altern, vergüten; *Wein etc.* ablagern lassen; *Käse etc.* reifen lassen; **III** *v/i.* **9.** alt werden, altern; **age brack·et** → *age group*; **aged** [eɪdʒd] *adj.* ... Jahre alt: ~ *twenty*; **a·ged** ['eɪdʒɪd] *adj.* bejahrt, betagt; **age group** *s.* Altersklasse *f*, Jahrgang *m*; **age·ing** → *aging*; **age·ism** ['eɪdʒɪzəm] *s.* Altersdiskriminierung *f*; **age·less** ['eɪdʒlɪs] *adj.* nicht alternd, zeitlos; **age lim·it** *s.* Altersgrenze *f*; **'age·long** *adj.* lebenslänglich, dauernd.

a·gen·cy ['eɪdʒənsɪ] *s.* **1.** (wirkende) Kraft *f*, (ausführendes) Or'gan, Werkzeug *n* (*fig.*); **2.** Tätigkeit *f*, Wirkung *f*; **3.** Vermittlung *f*, Mittel *n*, Hilfe *f*: *by od. through the* ~ *of*; **4.** ✝ Agen'tur *f*: a) (Handels)Vertretung *f*, b) Bü'ro *n od.* Amt *n* e-s A'genten; **5.** ⚖ ('Handlungs)Vollmacht *f*; **6.** ('Nachrichten-) Agen,tur *f*; **7.** Geschäfts-, Dienststelle *f*; Amt *n*, Behörde *f*; ~ **busi·ness** *s.* Kommissi'onsgeschäft *n*.

a·gen·da [ə'dʒendə] *s.* Tagesordnung *f*.

a·gent ['eɪdʒənt] *s.* **1.** Handelnde(r *m*) *f*, Urheber(in): *free* ~ selbstständig Handelnde(r), *weitS.* ein freier Mensch; **2.** 🜨, 🜊, *biol., phys.* 'Agens *n*, (be)wirkende Kraft *od.* Ursache, Mittel *n*, Werkzeug *n*: *protective* ~ Schutzmittel; **3.** a) ✝ (Handels)Vertreter *m*, A'gent *m*, a. Makler *m*, Vermittler *m*, b) ⚖ (Handlungs)Bevollmächtigte(r *m*) *f*, (Stell)Vertreter(in); **4.** *pol.* (Geheim)Agent(in).

a·gent pro·vo·ca·teur *pl.* **a·gents pro·vo·ca·teurs** ['æʒɑ̃ːŋ prə,vɒkə'tɜː] (*Fr.*) *s.* Lockspitzel *m*.

'age|-old *adj.* uralt; **'~-worn** *adj.* altersschwach.

ag·glom·er·ate I *v/t. u. v/i.* [ə'glɒməreɪt] **1.** (sich) zs.-ballen, (sich) an- *od.* aufhäufen; **II** *s.* [-rət] **2.** angehäufte Masse, Ballung *f*; **3.** 🜨, *geol., phys.* Agglome'rat *n*; **III** *adj.* [-rət] **4.** zs.-geballt, gehäuft; **ag·glom·er·a·tion** [ə,glɒmə'reɪʃn] *s.* **1.** Zs.-ballung *f*; Anhäufung *f*; (wirrer) Haufen.

ag·glu·ti·nate I *adj.* [ə'gluːtɪnət] **1.** zs.-geklebt, verbunden; **2.** *ling.* agglutiniert; **II** *v/t.* [-neɪt] **3.** zs.-kleben, verbinden; **4.** *biol., ling.* agglutinieren; **ag·glu·ti·na·tion** [ə,gluːtɪ'neɪʃn] *s.* **1.** Zs.-kleben *n*; anein'ander klebende Masse; **2.** *biol., ling.* Agglutinati'on *f*.

ag·gran·dize [ə'grændaɪz] *v/t.* **1.** Macht, Reichtum vermehren, -größern, erhöhen; **2.** verherrlichen, ausschmücken, *j-n* erhöhen; **ag·gran·dize·ment** [-dɪzmənt] *s.* Vermehrung *f*, Vergrößerung *f*, Erhöhung *f*, Aufstieg *m*.

ag·gra·vate ['ægrəveɪt] *v/t.* **1.** erschweren, verschärfen, verschlimmern, verstärken: ~*d larceny* ⚖ schwerer Diebstahl; **2.** F erbittern, ärgern; **'ag·gra·vat·ing** [-tɪŋ] *adj.* □ **1.** erschwerend *etc.*, gra'vierend; **2.** F ärgerlich, aufreizend; **ag·gra·va·tion** [ægrə'veɪʃn] *s.* **1.** Erschwerung *f*, Verschlimmerung *f*; **2.** F Ärger *m*.

ag·gre·gate ['ægrɪgət] **I** *adj.* □ **1.** ange-

häuft, vereinigt, gesamt, Gesamt...: ~ *amount* → II; **2.** zs.-gesetzt, Sammel...; **II** *s.* **3.** Anhäufung *f*; (Gesamt-) Menge *f*; Summe *f*: *in the* ~ insgesamt; **4.** 🜊, ⚙, *biol.* Aggre'gat *n*; **III** *v/t.* [-geɪt] **5.** anhäufen, ansammeln; vereinigen (*to* mit); **6.** sich insgesamt belaufen auf (*acc.*); **ag·gre·ga·tion** [ægrɪ'geɪʃn] *s.* **1.** Anhäufung *f*, Ansammlung *f*; Zs.-fassung *f*; **2.** *phys.* Aggre'gat *n*: *state of* ~ Aggregatzustand *m*.

ag·gres·sion [ə'greʃn] *s.* Angriff *m*, 'Überfall *m*; Aggressi'on *f* (*a. pol. u. psych.*); **ag·gres·sive** [-esɪv] *adj.* □ aggres'siv: a) streitsüchtig, angriffslustig, b) e'nergisch, draufgängerisch, dy'namisch, forsch; **ag·gres·sor** [-esə] *s.* Angreifer *m*.

ag·grieved [ə'griːvd] *adj.* **1.** bedrückt, betrübt; **2.** *bsd.* ⚖ geschädigt, beschwert, benachteiligt.

ag·gro ['ægrəʊ] *s. sl.* Randale *f*; Ärger *m*.

a·ghast [ə'gɑːst] *adj.* entgeistert, bestürzt, entsetzt (*at* über *acc.*).

ag·ile ['ædʒaɪl] *adj.* □ flink, be'händ(e) (*Verstand etc.*); **a·gil·i·ty** [ə'dʒɪlətɪ] *s.* Flinkheit *f*, Be'händigkeit *f*; Aufgewecktheit *f*.

ag·ing ['eɪdʒɪŋ] **I** *s.* **1.** Altern *n*; **2.** ⚙ Alterung *f*, Vergütung *f*; **II** *pres. p. u. adj.* **3.** alternd.

ag·i·o ['ædʒɪəʊ] *pl.* **ag·i·os** ✝ 'Agio *n*, Aufgeld *n*; **ag·i·o·tage** ['ædʒətɪdʒ] *s.* Agio'tage *f*.

ag·i·tate ['ædʒɪteɪt] **I** *v/t.* **1.** hin und her bewegen, schütteln; (um)rühren; **2.** *fig.* beunruhigen, auf-, erregen; **3.** aufwiegeln, aufregen, lebhaft erörtern; **II** *v/i.* **5.** agitieren, wühlen, hetzen; Propa'ganda machen (*for* für, *against* gegen); **'ag·i·tat·ed** [-tɪd] *adj.* □ aufgeregt; **ag·i·ta·tion** [,ædʒɪ'teɪʃn] *s.* **1.** Erschütterung *f*, heftige Bewegung; **2.** Aufregung *f*, Unruhe *f*; **3.** Agitati'on *f*, Hetze'rei *f*; Bewegung *f*, Gärung *f*; **'ag·i·ta·tor** [-tə] *s.* **1.** Agi'tator *m*, Aufwiegler *m*, Wühler *m*, Hetzer *m*; **2.** ⚙ 'Rührappa,rat *m*, -werk *n*, -arm *m*;

ag·it·prop [,ædʒɪt'prɒp] **1.** Agit'prop *f* (*kommunistische Agitation u. Propaganda*); **2.** Agit'propredner *m*.

a·glow [ə'gləʊ] *adv. u. adj. a. fig.* glühend (*with* vor *dat.*).

ag·nate ['ægneɪt] **I** *s.* **1.** A'gnat *m* (*Verwandter väterlicherseits*); **II** *adj.* **2.** väterlicherseits verwandt; **3.** stamm-, wesensverwandt; **ag·nat·ic** *adj.*; **ag·nat·i·cal** [æg'nætɪk(l)] *adj.* □ → agnate 2, 3.

ag·nos·tic [æg'nɒstɪk] **I** *s.* A'gnostiker *m*; **II** *adj.* → agnostical; **ag·nos·ti·cal** [-kl] *adj.* a'gnostisch; **ag·nos·ti·cism** [-tɪsɪzəm] *s.* Agnosti'zismus *m*.

a·go [ə'gəʊ] *adv. u. adj.* vor'über, her, vor: *ten years* ~ vor zehn Jahren; *long* ~ vor langer Zeit; *long, long* ~ lang, lang ists her; *no longer* ~ *than last month* erst vorigen Monat.

a·gog [ə'gɒg] *adv. u. adj.* gespannt, erpicht (*for* auf *acc.*): *all* ~ ganz aus dem Häuschen, ,gespannt wie ein Regenschirm'.

ag·o·nize ['ægənaɪz] **I** *v/t.* **1.** quälen, martern; **II** *v/i.* **2.** mit dem Tode ringen; **3.** Höllenqualen leiden; **4.** sich (ab-) quälen, verzweifelt ringen; **'ag·o·niz·ing** [-zɪŋ] *adj.* □ qualvoll, herzzerreißend; **'ag·o·ny** [-nɪ] *s.* **1.** heftiger Schmerz, Höllenqualen *pl.*, Qual *f*, Pein *f*, Seelenangst *f*: ~ *of despair*; ~ *column* F *Zeitung*: Seufzerspalte *f*; *pile on the* ~ F ,dick auftragen'; **2.** ⚥ Rin-

gen *n* Christi mit dem Tode; **3.** Todeskampf *m*, Ago'nie *f*.

ag·o·ra·pho·bi·a [,ægərə'fəʊbjə] *s.* 🜪 Platzangst *f*.

a·grar·i·an [ə'greərɪən] **I** *adj.* **1.** a'grarisch, landwirtschaftlich, Agrar...: ~ *unrest* Unruhe in der Landwirtschaft; **2.** gleichmäßige Landaufteilung betreffend; **II** *s.* **3.** Befürworter *m* gleichmäßiger Aufteilung des (Acker)Landes.

a·gree [ə'griː] **I** *v/i.* **1.** (*to*) zustimmen (*dat.*), einwilligen (in *acc.*), beipflichten (*dat.*), genehmigen (*acc.*), einverstanden sein (mit), eingehen (auf *acc.*), gutheißen (*acc.*): ~ *to a plan*; *I* ~ *to come with you* ich bin bereit mitzukommen; *you will* ~ *that* du musst zugeben, dass; **2.** (*on, upon, about*) sich einigen *od.* verständigen (über *acc.*); vereinbaren, verabreden (*acc.*): *they* ~*d about the price*; ~ *to differ* sich auf verschiedene Standpunkte einigen; *let us* ~ *to differ!* ich fürchte, wir können uns da nicht einigen!; **3.** über'einkommen, vereinbaren (*to inf.* zu *inf.*, *that* dass): *it is* ~*d* es ist vereinbart, es steht fest; → *agreed* 2; **4.** (*with* mit) über'einstimmen (*a. ling.*), (sich) einig sein, gleicher Meinung sein: *I* ~ *that your advice is best* auch ich bin der Meinung, dass Ihr Rat der beste ist; → *agreed* 1; **5.** sich vertragen, auskommen, zs.-passen, sich vereinigen (lassen); **6.** ~ *with j-m* bekommen, zuträglich sein: *wine does not* ~ *with me*; **II** *v/t.* **7.** ✝ *Konten etc.* abstimmen.

a·gree·a·ble [ə'griːəbl] *adj.* □ → *agreeably*; **1.** angenehm; gefällig, liebenswürdig; **2.** einverstanden (*to* mit): ~ *to the plan*; **3.** F bereit, gefügig; **4.** (*to*) über'einstimmend (mit), entsprechend (*dat.*): ~ *to the rules*; **a·gree·a·ble·ness** [-nɪs] *s.* angenehmes Wesen; Annehmlichkeit *f*; **a·gree·a·bly** [-lɪ] *adv.* **1.** angenehm: ~ *surprised*; **2.** einverstanden (*to* mit); entsprechend (*to dat.*): ~ *to his instructions*.

a·greed [ə'griːd] *adj.* **1.** einig (*on* über *acc.*); einmütig: ~ *decisions*; **2.** vereinbart: *the* ~ *price*; ~*!* abgemacht!, einverstanden!; **a·gree·ment** [-mənt] *s.* **1.** a) Abkommen *n*, Vereinbarung *f*, Einigung *f*, Verständigung *f*, Über'einkunft *f*, b) Vertrag *m*, c) (gütlicher) Vergleich: *by* ~ wie vereinbart; *come to an* ~ sich einigen, sich verständigen; *by mutual* ~ in gegenseitigem Einvernehmen; ~ *country* (*currency*) ✝ Verrechnungsland *n* (-währung *f*); **2.** Einigkeit *f*, Eintracht *f*; **3.** Über'einstimmung *f* (*a. ling.*), Einklang *m*; **4.** Genehmigung *f*, Zustimmung *f*.

ag·ri·cul·tur·al [,ægrɪ'kʌltʃərəl] *adj.* □ landwirtschaftlich, Landwirtschaft(s)...: ~ *country* Ag'rarland *n*; ~ *labo(u)rer* Landarbeiter *m*; ~ *levy* EU Abschöpfung *f*; ~ *market* Ag'rarmarkt; ~ *policy* Ag'rarpoli,tik *f*; ~ *show* Landwirtschaftsausstellung *f*; ,**ag·ri'cul·tur·al·ist** [-rəlɪst] → *agriculturist*; **ag·ri·cul·ture** ['ægrɪkʌltʃə] *s.* Landwirtschaft *f*, Ackerbau *m* (u. Viehzucht *f*); ,**ag·ri'cul·tur·ist** [-tʃərɪst] *s.* (Dip'lom)Landwirt *m*.

ag·ro·chem·i·cal [,ægrəʊ'kemɪkl] *s.* Ag'rarchemi,kalie *f* (*Spritz- od. Düngemittel*).

ag·ro·nom·ics [,ægrə'nɒmɪks] *s. pl. sg. konstr.* Agrono'mie *f*, Ackerbaukunde *f*; **a·gron·o·mist** [ə'grɒnəmɪst] *s.* Agro'nom *m*, (Dip'lom)Landwirt *m*; **a·gron·o·my** [ə'grɒnəmɪ] → *agronomics*.

a·ground [ə'graʊnd] *adv. u. adj.* ⚓ gestrandet: **run ~** a) auflaufen, stranden, b) auf Grund setzen; **be ~** a) aufgelaufen sein, b) *fig.* auf dem Trocknen sitzen.

a·gue ['eɪgjuː] *s.* Schüttelfrost *m*; (Wechsel)Fieber *n.*

ah [ɑː] *int.* ah, ach, oh, ha, ei!

a·ha [ɑːˈhɑː] I *int.* a'ha, ha'ha!; II *adj.*: ~ **experience** Aha-Erlebnis *n.*

a·head [əˈhed] *adv. u. adj.* **1.** vorn; voraus, vor'an; vorwärts, nach vorn; einen Vorsprung habend, an der Spitze; be'vorstehend: **right** (*od.* **straight**) ~ geradeaus; **the years ~** (**of us**) die bevorstehenden (*od.* vor uns liegenden) Jahre; **look** (**think, plan**) ~ vorausschauen (-denken, -planen); **look ~!** a) sieh dich vor!, b) *fig.* denk an die Zukunft!; → **get ahead, go ahead, speed** 1; **2. ~ of** vor (*dat.*), vor'aus (*dat.*): **be ~ of the others** vor den anderen sein *od.* liegen, den anderen voraus sein, (e-n) Vorsprung vor den anderen haben, die anderen übertreffen; **get ~ of s.o.** j-n überholen *od.* überflügeln; **~ of the times** der *od.* s-r Zeit voraus.

a·hem [mˈmm] *int.* hm!

a·hoy [əˈhɔɪ] *int.* ♨ ho!, a'hoi!

aid [eɪd] I *v/t.* **1.** unter'stützen, fördern; *j-m* helfen, behilflich sein (**in** bei, **to** *inf.* zu *inf.*): **~ and abet** 🕮 a) Beihilfe leisten (*dat.*), b) begünstigen (*acc.*); II *s.* **2.** Hilfe *f* (**to** für), -leistung *f* (**in** bei), Unter'stützung *f*: **he came to her ~** er kam ihr zu Hilfe; **by** *od.* **with** (**the**) **~ of** mithilfe von; **in ~ of** zugunsten von (*od. gen.*); **3.** Helfer(in), Beistand *m*, Assis'tent(in); **4.** Hilfsmittel *n*, (Hilfs-) Gerät *n*, Mittel *n*: → **hearing** 2.

aide [eɪd] *s.* **1.** Berater *m*; **2.** → **aid(e)- -de-camp** [ˌeɪddəˈkɑːŋ] *pl.* **ˌaid(e)s- -de-camp** [ˌeɪdzˈ-] *s.* ✕ Adju'tant *m.*

aide-mé·moire [ˌeɪdmemˈwɑː] (*Fr.*) *s. sg. u. pl.* **1.** Gedächtnisstütze *f*, No'tiz *f*; **2.** *pol.* Denkschrift *f.*

AIDS, Aids [eɪdz] *s.* Aids *n*: **~ risk** Aidsgefahr *f*; **~ sufferer** Aidskranke(r *m*) *f*; **~ victim** Aidskranke(r *m*) *f*, -opfer *n.*

ai·grette ['eɪgret] *s.* **1.** *orn.* kleiner, weißer Reiher; **2.** Ai'grette *f*, Kopfschmuck *m* (*aus Federn etc.*).

ail [eɪl] I *v/t.* schmerzen: **what ~s you?** *a. fig.* was hast du denn?; II *v/i.* kränkeln.

ai·ler·on ['eɪlərɒn] (*Fr.*) *s.* ✈ Querruder *n.*

ail·ing ['eɪlɪŋ] *adj.* kränklich, leidend; **ail·ment** ['eɪlmənt] *s.* Unpässlichkeit *f*, Leiden *n.*

aim [eɪm] I *v/i.* **1.** zielen (**at** auf *acc.*, nach); **2.** *mst* **~ at** *fig. et.* beabsichtigen, an-, erstreben, bezwecken: **~ing to please** zu gefallen suchend; **be ~ing to do** *Am.* vorhaben *et.* zu tun; **3.** abzielen (**at** auf *acc.*): **that was not ~ed at you** das war nicht auf dich gemünzt; II *v/t.* (**at**) **4.** Waffe *etc.*, *a.* Bestrebungen richten (auf *acc.*); **5.** *Bemerkungen* richten (gegen); III *s.* **6.** Ziel *n*, Richtung *f*: **take ~** at zielen auf (*acc.*) *od.* nach; **7.** Ziel *n*, Zweck *m*, Absicht *f*; **ˈaim·less** [-lɪs] *adj.* □ ziel-, zweck-, planlos.

ain't [eɪnt] F *abbr. für:* **am not, is not, are not, has not, have not.**

air¹ [eə] I *s.* **1.** Luft *f*, Atmo'sphäre *f*, Luftraum *m*: **by ~** auf dem Luftweg(e), mit dem Flugzeug; **in the open ~** im Freien; **hot ~** *sl.* leeres Geschwätz, blauer Dunst; → **beat** 11; **clear the ~** die Luft (*fig.* die Atmosphäre) reinigen; **vanish into thin ~** *fig.* sich in nichts auflösen; **change of ~** Luftveränderung *f*; **be in the ~** *fig.* a) in der

Luft liegen, b) in der Schwebe sein (*Frage etc.*), c) im Umlauf sein (*Gerücht etc.*); **be up in the ~** *fig.* a) (völlig) in der Luft hängen, b) völlig ungewiss sein, c) F ganz aus dem Häuschen sein (**about** wegen); **take the ~** a) frische Luft schöpfen, b) ✈ abheben, aufsteigen; **walk on ~** sich wie im Himmel fühlen, selig sein; **in the ~** *fig.* (völlig) ungewiss; **give s.o. the ~** *Am.* j-n an die (frische) Luft setzen; **2.** Brise *f*, Luftzug *m*, Lüftchen *n*; **3.** ⚒ Wetter *n*: **foul ~** schlagende Wetter *pl.*; **4.** *Radio, TV*: 'air: **on the ~** im Rundfunk *od.* Fernsehen; **be on the ~** a) senden, b) gesendet werden, c) auf Sendung sein (*Person*), d) zu hören *od.* zu sehen sein (*Person*); **go off the ~** a) die Sendung beenden (*Person*), b) sein Programm beenden (*Sender*); **put on the ~** senden, übertragen; **stay on the ~** auf Sendung bleiben; **5.** Art *f*, Stil *m*; **6.** Miene *f*, Aussehen *n*, Wesen *n*: **an ~ of importance** e-e gewichtige Miene; **7.** *mst pl.* Getue *n*; ‚Gehabe' *n*, Pose *f*: **~s and graces** affektiertes Getue; **put on** (*od.* **give o.s**) **~s** vornehm tun; II *v/t.* **8.** der Luft aussetzen, lüften; **9.** *Wäsche* trocknen, zum Trocknen aufhängen; **10.** *Ansicht etc.* an die Öffentlichkeit *od.* zur Sprache bringen, äußern: **~ one's grievances**; **12. ~ o.s.** frische Luft schöpfen; III *adj.* **13.** Luft..., pneu'matisch.

air² [eə] *s.* ♪ **1.** Lied *n*, Melo'die *f*, Weise *f*; **2.** Arie *f.*

air| a·lert *s.* 'Flieger-, 'Lufta‚larm *m*; **~ arm** *s.* ✈ *Brit.* Luftwaffe *f*; **~ bag** *s. mot.* Airbag *m*, Luftsack *m*; **~ bar·rage** *s.* ✈ Luftsperre *f*; **ˈ~·base** *s.* ✈ Luft-, Flugstützpunkt *m*, Fliegerhorst *m*; **ˈ~· bath** *s.* Luftbad *n*; **~ bea·con** *s.* ✈ Leuchtfeuer *n*; **ˈ~·bed** *s.* 'Luftma‚tratze *f*; **~ blad·der** *s. ichth.* Schwimmblase *f*; **ˈ~·borne** *adj.* **1.** a) im Flugzeug befördert *od.* eingebaut, Bord...: **~ transmitter** Bordfunkgerät *n*, b) Luftlande...: **~ troops**, c) auf dem Luftweg(e); **2.** in der Luft befindlich, aufgestiegen: **be ~**; **ˈ~·brake** *s.* ✈ Luft(druck)bremse *f*; **2.** ✈ Landeklappe *f*: **~ parachute** Landefallschirm *m*; **ˈ~·brick** *s.* ⊛ Luftziegel *m*; **ˈ~·bridge** *s.* ✈ **1.** Luftbrücke *f*; **2.** Fluggastbrücke *f*; **~ bub·ble** *s.* Luftblase *f*; **ˈ~·bump** *s.* ✈ Bö *f*, aufsteigender Luftstrom; **ˈ~·bus** *s.* ✈ Airbus *m*; **~ car·go** *s.* Luftfracht *f*; **~ car·ri·er** *s.* ✈ Fluggesellschaft *f*; **2.** Charterflugzeug *n*; **~ cas·ing** *s.* ⊛ Luftmantel *m*; **~ cham·ber** *s.* ♥, *zo.*, ⊛ Luftkammer *f*; **~ com·pres·sor** *s.* ⊛ Luftverdichter *m*; **ˈ~·con‚di·tion** *v/t.* mit Klimaanlage versehen, klimatisieren; **~ con‚di·tion·ing** *s.* ⊛ Klimatisierung *f*; *a.* **~ plant** Klimaanlage *f*; **ˈ~· -cooled** *adj.* luftgekühlt; **⚒ Corps** *s. hist. Am.* Luftwaffe *f*; **~ cor·ri·dor** *s.* 'Luft‚korridor *m*, Einflugschneise *f*; **~ cov·er** *s.* Luftsicherung *f.*

ˈair·craft *s.* Flugzeug *n*; *coll.* Luftfahrzeuge *pl.*; **~ car·ri·er** *s.* Flugzeugträger *m*; **~ en·gine** *s.* 'Flug‚motor *m*; **~ in·dus·try** *s.* 'Luftfahrt-, 'Flugzeugindu‚strie *f*; **~ man** [-mən] *s.* [*irr.*] *Brit.* Flieger *m* (*Dienstgrad*); **~ weap·ons** *pl.* Bordwaffen *pl.*

air| crash *s.* Flugzeugabsturz *m*; **ˈ~·crew** *s.* (Flugzeug)Besatzung *f*; **~ cush·ion** *s. a.* ⊛ Luftkissen *n*; **ˈ~·‚cush·ion ve·hi·cle** *s.* ⊛ Luftkissenfahrzeug *n*; **~ de·fence**, *Am.* **~ de·fense** *s.* ✕ Luftschutz *m*, -verteidigung *f*, Fliegerabwehr *f.*

air·drome ['eədrəʊm] *s. Am.* Flugplatz *m.*

ˈair|·drop I *s.* a) Fallschirmabwurf *m*, b) ✕ Luftlandung *f*; II *v/t.* a) mit dem Fallschirm abwerfen, b) ✕ *Fallschirmjäger etc.* absetzen; **ˈ~·dry** *v/t. u. v/i.* lufttrocknen; **ˈ~·field** *s.* Flugplatz *m*; **~ flap** *s.* ⊛ Luftklappe *f*; **ˈ~·foil** *s.* ✈ Tragfläche *f*; **~ force**, ⚒ **Force** *s.* ✕ Luftwaffe *f*, Luftstreitkräfte *pl.*; **ˈ~·frame** *s.* ✈ Flugwerk *n*, (Flugzeug-) Zelle *f*; **ˈ~·freight** *s.* Luftfracht *f*; **ˈ~·‚freight·er** *s.* **1.** Luftfrachter *m*; **2.** 'Luftspediti‚on *f*; **ˈ~·graph** [-grɑːf] *s.* 'Fotoluftpostbrief *m*; **ˈ~·ground** *adj.* ✈ Bord-Boden-...; **ˈ~·gun** *s.* Luftgewehr *n*; **~ host·ess** *s.* ✈ ('Luft)Stewardess *f*; **ˈ~·house** *s.* Traglufthalle *f.*

air·i·ly ['eərɪlɪ] *adv.* 'leicht'hin, unbekümmert; **ˈair·i·ness** [-nɪs] *s.* **1.** Luftigkeit *f*; luftige Lage; **2.** Leichtigkeit *f*; Munterkeit *f*; Leichtfertigkeit *f*; **ˈair·ing** [-rɪŋ] *s.* **1.** (Be)Lüftung *f*, Trocknen *n*: **give s.th. an ~** *et.* lüften; **2.** Spaziergang *m*: **take an ~** frische Luft schöpfen; **3.** Äußerung *f*; Erörterung *f.*

air| in·take *s.* ⊛ **1.** Lufteinlass *m*; Zuluftstutzen *m*; **~ jack·et** *s.* **1.** Schwimmweste *f*; **2.** ⊛ Luftmantel *m*; **~ jet** *s.* ⊛ Luftstrahl *m*, -düse *f*; **ˈ~·lane** *s.* Luftroute *f.*

air·less ['eəlɪs] *adj.* **1.** ohne Luft(zug); **2.** dumpf, stickig.

air| let·ter *s.* **1.** Luftpostbrief *m* (*auf Formular*); **2.** *Am.* Luftpostleichtbrief *m*; **~ lev·el** *s.* ⊛ Li'belle *f*, Setzwaage *f*; **ˈ~·lift** I *s.* Luftbrücke *f*; II *v/t.* über e-e Luftbrücke befördern; **ˈ~·line** *s.* Luft-, Flugverkehrsgesellschaft *f*; **ˈ~·lin·er** *s.* ✈ Verkehrs-, Linienflugzeug *n*; **ˈ~·lock** *s.* ⊛ **1.** Luftschleuse *f*; **2.** Druckstauung *f*; **ˈ~·mail** *s.* (**by ~** mit *od.* per) Luftpost *f*; **~ man** [-mən] *s.* [*irr.*] Flieger *m*; **~ me·chan·ic** *s.* ✈ 'Bordmon‚teur *m*; **ˈ~·‚mind·ed** *adj.* ✈ luft(fahrt)-, flug(sport)begeistert; **ˈ~·op·er·at·ed** *adj.* ⊛ pressluftbetätigt; **~ par·cel** *Brit.* 'Luftpostpa‚ket *n*; **~ pas·sage** *s.* **1.** *anat., biol.*, Luft-, Atemweg *m*; **2.** ⊛ Luftschlitz *m*; **~ pas·sen·ger** *s.* Fluggast *m*; **~ pho·to(·graph)** *s.* ✈ Luftbild *n*, -aufnahme *f*; **~ pi·ra·cy** *s.* 'Luftpirate‚rie *f*; **~ pi·rate** *s.* 'Luftpi‚rat *m*; **ˈ~·plane** *s.* ✈ Flugzeug *n*; **ˈ~·plane car·ri·er** *bsd. Am.* → **aircraft carrier**; **~ pock·et** *s.* Fallbö *f*, Luftloch *n*; **~ pol·lu·tion** *s.* Luftverschmutzung *f*; **ˈ~·port** *s.* ✈ Flughafen *m*; **ˈ~·proof** *adj.* luftbeständig, -dicht; **~ pump** *s.* ⊛ Luftpumpe *f*; **~ raft** *s.* Schlauchboot *n*; **~ raid** *s.* Luftangriff *m.*

ˈair·raid| pre·cau·tions *s. pl.* Luftschutz *m*; **~ shel·ter** *s.* Luftschutzraum *m*, -bunker *m*, -keller *m*; **~ ward·en** *s.* Luftschutzwart *m*; **~ warn·ing** *s.* Luft-, Fliegerwarnung *f*, 'Fliegera‚larm *m.*

air| res·cue *s.* Luftrettung *f*: **~ service** Luftrettungsdienst; **~ ri·fle** *s.* Luftgewehr *n*; **~ route** *s.* ✈ Flugroute *f*; **~ sched·ule** *s.* Flugplan *m*; **ˈ~·screw** *s.* ✈ Luftschraube *f*; **ˈ~·seal** *v/t.* ⊛ luftdicht verschließen; **ˈ~·ship** *s.* Luftschiff *n*; **ˈ~·sick** *adj.* luftkrank; **ˈ~·‚sick·ness** *s.* Luftkrankheit *f*; **ˈ~·space** *s.* Luftraum *m*; **~ speed** *s.* ✈ (Flug)Eigengeschwindigkeit *f*; **ˈ~·strip** *s.* ✈ **1.** Behelfslandeplatz *m*; **2.** *Am.* Roll-, Start-, Landebahn *f*; **~ tax·i** *s.* ✈ Lufttaxi *n*; **~ tee** *s.* ✈ Landekreuz *n*; **~ ter·mi·nal** *s.* ✈ **1.** Großflughafen *m*; **2.** Terminal *m*, *n*: a) (Flughafen)Abfertigungsgebäude, b) *Brit.* 'Endstati‚on *f* der 'Zubringer‚linie zum und vom Flughafen;

'~·tight adj. **1.** luftdicht; **2.** fig. todsicher, völlig klar; **,~-to-'air** adj. ✈ Bord-Bord-...; **,~-to-'ground** adj. ✈ Bord-Boden-...; **~ traf·fic** s. Luft-, Flugverkehr m; **'~-,traf·fic con·trol** s. ✈ Flugsicherung f; **'~-,traf·fic con·trol·ler** s. ✈ Fluglotse m; **~ tube** s. **1.** ⊙ Luftschlauch m; **2.** anat. Luftröhre f; **~ um·brel·la** s. ✈ Luftschirm m; **'~·way** s. **1.** ⊙, ✈ Wetterstrecke f, Luftschacht m; **2.** ✈ a) Luft(verkehrs)weg m, Luftroute f, b) → **airline**; **'~,wom·an** s. [irr.] Fliegerin f; **'~,wor·thi·ness** s. ✈ Lufttüchtigkeit f.

air·y ['eərɪ] adj. □ → **airily**; **1.** Luft...; **2.** luftig, a. windig; **3.** körperlos; **4.** grazi'ös; **5.** lebhaft, munter; **6.** über-'spannt, verstiegen: **~ plans**; **7.** lässig: **an ~ manner**; **8.** vornehmtuerisch.

aisle [aɪl] s. **1.** △ a) Seitenschiff n, -chor m (e-r Kirche), b) Schiff n, Abteilung f (e-r Kirche od. e-s Gebäudes); **2.** (Mittel)Gang m (zwischen Bänken etc.): **~ seat** ✈ etc. Gangplatz m; **3.** fig. Schneise f.

aitch [eɪtʃ] s. H n, h n (Buchstabe): **drop one's ~es** das H nicht aussprechen (Zeichen der Unbildung); **'aitch·bone** s. **1.** Lendenknochen m; **2.** Lendenstück n (vom Rind).

a·jar [ə'dʒɑː] adv. u. adj. **1.** halb offen, angelehnt (Tür); **2.** fig. im Zwiespalt.

a·kim·bo [ə'kɪmbəʊ] adv. die Arme in die Seite gestemmt.

a·kin [ə'kɪn] adj. **1.** (bluts- od. stamm-) verwandt (to mit); **2.** verwandt; sehr ähnlich (to dat.).

al·a·bas·ter ['æləbɑːstə] **I** s. min. Ala-'baster m; **II** adj. ala'bastern, ala'basterweiß, Alabaster...

a·lac·ri·ty [ə'lækrɪtɪ] s. **1.** Munterkeit f; **2.** Bereitwilligkeit f, Eifer m.

A·lad·din's lamp [ə'lædɪnz] s. 'Aladins Wunderlampe f; fig. Wunder wirkender 'Talisman.

à la mode [,ɑːlɑː'məʊd] (Fr.) adj. **1.** à la mode, modisch; **2.** gespickt u. geschmort u. mit Gemüse zubereitet: **beef ~**; **3.** Am. mit (Speise)Eis (serviert): **cake ~**.

a·larm [ə'lɑːm] **I** s. **1.** A'larm m, Warnruf m, Warnung f: **false ~** blinder Alarm, falsche Meldung; **give (raise, sound) the ~** Alarm geben od. fig. schlagen; **2.** a) Weckvorrichtung f b) Wecker m; **3.** A'larmvorrichtung f; **4.** Lärm m, Aufruhr m; **5.** Angst f, Unruhe f, Bestürzung f; **II** v/t. **6.** alarmieren, warnen; **7.** beunruhigen, erschrecken (at über acc., by durch): **be ~ed** sich ängstigen, bestürzt sein; **~ bell** s. A'larm-, Sturmglocke f; **~ clock** s. Wecker m (Uhr).

a·larm·ing [ə'lɑːmɪŋ] adj. □ beunruhigend, beängstigend; **a'larm·ist** [-mɪst] **I** s. Bangemacher m, Schwarzseher m, ,Unke' f; **II** adj. schwarzseherisch.

a·las [ə'læs] int. ach!, leider!

alb [ælb] s. eccl. Albe f, Chorhemd n.

Al·ba·ni·an [æl'beɪnjən] **I** adj. al'banisch; **II** s. Al'ban(i)er(in).

al·ba·tross ['ælbətrɒs] s. orn. 'Albatros m, Sturmvogel m.

al·be·it [ɔːl'biːɪt] cj. ob'gleich, wenn auch.

al·bert ['ælbət] s. a. ♀ **chain** Brit. (kurze) Uhrkette.

al·bi·no [æl'biːnəʊ] pl. **-nos** s. Al'bino m, 'Kakerlak m.

Al·bion ['ælbɪən] npr. poet. 'Albion n (Britannien od. England).

al·bum ['ælbəm] s. **1.** 'Album n, Stammbuch n; **2.** (Briefmarken-, Foto-, Schallplatten- etc.)Album n; **3.** a) 'Schallplattenkas,sette f, b) Album n

(Langspielplatte[n]); **4.** Gedichtsammlung etc. (in Buchform).

al·bu·men ['ælbjumɪn] s. **1.** zo. Eiweiß n, Al'bumen n; **2.** ♀, ♗, ♯ Eiweiß(stoff m) n, Albu'min n; **al·bu·min** ['ælbjumɪn] → **albumen** 2; **al·bu·mi·nous** [æl'bjuːmɪnəs] adj. eiweißartig, -haltig.

al·chem·ic adj., **al·chem·i·cal** [æl'kemɪk(l)] adj. □ alchi'mistisch; **al·che·mist** ['ælkɪmɪst] s. Alchi'mist m, Goldmacher m; **al·che·my** ['ælkɪmɪ] s. Alchi'mie f.

al·co·hol ['ælkəhɒl] s. 'Alkohol m: a) Sprit m, 'Spiritus m, Weingeist m: **ethyl ~** Äthylalkohol m, b) geistige od. alko-'holische Getränke pl.; **al·co·hol·ic** [,ælkə'hɒlɪk] **I** adj. **1.** alko'holisch, 'alkoholartig, -haltig, Alkohol...: **~ drinks**; **~ strength** Alkoholgehalt m; **II** s. **2.** (Gewohnheits)Trinker(in), Alko'holiker(in); **3.** pl. Alko'holika pl., alkoholische Getränke pl.; **'al·co·hol·ism** [-lɪzəm] s. Alkoho'lismus m: a) Trunksucht f, b) durch Trunksucht verursachte Organismusschädigungen.

al·cove ['ælkəʊv] s. Al'koven m, Nische f; (Garten)Laube f, Grotte f.

al·de·hyde ['ældɪhaɪd] s. ♯ Alde'hyd m.

al·der ['ɔːldə] s. ♀ Erle f.

al·der·man ['ɔːldəmən] s. [irr.] Ratsherr m, Stadtrat m; **'al·der·man·ry** [-rɪ] s. **1.** (von e-m Ratsherrn vertretener) Stadtbezirk; **2.** → **'al·der·man·ship** [-ʃɪp] s. Amt n e-s Ratsherrn; **al·der·wom·an** ['ɔːldə,wʊmən] s. [irr.] Stadträtin f.

ale [eɪl] s. Ale n (helles, obergäriges Bier).

a·leck ['ælɪk] s. Am. F → **smart aleck**.

a·lee [ə'liː] adv. u. adj. leewärts.

'ale·house s. 'Bierlo,kal n.

a·lem·bic [ə'lembɪk] s. **1.** Destillierkolben m; **2.** fig. Re'torte f.

a·lert [ə'lɜːt] **I** adj. □ **1.** wachsam, auf der Hut; achtsam: **~ to** klar bewusst (gen.); **2.** rege, munter; **3.** aufgeweckt, forsch, a'lert; **II** s. **4.** (A'larm)Bereitschaft f: **on the ~** auf der Hut, in Alarmbereitschaft; **5.** A'larm(si,gnal n) m, Warnung f; **III** v/t. **6.** alarmieren, warnen, ✗a. in A'larmzustand versetzen, weitS. mobilisieren: **~ s.o. to s.th.** fig. j-m et. zum Bewusstsein bringen; **a'lert·ness** [-nɪs] s. **1.** Wachsamkeit f; **2.** Munterkeit f, Flinkheit f; **3.** Aufgewecktheit f, Forschheit f.

A lev·el s. Brit. ped. (etwa) Abi'tur n: **take one's ~s** etwa: das Abitur machen; **he has three ~s** er hat das Abitur in drei Fächern gemacht.

Al·ex·an·drine [,ælɪg'zændraɪn] s. Alexan'driner m (Versart).

al·fal·fa [æl'fælfə] s. ♀ Lu'zerne f.

al·fres·co [æl'freskəʊ] (Ital.) adj. u. adv. im Freien: **~ lunch**.

al·ga ['ælgə] pl. **-gae** [-dʒiː] s. ♀ Alge f, Tang m.

al·ge·bra ['ældʒɪbrə] s. ♬ Algebra f; **,al·ge·bra·ic** [-'reɪɪk] adj. □ alge'braisch: **~ calculus** Algebra f.

Al·ge·ri·an [æl'dʒɪərɪən] **I** adj. al'gerisch; **II** s. Al'gerier(in).

Al·gol ['ælgɒl] s. ALGOL n (Computersprache).

al·go·rithm ['ælgərɪðəm] s. ♬ etc. Algo'rithmus m.

a·li·as ['eɪlɪæs] **I** adv. 'alias, sonst (... genannt); **II** s. pl. **-as·es** angenommener Name, Deckname m.

al·i·bi ['ælɪbaɪ] s. **1.** ♔ 'Alibi n: **establish one's ~** sein Alibi erbringen; **3.** F Ausrede f, 'Alibi n.

al·ien ['eɪljən] **I** adj. **1.** fremd; ausländisch: **~ subjects** ausländische Staatsangehörige; **2.** außerirdisch (Wesen); **3.**

fig. andersartig, fern liegend, fremd (to dat.); **4.** fig. zu'wider, 'unsym,pathisch (to dat.); **II** s. **5.** Fremde(r m) f, Ausländer(in): **enemy ~** feindlicher Ausländer; **~s police** Fremdenpolizei f; **6.** nicht naturalisierter Bewohner des Landes; **7.** fig. Fremdling m; **8.** außerirdisches Wesen; **9.** ling. Fremdwort n; **'al·ien·a·ble** [-nəbl] adj. veräußerlich; über'tragbar; **al·ien·age** [-nɪdʒ] s. Ausländertum n; **'al·ien·ate** [-neɪt] v/t. **1.** ♔ veräußern, über'tragen; **2.** entfremden, abspenstig machen (from dat.); **al·ien·a·tion** [,eɪljə'neɪʃn] s. **1.** ♔ Veräußerung f, Über'tragung f; **2.** Entfremdung f (a. psych., pol.) (from von), Abwendung f, Abneigung f: **~ of affections** ♔ Entfremdung (ehelicher Zuneigung); **3.** a. **mental ~** Alienati'on f, Psy'chose f; **4.** literarische Verfremdung: **~ effect** Verfremdungs-, V-Effekt m; **'al·ien·ist** [-nɪst] s. obs. Nervenarzt m.

a·light¹ [ə'laɪt] v/i. **1.** ab-, aussteigen; **2.** sich niederlassen, sich setzen (Vogel), fallen (Schnee): **~ on one's feet** auf die Füße fallen; **3.** ✈ niedergehen, landen; **4.** (on) (zufällig) stoßen (auf acc.), antreffen (acc.).

a·light² [ə'laɪt] adj. **1.** → **ablaze**; **2.** erleuchtet (with von).

a·lign [ə'laɪn] **I** v/t. **1.** ausfluchten, in e-e (gerade) 'Linie bringen; in gerader Linie od. in Reih und Glied aufstellen; ausrichten (with nach); **2.** fig. zu e-r Gruppe (Gleichgesinnter) zs.-schließen; **3.** ~ o.s. (with) sich anschließen, sich anpassen (an acc.); **II** v/i. **4.** sich in gerader Linie od. in Reih und Glied aufstellen; sich ausrichten (with nach); **a'lign·ment** [-mənt] s. **1.** Anordnung f in 'einer Linie, Ausrichten n; Anpassung f: **in ~ with** in 'einer Linie od. Richtung mit (a. fig.); **2.** ⊙ a) Ausfluchten n, Ausrichten n, b) 'Linien-, Zeilenführung f, c) 'Absteckungs,linie f, Trasse f, Flucht f, Gleichlauf m; **3.** fig. Ausrichtung f, Gruppierung f: **~ of political forces**.

a·like [ə'laɪk] **I** adj. gleich, ähnlich; **II** adv. gleich, ebenso, in gleichem Maße: **she helps enemies and friends ~**.

al·i·ment ['ælɪmənt] s. Nahrung(smittel n) f; **2.** et. Lebensnotwendiges; **al·i·men·ta·ry** [,ælɪ'mentərɪ] adj. **1.** nahrhaft; **2.** Nahrungs..., Ernährungs...: **~ canal** Verdauungskanal m; **al·i·men·ta·tion** [,ælɪmen'teɪʃn] s. Ernährung f, Unterhalt m.

al·i·mo·ny ['ælɪmənɪ] s. ♔ 'Unterhalt(szahlung f) m.

a·line etc. → **align** etc.

al·i·quant ['ælɪkwənt] adj. ♬ ali'quant, mit Rest teilend; **'al·i·quot** [-kwɒt] adj. ♬ ali'quot, ohne Rest teilend.

a·live [ə'laɪv] adj. **1.** lebend, (noch) am Leben: **the proudest man ~** der stolzeste Mann der Welt; **no man ~** kein Sterblicher; **man ~!** F Menschenskind!; **2.** tätig, in voller Kraft od. Wirksamkeit, im Gange: **keep ~** a) aufrechterhalten, bewahren, b) am Leben bleiben; **3.** lebendig, lebhaft, belebt: **~ and kicking** F gesund u. munter; **look ~!** F (mach) fix!, pass auf!; **4.** (to) empfänglich (für), bewusst (gen.), achtsam (auf acc.); **5.** voll, belebt, wimmelnd (with von); **6.** ♭ Strom führend, geladen, unter Strom stehend.

al·ka·li ['ælkəlaɪ] ♔ **I** pl. **-lies** od. **-lis** s. **1.** Al'kali n; **2.** (in wässriger Lösung) stark al'kalisch reagierende Verbindung: **caustic ~** Ätzalkali; **mineral ~**

kohlensaures Natron; **3.** *geol.* kalzinierte Soda; **II** *adj.* **4.** al'kalisch: **~** *soil*; **'al·ka·line** [-laɪn] *adj.* 🜍 al'kalisch, al'kalihaltig, basisch; **al·ka·lin·i·ty** [ˌælkə'lɪnətɪ] *s.* 🜍 Alkalini'tät *f*, al'kalische Eigenschaft; **'al·ka·lize** [-laɪz] *v/t.* 🜍 alkalisieren, auslaugen; **'al·ka·loid** [-lɔɪd] 🜍 **I** *s.* Alkalo'id *n*; **II** *adj.* al'kaliartig, laugenhaft.

all [ɔːl] **I** *adj.* **1.** all, sämtlich, vollständig, ganz: **~** *the wine* der ganze Wein; **~** *day* (*long*) den ganzen Tag; *for* **~** *that* dessen ungeachtet, trotzdem; **~** *the time* die ganze Zeit; *for* **~** *time* für immer; **~** *the way* die ganze Strecke, *fig.* völlig, rückhaltlos; *with* **~** *respect* bei aller Hochachtung; **2.** jeder, jede, jedes (beliebige); alle *pl.*: *at* **~** *hours* zu jeder Stunde; *beyond* **~** *question* fraglos; → *event* 3, *mean³* 3; **3.** ganz, rein: **~** *wool* reine Wolle; → *all-American*; **II** *s.* **4.** das Ganze, alles; Gesamtbesitz *m*: *his* **~** a) sein Hab u. Gut, b) sein Ein u. Alles; **III** *pron.* **5.** alles: **~** *of it* alles; **~** *of us* wir alle; **~'s** *well that ends well* Ende gut, alles gut; *when* **~** *is said* (*and done*) F letzten Endes, im Grunde genommen; *what is it* **~** *about?* um was handelt es sich?; *the best of* **~** *would be* das Allerbeste wäre; *in* **~** insgesamt; **~** *in* **~** alles in allem; *is that* **~***?* a) sonst noch et.?, b) F schöne Geschichte!; **IV** *adv.* **6.** ganz, gänzlich, völlig, höchst: **~** *wrong* ganz falsch, völlig im Irrtum; *that is* **~** *very well, but ...* das ist ja ganz schön u. gut, aber ...; *he was* **~** *ears* (*eyes*) er war ganz Ohr (Auge); *she is* **~** *kindness* sie ist die Güte selber; *the better* umso besser; **~** *one* einerlei, gleichgültig; **~** *the same* a) ganz gleich, gleichgültig, b) gleichwohl, trotzdem, immerhin; → *above* 2, *after* 1, *at¹* 7, *but* 13, *once* 4 b; **7.** *Sport:* *two* **~** zwei beide, zwei zu zwei;

Zssgn mit adv. u. prp.:

all| a·long a) der ganzen Länge nach, b) F die ganze Zeit, schon immer; **~** *in sl.* ‚fertig', ganz ‚erledigt'; **~** *out* a) ‚auf dem Holzweg', b) völlig ‚ka'putt', c) mit aller Macht: *be* **~** *for s.th.* mit aller Macht auf et. aus sein; → *go* 16; **~** *o·ver* a) *es ist* alles aus, b) gänzlich: *that is Max* **~** F das sieht Max ähnlich, das ist typisch Max, c) am ganzen Körper, d) über'all(hin); **~** *right* ganz richtig; in Ordnung(!), schön!, (na) gut!; **~** *round* 'ringsum'her, über'all; **~** *there:* *he is not* **~** F er ist nicht ganz bei Trost; **~** *up:* *it's* **~** *with him* mit ihm ists aus; *for* **~** a) trotz: **~** *his smartness*; **~** *that* trotzdem, b) so'viel: **~** *I know*; **~** *I care* F das ist mir doch egal!, meinetwegen!; *in* **~** insgesamt.

,all|-A'mer·i·can *adj.* rein ameri'kanisch, die ganzen USA vertretend; *Sport:* National...; **,~-a'round** *Am.* → *all-round*; **'all-,au·to'mat·ic** *adj.* ⊚ 'vollauto,matisch.

al·lay [ə'leɪ] *v/t.* beschwichtigen, beruhigen; *Streit* schlichten; mildern, lindern, *Hunger, Durst* stillen.

,all|-'clear *s.* Ent'warnung(ssi,gnal *n*) *f*; **2.** *fig.* ‚grünes Licht'; **'~-,du·ty** *adj.* ⊚ Allzweck...

al·le·ga·tion [ˌælɪ'geɪʃn] *s.* unerwiesene Behauptung, Aussage *f*, Vorbringen *n*; Darstellung *f*.

al·lege [ə'ledʒ] *v/t.* **1.** *Unerwiesenes* behaupten, erklären, vorbringen; **2.** vorgeben, vorschützen; **al'leged** [-dʒd] *adj*; **al'leg·ed·ly** [-dʒɪdlɪ] *adv.* an-, vorgeblich.

al·le·giance [ə'liːdʒəns] *s.* **1.** 'Untertanenpflicht *f*, -treue *f*, -gehorsam *m*: *oath of* **~** Treu-, ⚔ Fahneneid *m*; *change one's* **~** s-e Staats- od. Parteiangehörigkeit wechseln; **2.** (*to*) Treue *f* (zu), Loyali'tät *f*; Bindung *f* (an *acc.*); Ergebenheit *f*, Gefolgschaft *f*.

al·le·gor·ic, al·le·gor·i·cal [ˌælɪ'gɒrɪk(l)] *adj.* □ alle'gorisch, (sinn)bildlich; **al·le·go·rize** ['ælɪgəraɪz] **I** *v/t.* alle'gorisch darstellen; **II** *v/i.* in Gleichnissen reden; **al·le·go·ry** ['ælɪgərɪ] *s.* Allego'rie *f*, Sinnbild *n*, sinnbildliche Darstellung, Gleichnis *n*.

al·le·lu·ia [ˌælɪ'luːjə] **I** *s.* Halle'luja *n*, Loblied *n*; **II** *int.* halleluja!

al·ler·gen ['ælədʒen] *s.* 🝆 Aller'gen *n*; **al·ler·gic** [ə'lɜːdʒɪk] *adj.* 🝆 *u.* F *fig.* al'lergisch, äußerst empfindlich (*to* gegen); **al·ler·gist** ['ælədʒɪst] *s.* Allergologe *m*; **al·ler·gy** ['ælədʒɪ] *s.* **1.** ⚕, 🝆, *zo.* Aller'gie *f*, 'Überempfindlichkeit *f*; **2.** F ,Aller'gie' *f*, 'Widerwille *m* (*to* gegen).

al·le·vi·ate [ə'liːvɪeɪt] *v/t.* erleichtern, lindern, mildern, (ver)mindern; **al·le·vi·a·tion** [ə,liːvɪ'eɪʃn] *s.* Erleichterung *f* etc.

al·ley ['ælɪ] *s.* **1.** (schmale) Gasse, Verbindungsgang *m*, 'Durchgang *m* (*a. fig.*): *that's down* (*od. up*) *my* **~** F das ist et. für mich, das ist ganz mein Fall; → *blind alley*; **2.** Spielbahn *f*; → *bowling alley etc.*; **'~-way** *s.* → *alley* 1.

All| Fools' Day [ˌɔːl'fuːlzdeɪ] *s.* der 1. A'pril; **♀ fours** alle vier (*Kartenspiel*); → *four* 2; **~ Hal·lows** [ˌɔːl'hæləʊz] *s.* Aller'heiligen *n*.

al·li·ance [ə'laɪəns] *s.* **1.** Verbindung *f*, Verknüpfung *f*; **2.** Bund *m*, Bündnis *n*: *offensive and defensive* **~** Schutz- und Trutzbündnis; *form an* **~** ein Bündnis schließen; **3.** Heirat *f*, Verwandtschaft *f*, Verschwägerung *f*; **4.** *weitS.* Verwandtschaft *f*; **5.** *fig.* Bund *m*, (Inter'essen)Gemeinschaft *f*; **6.** Über'einkunft *f*; **al'lied** [ə'laɪd; *attr.* 'ælaɪd] *adj.* **1.** verbündet, alliiert (*with* mit): *the ♀ Powers*; **2.** *fig.* (art)verwandt (*to* mit); **Al·lies** ['ælaɪz] *s. pl.*: *the* **~** die Alliierten, die Verbündeten.

al·li·ga·tor ['ælɪgeɪtə] *s. zo.* Alli'gator *m*, 'Kaiman *m*; **~ pear** *s.* → *avocado*; **~ skin** *s.* Kroko'dilleder *n*.

'all|-in,por·tant *adj.* äußerst wichtig; **,~-'in, all-in,clu·sive** *adj. bsd. Brit.* alles inbegriffen, Gesamt..., Pauschal...: **~** *insurance* Generalversicherung *f*; **~** *wrestling sport* Catchen *n*.

al·lit·er·ate [ə'lɪtəreɪt] *v/t.* **1.** alliterieren; **2.** im Stabreim dichten; **al·lit·er·a·tion** [ə,lɪtə'reɪʃn] *s.* Alliterati'on *f*, Stabreim *m*; **al'lit·er·a·tive** [-rətɪv] *adj.* □ alliterierend.

,all|-'mains *adj.* ⚡ Allstrom..., mit Netzanschluss; **,~-'met·al** *s.* Ganzme'tall...

al·lo·cate ['æləʊkeɪt] *v/t.* ver-, zuteilen, an-, zuweisen (*to dat.*): **~** *costs* ✝ Kosten zuweisen *od.* 'umlegen; **~** *duties* die Pflichten (*od.* Aufgaben) verteilen; **~** *shares* Aktien zuteilen; **2.** → *allot* 3; **3.** den Platz bestimmen für; **al·lo·ca·tion** [ˌæləʊ'keɪʃn] *s.* **1.** Zu-, Verteilung *f*; An-, Zuweisung *f*, Kon'tin'gent *n*; Aufschlüsselung *f*; **2.** ✝ Bewilligung *f*, Zahlungsanweisung *f*.

al·lo·cu·tion [ˌæləʊ'kjuːʃn] *s.* feierliche *od.* ermahnende Ansprache.

al·lo·path ['æləʊpæθ] *s.* ⚕ Allo'path *m*; **al·lop·a·thy** [ə'lɒpəθɪ] *s.* ⚕ Allopa'thie *f*.

al·lot [ə'lɒt] *v/t.* **1.** zu-, aus-, verteilen, auslosen; **2.** bewilligen, abtreten; **3.** be-

stimmen (*to, for* für j-n *od.* e-n Zweck); **al'lot·ment** [-mənt] *s.* **1.** Ver-, Zuteilung *f*; Anteil *m*; zugeteilte 'Aktien *pl.*; **2.** *Brit.* Par'zelle *f*; (*a.* **~** *garden*) Schrebergarten *m*; **3.** Los *n*, Schicksal *n*.

,all-'out *adj.* **1.** to'tal, um'fassend, Groß...: **~** *effort*; **2.** kompro'misslos, radi'kal.

al·low [ə'laʊ] **I** *v/t.* **1.** erlauben, gestatten, zulassen: *he is not* **~***ed to go there* er darf nicht hingehen; **2.** gewähren, bewilligen, gönnen, zuerkennen: **~** *more time*; *we are* **~***ed two ounces a day* uns stehen täglich zwei Unzen zu; **~** *an item of expenditure* e-n Ausgabeposten billigen; **3.** a) zugeben: *I* **~** *I was rather nervous*, b) gelten lassen, *Forderung* anerkennen: **~** *a claim*; **4.** lassen, dulden, ermöglichen: *you must* **~** *the soup to get cold* du musst die Suppe abkühlen lassen; **5.** *Summe für gewisse Zeit* zuwenden, geben: *my father* **~***s me £100 a year* mein Vater gibt mir jährlich £ 100 (*Zuschuss od. Unterhaltsgeld*); **6.** ab-, anrechnen, abziehen, nachlassen, vergüten: **~** *a discount* e-n Rabatt gewähren; **~** *10% for inferior quality*; **7.** *Am.* a) meinen, b) beabsichtigen; **II** *v/i.* **8.** **~** *of* erlauben, zulassen, ermöglichen (*acc.*): *it* **~***s of no excuse* es lässt sich nicht entschuldigen; **9.** **~** *for* berücksichtigen, bedenken, in Betracht ziehen, anrechnen (*acc.*): → *for wear and tear*; **al'low·a·ble** [-əbl] *adj.* □ **1.** erlaubt, zulässig, rechtmäßig; **2.** abziehbar, -zugsfähig: **~** *expenses* ✝ abzugsfähige Ausgaben; **al'low·ance** [-əns] **I** *s.* **1.** Erlaubnis *f*, Be-, Einwilligung *f*, Anerkennung *f*; **2.** *geldliche* Zuwendung; Zuteilung *f*, Rati'on *f*, Maß *n*; Zuschuss *m*, Beihilfe *f*, Taschengeld *n*: *weekly* **~**; *family* **~** Familienunterstützung *f*; *dress* **~** Kleidergeld *n*; **3.** Nachsicht *f*: *make* **~** *for* berücksichtigen, bedenken, in Betracht ziehen; **4.** Entschädigung *f*, Vergütung *f*: *expense* **~** Aufwandsentschädigung; **5.** ✝ Nachlass *m*, Ra'batt *m*: **~** *for cash* Skonto *m, n*; *tax* **~** Steuerermäßigung *f*; **6.** ⊚, 🜊 Tole'ranz *f*, Spiel(raum *m*) *n*, zulässige Abweichung; **7.** *sport* Vorgabe *f*; **II** *v/t.* **8.** a) j-n auf Rationen setzen, b) *Waren* rationieren.

al·loy [ˈælɔɪ] **1.** Me'tallegierung *f*: **~** *wheels* Alufelgen *pl.*; **2.** ⊚ Legierung *f*, Gemisch *n*; **3.** [ə'lɔɪ] *fig.* (Bei)Mischung *f*: *pleasure without* **~** unge'trübte Freude; **II** *v/t.* [ə'lɔɪ] **4.** *Metalle* legieren, mischen; **5.** *fig.* beeinträchtigen, verschlechtern.

,all|-'par·ty *adj. pol.* Allparteien...; **,~-'pur·pose** *adj.* für jeden Zweck verwendbar, Allzweck..., Universal...: **~** *outfit*; **,~-'red** *adj. bsd. geogr.* rein 'britisch; **,~-'round** *adj.* all-, vielseitig, Allround...; **,~-'round·er** *s.* Alleskönner *m*; *sport* All'roundsportler *m*, -spieler *m*; **♀ Saints' Day** [ˌɔːl'seɪntsdeɪ] *s.* Aller'heiligen *n*; **♀ Souls' Day** [ˌɔːl'səʊlzdeɪ] *s.* Aller'seelen *n*; **,~-'star** *adj. thea.*, *sport* nur mit ersten Kräften besetzt: **~** *cast* Star-, Galabesetzung *f*; **,~-'steel** *adj.* Ganzstahl...; **,~-'ter'rain** *adj. mot.* geländegängig, Gelände...; **,~-'time** *adj.* **1.** bisher unerreicht, *der* (*die, das*) *beste etc.* aller Zeiten: **~** *high* Höchstleistung *f*, -stand *m*; **~** *low* Tiefststand *m*; **2.** hauptberuflich, Ganztags...: **~** *job*.

al·lude [ə'luːd] *v/i.* (*to*) anspielen, hinweisen (auf *acc.*); *et.* andeuten, erwähnen.

al·lure [ə'ljʊə] **I** *v/t.* **1.** (an-, ver)locken, gewinnen (*to* für); abbringen (*from*

von); **2.** anziehen, reizen; **II** s. **3.** →
al'lure·ment [-mənt] s. **1.** (Ver)Lockung f; **2.** Lockmittel n, Köder m; **3.**
Anziehungskraft f, Zauber m, Reiz m;
al'lur·ing [-ərɪŋ] adj. □ verlockend,
verführerisch.

al·lu·sion [ə'luːʒn] s. (to) Anspielung f,
Hinweis m (auf acc.); Erwähnung f,
Andeutung f (gen.); **al'lu·sive** [-uːsɪv]
adj. □ anspielend, verblümt, viel
sagend.

al·lu·vi·al [ə'luːvjəl] adj. geol. angeschwemmt, alluvi'al; **al'lu·vi·on** [-ən] s.
1. geol. Anschwemmung f, Alluvi'on
f, angeschwemmtes Land; **al'lu·vi·um**
[-əm] pl. **-vi·ums** od. **-vi·a** [-vjə] s.
geol. Al'luvium n, Schwemmland n.

,all·'·wave ⚡: **~ receiving set** Allwellenempfänger m; **,~·'weath·er** adj.
⊕ Allwetter...; **'~·wheel** adj. ⊕, mot.
Allrad...: **~ drive** Allradantrieb m.

al·ly [ə'laɪ] **I** v/t. **1.** (durch Heirat, Verwandtschaft, Ähnlichkeit) vereinigen,
verbinden (**to, with** mit); **2. ~ o.s.** sich
verbinden od. verbünden (**with** mit); **II**
v/i. **3.** sich vereinigen, sich verbinden,
sich verbünden (**to, with** mit); → **allied**; **III** s. ['ælaɪ] **4.** Alliierte(r m) f,
Verbündete(r m) f, Bundesgenosse m,
-genossin f (a. fig.); **5.** ♀, zo. verwandte
Sippe.

al·ma·nac ['ɔːlmənæk] s. 'Almanach m,
Ka'lender m, Jahrbuch n.

al·might·y [ɔːl'maɪtɪ] adj. **1.** allmächtig:
the ♗ der Allmächtige; **2.** a. adv. F
,riesig', ,mächtig'.

al·mond ['ɑːmənd] s. ♀ Mandel f; Mandelbaum m; **'~·eyed** adj. mandeläugig.

al·mon·er ['ɑːmənə] s. **1.** hist. 'Almosenpfleger m; **2.** Brit. Sozi'alarbeiter(in) im Krankenhaus.

al·most ['ɔːlməʊst] adv. fast, beinahe.

alms [ɑːmz] s. sg. u. pl. 'Almosen n;
'~·house s. **1.** Brit. a) pri'vates Altenheim, b) privates Wohnheim für sozi'al
Schwache; **2.** hist. Armenhaus n;
'~·man [-mən] s. [irr.] hist. 'Almosenempfänger m.

al·oe ['æləʊ] s. **1.** ♀ Aloe f; **2.** pl. sg.
konstr. ♀ Aloe f (Abführmittel).

a·loft [ə'lɒft] adv. **1.** poet. hoch (oben
od. hin'auf), em'por, droben, in der od.
die Höhe; **2.** ⚓ oben, in der od. die
Takelung.

a·lone [ə'ləʊn] **I** adj. al'lein, einsam; →
leave alone, let alone, let' Redew.; **II**
adv. allein, bloß, nur.

a·long [ə'lɒŋ] **I** prp. **1.** entlang, längs; **II**
adv. **2.** entlang, längs; **3.** vorwärts, weiter: → **get along**; **4.** zu'sammen (mit),
mit, bei sich: **take ~** mitnehmen; **come
~** komm mit!, ,komm doch schon!'; **I'll
be ~ in a few minutes** ich werde in ein
paar Minuten da sein; **5.** → **all along**;
a,long'shore adv. längs der Küste;
a,long'side I adv. **1.** ⚓ längsseits; **2.**
fig. (**of, with**) verglichen (mit), im Vergleich (zu); **II** prp. **3.** längsseits (gen.);
neben (dat.).

a·loof [ə'luːf] **I** adv. fern, abseits, von
fern: **keep ~** sich fern halten (**from**
von), Distanz wahren; **stand ~** für sich
bleiben; **II** adj. zu'rückhaltend, reser
'viert; **a'loof·ness** [-nɪs] s. Zu'rückhaltung f, Reser'viertheit f, Dis'tanz f.

a·loud [ə'laʊd] adv. laut, mit lauter
Stimme.

alp [ælp] s. Alp(e) f, Alm f.

al·pac·a [æl'pækə] s. **1.** zo. 'Pako n,
Al'paka n; **2.** a) Al'pakawolle f, b)
Al'pakastoff m.

'al·pen|·glow ['ælpən-] s. Alpenglühen n;
'~·horn (Ger.) s. Alphorn n; **'~·stock**
[-'ælpɪn-] (Ger.) s. Bergstock m.

al·pha ['ælfə] s. **1.** 'Alpha n: **the ~ and
omega** fig. das A u. O; **2. ~ particles
(rays)** pl. phys. 'Alphateilchen (-strahlen) pl.; **3.** univ. Brit. Eins f (beste Note): **~ plus** hervorragend.

al·pha·bet ['ælfəbɪt] s. **1.** Alpha'bet n,
Abc n; **2.** fig. Anfangsgründe pl., Abc
n; **al·pha·bet·ic, al·pha·bet·i·cal**
[,ælfə'betɪk(l)] adj. □ alpha'betisch: **~
order** alphabetische Reihenfolge.

al·pha·nu·mer·ic [,ælfənju:'merɪk] adj.
(□ **~ally**) EDV ,alphanu'merisch.

Al·pine ['ælpaɪn] adj. **1.** Alpen...; **2.** al
'pin, Hochgebirgs...: **~ sun** ☀ Höhensonne f; **~ combined** sport alpine
Kombination; **'Al·pin·ism** [-pɪnɪzəm] s.
1. Alpi'nismus m; **2.** al'piner Skisport;
'Al·pin·ist [-pɪnɪst] s. Alpi'nist(in);
Alps [ælps] s. pl. die Alpen pl.

al·read·y [ɔːl'redɪ] adv. schon, bereits.

al·right [,ɔːl'raɪt] adv. Brit. F od. Am. für
all right.

Al·sa·tian [æl'seɪʃjən] **I** adj. **1.** elsässisch; **II** s. **2.** Elsässer(in); **3.** a. **~ dog**
(Deutscher) Schäferhund.

al·so ['ɔːlsəʊ] adv. auch, ferner, außerdem, ebenfalls; **'al·so-ran** s. **1.** sport
Rennteilnehmer (a. Pferd), der sich
nicht platzieren kann: **she was an ~** sie
kam unter ,ferner liefen' ein; **2.** F Versager m, Niete f.

al·tar ['ɔːltə] s. Al'tar m: **lead to the ~**
zum Altar führen, heiraten; **~ boy** s.
Mini'strant m; **~ cloth** s. Al'tardecke f;
'~·piece s. Al'tarblatt n, -gemälde n;
~ screen s. reich verzierte Al'tarrückwand, Re'tabel n.

al·ter ['ɔːltə] **I** v/t. **1.** (ver)ändern, ab-,
'umändern; **2.** Am. dial. Tiere kastrieren; **II** v/i. **3.** sich (ver)ändern; **'al·
ter·a·ble** [-tərəbl] adj. veränderlich,
wandelbar; **al·ter·a·tion** [,ɔːltə'reɪʃn] s.
1. (Ab-, 'Um-, Ver)Änderung f; **2.** a.
pl. 'Umbau m.

al·ter·ca·tion [,ɔːltə'keɪʃn] s. heftige
Ausein'andersetzung.

al·ter e·go [,æltər'egəʊ] (Lat.) s. Alter
Ego n: a) das andere Ich, b) j-s Busenfreund(in).

al·ter·nate [ɔːl'tɜːneɪt] **I** adj. □ → **alternately**; **1.** (mitein'ander) abwechselnd,
wechselseitig: **on ~ days** jeden zweiten
Tag; **2.** ⚔ Ausweich...: **~ position**; **II** s.
3. pol. Am. Stellvertreter m; **III** v/t.
['ɔːltəneɪt] **4.** wechselweise tun; abwechseln lassen, *miteinander* vertauschen; **5.** ⚡, ⊕ peri'odisch verändern;
IV v/i. ['ɔːltəneɪt] **6.** abwechseln, alternieren; **7.** ⚡ wechseln; **al'ter·nate·ly**
[-lɪ] adv. abwechselnd, wechselweise;
al'ter·nat·ing ['ɔːltəneɪtɪŋ] adj. abwechselnd, Wechsel...: **~ current** ⚡
Wechselstrom m; **~ voltage** ⚡ Wechselspannung f; **al·ter·na·tion** [,ɔːltə
'neɪʃn] s. Abwechslung f, Wechsel m;
al·ter·na·tive [-nətɪv] **I** adj. □ → **alternatively**; **1.** alterna'tiv, die Wahl
lassend, ein'ander ausschließend, nur
'eine Möglichkeit lassend; **2.** ander(er,
-e, -es) (von zweien), Ersatz..., Ausweich...: **~ airport** Ausweichflughafen
m; **II** s. **3.** Alterna'tive f, Wahl f: **have
no (other) ~** keine andere Möglichkeit
od. Wahl od. keinen anderen Ausweg
haben; **al'ter·na·tive·ly** [-nətɪvlɪ] adv.
im anderen Falle, ersatz-, hilfsweise;
al·ter·na·tor ['ɔːltəneɪtə] s. ⚡ 'Wechselstroma,schine f.

al·tho [ɔːl'ðəʊ] Am. → **although**.

alt·horn ['ælthɔːn] s. ♪ Althorn n.

al·though [ɔːl'ðəʊ] cj. ob'wohl, ob
'gleich, wenn auch.

al·tim·e·ter ['æltɪmiːtə] s. phys. Höhenmesser m.

al·ti·tude ['æltɪtjuːd] s. **1.** Höhe f (bsd.
über dem Meeresspiegel, a. ⚷, ✈, ast.):
~ control Höhensteuerung f; **~ flight**
Höhenflug m; **~ of the sun** Sonnenstand m; **2.** mst pl. hoch gelegene Gegend, (Berg)Höhen pl.; **3.** fig. Erhabenheit f.

Alt (key) [ælt; ɔːlt] s. Computer: Alt
-Taste f: **hold down Alt** (od. **the Alt
key**) Alt (od. die Alt-Taste) gedrückt
halten.

al·to ['æltəʊ] pl. **'al·tos** (Ital.) s. ♪ **1.** Alt
m, Altstimme f; **2.** Al'tist(in), Altsänger(in).

al·to·geth·er [,ɔːltə'geðə] **I** adv. **1.** völlig, gänzlich, ganz u. gar schlecht etc.;
2. insgesamt, im Ganzen genommen; **II**
s. **3. in the ~** splitternackt.

al·to-re·lie·vo [,æltəʊrɪ'liːvəʊ] (Ital.) s.
'Hochreli,ef n.

al·tru·ism ['æltruɪzəm] s. Altru'ismus m,
Nächstenliebe f, Uneigennützigkeit f;
'al·tru·ist [-ɪst] s. Altru'ist(in); **al·truis·tic** [,æltru'ɪstɪk] adj. (□ **~ally**) altru
'istisch, uneigennützig, selbstlos.

al·um ['æləm] s. ♙ A'laun m.

a·lu·mi·na [ə'ljuːmɪnə] s. ♙ Tonerde f.

a·lu·min·i·um [,ælju'mɪnjəm], Am. **a·lumi·num** [ə'luːmɪnəm] s. ♙ Alu'minium
n.

a·lum·na [ə'lʌmnə] pl. **-nae** [-niː] s. ehemalige Stu'dentin od. Schülerin; **a'lumnus** [-nəs] pl. **-ni** [naɪ] s. ehemaliger
Stu'dent od. Schüler.

al·ve·o·lar [æl'vɪələ] adj. **1.** anat. alveo
'lär, das Zahnfach betreffend; **2.** ling.
alveo'lar, am Zahndamm artikuliert; **al·
ve·o·lus** [æl'vɪələs] pl. **-li** [-laɪ] s. anat.
Alve'ole f: a) Zahnfach n, b) Zungenbläs-chen n.

al·ways ['ɔːlweɪz] adv. **1.** immer, stets, jederzeit; **2.** F auf jeden Fall, immer'hin.

a·lys·sum ['ælɪsəm] s. ♀ Steinkraut n.

Alz·hei·mer's dis·ease ['æltshaɪməz] s.
☤ Alzheimerkrankheit f.

am [æm; əm] 1. sg. pres. von **be**.

a·mal·gam [ə'mælgəm] s. **1.** Amal'gam
n; **2.** fig. Mischung f, Gemenge n, Verschmelzung f; **a'mal·gam·ate** [-meɪt] **I**
v/t. **1.** amalgamieren; **2.** fig. vereinigen,
verschmelzen; zs.-legen, zs.-schließen,
⚕ fusionieren; **II** v/i. **3.** sich amalgamieren; **4.** sich vereinigen, verschmelzen, sich zs.-schließen, ⚕ fusionieren;
a·mal·gam·a·tion [ə,mælgə'meɪʃn] s.
1. Amalgamieren n; **2.** Vereinigung f,
Verschmelzung f, Mischung f; **3.** bsd.
⚕ Zs.-schluss m, Fusi'on f.

a·man·u·en·sis [ə,mænjʊ'ensɪs] pl. **-ses**
[-siːz] s. Amanu'ensis m, (Schreib)Gehilfe m, Sekre'tär(in).

am·a·ranth ['æmərænθ] s. **1.** ♀ Ama
'rant m, Fuchsschwanz m; **2.** poet. unverwelkliche Blume; **3.** Ama'rantfarbe
f, Purpurrot n.

am·a·ryl·lis [,æmə'rɪlɪs] s. ♀ Ama'ryllis f,
Nar'zissenlilie f.

a·mass [ə'mæs] v/t. bsd. Geld etc. an-,
aufhäufen, ansammeln.

am·a·teur ['æmətə] s. Ama'teur m: a)
(Kunst- etc.)Liebhaber m, b) Amateursportler(in): **~ flying** Sportfliegerei f,
c) Nichtfachmann m, contp. Dilet'tant
m, Stümper m (**at painting** im Malen),
d) Bastler m, e) Hobby...: **~ gardener**
Hobbygärtner(in); **am·a·teur·ish**
[,æmə'tɜːrɪʃ] adj. □ dilet'tantisch; **'am·
a·teur·ism** [-ərɪzəm] s. **1.** sport Amateu'rismus m; **2.** Dilet'tantentum n.

am·a·tive ['æmətɪv] adj., **'am·a·to·ry**
[-tərɪ] → **amorous**.

a·maze [ə'meɪz] v/t. in Staunen setzen, verblüffen, über'raschen; **a'mazed** [-zd] adj.; **a'maz·ed·ly** [-zɪdlɪ] adv. erstaunt, verblüfft (**at** über acc.); **a'maze·ment** [-mənt] s. (Er)Staunen n, Verblüffung f, Verwunderung f; **a'maz·ing** [-zɪŋ] adj. □ erstaunlich, verblüffend; unglaublich, ‚toll'.

Am·a·zon [ˈæməzən] s. **1.** antiq. Ama-'zone f; **2.** ♀ fig. Ama'zone f, Mannweib n; **Am·a·zo·ni·an** [ˌæməˈzəʊnjən] adj. **1.** ama'zonenhaft, Amazonen...; **2.** geogr. Amazonas...

am·bas·sa·dor [æmˈbæsədə] s. **1.** pol. a) Botschafter m (a. fig.), b) Gesandte(r) m; **2.** Abgesandte(r) m, Bote m (a. fig.): ~ **of peace**; **am·bas·sa·do·ri·al** [æmˌbæsəˈdɔːrɪəl] adj. Botschafts...; **am·'bas·sa·dress** [-drɪs] s. **1.** Botschafterin f; **2.** Gattin f e-s Botschafters.

am·ber [ˈæmbə] I s. **1.** min. Bernstein m; **2.** Gelb n, gelbes Licht (*Verkehrsampel*): **at** ~ bei Gelb; **the lights were at** ~ die Ampel stand auf Gelb; II adj. **3.** Bernstein...; **4.** bernsteinfarben.

am·ber·gris [ˈæmbəgriːs] s. (Graue) Ambra.

am·bi·dex·trous [ˌæmbɪˈdekstrəs] adj. □ **1.** beidhändig; **2.** mit beiden Händen gleich geschickt, *weitS*. ungewöhnlich geschickt; **3.** doppelzüngig, 'hinterhältig.

am·bi·ence [ˈæmbɪəns] s. Kunst: Ambi'ente n, fig. a. a) Mili'eu n, 'Umwelt f, b) Atmo'sphäre f; **'am·bi·ent** [-nt] adj. um'gebend, um'kreisend; ◎ Umgebungs...(*-temperatur etc.*), Neben... (*-geräusch*).

am·bi·gu·i·ty [ˌæmbɪˈɡjuːɪtɪ] s. Zwei-, Vieldeutigkeit f, Doppelsinn m; Unklarheit f; **am·big·u·ous** [æmˈbɪɡjʊəs] adj. □ zweideutig; unklar.

am·bit [ˈæmbɪt] s. **1.** 'Umkreis m; **2.** a) Um'gebung f, b) Grenzen pl.; **3.** fig. Bereich m.

am·bi·tion [æmˈbɪʃn] s. Ehrgeiz m, Ambiti'on f (*beide a. Gegenstand des Ehrgeizes*); Streben n, Begierde f, Wunsch m (**of** nach od. inf.), Ziel n, pl. Bestrebungen pl.; **am·bi·tious** [-ʃəs] adj. □ **1.** ehrgeizig (a. Plan etc.); **2.** strebsam; begierig (**of** nach); **3.** ambiti'ös, anspruchsvoll.

am·bi·va·lence [ˌæmbɪˈveɪləns] s. psych., phys. Ambiva'lenz f, Doppelwertigkeit f; fig. Zwiespältigkeit f; **am·bi·va·lent** [-nt] adj. bes. psych. ambiva·'lent.

am·ble [ˈæmbl] I v/i. im Passgang gehen od. reiten; fig. schlendern; II s. Pass (-gang) m (*Pferd*); fig. gemächlicher (Spazier)Gang, Schlendern n.

am·bro·si·a [æmˈbrəʊzjə] s. antiq. Ambrosia f, Götterspeise f (a. fig.); **am·'bro·si·al** [-əl] adj. □ am'brosisch; fig. köstlich (duftend).

am·bu·lance [ˈæmbjʊləns] s. **1.** Ambu'lanz f, Kranken-, Sani'tätswagen m; **2.** ✕ 'Feldlaza,rett n; ~ **bat·tal·ion** s. ✕ 'Krankentrans,portbatail,lon n; ~ **box** s. Verbandskasten m; ~ **sta·tion** s. Sani'tätswache f, 'Unfallstati,on f.

am·bu·lant [ˈæmbjʊlənt] adj. ambu'lant: a) wandernd: ~ **trade** Wandergewerbe n, b) ♣ gehfähig: ~ **patients**; ~ **treatment** ambulante Behandlung; **'am·bu·la·to·ry** [-ətərɪ] I adj. **1.** beweglich, (orts)veränderlich; **2.** → **ambulant**; II s. **3.** Ar'kade f, Wandelgang m.

am·bus·cade [ˌæmbəsˈkeɪd], **am·bush** [ˈæmbʊʃ] I s. **1.** 'Hinterhalt m; **2.** im 'Hinterhalt liegende Truppen pl.; II v/i. **3.** im 'Hinterhalt liegen; III v/t. **4.** in

e-n 'Hinterhalt legen; **5.** aus dem 'Hinterhalt über'fallen, auflauern (dat.).

a·me·ba, a·me·bic Am. → **amoeba, amoebic**.

a·mel·io·rate [əˈmiːljəreɪt] I v/t. verbessern (bsd. ✓); II v/i. besser werden, sich bessern; **a·mel·io·ra·tion** [əˌmiːljəˈreɪʃn] s. (✓ Boden)Verbesserung f.

a·men [ˌɑːˈmen; ˌeɪˈmen] I int. 'amen!; II s. 'Amen n.

a·me·na·ble [əˈmiːnəbl] adj. □ (**to**) **1.** zugänglich (dat.): ~ **to flattery**; **2.** gefügig; **3.** unter'worfen (dat.): ~ **to a fine**; **4.** verantwortlich (dat.).

a·mend [əˈmend] I v/t. **1.** (ver)bessern, berichtigen; **2.** Gesetz etc. (ab)ändern, ergänzen; II v/i. **3.** sich bessern (bsd. Betragen).

a·mende ho·no·ra·ble [aˌmɑːd ɔnɔrabl] (Fr.) s. öffentliche Ehrenerklärung od. Abbitte.

a·mend·ment [əˈmendmənt] s. **1.** (bsd. sittliche) Besserung; **2.** Verbesserung f, Berichtigung f, Neufassung f; **3.** bsd. ✡, parl. (Ab)Änderungs-, Ergänzungsantrag m (*zu e-m Gesetz*), Am. 'Zusatz,artikel m zur Verfassung, Nachtragsgesetz n: **the Fifth** ♀.

a·mends [əˈmendz] s. pl. sg. konstr. (Schaden)Ersatz m, Genugtuung f: **make** ~ Schadenersatz leisten, es wieder gutmachen.

a·men·i·ty [əˈmiːnɪtɪ] s. **1.** Annehmlichkeit f, angenehme Lage; **2.** Anmut f, Liebenswürdigkeit f; **3.** pl. Konventi'on f, Eti'kette f; Höflichkeiten pl.; **4.** pl. (na'türliche) Vorzüge pl., Reize pl., Annehmlichkeiten pl.

Am·er·a·sian [ˌæməˈreɪʃən] adj. u. s. (Per'son f) ameri'kanisch-asi'atischer Abstammung.

A·mer·i·can [əˈmerɪkən] I adj. **1.** a) ameri'kanisch, b) die USA betreffend: **the** ~ **navy**; II s. **2.** a) Ameri'kaner(in), b) Bürger(in) der USA; **3.** Ameri'kanisch n (*Sprache der USA*); **A·mer·i·ca·na** [əˌmerɪˈkɑːnə] s. pl. Ameri'kana pl. (*Schriften etc. über Amerika*).

A·mer·i·can| cloth s. Wachstuch n; ~ **foot·ball** s. sport American Football m (*rugbyähnliches Spiel*); ~ **In·di·an** s. Indi'aner(in).

A·mer·i·can·ism [əˈmerɪkənɪzəm] s. **1.** Ameri'kanertum n; **2.** Amerika'nismus m: a) ameri'kanische Spracheigentümlichkeit, b) ameri'kanischer Brauch; **A·mer·i·can·i·za·tion** [əˌmerɪkənaɪˈzeɪʃn] s. Amerikanisierung f; **A·mer·i·can·ize** [əˈmerɪkənaɪz] I v/t. amerikanisieren; II v/i. Ameri'kaner od. ameri'kanisch werden.

A·mer·i·can| leath·er → **American cloth**; ~ **Le·gion** s. Am. Frontkämpferbund m; ~ **or·gan** s. ♪ Har'monium n; ~ **plan** s. Am. 'Vollpensi,on f.

Am·er·ind [ˈæmərɪnd], **Am·er·in·di·an** [ˌæmərˈɪndjən] s. ameri'kanischer Indi'aner od. 'Eskimo.

am·e·thyst [ˈæmɪθɪst] s. min. Ame'thyst m.

a·mi·a·bil·i·ty [ˌeɪmjəˈbɪlətɪ] s. Freundlichkeit f, Liebenswürdigkeit f; **a·mi·a·ble** [ˈeɪmjəbl] adj. □ liebenswürdig, freundlich, gewinnend, reizend.

am·i·ca·ble [ˈæmɪkəbl] adj. □ freund-(schaft)lich, friedlich: ~ **settlement** gütliche Einigung; **'am·i·ca·bly** [-lɪ] adv. freundschaftlich, in Güte, gütlich.

a·mid [əˈmɪd] prp. in'mitten (gen.), (mitten) in od. unter (dat. od. acc.); **a'mid·ship(s)** [-ʃɪp(s)] ♣ I adv. mittschiffs; II adj. in der Mitte des Schiffes

(befindlich); **a'midst** [-st] → **amid**.

a·mine [ˈæmaɪn] s. ♣ A'min n.

a·mi·no- [əmiːnəʊ] ♣ in Zssgn Amino...: ~ **acid**.

a·miss [əˈmɪs] I adv. verkehrt, verfehlt, schlecht: **take** ~ übel nehmen; II adj. unpassend, verkehrt, falsch, übel: **there is s.th.** ~ etwas stimmt nicht; **it would not be** ~ es würde nicht schaden.

am·i·ty [ˈæmɪtɪ] s. Freundschaft f, gutes Einvernehmen.

am·me·ter [ˈæmɪtə] s. ⚡ Am'pere,meter n, Strom(stärke)messer m.

am·mo [ˈæməʊ] s. sl. Muniti'on f.

am·mo·ni·a [əˈməʊnjə] s. ♣ Ammoni'ak n: liquid ~ (od. ~ **solution**) Salmiakgeist m; **am·mo·ni·ac** [-nɪæk] adj. ammonia'kalisch: (**gum**) ~ Ammoniakgummi m, n; → **sal**.

am·mo·ni·um [əˈməʊnjəm] s. ♣ Am'monium n; ~ **car·bon·ate** s. ♣ Hirschhornsalz n; ~ **chlo·ride** s. ♣ Am'moniumchlo,rid n, 'Salmiak m; ~ **ni·trate** s. ♣ Am'moniumni,trat n, Ammoni'aksal,peter m.

am·mu·ni·tion [ˌæmjʊˈnɪʃn] s. Muniti'on f (a. fig.): ~ **belt** Patronengurt m; ~ **carrier** Munitionswagen m; ~ **dump** Munitionslager n.

am·ne·si·a [æmˈniːzjə] s. ✦ Amne'sie f, Gedächtnisschwund m.

am·nes·ty [ˈæmnɪstɪ] I s. Amne'stie f, allgemeiner Straferlass; II v/t. begnadigen, amnestieren.

am·ni·o·cen·te·sis [ˌæmnɪəʊsenˈtiːsɪs] pl. **-ses** [-siːz] s. ✦ Fruchtwasseruntersuchung f, ,Amniozen'tese f; **am·ni·ot·ic sac** [ˌæmnɪˈɒtɪk] s. ✦ Fruchtblase f.

a·moe·ba [əˈmiːbə] s. zo. A'möbe f; **a'moe·bic** [-bɪk] adj. a'möbisch: **dysentery** Amöbenruhr f.

a·mok [əˈmɒk] → **amuck**.

a·mong(st) [əˈmʌŋ(st)] prp. (mitten) unter (dat. od. acc.), in'mitten (gen.), zwischen (dat. od. acc.), bei: **who** ~ **you?** wer von euch?; **a custom** ~ **the savages** e-e Sitte bei den Wilden; **be** ~ **the best** zu den Besten gehören; ~ **other things** unter anderem; **from among** aus der Zahl (derer), aus ... heraus; **they had two pounds** ~ **them** sie hatten zusammen zwei Pfund.

a·mor·al [ˌeɪˈmɒrəl] adj. 'amo,ralisch.

am·o·rist [ˈæmərɪst] s. E'rotiker m: a) Herzensbrecher m, b) Verfasser m von 'Liebesro,manen etc.

am·o·rous [ˈæmərəs] adj. □ amou'rös: a) e'rotisch, sinnlich, Liebes..., b) liebebedürftig, verliebt (**of** in acc.); **'am·o·rous·ness** [-nɪs] s. amou'röse Art, Verliebtheit f.

a·mor·phous [əˈmɔːfəs] adj. a'morph: a) formlos, b) ungestalt, c) min. 'unkristal,linisch.

a·mor·ti·za·tion [əˌmɔːtɪˈzeɪʃn] s. **1.** Amortisierung f, Tilgung f (*von Schulden*); **2.** Abschreibung f (*von Anlagewerten*); **3.** ✡ Veräußerung f (*von Grundstücken*) an die tote Hand; **a·mor·tize** [əˈmɔːtaɪz] v/t. **1.** amortisieren, tilgen, abzahlen; **2.** ✡ an die tote Hand veräußern.

a·mount [əˈmaʊnt] I v/i. **1.** (**to**) sich belaufen (auf acc.), betragen (acc.): **his debts** ~ **to £120**; **2.** hin'auslaufen (**to** auf acc.), bedeuten: **it** ~**s to the same thing** es läuft od. kommt auf dasselbe hinaus; **that doesn't** ~ **to much** das ist unbedeutend; **you'll never** ~ **to much** F aus dir wird nie etwas werden; II s. **3.** Betrag m, Summe f, Höhe f (*e-r Summe*); Menge f: **to the** ~ **of** bis zur od.

Höhe von, im Betrag *od.* Wert von; *net* ~ Nettobetrag; ~ *carried forward* Übertrag *m;* **4.** *fig.* Inhalt *m,* Ergebnis *n,* Wert *m,* Bedeutung *f.*

a·mour [ə'muə] *(Fr.)* s. Liebschaft *f,* A'mour *f,* ,Verhältnis' *n;* **~·pro·pre** [,æmuə'prɔprə] *(Fr.) s.* Eigenliebe *f,* Eitelkeit *f.*

amp [æmp] *s.* F **1.** → *ampere;* **2.** → *amplifier.*

am·per·age [æm'peərɪdʒ] *s.* ⚡ Stromstärke *f,* Am'perezahl *f;* **am·pere, am·père** ['æmpeə] *(Fr.) s.* ⚡ Am'pere *n;* ~ **me·ter** → *ammeter.*

am·per·sand ['æmpəsænd] *s. typ.* das Zeichen & *(abbr. für and).*

am·phet·a·mine [æm'fetəmɪn] *s.* 🧪 Ampheta'min *n.*

am·phi- [æmfɪ] *in Zssgn* doppelt, zwei..., zweiseitig, beiderseitig, umher...

Am·phib·i·a [æm'fɪbɪə] *s. pl. zo.* Am'phibien *pl.,* Lurche *pl.;* **am·phib·i·an** [-ən] **I** *adj.* **1.** *zo., a.* ✕, ⊕ am'phibisch, Amphibien...; **II** *s.* **2.** *zo.* Am'phibie *f,* Lurch *m;* **3.** a) Am'phibienflugzeug *n,* b) Am'phibien-, Schwimmfahrzeug *n,* c) ✕ Schwimmkampfwagen *m;* **am·phib·i·ous** [-əs] *adj.* **1.** → *amphibian* 1: ~ *landing* amphibische Landung *od.* Operation; ~ *tank* → *amphibian* 3 c; ~ *vehicle* → *amphibian* 3 b; **3.** von gemischter Na'tur, zweierlei Wesen habend.

am·phi·the·a·tre, *Am.* **am·phi·the·a·ter** ['æmfɪ,θɪətə] *s.* Am'phithe,ater *n (a. fig.* Gebäudeteil *od.* Tal *etc. in der* Form *e-s* Amphitheaters).

am·pho·ra ['æmfərə] *pl.* **-rae** [-riː] *od.* **-ras** *(Lat.) s.* Am'phore *f.*

am·ple ['æmpl] *adj.* □ → *amply;* **1.** weit, groß, geräumig; weitläufig; stattlich *(Figur),* üppig *(Busen);* **2.** ausführlich, um'fassend; **3.** reich(lich), mehr als genug, (vollauf) genügend: ~ *means* reich(lich)e Mittel; **am·ple·ness** [-nɪs] *s.* **1.** Weite *f,* Geräumigkeit *f;* **2.** Reichlichkeit *f,* Fülle *f.*

am·pli·fi·ca·tion [,æmplɪfɪ'keɪʃn] *s.* **1.** Erweiterung *f,* Vergrößerung *f,* Ausdehnung *f;* **2.** weitere Ausführung, Weitschweifigkeit *f,* Ausschmückung *f;* **3.** ⚡, Radio, phys. Vergrößerung *f,* Verstärkung *f.*

am·pli·fi·er ['æmplɪfaɪə] *s.* **1.** *phys.* Vergrößerungslinse *f;* **2.** Radio, phys. Verstärker *m:* ~ *tube (od. valve)* Verstärkerröhre *f;* **am·pli·fy** ['æmplɪfaɪ] **I** *v/t.* **1.** erweitern, vergrößern, ausdehnen; **2.** ausmalen, -schmücken; weitläufig darstellen; näher ausführen *od.* erläutern; **3.** Radio, phys. verstärken; **II** *v/i.* **4.** sich weitläufig ausdrücken *od.* auslassen; **am·pli·tude** [-tjuːd] *s.* **1.** Weite *f,* 'Umfang *m (a. fig.),* Reichlichkeit *f,* Fülle *f;* **2.** *phys.* Ampli'tude *f,* Schwingungsweite *f (Pendel etc.).*

am·ply ['æmplɪ] *adv.* reichlich.

am·poule ['æmpuːl] *s.* Am'pulle *f.*

am·pul·la [æm'pʊlə] *pl.* **-lae** [-liː] *s.* **1.** *antiq.* Am'pulle *f,* Phi'ole *f,* Salbengefäß *n;* **2.** Blei-*od.* Glasflasche *f der* Pilger; **3.** *eccl.* Krug *m* für Wein u. Wasser *(Messe);* Gefäß *n* für das heilige Öl *(Salbung).*

am·pu·tate ['æmpjuteɪt] *v/t.* **1.** Bäume stutzen; **2.** 🩺 amputieren *(a. fig.),* ein Glied abnehmen; **am·pu·ta·tion** [,æmpjuˈteɪʃn] *s.* Amputati'on *f;* **am·pu·tee** [-tiː] *s.* Ampu'tierte(r *m) f.*

a·muck [ə'mʌk] *adv.:* **run** ~ Amok laufen, *fig. a.* blindwütig rasen *(at, on,* *against* gegen *et.).*

am·u·let ['æmjulɪt] *s.* Amu'lett *n.*

a·muse [ə'mjuːz] *v/t.* **(o.s.** sich) amüsieren, unter'halten, belustigen: *you* ~ *me!* da muss ich (über dich) lachen!; *be* ~*d* sich freuen *(at, by, in, with* über *acc.);* *it* ~*s them* es macht ihnen Spaß; *he* ~*s himself with gardening* er gärtnert zu s-m Vergnügen; **a'mused** [-zd] *adj.* amüsiert, belustigt, erfreut: *I am not* ~ ich finde das nicht lustig!; **a·'muse·ment** [-mənt] *s.* Unter'haltung *f,* Belustigung *f,* Vergnügen *n,* Freude *f,* Zeitvertreib *m:* *to the* ~ *of* zur Belustigung *(gen.);* ~ *arcade* Brit. Spielsalon *m;* ~ *park* Vergnügungspark *m;* **a'mus·ing** [-zɪŋ] *adj.* □ amü'sant, unter'haltsam; 'komisch.

am·yl ['æmɪl] *s.* 🧪 A'myl *n;* **am·y·la·ceous** [,æmɪ'leɪʃəs] *adj.* stärkemehlartig, stärkehaltig.

an [æn; ən] *unbestimmter Artikel (vor* Vokalen *od.* stummem H) ein, eine.

an·a·bap·tism [,ænə'bæptɪzəm] *s.* Anabap'tismus *m;* **an·a·bap·tist** [-ɪst] *s.* Wiedertäufer *m.*

an·a·bol·ic [,ænə'bɒlɪk] *adj.* 🧪 ana'bol; ~ **ster·e·oid** ['stɪərɔɪd; 'ster-] *s.* 🧪 Ana'bolikum *n.*

a·nach·ro·nism [ə'nækrənɪzəm] *s.* Anachro'nismus *m;* **a·nach·ro·nis·tic** [ə,nækrə'nɪstɪk] *adj.* (□ ~*ally*) anachro'nistisch.

a·nae·mi·a [ə'niːmjə] *s.* 🩺 Anä'mie *f,* Blutarmut *f,* Bleichsucht *f;* **a'nae·mic** [-mɪk] *adj.* 🩺 blutarm, bleichsüchtig, an'ämisch; **2.** *fig.* farblos, blass.

an·aes·the·si·a [,ænɪs'θiːzjə] *s.* 🩺 **1.** Anästhe'sie *f,* Nar'kose *f,* Betäubung *f;* **2.** Unempfindlichkeit *f (gegen Schmerz);* **an·aes·thet·ic** [-'θetɪk] **I** *adj.* (□ ~*ally*) nar'kotisch, betäubend, Narkose...; **II** *s.* Betäubungsmittel *n;* **an·aes·the·tist** [æ'niːsθɪtɪst] *s.* Anästhe'sist *m,* Nar'kosearzt *m;* **an·aesthe·tize** [æ'niːsθətaɪz] *v/t.* betäuben, narkotisieren.

an·a·gram ['ænəgræm] *s.* Ana'gramm *n.*

a·nal [eɪnl] *adj. anat.* a'nal, Anal...

an·a·lects ['ænəlekts] *s. pl.* Ana'lekten *pl.,* Lesefrüchte *pl.*

an·al·ge·si·a [,ænæl'dʒiːzjə] *s.* 🩺 Unempfindlichkeit *f* gegen Schmerz, Schmerzlosigkeit *f;* **an·al'ge·sic** [-'dʒesɪk] **I** *adj.* schmerzlindernd; **II** *s.* schmerzlinderndes Mittel.

an·a·log·ic, an·a·log·i·cal [,ænə'lɒdʒɪk(l)] *adj.* □, **a·nal·o·gous** [ə'næləgəs] *adj.* □ ana'log, ähnlich, entsprechend, paral'lel *(to dat.):* ~ *computer* Ana'logrechner *m;* **an·a·logue** ['ænəlɒg] *s.* A'nalogon *n,* Entsprechung *f:* ~ *computer* Analogrechner *m;* **a·nal·o·gy** [ə'nælədʒɪ] *s.* **1.** *a.* *ling.* Analo'gie *f,* Entsprechung *f:* *on the* ~ *of (od. by* ~ *with)* analog, nach, gemäß *(dat.);* **2.** 🔭 Proporti'on *f.*

an·a·lyse ['ænəlaɪz] *v/t.* **1.** analysieren: a) 🧪, 🔬, *psych. etc.* zergliedern, zerlegen, b) *fig.* genau unter'suchen, c) erläutern, darlegen; **a·nal·y·sis** [ə'næləsɪs] *pl.* **-ses** [-siːz] *s.* **1.** Ana'lyse *f:* a) 🧪 *etc.* Zerlegung *f,* ('kritische) Zergliederung, b) *fig.* gründliche Unter'suchung, Darlegung *f,* Deutung *f: in the last* ~ im Grunde, letzten Endes; **2.** 🔭 A'nalysis *f;* **3.** (Psycho)Ana'lyse *f;* **an·a·lyst** [-lɪst] *s.* **1.** 🧪, 🔬 Ana'lytiker(in); *fig.* Unter'sucher(in): *public* ~ (behördlicher) Lebensmittelchemiker; **2.** Psychoana'lytiker *m;* **3.** Sta'tistiker *m;* **an·a·lyt·ic, an·a·lyt·i·cal** [,ænə'lɪtɪk(l)] *adj.* □ **1.** ana'lytisch: *analytical chemist* Chemiker(in); **2.** psychoana'lytisch; **an·a·lyt·ics** [,ænə'lɪtɪks] *s. pl. sg. konstr.* Ana'lytik *f.*

an·a·lyze *bsd. Am.* → *analyse.*

an·am·ne·sis [,ænæm'niːsɪs] *pl.* **-ses** [-siːz] *s.* Anam'nese *f:* a) Wiedererinnerung *f,* b) 🩺 Vorgeschichte *f.*

an·aph·ro·dis·i·ac [æ,næfrəʊ'dɪzɪæk] 🩺 **I** *adj.* den Geschlechtstrieb hemmend; **II** *s.* Anaphrodi'siakum *n.*

an·ar·chic, an·ar·chi·cal [æ'nɑːkɪk(l)] *adj.* □ an'archisch, anar'chistisch, gesetzlos, zügellos.

an·arch·ism ['ænəkɪzəm] *s.* **1.** Anar'chie *f,* Regierungs-, Gesetzlosigkeit *f;* **2.** Anar'chismus *m;* **'an·arch·ist** [-ɪst] **I** *s.* Anar'chist(in), 'Umstürzler *m;* **II** *adj.* anar'chistisch, 'umstürzlerisch.

an·ar·cho- [ænɑːkəʊ] *in Zssgn* Anarcho...: ~*scene;* ~*situationist* Chaot *m.*

an·arch·y ['ænəkɪ] *s.* **1.** → *anarchism;* **2.** *fig.* 'Chaos *n.*

an·as·tig·mat·ic [ə,næstɪg'mætɪk] *adj. phys.* anastig'matisch *(Linse).*

a·nath·e·ma [ə'næθəmə] *(Greek) s.* **1.** *eccl.* A'nathema *n,* Kirchenbann *m; fig.* Fluch *m,* Verwünschung *f;* **2.** *eccl.* Exkommunizierte(r *m) f,* Verfluchte(r *m)* f; **3.** *fig.* etwas Verhasstes, Gräuel *m;* **a'nath·e·ma·tize** [-ətaɪz] *v/t.* in den Bann tun, verfluchen.

an·a·tom·ic, an·a·tom·i·cal [,ænə'tɒmɪk(l)] *adj.* □ ana'tomisch.

a·nat·o·mist [ə'nætəmɪst] *s.* **1.** Ana'tom *m;* **2.** Zergliederer *m (a. fig.);* **a'nat·o·mize** [-maɪz] *v/t.* **1.** 🩺 zerlegen, sezieren; **2.** *fig.* zergliedern; **a'nat·o·my** [-mɪ] *s.* **1.** Anato'mie *f (Aufbau, Wissenschaft, Abhandlung);* **2.** F a) ,Wanst' *m,* Körper *m,* b) ,Gerippe' *n,* Gestell *n.*

an·ces·tor ['ænsestə] *s.* **1.** Vorfahr *m,* Ahn(herr) *m,* Stammvater *m (a. fig.):* ~ *worship* Ahnenkult *m;* **2.** *fig.* Vorläufer *m;* **3.** ⚖ Vorbesitzer *m;* **an·ces·tral** [æn'sestrəl] *adj.* der Vorfahren, Ahnen..., angestammt, Erb..., Ur...; **'an·ces·tress** [-trɪs] *s.* Ahnfrau *f,* Stammmutter *f;* **'an·ces·try** [-trɪ] *s.* Abstammung *f,* hohe Geburt; Ahnen(reihe *f) pl; fig.* Vorgänger *pl.:* ~ *research* Ahnenforschung *f.*

an·chor ['æŋkə] **I** *s.* **1.** ⚓ Anker *m: at* ~ vor Anker; *weigh* ~ a) den Anker lichten, b) abfahren; *cast (od. drop)* ~ ankern, vor Anker gehen; *ride at* ~ vor Anker liegen; **2.** *fig.* Rettungsanker *m,* Zuflucht *f;* **3.** ⊕ Anker *m,* Schließe *f,* Klammer *f;* **4.** Radio, TV: *Am.* a) Mode'rator *m,* Modera'torin *f e-r Nachrichtensendung,* b) Diskussi'onsleiter (-in); **5.** *sport:* a) Schlussläufer(in), b) Schlussschwimmer(in); **II** *v/t.* **6.** verankern, vor Anker legen; **7.** ⊕ *u. fig.* verankern; **8.** Radio, TV: *Am.* a) *e-e* Nachrichtensendung moderieren, b) *e-e* *Diskussion* leiten; **9.** Schlussläufer(in) *od.* -schwimmer(in) *e-r Staffel* sein; **III** *v/i.* **10.** ankern, vor Anker gehen *od.* liegen; **11.** Radio, TV: *Am.* Moderator (-in) *od.* Diskussi'onsleiter(in) sein.

an·chor·age ['æŋkərɪdʒ] *s.* **1.** Ankerplatz *m;* **2.** *a.* ~ *dues* Anker-, Liegegebühr *f;* **3.** fester Halt, Verankerung *f;* **4.** *fig.* → *anchor* 2.

an·cho·ress ['æŋkərɪs] *s.* Einsiedlerin *f;* **'an·cho·ret** [-ret], **'an·cho·rite** [-raɪt] *s.* Einsiedler *m.*

'an·chor|·man [-mən] *s. [irr.],* **'~·wom·an** *s [irr.]* → *anchor* 4, 5.

an·cho·vy ['æntʃəvɪ] *s. ichth.* An'(s)chovis *f,* Sar'delle *f.*

an·cient ['eɪnʃənt] **I** *adj.* □ **1.** alt, aus alter Zeit, das Altertum betreffend, an'tik: ~ *Rome;* **2.** uralt *(a. humor.),* altberühmt; **3.** altertümlich; ehemalig; **II**

s. **4.** *the* ~s a) die Alten (*Griechen u. Römer*), b) die (antiken) Klassiker; **5.** Alte(r *m*) *f*, Greis(in); F ,Olle(r' *m*) *f*; **'an·cient·ly** [-lı] *adv.* vor'zeiten.

an·cil·lar·y [æn'sɪlərɪ] *adj.* 'untergeordnet (**to** *dat.*), Hilfs..., Neben...: ~ *agreement* Nebenabrede *f*; ~ *equipment* Zusatz-, Hilfsgerät *n*; ~ *industries* Zulieferbetriebe; ~ *road* Nebenstraße *f*.

and [ænd; ən(d)] *cj.* und: ~ *so forth* und so weiter; *there are books* ~ *books* es gibt gute und schlechte Bücher; *nice* ~ *warm* schön warm; ~ *all* F und so weiter; *skin* ~ *all* mitsamt der Haut; *a little more* ~ ... es fehlte nicht viel, so ...; *try* ~ *come* versuchen Sie zu kommen.

and·i·ron ['ændaıən] *s.* Feuer-, Brat-, Ka'minbock *m*.

An·drew ['ændruː] *npr.* An'dreas *m*: *St.* ~'s *cross* Andreaskreuz *n*.

an·drog·y·nous [æn'drɒdʒınəs] *adj.* zwitterartig, zweigeschlechtig; ♀ zwitterblütig.

an·droid ['ændrɔıd] *s.* Andro'id(e) *m* (*Kunstmensch*).

an·droph·a·gous [æn'drɒfəgəs] *adj.* Menschen fressend.

an·dro·pho·bi·a [,ændrəʊ'fəʊbjə] *s.* Andropho'bie *f*, Männerscheu *f*.

an·ec·do·tal [,ænek'dəʊtl] → *anecdotic*; **an·ec·dote** ['ænıkdəʊt] *s.* Anek'dote *f*; **an·ec·dot·ic, an·ec·dot·i·cal** [,ænek'dɒtık(l)] *adj.* □ anek'dotenhaft, anek'dotisch.

a·ne·mi·a, a·ne·mic *Am.* → *anaemia, anaemic.*

an·e·mom·e·ter [,ænı'mɒmıtə] *s. phys.* Windmesser *m*.

a·nem·o·ne [ə'nemənı] *s.* **1.** ♀ Ane'mone *f*; **2.** *zo.* 'Seeane,mone *f*.

an·er·oid ['ænərɔıd] *s. phys. a.* ~ *ba·rometer* Anero'idbaro,meter *n*.

an·es·the·si·a *etc. Am.* → *anaesthesia etc.*

a·new [ə'njuː] *adv.* von neuem, aufs Neue; auf neue Art und Weise.

an·gel ['eındʒəl] *s.* **1.** Engel *m*: ~ *of death* Todesengel; *rush in where* ~s *fear to tread* sich törichter- *od.* anmaßenderweise in Dinge einmischen, an die sich sonst niemand heranwagt; **2.** *fig.* Engel *m* (*Person*): *be an* ~ *and* ... sei doch so lieb und ...; **3.** *sl.* Geldgeber *m*, fi'nanzkräftiger 'Hintermann.

'an·gel|·food *Am.*, ~ *cake s.* Art Bis'kuitkuchen *m*.

an·gel·ic [æn'dʒelık] *adj.* (□ ~*ally*) engelhaft, -gleich, Engels...

an·gel·i·ca [æn'dʒelıkə] *s.* **1.** ♀ Brustwurz *f* (*als Gewürz*); **2.** kandierte An'gelikawurzel.

an·gel·i·cal [æn'dʒelıkl] *adj.* □ → *angelic.*

An·ge·lus ['ændʒıləs] *s. eccl.* 'Angelus (-gebet *n*, -läuten *n*) *m*.

an·ger ['æŋgə] **I** *s.* Ärger *m*, Zorn *m*, Wut *f* (*at* über *acc.*); **II** *v/t.* erzürnen, ärgern.

An·ge·vin ['ændʒıvın] **I** *adj.* **1.** aus An'jou (*in Frankreich*); **2.** die Plan'tagenets betreffend; **II** *s.* **3.** Mitglied *n* des Hauses Plan'tagenet.

an·gi·na [æn'dʒaınə] *s.* ✻ An'gina *f* 'pectoris; ~ *pec·to·ris* ['pektərıs] *s.* ✻ An'gina *f* 'pectoris.

an·gle¹ ['æŋgl] **I** *s.* **1.** *bsd.* ✚ Winkel *m*: *acute* (*obtuse, right*) ~ spitzer (stumpfer, rechter) Winkel; ~ *of incidence* Einfallswinkel; *at right* ~s *to* im rechten Winkel zu; **2.** ✪ a) Knie(stück

n, b) *pl.* Winkeleisen *pl.*; **3.** Ecke *f*, Vorsprung *m*, spitze Kante; **4.** *fig.* a) Standpunkt *m*, Gesichtswinkel *m*, As'pekt *m*, Seite *f*: *consider all* ~s *of a question*; **5.** *Am.* Me'thode *f* (*et. zu erreichen*); **6.** *sl.* Trick *m*, ,Tour' *f*, ,Masche' *f*; **II** *v/t.* **7.** 'umbiegen; **8.** *fig.* tendenzi'ös färben, verdrehen.

an·gle² ['æŋgl] *v/i.* angeln (*a. fig. for* nach).

an·gled ['æŋgld] *adj.* **1.** winklig, *mst in Zssgn*: *right-~* rechtwinklig; **2.** *fig.* tendenzi'ös.

'an·gle|,do·zer [-,dəʊzə] *s.* ✪ Pla'nierraupe *f*, Winkelräumer *m*; '~·park *v/t. u. v/i. mot.* schräg parken.

an·gle·poise *TM* (**lamp**) ['æŋglpɔız] *s.* Gelenkleuchte *f*, Arbeitsleuchte *f*.

an·gler ['æŋglə] *s.* **1.** Angler(in); **2.** *ichth.* Seeteufel *m*.

An·gles ['æŋglz] *s. pl. hist.* Angeln *pl.*; **'An·gli·an** [-glıən] **I** *adj.* englisch; **II** *s.* Angehörige(r *m*) *f* des Volksstammes der Angeln.

An·gli·can ['æŋglıkən] *eccl.* **I** *adj.* angli'kanisch, hochkirchlich; **II** *s.* Angli'kaner(in).

An·gli·cism ['æŋglısızəm] *s.* **1.** *ling.* Angli'zismus *m*; **2.** englische Eigenart; **'An·gli·cist** [-ıst] *s.* An'glist(in); **'An·gli·cize** [-saız], *a.* ⚨ *v/t. u. v/i.* (sich) anglisieren, englisch machen (werden).

an·gling ['æŋglıŋ] *s.* Angeln *n*.

An·glist ['æŋglıst] *s.* An'glist(in); **An·glis·tics** [æn'glıstıks] *s. pl. sg. konstr.* An'glistik *f*.

Anglo- [æŋgləʊ] *in Zssgn* Anglo..., anglo-..., englisch, englisch und; **,An·glo|-A'mer·i·can** [-əʊ-] **I** *s.* 'Angloameri'kaner(in); **II** *adj.* angloameri'kanisch; **,~-'In·di·an** [-əʊ-] **I** *s.* Anglo'inder(in); **II** *adj.* anglo'indisch; **,~'ma·ni·a** [-əʊ-] *s.* Angloma'nie *f*; **,~-'Nor·man** [-əʊ-] **I** *s.* **1.** Anglonor'manne *m*; **2.** *ling.* Anglonor'mannisch *n*; **II** *adj.* **3.** anglonor'mannisch; **'~·phile** [-əʊfaıl] **I** *s.* Anglo'phile *m*, Englandfreund *m*; **II** *adj.* anglo'phil, englandfreundlich; **'~·phobe** [-əʊfəʊb] **I** *s.* Anglo'phobe *m*, Englandfeind *m*; **II** *adj.* englandfeindlich; **,~'pho·bi·a** [-əʊ'fəʊbjə] *s.* Anglopho'bie *f*; **,~-'Sax·on** [-əʊ-] **I** *s.* **1.** Angelsachse *m*; **2.** *ling.* Altenglisch *n*, Angelsächsisch *n*; **3.** F urwüchsiges *u.* einfaches Englisch; **II** *adj.* **4.** angelsächsisch; **,~-'Scot** [-əʊ-] *s.* dauernd in England lebende Schotte.

an·go·ra [æŋ'gɔːrə], *a.* ⚨ *s.* Gewebe *n* aus An'gorawolle; **~ *cat*** *s. zo.* An'gorakatze *f*; **~ *goat*** *s. zo.* An'goraziege *f*; **~ *wool*** *s.* An'gorawolle *f*; Mo'här *m*.

an·gry ['æŋgrı] *adj.* □ **1.** (*at, about*) ärgerlich, ungehalten (über *acc.*), zornig, böse (auf *j-n*, über *et.*, *with* mit *j-m*): **~ *young man*** Literatur: ,zorniger junger Mann'; **2.** ✱ entzündet, schlimm; **3.** *fig.* drohend, stürmisch, finster.

angst [æŋst] *s. psych.* Angst *f*.

ang·strom [-], *a.* ⚨ ['æŋstrəm] *s. phys. a.* ~ *unit* Angström(einheit *f*) *n*.

an·guish ['æŋgwıʃ] *s.* Qual *f*, Pein *f*, Angst *f*, Schmerz *m*: ~ *of mind* Seelenqual(en *pl.*) *f*.

an·gu·lar ['æŋgjʊlə] *adj.* □ **1.** winklig, winkelförmig, eckig; Winkel...; **2.** *fig.* knochig, hager; **3.** *fig.* eckig, steif; barsch; **an·gu·lar·i·ty** [,æŋgjʊ'lærətı] *s.* **1.** Winkligkeit *f*; **2.** *fig.* Eckigkeit *f*, Steifheit *f*.

an·hy·drous [æn'haıdrəs] *adj.* ✿, *biol.* kalziniert, wasserfrei; getrocknet, Dörr... (*Obst etc.*).

an·il ['ænıl] *s.* ♀ 'Indigopflanze *f*; Indigo (-farbstoff) *m*.

an·i·line ['ænılıːn] *s.* Ani'lin *n*: ~ *dye* Anilinfarbstoff *m*, *weitS.* chemisch hergestellte Farbe.

an·i·mad·ver·sion [,ænımæd'vɜːʃn] *s.* Tadel *m*, Rüge *f*, Kri'tik *f*; ,an·i·mad·'vert [-'vɜːt] *v/i.* (*on, upon*) kritisieren; tadeln, rügen (*acc.*).

an·i·mal ['ænıml] **I** *s.* **1.** Tier *n*, ,Vierfüß(l)er' *m*; tierisches Lebewesen (*Ggs. Pflanze*, F *a. Ggs. Vogel*): *there's no such* ~! F so was gibts ja gar nicht!; **2.** *fig.* Tier *n*, viehischer Mensch, 'Bestie *f*; **II** *adj.* **3.** ani'malisch, tierisch (*beide a. fig.*); Tier...: ~ *kingdom* Tierreich *n*; ~ *magnetism* a) tierischer Magnetismus, b) *bsd. humor.* erotische Anziehungskraft; ~ *spirits* *pl.* Lebenskraft *f*, -geister *pl.*, Vitalität *f*; ~ *welfare* Tierschutz *m*; ~ *welfarist* Tierschützer *m*.

an·i·mal·cu·le [,ænı'mælkjuːl] *s.* mikro'skopisch kleines Tierchen: *infusorial* ~s.

an·i·mal·ism ['ænıməlızəm] *s.* **1.** Vertiertheit *f*; **2.** Sinnlichkeit *f*; **3.** Lebenstrieb *m*, -kraft *f*; **'an·i·mal·ist** [-ıst] *s.* Tiermaler(in), -bildhauer(in).

an·i·mate I *v/t.* ['ænımeıt] **1.** beseelen, beleben, mit Leben erfüllen (*alle a. fig.*); anregen, aufmuntern; **2.** lebendig gestalten: ~ *a cartoon* e-n Zeichentrickfilm herstellen; **II** *adj.* [-mət] **3.** belebt, lebend; lebhaft, munter; **'an·i·mat·ed** [-tıd] *adj.* □ **1.** lebendig, beseelt (*with, by* von), voll Leben: ~ *cartoon* Zeichentrickfilm *m*; **2.** ermutigt; **3.** lebhaft, angeregt; **an·i·ma·tion** [,ænı'meıʃn] *s.* **1.** Leben *n*, Feuer *n*, Lebhaftigkeit *f*, Munterkeit *f*; Leben *n* und Treiben *n*; **2.** a) Herstellung *f* von Zeichentrickfilmen, b) (Zeichen)Trickfilm *m*; **'an·i·ma·tor** [-tə] *s.* Zeichner *m* von Trickfilmen.

an·i·mos·i·ty [,ænı'mɒsətı] *s.* Feindseligkeit *f*, Erbitterung *f*, Animosi'tät *f*.

an·i·mus ['ænıməs] *s.* **1.** (innewohnender) Geist; **2.** *psych.* Animus *m*; **3.** ✻ Absicht *f*; **4.** → *animosity.*

an·ise ['ænıs] *s.* ♀ A'nis *m*; **'an·i·seed** [-siːd] *s.* A'nis(samen) *m*.

an·i·sette [,ænı'zet] *s.* Ani'sett *m*, A'nis,likör *m*.

an·kle ['æŋkl] **I** *s. anat.* **1.** (Fuß)Knöchel *m*: *sprain one's* ~ sich den Fuß verstauchen; **2.** Knöchelgegend *f* des Beins; **II** *v/i.* **3.** F marschieren; **'~·bone** *s.* Sprungbein *n*; ~ *boot* *s.* Halbstiefel *m*; **,~-'deep** *adj.* knöcheltief, bis zu den Knöcheln; **,~-'length** *adj.* knöchellang; ~ *sock s.* Knöchelsocke *f*, Söckchen *n*; ~ *strap s.* Schuhspange *f*: *ankle-strap shoes* Spangenschuhe.

an·klet ['æŋklıt] *s.* **1.** Fußkettchen *n*, -spange *f* (*als Schmuck od. Fessel*); **2.** → *anklesock.*

an·na ['ænə] *s.* An'na *m* (*ind. Münze*).

an·nal·ist ['ænəlıst] *s.* Chro'nist *m*; **an·nals** ['ænlz] *s. pl.* **1.** An'nalen *pl.*, Jahrbücher *pl.*; **2.** hi'storischer Bericht; **3.** regelmäßig erscheinende wissenschaftliche Berichte *pl.*; **4.** *a. sg. konstr.* (Jahres)Bericht *m*.

an·neal [ə'niːl] *v/t.* **1.** ✪ Metall ausglühen, anlassen, vergüten, tempern; *Glas* kühlen; **2.** *fig.* härten, stählen.

an·nex I *v/t.* [ə'neks] **1.** (*to*) beifügen (*dat.*), anhängen (an *acc.*); **2.** annektieren, (sich) einverleiben: *the province was* ~ed *to France* Frankreich verleibte sich das Gebiet ein; **3.** ~ *to* verknüpfen mit; **4.** F sich aneignen, ,sich unter den Nagel reißen'; **II** *s.* [æneks] **5.** Anhang *m*, Nachtrag *m*; Anlage *f zum Brief*; **6.** Nebengebäude *n*, Anbau *m*; **an·nex·a·tion** [ˌænekˈseɪʃn] *s*. **1.** Hin-'zufügung *f* (**to** zu); **2.** Annexi'on *f*, Einverleibung *f* (**to** in *acc.*); **3.** Aneignung *f*; **an·nexe** [ˈæneks] (*Fr.*) → *annex* 6; **an'nexed** [-kst] *adj.* ✝ beifolgend, beigefügt.

an·ni·hi·late [əˈnaɪəleɪt] *v/t.* **1.** vernichten (*a. fig.*); **2.** ✕ aufreiben; **3.** *sport* vernichtend schlagen; **4.** *fig.* zu'nichte machen, aufheben; **an·ni·hi·la·tion** [əˌnaɪəˈleɪʃn] *s*. Vernichtung *f*; Aufhebung *f*.

an·ni·ver·sa·ry [ˌænɪˈvɜːsərɪ] *s*. Jahrestag *m*, -feier *f*, jährlicher Gedenktag, Jubi'läum *n*: *wedding* ~ Hochzeitstag *m*; *the 50th* ~ *of his death* die 50. Wiederkehr s-s Todestages.

an·no Dom·i·ni [ˌænəʊˈdɒmɪnaɪ] (*Lat.*) im Jahre des Herrn, anno Domini.

an·no·tate [ˈænəʊteɪt] **I** *v/t.* e-e Schrift mit Anmerkungen versehen, kommentieren; **II** *v/i.* (**on**) Anmerkungen machen (zu), einen Kommen'tar schreiben (über *acc.*); **an·no·ta·tion** [ˌænəʊˈteɪʃn] *s*. Kommentieren *n*; Anmerkung *f*, Kommen'tar *m*; **'an·no·ta·tor** [-tə] *s*. Kommen'tator *m*.

an·nounce [əˈnaʊns] **I** *v/t.* **1.** ankündigen; **2.** bekannt geben, verkünden; **3.** a) *Radio*, *TV*: ansagen, b) (*über Lautsprecher*) 'durchsagen; **4.** *Besucher etc.* melden; **5.** *Geburt etc.* anzeigen, bekannt geben; **II** *v/i.* **6.** *pol. Am.* seine Kandida'tur bekannt geben (**for** für das Amt *gen.*); **7.** ~ *for Am.* sich aussprechen für; **an'nounce·ment** [-mənt] *s*. **1.** Ankündigung *f*; **2.** Bekanntgabe *f*; (*Geburts- etc.*)Anzeige *f*; **3.** a) *Radio*, *TV*: Ansage *f*, b) ('Lautsprecher-)Durchsage *f*; **an'nounc·er** [-sə] *s. Radio*, *TV*: Ansager(in), Sprecher(in).

an·noy [əˈnɔɪ] *v/t.* **1.** ärgern: *be ~ed* sich ärgern (*at s.th.* über et., *with s.o.* über j-n); **2.** belästigen, stören; schikanieren; **an'noy·ance** [-ɔɪəns] *s*. **1.** Störung *f*, Belästigung *f*, Ärgernis *n*; Ärger *m*; **2.** Plage(geist *m*) *f*; **an'noyed** [-ɔɪd] *adj.* ärgerlich; **an'noy·ing** [-ɔɪɪŋ] *adj.* □ ärgerlich (*Sache*), lästig; **an'noy·ing·ly** [-ɔɪɪŋlɪ] *adv.* ärgerlicherweise.

an·nu·al [ˈænjʊəl] **I** *adj.* □ **1.** jährlich, Jahres...; ~ *accounts* Jahresabschluss *m*; ~ *report* Jahresbericht *m*, Geschäftsbericht *m*; **2.** *bsd.* ♀ einjährig: ~ *ring* Jahresring *m*; **II** *s*. **3.** jährlich erscheinende Veröffentlichung, Jahrbuch *n*; **4.** einjährige Pflanze; → *hardy* 2.

an·nu·i·tant [əˈnjuːɪtənt] *s*. Empfänger (-in) e-r Jahresrente, Rentner(in); **an'nu·i·ty** [-tɪ] *s*. **1.** (Jahres)Rente *f*; **2.** Jahreszahlung *f*; **3.** ✝ *a.* ~ *bond* Rentenbrief *m*; **4.** *pl.* 'Rentenpa,piere *pl.*

an·nul [əˈnʌl] *v/t.* aufheben, für ungültig erklären, annullieren.

an·nu·lar [ˈænjʊlə] *adj.* □ ringförmig; **'an·nu·late** [-leɪt], **'an·nu·lat·ed** [-leɪtɪd] *adj.* geringelt, aus Ringen bestehend, Ring...

an·nul·ment [əˈnʌlmənt] *s*. Aufhebung *f*, Nichtigkeitserklärung *f*, Annullierung *f*; *action for* ~ Nichtigkeitsklage *f*.

an·nun·ci·ate [əˈnʌnʃɪeɪt] *v/t.* verkünden, ankündigen; **an·nun·ci·a·tion** [əˌnʌnsɪˈeɪʃn] *s*. **1.** An-, Verkündigung *f*; **2.** ♀, *a.* ♀ *Day eccl.* Ma'riä Verkündigung *f*; **an'nun·ci·a·tor** [-tə] *s*. ♭ Signalanlage *f*, -tafel *f*.

an·ode [ˈænəʊd] *s*. ♭ An'ode *f*, 'positiver Pol: ~ *potential* Anodenspannung *f*; *DC* ~ Anodenruhestrom *m*; **an·od·ize** [ˈænəʊdaɪz] *v/t.* eloxieren.

an·o·dyne [ˈænəʊdaɪn] **I** *adj.* schmerzstillend; *fig.* a) lindernd, beruhigend, b) verwässert, kraftlos; **II** *s*. schmerzstillendes Mittel; *fig.* Beruhigungspille *f*.

a·noint [əˈnɔɪnt] *v/t.* **1.** einölen, einschmieren; **2.** *bsd. eccl.* salben; **a-'noint·ment** [-mənt] *s*. Salbung *f*.

a·nom·a·lous [əˈnɒmələs] *adj.* □ 'anomal, ab'norm; ungewöhnlich, abweichend; **a'nom·a·ly** [-lɪ] *s*. Anoma'lie *f*.

a·non [əˈnɒn] *adv.* bald, so'gleich: *ever and* ~ immer wieder.

an·o·nym·i·ty [ˌænəˈnɪmətɪ] *s*. Anonymi'tät *f*; **a·non·y·mous** [əˈnɒnɪməs] *adj.* □ ano'nym, namenlos, ungenannt; unbekannten Ursprungs.

a·noph·e·les [əˈnɒfɪliːz] *s. zo.* Fiebermücke *f*.

a·no·rak [ˈænəræk] *s*. Anorak *m*.

an·o·rex·i·a [ˌænəˈreksɪə] *s*. ♯ Magersucht *f*, Anore'xie *f*; **an·o'rex·ic** [-sɪk] ♯ **I** *adj.* magersüchtig; **II** *s*. Magersüchtige(r *m*) *f*.

an·oth·er [əˈnʌðə] *adj. u. pron.* **1.** ein anderer, eine andere, ein anderes (*than* als): ~ *thing* etwas anderes; *one* ~ a) einander, b) uns (euch, sich) gegenseitig; *one after* ~ einer nach dem andern; *he is* ~ *man now* jetzt ist er ein (ganz) anderer Mensch; **2.** ein zweiter *od.* weiterer *od.* neuer, eine zweite *od.* weitere *od.* neue, ein zweites *od.* weiteres *od.* neues; **3.** *a. yet* ~ noch ein(er, e, es): ~ *cup of tea* noch eine Tasse Tee; ~ *five weeks* weitere *od.* noch fünf Wochen; *tell us* ~*!* F das glaubst du doch selbst nicht!; *you are* ~*!* F *iro.* danke gleichfalls!; ~ *Shakespeare* ein zweiter Shakespeare; *A.N.Other sport* ein ungenannter (Ersatz)Spieler.

an·ov·u·lant [ˌæˈnɒvjʊlənt] *s*. ♯ Ovulati'onshemmer *m*.

An·schluss [ˈɑːnʃlʊs] (*Ger.*) *s. pol.* Anschluss *m*.

ANSI code [ˈænsiː] *s. Computer*: ANSI-Code *m*.

an·swer [ˈɑːnsə] **I** *s*. **1.** Antwort *f*, Entgegnung *f* (**to** auf *acc.*): *in* ~ *to* a) in Beantwortung (*gen.*), b) auf *et.* hin; **2.** *fig.* Antwort *f*, Erwiderung *f*; Reakti'on *f* (*alle*: **to** auf *acc.*); **3.** Gegenmaßnahme *f*, -mittel *n*; **4.** ✝ Klagebeantwortung *f*, Gegenschrift *f*; *weitS.* Rechtfertigung *f*; **5.** Lösung *f* (**to** *e-s Problems etc.*); ♩ Auflösung *f*: *he knows all the* ~*s* a) ,er blickt voll durch', b) *contp.* er weiß immer alles besser; **II** *v/i.* **6.** antworten (**to** *j-m*, auf *acc.*): ~ *back* a) freche Antworten geben, b) widersprechen, sich (*mit Worten*) verteidigen *od.* wehren; **7.** sich verantworten, Rechenschaft ablegen (**for** für); **8.** verantwortlich sein, haften, bürgen (**for** für); **9.** die Folgen tragen, büßen (**for** für): *you have much to* ~ *for* du hast viel auf dem Kerbholz; **10.** *fig.* (**to**) reagieren (auf *acc.*), hören (auf *e-n Namen*): gehorchen, Folge leisten (*dat.*); **11.** ~ *to e-r Beschreibung* entsprechen; **12.** sich eignen, taugen, gelingen (*Plan*); **III** *v/t.* **13.** a) *j-m* antworten, b) *et.* beantworten, antworten auf (*acc.*); **14.** a) sich *j-m gegenüber* verantworten, *j-m* Rechenschaft ablegen (**for** für), b) sich gegen *e-e Anklage etc.* verteidigen; **15.** reagieren *od.* eingehen auf (*acc.*); *e-m Befehl etc.* Folge leisten; sich auf *eine Anzeige etc.* hin melden: ~ *the bell* (*od.* *door*) auf das Läuten *od.* Klopfen die Tür öffnen; ~ *the telephone* den Anruf entgegennehmen, ans Telefon gehen; **16.** *dem Steuer* gehorchen; *Gebet* erhören; *Zweck*, *Wunsch etc.* erfüllen;

Auftrag etc. ausführen: ~ *the call of duty* dem Ruf der Pflicht folgen; **17.** *bsd. Aufgabe* lösen; **18.** *e-r Beschreibung*, *e-m Bedürfnis* entsprechen; **19.** *j-m* genügen, *j-n* zu'frieden stellen; **'an·swer·a·ble** [-sərəbl] *adj.* verantwortlich (**for** für): *to be* ~ *to s.o. for s.th.* j-m für et. bürgen, sich vor j-m für et. verantworten müssen; **2.** (**to**) entsprechend, angemessen, gemäß (*dat.*); **3.** zu beantworten(d).

an·swer·ing ma·chine *s*. Anrufbeantworter *m*.

ant [ænt] *s. zo.* Ameise *f*.

an't [ɑːnt; ænt] → *ain't.*

ant·ac·id [ˌæntˈæsɪd] *adj. u. s.* ♯ gegen Magensäure wirkend(es Mittel).

an·tag·o·nism [ænˈtæɡənɪzəm] *s*. **1.** 'Widerstreit *m*, Gegensatz *m*, 'Widerspruch *m* (**between** zwischen *dat.*); **2.** Feindschaft *f* (**to** gegen); 'Widerstand *m* (**against**, **to** gegen); **an'tag·o·nist** [-ɪst] *s*. Gegner(in), 'Widersacher(in); **an·tag·o·nis·tic** [ænˌtæɡəˈnɪstɪk] *adj.* (□ ~*ally*) gegnerisch, feindlich (**to** gegen); wider'streitend (**to** *dat.*); **an'tag·o·nize** [-naɪz] *v/t.* ankämpfen gegen; sich *j-n* zum Feind machen, *j-n* gegen sich aufbringen.

ant·arc·tic [æntˈɑːktɪk] **I** *adj.* ant'arktisch, Südpol...: ♀ *Circle* südlicher Polarkreis; ♀ *Ocean* südliches Eismeer; **II** *s*. Ant'arktis *f*.

'ant·bear *s. zo.* Ameisenbär *m*.

an·te [ˈæntɪ] (*Lat.*) **I** *adv.* vorn, vo'ran; b) *zeitlich*: vorher, zu'vor; **II** *prp.* vor; **III** *s*. F *Poker*: Einsatz *m*: *raise the* ~ a) den Einsatz (*weitS.* den Preis *etc.*) erhöhen, b) F (*das nötige*) Geld beschaffen; **IV** *v/t. u. v/i. mst* ~ *up* (ein)setzen; *fig. Am.* a) (be)zahlen, ,blechen', b) (dazu) beisteuern.

'ant,eat·er *s. zo.* Ameisenfresser *m*.

an·te·ced·ence [ˌæntɪˈsiːdəns] *s*. **1.** Vortritt *m*, -rang *m*; **2.** *ast.* Rückläufigkeit *f*; **,an·te'ced·ent** [-nt] **I** *adj.* **1.** vor'hergehend, früher (**to** als); **II** *s*. **2.** *pl.* Vorgeschichte *f*: *his* ~*s* sein Vorleben; **3.** *fig.* Vorläufer *m*; **4.** *ling.* Beziehungswort *n*.

an·te|·cham·ber [ˈæntɪˌtʃeɪmbə] *s*. Vorzimmer *n*; ~·**date** [ˌæntɪˈdeɪt] *v/t.* **1.** vor- *od.* zu'rückdatieren, ein früheres Datum setzen auf (*acc.*); **2.** vor'wegnehmen; **3.** *zeitlich* vor'angehen (*dat.*); ~·**di·lu·vi·an** [ˌæntɪdɪˈluːvjən] **I** *adj.* vorsintflutlich (*a. fig.*); **II** *s*. vorsintflutliches Wesen; *contp.* a) rückständige Per'son, b) ,Fos'sil' *n* (*sehr alte Person*).

an·te·lope [ˈæntɪləʊp] *s*. **1.** *zo.* Anti'lope *f*; **2.** Anti'lopenleder *n*.

an·te me·rid·i·em [ˌæntɪməˈrɪdɪəm] (*Lat.*) *abbr.* **a.m.** vormittags.

an·te·na·tal [ˌæntɪˈneɪtl] **I** *adj.* präna'tal: ~ *care* Mutterschaftsfürsorge *f*; **II** *s*. F Mutterschaftsvorsorgeuntersuchung *f*.

an·ten·na [ænˈtenə] *s*. **1.** *pl.* **-nae** [-niː] *zo.* Fühler *m*; Fühlhorn *n*; *fig.* Gespür *n*, ,An'tenne' *f*; **2.** *pl.* **-nas** *bsd. Am.* ♭ Antenne *f*.

an·te|·nup·tial [ˌæntɪˈnʌpʃl] *adj.* vorhochzeitlich; ~·**pe·nul·ti·mate** [ˌæntɪpɪˈnʌltɪmət] **I** *adj.* drittletzt (*bsd. Silbe*); **II** *s*. drittletzte Silbe.

an·te·ri·or [ænˈtɪərɪə] *adj.* **1.** vorder; **2.** vor'hergehend, früher (**to** als).

an·te·room [ˈæntɪrʊm] *s*. Vor-, Wartezimmer *n*.

an·them [ˈænθəm] *s*. 'Hymne *f*, Cho'ral *m*: *national* ~ Nationalhymne *f*.

an·ther [ˈænθə] *s*. ♀ Staubbeutel *m*.

'ant·hill *s. zo.* Ameisenhaufen *m*.

an·thol·o·gy [ænˈθɒlədʒɪ] *s*. Antholo'gie

f, (Gedicht)Sammlung *f.*

an·thra·cite [ˈænθrəsaɪt] *s. min.* Anthra-'zit *m,* Glanzkohle *f.*

an·thrax [ˈænθræks] *s.* ✳ 'Anthrax *m,* Milzbrand *m.*

an·thro·poid [ˈænθrəʊpɔɪd] *zo.* **I** *adj.* menschenähnlich, Menschen...; **II** *s.* Menschenaffe *m;* **an·thro·po·log·i·cal** [ˌænθrəpəˈlɒdʒɪk(l)] *adj.* □ anthropo-'logisch; **an·thro·pol·o·gist** [ˌænθrəˈpɒlədʒɪst] *s.* Anthropo'loge *m;* **an·thro·pol·o·gy** [ˌænθrəˈpɒlədʒɪ] *s.* Anthropo'logie *f;* **an·thro·po·mor·phous** [ˌænθrəpəʊˈmɔːfəs] *adj.* anthropo-'morph(isch), von menschlicher *od.* menschenähnlicher Gestalt; **an·thro·poph·a·gi** [ˌænθrəʊˈpɒfəɡaɪ] *s. pl.* Menschenfresser *pl.;* **an·thro·poph·a·gous** [ˌænθrəʊˈpɒfəɡəs] *adj.* Menschen fressend.

an·ti [ˈæntɪ] F **I** *prp.* gegen; **II** *adj.:* **be ~** dagegen sein; **III** *s.* Gegner(in).

an·ti-a·bor·tion·ist [ˌæntɪ-] *s.* Abtreibungsgegner(in); **~-air·craft** *adj.* ✕ Fliegerabwehr...: **~ gun** Flakgeschütz *n,* Fliegerabwehrkanone *f;* **~-au·thor·i·tar·i·an** *adj.* antiautori'tär; **~-ba·by pill** *s.* ✳ Anti'babypille *f;* **~-bal·lis·tic** *adj.* ✕ antibal'listisch; **~-bi·ot·ic** [-baɪ-'ɒtɪk] **I** *s.* Antibi'otikum *n;* **II** *adj.* antibi'otisch; **~-bod·y** 🔬, *biol.* 'Antikörper *m,* Abwehrstoff *m;* **~-cath·ode** *s.* ⚡ Antika'thode *f;* **~-christ** *s. eccl.* 'Antichrist *m;* **~-Chris·tian I** *adj.* christenfeindlich; **II** *s.* Christenfeind(in).

an·tic·i·pate [ænˈtɪsɪpeɪt] *v/t.* **1.** vor'ausempfinden, -sehen, -ahnen; **2.** erwarten, erhoffen; **~d profit** voraussichtlicher Verdienst; **3.** im Vor'aus tun *od.* erwähnen, vor'wegnehmen; Ankunft beschleunigen; vor'auseilen *(dat.);* **4.** *j-m od. e-m* Wunsch *etc.* zu'vorkommen; **5.** *e-r* Sache vorbauen, verhindern; **6.** *bsd.* ✝ vorzeitig bezahlen *od.* verbrauchen; **an·tic·i·pa·tion** [ænˌtɪsɪ-ˈpeɪʃn] *s.* **1.** Vorgefühl *n,* Vorahnung *f,* Vorgeschmack *m;* **2.** Ahnungsvermögen *n,* Vor'aussicht *f;* **3.** Erwartung *f,* Hoffnung *f,* Vorfreude *f;* **4.** Zu'vorkommen *n,* Vorgreifen *n,* Vor'wegnahme *f:* **in ~** im Voraus; **5.** Verfrühtheit *f:* **payment by ~** Vorauszahlung *f;* **an·tic·i·pa·to·ry** [-tərɪ] *adj.* **1.** vor'wegnehmend, vorgreifend, erwartend, Vor...; **2.** *ling.* vor'ausdeutend; **3.** Patentrecht: neuheitsschädlich: **~ reference** Vorwegnahme *f.*

an·ti-cler·i·cal *adj.* kirchenfeindlich; **~-cli·max** *s.* (enttäuschendes) Abfallen, Abstieg *m;* **a. sense of ~** plötzliches Gefühl der Leere *od.* Enttäuschung; **~-clock·wise** *adv. u. adj.* entgegen dem Uhrzeigersinn: **~ rotation** Linksdrehung *f;* **~-cor·ro·sive** *adj.* rostfrei; Rostschutz...

an·tics [ˈæntɪks] *s. pl.* Possen *pl.,* *fig.* Mätzchen *pl.,* (tolle) Streiche *pl.*

an·ti-cy·cli·cal *adj.* ✝ anti'zyklisch, konjunk'turdämpfend; **~-cy·clone** *s. meteor.* Hoch(druckgebiet) *n;* **~-daz·zle** *adj.* Blendschutz...: **~ switch** Abblendschalter *m;* **~-de·pres·sant** *s.* ✳ Antidepres'sivum *n;* **~-dote** *adj.* ⊕ Klar(sicht)...; **~-dis·tor·tion** *s.* ⚡ Entzerrung *f;* **~-dot·al** [-dəʊtl] *adj.* als Gegengift dienend *(a. fig.);* **~-dote** [-dəʊt] *s.* Gegengift *n,* -mittel *n* (**against, for, to** gegen); **~-fad·ing** ⚡ *s.* Schwundausgleich *m;* **II** *adj.* schwundmindernd; **~-Fas·cist** *pol.* **I** *s.* Antifa'schist(in); **II** *adj.* antifa'schistisch; **~-fe·brile** *s.* ✳ Fiebermittel *n;* **~-fed·er·al·ist** *s. Am. hist.* Antiföderalist *m;* **~-freeze** **I**

adj. Gefrier-, Frostschutz...; **II** *s.* Frostschutzmittel *n;* **~-fric·tion** *s.* Schmiermittel *n:* **~ metal** Lagermetall *n;* **~-gas** *adj.* Gasschutz...

an·ti·gen [ˈæntɪdʒən] *s.* ✳ Anti'gen *n,* Abwehrstoff *m.*

an·ti-glare → **antidazzle;** **~-ha·lo** *adj. phot.* lichthoffrei; **~-he·ro** *s.* Antiheld *m;* **~-his·ta·mine** *s. physiol., pharm.* 'Antihista'min *n;* **~-im·pe·ri·al·ist** *s.* Gegner *m* des Imperia'lismus; **~-in·ter·fer·ence** *adj.* ⚡ Entstörungs..., Störschutz...; **~-jam** *v/t. u. v/i.* Radio entstören; **~-knock** 🔬, *mot.* **I** *adj.* klopffest; **II** *s.* Anti'klopfmittel *n;* **~-lock 'brak·ing sys·tem** *s.* Antiblockiersystem *n.*

an·ti-ma·cas·sar [ˌæntɪməˈkæsə] **I** *s.* Sofa- *od.* Sesselschoner *m;* **II** *adj. fig.* altmodisch; **~-ma'lar·i·al** *s.* ✳ Ma'lariamittel *n;* **~-mat·ter** *s. phys.* 'Antima,terie *f;* **~-mis·sile** *s.* ✕ Antira'ketenra,kete *f.*

an·ti·mo·ny [ˈæntɪmənɪ] *s.* 🔬, *min.* Anti'mon *n.*

an·tin·o·my [ænˈtɪnəmɪ] *s.* Antino'mie *f,* 'Widerspruch *m.*

an·ti·pa·thet·ic, **an·ti·pa·thet·i·cal** [-pəˈθetɪk(l)] *adj.* □ (**to**) **1.** zu'wider *(dat.);* **2.** abgeneigt *(dat.);* **an·tip·a·thy** [ænˈtɪpəθɪ] *s.* Antipa'thie *f,* Abneigung *f* (**against, to** gegen).

an·ti-per·son'nel *adj.:* ✕ **~ bomb** Splitterbombe *f;* **~ mine** Schützen-, Tretmine *f;* **~-phlo'gis·tic** [-fləʊˈdʒɪs-tɪk] **I** *adj.* **1.** 🔬 antiphlo'gistisch; **2.** ✳ entzündungshemmend; **II** *s.* **3.** ✳ Antiphlo'gistikum *n.*

an·tiph·o·ny [ænˈtɪfənɪ] *s.* Antipho'nie *f,* Wechselgesang *m.*

an·tip·o·dal [ænˈtɪpədl] *adj.* anti'podisch, *fig. a.* genau entgegengesetzt; **an·tip·o·de·an** [ænˌtɪpəˈdiːən] *s.* Anti-'pode *m,* Gegenfüßler *m;* **an·tip·o·des** [ænˈtɪpədiːz] *s. pl.* **1.** die diame'tral gegen'überliegenden Teile *pl.* der Erde; **2.** *sg. u. pl.* Gegenteil *n,* -satz *m,* -seite *f.*

an·ti-pol'lu·tion *adj.* umweltschützend; **~-pol'lu·tion·ist** [-pəˈluːʃənɪst] *s.* Umweltschützer *m;* **~-pope** *s.* Gegenpapst *m;* **~-py'ret·ic** ✳ **I** *adj.* Fieber verhütend; **II** *s.* Fiebermittel *n;* **~-py-rin(e)** [-ˈpaɪərɪn] *s.* ✳ Antipy'rin *n.*

an·ti·quar·i·an [ˌæntɪˈkweərɪən] **I** *adj.* altertümlich; **II** *s.* → **an·ti·quar·y** [ˈæntɪ-kwərɪ] *s.* **1.** Altertumskenner *m,* -forscher *m;* **2.** Antiqui'tätensammler *m,* -händler *m;* **an·ti·quat·ed** [ˈæntɪkweɪ-tɪd] *adj.* veraltet, altmodisch, über'holt, anti'quiert.

an·tique [ænˈtiːk] **I** *adj.* □ **1.** an'tik, alt; **2.** altmodisch, veraltet; **II** *s.* **3.** Antiqui'tät *f:* **~ dealer** Antiquitätenhändler *m;* **4.** *typ.* Egypti'enne *f;* **an·tiq·ui·ty** [ænˈtɪkwətɪ] *s.* **1.** Altertum *n,* Vorzeit *f;* **2.** die Alten *pl.* (*bsd. Griechen u. Römer*); **3.** *die* Antike; **4.** *pl.* Antiqui'täten *pl.,* Altertümer *pl.;* **5.** (ehrwürdiges) Alter.

an·ti-rust *adj.* Rostschutz...; **~-sab·ba'tar·i·an** *adj. u. s.* der strengen Sonntagsheiligung abgeneigt(e Person); **~-'Sem·ite** *s.* Antise'mit(in); **~-Se'mit·ic** *adj.* antise'mitisch; **~-Sem·i·tism** *s.* Antisemi'tismus *m;* **~-sep·tic** ✳ **I** *adj.* (□ **~ally**) anti'septisch; **II** *s.* Anti'septikum *n;* **~-skid** *mot.* ⊕, *mot.* gleit-, schleudersicher, Gleitschutz...; rutschfest; **~-smok·ing** *adj.:* **~ campaign** Kam'pagne *f* gegen das Rauchen; **~-so·cial** *adj.* 'unsozi,al, gesellschaftsfeindlich; ungesellig; **~-tank**

adj. ✕ Panzerabwehr... (**-kanone** *etc.*), Panzer... (**-sperre** *etc.*); Panzerjäger...: **~ battalion;** **~-tech·no'log·i·cal** *adj.* □ technolo'giefeindlich.

an·tith·e·sis [ænˈtɪθɪsɪs] *pl.* **-ses** [-siːz] *s.* Anti'these *f:* a) Gegensatz *m,* b) 'Widerspruch *m;* **an·ti·thet·ic, an·ti·thet·i·cal** [ˌæntɪˈθetɪk(l)] *adj.* □ im Widerspruch stehend, gegensätzlich, anti'thetisch; **an·tith·e·size** [-saɪz] *v/t.* in Gegensätzen ausdrücken; in 'Widerspruch bringen.

an·ti-tox·in *s.* ✳ Antito'xin *n,* Gegengift *n;* **~-trust** *adj.* kar'tell- u. mono-'polfeindlich, Antitrust...; **~-un·ion** *adj.* gewerkschaftsfeindlich; **~-vi·rus** *adj. Computer:* Anti'viren...; **~-world** *s.* Antiwelt *f.*

ant·ler [ˈæntlə] *s. zo.* **1.** Geweihsprosse *f;* **2.** *pl.* Geweih *n.*

an·to·nym [ˈæntənɪm] *s. ling.* Anto'nym *n.*

a·nus [ˈeɪnəs] *s.* After *m,* Anus *m.*

an·vil [ˈænvɪl] *s.* Amboss *m* (*a. anat. u. fig.*).

anx·i·e·ty [æŋˈzaɪətɪ] *s.* **1.** Angst *f,* Unruhe *f;* Bedenken *n,* Besorgnis *f,* Sorge *f* (**for** um); **2.** ✳ Angst(gefühl *n*) *f,* Beklemmung *f:* **~ neurosis** Angstneurose *f;* **~ state** Angstzustand *m;* **3.** starkes Verlangen, eifriges (Be)Streben *n* (**for** nach); **anx·ious** [ˈæŋkʃəs] *adj.* □ **1.** ängstlich, bange, besorgt, unruhig (*about* um, wegen): **~ about his health** um s-e Gesundheit besorgt; **2.** *fig.* (**for, to** *inf.*) begierig (auf *acc.,* nach, zu *inf.*), bestrebt (zu *inf.*), bedacht (auf *acc.*): **~ for his report** auf s-n Bericht begierig *od.* gespannt; **he is ~ to please** er gibt sich alle Mühe(, es recht zu machen); **I am ~ to see him** mir liegt daran, ihn zu sehen; **I am ~ to know** ich möchte zu gern wissen, ich bin begierig zu wissen.

an·y [ˈenɪ] **I** *adj.* **1.** (*fragend, verneinend od. bedingend*) (irgend)ein, (irgend)welch; etwaig; einige *pl.;* etwas: **have you ~ money on you?** haben Sie Geld bei sich?; **if I had ~ hope** wenn ich irgendwelche Hoffnung hätte; **not ~** kein; **there was not ~ milk in the house** es war keine Milch im Hause; **I cannot eat ~ more** ich kann nichts mehr essen; **2.** (*bejahend*) jeder, jede, jedes (beliebige): **~ cat will scratch** jede Katze kratzt; **~ amount** jede beliebige Menge, ein ganzer Haufen; **in ~ case** auf jeden Fall; **at ~ rate** jedenfalls, wenigstens; **at ~ time** jederzeit; **II** *pron. sg. u. pl.* **3.** irgendein; irgendwelche *pl.;* etwas: **no money and no prospect of ~** kein Geld und keine Aussicht auf welches; **I'm not having ~!** *sl.* ich pfeife drauf!; **it doesn't help ~** *sl.* es hilft einen Dreck; **III** *adv.* **4.** irgend(wie), (noch) etwas: **~ more?** noch (etwas) mehr?; **not ~ more than** ebenso wenig wie; **is he ~ happier now?** ist er denn jetzt glücklicher?; → **if; ~-bod·y** *pron.* irgendjemand, irgendeine(r), ein Beliebiger, eine Beliebige: **~ but you** jeder andere eher als du; **is he ~ at all?** ist er überhaupt jemand (von Bedeutung)?; **ask ~ you meet** frage den ersten Besten, den du triffst; **it's ~'s match** F das Spiel ist (noch) völlig offen; → **guess** 7; **~-how** *adv.* **1.** irgendwie; so gut wies geht, schlecht und recht; **2.** a) trotzdem, jedenfalls, b) sowie'so, ohne'hin, c) immer'hin: **you won't be late ~** jedenfalls wirst du nicht zu spät kommen; **who wants him to come ~?** wer will denn überhaupt, dass er kommt?; *I am going there* ~ ich gehe ohnehin dorthin; '**~ one** → *anybody*; '**~place** *Am.* → *anywhere*; '**~thing** *pron.* **1.** (irgend-) etwas, etwas Beliebiges: *not* ~ gar nichts; *not for* ~ um keinen Preis; *take* ~ *you like* nimm, was du willst; *my head aches like* ~ F mein Kopf schmerzt wie toll; *for* ~ *I know* soviel ich weiß; ~ *goes!* F alles ist ,drin'!; **2.** alles: ~ *but* alles andere (eher) als; '**~way** *adv.* **1.** irgendwie; **2.** → *anyhow* 2; '**~where** *adv.* **1.** irgendwo (-hin): *not* ~ nirgendwo; **2.** über'all: *from* ~ von überall her.

A one → *A 1.*

a·o·rist ['eərɪst] *s. ling.* Ao'rist *m.*

a·or·ta [eɪ'ɔːtə] *s. anat.* A'orta *f,* Hauptschlagader *f.*

a·pace [ə'peɪs] *adv.* schnell, rasch, zusehends.

A·pach·e *pl.* **-es** *od.* **-e** *s.* **1.** [ə'pætʃɪ] A'pache *m* (*Indianer*); **2.** ⚿ [ə'pæʃ] A'pache *m,* 'Unterweltler *m.*

ap·a·nage → *appanage.*

a·part [ə'pɑːt] *adv.* **1.** einzeln, für sich, (ab)gesondert (*from* von): *keep* ~ getrennt *od.* auseinander halten; *take* ~ zerlegen, auseinander nehmen (*a. fig.* F *j-n*); ~ *from* abgesehen von; **2.** abseits, bei'seite: *joking* ~ Scherz beiseite.

a·part·heid [ə'pɑːtheɪt] *s.* A'partheid *f,* (Poli'tik *f* der) Rassentrennung *f* in *Südafrika.*

a·part·ho·tel [ə,pɑːthəʊ'tel] *s. Brit.* Eigentumswohnanlage, deren Wohneinheiten bei Abwesenheit der Eigentümer als Hotelsuiten vermietet werden.

a·part·ment [ə'pɑːtmənt] *s.* **1.** Zimmer *n;* **2.** *Am.* (E'tagen)Wohnung *f;* **3.** *Brit.* große Luxuswohnung; ~ **block** *s.,* ~ **build·ing** *s.* Mietshaus *n;* ~ **ho·tel** *s. Am.* A'partho,tel *n* (*das Appartements mit Bedienung u. Verpflegung vermietet*); ~ **house** *s.* Mietshaus *n.*

ap·a·thet·ic, **ap·a·thet·i·cal** [,æpə'θetɪk(l)] *adj.* □ a'pathisch, teilnahmslos; **ap·a·thy** ['æpəθɪ] *s.* Apa'thie *f,* Teilnahmslosigkeit *f;* Gleichgültigkeit *f* (*to* gegen).

ape [eɪp] **I** *s. zo.* (*bsd.* Menschen)Affe *m; fig.* a) Nachäffer(in), b) ,Affe' *m,* ,Go'rilla' *m: go* ~ ,überschnappen'; **II** *v/t.* nachäffen.

a·pe·ri·ent [ə'pɪərɪənt] ⚕ **I** *adj.* abführend; **II** *s.* Abführmittel *n.*

a·pé·ri·tif [ɑː,perɪ'tiːf] *s.* Aperi'tif *m.*

ap·er·ture ['æpə,tjʊə] *s.* **1.** Öffnung *f,* Schlitz *m,* Loch *n;* **2.** *phot., phys.* Blende *f.*

a·pex ['eɪpeks] *pl.* **'a·pex·es** *od.* **'a·pi·ces** [-pɪsɪz] *s.* **1.** (*a. anat.* Lungen- *etc.*) Spitze *f,* Gipfel *m,* Scheitelpunkt *m;* **2.** *fig.* Gipfel *m,* Höhepunkt *m.*

a·phe·li·on [æ'fiːljən] *s.* **1.** *ast.* A'phelium *n;* **2.** *fig.* entferntester Punkt.

a·phid ['eɪfɪd], *a.* **a·phis** ['eɪfɪs] *pl.* **'aph·i·des** [-diːz] *s. zo.* Blattlaus *f.*

aph·o·rism ['æfərɪzəm] *s.* Apho'rismus *m,* Gedankensplitter *m;* '**aph·o·rist** [-ɪst] *s.* Apho'ristiker *m.*

aph·ro·dis·i·ac [,æfrəʊ'dɪzɪæk] ⚕ **I** *adj.* aphro'disisch, den Geschlechtstrieb steigernd; *weitS.* erotisierend, erregend; **II** *s.* Aphrodi'siakum *n.*

a·pi·ar·i·an [,eɪpɪ'eərɪən] *adj.* Bienen(zucht)...; **a·pi·a·rist** ['eɪpjərɪst] *s.* Bienenzüchter *m,* Imker *m;* **a·pi·ar·y** ['eɪpjərɪ] *s.* Bienenhaus *n.*

ap·i·cal ['æpɪkl] *adj.* □ Spitzen...: ~ *angle* ✿ Winkel *m* an der Spitze; ~ *pneumonia* ⚕ Lungenspitzenkatarr(h) *m.*

a·pi·cul·ture ['eɪpɪkʌltʃə] *s.* Bienenzucht *f.*

a·piece [ə'piːs] *adv.* für jedes Stück, je; pro Per'son, pro Kopf.

ap·ish ['eɪpɪʃ] *adj.* □ **1.** affenartig; **2.** nachäffend; albern, läppisch.

a·plomb [ə'plɒm] (*Fr.*) *s.* **1.** A'plomb *m,* (selbst)sicheres Auftreten, Selbstbewusstsein *n;* **2.** Fassung *f.*

A·poc·a·lypse [ə'pɒkəlɪps] *s.* **1.** *bibl.* Apoka'lypse *f,* Offen'barung *f* Jo'hannis; **2.** ⚿ a) Enthüllung *f,* Offen'barung *f,* b) Apoka'lypse *f,* ('Welt)kata,strophe *f;* **a·poc·a·lyp·tic** [ə,pɒkə'lɪp-tɪk] *adj.* (□ *~ally*) **1.** apoka'lyptisch (*a. fig.*); **2.** *fig.* dunkel, rätselhaft; **3.** *fig.* Unheil kündend.

a·poc·ry·pha [ə'pɒkrɪfə] *s. bibl.* Apo'kryphen *pl.;* **a·poc·ry·phal** [-fl] *adj.* apo'kryphisch, von zweifelhafter Verfasserschaft; zweifelhaft; unecht.

ap·o·gee ['æpəʊdʒiː] *s.* **1.** *ast.* Apo'gäum *n,* Erdferne *f;* **2.** *fig.* Höhepunkt *m,* Gipfel *m.*

a·po·lit·i·cal [,eɪpə'lɪtɪkl] *adj.* 'apolitisch.

A·pol·lo [ə'pɒləʊ] *npr. myth. u. s. fig.* A'poll(o) *m.*

a·pol·o·get·ic [ə,pɒlə'dʒetɪk] **I** *s.* **1.** Entschuldigung *f,* Verteidigung *f;* **2.** *mst pl. eccl.* Apolo'getik *f;* **II** *adj.* **3.** → *a,pol·o'get·i·cal* [-kl] *adj.* □ **1.** entschuldigend, rechtfertigend; **2.** kleinlaut, reumütig, schüchtern; **a·pol·o·gi·a** [,æpə-'ləʊdʒɪə] *s.* Verteidigung *f,* (Selbst-) Rechtfertigung *f,* Apolo'gie *f;* **a·pol·o·gist** [ə'pɒlədʒɪst] *s.* **1.** Verteidiger(in); **2.** *eccl.* Apolo'get *m;* **a·pol·o·gize** [ə'pɒlədʒaɪz] *v/i.* : ~ *to s.o.* (*for s.th.*) sich bei j-m (für et.) entschuldigen, j-n (für et.) um Verzeihung bitten; **a·pol·o·gy** [ə'pɒlədʒɪ] *s.* **1.** Entschuldigung *f,* Abbitte *f;* Rechtfertigung *f: make an* ~ *to s.o.* (*for s.th*) → *apologize;* **2.** Verteidigungsrede *f,* -schrift *f;* **3.** F minderwertiger Ersatz: *an* ~ *for a meal* ein armseliges Essen.

ap·o·phthegm → *apothegm.*

ap·o·plec·tic, **ap·o·plec·ti·cal** [,æpə-'plektɪk(l)] *adj.* □ apo'plektisch: a) Schlaganfall..., b) zum Schlaganfall neigend; *fig.* e-m Schlaganfall nahe (*vor* Wut): ~ *fit,* ~ *stroke* → **ap·o·plex·y** ['æpəpleksɪ] *s.* ⚕ Apople'xie *f,* Schlaganfall *m,* (Gehirn)Schlag *m.*

a·pos·ta·sy [ə'pɒstəsɪ] *s.* Abfall *m,* Abtrünnigkeit *f* (*vom Glauben, von e-r Partei etc.*); **a'pos·tate** [-teɪt] **I** *s.* Abtrünnige(r *m*) *f,* Rene'gat *m;* **II** *adj.* abtrünnig; **a'pos·ta·tize** [-tətaɪz] *v/i.* **1.** (*from*) abfallen (von), abtrünnig *od.* untreu werden (*dat.*); **2.** 'übergehen (*from ... to* von ... zu).

a·pos·tle [ə'pɒsl] *s.* **1.** *eccl.* A'postel *m:* ⚿*s' Creed* Apostolisches Glaubensbekenntnis; **2.** *fig.* A'postel *m,* Verfechter *m,* Vorkämpfer *m:* ~ *of Free Trade;* **a·pos·to·late** [ə'pɒstəʊlət] *s.* Aposto'lat *n,* A'postelamt *n,* -würde *f;* **ap·os·tol·ic,** *oft* ⚿ [,æpə'stɒlɪk] *adj.* (□ *~ally*) apo'stolisch: ~ *succession* apostolische Nachfolge; ⚿ *See* Heiliger Stuhl.

a·pos·tro·phe [ə'pɒstrəfɪ] *s.* **1.** (feierliche) Anrede; **2.** *ling.* Apo'stroph *m;* **a'pos·tro·phize** [-faɪz] *v/t.* apostrophieren: a) mit e-m Apo'stroph versehen, b) j-n besonders ansprechen, sich wenden an (*acc.*).

a·poth·e·car·y [ə'pɒθəkərɪ] *s. obs. bsd. Am.* Apo'theker *m.*

ap·o·thegm ['æpəʊθem] *s.* Denk-, Kern-, Lehrspruch *m;* Ma'xime *f.*

a·poth·e·o·sis [ə,pɒθɪ'əʊsɪs] *s.* **1.** Apothe'ose *f:* a) Vergöttlichung *f,* b) *fig.*

Verherrlichung *f,* Vergötterung *f;* **2.** *fig.* Ide'al *n.*

Ap·pa·lach·i·an [,æpə'leɪtʃjən] *adj.:* ~ *Mountains* die Appalachen (*Gebirge im Nordosten der USA*).

ap·pal, *Am. a.* **ap·pall** [ə'pɔːl] *v/t.* erschrecken, entsetzen: *be* ~*led* entsetzt sein (*at* über *acc.*); **ap'pal·ling** [-lɪŋ] *adj.* □ erschreckend, entsetzlich, beängstigend.

ap·pa·nage ['æpənɪdʒ] *s.* **1.** Apa'nage *f* *e-s Prinzen; fig.* Erbteil *n;* Einnahme (-quelle) *f;* **2.** abhängiges Gebiet; **3.** *fig.* Merkmal *n,* Zubehör *m.*

ap·pa·ra·tus [,æpə'reɪtəs] *pl.* **-tus** [-təs], **-tus·es** *s.* **1.** Appa'rat *m,* Gerät *n,* Vorrichtung *f; coll.* Apparat(e *pl.*) *m* (*a. fig.*), Appara'tur *f,* Maschine'rie *f* (*a. fig.*): ~ *work* Geräteturnen *n;* **2.** ⚿ System *n,* Appa'rat *m: respiratory* ~ Atmungsapparat, Atemwerkzeuge *pl.*

ap·par·el [ə'pærəl] *s.* **1.** Kleidung *f,* Tracht *f;* **2.** *fig.* Gewand *n,* Schmuck *m.*

ap·par·ent [ə'pærənt] *adj.* □ → *apparently;* **1.** sichtbar; **2.** augenscheinlich, offenbar; ersichtlich, einleuchtend: → *heir;* **3.** scheinbar, anscheinend, Schein...; **ap'par·ent·ly** [-lɪ] *adv.* anscheinend, wie es scheint; **ap·pa·ri·tion** [,æpə'rɪʃən] *s.* **1.** (plötzliches) Erscheinen; **2.** Erscheinung *f,* Gespenst *n,* Geist *m.*

ap·peal [ə'piːl] **I** *v/i.* **1.** (*to*) appellieren, sich wenden (an *acc.*); j-n *od. et.* (als Zeugen) anrufen, sich berufen (auf *acc.*): ~ *to the law* das Gesetz anrufen; ~ *to history* die Geschichte als Zeugen anrufen; ~ *to the country* *pol. Brit.* (das Parlament auflösen u.) Neuwahlen ausschreiben; **2.** (*to s.o. for s.th.*) (j-n) dringend (um et.) bitten, (j-n um et.) anrufen; **3.** Einspruch erheben; *bsd.* ⚖ Berufung *od.* Revisi'on *od.* Beschwerde einlegen (*against,* ⚖ *mst from* gegen); **4.** (*to*) wirken (auf *acc.*), reizen (*acc.*), gefallen, zusagen (*dat.*), Anklang finden (bei); **II** *s.* **5.** (*to*) dringende Bitte (an *acc., for* um); Aufruf *m,* Mahnung *f* (an *acc.*); Werbung *f* (bei); Aufforderung *f* (*gen.*); **6.** (*to*) Ap'pell *m* (an *acc.*), Anrufung *f* (*gen.*): ~ *to reason* Appell an die Vernunft; **7.** (*to*) Verweisung *f* (an *acc.*), Berufung *f* (auf *acc.*); **8.** ⚖ Rechtsmittel *n* (*from od. against* gegen): a) Berufung *f,* Revisi'on *f,* b) (Rechts)Beschwerde *f,* Einspruch *m: Court of* ⚿ Berufungs- *od.* Revisionsgericht *n;* **9.** (*to*) Wirkung *f,* Anziehung(skraft) *f* (auf *acc.*); ✝, *thea. etc.* Zugkraft *f;* Anklang *m,* Beliebtheit *f* (bei); **ap'peal·ing** [-lɪŋ] *adj.* □ **1.** flehend; **2.** ansprechend, reizvoll, gefällig.

ap·pear [ə'pɪə] *v/i.* **1.** erscheinen (*a. von Büchern*), sich zeigen; *öffentlich* auftreten; **2.** erscheinen, sich stellen (*vor Gericht etc.*); **3.** scheinen, den Anschein haben, aussehen, *j-m* vorkommen: *it* ~*s to me you are right* mir scheint, Sie haben Recht; *he* ~*s to be tired; it does not* ~ *that* es liegt kein Anhaltspunkt dafür vor, dass; **4.** sich her'ausstellen: *it* ~*s from this* hieraus ergibt sich *od.* geht hervor; **ap·pearance** [ə'pɪərəns] *s.* **1.** Erscheinen *n, öffentliches* Auftreten, Vorkommen *n: make one's* ~ sich einstellen, sich zeigen; *put in an* ~ (persönlich) erscheinen; **2.** (äußere) Erscheinung, Aussehen *n, das* Äußere: *at first* ~ beim ersten Anblick; **3.** äußerer Schein, (An)Schein *m: there is every* ~ *that* es hat ganz den Anschein, dass; *in* ~ anscheinend; *to all* ~(*s*) allem Anschein nach; ~*s are against* *him* der (Augen)Schein spricht gegen ihn; **keep up** (*od.* **save**) ⁓s den Schein wahren.

ap·pease [ə'piːz] *v/t.* **1.** *j-n od. j-s Zorn etc.* beruhigen, beschwichtigen; *Streit* schlichten, beilegen; *Leiden* mildern; *Durst etc.* stillen; *Neugier* befriedigen; **2.** *bsd. pol.* (durch Nachgiebigkeit *od.* Zugeständnisse) beschwichtigen; **ap·'pease·ment** [-mənt] *s.* Beruhigung *f etc.*; Be'schwichtigung(spoli,tik) *f*; **ap·'peas·er** [-zə] *s. pol.* Be'schwichtigungspo,litiker *m*.

ap·pel·lant [ə'pelənt] **I** *adj.* appellierend; **II** *s.* Appel'lant *m*, Berufungskläger(in); Beschwerdeführer(in); **ap·'pel·late** [-lət] *adj.* Berufungs...: ⁓ **court** Berufungsinstanz *f*, Revisions-, Appellationsgericht *n*.

ap·pel·la·tion [ˌæpə'leɪʃn] *s.* Benennung *f*, Name *m*; **ap·pel·la·tive** [ə'pelətɪv] **I** *adj.* □ *ling.* appella'tiv: ⁓ *name* Gattungsname *m*; **II** *s. ling.* Gattungsname *m*.

ap·pel·lee [ˌæpe'liː] *s.* ⚖ Berufungsbeklagte(r *m*) *f*.

ap·pend [ə'pend] *v/t.* **1.** (*to*) befestigen, anbringen (an *dat.*), anhängen (an *acc.*); **2.** hin'zu-, beifügen (*to dat.*, zu): ⁓ *the signature*; ⁓ *a price list*; **ap·'pend·age** [-dɪdʒ] *s.* **1.** Anhang *m*, Anhängsel *n*, Zubehör *n*, *m*; **2.** *fig.* Anhängsel *n*: a) Beigabe *f*, b) (ständiger) Begleiter; **ap·pen·dec·to·my** [ˌæpen'dektəmɪ] *s.* 'Blinddarmoperati,on *f*; **ap·pen·di·ces** *pl. von appendix*; **ap·pen·di·ci·tis** [əˌpendɪ'saɪtɪs] *s.* ☛ Blinddarmentzündung *f*; **ap·pen·dix** [ə'pendɪks] *pl.* **-dix·es**, **-di·ces** [-dɪsiːz] *s.* **1.** Anhang *m* *e-s Buches*; **2.** ⊙ Ansatz *m*; **3.** *anat.* Fortsatz *m*: (**vermiform**) ⁓ Wurmfortsatz *m*, Blinddarm *m*.

ap·per·tain [ˌæpə'teɪn] *v/i.* (*to*) gehören (zu), (zu)gehören (*dat.*); *j-m* zustehen, gebühren (*dat.*).

ap·pe·tence [ˈæpɪtəns], **'ap·pe·ten·cy** [-sɪ] *s.* **1.** Verlangen *n* (*of, for, after* nach); **2.** instink'tive Neigung; (Na'tur) Trieb *m*.

ap·pe·tite [ˈæpɪtaɪt] *s.* **1.** (*for*) Verlangen *n*, Gelüst *n* (nach); Neigung *f*, Trieb *m*, Lust *f* (zu), ,Appe'tit' (auf *acc.*); **2.** Appe'tit *m* (*for* auf *acc.*), Esslust *f*: *have an* ⁓ Appetit haben; *take away* (*od.* **spoil**) *s.o.'s* ⁓ *j-m* den Appetit nehmen *od.* verderben; *loss of* ⁓ Appetitlosigkeit *f*; ⁓ *suppressant* Appetitzügler *m*; **'ap·pe·tiz·er** [-aɪzə] *s.* appe'titanregendes Mittel *od.* Getränk *od.* Gericht, Aperi'tif *m*; **'ap·pe·tiz·ing** [-aɪzɪŋ] *adj.* □ appe'titanregend; appe'titlich, lecker (*beide a. fig.*); *fig.* reizvoll, ,zum Anbeißen'.

ap·plaud [ə'plɔːd] **I** *v/i.* applaudieren, Beifall spenden; **II** *v/t.* beklatschen, *j-m* Beifall spenden; *fig.* loben, billigen; *j-m* zustimmen; **ap·plause** [ə'plɔːz] *s.* **1.** Ap'plaus *m*, Beifall(klatschen *n*) *m*: *break into* ⁓ in Beifall ausbrechen; **2.** *fig.* Zustimmung *f*, Anerkennung *f*, Beifall *m*.

ap·ple [ˈæpl] *s.* Apfel *m*: ⁓ *of discord fig.* Zankapfel; ⁓ *of one's eye anat.* Augapfel (*a. fig.*); '⁓·cart *s.* Apfelkarren *m*: *upset the* ⁓ *od. s.o.'s* ⁓ *fig.* alle *od.* *j-s* Pläne über den Haufen werfen; ⁓ *char·lotte* [ˈʃɑːlət] *s.* 'Apfelchar,lotte *f* (*e-e Apfelspeise*); ⁓ *dump·ling s.* Apfel *m* im Schlafrock; ⁓ *frit·ters s. pl.* (in Teig gebackene) Apfelschnitten *pl.*; '⁓·jack *s. Am.* Apfelschnaps *m*; ⁓ *pie s.* (warmer) gedeckter Apfelkuchen; '⁓·pie or·der *s.* F schönste Ordnung:

everything is in ⁓ alles ,in Butter' *od.* in bester Ordnung; ⁓ *pol·ish·er s. Am.* F Speichellecker *m*; ⁓ *sauce s.* **1.** Apfelmus *n*; **2.** *Am. sl.* a) ,Schmus' *m*, Schmeiche'lei *f*, b) *int.* Quatsch!; ⁓ *tree s.* ❀ Apfelbaum *m*.

ap·pli·ance [ə'plaɪəns] *s.* Gerät *n*, Vorrichtung *f*, Appa'rat *m*.

ap·pli·ca·bil·i·ty [ˌæplɪkə'bɪlətɪ] *s.* (*to*) Anwendbarkeit *f* (auf *acc.*), Eignung *f* (für); **ap·pli·ca·ble** [ˈæplɪkəbl] *adj.* □ (*to*) anwendbar (auf *acc.*), passend, geeignet (für): *not* ⁓ *in Formularen*: nicht zutreffend, entfällt; **ap·pli·cant** [ˈæplɪkənt] *s.* (*for*) Bewerber(in) (um), Bestellter(in) (*gen.*); Antragsteller(in); (Pa'tent)Anmelder(in); **ap·pli·ca·tion** [ˌæplɪ'keɪʃn] *s.* **1.** ☛ Auf-, Anlegen *n* *e-s Verbandes etc.*; Anwendung *f* (*to* auf *acc.*); **2.** (*to* für) An-, Verwendung *f*, Gebrauch *m*: ⁓ *of poison*; ⁓ *of drastic measures*; **3.** (*to*) Anwendung *f*, Anwendbarkeit *f* (auf *acc.*); Beziehung *f* (zu): ⁓ *software* Anwendersoftware *f*; *have no* ⁓ keine Anwendung finden, unangebracht sein, nicht zutreffen; **4.** (*for*) Gesuch *n*, Bitte *f* (um); Antrag *m* (auf *acc.*): *an* ⁓ *for help*; *make an* ⁓ ein Gesuch einreichen, e-n Antrag stellen; ⁓ *for a patent* Anmeldung *f* zum Patent; *samples on* ⁓ Muster auf Verlangen *od.* Wunsch; **5.** Bewerbung *f* (*for* um): (*letter of*) ⁓ Bewerbungsschreiben *n*; **6.** Fleiß *m*, Eifer *m* (*in* bei): ⁓ *in one's studies*; **ap·plied** [ə'plaɪd] *adj.* angewandt: ⁓ *chemistry* (*psychology etc.*); ⁓ *art* Kunstgewerbe *n*, Gebrauchsgrafik *f*.

ap·pli·qué [ə'pliːkeɪ] *adj.* aufgelegt, -genäht, appliziert: ⁓ *work* Applikation(sstickerei) *f*.

ap·ply [ə'plaɪ] **I** *v/t.* **1.** (*to*) auflegen, -tragen, legen (auf *acc.*), anbringen (an, auf *dat.*): ⁓ *a plaster to a wound*; **2.** (*to*) a) verwenden (auf *acc.*, für), b) anwenden (auf *acc.*): ⁓ *a rule*; *applied to modern conditions* auf moderne Verhältnisse angewandt, c) gebrauchen (für): ⁓ *the brakes* bremsen, d) verwerten (zu, für); **3.** *Sinn* richten (*to* auf *acc.*); **4.** ⁓ *o.s.* sich widmen (*to dat.*): ⁓ *o.s. to a task*; **II** *v/i.* **5.** (*to*) sich wenden (an *acc.*, *for* wegen), sich melden (bei): ⁓ *to the manager*; **6.** (*for*) beantragen (*acc.*); sich bewerben, sich bemühen, ersuchen (um): ⁓ *for a job*; **7.** (*for*) (*bsd.* zum Pa'tent) anmelden (*acc.*); **8.** (*to*) Anwendung finden (bei, auf *acc.*), passen, zutreffen (auf *acc.*), gelten (für): *cross out that which does not* ⁓ Nichtzutreffendes (*od.* nicht Zutreffendes) bitte streichen.

ap·point [ə'pɔɪnt] *v/t.* **1.** ernennen, berufen, an-, bestellen: ⁓ *a teacher* e-n Lehrer anstellen; ⁓ *an heir* e-n Erben einsetzen; ⁓ *s.o. governor* *j-n* zum Gouverneur ernennen, *j-n* als Gouverneur berufen; ⁓ *s.o. to a professorship* *j-m* e-e Professur übertragen; **2.** festsetzen, bestimmen; vorschreiben; verabreden: ⁓ *a time*; *the* ⁓*ed day* der festgesetzte Tag *od.* Termin, der Stichtag; *the* ⁓*ed task* die vorgeschriebene Aufgabe; **3.** einrichten, ausrüsten: *a well-*⁓*ed house*; **ap·point·ee** [əpɔɪn'tiː] *s.* Ernannte(r *m*) *f*; **ap·'point·ment** [-mənt] *s.* **1.** Ernennung *f*, Anstellung *f*, Berufung *f*, Einsetzung *f* (*a. e-s Erben*), Bestellung *f* (*bsd. e-s Vormunds*); ②(s) Board Behörde *f* zur Besetzung höherer Posten; *by special* ⁓ *to the King* Königlicher Hoflieferant; **2.** Amt *n*, Stellung *f*; **3.** Festsetzung *f bsd. e-s* Ter-

mins; **4.** Verabredung *f*; Zs.-kunft *f*; geschäftlich, beim Arzt etc.: Ter'min *m*: *by* ⁓ nach Vereinbarung; *make an* ⁓ e-e Verabredung treffen; *keep* (*break*) *an* ⁓ eine Verabredung (nicht) einhalten; ⁓(*s*) *book* (*od.* *diary*) Terminkalender *m*; **5.** *pl.* Ausstattung *f*, Einrichtung *f* *e-r Wohnung etc.*

ap·por·tion [ə'pɔːʃn] *v/t.* e-n Anteil zuteilen, (proportio'nal *od.* gerecht) ein-, verteilen; *Lob* erteilen, zollen; *Aufgabe* zuteilen; *Schuld* beimessen; *Kosten* 'umlegen; **ap·'por·tion·ment** [-mənt] *s.* (gleichmäßige *od.* gerechte) Ver-, Zuteilung, Einteilung *f*; ('Kosten),Umlage *f*.

ap·po·site [ˈæpəʊzɪt] *adj.* □ (*to*) passend (für), angemessen (*dat.*), geeignet (für); angebracht, treffend; **'ap·po·site·ness** [-nɪs] *s.* Angemessenheit *f*; **ap·po·si·tion** [ˌæpə'zɪʃn] *s.* **1.** Bei-, Hin'zufügung *f*; **2.** *ling.* Appositi'on *f*, Beifügung *f*.

ap·prais·al [ə'preɪzl] *s.* (Ab)Schätzung *f*, Taxierung *f*; Schätzwert *m*, *a. ped.* Bewertung *f*; *fig.* Beurteilung *f*, Würdigung *f*; **ap·praise** [ə'preɪz] *v/t.* (ab-, ein)schätzen, taxieren, bewerten, beurteilen, würdigen; **ap·'praise·ment** [-mənt] → *appraisal*; **ap·'prais·er** [-zə] *s.* (Ab)Schätzer *m*.

ap·pre·ci·a·ble [ə'priːʃəbl] *adj.* □ merklich, spürbar, nennenswert; **ap·pre·ci·ate** [ə'priːʃɪeɪt] **I** *v/t.* **1.** (hoch)schätzen; richtig einschätzen, würdigen, zu schätzen *od.* würdigen wissen; **2.** aufgeschlossen sein für, Gefallen finden an (*dat.*), Sinn haben für: ⁓ *music*; **3.** dankbar sein für: *I* ⁓ *your kindness*; **4.** (richtig) beurteilen, einsehen, (klar) erkennen: ⁓ *a danger*; **5.** *bsd. Am.* a) den Wert *e-r Sache* erhöhen, b) aufwerten; **II** *v/i.* **6.** im Wert steigen; **ap·pre·ci·a·tion** [əˌpriːʃɪ'eɪʃn] *s.* **1.** Würdigung *f*, (Wert-, Ein)Schätzung *f*, Anerkennung *f*; **2.** Verständnis *n*, Aufgeschlossenheit *f*, Sinn *m* (*of* für): ⁓ *of music*; **3.** richtige Beurteilung, Einsicht *f*; **4.** (kritische) Würdigung, *bsd. günstige* Kri'tik; **5.** (*of*) Dankbarkeit *f* (für), (dankbare) Anerkennung (*gen.*); **6.** ♣ a) Wertsteigerung *f*, b) Aufwertung *f*; **ap·'pre·ci·a·tive** [-ʃətɪv] *adj.*; **ap·'pre·ci·a·to·ry** [-ʃɔətərɪ] *adj.* □ (*of*) **1.** anerkennend, würdigend (*acc.*); **2.** verständnisvoll, empfänglich, dankbar (für): *be* ⁓ *of* zu schätzen wissen.

ap·pre·hend [ˌæprɪ'hend] *v/t.* **1.** ergreifen, festnehmen, verhaften: ⁓ *a thief*; **2.** *fig.* wahrnehmen, erkennen; begreifen, erfassen; **3.** *fig.* (be)fürchten, ahnen, wittern; **ap·pre·hen·sion** [-nʃn] *s.* **1.** Festnahme *f*, Verhaftung *f*; **2.** *fig.* Begreifen *n*, Erfassen *n*; Verstand *m*, Fassungskraft *f*; **3.** Begriff *m*, Ansicht *f*: *according to popular* ⁓; **4.** (Vor)Ahnung *f*, Besorgnis *f*: *in* ⁓ *of etc.* befürchtend; **ap·pre·hen·sive** [-sɪv] *adj.* □ besorgt (*for* um; *of* wegen; *that* dass), ängstlich: *be* ⁓ *for one's life* um sein Leben besorgt; *be* ⁓ *of dangers* sich vor Gefahren fürchten.

ap·pren·tice [ə'prentɪs] **I** *s.* Lehrling *m*, Auszubildende(r) *m*; Prakti'kant(in); *fig.* Anfänger *m*, Neuling *m*; **II** *v/t.* in die Lehre geben: *be* ⁓*d to* in die Lehre kommen zu, in der Lehre sein bei; **ap·'pren·tice·ship** [-tɪʃɪp] *s.* a) *a.* figurative Lehrjahre *pl.*, -zeit *f*, Lehre *f*: *serve one's* ⁓ (*with*) in die Lehre gehen (bei), b) Lehrstelle *f*.

ap·prise [ə'praɪz] *v/t.* in Kenntnis setzen, unter'richten (*of* von).

ap·pro ['æprəʊ] *s.*: *on* ~ ✝ F zur Ansicht, zur Probe.

ap·proach [ə'prəʊtʃ] I *v/i.* **1.** sich nähern; (her'an)nahen, bevorstehen; **2.** *fig.* nahe kommen, ähnlich sein (*to dat.*); **3.** ✔ an-, einfliegen; II *v/t.* **4.** sich nähern (*dat.*): ~ *the city*; ~ *the end*; **5.** *fig.* nahe kommen (*dat.*), (fast) erreichen: ~ *the required sum*; **6.** her'angehen an (*acc.*): ~ *a task*; **7.** her'antreten *od.* sich her'anmachen an (*acc.*): ~ *a customer*; ~ *a girl*; **8.** *j-n* angehen, bitten; sich an *j-n* wenden (*for* um, *on* wegen); **9.** *auf et.* zu sprechen kommen; III *s.* **10.** (Heran)Nahen *n* (*a. e-s Zeitpunktes etc.*); Annäherung *f*, Anmarsch *m* (*a.* ✕), ✔ Anflug *m*; **11.** *fig.* (*to*) Nahekommen *n*, Annäherung *f* (an *acc.*); Ähnlichkeit *f* (mit): *an* ~ *to truth* annähernd die Wahrheit; **12.** Zugang *m*, Zufahrt *f*, Ein-, Auffahrt *f*; *pl.* ✕ Laufgräben *pl.*; **13.** (*to*) Einführung *f* (in *acc.*), erster Schritt (zu); Versuch *m* (*gen.*): *a good* ~ *to philosophy*; *an* ~ *to a smile* der Versuch e-s Lächelns; **14.** *oft pl.* Herantreten *n* (*to* an *acc.*), Annäherungsversuche *pl.*; **15.** *a.* **meth·od** *od.* **line of** ~ (*to*) a) Art *f* und Weise *f et.* anzupacken, Me'thode *f*, Verfahren *n*: (*basic*) ~ Ansatz *m*, b) Auffassung *f* (*gen.*), Haltung *f*, Einstellung *f* (zu), Stellungnahme *f* (zu); Behandlung *f e-s Themas etc.*; **ap'proach·a·ble** [-tʃəbl] *adj.* zugänglich (*a. fig.*).

ap·pro·ba·tion [ˌæprəʊ'beɪʃn] *s.* Billigung *f*, Genehmigung *f*; Bestätigung *f*; Zustimmung *f*, Beifall *m*.

ap·pro·pri·ate I *adj.* [ə'prəʊprɪət] □ **1.** (*to*, *for*) passend, geeignet (für, zu), angemessen (*dat.*), entsprechend (*dat.*), richtig (für); **2.** eigen, zugehörig (*to dat.*); II *v/t.* [-ɪeɪt] **3.** verwenden, bereitstellen; *parl. bsd.* Geld bewilligen (*to* zu, *for* für); **4.** sich *et.* aneignen (*a. widerrechtlich*); **ap·pro·pri·a·tion** [əˌprəʊprɪ'eɪʃn] *s.* **1.** Aneignung *f*, Besitzergreifung *f*; **2.** Verwendung *f*, Bereitstellung *f*; *parl.* (Geld)Bewilligung *f*.

ap·prov·a·ble [ə'pruːvəbl] *adj.* zu billigen(d), anerkennenswert; **ap'prov·al** [-vl] *s.* **1.** Billigung *f*, Genehmigung *f*: *the plan has my* ~; *on* ~ zur Ansicht, auf Probe; **2.** Anerkennung *f*, Beifall *m*: *meet with* ~ Beifall finden; **ap·prove** [ə'pruːv] I *v/t.* **1.** billigen, gutheißen, anerkennen, annehmen; bestätigen, genehmigen; **2.** ~ *o.s.* sich erweisen *od.* bewähren (*as* als); II *v/i.* **3.** billigen, anerkennen, gutheißen, genehmigen (*of acc.*): ~ *of s.o.* j-n akzeptieren; *be* ~*d of* Anklang finden; **ap'proved** [-vd] *adj.* **1.** erprobt, bewährt: *an* ~ *friend*; *in the* ~ *manner*; **2.** anerkannt: ~ *school Brit. hist.* (staatliche) Erziehungsanstalt; **ap'prov·er** [-və] *s.* ⚖ *Brit.* Kronzeuge *m*; **ap'prov·ing·ly** [-vɪŋlɪ] *adv.* zustimmend, beifällig.

ap·prox·i·mate I *adj.* [ə'prɒksɪmət] □ → **approximately**; **1.** annähernd, ungefähr; Näherungs... (-*formel*, *-rechnung*, *-wert*); **2.** *fig.* sehr ähnlich; II *v/t.* [-meɪt] **3.** sich *e-r* Menge *od.* *e-m* Wert nähern, nahe kommen (*dat.*); III *v/i.* [-meɪt] **4.** nahe od. näher kommen (*oft mit to dat.*); **ap'prox·i·mate·ly** [-lɪ] *adv.* annähernd, ungefähr, etwa; **ap·prox·i·ma·tion** [əˌprɒksɪ'meɪʃn] *s.* **1.** Annäherung *f* (*to* an *acc.*): *an* ~ *to the truth* annähernd die Wahrheit; **2.** Å a) (An)Näherung *f* (*to* an *acc.*), b) Näherungswert *m*; annähernde Gleichheit *f*; **ap'prox·i·ma·tive** [-ətɪv] *adj.* □

annähernd.

ap·pur·te·nance [ə'pɜːtɪnəns] *s.* **1.** Zubehör *n*, *m*; **2.** *pl.* ⚖ Re'alrechte *pl.* (*aus Eigentum an Liegenschaften*); **ap·'pur·te·nant** [-nt] *adj.* zugehörig (*to dat.*).

a·pri·cot ['eɪprɪkɒt] *s.* Apri'kose *f*.

A·pril ['eɪprəl] *s.* A'pril *m*: *in* ~ im April; ~ *fool* Aprilnarr *m*; ~ *Fools Day* der 1. April; *make a* ~ *fool of s.o.*, ~*fool s.o.* j-n in den April schicken.

a pri·o·ri [ˌeɪpraɪ'ɔːraɪ] *adv. u. adj. phls.* **1.** a pri'ori, deduk'tiv; **2.** F mutmaßlich, ohne (Über)'Prüfung.

a·pron ['eɪprən] *s.* **1.** Schürze *f*; Schurz (-fell *n*) *m*; **2.** Schurz *m* von Freimaurern *od.* engl. Bischöfen; **3.** ⚙ a) Schutzblech *n*, -haube *f*, b) mot. Blech-, Windschutz *m*, c) Schutzleder *n*, Kniedecke *f* an Fahrzeugen; **4.** ✔ (betoniertes) (Hallen)Vorfeld; **5.** *a.* ~ *stage thea.* Vorbühne *f*; ~ *strings pl.* Schürzenbänder *pl.*; *fig.* Gängelband *n*: *tied to one's mother's* ~ an Mutters Schürzenzipfel hängend; *tied to s.o.'s* ~ unter j-s Fuchtel stehend.

ap·ro·pos ['æprəpəʊ] I *adv.* **1.** angemessen, zur rechten Zeit: *he arrived very* ~ er kam wie gerufen; **2.** 'hinsichtlich (*of gen.*): ~ *of our talk*; **3.** apro'pos, nebenbei bemerkt; II *adj.* **4.** passend, angemessen, treffend: *his remark was very* ~.

apse [æps] *s.* Δ 'Apsis *f*.

apt [æpt] *adj.* □ **1.** passend, geeignet; treffend: *an* ~ *remark*; **2.** geneigt, neigend (*to inf.* zu *inf.*): *he is* ~ *to believe it* wird es wahrscheinlich glauben; ~ *to be overlooked* leicht zu übersehen; ~ *to rust* leicht rostend; **3.** (*at*) geschickt (in *dat.*), begabt (für): *an* ~ *pupil.*

ap·ter·ous ['æptərəs] *adj.* **1.** zo. flügellos; **2.** ♀ ungeflügelt.

ap·ti·tude ['æptɪtjuːd] *s.* (*ped.* Sonder-) Begabung *f*, Befähigung *f*, Ta'lent *n*; Fähigkeit *f*; Auffassungsgabe *f*; Eignung *f* (*for* für, zu): ~ *test Am.* Eignungsprüfung *f*; **apt·ness** ['æptnɪs] *s.* **1.** Angemessenheit *f*, Tauglichkeit *f* (*for* für, zu); **2.** (*for*, *to*) Neigung *f* (zu), Eignung *f* (für, zu), Geschicklichkeit *f* (in *dat.*).

aq·ua·cul·ture ['ækwəkʌltʃə] *s.* 'Aquakul,tur *f*.

aq·ua for·tis [ˌækwə'fɔːtɪs] *s.* 🜍 Scheidewasser *n*, Sal'petersäure *f*.

aq·ua·lung ['ækwəlʌŋ] *s.* Taucherlunge *f*, Atmungsgerät *n*; **'aq·ua·lun·ger** [-ŋə] *s.* Tiefsee-, Sporttaucher(in).

aq·ua·ma·rine [ˌækwəmə'riːn] *s.* **1.** min. Aquama'rin *m*; **2.** Aquama'rinblau *n*.

aq·ua·plane ['ækwəpleɪn] I *s.* **1.** *Wassersport:* Monoski *m*; II *v/i.* **2.** Monoski laufen; **3.** mot. a) aufschwimmen (*Reifen*), b) ‚schwimmen', die Bodenhaftung verlieren; **'aq·ua·plan·ing** *s.* **1.** Monoskilauf *m*; **2.** mot. Aqua'planing *n*.

aq·ua·relle [ˌækwə'rel] *s.* Aqua'rell(male,reif *f*) *n*; **'aq·ua·rel·list** [-lɪst] *s.* Aqua'rellmaler(in).

A·quar·i·an [ə'kweərɪən] *s. ast.* Wassermann *m* (*Person*).

a·quar·i·um [ə'kweərɪəm] *pl.* **-i·ums** *od.* **-i·a** [-ɪə] *s.* A'quarium *n*.

A·quar·i·us [ə'kweərɪəs] *s. ast.* Wassermann *m*.

aq·ua show ['ækwə] *s. Brit.* 'Wasserbal,lett *n*.

a·quat·ic [ə'kwætɪk] *adj.* **1.** Wasser...: ~ *plants*; ~ *sports* Wassersport *m*; II *s.* **2.** biol. Wassertier *n*, -pflanze *f*; **3.** *pl.* Wassersport *m*.

aq·ua·tint ['ækwətɪnt] *s.* Aqua'tinta *f*,

'Tuschma,nier *f*.

aq·ua vi·tae [ˌækwə'vaɪtiː] *s.* **1.** 🌿 hist. 'Alkohol *m*; **2.** Branntwein *m*.

aq·ue·duct ['ækwɪdʌkt] *s.* Aquä'dukt *m*, *n*.

a·que·ous ['eɪkwɪəs] *adj.* wäss(e)rig (*a. fig.*), wasserartig, -haltig.

Aq·ui·la ['ækwɪlə] *s. ast.* Adler *m*.

aq·ui·le·gi·a [ˌækwɪ'liːdʒə] *s.* ♀ Ake'lei *f*.

aq·ui·line ['ækwɪlaɪn] *adj.* gebogen, Adler..., Habichts...: ~ *nose*.

Ar·ab ['ærəb] I *s.* **1.** Araber(in); **2.** Araber *m* (*Pferd*); **3.** → *street Arab*; II *adj.* **4.** a'rabisch; Araber...; **ar·a·besque** [ˌærə'besk] I *s.* Ara'beske *f*; II *adj.* ara'besk; **A·ra·bi·an** [ə'reɪbjən] I *adj.* **1.** a'rabisch: *The* ~ *Nights* Tausendundeine Nacht; II *s.* **2.** → *Arab* 1; **3.** → *Arab* 2; **'Ar·a·bic** [-bɪk] I *adj.* a'rabisch: ~ *figures* (*od.* *numerals*) arabische Ziffern *od.* Zahlen; II *s.* ling. A'rabisch *n*; **'Ar·ab·ist** [-bɪst] *s.* Ara'bist *m*.

ar·a·ble ['ærəbl] I *adj.* pflügbar, anbaufähig; II *s.* Ackerland *n*.

Ar·a·by ['ærəbɪ] *s. poet.* A'rabien *n*.

ar·au·ca·ri·a [ˌærɔː'keərɪə] *s.* ♀ Zimmertanne *f*, Arau'karie *f*.

ar·bi·ter ['ɑːbɪtə] *s.* **1.** Schiedsrichter *m*; **2.** *fig.* Richter *m* (*of* über *acc.*); **3.** *fig.* Herr *m*, Gebieter *m*; **ar·bi·trage** [ɑːbɪ'trɑːʒ] *s.* ✝ Arbi'trage *f*; **ar·bi·tral** ['ɑːbɪtrəl] *adj.* schiedsrichterlich: ~ *award* Schiedsspruch *m*; ~ *body od.* ~ *court* Schiedsgericht *n*, -stelle *f*; ~ *clause* Schiedsklausel *f*; **ar·bi·trar·i·ness** ['ɑːbɪtrərɪnɪs] *s.* Willkür *f*, Eigenmächtigkeit *f*; **ar·bi·trar·y** ['ɑːbɪtrərɪ] *adj.* □ **1.** willkürlich, eigenmächtig, -willig; **2.** launenhaft; **3.** ty'rannisch; **ar·bi·trate** ['ɑːbɪtreɪt] I *v/t.* **1.** (als Schiedsrichter *od.* durch Schiedsspruch) entscheiden, schlichten, beilegen; **2.** e-m Schiedsspruch unter'werfen; II *v/i.* **3.** Schiedsrichter sein; **ar·bi·tra·tion** [ˌɑːbɪ'treɪʃn] *s.* **1.** Schieds(gerichts)verfahren *n*; Schiedsspruch *m*; Schlichtung *f*: *court of* ~ Schiedsgericht *n*, -hof *m*; ~ *board* Schiedsstelle *f*; *submit to* ~ e-m Schiedsgericht unterwerfen; *settle by* ~ schiedsgerichtlich beilegen; **2.** ✝ (~ *of exchange* Wechsel)Arbitrage *f*; **'ar·bi·tra·tor** [-reɪtə] *s.* ⚖ Schiedsrichter *m*, -mann *m*.

ar·bor¹ *Am.* → *arbour*; ⚘ *Day Am.* Tag *m* des Baums.

ar·bor² ['ɑːbə] *s.* ⚙ Achse *f*, Welle *f*; (Aufsteck)Dorn *m*, Spindel *f*.

ar·bo·re·al [ɑː'bɔːrɪəl] *adj.* baumartig; Baum...; auf Bäumen lebend; **ar'bo·re·ous** [-ɪəs] *adj.* **1.** baumreich, waldig. **2.** baumartig; Baum...; **ar·bo·res·cent** [ˌɑːbɔ'resnt] *adj.* baumartig, verzweigt; **ar·bo·re·tum** [ˌɑːbə'riːtəm] *pl.* **-ta** [-tə] *s.* Arbo'retum *n*; **ar·bo·ri·cul·ture** ['ɑːbərɪkʌltʃə] *s.* Baumzucht *f*.

ar·bor vi·tae [ˌɑːbə'vaɪtɪ] *s.* ♀ Lebensbaum *m*.

ar·bour ['ɑːbə] *s.* Laube *f*.

arc [ɑːk] I *s.* **1.** *a.* Å, ⚙, *ast.* Bogen *m*; **2.** ⚡ (Licht)Bogen *m*: ~ *welding* Lichtbogenschweißen *n*; II *v/i. a.* ~ *over* ⚡ e-n (Licht)Bogen bilden, ‚funken'.

ar·cade [ɑː'keɪd] *s.* Ar'kade *f*: a) Säulen-, Bogen-, Laubengang *m*, b) Pas'sage *f*; **ar'cad·ed** [-dɪd] *adj.* mit Arkaden (versehen).

Ar·ca·di·a [ɑː'keɪdjə] *s.* Ar'kadien *n*, ländliches Para'dies *od.* I'dyll; **Ar'ca·di·an** [-ən] *adj.* ar'kadisch, i'dyllisch.

ar·cane [ɑː'keɪn] *adj.* geheimnisvoll; **ar·'ca·num** [-nəm] *pl.* **-na** [-nə] *s.* **1.** hist. ⚕ Ar'kanum *n*; Eli'xier *n*; **2.** *mst pl.* Geheimnis *n*, My'sterium *n*.

arch¹ [ɑːtʃ] **I** s. **1.** mst △ (Brücken-, Fenster- etc.)Bogen m; über'wölbter (Ein-, 'Durch)Gang; ('Eisenbahn- etc.) Über,führung f; Tri'umphbogen m; **2.** Wölbung f, Gewölbe n: ~ of the instep (Fuß)Rist m, Spann m; ~ support Senkfußeinlage f; fallen ~es Senkfuß m; **II** v/t. **3.** a. ~ over mit Bogen versehen, über'wölben; **4.** wölben, krümmen: ~ the back e-n Buckel machen (Katze); **III** v/i. **5.** sich wölben; sich krümmen.

arch² [ɑːtʃ] adj. oft **arch-** erst, oberst, Haupt..., Erz...; schlimmst, Riesen...: ~ rogue Erzschurke m.

arch³ [ɑːtʃ] adj. □ schalkhaft, schelmisch: an ~ look.

arch- [ɑːtʃ] Präfix bei Titeln etc.: erst, oberst, Haupt..., Erz...

ar·chae·o·log·ic, ar·chae·o·log·i·cal [,ɑːkɪə'lɒdʒɪk(l)] adj. □ archäo'logisch, Altertums...; **ar·chae·ol·o·gist** [,ɑːkɪ-'ɒlədʒɪst] s. Archäo'loge m, Altertumsforscher m; **ar·chae·ol·o·gy** [,ɑːkɪ'ɒlə-dʒɪ] s. Archäolo'gie f, Altertumskunde f.

ar·cha·ic [ɑː'keɪɪk] adj. (□ ~ally) ar-'chaisch: a) altertümlich, b) bsd. ling. veraltet, altmodisch; **ar·cha·ism** ['ɑːkeɪɪzəm] s. **1.** ling. Archa'ismus m, veralteter Ausdruck; **2.** et. Veraltetes.

arch·an·gel ['ɑːk,eɪndʒəl] s. Erzengel m.

arch·bish·op [,ɑːtʃ-] s. Erzbischof m; **~'bish·op·ric** s. **1.** Erzbistum n; **2.** Amt n e-s Erzbischofs; **~'dea·con** s. Archidia'kon m; **~'di·o·cese** s. 'Erzdiö,zese f; **~'du·cal** adj. erzherzoglich; **~'duch·ess** s. Erzherzogin f; **~-'duch·y** s. Erzherzogtum n; **~'duke** s. Erzherzog m.

arched [ɑːtʃt] adj. gewölbt, gebogen, gekrümmt.

arch·en·e·my [,ɑːtʃ-] s. → archfiend.

arch·er ['ɑːtʃə] s. **1.** Bogenschütze m; **2.** 2 ast. Schütze m; **'arch·er·y** [-ərɪ] s. **1.** Bogenschießen n; **2.** coll. Bogenschützen pl.

ar·che·typ·al ['ɑːkɪtaɪpl] adj. arche'typisch; **'ar·che·type** [-taɪp] s. Urform f, -bild n, Arche'typ(us) m.

arch·fiend [,ɑːtʃ-] s. Erzfeind m: a) Todfeind m, b) 'Satan m, Teufel m.

ar·chi·e·pis·co·pal [,ɑːkɪɪ'pɪskəpl] adj. erzbischöflich; **ar·chi·e·pis·co·pate** [-pɪt] s. Amt n od. Würde f e-s Erzbischofs.

Ar·chi·pel·a·go [,ɑːkɪ'pelɪgəʊ] **I** npr. Ä'gäisches Meer; **II** 2 pl. **-gos** s. Archi-'pel m, Inselmeer n, -gruppe f.

ar·chi·tect ['ɑːkɪtekt] **I** s. **1.** Archi'tekt (-in); **2.** fig. Schöpfer(in), Urheber(in), Archi'tekt m: the ~ of one's fortunes des eigenen Glückes Schmied; **II** v/t. **3.** bauen, entwerfen; **ar·chi·tec·ton·ic** [,ɑːkɪtek'tɒnɪk] **I** adj. (□ ~ally) **1.** ar-chitek'tonisch, baulich; **2.** aufbauend, konstruk'tiv, planvoll, schöpferisch, syste'matisch; **II** s. mst pl. sg. konstr. **3.** Architek'tonik f: a) Baukunst f (als Fach), b) künstlerischer Aufbau; **ar·chi·tec·tur·al** [,ɑːkɪ'tektʃərəl] adj. □ architek'tonisch, Architektur..., Bau...; **'ar·chi·tec·ture** [-tʃə] s. Architek'tur f: a) Baukunst f, Bauart f, Baustil m, b) Konstrukti'on f, (Auf)Bau m, Struk'tur f, Anlage f (a. fig.), c) Bau(werk n) m, coll. Gebäude pl., Bauten pl.

ar·chi·trave ['ɑːkɪtreɪv] s. △ Archi'trav m, Tragbalken m.

ar·chive ['ɑːkaɪv] s. mst pl. Ar'chiv n; Urkundensammlung f; **ar·chi·vist** ['ɑːkɪvɪst] s. Archi'var m.

arch·ness ['ɑːtʃnɪs] s. Schalkhaftigkeit

f, Durch'triebenheit f.

arch·priest [,ɑːtʃ-] s. eccl. hist. Erzpriester m.

arch·way ['ɑːtʃ-] s. △ Bogengang m, über'wölbter Torweg; **'~·wise** [-waɪz] adv. bogenartig.

arc lamp s. ⚡ Bogenlampe f; ~ light s. Bogenlicht n, -lampe f.

arc·tic ['ɑːktɪk] **I** adj. **1.** 'arktisch, nördlich, Nord..., Polar...: 2 Circle Nördlicher Polarkreis; 2 Ocean Nördliches Eismeer; ~ fox Polarfuchs m; **2.** fig. sehr kalt, eisig; **II** s. **3.** die 'Arktis; **4.** pl. Am. gefütterte, wasserdichte 'Überschuhe pl.

ar·dent ['ɑːdənt] adj. □ **1.** bsd. fig. heiß, glühend, feurig: ~ eyes; ~ love; ~ spirits hochprozentige Spirituosen; **2.** fig. feurig, heftig, inbrünstig, leidenschaftlich: ~ wish; ~ admirer glühender Verehrer; **3.** fig. begeistert; **ar·dour**, Am. **ar·dor** ['ɑːdə] s. fig. **1.** Feuer n, Glut f, Inbrunst f, Leidenschaft f; **2.** Eifer m, Begeisterung f (for für).

ar·du·ous ['ɑːdjʊəs] adj. □ **1.** schwierig, anstrengend, mühsam: an ~ task; **2.** ausdauernd, zäh, e'nergisch: an ~ worker; **3.** steil, jäh (Berg etc.); **'ar·du·ous·ness** [-nɪs] s. Schwierigkeit f, Mühsal f.

are¹ [ɑː; ə] pres. pl. u. 2 sg. von be.

are² [ɑː] s. Ar n (Flächenmaß).

a·re·a ['eərɪə] s. **1.** (begrenzte) Fläche, Flächenraum m od. -inhalt m; Grundstück n, Are'al n; Ober-, Grundfläche f; **2.** Raum m, Gebiet n, Gegend f: danger ~ Gefahrenzone f; prohibited (od. restricted) ~ Sperrzone f; teleph. Am. Vorwahl f, Vorwählnummer f; in the Chicago ~ im (Groß-) Raum (von) Chikago; **3.** fig. Bereich m, Gebiet n; **4.** a. ~way Kellervorhof m; **5.** ✕ Operati'onsgebiet n: ~ bombing Bombenflächenwurf m; back ~ Etappe f; forward ~ Kampfgebiet n; **6.** anat. (Seh- etc.)Zentrum n; **a·re·al** [-əl] adj. Flächen(inhalts)...

a·re·na [ə'riːnə] s. A'rena f: a) Kampfplatz m, b) 'Stadion n, c) fig. Schauplatz m, Bühne f: political ~.

aren't [ɑːnt] F für are not.

a·rête [æ'reɪt] (Fr.) s. (Fels)Grat m.

ar·gent ['ɑːdʒənt] **I** s. Silber(farbe f) n; **II** adj. silberfarbig.

Ar·gen·tine ['ɑːdʒəntaɪn], **Ar·gen·tin·e·an** [,ɑːdʒən'tɪnɪən] **I** adj. argen'tinisch; **II** s. Argen'tinier(in).

ar·gil ['ɑːdʒɪl] s. Ton m, Töpfererde f; **ar·gil·la·ceous** [,ɑːdʒɪ'leɪʃəs] adj. tonartig, Ton...

ar·gon ['ɑːgɒn] s. 🜊 'Argon n.

Ar·go·naut ['ɑːgənɔːt] s. **1.** myth. Argo-'naut m; **2.** Am. Goldsucher m in Kali-'fornien (1848/49).

ar·got ['ɑːgəʊ] s. Ar'got n, Jar'gon m, Slang m, bsd. Gaunersprache f.

ar·gu·a·ble ['ɑːgjʊəbl] adj. □ disku-'tabel, vertretbar: it is ~ man könnte mit Recht behaupten; **'ar·gu·a·bly** [-lɪ] adv. vertretbarerweise; **ar·gue** ['ɑːgjuː] **I** v/i. **1.** argumentieren; Gründe (für od. wider) anführen: ~ for s.th. a) für et. eintreten, b) für et. sprechen (Sache); ~ against s.th. a) gegen et. Einwände machen, b) gegen et. sprechen (Sache); don't ~! keine Widerrede!; **2.** streiten, rechten (with mit); disputieren (about über acc., for für, against gegen, with mit); **II** v/t. **3.** e-e Angelegenheit erörtern, diskutieren; **4.** j-n über'reden od. (durch Argu'mente) bewegen: ~ s.o. into s.th. j-n zu et. überreden; ~ s.o. out of s.th. j-n von

et. abbringen; **5.** geltend machen, behaupten: ~ that black is white; **6.** begründen, beweisen; folgern (from aus); **7.** verraten, (an)zeigen, beweisen: his clothes ~ poverty; **ar·gu·ment** ['ɑːgjʊmənt] s. **1.** Argu'ment n, (Beweis)Grund m; Beweisführung f, Schlussfolgerung f; **2.** Behauptung f; Entgegnung f, Einwand m; **3.** Erörterung f, Besprechung f: hold an ~ diskutieren; **4.** F (Wort)Streit m, Auseinandersetzung f; Streitfrage f; **5.** 'Thema n, (Haupt)Inhalt m; **ar·gu·men·ta·tion** [,ɑːgjʊmen'teɪʃn] s. **1.** Beweisführung f, Schlussfolgerung f; **2.** Erörterung f; **ar·gu·men·ta·tive** [,ɑːgjʊ'mentətɪv] adj. □ **1.** streitlustig; **2.** strittig, um'stritten; **3.** 'kritisch; **4.** ~ of hindeutend auf (acc.).

Ar·gus ['ɑːgəs] npr. myth. 'Argus m; **'~-eyed** adj. 'argusäugig, wachsam, mit 'Argusaugen.

a·ri·a ['ɑːrɪə] s. ♪ 'Arie f.

Ar·i·an ['eərɪən] eccl. **I** adj. ari'anisch; **II** s. Ari'aner m.

ar·id ['ærɪd] adj. □ dürr, trocken, unfruchtbar; fig. trocken, öde; **a·rid·i·ty** [æ'rɪdətɪ] s. Dürre f, Trockenheit f, Unfruchtbarkeit f (a. fig.).

A·ri·es ['eərɪːz] s. ast. Widder m.

a·right [ə'raɪt] adv. recht, richtig: set ~ richtig stellen.

a·rise [ə'raɪz] v/i. [irr.] **1.** (from, out of) entstehen, entspringen, her'vorgehen (aus), herrühren, stammen (von); **2.** entstehen, sich ergeben (from aus); sich erheben, erscheinen, auftreten; **3.** aufstehen, sich erheben; **a·ris·en** [ə'rɪzn] p.p. von arise.

ar·is·toc·ra·cy [,ærɪ'stɒkrəsɪ] s. **1.** Aristo'kratie f, coll. a. Adel m; **2.** fig. E'lite f, Adel m; **a·ris·to·crat** ['ærɪstəkræt] s. Aristo'krat(in); Adlige(r m) f; fig. Pa'trizier(in); **a·ris·to·crat·ic, a·ris·to·crat·i·cal** [,ærɪstə'krætɪk(l)] adj. □ aristo'kratisch, Adels...; fig. adlig, vornehm.

a·rith·me·tic [ə'rɪθmətɪk] s. Arith'metik f, Rechnen n, Rechenkunst f; **ar·ith·met·ic, ar·ith·met·i·cal** [,ærɪθ'me-tɪk(l)] adj. □ arith'metisch, Rechen...; **a·rith·me·ti·cian** [ə,rɪθmə'tɪʃn] s. Rechner(in), Rechenmeister(in).

ark [ɑːk] s. **1.** Arche f: Noah's ~ Arche Noah(s); **2.** Schrein m: 2 of the Covenant bibl. Bundeslade f.

arm¹ [ɑːm] s. **1.** anat. Arm m: keep s.o. at ~'s length fig. sich j-n vom Leibe halten; within ~'s reach in Reichweite; with open ~s fig. mit offenen Armen; fly into s.o.'s ~s j-m in die Arme fliegen; take s.o. in one's ~s j-n in die Arme nehmen; infant (od. babe) in ~s Säugling m; **2.** Fluss-, Meeresarm m; **3.** Arm-, Seitenlehne f; **4.** Ast m, großer Zweig; **5.** Ärmel m; **6.** ⊛ Arm m e-r Maschine etc.: ~ of a balance Waagebalken m; **7.** fig. Arm m des Gesetzes etc.

arm² [ɑːm] **I** s. **1.** ✕ mst pl. Waffe(n pl.) f: do ~s drill Gewehrgriffe üben; in ~s bewaffnet; rise in ~s zu den Waffen greifen, sich empören; up in ~s a) in Aufruhr, b) fig. in Harnisch, in hellem Zorn; by force of ~s mit Waffengewalt; bear ~s a) Waffen tragen, b) als Soldat dienen; lay down ~s die Waffen strecken; take up ~s zu den Waffen greifen (a. fig.); ~s dealer Waffenhändler m; ~s control Rüstungskontrolle f; ~s race Wettrüsten n; ground ~s! Gewehr nieder!; order ~s! Gewehr ab!; pile ~s! setzt die Gewehre zusammen!; *port ~s!* fällt das Gewehr!; *present ~s!* präsentiert das Gewehr!; *slope ~s!* das Gewehr über!; *shoulder ~s!* das Gewehr an Schulter!; *to ~s!* zu den Waffen!, ans Gewehr!; → *passage at arms*; **2.** Waffengattung *f*, Truppe *f*: *the naval ~* die Kriegsmarine; **3.** *pl.* Wappen *n*; → *coat* 1; **II** *v/t.* **4.** bewaffnen: *~ed to the teeth* bis an die Zähne bewaffnet; **5.** ⊙ armieren, bewehren, befestigen, verstärken, *mit Metall* beschlagen; **6.** ✕ *Munition, Mine* scharf machen; **7.** (aus)rüsten, bereit machen, versehen: *be ~ed with an umbrella*; *be ~ed with arguments*; **III** *v/i.* **8.** sich bewaffnen, sich (aus)rüsten.

ar·ma·da [ɑːˈmɑːdə] *s.* **1.** ⚓ *hist.* Ar'mada *f*; **2.** Kriegsflotte *f*, Luftflotte *f*, Geschwader *n*.

ar·ma·dil·lo [ˌɑːməˈdɪləʊ] *s. zo.* **1.** Ar'madill *n*, Gürteltier *n*; **2.** Apo'thekerassel *f*.

Ar·ma·ged·don [ˌɑːməˈɡedn] *s.* **1.** *bibl.* Arma'geddon *n*, Entscheidungskampf *m (a. fig.)*; **2.** globale Kata'strophe; **3.** *fig.* totaler Zs.-bruch, De'saster *n*.

ar·ma·ment [ˈɑːməmənt] *s.* ✕ **1.** Kriegsstärke *f*, -macht *f e-s Landes*: *naval ~* Kriegsflotte *f*; **2.** Bewaffnung *f*, Bestückung *f e-s Kriegsschiffes etc.*; **3.** (Kriegsaus)Rüstung *f*: *~ race* Wettrüsten *n*; **ar·ma·ture** [ˈɑːməˌtjʊə] *s.* **1.** Rüstung *f*, Panzer *m*; **2.** ⊙ Panzerung *f*, Beschlag *m*, Bewehrung *f*, Armierung *f*, Arma'tur *f*; **3.** ⚡ Anker *m (a. e-s Magneten etc.)*, Läufer *m*: *~ shaft* Ankerwelle *f*; **4.** ♀, *zo.* Bewehrung *f*.

'arm|·band *s.* Armbinde *f*; **,~'chair I** *s.* Lehnstuhl *m*, (Lehn)Sessel *m*; **II** *adj.* vom (*od.* am) grünen Tisch; Stammtisch..., Salon...: *~ strategists*.

armed [ɑːmd] *adj.* **1.** bewaffnet: *~ conflict*; *~ neutrality*; *~ forces* (Gesamt-) Streitkräfte *pl.*; *~ robbery* schwerer Raub; **2.** ✕ scharf, zündfertig (*Munition etc.*), b) *a.* ⊙ → *armoured*.

Ar·me·ni·an [ɑːˈmiːnjən] **I** *adj.* ar'menisch; **II** *s.* Ar'menier(in).

'arm·ful [-fʊl] *s.* Armvoll *m*.

arm·ing [ˈɑːmɪŋ] *s.* **1.** Bewaffnung *f*, (Aus)Rüstung *f*; **2.** ⊙ Armierung *f*, Arma'tur *f*; **3.** Wappen *n*.

ar·mi·stice [ˈɑːmɪstɪs] *s.* Waffenstillstand *m (a. fig.)*; **♀ Day** *s.* Jahrestag *m* des Waffenstillstandes vom 11. November 1918.

arm·let [ˈɑːmlɪt] *s.* **1.** Armbinde *f als Abzeichen*; Armspange *f*; **2.** kleiner Meeres- *od.* Flussarm.

ar·mor *etc. Am.* → *armour etc.*

ar·mo·ri·al [ɑːˈmɔːrɪəl] **I** *adj.* Wappen..., he'raldisch: *~ bearings* Wappen(schild *m, n*) *n*; **II** *s.* Wappenbuch *n*; **ar·mor·y** [ˈɑːmərɪ] *s.* **1.** He'raldik *f*, Wappenkunde *f*; **2.** *Am.* → *armoury*.

ar·mour [ˈɑːmə] *s.* **1.** Rüstung *f*, Panzer *m (a. fig.)*; **2.** ✕, ⊙ Panzer(ung *f*) *m*, Armierung *f*; *coll.* Panzerfahrzeuge *pl.*, -truppen *pl.*; **3.** ♀, *zo.* Panzer *m*, Schutzdecke *f*; **'~-clad** → *armour-plated*.

ar·moured [ˈɑːməd] *adj.* ✕, ⊙ gepanzert, Panzer...: *~ cable* armiertes Kabel, Panzerkabel *n*; *~ car* a) Panzerkampfwagen *m*, b) gepanzerter (Geld-) Transportwagen; *~ infantry* Panzergrenadiere *pl*; *~ train* Panzerzug *m*; **'ar·mour·er** [-ərə] *s.* Waffenschmied *m*; ✕, ⚓ Waffenmeister *m*.

'ar·mour|·,pierc·ing *adj.* panzerbrechend, Panzer...: *~ ammunition*; **'~-,plat·ed** *adj.* gepanzert, Panzer...

ar·mour·y [ˈɑːmərɪ] *s.* **1.** Rüst-, Waffenkammer *f (a. fig.)*, Arse'nal *n*, Zeughaus *n*; **2.** *Am.* a) 'Waffenfa,brik *f*, b) Exerzierhalle *f*.

'arm|·pit *s.* Achselhöhle *f*; **'~·rest** *s.* Armlehne *f*, -stütze *f*; **'~-,twist·ing** *s.* F Druckausübung *f*.

ar·my [ˈɑːmɪ] *s.* **1.** Ar'mee *f*, Heer *n*; Mili'tär *n*: *~ contractor* Heereslieferant *m*; *join the ~* Soldat werden; *~ of occupation* Besatzungsarmee; *~ issue* die dem Soldaten gelieferte Ausrüstung, Heereseigentum *n*; **2.** Ar'mee *f (als militärische Einheit)*; **3.** *fig.* Heer *n*, Menge *f*: *a whole ~ of workmen*; *~ chap·lain* *s.* Mili'tärgeistliche(r) *m*; *~ corps* *s.* Ar'meekorps *n*.

ar·ni·ca [ˈɑːnɪkə] *s.* ♣ 'Arnika *f*.

A-road [ˈeɪrəʊd] *s. Brit. etwa:* Bundesstraße *f*.

a·ro·ma [əˈrəʊmə] *s.* **1.** A'roma *n*, Duft *m*, Würze *f*; Blume *f (Wein)*; **2.** *fig.* Würze *f*, Reiz *m*; **ar·o·mat·ic** [ˌærəʊˈmætɪk] *adj.* (□ *~ally*) aro'matisch, würzig, duftig: *~ bath* Kräuterbad *n*.

a·ro·ma·ther·a·py [əˌrəʊməˈθerəpɪ] *s.* ♣ A'romathera,pie *f*.

a·rose [əˈrəʊz] *pret. von arise.*

a·round [əˈraʊnd] **I** *adv.* **1.** 'ringsher'um, im Kreise; rundum, nach *od.* auf allen Seiten, über'all: *I've been ~* F *fig.* ich kenn mich aus; **2.** *bsd. Am.* F um'her, (in der Gegend) herum; in der Nähe, da'bei; **II** *prp.* **3.** um, um ... her(um), rund um; **4.** *bsd. Am.* F a) (rings- *od.* in der Gegend) herum; durch, hin und her, b) (nahe) bei, in, c) ungefähr, etwa; **a,round-the-'clock** *adj.* den ganzen Tag dauernd, 24-stündig; Dauer...

a·rouse [əˈraʊz] *v/t.* **1.** *j-n* (auf-) wecken; **2.** *fig.* aufrütteln; *Gefühle etc.* erregen.

ar·que·bus [ˈɑːkwɪbəs] → *harquebus.*

ar·rack [ˈærək] *s.* 'Arrak *m*.

ar·raign [əˈreɪn] *v/t.* **1.** ⚖ a) vor Gericht stellen, b) zur Anklage vernehmen; **2.** *öffentlich* beschuldigen, rügen; **3.** *fig.* anfechten; **ar·raign·ment** [-mənt] *s.* ⚖ Vernehmung *f* zur Anklage; *bsd. fig.* Anklage *f*.

ar·range [əˈreɪndʒ] **I** *v/t.* **1.** (an)ordnen, aufstellen; einteilen; ein-, ausrichten; erledigen: *~ one's ideas* s-e Gedanken ordnen; *~ one's affairs* s-e Angelegenheiten regeln; **2.** verabreden, vereinbaren; festsetzen, planen: *everything had been ~d beforehand*; *an ~d marriage* e-e (von den Eltern) arrangierte Ehe; **3.** *Streit etc.* beilegen, schlichten; **4.** ♪, *thea.* einrichten, bearbeiten; **II** *v/i.* **5.** sich verständigen (*about* über *acc.*); **6.** Anordnungen *od.* Vorkehrungen treffen (*for, about* für, zu, *to inf.* zu *inf.*); es einrichten, dafür sorgen, veranlassen (*that* dass): *~ for the car to be ready*; **7.** sich einigen (*with s.o. about s.th.* mit j-m über et.); **ar'range·ment** [-mənt] *s.* **1.** (An)Ordnung *f*, Einrichtung *f*, Einteilung *f*, Auf-, Zs.-stellung *f*; Sy'stem *n*; **2.** Vereinbarung *f*, Verabredung *f*, Abmachung *f*: *make an ~ with s.o.* mit j-m e-e Verabredung treffen; **3.** Ab-, Übereinkommen *n*; Schlichtung *f*: *come to an ~* e-n Vergleich schließen; **4.** *pl.* *make ~s* Vorkehrungen *od.* Vorbereitungen *od.* a-e Dispositionen treffen: *today's ~s* die heutigen Veranstaltungen; **5.** *thea.* Bearbeitung *f*, ♪ *a.* Arrange'ment *n*.

ar·rant [ˈærənt] *adj.* □ völlig, ausgesprochen, ,kom'plett: *an ~ fool*; *nonsense*; *an ~ rogue* ein Erzgauner.

ar·ray [əˈreɪ] **I** *v/t.* **1.** ordnen, aufstellen (*bsd. Truppen*); **2.** ⚖ *Geschworene* aufrufen; **3.** *fig.* aufbieten; **4.** (*o.s.* sich) kleiden, putzen; **II** *s.* **5.** Ordnung *f*; Schlachtordnung *f*; **6.** ⚖ Geschworenen(liste *f*) *pl.*; **7.** 'Phalanx *f*, stattliche Reihe, Menge *f*, Aufgebot *n*; **8.** Kleidung *f*, Staat *m*, Aufmachung *f*.

ar·rear [əˈrɪə] *s.* a) *mst pl.* Rückstand *m*, *bsd.* Schulden *pl.*: *~s of rent* rückständige Miete; *in ~(s)* im Rückstand *od.* Verzug, b) *et.* Unerledigtes, Arbeitsrückstände *pl.*

ar·rest [əˈrest] **I** *s.* **1.** Aufhalten *n*, Hemmung *f*, Stockung *f*; **2.** ⚖ a) Verhaftung *f*, Haft *f*: *under ~* verhaftet, in Haft, b) Beschlagnahme *f*, c) *a.* ~ *of judgment* Urteilssistierung *f*; **II** *v/t.* **3.** an-, aufhalten, hemmen, hindern: *~ progress*; *~ed growth* *biol.* gehemmtes Wachstum; *~ed tuberculosis* ♣ inaktive Tuberkulose; **4.** ⚖ feststellen, sperren, arretieren; **5.** ⚖ a) verhaften, b) beschlagnahmen, c) *~ judgment* das Urteil vertagen; **6.** *Geld etc.* einbehalten, konfiszieren; **7.** *Aufmerksamkeit etc.* fesseln, festhalten; **ar'rest·ing** [-tɪŋ] *adj.* fesselnd, interes'sant; **ar'restment** [-mənt] *s.* Beschlagnahme *f*.

ar·rière-pen·sée [ˌærɪeə(r)ˈpɒnseɪ] (*Fr.*) *s.* 'Hintergedanke *m*.

ar·riv·al [əˈraɪvl] *s.* **1.** Ankunft *f*, Eintreffen *n*; *fig.* Gelangen *n (at* zu); **2.** Erscheinen *n*, Auftreten *n*; **3.** a) Ankömmling *m*: *new ~* Neuankömmling, Familienzuwachs *m*, b) *et.* Angekommenes; **4.** *pl.* ankommende Züge *pl.* *od.* Schiffe *pl. od.* Flugzeuge *pl. od.* Per'sonen *pl.*; Zufuhr *f*; ♣ (Waren)Eingänge *pl.*; **ar·rive** [əˈraɪv] *v/i.* **1.** (an-) kommen, eintreffen; **2.** erscheinen, auftreten; **3.** *fig.* (*at*) erreichen (*acc.*), gelangen (zu): *~ at a decision*; **4.** kommen, eintreten (*Zeit, Ereignis*); **5.** Erfolg haben.

ar·ro·gance [ˈærəgəns] *s.* Arro'ganz *f*, Anmaßung *f*, Über'heblichkeit *f*; **'ar·ro·gant** [-nt] *adj.* □ arro'gant, anmaßend, über'heblich; **ar·ro·gate** [ˈærəʊgeɪt] *v/t.* **1.** *~ to o.s.* sich *et.* anmaßen, *et.* für sich in Anspruch nehmen; **2.** zuschreiben, zuschieben (*s.th. to s.o.* j-m et.); **ar·ro·ga·tion** [ˌærəʊˈgeɪʃn] *s.* Anmaßung *f*.

ar·row [ˈærəʊ] *s.* **1.** Pfeil *m*; *~ keys* Computer: Pfeiltasten *pl*; **2.** Pfeil (-zeichen *n*) *m*; **3.** *surv.* Zähl-, Markierstab *m*; **'ar·rowed** [-əʊd] *adj.* mit Pfeilen *od.* Pfeilzeichen (versehen).

'ar·row|·head *s.* **1.** Pfeilspitze *f*; **2.** (Zeichen *n der*) Pfeilspitze *f* (*brit. Regierungsgut kennzeichnend*); **'~·root** *s.* ♣ a) Pfeilwurz *f*, b) Pfeilwurzstärke *f*.

ar·roy·o [əˈrɔɪəʊ] *s. geol.* Ar'royo *m*, Erosi'onsrinne *f*, -schlucht *f*.

arse [ɑːs] **I** *s.* V Arsch *m*; **II** *v/i. sl.* *~ around* ,herumspinnen'; **'~·hole** *s.* V ,Arschloch' *n (a. fig. contp.)*; *~ lick·er* *s.* V ,Arschkriecher' *m*.

ar·se·nal [ˈɑːsənl] *s.* **1.** Arse'nal *n (a. fig.)*, Zeughaus *n*, Waffenlager *n*; **2.** 'Waffen-, Muniti'onsfa,brik *f*.

ar·se·nic **I** *s.* [ˈɑːsnɪk] Ar'sen(ik) *n*; **II** *adj.* [ɑːˈsenɪk] ar'senhaltig; Arsen...

ar·sis [ˈɑːsɪs] *s.* **1.** *poet.* Hebung *f*, betonte Silbe; **2.** ♪ Aufschlag *m*.

ar·son [ˈɑːsn] *s.* ⚖ Brandstiftung *f*; **'ar·son·ist** [-nɪst] *s.* Brandstifter *m*.

art¹ [ɑːt] **I** *s.* **1.** (*bsd.* bildende) Kunst: *the fine ~s* die schönen Künste; *brought to a fine ~* zu e-r wahren Kunst entwickelt; *work of ~* Kunstwerk n; **2.** Kunst(fertigkeit) f, Geschicklichkeit f; **the ~ of the painter**; **the ~ of cooking; industrial ~(s)** (od. **~s and crafts**) Kunstgewerbe n, -handwerk n; **the black ~** die schwarze Kunst, die Zauberei; **3.** pl. univ. Geisteswissenschaften pl.: **Faculty of ~s**, Am. **~s Department** philosophische Fakultät; **liberal ~s** humanistische Fächer; → **master** 10, **bachelor** 2; **4.** mst pl. Kunstgriff m, Kniff m, List f, Tücke f; **5.** Patentrecht: a) Fach(gebiet) n, b) Fachkenntnis f, c) (**state of the ~** Stand m der) Technik; → **prior** 1; **II** adj. **6.** Kunst...: **~ critic**; **~ director** a) thea. etc. Bühnenmeister m, b) Werbung: Art-Director m, künstlerischer Leiter; **7.** künstlerisch, dekora'tiv: **~ pottery**; **III** v/t. **8. ~ up** sl. (künstlerisch) 'aufmöbeln'.

art² [a:t] obs. 2. pres. sg. von **be**.

ar·te·fact → **artifact**.

ar·te·ri·al [a:'tɪərɪəl] adj. **1.** ♂ arteri'ell, Arterien...: **~ blood** Pulsaderblut n; **2.** fig. **~ road** Hauptverkehrsader f, Ausfall-, Durchgangs-, Hauptverkehrs-, a. Fernverkehrsstraße f.

ar·te·ri·o·scle·ro·sis [a:,tɪərɪəʊsklɪə'rəʊsɪs] s. ♂ Arterioskle'rose f, Ar'terienverkalkung f.

ar·ter·y ['a:tərɪ] s. **1.** Ar'terie f, Puls, Schlagader f; **2.** fig. Verkehrsader f, bsd. Hauptstraße f, -fluss m: **~ of traffic**; **~ of trade** Haupthandelsweg m.

ar·te·sian well [a:'ti:zjən] s. ar'tesischer (Am. tiefer) Brunnen.

art·ful ['a:tfʊl] adj. □ **1.** schlau, listig, verschlagen; **'art·ful·ness** [-nɪs] s. List f, Schläue f, Verschlagenheit f.

ar·thrit·ic, ar·thrit·i·cal [a:'θrɪtɪk(l)] adj. ♂ ar'thritisch, gichtisch; **ar·thri·tis** [a:'θraɪtɪs] s. ♂ Ar'thritis f; **ar·thro·sis** [a:'θrəʊsɪs] s. Ar'throse f.

Ar·thu·ri·an [a:'θʊərɪən] adj. (König) Arthur od. Artus betreffend, Arthur..., Artus...

ar·ti·choke ['a:tɪtʃəʊk] s. ♀ **1.** a. **globe ~** Arti'schocke f; **2. Jerusalem ~** 'Erdarti,schocke f.

ar·ti·cle ['a:tɪkl] **I** s. **1.** ('Zeitungs- etc.) Ar,tikel m, Aufsatz m; **2.** Ar'tikel m, Gegenstand m, Sache f; Posten m, Ware f: **~ of trade** Handelsware; **the genuine ~** F der 'wahre Jakob'; **3.** Abschnitt m, Para'graph m, Klausel f, Punkt m: **~s of apprenticeship** Lehrvertrag m; **~s (of association,** Am. **incorporation)** ♱ Satzung f; **the Thirty-nine ~s** die 39 Glaubensartikel der anglikanischen Kirche; **according to the ~s** ♱ satzungsgemäß; **4.** ling. Ar'tikel m, Geschlechtswort n; **II** v/t. **5.** vertraglich binden; in die Lehre geben (**to** bei); **'ar·ti·cled** [-ld] adj. **1.** vertraglich gebunden; **2.** in der Lehre (**to** bei): **~ clerk** Brit. Anwaltsgehilfe m.

ar·tic·u·late I v/t. [a:'tɪkjʊleɪt] **1.** artikulieren, deutlich (aus)sprechen; **2.** gliedern; **3.** Knochen zs.-fügen; **II** adj. [-lət] **4.** klar erkennbar, deutlich (gegliedert), artikuliert, verständlich (Wörter etc); **5.** fähig, sich klar auszudrücken, sich klar ausdrückend; **6.** sich Gehör verschaffend; **7.** ♂, ♀, zo. gegliedert; **ar·tic·u·lat·ed** [-tɪd] adj. ❂ Gelenk..., Glieder...: **~ lorry** Brit. Sattelschlepper m; **ar·tic·u·la·tion** [a:,tɪkjʊ'leɪʃn] s. **1.** bsd. ling. Artikulati'on f, deutliche Aussprache; Verständlichkeit f; **2.** Anein'anderfügung f; **3.** ❂ Gelenk(verbindung f) n; **4.** Gliederung f.

ar·ti·fact ['a:tɪfækt] s. Arte'fakt n: a) Werkzeug n od. Gerät n bsd. primitiver od. prähistorischer Kulturen, b) ♂ 'Kunstpro,dukt n; **'ar·ti·fice** [-fɪs] s. Kunstgriff m; Kniff m, List f; **ar·tif·i·cer** [a:'tɪfɪsə] s. **1.** → **artisan**; **2.** ✕ a) Feuerwerker m, b) Handwerker m; **3.** Urheber(in).

ar·ti·fi·cial [,a:tɪ'fɪʃl] adj. □ **1.** künstlich, Kunst...: **~ heart** Kunstherz n; **~ intelligence** künstliche Intelli'genz; **~ silk** Kunstseide f; **~ leg** Beinprothese f; **~ teeth** künstliche Zähne; **~ person** ♱ juristische Person; **~ turf** sport Kunststoffrasen m; **2.** fig. gekünstelt, falsch; **ar·ti·fi·ci·al·i·ty** [,a:tɪfɪʃɪ'ælətɪ] s. Künstlichkeit f; et. Gekünsteltes.

ar·til·ler·ist [a:'tɪlərɪst] s. Artille'rist m, Kano'nier m.

ar·til·ler·y [a:'tɪlərɪ] s. **1.** Artille'rie f; **2.** sl. ,Artille'rie' f, Schießeisen n od. pl.

ar·ti·san [,a:tɪ'zæn] s. (Kunst)Handwerker m.

art·ist ['a:tɪst] s. **1.** a) Künstler(in), bsd. Kunstmaler(in), b) → **artiste**; **2.** fig. Künstler(in), Könner(in); **ar·tiste** [a:'ti:st] (Fr.) s. Ar'tist(in), Künstler (-in), Sänger(in), Schauspieler(in), Tänzer(in); **ar·tis·tic, ar·tis·ti·cal** [a:'tɪstɪk(l)] adj. □ **1.** künstlerisch, Künstler..., Kunst...; **2.** kunstverständig; **3.** kunst-, geschmackvoll; **'art·ist·ry** [-trɪ] s. **1.** Künstlertum n, das Künstlerische; **2.** künstlerische Wirkung od. Voll'endung; **3.** Kunstfertigkeit f.

art·less ['a:tlɪs] adj. □ **1.** ungekünstelt, na'türlich, schlicht, unschuldig, na'iv; **2.** offen, arglos, ohne Falsch; **3.** unkünstlerisch, stümperhaft.

Art Nou·veau [,a:'rnu:'vəʊ] (Fr.) s. Kunst: Art f nou'veau, Jugendstil m.

art·sy ['a:tsɪ] → **arty**.

'art·work s. Artwork n: a) künstlerische Gestaltung, Illustrati'on(en pl.) f, Grafik f, b) (grafische etc.) Gestaltungsmittel pl.

art·y ['a:tɪ] adj. F **1.** (gewollt) künstlerisch od. bohemi'enhaft; **2.** ,kunstbeflissen'; **~(-and)-'craft·y** adj. **1.** iro. ,künstlerisch', mo'dern-verrückt; **2.** → **arty** 1.

Ar·y·an ['eərɪən] **I** s. **1.** Arier m, Indoger'mane m; **2.** ling. arische Sprachengruppe; **3.** Arier m, Nichtjude m (in der Nazi-Ideologie); **II** adj. **4.** arisch; **5.** arisch, nichtjüdisch.

as [æz; əz] **I** adv. **1.** (ebenso) wie, so: **~ usual** wie gewöhnlich od. üblich; **~ soft ~ butter** weich wie Butter; **twice ~ large** zweimal so groß; **just ~ good** ebenso gut; **2.** als: **he appeared ~ Macbeth**; **I knew him ~ a child**; **~ prose style this is bad** für Prosa ist das schlecht; **3.** wie (z. B.): **cathedral cities, ~ Ely**; **II** cj. **4.** wie, so wie: **~ follows; do ~ you are told!** wie man dir sagt!; **~ I said before; ~ you were!** ✕ Kommando zurück!; **~ it is** unter diesen Umständen, ohnehin; **~ it were** sozusagen, gleichsam; **5.** als, in'dem, während: **~ he entered** als er eintrat, bei s-m Eintritt; **6.** ob'gleich, wenn auch; wie, wie sehr, so sehr: **old ~ I am** so alt wie ich bin; **try ~ he would** sosehr er (es) auch versuchte; **7.** da, weil: **~ you are sorry I'll forgive you**; **III** pron. **8.** was, wie: **~ he himself admits**; → **such** 7;

Zssgn mit adv. u. prp.:

as|... ~ as (eben)so ... wie: **as fast as I could** so schnell ich konnte; **as sweet as can be** so süß wie möglich; **as cheap as five pence a bottle** schon

für (od. für nur) fünf Pence die Flasche; **as recently as last week** noch (od. erst) vorige Woche; **as good as** so gut wie, sozusagen; **not as bad as (all) that** gar nicht so schlimm; **as fine a song as I ever heard** ein Lied, wie ich kein schöneres je gehört habe; **~ far as** so weit (wie), so'weit, so'viel: **~ I know** soviel ich weiß; **~ Cologne** bis (nach) Köln; **as far back as 1890** schon im Jahre 1890; **~ for** was ... (an)betrifft, bezüglich (gen.); **~ from** vor Zeitangaben: von ... an, ab, mit Wirkung vom...; **~ if** od. **though** als ob, als wenn: **he talks ~ he knew them all**; **~ long as** a) so lange wie, solange: **~ he stays**, b) wenn (nur); vor'ausgesetzt, dass: **~ you have enough money**; **~ much** gerade (od. eben) das: **I thought ~**; **~ again** doppelt so viel; **~ much as** (neg. mst **not so much as**) a) (eben)so viel wie: **~ my son**, b) so sehr, so viel: **did he pay ~ that?** hat er so viel (dafür) bezahlt?, c) so'gar, über'haupt (neg. nicht einmal): **without ~ looking at him** ohne ihn über'haupt od. auch nur anzusehen; **~ per** laut, gemäß (dat.); **~ soon as** → **soon** 3; **~ to** 1. → **as for**; 2. (als od. so) dass: **be so kind ~ come** sei so gut und komm; **3.** nach, gemäß (dat.); **~ well** → **well¹** 11; **~ yet** → **yet** 2.

asap, ASAP ['eɪsæp] abbr. für **as soon as possible** möglichst bald.

as·bes·tos [æz'bestɒs] s. min. As'best m: **~ board** Asbestpappe f; **~-contaminated** asbestbelastet.

as·bes·to·sis [,æsbe'stəʊsɪs] s. Asbeststaublunge f.

as·cend [ə'send] **I** v/i. **1.** (auf-, em'por-, hin'auf)steigen; **2.** ansteigen, (schräg) in die Höhe gehen: **the path ~s here**; **3.** zeitlich hin'aufreichen, zu'rückgehen (**to** bis in acc., bis auf acc.); **4.** ♪ steigen (Ton); **II** v/t. **5.** be-, ersteigen: **~ a river** e-n Fluss hinauffahren; **~ the throne** den Thron besteigen; **as'cend·an·cy**, **as'cend·en·cy** [-dənsɪ] s. (**over**) Über'legenheit f, Herrschaft f, Gewalt f (über acc.); (bestimmender) Einfluss (auf acc.); **as'cend·ant, as'cend·ent** [-dənt] **I** s. **1.** ast. Aufgangspunkt m e-s Gestirns: **in the ~** fig. im Kommen od. Aufstieg; **2.** → **ascendancy**; **3.** Verwandte(r m) f (in aufsteigender Linie); Vorfahr m; **II** adj. **4.** aufgehend, aufsteigend; **5.** über'legen, (vor)herrschend; **as'cend·ing** [-dɪŋ] adj. (auf-) steigend (a. fig.): **~ air current** Aufwind m; **as'cen·sion** [-nʃn] s. **1.** Aufsteigen n (a. ast.), Besteigung f; **2. the ~** die Himmelfahrt Christi: **~ Day** Himmelfahrtstag m; **as'cent** [-nt] s. **1.** Aufstieg m (a. fig.), Besteigung f; **2.** bsd. ♂, ❂ Steigung f, Gefälle n, Abhang m; **3.** Auffahrt f, Rampe f, (Treppen)Aufgang m.

as·cer·tain [,æsə'teɪn] v/t. feststellen, ermitteln; in Erfahrung bringen; **,ascer'tain·a·ble** [-nəbl] adj. feststellbar, zu ermitteln(d); **,as·cer'tain·ment** [-mənt] s. Feststellung f, Ermittlung f.

as·cet·ic [ə'setɪk] **I** adj. (□ **~ally**) as'ketisch, Asketen...; **II** s. As'ket m; **as'cet·i·cism** [-ɪsɪzəm] s. As'kese f, Kasteiung f.

ASCII code ['æski:] s. Computer: ASCII-Code m; **ASCII file** s. Computer: ASCII-Datei f.

as·cor·bic ac·id [ə'skɔ:bɪk] s. Askor'binsäure f, Vitamin C n.

as·crib·a·ble [ə'skraɪbəbl] adj. zuzuschreiben(d), beizumessen(d); **as·cribe** [ə'skraɪb] v/t. (**to**) zuschreiben, beimes sen, beilegen (*dat.*); zu'rückführen (auf *acc.*).

a·sep·sis [æ'sepsɪs] *s.* ✵ A'sepsis *f*; keimfreie Wundbehandlung; **a'sep·tic** [-ptɪk] *adj.* (□ **~ally**) a'septisch, keimfrei, ste'ril.

a·sex·u·al [eɪ'seksjʊəl] *adj.* □ *biol.* asexual: a) geschlechtslos (*a. fig.*), b) ungeschlechtlich: **~ reproduction** ungeschlechtliche Fortpflanzung.

ash¹ [æʃ] *s.* ♀ **1.** *a.* **~ tree** Esche *f*: **weeping ~** Traueresche; **2.** *a.* **~ wood** Eschenholz *n*.

ash² [æʃ] *s.* **1.** Asche *f* (*a.* 🜍): **~ bin** (*Am.* **can**) Aschen-, Mülleimer *m*; **~ furnace** Glasschmelzofen *m*; **2.** *mst pl.* Asche *f*: **lay in ~es** niederbrennen; **3.** *pl. fig.* sterbliche 'Überreste *pl.*; Trümmer *pl.*, Staub *m*: **rise from the ~es** *fig.* (wie ein Phönix) aus der Asche aufsteigen; **4. win the ℒes** (*Kricket*) gegen Australien gewinnen.

a·shamed [ə'ʃeɪmd] *adj.* □ sich schämend, beschämt: **be** (*od.* **feel**) **~ of** sich e-r Sache *od.* j-s schämen; **be ~ to** (*inf.*) sich schämen zu (*inf.*); **I am ~ that** es ist mir peinlich, dass; **you ought to be ~ of yourself!** du solltest dich schämen!

ash·en¹ ['æʃn] *adj.* ♀ eschen, aus Eschenholz.

ash·en² ['æʃn] *adj.* Aschen...; *fig.* aschfahl, -grau.

Ash·ke·naz·im [,æʃkɪ'næzɪm] (*Hebrew*) *s. pl.* As(ch)ke'nasim *pl.*

ash·lar ['æʃlə] *s.* △ Quaderstein *m*.

a·shore [ə'ʃɔː] *adv. u. adj.* ans *od.* am Ufer *od.* Land: **go ~** an Land gehen; **run ~** a) stranden, auflaufen, b) auf Strand setzen.

'ash|·pit *s.* Aschengrube *f*; **'~·tray** *s.* Aschenbecher *m*; ℒ **Wednes·day** *s.* Ascher'mittwoch *m*.

ash·y ['æʃɪ] *adj.* **1.** aus Asche (bestehend); m⁺ Asche bedeckt; **2.** → **ashen²**.

A·sian ['eɪʃn], **A·si·at·ic** [,eɪʃɪ'ætɪk] **I** *adj.* asi'atisch; **II** *s.* Asi'at(in).

a·side [ə'saɪd] **I** *adv.* **1.** bei'seite, auf die *od.* zur Seite, seitwärts; abseits: **step** (**set**) **~**; **2.** *thea.* beiseite: **speak ~**; **3. ~ from** *Am.* abgesehen von; **II** *s.* **4.** *thea.* A'parte *n*, beiseite gesprochene Worte *pl.*; **5.** a) Nebenbemerkung *f*, b) geflüsterte Bemerkung.

as·i·nine ['æsɪnaɪn] *adj.* eselartig, Esels...; *fig.* eselhaft, dumm.

ask [ɑːsk] **I** *v/t.* **1.** a) j-n fragen: **~ the policeman**, b) nach *et.* fragen: **~ the way**; **~ the time** wie spät es ist; **~ a question of s.o.** e-e Frage an j-n stellen; **2.** j-n nach *et.* fragen, sich bei j-m nach *et.* erkundigen: **~ s.o. the way**; **may I ~ you a question?** darf ich Sie (nach) etwas fragen?; **~ me another!** F keine Ahnung!; **3.** j-n bitten (**for** um, **to** *inf.* zu *inf.*, **that** dass): **~ s.o. for advice; we were ~ed to believe** man wollte uns glauben machen; **4.** bitten um, erbitten: **~ his advice; be there for the ~ing** umsonst *od.* mühelos zu haben sein; **~ favour** ℒ; **5.** einladen, bitten: **~ s.o. to lunch; ~ s.o. in** j-n hereinbitten; **6.** fordern, verlangen: **~ a high price; that is ~ing too much!** das ist zu viel verlangt!; **7.** → **banns**; **II** *v/i.* **8.** (**for**) bitten (um), verlangen (*acc. od.* nach); fragen (nach), j-n zu sprechen wünschen; *et.* erfordern: **~ (s.o.) for help** (j-n) um Hilfe bitten; **s.o. has been ~ing for you** es hat jemand nach Ihnen gefragt; **the matter ~s for great care** die Angelegenheit erfordert große Sorgfalt; **9.** *fig.* her'beiführen: **you ~ed**

for it (*od.* **for trouble**) du wolltest es ja so haben; **10.** fragen, sich erkundigen (**after, about** nach, wegen).

a·skance [ə'skæns] *adv.* von der Seite; *fig.* schief, scheel, misstrauisch: **look ~ at s.o.** (*od.* **s.th.**).

a·skew [ə'skjuː] *adv.* schief, schräg (*a. fig.*).

a·slant [ə'slɑːnt] **I** *adv. u. adj.* schräg, quer; **II** *prp.* quer über *od.* durch.

a·sleep [ə'sliːp] *adv. u. adj.* **1.** schlafend, im *od.* in den Schlaf: **be ~** schlafen; **fall ~** einschlafen; **2.** *fig.* entschlafen, leblos; **3.** *fig.* schlafend, unaufmerksam; **4.** *fig.* eingeschlafen (*Glied*).

a·slope [ə'sləʊp] *adv. u. adj.* abschüssig, schräg.

a·so·cial [æ'səʊʃəl] *adj.* □ **1.** ungesellig, kon'taktfeindlich; **2.** → **antisocial**.

asp¹ [æsp] *s. zo.* Natter *f*.

asp² [æsp] → **aspen**.

as·par·a·gus [ə'spærəgəs] *s.* ♀ Spargel *m*: **~ tips** Spargelspitzen.

as·pect ['æspekt] *s.* **1.** Aussehen *n*, Äußere(s) *n*, Erscheinung *f*, Anblick *m*, Gestalt *f*; **2.** Gebärde *f*, Miene *f*; **3.** A'spekt *m* (*a. ast.*); Gesichtspunkt *m*, Seite *f*, Hinsicht *f*, (Be)Zug *m*: **in its true ~** im richtigen Licht; **4.** Aussicht *f*, Lage *f*: **the house has a southern ~** das Haus liegt nach Süden.

as·pen ['æspən] ♀ **I** *s.* Espe *f*, Zitterpappel *f*; **II** *adj.* espen: **tremble like an ~ leaf** wie Espenlaub zittern.

as·per·gill ['æspədʒɪl], **as·per·gil·lum** [,æspə'dʒɪləm] *s. eccl.* Weihwedel *m*.

as·per·i·ty [æ'sperətɪ] *s. bsd. fig.* Rauheit *f*, Schroffheit *f*; Schärfe *f*, Strenge *f*, Herbheit *f*.

as·perse [ə'spɜːs] *v/t.* verleumden, in schlechten Ruf bringen, schlecht machen, schmähen; **as'per·sion** [-ɜːʃn] *s.* **1.** *eccl.* Besprengung *f*; **2.** Verleumdung *f*, Anwurf *m*, Schmähung *f*: **cast ~s on** j-n verleumden *od.* mit Schmutz bewerfen.

as·phalt ['æsfælt] **I** *s. min.* As'phalt *m*; **II** *v/t.* asphaltieren.

as·phyx·i·a [æs'fɪksɪə] *s.* ✵ a) Erstickung(stod *m*) *f*, b) Scheintod *m*; **as·phyx·i·ant** [əs'fɪksɪənt] **I** *adj.* erstickend; **II** *s.* erstickender (✗ Kampf-)Stoff; **as·phyx·i·ate** [əs'fɪksɪeɪt] *v/t.* ersticken: **be ~d** ersticken; **as·phyx·i·a·tion** [əs,fɪksɪ'eɪʃn] *s.* Erstickung *f*.

as·pic ['æspɪk] *s.* A'spik *m*, Ge'lee *n*.

as·pir·ant [ə'spaɪərənt] *s.* (**to, after, for**) Aspi'rant(in), Kandi'dat(in) (für); (eifriger) Bewerber (um): **~ officer** Offiziersanwärter *m*.

as·pi·rate ['æspərət] *ling.* **I** *s.* Hauchlaut *m*; **II** *adj.* aspiriert; **III** *v/t.* [-pəreɪt] aspirieren; **as·pi·ra·tion** [,æspə'reɪʃn] *s.* **1.** Bestrebung *f*, Aspirati'on *f*, Trachten *n*, Sehnen *n* (**for, after** nach); **2.** *ling.* Aspirati'on *f*; Hauchlaut *m*; **3.** ⊕, ✵ An-, Absaugung *f*; **as·pi·ra·tor** ['æspəreɪtə] *s.* ⊕, ✵ 'Saugappa,rat *m*; **as·pire** [ə'spaɪə] *v/i.* **1.** streben, trachten, verlangen (**to, after** nach, **to** *inf.* zu *inf.*); **2.** *fig.* sich erheben.

as·pi·rin ['æspərɪn] *s.* ✵ Aspi'rin *n*: **two ~s** zwei Aspirintabletten.

as·pir·ing [ə'spaɪərɪŋ] *adj.* □ hochstrebend, ehrgeizig.

ass¹ [æs] *s. zo.* Esel *m*; *fig.* Esel *m*, Dummkopf *m*: **make an ~ of o.s.** sich lächerlich machen.

ass² [æs] *s. Am.* V Arsch *m*.

as·sail [ə'seɪl] *v/t.* **1.** angreifen, über'fallen, bestürmen (*a. fig.*): **~ a city; ~ s.o. with blows; ~ s.o. with questions** j-n

mit Fragen überschütten; **~ed by fear** von Furcht ergriffen; **~ed by doubts** von Zweifeln befallen; **2.** (eifrig) in Angriff nehmen; **as'sail·a·ble** [-ləbl] *adj.* angreifbar (*a. fig.*); **as'sail·ant** [-lənt], **as'sail·er** [-lə] *s.* Angreifer(in), Gegner(in); *fig.* 'Kritiker *m*.

as·sas·sin [ə'sæsɪn] *s.* (Meuchel)Mörder (-in); po'litischer Mörder, Atten'täter (-in); **as'sas·si·nate** [-neɪt] *v/t.* (meuchlings) (er)morden; **as·sas·si·na·tion** [ə,sæsɪ'neɪʃn] *s.* Meuchelmord *m*, Ermordung *f*, (politischer) Mord, Atten'tat *n*.

as·sault [ə'sɔːlt] **I** *s.* **1.** Angriff *m* (*a. fig.*), 'Überfall *m* (**upon, on** auf *acc.*); **2.** ✗ Sturm *m*: **carry** (*od.* **take**) **by ~** erstürmen; **~ boat** a) Sturmboot *n*, b) Landungsfahrzeug *n*; **~ troops** Stoßtruppen; **3.** ⚖ tätliche Bedrohung *od.* Beleidigung: **~ and battery** schwere tätliche Beleidigung, Misshandlung *f*; **indecent** *od.* **criminal ~** unzüchtige Handlung (*Belästigung*), Sittlichkeitsvergehen *n*; **II** *v/t.* **4.** angreifen, über'fallen (*a. fig.*); anfallen, tätlich werden gegen; **5.** ✗ bestürmen (*a. fig.*); **6.** ⚖ tätlich *od.* schwer beleidigen; **7.** vergewaltigen.

as·say [ə'seɪ] **I** *s.* **1.** ⊕, 🜍 Probe *f*, Ana·'lyse *f*, Prüfung *f*, Unter'suchung *f*, *bsd.* Me'tall-, Münzprobe *f*: **~ office** Prüfungsamt *n*; **II** *v/t.* **2.** *bsd.* (Edel)Metalle prüfen, unter'suchen; **3.** *fig.* versuchen, probieren; **III** *v/i.* **4.** *Am.* 'Edelme,tall enthalten; **as'say·er** [-eɪə] *s.* (Münz-)Prüfer *m*.

as·sem·blage [ə'semblɪdʒ] *s.* **1.** Zs.-kommen *n*, Versammlung *f*; **2.** Ansammlung *f*, Schar *f*, Menge *f*; **3.** ⊕ Zs.-setzen *n*, Mon'tage *f*; **4.** *Kunst:* Assem'blage *f*, **as·sem·ble** [ə'sembl] **I** *v/t.* **1.** versammeln, zs.-berufen; *Truppen* zs.-ziehen; **2.** ⊕ *Teile* zs.-setzen, -bauen, montieren; *Computer:* assemblieren; **II** *v/i.* **3.** sich versammeln, zs.-kommen; *parl.* zs.-treten; **as'sem·bler** [-lə] *s.* **1.** ⊕ Mon'teur *m*; **2.** *Computer:* As'sembler *m*; **as'sem·bly** [-lɪ] *s.* **1.** Versammlung *f*, Zs.-kunft *f*, Gesellschaft *f*: **~ point** Versammlungsort *m*; **~ hall, ~ room** a. Gesellschaftsraum *m*, Ballsaal *m*; **2.** *oft* ℒ *pol.* beratende *od.* gesetzgebende Körperschaft; *Am.* ℒ, *a.* **General ℒ** 'Unterhaus *n* (*in einigen Staaten*): **~ man** Abgeordnete(r) (→ 3); **3.** ⊕ Zs.-bau *m*, Mon'tage *f*; *a. Computer:* Baugruppe *f*: **~ line** Montage-, Fließband *n*, (Fertigungs)Straße *f*, laufendes Band; **~ man** Fließbandarbeiter *m* (→ 2); **~ plant** Montagewerk *n*; **~ shop** Montagehalle *f*; **4.** ✗ a) Bereitstellung *f*, b) 'Sammelsi,gnal *n*: **~ area** Bereitstellungsraum *m*.

as·sent [ə'sent] **I** *v/i.* (**to**) zustimmen (*dat.*), beipflichten (*dat.*), billigen (*acc.*); genehmigen (*acc.*); **II** *s.* Zustimmung *f*: **royal ~** *pol. Brit.* königliche Genehmigung.

as·sert [ə'sɜːt] *v/t.* **1.** behaupten, erklären; **2.** *Anspruch, Recht* behaupten, geltend machen; 'durchsetzen; bestehen auf (*acc.*); verteidigen, einstehen für: **~ one's liberties**; **3. ~ o.s.** a) sich behaupten, sich geltend machen *od.* 'durchsetzen, b) sich zu viel anmaßen; **as·ser·tion** [ə'sɜːʃn] *s.* **1.** Behauptung *f*, Erklärung *f*: **make an ~** e-e Behauptung aufstellen; **2.** Geltendmachung *f* *od.* 'Durchsetzung *f* *e-s Anspruches etc.*; **as·ser·tive** [-tɪv] *adj.* □ **1.** 'positiv, zur Geltung kommend, ausdrücklich; **2.** anspruchsvoll, anmaßend.

as·sess [ə'ses] *v/t.* **1.** besteuern, zur Steuer einschätzen *od.* veranlagen (*in od. at* [*the sum of*] mit); **2.** *Steuer, Geldstrafe etc.* auferlegen (*upon dat.*): **~ed value** Einheitswert *m*; **3.** *bsd. Wert zur Besteuerung od. e-s Schadens* schätzen, veranschlagen, festsetzen; **4.** *fig. Leistung etc.* bewerten, einschätzen, beurteilen, würdigen; **as'sess·a·ble** [-səbl] *adj.* □ **1.** (ab)schätzbar; **2.** (**~ to income tax** einkommens)steuerpflichtig; **as'sess·ment** [-mənt] *s.* **1.** (Steuer)Veranlagung *f*, Einschätzung *f*, Besteuerung *f*: **~ notice** Steuerbescheid *m*; **rate of ~** Steuersatz *m*; **2.** Festsetzung *f* e-r Zahlung (*als Entschädigung etc.*), (*Schadens*)Feststellung *f*; **3.** (*Betrag der*) Steuer *f*, Abgabe *f*, Zahlung *f*; **4.** *fig.* Bewertung *f*, Beurteilung *f*, Würdigung *f*; **as'ses·sor** [-sə] *s.* **1.** Steuereinschätzer *m*; **2.** ♓ (sachverständiger) Beisitzer *m*, Sachverständige(r) *m*.

as·set ['æset] *s.* **1.** ✝ Vermögen(swert *m*, -gegenstand *m*) *n*; *Bilanz:* Ak'tivposten *m*, *pl.* Ak'tiva *pl.*, (Aktiv-, Betriebs)Vermögen *n*; (Kapital)Anlagen *pl.*; Guthaben *n u. pl.*: **~s and liabilities** Aktiva u. Passiva; **concealed** (*od. hidden*) **~s** stille Reserven; **current ~s** 'Umlaufvermögen *n*; **fixed ~s** Sachanlagen *pl.*, Anlagevermögen *n*; **intangible ~s** 'immateri,elles Vermögen; **2.** *pl.* ♓ Vermögen(smasse *f*) *n*, Nachlass *m*; (**bankrupt's**) **~s** Kon'kursmasse *f*; **3.** *fig.* a) Vorzug *m*, -teil *m*, Plus *n*, Wert *m*, b) Gewinn (**to** für), wertvolle Kraft, guter Mitarbeiter *etc.*

as·sev·er·ate [ə'sevəreɪt] *v/t.* beteuern; **as·sev·er·a·tion** [ə,sevə'reɪʃn] *s.* Beteuerung *f*.

as·si·du·i·ty [,æsɪ'djuːətɪ] *s.* Emsigkeit *f*, (unermüdlicher) Fleiß; Dienstbeflissenheit *f*; **as·sid·u·ous** [ə'sɪdjʊəs] *adj.* □ **1.** emsig, fleißig, eifrig, beharrlich; **2.** aufmerksam, dienstbeflissen.

as·sign [ə'saɪn] **I** *v/t.* **1.** *Aufgabe etc.* zu-, anweisen, zuteilen, über'tragen (**to s.o.** j-m); **2.** j-n zu e-r *Aufgabe etc.* bestimmen, j-n mit et. beauftragen; e-m *Amt*, ✗ e-m *Regiment* zuteilen; **3.** *fig. et.* zuordnen (**to** *dat.*); **4.** *Zeit, Aufgabe* festsetzen, bestimmen; **5.** *Grund etc.* angeben, anführen; **6.** zuschreiben (**to** *dat.*); **7.** ♓ (**to**) über'tragen (auf *acc.*), abtreten (an *acc.*); **II** *s.* **8.** ♓ Rechtsnachfolger(in), Zessio'nar *m*; **as'sign·a·ble** [-nəbl] *adj.* bestimmbar, zuweisbar; zuzuschreiben(d); anführbar; ♓ über'tragbar; **as·sig·na·tion** [,æsɪg'neɪʃn] *s.* **1.** → **assignment** 1, 2, 4; **2.** *et.* Zugewiesenes, (Geld)Zuwendung *f*; **3.** Stelldichein *n*; **as·sign·ee** [,æsɪ'niː] *s.* ♓ **1.** → **assign** 8; **2.** Bevollmächtigte(r *m*) *f*; Treuhänder *m*: **~ in bankruptcy** Konkursverwalter *m*; **as'sign·ment** [-mənt] *s.* **1.** An-, Zuweisung *f*; **2.** Bestimmung *f*, Festsetzung *f*; **3.** Aufgabe *f*, Arbeit *f* (*a. ped.*); Auftrag *m*; *bes. Am.* Stellung *f*, Posten *m*; **4.** ♓ a) Übertragung *f*, Abtretung *f*, b) Abtretungsurkunde *f*; **as'sign·or** [,æsɪ'nɔː] *s.* ♓ Ze'dent(in), Abtretende(r *m*) *f*.

as·sim·i·late [ə'sɪmɪleɪt] **I** *v/t.* **1.** assimilieren: a) angleichen (*a. ling.*), anpassen (**to, with** *dat.*), b) *bsd. sociol.* aufnehmen, absorbieren, *a.* gleichsetzen (**to, with** mit), c) *biol. Nahrung* einverleiben, 'umsetzen; **2.** vergleichen (**to, with** mit); **II** *v/i.* **3.** sich assimilieren, gleich *od.* ähnlich werden, sich anpassen, sich angleichen; **4.** aufgenommen werden; **as·sim·i·la·tion** [ə,sɪmɪ'leɪʃn] *s.* (**to**) Assimilati'on *f* (an *acc.*): a) *a. sociol.* Angleichung *f* (an *acc.*), Gleichsetzung *f* (mit), b) *biol., sociol.* Aufnahme *f*, Einverleibung *f*, c) *bot.* Photosyn'these *f*, d) *ling.* Assimilierung *f*.

as·sist [ə'sɪst] **I** *v/t.* j-m helfen, beistehen; j-n *od. et.* unter'stützen: **~ed take-off** Abflug *m* mit Starthilfe; **2.** fördern, (*mit Geld*) unter'stützen: **~ed immigration** Einwanderung mit (staatlicher) Beihilfe; **II** *v/i.* **3.** Hilfe leisten, mithelfen (*in* bei): **~ in doing a job** bei e-r Arbeit (mit)helfen; **4.** (*at*) beiwohnen (*dat.*), teilnehmen (an *dat.*); **III** *s.* **5.** F → **assistance**; **6.** *Eishockey etc.*: Vorlage *f*; **as'sist·ance** [-təns] *s.* Hilfe *f*, Unter'stützung *f*, Beistand *m*: **economic** (**judicial**) **~** Wirtschafts-(Rechts)Hilfe; **social ~** Sozialhilfe *f*; **afford** (*od. lend*) **~** Hilfe gewähren *od.* leisten; **as'sist·ant** [-tənt] **I** *adj.* **1.** behilflich (**to** *dat.*); **2.** Hilfs..., Unter..., stellvertretend, zweite(r): **~ driver** Beifahrer *m*; **~ judge** ♓ Beisitzer *m*; **II** *s.* **3.** Assi'stent(in), Gehilfe *m*, Gehilfin *f*, Mitarbeiter(in); Angestellte(r *m*) *f*; **4.** Ladengehilfe *m*, -gehilfin *f*, Verkäufer(in).

as·size [ə'saɪz] *s. hist.* **1.** ♓ (Schwur-) Gerichtssitzung *f*, Gerichtstag *m*; **2.** **~s** *pl.* ♓ *Brit.* As'sisen *pl.*, peri'odische (Schwur)Gerichtssitzungen *pl.* des **High Court of Justice** in den einzelnen Grafschaften (*bis 1971*).

as·so·ci·a·ble [ə'səʊʃjəbl] *adj.* (gedanklich) vereinbar (**with** mit).

as·so·ci·ate [ə'səʊʃɪeɪt] **I** *v/t.* **1.** (**with**) vereinigen, verbinden, verknüpfen (mit); hin'zufügen, angliedern, -schließen, zugesellen (*dat.*): **~d company** ✝ *Brit.* Schwestergesellschaft *f*; **2.** *bsd. psych.* assoziieren, (gedanklich) verbinden, in Zs.-hang bringen, verknüpfen; **3. ~ o.s.** sich anschließen (**with** *dat.*); **II** *v/i.* (**with** mit) **4.** 'Umgang haben, verkehren; **5.** sich verknüpfen, sich verbinden; **III** *adj.* [-ʃɪət] **6.** eng verbunden, verbündet; verwandt (**with** mit); **7.** beigeordnet, Mit...: **~ editor** Mitherausgeber *m*; **~ judge** beigeordneter Richter; **8.** außerordentlich: **~ member**; **~ professor**; **IV** *s.* [-ʃɪət] **9.** ✝ Teilhaber *m*, Gesellschafter *m*; **10.** Gefährte *m*, Genosse *m*, Kol'lege *m*, Mitarbeiter(in); **11.** außerordentliches Mitglied, Beigeordnete(r *m*) *f*; **12.** *Am. univ.* Lehrbeauftragte(r *m*) *f*.

as·so·ci·a·tion [ə,səʊsɪ'eɪʃn] *s.* **1.** Vereinigung *f*, Verbindung *f*, An-, Zs.-schluss *m*; **2.** Verein(igung *f*) *m*, Gesellschaft *f*; Genossenschaft *f*, Handelsgesellschaft *f*, Verband *m*; **3.** Freundschaft *f*, Kame'radschaft *f*; 'Umgang *m*, Verkehr *m*; **4.** Zs.-hang *m*, Beziehung *f*, Verknüpfung *f*; (Gedanken)Verbindung *f*, (I'deen)Assoziati,on *f*: **~ of ideas**; **~ foot·ball** *s. sport* (Verbands-) Fußball(spiel *n*) *m* (*Ggs. Rugby*).

as·so·nance ['æsənəns] *s.* Asso'nanz *f*, vo'kalischer Gleichklang; **'as·so·nant** [-nt] **I** *adj.* anklingend; **II** *s.* Gleichklang *m*.

as·sort [ə'sɔːt] **I** *v/t.* **1.** sortieren, gruppieren, (passend) zs.-stellen; **2.** ✝ assortieren; **II** *v/i.* **3.** (**with**) passen (zu), über'einstimmen (mit); **4.** verkehren, 'umgehen (**with** mit); **as'sort·ed** [-tɪd] *adj.* **1.** sortiert, geordnet; **2.** ✝ assortiert, *a. fig.* gemischt, verschiedenartig, allerlei; **as'sort·ment** [-mənt] *s.* **1.** Sortieren *n*, Ordnen *n*; **2.** Zs.-stellung *f*, Sammlung *f*; **3.** *bsd.* ♓ Sorti'ment *n*,

werden; **as·sim·i·la·tion** [ə,sɪmɪ'leɪʃn] *s.* (**to**) Assimilati'on *f* (an *acc.*): a) *a. sociol.* Angleichung *f* (an *acc.*), Gleichsetzung *f* (mit), b) *biol., sociol.* Aufnahme *f*, Einverleibung *f*, c) *bot.* Photosyn'these *f*, d) *ling.* Assimilierung *f*.

Auswahl *f*, Mischung *f*, Kollekti'on *f*.

as·suage [ə'sweɪdʒ] *v/t.* **1.** erleichtern, lindern, mildern; **2.** besänftigen, beschwichtigen; **3.** *Hunger etc.* stillen.

as·sume [ə'sjuːm] *v/t.* **1.** annehmen, vor'aussetzen, unter'stellen: **assuming that** angenommen, dass; **2.** *Amt, Pflicht, Schuld etc.* über'nehmen, (*a. Gefahr*) auf sich nehmen: **~ office**; **3.** *Gestalt, Eigenschaft etc.* annehmen, bekommen; sich zulegen, sich geben, sich angewöhnen; **4.** sich anmaßen *od.* aneignen: **~ power** die Macht ergreifen; **5.** vorschützen, vorgeben, (er)heucheln; **6.** *Kleider etc.* anziehen; **as'sumed** [-md] *adj.* □ **1.** angenommen, vor'ausgesetzt; **2.** vorgetäuscht, unecht: **~ name** Deckname *m*; **as'sum·ed·ly** [-mɪdlɪ] *adv.* vermutlich; **as'sum·ing** [-mɪŋ] *adj.* □ anmaßend.

as·sump·tion [ə'sʌmpʃn] *s.* **1.** Annahme *f*, Vor'aussetzung *f*, Vermutung *f*: **on the ~ that** in der Annahme, dass; **2.** 'Übernahme *f*, Annahme *f*; **3.** ('widerrechtliche) Aneignung; **4.** Anmaßung *f*; **5.** Vortäuschung *f*; **6.** 2 (*Day*) *eccl.* Mariä Himmelfahrt *f*.

as·sur·ance [ə'ʃʊərəns] *s.* **1.** Ver-, Zusicherung *f*; **2.** Bürgschaft *f*, Garan'tie *f*; **3.** ✝ (*bsd.* Lebens)Versicherung *f*; **4.** Sicherheit *f*, Gewissheit *f*; Sicherheitsgefühl *n*, Zuversicht *f*; **5.** Selbstsicherheit *f*, -vertrauen *n*; sicheres Auftreten; *b.s.* Dreistigkeit *f*; **as·sure** [ə'ʃʊə] *v/t.* **1.** sichern, sicherstellen, bürgen für: **this will ~ your success**; **2.** ver-, zusichern: **~ s.o. of s.th.** j-n e-r Sache versichern, j-m et. zusichern; **~ s.o. that** j-m versichern, dass; **3.** beruhigen; **4.** (*o.s.* sich) über'zeugen *od.* vergewissern; **5.** *Leben* versichern: **~ one's life with** e-r Lebensversicherung abschließen bei e-r Gesellschaft; **as·sured** [ə'ʃʊəd] **I** *adj.* □ **1.** ge-, versichert; **2.** a) sicher, über'zeugt, b) selbstsicher, c) beruhigt, ermutigt; **3.** gewiss, zweifellos; **II** *s.* **4.** Versicherte(r *m*) *f*; **as'sur·ed·ly** [-rɪdlɪ] *adv.* ganz gewiss; **as·sur·ed·ness** [ə'ʃʊədnɪs] *s.* Gewissheit *f*; Selbstvertrauen *n*; *b.s.* Dreistigkeit *f*; **as'sur·er** [-rə] *s.* Versicherer *m*.

As·syr·i·an [ə'sɪrɪən] **I** *adj.* as'syrisch; **II** *s.* As'syrer(in).

as·ter ['æstə] *s.* ♀ Aster *f*.

as·ter·isk ['æstərɪsk] *s. typ.* Sternchen *n*.

a·stern [ə'stɜːn] *adv.* ⚓ **1.** achtern, hinten; **2.** achteraus.

as·ter·oid ['æstərɔɪd] *s. ast.* Astero'id *m* (*kleiner Planet*).

asth·ma ['æsmə] *s.* ⚕ 'Asthma *n*, Atemnot *f*; **asth·mat·ic** [æs'mætɪk] **I** *adj.* (□ **~ally**) asth'matisch; **II** *s.* Asth'matiker (-in); **asth·mat·i·cal** [æs'mætɪkl] → **asthmatic** I.

as·tig·mat·ic [,æstɪg'mætɪk] *adj.* (□ **~ally**) *phys.* astig'matisch; **a·stig·ma·tism** [æ'stɪgmətɪzəm] *s.* Astigma-'tismus *m*.

a·stir [ə'stɜː] *adv. u. adj.* **1.** auf den Beinen: a) in Bewegung, rege, b) auf(gestanden), aus dem Bett, munter; **2.** in Aufregung (**with** über *acc.*, wegen).

as·ton·ish [ə'stɒnɪʃ] *v/t.* **1.** in Erstaunen *od.* Verwunderung setzen; **2.** über'raschen, befremden: **be ~ed** erstaunt *od.* überrascht sein (*at* über *acc.*, *to inf.* zu *inf.*), sich wundern (*at* über *acc.*); **as'ton·ish·ing** [-ʃɪŋ] *adj.* □ erstaunlich, überraschend; **as'ton·ish·ing·ly** [-ʃɪŋlɪ] *adv.* erstaunlich(erweise); **as-'ton·ish·ment** [-mənt] *s.* Verwunderung *f*, (Er)Staunen *n*, Befremden *n* (*at* über *acc.*): **fill** (*od. strike*) **with ~** in

Erstaunen setzen.

as·tound [ə'staʊnd] *v/t.* verblüffen, in Erstaunen setzen, äußerst über'raschen; **as'tound·ing** [-dɪŋ] *adj.* □ verblüffend, höchst erstaunlich.

as·tra·chan → *astrakhan*.

a·strad·dle [ə'strædl] *adv.* rittlings.

as·tra·khan [ˌæstrə'kæn] *s.* 'Astrachan *m*, Krimmer *m* (*Pelzart*).

as·tral ['æstrəl] *adj.* Stern(en)..., Astral...: ~ *body* Astralleib *m*; ~ *lamp* Astrallampe *f.*

a·stray [ə'streɪ] **I** *adv.*: *go* ~ a) vom Weg abkommen, b) *fig.* auf Abwege geraten, c) *fig.* irre-, fehlgehen, d) das Ziel verfehlen (*Schuss etc.*); *lead* ~ *fig.* irreführen, verleiten; **II** *adj.* irregehend, abschweifend (*a. fig.*); irrig, falsch.

a·stride [ə'straɪd] *adv., adj. u. prp.* rittlings (*of* auf *dat.*), mit gespreizten Beinen: *ride* ~ im Herrensattel reiten; ~ (*of*) *a horse* zu Pferde; ~ (*of*) *a road* quer über die Straße.

as·tringe [ə'strɪndʒ] *v/t.* (*a.* 🜪) zs.-ziehen, adstringieren; **as'trin·gent** [-dʒənt] **I** *adj.* □ **1.** 🜪 adstringierend, zs.-ziehend; **2.** *fig.* streng, hart; **II** *s.* **3.** 🜪 Ad'stringens *n.*

as·tri·on·ics [ˌæstrɪ'ɒnɪks] *s. pl. sg.* konstr. Astri'onik *f*, 'Raumfahrtelekt-ˌronik *f.*

as·tro·dome ['æstrəʊdəʊm] *s.* ➣ Kuppel *f* für astro'nomische Navigati'on; **as·tro·labe** ['æstrəʊleɪb] *s. ast.* Astro'labium *n.*

as·trol·o·ger [ə'strɒlədʒə] *s.* Astro'loge *m*, Sterndeuter *m*; **as·tro·log·ic**, **as·tro·log·i·cal** [ˌæstrə'lɒdʒɪk(l)] *adj.* □ astro'logisch; **as·trol·o·gy** [ə'strɒlədʒɪ] *s.* Astrolo'gie *f*, Sterndeutung *f.*

as·tro·naut ['æstrənɔːt] *s.* (Welt-) Raumfahrer *m*, Astro'naut *m*; **as·tro·nau·tics** [ˌæstrə'nɔːtɪks] *s. pl. sg.* konstr. Raumfahrt *f.*

as·tron·o·mer [ə'strɒnəmə] *s.* Astro'nom *m*; **as·tro·nom·ic**, **as·tro·nom·i·cal** [ˌæstrə'nɒmɪk(l)] *adj.* □ **1.** astro'no-misch, Stern..., Himmels...; **2.** *fig.* riesengroß: ~ *figures* astronomische Zahlen; **as·tron·o·my** [ə'strɒnəmɪ] *s.* Astrono'mie *f*, Sternkunde *f.*

as·tro·phys·i·cist [ˌæstrəʊ'fɪzɪsɪst] *s.* Astro'physiker *m*; **as·tro·phys·ics** [ˌæstrəʊ'fɪzɪks] *s. pl. sg. konstr.* Astro-phy'sik *f.*

as·tute [ə'stjuːt] *adj.* □ **1.** scharfsinnig; **2.** schlau, gerissen, raffiniert; **as'tute·ness** [-nɪs] *s.* Scharfsinn *m*; Schlauheit *f.*

a·sun·der [ə'sʌndə] **I** *adv.* ausein'ander, ent'zwei, in Stücke: *cut s.th.* ~; **II** *adj.* ausein'ander (liegend); *fig.* verschieden.

a·sy·lum [ə'saɪləm] *s.* **1.** A'syl *n*, Heim *n*, (Pflege)Anstalt *f*: (*insane od. lunatic*) ~ Irrenanstalt *f*; **2.** A'syl *n*: a) Freistätte *f*, Zufluchtsort *m*, b) *fig.* Zuflucht *f*, Schutz *m*; po'litisches A'syl: *right of* ~ Asylrecht *n*; ~ *camp* Asylantenlager *n*; ~ *seeker* Asylbewerber *m.*

a·sym·met·ric, **a·sym·met·ri·cal** [ˌæsɪ-'metrɪk(l)] *adj.* □ asym'metrisch, 'unsym,metrisch, ungleichmäßig: *asymmetrical bars* Turnen: Stufenbarren *m*; **a·sym·me·try** [æ'sɪmətrɪ] *s.* Asymme'trie *f*, Ungleichmäßigkeit *f.*

a·syn·chro·nous [æ'sɪŋkrənəs] *adj.* □ 'asynchron, Asynchron...

at¹ [æt; *unbetont* ət] *prp.* **1.** (*Ort*) an (*dat.*), bei, zu, auf (*dat.*), in (*dat.*): ~ *the corner* an der Ecke; ~ *the door* an *od.* vor der Tür; ~ *home* zu Hause, *östr., schweiz.* zuhause; ~ *the baker's* beim Bäcker; ~ *school* in der Schule; ~ *a ball*

---

bei (*od.* auf) e-m Ball; ~ *Stratford* in Stratford (*at vor dem Namen jeder Stadt außer London u. dem eigenen Wohnort; vor den beiden Letzteren in*); **2.** (*Richtung*) auf (*acc.*), nach, gegen, zu, durch: *point* ~ *s.o.* auf j-n zeigen; **3.** (*Art u. Weise, Zustand*) in (*dat.*), bei, zu, unter (*dat.*), auf (*acc.*): ~ *work* bei der Arbeit; ~ *your service* zu Ihren Diensten; *good* ~ *Latin* gut in Latein; ~ *my expense* auf meine Kosten; ~ *a gallop* im Galopp; *he is still* ~ *it* er ist noch dabei *od.* dran *od.* damit beschäftigt; **4.** (*Zeit*) um, bei, zu, auf (*acc.*): ~ *3 o'clock* um 3 Uhr; ~ *dawn* bei Tagesanbruch; ~ *Christmas* zu Weihnachten; ~ (*the age of*) *21* im Alter von 21 Jahren; **5.** (*Grund*) auf (*acc.*), von, bei: *alarmed* ~ beunruhigt über; **6.** (*Preis, Maß*) für, um, zu: ~ *6 dollars*; *charged* ~ berechnet mit; **7.** ~ *all in neg. od. Fragesätzen*: über'haupt, gar *nichts etc.*: *is he suitable* ~ *all?* ist er überhaupt geeignet?; *not* ~ *all* überhaupt nicht; *not* ~ *all!* F nichts zu danken!, gern geschehen!

At² [æt] *s. Brit.* ✗ *hist.* F Angehörige *f* der Streitkräfte.

at·a·vism ['ætəvɪzəm] *s. biol.* Ata'vismus *m*, (Entwicklungs)Rückschlag *m*; **at·a·vis·tic** [ˌætə'vɪstɪk] *adj.* ata'vistisch.

a·tax·i·a [ə'tæksɪə], **a·tax·y** [-ksɪ] *s.* Ata-'xie *f*, Bewegungsstörung *f.*

ate [et] *pret. von* **eat**.

at·el·ier ['ætəlɪeɪ] (*Fr.*) *s.* Ateli'er *n.*

a·the·ism ['eɪθɪɪzəm] *s.* Athe'ismus *m*, Gottesleugnung *f*; **'a·the·ist** [-ɪst] *s.* **1.** Athe'ist(in); **2.** gottloser Mensch; **a-the·is·tic**, **a·the·is·ti·cal** [ˌeɪθɪ'ɪs-tɪk(l)] *adj.* □ **1.** athe'istisch; **2.** gottlos.

A·the·ni·an [ə'θiːnjən] **I** *adj.* a'thenisch; **II** *s.* A'thener(in).

a·thirst [ə'θɜːst] *adj.* **1.** durstig; **2.** begierig (*for* nach).

ath·lete ['æθliːt] *s.* **1.** Ath'let *m*: a) Sportler *m*, Wettkämpfer *m*, b) *fig.* Hüne *m*; **2.** *Brit.* 'Leichtath,let *m*; ~*'s foot* *s.* 🜪 Fußpilz *m*; ~*'s heart* *s.* Sportlerherz *n.*

ath·let·ic [æθ'letɪk] *adj.* (□ ~*ally*) ath'letisch: a) sportlich, b) von athletischem Körperbau, musku'lös, c) sportlich (gewandt); ~ *heart* 🜪 Sportlerherz *n.*

ath·let·i·cism [æθ'letɪsɪzəm] *s.* → *athletics*; **ath·let·ics** [-ɪks] *s. pl. sg. konstr.* **1.** a) Sport *m*, b) *Brit.* 'Leicht-ath,letik *f*; **2.** sportliche Betätigung *od.* Gewandtheit, Sportlichkeit *f.*

at-home [ət'həʊm] *s.* (zwangloser) Empfang(stag), At-'home *n.*

a·thwart [ə'θwɔːt] **I** *adv.* **1.** quer, schräg hin'durch; ⚓ dwars (über); **2.** *fig.* verkehrt, ungelegen, in die Quere; **II** *prp.* **3.** (quer) über (*acc.*) *od.* durch; ⚓ dwars (über *acc.*); **4.** *fig.* (ent)gegen.

a·tilt [ə'tɪlt] *adv. u. adj.* **1.** vorgebeugt, kippend; **2.** mit eingelegter Lanze: *run* (*od. ride*) ~ *at s.o.* *fig.* gegen j-n e-e Attacke reiten.

At·lan·tic [ət'læntɪk] **I** *adj.* at'lantisch; **II** *s.*: *the* ~ der At'lantik, der Atlantische Ozean; ~ *Char·ter* *s. pol.* At'lantik-,Charta *f*; ~ (*standard*) *time* *s.* at'lantische ('Standard)Zeit (*im Osten Kanadas*).

at·las ['ætləs] *s.* **1.** Atlas *m* (*Buch*); **2.** △ At'lant *m*, Atlas *m* (*Gebälkträger*); **3.** *fig.* Hauptstütze *f*; **4.** *anat.* Atlas *m* (*oberster Halswirbel*); **5.** *großes Papierformat*; **6.** Atlas(seide *f*) *m.*

at·mos·phere ['ætməˌsfɪə] *s.* **1.** Atmo-'sphäre *f*, Lufthülle *f*; **2.** Luft *f*: *a moist* ~; **3.** ⊚ Atmo'sphäre *f* (*Druckeinheit*);

---

4. *fig.* Atmo'sphäre *f*: a) Um'gebung *f*, b) Stimmung *f.*

at·mos·pher·ic [ˌætməs'ferɪk] *adj.* (□ ~*ally*) **1.** atmo'sphärisch, Luft...: ~ *pressure phys.* Luftdruck; **2.** Witterungs..., Wetter...; **3.** ⊚ mit (Luft-) Druck betrieben; **4.** *fig.* stimmungsvoll, Stimmungs...; **at·mos'pher·ics** [-ks] *s. pl.* **1.** ⊚ atmo'sphärische Störungen *pl.*; **2.** *fig.* (*bsd.* opti'mistische) Atmo-'sphäre.

at·oll ['ætɒl] *s. geogr.* A'toll *n.*

at·om ['ætəm] *s.* **1.** *phys.* A'tom *n*: ~ *bomb* Atombombe *f*; ~ *smashing* Atomzertrümmerung *f*; ~ *splitting* Atom(kern)spaltung *f*; **2.** *fig.* A'tom *n*, winziges Teilchen, bisschen *n*: *not an* ~ *of truth* kein Körnchen Wahrheit.

a·tom·ic [ə'tɒmɪk] *adj. phys.* (□ ~*ally*) ato'mar, a'tomisch, Atom...: ~ *age* Atomzeitalter *n*; ~ *bomb* Atombombe *f*; ~ *clock* Atomuhr *f*; ~ *decay*, ~ *disintegration* Atomzerfall *m*; ~ *energy* Atomenergie *f*; ~ *fission* Atomspaltung *f*; ~ *fuel* Kernbrennstoff *m*; ~ *index*, ~ *number* Atomzahl *f*; ~ *nucleus* Atomkern *m*; ~ *pile* Atombatterie *f*, -säule *f*, -meiler *m*; ~*-powered* mit Atomkraft getrieben, Atom...; ~ *power plant* Atomkraftwerk *n*; ~ *waste* A'tommüll *m*, ato'mare Abfälle *pl.*, ato'marer Abfall; ~ *weight* Atomgewicht *n.*

a·tom·i·cal [ə'tɒmɪkl] → *atomic*.

a·tom·ics [ə'tɒmɪks] *s. pl. mst sg. konstr.* A'tomphy,sik *f.*

at·om·ism ['ætəmɪzəm] *s. phls.* Ato'mismus *m*; **at·om·is·tic** [ˌætəʊ'mɪstɪk] *adj.* (□ ~*ally*) ato'mistisch.

at·om·ize ['ætəʊmaɪz] *v/t.* **1.** in A'tome auflösen; **2.** *Flüssigkeit* zerstäuben; **3.** in s-e Bestandteile auflösen, atomisieren; **4.** ✗ mit Atombomben belegen; **'at·om·iz·er** [-maɪzə] *s.* ⊚ Zerstäuber *m.*

at·o·my¹ ['ætəmɪ] *s.* **1.** A'tom *n*; **2.** *fig.* Zwerg *m*, Knirps *m.*

at·o·my² ['ætəmɪ] *s.* F ,Gerippe' *n.*

a·tone [ə'təʊn] *v/i.* (*for*) büßen (für); sühnen, wieder gutmachen (*acc.*); **a-'tone·ment** [-mənt] *s.* **1.** Buße *f*, Sühne *f*, Genugtuung *f* (*for* für): *Day of* ⚝ *eccl.* a) Buß- und Bettag *m*, b) Versöhnungstag *m* (*jüd. Feiertag*); **2.** *the* ⚝ *eccl.* das Sühneopfer Christi.

a·ton·ic [æ'tɒnɪk] *adj.* **1.** 🜪 a'tonisch, schlaff, schwächend; **2.** *ling.* a) unbetont, b) stimmlos; **at·o·ny** ['ætənɪ] *s.* 🜪 Ato'nie *f.*

a·top [ə'tɒp] **I** *adv.* oben(auf), zu'oberst; **II** *prp.* a. ~ *of* (oben) auf (*dat.*); *fig.* besser als.

a·trip [ə'trɪp] *adj.* ⚓ **1.** gelichtet (*Anker*); **2.** steif geheißt (*Segel*).

a·tri·um ['ɑːtrɪəm] *pl.* **-a** [-ə] *s.* 'Atrium *n*: a) *antiq.* Hauptraum *m*, b) △ Lichthof *m*, c) *anat.* (*bsd.* Herz)Vorhof *m*, Vorkammer *f.*

a·tro·cious [ə'trəʊʃəs] *adj.* □ scheußlich, grässlich, grausam, *fig.* F *a.* mise-'rabel; **a·troc·i·ty** [ə'trɒsətɪ] *s.* **1.** Scheußlichkeit *f*; **2.** Gräuel(tat *f*) *m*; **3.** F a) Ungeheuerlichkeit *f*, (grober) Verstoß, b) ,Gräuel' *m*, et. Scheußliches.

at·ro·phied ['ætrəfɪd] *adj.* 🜪 atrophiert, geschrumpft, verkümmert (*a. fig.*); **'at·ro·phy** [-fɪ] 🜪 **I** *s.* Atro'phie *f*, Abzehrung *f*, Schwund *m*, Verkümmerung *f* (*a. fig.*); **II** *v/t.* abzehren *od.* verkümmern lassen; **III** *v/i.* schwinden, verkümmern (*a. fig.*).

Ats [æts] *s. pl. Brit. hist.* F *statt* **A.T.S.** ['eɪˌtiː'es] *abbr. für* (*Women's*) *Auxiliary Territorial Service* Organisation *der weiblichen Angehörigen der Streit-kräfte.*

at sign *s.* E-mail etc. at-Zeichen *n*, F ‚Klameraffe‘ *m*.

at·ta·boy [ˈætəbɔɪ] *int. Am.* F bravo!, so ists recht!

at·tach [əˈtætʃ] **I** *v/t.* **1.** *(to)* befestigen, anbringen (an *dat.*), beifügen *(dat.)*, anheften, -binden, -kleben (an *acc.*), verbinden (mit); **2.** *fig. (to) Sinn etc.* verknüpfen, verbinden (mit); *Wert, Wichtigkeit, Schuld* beimessen *(dat.)*; *Namen* beilegen *(dat.)*: ~ **conditions (to)** Bedingungen knüpfen (an *acc.*); → **importance** 1; **3.** *fig. j-n* fesseln, gewinnen, für sich einnehmen: **be ~ed to s.o.** an j-m hängen; **be ~ed** ‚in festen Händen sein‘ *(Mädchen etc.)*; ~ **o.s.** sich anschließen (**to** *dat.*, an *acc.*); **4.** *(to) j-n* angliedern, zuteilen *(dat.)*; **5.** ⚖ a) *j-n* verhaften, b) *et.* beschlagnahmen, *Forderung, Konto etc.* pfänden; **II** *v/i.* **6.** *(to)* anhaften *(dat.)*, verknüpft *od.* verbunden sein (mit): **no blame ~es to him** ihn trifft keine Schuld; **7.** ⚖ als Rechtsfolge eintreten: **liability ~es**; **at·tach·a·ble** [-tʃəbl] *adj.* **1.** anfügbar, an-, aufsteckbar; **2.** *fig.* verknüpfbar (**to** mit); **3.** ⚖ zu beschlagnahmen(d); beschlagnahmefähig, pfändbar.

at·ta·ché [əˈtæʃeɪ] *(Fr.) s.* Atta'ché *m*: **commercial ~** Handelsattaché; ~ **case** *s.* Aktenkoffer *m*.

at·tached [əˈtætʃt] *adj.* **1.** befestigt, fest, da'zugehörig: **with collar ~** mit festem Kragen; **2.** angeschlossen, zugeteilt; **3.** anhänglich, *j-m* zugetan; **at·tach·ment** [-tʃmənt] *s.* **1.** Befestigung *f*, Anbringung *f*; Anschluss *m*; **2.** Verbindung *f*, Verknüpfung *f*; **3.** Anhängsel *n*, Beiwerk *n*; ◎ Zusatzgerät *n*; **4.** *fig. (to, for)* Bindung *f* (an *acc.*); Zugehörigkeit *f* (zu); Anhänglichkeit *f* (an *acc.*), Neigung *f*, Liebe *f* (zu); **5.** ⚖ a) Verhaftung *f*, b) Beschlagnahme *f*, Pfändung *f*; dinglicher Ar'rest: ~ **of a debt** Forderungspfändung; **order of ~** Beschlagnahmeverfügung *f*.

at·tack [əˈtæk] **I** *v/t.* **1.** angreifen, über'fallen; **2.** *fig.* angreifen, scharf kritisieren; **3.** *fig. Arbeit etc.* in Angriff nehmen, sich über *Essen etc.* hermachen; **4.** *fig.* befallen *(Krankheit)*; angreifen: **acid ~s metals**; **II** *s.* **5.** Angriff *m* (**on** auf *acc.*) (a. ♫ Einwirkung), 'Überfall *m*; **6.** *fig.* Angriff *m*, At'tacke *f*, (scharfe) Kri'tik: **be under ~** unter Beschuss stehen; **7.** ♥ Anfall *m*, At'tacke *f*; **8.** In'angriffnahme *f*; **at·tack·er** [-kə] *s.* Angreifer *m*.

at·tain [əˈteɪn] **I** *v/t. Zweck etc.* erreichen; erlangen; erzielen; **II** *v/i. (to)* gelangen (zu), erreichen *(acc.)*: **after ~ing the age of 18 years** nach Vollendung des 18. Lebensjahres; **at·tain·a·ble** [-nəbl] *adj.* erreichbar; **at·tain·der** [-ndə] *s.* ⚖ Verlust *m* der bürgerlichen Ehrenrechte u. Einziehung *f* des Vermögens; **at·tain·ment** [-mənt] *s.* **1.** Erreichung *f*, Erwerbung *f*; **2.** *pl.* Kenntnisse *pl.*, Fertigkeiten *pl.*; **at·taint** [-nt] **I** *v/t.* **1.** zum Tode und zur Ehrlosigkeit verurteilen; **2.** befallen *(Krankheit)*; **3.** *fig.* beflecken, entehren; **II** *s.* **4.** Makel *m*, Schande *f*.

at·tar [ˈætə] *s.* 'Blumenˌsenz *f*, *bsd.* ~ **of roses** Rosenöl *n*.

at·tempt [əˈtempt] **I** *v/t.* **1.** versuchen, probieren; **2.** ~ **s.o.'s life** e-n Mordanschlag auf j-n verüben; **~ed murder** Mordversuch *m*; **3.** in Angriff nehmen, sich wagen *od.* machen an *(acc.)*; **II** *s.* **4.** Versuch *m*, Bemühung *f* (**to** *inf.* zu

inf.): ~ **at explanation** Erklärungsver-such; **5.** Angriff *m*: ~ **on s.o.'s life** (Mord)Anschlag *m*, Attentat *n* auf j-n.

at·tend [əˈtend] **I** *v/t.* **1.** *j-m* aufwarten; als Diener *od.* dienstlich begleiten; **2.** *bsd. Kranke* pflegen; *ärztlich* behandeln; **3.** *fig.* begleiten: **~ed by** *od.* **with** begleitet von, verbunden mit *(Schwierigkeiten etc.)*; **4.** beiwohnen *(dat.)*, teilnehmen an *(dat.)*; *Vorlesung, Schule, Kirche etc.* besuchen; **5.** ◎ a) bedienen, b) warten, pflegen, über'wachen; **II** *v/i.* **6.** *(to)* beachten *(acc.)*, hören, achten *(auf acc.)*: ~ **to what I am saying**; **7.** *(to)* sich kümmern (um), sich widmen *(dat.)*; ✝ *j-n* bedienen *(im Laden)*, abfertigen; **8.** *(to)* sorgen (für); besorgen, erledigen *(acc.)*; **9.** *([up]on) j-m* aufwarten, zur Verfügung stehen; *j-n* bedienen; **10.** erscheinen, zu'gegen sein *(at* bei); **11.** *obs.* Acht geben; **at·'tend·ance** [-dəns] *s.* **1.** Bedienung *f*, Aufwartung *f*, Pflege *f* (**on**, **upon** *gen.*), Dienst(leistung *f*) *m*: **medical ~** ärztliche Hilfe; **hours of ~** Dienststunden; **in** ~ Dienst habend *od.* tuend; ~ **dance** 3; **2.** *(at)* Anwesenheit *f*, Erscheinen *n* (bei), Beteiligung *f*, Teilnahme *f* (an *dat.*), Besuch *m* *(gen.)*: ~: **compulsory** Anwesenheitspflicht *f*; ~ **list** Anwesenheitsliste *f*; **hours of ~** Besuchszeit *f*; **3.** ◎ Bedienung *f*; Wartung *f*; **4.** Begleitung *f*, Dienerschaft *f*, Gefolge *n*; **5.** a) Besucher(zahl *f*) *pl.*, b) Besuch *m*, Beteiligung *f*: **in ~ at** anwesend bei; **at·'tend·ant** [-dənt] **I** *adj.* **1.** (**on**, **upon**) begleitend *(acc.)*, Dienst tuend (bei); **2.** anwesend *(at* bei); **3.** *fig. (upon)* verbunden (mit); zugehörig *(dat.)*, Begleit...: ~ **circumstances** Begleitumstände; ~ **expenses** Nebenkosten; **II** *s.* **4.** Begleiter(in), Gefährte *m*, Gesellschafter(in); **5.** Diener(in), Bediente(r *m*) *f*; Aufseher(in), Wärter (-in); **6.** *pl.* Dienerschaft *f*, Gefolge *n*; **7.** ◎ Bedienungsmann *m*; **8.** Begleiterscheinung *f*, Folge *f*.

at·ten·tion [əˈtenʃn] *s.* **1.** Aufmerksamkeit *f*, Beachtung *f*: **call ~ to** die Aufmerksamkeit lenken auf *(acc.)*; **come to s.o.'s ~** j-m zur Kenntnis gelangen; **pay ~ to** j-m *od.* et. Beachtung schenken; **2.** Berücksichtigung *f*, Erledigung *f*: *(for* **the)** ~ **of** zu Händen von *(od. gen.)*; **for immediate ~** zur sofortigen Erledigung; **3.** Aufmerksamkeit *f*, Freundlichkeit *f*; *pl.* Aufmerksamkeiten *pl.*: **pay one's ~s to s.o.** j-m den Hof machen; **4.** ~! Achtung!; ✕ *a.* stillgestanden!; **stand at** *od.* **to** ~ ✕ stillstehen, Haltung annehmen; **5.** Bedienung *f*, Wartung *f*; **at·'ten·tive** [-ntɪv] *adj.* □ *(to)* aufmerksam: a) achtsam (auf *acc.*), b) *fig.* höflich (zu).

at·ten·u·ate **I** *v/t.* [əˈtenjʊeɪt] **1.** dünn *od.* schlank machen; verdünnen; ✝ dämpfen; **2.** *fig.* vermindern, abschwächen; **II** *adj.* [-jʊət] **3.** verdünnt, vermindert, abgeschwächt, abgemagert; **at·ten·u·a·tion** [əˌtenjʊˈeɪʃn] *s.* Verminderung *f*, Verdünnung *f*, Schwächung *f*, Abmagerung *f*; ✝ Dämpfung *f*.

at·test [əˈtest] **I** *v/t.* **1.** a) beglaubigen, bescheinigen, b) amtlich bestätigen *od.* attestieren: ~ **cattle**; **2.** bestätigen, beweisen; **3.** ✕ *Br.* vereidigen; **II** *v/i.* **4.** zeugen **(to** für); **at·tes·ta·tion** [ˌætesˈteɪʃn] *s.* **1.** Bezeugung *f*, Zeugnis *n*, Beweis *m*, Bescheinigung *f*, Bestätigung *f*; **2.** Eidesleistung *f*, Vereidigung *f*.

at·tic¹ [ˈætɪk] *s.* **1.** Dachstube *f*, Man'sarde *f*; *pl.* Dachgeschoss, *östr.* -geschoß *n*;

2. F *fig.* ‚Oberstübchen‘ *n*, Kopf *m*. **At·tic²** [ˈætɪk] *adj.* 'attisch: ~ **salt**, ~ **wit** attisches Salz, feiner Witz.

at·tire [əˈtaɪə] **I** *v/t.* **1.** kleiden, anziehen; **2.** putzen; **II** *s.* **3.** Kleidung *f*, Gewand *n*; **4.** Schmuck *m*.

at·ti·tude [ˈætɪtjuːd] *s.* **1.** Stellung *f*, Haltung *f*: **strike an** ~ e-e Pose annehmen; **2.** *fig.* Haltung *f*: a) Standpunkt *m*, Verhalten *n*: ~ **of mind** Geisteshaltung, b) Stellung(nahme) *f*, Einstellung *f* (**to**, **towards** zu, gegenüber); **3.** (a. ✈) Lage *f*; **at·ti·tu·di·nize** [ˌætɪˈtjuːdɪnaɪz] *v/i.* **1.** sich in Posi'tur setzen, posieren; **2.** affektiert tun.

at·tor·ney [əˈtɜːnɪ] *s.* ⚖ (Rechts)Anwalt *m* (*Am. a.* ~ **at law**); Bevollmächtigte(r *m*) *f*, (Stell)Vertreter *m*: **letter** *(od.* **warrant)** **of** ~ schriftliche Vollmacht; **power of** ~ Vollmacht(surkunde) *f*; **by** ~ im Auftrag; **At·tor·ney-'Gen·er·al** *s.* ⚖ *Brit.* Kronanwalt *m*, Gene'ralstaatsanwalt *m*; *Am.* Ju'stizmiˌnister *m*.

at·tract [əˈtrækt] *v/t.* **1.** anziehen (a. *phys.*); **2.** *fig.* anziehen, anlocken, fesseln, reizen; *Missfallen etc.* auf sich lenken *(od.* ziehen): ~ **attention** Aufmerksamkeit erregen; ~ **new members** neue Mitglieder gewinnen; **~ed by the music** von der Musik angelockt; **be ~ed to** eingenommen sein (für), liebäugeln (mit), sich hingezogen fühlen (zu); **at·'trac·tion** [-kʃn] *s.* **1.** *phys.* Anziehungskraft *f*: ~ **of gravity** Gravitationskraft *f*; **2.** *fig.* Anziehungskraft *f*, -punkt *m*, Reiz *m*, Attrakti'on *f*; *thea.* ('Haupt)Attrakti‚on *f*, Zugstück *n*, -nummer *f*; **at·'trac·tive** [-tɪv] *adj.* □ anziehend, (a. attrak'tiv, reizvoll, fesselnd, verlockend; zugkräftig; **at·'trac·tive·ness** [-tɪvnɪs] *s.* Reiz *m*, das Attrak'tive.

at·trib·ut·a·ble [əˈtrɪbjʊtəbl] *adj.* 'zuzuschreiben(d), beizumessen(d); **at·trib·ute** **I** *v/t.* [əˈtrɪbjuːt] *(to)* **1.** zuschreiben, beilegen, -messen *(dat.)*; *b.s. a.* unter'stellen *(dat.)*; **2.** zu'rückführen (auf *acc.*); **II** *s.* [ˈætrɪbjuːt] **3.** Attri'but *n* (a. *ling.*), Eigenschaft *f*, Merkmal *n*; **4.** (Kenn)Zeichen *n*, Sinnbild *n*; **at·tri·bu·tion** [ˌætrɪˈbjuːʃn] *s.* **1.** Zuschreibung *f*; **2.** beigelegte Eigenschaft; **3.** zuerkanntes Recht; **at·'trib·u·tive** [-tɪv] **I** *adj.* □ **1.** zugeschrieben, beigelegt; *2. ling.* attribu'tiv; **II** *s.* **3.** *ling.* Attri'but *n*.

at·trit·ed [əˈtraɪtɪd] *adj.* abgenutzt; **at·tri·tion** [əˈtrɪʃn] *s.* **1.** Abrieb *m*, Abnutzung *f*, ◎ a. Verschleiß *m*; **2.** Zermürbung *f*: **war of** ~ Zermürbungs-, Abnutzungskrieg *m*.

at·tune [əˈtjuːn] *v/t.* ♪ stimmen; *fig. (to)* in Einklang bringen (mit), anpassen *(dat.)*; abstimmen (auf *acc.*).

a·typ·i·cal [ˌeɪˈtɪpɪkl] *adj.* □ atypisch.

au·ber·gine [ˈəʊbəʒiːn] *s.* ♀ Auber'gine *f*.

au·burn [ˈɔːbən] *adj.* ka'stanienbraun *(Haar)*.

auc·tion [ˈɔːkʃn] **I** *s.* Aukti'on *f*, Versteigerung *f*: **sell by** *(Am. at)* ~, **put up for** *(od.* **to**, *Am.* **at)** ~ versteigern, versteigern; **Dutch** ~ Auktion, bei der der Preis so lange erniedrigt wird, bis sich ein Käufer findet; **sale by** *(od.* **at)** ~ Versteigerung; ~ **bridge** Kartenspiel: Auktionsbridge *n*; ~ **room** Auktionslokal *n*; **II** *v/t.* → **auction** II. **auc·tion·eer** [ˌɔːkʃəˈnɪə] **I** *s.* Auktio'nator *m*, Versteigerer *m*, *pl. a.* Aukti'onshaus *n*; **II** *v/t.* → **auction** II.

au·da·cious [ɔːˈdeɪʃəs] *adj.* □ kühn: a) verwegen, b) keck, dreist, unverfroren;

au·dac·i·ty [ɔːˈdæsətɪ] *s.* Kühnheit *f:* a) Verwegenheit *f*, Waghalsigkeit *f*, b) Dreistigkeit *f*, Unverfrorenheit *f*.

au·di·bil·i·ty [ˌɔːdɪˈbɪlətɪ] *s.* Hörbarkeit *f*, Vernehmbarkeit *f*; Lautstärke *f*; **au·di·ble** [ˈɔːdəbl] *adj.* □ hör-, vernehmbar, vernehmlich; ◎ aˈkustisch: ~ *signal*.

au·di·ence [ˈɔːdjəns] *s.* **1.** Anhören *n*, Gehör *n* (a. ⅄): *give* ~ *to s.o.* j-m Gehör schenken, j-n anhören; *right of* ~ ⅄ rechtliches Gehör; **2.** Audiˈenz *f* (*of*, *with* bei), Gehör *n*; **3.** ˈPublikum *n:* a) Zuhörer(schaft *f*) *pl.*, b) Zuschauer *pl.*, c) Besucher *pl.*, d) Leser(kreis *m*) *pl.*: ~ *rating* Radio, TV Einschaltquote *f*.

audio- [ˈɔːdɪəʊ] *in Zssgn* Hör..., Ton..., Audio...: ~ *frequency* Tonfrequenz *f*; ~ *range* Tonfrequenzbereich *m*.

au·di·on [ˈɔːdɪən] *s.* Radio: ˈAudion *n:* ~ *tube Am.*, ~ *valve Brit.* Verstärkerröhre *f*.

au·di·o·phile [ˈɔːdɪəʊfaɪl] *s.* Hi-Fi-Fan *m*.

au·di·o|·tape [ˈɔːdɪəʊteɪp] *s.* (besprochenes) Tonband; ~·**typ·ist** [ˈɔːdɪəʊˌtaɪpɪst] *s.* Phonotyˈpistin *f*; ~·**vis·u·al** [ˌɔːdɪəʊˈvɪzjʊəl] **I** *adj. ped.* audiovisuˈell: ~ *aids* → **II** *s. pl.* audiovisuˈelle ˈUnterrichtsmittel *pl.*

au·dit [ˈɔːdɪt] **I** *s.* **1.** ⁜ (Rechnungs-, Wirtschafts)Prüfung *f*, ˈBücherrevisiˌon *f:* ~ *year* Prüfungs-, Rechnungsjahr *n*; **2.** *fig.* Rechenschaftslegung *f*; **II** *v/t.* **3.** *Geschäftsbücher* (amtlich) prüfen, revidieren: ~ *accounts* die Konten (*od.* die Bücher, den Jahresabschluss) prüfen; ˈ**au·dit·ing** [-tɪŋ] *s.* → *audit* 1.

au·di·tion [ɔːˈdɪʃn] **I** *s.* **1.** ♪ Hörvermögen *n*, Gehör *n*; **2.** *thea.*, ♪ a) Vorsprechen *n od.* -singen *n od.* -spielen *n*, b) Anhörprobe *f*; **II** *v/t.* **3.** *thea. etc.* j-n vorsprechen *od.* vorsingen *od.* vorspielen lassen.

au·di·tor [ˈɔːdɪtə] *s.* **1.** Rechnungs-, Wirtschaftsprüfer *m*; **2.** *Am. univ.* Gasthörer(in); **au·di·to·ri·um** [ˌɔːdɪˈtɔːrɪəm] *s.* Audiˈtorium *n*, Zuhörer-, Zuschauerraum *m*, Hörsaal *m*; *Am.* Vortragssaal *m*, Festhalle *f*; ˈ**au·di·to·ry** [-tərɪ] **I** *adj.* **1.** Gehör..., Hör...; **II** *s.* **2.** Zuhörer(schaft *f*) *pl.*; **3.** → *auditorium*.

au fait [ˌəʊ ˈfeɪ] (*Fr.*) *adj.* auf dem Laufenden, vertraut (*with* mit).

au fond [ˌəʊ ˈfɔːŋ] (*Fr.*) *adv.* im Grunde.

Au·ge·an [ɔːˈdʒiːən] *adj.* Augias..., ˈüberaus schmutzig: *cleanse the* ~ *stables fig.* die Augiasställe reinigen.

au·ger [ˈɔːgə] *s.* ◎ *großer* Bohrer, Löffel-, Schneckenbohrer *m*; Förderschnecke *f*.

aught [ɔːt] *pron.* (irgend) etwas: *for* ~ *I care* meinetwegen; *for* ~ *I know* soviel ich weiß.

aug·ment [ɔːgˈment] **I** *v/t.* vermehren, vergrößern; **II** *v/i.* sich vermehren, zunehmen; **III** *s.* [ˈɔːgmənt] *ling.* Augˈment *n* (*Vorsilbe in griech. Verben*); **aug·men·ta·tion** [ˌɔːgmenˈteɪʃn] *s.* Vergrößerung *f*, Vermehrung *f*, Zunahme *f*, Wachstum *n*, Zuwachs *m*; Zusatz *m*; ˈ**aug·men·ta·tive** [-tətɪv] **I** *adj.* vermehrend, verstärkend; **II** *s. ling.* Verstärkungsform *f*.

au gra·tin [ˌəʊ ˈgrætæŋ] (*Fr.*) *adj.* Küche: au graˈtin, überˈkrustet.

au·gur [ˈɔːgə] **I** *s. antiq.* ˈAugur, Wahrsager *m*; **II** *v/t. u. v/i.* propheˈzeien, ahnen (lassen), verheißen: ~ *ill* (*well*) ein schlechtes (gutes) Zeichen sein (*for* für), Böses (Gutes) ahnen las-

sen; **au·gu·ry** [ˈɔːgjʊrɪ] *s.* **1.** Weissagung *f*, Propheˈzeiung *f*; **2.** Vorbedeutung *f*, Anzeichen *n*, Omen *n*; Vorahnung *f*.

au·gust¹ [ɔːˈgʌst] *adj.* □ erhaben, hehr, majeˈstätisch.

Au·gust² [ˈɔːgəst] *s.* Auˈgust *m:* *in* ~ im August.

Au·gus·tan age [ɔːˈgʌstən] *s.* **1.** Zeitalter *n* des (Kaisers) Auˈgustus; **2.** Blütezeit *f* e-r Natiˈon.

Au·gus·tine [ɔːˈgʌstɪn], *a.* ~ **fri·ar** *s.* Auguˈstiner(mönch) *m*.

auld [ɔːld] *adj. Scot.* alt; ~ *lang syne* [ˌɔːldlæŋˈsaɪn] *s. Scot.* die gute alte Zeit.

aunt [ɑːnt] *s.* Tante *f*; ˈ**aunt·ie** [-tɪ] *s.* F Tantchen *n*; **Aunt Sal·ly** [ˈsælɪ] *s.* **1.** volkstümliches Wurfspiel; **2.** *fig.* (gute) Zielscheibe *f*, *a.* Hassobjekt *n*.

au pair [ˌəʊ ˈpeə] **I** *adv.* als Auˈpair-Mädchen (*arbeiten etc.*); **II** *s. a.* ~ *girl* Auˈpair-Mädchen *n*; **III** *v/i.* als Auˈpair-Mädchen arbeiten.

au·ra [ˈɔːrə] *pl.* **-rae** [-riː] *s.* **1.** Hauch *m*, Duft *m*; Aˈroma *n*; **2.** ⚕ Vorgefühl *n* vor Anfällen; **3.** *fig.* Aura *f:* a) Fluidum *n*, Ausstrahlung *f*, b) Atmoˈsphäre *f*, c) ˈNimbus *m*.

au·ral [ˈɔːrəl] *adj.* □ Ohr..., Ohren..., Gehör...; Hör..., aˈkustisch: ~ *surgeon* Ohrenarzt *m*.

au·re·o·la [ɔːˈrɪəʊlə], **au·re·ole** [ˈɔːrɪəʊl] *s.* **1.** Strahlenkrone *f*, Aureˈole *f*; **2.** *fig.* ˈNimbus *m*; **3.** *ast.* Hof *m*.

au·ri·cle [ˈɔːrɪkl] *s. anat.* **1.** äußeres Ohr, Ohrmuschel *f*; **2.** Herzvorhof *m*; Herzohr *n*.

au·ric·u·la [əˈrɪkjʊlə] *s.* ♣ Auˈrikel *f*.

au·ric·u·lar [ɔːˈrɪkjʊlə] *adj.* □ **1.** Ohren..., Hör...: ~ *confession* Ohrenbeichte *f*; ~ *tradition* mündliche Überlieferung; ~ *witness* Ohrenzeuge *m*; **2.** *anat.* zu den Herzohren gehörig.

au·rif·er·ous [ɔːˈrɪfərəs] *adj.* goldhaltig.

au·rist [ˈɔːrɪst] *s.* ⚕ Ohrenarzt *m*.

au·rochs [ˈɔːrɒks] *s. zo.* Auerochs *m*, Ur *m*.

au·ro·ra [ɔːˈrɔːrə] *s.* **1.** *poet.* Morgenröte *f*; **2.** ♀ *myth.* Auˈrora *f*; ~ **bo·re·a·lis** *s. phys.* Nordlicht *n*.

aus·cul·tate [ˈɔːskəlteɪt] *v/t.* ⚕ *Lunge, Herz etc.* abhorchen; **aus·cul·ta·tion** [ˌɔːskəlˈteɪʃn] *s.* ⚕ Abhorchen *n*.

aus·pice [ˈɔːspɪs] *s.* **1.** (günstiges) Vor-, Anzeichen; **2.** *pl. fig.* Auˈspizien *pl.*; Schutzherrschaft *f:* *under the* ~*s of ...* unter der Schirmherrschaft von ...; **aus·pi·cious** [ɔːˈspɪʃəs] *adj.* □ günstig, verheißungsvoll, glücklich; **aus·pi·cious·ness** [ɔːˈspɪʃəsnɪs] *s.* günstige Aussicht, Glück *n*.

Aus·sie [ˈɒzɪ] F **I** *s.* Auˈstralier(in); **II** *adj.* ausˈtralisch.

aus·tere [ɒˈstɪə] *adj.* □ **1.** streng, herb; rau, hart; **2.** einfach, nüchtern; mäßig, enthaltsam, genügsam; **3.** dürftig, karg; **aus·ter·i·ty** [ɒˈsterətɪ] *s.* **1.** Strenge *f*, Ernst *m*; **2.** Asˈkese *f*, Enthaltsamkeit *f*; **3.** Herbheit *f*; **4.** Nüchternheit *f*, Strenge *f*, Schmucklosigkeit *f*; **5.** Einfachheit *f*, Nüchternheit *f*; **6.** Mäßigung *f*, Genügsamkeit *f*; *Brit.* strenge (wirtschaftliche) Einschränkung, Sparmaßnahmen *pl.* (*in Notzeiten*): ~ *program(me)* Sparprogramm *n*.

aus·tral [ˈɔːstrəl] *adj. ast.* südlich.

Aus·tral·a·sian [ˌɒstrəˈleɪʒn] **I** *adj.* ausˈtralˌasisch; **II** *s.* Auˈstralˌasier(in), Bewohner(in) Ozeˈaniens.

Aus·tral·ian [ɒˈstreɪljən] **I** *adj.* auˈstralisch; **II** *s.* Auˈstralier(in).

Aus·tri·an [ˈɒstrɪən] **I** *adj.* österreichisch; **II** *s.* Österreicher(in).

Aus·tro- [ɒstrəʊ] *in Zssgn* österreichisch: ~·*Hungarian Monarchy* österreichisch-ungarische Monarchie.

au·tar·chic, **au·tar·chi·cal** [ɔːˈtɑːkɪk(l)] *adj.* **1.** selbstregierend; **2.** → *autarkic*; **au·tar·chy** [ˈɔːtɑːkɪ] *s.* **1.** Selbstregierung *f*, volle Souveräniˈtät; **2.** → *autarky* 1.

au·tar·kic, **au·tar·ki·cal** [ɔːˈtɑːkɪk(l)] *adj.* auˈtark, wirtschaftlich unabhängig; **au·tar·ky** [ˈɔːtɑːkɪ] *s.* **1.** Autarˈkie *f*, wirtschaftliche Unabhängigkeit; **2.** → *autarchy*.

au·then·tic [ɔːˈθentɪk] *adj.* (□ ~*ally*) **1.** auˈthentisch: a) echt, verbürgt, b) glaubwürdig, zuverlässig, c) origiˈnal, urschriftlich: ~ *text* maßgebender Text, authentische Fassung; **2.** ⅄ rechtskräftig, -gültig, beglaubigt; **au·then·ti·cate** [-keɪt] *v/t.* **1.** die Echtheit (*gen.*) bescheinigen; **2.** beglaubigen, beurkunden, rechtskräftig machen; **au·then·ti·ca·tion** [ɔːˌθentɪˈkeɪʃn] *s.* Beglaubigung *f*, Legalisierung *f*; **au·then·tic·i·ty** [ˌɔːθenˈtɪsətɪ] *s.* **1.** Authentiziˈtät *f:* a) Echtheit *f*, b) Glaubwürdigkeit *f*; **2.** ⅄ (Rechts)Gültigkeit *f*.

au·thor [ˈɔːθə] *s.* **1.** Urheber(in); **2.** ˈAutor *m*, Auˈtorin *f*, Schriftsteller(in), Verfasser(in); **au·thor·ess** [ˈɔːθərɪs] *s.* Auˈtorin *f*, Schriftstellerin *f*, Verfasserin *f*.

au·thor·i·tar·i·an [ɔːˌθɒrɪˈteərɪən] *adj.* autoriˈtär; **au·thor·i·tar·i·an·ism** [-nɪzəm] *s. pol.* autoriˈtäres Reˈgierungssystem; **au·thor·i·ta·tive** [ɔːˈθɒrɪtətɪv] *adj.* □ **1.** gebieterisch, herrisch; **2.** autoriˈtativ, maßgebend, -geblich.

au·thor·i·ty [ɔːˈθɒrətɪ] *s.* **1.** Autoriˈtät *f*, (Amts)Gewalt *f:* *by* ~ mit amtlicher Genehmigung; *on one's own* ~ aus eigener Machtbefugnis; *be in* ~ die Gewalt in Händen haben; **2.** ˈVollmacht *f*, Ermächtigung *f*, Befugnis *f* (*for*, *to inf.* zu *inf.*): *on the* ~ *of ...* im Auftrage *od.* mit Genehmigung von (*od. gen.*) ...; → 4; **3.** Ansehen *n* (*with* bei), Einfluss *m* (*over* auf *acc.*); Glaubwürdigkeit *f:* *of great* ~ von großem Ansehen; **4.** a) Zeugnis *n* e-r *Persönlichkeit*, b) Gewährsmann *m*, Quelle *f*, Beleg *m:* *on good* ~ aus glaubwürdiger Quelle; *on the* ~ *of ...* a) nach Maßgabe *od.* aufgrund von (*od. gen.*) ..., b) mit ... als Gewährsmann; → 2; **5.** Autoriˈtät *f*, Sachverständige(r *m*) *f*, Fachmann *m* (*on* auf e-m *Gebiet*): *he is an* ~ *on the subject of Law*; **6.** *mst pl.* Behörde *f*, Obrigkeit *f:* *the local authorities* die Ortsbehörde(n); **au·thor·i·za·tion** [ˌɔːθəraɪˈzeɪʃn] *s.* Ermächtigung *f*, Genehmigung *f*, Befugnis *f*; **au·thor·ize** [ˈɔːθəraɪz] *v/t.* **1.** j-n ermächtigen, bevollmächtigen, berechtigen, autorisieren; **2.** *et.* gutheißen, billigen, genehmigen; *Handlung* rechtfertigen; **au·thor·ized** [ˈɔːθəraɪzd] *adj.* **1.** autorisiert, bevollmächtigt, befugt; zulässig: ~ *capital* ⁜ autorisiertes Kapital; ~ *person* Befugte(r *m*) *f*; ~ *to sign* unterschriftsberechtigt; ⁌ *Version eccl.* engl. Bibelübersetzung von 1611; **2.** ⅄ rechtsverbindlich; **au·thor·ship** [ˈɔːθəʃɪp] *s.* **1.** ˈAutorschaft *f*, Urheberschaft *f*; **2.** Schriftstellerberuf *m*.

au·tism [ˈɔːtɪzm] *s. psych.* Auˈtismus *m*; **au·tis·tic** [ɔːˈtɪstɪk] *adj.* (□ ~*ally*) *psych.* auˈtistisch.

au·to [ˈɔːtəʊ] *Am.* F *pl.* **-tos** *s.* Auto *n:* ~ *graveyard* Autofriedhof *m*; **II** *v/i.* (mit dem Auto) fahren.

auto- [ɔːtəʊ] *in Zssgn* a) selbsttätig, selbst..., Selbst..., auto..., Auto..., b)

Auto..., Kraftfahr...

au·to·bahn ['ɔːtəʊbɑːn] *pl.* **-bahnen** [-nən] (*Ger.*) *s.* Autobahn *f.*

au·to·bi·og·ra·pher [ˌɔːtəʊbaɪˈɒgrəfə] *s.* Autobio'graph(in); **au·to·bi·o·graph·ic** ['ɔːtəʊˌbaɪəʊˈgræfɪk] *adj.* (□ *~ally*) autobio'graphisch; **au·to·bi·og·ra·phy** [-fɪ] *s.* Autobiogra'phie *f,* 'Selbstbiogra,phie *f.*

au·to·bus ['ɔːtəʊbʌs] *s. Am.* Autobus *m.*

au·to·cade ['ɔːtəʊkeɪd] → *motorcade.*

au·to·car ['ɔːtəʊkɑː] *s.* Auto(mo'bil) *n,* Kraftwagen *m.*

'au·to,chang·er *s.* Plattenwechsler *m.*

au·toch·thon [ɔːˈtɒkθən] *s.* Autochthone *m,* Ureinwohner *m;* **au·'toch·tho·nous** [-θənəs] *adj.* autochthon, ureingesessen, bodenständig.

au·to·cide ['ɔːtəʊsaɪd] *s.* **1.** Selbstvernichtung *f;* **2.** Selbstmord *m* mit dem Auto.

au·to·clave ['ɔːtəʊkleɪv] *s.* **1.** Schnell-, Dampfkochtopf *m;* **2.** 🔧, ⚙ Auto'klav *m.*

au·to·code ['ɔːtəʊkəʊd] *s. Computer:* Autokode *m.*

au·toc·ra·cy [ɔːˈtɒkrəsɪ] *s.* Autokra'tie *f,* Selbstherrschaft *f;* **au·to·crat** ['ɔːtəʊkræt] *s.* Auto'krat(in), unumschränkter Herrscher; **au·to·crat·ic,** **au·to·crat·i·cal** [ˌɔːtəʊˈkrætɪk(l)] *adj.* □ auto'kratisch, selbstherrlich, unum'schränkt.

au·to·cue ['ɔːtəʊkjuː] *s. TV* 'Tele,prompter *m.*

au·to·da·fé [ˌɔːtəʊdɑːˈfeɪ] *pl.* **au·tos·da·fé** [ˌɔːtəʊzdɑːˈfeɪ] *s.* **1.** *hist.* Autoda'fé *n,* Ketzergericht *n,* -verbrennung *f;* **2.** *pol.* (Bücher- *etc.*)Verbrennung *f.*

au·to·di·dact ['ɔːtəʊdɪˌdækt] *s.* Autodi'dakt(in).

au·to·e·rot·ic [ˌɔːtəʊˈrɒtɪk] *adj. psych.* autoe'rotisch.

au·to·func·tion ['ɔːtəʊˌfʌŋkʃn] *s. Computer etc.* auto'matische Funkti'on.

au·tog·a·mous [ɔːˈtɒgəməs] *adj.* ♀ auto'gam, selbstbefruchtend.

au·tog·e·nous [ɔːˈtɒdʒɪnəs] *adj. allg.* auto'gen: **~ training;** **~ welding** ⚙ Autogenschweißen *n.*

au·to·gi·ro [ˌɔːtəʊˈdʒaɪərəʊ] *pl.* **-ros** *s.* ✈ Auto'giro *n,* Tragschrauber *m.*

au·to·graph ['ɔːtəgrɑːf] **I** *s.* **1.** Auto'gramm *n,* eigenhändige 'Unterschrift; **2.** eigene Handschrift; **3.** Urschrift *f;* **II** *adj.* **4.** eigenhändig unter'schrieben: *~ letter* Handschreiben *n;* **III** *v/t.* **5.** eigenhändig (unter)'schreiben; mit s-m Auto'gramm versehen: *~ing session* Autogrammstunde *f;* **6.** ⚙ autographieren, 'umdrucken; **au·to·graph·ic** [ˌɔːtəʊˈgræfɪk] *adj.* (□ *~ally*) auto'graphisch, eigenhändig geschrieben; **au·tog·ra·phy** [ɔːˈtɒgrəfɪ] *s.* **1.** ⚙ Autogra'phie *f,* 'Umdruck *m;* **2.** Urschrift *f.*

au·to·hy·phe·na·tion [ˌɔːtəʊˌhaɪfəˈneɪʃn] *s.* auto'matische Silbentrennung.

au·to·ig·ni·tion [ˌɔːtəʊɪgˈnɪʃn] *s.* ⚙ Selbstzündung *f.*

au·to·ist ['ɔːtəʊɪst] *s. Am.* F Autofahrer(in).

au·to·mat ['ɔːtəʊmæt] *s.* **1.** Auto'maten,restau,rant *n;* **2.** (Ver'kaufs)Auto,mat *m;* **3.** ⚙ Auto'mat *m* (*Maschine*); **'au·to·mate** [-meɪt] *v/t.* automatisieren: *~d teller* (*machine*) Geldautomat *m;* **au·to·mat·ic** [ˌɔːtəˈmætɪk] **I** *adj.* □ *~ automatically;* **1.** auto'matisch: a) selbsttätig, ⚙ *a.* Selbst..., zwangsläufig, 🗡 *a.* Selbstlade...: *~ gear change* (*Am. shift*) *mot.* Auto'matikschaltung *f;* **~ redial** *teleph.* automatische Wahlwiederholung, b) unwillkürlich,

me'chanisch; **II** *s.* **2.** 'Selbstladepi,stole *f,* -gewehr *n;* **3.** → *automat* 3; **4.** *mot.* Auto *n* mit Auto'matik; **au·to·mat·i·cal** [ˌɔːtəˈmætɪkl] → *automatic* 1; **au·to·mat·i·cal·ly** [ˌɔːtəˈmætɪkəlɪ] *adv.* auto'matisch; ohne weiteres.

au·to·mat·ic| lathe *s.* ⚙ 'Drehauto,mat *m;* **~ ma·chine** → *automat* 2; **~ pi·lot** *s.* ✈ → *autopilot;* **~ pis·tol** *s.* 'Selbstladepi,stole *f;* **~ start·er** *s.* ⚙ Selbstanlasser *m.*

au·to·ma·tion [ˌɔːtəˈmeɪʃn] *s.* ⚙ Automati'on *f;* **au·tom·a·ton** [ɔːˈtɒmətən] *pl.* **-ta** [-tə], **-tons** *s.* Auto'mat *m,* 'Roboter *m* (*beide a. fig.*).

au·to·mo·bile ['ɔːtəməʊbiːl] *s. bsd. Am.* Auto *n,* Automo'bil *n,* Kraftwagen *m;* **au·to·mo·bil·ism** [ˌɔːtəˈməʊbɪlɪzəm] *s.* Kraftfahrwesen *n;* **au·to·mo·bil·ist** [ˌɔːtəˈməʊbɪlɪst] *s.* Kraftfahrer *m;* **au·to·mo·tive** [ˌɔːtəˈməʊtɪv] *adj.* selbstbewegend, -fahrend; *bsd. Am.* 'kraftfahr,technisch, Auto(mobil)..., Kraftfahrzeug...

au·ton·o·mous [ɔːˈtɒnəməs] *adj.* auto'nom, sich selbst regierend; **au·'ton·o·my** [-mɪ] *s.* Autono'mie *f,* Selbstständigkeit *f.*

au·to·pi·lot ['ɔːtəʊˌpaɪlət] *s.* ✈ Autopi'lot *m,* auto'matische Steuervorrichtung.

au·top·sy ['ɔːtəpsɪ] **I** *s.* **1.** 🩺 Autop'sie *f,* Obdukti'on *f;* **2.** *fig.* kritische Ana'lyse; **II** *v/t.* **3.** 🩺 e-e Autop'sie vornehmen an (*dat.*).

au·to·sug·ges·tion [ˌɔːtəʊsəˈdʒestʃən] *s.* Autosuggesti'on *f.*

au·to·tell·er ['ɔːtəʊˌtelə] *s.* 'Bankauto,mat *m.*

au·to·trans·fu·sion [ˌɔːtəʊtrænsˈfjuːʒn] *s.* 🩺 'Eigenbluttransfusi,on *f.*

au·to·type ['ɔːtətaɪp] **I** *s. typ.* Autoty'pie *f:* a) Rasterätzung *f,* b) Fak'simileabdruck *m;* **II** *v/t.* mittels Autotypie vervielfältigen.

au·tumn ['ɔːtəm] *s. bsd. Brit.* Herbst *m* (*a. fig.*): *the ~ of life;* **au·tum·nal** [ɔːˈtʌmnəl] *adj.* herbstlich, Herbst... (*a. fig.*).

aux·il·ia·ry [ɔːgˈzɪljərɪ] **I** *adj.* **1.** helfend, mitwirkend, Hilfs...: *~ engine* Hilfsmotor *m;* *~ troops* Hilfstruppen; *~ verb* Hilfszeitwort *n;* **2.** ✗ Behelfs..., Ausweich...; **II** *s.* **3.** Helfer *m,* Hilfskraft *f, pl. a.* Hilfspersonal *n;* **4.** *pl.* ✗ Hilfstruppen *pl.;* **5.** *ling.* Hilfszeitwort *n.*

a·vail [əˈveɪl] **I** *v/t.* **1.** nützen (*dat.*), helfen (*dat.*), fördern; **2.** *~ o.s. of s.th.* sich e-r Sache bedienen, et. benutzen, Gebrauch von et. machen; **II** *v/i.* **3.** nützen, helfen; **III** *s.* **4.** Nutzen *m,* Vorteil *m,* Gewinn *m: of no ~* nutzlos; *of what ~ is it?* was nützt es?; *to no ~* vergeblich; **5.** *pl.* 🌾 *Am.* Ertrag *m;* **a·vail·a·bil·i·ty** [əˌveɪləˈbɪlətɪ] *s.* **1.** Vor'handensein *n;* **2.** Verfügbarkeit *f;* **3.** *Am.* verfügbare Per'son od. Sache; **4.** 🔧 Gültigkeit *f;* **a·vail·a·ble** [-ləbl] *adj.* □ **1.** verfügbar, erhältlich, vor'handen, vorrätig, zu haben(d): *make ~* bereitstellen, verfügbar machen; **2.** anwesend, abkömmlich; **3.** benutzbar; statthaft; **4.** 🔧 a) gültig, b) zulässig.

av·a·lanche ['ævəlɑːnʃ] *s.* La'wine *f, fig. a.* Unmenge *f.*

av·ant-garde [ˌævɑːˈɡɑːd] (*Fr.*) **I** *s. fig.* A'vantgarde *f;* **II** *adj.* avantgar'distisch; **,av·ant-'gard·ist(e)** [-dɪst] *s.* Avantgar'dist(in).

a·ve ['ɑːvɪ] **I** *int.* **1.** sei gegrüßt!; **2.** leb wohl!; **II** *s.* **3.** ♃ 'Ave(-Ma'ria) *n.*

a·venge [əˈvendʒ] *v/t.* **1.** rächen (*on, upon* an *dat.*): *~ one's friend* s-n Freund rächen; *~ o.s., be ~d* sich rächen; **2.** *et.* rächen, ahnden; **a'veng·er** [-dʒə] *s.* Rächer(in); **a'veng·ing** [-dʒɪŋ] *adj.* □ rächend, Rache...

av·e·nue ['ævənjuː] *s.* **1.** *mst fig.* Zugang *m,* Weg *m* (*to, of* zu): *~ to fame* Weg zum Ruhm; **2.** Al'lee *f;* **3.** a) Haupt-, Prachtstraße *f,* Ave'nue *f,* b) (Stadt)Straße *f.*

a·ver [əˈvɜː] *v/t.* **1.** behaupten, als Tatsache hinstellen (*that* dass); **2.** 🔧 beweisen.

av·er·age ['ævərɪdʒ] **I** *s.* **1.** 'Durchschnitt *m: on an* (*od. the*) *~* im Durchschnitt, durchschnittlich; *strike an ~* den Durchschnitt schätzen *od.* nehmen; **2.** ⚓, 🔧 Hava'rie *f,* Seeschaden *m: ~ adjuster* Dispacheur *m;* *general ~* große Havarie; *particular ~* besondere (*od.* partikulare) Havarie; *petty ~* kleine Havarie; *under ~* havariert; **3.** *Börse: Am.* 'Aktienindex *m;* **II** *adj.* □ **4.** 'durchschnittlich; Durchschnitts...: *~ access time Computer:* mittlere Zugriffszeit; *~ amount* Durchschnittsbetrag *m;* *~ Englishman* Durchschnittsengländer *m;* *~ useful life* durchschnittliche Nutzungsdauer; *be only ~* nur Durchschnitt sein; **III** *v/t.* **5.** den 'Durchschnitt schätzen (*at* auf *acc.*) *od.* nehmen von (*od. gen.*); **6.** † anteilsmäßig auf-, verteilen: *~ one's losses;* **7.** 'durchschnittlich betragen, haben, erreichen, verlangen, tun *etc.: I ~ £60 a week* ich verdiene durchschnittlich £ 60 die Woche; **IV** *v/i.* **8.** *~ out* sich im Durchschnitt belaufen auf (*acc.*).

a·ver·ment [əˈvɜːmənt] *s.* **1.** Behauptung *f;* **2.** 🔧 Beweisangebot *n,* Tatsachenbehauptung *f.*

a·verse [əˈvɜːs] *adj.* □ **1.** abgeneigt (*to, from dat., to inf.* zu *inf.*): *not ~ to a drink;* *~ from such methods;* **2.** zu'wider (*to dat.*); **a·ver·sion** [əˈvɜːʃn] *s.* **1.** (*to, for, from*) 'Widerwille *m,* Abneigung *f* (gegen), Abscheu *m* (vor *dat.*): *take an ~ (to)* e-e Abneigung fassen (gegen); **2.** Unlust *f,* Abgeneigtheit *f* (*to inf.* zu *inf.*); **3.** Gegenstand *m* des Abscheus: *beer is my pet* (*od. chief*) *~* Bier ist mir ein Gräuel.

a·vert [əˈvɜːt] *v/t.* **1.** abwenden, -kehren: *~ one's face;* **2.** *fig.* abwenden, -wehren, verhüten.

a·vi·ar·y ['eɪvjərɪ] *s.* Vogelhaus *n,* Voli'ere *f.*

a·vi·ate ['eɪvɪeɪt] *v/i.* ✈ fliegen; **a·vi·a·tion** [ˌeɪvɪˈeɪʃn] *s.* ✈ Luftfahrt *f,* Flugwesen *n,* Fliegen *n,* Flugsport *m: ~ industry* Flugzeugindustrie *f; Ministry of ⚕* Ministerium *n* für zivile Luftfahrt; **a·vi·a·tor** ['eɪvɪeɪtə] *s.* Flieger *m.*

a·vi·cul·ture ['eɪvɪkʌltʃə] *s.* Vogelzucht *f.*

av·id ['ævɪd] *adj.* □ (be)gierig (*of* nach, *for auf acc.*); *weitS.* leidenschaftlich, begeistert; **a·vid·i·ty** [əˈvɪdətɪ] *s.* Gier *f,* Begierde *f,* Habsucht *f.*

a·vi·on·ics [ˌeɪvɪˈɒnɪks] *s. pl. sg. konstr.* Avi'onik *f,* 'Flugelek,tronik *f.*

a·vi·ta·min·o·sis ['eɪˌvaɪtəmɪˈnəʊsɪs] *s.* Vita'minmangel(krankheit *f*) *m.*

av·o·ca·do [ˌævəʊˈkɑːdəʊ] *s.* ♀ Avo'cado(birne) *f.*

av·o·ca·tion [ˌævəʊˈkeɪʃn] *s. obs.* **1.** (Neben)Beschäftigung *f;* **2.** F (Haupt)Beruf *m.*

a·void [əˈvɔɪd] **1.** (ver)meiden, ausweichen (*dat.*), aus dem Wege gehen (*dat.*), *Pflicht etc.* um'gehen, *e-r Gefahr* entgehen: **~** *s.o.* j-n meiden; **~** *doing s.th.* es vermeiden, et. zu tun; **2.** ♻ a) aufheben, ungültig machen, b) anfechten; **a'void·a·ble** [-dəbl] *adj.* **1.** vermeidbar; **2.** ♻ a) annullierbar, b) anfechtbar; **a'void·ance** [-dəns] *s.* **1.** Vermeidung *f* (*Sache*), Meidung *f* (*Person*); Um'gehung *f*; **2.** ♻ a) Aufhebung *f*, Nichtigkeitserklärung *f*, b) Anfechtung *f*.

av·oir·du·pois [ˌævədə'pɔɪz] *s.* **1.** ✝ *a.* **~ weight** Handelsgewicht *n* (*1 Pfund = 16 Unzen*): **~** *pound* Handelspfund *n*; **2.** F ‚Lebendgewicht' *n e-r Person*.

a·vow [ə'vaʊ] *v/t.* (offen) bekennen, (ein)gestehen; rechtfertigen; anerkennen: **~** *o.s.* sich bekennen, sich erklären; **a·vow·al** [ə'vaʊəl] *s.* Bekenntnis *n*, Geständnis *n*, Erklärung *f*; **a·vowed** [ə'vaʊd] *adj.* □ erklärt: *his* **~** *principle*; *he is an* **~** *Jew* er bekennt sich offen zum Judentum; **a·vow·ed·ly** [ə'vaʊɪdlɪ] *adv.* eingestandenermaßen.

a·vun·cu·lar [ə'vʌŋkjʊlə] *adj.* **1.** Onkel...; **2.** *iro.* onkelhaft.

a·wait [ə'weɪt] *v/t.* **1.** erwarten (*acc.*), entgegensehen (*dat.*); **2.** *fig.* j-n erwarten: *a hearty welcome* **~***s you.*

a·wake [ə'weɪk] **I** *v/t.* [*irr.*] **1.** wecken; **2.** *fig.* erwecken, aufrütteln (*from* aus): **~** *s.o. to s.th.* j-m et. zum Bewusstsein bringen; **II** *v/i.* [*irr.*] **3.** auf-, erwachen; **4.** *fig. zu neuer Tätigkeit etc.* erwachen: **~** *to s.th.* sich e-r Sache bewusst werden; **III** *adj.* **5.** wach; **6.** *fig.* munter, wach(sam), auf der Hut: *be* **~** *to s.th.* sich e-r Sache bewusst sein; **a'wak·en** [-kən] → *awake* 1–4; **a'wak·en·ing** [-knɪŋ] *s.* Erwachen *n*: *a rude* **~** *fig.* ein unsanftes Erwachen.

a·ward [ə'wɔːd] **I** *v/t.* **1.** zuerkennen, zusprechen, ♻ *a.* (*durch Urteil od. Schiedsspruch*) zubilligen: *he was* **~***ed the prize* der Preis wurde ihm zuerkannt; **2.** gewähren, verleihen, zuwenden, zuteilen; **II** *s.* **3.** ♻ Urteil *n*, (Schieds)Spruch *m*; **4.** Belohnung *f*, Auszeichnung *f*, (*a. Film- etc.*)Preis *m*, (Ordens)Verleihung *f*, ✝ 'Prämie *f*; **5.** ✝ Zuschlag *m* (*auf ein Angebot*), (Auftrags)Vergabe *f*.

a·ware [ə'weə] *adj.* **1.** gewahr (*of gen., that* dass): *be* **~** sich bewusst sein, wissen, (er)kennen; *become* **~** *of s.th.* et. gewahr werden *od.* merken, sich e-r Sache bewusst werden; *not that I am* **~** *of*

nicht, dass ich wüsste; **2.** aufmerksam, ‚hellwach'; **a'ware·ness** [-nɪs] *s.* Bewusstsein *n*, Kenntnis *f*.

a·wash [ə'wɒʃ] *adv. u. adj.* ♻ **1.** über'flutet; **2.** über'füllt (*with* von).

a·way [ə'weɪ] **I** *adv.* **1.** weg, hin'weg, fort: *go* **~** weg-, fortgehen; **~** *with you!* fort mit dir!; **2.** (*from*) entfernt, (weit) weg (von), fern, abseits (*gen.*): **~** *from the question* nicht zur Frage *od.* Sache gehörend; **3.** fort, abwesend, verreist: **~** *from home* nicht zu Hause; **~** *on leave* auf Urlaub; **4.** *bei Verben oft* (drauf')los: *chatter* **~**; *work* **~**; **5.** *bsd. Am.* bei weitem: **~** *below the average*; **II** *adj.* **6.** *sport* Auswärts...: **~** *match* → **III** *s.* **7.** *sport* Auswärtsspiel *n.*

awe [ɔː] **I** *s.* **1.** Ehrfurcht *f*, (heilige) Scheu (*of* vor *dat.*): *hold s.o. in* **~** Ehrfurcht vor j-m haben; *stand in* **~** *of a)* e-e heilige Scheu haben *od.* sich fürchten vor (*dat.*), b) e-n gewaltigen Respekt haben vor (*dat.*); **2.** *fig.* Macht *f*, Maje'stät *f*; **II** *v/t.* **3.** (Ehr)Furcht einflößen (*dat.*), einschüchtern; **'awe-in·spir·ing** *adj.* Ehrfurcht gebietend, eindrucksvoll; **awe·some** ['ɔːsəm] *adj.* □ **1.** Furcht einflößend, schrecklich; **2.** → *awe-inspiring*; **3.** großartig, überwältigend, ‚gewaltig'; **4.** 'übergroß, gewaltig; **5.** F toll, irre; **'awe·struck** *adj.* von Ehrfurcht *od.* Scheu *od.* Schrecken ergriffen.

aw·ful ['ɔːfʊl] *adj.* □ **1.** → *awe-inspiring*; **2.** furchtbar, schrecklich; **3.** F ['ɔːfl] furchtbar: a) riesig, kolos'sal: *an* **~** *lot* e-e riesige Menge, b) scheußlich, schrecklich: *an* **~** *noise*; **aw·ful·ly** ['ɔːflɪ] *adv.* F furchtbar, schrecklich, äußerst: **~** *cold*; **~** *nice* furchtbar *od.* riesig nett; *I am* **~** *sorry* es tut mir schrecklich Leid; *thanks* **~***!* tausend Dank!; **'aw·ful·ness** [-nɪs] *s.* **1.** Schrecklichkeit *f*; **2.** Erhabenheit *f*.

a·while [ə'waɪl] *adv.* ein Weilchen.

awk·ward ['ɔːkwəd] *adj.* □ **1.** ungeschickt, unbeholfen, linkisch, tölpelhaft: *feel* **~** verlegen sein; → *squad* 1; **2.** peinlich, misslich, unangenehm: *an* **~** *silence* (*matter*); **3.** unhandlich, schwer zu behandeln, schwierig, lästig, ungünstig, ‚dumm': *an* **~** *door to open* e-e schwer zu öffnende Tür; *an* **~** *customer* ein unangenehmer Zeitgenosse; *it's a bit* **~** *on Sunday* am Sonntag passt es (mir) nicht so recht; **'awk·wardness** [-nɪs] *s.* **1.** Unge-

schicklichkeit *f*, Unbeholfenheit *f*; **2.** Peinlichkeit *f*, Unannehmlichkeit *f*; **3.** Lästigkeit *f*.

awl [ɔːl] *s.* ☉ Ahle *f*, Pfriem *m*.

awn [ɔːn] *s.* ♣ Granne *f*.

awn·ing ['ɔːnɪŋ] *s.* **1.** ♻ Sonnensegel *n*; **2.** Wagendecke *f*, Plane *f*; **3.** Mar'kise *f*; 'Baldachin *m*; Vorzelt *n*.

a·woke [ə'wəʊk] *pret. von* awake I u. II; **a'wok·en** *p.p. von* awake I u. II.

a·wry [ə'raɪ] *adv. u. adj.* **1.** schief, krumm: *look* **~** *fig.* schief *od.* scheel blicken; **3.** *fig.* verkehrt: *go* **~** fehlgehen (*Person*), schief gehen (*Sache*).

ax, *mst* **axe** [æks] **I** *s.* **1.** Axt *f*, Beil *n*: *have an* **~** *to grind* eigennützige Zwecke verfolgen, es auf et. abgesehen haben; **2.** F *fig.* a) rücksichtslose Sparmaßnahme, b) Abbau *m*, Entlassung *f*: *get the* **~** entlassen werden, ‚rausfliegen'; **3.** ♪ *Am. sl.* Instru'ment *n*; **II** *v/t.* **4.** F *fig.* drastisch kürzen *od.* zs.-streichen; *Beamte etc.* abbauen, *Leute* entlassen, ‚feuern'.

ax·i·al ['æksɪəl] *adj.* □ ☉ Achsen..., axi'al.

ax·il ['æksɪl] *s.* ♣ Blattachsel *f*.

ax·i·om ['æksɪəm] *s.* Ax'iom *n*, allgemein anerkannter Grundsatz: **~** *of law* Rechtsgrundsatz; **ax·i·o·mat·ic** [ˌæksɪəʊ'mætɪk] *adj.* (□ **~ally**) axio'matisch, 'unum,stößlich, selbstverständlich.

ax·is ['æksɪs] *pl.* **'ax·es** [-siːz] *s.* **1.** A, ☉, *phys.* Achse *f*, 'Mittel,linie *f*: **~** *of the earth* Erdachse; **2.** *pol.* Achse *f*: *the* ☽ die Achse Berlin-Rom-Tokio (*vor dem u. im 2. Weltkrieg*); *the* ☽ *powers* die Achsenmächte.

ax·le ['æksl] *s.* ☉ **1.** *a.* **~** *tree* (Rad-) Achse *f*, Welle *f*; **2.** Angel(zapfen *m*) *f*.

ay → *aye.*

a·yah ['aɪə] *s. Brit. Ind.* 'Aja *f*, indisches Kindermädchen.

aye [aɪ] **I** *int. bsd.* ♻ *u. parl.* ja: **~**, **~**, *Sir!* zu Befehl!; **II** *s. parl.* Ja *n*, Jastimme *f*: *the* **~***s have it* die Mehrheit ist dafür.

a·za·le·a [ə'zeɪljə] *s.* ♣ Aza'lee *f*.

az·i·muth ['æzɪməθ] *s. ast.* Azi'mut *m*, Scheitelkreis *m*.

a·zo·ic [ə'zəʊɪk] *adj. geol.* a'zoisch (*ohne Lebewesen*): *the* **~** *age.*

Az·tec ['æztek] *s.* Az'teke *m*.

az·ure ['æʒə] **I** *adj.* a'zur-, himmelblau; **II** *s.* a) A'zur(blau *n*) *m*, b) *poet.* das blaue Himmelszelt.

B, b [biː] *s.* **1.** B *n*, b *n* (*Buchstabe*); **2.** ♪
H *n*, h *n* (*Note*): **B flat** B *n*, b *n*; **B
sharp** His *n*, his *n*; **3.** *ped. Am.* Zwei *f*
(*Note*); **4. B flat** *Brit. sl.* Wanze *f*.
baa [baː] I *s.* Blöken *n*; II *v/i.* blöken; III
int. bäh!
Ba·al ['beɪəl] I *npr. bibl. Gott* Baal *m*; II
s. Abgott *m*, Götze *m*; **'Ba·al·ism**
[-lɪzəm] *s.* Götzendienst *m*.
baas [baːs] *s.* S. *Afr.* Herr *m*.
Bab·bitt ['bæbɪt] *s.* **1.** *Am.* (selbstzufrie-
dener) Spießer; **2.** ⚙ (*metal*) ⊚ 'Lager-
weiß,tall *n*.
bab·ble ['bæbl] I *v/t. u. v/i.* **1.** stammeln;
plappern, schwatzen; nachschwatzen,
ausplaudern; **2.** plätschern, murmeln
(*Bach*); II *s.* **3.** Geplapper *n*, Geschwätz *n*; **'bab·bler** [-lə] *s.* **1.** Schwät-
zer(in); **2.** *orn.* e-e Drossel *f*.
babe [beɪb] *s.* **1.** kleines Kind, Baby *n*,
fig. a. Na'ivling *m*; → **arm¹** 1; **2.** *Am.
sl.* ,Puppe' *f* (*Mädchen*).
Ba·bel ['beɪbl] I *npr. bibl.* Babel *n*; II *s.*
2 *fig.* Babel *n*, Wirrwarr *m*, Stimmengewirr *n*.
ba·boo ['baːbuː] *s. Brit.-Ind.* **1.** Herr *m*
(*bei den Hindus*); **2.** Inder *m* mit oberflächlicher engl. Bildung.
ba·boon [bə'buːn] *s. zo.* 'Pavian *m*.
ba·by ['beɪbɪ] I *s.* **1.** Baby *n*: a) Säugling
m, b) jüngstes Kind: **be left holding
the ~** F der Dumme sein, die Sache am
Hals haben; **2.** a) ,Kindskopf' *m*, b)
,Heulsuse' *f*; **3.** *sl.* ,Schatz' *m*, ,Kind-
chen' *n* (*Mädchen*); **4.** *sl.* Sache *f*:
it's your ~; II *adj.* **5.** Säuglings...,
Baby..., Kinder...; **6.** kindlich, kindisch:
plead the ~ act *Am.* F auf Unreife
plädieren; **7.** klein; **~ bond** *s.* ✝ *Am.*
BabyBond *m*, Kleinschuldverschrei-
bung *f*; **~ boom·er gen·er·a·tion** *s.*
geburtenstarke Jahrgänge *pl.*; **~ bot·tle**
s. (Saug)Flasche *f*; **~ car** *s.* Klein(st)-
wagen *m*; **~ car·riage** *s. Am.* Kinderwagen *m*; **~ farm·er** *s. mst contp.*
Frau, die gewerbsmäßig Kinder in
Pflege nimmt; **~ grand** *s.* ♪ Stutzflügel
m.
ba·by·hood ['beɪbɪhʊd] *s.* Säuglingsalter
n; **'ba·by·ish** [-ɪɪʃ] *adj.* **1.** kindlich; **2.**
kindisch.
Bab·y·lon ['bæbɪlən] I *npr.* 'Babylon *n*;
II *s. fig.* (Sünden)Babel *n*; **Bab·y·lo-
ni·an** [,bæbɪ'ləʊnjən] I *adj.* baby'lonisch; II *s.* Baby'lonier(in).
'ba·by|-,mind·er *s. Brit.* Tagesmutter *f*;
'~-sit *v/i.* [*irr.* → *sit*] babysitten; **'~-
,sit·ter** *s.* Babysitter *m*; **~ snatch·er** *s.*
ältere Person (*Mann od. Frau*), die mit
einem blutjungen Mädchen *od.* Mann
ein Verhältnis hat: **I'm no ~** ich vergreif
mich doch nicht an kleinen Kindern!; **~
spot** *s.* Baby-Spot *m* (*kleiner Suchscheinwerfer*); **~ talk** *s.* Babysprache *f*.
bac·ca·lau·re·ate [,bækə'lɔːrɪət] *s. univ.*
Bakkalaure'at *n*; **2.** *a.* **~ sermon** *Am.*
Predigt *f* an die promovierten Stu-
'denten.
bac·ca·ra(t) ['bækəraː] *s.* 'Bakkarat *n*

(*Glücksspiel*).
bac·cha·nal ['bækənl] I *s.* **1.** Bac'chant
(-in); **2.** ausgelassener *od.* trunkener
Zecher; **3.** *a. pl.* Baccha'nal *n* (*wüstes
Gelage*); II *adj.* **4.** 'bacchisch; **5.** bac-
'chantisch; **bac·cha·na·li·a** [,bækə'neɪl-
jə] → **bacchanal** 3; **bac·cha·na·li·an**
[,bækə'neɪljən] I *adj.* bac'chantisch,
ausschweifend; II *s.* Bac'chant(in);
bac·chant ['bækənt] I *s.* Bac'chant *m*;
fig. wüster Trinker *od.* Schwelger; II
adj. bac'chantisch; **bac·chan·te** [bə-
'kæntɪ] *s.* Bac'chantin *f*; **bac·chic** ['bæ-
kɪk] → **bacchanal** 4 u. 5.
bac·cy ['bækɪ] *s.* F *abbr. für* **tobacco**.
bach [bætʃ] F I *s.* → **bachelor** 1; II *v/i.
mst ~ it* ein Strohwitwerdasein führen.
bach·e·lor ['bætʃələ] *s.* **1.** Junggeselle
m; *in Urkunden:* ledig (*dem Namen
nachgestellt*); **2.** *univ.* Bakka'laureus *m*
(*Grad*): **2 of Arts** (*abbr.* **B.A.**) Bakka-
laureus der philosophischen Fakultät; **2
of Science** (*abbr.* **B.Sc.**) Bakkalau-
reus der Naturwissenschaften; **~ girl** *s.*
Junggesellin *f*.
bach·e·lor·hood ['bætʃələhʊd] *s.* **1.**
Junggesellenstand *m*; **2.** *univ.* Bakkalaure'at *n*.
ba·cil·lar·y [bə'sɪlərɪ] *adj.* **1.** stäbchen-
förmig; **2.** 🦠 Bazillen...; **ba·cil·lus**
[bə'sɪləs] *pl.* **-li** [-laɪ] *s.* 🦠 Ba'zillus *m* (*a.
fig.*).
back¹ [bæk] I *s.* **1.** Rücken *m* (*Mensch,
Tier*); **2.** 'Hinter-, Rückseite *f* (*Kopf,
Haus, Tür, Bild, Brief, Kleid etc*);
(Rücken)Lehne *f* (*Stuhl*); **3.** *untere od.
abgekehrte Seite:* (*Hand-, Buch-, Messer*)Rücken *m*, 'Unterseite *f* (*Blatt*), linke Seite (*Stoff*), Kehrseite *f* (*Münze*),
Oberteil *m*, *n* (*Bürste*); → **beyond** 6; **4.**
rückwärtiger od. entfernt gelegener Teil:
hinterer Teil (*Mund, Schrank, Wald
etc*), 'Hintergrund *m*; Rücksitz *m* (*Wagen*); **5.** Rumpf *m* (*Schiff*); **6. the 2s**
die Parkanlagen *pl.* hinter den Colleges
in Cambridge; **7.** *sport* Verteidiger *m*;
Besondere Redewendungen:
(**at the**) **~ of** hinter (*dat.*), hinten in
(*dat.*); **be at the ~ of s.th.** *fig.* hinter
e-r Sache stecken; **~ to front** die Rückseite nach vorn, falsch herum; **have
s.th. at the ~ of one's mind** a) insgeheim an et. denken, b) sich dunkel an
et. erinnern; **turn one's ~ on** *fig.* j-m
den Rücken kehren, *et.* aufgeben; **behind s.o.'s ~** hinter j-s Rücken; **on
one's ~** a) auf dem Körper (*Kleidungsstück*), b) bettlägerig, c) am Boden,
hilflos, verloren; **have one's ~ to the
wall** mit dem Rücken zur Wand stehen;
break s.o.'s ~ a) j-m das Kreuz brechen (*a. fig.*), b) j-n ,fertig machen' *od.*
zugrunde richten; **break the ~ of s.th.**
das Schwierigste e-r Sache hinter sich
bringen; **put one's ~ into s.th.** sich bei
e-r Sache ins Zeug legen, sich in et.
hineinknien; **put s.o.'s ~ up** j-n ,auf die
Palme bringen';
II *adj.* **8.** rückwärtig, letzt, hinter,

Rück..., Hinter..., Nach...: *the ~ left-
-hand corner* die hintere linke Ecke;
9. rückläufig; **10.** rückständig (*Zahlung*); **11.** zu'rückliegend, alt (*Zeitung
etc.*); **12.** fern, abgelegen; *fig.* finster;
III *adv.* **13.** zu'rück, rückwärts; zurückliegend; (wieder) zurück: **he is ~
again** er ist wieder da; **he is ~ home** er
ist wieder zu Hause; **~ home** *Am.* bei
uns (zu Lande); **~ and forth** hin und
her; **14.** zu'rück, 'vorher: **20 years ~**
vor 20 Jahren; **~ in 1900** (schon) im
Jahre 1900; IV *v/t.* **15.** Buch mit e-m
Rücken *od. Stuhl* mit e-r Lehne *od.*
Rückenverstärkung versehen; **16.** hinten grenzen an (*acc.*), den Hintergrund
e-r Sache bilden; **17.** *a.* **~ up** j-m den
Rücken decken *od.* stärken, j-n unter-
'stützen, eintreten für; **18.** *a.* **~ up** zu-
'rückbewegen; *Wagen, Pferd, Maschine*
rückwärts fahren *od.* laufen lassen: **~
one's car up** mit dem Auto zurückstoßen; **~ a car out of the garage** e-n
Wagen rückwärts aus der Garage fahren; **~ water** (*od. the oars*) rückwärts
rudern; **~ed up** (**with traffic**) *Am.* verstopft (*Straße*); **19.** auf der Rückseite
beschreiben; *Wechsel* verantwortlich
gegenzeichnen, avalieren; **20.** wetten
od. setzen auf (*acc.*); V *v/i.* **21.** *a.* **~ up**
sich rückwärts bewegen, zu'rückgehen
od. -fahren; **22.** **~ and fill** a) ⚓ lavieren,
b) *Am.* F unschlüssig sein; **~ down
(from)**, **~ out** (**of**) *v/i.* zu'rücktreten
od. sich zu'rückziehen (von), aufgeben
(*acc.*); F sich drücken (vor *dat.*), abspringen (von), ,aussteigen' (bei), kneifen (vor *dat.*); klein beigeben, ,den
Schwanz einziehen'.
back² [bæk] *s.* ⊚, *Brauerei, Färberei etc.*
Bottich *m*.
'back|·ache *s.* Rückenschmerzen *pl.*;
~ al·ley *s. Am.* finsteres Seitengäss-
chen; **,~'bench·er** *s. parl.* 'Hinter-
bänkler *m*; **'~·bend** *s. sport* Brücke *f*
(aus dem Stand); **'~·bite** *v/t. u. v/i.* [*irr.*
→ *bite*] j-n verleumden; **'~,bit·er** *s.*
Verleumder (-in); **'~·bone** *s.* **1.** Rückgrat *n*: **to the ~** bis auf die Knochen,
ganz u. gar; **2.** *fig.* Rückgrat *n*: a)
(Cha'rakter)Stärke *f*, Mut *m*, b) Hauptstütze *f*; **'~,break·ing** *adj.* ,mörde-
risch', zermürbend: **a ~ job**; **'~,burn-
er** *adj.* F nebensächlich, zweitrangig;
'~·chat *s. sl.* **1.** freche Antwort(en *pl.*);
2. *Brit.* schlagfertiges Hin und Her;
~·cloth → **backdrop**; **'~,cou·pled** *adj.*
🔌 rückgekoppelt; **,~'date** *v/t.* **1.** zu-
'rückdatieren; **2.** rückwirkend in Kraft
setzen; **~ door** *s.* 'Hintertür *f* (*a. fig.
Ausweg*); **,~'door** *adj.* heimlich, geheim; **'~·down** *s. Am.* F ,Rückzieher'
m; **'~·drop** *s. thea.* Prospekt *m*;
2. 'Hintergrund *m*, 'Folie *f*.
backed [bækt] *adj.* **1.** mit Rücken, Lehne *etc.* (versehen); **2.** gefüttert: **a curtain ~ with satin**; **3.** *in Zssgn:*
straight-~ mit geradem Rücken, ge-
radlehnig.

back·er ['bækə] s. **1.** Unter'stützer(in), Helfer(in), Förderer m; **2.** ✝ a) (Wechsel)Bürge m, b) 'Hintermann m, Geldgeber m; **3.** Wetter(in).

,**back**|'**fire I** v/i. **1.** mot. früh-, fehlzünden; **2.** fig. fehlschlagen, ,ins Auge gehen': *the plan ~d* der Schuss ging nach hinten los; **II** s. **3.** ⊙ Früh-, Fehlzündung f; ~ **for·ma·tion** s. ling. Rückbildung f; ~'**gam·mon** s. Back'gammon n, Puffspiel n; '~·**ground** s. **1.** 'Hintergrund m: ~ **noise** Nebengeräusch n; *keep in the ~* im Hintergrund bleiben; **2.** fig. 'Hintergrund m, 'Hintergründe pl., 'Umstände pl.; 'Umwelt f, Mili'eu n; 'Herkunft f; Werdegang m, Vorgeschichte f; Bildung f, Erfahrung f, Wissen n: *educational ~* Vorbildung f; '~·**hand I** s. **1.** nach links geneigte Handschrift; **2.** sport Rückhand(schlag m) f; **II** adj. **3.** sport Rückhand...: ~ **stroke** Rückhandschlag m; ,~'**hand·ed** adj. **1.** nach links geneigt (Schrift); **2.** Rückhand...; **3.** zweideutig; unredlich, 'indi,rekt; '~·**hand·er** s. **1.** a) → *backhand* 2, b) Schlag m mit dem Handrücken; **2.** F 'indi,rekter Angriff; **3.** F ,Schmiergeld' n.

back·ing ['bækɪŋ] s. **1.** Unter'stützung f, Hilfe f; Beifall m; Unter'stützer pl., 'Hintermänner pl.; **2.** rückwärtige Verstärkung; (Rock- etc.) Futter n; Stützung f; **3.** ✝ a) Wechselbürgschaft f, b) Gegenzeichnen n, c) Deckung f.

'**back**|·**lash** s. **1.** ⊙ toter Gang, Flankenspiel n; **2.** (heftige) Reakti'on, Rückwirkung f; '~·**log** s. **1.** großes Scheit hinten im Ka'min; **2.** (Arbeits-, Auftrags- etc.)Rückstand m, 'Überhang m (of an dat.): ~ **demand** Nachholbedarf m; **3.** Rücklage f, Re'serve f (of an dat., von); ~ **num·ber** s. **1.** alte Nummer e-r Zeitung etc.; **2.** fig. rückständige od. altmodische Per'son od. Sache; '~·**pack I** s. Rucksack m, Back Pack m; **II** v/i. ~ **it** F (mit dem Rucksack) trampen; '~·**pack·er** s. Rucksacktourist m; '~·**pack·ing** s. Rucksacktourismus m; ~ **pay** s. Lohn-, Gehaltsnachzahlung f; ,~'**ped·al** v/i. **1.** rückwärts treten (Radfahrer); **2.** F fig. e-n ,Rückzieher' machen; '~·**ped·al brake** s. Rücktrittbremse f; '~·**rest** s. Rückenstütze f; ~ **room** s. 'Hinterzimmer n; '~·**-room boy** s. Brit. F Wissenschaftler, der an Ge'heimpro,jekten arbeitet; ~ **sal·a·ry** → *back pay*; '~,**scratch·ing** s. F gegenseitige Unter'stützung; ~ **seat** s. Rücksitz m: *back-seat driver* fig. Besserwisser(in); *take a ~* fig. in den Hintergrund treten.

back·sheesh → *baksheesh*.

,**back**|'**side** s. **1.** F Hintern m; **2.** mst *back side* Kehr-, Rückseite f, hintere od. linke Seite; '~·**sight** s. **1.** ⊙ Visier n; **2.** ✗ (Visier)Kimme f; ~ **slang** s. 'Umkehrung f der Wörter (beim Sprechen); '~,**slap·per** s. Am. jovi'aler od. plumpvertraulicher Mensch; ,~'**slide** v/i. [irr. → *slide*] **1.** rückfällig werden; **2.** auf die schiefe Bahn geraten, abtrünnig werden; '~,**slid·er** s. Rückfällige(r m) f; '~·**space con·trol** s. Rückholtaste f (Tonbandgerät); '~·**space key** s. Computer: Rücktaste f; ,~'**spac·er** s. Rücktaste f (Schreibmaschine); ~·**stage I** s. ['bæksteɪdʒ] **1.** thea. Garde'robenräume pl. u. Bühne f hinter dem Vorhang; **II** adv. [,bæk'steɪdʒ] **2.** (hinten) auf der Bühne; **3.** hinter dem od. die Ku'lissen, hinter den od. die Ku'lissen (a. fig.); ,~'**stairs** s. 'Hintertreppe f: ~ **talk** (bös-

artige) Anspielungen pl.; ~ **influence** Protektion f; '~·**stop** s. **1.** Kricket: Feldspieler m, Fänger m; **2.** Baseball: Gitter n (hinter dem Fänger); **3.** Am. Schießstand: Kugelfang m; '~·**stroke** s. sport **1.** Rückschlag m des Balls; **2.** Rückenschwimmen n; '~·**swept** adj. **1.** ⊙, ✈ nach hinten verjüngt, pfeilförmig; **2.** zu'rückgekämmt (Haar); ~ **talk** s. sl. unverschämte Antwort(en pl.); '~·**track** v/i. Am. **1.** den'selben Weg zu'rückgehen; **2.** fig. a) → *back down* (from), b) e-e Kehrtwendung machen; '~·**up I** s. **1.** Unter'stützung f; **2.** → *backing* 2; **3.** mot. Am. (Rück)Stau m; **4.** fig. ,Rückzieher' m; **5.** ⊙ Ersatzgerät n; **6.** Computer: a) Datenströmung f: ~ **disk** 'Sicherungsdis,kette f, b) → *back-up copy*; **II** adj. **7.** Unterstützungs..., Hilfs..., ⊙ Ersatz..., Reserve...; ~ **copy** Sicherungskopie f.

back·ward ['bækwəd] **I** adj. **1.** rückwärts gerichtet, Rück(wärts)...; 'umgekehrt; **2.** hinten gelegen, Hinter...; **3.** langsam, schwerfällig, schleppend; **4.** zu'rückhaltend, schüchtern; **5.** in der Entwicklung zu'rückgeblieben (Kind etc.), rückständig (Land, Arbeit); **6.** vergangen; **II** adv. **7.** a. backwards [-dz] rückwärts, zu'rück: ~ **and forwards** vor u. zurück; **8.** fig. 'umgekehrt; zum Schlechten; **back·ward·a·tion** [,bækwə'deɪʃn] s. Brit. ✝ De'port m, Kursabschlag m; '**back·ward·ness** [-nɪs] s. **1.** Rückständigkeit f; **2.** Langsamkeit f, Trägheit f; **3.** Wider'streben n; '**back·wards** [-dz] → *backward* 7.

'**back**|·**wash** s. **1.** Rückströmung f, Kielwasser n; **2.** fig. Nachwirkung f; '~,**wa·ter** s. **1.** totes Wasser, Stauwasser n; **2.** Seitenarm m e-s Flusses; **3.** fig. a) tiefste Provinz, (kultu'relles) Notstandsgebiet, b) Rückständigkeit f, Stagnati'on f; '~·**woods I** s. pl. **1.** 'Hinterwälder pl., abgelegene Wälder; fig. (tiefste) Pro'vinz; **II** adj. **2.** 'hinterwäldlerisch (a. fig.), Provinz...; **3.** fig. rückständig; '~·**woods·man** [-mən] s. [irr.] **1.** 'Hinterwäldler m (a. fig.); **2.** Brit. parl. Mitglied n des Oberhauses, das selten erscheint; ~ **yard** s. 'Hinterhof m; Am. a. Garten m hinter dem Haus.

ba·con ['beɪkən] s. Speck m: ~ **and eggs** Speck mit (Spiegel)Ei; *he brought home the ~* F er hat es geschafft; *save one's ~* F a) mit heiler Haut davonkommen, b) s-e Haut retten.

Ba·co·ni·an [beɪ'kəʊnjən] adj. Sir Francis Bacon betreffend; ~ **the·o·ry** s. 'Bacon-Theo,rie f (dass Francis Bacon Shakespeares Werke verfasst habe).

bac·te·ri·a [bæk'tɪərɪə] s. pl. Bak'terien pl.; **bac'te·ri·al** [-əl] adj. Bakterien...; **bac·te·ri·cid·al** [bæk,tɪərɪ'saɪdl] adj. bakteri'zid, Bak'terien tötend; **bac·te·ri·cide** [bæk'tɪərɪsaɪd] s. Bakteri'zid n; **bac·te·ri·o·log·i·cal** [bæk,tɪərɪə'lɒdʒɪkl] adj. □ bakterio'logisch; **bac·te·ri·ol·o·gist** [bæk,tɪərɪ'ɒlədʒɪst] s. Bakterio'loge m; **bac·te·ri·ol·o·gy** [bæk,tɪərɪ'ɒlədʒɪ] s. Bak'terienkunde f; **bac·te·ri·um** [bæk'tɪərɪəm] sg. von *bacteria*.

Bac·tri·an cam·el ['bæktrɪən] s. zo. Trampeltier n, zweihöckriges Ka'mel.

bad [bæd] adj. □ → *badly*; **1.** allg. schlecht, schlimm: ~ **manners** schlechte Manieren; *from ~ to worse* immer schlimmer; **2.** böse, ungezogen: *a ~ boy*; *a ~ lot* F ein schlimmes Pack; **3.** lasterhaft, schlecht: *a ~ woman*; **4.** anstößig, hässlich: *a ~ word*; ~ **language**

a) hässliche Ausdrücke pl., b) lästerliche Reden pl.; **5.** unbefriedigend, ungünstig, schlecht: ~ **lighting** schlechte Beleuchtung; ~ **name** schlechter Ruf; *in ~ health* kränkelnd; *his ~ German* sein schlechtes Deutsch; *he is ~ at mathematics* er ist in Mathematik schwach; ~ **debts** ✝ zweifelhafte Forderungen; ~ **debt losses** ✝ Forderungsausfälle pl.; ~ **title** mangelhafter Rechtstitel; **6.** unangenehm, schlecht: *a ~ smell*; ~ **news**; *(that's) too ~!* F (das ist doch) zu dumm od. schade!; *not (half od. too) ~* (gar) nicht übel; **7.** schädlich: ~ **for the eyes**; ~ **for you**; **8.** schlecht, verdorben (Fleisch, Ei etc.): *go ~* schlecht werden; **9.** ungültig, falsch (Münze etc.); **10.** unwohl, krank: *he is (od. feels) ~*; *a ~ finger* ein schlimmer od. böser Finger; *he is in a ~ way* es geht ihm nicht gut, er ist schlecht d(a)ran; **11.** heftig, schlimm, arg: *a ~ cold*; *a ~ crime* ein schweres Verbrechen; **II** s. **12.** das Schlechte: *go to the ~* F auf die schiefe Bahn geraten; *~ worse* 4; **13.** ✝ 'Defizit n, Verlust m: *be £5 to the ~* £5 Defizit haben; **14.** *be in ~ with s.o.* Am. F bei j-m in Ungnade sein; **III** adv. **15.** → *badly*.

bad·die ['bædɪ] s. F Film etc.: Bösewicht m, Schurke m.

bad·dish ['bædɪʃ] adj. ziemlich schlecht.

bad·dy → *baddie*.

bade [beɪd] pret. von *bid* 7, 8, 9.

badge [bædʒ] s. Ab-, Kennzeichen n (a. fig.); (Dienst- etc.)Marke f; ✗ (Ehren-)Spange f; fig. Merkmal n, Stempel m.

badg·er ['bædʒə] **I** s. **1.** zo. Dachs m; **2.** Am. F Bewohner(in) von Wis'consin; **II** v/t. **3.** hetzen; **4.** fig. plagen, ,piesacken', j-m zusetzen.

bad·i·nage ['bædɪnɑːʒ] s. Necke'rei f, Schäke'rei f.

'**bad·lands** s. pl. Am. Ödland n.

bad·ly ['bædlɪ] adv. **1.** schlecht, schlimm: *he is ~* (Am. a. *bad*) *off* es geht ihm schlecht (mst finanziell); *do (od. come off) ~* schlecht fahren (in bei, mit); *be in ~ with (od. over)* Am. F über Kreuz stehen mit; *feel ~ (Am. a. bad) (about it)* ein ,mieses' Gefühl haben (deswegen); **2.** dringend, heftig, sehr: ~ **needed** dringend nötig; ~ **wounded** schwer verwundet.

bad·min·ton ['bædmɪntən] s. **1.** sport Badminton n; **2.** Federballspiel n.

'**bad·mouth** v/t. F j-n übel beschimpfen.

bad·ness ['bædnɪs] s. **1.** schlechte Beschaffenheit f; **2.** Schlechtigkeit f, Verderbtheit f; Bösartigkeit f.

,**bad-'tem·pered** adj. schlecht gelaunt, übellaunig.

Bae·de·ker ['beɪdɪkə] s. Baedeker m, Reiseführer m; weitS. Handbuch n.

baf·fle ['bæfl] v/t. **1.** j-n verwirren, verblüffen, narren, täuschen, j-m ein Rätsel aufgeben: *be ~d* vor e-m Rätsel stehen; **2.** Plan etc. durch'kreuzen, unmöglich machen: *it ~s description* es spottet jeder Beschreibung; ~ **paint** s. ✗ Tarnungsanstrich m; ~ **plate** s. Ablenk-, Prallplatte f; Schlingerwand f (im Kraftstoffbehälter).

baf·fling ['bæflɪŋ] adj. □ **1.** verwirrend, vertrackt, rätselhaft; **2.** vereitelnd, hinderlich; **3.** 'umspringend (Wind).

bag [bæg] s. **1.** Sack m, Beutel m, Tüte f, (Schul-, Hand- etc.)Tasche f; engS. a) Reisetasche f, b) Geldbeutel m: *mixed ~* fig. Sammelsurium n; ~ **and baggage** (mit) Sack u. Pack, mit allem Drum und Dran; *the whole ~ of tricks* alles, der ganze Krempel; *give s.o. the*

B

~ F j-m den Laufpass geben; *be left holding the* ~ *Am.* F die Sache ausbaden müssen; *that's (just) my* ~ *sl.* das ist genau mein Fall; *that's not my* ~ *sl.* das ist nicht ‚mein Bier'; *that's in the* ~ das haben wir (so gut wie) sicher; → *bone* 1; **2.** *hunt.* a) Jagdtasche *f,* b) Jagdbeute *f,* Strecke *f;* **3.** (*pair of*) ~**s** F Hose *f;* **4.** (*old*) ~ *sl.* Weibsbild *n,* ‚alte Ziege'; **II** *v/t.* **5.** in e-n Sack *etc.* tun, ☺ einsacken, abfüllen; **6.** *hunt.* zur Strecke bringen, fangen (*a. fig.*); **7.** *sl.* a) sich *et.* schnappen, b) ‚klauen', c) j-n ‚in die Tasche stecken', besiegen; **8.** bauschen; **III** *v/i.* **9.** sich bauschen.

bag·a·telle [ˌbægəˈtel] *s.* **1.** Baga'telle *f* (*a. ♪*), Kleinigkeit *f;* **2.** 'Tivolispiel *n.*

bag·gage ['bægɪdʒ] *s.* **1.** *bsd. Am.* (Reise)Gepäck *n;* **2.** ✕ Ba'gage *f,* Gepäck *n,* Tross *m;* **3.** V ‚Flittchen' *n;* **4.** F ‚Fratz' *m,* (kleiner) Racker (*Mädchen*); **~ al·low·ance** *s.* ✈ Freigepäck *n;* **~ car** *s. Am.* Gepäckwagen *m;* **~ check** *s. Am.* Gepäckschein *m;* **~ claim** *s.* ✈ Gepäckausgabe *f;* **~ hold** *s. Am.* Gepäckraum *m;* **~ in·sur·ance** *s. Am.* (Reise)Gepäckversicherung *f.*

bag·ging ['bægɪŋ] **I** *s.* **1.** Sack-, Packleinwand *f;* **II** *adj.* **2.** sich bauschend; **3.** → *bag·gy* ['bægɪ] *adj.* bauschig, zu weit, sackartig herabhängend; ausgebeult (*Hose*).

'bag·pipe *s. ♪* Dudelsack(pfeife *f*) *m;* **'~·pip·er** *s.* Dudelsackpfeifer *m;* **'~-·snatch·er** *s.* Handtaschenräuber *m.*

bah [bɑ(ː)] *int.* pah! (*Verachtung*).

bail¹ [beɪl] ⚖ **I** *s.* (*nur sg.*) **1.** a) Bürge *m:* *find* ~ sich e-n Bürgen verschaffen, b) Bürgschaft *f,* Sicherheitsleistung *f,* Kauti'on *f:* *admit to* ~ → 4; *allow* (*od. grant*) ~ a) → 4, b) Kaution zulassen; *be out on* ~ gegen Kaution auf freiem Fuß sein; *forfeit one's* ~ (*bsd. wegen Nichterscheinens*) die Kaution verlieren; *go* (*od. stand*) ~ *for s.o.* für j-n Sicherheit leisten *od.* Kaution stellen; *jump* ~ *Am.* F die Kaution ‚sausen lassen' (*u. verschwinden*); *release on* ~ → 4; *surrender to* (*od. save*) one's ~ vor Gericht erscheinen; **2.** a) *release on* ~ Freilassung *f* gegen Kauti'on *od.* Sicherheitsleistung *f;* **II** *v/t.* **3.** *mst* ~ *out* j-s Freilassung gegen Kauti'on erwirken; **4.** *j-n* gegen Kauti'on freilassen; **5.** *j-n* gegen Kauti'on freilassen; *Güter* (*zur treuhänderischen Verwahrung*) übergeben (*to s.o.* j-m); **6.** ~ *out fig.* j-n retten, j-m her'aushelfen (*of aus dat.*).

bail² [beɪl] **I** *v/t.* ⚓ ausschöpfen: ~ *out water* (*a boat*); **II** *v/i.* ~ *out* ‚aussteigen': a) ✈ mit dem Fallschirm abspringen, b) *fig.* nicht mehr mitmachen.

bail³ [beɪl] *s.* Bügel *m,* Henkel *m.*

bail·a·ble ['beɪləbl] *adj.* ⚖ kauti'onsfähig.

bail·ee [ˌbeɪˈliː] *s.* ⚖ Verwahrer *m* (*e-r beweglichen Sache*), *z.B.* Spedi'teur *m.*

bai·ley ['beɪlɪ] *s. hist.* Außenmauer *f,* Außenhof *m e-r Burg: Old* ♀ *Hauptkriminalgericht in London.*

bail·iff ['beɪlɪf] *s.* **1.** ⚖ a) Gerichtsvollzieher *m,* b) Gerichtsdiener *m,* c) *Am.* Jus'tizwachtmeister *m;* **2.** *bsd. Brit.* (Guts)Verwalter *m;* **3.** *hist. Brit.* königlicher Beamter.

bail·i·wick ['beɪlɪwɪk] *s.* ⚖ Amtsbezirk *m* e-s *bailiff.*

bail·ment ['beɪlmənt] *s.* ⚖ (vertragliche) Hinter'legung (*e-r beweglichen Sache*), Verwahrung(svertrag *m*) *f.*

bail·or ['beɪlə] *s.* ⚖ Hinter'leger *m.*

bairn [beən] *s. Scot.* Kind *n.*

bait [beɪt] **I** *s.* **1.** Köder *m;* *fig. a.* Lo-

ckung *f,* Reiz *m:* *take* (*od. rise to*) *the* ~ anbeißen, den Köder schlucken, *fig. a.* auf den Leim gehen; **2.** Rast *f,* Imbiss *m;* **3.** Füttern *n* (*Pferde*); **II** *v/t.* **4.** mit Köder versehen; **5.** *fig.* ködern, (an-)locken; **6.** *obs. Pferde unterwegs* füttern; **7.** mit Hunden hetzen; **8.** *fig.* j-n reizen, quälen, peinigen; **'bait·er** [-tə] *s.* Hetzer *m,* Quäler *m;* **'bait·ing** [-tɪŋ] *s.* **1.** *fig.* Hetze *f,* Quäle'rei *f;* **2.** Rast *f.*

baize [beɪz] *s.* Boi *m,* *mst grüner* Fries (*Wollstoff für Tischüberzug*).

bake [beɪk] **I** *v/t.* **1.** backen, im (Back-)Ofen braten: ~*d potatoes* Folien-, Ofenkartoffeln *pl.;* **2.** a) dörren, austrocknen, härten: *sun-baked ground,* b) *Ziegel* brennen, c) ☺ *Lack* einbrennen; **II** *v/i.* **3.** backen, braten (*a. fig. in der Sonne*); gebacken werden (*Brot etc.*); **4.** dörren, hart werden; **III** *s.* **5.** *Am.* gesellige Zs.-kunft; **'~·house** *s.* Backhaus *n,* -stube *f.*

ba·ke·lite ['beɪkəlaɪt] *s.* ☺ Bake'lit *n.*

bak·er ['beɪkə] *s.* **1.** Bäcker *m:* ~'*s dozen* dreizehn; **2.** *Am.* tragbarer Backofen; **'bak·er·y** [-ərɪ] *s.* Bäcke'rei *f.*

bakh·shish → *baksheesh.*

bak·ing ['beɪkɪŋ] **I** *s.* Backen *n;* Brennen *n* (*Ziegel*); **II** *adv. u. adj.* glühend heiß; **~ pow·der** *s.* Backpulver *n.*

bak·sheesh, bak·shish ['bækʃiːʃ] *s.* 'Bakschisch *n,* Trinkgeld *n;* Bestechungsgeld *n* (*im Orient*).

Ba·la·kla·va (**hel·met**) [ˌbæləˈklɑːvə] *s.* ✕ *Brit.* (wollener) Kopfschützer.

bal·a·lai·ka [ˌbæləˈlaɪkə] *s.* Bala'laika *f* (*russ. Zupfinstrument*).

bal·ance ['bæləns] **I** *s.* **1.** Waage *f* (*a. fig.*); **2.** Gleichgewicht *n* (*a. fig.*): ~ (*of mind*) inneres Gleichgewicht, Gelassenheit *f;* ~ *of nature* Gleichgewicht der Natur; ~ *of power* (politisches) Gleichgewicht der Kräfte; *loss of* ~ ⚕ Gleichgewichtsstörungen *pl.; hold the* ~ *fig.* das Zünglein an der Waage bilden; *turn the* ~ den Ausschlag geben; *lose one's* ~ das Gleichgewicht *od. fig.* die Fassung verlieren; *in the* ~ in der Schwebe; *tremble* (*od. hang*) *in the* ~ auf Messers Schneide stehen; **3.** Gegengewicht *n,* Ausgleich *m;* **4.** *on* ~ alles in allem, ‚unterm Strich'; **5.** → *balance-wheel;* **6.** ✝ 'Saldo *m,* Ausgleichsposten *m,* 'Überschuss *m,* Guthaben *n,* 'Kontostand *m;* Bi'lanz *f;* Rest (-betrag) *m: adverse* ~ Unterbilanz; ~ *brought* (*od. carried*) *forward* Saldovortrag *m;* ~ *due* Debetsaldo; ~ *at the bank* Bankguthaben; ~ *in hand* Kassenbestand *m;* ~ *of payments* Zahlungsbilanz; *strike a* ~ den Saldo *od.* (*a. fig.*) die Bilanz ziehen; **7.** Bestand *m;* F ('Über)Rest *m;* **II** *v/t.* **8.** *fig.* (er-, ab)wägen; **9.** (*a. o.s.*) sich) im Gleichgewicht halten; ins Gleichgewicht bringen, ausgleichen; ausbalancieren; ✝ *Rechnung od. Konto* ausgleichen, aufrechnen, saldieren, abschließen: ~ *the cash* Kasse(nsturz) machen; → *account* 5; **10.** *Kunstwerk* har'monisch gestalten; **III** *v/i.* **11.** balancieren, *fig. a.* ~ *out* sich im Gleichgewicht halten (*a. fig.*); **12.** sich (hin u. her) wiegen; *fig.* schwanken; **13.** ✝ sich ausgleichen; **14.** ~ *out* ☺ (sich) einspielen; **~ beam** *s.* Turnen: Schwebebalken *m.*

bal·anced ['bælənst] *adj. fig.* (gut) ausgewogen, wohlerwogen, ausgeglichen (*a. ✝ u. ♪*), gleichmäßig: ~ *diet* ausge-

glichene Kost; ~ *judg(e)ment* wohlerwogenes Urteil.

bal·ance| i·tem *s.* Bi'lanzposten *m;* ~ **sheet** *s.* ✝ Bi'lanz *f;* Rechnungsabschluss *m: first* (*od. opening*) ~ Eröffnungsbilanz; ~ **wheel** *s.* ☺ Hemmungsrad *n,* Unruh *f* (*Uhr*).

bal·co·ny ['bælkənɪ] *s.* Bal'kon *m* (*a. thea.*).

bald [bɔːld] *adj.* □ **1.** kahl (*ohne Haar, Federn, Laub, Pflanzenwuchs*): *as* ~ *as a coot* völlig kahl; **2.** *fig.* kahl, schmucklos, nüchtern, armselig, dürftig; **3.** *fig.* nackt, unverhüllt, trocken, unverblümt: *a* ~ *statement;* **4.** *zo.* weißköpfig (*Vögel*), mit Blesse (*Pferde*); **5.** ~ *tyre* (*Am. tire*) abgefahrener Reifen.

bal·da·chin, bal·da·quin ['bɔːldəkɪn] *s.* 'Baldachin *m,* Thron-, Traghimmel *m.*

bal·der·dash ['bɔːldədæʃ] *s.* ‚Quatsch' *m,* Unsinn *m.*

'bald·head *s.* Kahlkopf *m;* **‚~-'head·ed** *adj.* kahlköpfig: *go* ~ *into sl.* blindlings hineinrennen in (*acc.*).

bald·ing ['bɔːldɪŋ] *adj.* kahl werdend; **bald·ness** ['bɔːldnɪs] *s.* Kahlheit *f; fig.* Dürftigkeit *f,* Nacktheit *f;* **'bald·pate** *s.* **1.** Kahl-, Glatzkopf *m;* **2.** *orn.* Pfeifente *f.*

bale¹ [beɪl] **I** *s.* ✝ Ballen *m:* ~ *goods* Ballengüter *pl.,* Ballenware *f;* **II** *v/t.* in Ballen verpacken.

bale² [beɪl] → *bail².*

'bale·fire *s.* **1.** Si'gnalfeuer *n;* **2.** Freudenfeuer *n.*

bale·ful ['beɪlfʊl] *adj.* □ **1.** unheilvoll (*Einfluss*); **2.** a) bösartig, rachsüchtig, b) hasserfüllt (*Blick*); **3.** niedergeschlagen.

balk [bɔːk] **I** *s.* **1.** Hindernis *n;* **2.** Enttäuschung *f;* **3.** *dial. u. Am.* Auslassung *f,* Fehler *m,* Schnitzer *m;* **4.** (Furchen-)Rain *m;* **5.** Hindernis *n,* Hemmnis *n;* **6.** △ Hauptbalken *m;* **7.** *Billard:* Quartier *n;* **8.** *Am. Baseball:* vorgetäuschter Wurf; **II** *v/i.* **9.** stocken, stutzen; scheuen (*at* bei, vor. *dat.*) (*Pferd*); *Reitsport:* verweigern (*acc.*); **10.** ~ *at fig.* a) sich sträuben gegen, b) zu'rückschrecken vor (*dat.*); **III** *v/t.* **11.** (ver)hindern, vereiteln: ~ *s.o. of s.th.* j-n um et. bringen; **12.** ausweichen (*dat.*), um'gehen; **13.** sich entgehen lassen.

Bal·kan ['bɔːlkən] **I** *adj.* Balkan...; **II** *s.: the* ~**s** *pl.* die 'Balkanstaaten, der 'Balkan; **'Bal·kan·ize** [-naɪz] *v/t.* Gebiet balkanisieren.

ball¹ [bɔːl] **I** *s.* **1.** Ball *m,* Kugel *f;* Knäuel *m, n,* Klumpen *m,* Kloß *m,* Ballen *m: three* ~**s** drei Kugeln (*Zeichen des Pfandleihers*); **2.** Kugel *f* (*zum Spiel*); **3.** *sport* a) Ball *m,* b) *Am.* Ballspiel *n,* *bsd.* Baseball(spiel *n*) *m,* c) *Tennis:* Ball *m,* Schlag *m,* d) *Fußball:* Ball *m,* Schuss *m,* e) Wurf *m: be on the* ~ F ‚auf Draht' sein; *have a lot on the* ~ *Am.* ‚schwer was loshaben'; *have the* ~ *at one's feet* s-e große Chance haben; *keep the* ~ *rolling* das Gespräch *od.* die Sache in Gang halten; *the* ~ *is with you od. in your court!* jetzt bist 'du dran!; *play* ~ F mitmachen, ‚spuren'; **4.** ✕ *etc.* Kugel *f;* **5.** (Abstimmungs)Kugel *f;* → *black ball;* **6.** *ast.* Himmelskörper *m,* Erdkugel *f;* **7.** ~ *of the eye* Augapfel *m;* ~ *of the foot* Fußballen *m;* ~ *of the thumb* Handballen *m;* **8.** *pl.* V → *balls;* **II** *v/t.* **9.** (*v/i.* sich) zs.-ballen; **10.** ~ *up Am. sl.* a) (völlig) durcheinander bringen, b) ‚vermasseln'; **11.** (*a. v/i.*) V ‚bumsen'.

ball² [bɔːl] *s.* (Tanz- *etc.*)Ball *m: open*

the ~ a) den Ball (*mst fig.* den Reigen) eröffnen, b) *fig.* die Sache in Gang bringen; *have a* ~ *Am.* F sich (prima) amüsieren; *get a* ~ *out of s.th. Am.* F an et. Spaß haben.

ball³ [bɔːl] *s.* große Arz'neipille (*für Pferde etc.*).

bal·lad ['bæləd] *s.* Bal'lade *f*; **'bal·lad·mon·ger** *s.* Bänkelsänger *m*; Dichterling *m*; **'bal·lad·ry** [-drɪ] *s.* Bal'ladendichtung *f*.

,ball-and-'sock·et joint *s.* ☉, *anat.* Kugel-, Drehgelenk *n*.

bal·last ['bæləst] **I** *s.* **1.** ⚓, ✈ Ballast *m*, Beschwerung *f*: *in* ~ in Ballast; **2.** *fig.* (sittlicher) Halt; **3.** ☉ Schotter *m*, 'Bettungsmateri,al *n*; **II** *v/t.* **4.** ⚓, ✈ mit Ballast beladen; **5.** *fig.* j-m Halt geben; **6.** ☉ beschottern.

ball| bear·ing(s *pl.*) *s.* ☉ Kugellager *n*; **'~·boy** *s. Tennis etc.*: Balljunge *m*.

bal·le·ri·na [,bælə'riːnə] *s.* **1.** (Prima-)Balle'rina *f*; **2.** Bal'letttänzerin *f*.

bal·let ['bæleɪ] *s.* **1.** *allg.* Bal'lett *n*; **2.** Bal'lettkorps *n*; **~ danc·er** ['bælɪ] *s.* Bal'letttänzer(in); **~ danc·ing** ['bælɪ] *s.* Bal'letttanzen *n*; Tanzen *n*.

bal·let·o·mane ['bælɪtəʊmeɪn] *s.* Bal'lettfa,natiker(in).

'ball|,flow·er *s.* △ Ballenblume *f* (*gotische Verzierung*); ~ **game** *s.* **1.** *sport* (*Am.* Base)Ballspiel *n*; **2.** *Am.* F a) Situati'on *f*, b) Sache *f*; **'~·girl** *s. Tennis etc.*: Ballmädchen *s.*

bal·lis·tic [bə'lɪstɪk] *adj.* (□ *~ally*) *phys.*, ✕ bal'listisch; → *missile* 2; **bal·'lis·tics** [-ks] *s. pl. mst sg. konstr. phys.*, ✕ Bal'listik *f*.

ball joint *s. anat.*, ☉ Kugelgelenk *n*.

bal·lon d'es·sai [balɔ̃ desɛ] (*Fr.*) *s. bsd. fig.* Ver'suchsbal,lon *m*.

bal·loon [bə'luːn] **I** *s.* **1.** ✈ Bal'llon *m*: ~ *barrage* ✕ Ballonsperre *f*; *when the* ~ *goes up* F wenn es losgeht; **2.** Luftballon *m* (*Spielzeug*); **3.** △ (Pfeiler)Kugel *f*; **4.** 🜍 Bal'lon *m*, Rezipi'ent *m*; **5.** *in Comics etc.*: (Sprech-, Denk)Blase *f*; **6.** ~ (*glass*) 'Kognakschwenker *m*; **7.** *sl. sport* ,Kerze' *f* (*Hochschuss*); **II** *v/i.* **8.** im Ballon aufsteigen; **9.** sich blähen; **III** *v/t.* **10.** *sl. sport* den Ball ,in die Wolken jagen'; **11.** aufblasen; *fig.* aufblähen, über'treiben, steigern; **12.** ✝ *Am. Preise* in die Höhe treiben; **IV** *adj.* **13.** aufgebläht: ~ *sleeve* Puffärmel *m*; **bal·loon·ist** [bə'luːnɪst] *s.* Bal'lonfahrer *m*; **bal·loon tire** (*Brit.* **tyre**) *s.* ☉ Bal'lonreifen *m*.

bal·lot ['bælət] **I** *s.* **1.** *hist.* Wahlkugel *f*; *weitS.* Stimmzettel *m*; **2.** (geheime) Wahl: *voting is by* ~ die Wahl ist geheim; *at the first* ~ im ersten Wahlgang; **3.** Zahl *f* der abgegebenen Stimmen, *weitS.* Wahlbeteiligung *f*; **II** *v/i.* **4.** (geheim) abstimmen; **5.** losen (*for* um); ~ **box** *s.* Wahlurne *f*; ~ **pa·per** *s.* Stimmzettel *m*; ~ **rig·ging** *s.* 'Wahlmanipulati,on *f*; ~ **vote** *s.* Urabstimmung *f* (*bei Lohnkämpfern*).

'ball|(·point) pen *s.* Kugelschreiber *m*; ~ **race** *s.* ☉ Kugellager-, Laufring *m*; ~ **re·cep·tion** *s. TV* Ball-, Re'laisempfang *m*; **'~·room** *s.* Tanzsaal *m*: ~ *dancing* Gesellschaftstanz *m*, -tänze *pl.*

balls [bɔːlz] **I** *s. pl.* V **1.** ,Eier' *pl.* (*Hoden*); **II** *int.* ,Quatsch'!, Blödsinn!

'ball-up *s. Am. sl.* Durchein'ander *n*.

bal·ly·hoo [,bælɪ'huː] F **I** *s.* (Re'klame)Rummel *m*, Ballyhoo *n*, *a. weitS.* ,Tam'tam' *n*, ,Wirbel' *m*; **II** *v/i. u. v/t.* e-n Rummel machen (um), marktschreierisch anpreisen.

---

bal·ly·rag ['bælɪræg] *v/t.* mit *j-m* Possen *od.* Schindluder treiben.

balm [baːm] *s.* **1.** 'Balsam *m*: a) aro'matisches Harz, b) wohlriechende Salbe, c) *fig.* Trost *m*, *a.* Wohltat *f*; **2.** *fig.* bal'samischer Duft; **3.** ♀ ⚘ *of Gilead* 'Balsamstrauch *m od.* -harz *n*.

bal·mor·al [bæl'mɒrəl] *s.* Schottenmütze *f*.

balm·y ['baːmɪ] *adj.* □ **1.** bal'samisch; **2.** *fig.* mild; heilend; **3.** *Brit. sl.* ,bekloppt'.

bal·ne·ol·o·gy [,bælnɪ'ɒlədʒɪ] *s.* 🜍 Balneolo'gie *f*, Bäderkunde *f*.

bal·sam ['bɔːlsəm] *s.* **1.** → *balm* 1; **2.** ♀ a) Springkraut *n*, b) Balsa'mine *f*; **bal·sam·ic** [bɔːl'sæmɪk] *adj.* (□ *~ally*) **1.** 'balsamartig, Balsam...; **2.** bal'samisch (duftend); **3.** *fig.* mild, sanft; lindernd, heilend.

Balt [bɔːlt] *s.* Balte *m*, Baltin *f*; **'Bal·tic** [-tɪk] **I** *adj.* **1.** baltisch; **2.** Ostsee...; **II** *s.* **3.** *a.* ~ *Sea* Ostsee *f*.

bal·us·ter ['bæləstə] *s.* → *banister*; **bal·us·trade** [,bæləs'treɪd] *s.* Balu'strade *f*, Brüstung *f*; Geländer *n*.

bam·boo [bæm'buː] *s.* **1.** ♀ 'Bambus *m*: ~ *curtain pol.* Bambusvorhang *m* (*von Rotchina*); ~ *shoot* Bambussprosse *f*; **2.** 'Bambusrohr *n*, -stock *m*.

bam·boo·zle [bæm'buːzl] *v/t. sl.* **1.** beschwindeln (*out of* um), übers Ohr hauen; **2.** foppen, verwirren.

ban [bæn] **I** *v/t.* **1.** verbieten: ~ *a play*; ~ *s.o. from speaking* j-m verbieten zu sprechen; **2.** *sport j-n* sperren; **II** *s.* **3.** (amtliches) Verbot, Sperre *f* (*a. sport*): *travel* ~ Reiseverbot; *lift a* ~ ein Verbot aufheben; **4.** Ablehnung *f* durch die öffentliche Meinung: *under a* ~ allgemein missbilligt, geächtet; **5.** ⚡, *eccl.* Bann *m*, Acht *f*: *under the* ~ in die Acht erklärt, exkommuniziert.

ba·nal [bə'naːl] *adj.* banal, abgedroschen, seicht; **ba·nal·i·ty** [bə'nælətɪ] *s.* Banali'tät *f*; **ba·na·lize** [bə'naːlaɪz] *v/t.* banalisieren.

ba·nan·a [bə'naːnə] *s.* ♀ Ba'nane *f*: *go* ~*s sl.* ,überschnappen'; ~ *plug* ⚡ Ba'nanenstecker *m*; ~ *re·pub·lic s. iro.* Ba'nanenrepu,blik *f*.

band¹ [bænd] *s.* **1.** Schar, *f*, Gruppe *f*; Bande *f*: ~ *of robbers* Räuberbande; **2.** Band *f*, (Mu'sik)Ka,pelle *f*, ('Tanz-)Or,chester *n*: *big* ~ Big Band; → *beat* 12; **II** *v/t.* **3.** ~ *together* (zu e-r Gruppe *etc.*) vereinigen; **III** *v/i.* **4.** ~ *together* sich zs.-tun, *b.s.* sich zs.-rotten.

band² [bænd] **I** *s.* **1.** (flaches) Band; (Heft)Schnur *f*; ~ Gummiband; **2.** Band *n* (*an Kleidern*), Gurt *m*, Binde *f*, (Hosen- *etc.*)Bund *m*, Einfassung *f*; **3.** Band *n*, Ring *m* (*als Verbindung od. Befestigung*); Bauchbinde *f* (*Zigarre*); **4.** 🜍 (Gelenk)Band *n*; Verband *m*; **5.** (Me'tall)Reifen *m*; Ring *m*; Streifen *m*; **6.** ☉ Treibriemen *m*; **7.** *pl.* Beffchen *n der Geistlichen u. Richter*; **8.** andersfarbiger *od.* andersartiger Streifen, Querstreifen *m*; Schicht *f*; **9.** *Radio*: (Fre'quenz)Band *n*; **II** *v/t.* **10.** mit e-m Band *od.* e-r Binde versehen, zs.-binden; *Am. Vogel* beringen; **11.** mit (e-m) Streifen versehen; **band·age** ['bændɪdʒ] **I** *s.* **1.** 🜍 Verband *m*, Binde *f*, Ban'dage *f*: ~ *case* Verbandskasten *m*; **2.** Binde *f*, Band *n*; **II** *v/t.* **3.** *Wunde etc.* verbinden, *Bein etc.* bandagieren.

'Band-Aid *TM*, F **'band-aid** *Am.* **I** *s.* Heftpflaster *n*; **II** *adj.* F Behelfs...

ban·dan·(n)a [bæn'dænə] *s.* buntes Taschen- *od.* Halstuch.

---

band|·box ['bændbɒks] *s.* Hutschachtel *f*: *as if he* (*she*) *came out of a* ~ wie aus dem Ei gepellt; ~ **brake** *s.* ☉ Band-, Riemenbremse *f*.

ban·deau ['bændəʊ] *pl.* **-deaux** [-dəʊz] (*Fr.*) *s.* Haar- *od.* Stirnband *n*.

ban·de·rol(e) ['bændərəʊl] *s.* **1.** langer Wimpel, Fähnlein *n*; **2.** Inschriftenband *n*.

ban·dit ['bændɪt] *pl.* *a.* **-ti** [bæn'dɪtɪ] *s.* Ban'dit *m*, (Straßen)Räuber *m*, *weitS.* Gangster *m*: *a banditti coll.* e-e Räuberbande; ~ *one-armed*; **'ban·dit·ry** [-trɪ] *s.* Ban'ditentum *n*.

band·mas·ter ['bænd,maːstə] *s.* ♪ Ka'pellmeister *m*.

'ban·dog *s. Brit.* Kettenhund *m*.

ban·do·leer, **ban·do·lier** [,bændəʊ'lɪə] *s.* ✕ (*um die Brust geschlungener*) Patronengurt.

band|-pass fil·ter *s. Radio*: Bandfilter *n*, *m*; ~ **pul·ley** *s.* ☉ Riemenscheibe *f*, Schnurrad *n*; ~ **saw** *s.* ☉ Bandsäge *f*; ~ **shell** *s.* (muschelförmiger) Or'chester,pavillon.

bands·man ['bændzmən] *s.* [*irr.*] ♪ 'Musiker *m*, Mitglied *n* e-r (Mu'sik)Ka,pelle.

'band|·stand *s.* Mu'sik,pavillon *m*; Podium *n*; ~ **switch** *s. Radio*: Fre'quenz(band),umschalter *m*; **'~,wag·on** *s.* **1.** Wagen *m* mit e-r Mu'sikka,pelle; **2.** F *pol.* erfolgreiche Seite *od.* Par'tei: *climb on the* ~ mit ,einsteigen', sich der Erfolg versprechenden Sache anschließen; **'~·width** *s. Radio*: Bandbreite *f*.

ban·dy ['bændɪ] **I** *v/t.* **1.** sich *et.* zuwerfen; **2.** sich *et.* erzählen; **3.** sich (gegenseitig) *Vorwürfe, Komplimente etc.* machen, *Blicke, böse Worte, Schläge etc.* tauschen: ~ *words* sich streiten; **4.** *a.* ~ *about Gerüchte* in 'Umlauf setzen *od.* weitertragen; **5.** *a.* ~ *about j-s* Namen immer wieder erwähnen: *his name was bandied about a.* er war ins Gerede gekommen; **II** *s.* **6.** *sport* Bandy *n* (*Abart des Eishockey*).

'bandy-legged [-legd] *adj.* o- *od.* säbelbeinig.

bane [beɪn] *s.* Verderben *n*, Ru'in *m*: *the* ~ *of his life* der Fluch s-s Lebens; **'bane·ful** [-fʊl] *adj.* □ verderblich, tödlich, schädlich.

bang¹ [bæn] **I** *s.* **1.** Bums *m*, Schlag *m*, Krach *m*, Knall *m*: *go over with a* ~ *Am.* F ein Bombenerfolg sein; **2.** V ,Nummer' *f* (*Koitus*); **3.** *sl.* ,Schuss' *m* (*Rauschgift*); **II** *v/t.* **4.** dröhnend schlagen, knallen mit, *Tür etc.* zuknallen: ~ *one's head against* sich den Kopf anschlagen an (*dat.*); ~ *one's fist on the table* mit der Faust auf den Tisch schlagen; ~ *sense into s.o.* j-m Vernunft einbläuen; ~ *up* kaputtmachen, zerschlagen, *Auto* zu Schrott fahren; ~*ed(-)up* zerbeult, (arg) mitgenommen, demoliert; **5.** ~ *about fig.* j-n he'rumstoßen; **6.** V ,bumsen', ,vögeln'; **III** *v/i.* **7.** knallen: a) krachen, b) zuschlagen (*Tür etc.*), c) ballern, schießen: ~ *at* an die *Tür etc.* schlagen; ~ *away* drauflosballern; ~ *into* bumsen *od.* knallen gegen; **8.** V ,bumsen', ,vögeln'; **IV** *adv.* **9.** bums: a) mit e-m Knall *od.* Krach, b) F *fig.* ,zack', genau: ~ *in the eye*, c) F *fig.* plötzlich: ~ *off sl.* sofort, ,zack'; ~ *on sl.* (haar)genau; **V** *int.* **10.** bums!, peng!

bang² [bæn] *s. mst pl.* Pony *m*: 'Ponyfri,sur *f*.

bang·er ['bænə] *s.* **1.** Knallkörper *m*, Feuerwerkskörper *m*; **2.** ,Klapperkiste' *f* (*Auto*); **3.** (Brat)Würstchen *n*: ~*s*

B

pl. *and* **mash** Würstchen *pl.* mit Kartoffelbrei.

ban·gle ['bæŋgl] *s.* Armring *m*, -reif *m*; Fußring *m*, -spange *f*.

'bang|-on *adv.* F haargenau; genau (richtig); **'~-up** *adv. u. adj. Am. sl.* ‚prima'.

ban·ish ['bænɪʃ] *v/t.* **1.** verbannen, ausweisen (*from* aus); **2.** *fig.* (ver)bannen, verscheuchen, vertreiben: **~** *care*; **'banish·ment** [-mənt] *s.* **1.** Verbannung *f*, Ausweisung *f*; **2.** *fig.* Vertreiben *n*, Bannen *n*.

ban·is·ter ['bænɪstə] *s.* Geländersäule *f*; *pl.* Treppengeländer *n*.

ban·jo ['bændʒəʊ] *pl.* **-jos**, **-joes** *s.* ♪ Banjo *n*; **'ban·jo·ist** [-əʊɪst] *s.* Banjospieler *m*.

bank¹ [bæŋk] **I** *s.* **1.** ✝ Bank *f*, Bankhaus *n*: *the 2 Brit.* die Bank von England; **~** *of deposit* Depositenbank; **~** *of issue* (*od.* **circulation**) Noten-, Emissionsbank; **2.** (Spiel)Bank *f*: *break* (*keep*) *the* **~** die Bank sprengen (halten); *go* (*the*) **~** Bank setzen; **3.** Vorrat *m*, Re'serve *f*, Bank *f*: → *blood bank etc.*; **II** *v/i.* **4.** ✝ Geld auf e-r Bank haben: *I* **~** *with* ... ich habe mein Bankkonto bei ...; **5.** *Glücksspiel:* die Bank halten; **6.** **~** *on fig.* bauen *od.* s-e Hoffnung setzen auf (*acc.*); **III** *v/t.* **7.** Geld bei e-r Bank einzahlen *od.* hinter'legen.

bank² [bæŋk] **I** *s.* **1.** (Erd)Wall *m*, Damm *m*, (Straßen- *etc.*)Böschung *f*; Über'höhung *f* e-r Straße; **2.** Ufer *n*; **3.** (Sand)Bank *f*, Untiefe *f*: *Dogger 2* Doggerbank; **4.** Bank *f*, Wand *f*, Wall *m*; Zs.-ballung *f*: **~** *of clouds* Wolkenbank; *snow* **~** Schneewall; **5.** ✔ Querneigung *f in der Kurve*; **II** *v/t.* **6.** eindämmen, mit e-m Wall um'geben; *fig.* dämpfen; **7.** *e-e Straße in der Kurve* über'höhen; **8.** *a.* **~** *up* aufhäufen, zs.- ballen; **9.** ✔ *in die Kurve legen*, in Schräglage bringen; **10.** *a.* **~** *up ein Feuer* mit Asche belegen; **III** *v/i.* **11.** *a.* **~** *up* sich aufhäufen, sich zs.-ballen; **12.** ✔ in die Kurve gehen; **13.** *e-e* Über'höhung haben (*Straße in der Kurve*).

bank³ [bæŋk] *s.* **1.** Ruderbank *f od.* (Reihe *f* der) Ruderer *pl.* in e-r Galeere; **2.** ⊗ Reihe *f*, Gruppe *f*, Reihenanordnung *f*.

bank·a·ble ['bæŋkəbl] *adj.* ✝ bankfähig, diskontierbar; *fig.* verlässlich, zuverlässig.

bank| ac·count *s.* ✝ Bankkonto *n*; **~** *bill* → *bank draft*; **~** *book* *s.* Sparbuch *n*; **~** *clerk* *s.* Bankangestellte(r *m*) *f*, -beamte(r) *m*, -beamtin *f*; **~** *code num·ber* *s.* Bankleitzahl *f*; **~** *dis·count* *s.* 'Bankdis,kont *m*; **~** *draft* *s.* Bankwechsel *m* (*von e-r Bank auf e-e andere gezogen*).

bank·er ['bæŋkə] *s.* **1.** ✝ Banki'er *m*: **~'s** *discretion* Bankgeheimnis *n*; **~'s** *order* Dauerauftrag *m*; **2.** *Kartenspiel etc.:* Bankhalter *m*.

bank hol·i·day *s.* Bankfeiertag *m*.

bank·ing¹ ['bæŋkɪŋ] ✝ **I** *s.* Bankwesen *n*; **II** *adj.* Bank...

bank·ing² ['bæŋkɪŋ] *s.* ✔ Schräglage *f*.

bank·ing| ac·count *s.* 'Bank,konto *n*; **~** *charg·es* *s. pl.* Bankgebühren *pl.*; **~** *house* *s.* Bankhaus *n*; **~** *hours* *s.* Banköffnungszeiten *pl.*

bank| lend·ing rate *s.* Kreditzinssatz *m*; **~** *man·ag·er* *s.* 'Bankdi,rektor *m*; **~** *loan* *s.* 'Bankdarlehen *n*, -kre,dit *m*: *take out a* **~** in e-n Kre'dit bei der Bank aufnehmen; **'~-note** *s.* ✝ Banknote *f*; **~** *rate* *s.* ✝ Dis'kontsatz *m*; **~** *re·turn* *s.* Bankausweis *m*; **~** *rob·ber·y* *s.* Bank-

raub *m*; **'~-roll** *s. Am.* **1.** Bündel *n* Banknoten; **2.** Geld(mittel *pl.*) *n*.

bank·rupt ['bæŋkrʌpt] **I** *s.* **1.** 🔣 Kon'kurs-, Gemeinschuldner *m*, Bankrot'teur *m*: **~'s** *certificate* Dokument *n* über Einstellung des Konkursverfahrens; **~'s** *creditor* Konkursgläubiger *m*; **~'s** *estate* Konkursmasse *f*; *declare o.s. a* **~** (s-n) Konkurs anmelden; **2.** *fig.* bank'rotter *od.* her'untergekommener Mensch; **II** *adj.* **3.** 🔣 bank'rott: *go* **~** in Konkurs geraten, Bankrott machen; **4.** *fig.* bank'rott (*a. Politik, Politiker etc.*), ruiniert: *morally* **~** moralisch bankrott, sittlich verkommen; **~** *in intelligence* bar aller Vernunft; **III** *v/t.* **5.** 🔣 Bank'rott machen; **6.** *fig.* zu'grunde richten; **'bank·rupt·cy** [-rəptsɪ] *s.* **1.** 🔣 Bank'rott *m*, Kon'kurs *m*: *act of* **~** Konkurshandlung *f*; *2 Act* Konkursordnung *f*; *declaration of* **~** Konkursanmeldung *f*; *petition in* **~** Konkursantrag *m*; *referee in* **~** Konkursrichter *m*; **2.** *fig.* Ru'in *m*, Bank'rott *m*.

bank| sort code *s.* ✝ Bankleitzahl *f*; **~** *state·ment* *s.* ✝ **1.** Bankausweis *m*; **2.** *Brit.* Kontoauszug *m*.

ban·ner ['bænə] **I** *s.* **1.** Banner *n*, Fahne *f*, Heeres-, Kirchen-, Reichsfahne *f*; **2.** *fig.* Banner *n*, Fahne *f*: *the* **~** *of freedom*; **3.** Spruchband *n*, Transpa'rent *n* bei politischen Umzügen; **4.** *a.* **~** *headline* Balken,überschrift *f*, Schlagzeile *f*; **II** *adj. Am.* **5.** führend, 'prima: **~** *class* beste Sorte; **'~,bear·er** *s.* **1.** Fahnenträger *m*; **2.** Vorkämpfer *m*.

banns [bænz] *s. pl. eccl.* Aufgebot *n des Brautpaares vor der Ehe*: *ask the* **~** das Aufgebot bestellen; *publish* (*od.* *put up*) *the* **~** (*of*) (*das Brautpaar*) kirchlich aufbieten.

ban·quet ['bæŋkwɪt] **I** *s.* Ban'kett *n*, Festessen *n*; **II** *v/t.* festlich bewirten; **III** *v/i.* tafeln; **'ban·quet·er** [-tə] *s.* Ban'kettteilnehmer(in).

ban·shee ['bænʃiː] *s. Ir., Scot.* Todesfee *f*.

ban·tam ['bæntəm] **I** *s.* **1.** *zo.* 'Bantam-, Zwerghuhn *n*, -hahn *m*; **2.** *fig.* Zwerg *m*, Knirps *m*; **II** *adj.* **3.** klein, ⊗ Klein..., *a.* handlich; **'~-weight** *s. sport* 'Bantamgewicht(ler *m*) *n*.

ban·ter ['bæntə] **I** *v/t.* necken, hänseln; **II** *v/i.* necken, scherzen; **III** *s.* Necke'rei *f*, Scherz(e *pl.*) *m*; **'ban·ter·er** [-ərə] *s.* Spaßvogel *m*.

Ban·tu [,bænˈtuː] **I** *pl.* **-tu**, **-tus** *s.* 'Bantu(neger) *m*; **2.** 'Bantusprache *f*; **II** *adj.* **3.** Bantu...

ban·zai [,bænˈzaɪ] *int.* Banzai! (*japanischer Hoch- od. Hurraruf*).

ba·o·bab ['beɪəʊbæb] *s.* ♠ 'Baobab *m*, Affenbrotbaum *m*.

bap·tism ['bæptɪzəm] *s.* **1.** *eccl.* Taufe *f*: **~** *of blood* Märtyrertod *m*; **2.** *fig.* Taufe *f*, Einweihung *f*, Namensgebung *f*: **~** *of fire* ✗ Feuertaufe *f*; **bap·tis·mal** [bæpˈtɪzml] *adj. eccl.* Tauf...; **'bap·tist** [-ɪst] *s.* **1.** Bap'tist(in); **2.** *2* Baptist(in): *John the 2*; **'bap·tis·ter·y** [-ɪstərɪ], **'bap·tist·ry** [-ɪstrɪ] *s.* **1.** 'Taufka,pelle *f*; **2.** Taufbecken *n*; **bap·tize** [bæpˈtaɪz] *v/t. u. v/i. fig.* taufen.

bar [baː] **I** *s.* **1.** Stange *f*, Stab *m*: **~s** Gitter *n*; *prison* **~s** Gefängnis *n*; *behind* **~s** *fig.* hinter Schloss u. Riegel; **2.** Riegel *m*, Querbalken *m*, -holz *n*, -stange *f*, Schranke *f*, Sperre *f*; **3.** *fig.* (*to*) Hindernis *n* (für) (*a.* 🔣), Verhinderung *f* (*gen.*), Schranke *f* (gegen); 🔣 Ausschließungsgrund *m*: **~** *to progress* Hemmnis *n* für den Fortschritt; **~** *to marriage* Ehehindernis *n*; *as a* **~** *to, in*

~ *of* 🔣 zwecks Ausschlusses (*gen.*); **4.** Riegel *m*, Stange *f*: *a* **~** *of soap* ein Riegel Seife; **~** *soap* Stangenseife *f*; *a chocolate* **~** ein Riegel (*a.* e-e Tafel) Schokolade; *gold* **~** Goldbarren *m*; **5.** Barre *f*, Sandbank *f* (*am Hafeneingang*); **6.** Strich *m*, Streifen *m*, Band *n*; *Computer:* Leiste *f* (*auf Bildschirmdarstellung*); Strahl *m* (*Farbe, Licht*): **~** *chart* Säulendiagramm *n*; **~** *code* Strichkode *m*; **7.** 𝄞 La'melle *f*; **8.** ♪ a) Taktstrich *m*, b) *ein* Takt; **9.** Streifen *m*, Band *n an e-r Medaille*; Spange *f am Orden*; **10.** 🔣 a) Schranke *f* vor der Richterbank: *prisoner at the* **~** Angeklagte(r *m*) *f*; *trial at* **~** *Brit.* Verhandlung *f* vor dem vollen Strafsenat des *High Court of Justice* (*z.B. bei Landesverrat*), b) Schranke *f* in den *Inns of Court*: *be called* (*Am.* **admitted**) *to the* **~** als Anwalt *od. Brit.* als Barrister (*plädierender Anwalt*) zugelassen werden; *be at the* **~** Barrister sein; *read for the* **~** Jura studieren, c) *the* **~** die (gesamte) Anwaltschaft, *Brit.* die Barristers *pl.*: *2 Association Am.* (halbamtliche) Anwaltsvereinigung, -kammer; **11.** *parl.: the* **~** *of the House* Schranke im Brit. Unterhaus (*bis zu der geladene Zeugen vortreten dürfen*); **12.** *fig.* Gericht *n*, Tribu'nal *n*: *the* **~** *of public opinion* das Urteil der Öffentlichkeit; **13.** Bar *f*: a) Bü'fett *n*, Theke *f*, b) Schankraum *m*, Imbissstube *f*; → *ice-cream bar*; **II** *v/t.* **14.** verriegeln: **~** *in* (*out*) ein- (aus)sperren; **15.** *a.* **~** *up* vergittern, mit Schranken um'geben: **~** *red window* Gitterfenster *n*; **16.** versperren: **~** *the way* (*a. fig.*); **17.** hindern (*from* an *dat.*); hemmen, auf-, abhalten; **18.** ausschließen (*from* von; *a.* 🔣), verbieten; → *barred* 4; **19.** absehen von; **20.** *Brit. sl.* nicht leiden können; **21.** mit Streifen versehen; **III** *prp.* **22.** außer, abgesehen von: **~** *one* außer einem; **~** *none* (alle) ohne Ausnahme.

barb¹ [baːb] *s.* **1.** 'Widerhaken *m*; **2.** *fig.* a) Stachel *m*, b) Spitze *f*, spitze Bemerkung, Pfeil *m* des Spottes; **3.** *zo.* Bart (-faden) *m*; Fahne *f* e-r Feder.

barb² [baːb] *s.* Berberpferd *n*.

bar·bar·i·an [baːˈbeərɪən] **I** *s.* **1.** Bar'bar *m*; **2.** *fig.* Bar'bar *m*, roher u. ungesitteter Mensch; Unmensch *m*; **II** *adj.* **3.** bar'barisch, unzivilisiert; **4.** *fig.* roh, ungesittet, grausam; **bar·bar·ic** [baːˈbærɪk] *adj.* (□ **~ally**) bar'barisch, wild, roh, ungesittet; **bar·ba·rism** ['baːbərɪzəm] *s.* **1.** Barba'rismus *m*, Sprachwidrigkeit *f*; **2.** Barba'rei *f*, 'Unkul,tur *f*; **bar·bar·i·ty** [baːˈbærətɪ] *s.* Barba'rei *f*, Rohheit *f*, Grausamkeit *f*, Unmenschlichkeit *f*; **bar·ba·rize** ['baːbəraɪz] **I** *v/t.* **1.** verrohen *od.* verwildern lassen; **2.** *Sprache, Kunst etc.* barbarisieren, verderben; **II** *v/i.* **3.** verrohen; **bar·ba·rous** ['baːbərəs] *adj.* □ bar'barisch, roh, ungesittet, grausam.

bar·be·cue ['baːbɪkjuː] **I** *s.* **1.** Barbecue *n*: a) Grillfest *n* (*bei dem ganze Tiere gebraten werden*), b) Bratrost *m*, Grill *m*, c) gegrilltes *od.* gebratenes Fleisch; **2.** *Am.* in Essigsoße zubereitete Fleisch- *od.* Fischstückchen; **II** *v/t.* **3.** (*auf dem Rost od.* am Spieß) im Ganzen *od.* in großen Stücken) braten; **4.** braten, grillen; **5.** *Am.* in stark gewürzter (Essig)Soße zubereiten; **6.** *Am.* a) dörren, b) räuchern.

barbed [baːbd] *adj.* **1.** mit 'Widerhaken *od.* Stacheln (versehen), Stachel...; **2.** *fig.* bissig, spitz: **~** *remarks*; **~** *wire* *s.*

Stacheldraht *m*.
bar·bel ['bɑːbəl] *s*. *ichth*. Barbe *f*.
'**bar·bell** *s*. *sport* Hantel *f mit langer Stange*, Kugelstange *f*.
bar·ber ['bɑːbə] **I** *s*. Bar'bier *m*, ('Herren)Fri,seur *m*; **II** *v/t*. *Am*. rasieren; frisieren.
bar·ber·ry ['bɑːbərɪ] *s*. ♀ Berbe'ritze *f*.
'**bar·ber·shop** *s*. **1**. *bsd. Am*. Fri'seurgeschäft *n*; **2**. *a*. **~ singing** *Am*. F (zwangloses) Singen im Chor.
bar·ber's| itch ['bɑːbəz] *s*. ⚕ Bartflechte *f*; **~ pole** *s*. *spiralig bemalte Stange als Geschäftszeichen der Friseure*.
bar·bi·tal ['bɑːbɪtæl] *s*. *pharm. Am*. Barbi'tal *n*; **~ so·di·um** *s*. *pharm*. 'Natriumsalz *n* von Barbi'tal.
bar·bi·tone ['bɑːbɪtəʊn] *s*. *Brit*. → **barbital**; **bar·bi·tu·rate** [bɑː'bɪtjʊərət] *s*. *pharm*. □ Barbitu'rat *n*; **bar·bi·tu·ric** [,bɑːbɪ'tjʊərɪk] *adj. pharm*.: **~ acid** Barbitursäure *f*.
bar·ca·rol(l)e ['bɑːkərəʊl] *s*. ♪ Barka'role *f* (*Gondellied*).
bar cop·per *s*. ⊘ Stangenkupfer *n*.
bard [bɑːd] *s*. **1**. Barde *m* (*keltischer Sänger*); **2**. *fig*. Barde *m*, Sänger *m* (*Dichter*): ♀ **of Avon** Shakespeare; '**bard·ic** [-dɪk] *adj*. Barden...; **bard·ol·a·try** [bɑː'dɒlətrɪ] *s*. Shakespearevergötterung *f*.
bare [beə] **I** *adj*. □ → **barely**; **1**. nackt, unbekleidet, bloß: **in one's ~ skin** splitternackt; **2**. kahl, leer, nackt, unbedeckt: **~ walls** kahle Wände; **the ~ boards** der nackte Fußboden; **the larder was ~** *fig*. es war nichts zu essen im Hause; **~ sword** bloßes *od*. blankes Schwert; **3**. ♀, *zo*. kahl; **4**. unverhüllt, klar: **lay ~** zeigen, enthüllen (*a. fig*.); **the ~ facts** die nackten Tatsachen; **~ nonsense** barer *od*. reiner Unsinn; **5**. (*of*) entblößt (von), arm (an *dat*.), ohne; **6**. knapp, kaum hinreichend: **~ majority** a) knappe Mehrheit, b) (**of votes**) einfache Stimmenmehrheit; **a ~ ten pounds** gerade noch 10 Pfund; **7**. bloß, al'lein, nur: **the ~ thought** der bloße (*od*. allein der) Gedanke; **II** *v/t*. **8**. entblößen, entkleiden; **9**. *fig*. bloßlegen, enthüllen: **~ one's heart** sein Herz öffnen (**to** *j-m*); '**~·back(ed)** [-bæk(t)] *adj. u. adv*. ungesattelt; '**~·faced** [-feɪst] *adj*. □ schamlos, frech; '**~·foot** *adj. u. adv*. barfuß; '**~·foot·ed** [-'fʊtɪd] *adj*. barfuß, barfüßig; '**~·head·ed** [-'hedɪd] *adj. u. adv*. mit bloßem Kopf, barhäuptig; '**~·legged** [-'legd] *adj*. mit nackten Beinen.
bare·ly ['beəlɪ] *adv*. **1**. kaum, knapp, gerade (noch): **~ enough time**; **2**. ärmlich, spärlich; **bare·ness** ['beənɪs] *s*. **1**. Nacktheit *f*, Blöße *f*, Kahlheit *f*; **2**. Dürftigkeit *f*.
bare·sark ['beəsɑːk] **I** *s*. Ber'serker *m*; **II** *adv*. ohne Rüstung.
bar·gain ['bɑːgɪn] **I** *s*. **1**. (geschäftliches) Abkommen, Handel *m*, Geschäft *n*: **a good** (**bad**) **~**; **2**. *a*. **good ~** vorteilhaftes Geschäft, günstiger Kauf, Gelegenheitskauf *m* (*a. die gekaufte Sache*): **at £10 it is a** (**dead**) **~** für £10 ist es spottbillig; **it's a ~!** abgemacht!, topp!; **into the ~** obendrein, noch dazu; **strike** *od*. **make a ~** ein Abkommen treffen, e-n Handel abschließen; **make the best of a bad ~** so gut wie möglich aus der Affäre ziehen; **drive a hard ~** hart feilschen, ,mächtig rangehen'; **3**. *Brit. Börse*: (*einzelner*) Abschluss: **~ for account** Termingeschäft *n*; **II** *v/i*. **4**. handeln, feilschen (**for**, **about** um); **5**. verhandeln, über'einkommen (**for** über

acc., *that* dass): **~ing point** Verhandlungspunkt *m*; **~ing position** Verhandlungsposition *f*; **6**. **~ for** rechnen mit, erwarten (*acc.*) (*mst neg.*): **I did not ~ for that** darauf war ich nicht gefasst; **it was more than we had ~ed for** damit hatten wir nicht gerechnet; **7**. **~ on** *fig*. zählen auf (*acc.*); **III** *v/t*. **8**. (ein)tauschen (**for** gegen); **9**. **~ away** verschachern, *fig. a*. verschenken; **~ basement** *s*. Niedrigpreisabteilung *f im* Tiefgeschoss *e-s Warenhauses*; **~ count·er** *s*. **1**. ♈ Wühltisch *m*; **2**. *fig. pol*. 'Tauschob,jekt *n*.
bar·gain·er ['bɑːgɪnə] *s*. **1**. Feilscher (-in); **2**. Verhandler *m*.
bar·gain| hunt·er F *s*. Schnäppchenjäger(in); **~ hunt·ing** F *s*. Schnäppchenjagd *f*.
bar·gain·ing ['bɑːgɪnɪŋ] *s*. Handeln *n*, Feilschen *n*; Verhandeln *n*: → **collective bargaining**.
bar·gain| price *s*. Spott-, Schleuderpreis *m*; **~ sale** *s*. (Ramsch)Ausverkauf *m*.
barge [bɑːdʒ] **I** *s*. **1**. ⚓ a) flaches Flussod. Ka'nalboot, Lastkahn *m*, b) Bar'kasse *f*, c) Hausboot *n*; **II** *v/i*. **2**. F ungeschickt gehen *od*. fahren *od*. sich bewegen, torkeln, stürzen, prallen (*into* in *acc.*, *against* gegen); **3**. **~ in** her'einplatzen, sich einmischen; **bargee** [bɑː'dʒiː] *s. Brit*. Kahnführer *m*: **swear like a ~** fluchen wie ein Landsknecht.
'**barge| man** [-mən] *s*. [*irr.*] *Am*. Kahnführer *m*; '**~·pole** *s*. Bootsstange *f*: **I wouldn't touch him** (*it*) **with a ~** *Brit*. F a) den (das) würde ich nicht mal mit e-r Feuerzange anfassen, b) mit dem (damit) will ich nichts zu tun haben.
bar·ic ['beərɪk] *adj*. ♈ Barium...
bar i·ron *s*. ⊘ Stabeisen *n*.
bar·i·tone ['bærɪtəʊn] *s*. ♪ 'Bariton *m* (*Stimme u. Sänger*).
bar·i·um ['beərɪəm] *s*. ♈ 'Barium *n*; **~ meal** *s*. ♈ Kon'trastmittel *n*, -brei *m*.
bark¹ [bɑːk] **I** *s*. **1**. ♀ (Baum)Rinde *f*, Borke *f*; **2**. → **Peruvian** I; **3**. ⊘ (Gerber)Lohe *f*; **II** *v/t*. **4**. abrinden; **5**. abschürfen: **~ one's knees**.
bark² [bɑːk] **I** *v/i*. **1**. bellen, kläffen (*a. fig*.): **~ at s.o.** *fig*. j-n anschnauzen; **~ing dogs never bite** Hunde, die bellen, beißen nicht; **~ up the wrong tree** a) auf dem Holzweg sein, b) an der falschen Adresse sein; **2**. *fig*. ,bellen' (*husten*); ,bellen', krächzen (*Schusswaffe*); **3**. F Ware marktschreierisch anpreisen; **II** *s*. **4**. Bellen *n*: **his ~ is worse than his bite** er kläfft nur (aber beißt nicht); **5**. *fig*. ,Bellen' *n* (*Husten*); Krachen *n*.
bark³ [bɑːk] *s*. **1**. ⚓ Bark *f*; **2**. *poet*. Schiff *n*.
'**bark| keep** *Am*. F → '**~·keep·er** *s*. **1**. Barkellner *m*, -mixer *m*; **2**. Barbesitzer *m*.
bark·er ['bɑːkə] *s*. **1**. Beller *m*, Kläffer *m*; **2**. F ,Anreißer' *m* (*Kundenwerber*); Marktschreier *m*; *Am. a*. Fremdenführer *m*.
bark| pit *s*. *Gerberei*: Lohgrube *f*; **~ tree** *s*. ♀ 'Chinarindenbaum *m*.
bar·ley ['bɑːlɪ] *s*. ♀ Gerste *f*: **French ~**, **pearl ~** Perlgraupen *pl*.; **pot ~** ungeschälte Graupen *pl*.; '**~·corn** *s*. Gerstenkorn *n*: **John ♀** *scherzhafte Personifikation* (*der Gerste als Grundstoff*) *von Bier* (,Gerstensaft') *od*. *Whisky*; **~ sug·ar** *s*. Gerstenzucker *m*; **~ wa·ter** *s*. *aromatisiertes Getränk aus Gerstenextrakt*; **~ wine** *s*. *ein Starkbier*.

bar line *s*. ♪ Taktstrich *m*.
barm [bɑːm] *s*. Bärme *f*, (Bier)Hefe *f*.
'**bar| maid** *s. bsd. Brit*. Bardame *f*, -kellnerin *f*; '**~·man** [-mən] *s*. [*irr.*] → **barkeeper** 1.
barm·y ['bɑːmɪ] *adj*. **1**. heftig, gärend, schaumig; **2**. *Brit. sl*. ,bekloppt': **go ~** überschnappen.
barn [bɑːn] *s*. **1**. Scheune *f*; **2**. *Am*. (Vieh)Stall *m*.
bar·na·cle¹ ['bɑːnəkl] *s*. **1**. *orn*. Ber'nikel-, Ringelgans *f*; **2**. *zo*. Entenmuschel *f*; **3**. *fig*. a) ,Klette' *f* (*lästiger Mensch*), b) (lästige) Fessel.
bar·na·cle² ['bɑːnəkl] *s*. **1**. *mst pl*. Nasenknebel *m für unruhige Pferde*; **2**. *pl. Brit*. F Kneifer *m*, Zwicker *m*.
barn| dance *s. Am*. ländlicher Tanz; **~ door** *s*.: **as big as a ~** F (so) groß wie ein Scheunentor, nicht zu verfehlen; '**~·door fowl** *s*. Haushuhn *n*; **~ owl** *s*. Schleiereule *f*; '**~·storm** *v/i*. F ,auf die Dörfer gehen': a) *thea. etc.* auf Tour'nee (durch die Pro'vinz) gehen, b) *pol*. überall Wahlreden halten; '**~·storm·er** *s*. F **1**. Wander- *od*. Schmierenschauspieler *m*; **2**. her'umreisender Wahlredner; **~ swal·low** *s*. Rauchschwalbe *f*.
bar·o·graph ['bærəʊgrɑːf] *s. phys., meteor*. Baro'graph *m* (*selbstaufzeichnender Luftdruckmesser*).
ba·rom·e·ter [bə'rɒmɪtə] *s*. Baro'meter *n*: a) Wetterglas *n*, Luftdruckmesser *m*, b) *fig*. Grad-, Stimmungsmesser *m*; **bar·o·met·ric** [,bærəʊ'metrɪk] *adj*. (□ **~ally**) *phys*. baro'metrisch, Barometer...: **~ maximum** Hoch(druckgebiet) *n*; **~ pressure** Luftdruck *m*; '**bar·o·'met·ri·cal** [-'metrɪkl] *adj*. → **barometric**.
bar·on ['bærən] *s*. **1**. *hist*. Pair *m*, Ba'ron *m*; *jetzt*: Ba'ron *m* (*brit. Adelstitel*); **2**. *nicht-Brit*. Ba'ron *m*, Freiherr *m*; **3**. *fig*. (Indu'strie- *etc*.)Ba,ron *m*, Ma'gnat *m*; **4**. **~** (**of beef**) *Küche*: doppeltes Lendenstück.
bar·on·age ['bærənɪdʒ] *s*. **1**. *coll*. die Ba'rone *pl*.; **2**. Verzeichnis *n* der Ba'rone; **3**. Rang *m* e-s Ba'rons; '**bar·on·ess** [-nɪs] *s*. **1**. *Brit*. Ba'ronin *f*; **2**. *nicht-Brit*. Ba'ronin *f*, Freifrau *f*; '**bar·on·et** [-nɪt] **I** *s*. Baronet *m* (*brit. Adelstitel*; *abbr.* **Bart.**); **II** *v/t*. zum Baronet ernennen; '**bar·on·et·age** [-nɪtɪdʒ] *s*. **1**. *coll*. die Baronets *pl*.; **2**. Verzeichnis *n* der Baronets; '**bar·on·et·cy** [-nɪtsɪ] *s*. Titel *m od*. Rang *m* e-s Baronet; **ba·ro·ni·al** [bə'rəʊnjəl] *adj*. **1**. Barons..., freiherrlich; **2**. prunkvoll, großartig; '**bar·o·ny** [-nɪ] *s*. Baro'nie *f* (*Gebiet od. Würde*).
ba·roque [bə'rɒk] **I** *adj*. **1**. ba'rock (*a. von Perlen u. fig*.); **2**. *fig*. prunkvoll; über'steigert; bi'zarr, verschnörkelt; **II** *s*. **3**. *allg*. Ba'rock *n, m*.
bar par·lour *s. Brit*. Schank-, Gaststube *f*.
barque → **bark³**.
bar·rack ['bærək] **I** *s*. **1**. *mst pl*. Ka'serne *f*: *a ~s* e-e Kaserne; **2**. *mst fig*. 'Mietska,serne *f*; **II** *v/t*. **3**. in Ka'sernen *od*. Ba'racken 'unterbringen; **4**. F *sport, pol*. auspfeifen, -buhen; **III** *v/i*. **5**. F buhen, pfeifen: **~ for** (*laut*stark) anfeuern; **~ square** *s*. ✕ Ka'sernenhof *m*.
bar·rage¹ ['bærɑːʒ] *s*. **1**. ✕ Sperrfeuer *n*; **2**. ✕ Sperre *f*: **creeping ~** Feuerwalze *f*; **~ balloon** Sperrballon *m*; **3**. *fig*. über'wältigende Menge: **a ~ of questions** ein Schwall *od*. Kreuzfeuer von Fragen.
bar·rage² ['bærɑːʒ] *s*. Talsperre *f*, Stau-

B

damm *m*.

bar·ra·try ['bærətrɪ] *s*. **1.** ⚖, ⚓ Baratte-'rie *f* (*Veruntreuung*); **2.** ⚖ schika'nöses Prozessieren (*od*. Anstiftung *f* dazu); **3.** Ämterschacher *m*.

barred [baːd] *adj*. **1.** (ab)gesperrt, verriegelt; **2.** gestreift; **3.** ♪ durch Taktstriche abgeteilt; **4.** ⚖ verjährt.

bar·rel ['bærəl] *s*. **1.** Fass *n*, Tonne *f*; *im Ölhandel*: Barrel *n*: **have s.o. over a ~** F j-n in s-r Gewalt haben; **scrape the ~** F den letzten, schäbigen Rest zs.-kratzen; **2.** ⚙ Walze *f*, Rolle *f*, Trommel *f*, Zy'linder *m*, (rundes) Gehäuse; (Gewehr)Lauf *m*, (Geschütz)Rohr *n*; Kolbenrohr *n*; Rumpf *m* *e-s Dampfkessels*; Tintenbehälter *m* *e-r Füllfeder*; Walze *f der Drehorgel*; Kiel *m* *e-r Feder*; Zylinder *m* *e-r Spritze*; **3.** Rumpf *m* *e-s Pferdes etc.*; **II** *v/t*. **4.** in Fässer füllen *od*. packen; **III** *v/i*. **5.** F rasen, sausen; **~ chair** *s*. Lehnstuhl *m* mit hoher runder Lehne; **~ drain** *s*. ⚙, 🜂 gemauerter runder 'Abzugska,nal; **'~·house** *s*. *Am*. *sl*. Spe'lunke *f*, Kneipe *f*.

bar·rel(l)ed ['bærəld] *adj*. **1.** fassförmig; **2.** in Fässer gefüllt; **3.** ...läufig (*Gewehr*).

'bar·rel|,mak·er *s*. Fassbinder *m*; **~ organ** *s*. ♪ Drehorgel *f*; **~ roll** *s*. ✈ Rolle *f* (*im Kunstflug*); **~ roof** *s*. 🜂 Tonnendach *n*; **~ vault** *s*. 🜂 Tonnengewölbe *n*.

bar·ren ['bærən] **I** *adj*. □ **1.** unfruchtbar (*Lebewesen, Pflanze etc.*; *a. fig.*); **2.** öde, kahl, dürr; **3.** *fig*. trocken, langweilig, seicht; dürftig; **4.** 'unprodukˌtiv (*Geist*); tot (*Kapital*); **5.** leer, arm (*of* an *dat*.); **II** *s*. **6.** *mst pl*. Ödland *n*; **'bar·ren·ness** [-nɪs] *s*. **1.** Unfruchtbarkeit *f* (*a. fig.*); **2.** *fig*. Trockenheit *f*, geistige Leere, Dürftigkeit *f*, Dürre *f*.

bar·ri·cade [,bærɪ'keɪd] **I** *s*. **1.** Barri'kade *f*: **mount** (*od*. **go to**) **the ~s** auf die Barrikaden steigen (*a. fig.*); **2.** *fig*. Hindernis *n*; **II** *v/t*. **3.** (ver)barrikadieren, (ver)sperren (*a. fig.*).

bar·ri·er ['bærɪə] *s*. **1.** Schranke *f* (*a. fig.*), Barri'ere *f*, Sperre *f*: **~ cream** Schutzcreme *f*; **2.** Schlag-, Grenzbaum *m*; **3.** *sport* 'Startma,schine *f*; **4.** *fig*. Hindernis *n* (**to** für); Mauer *f*; (*Sprachetc.*)Barri'ere *f*; **5.** ⚲ 'Eisbarriˌere *f* der Ant'arktis: ⚲ **Reef** Barrierriff *n*.

bar·ring ['baːrɪŋ] *prp*. abgesehen von, ausgenommen: **~ errors** Irrtümer vorbehalten; **~ a miracle** wenn kein Wunder geschieht.

bar·ris·ter ['bærɪstə] *s*. ⚖ **1.** **~-at-law** *Brit*. Barrister *m*, plädierender Rechtsanwalt (vor höheren Gerichten); **2.** *Am*. *allg*. Rechtsanwalt *m*.

bar room *s*. Schankstube *f*.

bar·row¹ ['bærəʊ] *s*. **1.** 'Tumulus *m*, Hügelgrab *n*; **2.** Hügel *m*.

bar·row² ['bærəʊ] *s*. (Hand-, Schub-, Gepäck-, Obst)Karre(n *m*) *f*.

bar·row³ ['bærəʊ] *s*. ✎ Bork *m* (*im Ferkelalter kastriertes Schwein*).

bar·row| boy *s*., **'~·man** [-mən] *s*. [*irr*.] Straßenhändler *m*, ˌfliegender Händler‘.

bar| steel *s*. ⚙ Stangenstahl *m*; **'~·tender** *s*. → barkeeper *s*.

bar·ter ['baːtə] **I** *v/i*. Tauschhandel treiben; **II** *v/t*. *im Handel* (ein-, 'um)tauschen, austauschen (**for, against** gegen): **~ away** verschachern, -kaufen (*a. fig. Ehre etc.*); **III** *s*. Tauschhandel *m*, Tausch *m* (*a. fig.*): **~ shop** Tauschladen *m*; **~ trans·ac·tion** *s*. ✝ Tausch(handels-), Kompensati'onsgeschäft *n*.

bar·y·tone → baritone.

bas·al ['beɪsl] *adj*. □ **1.** an der Basis *od*.

Grundfläche befindlich; **2.** *mst fig*. grundlegend: **~ metabolism** ✳ Grundstoffwechsel *m*; **~ metabolic rate** ✳ Grundumsatz *m*; **~ cell** *biol*. Basalzelle *f*.

ba·salt ['bæsɔːlt] *s*. *geol*. Ba'salt *m*; **ba·sal·tic** [bə'sɔːltɪk] *adj*. ba'saltisch, Basalt...

base¹ [beɪs] **I** *s*. **1.** Basis *f*, 'Unterteil *m*, *n*, Boden *m*; 'Unterbau *m*, -lage *f*; Funda'ment *n*; **2.** Fuß *m*, Sockel *m*; Sohle *f*; **3.** *fig*. Basis *f*: a) Grund(lage *f*) *m*, b) Ausgangspunkt *m*, c) a. **~ camp** *mount*. Basislager *n*; **4.** Grundstoff *m*, Hauptbestandteil *m*; **5.** 🜂 Grundlinie *f*, -fläche *f*, -zahl *f*; **6.** 🜂 Base *f*; *Färberei*: Beize *f*; **7.** *sport* a) Grund-, Startlinie *f*, b) Mal *n*: **not to get to first ~** (**with s.o.**) F *fig*. keine Chance haben (bei j-m); **8.** ✕, ⚓ a) Standort *m*, Stati'on *f*, b) (Operati'ons)Basis *f*, Stützpunkt *m*, c) (Flug)Basis *f*, *Am*. (Flieger)Horst *m*: **naval ~** Flottenstützpunkt, d) E'tappe *f*; **II** *v/t*. **9.** stützen, gründen (**on, upon** auf *acc*.): **be ~d on** beruhen auf (*dat*.), sich stützen auf (*acc*.); **~ o.s. on** sich verlassen auf (*acc*.); **10.** *a*. ✕ stationieren; → **based** 2.

base² [beɪs] *adj*. □ **1.** gemein, niedrig, niederträchtig; **2.** minderwertig, unedel: **~ metals**; **3.** falsch, unecht (*Geld*): **~ coin** falsche Münze, *coll*. Falschgeld *n*, *Am*. Scheidemünze *f*; **4.** *ling*. unrein, unklassisch.

'base·ball *s*. *sport* **1.** Baseball(spiel *n*) *m*; **2.** Baseball *m*.

based [beɪst] *adj*. **1.** (**on**) gegründet (auf *acc*.), beruhend (auf *dat*.), mit e-r Grundlage (von); **2.** ✕ *in Zssgn* mit ... als Stützpunkt, stationiert in (*dat*.), *a*. (land- *etc*.)gestützt; **3.** *in Zssgn* mit Sitz in (*dat*.): **a London-~ company**.

base·less ['beɪslɪs] *adj*. grundlos, unbegründet.

base| line *s*. **1.** Grundlinie *f* (*a. sport*); **2.** *surv*. Standlinie *f*; **3.** ✕ Basislinie *f*; **~ load** *s*. ⚡ Grundlast *f*, -belastung *f*; **'~·man** [-mən] *s*. [*irr*.] *Baseball*: Malhüter *m*.

base·ment ['beɪsmənt] *s*. 🜂 **1.** Kellergeschoss, *östr*. -geschoß *n*; **2.** Grundmauer(n *pl*.) *f*.

base·ness ['beɪsnɪs] *s*. **1.** Gemeinheit *f*, Niederträchtigkeit *f*; **2.** Minderwertigkeit *f*; **3.** Unechtheit *f*.

ba·ses ['beɪsiːz] *pl. von* **basis**.

base wal·lah *s*. ✕ *Brit. sl*. E'tappenschwein *n*.

bash [bæʃ] F **I** *v/t*. **1.** heftig schlagen, einhauen auf (*acc*.) (*a*. F *fig*.): **~ in** a) einschlagen, b) verbeulen; **~ up** a) j-n zs.-schlagen, b) *Auto* zu Schrott fahren; **II** *s*. **2.** heftiger Schlag: **have a ~ at s.th.** es mit et. probieren; **3.** Beule *f* (*am Auto etc.*); **4.** *Brit*. (tolle) Party.

bash·ful ['bæʃfʊl] *adj*. □ schüchtern, verschämt, scheu; zu'rückhaltend; **'bash·ful·ness** [-nɪs] *s*. Schüchternheit *f*, blueing.

bash·ing ['bæʃɪŋ] *s*. F ˌSenge‘ *f*, Prügel *pl*.: **get** (*od*. **take**) **a ~** Prügel beziehen (*a. fig.*).

bas·ic ['beɪsɪk] **I** *adj*. (□ **~ally**) **1.** grundlegend, die Grundlage bildend; elemen'tar; Einheits..., Grund...; **2.** 🜂, *geol., min*. basisch; **3.** ⚡ ständig (*Belastung*); **II** *s*. **4.** *a*.) Grundlagen *pl*., b) das Wesentliche; **5.** → **Basic English**; **'bas·i·cal·ly** [-kəlɪ] *adv*. im Grunde, grundsätzlich.

Bas·ic| Eng·lish *s*. Basic English *n* (*vereinfachte Form des Englischen von C. K. Ogden*); ⚲ **for·mu·la** *s*. 🜂 Grundfor-

mel *f*; ⚲ **in·dus·try** *s*. 'Grund(stoff)-, 'Schlüsselinduˌstrie *f*; ⚲ **i·ron** *s*. ⚙ Thomaseisen *n*; ⚲ **load** *s*. ⚡ ständige Grundlast; ⚲ **ma·ter·i·als** *s. pl*. Grund-, Ausgangsstoffe *pl*.; ⚲ **ra·tion** *s*. ✕ Mindestverpflegungssatz *m*; ⚲ **research** *s*. Grundlagenforschung *f*; ⚲ **sal·a·ry** *s*. ✝ Grundgehalt *n*; ⚲ **size** *s*. ⚙ Sollmaß *n*; ⚲ **slag** *s*. 🜚 Thomasschlacke *f*; ⚲ **steel** *s*. ⚙ Thomasstahl *m*; ⚲ **train·ing** *s*. *a*. ✕ Grundausbildung *f*; ⚲ **wage** *s*. ✝ Grundlohn *m*.

bas·il ['bæzl] *s*. 🌿 Ba'silienkraut *n*, Ba'silikum *n*.

ba·sil·i·ca [bə'zɪlɪkə] *s*. 🜂 Ba'silika *f*.

bas·i·lisk ['bæzɪlɪsk] **I** *s*. **1.** Basi'lisk *m* (*Fabeltier*); **2.** *zo*. Legu'an *m*; **II** *adj*. **3.** Basilisken...: **~ eye**.

ba·sin ['beɪsn] *s*. **1.** (Wasser-, Wasch-*etc*.)Becken *n*, Schale *f*, Schüssel *f*; **2.** Fluss-, Hafenbecken *n*; Schwimmbecken *n*, Bas'sin *n*; **3.** a) Stromgebiet *n*, b) (kleine) Bucht; **4.** Wasserbehälter *m*; **5.** Becken *n*, Einsenkung *f*, Mulde *f*; **6.** (Kohlen- *etc*.)Lager *n* *od*. Revier *n*.

ba·sis ['beɪsɪs] *pl*. **-ses** [-siːz] *s*. **1.** Basis *f*, Grundlage *f*, Funda'ment *n*: **~ of discussion** Diskussionsbasis *f*; **take as a ~** zugrunde legen; **2.** Hauptbestandteil *m*; **3.** 🜂 Basis *f*, Grundlinie *f*, -fläche *f*; **4.** ✕, ⚓ (Operati'ons)Basis *f*, Stützpunkt *m*.

bask [baːsk] *v/i*. sich aalen, sich sonnen (*a. fig.*): **~ in the sun** ein Sonnenbad nehmen.

bas·ket ['baːskɪt] *s*. **1.** Korb *m*: 🜚 **~ of commodities** Warenkorb *m*; **2.** Korb *m* (voll); **3.** *Basketball*: a) Korb *m*, b) Treffer *m*, Korb *m*; **4.** (Passa'gier)Korb *m*, Gondel *f* (*e-s Luftballons od. Luftschiffes*); **5.** Säbelkorb *m*; **6.** Tastenfeld *n* (*der Schreibmaschine*); **'~·ball** *s*. *sport* **1.** Basketball(spiel *n*) *m*; **2.** Basketball *m*; **~ case** *Am*. F **1.** Arm- u. Beinamputierte(r *m*) *f*; **2.** to'tales ˌWrack‘; **~ chair** *s*. Korbsessel *m*; **~ din·ner** *s*. *Am*. Picknick *n*.

bas·ket·ful ['baːskɪtfʊl] *pl*. **-fuls** *s*. ein Korb (voll).

bas·ket| hilt *s*. Säbelkorb *m*; **~ lunch** *s*. *Am*. Picknick *n*.

bas·ket·ry ['baskɪtrɪ] *s*. Korbwaren *pl*.

Basque [bæsk] **I** *s*. Baske *m*, Baskin *f*; **II** *adj*. baskisch.

bas-re·lief ['bæsrɪ,liːf] *s*. *sculp*. 'Bas-, 'Flachreliˌef *n*.

bass¹ [beɪs] ♪ **I** *adj*. Bass...; **II** *s*. Bass *m* (*Stimme, Sänger, Instrument u. Partie*).

bass² [bæs] *pl. mst* **bass** *s*. *ichth*. Barsch *m*.

bass³ [bæs] *s*. **1.** (Linden)Bast *m*; **2.** Bastmatte *f*.

bas·set ['bæsɪt] *s*. *zo*. Basset *m* (*ein Dachshund*).

bas·si·net [,bæsɪ'net] *s*. Korbwiege *f*; Stubenwagen *m*; Korb(kinder)wagen *m* (*mit Verdeck*).

bas·soon [bə'suːn] *s*. ♪ Fa'gott *n*.

bas·so| pro·fun·do ['bæsəʊ prə'fʌndəʊ] (*Ital.*) *s*. ♪ tiefster Bass (*Stimme od. Sänger*); **,~-re·lie·vo** [-rɪ'liːvəʊ] *pl*. **-vos** → bas-relief.

'bass-re·lief ['bæs-] → bas-relief.

bass vi·ol [beɪs] *s*. ♪ 'Cello *n*.

'bass·wood ['bæs-] *s*. 🌿 **1.** Linde *f*; **2.** Lindenholz *n*.

bast [bæst] *s*. (Linden)Bast *m*.

bas·tard ['bæstəd] **I** *s*. **1.** Bastard *m*, *a*. ⚖ uneheliches Kind; **2.** *biol*. Bastard *m*, Mischling *m*; **3.** *fig*. a) Fälschung *f*, Nachahmung *f*, b) Scheußlichkeit *f*; **4.** a) V ˌSchwein‘ *n*, ˌScheißkerl‘ *m*, b) *iro*. alter Ha'lunke, c) Kerl *m*; **II** *adj*. **5.**

unehelich, Bastard...; **6.** *biol.* Bastard...; **7.** *fig.* unecht, falsch; **8.** ab-'norm; **'bas·tard·ize** [-daız] I *v/t.* **1.** 🌱 für unehelich erklären; **2.** verschlechtern, verfälschen; **II** *v/i.* **3.** entarten; **'bas·tard·ized** [-daızd] *adj.* entartet, Mischlings..., Bastard...

bas·tard| slip → *bastard* 1; **~ ti·tle** *s.* *typ.* Schmutztitel *m.*

bas·tar·dy ['bæstədı] *s.* uneheliche Geburt: **~ procedure** Verfahren *n* zur Feststellung der (unehelichen) Vaterschaft u. Unterhaltspflicht.

baste¹ [beıst] *v/t.* **1.** ,(ver)hauen', verprügeln; **2.** *fig.* beschimpfen, herfallen über (*acc.*).

baste² [beıst] *v/t.* **1.** Braten *etc.* mit Fett begießen; **2.** *Docht der Kerze* mit geschmolzenem Wachs begießen.

baste³ [beıst] *v/t.* lose (an)heften.

bast·ing ['beıstıŋ] *s.* (Tracht *f*) Prügel *pl.*

bas·tion ['bæstıən] *s.* Ba'stei *f*, Basti'on *f*, Bollwerk *n* (*a. fig.*).

bat¹ [bæt] I *s.* **1.** *sport* a) Schlagholz *n*, Schläger *m* (*bsd. Baseball u. Kricket*): **carry one's ~** *Kricket:* noch im Spiel sein; **off one's own ~** *Kricket u. fig.* selbstständig, ohne Hilfe, auf eigene Faust; **right off the ~** F auf Anhieb; **be at (the) ~** am Schlagen sein, dran sein; **go to ~ for s.o.** *Baseball:* für j-n einspringen, *fig.* → 6, b) → *batsman;* **2.** F Stockhieb *m;* **3.** *Brit. sl.* (Schritt)Tempo *n:* **at a rare ~** mit e-m ,Affenzahn'; **4.** *Am. sl.* ,Saufe'rei' *f:* **go on a ~** e-e ,Sauftour' machen; **II** *v/i.* **5.** a) (mit dem Schlagholz) schlagen, b) am Schlagen sein; → *batting* 3; **6.** **~ for s.o.** *fig.* für j-n eintreten.

bat² [bæt] *s.* **1.** *zo.* Fledermaus *f:* **have ~s in the belfry** verrückt sein, ,e-n Vogel haben'; → *blind* 1; **2.** ✈, ✕ 'radargelenkte Bombe.

bat³ [bæt] *v/t.:* **~ the eyes** mit den Augen blinzeln *od.* zwinkern; **without ~ting an eyelid** (*Am. eyelash*) ohne mit der Wimper zu zucken; **I never ~ted an eyelid** ich habe kein Auge zugetan.

ba·ta·ta [bə'tɑːtə] *s.* ♀ Ba'tate *f*, 'Süßkar,toffel *f.*

batch [bætʃ] *s.* **1.** Schub *m* (*die auf einmal gebackene Menge Brot*): **a ~ of bread**, **2.** ⊙ a) Schub *m*, b) Satz *m* (*Material*), Charge *f*, Füllung *f;* **3.** Schub *m;* ,Schwung' *m:* a) Gruppe *f* (*von Personen*), Trupp *m* (*Gefangener*), b) Schicht *f*, Satz *m* (*Muster*), Stapel *m*, Stoß *m* (*Briefe etc.*), Par'tie *f*, Posten *m* (*gleicher Dinge*), *Computer:* Stapel *m:* **in ~es** schubweise; **'~-,pro·cess** *v/t.* stapelweise verarbeiten; **~ pro·duc·tion** *s.* Serienfertigung *f.*

bate¹ [beıt] I *v/i.* abnehmen, nachlassen; **II** *v/t.* schwächen, *Hoffnung etc.* vermindern, *Neugier etc.* mäßigen, *Forderung etc.* her'absetzen: **with ~d breath** mit verhaltenem Atem, gespannt.

bate² [beıt] *s.* ⊙ *Gerberei:* Ätzlauge *f.*

bate³ [beıt] *s. Brit. sl.* Wut *f.*

ba·teau [bɑː'təʊ] *pl.* **-teaux** [-'təʊz] (*Fr.*) *s. Am.* leichtes langes Flussboot; **~ bridge** *s.* Pon'tonbrücke *f.*

bath [bɑːθ] I *pl.* **baths** [-ðz] *s.* **1.** (Wannen)Bad *n:* **take a ~** ein Bad nehmen, baden, *Am. sl.* (*bsd. finanziell*) ,baden gehen'; **2.** Badewasser *n;* **3.** Badewanne *f:* **enamelled ~;** **4.** Badezimmer *n;* **5.** *mst pl.* a) Badeanstalt *f*, b) Badeort *m;* **6.** 🗲 *phot.* a) Bad *n* (*Behandlungsflüssigkeit*), b) Behälter *m* dafür; **7.** *Brit.:* **order of the 𝓛** Bathorden *m;*

Knight of the 𝓛 Ritter *m* des Bathordens; **Knight Commander of the 𝓛** Komtur *m* des Bathordens; **II** *v/t.* **8.** *Kind etc.* baden; **III** *v/i.* **9.** baden, ein Bad nehmen.

Bath| brick *s.* Me'tallputzstein *m;* **~ bun** *s.* über'zuckertes Kuchenbrötchen; **~ chair** *s.* Rollstuhl *m.*

bathe [beıð] I *Auge, Hand,* (*verletzten*) *Körperteil* baden, in Wasser *etc.* tauchen; **2.** **~d in sunlight** (*perspiration*) in Sonne (Schweiß) gebadet; **~d in tears** in Tränen aufgelöst; **3.** *poet.* bespülen; **II** *v/i.* **4.** (sich) baden; **5.** schwimmen; **6.** (Heil)Bäder nehmen; **7.** *fig.* sich baden *od.* schwelgen (*in* in *dat.*); **III** *s.* **8.** *bsd. Brit.* Bad *n im Freien;* **'bath·er** [-ðə] *s.* **1.** Badende(r *m*) *f;* **2.** Badegast *m.*

'bath·house *s. Am.* **1.** Badeanstalt *f;* **2.** 'Umkleideka,binen *pl.*

bath·ing ['beıðıŋ] *s.* Baden *n;* **~ beau·ty** *s.,* **~ belle** *s.* F Badeschönheit *f;* **~ cos·tume** → *bathing suit;* **~ draw·ers** *s. pl.* Badehose *f;* **~ dress** → *bathing suit;* **~ gown** *s.* Badeanzug *m;* **~ ma·chine** *s. hist.* Badekarren *m* (*fahrbare Umkleidekabine*); **~ suit** *s.* Badeanzug *m.*

Bath met·al *s.* ⊙ 'Tombak *m.*

ba·thos ['beıθɒs] *s.* **1.** Abgleiten *n* vom Erhabenen zum Lächerlichen; **2.** Gemeinplatz *m*, Plattheit *f;* **3.** falsches Pathos; **4.** a) Null-, Tiefpunkt *m*, b) Gipfel *m der Dummheit etc.*

'bath|·robe *s.* Bademantel *m;* **'~·room** [-rʊm] *s.* Badezimmer *n; weitS.* Klo'sett *n;* **~ salts** *s. pl.* Badesalz *n;* **2 stone** *s.* Muschelkalkstein *m;* **~ tow·el** *s.* Badetuch *n;* **'~·tub** *s.* Badewanne *f* (*a.* F *Skisport*).

ba·thym·e·try [bə'θımıtrı] *s.* Tiefen- *od.* Tiefseemessung *f.*

bath·y·sphere ['bæθı,sfıə] *s.* ⊙ Tiefseetaucherkugel *f.*

ba·tik ['bætık] *s.* 'Batik(druck) *m.*

ba·tiste [bæ'tiːst] *s.* Ba'tist *m.*

bat·man ['bætmən] *s.* [*irr.*] ✕ *Brit.* Offi-'ziersbursche *m.*

ba·ton ['bætən] *s.* **1.** (Amts-, Kom'mando)Stab *m:* **Field-Marshal's ~** Marschallsstab *m;* **2.** ♪ Taktstock *m*, Stab *m;* **3.** *sport* (Staffel)Stab *m;* **4.** *Brit.* Schlagstock *m*, (Poli'zei)Knüppel *m.*

ba·tra·chi·an [bə'treıkjən] *zo.* I *adj.* frosch-, krötenartig; **II** *s.* Ba'trachier *m*, Froschlurch *m.*

bats·man ['bætsmən] *s.* [*irr.*] *Kricket, Baseball etc.:* Schläger *m*, Schlagmann *m.*

bat·tal·ion [bə'tæljən] *s.* ✕ Batail'lon *n.*

bat·tels ['bætlz] *s. pl.* (*Universität Oxford*) College-Rechnungen *pl.* für Lebensmittel *etc.*

bat·ten¹ ['bætn] *v/i.* **1.** fett werden (*on* von *dat.*), gedeihen; **2.** (*on*) *a. fig.* sich mästen (mit), sich gütlich tun (an *dat.*): **~ on others** auf Kosten anderer dick u. fett werden.

bat·ten² ['bætn] I *s.* **1.** Latte *f*, Leiste *f;* **2.** Diele *f*, (Fußboden)Brett *n;* **II** *v/t.* **3.** mit Latten verkleiden *od.* befestigen; **4.** **~ down the hatches** a) ♣ die Luken schalken, b) *fig.* dichtmachen.

bat·ter¹ ['bætə] ⚠ I *v/i.* sich nach oben verjüngen; **II** *s.* Böschung *f*, Verjüngung *f*, Abdachung *f.*

bat·ter² ['bætə] I *v/t.* **1.** mit heftigen Schlägen traktieren; (zer)schlagen, demolieren; *Ehefrau, Kind* (ständig) misshandeln *od.* schlagen *od.* prügeln: **~ed wives** misshandelte (Ehe)Frauen; **~**

down (*od.* **in**) *Tür* einschlagen; **2.** ✕ *u. weitS.* bombardieren: **~ down** zs.-schießen; **3.** beschädigen, zerbeulen, *a. j-n* böse zurichten, arg mitnehmen; **II** *v/i.* **4.** heftig *od.* wiederholt schlagen: **~ at the door** gegen die Tür hämmern; **'bat·tered** [-təd] *adj.* **1.** zerschlagen, zerschmettert, demoliert; **2.** a) abgenutzt, zerbeult, beschädigt, b) *a. fig.* arg mitgenommen, übel zugerichtet, c) miss'handelt (*Kind etc.*).

bat·ter·ing ram ['bætərıŋ-] *s.* ✕ *hist.* (Belagerungs)Widder *m*, Sturmbock *m.*

bat·ter·y ['bætərı] *s.* **1.** a) ✕ Batte'rie *f*, b) ♣ Geschützgruppe *f;* **2.** 🗲, ⊙ Batte-'rie *f* (*von Maschinen, Flaschen etc.*); **4.** ♪ 'Legebatte,rie *f;* **5.** ♪ Batte-'rie *f*, Schlagzeuggruppe *f;* **6.** *Baseball:* Werfer *m* u. Fänger *m;* **7.** 🌱 Tätlichkeit *f*, *a.* Körperverletzung *f;* → *assault* 3; **~ cell** *s.* Sammelzelle *f;* **'~-,charg·ing sta·tion** *s.* 🗲 'Ladestati,on *f;* **~ farm·ing** *s.* Massentierhaltung *f.;* **'~-,op·er·at·ed** *adj.* batteriebetrieben, Batterie...; **~ hen** *s.* Batte'riehenne *f.*

bat·ting ['bætıŋ] *s.* **1.** Schlagen *n bsd. der Rohbaumwolle zu Watte;* **2.** (Baumwoll)Watte *f;* **3.** *Kricket, Baseball etc.:* Schlagen *n*, Schlägerspiel *n:* **~ average** *a. fig.* Durchschnitt(sleistung *f*) *m.*

bat·tle ['bætl] I *s.* **1.** Schlacht *f* (**of** *mst* bei), Gefecht *n:* **~ of Britain** Schlacht um England (2. Weltkrieg); **2.** *fig.* Kampf *m*, Ringen *n* (**for** um, **against** gegen): **do ~** kämpfen, sich schlagen; **fight a ~** e-n Kampf führen; **fight a losing ~ against** e-n aussichtslosen Kampf führen gegen; **fight s.o.'s ~** j-s Sache vertreten; **give** (*od.* **join**) **~** e-e Schlacht liefern, sich zum Kampf stellen; **that is half the ~** damit ist es schon halb gewonnen; **line of ~** Schlachtlinie *f;* **~ of words** Wortgefecht *n;* **~ of wits** geistiges Duell; **II** *v/i.* **3.** *mst fig.* kämpfen, streiten, fechten (**with** mit, **for** um, **against** gegen); **~ ar·ray** *s.* ✕ Schlachtordnung *f;* **'~·ax(e)** *s.* **1.** ✕ *hist.* Streitaxt *f;* **2.** F ,alter Drachen' (*Frau*); **~ cruis·er** *s.* ✕ Schlachtkreuzer *m;* **~ cry** *s.* Schlachtruf *m* (*a. fig.*).

bat·tle·dore ['bætldɔː] *s.* **1.** Waschschlägel *m;* **2.** *sport hist.* a) Federballschläger *m*, b) **~ and shuttlecock** Art Federballspiel *n.*

bat·tle| dress *s. Brit.* ✕ Dienst-, Feldanzug *m;* **~ fa·tigue** *s.* 'Kriegsneu,rose *f;* **'~·field**, **'~·ground** *s.* Schlachtfeld *n* (*a. fig.*).

bat·tle·ment ['bætlmənt] *s. mst pl.* (Brustwehr *f* mit) Zinnen *pl.*

bat·tle| or·der *s.* **1.** Schlachtordnung *f;* **2.** Gefechtsbefehl *m;* **~ piece** *s.* Schlachtenszene *f* (*in Malerei od. Literatur*); **~ roy·al** *s.* erbitterter Kampf (*a. fig.*); Massenschläge'rei *f;* **'~·ship** *s.* ✕ Schlachtschiff *n.*

bat·tue [bæ'tuː] (*Fr.*) *s.* **1.** Treibjagd *f;* **2.** (auf e-r Treibjagd erlegte) Strecke; **3.** *fig.* Mas'saker *n.*

bat·ty ['bætı] *adj. sl.* ,bekloppt'.

bau·ble ['bɔːbl] *s.* **1.** Nippsache *f;* **2.** (protziger) Schmuck; **3.** (Kinder)Spielzeug *n*, *fig.* Spiele'rei *f*, Tand *m.*

baulk [bɔːk] → *balk.*

Ba·var·i·an [bə'veərıən] I *adj.* bay(e)risch; **II** *s.* Bayer(in).

bawd [bɔːd] *s. obs.* Kupplerin *f;* **'bawd·ry** [-drı] *s.* **1.** Kuppe'lei *f;* **2.** Unzucht *f;* **3.** Obszöni'tät *f.*

bawd·y ['bɔːdı] *adj.* unzüchtig, unflätig (*Rede*); **'~·house** *s.* Bor'dell *n.*

bawl [bɔːl] I *v/i.* schreien, grölen, brül-

B

len, *Am. a.* ‚heulen‘ (*weinen*): ~ **at s.o.** j-n anbrüllen; **II** *v/t. a.* ~ **out** F j-n anbrüllen, zs.-stauchen.

bay¹ [beɪ] *s.* **1.** ♀ *a.* ~ **tree** Lorbeer (-baum) *m*; **2.** *pl.* a) Lorbeerkranz *m*, b) *fig.* Lorbeeren *pl.*, Ehren *pl.*

bay² [beɪ] *s.* **1.** Bai *f*, Bucht *f*, Meerbusen *m*; **2.** Talbucht *f*.

bay³ [beɪ] *s.* **1.** △ Fach *n*, Abteilung *f*, Feld *n zwischen Pfeilern, Balken etc.*; Brückenglied *n*, Joch *n*; **2.** △ Fensternische *f*, Erker *m*; **3.** ✔ Abteilung *f od.* Zelle *f im Flugzeugrumpf*; **4.** ⚓ 'Schiffslaza,rett *n*; **5.** 🚂 *Brit.* Seitenbahnsteig *m, bsd.* 'Endstati͵on *f e-s* Nebengeleises.

bay⁴ [beɪ] *v/i.* **1.** (dumpf) bellen (*bsd. Jagdhund*): ~ **at s.o.** *od.* **s.th.** j-n *od.* et. anbellen; **II** *v/t.* **2.** *obs.* anbellen: ~ **the moon**; **III** *s.* **3.** dumpfes Gebell *der Meute*: **be** (*od.* **stand**) **at** ~ gestellt sein (*Wild*), *fig.* in die Enge getrieben sein; **bring to** ~ *Wild* stellen, *fig.* in die Enge treiben; **keep** (*od.* **hold**) **at** ~ a) sich j-n vom Leibe halten, b) j-n in Schach halten, fern halten; *Seuche, Feuer etc.* unter Kontrolle halten; **turn to** ~ sich stellen (*a. fig.*).

bay⁵ [beɪ] **I** *adj.* ka'stanienbraun (*Pferd*): ~ **horse** → **II** *s.* Braune(r) *m*.

bay leaf *s.* Lorbeerblatt *n*.

bay·o·net ['beɪənɪt] ⚔ **I** *s.* Bajo'nett *n*, Seitengewehr *n*: **at the point of the** ~ mit dem Bajo'nett, im Sturm; **fix the** ~ das Seitengewehr aufpflanzen; **II** *v/t.* mit dem Bajo'nett angreifen *od.* niederstechen; **III** *adj.* ⊙ Bajonett... (-*fassung, -verschluss*).

bay·ou ['baɪuː] *s. Am.* sumpfiger Flussarm (*Südstaaten der USA*).

bay| rum *s.* 'Bayrum *m*, Pi'mentrum *m*; ~ **salt** *s.* Seesalz *n*; ♀ **State** *s. Am.* (*Beiname von*) Massachusetts; ~ **window** *s.* **1.** Erkerfenster *n*; **2.** *Am. sl.*, ‚Vorbau‘ *m*, Bauch *m*; '~**work** *s.* △ Fachwerk *n*.

ba·zaar [bə'zɑː] *s.* **1.** (*Orient*) Ba'sar *m*; **2.** ♀ Warenhaus *n*; **3.** 'Wohltätigkeits-ba,sar *m*.

ba·zoo·ka [bə'zuːkə] *s.* ⚔ Ba'zooka *f* (*Panzerabwehrwaffe*).

B bat·ter·y *s.* ⚡ An'odenbatte,rie *f*.

be [biː; bɪ] [*irr.*] **I** *v/aux.* **1.** *bildet das Passiv transitiver Verben*: **I was cheated** ich wurde betrogen; **I was told** man sagte mir; **2.** *lit., bildet das Perfekt einiger intransitiver Verben*: **he is come** er ist gekommen *od.* da; **3.** *bildet die umschriebene Form* (*continuous od. progressive form*) *der Verben*: **he is reading** er liest gerade; **the house was being built** das Haus war im Bau; **what I was going to say** was ich sagen wollte; **4.** *drückt die* (*nahe*) *Zukunft aus*: **I am leaving for Paris tomorrow** ich reise morgen nach Paris (ab); **5.** *mit inf. zum Ausdruck der Absicht, Pflicht, Möglichkeit etc.*: **I am to go** ich soll gehen; **the house is to let** das Haus ist zu vermieten; **he is to be pitied** er ist zu bedauern; **it was not to be found** es war nicht zu finden; **6.** *Kopula*: **trees are green** (*die*) Bäume sind grün; **the book is mine** (**my brother's**) das Buch gehört mir (m-m Bruder); **II** *v/i.* **7.** (vor'handen *od.* anwesend) sein, bestehen, sich befinden, geschehen; werden: **I think, therefore I am** ich denke, also bin ich; **to be or not to be** sein oder nicht sein; **it was not to be** es hat nicht sollen sein; **so be it!** gut so!, es sei es!, gut so!; **how is it that ...?** wie kommt es, dass ...?; **what will you**

be when you grow up? was willst du werden, wenn du erwachsen bist?; **there is no substitute for wool** für Wolle gibt es keinen Ersatz; **8.** stammen (**from** aus): **he is from Liverpool**; **9.** gleichkommen, bedeuten: **seeing is believing** was man (selbst) sieht, glaubt man; **that is nothing to me** das bedeutet mir nichts; **10.** kosten: **the picture is £10** das Bild kostet 10 Pfund; **11.** **been** (*p.p.*): **have you been to Rome?** sind Sie (je) in Rom gewesen?; **has anyone been?** F ist j-d da gewesen?

beach [biːtʃ] **I** *s.* Strand *m*; **II** *v/t.* ⚓ *Schiff* auf den Strand setzen *od.* ziehen; ~ **ball** *s.* Wasserball *m*; ~ **bug·gy** *s. mot.* Strandbuggy *m*; '~,comb·er *s.* **1.** ⚓ F a) Strandgutjäger *m*, b) Her'umtreiber *m*, c) *fig.* Nichtstuer *m*; **2.** breite Strandwelle; '~**head** *s.* **1.** ⚔ Lande-, Brückenkopf *m*; **2.** *fig.* Ausgangsbasis *f*; ~ **wear** *s.* Strandkleidung *f*.

bea·con ['biːkən] **I** *s.* **1.** Leucht-, Signalfeuer *n*; (Feuer)Bake *f*, Seezeichen *n*; **2.** Leuchtturm *m*; **3.** ✔ Funkfeuer *n*, -bake *f*, Landelicht *n*; **4.** (*traffic*) ~ Verkehrsampel *f, bsd.* Blinklicht *n an Zebrastreifen*; **5.** *fig.* a) Fa'nal *n*, b) Leitstern *m*, c) 'Warnsig͵nal *n*; **II** *v/t.* **6.** mit Baken versehen; **7.** *fig.* a) erleuchten, b) j-n leiten.

bead [biːd] **I** *s.* **1.** (Glas-, Stick-, Holz-) Perle *f*; **2.** (*Blei- etc.*)Kügelchen *n*; **3.** *pl. eccl.* Rosenkranz *m*: **tell one's** ~**s** den Rosenkranz beten; **4.** (Schaum-) Bläs-chen *n*, (Tau-, Schweiß- *etc.*)Perle *f*, Tröpfchen *n*; **5.** △ perlartige Verzierung; **6.** ⊙ Wulst *m*; **7.** ⚔ (Perl)Korn *n am Gewehr*: **draw a** ~ **on** zielen auf (*acc.*); **II** *v/t.* **8.** mit Perlen *od.* perlartiger Verzierung *etc.* versehen; **9.** *wie Perlen* aufziehen, aufreihen; **III** *v/i.* **10.** perlen, Perlen bilden; '**bead·ed** [-dɪd] *adj.* **1.** mit Perlen versehen *od.* verziert; **2.** ⊙ mit Wulst; '**bead·ing** [-dɪŋ] *s.* **1.** 'Perlsticke͵rei *f*; **2.** △ Rundstab *m*; **3.** ⊙ Wulst *m*.

bea·dle ['biːdl] *s.* **1.** *bsd. Brit.* Kirchendiener *m*; **2.** *univ. Brit.* Pe'dell *m*, (*Fest- etc.*)Ordner *m*; **3.** *obs.* Büttel *m*, Gerichtsdiener *m*; '**bea·dle·dom** [-dəm] *s.* büttelhaftes Wesen.

bead mo(u)ld·ing *s.* △ Perl-, Rundstab *m*, Perlleiste *f*.

bead·y ['biːdɪ] *adj.* **1.** mit Perlen verziert; **2.** perlartig; **3.** perlend; **4.** ~ **eyes** glänzende Knopfaugen.

bea·gle ['biːgl] *s.* **1.** *zo.* Beagle *m* (*Hunderasse*); **2.** *fig.* Spi'on *m*.

beak¹ [biːk] *s.* **1.** *zo.* Schnabel *m*; **2.** F (scharfe) Nase, ‚Zinken‘ *m*; **3.** ⊙ *a.* Tülle *f*, Ausguss *m*, b) Schnauze *f*, Nase *f*, Röhre *f*.

beak² [biːk] *s. Brit. sl.* **1.** ‚Kadi‘ *m* (*Richter*); **2.** *ped.* ‚Rex‘ *m* (*Direktor*).

beaked [biːkt] *adj.* **1.** geschnäbelt, schnabelförmig; **2.** vorspringend, spitz.

beak·er ['biːkə] *s.* **1.** Becher *m*; **2.** ⚗ Becherglas *n*.

'be-all: **the** ~ **and end-all** F das A und O, das Wichtigste; j-s Ein und Alles.

beam [biːm] **I** *s.* **1.** △ Balken *m*; Tragbalken *m* (*Haus, Brücke*); *a.* ✔ Holm *m*; **2.** ⚓ a) Deckbalken *m*, b) größte Schiffsbreite: **in the** ~ in der Breite; **on the starboard** ~ querab an Steuerbord; **3.** *fig.* F Körperbreite *f e-s Menschen*: **broad in the** ~ breit (gebaut); **4.** ⊙ a) (Waage)Balken *m*, b) Weberbaum *m*, c) Pflugbaum *m*, d) Spindel *f der Drehbank*; **5.** *zo.* Stange *f am Geweih*; **6.** (Licht)Strahl *m*, (Strahlen)Bündel *n*;

mot. Fernlicht *n*; **7.** *Funk*: Richt-, Peil-, Leitstrahl *m*: **ride the** ~ ✔ genau auf dem Leitstrahl steuern; **on the** ~ a) auf dem richtigen Kurs, b) *fig.* F ‚auf Draht‘; **off the** ~ *fig.* auf dem Holzweg, (völlig) daneben (*abwegig*); **8.** strahlender Blick, Glanz *m*; **II** *v/t.* **9.** ⊙ *Weberei: Kette* aufbäumen; **10.** *a. phys.* (aus-)strahlen; **11.** a) ⚡ Funkspruch mit Richtstrahler senden, b) *Radio, TV*: ausstrahlen; **III** *v/i.* **12.** strahlen, glänzen (*a. fig.*): ~ (**up**)**on s.o.** j-n anstrahlen; ~**ing with joy** freudestrahlend; ~ **aer·i·al**, *bsd. Am.* ~ **an·ten·na** *s. Radio*: 'Richtstrahler *m*, -an͵tenne *f*; ‚~--'ends *s. pl.* **1.** ⚓ **on her** ~ mit starker Schlagseite, in Gefahr; **2.** *fig.*: **on one's** ~ ‚pleite‘; ~ **trans·mis·sion** *s.* Richtsendung *f*; ~ **trans·mit·ter** *s.* Richt(strahl)sender *m*.

bean [biːn] **I** *s.* **1.** ♀ Bohne *f*: **full of** ~**s** F ‚putzmunter‘, ‚aufgekratzt‘; **give s.o.** ~**s** *sl.* j-m ‚Saures geben‘ (*j-n schlagen, strafen, schelten*); **not to know** ~**s** *Am. sl.* keine Ahnung haben; **I haven't a** ~ *sl.* ich habe keinen roten Heller; **spill the** ~**s** *sl.* alles ausplaudern, ‚auspacken‘; **2.** bohnenförmiger Samen, (*Kaffee- etc.*)Bohne *f*; **3.** *sl.* a) Kerl *m*, b) ‚Birne‘ *f* (*Kopf*), c) ‚Grips‘ *m* (*Verstand*); **II** *v/t.* **4.** *Am. sl.* j-m ‚auf die Rübe hauen‘; ~ **curd** *s.* Tofu *m*; '~**feast** *s. Brit.* F **1.** jährliches Festessen für die Belegschaft; **2.** (feucht)fröhliches Fest.

bean·o ['biːnəʊ] *s.* F → **beanfeast** 2.

bean| pod *s.* Bohnenhülse *f*; ~ **pole** *s.* Bohnenstange *f* (*a.* F *Person*).

bean·y ['biːnɪ] *adj.* F ‚putzmunter‘, tempera'mentvoll.

bear¹ [beə] **I** *v/t.* [*irr.*] [*p.p.* **borne**; **born** (*bei Geburt*; → *a.* **borne** 2)] **1.** *Lasten etc.* tragen, befördern: ~ **a message** e-e Nachricht überbringen; → **borne** 1; **2.** *fig. Waffen, Namen etc.* tragen, führen; *Datum* tragen; **3.** *fig. Kosten, Verlust, Verantwortung, Folgen etc.* tragen, über'nehmen; → **blame** 4, **palm²** 2, **penalty** 1; **4.** *fig. Zeichen, Stempel etc.* tragen, zeigen; → **resemblance**; **5.** zur Welt bringen, gebären: ~ **children**; **he was born into a rich family** er kam als Kind reicher Eltern zur Welt; **there's one born every minute** F die Dummen werden nicht weniger; → **born** 6; **6.** *fig.* her'vorbringen: ~ **fruit** Früchte tragen (*a. fig.*); ~ **interest** Zinsen tragen; **7.** *fig. Schmerzen etc.* ertragen, (er)dulden, (er)leiden, aushalten; *e-r Prüfung etc.* standhalten: ~ **comparison** den Vergleich aushalten; *mst neg. od. interrog.*: **I cannot** ~ **him** ich kann ihn nicht leiden *od.* ausstehen; **I cannot** ~ **it** ich kann es nicht ausstehen *od.* aushalten; **his words won't** ~ **repeating** s-e Worte lassen sich unmöglich wiederholen; **it does not** ~ **thinking about** daran mag man gar nicht denken; **8.** *fig.*: ~ **a hand** zur Hand gehen, helfen (*dat.*); ~ **love** (**a grudge**) Liebe (Groll) hegen; ~ **a part in** e-e Rolle spielen bei; **9.** ~ **o.s.** sich betragen: ~ **o.s. well**; **II** *v/i.* [*irr.*] **10.** tragen, halten (*Balken, Eis etc.*): **will the ice** ~ **today?** wird das Eis heute tragen?; **11.** Früchte tragen; **12.** Richtung annehmen: ~ (**to the**) **left** sich links halten; ~ **to the north** sich nach Norden erstrecken; **13.** → **bring** 1.

Zssgn mit prp.:

bear| a·gainst *v/i.* drücken gegen; 'Widerstand leisten (*dat.*); ~ **on od.** **up·on** *v/i.* **1.** sich beziehen auf (*acc.*), betreffen (*acc.*); **2.** einwirken *od.* zielen

auf (*acc.*); **3.** drücken *od.* sich stützen auf (*acc.*), lasten auf (*dat.*); **4.** *bear hard on* j-m sehr zusetzen, j-n bedrücken; **5.** ✕ beschießen; **~ with** *v/i.* Nachsicht üben mit, Geduld haben mit; *Zssgn mit adv.*:
bear| a·way I *v/t.* forttragen, -reißen (*a. fig.*); **II** *v/i.* ♻ absegeln, abfahren; **~ down I** *v/t.* über'winden, über'wältigen; **II** *v/i.*: **~ on** a) sich wenden gegen, sich stürzen auf (*acc.*), überwältigen (*acc.*), b) sich (schnell) nähern (*dat.*), zusteuern auf (*acc.*); **~ in** *v/t.*: *it was borne in upon him* es wurde ihm klar, es drängte sich ihm auf; **~ out** *v/t.* **1.** bestätigen, bekräftigen: *bear s.o. out* j-m Recht geben; **2.** unter'stützen; **~ up I** *v/t.* **1.** stützen, ermutigen; **II** *v/i.* **2.** (*against*) (tapfer) standhalten (*dat.*), die Stirn bieten (*dat.*), mutig ertragen (*acc.*), *weitS.* sich fabelhaft halten; **3.** *Brit.* Mut fassen: **~!** Kopf hoch!
bear² [beə] **I** *s.* **1.** *zo.* Bär *m*; **2.** *fig.* a) Bär *m*, Tollpatsch *m*, b) 'Brummbär' *m*, Ekel *n*; **3.** ♰ 'Baissespeku,lant *m*, Baissi'er *m*: **~ market** Baissemarkt *m*; **4.** *ast.*: *Great(er)* ♎ Großer Bär; *Little od. Lesser* ♎ Kleiner Bär; **II** *v/i.* **5.** ♰ auf Baisse spekulieren; **III** *v/t.* **6.** ♰ **~ the market** die Kurse drücken (wollen).
bear·a·ble ['beərəbl] *adj.* □ tragbar, erträglich, zu ertragen(d).
'bear-bait·ing *s. hist.* Bärenhetze *f*.
beard [bɪəd] **I** *s.* **1.** Bart *m* (*a. von Tieren*); → *grow* 6; **2.** ♀ Grannen *pl.*; **3.** ⊙ 'Widerhaken *m* (*an Pfeil, Angel etc.*); **II** *v/t.* **4.** *fig.* mutig entgegentreten, Trotz bieten (*dat.*): **~ the lion in his den** sich in die Höhle des Löwen wagen; **'bearded** [-dɪd] *adj.* **1.** bärtig; **2.** ♀ mit Grannen; **3.** ⊙ mit (e-m) 'Widerhaken; **'beardless** [-lɪs] *adj.* **1.** bartlos; **2.** ♀ ohne Grannen; **3.** *fig.* jugendlich, unreif.
bear·er ['beərə] *s.* **1.** Träger(in); **2.** Über'bringer(in) *e-s Briefes, Schecks etc.*; **3.** ♰ Inhaber(in) *e-s Wechsels etc.*: **~ bond** Inhaberobligation *f*; **~ cheque** (*Am.* **check**) Inhaberscheck *m*; **~ securities** Inhaberpapiere *pl.*; **~ share** (*Am.* **stock**) Inhaberaktie *f*; → *payable* 1; **4.** ♀ **a good ~** ein Baum, der gut trägt; **5.** *her.* Schildhalter *m*.
bear| gar·den *s.* **1.** Bärenzwinger *m*; **2.** *fig.* 'Tollhaus' *n*; **~ hug** *s.* F heftige Um'armung.
bear·ing ['beərɪŋ] **I** *adj.* **1.** tragend; **2.** ⚛, *min.* ... enthaltend, ...haltig; **II** *s.* **3.** (Körper)Haltung *f*: *of noble ~*; **4.** Betragen *n*, Verhalten *n*: *his kindly ~*; **5.** (*on*) Bezug *m* (auf *acc.*), Beziehung *f* (zu), Verhältnis *n* (zu), Zs.-hang *m* (mit); Tragweite *f*, Bedeutung *f*: *have no ~ on* keinen Einfluss haben auf (*acc.*), nichts zu tun haben mit; *consider it in all its ~s* es in s-r ganzen Tragweite *od.* von allen Seiten betrachten; **6.** *pl.* ♻, ⚓, *surv.* Richtung *f*, Lage *f*; Peilung *f*; *fig.* Orientierung *f*: *take the ~s* die Richtung *od.* Lage feststellen, peilen; *take one's ~s* sich orientieren; *find* (*od.* *get*) *one's ~s* sich zurechtfinden; *lose one's ~s* die Orientierung verlieren, *fig.* in Verlegenheit *od.* 'ins Schwimmen' geraten; **7.** Ertragen *n*, Erdulden *n*, Nachsicht *f*: *beyond* (*all*) *~* unerträglich; *there is no ~ with such a fellow* solch ein Kerl ist unerträglich; **8.** *mst pl.* ⊙ a) (Zapfen-, Achsen- *etc.*)Lager *n*, b) Stütze *f*; **9.** *pl. her.* → *armorial* I; **10.** (Früchte)Tragen *n*: *beyond ~* ♀ nicht mehr tragend.
bear·ing| com·pass *s.* ♻ 'Peil,kompass

m; **~ line** *s.* ♻, ✐ 'Peil-, Vi'sier,linie *f*; **~ met·al** *s.* ⊙ 'Lagerme,tall *n*; **~ pin** *s.* ⊙ Lagerzapfen *m*.
bear·ish ['beərɪʃ] *adj.* **1.** bärenhaft; **2.** *fig.* plump; brummig, unfreundlich; **3.** ♰ flau, Baisse...: **~ operation** Baissespekulation *f*.
bear lead·er *s. hist.* Bärenführer *m* (*a. fig. Reisebegleiter*).
'bear|·skin *s.* **1.** Bärenfell *n*; **2.** ✕ Bärenfellmütze *f*; **'~·wood** *s.* ♀ Kreuz-, Wegdorn *m*.
beast [biːst] *s.* **1.** *bsd. vierfüßiges u. wildes Tier*: **~ of burden** Lasttier; **~s of the forest** Waldtiere; **~ of prey** Raubtier; *the ~ in us fig.* das Tier(ische) in uns; **2.** ✐ Vieh *n* (*Rinder*), *bsd.* Mastvieh *n*; **3.** *fig.* a) bru'taler Mensch, Rohling *m*, 'Bestie *f*, b) ,Biest' *n*, Ekel *n*; **beast·li·ness** ['biːstlɪnɪs] *s.* **1.** Brutali'tät *f*, Rohheit *f*; **2.** F a) Scheußlichkeit *f*, b) Gemeinheit *f*; **beast·ly** ['biːstlɪ] **I** *adj.* **1.** *fig.* viehisch, bru'tal, roh, gemein; **2.** F ab'scheulich, garstig, eklig, *Person*: *a.* ekelhaft, gemein; **II** *adv.* F scheußlich, ,verdammt': *it was ~ hot*.
beat [biːt] **I** *s.* **1.** (*regelmäßig wiederholter*) Schlag; Herz-, Puls-, Trommelschlag; Ticken *n* (*Uhr*); **2.** ♪ a) Takt (-schlag) *m*, b) Jazz: Beat *m*, 'rhythmischer Schwerpunkt, c) → *beat music*; **3.** *Versmaß*: Hebung *f*; **4.** *phys.*, *Radio*: Schwebung *f*; Schlag *f od.* Re'vier *n e-s Schutzmanns etc.*: *be on one's ~* die Runde machen; *be off* (*od.* *out of*) *one's ~ fig.* nicht in s-m Element sein; *that is outside my ~ fig.* das schlägt nicht in mein Fach *od.* ist mir ungewohnt; **6.** *Am.* (Verwaltungs)Bezirk *m*; **7.** *Am.* F a) *wer od. was alles übertrifft*: *I've never seen his ~* der schlägt alles, was ich je gesehen habe, b) (sensatio-'nelle) Erst- *od.* Al'leinmeldung *e-r Zeitung*, c) → *deadbeat*, d) → *beatnik*; **8.** *hunt.* Treibjagd *f*; **II** *adj.* **9.** F (wie) erschlagen: a) ,ganz ka'putt', erschöpft, b) verblüfft; **10.** *Am. sl.* 'antikonfor,mistisch, illusi'onslos: *the ♎ Generation* die Beat-Generation; **III** *v/t.* [*irr.*] **11.** (*regelmäßig od. häufig*) schlagen; *Teppich etc.* klopfen; *Metall* hämmern *od.* schmieden; *Eier, Sahne* (zu Schaum *od.* Schnee) schlagen: **~ a horse** ein Pferd schlagen; **~ a path** e-n Weg (durch Stampfen *etc.*) bahnen; **~ the wings** mit den Flügeln schlagen; **~ the air** *fig.* vergebliche Versuche machen, gegen Windmühlen kämpfen; **~ a charge** *Am. sl.* e-r Strafe entgehen; **~ s.th. into s.o.'s head** j-m et. einbläuen; **~ one's brains** sich den Kopf zerbrechen; → *it sl.* ,abhauen', ,verduften'; → *retreat* 1; **12.** *Gegner* schlagen, besiegen; über'treffen, -'bieten; zu viel sein für j-n: **~ s.o. at tennis** j-n im Tennis schlagen; **~ the record** den Rekord brechen; *to ~ the band* (*Wendung*) mit aller Macht, wie toll; **~ s.o. hollow** j-n vernichtend schlagen; **~ s.o. to it** j-m zuvorkommen; *that ~s me!* F das ist mir zu hoch!, da komme ich nicht mit!; *this poster takes some ~ing* dieses Plakat ist schwer zu überbieten; *that ~s everything!* F a) das ist die Höhe!, b) ist ja sagenhaft!; *can you ~ that!* F das darf doch nicht wahr sein!; *the journey ~ me* die Reise hat mich völlig erschöpft; *hock ~s claret* Weißwein ist besser als Rotwein; **13.** *Wild* aufstöbern, treiben: **~ the woods** e-e Treibjagd *od.* Suche durch die Wälder veranstalten; **14.** schlagen, verprügeln, (ver)hauen; **15.** abgehen, ,abklopfen',

e-n Rundgang machen um; **IV** *v/i.* [*irr.*] **16.** schlagen (*a. Herz etc.*); ticken (*Uhr*): **~ at** (*od.* **on**) *the door* (fest) an die Tür pochen; *rain ~ on the windows* der Regen schlug *od.* peitschte gegen die Fenster; *the hot sun was ~ing down on us* die heiße Sonne brannte auf uns nieder; **17.** *hunt.* treiben; → *bush¹* 1; **18.** ♻ lavieren: **~ against the wind** gegen den Wind kreuzen; *Zssgn mit adv.*:
beat| back *v/t.* zu'rückschlagen, -treiben, abwehren; **~ down I** *v/t.* **1.** ♰ niederschlagen, unter'drücken; **2.** ♰ a) *den Preis* drücken, b) j-n her'unterhandeln (*to* auf *acc.*); **II** *v/i.* **3.** a) her'unterbrennen (*Sonne*), b) niederprasseln (*Regen*); **~ off** *v/t. Angriff, Gegner* abschlagen, -wehren; **~ out** *v/t.* **1.** *Metall* (aus-) schmieden, hämmern; **~ s.o.'s brains** j-m den Schädel einschlagen; **2.** *Feuer* ausschlagen; **3.** *fig. et.* ,ausknobeln', her'ausarbeiten; **4.** F j-n ausstechen; **~ up** *v/t.* **1.** *Eier, Sahne* (zu Schaum *od.* Schnee) schlagen; **2.** ✕ *Rekruten* werben; **3.** j-n zs.-schlagen, verprügeln; **4.** *fig.* aufrütteln; **5.** *et.* auftreiben.
beat·en ['biːtn] *p.p. u. adj.* geschlagen; besiegt; erschöpft; ausgetreten, viel begangen (*Weg*): **~ gold** Blattgold *n*; *the ~ track fig.* das ausgefahrene Geleise; *off the ~ track* a) abgelegen, b) *fig.* ungewohnt; **~ biscuit** *Am.* ein Blätterteiggebäck *n*.
beat·er ['biːtə] *s.* **1.** Schläger *m*, Klopfer *m* (*Person od. Gerät*); Stößel *m*, Stampfe *f*; **2.** *hunt.* Treiber *m*.
be·a·tif·ic [,biːə'tɪfɪk] *adj.* **1.** glück'selig; **2.** selig machend; **be·at·i·fi·ca·tion** [biː,ætɪfɪ'keɪʃn] *s. eccl.* Seligsprechung *f*; **be·at·i·fy** [biː'ætɪfaɪ] *v/t.* **1.** beseligen, selig machen; **2.** *eccl.* selig sprechen, beatifizieren.
beat·ing ['biːtɪŋ] *s.* **1.** Schlagen *n* (*a. Herz, Flügel etc.*); **2.** Prügel *pl.*: *give s.o. a good ~* j-m e-e tüchtige Tracht Prügel verabreichen, *fig.* j-m e-e böse Schlappe bereiten; *give the enemy a good ~* den Feind aufs Haupt schlagen; *take a ~* Prügel beziehen, e-e Schlappe erleiden.
be·at·i·tude [biː'ætɪtjuːd] *s.* (Glück)'Seligkeit *f*: *the ~s bibl.* die Seligpreisungen.
beat mu·sic *s.* 'Beatmu,sik *f*.
beat·nik ['biːtnɪk] *s. hist.* Beatnik *m*, junger 'Antikonfor,mist.
beau [bəʊ] *pl.* **beaus** *od.* **beaux** [bəʊz] (*Fr.*) *s. obs.* **1.** Beau *m*, Geck *m*; **2.** Liebhaber *m*, ,Kava'lier' *m*.
beau i·de·al *s.* **1.** ('Schönheits)Ide,al *n*, Vorbild *n*; **2.** vollkommene Schönheit.
beaut [bjuːt] *s. sl.* → *beauty* 3.
beau·te·ous ['bjuːtjəs] *adj. mst poet.* (äußerlich) schön.
beau·ti·cian [bjuː'tɪʃn] *s.* Kos'metiker (-in).
beau·ti·ful ['bjuːtəfʊl] **I** *adj.* □ **1.** schön: *the ~ people* F die ,Schickeria'; **2.** wunderbar; **II** *s.* **3.** *the ~* das Schöne; die Schönen *pl.*; **'beau·ti·ful·ly** [-təflɪ] *adv.* F schön, wunderbar, ausgezeichnet: *~ warm* schön warm; **'beau·ti·fy** [-tɪfaɪ] *v/t.* verschönern, verzieren.
beau·ty ['bjuːtɪ] *s.* **1.** Schönheit *f*; **2.** *das* Schön(st)e, *et.* Schönes: *that is the ~ of it* das ist das Schönste daran; **3.** a) Prachtstück *n*: *a ~ of a vase* ein Gedicht von e-r Vase, b) F ,tolles Ding' schicke Sache: *that goal was a ~!* das Tor war Klasse!; **4.** Schönheit *f*, Per'son (*mst Frau*; *a. Tier*): **~ queen** Schönheitskönigin *f*; **5.** *iro.*: *you are a*

~! du bist mir ein Schöner od. ein Schlimmer!; ~ con·test s. Schönheitswettbewerb m; ~ par·lo(u)r, ~ sa·lon, ~ shop s. 'Schönheitssa,lon m; ~ sleep s. Schlaf m vor Mitternacht; ~ spot s. 1. Schönheitspflästerchen n; 2. schönes Fleckchen Erde, lohnendes Ausflugsziel.

beaux pl. von **beau.**

bea·ver¹ ['biːvə] I s. 1. zo. Biber m: work like a ~ → 5; 2. Biberpelz m; 3. ✝ Biber m (filziger Wollstoff); 4. sl. a) Bart(träger) m, b) Am. ,Muschi' f; II v/i. 5. mst ~ away (schwer) schuften.

bea·ver² ['biːvə] s. ✗ hist. Vi'sier n, Helmsturz m.

be·bop ['biːbɒp] s. ♪ Bebop m (Jazz).

be·calm [bɪ'kaːm] v/t. 1. beruhigen; 2. be ~ed ⚓ in e-e Flaute geraten.

be·came [bɪ'keɪm] pret. von **become.**

be·cause [bɪ'kɒz] I cj. weil, da; II ~ of prp. wegen (gen.), in'folge von (od. gen.).

bêche-de-mer [ˌbeɪʃdə'meə] (Fr.) s. zo. essbare Seewalze, 'Trepang m.

beck¹ [bek] s. Wink m, Nicken n: be at s.o.'s ~ and call j-m auf den (leisesten) Wink gehorchen, nach j-s Pfeife tanzen.

beck² [bek] s. Brit. (Wild)Bach m.

beck·on ['bekən] I v/t. j-m (zu)winken, zunicken, j-n her'anwinken, j-m ein Zeichen geben; II v/i. winken, fig. a. locken.

be·cloud [bɪ'klaʊd] v/t. um'wölken, verdunkeln, fig. a. verneblen.

be·come [bɪ'kʌm] [irr. → come] I v/i. 1. werden: ~ an actor; ~ warmer; what has ~ of him? a) was ist aus ihm geworden?, b) F wo steckt er nur?; II v/t. 2. sich schicken für, sich (ge)ziemen für: it does not ~ you; 3. j-m stehen, passen zu, j-n kleiden (Hut etc.); be·'com·ing [-mɪŋ] adj. □ 1. schicklich, geziemend, anständig; 2. kleidsam.

bed [bed] I s. 1. Bett n: ~ and breakfast Übernachtung f mit Frühstück; his life is no ~ of roses er ist nicht auf Rosen gebettet; marriage is not always a ~ of roses die Ehe hat nur angenehme Seiten; die in one's ~ e-s natürlichen Todes sterben; get out of ~ on the wrong side mit dem verkehrten od. linken Fuß zuerst aufstehen; go to ~ zu Bett od. schlafen gehen; keep one's ~ das Bett hüten; make the ~ das Bett machen; as you make your ~, so you must lie upon it wie man sich bettet, so schläft man; put to ~ j-n zu Bett bringen; take to one's ~ (krank) ins Bett legen; 2. Federbett n; 3. Ehebett n: ~ and board Tisch m u. Bett (Ehe); 4. Lager(statt f) n (a. e-s Tieres): ~ of straw Strohlager; 5. fig. letzte Ruhestätte; 6. 'Unterkunft f: ~ and breakfast Zimmer n mit Frühstück; 7. (Fluss- etc.)Bett n; 8. ♪ Beet n; 9. ⊕, 🔺 Bett n (a. e-r Werkzeugmaschine), Bettung f, 'Unterlage f, Stützlage f: ~ of concrete Betonunterlage f; 10. geol., ⚒ Bett n, Schicht f, Lage f, Lager n, Flöz n (Kohle); 11. 🏛 'Unterbau m; II v/t. 12. zu Bett bringen; 13. be bedded bettlägerig sein; 14. mst ~ down a) j-m das Bett machen, b) j-n für die Nacht 'unterbringen, c) Pferd etc. mit Streu versorgen; 15. mst ~ out in Beet pflanzen, auspflanzen; III v/i. 16. a. ~ down a) ins od. zu Bett gehen, b) sein Nachtlager aufschlagen; 17. (sich ein)nisten (a. fig.).

be·dad [bɪ'dæd] int. Ir. bei Gott!

be·daub [bɪ'dɔːb] v/t. beschmieren.

be·daz·zle [bɪ'dæzl] v/t. blenden.

'**bed|·bug** s. zo. Wanze f; ~ bun·ny s. F ,Betthäschen' n; '~,cham·ber s. (königliches) Schlafgemach: Gentleman od. Groom of the ⚮ königlicher Kammerherr; Lady of the ⚮ königliche Kammerzofe; '~·clothes s. pl. Bettwäsche f.

bed·der ['bedə] s. Brit. Zimmermädchen n (in Colleges).

bed·ding ['bedɪŋ] I s. 1. Bettzeug n, Bett n u. 'Zubehör n, m; 2. (Lager-) Streu f für Tiere; 3. ⊕ Bettung f, 'Unterschicht f, -lage f, Lager n; II adj. 4. ~ plants Beetpflanzen (Blumen etc.).

be·deck [bɪ'dek] v/t. (ver)zieren, schmücken.

be·del(l) [be'del] s. Brit. univ. Herold m.

be·dev·il [bɪ'devl] v/t. fig. 1. fig. verhexen; 2. a) plagen, peinigen, b) bedrücken, belasten; 3. fig. verwirren, durch-ein'ander bringen.

be·dew [bɪ'djuː] v/t. betauen, benetzen.

'**bed|·fast** adj. bettlägerig; '~,fel·low s. 1. 'Schlafkame,rad m, Bettgenosse m; 2. fig. Genosse m; '~·gown s. (Frauen)Nachthemd n.

be·dim [bɪ'dɪm] v/t. trüben.

be·diz·en [bɪ'daɪzn] v/t. (über'trieben) her'ausputzen.

bed·lam ['bedləm] s. fig. Tollhaus n: cause a ~ e-n Tumult auslösen; 'bed·lam·ite [-maɪt] s. obs. Irre(r m) f.

Bed·ou·in ['beduɪn] I s. Bedu'ine m; II adj. Beduinen...

'**bed|·pan** s. 🏥 Stechbecken n, Bettschüssel f; '~·plate s. ⊕ 'Unterlagsplatte f, -gestell n od. -rahmen m; '~·post s. Bettpfosten m: between you and me and the ~ F unter uns od. im Vertrauen (gesagt).

be·drag·gled [bɪ'drægld] adj. 1. a) verdreckt, b) durch'nässt; 2. fig. verwahrlost.

'**bed|·rid·den** adj. bettlägerig; '~·rock I s. 1. geol. unterste Felsschicht, Grundgestein n; 2. (mst fig.) Grundlage f: get down to ~ der Sache auf den Grund gehen; 3. fig. Tiefpunkt m; II adj. 4. F a) grundlegend, b) (felsen)fest, c) ✝ äußerst, niedrigst: ~ price; '~·roll s. zs.-gerolltes Bettzeug; '~·room [-rum] s. Schlafzimmer n: ~ eyes F ,Schlafzimmeraugen'; ~ suburb Schlafstadt f; '~-set·tee s. Schlafcouch f; '~·sheet s. Bettlaken n.

'**bed·side** s.: at the ~ am (Kranken-) Bett; good ~ manner gute Art, mit Kranken umzugehen; ~ lamp s. Nachttischlampe f; ~ read·ing s. 'Bettlektüre f; ~ rug s. Bettvorleger m; ~ stor·y s. Gutenachtgeschichte f; ~ ta·ble s. Nachttisch m.

,**bed|·'sit** Brit. I v/i. [irr.] ein möbliertes Zimmer bewohnen; II s. → ,~'sit·ter s., ,~·'sit·ting room s. Brit. 1. möbliertes Zimmer; 2. Ein'zimmerappartement m; '~·sore s. 🏥 wund gelegene Stelle; '~·space s. (An)Zahl f der Betten (in Klinik etc.); '~·spread s. (Zier-) Bettdecke f; Tagesdecke f; '~·stead s. Bettstelle f, -gestell n; '~·straw s. ♣ Labkraut n; '~·tick s. Inlett n; '~·time s. Schlafenszeit f; '~-,wet·ting s. Bettnässen n.

bee¹ [biː] s. 1. zo. Biene f: have a ~ in one's bonnet F ,e-n Vogel haben'; 2. fig. Biene f, fleißiger Mensch; → busy 2; 3. bsd. Am. a) Treffen n von Freunden zur Gemeinschaftshilfe od. Unterhaltung: sewing ~ Nähkränzchen n, b) Wettbewerb m.

bee² [biː] s. B, b n (Buchstabe).

Beeb [biːb] s.: the ~ Brit. F die BB'C.

beech [biːtʃ] s. ♣ Buche f; Buchenholz n; **beech·en** ['biːtʃən] adj. aus Buchenholz, Buchen...

beech| mar·ten s. zo. Steinmarder m; '~·mast s. Bucheckern pl.; '~·nut s. Buchecker f.

beef [biːf] pl. beeves [biːvz], a. beefs I s. 1. Mastrind n, -ochse m, -bulle m; 2. Rindfleisch n; 3. F a) Fleisch n (am Menschen), b) (Muskel)Kraft f; 4. sl. ,Mecke'rei' f, Beschwerde f; 5. Am. sl. ,dufte Puppe'; II v/i. 6. sl. nörgeln, ,meckern', sich beschweren; III v/t. 7. ~ up F et. ,aufmöbeln'; '~·cake s. Am. sl. Bild n e-s Muskelprotzen; '~,eat·er s. Brit. Beefeater m, Towerwächter m (in London); ,~'steak s. 'Beefsteak n; ~ tea s. (Rind)Fleisch-, Kraftbrühe f, Bouil'lon f.

beef·y ['biːfɪ] adj. 1. fleischig; 2. F bullig, kräftig.

'**bee|·hive** s. 1. Bienenstock m, -korb m; 2. fig. ,Taubenschlag' m; '~,keep·er s. Bienenzüchter m, Imker m; '~,keep·ing s. Bienenzucht f, Imke'rei f; '~·line s.: make a ~ for schnurgerade auf et. losgehen.

Be·el·ze·bub [biː'elzɪbʌb] I npr. Be'elzebub m; II s. Teufel m.

'**bee,mas·ter** s. → beekeeper.

been [biːn; bɪn] p.p. von **be.**

beep [biːp] s. 1. ♫ Piepton m; 2. mot. 'Hupsig,nal n; 'beep·er s. Piepser m (Gerät).

beer [bɪə] s. 1. Bier n: two ~s zwei Glas Bier; life is not all ~ and skittles Brit. F das Leben besteht nicht nur aus Vergnügen; → small beer; 2. bierähnliches Getränk (aus Pflanzen); ~ can s. Bierdose f; ~ en·gine s. 'Bier,druckappa,rat m; ~ gar·den s. Biergarten m; '~·house s. Brit. Bierschenke f; ~ mat s. Bierfilz m, -deckel m; '~·pull s. (Griff m der) Bierpumpe f.

beer·y ['bɪərɪ] adj. 1. bierartig; 2. bierselig; 3. nach Bier riechend.

beest·ings ['biːstɪŋz] s. Biestmilch f (erste Milch nach dem Kalben).

bees·wax ['biːzwæks] s. Bienenwachs n.

beet [biːt] s. ♣ 1. Runkelrübe f, Mangold m, Beete f; ~ greens Mangoldgemüse n; 2. Am. Rote Bete.

bee·tle¹ ['biːtl] I s. 1. zo. Käfer m; → blind 1.; II v/i F 2. ~ along F entlangflitzen, -pesen; 3. ~ off F abschwirren, sich davonmachen.

bee·tle² ['biːtl] I s. 1. Holzhammer m, Schlägel m; 2. ⊕ a) Erdstampfe f, b) 'Stampfka,lander m; II v/t. 3. mit e-m Schlägel bearbeiten, (ein)stampfen; 4. ⊕ ka'landern.

bee·tle³ ['biːtl] I adj. 'überhängend; II v/i. vorstehen, 'überhängen.

'**bee·tle|-browed** adj. 1. mit buschigen Augenbrauen; 2. finster blickend; '~,crush·ers s. pl. ,Elbkähne' pl. (riesige Schuhe).

'**beet|·root** s. ♣ 1. Brit. Wurzel f der Roten Bete; 2. Am. → beet 1; ~ sug·ar s. ♣ Rübenzucker m.

beeves [biːvz] pl. von beef.

be·fall [bɪ'fɔːl] [irr. → fall] obs. od. poet. I v/i. sich ereignen; II v/t. zustoßen, wider'fahren (dat.).

be·fit [bɪ'fɪt] v/t. sich ziemen od. schicken für: ~ s.o. j-m angemessen sein, sich für j-n ziemen; be·'fit·ting [-tɪŋ] adj. □ geziemend, schicklich.

be·fog [bɪ'fɒg] v/t. 1. in Nebel hüllen; 2. fig. a) um'nebeln, b) verwirren.

be·fool [bɪ'fuːl] v/t. zum Narren haben,

täuschen.

be·fore [bɪˈfɔː] **I** *prp.* **1.** *räumlich*: vor: *he sat ~ me*; *~ my eyes*; *the question ~ us* die (uns) vorliegende Frage; **2.** vor, in Gegenwart von: *~ witnesses*; **3.** *Reihenfolge, Rang*: vor'aus: *be ~ the others in class* den anderen in der Klasse voraus sein; **4.** *zeitlich*: vor, früher als: *~ lunch* vor dem Mittagessen; *an hour ~ the time* e-e Stunde früher *od.* zu früh; *~ long* in Kürze, bald; *~ now* schon früher *od.* vorher; *the day ~ yesterday* vorgestern; *the month ~ last* vorletzten Monat; *be ~ one's time* s-r Zeit voraus sein; **II** *cj.* **5.** be'vor, ehe: *he died ~ I was born*; *not ~* nicht früher *od.* eher als bis, erst als *od.* wenn; **6.** lieber ... als dass: *I would die ~ I lied*; **III** *adv.* **7.** *räumlich*: vorn, vo'ran: *go ~* vorangehen; *~ and behind* vorn u. hinten; **8.** *zeitlich*: 'vorher, vormals, früher, zu'vor; (schon) früher: *the year ~* das vorige *od.* vorhergehende Jahr, das Jahr zuvor; *an hour ~* e-e Stunde vorher *od.* früher *od.* zuvor; *long ~* lange vorher; *never ~* noch nie(mals), nie zuvor; **be·fore·hand** *adv.* zu'vor, im Voraus: *know s.th. ~* et. im Voraus wissen; *be ~ in one's suspicions* zu früh e-n Verdacht äußern; **be·fore-,men·tioned** *adj.* vorerwähnt; **be·'fore-tax** *adj.* ✝ vor Abzug der Steuern, Brutto...

be·foul [bɪˈfaʊl] *v/t.* besudeln, beschmutzen (*a. fig.*).

be·friend [bɪˈfrend] *v/t. j-m* Freundschaft erweisen; *j-m* behilflich sein, sich *j-s* annehmen.

be·fud·dle [bɪˈfʌdl] *v/t.* ,benebeln‘, berauschen.

beg [beg] **I** *v/t.* **1.** *et.* erbitten (*of s.o.* von j-m), bitten um: *~ leave* um Erlaubnis bitten; → *pardon* 4; **2.** betteln *od.* bitten um: *~ a meal*; **3.** *j-n* bitten (*to do s.th.* et. zu tun); **II** *v/i.* **4.** betteln: *go ~ging* a) betteln (gehen), b) keinen Interessenten finden; **5.** (dringend) bitten (*for* um, *of s.o. to inf.* j-n zu *inf.*): *~ off* sich entschuldigen, absagen; **6.** sich erlauben: *I ~ to differ* ich erlaube mir, anderer Meinung zu sein; *I ~ to inform you* ✝ *obs.* ich erlaube mir, Ihnen mitzuteilen; **7.** schönmachen, Männchen machen (*Hund*); **8.** → *question* 1.

be·gad [bɪˈgæd] *int.* F bei Gott!

be·gan [bɪˈgæn] *pret. von* **begin**.

be·gat [bɪˈgæt] *obs. pret. von* **beget**.

be·get [bɪˈget] *v/t.* [*irr.*] **1.** zeugen; **2.** *fig.* erzeugen, her'vorbringen; **be·'get·ter** [-tə] *s.* **1.** Erzeuger *m*, Vater *m*; **2.** *fig.* Urheber *m*.

beg·gar [ˈbegə] **I** *s.* **1.** Bettler(in); Arme(r *m*) *f*: *~s must not be choosers* arme Leute dürfen nicht wählerisch sein; **2.** F Kerl *m*, Bursche *m*: *lucky ~* Glückspilz *m*; *a naughty little ~* ein kleiner Schelm; **II** *v/t.* **3.** an den Bettelstab bringen; *a. fig.* erschöpfen; über'steigen: *it ~s description* a) es spottet jeder Beschreibung, b) es lässt sich nicht mit Worten beschreiben; **'beg·gar·ly** [-lɪ] *adj.* **1.** (sehr) arm; **2.** *fig.* armselig, lumpig; **,beg·gar-my-'neigh·bo(u)r** [-mɪ-] *s.* Bettelmann *m* (*Kartenspiel*); **'beg·gar·y** [-ərɪ] *s.* Bettelarmut *f*: *reduce to ~* an den Bettelstab bringen.

be·gin [bɪˈgɪn] [*irr.*] **I** *v/t.* **1.** beginnen, anfangen: *~ a new book*; **2.** (be-)gründen; **II** *v/i.* **3.** beginnen, anfangen: *~ with s.o. od. s.th* mit *od.* bei j-m *od.*

et. anfangen; *to ~ with* (*Wendung*) a) zunächst, b) erstens (einmal); *~ on s.th.* et. in Angriff nehmen; *he began by asking* zuerst fragte er; *... began to be put into practice* ... wurde bald in die Praxis umgesetzt; *he does not even ~ to try* er versucht es nicht einmal; *it doesn't ~ to do him justice* F es wird ihm nicht annähernd gerecht; **4.** entstehen; **be·'gin·ner** [-nə] *s.* Anfänger(in), Neuling *m*: *~'s luck* Anfängerglück *n*; **be·'gin·ning** [-nɪŋ] *s.* **1.** Anfang *m*, Beginn *m*: *from the (very) ~* (ganz) von Anfang an; *the ~ of the end* der Anfang vom Ende; **2.** Ursprung *m*; **3.** *pl.* a) Anfangsgründe *pl.*, b) Anfänge *pl.*

be·gone [bɪˈgɒn] *int.* fort (mit dir)!

be·go·ni·a [bɪˈgəʊnjə] *s.* Be'gonie *f*.

be·got [bɪˈgɒt] *pret. von* **beget**.

be·got·ten [bɪˈgɒtn] *p.p. von* **beget**: *God's only ~ son* Gottes eingeborener Sohn.

be·grime [bɪˈgraɪm] *v/t.* (*mit Ruß, Rauch etc.*) beschmutzen.

be·grudge [bɪˈgrʌdʒ] *v/t.* **1.** *~ s.o. s.th.* j-m et. missgönnen; **2.** *et.* nur ungern geben.

be·guile [bɪˈgaɪl] *v/t.* **1.** täuschen; betrügen (*of od. out of* um); **2.** verleiten (*into doing* zu tun); **3.** *Zeit* (angenehm) vertreiben; **4.** betören; **be·'guil·ing** [-lɪŋ] *adj.* □ verführerisch, betörend.

be·gun [bɪˈgʌn] *p.p. von* **begin**.

be·half [bɪˈhɑːf] *s.*: *on* (*od.* *in*) *~ of* zugunsten *od.* im Namen *od.* im Auftrag von (*od. gen.*), für *j-n*; *on* (*od. in*) *my ~* zu m-n Gunsten, für mich; *act on one's own ~* im eigenen Namen handeln.

be·have [bɪˈheɪv] **I** *v/i.* **1.** sich (gut) benehmen, sich zu benehmen wissen: *please ~!* bitte benimm dich!; *he doesn't know how to ~*, *he can't ~* er kann sich nicht (anständig) benehmen; **2.** sich verhalten; funktionieren (*Maschine etc.*); **II** *v/t.* **3.** *~ o.s.* sich (gut) benehmen: *~ yourself!* beninmm dich!; **be·'haved** [-vd] *adj.*: *he is well-~* er hat ein gutes Benehmen.

be·hav·io(u)r [bɪˈheɪvjə] *s.* Benehmen *n*, Betragen *n*; Verhalten *n* (*a.* ⚗, ⚙, *phys.*): *~ pattern psych.* Verhaltensmuster *n*; *~ therapy psych.* Verhaltenstherapie *f*; *during good ~ Am.* auf Lebenszeit (*Ernennung*); *be in office on one's good ~* ein Amt auf Bewährung innehaben; *be on one's best ~* sich von seiner besten Seite zeigen; *put s.o. on his good ~* j-m einschärfen, sich gut zu benehmen; **be·'hav·io(u)r·al** [-ərəl] *adj. psych.* Verhaltens...: *~ science* Verhaltensforschung *f*; **be·'hav·io(u)r·ism** [-ərɪzəm] *s. psych.* Behavio'rismus *m*.

be·head [bɪˈhed] *v/t.* enthaupten.

be·held [bɪˈheld] *pret. u. p.p. von* **behold**.

be·he·moth [bɪˈhiːməθ] **1.** *Bibl.* Behemoth; **2.** *fig.* Ko'loss *m*, Ungeheuer *n*.

be·hest [bɪˈhest] *s. poet.* Geheiß *n*: *at s.o.'s ~* auf j-s Geheiß *od.* Befehl *od.* Veranlassung.

be·hind [bɪˈhaɪnd] **I** *prp.* **1.** hinter: *~ the tree* hinter dem *od.* den Baum; *he looked ~ him* er blickte hinter sich; *be ~ s.o.* a) hinter j-m stehen, j-n unterstützen, b) j-m nachstehen, hinter j-m zurück sein; *what is ~ all this?* was steckt dahinter?; **II** *adv.* **2.** hinten, da-'hinter, hinter'her: *walk ~* hinterhergehen; **3.** nach hinten, zu'rück: *look ~*

zurückblicken; **4.** zu'rück, im Rückstand: *~ with one's work* mit s-r Arbeit im Rückstand; *my watch is ~* meine Uhr geht nach; → *time* 7; **5.** *fig.* da'hinter, verborgen: *there is more ~* da steckt (noch) mehr dahinter; **III** *s.* **6.** F ,Hintern‘ *m*, Gesäß *n*; **be·'hind·hand** *adv. u. pred. adj.* **1.** → *behind* 4; **2.** *fig.* rückständig; altmodisch.

be·hold [bɪˈhəʊld] **I** *v/t.* [*irr.* → *hold*] erblicken, anschauen; **II** *int.* siehe da!; **be·'hold·en** [-dən] *adj.* verpflichtet, dankbar (*to dat.*); **be·'hold·er** [-də] *s.* Beschauer(in), Betrachter(in).

be·hoof [bɪˈhuːf] *s. lit.*: *in* (*od. to, for, on*) (*the*) *~ of* um ... willen; *on her ~* zu ihren Gunsten.

be·hoove [bɪˈhuːv] *Am.*, **be·hove** [-ˈhəʊv] *Brit. v/t. impers.*: *it ~s you* (*to inf.*), a) es obliegt dir *od.* ist deine Pflicht (zu *inf.*), b) es gehört sich für dich (zu *inf.*).

beige [beɪʒ] **I** *s.* Beige *f* (*Wollstoff*); **II** *adj.* beige(farben).

be·ing [ˈbiːɪŋ] *s.* **1.** (Da)Sein *n*: *in ~* existierend, wirklich (vorhanden); *come into ~* entstehen; *call into ~* ins Leben rufen; **2.** *j-s* Wesen *n od.* Sein, Na'tur *f*; **3.** Wesen *n*; Geschöpf *n*: *living ~* Lebewesen.

be·la·bo(u)r [bɪˈleɪbə] *v/t.* **1.** (mit den Fäusten *etc.*) bearbeiten, 'durchprügeln; **2.** *fig. j-n* ,bearbeiten‘, *j-m* zusetzen.

be·lat·ed [bɪˈleɪtɪd] *adj.* **1.** verspätet; **2.** von der Nacht über'rascht.

be·laud [bɪˈlɔːd] *v/t.* preisen.

be·lay [bɪˈleɪ] *v/t.* [*irr.* → *lay*] **1.** ⚓ festmachen, *Tau* belegen; **2.** *mount. j-n* sichern.

belch [beltʃ] **I** *v/i.* **1.** aufstoßen, rülpsen; **II** *v/t.* **2.** *Rauch etc.* ausspeien; **III** *s.* **3.** Rülpsen *n*; **4.** *fig.* Ausbruch *m* (*Rauch etc.*).

bel·dam(e) [ˈbeldəm] *s. obs.* Ahnfrau *f*; alte Frau; Vettel *f*, Hexe *f*.

be·lea·guer [bɪˈliːgə] *v/t.* **1.** belagern (*a. fig.*); **2.** *fig.* a) heimsuchen, b) um-'geben.

bel es·prit [ˌbel esˈpriː] *pl.* **beaux es·prits** [ˌbəʊz esˈpriː] (*Fr.*) *s.* Schöngeist *m*.

bel·fry [ˈbelfrɪ] *s.* **1.** Glockenturm *m*; → *bat*² 1; **2.** Glockenstuhl *m*.

Bel·gian [ˈbeldʒən] **I** *adj.* belgisch; **II** *s.* Belgier(in).

be·lie [bɪˈlaɪ] *v/t.* **1.** Lügen erzählen über (*acc.*), et. falsch darstellen; **2.** *j-n od. et.* Lügen strafen; **3.** wider'sprechen (*dat.*); **4.** hin'wegtäuschen über (*acc.*); **5.** *Hoffnung etc.* enttäuschen, e-r Sache nicht entsprechen.

be·lief [bɪˈliːf] *s.* **1.** *eccl.* Glaube *m*, Religi'on *f*: *the ℬ* das Apostolische Glaubensbekenntnis; **2.** (*in*) a) Glaube *m* (an *acc.*): *beyond ~* unglaublich, b) Vertrauen *n* (auf *et. od.* zu *j-m*); **3.** Meinung *f*, Anschauung *f*, Über'zeugung *f*: *to the best of my ~* nach bestem Wissen u. Gewissen.

be·liev·a·ble [bɪˈliːvəbl] *adj.* glaubhaft; **be·lieve** [bɪˈliːv] **I** *v/i.* **1.** glauben (*in an acc.*); **2.** (*in*) Vertrauen haben (zu), viel halten (von): *not ~ in sports* F ich halte nicht viel von Sport; **II** *v/t.* **3.** glauben, meinen, denken: *~ it or not* ob Sie es glauben *od.* nicht!, ganz sicher; *do not ~ it* glaube es nicht; *would you ~ it!* nicht zu glauben!; *he is ~d to be a miser* man hält ihn für e-n Geizhals; **4.** Glauben schenken, glauben (*dat.*): *~ me* glaube mir; *not to ~ one's eyes* s-n Augen nicht trauen; **be·'liev·er**

B

[-və] *s.* **1.** *be a great od. firm ~ in* fest glauben an (*acc.*), viel halten von; **2.** *eccl.* Gläubige(r *m*) *f*: *a true ~* ein Rechtgläubiger; **be'liev·ing** [-vɪŋ] *adj.* □ gläubig: *a ~ Christian*.

Be·lish·a bea·con [bɪ'liːʃə] *s.* Brit. (gelbes) Blinklicht *n* an 'Fußgänger,überwegen.

be·lit·tle [bɪ'lɪtl] *v/t.* **1.** verkleinern; **2.** her'absetzen, schmälern; **3.** herabsetzen, schmähen; **4.** verharmlosen.

bell[1] [bel] **I** *s.* **1.** Glocke *f*, Klingel *f*, Schelle *f*: *carry away* (*od. bear*) *the ~* Sieger sein; *does that name ring a* (*od. the*) *~?* erinnert dich der Name an et.?; *the ~ has rung* es hat geklingelt; → *clear* 5, *sound*[1] 1; **2.** *pl.* ♪ (halbstündige Schläge *pl.* der) Schiffsglocke *f*; **3.** Taucherglocke *f*; **4.** ♀ glockenförmige Blumenkrone, Kelch *m*; **5.** △ Glocke *f*, Kelch *m* (*am Kapitell*); **II** *v/t.* **6.** *~ the cat fig.* der Katze die Schelle umhängen.

bell[2] [bel] *v/i.* röhren (*Hirsch*).

bel·la·don·na [,belə'dɒnə] *s.* ♀ Bella'donna *f* (*a. pharm.*), Tollkirsche *f*.

'bell|-,bot·tomed *adj.* unten weit auslaundend: *~ trousers*; **'~·boy** *s. Am.* Ho'telpage *m*; **~ buoy** *s.* ♪ Glockenboje *f*; **~ but·ton** *s.* ♫ Klingelknopf *m*.

belle [bel] (*Fr.*) *s.* Schöne *f*, Schönheit *f*: *~ of the ball* Ballkönigin *f*.

belles-let·tres [,bel'letrə] (*Fr.*) *s. pl. sg. konstr.* Belle'tristik *f*, Unter'haltungsliitera,tur *f*.

'bell|,flow·er *s.* ♀ Glockenblume *f*; **~ found·ry** *s.* Glockengieße'rei *f*; **~ glass** *s.* Glasglocke *f*; **'~·hop** *s. Am.* Ho'telpage *m*.

bel·li·cose ['belɪkəʊs] *adj.* □ kriegslustig, kriegerisch; **bel·li·cos·i·ty** [,belɪ'kɒsətɪ] *s.* **1.** Kriegslust *f*; **2.** → *belligerence* 2.

bel·lied ['belɪd] *adj.* bauchig; *in Zssgn* ...bauchig, ...bäuchig.

bel·lig·er·ence [bɪ'lɪdʒərəns] *s.* **1.** Kriegführung *f*; **2.** Kampfeslust *f*, Streitsucht *f*; **bel·lig·er·en·cy** [-rənsɪ] *s.* **1.** Kriegszustand *m*; **2.** → *belligerence*; **bel·'lig·er·ent** [-nt] **I** *adj.* □ **1.** Krieg führend: *the ~ powers*; *~ rights* Rechte der Krieg Führenden; **2.** *fig.* streitlustig; **II** *s.* **3.** Krieg führender Staat.

bell| lap *s. sport* letzte Runde; **'~·man** [-mən] *s.* [*irr.*] öffentlicher Ausrufer; **~ met·al** *s.* ♫ 'Glockenme,tall *n*, -speise *f*; **'~-mouthed** *adj.* (*a.* ✗) mit trichterförmiger Öffnung.

bel·low ['beləʊ] **I** *v/t. u. v/i.* brüllen; **II** *s.* Gebrüll *n*.

bel·lows ['beləʊz] *s. pl.* (*a. sg. konstr.*) **1.** ⊕ a) Gebläse *n*, b) a. *pair of ~* Blasebalg *m*; **2.** Lunge *f*; **3.** *phot.* Balg *m*.

bell| pull *s.* Klingelzug *m*; **~ push** *s.* Klingelknopf *m*; **~ ring·er** *s.* Glöckner *m*; **~ rope** *s.* **1.** Glockenstrang *m*; **2.** Klingelzug *m*; **'~-shaped** *adj.* glockenförmig; **~ tent** *s.* Rundzelt *n*; **'~,weth·er** *s.* Leithammel *m* (*a. fig.*, *mst contp.*).

bel·ly ['belɪ] **I** *s.* **1.** Bauch *m* (*a. fig.*); 'Unterleib *m*: *go ~ up* → 8; **2.** Magen *m*; **3.** *fig.* a) Appe'tit *m*, b) Schlemme-'rei *f*; **4.** Bauch *m*, Ausbauchung *f*, Höhlung *f*; **5.** 'Unterseite *f*; **6.** ♪ Reso'nanzboden *m*; Decke *f* (*Saiteninstrument*); **II** *v/i.* **7.** sich (aus)bauchen, (an)schwellen; **8.** *~ up* a) ,abkratzen' (*sterben*), b) ,Pleite' machen, ,eingehen'; **'~·ache** **I** *s.* Bauchweh *n*; **II** *v/i.* F ,meckern', nörgeln; **'~·band** *s.* Bauch-, Sattelgurt *m*; **~ but·ton** *s.* F (Bauch-)Nabel *m*; **~ danc·er** *s.* Bauchtänzerin *f*;

~ flop *s.* F ,Bauchklatscher' *m*; ✈ Bauchlandung *f*; **'~·ful** *s.*: *have had a ~* (*of*) F die Nase voll haben (von); **'~·hold** *s.* ✈ Frachtraum *m*; **~ land·ing** *s.* ✈ Bauchlandung *f*; **~ laugh** *s.* F dröhnendes Lachen; **~ tank** *s.* Rumpfabwurfbehälter *m*.

be·long [bɪ'lɒŋ] *v/i.* **1.** gehören (*to dat.*): *this ~s to me*; **2.** gehören (*to* zu), da'zugehören, am richtigen Platz sein: *this lid ~s to another pot* dieser Deckel gehört zu e-m anderen Topf; *where does this book ~?* wohin gehört dieses Buch?; *he does not ~* er gehört nicht dazu *od.* hierher; **3.** (*to*) sich gehören (für), j-m ziemen; **4.** *Am.* a) verbunden sein (*with* mit), gehören *od.* passen (*with* zu), b) wohnen (*in* in *dat.*); **5.** an-, zugehören (*to dat*): *~ to a club*; **be'long·ings** [-ŋɪŋz] *s. pl.* a) Habseligkeiten *pl.*, Habe *f*, Gepäck *n*, b) Zubehör *n*, c) F Angehörige *pl.*

be·lov·ed [bɪ'lʌvd] **I** *adj.* [*attr. a.* -vɪd] (innig) geliebt (*of*, *by* von); **II** *s.* [*mst* -vɪd] Geliebte(r *m*) *f*.

be·low [bɪ'ləʊ] **I** *adv.* **1.** unten: *he is ~* er ist unten (*im Haus*); *as stated ~* wie unten erwähnt; **2.** hin'unter; **3.** *poet.* hie'nieden; **4.** in der Hölle; **5.** (dar)'unter, niedriger: *the class ~*; **6.** strom'ab; **II** *prp.* **7.** unter, 'unterhalb, tiefer als: *the line* unter der *od.* die Linie; *~ cost* unter dem Kostenpreis; *~ s.o.* unter j-s Rang, Würde, Fähigkeit *etc.*; *20 ~* F 20 Grad Kälte.

belt [belt] **I** *s.* **1.** Gürtel *m*, Gurt *m*: *hit below the ~ a) Boxen u. fig.* j-m e-n Tiefschlag versetzen; *that was below the ~* a. *fig.* das war unter der Gürtellinie *od.* unfair; *tighten one's ~ fig.* den Gürtel enger schnallen; *the Black ε Judo:* der Schwarze Gürtel (→ 5); *under one's ~* F a) im Magen, b) *fig.* ,in der Tasche', c) hinter sich; **2.** ✗ Koppel *n*; Gehenk *n*; **3.** ♪ Panzergürtel *m* (*Kriegsschiff*); **4.** Gürtel *m*, Gebiet *n*, Zone *f*: *green ~* Grüngürtel (*um e-e Stadt*); *cotton ~ Am. geogr.* Baumwollgürtel *m*; **5.** *Am.* Gebiet *n* (*in dem ein Typus vorherrscht*): *the black ~* vorwiegend von Schwarzen bewohnte Staaten der USA; **6.** ⊕ a) (Treib)Riemen *m*: *~ drive* Riemenantrieb *m*; *a. conveyer ~* Förderband *n*, c) Streifen *m*, d) ✗ (Ma-'schinengewehr)Gurt *m*; **II** *v/t.* **7.** um'gürten, mit Riemen befestigen; zs.-halten; **8.** 'durchprügeln; *j-m* ,eine knallen'; **9.** *~ out sl.* Lied schmettern; **10.** a. *~ down* Schnaps etc. ,kippen'; **III** *v/i.* **11.** *~ up! sl.* (halt die) Schnauze!; **12.** *sl.* rasen: *~ down the road*; **~ con·vey·er** *s.* ⊕ Bandförderer *m*; **~ drive** *s.* ⊕ Riemenantrieb *m*; **~ line** *s. Am.* Verkehrsgürtel *m* um e-e Stadt; **~ pul·ley** *s.* ⊕ Riemenscheibe *f*; **~ saw** *s.* Bandsäge *f*; **~ trans·mis·sion** *s.* ⊕ 'Riementransmissi,on *f*; **'~·way** *s. Am.* Um'gehungsstraße *f*.

be·lu·ga [bɪ'luːgə] *s. ichth.* Be'luga *f*: a) Weißwal *m*, b) Hausen *m*.

be·moan [bɪ'məʊn] *v/t.* beklagen, betrauern, beweinen.

be·muse [bɪ'mjuːz] *v/t.* verwirren, benebeln, betäuben; nachdenklich stimmen; **be'mused** [-zd] *adj.* **1.** verwirrt *etc.*; **2.** nachdenklich; gedankenverloren.

bench [bentʃ] *s.* **1.** Bank *f* (*zum Sitzen*); **2.** ♫ (*oft ε*) a) Richterbank *f*, b) Gerichtshof *m*, c) *coll.* Richter *pl.*: *raised to the ~* zum Richter ernannt; *~ and bar* die Richter u. die Anwälte; *be on the ~* Richter sein; **3.** *parl. etc.* Platz *m*, Sitz *m*; **4.** ⊕ a) Werkbank *f*, -tisch *m*,

Experimentiertisch *m*: *carpenter's ~* Hobelbank, b) Bank *f*, Reihe *f* von Geräten; **5.** *geogr. Am.* a) Riff *n*, b) ter-'rassenförmiges Flussufer; **6.** *sport* a) (Teilnehmer-, Auswechsel-, Re'serve-) Bank *f*, b) Ruderbank *f*; **'bench·er** [-tʃə] *s.* **1.** *Brit.* Vorstandsmitglied *n* e-r Anwaltsinnung; **2.** *parl.* → *back-bencher*, *front-bencher*.

bench| lathe *s.* ⊕ Me'chanikerdrehbank *f*; **'~·mark** **I** *s.* **1.** *surv.* Fest-, Fixpunkt *m*; **2.** *fig.* a) Bezugspunkt *m*, -größe *f*; *~ problem Computer*: Bewertungsaufgabe *f*; *~ test Computer*: Benchmarktest *m* (*Leistungstest*), b) Maßstab *m* (*in* für); **II** *v/i.* **3.** s-e eigene Position bestimmen (*against* im Vergleich zu *od.* mit); **III** *v/t.* **4.** die Position von etw. bestimmen (*against* im Vergleich zu *od.* mit); **~ sci·en·tist** *s.* La'borwissenschaftler *m*; **'~,war·rant** *s.* ♫ richterlicher Haftbefehl.

bend [bend] **I** *v/t.* [*irr.*] **1.** biegen, krümmen: *~ out of shape* verbiegen; *~ s.o.'s ear* F *fig.* j-m sein Herz ausschütten, j-m die Ohren voll quatschen; **2.** beugen, neigen: *~ the knee* a) das Knie beugen, *fig.* sich unterwerfen, b) beten; **3.** *Bogen, Feder* spannen; **4.** ♪ *Tau, Segel* festmachen; **5.** *fig.* beugen: *~ the law* das Recht beugen; *~ s.o. to one's will* sich j-n gefügig machen; **6.** richten, (zu)wenden: *~ one's steps towards home* s-e Schritte heimwärts lenken; *~ o.s.* (*one's mind*) *to a task* sich (s-e Aufmerksamkeit) e-r Sache zuwenden, sich auf e-e Sache konzentrieren; **II** *v/i.* [*irr.*] **7.** sich biegen, sich krümmen, sich winden: *the road ~s here* die Straße macht hier e-e Kurve; **8.** sich neigen, sich beugen; **9.** (*to*) *fig.* sich beugen, sich fügen (*dat.*); **10.** (*to*) sich zuwenden, sich widmen (*dat.*); **III** *s.* **11.** Biegung *f*, Krümmung *f*, Windung *f*, Kurve *f*; **12.** Knoten *m*, Schlinge *f*: *drive s.o. round the ~ sl.* j-n verrückt machen; **14.** *the ~s pl.* ✗ Cais'sonkrankheit *f*; **'bend·ed** [-dɪd] *adj.* gebeugt: *on ~ knees* kniefällig; **'bend·er** [-də] *s. sl.* ,Saufe'rei' *f*, ,Bummel' *m*; **'bend·ing** [-dɪŋ] *adj.* ⊕ Biege...: *~ pressure*; *~ test*.

bend sin·is·ter *s. her* Schrägbalken *m*.

be·neath [bɪ'niːθ] **I** *adv.* dar'unter, 'unterhalb, (weiter) unten; **II** *prp.* unter, unterhalb (*gen.*): *~ a tree* unter e-m Baum; *it is ~ him* es ist unter s-r Würde; *~ notice* nicht der Beachtung wert; *~ contempt* unter aller Kritik.

Ben·e·dic·tine *s.* **1.** [,benɪ'dɪktɪn] Benedik'tiner *m* (*Mönch*); **2.** [-tiːn] Benedik'tiner *m* (*Likör*).

ben·e·dic·tion [,benɪ'dɪkʃn] *s. eccl.* Segnung *f*, Segen(sspruch) *m*.

ben·e·fac·tion [,benɪ'fækʃn] *s.* **1.** Wohltat *f*; **2.** Spende *f*, Geschenk *n*; Zuwendungen *pl.*; **3.** wohltätige Stiftung; **ben·e·fac·tor** ['benɪfæktə] *s.* **1.** Wohltäter *m*; **2.** Gönner *m*; Stifter *m*; **ben·e·fac·tress** ['benɪfæktrɪs] *s.* Wohltäterin *f etc.*

ben·e·fice ['benɪfɪs] *s. eccl.* Pfründe *f*; **'ben·e·ficed** [-st] *adj.* im Besitz e-r Pfründe; **be·nef·i·cence** [bɪ'nefɪsns] *s.* Wohltätigkeit *f*; **be·nef·i·cent** [bɪ'nefɪsnt] *adj.* □ wohltätig, gütig, wohltuend.

ben·e·fi·cial [,benɪ'fɪʃl] *adj.* □ **1.** (*to*) nützlich, wohltuend, förderlich (*dat.*); vorteilhaft (für); **2.** ♫ nutznießend: *~ owner* unmittelbarer Besitzer, Nießbraucher *m*; **ben·e·fi·ci·ar·y** [-'fɪʃərɪ] *s.* **1.** Nutznießer(in); Begünstigte(r *m*) *f*; Empfänger(in); **2.** Pfründner *m*.

ben·e·fit ['benɪfɪt] **I** *s.* **1.** Vorteil *m*, Nutzen *m*, Gewinn *m*: *for the ~ of* zum Besten *od.* zugunsten (*gen.*); *derive ~ from* Nutzen ziehen aus *od.* haben von; *give s.o. the ~ of* j-n in den Genuss *e-r Sache* kommen lassen, j-m *et.* gewähren; *~ of the doubt* Rechtswohltat *f* des Grundsatzes ,im Zweifel für den Angeklagten'; *give s.o. the ~ of the doubt* im Zweifelsfalle zu j-s Gunsten entscheiden; **2.** ✝ Zuwendung *f*, Beihilfe *f*: a) (*Sozial-, Versicherungs- etc.*)Leistung *f*, b) (*Alters- etc.*)Rente *f*, c) (*Arbeitslosen- etc.*)Unter'stützung *f*, d) (*Kranken-, Sterbe- etc.*)Geld *n*; **3.** Bene'fiz(vorstellung *f*, *sport* -spiel *n*) *n*, Wohltätigkeitsveranstaltung *f*; **4.** Wohltat *f*, Gefallen *m*, Vergünstigung *f*; **II** *v/t.* **5.** nützen (*dat.*), zu'gute kommen (*dat.*), fördern (*acc.*), begünstigen (*acc.*), *a.* j-m (gesundheitlich) gut tun; **III** *v/i.* **6.** (*by, from*) Vorteil haben (von, durch), Nutzen ziehen (aus).

Ben·e·lux ['benɪlʌks] *s.* Benelux-Länder *pl.* (*Belgien, Niederlande, Luxemburg*).

be·nev·o·lence [bɪ'nevələns] *s.* Wohlwollen *n*, Güte *f*; Wohltätigkeit *f*, Wohltat *f*; **be·nev·o·lent** [-nt] *adj.* □ wohl-, mildtätig, gütig; wohlwollend: *~ fund* Unterstützungsfonds *m*; *~ society* Hilfsverein *m* (auf Gegenseitigkeit).

Ben·gal [,beŋ'gɔːl] *npr.* Ben'galen *n*: *~ light* bengalisches Feuer; **Ben·ga·li** [-lɪ] **I** *s.* **1.** Ben'gale *m*, Ben'galin *f*; **2.** *ling.* das Ben'galische; **II** *adj.* **3.** ben'galisch.

be·night·ed [bɪ'naɪtɪd] *adj.* **1.** von der Dunkelheit über'rascht; **2.** *fig.* a) ,geistig um'nachtet', ,verblödet', b) unbedarft.

be·nign [bɪ'naɪn] *adj.* □ **1.** gütig; **2.** günstig, mild, zuträglich; **3.** ✚ gutartig; **be·nig·nant** [bɪ'nɪgnənt] *adj.* □ **1.** gütig, freundlich; **2.** günstig, wohltuend; **3.** → *benign* 3; **be·nig·ni·ty** [bɪ'nɪgnətɪ] *s.* Güte *f*, Freundlichkeit *f*.

ben·i·son ['benɪzn] *s. poet.* Segen *m*, Gnade *f*.

bent¹ [bent] **I** *pret. u. p.p. von bend* **I** *u.* **II**; **II** *adj.* a) entschlossen (*on doing zu tun*), b) erpicht (*on auf acc.*), darauf aus (*on doing zu tun*); **III** *s.* Neigung *f*, Hang *m*, Trieb *m* (*for zu*); Veranlagung *f*: *to the top of one's ~* nach Herzenslust; *allow full ~* freien Lauf lassen (*dat.*).

bent² [bent] *s.* ♀ **1.** *a.* **~ grass** Straußgras *n*; **2.** Sandsegge *f*.

'bent·wood *s.* Bugholz *n*: *~ chair* Wiener Stuhl *m*.

be·numb [bɪ'nʌm] *v/t.* betäuben: a) gefühllos machen, b) *fig.* lähmen; **be·'numbed** [-md] *adj.* betäubt, gelähmt (*a. fig.*), starr, gefühllos.

ben·zene ['benziːn] *s.* 🝆 Ben'zol *n*.

ben·zine ['benziːn] *s.* 🝆 Ben'zin *n*.

ben·zo·ic [ben'zəʊɪk] *adj.* 🝆 Benzoe...: *~ acid* Benzoesäure *f*; **ben·zo·in** ['benzəʊɪn] *s.* Ben'zoe,gummi *n*, *m*, -harz *n*, Ben'zoe *f*.

ben·zol(e) ['benzɒl] *s.* 🝆 Ben'zol *n*; **'ben·zo·line** [-zəʊliːn] → *benzine*.

be·queath [bɪ'kwiːð] *v/t.* **1.** *Vermögen* hinter'lassen, vermachen (*to s.o.* j-m); **2.** über'liefern, vererben (*fig.*).

be·quest [bɪ'kwest] *s.* Vermächtnis *n*, Hinter'lassenschaft *f*.

be·rate [bɪ'reɪt] *v/t.* heftig ausschelten, auszanken.

Ber·ber ['bɜːbə] **I** *s.* **1.** Berber(in); **2.** *ling.* Berbersprache(n *pl.*) *f*; **II** *adj.* **3.** Berber...

Ber·ber·is ['bɜːbərɪs], **ber·ber·ry**

['bɜːbərɪ] → *barberry*.

be·reave [bɪ'riːv] *v/t.* [*irr.*] **1.** berauben (*of gen.*); **2.** hilflos zu'rücklassen; **be·'reaved** [-vd] *adj.* durch den Tod beraubt, hinter'blieben: *the ~* die (trauernden) Hinterbliebenen; **be·'reave·ment** [-mənt] *s.* schmerzlicher Verlust (*durch Tod*); Trauerfall *m*.

be·reft [bɪ'reft] **I** *pret. u. p.p. von be·reave*; **II** *adj.* beraubt (*of gen.*) (*mst fig.*): *~ of hope* aller Hoffnung beraubt; *~ of reason* von Sinnen.

be·ret ['bereɪ] *s.* **1.** Baskenmütze *f*; **2.** ✗ *Brit.* 'Felduni,formmütze *f*.

berg [bɜːg] → *iceberg*.

ber·ga·mot ['bɜːgəmɒt] *s.* **1.** ♀ Berga'mottenbaum *m*; **2.** Berga'mottöl *n*; **3.** Berga'motte *f* (*Birnensorte*).

be·rib·boned [bɪ'rɪbənd] *adj.* mit (Ordens)Bändern geschmückt.

ber·i·ber·i [,berɪ'berɪ] *s.* 🝆 Beri'beri *f*, Reisesserkrankheit *f*.

Ber·lin| black [bɜː'lɪn] *s.* schwarzer Eisenlack; *~ wool s.* feine Strickwolle.

Ber·mu·das [bə'mjuːdəz] *pl.*, **Ber·mu·da shorts** *pl.* Ber'mudashorts *pl.*

ber·ry ['berɪ] **I** *s.* **1.** ♀ a) Beere *f*, b) Korn *n*, Kern *m* (*beim Getreide*); **2.** *zo.* Ei *n* (*vom Hummer od. Fisch*); **II** *v/i.* **3.** a) ♀ Beeren tragen, b) Beeren sammeln.

ber·serk [bə'sɜːk] *adj. u. adv.* wütend, rasend: *go ~* (*with*) rasend werden (vor), *fig. a.* wahnsinnig werden (vor); **ber·'serk·er** [-kə] *s. hist.* Ber'serker *m* (*a. fig. Wüterich*): *~ rage* Berserkerwut *f*; *go ~* wild werden, Amok laufen.

berth [bɜːθ] **I** *s.* **1.** ♣ (genügend) Seeraum (*an der Küste od. zum Ausweichen*): *give a wide ~ to* a) weit abhalten von (*Land, Insel etc.*), b) *fig.* um j-n e-n Bogen machen; **2.** ♣ Liegeplatz *m* (*e-s Schiffes am Kai*); **3.** a) ♣ (Schlaf-) Koje *f*, b) Bett *n* (*Schlafwagen*); **4.** *Brit.* F Stellung *f*, ,Pöstchen' *n*: *he has a good ~*; **II** *v/t.* **5.** ♣ am Kai festmachen; vor Anker legen, docken; **6.** *Brit* j-m einen (Schlaf)Platz anweisen; j-n 'unterbringen; **III** *v/i.* **7.** ♣ anlegen.

ber·yl ['berɪl] *s. min.* Be'ryll *m*; **be·ryl·li·um** [be'rɪljəm] *s.* 🝆 Be'ryllium *n*.

be·seech [bɪ'siːtʃ] *v/t.* [*irr.*] j-n dringend bitten (*for* um), ersuchen, anflehen (*to inf.* zu *inf.*, *that* dass); **be·'seech·ing** [-tʃɪŋ] *adj.* □ flehend, bittend; **be·'seech·ing·ly** [-tʃɪŋlɪ] *adv.* flehentlich.

be·seem [bɪ'siːm] *v/t.* sich ziemen *od.* schicken für.

be·set [bɪ'set] *v/t.* [*irr.* → *set*] *v/t.* **1.** um'geben, (von allen Seiten) bedrängen, verfolgen: *~ with difficulties* mit Schwierigkeiten überhäuft; **2.** *Straße* versperren; **be·'set·ting** [-tɪŋ] *adj.* **1.** hartnäckig, unausrottbar: *~ sin* Gewohnheitslaster *n*; **2.** ständig drohend (*Gefahr*).

be·side [bɪ'saɪd] *prp.* **1.** neben, dicht bei: *sit ~ me* setz dich neben mich; **2.** *fig.* außerhalb (*gen.*), außer, nicht gehörend zu: *~ the point* nicht zur Sache gehörig; *~ o.s.* außer sich (*with* vor *dat.*); **3.** im Vergleich zu; **be·'sides** [-dz] **I** *adv.* **1.** außerdem, ferner, über'dies, noch da'zu; **2.** *neg.* sonst; **II** *prp.* **3.** außer, neben (*dat.*); **4.** über ... hin'aus.

be·siege [bɪ'siːdʒ] *v/t.* **1.** belagern (*a. fig.*); **2.** *fig.* bestürmen, bedrängen.

be·slav·er [bɪ'slævə] *v/t.* **1.** begeifern; **2.** *fig.* j-m lobhudeln.

be·slob·ber [bɪ'slɒbə] *v/t.* **1.** → *be·slaver*; **2.** ,abschlecken', abküssen.

be·smear [bɪ'smɪə] *v/t.* beschmieren.

be·smirch [bɪ'smɜːtʃ] *v/t.* besudeln (*bsd. fig.*).

---

be·som ['biːzəm] *s.* (Reisig)Besen *m*.

be·sot·ted [bɪ'sɒtɪd] *adj.* □ **1.** töricht, dumm; **2.** (*on, about*) vernarrt (in *acc.*), verrückt (auf *acc.*); **3.** berauscht (*with* von).

be·sought [bɪ'sɔːt] *pret. u. p.p. von be·seech*.

be·spat·ter [bɪ'spætə] *v/t.* **1.** (mit Kot *etc.*) bespritzen, beschmutzen; **2.** *fig.* (mit Vorwürfen *etc.*) über'schütten.

be·speak [bɪ'spiːk] [*irr.* → *speak*] *v/t.* **1.** (vor'aus)bestellen, im Voraus bitten um: *~ a seat* e-n Platz bestellen; *~ s.o.'s help* j-n um Hilfe bitten; **2.** zeigen, zeugen von; **3.** *poet.* anreden.

be·spec·ta·cled [bɪ'spektəkld] *adj.* bebrillt.

be·spoke [bɪ'spəʊk] **I** *pret. von be·speak*; **II** *adj. Brit.* auf Bestellung *od.* nach Maß angefertigt, Maß...: *~ tailor* Maßschneider *m*; **be·'spo·ken** [-kən] *p.p. von bespeak*.

be·sprin·kle [bɪ'sprɪŋkl] *v/t.* besprengen, bespritzen, bestreuen.

Bes·se·mer steel ['besɪmə] *s.* 🔧 Bessemerstahl *m*.

best [best] **I** *sup. von good adj.* **1.** best: *the ~ of wives* die beste aller (Ehe-) Frauen; *be ~ at* hervorragend sein in (*dat.*); **2.** geeignetst; höchst; *~-before date* Mindesthaltbarkeitsdatum *n*; **3.** größt, meist: *the ~ part of* der größte Teil (*gen.*); **II** *sup. von well adv.* **4.** am besten (meisten, passendsten): *as ~ I can* so gut ich kann; *the ~ hated man of the year* der meist- *od.* bestgehasste Mann des Jahres; *~ used* meistgebraucht; *you had ~ go* es wäre das Beste, Sie gingen; **III** *v/t.* **5.** über'treffen; **6.** F über'vorteilen; **IV** *s.* **7.** *der (die, das)* Beste (Passendste *etc.*): *at ~* bestenfalls, höchstens; *with the ~* mindestens so gut wie jeder andere; *for the ~* zum Besten; *do one's (level) ~* sein Bestes geben, sein Möglichstes tun; *be at one's ~* in bester Verfassung (*od.* Form) sein, *a.* in seinem Element sein; *that is the ~ of ...* das ist der Vorteil (*gen. od.* wenn ...); *give s.o. ~* sich vor j-m beugen; *look one's ~* am vorteilhaftesten *od.* blendend aussehen; *have (od. get) the ~ of it* am besten dabei wegkommen; *make the ~ of* a) bestens ausnutzen, b) sich abfinden mit, c) *e-r Sache* die beste Seite abgewinnen, das Beste machen aus; *all the ~!* alles Gute!, viel Glück!; → *ability* 1, *belief* 3, *job'* 5.

bes·tial ['bestjəl] *adj.* □ **1.** tierisch (*a. fig.*); *fig.* besti'alisch, entmenscht, viehisch; **2.** *fig.* gemein, verderbt; **bes·ti·al·i·ty** [,bestɪ'ælətɪ] *s.* **1.** Bestiali'tät *f*: a) tierisches Wesen, b) *fig.* besti'alische Grausamkeit; **2.** 🐾 Sodo'mie *f*.

be·stir [bɪ'stɜː] *v/t.*: *~ o.s.* sich rühren, sich aufraffen; sich bemühen: *~ yourself!* tummle dich!

best man *s.* [*irr.*] *Freund des Bräutigams, der bei der Ausrichtung der Hochzeit e-e wichtige Rolle spielt.*

be·stow [bɪ'stəʊ] *v/t.* **1.** schenken, gewähren, geben, spenden, erweisen, verleihen (*s.th.* [*up*]*on s.o.* j-m et.): *~ one's hand on s.o.* j-m die Hand fürs Leben reichen; **2.** *obs.* 'unterbringen; **be·'stow·al** [-əʊəl] *s.* **1.** Gabe *f*, Schenkung *f*, Verleihung *f*; **2.** *obs.* 'Unterbringung *f*.

be·strew [bɪ'struː] [*irr.* → *strew*] *v/t.* **1.** bestreuen; **2.** verstreut liegen auf (*dat.*).

be·strid·den [bɪ'strɪdn] *p.p. von be·stride*; **be·stride** [bɪ'straɪd] *v/t.* [*irr.*] **1.**

B

rittlings sitzen auf (dat.), reiten; **2.** mit gespreizten Beinen stehen auf od. über (dat.); **3.** über'spannen, über'brücken; **4.** sich (schützend) breiten über (acc.); **be·strode** [bɪ'strəʊd] pret. von **bestride**.

'best|,sell·er s. 'Bestseller m, Verkaufsschlager m (Buch etc.); '**~-,sell·ing** adj. meistgekauft, Erfolgs..., Bestseller...

bet [bet] **I** s. Wette f; Wetteinsatz m; gewetteter Betrag od. Gegenstand: **the best ~** F das Beste(, was man tun kann), die sicherste Methode; **that's a better ~ than** das ist viel besser od. sicherer als...; **II** v/t. u. v/i. [irr.] wetten, (ein)setzen: **I ~ you ten pounds** ich wette mit Ihnen um zehn Pfund; (**I**) **you ~!** sl. aber sicher!; **~ one's bottom dollar** Am. sl. den letzten Heller wetten, a. sich s-r Sache völlig sicher sein.

be·ta ['biːtə] s. 'Beta n: a) griech. Buchstabe, b) Å, ast., phys. Symbol für 2. Größe, c) ped. Brit. Zwei f (Note): **~ rays** phys. Betastrahlen pl.; **~ block·er** s. 🟊, pharm. 'Beta,blocker m.

be·take [bɪ'teɪk] [irr. → **take**] v/t.: **~ o.s.** (**to**) sich begeben (nach); s-e Zuflucht nehmen (zu).

be·tel ['biːtl] s. 'Betel m; '**~-nut** s. ⚘ 'Betelnuss f.

bête noire [,beɪt'nwɑː] (Fr.) s. fig. Schreckgespenst n.

beth·el ['beθl] s. **1.** Brit. Dis'senterka-,pelle f; **2.** Am. Kirche f für Ma'trosen.

be·think [bɪθɪŋk] v/t. [irr. → **think**]: **~ o.s.** sich über'legen, sich besinnen; sich vornehmen; **~ o.s. to do** sich in den Kopf setzen zu tun.

be·thought [bɪ'θɔːt] pret. u. p.p. von **bethink**.

be·tide [bɪ'taɪd] v/i. u. v/t. (nur 3. sg. pres. subj.) (j-m) geschehen; v/t. j-m zustoßen; → **woe** II.

be·times [bɪ'taɪmz] adv. **1.** bei'zeiten, rechtzeitig; **2.** früh(zeitig).

be·to·ken [bɪ'təʊkən] v/t. **1.** bezeichnen, bedeuten; **2.** anzeigen.

be·took [bɪ'tʊk] pret. von **betake**.

be·tray [bɪ'treɪ] v/t. **1.** Verrat begehen an (dat.), verraten (**to** an acc.); **2.** j-n hinter'gehen; j-m die Treue brechen: **~ s.o.'s trust** j-s Vertrauen missbrauchen; **3.** fig. offen'baren; (a. o.s. sich) verraten; **4.** verleiten (**into, to** zu); **be·'tray·al** [-ɛrəl] s. Verrat m, Treubruch m.

be·troth [bɪ'trəʊð] v/t. j-n (od. o.s. sich) verloben (**to** mit); **be·'troth·al** [-ðl] s. Verlobung f; **be·'trothed** [-ðd] s. Verlobte(r m) f.

bet·ter¹ ['betə] **I** comp. von **good** adj. **1.** besser: **I am ~** es geht mir (gesundheitlich) besser; **get ~** a) besser werden, b) sich erholen; **~ late than never** besser spät als nie; **go one ~ than s.o.** j-n (noch) übertreffen; **~ off** a) besser daran, b) wohlhabender; **be ~ than one's word** mehr tun als man versprach; **my ~ half** m-e bessere Hälfte; **on ~ acquaintance** bei näherer Bekanntschaft; **II** s. **2.** das Bessere: **for ~ for worse** a) in Freud u. Leid (Trauformel), b) was auch geschehe; **get the ~ (of)** die Oberhand gewinnen (über acc.), j-n besiegen od. ausstechen, et. überwinden; **3.** pl. mit pers. pron. Vorgesetzte pl., Höherstehende pl., Über'legene pl.; **III** comp. von **well** adv. **4.** besser: **I know ~** ich weiß es besser; **think ~ of it** sich e-s Besseren besinnen, es sich anders überlegen; **think ~ of s.o.** e-e bessere Meinung von j-m ha-

ben; **so much the ~** desto besser; **you had ~** (od. F mst **you ~**) go es wäre besser, wenn du gingest; **you'd ~ not!** F lass das lieber sein!; **know ~ than to ...** gescheit genug sein, nicht zu ...; **5.** mehr: **like ~** lieber haben; **~ loved** IV v/t. **6.** allg. verbessern; **7.** über'treffen; **8. ~ o.s.** sich (finanziell) verbessern, vorwärts kommen; a. sich weiterbilden; **V** v/i. **9.** besser werden.

bet·ter² ['betə] s. Wetter(in).

bet·ter·ment ['betəmənt] s. **1.** (Ver-)Besserung f; **2.** Wertzuwachs m (bei Grundstücken), Meliorati'on f.

bet·ting ['betɪŋ] s. sport Wetten n; **~ man** s. [irr.] (regelmäßiger) Wetter; **~ of·fice** s., **~ shop** s. 'Wettbü,ro n.

bet·tor → better².

be·tween [bɪ'twiːn] **I** prp. **1.** zwischen: **~ the chairs** a) zwischen den Stühlen, b) zwischen die Stühle; **~ nine and ten at night** abends zwischen neun und zehn; **2.** unter: **they shared the money ~ them** sie teilten das Geld unter sich; **~ ourselves, ~ you and me unter uns** (gesagt); **we had fifty pence ~ us** wir hatten zusammen fünfzig Pence; **II** adv. **3.** da'zwischen: **the space ~** der Zwischenraum; **in ~** da'zwischen, zwischendurch; **~ decks** s. pl. ⚓ Zwischendeck n; **be-'tween·times; be·'tween·whiles** adv. zwischendurch.

be·twixt [bɪ'twɪkst] **I** adv. da'zwischen: **~ and between** halb u. halb, weder das e-e noch das andere; **II** prp. obs. zwischen.

bev·el ['bevl] ⚙ **I** s. **1.** Abschrägung f, Schräge f; **2.** Fase f, Fa'cette f; **2.** Schrägmaß n; **3.** Kegel m, Konus m; **II** v/t. **4.** abschrägen; **~(l)ed edge** abgeschrägte Kante; **~(l)ed glass** facettiertes Glas; **III** adj. **5.** abgeschrägt; **~ cut** s. Schrägschnitt m; **~ gear** s. ⚙ Kegelrad(getriebe) n, konisches Getriebe; **~ plane** s. ⚙ Schräghobel m; **~ wheel** s. ⚙ Kegelrad n.

bev·er·age ['bevərɪdʒ] s. Getränk n.

bev·y ['bevɪ] s. Schar f, Schwarm m (Vögel; a. fig. Mädchen etc.).

be·wail [bɪ'weɪl] **I** v/t. beklagen, betrauern; **II** v/i. wehklagen.

be·ware [bɪ'weə] v/i. sich in Acht nehmen, sich hüten (**of** vor dat., **lest** dass nicht): **~!** Achtung!; **~ of pickpockets!** vor Taschendieben wird gewarnt!; **~ of the dog!** Warnung vor dem Hunde!

be·wil·der [bɪ'wɪldə] v/t. **1.** irreführen; **2.** verwirren, verblüffen; **3.** bestürzen; **be·'wil·dered** [-əd] adj. verwirrt; verblüfft, bestürzt, verdutzt; **be·'wil·der·ing** [-dərɪŋ] adj. □ verwirrend; **be·'wil·der·ment** [-mənt] s. Verwirrung f, Bestürzung f.

be·witch [bɪ'wɪtʃ] v/t. berücken, betören, bezaubern; **be·'witch·ing** [-tʃɪŋ] adj. □ berückend etc.

bey [beɪ] s. Bei m (Titel e-s höheren türkischen Beamten).

be·yond [bɪ'jɒnd] **I** prp. **1.** jenseits: **~ the seas** in Übersee; **2.** außer, abgesehen von: **~ dispute** außer allem Zweifel, unstreitig; **3.** über ... (acc.) hin'aus; mehr als, weiter als: **~ the time** über die Zeit hinaus; **~ belief** unglaublich; **~ all blame** über jeden Tadel erhaben; **~ endurance** unerträglich; **~ hope** hoffnungslos; **~ measure** über die Maßen; **it is ~ my power** es übersteigt m-e Kraft; **~ praise** über alles Lob erhaben; **~ repair** nicht mehr zu reparieren; **~ reproach** untadelig; **that is ~ me** das ist mir zu hoch, das geht über m-n Ver-

stand; **~ me in Latin** weiter als ich in Latein; **II** adv. **4.** da'rüber hin'aus, jenseits; **5.** weiter weg; **III** s. **6.** Jenseits n: **at the back of ~** im entlegensten Winkel, am Ende der Welt.

'B-girl s. Am. Animierdame f.

bi·an·nu·al [,baɪ'ænjʊəl] adj. □ halbjährlich, zweimal jährlich.

bi·as ['baɪəs] **I** s. **1.** schiefe Seite, schräge Richtung; **2.** schräger Schnitt: **cut on the ~** diagonal geschnitten; **3.** Bowling: 'Überhang m der Kugel; **4.** (**towards**) fig. Hang m, Neigung f (zu); Vorliebe f (für); **5.** fig. a) Ten'denz f, b) Vorurteil n, c) ⚖ Befangenheit f: **free from ~** unvoreingenommen; **challenge a judge for ~** e-n Richter wegen Befangenheit ablehnen; **6.** Statistik etc.: Verzerrung f: **cause ~ to the figures** die Zahlen verzerren; **7.** ⚡ (Gitter-)Vorspannung f; **II** adj u. adv. **8.** schräg, schief; **III** v/t. **9.** (mst ungünstig) beeinflussen; gegen j-n einnehmen; **'bi·as(s)ed** [-st] adj. voreingenommen; ⚖ befangen; tendenzi'ös.

bi·ath·lete [,baɪ'æθliːt] s. sport 'Biath,let m, 'Biathlonkämpfer m; **bi'ath·lon** [-'æθlɒn] s. 'Biathlon n.

bi·ax·i·al [,baɪ'æksɪəl] adj. zweiachsig.

bib [bɪb] **I** s. **1.** Lätzchen n; **2.** Schürzenlatz m; → **tucker** 2; **II** v/i. **3.** (unmäßig) trinken.

Bi·ble ['baɪbl] s. **1.** Bibel f; **2.** 2 fig. Bibel f (maßgebendes Buch); **~ clerk** s. (in Oxford) Student, der in der College-Kapelle während des Gottesdienstes die Bibeltexte verliest; **~ thump·er** s. Mo'ralprediger m.

bib·li·cal ['bɪblɪkl] adj. □ biblisch, Bibel...

bib·li·og·ra·pher [,bɪblɪ'ɒgrəfə] s. Biblio'graph m; **bib·li·o·graph·ic** [,bɪblɪəʊ'græfɪk], **bib·li·o·graph·i·cal** [,bɪblɪəʊ'græfɪk(l)] adj. □ biblio'graphisch; **bib·li·og·ra·phy** [-fɪ] s. Bibliogra'phie f; **bib·li·o·ma·ni·a** [,bɪblɪəʊ'meɪnɪæk] s. Biblioma'nie f, (krankhafte) Bücherleidenschaft; **bib·li·o·ma·ni·ac** [,bɪblɪəʊ'meɪnɪæk] s. Büchernarr m; **bib·li·o·phil** ['bɪblɪəʊfɪl], **bib·li·o·phile** ['bɪblɪəʊfaɪl] s. Biblio'phile m, Bücherliebhaber(in); **bib·li·o·the·ca** [,bɪblɪəʊ'θiːkə] s. **1.** Biblio'thek f; **2.** 'Bücherkata,log m.

bib·u·lous ['bɪbjʊləs] adj. □ **1.** trunksüchtig; **2.** weinselig.

bi·cam·er·al [baɪ'kæmərəl] adj. pol. Zweikammer...

bi·car·bon·ate [baɪ'kɑːbənɪt] s. 🜔 Bikarbo'nat n: **~ of soda** doppel(t)kohlensaures Natrium.

bi·cen·te·nar·y [,baɪsen'tiːnərɪ] **I** adj. zweihundertjährig; **II** s. Zweihundertjahrfeier f; **bi·cen·ten·ni·al** [-'tenjəl] **I** adj. zweihundertjährig; alle zweihundert Jahre eintretend; **II** s. bsd. Am. → **bicentenary** II.

bi·ceph·a·lous [,baɪ'sefələs] adj. zweiköpfig.

bi·ceps ['baɪseps] s. anat. 'Bizeps m.

bick·er ['bɪkə] v/i. **1.** (sich) zanken; quengeln; **2.** plätschern (Fluss, Regen); **3.** zucken; **'bick·er·ing** [-ərɪŋ] s. a. pl. Gezänk n.

bi·cy·cle ['baɪsɪkl] **I** s. Fahrrad n, Zweirad n; **II** v/i. Rad fahren, radeln; **'bi·cy·cler** [-lə] Am., **'bi·cy·clist** [-lɪst] Brit. s. Radfahrer(in).

bid [bɪd] **I** s. **1.** a) Gebot n (bei Versteigerungen), b) 🟊 Angebot n (bei öffentlichen Ausschreibungen), c) Börse: Geld n (Nachfrage): **~ and asked** Geld u. Brief; **higher ~** Mehrgebot; **highest ~** Meistgebot; **invitation for**

~s Ausschreibung *f*; **2.** *Kartenspiel*: Reizen *n*, Melden *n*: ***no ~*** ich passe; **3.** Bemühung *f*, Bewerbung *f* (***for*** um); Versuch *m* (***to*** *inf.* zu *inf.*): ***~ for power*** Versuch, an die Macht zu kommen; ***make a ~ for*** sich bemühen um *et. od.* zu *inf.*; **4.** *Am.* F Einladung *f*; **II** *v/t.* [*irr.*] 5 *u.* 6 *pret. u. p.p.* **bid**; 7–9 *pret.* **bade** [beɪd], *p.p. mst* **bid·den** ['bɪdn] **5.** bieten (*bei Versteigerungen*): ***~ up den Preis*** in die Höhe treiben; **6.** *Kartenspiel*: melden, reizen; **7.** *Gruß* entbieten; wünschen: ***~ good morning*** e-n guten Morgen wünschen; ***~ farewell*** Lebewohl sagen; **8.** *lit. j-m et.* gebieten, befehlen; *j-n et. tun* lassen, heißen: ***~ him come in*** lass ihn hereinkommen; **9.** *obs.* einladen (***to*** zu); **III** *v/i.* [*irr., pret. u. p.p.* **bid**] **10.** ✝ ein (Preis)Angebot machen; **11.** *Kartenspiel*: melden, reizen; **12.** (***for***) werben, sich bemühen (um); '**bid·den** [-dn] *p.p. von* ***bid***; '**bid·der** [-də] *s.* **1.** Bieter *m* (*bei Versteigerungen*): ***highest ~*** Meistbietende(r); **2.** Bewerber *m bei Ausschreibungen*; '**bid·ding** [-dɪŋ] *s.* **1.** Gebot *n*, Bieten *n* (*bei Versteigerungen*); **2.** Geheiß *n*: ***do s.o.'s ~*** tun, was j-d will.

bide [baɪd] *v/t.* [*irr.*] er-, abwarten: ***~ one's time*** (den rechten Augenblick) abwarten.

bi·en·ni·al [baɪ'enɪəl] **I** *adj.* □ **1.** alle zwei Jahre eintretend; **2.** ⚘ zweijährig; **II** *s.* **3.** ⚘ zweijährige Pflanze; **bi'en·ni·al·ly** [-lɪ] *adv.* alle zwei Jahre.

bier [bɪə] *s.* (Toten)Bahre *f*.

biff [bɪf] *sl.* **I** *v/t.* ‚hauen', schlagen; **II** *s.* Schlag *m*, Hieb *m*.

bif·fin ['bɪfɪn] *s.* roter Kochapfel.

bi·fo·cal [ˌbaɪ'fəʊkl] **I** *adj.* **1.** Bifokal-, Zweistärken...; **II** *s.* **2.** Bifo'kal-, Zweistärkenlinse *f*; **3.** *pl.* Bifo'kal-, Zweistärkenbrille *f*.

bi·fur·cate ['baɪfəkeɪt] **I** *v/t.* gabelförmig teilen; **II** *v/i.* sich gabeln; **III** *adj.* gegabelt, gabelförmig; **bi·fur·ca·tion** [ˌbaɪfə'keɪʃn] *s.* Gabelung *f*.

big [bɪg] **I** *adj.* **1.** groß, dick; stark, kräftig (*a. fig.*): ***the ~ toe*** der große Zeh; ***~ business*** Großunternehmertum *n*, Großindustrie *f*; ***~ ideas*** F ‚große Rosinen im Kopf'; ***~ money*** ein Haufen Geld; ***a ~ voice*** e-e kräftige Stimme; **2.** groß, weit: ***get too ~ for one's boots*** (*od.* ***breeches***) *fig.* ‚üppig' *od.* größenwahnsinnig werden; **3.** groß, hoch: ***~ game*** Großwild *n*, *fig.* hoch gestecktes Ziel; **4.** groß, erwachsen: ***my ~ brother***; **5.** schwanger; *fig.* voll: ***~ with child*** hochschwanger; ***~ with fate*** schicksalsschwer; **6.** hochmütig, eingebildet: ***~ talk*** ‚große Töne', Angeberei *f*; **7.** F groß, bedeutend, wichtig, führend: ***the*** ♀ ***Three*** (***Five***) die großen Drei (Fünf) (*führende Staaten, Banken etc.*); **8.** großmütig, edel: ***a ~ heart***; ***that's ~ of you*** F das ist sehr anständig von dir; **II** *adv.* **9.** großspurig: ***talk ~*** ‚große Töne spucken', angeben; **10.** *sl.* a) ‚mächtig', b) *Am.* tapfer.

big·a·mist ['bɪgəmɪst] *s.* Biga'mist(in); '**big·a·mous** [-məs] *adj.* □ biga'mistisch; '**big·a·my** [-mɪ] *s.* Biga'mie *f*, Doppelehe *f*.

big| bang *s. phys.* Urknall *m*; ***~ dip·per*** *s.* **1.** *Brit.* Achterbahn *f*, Berg- und Talbahn *f*; **2.** *mst* ***Big Dipper*** *Am. ast.* Großer Wagen (*od.* Bär); ***~ game*** *s.* Großwild *n*; ***~ gun*** *s.* F **1.** ‚schweres Geschütz'; **2.** → ***bigwig***.

bight [baɪt] *s.* **1.** Bucht *f*, Einbuchtung *f*; **2.** Krümmung *f*; **3.** ⚓ Bucht *f* (*im Tau*).

'**big·mouth** *s.* F Großmaul *n*.

big·ness ['bɪgnɪs] *s.* Größe *f*.

big·ot ['bɪgət] *s.* **1.** blinder Anhänger, Fa'natiker *m*; **2.** Betbruder *m*, -schwester *f*, Frömmler(in); '**big·ot·ed** [-tɪd] *adj.* bi'gott, fa'natisch, frömmlerisch; '**big·ot·ry** [-trɪ] *s.* **1.** blinder Eifer, Fana'tismus *m*, Engstirnigkeit *f*; **2.** Bigotte'rie *f*, Frömme'lei *f*.

big| shot *s.* → ***bigwig***; ***~ stick*** *s.* F *pol.* ‚großer Knüppel': ***~ policy*** Politik *f* des Säbelrasselns; '***~-time*** *adj. sl.* ‚groß', Spitzen...; '***~-ˌtim·er*** *s.* ‚Spitzenmann' *m*, ‚großer Macher'; ***~ top*** *s. Am.* **1.** großes 'Zirkuszelt; **2.** 'Zirkus *m* (*a. fig.*).

'**big·wig** *s.* ‚großes' *od.* ‚hohes Tier', Bonze *m*.

bike [baɪk] F **I** *s.* a) (Fahr)Rad *n*, b) ‚Maschine' *f* (*Motorrad*); **II** *v/i.* a) radeln, b) (mit dem) Motorrad fahren; '***~·way*** *s. bsd. Am.* Rad(fahr)weg *m*.

bi·lat·er·al [ˌbaɪ'lætərəl] *adj.* □ zweiseitig, bilate'ral: a) ⚖ beiderseitig verbindlich, gegenseitig (*Vertrag etc.*), b) *biol.* beide Seiten betreffend, c) ⚙ doppelseitig (*Antrieb*).

bil·ber·ry ['bɪlbərɪ] *s.* ⚘ Heidel-, Blaubeere *f*.

bile [baɪl] *s.* **1.** ⚕ a) Galle *f*, b) Gallenflüssigkeit *f*; **2.** *fig.* Galle *f*, Ärger *m*.

bilge [bɪldʒ] *s.* **1.** ⚓ Kielraum *m*, Bilge *f*, Kimm *f*; **2.** → ***bilge water***; **3.** *sl.* ‚Quatsch' *m*, ‚Mist' *m*, Unsinn *m*; ***~ pump*** *s.* ⚓ Lenzpumpe *f*; ***~ wa·ter*** *s.* ⚓ Bilgenwasser *n*.

bi·lin·e·ar [ˌbaɪ'lɪnɪə] *adj.* doppellinig; ⩚ biline'ar.

bi·lin·gual [baɪ'lɪŋgwəl] *adj.* zweisprachig.

bil·ious ['bɪljəs] *adj.* □ **1.** ⚕ Gallen...: ***~ complaint*** Gallenleiden *n*; **2.** *fig.* gallig, gereizt, reizbar; '**bil·ious·ness** [-nɪs] *s.* **1.** Gallenkrankheit *f*; **2.** *fig.* Gereiztheit *f*.

bilk [bɪlk] **I** *v/t.* prellen, betrügen; **II** *s., a.* '**bilk·er** [-kə] *s.* Betrüger *m*.

bill[1] [bɪl] **I** *s.* **1.** *zo.* a) Schnabel *m*, b) schnabelähnliche Schnauze; **2.** Spitze *f am Anker, Zirkel etc.*; **3.** *geogr.* spitz zulaufende Halbinsel; **4.** *hist.* ⚔ Pike *f*; **5.** → ***billhook***; **II** *v/i.* **6.** (sich) schnäbeln; **7.** *fig., a.* ***~ and coo*** (mitein'ander) turteln.

bill[2] [bɪl] **I** *s.* **1.** *pol.* (Gesetzes)Vorlage *f*, Gesetzentwurf *m*: ♀ ***of Rights*** a) *Brit.* Staatsgrundgesetz *n*, Freiheitsurkunde *f* (*von 1689*), b) *USA*: die ersten 10 Zusatzartikel zur Verfassung; ***bring in a ~*** e-n Gesetzentwurf einbringen; **2.** ⚖ *a.* ***~ of indictment*** Anklageschrift *f*: ***find a true ~*** die Anklage für begründet erklären; **3.** ✝ *a.* ***~ of exchange*** Wechsel *m*, Tratte *f*: ***~s payable*** Wechselschulden; ***~s receivable*** Wechselforderungen; ***long*** (***-dated***) ***~*** langfristiger Wechsel; ***~ after date*** Datowechsel *m*; ***~ after sight*** Nachsichtwechsel *m*; ***~ at sight*** Sichtwechsel *m*; ***~ of lading*** Seefrachtbrief *m*, Konnossement *n*, *Am. a.* Frachtbrief *m*; **4.** Rechnung *f*: ***~ of costs*** Kostenberechnung *f*; ***~ of sale*** Kauf-, Übereignungsvertrag *m*; F *fig.* ***fill the ~*** den Ansprüchen genügen; ***sell s.o. a ~ of goods*** F j-n ‚verschaukeln'; **5.** Liste *f*, Schein *m*, Zettel *m*, Pla'kat *n*: ***~ of fare*** Speisekarte *f*; (***theatre***) ***~*** Theaterzettel *m*, -programm *n*; (***clean***) ***~ of health*** Gesundheitszeugnis *n*, -pass *m*, *fig.* Unbedenklichkeitsbescheinigung *f*; **6.** *Am.* Banknote *f*, (Geld-) Schein *m*; **II** *v/t.* **7.** ***~ s.o. for s.th.*** j-m et. in Rechnung stellen *od.* berechnen; **8.** (durch Pla'kate) ankündigen, *thea. etc. a. Am. Darsteller etc.* ‚bringen'.

'**bill|·board** *s.* Anschlagbrett *n*, Re'klamefläche *f*, -tafel *f*: ***~ advertising*** Plakatwerbung *f*; ***~ case*** *s.* ✝ 'Wechselporte,feuille *n e-r Bank*; ***~ dis·count*** *s.* ✝ 'Wechseldis,kont *m*.

bil·let[1] ['bɪlɪt] **I** *s.* **1.** ⚔ a) Quartierzettel *m*, b) Quartier *n*: ***in ~s*** privat einquartiert; **2.** 'Unterkunft *f*; **3.** F ‚Job' *m*, Posten *m*; **II** *v/t.* **4.** 'unterbringen, einquartieren (***on*** bei).

bil·let[2] ['bɪlɪt] *s.* **1.** Holzscheit *n*, -klotz *m*; **2.** *metall.* Knüppel *m*.

bil·let-doux [ˌbɪleɪ'duː] (*Fr.*) *s. humor.* Liebesbrief *m*.

'**bill|·fold** *s. Am.* Scheintasche *f*; '***~·head*** *s.* gedrucktes 'Rechnungsformu,lar; '***~·hook*** *s.* ⚒ Hippe *f*.

bil·liard ['bɪljəd] **I** *s.* **1.** *pl. mst sg. konstr.* Billard(spiel) *n*; **2.** *Billard*: Karambo'lage *f*; **II** *adj.* **3.** Billard...; ***~ ball*** *s.* Billardkugel *f*; ***~ cue*** *s.* Queue *n*, Billardstock *m*.

bill·ing ['bɪlɪŋ] *s.* **1.** ✝ a) Rechnungsschreibung *f*, b) Buchung *f*, *a.* (Voraus)Bestellung *f*; **2.** *thea.* a) Ankündigung *f*, b) Re'klame *f*.

Bil·lings·gate ['bɪlɪŋzgɪt] **I** *npr. Fischmarkt in London*; **II** ♀ *s.* wüstes Geschimpfe, Unflat *m*: ***talk ~*** keifen wie ein Fischweib.

bil·lion ['bɪljən] *s.* **1.** Milli'arde *f*; **2.** *Brit. obs.* Billi'on *f*.

'**bill|-ˌjob·ber** *s.* ✝ *Brit.* Wechselreiter *m*; '***~-ˌjob·bing*** *s.* ✝ *Brit.* Wechselreite'rei *f*.

bil·low ['bɪləʊ] **I** *s.* **1.** Woge *f* (*a. fig.*); **2.** (Nebel- *etc.*)Schwaden *m*; **II** *v/i.* **3.** wogen; **4.** *a.* ***~ out*** sich bauschen *od.* blähen; **III** *v/t.* bauschen, blähen; '**bil·low·y** [-əʊɪ] *adj.* **1.** wogend; **2.** gebauscht, gebläht.

'**bill|ˌpost·er**, '***~ˌstick·er*** *s.* Pla'kat-, Zettelankleber *m*.

bil·ly ['bɪlɪ] *s. Am.* (Poli'zei)Knüppel *m*; '***~·cock*** (***hat***) *s. Brit.* F ‚Me'lone' *f* (*steifer Filzhut*); ***~ goat*** *s.* F Ziegenbock *m*.

bim·bo ['bɪmbəʊ] *s. sl.* ‚Puppe' *f*, ‚Dummerchen' *n* (*Frau*).

bi·met·al·lism [ˌbaɪ'metəlɪzəm] Bimetal'lismus *m*, Doppelwährung *f* (*Gold u. Silber*).

bi·month·ly [ˌbaɪ'mʌnθlɪ] **I** *adj. u. adv.* **1.** a) zweimonatlich, alle zwei Monate ('wiederkehrend *od.* erscheinend), b) zweimal im Monat (erscheinend); **II** *s.* **2.** zweimonatlich erscheinende Veröffentlichung; **3.** Halbmonatsschrift *f*.

bi·mo·tored [ˌbaɪ'məʊtəd] *adj.* ✈ 'zweimo,torig.

bin [bɪn] *s.* **1.** (großer) Behälter, Kasten *m*; *a.* Silo *m*, *n*; **2.** Verschlag *m*; **3.** *sl.* ‚Klapsmühle' *f*.

bi·na·ry ['baɪnərɪ] *adj.* ⚗, ⚙, ⩚, *phys.* bi'när, aus zwei Einheiten bestehend: ***~ digit*** Binärziffer *f*; ***~*** (***number***) ⩚ Binär-, Dualzahl *f*; ***~*** (***star***) *ast.* Doppelstern *m*; ***~ fission*** *biol.* Zellteilung *f*.

bind [baɪnd] **I** *s.* **1.** Band *n*; **2.** ♪ Halte- *od.* Bindebogen *m*; **3.** F ***be in a ~*** in ‚Schwulitäten' sein; ***be in a ~ for*** *et. od. j-n* dringend brauchen, verlegen sein um; **II** *v/t.* [*irr.*] **4.** binden, an-, 'um-, festbinden, verbinden: ***~ to a tree*** an e-n Baum binden; ***bound hand and foot*** *fig.* an Händen u. Füßen gebunden; **5.** *Buch* (ein)binden; **6.** *Saum etc.* einfassen; **7.** *Rad etc.* (mit Me'tall) beschlagen; **8.** *Sand etc.* fest *od.* hart machen; zs.-fügen; **9.** (***o.s.*** sich) binden (*a. vertraglich*), verpflichten; zwingen:

B

~ *an apprentice* j-n in die Lehre geben (*to* bei); ~ *a bargain* e-n Handel (durch Anzahlung) verbindlich machen; → *bound¹* 1; **10.** 🔨, ❂ binden; **11.** 🪡 verstopfen; **II** v/i. **12.** binden, fest od. hart werden, zs.-halten; **o·ver** v/t. 🕮 **1.** zum Erscheinen verpflichten (*to* vor e-m *Gericht*); **2.** *Brit.* j-n auf Bewährung entlassen; ~ **up** v/t. **1.** vereinigen, zs.-binden; *Wunde* verbinden; **2.** *pass.* **be bound up** (**in** od. **with**) a) eng verknüpft sein (mit), b) ganz in Anspruch genommen werden (von).

bind·er ['baɪndə] s. **1.** a) (*Buch-*, *Garben*)Binder(in), b) Garbenbinder m (*Maschine*); **2.** Binde f, Band n, Schnur f; **3.** Aktendeckel m, 'Umschlag m; **4.** ❂ Bindemittel n; **5.** ✝ Vorvertrag m; **'bind·er·y** [-ərɪ] s. Buchbinde'rei f.

bind·ing ['baɪndɪŋ] **I** adj. **1.** bindend, (rechts)verbindlich ([*up*]*on* für): ~ *force* bindende Kraft; ~ *law* zwingendes Recht; **II** s. **2.** (Buch)Einband m; **3.** a) Einfassung f, Borte f, b) (Me'tall-)Beschlag m (*Rad*), c) (Ski)Bindung f; ~ **a·gent** → *binder* 4; ~ **post** s. ⚡ (Pol-, Anschluss)Klemme f.

'bind·weed s. ♀ e-e Winde f.

bine [baɪn] s. ♀ Ranke f.

binge [bɪndʒ] s. F 'Sauf- od. Fressgelage' n: **go on a** ~ ,einen draufmachen'.

bin·go ['bɪŋgəʊ] s. Bingo n (*ein Glücksspiel*): ~ *!* F Zack!, Volltreffer!

bin lin·er s. Müllbeutel m.

bin·na·cle ['bɪnəkl] s. ⚓ 'Kompasshaus n.

bin·oc·u·lar I adj. [,baɪ'nɒkjʊlə] binoku'lar, für beide od. mit beiden Augen; **II** s. [bɪ'n-] *mst pl.* Fernglas n; Opernglas n.

bi·no·mi·al [,baɪ'nəʊmjəl] adj. **1.** A bi'nomisch, zweigliedrig; **2.** ♀, zo. → *binominal*.

bi·nom·i·nal [,baɪ'nɒmɪnl] adj. ♀, zo. bi-nomi'nal, zweinamig: ~ *system* (System n der) Doppelbenennung f.

bi·nu·cle·ar [,baɪ'njuːklɪə], **bi'nu·cle·ate** [-ɪət] adj. *phys.* zweikernig.

bi·o·chem·i·cal [,baɪəʊ'kemɪkl] adj. ☐ bio'chemisch; **bi·o'chem·ist** [-ɪst] s. Bio'chemiker m; **bi·o'chem·is·try** [-ɪstrɪ] s. Bioche'mie f.

bi·o·de·gra·da·ble [,baɪəʊdɪ'greɪdəbl] adj. 🔨 (bio'logisch) abbaubar; **bi·o·deg·ra·da·tion** ['baɪəʊ,degrə'deɪʃn] s. biologischer Abbau, Rotte f.

bi·o·di·ver·si·ty ['baɪəʊdaɪ'vɜːsətɪ] s. Artenvielfalt f; ~ **con·ven·tion** s. Artenschutzabkommen n.

bio·dy·nam·ic [,baɪəʊdaɪ'næmɪk] adj. ☐ ,biody'namisch.

bi·o·en·er·get·ics ['baɪəʊ,enə'dʒetɪks] s. *pl. sg. konstr.* Bioener'getik f.

bi·o·en·gi·neer·ing ['baɪəʊ,endʒɪ'nɪərɪŋ] s. Biotechnik f.

bi·o·fu·el ['baɪəʊ,fjʊəl] s. Biotreibstoff m.

bi·og·ra·pher [baɪ'ɒgrəfə] s. Bio'graph m; **bi·o·graph·ic**, **bi·o·graph·i·cal** [,baɪəʊ'græfɪk(l)] adj. ☐ bio'graphisch; **bi·og·ra·phy** [-fɪ] s. Biogra'phie f, Lebensbeschreibung f.

bi·o·log·ic [,baɪəʊ'lɒdʒɪk] adj. (☐ ~ally) → **bi·o'log·i·cal** [-kl] adj. ☐ bio'logisch: ~ *warfare* Bakterienkrieg m; **bi·ol·o·gist** [baɪ'ɒlədʒɪst] s. Bio'loge m; **bi·ol·o·gy** [baɪ'ɒlədʒɪ] s. Biolo'gie f.

bi·ol·y·sis [baɪ'ɒləsɪs] s. *biol.* Bio'lyse f.

bi·on·ics [baɪ'ɒnɪks] s. *pl. sg. konstr. phys.* Bi'onik f.

bi·o·nom·ics [,baɪəʊ'nɒmɪks] s. *pl. sg. konstr. biol.* Ökolo'gie f; **bi·o·phys·ics** [,baɪəʊ'fɪzɪks] s. *pl. sg. konstr.* Biophy-

'sik f.

bi·op·ic [baɪ'ɒpɪk] s. biographisches Filmepos.

bi·op·sy ['baɪɒpsɪ] s. 🩺 Biop'sie f.

bi·o·rhythm ['baɪəʊ,rɪðəm] s. 🩺 'Biorhythmus m.

bi·o·sphere ['baɪəʊ,sfɪə] s. Bio'sphäre f.

bi·o·tech·nol·o·gy [,baɪəʊtək'nɒlədʒɪ] s. Biotechnik f.

bi·o·tope ['baɪəʊtəʊp] s. *biol. geogr.* Bio'top m, n.

bi·par·ti·san [,baɪpɑːtɪ'zæn] adj. zwei Par'teien vertretend, Zweiparteien...; **,bi·par·ti'san·ship** [-ʃɪp] s. Zugehörigkeit f zu zwei Parteien; **bi·par·tite** [,baɪ'pɑːtaɪt] adj. **1.** zweiteilig; **2.** pol., 🔨 a) zweiseitig (*Vertrag etc.*), b) in doppelter Ausfertigung (*Dokumente*).

bi·ped ['baɪped] s. zo. Zweifüß(l)er m.

bi·plane ['baɪpleɪn] s. ✈ Doppel-, Zweidecker m.

birch [bɜːtʃ] **I** s. **1.** a) ♀ Birke f, b) Birkenholz n; **2.** (Birken)Rute f; **II** v/t. **3.** mit der Rute züchtigen; **'birch·en** [-tʃən] adj. birken, Birken...; **'birch·ing** [-tʃɪŋ] s. (Ruten)Schläge pl.; **'birch·rod** → *birch* 2.

bird [bɜːd] s. **1.** Vogel m: ~ *of paradise* Paradiesvogel; ~ *of passage* Zugvogel (*a. fig.*); ~ *of prey* Raub-, Greifvogel; F *early* ~ Frühaufsteher m, wer früh kommt; *the early* ~ *catches the worm* Morgenstund hat Gold im Mund; ~*s of a feather flock together* Gleich u. Gleich gesellt sich gern; *kill two* ~*s with one stone* zwei Fliegen mit e-r Klappe schlagen; *a* ~ *in the hand is worth two in the bush* ein Spatz in der Hand ist besser als e-e Taube auf dem Dach; *fine feathers make fine* ~*s* Kleider machen Leute; *the* ~ *is* (*od. has*) *flown fig.* der Vogel ist ausgeflogen; *give s.o. the* ~ j-n auspfeifen *od.* ,abfahren lassen', j-m den Laufpass geben; F *a little* ~ *told me* mein kleiner Finger hat es mir gesagt; *tell a child about the* ~*s and the bees* ein Kind aufklären; *that's for the* ~*s* F das ist ,für die Katz'; **2.** a) F ,Knülch' m, Kerl m, b) *Brit. sl.* ,Puppe' f (*Mädchen*): *queer* ~ komischer Kauz; *old* ~ alter Knabe; *gay* ~ lustiger Vogel; **3.** *sl.* a) ,Vogel' m (*Flugzeug*), b) *Am.* Rangabzeichen n e-s Colonel etc.; **'~·brain** s. F ,Spatzen(ge)hirn' n; ~ **cage** s. Vogelbauer n, -käfig m; **'~·call** s. Vogelruf m; Lockpfeife f; ~ **dog** s. Hühnerhund m; ~ **fan·ci·er** s. Vogelliebhaber(in), -züchter(in), -händler(in).

bird·ie [bɜːdɪ] s. **1.** Vögelchen n; **2.** ,Täubchen n (*Kosewort*); **3.** Golf: 'Birdie n (*1 Schlag unter Par*).

bird| life s. Vogelleben n, -welt f; **'~·lime** s. Vogelleim m; **'~·man** s. [irr.] **1.** Vogelkenner m; **2.** ✈ F Flieger m; **'~·,nest·ing** s. Ausnehmen n von Vogelnestern; **'~·seed** s. Vogelfutter n.

'bird's·eye [bɜːdz] s. **1.** ♀ A'donisröschen n; **2.** Feinschnittabak m; **3.** ✝ Pfauenauge(nmuster) n; **II** adj. **4.** ~ *view* (Blick m aus der) Vogelperspektive f, allgemeiner Überblick; ~ *nest* s. (*a. essbares*) Vogelnest.

bird watch·er s. Vogelbeobachter m.

bi·ro ['baɪərəʊ] s. (*TM*) *Brit.* Kugelschreiber m.

birth [bɜːθ] s. **1.** Geburt f; Wurf m (*Hunde etc.*): *give* ~ *to* gebären, zur Welt bringen, *fig.* hervorbringen, -rufen; *by* ~ von Geburt; **2.** Abstammung f, Herkunft f; *engS.* edle Herkunft; **3.** Ursprung m, Entstehung f; ~ **cer·tif·i-**

cate s. Geburtsurkunde f; ~ **con·trol** s. Geburtenregelung f, -beschränkung f; **'~·day** s. Geburtstag m: ~ *honours Brit.* Titelverleihungen zum Geburtstag des Königs od. der Königin; *in one's* ~ *suit* im Adams- od. Evaskostüm; ~ *party* Geburtstagsparty f; **'~·mark** s. Muttermal n; **'~·place** s. Geburtsort m; ~ **rate** s. Geburtenziffer f: *falling* ~ Geburtenrückgang m; **'~·right** s. (Erst-)Geburtsrecht n.

bis·cuit ['bɪskɪt] **I** s. **1.** *Brit.* Keks m: *that takes the* ~! F a) das ist doch das Allerletzte!, b) das ist (einsame) Spitze!; **2.** *Am.* weiches Brötchen; **3.** → *biscuit ware*; **II** adj. **4.** a) blassbraun, b) graugelb; ~ **ware** s. ❂ Bis'kuit n (*Porzellan*).

bi·sect [baɪ'sekt] v/t. **1.** in zwei Teile zerschneiden; **2.** A halbieren; **bi·sec·tion** [,baɪ'sekʃn] s. A Halbierung f.

bi·sex·u·al [,baɪ'seksjʊəl] adj. *allg.* bisexu'ell.

bish·op ['bɪʃɒp] s. **1.** Bischof m; **2.** *Schach:* Läufer m; **3.** Bischof m (*Getränk*); **'bish·op·ric** [-rɪk] s. Bistum n, Diö'zese f.

bi·son ['baɪsn] s. zo. **1.** Bison m, amer. Büffel m; **2.** euro'päischer Wisent.

bis·sex·tile [bɪ'sekstaɪl] **I** s. Schaltjahr n; **II** adj. Schalt...: ~ *day* Schalttag m.

bit¹ [bɪt] s. **1.** Gebiss n (*am Pferdezaum*): *take the* ~ *between one's teeth* a) durchgehen (*Pferd*), b) störrisch werden (*a. fig.*), c) *fig.* ,rangehen'; → *champ¹*; **2.** *fig.* Zaum m, Zügel m u. pl.; **3.** ❂ a) Bohrerspitze f, b) Hobeleisen n, c) Maul n der Zange etc., d) Bart m des Schlüssels.

bit² [bɪt] s. **1.** Stückchen n: *a* ~ *of bread* ein bisschen, ein wenig, leicht; *a* ~ *of a ...* so et. wie ein(e) ...; *a* ~ *of a fool* etwas närrisch; ~ *by* ~ Stück für Stück, allmählich; *after a* ~ nach e-m Weilchen; *every* ~ *as good* ganz genauso gut; *not a* ~ *better* kein bisschen besser; *not a* ~ (*of it*) ,keine Spur', ganz und gar nicht; *do one's* ~ a) s-e Pflicht tun, b) s-n Beitrag leisten; *give s.o. a* ~ *of one's mind* j-m (gehörig) die Meinung sagen; **2.** kleine Münze: a) *Brit.* F *threepenny* ~, b) *Am.* F *two* ~*s* 25 Cent; **3.** F ,Mieze' f (*Mädchen*); **4.** a. ~ *part thea.* F kleine Rolle: ~ *player*.

bit³ [bɪt] s. *Computer:* Bit n.

bit⁴ [bɪt] *pret. von* bite.

bitch [bɪtʃ] s. **1.** Hündin f; **2.** a. ~ *fox* Füchsin f; a. ~ *wolf* Wölfin f; **3.** V *contp.* a) Schlampe f, b) ,Miststück' n; **4.** *sl.* ,Scheißding' n; **II** v/t. **5.** *sl.* a. ~ *up* ,versauen'; **III** v/i. **6.** *sl.* ,meckern'; **bitch·y** ['bɪtʃɪ] adj. F ,gemein'.

bite [baɪt] **I** s. **1.** Beißen n, Biss m; Stich m (*Insekt*): *put the* ~ *on s.o. Am. sl.* j-n unter Druck setzen; **2.** Bissen m, Happen m: *not a* ~ *to eat*; **3.** (An-)Beißen n (*Fisch*); **4.** ❂ Fassen n, Greifen n; **5.** *fig.* a) Bissigkeit f, Schärfe f, Spitze f, b) ,Biss' m (*Aggressivität*): *the* ~ *was gone*; **6.** *fig.* Würze f, Geist m; **II** v/t. [irr.] **7.** beißen: ~ *one's lips* sich auf die Lippen (*fig.* auf die Zunge) beißen; ~ *one's nails* an den Nägeln kauen; ~ *bitten with a desire fig.* von e-m Wunsch gepackt; *what's biting you? Am. sl.* was ist mit dir los? → *dust* 1; **8.** beißen, stechen (*Insekt*); **9.** ❂ fassen, greifen; schneiden in (*acc.*); **10.** 🔨 beizen, zerfressen, angreifen; beschädigen; **11.** F *pass.:* **be bitten** hereingefallen sein; *once bitten twice shy* ein gebranntes Kind scheut das

Feuer; **III** *v/i.* [*irr.*] **12.** beißen; **13.** (an-) beißen; *fig.* sich verlocken lassen; **14.** ⊙ fassen, greifen (*Rad, Bremse, Werkzeug*); **15.** *fig.* beißen, schneiden, brennen, stechen, scharf sein (*Kälte, Wind, Gewürz, Schmerz*); **16.** *fig.* beißend *od.* verletzend sein; ~ **off** *v/t.* abbeißen: ~ *more than one can chew* sich zu viel zumuten.

bit·er ['baɪtə] *s.*: *the* ~ *bit* der betrogene Betrüger; *the* ~ *will be bitten* wer andern e-e Grube gräbt, fällt selbst hinein.

bit·ing ['baɪtɪŋ] *adj.* □ *a. fig.* beißend, scharf, schneidend.

bit·ten ['bɪtn] *p.p. von* bite.

bit·ter ['bɪtə] **I** *adj.* □ → *a.* 4; **1.** bitter (*Geschmack*); **2.** *fig.* bitter (*Schicksal, Wahrheit, Tränen, Worte etc.*), schmerzlich, hart: *to the* ~ *end* bis zum bitteren Ende; **3.** *fig.* verärgert, böse, verbittert; streng, unerbittlich; rau, unfreundlich (*a. Wetter*); **II** *adv.* **4.** nur: ~ *cold* bitter kalt; **III** *s.* **5.** Bitterkeit *f* (*a. fig.*): *take the* ~ *with the sweet* das Leben (so) nehmen, wie es ist; **6.** *a.* ~ *beer Brit.* stark gehopftes Fassbier; **7.** *pl.* Magenbitter *m*.

bit·tern[1] ['bɪtən] *s. orn.* Rohrdommel *f*.

bit·tern[2] ['bɪtən] *s.* **1.** 🜍 Mutterlauge *f*; **2.** Bitterstoff *m* (*für Bier*).

bit·ter·ness ['bɪtənɪs] *s.* **1.** Bitterkeit *f*; **2.** *fig.* Bitterkeit *f*, Schmerzlichkeit *f*; **3.** *fig.* Verbitterung *f*, Härte *f*, Grausamkeit *f*.

'**bit·ter·sweet I** *adj.* bittersüß; halbbitter; **II** *s.* ♀ Bittersüß *n*.

bi·tu·men ['bɪtjʊmɪn] *s.* **1.** *min.* Bi'tumen *n*, Erdpech *n*, As'phalt *m*; **2.** *geol.* Bergteer *m*.

bi·tu·mi·nous [bɪ'tjuːmɪnəs] *adj. min.* bitumi'nös, as'phalt-, pechhaltig; ~ *coal s.* Stein-, Fettkohle *f*.

bi·va·lent ['baɪ,veɪlənt] *adj.* 🜍 zweiwertig.

bi·valve ['baɪvælv] *s. zo.* zweischalige Muschel (*z.B. Auster*).

biv·ouac ['bɪvʊæk] **I** *s.* 'Biwak *n*; **II** *v/i.* biwakieren.

bi·week·ly [,baɪ'wiːklɪ] **I** *adj. u. adv.* **1.** zweiwöchentlich, vierzehntägig, halbmonatlich; **2.** zweimal die Woche; **II** *s.* **3.** Halbmonatsschrift *f*.

biz [bɪz] *s.* F *für* business.

bi·zarre [bɪ'zɑː] *adj.* bi'zarr, fan'tastisch, ab'sonderlich.

blab [blæb] **I** *v/t.* ausplaudern; **II** *v/i.* schwatzen; **III** *s.* Schwätzer(in), Klatschbase *f*, -weib *n*; **blab·ber** [-bə] *s.* Schwätzer(in).

black [blæk] **I** *adj.* **1.** schwarz (*a. Tee, Kaffee*): ~ *as coal* (*od. the devil od.* *ink od.* *night od.* *pitch*) kohlraben-, pechschwarz; → *black eye, belt* 1, 5, *diamond* 1; **2.** dunkel: ~ *in the face* dunkelrot im Gesicht (*vor Aufregung etc.*); **3.** dunkel(häutig): ~ *man* Schwarzer *m*, Neger *m*; **4.** schwarz, schmutzig: ~ *hands*; **5.** *fig.* dunkel, trübe, düster (*Gedanken, Wetter*); **6.** böse, schlecht: ~ *soul* schwarze Seele; *not so* ~ *as he is painted* besser als sein Ruf; **7.** ,schwarz', ungesetzlich: ~ *economy* Schattenwirtschaft *f*; **8.** ärgerlich, böse: ~ *look(s)* böser Blick; *look* ~ *at s.o.* j-n böse anblicken; **9.** schlimm: ~ *despair* völlige Verzweiflung; **10.** *Am.* eingefleischt; **11.** ,schwarz' (*makaber*): ~ *humo(u)r*; **12.** *TV* schwarz/weiß; **II** *s.* **13.** Schwarz *n*; **14.** *et.* Schwarzes, schwarzer Fleck: *wear* ~ Trauer(kleidung) tragen; **15.** Schwarze(r *m*) *f*, Neger(in); **16.** Schwärze *f*, schwarze

Schuhcreme; **17.** *be in the* ~ bsd. 🜪 a) mit Gewinn arbeiten, b) aus den roten Zahlen heraus sein; **III** *v/t.* **18.** schwärzen, *Schuhe* wichsen; ~ **out I** *v/t.* **1.** (völlig) abdunkeln, *a.* ✕ verdunkeln; **2.** ⊙ *u. fig.* ausschalten, außer Betrieb setzen; *Funkstation* (durch Störgeräusche) ausschalten; **3.** *j-n* bewusstlos machen; **4.** *fig.* (*a. durch Zensur*) unter-'drücken; **II** *v/i.* **5.** sich verdunkeln; **6.** a) das Bewusstsein verlieren, b) e-n ,Black-out' haben; **7.** ⊙ *etc.* ausfallen.

black Af·ri·ca *s. pol.* Schwarzafrika *n*.

black·a·moor ['blækə,mʊə] *s. obs.* Neger(in *f*) *m*, Mohr(in *f*) *m*.

black| and blue *adj.*: *beat s.o.* ~ j-n grün und blau schlagen; ~ **and tan** *adj.* schwarz mit braunen Flecken; ~ **and white** *s.* **1.** Schwarz'weißzeichnung *f*; **2.** *in* ~ schwarz auf weiß, schriftlich, gedruckt; **3.** *TV etc.* schwarz/weiß; ~ **art** → *black magic*; ~ **ball** *s.* schwarze (Wahl)Kugel; *fig.* Gegenstimme *f*; '~**ball** *v/t.* gegen *j-n* stimmen, *j-n* ausschließen; ~ **bee·tle** *s. zo.* Küchenschabe *f*; '~**ber·ry** [-bərɪ] *s.* ♀ Brombeere *f*; '~**bird** *s. orn.* Amsel *f*; '~**board** *s.* (Schul-, Wand)Tafel *f*; ~ **box** *s.* ✈ Flugschreiber *m*; ~ **cap** *s.* schwarze Kappe (*des Richters bei Todesurteilen*); '~**cap** *s. orn.* a) Kohlmeise *f*, b) Schwarzköpfige Grasmücke; ~ **cat·tle** *s. zo.* schwarze Rinderrasse; '~-**coat**(·**ed**) *adj.* ~ *worker* Büroangestellte(r) *m* (*Ggs. Arbeiter*); '~**cock** *s. orn.* Schwarzes Schottisches Moorhuhn (*Hahn*); ⚲ **Coun·try** *s.* Indu'striegebiet *n* in Staffordshire u. Warwickshire; ,~**cur·rant** [-'kʌrənt] *s.* ♀ Schwarze Jo'hannisbeere; ⚲ **Death** *s.* der schwarze Tod, Pest *f*; ~ **dog** *s.* F schlechte Laune.

black·en ['blækən] **I** *v/t.* **1.** schwärzen, wichsen; **2.** *fig.* anschwärzen: ~*ing the memory of the deceased* 🜪 Verunglimpfung *f* Verstorbener; **II** *v/i.* **3.** schwarz werden.

black| eye *s.* ,blaues Auge': *get away with a* ~ mit e-m blauen Auge davonkommen; '~**face** *s. typ.* (halb)fette Schrift; ~ **flag** *s.* schwarze (Pi'raten-) Flagge; ⚲ **Fri·ar** *s. eccl.* Domini'kaner *m*; ~ **frost** *s.* strenge, aber trockene Kälte; ~ **game** *s. orn.* schwarzes Rebhuhn; ~ **grouse** *s. orn.* Birkhuhn *n*.

black·guard ['blægɑːd] **I** *s.* Lump *m*, Schuft *m*; **II** *v/t. j-n* beschimpfen; '**black·guard·ly** [-lɪ] *adj.* gemein, unflätig.

'**black|·head** *s.* ✿ Mitesser *m*; ~ **hole** *s. ast.* schwarzes Loch; ~ **ice** *s.* Glatteis *n*.

black·ie ['blækɪ] *s.* → *blacky*.

black·ing ['blækɪŋ] *s.* **1.** schwarze (Schuh)Wichse; **2.** (Ofen)Schwärze *f*.

black·ish ['blækɪʃ] *adj.* schwärzlich.

'**black|·jack** *s.* **1.** → *black flag*; **2.** *Am.* Totschläger *m* (*Waffe*); **3.** 'Siebzehnund'vier *n* (*Kartenspiel*); **II** *v/t.* **4.** *Am.* mit e-m Totschläger zs.-schlagen; ~ **lead** [led] *s. min.* Gra'phit *m*, Reißblei *n*; ,~-'lead pen·cil *s.* Graphitstift *m*; '~**leg I** *s.* **1.** a) Falschspieler *m*, b) Wettbetrüger *m*; **2.** *Brit.* Streikbrecher *m*; **II** *v/i.* **3.** als Streikbrecher auftreten; ~ **let·ter** *s. typ.* Frak'tur *f*, gotische Schrift; ,~-'let·ter *adj.*: ~ *day* schwarzer Tag, Unglückstag *m*; '~**list I** *s.* schwarze Liste; **II** *v/t. j-n* auf die schwarze Liste setzen; ~ **mag·ic** *s.* schwarze Ma'gie; '~**mail I** *s.* **1.** 🜪 Erpressung *f*; **2.** Erpressungsgeld *n*; **II** *v/t.* **3.** *j-n* erpressen, von *j-m* Geld erpressen: ~ *s.o. into s.th* j-n durch Erpres-

sung zu et. zwingen; '~,**mail·er** *s.* Erpresser *m*; ⚲ **Ma·ri·a** [mə'raɪə] *s.* F ,Grüne Minna', (Poli'zei)Gefangenenwagen *m*; ~ **mark** *s.* schlechte Note, Tadel *m*; ~ **mar·ket** *s.* schwarzer Markt, Schwarzmarkt *m*, -handel *m* (*in* mit); ~ **mar·ket·eer** *s.* Schwarzhändler(in); ~ **mass** *s.* schwarze Messe, Teufelsmesse *f*; ~ **monk** *s.* Benedik'tiner(mönch) *m*.

black·ness ['blæknɪs] *s.* **1.** Schwärze *f*, Dunkelheit *f*; **2.** *fig.* Verderbtheit *f*, Ab'scheulichkeit *f*.

'**black|·out** *s.* **1.** *bsd.* ✕ Verdunkelung *f*; **2.** (*Nachrichten- etc.*)Sperre *f*: *news* ~; **3.** ✈ a) Black-out *n, m* (*kurze Ohnmacht, Bewusstseinsstörung etc.*), b) Bewusstlosigkeit *f*, Ohnmacht *f*; **4.** ⊙ *u. fig.* Ausfall *m*; ⚡ to'taler Stromausfall; **5.** *TV* a) Austasten *n*, b) Pro'grammod. Bildausfall *m*; **6.** *phys. etc., a. thea.* Black-out *n, m*; ⚲ **Prince** *s. der* Schwarze Prinz (*Eduard, Prinz von Wales*); ~ **pud·ding** *s. Brit.* Blutwurst *f*; ⚲ **Rod** *s.* **1.** oberster Dienstbeamter des brit. Oberhauses; **2.** erster Zere'monienmeister des Hosenbandordens; ~ **sheep** *s. fig.* schwarzes Schaf; '~**shirt** *s.* Schwarzhemd *n* (*italienischer Faschist*); '~**smith** *s.* (Grob-, Huf)Schmied *m*; ~ **spot** *s. mot.* schwarzer Punkt, Gefahrenstelle *f*; '~**strap** *s. Am.* **1.** Getränk aus Rum u. Sirup; **2.** F Rotwein *m* aus dem Mittelmeergebiet; '~**thorn** *s.* ♀ Schwarz-, Schlehdorn *m*; ~ **tie** *s.* **1.** schwarze Fliege; **2.** Smoking *m*; '~**top** *s.* Asphaltbelag *m od.* -straße *f*; '~,**wa·ter fe·ver** *s.* 🜪 Schwarzwasserfieber *n*; ~ **wid·ow** *s.* 🜪 Schwarze Witwe (*Spinne*).

black·y ['blækɪ] *s.* F Schwarze(r *m*) *f* (*Neger od. Schwarzhaarige[r]*).

blad·der ['blædə] *s.* **1.** *anat.* (Gallen-, *engS.* Harn)Blase *f*; **2.** (*Fußball- etc.*) Blase *f*; **3.** *zo.* Schwimmblase *f*; ~ **wrack** *s.* ♀ Blasentang *m*.

blade [bleɪd] *s.* **1.** ♀ Blatt *n* (*mst poet.*), Spreite *f* (*e-s Blattes*), Halm *m*: *in the* ~ auf dem Halm; ~ *of grass* Grashalm; **2.** ⊙ Blatt *n* (*Säge, Axt, Schaufel, Ruder*); **3.** ⊙ a) Flügel *m* (*Propeller*): *Hubschrauber*: Rotor *m*, Drehflügel *m*, b) Schaufel *f* (*Schiffsrad, Turbine*); **4.** ⊙ Klinge *f* (*Messer, Degen etc.*); **5.** → *shoulder blade*; **6.** *poet.* a) Degen *m*, Klinge *f*, b) Kämpfer *m*; **7.** F (forscher) Kerl, Bursche *m*.

blae·ber·ry ['bleɪbərɪ] → *bilberry*.

blah[1] [blɑː] *a.* ,**blah·'blah** F I *s.* ,Bla'bla' *n*, Geschwafel *n*; **II** *v/i.* schwafeln.

blah[2] [blɑː] F I *adj.* (stink)fad; **II** *s. pl. Am.* a) Langeweile *f*, b) ,mieses Gefühl'.

blain [bleɪn] *s.* ✿ Pustel *f*.

blam·a·ble ['bleɪməbl] *adj.* □ zu tadeln(d), schuldig; **blame** [bleɪm] **I** *v/t.* **1.** tadeln, rügen, *j-m* Vorwürfe machen (*for* wegen); **2.** (*for*) verantwortlich machen (für), *j-m* die Schuld geben (an *dat.*): *he is to* ~ *for it* er ist daran schuld; *he has only himself to* ~ das hat er sich selbst zuzuschreiben; *I cannot* ~ *him for it* ich kann es ihm nicht verübeln; **II** *s.* **3.** Tadel *m*, Vorwurf *m*, Rüge *f*; **4.** Schuld *f*, Verantwortung *f*: *lay* (*od.* *put*) *the* ~ *on s.o.* j-m die Schuld geben; *bear* (*od.* *take*) *the* ~ die Schuld auf sich nehmen; '**blame·less** [-lɪs] *adj.* □ untadelig, schuldlos (*of* an *dat.*); '**blame·less·ness** [-lɪsnɪs] *s.* Schuldlosigkeit *f*, Unschuld *f*; '**blame,wor·thy** *adj.* tadelnswert, schuldig.

B

blanch [blɑːntʃ] **I** v/t. **1.** bleichen, weiß machen; fig. erbleichen lassen; **2.** ♪ (durch Ausschluss von Licht) bleichen; **3.** Küche: Mandeln etc. blanchieren, brühen; **4.** ◎ weiß sieden; brühen; **5.** ~ over fig. beschönigen; **II** v/i. **6.** erbleichen.

blanc·mange [blə'mɒnʒ] s. Küche: Pudding m.

bland [blænd] adj. □ **1.** a) mild, sanft, b) höflich, verbindlich, c) (ein)schmeichelnd; **2.** a) kühl, b) i'ronisch.

blan·dish ['blændɪʃ] v/t. schmeicheln, zureden (dat.); **'blan·dish·ment** [-mənt] s. Schmeiche'lei f, Zureden n; pl. Über'redungskünste pl.

blank [blæŋk] **I** adj. □ **1.** leer, nicht ausgefüllt, unbeschrieben; Blanko... (bsd. ✝): a ~ page; ~ space Computer etc.: Leerzeichen n; a ~ space a. ein leerer Raum; ~ tape Leerband n; in ~ blanko; leave ~ frei lassen; ~ acceptance Blankoakzept n; ~ signature Blankounterschrift f; → cheque; **2.** leer, unbebaut; **3.** blind (Fenster, Tür); **4.** leer, ausdruckslos; **5.** verdutzt, verblüfft, verlegen: a ~ look; **6.** bar, rein, völlig: ~ astonishment sprachloses Erstaunen; ~ despair helle Verzweiflung; **7.** → cartridge 1, fire 13, verse 3; **II** s. **8.** Formblatt n, Formu'lar n, Vordruck m; unbeschriebenes Blatt (a. fig.); **9.** leerer od. freier Raum (bsd. für Wort[e] od. Buchstaben); Lücke f, Leere f (a. fig.): leave a ~ e-n freien Raum lassen (beim Schreiben etc.); his mind was a ~ a) er hatte alles vergessen, b) in s-m Kopf herrschte völlige Leere; **10.** Lotterie: Niete f: draw a ~ a) e-e Niete ziehen, b) fig. kein Glück haben; **11.** bsd. sport Null f; **12.** das Schwarze (Zielscheibe); **13.** Öde f, Nichts n; **14.** ◎ unbearbeitetes Werkstück, Rohling m; ungeprägte Münzplatte; **15.** Gedankenstrich m (an Stelle e-s [unanständigen] Wortes), 'Pünktchen' pl.; **III** v/t. **16.** mst ~ out a) verhüllen, auslöschen, b) fig. 'erledigen', abtun; **17.** ~ out typ. gesperrt drucken; **18.** Wort durch e-n Gedankenstrich od. Pünktchen ersetzen; **19.** TV Brit. austasten; **20.** sport zu null schlagen.

blan·ket ['blæŋkɪt] **I** s. **1.** (wollene) Decke, Bettdecke f: get between the ~s F in die Federn kriechen; born on the wrong side of the ~ F unehelich; → wet 1; **2.** fig. Decke f, Hülle f: ~ of snow Schneedecke; **3.** ◎ 'Filz,unterlage f; **II** v/t. **4.** zudecken; **5.** ⚓ den Wind abfangen (dat.); **6.** fig. verdecken, unter'drücken, ersticken, vertuschen; **7.** ⚡, ✗ abschirmen; **8.** Radio: stören, über'lagern; **9.** prellen; **10.** Am. zs.-fassen, um'fassen; **III** adj. **11.** alles einschließend, gene'rell: ~ clause Generalklausel f; ~ insurance Kollektivversicherung f; ~ mortgage Gesamthypothek f; ~ policy Pauschalpolice f; ~ sheet Am. Zeitung f in Großfolio.

blan·ket·ing ['blæŋkɪtɪŋ] s. Stoff m für Wolldecken.

blare [bleə] **I** v/i. u. v/t. a) schmettern (Trompete), b) brüllen, plärren (a. Radio etc.); **II** s. a) Schmettern n, b) Brüllen n, Plärren n, c) Lärm m.

blar·ney ['blɑːnɪ] F **I** (plumpe) Schmeiche'lei, 'Schmus' m; **II** v/t. u. v/i. (j-m) schmeicheln.

bla·sé ['blɑːzeɪ] (Fr.) adj. gleichgültig, gelangweilt.

blas·pheme [blæs'fiːm] **I** v/t. (engS. Gott) lästern; schmähen; **II** v/i.: ~ against j-m fluchen, j-n lästern; **blas-**

'phem·er [-mə] s. (Gottes)Lästerer m; **blas·phe·mous** ['blæsfəməs] adj. □ blas'phemisch; **blas·phe·my** ['blæsfəmɪ] s. **1.** Blasphe'mie f, (Gottes)Lästerung f; **2.** Fluchen n.

blast [blɑːst] **I** s. **1.** (heftiger) Windstoß m; **2.** ♪ Schmettern n, Schall m: ~ of a trumpet Trompetenstoß m; **3.** Si'gnal n, (Heul-, Pfeif)Ton m; Tuten n; **4.** fig. Pesthauch m, Fluch m; **5.** ♀ Brand m, Mehltau m; Verdorren n; **6.** ◎ a) Sprengladung f, b) Sprengung f; **7.** a) Explosi'on f, Detonati'on f, b) a. ~ wave Druckwelle f; **8.** ◎ Gebläse(luft f) n: (at) full ~ a. fig. auf Hochtouren, a. mit voller Lautstärke; **9.** F a) heftige At'tacke n, b) 'Anschiss' m; **10.** Am. sl. Party f; **II** v/t. **11.** sprengen; **12.** a. ~ vernichten (a. F sport), fig. a. zu'nichte machen; **13.** ✗ unter Beschuss nehmen, fig. a. heftig attackieren, F ,anscheißen'; Science Fiction: durch Strahler(schuss) töten; **14.** verfluchen; ~ed verflucht; ~ it! verdammt!; ~ him! der Teufel soll ihn holen!; **15.** ~ off in den Weltraum schießen; **III** v/i. **16.** sprengen; **17.** ,knallen': ~ away at ballern auf (acc.), fig. heftig attackieren; **18.** ~ off abheben (Rakete); ~ fur·nace s. ◎ Hochofen m; '~·hole s. ◎ Sprengloch n; '~·off s. (Ra'keten)Start m.

bla·tan·cy ['bleɪtənsɪ] s. lärmendes Wesen, Angebe'rei f; **'bla·tant** [-nt] adj. □ **1.** brüllend; **2.** marktschreierisch, lärmend; **3.** aufdringlich; **4.** offenkundig, ekla'tant: ~ lie.

blath·er ['blæðə] **I** v/i. ,(blöd) quatschen, ,Gewäsch' n; Quatsch m; **'~·skite** [-skaɪt] s. F **1.** ,Quatschkopf' m; **2.** → blather II.

blaze [bleɪz] **I** s. **1.** lodernde Flamme, Feuer n, Glut f: be in a ~ in Flammen stehen; **2.** pl. Hölle f: go to ~s! sl. scher dich zum Teufel!; like ~s F wie verrückt od. toll; what the ~s is the matter? F was zum Teufel ist denn los?; **3.** Leuchten n, Glanz m (a. fig.): ~ of noon Mittagshitze f; ~ of fame Ruhmesglanz m; ~ of colo(u)r Farbenpracht f; ~ of publicity volles Licht der Öffentlichkeit; **4.** fig. (plötzlicher) Ausbruch, Auflodern n (Gefühl): ~ of anger Wutanfall m; **5.** Blesse f (bei Rind od. Pferd); Anschalmung f, Markierung f an Waldbäumen; **II** v/i. **7.** (auf)flammen, (auf)lodern, (ent)brennen (alle a. fig.): ~ into prominence fig. e-n kometenhaften Aufstieg erleben; ~ with anger vor Zorn glühen; in a blazing temper in heller Wut; **8.** leuchten, strahlen (a. fig.); **III** v/t. **9.** Bäume anschalmen; → trail 15;

Zssgn mit adv.:

blaze| a·broad v/t. verkünden, 'auspo,saunen; **~ a·way** v/i. drauf'losschießen; fig. F losgelen (at mit et.), herziehen (about über acc.); ~ out, ~ up v/i. **1.** auflodern, -flammen, **2.** fig. in Wut geraten, (wütend) auffahren.

blaz·er ['bleɪzə] s. Blazer m, Klub-, Sportjacke f.

blaz·ing ['bleɪzɪŋ] adj. **1.** lodernd (a. fig.); **2.** fig. a) schreiend, auffallend: ~ colo(u)rs, b) offenkundig, ekla'tant: ~ lie, c) hunt. warm (Fährte); → scent 3; **3.** F verteufelt: ~ star s. Gegenstand m allgemeiner Bewunderung.

bla·zon ['bleɪzn] **I** s. **1.** a) Wappenschild m, n b) Wappenkunde f; **2.** lautes Lob; **II** v/t. **3.** Wappen ausmalen; **4.** fig. schmücken, zieren; **5.** fig. her'ausstreichen, rühmen; **6.** mst ~ abroad, ~ out 'auspo,saunen; **'bla·zon·ry** [-rɪ] s. **1.** a)

Wappenzeichen n, b) He'raldik f; **2.** fig. Farbenschmuck m.

bleach [bliːtʃ] **I** v/t. bleichen (a. fig.); **II** s. Bleichmittel n; **'bleach·er** [-tʃə] s. **1.** Bleicher(in); **2.** mst pl. Am. sport 'un,über,dachte Tri'büne.

bleak [bliːk] adj. □ **1.** kahl, öde; **2.** ungeschützt, windig (gelegen); **3.** rau (Wind, Wetter); **4.** fig. trost-, freudlos, trübe, düster: ~ prospects trübe Aussichten.

blear [blɪə] **I** adj. verschwommen, trübe (a. Augen); **II** v/t. trüben; **~-eyed** ['blɪəraɪd] adj. **1.** a) mit trüben Augen, b) verschlafen; **2.** kurzsichtig, fig. a. einfältig.

bleat [bliːt] v/i. **1.** blöken (Schaf, Kalb), meckern (Ziege); **2.** in weinerlichem Ton reden; **II** s. **3.** Blöken n, Gemecker n (a. fig.).

bled [bled] pret. u. p.p. von bleed.

bleed [bliːd] [irr.] **I** v/i. **1.** (ver)bluten (a. Pflanze): ~ to death verbluten; **2.** sein Blut vergießen, sterben (for für); **3.** fig. (for) bluten (um) (Herz), (tiefes) Mitleid empfinden (mit); **4.** F ,bluten' (zahlen): ~ for s.th. für et. schwer bluten müssen; **5.** auslaufen, ,bluten' (Farbe); zerlaufen (Teer etc.); leck sein, lecken; **6.** typ. angeschnitten od. bis eng an den Druck beschnitten sein (Buch, Bild); **II** v/t. **7.** ✂ zur Ader lassen; **8.** Flüssigkeit, Dampf etc. ausströmen lassen, abzapfen: ~ a valve Ablassventil n; **9.** ⊕, bsd. mot. Bremsleitung entlüften; **10.** F ,bluten lassen', schröpfen: ~ white j-n bis zum Weißbluten auspressen; **'bleed·er** [-də] s. ✂ **1.** Bluter m; **2.** F a) Erpresser m, b) (blöder etc.) Kerl, c) ,Scheißding' n; **3.** ◎ 'Ablassven,til n; **4.** ⚡ 'Vorbelastungs,widerstand m.

bleed·ing ['bliːdɪŋ] s. **1.** Blutung f, Aderlass m (a. fig.): ~ of the nose Nasenbluten n; **2.** ◎ ,Bluten' n, Auslaufen n (Farbe, Teer); **3.** ◎ Entlüften n; **II** adj. **4.** sl. verdammt; ~ heart s. ♀ F Flammendes Herz.

bleep [bliːp] s. **1.** Piepton m; **2.** → bleeper; **II** v/i. **3.** piepen; **'bleep·er** [-pə] s. F ,Piepser' m (Funkrufempfänger).

blem·ish ['blemɪʃ] **I** v/t. verunstalten, schaden (dat.); fig. beflecken; **II** s. **1.** Fehler m, Mangel m; Makel m, Schönheitsfehler m.

blench¹ [blentʃ] **I** v/i. **1.** verzagen; **2.** zu'rückschrecken (at vor dat.); **II** v/t. (ver)meiden.

blench² [blentʃ] → blanch 6.

blend [blend] **I** v/t. **1.** (ver)mengen, (ver)mischen, verschmelzen; **2.** mischen, mixen; e-e (Tee-, Tabak-, Whisky)Mischung zs.-stellen; Wein etc. verschneiden; **II** v/i. **3.** (with) sich mischen od. har'monisch verbinden (mit); **4.** verschmelzen, inein'ander 'übergehen (Farben); **III** s. **5.** Mischung f, (harmonische) Zs.-stellung (Getränke, Tabak, Farben); (Wein)Verschnitt m; ~ word s. ling. Misch-, Kurzwort n.

blende [blend] s. min. Blende f, engS. Zinkblende f.

blend·er ['blendə] s. Mixer m, 'Mixma,schine f.

Blen·heim or·ange ['blenɪm] s. Brit. eine Apfelsorte.

blent [blent] obs. pret. u. p.p. von blend.

bless [bles] v/t. **1.** segnen; **2.** segnen, preisen; glücklich machen: ~ed with gesegnet mit (Talent, Reichtum etc.); I ~ the day I met you ich segne od. preise den Tag, an dem ich dich kennen lernte; **~ one's stars** sich glücklich schätzen; **3. ~ o.s.** sich bekreuzigen; *Besondere Redewendungen:* (**God**) **~ you!** a) alles Gute!, b) *beim Niesen:* Gesundheit!; **well, I'm ~ed!** F na, so was!; **I'm ~ed if I know** F ich weiß es wirklich nicht; **Mr. Brown, ~ him** Herr Brown, der Gute; **~ my soul!** F du meine Güte!; **not at all, ~ you!** *iro.* o nein, mein Verehrtester! *od.* meine Beste!; **~ that boy, what is he doing there?** F was zum Kuckuck stellt der Junge dort an?; **not to have a penny to ~ o.s. with** keinen roten Heller besitzen.

bless·ed ['blesɪd] **I** *adj.* **1.** gesegnet, selig, glücklich: **of ~ memory** seligen Angedenkens; **~ event** freudiges Ereignis (*Geburt e-s Kindes*); **2.** gepriesen, selig, heilig: **the 2 Virgin** die Heilige Jungfrau (Maria); **3. the whole ~ day** F den lieben langen Tag; **not a ~ soul** keine Menschenseele; **II** *s.* **4. the ~** (**ones**) die Seligen; '**bless·ed·ness** [-nɪs] *s.* Glück'seligkeit f, Glück n; Seligkeit f: **live in single ~** Junggeselle sein; '**blessing** [-sɪŋ] *s.* Segen m, Segnung f, Wohltat f, Gnade f: **ask a ~** a) Segen erbitten, b) das Tischgebet sprechen; **what a ~ that …** welch ein Segen, dass …; **it turned out to be a ~ in disguise** es stellte sich im nachhinein als Segen heraus; **count one's ~s** dankbar sein für das, was e-m beschert ist; **give one's ~ to** s-n Segen geben zu, *fig. a. et.* absegnen.

blest [blest] **I** *poet. pret. u. p.p. von* **bless**; **II** *pred. adj. poet.* → **blessed**; **III** *s.:* **the Isles of the 2** die Inseln der Seligen.

bleth·er ['bleðə] → **blather**.

blew [blu:] *pret. von* **blow¹** II u. III u. **blow³**.

blight [blaɪt] **I** *s.* **1.** 🌿 Mehltau m, Fäule f, Brand m (*Pflanzenkrankheit*); **2.** *fig.* Gift-, Pesthauch m; Vernichtung f; Fluch m; Enttäuschung f, Schatten m; **3.** Verwahrlosung f *e-r Wohngegend*; **II** *v/t.* **4.** *fig.* im Keim ersticken, zu'nichte machen, vereiteln; '**blight·er** [-tə] *s. Brit.* F a) Kerl m, ‚Knülch' m, b) ‚Mistkerl' m, c) ‚Mistding' n.

Blight·y ['blaɪtɪ] *s.* ✕ *Brit. sl.* **1.** die Heimat, England n; **2.** a) a. **a ~ one** ‚Heimatschuss' m, b) Heimaturlaub m.

bli·mey ['blaɪmɪ] *int.* F *Brit.* a) ich werd' verrückt! (*überrascht*), b) verdammt!

blimp¹ [blɪmp] *s.* F **1.** unstarres Kleinluftschiff; **2.** *phot.* schalldichte Kamerahülle.

Blimp² [blɪmp] *s.:* (**Colonel**) **~** *Brit.* selbstgefälliger Erzkonservativer.

blind [blaɪnd] **I** *adj.* ☐ → *a.* 9 **1.** blind: **~ in one eye** auf 'einem Auge blind; **struck ~** mit Blindheit geschlagen; **as ~ as a bat** (*od.* **beetle**) stockblind; **2.** *fig.* blind, verständnislos (**to** gegen['über]): **~ to s.o.'s faults** j-s Fehlern gegenüber blind; **~ chance** blinder Zufall; **~ with rage** blind vor Wut; **~ side** *fig.* schwache Seite; **turn a ~ eye** *fig.* ein Auge zudrücken, *et.* absichtlich übersehen; **3.** unbesonnen; **~ bargain** *etc.* zweck-, ziellos, leer: **~ excuse** Ausrede f; **5.** verborgen, geheim: **~ staircase** Geheimtreppe; **6.** schwer erkennbar: **~ corner** unübersichtliche Ecke *od.* Kurve; **~ copy** *typ.* unleserliches Manuskript; **7.** △ blind: **~ window**; **8.** 🌿 blütenlos, taub; **II** *adv.* **9. ~ drunk** sinnlos betrunken, ‚blau'; *fig.* **go it ~** blindlings handeln; **III** *v/t.* **10.** blenden,

blind machen; *j-m* die Augen verbinden: **~ing rain** alles verhüllender Regen; **11.** verblenden, täuschen; blind machen (**to** gegen); **12.** *fig.* verdunkeln, verbergen, vertuschen, verwischen; **IV** *v/i.* **13.** *Brit. sl.* blind drauf-'lossausen; **V** *s.* **14. the ~** die Blinden *pl.*; **15.** a) Rollladen m, b) Rou'leau n, Rollo n, c) Mar'kise f; → **Venetian** I; **16.** *pl.* Scheuklappen *pl.*; **17.** *fig.* a) Vorwand m, b) (Vor)Täuschung f, c) Tarnung f, d) F Strohmann m; **18.** *hunt.* Deckung f; **19.** *Brit. sl.* Saufe'rei f; **~ al·ley** *s.* Sackgasse f (*a. fig.*); **~-'al·ley** *adj.:* **~ occupation** Stellung f ohne Aufstiegsmöglichkeit; **~ coal** *s.* Anthra'zit m; **~ date** *s.* F a) Verabredung f mit e-r *od.* e-m Unbekannten, b) unbekannter Partner bei e-m solchen Rendezvous.

blind·er ['blaɪndə] *s. Am.* Scheuklappe f (*a. fig.*).

blind│ flight *s.* ✈ Blindflug m; '**~·fold I** *adj. u. adv.* **1.** mit verbundenen Augen: **~ chess** Blindschach n; **2.** blind (-lings) (*a. fig.*): **~ rage** blinde Wut; **II** *v/t.* **3.** *j-m* die Augen verbinden; **4.** *fig.* blind machen; **~ gut** *s. anat.* Blinddarm m; '**~-man's-'buff** [ˌblaɪndmænz-] *s.* Blindekuh(spiel n) f.

blind·ness ['blaɪndnɪs] *s.* **1.** Blindheit f (*a. fig.*); **2.** *fig.* Verblendung f.

blind│ shell *s.* ✕ Blindgänger m; **~ spot** *s.* **1.** ⚕ blinder Fleck *auf der Netzhaut*; **2.** *fig.* schwacher *od.* wunder Punkt; **3.** *mot.* toter Winkel *im Rückspiegel*; **4.** *Radio:* Empfangsloch n; **~ stitch** *s.* blinder (*unsichtbarer*) Stich; '**~-worm** *s. zo.* Blindschleiche f.

blink [blɪŋk] **I** *v/i.* **1.** blinken, blinzeln, zwinkern: **~ at** a) *j-m* zublinzeln, b) → 2 *u.* 5; **2.** erstaunt *od.* verständnislos dreinblicken: **~ at** *fig.* sich maßlos wundern über (*acc.*); **3.** flimmern, schimmern; **II** *v/t.* **4. ~ one's eyes** mit den Augen zwinkern; **5.** *et.* ignorieren, die Augen verschließen vor (*dat.*): **there is no ~ing the fact** (**that**) es ist nicht zu leugnen (, dass); **6.** *Meldung* blinken; **III** *s.* **7.** Blinzeln n; **8.** (Licht)Schimmer m; **9.** flüchtiger Blick; **10.** Augenblick m; **11. on the ~** *sl.* a) de'fekt, nicht in Ordnung, b) ‚am Eingehen' (*Gerät etc.*); '**blink·er** [-kə] **I** *s.* **1.** *pl.* Scheuklappen (*a. fig.*); **2.** *pl.* F Schutzbrille f; **3.** F ‚Gucker' *pl.* (*Augen*); **4.** a) Blinklicht n, b) *mot.* Blinker m; **5.** a) Blinkgerät n, b) Blinkspruch m; **II** *v/t.* **6.** *e-m Pferd* Scheuklappen anlegen: **~ed** mit Scheuklappen (*a. fig.*); **7.** → **blink** 6.

'**blink·ing** [-kɪŋ] *adj. u. adv. Brit. sl.* verdammt.

blip [blɪp] *s.* **1.** Klicken n; **2.** *Radar:* 'Echoim,puls m, -zeichen n.

bliss [blɪs] *s.* Freude f, Entzücken n, (Glück)'Seligkeit f, Wonne f; '**bliss·ful** [-fʊl] *adj.* ☐ (glück)'selig, völlig glücklich; '**bliss·ful·ness** [-fʊlnɪs] *s.* Wonne f.

blis·ter ['blɪstə] **I** *s.* **1.** ⚕ (*Haut*)Blase f, Pustel f; **2.** Blase f (*auf bemaltem Holz, in Glas etc.*); **3.** ⚕ Zugpflaster n; **4.** ✕, ✈ a) Bordwaffen- *od.* Beobachterstand m, b) Radarkuppel f; **II** *v/t.* **5.** Blasen her'vorrufen auf (*dat.*); **6.** *fig.* scharf kritisieren, ‚fertig machen'; **7.** brennenden Schmerz her'vorrufen auf (*dat.*): **~ing heat** glühende Hitze; **III** *v/i.* **8.** Blasen ziehen *od.* ⊙ werfen.

blithe [blaɪð] *adj.* ☐ vergnügt.

blith·er·ing ['blɪðərɪŋ] *adj. Brit.* F verdammt: **~ idiot** Vollidiot m.

blitz [blɪts] ✕ **I** *s.* **1.** Blitzkrieg m; **2.** schwerer Luftangriff; schwere Luftangriffe *pl.*; **II** *v/t.* **3.** schwer bombardieren: **~ed area** zerbombtes Gebiet; '**~·krieg** [-kri:g] → **blitz** 1.

bliz·zard ['blɪzəd] *s.* Schneesturm m.

bloat¹ [bləʊt] **I** *v/t. a.* **~ up** aufblasen, -blähen (*a. fig.*); **II** *v/i. a.* **~ out** auf-, anschwellen; '**bloat·ed** [-tɪd] *adj.* aufgebläht (*a. fig.*), (auf)gedunsen.

bloat·er ['bləʊtə] *s.* Räucherhering m.

blob [blɒb] *s.* **1.** Tropfen m, Klümpchen n, Klecks m; **2.** *Kricket:* null Punkte; **3.** F ‚Kloß' (*Person*).

bloc [blɒk] *s. pol.* Block m: **sterling ~** ✝ Sterlingblock.

block [blɒk] **I** *s.* **1.** Block m, Klotz m (*mst Holz, Stein*): **on the ~** zur Versteigerung anstehend, unterm Hammer; **2.** Hackklotz m; **3. the ~** der Richtblock: **go to the ~** das Schafott besteigen; **4.** ⊙ Block m, Rolle f; **pulley** 1, **tackle** 3; **5.** *typ.* Kli'schee n, Druckstock m; Prägestempel m; **6.** a) **~ of flats** *Brit.* Wohnhaus n, b) → **office block**, c) *Am.* Zeile f (*Reihenhäuser*), d) *bsd. Am.* Häuserblock m: **three ~s from here** drei Straßen weiter; **7.** Block m, Masse f, Gruppe f; *attr.* Gesamt…: **~ of shares** Aktienpaket n; (**data**) **~** *Computer:* (Daten)Block m; **the new kid on the ~** F der Neuling, der Newcomer; **8.** Abreißblock m: **scribbling ~** Notiz-, Schmierblock; **9.** *fig.* Klotz m, Tölpel m; **10.** a) Verstopfung f, Hindernis n, Stockung f, b) Sperre f, Absperrung f: **traffic ~** Verkehrsstockung f; **mental ~** *fig.* ‚geistige Ladehemmung'; **11.** 🚂 Blockstrecke f; **12.** *sport:* a) Sperren n, b) *Volleyball etc.:* Block m; **II** *v/t.* **13.** (auf e-m Block) formen; **~ a hat**; **14.** hemmen, hindern, blockieren, *fig. a.* durch'kreuzen: **~ a bill** *Brit. pol.* die Beratung e-s Gesetzentwurfs verhindern; **15.** *oft* **~ up** (ab-, ver)sperren, verstopfen, blockieren: **road** *od.* Straße ge-, versperrt; **16.** ✝ Konto, 🚂 Röhre, Leitung sperren; ✝ Kredit etc. einfrieren: **~ed account** Sperrkonto n; **17.** *sport* a) Gegner sperren, *a. Schlag etc.* abblocken, b) Ball stoppen, halten; **~ in** *v/t.* skizzieren, entwerfen; **~ out** *v/t.* **1.** → **block in**; **2.** Licht nehmen (*Bäume etc.*); **3.** *phot.* Negativteil abdecken; **~ up** *v/t.* → **block** 15.

block·ade [blɒ'keɪd] **I** *s.* Bloc'kade f, (Hafen)Sperre f: **impose a ~** e-e Blockade verhängen; **raise a ~** e-e Blockade aufheben; **run the ~** die Blockade brechen; **II** *v/t.* blockieren, absperren; **block'ad·er** [-də] *s.* Bloc'kadeschiff n; **block'ade-,run·ner** *s.* Bloc'kadebrecher m.

block│ brake *s.* Backenbremse f; '**~-buster** *s.* F **1.** ✕ Minenbombe f; **2.** *fig.* ‚Knüller' m, ‚Hammer' m, tolles Ding; **~ di·a·gram** *s.* ⊙, 🚂 'Blockdia-,gramm n, -schaltbild n; '**~-head** *s.* Dummkopf m; '**~-house** *s.* Blockhaus n; **~ let·ters** *s. pl. typ.* Blockschrift f; **~ print·ing** *s.* Handdruck m; **~ sys·tem** *s.* 🚂 'Blocksy,stem n; **2.** 🚂 Blockschaltung f; **~ vote** *s.* Sammelstimme f (*e-e ganze Organisation vertretend*).

bloke [bləʊk] *s.* F Kerl m.

blond [blɒnd] *adj.* **1.** blond (*Haar*), hell (*Gesichtsfarbe*); **2.** blond(haarig); **blonde** [blɒnd] *s.* **1.** Blon'dine f; **2.** ✝ Blonde f (*seidene Spitze*).

blood [blʌd] *s.* **1.** Blut n: **spill ~** Blut vergießen; **give one's ~** (**for**) sein Blut (*od.* Leben) lassen (für); **taste ~** *fig.* Blut lecken; **fresh ~** *fig.* frisches Blut;

~-and-thunder (*story*) *Brit.* F ‚Reißer‘ *m* (*Roman*); Schauergeschichte *f*; **2.** *fig.* Blut *n*, Tempera'ment *n*, Wesen *n*: **it made his ~ boil, his ~ was up** er kochte vor Wut; **his ~ froze** (*od.* **ran cold**) das Blut erstarrte ihm in den Adern; **breed** (*od.* **make**) **bad ~** böses Blut machen; → **cold blood, curdle** II; **3.** (edles) Blut, Geblüt; *n* Abstammung *f*; Rasse *f* (*Mensch*), 'Vollblut *n* (*bes. Pferd*): **prince of the ~ royal** Prinz *m* von königlichem Geblüt; **noble ~** → **blue blood**; **related by ~** blutsverwandt; **it runs in the ~** es liegt im Blut *od.* in der Familie; **~ will out** Blut bricht sich Bahn; **~ al·co·hol** (**con·cen·tra·tion**) *s.* Blutalkohol(gehalt) *m*; **~ bank** *s.* ♣ Blutbank *f*; **~ broth·er** *s.* **1.** leiblicher Bruder; **2.** Blutsbruder *m*; **~ cir·cu·la·tion** *s.* ♣ Blutkreislauf *m*; **~ clot** *s.* ♣ Blutgerinnsel *n*; '**~,cur·dler** *s.* F ‚Reißer‘ *m* (*Roman etc.*); '**~,cur·dling** *adj.* grauenhaft; **~ do·nor** *s.* ♣ Blutspender *m*.

blood·ed ['blʌdɪd] *adj.* **1.** Vollblut...; **2.** *in Zssgn* ...blütig.

blood| **feud** *s.* Blut-, Todfehde *f*; **~ group** *s.* ♣ Blutgruppe *f*; **~ group·ing** *s.* ♣ Blutgruppenbestimmung *f*; '**~,guilt** *s.* Blutschuld *f*; **~ heat** *s.* ♣ Blutwärme *f*, 'Körpertempera,tur *f*; **~ horse** *s.* 'Vollblut(pferd) *n*; '**~-hound** *s.* **1.** Schweiß-, Bluthund *m*; **2.** F ‚Schnüffler‘ *m* (*Detektiv*).

blood·less ['blʌdlɪs] *adj.* □ **1.** blutlos, -leer (*a. fig.*); **2.** bleich; **3.** *fig.* kalt; **4.** unblutig (*Kampf etc.*).

'**blood**|**,let·ting** *s.* Aderlass *m* (*a. fig.*); **2.** → **bloodshed**; **~ mon·ey** *s.* Blutgeld *n*; **~ poi·son·ing** *s.* ♣ Blutvergiftung *f*; **~ pres·sure** *s.* ♣ Blutdruck *m*; **~ re·la·tion** *s.* Blutsverwandte(r *m*) *f*; **~ re·venge** *s.* Blutrache *f*; **~ sam·ple** *s.* ♣ Blutprobe *f*; '**~·shed** *s.* Blutvergießen *n*; '**~·shot** *adj.* 'blutunter,laufen; **~ spec·i·men** *s.* ♣ Blutprobe *f*; **~ sports** *s.* Hetz-, *bsd.* Fuchsjagd *f*; '**~·stained** *adj.* blutbefleckt (*a. fig.*); '**~·stock** *s.* 'Vollblutpferde *pl.*; '**~·stream** *s.* **1.** ♣ Blut(kreislauf *m*) *n*; **2.** *fig.* Lebensstrom *m*; '**~,suck·er** *s.* Blutsauger *m* (*a. fig.*); **~ sug·ar** *s.* ♣ Blutzucker *m*; **~ test** *s.* ♣ Blutprobe *f*, 'Blutunter,suchung *f*; '**~,thirst·i·ness** *s.* Blutdurst *m*; '**~,thirst·y** *adj.* blutdürstig; **~ trans·fu·sion** *s.* ♣ 'Blutüber,tragung *f*; **~ typ·ing** *s.* → **blood grouping**; **~ ven·geance** *s.* Blutrache *f*; **~ ves·sel** *s. anat.* Blutgefäß *n*.

blood·y ['blʌdɪ] **I** *adj.* □ **1.** blutig, blutbefleckt: **~ flux** ♣ rote Ruhr; **2.** blutdürstig, mörderisch, grausam: **a ~ battle** e-e blutige Schlacht; **3.** *Brit. sl.* verdammt, saumäßig, Scheiß... (*oft nur verstärkend*): **not a ~ soul** kein Schwanz; **a ~ fool** ein Vollidiot *m*; **~ thing** ‚Scheißding‘ *n*; **II** *adv.* **~** *Brit. sl.* mordsmäßig, verdammt: **~ awful** ‚beschissen‘; **you ~ well know** du weißt ganz genau; ♀ **Ma·ri·a** [məˈraɪə; məˈrɪə] *s. Am.* Getränk aus Tequila u. Tomatensaft; ♀ **Mar·y** ['meərɪ] *s. Getränk aus Wodka u. Tomatensaft*; *Br.* F **1.** gemein, ekelhaft; **2.** störrisch, stur.

bloom¹ [bluːm] **I** *s.* **1.** Blüte *f*, Blume *f*: **in full ~** in voller Blüte; **2.** *fig.* Blüte (-zeit) *f*, Jugendfrische *f*; **3.** Flaum *m* (*auf Pfirsichen etc.*); **4.** *fig.* Schmelz *m*, Glanz *m*; **II** *v/i.* **5.** (er)blühen (*a. fig.*).

bloom² [bluːm] *metall.* **I** *s.* **1.** Walzblock *m*; **2.** Puddelluppe *f*: **~ steel** Puddel-

stahl *m*; **II** *v/t.* **3.** luppen; **~ing mill** Luppenwalzwerk *n*.

bloom·er ['bluːmə] *s. sl.* grober Fehler, Schnitzer *m*, (Stil)Blüte *f*.

bloom·ers ['bluːməz] *s. pl.* a) *obs.* (Damen)Pumphose *f*, b) Schlüpfer *m* mit langem Bein, ‚Liebestöter‘ *m*.

bloom·ing ['bluːmɪŋ] *pres. p. u. adj.* **1.** blühend (*a. fig.*); **2.** *sl.* → **bloody** 3.

blos·som ['blɒsəm] **I** *s.* (*bsd.* Obst)Blüte *f*, Blütenfülle *f*: **in ~** in (voller) Blüte; **II** *v/i. a. fig.* blühen, Blüten treiben: **~** (**out**) (**into**) erblühen, gedeihen (zu).

blot [blɒt] **I** *s.* **1.** (Tinten)Klecks *m*, Fleck *m*; **2.** *fig.* Schandfleck *m*, Makel *m*; → **escutcheon** 1; **3.** Verunstaltung *f*, Schönheitsfehler *m*; **II** *v/t.* **4.** mit Tinte beschmieren, beklecksen; **5. ~ out** Schrift ausstreichen; **6. ~ out** *fig.* a) *Erinnerungen etc.* auslöschen, b) verdunkeln, verhüllen: **fog ~ted out the view** Nebel verhüllte die Aussicht; **7.** mit Löschpapier (ab)löschen.

blotch [blɒtʃ] **I** *s.* **1.** Fleck *m*, Klecks *m*; **2.** *fig.* → **blot** 2; **3.** ♣ Hautfleck *m*; **II** *v/t.* **4.** beklecksen; **III** *v/i.* **5.** klecksen; '**blotch·y** [-tʃɪ] *adj.* **1.** klecksig; **2.** ♣ fleckig.

blot·ter ['blɒtə] *s.* **1.** (Tinten)Löscher *m*; **2.** *Am.* Kladde *f*, Berichtsliste *f* (*bsd. der Polizei*).

blot·ting **pad** ['blɒtɪŋ] *s.* 'Schreib,unterlage *f od.* Block *m* aus 'Löschpa,pier; **~ pa·per** *s.* Löschpapier *n*.

blot·to ['blɒtəʊ] *adj. sl.* ‚sternhagelvoll‘, ‚stinkbesoffen‘.

blouse [blaʊz] *s.* **1.** Bluse *f*; **2.** ✂ a) Uni'formjacke *f*, b) Feldbluse *f*.

blow¹ [bləʊ] **I** *s.* **1.** Blasen *n*, Luftzug *m*, Brise *f*: **go for a ~** an die frische Luft gehen; **2.** Blasen *n*, Schall *m*: **a ~ on a whistle** ein Pfiff; **3.** *Am.* F a) Angebe'rei *f*, b) Angeber *m*; **II** *v/i.* [*irr.*] **4.** blasen, wehen, pusten: **it is ~ing hard** es weht ein starker Wind; **~ hot and cold** *fig.* ‚mal so, mal so‘ *od.* wetterwendisch sein; **5.** ertönen: **the horn is ~ing**; **6.** keuchen, schnaufen; **7.** spritzen, blasen (*Wal*); **8.** *Am.* F ‚angeben‘; **9.** a) explodieren, b) platzen (*Reifen*), c) ⚡ 'durchbrennen (*Sicherung*), d) ausbrechen (*Erdöl etc.*); **III** *v/t.* [*irr.*] **10.** wehen, treiben (*Wind*): **~n ashore** an Strand geworfen; **11.** anfachen: **~ the fire**; **12.** (an)blasen: **~ the soup**; **13.** blasen, ertönen lassen: **~ the horn** ins Horn stoßen; **14.** auf-, ausblasen: **~ bubbles** Seifenblasen machen; **~ glass** Glas blasen; **~ one's nose** sich die Nase putzen, sich schnauben; **~ an egg** ein Ei ausblasen; **15.** *sl.* Geld ‚verpulvern‘; **16.** zum Platzen bringen: **blew itself to pieces** zersprang in Stücke; → **top** 4; **17.** F (*p.p.* **blowed**) verfluchen: **~ it!** verflucht!; **I'll be ~ed** (**if**) ...**!** zum Teufel (wenn) ...!; **18.** *sl.* a) ‚verpfeifen‘, verraten, b) aufdecken, c) ‚verduften‘ aus (*dat.*); **19.** *sl.* ‚vermasseln‘; **20.** V *j-m ein* blasen‘;

Zssgn mit adv.:

blow| **a·way** *v/t.* **1.** wegblasen; **2.** F *j-n* ‚wegpusten‘ (*töten*); **~ down** *v/t.* herunter-, 'umwehen; **~ in** I *v/i. fig.* auftauchen, her'einschneien; **II** *v/t.* Scheiben eindrücken; **~ off** I *v/i.* **1.** fortwehen; **2.** abziehen (*Schiff*); **II** *v/t.* **1.** fortblasen; verjagen; **2.** *Dampf etc.* ablassen; → **steam** 1; **~ out** I *v/i.* **1.** verlöschen; **2.** platzen; **3.** ⚡ 'durchbrennen (*Sicherung*); **II** *v/t.* **4.** *Licht* ausblasen; *Feuer* (aus)löschen; **5.** her'ausblasen, -treiben: **~ one's brains** sich e-e Kugel

durch den Kopf jagen; **6.** sprengen, zertrümmern; **~ o·ver** I *v/i. fig.* vor'beigehen, sich legen; **II** *v/t.* 'umwehen; **~ up** I *v/t.* **1.** a) (in die Luft) sprengen, b) vernichten, *fig. a.* ruinieren; **2.** aufblasen, -pumpen; *fig. et.* aufbauschen; **3.** *Foto* (stark) vergrößern; **4.** F *j-n* ‚anschnauzen‘; **II** *v/i.* **5.** a) in die Luft fliegen, b) explodieren (*a.* F *fig. Person*): **~ at s.o.** *j-m* ‚ins Gesicht springen‘; **6.** aus-, losbrechen; **7.** *fig.* eintreten, auftauchen.

blow² [bləʊ] *s.* **1.** Schlag *m*, Streich *m*, Stoß *m*: **at a** (*od.* **one**) **~** mit ‚einem Schlag *od.* Streich; **without striking a ~** *fig.* ohne jede Gewalt(anwendung), mühelos; **come to ~s** handgemein werden; **strike a ~** at e-n Schlag führen gegen (*a. fig.*); **strike a ~** (**for**) sich einsetzen (für), helfen (*dat.*); **2.** *fig.* (Schicksals)Schlag *m*, Unglück *n*: **it was a ~ to his pride** es traf ihn schwer in s-m Stolz.

blow³ [bləʊ] *v/i.* [*irr.*] (auf)blühen, sich entfalten (*a. fig.*).

'**blow**|**·ball** *s.* ♣ Pusteblume *f*; '**~-dry** *v/t.* (*j-m die Haare*) föhnen; **~ dry·er** *s.* Haartrockner *m*.

blowed [bləʊd] *p.p. von* **blow¹** 17.

blow·er ['bləʊə] *s.* **1.** Bläser *m*: **glass-~**; **~ of a horn**; **2.** ☉ a) Gebläse *n*, b) *mot.* Vorverdichter *m*; **3.** F Telefon *n*.

'**blow**|**·fly** *s. zo.* Schmeißfliege *f*; '**~-gun** *s.* **1.** Blasrohr *n*; **2.** ☉ 'Spritzpis,tole *f*; '**~-hard** *s. Am.* F Angeber *m*; '**~-hole** *s.* **1.** Luft-, Zugloch *n*; **2.** Nasenloch *n* (*Wal*); **~ job** *s.* F: **give s.o. a ~** *j-m* e-n blasen (*Sex*); '**~-lamp** *s.* ☉ Lötlampe *f*.

blown¹ [bləʊn] **I** *p.p. von* **blow¹** II u. III; **II** *adj.* **1.** *oft* **~ up** aufgeblasen, -gebläht (*a. fig.*); **2.** außer Atem.

blown² [bləʊn] **I** *p.p. von* **blow³**; **II** *adj. a. fig.* blühend, aufgeblüht.

'**blow**|**-out** *s.* **1.** a) Zerplatzen *n*, b) Reifenpanne *f*; **2.** F Koller *m*, (Wut)Ausbruch *m*; **3.** *sl.* a) große Party, b) ('Fress),Orgie *f*; '**~-pipe** *s.* **1.** ☉ Lötrohr *n*, Schweißbrenner *m*; **2.** Puste-, Blasrohr *n*; '**~-torch** *s.* ☉ *Am.* Lötlampe *f*; '**~-up** *s.* **1.** Explosi'on *f*; **2.** *fig. a)* ‚Krach‘, b) Koller *m*; **3.** *phot.* Vergrößerung *f*, Großfoto *n*.

blow·y ['bləʊɪ] *adj.* windig, luftig.

blowz·y ['blaʊzɪ] *adj.* **1.** schlampig (*bsd. Frau*); **2.** rotgesichtig (*Frau*).

blub·ber ['blʌbə] **I** *s.* Tran *m*, Speck *m*; **II** *v/i.* heulen, ‚flennen‘.

bludg·eon ['blʌdʒən] **I** *s.* **1.** Knüppel *m*, Keule *f*; **II** *v/t.* **2.** 'niederknüppeln; **3.** *j-n* zwingen (**into** zu).

blue [bluː] **I** *adj.* **1.** blau: **till you are ~ in the face** F bis Sie schwarz werden; → **moon** 1; **2.** F trübe, schwermütig, traurig: **feel ~** niedergeschlagen sein; **look ~** trübe aussehen (*Person, Umstände*); **3.** *pol. Brit.* ‚schwarz‘, konserva'tiv; **4.** *Brit.* F nicht sa'lonfähig, ordi'när: **~ jokes**; **~ movie** Pornofilm *m*; **5.** F schrecklich; → **funk** 1, **murder** 1; **II** *s.* **6.** Blau *n*, blaue Farbe; **7.** Waschblau *n*; **8.** blaue Kleidung, *mst poet.* **the ~** a) der Himmel, b) das Meer: **out of the ~** aus heiterem Himmel, völlig unerwartet; **10.** *pol. Brit.* Konserva'tive(r *m*) *f*; **11. the dark** (**light**) **~s** *pl. Studenten von Oxford* (*Cambridge*), *die bei Wettkämpfen ihre Universität vertreten*: **get one's ~** in die Universitätsmannschaft aufgenommen werden; **12.** *pl.* F Trübsinn *m*: **have the ~s** ‚den Moralischen haben‘; **13.** *pl.* ♪ Blues *m*; **III** *v/t.* **14.** *Wäsche* bläuen; **15.** *sl.* Geld ‚verjuxen‘;

~ ba·by s. ✴ Blue Baby n (*mit angeborenem Herzfehler*); '~beard s. (Ritter) Blaubart m (*Frauenmörder*); '~·bell s. ⚘ **1.** 'Sternhya,zinthe f (*England*); **2.** e-e Glockenblume f (*Schottland*); ~ be·rets s. pl. Blauhelme pl.; '~·ber·ry [-bərı] s. ⚘ Blau-, Heidelbeere f; ~ blood s. **1.** blaues Blut, alter Adel; **2.** Aristo'krat(in), Adlige(r m) f; ~ book s. Blaubuch n: a) Brit. amtliche politische Veröffentlichung, b) F Am. Verzeichnis prominenter Persönlichkeiten; '~·bot·tle s. **1.** zo. Schmeißfliege f; **2.** ⚘ Kornblume f; **3.** F Brit. ‚Bulle‘ m (*Polizist*); ~ chips s. pl. ✝ Spitzenwerte pl.; '~-,col·lar worker s. Fa'brikarbeiter m; '~-eyed adj. blauäugig (a. fig.): ~ boy F ‚Liebling‘ m des Chefs etc.; '~,jack·et s. fig. Blaujacke f, Matrose m; ~ laws s. pl. Am. strenge puri'tanische Gesetze pl. (bsd. gegen die Entheiligung des Sonntags).

blue·ness ['bluːnıs] s. Bläue f.
blue| pen·cil s. **1.** Blaustift m; **2.** fig. Zen'sur f; **~-'pen·cil** v/t. **1.** Manuskript etc. (mit Blaustift) korrigieren od. (zs.-, aus)streichen; **2.** fig. zensieren, unter'sagen; '~·print s. **1.** Blaupause f; **2.** fig. Plan m, Entwurf m: *do you need a ~? iro.* ‚brauchst du e-e Zeichnung‘?; '~·print I v/t. entwerfen, planen; II adj.: ~ stage Planungsstadium n; ~ rib·bon s. blaues Band: a) des Hosenbandordens, b) als Auszeichnung für e-e Höchstleistung, bsd. ♣ das Blaue Band des 'Ozeans; '~,stock·ing s. fig. Blaustrumpf m; '~·stone s. ♠ 'Kupfervitri,ol n; '~·throat s. orn. Blaukehlchen n; ~ tit (-mouse) s. orn. Blaumeise f.
bluff¹ [blʌf] I v/t. **1.** a) j-n bluffen, b) ~ it out sich (kühn) herausreden od. ‚durchmogeln‘; **2.** et. vortäuschen; II v/i. **3.** bluffen; III s. **4.** Bluff m: call s.o.'s ~ j-n zwingen, Farbe zu bekennen.
bluff² [blʌf] I adj. **1.** ♣ breit (Bug); **2.** schroff, steil (Felsen, Küste); **3.** rau, aber herzlich; gutmütig-derb; II s. **4.** Steilufer n, Klippe f.
bluff·er ['blʌfə] s. Bluffer m.
blu·ish ['bluːıʃ] adj. bläulich.
blun·der ['blʌndə] I s. **1.** (grober) Fehler, Schnitzer m; II v/i. **2.** e-n (groben) Fehler od. Schnitzer machen; e-n Bock schießen; **3.** pfuschen, unbesonnen handeln; **4.** stolpern (a. fig.): ~ into a dangerous situation; ~ about umhertappen; ~ on fig. weiterwursteln; ~ upon s.th. zufällig auf et. stoßen; III v/t. **5.** verpfuschen, verpatzen; **6.** ~ out her'ausplatzen mit.
blun·der·buss ['blʌndəbʌs] s. ✗ hist. Donnerbüchse f.
blun·der·er ['blʌndərə] s. Stümper m, Pfuscher m, Tölpel m; '**blun·der·ing** [-dərıŋ] adj. stümper-, tölpelhaft, ungeschickt.
blunt [blʌnt] I adj. □ **1.** stumpf: ~ instrument ⚖ stumpfer Gegenstand (Mordwaffe); **2.** fig. unempfindlich (to gegen); **3.** fig. ungeschliffen, derb, ungehobelt (Manieren etc.); **4.** schonungslos, offen; schlicht; II v/t. **5.** stumpf machen, abstumpfen (a. fig.); **6.** Gefühle etc. mildern, schwächen; III s. **7.** pl. kurze Nähnadeln pl.; '**blunt·ly** [-lı] adv. fig. freiher'aus, grob: to put it ~ um es ganz offen zu sagen; refuse ~ glatt ablehnen; '**blunt·ness** [-nıs] s. **1.** Stumpfheit f (a. fig.); **2.** fig. Grobheit f; schonungslose Offenheit.
blur [blɜː] I v/t. **1.** Schrift verwischen, verschmieren; Bild verschwommen ma-

chen; verschleiern; **2.** verdunkeln, verwischen, Sinne trüben; **3.** fig. besudeln, entstellen; II v/i. **4.** verschwimmen; III s. **5.** Fleck m, verwischte Stelle; **6.** fig. Makel m; **7.** undeutlicher od. nebelhafter Eindruck; **8.** (huschender) Schatten; **9.** Schleier m (vor den Augen).
blurb [blɜːb] s. F Buchhandel: a) ‚Waschzettel‘ m, Klappentext m, b) ‚Bauchbinde‘ f (Reklamestreifen).
blurred [blɜːd] adj. unscharf, verschwommen, verwischt; schattenhaft; fig. nebelhaft.
blurt [blɜːt] v/t. ~ out (‚voreilig od. unbesonnen‘) her'ausplatzen mit, ausschwatzen.
blush [blʌʃ] I v/i. erröten, rot werden, in Verwirrung geraten (at, for über acc.); sich schämen (to do zu tun); II s. Erröten n, (Scham)Röte f: at first ~ obs. auf den ersten Blick; put to (the) ~ j-n zum Erröten bringen; '**blush·er** [-ʃə] s. F Rouge n; '**blush·ing** [-ʃıŋ] adj. □ errötend; fig. züchtig.
blus·ter ['blʌstə] I v/i. **1.** brausen, tosen, stürmen; **2.** fig. poltern, toben, schimpfen; **3.** prahlen, bramarbasieren: ~ing fellow Bramarbas m, Großmaul n; II s. **4.** Brausen n, Getöse f, Toben n (a. fig.); **5.** Schimpfen n; **6.** Prahlen n, ‚große Töne‘ pl.
bo [bəʊ] int. hu!: he can't say ~ to a goose er ist ein Hasenfuß.
bo·a ['bəʊə] s. **1.** zo. Boa f, Riesenschlange f; **2.** Mode: Boa f.
boar [bɔː] s. zo. Eber m, Keiler m: wild ~ Wildschwein n.
board [bɔːd] I s. **1.** Brett n, Planke f; **2.** (Schach-, Bügel)Brett n: ~ game Brettspiel n; sweep the ~ alles gewinnen; **3.** Anschlagbrett n; **4.** ped. → blackboard; **5.** sport a) (Surf)Board n, b) pl. ,Bretter‘ pl., Skier pl.; **6.** pl. fig. Bretter pl., Bühne f: tread (od. walk) the ~s auf den Brettern stehen, Schauspieler sein; **7.** Tisch m, Tafel f (nur in festen Ausdrücken): → above-board, bed 3, groan 2; **8.** Kost f, Verpflegung f: ~ and lodging Kost und Logis, Wohnung u. Verpflegung; **9.** fig. oft ♀ Ausschuss m, Behörde f, Amt n: ♀ of Admiralty Admiralität f; ♀ of Examiners Prüfungskommission f; ♀ of Governors Verwaltungsrat m, (Schul- etc.)Behörde f; ♀ of Trade a) Brit. Handelsministerium n, b) Am. Handelskammer f; **10.** ~ of directors, (the) ♀ ✝ Verwaltungsrat m, Direkti'on f (Vorstand u. Aufsichtsrat in einem); ~ of management ✝ Vorstand m e-r AG; **11.** ♣ Bord m, Bordwand f (nur in festen Ausdrücken): on ~ a) an Bord e-s Schiffs, Flugzeugs, b) im Zug od. Bus; on ~ a ship an Bord e-s Schiffes; free on ~ (abbr. f.o.b.) ✝ frei an Bord (geliefert); go by the ~ über Bord gehen od. fallen, fig. a. zugrunde gehen, verloren gehen, verschwinden; take s.th. on ~ F fig. a) et. akzeptieren od. anerkennen, verstehen, b) et. annehmen (Arbeit, Aufgabe); **12.** Pappe f: in ~s kartoniert (Buch); II v/t. **13.** täfeln; mit Brettern bedecken od. absperren, dielen, verschalen; **14.** beköstigen, in Kost nehmen od. geben (with bei); **15.** a) an Bord e-s Schiffs od. Flugzeugs gehen, b) in e-n Zug etc. einsteigen, c) ✗, ♣ entern; III v/i. **16.** sich in Kost od. Pensi'on befinden, wohnen (with bei); ~ out v/i. außerhalb in Kost geben; II v/i. auswärts essen; ~ up v/t. mit Brettern vernageln.

board·er ['bɔːdə] s. **1.** a) Kostgänger (-in), b) Pensi'onsgast m; **2.** Inter'natsschüler(in).
board·ing ['bɔːdıŋ] s. **1.** Bretterverschalung f, Dielenbelag m, Täfelung f; **2.** Kost f, Verpflegung f; ~ card s. ✈ Bordkarte f; '~·house s. Pensi'on f; ~ school s. Inter'nat n, Pensio'nat n.
board| meet·ing s. Vorstandssitzung f; ~ room s. Sitzungssaal m; ~ wag·es s. pl. Kostgeld n des Personals; '~·walk s. Am. Plankenweg m, (hölzerne) 'Strandprome,nade.
boast [bəʊst] I s. **1.** Prahle'rei f, Großtue'rei f; **2.** Stolz m (Gegenstand des Stolzes): it was his proud ~ that ... es war sein ganzer Stolz, dass ...; he was the ~ of his age er war der Stolz s-r Zeit; II v/i. **3.** (of, about) prahlen, großtun (mit): he ~s of his riches; it is not much to ~ of damit ist es nicht weit her; **4.** (of) sich rühmen (gen.), stolz sein (auf acc.): our village ~s of a fine church; III v/t. **5.** sich (des Besitzes) e-r Sache rühmen, aufzuweisen haben: our street ~s the tallest house in the town; '**boast·er** [-tə] s. Prahler(in); '**boast·ful** [-fʊl] adj. □ prahlerisch, über'heblich.
boat [bəʊt] I s. **1.** Boot n, Kahn m; allg. Schiff n; Dampfer m: we are all in the same ~ fig. wir sitzen alle in 'einem Boot; miss the ~ fig. den Anschluss verpassen; burn one's ~s alle Brücken hinter sich abbrechen; **2.** bootförmiges Gefäß, (bsd. Soßen)Schüssel f; II v/i. **3.** (in e-m) Boot fahren: go ~ing e-e Bootsfahrt machen (mst rudern).
boat·er ['bəʊtə] s. Brit. steifer Strohhut, ‚Kreissäge‘ f.
boat·ing ['bəʊtıŋ] s. Bootfahren n; Rudersport m; Bootsfahrt f.
'**boat·man** [-mən] s. [irr.] Bootsführer m, -verleiher m; ~ race s. 'Ruderre,gatta f; ~·swain ['bəʊsn] s. ♣ Bootsmann m; ~ train s. Zug m mit Schiffsanschluss.
bob¹ [bɒb] I s. **1.** Haarschopf m, Büschel n; Bubikopf(haarschnitt) m; gestutzter Pferdeschwanz; Quaste f; **2.** Ruck m; Knicks m; **3.** sg. u. pl. obs. Brit. F Schilling m: five ~; a job e-n Schilling für jede Arbeit; **4.** abbr. für bobsled; II v/t. **5.** ruckweise (hin u. her, auf u. ab) bewegen; **6.** Haare, Pferdeschwanz etc. kurz schneiden, stutzen: ~bed hair Bubikopf m; III v/i. **7.** sich auf u. ab od. hin u. her bewegen, baumeln, tänzeln; **8.** schnappen (for nach); **9.** knicksen; **10.** Bob fahren; **11.** ~ up (plötzlich) auftauchen: ~ up like a cork fig. immer wieder hochkommen, sich nicht unterkriegen lassen.
Bob² [bɒb] npr., abbr. für Robert: ~'s your uncle ‚fertig ist die Laube‘.
bob·bin ['bɒbın] s. **1.** ⊕ Spule f, (Garn-) Rolle f; **2.** ⚡ Indukti'onsspule f; **3.** Klöppel(holz n) m; ~ lace s. Klöppelspitze f.
bob·by ['bɒbı] s. Brit. F ‚Bobby‘ m (Polizist); ~ pin s. Haarklemme f (aus Metall); ~ socks s. pl. Am. F Söckchen pl.; '~,sox·er [-,sɒksə] s. Am. F hist. ‚Backfisch‘ m.
'**bob·sled**, '~·sleigh s. Bob m (Rennschlitten); '~·tail s. **1.** Stutzschwanz m; **2.** Pferd n od. Hund m mit Stutzschwanz.
bock (beer) [bɒk] s. Bockbier n.
bode¹ [bəʊd] I v/t. ahnen lassen: this ~s you no good das bedeutet nichts Gutes für dich; II v/i.: ~ well Gutes versprechen; ~ ill Schlimmes ahnen lassen.

B

bode² [bəʊd] *pret. von* **bide**.
bod·ice ['bɒdɪs] *s.* **1.** *allg.* Mieder *n*; **2.** Oberteil *n*.
bod·ied ['bɒdɪd] *adj. in Zssgn* ...gebaut, von ... Körperbau *od.* Gestalt: *small-~* klein von Gestalt.
bod·i·less ['bɒdɪlɪs] *adj.* **1.** körperlos; **2.** unkörperlich, wesenlos; **'bod·i·ly** [-ɪlɪ] **I** *adj.* körperlich, leiblich: *~ injury* (å *harm*) Körperverletzung *f*; **II** *adv.* leib-'haftig, per'sönlich.
bod·kin ['bɒdkɪn] *s.* **1.** ◎ Ahle *f*, Pfriem *m*: *sit ~* eingepfercht sitzen; **2.** 'Durch-zieh-, Schnürnadel *f*; **3.** *obs.* lange Haarnadel.
bod·y ['bɒdɪ] **I** *s.* **1.** Körper *m*, Leib *m*: *heir of one's ~* Leibeserbe *m*; *in the ~* lebend; *~ and soul* mit Leib u. Seele; *keep ~ and soul together* Leib u. Seele zs.-halten; **2.** *engS.* Rumpf *m*, Leib *m*: *one wound in the leg and one in the ~*; **3.** *oft dead ~* Leiche *f*; **4.** Hauptteil *m*, *das* Wesentliche, Kern *m*, Stamm *m*, Rahmen *m*, Gestell *n*; Rumpf *m* (*Schiff, Flugzeug*); eigentlicher Inhalt, Sub'stanz *f* (*Schriftstück, Rede*): *car ~* Karosserie *f*; *hat ~* Hutstumpen *m*; **5.** Gesamtheit *f*, Masse *f*: *in a ~* zusammen, geschlossen, wie 'ein Mann; *~ of water* Wassermasse *f*, -fläche *f*, Gewässer *n*; *~ of facts* Tatsachenmaterial *n*; *~ of laws* Gesetz(es)sammlung *f*; **6.** Körper(schaft *f*) *m*, Gesellschaft *f*; Gruppe *f*; Gremium *n*: *~ politic* a) juristische Person, b) Gemeinwesen *n*; *diplomatic ~* diplomatisches Korps; *governing ~* Verwaltungskörper *m*; *a ~ of unemployed* e-e Gruppe Arbeitsloser; *student ~* Studentenschaft *f*; **7.** × Truppenkörper *m*, Trupp *m*, Ab'teilung *f*; **8.** *phys.* Körper *m*: *solid ~* fester Körper; *heavenly ~ ast.* Himmelskörper; **9.** ⚓ Masse *f*, Sub'stanz *f*; **10.** F Bursche *m*, Kerl *m*; **11.** *fig.* Güte *f*, Stärke *f*, Festigkeit *f*, Gehalt *m*, Körper *m* (*Wein*), (Klang-) Fülle *f*; **II** *v/t.* **12.** *mst ~ forth fig.* verkörpern; *~ blow s.* Boxen: Körperschlag *m*; *fig.* harter Schlag; *~ build s. biol.* Körperbau *m*; *~ build·er s.* Bodybuilder *m*; *~ build·ing s.* Bodybuilding *n*; *'~·check s. sport* Bodycheck *m*; *'~ guard s.* **1.** Leibwächter *m*; **2.** Leibgarde *f*; *~ lan·guage s. psych.* Körpersprache *f*; *'~·,mak·er s.* ◎ Karosse'riebauer *m*; *~ o·do(u)r s.* Körpergeruch *m*; *~ pierc·ing s.* Mode: Piercing *n*; *~ plasm s. biol.* 'Körper,plasma *n*; *~ search s.* 'Leibesvisitati,on *f*; *~ seg·ment s. biol.* 'Rumpfseg,ment *n*; *~ serv·ant s.* Leib-, Kammerdiener *m*; *~ snatch·er s.* å Leichenräuber *m*; *~ stock·ing s.*, *'~·suit s.* Body(stocking) *m* (*einteilige Unterkleidung [mit Strümpfen]*); *'~·work s.* ◎ Karosse'rie *f*.
bof·fin ['bɒfɪn] *s. Brit. sl.* (Geheim)Wissenschaftler *m*.
Boer ['bəʊə] **I** *s.* Bur(e) *m*, Boer *m* (*Südafrika*); **II** *adj.* burisch: *~ War* Burenkrieg *m*.
bog [bɒg] **I** *s.* **1.** Sumpf *m*, Mo'rast *m* (*a. fig.*); Moor *n*; **2.** V Scheißhaus *n*; **II** *v/t.* **3.** im Sumpf versenken; *fig. a. ~ down* zum Stocken bringen, versanden lassen; **III** *v/i.* **4.** *a. ~ down* im Sumpf *od.* Schlamm versinken; *a. fig.* stecken bleiben, sich festfahren, versanden.
bo·gey ['bəʊgɪ] *s.* **1.** *Golf:* a) Par *n*, b) Bogey *n* (*1 Schlag über Par*); **2.** → **bogy**.
bog·gle ['bɒgl] *v/i.* **1.** (*at*) zu'rückschrecken (vor *dat.*): *imagination ~s at the thought* es wird einem schwind-

lig bei dem Gedanken; **2.** stutzen (*at* vor, bei *dat.*); zögern (*at doing* zu tun): *the mind ~s* F da bist du platt, es ist nicht zu fassen; **3.** pfuschen.
bog·gy ['bɒgɪ] *adj.* sumpfig.
bo·gie ['bəʊgɪ] *s.* **1.** ◎ *Brit.* a) Blockwagen *m*, b) ⛏ Dreh-, Rädergestell *n*; **2.** ⚒ *Art* Förderkarren *m*; **3.** → **bogy**; *~ wheel s.* × (Ketten)Laufrad *n*.
'bog,trot·ter *s. contp.* Ire *m*.
bo·gus ['bəʊgəs] *adj.* falsch, unecht, Schein..., Schwindel...: *~ asylum seeker* 'Scheinasy,lant(in).
bo·gy ['bəʊgɪ] *s.* **1.** 'Kobold *m*, 'Popanz *m* **2.** (*a. fig.* Schreck)Gespenst *n*; *~ man s.* [*irr.*] **1.** Butzemann *m*, *der* schwarze Mann (*Kindersprache*); **2.** *fig.* 'Buhmann' *m*.
Bo·he·mi·an [bəʊ'hiːmjən] **I** *s.* **1.** Böhme *m*, Böhmin *f*; **2.** Bohemi'en *m* (*bsd. Künstler*); **II** *adj.* **3.** böhmisch; **4.** *fig.* bo'hemehaft; **bo·he·mi·an·ism** [-nɪzəm] *s.* Bo'heme *f*, 'Künstlerleben' *n*.
boil¹ [bɔɪl] *s.* å Geschwür *n*, Fu'runkel *m*; Eiterbeule *f*.
boil² [bɔɪl] *s.* **1.** Kochen *n*, Sieden *n*: *bring to the ~* zum Kochen bringen; *come to the ~* zu kochen anfangen; *fig.* F sich zuspitzen, s-n Höhepunkt erreichen; *come off the ~* F sich 'legen' *od.* beruhigen; **2.** Wallen *n*, Wogen *n*, Schäumen *n* (*Gewässer*); **3.** *fig.* Erregung *f*, Wut *f*, Wallung *f*; **II** *v/i.* **4.** kochen, sieden; **5.** wallen, wogen, brausen, -laufen, -schäumen (*alle a. fig.*); **III** *v/t.* **7.** kochen (lassen), zum Kochen bringen, ab-, einkochen: *~ eggs* Eier kochen; *~ clothes* Wäsche kochen; *go ~ your head!* F häng dich doch auf!; *~ a·way v/i.* **1.** verdampfen; **2.** weiterkochen; *~ down* **I** *v/t.* verdampfen, einkochen; *fig.* zs.-fassen, kürzen, **II** *v/i.*: *~ to* hinauslaufen auf (*acc.*); *~ o·ver v/i.* 'überkochen, -laufen, -schäumen (*alle a. fig.*).
boiled | **din·ner** [bɔɪld] *s. Am.* Eintopf(-gericht *n*) *m*; *~ po·ta·toes s. pl.* Salzkartoffeln *pl.*; *~ shirt s.* F Frackhemd *n*; *~ sweet s.* Bon'bon *m*, *n*.
boil·er ['bɔɪlə] *s.* **1.** Sieder *m*: *soap ~*; **2.** ◎ Dampfkessel *m*; **3.** 'Boiler *m*, Heißwasserspeicher *m*; **4.** Siedepfanne *f*; **5.** *be a good ~* sich (gut) zum Kochen eignen; **6.** Suppenhuhn *n*; *~ suit s.* 'Overall *m*.
boil·ing ['bɔɪlɪŋ] **I** *adj.* kochend, heiß; *fig.* kochend, schäumend (*with rage* vor Wut); **II** *adv.*: *~ hot* kochend heiß; *~ point s.* Siedepunkt *m* (*a. fig.*).
bois·ter·ous ['bɔɪstərəs] *adj.* □ **1.** stürmisch, ungestüm, rau; **2.** ausgelassen, lärmend, turbu'lent; **'bois·ter·ous·ness** [-nɪs] *s.* Ungestüm *n*.
bold [bəʊld] *adj.* □ **1.** kühn, zuversichtlich, mutig, unerschrocken; **2.** keck, verwegen, dreist, frech; anmaßend: *make ~ to ...* sich erdreisten *od.* es wagen zu ...; *make ~ (with)* sich Freiheiten herausnehmen (gegen); *as ~ as brass* F frech wie Oskar, unverschämt; **3.** kühn, gewagt: *a ~ plan* **4.** a) kühn (*Entwurf etc.*), b) scharf her'vortretend, ins Auge fallend: *in ~ outline* in deutlichen Umrissen; *a few ~ strokes of the brush* ein paar kühne Pinselstriche; **5.** steil (*Küste*); **6.** → **'bold·face** *adj. typ.* (halb)fett; *'~·faced adj.* **1.** kühn, frech; **2.** *typ.* → **boldface**.
bold·ness ['bəʊldnɪs] *s.* **1.** Kühnheit *f*: a) Mut *m*, Beherztheit *f*, b) Keckheit *f*, Dreistigkeit *f*; **2.** scharfes Her'vortreten.
bole [bəʊl] *s.* starker Baumstamm.

bo·le·ro¹ [bə'leərəʊ] *s.* Bo'lero *m* (*spanischer Tanz*).
bo·le·ro² ['bɒlərəʊ] *s.* Bo'lero *m* (*kurzes Jäckchen*).
boll [bəʊl] *s.* ♀ Samenkapsel *f*.
bol·lard ['bɒləd] *s.* ⚓ Poller *m* (*a. weitS.* Sperrpfosten an Verkehrsinseln etc.*).
bol·lix ['bɒlɪks] *sl. v/t.*: *~ s.th. up* et. verpfuschen (*od.* versauen).
'bol·lock·ing ['bɒləkɪŋ] *s. sl.* Anschiss *m*.
bol·locks ['bɒləks] *s. pl.* V ,Eier' *pl.* (*Hoden*).
Bo·lo·gna sau·sage [bə'ləʊnjə] *s. bsd. Am.* Morta'della *f*.
bo·lo·ney [bə'ləʊnɪ] *s.* **1.** *sl.* ,Quatsch' *m*, Geschwafel *n*; **2.** *bsd. Am.* Morta'della *f*; → **polony**.
Bol·she·vik ['bɒlʃɪvɪk] **I** *s.* Bolsche'wik *m*; **II** *adj.* bolsche'wistisch; **'Bol·she·vism** [-ɪzəm] *s.* Bolsche'wismus *m*; **'Bol·she·vist** [-ɪst] **I** *s.* Bolsche'wist *m*; **II** *adj.* bolsche'wistisch; **'Bol·she·vize** [-vaɪz] *v/t.* bolschewisieren.
bol·ster ['bəʊlstə] **I** *s.* **1.** Kopfpolster *n* (*unter dem Kopfkissen*), Keilkissen *n*; **2.** Polster *n*, Polsterung *f*, 'Unterlage *f* (*a.* ◎); **II** *v/t.* **3.** j-m Kissen 'unterlegen; **4.** (aus)polstern; **5.** *~ up* unter'stützen, stärken, künstlich aufrechterhalten.
bolt¹ [bəʊlt] **I** *s.* **1.** Schraube *f* (*mit Mutter*), Bolzen *m*: *~ nut* Schraubenmutter *f*; **2.** Bolzen *m*, Pfeil *m*: *shoot one's ~* e-n (letzten) Versuch machen; *he has shot his ~* er hat sein Pulver verschossen; *~ upright* kerzengerade; **3.** ◎ (Tür-, Schloss)Riegel *m*: *behind ~ and bar* hinter Schloss u. Riegel; **4.** Schloss *n* an Handfeuerwaffen; **5.** Blitzstrahl *m*: *a ~ from the blue* ein Blitz aus heiterem Himmel; **6.** plötzlicher Sprung, Flucht *f*: *he made a ~ for the door* er machte e-n Satz zur Tür; *he made a ~ for it* F er machte sich aus dem Staube; **7.** *pol. Am.* Abtrünnigkeit *f* von der Poli'tik der eigenen Par'tei; **8.** ✝ a) (Stoff)Ballen *m*, b) (Ta'peten- *etc.*)Rolle *f*; **II** *v/t.* **9.** Tür etc. ver-, zuriegeln; **10.** Essen hin'unterschlingen; **11.** *Am. pol.* sich von s-r Partei lossagen; **III** *v/i.* **12.** 'durchgehen (*Pferd*); **13.** da'vonlaufen, ausreißen, ,'durchbrennen'.
bolt² [bəʊlt] *v/t.* Mehl sieben.
bolt·er ['bəʊltə] *s.* **1.** 'Durchgänger *m* (*Pferd*); **2.** *pol. Am.* Abtrünnige(r *m*)
bo·lus ['bəʊləs] *s.* å Bolus *m*, große Pille.
bomb [bɒm] **I** *s.* **1.** Bombe *f*: *the ⚓* die (Atom)Bombe; **2.** ◎ a) Gasflasche *f*, b) Zerstäuberflasche *f*; **3.** F a) Bombenerfolg *m*, b) Heidengeld *n*, c) *thea. etc. Am.* ,'Durchfall' *m*, ,'Flop' *m*; **II** *v/t.* **4.** mit Bomben belegen, bombardieren; zerbomben: *~ed out* ausgebombt; *~ed site* Ruinengrundstück *n*; **5.** *~ up* ✈ mit Bomben beladen; **III** *v/i.* **6.** *sl.* e-e ,Pleite' sein, *thea.* ,'durchfallen', *bsd. Am.* (*im Examen*) ,'durchrasseln'.
bom·bard [bɒm'bɑːd] *v/t.* **1.** × bombardieren, Bomben werfen auf (*acc.*), beschießen; **2.** *fig.* (*with*) bombardieren, bestürmen (mit); **3.** *phys.* bombardieren, beschießen; **bom·bard·ier** [,bɒmbə'dɪə] *s.* × **1.** *Brit.* Artille'rie,unteroffi,zier *m*; **2.** Bombenschütze *m* (*im Flugzeug*); **bom'bard·ment** [-mənt] *s.* Bomberde'ment *n*, Beschießung *f* (*a. phys.*), Belegung *f* mit Bomben, Bombardierung *f*.
bom·bast ['bɒmbæst] *s. fig.* Bom'bast *m*, (leerer) Wortschwall, Schwulst *m*; **bom·bas·tic** [bɒm'bæstɪk] *adj.* (□ *~ally*) bom'bastisch, schwülstig.
bomb| at·tack *s.* Bombenanschlag *m*; *~*

bay *s.* ✈ Bombenschacht *m*; ~ **dis·pos·al** *s.* ⚔ Bombenräumung *f*: ~ **squad** Bombenräumungs-, Sprengkommando *n*.

bom·be [bɔ̃:mb] (*Fr.*) *s.* Eisbombe *f*.

bombed [bɒmd] *adj. sl.* **1.** ,besoffen'; **2.** ,high' (*im Drogenrausch*).

bomb·er ['bɒmə] *s.* **1.** Bomber *m*, Bombenflugzeug *n*; **2.** Bombenleger *m*.

bomb·ing ['bɒmɪŋ] *s.* Bombenabwurf *m*: ~ **raid** Bombenangriff *m*.

'bomb'·proof ⚔ **I** *adj.* bombensicher; **II** *s.* Bunker *m*; ~ **scare** *s.* Bombendrohung *f*; **'~·shell** *s. fig.* Bombe *f*: **the news came like a ~** die Nachricht schlug ein wie e-e Bombe.

bo·na fi·de [,bəʊnə'faɪdɪ] *adj. u. adv.* **1.** in gutem Glauben, auf Treu u. Glauben: ~ **owner** ⚖ gutgläubiger Besitzer; **2.** ehrlich; echt; **,bo·na 'fi·des** [-di:z] *s. pl.* guter Glaube, Treu *f* und Glauben *m*, ehrliche Absicht; Rechtmäßigkeit *f*.

bo·nan·za [bəʊ'nænzə] **I** *s.* **1.** *min.* reiche Erzader (*bsd. Edelmetalle*); **2.** F Goldgrube *f*, Glücksquelle *f, a.* Fundgrube *f*; **3.** Fülle *f*, Reichtum *m*; **II** *adj.* **4.** sehr einträglich *od.* lukra'tiv.

bon·bon ['bɒnbɒn] *s.* Bon'bon *m, n; fig.* Zuckerl *n*.

bond [bɒnd] **I** *s.* **1.** *pl. obs.* Fesseln *pl.*: **in ~s** in Fesseln, gefangen, versklavt; **burst one's ~s** s-e Ketten sprengen; **2.** *sg. od. pl. fig.* Bande *pl.*: **~s of love**; **3.** Verpflichtung *f*; Bürgschaft *f*; (*a.* 'Haft)Kauti,on *f*; Vertrag *m*; Urkunde *f*; Garan'tie(schein *m*) *f*: **enter into a ~** e-e Verpflichtung eingehen; **his word is as good as his ~** er ist ein Mann von Wort; **4.** ✝ a) Schuldschein *m*, b) öffentliche Schuldverschreibung, (festverzinsliches) 'Wertpa,pier *n*, Obligati'on *f*, (Schuld- Staats)Anleihe *f*: **industrial ~** Industrieobligation, -anleihe; → **mortgage bond**; **5.** ✝ Zollverschluss *m*: **in ~** unter Zollverschluss; **6.** ⚔ a) Verband *m*, Verbindungsstück *n*; **7.** ♠ A a) Bindung *f*, b) Bindemittel *n*, c) Wertigkeit *f*; **8.** → **bond paper**; **II** *v/t.* **9.** verpfänden; **10.** ✝ unter Zollverschluss legen; **11.** ⊕ Lack *etc.* binden (*a. v/i.*): **~ing agent** Bindemittel *n*; **'bond·age** [-dɪdʒ] *s. hist.* Knechtschaft *f*, Sklave·'rei *f* (*a. fig.*); *fig. a.* Hörigkeit *f*: **in the ~ of vice** dem Laster verfallen; **'bond·ed** [-dɪd] *adj.* ✝: ~ **debt** fundierte Schuld; ~ **goods** Waren unter Zollverschluss; ~ **warehouse** Zollspeicher *m*.

'bond'·hold·er *s.* Obligati'onsinhaber *m*; **'~·man** [-mən] *s.* [*irr.*] Sklave *m*, Leibeigene(r) *m*; ~ **mar·ket** *s.* ✝ Rentenmarkt *m*; ~ **pa·per** *s.* Bankpost *f*, 'Post-, 'Banknotenpa,pier *n*; ~ **slave** *s. fig.* Sklave *m*.

bonds·man ['bɒndzmən] *s.* [*irr.*] **1.** → **bondman**; **2.** ⚖ a) Bürge *m*, b) *Am.* gewerblicher Kauti'onssteller.

bone [bəʊn] **I** *s.* **1.** Knochen *m*; Bein *n*: ~ **of contention** Zankapfel *m*; **to the ~** bis auf die Knochen *od.* die Haut, durch u. durch (*nass od. kalt*); **price cut to the ~** aufs Äußerste reduzierter Preis, Schleuderpreis; **I feel it in my ~s** *fig.* ich spüre es in den Knochen (*ahne es*); **a bag of ~s** F nur (noch) Haut u. Knochen, ein Skelett; **my old ~s** m-e alten Knochen; **bred in the ~** angeboren; **make no ~s about it** nicht viel Federlesens machen, nicht lange (damit) fackeln; **have a ~ to pick with s.o.** ein Hühnchen mit j-m zu rupfen haben; **2.** *pl.* Gebeine *pl.*; **3.** (Fisch)Gräte *f*; **4.** *pl.* Kor'settstangen *pl.*; **5.** *pl. Am.* a) Würfel *pl.*, b) 'Dominosteine *pl.*; **II** *v/t.*

6. die Knochen her'ausnehmen aus (*dat.*), *Fisch* entgräten; **III** *v/i.* **7.** *oft* ~ **up on** *sl. et.* ,büffeln', ,ochsen', ,pauken'; **IV** *adj.* **8.** beinern, knöchern, aus Bein *od.* Knochen; **'~·black** *s.* 🔥 Knochenkohle *f*; **2.** Beinschwarz *n* (*Farbe*); ~ **chi·na** *s.* 'Knochenporzel,lan *n*.

boned [bəʊnd] *adj.* **1.** *in Zssgn* ...knochig: **strong-~** starkknochig; **2.** *Küche:* a) ohne Knochen: ~ **chicken**, b) entgrätet: ~ **fish**.

,bone'-'dry *adj.* **1.** staubtrocken; **2.** F völlig ,trocken': a) streng 'antialko,holisch, b) ohne jeden Alko'hol (*Party etc.*); ~ **glue** *s.* Knochenleim *m*; **'~·head** *s. sl.* Holz-, Dummkopf *m*; **'~,head·ed** *adj. sl.* dumm; ~ **lace** *s.* Klöppelspitze *f*; **,~'la·zy** *adj.* F ,stinkfaul'; ~ **meal** *s.* Knochenmehl *n*.

bon·er ['bəʊnə] *s. Am. sl.* Schnitzer *m*, (grober) Fehler.

'bone',shak·er *s. sl.* ,Klapperkasten' *m* (*Bus etc.*); **'~·yard** *s. Am.* **1.** Schindanger *m*; **2.** F (*a.* Auto- *etc.*)Friedhof *m*.

bon·fire ['bɒnfaɪə] *s.* **1.** Freudenfeuer *n*; **2.** Feuer *n* im Freien (*zum Unkrautverbrennen etc.*); **3.** *allg.* Feuer *n*, ,Scheiterhaufen' *m*: **make a ~ of s.th.** *et.* vernichten.

bon·ho·mie ['bɒnɒmi:] (*Fr.*) *s.* Gutmütigkeit *f*, Joviali'tät *f*.

bonk [bɒŋk] V *v/i. u. v/t.* V vögeln.

bon·kers ['bɒŋkəz] *adj. sl.* verrückt.

bon·net ['bɒnɪt] **I** *s.* **1.** (*bsd.* Schotten)Mütze *f*, Kappe *f*; → **bee¹** 1; **2.** (Damen)Hut *m*, (Damen- *od.* Kinder-) Haube *f* (*mst randlos*); **3.** Kopfschmuck *m* der Indi'aner; **4.** ⊕ Schornsteinkappe *f*; **5.** *mot. Brit.* 'Motorhaube *f*; **6.** ⊕ Schutzkappe *f* (*für Ventil, Zylinder etc.*); **II** *v/t.* **7.** *j-m* den Hut über die Augen drücken; **'bon·net·ed** [-tɪd] *adj.* e-e Mütze *etc.* tragend.

bon·ny ['bɒnɪ] *adj. bsd. Scot.* **1.** hübsch, nett (*a. iron.*), *fig.* ,prima'; **2.** F drall.

bo·nus ['bəʊnəs] *s.* ✝ **1.** 'Bonus *m*, 'Prämie *f*, Gratifikati'on *f*, Sondervergütung *f*, (Sonder)Zulage *f*, Tanti'eme *f*: **Christmas ~** Weihnachtsgratifikation; ~ **number** *Lotto:* Zusatzzahl *f*; **2.** 'Prämie *f*, 'Extravi,dende *f*, Sonderausschüttung *f*: ~ **share** Gratisaktie *f*; **3.** *Am.* Dreingabe *f* (*beim Kauf*); **4.** Vergünstigung *f*.

bon·y ['bəʊnɪ] *adj.* **1.** knöchern, Knochen...; **2.** starkknochig; **3.** voll Knochen *od.* Gräten; **4.** knochendürr.

bonze [bɒnz] *s.* Bonze *m* (*buddhistischer Mönch od. Priester*).

boo [bu:] **I** *int.* **1.** huh! (*um j-n zu erschrecken*); **he can't say ~ to a goose** er ist ein Hasenfuß; **2.** buh!, pfui!; **II** *s.* **3.** Buh(ruf *m*) *n*, Pfui(ruf *m*) *n*; **III** *v/i.* **4.** buh! *od.* pfui! schreien, buhen; **IV** *v/t.* **5.** durch Pfui- *od.* Buhrufe ver-höhnen; auspfeifen, ausbuhen, niederbrüllen.

boob [bu:b] *sl.* **I** *s.* **1.** ,Schnitzer' *m*, Fehler *m*; **2.** → **booby** 1; **3.** *pl.* ,Titten' *pl.* (*Brüste*); **II** *v/i.* **4.** e-n ,Schnitzer' machen, ,Mist bauen'.

boo-boo ['bu:bu:] *s. Am. sl.* → **boob** 1.

boob tube *s. sl. TV* ,Röhre' *f*, ,Glotze' *f* (*Fernseher*).

boo·by ['bu:bɪ] *s.* **1.** ,Dussel' *m*, Trottel *m*; **2.** Letzte(r *m*) *f*, Schlechteste(r *m*) *f* (*in Wettkämpfen etc.*); **3.** *orn.* Tölpel *m*, Seerabe *m*; ~ **hatch** *s. Am. sl.* ,Klapsmühle' *f* (*Irrenanstalt*); ~ **prize** *s.* Trostpreis *m*; ~ **trap** *s.* (versteckte) Sprengladung *od.* Bombe; *allg. (bsd.* Todes)Falle *f*; **'~·trap** *v/t.* a) e-e Bombe *etc.* verstecken in (*dat.*), b) durch e-e

versteckte Bombe *etc.* e-n Anschlag verüben auf (*acc.*).

boo·dle ['bu:dl] *s. Am. sl.* **1.** → **caboodle**; **2.** Falschgeld *n*; **3.** Schmiergelder *pl.*

boo·gie-woo·gie [,bu:gɪ'wu:gɪ] *s.* ♪ Boogie-Woogie *m* (*Tanz*).

boo·hoo [,bu:'hu:] **I** *s.* lautes Geschluchze; **II** *v/i.* laut schluchzen, plärren.

book [bʊk] **I** *s.* **1.** Buch *n*: **be at one's ~s** über s-n Büchern sitzen; **without the ~** auswendig; **he talks like a ~** er redet sehr gestelzt; **the ~ of life** (*nature*) *fig.* das Buch des Lebens (der Natur); **a closed ~** a) ein Buch mit sieben Siegeln, b) e-e erledigte Sache; **the 2** (*of 2s*) die Bibel; **kiss the 2** die Bibel küssen; **swear on the 2** bei der Bibel schwören; **suit s.o.'s ~** *fig.* j-m passen *od.* recht sein; **throw the ~ at s.o.** F a) j-n (zur Höchststrafe) verdonnern', b) j-n wegen sämtlicher einschlägigen Delikte belangen; **by the ~** a) ganz korrekt *od.* genau, b) ,nach allen Regeln der Kunst'; **in my ~** F wie 'ich es sehe; → **leaf** 3; **2.** Buch *n* (*Teil e-s Gesamtwerkes*); **3.** ✝ Geschäfts-, Handelsbuch *n*: **close the ~s** die Bücher abschließen; **keep ~s** Bücher führen; **be deep in s.o.'s ~s** bei j-m tief in der Kreide stehen; **bring to ~** a) j-n zur Rechenschaft ziehen, b) ✝ (ver)buchen; **be in s.o.'s good** (*bad od.* **black**) **~s** bei j-m gut (schlecht) angeschrieben sein; **4.** (Schreib)Heft *n*, No·'tizblock *m*; **5.** (Namens)Liste *f*, Verzeichnis *n*, Buch *n*: **visitors' ~** Gästebuch; **be on the ~s** auf der Mitgliedsliste (*univ.* Liste der Immatrikulierten) stehen; **6.** Heft(chen) *n*, Block *m*: ~ **of stamps** Briefmarkenheft; **7.** Wettbuch *n*: **you can make a ~ on that!** F darauf kannst du wetten!; **8.** a) *thea.* Text *m*, b) ♪ Textbuch *n*, Lib'retto *n*; **II** *v/t.* **9.** ✝ (ver)buchen, eintragen; **10.** *j-n* verpflichten, engagieren; **11.** *j-n als* (*Fahr*)Gast, Teilnehmer *etc.* einschreiben, vormerken; **12.** *Platz, Zimmer* bestellen, *a.* Überfahrt *etc.* buchen; *Eintritts-, Fahrkarte* lösen; *Auftrag* notieren; *Güter, Gepäck* (*zur Beförderung*) aufgeben; *Ferngespräch* anmelden; → **booked**; **13.** *j-n* polizeilich aufschreiben *od. sport* notieren (**for** wegen); **III** *v/i.* **14.** eine Fahrkarte *etc.* lösen *od.* nehmen: ~ **through** (**to**) durchlösen (bis, nach); **15.** Platz *etc.* bestellen; **16.** ~ **in** sich (*im Hotel*) eintragen: → **in at** absteigen in (*dat.*); **'book·a·ble** [-kəbl] *adj.* im Vorverkauf erhältlich (*Karten etc.*).

'book'·bind·er *s.* Buchbinder *m*; **'~,bind·ing** *s.* Buchbinderhandwerk *n*, Buchbinde'rei *f*; **'~·case** *s.* 'Bücherschrank *m*, -re,gal *n*; ~ **cloth** *s.* Buchbinderleinwand *f*; ~ **club** *s.* Buchgemeinschaft *f*; ~ **cov·er** *s.* 'Buchdecke *f*, -,umschlag *m*; ~ **debt** *s.* ✝ Buchschuld *f*.

booked [bʊkt] *adj.* **1.** gebucht, eingetragen; **2.** vorgemerkt, bestimmt, bestellt: **all ~** (**up**) voll besetzt *od.* belegt, ausverkauft.

book end *s. mst pl.* Bücherstütze *f*.

book·ie ['bʊkɪ] *sl.* → **bookmaker**.

book·ing ['bʊkɪŋ] *s.* **1.** Buchung *f*, Eintragung *f*; **2.** Bestellung *f*; ~ **clerk** *s.* Schalterbeamte(r) *m*, Fahrkartenverkäufer *m*; ~ **hall** *s.* Schalterhalle *f*; ~ **of·fice** *s.* **1.** Fahrkartenschalter *m*; **2.** *thea. etc.* Kasse *f*, Vorverkaufsstelle *f*; **3.** *Am.* Gepäckschalter *m*.

book·ish ['bʊkɪʃ] *adj.* □ **1.** belesen,

B

gelehrt; **2.** voll Bücherweisheit: **~ person** a) Büchernarr *m*, b) Stubengelehrte(r) *m*; **~ style** papierener Stil; **'book·ish·ness** [-nɪʃ] *s.* trockene Gelehrsamkeit.

'book|,keep·er *s.* Buchhalter(in); **'~,keep·ing** *s.* Buchhaltung *f*, -führung *f*: **~ by single** (**double**) **entry** einfache (doppelte) Buchführung; **~ knowl·edge**, **~ learn·ing** *s.* Buchwissen *n*, Bücherweisheit *f*.

book·let ['bʊklɪt] *s.* Büchlein *n*, Bro'schüre *f*.

'book|,mak·er *s.* Buchmacher *m*; **'~·man** [-mən] *s.* [*irr.*] Büchermensch *m*, Gelehrte(r) *m*; **'~·mark** *s.* Lesezeichen *n*, *Computer a.* 'Bookmark *f*; **'~·mo,bile** [-məʊˌbiːl] *s. Am.* 'Auto-, 'Wanderbüche,rei *f*; **'~·plate** *s.* Ex'libris *n*; **~ post** *s. Brit.* (**by ~** als) Büchersendung *f*; **~ prof·it** *s.* ✝ Buchgewinn *m*; **'~·rack** *s.* 'Büchergestell *n*, -re,gal *n*; **'~·rest** *s.* **1.** Buchstütze *f*; **2.** (kleines) Lesepult; **~ re·view** *s.* Buchbesprechung *f*; **~ re·view·er** *s.* 'Buch,kritiker *m*; **'~,sell·er** *s.* Buchhändler(in); **'~·shelf** *s.* Bücherbrett *n*, -gestell *n*; **'~·shop** *s.* Buchhandlung *f*; **'~·stack** *s.* Bücherregal *n*; **'~·stall** *s.* **1.** Bücher-(verkaufs)stand *m*; **2.** Zeitungsstand *m*; **'~·stand** → **bookrack**; **'~·store** *s. Am.* Buchhandlung *f*.

book·sy ['bʊksɪ] *adj. Am.* F ,hochgestochen'.

book| to·ken *s. Brit.* Büchergutschein *m*; **~ trade** *s.* Buchhandel *m*; **~ val·ue** *s.* ✝ Buchwert *m*; **'~·worm** *s. zo. u. fig.* Bücherwurm *m*.

boom¹ [buːm] **I** *s.* Dröhnen *n*, Donnern *n*, Brausen *n*; **II** *v/i.* dröhnen, donnern, brausen; **III** *v/t. a.* **~ out** dröhnen(d äußern).

boom² [buːm] *s.* **1.** ♻ Baum *m* (*Hafen- od. Flusssperrgerät*); **2.** ♻ Baum *m*, Spiere *f* (*Stange am Segel*); **3.** *Am.* Schwimmbaum *m* (*zum Auffangen des Floßholzes*); **4.** *Film, TV:* (Mikro'fon)Galgen *m*.

boom³ [buːm] **I** *s.* **1.** Aufschwung *m*; Berühmtheit *f*, *das Berühmtwerden*, Blüte(zeit) *f*; **2.** ✝ Boom *m*: a) ('Hoch-)Konjunk,tur *f*: **building ~** Bauboom, b) Aufschwung *m*, c) Börse: Hausse *f*; **3.** Re'klamerummel *m*, aufdringliche Propa'ganda; **II** *v/i.* **4.** e-n (ra'piden) Aufschwung nehmen, in die Höhe schnellen, anziehen (*Preise, Kurse*), blühen; **~ing** florierend, blühend; **III** *v/t.* **5.** die Werbetrommel rühren für; *Preise* in die Höhe treiben; **'~-and-'bust** *s. Am.* F außergewöhnlicher Aufstieg, dem e-e ernste Krise folgt.

boom·er·ang ['buːməræŋ] **I** *s.* Bumerang *m* (*a. fig.*); **II** *v/i. fig.* (**on**) sich als Bumerang erweisen (für), zurückschlagen (auf *acc.*).

boon¹ [buːn] *s.* **1.** Wohltat *f*, Segen *m*; **2.** Gefälligkeit *f*.

boon² [buːn] *adj. lit.* freundlich, munter: **~ companion** lustiger Kumpan *od.* Zechbruder.

boon·docks ['buːndɒks] *s. pl. Am. sl.* die Pro'vinz.

boor [bʊə] *s. fig.* a) ,Bauer' *m*, ungehobelter Kerl, b) Flegel *m*; **boor·ish** ['bʊərɪʃ] *adj.* □ *fig.* ungehobelt, flegelhaft; **'boor·ish·ness** ['bʊərɪʃnɪs] *s.* ungehobeltes Benehmen *od.* Wesen.

boost [buːst] **I** *v/t.* **1.** hochschieben, -treiben; nachhelfen (*dat.*) (*a. fig.*); **2.** ✝ F a) fördern, Auftrieb geben (*dat.*) (*a. fig.*), *Produktion etc.* ,ankurbeln'; *Preise* in die Höhe treiben: **~ the mo-**

rale die (*Arbeits- etc.*)Moral heben, b) anpreisen, Re'klame machen für; **3.** ♻, ⚡ *Druck, Spannung* erhöhen, verstärken; **II** *s.* **4.** Förderung *f*, Erhöhung *f*; Auftrieb *m*; **5.** *fig.* Re'klame *f*.

boost·er ['buːstə] *s.* **1.** F Förderer *m* Re'klamemacher *m*; Preistreiber *m*; **2.** ♻, ⚡ 'Zusatz(aggre,gat *n*, -dy,namo *m*, -verstärker *m*) *m*; Kom'pressor *m*; Servomotor *m*; *Rakete*: a) 'Antriebssag-gre,gat *n*, b) Zündstufe *f*, c) 'Trägerra-,kete *f*; **~ bat·ter·y** *s.* ⚡ 'Zusatzbatte,rie *f*; **~ rock·et** *s.* 'Startra,kete *f*; **~ shot** *s.* ✚ Wieder'holungsimpfung *f*.

boot¹ [buːt] **I** *s.* **1.** (*Am.* Schaft)Stiefel *m*; *pl.* Mode: Boots *pl.*: **the ~ is on the other leg** a) der Fall liegt umgekehrt, b) die Verantwortung liegt bei der anderen Seite; **die in one's ~s** a) *am Ende e-s langen Arbeitslebens* ,am Schreibtisch' sterben b) e-s plötzlichen *od.* gewaltsamen Todes sterben; **get the ~** *sl.* ,rausgeschmissen' (*entlassen*) werden; → **big** 2; **2.** *Brit. mot.* Kofferraum *m*; **3.** ♻ Schutzkappe *f*, -hülle *f*; **II** *v/i.* **4.** *sl.* j-m e-n Fußtritt geben; **5.** *sl. fig.* j-n ,rausschmeißen' (*entlassen*); **6.** F *Fußball* treten; **7.** *Computer*: Programm booten, starten.

boot² [buːt] *s. nur noch in*: **to ~** obendrein, noch dazu.

'boot|·black *s. Am.* Schuhputzer *m*; **~ camp** *s.* ✕ Ausbildungslager *n* (*der Navy u. Marines*).

boot·ed ['buːtɪd] *adj.* Stiefel tragend: **~ and spurred** gestiefelt u. gespornt.

booth [buːð] *s.* **1.** (Markt)Bude *f*; (Messe)Stand *m*; **2.** (Fernsprech-, *pol.* Wahl)Zelle *f*; **3.** a) *Radio, TV:* ('Über)tragungs)Ka,bine *f*, b) ('Abhör-)Ka,bine *f* (*Schallplattengeschäft*); **4.** Nische *f*, Sitzgruppe *f im Restaurant*.

'boot|·jack *s.* Stiefelknecht *m*; **'~·lace** *s. bsd. Brit.* Schnürsenkel *m*.

boot·leg ['buːtleg] *v/t. u. v/i. Am. sl. bsd. Spirituosen* 'illegal herstellen, schwarz verkaufen, schmuggeln; **'boot-,leg·ger** [-gə] *s. Am. sl.* ('Alkohol-)Schmuggler *m*, (-)Schwarzhändler *m*; **'boot,leg·ging** [-gɪŋ] *s. Am. sl.* ('Alkohol)Schmuggel *m*.

boot·less ['buːtlɪs] *adj.* □ nutzlos, vergeblich.

'boot|·lick *v/t. u. v/i.* F (vor *j-m*) kriechen; **'~,lick·er** *s.* F ,Kriecher' *m*.

boots [buːts] *s. sg.* Hausdiener *m* (*im Hotel*).

'boot|·strap **I** *s.* **1.** Stiefelstrippe *f*, -schlaufe *f*: **pull o.s. up by one's own ~s** sich aus eigener Kraft hocharbeiten; **2.** *Computer*: 'Bootstrap *m*, 'Boot,strapping *n*; **II** *v/t.* **3.** sich aus eigener Kraft von *et.* befreien, aus eigener Kraft *et.* erreichen; **4.** e-n *Computer*, ein Programm booten; **~ top** *s.* Stiefelstulpe *f*; **~ tree** *s.* Schuh-, Stiefelleisten *m*.

boot·y ['buːtɪ] *s.* **1.** (Kriegs)Beute *f*, Raub *m*; **2.** *fig.* Beute *f*, Fang *m*.

booze [buːz] F **I** *v/i.* ,saufen'; **II** *s.* a) Schnaps *m*, 'Alkohol *m*, ,Saufe'rei' *f*, Besäufnis *n*: **go on** (*od.* **hit**) **the ~** → I; b) alko'holisches Getränk; **boozed** [-zd] *adj.* F ,blau', ,voll', besoffen; **'booz·er** [-zə] *s.* **1.** F Säufer *m*; **2.** *Brit. sl.* Kneipe *f*.

'booze-up → **booze** II b.

booz·y ['buːzɪ] *adj.* F **1.** → **boozed**; **2.** versoffen.

bo·rac·ic [bə'ræsɪk] *adj.* ✚ 'boraxhaltig, Bor...: **~ acid** Borsäure *f*.

bor·age ['bɒrɪdʒ] *s.* ✿ Borretsch *m*, Gurkenkraut *n*.

bo·rax ['bɔːræks] *s.* ✚ 'Borax *m*.

bor·der ['bɔːdə] **I** *s.* **1.** Rand *m*, Kante *f*;

2. (*Landes- od. Gebiets*)Grenze *f*; *a.* **~ area** Grenzgebiet *n*: **the ☾** Grenze *od.* Grenzgebiet zwischen England u. Schottland; **north of the ☾** in Schottland; **~ incident** Grenzzwischenfall *m*; **3.** Um'randung *f*, Borte *f*, Einfassung *f*, Saum *m*; Zierleiste *f*; **4.** Randbeet *n*, Ra'batte *f*; **II** *v/t.* **5.** einfassen, besetzen; **6.** begrenzen, (um)'säumen: **a lawn ~ed by trees**; **7.** grenzen an (*acc.*): **my park ~s yours**; **III** *v/i.* **8.** grenzen (**on** an *acc.*) (*a. fig.*); **'bor·der·er** [-ərə] *s.* **1.** Grenzbewohner *m*; **2.** **☾s** *pl.* ✕ 'Grenzregi,ment *n*.

'bor·der·land *s.* Grenzgebiet *n* (*a. fig.*); **'~·line** **I** *s.* 'Grenz,linie *f*; *fig.* Grenze *f*; **II** *adj.* auf *od.* an e-r Grenze: **~ case** Grenzfall *m*.

bor·dure ['bɔːˌdjʊə] *s. her.* 'Schild-, 'Wappenum,randung *f*.

bore¹ [bɔː] **I** *v/t.* **1.** (durch)'bohren: **~ a well** e-n Brunnen bohren; **~ one's way** *fig.* sich (mühsam) e-n Weg bahnen; **II** *v/i.* **2.** (**for**) bohren, Bohrungen machen (nach); **~ schürfen** (nach); **3.** ♻ *bei Holz*: (ins Volle) bohren; *bei Metall*: (aus-, auf)bohren; **4.** sich einbohren (**into** in *acc.*); **III** *s.* **5.** ♻ Bohrung *f*, Bohrloch *n*; **6.** ✕, ♻ Bohrung *f*, Seele *f*, Ka'liber *n* (*e-r Schusswaffe*).

bore² [bɔː] **I** *s.* **1.** *et.* Langweiliges *od.* Lästiges *od.* Stumpfsinniges: **what a ~** a) wie langweilig, b) wie dumm; **the book is a ~ to read** das Buch ist ,stinkfad'; **2.** a) fader Kerl, b) unangenehmer Kerl, (altes) Ekel; **II** *v/t.* **3.** langweilen: **be ~d** sich langweilen; **look ~d** gelangweilt aussehen.

bore³ [bɔː] *s.* Springflut *f*.

bore⁴ [bɔː] *pret. von* **bear¹**.

bo·re·al ['bɔːrɪəl] *adj.* nördlich, Nord...; **bo·re·a·lis** [bɔːrɪ'eɪlɪs] → **aurora borealis**; **Bo·re·as** ['bɒrɪæs] **I** *npr.* 'Boreas *m*; **II** *s. poet.* Nordwind *m*.

bore·dom ['bɔːdəm] *s.* **1.** Langeweile *f*, Gelangweiltsein *n*; **2.** Langweiligkeit *f*, Stumpfsinn *m*.

bor·er ['bɔːrə] *s.* **1.** ♻ Bohrer *m*; **2.** *zo.* Bohrer *m* (*Insekt*).

bo·ric ['bɔːrɪk] *adj.* ✚ Bor...: **~ acid** Borsäure *f*.

bor·ing ['bɔːrɪŋ] *adj.* **1.** bohrend, Bohr...; **2.** langweilig.

born [bɔːn] **I** *p.p. von* **bear¹**; **II** *adj.* geboren: **~ of ...** geboren von ..., Kind des *od.* der ...; **a ~ poet**, **~ a poet** ein geborener Dichter, zum Dichter geboren; **a ~ fool** ein völliger Narr; **an Englishman ~ and bred** ein echter Engländer; **never in all my ~ days** mein Lebtag (noch) nie; **~-a·gain** *adj. relig. u. fig.* spätberufen.

borne [bɔːn] *p.p. von* **bear¹** **1.** getragen *etc.*: **lorry-~** mit (e-m) Lastwagen befördert; **2.** geboren (*in Verbindung mit* **by** *und dem Namen der Mutter*): **Elizabeth I was ~ by Anne Boleyn**.

bor·né ['bɔːneɪ] (*Fr.*) *adj.* borniert.

bo·ron ['bɔːrɒn] *s.* ✚ Bor *n*.

bor·ough ['bʌrə] *s.* **1.** *Brit.* a) Stadt *f od.* im Parla'ment vertretener städtischer Wahlbezirk, b) Stadtteil *m* (*von Groß-London*): **☾ Council** Stadtrat *m*; **2.** *Am.* a) Stadt- *od.* Dorfgemeinde *f*, b) Stadtbezirk *m* (*in New York*).

bor·row ['bɒrəʊ] *v/t.* **1.** (aus)borgen, (ent)leihen (**from**, **of** von): **~ed funds** ✝ Fremdmittel *pl.*; **2.** *fig.* entlehnen, *humor.* ,borgen': **~ed word** Lehnwort *n*; **'bor·row·er** [-əʊə] *s.* **1.** Entleiher (-in), Borger(in); **2.** ✝ Kre'ditnehmer (-in); **'bor·row·ing** [-əʊɪŋ] *s.* (Aus)Borgen *n*; Darlehns-, Kre'ditaufnahme *f*,

Anleihe f: ~ **power** ✝ Kreditfähigkeit f.

Bor·stal (**In·sti·tu·tion**) ['bɔːstl] s. Brit. erzieherisch gestaltete Jugendstrafanstalt: **Borstal training** Strafvollzug m in e-m **Borstal**.

bosh [bɒʃ] s. F 'Quatsch' m.

bos·om ['buzəm] s. **1.** Busen m, Brust f, fig. a. Herz n: ~ **friend** Busenfreund (-in); **keep** (od. **lock**) **in one's** (**own**) ~ in s-m Busen verschließen; **take s.o. to one's** ~ j-n ans Herz drücken; **3.** fig. Schoß m: **in the** ~ **of one's family** (**the Church**); → **Abraham**; **4.** Brustteil m (Kleid etc.); bsd. Am. Hemdbrust f; **5.** Tiefe f, das Innere: **in the** ~ **of the earth** im Erdinnern; '**bos·omed** [-md] adj. in Zssgn ...busig; '**bos·om·y** [-mɪ] adj. vollbusig.

boss¹ [bɒs] **I** s. Beule f, Buckel m, Knauf m, Knopf m, erhabene Verzierung; ◉ (Rad-, Schiffsschrauben)Nabe f; **II** v/t. mit Buckeln etc. verzieren, bosseln, treiben.

boss² [bɒs] F **I** s. **1.** a. ~ **man** Chef m, Vorgesetzte(r) m, 'Boss' m; **2.** fig. 'Macher' m, 'Boss' m, Tonangebende(r) m; **3.** Am. pol. (Par'tei)Bonze m, (-)Boss m; **II** v/t. **4.** Herr sein über (acc.): ~ **the show** der Chef vom Ganzen sein; **III** v/i. **5.** den Chef od. Herrn spielen, kommandieren; **6.** ~ **about** herumkommandieren; **boss·y** ['bɒsɪ] adj. F **1.** herrisch, dikta'torisch; **2.** rechthaberisch.

bo·sun ['bəʊsn] → **boatswain**.

bo·tan·ic, **bo·tan·i·cal** [bə'tænɪk(l)] adj. □ bo'tanisch.

bot·a·nist ['bɒtənɪst] s. Bo'taniker m, Pflanzenkenner m; '**bot·a·nize** [-naɪz] v/i. botanisieren; '**bot·a·ny** [-nɪ] s. Bo'tanik f, Pflanzenkunde f.

botch [bɒtʃ] **I** s. Flickwerk n, fig. a. Pfuscharbeit f: **make a** ~ **of s.th** et. verpfuschen; **II** v/t. zs.-schustern od. -stoppeln; verpfuschen; **III** v/i. pfuschen, stümpern; '**botch·er** [-tʃə] s. **1.** Flickschneider m, -schuster m (a. fig.); **2.** Pfuscher m, Stümper m.

both [bəʊθ] **I** adj. u. pron. beide, beides: ~ **my sons** m-e beiden Söhne; ~ **parents** beide Eltern; ~ **of them** sie (od. alle) beide; **you can't have it** ~ **ways** du kannst nicht beides od. nur eins von beiden haben; **II** adv. od. cj.: ~ **... and** sowohl ... als (auch): ~ **boys and girls**.

both·er ['bɒðə] **I** s. **1.** a) Last f, Plage f, Mühe f, Ärger m, Schere'rei f, b) Aufregung f, 'Wirbel' m, Getue n: **this boy is a great** ~ dieser Junge ist e-e große Plage; **II** v/t. **2.** belästigen, quälen, stören, beunruhigen, ärgern: **don't** ~ **me!** lass mich in Frieden!; **be** ~**ed about s.th.** über et. beunruhigt sein; **I can't be** ~**ed with it** ich kann mich nicht damit abgeben; ~ **one's head about s.th.** sich über et. den Kopf zerbrechen; ~ (**it**)**!** F verflixt!; **III** v/i. **3.** (**about**) sich sorgen (um), sich aufregen (über acc.); **4.** sich Mühe geben: **don't** ~**!** bemüh dich nicht!; **5.** (**about**) sich kümmern (um), sich befassen (mit) sich Gedanken machen (wegen): **I shan't** ~ **about it**; **both·er·a·tion** [ˌbɒðə'reɪʃn] F **I** s. Belästigung f; **II** int. 'Mist'!

bo tree ['bəʊtriː] s. der heilige Feigenbaum (Buddhas).

bot·tle ['bɒtl] **I** s. **1.** Flasche f (a. ◉): **wine in** a ~ Flaschenwein m; **bring up on the** ~ Säugling mit der Flasche aufziehen; **be fond of the** ~ gern 'einen heben'; **II** v/t. **2.** in Flaschen abfüllen; **3.** bsd. Brit. Früchte etc. in Gläsern einmachen; ~ **up** v/t. **1.** fig. Gefühle etc.

---

unter'drücken: **bottled-up** aufgestaut; **2.** einschließen: ~ **the enemy's fleet**.

bot·tle bank s. (Alt)Glascontainer m.

bot·tled ['bɒtld] adj. in Flaschen od. (Einmach)Gläser (ab)gefüllt: ~ **beer** Flaschenbier n; → **bottle up** 1.

'**bot·tle**|**-feed** v/t. [irr.] mit der Flasche aufziehen, aus der Flasche ernähren: **bottle-fed child**; ~ **gourd** s. ♀ Flaschenkürbis m; '~**-green** adj. flaschen-, dunkelgrün; '~**-,hold·er** s. **1.** Boxen: Sekun'dant m; **2.** fig. Helfershelfer m; ~ **imp** s. Flaschenteufelchen n; '~**-neck** s. Engpass m (a. fig.); '~**-nosed** adj. mit e-r Säufernase; ~ **par·ty** s. Bottle--Party f (zu der jeder Gast e-e Flasche Wein etc. mitbringt); ~ **post** s. Flaschenpost f.

bot·tler ['bɒtlə] s. 'Abfüllma,schine f od. -betrieb m.

'**bot·tle,wash·er** s. **1.** Flaschenreiniger m; **2.** humor. Fak'totum n, 'Mädchen n für alles'.

bot·tom ['bɒtəm] **I** s. **1.** der unterste Teil, 'Unterseite f, Boden m (Gefäß etc.), Fuß m (Berg, Treppe, Seite etc.), Sohle f (Brunnen, Tal etc.): ~**s up!** sl. ex! (beim Trinken); **2.** Boden m, Grund m (Gewässer): **go to the** ~ versinken; **send to the** ~ versenken; **touch** ~ a) auf Grund geraten, b) fig. den Tiefpunkt erreichen; **the** ~ **has fallen out of the market** der Markt hat e-n Tiefstand erreicht; **3.** fig. Grund(lage f) m: **what is at the** ~ **of it?** was ist der Grund dafür?, was steckt dahinter?; **knock the** ~ **out of s.th.** et. gründlich widerlegen; **get to the** ~ **of s.th.** e-r Sache auf den Grund gehen od. kommen: **from the** ~ **up** von Grund auf; **4.** fig. das Innere, Tiefe f: **from the** ~ **of my heart** aus tiefstem Herzen; **at** ~ im Grunde; **5.** ⚓ Schiffsboden m; Schiff n: ~ **up(wards)** kieloben; **shipped in British** ~**s** in brit. Schiffen verladen; **6.** (Stuhl)Sitz m; **7.** F der Hintern, Po (-'po)' m: **smack the boy's** ~ den Jungen 'versohlen'; **smooth as a baby's** ~ glatt wie ein Kinderpopo; **8.** (unteres) Ende (Tisch, Klasse, Garten); **II** adj. **9.** unterst, letzt, äußerst: ~ **shelf** unterstes (Bücher)Brett; ~ **drawer** a) unterste Schublade (a. fig.), b) Brit. Aussteuer (-truhe) f; ~ **price** äußerster Preis; ~ **line** letzte Zeile; **III** v/t. **10.** mit e-m Boden od. Sitz versehen; **11.** ergründen; **IV** v/i. ~ **out** Rezession: die Talsohle durchschritten haben; '**bot·tomed** [-md] adj.: ~ **on** beruhend auf (dat.); **double-**~ mit doppeltem Boden; **cane-**~ mit Rohrsitz (Stuhl); '**bot·tom·less** [-lɪs] adj. bodenlos (a. fig.); unergründlich; unerschöpflich; '**bot·tom·ry** [-rɪ] s. ⚓ Bodme'rei(geld n) f.

bot·u·lism ['bɒtjʊlɪzəm] s. ✻ Botu'lismus m (Fleischvergiftung etc.).

bou·doir ['buːdwaː] (Fr.) s. Bou'doir n.

bough [baʊ] s. Ast m, Zweig m.

bought [bɔːt] pret. u. p.p. von **buy**.

boul·der ['bəʊldə] s. Fels-, Geröllblock m; geol. er'ratischer Block: ~ **period** Eiszeit f.

bou·le·vard ['buːlvaː] s. Boule'vard m, Prachtstraße f, Am. a. Hauptverkehrsstraße f.

boult → **bolt²**.

bounce [baʊns] **I** v/i. **1.** springen, (hoch)schnellen, hüpfen: **the ball** ~**d**; **he** ~**d out of his chair**; ~ **about** herumhüpfen; **2.** stürzen, stürmen: ~ **into a room**; **3.** auf-, anprallen (**against** gegen): ~ **off** abprallen; **4.** ✝ 'platzen' (Scheck); **II** v/t. **5.** Ball (auf)springen

---

lassen; **6.** Brit. F j-n drängen (**into** zu); **7.** Am. sl. j-n 'rausschmeißen' (a. fig. entlassen); **III** s. **8.** Sprungkraft f; **9.** Sprung m, Schwung m, Stoß m; **10.** Unverfrorenheit f; **11.** F 'Schwung' m, E'lan m; **12.** Am. sl. 'Rausschmiss' m (Entlassung); '**bounc·er** [-sə] s. F **1.** a) Angeber m, b) Lügner m; **2.** freche Lüge; **3.** a) 'Mordskerl' m, b) 'Prachtweib' n, c) 'Mordssache' f; **4.** Am. 'Rausschmeißer' m (in Nachtlokalen etc.); **5.** ungedeckter Scheck; '**bounc·ing** [-sɪŋ] adj. **1.** stramm (kräftig): ~ **baby**; ~ **girl**; **2.** munter, lebhaft; **3.** Mords...

bound¹ [baʊnd] **I** pret. u. p.p. von **bind**; **II** adj. **1.** **be** ~ **to do** zwangsläufig et. tun müssen; **he is** ~ **to tell me** er ist verpflichtet, es mir zu sagen; **he is** ~ **to be late** er muss ja zu spät kommen; **he is** ~ **to come** er kommt bestimmt; **I'll be** ~ ich bürge dafür, ganz gewiss; **2.** in Zssgn festgehalten od. verhindert durch: **ice-**~; **storm**~.

bound² [baʊnd] adj. (**for**) bestimmt, unter'wegs (nach): ~ **for London**; **homeward** (**outward**) ~ ⚓ auf der Heimreise (Hin-, Ausreise) (befindlich); **where are you** ~ **for?** wohin reisen od. gehen Sie?

bound³ [baʊnd] **I** s. **1.** Grenze f, Schranke f, Bereich m: **beyond all** ~**s** maß-, grenzenlos; **keep within** ~**s** in vernünftigen Grenzen halten; **set** ~**s to** Grenzen setzen (dat.), in Schranken halten; **within the** ~**s of possibility** im Bereich des Möglichen; **out of** ~**s** a) sport aus, im Aus, b) (**to**) Zutritt verboten (für); **II** v/t. **2.** be-, abgrenzen, die Grenze von et. bilden; **3.** fig. beschränken, in Schranken halten.

bound⁴ [baʊnd] **I** v/i. **1.** (hoch)springen, hüpfen (a. fig.); **2.** lebhaft gehen, laufen; **3.** an-, abprallen; **II** s. **4.** Sprung m, Satz m, Schwung m: **at a single** ~ mit 'einem Satz; **on the** ~ beim Aufspringen (Ball).

bound·a·ry ['baʊndərɪ] s. **1.** a. fig. Grenze f, a. ~ **line** 'Grenz,linie f; **2.** fig. Bereich m; **4.** ✈, phys. a) Begrenzung f, b) Rand m, c) 'Umfang m.

bound·en ['baʊndən] adj.: **my** ~ **duty** m-e Pflicht u. Schuldigkeit.

bound·er ['baʊndə] s. sl. 'Stromer' m, Kerl m.

bound·less ['baʊndlɪs] adj. □ grenzenlos, unbegrenzt, fig. a. 'übermäßig.

boun·te·ous ['baʊntɪəs] adj. □ **1.** freigebig, großzügig; **2.** (allzu) reichlich; '**boun·ti·ful** [-tɪfʊl] adj. □ → **bounteous**; **boun·ty** ['baʊntɪ] s. **1.** Freigebigkeit f; **2.** (milde) Gabe; Spende f (bsd. e-s Herrschers); **3.** ✕ Handgeld n; **4.** ✝ (bsd. Ex'port)Prämie f, Zuschuss m (**on** auf, für); **5.** Belohnung f.

bou·quet [bu'keɪ] s. **1.** Bu'kett n, (Blumen)Strauß m; **2.** A'roma n, Blume f (Wein); **3.** bsd. Am. Kompli'ment n.

Bour·bon ['buəbən] s. **1.** pol. Am. Reaktio'när m; **2.** 2 ['bɜːbən] 'Bourbon m (amer. Whiskey aus Mais).

bour·geois¹ ['buəʒwaː] contp. **I** s. Bour'geois m; **II** adj. bour'geois, (spieß)bürgerlich.

bour·geois² [bɜː'dʒɔɪs] typ. **I** s. 'Borgis f; **II** adj. in 'Borgis,lettern gedruckt.

bourn(e)¹ [buən] s. (Gieß)Bach m.

bourn(e)² [buən] s. **1.** obs. Grenze f; **2.** poet. Ziel n; Gebiet n, Bereich m.

bourse [buəs] s. ✝ Börse f.

bout [baʊt] s. **1.** Arbeitsgang m; Fechten, Tanz: Runde f: **drinking** ~ Zecherei f; **2.** (Krankheits)Anfall m, At'tacke

B

f; **3.** Zeitspanne *f*; **4.** Kraftprobe *f*, Kampf *m*; **5.** (*bsd.* Box-, Ring)Kampf *m*.

bo·vine ['bəʊvaɪn] *adj*. **1.** *zo*. Rinder...; **2.** *fig*. (*a*. *geistig*) träge, schwerfällig, dumm.

bov·ver ['bɒvə] *s*. *Brit*. *sl*. Schläge'rei *f bsd*. zwischen Rockern: ~ *boots* Rockerstiefel *pl*.

bow¹ [baʊ] **I** *s*. **1.** Verbeugung *f*, Verneigung *f*: *make one's* ~ a) sich vorstellen, b) sich verabschieden; *take a* ~ sich verbeugen, sich für den Beifall bedanken; **II** *v/t*. **2.** beugen, neigen: ~ *one's head* den Kopf neigen; ~ *one's neck fig*. den Nacken beugen; ~*ed with grief* grambgebeugt; → *knee* 1; **3.** biegen: *the wind has ~ed the branches*; **III** *v/i*. **4.** (*to*) sich verbeugen *od*. verneigen (vor *dat*.), grüßen (*acc*.): *a ~ing acquaintance* e-e Gußbekanntschaft; *on ~ing terms* auf dem Grußfuße, flüchtig bekannt; ~ *and scrape* Kratzfüße machen, *fig*. katzbuckeln; **5.** *fig*. sich beugen *od*. unter'werfen (*to dat*.): ~ *to the inevitable* sich in das Unvermeidliche fügen; ~ *down v/i*. (*to*) **1.** verehren, anbeten (*acc*.); **2.** sich unter'werfen (*dat*.); ~ *in v/t*. j-n unter Verbeugungen hin'eingeleiten; ~ *out* **I** *v/t*. j-n hin'auskomplimentieren; **II** *v/i*. sich verabschieden.

bow² [baʊ] **I** *s*. **1.** (Schieß)Bogen *m*: *have more than one string to one's* ~ *fig*. mehrere Eisen im Feuer haben; *draw the long* ~ *fig*. aufschneiden, übertreiben; **2.** ♪ (*Violin- etc.*)Bogen *m*; **3.** ♪, ⊛ a) Bogen *m*, Kurve *f*, b) *pl*. 'Bogen,zirkel *m*; **4.** Bügel *m* (*der Brille*); **5.** Knoten *m*, Schleife *f*; **II** *v/i*. **6.** ♪ den Bogen führen.

bow³ [baʊ] *s*. ♻ **1.** *a*. *pl*. Bug *m*; **2.** Bugmann *m* (*im Ruderboot*).

Bow| bells [baʊ] *s*. *pl*. Glocken *pl*. der Kirche *St. Mary le Bow* (*London*): *be born within the sound of* ~ ein echter Cockney sein; ☿ **com·pass(·es)** *s*. *sg*. *od*. *pl*. ♪, ⊛ → *bow²* 3b.

bowd·ler·ize ['baʊdləraɪz] *v/t*. Bücher (von anstößigen Stellen) säubern; *fig*. verwässern.

bow·els ['baʊəlz] *s*. *pl*. **1.** *anat*. Darm *m*; Gedärm *n*, Eingeweide *pl*.: *open* ~ ♂ offener Leib; *have open* ~ regelmäßig Stuhlgang haben; **2.** *das* Innere, Mitte *f*: *the* ~ *of the earth* das Erdinnere.

bow·er¹ ['baʊə] *s*. (Garten)Laube *f*, schattiges Plätzchen; *obs*. (Frauen)Gemach *n*.

bow·er² ['baʊə] *s*. ♻ Buganker *m*.

bow·er·y ['baʊərɪ] *s*. *hist*. *Am*. Farm *f*, Pflanzung *f*: *the* ☿ die Bowery (*heruntergekommene Straße u. Gegend in New York City*).

'bow·head ['baʊ-] *s*. *zo*. Grönlandwal *m*.

bow·ie knife ['baʊɪ-] *s*. [*irr*.] 'Bowiemesser *n* (*langes Jagdmesser*).

bowl¹ [baʊl] *s*. **1.** Napf *m*, Schale *f*; Bowle *f* (*Gefäß*); **2.** Schüssel *f*, Becken *n*; **3.** *poet*. Gelage *n*; **4.** a) (Pfeifen-) Kopf *m*, b) Höhlung *f* (*Löffel etc.*); **5.** *Am*. 'Stadion *n*.

bowl² [baʊl] **I** *s*. **1.** a) (*Bowling-, Bowls-, Kegel*)Kugel *f*, b) ~ *bowls* 1, c) Wurf *m*; **II** *v/t*. **2.** *allg*. rollen (lassen); *Bowling etc*: *die Kugel* werfen; *Ball* rollen, werfen (*a. Kricket*); *Reifen* schlagen, treiben; **III** *v/i*. **3.** a) bowlen, Bowls spielen, bowlen, Bowling spielen, c) kegeln, d) werfen; **4.** *mst* ~ *along*, (da-

'hin)gondeln' (*Wagen*); ~ *out v/t*. *Kricket*: *den Schläger* (durch Treffen des Dreistabes) ,ausmachen'; *fig*. j-n ,erledigen', schlagen; ~ *o·ver v/t*. 'umwerfen (*a*. *fig*.).

'bow-legged ['baʊ-] *adj*. säbel-, o-beinig; **'bow·legs** *s*. *pl*. Säbel-, O-Beine *pl*.

bowl·er ['baʊlə] *s*. **1.** a) Bowlsspieler (-in), b) Bowlingspieler(in), c) Kegler (-in); **2.** *Kricket*: Werfer *m*; **3.** *a*. ~ *hat* Brit. ,Me'lone' *f*.

bow·line ['baʊlɪn] *s*. ♻ Bu'lin *f*.

bowl·ing ['baʊlɪn] *s*. **1.** Bowling *n*; **2.** Kegeln *n*; ~ *al·ley s*. **1.** Bowlingbahn *f*; **2.** Kegelbahn *f*; ~ *green s*. Bowls *etc*: Rasenplatz *m*.

bowls [baʊlz] *s*. *pl*. *sg*. *konstr*. **1.** Bowls (-spiel) *n*; **2.** Kegeln *n*.

bow·man ['baʊmən] *s*. [*irr*.] Bogenschütze *m*; **'~·shot** *s*. Bogenschussweite *f*; **'~·sprit** *s*. ♻ Bugspriet *m*; ☿ *Street npr*. Straße in London mit dem Polizeigericht; **'~·string** **I** *s*. Bogensehne *f*; **II** *v/t*. erdrosseln; ~ *tie s*. (Frack)Schleife *f*, Fliege *f*; ~ *win·dow s*. Erkerfenster *n*.

bow-wow **I** *int*. [,baʊ'waʊ] wau'wau!; **II** *s*. ['baʊwaʊ] *Kindersprache*: Wau'wau *m* (*Hund*).

box¹ [bɒks] **I** *s*. **1.** Kasten *m*, Kiste *f*, *Brit*. *a*. Koffer *m*; **2.** Büchse *f*, Schachtel *f*, Etu'i *n*, Dose *f*, Kästchen *n*; **3.** Behälter *m*, (*a. Buch-, Film- etc.*)Kas'sette *f*, Hülse *f*, Gehäuse *n*, Kapsel *f*; **4.** Häus·chen *n*; Ab'teil *n*, Ab'teilung *f*, Loge *f* (*Theater etc.*); ₮₮ a) Zeugenstand *m*, b) (Geschworenen)Bank *f*; **5.** Box *f*: a) *Pferdestand*, b) *mot*. *Einstellplatz m in e-r Großgarage*; **6.** Fach *n* (*a*. *für Briefe etc.*); **7.** Kutschbock *m*; **8.** *Am*. Wagenkasten *m*; **9.** *Baseball*: Standplatz *m* (*des Schlägers*); **10.** a) Postfach *n*, b) → *box number*, c) Briefkasten *m*; **11.** *pol*. (Wahl)Urne *f*; **12.** *typ*. Kasten *m*, Kästchen *n* (*eingeschobener, umrandeter Text*), Rub'rik *f*; **13.** F ,Kasten' *m* (*Fernsehapparat, Fußballtor etc.*); **II** *v/t*. **14.** in Schachteln, Kasten *etc*. legen, packen, einschließen; **15.** ~ *the compass* a) ♻ alle Kompasspunkte aufzählen, b) *fig*. alle Gesichtspunkte vorbringen u. schließlich zum Ausgangspunkt zurückkehren, e-e völlige Kehrtwendung machen; ~ *in v/t*. **1.** → *box¹* 14; **2.** = ~ *up v/t*. einschließen, -klemmen.

box² [bɒks] **I** *s*. **1.** Schlag *m* mit der Hand: ~ *on the ear* Ohrfeige *f*; **II** *v/t*. **2.** ~ *s.o.'s ears* j-n ohrfeigen; **3.** gegen j-n boxen; **III** *v/i*. **4.** *sport* boxen.

box³ [bɒks] *s*. ♀ Buchsbaum(holz *n*) *m*.

box| bar·rage *s*. ✗Abriegelungsfeuer *n*; **'~·calf** *s*. 'Boxkalf *n* (*Leder*); ~ **cam·er·a** *s*. *phot*. 'Box(,kamera) *f*; **'~·car** *s*. ⛟ *Am*. geschlossener Güterwagen.

box·er ['bɒksə] *s*. **1.** *sport* Boxer *m*; **2.** *zo*. Boxer *m* (*Hunderasse*). **3.** ☿ *hist*. Boxer *m* (*Anhänger e-s chinesischen Geheimbundes um 1900*); ~ *shorts pl*. 'Boxershorts *pl*. (*Hose*).

box·ing ['bɒksɪŋ] *s*. **1.** *sport* Boxen *n*; **2.** Ver-, Einpacken *n*; ☿ *Day s*. *Brit*. der zweite Weihnachtsfeiertag; ~ *gloves pl*. Boxhandschuhe *pl*.; ~ *match s*. *sport* Boxkampf *m*.

box| i·ron *s*. Bolzen(bügel)eisen *n*; ~ **junc·tion** *s*. *Brit*. markierte Kreuzung, in die bei stehendem Verkehr nicht eingefahren werden darf; **'~·keep·er** *s*. *thea*. 'Logenschließer(in); ~ *num·ber s*. 'Chiffre(nummer) *f* (*in Zeitungsan-*

zeigen); ~ *of·fice s*. **1.** (The'ater- *etc*.) Kasse *f*; **2.** *be good* ~ ein Kassenerfolg *od*. -schlager sein; **3.** Einspielergebnis *n*; **'~·,of·fice** *adj*. Kassen...: ~ *success od*. *draw* Kassenschlager *m*; ~ *ra·di·o s*. F Dampfradio *n*; **'~·room** *s*. Abstellraum *m*; **'~·,wal·lah** *s*. *Brit.-Ind*. **1.** F indischer Hausierer; **2.** *contp*. Handlungsreisende(r) *m*; **'~·wood** →*box³*.

boy [bɔɪ] **1.** Knabe *m*, Junge *m*, Bursche *m*, ,Mann' *m*: *the* (*od*. *our*) ~*s* unsere Jung(en)s (*z. B. Soldaten*); *old* ~ a) ,alter Knabe', b) → *old boy*; *a* ~ *child* ein fest männlichen Geschlechts, ein Junge; ~ *singer* Sängerknabe; ~ *wonder* oft *iro*. Wunderknabe; **2.** Laufbursche *m*; **3.** Boy *m*, (*bsd*. eingeborener) Diener.

boy·cott ['bɔɪkət] **I** *v/t*. boykottieren; **II** *s*. Boy'kott *m*.

'boy·friend *s*. Freund *m* (*e-s Mädchens*).

boy·hood ['bɔɪhʊd] *s*. Knabenalter *n*, Kindheit *f*, Jugend *f*.

boy·ish ['bɔɪɪʃ] *adj*. □ a) jungenhaft: ~ *laughter*, b) knabenhaft.

boy scout *s*. Pfadfinder *m*.

bo·zo ['bəʊzəʊ] *s*. *Am*. *sl*. a) Kerl *m*, b) *contp*. Blödmann *m*.

B pow·er sup·ply *s*. ⚡ Ener'gieversorgung *f* des An'odenkreises.

bra [brɑː] *s*. F für *brassière*: B'H *m*.

brace [breɪs] **I** *s*. **1.** ⊛ Stütze *f*, Strebe *f*, (*a*. ✗ Zahn)Klammer *f*, Anker *m*, Versteifung *f*; (Trag)Band *n*, Gurt *m*; ✗ Stützband *f*; **2.** ⊛ Griff *m* der Bohrkurbel: ~ *and bit* Bohrkurbel *f*; **3.** △, ♪, ♪, *typ*. (geschweifte) Klammer *f*; **4.** ♻ Brasse *f*; **5.** (*a pair of*) ~ *s pl*. *Brit*. Hosenträger *m od*. *pl*.; **6.** (*pl*. *brace*) ein Paar, zwei (*bsd*. *Hunde, Kleinwild, Pistolen; contp. Personen*); **II** *v/t*. **7.** ⊛ versteifen, -streben, stützen, verankern, befestigen; **8.** ⊛, ♪, *typ*. klammern; **9.** ♻ brassen; **10.** *fig*. stärken, erfrischen; **11.** *a*. ~ *up* s-e Kräfte, s-n Mut zs.-nehmen; **12.** ~ *o.s.* (*up*) a) → 11, b) *for s.th*. sich auf et. gefasst machen; **brace·let** ['breɪslɪt] *s*. **1.** Armband *n*, -reif *m*, -spange *f*; **2.** *pl*. *humor*. Handschellen *pl*.; **'brac·er** [-sə] *s*. *Am*. F Stärkung *f*, *bsd*. Schnäpschen *n*; *fig*. Ermunterung *f*.

bra·chi·al ['breɪkjəl] *adj*. Arm...; **'brachi·ate** [-kɪeɪt] *adj*. ♀ paarweise gegenständig.

brach·y·ce·phal·ic [,brækɪke'fælɪk] *adj*. kurzköpfig.

brac·ing ['breɪsɪŋ] *adj*. stärkend, kräftigend, erfrischend (*bsd. Klima*).

brack·en ['brækən] *s*. **1.** Farnkraut *n*; **2.** farnbewachsene Gegend.

brack·et ['brækɪt] *s*. **1.** ⊛ Träger *m*, Halter *m*; **2.** Kon'sole *f*, Krag-, Tragstein *m*, Stützbalken *m*, Winkelstütze *f*; **3.** Wandarm *m*; **4.** ✗Gabel *f* (*Einschießen*); **5.** ♪, *typ*. *Am*. *mst* eckige) Klammer: *in* ~*s*; *square* ~*s* eckige Klammern; **6.** Gruppe *f*, Klasse *f*, Stufe *f*: *lower income* ~ niedrige Einkommensstufe; **II** *v/t*. **7.** einklammern; **8.** *a*. ~ *together* in dieselbe Gruppe einordnen; auf gleiche Stufe stellen; **9.** ✗eingabeln.

brack·ish ['brækɪʃ] *adj*. brackig.

bract [brækt] *s*. ♀ Deckblatt *n*.

brad [bræd] *s*. ⊛ Nagel *m* ohne Kopf; (Schuh)Zwecke *f*.

Brad·shaw ['brædʃɔː] *s*. *Brit*. (Eisenbahn)Kursbuch *n* (*1839–1961*).

brae [breɪ] *s*. *Scot*. Abhang *m*, Böschung *f*.

brag [bræg] **I** *s*. **1.** Prahle'rei *f*; **2.** → *braggart* I; **II** *v/i*. **3.** (*about, of*) prahlen (mit), sich rühmen (*gen.*).

brag·ga·do·ci·o [ˌbrægəˈdəʊtʃɪəʊ] *s.* Prahle'rei *f*, Aufschneide'rei *f*.

brag·gart [ˈbrægət] **I** *s.* Prahler *m*, Aufschneider *m*; **II** *adj.* prahlerisch.

Brah·man [ˈbrɑːmən] *s.* Brah'mane *m*; **'Brah·ma·ni** [-nɪ] *s.* Brah'manin *f*; **Brah·man·ic, Brah·man·i·cal** [brɑːˈmænɪk(l)] *adj.* brah'manisch.

Brah·min [ˈbrɑːmɪn] *s.* **1.** → **Brahman**; **2.** gebildete, kultivierte Per'son; **3.** *Am. iro.* dünkelhafte(r) Intellektu'elle(r).

braid [breɪd] **I** *v/t.* **1.** *bsd. Haar, Bänder* flechten; **2.** mit Litze, Band, Borte besetzen, schmücken; **3.** ⊕ um'spinnen; **II** *s.* **4.** (*Haar*)Flechte *f*; **5.** Borte *f*, Litze *f*, Tresse *f* (*bsd.* ✗): **gold ~** goldene Tresse(n); **'braid·ed** [-dɪd] *adj.* geflochten; mit Litze *etc.* besetzt; um-'sponnen; **'braid·ing** [-dɪŋ] *s.* Litzen *pl.*, Borten *pl.*, Tressen *pl.*, Besatz *m*.

braille [breɪl] *s.* Blindenschrift *f*.

brain [breɪn] **I** *s.* **1.** Gehirn *n*; → **blow out** 5; **2.** *fig.* (*oft pl.*) a) ‚Köpfchen' *n*, ‚Grips' *m*, Verstand *m*, b) Kopf *m* (*Leiter*), *b.s.* ‚Drahtzieher' *m*: **a clear ~** ein klarer Kopf; **who is the ~ behind it?** wessen Idee ist das?; **have ~s** intelligent sein, ‚Köpfchen' haben; **have (got) s.th on the ~** et. dauernd im Kopf haben; **cudgel** (*od.* **rack**) **one's ~s** sich den Kopf zerbrechen, sich das Hirn zermartern; **pick s.o.'s ~s** a) geistigen Diebstahl an j-m begehen, b) j-n ‚ausholen'; **II** *v/t.* **3.** j-m den Schädel einschlagen; **~ child** *s.* 'Geistespro,dukt *n*; **'~-dead** *adj.* **1.** ✝ gehirntot; **2.** *iro.* ge'hirnampu,tiert; **~ death** *s.* ✝ Hirntod *m*; **~ drain** *s.* Abwanderung *f* von Wissenschaftlern, Brain-Drain *m*.

brained [breɪnd] *adj.*, *nur in Zssgn* ...köpfig, mit e-m ... Gehirn: **feeble-~** schwachköpfig.

'brain|·fag *s.* geistige Erschöpfung; **~ fe·ver** *s.* ✝ Gehirnentzündung *f*.

brain·less [ˈbreɪnlɪs] *adj.* **1.** hirnlos, dumm; **2.** gedankenlos.

'brain|·pan *s. anat.* Hirnschale *f*, Schädeldecke *f*; **'~-storm** *s.* **1.** geistige Verwirrung; **2.** verrückter Einfall; **3.** *Am.* F → **brain wave** 2; **'~-storm·ing** *s.* Brainstorming *n* (*Problemlösung durch Sammeln spontaner Einfälle*).

brains trust [breɪnz] *s.* **1.** *Brit.* Teilnehmer *pl.* an e-r 'Podiumsdiskussi,on; **2.** → **brain trust**.

brain| trust *s. Am.* F po'litische *od.* wirtschaftliche Beratergruppe, Brain-Trust *m*; **~ trust·er** *s. Am.* F Brain-Truster *m*, Mitglied *n* e-s **brain trust**; **~ twist·er** *s.* ‚(harte) Nuss', schwierige Aufgabe; **'~-wash** *v/t. bsd. pol.* j-n e-r Gehirnwäsche unter'ziehen; *weitS.* verdummen; **'~-wash·ing** *s. pol.* Gehirnwäsche *f*; **~ wave** *s.* **1.** Hirn(strom)welle *f*; **2.** F Geistesblitz *m*, ‚tolle I'dee'; **'~-work·er** *s.* Kopf-, Geistesarbeiter *m*.

brain·y [ˈbreɪnɪ] *adj.* gescheit.

braise [breɪz] *v/t. Küche:* schmoren: **~d beef** Schmorbraten *m*.

brake¹ [breɪk] **I** *s.* ⊕ Bremse *f*, Hemmschuh *m* (*a. fig.*): **put on** (*od.* **apply**) **the ~** bremsen, die Bremse ziehen, *fig. a.* der Sache Einhalt gebieten; **II** *v/t.* bremsen.

brake² [breɪk] **I** *s.* (*Flachs- etc.*)Breche *f*; **II** *v/t. Flachs etc.* brechen.

brake³ → **break** 11.

brake| block → **brake shoe**; **~ horse·pow·er** *s.* ⊕ (*abbr.* **b.h.p.**) Nutz-, Bremsleistung *f*; **~ flu·id** *s.* Bremsflüs-

---

sigkeit *f*; **~ lin·ing** *s.* Bremsbelag *m*; **'~-man** *Am.* → **brakesman**; **~ par·a·chute** *s.* ✈ Bremsfallschirm *m*; **~ shoe** *s.* ⊕ Bremsbacke *f*, -klotz *m*.

brakes·man [ˈbreɪksmən] *s.* [*irr.*] ⚅ *Brit.* Bremser *m*.

brak·ing dis·tance [ˈbreɪkɪŋ] *s. mot.* Bremsweg *m*.

bra·less [ˈbrɑːlɪs] *adj.* F ohne B'H.

bram·ble [ˈbræmbl] *s.* **1.** ⚘ Brombeerstrauch *m*; **~ jelly** Brombeergelee *n*; **2.** Dornenstrauch *m*, -gestrüpp *n*; **~ rose** *s.* ⚘ Hundsrose *f*.

bram·bly [ˈbræmblɪ] *adj.* dornig.

bran [bræn] *s.* Kleie *f*.

branch [brɑːntʃ] **I** *s.* **1.** ⚘ Zweig *m*; **2.** *fig.* a) Zweig *m*, ('Unter)Abteilung *f*, Sparte *f*, b) Branche *f*, Wirtschafts-, Geschäftszweig *m*, c) *a.* **~ of service** ✗ Waffen-, Truppengattung *f*; **3.** *fig.* Zweig *m*, 'Linie *f* (*Familie*); **4.** *a.* **~ establishment** ✝ Außen-, Zweig-, Nebenstelle *f*, Fili'ale *f*, Niederlassung *f*: **~ bank** Filialbank *f*; **5.** ⚅ Zweigbahn *f*; 'Neben,linie *f*; **6.** *geogr.* a) Arm *m* (*Gewässer*), b) Ausläufer *m* (*Gebirge*), c) *Am.* Nebenfluss *m*, Flüsschen *n*; **II** *adj.* **7.** Zweig..., Tochter..., Filial..., Neben...; **III** *v/i.* **8.** Zweige treiben; **9.** *oft* **~ off** (*od.* **out**) sich verzweigen, sich ausbreiten; abzweigen: **here the road ~es** hier gabelt sich die Straße; **~ out** *v/i.* s-e Unter'nehmungen ausdehnen, sich vergrößern; → **branch** 9.

bran·chi·a [ˈbræŋkɪə] *pl.* **-chi·ae** [-kɪiː] *s. zo.* Kieme *f*; **'bran·chi·ate** [-kɪeɪt] *adj. zo.* Kiemen tragend.

branch| line *s.* ⚅ 'Zweig-, 'Neben,linie *f*, **2.** 'Seiten,linie *f* (*Familie*); **~ man·ag·er** *s.* Fili'al-, Zweigstellenleiter *m*; **~ of·fice** *s.* Fili'ale *f*; **~ road** *s. Am.* Nebenstraße *f*.

brand [brænd] **I** *s.* **1.** Feuerbrand *m*; *fig.* Fackel *f*, **2.** Brandmal *n* (*auf Tieren*); **3.** *fig.* Schandmal *n*, -fleck *m*: **~ of Cain** Kainszeichen *n*; **4.** Brand-, Brenneisen *n*; **5.** a) ✝ (Handels-, Schutz)Marke *f*, Warenzeichen *n*, Markenbezeichnung *f*, Sorte *f*, Klasse *f*; **~ awareness** Markenbewusstsein *n*; **~ leader** Markenführer *m*; **~ loyalty** Markentreue *f*; **~ name** Markenname *m*; **best ~ of tea** beste Sorte Tee, b) *fig.* ‚Sorte' *f*, Art *f*: **his ~ of humour** *iro.*; **6.** ⚘ Brand *m* (*Getreidekrankheit*); **II** *v/t.* **7.** mit e-m Brandmal *od.* -zeichen *od.* ✝ mit e-r Schutzmarke *etc.* versehen: **~ed goods** Markenartikel; **8.** *fig.* brandmarken; **9.** einprägen (**on s.o's mind** j-m).

brand·ing i·ron [ˈbrændɪŋ] → **brand** 4.

bran·dish [ˈbrændɪʃ] *v/t.* (*bsd. drohend*) schwingen.

brand·ling [ˈbrændlɪŋ] *s. ichth.* junger Lachs.

brand-new [ˌbrændˈnjuː] *adj.* (funkel-)nagelneu.

bran·dy [ˈbrændɪ] *s.* Weinbrand *m*, Kognak *m*; **'~-ball** *s. Brit.* 'Weinbrandbon,bon *m*.

bran-new [ˌbrænˈnjuː] → **brand-new**.

brant [brænt] *s. orn.* e-e Wildgans *f*.

brash [bræʃ] **I** *s.* **1.** *geol.* Trümmergestein *n*; **2.** ⚕ Eisträmmer *pl.*; **II** *adj. Am.* **3.** brüchig, bröckelig; **4.** *fig.* a) (nass)forsch, frech, unverfroren, b) ungestüm, c) grell, aufdringlich.

brass [brɑːs] **I** *s.* **1.** Messing *n*; **2.** *Brit.* ziselierte Gedenktafel (*aus Messing od. Bronze, bsd. in Kirchen*); **3.** Messingzierrat *m*; **4.** ♪ die 'Blechinstru,mente *pl.* (*e-s Orchesters*), Blechbläser *pl.*; **5.** F *coll.* ‚hohe Tiere' *pl.*, *a.* hohe

---

Offi'ziere *pl.*: **top ~** die höchsten ‚Tiere' (*e-s Konzerns etc.*) *od.* Offiziere; **6.** *Brit. sl.* ‚Moos' *n*, ‚Kies' *m* (*Geld*); **7.** F Unverschämtheit *f*, Frechheit *f*; → **bold** 2; **II** *adj.* **8.** Messing...; **III** *v/t.* **9.** mit Messing über'ziehen.

bras·sard [ˈbræsɑːd] *s.* Armbinde *f* (*als Abzeichen*).

brass band *s.* ♪ 'Blaska,pelle *f*; 'Blechmu,sik *f*; Mili'tärka,pelle *f*.

bras·se·rie [ˈbræsərɪ] (*Fr.*) *s.* 'Bierstube *f*, -lo,kal *n*; Restau'rant *n*.

brass| far·thing *s.* F ‚roter Heller': **I don't care a ~** das kümmert mich e-n Dreck; **~ hat** *s.* ✗ *sl.* ‚hohes Tier', hoher Offi'zier.

bras·sière [ˈbræsɪə] (*Fr.*) *s.* Büstenhalter *m*, F B'H *m*.

brass| knuck·les *s. pl. Am.* Schlagring *m*; **~ plate** *s.* Messingschild *n* (*mit Namen*), Türschild *n*; **~ tacks** *s. pl.:* **get down to ~** zur Sache kommen; **'~-ware** *s.* Messinggeschirr *n*, -gegenstände *pl.*; **~ winds** *bsd. Am.* → **brass** 4.

brass·y [ˈbrɑːsɪ] *adj.* □ **1.** messingartig, -farbig; **2.** blechern (*Klang*); **3.** *fig.* unverschämt, frech.

brat [bræt] *s.* Balg *m, n*, Gör *n*, Racker *m* (*Kind*).

bra·va·do [brəˈvɑːdəʊ] *s.* gespielte Tapferkeit, her'ausforderndes Benehmen.

brave [breɪv] **I** *adj.* □ **1.** tapfer, mutig, unerschrocken: **as ~ as a lion** mutig wie ein Löwe; **2.** *obs.* stattlich, ansehnlich; **II** *s.* **3.** *poet.* Tapfere(r) *m*: **the ~** *coll.* die Tapferen; **III** *v/t.* **4.** mutig begegnen, trotzen, die Stirn bieten (*dat.*): **~ death**; **~ it out** es (trotzig) durchstehen; **5.** her'ausfordern; **'brav·er·y** [-vərɪ] *s.* **1.** Tapferkeit *f*, Mut *m*; **2.** Pracht *f*, Putz *m*, Staat *m*.

bra·vo¹ [ˌbrɑːˈvəʊ] **I** *int.* 'bravo!; **II** *pl.* **-vos** *s.* 'Bravo(ruf *m*) *n*.

bra·vo² [ˈbrɑːvəʊ] *s.* 'Bravo *m*, Ban'dit *m*.

bra·vu·ra [brəˈvʊərə] *s.* ♪ *od. fig.* **1.** Bra'vour *f*, Meisterschaft *f*; **2.** Bra-'vourstück *n*.

brawl [brɔːl] **I** *s.* **1.** Streite'rei *f*, Kra'keel *m*, Lärm *m*; **2.** Raufe'rei *f*, Kra'wall *m*, ⚖ Raufhandel *m*; **II** *v/i.* **3.** kra'keelen, zanken, keifen, lärmen; **4.** rauschen (*Fluss*); **'brawl·er** [-lə] *s.* Raufbold *m*, Kra'keeler(in); **'brawl·ing** [-lɪŋ] *s.* **1.** → **brawl** 1, 2; **2.** ⚖ *Brit.* Ruhestörung *f* *bsd. in Kirchen*.

brawn [brɔːn] *s.* **1.** Muskeln *pl.*; **2.** *fig.* Muskelkraft *f*, Stärke *f*; **3.** Presskopf *m*, (Schweine)Sülze *f*; **'brawn·y** [-nɪ] *adj.* musku'lös; *fig.* kräftig, stämmig, stark.

bray¹ [breɪ] **I** *s.* **1.** (*bsd. Esels*)Schrei *m*; **2.** Schmettern *n* (*Trompete*); gellender *od.* 'durchdringender Ton; **II** *v/i.* **3.** schreien (*bsd. Esel*); **4.** schmettern; kreischen, gellen.

bray² [breɪ] *v/t.* zerstoßen, -reiben, -stampfen (*im Mörser*).

braze [breɪz] *v/t.* ⊕ (hart)löten.

bra·zen [ˈbreɪzn] **I** *adj.* □ **1.** ehern, bronzen, Messing...; **2.** *fig.* me'tallisch, grell (*Ton*); **3.** *a.* **~-faced** *fig.* unverschämt, frech, schamlos; **II** *v/t.* **4.** *s.a.* **~ it out** die Sache ‚frech wie Oskar' durchstehen; **'bra·zen·ness** [-nɪs] *s.* Unverschämtheit *f*.

bra·zier [ˈbreɪzjə] *s.* **1.** Kupferschmied *m*, Gelbgießer *m*; **2.** große Kohlenpfanne *f*.

Bra·zil [brəˈzɪl] → **brazilwood**; **Bra·zil·ian** [-ljən] **I** *adj.* brasili'anisch; **II** *s.* Brasili'aner(in).

Bra·zil| nut *s.* ⚘ 'Paranuss *f*; **⚹-wood** *s.*

B

✝ Bra'sil-, Rotholz *n*.

breach [bri:tʃ] **I** *s*. **1.** *fig.* Bruch *m*, Über'tretung *f*, Verletzung *f*, Verstoß *m*: **~ of contract** Vertragsbruch; **~ of duty** Pflichtverletzung; **~ of etiquette** Verstoß gegen den guten Ton; **~ of faith** (*od.* **trust**) Vertrauensbruch, Untreue *f*; **~ of the law** Übertretung des Gesetzes; **~ of the peace** öffentliche Ruhestörung, Aufruhr *m*, *oft* grober Unfug; **~ of promise** (**to marry**) ⚖ Bruch des Eheversprechens; **~ of prison** Ausbruch *m* aus dem Gefängnis; **2.** *fig.* Bruch *m*, Riss *m*, Zwist *m*; **3.** ✗ *u. fig.* Bresche *f*, Lücke *f*: **stand in** (*od.* **step into**) **the ~** in die Bresche springen, (aus)helfen; **4.** ⚓ Einbruch *m* der Wellen; **5.** ◉ 'Durchbruch *m*; **II** *v/t.* **6.** ✗ e-e Bresche schlagen in (*acc.*), durch'brechen; **7.** *Vertrag etc.* brechen.

bread [bred] **I** *s*. **1.** Brot *n*; **2.** *fig.* **daily ~** (tägliches) Brot, 'Lebens,unterhalt *m*: **earn one's ~** sein Brot verdienen; **~ and butter** a) Butterbrot, b) Lebensunterhalt, 'Brötchen' *pl.*; **quarrel with one's ~ and butter** a) mit s-m Los hadern, b) sich ins eigene Fleisch schneiden; **~ buttered both sides** großes Glück, Wohlstand *m*; **know which side one's ~ is buttered** s-n Vorteil (er)kennen; **take the ~ out of s.o.'s mouth** j-n brotlos machen; **cast one's ~ upon the waters** et. ohne Aussicht auf Erfolg tun; **~ and water** Wasser u. Brot; **~ and wine** *eccl.* Abendmahl *n*; **3.** *sl.* ‚Kies‘ *m*, ‚Kohlen‘ *pl.* (*Geld*); **II** *v/t.* **4.** *Am. Küche:* panieren.

,**bread**-**and**-'**but·ter** *adj.* F **1.** einträglich, Brot...: **~ education** Brotstudium *n*; **2.** praktisch, sachlich; **3.** **~ letter** Dankesbrief *m* für erwiesene Gastfreundschaft; '**~,bas·ket** *s*. **1.** Brotkorb *m*; **2.** *sl.* Magen *m*; **~ bin** *s*. Brotkasten *m*; '**~·board** *s*. *Brit.* Brotschneidebrett *n*: **~ circuit** ⚡ Brettschaltung *f*; '**~·crumb I** *s*. **1.** Brotkrume *f*; **2.** *das* Weiche des Brotes (*ohne Rinde*); **II** *v/t.* **3.** *Küche:* panieren; '**~·fruit** *s*. ⚘ **1.** Brotfrucht *f*; **2.** → **bread tree**; **~ grain** *s*. Brotgetreide *n*; '**~·line** *s*. Schlange *f* von Bedürftigen (*an die Nahrungsmittel verteilt werden*): **live on the ~** an der Armutsgrenze leben; **~ sauce** *s*. Brottunke *f*; '**~·stuffs** *s. pl.* Brotgetreide *n*.

breadth [bredθ] *s*. **1.** Breite *f*, Weite *f*; **2.** ◉ Bahn *f*, Breite *f* (*Stoff*); **3.** *fig.* Ausdehnung *f*, Größe *f*; **4.** *fig., a. Kunst:* Großzügigkeit *f*.

bread| tree *s*. ⚘ Brotfruchtbaum *m*; '**~,win·ner** *s*. Ernährer *m*, Geldverdiener *m* (*e-r Familie*).

break [breɪk] **I** *s*. **1.** (Ab-, Zer-, 'Durch)Brechen *n*, Bruch *m* (*a. fig.*), Abbruch *m* (*a. fig. von Beziehungen*), Bruchstelle *f*: **~ in the voice** Umschlagen *n* der Stimme; **~ of day** Tagesanbruch *m*; **a ~ with tradition** ein Bruch mit der Tradition; **make a ~ for it** (sich) flüchten, das Weite suchen; **2.** Lücke *f* (*a. fig.*), Zwischenraum *m*; Lichtung *f*; **3.** Pause *f*, Ferien *pl.*; Unter'brechung *f* (*a. ⚡*), Aufhören *n*, *fig. u. Metrik: a.* Zä'sur *f*: **without a ~** ununterbrochen; **tea ~** Teepause; **4.** Wechsel *m*, Abwechslung *f*; 'Umschwung *m*; Sturz *m* (*Wetter, Preis*); **5.** *typ.* Absatz *m*; **6.** *Billard:* Serie *f*; *Tennis:* Break *m, n* (*Durchbrechen des gegnerischen Aufschlagspiels*); **8.** *Jazz:* Break *m, n*; **9.** *Am. sl.* Chance *f*, Gelegenheit *f*: **bad ~**, ‚Pech‘ *n*; **give s.o. a ~** j-m e-e Chance geben; **10.** *Am. sl.*

Schnitzer *m*, Faux'pas *m*; **11.** a) Kremser *m*, b) Wagen *m* zum Einfahren von Pferden; **12.** ◉ → **brake**[1]; **II** *v/t.* [*irr.*] **13.** brechen (*a. fig.*), auf-, 'durch-, zerbrechen, ent'zweibrechen: **~ one's arm** (sich) den Arm brechen; **~ s.o.'s heart** j-m das Herz brechen; **~ jail** aus dem Gefängnis ausbrechen; **~ a seal** ein Siegel erbrechen; **~ s.o.'s resistance** j-s Widerstand brechen; **14.** *Geldschein* klein machen, wechseln; **15.** zerreißen, -schlagen, -trümmern, ka'puttmachen: **I've broken my watch** m-e Uhr ist kaputt; **16.** unter'brechen (*a. ⚡*), aufheben, -geben: **~ a journey** e-e Reise unterbrechen; **~ the circuit** ⚡ den Stromkreis unterbrechen; **~ the silence** das Schweigen brechen; **~ a custom** e-e Gewohnheit aufgeben; **17.** *Vorrat etc.* anbrechen; **18.** *fig.* brechen, verletzen, verstoßen gegen, nicht (ein-) halten: **~ a contract** e-n Vertrag brechen; **~ the law** das Gesetz übertreten; **19.** *fig.* zu'grunde richten, ruinieren, *a. j-n* ka'puttmachen: **~ the bank** die Bank sprengen; **20.** vermindern, abschwächen; **21.** *Tier* zähmen, abrichten; gewöhnen (**to** an *acc.*): **~ a horse to harness** ein Pferd einfahren *od.* zureiten; **22.** *Nachricht* eröffnen: **~ that news gently to her** bring ihr diese (*schlechte*) Nachricht schonend bei; **23.** ⚡ pflügen, urbar machen: **~ ground**[1] 1; **24.** *Flagge* aufziehen; **III** *v/i.* [*irr.*] **25.** brechen, zerbrechen, -springen, -reißen, platzen, ent'zwei-, ka'puttgehen: **glass ~s easily** Glas bricht leicht; **the rope broke** das Seil zerriss; **26.** *fig.* brechen (*Herz, Kraft*); **27.** sich brechen (*Wellen*); **28.** unter'brochen werden; **29.** sich (zer)teilen (*Wolken*); sich auflösen (*Heer*); **30.** nachlassen (*Gesundheit*); zu'grunde gehen (*Geschäft*); vergehen, aufhören; **31.** anbrechen (*Tag*); aus-, losbrechen (*Sturm, Gelächter*); **32.** brechen (*Stimme*): **his voice broke** a) er befand sich im Stimmwechsel, er mutierte; **33.** sich verändern, 'umschlagen (*Wetter*); **34.** ✝ im Preise fallen; **35.** bekannt (gegeben) werden (*Nachricht*); **36.** *Boxen:* brechen;

Zssgn mit adv. u. prp.:

break| a·way *v/i.* **1.** ab-, losbrechen; **2.** sich losreißen, ausreißen; **3.** sich trennen, sich lossagen, absplittern; **4.** *sport* a) sich absetzen (**from, of** von), ausreißen, b) *Am.* e-n Fehlstart verursachen; **~ down I** *v/t.* **1.** niederreißen, abbrechen; **2.** *fig. j-n, j-s Widerstand* brechen; **3.** *einteilen (a. ⚡);* auflösen; *Statistik:* aufgliedern, -schlüsseln; **II** *v/i.* **4.** zs.-brechen (*a. fig.*); **5.** zerbrechen (*a. fig.*); **6.** versagen, scheitern; stecken bleiben; *mot.* e-e Panne haben; **7.** *fig.* zerfallen (*in einzelne Gruppen etc.*); **~ e·ven** *v/i.* ✝ kostendeckend arbeiten; **~ forth** *v/i.* **1.** her'vorbrechen; **2.** sich erheben (*Geschrei etc.*); **~ in I** *v/t.* **1.** einschlagen; **2.** *Tier* abrichten; *Pferd* zureiten; *Auto etc.* einfahren; *Person* einarbeiten; *j-n* gewöhnen (**to** an *acc.*); **II** *v/i.* **3.** einbrechen; **~ on** sich einmischen in (*acc.*), *Unterhaltung etc.* unterbrechen; **~ in·to** *v/i.* **1.** einbrechen *od.* -dringen in (*acc.*); **2.** *fig.* in Gelächter etc. ausbrechen; **3.** *Vorrat etc.* anbrechen; **~ off** *v/t. u. v/i.* abbrechen (*a. fig.*); **~ out** *v/i.* ausbrechen (*a. fig.*): **~ in a rash** ✚ e-n Ausschlag bekommen; **~ through I** *v/t.* (durch)'brechen, über'winden; **II** *v/i.* 'durchbrechen, erschei

nen; **~ up I** *v/t.* **1.** zer-, aufbrechen; zerlegen (*a. hunt. Wild*); weitS. zerstören, ka'puttmachen, *fig. a.* zerrütten: **that breaks me up!** F ich lach mich tot!; **2.** abbrechen, *Sitzung etc.* aufheben, *Versammlung, Menge, a. Haushalt* auflösen; **II** *v/i.* **3.** aufgehoben werden, sich auflösen (*Versammlung etc., a. Nebel etc.*); **4.** aufhören; schließen (*Schule etc.*); **5.** zerbrechen (*Ehe etc.*); sich trennen, Schluss machen (*Paar*); zerfallen (*Reich etc.*); **6.** *fig.* zs.-brechen (*Person*); **7.** aufklaren (*Wetter, Himmel*); **8.** aufbrechen (*Straße, Eis*); **~ with** *v/i.* brechen *od.* Schluss machen mit (*e-m Freund, e-r Gewohnheit*).

break·a·ble ['breɪkəbl] **I** *adj.* zerbrechlich; **II** *s. pl.* zerbrechliche Ware *sg.*; '**break·age** [-kɪdʒ] *s*. **1.** Bruch(stelle *f*) *m*; **2.** Bruchschaden *m*; '**break·a·way** *s*. **1.** (*from*) *pol.* Absplitterung *f*, Lossagung *f* (von), Bruch *m* (mit): **~ group** Splittergruppe *f*; **2.** *sport* a) Ausreißen *n*, b) 'Durchbruch *m*, c) *Am.* Fehlstart *m*.

'**break·down** *s*. **1.** Zs.-bruch *m*, Scheitern *n*: **nervous ~** Nervenzusammenbruch; **~ of marriage** ⚖ Zerrüttung *f* der Ehe; **2.** Panne *f*, (Ma'schinen)Schaden *m*, (Betriebs)Störung *f*; ⚡ 'Durchschlag *m*; **3.** Zerlegung *f*, *bsd. statistische* Aufgliederung, Aufschlüsselung *f*, Ana'lyse *f* (*a.* 🧪); **~ serv·ice** *s. mot. Brit.* Pannendienst *m*; **~ truck, ~ van** *s. Brit.* Abschleppwagen *m*; **~ volt·age** *s*. ⚡ 'Durchschlagspannung *f*.

break·er ['breɪkə] *s*. **1.** Brecher *m* (*bsd. in Zssgn Person od. Gerät*); 'Abbruchunter,nehmer *m*, Verschrotter *m*; **2.** Abrichter *m*, Dres'seur *m*; **3.** Brecher *m*, Sturzwelle *f*: **~s** Brandung *f*.

,**break·'e·ven| point** *s*. ✝ Rentabili'tätsgrenze *f*, Gewinnschwelle *f*; **~ price** *s*. Selbstkostenpreis *m*.

break·fast ['brekfəst] **I** *s*. Frühstück *n*: **~ television** Frühstücksfernsehen *n* (*am frühen Morgen*); **have ~** → **II** *v/i.* frühstücken.

'**break-in** → **breaking-in**.

break·ing ['breɪkɪŋ] *s*. Bruch *m*: **~ of the voice** Stimmbruch, -wechsel *m*; **~ and entering** ⚖ Einbruch *m*; '**~-in** *s*. **1.** ⚖ Einbruch *m*; **2.** Abrichten *n*; Zureiten *n*; *mot.* Einfahren *n*; Einarbeitung *f*, Anlernen *n von Personen*; **~ point** *s*. ◉, *phys.* Bruch-, Festigkeitsgrenze *f*: **to ~** *fig.* bis zur (totalen) Erschöpfung: **have reached ~** kurz vor dem Zs.bruch stehen; **~ strength** *s*. ◉, *phys.* Bruch-, Reißfestigkeit *f*.

'**break·neck** *adj.* halsbrecherisch; '**~-out** *s*. Ausbruch *m* (*aus Gefängnis etc.*); '**~·through** *s. bsd.* ✗ 'Durchbruch *m* (*a. fig. Erfolg*); '**~·up** *s*. **1.** Zerbrechen *n*, -bersten *n*; Bersten *n* (*von Eis*); **2.** *fig.* Zerrüttung *f*, Zs.bruch *m*, Zerfall *m*; **3.** Bruch *m* (*e-r Freundschaft etc.*); **4.** Auflösung *f* (*e-r Versammlung etc.*); '**~,wa·ter** *s*. Wellenbrecher *m*.

bream[1] [bri:m] *s. ichth.* Brassen *m*.

bream[2] [bri:m] *v/t.* ⚓ den Schiffsboden rein kratzen u. brennen.

breast [brest] **I** *s*. **1.** Brust *f*; (*weibliche*) Brust, Busen *m*; **2.** *fig.* Brust *f*, Herz *n*, Busen *m*: **make a clean ~ of s.th.** et. gestehen; **3.** Brust(stück *n*) *f e-s Kleides etc.*; **4.** Wölbung *f e-s Berges*; **II** *v/t.* **5.** mutig auf et. losgehen; gegen et. ankämpfen, mühsam bewältigen: **~ the waves** gegen die Wellen ankämpfen; **6.** *sport* das Zielband durch'reißen; '**~·bone** ['brest-] *s*. Brustbein *n*; ,**~-**

-'deep *adj.* brusthoch.
breast·ed ['brestɪd] *adj. in Zssgn* ...brüstig.
'breast|-feed *v/t. u. v/i.* [*irr.*] stillen: **breast-fed child** Brustkind *n*; **'~·pin** ['brest-] *s.* Ansteck-, Kra'wattennadel *f*; **'~·stroke** *s. sport* Brustschwimmen *n*; **'~·work** *s.* ✕, ⚞ Brustwehr *f*.
breath [breθ] *s.* **1.** Atem(zug) *m*: *bad* ~ (übler) Mundgeruch; *draw one's first* ~ das Licht der Welt erblicken; *draw one's last* ~ den letzten Atemzug tun (*sterben*); *it took my* ~ *away fig.* es verschlug mir den Atem; *take* ~ Atem schöpfen (*a. fig.*); *catch one's* ~ den Atem anhalten; *save your* ~*!* spar dir die Worte!; *waste one's* ~ *fig.* in den Wind reden; *out of* ~ außer Atem; *under one's* ~ leise, im Flüsterton; *with his last* ~ mit s-m letzten Atemzug, als Letztes; *in the same* ~ im gleichen Atemzug; **2.** *fig.* Spur *f*, Anflug *m*; **3.** Hauch *m*, Lüftchen *n*: *a* ~ *of air*, **4.** Duft *m*.
breath·a·lyz·er ['breθəlaɪzə] *s. mot.* Alkoholtestgerät *n*.
breathe [bri:ð] **I** *v/i.* **1.** atmen; *fig.* leben; **2.** Atem holen; *fig.* sich verschnaufen: ~ *again* (*od. freely*) (erleichtert) aufatmen; **3.** ~ *upon* anhauchen; *fig.* besudeln; **4.** duften (*of* nach); **II** *v/t.* **5.** (ein- u. aus)atmen; *fig.* ausströmen: ~ *a sigh* seufzen; **6.** hauchen, flüstern: *not to* ~ *a word* kein Sterbenswörtchen sagen; **'breath·er** [-ðə] *s.* **1.** Atem-, Verschnaufpause *f* (*a. fig.*): *take a* ~ sich verschnaufen; **2.** *sport* F 'Spa'ziergang' *m*; **3.** F Stra'paze *f*; **'breath·ing** [-ðɪŋ] *s.* **1.** Atmen *n*, Atmung *f*; **2.** (Luft)Hauch *m*: ~ *space* Atempause *f*.
breath·less ['breθlɪs] *adj.* ☐ **1.** außer Atem; atemlos (*a. fig.*); **2.** *fig.* atemberaubend; **3.** windstill.
'breath|tak·ing *adj.* ☐ atemberaubend; ~ *test s. Brit.* (an e-m Verkehrsteilnehmer vorgenommener) Alkoholtest.
bred [bred] *pret. u. p.p. von breed.*
breech [bri:tʃ] *s.* **1.** Hosenboden *m*; **2.** ✕ Verschluss *m* (*Geschütz, Hinterlader*); ~ *de·liv·er·y s.* 💊 Steißgeburt *f*.
breech·es ['brɪtʃɪz] *s. pl.* Knie-, Reithose(n *pl.*) *f*, Breeches *pl.*; → *big* 1, *wear* 1.
'breech|load·er *s.* ✕ 'Hinterlader *m*.
breed [bri:d] **I** *v/t.* [*irr.*] **1.** her'vorbringen, gebären; **2.** *Tiere* züchten; *Pflanzen* züchten, ziehen: *French-bred* in Frankreich gezüchtet; **3.** *fig.* her'vorrufen, verursachen, erzeugen: *war* ~*s misery*; **4.** auf-, erziehen; ausbilden; **II** *v/i.* [*irr.*] **5.** zeugen, brüten, sich paaren, sich fortpflanzen, sich vermehren; **6.** entstehen; **III** *s.* **7.** Rasse *f*, Zucht *f*, Stamm *m*; **8.** Art *f*, Schlag *m*, Herkunft *f*; **'breed·er** [-də] *s.* **1.** Züchter(in); **2.** Zuchttier *n*; **3.** *a.* ~ *reactor phys.* Brüter *m*, 'Brutre,aktor *m*; **'breed·ing** [-dɪŋ] *s.* **1.** Fortpflanzung *f*; Züchtung *f*, Zucht *f*: ~ *place* ⚞ Brutstätte *f*; **2.** Erziehung *f*, Ausbildung *f*; **3.** Benehmen *n*; Bildung *f*, (gute) Lebensart *od.* 'Kinderstube'.
breeze¹ [bri:z] **I** *s.* **1.** Brise *f*, leichter Wind; **2.** F Krach *m*: a) Lärm *m*, b) Streit *m*; **3.** *Am.* 'Kinderspiel' *n*, 'Spa'ziergang' *m*; **II** *v/i.* **4.** wehen; **5.** F a) 'schweben' (*Person*), b) sausen.
breeze² [bri:z] *s.* ☉ Kohlenlösche *f*.
breez·y ['bri:zɪ] *adj.* ☐ **1.** luftig, windig; **2.** F a) forsch, flott, unbeschwert, b) oberflächlich.
Bren gun [bren] *s.* leichtes Ma'schinen-

gewehr.
brent goose [brent] → *brant*.
breth·ren ['breðrən] *pl. von brother* 2.
Bret·on ['bretən] **I** *adj.* bre'tonisch; **II** *s.* Bre'tone *m*, Bre'tonin *f*.
breve [bri:v] *s. typ.* Kürzezeichen *n*.
bre·vet ['brevɪt] ✕ **I** *s.* Bre'vet *n* (*Offizierspatent zu e-m Titularrang*): ~ *major* Hauptmann *m* im Range e-s Majors (*ohne entsprechendes Gehalt*); **II** *adj.* Brevet...: ~ *rank* Titularrang *m*.
bre·vi·a·ry ['bri:vjərɪ] *s.* Bre'vier *n*.
bre·vier [brə'vɪə] *s. typ.* Pe'titschrift *f*.
brev·i·ty ['brevətɪ] *s.* Kürze *f*.
brew [bru:] **I** *v/t.* **1.** *Bier* brauen; **2.** *Getränke* (*a. Tee*) (zu)bereiten; **3.** *fig.* aushecken, -brüten; **II** *v/i.* **4.** brauen, Brauer sein; **5.** sich zs.-brauen, in der Luft liegen, im Anzuge sein (*Gewitter, Unheil*); **III** *s.* **6.** Gebräu *n* (*a. fig.*); **brew·age** ['bru:ɪdʒ] *s.* Gebräu *n* (*a. fig.*); **brew·er** ['bru:ə] *s.* Brauer *m*: ~*'s yeast* Bierhefe *f*; **brew·er·y** ['bruərɪ] *s.* Braue'rei *f*.
bri·ar → *brier*.
brib·a·ble ['braɪbəbl] *adj.* bestechlich;
bribe [braɪb] **I** *v/t.* **1.** bestechen; **2.** *fig.* verlocken; **II** *s.* **3.** Bestechung *f*; **4.** Bestechungsgeld *n*, -geschenk *n*: *taking* (*of*) ~*s* 𝔥 Bestechlichkeit *f*, passive Bestechung, *pol.* Vorteilsnahme *f*; **'brib·er** [-bə] *s.* Bestecher *m*; **'brib·er·y** [-bərɪ] *s.* Bestechung *f*.
bric-à-brac ['brɪkəbræk] *s.* **1.** Antiqui'täten *pl.*; **2.** Nippsachen *pl.*
brick [brɪk] **I** *s.* **1.** Ziegel-, Backstein *m*: *drop a* ~ F 'ins Fettnäpfchen treten'; *swim like a* ~ wie e-e bleierne Ente schwimmen; **2.** (Bau)Klötzchen *n* (*Spielzeug*): *box of* ~*s* Baukasten *m*; **3.** F prima Kerl; **II** *adj.* **4.** Ziegel..., Backstein...: *red-*~ *university Brit.* moderne Universität (*ohne jahrhundertealte Tradition*); **III** *v/t.* **5.** mit Ziegelsteinen belegen *od.* pflastern: *to* ~ *in* (*od. up*) zumauern; **'~·bat** *s.* Ziegelbrocken *m* (*bsd. als Wurfgeschoss*); **'~,lay·er** *s.* Maurer *m*; **'~,lay·ing** *s.* Maure'rei *f*; **'~,mak·er** *s.* Ziegelbrenner *m*; **~ tea** *s.* (*chinesischer*) Ziegeltee; **~ wall** *s.* Backsteinmauer *f*; *fig.* Wand *f*: *see through a* ~ das Gras wachsen hören; **'~·work** *s.* **1.** Mauerwerk *n*; **2.** *pl. sg. konstr.* Ziege'lei *f*.
brid·al ['braɪdl] **I** *adj.* ☐ bräutlich; Braut...; Hochzeits...; **II** *s. poet.* Hochzeit *f*.
bride [braɪd] *s.* Braut *f* (*am u. kurz vor u. nach dem Hochzeitstage*), Neuvermählte *f*: *give away the* ~ Brautvater sein.
bride·groom ['braɪdgrʊm] *s.* Bräutigam *m*; **brides·maid** ['braɪdzmeɪd] *s.* Brautjungfer *f*.
bride·well ['braɪdwəl] *s.* Gefängnis *n*, Besserungsanstalt *f*.
bridge¹ [brɪdʒ] **I** *s.* **1.** Brücke *f*: *burn one's* ~*s* (*behind one*) *fig.* alle Brücken hinter sich abbrechen; *don't cross your* ~*s before you come to them fig.* lass doch die Dinge einfach auf dich zukommen; **2.** ⚓ Kom'mandobrücke *f*; **3.** ♪ (Vio'linen- *etc.*)Steg *m*; ⚒ (Zahn-)Brücke *f*; (Brillen)Steg *m*; **4.** *a.* ~ *of the nose* Nasenrücken *m*; **5.** ('Straßen)Über,führung *f*; **6.** *Turnen*: Ringen: Brücke *f*; **7.** ⚡ (Mess)Brücke *f*; Brückenschaltung *f*; **II** *v/t.* **8.** e-e Brücke schlagen über (*acc.*); **9.** *fig.* über'brücken: *bridging loan* ✝ Überbrückungskredit *m*.
bridge² [brɪdʒ] *s.* Bridge *n* (*Kartenspiel*).

'bridge|·head *s.* ✕ Brückenkopf *m*; ~ *toll* *s.* Brückenmaut *f*; **'~·work** *s.* ⚒ (Zahn)Brücke *f*.
bri·dle ['braɪdl] **I** *s.* **1.** Zaum *m*, Zaumzeug *n*; **2.** Zügel *m*: *give a horse the* ~ e-m Pferd die Zügel schießen lassen; **II** *v/t.* **3.** *Pferd* (auf)zäumen; **4.** *Pferd* (*a. fig. Leidenschaft etc.*) zügeln, im Zaum halten; **III** *v/i.* **5.** *a.* ~ *up* (*verächtlich od. stolz*) den Kopf zu'rückwerfen, *weitS.* hochfahren, ärgerlich werden; **6.** Anstoß nehmen (*at* an *dat.*); ~ *hand s.* Zügelhand *f* (*Linke des Reiters*); ~ *path s.* schmaler Reitweg, Saumpfad *m*; ~ *rein s.* Zügel *m*.
brief [bri:f] **I** *adj.* ☐ **1.** kurz: *be* ~*!* fasse dich kurz!; **2.** kurz, gedrängt: *in* ~ kurz (gesagt); **3.** kurz angebunden, schroff; **II** *s.* **4.** (päpstliches) Breve; **5.** 𝔥 a) Schriftsatz *m*, b) *Brit.* Beauftragung *f* u. Informierung *f* (*des barrister durch den solicitor*) zur Vertretung vor Gericht, *weitS.* Man'dat *n*, c) *Am.* (schriftliche) Informierung des Gerichts (*durch den Anwalt*): *abandon* (*od. give up*) *one's* ~ sein Mandat niederlegen; *hold a* ~ *for s.o.* 𝔥 j-s Sache vertreten, *fig.* für j-n e-e Lanze brechen; *I hold no* ~ *for* ich halte nichts von ...; *hold a watching* ~ j-s Interessen (*bei Gericht*) als Beobachter vertreten; **6.** → *briefing*; **III** *v/t.* **7.** j-n instruieren *od.* einweisen, j-m genaue Anweisungen geben; **8.** 𝔥 a) *e-m Anwalt* e-e Darstellung des Sachverhalts geben, b) *e-n Anwalt* mit s-r Vertretung beauftragen; **'~·case** *s.* Aktentasche *f*.
brief·ing ['bri:fɪŋ] *s.* **1.** 𝔥 Beauftragung *f* e-s Anwalts; **2.** *a.* ✕ (genaue) Anweisung, Instrukti'on *f*, Einweisung *f*; **3.** ✕ Lage-, Einsatzbesprechung *f*, Befehlsausgabe *f*; **'brief·less** [-lɪs] *adj.* unbeschäftigt (*Anwalt*); **'brief·ness** [-nɪs] *s.* Kürze *f*.
briefs [bri:fs] *s. pl.* Slip *m* (*kurze Unterhose*).
bri·er ['braɪə] *s.* ⚘ **1.** Dornstrauch *m*; **2.** wilde Rose: *sweet* ~ Weinrose; **3.** Bruy'èreholz *n*: ~ (*pipe*) Bruyèrepfeife *f*.
brig [brɪg] *s.* **1.** ⚓ Brigg *f*; **2.** ✕ F 'Bau' *m*.
Bri·gade [brɪ'geɪd] *s.* **1.** ✕ Bri'gade *f*; **2.** (*mst* uniformierte) Vereinigung; *contp.* 'Verein' *m*; **brig·a·dier** [,brɪgə'dɪə] *s.* ✕ a) *Brit.* Bri'gadekomman,deur *m*, -gene,ral *m*, b) *Am. a.* ~ *general* Brigadegeneral *m*.
brig·and ['brɪgənd] *s.* Ban'dit *m*, (Straßen)Räuber *m*; **'brig·and·age** [-dɪdʒ] *s.* Räuberunwesen *n*.
bright [braɪt] *adj.* ☐ **1.** hell, glänzend, blank, leuchtend; strahlend (*Wetter, Augen*): ~ *red* leuchtend rot; **2.** klar, 'durchsichtig; heiter (*Wetter*); **3.** *fig.* ,hell', gescheit, klug; **4.** munter, fröhlich; **5.** glänzend, berühmt; **6.** günstig; **7.** ☉ blank, Blank...: ~ *wire*; **'bright·en** [-tn] **I** *v/t.* **1.** hell(er) machen; *a. fig.* auf-, erhellen; **2.** *fig.* a) heiter(er) machen, beleben, b) fröhlich stimmen; **3.** polieren, blank putzen; **II** *v/i. oft* ~ *up* **4.** sich aufhellen (*Gesicht, Wetter etc.*), aufleuchten (*Gesicht*); **5.** *fig.* a) sich beleben, b) besser werden (*Aussichten etc.*); **'bright·ness** [-nɪs] *s.* **1.** Glanz *m*, Helle *f*, Klarheit *f*: ~ *control TV* Helligkeitssteuerung *f*; **2.** Aufgewecktheit *f*, Gescheitheit *f*; **3.** Munterkeit *f*.
Bright's dis·ease [braɪts] *s.* 💊 brightsche Krankheit, Nierenentzündung *f*.
brill [brɪl] *adj. Brit.* F super, ,geil'.
bril·liance ['brɪljəns], **'bril·lian·cy** [-sɪ]

s. **1.** Leuchten n, Glanz m; Helligkeit f (a. TV); **2.** fig. a) Scharfsinn m, b) Bril'lanz f, (das) Her'vorragende; **'bril·li·ant** [-nt] **I** adj. □ **1.** leuchtend, glänzend; **2.** fig. bril'lant, glänzend, her'vorragend; **II** s. **3.** Bril'lant m (Diamant); **4.** typ. Bril'lant f (Schriftgrad).

bril·li·an·tine [ˌbrɪljənˈtiːn] s. **1.** Brillan'tine f, 'Haarpˌmade f; **2.** Am. al'paka-artiger Webstoff.

brim [brɪm] **I** s. **1.** Rand m (bsd. Gefäß); **2.** (Hut)Krempe f; **II** v/i. **3.** voll sein (with von; a. fig.): **~ over** übervoll sein, überfließen, -sprudeln; **ˌbrim'ful** [-'fʊl] adj. rand-, 'übervoll (a. fig.); **brimmed** [-md] adj. mit Rand, mit Krempe.

brim·stone ['brɪmstən] s. **1.** Schwefel m; **2.** → **~ but·ter·fly** s. zo. Zi'tronenfalter m.

brin·dled ['brɪndld] adj. gestreift, scheckig.

brine [braɪn] s. **1.** Sole f, (Salz)Lake f; **2.** poet. Meer(wasser) n; **~ pan** s. Salzpfanne f.

bring [brɪŋ] v/t. [irr.] **1.** bringen, mit-, herbringen, her'beischaffen: **~ him (it) with you** bring ihn (es) mit; **~ before the judge** vor den Richter bringen; **~ good luck** Glück bringen; **~ to bear** Einfluss etc. zur Anwendung bringen, geltend machen, Druck etc. ausüben; **2.** Gründe, Beschuldigung etc. vorbringen; **3.** her'vorbringen; Gewinn einbringen; mit sich bringen, her'beiführen: **~ into being** ins Leben rufen, entstehen lassen; **~ to pass** zustande bringen; **4.** j-n veranlassen, bewegen, dazu bringen (**to inf.** zu inf.): **I can't ~ myself to do it** ich kann mich nicht dazu durchringen (, es zu tun); Zssgn mit adv.:

bring| a·bout v/t. **1.** zu'stande bringen; **2.** bewirken, verursachen; **3.** ♺ wenden; **~ a·long** v/t. **1.** → **bring** 1; **2.** fig. mit sich bringen; **~ back** v/t. zu'rück-, a. fig. wiederbringen; fig. a) Erinnerungen wachrufen (of an acc.), b) Erinnerungen wachrufen an (acc.); **~ down** v/t. **1.** a. Flugzeug her'unterbringen; **2.** hunt. Wild erlegen; **3.** ✕ Flugzeug abschießen; **4.** sport j-n ˌlegen'; **5.** Regierung etc. stürzen, zu Fall bringen; **6.** Preise drücken; **7.** **~ on one's head** sich j-s Zorn zuziehen; **8.** **~ the house** F a) stürmischen Beifall auslösen, b) Lachstürme entfesseln; **~ forth** v/t. **1.** her'vorbringen, gebären; **2.** verursachen, zeitigen; **~ for·ward** v/t. **1.** Wunsch etc. vorbringen; **2.** ✝ Betrag über'tragen (amount) brought forward Übertrag m; **~ in** v/t. **1.** hereinbringen; **2.** Ernte, a. ✝ Gewinn, Kapital, a. parl. Gesetzesentwurf einbringen; **3.** a) j-n einschalten, b) j-n beteiligen (on an dat.); **4.** ⚖ Schuldspruch etc. fällen: **~ a verdict of guilty**; **~ off** v/t. **1.** retten; **2.** ˌschaffen', fertig bringen; **~ on** v/t. **1.** her'beibringen; **2.** her'beiführen, verursachen; **3.** in Gang bringen; **4.** zur Sprache bringen; **5.** thea. Stück ˌbringen', aufführen; **~ out** v/t. **1.** a) Buch, Theaterstück her'ausbringen, b) ✝ Waren auf den Markt bringen; **2.** Sinn etc. her'ausarbeiten; **3.** **bring s.o. out of himself** j-n dazu bringen, mehr aus sich her'auszugehen; **4.** j-n in die Gesellschaft einführen; **~ o·ver** v/t. 'umstimmen, bekehren; **~ round** v/t. **1.** Ohnmächtigen wieder zu sich bringen, Patienten 'durchbringen; **2.** j-n umstimmen, ˌher'umkriegen'; **3.** das Gespräch brin-

gen (to auf acc.); **~ through** v/t. Kranken od. Prüfling 'durchbringen; **~ to** v/t. **1.** Ohnmächtigen wieder zu sich bringen; **2.** ♺ stoppen; **~ up** v/t. **1.** Kind auf-, erziehen; **2.** zur Sprache bringen; **3.** ✕ Truppen her'anführen; **4.** zum Stillstand bringen; **5.** et. (er)brechen: **~ one's lunch**; **6.** **~ short** zum Halten bringen; **7.** → **date²** 3, **rear²** 3.

bring·ing-up [ˌbrɪŋɪŋˈʌp] s. **1.** Auf-, Großziehen n; **2.** Erziehung f.

brink [brɪŋk] s. Rand m (mst fig.): **on the ~ of** am Rande (e-s Krieges, des Ruins etc.); **be on the ~ of the grave** mit e-m Fuß im Grabe stehen; **'~·man·ship** [-mənʃɪp] s. pol. Poli'tik f des äußersten 'Risikos.

brin·y ['braɪnɪ] **I** adj. salzig, solehaltig; **II** s. Brit. F: **the ~** die See.

bri·oche [briːˈɒʃ] (Fr.) s. Bri'oche f (süßes Hefegebäck).

bri·quet(te) [brɪˈket] (Fr.) s. Bri'kett n.

brisk [brɪsk] **I** adj. □ **1.** lebhaft, flott, flink; **2.** frisch (Wind), lustig (Feuer); schäumend (Wein); **3.** a) rüstig, munter, b) forsch, e'nergisch; **4.** ✝ lebhaft, flott; **II** v/t. **5.** mst **~ up** anfeuern, beleben.

bris·ket ['brɪskɪt] s. Küche: Brust(stück n) f (Rind).

bris·ling ['brɪslɪŋ] s. ichth. Sprotte f.

bris·tle ['brɪsl] **I** s. **1.** Borste f; (Bart-)Stoppel f; **II** v/i. **2.** sich sträuben (Haar); **3.** a. **~ up** (with anger) hochfahren, zornig werden: **~ with anger**; **4.** (with) strotzen, starren, voll sein (von).

bris·tling → **brisling**.

bris·tly ['brɪslɪ] adj. stachelig, rau; struppig; stoppelig, Stoppel...

Brit [brɪt] s. F Brite m, Britin f.

Bri·tan·nic [brɪˈtænɪk] adj. bri'tannisch.

Brit·i·cism ['brɪtɪsɪzəm] s. Angli'zismus m; **'Brit·ish** [-tɪʃ] **I** adj. britisch: **~ subject** britischer Staatsangehöriger; **II** s.: **the ~** die Briten pl.; **'Brit·ish·er** [-tɪʃə] s. Brite m; **'Brit·on** [-tn] s. **1.** Brite m, Britin f; **2.** hist. Bri'tannier(in).

brit·tle ['brɪtl] adj. **1.** spröde, zerbrechlich; bröckelig; brüchig (metall etc.; a. fig.); **2.** reizbar.

broach [brəʊtʃ] **I** s. **1.** Stecheisen n; Räumnadel f; **2.** Bratspieß m; **3.** Turmspitze f; **II** v/t. **4.** Fass anstechen; **5.** ⊚ räumen; **6.** fig. Thema anschneiden.

B-road ['biːrəʊd] s. Brit. etwa: Staatsstraße f, Landstraße f.

broad [brɔːd] **I** adj. □ → **broadly**; **1.** breit: **it is as ~ as it is long** fig. es ist gehüpft wie gesprungen; **2.** weit, ausgedehnt; weit reichend, 'umfassend, voll: **~ jump** sport Weitsprung m; **in the ~est sense** im weitesten Sinne; **in ~ daylight** am helllichten Tage; **3.** deutlich, ausgeprägt; breit (Akzent, Dialekt); → **hint** 1; **4.** ungeschminkt, offen, derb: **a ~ joke** ein derber Witz; **5.** allgemein, einfach: **the ~ facts** die allgemeinen Tatsachen; **in ~ outline** in groben Umrissen, in großen Zügen; großzügig: **a ~ outlook** e-e tolerante Auffassung; **7.** Radio: unscharf; **II** s. **8.** sl. a) ˌWeib(sbild)' n, b) ˌNutte' f; **ar·row** s. breitköpfiger Pfeil (amtliches Zeichen auf brit. Regierungsgut u. auf Sträflingskleidung); **'~·ax(e)** s. **1.** Breitbeil n; **2.** hist. Streitaxt f; **~ beam** s. ✝ Breitstrahler m; **~ bean** s. ♦ Saubohne f; **'~·brush** adj. (ganz) grob, ganz allgemein.

broad·cast ['brɔːdkɑːst] **I** v/t. [irr. → **cast**; pret. u. p.p. a. **~ed**] **1.** breitwürfig säen; **2.** fig. Nachricht verbreiten,

iro. 'auspoˌsaunen; **3.** durch Rundfunk od. Fernsehen verbreiten, über'tragen, senden, ausstrahlen; **II** v/i. **4.** im Rundfunk od. Fernsehen auftreten; **5.** senden; **III** s. **6.** Rundfunk-, Fernsehsendung f, Über'tragung f; **IV** adj. **7.** Rundfunk..., Fernseh...; **'broad·cast·er** [-tə] s. **1.** Rundfunk-, Fernsehsprecher(in); **2.** → **broadcasting station**.

broad·cast·ing ['brɔːdkɑːstɪŋ] **I** s. **1.** → **broadcast** 6; **2.** a) Rundfunk m od. Fernsehen n: **~ area** Sendebereich m, b) Sendebetrieb m; **II** adj. **3.** Rundfunk..., Fernseh...; **~ sta·tion** s. 'Rundfunk-, 'Fernsehstatiˌon f, Sender m; **~ stu·di·o** s. Senderaum m, 'Studio n.

Broad| Church s. liberale Richtung in der anglikanischen Kirche; **'2·cloth** s. feiner Wollstoff.

broad·en ['brɔːdn] v/t. u. v/i. (sich) verbreitern, (sich) erweitern: **~ one's mind** fig. sich bilden, s-n Horizont erweitern; **travel(l)ing ~s the mind** Reisen bildet.

'broad-ga(u)ge adj. ₲ Breitspur...

broad·ly ['brɔːdlɪ] adv. **1.** weitgehend (etc., → **broad** I); **2.** allgemein (gesprochen), in großen Zügen.

ˌbroad'mind·ed adj. großzügig, tole'rant.

'broad|·sheet s. **1.** typ. Planobogen m; **2.** hist. große, einseitig bedruckte Flugschrift; Flugblatt n; **'~·side** s. **1.** ♺ Breitseite f (Geschütze u. Salve): **fire a ~** e-e Breitseite abgeben; **2.** F ˌBreitseite' f, mas'sive At'tacke; **3.** → **broadsheet**; **'~·sword** s. breites Schwert, 'Pallasch m.

bro·cade [brəʊˈkeɪd] s. ✝ **1.** Bro'kat m; **2.** Broka'tell(e f) m.

broc·co·li ['brɒkəlɪ] pl. (als sg. konstr.) 'Brokkoli pl.

bro·chure [brəʊˈʃə] s. Bro'schüre f.

brock·et ['brɒkɪt] s. hunt. Spießer m, zweijähriger Hirsch.

brogue [brəʊg] s. **1.** a) irischer Ak'zent (des Englischen), b) dia'lektisch gefärbte Aussprache; **2.** derber Straßenschuh.

broil¹ [brɔɪl] **I** v/t. auf dem Rost braten, grillen; **II** v/i. schmoren, braten, kochen (alle a. fig.).

broil² [brɔɪl] s. Krach m, Streit m.

broil·er¹ ['brɔɪlə] s. **1.** Bratrost m; Bratofen m mit Grillvorrichtung; **2.** Brathühnchen n (bratfertig); **3.** F glühend heißer Tag.

broil·er² ['brɔɪlə] s. Streithammel m.

broil·ing ['brɔɪlɪŋ] adj. a. **~ hot** glühend heiß.

broke¹ [brəʊk] pret. von **break**.

broke² [brəʊk] adj. F pleite: a) bank'rott, ruiniert, b) ˌabgebrannt', ˌblank': **go ~** Pleite gehen; **go for ~** alles riskieren.

bro·ken ['brəʊkən] **I** p.p. von **break**; **II** adj. □ → **brokenly**; **1.** zerbrochen, entzwei, ka'putt; zerrissen; **2.** gebrochen; **3.** unter'brochen (Schlaf); angebrochen, unvollständig: **~ line** gestrichelte od. punktierte Linie; **4.** fig. (seelisch) gebrochen: **a ~ man**; **5.** zerrüttet (Ehe, Gesundheit): **~ home** zerrüttete Familienverhältnisse pl.; **6.** uneben, holperig (Boden); zerklüftet (Gelände); bewegt (Meer); **7.** ling. gebrochen: **~ German**; **ˌ~'down** adj. **1.** ruiniert, unbrauchbar; **2.** erschöpft, geschwächt, zerrüttet, ˌka'putt'; **3.** zs.-gebrochen (a. fig.); **ˌ~'heart·ed** adj. un'tröstlich, (ganz) gebrochen.

bro·ken·ly ['brəʊkənlɪ] adv. **1.** stoßweise, mit Unter'brechungen; **2.** mit gebrochener Stimme.

bro·ken| num·ber s. ₳ gebrochene Zahl, Bruch m; **~ stone** s. Split m,

Schotter *m*; ̰~-'**wind·ed** *adj.* dämpfig, kurzatmig (*Pferd*).

bro·ker ['brəʊkə] *s.* a) (Handels)Makler *m*, (*weitS. a.* Heirats)Vermittler *m*: *honest ~ pol.*, *fig.* ehrlicher Makler, b) (Börsen)Makler *m*, Broker *m* (*der im Kundenauftrag Geschäfte tätigt*); '**bro·ker·age** [-ərɪdʒ] *s.* **1.** Maklergebühr *f*, Cour'tage *f*; **2.** Maklergeschäft *n*.

brol·ly ['brɒlɪ] *s. Brit.* F Schirm *m*.

bro·mide ['brəʊmaɪd] *s.* **1.** 🜊 Bro'mid *n*: **~ paper** *phot.* Bromsilberpapier *n*; **2.** *fig.* a) Plattheit *f*, Banali'tät *f*, b) langweiliger Mensch; '**bro·mine** [-miːn] *s.* 🜊 Brom *n*.

bron·chi ['brɒŋkaɪ], '**bron·chi·a** [-kɪə] *s. pl. anat.* 'Bronchien *pl.*; '**bron·chi·al** [-kjəl] *adj.* Bronchial...; **bron·chi·tis** [brɒŋ'kaɪtɪs] *s.* ⚕ Bron'chitis *f*, Bron·chi'alka,tarr(h) *m*.

bron·co ['brɒŋkəʊ] *pl.* **-cos** *s.* kleines, halbwildes Pferd (*Kaliforniens*); '~,**bust·er** *s.* Zureiter *m* (von wilden Pferden).

Bronx cheer [brɒŋks] *s. Am. sl.* ,'Pfeif-kon,zert' *n*.

bronze [brɒnz] **I** *s.* **1.** Bronze *f*: **~ age** Bronzezeit *f*; **~ medal(l)ist** Bronzeme-daillengewinner(in); **2.** ('Statue *f etc.* aus) Bronze *f*; **II** *v/t.* **3.** bronzieren; **III** *adj.* **4.** bronzefarben, Bronze...; **bronzed** [-zd] *adj.* **1.** bronziert; **2.** (sonnen)gebräunt.

brooch [brəʊtʃ] *s.* Brosche *f*, Spange *f*.

brood [bruːd] **I** *s.* **1.** Brut *f*; **2.** Nach-kommenschaft *f*; **3.** *contp.* Brut *f*, Hor-de *f*; **II** *v/i.* **4.** brüten; **5.** *fig.* (**on**, **over**) brüten (über *dat.*), grübeln (über *acc.*); **6.** brüten, lasten (*Hitze etc.*); **II** *adj.* **7.** Brut..., Zucht...: **~ mare** Zuchtstute *f*; '**brood·er** [-də] *s.* **1.** Bruthenne *f*; **2.** Brutkasten *m*; '**brood·y** [-dɪ] *adj.* **1.** brütig (*Henne*); **2.** *fig.* brütend, grüble-risch; trübsinnig.

brook¹ [brʊk] *s.* Bach *m*.

brook² [brʊk] *v/t.* erdulden: *it ~s no delay* es duldet keinen Aufschub.

broom [bruːm] *s.* **1.** Besen *m*: *a new ~ sweeps clean* neue Besen kehren gut; **2.** ♀ (Besen)Ginster *m*; '~·**stick** ['brʊm-] *s.* Besenstiel *m*.

broth [brɒθ] *s.* (Fleisch-, Kraft)Brühe *f*, Suppe *f*.

broth·el ['brɒθl] *s.* Bor'dell *n*.

broth·er ['brʌðə] *s.* **1.** Bruder *m*: *~s and sisters* Geschwister; *Smith ~s* ✝ Ge-brüder Smith; **2.** *eccl. pl.* **brethren** Bruder *m*, Nächste(r) *m*, Mitglied *n* e-r (reli'giösen) Gemeinschaft; **3.** Amts-bruder *m*, Kol'lege *m*: **~ in arms** Waf-fenbruder; **~ student** Kommilitone, Studienkollege *m*; **~ officer** Regiments-kamerad *m*; **~!** F Mann!, Mensch!; ,**broth·er·'ger·man** *s.* leiblicher Bru-der; '**broth·er·hood** [-hʊd] *s.* **1.** Bru-derschaft *f*; **2.** Brüderlichkeit *f*; **broth·er-in-law** ['brʌðərɪnlɔː] *s.* Schwager *m*. **broth·er·ly** ['brʌðəlɪ] *adj.* brüderlich.

brough·am ['bruːəm] *s.* **1.** Brougham *m* (*geschlossener, vierrädriger, zweisitzi-ger Wagen*); **2.** *hist. mot.* Limou'sine *f* mit offenem Fahrersitz.

brought [brɔːt] *pret. u. p.p. von* **bring**.

brou·ha·ha [bruː'hɑːhɑː] *s.* Getue *n*, Wirbel *m*, Lärm *m*.

brow [braʊ] *s.* **1.** (Augen)Braue *f*: *knit* (*od.* *gather*) *one's ~s* die Stirn run-zeln; **2.** Stirn *f*; **3.** Vorsprung *m*, Ab-hang *m*, (Berg)Kuppe *f*; '~·**beat** *v/t.* [*irr.* → **beat**] einschüchtern, tyranni-sieren.

brown [braʊn] **I** *adj.* braun: *do s.o.* (*up*) *~* F j-n ,anschmieren' *od.* ,reinlegen'; **II** *s.* Braun *n*; **III** *v/t.* Haut *etc.* bräunen,

---

Fleisch etc. (an)bräunen; ⊗ brünieren: *~ed off* F ,restlos bedient', ,sauer'; **IV** *v/i.* braun werden; **~ bear** *s. zo.* Braun-bär *m*; **~ bread** *s.* Vollkorn- *od.* Schwarzbrot *n*; **~ coal** *s.* Braunkohle *f*.

brown·ie ['braʊnɪ] *s.* **1.** Heinzelmänn-chen *n*; **2.** *Am.* kleiner Schoko'laden-kuchen mit Nüssen; **3.** ,Wichtel' *m* (*junge Pfadfinderin*).

Brown·ing ['braʊnɪŋ] *s.* Browning *m* (*e-e Pistole*).

'**brown|-nose** *Am.* V **I** *s.* ,Arschkrie-cher' *m*; **II** *v/t.* j-m ,in den Arsch krie-chen'; **~ pa·per** *s.* 'Packpa,pier *n*; '~·**shirt** *s. hist.* Braunhemd *n* (*SA-Mann od. Nazi*); '~·**stone** *Am.* **I** *s.* brauner Sandstein; **II** *adj.* F wohlha-bend, vornehm.

browse [braʊz] *v/i.* **1.** grasen, weiden; *fig.* naschen (**on** von); **2.** *in Büchern* blättern *od.* schmökern; *im Internet* browsen; **3.** *a.* **~ around** sich (unver-bindlich) 'umsehen (*in e-m Laden*); '**browser** *s.* **1.** *Internet:* Browser *m* (*Programm, mit dem man sich im Inter-net bewegt*); **2.** a) j-d, der *in Büchern etc.* herumblättert, b) j-d, der sich in e-m *Geschäft unverbindlich umsieht.*

bru·in ['bruːɪn] *s. poet.* (Meister) Petz *m* (*Bär*).

bruise [bruːz] **I** *v/t.* **1.** *Körperteil* quet-schen; *Früchte* anstoßen; **2.** zerstamp-fen, schroten; **3.** *j-n* grün u. blau schla-gen; **II** *v/i.* **4.** e-e Quetschung *od.* e-n blauen Fleck bekommen; **III** *s.* **5.** ⚕ Quetschung *f*, Bluterguss *m*; blauer Fleck; **6.** Druckstelle *f* (*auf Obst*); '**bruis·er** [-zə] *s.* F Boxer *m*; **2.** a) ,Schläger' *m*, b) ,Schrank' *m* (*Hüne*).

bruit [bruːt] *v/t.*: **~ about** *obs.* Gerücht verbreiten.

Brum·ma·gem ['brʌmədʒəm] F **I** *s.* **1.** *npr.* Birmingham (*Stadt*); **2.** ♀ Schund (-ware *f*) *m* (*bsd. in Birmingham herge-stellt*); **II** *adj.* **3.** billig, kitschig, Schund..., unecht.

brunch [brʌntʃ] *s.* F (*aus breakfast u.* *lunch*) Brunch *m*.

bru·nette [bruː'net] **I** *adj.* brü'nett, dun-kelbraun; **II** *s.* Brü'nette *f*.

brunt [brʌnt] *s.* Hauptstoß *m*, -last *f*, volle Wucht *des Angriffs* (*a. fig.*): *bear the ~* die Hauptlast tragen.

brush [brʌʃ] **I** *s.* **1.** Bürste *f*; Besen *m*: *tooth~* Zahnbürste *f*; **2.** Pinsel *m*: *shaving ~*; **3.** a) Pinselstrich *m* (*Ma-ler*), b) Maler *m*, c) *the ~* die Malerei; **4.** Bürsten *n*: *give a ~* (*to*) *et.* abbür-sten; **5.** buschiger Schwanz (*bsd. Fuchs*); **6.** ⚡ (Kon'takt)Bürste *f*; **7.** *phys.* Strahlenbündel *n*; **8.** ⚔ Feindbe-rührung *f*; Schar'mützel *n* (*a. fig.*): *have a ~ with s.o.* mit j-m aneinander geraten; **9.** → **brushwood**; **II** *v/t.* **10.** bürsten; **11.** fegen: **~ away** (*od.* **off**) abwischen, -streifen (*a. mit der Hand*); **~ off** *fig.* j-n abwimmeln *od.* abweisen; **~ aside** *fig.* beiseite schieben, abtun; **12. ~ up** *fig.* ,aufpolieren', auffrischen; **13.** streifen, leicht berühren; **III** *v/i.* **14. ~ against** streifen (*acc.*); **15.** da-'hinrasen: **~ past** vorbeisausen; '**brush·ing** [-ʃɪŋ] *s. mst pl.* Kehricht *m*, *n*; '**brush·less** [-lɪs] *adj.* **1.** ohne Bürste; **2.** ohne Schwanz (*Fuchs*); '**brush-off** *s.* F Abfuhr *f*; '**brush-wood** *s.* **1.** 'Unter-holz *n*, Gestrüpp *n*; Busch *m* (*USA u. Australien*); **2.** Reisig *n*.

brusque [brʊsk] *adj.* □ brüsk, barsch, schroff.

Brus·sels ['brʌslz] *npr.* Brüssel *n*; **~ lace** *s.* Brüsseler Spitzen *pl.*; **~ sprouts** [,brʌsl'spraʊts] *s. pl.* Rosen-

---

kohl *m*.

bru·tal ['bruːtl] *adj.* □ **1.** viehisch; bru-'tal, roh, unmenschlich; **2.** scheußlich; **bru·tal·i·ty** [bruː'tælətɪ] *s.* Brutali'tät *f*, Rohheit *f*; '**bru·tal·ize** [-təlaɪz] **I** *v/t.* **1.** zum Tier machen, verrohen lassen; **2.** brutal behandeln; **II** *v/i.* verrohen, zum Tier werden.

brute [bruːt] **I** *s.* (*unvernünftiges*) Tier, Vieh *n*, *fig. a.* Untier *n*, Scheusal *n*: *the ~ in him* das Tier in ihm; **II** *adj.* tierisch (*a. = triebhaft, unvernünftig, brutal*); viehisch, roh; hirnlos, dumm; gefühl-los: **~ force** rohe Gewalt; '**brut·ish** [-tɪʃ] *adj.* □ → **brute** II.

Bry·thon·ic [brɪ'θɒnɪk] *s.* Ursprache *f* der Kelten in Wales, 'Cornwall u. der Bre'tagne.

bub·ble ['bʌbl] **I** *s.* **1.** (*Luft-, Gas-, Seifen*)Blase *f*; **2.** *fig.* Seifenblase *f*; Schwindel(geschäft *n*) *m*: *prick the ~* den Schwindel aufdecken; **~ company** Schwindelfirma *f*; **3.** Sprudeln *n*, Bro-deln *n*, (Auf)Wallen *n*; **4.** *Am.* Trag-lufthalle *f*; **II** *v/i.* sprudeln, brodeln, wallen; perlen: **~ over** übersprudeln (*a. fig.* **with** vor *dat.*); **~ up** aufsprudeln; Blasen aufsteigen; **~ bath** *s.* Schaum-bad *n*; **~ car** *s.* **1.** Kleinstauto *n*, Ka'bi-nenroller *m*; **2.** Wagen *m* mit kugelsi-cherer Kuppel; **~ gum** *s.* Bal'lon-, Knallkaugummi *m*.

bu·bo ['bjuːbəʊ] *pl.* **-boes** ⚕ 'Bubo *m* (*Drüsenschwellung*); Beule *f*; **bu·bon·ic** [bjuː'bɒnɪk] *adj.*: **~ plague** ⚕ Beu-lenpest *f*.

buc·ca·neer [,bʌkə'nɪə] **I** *s.* Seeräuber *m*, Freibeuter *m*; **II** *v/i.* Seeräube'rei betreiben.

buck¹ [bʌk] **I** *s.* **1.** *zo.* Bock *m* (*Hirsch, Reh, Ziege etc.*; *a. Turnen*); Rammler *m* (*Hase, Kaninchen*); *engS.* Rehbock *m*; **2.** *obs.* Stutzer *m*, Geck *m*; Lebe-mann *m*; **3.** *Am. obs. contp.* a) Rothaut *f*, b) Nigger *m*; **4.** *Am. Poker:* Spiel-marke, die e-n Spieler daran erinnern soll, dass er am Geben ist: *pass the ~ to* F j-m ,den schwarzen Peter (*die Verant-wortung*) zuschieben'; **II** *v/i.* **5.** bocken (*Pferd, Esel etc.*); **6.** *Am.* ,meutern', sich sträuben (**at**, **against** bei, gegen); **7. ~ up** F a) sich ranhalten, b) sich zs.-reißen: **~ up!** Kopf hoch!; **III** *v/t.* **8.** *Reiter* durch Bocken abwerfen (wol-len); **9.** *Am.* wütend angreifen; ange-hen gegen; **10.** *a.* **~ up** F aufmuntern: *greatly ~ed* hocherfreut; **IV** *adj.* **11.** männlich; **12. ~ private** ✕ *Am.* F ein-facher Soldat.

buck² [bʌk] *s. Am.* F Dollar *m*: *earn a fast ~* schnelles Geld verdienen (*od.* machen).

buck·et ['bʌkɪt] **I** *s.* **1.** Eimer *m*, Kübel *m*: *champagne ~* Sektkühler *m*; *kick the ~* F ,abkratzen' (*sterben*); **2.** ⊗ a) Schaufel *f e-s Schaufelrades*, b) Eimer *m od.* Löffel *m e-s Baggers*, c) (Pum-pen)Kolben *m*; **II** *v/t.* **3.** (aus)schöpfen; **4.** *Pferd* zu'schanden reiten; **III** *v/i.* **5.** F (da'hin)rasen; **~ con·vey·or** *s.* Becherwerk *n*; **~ dredg·er** *s.* Löffel-bagger *m*; '~·**ful** [-fʊl] *pl.* **-fuls** *s.* ein Eimer (voll).

buck·et| seat *s.* **1.** *mot.*, ✈ Klapp-, Notsitz *m*; **2.** *mot.* Schalensitz *m*; **~ shop** *s.* **1.** 'unre,elle Maklerfirma; **2.** ,Klitsche' *f*, kleiner ,Laden'.

'**buck·eye** *s. Am.* **1.** ♀ e-e 'Rosska,stanie *f*; **2.** ♀ F Bewohner(in) von Ohio; '~·**horn** *s.* Hirschhorn *n*; '~·**hound** *s. zo.* Jagdhund *m*; '~·**jump·er** *s.* störri-sches Pferd

buck·le ['bʌkl] **I** *s.* **1.** Schnalle *f*, Spange

f; **2.** ⚔ Koppelschloss n; **3.** ⊕ verbogene od. verzogene Stelle; **II** v/t. **4.** a. ~ **on**, ~ **up** an-, 'um-, zuschnallen; **5.** ⊕ (ver)biegen, krümmen; **6.** ~ **o.s. to** → 9; **III** v/i. **7.** ⊕ sich (ver)biegen od. verziehen, sich wölben od. krümmen; **8.** nachgeben unter e-r Last: ~ (**under**) fig. zs.-brechen; **9.** ~ **down to** F sich hinter e-e Aufgabe ,klemmen'.

buck·ling ['bʌklɪŋ] (Ger.) s. Bückling m (geräucherter Hering).

buck·ling strength ['bʌklɪŋ] s. ⊕ Knickfestigkeit f.

buck·ram ['bʌkrəm] **I** s. **1.** Steifleinen n; **2.** fig. Steifheit f, Förmlichkeit f; **II** adj. **3.** fig. steif, for'mell.

buck·saw ['bʌksɔː] s. Am. Bocksäge f.

Buck's Fizz [,bʌks'fɪz] npr. Brit. Sekt m orange (Mischung aus Sekt u. Orangensaft).

'**buck|·shot** s. hunt. grober Schrot, Rehposten m; '~·**skin** s. **1.** a) Wildleder n, b) pl. Lederhose f; **2.** Buckskin m (Wollstoff); '~·**thorn** s. ⚘ Kreuzdorn m; '~·**tooth** [irr.] vorstehender Zahn; '~·**wheat** s. ⚘ Buchweizen m.

bu·col·ic [bjuː'kɒlɪk] **I** adj. (□ ~**ally**) **1.** bu'kolisch: a) Hirten..., b) ländlich, i'dyllisch; **II** s. **2.** I'dylle f, Hirtengedicht n; **3.** humor. Landmann m.

bud [bʌd] **I** s. **1.** ⚘ Knospe f; Auge n (Blätterknospe): **be in** ~ knospen; **2.** Keim m; **3.** fig. Keim m, Ursprung m; → **nip¹** 2; **4.** unentwickeltes Wesen; **5.** Am. F Debü'tantin f; **II** v/i. **6.** knospen, sprossen; **7.** sich entwickeln od. entfalten: ~**ding lawyer** angehender Jurist; **III** v/t. **8.** ✐ okulieren.

Bud·dha ['budə] s. 'Buddha m; '**Bud·dhism** [-dɪzəm] s. Bud'dhismus m; '**Bud·dhist** [-dɪst] **I** s. Bud'dhist m; **II** adj. → **Bud·dhis·tic** [bu'dɪstɪk] adj. bud'dhistisch.

bud·dy ['bʌdɪ] s. F **1.** ,Kumpel' m, ,Spezi' m, Kame'rad m; **2.** Anrede: Freundchen n.

budge [bʌdʒ] mst neg. **I** v/i. sich (von der Stelle) rühren, (im Geringsten) bewegen: ~ **from** fig. von et. abrücken; **II** v/t. (vom Fleck) bewegen.

budg·er·i·gar ['bʌdʒərɪgɑː] s. orn. Wellensittich m.

budg·et ['bʌdʒɪt] **I** s. **1.** bsd. pol. Bud-'get n, (Staats)Hauhalt m, E'tat m, (a. pri'vater) Haushaltsplan: **open the** ~ das Budget vorlegen; ~ **cut** Etatkürzung f; **for the low** ~ für den schmalen Geldbeutel; ~(**-priced**) preisgünstig; **2.** fig. Vorrat m: **a** ~ **of news** ein Sack voll Neuigkeiten; **II** v/t. **3.** a) Mittel bewilligen, vorsehen, Ausgaben einplanen; **III** v/i. **4.** planen, ein Bud-'get machen: ~ **for s.th.** et. im Haushaltsplan vorsehen, die Kosten für et. veranschlagen; '**budg·et·ar·y** [-tərɪ] adj. Budget..., Etat..., Haushalts...: ~ **deficit**.

bud·gie ['bʌdʒɪ] s. F für **budgerigar**.

buff¹ [bʌf] s. **1.** starkes Ochsen- od. Büffelleder; **2.** F bloße Haut: **in the** ~ im Adams- od. Evaskostüm (nackt); **3.** Lederfarbe f; **4.** F ,Fex' m, Fan m: **hi-fi** ~; **II** adj. **5.** lederfarben.

buff² [bʌf] v/t. ⊕ schwabbeln, polieren.

buf·fa·lo ['bʌfələu] pl. **-loes**, Am. a. **-los** **I** s. **1.** zo. Büffel m; nordamer. 'Bison m; **2.** ⚔ am'phibischer Panzerwagen; **II** v/t. **3.** Am. F j-n täuschen od. einschüchtern.

buf·fer ['bʌfə] **I** s. ⊕ a) Stoßdämpfer m, b) Puffer m (a. Computer u. fig.), c) Prellbock (a. fig.): ~ **solution** 🜊 Pufferlösung f; ~ **state** pol. Pufferstaat m;

3. a. ~ **memory** Computer: Pufferspeicher m; **II** v/t. **4.** als Puffer wirken gegen; **5.** Computer: puffern, zwischenspeichern.

buf·fet¹ ['bʌfɪt] **I** s. **1.** Puff m, Stoß m; Schlag m (a. fig.); **II** v/t. **2.** a) j-m e-n Schlag versetzen, b) j-n od. et. her'umstoßen: ~ (**about**) durchrütteln; **3.** gegen Wellen etc. (an)kämpfen.

buf·fet² s. **1.** ['bʌfɪt] Bü'fett n, Anrichte f; **2.** ['bufeɪ] Bü'fett n: a) Theke f, b) Tisch mit Speisen, c) Erfrischungsbar f, Imbissstube f: ~ **car** 🚉 Büfettwagen m; ~ **dinner** kaltes Büfett.

buf·foon [bʌ'fuːn] s. **1.** Possenreißer m, Hans'wurst m (a. fig. contp.); **2.** derber Witzbold; **buf'foon·er·y** [-nərɪ] s. Possen(reißen n) pl.

bug [bʌg] **I** s. **1.** zo. (Bett)Wanze f; **2.** zo. bsd. Am. allgemein In'sekt n (Ameise, Fliege, Spinne, Käfer); **3.** F Ba'zillus m (a. fig.): **the golf** ~ die Golfleidenschaft; **4.** ⊕ Am. F De'fekt m, mst pl. ,Mucken' pl.; Computer: (Pro-gramm[ier])Fehler m, F Bug m: ~ **report** Fehlerbericht m; **5.** big ~ F ,großes' od. ,hohes Tier' (Person); **6.** Am. F Fan m, Fa'natiker m: **baseball** ~; **7.** sl. ,Wanze' f (Abhörgerät); **II** v/t. sl. **8.** a) ,Wanzen' anbringen in e-m Raum etc., b) (heimlich) abhören; **9.** Am. F j-n nerven: **what's** ~**ging you?** was hast du denn?

bug·a·boo ['bʌgəbuː] s. **1.** → **bugbear**; **2.** ,Quatsch' m.

'**bug|·bear** s. a) ,Buhmann' m, b) Schreckgespenst n; '~-**eyed** adj. mit her'vorquellenden Augen.

bug·ger ['bʌgə] **I** s. **1.** a) Sodo'mit m, b) Homosexu'elle(r) m; **2.** V a) ,Scheißkerl' m, b) Kerl m, ,Knülch' m, c) ,Scheißding' n; **II** v/t. **3.** a) Sodo'mie treiben mit, b) a'nal verkehren mit: ~ (**it**)! V Scheiße!; ~ **you!** V leck mich!; **4.** a) j-n ,fertig machen', b) j-n ,nerven'; **5.** ~ (**up**) V et. versauen od. vermasseln; **III** v/i. **6.** ~ **around** V he'rumgammeln; **7.** ~ **off** V ,abhauen'; '**bug·ger·y** [-ərɪ] s. **1.** Sodo'mie f, 'widerna,türliche Unzucht; **2.** Homosexuali'tät f.

bug·ging| af·fair ['bʌgɪŋ] s. Abhöraffäre f; ~ **system** s. Abhöranlage f.

bug·gy¹ ['bʌgɪ] s. **1.** leichter (Pferde-) Wagen; **2.** mot. Buggy m (geländegängiges, offenes Freizeitauto); **3.** Am. Kinderwagen m.

bug·gy² ['bʌgɪ] adj. **1.** verwanzt; **2.** Am. sl. ,bekloppt', verrückt.

'**bug|·house** Am. sl. **I** s. ,Klapsmühle' f (Nervenheilanstalt); **II** adj. verrückt; '~-,**hunt·er** s. sl. In'sektensammler m.

bu·gle ['bjuːgl] **I** s. **1.** Wald-, Jagdhorn n; **2.** ⚔ Si'gnalhorn n: **sound the** ~ ein Hornsignal blasen; **bu·gle call** s. 'Hornsi,gnal n; '**bu·gler** [-lə] s. Hor'nist m.

buhl [buːl] s. Einlege-, Boulearbeit f.

build [bɪld] **I** v/t. [irr.] **1.** (er)bauen, errichten: ~ **a fire** (ein) Feuer machen; ~ **in** a) einbauen (a. fig.), b) zubauen; **2.** ⊕ bauen: a) konstruieren, b) herstellen: ~ **cars**; **3.** mst ~ **up** aufbauen, gründen, (er)schaffen: ~ **up a business** ein Geschäft aufbauen; ~ **up one's health** s-e Gesundheit festigen; ~ **up a reputation** sich e-n Namen machen; ~ **up a case** bsd. 🜊 (Beweis)Material zs.-tragen; **4.** ~ **up** a) zubauen, vermauern: ~ **up a window**, b) Gelände aus-, bebauen; **5.** ~ **up** fig. j-n ,aufbauen' od. groß her'ausstellen, Re'klame machen für; **6.** fig. gründen, setzen: ~ **one's hopes on s.th.**; **II** v/i. [irr.] **7.**

bauen; gebaut werden: **the house is** ~**ing** das Haus ist im Bau; **8.** fig. bauen, sich verlassen (**on** auf acc.); **9.** ~ (**up**) a) sich entwickeln, b) zunehmen, wachsen; **III** s. **10.** Bauart f, Gestalt f; **11.** Körperbau m, Fi'gur f; **12.** Schnitt m (Kleid); '**build·er** [-də] s. **1.** Erbauer m; **2.** Baumeister m; **3.** 'Bauunter,nehmer m, Bauhandwerker m: ~'**s merchant** Baustoffhändler m.

build·ing ['bɪldɪŋ] s. **1.** Bauen n, Bauwesen n; **2.** Gebäude n, Bau m, Bauwerk n; ~ **block** s. **1.** ⊕ u. fig. Baustein m; **2.** Bauklötzchen n für Kinder; ~ **con-trac·tor** s. 'Bauunter,nehmer m; ~ **lease** s. 🜊 Brit. Baupacht(vertrag m) f; ~ **line** s. ⊕ 'Baufluchtlinie f; ~ **lot**, ~ **plot**, ~ **site** s. **1.** Baugrund m; **2.** Baugrundstück n, Baugelände n; ~ **own·er** s. Bauherr m; ~ **so·ci·e·ty** s. Brit. Bausparkasse f.

'**build-up** s. **1.** Aufbau m, Zs.-stellung f; **2.** Zunahme f; **3.** ,Aufbau(en)' n, Re'klame f, Propa'ganda f; **4.** dra'matische Steigerung.

built [bɪlt] pret. u. p.p. von **build** I u. II; **II** adj. gebaut, geformt: **he is** ~ **that way** F so ist er eben; ~**-'in** adj. eingebaut (a. fig.), Einbau...; '~**-up a·re·a** s. **1.** bebautes Gelände; **2.** Verkehr: geschlossene Ortschaft.

bulb [bʌlb] **I** s. **1.** ⚘ Knolle f, Zwiebel f (e-r Pflanze); **2.** Zwiebelgewächs n; **3.** (Glas- etc.)Bal'lon m od. Kolben m; Kugel f (Thermometer); **4.** 🜊 Glühbirne f, -lampe f; **II** v/i. **5.** rundlich anschwellen; Knollen bilden; **bulbed** [-bd] adj. knollenförmig; '**bulb·ous** [-bəs] adj. knollig, Knollen...: ~ **nose**.

Bul·gar ['bʌlgɑː] s. Bul'gare m, Bul'garin f; **Bul·gar·i·an** [bʌl'geərɪən] **I** adj. bul'garisch; **II** s. → **Bulgar**.

bulge [bʌldʒ] **I** s. **1.** (Aus)Bauchung f, (a. ⚔ Front)Ausbuchtung f; Anschwellung f, Beule f; Vorsprung m, Buckel m; Rundung f, Bauch m, Wulst m: **the battle of the** ~ fig. der Kampf um die Pfunde, der Versuch, abzunehmen; **Battle of the** ⚲ Ardennenschlacht f (1944); **2.** ⚓ ↓ bilge; **3.** Anschwellen n, Zunahme f, plötzliches Steigen (bsd. der Börsenkurse); **4.** a. ~ **age group** geburtenstarker Jahrgang; **5. have a** ~ **on** s.o. sl. j-m gegenüber im Vorteil sein; **II** v/i. **6.** sich (aus)bauchen, her-'vortreten, -ragen, -quellen, sich blähen od. bauschen; '**bulg·ing** [-dʒɪŋ] adj. (zum Bersten) voll (**with** von).

bu·lim·i·a [bjuː'lɪmɪə] s. Bulimie f, Fresssucht f.

bulk [bʌlk] **I** s. **1.** 'Umfang m, Größe f, Masse f; **2.** große od. massige Gestalt; 'Körper,umfang m, -fülle f; **3.** Hauptteil m, -masse f, Großteil m, Mehrheit f; **4.** ✝ (gekaufte) Gesamtheit; ⚓ (unverpackte) Schiffsladung: **in** ~ a) unverpackt, lose, b) in großen Mengen, en gros; **break** ~ ⚓ zu löschen anfangen; ~ **cargo**, ~ **goods** ✝ Schüttgut n, Massengüter pl.; ~ **buying** ✝ Mengeneinkauf m; ~ **discount** 'Mengenra,batt m; ~ **mail** Postwurfsendung f; ~ **mortgage** Am. Fahrnishypothek f; **II** v/i. **5.** 'umfangreich od. sperrig sein; **6.** fig. wichtig sein: ~ **large** e-e große Rolle spielen; **III** v/t. **7.** bsd. Am. aufstapeln; '~**·head** s. **1.** ⚓ Schott n; **2.** ⊕ a) Schutzwand f, b) Spant m.

bulk·y ['bʌlkɪ] adj. **1.** (sehr) 'umfangreich, massig; **2.** sperrig: ~ **goods** ✝ Sperrgut m.

bull¹ [bʊl] **I** s. **1.** zo. Bulle m, Stier m: **like a** ~ **in a china shop** wie ein Elefant im Porzellanladen; **take the ~ by the horns** den Stier bei den Hörnern packen; **2.** *zo.* (*Elefanten-, Elch-, Wal- etc.*)Bulle *m*; **3.** ✝ Haussi'er *m*, 'Haussespeku,lant *m*; **4.** *Am. sl.* ‚Bulle' *m* (*Polizist*); **5.** *ast.* Stier *m*; **6.** → **bull's-eye** 3 *u.* 4; **II** *v/t.* **7.** ✝ Preise in die Höhe treiben für *et.*: **~ the market** auf Hausse kaufen; **III** *v/i.* **8.** ✝ auf Hausse spekulieren; **IV** *adj.* **9.** männlich; **10.** ✝ steigend, Hausse...: **~ market**.

bull² [bʊl] *s.* (päpstliche) Bulle.

bull³ [bʊl] *s. sl.* **1.** *a. Irish* ~ ungereimtes Zeug, 'widersprüchliche Behauptung; **2.** Schnitzer *m*, Faux'pas *m*; **3.** *Am.* Quatsch *m*, Blödsinn *m*.

'**bull|-,bait·ing** *s.* Stierhetze *f*; **~ bars** *s. pl. mot.* Schutzgitter *n* (*an Vorderseite von Fahrzeugen*); '**~·dog** **I** *s.* **1.** *zo.* Bulldogge *f*; **2.** *Brit. univ.* Begleiter *m* des 'Proctors; **3.** *e-e* Pi'stole (*f*; **II** *adj.* **4.** mutig, zäh, hartnäckig; '**~·doze** *v/t.* **1.** planieren, räumen; **2.** F ‚über'fahren', einschüchtern, terrorisieren; zwingen (*into* zu); '**~·doz·er** [-,dəʊzə] *s.* **1.** ⊙ Planierraupe *f*, Bulldozer *m*; **2.** *fig.* F → **bully²** 1.

bul·let ['bʊlɪt] *s.* **1.** (Gewehr- *etc.*)Kugel *f*, Geschoss *n*, östr. Geschoß *n*: **bite the ~** *fig.* die bittere Pille schlucken; **2.** *Computer*: Aufzählungszeichen *n*; **~ head** *s.* **1.** Rundkopf *m*; **2.** *Am.* F Dickkopf *m*.

bul·le·tin ['bʊlɪtɪn] *s.* **1.** Bulle'tin *n*: a) Tagesbericht *m* (*a.* ✕), b) Krankenbericht *m*, c) offizi'elle Bekanntmachung: **~ board** *Am.* schwarzes Brett (*für Anschläge*); **2.** Mitteilungsblatt *n*; **3.** *Am.* Kurznachricht *f*.

'**bul·let·proof** *adj.* kugelsicher.

'**bull|·fight** *s.* Stierkampf *m*; '**~·,fight·er** *s.* Stierkämpfer *m*; '**~·finch** *s.* **1.** *orn.* Dompfaff *m*; **2.** hohe Hecke; '**~·frog** *s. zo.* Ochsenfrosch *m*; ‚**~·'head·ed** *adj.* starrköpfig.

bul·lion ['bʊljən] *s.* **1.** ungemünztes Gold *od.* Silber: **~ point** ✝ Goldpunkt *m*; **2.** Gold *n od.* Silber *n* in Barren; **3.** Gold-, Silberlitze *f*, -schnur *f*, -troddel *f*.

bull·ish ['bʊlɪʃ] *adj.* **1.** dickköpfig; **2.** ✝ steigend, Hausse...

‚**bull·'necked** *adj.* stiernackig.

bull·ock ['bʊlək] *s. zo.* Ochse *m*.

bull| pen *s. Am.* **1.** *sl.* Ba'racke *f* für Holzfäller; **2.** F a) ‚Kittchen' *n*, b) große (Gefängnis)Zelle; **3.** *Baseball*: Übungsplatz *m* für Re'servewerfer; '**~·ring** *s.* 'Stierkampfa,rena *f*.

bull's-eye ['bʊlzaɪ] *s.* **1.** ♣, ⌂ Bullauge *n*, rundes Fensterchen; **2.** *a.* **~ pane** Ochsenauge *n*, Butzenscheibe *f*; **3.** Zentrum *n od.* das Schwarze *der Zielscheibe*; **4.** *a. fig.* Schuss *m* ins Schwarze, 'Volltreffer *m*; **5.** 'Blendla,terne *f*; **6.** großer runder 'Pfefferminz,bon,bon.

'**bull|·shit** *s. u. int.* V Scheiß(dreck) *m*; **~ ter·ri·er** *s. zo.* 'Bull,terrier *m*.

bul·ly¹ ['bʊlɪ] *s. a.* **~ beef** Rinderpökelfleisch *n* (in Büchsen).

bul·ly² ['bʊlɪ] **I** *s.* **1.** bru'taler Kerl, ‚Schläger' *m*; Ty'rann *m*; Maulheld *m*; **2.** *obs.* Zuhälter *m*; **3.** *Hockey*: Bully *n*, Anspiel *n*; **II** *v/t.* **4.** tyrannisieren, schikanieren, einschüchtern, piesacken; **III** *adj.* **5.** F ‚prima' (*a. int.*); **IV** *int.* **6.** F bravo!, Klasse!

bul·ly| beef → **bully¹**; '**~·rag** → **ballyrag**.

bul·rush ['bʊlrʌʃ] *s.* ♀ *große* Binse.

bul·wark ['bʊlwək] *s.* **1.** Bollwerk *n*, Wall *m* (*beide a. fig.*); **2.** ♣ a) Hafen-

---

damm *m*, b) Schanzkleid *n*.

bum¹ [bʌm] *bsd. Brit.* F **1.** ‚Hintern' *m*; **2.** ‚Niete' *f*, ‚Flasche' *f*.

bum² [bʌm] *bsd. Am.* F **I** *s.* **1.** a) ‚Stromer' *m*, ‚Gammler' *m*, He'rumtreiber *m*, b) Tippelbruder *m*, c) Schnorrer *m*, d) Mistkerl *m*; **II** *v/i.* **2.** *mst* **~ around** ‚he'rumgammeln'; **3.** schnorren (*off* bei); **III** *v/t.* **4.** *et.* schnorren (*of* bei, *von*); **IV** *adj.* **5.** a) ‚mies', schlecht, b) ka'putt.

bum·ble-bee ['bʌmblbiː] *s. zo.* Hummel *f*.

bum·ble·dom ['bʌmbldəm] *s.* Wichtigtue'rei *f* der kleinen Beamten.

bumf [bʌmf] *s. Brit. sl.* **1.** *contp.* ‚Papierkram' *m* (*Akten, Formulare etc.*); **2.** ‚Klopa,pier' *n.*

bum·mer ['bʌmə] → **bum²** 1.

bump [bʌmp] **I** *v/t.* **1.** (heftig) stoßen, (an)prallen: **~ one's head** sich den Kopf anstoßen; *I* **~ed my head against** (*od. on*) **the door** ich stieß *od.* rannte mit dem Kopf gegen die Tür; **~ a car** auf ein Auto auffahren; **2.** *Rudern*: *Boot* über'holen u. anstoßen; **3.** *~ off sl.* ‚umlegen', ‚kaltmachen'; **4.** **~ up** F *Preise etc.* hochtreiben, *Gehalt etc.* aufbessern; **II** *v/i.* **5.** (**against**, **into**) stoßen, prallen, bumsen (gegen), zs.-stoßen (mit): **~ into** *fig. j-n* zufällig treffen, zufällig stoßen auf (*acc.*); **6.** rütteln, holpern (*Wagen*); **III** *s.* **7.** heftiger Stoß, Bums *m*; **8.** ✱ Beule *f*, Höcker *m*; **9.** Unebenheit *f* (*Straße*); **10.** Sinn *m* (*für et.*): **~ of locality** Ortssinn; **11.** ✈ (Steig)Bö *f*; **IV** *adv.* **12.** bums!

bump·er ['bʌmpə] *s.* **1.** randvolles Glas (*Wein etc.*); **2.** F *et.* Riesiges: **~ crop** Rekordernte *f*; **~ house** *thea.* volles Haus; **3.** ✱ *Am.* Puffer *m*; **4.** *mot.* Stoßstange *f*: **~ car** (Auto)Skooter *m*; **~ guard** Stoßstangenhorn *n*; **~ sticker** Autoaufkleber *m*.

bump·kin ['bʌmpkɪn] *s.* Bauernlackel *m.*

'**bump-start** *s. Brit. mot.* **I** *s.* Anschieben *n*; **II** *v/t. Auto* anschieben.

bump·tious ['bʌmpʃəs] *adj.* □ aufgeblasen.

bump·y ['bʌmpɪ] *adj.* **1.** holperig, uneben; **2.** ✈ ‚bockig', böig.

bum| steer *s. Am. sl.*: **give s.o. the ~** j-n ‚verschaukeln'; '**~·,suck·er** *s.* V ‚Arschkriecher' *m.*

bun¹ [bʌn] *s.* **1.** süßes Brötchen: **she has a ~ in the oven** *sl.* bei ihr ist was unterwegs; **2.** (Haar)Knoten *m.*

bun² [bʌn] *s. Brit.* Ka'ninchen *n.*

bunch [bʌntʃ] **I** *s.* **1.** Bündel *n* (*a.* ⚡), Bund *n*, Büschel *n*: **~ of flowers** Blumenstrauß *m*; **~ of grapes** Weintraube *f*; **~ of keys** Schlüsselbund; **2.** F a) Haufen *m*, ‚Verein' *m*: **the best of the ~** der Beste von allen; **II** *v/t.* **3.** bündeln (*a.* ⚡), zs.-fassen, -binden; falten: **~ed circuit** *f* Leitungsbündel *n*; **III** *v/i.* **4.** sich zs.-legen, -schließen; **5.** sich bauschen; **6.** *oft* **~ up** (*od.* **together**) Grüppchen (*od.* Haufen) bilden; **7.** *oft* **~ up** sich zs.-knüllen (*Kleid etc.*); '**bunch·ing** *s. mot.* Ko'lonnenbildung *f*, -fahren *n*; '**bunch·y** [-tʃɪ] *adj.* büschelig, bauschig, in Bündeln.

bunc·ing ['bʌnsɪŋ] *s. Brit.* F *Preiserhöhungen als Ausgleich für Verluste durch Ladendiebstahl.*

bun·co ['bʌŋkəʊ] *v/t. Am. sl.* ‚reinlegen', betrügen.

bun·dle ['bʌndl] **I** *s.* **1.** Bündel *n*, Bund *n*; Pa'ket *n*; Ballen *m*: **~ of energy** (**nerves**) *fig.* Kraft-(Nerven)Bündel *n*; **2.** *fig.* a) Menge *f*, Haufen *m*, b) F ‚Batzen' *m* Geld; **3.** in Bündel

---

zs.-binden, -packen; **4.** *et. wohin* stopfen; **5.** *mst* **~ off** (*od.* **out**) zs.-schieben, (eilig) fortschaffen: **he was ~d into a taxi** er wurde in ein Taxi verfrachtet *od.* gepackt; **III** *v/i.* **6.** **~ off** (*od.* **out**) sich packen *od.* da'vonmachen.

bung [bʌŋ] **I** *s.* **1.** Spund(zapfen) *m*, Stöpsel *m*; **2.** ✕ Mündungspfropfen *m* (*Geschütz*); **II** *v/t.* **3.** verspunden, verstopfen; zupfropfen; **4.** F ‚schmeißen', werfen; **5.** **~ up** Röhre, Öffnung verstopfen (*mst pass.*): **~ed up** verstopft; **6.** *mst* **~ up** *Am.* F *Auto etc.* schwer beschädigen, verbeulen.

bun·ga·low ['bʌŋgələʊ] *s.* 'Bungalow *m.*

bun·gee jump·ing ['bʌndʒiː] *s.* 'Bungee,jumping *n.*

bung·hole ['bʌŋhəʊl] *s.* Spund-, Zapfloch *n.*

bun·gle ['bʌŋgl] **I** *v/i.* **1.** stümpern, pfuschen; **II** *v/t.* **2.** verpfuschen; **III** *s.* **3.** Stümpe'rei *f*; **4.** Fehler *m*, ‚Schnitzer' *m*; '**bun·gler** [-lə] *s.* Stümper *m*, Pfuscher *m*; '**bun·gling** [-lɪŋ] *adj.* □ ungeschickt, stümperhaft.

bun·ion ['bʌnjən] *s.* ✱ entzündeter Fußballen.

bunk¹ [bʌŋk] **I** *s.* a) ♣ (Schlaf)Koje *f*, b) Schlafstelle *f*, Bett *n*, ‚Falle' *f*: **~ bed** Etagenbett *n*; **II** *v/i.* a) in e-r Koje schlafen, b) *oft* **~ down** F ‚kampieren'.

bunk² [bʌŋk] *abbr. für* **bunkum**.

bunk³ [bʌŋk] *Brit.* F **I** *s.*: **do a ~** → **II** *v/i.* ‚ausreißen', ‚türmen'.

bunk·er ['bʌŋkə] **I** *s.* **1.** ♣ (Kohlen)Bunker *m*; **2.** ✕ Bunker *m*, bombensicherer 'Unterstand; **3.** *Golf*: Bunker *m* (*Hindernis*); **II** *v/t.* **4.** ♣ bunkern; **5.** *Golf*: *Ball* in e-n Bunker schlagen; '**bunk·ered** [-əd] *adj.* F in der Klemme.

bun·kum ['bʌŋkəm] *s.* ‚Blech' *n*, Blödsinn *m*, Quatsch *m.*

bun·ny ['bʌnɪ] *s.* Häs-chen *n* (*a.* F *süßes Mädchen*).

bun·ting¹ ['bʌntɪŋ] *s.* **1.** Flaggentuch *n*; **2.** *coll.* Flaggen *pl.*

bun·ting² ['bʌntɪŋ] *s. orn.* Ammer *f.*

buoy [bɔɪ] **I** *s.* **1.** ♣ Boje *f*, Bake *f*, Seezeichen *n*; **II** *v/t.* **2.** *a.* **~ out** Fahrrinne durch Bojen markieren; **3.** *mst* **~ up** flott erhalten; **4.** *fig.* Auftrieb geben (*dat.*), beleben: **~ed up** hoffnungsvoll; **buoy·an·cy** ['bɔɪənsɪ] *s.* **1.** *phys.* Schwimm-, Tragkraft *f*; **2.** ✈ Auftrieb *m* (*a. fig.*); **3.** *fig.* Schwung *m*, Spann-, Lebenskraft *f*; **buoy·ant** ['bɔɪənt] *adj.* □ **1.** schwimmend, tragend (*Wasser etc.*); **2.** *fig.* schwungvoll, lebhaft; **3.** ✝ steigend; lebhaft.

bur [bɜː] *s.* **1.** ♀ Klette *f* (*a. fig.*): **cling to s.o. like a ~** *fig.* wie e-e Klette an j-m hängen; **2.** → **burr¹** I.

bur·ble ['bɜːbl] **I** *v/i.* **1.** brodeln, sprudeln; **2.** plappern; **II** *s.* **3.** ⊙, ✈ Wirbel *m.*

bur·bot ['bɜːbət] *s. ichth.* Quappe *f.*

bur·den¹ ['bɜːdn] *s.* **1.** Re'frain *m*, Kehrreim *m*; **2.** Hauptgedanke *m*, Kern *m.*

bur·den² ['bɜːdn] **I** *s.* **1.** Last *f*, Ladung *f*; *fig.* Last *f*, Bürde *f*, (*a. finanzi'elle*) Belastung, Druck *m*: **~ of proof** ✝ Beweislast; **~ of years** Last der Jahre; **he is a ~ on me** er fällt mir zur Last; **3.** ⊙ Traglast *f*; **4.** ♣ Tragfähigkeit *f*, Ladung *f*; **II** *v/t.* **5.** belasten: **~ s.o. with s.th.** j-m et. aufbürden; '**bur·den·some** [-səm] *adj.* lästig, drückend.

bur·dock ['bɜːdɒk] *s.* ♀ Große Klette.

bu·reau ['bjʊərəʊ] *pl.* **-reaus**, **-reaux** [-rəʊz] *s.* **1.** Bü'ro *n*; Geschäfts-, Amtszimmer *n*; **2.** Behörde *f*; **3.** *Brit.* Schreibpult *n*; **4.** *Am.* ('Spiegel)Kom,mode *f*; **bu·reauc·ra·cy** [bjʊəˈrɒkrəsɪ]

s. **1.** Bürokra'tie f; **2.** coll. Beamtenschaft f; **'bu·reau·crat** [-əʊkræt] s. Büro'krat m; **bu·reau·crat·ic** [‚bjʊərəʊ-'krætɪk] adj. (□ **~ally**) büro'kratisch; **bu·reauc·ra·tize** [bjʊə'rɒkrətaɪz] v/t. bürokratisieren.

bu·reau de change [‚bjʊərəʊdə'ʃɑ̃:ʒ] s. Wechselstube f.

bu·rette [bjʊə'ret] s. Bü'rette f.

burg [bɜːg] s. Am. F Stadt f.

bur·geon ['bɜːdʒən] I s. ♀ Knospe f; II v/i. knospen, (her'vor)sprießen (a. fig.).

bur·gess ['bɜːdʒɪs] s. hist. **1.** Bürger m; **2.** Abgeordnete(r) m.

burgh ['bʌrə] s. Scot. Stadt f (= Brit. **borough**); **burgh·er** ['bɜːgə] s. **1.** (konserva'tiver) Bürger; **2.** Städter m.

bur·glar ['bɜːglə] s. Einbrecher: **we had ~s last night** bei uns wurde letzte Nacht eingebrochen; **~ a·larm** s. A'larmanlage f.

bur·glar·i·ous [bɜː'gleərɪəs] adj. □ Einbruchs..., einbrecherisch; **bur·glar·ize** ['bɜːgləraɪz] → **burgle**.

'bur·glar·proof adj. einbruchsicher.

bur·gla·ry ['bɜːglərɪ] s. (nächtlicher) Einbruch; Einbruchdiebstahl m; **bur·gle** ['bɜːgl] v/t. einbrechen in (acc.).

bur·go·mas·ter ['bɜːgəʊ‚mɑːstə] s. Bürgermeister m (in Deutschland, Holland etc.).

bur·gun·dy ['bɜːgəndɪ] s. a. **~ wine** Bur'gunder m.

bur·i·al ['berɪəl] s. **1.** Begräbnis n, Beerdigung f; **2.** Leichenfeier f; **3.** Ein-, Vergraben n; **~ ground** s. Begräbnisplatz m, Friedhof m; **~ mound** s. Grabhügel m; **~ place** s. Grabstätte f; **~ serv·ice** s. Trauerfeier f.

burke [bɜːk] v/t. fig. a) vertuschen, b) vermeiden.

bur·lap ['bɜːlæp] s. Sackleinwand f, Rupfen m, Juteleinen n.

bur·lesque [bɜː'lesk] I adj. **1.** bur'lesk, possenhaft; II s. **2.** Bur'leske f, Posse f; **3.** Am. Varie'tee n.

bur·ly ['bɜːlɪ] adj. stämmig.

Bur·man ['bɜːmən] s. Bir'mane m, Bir'manin f; **Bur·mese** [‚bɜː'miːz] I adj. bir'manisch; II s. a) → **Burman**, b) Bir'manen pl.

burn¹ [bɜːn] I s. **1.** verbrannte Stelle; **2.** Brandwunde f, -mal n; II v/i. [irr.] **3.** (ver)brennen, in Flammen stehen, in Brand geraten: **the house is ~ing** das Haus brennt; **the stove ~s well** der Ofen brennt gut; **all the lights were ~ing** alle Lichter brannten; **4.** fig. (ent)brennen, dar'auf brennen (to inf. zu inf.): **~ing with anger** wutentbrannt; **~ing with love** von Liebe entflammt; **5.** an-, verbrennen, versengen: **the meat is ~t** das Fleisch ist angebrannt; **6.** brennen (Gesicht, Zunge etc.); **7.** verbrannt werden, in den Flammen 'umkommen; → 9; III v/t. [irr.] **8.** (ver)brennen: **our boiler ~s coke; his house was ~t** sein Haus brannte ab; **9.** ver-, anbrennen, versengen, durch Feuer od. Hitze verletzen: **~ a hole** ein Loch brennen; **the soup is ~t** die Suppe ist angebrannt; **I have ~t my fingers** ich habe mir die Finger verbrannt (a. fig.); **~ to death** verbrennen; → 7; **10.** ⊙ e-e CD, Porzellan, (Holz-) Kohle, Ziegel brennen; **~ down** v/t. u. v/i. ab-, niederbrennen; **~ out** I v/i. ausbrennen, ⚡ 'durchbrennen; II v/t. ausbrennen, -räuchern: **~ o.s. out** fig. sich kaputtmachen od. völlig verausgaben; **~ up** I v/t. **1.** ganz verbrennen; **2.** Am.

F j-n wütend machen; II v/i. **3.** auflodern; **4.** a) ab-, aus-, verbrennen, b) verglühen (Rakete etc.).

burn² [bɜːn] s. Scot. Bach m.

burn·er ['bɜːnə] s. Brenner m (Person u. Gerät): **gas ~.**

burn·ing ['bɜːnɪŋ] adj. brennend, heiß, glühend (a. fig.): **a ~ question** e-e brennende Frage; **~ glass** s. Brennglas n.

bur·nish ['bɜːnɪʃ] I v/t. **1.** polieren, blank reiben; **2.** ⊙ brünieren; II v/i. **3.** blank od. glatt werden; **'bur·nish·er** [-ʃə] s. Polierer m, Brünierer m; **bur·nouse** [bɜː'nuːz] s. 'Burnus m.

'burn·out s. **1.** ⚡ 'Durchbrennen n; **2.** Brennschluss m (e-r Rakete).

burnt| al·monds [bɜːnt] s. pl. gebrannte Mandeln pl.; **~ lime** s. ⊙ gebrannter Kalk; **~ of·fer·ing** s. bibl. Brandopfer n.

burp [bɜːp] I rülpsen, aufstoßen, ein 'Bäuerchen' machen (Baby); II v/t. Baby ein 'Bäuerchen' machen lassen.

burr¹ [bɜː] I s. **1.** ⊙ Grat m (raue Kante); **2.** ⊙ Schleif-, Mühlstein m; **3.** ⚒ (Zahn)Bohrer m; II v/t. **4.** ⊙ abgraten.

burr² [bɜː] I s. **1.** Zäpfchenaussprache f des R; II v/t. u. v/i. **2.** (das R) schnarren; **3.** undeutlich sprechen.

burr³ [bɜː] → **bur** 1.

burr drill s. ⊙, ⚒ Drillbohrer m.

bur·row ['bʌrəʊ] I s. **1.** (Fuchs- etc.)Bau m, Höhle f; II v/i. **2.** sich eingraben; **3.** fig. sich verkriechen od. verbergen; sich vertiefen (**into** in acc.); III v/t. **4.** Bau graben.

bur·sar ['bɜːsə] s. univ. **1.** 'Quästor m, Fi'nanzverwalter m; **2.** Stipendi'at m; **'bur·sa·ry** [-ərɪ] s. univ. **1.** Quä'stur f; **2.** Sti'pendium n.

bur·si·tis [bɜː'saɪtɪs] s. ⚕ Schleimbeutelentzündung f.

burst [bɜːst] I v/i. [irr.] **1.** bersten, (auf- od. zer)platzen, (auf-, zer)springen; explodieren; sich entladen (Gewitter); aufspringen (Knospe); aufgehen (Geschwür): **~ open** aufplatzen, -springen; **2. ~ in (out)** herein-, (hinaus)stürmen: **~ in (up)on** a) hereinplatzen bei j-m, b) sich einmischen in (acc.); **3.** fig. ausbrechen, her'ausplatzen: **~ into tears** in Tränen ausbrechen; **~ into laughter, ~ out laughing** in Gelächter ausbrechen; **~ out** herausplatzen (sagen); **4.** fig. platzen, bersten (**with** vor dat.); gespannt sein, brennen: **~ with envy** vor Neid platzen; **I am ~ing to tell you** ich brenne darauf, es dir zu sagen; **5.** zum Bersten voll sein (**with** von): **a larder ~ing with food** e-e zum Bersten volle Speisekammer; **~ with health (energy)** vor Gesundheit (Kraft) strotzen; **6.** **~ up** zs.-brechen, Bank'rott gehen; **7.** plötzlich sichtbar werden: **~ into view**; **~ forth** hervorbrechen, -sprudeln; **~ upon s.o.** j-m plötzlich klar werden; II v/t. [irr.] **8.** sprengen, auf-, zerbrechen, zum Platzen bringen (a. fig.): **~ open** sprengen, aufbrechen; **I have ~ a bloodvessel** mir ist e-e Ader geplatzt; **the river ~ its banks** a) der Fluss trat über die Ufer, b) der Fluss durchbrach die Dämme; **the car ~ a tyre** ein Reifen am Wagen platzte; **~ one's sides with laughter** sich vor Lachen ausschütten; **9.** fig. zum Scheitern bringen, auffliegen lassen, ruinieren; III s. **10.** Bersten n, Platzen n, Explosi'on f; ⚒ Feuerstoß m (Maschinengewehr); Auffliegen n, Ausbruch m: **~ of laughter** Lachsalve f; **~ of applause** Beifallssturm m; **~ of hospitality** plötzliche Anwendung von Gastfreundschaft;

11. Bruch m, Riss m, Sprung m (a. fig.); **12.** plötzliches Erscheinen; **13.** sport (Zwischen)Spurt m.

'burst-up s. sl. **1.** Bank'rott m, Zs.-bruch m, Pleite f; **2.** Krach m, Streit m; **3.** Saufe'rei f.

bur·y ['berɪ] v/t. **1.** begraben, beerdigen; **2.** ein-, vergraben, verschütten, versenken (a. fig.): **buried cable** ⚡ Erdkabel n; **3.** verbergen; **4.** fig. begraben, vergessen; **5. ~ o.s.** sich verkriechen, fig. sich vertiefen: **~ o.s. in books** sich in Büchern vergraben.

bus [bʌs] I pl. **'bus·es** [-sɪz] s. **1.** Omnibus m, (Auto)Bus m: **miss the ~** F den Anschluss (Gelegenheit) verpassen; **2.** sl. ‚Kiste' f (Auto od. Flugzeug); II v/i. **3.** a. **~ it** mit dem Omnibus fahren; III v/t. **4.** mit dem Bus transportieren; **~ bar** s. ⚡ Sammel-, Stromschiene f; **~ boy** s. Am. 'Pikkolo m, Hilfskellner m.

bus·by ['bʌzbɪ] s. ✕ Bärenmütze f.

bush¹ [bʊʃ] s. **1.** Busch m, Strauch m: **beat about the ~** fig. wie die Katze um den heißen Brei herumgehen, um die Sache herumreden; **2.** Gebüsch n, Dickicht n; **3.** Busch m, Urwald m; **4.** (Haar)Schopf m.

bush² [bʊʃ] s. ⊙ Lagerfutter n.

bushed [bʊʃt] adj. ‚erledigt', erschöpft.

bush·el¹ ['bʊʃl] s. Scheffel m (36,37 l); → **light** ¹ 1.

bush·el² ['bʊʃl] v/t. Am. Kleidung ausbessern, flicken, ändern.

bush| fight·er s. Gue'rillakämpfer m; **~ league** s. bsd. Baseball: Am. F a) untere Spielklasse, b) Pro'vinzliga f; **'~-league** adj. Am. F Schmalspur...; Provinz...; **'~-man** [-mən] s. [irr.] **1.** Buschmann m; **2.** 'Hinterwäldler m.

bush·y ['bʊʃɪ] adj. buschig.

busi·ness ['bɪznɪs] s. **1.** Geschäft n, Tätigkeit f, Arbeit f, Beruf m, Gewerbe n: **what is his ~?** was ist er von Beruf?; → a. 5; **on ~** beruflich, geschäftlich; **~ of the day** Tagesordnung f; **2.** a) Handel m, Kaufmannsberuf m, Geschäftsleben n, b) a. **~ activity** Ge'schäftsvo‚lumen n, 'Umsatz m: **go into ~** Kaufmann werden; **be in ~** Kaufmann sein; **go out of ~** das Geschäft od. den Beruf aufgeben; **do good ~ (with)** gute Geschäfte machen (mit); **lose ~** Kundschaft od. Aufträge verlieren; **~ as usual!** nichts Besonderes!; → **big** 1; **3.** Geschäft n, Firma f, Unter'nehmen n, Laden m, Ge'schäftslo‚kal n; **4.** Aufgabe f, Pflicht f; Recht n: **make it one's ~ (to inf.)** es sich zur Aufgabe machen (zu inf.); **have no ~ (to inf.)** kein Recht haben (zu inf.); **what ~ had you (to inf.)?** wie kamst du dazu (zu inf.)?; **send s.o. about his ~** j-m heimleuchten; **he means ~** er meint es ernst; **5.** Sache f, Angelegenheit f: **that is none of your ~** das geht dich nichts an; **mind your own ~** kümmere dich um d-e eigenen Angelegenheiten; **what is your ~?** was ist dein Anliegen?; → a. 1; **what a ~ it is!** das ist ja e-e schreckliche Geschichte!; **like nobody's ~** F ‚wie nichts', ‚ganz toll'; **get down to ~** zur Sache kommen; **~ ad·dress** s. Ge'schäfts‚adresse f; **~ ad·min·is·tra·tion** → **business economics**; **~ al·low·ance** s. Werbungskosten pl.; **~ as·so·ci·ate** [-ʃiət] s. **1.** Geschäftspartner(in); **2.** Teilhaber(in); **3.** weitS. Ge'schäftsfreund (-in); **~ cap·i·tal** s. Be'triebskapi‚tal n; **~ card** s. Geschäftskarte f; **~ class** s. 'Business-Class f; **~ col·lege** s. Wirtschaftsoberschule f; **~ con·fi·dence** s. optimistische Grundhaltung der Wirtschaft; **~ con·sult·ant** s. Betriebsberater m; **~ cy·cle** s. Konjunk'tur(zyklus m) f; **~ down·turn** s. Konjunkturrückgang m; **~ e·co·nom·ics** s. pl. sg. konstr. Brit. Betriebswirtschaft(slehre) f; **~ end** s. F wesentlicher Teil, z.B. Spitze f e-s Bohrers od. Dolches, Mündung f e-s Gewehres; **~ hours** s. pl. Geschäftsstunden pl., -zeit f; **~ let·ter** s. Geschäftsbrief m; **'~-like** adj. **1.** geschäftsmäßig, sachlich, nüchtern; **2.** (geschäfts-) tüchtig; **~ line** s. Branche f; **~ lunch** s. Arbeitsessen n; **'~-man** s. [irr.] Geschäfts-, Kaufmann m; **~ practic·es** s. pl. Geschäftsmethoden pl., -gebaren n; **~ prem·is·es** s. pl. Geschäftsräume pl.; **~ re·search** s. Konjunk'turforschung f; **~ re·viv·al** s. Konjunkturbelebung f; **~ suit** Am. → lounge suit; **~ trip** s. Geschäfts-, Dienstreise f; **'~-wom·an** s. [irr.] Geschäftsfrau f; **~ year** s. Geschäftsjahr n.

busk¹ [bʌsk] s. Kor'settstäbchen n.

busk² [bʌsk] v/i. Brit. F auf der Straße musizieren etc.; **'busk·er** [-kə] s. Brit. 'Straßenmusi,kant m od. -akro,bat m.

bus·kin ['bʌskɪn] s. **1.** Halbstiefel m; **2.** Ko'thurn m; **3.** fig. Tra'gödie f.

'bus|·man [-mən] s. [irr.] Omnibusfahrer m: **~'s holiday** mit der üblichen Berufsarbeit verbrachter Urlaub; **~ shel·ter** s. (Bus)Wartehäuschen n.

bus·sing ['bʌsɪŋ] s. Am. Beförderung von Schülern mit Bussen in andere Schulen, um Rassenintegration zu erreichen.

bust¹ [bʌst] s. Büste f: a) Brustbild n, Kopf m (aus Marmor, Bronze etc.), b) anat. Busen m.

bust² [bʌst] sl. **I** v/i. **1.** oft **~ up** ,ka'puttgehen', ,eingehen', **♥** a. ,Pleite' gehen; **2.** ,auffliegen', ,platzen'; **II** v/t. **3.** ,ka'puttmachen': a) sprengen, b) ruinieren; **4.** ,auffliegen' lassen, zerschlagen; **5.** Am. ,knallen', hauen; **6.** einbrechen in (acc.); **7.** einsperren; **8.** ✕ degradieren; **III** s. **9.** Sauftour f: **go on the ~** ,einen draufmachen'; **10.** ,Pleite' f, Bank'rott m; **11.** Razzia f; **IV** adv. **12.** **go ~** → 1.

bus·tard ['bʌstəd] s. orn. Trappe f.

bust·er ['bʌstə] s. sl. a) ,Mordsding' n, b) Kerl m, Bursche m, ,Kumpel' m; **2.** in Zssgn ...knacker m: **safe ~** Geldschrankknacker; **3.** → bust² 9.

bus·ti·er ['bʌstɪə; Am. 'buːstɪeɪ] s. Kleidungsstück: Busti'er n.

bus·tle¹ ['bʌsl] s. hist. Tur'nüre f.

bus·tle² ['bʌsl] **I** v/i. a. **~ about** geschäftig hin u. her rennen, ,her'umfuhrwerken', hasten, sich tummeln; **II** v/t. **~ up** hetzen; **III** s. Geschäftigkeit f, geschäftiges Treiben, Getriebe n, Gewühl n; Gehetze n; Getue n; **'bus·tler** [-lə] s. geschäftiger Mensch; **'bus·tling** [-lɪŋ] adj. geschäftig.

'bust-up s. F ,Krach' m.

bus·y ['bɪzɪ] **I** adj. ☐ **1.** beschäftigt, tätig: **be ~ packing** mit Packen beschäftigt sein; **get ~** F sich ,ranmachen'; **2.** geschäftig, rührig, fleißig: **as ~ as a bee** bienenfleißig; **3.** belebt (Straße etc.); ereignis-, arbeitsreich (Zeit); **4.** auf-, zudringlich; **5.** teleph. Am. besetzt (Leitung): **~ signal** Besetztzeichen n; **II** v/t. **6.** (o.s. sich) beschäftigen (with, in, at, about ger. mit); **'~,bod·y** s. ,Gschaftlhuber' m, 'Übereifrige(r) m, Wichtigtuer m.

bus·y·ness ['bɪzɪnɪs] s. Geschäftigkeit f.

but [bʌt; bət] **I** cj. **1.** aber, je'doch, sondern: **small ~ select** klein, aber fein; **I wished to go ~ I couldn't** ich wollte

gehen, aber ich konnte nicht; **not only ... ~ also** nicht nur ..., sondern auch; **2.** außer, als: **what could I do ~ refuse** was blieb mir übrig, als abzulehnen; **he couldn't ~ laugh** er musste einfach lachen; **3.** ohne dass: **justice was never done ~ someone complained**; **4.** **~ that** a) wenn nicht: **I would do it ~ that I am busy**, b) dass: **you cannot deny ~ that it was you**, c) dass nicht: **I am not so stupid ~ that I can learn it** ich bin nicht so dumm, dass ich es nicht lernen könnte; **5.** **~ then** andererseits, immer'hin; **6.** **~ yet** → **for all that** (aber) trotzdem; **II** prp. **7.** außer: **~ that** außer dass; **all ~ me** alle außer mir; → 13; **anything ~ clever** alles andere als klug: **the last ~ one** der Vorletzte; **the last ~ two** der Drittletzte; **8.** **~ for** ohne, wenn nicht: **~ for the war** ohne den Krieg, wenn der Krieg nicht (gewesen od. gekommen) wäre; **III** adv. **9.** nur, bloß: **~ a child**; **I did ~ glance** ich blickte nur flüchtig hin; **~ once** nur 'einmal; **10.** erst, gerade: **he left ~ an hour ago**; **11.** immerhin, wenigstens: **you can ~ try**; **12.** **nothing ~, none ~** nur; **13.** **all ~** fast: **he all ~ died** er wäre fast gestorben; → 7; **IV** neg. rel. pron. **14.** **few of them ~ rejoiced** es gab wenige, die sich nicht freuten; **V** s. **15.** Aber n; → **if** 5.

bu·tane ['bjuːteɪn] s. 🜊 Bu'tan n.

butch [bʊtʃ] s. sl. Mannweib, (Lesbierin) kesser Vater.

butch·er ['bʊtʃə] **I** s. **1.** Fleischer m, Schlachter m, Metzger m: **~'s meat** Schlachtfleisch n; **2.** fig. Mörder m, Schlächter m; **3.** 🜉 Am. (Süßwarenetc.)Verkäufer m; **II** v/t. **4.** schlachten; **5.** fig. morden, abschlachten; **'butcher·ly** [-lɪ] adj. blutdürstig; **'butch·er·y** [-ərɪ] s. **1.** Schlachterhandwerk n; **2.** Schlachthaus n, -hof m; **3.** fig. Gemetzel n.

but·ler ['bʌtlə] s. **1.** Butler m; **2.** Kellermeister m.

butt [bʌt] **I** s. **1.** (dickes) Ende (e-s Werkzeugs etc.); **2.** (Gewehr)Kolben m; **3.** (Zigaretten- etc.)Stummel m; **4.** 🜉 unteres Ende (von Stiel od. Stamm); **5.** 🜊 Stoß m; → **butt joint**; **6.** ✕ Kugelfang m; pl. Schießstand m; **7.** fig. Zielscheibe f (des Spottes etc.); **8.** (Kopfetc.)Stoß m; **9.** sl. ,Hintern' m; **II** v/t. **10.** (bsd. mit dem Kopf) stoßen; **11.** 🜊 anein'ander fügen; **III** v/i. **12.** (an-) stoßen, angrenzen (**on, against** an acc.); **13.** **~ in** F sich einmischen: **~ in on, ~ into** sich einmischen in (acc.); **~ end** s. **1.** (Gewehr)Kolben m; **2.** dickes Endstück; Ende f.

but·ter ['bʌtə] **I** s. **1.** Butter f: **melted ~** zerlassene Butter; **he looks as if ~ would not melt in his mouth** er sieht aus, als könnte er nicht bis drei zählen; **2.** (Erdnuss-, Kakao- etc.)Butter f; **3.** F ,Schmus' m, Schmeiche'lei(en pl.) f; **II** v/t. **4.** mit Butter bestreichen od. zubereiten; **5.** **~ up** F j-n ,einwickeln', j-m schmeicheln; **~ bean** s. 🜉 Wachsbohne f; **~ churn** s. 🜉 Butterfass n (zum Buttern); **'~-cup** s. 🜉 Butterblume f; **~ dish** s. Butterdose f; **'~,fin·gers** s. pl. sg. konstr. F Tollpatsch m, ,Tapps' m.

but·ter·fly ['bʌtəflaɪ] s. **1.** zo. Schmetterling m: a. fig. flatterhafter Mensch); **2.** sport a. **~ stroke** Schmetterlingsstil m; **~ nut** s. 🜊 Flügelmutter f; **~ valve** s. 🜊 Drosselklappe f.

but·ter·ine ['bʌtəriːn] s. Kunstbutter f.

'but·ter|·milk s. Buttermilch f; **~ mountain** s. Butterberg m; **'~-scotch** s. Ka

ra'mellbon,bon m, n.

but·ter·y ['bʌtərɪ] **I** adj. **1.** butterartig, Butter...; **2.** F schmeichlerisch; **II** s. **3.** Speisekammer f; **4.** Brit. univ. Kan'tine f.

butt joint s. 🜊 Stoßfuge f, -verbindung f.

but·tock ['bʌtək] s. **1.** anat. 'Hinterbacke f; mst pl. 'Hinterteil n, Gesäß n; **2.** Ringen: Hüftschwung m.

but·ton ['bʌtn] **I** s. **1.** (Kleider)Knopf m: **not worth a ~** keinen Pfifferling wert; **not to care a ~ (about)** F sich nichts machen (aus); **a ~ short** F ,leicht beknackt'; (**boy in**) **~s** (Hotel)Page m; **take by the ~** a) j-n fest-, aufhalten, b) sich j-n vorknöpfen; **2.** (Klingel-, Lichtetc.)Knopf m; → **press** 2; **3.** Knopf m (Gegenstand), z.B. a) Abzeichen n, Pla'kette f, b) (Mikro'fon)Kapsel f; **4.** 🌢 Knospe f, Auge n; **5.** sport sl. ,Punkt' m, Kinnspitze f; **II** v/t. **6.** a. **~ up** (zu-) knöpfen: **~ one's mouth** den Mund halten; **~ed up** fig. a) ,zugeknöpft' (Person), b) ,in der Tasche', unter Dach und Fach (Sache); **III** v/i. **7.** sich knöpfen lassen, geknöpft werden; **'~-cell** (**bat·ter·y**) s. Knopfzelle f; **'~-hole I** s. **1.** Knopfloch n; **2.** Brit. Knopflochsträußchen n, Blume f im Knopfloch; **II** v/t. **3.** j-n festhalten (u. auf ihn einreden); **4.** mit Knopflöchern versehen; **~ mush·room** s. (junger) Champignon.

but·tress ['bʌtrɪs] **I** s. **1.** 🜂 Strebepfeiler m, -bogen m; **2.** Stütze f (a. fig.); **II** v/t. a. **~ up** **3.** (durch Strebepfeiler) stützen; **4.** fig. stützen.

'butt-weld v/t. 🜊 stumpfschweißen.

but·ty ['bʌtɪ] s. Brit. F **1.** Butterbrot n, Stulle f: **jam ~** Marmeladenbrot n; **2.** ⚒ Kumpel m.

bu·tyl ['bjuːtɪl] s. 🜊 Bu'tyl n.

bu·tyr·ic [bjuː'tɪrɪk] adj. 🜊 Butter...

bux·om ['bʌksəm] adj. drall.

buy [baɪ] **I** s. **1.** F Kauf m, das Gekaufte: **a good ~** ein günstiger Kauf; **II** v/t. [irr.] **2.** (an-, ein)kaufen (**of, from** von, **at** bei): **money cannot ~** es ist für Geld nicht zu haben; **~ing habit** Kaufgewohnheit f; **~ing power** (überschüssige) Kaufkraft; **3.** fig. erkaufen: **dearly bought** teuer erkauft; **4.** j-n kaufen, bestechen; **5.** loskaufen, auslösen; **6.** Am. sl. et. ,abkaufen', glauben; **7.** **~ it** Brit. sl. ,dran glauben müssen'; **III** v/i. [irr.] **8.** kaufen; **~ into** 🜊 sich einkaufen in (acc.);

Zssgn mit adv.:

buy| in v/t. **1.** sich eindecken mit; **2.** (auf Auktionen) zu'rückkaufen; **3. buy o.s. in** 🜊 sich einkaufen; **~ off** v/t. → **buy** 4; **~ out** v/t. **1.** Teilhaber etc. auszahlen, abfinden; **2.** Firma etc. aufkaufen; **~ o·ver** v/t. → **buy** 4; **~ up** v/t. aufkaufen.

buy·er ['baɪə] s. **1.** Käufer(in), Abnehmer(in): **~-up** Aufkäufer; **~s' market** 🜊 Käufermarkt m; **~s' strike** Käuferstreik m; **2.** ⚒ Einkäufer(in).

buy·out ['baɪaʊt] s. a. **management ~** Aufkauf m e-r Firma durch deren Manager (der damit neuer Eigentümer wird).

buzz [bʌz] **I** v/i. **1.** summen, brummen, surren, schwirren: **~ about** (od. **around**) herumschwirren (a. fig.); **~ing with excitement** in heller Aufregung; **~ off** sl. ,abschwirren', ,abhauen'; **2.** säuseln, sausen; **3.** murmeln, durcheinander reden; **II** v/t. **4.** F a) j-n mit dem Pieper rufen, b) teleph. j-n anrufer **5.** ✈ a) in geringer Höhe über'fliege b) (bedrohlich) anfliegen; **III** s. **6.** ꜱ

B

men *n*, Brummen *n*, Schwirren *n*; **7.** F *teleph.* Anruf *m*: *give s.o. a ~* j-n anrufen; **8.** Stimmengewirr *n*; **9.** Gerücht *n*.

buz·zard ['bʌzəd] *s. orn.* Bussard *m*.

buzz·er ['bʌzə] *s.* **1.** Summer *m, bsd.* summendes In'sekt; **2.** Summer *m*, Summpfeife *f*; **3.** ♂ Summer *m*; **4.** ✕ a) 'Feldtele,graf *m*, b) *sl.* Telegra'fist *m*; **5.** *Am. sl.* Poli'zeimarke *f*.

buzz saw *s. Am.* Kreissäge *f*.

buzz·word ['bʌzwɜːd] *s.* **1.** Modewort *n*; **2.** Parole *f*.

by [baɪ] **I** *prp.* **1.** (*Raum*) (nahe) bei *od.* an (*dat.*), neben (*dat.*): *~ the window* beim *od.* am Fenster; **2.** durch (*acc.*), über (*acc.*), via, an (*dat.*) ... entlang *od.* vor'bei: *he came ~ Park Road* er kam über *od.* durch die Parkstraße; *we drove ~ the park* wir fuhren am Park entlang; *~ land* zu Lande; **3.** (*Zeit*) während, bei: *~ day* bei Tage; *day ~ day* Tag für Tag; *~ lamplight* bei Lampenlicht; **4.** bis (zu *od.* um *od.* spätestens): *be here ~ 4.30* sei um 4 Uhr 30 hier; *~ the allotted time* bis zum festgesetzten Zeitpunkt; *~ now* nunmehr, inzwischen, schon; **5.** (*Urheber*) von, durch: *a book ~ Shaw* ein Buch von Shaw; *settled ~ him* durch ihn *od.* von ihm geregelt; *~ nature* von Natur (aus); *~ oneself* aus eigener Kraft, selbst, al-

lein; **6.** (*Mittel*) durch, mit, vermittels: *~ listening* durch Zuhören; *driven ~ steam* mit Dampf betrieben; *~ rail* per Bahn; *~ letter* brieflich; **7.** gemäß, nach: *~ my watch it is now ten* nach m-r Uhr ist es jetzt zehn; **8.** (*Menge*) um, nach: *too short ~ an inch* um einen Zoll zu kurz; *sold ~ the metre* meterweise verkauft; **9.** ⅍ a) mal: *3 (multiplied) ~ 4*; *the size is 9 feet ~ 6* die Größe ist 9 mal 6 Fuß, b) durch: *6 (divided) ~ 2*; **10.** *~ the way od. ~ the ~(e)* übrigens; **II** *adv.* **11.** da'bei: *close ~, hard ~* dicht dabei; **12.** *~ and large* im Großen u. Ganzen; *~ and ~* demnächst, nach u. nach; **13.** vor'bei, -'über: *pass ~* vorübergehen; **14.** bei'seite: *put ~*.

by- [baɪ] *Vorsilbe* **1.** Neben..., Seiten...; **2.** geheim.

bye [baɪ] **I** *s. sport* a) *Kricket*: durch einen vor'beigelassenen Ball ausgelöster Lauf, b) Freilos *n*: *draw a ~* ein Freilos ziehen; **II** *adj.* 'untergeordnet, Neben...

bye- → *by-*.

bye-bye I *s.* ['baɪbaɪ] *Kindersprache*: ‚Heia' *f*, Bett *n*, Schlaf *m*; **II** *int.* [ˌbaɪ-'baɪ] F Wiedersehen!, Tschüss!

'bye-law → *bylaw*.

'by|-e,lec·tion *s.* Ersatz-, Nachwahl *f*;

'*~*·**gone I** *adj.* vergangen; **II** *s. das* Vergangene: *let ~s be ~s* lass(t) das Vergangene ruhen; '*~*·**law** *s.* **1.** Gemeindeverordnung *f*, -satzung *f*; **2.** *pl.* Sta'tuten *pl.*, Satzung *f*; **3.** 'Durchführungsverordnung *f*; '*~*·**line** *s.* **1.** ⅊ 'Neben,linie *f*; **2.** Verfasserangabe *f* (*unter der Überschrift e-s Zeitungsartikels*); **3.** Nebenbeschäftigung *f*; '*~*·**name** *s.* **1.** Beiname *m*; **2.** Spitzname *m*; '*~*·**pass I** *s.* **1.** 'Umleitung *f*, Um'gehungsstraße *f*; **2.** Nebenleitung *f*; **3.** *Gasbrenner*: Dauerflamme *f*; **4.** ♂ Nebenschluss *m*; **5.** ♂ Bypass *m*; **II** *v/t.* **6.** 'umleiten; **7.** um'gehen (*a. fig.*); **8.** vermeiden, über'gehen; '*~*·**path** *s.* Seitenweg *m* (*a. fig.*); '*~*·**play** *s. thea.* Nebenhandlung *f*; '*~*·,**prod·uct** *s.* 'Nebenpro,dukt *n*, *fig. a.* Nebenerscheinung *f*.

byre ['baɪə] *s. Brit.* Kuhstall *m*.

'**by|·road** *s.* Seiten-, Nebenstraße *f*; '*~*·,**stand·er** *s.* Zuschauer(in); '*~*·**street** → *byroad*.

byte [baɪt] *s. Computer*: Byte *n*.

'**by|·way** *s.* **1.** Seiten-, Nebenweg *m*; **2.** *fig.* 'Nebenas,pekt *m*; '*~*·**word** *s.* **1.** Sprichwort *n*; **2.** (*for*) Inbegriff *m* (*gen.*), Musterbeispiel *n* (für); **3.** Schlagwort *n*.

By·zan·tine [bɪ'zæntaɪn] *adj.* byzan'tinisch.

C, c [si:] *s.* **1.** C *n*, c *n* (*Buchstabe*); **2.** ♪ C *n*, c *n* (*Note*); **3.** *ped. Am.* Drei *f*, Befriedigend *n* (*Note*); **4.** *Am. sl.* ‚Hunderter' *m* (*Banknote*).

cab [kæb] **I** *s.* **1.** a) Droschke *f*, b) Taxi *n*; **2.** a) 🚂 Führerstand *m*, b) Führersitz *m* (*Lastauto*), c) Lenkerhäus-chen *n* (*Kran*); **II** *v/i.* **3.** mit e-r Droschke *od.* e-m Taxi fahren.

ca·bal [kə'bæl] **I** *s.* **1.** Ka'bale *f*, In'trige *f*; **2.** Clique *f*, Klüngel *m*; **II** *v/i.* **3.** intrigieren, Ränke schmieden, sich verschwören.

cab·a·ret ['kæbəreɪ] *s.* **1.** (*a. politisches*) Kaba'rett, Kleinkunstbühne *f*; ~ *performer* Kabarettist(in) *f*; **2.** Restau'rant *n od.* Nachtklub *m* mit Varie'teedarbietungen.

cab·bage ['kæbɪdʒ] *s.* ♀ **1.** Kohl(pflanze *f*) *m*: *become a* ~ *F* verblöden, dahinvegetieren; **2.** Kohlkopf *m*; ~ *but·ter·fly s. zo.* Kohlweißling *m*; '~·head *s.* **1.** Kohlkopf *m*; **2.** *F* Dummkopf *m*; '~-*white* → *cabbage butterfly*.

ca(b)·ba·la [kə'bu:lə] *s.* 'Kabbala *f*, Geheimlehre *f* (*a. fig.*).

cab·by ['kæbɪ] *F* → *cab driver*.

cab driv·er *s.* **1.** Droschkenkutscher *m*; **2.** Taxifahrer *m*.

ca·ber ['keɪbə] *s. Scot.* Baumstamm *m*: *tossing the* ~ Baumstammwerfen *n*.

cab·in ['kæbɪn] *s.* **1.** Häus-chen *n*, Hütte *f*; **2.** ♣ Ka'bine *f*, Ka'jüte *f*; **3.** ✈ Ka'bine *f*: a) Fluggastraum *m*, b) Kanzel *f*; **4.** *Brit.* 🚂 Stellwerk *n*; ~ *boy s.* ♣ Ka'binensteward *m*; ~ *class s.* ♣ Ka'jütenklasse *f*; ~ *cruis·er s.* Ka'binenkreuzer *m*.

cab·i·net ['kæbɪnɪt] *s.* **1.** *oft* ♀ *pol.* Kabi'nett *n*: ~ *council*, ~ *meeting* Kabinettssitzung *f*; ~ *crisis* Regierungskrise *f*; **2.** (Schau-, Sammlungs-, *a.* Bü'ro-, Kar'tei- *etc.*)Schrank *m*, (Wand-) Schränkchen *n*, Vi'trine *f*; **3.** *Radio etc.*: Gehäuse *n*; **4.** *phot.* Kabi'nettfor‚mat *n*; '~‚mak·er *s.* **1.** Kunsttischler *m*; **2.** *humor.* Mi'nisterpräsi‚dent *m* bei der Regierungsbildung; '~‚mak·ing *s.* ♀ Min·is·ter *s. pol.* Kabi'nettsmi‚nister *m*; ~ *size* → *cabinet* 4.

cab·in scoot·er *s. mot.* Ka'binenroller *m*.

ca·ble ['keɪbl] **I** *s.* **1.** Kabel *n*, Tau *n*, (Draht)Seil *n*; **2.** ♣ Trosse *f*, Ankertau *n*, -kette *f*; **3.** ⚡ (Leitungs)Kabel *n*; **4.** → *cablegram*; **II** *v/t. u. v/i.* **5.** kabeln, telegrafieren; ~ *car Seilbahn:* a) Ka'bine *f*, b) Wagen *m*; '~·cast **I** *v/t.* [*irr.* → *cast*] per Kabelfernsehen über'tragen; **II** *s.* Sendung *f* im Kabelfernsehen; ~ *chan·nel s.* TV Kabelkanal *m*.

ca·ble·gram ['keɪblgræm] *s.* Kabel *n*, ('Übersee)Tele‚gramm *n*.

ca·ble rail·way s.* **1. Drahtseilbahn *f*; **2.** *Am.* Drahtseilstraßenbahn *f*.

ca·blese [keɪ'bli:z] *s.* Tele'grammstil *m*.

'ca·ble's-length ['keɪblz-] *s.* ♣ Kabellänge *f* (*100 Faden*).

ca·ble| tel·e·vi·sion *s.* Kabelfernsehen

n; '~·way *s.* Drahtseilbahn *f*.

'cab·man [-mən] *s.* [*irr.*] → *cab driver*.

ca·boo·dle [kə'bu:dl] *s. sl.*: *the whole* ~ a) der ganze Klimbim, b) die ganze Sippschaft.

ca·boose [kə'bu:s] *s.* **1.** ♣ Kom'büse *f*, Schiffsküche *f*; **2.** 🚂 *Am.* Dienst-, Bremswagen *m*.

cab rank *s. Brit.* Taxi-, Droschkenstand *m*.

cab·ri·o·let ['kæbrɪəleɪ] *s. a. mot.* Kabrio'lett *n*.

ca'can·ny [‚ka:'kænɪ] *s. Scot.* ✝ Bummelstreik *m*.

ca·ca·o [kə'ka:əʊ] *s.* **1.** ♀ *a.* ~-*tree* Ka'kaobaum *m*; **2.** Ka'kaobohnen *pl.*; ~ *bean s.* Ka'kaobohne *f*; ~ *but·ter s.* Ka'kaobutter *f*.

cache [kæʃ] **I** *s.* **1.** *Computer:* Cache *m*, Zwischenspeicher *m*; **2.** geheimes (Waffen- *od.* Provi'ant- *etc.*)Lager, Versteck *n*; **II** *v/t.* **3.** verstecken.

ca·chet ['kæʃeɪ] *s.* **1.** a) Siegel *n*, b) *fig.* Stempel *m*, Merkmal *n*; **2.** ♣ Kapsel *f*.

cack·le ['kækl] **I** *v/i.* gackern (*a. fig. lachen*), schnattern (*a. fig. schwatzen*); **II** *s.* (*a. fig.*) Gegacker *n*, Geschnatter *n*: *cut the* ~! *F* quatsch nicht!

ca·coph·o·nous [kæ'kɒfənəs] *adj.* 'misstönend; **ca·coph·o·ny** [-nɪ] *s.* Kakopho'nie *f* (*Missklang*).

cac·tus ['kæktəs] *pl.* **-ti** [-taɪ], **-tus·es** *s.* ♀ 'Kaktus *m*.

cad [kæd] *s.* **1.** ordi'närer Kerl; **2.** gemeiner Kerl.

ca·das·tral [kə'dæstrəl] *adj.*: ~ *survey* Katasteraufnahme *f*.

ca·dav·er·ous [kə'dævərəs] *adj.* leichenhaft.

cad·die ['kædɪ] *s.* a) 'Caddie *m* (*Golfjunge*), b) → '~·*cart s.* 'Caddie *m* (*Golfschlägerwagen*).

cad·dish ['kædɪʃ] *adj.* **1.** pro'letenhaft; **2.** gemein, niederträchtig.

cad·dy¹ → *caddie*.

cad·dy² ['kædɪ] *s.* Teedose *f*; ~ *spoon s.* Tee-, Messlöffel *m*.

ca·dence ['keɪdəns] *s.* **1.** ('Vers-, 'Sprech‚)Rhythmus *m*; **2.** ♪ Ka'denz *f*; **3.** Tonfall *m* (*am Satzende*); '**ca·denced** [-st] *adj.* rhythmisch.

ca·det [kə'det] *s.* **1.** ✕ Ka'dett *m*; **2.** (Poli'zei- *etc.*)Schüler *m*; **3.** jüngerer Sohn *od.* Bruder; **4.** *in Zssgn a.* Nachwuchs...: ~ *researcher*; ~ *nurse* Lernschwester *f*.

cadge [kædʒ] *v/i. u. v/t.* ‚schnorren'; '**cadg·er** [-dʒə] *s.* ‚Schnorrer', ‚Nassauer' *m*.

ca·di ['ka:dɪ] *s.* Kadi *m*, Bezirksrichter *m* (*im Orient*).

cad·mi·um ['kædmɪəm] *s.* 🜨 'Kadmium *n*; '~-,plate *v/t.* ⊙ kadmieren.

ca·dre ['ka:də] *s.* **1.** Kader *m*: a) ✕ (Truppen)Stamm *m*, b) *pol.* Führungsgruppe *f*, c) 'Rahmenorganisati‚on *f*; **2.** *fig.* Grundstock *m*.

ca·du·ce·us [kə'dju:sjəs] *pl.* **-ce·i** [-sjaɪ] *s.* Mer'kurstab *m* (*a. ärztliches Abzei-*

chen).

cae·cum ['si:kəm] *s. anat.* Blinddarm *m*.

Cae·sar ['si:zə] *s.* **1.** 'Cäsar *m* (*Titel römischer Kaiser*); **2.** Auto'krat *m*.

Cae·sar·e·an, Cae·sar·i·an [si:'zeərɪən] *adj.* cä'sarisch: ~ (*operation od. section*) ♣ Kaiserschnitt *m*.

Cae·sar·ism ['si:zərɪzəm] *s.* Dikta'tur *f*; Herrschsucht *f*.

cae·su·ra [si:'zjʊərə] *s.* Zä'sur *f*: a) (Vers)Einschnitt *m*, b) ♪ Ruhepunkt *m*.

ca·fé ['kæfeɪ] *s.* **1.** a) Ca'fé *n*, b) Restau'rant *n*; **2.** *Am.* Bar *f*.

caf·e·te·ri·a [‚kæfɪ'tɪərɪə] *s.* 'Selbstbedienungsrestau‚rant *n*, Cafete'ria *f*.

caf·fe·ine ['kæfi:n] *s.* 🜏 Koffe'in *n*; '~-*free adj.* koffe'infrei.

caf·tan ['kæftæn] *s.* 'Kaftan *m* (*a. Damenmode*).

cage [keɪdʒ] **I** *s.* **1.** Käfig *m* (*a. fig.*); (Vogel)Bauer *n*; **2.** Gefängnis *n* (*a. fig.*); **3.** Kriegsgefangenenlager *n*; **4.** Ka'bine *f* *e-s Aufzuges*; **5.** ✕ Förderkorb *m*; **6.** a. △ Stahlgerüst *n*; **7.** a) *Baseball:* abgegrenztes Trainingsfeld, b) *Eishockey:* Tor *n*, c) *Basketball:* Korb *m*; **II** *v/t.* **8.** (in e-n Käfig) einsperren; **9.** *Eishockey:* den Puck ins Tor schießen; ~ *aer·i·al s. Brit.*, ~ *an·ten·na s. Am.* ♀ 'Käfigan‚tenne *f*.

ca·gey ['keɪdʒɪ] *adj. F* **1.** verschlossen; **2.** vorsichtig, berechnend; **3.** ‚gerissen', schlau.

ca·goule [kə'gu:l] *s.* Windjacke *f*, leichter 'Anorak.

ca·hoot [kə'hu:t] *s.*: *be in* ~*s* (*with*) *F* unter e-r Decke stecken (mit).

Cain [keɪn] *s.*: *raise* ~ *F* Krach schlagen.

cairn [keən] *s.* **1.** Steinhaufen *m* (*als Grenz- od. Grabmal*); **2.** *mount.* Steinmann *m*; **3.** a. ~ *terrier zo.* 'Cairn-‚Terrier *m* (*Hund*).

cais·son [kə'su:n] *s.* **1.** ⊙ Cais'son *m*, Senkkasten *m*; **2.** ✕ Muniti'onswagen *m*; ~ *dis·ease s.* ♣ Cais'sonkrankheit *f*.

ca·jole [kə'dʒəʊl] *v/t. j-m* schmeicheln *od.* schöntun; *j-n* beschwatzen, verleiten (*into* zu): ~ *s.th. out of s.o.* j-m et. abbetteln; **ca'jol·er·y** [-lərɪ] *s.* Schmeiche'lei *f*, gutes Zureden; Liebediene'rei *f*.

cake [keɪk] **I** *s.* **1.** Kuchen *m* (*a. fig.*): *parcel out the* ~ *fig.* den (*finanziellen*) Kuchen verteilen; *take the* ~ den Preis davontragen, *fig.* den Vogel abschießen; *that takes the* ~! *F* a) das ist (einsame) Spitze!, b) *contp.* das ist die Höhe!; *be selling like hot* ~*s* weggehen wie warme Semmeln; *you can't eat your* ~ *and have it!* du kannst nur eines von beiden tun *od.* haben!, entweder – oder!; ~*s and ale* Lustbarkeit(en *pl.*) *f*, ‚süßes Leben'; **2.** Kuchen *m* (*Masse*); Tafel *f* *Schokolade*, Riegel *m* *Seife etc.*; **3.** (Schmutz- *etc.*)Kruste *f*; **II** *v/i.* **4.** zs.-backen, -ballen, verkrusten: ~*d with*

C

filth mit e-r Schmutzkruste (überzogen *od.* bedeckt); ~ **mix** *s.* Backmischung *f*; '~**walk** *s.* 'Cakewalk *m* (*Tanz*).

cal·a·bash ['kæləbæʃ] *s.* ♀ Kale'basse *f*: a) Flaschenkürbis *m*, b) *daraus gefertigtes Trinkgefäß.*

ca·lam·i·tous [kə'læmɪtəs] *adj.* □ katastro'phal, unheilvoll, Unglücks...

ca·lam·i·ty [kə'læmətɪ] *s.* **1.** Unglück *n*, Unheil *n*, Kata'strophe *f*; **2.** Elend *n*, Mi'sere *f*; ~ **howl·er** *s. bsd. Am.* Schwarzseher *m*, 'Panikmacher *m*; ⚥ **Jane** *s.* F Pechmarie *f*, Unglückswurm *m*.

cal·car·e·ous [kæl'keərɪəs] *adj.* ⚘ kalkartig, Kalk...; kalkhaltig.

cal·cif·er·ous [kæl'sɪfərəs] *adj.* ⚘ kalkhaltig; **cal·ci·fi·ca·tion** [,kælsɪfɪ'keɪʃn] *s.* **1.** ⚕ Verkalkung *f*; **2.** *geol.* Kalkablagerung *f*; **cal·ci·fy** ['kælsɪfaɪ] *v/t. u. v/i.* verkalken; **cal·ci·na·tion** [,kælsɪ-'neɪʃn] *s.* ⚙ Kalzinierung *f*, Glühen *n*; **cal·cine** ['kælsaɪn] *v/t.* ⚙ kalzinieren, (aus)glühen, zu Asche verbrennen.

cal·ci·um ['kælsɪəm] *s.* ⚘ 'Kalzium *n*; ~ **car·bide** *s.* ⚘ ('Kalzium)Kar,bid *n*; ~ **chlo·ride** *s.* ⚘ Chlor'kalzium *n*; ~ **light** *s.* Kalklicht *n*.

cal·cu·la·ble ['kælkjʊləbl] *adj.* berechenbar, kalkulierbar (*Risiko*).

cal·cu·late ['kælkjʊleɪt] **I** *v/t.* **1.** aus-, er-, berechnen; ✝ kalkulieren; **2.** *mst pass.* berechnen, planen; → **calculated**; **3.** *Am.* F vermuten, glauben; **II** *v/i.* **4.** rechnen; ✝ kalkulieren; **5.** über'legen; **6.** (**upon**) rechnen (mit, auf *acc.*), sich verlassen (auf *acc.*); '**cal·cu·lat·ed** [-tɪd] *adj.* berechnet, gewollt, beabsichtigt: ~ **indiscretion** gezielte Indiskretion; ~ **risk** kalkuliertes Risiko; ~ **to deceive** darauf angelegt zu täuschen; **not** ~ **for** nicht geeignet *od.* bestimmt für; '**cal·cu·lat·ing** [-tɪŋ] *adj.* **1.** (schlau) berechnend, (kühl) über'legend; **2.** Rechen...: ~ **machine** *cal*; **cu·la·tion** [,kælkjʊ'leɪʃn] *s.* **1.** Kalkulati'on *f*, Berechnung *f*: **be out in one's** ~ sich verrechnet haben; **2.** Voranschlag *m*; **3.** Über'legung *f*; **4.** *fig. a.)* Berechnung *f*, b) Schläue *f*; '**cal·cu·la·tor** [-tə] *s.* **1.** Kalku'lator *m*; **2.** 'Rechenta,belle *f*; **3.** 'Rechenma,schine *f*, Rechner *m*.

cal·cu·lus ['kælkjʊləs] *pl.* **-li** [-laɪ] *s.* **1.** ⚕ (*Blasen-, Gallen-, Nieren- etc.*)Stein *m*; **2.** Ⱥ a) (*bsd. Differenzial-, Integral-*) Rechnung *f*, Rechnungsart *f*, b) höhere A'nalysis: ~ **of probabilities** Wahrscheinlichkeitsrechnung *f*.

cal·dron ['kɔːldrən] → **cauldron**.

Cal·e·do·ni·an [,kælɪ'dəʊnjən] *poet.* **I** *adj.* kale'donisch (*schottisch*); **II** *s.* Kale'donier *m* (*Schotte*).

cal·e·fac·tion [,kælɪ'fækʃn] *s.* Erwärmung *f*, Erhitzung *f*.

cal·en·dar ['kælɪndə] *s.* **1.** Ka'lender *m*; **2.** *fig.* Zeitrechnung *f*; **3.** Jahrbuch *n*; **4.** Liste *f*, Re'gister *n*; **5.** *Brit. univ.* Vorlesungsverzeichnis *n*; **6.** ✝, *Am.* ⚖ Ter'mina,lender *m*; **II** *v/t.* **7.** registrieren; ~ **month** *s.* Ka'lendermonat *m*.

cal·en·der ['kælɪndə] ⚙ **I** *s.* Ka'lander *m*; **II** *v/t.* ka'landern.

cal·ends ['kælɪndz] *s. pl. antiq.* Ka'lenden *pl.*: **on the Greek** ~ am St.-Nimmerleins-Tag.

calf¹ [kɑːf] *pl.* **calves** [-vz] *s.* **1.** Kalb *n* (*der Kuh, von Elefant, Wal, Hirsch etc.*): **with** (*od. in*) ~ trächtig (*Kuh*); **2.** Kalbleder *n*: ~**bound** in Kalbleder gebunden (*Buch*); **3.** F ,Kalb' *n*, ,Schaf' *n*; **4.** treibende Eisscholle.

calf² [kɑːf] *pl.* **calves** [-vz] *s.* Wade *f* (*Bein, Strumpf etc.*).

'**calf**|·**love** *s.* F erste, junge Liebe; '~**'s-foot jel·ly** ['kɑːvz-] *s.* Kalbsfußsülze *f*; '~**skin** *s.* Kalbleder *n*.

cal·i·ber *Am.* → **calibre**; '**cal·i·bered** *Am.* → **calibred**; **cal·i·brate** ['kælɪbreɪt] *v/t.* ⚙ kalibrieren: a) mit e-r Gradeinteilung versehen, b) eichen; **cal·i·bra·tion** [,kælɪ'breɪʃn] *s.* ⚙ Kalibrierung *f*, Eichung *f*; **cal·i·bre** ['kælɪbə] *s.* ✕ Ka'liber *n*; **2.** ⚙ a) ('Innen)Durchmesser *m*, b) Ka'liberlehre *f*; **3.** *fig.* Ka'liber *n*, For'mat *n*; '**cal·i·bred** [-bəd] *adj.* ...kalibrig.

cal·i·ces ['kælɪsiːz] *pl. von* **calix**.

cal·i·co ['kælɪkəʊ] **I** *pl.* **-coes**, *Am. a.* **-cos** *s.* **1.** 'Kaliko *m*, (bedruckter) Kat'tun; **2.** *Brit.* weißer *od.* ungebleichter Baumwollstoff; **II** *adj.* **3.** Kattun...; **4.** F bunt.

ca·lif, cal·if·ate → **caliph, caliphate**.

Cal·i·for·ni·an [,kælɪ'fɔːnjən] **I** *adj.* kali'fornisch; **II** *s.* Kali'fornier(in).

cal·i·pers ['kælɪpəz] *s. pl.* Greif-, Tastzirkel *m*; ⚙ Tast(er)lehre *f*.

ca·liph ['keɪlɪf] *s.* Ka'lif *m*; '**cal·iph·ate** [-feɪt] *s.* Kali'fat *n*.

cal·is·then·ics → **callisthenics**.

ca·lix ['keɪlɪks] *pl.* **cal·i·ces** ['kælɪsiːz] *s. anat., zo., eccl.* Kelch *m*; → **calyx**.

calk¹ [kɔːk] **I** *s.* **1.** Stollen *m* (*am Hufeisen*); **2.** Gleitschutzbeschlag *m* (*an der Schuhsohle*); **II** *v/t.* **3.** mit Stollen *od.* Griffeisen versehen.

calk² [kɔːk] *v/t.* ('durch)pausen.

calk³ [kɔːk] → **caulk**.

cal·kin ['kælkɪn] *Brit.* → **calk¹** I.

call [kɔːl] **I** *s.* **1.** Ruf *m* (*a. fig.*); Schrei *m*: **within** ~ in Rufweite; **the** ~ **of duty**; **the** ~ **of nature** *humor.* ,ein dringendes Bedürfnis'; **2.** (Tele'fon)Anruf *m*, (-)Gespräch *n*: **give s.o. a** ~ j-n anrufen; → **local** 1, **personal** 1; **3.** *thea.* Her'vorruf *m*; **4.** Lockruf *m* (*Tier*); *fig.* Ruf *m*, Lockung *f*: **the** ~ **of the East**; **5.** Namensaufruf *m*; **6.** Ruf *m*, Berufung *f* (**to** in *ein Amt etc.*, auf *e-n Lehrstuhl*); **7.** (innere) Berufung, Drang *m*, Missi'on *f*; **8.** Si'gnal *n*; **9.** (Auf)Ruf *m*; (✝ Zahlungs)Aufforderung *f*: ~ **loan** *m*, Kündigung *f von Geldern*; 'Kaufopti,on *f*; *Brit.* Vorprämie *f*, Vorprämiengeschäfte *pl.*; *a.* Nachfrage *f* (**for** nach): ~ **on shares** Aufforderung zur Einzahlung auf Aktien; **at** ~, **on** ~ auf Abruf *od.* sofort bereit(stehend), ✝ *a.* jederzeit kündbar; **money at** ~ ✝ Tagesgeld *n*; **10.** a) Veranlassung *f*, Grund *m*, b) Recht *n*: **he had no** ~ **to do that**; **11.** In'anspruchnahme *f*: **many** ~**s on my time** starke Beanspruchung m-r Zeit; **have the first** ~ den Vorrang haben; **12.** kurzer Besuch (**at** in *e-m Ort*, **on** bei *j-m*); ⚓ Anlaufen *n*: **port of** ~ Anlaufhafen *m*; **II** *v/t.* **13.** j-n (her'bei)rufen: *et.* (*a. weitS. Streik*) ausrufen; *Versammlung* einberufen; *teleph.* anrufen; *thea.* Schauspieler her'vorrufen: ~ **into being** *fig.* ins Leben rufen; **14.** berufen (**to** in *ein Amt*); **15.** ⚖ a) *Zeugen, Sache* aufrufen, b) *als Zeugen* vorladen; **16.** *Arzt, Auto* kommen lassen; **17.** nennen, bezeichnen als; **18.** *pass.* heißen (*after* nach): **he is** ~**ed Max**; **what is it** ~**ed in English?** wie heißt es auf Englisch?; **19.** nennen, heißen (*lit.*), halten für: **I** ~ **that a blunder**; **we'll** ~ **it a pound** wir wollen es bei einem Pfund bewenden lassen; **20.** wecken: ~ **me at 6 o'clock**; **21.** *Kartenspiel:* a) *Farbe* ansagen, b) ~ **s.o.'s hand** *Poker:* j-n auffordern, s-e Karten vorzuzeigen; **III** *v/i.* **22.** rufen: **you must come when I** ~; **duty** ~**s**; **he** ~**ed for help** er rief um

Hilfe; → **call for**; **23.** *teleph.* anrufen: **who is** ~**ing?** wer ist dort?; **24.** (kurz) vor'beischauen (**on s.o.** bei j-m); *Zssgn mit prp. u. adv.*:

call | **at** *v/i.* **1.** besuchen (*acc.*), vorsprechen bei *od.* in (*dat.*), gehen *od.* kommen zu; **2.** ⚓ *Hafen* anlaufen; anlegen in (*dat.*); ⚓ halten in (*dat.*); ~ **a·way** *v/t.* ab-, wegrufen; *fig.* ablenken; ~ **back I** *v/t.* **1.** zu'rückrufen; **2.** wider'rufen; **II** *v/i.* **3.** *teleph.* zu'rückrufen; ~ **down** *v/t.* **1.** *Segen etc.* her'abrufen, -flehen; *Zorn etc.* auf sich ziehen; **2.** *Am.* F ,zs.-stauchen'; ~ **for** *v/i.* **1.** nach j-m rufen; *Waren* abrufen; *thea.* herausrufen; **2.** *et.* erfordern, verlangen: ~ **courage**; **your remark was not called for** Ihre Bemerkung war unnötig; **3.** j-n *od. et.* abholen: **to be called for** a) abzuholen(d), b) postlagernd; ~ **forth** *v/t.* **1.** her'vorrufen, auslösen; **2.** *Kraft* aufbieten; ~ **in** *v/t.* **1.** her'ein-, her'beirufen; hin'zu-, zurate ziehen; **2.** zu'rückfordern; *Geld* kündigen; *Schulden* einziehen; *Banknoten etc.* einziehen: ~ **a loan** e-n Kredit einfordern (*od.* kündigen); **II** *v/i.* **3.** vorsprechen (**on** bei j-m; **at** in *dat.*); ~ **off** *v/t.* **1.** ab(be)rufen: ~ **goods** Waren abrufen; **2.** *fig. et.* abbrechen, absagen, abblasen: ~ **a strike**; **3.** *Aufmerksamkeit, Gedanken* ablenken; ~ **on** *od.* **up·on** *v/i.* **1.** j-n besuchen; bei j-m vorsprechen; **2.** j-n auffordern; **3.** ~ **s.o. for s.th.** *et.* von j-m fordern, sich an j-n um *et.* wenden: **I am** (*od.* **I feel**) **called upon** ich bin *od.* fühle mich genötigt (**to** *inf.* zu *inf.*); ~ **out I** *v/t.* **1.** her'ausrufen; **2.** *Polizei, Militär* aufbieten; **3.** *zum Kampf* herausfordern; *zum Streik* auffordern; **II** *v/i.* **4.** aufschreien; laut rufen; ~ **o·ver** *v/t.* **1.** *Namen* verlesen; **2.** *Zahlen, Text* kollationieren; ~ **to** *v/i.* j-m zurufen, j-n anrufen; ~ **up** *v/t.* **1.** auf-, her'beirufen; *teleph.* anrufen; **2.** ✕ einberufen; **3.** *fig.* her'vor-, wachrufen, her'aufbeschwören; **4.** sich ins Gedächtnis zu'rückrufen; ~ **up·on** → **call on**.

call·a·ble ['kɔːləbl] *adj.* ✝ kündbar (*Geld, Kredit*); einziehbar (*Forderungen etc.*).

'**call**|·**back** *s.* ✝, ⚙ 'Rückrufakti,on *f in die Werkstatt*; ~ **box** *s.* **1.** *Brit.* Fernsprechzelle *f*; **2.** *Am.* a) Postfach *n*, b) Notrufsäule *f*; '~**boy** *s.* **1.** Ho'telpage *m*; **2.** *thea.* Inspizi'entengehilfe *m*; ~ **but·ton** *s.* Klingelknopf *m*; ~ **card** *s.* Tele'fonkarte *f* (*bsd. in Irland*); ~ **charge** *s. teleph.* Anrufgebühr *f*.

called [kɔːld] *adj.* genannt, namens.

call·er ['kɔːlə] *s.* **1.** *teleph.* Anrufer(in). **2.** Besucher(in); **3.** Abholer(in).

call | **girl** *s.* Callgirl *n* (*Prostituierte*); ~ **house** *s. Am.* Bor'dell *n*.

cal·lig·ra·phy [kə'lɪgrəfɪ] *s.* Kalligra'phie *f*, Schönschreibkunst *f*.

'**call-in** *s. Radio, TV:* Sendung *f* mit tele'fonischer Publikumsbeteiligung.

call·ing ['kɔːlɪŋ] *s.* **1.** Beruf *m*, Geschäft *n*, Gewerbe *n*; **2.** *eccl.* Berufung *f*; **3.** Einberufung *f* *e-r Versammlung*; ~ **card** *s.* Vi'sitenkarte *f*.

cal·li·pers → **calipers**.

cal·lis·then·ics [,kælɪs'θenɪks] *s. pl. mst sg. konstr.* Freiübungen *pl.*

call | **loan** *s.* ✝ täglich kündbares Darlehen; ~ **mon·ey** *s.* ✝ Tagesgeld *n*; ~ **num·ber** *s. teleph.* Rufnummer *f*; ~ **of·fice** *s.* Fernsprechstelle *f*, -zelle *f*.

cal·los·i·ty [kæ'lɒsətɪ] *s.* Schwiele *f*, Hornhautbildung *f*; **cal·lous** ['kæləs] **I** *adj.* □ schwielig; *fig.* abgebrüht, gefühllos; **II** *v/i.* sich verhärten, schwielig

werden; *fig.* abstumpfen; **cal·lous·
ness** ['kæləsnɪs] *s.* Schwieligkeit *f*; *fig.*
Abgebrühtheit *f*, Gefühllosigkeit *f*.
cal·low ['kæləʊ] *adj.* **1.** ungefiedert,
nackt; **2.** *fig.* ‚grün‘, unreif.
call| sign, ~ sig·nal *s. teleph. etc.* Ruf-
zeichen *n*; **~ u·nit** *s. teleph.* Gesprächs-
einheit *f*; **'~-up** *s.* ✕ a) Einberufung,
b) Mobilisierung *f*.
cal·lus ['kæləs] *pl.* **-li** [-laɪ] *s.* ✊ **1.** Kno-
chennarbe *f*; **2.** Schwiele *f*.
calm [kɑːm] **I** *s.* **1.** Stille *f*, Ruhe *f* (*a.
fig.*); **2.** Windstille *f*, Flaute *f*; **II** *adj.* ☐
3. still, ruhig; friedlich; **4.** windstill; **5.**
fig. ruhig, gelassen: **~ and collected**
ruhig u. gefasst; **6.** F unverfroren,
‚kühl‘; **III** *v/t.* **7.** beruhigen, besänftigen; **IV** *v/i.* **8.** a. **~ down** sich beruhigen; **'calm·ness** [-nɪs] *s.* **1.** Ruhe *f*,
Stille *f*; **2.** Gemütsruhe *f*, Gelassenheit *f*.
ca·lor·ic [kə'lɒrɪk] *phys.* **I** *s.* Wärme *f*; **II**
adj. ka'lorisch, Wärme...: **~ engine**
Heißluftmaschine *f*; **cal·o·rie** ['kælərɪ]
s. Kalo'rie *f*, Wärmeeinheit *f*; **cal·o·rif-
ic** [‚kælə'rɪfɪk] *adj.* (☐ **~ally**) Wärme
erzeugend; Wärme..., Heiz...; **cal·o·ry**
→ **calorie**.
cal·u·met ['kæljʊmet] *s.* Kalu'met *n*, (indi'anische) Friedenspfeife.
ca·lum·ni·ate [kə'lʌmnɪeɪt] *v/t.* verleumden; **ca·lum·ni·a·tion** [kə‚lʌmnɪ-
'eɪʃn] *s.* Verleumdung *f*; **ca'lum·ni·a·
tor** [-tə] *s.* Verleumder(in); **ca'lum-
ni·ous** [-ɪəs] *adj.* ☐ verleumderisch;
cal·um·ny ['kæləmnɪ] *s.* Verleumdung
f.
Cal·va·ry ['kælvərɪ] *s.* **1.** *bibl.* 'Golgatha
n; **2.** *eccl.* Kal'varienberg *m*; **3.** ⚱ Bild-
stock *m*, Marterl *n*; **4.** ⚱ *fig.* Mar'tyrium
n.
calve [kɑːv] *v/i.* zo. kalben; **2.** kalben, Eisstücke abstoßen (*Eisberg, Gletscher*).
calves [kɑːvz] *pl. von* **calf**; **'~-foot jel·ly**
→ **calf's-foot jelly**.
Cal·vin·ism ['kælvɪnɪzəm] *s. eccl.* Kalvi-
'nismus *m*; **'Cal·vin·ist** [-ɪst] *s.* Kalvi-
'nist(in).
ca·lyx ['keɪlɪks] *pl.* **ca·lyx·es** [-ɪksɪz],
'ca·ly·ces [-ɪsiːz] *s.* ♣ (*Blüten*)Kelch *m*;
→ **calix**.
cam [kæm] *s.* ⊙ Nocken *m*, Mitnehmer
m, (Steuer)Kurve *f*: **~ gear** Nocken-
steuerung *f*, Kurvengetriebe *n*; **~shaft**
Nocken-, Steuerwelle *f*; **~control(l)ed**
nockengesteuert.
ca·ma·ra·de·rie [‚kæmə'rɑːdərɪ] *s.* Kame'radschaft(lichkeit) *f*; *b.s.* Kumpa-
'nei *f*.
cam·ber ['kæmbə] **I** *v/t. u. v/i.* (sich)
wölben; **II** *s.* leichte Wölbung, Krümmung *f*; *mot.* (Rad)Sturz *m*; **'cam-
bered** [-əd] *adj.* **1.** gewölbt, geschweift; **2.** gestürzt (*Achse, Rad*).
Cam·bo·di·an [kæm'bəʊdjən] **I** *s.* Kambo'dschaner(in); **II** *adj.* kambo'dscha-
nisch.
Cam·bri·an ['kæmbrɪən] **I** *s.* **1.** Wa'liser
(-in); **2.** *geol.* 'Kambrium *n*; **II** *adj.* **3.**
wa'lisisch; **4.** *geol.* 'kambrisch.
cam·bric ['keɪmbrɪk] *s.* Ba'tist *m*.
cam·cor·der ['kæmkɔːdə] *s.* 'Camcorder *m*.
came [keɪm] *pret. von* **come**.
cam·el ['kæml] *s.* **1.** *zo.* Ka'mel *n*: **Arabian ~** Dromedar *n*; → **Bactrian cam-
el**; **2.** ♎, ⊙ Ka'mel *n*, Hebeleichter *m*;
cam·el·eer [‚kæmɪ'lɪə] *s.* Ka'meltreiber
m; **cam·el's hair** → **camel's hair**.
ca·mel·li·a [kə'miːljə] *s.* ♣ Ka'melie *f*.
cam·el's| hair ['kæmlz] *s.* Ka'melhaar

(-stoff *m*) *n*; **'~-hair** *adj.* Kamelhaar...
cam·e·o ['kæmɪəʊ] **I** *s.* Ka'mee *f*; **II** *adj.*
fig. Miniatur...
cam·er·a ['kæmərə] *s.* **1.** 'Kamera *f*: a)
'Fotoappa‚rat *m*, b) 'Film- *od.* 'Fernseh-
‚kamera *f*: **be on ~** a) auf Sendung *od.*
im Bild sein, b) vor der Kamera stehen;
2. in ~ ✄ unter Ausschluss der Öffentlichkeit, nicht öffentlich; *fig.* geheim;
'~·man [-mæn] *s.* [*irr.*] **1.** 'Pressefoto-
‚graf *m*; **2.** *Film:* 'Kameramann *m*; **~
ob·scu·ra** [ɒb'skjʊərə] *s. opt.* 'Loch‚kamera *f*, 'Camera *f* ob'scura; **'~-shy** *adj.*
'kamerascheu.
cam·i·knick·ers ['kæmɪ‚nɪkəz] *s. pl.*
Brit. (Damen)Hemdhose *f*.
cam·i·sole ['kæmɪsəʊl] *s.* **1.** Bett-, Mor-
genjäckchen *n*; **2.** (Trachten- *etc.*)Mie-
der *n*.
cam·o·mile ['kæməʊmaɪl] *s.* ♣ Ka'mille
f: **~ tea** Kamillentee *m*.
cam·ou·flage ['kæmʊflɑːʒ] **I** *s.* ✕ Tarnung *f* (*a. fig.*): **~ paint** Tarnanstrich *m*;
II *v/t.* tarnen, *fig. a.* verschleiern.
camp[^1] [kæmp] **I** *s.* **1.** (Zelt-, Ferien)La-
ger *n*, Lagerplatz *m*, Camp *n*: **break**
od. **strike ~** das Lager abbrechen, aufbrechen; **2.** ✕ Feld-, Heerlager *n*; **3.**
fig. Lager *n*, Par'tei *f*, Anhänger *pl.* e-r
Richtung: **the rival ~** das gegnerische
Lager; **II** *adj.* **4.** Lager..., Camping...:
~ bed a) Feldbett *n*, b) Campingliege *f*;
III *v/i.* **5.** *a.* **~ out** zelten, campen, kampieren.
camp[^2] [kæmp] F **I** *adj.* **1.** a) ‚schwul‘,
‚tuntenhaft‘, b) über'zogen, über'trie-
ben, ‚irr‘, c) verkitscht; **II** *v/i.* **2.** → **4**;
III *v/t.* **3.** *et.* ‚aufmotzen‘, *thea. etc. a.*
über'ziehen, über'trieben darstellen, *a.*
verkitschen; **4.** **~ it up** a) die Sache
‚aufmotzen‘, *thea. etc. a.* über'ziehen,
b) sich ‚tuntenhaft‘ benehmen.
cam·paign [kæm'peɪn] **I** *s.* **1.** ✕ Feldzug *m*; **2.** *pol. u. fig.* Schlacht *f*, Kam-
'pagne *f*, (*a.* Werbe)Feldzug *m*, Akti'on
f; **3.** *pol.* 'Wahlkampf *m*, -kam‚pagne *f*:
~ button Wahlkampfplakette *f*; **II** *v/i.*
4. ✕ an e-m Feldzug teilnehmen,
kämpfen; **5.** *fig.* kämpfen, zu Felde ziehen (**for** für; **against** gegen); **6.** *pol.* a)
sich am Wahlkampf beteiligen, im
Wahlkampf stehen, b) Wahlkampf machen (**for** für); *c) Am.* kandidieren;
cam'paign·er [-nə] *s.* **1.** Feldzugteil-
nehmer *m*: **old ~** *fig.* alter Praktikus *od.*
Hase; **2.** *fig.* Kämpfer *m* (**for** für).
cam·pan·u·la [kəm'pænjʊlə] *s.* ♣ Glockenblume *f*.
camp·er ['kæmpə] *s.* **1.** Camper(in); **2.**
Am. a) Wohnanhänger *m*, -wagen *m*,
b) 'Wohnmo‚bil *n*.
camp| fe·ver *s.* ✊ 'Typhus *m*; **'~-‚fire** *s.*
Lagerfeuer *n*: **~ girl** Pfadfinderin *f*; **~
fol·low·er** *s.* **1.** Sol'datenprostituierte
f; **2.** *pol. etc.* Sympathi'sant(in), Mitläu-
fer(in); **'~ground** → **camping ground**.
cam·phor ['kæmfə] *s.* 🜊 Kampfer *m*;
'cam·phor·at·ed [-əreɪtɪd] *adj.* mit
Kampfer behandelt, Kampfer...
cam·phor| ball *s.* Mottenkugel *f*;
'~-wood *s.* Kampferholz *n*.
camp·ing ['kæmpɪŋ] *s.* Camping *n*, Zelten *n*; Kampieren *n*; **~ ground, ~ site**
s. Zelt-, Campingplatz *m*.
cam·pi·on ['kæmpjən] *s.* ♣ Lichtnelke *f*.
camp meet·ing *s. Am.* religi'öse Versammlung im Freien; 'Zeltmissi‚on *f*.
cam·po·ree [‚kæmpə'riː] *s. Am.* regio-
'nales Pfadfindertreffen.
cam·pus ['kæmpəs] *s.* Campus *m* (*Ge-
samtanlage e-r Universität od. Schule*),
weitS. 'Uni *f od.* Gym'nasium *n*: **live
on ~** auf dem Campus wohnen.

'cam·wood *s.* Kam-, Rotholz *n*.
can[^1] [kæn; kən] *v/aux.* [*irr.*], *pres. neg.*
'can·not 1. können: **~ you do it?**; **he
cannot read**; **we could do it now** wir
könnten es jetzt tun; **how could you?**
wie konntest du nur (so etwas tun)?; **~
do!** *sl.* (wird) gemacht!; **no ~ do!** *sl.* das
geht nicht!; **2.** dürfen, können: **you ~
go away now**.
can[^2] [kæn] **I** *s.* **1.** (Blech)Kanne *f*; (Öl-)
Kännchen *n*: **carry the ~** *sl.* der Sündenbock sein, dran sein; **2.** (Kon'serven)Dose *f*, (-)Büchse *f*: **~ opener**
Büchsenöffner *m*; **in the ~** F ‚abgedreht‘, ‚im Kasten‘ (*Film*), *allg.* unter
Dach u. Fach; **3.** (Blech)Trinkgefäß *n*;
4. Ka'nister *m*; **5.** *Am. sl.* a) ‚Kittchen‘
n, ‚Knast‘ *m*, b) ‚Klo‘ *n*, c) ‚Arsch‘ *m*;
II *v/t.* **6.** in Büchsen konservieren, eindosen; **7.** F auf Schallplatte *od.* Band
aufnehmen; **8.** *Am sl.* a) ‚rausschmeißen‘, entlassen, b) ‚einlochen‘, c) aufhören mit.
Ca·na·di·an [kə'neɪdjən] **I** *adj.* ka'nadisch; **II** *s.* Ka'nadier(in).
ca·naille [kə'nɑːiː] (*Fr.*) *s.* Pöbel *m*.
ca·nal [kə'næl] *s.* **1.** Ka'nal *m* (*für Schifffahrt etc.*): **~s of Mars** Marskanäle *f*; **2.**
anat., zo. Ka'nal *m*, Gang *m*, Röhre *f*;
ca·nal·i·za·tion [‚kænəlaɪ'zeɪʃn] *s.* Kanalisierung *f*; Ka'nalnetz *n*; **ca·nal·ize**
['kænəlaɪz] *v/t.* **1.** kanalisieren, schiffbar machen; **2.** *fig.* (in bestimmte Bahnen) lenken, kanalisieren.
can·a·pé ['kænəpeɪ] (*Fr.*) *s.* Appe'tithappen *m*, Cocktailhappen *m*.
ca·nard [kæ'nɑːd] (*Fr.*) *s.* (Zeitungs)En-
te *f*, Falschmeldung *f*.
ca·nar·y [kə'neərɪ] **I** *s.* **1.** *a.* **~ bird** *orn.*
Ka'narienvogel *m*; **2.** *a.* ⚱ **wine** Ka'na-
rienwein *m*; **II** *adj.* **3.** hellgelb.
can·cel ['kænsl] **I** *v/t.* **1.** (durch-, aus-)
streichen; **2.** wider'rufen, aufheben (*a.*
♪), annullieren (*a.* ♱), rückgängig machen, absagen; ♱ stornieren; *Computer:*
Programm abbrechen; **3.** ungültig machen, tilgen; erlassen; *Briefmarke, Fahrschein etc.* entwerten; *fig.* zu'nichte
machen; *a.* **~ out** ausgleichen, kompensieren; **4.** ♪ heben, streichen; **II** *v/i.* **5.**
mst **~ out** sich (gegenseitig) aufheben
od. ausgleichen **6.** **~ out** absagen, die
Sache abblasen; **III** *s.* **7.** Streichung
f; **can·cel·la·tion** [‚kænsə'leɪʃn] *s.* **1.**
Streichung *f*; Aufhebung *f*; 'Widerruf
m; Absage *f*; **2.** ♱ Annullierung *f*,
Stornierung *f*: **~ clause** Rücktrittsklausel *f*; **~ charge, ~ fee** Rücktrittsgebühr
f; **3.** Entwertung *f* (*Briefmarke etc.*).
can·cer ['kænsə] *s.* **1.** ✊ Krebs *m*; Karzi'nom *n*; **2.** *fig.* Krebsgeschwür *n*, Übel
n; **3.** ⚱ *ast.* Krebs *m*; **'can·cer·ous**
[-sərəs] *adj.* ✊ a) krebsbefallen: **~ lung**
b) Krebs...: **~ tumo(u)r**, c) krebsartig:
~ growth *fig.* Krebsgeschwür *n*.
can·de·la·bra [‚kændɪ'lɑːbrə] *pl.* **-bras**,
can·de·la·brum [-brəm] *pl.* **-bra**, *Am.*
a. **-brums** *s.* Kande'laber *m*; (Arm-,
Kron)Leuchter *m*.
can·des·cence [kæn'desns] *s.* Weißglut
f.
can·did ['kændɪd] *adj.* ☐ **1.** offen (u.
ehrlich), freimütig; **2.** aufrichtig, unvoreingenommen, objek'tiv; **3.** freizügig, (ta'bu)frei: **a ~ film**; **4.** *phot.* unge-
stellt, unbemerkt aufgenommen: **~
camera** a) Kleinstbildkamera *f*, b) versteckte Kamera *f*: **~ shot** Schnappschuss
m.
can·di·da·cy ['kændɪdəsɪ] *s.* Kandida'tur
f, Bewerbung *f*, Anwartschaft *f*; **can-
di·date** ['kændɪdət] *s.* **1.** (**for**) Kandi-
'dat *m* (für) (*a. fig.*), Bewerber *m* (um),

Anwärter (auf *acc.*): ~ *country* 'Bei-trittskandi,dat *m* (*zur EU etc.*); **2.** ('Prü-fungs)Kandi,dat(in); **'can·di·dature** [-dətʃə] → **candidacy**.

can·died ['kændɪd] *adj.* **1.** kandiert, über'zuckert: ~ *peel* Zitronat *n*; **2.** *fig. contp.* ,honigsüß'.

can·dle ['kændl] *s.* **1.** (Wachs- *etc.*)Ker-ze *f*, Licht *n*: *burn the* ~ *at both ends fig.* Raubbau mit s-r Gesundheit trei-ben; *not to be fit to hold a* ~ *to* das Wasser nicht reichen können (*dat.*); → *game*[1] 4; **2.** → *candlepower*; '~,berry [-,bərɪ] *s.* ♀ Wachsmyrtenbeere *f*; '~-end *s.* **1.** Kerzenstummel *m*; **2.** *pl. fig.* Abfälle *pl.*, Krimskrams *m*; '~·light *s.* **1.** (*by* ~ bei) Kerzenlicht *n*; **2.** Abend-dämmerung *f*.

Can·dle·mas ['kændlməs] *s. R.C.* (Ma-'riä) Lichtmess *f*.

'can·dle|,pow·er *s. phys.* (Nor'mal)Ker-ze *f* (*Lichteinheit*); '~·stick *s.* (Kerzen-)Leuchter *m*; '~·wick *s.* Kerzendocht *m*.

can·do(u)r ['kændə] *s.* **1.** Offenheit *f*, Aufrichtigkeit *f*; **2.** 'Unpar,teilichkeit *f*, Objektivi'tät *f*.

can·dy ['kændɪ] **I** *s.* **1.** Kandis(zucker) *m*; **2.** *Am.* a) Süßigkeiten *pl.*, Kon'fekt *n*, b) a. *hard* ~ Bon'bon *m*, *n*; **II** *v/t.* **3.** kandieren, glacieren; mit Zucker ein-machen; **4.** *Zucker* kristallisieren las-sen; **III** *v/i.* **5.** kristallisieren (*Zucker*); '~·floss *s.* Zuckerwatte *f*; ~ *store s. Am.* Süßwarengeschäft *n*.

cane [keɪn] **I** *s.* **1.** ♀ (Bambus-, Zucker-, Schilf)Rohr *n*; **2.** spanisches Rohr; **3.** Rohrstock *m*; **4.** Spazierstock *m*; **II** *v/t.* **5.** (mit dem Stock) züchtigen *od.* prü-geln; **6.** *Stuhl* mit Rohrgeflecht verse-hen: ~·*bottomed* mit Sitz aus Rohr; ~ *chair s.* Rohrstuhl *m*; ~ *sug·ar s.* Rohrzucker *m*; '~·work *s.* Rohrgeflecht *n*.

ca·nine **I** *adj.* ['keɪnaɪn] Hunde...; *fig. contp.* hündisch; **II** *s.* ['kænaɪn] *anat. a.* ~ *tooth* Eckzahn *m*.

can·ing ['keɪnɪŋ] *s.*: *give s.o. a* ~ → *cane* 5.

can·is·ter ['kænɪstə] *s.* **1.** Ka'nister *m*, Blechdose *f*; **2.** ✕ *a.* ~ *shot* Kar'tät-sche *f*.

can·ker ['kæŋkə] **I** *s.* **1.** ✿ Mund- *od.* Lippengeschwür *n*; **2.** *vet.* Strahlfäule *f*; **3.** ♀ Rost *m*, Brand *m*; **4.** *fig.* Krebs-geschwür *n*; **II** *v/t.* **5.** *fig.* an-, zerfressen, verderben; **III** *v/i.* **6.** angefressen wer-den, verderben; **'can·kered** [-əd] *adj.* **1.** ♀ a) brandig, b) (von Raupen) zer-fressen; **2.** *fig.* a) bösartig, b) mürrisch; **'can·ker·ous** [-ərəs] *adj.* **1.** → *can-kered* 1; **2.** fressend, schädlich, vergif-tend.

can·na·bis ['kænəbɪs] *s.* 'Cannabis *m*: a) ♀ Hanf *m*, b) Haschisch *n*.

canned [kænd] *adj.* konserviert, Dosen..., Büchsen...: ~ *food* Konserven *pl.*; ~ *meat* Büchsenfleisch *n*; **2.** F ,aus der Konserve': ~ *music*; ~ *film* TV Aufzeichnung *f*; **3.** *sl.* ,blau', betrun-ken; **4.** *Am.* stereo'typ, scha'blonenhaft; **can·ner** ['kænə] *s.* **1.** Kon'servenfabri-,kant *m*; **2.** Arbeiter(in) in e-r Kon'ser-venfa,brik; **'can·ner·y** [-ərɪ] *s.* Kon'ser-venfa,brik *f*.

can·ni·bal ['kænɪbl] **I** *s.* Kanni'bale *m*, Menschenfresser *m*; **II** *adj.* kanni'ba-lisch (*a. fig.*); **'can·ni·bal·ism** [-bəlɪ-zəm] *s.* Kanniba'lismus *m* (*a. zo.*); *fig.* Unmenschlichkeit *f*; **can·ni·bal·is·tic** [,kænɪbə'lɪstɪk] *adj.* (□ ~*ally*) kanni'ba-lisch (*a. fig.*); **'can·ni·bal·ize** [-bəlaɪz] *v/t. altes Auto etc.* ,ausschlachten'.

can·ning ['kænɪŋ] *s.* Kon'servenfabrika-

ti,on *f*: ~ *factory od. plant* → *cannery*.

can·non ['kænən] **I** *s.* **1.** ✕ a) Ka'none *f*, Geschütz *n*, b) *coll.* Ka'nonen *pl.*, Artille'rie *f*; **2.** Wasserwerfer *m*; **3.** ❁ Zy'linder *m* um e-e Welle; **4.** *Billard: Brit.* Karambo'lage *f*; **II** *v/i.* **5.** *Billard: Brit.* karambolieren; **6.** (*against, into, with*) rennen, prallen (gegen), karam-bolieren (mit); **can·non·ade** [,kænə-'neɪd] **I** *s.* **1.** Kano'nade *f*; **2.** *fig.* Dröh-nen *n*; **II** *v/t.* **3.** beschießen.

'can·non|·ball *s.* **1.** Ka'nonenkugel *f*; **2.** *Fußball:* F Bombe(nschuss *m*) *f*; '~·bone *s. zo.* Ka'nonenbein *n* (*Pferd*); '~-,fod·der *s. fig.* Ka'nonenfutter *n*.

can·not ['kænɒt] → *can*[1].

can·nu·la ['kænjʊlə] *s.* ✿ Ka'nüle *f*.

can·ny ['kænɪ] *adj.* □ *Scot.* **1.** schlau, gerissen; **2.** nett.

ca·noe [kə'nuː] **I** *s.* Kanu *n* (*a. sport*), Paddelboot *n*: ~ *slalom* Kanu-, Wild-wasserslalom *m*; *paddle one's own* ~ auf eigenen Füßen stehen, selbstständig sein; **II** *v/i.* Kanu fahren, paddeln; **ca·'noe·ist** [-uːɪst] *s.* Ka'nute *m*, Ka'nutin *f*.

can·on[1] ['kænən] *s.* **1.** Regel *f*, Richt-schnur *f*, Grundsatz *m*, 'Kanon *m*; **2.** *eccl.* 'Kanon *m*: a) ka'nonische Bücher *pl.*, b) 'Mess,kanon *m*, c) Ordensregeln *pl.*, d) → *canon law*; **3.** ♪ 'Kanon *m*; **4.** *typ.* 'Kanon(schrift) *f*.

can·on[2] ['kænən] *s. eccl.* Ka'noniker *m*, Dom-, Stiftsherr *m*.

ca·ñon ['kænjən] → *canyon*.

can·on·ess ['kænənɪs] *s. eccl.* Kano'nis-sin *f*, Stiftsdame *f*.

ca·non·i·cal [kə'nɒnɪkl] **I** *adj.* □ ka'no-nisch, vorschriftsmäßig; *bibl.* au'then-tisch; **II** *s. pl. eccl.* kirchliche Amts-tracht; ~ *books* → *canon*[1] 2 a; ~ *hours s. pl.* a) regelmäßige Gebetszei-ten *pl.*, b) *Brit.* Zeiten *pl.* für Trau-ungen.

can·on·ist ['kænənɪst] *s.* Kirchenrechts-lehrer *m*; **can·on·i·za·tion** [,kænənaɪ-'zeɪʃn] *s. eccl.* Heiligsprechung *f*; **'can·on·ize** [-naɪz] *v/t. eccl.* heilig spre-chen; **can·on law** *s.* ka'nonisches Recht, Kirchenrecht *n*.

ca·noo·dle [kə'nuːdl] *v/t. u. v/i. sl.* ,schmusen', ,knutschen'.

can·o·py ['kænəpɪ] **I** *s.* **1.** 'Baldachin *m*, (Bett-, Thron-, Trag)Himmel *m*: ~ *of heaven* Himmelszelt *n*; **2.** Schutz-, Ka-'binendach *n*, Verdeck *n*; **3.** Fallschirm (-kappe *f*) *m*; **4.** △ Über'dachung *f*; **II** *v/t.* **5.** über'dachen; *fig.* bedecken.

canst [kænst; kənst] *obs. 2. sg. pres. von can*[1].

cant[1] [kænt] **I** *s.* **1.** Fach-, Zunftsprache *f*; **2.** Jar'gon *m*, Gaunersprache *f*; **3.** Gewäsch *n*, Frömme'lei *f*, scheinhei-liges Gerede; **4.** (leere) Phrase(n *pl.*) *f*; **II** *v/i.* **6.** frömmeln, scheinheilig reden; **7.** Phrasen dreschen.

cant[2] [kænt] **I** *s.* **1.** (Ab)Schrägung *f*, schräge Lage; **2.** Ruck *m*, Stoß *m*; plötzliche Wendung; **II** *v/t.* **3.** (ver)kan-ten, kippen; **4.** ✪ abschrägen; **II** *v/i.* **5.** *a.* ~ *over* sich neigen, sich auf die Seite legen; 'umkippen.

can't [kɑːnt] F *für cannot*; → *can*[1].

Can·tab ['kæntæb] *abbr. für* **Can·ta-brig·i·an** [,kæntə'brɪdʒɪən] *s.* Stu'dent (-in) *od.* Absol'vent(in) der Universi'tät Cambridge (*England*) *od.* der Harvard University (*USA*).

can·ta·loup(e) ['kæntəluːp] *s.* ♀ Kanta-'lupe *f*, 'Warzenme,lone *f*.

can·tan·ker·ous [kæn'tæŋkərəs] *adj.* □ streitsüchtig.

can·ta·ta [kæn'tɑːtə] *s.* ♪ Kan'tate *f*.

can·teen [kæn'tiːn] *s.* **1.** (Mili'tär-, Be-

'triebs- *etc.*)Kan,tine *f*; **2.** ✕ a) Feldfla-sche *f*, b) Kochgeschirr *n*; **3.** Besteck-, Silberkasten *m*.

can·ter ['kæntə] **I** *s.* 'Kanter *m*, kurzer Ga'lopp: *win in a* ~ mühelos siegen; **II** *v/i.* im kurzen Galopp reiten.

can·ti·cle ['kæntɪkl] *s. eccl.* Lobgesang *m*: ⨀*s bibl. das* Hohelied (Salo'monis).

can·ti·le·ver ['kæntɪliːvə] **I** *s.* **1.** △ Kon-'sole *f*, ❁ freitragender Arm, vor-springender Träger, Ausleger *m*; **II** *adj.* **3.** freitragend; ~ *bridge s.* Ausleger-brücke *f*; ~ *wing s.* ✈ unverspreizte Tragfläche.

can·to ['kæntəʊ] *pl.* **-tos** *s.* Gesang *m* (*Teil e-r größeren Dichtung*).

can·ton[1] ['kæntən] *s.* Kan'ton *m*, (Ver-waltungs)Bezirk *m*; **II** *v/t.* in Kan'tone *od.* Bezirke einteilen.

can·ton[2] ['kæntən] **I** *s.* **1.** *her.* Feld *n*; **2.** Gösch *f* (*Obereck an Flaggen*); **II** *v/t.* **3.** *her.* in Felder einteilen.

can·ton[3] [kæn'tuːn] *v/t.* ✕ einquar-tieren.

Can·ton·ese [,kæntə'niːz] **I** *adj.* kanto-'nesisch; **II** *s.* Bewohner(in) 'Kantons.

can·ton·ment [kæn'tuːnmənt] *s.* ✕ *oft pl.* Quar'tier *n*, 'Orts,unterkunft *f*.

Ca·nuck [kə'nʌk] *s. a)* Ka'nadier(in) (*französischer Abstammung*), b) *Am. contp.* Ka'nadier(in).

can·vas ['kænvəs] *s.* **1.** a) Segeltuch *n*: ~ *shoes* Segeltuchschuhe, b) *coll.* (*alle*) Segel *pl.*: *under* ~ unter Segel; **2.** Pack-, Zeltleinwand *f*: *under* ~ in Zel-ten; **3.** 'Kanevas *m*, Stra'min *m* (*zum Sticken*); **4.** a) (Maler)Leinwand *f*, b) (Öl)Gemälde *n*.

can·vass ['kænvəs] **I** *v/t.* **1.** gründlich erörtern *od.* prüfen; **2.** a) *pol.* Stimmen werben, b) *Am.* Wahlresultate prüfen, c) ✝ Aufträge her'einholen, *Abonnen-ten, Inserate* sammeln; **3.** *Wahlkreis od. Geschäftsbezirk* bereisen, bearbeiten; **4.** *um et.* werben, *Am.* für et. *pol.* et. anpreisen; **II** *v/i.* **5.** e-n Wahlfeldzug veranstalten; **6.** *Am.* 'Wahlresul,tate prüfen; **7.** wer-ben (*for* um); **III** *v/t.* **8.** *pol.* a) Stimmen-werbung *f*, Wahlfeldzug *m*, b) *Am.* Wahl(stimmen)prüfung *f*; **9.** ✝ Kun-denwerbung *f*; He'reinholen *n* von Auf-trägen; **can·vass·er** [-sə] *s.* **1.** ✝ Kun-denwerber *m*, b) *Am.* Wahleinpeit-scher *m*, b) *Am.* Wahl(stimmen)prüfer *m*; **'can·vass·ing** [-sɪŋ] *s.* **1.** 'Wahlpro-pa,ganda *f*; **2.** ✝ Kundenwerbung *f*.

can·yon ['kænjən] *s.* 'Cañon *m*, Fels-schlucht *f*.

caou·tchouc ['kaʊtʃʊk] *s.* 'Kautschuk *m*, 'Gummi *n*, *m*.

cap[1] [kæp] **I** *s.* **1.** Mütze *f*, Kappe *f*, Haube *f*: ~ *and bells* Schellen-, Nar-renkappe; ~ *in hand* mit der Mütze in der Hand, demütig; *if the* ~ *fits wear it fig.* wen's juckt, der kratze sich; *set one's* ~ *at s.o.* F hinter j-m her sein, sich j-n zu angeln suchen (*Frau*); **2.** *univ.* Ba'rett *n*: ~ *and gown univ.* Ba-rett u. Talar; **3.** (Sport-, Stu'denten-, Klub-, Dienst)Mütze *f*; **4.** *sport Brit.* Auswahl-, Natio'nalspieler(in): *get od. win one's* ~ in die Nationalmannschaft berufen werden; **5.** (Schutz-, Ver-schluss)Kappe *f od.* (-)Kapsel *f*, Deckel *m*, Aufsatz *m*; ✕ Zündkapsel *f*; **6.** *mot.* (Reifen)Auflage *f*: *full* ~ Runderneue-rung *f*; **7.** ♂ Pes'sar *n*; **8.** Spitze *f*, Gip-fel *m*; **II** *v/t.* **9.** (mit *od.* wie mit e-r Kappe) bedecken; **10.** mit (Schutz-)Kappe, Kapsel, Deckel, Aufsatz *etc.* versehen; *mot.* Reifen runderneuern; **11.** *Brit. univ.* j-m e-n aka'demischen Grad verleihen; **12.** oben liegen auf (dat.), krönen (a. fig. abschließen); **13.** fig. über'treffen, -'trumpfen; **14.** sport Brit. j-n in die Natio'nalmannschaft berufen.

cap² [kæp] abbr. für **capital¹** 2.

ca·pa·bil·i·ty [ˌkeɪpə'bɪlətɪ] s. **1.** Fähigkeit f (**of** zu); **2.** Tauglichkeit f (**for** zu); **3.** a. pl. Ta'lent n, Begabung f; **ca·pa·ble** ['keɪpəbl] adj. □ **1.** (Personen) a) fähig, tüchtig, b) (**of**) fähig (zu od. gen.), im'stande (zu inf.) (mst b.s.): **legally ~** rechts-, geschäftsfähig; **2.** (Sachen) a) geeignet, tauglich (**for** zu), b) (**of**) (et.) zulassend, (zu et.) fähig: **~ of being divided** teilbar.

ca·pa·cious [kə'peɪʃəs] adj. □ geräumig, weit; um'fassend (a. fig.).

ca·pac·i·tance [kə'pæsɪtəns] s. ⚡ kapazi'tiver ('Blind), Widerstand, Kapazi'tät f; **ca'pac·i·tate** [-teɪt] v/t. befähigen, ermächtigen (a. ⚖️); **ca'pac·i·tor** [-tə] s. ⚡ Konden'sator m; **ca'pac·i·ty** [-sətɪ] I s. **1.** (Raum)Inhalt m, Fassungsvermögen n; Kapazi'tät f (a. ⚡, phys.): **measure of ~** Hohlmaß n; **seating ~** Sitzgelegenheit f (**of** für); **full to ~** ganz voll, thea. etc. ausverkauft; **2.** Leistungsfähigkeit f, Vermögen n; **3.** ⚡, ⚙ Kapazi'tät f, Leistungsfähigkeit f, (Nenn)Leistung f: **~ utilization** Kapazitätsauslastung f; **working to ~** mit Höchstleistung arbeitend, voll ausgelastet; **4.** fig. Auffassungsgabe f, geistige Fähigkeit f; **5.** ⚖️ (Geschäfts-, Test'tier etc.)Fähigkeit f: **~ to sue and to be sued** Prozeßfähigkeit f; **6.** Eigenschaft f, Stellung f: **in my ~ as** in m-r Eigenschaft als; **in an advisory ~** in beratender Funktion; **II** adj. **7.** maxi'mal, Höchst...: **~ business** Rekordgeschäft n; **8.** thea. etc. voll, ausverkauft: **~ house, ~ crowd** sport ausverkauftes Stadion.

ca·par·i·son [kə'pærɪsn] s. **1.** Scha'bracke f; **2.** fig. Aufputz m.

cape¹ [keɪp] s. Cape n, 'Umhang m; Schulterkragen m.

cape² [keɪp] s. Kap n, Vorgebirge n: **the ⚬** das Kap der Guten Hoffnung; **⚬ Dutch** Kapholländisch n; **⚬ wine** Kapwein m.

ca·per¹ ['keɪpə] I s. **1.** Kapri'ole f: a) Freuden-, Luftsprung m, b) Streich m, Schabernack m: **cut ~s** → 3; **2.** F fig. ,Ding' n, ,Spaß' m, Sache f; **II** v/i. **3.** a) Luftsprünge machen, b) he'rumtollen.

ca·per² ['keɪpə] s. **1.** ♀ Kapernstrauch m; **2.** Kaper f.

cap·er·cail·lie [ˌkæpə'keɪlɪ], **cap·er·'cail·zie** [-lɪ] s. orn. Auerhahn m.

ca·pi·as ['keɪpɪæs] s. ⚖️ Haftbefehl m (bsd. im Vollstreckungsverfahren).

cap·il·lar·i·ty [ˌkæpɪ'lærətɪ] s. phys. Kapillari'tät f; **cap·il·lar·y** [kə'pɪlərɪ] I adj. haarförmig, -fein, kapil'lar: **~ attraction** Kapillaranziehung f; **~ tube** → II; **II** s. anat. Kapil'largefäß n.

cap·i·tal¹ ['kæpɪtl] I s. **1.** Hauptstadt f; **2.** Großbuchstabe m; **3.** ✝ Kapi'tal n: a) Vermögen n, b) Unter'nehmer(tum n) pl.: **⚬ and Labo(u)r**; **4.** Vorteil m, Nutzen m: **make ~ out of** aus et. Kapital schlagen; **II** adj. **5.** ⚖️ a) kapi'tal, todeswürdig: **~ crime** Kapitalverbrechen n, b) Todes...: **~ punishment** Todesstrafe f; **6.** größt, wichtigst, Haupt...: **~ city** Hauptstadt f; **~ ship** Großkampfschiff n; **7.** verhängnisvoll: **a ~ error** ein Kapitalfehler m; **8.** großartig: **a ~ joke; a ~ fellow** ein Prachtkerl m; **9.** ✝ Kapital...: **~ fund** Stamm-, Grundkapital n; **10.** **~ letter** → 2; **~ B** großes B.

cap·i·tal² ['kæpɪtl] s. △ Kapi'tell n.

cap·i·tal| ac·count s. ✝ Kapi'talkonto n; **~ ac·cu·mu·la·tion** s. Kapi'talakkumulati,on f; **~ as·sets** s. pl. Anlagevermögen n; **~ ex·pend·i·ture** s. Investiti'onsaufwand m; **~ flight** s. Kapi'talflucht f; **~ gain(s** pl.) s. Kapi'talertrag m, -zuwachs m, Wertzuwachs m; **~ gains tax** s. Kapi'talertragssteuer f; **~ gen·er·a·tion** s. Kapi'talbeschaffung f; **~ goods** s. pl. Investiti'onsgüter pl.; **'~-in,ten·sive** adj. kapi'talinten,siv; **~ in·vest·ment** s. Kapi'talanlage f.

cap·i·tal·ism ['kæpɪtəlɪzəm] s. Kapita-'lismus m; **'cap·i·tal·ist** [-ɪst] I Kapita-'list m; **II** adj. → **cap·i·tal·is·tic** [ˌkæpɪtə'lɪstɪk] adj. (□ **~ally**) kapita'listisch; **cap·i·tal·i·za·tion** [ˌkæpɪtəlaɪ-'zeɪʃn] s. **1.** ✝ allg. Kapitalisierung f; **2.** Großschreibung f; **'cap·i·tal·ize** [-laɪz] I v/t. **1.** ✝ kapitalisieren; **2.** fig. sich et. zu'nutze machen; **3.** großschreiben (mit Großbuchstaben od. mit großen Anfangsbuchstaben schreiben); **II** v/i. **4.** Kapi'tal anhäufen; **5.** e-n Kapi'talwert haben (**at** von); **6.** fig. Kapital schlagen (**on** aus).

cap·i·tal| lev·y s. ✝ Vermögensabgabe f; **~ mar·ket** s. Kapi'talmarkt m; **~ re·quire·ments** s. pl. Kapitalbedarf m; **~ re·serves** s. pl. Kapitalrücklagen pl.; **~ stock** s. ✝ 'Aktienkapi,tal n; **~ tie-up** s. Kapitalbindung f.

cap·i·ta·tion [ˌkæpɪ'teɪʃn] s. **1.** a. **~ tax** Kopfsteuer f; **2.** Zahlung f pro Kopf: **~ grant** Zuschuss m pro Kopf.

Cap·i·tol ['kæpɪtl] s. Kapi'tol n: a) im alten Rom, b) in Washington.

ca·pit·u·lar [kə'pɪtjʊlə] eccl. I adj. kapitu'lar, zum Ka'pitel gehörig; **II** s. Kapitu'lar m, Domherr m.

ca·pit·u·late [kə'pɪtjʊleɪt] v/i. ✗ u. fig. kapitulieren (**to** vor dat); **ca·pit·u·la·tion** [kəˌpɪtjʊ'leɪʃn] s. ✗ a) Kapitulati'on f, 'Übergabe f, b) Kapitulati'onsurkunde f.

ca·pon ['keɪpən] s. Ka'paun m; **'ca·pon·ize** [-naɪz] v/t. Hahn kastrieren, ka'paunen.

capped [kæpt] adj. mit e-r Kappe od. Mütze bedeckt: **~ and gowned** in vollem Ornat.

ca·price [kə'priːs] s. Ka'prize f, Laune f, Grille f; Launenhaftigkeit f; **ca'pricious** [-ɪʃəs] adj. □ launenhaft, launisch; kaprizi'ös; **ca'pri·cious·ness** [-ɪʃəsnɪs] s. Launenhaftigkeit f; kaprizi'öse Art.

Cap·ri·corn ['kæprɪkɔːn] s. ast. Steinbock m.

cap·ri·ole ['kæprɪəʊl] I s. Kapri'ole f (a. Reiten), Bock-, Luftsprung m; **II** v/i. Kapri'olen machen.

cap·si·cum ['kæpsɪkəm] s. ♀ 'Paprika m, Spanischer Pfeffer.

cap·size [kæp'saɪz] I v/i. **1.** ⚓ kentern; **2.** fig. 'umschlagen; **II** v/t. **3.** ⚓ zum Kentern bringen.

cap·stan ['kæpstən] s. ⚓ Gangspill n, Ankerwinde f; **~ lathe** s. ⚙ Re'volverdrehbank f.

cap·su·lar ['kæpsjʊlə] adj. kapselförmig, Kapsel...; **cap·sule** ['kæpsjuːl] I s. **1.** anat. (Gelenk- etc.)Kapsel f, Hülle f, Schale f; **2.** ♀ a) Kapselfrucht f, Sporenkapsel f; **3.** pharm. (Arz'nei-)Kapsel f; **4.** (Me'tall-, Verschluss)Kapsel f; **5.** (Raum)Kapsel f; **6.** ♞ Abdampfschale f; **7.** fig. kurze 'Übersicht od. Beschreibung etc.; **II** adj. **8.** fig. kurz, gedrängt, Kurz...

cap·tain ['kæptɪn] I s. **1.** Führer m, Oberhaupt n: **~ of industry** Industriekapitän m; **2.** ✗ a) Hauptmann m, b) Kavallerie: hist. Rittmeister m; **3.** ⚓ a) Kapi'tän m, Komman'dant m, b) Kriegsmarine: Kapitän m zur See; **4.** 'Flugkapi,tän m; **5.** sport ('Mannschafts)Kapi,tän m; **6.** ped. Klassensprecher(in); **7.** Vorarbeiter m; ⚒ Obersteiger m; **8.** Am. (Poli'zei-),Hauptkommis,sar m; **II** v/t. **9.** (an)führen; **'cap·tain·cy** [-sɪ], **'cap·tain·ship** [-ʃɪp] s. **1.** ✗ Hauptmanns-, Kapi'tänsposten m, -rang m; **2.** Führerschaft f.

cap·tion ['kæpʃn] I s. **1.** a) 'Überschrift f, Titel m, b) ('Bild),Unterschrift f, c) Film: 'Untertitel m; **2.** ⚖️ a) Prä'ambel f, b) Prozessrecht: 'Rubrum n; **II** v/t. **3.** mit e-r Überschrift etc. versehen; Film unter'titeln.

cap·tious ['kæpʃəs] adj. □ **1.** verfänglich; **2.** spitzfindig; **3.** krittelig, pe'dantisch.

cap·ti·vate ['kæptɪveɪt] v/t. fig. gefangen nehmen, fesseln, bestricken, bezaubern; **'cap·ti·vat·ing** [-tɪŋ] adj. fig. fesselnd, bezaubernd; **cap·ti·va·tion** [ˌkæptɪ'veɪʃn] s. fig. Bezauberung f.

cap·tive ['kæptɪv] I adj. **1.** gefangen, in Gefangenschaft: **be held ~** gefangen gehalten werden; **take ~** gefangen nehmen (a. fig.); **2.** festgehalten, ,gefangen': **~ balloon** Fesselballon m; **~ market** ✝ monopolistisch beherrschter Markt; **3.** fig. gefangen, gefesselt (**to** von); **II** s. **4.** Gefangene(r) m, f (a. phys. Neutronen) einfangen; erobern, für sich einnehmen, gewinnen, erlangen; an sich reißen; **II** s. **5.** Gefangennahme f, Fang m; **6.** ✗ Eroberung f (a. fig.); Erbeutung f, Beute f; **7.** ⚓ a) Kapern n, Aufbringung f, b) Prise f.

Cap·u·chin ['kæpjʊʃɪn] s. **1.** eccl. Kapu-'ziner(mönch) m; **2.** ♀ 'Umhang m mit Ka'puze; **3.** a. **~ monkey** zo. Kapu'zineraffe m.

car [kɑː] s. **1.** Auto n, Wagen m: **by ~** mit dem (od. im) Auto; **2.** (Eisenbahn etc.)Wagen m, Wag'gon m; **3.** Wagen m, Karren m; **4.** (Luftschiff- etc.)Gondel f; **5.** Ka'bine f e-s Aufzuges; **6.** poet. Kriegs- od. Tri'umphwagen m.

ca·rafe [kə'ræf] s. Ka'raffe f.

car·a·mel ['kærəmel] s. **1.** Kara'mel m, gebrannter Zucker; **2.** Kara'melle f (Bonbon).

car·a·pace ['kærəpeɪs] s. zo. Rückenschild m (Schildkröte, Krebs).

car·at ['kærət] s. Ka'rat n: a) Juwelenod. Perlengewicht, b) Goldfeingehalt: **18-~ gold** 18-karätiges Gold.

car·a·van ['kærəvæn] I s. **1.** Kara'wane f (a. fig.); **2.** a) Wohnwagen m (von Schaustellern etc.), b) Brit. Caravan m, Wohnwagen m, -anhänger m: **~ park** od. **site** Campingplatz m für Wohnwagen; **II** v/i. **3.** im Wohnwagen etc. reisen; **'car·a·van·ner** [-nə] s. **1.** Reisende(r) in e-r Kara'wane; **2.** mot. Brit. Caravaner m; **car·a·van·sa·ry** [-sərɪ], **car·a·van·se·rai** [-səraɪ] s. Karawanse'rei f.

car·a·vel ['kærəvəl] s. ⚓ Kara'velle f.

car·a·way ['kærəweɪ] s. ♀ Kümmel m; **~ seeds** s. pl. Kümmelkörner pl.

car·bide ['kɑːbaɪd] s. ♞ Kar'bid n.

car·bine ['kɑːbaɪn] s. ✗ Kara'biner m.

car bod·y s. ⚙ Karosse'rie f.

C

car·bo·hy·drate [ˌkɑːbəʊˈhaɪdreɪt] *s.* 🦅 'Kohle(n)hy,drat *n*.
car·bol·ic ac·id [kɑːˈbɒlɪk] *s.* 🦅 Kar'bol(säure *f*) *n*, Phe'nol *n*.
car·bo·lize [ˈkɑːbəlaɪz] *v/t.* 🦅 mit Kar'bolsäure behandeln.
car bomb [bɒm] *s.* 'Auto,bombe *f*.
car·bon [ˈkɑːbən] *s.* **1.** 🦅 Kohlenstoff *m*; **2.** ⚡ Kohle(elek,trode) *f*; **3.** a) 'Kohlepa,pier *n*, b) 'Durchschlag *m*; **car·bo·na·ceous** [ˌkɑːbəʊˈneɪʃəs] *adj.* kohlenstoff-, kohleartig; Kohlen...; **'car·bon·ate** [-nɪt] **I** *s.* [-nɪt] **1.** kohlensaures Salz: ~ *of lime* Kalziumkarbonat *n*, Kreide *f*; ~ *of soda* Natriumkarbonat *n*, kohlensaures Natrium, Soda *f*; **II** *v/t.* [-neɪt] **2.** mit Kohlensäure *od.* Kohlen'dio,xid behandeln; ~*d water* kohlensäurehaltiges Wasser, Sodawasser; **3.** karbonisieren, verkohlen.
car·bon| brush *s.* ⚡ Kohlebürste *f*; ~ **cop·y** *s.* **1.** 'Durchschlag *m*, -schrift *f*, Ko'pie *f*; **2.** *fig.* Abklatsch *m*, Dupli'kat *n*; ~ **dat·ing** *s.* Radiokar'bonme,thode *f*, 'C-'14-Me,thode *f* (*zur Altersbestimmung*); ~ **di·ox·ide** *s.* 🦅 Kohlen'dio,xid *n*; ~ **fil·a·ment** *s.* ⚡ Kohlefaden *m*.
car·bon·ic [kɑːˈbɒnɪk] *adj.* 🦅 kohlenstoffhaltig; Kohlen...; ~ **ac·id** *s.* 🦅 Kohlensäure *f*; ~·**'ac·id gas** *s.* 🦅 Kohlen'dio,xid *n*, Kohlensäuregas *n*; ~ **ox·ide** *s.* 🦅 Kohlen('mon)o,xid *n*.
car·bon·if·er·ous [ˌkɑːbəˈnɪfərəs] *adj.* kohlehaltig, Kohle führend: ♃ *Period geol.* Karbon *n*, Steinkohlenzeit *f*; **car·bon·i·za·tion** [ˌkɑːbənaɪˈzeɪʃn] *s.* **1.** Verkohlung *f*; **2.** Verkokung *f*: ~ *plant* Kokerei *f*; **'car·bon·ize** [-naɪz] *v/t.* **1.** verkohlen; **2.** verkoken.
car·bon| mi·cro·phone *s.* 'Kohlemikro-,fon *n*; ~ **pa·per** *s.* 'Kohlepa,pier *n* (*a. phot.*); ~ **print** *s. typ.* Kohle-, Pig'mentdruck *m*; ~ **steel** *s.* Kohlenstoff-, Flussstahl *m*.
car·bo·run·dum [ˌkɑːbəˈrʌndəm] *s.* ⚙ Karbo'rundum *n* (*Schleifmittel*).
car·boy [ˈkɑːbɔɪ] *s.* Korbflasche *f*, ('Glas)Bal,lon *m* (*bsd. für Säuren*).
car·bun·cle [ˈkɑːbʌŋkl] *s.* **1.** 🦟 Kar'bunkel *m*; **2.** Kar'funkel *m*, geschliffener Gra'nat.
car·bu·ret [ˈkɑːbjʊret] *v/t.* ⚙ karburieren; *mot.* vergasen; **'car·bu·ret·(t)ed** [-tɪd] *adj.* karburiert; **'car·bu·ret·ter**, **-ret·tor** [-tə], *Am. mst* **-ret·or** [-reɪtə] *s.* ⚙, *mot.* Vergaser *m*.
car·bu·rize [ˈkɑːbjʊraɪz] *v/t.* **1.** 🦅 a) mit Kohlenstoff verbinden, b) karburieren; **2.** ⚙ einsatzhärten.
car·cass, car·case [ˈkɑːkəs] *s.* **1.** Ka'daver *m*, (Tier-, Menschen)Leiche *f*; *humor.* ,Leichnam' *m* (*Körper*); **2.** Rumpf *m* (*e-s geschlachteten Tieres*): ~ *meat* frisches Fleisch (*Ggs. konserviertes*); **3.** Gerippe *n*, Ske'lett *n*, △ a. Rohbau *m*; **4.** ⚙ Kar'kasse *f e-s Gummireifens*; **5.** *fig.* Ru'ine *f*.
car·cin·o·gen [kɑːˈsɪnədʒən] *s.* Karzino'gen *n*, Krebserreger *m*; **car·cin·o·gen·ic** [ˌkɑːsɪnəˈdʒenɪk] *adj.* karzino'gen, Krebs erzeugend; **car·ci·nol·o·gy** [ˌkɑːsɪˈnɒlədʒɪ] *s.* 🦐, *a. zo.* Karzinolo'gie *f*; **car·ci·no·ma** [ˌkɑːsɪˈnəʊmə] *pl.* **-ma·ta** [-mətə] *od.* **-mas** *s.* 🦟 Karzi'nom *n*, Krebsgeschwür *n*.
card¹ [kɑːd] *s.* **1.** (*Spiel*)Karte *f*: *play* (*at*) ~*s* Karten spielen; *game of* ~*s* Kartenspiel *n*; *a pack of* ~*s* ein Spiel Karten; *house of* ~*s fig.* Kartenhaus *n*; *a safe* ~ *fig.* eine sichere Sache, et. auf das (*a.* j-d, auf den) man sich verlassen kann; *play one's* ~*s well fig.* geschickt

vorgehen; *put one's* ~*s on the table fig.* s-e Karten auf den Tisch legen; *show one's* ~*s fig.* s-e Karten aufdecken; *on the* ~*s fig.* (durchaus) möglich, ,drin'; **2.** (*Post-, Glückwunsch etc., Geschäfts-, Visiten-, Eintritts-, Einladungs*)Karte *f*; **3.** Mitgliedskarte *f*: ~-*carrying member* eingeschriebenes Mitglied; **4.** *pl.* (*'Arbeits*)Pa,piere *pl.*: *get one's* ~*s* F entlassen werden; **5.** ⚙ (Loch)Karte *f*; **6.** *sport* Pro'gramm *n*; **7.** Windrose *f* (*Kompass*); **8.** F ,Type' *f*, Witzbold *m*.
card² [kɑːd] ⚙ **I** *s.* Wollkratze *f*, Krempel *f*; **II** *v/t.* Wolle krempeln, kämmen: ~*ed yarn* Streichgarn *n*.
car·dan| joint [ˈkɑːdən] *s.* ⚙ Kar'dangelenk *n*; ~ **shaft** *s.* ⚙ Kar'dan-, Gelenkwelle *f*.
'card|-,bas·ket *s.* Vi'sitenkartenschale *f*; **'~·board** *s.* **1.** Kar'ton(pa,pier *n*) *m*, Pappe *f*; **II** *adj.* **2.** Karton..., Papp...: ~ *box* Pappschachtel *f*, Karton *m*; **3.** *fig. contp.* ,nachgemacht', Pappmaschee-...; **~ cat·a·logue** → *card index*.
card·er [ˈkɑːdə] *s.* ⚙ **1.** Krempler *m*, Wollkämmer *m*; **2.** 'Krempelma,schine *f*.
card·hold·er [ˈkɑːd,həʊldə] *s.* Kre'ditkarteninhaber(in).
car·di·ac [ˈkɑːdɪæk] 🦟 **I** *adj.* **1.** Herz...: ~ *arrest* Herzstillstand *m*; **II** *s.* **2.** Herzmittel *n*; **3.** 'Herzpati,ent *m*.
car·di·gan [ˈkɑːdɪgən] *s.* Strickjacke *f*.
car·di·nal [ˈkɑːdɪnl] **I** *adj.* **1.** grundsätzlich, grundlegend, hauptsächlich, Haupt..., Kardinal...: ~ *points* die vier (Haupt)Himmelsrichtungen; ~ *principles* Grundprinzipien; ~ *number* Kardinalzahl *f*; **2.** *eccl.* Kardinals...; **3.** scharlachrot, hochrot: ~·*flower* 🌼 hochrote Lobelie; **II** *s.* **4.** *eccl.* Kardi'nal *m*; **5.** *orn. a.* ~·*bird* Kardi'nal *m*; **'car·di·nal·ship** [-ʃɪp] *s.* Kardi'nalswürde *f*.
card in·dex *s.* Karto'thek *f*, Kar'tei *f*; **'card-,in·dex** *v/t.* **1.** e-e Kartei anlegen von, verzetteln; **2.** in e-e Kartei eintragen.
card·ing [ˈkɑːdɪŋ] *s.* ⚙ Krempeln *n*, Kratzen *n* (*Wolle*): ~ *machine* Krempel-, Kratzmaschine *f*.
cardio- [ˈkɑːdɪəʊ] *in Zssgn* Herz...
car·di·o·gram [ˈkɑːdɪəʊgræm] *s.* 🦟 Kardio'gramm *n*; **car·di·ol·o·gy** [ˌkɑːdɪˈɒlədʒɪ] *s.* Kardiolo'gie *f*, Herz(heil)kunde *f*.
card| room *s. Brit.* 'Kartenele,fon *m*; ~ **room** *s.* (Karten)Spielzimmer *n*; **'~·sharp**, **'~·sharp·er** *s.* Falschspieler *m*; ~ **ta·ble** *s.* Spieltisch *m*; ~ **trick** *s.* Kartenkunststück *n*; ~ **vote** *s. Brit.* (*mst gewerkschaftliche*) Abstimmung durch Wahlmänner.
care [keə] **I** *s.* **1.** Sorge *f*, Kummer *m*: *be free from* ~(*s*) keine Sorgen haben; *without a* ~ *in the world* völlig sorgenfrei; **2.** Sorgfalt *f*, Aufmerksamkeit *f*, Vorsicht *f*: *ordinary* ~ 🚗 verkehrsübliche Sorgfalt; *with due* ~ mit der erforderlichen Sorgfalt; *have a* ~*! Brit.* F a) pass doch auf!, b) ich bitte dich!; *take* ~ a) vorsichtig sein, aufpassen, b) sich Mühe geben, *od.* darauf achten *od.* nicht vergessen (*to do* zu tun; *that* dass); *take* ~ *not to do s.th.* sich hüten, et. zu tun; et. ja nicht tun; *take* ~ *not to drop it!* lass es ja nicht fallen; *take* ~*!* machs gut!; **3.** a) Obhut *f*, Schutz *m*, Fürsorge *f*, Betreuung *f*, (*Kinder- etc., a.Körper- etc.*)Pflege *f*, b) Aufsicht *f*, Leitung *f*: ~ *and custody* (*od. control*) 🦟 Sorgerecht *n* (*of* für *j-n*); *take* ~ *of* a) → 6, b) aufpassen auf (*acc.*), c) et.

erledigen *od.* besorgen; *take* ~ *of yourself!* pass auf dich auf!, machs gut!; *that takes* ~ *of that!* F das wäre (damit) erledigt!; **4.** Pflicht *f*: *his special* ~*s*; **II** *v/i.* **5.** sich sorgen (*about* über *acc.*, um); **6.** ~ *for* sorgen für, sich kümmern um, betreuen, pflegen: (*well*) ~*d-for* (gut) gepflegt; **7.** (*for*) (*j-n*) gern haben *od.* mögen: *he doesn't* ~ *for her* er macht sich nichts aus ihr, er mag sie nicht; *he does* ~ (*for her*) er mag sie wirklich; **8.** sich etwas daraus machen: *I don't* ~ *for whisky* ich mache mir nichts aus Whisky; *he* ~*s a great deal* es ist ihm sehr daran gelegen, es macht ihm schon etwas aus; *she doesn't really* ~ in Wirklichkeit liegt ihr nicht viel daran: *I don't* ~ *a damn* (*od. fig. pin, straw*), *I couldn't* ~ *less* es ist mir völlig gleich(gültig) *od.* egal *od.* ,schnuppe'; *who* ~*s?* na, und?, (und) wenn schon?; *for all I* ~ meinetwegen, von mir aus; *for all you* ~ wenn es nach dir ginge; *I don't* ~ *to do it now* ich habe keine Lust, es jetzt zu tun; *I don't* ~ *to be seen with you* ich lege keinen Wert darauf, mit dir gesehen zu werden; *would you* ~ *for a drink?* möchtest du et. zu trinken?; *we don't* ~ *if you stay here* wir haben nichts dagegen *od.* es macht uns nichts aus, wenn du hierbleibst; *I don't* ~ *if I do!* F von mir aus!
ca·reen [kəˈriːn] **I** *v/t.* **1.** ⚓ *Schiff* kielholen; **II** *v/i.* **2.** ⚓ krängen, sich auf die Seite legen; **3.** *fig.* (hin u. her) schwanken, torkeln.
ca·reer [kəˈrɪə] **I** *s.* **1.** Karri'ere *f*, Laufbahn *f*, Werdegang *m*: *enter upon a* ~ e-e Laufbahn einschlagen; **2.** (*erfolgreiche*) Karri'ere: *make a* ~ na. Karriere machen; **3.** (Lebens)Beruf *m*: ~ *diplomat* Berufsdiplomat *m*; ~ *girl od. woman* Karrierefrau *f*; ~ *prospects* Aufstiegsmöglichkeiten *pl.*; ~*s guidance Brit.* Berufsberatung *f*; ~*s officer Brit.* Berufsberater *m*; **4.** gestreckter Ga'lopp, Karri'ere *f*: *in full* ~ in vollem Galopp (*a. weitS.*); **II** *v/i.* **5.** galoppieren; **6.** rennen, rasen, jagen;
ca·reer·ist [kəˈrɪərɪst] *s.* Karri'eremacher *m*; **ca'reer·,mind·ed** *adj.* karri'erebe,wusst.
'care·free *adj.* sorgenfrei.
care·ful [ˈkeəfʊl] *adj.* □ **1.** vorsichtig, achtsam: *be* ~*!* nimm dich in Acht!; *be* ~ *to inf.* darauf achten zu *inf.*, nicht vergessen zu *inf.*; *be* ~ *not to inf.* sich hüten zu *inf.*; aufpassen, dass nicht; *be* ~ *of your clothes!* gib Acht auf deine Kleidung!; **2.** bedacht, achtsam (*of, for, about* auf *acc.*), ,umsichtig; **3.** sorgfältig, genau, gründlich: *a* ~ *study*; **4.** *Brit.* sparsam; **'care·ful·ness** [-nɪs] *s.* Vorsicht *f*, Sorgfalt *f*; Gründlichkeit *f*; 'Umsicht *f*.
care·less [ˈkeəlɪs] *adj.* □ **1.** nachlässig, unvorsichtig, unachtsam; leichtsinnig; **2.** (*of, about*) unbekümmert (um), unbesorgt (um), gleichgültig (gegenüber): ~ *of danger*; **3.** unbedacht, unbesonnen: *a* ~ *remark*; *a* ~ *mistake* ein Flüchtigkeitsfehler; **4.** sorgenfrei, fröhlich: ~ *youth*; **'care·less·ness** [-nɪs] *s.* Nachlässigkeit *f*; Unbedachtheit *f*; Sorglosigkeit *f*, Unachtsamkeit *f*.
ca·ress [kəˈres] **I** *s.* Liebkosung *f*, *pl. a.* Zärtlichkeiten *pl.*; **II** *v/t.* liebkosen, streicheln; *fig. der Haut etc.* schmeicheln; **ca'ress·ing** [-sɪŋ] *adj.* □ zärtlich; schmeichelnd.
car·et [ˈkærət] *s.* Einschaltungszeichen *n* (*für Auslassung im Text*).

'care|,tak·er s. 1. a) Hausmeister m, b) (Haus- etc.)Verwalter m; 2. ~ government geschäftsführende Regierung, 'Übergangskabi,nett n; '~·worn adj. vergrämt, abgehärmt.

car ex·haust fumes pl. 'Auto,abgase pl.

Ca·rey Street ['keərɪ] s.: in ~ Brit. F ,pleite', bankrott.

'car·fare s. Am. Fahrgeld n, -preis m.

car·go ['kɑ:gəʊ] pl. -goes, Am. a. -gos s. ♣, ✈ Ladung f, Fracht(gut n) f; ~ boat s. ♣ Frachtschiff n; '~-,car·ry·ing adj. Fracht..., Transport...: ~ glider Lastensegler m; ~ hold s. Laderaum m; ~ par·a·chute s. Lastenfallschirm m; ~ plane s. ✈ Trans'portflugzeug n.

car hire s. Autovermietung f: ~ booking Mietwagenbuchung f; ~ company (od. firm) Autoverleih m, Mietwagenfirma f.

'car·hop s. Am. Kellner(in) in e-m Drive-'in-Restau,rant.

Car·ib·be·an [,kærɪ'bi:ən] I adj. ka'ribisch; II s. geogr. Ka'ribisches Meer.

car·i·bou, car·i·boo ['kærɪbu:] s. zo. 'Karibu m.

car·i·ca·ture ['kærɪkə,tjʊə] I s. Karika'tur f (a. fig.); II v/t. karikieren; 'car·ica,tur·ist [-ʊərɪst] s. Karikatu'rist m.

car·i·es ['keəri:z] s. ♣ 'Karies f: a) Knochenfraß m, b) Zahnfäule f.

car·il·lon ['kærɪljən] s. (Turm)Glockenspiel n, 'Glockenspielmu,sik f.

car·ing ['keərɪŋ] adj. liebevoll, mitfühlend; sozi'al (engagiert).

car in·sur·ance s. Kraftfahrzeugversicherung f.

Ca·rin·thi·an [kə'rɪnθɪən] I adj. kärntnerisch; II s. Kärntner(in).

car·i·ous ['keərɪəs] adj. ✿ kari'ös, angefressen, faul.

car| jack s. ⊙ Wagenheber m; '~,jacking s. bsd. Am. 'Car,jacking n, Autoentführung f; '~·load s. 1. Wagenladung f; 2. Am. a) Güterwagenladung f, b) Mindestladung f (für Frachtermäßigung); 3. Am. fig. 'Haufen' m, Menge f; '~·man [-mən] s. [irr.] 1. Fuhrmann m; 2. (Kraft)Fahrer m; 3. Spedi'teur m.

car·mine ['kɑ:maɪn] I s. Kar'minrot n; II adj. kar'minrot.

car·nage ['kɑ:nɪdʒ] s. Blutbad n, Gemetzel n.

car·nal ['kɑ:nl] adj. □ fleischlich, sinnlich; geschlechtlich: ~ knowledge ⚖ Geschlechtsverkehr (of mit); car·nal·ity [kɑ:'nælətɪ] s. Fleischeslust f, Sinnlichkeit f.

car·na·tion [kɑ:'neɪʃn] s. 1. ♀ (Garten-) Nelke f; 2. Blassrot n.

car·net ['kɑ:neɪ] s. mot. Car'net n, 'Zollpas,sierschein m.

car·ni·val ['kɑ:nɪvl] s. 1. 'Karneval m, Fasching m; 2. Volksfest n; 3. ausgelassenes Feiern; 4. Am. (Sport- etc.)Veranstaltung f.

car·niv·o·ra [kɑ:'nɪvərə] s. pl. zo. Fleischfresser pl.; car·ni·vore ['kɑ:nɪvɔ:] s. zo. Fleischfresser m, bsd. Raubtier n; car'niv·o·rous [-rəs] adj. zo. Fleisch fressend.

car·ob ['kærəb] s. ♀ Jo'hannisbrot(baum m) n.

car·ol ['kærəl] I s. 1. Freuden-, bsd. Weihnachtslied n; II v/i. 2. Weihnachtslieder singen; 3. jubilieren.

Car·o·lin·gi·an [,kærəʊ'lɪndʒɪən] hist. I adj. 'karolingisch; II s. 'Karolinger m.

car·om ['kærəm] bsd. Am. I s. 1. Billard: Karambo'lage f; II v/i. 2. karambolieren; 3. abprallen.

ca·rot·id [kə'rɒtɪd] s. u. adj. anat. (die) Halsschlagader (betreffend).

ca·rous·al [kə'raʊzl] s. Trinkgelage n, Zeche'rei f; ca·rouse [kə'raʊz] I v/i. (lärmend) zechen; II s. → carousal.

carp¹ [kɑ:p] v/i. (at) nörgeln (an dat.), kritteln (über acc.).

carp² [kɑ:p] s. ichth. Karpfen m.

car·pal ['kɑ:pl] anat. I adj. Handwurzel...; II s. Handwurzelknochen m.

car park s. Parkplatz m, -haus n: underground ~ Tiefgarage f.

car·pel ['kɑ:pel] s. ♀ Fruchtblatt n.

car·pen·ter ['kɑ:pəntə] I s. Zimmermann m; II v/t. u. v/i. zimmern; ~ ant s. zo. Holzameise f; ~ bee s. zo. Holzbiene f.

car·pen·ter's| bench ['kɑ:pəntəz] s. Hobelbank f; ~ lev·el s. ⊙ Setzwaage f.

car·pen·try ['kɑ:pəntrɪ] s. Zimmerhandwerk n; Zimmerarbeit f.

car·pet ['kɑ:pɪt] I s. 1. Teppich m (a. fig.), (Treppen- etc.)Läufer m: be on the ~ fig. a) zur Debatte stehen, auf dem Tapet sein, b) F ,zs.-gestaucht' werden; sweep under the ~ a. fig. unter den Teppich kehren; ~ red carpet; II v/t. 2. mit (od. wie mit) e-m Teppich belegen; 3. Brit. F ,zs.-stauchen'; ~ bag s. Reisetasche f; '~·bag·ger s. Am. F 1. (po'litischer) Abenteurer (ursprünglich nach dem Bürgerkrieg); 2. allg. Schwindler m; ~ bomb·ing s. ✕ Bombenteppichwurf m; ~ dance s. zwangloses Tänzchen; '~·knight s. Brit. Sa'lonlöwe m; ~ sweep·er s. 'Teppichkehrma,schine f.

car·phone ['kɑ:fəʊn] s. Autotelefon n.

carp·ing ['kɑ:pɪŋ] I s. Kritte'lei f; II adj. □ krittelig: ~ criticism → I.

car| pool s. 1. Fuhrpark m; 2. Fahrgemeinschaft f; '~·port s. Einstellplatz m (im Freien).

car·pus ['kɑ:pəs] pl. -pi [-paɪ] s. anat. Handgelenk n, -wurzel f.

car·rel ['kærəl] s. Lesenische f (in e-r Bibliothek).

car rent·al s. Autovermietung f: ~ company (od. firm) Autoverleih m, Mietwagenfirma f.

car·riage ['kærɪdʒ] s. 1. Wagen m, Kutsche f: ~ and pair Zweispänner m; 2. Brit. Eisenbahnwagen m; 3. Beförderung f, Trans'port m: ~ by sea Seetransport; ~ 'Trans'portkosten pl., Fracht(gebühr) f; Fuhrlohn m, Rollgeld n: ~ paid frachtfrei, franko; ~ forward Brit. Fracht gegen Nachnahme; 5. ✕ La'fette f; 6. ✈ Fahrgestell n; 7. a) Karren m, Laufbrett n (e-r Druckerpresse), b) Wagen m (e-r Schreibmaschine etc.), c) Schlitten m (e-r Werkzeugmaschine); 8. (Körper)Haltung f, Gang m: a graceful ~; 9. pol. 'Durchbringen n, Annahme f (Gesetz etc.); 'car·riage·a·ble [-dʒəbl] adj. befahrbar.

car·riage| bod·y s. Wagenkasten m, Karosse'rie f; '~·drive s. Fahrweg m; '~·road, '~·way s. Brit. Fahrbahn f.

car·ri·er ['kærɪə] s. 1. Über'bringer m, Bote m; 2. Spedi'teur m, a. ~s pl. Spediti'onsfirma f: common ~ ✚ Frachtführer m, Transportunternehmer m, -unternehmen n (a. 🚅, ♣ etc.); 3. ⚕ ('Krankheits)Über,träger m; Keimträger m; 4. 🐎 (Über')Träger m, Kataly'sator m; 5. ⚡ Träger(strom m, -welle f) m; 6. Träger m, Tragbehälter m, -netz n, -kiste f, -gestell n; Gepäckhalter m am Fahrrad; mot. Dachgepäckträger m; 7. ⊙ a) Schlitten m, Trans'port m, b) Mitnehmer m; 8. abbr. für aircraft carrier; ~ bag s. Tragtasche f, -tüte f; ~ pi·geon s. Brieftaube f; ~ rock·et s.

'Trägerra,kete f.

car ring·ing [kɑ:,rɪŋɪŋ] s. betrügerisches Abändern der Identität e-s Kfz durch Anbringen e-s falschen Kennzeichens.

car·ri·on ['kærɪən] s. 1. Aas n; 2. verdorbenes Fleisch; 3. fig. Unrat m, Schmutz m; ~ bee·tle s. zo. Aaskäfer m.

car·rot ['kærət] s. 1. ♀ Ka'rotte f, Mohrrübe f: ~ or stick fig. Zuckerbrot oder Peitsche; hold out a ~ to s.o. fig. j-n zu ködern versuchen; 2. F a) pl. rotes Haar, b) Rotkopf m; 'car·rot·y [-tɪ] adj. 1. gelbrot; 2. rothaarig.

car·rou·sel [,kærʊ'zel] s. bsd. Am. Karus'sell n.

car·ry ['kærɪ] I s. 1. Trag-, Schussweite f; 2. Flugstrecke f (Golfball); 3. → portage 2; II v/t. 4. tragen: ~ a burden; ~ o.s. (od. one's body) well e-e gute (Körper)Haltung haben; 5. bei sich haben, (an sich) haben: ~ money about one Geld bei sich haben; ~ in one's head im Kopf haben od. behalten; ~ authority großen Einfluss ausüben; ~ conviction überzeugen(d sein od. klingen); ~ a moral e-e Moral (zum Inhalt) haben; 6. befördern, bringen; mit sich bringen od. führen; (ein)bringen: railways ~ goods die Eisenbahnen befördern Waren; ~ a message e-e Nachricht überbringen; ~ interest Zinsen tragen od. bringen; ~ insurance versichert sein; ~ consequences Folgen haben; 7. (hin'durch-, he'rum)führen; fortsetzen, ausdehnen: ~ a wall around the park e-e Mauer um den Park ziehen; ~ to excess übertreiben; you ~ things too far du treibst die Dinge zu weit; 8. erlangen, gewinnen; erobern (a. ✕): ~ all before one auf der ganzen Linie siegen, vollen Erfolg haben; ~ the audience with one die Zuhörer mitreißen; ~ an election e-e Wahl gewinnen; ~ a district Am. e-n Wahlkreis od. -bezirk erobern, den Wahlsieg in e-m Bezirk davontragen; 9. 'durchbringen, -setzen: ~ a motion e-n Antrag durchbringen; carried unanimously einstimmig angenommen; ~ one's point s-e Ansicht durchsetzen, sein Ziel erreichen; 10. Waren führen; Zeitungsmeldung bringen; 11. Rechnen: über'tragen, ,sich merken': ~ two gemerkt zwei; ~ to a new account ✚ auf neue Rechnung vortragen; III v/i. 12. weit tragen, reichen (Stimme, Schall; Schusswaffen);

Zssgn mit adv.:

car·ry| a·way v/t. 1. wegtragen; fortreißen (a. fig.); 2. fig. hinreißen: a) begeistern, b) verleiten: get carried away a) in Verzückung geraten, b) die Selbstkontrolle verlieren, sich hinreißen lassen (into doing et. zu tun); ~ for·ward v/t. 1. fortsetzen, vor'anbringen; 2. ✚ Summe od. Saldo vortragen: amount carried forward a) Vor-, Übertrag m, b) Rechnen: Transport m; ~ off v/t. forttragen, -schaffen; ab-, entführen, verschleppen; j-n hinweggraffen (Krankheit); Preis etc. gewinnen, erringen; ~ on I v/t. 1. fig. fortführen, -setzen; Plan verfolgen; Geschäft betreiben; Gespräch führen; II v/i. 2. fortfahren; weitermachen; 3. fortbestehen; 4. F a) ein ,The'ater' od. e-e Szene machen, sich schlecht aufführen, es wild od. wüst treiben, b) ,es (ein Verhältnis) haben' (with mit); ~ out v/t. aus-, 'durchführen, erfüllen; ~ o·ver v/t. 1. → carry forward 2; 2. Waren übrig behalten; 3. Börse: prolongieren; ~

c

through *v/t.* 'durchführen; *j-m* 'durchhelfen, *j-n* 'durchbringen.

'car·ry|·all *s. Am.* **1.** Per'sonen,auto *n* mit Längssitzen; **2.** große (Einkaufs-, Reise)Tasche; **'~·cot** *s.* (Baby)Tragetasche *f*; **'~·,for·ward** *s.* ✝ *Brit.* ('Saldo-) Vortrag *m*, 'Übertrag *m*.

car·ry·ing ['kærɪɪŋ] *s.* Beförderung *f*; Trans'port *m*; ~ **a·gent** *s.* Spedi'teur *m*; ~ **ca·pac·i·ty** *s.* Lade-, Tragfähigkeit *f*; **,~·'on** *pl.* **,~·s·'on** *s.* F **1.** ,The'ater' *n*: a) Getue *n*, b) Af'färe *f*; **2.** schlechtes Benehmen; ~ **trade** *s.* Spediti'onsgewerbe *n*.

,car·ry·'o·ver *s.* ✝ **1.** → *carry-forward*; **2.** *Brit. Börse:* Prolongati'on *f*: ~ *rate* Reportsatz *m*.

'car·sick *adj.* eisenbahn- *od.* autokrank; **'~·,sick·ness** *s.* Autokrankheit *f*, Übelkeit *f* beim Autofahren.

cart [kɑːt] **I** *s.* (Fracht)Karren *m*, Lieferwagen *m*; Handwagen *m*, Einkaufswagen *m* (*im Supermarkt*): *put the ~ before the horse fig.* das Pferd beim Schwanz aufzäumen; *in the ~ Brit.* F in der Klemme; **II** *v/t.* karren, fördern, fahren; ~ *about* umherschleppen; **'cart·age** [-tɪdʒ] *s.* Fuhrlohn *m*, Rollgeld *n*.

carte blanche [,kɑːt'blɑː/nʃ] *s.* **1.** ✝ Blan'kett *n*; **2.** *fig.* unbeschränkte Vollmacht: *have ~* (völlig) freie Hand haben.

car·tel [kɑː'tel] *s.* **1.** ✝, *a. pol.* Kar'tell *n*; **2.** ✕ Abkommen *n* über den Austausch von Kriegsgefangenen; **car·tel·i·za·tion** [,kɑːtəlɑɪ'zeɪʃn] *s.* ✝ Kartellierung *f*; **car·tel·ize** ['kɑːtəlɑɪz] *v/t. u. v/i.* ✝ kartellieren.

cart·er ['kɑːtə] *s.* ('Roll)Fuhrunter,nehmer *m*.

Car·te·sian [kɑː'tiːzjən] **I** *adj.* kartesi'anisch; **II** *s.* Kartesi'aner *m*, Anhänger *m* der Lehre Des'cartes'.

'cart-horse *s.* Zugpferd *n*.

Car·thu·sian [kɑː'θjuːzjən] *s.* **1.** Kar'täuser(mönch) *m*; **2.** Schüler *m* der Charterhouse-Schule (*in England*).

car·ti·lage ['kɑːtɪlɪdʒ] *s. anat., zo.* Knorpel *m*; **car·ti·lag·i·nous** [,kɑːtɪ'lædʒɪnəs] *adj.* knorpelig.

'cart·load *s.* Wagenladung *f*, Fuhre *f*; *fig.* Haufen *m*.

car·tog·ra·pher [kɑː'tɒgrəfə] *s.* Karto'graph *m*, Kartenzeichner *m*; **car'tog·ra·phy** [-fɪ] *s.* Kartogra'phie *f*.

car·ton ['kɑːtən] *s.* **1.** (Papp)Schachtel *f*, Kar'ton *m*: *a ~ of cigarettes* e-e Stange Zigaretten; **2.** das ,Schwarze' (*der Zielscheibe*).

car·toon [kɑː'tuːn] *s.* **1.** Karika'tur *f*: ~ (*film*) Zeichentrickfilm *m*; **2.** *mst pl.* Cartoon(s *pl.*) *m*, Comics-Serie *f*, Bilder(fortsetzungs)geschichte *f*; **3.** *paint.* Kar'ton *m*, Entwurf *m* (*in natürlicher Größe*); **car'toon·ist** [-nɪst] *s.* Karikatu'rist *m*.

car·touch(e) [kɑː'tuːʃ] *s.* △ Kar'tusche *f* (*Ornament*).

car·tridge ['kɑːtrɪdʒ] *s.* **1.** ✕ a) Pat,rone *f*, b) *Artillerie:* Kar'tusche *f*: *blank ~* Platzpatrone *f*; **2.** *phot.* ('Film-) Pa,trone *f* (*Kleinbildkamera*), (-)Kas,sette *f* (*Film- od. Kassettenkamera*); **3.** Tonabnehmer *m*; **4.** ('Füllhalter-) Pa,trone *f*, ~ *belt* ✕ Pa'tronengurt *m*; ~ *case* s. Pa'tronenhülse *f*; ~ *clip* *s.* Ladestreifen *m*; ~ *pa·per* *s.* 'Zeichenpa,pier *n*; ~ *pen* *s.* Pa'tronenfüllhalter *m*.

'cart|·wheel *s.* **I** *s.* **1.** Wagenrad *n*; **2.** *turn a ~ sport* Rad schlagen; **II** *v/i.* **3.** Rad schlagen; **4.** sich mehrmals (seit

---

lich) über'schlagen; **'~·wright** *s.* Stellmacher *m*, Wagenbauer *m*.

carve [kɑːv] **I** *v/t.* **1.** (*in*) Holz schnitzen, (*in*) Stein meißeln: ~ *out of stone* aus Stein meißeln *od.* hauen; ~ *one's name on a tree* s-n Namen in e-n Baum einritzen *od.* -schneiden; **2.** mit Schnitze'reien *etc.* verzieren: ~ *the leg of a table*; **3.** Fleisch vorschneiden, zerlegen, tranchieren; **4.** *fig. oft* ~ *out* gestalten: ~ *out a fortune* ein Vermögen machen; ~ *out a career for o.s.* sich e-e Karriere aufbauen; **5.** ~ *up* aufteilen, zerstückeln; **6.** ~ *up* F *j-n* mit dem Messer übel zurichten; **II** *v/i.* **7.** schnitzen, meißeln; **8.** (Fleisch) vorschneiden.

car·vel ['kɑːvl] → *caravel*; **'~·built** *adj.* ⚓ kra'weelgebaut.

carv·er ['kɑːvə] *s.* **1.** (Holz)Schnitzer *m*, Bildhauer *m*; **2.** Carver *m*, Carving-Ski *m*; **3.** Tranchierer *m*; **4.** a) Tranchiermesser *m*, b) *pl.* Tranchierbesteck *n*; **'carv·er·y** [-ərɪ] *s. Lokal, in dem man für e-n Einheitspreis so viel Fleisch essen kann, wie man will.*

carv·ing ['kɑːvɪŋ] *s.* Schnitze'rei *f*, Schnitzwerk *n*; ~ *knife* → *carver* 4 a; ~ *ski* *s.* Carving-Ski *m*.

'car·wash *s.* **1.** Autowäsche *f*; **2.** (Auto)Waschanlage *f*.

car·y·at·id [,kærɪ'ætɪd] *s.* △ Karya'tide *f*.

cas·cade [kæ'skeɪd] **I** *s.* **1.** Kas'kade *f*, Wasserfall *m*; **2.** *fig.* Kas'kade *f*, *z.B.* Feuerregen *m* (*Feuerwerk*), Faltenbesatz *m*, Faltenwurf *m* (*Kleidung*), *chem.* Tandemanordnung von Gefäßen *od. Geräten*; **3.** ⚡ *a.* ~ *connection* Kas'kade(nschaltung) *f*; **II** *adj.* **4.** ⚡ Kaskaden...(*-motor, -verstärker etc.*); **III** *v/i.* **5.** kas'kadenartig her'abstürzen; wellig fallen; **cas·cad·ing men·u** [kæ'skeɪdɪŋ] *s. Computer:* Untermenü *n.*

case¹ [keɪs] **I** *s.* **1.** Fall *m*, 'Umstand *m*, Vorfall *m*, Sache *f*, Frage *f*: *a ~ in point* ein typischer Fall, ein treffendes Beispiel; *a ~ of fraud* ein Fall von Betrug; *a ~ of conscience* e-e Gewissensfrage; *a hard ~* a) ein schwieriger Fall, b) ein schwerer Gegner, c) F ein ,schwerer Junge'; *that alters the ~* das ändert die Sache *od.* Lage; *in ~* im Falle, falls; *in ~ of* im Falle von (*od. gen.*); *in ~ of need* im Notfall; *in any ~* auf jeden Fall, jedenfalls; *in that ~* in dem Falle; *if that is the ~* wenn das der Fall ist, wenn das zutrifft; *as the ~ may be* je nachdem; *it is a ~ of* es handelt sich um; *the ~ is this* die Sache liegt so; *state one's ~* s-e Sache *od.* s-n Standpunkt vortragen *od.* vertreten (*a. ✝*); → 3; *come down to ~s* zur Sache kommen; **2.** 🏛 (Rechts)Fall *m*, Pro'zess *m*: *leading ~* Präzedenzfall; **3.** 🏛 Sachverhalt *m*; Begründung *f*, Be'weismateri,al *n*; (*a.* begründeter) Standpunkt *e-r Partei*: ~ *for the Crown* Anklage *f*; ~ *for the defence* Verteidigung *f*; *make out a* (*od.* one's) ~ *for* (*against*) alle Rechtsgründe *od.* Argumente vorbringen für (gegen); *he has a strong ~* er hat schlüssige Beweise, s-e Sache steht günstig; *he has no ~* s-e Sache ist unbegründet; *there is a ~ for s.th.* et. ist begründet *od.* berechtigt, es gibt triftige Gründe für et.; **4.** *ling.* 'Kasus *m*, Fall *m*; **5.** ✝ (Krankheits)Fall *m*; Pati'ent(in): *two ~s of typhoid* zwei Typhusfälle *od.* Typhuskranke; *a mental ~* F ein Geisteskranker; **6.** *Am.* F komischer Kauz; **II** *v/t.* **7.** ~ *the joint sl.* ,den Laden ausbaldowern'.

---

case² [keɪs] **I** *s.* **1.** Kiste *f*, Kasten *m*; Koffer *m*; (*Schmuck*)Kästchen *n*; Schachtel *f*, Behälter *m*; **2.** (*Bücher-, Glas*)Schrank *m*; (*Uhr*)Gehäuse *n*; (*Patronen*)Hülse *f*, (*Samen*)Kapsel *f* (*Zigaretten*)E'tui *n*; (*Brillen-, Messer*)Futte'ral *n*; (*Schutz*)Hülle *f* (*für Bücher, Messer etc.*); (*Akten*)Tasche *f*; (*Schreib*)Mappe *f*, (*Kissen*)Bezug *m*, 'Überzug *m*: *pencil ~* Federmäppchen *n*; **3.** ⊙ Verkleidung *f*, Einfassung *f*, Mantel *m*, Rahmen *m*; Scheide *f*: *lower* (*upper*) ~ *typ.* (Setzkasten *m* für) kleine (große) Buchstaben *pl.*; **II** *v/t.* **4.** in ein Gehäuse *od.* Futte'ral *etc.* stecken; **5.** ver-, um'kleiden, um'geben (*in, with* mit); **6.** *Buchbinderei:* Buch einhängen.

'case|·book *s.* **1.** 🏛 kommentierte Entscheidungssammlung; **2.** ✝ Pati'entenbuch *n*; ~ **end·ing** *s. ling.* 'Kasusendung *f*; **'~·,hard·ened** *adj.* **1.** *metall.* schalenhart, im Einsatz gehärtet; **2.** *fig.* abgehärtet, hartgesotten; ~ **his·to·ry** *s.* **1.** Vorgeschichte *f* (*e-s Falles*); **2.** ✝ Krankengeschichte *f*, Ana'mnese *f*; **3.** typisches Beispiel.

ca·se·in ['keɪsiːɪn] *s.* Kase'in *n.*

case law *s.* 🏛 ,Fallrecht' *n* (*auf Präzedenzfällen beruhend*).

case-mate ['keɪsmeɪt] *s.* ✕ Kase'matte *f*.

case·ment ['keɪsmənt] *s.* a) Fensterflügel *m*, b) *a.* ~ *window* Flügelfenster *n.*

ca·se·ous ['keɪsɪəs] *adj.* käsig, käseartig.

case| shot *s.* ✕ Schrap'nell *n*, Kar'tätsche *f*; ~ **stud·y** *s.* (Einzel)Fallstudie *f*; **'~·work** *s. sociol.* Einzelfallhilfe *f*, sozi'ale Einzelarbeit; **'~·,work·er** *s.* Sozi'alarbeiter(in) (für Individu'albetreuung).

cash¹ [kæʃ] **I** *s.* **1.** (Bar)Geld *n*; **2.** ✝ Barzahlung *f*, Kasse *f*: ~ *down, for ~* gegen Barzahlung, in bar; ~ *in ad·vance* gegen Vorauszahlung; → *cash and carry*; ~ *at bank* Bankguthaben *n*; ~ *in hand* Bar-, Kassenbestand *m*; ~ *on delivery* per Nachnahme, zahlbar bei Lieferung; ~ *with order* zahlbar bei Bestellung; *be in (out of) ~* bei (nicht bei) Kasse sein; *he is rolling in ~* er hat Geld wie Heu; **II** *v/t.* **3.** Scheck *etc.* einlösen, -kassieren; ~ *in* **I** *v/t.* **1.** *Poker etc.:* s-e Spielmarken einlösen; **II** *v/i.* **2.** F ,abkratzen', sterben; **3.** F ~ (*on*) ,absahnen' (bei), profitieren (von).

cash² [kæʃ] *s. sg. u. pl.* Käsch *n* (*kleine Münze in Indien u. China*).

cash| ac·count *s.* ✝ Kassenkonto *n*; ~ **ad·vance** *s.* Barkredit *m*; ~ **and car·ry** **I** *s.* **1.** Selbstabholung *f* gegen Barzahlung; **2.** Cash-and-carry-Geschäft *n*; **II** *adv.* **3.** (nur) gegen Barzahlung u. Selbstabholung; **,~·and-'car·ry** *adj.* Cash-and-carry-...; ~ **au·dit** *s.* Kassenprüfung *f*; ~ **bal·ance** *s.* Kassenbestand *m*; Barguthaben *n*; ~ **book** *s.* Kassenbuch *n*; ~ **card** *s.* Geldautomatenkarte *f*; ~ **cheque** *s. Brit.* Barscheck *m*; ~ **cow** *s. fig.* Melkkuh *f*, ✝ Cash-Cow *f*; ~ **crop** *s.* für den Verkauf bestimmte Anbaufrucht; ~ **desk** *s.* Kasse *f* im Warenhaus *etc.*; ~ **dis·count** *s.* 'Barzahlungsra,batt *m*; ~ **dis·pens·er** *s.* 'Geldauto,mat *m*; ~ **div·i·dend** *s.* Barausschüttung *f*.

ca·shew [kæ'ʃuː] *s.* **1.** Aca'joubaum *m*; **2.** *a.* ~ *nut* Aca'jou-, 'Cashewnuss *f.*

cash flow *s.* ✝ Cash-Flow *m*, Kassenzufluss *m.*

cash·ier¹ [kæ'ʃɪə] *s.* Kassierer(in): ~*'s check Am.* Bankscheck *m*; ~*'s desk od.* **office** Kasse *f.*

cash·ier² [kəˈʃɪə] v/t. ✕ (unehrenhaft) entlassen.
cash·less [ˈkæʃlɪs] adj. † bargeldlos.
cash·mere [ˈkæʃmɪə] s. **1.** ˈKaschmir m (feiner Wollstoff); **2.** ˈKaschmirwolle f.
cash·o·mat [ˈkæʃəʊmæt] → cash dispenser.
cash| pay·ment s. Barzahlung f; '~-point s. Brit. Geldautomat m; ~ price s. Bar(zahlungs)preis m; ~ prob·lem s. Liquiditätsproblem n; ~ po·si·tion s. Liquiditätslage f; ~ re·ceipts s. pl. Bareinnahmen pl; ~ reg·is·ter s. Registrierkasse f; ~ sale s. Barverkauf m; ~ set·tle·ment s. Barausgleich m, Barabgeltung f; ~ sur·ren·der val·ue s. Rückkaufswert m (e-r Police); ~ vouch·er s. Kassenbeleg m.
cas·ing [ˈkeɪsɪŋ] s. **1.** Be-, Umˈkleidung f, Umˈhüllung f; **2.** (Fenster)Futter n; (Tür)Verkleidung f; **3.** Gehäuse n, Futˈteˈral n; mot. Mantel m e-s Reifens; **4.** (Wurst)Darm m, (-)Haut f.
ca·si·no [kəˈsiːnəʊ] pl. **-nos** s. ('Spiel-, Unterˈhaltungs)Kaˌsino n.
cask [kɑːsk] s. Fass n; (hölzerne) Tonne: a ~ of wine ein Fass Wein; '~-con·di·tioned adj. fassvergoren, ungefiltert u. nicht pasteurisiert (Bier, Real Ale).
cas·ket [ˈkɑːskɪt] s. **1.** (Schmuck)Kästchen n; **2.** (Bestattungs)Urne f; **3.** Am. Sarg m.
Cas·pi·an [ˈkæspɪən] adj. kaspisch: ~ Sea Kaspisches Meer.
Cas·san·dra [kəˈsændrə] s. fig. Kasˈsandra f (Unglücksprophetin).
cas·sa·tion [kæˈseɪʃn] s. ✠ Kassatiˈon f: Court of £ Kassationshof m.
cas·se·role [ˈkæsərəʊl] s. Kasseˈrolle f, Schmortopf m (mit Griff).
cas·sette [kæˈset] s. ('Film-, 'Tonband-etc.)Kasˌsette f; ~ re·cord·er s. Kasˈsettenreˌkorder m.
cas·sock [ˈkæsək] s. eccl. Souˈtane f.
cast [kɑːst] **I** s. **1.** Wurf m (a. mit Würfeln); **2.** a) Auswerfen n (Angel, Netz, Lot), b) Angelhaken m; **3.** a) Auswurf m (gewisser Tiere), bsd. Gewölle n (von Raubvögeln), b) abgestoßene Haut (Schlange, Insekt); **4.** ~ in the eye Schielen n; **5.** Aufrechnung f, Additiˈon f; **6.** ◉ Gussform f, Abguss m, -druck m; ✄ Gipsverband m; fig. Zuschnitt m, Anordnung f; **7.** thea. (Rollen)Besetzung f; Mitwirkende pl.; Truppe f; **8.** Farbton m; fig. Anflug m; **9.** Typ m, Art f, Schlag m: ~ of mind Geistesart f; ~ of features Gesichtsausdruck m; **II** v/t. [irr.] **10.** werfen: the die is ~ die Würfel sind gefallen; ~ s.th. in s.o.'s teeth j-m et vorwerfen; **11.** Angel, Netz, Anker, Lot (aus)werfen; **12.** zo. a) Haut, Geweih abwerfen, b) Junge vorzeitig werfen; **13.** fig.Blick, Licht, Schatten werfen; Horoskop stellen: ~ the blame die Schuld zuschieben (on dat.); ~ a slur (on) verunglimpfen (acc.); ~ one's vote s-e Stimme abgeben; ~ lots losen; **14.** thea. a) Stück besetzen: the play is well ~, b) Rollen besetzen, verteilen: he was badly ~ er war e-e Fehlbesetzung; **15.** Metall, Statue etc. gießen; fig. formen, bilden, anordnen; **16.** ✠ pass. be ~ in costs zu den Kosten verurteilt werden; **17.** a. ~ up aus-, zs.-rechnen: to ~ accounts Abrechnung machen; **III** v/i. [irr.] **18.** sich werfen, sich (ver)ziehen; **19.** die Angel auswerfen.
Zssgn mit adv.:
cast| a·bout, ~ a·round v/i. **1.** ~ for suchen nach, fig. a. sich 'umsehen nach; **2.** ⚓ um'herlavieren; ~ **a·way** v/t. **1.**

wegwerfen; **2.** verschwenden; **3.** be ~ ⚓ verschlagen werden; ~ **back** v/t.: ~ one's mind (to) zu'rückdenken (an acc.); ~ **down** v/t. **1.** fig. entmutigen: be ~ niedergeschlagen sein; **2.** die Augen niederschlagen; ~ **in** v/t.: ~ one's lot with s.o. sein Los mit j-m teilen, sich j-m anschließen; ~ **off I** v/t. **1.** ab-, wegwerfen; Kleider etc. ablegen, ausrangieren; **2.** sich befreien von, sich entledigen (gen.); **3.** Freund etc. fallen lassen; **4.** Stricken: Maschen abketten; **5.** typ. den 'Umfang (gen.) berechnen; **II** v/i. **6.** ⚓ ablegen, losmachen; ~ **on** v/t. u. v/i. Stricken: die ersten Maschen aufnehmen; ~ **out** v/t. vertreiben, ausstoßen; ~ **up** v/t. **1.** die Augen aufschlagen; **2.** anspülen; **3.** → cast 17.
cas·ta·net [ˌkæstəˈnet] s. Kastaˈgnette f.
'cast·a·way I s. **1.** Ausgestoßene(r m) f; **2.** ⚓ Schiffbrüchige(r m) f (a. fig.); **3.** et. Ausrangiertes, bsd. abgelegtes Kleidungsstück; **II** adj. **4.** ausgestoßen; **5.** ausrangiert (Möbel etc.), abgelegt (Kleider); **6.** ⚓ schiffbrüchig.
caste [kɑːst] s. **1.** (indische) Kaste: ~ feeling Kastengeist m; **2.** Kaste f, Gesellschaftsklasse f; **3.** Rang m, Stellung f, Ansehen n: lose ~ an gesellschaftlichem Ansehen verlieren (with bei).
cas·tel·lan [ˈkæstələn] s. Kastelˈlan m; **'cas·tel·lat·ed** [-leɪtɪd] adj. **1.** mit Türmen u. Zinnen; **2.** burgenreich.
cast·er [ˈkɑːstə] s. → castor³.
cas·ti·gate [ˈkæstɪgeɪt] v/t. **1.** züchtigen; **2.** fig. geißeln; **3.** fig. Text verbessern; **cas·ti·ga·tion** [ˌkæstɪˈgeɪʃn] s. **1.** Züchtigung f; **2.** Geißelung f; scharfe Kriˈtik; **3.** Textverbesserung f.
cast·ing [ˈkɑːstɪŋ] s. **1.** ◉ a) Guss m, Gießen n, b) Gussstück n; pl. Gusswaren pl.; **2.** ⚠ (roher) Bewurf; **3.** thea. Rollenverteilung f; **4.** a. ~-up Additiˈon f; **5.** Fischen n (mit dem Netz); ~ net s. Wurfnetz n; ~ vote s. entscheidende Stimme.
cast| i·ron s. Gusseisen n; '~-'i·ron adj. **1.** gusseisern; **2.** fig. eisern (Konstitution, Wille etc.); hart (Gesetze etc.); hieb- u. stichfest (Alibi), 'unanˌstößlich, unbeugsam: ~ constitution eiserne Gesundheit.
cas·tle [ˈkɑːsl] **I** s. **1.** Burg f, Schloss n: ~s in the air (od. in Spain) fig. Luftschlösser; **2.** Schach: Turm m; **II** v/i. **3.** Schach: rochieren; ~ nut s. ◉ Kronenmutter f.
cas·tling [ˈkɑːslɪŋ] s. Schach: Roˈchade f.
'cast| off s. **1.** ausrangiertes Kleidungsstück; **2.** typ. 'Umfangsberechnung f; '~-'off adj. **1.** abgelegt, ausrangiert: ~ clothes; **2.** et. Abgelegtes od. Weggeworfenes.
Cas·tor¹ [ˈkɑːstə] s. ast. ˈKastor m.
cas·tor² [ˈkɑːstə] s. vet. Spat m.
cas·tor³ [ˈkɑːstə] s. **1.** (Salz- etc.)Streuer m; **2.** pl. Meˈnage f, Gewürzständer m; **3.** (schwenkbare) Laufrolle.
cas·tor| oil s. ✄ 'Rizinus-, ˈKastoröl n; ~ sug·ar s. 'Kastorzucker m.
cas·trate [kæˈstreɪt] v/t. **1.** ✄, vet. kastrieren (a. fig. iro.); **2.** Buch zensieren; **cas·tra·tion** [-eɪʃn] s. Kastrierung f, Kastratiˈon f.
cast steel s. Gussstahl m.
cas·u·al [ˈkæʒjʊəl] **I** adj. □ **1.** zufällig, unerwartet; **2.** gelegentlich, unregelmäßig: ~ labo(u)r(er) Gelegenheitsarbeit(er m) f; **3.** unbestimmt, ungenau; **4.** lässig od. nachlässig, gleichgültig, b) ungezwungen, zwanglos, bsd. Mode:

sa'lopp, sportlich: ~ wear Freizeitkleidung f; **5.** beiläufig: a ~ remark; ~ glance flüchtiger Blick; **II** s. **6.** a) sportliches Kleidungsstück, Straßenanzug m, b) pl. Slipper pl. (flache Schuhe); **7.** Brit. a) Gelegenheitsarbeiter m, b) gelegentlicher Kunde od. Besucher; **'cas·u·al·ism** [-lɪzəm] s. philos. Kasua-ˈlismus m; **'cas·u·al·ness** [-nɪs] s. (Nach)Lässigkeit f, Gleichgültigkeit f.
cas·u·al·ty [ˈkæʒjʊəltɪ] s. **1.** Unfall m (e-r Person); **2.** a) Verunglückte(r m) f, (Unfall)Opfer n, ✕ Verwundete(r) m od. Gefallene(r) m: casualties Opfer pl. e-r Katastrophe etc., ✕ mst Verluste pl.; ~ list Verlustliste f; **3.** a. ~ department od. ward ✚ Notaufnahme f.
cas·u·ist [ˈkæzjʊɪst] s. Kasu'ist m; **cas·u·is·tic, cas·u·is·ti·cal** [ˌkæzjʊˈɪstɪk(l)] adj. □ **1.** kasuˈistisch; **2.** spitzfindig; **'cas·u·ist·ry** [-trɪ] s. **1.** Kasuˈistik f; **2.** Spitzfindigkeit f.
cat [kæt] s. **1.** zo. Katze f: let the ~ out of the bag die Katze aus dem Sack lassen; it's raining ~s and dogs F es gießt wie mit Kübeln; has the ~ got your tongue? hat es dir die Sprache verschlagen?; wait for the ~ to jump od. see which way the ~ jumps fig. sehen, wie der Hase läuft; that ~ won't jump! F so gehts nicht!; set the ~ among the pigeons für helle Aufregung sorgen; think one is the cat's whiskers od. pyjamas sich für was Besonderes halten; not room to swing a ~ sl. kaum Platz zum Umdrehen; they lead a ~-and-dog life sie leben wie Hund u. Katze; it's enough to make a ~ laugh F da lachen ja die Hühner; **2.** zo. große pl. (Fa'milie f der) Katzen pl.; **3.** fig. falsche Katze (Frau): old ~ alte Hexe; **4.** Am. sl. a) 'Jazzfaˌnatiker m, b) a. cool ~ ‚dufter Typ'; **5.** ⚓ Kattanker m; **6.** mot. F Kat m (Katalysator): ~ car F Katauto n.
cat·a·clysm [ˈkætəklɪzəm] s. **1.** geol. Kata'klysmus m, erdgeschichtliche Kata'strophe; **2.** Über'schwemmung f; **3.** fig. (gewaltige) 'Umwälzung.
cat·a·comb [ˈkætəkuːm] s. Kata'kombe f.
cat·a·falque [ˈkætəfælk] s. **1.** Kata'falk m; **2.** offener Leichenwagen.
Cat·a·lan [ˈkætələn] **I** adj. kata'lanisch; **II** s. Kata'lane m, Kata'lanin f.
cat·a·lep·sis [ˌkætəˈlepsɪs], **cat·a·lep·sy** [ˈkætəlepsɪ] s. ✚ Starrkrampf m.
cat·a·logue, Am. a. **cat·a·log** [ˈkætəlɒg] **I** s. **1.** Kata'log m; **2.** Verzeichnis n, (Preis- etc.)Liste f; **3.** Am. univ. Vorlesungsverzeichnis n; **II** v/t. **4.** katalogisieren.
ca·tal·y·sis [kəˈtælɪsɪs] s. ✺ Kata'lyse f; **cat·a·lyst** [ˈkætəlɪst] s. ✺ u. fig. Kataly'sator m; **cat·a·lyt·ic** [ˌkætəˈlɪtɪk] **I** adj. ✺ kata'lytisch: ~ converter Kataly'sator m; **II** s. → catalyst; **cat·a·lyze** [ˈkætəlaɪz] v/t. katalysieren (a. fig.); **cat·a·lyz·er** [ˈkætəlaɪzə] → catalyst.
cat·a·ma·ran [ˌkætəməˈræn] s. **1.** ⚓ a) Floß n, b) Auslegerboot n; **2.** F ‚Kratzbürste' f, Xan'thippe f.
cat·a·mite [ˈkætəmaɪt] s. Lustknabe m.
cat·a·plasm [ˈkætəplæzəm] s. ✄ 'Breiˌumschlag m, Kata'plasma n.
cat·a·pult [ˈkætəpʌlt] s. **1.** Kata'pult m, n; a) hist. 'Wurfmaˌschine f, b) (Spiel)Schleuder f, c) ✈ Startschleuder f; **II** adj. **2.** ✈ Schleuder...(-sitz, -start); **III** v/t. **3.** schleudern, katapultieren (a. ✈); **4.** mit e-r Schleuder beschießen.
cat·a·ract [ˈkætərækt] s. **1.** Kata'rakt m:

C

a) Wasserfall *m*, b) Stromschnelle *f*, c) *fig.* Flut *f*; **2.** ✶ grauer Star.

ca·tarrh [kə'tɑː] *s.* ✶ Ka'tarr(h) *m*; Schnupfen *m*; **ca'tarrh·al** [-ɑːrəl] *adj.* katar'r(h)alisch: ~ *syringe* Nasenspritze *f.*

ca·tas·tro·phe [kə'tæstrəfɪ] *s.* Kata'strophe *f* (*a. im Drama u. geol.*), Verhängnis *n*, Unheil *n*, Unglück *n*; **cat·a·stroph·ic, cat·a·stroph·i·cal** [,kætə'strɒfɪk(l)] *adj.* katastro'phal.

'cat|·bird *s. orn. amer.* Spottdrossel *f*; **'~·boat** *s.* ⛵ kleines Segelboot (*mit einem Mast*); ~ **bur·glar** *s.* Fas'sadenkletterer *m*, Einsteigdieb *m*; **'~·call** I *s.* a) Buh(ruf *m*) *n*, b) Pfiff *m*; II *v/i.* buhen, pfeifen; III *v/t.* j-n ausbuhen, -pfeifen.

catch [kætʃ] I *s.* **1.** Fangen *n*, Fang *m*; *fig.* Fang *m*, Beute *f*, Vorteil *m*: *a good* ~ a) ein guter Fang (*beim Fischen u. fig.*), b) e-e gute Partie (*Heirat*); *no* ~ kein gutes Geschäft; **2.** *Kricket, Baseball*: a) Fang *m*, b) Fänger *m*; **3.** Halter *m*, Griff *m*, Klinke *f*; Haken *m*; **4.** Sperr-, Schließhaken *m*, Schnäpper *m*; Sicherung *f*; Verschluss *m*; **5.** Stocken *n*, Anhalten *n*; **6.** *fig.* a) Haken *m*, Schwierigkeit *f*, b) Falle *f*, Trick *m*, Kniff *m*: *there is a ~ in it* die Sache hat e-n Haken; *~-22* F gemeiner Trick; II *v/t.* [*irr.*] **7.** *Ball, Tier etc.* fangen; *Dieb etc. a.* fassen, ‚schnappen', *a. Blick* erhaschen; *Tropfendes* auffangen; *a.* erwischen, ‚kriegen': ~ *a train* e-n Zug erreichen *od.* kriegen; → *glimpse* 1, *sight* 3; **8.** ertappen, über'raschen (*s.o. at* j-n bei): *be caught in the act* auf frischer Tat ertappt werden; ~ *me* (*doing that*)*!* F ich denke (ja) nicht dran!, ‚denkste'!; *I caught myself lying* ich ertappte mich beim Lügen; *caught in a storm* vom Unwetter überrascht; **9.** ergreifen, packen, *Gewohnheit, Aussprache* annehmen; → *hold²* 1; **10.** *fig.* fesseln, packen, gewinnen; einfangen; → *eye* 2, *fancy* 5; **11.** *fig.* ‚mitkriegen', verstehen: *I didn't ~ what you said*; **12.** einholen: *I soon caught him*; → *catch up* 2; **13.** sich holen *od.* zuziehen, angesteckt werden von (*Krankheit etc.*); → *cold* 8, *fire* 1; **14.** sich zuziehen, *Strafe, Tadel* bekommen: ~ *it* F ‚sein Fett abbekommen'; **15.** streifen, mit *et.* hängen bleiben: *a nail caught my dress* mein Kleid blieb an e-m Nagel hängen; ~ *one's finger in the door* sich den Finger in der Tür klemmen; **16.** a) schlagen: ~ *s.o. a blow* j-m e-n Schlag versetzen, b) mit e-m Schlag treffen *od.* ‚erwischen': *the blow caught him on the chin*; III *v/i.* [*irr.*] **17.** greifen: ~ *at* greifen *od.* schnappen nach, (*fig. Gelegenheit* gern) ergreifen; → *straw* 1; **18.** ⚙ (ein)greifen (*Räder*), einschnappen (*Schloss etc.*); **19.** sich verfangen, hängen bleiben: *the plane caught in the trees*; **20.** klemmen; **21.** *mot.* anspringen; *Zssgn mit adv.:*

catch| on *v/i.* F **1.** ‚kapieren' (*to s.th.* et.); **2.** Anklang finden, einschlagen; ~ **out** *v/t.* **1.** ertappen; **2.** *Kricket*: (durch Fangen des Balles) *den Schläger* ‚ausmachen'; ~ **up** I *v/t.* **1.** j-n unter'brechen; **2.** j-n einholen; **3.** *et.* schnell ergreifen; *Kleid* aufraffen; **4.** *be caught up in* et. vertieft sein in (*acc.*), b) verwickelt sein in (*acc.*); II *v/i.* **5.** aufholen: ~ *with* einholen (*a. fig.*); ~ *on od. with* et. auf- *od.* nachholen.

'catch|·all *s. Am.* **1.** Tasche *f* od. Behälter *m* für alles Mögliche; **2.** *fig.* Sammelbezeichnung *f*, -begriff *m*; **'~·as-**

-,catch-'can *s. sport* Catchen *n*; ~ *wrestler* Catcher *m.*

catch·er ['kætʃə] *s.* Fänger *m*; **'catch·ing** [-tʃɪŋ] *adj.* **1.** ✶ ansteckend (*a. fig.*); **2.** *fig.* anziehend, fesselnd; **3.** eingängig (*Melodie*); **4.** verfänglich; arglistig.

catch·ment ['kætʃmənt] *s.* **1.** Auffangen *n von Wasser etc.*; **2.** *geol.* Reservo'ir *n*; ~ **a·re·a** *s.* Einzugsgebiet *n* (*e-s Flusses; a. fig.*).

'catch|,pen·ny I *adj.* Schund...; auf Kundenfang berechnet, Lock..., Schleuder...: ~ *title* reißerischer Titel; II *s.* Schundware *f*, 'Ramschar,tikel *m*; **'~·phrase** *s.* Schlagwort *n*, (hohle) Phrase; **'~·pole, '~·poll** *s.* Gerichtsdiener *m*; ~ **ques·tion** *s.* Fangfrage *f*; **'~·up** → *ketchup*; **'~·weight** *s. sport* durch keinerlei Regeln beschränktes Gewicht (*es* Wettkampfteilnehmers; **'~·word** *s.* **1.** *bsd. thea.* Stichwort *n*; **2.** Schlagwort *n*; **3.** *typ.* a) *hist.* 'Kustos *m*, b) Ko'lumnentitel *m.*

catch·y ['kætʃɪ] *adj.* F **1.** → *catching* 2, 3; **2.** unregelmäßig; **3.** schwierig.

cat·e·chism ['kætɪkɪzəm] *s.* **1.** ☒ *eccl.* Kate'chismus *m*; **2.** *fig.* Reihe *f od.* Folge *f* von Fragen; **'cat·e·chist** [-kɪst] *s.* Kate'chet *m*, Religi'onslehrer *m*; **'cat·e·chize** [-kaɪz] *v/t.* **1.** *eccl.* katechisieren; **2.** gründlich ausfragen, examinieren.

cat·e·chu ['kætɪtʃuː] *s.* 🌿 'Katechu *n.*

cat·e·chu·men [,kætɪ'kjuːmen] *s.* **1.** *eccl.* Konfir'mand(in); **2.** *fig.* Neuling *m.*

cat·e·gor·i·cal [,kætɪ'gɒrɪkl] *adj.* ☐ kate'gorisch, bestimmt, unbedingt; **cat·e·go·ry** ['kætɪgərɪ] *s.* Katego'rie *f*, Klasse *f*, Gruppe *f.*

ca·ter ['keɪtə] I *v/i.* **1.** (*for*) Speisen u. Getränke liefern (für): *~ing industry od. trade* Gaststättengewerbe *n*; **2.** sorgen (*for* für); **3.** *fig.* befriedigen (*for, to acc.*); etwas bieten (*to dat.*); II *v/t.* **4.** mit Speisen u. Getränken beliefern; **'ca·ter·er** [-ərə] *s.* Liefe'rant *m* für Speisen u. Getränke; **ca·ter·ing serv·ice** *s.* 'Party,service *m.*

cat·er·pil·lar ['kætəpɪlə] *s.* **1.** *zo.* Raupe *f*; **2.** ⚙ (*Warenzeichen*) Raupenfahrzeug *n.*

cat·er·waul ['kætəwɔːl] I *v/i.* **1.** jaulen (*Katze etc.*); **2.** kreischen; keifen; II *s.* **3.** Jaulen *n*; **4.** Keifen *n*, Kreischen *n.*

'cat|·eyed *adj.* katzenäugig; *weitS.* im Dunkeln sehend; **'~·fish** *s. ichth.* Katzenfisch *m*, Wels *m*; **'~·foot** *v/i. a. ~ it* F schleichen; **'~·gut** *s.* **1.** Darmsaite *f*; **2.** ✶ 'Katgut *n*; **3.** *Art* Steifleinen *n.*

ca·thar·sis [kə'θɑːsɪs] *s.* **1.** Ästhetik, *a. psych.*: 'Katharsis *f*; **2.** ✶ Abführung *f.*

ca·the·dral [kə'θiːdrəl] I *s.* Kathe'drale *f*, Dom *m*; II *adj.* Dom...: ~ *church* I; ~ *town* → *city* 2.

Cath·er·ine wheel ['kæθərɪnwiːl] *s.* **1.** △ Katha'rinenrad *n* (*Radfenster*); **2.** *Feuerwerk*: Feuerrad *n*; **3.** *sport turn* **~s** Rad schlagen.

cath·e·ter ['kæθɪtə] *s.* ✶ Ka'theter *m.*

cath·ode ['kæθəud] *s.* ⚡ Ka'thode *f*; ~ **ray** *s.* Ka'thodenstrahl *m*; **'~-ray tube** *s.* Ka'thodenstrahlröhre *f.*

cath·o·lic ['kæθəlɪk] I *adj.* (☐ *~ally*) **1.** ('all)um,fassend, univer'sal: ~ *interests* vielseitige Interessen; **2.** großzügig, tole'rant; **3.** ☒ ka'tholisch; II *s.* **4.** ☒ katho'lik(in); **Ca·thol·i·cism** [kə'θɒlɪsɪzəm] *s.* Katholi'zismus *m*; **cath·o·lic·i·ty** [,kæθə'lɪsətɪ] *s.* **1.** Universali'tät *f*; **2.** Großzügigkeit *f*, Tole'ranz *f*; **3.** a) ka'tholischer Glaube, b) ☒ Katholizi'tät

f (*Gesamtheit der katholischen Kirche*).

cat ice *s.* dünne Eisschicht.

cat·kin ['kætkɪn] *s.* 🌿 (Blüten)Kätzchen *n* (*an Weiden etc.*).

'cat|·lick *s.* F ‚Katzenwäsche' *f*; **'~·nap** *s.* ‚Nickerchen' *n*, kurzes Schläfchen.

cat-o'-nine-tails [,kætə'naɪnteɪlz] *s.* neunschwänzige Katze (*Peitsche*).

'cat's|-eye ['kæts-] *s.* **1.** *min.* Katzenauge *n*; **2.** a) Katzenauge *n*, Rückstrahler *m*, b) Leuchtnagel *m*; **'~·paw** *s. fig.* Handlanger *m*, j-s Werkzeug *n.*

cat suit *s.* einteiliger Hosenanzug, Overall *m.*

cat·sup ['kætsəp] → *ketchup*.

cat·tish ['kætɪʃ] *adj.* katzenhaft; *fig.* boshaft, gehässig, gemein.

cat·tle ['kætl] *s. coll.* (*mst pl. konstr.*) **1.** (Rind)Vieh *n*, Rinder *pl.*; **2.** *contp.* Viehzeug *n* (*Menschen*); ~ **car** *s.* 🚃 *Am.* Viehwagen *m*; **'~,feed·er** *s.* ✶ 'Futterma,schine *f*; **'~·lead·er** *s.* Nasenring *m*; **'~,lift·er** *s.* Viehdieb *m*; ~ **plague** *s. vet.* Rinderpest *f*; ~ **ranch,** ~ **range** *s.* Viehweide(land *n*) *f.*

cat·ty ['kætɪ] → *cattish*.

'cat|·walk *s.* **1.** ⚙ Laufplanke *f*, Steg *m*; **2.** *Mode*: Laufsteg *m*; ~ **whisk·er** *s.* ⚡ De'tektornadel *f.*

Cau·ca·sian [kɔː'keɪzjən] I *adj.* kau'kasisch; II *s.* Kau'kasier(in).

cau·cus ['kɔːkəs] *s. pol. bsd. Am.* **1.** Par'teiausschuss *m* zur Wahlvorbereitung; **2.** Par'teikonfe,renz *f*, -tag *m*; **3.** Par'teiclique *f.*

cau·dal ['kɔːdl] *adj. zo.* Schwanz...; **'cau·date** [-deɪt] *adj.* geschwänzt.

caught [kɔːt] *pret. u. p.p. von catch.*

caul·dron ['kɔːldrən] *s.* (großer) Kessel.

cau·li·flow·er ['kɒlɪflauə] *s.* 🌿 Blumenkohl *m*; ~ **ear** *s. Boxen:* ‚Blumenkohlohr' *n.*

caulk [kɔːk] *v/t.* ⛵ kal'fatern, *a. allg.* abdichten; **'caulk·er** [-kə] *s.* ⛵, ⚙ Kal'faterer *m.*

caus·al ['kɔːzl] *adj.* ☐ ursächlich, kau'sal: ~ *connection* → *causality* 2; **cau·sal·i·ty** [kɔː'zælətɪ] *s.* **1.** Ursächlichkeit *f*, Kausali'tät *f*: *law of* ~ Kausalgesetz *n*; **2.** Kau'salzu,sammenhang *m*; **cau·sa·tion** [kɔː'zeɪʃn] *s.* **1.** Verursachung *f*; **2.** Ursächlichkeit *f*; **3.** Kau'salprin,zip *n*; **'caus·a·tive** [-zətɪv] *adj.* ☐ **1.** kau'sal, begründend, verursachend; **2.** *ling.* 'kausativ.

cause [kɔːz] I *s.* **1.** Ursache *f*: ~ *of death* Todesursache; **2.** Grund *m*; Veranlassung *f*, Anlass *m*: ~ *for complaint* Grund *od.* Anlass zur Klage; ~ *to be thankful* Grund zur Dankbarkeit; *without* ~ ohne (triftigen) Grund, grundlos (*entlassen etc.*); **3.** (gute) Sache: *fight for one's* ~ für s-e Sache kämpfen; *make common* ~ *with* gemeinsame Sache machen mit; **4.** ⚖ a) (Streit)Sache *f*, Rechtsstreit *m*, Pro'zess *m*, b) Gegenstand *m*; Rechtsgründe *pl.*: ~*list* Terminliste *f*; *show* ~ s-e Gründe darlegen *od.* dartun (*why* warum); *upon good* ~ *shown* bei Vorliegen von triftigen Gründen; ~ *of action* Klagegrund *m*; **5.** Sache *f*, Angelegenheit *f*, Gegenstand *m*, 'Thema *n*, Frage *f*, Problem *n*: *lost* ~ verlorene *od.* aussichtslose Sache; *in the* ~ *of* um ... (*gen.*) willen, für; II *v/t.* **6.** veranlassen, (*j-n et.*) lassen: *I caused him to sit down* ich ließ ihn sich setzen; *he ~ed the man to be arrested* er ließ den Mann verhaften, er veranlasste, dass der Mann verhaftet wurde; **7.** verursachen, bewirken, her'vorrufen, her'beiführen: ~ *a fire* e-n Brand verursachen; **8.** berei-

ten, zufügen: **~** *s.o.* *a loss* j-m e-n Verlust zufügen; **~** *s.o.* *trouble* j-m Schwierigkeiten bereiten.
cause cé·lè·bre [ˌkəʊz seˈlebrə] (*Fr.*) *s.* Cause *f* célèbre.
cause·less [ˈkɔːzlɪs] *adj.* □ grundlos.
cau·se·rie [ˈkəʊzərɪ] (*Fr.*) *s.* Plaude'rei *f.*
cause·way [ˈkɔːzweɪ], *Brit. a.* 'cau·sey [-zeɪ] *s.* erhöhter Fußweg, Damm *m* (*durch e-n See od. Sumpf*).
caus·tic [ˈkɔːstɪk] **I** *adj.* (□ ~*ally*) **1.** 🜍 kaustisch, ätzend, beizend, brennend: **~** *potash* Ätzkali *n*; **~** *soda* Ätznatron *n*; ~*soda solution* Ätzlauge *f*; **2.** *fig.* ätzend, beißend, sar'kastisch (*Worte etc.*); **II** *s.* **3.** 🜍 Beiz-, Ätzmittel *n*: *lunar* **~** 🜍 Höllenstein *m*; **caus·tic·i·ty** [kɔːˈstɪsətɪ] *s.* **1.** Ätz-, Beizkraft *f*; **2.** *fig.* Sar'kasmus *m*, Schärfe *f.*
cau·ter·i·za·tion [ˌkɔːtəraɪˈzeɪʃn] *s.* 🜍, ⚕ (Aus)Brennen *n*; Ätzen *n*; **cau·ter·ize** [ˈkɔːtəraɪz] *v/t.* **1.** 🜍, ⚕ (aus)brennen, ätzen; **2.** *fig. Gefühl etc.* abstumpfen; **cau·ter·y** [ˈkɔːtərɪ] *s.* Brenneisen *n*; Ätzmittel *n.*
cau·tion [ˈkɔːʃn] **I** *s.* **1.** Vorsicht *f*, Behutsamkeit *f*: *proceed with* **~** Vorsicht walten lassen; **2.** Warnung *f*; *a. sport* Verwarnung; **3.** ⚖ Eides- *od.* Rechtsmittelbelehrung *f*; **4.** ⚔ 'Ankündigungskom,mando *n*; **5.** F a) *et.* Origi'nelles, ,tolles Ding‘, b) ulkige ,Nummer‘ (*Person*), c) unheimlicher Kerl; **II** *v/t.* **6.** warnen (*against* vor *dat.*); **7.** verwarnen; **8.** ⚖ belehren (*as to* über *acc.*); 'cau·tion·ar·y [-ʃnərɪ] *adj.* warnend, Warnungs...: **~** *tale* Geschichte *f* mit e-r Moral.
cau·tious [ˈkɔːʃəs] *adj.* □ vorsichtig, behutsam, auf der Hut; 'cau·tious·ness [-nɪs] → *caution* 1.
cav·al·cade [ˌkævlˈkeɪd] *s.* Kaval'kade *f*, Reiterzug *m*, *a.* Zug *m* von Autos *etc.*
cav·a·lier [ˌkævəˈlɪə] **I** *s.* **1.** *hist.* Ritter *m*; **2.** Kava'lier *m*; **3.** ⚘ *hist.* Roya'list *m* (*Anhänger Karls I. von England*); **II** *adj.* □ **4.** anmaßend, rücksichtslos; **5.** unbekümmert, ,eiskalt‘, keck.
cav·al·ry [ˈkævlrɪ] *s.* ⚔ Kavalle'rie *f*, Reite'rei *f*; '~·man [-mən] *s.* [*irr.*] Kavalle'rist *m.*
cave[1] [keɪv] **I** *s.* **1.** Höhle *f*; **2.** *pol. Brit.* a) Abspaltung *f* e-s Teils e-r Partei, b) Sezessi'onsgruppe *f*; **II** *v/t.* **3.** *mst* **~** *in* eindrücken, zum Einsturz bringen; **III** *v/i.* **4.** *mst* **~** *in* einstürzen, -sinken; **5.** *mst* **~** *in* F a) nachgeben, klein beigeben (*to dat.*), b) zs.-brechen, ,zs.-klappen‘; **6.** *pol. Brit.* sich *von der Partei* absondern.
ca·ve[2] [ˈkeɪvɪ] (*Lat.*) *ped. sl.* **I** *int.* Vorsicht!, Achtung!; **II** *s.*: *keep* **~** ,Schmiere stehen‘, aufpassen.
ca·ve·at [ˈkævɪæt] *s.* **1.** ⚖ Einspruch *m*, Verwahrung *f*: *enter a* **~** Verwahrung einlegen; **~** *emptor* Mängelausschluss *m*; **2.** Warnung *f.*
cave| **bear** [keɪv] *s. zo.* Höhlenbär *m*; **~ dwell·er** → *caveman* 1; '~·man [-mən] *s.* [*irr.*] **1.** Höhlenbewohner *m*, -mensch *m*; **2.** F Na'turbursche *m*, ,Bär‘ *m*, b) ,Tier‘ *n.*
cav·ern [ˈkævən] *s.* **1.** Höhle *f*; **2.** ⚕ Ka'verne *f*; **'cav·ern·ous** [-nəs] *adj.* **1.** voller Höhlen; **2.** po'rös; **3.** tief liegend, hohl (*Augen*); eingefallen (*Wangen*); tief (*Dunkelheit*); **4.** ⚕ kaver'nös.
cav·i·ar(e) [ˈkævɪɑ:] *s.* 'Kaviar *m*: **~** *to the general* Kaviar fürs Volk.
cav·il [ˈkævɪl] **I** *v/i.* nörgeln, kritteln (*at* an *dat.*); **II** *s.* Nörge'lei *f*; **'cav·il·(l)er** [-lə] *s.* Nörgler(in).
cav·i·ty [ˈkævətɪ] *s.* **1.** (Aus)Höhlung *f*,

Hohlraum *m*; **2.** *anat.* Höhle *f*, Raum *m*, Grube *f*: *abdominal* **~** Bauchhöhle; *mouth* **~** Mundhöhle; **3.** 🦷 Loch *n* (*im Zahn*).
ca·vort [kəˈvɔːt] *v/i.* F he'rumtollen, -tanzen.
ca·vy [ˈkeɪvɪ] *s. zo.* Meerschweinchen *n.*
caw [kɔː] **I** *s.* Krächzen *n* (*Rabe, Krähe etc.*); **II** *v/i.* krächzen.
cay·enne [keɪ'en], *a.* **~** *pep·per* [ˈkeɪən] *s.* Cay'ennepfeffer *m.*
cay·man [ˈkeɪmən] *pl.* **-mans** *s. zo.* 'Kaiman *m.*
CD [ˌsiːˈdiː] *s.* CD *f*; **~** *burn·er* *s.* CD-Brenner *m* (*Gerät*); **~** *play·er* *s.* C'D-,Player *m*, CD-Spieler *m*; ,~-'ROM *s. Computer:* ,CD-'ROM *f*; ,~-'ROM drive *s.* ,CD-'ROM-Laufwerk *n*; **~** *writer* → *CD burner.*
cease [siːs] **I** *v/i.* **1.** aufhören, enden: *the noise* ~*d*; **2.** (*from*) ablassen (von), aufhören (mit): **~** *and desist order* ⚖ *Am.* Unterlassungsanordnung *f*; **II** *v/t.* **3.** aufhören (*doing od. to do* mit *et. od. et.* zu tun); **4.** einstellen: **~** *fire* ⚔ das Feuer einstellen; **~** *payment* ✝ die Zahlungen einstellen; ,**cease·fire** *s.* ⚔ **1.** (Befehl *m* zur) Feuereinstellung *f*; **2.** Waffenruhe *f*; **'cease·less** [-lɪs] *adj.* □ unaufhörlich.
ce·dar [ˈsiːdə] *s.* **1.** ⚘ Zeder *f*; **2.** Zedernholz *n.*
cede [siːd] **I** *v/t.* (*to*) abtreten (*dat. od.* an *acc.*), über'lassen (*dat.*); **II** *v/i.* nachgeben, weichen.
ce·dil·la [sɪˈdɪlə] *s.* Ce'dille *f.*
cee [siː] *s.* C *n*, *c* (*Buchstabe*).
ceilidh [ˈkeɪlɪ] *s. Scot., Ir.* gemütlicher Abend mit Musik, Tanz u. Gedichtvorträgen etc.
ceil·ing [ˈsiːlɪŋ] *s.* **1.** Decke *f* e-s Raumes; **2.** ⚓ Innenbeplankung *f*; **3.** Höchstmaß *n*, -grenze *f*, ✝ *a.* Pla'fond *m* e-s Kredits: **~** *price* ✝ Höchstpreis *m*; **4.** ✈ a) Gipfelhöhe *f*, b) Wolkenhöhe *f.*
cel·e·brant [ˈselɪbrənt] *s. eccl.* Zelebrant *m*; **cel·e·brate** [ˈselɪbreɪt] **I** *v/t.* **1.** *Fest etc.* feiern, begehen; **2.** j-n feiern (*preisen*); **3.** *R. C. Messe* zelebrieren, lesen; **II** *v/i.* **4.** feiern; *R. C.* zelebrieren; **'cel·e·brat·ed** [-breɪtɪd] *adj.* gefeiert, berühmt (*for* für, wegen); **cel·e·bra·tion** [ˌselɪˈbreɪʃn] *s.* **1.** Feier *f*; Feiern *n*: *in* **~** *of* zur Feier (*gen.*); **2.** *R. C.* Zelebrieren *n*, Lesen *n* (*Messe*); **ce·leb·ri·ty** [sɪˈlebrətɪ] *s.* **1.** Berühmtheit *f*, Ruhm *m*; **2.** Berühmtheit *f* (*Person*).
ce·ler·i·ac [sɪˈlerɪæk] *s.* ⚘ Knollensellerie *m, f.*
ce·ler·i·ty [sɪˈlerɪtɪ] *s.* Geschwindigkeit *f.*
cel·er·y [ˈselərɪ] *s.* ⚘ (Stauden)Sellerie *m, f.*
ce·les·tial [sɪˈlestjəl] **I** *adj.* □ **1.** himmlisch, Himmels..., göttlich; selig; **2.** *ast.* Himmels...: **~** *body* Himmelskörper *m*; **~** *map* Himmelskarte *f*; **3.** ⚘ chi'nesisch: ⚘ *Empire* China (*alter Name*); **II** *s.* **4.** Himmelsbewohner(in), Selige(r *m*) *f*; **5.** ⚘ F Chi'nese *m*, Chi'nesin *f*; ⚘ *Cit·y* *s.* das himmlische Je'rusalem.
cel·i·ba·cy [ˈselɪbəsɪ] *s.* Zöli'bat *n, m*, Ehelosigkeit *f*; **'cel·i·bate** [-bət] **I** *s.* Unverheiratete(r *m*) *f*, Zöliba'tär *m*; **II** *adj.* unverheiratet, zöliba'tär.
cell [sel] *s.* **1.** (*Kloster-, Gefängnis- etc.*) Zelle *f*: *condemned* **~** Todeszelle; **2.** *allg., a. biol., phys., pol.* Zelle *f, a.* Kammer *f*, Fach *n*: **~** *division* Zellteilung *f*; **3.** ⚡ Zelle *f*, Ele'ment *n.*
cel·lar [ˈselə] *s.* **1.** Keller *m*; **2.** Weinkel-

---

ler *m*: *he keeps a good* **~** er hat e-n guten Keller; **'cel·lar·age** [-ərɪdʒ] *s.* **1.** Keller(räume *pl.*) *m*; **2.** Einkellerung *f*; **3.** Kellermiete *f*; **'cel·lar·er** [-ərə] *s.* Kellermeister *m.*
-celled [seld] *adj.* *in Zssgn* ...zellig.
cel·list [ˈtʃelɪst] *s.* ♪ Cel'list(in); **cel·lo** [ˈtʃeləʊ] *pl.* **-los** *s.* (Violon)'Cello *n.*
cel·lo·phane [ˈseləʊfeɪn] *s.* ⊚ Zello'phan *n*, Zellglas *n.*
cell·phone [ˈselfəʊn] *s. bsd. Am.* Mo'biltele,fon *n*, Handy *n.*
cel·lu·lar [ˈseljʊlə] *adj.* **1.** zellig, Zell(en)...: **~** *phone bsd. Am.* Mo'biltele,fon *n*, Handy *n*; **~** *tissue* Zellgewebe *n*; **~** *therapy* ⚕ Zelltherapie *f*; **2.** netzartig: **~** *shirt* Netzhemd *n*; **'cel·lule** [-juːl] *s.* kleine Zelle.
cel·lu·loid [ˈseljʊlɔɪd] *s.* ⊚ Zellu'loid *n.*
cel·lu·lose [ˈseljʊləʊs] *s.* Zellu'lose *f*, Zellstoff *m.*
Cel·si·us [ˈselsjəs], **~** *ther·mom·e·ter* *s. phys.* 'Celsiusthermo,meter *n.*
Celt [kelt] *s.* Kelte *m*, Keltin *f*; **'Celt·ic** [-tɪk] **I** *adj.* keltisch; **II** *s. ling.* das Keltische; **'Celt·i·cism** [-tɪsɪzəm] *s.* Kelti'zismus *m* (*Brauch od. Spracheigentümlichkeit*).
ce·ment [sɪˈment] **I** *s.* **1.** Ze'ment *m*, (Kalk)Mörtel *m*; **2.** Klebstoff *m*, Kitt *m*; Bindemittel *n*; **3.** a) *biol.* 'Zahnze-,ment *m*, b) 🦷 Ze'ment *m* zur Zahnfüllung; **4.** *fig.* Band *n*, Bande *pl.*; **II** *v/t.* **5.** a) zementieren, b) kitten; **6.** *fig.* festigen, ,zementieren‘; **ce·men·ta·tion** [ˌsiːmenˈteɪʃn] *s.* **1.** Zementierung *f* (*a. fig.*); **2.** Kitten *n*; **3.** *metall.* Einsatzhärtung *f*; **4.** *fig.* Bindung *f.*
cem·e·ter·y [ˈsemɪtrɪ] *s.* Friedhof *m.*
cen·o·taph [ˈsenəʊtɑ:f] *s.* (leeres) Ehren(grab)mal: *the* ⚷ *das brit. Ehrenmal in London für die Gefallenen beider Weltkriege.*
cense [sens] *v/t.* (mit Weihrauch) beräuchern; **'cen·ser** [-sə] *s.* (Weih-)Rauchfass *n.*
cen·sor [ˈsensə] **I** *s.* **1.** ('Kunst-, 'Schrifttums),Zensor *m*; **2.** 'Brief,zensor *m*; **3.** *antiq.* 'Zensor *m*, Sittenrichter *m*; **II** *v/t.* **4.** zensieren; **cen·so·ri·ous** [senˈsɔː-rɪəs] *adj.* □ **1.** 'kritisch, streng; **2.** tadelsüchtig, krittelig; **'cen·sor·ship** [-ʃɪp] *s.* **1.** Zen'sur *f*; **2.** 'Zensoramt *n*; **cen·sur·a·ble** [ˈsenʃərəbl] *adj.* tadelnswert, sträflich; **cen·sure** [ˈsenʃə] **I** *s.* **1.** Tadel *m*, Verweis *m*; Kri'tik *f*, 'Missbilligung *f*: *motion of* **~** *parl.* Misstrauensantrag *m*; **~** *vote* 1; **II** *v/t.* tadeln, miss-'billigen, kritisieren.
cen·sus [ˈsensəs] *s.* 'Zensus *m*, (*bsd.* Volks)Zählung *f*, Erhebung *f*: *live-stock* **~** Viehzählung *f*; ~*taker* Volkszähler *m*; *take a* **~** e-e (Volks- *etc.*) Zählung vornehmen.
cent [sent] *s.* **1.** Hundert *n* (*nur noch in*): *per* **~** Prozent, vom Hundert; **2.** Cent *m*: a) ¹/₁₀₀ *Dollar*: *not worth a* **~** keinen (roten) Heller wert, b) ¹/₁₀₀ *Euro.*
cen·taur [ˈsentɔː] *s.* **1.** *myth.* Zen'taur *m*; **2.** *fig.* Zwitterwesen *n*; **Cen·tau·rus** [senˈtɔːrəs] *s. ast.* Zen'taur *m.*
cen·te·nar·i·an [ˌsentɪˈneərɪən] **I** *adj.* hundertjährig; **II** *s.* Hundertjährige(r *m*) *f*; **cen·te·nar·y** [senˈtiːnərɪ] **I** *adj.* **1.** hundertjährig; **2.** hundert betragend; **II** *s.* **3.** Jahr'hundert *n*; **4.** Hundert'jahrfeier *f.*
cen·ten·ni·al [senˈtenjəl] **I** *adj.* hundertjährig; **II** *s. bsd. Am.* Hundert'jahrfeier *f.*
cen·ter *etc. Am.* → *centre etc.*
cen·tes·i·mal [senˈtesɪml] *adj.* □ zente-si'mal, hundertteilig.
cen·ti·grade [ˈsentɪgreɪd] *adj.* hundert-

C

teilig, -gradig: **~ thermometer** Celsius-thermometer *n*; **degree(s) ~** Grad Celsius; **'cen·ti·gram(me)** [-græm] *s.* Zenti'gramm *n*; **'cen·ti,me·tre,** *Am.* **'cen·ti,me·ter** [-,miːtə] *s.* Zenti'meter *m*, *n*; **'cen·ti·pede** [-piːd] *s. zo.* Hundertfüßer *m*.

cen·tral ['sentrəl] **I** *adj.* □ **1.** zen'tral (gelegen); **2.** Haupt..., Zentral...: **~ of·fice** Hauptbüro *n*, Zentrale *f*; **~ idea** Hauptgedanke *m*; **II** *s.* **3.** *Am.* a) (Tele'fon)Zen,trale *f*, b) Telefo'nist(in) (*in e-r Zentrale*); **Ⓢ A·mer·i·can** *adj.* 'mittelameri,kanisch; **~ cit·y** *s. Am.* Stadtkern *m*, Innenstadt *f*; **Ⓢ Eu·ro·pe·an time** *s.* 'mitteleuro,päische Zeit (*abbr. MEZ*); **~ heat·ing** *s.* Zen'tralheizung *f*.

cen·tral·ism ['sentrəlizəm] *s.* Zentra'lismus *m*, (Sy'stem *n* der) Zentralisierung *f*; **'cen·tral·ist** [-ist] *s.* Verfechter *m* der Zentralisierung; **cen·tral·i·za·tion** [,sentrəlar'zeiʃn] *s.* Zentralisierung *f*; **'cen·tral·ize** [-laiz] *v/t.* (*v/i.* sich) zentralisieren.

cen·tral‖ lock·ing *s. mot.* Zen'tralverriegelung *f*; **~ nerv·ous sys·tem** *s. anat.* Zen'tral,nervensy,stem *n*; **~ point** *s.* Ⓐ Mittelpunkt *m*; **⚡** Nullpunkt *m*; **Ⓢ Pow·ers** *s. pl. pol. hist.* Mittelmächte *pl.*; **~ pro·cess·ing u·nit** *s. Computer:* Zen'traleinheit *f*; **~ re·serve** *s. mot. Brit.* Mittelstreifen *m*; **~ sta·tion** *s.* **1.** ⚓ ('Bord)Zen,trale *f*, Kom'mandostand *m*; **2.** Haupt-, Zen'tralbahnhof *m*; **3.** **⚡** Zen'trale *f*.

cen·tre ['sentə] **I** *s.* **1.** 'Zentrum *n*, Mittelpunkt *m* (*a. fig.*): **~ of attraction** *fig.* Hauptanziehungspunkt *m*; **~ of gravity** *phys.* Schwerpunkt *m*; **~ of motion** *phys.* Drehpunkt *m*; **~ of trade** Handelszentrum; **2.** Hauptstelle *f*, -gebiet *n*, Sitz *m*: **amusement ~** Vergnügungszentrum *n*; **~ of interest** Hauptinteresse *n*; → **shopping, train·ing centre**; **3.** *pol.* Mitte *f*, 'Mittelpar,tei *f*; **4.** Ⓢ Spitze *f*: **~ lathe** Spitzendrehbank *f*; **5.** *sport* Flanke *f*; **6.** (Pra'linen- *etc.*)Füllung *f*; **II** *v/t.* **7.** in den Mittelpunkt stellen (*a. fig.*); konzentrieren, vereinigen (**on, in** auf *acc.*); Ⓢ einmitten, zentrieren; ankörnen: **~ the bubble** die Libelle einspielen lassen; **III** *v/i.* **8.** im Mittelpunkt stehen (*a. fig.*); *fig.* sich drehen (**round** um); **9.** (**in, on**) sich konzentrieren, sich gründen (auf *acc.*); **10.** *Fußball:* flanken; **~ bit** *s.* Ⓢ 'Zentrumsbohrer *m*; **'~·board** *s.* ⚓ (Kiel)Schwert *n*; **~ cir·cle** *s. Fußball:* Anstoßkreis *m*; **~ court** *s. Tennis:* 'Centre-Court *m*; **~ for·ward** *s. Fußball:* Mittelstürmer *m*; **~ half** *s. Fußball:* 'Vor,stopper *m*; **~ par·ty** *s. pol.* 'Mittelpar,tei *f*, 'Zentrum *n*; **'~·piece** *s.* **1.** Mittelstück *n*; **2.** (mittlerer) Tafelaufsatz; **3.** *fig.* Hauptstück *n*; **~ punch** *s.* Ⓢ (An)Körner *m*; **~ sec·ond** *s.* Zent'ralse,kundenzeiger *m*; **~ strip** *s. mot.* Mittelstreifen *m*, Grünstreifen *m*.

cen·tric, cen·tri·cal ['sentrik(l)] *adj.* □ zen'tral, zentrisch.

cen·trif·u·gal [sen'trifjugl] *adj. phys.* zentrifu'gal; Schleuder..., Schwung...: **~ force** Zentrifugal-, Fliehkraft *f*; **~ governor** Fliehkraftregler *m*; **cen·tri·fuge** ['sentrifjuːdʒ] **I** *s.* Zentri'fuge *f*, Trennschleuder *f*; **II** *v/t.* zentrifugieren, schleudern.

cen·trip·e·tal [sen'tripitl] *adj.* zentripe-'tal: **~ force** Zentripetalkraft *f*.

cen·tu·ple ['sentjupl], **cen·tu·pli·cate** [sen'tjuːpliːkət] **I** *adj.* hundertfach; **II** *v/t.* verhundertfachen; **III** *s.* (das) Hundertfache.

cen·tu·ri·on [sen'tjuəriən] *s. antiq.* (*Rom*) ⚔ Zen'turio *m*.

cen·tu·ry ['sentʃuri] *s.* **1.** Jahr'hundert *n*: **centuries-old** jahrhundertealt; **2.** Satz *m* od. Gruppe *f* von hundert; *bsd. Kricket:* 100 Läufe *pl.*; **3.** *Am. sl.* hundert Dollar *pl.*; **4.** *antiq.* (*Rom*) Zen'turie *f*, Hundertschaft *f*.

ce·phal·ic [ke'fælik] *adj. anat., zo.* Schädel..., Kopf...; **ceph·a·lo·pod** ['sefələupɒd] *s. zo.* Kopffüßer *m*; **ceph·a·lous** ['sefələs] *adj. zo.* mit e-m ... Kopf, ...köpfig.

ce·ram·ic [si'ræmik] **I** *adj.* **1.** ke'ramisch; **II** *s.* **2.** Ke'ramik *f* (*einzelnes Produkt*); **3.** *pl. mst sg. konstr.* Ke'ramik *f* (*Technik*); **4.** *pl.* Ke'ramik *f*, ke'ramische Erzeugnisse; **cer·a·mist** ['serəmist] *s.* Ke'ramiker *m*.

Cer·ber·us ['sɜːbərəs] *s. fig.* 'Zerberus *m* (*a. ast.*), grimmiger Wächter: **sop to ~** Beschwichtigungsmittel *n*.

ce·re·al ['siəriəl] **I** *adj.* **1.** Getreide...; **II** *s.* **2.** *mst pl.* Zere'alien *pl.*, Getreidepflanzen *pl.*, -früchte *pl.*; **3.** Frühstückskost *f aus Weizen, Hafer etc.*

cer·e·bel·lum [,seri'beləm] *s. anat.* Kleinhirn *n*; **cer·e·bral** ['seribrəl] *adj.* **1.** *anat.* Gehirn...: **~ death ⚕** Hirntod *m*; **2.** *ling.* alveo'lar; **,cer·e·bra·tion** [-'breiʃn] *s.* Gehirntätigkeit *f*; Denken *n*, 'Denkpro,zess *m*; **cer·e·brum** ['seribrəm] *s. anat.* Großhirn *n*, Ze'rebrum *n*.

cere·cloth ['siəklɒθ] *s.* Wachsleinwand *f*, *bsd. als* Leichentuch *n*.

cere·ment ['siəmənt] *s. mst pl.* Leichentuch *n*, Totenhemd *n*.

cer·e·mo·ni·al [,seri'məunjəl] **I** *adj.* □ **1.** feierlich, förmlich; **2.** ritu'ell; **II** *s.* **3.** Zeremoni'ell *n*; **,cer·e·mo·ni·ous** [-jəs] *adj.* □ **1.** → **ceremonial** 1 *u.* 2; **2.** 'umständlich, steif; **cer·e·mo·ny** ['seriməni] *s.* **1.** Zeremo'nie *f*, Feierlichkeit *f*, feierlicher Brauch; Feier *f*; → **master** 12; **2.** Förmlichkeit(en *pl.*) *f*: **with·out ~** ohne Umstände; **stand on ~** a) sehr förmlich sein, b) Umstände machen; **3.** Höflichkeit *f*.

ce·rise [sə'riːz] *adj.* kirschrot, ce'rise.

cert [sɜːt] *s. a.* **dead ~** *Brit. sl.* ,todsichere Sache'.

cer·tain ['sɜːtn] *adj.* □ **1.** (*von Sachen*) sicher, gewiss, bestimmt: **it is ~ to happen** es wird gewiss geschehen; **I know for ~** ich weiß ganz bestimmt; **2.** (*von Personen*) über'zeugt, sicher, gewiss: **to make ~ of s.th.** sich e-r Sache vergewissern; **3.** bestimmt, zuverlässig, sicher: **a ~ cure** e-e sichere Kur; **a ~ day** ein (ganz) bestimmter Tag; **4.** gewiss: **a ~ Mr. Brown** ein gewisser Herr Brown; **for ~ reasons** aus bestimmten Gründen; **'cer·tain·ly** [-li] *adv.* **1.** sicher, zweifellos, bestimmt; **2.** sicherlich, (aber) sicher *od.* na'türlich; **'cer·tain·ty** [-ti] *s.* **1.** Sicherheit *f*, Bestimmtheit *f*, Gewissheit *f*: **know for a ~** mit Sicherheit wissen; **2.** Über'zeugung *f*.

cer·ti·fi·a·ble [,sɜːti'faiəbl] *adj.* □ **1.** feststellbar; **2.** ⚕ *Brit.* a) meldepflichtig (*Krankheit*), b) geisteskrank, c) F verrückt.

cer·tif·i·cate I *s.* [sə'tifikət] Bescheinigung *f*, At'test *n*, Zeugnis *n*, Schein *m*, Urkunde *f*: **death ~** Sterbeurkunde; **school ~** Schul(abgangs)zeugnis; **~ of baptism ✝** Taufschein; **~ of identification ✝** Nämlichkeitsbescheinigung *f*; **~ of origin ✝** Ursprungszeugnis; **share ~** (*Am. stock*) **~** Aktienzertifikat *n*; **~ of health 1, master 7, medical 1; II** *v/t.* [-keit] j-m e-e Bescheinigung *od.* ein

Zeugnis geben; *et.* attestieren, bescheinigen; **~d** amtlich anerkannt *od.* zugelassen; **~d bankrupt** rehabilitierter Konkursschuldner; **~d engineer** Diplomingenieur *m*; **cer·ti·fi·ca·tion** [,sɜːtifi'keiʃn] *s.* **1.** Bescheinigung *f* (*Am.* ✝ *a. e-s Schecks*); **2.** (amtliche) Beglaubigung *od.* beglaubigte Erklärung.

cer·ti·fied ['sɜːtifaid] *adj.* **1.** bescheinigt, beglaubigt, garantiert: **~ copy** beglaubigte Abschrift; **2.** staatlich zugelassen *od.* anerkannt, *Am.* Diplom...; **3.** ⚕ *Brit.* für geisteskrank erklärt; **~ ac·count·ant** *s.* ✝ *Brit.* konzessionierter Buch- *od.* Steuerprüfer; **~ cheque,** *Am.* **check** *s.* (*als gedeckt*) bestätigter Scheck; **~ mail** *s. Am.* eingeschriebene Sendung (*on pl.*) *f*; **~ milk** *s.* amtlich geprüfte Milch; **~ pub·lic ac·count·ant** *s.* ✝ *Am.* amtlich zugelassener 'Bücherre,visor *od.* Wirtschaftsprüfer.

cer·ti·fy ['sɜːtifai] **I** *v/t.* **1.** bescheinigen: **this is to ~** hiermit wird bescheinigt; **2.** beglaubigen; **3.** *Scheck* (als gedeckt) bestätigen (*Bank*); **4.** **~ s.o.** (**insane**) ⚖ *Brit.* j-n für geisteskrank erklären; **5.** ⚖ *Sache* verweisen (**to** an *ein anderes Gericht*); **II** *v/i.* **6.** (**to**) bezeugen (*acc.*).

cer·ti·tude ['sɜːtitjuːd] *s.* Sicherheit *f*, Gewissheit *f*.

ce·ru·men [si'ruːmen] *s.* Ohrenschmalz *n*.

ce·ruse [si'ruːs] *s.* **1.** 🜍 Bleiweiß *n*; **2.** weiße Schminke.

cer·vi·cal [sɜː'vaikl] *anat.* **I** *adj.* Hals..., Nacken...: **~ smear ⚕** Abstrich *m* (*vom Gebärmutterhals*); **II** *s.* Halswirbel *m*; **cer·vix** ['sɜːviks] *pl.* **-vi·ces** [-visiːz] *s.* ⚕, *anat.* Gebärmutterhals *m*.

Ce·sar·e·vitch [si'zɑːrəvitʃ] *s. hist.* Za'rewitsch *m*.

ces·sa·tion [se'seiʃn] *s.* Aufhören *n*, Ende *n*; Stillstand *m*, Einstellung *f*.

ces·sion ['seʃn] *s.* Abtretung *f*, Zessi'on *f*.

cess·pit ['sespit], **'cess·pool** [-puːl] *s.* **1.** Jauche-, Senkgrube *f*; **2.** *fig.* (Sünden)Pfuhl *m*.

ce·ta·cean [si'teiʃən] *zo.* **I** *s.* Wal (-fisch) *m*; **II** *adj.* Wal(fisch)...

ce·tane ['siːtein] *s.* 🜍 Ce'tan *n*: **~ num·ber** Cetanzahl *f*.

chafe [tʃeif] **I** *v/t.* **1.** warm reiben, frottieren; **2.** ('durch)reiben, wund reiben, scheuern; **3.** *fig.* ärgern, reizen; **II** *v/i.* **4.** sich ('durch)reiben, sich wund reiben, scheuern (**against** an *dat.*); **5.** Ⓢ verschleißen; **6.** a) sich ärgern, b) toben, wüten.

chaf·er ['tʃeifə] *s. zo.* Käfer *m*.

chaff [tʃɑːf] **I** *s.* **1.** Spreu *f*: **separate the ~ from the wheat** die Spreu vom Weizen trennen; **as ~ before the wind** wie Spreu im Winde; **2.** Häcksel *m*, *n*; **3.** ✕ Stör,folie *f* (*Radar*); **4.** *fig.* wertloses Zeug; **5.** Necke'rei *f*; **II** *v/t.* **6.** zu Häcksel schneiden; **7.** *fig.* necken, aufziehen; **'~·cut·ter** *s.* ⚘ Häckselbank *f*.

chaf·fer ['tʃæfə] **I** *s.* Feilschen *n*; **II** *v/i.* feilschen, schachern.

chaf·finch ['tʃæfintʃ] *s.* Buchfink *m*.

chaf·ing dish ['tʃeifiŋ] *s.* Re'chaud *m*, *n*.

cha·grin ['ʃægrin] **I** *s.* **1.** Ärger *m*, Verdruss *m*; **2.** Kränkung *f*; **II** *v/t.* **3.** ärgern, verdrießen: **~ed** ärgerlich, gekränkt.

chain [tʃein] **I** *s.* **1.** Kette *f* (*a.* 🜍, ⚡, Ⓢ, *phys.*): **~ of office** Amtskette; **human ~** Menschenkette *f*; **2.** *fig.* Kette *f*,

Fessel f: **in** ~s in Ketten, gefangen; **3.** *fig.* Kette f, Reihe f: ~ **of events**; **4.** a. ~ **of mountains** Gebirgskette f; **5.** ✝ (Laden- *etc.*)Kette f; **6.** ⊕ Messkette f (66 *engl. Fuß*); **II** *v/t.* **7.** (an)ketten, mit e-r Kette befestigen: ~ (**up**) **a dog** e-n Hund an die Kette legen; ~ **a prisoner** e-n Gefangenen in Ketten legen; ~ **a door** e-e Tür durch e-e Kette sichern; **8.** *fig.* (**to**) verketten (mit), ketten *od.* fesseln (an *acc.*); **9.** *Land* mit der Messkette messen; ~ **armo(u)r** s. Kettenpanzer m; ~ **belt** s. ⊕ endlose Kette, 'Kettentransmissi,on f; ~ **bridge** s. Hängebrücke f; ~ **drive** s. ⊕ Kettenantrieb m; ~ **gang** s. Trupp m anein'ander geketteter Sträflinge; '~·**less** ['tʃeɪnlɪs] adj. ⊕ kettenlos; ~ **let·ter** s. Kettenbrief m; ~ **mail** → **chain armo(u)r**; ~ **pump** s. Pater'nosterwerk n; ~ **re·ac·tion** s. *phys. u. fig.* 'Kettenreakti,on f; '~·**smoke** v/i. u. v/t. Kette rauchen; '~·,**smok·er** s. Kettenraucher m; ~ **stitch** s. *Nähen:* Kettenstich m; ~ **store** s. ✝ Kettenladen m.

chair [tʃeə] **I** s. **1.** Stuhl m, Sessel m: **take a** ~ sich setzen; **2.** *fig.* a) Vorsitz m: **be in** (**take**) **the** ~ den Vorsitz führen (übernehmen); **leave the** ~ die Sitzung aufheben, b) Vorsitzende(r) m: **address the** ~ sich an den Vorsitzenden wenden; ~! ~! *parl. Brit.* zur Ordnung!; **3.** Lehrstuhl m, Profes'sur f (**of German** für Deutsch); **4.** *Am.* F der e'lektrische Stuhl; **5.** ⬚ Schienenstuhl m; **6.** Sänfte f; **II** v/t. **7.** (in ein Amt) einsetzen, auf e-n *Lehrstuhl etc.* berufen; **8.** den Vorsitz führen von (*od.* gen.); **9.** ~ **s.o. off** j-n (im Tri'umph) auf den Schultern (da'von)tragen; ~ **back** s. Stuhllehne f; ~ **bot·tom** s. Stuhlsitz m; ~ **car** s. 🚃 Sa'lonwagen m; ~ **lift** s. Sesselbahn f, -lift m.

chair·man ['tʃeəmən] s. [irr.] **1.** Vorsitzende(r) m, Präsi'dent m; **2.** Sänftenträger m; '**chair·man·ship** [-ʃɪp] s. Vorsitz m.

chair·o·plane ['tʃeərəpleɪn] s. 'Kettenkarus,sell n.

'**chair|·per·son** s. Vorsitzende(r m) f; '~·**wom·an** s. [irr.] Vorsitzende f.

chaise [ʃeɪz] s. Chaise f, Halbkutsche f; ~ **longue** [lɔ̃:ŋg] s. Chaise'longue f, Liegesofa n.

chal·cog·ra·pher [kæl'kɒgrəfə] s. Kupferstecher m.

cha·let ['ʃæleɪ] s. Cha'let n: a) Sennhütte f, b) Landhaus n.

chal·ice ['tʃælɪs] s. **1.** *poet.* (Trink)Becher m; **2.** *eccl.* (Abendmahls)Kelch m; **3.** ♀ Blütenkelch m.

chalk [tʃɔ:k] **I** s. **1.** *min.* Kreide f; **2.** (Zeichen)Kreide f, Kreidestift m: **col·o(u)red** ~ Buntstift; **red** ~ a) Rötel m, b) Rotstift; **as different as** ~ **and cheese** grundverschieden; **3.** Kreidestrich m: a) (Gewinn)Punkt m (*bei Spielen*), b) *Brit.* (angekreidete) Schuld: **by a long** ~ bei weitem; **II** v/t. **4.** mit Kreide (be)zeichnen; **5.** ~ **out** entwerfen; *fig.* Weg vorzeichnen; **6.** ~ **up** anschreiben; ankreiden, auf die Rechnung setzen: ~ **it up to s.o.** es j-m ankreiden; ~ **mark** s. Kreidestrich m; ~ **pit** s. Kreidegrube f; '~·**stone** s. ✻ Gichtknoten m.

chalk·y ['tʃɔ:kɪ] adj. kreidig; kreidehaltig.

chal·lenge ['tʃælɪndʒ] **I** s. **1.** Her'ausforderung f (*a. sport u. fig.*), Forderung f (*zum Duell etc.*); (Auf-, An)Forderung f; Aufruf m; **2.** ✕ Anruf m (*Wachtpos-*

ten); **3.** *hunt.* Anschlagen n (*Hund*); **4.** *bsd.* 🏛 a) Ablehnung f (*e-s Geschworenen od. Richters*), b) Anfechtung f (*e-s Beweismittels*); **5.** 'Widerspruch m, Kri-'tik f, Bestreitung f, Kampfansage f; Angriff m; Streitfrage f; **6.** Her'ausforderung f: a) Bedrohung f, kritische Lage, b) Schwierigkeit f, Pro'blem n, c) (schwierige *od.* lockende) Aufgabe; **7.** ✻ Immuni'tätstest m; **II** v/t. **8.** her'ausfordern (*a. sport u. fig.*); ✕ anrufen; **9.** Anforderungen an j-n stellen; auf die Probe stellen; **10.** bestreiten, anzweifeln; *bsd.* 🏛 anfechten, *Geschworenen etc.* ablehnen; → **bias** 5; **11.** trotzen (*dat.*); angreifen; **12.** j-n reizen, locken, fordern (*Aufgabe*); **13.** j-m *Bewunderung etc.* abnötigen; '**chal·lenge·a·ble** [-dʒəbl] adj. her'auszufordern(d); anfechtbar; **chal·lenge cup** s. *sport* 'Wanderpo,kal m; '**chal·leng·er** [-dʒə] s. Her'ausforderer m; **chal·lenge tro·phy** s. Wanderpreis m; '**chal·leng·ing** [-dʒɪŋ] adj. □ **1.** herausfordernd; **2.** *fig.* lockend *od.* schwierig (*Aufgabe*).

cha·lyb·e·ate [kə'lɪbɪət] min. **I** adj. stahl-, eisenhaltig: ~ **spring** Stahlquelle f; **II** s. Stahlwasser n.

cham·ber ['tʃeɪmbə] s. **1.** *obs.* Zimmer n, Kammer f, Gemach n; **2.** *pl. Brit.* a) (*zu vermietende*) Zimmer *pl.*: **live in** ~s privat wohnen, b) Geschäftsräume *pl.*; **3.** (*Empfangs*)Zimmer n (*im Palast etc.*); **4.** *parl.* a) Ple'narsaal m, b) Kammer f; **5.** *pl. Brit.* a) 'Anwaltsbü,ro n, b) Amtszimmer n des Richters: **in** ~s in nichtöffentlicher Sitzung; **6.** ⊕ Kammer f; Raum m; (Gewehr)Kammer f; **con·cert** s. 'Kammerkon,zert n; ~ **coun·sel** s. *Brit.* (nur) beratender Anwalt.

cham·ber·lain ['tʃeɪmbəlɪn] s. **1.** Kammerherr m; **2.** Schatzmeister m.

'**cham·ber|·maid** s. Zimmermädchen n (*in Hotels*); ~ **mu·sic** s. 'Kammermu,sik f; ⅃ **of Com·merce** s. Handelskammer f; ~ **pot** s. Nachtgeschirr n.

cha·me·le·on [kə'mi:ljən] s. *zo.* Cha-'mäleon n (*a. fig.*).

cham·fer ['tʃæmfə] **I** s. **1.** △ Auskehlung f; **2.** ⊕ Schrägkante f, Fase f; **II** v/t. **3.** △ auskehlen; **4.** ⊕ abfasen, abschrägen.

cham·ois ['ʃæmwɑ:] *pl.* ~ [-ɑ:z] s. **1.** *zo.* Gämse f; **2.** a. ~ **leather** [mst 'ʃæmɪ] a) Sämischleder n, b) ⊕ Polierleder m.

champ¹ [tʃæmp] v/i. u. v/t. (heftig *od.* geräuschvoll) kauen: ~ **at the bit** a) am Gebiss kauen (*Pferd*), b) *fig.* vor Ungeduld (fast) platzen, c) mit den Zähnen knirschen.

champ² [tʃæmp] *sl.* → **champion** 3.

cham·pagne [,ʃæm'peɪn] s. **1.** Cham'pagner m, Sekt m, Schaumwein m: ~ **cup** Sektkelch m, -schale f; **2.** Cham'pagnerfarbe f.

cham·pi·on ['tʃæmpjən] **I** s. **1.** Kämpe m, (Tur'nier)Kämpfer m; **2.** *fig.* Vorkämpfer m, Verfechter m, Fürsprecher m; **3.** a) *sport* Meister m, Titelhalter m, b) Sieger m (*Wettbewerb*); **II** v/t. **4.** verfechten, eintreten für, verteidigen; **III** adj. **5.** Meister..., best, preisgekrönt; '**cham·pi·on·ship** [-ʃɪp] s. **1.** Meisterschaft f, -titel m; **2.** *pl.* Meisterschaftskämpfe *pl.*, Meisterschaften *pl.*; **3.** Verfechten n, Eintreten n für etwas.

chance [tʃɑ:ns] **I** s. **1.** Zufall m: **by** ~ zufällig; **2.** Glück n; Schicksal n; 'Risiko n: **game of** ~ Glücksspiel n; **take one's** ~ sein Glück versuchen; **take a**

(*od. one's*) ~ es darauf ankommen lassen, es riskieren; **take no** ~s nichts riskieren (wollen); **3.** Chance f: a) Glücksfall m, (günstige) Gelegenheit: **the** ~ **of his lifetime** die Chance s-s Lebens, e-e einmalige Gelegenheit; **give him a** ~! gib ihm e-e Chance!, versuchs mal mit ihm!; → **main chance**, b) Aussicht f (**of** auf acc.): **stand a** ~ Aussichten haben, c) Möglichkeit f, Wahrscheinlichkeit f: **the** ~s **are that** aller Wahrscheinlichkeit nach; **the** ~s **are against you** die Umstände sind gegen dich; ~ **of rain** vereinzelt Regen; **on the** (**off**) ~ auf gut Glück, ,auf Verdacht', für den Fall (*dass*); **II** v/t. **4.** riskieren: ~ **it** es darauf ankommen lassen, es wagen; **III** v/i. **5.** (unerwartet) geschehen: **I** ~**ed to meet her** zufällig traf ich sie; **6.** ~ **upon** auf j-n *od.* et. stoßen; **IV** adj. **7.** zufällig, Zufalls..., gelegentlich, ✝ a. Gelegenheits...: unerwartet: ~ **customers** Laufkundschaft f.

chan·cel ['tʃɑ:nsl] s. △ Al'tarraum m, hoher Chor.

chan·cel·ler·y ['tʃɑ:nsələrɪ] s. 'Botschafts- *od.* Konsu'latskanz,lei f.

chan·cel·lor ['tʃɑ:nsələ] s. **1.** Kanzler m (*a. univ.*); *univ. Am.* Rektor m; ⅃ **of the Exchequer** *Brit.* Schatzkanzler m, Finanzminister m; → **Lord** 2; **2.** Kanz'leivorstand m; '**chan·cel·lor·ship** [-ʃɪp] s. Kanzleramt n, -würde f.

chan·cer·y ['tʃɑ:nsərɪ] s. Kanz'leigericht n (*Brit. Gerichtshof des Lordkanzlers*; *Am. Billigkeitsgericht*): **in** ~ a) unter gerichtlicher Verwaltung, b) F in der Klemme; **ward in** ~ Mündel n unter Amtsvormundschaft; ⅃ **Di·vi·sion** 🏛 *Brit.* Kammer f für Billigkeitsrechtsprechung des **High Court of Justice**.

chan·cre ['ʃæŋkə] s. ✻ Schanker m.

chan·de·lier [,ʃændə'lɪə] s. Arm-, Kronleuchter m, Lüster m.

chan·dler ['tʃɑ:ndlə] s. Krämer m; ⅃ **Act** s. *Am.* Kon'kursordnung f.

change [tʃeɪndʒ] **I** v/t. **1.** (ver)ändern, 'umändern, verwandeln (**into** in acc.): ~ **one's lodgings** umziehen; ~ **the subject** das Thema wechseln, von et. anderem reden; ~ **one's position** die Stellung wechseln, sich beruflich verändern; → **mind** 4, **colour** 3; **2.** ('um-, ver)tauschen (**for** gegen), wechseln: **one's shirt** ein anderes Hemd anziehen; ~ **hands** den Besitzer wechseln; ~ **places with s.o.** den Platz mit j-m tauschen; ~ **trains** umsteigen; → **side** 9; **3.** Geld, Banknoten (ein)wechseln; *Scheck* einlösen; **4.** j-m andere Kleider anziehen; *Säugling* trockenlegen; *Bett* frisch über'ziehen *od.* beziehen; **5.** ⊕ schalten: ~ **up** (**down**) hinauf- (herunter)schalten; ~ **over** Betrieb, *Maschinen etc.* umstellen; **II** v/i. **6.** sich (ver)ändern, wechseln; **7.** sich verwandeln (**to** *od.* **into** in acc.); **8.** 🚃 *etc.* 'umsteigen: **all** ~! alles umsteigen *od.* aussteigen!; **9.** sich 'umziehen: ~ **into evening dress** sich für den Abend umziehen; **10.** ~ **to** 'übergehen zu: ~ **to cigars**; **III** s. **11.** (Ver)Änderung f, Wechsel m; Wandlung f, Wendung f, 'Umschwung m: **no** ~ unverändert; ~ **for the better** Besserung f; ~ **of heart** Sinnesänderung f; ~ **of life** Wechseljahre *pl.*; ~ **of moon** Mondwechsel m; ~ **of voice** Stimmwechsel m; ~ **in the weather** Witterungsumschlag m; **12.** Abwechs(e)lung f, et. Neues; Tausch m: **for a** ~ zur Abwechs(e)lung; **a** ~ **of clothes** Wäsche zum Wechseln; **you need a** ~ Sie müssen mal ausspannen; **13.** Wech-

C

selgeld *n*: (*small*) ~ Kleingeld; ~ *dispenser* (od. *machine*) Wechselautomat *m*; *can you give me* ~ *for a pound?* a) können Sie mir auf ein Pfund herausgeben?, b) können Sie mir ein Pfund wechseln?; *get no* ~ *out of s.o. fig.* nichts (*keine Auskunft od. keinen Vorteil*) aus j-m herausholen können, bei j-m nicht ‚landen' können; **14.** ♙ *Brit.* Börse *f*; **change·a·bil·i·ty** [ˌtʃeɪndʒə-ˈbɪlətɪ] *s.* Veränderlichkeit *f*; *fig.* Wankelmut *m*; **'change·a·ble** [-dʒəbl] *adj.* □ **1.** veränderlich; **2.** wankelmütig; **'change·ful** [-fʊl] *adj.* □ veränderlich, wechselvoll; **change gear** *s.* ⊛ Wechselgetriebe *n*; **'change·less** [-lɪs] *adj.* unveränderlich, beständig; **'change·ling** [-lɪŋ] *s.* Wechselbalg *m*; ‚untergeschobenes Kind'; **'change·o·ver** *s.* **1.** (*to*) ‚Übergang *m* (zu), Wechsel *m* (zu), 'Umstellung *f* (auf *acc.*) (a. ⊛ *von Maschinen, e-s Betriebs etc.*); **2.** ⊛ 'Umschaltung *f*; **3.** *sport* (Stab)Wechsel *m*; **'chang·er** [-dʒə] *s. in Zssgn* ...wechsler *m* (*Person od. Gerät*); **'chang·ing** [-dʒɪŋ] *s.* Wechsel *m*, Änderung *f*: ~ *of the guard* ⚔ Wachablösung *f*; ~ *room* Umkleidezimmer *n*; ~ *cubicle* Umkleidekabine *f*.

chan·nel [ˈtʃænl] **I** *s.* **1.** Flussbett *n*; **2.** Fahrrinne *f*, Ka'nal *m*; **3.** Rinne *f*, 'Durchlassröhre *f*; **4.** breite Wasserstraße: *the* (*English*) ♙ *geogr.* der (Ärmel-) Kanal; **5.** Rille *f*, Riefe *f*; **6.** *fig.* Weg *m*, Ka'nal *m*: ~*s of distribution* Vertriebswege *pl.*; ~*s of trade* Handelswege, *a.* Absatzgebiete; *official* ~ Dienstweg; *through the usual* ~*s* auf dem üblichen Wege; **7.** *Radio, TV:* Pro'gramm *n*, Ka'nal *m*: ~ *hopping* Zappen *n*, dauerndes 'Umschalten; ~ *selector* Kanalwähler *m*; **II** *v/t.* **8.** *fig.* leiten, lenken; **9.** ⊛ furchen, riefeln; △ kannelieren, auskehlen.

chant [tʃɑːnt] **I** *s.* **1.** *eccl.* Kirchengesang *m*, -lied *n*; **2.** Singsang *m*, eintöniger Gesang *od.* Tonfall; **3.** Sprechchor *m* (*als Geschrei*); **II** *v/t.* **4.** *Kirchenlied* singen; **5.** absingen, 'herleiern; **6.** im Sprechchor rufen.

chan·te·relle [ˌtʃæntəˈrel] *s.* ♠ Pfifferling *m*.

chan·ti·cleer [ˌtʃæntɪˈklɪə] *s. poet.* Hahn *m*.

chan·try [ˈtʃɑːntrɪ] *s. eccl.* **1.** Stiftung *f* von Seelenmessen; **2.** Vo'tivka‚pelle *f od.* -al‚tar *m*.

chant·y [ˈtʃɑːntɪ] *s.* Ma'trosenlied *n*, Shanty *n*.

cha·os [ˈkeɪɒs] *s.* 'Chaos *n*, *fig. a.* Wirrwarr *m*, Durchein'ander *n*; **cha·ot·ic** [keɪˈɒtɪk] *adj.* (□ ~*ally*) cha'otisch, wirr.

chap¹ [tʃæp] *s.* F Bursche *m*, Junge *m*: *a nice* ~ ein netter Kerl; *old* ~ ‚alter Knabe'.

chap² [tʃæp] *s.* Kinnbacken *m* (*bsd. Tier*), *pl.* Maul *n*.

chap³ [tʃæp] **I** *v/t. u. v/i.* rissig machen *od.* werden: ~*ped hands* aufgesprungene Hände; **II** *s.* Riss *m*, Sprung *m*.

chap·el [ˈtʃæpl] *s.* **1.** Ka'pelle *f*; Gotteshaus *n* (der Dis'senters): *I am* ~ F ich bin ein Dissenter; **2.** ('Seiten)Ka‚pelle *f* in e-r Kathe'drale; **3.** Gottesdienst *m*; **4.** *typ.* betriebliche Ge'werkschaftsorganisati‚on der Drucker; **'chap·el·ry** [-rɪ] *s. eccl.* Sprengel *m*.

chap·er·on [ˈʃæpərəʊn] **I** *s.* **1.** Anstandsdame *f*; **2.** Be'gleiter‚son *f*; **II** *v/t.* (als Anstandsdame) begleiten.

'chap‚fall·en *adj.* niedergeschlagen.

chap·lain [ˈtʃæplɪn] *s.* **1.** Ka'plan *m*,

Geistliche(r) *m* (*an e-r Kapelle*); **2.** Hof-, Haus-, Anstalts-, Mili'tär-, Ma'rinegeistliche(r) *m*; **'chap·lain·cy** [-sɪ] *s.* Ka'plans‚amt *n*, -pfründe *f*.

chap·let [ˈtʃæplɪt] *s.* **1.** Kranz *m*; **2.** *eccl.* Rosenkranz *m*.

chap·py [ˈtʃæpɪ] *adj.* rissig, aufgesprungen: ~ *hands*.

Chap Stick *npr.* (*Warenzeichen*), F *a.* **chap·stick** [ˈtʃæpstɪk] *s.* La'bello *npr.* (*Warenzeichen*), Lippenpflegestift *m*.

chap·ter [ˈtʃæptə] *s.* **1.** Ka'pitel *n* (*Buch u. fig.*): ~ *and verse* a) *bibl.* Kapitel u. Vers, b) genaue Einzelheiten; *give* ~ *and verse a.* genau zitieren; *to the end of the* ~ bis ans Ende; **2.** *eccl.* 'Dom-, 'Ordenska‚pitel *n*; **3.** *Am.* Orts-, 'Untergruppe *f* e-r Vereinigung; ~ *house s.* 'Domka‚pitel *n*, Stiftshaus *n*; **2.** *Am.* Verbindungshaus *n* (*Studenten*).

char¹ [tʃɑː] *v/t. u. v/i.* verkohlen.

char² [tʃɑː] *s. ichth.* 'Rotfo‚relle *f*.

char³ [tʃɑː] *Brit.* **I** *v/i.* **1.** als Putzfrau *od.* Raumpflegerin arbeiten; **II** *s.* **2.** Putzen *n* (*als Lebensunterhalt*); **3.** → *charwoman*.

char-à-banc [ˈʃærəbæŋ] *pl.* **-bancs** [-z] *s.* **1.** Kremser *m* (*Kutsche*); **2.** Ausflugsautobus *m*.

char·ac·ter [ˈkærəktə] *s.* **1.** Cha'rakter *m*, Wesen *n*, Na'tur *f* (*e-s Menschen*): *a bad* ~ a) ein schlechter Charakter, b) ein schlechter Kerl; *a strange* ~ ein eigenartiger Mensch; *quite a* ~ ein Original; **2.** Cha'rakter(stärke *f*) *m*, (ausgeprägte) Per'sönlichkeit: *a man of* ~; *a public* ~ e-e bekannte Persönlichkeit; ~ *actor thea.* Charakterdarsteller *m*; ~ *part thea.* Charakterrolle *f*; ~ *assassination* Rufmord *m*; ~ *building* Charakterbildung *f*; ~ *defect* Charakterfehler *m*; **3.** Cha'rakter *m*, Gepräge *n*, Eigenart *f*; Merkmal *n*, Kennzeichen *n*; **4.** Stellung *f*, Rang *m*, Eigenschaft *f*: *he came in the* ~ *of a friend* er kam (in s-r Eigenschaft) als Freund; **5.** Leumund *m*, Ruf *m*, Name *m*: *have a good* ~ in gutem Ruf stehen; ~ *witness* ♐ Leumundszeuge *m*; **6.** Zeugnis *n* (*für Personal*): *give s.o. a good* ~ a) j-m ein gutes Zeugnis geben, b) gut von j-m sprechen; **7.** *thea.* Per'son *f*, Rolle *f*: *in* ~ a) der Rolle gemäß, b) (zs.-)passend; *it is out of* ~ es passt nicht (dazu, zu ihm *etc.*); **8.** *Roman:* Fi'gur *f*, Gestalt *f*; **9.** Schriftzeichen *n* (*a. Computer*), Schrift *f*; Handschrift *f*: ~ *set* Computer, *typ.* Zeichensatz *m*.

char·ac·ter·is·tic [ˌkærəktəˈrɪstɪk] **I** *adj.* □ → *characteristically*; charakte'ristisch, bezeichnend, typisch (*of* für): ~ *curve* ⊛ Leistungskurve *f*; **II** *s.* charakte'ristisches Merkmal, Eigentümlichkeit *f*, Kennzeichen *n*, Eigenschaft *f*: (*performance*) ~ ⊛ (Leistungs)Angabe *f*, (-)Kennwert *m*; **char·ac·ter·is·ti·cal** [-kl] → *characteristic* **I**; **char·ac·ter·is·ti·cal·ly** [-kəlɪ] *adv.* bezeichnenderweise; **char·ac·ter·i·za·tion** [ˌkærəktəraɪˈzeɪʃn] *s.* Charakterisierung *f*, Kennzeichnung *f*; **char·ac·ter·ize** [ˈkærəktəraɪz] *v/t.* charakterisieren: a) beschreiben, b) kennzeichnen, charakte'ristisch sein für; **char·ac·ter·less** [ˈkærəktəlɪs] *adj.* nichts sagend.

cha·rade [ʃəˈrɑːd] *s.* **1.** Scha'rade *f* (*Ratespiel mit Verkleidungsszenen*); **2.** *fig.* Farce *f*.

'char·broil *v/t.* auf Holzkohle grillen.

char·coal [ˈtʃɑːkəʊl] *s.* **1.** Holzkohle *f*; **2.** (Zeichen)Kohle *f*, Kohlestift *m*; **3.** Kohlezeichnung *f*; ~ *burn·er s.* Köhler

m, Kohlenbrenner *m*; ~ **draw·ing** *s.* Kohlezeichnung *f*.

chard [tʃɑːd] *s.* ♠ Mangold(gemüse *n*) *m*.

charge [tʃɑːdʒ] **I** *v/t.* **1.** belasten, beladen, beschweren (*with* mit) (*mst fig.*); **2.** *Gewehr etc.* laden; *Batterie* aufladen: (*emotionally*) ~*d atmosphere fig.* geladene (*od.* angeheizte) Stimmung; **3.** (an)füllen; ⊛, ⚒ beschicken; ♞ sättigen; **4.** beauftragen, betrauen: ~ *s.o. with a task*; **5.** ermahnen: *I* ~*d him not to forget* ich schärfte ihm ein, es nicht zu vergessen; **6.** Weisungen geben (*dat.*); belehren: ~ *the jury* ♐ den Geschworenen Rechtsbelehrung geben; **7.** zur Last legen, vorwerfen, anlasten (*on dat.*): *he* ~*d the fault on me* er schrieb mir die Schuld zu; **8.** beschuldigen, anklagen (*with gen.*): ~ *s.o. with murder*; **9.** angreifen, *sport a.* ‚angehen', rempeln; anstürmen gegen: ~ *the enemy*; **10.** *Preis etc.* fordern, berechnen: *he* ~*d (me) a dollar for it* er berechnete (mir) e-n Dollar dafür; **11.** ♐ j-n mit *et.* belasten, j-m et. in Rechnung stellen: ~ *these goods to me* (*od. to my account*); **II** *v/i.* **12.** angreifen; stürmen: *the lion* ~*d at me* der Löwe fiel mich an; **13.** (e-n Preis) fordern, (Kosten) berechnen: ~ *too much* zu viel berechnen; *I shall not* ~ *for it* ich werde es nicht berechnen; **III** *s.* **14.** ⚔, ♐, *mot.* Ladung *f*; ⊛ (Spreng)Ladung *f*; Füllung *f*, Beschickung *f*; *metall.* Einsatz *m*; **15.** Belastung *f*, Forderung *f* (*beide a.* ♐), Last *f*, Bürde *f*; Anforderung *f*, Beanspruchung *f*: ~ (*on an estate*) (Grundstücks)Belastung; *real* ~ Grundschuld *f*; *be a* ~ *on s.o.* j-m zur Last fallen; *a first* ~ *on s.th.* e-e erste Forderung an et. (*acc.*); **16.** (*a. pl.*) Preis *m*, Kosten *pl.*, Spesen *pl.*, Unkosten *pl.*; Gebühr *f*: *no* ~, *free of* ~ kostenlos, gratis; ~*s forward* per Nachnahme; ~*s* (*to be*) *deducted* abzüglich der Unkosten; **17.** Aufgabe *f*, Amt *n*, Pflicht *f*, Verantwortung *f*; **18.** Aufsicht *f*, Obhut *f*, Pflege *f*, Sorge *f*; Verwahrung *f*; Verwaltung *f*: *person in* ~ verantwortliche Person, Verantwortliche(r), Leiter(in); *be in* ~ *of* verantwortlich sein für, die Aufsicht *od.* den Befehl führen über (*acc.*), leiten; *have* ~ *of* in Obhut *od.* Verwahrung haben, betreuen, versorgen; *put s.o. in* ~ *of* j-m die Leitung *od.* Aufsicht *etc.* übertragen (*gen.*); *take* ~ die Leitung *etc.* übernehmen, die Sache in die Hand nehmen; **19.** Gewahrsam *m*: *give s.o. in* ~ j-n der Polizei übergeben; *take s.o. in* ~ j-n festnehmen; **20.** ♐ Mündel *m*; Pflegebefohlene(r *m*) *f*, Schützling *m*; *a.* anvertraute Sache; **21.** Befehl *m*, Anweisung *f*, Mahnung *f*; ♐ Rechtsbelehrung *f*; **22.** Vorwurf *m*, Beschuldigung *f*; ♐ (Punkt *m* der) Anklage *f*: *on a* ~ *of murder* wegen Mord; *return to the* ~ *fig.* noch einmal ‚einhaken' (*Diskussion*); **23.** Angriff *m*, (An)Sturm *m*; **24.** *get a* ~ *out of Am. sl.* an e-r Sache mächtig Spaß haben.

charge·a·ble [ˈtʃɑːdʒəbl] *adj.* □ **1.** anzurechnen(d), zulasten gehen(d) (*to* von); zu berechnen(d) (*on dat.*); zu belasten(d) (*with* mit); *teleph.* gebührenpflichtig; **2.** zahlbar; **3.** strafbar.

charge| ac·count *s.* **1.** ('Kunden-) Kre‚ditkonto *n*; **2.** Abzahlungskonto *n*; ~ **card** *s.* Kunden(kredit)karte *f*.

char·gé (d'af·faires) [ˌʃɑːʒeɪ(dæˈfeə)] *pl.* **char·gés (d'af·faires)** [-ʒeɪdæˈfeəz] (*Fr.*) *s. pol.* Geschäftsträger *m*.

charge nurse s. ✚ Stati'ons-, Oberschwester f.

charg·er ['tʃɑːdʒə] s. **1.** ✕ Dienstpferd n (es Offiziers); **2.** poet. Schlachtross n; **3.** ⊕ Aufgeber m.

charge sheet s. Brit. **1.** polizeiliches Aktenblatt über den Beschuldigten u. die ihm zur Last gelegte Tat; **2.** ✕ Tatbericht m.

char·i·ness ['tʃeərɪnɪs] s. **1.** Behutsamkeit f; **2.** Sparsamkeit f.

char·i·ot ['tʃærɪət] s. antiq. zweirädriger Streit- od. Tri'umphwagen; **char·i·ot·eer** [ˌtʃærɪə'tɪə] s. poet. Wagen-, Rosselenker m.

cha·ris·ma [kə'rɪzmə] pl. **-ma·ta** [-mətə] s. eccl. 'Charisma n (a. fig. persönliche Ausstrahlung); **char·is·mat·ic** [ˌkærɪz'mætɪk] adj. charis'matisch.

char·i·ta·ble ['tʃærətəbl] adj. □ **1.** mild-, wohltätig, karita'tiv, Wohltätigkeits...; **2.** mild, nachsichtig; **'char·i·ta·ble·ness** [-nɪs] s. Wohltätigkeit f; Güte f, Milde f, Nachsicht f; **char·i·ty** ['tʃærətɪ] s. **1.** Nächstenliebe f; **2.** Wohltätigkeit f; Freigebigkeit f; ~ **performance** Wohltätigkeits-, Benefizveranstaltung f; ~ **stamp** Wohlfahrtsmarke f; ~ **begins at home** zuerst kommt die eigene Familie od. das eigene Land; → **cold** 3; **3.** Güte f; Milde f, Nachsicht f; **4.** Almosen n, milde Gabe; Wohltat f, gutes Werk; **5.** Wohlfahrtseinrichtung f.

cha·ri·va·ri [ˌʃɑːrɪ'vɑːrɪ] s. **1.** 'Katzenmu,sik f; **2.** Lärm m, Getöse n.

char·la·dy ['tʃɑːˌleɪdɪ] → **charwoman.**

char·la·tan ['ʃɑːlətən] s. 'Scharlatan m: a) Quacksalber m, Marktschreier m, b) Schwindler m; **'char·la·tan·ry** [-tənrɪ] s. Scharlatane'rie f.

Charles's Wain [ˌtʃɑːlzɪz'weɪn] s. ast. Großer Bär.

char·ley horse ['tʃɑːlɪ] s. Am. F Muskelkater m.

char·lock ['tʃɑːlɒk] s. ♣ Hederich m.

charm [tʃɑːm] I s. **1.** Anmut f, Charme m, (Lieb)Reiz m, Zauber m: (feminine) ~**s** weibliche Reize; ~ **of style** reizvoller Stil; **turn on the old** ~ s-n Charme spielen lassen; **2.** Zauber m, Bann m; Zauberformel f: **it worked like a** ~ fig. es klappte fantastisch; **3.** Amu'lett n, 'Talisman m; **II** v/t. **4.** bezaubern, reizen, entzücken: **be** ~**ed to meet s.o.** entzückt od. erfreut sein, j-n zu treffen; ~**ed with** entzückt von; **5.** be-, verzaubern: ~**ed against** gefeit gegen; ~ **away** wegzaubern; **III** v/i. **6.** bezaubern(d wirken), entzücken; **'charm·er** [-mə] s. **1.** fig. Zauberer m, Zauberin f; **2.** a) bezaubernder Mensch, Char'meur m, b) reizvolles Geschöpf, ,Circe'; **'charm·ing** [-mɪŋ] adj. □ char'mant; a. Sache: bezaubernd, entzückend, reizend.

char·nel house ['tʃɑːnl] s. Leichen-, Beinhaus n.

chart [tʃɑːt] I s. **1.** (bsd. See-, Himmels)Karte f: ~**room** ♣ Kartenhaus n; **2.** Ta'belle f. **3.** a) grafische Darstellung, z.B. (Farb)Skala f, (Fieber)Kurve f, (Wetter)Karte f, b) bsd. ⊕ Dia'gramm n, Schaubild n, Kurve(nblatt n) f; **II** v/t. **4.** auf e-r (See- etc.)Karte einzeichnen; **5.** grafisch darstellen, skizzieren; **6.** fig. planen, entwerfen.

char·ta ['tʃɑːtə] s. → **Magna C(h)arta.**

char·ter ['tʃɑːtə] I s. **1.** Urkunde f; Freibrief m; Privi'leg n; **2.** a) Gründungsurkunde f, b) Am. Satzung f (e-r AG etc.), c) Konzessi'on f; **3.** pol. Charta f; **4.** ♣, ✈ a) Chartern n, b) → **charter**

---

party; **II** v/t. **5.** Bank etc. konzessionieren: ~**ed company** zugelassene Gesellschaft; → **accountant** 2; **6.** chartern: a) ♣, ✈ mieten, b) befrachten; **'charter·er** [-ərə] s. ♣ Befrachter m.

char·ter flight s. Charterflug m; ~ **party** s. 'Charterpar,tie f, Miet-, Frachtvertrag m; ~ **plane** s. Charterflugzeug n.

char·wom·an ['tʃɑːˌwumən] s. [irr.] Reinemach-, Putzfrau f, Raumpflegerin f.

char·y ['tʃeərɪ] adj. □ **1.** vorsichtig, behutsam (in, of in dat., bei); **2.** sparsam, zu'rückhaltend (of mit).

chase¹ [tʃeɪs] I v/t. **1.** jagen, nachjagen (dat.), verfolgen; **2.** hunt. hetzen, jagen; **3.** fig. verjagen, vertreiben; **II** v/i. **4.** nachjagen (after dat.); F sausen, rasen; **III** s. **5.** Verfolgung f: **give** ~ die Verfolgung aufnehmen; **give** ~ **to** → 1; **6.** hunt. **the** ~ die Jagd; **7.** Brit. 'Jagdre,vier n; **8.** gejagtes Wild (a. fig.) od. Schiff etc.

chase² [tʃeɪs] I s. **1.** typ. Formrahmen m; **2.** Rinne f, Furche f; **II** v/t. **3.** ziselieren, ausmeißeln, punzen: ~**d work** getriebene Arbeit; **4.** ⊕ Gewinde strehlen, schneiden.

chas·er¹ ['tʃeɪsə] s. **1.** Jäger m; Verfolger m; **2.** ♣ a) 'Verfolgungsschiff n, (bsd. U-Boot-)Jäger m, b) Jagdgeschütz n; **3.** ✈ Jagdflugzeug n; **4.** F ,Schluck m zum Nachspülen'; **5.** sl. a) Schürzenjäger m, b) mannstolles Weib.

chas·er² ['tʃeɪsə] s. ⊕ **1.** Zise'leur m; **2.** Gewindestahl m; Treibpunzen m.

chasm ['kæzəm] s. **1.** Kluft f, Abgrund m (beide a. fig.) **2.** Schlucht f; **3.** Riss m, Spalte f; **4.** Lücke f.

chas·sis ['ʃæsɪ] pl. **'chas·sis** [-sɪz] s. **1.** Chas'sis n: a) ✈, mot. Fahrgestell n, b) Radio: Grundplatte f; **2.** ✕ La'fette f.

chaste [tʃeɪst] adj. □ **1.** keusch (a. fig. schamhaft; anständig, tugendhaft); rein, unschuldig; **2.** rein, von edler Schlichtheit: ~ **style.**

chas·ten ['tʃeɪsn] v/t. **1.** züchtigen, strafen; **2.** läutern; **3.** mäßigen, dämpfen; ernüchtern.

chas·tise [tʃæ'staɪz] v/t. **1.** züchtigen, strafen; **2.** geißeln, tadeln; **chas·tise·ment** ['tʃæstɪzmənt] s. Züchtigung f, Strafe f.

chas·ti·ty ['tʃæstətɪ] s. **1.** Keuschheit f: ~ **belt** Keuschheitsgürtel m; **2.** Reinheit f; **3.** Schlichtheit f.

chas·u·ble ['tʃæzjubl] s. eccl. Messgewand n.

chat [tʃæt] I v/i. plaudern, schwatzen, Internet: chatten; **II** v/t. ~ **s.o.** (**up**) F a) auf j-n einreden, b) j-n ,anquatschen'; **III** s. Plaude'rei f, Internet: Chat m: ~ **show** Brit. Talkshow f; **have a** ~ → I.

chat·e·laine ['ʃætəleɪn] s. **1.** Schlossherrin f; **2.** Kastel'lanin f; **3.** (Gürtel)Kette f (für Schlüssel etc.).

chat·tel ['tʃætl] s. **1.** mst pl. bewegliches Eigentum, Habe f: ~ **mortgage** Mobiliarhypothek f; ~ **paper** Am. Verkehrspapier n; → **good** 18; **2.** mst ~ **slave** Leibeigene(r) m.

chat·ter ['tʃætə] I v/i. **1.** plappern, schwatzen; **2.** schnattern; **3.** klappern (a. Zähne), rattern; **II** s. **5.** Geplapper n, Geschnatter n; Klappern n; **'chat·ter·box** s. Plappermaul n; **'chat·ter·er** [-ərə] s. Schwätzer(in).

chat·ty ['tʃætɪ] adj. **1.** gesprächig; **2.** unter'haltsam (Person, Brief), im Plauderton (geschrieben etc.).

chauf·feur ['ʃəufə] (Fr.) s. Chauf'feur m, Fahrer m; **chauf·feuse** [ʃəu'fɜːz] s. Fahrerin f.

---

chau·vie ['ʃəuvɪ] s. F ,Chauvie' m (→ **chauvinist** 2).

chau·vin·ism ['ʃəuvɪnɪzəm] s. Chauvi'nismus m; **'chau·vin·ist** [-ɪst] s. **1.** Chauvi'nist m; **2.** male ~ sociol. männlicher Chauvinist; **chau·vin·is·tic** [ˌʃəuvɪ'nɪstɪk] adj. (□ ~**ally**) chauvi'nistisch.

cheap [tʃiːp] I adj. □ **1.** billig, preiswert: **get off** ~ mit e-m blauen Auge davonkommen; **hold** ~ wenig halten von; ~ **as dirt** spottbillig; **2.** billig, minderwertig; schlecht, kitschig: ~ **and nasty** billig u. schlecht; **3.** verbilligt, ermäßigt: ~ **fare**; ~ **money** billiges Geld; **4.** fig. billig, mühelos; **5.** fig. ,billig', schäbig: **feel** ~ a) sich ,billig' od. ärmlich vorkommen, b) sl. sich elend fühlen; **II** adv. **6.** billig; **III** s. **7. on the** ~ F billig; **'cheap·en** [-pən] v/t. (v/i. sich) verbilligen; her'absetzen (a. fig.): ~ **o.s.** sich herabwürdigen; **'cheap·jack** I s. billiger Jakob; **II** adj. Ramsch...; **'cheap·ness** [-nɪs] s. Billigkeit f (a. fig.); **'cheap·skate** s. Am. sl. ,Knicker' m, Geizhals m.

cheat [tʃiːt] I s. **1.** Betrüger(in), Schwindler(in); ,Mogler(in)'; **2.** Betrug m, Schwindel m; Moge'lei f; **II** v/t. **3.** betrügen (of, out of um); **4.** durch List bewegen (into zu); **5.** sich entziehen (dat.), ein Schnippchen schlagen (dat.): ~ **justice**; **III** v/i. **6.** betrügen, schwindeln, mogeln.

check [tʃek] I s. **1.** Schach(stellung f) n: **in** ~ im Schach (stehend); **give** ~ Schach bieten; **hold** (od. **keep**) **in** ~ fig. in Schach halten; **2.** Hemmnis n, Hindernis n (on für): **put a** ~ **upon s.o.** j-m e-n Dämpfer aufsetzen, j-n zurückhalten; **3.** Unter'brechung f, Rückschlag m: **give a** ~ **to** Einhalt gebieten (dat.); **4.** Kon'trolle f, Über'prüfung f, Nachprüfung f, Über'wachung f: **keep a** ~ **upon s.th.** etwas unter Kontrolle halten; **5.** Kon'trollzeichen n, bsd. Häkchen n (auf Listen etc.); **6.** ✝ Am. Scheck m (for über acc.); **7.** bsd. Am. Kassenschein m, -zettel m, Rechnung f (im Kaufhaus od. Restaurant); **8.** Kon'trollabschnitt m, -marke f, -schein m; **9.** bsd. Am. Aufbewahrungsschein m: a) Garde'robenmarke f, b) Gepäckschein m; **10.** (Essens- etc.)Bon m, Gutschein m; **11.** a) Schachbrett-, Würfel-, Karomuster n, b) Karo n, Viereck n, c) karierter Stoff; **12.** Spielmarke f: **to pass** (od. **hand**) **in one's** ~**s** Am. F ,abkratzen' (sterben); **13.** Eishockey: Check m; **II** v/t. **14.** Schach bieten (dat.): ~ **!** Schach!; **15.** hemmen, hindern, aufhalten, eindämmen; **16.** ⊕, a. fig. ✝ etc. drosseln, bremsen; **17.** zu'rückhalten, bremsen, zügeln, dämpfen: ~ **o.s.** (plötzlich) innehalten, sich e-s anderen besinnen; **18.** Eishockey: Gegner checken; **19.** kontrollieren, über'prüfen, nachprüfen, ,checken' (for auf e-e Sache hin): ~ **against** vergleichen mit; **20.** Am. (auf e-r Liste etc.) abhaken, ankreuzen; **21.** bsd. Am. a) (zur Aufbewahrung od. in der Garde'robe) abgeben, b) (als Reisegepäck) aufgeben; **22.** bsd. Am. a) (zur Aufbewahrung) annehmen, b) zur Beförderung (als Reisegepäck) über'nehmen od. annehmen; **23.** karieren, mit e-m Karomuster versehen; **III** v/i. **24.** a) stimmen, b) (**with**) über'einstimmen (mit); **25.** oft ~ **up** (**on**) nachprüfen, (e-e Sache od. j-n) über'prüfen: ~**!** Am. F klar!; **26.** Am. e-n Scheck ausstellen

C

(*for* über *acc.*); **27.** (plötzlich) inne- *od.* anhalten, stutzen. *Zssgn mit adv.*:

check| back *v/i.* rückfragen (**with** bei); **~ in I** *v/i.* **1.** sich anmelden; **2.** ✈ einstempeln; **3.** ✔ einchecken; **II** *v/t.* **4.** anmelden; **5.** ✔ einchecken, abfertigen; **~ off** → *check* 20; **~ out I** *v/t.* **1.** → *check* 19; **II** *v/i.* **2.** (*aus e-m Hotel*) abreisen; **3.** ✈ ausstempeln; **4.** *Am. sl.* ‚abkratzen‘; **~ o·ver** → *check* 19; **~ up** → *check* 25.

'check|·back *s.* Rückfrage *f*; **~ bit** *s.* Computer: Kon'trollbit *n*; **'~·book** → *chequebook*; **'~·card** *s. Am.* Scheckkarte *f*; **~ clock** *s.* Stechuhr *f*.

checked [tʃekt] *adj.* kariert; **~ pattern** Karomuster *n*.

check·er ['tʃekə] *etc. Am.* → *chequer etc.*

'check·in *s.* **1.** Anmeldung *f* in e-m Hotel; **2.** ✈ Einstempeln *n*; **3.** ✔ Einchecken *n*: **~ counter** Abfertigungsschalter *m*; **~ desk** ✔ Abflug-, Abfertigungsschalter *m*; **~ time** Eincheckzeit *f*.

check·ing ac·count ['tʃekɪŋ] *s. econ. Am.* Girokonto *n*.

check| list *s.* Kon'trolliste *f*; **~ lock** *s.* kleines Sicherheitsschloss; **'~·mate I** *s.* **1.** (Schach)'Matt *n*, Mattstellung *f*; **2.** *fig.* Niederlage *f*; **II** *v/t.* **3.** (schach)'matt setzen (*a. fig.*); **III** *int.* **4.** schach'matt!; **~ nut** *s.* ⚙ Gegenmutter *f*; **'~·out** *s.* **1.** Abreise *f aus e-m Hotel*; **2.** ✈ Ausstempeln *n*; **3.** *a.* **~ counter** Kasse *f im Kaufhaus*; **'~·out test** *s.* ✔ Tauglichkeitstest *m für ein Produkt*; **'~·o·ver** → *checkup* 1; **'~·point** *s. pol.* Kon'trollpunkt *m* (*an der Grenze*); **'~·room** *s. Am.* **1.** ⚓ Gepäckaufbewahrung(sstelle) *f*; **2.** Garde'robe(nraum *m*) *f*; **'~·up** *s.* **1.** Über'prüfung *f*, Kon'trolle *f*; **2.** ✘ 'Vorsorgeunter‚suchung *f*, Check-up *m*; **~ valve** *s.* ⚙ 'Absperr- *od.* 'Rückschlagven‚til *n*.

Ched·dar (**cheese**) ['tʃedə] *s.* 'Cheddarkäse *m*.

cheek [tʃiːk] **I** *s.* **1.** Backe *f*, Wange *f*: **~ by jowl** dicht *od.* vertraulich beisammen; **2.** ⚙ Backe *f*; **3.** F Frechheit *f*, Unverfrorenheit *f*: **have the ~** die Frechheit *od.* Stirn besitzen (**to** *inf.* zu *inf.*); **II** *v/t.* **4.** frech sein zu; **'cheekbone** *s.* Backenknochen *m*; **cheeked** [-kt] *adj.* ...wangig, ...bäckig; **'cheek·i·ness** [-kɪnɪs] *s.* F Frechheit *f*; **'cheek·y** [-kɪ] *adj.* □ frech.

cheep [tʃiːp] **I** *v/i. u. v/t.* piep(s)en; **II** *s.* Pieps(er) *m* (*a. fig.*).

cheer [tʃɪə] **I** *s.* **1.** Beifall(sruf) *m*, Hur'ra(ruf *m*) *n*, Hoch(ruf *m*) *n*: **three ~s for him!** ein dreifaches Hoch auf ihn!, er lebe hoch, hoch, hoch!; **to the ~s of** unter dem Beifall *etc.* (*gen.*); **2.** Ermunterung *f*, Trost *m*: **words of ~** aufmunternde Worte; **3.** a) gute Laune, vergnügte Stimmung, Fröhlichkeit *f*, b) Stimmung *f*: **good ~** → a); **be of good ~** guter Laune *od.* Dinge sein, vergnügt sein; **be of good ~!** sei guten Mutes!; **make good ~** sich amüsieren, *a.* gut essen u. trinken; **II** *v/t.* **4.** Beifall spenden (*dat.*), zujubeln (*dat.*), mit Hoch- *od.* Bravorufen begrüßen, hochleben lassen; **5.** *a.* **~ on** anspornen, anfeuern; **6.** *a.* **~ up** *j-n* er-, aufmuntern, aufheitern; **III** *v/i.* **7.** Beifall spenden, hoch *od.* hur'ra rufen, jubeln; **8.** *meist* **~ up** Mut fassen, (wieder) fröhlich werden: **~ up!** Kopf hoch!; → *cheers.*

cheer·ful ['tʃɪəfʊl] *adj.* □ **1.** heiter, fröhlich; (*iro.* quietsch)vergnügt; **2.** erfreulich, freundlich; **3.** freudig, gern;

'cheer·ful·ness [-nɪs], **cheer·i·ness** ['tʃɪərɪnɪs] *s.* Heiterkeit *f*, Frohsinn *m*; **cheer·i·o** [‚tʃɪərɪ'əʊ] *int.* F *bsd. Brit.* a) machs gut!, tschüs!, b) 'prosit!; **'cheer‚lead·er** *s. sport Am.* Einpeitscher *m* (*beim Anfeuern*); **cheer·less** ['tʃɪəlɪs] *adj.* □ freudlos, trüb, trostlos; unfreundlich (*Zimmer, Wetter etc.*); **cheers** [tʃɪəz] *pl.*, *int. Brit.* **1.** prost!, 'prosit!; **2.** F tschüs(s)!; **3.** F danke; **cheer·y** ['tʃɪərɪ] *adj.* □ fröhlich, heiter, vergnügt.

cheese [tʃiːz] **I** *s.* **1.** Käse *m*; → *chalk* 2; **2.** käseartige Masse; Ge'lee *n*, *m*; **3.** **big ~** *sl.* ‚hohes Tier‘; **4.** *sl.* das Richtige *od.* einzig Wahre: **that's the ~!** so ists richtig!; **hard ~!** schöne Pleite!; **II** *v/t.* **5.** *sl.*: **~ it!** ‚hau ab‘!; **'~·cake** *s.* **1.** Käsekuchen *m*, -törtchen *n*; **2.** *Am.* Pin-up-Girl *n*, Sexbombe *f* (*Bild*); **'~·cloth** *s.* Mull *m*, Gaze *f*; **'~‚mon·ger** *s.* Käsehändler *m*; **'~‚par·ing I** *s.* **1.** wertlose Sache; **2.** Knause'rei *f*; **II** *adj.* **3.** knauserig; **~ straws** *s. pl.* Käsestangen *pl.*

chee·tah ['tʃiːtə] *s. zo.* 'Gepard *m*.

chef [ʃef] (*Fr.*) *s.* Küchenchef *m*.

chem·i·cal ['kemɪkl] **I** *adj.* □ chemisch, Chemie...: **~ agent** ✘ Kampfstoff *m*; **~ engineer** Chemotechniker *m*; **~ fibre** Chemie-, Kunstfaser *f*; **~ warfare** chemische Kriegführung; **II** *s.* Chemi'kalie, chemisches Präpa'rat.

che·mise [ʃɪ'miːz] *s.* **1.** (Damen)Hemd *n*; **2.** *a.* **~ dress** Hängekleid *n*.

chem·ist ['kemɪst] *s.* **1.** *a.* **analytical ~** Chemiker *m*; **2.** *Brit. a.* **dispensing ~** Apo'theker *m*: **~'s shop** *Brit.* Apotheke *f*, Drogerie *f*; **'chem·is·try** [-trɪ] *s.* **1.** Che'mie *f*; **2.** chemische Zs.-setzung; **3.** *fig.* Na'tur *f*, Wirken *n*.

chem·o·ther·a·py [‚kiːməʊ'θerəpɪ] *s.* ✘ 'Chemothera‚pie *f*.

cheque [tʃek] *s.* ✈ *Brit.* Scheck *m* (*for* über *e-e Summe*): **blank ~** Blankoscheck, *fig.* unbeschränkte Vollmacht; **crossed ~** Verrechnungsscheck; **write out** (*od. cash*) **a ~** e-n Scheck ausstellen (*od.* einlösen); **~ account** *s.* ✈ *Brit.* 'Giro‚konto *n*; **'~·book** *s. Brit.* Scheckbuch *n*; **~ card** *s.* Scheckkarte *f*; **~ fraud** *s.* Scheckbetrug *m*.

cheq·uer ['tʃekə] *Brit.* **I** *s.* **1.** Schach-, Karomuster *n*; **2.** *pl. sg. konstr.* Damespiel *n*; **II** *v/t.* **3.** karieren; **4.** bunt *od.* unregelmäßig gestalten; **'cheq·uer·board** *s. Brit.* Damebrett *n*; **'cheq·uered** [-əd] *adj. Brit.* kariert; *fig.* bunt; wechselvoll, bewegt.

cher·ish ['tʃerɪʃ] *v/t.* **1.** schätzen, hochhalten; **2.** sorgen für, pflegen; **3.** Gefühle *etc.* hegen; bewahren; **4.** *fig.* festhalten an (*dat.*).

che·root [ʃə'ruːt] *s.* Stumpen *m* (*Zigarre*).

cher·ry ['tʃerɪ] **I** *s.* **1.** ♀ Kirsche *f* (*Frucht od. Baum*); **2.** *sl.* a) Jungfräulichkeit *f*, b) Jungfernhäutchen *n*; **II** *adj.* **3.** kirschrot; **~ bran·dy** *s.* Cherry Brandy *m*, 'Kirschli‚kör *m*; **~ pie** *s.* **1.** Kirschtorte *f*; **2.** ♀ Helio'trop *n*; **~ stone** *s.* Kirschkern *m*; **~ to·ma·to** *s.* 'Cocktailto‚mate *f*, 'Cherryto‚mate *f*; **'~·wood** *s.* Kirschbaumholz *n*.

chert [tʃɜːt] *s.* **1.** *min.* Kieselschiefer *m*, Feuerstein *m*, Hornstein *m*; **2.** *Bauwesen*: Gneiszuschlag(stoff) *m*, 'Feingranit‚zuschlag *m* (*für Sichtbeton*).

cher·ub ['tʃerəb] *pl.* **-ubs**, **-u·bim** [-əbɪm] *s.* **1.** *bibl.* 'Cherub *m*, Engel *m*; **2.** geflügelter Engelskopf; **3.** a) pausbäckiges Kind, b) *fig.* Engel(chen *n*) *n* (*Kind*).

cher·vil ['tʃɜːvɪl] *s.* ♀ Kerbel *m*.

Chesh·ire cat ['tʃeʃə] *s.*: **grin like a ~** grinsen wie ein Affe; **~ cheese** *s.* 'Chesterkäse *m*.

chess [tʃes] *s.* Schach(spiel) *n*: **a game of ~** e-e Partie Schach; **'~·board** *s.* Schachbrett *n*; **'~·man** [-mæn] *s.* [*irr.*] 'Schachfi‚gur *f*; **~ prob·lem** *s.* Schachaufgabe *f*.

chest [tʃest] *s.* **1.** Kiste *f*, Kasten *m*, Truhe *f*: **~ of drawers** Kommode *f*; **2.** kastenartiger Behälter; **3.** Brust(kasten *m*) *f*: **have a weak ~** schwach auf der Brust sein; **~ expander** Expander *m*; **~ note** Brustton *m*; **~ trouble** Lungenleiden; **beat one's ~** *fig.* sich reuig an die Brust schlagen; **get s.th. off one's ~** F sich *et.* von der Seele schaffen; **play** (**one's cards**) **close to one's** *a. fig.* sich nicht in die Karten gucken lassen; **4.** Kasse *f*, Kassenverwaltung *f*; **'chest·ed** [-tɪd] *adj. in Zssgn* ...brüstig.

ches·ter·field ['tʃestəfiːld] *s.* **1.** Chesterfield *m* (*Herrenmantel*); **2.** 'Polster‚sofa *n*.

chest·nut ['tʃesnʌt] **I** *s.* **1.** ♀ Ka'stanie *f* (*Frucht, Baum od. Holz*); **2.** Braune(r) *m* (*Pferd*); **3.** alter Witz, ‚alte Ka'melle‘; **II** *adj.* **4.** ka'stanienbraun.

chest·y ['tʃestɪ] *adj.* **1.** F tief (sitzend) (*Husten*); **2.** F dickbusig; **3.** *sl.* eingebildet, arro'gant.

chev·a·lier [‚ʃevə'lɪə] *s.* **1.** (Ordens)Ritter *m*; **2.** *fig.* Kava'lier *m*.

chev·ron ['ʃevrən] *s.* **1.** *her.* Sparren *m*; **2.** ✘ Winkel *m* (*Rangabzeichen*); **3.** △ Zickzackleiste *f*.

chev·y ['tʃevɪ] → *chiv(v)y*.

chew [tʃuː] **I** *v/t.* **1.** kauen: **~ the rag** *od.* **fat** a) ‚quatschen‘, plaudern, b) ‚meckern‘; **~ cud** **2.** *fig.* sinnen auf (*acc.*), über'legen, brüten; **3.** *a.* **~ over** F *et.* besprechen; **4.** **~ up** *Am. sl.* *j-n* ‚anscheißen‘; **II** *v/i.* **5.** kauen; **6.** F 'Tabak kauen; **7.** nachsinnen, grübeln (**on, over** über *acc.*); **III** *s.* **8.** Kauen *n*; **9.** Priem *m*; **'chew·ing·gum** ['tʃuːɪŋ-] *s.* 'Kau‚gummi *m*.

chi·a·ro·scu·ro [kɪ‚ɑːrəs'kʊərəʊ] *pl.* **-ros** (*Ital*) *s. paint.* Helldunkel *n*.

chic [ʃiːk] **I** *s.* Schick *m*, Ele'ganz *f*, Geschmack *m*; **II** *adj.* schick, ele'gant.

chi·cane [ʃɪ'keɪn] **I** *s.* **1.** Schi'kane *f* (*a. Motorsport*); **2.** Bridge: Blatt *n* ohne Trümpfe; **II** *v/t. u. v/i.* **3.** schikanieren; **4.** betrügen (**out of** um); **chi·can·er·y** [-nərɪ] *s.* Schi'kane *f*, (*bsd. Rechts-*) Kniff *m*.

chi·chi ['ʃiːʃiː] *adj.* F **1.** (tod)schick; **2.** *contp.* auf schick gemacht.

chick [tʃɪk] *s.* **1.** Küken *n* (*a. fig. Kind*); junger Vogel; **2.** *sl.* ‚Biene‘, ‚Puppe‘ *f*.

chick·en ['tʃɪkɪn] **I** *s.* **1.** Küken *n*; Hühnchen *n*, Hähnchen *n*: **count one's ~s before they are hatched** das Fell des Bären verkaufen, ehe man ihn hat; **2.** Huhn *n*; **3.** Hühnerfleisch *n*; **4.** F ‚Küken‘ *n*: **she is no ~** sie ist auch nicht mehr die Jüngste; **5.** *sl.* Mutprobespiel *n*; **6.** **give s.o. ~** ✘ *sl.* ‚mit j-m Schlitten fahren‘; **II** *adj.* **7.** *sl.* feig(e); **III** *v/i.* **8.** *sl.* ‚Schiss‘ bekommen: **~ out** ‚kneifen‘; **'~‚breast·ed** *adj.* hühnerbrüstig; **~ broth** *s.* Hühnerbrühe *f*; **'~ feed** *s.* **1.** Hühnerfutter *n*; **2.** *sl.* ‚ein paar Groschen‘, lächerliche Summe: **no ~** kein Pappenstiel; **'~‚heart·ed**, **'~‚liv·ered** *adj.* feig(e); **~ pox** *s.* ✘ Windpocken *pl.*; **~ run** *s.* Hühnerauslauf *m*.

'chick·pea *s.* ♀ Kichererbse *f*.

chic·le ['tʃɪkl] *a.* **~ gum** *s.* (Rohstoff *m* von) 'Kau‚gummi *m*.

chic·o·ry ['tʃɪkərɪ] s. ♥ **1.** Zi'chorie f; **2.** Chicorée m, f.

chid [tʃɪd] pret. u. p.p. von **chide**; **chid·den** [-dn] p.p. von **chide**; **chide** [tʃaɪd] v/t. u. v/i. [irr.] schelten, tadeln, (aus-) schimpfen.

chief [tʃiːf] **I** s. **1.** Haupt n, Oberhaupt n, Anführer m; Chef m, Vorgesetzte(r) m; Leiter m: ⚳ **of Staff** ✕ (General-) Stabschef m; ⚳ **of State** Staatschef m, -oberhaupt n; **in ~** hauptsächlich; **2.** Häuptling m; **3.** her. Schildhaupt n; **II** adj. □ → **chiefly**; **4.** erst, oberst, höchst; bedeutendst, Ober..., Höchst..., Haupt...: **~ designer** Chefkonstrukteur m; **~ mourner** Hauptleidtragende(r m) f; **~ part** Hauptrolle f; **~ clerk** s. **1.** Bü'rovorsteher m; erster Buchhalter; **2.** Am. erster Verkäufer; ⚳ **Con·sta·ble** s. Poli'zeipräsi,dent m; **~ en·gi·neer** s. **1.** 'Chefingeni,eur m; **2.** ⚓ erster Ma·schi'nist; ⚳ **Ex·ec·u·tive** s. Am. Leiter m der Verwaltung, bsd. Präsi'dent m der U.S.A.; ⚳ **Jus·tice** s. Oberrichter m.

chief·ly ['tʃiːflɪ] adv. hauptsächlich.

chief·tain ['tʃiːftən] s. Häuptling m (Stamm); Anführer m (Bande); **'chief·tain·cy** [-sɪ] s. Stellung f e-s Häuptlings.

chif·fon ['ʃɪfɒn] Chif'fon m.

chil·blain ['tʃɪlbleɪn] s. Frostbeule f.

child [tʃaɪld] pl. **chil·dren** ['tʃɪldrən] s. **1.** Kind n: **with ~** schwanger; **from a ~** von Kindheit an; **be a good ~!** sei artig!; **~'s play** fig. ein Kinderspiel (**to** für); **2.** fig. Kind n, kindische od. kindliche Per'son; **3.** Kind n, Nachkomme m: **the children of Israel**; **4.** fig. Kind n, Pro'dukt n; **5.** Jünger m; **~ a·buse** s. **1.** Kindesmisshandlung f; **2.** sexueller Kindesmissbrauch; **~ al·low·ance** s. Kinderfreibetrag m; **'~,bear·ing** s. Gebären n; **'~-bed** s. Kind-, Wochenbett n; **~ ben·e·fit** s. Brit. Kindergeld n; **'~-birth** s. Geburt f, Entbindung f, Niederkunft f; **~ care** s. Jugendfürsorge f, **~ guidance** s. 'heilpäda,gogische Betreuung (des Kindes).

child·hood ['tʃaɪldhʊd] s. Kindheit f: **second ~** zweite Kindheit (Senilität); **'child·ish** [-dɪʃ] adj. □ **1.** kindisch; **2.** kindlich; **'child·ish·ness** [-dɪʃnɪs] s. **1.** Kindlichkeit f; **2.** kindisches Wesen; **'child·less** [-lɪs] adj. kinderlos; **'child·like** adj. kindlich; **child mind·er** s. Tagesmutter f; **child prod·i·gy** s. Wunderkind n; **'child·proof** [-pruːf] adj. kindersicher.

chil·dren ['tʃɪldrən] pl. von **child**: **~'s allowance** Kindergeld n; **~'s channel** TV 'Kinderka,nal m; **~'s hour** Radio, TV: Kinderstunde f.

child seat s. mot. Kindersitz m; **child's seat** s. allg. Kindersitz m.

child| wel·fare s. Jugendfürsorge f: **~ worker** Jugendfürsorger(in), Jugendpfleger(in); **~ wife** s. Kindweib n, sehr junge Ehefrau.

chil·e → **chilli**.

Chil·e·an ['tʃɪlɪən] **I** s. Chi'lene m, Chi'lenin f; **II** adj. chi'lenisch.

Chil·e| pine ['tʃɪlɪ] s. ♥ Chiletanne f, Arau'karie f; **~ salt·pe·tre**, Am. **salt·pe·ter** s. ♔ 'Chilesal,peter m.

chil·i Am. → **chilli**.

chil·i·asm ['kɪlɪæzəm] s. Religion: Chili'asmus m.

chill [tʃɪl] **I** s. **1.** Kältegefühl n, Frösteln n; (a. Fieber)Schauer m: **~ of fear** eisiges Gefühl der Angst; **2.** Kälte f: **take the ~ off** leicht anwärmen, überschlagen lassen; **3.** Erkältung f: **catch a ~** sich erkälten; **4.** fig. Kälte f, Lieblosig-

keit f, Entmutigung f: **cast a ~ upon** → 9; **5.** ⚙ Ko'kille f, Gussform f; **II** adj. **6.** kalt, frostig, kühl (a. fig.); entmutigend; **III** v/i. **7.** abkühlen; **IV** v/t. **8.** (ab)kühlen; erstarren lassen; **~ed meat** Kühlfleisch n; **9.** fig. abkühlen, dämpfen, entmutigen; **10.** ⚙ abschrecken, härten; **~ed (cast) iron** Hartguss m; **chil·ler** ['tʃɪlə] s. Film: Gruselschocker m.

chil·li ['tʃɪlɪ] s. ♥ Chili m.

chill·i·ness ['tʃɪlɪnɪs] s. Kälte f, Frostigkeit f (beide a. fig.); **chill·ing** ['tʃɪlɪŋ] adj. kalt, frostig; fig. niederdrückend; **chill·y** ['tʃɪlɪ] adj. a) kalt, frostig, kühl (alle a. fig.), b) fröstelnd: **feel ~** frösteln.

Chil·tern Hun·dreds ['tʃɪltən] s. Brit. parl.: **apply for the ~** s-n Sitz im Unterhaus aufgeben.

chi·mae·ra [kaɪ'mɪərə] s. **1.** zo. a) Chi'märe f, Seehase m, b) Seedrachen m; **2.** → **chimera**.

chime [tʃaɪm] **I** s. **1.** oft pl. Glockenspiel n, Geläut(e) n; **2.** fig. Einklang m, Harmo'nie f; **II** v/i. **3.** läuten; ertönen; schlagen (Uhr); **4.** fig. über'einstimmen, harmonieren: **~ in** einfallen, -stimmen, weitS. sich (ins Gespräch) einmischen; **~ in with** a) beipflichten (dat.), b) übereinstimmen mit; **III** v/t. **5.** läuten, ertönen lassen; **die Stunde** schlagen.

chi·me·ra [kaɪ'mɪərə] s. **1.** myth. Chi'mära f; **2.** Schi'märe f: a) Schreckgespenst n, b) Hirngespinst n; **chi'mer·i·cal** [-'merɪkl] adj. □ schi'märisch, fan'tastisch.

chim·ney ['tʃɪmnɪ] s. **1.** Schornstein m, Schlot m, Ka'min m; Rauchfang m: **smoke like a ~** F rauchen wie ein Schlot; **2.** (Lampen)Zy'linder m; **3.** a) geol. Vul'kanschlot m, b) mount. Ka'min m; **~ cor·ner** s. Sitzecke f am Ka'min; **~ piece** s. Ka'minsims m, n; **~ pot** s. Schornsteinaufsatz m: **~ hat** F ,Angströhre' f (Zylinderhut); **~ stack** s. Schornstein(kasten) m; **~ sweep (-er)** s. Schornsteinfeger m.

chimp [tʃɪmp] s. F, **chim·pan·zee** [,tʃɪmpən'ziː] s. zo. Schim'panse m.

chin [tʃɪn] **I** s. Kinn n: **up to the ~** fig. bis über die Ohren; **take it on the ~** fig. a) schwer einstecken müssen, b) e-e böse ,Pleite' erleben, c) es standhaft ertragen; **(keep your) ~ up!** halt die Ohren steif!; **II** v/i. sl. ,quasseln'; **III** v/t. **~ o.s. (up)** Am. e-n Klimmzug od. Klimmzüge machen.

chi·na ['tʃaɪnə] **I** s. **1.** Porzel'lan n; **2.** (Porzel'lan)Geschirr n; **II** adj. **3.** Porzellan...; ⚳ **bark** s. ♥ Chinarinde f; **~ clay** s. min. Kao'lin n, Porzel'lanerde f; **'⚳-man** [-mən] s. [irr.] Chi'nese m; **'⚳-tea** s. chi'nesischer Tee; **'⚳-town** s. Chi'nesenviertel n; **'~-ware** s. Porzel'lan(waren n) n.

chinch [tʃɪntʃ] s. Am. Wanze f.

chin-chin [,tʃɪn'tʃɪn] int. (Pidgin-English) **1.** a) (guten) Tag!, b) tschüss!; **2.** 'prosit!, prost!

chine [tʃaɪn] s. **1.** Rückgrat n, Kreuz n (Tier); **2.** Küche: Kammstück n; **3.** (Berg)Grat m, Kamm m.

Chi·nese [,tʃaɪ'niːz] **I** adj. **1.** chi'nesisch; **II** s. Chi'nese m, Chi'nesin f, Chi'nesen pl.; **3.** ling. Chi'nesisch n; **~ cabbage** s. ♥ Chinakohl m; **~ lan·tern s. 1.** Lampi'on m, n; **2.** ♥ Lampi'onpflanze f; **~ puz·zle** s. Ve'xier-, Geduldspiel n; **2.** fig. schwierige Sache.

Chink¹ [tʃɪŋk] s. sl. Chi'nese m.

chink² [tʃɪŋk] s. **1.** Riss m, Ritz m, Ritze f, Spalt m, Spalte f: **the ~ in his ar-**

mo(u)r fig. sein schwacher Punkt; **2.** **~ of light** dünner Lichtstrahl.

chink³ [tʃɪŋk] **I** v/i. u. v/t. klingen od. klirren (lassen), klimpern (mit) (Geld etc.); **II** s. Klirren n, Klang m.

chin strap s. Kinnriemen m.

chintz [tʃɪnts] s. Chintz m, bunt bedruckter 'Möbelkat,tun; **'chintz·y** [-sɪ] adj. **1.** Plüsch...; **2.** fig. kleinbürgerlich, spießig.

'chin·wag I s. **1.** Plausch m; **2.** Tratsch m; **II** v/i. **3.** plauschen; **2.** tratschen.

chip [tʃɪp] **I** s. **1.** (Holz- od. Metall)Splitter m, Span m, Schnitzel n, m; Scheibchen n; abgebrochenes Stückchen n; pl. Abfall m: **dry as a ~** fade, fig. a. trocken, ledern; **a ~ of the old block** ganz (wie) der Vater; **have a ~ on one's shoulder** F sehr empfindlich sein; **2.** angeschlagene Stelle; **3.** pl. a) Brit. Pommes 'frites pl.: **fish and ~s**, b) Am. (Kar'toffel)Chips pl.; **4.** Spielmarke f: **when the ~s are down** fig. wenn es hart auf hart geht; **hand in one's ~s** Am. sl. ,abkratzen'; **have had one's ~s** sl. ,fertig' sein; **5.** pl. sl. ,Zaster' m (Geld): **in the ~s** (gut) bei Kasse; **6.** Computer: Chip m (Mikrobaustein); **II** v/t. **7.** (ab)schnitzeln; abraspeln; **8.** Kante von Geschirr etc. ab-, anschlagen; Stückchen ausbrechen; **9.** F hänseln; **III** v/i. **10.** (leicht) abbrechen; **~ in** v/i. **1.** sich (in ein Gespräch) einmischen; **2.** F beisteuern (a. v/t.); **~ off** v/i. abblättern, abbröckeln.

chip| bas·ket s. Spankorb m; **~ hat** s. Basthut m; **'~-board** s. (Holz)Spanplatte f.

chip·muck ['tʃɪpmʌk], **'chip·munk** [-mʌŋk] s. zo. amer. gestreiftes Eichhörnchen.

chip pan s. Küche: Frit'teuse f.

Chip·pen·dale ['tʃɪpəndeɪl] s. Chippendale(stil m) n (Möbelstil).

chip·per ['tʃɪpə] Am. **I** v/i. zwitschern; schwatzen; **II** adj. F munter, vergnügt.

chip·ping ['tʃɪpɪŋ] s. Schnitzel n, m, abgeschlagenes Stück, angestoßene Ecke; Span m; pl. Splitt m.

chip·py ['tʃɪpɪ] **I** adj. **1.** angeschlagen (Geschirr etc.); schartig; **2.** fig. trocken, fade; **3.** sl. verkatert; **II** s. **4.** Brit. F Frittenbude f, Fish-and-Chips-Laden m; **5.** Brit. F Tischler m, Schreiner m; **6.** Am. sl. a) ,Flittchen' n, b) ,Prosti'tuierte f.

chip shop [tʃɪp] s. Brit. Imbissstand m, -bude f, F Frittenbude f.

chi·ro·man·cer ['kaɪərəʊmænsə] s. Handleser m; **'chi·ro·man·cy** [-sɪ] s. Handlesekunst f.

chi·rop·o·dist [kɪ'rɒpədɪst] s. Fußpfleger(in), Pedi'küre f; **chi·rop·o·dy** [-dɪ] s. Fußpflege f, Pedi'küre f.

chi·ro·prac·tor ['kaɪərəʊ,præktə] s. Chiro'praktiker(in).

chirp [tʃɜːp] **I** v/i. u. v/t. zirpen, zwitschern; schilpen (Spatz); **II** s. Gezirp n, Zwitschern n; **'chirp·y** [-pɪ] adj. F munter, vergnügt.

chirr [tʃɜː] v/i. zirpen (Heuschrecke).

chir·rup ['tʃɪrəp] v/i. **1.** zwitschern; **2.** schnalzen.

chis·el ['tʃɪzl] **I** s. **1.** Meißel m; **2.** ⚙ Beitel m, Grabstichel m; **II** v/t. **3.** meißeln; **4.** fig. sti'listisch ausfeilen; **5.** sl. a) betrügen, ,reinlegen', b) ergaunern, her'ausschinden; **'chis·el·(l)ed** [-ld] adj. fig. **1.** ausgefeilt: **~ style**; **2.** scharf geschnitten: **~ face**; **'chis·el·(l)er** [-lə] s. F Gauner(in); ,Nassauer' m.

chit¹ [tʃɪt] s. Kindchen n: **a ~ of a girl**

C

ein junges Ding, ein Fratz.

chit² [tʃɪt] *s.* **1.** kurzer Brief; Zettel *m*; **2.** vom Gast abgezeichnete (Speise-) Rechnung.

chit-chat ['tʃɪttʃæt] → *chinwag*.

chit-ter-ling ['tʃɪtəlɪŋ] *s. mst pl.* Gekröse *n*, Inne'reien *pl.* (*bsd. Schwein*).

chiv-al-rous ['ʃɪvlrəs] *adj.* □ ritterlich, ga'lant; **'chiv-al-ry** [-rɪ] *s.* **1.** Ritterlichkeit *f*; **2.** Tapferkeit *f*; **3.** Rittertum *n*; **4.** Ritterdienst *m*.

chive¹ [tʃaɪv] *s.* ♀ Schnittlauch *m*.

chive² [tʃaɪv] *sl.* **I** *s.* Messer *n*; **II** *v/t.* (er)stechen.

chiv-(v)y ['tʃɪvɪ] *v/t.* **1.** *j-n* her'umjagen, hetzen; **2.** schikanieren.

chlo-ral ['klɔːrəl] *s.* ♒ Chlo'ral *n*: ~ *hydrate* Chloralhydrat *n*; **'chlo-rate** [-reɪt] *s.* ♒ chlorsaures Salz; **'chlo-ric** [-rɪk] *adj.* ♒ Chlor...: ~ *acid* Chlorsäure *f*; **'chlo-ride** [-raɪd] *s.* ♒ Chlo'rid *n*, Chlorverbindung *f*: ~ *of lime* Chlorkalk *m*; **'chlo-rin-ate** [-rɪneɪt] *v/t.* chloren, chlorieren; **chlo-rin-a-tion** [ˌklɔːrɪ-'neɪʃn] *s.* Chloren *n*; **'chlo-rine** [-riːn] *s.* ♒ Chlor *n*.

chlo-ro-flu-o-ro-car-bon ['klɔːrəʊ,fluərəʊ'kɑːbən] *s.* Fluorchlorkohlenwasserstoff *m*, FCKW.

chlo-ro-form ['klɔrəfɔːm] **I** *s.* ♒, ⚕ Chloro'form *n*; **II** *v/t.* chloroformieren; **'chlo-ro-phyll** [-fɪl] *s.* ♀ Chloro'phyll *n*, Blattgrün *n*.

chlo-ro-sis [kləˈrəʊsɪs] *s.* ⚕, ♀ Bleichsucht *f*; **chlo-rous** ['klɔːrəs] *adj.* chlorig.

choc [tʃɒk] *s.* F *abbr. für chocolate*: ~ *ice* Eis *n* mit Schokoladenüberzug.

chock [tʃɒk] **I** *s.* **1.** (Brems-, Hemm-) Keil *m*; **2.** ⚓ Klampe *f*; **II** *v/t.* **3.** festkeilen; **4.** *fig.* voll pfropfen; **III** *adv.* **5.** dicht; **~-a-block** [ˌtʃɒkə'blɒk] *adj.* voll gepfropft; **'~-'full** *adj.* zum Bersten voll.

choc-o-late ['tʃɒkələt] **I** *s.* **1.** Schoko'lade *f* (*a. als Getränk*); **2.** Pra'line *f*: ~*s* Pralinen, Konfekt *n*; **II** *adj.* **3.** schoko-'ladenbraun; ~ *bar* 'Schoko,riegel *m*; '~-,box(·y) *adj.* F kitschig, ,süßlich-,sentimen'tal; ~ *cream s.* 'Creme-pra,line *f*; ~ *sauce s.* Schoko'laden-,soße *f*.

choice [tʃɔɪs] **I** *s.* **1.** Wahl *f*: *make a* ~ wählen, e-e Wahl treffen; *take one's* ~ s-e Wahl treffen; *this is my* ~ dies habe ich gewählt; **2.** freie Wahl: *at* ~ nach Belieben; *by* (*od. for*) ~ vorzugsweise; *from* ~ aus Vorliebe; **3.** (große) Auswahl; Sorti'ment *n*: *a* ~ *of colours*; **4.** Wahl *f*, Möglichkeit *f*: *I have no* ~ ich habe keine (andere) Wahl, *a.* es ist mir einerlei; **5.** Auslese *f*, das Beste; **II** *adj.* □ **6.** auserlesen, vor'züglich; ♣ Quali-täts...: ~ *fruit* feinstes Obst; ~ *words* a) gewählte Worte, b) *humor.* deftige Sprache; ~ *quality* ♣ ausgesuchte Qualität; **'choice-ness** [-nɪs] *s.* Erlesenheit *f*.

choir ['kwaɪə] **I** *s.* **1.** (Kirchen-, Sänger-) Chor *m*; **2.** Chor *m*, ('Chor)Em,pore *f*; **II** *v/i. u. v/t.* **3.** im Chor singen; '~-boy *s.* Chor-, Sängerknabe *m*; '~,mas-ter *s.* Chorleiter *m*; ~ *stalls s. pl.* Chorgestühl *n*.

choke [tʃəʊk] **I** *s.* **1.** Würgen *n*; **2.** *mot.* Luftklappe *f*, Choke *m*: *pull out the* ~ den Choke ziehen; **3.** → *choke coil*; **4.** → *chokebore*; **II** *v/i.* **5.** würgen; ersticken (*a. fig.*): *with a choking voice* mit erstickter Stimme; **III** *v/t.* **6.** ersticken (*a. fig.*); erwürgen; würgen (*a. weitS.* Kragen etc.); **7.** hindern; dämpfen, drosseln (*a.* ♫, ⚙); **8.** *a.* ~ *up* a) verstopfen, b) voll stopfen; ~ *back v/t.* **1.**

Lachen *etc.* ersticken, unter'drücken; **2.** → *choke off*; ~ *down v/t.* **1.** hin'unterwürgen (*a. fig.*); **2.** → *choke back* 1; ~ *off v/t. fig.* ,abwürgen', nicht aufkommen lassen; *Konjunktur etc.* drosseln; ~ *up* → *choke* 8.

'choke|-bore *s.* ⚙ Chokebohrung *f*; ~ *coil s.* ♫ Drosselspule *f*; '~-damp *s.* ⚒ Nachschwaden *m*.

chok-er ['tʃəʊkə] *s.* F enger Kragen *od.* Schal; enge Halskette.

chol-er ['kɒlə] *s.* **1.** *obs.* Galle *f*; **2.** *fig.* Zorn *m*.

chol-er-a ['kɒlərə] *s.* ⚕ 'Cholera *f*.

chol-er-ic ['kɒlərɪk] *adj.* cho'lerisch.

cho-les-ter-ol [kə'lestərɒl] *s. physiol.* Choleste'rin *n*; ~ *lev-el s.* Cholesterinspiegel *m*.

choose [tʃuːz] **I** *v/t.* [*irr.*] **1.** (aus)wählen, aussuchen: *to* ~ *a hat*; *he was chosen king* er wurde zum König gewählt; *the chosen people bibl.* das auserwählte Volk; **2.** belieben (*a. iro.*), (es) vorziehen, lieber wollen; beschlie-ßen: *he chose to go* er zog es vor *od.* er beschloss fortzugehen; *do as you* ~ tu, wie *od.* was du willst; **II** *v/i.* [*irr.*] **3.** wählen: *not much to* ~ kaum ein Unterschied; *he cannot* ~ *but come* er hat keine andere Wahl als zu kommen; **'choos-er** [-zə] *s.* (Aus)Wählende(r *m*) *f*; → *beggar* 1; **'choos-y** [-zɪ] *adj.* F wählerisch.

chop¹ [tʃɒp] **I** *s.* **1.** Hieb *m*, Schlag *m* (*a.* Karate); *Boxen, Tennis:* Chop *m*; **2.** *Küche:* Kote'lett *n*; **3.** *pl.* a) (Kinn)Backen *pl.*: *lick one's* ~*s* sich die Lippen lecken, b) *fig.* Maul *n*, Rachen *m*; **II** *v/t.* **4.** (zer)hacken, hauen, spalten: ~ *wood* Holz hacken; ~ *one's words* abgehackt sprechen; **5.** *Tennis:* den Ball choppen; ~ *down v/t.* fällen; ~ *in v/i.* sich einmischen; ~ *off v/t.* abhauen; ~ *up v/t.* zerhacken, klein hacken.

chop² [tʃɒp] **I** *v/i. a.* ~ *about*, ~ *round* sich drehen, 'umschlagen (*Wind*): ~ *and change* s-n Standpunkt dauernd ändern, hin u. her schwanken; **II** *v/t.* *Worte* wechseln; **III** *s. pl.* ~*s and changes* ewiges Hin und Her.

chop³ [tʃɒp] *s.* (*Indien u. China*) **1.** Stempel *m*, Siegel *n*; **2.** Urkunde *f*; **3.** (Handels)Marke *f*; **4.** Quali'tät *f*: *first*- ~ erste Sorte, erstklassig.

'chop-house *s.* Steakhaus *n*.

chop-per ['tʃɒpə] *s.* **1.** Hackmesser *n*, -beil *n*; **2.** ♫ Zerhacker *m*; **3.** *Am. sl.* Hubschrauber *m*; **4.** *pl. sl.* Zähne *pl.*

chop-ping¹ ['tʃɒpɪŋ] *adj.* stramm (*Kind*).

chop-ping² ['tʃɒpɪŋ] *s.* Wechsel *m*: ~ *and changing* ewiges Hin und Her.

chop-ping| block ['tʃɒpɪŋ] *s.* Hackblock *m*, -klotz *m*; ~ *board s.* Hackbrett *n*; ~ *knife s.* [*irr.*] Hackmesser *n*.

chop-py ['tʃɒpɪ] *adj.* **1.** kabbelig (*Meer*); **2.** böig (*Wind*); **3.** *fig.* wechselnd; **4.** *fig.* abgehackt.

'chop|-stick *s.* Essstäbchen *n* (*China etc.*); ~ *su-ey* [suː'suːɪ] *s.* Chopsuey *n* (*chinesisches Mischgericht*).

cho-ral ['kɔːrəl] *adj.* □ Chor..., im Chor gesungen: ~ *service* Gottesdienst *m* mit Chorgesang; ~ *society* Chor *m*; **cho-rale** [kɒ'rɑːl] *s.* Cho'ral *m*.

chord [kɔːd] *s.* **1.** ♪, *poet., fig.* Saite *f*; **2.** ♪ Ak'kord *m*; *fig.* Ton *m*: *break into a* ~ e-n Tusch spielen; *strike the right* ~ bei *j-m* die richtige Saite anschlagen; *does that strike a* ~? erinnert *dich* das an etwas?; **3.** ♗ Sehne *f*; **4.** *anat.* Band *n*, Strang *m*; **5.** ✈ Pro'filsehne *f*; **6.** ⚙ Gurt *m*.

chore [tʃɔː] *s.* **1.** (Haus)Arbeit *f*; **2.** schwierige Aufgabe.

cho-re-a [kɒ'rɪə] *s.* ⚕ Veitstanz *m*.

cho-re-og-ra-pher [ˌkɒrɪ'ɒgrəfə] *s.* Choreo'graph *m*; **cho-re-og-ra-phy** [-fɪ] *s.* Choreogra'phie *f*.

chor-is-ter ['kɒrɪstə] *s.* **1.** Chorsänger (-in), *bsd.* Chorknabe *m*; **2.** *Am.* Kirchenchorleiter *m*.

chor-tle ['tʃɔːtl] **I** *v/i.* glucksen(d lachen); **II** *s.* Glucksen *n*.

cho-rus ['kɔːrəs] **I** *s.* **1.** Chor *m* (*a. antiq.*), Sängergruppe *f*; **2.** Tanzgruppe *f* (*e-r Revue*); **3.** *a. thea.* Chor *m*, gemeinsames Singen: ~ *of protest* Protestgeschrei *n*; *in* ~ im Chor (*a. fig.*); **4.** Chorsprecher *m* (*im elisabethanischen Theater*); **5.** (im Chor gesungener) Kehrreim; **6.** Chorwerk *n*; **II** *v/i. u. v/t.* **7.** im Chor singen *od.* sprechen *od.* rufen; ~ *girl s.* (Re'vue)Tänzerin *f*.

chose [tʃəʊz] *pret. von choose*.

cho-sen ['tʃəʊzn] *p.p. von choose*.

chough [tʃʌf] *s. orn.* Dohle *f*.

chow [tʃaʊ] *s.* **1.** *zo.* Chow-'Chow *m* (*Hund*); **2.** *sl.* ,Futter' *n*, Essen *n*.

chow-chow [ˌtʃaʊ'tʃaʊ] (*Pidginenglisch*) *s.* **1.** chi'nesische Mixed Pickles *pl. od.* 'Fruchtkonfi,türe *f*; **2.** → *chow 1*.

chow-der ['tʃaʊdə] *s. Am.* dicke Suppe aus Meeresfrüchten.

Christ [kraɪst] **I** *s.* der Gesalbte, 'Christus *m*: ~ *before* ~ (*B.C.*) vor Christi Geburt (*v. Chr.*); **II** *int. sl.* verdammt noch mal!; ~ *child s.* Christkind *n*.

chris-ten ['krɪsn] *v/t. eccl.*, ⚓ *u. fig.* taufen; **'Chris-ten-dom** [-dəm] *s.* Christenheit *f*; **'chris-ten-ing** [-nɪŋ] **I** *s.* Taufe *f*; **II** *adj.* Tauf...

Chris-tian ['krɪstjən] **I** *adj.* □ **1.** christlich; **2.** F anständig; **II** *s.* **3.** Christ(in); **4.** guter Mensch; **5.** Mensch *m* (*Ggs. Tier*); ~ *e-ra s.* christliche Zeitrechnung.

Chris-ti-an-i-ty [ˌkrɪstɪ'ænətɪ] *s.* Christentum *n*; **Chris-tian-ize** ['krɪstjənaɪz] *v/t.* zum Christentum bekehren, christianisicrn.

Chris-tian| name *s.* Tauf-, Vorname *m*; ~ **Sci-ence** *s.* Christian Science *f*; ~ **Sci-en-tist** *s.* Anhänger(in) der Christian Science.

Christ-mas ['krɪsməs] *s.* Weihnachten *n u. pl.*: *at* ~ zu *od.* an Weihnachten; *merry* ~*!* frohe Weihnachten!; ~ **bo-nus** *s.* ♣ 'Weihnachtsgratifikati,on *f*; ~ **card** *s.* Weihnachtskarte *f*; ~ **car-ol** *s.* Weihnachtslied *n*; ~ **Day** *s.* der erste Weihnachtsfeiertag; ~ **Eve** *s.* der Heilige Abend; ~ **pres-ent** ['preznt] *s.* Weihnachtsgeschenk *n*; ~ **pud-ding** *s. Brit.* Plumpudding *m*; '~-tide, '~-time *s.* Weihnachtszeit *f*; ~ **tree** *s.* Weihnachts-, Christbaum *m*.

Christ-mas-y ['krɪsməsɪ] *adj.* F weihnachtlich.

chro-mate ['krəʊmeɪt] *s.* ♒ Chro'mat *n*, chromsaures Salz.

chro-mat-ic [krəʊ'mætɪk] *adj.* (□ ~ally) **1.** *phys.* chro'matisch, Farben...; **2.** ♪ chromatisch; **chro'mat-ics** [-ks] *s. pl. sg. konstr.* **1.** Farbenlehre *f*; **2.** ♪ Chro-'matik *f*.

chrome [krəʊm] **I** *s.* **1.** ♒ a) Chrom *n*, b) Chromgelb *n*; **2.** Chromleder *n*; **II** *v/t.* **3.** *a.* ~*-plate* verchromen.

chro-mi-um ['krəʊmjəm] *s.* ♒ Chrom *n*; ,~-'plat-ed *adj.* verchromt; ,~-'plat-ing *s.* Verchromung *f*; ~ **steel** *s.* Chromstahl *m*.

chro-mo-lith-o-graph [ˌkrəʊməʊ'lɪθəʊgrɑːf] *s.* Chromolithogra'phie *f*, Mehrfarbensteindruck *m* (*Bild*); ,chro-

C

mo·li'thog·ra·phy [-lɪ'θɒɡrəfɪ] *s.* Mehrfarbensteindruck *m* (*Verfahren*). **chro·mo·some** ['krəʊməsəʊm] *s. biol.* Chromo'som *n*; **'chro·mo·type** [-məʊtaɪp] *s.* **1.** Farbdruck *m*; **2.** Chromoty'pie *f*. **chron·ic** ['krɒnɪk] *adj.* (□ *~ally*) **1.** ständig, (an)dauernd, 'chronisch': ~ *unemployment* Dauerarbeitslosigkeit *f*; **2.** *mst* ✻ chronisch, langwierig; **3.** *sl.* scheußlich. **chron·i·cle** ['krɒnɪkl] **I** *s.* **1.** Chronik *f*; **2.** *~s pl. bibl.* (*das* Buch der) Chronik *f*; **II** *v/t.* **3.** aufzeichnen; **'chron·i·cler** [-lə] *s.* Chro'nist *m*. **chron·o·gram** ['krɒnəʊɡræm] *s.* Chrono'gramm *n*; **'chron·o·graph** [-ɡrɑːf] *s.* Chrono'graph *m*, Zeitmesser *m*; **chron·o·log·i·cal** [ˌkrɒnə'lɒdʒɪkl] *adj.* □ chrono'logisch: ~ *order* zeitliche Reihenfolge; **chro·nol·o·gize** [krə'nɒlədʒaɪz] *v/t.* chronologisieren; **chro·nol·o·gy** [krə'nɒlədʒɪ] *s.* **1.** Chronolo'gie *f*, Zeitbestimmung *f*; **2.** Zeittafel *f*; **chro·nom·e·ter** [krə'nɒmɪtə] *s.* Chro'nometer *n*; **chro·nom·e·try** [krə'nɒmɪtrɪ] *s.* Zeitmessung *f*. **chrys·a·lis** ['krɪsəlɪs] *pl.* **-lis·es** [-lɪsɪz] *s. zo.* (*Insekten*)Puppe *f*. **chrys·an·the·mum** [krɪ'sænθəməm] *s.* ✿ Chrysan'theme *f*. **chub** [tʃʌb] *s. ichth.* Döbel *m*. **chub·by** ['tʃʌbɪ] *adj.* a) pausbäckig, b) rundlich. **chuck¹** [tʃʌk] **I** *s.* **1.** F Wurf *m*; **2.** zärtlicher Griff unters Kinn; **3.** *give s.o. the* ~ F j-n ‚rausschmeißen' (*entlassen*); **II** *v/t.* **4.** F schmeißen, werfen; **5.** ~ *s.o. under the chin* j-n unters Kinn fassen; **6.** F a) Schluss machen mit: ~ *it!* lass das!, b) → *chuck up*; ~ *a·way v/t.* F **1.** ‚wegschmeißen'; **2.** *Geld* verschwenden; **3.** *Gelegenheit* ‚verschenken'; ~ *out v/t.* F ‚rausschmeißen'; ~ *up v/t.* F *Job etc.* ‚hinschmeißen'. **chuck²** [tʃʌk] **I** *s.* **1.** Glucken *n* (*Henne*); **2.** F ‚Schnuckie' *m* (*Kosewort*); **II** *v/i. u. v/t.* **3.** glucken; **III** *int.* **4.** put, put! (*Lockruf für Hühner*). **chuck³** [tʃʌk] **I** *s.* ⊙ Spann- *od.* Bohrfutter *n*; **II** *v/t.* (in das Futter) einspannen. **chuck·er-out** [ˌtʃʌkər'aʊt] *s.* F ‚Rausschmeißer' *m* (*in Lokalen etc.*). **chuck·le** ['tʃʌkl] **I** *v/i.* **1.** glucksen, in sich hin'einlachen; **2.** sich (insgeheim) freuen (*at, over* über *acc.*); **3.** glucken (*Henne*); **II** *s.* **4.** leises Lachen, Glucksen *n*; **'~·head** *s.* Dummkopf *m*. **chuffed** [tʃʌft] *adj. Brit.* F froh. **chug** [tʃʌɡ] **chug-chug** [ˌtʃʌɡ'tʃʌɡ] **I** *s.* Tuckern *n* (*Motor*); **II** *v/i.* tuckern(d fahren). **chuk·ker** ['tʃʌkə] *s. Polospiel:* Chukker *m* (*Spielabschnitt*). **chum** [tʃʌm] F **I** *s.* **1.** ‚Kumpel' *m*, ‚Spezi' *m*, Kame'rad *m*: *be great* ~ *s* dicke Freunde sein; **2.** Stubengenosse *m*; **II** *v/i.* **3.** gemeinsam wohnen (*with* mit); **4.** ~ *up with s.o.* sich mit j-m anfreunden; **'chum·my** [-mɪ] *adj.* **1.** ‚dick' befreundet; **2.** gesellig; **3.** *contp.* plumpvertraulich. **chump** [tʃʌmp] *s.* **1.** Holzklotz *m*; **2.** dickes Ende (*bsd. Hammelkeule*); **3.** F Dummkopf *m*; **4.** *bsd. Brit. sl.* ‚Kürbis' *m*, ‚Birne' *f* (*Kopf*): *off one's* ~ (total) verrückt. **chunk** [tʃʌnk] *s.* F **1.** (Holz)Klotz *m*; Klumpen *m*, dickes Stück (*Fleisch etc.*), ‚Runken' *m* (*Brot*); *weitS.* ‚großer Brocken'; **2.** *Am.* a) unter'setzter Mensch, b) kleines, stämmiges Pferd;

'chunk·y [-kɪ] *adj.* **1.** *Am.* unter'setzt, stämmig; **2.** klobig, klotzig. **Chun·nel** ['tʃʌnl] *npr.* Ka'nal,tunnel *m*, Eurotunnel *m*. **church** [tʃɜːtʃ] **I** *s.* **1.** Kirche *f*: *in* ~ in der Kirche, beim Gottesdienst; ~ *is over* die Kirche ist aus; **2.** Kirche *f*, Religi'onsgemeinschaft *f*, *bsd.* Christenheit *f*; **3.** Geistlichkeit *f*: *enter the* ~ Geistlicher werden; **II** *adj.* **4.** Kirch(en)...; kirchlich; '**~·go·er** *s.* Kirchgänger(in); ⚯ **of Eng·land** *s.* englische Staatskirche, anglikanische Kirche; ~ *rate s.* Kirchensteuer *f*; '~**·ward·en** *s.* **1.** *Brit.* Kirchenvorsteher *m*: ~ *pipe* langstielige Tonpfeife; **2.** *Am.* Verwalter *m* der weltlichen Angelegenheiten e-r Kirche; ~ *wed·ding s.* kirchliche Trauung. **church·y** ['tʃɜːtʃɪ] *adj.* F kirchlich (gesinnt). '**church·yard** *s.* Kirchhof *m*. **churl** [tʃɜːl] *s.* **1.** Flegel *m*, Grobian *m*; **2.** Geizhals *m*, Knauser *m*; '**churl·ish** [-lɪʃ] *adj.* □ **1.** grob, ungehobelt, flegelhaft; **2.** geizig, knauserig; **3.** mürrisch. **churn** [tʃɜːn] **I** *s.* **1.** Butterfass *n* (*Maschine*); **2.** *Brit.* (große) Milchkanne; **II** *v/t.* **3.** verbuttern; **4.** ('durch)schütteln, aufwühlen; **5.** *fig.* ~ *out* am laufenden Band produzieren, ausstoßen; **III** *v/i.* **6.** buttern; **7.** schäumen; **8.** sich heftig bewegen. **chute** [ʃuːt] *s.* **1.** Stromschnelle *f*, starkes Gefälle; **2.** ⊙ a) Rutsche *f*, b) Schacht *m*, c) Müllschlucker *m*; **3.** Rutsche *f*, Rutschbahn *f* (*auf Spielplätzen etc.*); **4.** Rodelbahn *f*; **5.** F → *para·chute* 1; ~*-the-~chute(s)* → *chute* 3. **chutz·pa(h)** ['hʊtspə] *s.* F Chuzpe *f*, Frechheit *f*. **ci·bo·ri·um** [sɪ'bɔːrɪəm] *s. eccl.* **1.** 'Hostienkelch *m*, Zi'borium *n*; **2.** Al'tar,baldachin *m*. **ci·ca·da** [sɪ'kɑːdə], **ci'ca·la** [-ɑːlə] *s. zo.* Zi'kade *f*. **cic·a·trice** ['sɪkətrɪs] *s.* Narbe *f*; ✿ Blattnarbe *f*; '**cic·a·triced** [-st] *adj.* ✻ vernarbt; '**cic·a·trize** [-raɪz] *v/i. u. v/t.* vernarben (lassen). **cic·er·o** ['sɪsərəʊ] *s. typ.* Cicero *f* (*Schriftgrad*). **ci·ce·ro·ne** [ˌtʃɪtʃə'rəʊnɪ] *pl.* **-ni** [-niː] *s.* Cice'rone *m*, Fremdenführer *m*. **ci·der** ['saɪdə] *s.* (*Am. hard ~*) Apfelwein *m*: (*sweet*) ~ *Am.* Apfelmost *m*. **ci·gar** [sɪ'ɡɑː] *s.* Zi'garre *f*; ~ *box s.* Zi'garrenkiste *f*; ~ *case s.* Zi'garren,tui *n*, -tasche *f*; ~ *cut·ter s.* Zi'garrenabschneider *m*. **cig·a·ret(te)** [ˌsɪɡə'ret] *s.* Ziga'rette *f*; ~ *case s.* Ziga'rettene,tui *n*; ~ *end s.* Ziga'rettenstummel *m*; ~ *hold·er s.* Ziga'rettenspitze *f* (*Halter*). **cil·i·a** ['sɪlɪə] *s. pl.* **1.** (Augen)Wimpern *pl.*; **2.** ✿, *zo.* Wimper-, Flimmerhärchen *pl.*; '**cil·i·ar·y** [-ərɪ] *adj.* Wimper...; '**cil·i·at·ed** [-ɪeɪtɪd] *adj.* ✿, *zo.* bewimpert. **cinch** [sɪntʃ] *s.* **1.** *Am.* Sattelgurt *m*; **2.** *sl.* a) ‚todsichere Sache', ‚klarer Fall', b) ‚Kinderspiel' *n*. **cin·cho·na** [sɪŋ'kəʊnə] *s.* **1.** ✿ 'Chinarindenbaum *m*; **2.** 'Chinarinde *f*. **cinc·ture** ['sɪŋktʃə] **I** *s.* **1.** Gürtel *m*, Gurt *m*; **2.** (Säulen)Kranz *m*; **II** *v/t.* **3.** um'gürten, um'geben. **cin·der** ['sɪndə] *s.* **1.** Schlacke *f*: *burnt to a* ~ verkohlt, völlig verbrannt; **2.** *pl.* Asche *f*. **Cin·der·el·la** [ˌsɪndə'relə] *s.* Aschenbrödel *n*, -puttel *n* (*a. fig.*). **cin·der| path** *s.* **1.** Schlackenweg *m*; **2.**

→ ~ *track s. sport* Aschenbahn *f*. **cine-** [sɪnɪ] *in Zssgn* Kino..., Film...: ~ *camera* (Schmal)Filmkamera *f*; ~ *film* Schmalfilm *m*; ~*-record* filmen, mit der Schmalfilmkamera aufnehmen. **cin·e·aste** ['sɪnɪæst] *s.* Cine'ast *m*, Filmliebhaber(in). **cin·e·ma** ['sɪnɪmə] *s.* **1.** 'Lichtspielthe,ater *n*, 'Kino *n*; **2.** *the* ~ Film(kunst *f*) *m*; '~**,go·er** *s.* 'Kinobesucher(in). **cin·e·mat·ic** [ˌsɪnɪ'mætɪk] *adj.* (□ *~ally*) filmisch, Film...; **cin·e·mat·o·graph** [ˌsɪnə'mætəɡrɑːf] **I** *s.* Kinemato'graph *m*; **II** *v/t.* (ver)filmen; **cin·e·ma·tog·ra·pher** [ˌsɪnəmə'tɒɡrəfə] *s.* 'Kameramann *m*; **cin·e·mat·o·graph·ic** [ˌsɪnəmætə'ɡræfɪk] (□ *~ally*) kinemato'graphisch; **cin·e·ma·tog·ra·phy** [ˌsɪnəmə'tɒɡrəfɪ] *s.* Kinematogra'phie *f*. **cin·e·ra·ri·um** [ˌsɪnə'reərɪəm] *s.* Urnennische *f od.* -friedhof *m*. **cin·er·ar·y** ['sɪnərərɪ] *adj.* Aschen...; ~ *urn s.* Totenurne *f*. **cin·er·a·tor** ['sɪnəreɪtə] *s.* Feuerbestattungsofen *m*. **cin·na·bar** ['sɪnəbɑː] *s.* Zin'nober *m*. **cin·na·mon** ['sɪnəmən] **I** *s.* **1.** Zimt *m*, Ka'neel *m*; **2.** Zimtbaum *m*; **II** *adj.* **3.** zimtfarbig. **cinque** [sɪŋk] (*Fr.*) *s.* Fünf *f* (*Würfel od. Spielkarten*); '~**-foil** [-fɔɪl] *s.* **1.** ✿ Feingerkraut *n*; **2.** △ Fünfpass *m*; ⚯ **Ports** ['sɪŋkpɔːts] *s. pl. Gruppe von ursprünglich fünf südenglischen Seestädten.* **ci·on** ['saɪən] → *scion.* **ci·pher** ['saɪfə] *s.* **1.** ⚿ die Ziffer Null *f*; **2.** (a'rabische) Ziffer, Zahl *f*; **3.** *fig.* a) Null *f* (*Person*), b) Nichts *n*; **4.** Chiffre *f*, Geheimschrift *f*: *in* ~ chiffriert; **5.** *fig.* Schlüssel *m*, Kennwort *n*; **6.** Mono'gramm *n*; **II** *v/i.* **7.** rechnen; **III** *v/t.* **8.** chiffrieren; **9.** *a.* ~ *out* be-, ausrechnen; entziffern; *Am.* ‚ausknobeln'; ~ *code s.* Kodechiffre *f*, Tele'gramm-, Chiffrierschlüssel *m*. **cir·ca** ['sɜːkə] *prp.* um (*vor Jahreszahlen*). **Cir·ce** ['sɜːsɪ] *npr. myth.* 'Circe *f* (*a. fig. Verführerin*). **cir·cle** ['sɜːkl] **I** *s.* **1.** ⚿ Kreis *m*: *full* ~ im Kreise herum, volle Wendung, wieder da, wo *man* angefangen hat; *run* (*a. talk*) *in* ~*s fig.* sich im Kreis bewegen; *square the* ~ ⚿ den Kreis quadrieren (*a. fig.* das Unmögliche vollbringen); → *vicious circle*; **2.** *ast.*, *geogr.* Kreis *m*; **3.** Kreis *m*, Gruppe *f*: ~ *of friends* Freundeskreis; → *upper* I; **4.** Ring *m*, Kranz *m*, Reif *m*; **5.** Kreislauf *m*, 'Umlauf *m*, Runde *f*; Wiederkehr *f*, 'Zyklus *m*; **6.** *thea.* Rang *m*; **7.** Kreis *m*, Gebiet *n*; **8.** a) *Turnen*: Welle *f*, b) *Hockey*: (Schuss)Kreis *m*; **II** *v/t.* **9.** um'kreisen; um'zingeln; **10.** um'winden; **III** *v/i.* **11.** sich im Kreise bewegen, kreisen; die Runde machen; **12.** ✕ schwenken. **cir·clet** ['sɜːklɪt] *s.* **1.** kleiner Kreis, Reif, Ring; **2.** Dia'dem *n*. **circs** [sɜːks] *s. pl.* F *für* **circumstances**. **cir·cuit** ['sɜːkɪt] **I** *s.* **1.** 'Kreis,linie *f*, 'Um-, Kreislauf *m*; Bahn *f*; **2.** 'Umkreis *m*; **3.** 'Umweg *m*; **4.** Rundgang *m*, -flug *m*; *mot.* Rennstrecke *f*; **5.** 🛠 a) *Brit. hist.* Rundreise *f* der Richter e-s Bezirks (*zur Abhaltung der assizes*), b) Anwälte *pl.* e-s Gerichtsbezirks, c) Gerichtsbezirk *m*; **6.** ⚡ a) Strom-, Schaltkreis *m*: → *short* (*closed*) *circuit*, b) Schaltung *f*, 'Schaltsy,stem *n*; **7.** *Am.* (Per'sonen)Kreis *m*; **8.** *sport* ‚Zirkus' *m*: *the tennis* ~; **II** *v/t.* **9.** um'kreisen; **III** *v/i.* **10.** kreisen; '~**·board** *s.* ⚡, Com-

c

puter: Pla'tine *f*; ~ **break·er** *s.* ⚡ Ausschalter *m*; ~ **di·a·gram** *s.* ⚡ Schaltbild *n*, -plan *m*.

cir·cu·i·tous [sə'kjuːɪtəs] *adj.* □ weitschweifig, -läufig: ~ *route* Umweg *m*; **cir·cuit·ry** ['sɜːkɪtrɪ] *s.* ⚡ **1.** 'Schaltsys,tem *n*; **2.** Schaltungen *pl.*; **3.** Schaltbild *n*.

cir·cu·lar ['sɜːkjʊlə] **I** *adj.* □ **1.** (kreis)rund, kreisförmig; **2.** Rund..., Kreis..., Ring...; **II** *s.* **3.** a) Rundschreiben *n*, b) (Post)Wurfsendung *f*; **'cir·cu·lar·ize** [-əraɪz] *v/t.* a. (Post)Wurfsendungen verschicken an (*acc.*); Fragebogen schicken an (*acc.*); durch (Post)Wurfsendungen werben für.

cir·cu·lar| let·ter → *circular* 3a; ~ **letter of cred·it** *s.* ♥ 'Reiskre,ditbrief *m*; ~ **note** *s.* **1.** *pol.* Zirku'larnote *f*; **2.** 'Reiskre,ditbrief *m*; ~ **saw** *s.* ⊕ Kreissäge *f*; ~ **skirt** *s.* Glockenrock *m*; ~ **tick·et** *s.* Rundreisekarte *f*; ~ **tour**, ~ **trip** *s.* Rundreise *f*, -fahrt *f*.

cir·cu·late ['sɜːkjʊleɪt] **I** *v/i.* **1.** zirkulieren: a) 'umlaufen, kreisen, b) im 'Umlauf sein, kursieren (*Geld, Gerücht etc.*); **2.** her'umreisen, -gehen; **II** *v/t.* **3.** in Umlauf setzen, zirkulieren lassen.

cir·cu·lat·ing ['sɜːkjʊleɪtɪŋ] *adj.* zirkulierend, 'umlaufend; ~ **cap·i·tal** *s.* 'Umlauf-, Be'triebskapi,tal *n*; ~ **dec·i·mal** *s.* ⅍ peri'odischer Dezi'malbruch; ~ **li·brar·y** *s.* 'Leihbüche,rei *f*.

cir·cu·la·tion [,sɜːkjʊ'leɪʃn] *s.* **1.** Kreislauf *m*, Zirkulati'on *f*; **2.** *physiol.* ('Blut)Zirkulati,on *f*, (-)Kreislauf *m*; **3.** ♥ a) 'Umlauf *m*, Verkehr *m*, b) Verbreitung *f*, Absatz *m*, c) Auflage(nziffer) *f* (*Zeitung etc.*), d) 'Zahlungsmittel,umlauf *m*: *out of* ~ außer Kurs (gesetzt); *put into* ~ in Umlauf setzen; *withdraw from* ~ aus dem Verkehr ziehen (*a. fig.*); **4.** Strömung *f*, 'Durchzug *m*, -fluss *m*; **cir·cu·la·tor** ['sɜːkjʊleɪtə] *s.* Verbreiter(in); **cir·cu·la·to·ry** [,sɜːkjʊ'leɪtərɪ] *adj.* zirkulierend, 'umlaufend; *physiol.* Kreislauf...: ~ *collapse*; ~ *system* (Blut)Kreislauf *m*.

cir·cum·cise ['sɜːkəmsaɪz] *v/t.* **1.** ⚕, *eccl.* beschneiden; **2.** *fig.* läutern; **cir·cum·ci·sion** [,sɜːkəm'sɪʒn] *s.* **1.** ⚕, *eccl.* Beschneidung *f*; **2.** *fig.* Läuterung *f*; **3.** ⚷ Fest *n* der Beschneidung Christi; **4.** *the* ~ *bibl.* die Beschnittenen *pl.* (*Juden*).

cir·cum·fer·ence [sə'kʌmfərəns] *s.* 'Umkreis *m*, 'Umfang *m*, Periphe'rie *f*; **cir·cum·flex** ['sɜːkəmfleks] *s.* a. ~ *accent ling.* Zirkum'flex *m*; **cir·cum·ja·cent** [,sɜːkəm'dʒeɪsənt] *adj.* 'umliegend.

cir·cum·lo·cu·tion [,sɜːkəmlə'kjuːʃn] *s.* **1.** Um'schreibung *f*; **2.** a) 'Umschweife *pl.*, b) Weitschweifigkeit *f*; **cir·cum·loc·u·to·ry** [,sɜːkəm'lɒkjʊtərɪ] *adj.* weitschweifig.

cir·cum·nav·i·gate [,sɜːkəm'nævɪgeɪt] *v/t.* um'schiffen, um'segeln; **cir·cum·nav·i·ga·tion** ['sɜːkəm,nævɪ'geɪʃn] *s.* Um'segelung *f*; **cir·cum·nav·i·ga·tor** [-tə] *s.* Um'segler *m*.

cir·cum·scribe ['sɜːkəmskraɪb] *v/t.* **1.** a) um'schreiben (*a.* ⅍), b) definieren; **2.** begrenzen, einschränken; **cir·cum·scrip·tion** [,sɜːkəm'skrɪpʃn] *s.* **1.** Um'schreibung *f* (*a.* ⅍) **2.** 'Umschrift *f* (*Münze etc.*); **3.** Begrenzung *f*, Beschränkung *f*.

cir·cum·spect ['sɜːkəmspekt] *adj.* □ 'um-, vorsichtig; **cir·cum·spec·tion** [,sɜːkəm'spekʃn] *s.* 'Um-, Vorsicht *f*, Behutsamkeit *f*.

cir·cum·stance ['sɜːkəmstəns] *s.* **1.**

'Umstand *m*, Tatsache *f*; Ereignis *n*; Einzelheit *f*: *a fortunate* ~ ein glücklicher Umstand; **2.** *pl.* 'Umstände *pl.*, Lage *f*, Sachverhalt *m*, Verhältnisse *pl.*: *in* (*od.* *under*) *the* ~*s* unter diesen Umständen; *under no* ~*s* auf keinen Fall; **3.** *pl.* Verhältnisse *pl.*, Lebenslage *f*: *in good* ~*s* gut situiert; **4.** 'Umständlichkeit *f*, Weitschweifigkeit *f*; **5.** Förmlichkeit(en *pl.*) *f*, Umstände *pl.*: *without* ~ ohne (alle) Umstände; **'cir·cum·stanced** [-st] *adj.* in e-r ... Lage; ... situiert; gelagert (*Sache*): *poorly* ~ in ärmlichen Verhältnissen; *well timed and* ~ zur rechten Zeit u. unter günstigen Umständen; **cir·cum·stan·tial** [,sɜːkəm'stænʃl] *adj.* □ **1.** 'umständlich; **2.** ausführlich, genau; **3.** zufällig; **4.** ~ *evidence* ♣ Indizienbeweis *m*; **cir·cum·stan·ti·ate** [,sɜːkəm'stænʃɪeɪt] *v/t.* **1.** genau beschreiben; **2.** ♣ durch In'dizien beweisen.

cir·cum·vent [,sɜːkəm'vent] *v/t.* **1.** über'listen; **2.** vereiteln, verhindern; **3.** um'gehen; **cir·cum·ven·tion** [-nʃn] *s.* **1.** Vereitelung *f*; **2.** Um'gehung *f*.

cir·cum·vo·lu·tion [,sɜːkəmvə'ljuːʃn] *s.* **1.** 'Umdrehung *f*; 'Umwälzung *f*; **2.** Windung *f*.

cir·cus ['sɜːkəs] *s.* **1.** a) 'Zirkus *m*, b) 'Zirkustruppe *f*, c) ('Zirkus)Vorstellung *f*, d) A'rena *f*; **2.** *Brit. runder Platz mit Straßenkreuzungen*; **3.** *Brit. sl.* ✕ a) im Kreis fliegende Flugzeugstaffel, b) ,fliegende' Einheit; **4.** F ,'Zirkus' *m*, Rummel *m*.

cir·rho·sis [sɪ'rəʊsɪs] *s.* ✍ Zir'rhose *f*, (*Leber*)Schrumpfung *f*.

cir·rose [sɪ'rəʊs], **cir·rous** ['sɪrəs] *adj.* **1.** ♀ mit Ranken; **2.** *zo.* mit Haaren *od.* Fühlern; **3.** federartig.

cir·rus ['sɪrəs] *pl.* -ri [-raɪ] *s.* **1.** ♀ Ranke *f*; **2.** *zo.* Rankenfuß *m*; **3.** 'Zirrus *m*, Federwolke *f*.

cis·al·pine [sɪs'ælpaɪn] *adj.* diesseits der Alpen; **cis·at·lan·tic** [sɪsət'læntɪk] *adj.* diesseits des At'lantischen 'Ozeans.

cis·sy → *sissy*.

Cis·ter·cian [sɪ'stɜːʃjən] **I** *s.* Zisterzi'enser(mönch) *m*; **II** *adj.* Zisterzienser...

cis·tern ['sɪstən] *s.* **1.** Wasserbehälter *m*; **2.** Zi'sterne *f*, ('unterirdischer) Regenwasserspeicher.

cit·a·del ['sɪtədəl] *s.* **1.** Zita'delle *f* (*a. fig.*); **2.** Burg *f*; *fig.* Zuflucht *f*.

ci·ta·tion [saɪ'teɪʃn] *s.* **1.** Anführung *f*; **2.** a) Zi'tat *n* (*zitierte Stelle*), b) ♣ (*of*) Berufung *f* (auf *acc.*), Her'anziehung *f* (*gen.*), c) ♣ Vorladung *f*; **3.** *bsd.* ✕ ehrenvolle Erwähnung.

cite [saɪt] *v/t.* **1.** zitieren; **2.** (als Beispiel *od.* Beweis) anführen; **3.** ♣ vorladen; **4.** ✕ lobend erwähnen.

cith·er ['sɪθə] *poet.* → *zither*.

cit·i·fy ['sɪtɪfaɪ] *v/t.* verstädtern.

cit·i·zen ['sɪtɪzn] *s.* **1.** Bürger *m*, Staatsangehörige(r *m*) *f*: ~ *of the world* Weltbürger; **2.** Städter(in); **3.** Einwohner(in): ~*s' band* CB-Funk *m*; **4.** Zivi'list *m*; **cit·i·zen·ry** [-rɪ] *s.* Bürgerschaft *f* (*e-s Staates*); **'cit·i·zen·ship** [-ʃɪp] *s.* **1.** Staatsangehörigkeit *f*; **2.** Bürgerrecht *n*.

cit·rate ['sɪtreɪt] *s.* ♣ Zi'trat *n*.

cit·ric ac·id ['sɪtrɪk] *s.* ♣ Zi'tronensäure *f*.

cit·ri·cul·ture ['sɪtrɪkʌltʃə] *s.* Anbau *m* von 'Zitrusfrüchten.

cit·rus ['sɪtrəs] *s.* ♀ 'Zitrusgewächs *n*, -frucht *f*.

cit·y ['sɪtɪ] *s.* **1.** (Groß)Stadt *f*: ⚷ *of God fig.* Himmelreich *n*; **2.** *Brit.* inkorporierte Stadt (*mst mit Kathedrale*); **3.** *the*

⚷ die (Londoner) City (*Altstadt od. Geschäftsviertel od. Geschäftswelt*); **4.** *Am.* inkorporierte Stadtgemeinde; ~ **ar·ti·cle** *s.* Börsenbericht *m*; ⚷ **Com·pa·ny** *s. Brit.* e-e der großen Londoner Gilden; ~ **coun·cil** *s.* Stadtrat *m*; ~ **desk** *s. Brit.* 'Wirtschafts-, *Am.* Lo'kalredakti,on *f*; ~ **ed·i·tor** *s.* **1.** *Am.* Lo'kalredak,teur *m*; **2.** *Brit.* Redak'teur *m* des Handelsteiles; ~ **fa·ther** *s.* Stadtrat *m*; *pl.* Stadtväter *pl.*; ~ **hall** *s.* Rathaus *n*; ⚷ **man** *s. Brit.* Fi'nanz-, Geschäftsmann *m* der City; ~ **man·ag·er** *s. Am.* 'Stadt,rektor *m*; ~ **per·son** *s.* Stadtmensch *m*; ~ **state** *s.* Stadtstaat *m*.

civ·et (**cat**) ['sɪvɪt] *s. zo.* 'Zibetkatze *f*.

civ·ic ['sɪvɪk] *adj.* (□ ~*ally*) **1.** städtisch, Stadt...; **2.** → *civil* 2; ~ **cen·tre**, *Am.* **cen·ter** *s.* Behördenviertel *n*, Verwaltungszentrum *n*.

civ·ics ['sɪvɪks] *s. pl. sg. konstr.* Staatsbürgerkunde *f*.

civ·ies ['sɪvɪz] *bsd. Am.* → *civvies*.

civ·il ['sɪvl] *adj.* (□ *nur für* 6.) **1.** staatlich: ~ *affairs* Verwaltungsangelegenheiten; **2.** (staats)bürgerlich, Bürger...: ~ *duty*, ~ *commotion* Aufruhr *m*, innere Unruhen *pl.*; ~ *death* bürgerlicher Tod; ~ *liberties* bürgerliche Freiheiten; ~ *list Brit.* Zivilliste *f*; ~ *rights* Bürgerrechte, bürgerliche Ehrenrechte; ~ *rights activist* Bürgerrechtler(in); ~ *rights movement* Bürgerrechtsbewegung *f*; ⚷ *Servant* Staatsbeamte(r); ⚷ *Service* Staats-, Verwaltungsdienst *m*; ~ *war* Bürgerkrieg *m*; → *disobedience* 1; **3.** zi'vil (*Ggs. militärisch*): ~ *aviation* Zivilluftfahrt *f*; ~ *defence*, *Am.* ~ *defense* Zivilverteidigung *f*, -schutz *m*; ~ *government* Zivilverwaltung *f*; ~ *life* Zivilleben *n*; **4.** zi'vil (*Ggs. kirchlich*): ~ *marriage* Ziviltrauung *f*; **5.** ♣ zi'vil(rechtlich), bürgerlich: ~ *case od. suit* Zivilprozess *m*; ~ *code* Bürgerliches Gesetzbuch; ~ *year* bürgerliches Jahr; ~ *law* a) römisches *od.* kontinentales Recht, b) Zivilrecht *n*, bürgerliches Recht; **6.** höflich: ~*spoken* höflich; ~ **en·gi·neer** *s.* 'Bauinge,nieur *m*; ~ **en·gi·neer·ing** *s.* Tiefbau *m*.

ci·vil·ian [sɪ'vɪljən] **I** *s.* Zivi'list *m*; **II** *adj.* zi'vil, Zivil...: ~ *life*; ~ *casualties* Verluste unter der Zivilbevölkerung; **ci'vil·i·ty** [-lətɪ] *s.* Höflichkeit *f*, Artigkeit *f*.

civ·i·li·za·tion [,sɪvɪlaɪ'zeɪʃn] *s.* Zivilisati'on *f*, Kul'tur *f*; **civ·i·lize** ['sɪvɪlaɪz] *v/t.* zivilisieren; **civ·i·lized** ['sɪvɪlaɪzd] *adj.* **1.** zivilisiert: ~ *nations* Kulturvölker; **2.** gebildet, kultiviert.

civ·vies ['sɪvɪz] *s. pl. sl.* Zi'vil(kla,motten *pl.*) *n*; **civ·vy street** ['sɪvɪ] *s. sl.* Zi'villeben *n*.

clack [klæk] **I** *v/i.* **1.** klappern, knallen; **2.** plappern; **II** *s.* **3.** Klappern *n*; **4.** Plappern *n*; **5.** ⊕ (Ven'til)Klappe *f*.

clad [klæd] *adj.* gekleidet.

claim [kleɪm] **I** *v/t.* **1.** fordern, verlangen: ~ *damages* Schadenersatz fordern; **2.** a) Anspruch erheben auf (*acc.*), beanspruchen: ~ *the crown*, b) *fig.* in Anspruch nehmen, erfordern: ~ *attention*; **3.** für sich in Anspruch nehmen: ~ *victory*; **4.** (*a.* von sich) behaupten (*a. to inf. u. inf., that* dass): ~ *accuracy* die Richtigkeit behaupten; *the club* ~*s 200 members* der Klub behauptet, 200 Mitglieder zu haben; **5.** zu'rück-, einfordern; *Opfer, Leben* fordern: *death* ~*ed him* der Tod ereilte ihn; **II** *v/i.* **6.** ♥ reklamieren; **7.** ~ *against s.o.* j-n verklagen; **III** *s.* **8.** Forderung *f* (*on s.o.* gegen *od.* an j-n), (*a.* Rechts- *od.* Pa'tent)Anspruch *m*: ~ **for damages** Schaden(s)ersatzanspruch; ~ **under a contract** Anspruch aus e-m Vertrag; **lay** (*od.* **make a**) ~ **to** Anspruch erheben auf (*acc.*); **put in a** ~ **for** e-e Forderung auf *et.* stellen; **make** **~s upon** *fig.* *j-n od. j-s* Zeit (stark) in Anspruch nehmen; **9.** (An)Recht *n* (**to** auf *acc.*); **10.** Behauptung *f*; **11.** ✝ Reklamati'on *f*; **12.** Versicherungssumme *f*; Schaden(sfall) *m*; **13.** ⚖ Klage(begehren *n*) *f*; → **statement** 4; **14.** ⚒ Mutung *f*; *bsd. Am.* zugeteiltes *od.* beanspruchtes Stück Land; **'claim·a·ble** [-məbl] *adj.* zu beanspruchen(d); **'claim·ant** [-mənt] *s.* **1.** Antragsteller (-in), ⚖ *a.* Kläger(in); (Pa'tent)Anmelder(in); **2.** (**for**) Anwärter(in) (auf *acc.*), Bewerber(in) (für): **rightful** ~ Anspruchsberechtigte(r).

clair·voy·ance [kleə'vɔiəns] *s.* Hellsehen *n*; **clair'voy·ant** [-nt] **I** *adj.* hellseherisch; **II** *s.* Hellseher(in).

clam [klæm] *s.* **1.** *zo.* essbare Muschel: **hard** *od.* **round** ~ 'Venusmuschel *f*; **2.** *Am.* F ,zugeknöpfter' Mensch; '~·**bake** *s. Am.* **1.** Picknick *n*; **2.** große Party; **3.** ,Gaudi' *f*.

cla·mant ['kleimənt] *adj.* **1.** lärmend, schreiend (*a. fig.*); **2.** dringend.

clam·ber ['klæmbə] *v/i.* (mühsam) klettern, klimmen.

clam·my ['klæmi] *adj.* ☐ feuchtkalt (u. klebrig), klamm.

clam·or·ous ['klæmərəs] *adj.* ☐ lärmend, schreiend, laut; tobend; *fig.* lautstark; **clam·o(u)r** ['klæmə] **I** *s.* **1.** *a. fig.* Lärm *m*, (zorniges) Geschrei, Tu'mult *m*; **2.** *bsd. fig.* (Auf)Schrei *m* (**for** nach); Schimpfen; **3.** Tu'mult *m*; **II** *v/i.* **4.** (laut) schreien (**for** nach; *a. fig.* wütend verlangen); heftig protestieren, toben; **III** *v/t.* **5.** ~ **down** niederbrüllen.

clamp¹ [klæmp] *s.* **1.** Haufen *m*; **2.** (Kar'toffel- *etc.*)Miete *f*.

clamp² [klæmp] **I** *s.* **1.** ⊙ Klammer *f*, Krampe *f*, Klemmschraube *f*, Zwinge *f*, ⚡ Erdungsschelle *f*; **2.** *sport* Strammer *m* (*Ski*); **II** *v/t.* **3.** festklammern, -klemmen; befestigen; **4.** *fig. a.* ~ **down** als Strafe auferlegen; **III** *v/i.* **5.** ~ **down** *fig.* zuschlagen, einschreiten, scharf vorgehen (**on** gegen); '**clamp·down** *s.* F scharfes Vorgehen (**on** gegen).

clan [klæn] *s.* **1.** *Scot.* Clan *m*, Stamm *m*, Sippe *f*; **2.** *fig.* Clan *m*, Sippschaft *f*, Clique *f*.

clan·des·tine [klæn'destin] *adj.* ☐ heimlich, verstohlen, Schleich...

clang [klæŋ] **I** *v/i.* schallen, klingen, klirren; **II** *v/t.* laut schallen *od.* erklingen lassen; **III** *s.* → **clango(u)r; clang·er** ['klæŋə] *s. sl.* Faux'pas *m*: **drop a** ~ ,ins Fettnäpfchen treten'; **clang·or·ous** ['klæŋgərəs] *adj.* ☐ schallend, schmetternd; klirrend; **clang·o(u)r** ['klæŋgə] → **clank**.

clank [klæŋk] **I** *s.* Klirren *n*, Gerassel *n*, harter Klang; **II** *v/i. u. v/t.* rasseln *od.* klirren (mit).

clan·nish ['klæniʃ] *adj.* **1.** Sippen...; **2.** stammesbewusst; **3.** (unter sich) zs.-haltend, *contp.* cliquenhaft; '**clan·nish·ness** [-nis] *s.* **1.** Stammesbewusstsein *n*; **2.** Zs.-halten *n*, *contp.* Cliquenwesen *n*; **clan·ship** ['klænʃip] *s.* **1.** Vereinigung *f* in e-m Clan; **2.** → **clannishness** 1; **clans·man** ['klænzmən] *s.* [*irr.*] Mitglied *n* e-s Clans.

clap¹ [klæp] **I** *s.* **1.** (Hände)Klatschen *n*; **2.** (Beifall)Klatschen *n*; **3.** Klaps *m*; **4.** Knall *m*, Krach *m*: ~ **of thunder** Donnerschlag *m*; **II** *v/t.* **5.** a) klatschen: ~

---

one's hands in die Hände klatschen, b) schlagen: ~ **the wings** mit den Flügeln schlagen; **6.** klopfen; **7.** *j-m* Beifall klatschen; **8.** hastig an-, auflegen *od.* ausführen: ~ **eyes on** erblicken; ~ **a hat on one's head** den Hut auf den Kopf stülpen; **9.** ~ **on** F *j-m et.* ,aufbrummen'; **III** *v/i.* **10.** (Beifall) klatschen.

clap² [klæp] *s.* V (*a.* **dose of** ~) Tripper *m*.

'**clap**|·**board** **I** *s.* **1.** *Brit.* Fassdaube *f*; **2.** *Am.* Verschalungsbrett *n*; **II** *v/t.* **3.** *Am.* verschalen; '~·**net** *s.* Fangnetz *n* (*für Vögel etc.*).

clap·per ['klæpə] *s.* **1.** Klöppel *m* (*Glocke*); **2.** Klapper *f*; **3.** Beifallsklatscher *m*; '~·**board** *s. Am. Film*: Klappe *f*.

clap·trap ['klæptræp] **I** *s.* Ef'fekthasche,rei *f*; Klim'bim *m*; Re'klame(rummel *m*) *f*; Gewäsch *n*, Unsinn *m*; **II** *adj.* ef'fekthaschend; hohl.

claque [klæk] *s.* Claque *f*.

clar·en·don ['klærəndən] *s. typ.* halbfette Egypti'enne.

clar·et ['klærət] *s.* **1.** roter Bor'deaux (-wein); *weitS.* Rotwein *m*; **2.** Weinrot *n*; **3.** *sl.* Blut *n*; ~ **cup** *s.* Rotweinbowle *f*.

clar·i·fi·ca·tion [,klærifi'keiʃn] *s.* **1.** ⊙ (Ab)Klärung *f*, Läuterung *f*; **2.** Aufklärung *f*, Klarstellung *f*; **clar·i·fy** ['klærifai] **I** *v/t.* **1.** ⊙ (ab)klären, läutern, reinigen; **2.** (auf-, er)klären; **II** *v/i.* **3.** ⊙ sich (ab)klären; **4.** sich (auf)klären, klar werden.

clar·i·net [,klæri'net] *s.* ♪ Klari'nette *f*; ,**clar·i'net·(t)ist** [-tist] *s.* Klarinet'tist *m*.

clar·i·on ['klæriən] *s.* **1.** ♪ Cla'rino *n*; **2.** *poet.* Trom'petenschall *m*: ~ **call** *fig.* Auf-, Weckruf *m*; Fan'fare *f*; ~ **voice** Trompetenstimme *f*; **II** *v/t.* **3.** laut verkünden, 'auspo,saunen.

clar·i·ty ['klærəti] *s. allg.* Klarheit *f*.

clash [klæʃ] **I** *v/i.* **1.** klirren, rasseln; **2.** prallen (**into** gegen), (*a. feindlich u. fig.*) zs.-prallen, -stoßen (**with** mit); **3.** *fig.* (**with**) kollidieren: a) (zeitlich) zs.-fallen (mit), b) im 'Widerspruch stehen (zu), unvereinbar sein (mit); **4.** nicht zs.-passen (**with** mit), sich ,beißen' (*Farben*); **II** *v/t.* **5.** klirren *od.* rasseln mit; klirrend zs.-schlagen; **III** *s.* **6.** Geklirr *n*, Getöse *n*, Krach *m*; **7.** Zs.-prall *m*, Kollisi'on *f*; **8.** (feindlicher) Zs.-stoß; **9.** (zeitliches) Zs.-fallen; **10.** Kon'flikt *m*, 'Widerstreit *m*.

clasp [klɑːsp] **I** *v/t.* **1.** ein-, zuhaken, zuschnallen; **2.** fest ergreifen, um'klammern, fest um'fassen; um'ranken: ~ **s.o.'s hand** *j-m* die Hand drücken; ~ **s.o. in one's arms** *j-n* umarmen; ~ **one's hands** die Hände falten; **II** *v/i.* **3.** sich die Hand reichen; **III** *s.* **4.** Klammer *f*, Haken *m*; Schnalle *f*, Spange *f*, Schließe *f*; Schloss *n* (*Buch etc.*); **5.** Um'klammerung *f*, Um'armung *f*; Händedruck *m*; **6.** ⚔ (Ordens)Spange *f*; ~ **knife** *s.* [*irr.*] Klapp-, Taschenmesser *n*.

class [klɑːs] **I** *s.* **1.** Klasse *f* (*a.* 🐟 *etc.*, ♀, *zo.*), Gruppe *f*; **2.** Klasse *f*, Sorte *f*, Güte *f*, Quali'tät *f*; *engS.* Erstklassigkeit *f*: **in the same** ~ **with** gleichwertig mit; **in a** ~ **of one's** (*od.* **its**) **own** e-e Klasse für sich (*überlegen*); **no** ~ F minderwertig; **3.** Stand *m*, Rang *m*, Schicht *f*: **the** (**upper**) ~**es** die oberen (Gesellschafts)Klassen; **pull** ~ **on s.o.** F *j-n* s-e gesellschaftliche Überlegenheit fühlen lassen; **4.** *ped., univ.* a) Klasse *f*: **top of the** ~ Klassenerste(r), b) 'Unterricht *m*, Stunde *f*: **a** ~ **in cookery** Kochstunde, c) *pl.* 'Kurs(us) *m*, d) Semi'nar *n*, e) *Brit.* Stufe *f* bei der Universi'tätsprü-

---

fung: **take a** ~ e-n **honours degree** erlangen; **5.** *univ. Am.* Jahrgang *m*; **II** *v/t.* **6.** klassifizieren: a) in Klassen einteilen, b) einordnen, einstufen: ~ **with** gleichstellen mit; **be ~ed as** angesehen werden als; '~·**book** *s. ped.* **1.** *Brit.* Lehrbuch *n*; **2.** *Am.* Klassenbuch *n*; '~-,**con·scious** *adj.* klassenbewusst; ~ **dis·tinc·tion** *s. sociol.* 'Klassen,unterschied *m*; ~ **ha·tred** *s.* Klassenhass *m*.

clas·sic ['klæsik] **I** *adj.* (☐ **~ally**) **1.** erstklassig, ausgezeichnet; **2.** klassisch, mustergültig, voll'endet; **3.** klassisch: a) griechisch-römisch, b) die klassische Lite'ra'tur *od.* Kunst *etc.* betreffend, c) berühmt, d) edel (*Stil etc.*); **4.** klassisch: a) 'herkömmlich, b) zeitlos; **II** *s.* **5.** Klassiker *m*; **6.** klassisches Werk; **7.** Jünger(in) der Klassik; **8.** *pl.* a) klassische Litera'tur, b) *die* alten Sprachen; '**clas·si·cal** [-kl] *adj.* ☐ **1.** → **classic** 1, 2, 3: ~ **music** klassische Musik; **2.** a) altsprachlich, b) huma'nistisch (gebildet): ~ **education** humanistische Bildung; **the** ~ **languages** die alten Sprachen; ~ **scholar** Altphilologe *m*, Humanist *m*; '**clas·si·cism** [-isizəm] *s.* **1.** Klassi'zismus *m*; **2.** klassische Redewendung; '**clas·si·cist** [-isist] *s.* Kenner *m od.* Anhänger *m* des Klassischen u. der Klassiker.

clas·si·fi·ca·tion [,klæsifi'keiʃn] *s.* Klassifizierung *f* (*a.* ♣), Einteilung *f*, -stufung *f*, Anordnung *f*; Ru'brik *f*: (**security**) ~ *pol.* a) Geheimhaltungseinstufung *f*, b) Geheimhaltungsstufe *f*; **clas·si·fied** ['klæsifaid] *adj.* **1.** klassifiziert, eingeteilt: ~ **advertisements** Kleinanzeigen (*Zeitung*); ~ **directory** Branchenverzeichnis *n*; **2.** ⚔, *pol.* geheim, Geheim...: ~ **material**; ~ **information** Verschlusssache (*n pl.*) *f*; **clas·si·fy** ['klæsifai] *v/t.* klassifizieren, einteilen; einstufen; ⚔, *pol.* für geheim erklären.

class·less ['klɑːslis] *adj.* klassenlos: ~ **society**.

'**class**|·**mate** *s.* 'Klassenkame,rad(in); ~ **re·un·ion** *s.* Klassentreffen *n*; '~·**room** *s.* Klassenzimmer *n*; ~ **war** *s. pol.* Klassenkampf *m*.

class·y ['klɑːsi] *adj. sl.* ,klasse' (*od.* ,Klasse'), ,Klasse...'.

clat·ter ['klætə] **I** *v/i.* **1.** klappern, rasseln; **2.** trappeln, trampeln; **II** *v/t.* **3.** klappern *od.* rasseln mit; **III** *s.* **4.** Klappern *n*, Rasseln *n*, Krach *m*; **5.** Getrappel *n*; **6.** Lärm *m*; Stimmengewirr *n*.

clause [klɔːz] *s.* **1.** *ling.* Satz(teil *m*, -glied *n*) *m*; **2.** *jur.* a) 'Klausel *f*, Bestimmung *f*, Vorbehalt *m*, b) Absatz *m*, Para'graph *m*.

claus·tro·pho·bi·a [,klɔːstrə'fəubjə] *s.* Klaustropho'bie *f*.

clav·i·chord ['klævikɔːd] *s.* ♪ Clavi'chord *n*.

clav·i·cle ['klævikl] *s. anat.* Schlüsselbein *n*.

claw [klɔː] **I** *s.* **1.** *zo.* a) Klaue *f*, Kralle *f* (*beide a. fig.*), b) Schere *f* (*Krebs etc.*), c) Pfote *f* (*a. fig.* F Hand): **get one's ~s into s.o.** *fig.* *j-n* in s-e Klauen bekommen; **pare s.o.'s ~s** *fig.* *j-m* die Krallen beschneiden; **2.** ⊙ Klaue *f*, (Greif)Haken *m*; **II** *v/t.* **3.** (zer)kratzen, zerreißen, zerren; **4.** *a.* ~ **hold of** um'krallen, packen; **5.** ~ **back** *fig.* a) zurückgewinnen, b) zurücknehmen; **III** *v/i.* **6.** kratzen; **7.** reißen, zerren (**at** an); **8.** packen, greifen (**at** nach); **9.** ♣ ~ **off** vom Ufer abhalten; '~-,**ham·mer** *s.* **1.** ⊙ Klauenhammer *m*; **2.** *a.* ~ **coat** F Frack *m*.

C

clay [kleɪ] s. **1.** Ton m, Lehm m: **~ hut** Lehmhütte f; **feet of ~** fig. tönerne Füße; → **potter²** 1; **2.** fig. Erde f, Staub m u. Asche f; **3.** → **clay pipe**; **~ court** s. Tennis: Rotgrantplatz m.

clay·ey ['kleɪɪ] adj. lehmig, Lehm...

clay·more ['kleɪmɔː] s. hist. schottisches Breitschwert.

clay| pi·geon s. sport Wurf-, Tontaube f; **~ pipe** s. Tonpfeife f; **~ pit** s. Lehmgrube f.

clean [kliːn] I adj. □ **1.** rein, sauber; → **breast** 2; **2.** sauber, frisch, neu (Wäsche); unbeschrieben (Papier); **3.** reinlich; stubenrein; **4.** einwandfrei, makellos (a. fig.); astfrei (Holz); fast fehlerlos (Korrekturbogen); → **copy** 1; **5.** (moralisch) lauter, sauber; anständig, gesittet; schuldlos: **~ record** tadelloser Ruf; **keep it ~!** keine Ferkeleien!; **~ living!** bleib sauber!; **Mr. ♀** Saubermann m; **6.** ebenmäßig, von schöner Form; glatt (Schnitt, Bruch); **7.** sauber, geschickt (ausgeführt), tadellos; **8.** F 'sauber' (ohne Waffen, Schmuggelware etc.); II adv. **9.** rein, sauber: **sweep ~** rein ausfegen; **come ~** F alles gestehen; **10.** rein, glatt, völlig, to'tal: **I ~ forgot** ich vergaß ganz; **~ gone** a) spurlos verschwunden, b) sl. total übergeschnappt; **~ through the wall** glatt durch die Wand; III v/t. **11.** reinigen, säubern; Kleider ('chemisch) reinigen; **12.** Fenster, Schuhe, Zähne putzen; IV v/i. **13.** sich reinigen lassen; **~ down** v/t. gründlich reinigen; abwaschen; **~ out** v/t. **1.** reinigen; **2.** auslesen, -räumen; räumen; **3.** sl. a) 'ausnehmen', 'schröpfen', b) Am. a. j-n 'fertig machen'; **4.** F Kasse etc. leer machen; Laden etc. leer kaufen; **5.** F Bank etc. 'ausräumen'; **~ up** v/t. **1.** gründlich reinigen; **2.** aufräumen (mit fig.); in Ordnung bringen, erledigen, fig. a. bereinigen; Stadt etc. säubern; **3.** sl. (v/i. schwer) einheimsen.

clean| and jerk s. Gewichtheben: Stoßen n; **~ bill of lad·ing** s. ♏ reines Konosse'ment; **,~·'bred** adj. reinrassig; **,~·'cut** adj. **1.** klar um'rissen; klar, deutlich; **2.** regelmäßig; wohlgeformt; **3.** scharf geschnitten: **~ face**.

clean·er ['kliːnə] s. **1.** Reiniger m (Person, Gerät od. Mittel); Reinemachfrau f, Raumpflegerin f; (Fenster- etc.)Putzer m; **2.** pl. Reinigung(sanstalt) f: **take s.o. to the ~s** sl. a) j-n total 'ausnehmen', b) j-n 'fertig machen'.

,clean|-'hand·ed adj. schuldlos; **,~·'limbed** adj. wohlproportioniert.

clean·li·ness ['klenlɪnɪs] s. Reinlichkeit f; **clean·ly** ['klenlɪ] adj. □ reinlich.

cleanse [klenz] v/t. **1.** (a. fig.) reinigen, säubern, rein waschen (from von); **2.** läutern; **'cleans·er** [-zə] s. Reinigungsmittel n; **cleans·ing** [-zɪŋ] adj. Reinigungs...: **~ cream**.

,clean|-'shav·en adj. glatt rasiert; **'~·up** s. **1.** (gründliche) Reinigung f; **2.** F 'Säuberungsakti,on f; Ausmerzung f; **3.** Am. sl. 'Schnitt' m, (großer) Pro'fit.

clear [klɪə] I adj. □ → **clearly**; **1.** klar, hell, 'durchsichtig, rein (a. fig.): **a ~ day** ein klarer Tag; **as ~ as day(light)**, **~ as mud** sonnenklar; **a ~ conscience** ein reines Gewissen; **2.** klar, deutlich; 'übersichtlich; scharf (Foto, Sprache, Verstand): **a ~ head** ein klarer Kopf; **~ judgment** gesundes Urteil; **be ~ in one's mind** sich klar darüber sein: **make o.s. ~** sich verständlich machen; **3.** klar, offensichtlich; sicher, zweifellos: **I am quite ~ (that)** ich bin ganz

sicher (dass); **4.** klar, rein; unvermischt; ♏ netto: **~ amount** Nettobetrag m; **~ profit** Reingewinn m; **~ loss** reiner Verlust; **~ skin** reine Haut; **~ soup** klare Suppe; **~ water** (nur) reines Wasser; **5.** klar, hell (Ton): **as ~ as a bell** glockenrein; **6.** frei (of von), offen; unbehindert; ohne: **keep the roads ~** die Straßen offen halten; **~ of debt** schuldenfrei; **~ title** jur. unbestrittenes Recht; **see one's way ~** freie Bahn haben; **keep ~ of** a) (ver)meiden, b) sich fern halten von: **keep ~ of the gates!** Eingang (Tor) freihalten!; **be ~ of s.th.** et. los sein; **get ~ of** loskommen von; **7.** ganz, voll: **a ~ month** ein voller Monat; **8.** ☉ licht (Höhe, Weite); II adv. **9.** hell; klar, deutlich; **10.** frei, los, fort; **11.** völlig, glatt: **~ over the fence** glatt über den Zaun; III s. **12.** ☉ lichte Weite; **13. in the ~** a) frei, heraus, b) sport frei stehend, c) aus der Sache heraus, vom Verdacht gereinigt, d) Funk etc.: im Klartext; IV v/t. **14.** a. **~ up** (auf)klären, erläutern; **15.** säubern, reinigen (a. fig.), befreien; losmachen (of von): **~ the street of snow** die Straße von Schnee reinigen; **16.** Saal etc. räumen, leeren; ♏ Waren(lager) räumen (→ 23); Tisch abräumen, abdecken; Straße freimachen; Land, Wald roden: **~ the way** Platz machen, den Weg bahnen; **~ out of the way** fig. beseitigen; **17.** reinigen, säubern: **~ the air** a. fig. die Atmosphäre reinigen; **~ one's throat** sich räuspern; **18.** frei-, lossprechen; entlasten (of, from von e-m Verdacht etc.); Am. j-m (po'litische) Unbedenklichkeit bescheinigen; Am. die Genehmigung für et. einholen (with bei): **~ one's conscience** sein Gewissen entlasten; **~ one's name** s-n Namen rein waschen; **19.** (knapp od. heil) vor'beikommen an (dat.): **my car just ~ed the bus**; **20.** Hindernis nehmen, glatt springen über (acc.): **~ the hedge**; **~ 6 feet** 6 Fuß hoch springen; **21.** Gewinn erzielen, einheimsen: **~ expenses** die Unkosten einbringen; **22.** ♏ Schiff klarmachen (for action zum Gefecht), b) Schiff ausklarieren, c) Ladung löschen, d) aus e-m Hafen auslaufen; **23.** ♏ bereinigen, bezahlen; verrechnen; Scheck einlösen; Hypothek tilgen; Ware verzollen (→ 16); abfertigen; V v/i. **24.** sich klären, klar werden; **25.** sich aufklären (Wetter): **~ (away)** sich verziehen (Nebel etc.); **26.** sich klären (Wein etc.); **27.** ♏ a) die 'Zollformali,täten erledigen, b) ausklarieren;

Zssgn mit adv.:

clear| a·way I v/t. **1.** wegräumen, beseitigen; II v/i. **2.** verschwinden; → **clear** 25; **3.** (den Tisch) abdecken; **~ off** I v/t. **1.** beseitigen, loswerden; **2.** erledigen; II v/i. **3.** → **clear out** 3; **~ out** I v/t. **1.** ausräumen, reinigen; **2.** ♏ ausverkaufen; II v/i. **3.** verschwinden, 'sich verziehen', 'abhauen'; **~ up** I v/t. **1.** ab-, forträumen; **2.** bereinigen, erledigen; **3.** aufklären, lösen; II v/i. **4.** sich aufklären (Wetter).

clear·ance ['klɪərəns] s. **1.** Räumung f (a. ♏), Beseitigung f; Leerung f; Freilegung f; **2.** a) Rodung f, b) Lichtung f; **3.** ☉ lichter Raum, Zwischenraum m; Spiel(raum m n); mot. etc. Bodenfreiheit f; **4.** allg. Abfertigung f, bsd. a) ✈ Freigabe f, Start- od. 'Durchflugerlaubnis f, b) ♏ Auslaufgenehmigung f (→ 7); **5.** ♏ a) Tilgung f, volle Bezahlung f, b) Verrechnung f (→ **clearing** 2), c) →

clearance sale; **6.** ♏ a) (Ein-, Aus-) Klarierung f, Zollabfertigung f, b) Zollschein m: **~ (papers)** Zollpapiere; **7.** pol. etc. Unbedenklichkeitsbescheinigung f; **~ sale** s. Brit. (Räumungs)Ausverkauf m.

,clear|-'cut adj. scharf um'rissen; klar, eindeutig; **,~·'head·ed** adj. klar denkend, intelli'gent.

clear·ing ['klɪərɪŋ] s. **1.** Lichtung f, Rodung f; **2.** ♏ Clearing n, Verrechnungsverkehr m (Bank); **~ bank** s. 'Girobank f; **♀ Hos·pi·tal** s. ✕ Brit. 'Feldlaza,rett n; **~ house** s. ♏ 'Clearinginsti,tut n, Verrechnungsstelle f; **~ of·fice** s. Verrechnungsstelle f; **~ sys·tem** s. ♏ Clearingverkehr m.

clear·ly ['klɪəlɪ] adv. **1.** klar, deutlich; **2.** **~, that is wrong** offensichtlich ist das falsch; **3.** zweifellos, 'klar'; **clear·ness** ['klɪənɪs] s. **1.** Klarheit f, Deutlichkeit f; **2.** fig. reine Haut f; Schärfe f.

,clear|-'sight·ed adj. **1.** scharfsichtig; **2.** fig. klar denkend, hellsichtig, klug; **'~·starch** v/t. Wäsche stärken; **'~·way** s. Brit. Schnellstraße f.

cleat [kliːt] s. **1.** ♏ Klampe f; **2.** Keil m, Pflock m; **3.** ⚡ Isolierschelle f; **4.** ☉ Querleiste f; **5.** breiter Schuhnagel.

cleav·age ['kliːvɪdʒ] s. **1.** Spaltung f (a. ⚛ u. fig.); Spaltbarkeit f; **2.** Zwiespalt m; **3.** biol. (Zell)Teilung f; **4.** Brustansatz m, Dekolletee n.

cleave¹ [kliːv] v/i. **1.** kleben (to an dat.); **2.** fig. (to) festhalten (an dat.), halten (zu j-m), treu bleiben (dat.), anhängen (dat.).

cleave² [kliːv] I v/t. [irr.] **1.** (zer)spalten; **2.** hauen, reißen; Weg bahnen; **3.** Wasser, Luft etc. durch'schneiden; (zer)teilen; II v/i. [irr.] **4.** sich spalten, bersten; **'cleav·er** [-və] s. Hackmesser n, -beil n.

clef [klef] s. ♪ (Noten)Schlüssel m.

cleft¹ [kleft] pret. u. p.p. von **cleave²**.

cleft² [kleft] I s. Spalte f, Kluft f, Riss m; II adj. gespalten, geteilt; **~ pal·ate** s. Gaumenspalte f, Wolfsrachen m; **~ stick** s.: **be in a ~** 'in der Klemme' sitzen.

clem·a·tis ['klemətɪs] s. ♣ Kle'matis f.

clem·en·cy ['klemənsɪ] I s. Milde f (a. Wetter), Nachsicht f; II adj. Gnaden... (-behörde etc.); **'clem·ent** [-nt] adj. □ mild (a. Wetter), nachsichtig, gnädig.

clem·en·tine ['kleməntiːn, -taɪn] s. Obst: Klemen'tine f.

clench [klentʃ] I v/t. **1.** bsd. Lippen zs.-pressen; Zähne zs.-beißen; Faust ballen: **~ one's fist**; **2.** fest anpacken; (an)spannen (a. fig.); **3.** → **clinch** 1, 2, 3; II v/i. **4.** sich fest zs.-pressen; sich ballen.

cler·gy ['kləːdʒɪ] s. eccl. Geistlichkeit f, Klerus m, die Geistlichen pl.: **20 ~** 20 Geistliche; **'~·man** [-mən] s. [irr.] Geistliche(r) m.

cler·ic ['klerɪk] s. Kleriker m; **'cler·i·cal** [-kl] I adj. **1.** geistlich: **~ collar** Kragen m des Geistlichen; **2.** pol. kleri'kal; **3.** Schreib..., Büro...: **~ error** Schreibfehler m; **~ work** Büroarbeit f; II s. **4.** pol. Kleri'kale(r) m; **'cler·i·cal·ism** [-kəlɪzəm] s. pol. Klerika'lismus m, kleri'kale Poli'tik.

cler·i·hew ['klerɪhjuː] s. 'Clerihew n (witziger Vierzeiler).

clerk [klɑːk] I s. **1.** Sekre'tär m; Schriftführer m; (Bü'ro)Schreiber m: **~ of the court** Urkundsbeamte(r) m; → **articled** 2, **town clerk**; **2.** Bü'roangestellte(r m) f; Buchhalter(in); (Bank)Beamte(r) *m*, (-)Beamtin *f*; **3.** *Brit.* Vorsteher *m*, Leiter *m*: **~** *of* (*the*) *works* Bauleiter; **~** *of the weather* *fig.* Wettergott, Petrus; **4.** *Am.* a) Verkäufer(in) *im Laden*, b) (Ho'tel)Porti,er *m*, Empfangschef *m*, -dame *f*; **5.** **~** *in holy orders* *eccl.* Geistliche(r) *m*; **II** *v/i.* **6.** als Schreiber *etc.* *od.* *Am.* als Verkäufer (-in) tätig sein; '**clerk·ship** [-ʃɪp] *s.* Stellung *f* e-s Bü'roangestellten *etc. od. Am.* Verkäufers.

clev·er ['klevə] *adj.* □ **1.** geschickt, raffiniert (*Person u. Sache*); gewandt: **~** *dick* F ,Klugscheißer' *m*; **2.** klug, gescheit; begabt (*at* in); **3.** geistreich (*Worte, Buch*); **4.** a. '~'~ *contp.* ,superklug'; '**clev·er·ness** [-nɪs] *s.* Geschicklichkeit *f*; Klugheit *f etc.*

clew [kluː] I *s.* **1.** Knäuel *m*, *n* (*Garn*); **2.** → *clue* 1, 2; **3.** ♣ Schothorn *n*; **II** *v/t.* **4.** **~** *up* Segel aufgeien; **~** *gar·net* *s.* ♣ Geitau *n*.

cli·ché ['kliːʃeɪ] *s.* Kli'schee *n*: a) *typ.* Druckstock *m*, b) *fig.* Gemeinplatz *m*, abgedroschene Phrase.

click [klɪk] I *s.* **1.** Klicken *n*, Knipsen *n*, Knacken *n*, Ticken *n*; Einschnappen *n*; *Computer*: (Maus)Klick *m*; **2.** ⊚ Schnapp-, Sperrvorrichtung *f*; Sperrhaken *m*, Klinke *f*; **3.** Schnalzen *n*; **II** *v/i.* **4.** klicken, knacken, ticken; **5.** schnalzen; **6.** (zu-, ein)schnappen: **~** *into place* einrasten, *fig.* sein (richtiges) Plätzchen finden; **7.** *sl.* F ,einschlagen', Erfolg haben (*with* mit); **8.** sofort Gefallen aneinander finden, *engS.* sich ineinander ,verknallen'; **9.** F über'einstimmen (*with* mit); **10.** *it ~ed* F bei mir *etc.* ,klingelte' es (*als ich hörte etc.*); **III** *v/t.* **11.** klicken *od.* ticken *od.* knacken *od.* einschnappen lassen: **~** *the door* (*to*) die Tür zuklinken; **~** (*on*) *s.th. Computer*: et. anklicken, auf et. klicken; **~** *one's heels* die Hacken zs.-schlagen; **12.** schnalzen mit: **~** *one's tongue*.

cli·ent ['klaɪənt] *s.* **1.** ⚖ Kli'ent(in), Man'dant(in): **~** (*state*) *pol.* abhängiger Staat; **2.** † Kunde *m*, Kundin *f*; **3.** Pati'ent(in) (*e-s Arztes*); **cli·en·tele** [ˌkliːɑːn'tel] *s.* **1.** Klien'tel *f*, Kli'enten *pl.*; **2.** Pa'tienten(kreis *m*) *pl.*; **3.** Kunden(kreis *m*) *pl.*, Kundschaft *f*.

cliff [klɪf] *s.* Klippe *f*, Felsen *m*: **go over the ~** F *fig.* ,eingehen', Pleite gehen; **~ dwell·ing** *s.* Felsenwohnung *f*; '**~-** ,**hang·er** *s.* F **1.** 'Fortsetzungsro,man *m* (*etc.*), der jeweils im spannendsten Mo'ment abbricht; **2.** äußerst spannende Sache.

cli·mac·ter·ic [klaɪ'mæktərɪk] I *adj.* **1.** entscheidend, ,kritisch; **2.** ✿ klimak'terisch; **II** *s.* **3.** ♣ Klimak'terium *n*, Wechseljahre *pl.*; **4.** a) kritische Zeit, b) (Lebens)Wende *f*.

cli·mate ['klaɪmɪt] *s.* **1.** 'Klima *n*; **~** *change* Klimaveränderung *f*; **2.** Gegend *f*; **3.** *fig.* (*politisches, Betriebs-etc.*)'Klima *n*, Atmo'sphäre *f*; **cli·mat·ic** [klaɪ'mætɪk] *adj.* (□ *~ally*) kli'matisch; **cli·ma·to·log·ic** [ˌklaɪmətə'lɒdʒɪk(l)] *adj.* □ klimato'logisch; **cli·ma·tol·o·gy** [ˌklaɪmə'tɒlədʒɪ] *s.* Klimatolo'gie *f*, 'Klimakunde *f*.

cli·max ['klaɪmæks] I *s.* **1.** Steigerung *f*; **2.** Gipfel *m*, Höhepunkt *m*; 'Krisis *f*; **3.** (sexu'eller) Höhepunkt, Or'gasmus *m*; **II** *v/t.* **4.** auf e-n Höhepunkt bringen; *Laufbahn etc.* krönen; **III** *v/i.* **5.** e-n Höhepunkt erreichen; **6.** e-n Or'gasmus haben.

climb [klaɪm] I *s.* **1.** Aufstieg *m*, Bestei-

gung *f*; 'Kletterpar,tie *f*; **2.** ✈ Steigen *n*, Steigflug *m*; **II** *v/i.* **3.** klettern; **4.** steigen (*Straße, Flugzeug*); **5.** (auf-, em-por)steigen, (hoch)klettern (*a. fig. Preise etc.*); **6.** ♀ sich hin'aufranken; **III** *v/t.* **7.** be-, ersteigen; steigen *od.* klettern auf (*acc.*), erklimmen; **~** *down* *v/i.* **1.** hin'untersteigen, -klettern; **2.** *fig.* e-n ,Rückzieher' machen, klein beigeben; **~** *up* *v/t. u. v/i.* hin'aufsteigen, -klettern.

climb·a·ble ['klaɪməbl] *adj.* ersteigbar; '**climb-down** *s.* F ,Rückzieher' *m*, Nachgeben *n*; '**climb·er** [-mə] *s.* **1.** Kletterer *m*; Bergsteiger(in); **2.** ♀ Kletter-, Schlingpflanze *f*; **3.** *orn.* Klettervogel *m*; **4.** F (gesellschaftlicher) Streber, Aufsteiger *m*.

climb·ing| a·bil·i·ty ['klaɪmɪŋ] *s.* **1.** ✈ Steigvermögen *n*; **2.** *mot.* Bergfreudigkeit *f*; **~ i·rons** *s. pl. mount.* Steigeisen *pl.*

clime [klaɪm] *s. poet.* Gegend *f*, Landstrich *m*; *fig.* Gebiet *n*, Sphäre *f*.

clinch [klɪntʃ] I *v/t.* **1.** entscheiden, zum Abschluss bringen; *Handel* festmachen: *that ~ed it* damit war die Sache entschieden; **~** *an argument* den Streit für sich entscheiden; **2.** ⊚ a) sicher befestigen, b) vernieten; **3.** *Boxen*: um'klammern; **II** *v/i.* **4.** *Boxen*: clinchen; **III** *s.* **5.** fester Griff *od.* Halt; **6.** *Boxen*: Clinch *m* (*a. sl. Umarmung*); **7.** ⊚ Vernietung *f*; Niet *m*; '**clinch·er** [-tʃə] *s.* F entscheidender 'Umstand *od.* Beweis *etc.*, Trumpf *m*.

cling [klɪŋ] *v/i.* [*irr.*] **1.** (*to*) *a. fig.* kleben, haften (an *dat.*); anhaften (*dat.*): **~** *together* zs.-halten; **2.** (*to*) *a. fig.* sich klammern (an *j-n, e-e Hoffnung etc.*), festhalten (an *e-r Sitte, Meinung etc.*): **~** *to the text* am Text kleben; **3.** sich (an)schmiegen (*to* an *acc.*); **4.** *fig.* (*to*) hängen (an *dat.*), anhängen (*dat.*); **cling film** *s.* Frischhaltefolie *f*; '**cling·ing** [-ŋɪŋ] *adj.* eng anliegend, hauteng (*Kleid*).

clin·ic ['klɪnɪk] *s.* **1.** Klinik *f*, (Pri'vat *od.* Universi'täts)Krankenhaus *n*; **2.** Klinikum *n*, klinischer 'Unterricht; **3.** 'Poliklinik *f*, Ambu'lanz *f etc.*; **4.** *Am.* Fachkurs(us) *m*, Semi'nar *n*; '**clin·i·cal** [-kl] *adj.* □ **1.** klinisch: **~** *instruction* Unterweisung *f* am Krankenbett; **~** *thermometer* Fieberthermometer *n*; **2.** *fig.* nüchtern, kühl analysierend; **clin·i·car** ['klɪnɪkɑː] *s.* Notarztwagen *m*; **cli·ni·cian** [klɪ'nɪʃn] *s.* Kliniker *m*.

clink¹ [klɪŋk] I *v/i.* klingen, klimpern, klirren; **II** *v/t.* klingen *od.* klirren lassen: **~** *glasses* (mit den Gläsern) anstoßen; **III** *s.* Klingen *n etc.*

clink² [klɪŋk] *s. sl.* ,Knast' *m*, ,Kittchen' *n* (*Gefängnis*): *in ~*.

clink·er¹ ['klɪŋkə] *s.* **1.** Klinker *m*, Hartziegel *m*; **2.** Schlacke *f*.

clink·er² ['klɪŋkə] *bsd. Am. sl.* **1.** ,Patzer' *m*; **2.** ,Pleite' *f* (*Misserfolg*).

'**clink·er-built** *adj.* ♣ in Klinkerbauweise.

cli·nom·e·ter [klaɪ'nɒmɪtə] *s.* Neigungs-, Winkelmesser *m*.

Cli·o ['klaɪəʊ] *s. Am.* alljährlicher Preis für die beste Leistung im Werbefernsehen.

clip¹ [klɪp] I *v/t.* **1.** abschneiden; *a. fig.* beschneiden; *Schwanz, Flügel, Hecke* stutzen: **~** *s.o.'s wings* j-m die Flügel beschneiden; **2.** *Haare* (*mit der Maschine*) schneiden; *Tiere* scheren; **3.** *aus der Zeitung* ausschneiden; *Fahrschein* lochen; **4.** *Silben od. Buchstaben* ver-

schlucken: **~ped speech** a) undeutliche (Aus)Sprache, b) knappe *od.* schneidige Sprechweise; **5.** *j-m* e-n Schlag ,verpassen'; **6.** F a) *j-n* ,erleichtern' (*for* um), b) *j-n* ,neppen'; **II** *s.* **7.** Haarschnitt *m*; **8.** Schur *f*; **9.** Wollertrag *m* *e-r Schur*; **10.** F Hieb *m*; **11.** F Tempo *n*: *at a good ~* in scharfem Tempo.

clip² [klɪp] I *s.* **1.** (Bü'ro-, Heft)Klammer *f*, Klemme *f*, Spange *f*, Halter *m*; **2.** ✕ (*Patronen*)Rahmen *m*, Ladestreifen *m*; **II** *v/t.* **3.** festhalten; befestigen, (an)klammern.

'**clip|-board** [-bɔːd] *s. Computer*: Zwischenablage *f*; **~ joint** *s. sl.* 'Nepplo,kal *n*.

clip·per ['klɪpə] *s.* **1.** ♣ Klipper *m*, Schnellsegler *m*; **2.** ✈ Clipper *m*; **3.** Renner *m* (*schnelles Pferd*); **4.** *pl.* 'Haarschneide-, 'Scherma,schine *f*, Schere *f*.

clip·pie ['klɪpɪ] *s.* F *Brit.* Busschaffnerin *f*.

clip·ping ['klɪpɪŋ] *s.* **1.** *Am.* (Zeitungs-) Ausschnitt *m*: **~** *bureau* Zeitungsausschnittsdienst *m*; **2.** *mst pl.* Schnitzel *pl.*, Abfälle *pl.*

clique [kliːk] *s.* Clique *f*, Klüngel *m*; '**cli·quish** [-kɪʃ] *adj.* cliquenhaft.

clit [klɪt] *sl. für* **cli·to·ris** ['klɪtərɪs] *s. anat.* 'Klitoris *f*, Kitzler *m*.

clo·a·ca [kləʊ'eɪkə] *pl.* **-s**, **-cae** [-kiː] *s.* Klo'ake *f* (*a. zo.; a. fig.* Sündenpfuhl).

cloak [kləʊk] I *s.* **1.** (loser) Mantel, 'Umhang *m*; **2.** *fig.* Deckmantel *m*: *under the ~ of night* im Schutz der Nacht; **II** *v/t.* **3.** (wie) mit e-m Mantel bedecken; **4.** *fig.* bemänteln, verhüllen; ,**~-and-'dag·ger** *adj.* **1.** ,Mantel-und-Degen-...': **~** *drama*; **2.** Spionage-...: **~** *story*; '**~-room** *s.* **1.** Garde'robe *f*; **2.** *Brit.* F Toi'lette *f*.

clob·ber ['klɒbə] *v/t. sl.* **1.** verprügeln, *fig.* ,fertig machen'; **2.** *sport* ,über'fahren', ,vernaschen'.

cloche [kləʊʃ] *s.* **1.** Glasglocke *f* (*für Pflanzen*); **2.** Glocke *f* (*Damenhut*).

clock¹ [klɒk] I *s.* **1.** (Wand-, Turm-, Stand)Uhr *f*: *five o'clock* fünf Uhr; (*a*)*round the ~* rund um die Uhr, den ganzen Tag (*arbeiten etc.*); *put the ~ back fig.* das Rad zurückdrehen; **2.** F a) Kon'troll-, Stoppuhr, b) Fahrpreisanzeiger *m* (*Taxi*); **3.** *Computer*: Taktgeber *m*; **4.** ♀ Pusteblume *f*; **II** *v/t.* **5.** *bsd. sport* a) (*mit der Uhr*) (ab)stoppen, b) *Zeit* nehmen, c) *Zeit* erreichen; **6.** a. **~** *up* F *Zeit, Zahlen etc.* registrieren; **7.** a. **~** *back Brit. mot.* den Kilometerstand von et. verändern, F *den Tacho* ,frisieren' *od.* zurückstellen: **~ed vehicle** Fahrzeug *n* mit ,frisiertem' Tacho; **III** *v/i.* **8.** **~** *in od.* **on** (**off** *od.* **out**) einstempeln (ausstempeln) (*Arbeitnehmer*); **9.** **~** *back Brit. mot.* den Kilometerstand verändern, den Tacho ,frisieren' *od.* zurückstellen.

clock² [klɒk] *s.* (Strumpf)Verzierung *f*.

clock·er ['klɒkə] *s. Brit. mot.* F *j-d, der den Tacho zurückgestellt hat.*

clock face *s.* Zifferblatt *n*.

'**clock·ing** *s. Brit. mot.* F betrügerisches Zurückstellen des Tachos.

clock| ra·di·o *s.* 'Radiowecker *m*; '**~-** ,**watch·er** *s.* F Angestellte(r), der *od.* die immer nach der Uhr sieht; '**~-wise** *adj. u. adv.* im Uhrzeigersinn; rechtsläufig, Rechts...: **~** *rotation*; **~ work** *s.* Uhrwerk *n*: *like ~* a) wie am Schnürchen, b) (pünktlich) wie die Uhr; **~ toy** mechanisches Spielzeug; **~ fuse** ✕ Uhrwerkzünder *m*.

clod [klɒd] *s.* **1.** Erdklumpen *m*, Scholle

C

f; **2.** *fig.* ‚Heini‘ *m,* Trottel *m;* '~‚**hop·per** *s.* Bauerntölpel *m;* '~‚**hop·ping** *adj.* F ungehobelt.

clog [klɒg] **I** *s.* **1.** Holzklotz *m;* **2.** Pan'tine *f,* Holzschuh *m;* **3.** *fig.* Hemmnis *n,* Hindernis *n;* **II** *v/t.* **4.** (be)hindern, hemmen; **5.** verstopfen; **6.** *fig.* belasten, voll pfropfen; **III** *v/i.* **7.** sich verstopfen; stocken; **8.** klumpig werden, sich zs.-ballen; ~ **dance** *s.* Holzschuhtanz *m.*

clois·ter ['klɔɪstə] **I** *s.* **1.** Kloster *n;* **2.** △ a) Kreuzgang *m,* b) *oft pl.* gedeckter (Säulen)Gang *um e-n Hof;* **II** *v/t.* **3.** in ein Kloster stecken; **4.** *fig.* (*a. o.s.* sich) von der Welt abschließen; '**clois·tered** [-əd] *adj.* zu'rückgezogen, abgeschieden; '**clois·tral** [-trəl] *adj.* klösterlich.

clone [kləʊn] **I** *s.* **1.** *biol.* Klon *m;* **2.** *fig.* baugleiches Modell; **II 3.** *v/t.* klonen (*a. fig.*).

close¹ [kləʊs] **I** *adj.* □ → **closely;** **1.** geschlossen (*a. ling.*): ~ **formation** (*od.* **order**) ✗ (Marsch)Ordnung *f;* ~ **company** *Brit.,* ~ **corporation** † *Am.* GmbH *f;* **2.** zu'rückgezogen, abgeschlossen; **3.** verschlossen, verschwiegen, zu'rückhaltend; **4.** verborgen, geheim; **5.** geizig; sparsam; **6.** knapp (*Geld; Sieg*): ~ **election** knapper Wahlsieg; ~ **price** *†* scharf kalkulierter Preis; **7.** eng, beschränkt (*Raum*); **8.** nahe, dicht; *fig.* eng, vertraut: ~ **friend;** ~ **combat** ✗ Nahkampf *m;* ~ **proximity** nächste Nähe; ~ **fight** zähes Ringen, Handgemenge *n;* ~ **finish** scharfer Endkampf; ~ **shave** (*od.* **call**) F knappes Entrinnen; *that was ~!* F das war knapp!; ~ **shot** *phot.* Nahaufnahme *f;* → **quarter** 10; **9.** dicht, eng; fest; eng anliegend (*Kleid*): ~ **texture** dichtes Gewebe; ~ **writing** gedrängte Schrift; **10.** genau, gründlich, streng, eingehend (*Prüfung, Verhör etc.*); scharf (*Aufmerksamkeit, Bewachung*); streng (*Haft*); scharf (*Wettbewerb*); stark (*Ähnlichkeit*); (wort)getreu (*Übersetzung, Abschrift*); **11.** schwül, dumpf; **II** *adv.* **12.** nahe, eng, dicht, gedrängt: ~ **by** nahe (da)bei; ~ **at hand** nahe bevorstehend; ~ **to the ground** dicht am Boden; ~ **on 40** beinahe 40; **come ~ to** *fig.* dicht herankommen an (*acc.*); *cut ~* sehr kurz schneiden; *keep ~* in der Nähe bleiben; *keep o.s. ~* sich zurückhalten; *press s.o. ~* j-n (be)drängen; *run s.o. ~* j-m fast gleichkommen; **III** *s.* **13.** Einfriedigung *f,* (eingefriedetes) Grundstück; **14.** (Schul)Hof *m;* **15.** Sackgasse *f;* **16.** *Scot.* 'Haus‚durchgang *m zum Hof.*

close² [kləʊz] **I** *s.* **1.** (Ab)Schluss *m,* Ende *n: bring to a ~* beendigen; *draw to a ~* sich dem Ende nähern; **2.** a) Schlusswort *n,* b) Briefschluss *m;* **3.** ♪ Ka'denz *f;* **II** *v/t.* **4.** *Augen, Tür etc.* schließen, zumachen (→ **door** 1, **eye** 2); *Straße* sperren; *Loch* verstopfen; *Computer: Programm etc.* beenden, abbrechen: ~ *a shop* a) e-n Laden schließen, b) ein Geschäft aufgeben; ~ *an application Computer:* e-e Anwendung beenden (*od.* abbrechen); ~ *about s.o.* j-n umschließen *od.* umgeben; **5.** beenden, ab-, beschließen; zum Abschluss bringen, erledigen: ~ *the books* † die Bücher abschließen; ~ *an account* ein Konto auflösen; **III** *v/i.* **6.** schließen, geschlossen werden; sich schließen; **7.** enden, aufhören; **8.** sich nähern, heranrücken; **9.** ~ *with* a) (handels)einig werden mit *j-m,* sich mit *j-m* einigen (*on* über *acc.*), b) handge-

mein mit *j-m* werden; ~ **down I** *v/t.* **1.** schließen; *Geschäft* aufgeben; *Betrieb* stilllegen; **II** *v/i.* **2.** schließen, stillgelegt werden; **3.** *Radio, TV:* Sendeschluss haben; **4.** ~ **on** scharf vorgehen gegen; ~ **in** *v/i.* (**upon**) her'einbrechen (über *acc.*), sich her'anarbeiten (an *acc.*); ~ **out** *v/t.* **1.** † a) *Lager* räumen, b) → *wind up* 4; **2.** *fig. Am.* abwickeln, erledigen; ~ **up I** *v/t.* (ver)schließen, verstopfen, ausfüllen; **II** *v/i.* näher rücken, aufschließen; sich schließen *od.* füllen.

‚**close·'bod·ied** [‚kləʊs-] *adj.* eng anliegend (*Kleider*); ~-'**cropped** *adj.* kurz geschoren.

closed| **cir·cuit** [kləʊzd] *s.* ⚡ geschlossener Stromkreis; '~-‚**cir·cuit tel·e·vi·sion** *s.* Kurzschluss-, Betriebsfernsehen *n.*

'**close-down** ['kləʊz-] *s.* **1.** Schließung *f,* Stilllegung *f;* **2.** *Radio, TV:* Sendeschluss *m.*

closed shop *s.* gewerkschaftspflichtiger Betrieb.

‚**close·'fist·ed** [‚kləʊs-] *adj.* geizig, knauserig; ~ **fit** *s.* enge Passform; ❂ Edelpassung *f;* ~-'**fit·ting** *adj.* eng anliegend; ~-'**grained** *adj.* feinkörnig (*Holz etc.*); ~-'**hauled** *adj.* ♣ hart am Winde; ~-'**knit** *adj. fig.* eng verbunden; ‚~-'**mouthed** *adj.* verschlossen.

close·ly ['kləʊslɪ] *adv.* **1.** dicht, eng, fest; **2.** aus der Nähe; **3.** genau; **4.** scharf, streng; '**close·ness** [-snɪs] *s.* **1.** Nähe *f;* **2.** Enge *f,* Knappheit *f;* **3.** Dichte *f,* Festigkeit *f;* **4.** Genauigkeit *f,* Schärfe *f,* Strenge *f;* **5.** Verschlossenheit *f;* **6.** Schwüle *f;* **7.** Geiz *m.*

'**close-out** ['kləʊz-] *s. a.* ~ *sale* Ausverkauf *m* wegen Geschäftsaufgabe; '~-**range** ['kləʊs-] *adj.* aus nächster Nähe, Nah...; ~ **sea·son** [kləʊs] *s. hunt.* Schonzeit *f.*

clos·et ['klɒzɪt] **I** *s.* **1.** kleine Kammer; Gelass *n,* Kabi'nett *n;* Geheimzimmer *n:* ~ **drama** Lesedrama *n;* **2.** *Am.* (Wand)Schrank *m;* **3.** ('Wasser)Klo‚sett *n;* **II** *adj.* **4.** pri'vat, geheim; **III** *v/t.* **5.** einschließen: *be ~ed together with s.o.* e-e vertrauliche Besprechung mit *j-m* haben.

close| **time** [kləʊs] *s. hunt.* Schonzeit *f;* ‚~-'**tongued** *adj.* verschlossen; '~-**up** *s.* **1.** *Film:* Nah-, Großaufnahme *f;* **2.** *fig.* genaue Betrachtung, scharfes Bild.

clos·ing| **date** ['kləʊzɪŋ] *s.* letzter Ter'min; ‚~-'**down sale** *s.* Räumungsverkauf *m;* ~ **price** *s. Börse:* 'Schlussno‚tierung *f;* ~ **speech** *s.* Schlussrede; 'Schlussplädo‚yer *n;* ~ **time** *s.* **1.** Geschäftsschluss *m;* **2.** Poli'zeistunde *f.*

clo·sure ['kləʊʒə] **I** *s.* **1.** Verschluss *m* (*a. Vorrichtung*); **2.** Schließung *f* (*e-s Betriebs*), Stilllegung *f;* **3.** *parl.* Schluss *m* der De'batte: *apply* (*od.* **move**) *the ~* Antrag auf Schluss der Debatte stellen; **II** *v/t.* **4.** *Debatte etc.* schließen.

clot [klɒt] **I** *s.* **1.** Klumpen *m,* Klümpchen *n:* ~ *of blood* Blutgerinnsel *n;* **2.** F ‚Blödmann‘ *m;* **II** *v/i.* **3.** gerinnen, Klumpen bilden; ~*ted hair* verklebtes Haar.

cloth [klɒθ] *pl.* **cloths** [-θs] *s.* **1.** Tuch *n,* Stoff *m; engS.* Wollstoff *m:* ~ *of gold* Goldbrokat *m;* → *coat* 1, *whole* 3; **2.** Tuch *n,* Lappen *m: lay the ~* den Tisch decken; **3.** geistliche Amtstracht: *the ~* die Geistlichkeit; **4.** ♣ a) Segeltuch *n,* b) Segel *pl.;* **5.** (Buchbinder)Leinwand *f:* ~ *binding* Leinenband *m;* ~-*bound* in Leinen gebunden; ~-*cap* *adj.* F Arbeiterklassen . . ., Proleten . . .

clothe [kləʊð] *v/t.* **1.** (an- be)kleiden; **2.**

einkleiden, mit Kleidung versehen; **3.** *fig. in Worte* kleiden; **4.** *fig.* einhüllen; um'hüllen.

clothes [kləʊðz] *s. pl.* **1.** Kleider *pl.,* Kleidung *f;* **2.** (Leib-, Bett)Wäsche *f;* ~ **hang·er** *s.* Kleiderbügel *m;* '~-**horse** *s.* Wäscheständer *m;* ~ **line** *s.* Wäscheleine *f;* ~ **peg,** '~-**pin** *s.* Wäscheklammer *f;* '~-**press** *s.* Wäsche-, Kleiderschrank *m;* ~ **tree** *s.* Kleiderständer *m.*

cloth hall *s. hist.* Tuchbörse *f.*

cloth·ier ['kləʊðɪə] *s.* Tuch-, Kleiderhändler *m;* '**cloth·ing** [-ðɪŋ] *s.* Kleidung *f: article of* ~ Kleidungsstück *n;* ~ **industry** Bekleidungsindustrie *f.*

clo·ture ['kləʊtʃə] *Am.* → **closure** 3.

cloud [klaʊd] **I** *s.* **1.** Wolke *f* (*a. fig.*); Wolken *pl.:* ~ *of dust* Staubwolke; *have one's head in the ~s fig.* a) in höheren Regionen schweben, b) geistesabwesend sein; *be on ~ nine* F im siebten Himmel schweben; → *silver lining;* **2.** *fig.* Schwarm *m,* Haufen *m:* a ~ *of flies;* **3.** dunkler Fleck, Fehlstelle *f;* **4.** *fig.* Schatten *m:* ~ *of title* ⚖ (geltend gemachter) Fehler im Besitz; *cast a ~ on s.th.* e-n Schatten auf et. werfen; *under the ~ of night* im Schatten der Nacht; *under a ~* a) unter Verdacht, b) in Ungnade, c) in Verruf; **II** *v/t.* **5.** be-, um'wölken; **6.** *fig.* verdunkeln, trüben: ~ *the issue* die Sache vernebeln; **7.** ädern, flecken; **8.** ❂ Stoff moirieren; **III** *v/i.* **9.** *a.* ~ *over* sich beod. um'wölken, sich trüben (*a. fig.*); '~-**burst** *s.* Wolkenbruch *m;* ‚~-'**cuck·oo-land** *s.* Wolken'kuckucksheim *n.*

cloud·ed ['klaʊdɪd] *adj.* **1.** be-, um'wölkt; *fig.* nebelhaft; **2.** trübe, wolkig (*Flüssigkeit etc.*); beschlagen (*Glas*); **3.** gefleckt, geädert; '**cloud·ing** [-dɪŋ] *s.* **1.** Wolkigkeit *f;* Trübung *f* (*a. fig.*); **2.** Wolken-, Moirémuster *n;* '**cloud·less** [-lɪs] *adj.* □ **1.** wolkenlos; **2.** *fig.* ungetrübt; '**cloud·y** [-dɪ] *adj.* □ **1.** wolkig, bewölkt; **2.** geädert; moiriert (*Stoff*); **3.** trübe (*Flüssigkeit*); unklar, verschwommen; **4.** düster.

clout [klaʊt] F **I** *s.* **1.** Schlag *m;* **2.** *fig.* a) Macht *f,* Einfluss *m,* b) Wucht *f;* **II** *v/t.* **3.** hauen, schlagen; ~ **nail** *s.* (Schuh)Nagel *m.*

clove¹ [kləʊv] *s.* ♣ Gewürznelke *f.*

clove² [kləʊv] *s.* ♣ Brut-, Nebenzwiebel *f:* ~ *of garlic* Knoblauchzehe *f.*

clove³ [kləʊv] *pret. von* **cleave².**

clove⁴ [kləʊv] *s. Am.* Bergschlucht *f.*

clo·ven ['kləʊvn] **I** *p.p. von* **cleave²;** **II** *adj.* gespalten; ~ **foot** → **hoof** 1; ~ **hoof** *s.* **1.** Huf *m* der Paarhufer; **2.** *fig.* ‚Pferdefuß‘ *m: show the* ~ *fig.* den Pferdefuß *od.* sein wahres Gesicht zeigen; ‚~-'**hoofed** *adj.* **1.** *zo.* paarzehig, -hufig; **2.** teuflisch.

clove pink *s.* ♣ Gartennelke *f.*

clo·ver ['kləʊvə] *s.* ♣ Klee *m: be* (*od.* **live**) *in* ~ ‚in der Wolle‘ sitzen, üppig leben; '~-**leaf** *s.* Kleeblatt *n:* ~ (**intersection**) Kleeblatt (*Autobahnkreuzung*).

clown [klaʊn] **I** *s.* **1.** Clown *m,* Hans'wurst *m,* Kasper *m* (*alle a. fig.*); **2.** Bauerlümmel *m,* 'Grobian *m;* **II** *v/i.* **3.** *a.* ~ *around* he'rumkaspern; '**clown·er·y** [-nərɪ] *s.* **1.** Clowne'rie *f;* **2.** Posse *f;* '**clown·ish** [-nɪʃ] *adj.* □ **1.** bäurisch, tölpelhaft; **2.** närrisch.

cloy [klɔɪ] *v/t.* **1.** über'sättigen; **2.** anwidern; **cloy·ing** ['klɔɪɪŋ] *adj.* widerlich.

club [klʌb] **I** *s.* **1.** Keule *f,* Knüppel *m;* **2.** *sport* a) Schlagholz *n,* Schläger *m,* b) *a. Indian* ~ (Schwing)Keule *f;* **3.** Klub *m*: a) Verein *m*, Gesellschaft *f*, b) Klub-, Vereinshaus *n*, c) *fig., a. pol.* Klub *m*; **4.** *Spielkarten:* Treff *n*, Kreuz *n*, Eichel *f*; **II** *v/t.* **5.** mit e-r Keule *od.* mit dem Gewehrkolben schlagen; **6.** *Geld* zs.-legen, -schießen; sich teilen in (*acc.*); **III** *v/i.* **7.** *mst* ~ *together* (Geld) zs.-legen, sich zs.-tun; **club·(b)a·ble** ['klʌbəbl] *adj.* **1.** klub-, gesellschaftsfähig; **2.** → **'club·by** [-bɪ] *adj.* gesellig.

club| car s. *Am.* Sa'lonwagen *m*; **,~- 'foot** s. *✻* Klumpfuß *m*; **,~- 'foot·ed** *adj.* klumpfüßig; **'~·house** → *club* 3b; **'~·land** s. Klubviertel *n* (*bsd. in London*); **'~·man** [-mən] s. [*irr.*] **1.** Klubmitglied *n*; **2.** Klubmensch *m*; ~ **sand·wich** s. *Am.* 'Sandwich *n* (*aus drei Lagen bestehend*); ~ **steak** s. Klubsteak *n*.

cluck [klʌk] **I** *v/i.* **1.** glucken, locken; ~*ing hen* Glucke *f*; **II 2.** Glucken *n*; **3.** *Am. sl.* ,Blödmann' *m*.

clue [kluː] **I 1.** Anhaltspunkt *m*, Fingerzeig *m*, Spur *f*: *I haven't a ~!* keine Ahnung!; **2.** *fig.* a) Faden *m*, b) Schlüssel *m* (*e-s Rätsels etc.*); **3.** → *clew* 1, 3; **II** *v/t.* **4.** ~ *s.o.* (*in od. up*) *sl.* j-n ins Bild setzen *od.* informieren.

clump [klʌmp] **I** s. **1.** Klumpen *m* (*Erde*), (*Holz*)Klotz *m*; **2.** (Baum)Gruppe *f*; **3.** Doppelsohle *f*; **4.** schwerer Tritt; **II** *v/i.* **5.** trampeln; **III** *v/t.* **6.** zs.-ballen; **7.** doppelt besohlen; **8.** F *j-m* e-n Schlag ,verpassen'.

clum·si·ness ['klʌmzɪnɪs] s. Plumpheit *f*: a) Ungeschicklichkeit *f*, b) Unbeholfenheit *f*, Schwerfälligkeit *f*, c) Taktlosigkeit *f*, d) Unförmigkeit *f*; **clum·sy** ['klʌmzɪ] *adj.* □ plump: a) ungeschickt, unbeholfen, schwerfällig (*a. Stil*), b) taktlos, c) unförmig.

clung [klʌŋ] *pret. u. p.p. von* **cling**.

clus·ter ['klʌstə] **I** s. **1.** *♀* Büschel *n*, Traube *f*; **2.** Haufen *m* (*a. ast.*), Menge *f*, Schwarm *m*, Gruppe *f*; *a.* ⊕ Bündel *n*, traubenförmige Anordnung; **3.** ✕ *Am.* (Ordens)Spange *f*; **II** *v/i.* **4.** in Büscheln *od.* Trauben wachsen; **5.** sich sammeln *od.* häufen *od.* drängen *od.* ranken (*round* um); in Gruppen stehen.

clutch¹ [klʌtʃ] **I** *v/t.* **1.** fest (er)greifen, packen; drücken; **2.** ⊕ kuppeln; **II** *v/i.* **3.** (gierig) greifen (*at* nach); **III** s. **4.** fester Griff: *make a ~ at* (gierig) greifen nach; **5.** *pl., mst. fig.* Klauen *pl.*; Gewalt *f*, Macht *f*, Bande *pl.*: *in* (*out of*) *s.o.'s ~es* in (aus) j-s Klauen *od.* Gewalt; **6.** ⊕ (Schalt-, Ausrück)Kupplung *f*; Kupplungshebel *m*: *let in the ~* einkuppeln; *disengage the ~* auskuppeln; **7.** ⊕ Greifer *m*.

clutch² [klʌtʃ] s. **1.** Gelege *n*; Brut *f*; **2.** *fig.* F Schwarm *m von Leuten*.

clutch| disk s. Kupplungsscheibe *f*; ~ **le·ver** s., ~ **ped·al** s. 'Kupplungspe,dal *n*, -hebel *m*.

clut·ter ['klʌtə] **I** *v/t.* **1.** *a.* ~ *up* in Unordnung bringen; **2.** voll stopfen, anfüllen, über'häufen; um'herstreuen; **II** s. **3.** Wirrwarr *m*.

clys·ter ['klɪstə] s. *✻* *obs.* Kli'stier *n*.

coach [kəʊtʃ] **I** s. **1.** Kutsche *f*: ~ *and four* Vierspänner *m*; **2.** *✿ Brit.* (Personen)Wagen *m*; **3.** *mot. a)* (Fern-, Reise)Omnibus *m*, b) *Am.* Limou'sine *f*, c) → *coachwork*; **4.** Nachhilfe-, Pri'vatlehrer *m*, Einpauker *m*; **5.** *sport* 'Trainer *m*, Betreuer *m*; **II** *v/t.* **6.** 'Nachhilfe,unterricht *od.* Anweisungen geben (*dat.*), instruieren, einarbeiten: ~ *s.o. in s.th.* j-m et. einpauken; **7.** *sport* trainieren; **III** *v/i.* **8.** in e-r Kutsche reisen; **9.** Nachhilfeunterricht erteilen; ~ **box**

---

s. Kutschbock *m*; '~·**build·er** s. **1.** Stellmacher *m*; **2.** *mot. Brit.* Karosse'riebauer *m*; ~ **horse** s. Kutschpferd *n*; ~ **house** s. Wagenschuppen *m*.

coach·ing ['kəʊtʃɪŋ] s. **1.** Reisen *n* in e-r Kutsche; **2.** 'Nachhilfe,unterricht *m*; **3.** Unter'weisung *f*, Anleitung *f*.

'**coach·work** s. *mot.* Karosse'rie *f*.

co·ac·tion [kəʊ'ækʃn] s. **1.** Zs.-wirken *n*; **2.** Zwang *m*.

co·ag·u·late [kəʊ'ægjʊleɪt] **I** *v/i.* **1.** gerinnen; **2.** flockig *od.* klumpig werden; **II** *v/t.* **3.** gerinnen lassen; **co·ag·u·la·tion** [kəʊ,ægjʊ'leɪʃn] s. Gerinnen *n*; Flockenbildung *f*.

coal [kəʊl] **I** s. **1.** Kohle *f*, *engS.* Steinkohle *f*; *a* (ein) Stück Kohle; **2.** *pl. Brit.* Kohle *f*, Kohlen *pl.*, Kohlenvorrat *m*: *lay in ~s* sich mit Kohlen eindecken; *carry ~s to Newcastle fig.* Eulen nach Athen tragen; *call* (*od. haul*) *s.o. over the ~s* j-n ,fertig machen'; *heap ~s of fire on s.o.'s head fig.* feurige Kohlen auf j-s Haupt sammeln; **3.** glimmendes Stück Kohle *od.* Holz; **II** *v/t.* **4.** *✿, ♨* bekohlen, mit Kohle versorgen, **III** *v/i.* **5.** *✿, ♨* Kohle einnehmen, bunkern; '~·**bed** s. *geol.* Kohlenflöz *n*; '~·**box** s. Kohlenkasten *m*; ~ **car** s. *✿ Am.* Kohlenwagen *m*; '~·**dust** s. Kohlengrus *m*.

coal·er ['kəʊlə] s. *✿* Kohlenschiff *n*; 'Kohlenzug *m*, -wag,gon *m*.

co·a·lesce [,kəʊə'les] *v/i.* **1.** verschmelzen, sich verbinden *od.* vereinigen; **2.** *fig.* zs.-passen; ,**co·a'les·cence** [-sns] s. Verschmelzung *f*, Vereinigung *f*.

'**coal·field** s. 'Kohlenre,vier *n*; ~ **gas** s. Leuchtgas *n*.

coal·ing sta·tion ['kəʊlɪŋ] s. *♨* 'Bunker-, 'Kohlenstati,on *f*.

co·a·li·tion [,kəʊə'lɪʃn] s. Zs.-schluss *m*, Vereinigung *f*; *pol.* Koaliti'on *f*; ~ **part·ner** s. *pol.* Koaliti'onspartner *m*.

coal| mine s. Kohlenbergwerk *n*, Kohlengrube *f*, -zeche *f*; ~ **min·er** s. Grubenarbeiter *m*, Bergmann *m*; ~ **min·ing** s. Kohlenbergbau *m*; ~ **oil** s. *Am.* Petroleum *n*; '~·**pit** s. Kohlengrube *f*; ~ **seam** s. *geol.* Kohlenflöz *n*; ~ **tar** s. Steinkohlenteer *m*; ~ **wharf** s. *♨* Bunkerkai *m*.

coarse [kɔːs] *adj.* □ **1.** grob (*Ggs. fein*): ~ *texture* grobes Gewebe; **2.** grobkörnig: ~ *bread* Schrotbrot *n*; **3.** *fig.* grob, derb, ungehobelt; unanständig, anstößig; **4.** einfach, gemein: ~ *fare* grobe *od.* einfache Kost; '~·**grained** *adj.* **1.** grobkörnig, -faserig; grob (*Gewebe*); **2.** → *coarse* 3.

coars·en ['kɔːsn] **I** *v/t.* grob machen, vergröbern (*a. fig.*); **II** *v/i.* grob werden (*bsd. fig.*); '**coarse·ness** [-nɪs] s. **1.** grobe Quali'tät; **2.** *fig.* Grob-, Derbheit *f*; Unanständigkeit *f*.

coast [kəʊst] **I** s. **1.** Küste *f*, Meeresufer *n*: *the ~ is clear fig.* die Luft ist rein, die Bahn ist frei; **2.** Küstenlandstrich *m*; **3.** *Am. a)* Rodelbahn *f*, b) (Rodel-)Abfahrt *f*; **II** *v/i.* **4.** *♨ a)* die Küste entlangfahren, b) Küstenschifffahrt treiben; **5.** *Am.* rodeln; **6.** *mit e-m Fahrzeug* (berg'ab) rollen; im Freilauf (*Fahrrad*) *od.* im Leerlauf (*Auto*) fahren: ~ *on sl.* im Trick etc. ,reisen'; **7.** *sl.* mühelos vor'ankommen; '**coast·al** [-tl] *adj.* Küsten...

coast·er ['kəʊstə] s. **1.** *♨* Küstenfahrer *m* (*bsd. Schiff*); **2.** *Am.* Rodelschlitten *m*; **3.** *Am.* Achterbahn *f*; **4.** Ta'blett *n*, *bsd.* Serviertischchen *n*; ~ **brake** s. *Am.* Rücktrittbremse *f*.

coast guard s. **1.** *Brit.* Küstenwache *f* (*a.* ✕); Küstenzollwache *f*; **2.** *Am. ⚓*

(staatlicher) Küstenwach- u. Rettungsdienst; **3.** Angehörige(r) *m* von 1 u. 2.

coast·ing ['kəʊstɪŋ] s. **1.** Küstenschifffahrt *f*; **2.** *Am.* Rodeln *n*; **3.** Berg'abfahren *n* (*im Freilauf od. bei abgestelltem Motor*); ~ **trade** s. Küstenhandel *m*.

'**coast·line** s. Küstenlinie *f*, -strich *m*; '~·**wise** *adj. u. adv.* längs der Küste; Küsten...

coat [kəʊt] **I** s. **1.** Jac'kett *n*, Jacke *f*: *wear the king's* ~ *hist.* des Königs Rock tragen (*Soldat sein*); ~ *and skirt* (Schneider)Kostüm *n*; ~ *of arms* Wappen *n*; ~ *armo(u)r* Familienwappen *n*; ~ *of mail* Panzerhemd *n*; *cut one's ~ according to one's cloth* sich nach der Decke strecken; **2.** Mantel *m*: *turn one's* ~ sein Mäntelchen nach dem Wind hängen; **3.** Fell *n*, Pelz *m* (*Tier*); **4.** Schicht *f*, Lage *f*; Decke *f*, Hülle *f*, (*a. Farb-, Metall- etc.*)'Überzug *m*, Belag *m*, Anstrich *m*; Bewurf *m*: *a second* ~ *of paint* ein zweiter Anstrich; **II** *v/t.* **5.** anstreichen, über'streichen, -'ziehen, beschichten: ~ *with silver* plattieren; **6.** um'hüllen, -'kleiden, bedecken; auskleiden (*with* mit); '**coat·ed** [-tɪd] *adj.* **1.** mit e-m (...) Rock *od.* Mantel *od.* Fell (versehen): *black-~* schwarz gekleidet; **2.** mit ... über'zogen *od.* gestrichen *od.* bedeckt: *sugar-~* mit Zuckerüberzug; **3.** *✻* belegt (*Zunge*); **coat·ee** [kəʊ'tiː] s. kurzer (Waffen)Rock.

coat hang·er s. Kleiderbügel *m*.

coat·ing ['kəʊtɪŋ] s. **1.** Mantelstoff *m*; **2.** ⊕ Anstrich *m*, 'Überzug *m*, Schicht *f*; Bewurf *m*; **3.** ⊕ Auskleidung *f*, Futter *n*.

coat| stand s. Garde'robenständer *m*; '~·**tail** s. Rockschoß *m*; '~·**trail·ing** *adj.* provoka'tiv.

co·au·thor [kəʊ'ɔːθə] s. Mitverfasser *m*, -autor *m*.

coax [kəʊks] **I** *v/t.* **1.** schmeicheln (*dat.*); gut zureden (*dat.*), beschwatzen (*to do od. into doing* zu tun): ~ *s.th. out of s.o.* j-m et. abschwatzen; **2.** *et.* mit Gefühl *od.* ,mit Geduld und Spucke' bringen (*into* in *acc.*); **II** *v/i.* **3.** schmeicheln.

co·ax·al [,kəʊ'æksl], **co·ax·i·al** [-sɪəl] *⚡*, ⊕ koaxi'al, kon'zentrisch.

cob [kɒb] s. **1.** *a.* ~ *swan orn.* männlicher Schwan; **2.** *zo.* kleineres Reitpferd; **3.** Klumpen *m*, Stück *n* (*z. B.* Kohle); **4.** Maiskolben *m*; **5.** *Brit.* Strohlehm *m* (*Baumaterial*); **6.** → *cobloaf*; **7.** → *cobnut*.

co·balt [kəʊ'bɔːlt] s. *min.*, *✿* Kobalt *m*; ~ **blue** s. Kobaltblau *n*; ~ **bomb** s. **1.** ✕ Kobaltbombe *f*; **2.** *✻* 'Kobaltka,none *f*.

cob·ble¹ ['kɒbl] **I** s. **1.** runder Pflasterstein, Kopfstein *m*; **2.** *pl.* → *cob coal*; **II** *v/t.* **3.** mit Kopfsteinen pflastern.

cob·ble² ['kɒbl] *v/t.* Schuhe flicken; *fig.* zs.-flicken, zs.-schustern; '**cob·bler** [-lə] s. **1.** (Flick)Schuster *m*: ~'*s wax* Schusterpech *n*; **2.** *fig.* Stümper *m*; **3.** *Am.* Cobbler *m* (*ein Cocktail*).

'**cob·ble·stone** → *cobble¹* 1: ~ *pavement* Kopfsteinpflaster *n*, -pflasterung *f*.

cob coal s. Nuss-, Stückkohle *f*.

Cob·den·ism ['kɒbdənɪzəm] s. *✝* 'Manchestertum *n*, Freihandelslehre *f*.

co·bel·lig·er·ent [,kəʊbɪ'lɪdʒərənt] s. mit Krieg führender Staat.

'**cob·loaf** s. rundes Brot; '~·**nut** s. *♀* Haselnuss *f*.

Co·bol ['kəʊbɒl] s. COBOL *n* (*Computersprache*).

co·bra ['kəʊbrə] *s. zo.* Brillenschlange *f*, 'Kobra *f*.

cob·web ['kɒbweb] *s.* **1.** Spinn(en)gewebe *n*; Spinnenfaden *m*; **2.** feines, zartes Gewebe; **3.** *fig.* Hirngespinst *n*: ***blow away the ~s*** sich e-n klaren Kopf schaffen; **4.** *fig.* Netz *n*, Schlinge *f*; **5.** *fig.* alter Staub; '**cob·webbed** [-bd], '**cob,web·by** [-bɪ] *adj.* voller Spinnweben.

co·ca ['kəʊkə] *s.* 'Koka(blätter *pl.*) *f*.

co·cain(e) [kəʊ'keɪn] *s.* ⚗ Koka'in *n*; **co'cain·ism** [-nɪzəm] *s.* **1.** Koka'invergiftung *f*; **2.** Koka'insucht *f*.

coc·cus ['kɒkəs] *pl.* **-ci** [-kaɪ] *s.* ⚕ 'Kokkus *m*, 'Kokke *f* (*a.* ⚘).

coch·i·neal ['kɒtʃɪniːl] *s.* Kosche'nille (-laus) *f*; Kosche'nille(rot *n*) *f*.

coch·le·a ['kɒklɪə] *s. anat.* Cochlea *f*, Schnecke *f* (*im Ohr*).

cock[1] [kɒk] **I** *s.* **1.** *orn.* Hahn *m*: ***old ~*** F alter Knabe; ***that ~ won't fight*** F a) so geht das nicht, b) das zieht nicht; **2.** Vogelmännchen *n*: ***~ sparrow*** Sperlingsmännchen; **3.** Wetterhahn *m*; **4.** ⚙ (*Absperr*)Hahn *m*; **5.** (*Gewehr- etc.*) Hahn *m*: ***full ~*** Hahn gespannt; ***half ~*** Hahn in Ruh; **6.** Anführer *m*: ***~ of the roost*** (*od.* ***walk***) *oft contp.* der Größte; ***~ of the school*** Anführer *m* unter den Schülern; **7.** Aufrichten *n*: ***~ of the eye*** (bedeutsames) Augenzwinkern; ***give one's hat a saucy ~*** s-n Hut keck aufs Ohr setzen; **8.** V ,Schwanz' *m* (*Penis*); **9.** F Quatsch *m*; **II** *v/t.* **10.** *Gewehrhahn* spannen; **11.** aufrichten: ***~ one's ears*** die Ohren spitzen; ***~ one's eye at s.o.*** j-n viel sagend *od.* verächtlich ansehen; ***~ one's hat*** den Hut schief *od.* keck aufsetzen; → ***cocked hat***; **12.** ***~ up*** *sl.* ,versauen'.

cock[2] [kɒk] *s.* kleiner Heuhaufen.

cock·ade [kɒ'keɪd] *s.* Ko'karde *f*.

cock·a·doo·dle·doo [,kɒkəduːdl'duː] *s.* a) Kikeri'ki *n* (*Hahnenschrei*), b) *humor.* Kikeri'ki *m* (*Hahn*).

Cock·aigne [kɒ'keɪn] *s.* Schla'raffenland *n*.

,cock-and-'bull sto·ry *s.* Ammenmärchen *n*, Lügengeschichte *f*.

cock·a·too [,kɒkə'tuː] *s.* 'Kakadu *m*.

cock·a·trice ['kɒkətraɪs] *s.* Basi'lisk *m*.

Cock·ayne → ***Cockaigne***.

'**cock|·boat** *s.* ⚓ Jolle *f*; '~,**chaf·er** *s.* Maikäfer *m*; '~·**crow** *s.* Hahnenschrei *m*; *fig.* Tagesanbruch *m*.

cocked hat [kɒkt] *s.* Zwei-, Dreispitz *m* (*Hut*): ***knock into a ~*** a) zu Brei schlagen, b) (restlos) ,fertig machen'.

cock·er[1] ['kɒkə] → ***cocker spaniel***.

cock·er[2] ['kɒkə] *v/t.* verhätscheln, verwöhnen: ***~ up*** aufpäppeln.

Cock·er[3] ['kɒkə] *npr.*: ***according to ~*** nach Adam Riese, genau.

cock·er·el ['kɒkərəl] *s.* Hähnchen *n*.

cock·er span·iel *s.* 'Cocker,spaniel *m*.

'**cock|·eyed** *adj. sl.* **1.** schielend; **2.** (krumm u.) schief; **3.** ,doof'; **4.** ,blau' (*betrunken*); '~,**fight·ing** *s.* Hahnenkampf *m*: ***that beats ~!*** F das ist 'ne Wucht!

cock·i·ness ['kɒkɪnɪs] *s.* F Großspurigkeit *f*, Anmaßung *f*.

cock·le[1] ['kɒkl] **I** *s.* **1.** *zo.* (essbare) Herzmuschel: ***that warms the ~s of my heart*** das tut mir gut; **2.** → ***cockleshell***; **II** *v/i.* **3.** sich bauschen *od.* kräuseln *od.* werfen; **III** *v/t.* **4.** kräuseln.

cock·le[2] ['kɒkl] → ***corncockle***.

'**cock·le|·boat** → ***cockboat***; '~·**shell** *s.* **1.** Muschelschale *f*; **2.** ,Nussschale' *f*, kleines Boot.

cock·ney ['kɒknɪ] *s. oft* ♀ **1.** Cockney *m*, (waschechter) Londoner; **2.** 'Cockney (-dia,lekt *m*, -aussprache *f*) *n*; '**cockney·dom** [-dəm] *s.* **1.** Cockneybezirk *m*; **2.** *coll.* die Cockneys *pl.*; '**cockney·ism** [-ɪɪzəm] *s.* Cockneyausdruck *m*.

'**cock|·pit** *s.* **1.** Hahnenkampfplatz *m*; **2.** *fig.* Kampfplatz *m*; **3.** ⚓, ✈, *mot.* Cockpit *n*; '~·**roach** *s.* Kaker'lak *m*, (Küchen)Schabe *f*.

cocks·comb ['kɒkskəʊm] *s.* **1.** *zo.* Hahnenkamm *m*; **2.** ⚘ Hahnenkamm *m*; **3.** → ***coxcomb*** 1.

'**cock|·shy** Wurfziel *n*; *fig.* Zielscheibe *f*; '~·**spur** *s.* **1.** *zo.* Hahnensporn *m*; **2.** ⚘ Hahnen-, Weißdorn *m*; ,~'**sure** *adj.* **1.** todsicher, 'vollkommen über'zeugt; **2.** über'trieben selbstsicher, anmaßend; '~·**tail** *s. allg.* Cocktail *m*: ***~ cabinet*** Hausbar *f*; ***~ dress*** Cocktailkleid *n*; ***~ tomato*** 'Cocktailto,mate *f*.

'**cock-up** *s. Brit. sl.* 'Durcheinander *n*: ***make a ~ of s.th.*** et. vermasseln.

cock·y ['kɒkɪ] *adj.* F großspurig, anmaßend.

co·co ['kəʊkəʊ] *pl.* **-cos I** *s. mst in Zssgn* ⚘ 'Kokospalme *f*; **II** *adj.* Kokos...; aus 'Kokosfasern.

co·coa ['kəʊkəʊ] *s.* **1.** Ka'kao(pulver *n*) *m*; **2.** Ka'kao *m* (*Getränk*); ***~ bean*** *s.* Ka'kaobohne *f*.

co·co·nut ['kəʊkənʌt] *s.* **1.** ⚘ 'Kokosnuss *f*: ***that accounts for the milk in the ~*** F daher der Name!; **2.** *sl.* ,Kürbis' *m* (*Kopf*); ***~ but·ter*** *s.* 'Kokosbutter *f*; ***~ milk*** *s.* 'Kokosmilch *f*; ***~ palm***, ***~ tree*** *s.* 'Kokospalme *f*.

co·coon [kə'kuːn] **I** *s. zo.* Ko'kon *m*, Puppe *f der Seidenraupe*; *weitS.* Gespinst *n*; ⚔, ⚙ Schutzhülle *f*; **II** *v/t. u. v/i.* (sich) einspinnen *od.* (*fig.*) einhüllen; *Gerät etc.* ,einmotten'.

co·cotte [kɒ'kɒt] *s.* Ko'kotte *f*.

cod[1] [kɒd] *s. ichth.* Kabeljau *m*, Dorsch *m*: ***dried ~*** Stockfisch *m*; ***cured ~*** Klippfisch *m*.

cod[2] [kɒd] *v/t. j-n* foppen.

co·da ['kəʊdə] *s.* ♪ 'Koda *f*.

cod·dle ['kɒdl] *v/t.* verhätscheln, verzärteln, verwöhnen: ***~ up*** aufpäppeln.

code [kəʊd] **I** *s.* **1.** *bsd.* ⚖ 'Kodex *m*, Gesetzbuch *n*; *weitS.* Regeln *pl.*: ***~ of hono(u)r*** Ehrenkodex; **2.** ⚓, ⚔ Signalbuch *n*; **3.** (Tele'grafen)Kode *m*, (-)Schlüssel *m*; **4.** a) Kode *m* (*a. Computer*), Schlüssel(schrift *f*) *m*, b) Chiffre *f*: ***~ name*** Deckname *m*; ***~ number*** Kode-, Kennzahl *f*; ***~ word*** Kodewort *n*; **II** *v/t.* **5.** kodieren, chiffrieren, verschlüsseln: ***~d message***; ***coding device*** → ***coder***.

co·de·ine ['kəʊdiːn] *s. pharm.* Kode'in *n*.

cod·er ['kəʊdə] *s.* Kodiergerät *n*, Kodierer *m*, Verschlüssler *m*.

co·de·ter·mi·na·tion ['kəʊdɪ,tɜːmɪ'neɪʃn] *s.* ✝ (***parity ~*** pari'tätische) Mitbestimmung.

co·dex ['kəʊdeks] *pl.* '**co·di·ces** [-dɪsiːz] *s.* 'Kodex *m*, alte Handschrift (*Bibel, Klassiker*).

'**cod|·fish** → ***cod***[1]; '~,**fish·er** *s.* Kabeljaufischer *m*.

codg·er ['kɒdʒə] *s.* F alter Kauz.

co·di·ces *pl. von* ***codex***.

cod·i·cil ['kɒdɪsɪl] *s.* ⚖ Kodi'zill *n*.

cod·i·fi·ca·tion [,kəʊdɪfɪ'keɪʃn] *s.* Kodifizierung *f*; **cod·i·fy** ['kəʊdɪfaɪ] *v/t.* **1.** *bsd.* ⚖ kodifizieren; **2.** *Nachricht* verschlüsseln; '**cod·ing** *s.* Verschlüsselung *f*, Kodierung *f*.

cod·ling[1] ['kɒdlɪŋ] *s.* junger Dorsch.

cod·ling[2] ['kɒdlɪŋ] *s. ein* Kochapfel *m*; ***~ moth*** *s. zo.* Obstmade *f*.

cod liv·er oil [,kɒdlɪvər'ɔɪl] *s.* Lebertran *m*.

co·driv·er ['kəʊ,draɪvə] *s.* Beifahrer *m*.

co·ed [,kəʊ'ed] *s. ped.* Stu'dentin *f od.* Schülerin *f* e-r gemischten Schule; **co·ed·u·ca·tion** [,kəʊedjuː'keɪʃn] *s. ped.* Koedukati'on *f*, Gemeinschaftserziehung *f*.

co·ef·fi·cient [,kəʊɪ'fɪʃnt] **I** *s.* **1.** ⩘, *phys.* Koeffizi'ent *m*; **2.** mitwirkende Kraft, 'Faktor *m*; **II** *adj.* **3.** mitwirkend.

coe·li·ac ['siːlɪæk] *adj. anat.* Bauch...

co·erce [kəʊ'ɜːs] *v/t.* **1.** nötigen, zwingen (***into*** zu); **2.** erzwingen; **co'er·ci·ble** [-sɪbl] *adj.* ☐ zu (er)zwingen(d); **co'er·cion** [-'ɜːʃn] *s.* **1.** Zwang *m*; Gewalt *f*; ⚖ Nötigung *f*; **2.** *pol.* Zwangsherrschaft *f*; **co'er·cive** [-sɪv] **I** *adj.* ☐ zwingend (*a. fig.*), Zwangs...; **II** *s.* Zwangsmittel *n*.

co·es·sen·tial [,kəʊɪ'senʃl] *adj.* wesensgleich.

co·e·val [kəʊ'iːvl] *adj.* ☐ **1.** gleichzeitig; **2.** gleichaltrig; **3.** von gleicher Dauer.

co·ex·ist [,kəʊɪg'zɪst] *v/i.* gleichzeitig *od.* nebenein'ander bestehen *od.* leben, koexistieren; **,co·ex'ist·ence** [-təns] *s.* Koexi'stenz *f*; **,co·ex'ist·ent** [-tənt] *adj.* gleichzeitig *od.* nebenein'ander bestehend, koexi'stent.

cof·fee ['kɒfɪ] *s.* **1.** 'Kaffee *m* (*Getränk, Bohnen od. Baum*): ***black ~*** schwarzer Kaffee; ***white ~*** Milchkaffee; **2.** 'Kaffeebraun *n*; ***~ bar*** *s.* **1.** Ca'fé *n*; **2.** Imbissstube *f*; ***~ bean*** *s.* 'Kaffeebohne *f*; ***~ break*** *s.* 'Kaffeepause *f*; ***~ grounds*** *s. pl.* 'Kaffeesatz *m*; '~·**house** *s.* 'Kaffeehaus *n*; '~,**mak·er** *s. Am.* 'Kaffeema,schine *f*; ***~ mill*** *s.* 'Kaffeemühle *f*; '~·**pot** *s.* 'Kaffeekanne *f*; ***~ set*** *s.* 'Kaffeeser,vice *n*; ***~ shop*** *s. Am. für* ***coffee bar***; ***~ ta·ble*** *s.* Couchtisch *m*; ***~ book*** prächtiger Bildband; ***~ urn*** *s.* ('Groß)-,Kaffeema,schine *f*.

cof·fer ['kɒfə] **I** *s.* **1.** Kasten *m*, Kiste *f*, Truhe *f*, Kas'sette *f* (*für Wertsachen*); **2.** *pl.* a) Schatz *m*, Gelder *pl.*, b) Schatzkammer *f*, Tre'sor *m*; **3.** ⚠ Deckenfeld *n*, Kas'sette *f*; **4.** → ***cofferdam***; **II** *v/t.* **5.** verwahren; '~·**dam** *s.* ⚙ Kastendamm *m*, Senkkasten *m*, Cais'son *m*.

cof·fin ['kɒfɪn] **I** *s.* Sarg *m* (*a.* F *schlechtes Schiff*); **II** *v/t.* einsargen; ***~ bone*** *s. zo.* Hufbein *n* (*Pferd*); ***~ joint*** *s.* Hufgelenk *n* (*Pferd*).

cog[1] [kɒg] *s.* **1.** ⚙ (Rad)Zahn *m*; **2.** *fig.* ***he's just a ~ in the machine*** er ist nur ein Rädchen im Getriebe.

cog[2] [kɒg] **I** *v/t.* *Würfel* beschweren: ***~ the dice*** beim Würfeln mogeln; **II** *v/i.* betrügen.

co·gen·cy ['kəʊdʒənsɪ] *s.* Schlüssigkeit *f*, Triftigkeit *f*; '**co·gent** [-nt] *adj.* ☐ zwingend, triftig.

cogged [kɒgd] *adj.* ⚙ gezahnt, Zahn(rad)...: ***~ railway*** Zahnradbahn *f*.

cog·i·tate ['kɒdʒɪteɪt] **I** *v/i.* **1.** (nach-) denken, (nach)sinnen (***upon*** über *acc.*); **2.** *phls.* denken; **II** *v/t.* **3.** ersinnen; **cog·i·ta·tion** [,kɒdʒɪ'teɪʃn] *s.* **1.** (Nach)Denken *n*; **2.** Denkfähigkeit *f*; **3.** Gedanke *m*.

co·gnac ['kɒnjæk] *s.* 'Kognak *m*.

cog·nate ['kɒgneɪt] **I** *adj.* **1.** (*selten*) (bluts)verwandt; **2.** verwandt (*Wörter etc.*); **3.** *ling.* (sinn)verwandt: ***~ object*** Objekt *n* des Inhalts; **II** *s.* **4.** ⚖ Blutsverwandte(r *m*) *f*; **5.** verwandtes Wort.

cog·ni·tion [kɒg'nɪʃn] *s. bsd. phls.* Erkennen *n*, Wahrnehmung *f*; Kenntnis *f*; **cog·ni·tive** ['kɒgnɪtɪv] *adj.* kogni'tiv, erkenntnismäßig.

cog·ni·za·ble ['kɒgnɪzəbl] *adj.* ☐ **1.** erkennbar; **2.** ⚖ a) der Gerichtsbarkeit unter'worfen, b) gerichtlich verfolgbar, c) zu verhandeln(d); **'cog·ni·zance** [-zəns] s. **1.** Kenntnis f, Erkenntnis f; **2.** ⚖ a) Zuständigkeit f, b) (richterliche) Verhandlung, c) (richterliches) Erkenntnis, d) *Brit.* Anerkenntnis n: **take ~ of** sich zuständig mit e-m *Fall* befassen, *weitS.* zur Kenntnis nehmen; **beyond my ~** außerhalb m-r Befugnis; **3.** *her.* Ab-, Kennzeichen n; **'cog·ni·zant** [-zənt] adj. **1.** unter'richtet (*of* über acc. od. von); **2.** *phls.* erkennend.

cog·no·men [kɒgˈnəʊmen] s. **1.** Fa'milien-, Zuname m; **2.** Bei-, bsd. Spitzname m.

'cog·wheel s. ⚙ Zahnrad n; **~ drive** s. ⚙ Zahnradantrieb m; **~ rail·way** s. Zahnradbahn f.

co·hab·it [kəʊˈhæbɪt] v/i. (bsd. unverheiratet) zs.-leben; **co·hab·i·ta·tion** [ˌkəʊhæbɪˈteɪʃn] s. **1.** Zs.-leben n; **2.** Beischlaf m, Beiwohnung f.

co·heir [ˌkəʊˈeə] s. Miterbe m; **co·heir·ess** [ˌkəʊˈeərɪs] s. Miterbin f.

co·here [kəʊˈhɪə] v/i. **1.** zs.-hängen (a. fig.); **2.** fig. in Zs.-hang stehen; **3.** zs.-halten, **4.** zs.-passen, über'einstimmen (*with* mit); **5.** *Radio:* fritten; **co'her·ence** [-ərəns], **co'her·en·cy** [-ərənsɪ] s. **1.** phys. Kohäsi'on f; **2.** fig. a) Zs.-hang m, b) Klarheit f, c) Über'einstimmung f; **3.** Radio: Frittung f; **co'her·ent** [-ərənt] adj. □ **1.** zs.-hängend (a. fig.), -haftend; phys. kohä'rent; **2.** einheitlich, verständlich, klar; **3.** über'einstimmend, zs.-passend; **co'her·er** [-ərə] s. Radio: Fritter(empfänger) m.

co·he·sion [kəʊˈhiːʒn] s. **1.** Zs.-halt m, -hang m (a. fig.); **2.** Bindekraft f; **3.** phys. Kohäsi'on f; **co'he·sive** [-iːsɪv] adj. □ **1.** zs.-haltend od. -hängend, fig. a. bindend; **2.** Kohäsions...; **co'he·sive·ness** [-iːsɪvnɪs] s. **1.** phys. Kohäsi'ons-, Bindekraft f; **2.** Festigkeit f.

co·hort [ˈkəʊhɔːt] s. **1.** antiq. ✕ Ko'horte f; **2.** Schar f, Haufen m.

coif [kɔɪf] s. Kappe f, Haube f.

coif·feur [kwɑːˈfɜː] (Fr.) s. Fri'seur m; **coif·fure** [kwɑːˈfjʊə; kwafyːr] (Fr.) s. Fri'sur f.

coil¹ [kɔɪl] **I** v/t. **1.** a. **~ up** auf-, zs.-rollen, winden; **2.** ⚓ wickeln; **II** v/i. **3.** a. **~ up** sich winden, sich zs.-rollen; **4.** sich schlängeln; **III** s. **5.** Rolle f, Spi'rale f (a. Pessar), Knäuel m, n; **6.** ⚓ Wicklung f; Spule f; **7.** Windung f; **8.** ⚙ (Rohr)Schlange f; **9.** Locke f, Wickel m (Haar).

coil² [kɔɪl] s. poet. Tu'mult m, Wirrwarr m; Plage f: **mortal ~** Drang m od. Mühsal f des Irdischen.

coil ig·ni·tion s. ⚡ Abreißzündung f; **~ spring** s. ⚙ Spi'ralfeder f.

coin [kɔɪn] **I** s. **1.** a) Münze f, Geldstück n, b) Münzgeld n; c) Geld n: **the other side of the ~** fig. die Kehrseite (der Medaille); **pay s.o. back in his own ~** fig. es j-m mit gleicher Münze heimzahlen; **II** v/t. **2.** a) Metall münzen, b) Münzen prägen: **be ~ing money** F Geld wie Heu verdienen; **3.** fig. Wort prägen; **'coin·age** [-nɪdʒ] s. **1.** Prägen n; **2.** coll. Münzgeld n; **3.** 'Münzsy,stem n; **4.** fig. Prägung f (Wörter); **'coin-box tel·e·phone** s. Münzfernsprecher m.

co·in·cide [ˌkəʊɪnˈsaɪd] v/i. (*with*) **1.** örtlich od. zeitlich zs.-treffen, -fallen (mit); **2.** über'einstimmen, sich decken (mit); genau entsprechen (dat.); **co·in·ci·dence** [kəʊˈɪnsɪdəns] s. **1.** Zs.-treffen n (Raum od. Zeit); **2.** zufälliges Zs.-treffen: **mere ~** bloßer Zufall; **3.** Über-

'einstimmung f; **co·in·ci·dent** [kəʊˈɪnsɪdent] adj. □ (*with* mit); **1.** zs.-fallend, -treffend; **2.** über'einstimmend, sich deckend; **co·in·ci·den·tal** [kəʊˌɪnsɪˈdentl] adj. **1.** → **coincident** 2; **2.** zufällig; **3.** bsd. ⚙ gleichzeitig.

coin·er [ˈkɔɪnə] s. **1.** Münzer m; **2.** bsd. Brit. Falschmünzer m; **3.** fig. Präger m, (Wort)Schöpfer m.

coin|-op [ˈkɔɪnɒp] F **1.** 'Waschsa,lon m; **2.** Münztankstelle f; **'~-,op·er·at·ed** adj. Münz...

coir [ˈkɔɪə], a. **~ fi·bre** s. 'Kokosfaser f; **~ mat** s. 'Kokosmatte f.

co·i·tal [ˈkəʊɪtl] adj. (den) Geschlechtsverkehr betreffend; **co·i·tion** [kəʊˈɪʃn], **'co·i·tus** [-təs] s. 'Koitus m, Geschlechtsverkehr m.

coke¹ [kəʊk] **I** s. **1.** Koks m; **2.** sl. ˌKoks' m, Koka'in n; **II** v/t. **3.** verkoken.

coke² [kəʊk] s. F a) ⚓ 'Cola' f, n, (Coca-Cola), b) Limo'nade f etc.

co·ker [ˈkəʊkə] ⚓ Brit. → **coco**; **'~-nut** s. sl. 'Kokosnuss f.

col [kɒl] s. Gebirgspass m, Joch n.

co·la [ˈkəʊlə] s. ♀ 'Kolabaum m.

col·an·der [ˈkʌləndə] s. Sieb n, 'Durchschlag m.

co·la nut s. ♀ 'Kolanuss f.

col·chi·cum [ˈkɒltʃɪkəm] s. **1.** ♀ Herbstzeitlose f; **2.** pharm. 'Colchicum n.

cold [kəʊld] **I** adj. □ **1.** kalt: **as ~ as ice** eiskalt; **~ meat** od. **cuts** kalte Platte, Aufschnitt m; **I feel** (od. **am**) **~** mir ist kalt, mich friert; **2.** kalt, kühl, ruhig, gelassen; trocken: **that leaves me ~** das lässt mich kalt; **~ reason** kalter Verstand; **the ~ facts** die nackten Tatsachen; **~ scent** kalte Fährte (a. fig.); → **comfort** 6, **print** 12; **3.** kalt (Blick, Herz etc.; a. Frau), kühl, frostig, unfreundlich, gefühllos: **a ~ reception** ein kühler Empfang; **give s.o. the ~ shoulder** → **cold-shoulder**; **have** (**get**) **~ feet** F kalte Füße (Angst) haben (kriegen); **as ~ as charity** hart wie Stein, lieblos; **4.** kalt (noch nicht in Schwung): **~ player**; **~ motor**; **5.** ˌkalt' (im Suchspiel u. fig.); **6.** Am. sl. a) bewusstlos, b) (tod)sicher; **II** s. **7.** Kälte f; Frost m: **leave s.o. out in the ~** fig. a) j-n übergehen od. ignorieren od. kaltstellen, b) im Stich lassen; **8.** ⚕ Erkältung f: **common ~, ~ in the head** Schnupfen m; **~ on the chest** Bronchialkatarr(h) m; **catch** (**a**) **~** sich erkälten.

cold| blood s. fig. kaltes Blut, Kaltblütigkeit f: **murder s.o. in ~** j-n kaltblütig od. kalten Blutes ermorden; **,~-'blood·ed** adj. □ **1.** zo. kaltblütig; **2.** kälteempfindlich; **3.** fig. kaltblütig (begangen): **~ murder**; **~ boot** s. Computer: Kaltstart m; **~ box** s. Kühlbox f; **~ cream** s. Cold Cream f, m; **,~-'drawn** adj. ⚙ kaltgezogen; kaltgepresst; **~ duck** s. kalte Ente (Getränk); **~ front** s. Kaltfront f; **,~-'ham·mer** v/t. ⚙ kalthämmern, -schmieden; **,~-'heart·ed** adj. □ kalt-, hartherzig.

cold·ish [ˈkəʊldɪʃ] adj. ziemlich kalt.

cold·ness [ˈkəʊldnɪs] s. Kälte f (a. fig.).

,cold-'shoul·der v/t. j-m die kalte Schulter zeigen, j-n kühl behandeln od. abweisen; **~ steel** s. blanke Waffe (Bajonett etc.); **~ stor·age** s. Kühllagerung f; Kühlraum m: **put in ~** fig. ˌauf Eis legen' (aufschieben); **,~-'stor·age** adj. Kühl(haus)...; **~ store** s. Kühlhalle f; Kühlanlage f; ⚔ **War** s. pol. kalter Krieg; ⚔ **War·ri·or** s. pol. kalter Krieger; **~ wave** s. **1.** Kältewelle f; **2.** Kalt-

welle f (Frisur); **'~-,work·ing** s. ⚙ Kaltverformung f.

cole [kəʊl] s. ♀ **1.** (Blätter)Kohl m; **2.** Raps m.

co·le·op·ter·a [ˌkɒlɪˈɒptərə] s. pl. zo. Käfer pl.

'cole|·seed s. ♀ Rübsamen m; **'~-slaw** s. Am. 'Kohlsa,lat m.

col·ic [ˈkɒlɪk] s. ⚕ 'Kolik f; **'col·ick·y** [-ɪkɪ] adj. ⚕ 'kolikartig.

col·i·se·um [ˌkɒlɪˈsɪəm] s. **1.** a) Sporthalle f, b) 'Stadion n; **2.** ⚓ Kolos'seum n (Rom).

co·li·tis [kɒˈlaɪtɪs] s. ⚕ Ko'litis f, 'Dickdarmka,tarr(h) m.

col·lab·o·rate [kəˈlæbəreɪt] v/i. **1.** zs.-, mitarbeiten; **2.** behilflich sein; **3.** pol. mit dem Feind zs.-arbeiten, kollaborieren; **col·lab·o·ra·tion** [kəˌlæbəˈreɪʃn] s. **1.** Zs.-arbeit f: **in ~ with** gemeinsam mit; **2.** pol. Kollaborati'on f; **col·lab·o·ra·tion·ist** [kəˌlæbəˈreɪʃnɪst] s. pol. Kollabora'teur m; **col·lab·o·ra·tor** [-tə] s. **1.** Mitarbeiter m; **2.** pol. Kollabora'teur m.

col·lage [kɒˈlɑːʒ] s. Kunst: Col'lage f.

col·lapse [kəˈlæps] **I** v/i. **1.** zs.-brechen, einfallen, einstürzen; **2.** fig. zs.-brechen, scheitern, versagen; **3.** (körperlich od. seelisch) zs.-brechen, ˌzs.-klappen'; **II** s. **4.** Zs.-fallen n, Einsturz m; **5.** Zs.-bruch m, Versagen n; Sturz m: **~ of a bank** Bankkrach m; **~ of prices** Preissturz m; **6.** ⚕ Kol'laps m, Zs.-bruch m; **col·laps·i·ble** [-səbl] adj. zs.-klappbar, Klapp..., Falt...: **~ boat** Faltboot n; **~ chair** Klappstuhl m; **~ hood**, **~ roof** Klappverdeck n.

col·lar [ˈkɒlə] **I** s. **1.** Kragen m: **double ~, turn-down ~** (Steh)Umlegekragen; **stand-up ~** Stehkragen; **wing ~** Eckenkragen; **get hot under the ~** F wütend werden; **2.** Halsband n (Tier); **3.** Kummet n (Pferd etc.): **against the ~** fig. angestrengt; **4.** Kolli'er n, Halskette f; Amts-, Ordenskette f; **5.** zo. Halsstreifen m; **6.** ⚙ Ring m, Bund m, Man'schette f, Muffe f; **II** v/t. **7.** sport den Gegner aufhalten; **8.** j-n beim Kragen packen; fassen, festnehmen; **9.** F et. ergattern, sich aneignen; **10.** Fleisch etc. rollen u. zs.-binden; **'~-bone** s. Schlüsselbein n; **~ stud** s. Kragenknopf m.

col·late [kɒˈleɪt] v/t. **1.** Texte vergleichen, kollationieren; zs.-stellen (u. vergleichen); **2.** typ. Fahnen kollationieren, auf richtige Anzahl prüfen.

col·lat·er·al [kɒˈlætərəl] **I** adj. □ **1.** seitlich, Seiten...; **2.** begleitend, paral'lel, zusätzlich, Neben...: **~ acceptance** ✝ Avalakzept n; **~ circumstances** Begleitumstände; **~ credit** Lombardkredit m; **3.** 'indirekt; **4.** in der Seitenlinie verwandt; **II** s. **5.** a. **~ security** zusätzliche Sicherheit, Nebenbürgschaft f; **6.** Seitenverwandte(r m) f.

col·la·tion [kɒˈleɪʃn] s. **1.** Vergleichung f von Texten, Über'prüfung f; **2.** leichte (Zwischen)Mahlzeit: **cold ~** kalter Imbiss.

col·league [ˈkɒliːg] s. Kol'lege m, Kol'legin f; Mitarbeiter(in).

col·lect¹ [kəˈlekt] **I** v/t. **1.** Briefmarken, Bilder etc. sammeln: **~ed work(s)** gesammelte Werke; **2.** versammeln; **3.** einsammeln, auflesen; zs.-bringen, ansammeln; auffangen; **4.** Sachen od. Personen (ab)holen: **we ~ and deliver** ✝ wir holen ab und bringen zurück; **5.** fig. **~ one's thoughts** s-e Gedanken sammeln od. zs.-nehmen; **~ courage** Mut fassen; **6. ~ o.s.** sich fassen; **7.**

C

Geld etc. einziehen, (ein)kassieren; **8.** *Pferd* versammeln; **II** *v/i.* **9.** sich versammeln; sich ansammeln; **10.** **~ on delivery** ✝ *Am.* per Nachnahme; **III** *adj.* **11.** *Am.* Nachnahme...: **~ call** *teleph.* R-Gespräch *n*; **IV** *adv.* **12.** *Am.* gegen Nachnahme: **telegram sent ~** Nachnahmetelegramm *n*; **call ~** *Am.* ein R-Gespräch führen.

col·lect² ['kɒlekt] *s. eccl.* Kol'lekte *f*, *ein* Kirchengebet *n*.

col·lect·ed [kə'lektɪd] *adj.* □ *fig.* gefasst; → **calm** 5; **col'lect·ed·ness** [-nɪs] *s. fig.* Sammlung *f*, Gefasstheit *f*.

col·lect·ing | a·gent [kə'lektɪŋ] *s.* ✝ In'kassovertreter *m*; **~ bar** *s.* ⚡ Sammelschiene *f*; **~ cen·tre** (*Am.* **·ter**) *s.* Sammelstelle *f*.

col·lec·tion [kə'lekʃn] *s.* **1.** Sammeln *n*; **2.** Sammlung *f*; **3.** Kol'lekte *f*, (Geld-)Sammlung *f*; **4.** *bsd.* ✝ Einziehung *f*, In'kasso *n*; (Steuer-, *a.* sta'tistische) Erhebung(en *pl.*) *f*; **forcible ~** Zwangsbeitreibung *f*; **5.** ✝ Kollekti'on *f*, Auswahl *f*; **6.** Abholung *f*, Leerung *f* (*Briefkasten*); **7.** Ansammlung *f*, Anhäufung *f*; **8.** *Brit.* Steuerbezirk *m*; **9.** *pl. Brit. univ.* Prüfung *f* am Ende des Tri'mesters.

col·lec·tive [kə'lektɪv] **I** *adj.* □ → *collectively*; **1.** gesammelt, vereint, zs.-gefasst; gesamt, kollek'tiv, Sammel..., Gemeinschafts...: **~ (wage) agreement** Kollektiv-, Tarifvertrag *m*; **~ guilt** *pol.* Kollektivschuld *f*; **~ interests** Gesamtinteressen; **~ name** Sammelbegriff *m*; **~ order** ✝ Sammelbestellung *f*; **~ ownership** gemeinsamer Besitz *m*; **~ security** kollektive Sicherheit; **~ subscription** Sammelabonnement *n*; **II** *s.* **2.** *ling. a.* **~ noun** Kollek'tivum *n*, Sammelwort *n*; **3.** Gemeinschaft *f*, Gruppe *f*; **4.** *pol.* a) Kollek'tiv *n*, Produkti'onsgemeinschaft *f*, b) → *collective farm*; **~ bar·gain·ing** *s.* Ta'rifverhandlungen *pl.* (*zwischen Arbeitgeber*[*n*] *u.* Gewerkschaften); **~ con·sign·ment** *s.* Sammelladung *f*; **~ farm** *s.* Kol'chose *f*.

col·lec·tive·ly [kə'lektɪvlɪ] *adv.* insgesamt, gemeinschaftlich, zu'sammen, kollek'tiv.

col·lec·tiv·ism [kə'lektɪvɪzəm] *s.* ✝, *pol.* Kollekti'vismus *m*; **col'lec·tiv·ist** [-ɪst] *s.* Anhänger *m* des Kollekti'vismus; **col·lec·tiv·i·ty** [ˌkɒlek'tɪvətɪ] *s.* **1.** das Ganze; **2.** Gesamtheit *f* des Volkes; **3.** → *collectedness*; **col·lec·tiv·i·za·tion** [kəˌlektɪvaɪ'zeɪʃn] *s.* Kollektivierung *f*.

col·lec·tor [kə'lektə] *s.* **1.** Sammler *m*: **~'s item** Sammlerstück *n*; **~'s value** Liebhaberwert *m*; **2.** ✝ (Ein)Kassierer *m*, Einnehmer *m*: **~ of taxes** Steuereinnehmer; **3.** Einsammler *m*, Abnehmer *m* (*Fahrkarten*); **4.** ⚡ Stromabnehmer *m*, 'Auffangelek,trode *f*; **5.** ⚡ 'Sammel,appa,rat *m*.

col·leen ['kɒliːn] *s. Ir.* Mädchen *n*.

col·lege ['kɒlɪdʒ] *s.* **1.** College *n* (*Wohngemeinschaft von Dozenten u. Studenten innerhalb e-r Universität*): **~ of education** *Brit.* pädagogische Hochschule; **2.** höhere Lehranstalt, College *n*; Insti'tut *n*, Akade'mie *f* (*oft für besondere Studienzweige*): **Naval ⚓** Marineakademie; **3.** (*anmaßender*) *Name mancher Schulen*; **4.** College *n* (*Gebäude*) *od.* **5.** Kol'legium *n*, Vereinigung *f*: **~ of cardinals** Kardinalskollegium; **electoral ~** Wahlausschuss *m*; **~ pud·ding** *s.* kleiner 'Plumpudding.

col·leg·er ['kɒlɪdʒə] *s.* **1.** *Brit.* (im College wohnender) Stipendi'at (*in Eton*); **2.** *Am.* → **col·le·gi·an** [kə'liːdʒjən] *s.* Mitglied *n od.* Stu'dent *m* e-s College; höherer Schüler.

col·le·gi·ate [kə'liːdʒɪət] *adj.* □ **1.** College..., Universitäts..., aka'demisch: **~ dictionary** Schulwörterbuch *n*; **2.** Kollegial...; **~ church** *s.* **1.** *Brit.* Kollegi'at-, Stiftskirche *f*; **2.** *Am.* Vereinigung *f* mehrerer Kirchen (*unter gemeinsamem Pastorat*); **~ school** *s. Brit.* höhere Schule.

col·lide [kə'laɪd] *v/i.* (**with**) kollidieren (mit): a) zs.-stoßen (mit) (*a. fig.*), stoßen (gegen), b) *fig.* im 'Widerspruch stehen (zu).

col·lie ['kɒlɪ] *s. zo.* Collie *m*, Schottischer Schäferhund.

col·lier ['kɒlɪə] *s.* **1.** Kohlenarbeiter *m*, Bergmann *m*; **2.** ⚓ a) Kohlenschiff *n*, b) Ma'trose *m* auf e-m Kohlenschiff; **col·liery** ['kɒljərɪ] *s.* Kohlengrube *f*, (Kohlen)Zeche *f*.

col·li·mate ['kɒlɪmeɪt] *v/t. ast., phys.* **1.** *zwei Linien* zs.-fallen lassen; **2.** *Fernrohr* einstellen.

col·li·sion [kə'lɪʒn] *s.* **1.** Zs.-stoß *m*, Kollisi'on *f*: **be on (a) ~ course** auf Kollisionskurs sein (*a. fig.*); **2.** *fig.* 'Widerspruch *m*, Gegensatz *m*, Kon'flikt *m*.

col·lo·cate ['kɒləʊkeɪt] *v/t.* zs.-stellen, ordnen; **col·lo·ca·tion** [ˌkɒləʊ'keɪʃn] *s.* **1.** Zs.-stellung *f*; **2.** *ling.* Kollokati'on *f*.

col·loc·u·tor ['kɒləkjuːtə] *s.* Gesprächspartner(in).

col·lo·di·on [kə'ləʊdjən] *s.* 🜍 Kol'lodium *n*.

col·loid ['kɒlɔɪd] 🜍 **I** *s.* Kollo'id *n*; **II** *adj.* kolloi'dal, gallertartig.

col·lop ['kɒləp] *s. Scot.* Klops *m*.

col·lo·qui·al [kə'ləʊkwɪəl] *adj.* □ 'umgangssprachlich, famili'är: **~ English** Umgangsenglisch *n*; **~ expression** → **col·lo·qui·al·ism** [-ɪzəm] *s.* Ausdruck *m* der 'Umgangssprache.

col·lo·quy ['kɒləkwɪ] *s.* (förmliches) Gespräch; Konfe'renz *f*.

col·lo·type ['kɒləʊtaɪp] *s. phot.* **1.** Lichtdruckverfahren *n od.* -platte *f*; **2.** Farbenlichtdruck *m*.

col·lude [kə'luːd] *v/i. obs.* in geheimem Einverständnis stehen; unter 'einer Decke stecken; **col'lu·sion** [-uːʒn] *s.* 🜨 **1.** Kollusi'on *f*, geheimes *od.* betrügerisches Einverständnis; **2.** Verdunkelung *f des Sachverhalts*: **danger of ~** Verdunkelungsgefahr *f*; **3.** abgekartete Sache, Schwindel *m*; **col'lu·sive** [-uːsɪv] *adj.* □ geheim *od.* betrügerisch verabredet.

col·ly·wob·bles ['kɒlɪˌwɒblz] *s. pl.*: **have the ~** F ein flaues Gefühl in der Magengegend haben.

Co·lom·bi·an [kə'lɒmbɪən] **I** *adj.* ko'lumbisch; **II** *s.* Ko'lumbier(in).

co·lon¹ ['kəʊlən] *s.* Dickdarm *m*.

co·lon² ['kəʊlən] *s.* Doppelpunkt *m*.

colo·nel ['kɜːnl] *s.* ✕ Oberst *m*; **'colo·nel·cy** [-sɪ] *s.* Stelle *f od.* Rang *m* e-s Obersten.

co·lo·ni·al [kə'ləʊnjəl] **I** *adj.* □ **1.** koloni'al, Kolonial...: **⚓ Office** *Brit.* Kolonialministerium *n*; **⚓ Secretary** Kolonialminister *m*; **2.** *Am. hist.* die ersten 13 Staaten der heutigen USA *od.* die Zeit vor 1776 *od.* des 18. Jahrhunderts betreffend; **II** *s.* **3.** Bewohner(in) e-r Kolo'nie; **co·lo·ni·al·ism** [-lɪzəm] *s.* **1.** Kolonia'lismus *m*; **2.** koloni'aler (*Wesens*)Zug *od.* Ausdruck.

col·o·nist ['kɒlənɪst] *s.* Kolo'nist(in), (An)Siedler(in); **col·o·ni·za·tion** [ˌkɒlənaɪ'zeɪʃn] *s.* Kolonisati'on *f*, Besiedlung *f*; **'col·o·nize** [-naɪz] *I v/t.* **1.** kolo-

nisieren, besiedeln; **2.** ansiedeln; **II** *v/i.* **3.** sich ansiedeln; **4.** e-e Kolo'nie bilden; **'col·o·niz·er** [-naɪzə] *s.* Koloni'sator *m*, An-, Besiedler *m*.

col·on·nade [ˌkɒlə'neɪd] *s.* **1.** Kolon'nade *f*, Säulengang *m*; **2.** Al'lee *f*.

col·o·ny ['kɒlənɪ] *s.* **1.** Kolo'nie *f* (*Siedlungsgebiet*): **the Colonies** *Am.* die ersten 13 Staaten der heutigen USA; **2.** Gruppe *f* von einzelnen: **the German ~ in Rome** die deutsche Kolonie in Rom; **a ~ of artists** e-e Künstlerkolonie; **3.** *biol.* (*Pflanzen-, Bakterien-, Zellen*)Kolo'nie *f*.

co·loph·o·ny [kə'lɒfənɪ] *s.* Kolo'phonium *n*, Geigenharz *n*.

col·or *etc. Am.* → *colour etc.*

Col·o·ra·do bee·tle [ˌkɒlə'rɑːdəʊ] *s. zo.* Kar'toffelkäfer *m*.

col·o·ra·tu·ra [ˌkɒlərə'tʊərə] *s.* ♪ **1.** Kolora'tur *f*; **2.** Kolora'tursängerin *f*; **~ so·pran·o** *s.* **2.** Kolora'turso,pran *m* (*Stimme u. Sängerin*).

col·or·if·ic [ˌkɒlə'rɪfɪk] *adj.* farbgebend; **col·or·im·e·ter** [-'rɪmɪtə] *s. phys.* Farbmesser *m*, Kolori'meter *n*.

co·los·sal [kə'lɒsl] *adj.* □ **1.** kolos'sal, riesig, Riesen..., ungeheuer (*alle a. fig.*); riesenhaft; **2.** F kolos'sal, e'norm; **col·os·se·um** [ˌkɒlə'sɪəm] → *coliseum*; **Co·los·sians** [-ɒʃənz] *s. pl. bibl.* (Brief *m* des Paulus an die) Ko'losser *pl.*; **co·los·sus** [-səs] *s.* **1.** Ko'loss *m*: a) Riese *m*, b) *et.* Riesengroßes; **2.** Riesenstandbild *n*.

col·our ['kʌlə] **I** *s.* **1.** Farbe *f*; Färbung *f*; **what ~ is ...?** welche Farbe hat ...?; **2.** *mst pl. Malerei*: Farbe *f*, Farbstoff *m*: **lay on the ~s too thickly** *fig.* zu dick auftragen; **paint in bright** (**dark**) **~s** *fig.* in rosigen (düsteren) Farben schildern; **3.** (*a. gesunde*) Gesichtsfarbe: **she has little ~** sie ist blass; **change** (**lose**) **~** die Farbe wechseln (verlieren); → *off-colo(u)r*; **4.** Hautfarbe *f*: **~ problem** Rassenfrage *f*; **5.** Anschein *m*, Anstrich *m*, Vorwand *m*, Deckmantel *m*: **~ of law** 🜨 Amtsmissbrauch *m*; **~ of title** 🜨 unzureichender Eigentumsanspruch; **give ~ to** den Anstrich der Wahrscheinlichkeit geben (*dat.*); **under ~ of** unter dem Vorwand *od.* Anschein von; **6.** a) Färbung *f*, Ton *m*, b) Farbe *f*, Lebendigkeit *f*, Kolo'rit *n*: **lend** (*od.* **add**) **~ to** beleben, lebendig gestalten, e-r *Sache* Farbe verleihen; **in one's true ~s** in s-m wahren Licht; **local ~** Lokalkolorit; **7.** ♪ Klangfarbe *f*; **8.** *pl.* Farben *pl.*, Abzeichen *n* (*Klub, Schule, Partei, Jockei*): **show one's ~s** a) sein wahres Gesicht zeigen, b) Farbe bekennen; **to get one's ~s** sein Mitgliedsabzeichen bekommen; **9.** *pl.* bunte Kleider; **10.** *oft pl.* ✕ *od. fig.* Fahne *f*, Flagge *f* (*oft für die ~s* einberufen; **join the ~s** Soldat werden; **with flying ~s** *fig.* mit fliegenden Fahnen; **come off with flying ~s** e-n glänzenden Sieg *od.* Erfolg erzielen; **nail one's ~s to the mast** nicht kapitulieren (wollen), standhaft bleiben; **sail under false ~s** unter falscher Flagge segeln; **stick to one's ~s** e-r Sache treu bleiben; → *troop* 6; **11.** *Kartenspiel*: rote u. schwarze Farbe; **II** *v/t.* **12.** färben, kolorieren; anstreichen; **13.** *fig.* färben, e-n Anstrich geben (*dat.*); **14.** a) schönfärben, b) entstellen; **III** *v/i.* **15.** sich (ver)färben; e-e Farbe annehmen; *a.* **~ up** erröten.

col·o(u)r·a·ble ['kʌlərəbl] *adj.* □ *fig.* **1.** vor-, angeblich; fingiert: **~ title** 🜨 unzureichender Eigentumsanspruch; **2.** glaubhaft, plau'sibel; **'col·o(u)r·ant** [-rənt] s. Farbstoff m.

col·o(u)r·a·tion [ˌkʌləˈreɪʃn] s. Färben n; Färbung f; Farbgebung f.

col·o(u)r| bar s. Rassenschranke f; **'~ -blind** adj. farbenblind; **~ chart** s. Farbenskala f; **'~-code** v/t. mit Kennfarben versehen; **~ cop·y** s. 'Farbko,pie f.

col·o(u)red ['kʌləd] adj. **1.** farbig, bunt (beide a. fig.), koloriert; in Zssgn ...farbig: **~ pencil** Bunt-, Farbstift m; **~ plate** → colo(u)r plate; **2.** farbig, Am. bsd. Neger...: **a ~ man** ein Farbiger; **3.** fig. gefärbt: a) beschönigt, b) tendenzi'ös entstellt; **4.** fig. angeblich, falsch; **'col·o(u)r·fast** adj. farbecht; **'col· o(u)r·ful** [-ʊl] adj. **1.** farbenfreudig; **2.** fig. farbig, bunt, lebhaft, abwechslungsreich; **'col·o(u)r·ing** [-ərɪŋ] I s. **1.** Farbe f, Farbton m; **2.** Farbgebung f; **3.** Gesichts- (u. Haar)farbe f; **4.** fig. Anstrich m, Färbung f; II adj. **5.** Farbe...: **~ matter** Farbstoff m; **'col·o(u)r·ist** [-ərɪst] s. Farbenkünstler m, engS. Kolo'rist m; **'col·o(u)r·less** [-əlɪs] adj. □ farblos (a. fig.).

col·o(u)r| line s. Rassenschranke f; **~ pho·tog·ra·phy** s. 'Farbfotogra,fie f; **~ plate** s. Farben(kunst)druck m; **~ print** s. ein Farbendruck m; **~ prin·ter** s. Farbdrucker m; **~ print·ing** s. Bunt-, Farbendruck m (Verfahren); **~ scheme** s. Farbgebung f, Farbenanordnung f; **~ screen** s. Farbbildschirm m; **~ ser·geant** s. ✕ (etwa) Oberfeldwebel m; **~ set** s. Farbfernseher m; **~ sup·ple·ment** s. Farbbeilage f (Zeitung); **~ tel·e·vi·sion** s. Farbfernsehen n; **'~-wash** I s. farbige Tünche; II v/t. farbig tünchen.

colt¹ [kəʊlt] I s. **1.** Füllen n, Fohlen n; **2.** fig. 'Grünschnabel' m, sport F a. 'Fohlen' n; **3.** ♣ Tauende n; II v/t. **4.** mit dem Tauende prügeln.

colt² [kəʊlt] s. Colt m (Revolver).

col·ter ['kəʊltə] Am. → coulter.

'colts·foot s. ♀ Huflattich m.

col·um·bine ['kɒləmbaɪn] s. **1.** ♀ Ake'lei f; **2.** ♀ thea. Kolom'bine f.

col·umn ['kɒləm] s. **1.** △ Säule f, Pfeiler m; **2.** (Rauch-, Wasser-, Luft- etc.)Säule f; **3.** typ. (Zeitungs-, Buch)Spalte f; Ru'brik f: in double ~s zweispaltig; **4.** Spalte f, Ko'lumne f (regelmäßig erscheinender Meinungsbeitrag); **5.** ✕ Ko'lonne f; → fifth column; **6.** Ko'lonne f, senkrechte Zahlenreihe; **co·lum·nar** [kəˈlʌmnə] adj. säulenartig, -förmig; Säulen...; **'col·um·nist** [-mnɪst] s. Zeitung: Kolum'nist(in).

col·za ['kɒlzə] s. ♀ Raps m: **~ oil** Rüb-, Rapsöl n.

co·ma¹ ['kəʊmə] pl. -mae [-miː] s. **1.** ♀ Haarbüschel n (an Samen); **2.** ast. Nebelhülle f e-s Kometen.

co·ma² ['kəʊmə] s. ♣ Koma n, tiefe Bewusstlosigkeit: be in (fall into) a ~ im Koma liegen (ins Koma fallen); **'co·ma·tose** [-ətəʊs] adj. koma'tös, im Koma (befindlich).

comb [kəʊm] I s. **1.** Kamm m; **2.** ⊙ a) (Wollweber)Kamm m, b) (Flachs)Hechel f, c) Gewindeschneider m, d) ♫ (Kamm)Stromabnehmer m; **3.** zo. Hahnenkamm m; **4.** Kamm m (Berg; Woge); **5.** → honeycomb 1; II v/t. **6.** Haar kämmen; ⊙ a) Wolle kämmen, krempeln, b) Flachs hecheln; **8.** Pferd striegeln; **9.** fig. 'durchkämmen, durch'kämmen, absuchen; **10.** fig. a. ~ out a) sieben, sichten, b) aussondern, c) ✕ ausmustern.

com·bat ['kɒmbæt] I v/t. bekämpfen, kämpfen gegen; II v/i. kämpfen; III s. Kampf m; Streit m; ✕ a. Einsatz m: **single ~** Zweikampf; **'com·bat·ant** [-bətənt] I s. **1.** Kämpfer m; **2.** ✕ Frontkämpfer m; II adj. **3.** kämpfend; **4.** ✕ zur Kampftruppe gehörig; Kampf...

com·bat| car s. ✕ Am. Kampfwagen m; **~ fa·tigue** s. ✕ psych. 'Kriegsneu-,rose f.

com·ba·tive ['kɒmbətɪv] adj. □ **1.** kampfbereit; **2.** kampflustig, streitsüchtig.

com·bat| plane s. ✈ Am. Kampfflugzeug n; **~ sport** s. Kampfsport m; **~ train·ing** s. Gefechtsausbildung f; **~ troops** s. pl. Kampftruppen pl.; **~ u·nit** s. ✕ Am. Kampfverband m.

combe [kuːm] → coomb(e).

comb·er ['kəʊmə] s. **1.** ⊙ a) 'Krempelma,schine f, b) 'Hechelma,schine f; **2.** Sturzwelle f.

comb hon·ey s. Scheibenhonig m.

com·bi·na·tion [ˌkɒmbɪˈneɪʃn] s. **1.** Verbindung f, Vereinigung f; Zs.-setzung f; Kombinati'on f (a. sport, ✗ etc.); **2.** Zs.-schluss m, Bündnis n; b.s. Kom'plott n; **3.** ⚕ etc. → combine 6, 7, 8; **4.** 🚗 Verbindung f; **5.** mot. Gespann n, 'Motorrad n mit Beiwagen; **6.** mst. pl. Kombinati'on f: a) Hemdhose f, b) Mon'tur f; **7.** ♪ → combo; **~ lock** s. ⊙ Kombinati'ons-, Ve'xierschloss n; **~ room** s. Brit. univ. Gemeinschaftsraum m.

com·bine [kəmˈbaɪn] I v/t. **1.** verbinden (a. 🚗), vereinigen, kombinieren; **2.** in sich vereinigen; II v/i. **3.** sich verbinden (a. 🚗), sich vereinigen; **4.** sich zs.-schließen; **5.** zs.-wirken; III s. ['kɒmbaɪn] **6.** Verbindung f, Vereinigung f; **7.** ♣ Kon'zern m, Verband m; **8.** po'litische od. wirtschaftliche Interessengemeinschaft; **9.** a. **~ harvester** ✂ Mähdrescher m.

com·bined [kəmˈbaɪnd] adj. vereinigt, verbunden; vereint, gemeinsam, Gemeinschafts...; kombiniert: **~ arms** ✕ gemischte Verbände; **~ event** sport Mehrkampf m.

comb·ings ['kəʊmɪŋz] s. pl. ausgekämmte Haare pl.

com·bo ['kɒmbəʊ] s. Combo f, kleine Jazzband.

'comb-out s. Auskämmen n; fig. Siebung f, Sichtung f.

com·bus·ti·bil·i·ty [kəmˌbʌstɪˈbɪlətɪ] s. Brennbarkeit f, Entzündlichkeit f; **com·bus·ti·ble** [kəmˈbʌstəbl] I adj. **1.** brennbar, leicht entzündlich; **2.** fig. erregbar; II s. **3.** Brenn-, Zündstoff m; 'Brennmateri,al n.

com·bus·tion [kəmˈbʌstʃən] s. Verbrennung f (a. 🚗, biol.): **spontaneous ~** Selbstentzündung f; **~ cham·ber** s. ⊙ Verbrennungsraum m; **~ en·gine** s. ⊙ Ver'brennungs,motor m.

come [kʌm] I v/i. [irr.] **1.** kommen: **be long in coming** lange auf sich warten lassen; **he came to see us** er besuchte uns, er suchte uns auf; **that ~s on page 4** das kommt auf Seite 4; **~ what may!** komme, was da wolle!; **a year ago ~ March** im März vor e-m Jahr; **as stupid as they ~** dumm wie Bohnenstroh; **the message has ~** die Nachricht ist gekommen od. eingetroffen; **a year ago ~ coming to that** darauf wollte ich gerade hinaus; **~ to that** was das betrifft; **~ again!** F sags noch mal!; **2.** (dran)kommen, an die Reihe kommen: **who ~s first?**; **3.** kommen, erscheinen, auftre-

ten: **~ and go** a) kommen u. gehen, b) erscheinen u. verschwinden; **love will ~ in time** mit der Zeit wird die Liebe sich einstellen; **~ (to pass)** geschehen, sich ereignen, kommen; **how ~?** wie kommt das?, wieso (denn)?; **4.** kommen, gelangen (to zu): **~ to the throne** den Thron besteigen; **~ into danger** in Gefahr geraten; **5.** kommen, abstammen (of, from von): **he ~s of a good family** er kommt od. stammt aus gutem Hause; **I ~ from Leeds** ich stamme aus Leeds; **6.** kommen, 'herrühren (of von): **that's what ~s of your hurry** das kommt von deiner Eile; **nothing came of it** es wurde nichts daraus; **7.** sich erweisen: **it ~s expensive** es kommt teuer; **the expenses ~ rather high** die Kosten kommen recht hoch; **it ~s to this that** es läuft darauf hinaus, dass; **it ~s to the same thing** es läuft auf dasselbe hinaus; → a. **come** to 4; **8.** fig. ankommen (to s.o. j-n): **it ~s hard (easy) to me** es fällt mir schwer (leicht); **9.** werden, sich entwickeln, dahin od. dazu kommen: **he has ~ to be a good musician** er ist ein guter Musiker geworden; **it has ~ to be the custom** es ist Sitte geworden; **~ to know s.o.** j-n kennen lernen; **I have ~ to believe that** ich bin zu der Überzeugung gekommen, dass; **how did you ~ to do that?** wie kamen Sie dazu, das zu tun?; **~ true** wahr werden, sich erfüllen; **~ undone** auf-, ab-, losgehen, sich lösen; **10.** ♀ (her'aus)kommen, sprießen, keimen; **11.** erhältlich od. zu haben sein: **these shirts ~ in three sizes**; **12.** to ~ (als adj. gebraucht) (zu)künftig, kommend: **the life to ~** das zukünftige Leben; **for all time to ~** für alle Zukunft; **in the years to ~** in den kommenden Jahren; **13.** sport etc. ,kommen' (angreifen, stärker werden); **14.** sl. ,kommen' (e-n Orgasmus haben); II v/t. **15.** F sich aufspielen als, j-n od. etwas spielen, her'auskehren: **don't try to ~ the great scholar over me!** versuche nicht, mir gegenüber den großen Gelehrten zu spielen!; III int. **16.** na (hör mal)!, komm!, bitte!: **~, ~!** a) **~ now!** nanu!, nicht so wild!, immer langsam!, b) (ermutigend) na komm schon!, auf gehts!; IV s. **17.** V ,Saft' m (Sperma); Zssgn mit prp.:

come| a·cross v/i. zufällig treffen od. finden, stoßen auf (acc.); **~ af·ter** v/i. **1.** j-m folgen; **2.** et. holen kommen; **3.** suchen, sich bemühen um; **~ at** v/i. **1.** erreichen, bekommen; **2.** angreifen, auf j-n losgehen; **~ by** v/i. zu et. kommen, bekommen; **2.** → **come at** 2; **~ in·to** v/i. **1.** eintreten in (acc.); **2.** e-m Klub etc. beitreten; **3.** (rasch od. unerwartet) zu et. kommen: **~ a fortune** ein Vermögen erben; **~ near** v/i. **1.** nahe kommen (dat.); **2.** **~ doing (s.th.)** beinahe (et.) tun; **~ on** → **come upon**; **~ o·ver** v/i. **1.** über'kommen, beschleichen, befallen: **what has ~ you?** was ist mit dir los?, was fällt dir ein?; **2.** sl. j-n reinlegen; **3.** → **come** 15; **~ to** v/i. **1.** j-m zufallen (bsd. durch Erbschaft); **2.** j-m zukommen, zustehen: **he had it coming to him** F er hatte das längst verdient; **3.** zum Bewusstsein etc. kommen; **4.** kommen od. gelangen zu: **what are things coming to?** wohin sind wir (od. ist die Welt) geraten?; **when it comes to paying** wenn es ans Bezahlen geht; **5.** sich belaufen auf (acc.): **it comes to £100**; → a. **come** 7; **~ un·der** v/i. **1.**

C

kommen *od.* fallen unter (*acc.*): **~ a law**; **2.** geraten unter (*acc.*); **~ up·on** *v/i.* **1.** *j-n* befallen, über'kommen, *j-m* zustoßen; **2.** über *j-n* 'herfallen; **3.** (*zufällig*) treffen, stoßen auf (*acc.*); **4.** *j-m* zur Last fallen; **~ with·in** → come under.
Zssgn mit adv.:
come| a·bout *v/i.* **1.** geschehen, pas'sieren; **2.** entstehen; **3.** ♪ 'umspringen (*Wind*); **~ a·cross** *v/i.* **1.** her'überkommen; **2.** a) verstanden werden, b) ,an-kommen' (*Rede etc.*), c) ,rüberkom-men' (*Filmszene etc.*); **3.** ~ **with** F ,rü-berkommen' mit, *Geld etc.* her'ausrük-ken; **~ a·long** *v/i.* **1.** mitkommen, -ge-hen: ~*!* ,dalli'!, komm schon!; **2.** sich ergeben (*Chance etc.*); **3.** F vorankom-men, Fortschritte machen; **~ a·part** *v/i.* ausein'ander fallen, in Stücke gehen; **~ a·way** *v/i.* **1.** ab-, losgehen (*Knopf etc.*); **2.** weggehen (*Person*); **~ back** *v/i.* **1.** zu'rückkommen, *a. fig.* 'wieder-kehren: ~ **to s.th.** auf e-e Sache zurück-kommen; **2.** *sl.* ein ,Come-back' feiern; **3.** wieder einfallen (**to s.o.** *j-m*); **4.** (*bsd.* schlagfertig) antworten (**at s.o.** *j-m*); **~ by** *v/i.* vor'beikommen, ,rein-schauen'; **~ down** *v/i.* **1.** her'ab-, he-runterkommen; **2.** (ein)stürzen, fallen; **3.** ✈ niedergehen; **4.** *a.* **~ in the world** *fig.* her'unterkommen (*Person*); **5.** *ped. univ. Brit.* a) die Universi'tät verlassen, b) in die Ferien gehen; **6.** über'liefert werden; **7.** her'untergehen, sinken (*Preis*), billiger werden (*Dinge*); **8.** nachgeben, kleinlaut werden; **9.** **~ on** a) sich stürzen auf (*acc.*), b) 'herfallen über (*acc.*), *j-m* ,aufs Dach steigen'; **10.** **~ with** F her'ausrücken mit: **~ handsome(ly)** sich spendabel zeigen; **11.** **~ with** erkranken an (*dat.*); **12.** **~ to** hin'auslaufen auf (*acc.*); **~ forth** *v/i.* her'vorkommen; **~ for·ward** *v/i.* **1.** her'vortreten; **2.** sich melden (*Zeuge etc.*); **~ home** *v/i.* **1.** nach Hause, *östr. schweiz.* nachhause kommen; **2.** *fig.* Ein-druck machen, wirken, ,einschlagen', ,ziehen'; **~ in** *v/i.* **1.** hereinkommen: ~*!* a) herein!, b) (*Funk*) bitte kommen!; **2.** eingehen, -treffen (*Nachricht, Geld etc.*), ♪, ✠ *sport* einlaufen; **~ second** den zweiten Platz belegen; **3.** aufkommen, in Mode kommen: **long skirts ~ again**; **4.** an die Macht kommen; **5.** sich *als nützlich etc.* erweisen: **this will ~ use-ful**; **6.** Berücksichtigung finden: **where do I ~?** wo bleibe ich?; **that's were you ~** da bist dann du dran; **where does the joke ~?** was ist daran so witzig?; **7.** **~ for** a) bekommen, ,kriegen', b) Be-wunderung etc. erregen: **~ for it** F ,sein Fett abkriegen'; **~ off** *v/i.* **1.** ab-, losge-hen, sich lösen; **2.** *fig.* stattfinden, ,über die Bühne gehen'; **3.** a) abschneiden: **he came off best**, b) erfolgreich ver-laufen, glücken; **4.** **~ it!** F hör schon auf damit!; **~ on** *v/i.* **1.** her'ankommen: ~*!* a) komm (mit)!, b) komm her!, c) na, komm schon!, los!, d) F na, na!; **2.** be-ginnen, einsetzen: **it came on to rain** es begann zu regnen; **3.** an die Reihe kommen; **4.** *thea.* a) auftreten, b) aufge-führt werden; **5.** stattfinden; ✠ verhan-delt werden; **6.** a) wachsen, gedeihen, b) vor'ankommen, Fortschritte ma-chen; **~ out** *v/i.* **1.** her'aus-, her'vor-kommen, sich zeigen; **2.** *a.* **~ on strike** streiken; **3.** her'auskommen: a) erschei-nen (*Bücher*), b) bekannt werden, ans Licht kommen; **4.** ausgehen (*Haare*), her'ausgehen (*Farbe*); **5.** F werden, sich *gut etc.* entwickeln; *phot. etc.* gut *etc.*

werden (*Bild*); **6.** debü'tieren: a) zum ersten Mal auftreten (*Schauspieler*), b) in die Gesellschaft eingeführt wer-den; **7.** sich outen (*Homosexueller*); **8.** **~ with** F mit *et.* her'ausrücken (*sagen*); **9.** **~ against** sich aussprechen gegen, den Kampf ansagen (*dat.*); **~ o·ver** *v/i.* **1.** her'überkommen; **2.** 'übergehen (**to** zu); **3.** verstanden werden; **~ round** *v/i.* **1.** ,vor'beikommen' (*Besucher*); **2.** 'wiederkehren (*Fest, Zeitabschnitt*); **3.** **~ to s.o.'s way of thinking** sich zu j-s Meinung bekehren; **4.** → come to 1; **~ through** *v/i.* **1.** 'durchkommen (*a. allg. fig. Kranker, Meldung etc.*); **2.** *fig.* a) es ,schaffen', b) → come across 3; **~ to** *v/i.* **1.** a) wieder zu sich kommen, das Bewusstsein 'wiedererlangen, b) sich er-holen; **2.** ♪ vor Anker gehen; **~ up** *v/i.* **1.** her'aufkommen; **2.** her'ankommen: **~ to s.o.** an j-n herantreten; **coming up!** kommt gleich!; **3.** ✠ zur Verhand-lung kommen; **4.** *a.* **~ for discussion** zur Sprache kommen, angeschnitten werden; **5.** **~ for** zur *Abstimmung, Ent-scheidung* kommen; **6.** aufkommen, Mode werden; **7.** *Brit.* sein Studium aufnehmen; **8.** *Brit.* nach London kom-men; **9.** **~ to** a) reichen bis an (*acc.*) od. zu, b) erreichen (*acc.*), c) *fig.* her'anrei-chen an (*acc.*); **10.** **~ with** a) *j-n* einho-len, b) *fig.* es *j-m* gleichtun; **11.** **~ with** ,da'herkommen' mit, *e-e Idee etc.* prä-sentieren.
come-at-a·ble [,kʌm'ætəbl] *adj.* F **1.** zugänglich; **2.** erreichbar.
'come-back *s.* **1.** *sport, thea. etc.* Come-'back *n*: **make** *od.* **stage a ~** ein Come-back feiern; **2.** (schlagfertige) Antwort.
co·me·di·an [kə'mi:djən] *s.* **1.** a) Ko'mödienschauspieler *m*, b) Komiker *m (a. contp.)*; **2.** Lustspieldichter *m*; **3.** Witzbold *m (a. contp.)*; **co·me·di·enne** [kə,mi:di'en] *s.* a) Ko'mödienschauspie-lerin *f*, b) Komikerin *f*.
com·e·do ['kɒmədəʊ] *pl.* **-dos** *s.* ✠ Mit-esser *m*.
'come-down *s.* **1.** *fig.* Abstieg *m*, Abfall *m (from* gegenüber); **2.** F Enttäu-schung *f*.
com·e·dy ['kɒmɪdɪ] *s.* **1.** Ko'mödie *f*: a) Lustspiel *n*: **light ~** Schwank *m*, b) *fig.* komische Sache; **2.** Komik *f*.
,come-'hith·er *adj.*: **~ look** F einladen-der Blick.
come·li·ness ['kʌmlɪnɪs] *s.* Anmut *f*, Schönheit *f*; **come·ly** ['kʌmlɪ] *adj.* at-trak'tiv, hübsch.
'come-on *s. Am. sl.* **1.** Köder *m (bsd.* für Käufer*)*; **2.** Schwindler *m*; **3.** Gim-pel *m (einfältiger Mensch)*.
com·er ['kʌmə] *s.* **1.** Ankömmling *m*: **first ~** wer zuerst kommt, *weitS.* (*der od. die*) erste Beste; **all ~s** jedermann; **2. he is a ~** F er ist der kommende Mann.
co·mes·ti·ble [kə'mestɪbl] **I** *adj.* genieß-bar; **II** *s. pl.* Nahrungs-, Lebensmittel *pl.*
com·et ['kɒmɪt] *s. ast.* Ko'met *m*.
come-up·pance [,kʌm'ʌpəns] *s.* F wohl-verdiente Strafe.
com·fit ['kʌmfɪt] *s. obs.* Zuckerwerk *n*, kan'dierte Früchte *pl.*
com·fort ['kʌmfət] **I** *v/t.* **1.** trösten, *j-m* Trost spenden; **2.** beruhigen; **3.** erfreu-en; **4.** *j-m* Mut zusprechen; **5.** *obs.* un-ter'stützen, *j-m* helfen; **II** *s.* **6.** Trost *m*, Erleichterung *f* (**to** für): **derive** *od.* **take ~ from s.th.** aus etwas Trost schöpfen; **what a ~!** Gott sei Dank!; welch ein Trost!; **he was a great ~ to her** er war ihr ein großer Trost *od.* Bei-stand; **cold ~** ein schwacher *od.*

schlechter Trost; **7.** Wohltat *f*, Labsal *n*, Erquickung *f* (**to** für); **8.** Behaglich-keit *f*, Wohlergehen *n*: **live in ~** ein be-hagliches u. sorgenfreies Leben führen; **9.** *a. pl.* Kom'fort *m*: **with all modern ~s**; **10.** *a.* **soldiers' ~s** *pl.* Liebesgaben *pl.* (für Sol'daten); **11.** *obs.* Hilfe *f*.
com·fort·a·ble ['kʌmfətəbl] *adj.* (*adv.* **comfortably**) **1.** komfor'tabel, be-quem, behaglich, gemütlich: **make o.s. ~** es sich bequem machen; **are you ~?** haben Sie es bequem?, sitzen *od.* liegen *etc.* Sie bequem?; **feel ~** sich wohl füh-len; **2.** bequem, sorgenfrei: **live in ~ circumstances** in guten Verhältnissen leben; **3.** gut, reichlich: **a ~ income**; **4.** *bsd. sport* beruhigend (*Vorsprung etc.*); **5.** ohne Beschwerden (*Patient*); **'com-fort·er** [-tə] *s.* **1.** Tröster *m*: → **Job²**; **2. the ~** *eccl.* der Heilige Geist; **3.** *bsd. Brit.* Wollschal *m*; **4.** *Am.* Steppdecke *f*; **5.** *bsd. Brit.* Schnuller *m (für Babys)*; **'com·fort·ing** [-tɪŋ] *adj.* tröstlich; **'com·fort·less** [-lɪs] *adj.* **1.** unbequem; **2.** trostlos; **3.** unerfreulich.
com·frey ['kʌmfrɪ] *s.* ♣ Schwarzwurz *f*.
com·fy ['kʌmfɪ] F → **comfortable** 1.
com·ic ['kɒmɪk] **I** *adj.* □ → **comically**; **1.** komisch, Lustspiel...: **~ actor** Komi-ker *m*; **~ opera** komische Oper; **~ writ-er** Lustspieldichter *m*; **2.** komisch, hu-mo'ristisch: **~ paper** Witzblatt *n*; **~ strips** Comic Strips, Comics; **3.** drollig, spaßig; *II s.* **4.** Komiker *m*; **5.** Witzblatt *n*; *pl. Zeitung:* Comics *pl.*; **6.** 'Filmko-,mödie *f*; **'com·i·cal** [-kəl] *adj.* □ **1.** komisch, ulkig; **2.** F komisch, sonder-bar; **comi·cal·i·ty** [,kɒmɪ'kælətɪ] *s.* Spaßigkeit *f*; **'com·i·cal·ly** [-kəlɪ] *adv.* komisch(erweise).
com·ing ['kʌmɪŋ] **I** *adj.* kommend, (zu)künftig: **the ~ man** der kommende Mann; **~ week** nächste Woche; **II** *s.* Kommen *n*, Ankunft *f*; Beginn *m*: **~ of age** Mündigwerden *n*; **the Second ~** *(of Christ)* die Wiederkunft Christi.
com·i·ty ['kɒmɪtɪ] *s.* **1.** Höflichkeit *f*; **2.** **~ of nations** gutes Einvernehmen der Nationen.
com·ma ['kɒmə] *s.* Komma *n*; **~ ba·cil·lus** *s.* [*irr.*] ✠ 'Kommaba,zillus *m*.
com·mand [kə'mɑ:nd] **I** *v/t.* **1.** *j-m* be-fehlen, gebieten; **2.** gebieten, fordern, verlangen: **~ silence** Ruhe gebieten; **3.** beherrschen, gebieten über (*acc.*): **the hill ~s the plain** der Hügel beherrscht die Ebene; **4.** ✗ kommandieren: a) *j-m* befehlen, b) *Truppe* befehligen, füh-ren; **5.** *Gefühle, die Lage* beherrschen: **~ o.s.** sich beherrschen; **6.** verfügen über (*acc.*) (*Dienste, Gelder*); **7.** *Ver-trauen, Liebe* einflößen: **~ respect** Achtung gebieten; **~ admiration** Be-wunderung abnötigen *od.* verdienen; **8.** *Aussicht* gewähren, bieten; **9.** ✝ *Preis* erzielen; *Absatz* finden; **II** *v/i.* **10.** be-fehlen, herrschen; **11.** ✗ kommandie-ren; **III** *s.* **12.** *allg.* Befehl *m*: **by ~** auf Befehl; **~ key** *Computer:* Befehlstaste *f*; **~ menu** Befehlsmenü *n*; **13.** ✗ Kom'mando *n*: a) Befehl *m*: **word of ~** Kommando(wort) *n*, b) (Ober)Befehl *m*, Befehlsgewalt *f*, Führung *f*: **be in ~** a) (*of*) das Kommando führen (über *acc.*), b) *sport* den Gegner beherr-schen; **take ~** das Kommando überneh-men; **14.** ✗ a) Oberkom'mando *n*, Führungsstab *m*, b) Befehls-, Kom-'mandobereich *m*; **15.** *fig.* Gewalt *f*, Herrschaft *f* (**of** über *acc.*); Beherr-schung *f*, Meisterung *f* (*Gefühle*): **have ~ of** Fremdsprache *etc.* beherrschen; **his ~ of English** s-e Englischkenntnisse

pl.; **16.** Verfügung *f* (*of* über *acc.*): *at your* ~ zu Ihrer Verfügung; *be* (*have*) *at* ~ zur Verfügung stehen (haben).

com·man·dant [ˌkɒmənˈdænt] *s.* ✕ Komman'dant *m*, Befehlshaber *m*.

com·mand car *s.* ✕ *Am.* Befehlsfahrzeug *n*.

com·man·deer [ˌkɒmənˈdɪə] *v/t.* **1.** zum Mili'tärdienst zwingen; **2.** ✕ requirieren, beschlagnahmen; **3.** F ‚organisieren', sich aneignen.

com·mand·er [kəˈmɑːndə] *s.* **1.** ✕ Komman'dant *m* (*e-r Festung, e-s Flugzeugs etc.*), Befehlshaber *m*; Komman'deur *m* (*e-r Einheit*), Führer *m*; *Am.* ♣ Fre'gattenkapi‚tän *m*: ~-*in-chief* Oberbefehlshaber; **2.** ♘ *of the Faithful hist.* Beherrscher *m* der Gläubigen (*Sultan*); **3.** *hist.* (*Ordens*)Kom'tur *m*; **com-'mand·ing** [-dɪŋ] *adj.* □ **1.** herrschend, gebietend; **2.** *die Gegend* beherrschend: ~ *point* strategischer Punkt; **3.** ✕ kommandierend, befehlshabend; **4.** imponierend, eindrucksvoll; **5.** gebieterisch; **com'mand·ment** [-dmənt] *s.* Gebot *n*, Vorschrift *f*: *the Ten* ♘s *bibl.* die Zehn Gebote.

com·mand mod·ule *s. Raumfahrt*: Kom'mandokapsel *f*.

com·man·do [kəˈmɑːndəʊ] *pl.* -*dos s.* ✕ **1.** Kom'mando(truppe *f*, -einheit *f*) *n*: ~ *squad*; ~ *raid* Kommandoüberfall *m*; **2.** Angehörige(r) *m* e-s Kom-'mandos.

com·mand| **pa·per** *s. pol. Brit.* (*dem Parlament vorgelegter*) Kabi'nettsbeschluss *m*; ~ **per·form·ance** *s. thea.* Aufführung *f* auf königlichen Befehl *od.* Wunsch; ~ **post** *s.* ✕ Befehls-, Gefechtsstand *m*.

com·mem·o·rate [kəˈmeməreɪt] *v/t.* (ehrend) gedenken (*gen.*); erinnern an (*acc.*): *a monument to* ~ *a victory* ein Denkmal zur Erinnerung an e-n Sieg; **com·mem·o·ra·tion** [kəˌmeməˈreɪʃn] *s.* **1.** Gedenk-, Gedächtnisfeier *f*: *in* ~ *of* zum Gedächtnis an (*acc.*); **2.** *Brit. univ.* Stiftergedenkfest *n* (*Oxford*); **com'mem·o·ra·tive** [-rətɪv] *adj.* Gedächtnis..., Erinnerungs...: ~ *issue* Gedenkausgabe *f* (*Briefmarken etc.*); ~ *plaque* Gedenktafel *f*.

com·mence [kəˈmens] *v/t. u. v/i.* **1.** beginnen, anfangen; ☆ *Klage* anhängig machen; **2.** *Brit. univ.* promovieren (*M.A.* zum M.A.); **com'mence·ment** [-mənt] *s.* **1.** Anfang *m*, Beginn *m*; **2.** *Am.* (Tag *m* der) Feier *f* der Verleihung aka'demischer Grade; **com'menc·ing** [-sɪŋ] *adj.* Anfangs...: ~ *salary*.

com·mend [kəˈmend] *v/t.* **1.** empfehlen, loben: ~ *me to* ... F da lobe ich mir ...; **2.** empfehlen, anvertrauen (*to dat.*); **3.** ~ *o.s.* sich (*als geeignet*) empfehlen; **com'mend·a·ble** [-dəbl] *adj.* □ empfehlens-, lobenswert; **com·men·da·tion** [ˌkɒmenˈdeɪʃn] *s.* **1.** Empfehlung *f*; **2.** Lob *n*; **com'mend·a·to·ry** [-dətərɪ] *adj.* **1.** empfehlend, Empfehlungs...; **2.** lobend.

com·men·sal [kəˈmensəl] *s.* **1.** Tischgenosse *m*; **2.** *biol.* Kommen'sale *m*.

com·men·su·ra·ble [kəˈmenʃərəbl] *adj.* □ **1.** kommensu'rabel, vergleichbar (*with, to*); **2.** angemessen, im richtigen Verhältnis; **com'men·su·rate** [-rət] *adj.* □ **1.** gleich groß, von gleicher Dauer (*with* wie); **2.** (*with, to*) im Einklang stehend (mit), angemessen *od.* entsprechend (*dat.*).

com·ment [ˈkɒment] **I** *s.* **1.** Be-, Anmerkung *f*, Stellungnahme *f*, Kommen-'tar *m* (*on* zu): *no* ~*!* kein Kommentar!;

2. Erläuterung *f*, Kommen'tar *m*, Deutung *f*; Kri'tik *f*; **3.** Gerede *n*; **II** *v/i.* **4.** (*on*) kommentieren (*acc.*), Erläuterungen *od.* Anmerkungen machen (zu); **5.** sich (kritisch) äußern (*on* über *acc.*); **'com·men·tar·y** [-təri] *s.* Kommen'tar *m* (*on* zu): *radio* ~ Rundfunkkommentar; **'com·men·tate** [-teɪt] *v/i.* → *comment* 4; **'com·men·ta·tor** [-teɪtə] *s. allg., a. TV etc.*: Kommen'tator *m*.

com·merce [ˈkɒmɜːs] *s.* **1.** Handel *m*, Handelsverkehr *m*; **2.** Verkehr *m*, 'Umgang *m*.

com·mer·cial [kəˈmɜːʃl] **I** *adj.* □ **1.** kommerzi'ell (*a. Theaterstück etc.*), kaufmännisch, geschäftlich, gewerblich, Handels..., Geschäfts...; ~ *enterprise* gewerbliches Unternehmen; ~ *practice* kaufmännische Praxis; ~ *station* kommerzieller Sender; **2.** Handel treibend; **3.** für den Handel bestimmt, Handels...; **4.** a) in großen Mengen erzeugt, b) mittlerer *od.* niederer Quali'tät, c) nicht (ganz) rein (*Chemikalien*); **5.** handelsüblich: ~ *quality*; **6.** *Radio, TV*: Werbe...: ~ *television* a) Werbefernsehen *n*, b) kommerzielles Fernsehen; **II** *s.* **7.** *Radio, TV*: a) von e-m Sponsor finanzierte Sendung, b) Werbespot *m*; ~ **al·co·hol** *s.* handelsüblicher Alkohol, Sprit *m*; ~ **art** *s.* Werbegrafik *f*; ~ **a·vi·a·tion** *s.* Verkehrsluftfahrt *f*; ~ **code** *s.* Handelsgesetzbuch *n*; ~ **col·lege** *s.* Wirtschafts-(ober)schule *f*; ~ **cor·re·spond·ence** *s.* 'Handelskorrespon‚denz *f*; ~ **court** *s.* ☆ Handelsgericht *n*; ~ **ge·og·ra·phy** *s.* 'Wirtschaftsgeogra‚phie *f*.

com·mer·cial·ism [kəˈmɜːʃəlɪzəm] *s.* **1.** Handels-, Geschäftsgeist *m*; **2.** Handelsgepflogenheit *f*; **3.** kommerzi'elle Ausrichtung; **com·mer·cial·i·za·tion** [kəˌmɜːʃəlaɪˈzeɪʃn] *s.* Kommerzialisierung *f*, Vermarktung *f*, kaufmännische Verwertung *od.* Ausnutzung; **com·mer·cial·ize** [kəˈmɜːʃəlaɪz] *v/t.* kommerzialisieren, vermarkten, verwerten, ein Geschäft machen aus; in den Handel bringen.

com·mer·cial| **let·ter of cred·it** *s.* Akkredi'tiv *n*; ~ **loan** *s.* 'Warenkre‚dit *m*; ~ **man** *s.* [*irr.*] Geschäftsmann *m*; ~ **man·ag·er** *s.* Geschäftsführer(in); ~ **pa·per** *s.* 'Inhaberpa‚pier *n* (*bsd. Wechsel*); ~ **plane** *s.* Verkehrsflugzeug *n*; ~ **room** *s. Brit.* Hotelzimmer, *in dem Handlungsreisende Kunden empfangen können*; ~ **school** *s.* Handelsschule *f*; ~ **trav·el·(l)er** *s.* Handlungsreisende(r) *m*; ~ **trea·ty** *s.* Handelsvertrag *m*; ~ **val·ue** *s.* Handels-, Marktwert *m*; ~ **ve·hi·cle** *s.* Nutzfahrzeug *n*.

com·mie [ˈkɒmɪ] *s.* F Kommu'nist(in).

com·mi·na·tion [ˌkɒmɪˈneɪʃn] *s.* Drohung *f*; *bsd. eccl.* Androhung *f* göttlicher Strafe; *a.* ~ *service* Bußgottesdienst *m*.

com·mi·nute [ˈkɒmɪnjuːt] *v/t.* zerkleinern, zerstückeln; zerreiben: ~*d fracture* ✄ Splitterbruch *m*; **com·mi·nu·tion** [ˌkɒmɪˈnjuːʃn] *s.* **1.** Zerkleinerung *f*; Zerreibung *f*; **2.** ✄ Splitterung *f*; **3.** Abnutzung *f*.

com·mis·er·ate [kəˈmɪzəreɪt] **I** *v/t.* j-n bemitleiden, bedauern; **II** *v/i.* Mitleid haben (*with* mit); **com·mis·er·a·tion** [kəˌmɪzəˈreɪʃn] *s.* Mitleid *n*, Erbarmen *n*.

com·mis·sar [ˌkɒmɪˈsɑː] *s.* Kommis'sar *m* (*bsd. Russland*): *People's* ♘ Volkskommissar; **com·mis·sar·i·at** [-ˈseə-rɪət] *s.* ✕ a) Intendan'tur *f*, b) Ver'pflegungsorganisati‚on *f*; **com·mis·sar·y** [ˈkɒmɪsərɪ] *s.* **1.** Kommis'sar *m*, Beauf-

tragte(r) *m*; **2.** *eccl.* bischöflicher Kommis'sar; **3.** 'Volkskommis‚sar *m*; **4.** *Am.* a) ✕ Verpflegungsstelle *f*, b) Restau-'rant *n im Filmstudio etc.*

com·mis·sion [kəˈmɪʃn] **I** *s.* **1.** Auftrag *m*, Vollmacht *f*; **2.** Bestallung *f*; Bestallungsurkunde *f*; **3.** ✕ Offi'zierspa‚tent *n*: *hold a* ~ Offizier sein; *receive one's* ~ Offizier werden; **4.** (An)Weisung *f*, Aufgabe *f*; **5.** Auftrag *m*, Bestellung *f*; **6.** Amt *n*, Dienst *m*, Tätigkeit *f*, Betrieb *m*: *put into* ~ *Schiff* in Dienst stellen (F *a. Maschine etc.*); *in* ~ im Dienst, in Betrieb; *out of* ~ a) außer Dienst (*bsd. Schiff*), b) außer Betrieb, nicht funktionierend, kaputt; **7.** ♣ a) Kommissi'on *f*: *have on* ~ in Kommission *od.* Konsignation haben, b) Provisi'on *f*, Vergütung *f*: ~ *agent* Kommissionär *m*, Provisionsvertreter *m*; *goods on* ~ Kommissionswaren; *on a* ~ *basis* in Kommission, auf Provisionsgrundlage; *sell on* ~ gegen Provision verkaufen; **8.** Ausführung *f*, Verübung *f*; → *sin* 1; **9.** Kommissi'on *f*, Ausschuss *m*; Vorstand *m* (*Klub*): *Royal* ♘ *Brit.* Untersuchungsausschuss; **II** *v/t.* **10.** beauftragen, be'vollmächtigen; **11.** j-m e-e Bestellung *od.* e-n Auftrag geben; **12.** in Auftrag geben, bestellen: ~ *a statue*; ~*ed work* Auftragsarbeit *f*; **13.** ✕ zum Offi'zier ernennen: ~*ed officer* (durch Patent bestallter) Offizier; **14.** *Schiff* in Dienst stellen.

com·mis·sion·aire [kəˌmɪʃəˈneə] *s.* **1.** *Brit.* (livrierter) Porti'er; **2.** † *Am.* Vertreter *m*, Einkäufer *m*.

com·mis·sion·er [kəˈmɪʃnə] *s.* **1.** Be-'vollmächtigte(r) *m*, Beauftragte(r) *m*: ♘ *for data protection* Datenschutzbeauftragte *m*; **2.** (Re'gierungs)Kommis‚sar *m*: *High* ♘ Hochkommissar; **3.** Leiter *m* des Amtes: ~ *of police* Polizeichef *m*; ♘ *for Oaths* (*etwa*) Notar *m*; **4.** ☆ beauftragter Richter; **5.** a) Mitglied *n* e-r (Re'gierungs)Kommissi‚on, Kommis'sar *m*, b) *pl.* Kommissi'on *f*, Behörde *f*.

com·mis·sure [ˈkɒmɪˌsjʊə] *s.* **1.** Naht *f*; Band *n* (*bsd. anat.*); **2.** *anat.* Nervenstrang *m*.

com·mit [kəˈmɪt] *v/t.* **1.** anvertrauen, über'geben, über'tragen: ~ *to the ground* beerdigen; ~ *to memory* auswendig lernen; ~ *to paper* zu Papier bringen; ☆ ~ *s.o. to prison* (*to an institution*) j-n in e-e Strafanstalt (Heil- u. Pflegeanstalt) einweisen; ~ *for trial* dem zuständigen Gericht zur Hauptverhandlung überstellen; **2.** anvertrauen, empfehlen; **3.** *pol.* an e-n Ausschuss über'weisen; **4.** (*to*) *pol. etc.* verpflichten (zu), binden (an *acc.*); festlegen (auf *acc.*) (*alle a.* ~ *o.s.* sich): *be* ~*ted* sich festgelegt haben, gebunden sein; ~*ted writer* engagierter Schriftsteller; **5.** *Verbrechen etc.* begehen, verüben; **6.** (*o.s.* sich) kompromittieren; **com'mit·ment** [-mənt] *s.* **1.** (*to*) Verpflichtung *f* (zu), Bindung *f* (an *acc.*): *without* ~ unverbindlich; **2.** † Verbindlichkeit *f*; *Am. engS.* Börsengeschäft *n*; **3.** → *committal* 2; **4.** *fig.* Engage'ment *n*; **com'mit·tal** [-tl] *s.* **1.** → *commitment* 1; **2.** 'Übergabe *f*, Über'weisung *f* (*to* an *acc.*): ~ *to prison* (*an institution*) Einlieferung *f* in e-e Strafanstalt (Einweisung *f* in e-e Heil- und Pflegeanstalt); ~ *order* Haftbefehl *m*, Einweisungsbeschluss *m*; ~ *service* Bestattung(sfeier) *f*; **3.** Verübung *f*, Begehung *f* (*von Verbrechen etc.*).

com·mit·tee [kəˈmɪtɪ] *s.* Komi'tee *n*,

C

Ausschuss *m*, Kommissi'on *f*: *be* (*od.* *sit*) *on a* ~ in e-m Ausschuss sein; *the House goes into* (*od.* *resolves itself into a*) ♀ *parl.* das Haus konstituiert sich als Ausschuss; ~ *stage parl.* Stadium *n* der Ausschussberatung (*zwischen 2. u. 3. Lesung e-s Gesetzentwurfes*); ~*man*, ~*woman* Komiteemitglied *n.*

com·mo·di·ous [kəˈməʊdjəs] *adj.* □ geräumig.

com·mod·i·ty [kəˈmɒdətɪ] *s.* ✝ Ware *f*, ('Handels-, *bsd.* Ge'brauchs)Ar,tikel *m*; *oft pl.* Waren *pl.*: ~ *value* Waren-, Sachwert *m*; ~ *dol·lar s. Am.* Warendollar *m*; ~ *ex·change s.* Warenbörse *f*; ~ *mar·ket s.* **1.** Warenmarkt *m*; **2.** Rohstoffmarkt *m*; ~ *pa·per s.* Doku'mententratte *f.*

com·mo·dore [ˈkɒmədɔː] *s.* ♣ **1.** *allg.* Kommo'dore *m*; **2.** Präsi'dent *m* e-s Jachtklubs; **3.** Leitschiff *n* (*Geleitzug*).

com·mon [ˈkɒmən] **I** *adj.* □ → *commonly*; **1.** gemeinsam (*a.* ♣), gemeinschaftlich: *make* ~ *cause* gemeinsame Sache machen; ~ *ground* gleiche Grundlage, Gemeinsamkeit *f* (der Interessen *etc.*); *that's* ~ *ground* darüber besteht Einigkeit; ~ *pricing* Preisabsprache *f*; **2.** allgemein, öffentlich: ~ *knowledge* allgemein bekannt; ~ *rights* Menschenrechte; ~ *talk* Stadtgespräch *n*; ~ *usage* allgemein üblich; **3.** gewöhnlich, üblich, häufig, alltäglich: ~ *coin of the realm* übliche Landesmünze; ~ *event* normales Ereignis; ~ *sight* alltäglicher Anblick; *a very* ~ *name* ein sehr häufiger Name; ~ *as dirt* häufig, gewöhnlich; **4.** einfach, gewöhnlich: ~ *looking* von gewöhnlichem Aussehen; *the* ~ *people* das (einfache) Volk; ~ *salt* Kochsalz *n*; ~ *soldier* einfacher Soldat; ~ *or garden* ... F Feld-Wald-u.-Wiesen-...; → *cold* 8; **5.** gewöhnlich, gemein: ~ *accent* ordinäre Aussprache; ~ *herd* die große Masse; ~ *manners* schlechtes Benehmen; **6.** *ling.* ~ *gender* doppeltes Geschlecht; ~ *noun* Gattungsname *m*; **II** *s.* **7.** Gemeindeland *n* (*heute oft mit Parkanlage*): (*right of*) ~ Mitbenutzungsrecht *n*; ~ *of pasturage* Weiderecht *n*; **8.** *fig. in* ~ gemeinsam; *in* ~ *with* (genau) wie; *have s.th. in* ~ *with* et. gemein haben mit; *out of the* ~ außergewöhnlich, besonders; **9.** → *commons*.

com·mon·al·ty [ˈkɒmənltɪ] *s. das* gemeine Volk, Allgemeinheit *f.*

com·mon‖ car·ri·er → *carrier* 2; ~ **chord** *s.* ♩ Dreiklang *m*; ~ **de·nom·i·na·tor** *s.* ♣ gemeinsamer Nenner (*a. fig.*).

com·mon·er [ˈkɒmənə] *s.* **1.** Bürger(licher) *m*; **2.** *Brit.* Stu'dent (*Oxford*), der s-n 'Unterhalt selbst bezahlt; **3.** *Brit.* a) Mitglied *n* des 'Unterhauses, b) Mitglied *n* des Londoner Stadtrats.

com·mon‖ frac·tion *s.* ♣ gemeiner Bruch; ~ **law** *s.* a) *das gesamte anglo-amerikanische Rechtssystem* (*Ggs. civil law*), b) *obs. das engl. Gewohnheitsrecht*; ~*·'law adj.* gewohnheitsrechtlich: ~ *marriage* Konsensehe *f*, eheähnliches Zs.-leben; ~ *wife* Lebensgefährtin *f.*

com·mon·ly [ˈkɒmənlɪ] *adv.* gewöhnlich, im Allgemeinen.

Com·mon Mar·ket *s.* ✝ Gemeinsamer Markt.

com·mon·ness [ˈkɒmənnɪs] *s.* **1.** All'täglichkeit *f*, Häufigkeit *f*; **2.** Gewöhnlichkeit *f*, ordi'näre Art.

'com·mon‖·place I *s.* **1.** Gemeinplatz *m*, Platti'tüde *f*; **2.** *et.* All'tägliches; **II** *adj.* all'täglich, 'uninteres,sant, abgedroschen, platt; ♀ **Prayer** *s. eccl.* **1.** die angli'kanische Litur'gie; **2.** (*Book of*) ~ Gebetbuch *n* der angli'kanischen Kirche; ~ **room** [rʊm] *s.* **1.** *univ.* Gemeinschaftsraum *m*: a) *junior* ~ für Studenten, b) *senior* ~ für Dozenten; **2.** *Schule*: Lehrerzimmer *n.*

com·mons [ˈkɒmənz] *s. pl.* **1.** *das* gemeine Volk, *die* Bürgerlichen: *the* ♀ *parl. Brit.* das Unterhaus; **2.** *bsd. Brit. univ.* Gemeinschaftskost *f*, -essen *n*: *kept on short* ~ auf schmale Kost gesetzt.

com·mon‖ school *s.* staatliche Volksschule; ~ **sense** *s.* gesunder Menschenverstand; ~*·'sen·si·cal* [-ˈsensɪkl] *adj.* vernünftig; ~ **ser·geant** *s.* Richter *m* u. Rechtsberater *m* des Magi'strats der *City of London*; ~ **stock** *s.* ✝ *Am.* 'Stamm,aktie(n *pl.*) *f*; ~*·'weal s.* **1.** Gemeinwohl *n*; **2.** → *'·'wealth s.* **1.** Gemeinwesen *n*, Staat *m*; **2.** Repu'blik *f*: *the* ♀ *Brit. hist.* die engl. Republik unter Cromwell; **3.** *British* ♀ (*of Nations*) *das* Commonwealth, *die* Britische Nationengemeinschaft; ♀ *of Australia* der Australische Staatenbund; **4.** *Am. Bezeichnung für einige Staaten der USA.*

com·mo·tion [kəˈməʊʃn] *s.* **1.** Erschütterung *f*, Aufregung *f*; Aufsehen *n*; **2.** Aufruhr *m*, Tu'mult *m*; → *civil* 2; **3.** Wirrwarr *m.*

com·mu·nal [ˈkɒmjʊnl] *adj.* **1.** Gemeinde-..., Kommunal-...: ~ *tax*; **2.** Gemeinschafts-...; Volks-...: ~ *aerial* (*bsd. Am. antenna*) *TV* Gemeinschaftsantenne *f*; ~ *kitchen* Volksküche *f*; **3.** *Indien*: Volksgruppen betreffend; **'com·mu·nal·ism** [-nəlɪzəm] *s.* Kommuna'lismus *m* (*Regierungssystem nach Gemeindegruppen*); **'com·mu·nal·ize** [-nəlaɪz] *v/t.* in Gemeindebesitz über'führen, kommunalisieren.

com·mu·nard [ˈkɒmjʊnəd] *s. sociol.* Kommu'narde *m.*

com·mune¹ [kəˈmjuːn] *v/i.* **1.** sich vertraulich besprechen: ~ *with o.s.* mit sich zurate gehen; **2.** *eccl.* kommunizieren, die (heilige) Kommuni'on *od.* das Abendmahl empfangen.

com·mune² [ˈkɒmjuːn] *s.* Kom'mune *f* (*a. sociol.*).

com·mu·ni·ca·ble [kəˈmjuːnɪkəbl] *adj.* □ **1.** mitteilbar; **2.** ✝ über'tragbar, ansteckend; **com'mu·ni·cant** [-ənt] **I** *s.* **1.** *eccl.* Kommuni'kant(in); **2.** Gewährsmann *m*, Informant(in); **II** *adj.* **3.** mitteilend; **4.** teilhabend; **com'mu·ni·cate** [-keɪt] **I** *v/t.* **1.** mitteilen (*to dat.*); **2.** (*a.* ✝) über'tragen (*to auf acc.*); **II** *v/i.* **3.** sich besprechen, Gedanken *etc.* austauschen, in Verbindung stehen, kommunizieren (*with* mit), sich mitteilen (*with dat.*); **4.** sich in Verbindung setzen (*with* mit); **5.** in Verbindung stehen, zs.-hängen (*with* mit): *these two rooms* ~ diese beiden Räume haben e-e Verbindungstür; **6.** sich mitteilen (*Erregung etc.*) (*to dat.*); **7.** *eccl.* → *commune¹* 2.

com·mu·ni·ca·tion [kə,mjuːnɪˈkeɪʃn] *s.* **1.** (*to*) *allg.* Mitteilung *f* (*an acc.*): a) Verständigung *f* (*gen. od.* von), b) Über'mittlung *f* e-r Nachricht (*an acc.*), c) Nachricht *f* (*an acc.*), d) Kommuni'kati'on *f* (*e-r Idee etc.*); **2.** Kommunikati'on *f*, Gedankenaustausch *m*, Verständigung *f*; (*Brief-, Nachrichten)Verkehr *m*; Verbindung *f*: *be in* ~ *with s.o.* mit j-m in Verbindung stehen; **3.** (*a.*

---

phys.) Über'tragung *f*, Fortpflanzung *f* (*to auf acc.*); **4.** Kommunikati'on *f*, Verkehrsweg *m*, Verbindung *f*, 'Durchgang *m*; **5.** *pl.* a) Fernmelde-, Nachrichtenwesen *n* (*a.* ✗): ~ *net* Fernmeldenetz *n*; ~ *officer* Fernmeldeoffizier *m*, b) Verbindungswege *pl.*, Nachschublinien *pl.*; **6.** *pl.* Kommunikati'onswissenschaft *f*; ~ **cen·tre** (*Am.* **cen·ter**) *s.* ✗ 'Fernmeldezen,trale *f*; ~ **cord** *s.* 🚂 Notleine *f*, -bremse *f*; ~ **en·gi·neer·ing** *s.* 'Nachrichten,technik *f*; ~*s* **gap** *s.* Kommunikati'onslücke *f*; ~*s* **sat·el·lite** *s.* Kommunikati'onssatel,lit *m*; ~*s* **sys·tem** *s.* Kommunikati'onssys,tem *n*; ~ **trench** *s.* ✗ Verbindungs-, Laufgraben *m.*

com·mu·ni·ca·tive [kəˈmjuːnɪkətɪv] *adj.* □ mitteilsam, kommunika'tiv; **com'mu·ni·ca·tor** [-keɪtə] *s.* **1.** Mitteilende(r *m*) *f*; **2.** *tel.* (Zeichen)Geber *m.*

com·mun·ion [kəˈmjuːnjən] *s.* **1.** Gemeinschaft *f*; **2.** enge Verbindung; 'Umgang *m*: *hold* ~ *with o.s.* Einkehr bei sich selbst halten; **3.** Religi'onsgemeinschaft *f*; **4.** *eccl.* ♀, *a. Holy* ♀ (heilige) Kommuni'on, (heiliges) Abendmahl: ♀ *cup* Abendmahlskelch *m*; ♀ *table* Abendmahlstisch *m.*

com·mu·ni·qué [kəˈmjuːnɪkeɪ] (*Fr.*) *s.* Kommuni'qué *n.*

com·mu·nism [ˈkɒmjʊnɪzəm] *s.* Kommu'nismus *m*; **'com·mu·nist** [-nɪst] **I** *s.* Kommu'nist(in); **II** *adj.* → **com·mu·nis·tic** [,kɒmjʊˈnɪstɪk] *adj.* kommu'nistisch.

com·mu·ni·ty [kəˈmjuːnətɪ] *s.* **1.** Gemeinschaft *f*: ~ *aerial* (*bsd. Am. antenna*) Gemeinschaftsantenne *f*; ~ *spirit* Gemeinschaftsgeist *m*; ~ *singing* Gemeinschaftssingen *n*; **2.** Gemeinde *f*, Körperschaft *f*: *the mercantile* ~ die Kaufmannschaft; ~ *centre* (*Am. center*) Gemeindezentrum *n*; ~ *chest*, ~ *fund Am.* Wohlfahrtsfonds *m*; ~ *home Brit.* Erziehungsheim *n*; **3.** Gemeinwesen *n*: *the* ~ a) die Allgemeinheit, das Volk, b) der Staat; ~ *ownership* öffentliches Eigentum; **4.** Gemeinschaft *f*, Gemeinsamkeit *f*; Gleichheit *f*: ~ *of goods od. property* (eheliche) Gütergemeinschaft; ~ *of interest* Interessengemeinschaft; ~ *of goods acquired during marriage* Errungenschaftsgemeinschaft; ~ *of heirs* ⚖ Erbengemeinschaft.

com·mu·nize [ˈkɒmjʊnaɪz] *v/t.* **1.** in Gemeineigentum 'überführen, sozialisieren; **2.** kommu'nistisch machen.

com·mut·a·ble [kəˈmjuːtəbl] *adj.* **1.** austauschbar, 'umwandelbar; **2.** *durch Geld* ablösbar; **com·mu·tate** [ˈkɒmjʊteɪt] *v/t.* ⚡ *Strom* a) wenden, b) gleichrichten; **com·mu·ta·tion** [,kɒmjuːˈteɪʃn] *s.* **1.** 'Um-, Austausch *m*, 'Umwandlung *f*; **2.** Ablösung *f*, Abfindung *f*; **3.** ⚖ 'Straf,umwandlung *f*, -milderung *f*; **4.** ⚡ 'Umschaltung *f*, Stromwendung *f*; **5.** 🚂 *etc.* Pendelverkehr *m*: ~ *ticket* Zeitkarte *f*; **com·mu·ta·tive** [-ətɪv] *adj.* □ **1.** auswechselbar, Ersatz-..., Tausch-...; **2.** wechselseitig; **com·mu·ta·tor** [ˈkɒmjʊteɪtə] *s.* ⚡ a) Kommu'tator *m*, Pol-, Stromwender *m*, b) Kol'lektor *m*, c) *mot.* Zündverteiler *m*; Gleichrichter *m*; **com·mute** [kəˈmjuːt] **I** *v/t.* **1.** ein-, 'umtauschen, auswechseln; **2.** *Zahlung* 'umwandeln (*into* in *acc.*), ablösen (*for, into* durch); **3.** ⚖ *Strafe* umwandeln (*to, into* in *acc.*); **4.** → *commutate*; **II** *v/i.* **5.** 🚂 *etc.* pendeln; **com'mut·er** [-tə] *s.* **1.** 🚂 *etc.* Zeitkarteninhaber(in), Pendler *m*: ~ *belt* Einzugsbereich *m* (*e-r Stadt*);

~ ***traffic*** Pendlerverkehr *m*; ~ ***train*** Nahverkehrszug *m*; **2.** → ***commutator***.

com·pact¹ ['kɒmpækt] *s.* Pakt *m*, Vertrag *m*.

com·pact² [kəm'pækt] **I** *adj.* □ **1.** kom'pakt, fest, dicht (zs.-)gedrängt; mas'siv: ~ ***car*** → 6; ~ ***camera*** Kom'pakt‚kamera *f*; ~ ***cassette*** Kompaktkassette *f*; ~ ***disk*** CD *f*; **2.** gedrungen; **3.** knapp, gedrängt (*Stil*); **II** *v/t.* **4.** zs.-drängen, -pressen, fest verbinden; zs.-fügen: ~***ed of*** zs.-gesetzt aus; **III** *s.* ['kɒmpækt] **5.** Kom'paktpuder(dose *f*) *m*; **6.** *Am.* Kom'paktwagen *m*; **com'pact·ness** [-nɪs] *s.* **1.** Kom'paktheit *f*, Festigkeit *f*; **2.** *fig.* Knappheit *f*, Gedrängtheit *f* (*Stil*).

com·pan·ion¹ [kəm'pænjən] **I** *s.* **1.** Begleiter(in), Gesellschafter(in); *engS.* Gesellschafterin *f e-r Dame*; **2.** Kame'rad(in), Genosse *m*, Genossin *f*, Gefährte *m*, Gefährtin *f*: ~***-in-arms*** Waffenbruder *m*; ~ ***in misfortune*** Leidensgefährte; ***constant*** ~ ‚ständiger Begleiter' (*e-r Dame*); **3.** Gegen-, Seitenstück *n*, Pen'dant *n*: ~ ***volume*** Begleitband *m*; **4.** Handbuch *n*; **5.** Ritter *m*: ♀ ***of the Bath*** Ritter des Bath-Ordens; **II** *v/t.* **6.** begleiten; **III** *v/i.* **7.** verkehren (***with*** mit); **IV** *adj.* **8.** (dazu) passend, da'zugehörig.

com·pan·ion² [kəm'pænjən] *s.* ⚓ **1.** → ***companion hatch***; **2.** Ka'jütstreppe *f*; **3.** Deckfenster *n*.

com·pan·ion·a·ble [kəm'pænjənəbl] *adj.* □ 'umgänglich, gesellig; **com'pan·ion·a·ble·ness** [-nɪs] *s.* 'Umgänglichkeit *f*; **com'pan·ion·ate** [-nɪt] *adj.* kame'radschaftlich: ~ ***marriage*** Kameradschaftsehe *f*.

com·pan·ion| hatch *s.* ⚓ Ka'jütsklappe *f*, -luke *f*; ~ **lad·der** → ***companion²*** 2.

com·pan·ion·ship [kəm'pænjənʃɪp] *s.* **1.** Kame'radschaft *f*; Gesellschaft *f*; **2.** *typ. Brit.* Ko'lonne *f* von Setzern.

com'pan·ion·way → ***companion²*** 2.

com·pa·ny ['kʌmpənɪ] *s.* **1.** Gesellschaft *f*, Begleitung *f*: ***for*** ~ zur Gesellschaft; ***in*** ~ ***with*** in Gesellschaft von, zusammen mit; ***he is good*** ~ man ist gern mit ihm zusammen; ***I am*** (*od.* ***err***) ***in good*** ~ ich bin in guter Gesellschaft (*wenn ich das tue*); ***keep*** (*od.* ***bear***) ***s.o.*** ~ j-m Gesellschaft leisten; ***part*** ~ a) sich trennen (***with*** von), b) uneinig werden; **2.** Gesellschaft *f*, Besuch *m*, Gäste *pl.*: ***have*** ~ Besuch haben; ***be fond of*** ~ die Geselligkeit lieben; ***see much*** ~ a) viel Besuch haben, b) oft in Gesellschaft gehen; **3.** Gesellschaft *f*, 'Umgang *m*: ***avoid bad*** ~ schlechte Gesellschaft meiden; ***keep*** ~ ***with*** verkehren mit; **4.** ✝ (Handels)Gesellschaft *f*, Firma *f*: ~ ***assets*** Betriebsvermögen *n*; ~ ***car*** Firmenwagen *m*; ~ ***failure*** Insolvenz *f*; ~ ***law*** Gesellschaftsrecht *n*; ~ ***pension plan*** betriebliche Altersversorgung; ~ ***store*** *Am.* betriebseigenes (Laden)Geschäft; ~ ***union*** *Am.* Betriebsgewerkschaft *f*; ~***'s water*** Leitungswasser *n*; → ***private*** 2, ***public*** 3; **5.** Innung *f*, Zunft *f*, Gilde *f*; **6.** *thea.* Truppe *f*; **7.** ⚔ Kompa'nie *f*; **8.** ⚓ Mannschaft *f*.

com·pa·ra·ble ['kɒmpərəbl] *adj.* □ (***to***, ***with***) vergleichbar (mit): ~ ***period*** Vergleichszeitraum *m*; **com·par·a·tive** [kəm'pærətɪv] **I** *adj.* □ **1.** vergleichend: ~ ***literature*** vergleichende Literaturwissenschaft; **2.** Vergleichs...; **3.** verhältnismäßig, rela'tiv; **4.** beträchtlich, ziemlich: ***with*** ~ ***speed***; **5.** *ling.* komparativ, Komparativ...; **II** *s.* **6.** *a.* ~ ***degree*** Komparativ *m*; **com·par·a·tive·ly** [kəm'pærətɪvlɪ] *adv.* verhältnismäßig, ziemlich.

com·pare [kəm'peə] **I** *v/t.* **1.** vergleichen (***with*** mit): ***as*** ~***d with*** im Vergleich zu; → ***note*** 2; **2.** vergleichen, gleichstellen, -setzen: ***not to be*** ~***d to*** (*od.* ***with***) nicht zu vergleichen mit; **3.** *ling.* steigern; **II** *v/i.* **4.** sich vergleichen (lassen), e-n Vergleich aushalten (***with*** mit): ~ ***favo(u)rably with*** den Vergleich mit ... nicht zu scheuen brauchen; besser sein als; **III** *s.* **5.** ***beyond*** ~ unvergleichlich; **com'par·i·son** [-'pærɪsn] *s.* **1.** Vergleich *m*: ***by*** ~ vergleichsweise; ***in*** ~ ***with*** im Vergleich mit *od.* zu; ***bear*** ~ ***with*** e-n Vergleich aushalten mit; ***beyond*** (***all***) ~ unvergleichlich; **2.** Ähnlichkeit *f*; **3.** *ling.* Steigerung *f*; **4.** Gleichnis *n*.

com·part·ment [kəm'pɑːtmənt] *s.* **1.** Ab'teilung *f*; Fach *n*, Feld *n*; **2.** 🚃 (Wagen)Abteil *n*; **3.** ⚓ Schott *n*: → ***watertight***; **4.** *parl. Brit.* Punkt *m* der Tagesordnung; **com·part·men·tal·ize** [ˌkɒmpɑːt'mentəlaɪz] *v/t. bsd. fig.* (auf)teilen.

com·pass ['kʌmpəs] **I** *s.* **1.** *phys.* Kompass *m*: ***mariner's*** ~ ⚓ Schiffskompass; ***points of the*** ~ *die* Himmelsrichtungen; **2.** *pl. oft* ***pair of*** ~***es*** Zirkel *m*; **3.** 'Umkreis *m*, 'Umfang *m*, Ausdehnung *f* (*a. fig.*): ***within the*** ~ ***of*** innerhalb; ***it is beyond my*** ~ es geht über m-n Horizont; **4.** Bereich *m*, Gebiet *n*; **5.** ♪ 'Umfang *m* (*Stimme etc.*); **6.** Grenzen *pl.*, Schranken *pl.*: ***to keep within*** ~ in Schranken halten; **II** *v/t.* **7.** erreichen, zu'stande bringen; **8.** planen; *b.s.* anzetteln; **9.** → ***encompass***; ~ **bear·ing** *s.* ⚓ Kompasspeilung *f*; ~ **box** *s.* ⚓ Kompassgehäuse *n*; ~ **card** *s.* ⚓ Kompassscheibe *f*, Windrose *f*.

com·pas·sion [kəm'pæʃn] *s.* Mitleid *n*, Erbarmen *n* (***for*** mit): ***to have*** (*od.* ***take***) ~ (***on***) Mitleid haben (mit), sich erbarmen (*gen.*); **com'pas·sion·ate** [-ʃənət] *adj.* □ mitleidsvoll: ~ ***allowance*** (gesetzlich nicht verankerte Beihilfe als) Härteausgleich *m*; ~ ***leave*** ⚔ Sonderurlaub *m* aus familiären Gründen.

com·pass| nee·dle *s.* Kompassnadel *f*; ~ **plane** *s.* ⚙ Rundhobel *m*; ~ **rose** *s.* ⚓ Windrose *f*; ~ **saw** *s.* Stichsäge *f*; ~ **win·dow** *s.* ⚠ Rundbogenfenster *n*.

com·pat·i·bil·i·ty [kəmˌpætə'bɪlətɪ] *s.* **1.** Vereinbarkeit *f*; **2.** Verträglichkeit *f*; **3.** *Nachrichtentechnik*: Kompatibili'tät *f*; **com·pat·i·ble** [kəm'pætəbl] *adj.* □ **1.** (mitein'ander) vereinbar, im Einklang (***with*** mit); **2.** angemessen (***with*** *dat.*); **3.** ⚕ verträglich; **4.** *Nachrichtentechnik*, *Computer etc.*: kompa'tibel.

com·pa·tri·ot [kəm'pætrɪət] *s.* Landsmann *m*, -männin *f*.

com·peer [kɒm'pɪə] *s.* **1.** Standesgenosse *m*; Gleichgestellte(r *m*) *f*: ***have no*** ~ nicht seinesgleichen haben; **2.** Kame'rad(in).

com·pel [kəm'pel] *v/t.* **1.** zwingen, nötigen; **2.** *et.* erzwingen; *a. Bewunderung etc.* abnötigen (***from s.o.*** j-m); **3.** ~ ***s.o. to s.th.*** j-m et. aufzwingen; **com'pel·ling** [-lɪŋ] *adj.* **1.** zwingend, stark; **2.** 'unwider‚stehlich; verlockend.

com·pen·di·ous [kəm'pendɪəs] *adj.* □ kurz (gefasst), gedrängt; **com'pen·di·um** [-əm] *pl.* **-ums, -a** [-ə] *s.* **1.** Kom'pendium *n*, Handbuch *n*; **2.** Zs.-fassung *f*, Abriss *m*.

com·pen·sate ['kɒmpenseɪt] **I** *v/t.* **1.** *j-n* entschädigen (***for*** für, ***by*** durch), *Am. a.* bezahlen, entlohnen; **2.** *et.* ersetzen, vergüten (***to s.o.*** j-m); **3.** aufwiegen, ausgleichen (*a.* ⚙), *bsd. psych. u.* ⚙ kompensieren; **II** *v/i.* **4.** (***for***) ersetzen (*acc.*); Ersatz leisten (für); wettmachen (*acc.*); **5.** ~ ***for*** → 3; **6.** sich ausgleichen *od.* aufheben; **com·pen·sa·tion** [ˌkɒmpen'seɪʃn] *s.* **1.** Entschädigung *f*, (Schaden)Ersatz *m*; **2.** *Am.* Vergütung *f*, Entgelt *n*; **3.** Belohnung *f*; **4.** *pl.* Vorteile *pl.*; **5.** ⚖ Abfindung *f*; Aufrechnung *f*; **6.** ⚗, ⚡, ⚙, *psych.* Kompensati'on *f*; **com·pen·sa·tive** [kəm'pensətɪv] *adj.* **1.** entschädigend, Entschädigungs...; vergütend; **2.** Ersatz...; **3.** kompensierend, ausgleichend; **'com·pen·sa·tor** [-tə] *s.* ⚙ Kompen'sator *m*, Ausgleichsvorrichtung *f*; **com·pen·sa·to·ry** [kəm'pensətərɪ] → ***compensative***.

com·père ['kɒmpeə] (*Fr.*) *bsd. Brit.* **I** *s.* Conférenci'er *m*, Ansager(in); **II** *v/t. u. v/i.* konferieren, ansagen (bei).

com·pete [kəm'piːt] *v/i.* **1.** in Wettbewerb treten, sich (mit)bewerben (***for*** um); **2.** konkurrieren (*a.* ✝), wetteifern, sich messen (***with*** mit); sich behaupten; **3.** *sport* am Wettkampf teilnehmen; kämpfen (***for*** um).

com·pe·tence ['kɒmpɪtəns], **'com·pe·ten·cy** [-sɪ] *s.* **1.** (***for***) Befähigung *f* (zu), Tauglichkeit *f* (für); **2.** ⚖ a) Kompe'tenz *f*, Zuständigkeit *f*, Befugnis *f*, b) Zurechnungsfähigkeit *f*; **3.** Auskommen *n*; **'com·pe·tent** [-nt] *adj.* □ **1.** (leistungs)fähig, tüchtig; fachkundig, qualifiziert; **2.** ausreichend, angemessen; **3.** ⚖ a) zuständig, befugt, b) zulässig (*Zeuge*), c) zurechnungs-, geschäftsfähig; **4.** statthaft.

com·pe·ti·tion [ˌkɒmpɪ'tɪʃn] *s.* **1.** Wettbewerb *m*, -kampf *m* (***for*** um), *sport a.* Ver'anstaltung *f*, Konkur'renz *f*; **2.** ✝ Konkur'renz *f*: a) Wettbewerb *m*: ***open*** (***unfair***) ~ freier (unlauterer) Wettbewerb; ***destructive*** ~ ruinöser Wettbewerb, b) Konkur'renzkampf *m*, c) Konkur'renzfirmen *pl.*; **3.** Preisausschreiben *n*; **4.** Gegner *pl.*, Ri'valen *pl.*, Konkur'renz *f*; **com·pet·i·tive** [kəm'petətɪv] *adj.* □ **1.** konkurrierend, Konkurrenz..., Wettbewerbs...: ~ ***advantage*** Wettbewerbsvorteil *m*; ~ ***capacity*** ✝ Konkurrenzfähigkeit *f*; ~ ***disadvantage*** Wettbewerbsnachteil *m*; ~ ***edge*** Wettbewerbsvorteil *m*; ~ ***pressure*** Wettbewerbsdruck *m*; ~ ***sport***(***s***) Kampfsport *m*; **2.** konkur'renz-, wettbewerbsfähig (*Preise etc.*); **com·pet·i·tive·ness** [kəm'petətɪvnɪs] *s.* ✝ Konkur'renz-, Wettbewerbsfähigkeit *f*; **com·pet·i·tor** [kəm'petɪtə] *s.* **1.** Mitbewerber(in) (***for*** um); **2.** ✝ Konkur'rent(in); **3.** *sport* Teilnehmer(in), Ri'vale *m*, Ri'valin *f*.

com·pi·la·tion [ˌkɒmpɪ'leɪʃn] *s.* Kompilati'on *f*: a) Zs.-stellung *f*, b) Sammelwerk *n* (*Buch*); **com·pile** [kəm'paɪl] *v/t.* **1.** zs.-stellen, kompilieren; **2.** *Material* zs.-tragen; **com·pil·er** [kəm'paɪlə] *s.* **1.** Bearbeiter(in), Verfasser(in); **2.** *Computer*: Com'piler *m*.

com·pla·cence [kəm'pleɪsns], **com'pla·cen·cy** [-sɪ] *s.* 'Selbstzu‚friedenheit *f*, -gefälligkeit *f*; **com'pla·cent** [-nt] *adj.* □ 'selbstzu‚frieden, -gefällig.

com·plain [kəm'pleɪn] *v/i.* **1.** sich beklagen, sich beschweren (***of***, ***about*** über *acc.*, ***to*** bei, ***that*** dass); **2.** klagen (***of*** über *acc.*); **3.** ✝ reklamieren: ~ ***about*** *a. et.* beanstanden; **4.** ⚖ a) klagen, b) (Straf)Anzeige erstatten (***of*** gegen); **com'plain·ant** [-nənt] *s.* ⚖ Kläger(in); Beschwerdeführer *m*; **com'plaint** [-nt] *s.* **1.** Klage *f*, Beschwerde *f*, Beanstandung *f*: ***make a*** ~ ***about*** Klage führen

C

über (*acc.*); **2.** ⚖ Klage *f*, *a.* Strafanzeige *f*; **3.** ♥ Reklamati'on *f*, Beanstandung *f*; **4.** ⚓ Beschwerde *f*, Leiden *n*. **com·plai·sance** [kəm'pleɪzəns] *s.* Gefälligkeit *f*, Willfährigkeit *f*, Höflichkeit *f*; **com'plai·sant** [-nt] *adj.* □ gefällig, entgegenkommend.

com·ple·ment I *v/t.* ['kɒmplɪment] **1.** ergänzen, ver'vollständigen: ~ *each other* sich (gegenseitig) ergänzen; **II** *s.* [-mənt] **2.** Ergänzung *f*, Ver'vollständigung *f*; **3.** 'Vollständigkeit *f*, -zähligkeit *f*; **4.** *a.* **full** ~ volle Anzahl *od.* Menge; ⚓ volle Besatzung; **5.** *ling.* Ergänzung *f*; **6.** Å Komple'ment *n*; **com·ple·men·tal** [ˌkɒmplɪ'mentl] *adj.* □, **com·ple·men·ta·ry** [ˌkɒmplɪ'mentərɪ] *adj.* Ergänzungs... (*a.* Å, *Farben*); (sich) ergänzend.

com·plete [kəm'pliːt] **I** *adj.* □ **1.** 'vollständig, voll'kommen, völlig, ganz, kom'plett: ~ *with ...* samt (*dat.*), ... eingeschlossen; **2.** 'vollzählig, sämtlich; **3.** beendet, fertig; **4.** völlig: *a* ~ *surprise*; **5.** *obs.* per'fekt; **II** *v/t.* **6.** ver'vollständigen, ergänzen; **7.** beenden, abschließen, fertig stellen, erledigen; **8.** voll'enden, ver'vollkommnen; *Formular* ausfüllen; **com'plete·ly** [-lɪ] *adv.*: ~ *automatic* vollautomatisch; **com'plete·ness** [-nɪs] *s.* 'Vollständigkeit *f*, Voll-'kommenheit *f*; **com'ple·tion** [-iːʃn] *s.* **1.** Voll'endung *f*, Fertigstellung *f*, Abschluss *m*, Ablauf *m*: (*up*)*on* ~ *of* nach Vollendung *od.* Ablauf von *od.* gen.: *bring to* ~ zum Abschluss bringen, fertig stellen; ~ *date* Fertigstellungstermin *m*; **2.** Ver'vollständigung *f*; **3.** (*Vertrags- etc.*)Erfüllung *f*; **4.** Ausfüllung *f* (*e-s Formulars*).

com·plex ['kɒmpleks] **I** *adj.* □ **1.** zs.-gesetzt (*a. ling.*); **2.** kompliziert, verwickelt; **II** *s.* **3.** Kom'plex *m* (*a. psych.*), Gesamtheit *f*, *das Ganze*; **4.** (Ge'bäude- *etc.*)Kom,plex *m*; **5.** ⚙ Kom'plexverbindung *f*; **com·plex·ion** [kəm'plekʃn] *s.* **1.** Gesichtsfarbe *f*, Teint *m*; **2.** *fig.* Aussehen *n*, Anstrich *m*, Cha-'rakter *m*: *that puts a different* ~ *on it* das gibt der Sache ein (ganz) anderes Gesicht; **3.** *fig.* Cou'leur *f*, (po'litische) Richtung; **com·plex·i·ty** [kəm'pleksɪtɪ] *s.* **1.** Komplexi'tät *f* (*a.* Å), Kompliziertheit *f*, Vielschichtigkeit *f*; **2.** *et.* Kom'plexes.

com·pli·ance [kəm'plaɪəns] *s.* **1.** Einwilligung *f*, Erfüllung *f*, Befolgung *f* (*with gen.*): *in* ~ *with* gemäß *dat.*; **2.** Willfährigkeit *f*; **com'pli·ant** [-nt] *adj.* □ willfährig.

com·pli·ca·cy ['kɒmplɪkəsɪ] *s.* Kompliziertheit *f*; **com·pli·cate** ['kɒmplɪkeɪt] *v/t.* komplizieren; **'com·pli·cat·ed** [-keɪtɪd] *adj.* kompliziert; **com·pli·ca·tion** [ˌkɒmplɪ'keɪʃn] *s.* **1.** Komplikati'on *f* (*a.* ⚕); **2.** Kompliziertheit *f*.

com·plic·i·ty [kəm'plɪsətɪ] *s.* Mitschuld *f*, Mittäterschaft *f*: *look of* ~ komplizenhafter Blick.

com·pli·ment I *s.* ['kɒmplɪmənt] **1.** Kompli'ment *n*: *pay s.o. a* ~ j-m ein Kompliment machen; → *fish* 8; **2.** Ehrenbezeigung *f*, Lob *n*: *do s.o. the* ~ j-m die Ehre erweisen (*of a. inf. od. gen.*); **3.** Empfehlung *f*, Gruß *m*: *my best* ~*s* m-e Empfehlung; *with the* ~*s of the season* mit den besten Wünschen zum Fest; **II** *v/t.* [-ment] **4.** (*on*) beglückwünschen (zu); j-m Kompli'mente machen (über *acc.*); **com·pli·men·ta·ry** [ˌkɒmplɪ'mentərɪ] *adj.* **1.** höflich, Höflichkeits...; schmeichelhaft: ~ *close* Gruß-,

Schlussformel *f* (*in Briefen*); **2.** Ehren...: ~ *ticket* Ehren-, Freikarte *f*; ~ *dinner* Festessen *n*; **3.** Frei..., Gratis...: ~ *copy* Freiexemplar *n*; ~ *meals* kostenlose Mahlzeiten.

com·plot ['kɒmplɒt] **I** *s.* Kom'plott *n*, Verschwörung *f*; **II** *v/i.* sich verschwören.

com·ply [kəm'plaɪ] *v/i.* (*with*) e-r Bitte *etc.* nachkommen *od.* entsprechen, erfüllen (*acc.*), *Regel etc.* befolgen, einhalten: *he would not* ~ er wollte nicht einwilligen.

com·po ['kɒmpəʊ] (*abbr. für composition*) *s.* Putz *m*, Gips *m*, Mörtel *m etc.*

com·po·nent [kəm'pəʊnənt] **I** *adj.* e-n Teil bildend, Teil...: ~ *part* → **II** *s.* (Bestand)Teil *m*, ⚙ a. 'Bauele,ment *n*.

com·port [kəm'pɔːt] **I** *v/t.* ~ *o.s.* sich betragen; **II** *v/i.* ~ *with* passen zu.

com·pos ['kɒmpəs] → *compos mentis*.

com·pose [kəm'pəʊz] **I** *v/t.* **1.** *mst pass.* zs.-setzen: *be* ~*d of* bestehen aus; **2.** bilden; **3.** entwerfen, ordnen, zurechtlegen; **4.** aufsetzen, verfassen; **5.** ♪ komponieren; **6.** *typ.* setzen; **7.** *Streit* schlichten; *s-e Gedanken* sammeln; **8.** besänftigen: ~ *o.s.* sich beruhigen, sich fassen; **9.** ~ *o.s.* sich anschicken (*to* zu); **II** *v/i.* **10.** schriftstellern, dichten; **11.** komponieren; **com'posed** [-zd] *adj.*, **com'pos·ed·ly** [-zɪdlɪ] *adv.* ruhig, gelassen; **com'pos·ed·ness** [-zɪdnɪs] *s.* Gelassenheit *f*, Ruhe *f*; **com'pos·er** [-zə] *s.* ♪ Kompo'nist(in); **2.** Verfasser(in).

com·pos·ing [kəm'pəʊzɪŋ] *adj.* **1.** beruhigend, Beruhigungs...; **2.** *typ.* Setz...: ~ *machine*; ~ *room* Setzerei *f*; ~ *stick* Winkelhaken *m*.

com·pos·ite ['kɒmpəzɪt] **I** *adj.* □ **1.** zs.-gesetzt (*a.* Å), gemischt; vielfältig; Misch...: ~ *construction* △ Gemischtbauweise *f*; ~ *metal* Verbundmetall *n*; **2.** ♀ Korbblütler...; **II** *s.* **3.** Zs.-setzung *f*, Mischung *f*; **4.** *Kriminalistik:* Phan'tombild *n*; **5.** ♀ Korbblütler *m*; ~ **pho·to·graph** *s.* 'Fotomon,tage *f*.

com·po·si·tion [ˌkɒmpə'zɪʃn] *s.* **1.** Zs.-setzung *f* (*a. ling.*), Bildung *f*; **2.** Abfassung *f*, Entwurf *m*, Anordnung *f*, Gestaltung *f*, Aufbau *m*; **3.** Satzbau *m*; Stilübung *f*, Aufsatz *m*, *a.* Über'setzung *f*: *English* ~; **4.** ♪ Kompositi'on *f*, Mu'sikstück *n*; **5.** *typ.* Setzen *n*, Satz *m*; **7.** *a.* ⚙, ⚒ Zs.-setzung *f*, Verbindung *f*, 'Mischmateri,al *n*; **8.** Über'einkunft *f*, Abkommen *n*; **9.** ⚖, ♥ Vergleich *m* *mit Gläubigern*: ~ *proceedings* (Konkurs)Vergleichsverfahren *n*; **10.** Wesen *n*, Na'tur *f*, Anlage *f*; **com·pos·i·tor** [kəm'pɒzɪtə] *s. typ.* (Schrift)Setzer *m*.

com·pos men·tis [ˌkɒmpəs'mentɪs] (*Lat.*) *adj.* ⚖ bei klarem Verstand, geschäftsfähig.

com·post ['kɒmpɒst] **I** *s.* Mischdünger *m*, Kom'post *m*; **II** *v/t.* kompostieren.

com·po·sure [kəm'pəʊʒə] *s.* (Gemüts-) Ruhe *f*, Gelassenheit *f*, Fassung *f*.

com·pote ['kɒmpɒt] *s.* **1.** Kom'pott *n*; **2.** Kom'pottschale *f*.

com·pound[1] ['kɒmpaʊnd] *s.* **1.** Lager *n*; **2.** Gefängnishof *m*; **3.** (Tier)Gehege *n*.

com·pound[2] [kəm'paʊnd] **I** *v/t.* **1.** mischen, mengen; zs.-setzen, vereinigen, verbinden; **2.** (zu)bereiten, herstellen; **3.** in Güte *od.* durch Vergleich beilegen; erledigen; **4.** ⚖, ♥ a) in Raten abzahlen, b) durch einmalige Zahlung regeln: ~ *creditors* Gläubiger befriedigen; **5.** gegen Schadloshaltung auf Strafverfolgung (*gen.*) verzichten; **6.** verschlim-

mern, steigern; **II** *v/i.* **7.** *a.* ⚖, ♥ sich (durch Abfindung) einigen *od.* vergleichen (*with mit*, *for* über *acc.*); **III** *s.* ['kɒmpaʊnd] **8.** Zs.-setzung *f*, Mischung *f*; Masse *f*; Präpa'rat *n*; **9.** ⚒ Verbindung *f*; **10.** *ling.* Kompositum *n*; **IV** *adj.* ['kɒmpaʊnd] **11.** zs.-gesetzt (*a.* ♀, Å, *ling.*); ⚑, ⚙ Verbund...(*-dynamo, -motor, -stahl etc.*): ~ *eye* *zo.* Netz-, Facettenauge *n*; ~ *fracture* ⚒ komplizierter Bruch; ~ *fruit* ♀ Sammelfrucht *f*; ~ *interest* Staffel-, Zinseszinsen *pl.*; ~ *sentence* *ling.* zs.-gesetzter Satz.

com·pre·hend [ˌkɒmprɪ'hend] *v/t.* **1.** um'fassen, einschließen; **2.** begreifen, verstehen; **com·pre'hen·si·ble** [-nsəbl] *adj.* begreiflich, verständlich; **com·pre'hen·sion** [-nʃən] *s.* **1.** 'Umfang *m*; **2.** Einbeziehung *f*; **3.** Begriffsvermögen *n*; Verstand *m*; Verständnis *n*, Einsicht *f*: *quick* (*slow*) *of* ~ schnell (schwer) von Begriff; **4.** *bsd. eccl.* Duldung *f* (*anderer Ansichten*); **com·pre-'hen·sive** [-nsɪv] **I** *adj.* □ **1.** um'fassend; inhaltsreich: (*fully*) ~ *insurance* *mot.* Vollkaskoversicherung *f*; ~ *school* Gesamtschule *f*; *go* ~ F a) die Gesamtschule einführen, b) in e-e Gesamtschule umgewandelt werden; **2.** verstehend: ~ *faculty* Begriffsvermögen *n*; **II** *s.* *Brit.* Gesamtschule *f*; **com·pre'hen·sive·ness** [-nsɪvnɪs] *s.* 'Umfang *m*, Weite *f*; Reichhaltigkeit *f*; *das* Um'fassende.

com·press I *v/t.* [kəm'pres] zs.-drü-cken, -pressen, komprimieren; **II** *s.* ['kɒmpres] ⚒ Kom'presse *f*, 'Umschlag *m*; **com'pressed** [-st] *adj.* **1.** komprimiert, zs.-gepresst: ~ *air* Press-, Druckluft *f*; **2.** *fig.* zs.-gefasst, gedrängt, gekürzt; **com'press·i·ble** [-səbl] *adj.* komprimierbar; **com'pres·sion** [-eʃn] *s.* **1.** Zs.-pressen *n*, -drücken *n*; Verdichtung *f*, Druck *m*; **2.** *fig.* Zs.-drängung *f*; **3.** ⚙ Druck *m*, Kompressi'on *f*: ~ *mo(u)lding* Formpressen *n*; ~ *-mo(u)lded* formgepresst (*Plastik*); **com'pres·sive** [-sɪv] *adj.* zs.-pressend, Press..., Druck...; **com'pres·sor** [-sə] *s.* ⚙ Kom'pressor *m*, Verdichter *m*; ⚙ Lader *m*; **2.** *anat.* Schließmuskel *m*; **3.** ⚒ Druckverband *m*.

com·prise [kəm'praɪz] *v/t.* einschließen, um'fassen, enthalten, bestehen aus.

com·pro·mise ['kɒmprəmaɪz] **I** *s.* **1.** Kompro'miss *m*, (gütlicher) Vergleich; Über'einkunft *f*; **II** *v/t.* **2.** durch Kompro'miss regeln; **3.** gefährden, aufs Spiel setzen; beeinträchtigen; **4.** (*a. o.s.* sich) bloßstellen *od.* kompromittieren; **III** *v/i.* **5.** e-n Kompro'miss schließen, zu e-r Über'einkunft gelangen (*on* über *acc.*).

comp·trol·ler [kən'trəʊlə] *s.* (staatlicher) Rechnungsprüfer: ⚔ *General Am.* Präsident *m* des Rechnungshofes.

com·pul·sion [kəm'pʌlʃn] *s.* Zwang *m* (*a. psych.*): *under* ~ unter Zwang *od.* Druck, gezwungen; **com'pul·sive** [-sɪv] *adj.* □ zwingend, (*a. psych.*) Zwangs...; **com'pul·so·ry** [-sərɪ] *adj.* □ obliga'torisch, zwangsmäßig, Zwangs...; bindend; Pflicht...: ~ *auction* ⚖ Zwangsversteigerung *f*; ~ *education* allgemeine Schulpflicht; ~ *insurance* Pflichtversicherung *f*; ~ *military service* allgemeine Wehrpflicht; ~ *purchase* Enteignung *f*; ~ *subject ped.* Pflichtfach *n*.

com·punc·tion [kəm'pʌŋkʃn] *s.* a) Gewissensbisse *pl.*, b) Reue *f*, c) Bedenken *pl.*: *without* ~.

com·put·a·ble [kəm'pjuːtəbl] *adj.* berechenbar; **com·put·a·hol·ic** [kəm,pju:tə'hɒlɪk] *s.* Computerfreak *m*; **com·pu·ta·tion** [,kɒmpju:'teɪʃn] *s.* Berechnung *f*, 'Überschlag *m*, Schätzung *f*; ,**com·pu'ta·tion·al** [-ʃənl] *adj.* Computer...; **compute** [kəm'pju:t] **I** *v/t.* berechnen, schätzen, veranschlagen (*at* auf *acc.*); **II** *v/i.* rechnen; **com'put·er** [-tə] *s.* **1.** (Be)Rechner *m*; **2.** ⚡ Com'puter *m*: ~*-aided* computergestützt; ~ *animation* Com'puteranimati͵on *f*; ~ *centre* (*Am.* **center**) Rechenzentrum *n*; ~*-control(l)ed* computergesteuert; ~ *crash* Computerabsturz *m*; ~ *expert* Computerfachmann *m*; ~ *game* Computerspiel *n*; ~ *graphics pl.* (*als sg. konstr.*) Com'puter͵grafik *f*; ~*-literate* mit Computerkenntnissen; ~ *meltdown* Computer-GAU *m*; ~ *printout* Computerausdruck *m*; ~ *program* Com'puterpro͵gramm *n*; ~ *room* Computerraum *m*; ~ *skills* (*pl.* 'Kenntnisse *pl.*; ~ *science* Informatik *f*; ~ *scientist* Informatiker(in); ~ *tomography* Com'putertomogra͵phie *f*; ~ *virus* Com'puter͵virus *m*; **com'put·er·ize** [-təraɪz] *v/t.* a) auf Com'puter 'umstellen, b) mit Com'putern betreiben.

com·rade ['kɒmrɪd] *s.* **1.** Kame'rad *m*, Genosse *m*, Gefährte *m*; ~*-in-arms* Waffenbruder *m*; **2.** *pol.* Genosse *m*; '**com·rade·ly** [-lɪ] *adj.* kame'radschaftlich; '**com·rade·ship** [-ʃɪp] *s.* Kame'radschaft *f*.

com·sat ['kɒmsæt] → *communications satellite.*

con¹ [kɒn] *v/t.* (auswendig) lernen, sich (*dat.*) et. einprägen.

con² → *conn.*

con³ [kɒn] **I** *s.* **1.** Neinstimme *f*; **2.** 'Gegenargu͵ment *n*; → *pro¹* I; **II** *adv.* (da-) 'gegen.

con⁴ [kɒn] *sl.* **I** *adj.* **1.** betrügerisch: ~ *game* → *confidence game*; ~ *man* → 3; **II** *v/t.* **2.** ͵reinlegen': ~ *s.o. out of* j-n betrügen um; ~ *s.o. into doing s.th.* j-n (durch Schwindel) dazu bringen, et. zu tun; **III** *s.* **3.** Betrüger *m*; Hochstapler *m*; Ga'nove *m*; **4.** Sträfling *m*.

con·cat·e·nate [kɒn'kætɪneɪt] *v/t.* verketten, verknüpfen; **con·cat·e·na·tion** [kɒn,kætɪ'neɪʃn] *s.* **1.** Verkettung *f*; **2.** Kette *f*.

con·cave [,kɒn'keɪv] **I** *adj.* □ **1.** kon'kav, hohl, ausgehöhlt; **2.** ◉ hohlgeschliffen, Hohl...: ~ *lens* Zerstreuungslinse *f*; ~ *mirror* Hohlspiegel *m*; **II** *s.* **3.** (Aus)Höhlung *f*, Wölbung *f*; **con·cav·i·ty** [kɒn'kævətɪ] → *concave* 3.

con·ceal [kən'si:l] *v/t.* (*from* vor *dat.*) verbergen: a) (*a.* ◉) verdecken, kaschieren, b) verhehlen, verschweigen, verheimlichen, *a.* ✕ verschleiern, tarnen, c) verstecken: ~*ed assets* ⊤ verschleierte Vermögenswerte, *Bilanz*: unsichtbare Aktiva; **con'ceal·ment** [-mənt] *s.* **1.** Verbergung *f*, Verheimlichung *f*, Geheimhaltung *f*; **2.** Verborgenheit *f*; **3.** Versteck *n*.

con·cede [kən'si:d] **I** *v/t.* **1.** zugestehen, einräumen, zugeben, anerkennen (*a. that* dass); **2.** gewähren, einräumen: ~ *a point* a) in e-m Punkt nachgeben, b) (*to*) *sport* dem *Gegner* e-n Punkt abgeben; ~ *a goal* ein Tor zulassen; **II** *v/i.* **3.** *sport, pol.* F sich geschlagen geben; **con'ced·ed·ly** [-dɪdlɪ] *adv.* zugestandenermaßen.

con·ceit [kən'si:t] *s.* **1.** Eingebildetheit *f*, Einbildung *f*, (Eigen)Dünkel *m*: *in my own* ~ nach m-r Ansicht; *out of* ~ *with* überdrüssig (*gen.*); **2.** *obs.* guter *od.* seltsamer Einfall; **con'ceit·ed**

[-tɪd] *adj.* □ eingebildet, dünkelhaft, eitel.

con·ceiv·a·ble [kən'si:vəbl] *adj.* □ denkbar, erdenklich, begreiflich, vorstellbar: *the best plan* ~ der denkbar beste Plan; **con'ceiv·a·bly** [-blɪ] *adv.* es ist denkbar, dass; **con·ceive** [kən'si:v] **I** *v/t.* **1.** *biol.* Kind empfangen; **2.** begreifen; sich denken *od.* vorstellen: ~ *an idea* auf e-n Gedanken kommen; **3.** er-, ausdenken, ersinnen; **4.** *in Worten* ausdrücken; **5.** *Wunsch* hegen, (*Ab*)*Neigung* fassen, entwickeln; **II** *v/i.* **6.** (*of*) sich et. vorstellen; **7.** empfangen (*schwanger werden*); *zo.* aufnehmen (*trächtig werden*).

con·cen·trate ['kɒnsəntreɪt] **I** *v/t.* **1.** konzentrieren (*on, upon* auf *acc.*): a) zs.-ziehen, -ballen, massieren, b) *Gedanken etc.* richten; **2.** *fig.* zs.-fassen (*in* in *dat.*); **3.** ⚗ a) sättigen, konzentrieren, b) verstärken, *bsd. Metall* anreichern; **II** *v/i.* **4.** sich konzentrieren (*etc.*; → 1); **5.** sich *an e-m Punkt* sammeln; **III** *s.* **6.** ⚗ Konzen'trat *n*; '**con·cen·trat·ed** [-tɪd] *adj.* konzentriert; **con·cen·tra·tion** [,kɒnsən'treɪʃn] *s.* **1.** Konzentrierung *f*, Konzentrati'on *f*: a) Zs.-ziehung *f*, -fassung *f*, (Zs.-)Ballung *f*, Massierung *f*, (An)Sammlung *f* (*alle a.* ✕): ~ *camp* Konzentrationslager *n*, b) Hinlenkung *f* auf 'einen Punkt, c) (geistige) Sammlung, gespannte Aufmerksamkeit; **2.** ⚗ Konzentrati'on *f*, Dichte *f*, Sättigung *f*.

con·cen·tric [kɒn'sentrɪk] *adj.* (□ ~*ally*) kon'zentrisch.

con·cept ['kɒnsept] *s.* **1.** Begriff *m*; **2.** Gedanke *m*, Auffassung *f*, Konzepti'on *f*; **con·cep·tion** [kən'sepʃn] *s.* **1.** *biol.* Empfängnis *f*; **2.** Begriffsvermögen *n*, Verstand *m*; **3.** Begriff *m*, Auffassung *f*, Vorstellung *f*: *no* ~ *of* ... keine Ahnung von ...; **4.** Gedanke *m*, I'dee *f*; **5.** Plan *m*, Anlage *f*, Kon'zept *n*, Entwurf *m*; Schöpfung *f*; **con·cep·tion·al** [kən'sepʃənl] *adj.* begrifflich, ab'strakt; **con·cep·tive** [kən'septɪv] *adj.* **1.** begreifend, Begriffs...; **2.** ♂ empfängnisfähig; **con·cep·tu·al** [kən'septjʊəl] → *conceptive* 1; **con͵cep·tu·al·i'za·tion** [-laɪ'zeɪʃn] *s.* begriffliche Erfassung (u. Kategorisierung); **con'cep·tu·al·ize** [-laɪz] **I** *v/t.* begrifflich erfassen, auffassen (*as* als); **II** *v/i.* begrifflich denken.

con·cern [kən'sɜ:n] **I** *v/t.* **1.** betreffen, angehen; interessieren, von Belang sein für: *it does not* ~ *me od. I am not* ~*ed* es geht mich nichts an; *to whom it may* ~ an alle, die es angeht; Bescheinigung (*Überschrift auf Urkunden*); *his hono(u)r is* ~*ed* es geht um s-e Ehre; → *concerned* 1; **2.** beunruhigen: *don't let that* ~ *you* mache dir deswegen keine Sorgen!; → *concerned* 4; **3.** ~ *o.s.* (*with, about*) sich beschäftigen *od.* befassen (mit); sich kümmern (um); **II** *s.* **4.** Angelegenheit *f*, Sache *f*: *that is no* ~ *of mine* das ist nicht meine Sache, das geht mich nichts an; **5.** ⊤ Geschäft *n*, Unter'nehmen *n*, Betrieb *m*; → *going* 4; **6.** Beziehung *f*: *have no* ~ *with* nichts zu tun haben mit; **7.** Inter'esse *n* (*for* für, *in* an *dat.*); **8.** Wichtigkeit *f*, Bedeutung *f*; **9.** Unruhe *f*, Sorge *f*; Bedenken *pl.* (*at, about, for* um, wegen); **10.** F Ding *n*, Geschichte *f*; **con'cerned** [-nd] *adj.* □ **1.** betroffen, berührt; **2.** (*in*) beteiligt, interessiert (an *dat.*); verwickelt (in *acc.*): *the parties* ~ die Beteiligten; **3.** (*with, in*) beschäftigt (mit); handelnd (von);

4. besorgt (*about, at, for* um, *that* dass), *a.* (po'litisch *od.* sozi'al) engagiert; **5.** betrübt, sorgenvoll; **con'cerning** [-nɪŋ] *prp.* betreffend, betreffs, hinsichtlich (*gen.*), was ... betrifft, über (*acc.*), wegen.

con·cert I *s.* ['kɒnsət] **1.** ♪ Kon'zert *n*: ~ *hall* Konzertsaal *m*; ~ *pitch* Kammerton *m*; *at* ~ *pitch fig.* in Höchstform; *screw o.s. up to* ~ *pitch fig.* sich enorm steigern; *up to* ~ *pitch fig.* auf der Höhe, in Form; **2.** [-sɜ:t] Einvernehmen *n*, Über'einstimmung *f*, Harmo'nie *f*: *in* ~ *with* im Einvernehmen *od.* gemeinsam mit; *♫ of Europe pol. hist.* Europäisches Konzert; **II** *v/t.* [kən'sɜ:t] **3.** *et.* verabreden, vereinbaren; *Kräfte etc.* vereinigen; **4.** planen; **III** *v/i.* [kən'sɜ:t] **5.** zs.-arbeiten; **con·cert·ed** [kən'sɜ:tɪd] *adj.* **1.** gemeinsam, gemeinschaftlich: ~ *action* gemeinsames Vorgehen, konzertierte Aktion; **2.** ♪ mehrstimmig arrangiert.

'**con·cert**͵**go·er** *s.* Kon'zertbesucher *m*; ~ *grand s.* Kon'zertflügel *m*.

con·cer·ti·na [,kɒnsə'ti:nə] *s.* Konzer'tina *f* (*Ziehharmonika*): ~ *door* Falttür *f*; **con·cer·to** [kən'tʃeətəʊ] *pl.* **-tos** *s.* ♪ ('Solo)Kon͵zert *n*.

con·ces·sion [kən'seʃn] *s.* **1.** Zugeständnis *n*, Entgegenkommen *n*; **2.** Genehmigung *f*, Erlaubnis *f*, Gewährung *f*; **3.** amtliche *od.* staatliche Konzessi'on, Privi'leg *n*: a) Genehmigung *f*: *mining* ~ Bergwerkskonzession *f*, b) *Am.* Gewerbeerlaubnis *f*, c) über'lassenes Siedlungs- *od.* Ausbeutungsgebiet; **con·ces·sion·aire** [kən,seʃə'neə] *s.* ⊤ Konzessi'onsinhaber *m*; **con'ces·sion·ar·y** [-ʃnərɪ] *adj.* Konzessions...; bewilligt; **con'ces·sive** [-esɪv] *adj.* **1.** einräumend; **2.** *ling.* ~ *clause* Konzes'sivsatz *m*.

conch [kɒŋk] *s. zo.* (Schale *f* der) See*od.* Schneckenmuschel *f*; **con·cha** ['kɒŋkə] *pl.* **-chae** [-ki:] *s.* **1.** *anat.* Ohrmuschel *f*; **2.** △ Kuppeldach *n*.

con·chy ['kɒntʃɪ] *s. Brit. sl.* Kriegs-, Wehrdienstverweigerer *m* (*von conscientous objector*).

con·cil·i·ate [kən'sɪlɪeɪt] *v/t.* **1.** aus-, versöhnen; beschwichtigen; **2.** *Gunst etc.* gewinnen; **3.** ausgleichen; in Einklang bringen; **con·cil·i·a·tion** [kən,sɪlɪ'eɪʃn] *s.* **1.** Versöhnung *f*, Schlichtung *f*: ~ *board* Schlichtungsausschuss *m*; **2.** Ausgleich *m*: *debt* ~ Schuldenausgleich; **con'cil·i·a·tor** [-tə] *s.* Vermittler *m*, Schlichter *m*; **con'cil·i·a·to·ry** [-ɪətərɪ] *adj.* versöhnlich, vermittelnd, Versöhnungs...

con·cin·ni·ty [kən'sɪnətɪ] *s.* Feinheit *f*, Ele'ganz *f* (*Stil*).

con·cise [kən'saɪs] *adj.* □ kurz, gedrängt, knapp, prä'gnant: ~ *dictionary* Handwörterbuch *n*; **con'cise·ness** [-nɪs] *s.* Kürze *f*, Prä'gnanz *f*.

con·clave ['kɒnkleɪv] *s.* **1.** *R.C.* Kon'klave *n*; **2.** geheime Sitzung.

con·clude [kən'klu:d] **I** *v/t.* **1.** beenden, zu Ende führen; (be-, ab)schließen: *to be* ~*d* Schluss folgt; *he* ~*d by saying* zum Schluss sagte er (noch); **2.** *Vertrag etc.* (ab)schließen; **3.** schließen, folgern (*from* aus); **4.** beschließen, entscheiden; **II** *v/i.* **5.** schließen, enden, aufhören (*with* mit); **con'clud·ing** [-dɪŋ] *adj.* (ab)schließend, End..., Schluss...; **con'clu·sion** [-u:ʒn] *s.* **1.** (Ab)Schluss *m*, Ende *n*: *bring to a* ~ zum Abschluss bringen; *in* ~ zum Schluss, schließlich; **2.** (*Vertrags- etc.*)Abschluss *m*: ~ *of peace* Friedensschluss *m*; **3.** Schluss *m*,

C

(Schluss)Folgerung *f*: *come to the* ~ zu dem Schluss *od.* der Überzeugung kommen; *draw a* ~ e-n Schluss ziehen; *jump od. rush to* ~s voreilige Schlüsse ziehen; **4.** Beschluss *m*, Entscheidung *f*; **5.** Ausgang *m*, Folge *f*, Ergebnis *n*; **6.** *try* ~s *with* sich *od.* s-e Kräfte messen mit; **con·clu·sive** [-uːsɪv] *adj.* □ schlüssig, endgültig, entscheidend, über'zeugend, maßgebend: ~ *evidence* ‡ schlüssiger Beweis; **con·clu·sive·ness** [-uːsɪvnɪs] *s.* Endgültigkeit *f*, Triftigkeit *f*; Schlüssigkeit *f*, Beweiskraft *f*.

con·coct [kən'kɒkt] *v/t.* zs.-brauen (*a. fig.*); *fig.* ausdenken, sich ausdenken; **con·coc·tion** [-kʃn] *s.* **1.** (Zs.-)Brauen *n*, Bereiten *n*; **2.** Mischung *f*, Trank *m*; Gebräu *n*; **3.** *fig.* Aushecken *n*, Ausbrüten *n*; **4.** *fig.* Gebräu *n*; Erfindung *f*: ~ *of lies* Lügengewebe *n*.

con·com·i·tance [kən'kɒmɪtəns], **con·'com·i·tan·cy** [-sɪ] *s.* **1.** Zs.-bestehen *n*, Gleichzeitigkeit *f*; **2.** *eccl.* Konkomi'tanz *f*; **con·com·i·tant** [-nt] **I** *adj.* □ begleitend, Begleit..., gleichzeitig; **II** *s.* Begleiterscheinung *f*, -umstand *m*.

con·cord ['kɒŋkɔːd] *s.* **1.** Eintracht *f*, Einklang *m*; Über'einstimmung *f* (*a. ling.*); **2.** ♪ Zs.-klang *m*, Harmo'nie *f*.

con·cord·ance [kən'kɔːdəns] *s.* **1.** Über'einstimmung *f*; **2.** Konkor'danz *f*; **con·cord·ant** [kən'kɔːdənt] *adj.* □ (*with*) über'einstimmend (mit), entsprechend (*dat.*); har'monisch (*a.* ♪); **con·cor·dat** [kɒn'kɔːdæt] *s. eccl.* Konkor'dat *n*.

con·course ['kɒŋkɔːs] *s.* **1.** Zs.-treffen *n*; **2.** Ansammlung *f*, Auflauf *m*, Menge *f*; **3.** a) *Am.* Fahrweg *m od.* Prome'nadeplatz *m* (*im Park*), b) Bahnhofshalle *f*, c) freier Platz.

con·crete [kən'kriːt] **I** *v/t.* **1.** zu e-r festen Masse verbinden, zs.-ballen *od.* vereinigen; **2.** ['kɒnkriːt] ⊙ betonieren; **II** *v/i.* **3.** sich zu e-r festen Masse verbinden; **III** *adj.* □ ['kɒnkriːt] **4.** kon'kret (*a. ling., phls.,* ♪ *etc.*), greifbar, wirklich, dinglich; **5.** fest, dicht, kom'pakt; **6.** ⚐ benannt; **7.** ⊙ betoniert, Beton...; **IV** *s.* ['kɒnkriːt] **8.** kon'kreter Begriff: *in the* ~ im konkreten Sinne, in Wirklichkeit; **9.** ⊙ Be'ton *m*: ~ *jungle* Betonwüste *f*; **con·cre·tion** [-iːʃn] *s.* **1.** Zs.-wachsen *n*, Verwachsung *f*; **2.** Festwerden *n*; Verhärtung *f*, feste Masse; **3.** Häufung *f*; **4.** ⚕ Absonderung *f*, Stein *m*, Knoten *m*; **con·cre·tize** ['kɒnkriːtaɪz] *v/t.* konkretisieren.

con·cu·bi·nage [kɒn'kjuːbɪnɪdʒ] *s.* Konkubi'nat *n*, wilde Ehe; **con·cu·bine** ['kɒŋkjubaɪn] *s.* **1.** Konku'bine *f*, Mätresse *f*; **2.** Nebenfrau *f*.

con·cu·pis·cence [kən'kjuːpɪsns] *s.* Begierde *f*, Lüsternheit *f*; **con·cu·pis·cent** [-nt] *adj.* lüstern.

con·cur [kən'kɜː] *v/i.* **1.** zs.-treffen, -fallen; **2.** mitwirken, beitragen (*to* zu); **3.** (*with s.o., in s.th.*) über'einstimmen, gleicher Meinung sein (mit j-m, in e-r Sache), beipflichten (j-m, e-r Sache); **con·cur·rence** [-'kʌrəns] *s.* **1.** Zs.-treffen *n*; **2.** Mitwirkung *f*; **3.** Zustimmung *f*, Einverständnis *n*; **4.** Å Schnittpunkt *m*; **con·cur·rent** [-'kʌrənt] **I** *adj.* □ **1.** gleichzeitig: ~ *condition* ✝ Zug um Zug zu erfüllende Bedingung; ~ *sentence* ‡ gleichzeitige Verbüßung zweier Freiheitsstrafen; **2.** gemeinschaftlich; **3.** mitwirkend; **4.** über'einstimmend; **5.** Å durch 'einen Punkt laufend; **II** *s.* **6.** Be'gleit,umstand *m*.

con·cuss [kən'kʌs] *v/t. mst fig.* erschüttern; **con·cus·sion** [-ʌʃn] *s.* (*a.* ⚕ Ge-

---

hirn)Erschütterung *f*: ~ *fuse* ✕ Aufschlagzünder *m*; ~ *spring* ⊙ Stoßdämpfer *m*.

con·demn [kən'dem] *v/t.* **1.** verdammen, verurteilen, miss'billigen, tadeln: *his looks* ~ *him* sein Aussehen verrät ihn; **2.** ‡ verurteilen (*to death* zum Tode); *fig. a.* verdammen (*to* zu): ~*ed cell* Todeszelle *f*; → *cost* 4; **3.** ‡ als verfallen erklären, beschlagnahmen; *Am.* (zu öffentlichen Zwecken) enteignen; **4.** verwerfen; für gebrauchsunfähig *od.* unbewohnbar *od.* gesundheitsschädlich *od.* baufällig erklären; *Schwerkranke* aufgeben: ~*ed building* abbruchreifes Gebäude; **con·dem·na·ble** [-mnəbl] *adj.* verdammenswert, verwerflich, sträflich; **con·dem·na·tion** [ˌkɒndem'neɪʃn] *s.* **1.** Verurteilung *f* (*a.* ‡), Verdammung *f*, 'Missbilligung *f*; **2.** Verwerfung *f*; Untauglichkeitserklärung *f*; **3.** Beschlagnahme *f*; *Am.* Enteignung *f*; **con·dem·na·to·ry** [-mnətərɪ] *adj.* verurteilend; verdammend.

con·den·sa·ble [kən'densəbl] *adj. phys.* kondensierbar; **con·den·sa·tion** [ˌkɒnden'seɪʃn] *s.* **1.** *bsd. phys.* Verdichtung *f*, Kondensati'on *f* (*Gase etc.*); Konzentrati'on *f* (*Licht*); **2.** Zs.-drängung *f*, Anhäufung *f*; **3.** *fig.* Zs.-fassung *f*, (Ab-)Kürzung *f*; **con·dense** [kən'dens] **I** *v/t.* **1.** *bsd. phys. Gase etc.* verdichten, kondensieren, niederschlagen; eindicken: ~*d milk* Kondensmilch *f*; **2.** *fig.* zs.-drängen, -fassen; zs.-streichen, kürzen; **II** *v/i.* **3.** sich verdichten; flüssig werden; **con·dens·er** [kən'densə] *s.* **1.** ✦, ⊙, *phys.* Konden'sator *m*; **2.** Kühlrohr *n*.

con·dens·ing| coil [kən'densɪŋ] *s.* ⊙ Kühlschlange *f*; ~ *lens* *s. opt.* Sammel-, Kondensati'onslinse *f*.

con·de·scend [ˌkɒndɪ'send] *v/i.* **1.** sich her'ablassen, geruhen (*to* [*mst inf.*]) zu [*mst inf.*]); **2.** *b.s.* sich (so weit) erniedrigen (*to do* zu tun); **3.** leutselig sein (*to* gegen), **con·de·scend·ing** [-dɪŋ] *adj.* □ her'ablassend, gönnerhaft; **con·de·scen·sion** [-nʃn] *s.* Her'ablassung *f*, gönnerhaftes Wesen.

con·dign [kən'daɪn] *adj.* □ gebührend, angemessen (*Strafe*).

con·di·ment ['kɒndɪmənt] *s.* Würze *f*, Gewürz *n*.

con·di·tion [kən'dɪʃn] **I** *s.* **1.** Bedingung *f*; Vor'aussetzung *f*: *on* ~ *that* unter der Bedingung, dass; vorausgesetzt, dass; *on no* ~ unter keinen Umständen, keinesfalls; *to make it a* ~ es zur Bedingung machen; **2.** ‡, ✝ (*Vertrags- etc.*) Bedingung *f*, Bestimmung *f*; Vorbehalt *m*, Klausel *f*; **3.** Zustand *m*, Verfassung *f*, Beschaffenheit *f*; *sport* Kondi'tion *f*, Form *f*: *out of* ~ in schlechter Verfassung; *in good* ~ gut in Form (*Person, Pferd etc.*), in gutem Zustand (*Sachen*); **4.** (*a.* Fa'milien)Stand *m*, Stellung *f*, Rang *m*: *change one's* ~ heiraten; **5.** *pl.* 'Umstände *pl.*, Verhältnisse *pl.*, Lage *f*: *weather* ~s Witterung *f*; *working* ~s Arbeitsbedingungen *f*; **6.** *Am. ped.* (Gegenstand *m* der) Nachprüfung *f*; **II** *v/t.* **7.** bedingen, bestimmen; regeln, abhängig machen: → *conditioned* 2; **8.** *fig.* formen, gestalten; **9.** gewöhnen (*to* an *acc.*, zu tun); **10.** *Tiere* in Form bringen; *Sachen* herrichten, instand setzen; ⊙ konditionieren, in den *od.* e-n (*gewünschten*) Zustand bringen; *fig.* j-n programmieren (*to, for* auf *acc.*); **11.** ✝ (*bsd. Textil*)*Waren* prüfen; **12.** *Am. ped.* e-e Nachprüfung auferlegen (*dat.*); **con·di·tion·al** [-ʃənl] **I** *adj.* □

---

1. (*on*) bedingt (durch), abhängig (von), eingeschränkt (durch); unverbindlich; ✝ unter Eigentumsvorbehalt (*Verkauf*): ~ *discharge* ‡ bedingte Entlassung; *make* ~ *on* abhängig machen von; **2.** *ling.* konditio'nal: ~ *clause* → 3 a; ~ *mood* → 3 b; **II** *s.* **3.** *ling.* a) Bedingungs-, Konditio'nalsatz *m*, b) Bedingungsform *f*, Konditio'nalis *m*, c) Be'dingungspar,tikel *f*; **con·di·tion·al·ly** [-nəlɪ] *adv.* bedingungsweise; **con·di·tioned** [-nd] *adj.* **1.** (*by*) bedingt (durch), abhängig (von): ~ *reflex psych.* bedingter Reflex; **2.** (so) beschaffen *od.* geartet; in ... Verfassung; **con·di·tion·er** [-nə] *s.* **1.** Weichspüler *m* (*für Wäsche*); **2.** Pflegespülung *f* (*für Haare*).

con·do ['kɒndəʊ] *s. Am.* F Eigentumswohnung *f*.

con·do·la·to·ry [kən'dəʊlətərɪ] *adj.* Beileids..., Kondolenz...; **con·dole** [kən'dəʊl] *v/i.* Beileid bezeigen, kondolieren (*with s.o. on s.th.* j-m zu et.); **con·do·lence** [-əns] *s.* Beileid *n*, Kondo'lenz *f*.

con·dom ['kɒndəm] *s.* Kon'dom *n*, *m*, Präserva'tiv *n*.

con·do·min·i·um [ˌkɒndə'mɪnɪəm] *s.* **1.** *pol.* Kondo'minium *n*; **2.** *Am.* a) Eigentumswohnanlage *f*, b) a. ~ *apartment* Eigentumswohnung *f*.

con·do·na·tion [ˌkɒndəʊ'neɪʃn] *s.* Verzeihung *f* (*bsd. ehelicher Untreue*); stillschweigende Duldung; **con·done** [kən'dəʊn] *v/t.* verzeihen.

con·dor ['kɒndɔː] *s. orn.* 'Kondor *m*.

con·duce [kən'djuːs] *v/i.* (*to*) dienen, führen, beitragen (zu); förderlich sein (*dat.*); **con·du·cive** [-sɪv] *adj.* dienlich, förderlich (*to dat.*).

con·duct I *v/t.* [kən'dʌkt] **1.** führen, (ge)leiten; → *tour* 1; **2.** (be)treiben, handhaben; führen, leiten, verwalten; **3.** *Feldzug, Krieg, Prozess etc.* führen; **4.** ♪ dirigieren; **5.** ✦, *phys.* leiten; **6.** ~ *o.s.* sich betragen *od.* benehmen, sich (auf)führen; **II** *s.* ['kɒndʌkt] **7.** Führung *f*, Leitung *f*, Verwaltung *f*; Handhabung *f*; **8.** *fig.* Führung *f*, Betragen *n*; Verhalten *n*, Haltung *f*: ~ *sheet* Strafregister(auszug *m*) *n*; **con·duct·ance** [-təns], **con·duct·i·bil·i·ty** [kənˌdʌktɪ'bɪlətɪ] *s. phys.* Leitfähigkeit *f*; **con·duct·i·ble** [-tɪbl] *adj.* ✦, *phys.* leitfähig; **con·duct·ing** [-tɪŋ] *adj.* ✦, *phys.* Leit..., Leitungs...: ~ *wire* Leitungsdraht *m*; **con·duc·tion** [-kʃn] *s. oft* ⊙, *phys.* Leitung *f*, (Zu)Führung *f*, Über'tragung *f*; **con·duc·tive** [-tɪv] *adj. phys.* leitend, leitfähig; **con·duc·tiv·i·ty** [ˌkɒndʌk'tɪvətɪ] *s.* ✦, *phys.* spe'zifische Leitfähigkeit; **con·duc·tor** [-tə] *s.* **1.** Führer *m*, Leiter *m*; **2.** ♪ Diri'gent *m*; **3.** (Bus- *etc.*)Schaffner *m*; *Am.* 🚋 Zugbegleiter *m*; **4.** ✦, *phys.* Leiter *m*; Ader *f* (*Kabel*); *Am. a.* Blitzableiter *m*; **con·duc·tress** [-trɪs] *s.* Schaffnerin *f*.

con·duit ['kɒndɪt] *s.* **1.** Rohrleitung *f*, Röhre *f*; Ka'nal *m* (*a. fig.*); **2.** Leitung *f* (*a. fig.*); **3.** ✦ a) Rohrkabel *n*, b) Isolierrohr *n* (*für Leitungsdrähte*); ~ *pipe s.* Leitungsrohr *n*.

cone [kəʊn] *s.* **1.** Å u. *fig.* Kegel *m*: ~ *of fire* Feuergarbe *f*; ~ *of rays* Strahlenbündel *n*; ~ *sugar* Zuckerhut *m*; **2.** ⊙ Kegel *m*, Konus *m* (*a.* ♪): ~ *drive* Stufen(scheiben)antrieb *m*; ~ *friction clutch* Reibungskupplung *f*; ~ *valve* Kegelventil *n*; **3.** Bergkegel *m*; **4.** ♣ (Tannen- *etc.*)Zapfen *m*; **5.** Waffeltüte *f für Speiseeis*; **coned** [-nd] *adj.* kegelförmig.

con·fab ['kɒnfæb] F *abbr. für* **confabulation** *u.* **confabulate**; **con·fab·u·late** [kən'fæbjʊleɪt] *v/i.* plaudern; **con·fab·u·la·tion** [kən,fæbjʊ'leɪʃn] *s.* **1.** Plaude'rei *f*; **2.** *psych.* Konfabulati'on *f*.

con·fec·tion [kən'fekʃn] *s.* **1.** Kon'fekt *n*, Süßwaren *pl.*, *mit Zucker* Eingemachtes *n*; **2.** 'Damen,modear,tikel *m* (*Kleid, Hut etc.*); **con·fec·tion·er** [-nə] *s.* Kon'ditor *m*: *~'s sugar Am.* Puderzucker *m*; **con·fec·tion·er·y** [-nərɪ] *s.* **1.** Süßigkeiten *pl.*, Kon'ditorwaren *pl.*; **2.** Süßwarengeschäft *n*, Kondito'rei *f*.

con·fed·er·a·cy [kən'fedərəsɪ] *s.* **1.** Bündnis *n*, Bund *m*; **2.** Staatenbund *m*; **3.** *♈ Am.* Konföderati'on *f* (*der Südstaaten im Bürgerkrieg*); **4.** Verschwörung *f*; **con·fed·er·ate** [-rət] **I** *adj.* **1.** verbündet, verbunden, Bundes...: *♈ Am.* zur Konföderation der Südstaaten gehörig; **2.** mitschuldig; **II** *s.* **3.** Verbündete(r) *m*, Bundesgenosse *m*; **2** *Am. hist.* Konföderierte(r) *m*, Südstaatler *m*; **4.** Kom'plize *m*, Helfershelfer *m*; **III** *v/t. u. v/i.* [-dəreɪt] **5.** (sich) verbünden *od.* vereinigen *od.* zu-schließen; **con·fed·er·a·tion** [kən,fedə'reɪʃn] *s.* **1.** Bund *m*, Bündnis *n*; Zs.-schluss *m*; **2.** Staatenbund *m*: *Swiss ♈* (Schweizer) Eidgenossenschaft *f*.

con·fer [kən'fɜː] **I** *v/t.* **1.** *Titel etc.* verleihen, er-, zuteilen, über'tragen, *Gunst* erweisen (*on, upon dat.*); **2.** *nur noch Imperativ, abbr.* **cf.** vergleiche; **II** *v/i.* **3.** sich beraten, Rücksprache nehmen, verhandeln (*with* mit); **con·fer·ee** [,kɒnfə'riː] *s. Am.* **1.** Konfe'renzteilnehmer *m*; **2.** Empfänger *m* *eines Titels etc.*; **con·fer·ence** ['kɒnfərəns] *s.* **1.** Konfe'renz *f*: a) Tagung *f*, Sitzung *f*, Zs.-kunft *f*, b) Besprechung *f*, Beratung *f*, Verhandlung *f*: *at the ~* auf der Konferenz *od.* Tagung; *in ~* bei e-r Besprechung (*with* mit); *~ call teleph.* Sammel-, Konferenzgespräch *n*; **2.** Verband *m*; *Am. sport* Liga *f*; **con·fer·ment** [-mənt] *s.* Verleihung *f* (*on, upon* an *acc.*).

con·fess [kən'fes] **I** *v/t.* **1.** *Schuld etc.* bekennen, (ein)gestehen; anerkennen, zugeben (*a. that* dass); **2.** *eccl.* a) beichten, b) *j-m* die Beichte abnehmen; **II** *v/i.* **3.** (*to*) (ein)gestehen (*acc.*), sich schuldig bekennen (*gen. od. an acc.*); **4.** *eccl.* beichten; **con·fessed** [-st] *adj.* □ zugestanden; erklärt: *a ~ enemy* ein erklärter Gegner; **con·fess·ed·ly** [-sɪdlɪ] *adv.* zugestandenermaßen; **con·fes·sion** [-eʃn] *s.* **1.** Geständnis *n* (*a. ♈*), Bekenntnis *n*: *by* (*od. on*) *his own ~* nach (s-m) eigenen Geständnis; **2.** Einräumung *f*, Zugeständnis *n*; **3.** *♈ Zivilrecht:* Anerkenntnis *n*; **4.** *eccl.* Beichte *f*: *dying ~* Geständnis *n* auf dem Sterbebett; **5.** *eccl.* Konfessi'on *f*: a) Glaubensbekenntnis *n*, b) Glaubensgemeinschaft *f*; **con·fes·sion·al** [-eʃənl] **I** *adj.* konfessio'nell, Bekenntnis...; Beicht...; **II** *s.* Beichtstuhl *m*; **con·fes·sor** [-sə] *s.* **1.** (Glaubens)Bekenner *m*; **2.** *eccl.* Beichtvater *m*.

con·fet·ti [kən'fetɪ] (*Ital.*) *s. pl. sg. konstr.* Kon'fetti *n*.

con·fi·dant [,kɒnfɪ'dænt] *s.* Vertraute(r) *m*, Mitwisser *m*; **,con·fi'dante** [-'dænt] *s.* Vertraute *f*, Mitwisserin *f*.

con·fide [kən'faɪd] **I** *v/i.* **1.** sich anvertrauen; (ver)trauen (*in dat.*); **II** *v/t.* (*to*) **2.** vertraulich mitteilen, anvertrauen (*dat.*); **3.** *j-n* betrauen mit.

con·fi·dence ['kɒnfɪdəns] *s.* **1.** (*in*) Vertrauen *n* (auf *acc.*, zu), Zutrauen *n* (zu): *have* (*od. place*) *~ in s.o.* zu j-m

---

Vertrauen haben; *take s.o. into one's ~* j-n ins Vertrauen ziehen; *be in s.o.'s ~* j-s Vertrauen genießen; *in ~* vertraulich; **2.** Selbstvertrauen *n*, Zuversicht *f*; Über'zeugung *f*; **3.** vertrauliche Mitteilung, Geheimnis *n*; → *vote* 1; *~ game s.*, *~ trick s.* **1.** a) (aufgelegter) Schwindel, b) Hochstape'lei *f*; *~ man s.* [*irr.*], *~ trick·ster s.* **1.** a) Betrüger *m*, b) Hochstapler *m*; **2.** *weitS.* Ga'nove *m*.

con·fi·dent ['kɒnfɪdənt] *adj.* □ **1.** (*of, that*) über'zeugt (von, dass), gewiss, sicher (*gen.*, dass); **2.** vertrauensvoll; **3.** zuversichtlich, getrost; **4.** selbstsicher; **5.** eingebildet, kühn; **con·fi·den·tial** [,kɒnfɪ'denʃəl] *adj.* □ **1.** vertraulich, geheim; **2.** in'tim, vertraut, Vertrauens...: *~ agent* Geheimagent *m*; *~ clerk* † Prokurist *m*; *~ secretary* Privatsekretär(in); **con·fi·den·tial·ly** [,kɒnfɪ'denʃəlɪ] *adv.* im Vertrauen: *~ speaking* unter uns gesagt; **con·fid·ing** [kən'faɪdɪŋ] *adj.* □ vertrauensvoll, zutraulich.

con·fig·u·ra·tion [kən,fɪgjʊ'reɪʃn] *s.* **1.** Gestalt(ung) *f*, Bau *m*, Struk'tur *f*; Anordnung *f*, Stellung *f*; **2.** *ast.* Konfigurati'on *f*, A'spekt *m*; **3.** *Computer etc.:* Konfigurati'on *f*; **con'fig·ure** [-'fɪgə] *v/t.* kon,figu'rieren (*a. Computersystem*).

con·fine **I** *s.* ['kɒnfaɪn] *mst pl.* **1.** Grenze *f*, Grenzgebiet *n*; *fig.* Rand *m*, Schwelle *f*; **II** *v/t.* [kən'faɪn] **2.** begrenzen; be-, einschränken (*to auf acc.*): *~ o.s. to* sich beschränken auf; *be ~d to* beschränkt sein auf (*acc.*); **3.** einsperren, einschließen: *~d to bed* bettlägerig; *~d to one's room* ans Zimmer gefesselt; *be ~d to barracks* Kasernenarrest haben, die Kaserne nicht verlassen dürfen; **4.** *pass.* (*of*) niederkommen (mit), entbunden werden (von); **con'fined** [-nd] *adj.* **1.** beschränkt *etc.* (→ *confine* 2, 3); **2.** ✚ verstopft; **con'fine·ment** [-mənt] *s.* **1.** Beschränkung *f* (*to* auf *acc.*); Beengtheit *f*; Gebundenheit *f*; **2.** Haft *f*, Gefangenschaft *f*; Ar'rest *m*: *close ~* strenge Haft; *solitary ~* Einzelhaft; **3.** Niederkunft *f*, Wochenbett *n*.

con·firm [kən'fɜːm] *v/t.* **1.** *Nachricht, Auftrag, Wahrheit etc.* bestätigen; **2.** *Entschluss* bekräftigen; bestärken (*s.o. in s.th.* j-n in e-r Sache); **3.** *Macht etc.* festigen; **4.** *eccl.* konfirmieren; *R.C.* firmen; **con'firm·a·ble** [-məbl] *adj.* zu bestätigen(d); **con·firm·and** ['kɒnfəmænd] *s. eccl.* a) Konfir'mand(in), b) *R.C.* Firmling *m*; **con·fir·ma·tion** [,kɒnfə'meɪʃn] *s.* **1.** Bestätigung *f*; Bekräftigung *f*; **2.** Festigung *f*; **3.** *eccl.* Konfirmati'on *f*; *R.C.* Firmung *f*; **con'firm·a·tive** [-mətɪv] *adj.* □, **con'firm·a·to·ry** [-mətərɪ] *adj.* bestätigend: *~ letter* Bestätigungsschreiben *n*; **con'firmed** [-md] *fig.* fest, hartnäckig, eingewurzelt, unverbesserlich, Gewohnheits...; chronisch: *~ bachelor* eingefleischter Junggeselle.

con·fis·cate ['kɒnfɪskeɪt] *v/t.* beschlagnahmen, einziehen, konfiszieren; **con·fis·ca·tion** [,kɒnfɪ'skeɪʃn] *s.* Einziehung *f*, Beschlagnahme *f*, Konfiszierung *f*; † Plünderung *f*; **con·fis·ca·to·ry** [kən'fɪskətərɪ] *adj.* konfiszierend, Beschlagnahme...; † räuberisch.

con·fla·gra·tion [,kɒnflə'greɪʃn] *s.* Feuersbrunst *f*, (großer) Brand.

con·flict **I** *s.* ['kɒnflɪkt] **1.** Kon'flikt *m*: a) Zs.-prall *m*, Zs.-stoß *m*, Kampf *m*, Ausein'andersetzung *f*, Kollisi'on *f*, Streit *m*, b) 'Widerstreit *m*, -spruch *m*: *armed ~* bewaffnete Auseinanderset-

---

zung; *inner ~* innerer (*od.* seelischer) Konflikt; *~ of interests* Interessenkonflikt, -kollision; *~ of laws* Gesetzeskollision, *weitS.* internationales Privatrecht; **II** *v/i.* [kən'flɪkt] **2.** (*with*) kollidieren, im 'Widerspruch *od.* Gegensatz stehen (zu); **3.** sich wider'sprechen; **con·flict·ing** [kən'flɪktɪŋ] *adj.* wider'streitend, gegensätzlich; *a. ♈* entgegenstehend, kollidierend.

con·flu·ence ['kɒnflʊəns] *s.* **1.** Zs.-fluss *m*; **2.** Zustrom *m*, Zulauf *m* (*Menschen*); **3.** (Menschen)Menge *f*; **'con·flu·ent** [-nt] *adj.* zs.-fließend, -laufend; **II** *s.* Nebenfluss *m*; **con·flux** ['kɒnflʌks] → *confluence*.

con·form [kən'fɔːm] **I** *v/t.* **1.** (*a. o.s.*) sich anpassen (*to dat. od. an acc.*); **II** *v/i.* **2.** (*to*) sich anpassen (*dat.*), sich richten (nach); sich fügen (*dat.*); entsprechen (*dat.*); **3.** *eccl. Brit.* sich der engl. Staatskirche unter'werfen; **con'form·a·ble** [-məbl] *adj.* □ (*to*) **1.** kon'form, gleichförmig (mit); entsprechend, gemäß (*dat.*); **2.** vereinbar (mit); **3.** fügsam, nachgiebig; **con'form·ance** [-məns] *s.* Anpassung *f* (*to* an *acc.*); Über'einstimmung *f* (*with* mit): *in ~ with* gemäß (*dat.*); **con·for·ma·tion** [,kɒnfɔː'meɪʃn] *s.* **1.** Anpassung *f*, Angleichung *f* (*to* an *acc.*); **2.** Gestalt (-ung) *f*, Anordnung *f*, Bau *m*; **con'form·ism** [-mɪzəm] *s.* Konfor'mismus *m*; **con'form·ist** [-mɪst] *s.* Konfor'mist (-in): a) Angepasste(r *m*) *f*), b) Anhänger(in) der engl. Staatskirche; **con'form·i·ty** [-mətɪ] *s.* **1.** Gleichförmigkeit *f*, Ähnlichkeit *f*, Über'einstimmung *f*: *in ~ with* in Übereinstimmung mit, gemäß (*dat.*); **2.** (*to*) Anpassung *f* (an *acc.*); Befolgung *f* (*gen.*); **3.** *hist.* Zugehörigkeit *f* zur englischen Staatskirche.

con·found [kən'faʊnd] *v/t.* **1.** vermengen, verwechseln (*with* mit); **2.** in Unordnung bringen, verwirren; **3.** bestürzen, verblüffen; **4.** vereiteln; **5.** [*a.* ,kɒn-] F *~ him!* zum Teufel mit ihm!; *~ it!* verdammt!; **con'founded** [-dɪd] F **I** *adj.* □ (*a. int.*) verwünscht, verflixt; scheußlich; **II** *adv.*, *a. ~·ly* 'verdammt' (*kalt, etc.*).

con·fra·ter·ni·ty [,kɒnfrə'tɜːnətɪ] *s.* **1.** *bsd. eccl.* Bruderschaft *f*, Gemeinschaft *f*; **2.** Brüderschaft *f*; **con·frère** ['kɒnfreə] (*Fr.*) *s.* Amtsbruder *m*, Kol'lege *m*.

con·front [kən'frʌnt] *v/t.* **1.** (*oft feindlich*) gegen'übertreten, -stehen (*dat.*); **2.** mutig begegnen (*dat.*); **3.** *~ s.o. with* j-n konfrontieren mit, j-m *et.* entgegenhalten; *be ~ed with* sich gegenübersehen, gegenüberstehen (*dat.*); **con·fron·ta·tion** [,kɒnfrʌn'teɪʃn] *s.* Gegen'überstellung *f*, (*a. feindliche*) Konfrontati'on.

Con·fu·cian [kən'fjuːʃən] **I** *adj.* konfuzi'anisch; **II** *s.* Konfuzi'aner(in); **Con'fu·cian·ism** [-nɪzəm] *s.* Konfuzia'nismus *m*.

con·fuse [kən'fjuːz] *v/t.* **1.** verwechseln, durchein'ander bringen (*with* mit); **2.** verwirren: a) verlegen machen, aus der Fassung bringen, b) in Unordnung bringen; **3.** verworren *od.* undeutlich machen; **con'fused** [-zd] *adj.* □ **1.** verwirrt: a) kon'fus, verworren, wirr, b) verlegen, bestürzt; **2.** undeutlich, verworren: *~ sounds*; **con'fus·ing** [-zɪŋ] *adj.* verwirrend; **con'fu·sion** [-uːʒn] *s.* **1.** Verwirrung *f*, Durchein'ander *n*, Unordnung *f*, Wirrwarr *m*; **2.** Aufruhr *m*, Lärm *m*; **3.** Bestürzung *f*: *put s.o. to ~* j-n in Verlegenheit brin-

C

gen; **4.** Verworrenheit f; **5.** geistige Verwirrung; **6.** Verwechslung f.

con·fut·a·ble [kən'fju:təbl] adj. wider-'legbar; **con·fu·ta·tion** [‚kɒnfjuː'teɪʃn] s. Wider'legung f; **con·fute** [kən'fjuːt] v/t. **1.** et. wider'legen; **2.** j-n wider'legen, e-s Irrtums über'führen.

con·geal [kən'dʒiːl] **I** v/t. gefrieren od. gerinnen od. erstarren lassen (a. fig.); **II** v/i. gefrieren, gerinnen, erstarren (a. fig.); fest werden; **con'geal·ment** [-mənt] → congelation 1.

con·ge·la·tion [‚kɒndʒɪ'leɪʃn] s. **1.** Gefrieren n, Gerinnen n, Erstarren n, Festwerden n; **2.** gefrorene (etc.) Masse.

con·ge·ner ['kɒndʒɪnə] bsd. biol. **I** s. gleichartiges od. verwandtes Ding od. Wesen; **II** adj. (art- od. stamm)verwandt (**to** mit); **con·gen·er·ous** [kən'dʒenərəs] adj. gleichartig, verwandt.

con·gen·ial [kən'dʒiːnjəl] adj. □ **1.** (**with**) kongeni'al (dat.), (geistes)verwandt (mit od. dat.); **2.** sym'pathisch, zusagend, angenehm (**to** dat.): be ~ zusagen; **3.** zuträglich (**to** dat.); **4.** freundlich; **5.** passend, angemessen, entsprechend (**to** dat.); **con·ge·ni·al·i·ty** [kən-‚dʒiːnɪ'ælətɪ] s. **1.** Geistesverwandtschaft f; **2.** Zuträglichkeit f.

con·gen·i·tal [kən'dʒenɪtl] adj. □ angeboren: ~ **defect** Geburtsfehler m; **con'gen·i·tal·ly** [-təlɪ] adv. von Geburt (an); von Na'tur.

con·ger ['kɒŋgə], ~ **eel** [‚kɒŋgər'iːl] s. Meeral m.

con·ge·ries [kɒn'dʒɪərɪːz] s. sg. u. pl. Anhäufung f, (wirre) Masse.

con·gest [kən'dʒest] **I** v/t. **1.** zs.-drängen, über'füllen, anhäufen, stauen; **2.** fig. über'schwemmen; **3.** verstopfen; **II** v/i. **4.** sich ansammeln, sich stauen, sich verstopfen; **con'gest·ed** [-tɪd] adj. **1.** über'füllt (**with** von); über'völkert: ~ **area** Ballungsraum m; **2.** ✽ mit Blut über'füllt; **con'ges·tion** [-tʃən] s. **1.** Anhäufung f, Andrang m, Stauung f, Über'füllung f: ~ **of population** Übervölkerung f; **traffic** ~ Verkehrsstauung; **2.** ✽ Blutandrang m (**of the brain** zum Gehirn), (Gefäß)Stauung f.

con·glo·bate ['kɒŋgləʊbeɪt] **I** adj.(zs.-) geballt, kugelig; **II** v/t. u. v/i. (sich) zs.-ballen (**into** zu).

con·glom·er·ate [kən'glɒməreɪt] **I** v/t. u. v/i. (sich) zs.-ballen, verbinden, anhäufen; **II** adj. [-rət] zs.-geballt; fig. zs.-gewürfelt; **III** s. [-rət] fig. (An)Häufung f, Gemisch n, zs.-gewürfelte Masse, Konglome'rat n (a. geol.); **con·glom·er·a·tion** [kən‚glɒmə'reɪʃn] → conglomerate III.

con·glu·ti·nate [kən'gluːtɪneɪt] **I** v/t. zs.- leimen, -kitten; **II** v/i. zs.-kleben, -haften; **con·glu·ti·na·tion** [kən-‚gluːtɪ'neɪʃn] s. Zs.-kleben n; Verbindung f.

Con·go·lese [‚kɒŋgəʊ'liːz] hist. **I** adj. Kongo..., kongo'lesisch; **II** s. Kongo'lese m, Kongo'lesin f.

con·grat·u·late [kən'grætjʊleɪt] v/t. j-m gratulieren, Glück wünschen (j-n beglückwünschen (**on** zu) (alle a. o.s. sich); **con·grat·u·la·tion** [kən‚grætjʊ'leɪʃn] s. Glückwunsch m: ~**s!** ich gratuliere!; **con·grat·u·la·tor** [-tə] s. Gratu'lant (-in); **con·grat·u·la·to·ry** [-lətərɪ] adj. Glückwunsch..., Gratulations...

con·gre·gate ['kɒŋgrɪgeɪt] v/t. u. v/i. (sich) (ver)sammeln.

con·gre·ga·tion [‚kɒŋgrɪ'geɪʃn] s. **1.** (Kirchen)Gemeinde f; **2.** Versammlung f; **3.** Brit. univ. Versammlung f des Lehrkörpers od. des Se'nats; **con·gre-'ga·tion·al** [-ʃənl] adj. eccl. **1.** Gemeinde...; **2.** ♉ unabhängig; ♉ **chapel** Kapelle f der ‚freien' Gemeinden; **‚Con·gre'ga·tion·al·ism** [-ʃnəlɪzəm] s. eccl. Selbstverwaltung f der ‚freien' Kirchengemeinden, Independen'tismus m; **‚Con·gre'ga·tion·al·ist** [-ʃnəlɪst] s. Mitglied n e-r ‚freien' Kirchengemeinde.

con·gress ['kɒŋgres] s. **1.** Kon'gress m, Tagung f; **2.** pol. Am. ♉ Kon'gress m, gesetzgebende Versammlung; **3.** Geschlechtsverkehr m.

con·gres·sion·al [kən'greʃənl] adj. **1.** Kongress...; **2.** pol. Am. ♉ Kongress...: ♉ **medal** Verdienstmedaille f.

'Con·gress·man [-mən] s. [irr.] pol. Mitglied n des amer. Repräsen'tantenhauses, Kon'gressabgeordnete(r) m.

con·gru·ence ['kɒŋgruəns] s. **1.** Über-'einstimmung f; **2.** ♉ Kongru'enz f; **'con·gru·ent** [-nt] adj. kongru'ent: a) (**with**) über'einstimmend (mit), entsprechend (dat.), b) ♉ deckungsgleich; **con·gru·i·ty** [kɒŋ'gruːɪtɪ] s. **1.** Über-'einstimmung f; Angemessenheit f; **2.** Folgerichtigkeit f; **3.** ♉ Kongru'enz f; **'con·gru·ous** [-ʊəs] adj. □ **1.** (**to, with**) über'einstimmend (mit), entsprechend (dat.); **2.** folgerichtig; passend.

con·ic ['kɒnɪk] **I** adj. → conical; **II** s. a. ~ **section** ♉ a) Kegelschnitt m, b) pl. → conics; **'con·i·cal** [-kl] adj. □ konisch, kegelförmig: ~ **frustrum** ♉ Kegelstumpf m; **co·nic·i·ty** [kə'nɪsətɪ] s. Konizi'tät f, Kegelform f; **'con·ics** [-ks] s. pl. sg. konstr. ♉ Lehre f von den Kegelschnitten.

co·ni·fer ['kɒnɪfə] s. ♉ Koni'fere f, Nadelbaum m; **co·nif·er·ous** [kəʊ'nɪfərəs] adj. ♉ a) Zapfen tragend, b) Nadel...: ~ **tree**.

con·jec·tur·a·ble [kən'dʒektʃərəbl] adj. □ zu vermuten(d); **con'jec·tur·al** [-rəl] adj. □ mutmaßlich; **con·jec·ture** [kən'dʒektʃə] **I** s. **1.** Vermutung f, Mutmaßung f, (vage) I'dee; **II** v/t. **2.** vermuten, mutmaßen; **III** v/i. **3.** Mutmaßungen anstellen, mutmaßen.

con·join [kən'dʒɔɪn] v/t. u. v/i. (sich) verbinden od. vereinigen.

con·joint ['kɒndʒɔɪnt] adj. □ verbunden, vereinigt, gemeinsam, Mit...; **'con·joint·ly** [-lɪ] adv. zu'sammen, gemeinsam.

con·ju·gal ['kɒndʒʊgl] adj. □ ehelich, Ehe..., Gatten...

con·ju·gate ['kɒndʒʊgeɪt] **I** v/t. **1.** ling. konjugieren, beugen; **II** v/i. **2.** biol. sich paaren; **III** adj. [-gɪt] **3.** verbunden, gepaart; **4.** ling. wurzelverwandt; **5.** ♉ zugeordnet; **6.** ♉ paarig; **IV** s. [-gɪt] **7.** ling. wurzelverwandtes Wort; **con·ju·ga·tion** [‚kɒndʒʊ'geɪʃn] s. ling., biol., ✽ Konjugati'on f, ling. a. Beugung f.

con·junct [kən'dʒʌŋkt] adj. □ verbunden, vereint, gemeinsam; **con'junc·tion** [-kʃən] s. **1.** Verbindung f: **in** ~ **with** zusammen mit; **2.** Zs.-treffen n; **3.** ast., ling. Konjunkti'on f; **con·junc·ti·va** [‚kɒndʒʌŋk'taɪvə] s. anat. Bindehaut f; **con'junc·tive** [-tɪv] **I** adj. □ **1.** verbindend, Verbindungs...: ~ **tissue** anat. Bindegewebe n; **2.** ling. 'konjunktivisch: ~ **mood** Konjunktiv m; **II** s. **3.** ling. 'Konjunktiv m; **con'junc·tive·ly** [-tɪvlɪ] adv. verbindend; **con·junc·ti·vi·tis** [kən‚dʒʌŋktɪ'vaɪtɪs] s. ✽ Bindehautentzündung f; **con'junc·ture** [-tʃə] s. **1.** Zs.-treffen n (von Umständen); **2.** 'Umstände pl.; **3.** Krise f; **4.** ast. Konjunkti'on f.

con·ju·ra·tion [‚kɒndʒʊə'reɪʃn] s. **1.** feierliche Anrufung; Beschwörung f; **2.** a) Zauberformel f, b) Zaube'rei f.

con·jure¹ [kən'dʒʊə] v/t. beschwören, inständig bitten (**to** inf. zu inf.).

con·jure² ['kʌndʒə] **I** v/t. **1.** Geist etc. beschwören: ~ **up** heraufbeschwören (a. fig.), zitieren, hervorzaubern; **2.** behexen, (be)zaubern; ~ **away** wegzaubern, bannen; **II** v/i. **3.** zaubern, hexen: **a name to** ~ **with** ein Name, der Wunder wirkt; **'con·jur·er**, **'con·jur·or** [-dʒərə] s. **1.** Zauberer m, Zauberin f; **2.** Zauberkünstler m, Taschenspieler m; **'con·jur·ing trick** [-dʒərɪŋ] s. Zauberkunststück n.

conk¹ [kɒŋk] s. sl. ‚Riecher' m (Nase); Am. a. ‚Birne' (Kopf).

conk² [kɒŋk] v/i. sl. mst ~ **out 1.** ‚streiken', ‚den Geist aufgeben' (Fernseher etc.), ‚absterben' (Motor); **2.** ‚umkippen', ohnmächtig werden; **3.** ‚abkratzen', sterben.

con·ker ['kɒŋkə] s. F Ka'stanie f.

conn [kɒn] v/t. ♉ Schiff steuern.

con·nate ['kɒneɪt] adj. **1.** angeboren; **2.** biol. verwachsen.

con·nat·u·ral [kə'nætʃrəl] adj. □ **1.** (**to**) gleicher Na'tur (wie); verwandt (dat.); **2.** angeboren.

con·nect [kə'nekt] **I** v/t. **1.** verbinden, verknüpfen (mst **with** mit): **be** ~**ed** (**with**) in Verbindung (mit) od. in Beziehungen (zu) treten od. stehen; **be well** ~**ed** fig. gute Beziehungen haben; **2.** ⚡ (**to**) anschließen (an acc.), verbinden (mit) (a. teleph.), zuschalten (dat.), Kon'takt herstellen zwischen (dat.); **3.** ⚙ (**to**) verbinden, zs.-fügen, koppeln (mit), ankuppeln (an acc.); **II** v/i. **4.** in Verbindung od. Zs.-hang treten od. stehen; **5.** 🚂 etc. Anschluss haben (**with** an acc.); **6.** Boxen: ‚landen' (**with a blow** e-n Schlag); **con'nect·ed** [-tɪd] adj. □ **1.** zs.-hängend; **2.** verwandt: ~ **by marriage** verschwägert; → **connect 1**; **3.** (**with**) beteiligt (an dat., bei), verwickelt (in acc.); **con'nect·ed·ly** [-tɪdlɪ] adv. zs.-hängend; logisch; **con'nect·ing** [-tɪŋ] s. Binde..., Verbindungs..., Anschluss...: ~ **flight** Anschlussflug m; ~ **link** Bindeglied n; ~ **rod** ⚙ Kurbel-, Pleuelstange f; ~ **shaft** Transmissionswelle f; ~ **train** Anschlusszug m.

con·nec·tion [kə'nekʃn] s. **1.** Verbindung f; **2.** ⚡ Verbindung f, Bindeglied n: **hot-water** ~**s** Heißwasseranlage f; **3.** Zs.-hang m, Beziehung f: **in this** ~ in diesem Zs.-hang; **in** ~ **with** mit Bezug auf; **4.** per'sönliche Beziehung od. Verbindung; Verwandtschaft f, Verwandte(r m) f; **5.** pl. gute od. nützliche Beziehungen; Bekannten-, Kundenkreis m; **6.** ⚡ allg. Verbindung f, Anschluss m (beide a. ⚙, 🚂, teleph. etc.), Verbindungs-, Bindeglied n, ⚡ Schaltung f, Schaltverbindung f: ~ **fee** Anschlussgebühr f; ~ **plug** Anschlussstecker m; **catch one's** ~ 🚂 Anschluss erreichen; **run in** ~ **with** Anschluss haben an (acc.); **7.** (bsd. religiöse) Gemeinschaft f.

con'nec·tive [-ktɪv] **I** adj. verbindend: ~ **tissue** anat. Binde-, Zellgewebe n; **II** s. ling. Bindewort n.

con·nex·ion → connection.

con·ning tow·er ['kɒnɪŋ] s. ♉, ✕ Kom'mandoturm m.

con·niv·ance [kə'naɪvəns] s. stillschweigende Duldung od. Einwilligung (a. ⚖), bewusstes Über'sehen (**at, in** gen.); ⚖ Begünstigung f; **con·nive** [kə'naɪv] v/i. (**at**) stillschweigend dulden (acc.), ein Auge zudrücken (bei), Vorschub leisten (*dat.*).

con·nois·seur [ˌkɒnəˈsɜː] (*Fr.*) *s.* (Kunst- *etc.*)Kenner *m*: ***~ of*** (*od.* ***in***) ***wines*** Weinkenner.

con·no·ta·tion [ˌkɒnəʊˈteɪʃn] *s.* **1.** Mitbezeichnung *f*; (Neben)Bedeutung *f*; **2.** *phls.* Begriffsinhalt *m*; **con·note** [kɒˈnəʊt] *v/t.* mitbezeichnen, (zu'gleich) bedeuten.

con·nu·bi·al [kəˈnjuːbjəl] *adj.* □ ehelich, Ehe...; **con·nu·bi·al·i·ty** [kəˌnjuːbɪˈælətɪ] *s.* **1.** Ehestand *m*; **2.** eheliche Zärtlichkeiten *pl.*

co·noid [ˈkəʊnɔɪd] **I** *adj.* kegelförmig; **II** *s.* 𝔸 a) Kono'id *n*, b) Kono'ide *f* (*Fläche*).

con·quer [ˈkɒŋkə] **I** *v/t.* **1.** erobern, einnehmen, Besitz ergreifen von; **2.** *fig.* erobern, gewinnen; **3.** besiegen, über'winden; unter'werfen; **4.** *fig.* über'winden, bezwingen, Herr werden über (*acc.*); **II** *v/i.* **5.** siegen; Eroberungen machen; **'con·quer·ing** [-kərɪŋ] *adj.* siegreich; **'con·quer·or** [-kərə] *s.* **1.** Eroberer *m*; Sieger *m*: ***the ℒ*** *hist.* Wilhelm der Eroberer; **2.** F Entscheidungsspiel *n*.

con·quest [ˈkɒŋkwest] *s.* **1.** Eroberung *f*: a) Einnahme *f*: ***the ℒ*** *hist.* die normannische Eroberung, b) erobertes Gebiet, c) *fig.* Erringung *f*; **2.** Bezwingung *f*; **3.** *fig.* ,Eroberung' *f*: ***make a ~ of s.o.*** j-n erobern.

con·san·guine [kɒnˈsæŋgwɪn] *adj.* blutsverwandt; **con·san·guin·i·ty** [ˌkɒnsæŋˈgwɪnətɪ] *s.* Blutsverwandtschaft *f*.

con·science [ˈkɒnʃəns] *s.* Gewissen *n*: ***guilty ~*** schlechtes Gewissen; ***for ~ sake*** um das Gewissen zu beruhigen; ***in all ~*** F wahrhaftig; ***have s.th. on one's ~*** ein schlechtes Gewissen haben wegen e-r Sache; **~ clause** *s.* ⚖ Gewissensklausel *f*; **~ mon·ey** *s.* ano'nyme Steuernachzahlung; **'~-proof** *adj.* ,abgebrüht'; **'~-ˌstrick·en** *adj.* von Gewissensbissen gepeinigt, reuevoll.

con·sci·en·tious [ˌkɒnʃɪˈenʃəs] *adj.* □ gewissenhaft, Gewissens...: ***~ objector*** Kriegs-, Wehrdienstverweigerer *m* (*aus Gewissensgründen*); **ˌcon·sci'en·tious·ness** [-nɪs] *s.* Gewissenhaftigkeit *f*.

-conscious [kɒnʃəs] *adj.* in *Zssgn* ...bewusst; ...freudig, ...begeistert.

con·scious [ˈkɒnʃəs] *adj.* □ **1.** *pred.* bei Bewusstsein; **2.** bewusst: ***be ~ of*** sich bewusst sein (*gen.*), wissen von; ***be ~ that*** wissen *od.* überzeugt sein, dass; ***she became ~ that*** es kam ihr zum Bewusstsein, dass; **3.** wissentlich, bewusst: ***a ~ liar*** ein bewusster Lügner; **4.** (selbst)bewusst, über'zeugt: ***a ~ artist*** ein überzeugter Künstler; **5.** denkend: ***man is a ~ being***; **'con·scious·ly** [-lɪ] *adv.* bewusst, wissentlich; gewollt; **'con·scious·ness** [-nɪs] *s.* **1.** Bewusstsein *n*: ***lose ~*** das Bewusstsein verlieren; ***regain ~*** wieder zu sich kommen; **2.** (***of***) Bewusstsein *n* (*gen.*), Wissen *n* (um), Kenntnis *f* (von *od. gen.*): ***~-expanding*** bewusstseinserweiternd (*Droge*); ***~-raising*** Bewusstwerdung *f od.* -machung *f*; **3.** Denken *n*, Empfinden *n*.

con·script [ˈkɒnskrɪpt] **I** *adj.* zwangsweise eingezogen (*Soldat etc.*) *od.* verpflichtet (*Arbeiter*); **II** *s.* ⚔ Dienst-, Wehrpflichtige(r) *m*; ausgehobener Rekrut; **III** *v/t.* [kənˈskrɪpt] *bsd.* ⚔ (zwangsweise) ausheben, einziehen; **con·scrip·tion** [kənˈskrɪpʃn] *s.* **1.** *bsd.* ⚔ Zwangsaushebung *f*, Wehrpflicht *f*: ***industrial ~*** Arbeitsverpflichtung *f*; **2.** *a.* ***~ of wealth*** (Her'anziehung *f* zur) Vermögensabgabe *f*.

con·se·crate [ˈkɒnsɪkreɪt] **I** *v/t.* **1.** *eccl.* weihen; **2.** widmen; **3.** heiligen; **II** *adj.* **4.** geweiht, geheiligt; **con·se·cra·tion** [ˌkɒnsɪˈkreɪʃn] *s.* **1.** *eccl.* Weihung *f*, Einsegnung *f*; **2.** Heiligung *f*; **3.** Widmung *f*, Hingabe *f* (***to*** an *acc.*).

con·se·cu·tion [ˌkɒnsɪˈkjuːʃn] *s.* **1.** (Aufein'ander)Folge *f*, Reihe *f*; logische Folge; **2.** *ling.* Wort-, Zeitfolge *f*; **con·sec·u·tive** [kənˈsekjʊtɪv] *adj.* □ **1.** aufein'ander folgend, fortlaufend: ***six ~ days*** sechs Tage hintereinander; **2.** *ling.* ***~ clause*** Konsekutiv-, Folgesatz *m*; **con·sec·u·tive·ly** [kənˈsekjʊtɪvlɪ] *adv.* nachein'ander, fortlaufend.

con·sen·sus [kənˈsensəs] *s.* **1.** Über'einstimmung *f* (der Meinungen): ***~ of opinion*** übereinstimmende Meinung, allseitige Zustimmung; **2.** ⚕ Wechselwirkung *f* (*Organe*).

con·sent [kənˈsent] **I** *v/i.* **1.** (***to***) zustimmen (*dat.*), einwilligen (in *acc.*); **2.** sich bereit erklären (***to*** *inf.* zu *inf.*); **II** *s.* **3.** (***to***) Zustimmung *f* (zu), Einwilligung *f* (in *acc.*), Genehmigung *f* (für), Einverständnis *n* (zu): ***age of ~*** ⚖ (*bsd.* Ehe-) Mündigkeit *f*; ***with one ~*** einstimmig; ***by common ~*** mit allgemeiner Zustimmung; → ***silence*** 1; **con'sen·tient** [-nʃənt] *adj.* zustimmend.

con·se·quence [ˈkɒnsɪkwəns] *s.* **1.** Konse'quenz *f*, Folge *f*, Resul'tat *n*, Wirkung *f*: ***in ~*** folglich, daher; ***in ~ of*** infolge von (*od. gen.*), wegen; ***in ~ of which*** weswegen; ***take the ~s*** die Folgen tragen; ***with the ~ that*** mit dem Ergebnis, dass; **2.** (Schluss)Folgerung *f*, Schluss *m*; **3.** Wichtigkeit *f*, Bedeutung *f*, Einfluss *m*: ***of no ~*** ohne Bedeutung, unwichtig; ***a man of ~*** ein bedeutender *od.* einflussreicher Mann; **4.** *pl. mst sg. konstr.* ein Erzählspiel; **'con·se·quent** [-nt] **I** *adj.* □ → ***consequently***; **1.** (***on***) folgend (auf *acc.*), sich ergebend (aus); **2.** *phls.* logisch (richtig); **II** *s.* **3.** Folge(-erscheinung) *f*, Folgerung *f*, Schluss *m*; **4.** *ling.* Nachsatz *m*; **con·se·quen·tial** [ˌkɒnsɪˈkwenʃl] *adj.* □ **1.** sich ergebend (***on*** aus): ***~ damage*** ⚖ Folgeschaden *m*; **2.** logisch (richtig); **3.** 'indiˌrekt; **4.** wichtigtuerisch; **'con·se·quent·ly** [-ntlɪ] *adv.* **1.** folglich, deshalb; **2.** als Folge.

con·serv·an·cy [kənˈsɜːvənsɪ] *s.* **1.** Aufsichtsbehörde *f* für Flüsse, Häfen *etc.*; **2.** Forstbehörde *f*: ***nature ~*** Naturschutz(amt *n*) *m*; **con·ser·va·tion** [ˌkɒnsəˈveɪʃn] *s.* **1.** Erhaltung *f*, Bewahrung *f*; Instandhaltung *f*, Schutz *m* (*von Forsten, Flüssen, Boden*); Na'tur-, Umweltschutz *m*: ***~ of energy*** *phys.* Erhaltung der Energie; **2.** Haltbarmachung *f*, Konservierung *f*; **con·ser·va·tion·ist** [ˌkɒnsəˈveɪʃənɪst] *s.* Na'tur- *od.* 'Umweltschützer *m*.

con·serv·a·tism [kənˈsɜːvətɪzəm] *s.* Konserva'tismus *m* (*a. pol.*); **con'serv·a·tive** [-tɪv] **I** *adj.* **1.** erhaltend, konservierend; **2.** konserva'tiv (*a. pol., mst ℒ*); **3.** zu'rückhaltend, vorsichtig (*Schätzung etc.*); **4.** unauffällig: ***~ dress***; **II** *s.* **5.** *ℒ pol.* Konserva'tive(r) *m*.

con·ser·va·toire [kənˈsɜːvətwɑː] (*Fr.*) *s. bsd. Brit.* Konserva'torium *n*, Hochschule *f* für Mu'sik (*etc.*).

con·ser·va·tor [kənˈsɜːvətə] *s.* **1.** Konser'vator *m*, Mu'seumsdiˌrektor *m*; **2.** ⚖ *Am.* Vormund *m*; **con'serv·a·to·ry** [-trɪ] *s.* **1.** Treib-, Gewächshaus *n*, Wintergarten *m*; **2.** → ***conservatoire***;

con·serve [kənˈsɜːv] **I** *v/t.* **1.** erhalten, bewahren; beibehalten; **2.** schonen, sparsam 'umgehen mit; **3.** einmachen, konservieren; **II** *s.* **4.** *mst pl.* Eingemachtes *n*, Konfi'türe *f*.

con·sid·er [kənˈsɪdə] **I** *v/t.* **1.** nachdenken über (*acc.*), (sich) über'legen, erwägen: ***~ a plan***; **2.** in Betracht ziehen, berücksichtigen, beachten, bedenken: ***~ his age!*** bedenken Sie sein Alter!; ***all things ~ed*** wenn man alles in Betracht zieht; → ***considered, considering***; **3.** Rücksicht nehmen auf (*acc.*): ***he never ~s others***; **4.** betrachten *od.* ansehen als, halten für: ***~ s.o.*** (***to be***) ***a fool*** j-n für e-n Narren halten; ***be ~ed rich*** als reich gelten; ***you may ~ yourself lucky*** du kannst dich glücklich schätzen; ***~ yourself at home*** tun Sie, als ob Sie zu Hause wären; ***~ yourself dismissed!*** betrachten Sie sich als entlassen!; **5.** denken, meinen, annehmen, finden (*a.* ***that*** dass); **II** *v/i.* **6.** nachdenken, über'legen; **con'sid·er·a·ble** [-dərəbl] **I** *adj.* □ beträchtlich, erheblich; bedeutend (*a. Person*); **II** *s. bsd. Am.* F e-e Menge, viel.

con·sid·er·ate [kənˈsɪdərət] *adj.* □ rücksichtsvoll, aufmerksam (***towards***, ***of*** gegen): ***be ~ of*** Rücksicht nehmen auf (*acc.*); **con'sid·er·ate·ness** [-nɪs] *s.* Rücksichtnahme *f*; **con·sid·er·a·tion** [kənˌsɪdəˈreɪʃn] *s.* **1.** Erwägung *f*, Über'legung *f*: ***take into ~*** in Betracht *od.* Erwägung ziehen; ***leave out of ~*** außer Betracht lassen, ausklammern; ***the matter is under ~*** die Sache wird (noch) erwogen *od.* geprüft; ***upon ~*** nach Prüfung; **2.** Berücksichtigung *f*; Begründung *f*: ***in ~ of*** in Anbetracht (*gen.*); ***on*** (*od.* ***under***) ***no ~*** unter keinen Umständen; ***that is a ~*** das ist ein triftiger Grund; ***money is no ~*** Geld spielt keine Rolle; **3.** Rücksicht(-nahme) *f* (***for*** auf *acc.*): ***lack of ~*** Rücksichtslosigkeit *f*; **4.** Entgelt *n*, Entschädigung *f*, (vertragliche) Gegenleistung: ***for a ~*** gegen Entgelt; **con'sid·ered** [-dəd] *adj. a.* ***well-~*** wohl überlegt; **con'sid·er·ing** [-rɪŋ] **I** *prp.* in Anbetracht (*gen.*); **II** *adv.* F den 'Umständen nach.

con·sign [kənˈsaɪn] *v/t.* **1.** über'geben, über'liefern; **2.** anvertrauen; **3.** bestimmen (***for, to*** für); **4.** ☤ *Waren* a) (***to***) versenden (an *acc.*), zu-, über'senden (*dat.*), verfrachten (an *acc.*), b) in Kommissi'on *od.* Konsignati'on geben, konsignieren; **con·sign·ee** [ˌkɒnsaɪˈniː] *s.* ☤ **1.** Empfänger *m*, Adres'sat *m*; **2.** *Überseehandel*: Konsigna'tar *m*; **con'sign·ment** [-mənt] *s.* ☤ **1.** a) Über'sendung *f*, b) *Überseehandel*: Konsignati'on *f*: ***~ note*** Frachtbrief *m*; ***in ~*** in Konsignation *od.* Kommission; **2.** a) (Waren)Sendung *f*, b) *Überseehandel*: Konsignati'onsware(n *pl.*) *f*; **con'sign·or** [-nə] *s.* ☤ **1.** Über'sender *m*; **2.** *Überseehandel*: Konsi'gnant *m*.

con·sist [kənˈsɪst] *v/i.* **1.** bestehen, sich zs.-setzen (***of*** aus); **2.** bestehen (***in*** in *dat.*); **con'sist·ence** [-təns] → ***consistency*** 1 *u.* 2; **con'sist·en·cy** [-tənsɪ] *s.* **1.** Konsi'stenz *f*, Beschaffenheit *f*; **2.** Festigkeit *f*, Dichtigkeit *f*, Dicke *f*; **3.** Konse'quenz *f*, Folgerichtigkeit *f*; **4.** Stetigkeit *f*; **5.** Über'einstimmung *f*, Vereinbarkeit *f*; **con'sist·ent** [-tənt] *adj.* □ **1.** konse'quent: a) folgerichtig, logisch, b) gleichmäßig, stetig, unbeirrbar (*a. Person*); **2.** über'einstimmend, vereinbar, im Einklang stehend (***with*** mit); **3.** beständig, kon'stant (*Leistung etc.*); **con'sist·ent·ly** [-təntlɪ] *adv.* **1.** im Einklang (***with*** mit); **2.** 'durchweg;

3. logischerweise.

con·sis·to·ry [kən'sɪstərɪ] *s. eccl.* Konsistorium *n*.

con·so·la·tion [ˌkɒnsə'leɪʃn] *s.* Trost *m*, Tröstung *f*: **poor** ~ schwacher Trost; ~ **goal** *sport* Ehrentor *n*; ~ **prize** Trostpreis *m*.

con·sole¹ [kən'səʊl] *v/t.* j-n trösten: ~ **o.s.** sich trösten (**with** mit).

con·sole² ['kɒnsəʊl] *s.* **1.** Kon'sole *f*: a) △ Krag-, Tragstein *m*, b) Wandgestell *n*: ~ (**table**) Wandtischchen *n*; **2.** (Fernseh-, Mu'sik)Truhe *f*, (Radio)Schrank *m*; **3.** ◎, ♫ Schalt-, Steuerpult *n*, Kon'sole *f*.

con·sol·i·date [kən'sɒlɪdeɪt] **I** *v/t.* **1.** (ver)stärken, festigen, *fig. a.* konsolidieren; **2.** vereinigen: a) zs.-legen, zs.-schließen, b) *Truppen* zs.-ziehen; **3.** ✝ a) *Schulden* konsolidieren, fundieren, b) *Aktien, a.* 🕇 *Klagen* zs.-legen, c) *Gesellschaften* zs.-schließen; **4.** ◎ verdichten; **II** *v/i.* **5.** fest werden; sich festigen (*a. fig.*); **con·sol·i·dat·ed** [-tɪd] *adj.* **1.** fest, dicht, kom'pakt; **2.** *bsd.* ✝ vereinigt, konsolidiert: ~ **annuities** → **consols**; ~ **debt** fundierte Schuld; ♫ **Fund** *Brit.* konsolidierter Staatsfonds; **con·sol·i·da·tion** [kən‚sɒlɪ'deɪʃn] *s.* **1.** (Ver)stärkung *f*, Festigung *f* (*beide a. fig.*); **2.** ✕ a) Zs.-ziehung *f*, b) Ausbau *m*; **3.** ✝ a) Konsolidierung *f*, b) Zs.-legung *f*, Vereinigung *f*, c) Zs.-schluss *m*; **4.** ◎ Verdichtung *f*; **5.** ✓ Flurbereinigung *f*.

con·sols ['kɒnsɒlz] *s. pl.* ✝ *Brit.* Kon'sols *pl.*, konsolidierte Staatsanleihen *pl.*

con·som·mé [kən'sɒmeɪ] (*Fr.*) *s.* Consom'mé *f*, *n* (*klare Kraftbrühe*).

con·so·nance ['kɒnsənəns] *s.* **1.** Zs.-, Gleichklang *m*; **2.** ♪ Konso'nanz *f*; **3.** *fig.* Über'einstimmung *f*, Harmo'nie *f*; **'con·so·nant** [-nt] **I** *adj.* □ **1.** ♪ konso'nant; **2.** über'einstimmend, vereinbar (**with** mit); **3.** gemäß (**to** dat.); **II** *s.* **4.** *ling.* Konso'nant *m*; **con·so·nan·tal** [ˌkɒnsə'næntl] *adj. ling.* konso'nantisch.

con·sort **I** *s.* ['kɒnsɔːt] **1.** Gemahl(in); **2.** ⚓ Geleitschiff *n*; **II** *v/i.* [kən'sɔːt] **3.** (**with**) verkehren (mit), sich gesellen (zu); **4.** (**with**) über'einstimmen (mit), passen (zu); **con·sor·ti·um** [kən'sɔːtjəm] *s.* **1.** Vereinigung *f*, Gruppe *f*, Kon'sortium *n* (*a.* ✝): ~ **of banks** Bankenkonsortium; **2.** 🕇 eheliche Gemeinschaft.

con·spi·cu·i·ty [ˌkɒnspɪ'kjuːətɪ] → **conspicuousness**; **con·spic·u·ous** [kən'spɪkjʊəs] *adj.* □ **1.** deutlich sichtbar; **2.** auffallend: **be** ~ **by** one's **absence** durch Abwesenheit glänzen; **make o.s.** ~ sich auffällig benehmen, auffallen; **render o.s.** ~ sich hervortun; ~ **consumption** Prestigekonsum; **3.** *fig.* bemerkenswert, her'vorragend; **con·spic·u·ous·ness** [kən'spɪkjʊəsnɪs] *s.* **1.** Deutlichkeit *f*; **2.** Auffälligkeit *f*, Augenfälligkeit *f*.

con·spir·a·cy [kən'spɪrəsɪ] *s.* Verschwörung *f*, Kom'plott *n*: ~ **of silence** verabredetes Stillschweigen; ~ (**to commit a crime**) (*strafbare*) Verabredung zur Verübung e-r Straftat; **con·spir·a·tor** [-ətə] *s.* Verschwörer *m*; **con·spir·a·to·ri·al** [kən‚spɪrə'tɔːrɪəl] *adj.* verschwörerisch, Verschwörungs...; **con·spire** [kən'spaɪə] **I** *v/i.* **1.** sich verschwören; sich (heimlich) zs.-tun; 🕇 sich *zu e-r Tat* verabreden; **2.** *fig.* zs.-wirken, (insgeheim) dazu beitragen, sich verschworen haben; **II** *v/t.* **3.** (heimlich) planen, anzetteln.

con·sta·ble ['kʌnstəbl] *s. bsd. Brit.* Poli'zist *m*, Wachtmeister *m*: **special** ~ Hilfspolizist; → **Chief Constable**; **con·stab·u·lar·y** [kən'stæbjʊlərɪ] *s.* Poli'zei(truppe) *f*.

con·stan·cy ['kɒnstənsɪ] *s.* **1.** Beständigkeit *f*, Unveränderlichkeit *f*; **2.** Bestand *m*, Dauer *f*; **3.** *fig.* Standhaftigkeit *f*; Treue *f*; **'con·stant** [-nt] **I** *adj.* □ **1.** (be)ständig, unveränderlich, gleich bleibend, kon'stant; **2.** dauernd, unaufhörlich, stetig, regelmäßig: ~ **rain** anhaltender Regen; → **companion¹**; **3.** standhaft, beharrlich, fest; **4.** verlässlich, treu; **5.** ♃, ⚡, *phys.* kon'stant; **II** *s.* **6.** ♃, *phys.* kon'stante Größe, Kon'stante *f*.

con·stel·la·tion [ˌkɒnstə'leɪʃn] *s.* **1.** Konstellati'on *f*: a) *ast.* Sternbild *n*, b) *fig.* Gruppierung *f*; **2.** glänzende Versammlung.

con·ster·nat·ed ['kɒnstəneɪtɪd] *adj.* bestürzt, konsterniert; **con·ster·na·tion** [ˌkɒnstə'neɪʃn] *s.* Bestürzung *f*.

con·sti·pate ['kɒnstɪpeɪt] *v/t.* ⚚ verstopfen; **con·sti·pa·tion** [ˌkɒnstɪ'peɪʃn] *s.* ⚚ Verstopfung *f*.

con·stit·u·en·cy [kən'stɪtjʊənsɪ] *s.* **1.** Wählerschaft *f*, Wahlkreis *m*; **3.** *Am.* F Kundenkreis *m*; **con·stit·u·ent** [-nt] **I** *adj.* **1.** e-n (Bestand)Teil bildend: ~ **part** Bestandteil *m*; **2.** *pol.* Wähler..., Wahl...: ~ **body** Wählerschaft *f*; **3.** *pol.* konstituierend, verfassunggebend: ~ **assembly** verfassunggebende Versammlung; **II** *s.* **4.** Bestandteil *m*; **5.** 🕇 Vollmachtgeber(in); **6.** *pol.* Wähler (-in); **7.** *ling.* Satzteil *m*; **8.** ♃, *phys.* Kompo'nente *f*.

con·sti·tute ['kɒnstɪtjuːt] *v/t.* **1.** ernennen, einsetzen: ~ **s.o. president** j-n als Präsidenten einsetzen; **2.** *Gesetz* in Kraft setzen; **3.** *oft pol.* gründen, einsetzen, konstituieren: ~ **a committee** e-n Ausschuss einsetzen; **the** ~**d authorities** die verfassungsmäßigen Behörden; **4.** ausmachen, bilden: ~ **a precedent** e-n Präzedenzfall bilden; **be so** ~**d** that so geartet sein, dass.

con·sti·tu·tion [ˌkɒnstɪ'tjuːʃn] *s.* **1.** Zs.-setzung *f*, (Auf)Bau *m*, Beschaffenheit *f*; **2.** Einsetzung *f*, Bildung *f*, Gründung *f*; **3.** Konstituti'on *f*, Körperbau *m*, Na'tur *f*: **by** ~ von Natur; **strong** ~ starke Konstitution; **4.** Gemütsart *f*, Wesen *n*, Veranlagung *f*; **5.** *pol.* Verfassung *f*, Grundgesetz *n*, Satzung *f*; **con·sti·tu·tion·al** [-ʃənl] **I** *adj.* □ **1.** körperlich bedingt, angeboren, veranlagungsgemäß; **2.** *pol.* verfassungsmäßig, rechtsstaatlich, Verfassungs...: ~ **monarchy** konstitutionelle Monarchie; ~ **state** Rechtsstaat *m*; **II** *s.* **3.** F (Verdauungs-) Spaziergang *m*; **con·sti·tu·tion·al·ism** [-ʃnəlɪzəm] *s. pol.* verfassungsmäßige Regierungsform; **con·sti·tu·tion·al·ist** [-ʃnəlɪst] *s. pol.* Anhänger *m* der verfassungsmäßigen Regierungsform.

con·strain [kən'streɪn] *v/t.* **1.** zwingen, nötigen, drängen: **be** (*od.* **feel**) ~**ed** sich genötigt sehen; **2.** erzwingen; **3.** einzwängen; einsperren; **con'strained** [-nd] *adj.* □ gezwungen, steif, verkrampft, verlegen, befangen; **con'strain·ed·ly** [-nɪdlɪ] *adv.* gezwungen; **con'straint** [-nt] *s.* **1.** Zwang *m*, Nötigung *f*: **under** ~ unter Zwang, zwangsweise; **2.** Beschränkung *f*; **3.** a) Befangenheit *f*, b) Gezwungenheit *f*; **4.** Zu-'rückhaltung *f*.

con·strict [kən'strɪkt] *v/t.* zs.-ziehen, -pressen, -schnüren, einengen; **con'strict·ed** [-tɪd] *adj.* eingeengt, be-

schränkt; **con'stric·tion** [-kʃn] *s.* Zs.-ziehung *f*, Einschnürung *f*; Beengtheit *f*; **con'stric·tor** [-tə] *s.* **1.** *anat.* Schließmuskel *m*; **2.** *zo.* 'Boa *f*, Riesenschlange *f*.

con·strin·gent [kən'strɪndʒənt] *adj.* zs.-ziehend.

con·struct [kən'strʌkt] *v/t.* **1.** bauen, errichten; **2.** ◎, ♃, *ling.* konstruieren; **3.** *fig.* aufbauen, gestalten, formen; ausarbeiten, entwerfen, ersinnen; **con-'struc·tion** [-kʃn] *s.* **1.** (Er)Bauen *n*, Bau *m*, Errichtung *f*: **under** ~ im Bau; **2.** Bauwerk *n*, Bau *m*, Gebäude *n*; **3.** Bauweise *f*, *fig.* Aufbau *m*, Anlage *f*, Gestaltung *f*, Form *f*; **4.** ◎, ♃ Konstrukti'on *f*; **5.** *ling.* Konstrukti'on *f*; **6.** Auslegung *f*, Deutung *f*: **put a wrong** ~ **on s.th.** et. falsch auslegen *od.* auffassen; **con'struc·tion·al** [-kʃənl] *adj.* Bau..., Konstruktions..., baulich; **con'struc·tion pit** *s.* Baugrube *f*; **con'struc·tive** [-tɪv] *adj.* □ **1.** aufbauend, schaffend, schöpferisch, konstruk'tiv; **2.** konstruk'tiv, positiv: ~ **criticism**; **3.** Bau..., Konstruktions...; **4.** a) *a.* 🕇 abgeleitet, angenommen, b) 🕇 mittelbar: ~ **dismissal** unfreiwillige Kündigung seitens des Arbeitnehmers; **con'struc·tor** [-tə] *s.* Erbauer *m*, Konstruk'teur *m*.

con·strue [kən'struː] **I** *v/t.* **1.** *ling.* a) *Satz* zergliedern, konstruieren, b) (*Wort für Wort*) über'setzen; **2.** auslegen; deuten; auffassen; **II** *v/i.* **3.** *ling.* sich konstruieren *od.* zergliedern lassen.

con·sub·stan·ti·al·i·ty ['kɒnsəb‚stænʃɪ-'ælətɪ] *s. eccl.* Wesensgleichheit *f* (*der drei göttlichen Personen*); **con·sub·stan·ti·ate** [ˌkɒnsəb'stænʃɪeɪt] *v/t.* (*v/i.* sich) zu e-m einzigen Wesen vereinigen; **'con·sub‚stan·ti·a·tion** [-ɪ'eɪʃn] *s. eccl.* Konsubstantiati'on *f* (*Mitgegenwart des Leibes u. Blutes Christi beim Abendmahl*).

con·sue·tude ['kɒnswɪtjuːd] *s.* Gewohnheit *f*, Brauch *m*; **con·sue·tu·di·nar·y** [ˌkɒnswɪ'tjuːdɪnərɪ] *adj.* gewohnheitsmäßig, Gewohnheits...

con·sul ['kɒnsəl] *s.* Konsul *m*: ~-**general** Generalkonsul; **'con·su·lar** [-sjʊlə] *adj.* Konsulats..., Konsular...: ~ **invoice** ✝ Konsulatsfaktura *f*; **'con·su·late** [-sjʊlət] *s.* Konsu'lat *n* (*a. Gebäude*): ~-**general** Generalkonsulat; **'con·sul·ship** [-ʃɪp] *s.* Amt *n* e-s Konsuls.

con·sult [kən'sʌlt] **I** *v/t.* **1.** um Rat fragen, befragen, *Arzt etc.* zurate ziehen, konsultieren: ~ **one's watch** auf die Uhr sehen; ~ **the dictionary** im Wörterbuch nachschlagen; **2.** beachten, berücksichtigen: ~ **s.o.'s wishes**; **II** *v/i.* **3.** sich beraten *od.* besprechen (**with** mit, **about** über *acc.*); **con'sult·ant** [-tənt] *s.* **1.** (*Fach-, Betriebs- etc.*)Berater *m*; **2.** ⚚ a) Facharzt *m*, b) fachärztlicher Berater; **con·sul·ta·tion** [ˌkɒnsəl-'teɪʃn] *s.* Beratung *f*, Rücksprache *f* (**on** über *acc.*), Konsultati'on *f* (*a.* ⚚): ~ **hour** ⚚ Sprechstunde *f*; **con'sult·a·tive** [-tətɪv] *adj.* beratend; **con'sult·ing** [-tɪŋ] *adj.* beratend: ~ **engineer** technischer (Betriebs)Berater; ~ **room** ⚚ Sprechzimmer *n*.

con·sum·a·ble [kən'sjuːməbl] **I** *adj.* verzehrbar, verbrauchbar, zerstörbar; **II** *s. mst pl.* Ver'brauchsar‚tikel *m*; **con·sume** [kən'sjuːm] **I** *v/t.* **1.** verzehren (*a. fig.*), verbrauchen: **be** ~**d** *fig.* erfüllt sein von, von *Hass, Verlangen* verzehrt werden, vor *Neid* vergehen; **consuming desire** brennende Begierde; **2.** zerstören: **~d by fire** ein Raub der Flammen; **3.** (auf)essen, trinken; **4.** verschwenden; *Zeit* rauben *od.* benötigen; **II** *v/i.* **5.** *a.* **~ away** sich verzehren (*a. fig.*); sich verbrauchen *od.* abnutzen; **con'sum·er** [-mə] *s.* Verbraucher *m*, Abnehmer *m*, Konsu'ment *m*: **~ advice centre** (*Am. center*) Ver-'braucherzent‚rale *f*; **~ counselling** Verbraucherberatung *f*; **~ goods** Konsumgüter; **~ prices** *pl.* Verbraucherpreise *pl.*; **~ protection** Verbraucherschutz *m*; **~ resistance** Kaufunlust *f*; **~ society** Konsumgesellschaft *f*; **~ spending** Ausgaben der Privathaushalte; **~ survey** Konsumentenbefragung *f*; **~ ultimate ~** Endverbraucher *m*; **con'sum·er·ism** [-mərɪzəm] *s.* **1.** Verbraucherschutzbewegung *f*; **2.** kritische Verbraucherhaltung.

con·sum·mate I *v/t.* ['kɒnsəmeɪt] voll-'enden; *bsd. Ehe* voll'ziehen; **II** *adj.* □ [kən'sʌmɪt] voll'endet, 'vollkommen, völlig: **~ skill** höchste Geschicklichkeit; **con·sum·ma·tion** [‚kɒnsə'meɪʃn] *s.* **1.** Voll'endung *f*, Ziel *n*, Ende *n*; **2.** Erfüllung *f*; **3.** ⅌ Voll'ziehung *f* (*Ehe*). **con·sump·tion** [kən'sʌmpʃn] *s.* **1.** Verbrauch *m*, Kon'sum *m* (**of** an *dat. od.* von); **2.** Verzehrung *f*; Zerstörung *f*; **3.** Verzehr *m*: **unfit for human ~** für menschlichen Verzehr ungeeignet; **for public ~** *fig.* für die Öffentlichkeit bestimmt; **4.** ℱ *obs.* Schwindsucht *f*; **con-'sump·tive** [-ptɪv] **I** *adj.* □ **1.** verbrauchend, Verbrauchs...; **2.** (ver)zehrend; **3.** ℱ *obs.* schwindsüchtig; **II** *s.* **4.** ℱ *obs.* Schwindsüchtige(r *m*) *f*.

con·tact ['kɒntækt] **I** *s.* **1.** Berührung *f* (*a. fig.*), Kon'takt *m*; ✗ Feindberührung *f*; **2.** *fig.* Kon'takt *m*: a) Verbindung *f*, Beziehung *f*, Fühlung *f* (*a.* ✗), b) Verbindungs-, Gewährsmann *m*, c) *pol.* Kon'taktmann *m* (*Agent*): **make ~s** Verbindungen anknüpfen; **business ~** Geschäftsverbindung; **3.** ⚡ Kon'takt *m*: a) Anschluss *m*, b) Kon'taktstück *n*: **make** (**break**) **~** Kontakt herstellen (unterbrechen); **4.** ⚡ Kon'taktper‚son *f*; **II** *v/t.* **5.** in Berührung kommen mit; Kon'takt haben mit, berühren; **6.** *fig.* sich in Verbindung setzen mit, Beziehungen *od.* Kon'takt aufnehmen zu, sich an *j-n* wenden; **~ box** *s.* ⚡ Anschlussdose *f*; **~ break·er** *s.* ⚡ ('Strom-) Unter‚brecher *m*; **~ flight** *s.* ✈ Sichtflug *m*; **~ lens** *s.* Haft-, Kon'taktschale *f*, Kon'taktlinse *f*; **~ light** *s.* ✈ Lande-(bahn)feuer *n*; **'~-‚mak·er** *s.* ⚡ Einschalter *m*, Stromschließer *m*; **~ man** *s.* [*irr.*] → **contact** 2 b, c; **~ mine** *s.* ✗ Tretmine *f*.

con·tac·tor ['kɒntæktə] *s.* ⚡ (Schalt-) Schütz *m* → **switch** Schütz(schalter *m*). **con·tact| print** *s.* phot. Kon'taktabzug *m*; **~ rail** *s.* ⚡ Kon'taktschiene *f*. **con·ta·gion** [kən'teɪdʒən] *s.* **1.** ℱ a) Ansteckung *f* (*durch Berührung*), b) ansteckende Krankheit; **2.** *fig.* Vergiftung *f*; verderblicher Einfluss; **con'ta·gious** [-dʒəs] *adj.* □ **1.** ℱ a) ansteckend (*a. fig. Stimmung etc.*), b) infiziert; → **matter** Krankheitsstoff *m*; **2.** *fig. obs.* verderblich.

con·tain [kən'teɪn] *v/t.* **1.** enthalten; *fig. a.* beinhalten; **2.** (um)'fassen, einschließen, aufnehmen, Raum haben für; **3.** bestehen aus, messen; **4.** zügeln, im Zaum halten, bändigen; **~ one's anger;** **5.** **~ o.s.** sich beherrschen *od.* mäßigen: **be unable to ~ o.s. for** sich nicht fassen können vor; **6.** *a.* ✗ fest-,

zu'rückhalten; ✗ *Feindkräfte* fesseln, binden; *a. pol.* eindämmen; **~ the attack** den Angriff abriegeln; **~ a fire** e-n Brand unter Kontrolle bringen *od.* eindämmen; **7.** ⚹ teilbar sein durch; **con-'tain·er** [-nə] *s.* **1.** Behälter *m*; Gefäß *n*; Ka'nister *m*; **2.** ⚓ Con'tainer *m* (*Großbehälter*): **~ port** Containerhafen *m*; **~ ship** Containerschiff *n*; **con'tain·er·ize** [-nəraɪz] *v/t.* **1.** auf Con'tainerbetrieb 'umstellen; **2.** in Con'tainern transportieren; **con'tain·ment** [-mənt] *s. fig.* Eindämmung *f*, In-'Schach-Halten *n*: **policy of ~** Eindämmungspolitik *f*.

con·tam·i·nant [kən'tæmɪnənt] *s.* Verseuchungsstoff *m*; **con'tam·i·nate** [-neɪt] *v/t.* **1.** verunreinigen; **2.** *a. fig.* infizieren, vergiften, (*a.* radioak'tiv) verseuchen: **~d area** verseuchtes Gelände; **con·tam·i·na·tion** [kən‚tæmɪ-'neɪʃn] *s.* **1.** Verunreinigung *f*; **2.** (*a.* radioak'tive *etc.*) Verseuchung: **~ meter** Geigerzähler *m*; **3.** *ling.* Kontami-nati'on *f*.

con·tan·go [kən'tæŋɡəʊ] *s.* ⚹ *Börse:* Re'port *m* (*Kurszuschlag*).

con·temn [kən'tem] *v/t. poet.* verachten; **con'tem·nor** [-nə] *s.* ⅌ j-d der **contempt of court** begeht (→ **contempt** 4).

con·tem·plate ['kɒntempleɪt] **I** *v/t.* **1.** (nachdenklich) betrachten; nachdenken über (*acc.*); über'denken; **2.** ins Auge fassen, erwägen, beabsichtigen; **3.** erwarten, rechnen mit; **II** *v/i.* **4.** nachsinnen; **con·tem·pla·tion** [‚kɒntem'pleɪʃn] *s.* **1.** (nachdenkliche) Betrachtung; **2.** Nachdenken *n*, -sinnen *n*; **3.** *bsd. eccl.* Meditati'on *f*, innere Einkehr, Versunkenheit *f*; **4.** Erwägung *f*: **have in ~** → **contemplate** 2; **be in ~** erwogen *od.* geplant werden; **5.** Absicht *f*; **'con·tem·pla·tive** [-tɪv] *adj.* □ **1.** nachdenklich; **2.** beschaulich, besinnlich, kontempla'tiv.

con·tem·po·ra·ne·ous [kən‚tempə-'reɪnjəs] *adj.* □ gleichzeitig (**with** mit); **con‚tem·po'ra·ne·ous·ness** [-nɪs] *s.* Gleichzeitigkeit *f*; **con·tem·po·rar·y** [kən'tempərərɪ] **I** *adj.* **1.** zeitgenössisch: a) heutig, unserer Zeit, b) der damaligen Zeit: **~ history** Zeitgeschichte *f*; **2.** gleichalt(e)rig; **II** *s.* **3.** Zeitgenosse *m*, -genossin *f*; **4.** Altersgenosse *m*, -genossin *f*; **5.** gleichzeitig erscheinende Zeitung, Konkur'renz(blatt *n*) *f*.

con·tempt [kən'tem*p*t] *s.* **1.** Verachtung *f*, Geringschätzung *f*: **feel ~ for s.o.**, **hold s.o. in ~** j-n verachten; **bring into ~ verächtlich machen**; → **beneath** II; **2.** Schande *f*, Schmach *f*: **fall into ~** in Schande geraten; **3.** 'Missachtung *f*; **4.** **~** (**of court**) ⅌ 'Missachtung des Gerichts (*Ungebühr, Nichterscheinen etc.*); **con-tempt·i·bil·i·ty** [kən‚temptə'bɪlətɪ] *s.* Verächtlichkeit *f*; **con'tempt·i·ble** [-təbl] *adj.* □ **1.** verächtlich, verachtenswert, nichtswürdig: **Old ⅋s** *brit. Expeditionskorps in Frankreich 1914*; **2.** gemein, niederträchtig; **con'tempt·u·ous** [-tjʊəs] *adj.* □ verachtungsvoll, geringschätzig: **~ of s.th.** et. verachten; **con'temp·tu·ous·ness** [-tjʊəsnɪs] *s.* Verachtung *f*, Geringschätzigkeit *f*.

con·tend [kən'tend] **I** *v/i.* **1.** kämpfen, ringen (**with** *dat.*, **for** um); **2.** *mit Worten* streiten, disputieren (**about** über *acc.*, **against** gegen); **3.** wetteifern, sich bewerben (**for** um); **II** *v/t.* **4.** behaupten, geltend machen (**that** dass); **con'tend·er** [-də] *s.* Kämpfer(in); Bewerber(in) (**for** um); Konkur'rent(in);

con'tend·ing [-dɪŋ] *adj.* **1.** streitend, kämpfend; **2.** wider'streitend; **3.** konkurrierend; **con·tent**[1] ['kɒntent] *s.* **1.** *mst pl.* (*Raum*)Inhalt *m*, Fassungsvermögen *n*; 'Umfang *m*; **2.** *pl. a. fig.* Inhalt *m* (*Buch etc.*); **3.** *mst* 🜨 Gehalt *m*: **gold ~** Goldgehalt.

con·tent[2] [kən'tent] **I** *pred. adj.* **1.** zu-'frieden; **2.** bereit, willens (**to** *inf.* zu *inf.*); **3.** *parl. Brit.* (*nur House of Lords*) einverstanden: **not ~** dagegen; **II** *v/t.* **4.** befriedigen, zu'frieden stellen; **5.** **~ o.s.** zu'frieden sein, sich zufrieden geben *od.* begnügen *od.* abfinden (**with** mit); **III** *s.* **6.** Zu'friedenheit *f*, Befriedigung *f*: **to one's heart's ~** nach Herzenslust; **7.** *mst pl. parl. Brit.* Jastimmen *pl.*; **con'tent·ed** [-tɪd] *adj.* □ zu'frieden (**with** mit); **con'tent·ed·ness** [-tɪdnɪs] *s.* Zu'friedenheit *f*.

con·ten·tion [kən'tenʃn] *s.* **1.** Streit *m*, Zank *m*; **2.** Wortstreit *m*; **3.** Behauptung *f*: **my ~ is that** ich behaupte, dass; **4.** Streitpunkt *m*; **con'ten·tious** [-ʃəs] *adj.* □ **1.** streitsüchtig; **2.** streitig (*a.* ⅌), strittig, um'stritten; **con'ten·tious·ness** [-ʃəsnɪs] *s.* Streitsucht *f*.

con·tent·ment [kən'tentmənt] *s.* Zu-'friedenheit *f*.

con·test I *s.* ['kɒntest] **1.** Kampf *m*, Streit *m*; **2.** Wettkampf *m*, -streit *m*, -bewerb *m* (**for** um); **II** *v/t.* [kən'test] **3.** ✗ *u. fig.* kämpfen um; **4.** konkurrieren *od.* sich bewerben um; **5.** *pol.* **~ a seat** *od.* **an election** für e-e Wahl kandidieren; **6.** bestreiten; *a.* ⅌ *Aussage, Testament, Wahl(ergebnis) etc.* anfechten; **III** *v/i.* [kən'test] **7.** wetteifern (**with** mit); **con'test·a·ble** [kən'testəbl] *adj.* strittig; anfechtbar; **con·test·ant** [kən'testənt] *s.* **1.** (Wett)Bewerber(in); **2.** Wettkämpfer(in); **3.** Kandi'dat(in); **4.** ⅌ a) streitende Par'tei, b) Anfechter(in); **con·tes·ta·tion** [‚kɒntes'teɪʃn] *s.* Streit *m*; Dis'put *m*.

con·text ['kɒntekst] *s.* **1.** (*inhaltlicher*) Zs.-hang, Kontext *m*: **out of ~** aus dem Zs.-hang gerissen; **2.** Um'gebung *f*, Mili'eu *n*; **con·tex·tu·al** [kɒn'tekstjʊəl] *adj.* □ dem Zs.-hang gemäß; **con-tex·ture** [kɒn'tekstʃə] *s.* **1.** (Auf-) Bau *m*, Gefüge *n*, Struk'tur *f*; **2.** Gewebe *n*.

con·ti·gu·i·ty [‚kɒntɪ'ɡjuːətɪ] *s.* **1.** (**to**) Angrenzen *n* (an *acc.*), Berührung *f* (mit); **2.** Nähe *f*, Nachbarschaft *f*; **con-tig·u·ous** [kən'tɪɡjʊəs] *adj.* □ (**to**) **1.** angrenzend (an *acc.*), berührend (*acc.*); **2.** nahe, benachbart (*dat.*).

con·ti·nence ['kɒntɪnəns] *s.* Mäßigkeit *f*, (*bsd. sexuelle*) Enthaltsamkeit; **'con-ti·nent** [-nənt] **I** *adj.* □ **1.** mäßig; enthaltsam, keusch; **II** *s.* **2.** Konti'nent *m*, Erdteil *m*; **3.** Festland *n*: **the ⅋** *Brit.* das europäische Festland.

con·ti·nen·tal [‚kɒntɪ'nentl] **I** *adj.* □ **1.** kontinen'tal, Kontinental...: **~ shelf** Festlandsockel *m*; **~ ⅋** *Brit.* kontinen'tal (*das europäische Festland etreffend*); ausländisch: **~ quilt** *Brit.* Federbett *n*; **~ tour** Europareise *f*; **II** *s.* **3.** Festländer(in); **4.** ⅋ *Brit.* Kontinen'taleuro‚päer(in); **‚con·ti'nen·tal·ize** [-təlaɪz] *v/t.* kontinen'talen Cha'rakter geben (*dat.*): **~d** *Brit.* ‚euro-päisiert'.

con·tin·gen·cy [kən'tɪndʒənsɪ] *s.* **1.** Eventuali'tät *f*, Möglichkeit *f*, unvorhergesehener Fall: **~ insured against** Versicherungsfall *m*; **2.** Zufälligkeit *f*, Zufall *m*; **3.** *pl.* ⅌ unvorhergesehene

C

Ausgaben *pl.*; **con'tin·gent** [-nt] **I** *adj.* □ **1.** eventu'ell, möglich; zufällig, ungewiss; gelegentlich; **2.** (*on, upon*) abhängig (von), bedingt (durch), verbunden (mit): ~ *fee* Erfolgshonorar *n*; ~ *reserve* ✝ Sicherheitsrücklage *f*; **II** *s.* **3.** Anteil *m*, Beitrag *m*, Quote *f*, (✕ 'Truppen)Kontin,gent *n*; ~ *duty* EU Ausgleichsabgabe *f*; **con'tin·gent·ly** [-ntlɪ] *adv.* möglicherweise.

con·tin·u·al [kən'tɪnjʊəl] *adj.* □ **1.** fortwährend, 'ununter,brochen, (an)dauernd, (be)ständig; **2.** immer 'wiederkehrend, (sehr) häufig, oft wieder'holt; **3.** *a.* ↯ kontinuierlich, stetig; **con·'tin·u·al·ly** [-lɪ] *adv.* **1.** fortwährend *etc.*; **2.** immer wieder; **con'tin·u·ance** [-əns] *s.* **1.** → *continuation* 1, 2; **2.** Dauer *f*, Beständigkeit *f*; **3.** (Ver)Bleiben *n*; **con'tin·u·ant** [-ənt] *s.* **1.** *ling.* Dauerlaut *m*; **2.** ↯ Kontinu'ante *f*; **con·tin·u·a·tion** [kən,tɪnjʊ'eɪʃn] *s.* **1.** Fortsetzung *f* (*a. e-s Romans etc.*), Weiterführung *f*: ~ *school* Fortbildungsschule *f*; **2.** Fortbestand *m*, -dauer *f*; **3.** Erweiterung *f*; **4.** Verlängerung(sstück *n*) *f*; **5.** ✝ Prolongati'on *f*; **con·tin·ue** [kən'tɪnjuː] **I** *v/i.* **1.** fortfahren, weitermachen; **2.** fortdauern: a) (an)dauern, anhalten, b) sich fortsetzen, weitergehen, c) (fort)bestehen; **3.** (ver)bleiben: ~ *in office* im Amt bleiben; **4.** verbeharren (*in* bei, *in dat.*); **5.** ~ *doing*, ~ *to do* weiter *od.* auch weiterhin tun; ~ *talking* weiterreden; ~ (*to be*) *obstinate* eigensinnig bleiben; **II** *v/t.* **6.** fortsetzen, -führen, fortfahren mit: *to be* ~**d** Fortsetzung folgt; **7.** verlängern, weiterführen; **8.** aufrechterhalten; beibehalten, erhalten; belassen; **9.** vertagen; **con'tin·ued** [-juːd] *adj.* □ **1.** → *continuous* 1,3.; **2.** → *existence* Fortbestand *m*; **2.** in Fortsetzungen erscheinend; **con·ti·nu·i·ty** [,kɒntɪ'njuːətɪ] *s.* **1.** Fortbestand *m*, Stetigkeit *f*; **2.** Zs.-hang *m*; enge Verbindung; **3.** 'ununter,brochene Folge; **4.** *fig.* roter Faden; **5.** *Film:* Drehbuch *n*; *Radio, TV:* Manu'skript *n*: ~ *girl* Skriptgirl *n*; ~ *writer* a) Drehbuchautor *m*, b) Textschreiber *m*.

con·tin·u·ous [kən'tɪnjʊəs] *adj.* □ **1.** 'ununter,brochen, (fort)laufend; zs.-hängend; **2.** unaufhörlich, andauernd, fortwährend; **3.** kontinuierlich (*a.* ↻, *phys.*): ~ *function*; **4.** *ling.* progres'siv: ~ *form* Verlaufsform *f*; ~ *cur·rent s.* ⚡ Gleichstrom *m*; ~ *fire s.* ✕ Dauerfeuer *n*; ~ *form s.* Endlos-, EDV-Papier *n*; ~ **op·er·a·tion** *s.* ⊙ Dauerbetrieb *m*; ~ **pa·per** *s.* 'Endlospa,pier *n*; ~ **per·form·ance** *s. thea.* Non'stopvorstellung *f*.

con·tin·u·um [kən'tɪnjʊəm] **1.** ↯ Kon'tinuum *n*; **2.** → *continuity* 3.

con·tort [kən'tɔːt] *v/t.* **1.** (*a. Worte etc.*) verdrehen; **2.** *Gesicht etc.* verzerren, verziehen; **con'tor·tion** [-ɔːʃn] *s.* **1.** Verzerrung *f*; **2.** Verrenkung *f*; **con·'tor·tion·ist** [-ɔːʃnɪst] *s.* **1.** Schlangenmensch *m*; **2.** Wortverdreher(in).

con·tour [ˈkɒn,tʊə] **I** *s.* Kon'tur *f*, 'Umriss(linie *f*) *m*; **II** *v/t.* um'reißen, den 'Umriss zeichnen von; profilieren; *Straße* e-r Höhenlinie folgen lassen; ~ **chair** *s.* körpergerecht gestalteter Sessel; ~ **lathe** *s.* ⊙ Kopierdrehbank *f*; ~ **line** *s. surv.* Höhenlinie *f*; ~ **map** *s.* Höhenlinienkarte *f*.

con·tra [ˈkɒntrə] **I** *prp.* gegen, kontra (*acc.*); **II** *adv.* da'gegen; **III** *s.* ✝ Gegen-, 'Kreditseite *f*: ~ *account* Gegenrechnung *f*.

'con·tra|**·band** **I** *s.* **1.** 'Konterbande *f*,

Bann-, Schmuggelware *f*: ~ *of war* Kriegskonterbande; **2.** Schmuggel *m*, Schleichhandel *m*; **II** *adj.* **3.** Schmuggel..., gesetzwidrig; **~·bass** [-'beɪs] *s.* ♪ 'Kontrabass *m*; **~·bas·soon** *s.* ♪ 'Kontrafa,gott *n*.

con·tra·cep·tion [,kɒntrə'sepʃn] *s.* Empfängnisverhütung *f*; **con·tra·cep·tive** [-ptɪv] *adj. u. s.* empfängnisverhütend(es Mittel).

con·tract I *s.* [ˈkɒntrækt] **1.** *a.* ⚖ Vertrag *m*, Kon'trakt *m*: *by* ~ vertraglich; *under* ~ a) (*to*) vertraglich verpflichtet (*dat.*), b) ✝ in Auftrag gegeben (*Arbeit*); ~ (*to kill*) Mordauftrag *m*; **2.** Vertragsurkunde *f*; **3.** ✝ (Liefer-, Werk-)Vertrag *m*, (fester) Auftrag: ~ *note* Schlussschein *m*, -note *f*; ~ *processing* Lohnveredelung *f*; ~ *work* a) durch Subunternehmer ausgeführte Arbeiten, b) Leiharbeit *f*; **4.** Ak'kord(arbeit *f*) *m*; **5.** *a. marriage* ~ Ehevertrag *m*; **6.** a) *a.* ~ *bridge* Kontrakt-Bridge *n* (*Kartenspiel*), b) höchstes Gebot; **II** *v/t.* [kən'trækt] **7.** *Muskel* zs.-ziehen; *Stirn* runzeln; **8.** *ling.* zs.-ziehen, verkürzen; **9.** ein-, verengen, be-, einschränken; **10.** *Gewohnheit* annehmen, sich *e-e Krankheit* zuziehen; *Vertrag, Ehe, Freundschaft* schließen; *Schulden* machen; **III** *v/i.* [kən'trækt] **11.** sich zs.-ziehen, (ein)schrumpfen; **12.** enger *od.* kürzer *od.* kleiner werden; **13.** e-n Vertrag schließen, sich vertraglich verpflichten (*to inf.* zu *inf.*, *for* zu): ~ *for s.th.* et. vertraglich übernehmen; *as* ~*ed* wie (vertraglich) vereinbart; *the* ~*ing parties* die vertragschließenden Parteien; ~ *in v/i. pol. Brit.* sich zur Bezahlung des Par'teibeitrages (*für die Labour Party*) verpflichten; ~ *out v/i.* sich freizeichnen, sich von der Verpflichtung befreien; **II** *v/t.* (*Arbeiten*) außer Haus vergeben.

con·tract·ed [kən'træktɪd] *adj.* □ **1.** zs.-gezogen; verkürzt; **2.** *fig.* engherzig; beschränkt; **con'tract·i·ble** [-təbl]; **con'trac·tile** [-taɪl] *adj.* zs.-ziehbar.

con·trac·tion [kən'trækʃn] *s.* **1.** Zs.-ziehung *f*; **2.** *ling.* Ver-, Abkürzung *f*; Kurzwort *n*; **3.** Verkleinerung *f*, Einschränkung *f*; **4.** Zuziehung *f* (*Krankheit*); Eingehen *n* (*Schulden*); Annahme *f* (*Gewohnheit*); **5.** *contractions pl.* ✚ Wehen *pl.*; *the contractions are coming strong* die Wehen sind stark; **con'trac·tive** [-ktɪv] *adj.* zs.-ziehend; **con'trac·tor** [-ktə] *s.* **1.** (*bsd.* 'Bau-*etc.*)Unter,nehmer *m*; **2.** Unter'nehmer *m* (*Dienst-, Werkvertrag*), (Ver'trags-)Liefe,rant *m*; **3.** *anat.* Schließmuskel *m*; **con'trac·tu·al** [-ktʃʊəl] *adj.* vertraglich, Vertrags...: ~ *capacity* ⚖ Geschäftsfähigkeit *f*.

con·tra·dict [,kɒntrə'dɪkt] *v/t.* **1.** (*a. o.s.* sich) wider'sprechen (*dat.*); im 'Widerspruch stehen zu; **2.** *et.* bestreiten, in Abrede stellen; **con·tra·dic·tion** [-kʃn] *s.* **1.** 'Widerspruch *m*, -rede *f*: *spirit of* ~ Widerspruchsgeist *m*; **2.** 'Widerspruch *m*, Unvereinbarkeit *f*: *in* ~ *to* im Widerspruch zu; ~ *in terms* Widerspruch in sich; **3.** Bestreitung *f*; **con·tra·dic·tious** [-kʃəs] *adj.* □ zum 'Widerspruch geneigt, streitsüchtig; **con·tra·dic·to·ri·ness** [-tərɪnɪs] *s.* **1.** 'Widerspruch *m*; **2.** 'Widerspruchsgeist *m*; **con·tra·dic·to·ry** [-tərɪ] **I** *adj.* □ (sich) wider'sprechend, entgegengesetzt; unvereinbar; **II** *s.* 'Widerspruch *m*, Gegensatz *m*.

con·tra·dis·tinc·tion [,kɒntrədɪ'stɪŋkʃn] *s.* Gegensatz *m*: *in* ~ *to* (*od.*

from) im Gegensatz zu.

con·trail [ˈkɒntreɪl] *s.* ✈ Kon'densstreifen *m*.

con·tra·in·di·cate [,kɒntrə'ɪndɪkeɪt] *v/t.* ✚ kontraindizieren; **con·tra·in·di·ca·tion** *s.* ✚ 'Kontraindikati,on *f*, Gegenanzeige *f*.

con·tral·to [kən'træltəʊ] *pl.* **-tos** *s.* ♪ Alt *m*: a) Altstimme *f*, b) Al'tist(in), c) 'Altpar,tie *f*.

con·trap·tion [kən'træpʃn] *s.* F (neumodischer) Appa'rat, (komisches) Ding(s).

con·tra·pun·tal [,kɒntrə'pʌntl] *adj.* ♪ 'kontrapunktisch.

con·tra·ri·e·ty [,kɒntrə'raɪətɪ] *s.* **1.** Gegensätzlichkeit *f*, Unvereinbarkeit *f*; **2.** 'Widerspruch *m*, Gegensatz *m* (*to* zu); **con·tra·ri·ly** [ˈkɒntrərəlɪ] *adv.* **1.** entgegen (*to dat.*); **2.** andererseits; **con·tra·ri·ness** [ˈkɒntrərɪnɪs] *s.* **1.** Gegensätzlichkeit *f*, 'Widerspruch *m*; **2.** Widrigkeit *f*, Ungunst *f*; **3.** F [*a.* kən'treər-] 'Widerspenstigkeit *f*, Eigensinn *m*; **con·tra·ri·wise** [ˈkɒntrərɪwaɪz] *adv.* im Gegenteil; 'umgekehrt; and(e)rerseits.

con·tra·ry [ˈkɒntrərɪ] **I** *adj.* □ → *contrarily*; **1.** entgegengesetzt, gegensätzlich, -teilig; **2.** (*to*) wider'sprechend (*dat.*), im 'Widerspruch (zu); gegen (*acc.*), entgegen (*dat.*): ~ *to expectations* wider Erwarten; **3.** F [*a.* kən'treərɪ] 'widerspenstig, aufsässig; **II** *adv.* **4.** ~ *to* gegen, wider: *act* ~ *to nature* wider die Natur handeln; **III** *s.* **5.** Gegenteil *n* (*to* von *od. gen.*): *on the* ~ im Gegenteil; *unless I hear to the* ~ falls ich nichts Gegenteiliges höre; *proof to the* ~ Gegenbeweis *m*.

con·trast I *s.* [ˈkɒntrɑːst] Kon'trast *m*, Gegensatz *m*: ~ *control* TV Kontrastregler *m*; *by* ~ *with* im Vergleich mit; *in* ~ *to* im Gegensatz zu; *be a great* ~ *to* grundverschieden sein von; **II** *v/t.* [kən'trɑːst] (*with*) entgegensetzen, gegen'überstellen (*dat.*); vergleichen (*mit*); **III** *v/i.* [kən'trɑːst] (*with*) e-n Gegensatz bilden (zu), sich scharf unter'scheiden (von); sich abheben, abstechen (von): ~*ing colo(u)rs* Kontrastfarben; **con·trast·y** [kən'trɑːstɪ] *adj.* kon'trastreich.

con·tra·vene [,kɒntrə'viːn] *v/t.* **1.** zu'widerhandeln (*dat.*), verstoßen gegen, über'treten, verletzen; **2.** im 'Widerspruch stehen zu; **3.** bestreiten; **con·tra·ven·tion** [-'venʃn] *s.* (*of*) Über'tretung *f* (von *od. gen.*); Verstoß *m*, Zu'widerhandlung *f* (gegen): *in* ~ *of the rules* entgegen den Vorschriften.

con·tre·temps [ˈkɔ̃ːntrətɑ̃ː] (*Fr.*) *s.* unglücklicher Zufall, Widrigkeit *f*, ‚Panne' *f*.

con·trib·ute [kən'trɪbjuːt] **I** *v/t.* **1.** beitragen, beisteuern (*to* zu) (*beide a. fig.*); spenden (*to* für); ✝ a) *Kapital in e-e Firma* einbringen, b) *Brit. Geld* nachschießen; **2.** *Zeitungsartikel* beitragen; **II** *v/i.* **3.** (*to*) beitragen, e-n Beitrag leisten (zu), mitwirken (an *dat.*, bei): ~ *to a newspaper* für e-e Zeitung schreiben; **con·tri·bu·tion** [,kɒntrɪ'bjuːʃn] *s.* **1.** Beitragen *n*; **2.** Beitrag *m* (*a. für Zeitung*), Beisteuer *f*, Beihilfe *f* (*to* zu); Spende *f* (*to* für): *make a* ~ e-n Beitrag liefern; **3.** Mitwirkung *f* (*to* an *dat.*); **4.** ✝ a) Einlage *f*: ~ *in kind* (*cash*) Sach-(Bar-)einlage, b) Nachschuss *m*, c) Sozi'alversicherungsbeitrag *m*: *employer's* ~ Arbeitgeberanteil *m*, Sozialleistung *f*; **con·trib·u·tive** [-jʊtɪv] *adj.* → *contributory* 1, 2; **con'trib·u·tor** [-jʊtə] *s.* **1.** Beitragende(r *m*) *f*; Beisteuernde(r *m*) *f*; **2.** Mitwirkende(r *m*) *f*; Mitarbeiter(in) (*bsd. Zeitung*); **con-'trib·u·to·ry** [-jʊtərɪ] **I** *adj.* **1.** beisteuernd, beitragend (**to** zu); Beitrags...; **2.** mitwirkend (**to** an *dat.*, bei); Mit...: ~ *causes* ⚖ mitverursachende Umstände; ~ *negligence* mitwirkendes Verschulden; **3.** beitragspflichtig; **4.** ✝ *Brit.* nachschusspflichtig; **II** *s.* **5.** Beitrags- *od.* ✝ *Brit.* Nachschusspflichtige(r *m*) *f*.

con·trite ['kɒntraɪt] *adj.* □ zerknirscht, reuevoll; **con·tri·tion** [kən'trɪʃn] *s.* Zerknirschung *f*, Reue *f*.

con·triv·ance [kən'traɪvns] *s.* **1.** Ein-, Vorrichtung *f*; Appa'rat *m*; **2.** Kunstgriff *m*, Erfindung *f*, Plan *m*; **3.** Findigkeit *f*, Scharfsinn *m*; **4.** Bewerkstelligung *f*; **con·trive** [kən'traɪv] **I** *v/t.* **1.** erfinden, ersinnen, (sich) ausdenken, entwerfen; **2.** *Pläne* schmieden, aushecken; **3.** zu'stande bringen; **4.** es fertig bringen, es verstehen, es bewerkstelligen (**to** *inf.* zu *inf.*); **II** *v/i.* **5.** Pläne *od.* Ränke schmieden; **6.** Haus halten, auskommen.

con·trol [kən'trəʊl] **I** *v/t.* **1.** beherrschen, die Herrschaft *od.* Kon'trolle haben über (*acc.*), *et.* in der Hand haben *od.* kontrollieren; **~·ling company** Muttergesellschaft *f*; **~·ling share** (*od.* *interest*) ✝ maßgebliche Beteiligung; **2.** verwalten, beaufsichtigen, über'wachen; *Preise etc.* kontrollieren, nachprüfen; **3.** lenken, steuern, leiten, regeln, regulieren: *radio-~·led* funkgesteuert; **~·led ventilation** regulierbare Lüftung; **4.** (*a. o.s.* sich) beherrschen, meistern, im Zaum halten, Einhalt gebieten (*dat.*); zügeln; **5.** in Schranken halten, bekämpfen; **6.** (staatlich) bewirtschaften, planen, binden: **~·led economy** Planwirtschaft *f*, **~·led prices** gebundene Preise; **II** *s.* **7.** Macht *f*, Gewalt *f*, Herrschaft *f*, Kon'trolle *f* (*of*, *over* über *acc.*): *foreign* ~ Überfremdung *f*; *bring under* ~ Herr werden über (*acc.*); *have the situation under* ~ Herr der Lage sein; *get* ~ *over* in s-e Gewalt bekommen; *get beyond s.o.'s* ~ j-m über den Kopf wachsen; *get out of* ~ außer Kontrolle geraten; *have* ~ *over* a) → 1, b) Gewalt haben über (*acc.*); *keep under* ~ im Zaume halten; *lose* ~ *over* die Herrschaft *od.* Gewalt *od.* Kontrolle verlieren über (*acc.*); *circumstances beyond our* ~ unvorhersehbare Umstände; **8.** Machtbereich *m*, Verantwortung *f*; **9.** Aufsicht *f*, Kontrolle *f* (*of* über *acc.*); Leitung *f*, Über'wachung *f*, (Nach)Prüfung *f*; ⚖ (*of*) a) Verfügungsgewalt (über *acc.*), b) (Per'sonen)Sorge *f* (für): *be in* ~ *of s.th.* et. unter sich haben, et. leiten; *be under s.o.'s* ~ j-m unterstellt sein *od.* unterstehen; *traffic* ~ Verkehrsregelung *f*; **10.** Bekämpfung *f*, Eindämmung *f*: *without* ~ uneingeschränkt, frei; *beyond* ~ nicht einzudämmen, nicht zu bändigen; *be out of* ~ nicht zu halten sein; *get under* ~ eindämmen, bewältigen; *noise* ~ Lärmbekämpfung *f*; **11.** *mst pl.* ☻ a) Steuerung *f*, 'Steueror,gan *n*, b) Reguliervorrichtung *f*, Regler *m*, Kon'trollhebel *m*: *be at the* ~*s* od. am Hebeln der Macht sitzen; **12.** ⚡, ☻ Regelung *f*; **13.** *pl.* ✈ Steuerung *f*, Leitwerk *n*; **14.** ✝ a) (*Kapital-*, *Konsum- etc.*) Lenkung *f*, b) (Zwangs)Bewirtschaftung *f*: *foreign exchange* ~ Devisenkontrolle *f*; **15.** a) Kon'trolle *f*, An-

haltspunkt *m*, b) Vergleichswert *m*, c) Kon'troll-, Gegenversuch *m*.

con·trol| board *s.* ⚡ Schalttafel *f*; ~ **char·ac·ter** *s.* *Computer*: Steuerzeichen *n*; ~ **col·umn** *s.* **1.** ✈ Steuersäule *f*; **2.** ☻ Lenksäule *f*; ~ **com·mand** *s.* *Computer*: Steuerbefehl *m*; ~ **desk** *s.* ⚡ Steuer-, Schaltpult *n*; *Radio*, *TV*: Re'giepult *n*; ~ **en·gi·neer·ing** *s.* 'Steuerungs-, 'Regel,technik *f*; ~ **ex·per·i·ment** → *control* 15 c; ~ **key** *s.* *Computer etc.*: Control-Taste *f*, Steuerungstaste *f*; ~ **knob** *s.* ☻, ⚡ Bedienungsknopf *m*.

con·trol·la·ble [kən'trəʊləbl] *adj.* **1.** kontrollierbar, regulierbar, lenkbar; **2.** zu beaufsichtigen(d); zu beherrschen(d); **con'trol·ler** [-lə] *s.* **1.** Kon'trol'leur *m*, Aufseher *m*; Leiter *m*; Kon'trollbe,amte(r) *m*, ✈ *a.* Fluglotse *m*; **2.** Rechnungsprüfer *m* (*Beamter*); **3.** ⚡, ☻ Regler *m*; *mot.* Fahrschalter *m*; **4.** *sport* Kon'trollposten *m*.

con·trol| le·ver *s.* *mot.* Schalthebel *m*; ✈ Steuerknüppel *m*; ~ **light** *s.* Kon-'troll,lampe *f*.

con·trol·ling com·pa·ny ['kʌmpənɪ] *s.* ✝ Muttergesellschaft *f*.

con·trol| pan·el *s.* **1.** ☻ Bedienungsfeld *n*; **2.** *Computer*: Sys'tem,steuerung *f*; ~ **post** *s.* ✕ Kon'trollposten *m*; ~ **room** *s.* **1.** Kon'trollraum *m*, (✕ Be'fehls-) Zen,trale *f*; **2.** *Radio*, *TV*: Re'gieraum *m*; ~ **stick** *s.* ✈ Steuerknüppel *m*; ~ **sur·face** *s.* ✈ Steuerfläche *f*; ~ **tow·er** *s.* ✈ Kon'trollturm *m*, Tower *m*; ~ **u·nit** *s.* ☻ Steuergerät *n*.

con·tro·ver·sial [ˌkɒntrə'vɜːʃl] *adj.* □ **1.** strittig, um'stritten: ~ *subject* Streitfrage *f*; **2.** po'lemisch; streitlustig; **con·tro·ver·sial·ist** [-ʃəlɪst] *s.* Po'lemiker *m*; **con·tro·ver·sy** ['kɒntrəvɜːsɪ] *s.* **1.** Kontro'verse *f*, Meinungsstreit *m*; Debatte *f*; Aussprache *f*: *beyond* (*od.* *without*) ~ fraglos, unstreitig; **2.** Streitfrage *f*; **3.** Streit *m*; **con·tro·vert** ['kɒntrəvɜːt] *v/t.* **1.** bestreiten, anfechten; **2.** wider'sprechen (*dat.*); **con·tro·vert·i·ble** [-ɜːtəbl] *adj.* □ strittig; anfechtbar.

con·tu·ma·cious [ˌkɒntjuː'meɪʃəs] *adj.* □ **1.** 'widerspenstig, halsstarrig; **2.** ⚖ ungehorsam; **con·tu·ma·cy** ['kɒntjuːməsɪ] *s.* **1.** 'Widerspenstigkeit *f*, Halsstarrigkeit *f*; **2.** ⚖ Ungehorsam *m od.* (absichtliches) Nichterscheinen vor Gericht: *condemn for* ~ gegen j-n ein Versäumnisurteil fällen.

con·tume·ly ['kɒntjuːmlɪ] *s.* **1.** Unverschämtheit *f*; **2.** Beleidigung *f*.

con·tuse [kən'tjuːz] *v/t.* ✚ quetschen: ~*d wound* Quetschwunde *f*; **con'tu·sion** [-uːʒn] *s.* ✚ Quetschung *f*.

co·nun·drum [kə'nʌndrəm] *s.* **1.** Scherzfrage *f*, -rätsel *n*; **2.** *fig.* Rätsel *n*.

con·ur·ba·tion [ˌkɒnɜː'beɪʃn] *s.* Ballungsraum *m*, -zentrum *n*, Stadtgroßraum *m*.

con·va·lesce [ˌkɒnvə'les] *v/i.* gesund werden, genesen; **con·va'les·cence** [-sns] *s.* Rekonvales'zenz *f*, Genesung *f*; **con·va'les·cent** [-snt] **I** *adj.* genesend, auf dem Wege der Besserung: ~ *home* Genesungsheim *n*; **II** *s.* Rekonvales'zent(in).

con·vec·tion [kən'vekʃn] *s.* *phys.* Konvekti'on *f*; **con'vec·tor** [-ktə] *s.* *phys.* Konvekti'ons(strom)leiter *m*.

con·vene [kən'viːn] **I** *v/t.* **1.** zs.-rufen, (ein)berufen; versammeln; **2.** ⚖ vorladen; **II** *v/i.* **3.** zs.-kommen, sich versammeln.

con·ven·ience [kən'viːnjəns] *s.* **1.** Annehmlichkeit *f*, Bequemlichkeit *f*: *all*

(*modern*) ~*s* alle Bequemlichkeiten *od.* aller Komfort (der Neuzeit); *at your* ~ wenn es Ihnen passt; *at your earliest* ~ möglichst bald; *at one's own* ~ nach (eigenem) Gutdünken; *suit your own* ~ handeln Sie ganz nach Ihrem Belieben; ~ *food* Fertignahrung *f*; ~ *goods* ✝ *Am.* bequem erhältliche Waren des täglichen Bedarfs; **2.** Vorteil *m*, Nutzen *m*: *it is a great* ~ es ist sehr nützlich; → *flag*[1] 1, *marriage* 2; **3.** Angemessenheit *f*, Eignung *f*; **4.** *Brit.* Klo-'sett *n*: *public* ~ öffentliche Bedürfnisanstalt; **con'ven·ient** [-nt] *adj.* □ **1.** bequem, geeignet, günstig, passend: *if it is* ~ *to you* wenn es Ihnen passt; *it is not* ~ *for me* (*to inf.*) es passt mir schlecht (zu *inf.*); *make it* ~ es (so) einrichten; **2.** (zweck)dienlich, praktisch, brauchbar; **3.** günstig gelegen.

con·vent ['kɒnvənt] *s.* (*bsd.* Nonnen-) Kloster *n*: ~ (*school*) Klosterschule *f*.

con·ven·ti·cle [kən'ventɪkl] *s.* *eccl.* Konven'tikel *n*.

con·ven·tion [kən'venʃn] *s.* **1.** Zs.-kunft *f*, (*Am. a.* Par'tei)Versammlung *f*, Kon-'vent *m*, (*a.* Be'rufs-, 'Fach)Kon,gress *m*, (-)Tagung *f*; **2.** *a. pol.* Vertrag *m*, Abkommen *n*, Konventi'on *f* (*a.* ✕); **3.** *oft pl.* (gesellschaftliche) Konventi'on, Sitte *f*, Gewohnheits- *od.* Anstandsregel *f*, (stillschweigende) Gepflogenheit *od.* Über'einkunft *f*; **con'ven·tion·al** [-ʃənl] *adj.* □ **1.** herkömmlich, konventio'nell (*beide a.* ✕), üblich, traditio-'nell: ~ *weapons*; ~ *sign* (*bsd.* Karten)Zeichen *n*, Symbol *n*; **2.** förmlich, for'mell; **3.** vereinbart, Vertrags...; **4.** *contp.* 'unorigi,nell; **con'ven·tion·al·ism** [-ʃnəlɪzəm] *s.* Festhalten *n* am Hergebrachten; **con·ven·tion·al·i·ty** [kən-ˌvenʃə'nælətɪ] *s.* **1.** Herkömmlichkeit *f*, Üblichkeit *f*; **2.** Scha'blonenhaftigkeit *f*; **con'ven·tion·al·ize** [-ʃnəlaɪz] *v/t.* konventio'nell machen *od.* darstellen, den Konventi'onen unter'werfen.

con·verge [kən'vɜːdʒ] *v/i.* zs.-laufen, sich (ein'ander) nähern, ⅋ *u. fig.* konvergieren; **con'ver·gence** [-dʒəns] *s.* **1.** Zs.-laufen *n*; **2.** ⅋ a) Konver'genz *f* (*a. biol.*, *phys.*), b) Annäherung *f*: ~ *criteria pl. EU* Konver'genzkri,terien *pl.*; **con'ver·gen·cy** [-dʒənsɪ] *s.* → *convergence*; **con'ver·gent** [-dʒənt] *adj. bsd.* ⅋ konver'gent; **con'verg·ing** [-dʒɪŋ] *adj.* zs.-laufend, konvergierend: ~ *lens* Sammellinse *f*; ~ *point* Konver'genzpunkt *m*.

con·vers·a·ble [kən'vɜːsəbl] *adj.* □ unter'haltend, gesprächig; gesellig; **con-'ver·sance** [-səns] *s.* Vertrautheit *f* (*with* mit); **con'ver·sant** [-sənt] *adj.* **1.** bekannt, vertraut (*with* mit); **2.** geübt, bewandert, erfahren (*with*, *in* in *dat.*).

con·ver·sa·tion [ˌkɒnvə'seɪʃn] *s.* **1.** Unter'haltung *f*, Gespräch *n*, Konversati'on *f*: *enter into a* ~ ein Gespräch anknüpfen; **2.** *obs.* (*a.* Geschlechts-) Verkehr *m*; → *criminal conversation*; **3.** *a.* ~ *piece* a) *paint.* Genrebild *n*, b) *thea.* Konversati'onsstück *n*; **con·ver-'sa·tion·al** [-ʃənl] *adj.* □ → *conversationally*; **1.** gesprächig; **2.** Unterhaltungs..., Gesprächs...: ~ *grammar* Konversationsgrammatik *f*; ~ *tone* Plauderton *m*; **con·ver'sa·tion·al·ist** [-ʃənlɪst] *s.* gewandter Unter'halter, guter Gesellschafter; **con·ver'sa·tion·al·ly** [-ʃnəlɪ] *adv.* **1.** gesprächsweise; **2.** im Plauderton.

con·ver·sa·zi·o·ne [ˌkɒnvəsætsɪ'əʊnɪ] *pl.* **-ni** [-niː], **-nes** (*Ital.*) *s.* **1.** 'Abendunter,haltung *f*; **2.** lite'rarischer Gesell-

C

schaftsabend.

con·verse¹ [kən'vɜːs] *v/i.* sich unter'halten, sprechen (**with** mit, **on**, **about** über *acc.*).

con·verse² ['kɒnvɜːs] **I** *adj.* □ gegenteilig, 'umgekehrt, wechselseitig; **II** *s.* 'Umkehrung *f*; Gegenteil *n*; **'con·verse·ly** [-lɪ] *adv.* 'umgekehrt.

con·ver·sion [kən'vɜːʃn] *s.* **1.** *allg.* 'Um-, Verwandlung *f* (**from** von, **into** in *acc.*); **2.** ♥ a) Konvertierung *f*, 'Umwandlung *f* (*Effekten, Schulden*), b) Zs.-legung *f* (*von Aktien*), c) ('Währungs),Umstellung *f*, d) (Ge'schäfts-, a. Ver'mögens),Umwandlung *f*; **3.** ♪ a) a. *Währung*: 'Umrechnung *f* (**into** in *acc.*): ~ **table** Umrechnungstabelle *f*; ~ **rate** *Währung*: Umrechnungskurs *m*, b) *EDV, Computer*: Konver'tierung *f*, c) a. *phls.* 'Umkehrung *f*; **4.** ⊙, a. ♥ 'Umstellung *f* (**to** auf e-e andere Produktion etc.); **5.** ⊙, △ 'Umbau *m* (**into** in *acc.*); **6.** ♭ 'Umformung *f*; **7.** ♫, *phys.* 'Umsetzung *f*; **8.** geistige Wandlung; Meinungsänderung *f*; **9.** 'Übertritt *m*, *bsd. eccl.* Bekehrung *f* (**to** zu); **10.** ♭ a. ~ **to one's own use** 'widerrechtliche Aneignung *od.* Verwendung, *a.* Veruntreuung *f*; **11.** *sport* Verwandlung *f* (*Torschuss*).

con·vert **I** *v/t.* [kən'vɜːt] **1.** *allg.* 'um-, verwandeln (*a.* ♫), 'umformen (*a.* ♭), 'umändern (**into** in *acc.*); **2.** ⊙, △ 'umbauen (**into** zu); **3.** ♥, ⊙ *Betrieb, Maschine, Produktion* 'umstellen (**to** auf *acc.*); **4.** *metall.* frischen; **5.** ♥ a) *Geld* 'um-, einwechseln, *a.* 'umrechnen: ~ **into cash** zu Geld machen, flüssig machen, b) *Wertpapiere, Schulden* konvertieren, 'umwandeln, c) *Aktien* zs.-legen, d) *Währung* 'umstellen (**to** auf *acc.*), e) *EDV:* (*Daten*) konver'tieren; **6.** ♪ a) 'umrechnen (**into** in *acc.*), b) *Gleichung* auflösen, c) *Proportionen* 'umkehren (*a. phls.*); **7.** *Computer:* 'umsetzen; **8.** *eccl.* bekehren (**to** zu); **9.** (**to**) (zu e-r anderen Ansicht) bekehren, a. zum 'Übertritt (in e-e andere Partei etc.) veranlassen; **10.** ♭ a. ~ **to one's own use** sich 'widerrechtlich aneignen, veruntreuen; **11.** *sport* (zum Tor) verwandeln; **II** *v/i.* **12.** 'umgewandelt (*etc.*) werden (→ I); **13.** sich verwandeln *od.* 'umwandeln (**into** zu); **14.** sich verwandeln (*etc.*) lassen (**into** in *acc.*); **III** *s.* ['kɒnvɜːt] **15.** *bsd. eccl.* Bekehrte(r *m*) *f*, Konver'tit(in): **become a ~ to** sich bekehren zu; **con'vert·ed** [-tɪd] *adj.* 'umge-, verwandelt *etc.*: ~ **cruiser** ♣ Hilfskreuzer *m*; ~ **flat** in Teilwohnungen umgebaute große Wohnung; ~ **steel** Zementstahl *m*; **con'vert·er** [-tə] *s.* **1.** ⊙ 'Bessemerbirne *f*; **2.** ♭ 'Umformer *m*; **3.** *TV* Wandler *m*; **4.** *Computer:* Con'verter *m*, 'Umrechner *m*; **5.** ⊙ Bleicher *m*, *bsd. eccl.* Bekehrer *m*; **con·vert·i·bil·i·ty** [kən,vɜːtə'bɪlətɪ] *s.* **1.** 'Um-, Verwandelbarkeit *f*; **2.** ♥ Konvertierbar-, 'Umwandelbarkeit *f*; **con'vert·i·ble** [-təbl] **I** *adj.* □ **1.** 'um-, verwandelbar; **2.** ♥ konvertierbar, 'umwandelbar: ~ **bond** Wandelobligation *f*; **3.** auswechselbar, gleichbedeutend; **4.** bekehrbar; **5.** *mot.* mit Klappverdeck; **II** *s.* **6.** *mot.* Kabrio'lett *n*.

con·vex [kɒn'veks] *adj.* □ kon'vex, nach außen gewölbt; ♪ ausspringend (*Winkel*); **con·vex·i·ty** [kɒn'veksətɪ] *s.* kon'vexe Form.

con·vey [kən'veɪ] *v/t.* **1.** *Waren etc.* befördern, (ver)senden, (fort)schaffen, bringen; **2.** *bsd.* ⊙ (zu)führen, fördern; **3.** über'bringen, -'mitteln, bringen, geben: ~ **greetings** Grüße übermitteln;

4. *phys. Schall* fortpflanzen, leiten, über'tragen; **5.** *Nachricht etc.* mitteilen, vermitteln; *Meinung, Sinn* ausdrücken; andeuten; (be)sagen: ~ **an idea** e-n Begriff geben; **this word ~s nothing to me** dieses Wort sagt mir nichts; **6.** über'tragen, abtreten (**to** an *acc.*); **con'vey·ance** [-erəns] *s.* **1.** Beförderung *f*, Über'sendung *f*, Trans'port *m*, Spediti'on *f*: **means of** ~ Transportmittel *n*; **2.** Über'bringung *f*, -'mittlung *f*; Vermittlung *f*, Mitteilung *f*; **3.** *phys.* Fortpflanzung *f*, Über'tragung *f*; **4.** ⊙ (Zu-)Leitung *f*, Zufuhr *f*; **5.** Beförderungs-, Trans'port-, Verkehrsmittel *n*; **6.** ♭ a) Über'tragung *f*, Abtretung *f*, Auflassung *f*, b) Abtretungsurkunde *f*; **con'vey·anc·er** [-erənsə] *s.* ♭ No'tar *m* für 'Eigentumsüber,tragungen.

con·vey·er, con·vey·or [kən'veɪə] *s.* **1.** Beförderer *m*, (Über)'Bringer(in); **2.** ⊙ Fördergerät *n*, -band *n*, Förderer *m*; ~ **band**, ~ **belt** *s.* laufendes Band, Förder-, Fließband *n*; ~ **chain** *s.* Becher-, Förderkette *f*; ~ **spi·ral** *s.* Förder-, Trans'portschnecke *f*.

con·vict **I** *v/t.* [kən'vɪkt] **1.** ♭ über'führen, für schuldig erklären (**of** *gen.*); **2.** verurteilen; **3.** über'zeugen (**of** von e-m *Unrecht, Fehler etc.*); **II** *s.* ['kɒnvɪkt] **1.** ♭ a) Verurteilte(r *m*) *f*, b) Strafgefangene(r *m*) *f*, Sträfling *m*: ~ **colony** Sträflingskolonie *f*; ~ **labo(u)r** Sträflingsarbeit *f*; **con'vic·tion** [-kʃn] *s.* **1.** ♭ a) Über'führung *f*, Schuldspruch *m*, b) Verurteilung *f*: **previous ~** Vorstrafe *f*; **2.** Über'zeugung *f*: **carry ~** überzeugend wirken *od.* klingen; **live up to one's ~s** s-r Überzeugung gemäß leben; **3.** Anschauung *f*, Gesinnung *f*; **4.** (*Schuld- etc.*)Bewusstsein *n*.

con·vince [kən'vɪns] *v/t.* **1.** (*a. o.s.* sich) über'zeugen (**of** von, **that** dass); **2.** ~ **s.o. of s.th.** j-m et. zum Bewusstsein bringen; **con'vinc·ing** [-sɪŋ] *adj.* □ über'zeugend: ~ **proof** schlagender Beweis; **be ~** überzeugen.

con·viv·i·al [kən'vɪvɪəl] *adj.* □ **1.** gastlich, festlich, Fest...; **2.** gesellig, gemütlich, lustig; **con·viv·i·al·i·ty** [kən,vɪvɪ'ælətɪ] *s.* Geselligkeit *f*, Gemütlichkeit *f*, unbeschwerte Heiterkeit.

con·vo·ca·tion [,kɒnvəʊ'keɪʃn] *s.* **1.** Ein-, Zs.-berufung *f*; **2.** *eccl. Brit.* Provinzi'alsy,node *f*; Kirchenversammlung *f*; **3.** *univ.* a) *Brit.* gesetzgebende Versammlung (*Oxford etc.*); außerordentliche Se'natssitzung, b) *Am.* Promoti'ons- *od.* Eröffnungsfeier *f*.

con·voke [kən'vəʊk] *v/t.* (*bsd. amtlich*) ein-, zs.-berufen.

con·vo·lute ['kɒnvəluːt] *adj. bsd.* ♀ zs.-gerollt, ringelförmig; **'con·vo·lut·ed** [-tɪd] *adj. bsd. zo.* zs.-gerollt, gebogen, gewunden, spi'ralig; **con·vo·lu·tion** [,kɒnvə'luːʃn] *s.* Zs.-rollung *f*, -wicklung *f*, Windung *f*.

con·voy ['kɒnvɔɪ] **I** *s.* **1.** Geleit *n*, (Schutz)Begleitung *f*; **2.** ✕ a) Es'korte *f*, Bedeckung *f*, b) (bewachter) Trans'port; **3.** ♣ Geleitzug *m*; **4.** a. ✕ 'Lastwagen,ko,lonne *f*; **II** *v/t.* **5.** Geleitschutz geben (*dat.*), eskortieren.

con·vulse [kən'vʌls] *v/t.* **1.** erschüttern, in Zuckungen versetzen: **be ~d with pain** sich vor Schmerzen krümmen; **be ~d (with laughter)** in e-n Lachkrampf bekommen; **2.** krampfhaft zs.-ziehen *od.* verzerren; **3.** *fig.* erschüttern, in Aufruhr versetzen; **con'vul·sion** [-lʃn] *s.* **1.** ♣ Krampf *m*, Zuckung *f*: **be seized with ~s** (**of laughter**) *fig.* Lachkrämpfe; **2.** *pol.*,

fig. Erschütterung *f* (*a. geol.*), Aufruhr *m*; **con'vul·sive** [-sɪv] *adj.* □ **1.** *a. fig.* krampfhaft, -artig, konvul'siv; **2.** *fig.* erschütternd.

co·ny ['kəʊnɪ] *s.* **1.** *zo.* Ka'ninchen *n*; **2.** Ka'ninchenfell *n*.

coo [kuː] **I** *v/i.* gurren (*a. fig.*); **II** *v/t. fig. et.* gurren; **III** *s.* Gurren *n*; **IV** *int. Brit. sl.* Mann!

cook [kʊk] **I** *s.* **1.** Koch *m*, Köchin *f*: **too many ~s spoil the broth** viele Köche verderben den Brei; **II** *v/t.* **2.** *Speisen* kochen, zubereiten, braten, backen: **be ~ed alive** F vor Hitze umkommen; **3.** *a.* ~ **up** *fig.* a) zs.-brauen, erdichten, b) ,frisieren', verfälschen: **~ed account** ♥ F frisierte Abrechnung; ~ **the books** ♥ F die Bi'lanzen *pl.* frisieren; ~ **up a story** e-e Geschichte erfinden; **he is ~ed** *sl.* der ist ,erledigt'; **III** *v/i.* **4.** kochen, sich kochen lassen: ~ **well**; **5.** **what's ~ing** F was tut sich?, was ist los?; **'~·book** *s. Am.* Kochbuch *n*.

cook·er ['kʊkə] *s.* **1.** Kocher *m*, Kochgerät *n*; Herd *m*; **2.** Kochgefäß *n*; **3.** *pl.* Kochobst *n*: **these apples are good ~s** das sind gute Kochäpfel.

cook·er·y ['kʊkərɪ] *s.* Kochen *n*; Kochkunst *f*; ~ **book** *s. Brit.* Kochbuch *n*.

,cook-'gen·er·al *s. Brit.* Mädchen *n* für alles; **'~-house** *s.* **1.** Küche(ngebäude *n*) *f* (a. ✕); **2.** ♣ Schiffsküche *f*.

cook·ie ['kʊkɪ] *s. Am.* **1.** (süßer) Keks, Plätzchen *n*: **that's the way the ~ crumbles** F so gehts (*od.* so ist das) nun mal; **2.** *Internet:* Cookie *n* (aus dem Internet auf die Festplatte zu übertragende kleine Datei); **3.** *sl.* a) Kerl *m*, b) ,Puppe' *f*; ~ **cut·ter** *s.* Ausstechform *f*, Plätzchenform *f*.

cook·ing ['kʊkɪŋ] **I** *s.* **1.** Kochen *n*, Kochkunst *f*; **2.** Küche *f*, Kochweise *f*; **II** *adj.* **3.** Koch...: ~ **apple**; ~ **range** *s.* Kochherd *m*; ~ **so·da** *s.* ♫ 'Natron *n*.

'cook·out *s. Am.* Abkochen *n* (am Lagerfeuer).

cook·y ['kʊkɪ] → **cookie.**

cool [kuːl] **I** *adj.* □ **1.** kühl, frisch; **2.** kühl, gelassen, kalt(blütig), F ,cool': **as ~ as a cucumber** ,eiskalt', kaltblütig; **keep ~!** reg dich nicht auf!; ♪ ♫ *Jazz* ,Cool Jazz' *m*; **3.** kühl, gleichgültig, lau; **4.** kühl, kalt, abweisend: **a ~ reception** ein kühler Empfang; **5.** unverfroren, frech: ~ **cheek** Frechheit *f*; **a ~ customer** ein geriebener Kunde; **6.** *fig.* glatt, rund: **a ~ thousand pounds** glatte *od.* die Kleinigkeit von tausend Pfund; **7.** *sl.* ,dufte', ,Klasse', ,toll': **that's ~!**; **II** *s.* **8.** Kühle *f*, Frische *f* (*bsd. Luft*): **the ~ of the evening** die Abendkühle; **9.** *sl.* (Selbst)Beherrschung *f*: **blow** (*od.* **lose**) **one's ~** hochgehen, die Beherrschung verlieren; **keep one's ~** ruhig bleiben, die Nerven behalten; **III** *v/t.* **10.** (ab)kühlen; → **heel¹** Redew.; **11.** *fig. Leidenschaften etc.* (ab)kühlen, beruhigen; *Zorn etc.* mäßigen; **IV** *v/i.* **12.** kühl werden, sich abkühlen; **13.** *a.* ~ **down** *fig.* sich abkühlen, erkalten, nachlassen, sich beruhigen; **14.** ~ **down** F ruhiger werden, sich abregen; **15.** *sl.* ruhig bleiben, die Nerven behalten: ~ **it!** immer mit der Ruhe!, reg dich ab!; **'cool·ant** [-lənt] *s.* ⊙ Kühlmittel *n*; **'cool·er** [-lə] *s.* **1.** (*Wein- etc.*)Kühler *m*; **2.** Kühlraum *m*; **3.** *sl.* ,Kittchen' *n*, ,Knast' *m*; **,cool-'head·ed** *adj.* **1.** besonnen, kaltblütig; **2.** leidenschaftslos.

cool·ie ['kuːlɪ] *s.* Kuli *m*.

cool·ing ['kuːlɪŋ] **I** *adj.* kühlend, erfrischend; Kühl...; **II** *s.* (Ab)Kühlung *f*; ~

coil s. Kühlschlange f; ,~·'off pe·ri·od s. Friedenspflicht f; ~ **plant** s. Kühlanlage f.

cool·ness ['kuːlnɪs] s. **1.** Kühle f (a. fig.); **2.** Kaltblütigkeit f; **3.** Unfreundlichkeit f; **4.** Frechheit f.

coomb(e) [kuːm] s. Talmulde f.

coon [kuːn] s. **1.** zo. → **raccoon**; **2.** Am. sl. a) contp. Schwarze(r m) f; ~ **song** Negerlied n, b) ,schlauer Hund'.

coop [kuːp] **I** s. **1.** Hühnerstall m; **2.** Fischkorb m (zum Fangen); **3.** F ,Kabuff' n; **4.** F ,Knast' m; **II** v/t. **5.** oft ~ **up**, ~ **in** einsperren, einpferchen.

co-op ['kəʊɒp] s. F Co-op m (Genossenschaft u. Laden) (abbr. für **cooperative**).

coop·er ['kuːpə] **I** s. **1.** Küfer m, Böttcher m; **2.** Mischbier n; **II** v/t. **3.** Fässer machen, ausbessern; '**coop·er·age** [-ərɪdʒ] s. Böttche'rei f.

co·op·er·ate [kəʊ'ɒpəreɪt] v/t. **1.** zs.-arbeiten (**with** mit, **to** zu e-m Zweck, **in** an dat.); **2.** (**to**) mitwirken (an dat.), beitragen (zu), helfen (bei); **co·op·er·a·tion** [kəʊ,ɒpə'reɪʃn] s. **1.** Zs.-arbeit f, Mitwirkung f; **2.** ✝ a) Kooperati'on f, Zs.-arbeit f, b) Zs.-schluss m, Vereinigung f (zu e-r Genossenschaft); **co-** '**op·er·a·tive** [-pərətɪv] **I** adj. □ **1.** zs.-arbeitend, mitwirkend; **2.** koopera'tiv, hilfsbereit; **3.** genossenschaftlich: ~ **movement** Genossenschaftsbewegung f; ~ **society** Konsumgenossenschaft f; ~ **store** → 4; **II** s. **4.** Co-op m, Kon'sumladen m; **co'op·er·a·tive·ness** [-pərətɪvnɪs] s. Hilfsbereitschaft f; **co'op·er·a·tor** [-tə] s. **1.** Mitarbeiter(in), Mitwirkende(r m) f, Helfer(in); **2.** Mitglied n e-r Kon'sumgenossenschaft f.

co-opt [kəʊ'ɒpt] v/t. hin'zuwählen; **co-op·ta·tion** [,kəʊɒp'teɪʃn] s. Zuwahl f.

co·or·di·nate **I** v/t. [kəʊ'ɔːdɪneɪt] **1.** koordinieren, bei-, gleichordnen, gleichschalten; zs.-fassen; **2.** in Einklang bringen, aufein'ander abstimmen; richtig anordnen, anpassen; **II** adj. [-dnət] **3.** koordiniert, bei-, gleichgeordnet; gleichrangig, -wertig, -artig: ~ **clause** ling. beigeordneter Satz; **4.** Å Koordinaten...; **III** s. [-dnət] **5.** Beigeordnetes n, Gleichwertiges m; **6.** Å Koordi'nate f; **co·or·di·na·tion** [kəʊ- ,ɔːdɪ'neɪʃn] s. **1.** Koordinati'on f (a. physiol. der Muskeln etc.), Gleich-, Beiordnung f, Gleichstellung f, -schaltung f; richtige Anordnung f; **2.** Zs.-fassung f; Zs.-arbeit f; **co'or·di·na·tor** [-tə] s. Koordi'nator m.

coot [kuːt] s. orn. Bläss-, Wasserhuhn n; → **bald** 1.

cop¹ [kɒp] s. Garnwickel m.

cop² [kɒp] sl. **I** v/t. **1.** erwischen (**at** bei): ~ **it** ,sein Fett kriegen'; **2.** klauen; **II** v/i. **3.** ~ **out** ,aussteigen' (**of**, **on** aus), b) ,sich drücken'; **III** s. **4.** **it's a fair** ~ jetzt bin ich ,dran'.

cop³ [kɒp] s. sl. ,Bulle' m (Polizist).

co·pal ['kəʊpəl] s. Ko'pal(harz n) m.

co·par·ce·nar·y [,kəʊ'pɑːsənərɪ] s. ✝ gemeinschaftliches (Grund)Eigentum (gesetzlicher Erben); **co·par·ce·ner** [,kəʊ'pɑːsənə] s. ✝ Miterbe m, -erbin f.

co·part·ner [,kəʊ'pɑːtnə] s. Teilhaber m, Mitinhaber m; ,**co'part·ner·ship** [-ʃɪp] s. **1.** Teilhaberschaft f; **2.** a) Gewinnbeteiligung f, b) Mitbestimmungsrecht n (der Arbeitnehmer).

cope¹ [kəʊp] v/i. **1.** (**with**) gewachsen sein (dat.), fertig werden (mit), bewältigen (acc.), meistern (acc.); **2.** die Lage meistern, zurande kommen, ,es

schaffen'.

cope² [kəʊp] **I** s. **1.** eccl. Chorrock m; **2.** fig. Mantel m, Gewölbe n: ~ **of heaven** Himmelszelt n; **3.** → **coping**; **II** v/t. **4.** bedecken.

co·peck ['kəʊpek] s. Ko'peke f (russische Münze).

cop·er ['kəʊpə] s. Pferdehändler m.

Co·per·ni·can [kəʊ'pɜːnɪkən] adj. koperni'kanisch.

'**cope·stone** → **coping stone**.

cop·i·er ['kɒpɪə] s. **1.** → **copyist**; **2.** ◎ Kopiergerät n, Kopierer m.

co·pi·lot ['kəʊ,paɪlət] s. ✈ 'Kopi,lot m.

cop·ing ['kəʊpɪŋ] s. Mauerkappe f, -krönung f; ~ **saw** s. Laubsäge f; ~ **stone** s. **1.** Deck-, Kappenstein m; **2.** fig. Krönung f, Schlussstein m.

co·pi·ous ['kəʊpjəs] adj. □ **1.** reichlich, aus-, ergiebig, reich, um'fassend; **2.** produk'tiv, fruchtbar: ~ **writer**; **3.** wortreich; 'überschwänglich; '**co·pi·ous·ness** [-nɪs] s. **1.** Fülle f; 'Überfluss m; **2.** Wortreichtum m.

'**cop-out** s. sl. **1.** Vorwand m; **2.** ,Rückzieher' m; **3.** a) ,Aussteigen' n, b) a. ~ **artist** ,Aussteiger(in)'.

cop·per¹ ['kɒpə] **I** s. **1.** min. Kupfer n; **2.** Kupfermünze f: ~**s** Kupfer-, Kleingeld n; **3.** Kupferbehälter m, -gefäß n, -kessel m; bsd. Brit. Waschkessel m; **II** adj. **4.** kupfern, Kupfer...; **5.** kupferrot; **III** v/t. **6.** verkupfern; **7.** mit Kupferblech beschlagen.

cop·per² ['kɒpə] → **cop³**.

cop·per·as ['kɒpərəs] s. 🜍 Vitri'ol n.

cop·per| beech s. 🜍 Blutbuche f; ,~- -'bot·tomed adj. **1.** ⚓ a) mit Kupferbeschlag, b) seetüchtig; **2.** fig. kerngesund; ~ **en·grav·ing** s. **1.** Kupferstich m; **2.** Kupferstechkunst f; ~ **glance** s. min. Kupferglanz m; '~-**head** s. zo. Mokas'sinschlange f; '~-**plate** s. ◎ **1.** Kupferstichplatte f; **2.** Kupferstich m; **3.** fig. gestochene Handschrift; '~,**plat-ed** adj. verkupfert; '~-**smith** s. Kupferschmied m.

cop·per·y ['kɒpərɪ] adj. kupferartig, -farbig, -haltig.

cop·pice ['kɒpɪs] s. **1.** 'Unterholz n, Gestrüpp n; Gebüsch n, Dickicht n; **2.** Gehölz n, niedriges Wäldchen.

cop·ra ['kɒprə] s. Kopra f.

copse [kɒps] → **coppice**.

Copt [kɒpt] s. Kopte m, Koptin f.

'**cop·ter** ['kɒptə] F für **helicopter**.

cop·u·la ['kɒpjʊlə] s. **1.** ling. u. phls. 'Kopula f; **2.** anat. Bindeglied n; '**cop·u·late** [-leɪt] v/i. kopulieren: a) koitieren, b) zo. sich paaren; **cop·u·la·tion** [,kɒpjʊ'leɪʃn] s. **1.** ling. u. phls. Verbindung f; **2.** Kopulati'on f: a) 'Koitus m, b) Paarung f; '**cop·u·la·tive** [-lətɪv] **I** adj. □ **1.** verbindend, Binde...; **2.** ling. kopula'tiv; **3.** biol. Kopulations...; **II** s. **4.** ling. 'Kopula f.

cop·y ['kɒpɪ] **I** s. **1.** Ko'pie f, Abschrift f: **fair** (od. **clean**) ~ Reinschrift f; **rough** ~ erster Entwurf, Konzept n, Kladde f; **true** ~ (wort)getreue Abschrift; **2.** 'Durchschlag m, -schrift f; **3.** Abzug m (a. phot.), Abdruck m, Pause f; **4.** Nachahmung f, -bildung f; Reproduktion f, Ko'pie f, 'Wiedergabe f; **5.** Muster n, Mo'dell n, Vorlage f; Urschrift f; **6.** druckfertiges Manu'skript, lite'rarisches Materi'al; (Zeitungs- etc.)Stoff m, Text m; **7.** Ausfertigung f, Exem'plar n, Nummer f (Zeitung etc.); **8.** Urkunde f; **II** v/t. **9.** abschreiben, -drucken, -zeichnen, e-e Ko'pie anfertigen von: Computer: Daten über'tragen; ~ **out** ins Reine schreiben, abschreiben; **10.** phot.

e-n Abzug machen von; **11.** nachbilden, reproduzieren, kopieren; **12.** nachahmen, -machen; **13.** 'wiedergeben, Zeitungstext wieder'holen; **III** v/i. **14.** kopieren, abschreiben; **15.** (vom Nachbarn) abschreiben (Schule); **16.** nachahmen; '~-**book** **I** s. **1.** (Schön-)Schreibheft n: **blot one's** ~ F ,sich danebenbenehmen'; **2.** ✝ Kopierbuch n; **II** adj. **3.** alltäglich; **4.** nor'mal; '~-**cat** F **I** s. (sklavischer) Nachahmer; **II** v/t. (sklavisch) nachahmen; ~ **desk** s. Redakti'onstisch m; ~ **ed·i·tor** s. 'Zeitungsredak,teur(in), b) 'Lektor m, Lek'torin f; '~-**hold** s. ⚖ Brit. Zinslehen n, -gut n; '~,**hold·er** s. **1.** ⚖ Brit. Zinslehenbesitzer m; **2.** typ. a) Manu'skripthalter m, b) Kor'rektorgehilfe m.

cop·y·ing| ink ['kɒpɪɪŋ] s. Kopiertinte f; ~ **ma·chine** s. → **copier** 2; ~ **pa·per** s. Ko'pierpa,pier n; ~ **pen·cil** s. Tintenstift m; ~ **press** s. ◎ Kopierpresse f; ~ **test** s. Copytest m (werbepsychologischer Test).

cop·y·ist ['kɒpɪɪst] s. **1.** Abschreiber m, Ko'pist m; **2.** Nachahmer m.

'**cop·y| pro·tec·tion** s. Kopierschutz m; ~ **read·er** Am. → **copy editor**; '~-**right** ⚖ **I** s. 'Copyright n, Urheberrecht n (**in** an dat.): ~ **in designs** Musterschutz m; ~ **reserved** alle Rechte vorbehalten; **II** v/t. das Urheberrecht erwerben an (dat.); urheberrechtlich schützen; **III** adj. urheberrechtlich (geschützt); '~,**writ·er** s. (a. Werbe)Texter m.

co·quet [kɒ'ket] **I** v/i. kokettieren, flirten; fig. liebäugeln (**with** mit); **II** adj. → **coquettish**; **co·quet·ry** ['kɒkɪtrɪ] s. Kokette'rie f; **co·quette** [kɒ'ket] s. ko'kette Frau; **co'quet·tish** [-tɪʃ] adj. □ ko'kett.

cor·al ['kɒrəl] **I** s. **1.** zo. Ko'ralle f; **2.** Ko'rallenstück n; **3.** Ko'rallenrot n; **4.** Beißring m od. Spielzeug n (für Babys) aus Ko'ralle; **II** adj. **5.** Korallen...; **6.** ko'rallenrot; ~ **bead** s. Ko'rallenperle f; **2.** pl. Ko'rallenkette f; ~ **is·land** s. Ko'ralleninsel f.

cor·al·lin ['kɒrəlɪn] s. 🜍 Koral'lin n; '**cor·al·line** [-laɪn] **I** adj. **1.** ko'rallenartig, -haltig; ko'rallenrot; **II** s. **2.** ♀ Ko'rallenalge f; **3.** → **corallin**; '**cor·al·lite** [-laɪt] s. **1.** Ko'rallenske,lett n; **2.** versteinerte Ko'ralle.

cor·al reef s. Ko'rallenriff n.

cor an·glais [,kɔːr'ɑ̃ːŋgleɪ] (Fr.) s. ♪ Englischhorn n.

cor·bel ['kɔːbəl] △ **I** s. Kragstein m, Kon'sole f; **II** v/t. durch Kragsteine stützen.

cor·bie ['kɔːbɪ] s. Scot. Rabe m; '~-**steps** s. pl. △ Giebelstufen pl.

cord [kɔːd] **I** s. **1.** Schnur f, Kordel f, Strick m, Strang m; **2.** anat. Band n, Schnur f, Strang m: → **spinal cord** etc.; **3.** ⚡ (Leitungs-, Anschluss)Schnur f; **4.** a) Rippe f (e-s Stoffes), b) gerippter Stoff, Rips m, bsd. → **corduroy** 1, pl. → **corduroy** 2; **5.** Klafter m, n (Holz); **II** v/t. **6.** (zu)schnüren, (fest)binden, befestigen; **7.** Bücherrücken rippen; '**cord·age** [-dɪdʒ] s. ⚓ Tauwerk n.

cor·date ['kɔːdeɪt] adj. ♀, zo. herzförmig (Blatt, Muschel etc.).

cord·ed ['kɔːdɪd] adj. **1.** ge-, verschnürt; **2.** gerippt (Stoff); **3.** Strick...; **4.** in Klaftern gestapelt (Holz).

cor·de·lier [,kɔːdɪ'lɪə] s. eccl. Franzis'kaner(mönch) m.

cor·dial ['kɔːdjəl] **I** adj. □ **1.** fig. herzlich, freundlich, warm, aufrichtig; **2.** ✿ belebend, stärkend; **II** s. **3.** ✿ belebendes Mittel, Stärkungsmittel n; **4.** Li'kör

m; **cor·di·al·i·ty** [ˌkɔːdɪˈælətɪ] *s.* Herzlichkeit *f*, Wärme *f*.
cord·ite [ˈkɔːdaɪt] *s.* ✕ Kor'dit *m*.
cord·less *adj. teleph.* schnurlos: ~ **(tele-) phone** schnurloses Tele'fon.
cor·don [ˈkɔːdn] **I** *s.* **1.** Kor'don *m*: a) ✕ Postenkette *f*, b) Absperrkette *f*: ~ *of police*; **2.** Kette *f*, Spa'lier *n* (*Personen*); **3.** Spa'lier(obst)baum *m*; **4.** △ Mauerkranz *m*, -sims *m*, *n*; **5.** Ordensband *n*; **II** *v/t.* **6.** *a.* ~ *off* (mit Posten *etc.*) absperren, abriegeln; ~ **bleu** [ˌkɔːdɔ̃ːmˈblɜː] (*Fr.*) *s.* **1.** Cordon *m* bleu; **2.** hohe Per'sönlichkeit; **3.** *humor.* erstklassiger Koch.
cor·do·van [ˈkɔːdəvən] *s.* 'Korduan(leder) *n*.
cord| tire *Am.*, ~ **tyre** *Brit. s. mot.* Kordreifen *m*.
cor·du·roy [ˈkɔːdərɔɪ] **I** *s.* **1.** Kord-, Ripssamt *m*; **2.** *pl.* Kordsamthose *f*; **II** *adj.* **3.** Kordsamt...; ~ **road** *s. Am.* Knüppeldamm *m*.
cord·wain·er [ˈkɔːdˌweɪnə] *s.* Schuhmacher *m*: ♄**s' Company** Schuhmachergilde *f* (*London*).
'cord·wood *s. bsd. Am.* Klafterholz *n*.
core [kɔː] **I** *s.* **1.** ♀ Kerngehäuse *n*, Kern *m* (*Obst*); **2.** *fig.* Kern *m* (*a.* ⊕, ⚡), das Innerste, Herz *n*, Mark *n*, Seele *f* (*a. Kabel, Seil*): *to the* ~ bis ins Mark *od.* Innerste, durch u. durch; ~ *meltdown* Kernschmelze *f*; ~ *memory* Computer: Kernspeicher *m*; ~ *time* Kernzeit *f*; → *hard core*; **3.** (Eiter)Pfropf *m* (*Geschwür*); **II** *v/t.* **4.** Äpfel *etc.* entkernen.
co·re·late *etc.* → **correlate** *etc.*
co·re·li·gion·ist [ˌkəʊrɪˈlɪdʒənɪst] *s.* Glaubensgenosse *m*, -genossin *f*.
cor·er [ˈkɔːrə] *s.* Fruchtentkerner *m*.
co·re·spond·ent [ˌkəʊrɪˈspɒndənt] *s.* ⚖ Mitbeklagte(r *m*) *f* (*im Ehebruchsprozess*).
core time *s.* Kernzeit *f* (*Ggs. Gleitzeit*).
cor·gi, cor·gy [ˈkɔːgɪ] → *Welsh corgi*.
co·ri·a·ceous [ˌkɒrɪˈeɪʃəs] *adj.* **1.** ledern, Leder...; **2.** lederartig, zäh.
Co·rin·thi·an [kəˈrɪnθɪən] **I** *adj.* **1.** ko'rinthisch: ~ *column* korinthische Säule; **II** *s.* **2.** Ko'rinther(in); **3.** *pl. bibl.* (Brief *m* des Paulus an die) Ko'rinther *pl.*
cork [kɔːk] **I** *s.* **1.** ♀ Kork *m*, Korkrinde *f*; Korkeiche *f*; **2.** Kork(en) *m*, Stöpsel *m*, Pfropfen *m*; **3.** Angelkork *m*, Schwimmer *m*; **II** *adj.* **4.** Kork...; **III** *v/t.* **5.** ver-, zukorken; **6.** *Gesicht* mit gebranntem Kork schwärzen; **'cork·age** [-kɪdʒ] *s.* **1.** Verkorken *n*; **2.** Entkorken *n*; **3.** Korkengeld *n*; **corked** [-kt] *adj.* **1.** ver-, zugekorkt, verstöpselt; **2.** korkig, nach Kork schmeckend; **3.** mit Korkschwarz gefärbt; **'cork·er** [-kə] *s. sl.* **1.** das Entscheidende; **2.** entscheidendes Argu'ment; **3.** a) ‚Knüller', ‚tolles Ding', ‚toller Kerl'; **'cork·ing** [-kɪŋ] *adj. sl.* ‚toll', ‚prima'.
cork| jack·et *s.* Kork-, Schwimmweste *f*; ~ **oak** *s.* ♀ Korkeiche *f*; **'~·screw** **I** *s.* Korkenzieher *m*: ~ **curls** Korkenzieherlocken; **II** *v/i.* sich schlängeln *od.* winden; **III** *v/t.* 'durchwinden, spi'ralig bewegen; F *fig.* mühsam her'ausziehen (*out of* aus); ~ **sole** *s.* Korkeinlegesohle *f*; ~ **tree** → *cork oak*; **'~·wood** *s.* **1.** ♀ Korkholzbaum *m*; **2.** Korkholz *n*.
cork·y [ˈkɔːkɪ] *adj.* **1.** korkartig, Kork...; **2.** → *corked* 2; **3.** F ‚putzmunter'.
cor·mo·rant [ˈkɔːmərənt] *s.* **1.** *orn.* Kormo'ran *m*, Scharbe *f*, Seerabe *m*; **2.** *fig.* Vielfraß *m*.
corn¹ [kɔːn] **I** *s.* **1.** *coll.* Getreide *n*, Korn *n* (*Pflanze od. Frucht*); *engS.* a)

England: Weizen *m*, b) *Scot., Ir.* Hafer *m*, c) *Am.* Mais *m*, d) Hafer *m* (*Pferdefutter*): ~ *on the cob* Mais *m* am Kolben (*als Gemüse*); **2.** Getreide- *od.* Samenkorn *n*; **3.** *Am.* → *corn whisky*; **II** *v/t.* **4.** pökeln, einsalzen: ~*ed beef* Corned beef *n*, Büchsenfleisch *n*.
corn² [kɔːn] *s.* ♣ Hühnerauge *n*: *tread on s.o.'s* ~*s fig.* j-m auf die Hühneraugen treten.
corn| belt *s. Am.* Maisgürtel *m* (*im Mittleren Westen*); **'~·bind** *s.* ♀ Ackerwinde *f*; ~ **bread** *s. Am.* Maisbrot *n*; ~ **cake** *s. Am.* (Pfann)Kuchen *m* aus Maismehl; ~ **chan·dler** *s. Brit.* Korn-, Saathändler *m*; **'~·cob** *s.* **1.** Maiskolben *m*; **2.** *a.* ~ *pipe* Maiskolbenpfeife *f*; **'~·cock·le** *s.* ♀ Kornrade *f*.
cor·ne·a [ˈkɔːnɪə] *s. anat.* Hornhaut *f* (*des Auges*), 'Kornea *f*.
cor·nel [ˈkɔːnəl] *s.* ♀ Kor'nelkirsche *f*.
cor·ne·ous [ˈkɔːnɪəs] *adj.* hornig.
cor·ner [ˈkɔːnə] **I** *s.* **1.** (Straßen-, Häuser)Ecke *f*, *bsd. mot.* Kurve *f*: *round the* ~ um die Ecke; *blind* ~ unübersichtliche (Straßen)Biegung; *cut* ~*s a*) *mot.* die Kurven schneiden, b) *fig.* die Sache abkürzen; *take a* ~ e-e Kurve nehmen (*Auto*); *cut off a* ~ ein Stück (*Weges*) abschneiden; *turn the* ~ um die (Straßen)Ecke biegen; *he's turned the* ~ *fig.* er ist über den Berg; **2.** Winkel *m*, Ecke *f*: *put a child in the* ~ ein Kind in die Ecke stellen; *in a tight* ~ *fig.* in der Klemme, in Verlegenheit; *drive s.o. into a* ~ j-n in die Enge treiben; *look at s.o. from the* ~ *of one's eye* j-n aus den Augenwinkeln ansehen; **3.** verborgener *od.* geheimer Winkel, entlegene Stelle; **4.** Gegend *f*, ‚Ecke': *from the four* ~*s of the earth* aus allen Himmelsrichtungen, von überall her; **5.** ♣ a) spekula'tiver Aufkauf, b) (Aufkäufer)Ring *m*, Mono'pol(gruppe *f*) *n*: ~ *in wheat* Weizenkorner *m*; **6.** *sport* a) Fußball *etc.*: Eckball *m*, Ecke *f*, b) Boxen: (Ring)Ecke *f*; **II** *v/t.* **7.** in die Enge treiben; in Bedrängnis bringen; **8.** ♣ *Ware* (spekula'tiv) aufkaufen, *fig.* mit Beschlag belegen: ~ *the market* den Markt *od.* alles aufkaufen; **III** *v/i.* **9.** *Am.* a) e-e Ecke *od.* e-n Winkel bilden, b) an e-r Ecke gelegen sein; **IV** *adj.* **10.** Eck...: ~ *house*; **'~·chis·el** *s.* ⊕ Winkelmeißel *m.*
cor·nered [ˈkɔːnəd] *adj.* **1.** *in Zssgn:* ...eckig; **2.** in die Enge getrieben, in der Klemme.
cor·ner| kick *s.* Fußball: Eckstoß *m*; ~ **seat** *s.* Eckplatz *m*; ~ **shop** *s.* Tante-Emma-Laden *m*; **'~·stone** *s.* △ Eck-*od.* Grundstein *m*; *fig.* Eckpfeiler *m*, Grundstein *m*; **'~·ways, '~·wise** *adv.* **1.** mit der Ecke nach vorn; **2.** diago'nal.
cor·net [ˈkɔːnɪt] *s.* **1.** ♪ a) (Pi'ston)Kor'nett *n* (*a.* Orgelregister), b) Kornet'tist *m*; **2.** spitze Tüte; **3.** a) *Brit.* Eistüte *f*, b) Cremerolle *f*; **4.** Schwesternhaube *f*; **5.** ✕ *hist.* a) Fähnlein *n*, b) Kor'nett *m*, Fähnrich *m*; **'cor·net·(t)ist** [-tɪst] *s.* ♪ Kornet'tist *m.*
corn| ex·change *s.* Getreidebörse *f*; ~ **field** *s.* Getreidefeld *n*; *Am.* Maisfeld *n*; **'~·flakes** *s. pl.* Cornflakes *pl.*; ~ **flour** *s.* Stärkemehl *n*; **'~·flow·er** *s.* ♀ Kornblume *f*.
cor·nice [ˈkɔːnɪs] *s.* **1.** △ Gesims *n*, Sims *m*, *n*; **2.** Kranz-, Randleiste *f*; **3.** Bilderleiste *f*; **4.** (Schnee)Wechte *f*.
Cor·nish [ˈkɔːnɪʃ] **I** *adj.* aus Cornwall, kornisch; **II** *s.* kornische Sprache; **'~·man** [-mən] *s.* [irr.] Einwohner *m*

von Cornwall.
'corn·loft *s.* Getreidespeicher *m*; **~ pop·py, ~ rose** *s.* ♀ Klatschmohn *m*, -rose *f*; **'~·stalk** *s.* **1.** Getreidehalm *m*; **2.** *Am.* Maisstängel *m*; **3.** F Bohnenstange *f* (*lange, dünne Person*); **'~·starch** *s. Am.* Stärkemehl *n.*
cor·nu·co·pi·a [ˌkɔːnjuˈkəʊpjə] *s.* **1.** Füllhorn *n* (*a. fig.*); **2.** *fig.* (*of*) Fülle *f* (von), 'Überfluss *m* (an *dat.*).
corn whis·ky *s. Am.* Maiswhisky.
corn·y [ˈkɔːnɪ] *adj.* **1.** a) *Brit.* Korn..., b) *Am.* Mais...; **2.** getreidereich; **3.** körnig; **4.** *Am. sl.* a) schmalzig, sentimen'tal (*bsd.* ♪), b) kitschig, abgedroschen, c) ländlich.
co·rol·la [kəˈrɒlə] *s.* Blumenkrone *f.*
co·rol·lar·y [kəˈrɒlərɪ] *s.* **1.** ⋀, *phls.* Folgesatz *m*; **2.** logische Folge *f* (*of, to* von *od. gen.*).
co·ro·na [kəˈrəʊnə] *pl.* **-nae** [-niː] *s.* **1.** *ast.* a) Krone *f* (*Sternbild*), b) Hof *m*, Ko'rona *f*, Strahlenkranz *m*; **2.** *a.* ~ *discharge* ⚡ Glimmentladung *f*, Ko'rona *f*; **3.** ♀ Kranzleiste *f*; **4.** *anat.* Zahnkrone *f*; **5.** ♀ Nebenkrone *f*; **6.** Kronleuchter *m.*
cor·o·nach [ˈkɒrənək] *s. Scot. u. Ir.* Totenklage *f.*
cor·o·nal [ˈkɒrənl] *s.* **1.** Stirnreif *m*, Dia'dem *n*; **2.** (Blumen)Kranz *m.*
cor·o·nar·y [ˈkɒrənərɪ] **I** *adj.* **1.** kronen-, kranzartig; **2.** ♣ koro'nar, (Herz-)Kranz...: ~ *artery* Kranzarterie *f*; ~ *thrombosis* → **II** *s.* **3.** ♣ Koro'narthrom,bose *f*; **,~·risk** *adj.* in'farktgefährdet;
cor·o·na·tion [ˌkɒrəˈneɪʃn] *s.* **1.** Krönung *f*; **2.** Krönungsfeier *f.*
cor·o·ner [ˈkɒrənə] *s.* ⚖ Coroner *m* (*richterlicher Beamter zur Untersuchung der Todesursache in Fällen unnatürlichen Todes*); → *inquest* 1.
cor·o·net [ˈkɒrənɪt] *s.* **1.** kleine Krone; **2.** Adelskrone *f*; **3.** Dia'dem *n*; **4.** *zo.* Hufkrone *f* (*Pferd*); **'cor·o·net·ed** [-tɪd] *adj.* **1.** e-e Adelskrone *od.* ein Dia'dem tragend; **2.** adelig; **3.** mit Adelswappen (*Briefpapier*).
cor·po·ral¹ [ˈkɔːpərəl] *s.* ✕ 'Unteroffi,zier *m.*
cor·po·ral² [ˈkɔːpərəl] *adj.* ☐ **1.** körperlich, leiblich: ~ *punishment* körperliche Züchtigung; **2.** per'sönlich; **cor·po·ral·i·ty** [ˌkɔːpəˈrælətɪ] *s.* Körperlichkeit *f.*
cor·po·rate [ˈkɔːpərət] *adj.* ☐ **1.** vereinigt, körperschaftlich, korpora'tiv, Körperschafts...; inkorporiert: ~ *body* → *corporation* 1; ~ *seal* a) *Brit.* Siegel *n* e-r juristischen Person, b) *Am.* Firmensiegel *n*; ~ *stock Am.* (Gesellschafts)Aktien *pl.*; ~ *tax Am.* Körperschaftssteuer *f*; ~ *town* Stadt *f* mit eigenem Recht; **2.** gemeinsam, kollek'tiv;
cor·po·ra·tion [ˌkɔːpəˈreɪʃn] *s.* **1.** ⚖ ju'ristische Per'son: ~ *tax* Körperschaftssteuer *f*; **2.** *Brit.* (rechtsfähige) Handelsgesellschaft *f*; **3.** *a.* **stock** ~ ♣ *Am.* 'Aktiengesellschaft *f*; **4.** Vereinigung *f*, Gilde *f*, Innung *f*, Zunft *f*; **5.** Stadtbehörde *f*; inkorporierte Stadtgemeinde; **6.** F Schmerbauch *m*; **'cor·po·ra·tive** [-tɪv] *adj.* **1.** korpora'tiv, körperschaftlich; *Am.* ♣ Gesellschafts...; **2.** *pol.* korpora'tiv (*Staat etc.*).
cor·po·re·al [kɔːˈpɔːrɪəl] *adj.* ☐ **1.** körperlich, leiblich; **2.** materi'ell, dinglich, greifbar; **cor·po·re·al·i·ty** [kɔːˌpɔːrɪˈælətɪ] *s.* Körperlichkeit *f.*
cor·po·sant [ˈkɔːpəzənt] *s.* ⚡ Elmsfeuer *n.*
corps [kɔː] *pl.* **corps** [kɔːz] *s.* **1.** ✕ a)

(Ar'mee)Korps *n*, b) Korps *n*, Truppe *f*: *volunteer* ~ Freiwilligentruppe; **2.** Körperschaft *f*, Korps *n*; **3.** Korps *n*, Korporati'on *f*, (Stu'denten)Verbindung *f*; ~ **de bal·let** [ˌkɔːdə'bæleɪ] (*Fr.*) *s.* Bal'lettgruppe *f*; ♫ **Di·plo·ma·tique** ['kɔːˌdɪpləmæ'tɪk] (*Fr.*) *s.* diplo'matisches Korps.

corpse [kɔːps] *s.* Leichnam *m*, Leiche *f*.

cor·pu·lence ['kɔːpjʊləns], **'cor·pu·len·cy** [-sɪ] *s.* Korpu'lenz *f*, Beleibtheit *f*; **'cor·pu·lent** [-nt] *adj.* ☐ korpu'lent, beleibt.

cor·pus ['kɔːpəs] *pl.* **'cor·po·ra** [-pərə] *s.* **1.** Korpus *n*, Sammlung *f* (*Werk*, *Gesetz etc.*); **2.** Groß-, Hauptteil *m*; **3.** ♱ ('Stamm)Kapi,tal *n* (*Ggs. Zinsen etc.*); ♫ **Chris·ti** ['krɪstɪ] *s. eccl.* Fron'leichnam(sfest *n*) *m*.

cor·pus·cle ['kɔːpʌsl] *s.* **1.** *biol.* (Blut-) Körperchen *n*; **2.** *phys.* Kor'puskel *n*, *f*, Elemen'tarteilchen *n*; **cor·pus·cu·lar** [kɔː'pʌskjʊlə] *adj. phys.* Korpuskular...; **cor·pus·cule** [kɔː'pʌskjuːl] → *corpuscle.*

cor·pus| de·lic·ti [dɪ'lɪktaɪ] *s.* ⚖ 'Corpus *n* De'licti: a) ⚖ Tatbestand *m*, b) Beweisstück *n*, *bsd.* Leiche *f* (*des Ermordeten*); ~ **ju·ris** ['dʒʊərɪs] *s.* ⚖ Corpus *n* Juris, Gesetzessammlung *f*.

cor·ral [kɒ'rɑːl] **I** *s.* **1.** Kor'ral *m*, (Vieh)Hof *m*, Pferch *m*, Einzäunung *f*; **2.** Wagenburg *f*; **II** *v/t.* **3.** Wagen zu e-r Wagenburg zs.-stellen; **4.** in e-n Pferch treiben; **5.** *fig.* einsperren; **6.** *Am.* F sich *et.* ,schnappen'.

cor·rect [kə'rekt] **I** *v/t.* **1.** korrigieren, verbessern, berichtigen, richtig stellen; **2.** regulieren, regeln, ausgleichen; **3.** *Mängel* abstellen, beheben; **4.** zu'rechtweisen, tadeln: *I stand* ~*ed* ich gebe m-n Fehler zu; **5.** *j-n od. et.* bestrafen; **II** *adj.* ☐ **6.** richtig, fehlerfrei: *be* ~ a) stimmen, b) Recht haben; **7.** kor'rekt, schicklich, einwandfrei: *it is the* ~ *thing* es gehört sich; ~ *behavio(u)r* korrektes Benehmen; **8.** genau, ordentlich; **cor'rec·tion** [-kʃn] *s.* **1.** Verbesserung *f*, Richtigstellung *f*, Berichtigen *n* (*a.* ☯, *phys.*): *I speak under* ~ ich kann mich natürlich (auch) irren; **2.** Korrek'tur *f* (*a.* 🎨, *phys.*, *typ. etc.*), (Fehler)Verbesserung *f*: ~ *fluid* Korrek-'turflüssigkeit *f*; ~ *tape* Schreibmaschine: Korrek'turband *n*; **3.** Zu'rechtweisung *f*; **4.** Bestrafung *f*, ⚖ *a.* Besserung *f*: *house of* ~ ⚖ Strafanstalt *f*; **5.** Bereinigung *f*, Abstellung *f*, Regulierung *f*; **cor'rec·tion·al** [-kʃənl] → *corrective*; **cor'rect·i·tude** [-tɪtjuːd] *s.* Kor'rektheit *f* (*Benehmen*); **cor'rec·tive** [-tɪv] **I** *adj.* ☐ **1.** verbessernd, Verbesserungs..., Berichtigungs..., Korrektur...: ~ *measure* Abhilfemaßnahme *f*; **2.** mildernd, lindernd; **3.** ⚖ Besserungs..., Straf...: ~ *training* Besserungsmaßregel *f*; **II** *s.* **4.** Korrek'tiv *n*, Abhilfe *f*, Heil-, Gegenmittel *n*: **cor'rect·ness** [-nɪs] *s.* Richtigkeit *f*; Kor'rektheit *f*; **cor'rec·tor** [-tə] *s.* **1.** Verbesserer *m*; **2.** 'Kritiker(in); **3.** *mst* ~ *of the press Brit. typ.* Kor'rektor *m*; **4.** Besserungsmittel *n*.

cor·re·late ['kɒrəleɪt] **I** *v/t.* in Wechselbeziehung bringen (*with* mit), aufeinander beziehen; in Über'einstimmung bringen (*with* mit); **II** *v/i.* in Wechselbeziehung stehen (*with* mit), sich aufeinander beziehen; entsprechen (*with dat.*); **III** *s.* Korre'lat *n*, Gegenstück *n*; **cor·re·la·tion** [ˌkɒrə'leɪʃn] *s.* Wechselbeziehung *f*, gegenseitige Abhängigkeit, Entsprechung *f*; **cor·rel·a·tive** [kɒ'relətɪv] **I** *adj.* ☐ korrela'tiv, in

Wechselbeziehung stehend, sich ergänzend; entsprechend; **II** *s.* Korre'lat *n*, Gegenstück *n*, Ergänzung *f*.

cor·re·spond [ˌkɒrɪ'spɒnd] *v/i.* **1.** (*with*, *to*) entsprechen (*dat.*), über'einstimmen, in Einklang stehen (mit); **2.** (*with*, *to*) passen (zu), sich eignen (für); **3.** (*to*) entsprechen (*dat.*), das Gegenstück sein (von), ana'log sein (zu); **4.** in Briefwechsel (♱ in Geschäftsverkehr) stehen (*with* mit). **cor·re·spond·ence** [ˌkɒrɪ'spɒndəns] *s.* **1.** Über'einstimmung *f* (*with* mit, *between* zwischen *dat.*); **2.** Angemessenheit *f*, Entsprechung *f*; **3.** Korrespon-'denz *f*: a) Briefwechsel *m*, b) Briefe *pl.*; **4.** *Zeitung:* Beiträge *pl.*; ~ *clerk s.* ♱ Korrespon'dent(in); ~ *col·umn s.* Leserbriefspalte *f*; ~ *chess s.* Fernschach *n*; ~ *course s.* Fernkurs *m*; ~ *school s.* 'Fernlehrinsti,tut *n*.

cor·re·spond·ent [ˌkɒrɪ'spɒndənt] **I** *s.* Korrespon'dent(in): a) (Brief)Schreiber(in); Briefpartner(in), b) ♱ Geschäftsfreund *m*, c) *Zeitung:* Mitarbeiter(in); Einsender(in): *foreign* ~ Auslandskorrespondent; *special* ~ Sonderberichterstatter *m*; **II** *adj.* → ,**corre-**'**spond·ing** [-dɪŋ] *adj.* ☐ **1.** entsprechend, gemäß (*to dat.*); **2.** in Briefwechsel stehend (*with* mit): ~ *member* korrespondierendes Mitglied; ,**corre-**'**spond·ing·ly** [-dɪŋlɪ] *adv.* entsprechend, demgemäß.

cor·ri·dor ['kɒrɪdɔː] *s.* **1.** 'Korridor *m*, Gang *m*, Flur *m*; **2.** 🚆 'Korridor *m*, Seitengang *m*: ~ *train* D-Zug *m*; **3.** *geogr.*, *pol.* 'Korridor *m* (*Landstreifen durch fremdes Gebiet*).

cor·ri·gen·dum [ˌkɒrɪ'dʒendəm] *pl.* **-da** [-də] *s.* **1.** zu verbessernder Druckfehler; **2.** *pl.* Druckfehlerverzeichnis *n*; **cor·ri·gi·ble** ['kɒrɪdʒəbl] *adj.* **1.** zu verbessern(d); **2.** lenksam, fügsam.

cor·rob·o·rate [kə'rɒbəreɪt] *v/t.* bekräftigen, bestätigen, erhärten; **cor·rob·o·ra·tion** [kəˌrɒbə'reɪʃn] *s.* Bekräftigung *f*, Bestätigung *f*, Erhärtung *f*; **cor'rob·o·ra·tive** [-bərətɪv], **cor'rob·o·ra·to·ry** [-bərətərɪ] *adj.* bestärkend, bestätigend.

cor·rode [kə'rəʊd] **I** *v/t.* **1.** 🎨, ☯ zer-, anfressen, angreifen, korrodieren; weg-ätzen, -beizen; **2.** *fig.* zerfressen, zerstören, unter'graben, aushöhlen: *corroding care* nagende Sorge; **II** *v/i.* **3.** zerfressen werden, korrodieren, rosten; **4.** sich einfressen; **5.** verderben, verfallen; **cor·ro·dent** [-dənt] *Am.* **I** *adj.* ätzend; **II** *s.* Ätzmittel *n*; **cor·ro·sion** [-əʊʒn] *s.* **1.** 🎨, ☯ Korrosi'on *f*, An-, Zerfressen *n*; Rostfraß *m*; Ätzen *n*, Beizen *n*; **2.** *fig.* Zerstörung *f*; **cor·ro·sive** [-əʊsɪv] **I** *adj.* ☐ **1.** 🎨, ☯ zerfressend, ätzend, beizend, angreifend, Korrosions...; **2.** *fig.* nagend, quälend; **II** *s.* **3.** 🎨, ☯ Ätz-, Beizmittel *n*; **cor·'ro·sive·ness** [-əʊsɪvnɪs] *s.* ätzende Schärfe.

cor·ru·gate ['kɒrʊgeɪt] **I** *v/t.* wellen, riefen, runzeln, furchen; **II** *v/i.* sich wellen *od.* runzeln, runz(e)lig werden; '**cor·ru·gat·ed** [-tɪd] *adj.* runz(e)lig, gefurcht; gewellt, gerieft: ~ *iron* (*od.* *sheet*) Wellblech *n*; ~ *cardboard*, ~ *paper* Wellpappe *f*; **cor·ru·ga·tion** [ˌkɒrʊ'geɪʃn] *s.* **1.** Runzeln *n*, Furchen *n*; Wellen *n*, Riefen *n*; **2.** Furche *f*, Falte *f* (*auf der Stirn*).

cor·rupt [kə'rʌpt] **I** *adj.* ☐ **1.** (*moralisch*) verdorben, schlecht, verworfen; **2.** unredlich, unlauter; **3.** kor'rupt, bestechlich, käuflich: ~ *practices* Beste-

chungsmanöver *pl.*, Korruption *f*; **4.** faul, verdorben, schlecht; **5.** unrein, unecht, verfälscht, verderbt (*Text*); **II** *v/t.* **6.** verderben, zu'grunde richten: ~*ing influences* verderbliche Einflüsse; **7.** verleiten, verführen; **8.** korrumpieren, bestechen; **9.** *Texte etc.* verderben, verfälschen, verunstalten; **10.** *fig.* anstecken, infizieren; **III** *v/i.* **11.** (*moralisch*) verderben, verkommen; **12.** schlecht werden, verderben; **cor'rupt·ed** [-tɪd] *adj. Computer:* fehlerhaft; **cor'rupt·i·ble** [-təbl] *adj.* ☐ **1.** zum Schlechten neigend; **2.** bestechlich; **3.** verderblich; vergänglich; **cor'rup·tion** [-pʃn] *s.* **1.** Verdorbenheit *f*, Verworfenheit *f*; **2.** verderblicher Einfluss; **3.** Korrupti'on *f*: a) Kor'ruptheit *f*, Bestechlichkeit *f*, Käuflichkeit *f*, b) kor'rupte Me'thoden *pl.*, Bestechung *f*; **4.** Verfälschung *f*, Korrumpierung *f* (*Text etc.*); **5.** Fäulnis *f*; **cor'rup·tive** [-tɪv] *adj.* **1.** zersetzend, verderblich; **2.** *fig.* ansteckend; **cor'rupt·ness** [-nɪs] → *corruption* 1, 3 a.

cor·sage [kɔː'sɑːʒ] *s.* **1.** Mieder *n*; **2.** 'Ansteckbu,kett *n*.

cor·sair ['kɔːseə] *s.* **1.** *hist.* Kor'sar *m*, Seeräuber *m*; **2.** Kaperschiff *n*.

corse·let ['kɔːslɪt] *s. Am. mst* **cor·se·let** [ˌkɔːsə'let] Korse'lett *n*, Mieder *n*; **2.** *hist.* Harnisch *m*.

cor·set ['kɔːsɪt] *s. oft pl.* Kor'sett *n*; '**cor·set·ed** [-tɪd] *adj.* (ein)geschnürt; '**cor·set·ry** [-trɪ] *s.* Miederwaren *pl.*

Cor·si·can ['kɔːsɪkən] **I** *adj.* korsisch; **II** *s.* Korse *m*, Korsin *f*.

cor·tège [kɔː'teɪʒ] (*Fr.*) *s.* **1.** Gefolge *n* e-s *Fürsten etc.*; **2.** Zug *m*, Prozessi'on *f*: *funeral* ~ Leichenzug *m*.

cor·tex ['kɔːteks] *pl.* **-ti·ces** [-tɪsiːz] *s. ♧, zo., anat.* Rinde *f*: *cerebral* ~ Großhirnrinde.

cor·ti·sone ['kɔːtɪzəʊn] *s.* 💊 Korti'son *n*.

co·run·dum [kə'rʌndəm] *s. min.* Ko-'rund *m*.

cor·us·cate ['kɒrəskeɪt] *v/i.* (auf)blitzen, funkeln, glänzen (*a. fig.*).

cor·vée ['kɔːveɪ] (*Fr.*) *s.* Fronarbeit *f*, -dienst *m* (*a. fig.*).

cor·vette [kɔː'vet] *s.* ⚓ Kor'vette *f*.

cor·vine ['kɔːvaɪn] *adj.* raben-, krähenartig.

Cor·y·don ['kɒrɪdən] *s.* **1.** *poet.* 'Korydon *m*, Schäfer *m*; **2.** schmachtender Liebhaber.

cor·ymb ['kɒrɪmb] *s.* ♧ Doldentraube *f*.

co·ry·phae·us [ˌkɒrɪ'fiːəs] *pl.* **-phae·i** [-'fiːaɪ] *s. antiq. u. fig.* Kory'phäe *f*; **co·ry·phée** ['kɒrɪfeɪ] *s.* Primaballe'rina *f*.

cos¹ [kɒs] *s.* ♧ Lattich *m*.

cos² [kɒz] *cj.* F weil, da.

co·se·cant [ˌkəʊ'siːkənt] *s.* ♱ 'Kosekans *m*.

cosh [kɒʃ] *Brit.* F **I** *s.* Totschläger *m*; **II** *v/t.* mit e-m Totschläger schlagen, *j-m* ,eins über den Schädel hauen'.

cosh·er ['kɒʃə] *v/t.* verhätscheln.

co·sig·na·to·ry [ˌkəʊ'sɪgnətərɪ] *s.* 'Mitunter,zeichner(in).

co·sine ['kəʊsaɪn] *s.* ♱ 'Kosinus *m*.

co·si·ness ['kəʊzɪnɪs] *s.* Behaglichkeit *f*, Gemütlichkeit *f*.

cos·met·ic [kɒz'metɪk] **I** *adj.* (☐ ~*ally*) **1.** kos'metisch (*a. fig.*): ~ *treatment* → 4; ~ (*plastic*) *surgery* Schönheitschirurgie *f od.* -operation *f*; **2.** *fig.* kosmetisch, optisch; **II** *s.* **3.** kosmetisches Mittel, Schönheitsmittel *n*, *pl. a.* Kos'metika; **4.** *pl.* Kos'metik *f*, Schönheitspflege *f*; **cos·me·ti·cian** [ˌkɒzmə'tɪʃn] *s.*, **cos·me·tol·o·gist** [ˌkɒzmə'tɒlədʒɪst] *s.* Kos'metiker(in).

c

cos·mic, cos·mi·cal ['kɒzmɪk(l)] *adj.* □ kosmisch (*a. fig.*).

cos·mog·o·ny [kɒz'mɒgənɪ] *s.* Kosmogo'nie *f* (*Theorie über die Entstehung des Weltalls*); **cos'mog·ra·phy** [-grəfɪ] *s.* Kosmogra'phie *f*, Weltbeschreibung *f*; **cos'mol·o·gy** [-ɒlədʒɪ] *s.* Kosmolo'gie *f*.

cos·mo·naut ['kɒzmənɔːt] *s.* (Welt-)Raumfahrer *m*, Kosmo'naut *m*.

cos·mo·pol·i·tan [ˌkɒzmə'pɒlɪtən] I *adj.* kosmopo'litisch; *weitS.* weltoffen; II *s.* Kosmopo'lit *m*, Weltbürger(in); **cos·mo'pol·i·tan·ism** [-tənɪzəm] *s.* Weltbürgertum *n*; *weitS.* Weltoffenheit *f*.

cos·mos ['kɒzmɒs] *s.* **1.** 'Kosmos *m*: a) Weltall *n*, b) Weltordnung *f*; **2.** Welt *f* für sich; **3.** ♀ 'Kosmos *m* (*Blume*).

Cos·sack ['kɒsæk] *s.* Ko'sak *m*.

cos·set ['kɒsɪt] *v/t.* verhätscheln.

cost [kɒst] I *s.* **1.** *stets sg.* Kosten *pl.*, Preis *m*, Aufwand *m*: ~ *of living* Lebenshaltungskosten; ~*-of-living allowance* Teuerungszulage *f*; ~*-of-living index* Lebenshaltungsindex *m*; **2.** † *a.*) *a.* ~ *price* (Selbst-, Gestehungs)Kosten *pl.*, Selbstkosten-, (Netto)Einkaufspreis *m*, b) (Un)Kosten *pl.*, Auslagen *pl.*, Spesen *pl.*: *at* ~ zum Selbstkostenpreis; ~ *accounting* → *costing*; ~ *accountant* (Betriebs)Kalkulator *m*; ~ *allocation* Kostenumlage *f*; ~*-benefit analysis* Kosten-Nutzen-Analyse *f*; ~ *breakdown* Kostenaufgliederung *f*; ~*-covering* kostendeckend; ~ *free* kostenlos; ~ *plus* Gestehungskosten plus Unternehmergewinn; ~ *of construction* Baukosten *pl.*; **3.** *fig.* Kosten *pl.*, Schaden *m*, Nachteil *m*: *at my* ~ auf m-e Kosten; *at a heavy* ~ unter schweren Opfern; *at the* ~ *of his health* auf Kosten s-r Gesundheit; *to my* ~ zu m-m Schaden; *I know to my* ~ ich weiß aus eigener (bitterer) Erfahrung; *at all* ~*s*, *at any* ~ um jeden Preis; **4.** *pl.* ♫ (Gerichts)Kosten *pl.*, Gebühren *pl.*; *condemn s.o. in the* ~*s* j-n zu den Kosten verurteilen; *dismiss with* ~*s* kostenpflichtig abweisen; *allow* ~*s* die Kosten bewilligen; II *v/t.* [*irr.*] **5.** kosten: *it* ~ *me one pound* es kostete mich ein Pfund; **6.** kosten, bringen um: *it* ~ *him his life* es kostete ihn das Leben; **7.** kosten, verursachen: *it* ~ *me a lot of trouble* es verursachte mir (*od.* kostete mich) große Mühe; **8.** [*pret. u. p.p.* **cost·ed**] † kalkulieren, den Preis berechnen von: ~*ed at* mit e-m Kostenanschlag von; III *v/i.* [*irr.*] **9.** *it* ~ *him dearly fig.* es kam ihm teuer zu stehen.

cos·tal ['kɒstl] *adj.* **1.** *anat.* Rippen..., kos'tal; **2.** ♀ (Blatt)Rippen...; **3.** *zo.* (Flügel)Ader...

co-star ['kəʊstɑː] *thea.*, *Film* I *s.* e-r der Hauptdarsteller; II *v/i.* e-e der Hauptrollen spielen; ~*ring* in e-r der Hauptrollen.

cos·ter·mon·ger ['kɒstəˌmʌŋgə], *a.* **cos·ter** ['kɒstə] *s. Brit.* Straßenhändler(in) für Obst u. Gemüse *etc.*

cost·ing ['kɒstɪŋ] *s.* † *Brit.* Kosten(be)rechnung *f*, Kalkulati'on *f*.

cos·tive ['kɒstɪv] *adj.* □ **1.** ♫ verstopft, hartleibig; **2.** *fig.* geizig; '**cos·tive·ness** [-nɪs] *s.* **1.** ♫ Verstopfung *f*; **2.** *fig.* Geiz *m*.

cost·li·ness ['kɒstlɪnɪs] *s.* **1.** Kostspieligkeit *f*; **2.** Pracht *f*; **cost·ly** ['kɒstlɪ] *adj.* **1.** kostspielig, teuer; **2.** kostbar, wertvoll; prächtig.

cost price → *cost* 2 a.

cos·tume ['kɒstjuːm] *s.* **1.** Ko'stüm *n*, Kleidung *f*, Tracht *f*: ~ *jewel(le)ry* Mo-

deschmuck *m*; **2.** *obs.* Ko'stüm(kleid) *n* (*für Damen*); **3.** ('Masken-, 'Bühnen-)Ko,stüm *n*: ~ *piece thea.* Kostümstück *n*; **4.** Badeanzug *m*; **cos·tum·er** [kɒs'tjuːmə], **cos·tum·i·er** [kɒs'tjuːmɪə] *s.* **1.** Ko'stümverleiher(in); **2.** *thea.* Kostümi'er *m*.

co·sy ['kəʊzɪ] I *adj.* □ behaglich, gemütlich, traulich, heimelig; II *s.* Teehaube *f*, -wärmer *m*; Eierwärmer *m*.

cot¹ [kɒt] *s.* **1.** *Brit.* Kinderbettchen *n*: ~ *death* ♫ plötzlicher Kindstod; **2.** Feldbett *n*; **3.** leichte Bettstelle; **4.** ♪ Schwingbett *n*, Koje *f*.

cot² [kɒt] *s.* **1.** (Schaf- *etc.*)Stall *m*; **2.** *obs.* Häus·chen *n*, Hütte *f*.

co·tan·gent [ˌkəʊ'tændʒənt] *s.* ℞ 'Kotangens *m*.

cote [kəʊt] *s.* Stall *m*, Hütte *f*, Häuschen *n* (*für Kleinvieh etc.*).

co·te·rie ['kəʊtərɪ] *s.* **1.** *contp.* Kote'rie *f*, Klüngel *m*, 'Clique *f*; **2.** exklu'siver Zirkel.

co·thur·nus [kə'θɜːnəs] *pl.* **-ni** [-naɪ] *s.* **1.** *antiq.* Ko'thurn *m*; **2.** erhabener, pa'thetischer Stil.

co·tid·al lines [kəʊ'taɪdl] *s. pl.* ♪ Isor'rhachien *pl.*

co·trus·tee *Am.* **co·trus·tee** [ˌkəʊtrʌs'tiː] *s.* Mittreuhänder *m*.

cot·tage ['kɒtɪdʒ] *s.* **1.** (kleines) Landhaus, Cottage *n*; **2.** *Am.* Ferienhaus *n*; **3.** *Am.* Wohngebäude *n* (*bsd. in e-m Heim*); *Hotel*: Depen'dance *f*; ~ *cheese s.* Hüttenkäse *m*; ~ *hos·pi·tal s.* **1.** kleines Krankenhaus; **2.** *Am.* aus Einzelgebäuden bestehendes Krankenhaus; ~ *in·dus·try s.* 'Heimindu,strie *f*; ~ *pi·a·no s.* Pia'nino *n*; ~ *pud·ding s.* Kuchen *m* mit süßer Soße.

cot·tag·er ['kɒtɪdʒə] *s.* **1.** Cottagebewohner(in); **2.** *Am.* Urlauber(in) in e-m Ferienhaus.

cot·ter ['kɒtə] *s.* ⊕ a) (Schließ)Keil *m*, b) → ~ *pin s.* Splint *m*.

cot·ton ['kɒtn] I *s.* **1.** Baumwolle *f*: *absorbent* ~ Watte *f*; **2.** Baumwollpflanze *f*; **3.** Baumwollstoff *m*; **4.** *pl.* a) Baumwollwaren *pl.*, b) Baumwollkleidung *f*; **5.** (Näh-, Stick)Garn *n*; II *adj.* **6.** baumwollen, Baumwoll...; III *v/i.* **7.** *Am.* F (**with**) a) sich anfreunden (mit), b) gut auskommen (mit); **8.** ~ *on to* F a) *et.* ,kapieren', b) *Am.* → 7 a; ~ *belt s. Am.* Baumwollzone *f*; ~ *bud s.* Wattestäbchen *n*; ~ *can·dy s. Am.* Zuckerwatte *f*; ~ *gin s.* ⊕ Ent'körnungsma,schine *f* (*für Baumwolle*); ~ *grass s.* ♀ Wollgras *n*; ~ *mill s.* 'Baumwollspinne,rei *f*; ~ *pad s.* 'Wattepad *m*; ~ *pick·er s.* Baumwollpflücker *m*; ~ *press s.* Baumwollballenpresse *f*; ~ *print s.* bedruckter Kat'tun; '~-*seed s.* ♀ Baumwollsamen *m*: ~ *oil* Baumwollsamenöl *n*; '~-*tail s. zo. amer.* 'Wildka,ninchen *n*; ~ *waste s.* **1.** Baumwollabfall *m*; **2.** ⊕ Putzwolle *f*; '~-*wood s.* ♀ e-e amer. Pappel; ~ *wool s.* **1.** Rohbaumwolle *f*; **2.** (Verband)Watte *f*: ~ *ball* Wattebausch *m*.

cot·ton·y ['kɒtnɪ] *adj.* **1.** baumwollartig; **2.** flaumig, weich.

cot·y·le·don [ˌkɒtɪ'liːdən] *s.* ♀ **1.** Keimblatt *n*; **2.** ♀ Nabelkraut *n*.

couch¹ [kaʊtʃ] I *s.* **1.** Couch *f* (*a. des Psychoanalytikers*), 'Liege(,sofa *n*) *f*; **2.** Bett *n*, Lager *n* (*a. obs. hunt.*), Lagerstätte *f*; **3.** ⊕ Lage *f*, Schicht *f*, erster Anstrich; II *v/t.* **4.** *Gedanken etc.* in Worte fassen *od.* kleiden, ausdrücken; **5.** *Lanze* einlegen; **6.** ♫ *Star* stechen; **7.** *be* ~*ed* liegen; III *v/i.* **8.** liegen, lagern (*Tier*); **9.** (sich) kauern *od.*

ducken.

couch² [kaʊtʃ] → *couch grass*.

couch·ant ['kaʊtʃənt] *adj. her.* mit erhobenem Kopf liegend.

cou·chette [kuː'ʃet] *s.* 🚃 (Platz *m* in e-m) Liegewagen.

couch grass *s.* ♀ Quecke *f*.

couch po·ta·to *s.* F Dauerglotzer(in) (*der/die nie Sport treibt*).

cou·gar ['kuːgə] *s. zo.* 'Puma *m*.

cough [kɒf] I *s.* **1.** Husten *m*: *give a* ~ (einmal) husten; II *v/i.* **2.** husten; **3.** *mot.* F ,stottern', husten (*Motor*); III *v/t.* **4.** ~ *out od. up* aushusten; **5.** ~ *up sl.* her'ausrücken mit (*Geld, der Wahrheit etc.*); ~ *drop s.* 'Hustenbon,bon *m*, *n*; ~ *mix·ture s.* Hustensaft *m*.

could [kʊd] *pret. von* **can¹**.

cou·loir ['kuːlwɑː] (*Fr.*) *s.* **1.** Bergschlucht *f*; **2.** ⊕ 'Baggerma,schine *f*.

cou·lomb ['kuːlɒm] *s.* ⚡ Cou'lomb *n*, Am'perese,kunde *f*.

coul·ter ['kəʊltə] *s.* ♪ Kolter *n*, Pflugmesser *n*.

coun·cil ['kaʊnsl] *s.* **1.** Rat *m*, Ratsversammlung *f*, beratende Versammlung; Beratung *f*: *be in* ~ zu Rate sitzen; *meet in* ~ e-e (Rats)Sitzung abhalten; *Queen in* ⅋ *Brit.* Königin und Kronrat; ⅋ *of Europe* Europarat *m*; ⅋ *of the European Union* Rat *m* der Europäischen Union; ~ *of war* Kriegsrat (*a. fig.*); **2.** Rat *m* (*Körperschaft*); *engS.* Gemeinderat *m*: *municipal* ~ Stadtrat (*Behörde*); ~ *school* Gemeindeschule *f*; **3.** Kirchenrat *m*, Syn'ode *f*, Kon'zil *n*; **4.** Vorstand *m*, Komi'tee *n*; ~ *cham·ber s.* Ratszimmer *n*; ~ *es·tate s. Brit.* städtische (sozi'ale Wohn)Siedlung; ~ *flat s. Brit.* gemeindeeigene Wohnung (*mit niedriger Miete*), *etwa:* Sozi'alwohnung *f*; ~ *house s. Brit.* stadteigenes (Sozi'al)Wohnhaus.

coun·ci(l)·lor ['kaʊnsələ] *s.* Ratsmitglied *m*, -herr *m*, Stadtrat *m*, -rätin *f*.

coun·cil tax *s. Brit.* e-e Art Haushaltssteuer, *abhängig vom Wert des (privaten) Haushalts u. der Anzahl s-r Mitglieder.*

coun·sel ['kaʊnsl] I *s.* **1.** Rat(schlag) *m*: *take* ~ *of s.o.* von j-m (e-n) Rat annehmen; **2.** Beratung *f*, Über'legung *f*: *take* (*od.* **hold**) ~ *with* a) sich beraten mit, b) sich Rat holen bei; *take* ~ *together* zusammen beratschlagen; ~ *of Plan m*, Absicht *f*; Meinung *f*, Ansicht *f*: *divided* ~*s* geteilte Meinungen; *keep one's* (*own*) ~ s-e Meinung *od.* Absicht für sich behalten; **4.** ♫ (*ohne Artikel*) a) *Brit.* (Rechts)Anwalt *m*, b) *Am.* Rechtsberater *m*, -beistand *m*: ~ *for the defence* Anwalt des Beklagten, *Strafprozess:* Verteidiger *m*; ~ *for the prosecution* Anklagevertreter *m*; **5.** ♫ *coll.* ju'ristische Berater *pl.*; II *v/t.* **6.** *j-m* raten *od.* e-n Rat geben; **7.** zu *et.* raten: ~ *delay* Aufschub empfehlen; '**coun·se(l)·lor** [-lə] *s.* **1.** Berater(in), Ratgeber *m*; **2.** *a.* ~*-at-law Am.* (Rechts)Anwalt *m*; **3.** (Studien-, Berufs)Berater *m*.

count¹ [kaʊnt] I *s.* **1.** Zählen *n*, (*a. Volks- etc.*)Zählung *f*, (Be)Rechnung *f*: *keep* ~ *of s.th.* et. genau zählen (können); *lose* ~ a) die Übersicht verlieren (*of* über), b) sich verzählen; *by my* ~ nach m-r Schätzung; *take the* ~ *Boxen:* ausgezählt werden; *take a* ~ *of nine Boxen:* bis neun angezählt werden; **2.** (End)Zahl *f*, Anzahl *f*, Ergebnis *n*; *sport* Punktzahl *f*; **3.** Berücksichtigung *f*: *take* (**no**) ~ *of* (nicht) zählen *od.* (nicht) berücksichtigen (*acc.*); **4.** ♫ (An)Klagepunkt *m*; II *v/t.* **5.** (ab-, auf-)

C

zählen, (be)rechnen: **~** *the cost* a) die Kosten berechnen, b) *fig.* die Folgen bedenken; **6.** (mit)zählen, einschließen, berücksichtigen: *I* **~** *him among my friends* ich zähle ihn zu m-n Freunden; **~***ing those present* die Anwesenden eingeschlossen; *not* **~***ing* abgesehen von; **7.** erachten, schätzen, halten für: **~** *o.s. lucky* sich glücklich schätzen; **~** *for* (*od. as*) *lost* als verloren ansehen; **~** *it a great hono(u)r* es als große Ehre betrachten; **III** *v/i.* **8.** zählen, rechnen: *he* **~***s among my friends* er zählt zu m-n Freunden; **~***ing from today* von heute an (gerechnet); *I* **~** *on you* ich rechne (*od.* verlasse mich) auf dich; **9.** mitzählen, gelten, von Wert sein: **~** *for nothing* nichts wert sein, nicht von Belang sein; *every little* **~***s* auf jede Kleinigkeit kommt es an; *he simply doesn't* **~** er zählt überhaupt nicht;

Zssgn mit adv.:

count| down *v/t.* **1.** *Geld* hinzuzählen; **2.** *a. v/i.* den Count-down 'durchführen (für); *a. weitS.* letzte (Start)Vorbereitungen treffen (für); **~** *in* *v/t.* mitzählen, einschließen: *count me in!* ich bin dabei *od.* mache mit!; **~** *off* *v/t. u. v/i.* abzählen; **~** *out* *v/t.* **1.** (langsam) abzählen; **2.** ausschließen: *count me out!* ohne mich!; **3.** *Boxen u. Kinderspiel:* auszählen; **4.** *parl. Brit.* a) Gesetzesvorlage zu Fall bringen, b) *Unterhaussitzung* wegen Beschlussunfähigkeit vertagen; **~** *o·ver* *v/t.* nachzählen; **~** *up* *v/t.* zs.-zählen, 'durchrechnen.

count² [kaʊnt] *s.* (nichtbrit.) Graf *m*; → *palatine¹* 1.

count·down ['kaʊntdaʊn] *s.* 'Count--down *m, n* (*a. fig.*).

coun·te·nance ['kaʊntənəns] **I** *s.* **1.** Gesichtsausdruck *m*, Miene *f*: *his* **~** *fell* er machte ein langes Gesicht; *change one's* **~** s-n Gesichtsausdruck ändern, die Farbe wechseln; **2.** Fassung *f*, Haltung *f*, Gemütsruhe *f*: *keep one's* **~** die Fassung bewahren; *keep s.o. in* **~** j-n ermuntern, j-n unterstützen; *put s.o. out of* **~** j-n aus der Fassung bringen; **3.** Ermunterung *f*, Unter'stützung *f*: *give* (*od. lend*) **~** *to* j-n ermutigen, j-n *od. et.* unterstützen, Glaubwürdigkeit verleihen (*dat.*); **II** *v/t.* **4.** j-n ermuntern, (unter)'stützen; **5.** *et.* gutheißen.

count·er¹ ['kaʊntə] *s.* **1.** Ladentisch *m*, *a.* Theke *f* (*im Wirtshaus etc.*): *under the* **~** unter dem Ladentisch (*verkaufen etc.*), unter der Hand, heimlich; **2.** Schalter *m* (*Bank etc.*); **3.** Spielmarke *f*; **4.** Zählperle *f*, -kugel *f* (*Kinderrechenmaschine*); **5.** ☉ Zähler *m*, Zählgerät *n*, -werk *n*.

count·er² ['kaʊntə] **I** *adv.* **1.** entgegengesetzt; (*to*) entgegen, zu'wider (*dat.*): *run* (*od. go*) **~** *to* zuwiderlaufen (*dat.*); **~** *to all rules* entgegen allen *od.* wider alle Regeln; **II** *adj.* **2.** Gegen..., entgegengesetzt; **III** *s.* **3.** Abwehr *f, Boxen etc., a. fig.:* Konter(schlag) *m; fenc.* Pa'rade *f; Eislauf:* Gegenwende *f;* **4.** *zo.* Brustgrube *f* (*Pferd*); **IV** *v/t. u. v/i.* **5.** entgegenwirken, entgegnen; wider'sprechen, zu'widerhandeln (*dat.*); **6.** *Boxen, Fußball etc., a. fig.:* kontern.

coun·ter·|act [-tə'ræ-] *v/t.* **1.** entgegenwirken (*dat.*); bekämpfen, vereiteln; **2.** kompensieren, neutralisieren; **~·'ac·tion** [-tə'ræ-] *s.* **1.** Gegenwirkung *f,* -maßnahme *f;* **2.** 'Widerstand *m,* Oppositi'on *f;* **3.** Durch'kreuzung *f;* **~·'ac·tive** [-tə'ræ-] *adj.* ☐ entgegenwirkend; **'~·at,tack** [-təræ-] **I** *s.* Gegenangriff *m*

(*a. fig.*), *sport* Konter *m;* **II** *v/i. u. v/t.* e-n Gegenangriff machen (gegen), *sport* kontern; **'~·at,trac·tion** [-tərə-] *s.* **1.** *phys.* entgegengesetzte Anziehungskraft; **2.** *fig.* 'Gegenattrakti,on *f;* **'~·bal·ance I** *s.* Gegengewicht *n* (*a. fig.*); **II** *v/t.* [,kaʊntə'bæləns] ein Gegengewicht bilden zu, ausgleichen, aufwiegen; die Waage halten (*dat.*); **'~·blast** *s. fig.* Gegenschlag *m*, heftige Reakti'on; **'~·blow** *s.* Gegenschlag *m* (*a. fig.*): **'~·charge I** *s.* **1.** 🏛 Gegenklage *f;* **2.** ⚔ Gegenangriff *m;* **II** *v/t.* **3.** 🏛 e-e Gegenklage erheben gegen; **4.** ⚔ e-n Gegenangriff führen gegen; **'~·check** *s.* **1.** a) Gegenwirkung *f,* b) Hindernis *n;* **2.** Gegen-, Nachprüfung *f;* **'~·claim** 🏛, 🏛 **I** *s.* Gegenforderung *f;* **II** *v/t.* als Gegenforderung verlangen; **'~·clock·wise** → *anticlockwise;* **'~·cy·cli·cal** *adj.* ☐ ♣ konjunk'turdämpfend; **'~·es·pi·o·nage** [-tər'e-] *s.* Spio'nageabwehr *f,* Abwehr(dienst *m*) *f;* **'~·feit** [-fɪt] **I** *adj.* **1.** nachgemacht, gefälscht, unecht, falsch: **~** *coin* Falschgeld *n;* **2.** vorgetäuscht, falsch; verstellt; **II** *s.* **3.** Fälschung *f;* **4.** Falschgeld *n;* **III** *v/t.* **5.** fälschen; **6.** heucheln, vorgeben, vortäuschen; **'~·feit·er** [-,fɪtə] *s.* **1.** Fälscher *m,* Falschmünzer *m;* **2.** Heuchler(in); **'~·foil** *s.* **1.** (Kon'troll-) Abschnitt *m* (*Scheckbuch etc.*), Ku'pon *m;* **2.** a) Ku'pon *m,* Zins-, Divi'dendenschein *m,* b) Ta'lon *m* (*Erneuerungsschein*); **'~·in,tel·li·gence** [-tərɪn-] Spio'nageabwehr(dienst *m*) *f;* **'~·jump·er** *s.* F Ladenschwengel *m* (*Verkäufer*); **'~·man** [-mən] *s.* [*irr.*] Verkäufer *m;* **~·mand** [,kaʊntə'maːnd] **I** *v/t.* **1.** widerrufen, rückgängig machen, 🏛 stornieren: *until* **~***ed* bis auf Widerruf; **2.** absagen, abbestellen; **II** *s.* **3.** Gegenbefehl *m;* **4.** Wider'rufung *f,* Aufhebung *f;* 🏛 Stornierung *f;* **'~·march** *s.* **1.** ⚔ Rückmarsch *m;* **2.** *fig.* völlige 'Umkehr; **'~·mark** *s.* Gegen-, Kon'trollzeichen *n* (*bsd. für die Echtheit*); **'~·meas·ure** *s.* **1.** Gegenmaßnahme *f;* **'~·mo·tion** *s.* **1.** Gegenbewegung *f;* **2.** *pol.* Gegenantrag *m;* **'~·move** *s.* Gegenzug *m;* **'~·of·fer** [-tər,ɒ-] *s.* 🏛 Gegenangebot *n;* **'~·or·der** [-tər,ɔː-] **1.** 🏛 Abbestellung *f;* **2.** ⚔ Gegenbefehl *m;* **'~·pane** *s.* Tagesdecke *f;* **'~·part** *s.* **1.** Gegen-, Seitenstück *n;* **2.** genaue Ergänzung; **3.** Ebenbild *n;* **4.** Dupli'kat *n;* **5.** *fig.* ,Gegen'über' *n,* Kol'lege *m: his Soviet* **~***;* **'~·plot** *s.* Gegenanschlag *m;* **'~·point I** *s.* ♪ 'Kontrapunkt *m;* **II** *v/t.* kontrapunktieren; **'~·poise I** *s.* **1.** Gegengewicht *n* (*a. fig.*); Gleichgewicht *n;* **II** *v/t.* **2.** als Gegengewicht wirken zu, ausgleichen; **3.** *fig.* im Gleichgewicht halten, ausgleichen, aufwiegen; **'~·pro'duct·ive** *adj.* 'kontraprodu,ktiv, das Gegenteil bewirkend; **'~·ref·or,ma·tion** *s.* 'Gegenreformati,on *f;* **'~·rev·o,lu·tion** *s.* 'Gegenrevoluti,on *f;* **'~·shaft** *s.* ☉ Vorlegewelle *f:* **~** *gear* Vorgelege *n;* **'~·sign I** *s.* **1.** ⚔ Losungswort *n;* **2.** Gegenzeichen *n;* **II** *v/t.* **3.** gegenzeichnen; **4.** *fig.* bestätigen; **'~·sig·na·ture** *s.* Gegenzeichnung *f;* **'~·sink I** *s.* **1.** Versenkbohrer *m;* **2.** Senkschraube *f;* **II** *v/t.* [*irr.* → *sink*] ☉ **3.** *Loch* ausfräsen; **4.** *Schraubenkopf* versenken; **'~·ten·or** *s.* ♪ hoher Te'nor (*Stimme u. Sänger*); **~·vail** ['kaʊntəveɪl] **I** *v/t.* aufwiegen, ausgleichen; **II** *v/i.* stark genug sein, ausreichen (*against* gegen): **~***ing duty* Ausgleichszoll *m;* **'~·weight** *s.* Gegengewicht *n* (*a. fig. to* gegen); **'~·word** *s.* Aller'weltswort *n.*

count·ess ['kaʊntɪs] *s.* **1.** Gräfin *f;* **2.**

Kom'tesse *f.*

count·ing| glass ['kaʊntɪŋ] *s.* ☉ Zählglas *n,* -lupe *f;* **~** *house* *s. bsd. Brit.* 🏛 Bü'ro *n; engS.* Buchhaltung *f;* **~** *tube* *s.* Zählrohr *n.*

count·less ['kaʊntlɪs] *adj.* zahllos, unzählig.

'count-out *s. parl. Brit.* Vertagung *f* wegen Beschlussunfähigkeit.

coun·tri·fied ['kʌntrɪfaɪd] *adj.* **1.** ländlich, bäuerlich; **2.** *contp.* bäurisch, verbauert.

coun·try ['kʌntrɪ] **I** *s.* **1.** Land *n,* Staat *m: in this* **~** hierzulande; **~** *of destination* Bestimmungsland; **~** *of origin* Ursprungsland; **~** *of adoption* Wahlheimat *f;* **2.** Nati'on *f,* Volk *n: appeal* (*od. go*) *to the* **~** *pol.* an das Volk appellieren, Neuwahlen ausschreiben; **3.** Vaterland *n,* Heimat(land *n*) *f: the old* **~** die alte Heimat; **4.** Gelände *n,* Landschaft *f;* Gebiet *n* (*a. fig.*): *flat* **~** Flachland *n; wooded* **~** waldige Gegend; *unknown* **~** unbekanntes Gebiet (*a. fig.*); *new* **~** *fig.* Neuland *n* (*to me* für mich); *go up* **~** ins Innere reisen; **5.** Land *n* (*Ggs. Stadt*), Pro'vinz *f: in the* **~** auf dem Lande; *go* (*down*) *into the* **~** aufs Land *od.* in die Provinz gehen; **6.** *a.* **~***-and-western* → *country music;* **II** *adj.* **7.** Land...; Provinz...; ländlich: **~** *life* Landleben *n;* **~** *beam* *s. mot. Am.* Fernlicht *n;* **'~·bred** *adj.* auf dem Lande aufgewachsen; **~** *bump·kin* *s.* Bauerntölpel *m;* **~** *club* *s. Am.* Klub *m* auf dem Land (*für Städter*); **~** *code* *s.* internationale Vorwahl; **~** *cous·in* *s.* **1.** Vetter *m od.* Base *f* vom Lande; **2.** ,Unschuld *f* vom Lande'; **~** *dance* *s.* englischer Volkstanz; **'~·folk** *s.* Landbevölkerung *f;* **~** *gen·tle·man* *s.* [*irr.*] **1.** Landedelmann *m;* **2.** Gutsbesitzer *m;* **~** *house* *s.* Landhaus *n,* Landsitz *m;* **'~·man** [-mən] *s.* [*irr.*] **1.** *a. fellow* **~** Landsmann *m;* **2.** Landmann *m,* Bauer *m;* **~** *mu·sic* *s.* Country-Music *m;* **'~·side** *s.* **1.** ländliche Gegend; Land (-schaft *f*) *n;* **2.** (Land)Bevölkerung *f;* **'~·wide** *adj.* landesweit, im ganzen Land; **'~·wom·an** *s.* [*irr.*] **1.** *a. fellow* **~** Landsmännin *f;* **2.** a) Landbewohnerin *f,* b) Bäuerin *f.*

coun·ty ['kaʊntɪ] *s.* **1.** *Brit.* a) Grafschaft *f* (*Verwaltungsbezirk*), b) *county palatine,* b) *the* **~** die Bewohner *pl. od.* die Aristokra'tie e-r Grafschaft; **2.** *Am.* (Land)Kreis *m,* (Verwaltungs)Bezirk *m;* **~** *bor·ough* *s.* **~** *cor·po·rate* *s. Brit.* Stadt *f,* die e-e eigene Grafschaft bildet; **~** *coun·cil* *s. Brit.* Grafschaftsrat *m* (*Behörde*); **~** *court* *s.* 🏛 **1.** *Brit.* Grafschaftsgericht *n* (*erstinstanzliches Zivilgericht*); **2.** *Am.* Kreisgericht *n;* **~** *fam·i·ly* *s. Brit.* vornehme Fa'milie mit Ahnensitz in e-r Grafschaft; **~** *hall* *s. Brit.* Rathaus *n* e-r Grafschaft; **~** *pal·a·tine* *s. Brit. hist.* Pfalzgrafschaft *f;* **~** *seat* *s.,* **~** *town* *s. Am.* Kreishauptstadt *f.*

coup [kuː] *s.* Coup *m:* a) Bra'vourstück *n,* Handstreich *m,* b) Staatsstreich *m,* Putsch *m;* **~** *de grâce* [,kuːdə'graːs] (*Fr.*) *s.* Gnadenstoß *m* (*a. fig.*); **~** *de main* [,kuːdə'mɛ̃ːŋ] (*Fr.*) *s. bsd.* ⚔ Handstreich *m;* **~** *d'é·tat* [,kuːdeɪ'taː] (*Fr.*) → *coup* b.

cou·pé ['kuːpeɪ] *s.* **1.** Cou'pé *n:* a) *mst zweisitzige Limousine,* b) *geschlossene Kutsche für zwei Personen;* **2.** 🚂 *Brit.* Halbabteil *n.*

cou·ple ['kʌpl] **I** *s.* **1.** Paar *n: in* **~***s* paarweise; *a* **~** *of* ein paar *Tage etc.;* **2.** (Braut-, Ehe-, Liebes)Paar *n,* Pärchen *n;* **3.** Koppel *f* (*Jagdhunde*): *go* (*od.*

C

hunt) *in* ~s *fig.* stets gemeinsam handeln; **II** *v/t.* **4.** (zs.-, ver)koppeln, verbinden; ~*d with fig.* gepaart (*od.* verbunden, gekoppelt) mit; **5.** ehelich verbinden; paaren; **6.** *in Gedanken* verbinden, zs.-bringen; **7.** ♂ (an-, ein-, ver-)kuppeln; **8.** ♪, ♪ koppeln; **III** *v/i.* **9.** heiraten; sich paaren; **cou·pler** ['kʌplə] *s.* **1.** ♪ Kopplung *f* (*Orgel*); **2.** *Radio:* Koppler *m*; **3.** ⚙ Kupplung *f*; **4.** a) Koppel(glied *n*) *f,* b) (Leitungs)Muffe *f*: ~ *plug* Gerätestecker *m*.
cou·ple skat·ing *s.* Paarlauf(en *n*) *m*.
cou·plet ['kʌplɪt] *s.* Reimpaar *n*.
cou·pling ['kʌplɪŋ] *s.* **1.** Verbindung *f*; **2.** Paarung *f*; **3.** ⚙ (*feste*) Kupplung; **4.** ♪, *Radio:* Kopplung *f*; ~ **box** *s.* ⚙ Kupplungsmuffe *f*; ~ **chain** *s.* ⚙ Kupplungskette *f; pl.* 🔗 Kettenkupplung *f*; ~ **coil** *s.* ♪, *Radio:* Kopplungsspule *f*.
cou·pon ['kuːpɒn] *s.* **1.** ✝ Cou'pon *m*, Ku'pon *m*, Zinsschein *m*: *dividend* ~ Dividendenschein; ~ *bond Am.* Inhaberschuldverschreibung *f* mit Zinsschein; ~ *sheet* Couponbogen *m*; **2.** a) Kassenzettel *m*, Gutschein *m*, Bon *m*, b) Berechtigungs-, Bezugsschein *m*; **3.** Abschnitt *m der Lebensmittelkarte etc.*, Marke *f*; **4.** Kon'trollabschnitt *m*; **5.** *Brit.* Tippzettel *m* (*Fußballtoto*).
cour·age ['kʌrɪdʒ] *s.* Mut *m*, Tapferkeit *f*: *have the ~ of one's convictions* stets s-r Überzeugung gemäß handeln, Zivilcourage haben; *pluck up* (*od.* *take*) ~ Mut fassen; *screw up* (*od.* *summon up*) *one's ~, take one's ~ in both hands* sein Herz in beide Hände nehmen; **cou·ra·geous** [kə'reɪdʒəs] *adj.* ☐ mutig, beherzt, tapfer.
cour·gette [ˌkʊə'ʒet] *s.* Zuc'chini *f*.
cour·i·er ['kʊrɪə] *s.* **1.** Eilbote *m*, (*a. diplomatischer etc.*) Ku'rier *m*; **2.** Reiseleiter(in); **3.** *Am.* Verbindungsmann *m* (*Agent*).
course [kɔːs] **I** *s.* **1.** Lauf *m*, Bahn *f*, Weg *m*, Gang *m*; Ab-, Verlauf *m*, Fortgang *m*: *the ~ of life* der Lauf des Lebens; ~ *of events* Gang der Ereignisse, Lauf der Dinge; *the ~ of a disease* der Verlauf e-r Krankheit; *the ~ of nature* der natürliche (Ver)Lauf; *a matter of* ~ e-e Selbstverständlichkeit; *of* ~ natürlich, gewiss, bekanntlich; *in the ~ of* im (Ver)Lauf (*gen.*), während (*gen.*); *in* ~ *of construction* im Bau (befindlich); *in* ~ *of time* im Laufe der Zeit; *in due* ~ zur gegebenen *od.* rechten Zeit; *in the ordinary* ~ *of things* normalerweise; *let things take* (*od.* *run*) *their* ~ den Dingen ihren Lauf lassen; *the disease took its* ~ die Krankheit nahm ihren (natürlichen) Verlauf; **2.** (feste) Bahn, Strecke *f*, *sport* (Renn)Bahn *f*, (-)Strecke *f*, Piste *f*: *golf* ~ Golfbahn *f od.* -platz *m*; *clear the* ~ die Bahn frei machen; **3.** Fahrt *f*, Weg *m*; Richtung *f* ⚓, ✈ Kurs *m* (*a. fig.*): *on* (*off*) ~ (nicht) auf Kurs; *be on* ~ *for* (*od.* *to do*) *s.th.* auf et. zusteuern, auf dem besten Weg zu et. sein; *stand upon the* ~ Kurs halten; *steer a* ~ e-n Kurs steuern (*a. fig.*); *change one's* ~ s-n Kurs ändern (*a. fig.*); *keep to one's* ~ *fig.* beharrlich s-n Weg verfolgen; *take a new* ~ e-n neuen Weg einschlagen; ~ *computer* Kursrechner *m*; ~ *recorder* Kursschreiber *m*; **4.** Lebensbahn *f*, -weise *f*: *evil* ~s üble Gewohnheiten; **5.** Handlungsweise *f*, Verfahren *n*: *a dangerous* ~ ein gefährlicher Weg; → *action* 1; **6.** Gang *m*, Gericht *n* (*Speisen*); **7.** Reihe *f*, (Reihen)Folge *f*; 'Zyklus *m*: ~ *of lectures* Vortragsreihe; ~ *of treatment* 🜪

längere Behandlung, Kur *f*; **8.** *a.* ~ *of instruction* Kurs(us) *m*, Lehrgang *m*: *a German* ~ ein Deutschkurs, ein deutsches Lehrbuch; **9.** △ Schicht *f*, Lage *f* (*Ziegel etc.*); **10.** ⚓ unteres großes Segel: *main* ~ Großsegel; **11.** (*monthly*) ~s ♀ Regel *f*, Periode *f*; **II** *v/t.* **12.** *bsd. Hasen* mit Hunden hetzen *od.* jagen; **III** *v/i.* **13.** rennen, eilen, jagen; **14.** an e-r Hetzjagd teilnehmen.
cours·er ['kɔːsə] *s. poet.* Renner *m*, schnelles Pferd; '**cours·ing** [-sɪŋ] *s.* (*bsd. Hasen*)Hetzjagd *f* mit Hunden.
court [kɔːt] *s.* **1.** (Vor-, 'Hinter-, Innen)Hof *m*; **2.** 'Hintergässchen *n*; Sackgasse *f*; kleiner Platz; **3.** *bsd. Brit.* stattliches Wohngebäude; **4.** (abgesteckter) Spielplatz: *tennis* ~ Tennisplatz; *grass* ~ Rasentennisplatz; **5.** Hof *m*, Resi'denz *f* (*Fürst etc.*): *the* ☾ *of St. James* der britische Königshof; *be presented at* ~ bei Hofe vorgestellt werden; **6.** a) fürstlicher Hof *od.* Haushalt, b) fürstliche Fa'milie, c) Hofstaat *m*; **7.** (Empfang *m* bei) Hof *m*: *hold* ~ Hof halten (*a. fig.*); **8.** fürstliche Regierung; **9.** 🕸 a) *a.* ~ *of justice, law* ~ Gericht(shof *m*) *n*; ~ *of auditors* EU Rechnungshof *m*, b) Gerichtshof *m, der od. die* Richter, c) Gerichtssitzung *f,* d) Gerichtssaal *m: in* ~ vor Gericht; *out of* ~ a) außergerichtlich, gütlich, b) nicht zur Sache gehörig, c) indiskutabel; *bring into* ~, *take to* ~ vor Gericht bringen; *go to* ~ klagen; *laugh out of* ~ *fig.* verlachen; → *appeal* 8, *arbitration etc.*; **10.** *fig.* Hof *m*, Cour *f*, Aufwartung *f*: *pay* (*one's*) ~ *to* a) e-r Dame den Hof machen, b) *j-m* s-e Aufwartung machen; **11.** Rat *m*, Versammlung *f*: ~ *of directors* Direktion *f*, Vorstand *m*; **II** *v/t.* **12.** *der* Hof machen, huldigen (*dat.*); **13.** um'werben (*a. fig.*), werben *od.* freien um: ,*poussieren*' mit: ~*ing couple* Liebespaar *n*; **14.** *fig.* werben *od.* buhlen *od.* sich bemühen um et.; suchen: ~ *disaster* das Schicksal herausfordern, mit dem Feuer spielen.
court| card *s. Kartenspiel:* Bildkarte *f*; ☾ **Cir·cu·lar** *s.* (*tägliche*) Hofnachrichten *pl.*; ~ **dress** *s.* Hoftracht *f*.
cour·te·ous ['kɜːtjəs] *adj.* ☐ höflich, liebenswürdig.
cour·te·san [ˌkɔːtɪ'zæn] *s.* Kurti'sane *f*.
cour·te·sy ['kɜːtɪsɪ] *s.* Höflichkeit *f*, Verbindlichkeit *f*, Liebenswürdigkeit *f* (*alle a. als Handlung*); Gefälligkeit *f*: *by* ~ aus Höflichkeit *od.* Gefälligkeit; *by* ~ *of* a) mit freundlicher Genehmigung von (*od. gen.*), b) durch, mittels; ~ *light mot.* Innenlampe *f*; ~ *title* Höflichkeits- *od.* Ehrentitel *m*; ~ *call*, ~ *visit* Höflichkeits- *od.* Anstandsbesuch *m*.
cour·te·zan → *courtesan.*
court| guide *s.* 'Hof-, 'Adelska,lender *m* (*Verzeichnis der hoffähigen Personen*); ~ **hand** *s.* gotische Kanz'leischrift; '~**house** *s.* **1.** Gerichtsgebäude *n*; **2.** *Am.* Kreis(haupt)stadt *f*.
cour·ti·er ['kɔːtjə] *s.* Höfling *m*.
court·ly ['kɔːtlɪ] *adj.* **1.** vornehm, gepflegt, höflich; **2.** höfisch.
court| mar·tial *pl.* **courts mar·tial** *s.* Kriegsgericht *n*; ,~-'**mar·tial** *v/t.* vor ein Kriegsgericht stellen; ~ **mourn·ing** *s.* Hoftrauer *f*; ~ **or·der** *s.* 🕸 Gerichtsbeschluss *m*; ~ **plas·ter** *n, hist.* Heftpflaster *n*; ~ **room** *s.* Gerichtssaal *m*.
court·ship ['kɔːtʃɪp] *s.* **1.** Hofmachen *n*, Werben *n*, Freien *n*; **2.** *fig.* Werben *n* (*of* um).
court| shoes *s. pl.* Pumps *pl.*; '~**yard** *s.*

Hof(raum) *m*.
cous·in ['kʌzn] *s.* **1.** a) Vetter *m*, Cou'sin *m*, b) Base *f*, Ku'sine *f*: *first* ~, ~ *german* leiblicher Vetter *od.* leibliche Base; *second* ~ Vetter *od.* Base zweiten Grades; **2.** *weitS.* Verwandte(r *m*) *f*.
cou·tu·rier [kuː'tjʊrɪeɪ] (*Fr.*) *s.* (Haute) Couturi'er *m*, Modeschöpfer *m*; **cou·tu·rière** [-ɪeə] (*Fr.*) *s.* Modeschöpferin *f*.
cove[1] [kəʊv] **I** *s.* **1.** kleine Bucht; **2.** *fig.* Schlupfwinkel *m*; **3.** △ Wölbung *f*; **II** *v/t.* **4.** △ (über)'wölben.
cove[2] [kəʊv] *s. sl.* Bursche *m*, Kerl *m*.
cov·en ['kʌvn] *s.* Hexensabbat *m*.
cov·e·nant ['kʌvənənt] **I** *s.* **1.** Vertrag *m*; feierliches Abkommen; **2.** 🕸 a) Vertrag *m*, b) Ver'trags,klausel *f*, c) bindendes Versprechen, Zusicherung *f*, d) Satzung *f*; **3.** *bibl.* a) Bund *m*; → *ark* 2, b) Verheißung *f*: *the land of the* ~ das Gelobte Land; **II** *v/i.* **4.** e-n Vertrag schließen, über'einkommen (*with* mit, *for* über *acc.*); **5.** sich feierlich verpflichten, geloben; **III** *v/t.* **6.** vertraglich zusichern; '**cov·e·nant·ed** [-tɪd] *adj.* **1.** vertragsmäßig; **2.** vertraglich gebunden.
cov·en·trize ['kɒvəntraɪz] *v/t.* to'tal zerbomben, dem Erdboden gleichmachen; **Cov·en·try** ['kɒvəntrɪ] *npr. englische Stadt:* *send s.o. to* ~ *fig.* j-n gesellschaftlich ächten.
cov·er ['kʌvə] **I** *s.* **1.** Decke *f*; Deckel *m*; **2.** a) (Buch)Decke *f*, Einband *m*, b) 'Umschlag- *od.* Titelseite *f*: ~ *design* Titelbild *n*; ~ *girl* Covergirl *n*, Titelblattmädchen *n*; *from* ~ *to* ~ von Anfang bis Ende; **3.** a) 'Brief,umschlag *m*, b) *Philatelie:* Ganzsache *f*: *under* (*the*) *same* ~ beiliegend; *under separate* ~ mit getrennter Post; *under* ~ *of* unter der (Deck)Adresse von; **4.** 'Schutz,umschlag *m*, Hülle *f*, Futte'ral *n*; 'Überzug *m*, (Bett-, Möbel- *etc.*)Bezug *m*; ⚙ Schutzhaube *f*, -platte *f*, -mantel *m*; *mot.* (Reifen)Decke *f*, Mantel *m*; **5.** Gedeck *n* (*bei Tisch*): ~ *charge* (Kosten *pl.* für das) Gedeck; **6.** × a) Deckung *f*: *take* ~ Deckung nehmen; b) Feuerschutz *m*, c) (Luft)Sicherung *f*, Abschirmung *f*: *air* ~; **7.** *hunt.* Dickicht *n*, Lager *n*: *break* ~ ins Freie treten; **8.** Ob-, Schutzdach *n*: *get under* ~ sich unterstellen; **9.** *fig.* Schutz *m*: *under* ~ *of night* im Schutz der Nacht; **10.** *fig.* Deckmantel *m*, Tarnung *f*, Vorwand *m*: *under* ~ *of friendship*; ~ *address* Deckadresse *f*; ~ *name* Deckname *m*; *blow one's* ~ ,auffliegen'; **11.** ✝ Deckung *f*, Sicherheit *f*; (Schadens-) Deckung *f*, Versicherungsschutz *m*; **II** *v/t.* **12.** be-, zudecken: *remain* ~*ed* den Hut aufbehalten; ~ *o.s. with glory fig.* sich mit Ruhm bedecken; ~*ed with* voll von, über u. über bedeckt mit; **13.** einhüllen, -wickeln (*with* in *acc.*); **14.** be-, über'ziehen: ~*ed button* bezogener Knopf; ~*ed wire* umsponnener Draht; **15.** *fig.* decken, schützen, sichern (*from* vor *dat.*, gegen): ~ *o.s.* sich absichern (*against* gegen); **16.** ✝ decken: a) *Kosten* bestreiten, b) *Schulden, Verlust* abdecken, c) versichern; **17.** decken, genügen für; **18.** enthalten, einschließen, um'fassen, behandeln; *a. statistisch, durch Werbung etc.* erfassen; *Thema* (erschöpfend) behandeln; → *ground* 2; **19.** *Presse, TV etc.:* berichten über (*acc.*); **20.** *Gebiet* bereisen, bereisen; **21.** sich über e-e Fläche *od. Zeitspanne* erstrecken; **22.** e-e Strecke

zu'rücklegen; **23.** a) be-, verdecken, verhüllen, verbergen, b) *fig.* → *cover up* 2; **24.** ✕ decken, schützen, sichern (*from* vor *dat.* gegen); **25.** ✕ a) *ein Gebiet* beherrschen, im Schussfeld haben, b) *Gelände* bestreichen, mit Feuer belegen; **26.** *mit e-r Waffe* zielen auf (*acc.*), j-n in Schach halten; **27.** *sport den Gegner* decken; **28.** *j-n* ,beschatten'; **29.** *Hündin etc.* decken, *Stute a.* beschälen; **~ in** *v/t.* **1.** decken, bedachen; **2.** füllen; **~ o·ver** *v/t.* **1.** über-'decken; **2.** ✝ *Emission* über'zeichnen; **~ up I** *v/t.* **1.** zu-, verdecken; **2.** *fig.* vertuschen, verheimlichen, verbergen; **II** *v/i.* **3.** **~ for s.o.** j-n decken; **4.** *Boxen:* sich decken.

cov·er·age ['kʌvərɪdʒ] *s.* **1.** Erfassung *f*, Einschluss *m*; erfasstes Gebiet, erfasste Menge; *Werbung:* erfasster Per'sonenkreis; **2.** 'Umfang *m*; Reichweite *f*; Geltungsbereich *m*; **3.** ✝ a) → *cover* 11, b) Ver'sicherungs,umfang *m*; **4.** *Zeitung etc.:* Berichterstattung *f* (*of* über *acc.*); **5.** ✕ → *cover* 6 c; 'cov·ered [-əd] *adj.* be-, gedeckt; **~ court** *Tennis:* Hallenplatz *m*; **~ market** Markthalle *f*; **~ wag(g)on** a) Planwagen *m*, b) geschlossener Güterwagen; → *cover* 14; 'cov·er·ing [-ərɪŋ] *s.* **1.** Bedeckung *f*; Be-, Ver-, Um'kleidung *f*; (*Fußboden-*) Belag *m*; → a. *cover* 4; **2.** *fig.* Schutz *m*, Deckung *f*; **3.** ✕ → *cover* 6; **II** *adj.* **4.** deckend, Deck(ungs)...; **~ letter** Begleitbrief *m*; **~ note** → *cover note*; **cov·er·let** ['kʌvəlɪt], *a.* 'cov·er·lid [-lɪd] *s.* Tagesdecke *f*.

cov·er| **note** → ✝ Deckungsbrief *m* (*Versicherung*); **~ shot** *s. Film:* To'tale *f*; **~ sto·ry** *s.* Titelgeschichte *f*.

cov·ert I *adj.* ☐ ['kʌvət] **1.** heimlich, versteckt, verborgen; verschleiert; **2.** → *feme covert;* **II** *s.* ['kʌvə] **3.** Obdach *n*; Schutz *m*; **4.** Versteck *n*; **5.** *hunt.* Dickicht *n*; Lager *n*; **~ coat** ['kʌvət] *s.* Covercoat *m* (*Sportmantel*).

cov·er·ture ['kʌvə,tjʊə] *s.* ⚖ Ehestand *m der Frau.*

'**cov·er-up** *s. Am.* Tarnung *f*, Vertuschung *f* (*for gen.*).

cov·et ['kʌvɪt] *v/t.* begehren, trachten nach; '**cov·et·a·ble** [-təbl] *adj.* begehrenswert; '**cov·et·ous** [-təs] *adj.* ☐ **1.** begehrlich, lüstern (*of* nach); **2.** habsüchtig; '**cov·et·ous·ness** [-təsnɪs] *s.* **1.** Begehrlichkeit *f*; **2.** Habsucht *f*.

cov·ey ['kʌvɪ] *s.* **1.** *orn.* Brut *f*, Hecke *f*; **2.** *hunt.* Volk *n*, Kette *f*; **3.** Schar *f*, Schwarm *m*, Trupp *m*.

cov·ing ['kəʊvɪŋ] *s.* △ **1.** Wölbung *f*; **2.** 'überhängendes Obergeschoss, *östr.* -geschoss; **3.** schräge Seitenwände *pl.* (*Kamin*).

cow¹ [kaʊ] *s. zo.* **1.** Kuh *f*; **2.** Weibchen *n* (*bsd. Elefant, Wal etc.*).

cow² [kaʊ] *v/t.* einschüchtern; **~ s.o. into** j-n zwingen zu.

cow·ard ['kaʊəd] **I** *s.* Feigling *m*; **II** *adj.* feig(e); '**cow·ard·ice** [-dɪs] *s.* Feigheit *f*; '**cow·ard·li·ness** [-lɪnɪs] *s.* **1.** Feigheit *f*; **2.** Gemeinheit *f*; '**cow·ard·ly** [-lɪ] **I** *adj.* **1.** feig(e); **2.** gemein, 'hinterhältig; **II** *adv.* feig(e).

'**cow**|·**ber·ry** [-bərɪ] *s.* ♀ Preiselbeere *f*; '**~·boy** *s.* **1.** *Am.* Cowboy *m*; **2.** Kuhjunge *m*; '**~·catch·er** *s.* 🚂 *Am.* Schienenräumer *m*.

cow·er ['kaʊə] *v/i.* **1.** kauern, hocken; sich ducken (*aus Angst etc.*).

cow| **hand** → *cowboy* 1; '**~·herd** *s.* Kuhhirt *m*; '**~·hide** *s.* Rindsleder *n*; **2.** Ochsenziemer *m*; '**~·house** *s.* Kuhstall *m*.

cowl [kaʊl] *s.* **1.** Mönchskutte *f* (*mit Kapuze*); **2.** Ka'puze *f*; **3.** ⊛ Schornsteinkappe *f*; **4.** ⊛ a) *mot.* Haube *f*, b) Verkleidung *f*, c) → '**cowl·ing** [-lɪŋ] *s.* ✈ 'Motorhaube *f*.

'**cow·man** [-mən] *s. [irr.]* **1.** *Am.* Rinderzüchter *m*; **2.** Kuhknecht *m*.

'**co·,work·er** *s.* Mitarbeiter(in).

cow| **pars·nip** *s.* ♀ Bärenklau *f, m;* **~ pat** *s.* Kuhfladen *f;* '**~·pox** *s.* ♣ Kuhpocken *pl.;* '**~,punch·er** *s. Am.* F Cowboy *m.*

cow·rie, cow·ry ['kaʊrɪ] *s.* **1.** *zo.* 'Kaurischnecke *f;* **2.** 'Kauri(muschel *f*) *m, f,* Muschelgeld *n.*

'**cow**|·**shed** *s.* Kuhstall *m;* '**~·slip** *s.* ♀ **1.** *Brit.* Schlüsselblume *f;* **2.** *Am.* Sumpfdotterblume *f.*

cox [kɒks] F **I** *s.* → *coxswain;* **II** *v/t. Rennboot* steuern: **~ed four** Vierer *m* mit (Steuermann).

cox·comb ['kɒkskəʊm] *s.* **1.** Geck *m*, Stutzer *m;* **2.** → *cockscomb* 1, 2.

cox·swain ['kɒkswem] ⚓ 'kɒksn] **I** *s.* **1.** *Rudern:* Steuermann *m;* **2.** Bootsführer *m;* **II** *v/t.* **3.** → *cox* II.

coy [kɔɪ] *adj.* ☐ **1.** schüchtern, bescheiden, scheu; **2.** spröde, zimperlich (*Mädchen*); '**coy·ness** [-nɪs] *s.* Schüchternheit *f;* Sprödigkeit *f.*

coy·ote ['kɔɪəʊt] *s. zo.* Ko'jote *m*, Prä'rie-, Steppenwolf *m.*

coz·en ['kʌzn] *v/t. u. v/i.* **1.** betrügen, prellen (*out of* um); **2.** betören; verleiten (*into doing* zu).

co·zi·ness *etc.* → *cosiness etc.*

crab¹ [kræb] **I** *s.* **1.** *zo.* a) Krabbe *f*, b) Taschenkrebs *m:* **catch a ~** *Rudern:* ,e-n Krebs fangen', mit dem Ruder im Wasser stecken bleiben; **2.** ♌ *ast.* Krebs *m;* **3.** ⊛ Winde *f*, Hebezeug *n*, Laufkatze *f;* **4.** *pl. Würfeln:* niedrigster Wurf; **5.** → *crab louse;* **II** *v/t.* **6.** ✈ schieben.

crab² [kræb] **I** *s.* **1.** a) Nörgler *m*, b) Nörge'lei *f;* **II** *v/t.* **2.** F (her'um)nörgeln an (*dat.*); **3.** F verderben, -patzen; **III** *v/i.* **4.** nörgeln.

crab ap·ple *s.* ♀ Holzapfel(baum) *m.*

crab·bed ['kræbɪd] *adj.* ☐ **1.** a) mürrisch, b) boshaft, bitter, c) halsstarrig; **2.** verworren; kraus; **3.** kritzelig, unleserlich (*Schrift*); **crab·by** ['kræbɪ] → *crabbed* 1, 2.

crab louse *s. [irr.] zo.* Filzlaus *f.*

crack [kræk] **I** *s.* **1.** Krach *m*, Knall *m* (*Peitsche, Gewehr etc.*): **the ~ of doom** die Posaunen des Jüngsten Gerichts; **~ of dawn** Morgengrauen *n;* **2.** (heftiger) Schlag: **in a ~** im Nu; **take a ~ at s.th.** *sl.* es mit et. versuchen; **3.** Riss *m*, Sprung *m*; Spalt(e *f*) *m*, Schlitz *m;* **4.** F ,Knacks' (*geistiger Defekt*); **5.** *sl.* a) Witz *m*, b) Stiche'lei *f;* **6.** *sport* ,Ka'none', ,As' *n;* **7.** F Crack *n* (*Rauschgift*); **II** *adj.* **8.** F erstklassig, großartig: **~ shot** Meisterschütze *m;* **~ regiment** Eliteregiment *n;* **III** *int.* **9.** krach!; **IV** *v/i.* **10.** krachen, knallen, knacken; (auf)brechen; **11.** platzen, bersten, (auf-, zer)springen, Risse bekommen, (auf)reißen: **get ~ing** F loslegen (*anfangen*); **~ing pace** tolles Tempo; **12.** 'überschnappen (*Stimme*): **his voice is ~ing** er ist im Stimmbruch; **13.** *fig. zs.*-brechen; **V** *v/t.* **14.** knallen mit (*Peitsche*); knacken mit (*Fingern*): **~ jokes** Witze reißen; **15.** zerbrechen, (zer)spalten, ein-, zerschlagen; **16.** *Nuss* (auf)knacken, *Ei* aufschlagen: **~ a bottle** e-r Flasche den Hals brechen; **~ a code** e-n Kode ,knacken'; **~ a crib** *sl.* in ein Haus einbrechen; **~ a safe** e-n Geldschrank knacken; **17.** a) e-n Sprung machen in (*acc.*), b) sich e-e

Rippe *etc.* anbrechen; **18.** *fig.* erschüttern, zerrütten, zerstören; **19.** ⊛ *Erdöl* kracken, spalten; **~ down** *v/i.* F (*on*) a) scharf vorgehen (gegen), 'durchgreifen (bei), b) 'Razzia abhalten (bei); **~ up I** *v/i.* **1.** *fig.* (*körperlich od. seelisch*) zs.-brechen; **2.** ✈ abstürzen; **3.** sein Auto zu Schrott fahren; **4.** *Am.* F sich ,ka-'puttlachen'; **II** *v/t.* **5.** *Fahrzeug* zu Schrott fahren; **6.** F ,hochjubeln', (an-) preisen.

'**crack**|·**brained** *adj.* verrückt; '**~·down** *s.* F (*on*) scharfes Vorgehen (gegen), 'Durchgreifen *n* (bei).

cracked [krækt] *adj.* **1.** zer-, gesprungen, geborsten, rissig: **the cup is ~** die Tasse hat e-n Sprung; **2.** F ,angeknackst' (*Ruf etc.*); **3.** F verrückt.

crack·er ['krækə] *s.* **1.** Cracker *m*, Kräcker *m:* a) (Knusper)Keks *m*, b) Schwärmer *m*, Frosch *m* (*Feuerwerk*), *a.* 'Knallbon,bon *m, n;* **2.** Nussknacker *m;* **3.** *Computer:* Cracker(in) (*j-d, der in Computersysteme eindringt*); **4.** *Brit.* F a) toller Kerl, tolle Frau, b) tolles Ding, 'Überflieger *m;* '**~·jack** *Am.* F **I** *adj.* 'prima, toll; **II** *s.* a) tolle Sache, b) toller Kerl; '**crack·ers** *adj. Brit. sl.* verrückt, 'übergeschnappt: **go ~** überschnappen.

'**crack·jaw** F **I** *adj.* zungenbrecherisch; **II** *s.* Zungenbrecher *m.*

crack·le ['krækl] **I** *v/i.* **1.** knistern, prasseln, knattern; **II** *v/t.* **2.** ⊛ *Glas od. Glasur* krakelieren; **III** *s.* **3.** Knistern *n*, Knattern *n;* **4.** ⊛ Krakelierung *f*, Krake'lee *f, n:* **~ finish** Eisblumenlackierung *f;* **5.** ⊛ Haarrissbildung *f;* '**crack·ling** [-lɪŋ] *s.* **1.** → *crackle* 3; **2.** a) knusprige Kruste des Schweinebratens, b) *mst pl. Am.* Schweinegrieben *pl.*

crack·nel ['kræknl] *s.* **1.** Knusperkeks *m;* **2.** → *crackling* 2 a.

'**crack·pot** *sl.* **I** *s.* ,Spinner' *m*, Verrückte(r *m*) *f,* **II** *adj.* verrückt.

cracks·man ['kræksmən] *s. [irr.] sl.* **1.** Einbrecher *m;* **2.** ,Schränker' *m*, Geldschrankknacker *m.*

'**crack-up** *s.* F *pol.,* ✝ (*a. körperlicher od. seelischer*) Zs.-bruch.

crack·y ['krækɪ] → *cracked* 1, 3.

cra·dle ['kreɪdl] **I** *s.* **1.** Wiege *f* (*a. fig.*): **the ~ of civilization;** **from the ~ to the grave** von der Wiege bis zur Bahre; **2.** *fig.* Wiege *f*, Kindheit *f*, 'Anfangs,stadium *n*, Ursprung *m:* **from the ~** von Kindheit an; **in the ~** in den ersten Anfängen (steckend); **3.** wiegenartiges Gerät, *bsd.* ⊛ a) Hängegerüst *n* (*Bau*), b) Gründungseisen *n* (*Graveur*), c) Räderschlitten *m* (*für Arbeiten unter e-m Auto*), d) Schwingtrog *m* (*Goldwäscher*), e) (Tele'fon)Gabel *f*, *f*) ✕ Rohrwiege *f;* **4.** ⚓ Stapelschlitten *m;* **5.** 🗡 (Draht-) Schiene *f*, Schutzgestell *n;* **II** *v/t.* **6.** in die Wiege legen; **7.** in (den) Schlaf wiegen; **8.** auf-, großziehen; **9.** *den Kopf in den Armen etc.* bergen, betten.

craft [krɑːft] *s.* **1.** (Hand- *od.* Kunst-) Fertigkeit *f*, Kunst *f*, Geschicklichkeit *f;* → *gentle* 2; **2.** a) Gewerbe *n*, Handwerk *n*, b) Zunft *f:* **film ~** Filmgewerbe; **be one of the ~** F vom ,Bau' sein; **3.** **the ~** die Königliche Kunst (*Freimaurerei*); **4.** List *f*, Verschlagenheit *f;* **5.** ⚓ Fahrzeug *n*, Schiff *n;* *coll.* Fahrzeuge *pl.*, Schiffe *pl.;* **6.** a) ✈ Flugzeug *n,* *coll.* Flugzeuge *pl.*, b) Raumschiff *n,* -fahrzeug *n;* '**craft·i·ness** [-tɪnɪs] *s.* List *f*, Schlauheit *f.*

crafts·man ['krɑːftsmən] *s. [irr.]* **1.** gelernter Handwerker; **2.** Kunsthandwerker *m;* **3.** *fig.* Könner *m;* '**crafts·man·ship** [-ʃɪp] *s.* Kunstfertigkeit *f,*

C

handwerkliches Können *od.* Geschick.
craft·y ['krɑːftɪ] *adj.* ☐ listig, schlau, verschlagen.
crag [kræg] *s.* Felsenspitze *f*, Klippe *f*; **'crag·ged** [-gɪd], **'crag·gy** [-gɪ] *adj.* **1.** felsig, schroff; **2.** *fig.* knorrig (*Person*); **crags·man** ['krægzmən] *s.* [*irr.*] geübter Bergsteiger, Kletterer *m*.
cram [kræm] **I** *v/t.* **1.** *a. fig.* voll stopfen *od.* packen *od.* pfropfen, über'füllen (**with** mit); **2.** über'füttern, voll stopfen; **3.** *Geflügel* stopfen, mästen; **4.** (hin'ein-) stopfen, (-)zwängen (**into** in *acc.*); **5.** F a) mit *j-m* ,pauken', b) *et.* ,pauken' *od.* ,büffeln'; **II** *v/i.* **6.** sich (gierig) voll essen *od.* stopfen; **7.** F ,pauken', ,büffeln': ~ *up on* → 5 b; **III** *s.* **8.** F Gedränge *n*; **9.** F ,Pauken' *n*: ~ *course* Paukkurs *m*.
,cram-'full *adj.* zum Bersten voll.
cram·mer ['kræmə] *s.* F **1.** ,Einpauker' *m*; **2.** ,Paukstudio' *n*; **3.** ,Paukbuch' *n*.
cramp¹ [kræmp] **I** *s.* **1.** ⊕ Krampe *f*, Klammer *f*; Schraubzwinge *f*; **2.** *fig.* Zwang *m*, Fessel *f*; Einengung *f*; **II** *v/t.* **3.** ver-, anklammern, befestigen; **4.** *a.* ~ *up fig.* einengen, einzwängen; hemmen: *be* ~*ed for space* (zu) wenig Platz haben; → *style* 1 b.
cramp² [kræmp] **I** *s.* ✸ Krampf *m*; **II** *v/t.* Krämpfe auslösen in (*dat.*); **cramped** [-pt] *adj.* **1.** verkrampft; **2.** eng, beengt.
'cramp|·fish *s.* Zitterrochen *m*; ~ **i·ron** *s.* **1.** (Stahl)Klammer *f*, Krampe *f*; **2.** △ Steinanker *m*.
cram·pon ['kræmpən], *Am. a.* **cram-poon** [kræm'puːn] *s. oft pl.* **1.** ⊕ Kanthaken *m*; **2.** *mount.* Steigeisen *n*.
cran·ber·ry ['krænbərɪ] *s.* ♀ Preisel-, Kranbeere *f*.
crane [kreɪn] *s.* **1.** *orn. u.* ♌ *astr.* Kranich *m*; **2.** ⊕ Kran *m*: ~ *truck* Kranwagen *m*; **II** *v/t.* **3.** mit e-m Kran heben; **4.** ~ *one's neck* sich den Hals verrenken (*for* nach); ~ *fly s. zo.* (Erd)Schnake *f*.
cra·ni·a ['kreɪnjə] *pl. von* **cranium**; **'cra·ni·al** [-jəl] *adj. anat.* Schädel...; **cra·ni·ol·o·gy** [ˌkreɪnɪ'ɒlədʒɪ] *s.* Schädellehre *f*; **'cra·ni·um** [-jəm] *pl.* **-ni·a** [-jə] *Am. a.* **-ni·ums** *s. anat.* Schädel *m*.
crank [kræŋk] **I** *s.* **1.** ⊕ Kurbel *f*, Schwengel *m*: ~ *case* Kurbelgehäuse *n*, -kasten *m*; ~ *handle* Kurbelgriff *m*; ~ *pin* Kurbelzapfen *m*; ~ *shaft* Kurbelwelle *f*; **2.** Wortspiel *n*; **3.** Ma'rotte *f*, Grille *f*, fixe I'dee; **4.** ,Spinner' *m*, (harmloser) Verrückter: ~ *letter* Brief *m* von e-m ,Spinner'; **II** *v/t.* **5.** ⊕ kröpfen, krümmen; **6.** *oft* ~ *up* ankurbeln, *Motor* anlassen; *Maschine* 'durchdrehen; **III** *adj.* **7.** wack(e)lig, schwach; **8.** ♧ rank; **'crank·i·ness** [-kɪnɪs] *s.* Wunderlichkeit *f*, Verschrobenheit *f*; **'crank·y** [-kɪ] *adj.* ☐ **1.** wunderlich, verschroben; **2.** → *crank* 7, 8.
cran·ny ['krænɪ] *s.* **1.** Ritze *f*, Spalte *f*, Riss *m*; **2.** Schlupfwinkel *m*.
crap¹ [kræp] *s. Am.* Fehlwurf *m* beim *craps.*
crap² [kræp] V **I** *s.* a) Scheiße *f*: *have a* ~ → II, b) *fig.* ,Mist' *m*, ,Scheiß' *m*; **II** *v/i.* scheißen.
crape [kreɪp] *s.* **1.** Krepp *m*; **2.** Trauerflor *m*.
crap·py ['kræpɪ] *adj. sl.* ,mistig', Scheiß...
craps [kræps] *s. pl. sg. konstr. Am.* ein Würfelspiel *n*: *shoot* ~ Craps spielen.
crap·u·lence ['kræpjʊləns] *s.* Unmäßigkeit *f*, *bsd.* unmäßiger Alko'holgenuss.
crash¹ [kræʃ] **I** *v/i.* **1.** zs.-krachen, zerbrechen, *Computer*: ,abstürzen'; **2.** (kra-

chend) ab-, einstürzen; **3.** ✈ abstürzen, Bruch machen; *mot.* a) zs.-stoßen, b) verunglücken: ~ *into* krachen gegen; **4.** poltern, platzen, rasen, stürzen: ~ *in* hereinplatzen; ~ *in on* → 9; **5.** *fig. bsd.* ♆ zs.-brechen; **II** *v/t.* **6.** zertrümmern, zerschmettern; **7.** ✈ abstürzen *od.* e-e Bruchlandung machen mit; **8.** *mot.* zu Bruch fahren; **9.** *sl.* uneingeladen kommen zu e-r Party; **III** *s.* **10.** Krach(en *n*) *m*; **11.** Zs.-stoß *m*; Unfall *m*; **12.** ✈ Absturz *m*; **13.** ♆ (Börsen)Krach *m, allg.* Zs.-bruch; **14.** *Computer*: ,Absturz'; **IV** *adj.* **15.** *fig.* Schnell..., Sofort...
crash² [kræʃ] *s.* grober Leinendrell.
crash| bar·ri·er *s. Brit.* Leitplanke *f*; ~ **course** *s.* Schnell-, Inten'sivkurs *m*; ~ **di·et** *s.* radi'kale Abmagerungskur *f*; **'~-dive** *v/i.* ♧ schnelltauchen (*U-Boot*); ~ **halt** *s.* 'Vollbremsung *f*; ~ **hel·met** *s.* Sturzhelm *m*; ~ **job** *s.* brandeilige Arbeit, Eilauftrag *m*; **'~-land** *v/i.* ✈ e-e Bruchlandung machen; ~ **land·ing** *s.* ✈ Bruchlandung *f*; ~ **test** *s. mot.* 'Crashtest *m*; ~ **truck** *s.* Rettungswagen *m*.
crass [kræs] *adj.* ☐ *fig.* krass, grob; **'crass·ness** [-nɪs] *s.* **1.** Krassheit *f*; **2.** krasse Dummheit.
crate [kreɪt] **I** *s.* **1.** Lattenkiste *f*, (Bieretc.)Kasten *m*; **2.** großer Packkorb; **3.** *sl.* ,Kiste' *f* (*Auto od. Flugzeug*); **II** *v/t.* **4.** in e-e Lattenkiste *etc.* verpacken.
cra·ter ['kreɪtə] *s.* **1.** *geol. etc. a.* ✸ 'Krater *m*; **2.** (Bomben-, Gra'nat)Trichter *m*, -krater *m*.
cra·vat [krə'væt] *s.* Halstuch *n*; Kra'watte *f*.
crave [kreɪv] **I** *v/t.* **1.** flehen *od.* dringend bitten um; **II** *v/i.* **2.** sich (heftig) sehnen (**for** nach); **3.** flehen, inständig bitten (**for** um).
cra·ven ['kreɪvən] **I** *adj.* feige, zaghaft; **II** *s.* Feigling *m*, Memme *f*.
crav·ing ['kreɪvɪŋ] *s.* heftiges Verlangen, Sehnsucht *f*, (krankhafte) Begierde (**for** nach).
craw [krɔː] *s. zo.* Kropf *m* (*Vogel*).
craw·fish ['krɔːfɪʃ] **I** *s. zo.* → **crayfish**; **II** *v/i. Am.* F sich drücken, ,kneifen'.
crawl [krɔːl] **I** *v/i.* **1.** kriechen: a) krabbeln, b) sich da'hinschleppen, schleichen (*a. Arbeit, Zeit*), c) im ,Schneckentempo' gehen *od.* fahren; **2.** *fig.* (unter'würfig) kriechen (**to s.o.** vor j-m); **3.** wimmeln (**with** von); **4.** kribbeln, prickeln; **5.** *Schwimmen*: kraulen; **II** *s.* **6.** Kriechen *n*, Schleichen *n*: *go at a* ~ → 1 c; **7.** *Schwimmen*: Kraulstil *m*, Kraul(en) *n*; **'crawl·er** [-lə] *s.* **1.** Kriechtier *n*, Gewürm *n*; **2.** *fig.* Kriecher(in); **3.** F a) ,Schnecke' *f*, b) Taxi *n* auf Fahrgastsuche; **4.** *pl.* Krabbelanzug *m* für Kleinkinder; **5.** *a.* ~ *tractor* ⊕ Raupen-, Gleiskettenfahrzeug *n*; **6.** *Schwimmen*: Krauler(in); **crawl·er lane** *s. Brit. mot.* Kriechspur *f*; **'crawl·y** [-lɪ] *adj.* F grus(e)lig.
cray·fish ['kreɪfɪʃ] *s. zo.* **1.** Flusskrebs *m*; **2.** Lan'guste *f*.
cray·on ['kreɪən] **I** *s.* **1.** Zeichen-, Bunt-, Pa'stellstift *m*: *blue* ~ Blaustift; **2.** Kreide-, Pa'stellzeichnung *f*; **II** *v/t.* **3.** mit Kreide *etc.* zeichnen; **4.** *fig.* skizzieren.
craze [kreɪz] **I** *v/t.* **1.** verrückt machen; **2.** *Töpferei*: krakelieren; **II** *s.* **3.** a) Ma'nie *f*, fixe I'dee, Verrücktheit *f*, b) ,Fimmel' *m*: *be the* ~ die große Mode sein; *the latest* ~ der letzte Schrei; **crazed** [-zd] *adj.* **1.** wahnsinnig (**with** vor *dat.*); **2.** (wild) begeistert, hingerissen (**about** von); **'cra·zi·ness** [-zɪnɪs] *s.* Verrücktheit *f*.

cra·zy ['kreɪzɪ] *adj.* ☐ **1.** verrückt, wahnsinnig: ~ *with pain* vor; **2.** F (**about**) begeistert (von); versessen (auf *acc.*); **3.** baufällig, wackelig; ♧ seeuntüchtig; **4.** zs.-gestückelt; ~ *bone Am.* → *funny bone*; ~ *pav·ing*, ~ *pave·ment s.* Mosa'ikpflaster *n*; ~ *quilt s.* Flickendecke *f*.
creak [kriːk] **I** *v/i.* knarren, kreischen, quietschen, knirschen: ~ *along fig.* sich dahinschleppen (*Handlung etc.*); **II** *s.* Knarren *n*, Knirschen *n*, Quietschen *n*; **'creak·y** [-kɪ] *adj.* ☐ knarrend, knirschend.
cream [kriːm] **I** *s.* **1.** Rahm *m*, Sahne *f*; **2.** Creme(speise) *f*; **3.** (Haut-, Schuhetc.)Creme *f*; **4.** Cremesuppe *f*; **5.** *fig.* Creme *f*, Auslese *f*, E'lite *f*: *the* ~ *of society*; **6.** Kern *m*, Po'inte *f* (*Witz*); **7.** Cremefarbe *f*; **II** *v/i.* **8.** Sahne bilden; **9.** schäumen; **III** *v/t.* **10.** absahnen, den Rahm abschöpfen von (*a. fig.*); **11.** Sahne bilden lassen; **12.** schaumig rühren; **13.** (*dem Tee od. Kaffee*) Sahne zugießen: *do you* ~ *your tea?* nehmen Sie Sahne?; **14.** *Am. sl.* j-n ,fertig machen'; **IV** *adj.* **15.** creme(farben); ~ **cake** *s.* Creme- *od.* Sahnetorte *f*; ~ **cheese** *s.* Rahm-, Vollfettkäse *m*; **'~-,col·o(u)red** *adj.* creme(farben).
cream·er·y ['kriːmərɪ] *s.* **1.** Molke'rei *f*; **2.** Milchhandlung *f*.
cream| ice *s. Brit.* Sahneeis *n*, Speiseeis *n*; ~ **jug** *s.* Sahnekännchen *n*, -gießer *m*; **,~-'laid** *adj.* cremefarben und gerippt (*Papier*); ~ *of tar·tar s.* ✸ Weinstein *m*; **,~-'wove** → **cream-laid**.
cream·y ['kriːmɪ] *adj.* sahnig; *fig.* weich, samten.
crease [kriːs] **I** *s.* **1.** Falte *f*, Kniff *m*; **2.** Bügelfalte *f*; Eselsohr *n* (*Buch*); **4.** *Eishockey*: Torraum *m*; **II** *v/t.* **5.** falten, knicken, kniffen, 'umbiegen; **6.** zerknittern; **7.** *hunt. etc.* streifen, anschießen; **III** *v/i.* **8.** Falten bekommen *od.* werfen; knittern; **9.** sich falten lassen; **creased** [-st] *adj.* **1.** in Falten gelegt, gefaltet; **2.** mit Bügelfalte, gebügelt; **3.** zerknittert.
'crease|-proof, '~-re,sist·ant *adj.* knitterfrei.
cre·ate [kriː'eɪt] *v/t.* **1.** (er)schaffen; **2.** schaffen, erzeugen: a) her'vorbringen, ins Leben rufen, b) her'vorrufen, verursachen; **3.** *thea., Mode*: kre'ieren, gestalten; **4.** gründen, ein-, errichten; **5.** ♃ *Recht etc.* begründen; **6.** j-n ernennen zu: ~ *s.o. a peer*, **cre·a·tion** [-'eɪʃn] *s.* **1.** (Er)Schaffung *f*; **2.** Erzeugung *f*, Schaffung *f*: a) Her'vorbringung *f*; ~ *of needs* Bedarfsweckung *f*, b) Verursachung *f*, c) *the* ♌ *eccl.* die Schöpfung, die Erschaffung (der Welt): *the whole* ~ alle Geschöpfe, die ganze Welt; **3.** Geschöpf *n*, Krea'tur *f*; **4.** (Kunst-, Mode)Schöpfung *f*, Kreati'on *f*; Werk *n*; **5.** *thea.* Kre'ierung *f*, Gestaltung *f*; **6.** Gründung *f*, Errichtung *f*, Bildung *f*; **7.** Ernennung *f* (*zu e-m Rang*); **cre·a·tive** [-tɪv] *adj.* ☐ **1.** schöpferisch, (er)schaffend, *a.* krea'tiv; **2.** (**of s.th.**) *et.* verursachend; **cre·a·tive·ness** [-tɪvnɪs], **cre·a·tiv·i·ty** [ˌkriː-eɪ'tɪvətɪ] *s.* Kreativi'tät *f*, schöpferische Kraft; **cre·a·tor** [-tə] *s.* Schöpfer *m*, Erschaffer *m*, Erzeuger *m*, Urheber *m*: *the* ♌ der Schöpfer, Gott *m*.
crea·ture ['kriːtʃə] *s.* **1.** Geschöpf *n*, (Lebe)Wesen *n*, Krea'tur *f*: *fellow* ~ Mitmensch *m*; *dumb* ~ stumme Kreatur; *lovely* ~ süßes Geschöpf (*Frau*); *silly* ~ dummes Ding; ~ *of habit* Gewohnheitstier *n*; **2.** *fig.* j-s Krea'tur *f*,

Werkzeug *n*; ~ **com·forts** *s. pl. die* leiblichen Genüsse, *das* leibliche Wohl.

crèche [kreɪʃ] (*Fr.*) *s.* **1.** Kinderhort *m*, -krippe *f*; **2.** *Am.* (Weihnachts)Krippe *f*.

cre·dence ['kriːdəns] *s.* **1.** Glaube *m*: *give ~ to* Glauben schenken (*dat.*); **2.** *a. ~ table eccl.* Kre'denz *f*.

cre·den·tials [krɪ'denʃlz] *s. pl.* **1.** Beglaubigungs- *od.* Empfehlungsschreiben *n*; **2.** (Leumunds)Zeugnis *n*; **3.** 'Ausweis(pa,piere *pl.*) *m*.

cred·i·bil·i·ty [,kredɪ'bɪlətɪ] *s.* Glaubwürdigkeit *f*; ~ **gap** *s.* Glaubwürdigkeitslücke *f*; **cred·i·ble** ['kredəbl] *adj.* □ glaubwürdig; zuverlässig: *show credibly that* ⚖ glaubhaft machen, dass.

cred·it ['kredɪt] **I** *s.* **1.** ✝ a) Kre'dit *m*, b) Ziel *n*: (*letter of*) ~ Akkredi'tiv *n*; *on ~* auf Kredit; *open a ~* e-n Kredit *od.* ein Akkreditiv eröffnen; *30 days' ~* 30 Tage Ziel; **2.** ✝ a) Haben *n*, 'Kredit(seite *f*) *n*, b) Guthaben *n*, 'Kreditposten *m*, *pl. a.* Ansprüche: *enter* (*od. place*) *it to my ~* schreiben Sie es mir gut; ~ *advice* Gutschriftsanzeige *f*; (*tax*) ~ *Am.* (Steuer)Freibetrag *m*; **3.** ✝ Kre'ditwürdigkeit *f*; **4.** Glaube(n) *m*, Ver-, Zutrauen *n*: *give ~ to* → 10; **5.** Glaubwürdigkeit *f*, Zuverlässigkeit *f*; **6.** Ansehen *n*, Achtung *f*, guter Ruf, Ehre *f*: *be a ~ to s.o.*, *reflect ~ on s.o.*, *do s.o. ~*, *be to s.o.'s ~* j-m Ehre machen *od.* einbringen; *he does me ~* mit ihm lege ich Ehre ein; *to his ~ it must be said* a) zu s-r Ehre muss man sagen, b) man muss es ihm hoch anrechnen; *add to s.o.'s ~* j-s Ansehen erhöhen; *with ~* ehrenvoll, mit Lob; **7.** Verdienst *n*, Anerkennung *f*, Lob *n*: *get ~ for* Anerkennung finden für; *very much to his ~* sehr anerkennenswert von ihm; *give s.o. (the) ~ for s.th.* a) j-m et. hoch anrechnen, b) j-m et. zutrauen, c) j-m et. verdanken; *take (the) ~ for* sich et. als Verdienst anrechnen, den Ruhm *od.* alle Lorbeeren für et. in Anspruch nehmen; **8.** (*title and*) ~s *pl.* Film, TV: Vor- *od.* Abspann *m*, Erwähnungen *pl.*; **9.** *ped. Am.* a) Anrechnungspunkt *m*, b) Abgangszeugnis *n*; **II** *v/t.* **10.** Glauben schenken (*dat.*), j-m *od.* et. glauben; j-m trauen; **11.** ~ *s.o. with s.th.* a) j-m et. zutrauen, b) j-m et. zuschreiben; **12.** ✝ *Betrag* gutschreiben, kreditieren (*to s.o.* j-m); *j-n erkennen* (*with* für): ~ *an account with ... e-m Konto ... gutschreiben*; **13.** *ped. Am.* (*s.o. with*) (j-m) Punkte anrechnen (für); '**cred·it·a·ble** [-təbl] *adj.* □ **1.** rühmlich, lobens-, anerkennenswert, ehrenvoll (*to* für): *be ~ to s.o.* j-m Ehre machen; **2.** glaubwürdig.

cred·it| a·gen·cy *s.* Kre'ditauskun,tei *f*; ~ **bal·ance** *s.* ✝ 'Kredit,saldo *m*, Guthaben *n*; ~ **card** *s.* ✝ Kre'ditkarte *f*; ~ **in·ter·est** *s.* ✝ Habenzinsen *pl.*; ~ **note** *s.* ✝ Gutschriftsanzeige *f*.

cred·i·tor ['kredɪtə] *s.* ✝ **1.** Gläubiger (-in); **2.** a) *a. ~ side* Haben *n*, 'Kreditseite *f* e-s Kontobuchs, b) *pl.* Bilanz: Verbindlichkeiten *pl.*

cred·it| rat·ing *s. Am.* Kre'ditfähigkeit *f*; ~ **risk** *s.* ✝ Kre'dit,risiko *n*; 'Gegenpartei,risiko *n*; ~**slip** *s.* Einzahlungsschein *m*; ~ **squeeze** *s.* ✝ Kre'ditzwange *f*; ~ **stand·ing** *s.* Bonität *f*; ~ **tit·les** *pl.* → *credit* 8; ~ **trans·fer** *s.* Über'weisung *f* (*von Geld*); '~,**wor·thi·ness** *s.* ✝ Kre'ditwürdigkeit *f*; '~,**wor·thy** *adj.* ✝ kre'ditwürdig.

cre·do ['kriːdəʊ] *pl.* -**dos** *s.* **1.** *eccl.*

'Kredo *n*, Glaubensbekenntnis *n*; **2.** → *creed* 2.

cre·du·li·ty [krɪ'djuːlətɪ] *s.* Leichtgläubigkeit *f*; **cred·u·lous** ['kredjuləs] *adj.* □ leichtgläubig.

creed [kriːd] *s.* **1.** a) Glaubensbekenntnis *n*, b) Glaube *m*, Konfessi'on *f*; **2.** *fig.* (*a. politische etc.*) Über'zeugung, 'Kredo *n*.

creek [kriːk] *s.* **1.** Flüsschen *n*; kleiner Wasserlauf (*nur von der Flut gespeist*): *up the ~ fig.* in der Klemme (sitzend); **2.** kleine Bucht.

creel [kriːl] *s.* Fischkorb *m*.

creep [kriːp] **I** *v/i.* [*irr.*] **1.** *a. fig.* kriechen, (da'hin)schleichen: ~ *up on* sich heranschleichen an (*acc.*); ~ *into s.o.'s favo(u)r fig.* sich bei j-m einschmeicheln; ~ *in* sich einschleichen (*Fehler*); *old age is ~ing upon me* das Alter naht heran; **2.** ♀ kriechen, sich ranken; **3.** ⊙ kriechen; ♂ nacheilen; **4.** kribbeln: *it made my flesh ~* dabei überlief es mich kalt, ich bekam eine Gänsehaut dabei; **II** *s.* **5.** → *crawl* 6; **6.** → *creep·age*; **7.** Schlupfloch *n*; **8.** *geol.* (Erd-) Rutsch *m*; **9.** *pl.* F Gruseln *n*, Gänsehaut *f*: *the sight gave me the ~s* bei dem Anblick überlief es mich kalt; **10.** *sl.* ‚Fiesling' *m*, ‚Scheißtyp' *m*; '**creep·age** [-pɪdʒ] *s.* ⊙, ♂ Kriechen *n*; '**creep·er** [-pə] *s.* **1.** *fig.* Kriecher(in); **2.** Kriechtier *n* (*Insekt, Wurm*); **3.** ♀ Kriech- *od.* Kletterpflanze *f*; **4.** *orn.* Baumläufer *m*; **5.** *mount.* Steigeisen *n*; **6.** ♣ Dragganker *m*; **7.** *pl. Am.* (einteiliger) Spielanzug; **8.** F weichsohliger Schuh; '**creep·ing** [-pɪŋ] *adj.* □ **1.** kriechend, schleichend (*a. fig.*); **2.** ♀ kriechend, kletternd; **3.** a) kribbelnd, b) grus(e)lig; **4.** → *barrage*¹; '**creep·y** [-pɪ] *adj.* **1.** kriechend: a) krabbelnd, b) schleichend; **2.** grus(e)lig.

cre·mate [krɪ'meɪt] *v/t. bsd.* Leichen verbrennen, einäschern; **cre·ma·tion** [-eɪʃn] *s.* Feuerbestattung *f*, Einäscherung *f*; **cre·ma·to·ri·um** [,kremə'tɔːrɪəm] *pl.* -**ri·ums**, -**ri·a** [-rɪə], **cre·ma·to·ry** ['kremətərɪ] *s.* Krema'torium *n*.

crème [kreɪm] (*Fr.*) *s.* Creme *f*: ~ **de menthe** [,kreɪmdə'mɑːnt] *s.* 'Pfefferminzli,kör *m*; ~ **de la** [-dlɑː-] *s. fig.* a) *das Beste vom Besten*; *die* E'lite (*der* Gesellschaft), Crème *f* der La Crème.

cre·nate ['kriːneɪt], '**cre·nat·ed** [-tɪd] *adj.* ♀, ♂ gekerbt, gefurcht; **cre·na·tion** [krɪ'neɪʃn] *s.* ♀, ♂ Kerbung *f*, Furchung *f*.

cren·el ['krenl] *s.* Schießscharte *f*; '**cren·el(l)ate** [-nəleɪt] *v/t.* krenelieren, mit Zinnen *od.* zinnenartigem Orna'ment versehen; **cren·el(l)a·tion** [,krenə'leɪʃn] *s.* Krenelierung *f*.

Cre·ole ['kriːəʊl] **I** *s.* Kre'ole *m*, Kre'olin *f*; **II** *adj.* kre'olisch.

cre·o·sote ['kriːəsəʊt] *s.* 🜚 Kreo'sot *n*.

crêpe [kreɪp] *s.* **1.** Krepp *m*; **2.** → ~ **rubber**; ~ **de Chine** [,kreɪpdə'ʃiːn] *s.* Crêpe *m* de Chine; ~ **pa·per** *s.* 'Kreppa,pier *n*; ~ **rub·ber** *s.* 'Krepp,gummi *n*, *m*; ~ **su·zette** [suː'zet] *s.* Crêpe *f* Su'zette.

crep·i·tate ['krepɪteɪt] *v/i.* knarren, knirschen, knacken, rasseln; **crep·i·ta·tion** [,krepɪ'teɪʃn] *s.* Knarren *n*, Knirschen *n*, Knacken *n*, Rasseln *n*.

crept [krept] *pret. u. p.p. von creep.*

cre·pus·cu·lar [krɪ'pʌskjʊlə] *adj.* **1.** Dämmerungs..., dämmerig; **2.** *zo.* im Zwielicht erscheinend.

cre·scen·do [krɪ'ʃendəʊ] (*Ital.*) ♪ **I** *pl.* -**dos** *s.* Cre'scendo *n* (*a. fig.*); **II** *adv.* cre'scendo, stärker werdend.

cres·cent ['kresnt] **I** *s.* **1.** Halbmond *m*, Mondsichel *f*; **2.** *hist. pol.* Halbmond *m* (*Türkei od. Islam*); **3.** halbmondförmiger Gegenstand, Straßenzug *etc.*; **4.** ♪ Schellenbaum *m*; **5.** Hörnchen *n* (*Gebäck*); **II** *adj.* **6.** halbmondförmig; **7.** zunehmend.

cress [kres] *s.* ♀ Kresse *f*.

crest [krest] **I** *s.* **1.** *zo.* Kamm *m* (*Hahn*); **2.** *zo.* a) (Feder-, Haar)Schopf *m*, Haube *f* (*Vögel*), b) Mähne *f*; **3.** Helmbusch *m*, -schmuck *m*; **4.** Helm *m*; **5.** Bergrücken *m*, Kamm *m*; **6.** Kamm *m* (*Welle*): *he's riding (along) a ~ of the wave fig.* er schwimmt momentan ganz oben; **7.** Gipfel *m*, Krone *f*, Scheitelpunkt *m*; **8.** Verzierung *f* über dem (Fa'milien)Wappen: *family ~* Familienwappen *n*; **9.** △ Bekrönung *f*; **II** *v/t.* **10.** erklimmen; **III** *v/i.* **11.** hoch aufwogen; '**crest·ed** [-tɪd] *adj.* mit e-m Kamm *od.* Schopf *od.* e-r Haube (versehen): ~ *lark* Haubenlerche *f*; '**crest·, fall·en** *adj. fig.* geknickt, niedergeschlagen.

cre·ta·ceous [krɪ'teɪʃəs] *adj.* kreideartig, -haltig: ~ *period* Kreide(zeit) *f*.

Cre·tan ['kriːtn] **I** *adj.* kretisch, aus Kreta; **II** *s.* Kreter(in).

cre·tin ['kretɪn] *s.* ♣ Kre'tin *m* (*a. contp.*); '**cre·tin·ism** [-nɪzəm] *s.* Kreti'nismus *m*; '**cre·tin·ous** [-nəs] *adj.* kre'tinhaft.

Creutz·feld(t)-Ja·kob dis·ease [,krɔɪtsfelt'jækɒb] *s.* ♣ Creutzfeld(t)-Jakob-Krankheit *f* (= *BSE*).

cre·vasse [krɪ'væs] *s.* **1.** tiefer Spalt *od.* Riss; **2.** Gletscherspalte *f*; **3.** *Am.* Bruch *m* im Deich.

crev·ice ['krevɪs] *s.* Riss *m*, (Fels)Spalte *f*.

crew¹ [kruː] *pret. von crow².*

crew² [kruː] *s.* **1.** ♣, ✈ *etc.* Besatzung *f*, (*a. sport* Boots)Mannschaft *f*; **2.** (Arbeits)Gruppe *f*, ('Arbeiter)Ko,lonne *f*; **3.** 🜚 (Bedienungs)Mannschaft *f*; **4.** ('Dienst)Perso,nal *m*; **5.** *Am.* Pfadfindergruppe *f*; **6.** *contp.* Bande *f*; ~ **cut** *s.* Bürste(nschnitt *m*) *f*.

crib [krɪb] **I** *s.* **1.** a) (Futter)Krippe *f*, b) Hürde *f*, Stall *m*; **2.** Kinderbettchen *n*; **3.** a) Hütte *f*, b) kleiner Raum; **4.** Weidenkorb *m* (*Fischfalle*); **5.** F a) kleiner Diebstahl, b) ‚Anleihe' *f*, Plagi'at *n*; **6.** *ped.* F a) ‚Eselsbrücke' *f*, b) Spickzettel *m*; **7.** *Cribbage:* abgelegte Karten *pl.*; **II** *v/t.* **8.** ein-, zs.-pferchen; **9.** F ‚klauen' (*a. fig. plagiieren*), *ped.* abschreiben; **III** *v/i.* **10.** F abschreiben; '**crib·bage** [-bɪdʒ] *s.* 'Cribbage *n* (*Kartenspiel*).

crick [krɪk] **I** *s.* Muskelkrampf *m*: ~ *in one's back* (*neck*) steifer Rücken (Hals); **II** *v/t.* ~ *one's back* (*neck*) sich e-n steifen Rücken (Hals) holen.

crick·et¹ ['krɪkɪt] *s. zo.* Grille *f*, Heimchen *n*; → *merry* 1.

crick·et² ['krɪkɪt] *s. sport* Kricket *n*: ~ *bat* Kricketschläger *m*; ~ *field*, ~ *ground* Kricket(spiel)platz *m*; ~ *pitch* Feld *n* zwischen den beiden Dreistäben; *not ...* F nicht fair *od.* anständig; '**crick·et·er** [-tə] *s.* Kricketspieler *m*.

cri·er ['kraɪə] *s.* **1.** Schreier *m*; **2.** (öffentlicher) Ausrufer.

cri·key ['kraɪkɪ] *int. sl.* Mann!

crime [kraɪm] **I** *s.* **1.** ⚖ *u. fig.* a) Verbrechen *n*, b) → *criminality* 1: ~ *novel* Kriminalroman *m*; ~ *rate* Verbrechensquote *f*; ~ *wave* Welle *f* von Verbrechen; **2.** Frevel *m*, Übeltat *f*, Sünde *f*; **3.** *coll.* Krimi'nalro,mane *f*: ~ *writer* ,Krimi-Schreiber(in)'; **4.** F ‚Verbrechen' *n*, ‚Jammer' *m*, ‚Schande' *f*; **II** *v/t.*

5. ✗ beschuldigen.
Cri·me·an [kraɪˈmɪən] *adj.* die Krim betreffend: **~ War** Krimkrieg *m.*
crim·i·nal [ˈkrɪmɪnl] **I** *adj.* **1.** verbrecherisch, krimi'nell, strafbar: **~ act; 2.** ⚖ strafrechtlich, Straf..., in Strafsachen: **~ jurisdiction; ~ lawyer** Strafrechtler *m,* Anwalt *m* für Strafsachen; **II** *s.* **3.** Verbrecher(in); **~ ac·tion** *s.* 'Strafpro,zess *m;* **~ code** *s.* Strafgesetzbuch *n;* **~ con·ver·sa·tion** *s.* ⚖ *Brit. obs. u. Am.* Ehebruch *m (als Schadensersatzgrund);* ♀ **In·ves·ti·ga·tion De·part·ment** *s. (abbr. CID) Brit.* Krimi-'nalpoli,zei *f.*
crim·i·nal·ist [ˈkrɪmɪnəlɪst] *s.* **1.** Krimina'list *m,* Strafrechtler *m;* **2.** Krimino'loge *m;* **crim·i·nal·i·ty** [ˌkrɪmɪˈnælətɪ] *s.* **1.** Kriminali'tät *f,* Verbrechertum *n;* **2.** Schuld *f;* Strafbarkeit *f;* **'crim·i·nal·ize** *v/t.* **1.** *et.* unter Strafe stellen; **2.** *j-n, et.* kriminalisieren.
crim·i·nal| law *s.* Strafrecht *n;* **~ neg·lect** *s.* grobe Fahrlässigkeit; **~ of·fence,** *Am.* **~ of·fense** *s.* strafbare Handlung; **~ pro·ceed·ings** *s. pl.* Strafverfahren *n;* **~ re·spon·si·bil·i·ty** *s.* a) Strafbarkeit *f:* **age of ~** Strafmündigkeit *f,* b) Zurechnungsfähigkeit *f.*
crim·i·nate [ˈkrɪmɪneɪt] *v/t.* anklagen, (e-s Verbrechens) beschuldigen; **crim·i·na·tion** [ˌkrɪmɪˈneɪʃn] *s.* Anklage *f,* Beschuldigung *f;* **crim·i·nol·o·gist** [ˌkrɪmɪˈnɒlədʒɪst] *s.* Krimino'loge *m;* **crim·i·nol·o·gy** [ˌkrɪmɪˈnɒlədʒɪ] *s.* Kriminolo'gie *f.*
crimp¹ [krɪmp] **I** *v/t.* **1.** kräuseln, knittern, fälteln, wellen; **2.** *Leder* zu'rechtbiegen; **3.** ⊕ bördeln; **4.** *Küche: Fisch, Fleisch* schlitzen; **5.** *Am. sl.* hindern, stören; **II** *s.* **6.** Kräuselung *f,* Welligkeit *f;* Krause *f,* Falte *f;* **7.** ⊕ Falz *m;* **8.** (Haar)Welle *f,* Locke *f;* **9.** *Am.* F Behinderung *f.*
crimp² [krɪmp] *v/t.* ⚓, ✗ gewaltsam anwerben, pressen.
crim·son [ˈkrɪmzn] **I** *s.* Karme'sin-, Hochrot *n;* **II** *adj.* karme'sin-, hochrot; *fig.* puterrot *(from* vor *Zorn etc.);* **III** *v/t.* hochrot färben; **IV** *v/i.* puterrot werden; **~ ram·bler** *s.* ♀ blutrote Kletterrose.
cringe [krɪndʒ] *v/i.* **1.** sich ducken, sich krümmen: **~ at** zurückschrecken vor *(dat.);* **2.** *fig.* kriechen, ,katzbuckeln' *(to* vor *dat.);* **'cring·ing** [-dʒɪŋ] *adj.* □ kriecherisch, unter'würfig.
crin·kle [ˈkrɪŋkl] **I** *v/i.* **1.** sich kräuseln *od.* krümmen *od.* biegen; **2.** Falten werfen, knittern; **II** *v/t.* **3.** kräuseln, krümmen; **4.** faltig machen, knittern; **III** *s.* **5.** Fältchen *n,* Runzel *f;* **'crin·kly** [-lɪ] *adj.* **1.** kraus, faltig; **2.** zerknittert.
crin·o·line [ˈkrɪnəliːn] *s. hist.* Krino'line *f,* Reifrock *m.*
crip·ple [ˈkrɪpl] **I** *s.* **1.** Krüppel *m;* **II** *v/t.* **2.** a) zum Krüppel machen, b) lähmen; **3.** *fig.* lähmen, lahm legen; **4.** ✗ aktions- *od.* kampfunfähig machen; **'crip·pled** [-ld] *adj.* **1.** verkrüppelt; **2.** *fig.* lahm gelegt; **'crip·pling** [-lɪŋ] *adj. fig.* lähmend.
cri·sis [ˈkraɪsɪs] *pl.* **-ses** [-siːz] *s.* 💊, *thea. u. fig.* 'Krise *f,* 'Krisis *f:* **~ man·agement** Krisenmanagement *n;* **~-prone** krisenanfällig; **~ staff** Krisenstab *m.*
crisp [krɪsp] **I** *adj.* □ **1.** knusp(e)rig, mürbe: **~bread** Knäckebrot *n;* **2.** kraus, gekräuselt; **3.** frisch, fest *(Gemüse);* steif, unzerknittert *(Papier);* **4.**

a) forsch, schneidig, b) flott, lebhaft; **5.** klar, knapp *(Stil etc.);* **6.** scharf, frisch *(Luft);* **II** *s.* **7.** *pl. bsd. Brit.* (Kar'toffel) Chips *pl.;* **III** *v/t.* **8.** knusp(e)rig machen; **9.** kräuseln; **IV** *v/i.* **10.** knusp(e)rig werden; **11.** sich kräuseln; **'crisp·ness** [-nɪs] *s.* **1.** Knusp(e)rigkeit *f;* **2.** Frische *f,* Schärfe *f,* Le'bendigkeit *f;* **'crisp·y** [-pɪ] → **crisp** 1, 2, 4.
criss-cross [ˈkrɪskrɒs] **I** *adj.* **1.** gekreuzt, kreuz u. quer (laufend); Kreuz...; **II** *adv.* **2.** kreuzweise, kreuz u. quer, durchein'ander; **3.** *fig.* in die Quere, verkehrt; **III** *s.* **4.** Gewirr *n* von Linien; **5.** Kreuzzeichen *n (als Unterschrift);* **IV** *v/t.* **6.** (wieder'holt 'durch-) kreuzen, kreuz u. quer durch'ziehen; **V** *v/i.* **7.** sich kreuzen; kreuz u. quer verlaufen.
cri·te·ri·on [kraɪˈtɪərɪən] *pl.* **-ri·a** [-rɪə] *s.* **1.** Kri'terium *n,* Maßstab *m,* Prüfstein *m: that is no ~* das ist nicht maßgebend *(for* für); **2.** (Unter'scheidungs)Merkmal *n.*
crit·ic [ˈkrɪtɪk] *s.* **1.** Kritiker(in); **2.** (Kunst- *etc.*)Kritiker(in), Rezen'sent (-in); **3.** Krittler *m,* Tadler *m;* **'crit·i·cal** [-kl] *adj.* □ **1.** kritisch, tadelsüchtig *(of s.o.* j-m gegen'über): *be ~ of s.th.* et. kritisieren *od.* beanstanden, Bedenken gegen et. haben; **2.** kritisch, kunstverständig; sorgfältig: **~ edition** kritische Ausgabe; **3.** kritisch, entscheidend: *the ~ moment;* **4.** kritisch, bedenklich, gefährlich: **~ situation; ~ supplies** Mangelgüter; **5.** *phys.* kritisch: **~ speed; ~ load** Grenzbelastung *f;* **'crit·i·cism** [-ɪsɪzəm] *s.* Kri'tik *f:* a) kritische Beurteilung, b) (Buch- *etc.*)Besprechung *f,* Rezensi'on *f,* c) kritische Unter'suchung, d) Tadel *m:* **textual ~** Textkritik; **open to ~** anfechtbar; **above ~** über jede Kritik *od.* jeden Tadel erhaben; **'crit·i·cize** [-ɪsaɪz] *v/t.* kritisieren *(a. v/i.):* a) kritisch beurteilen, b) besprechen, rezensieren; c) Kri'tik üben an *(dat.),* tadeln, rügen; **cri·tique** [krɪˈtiːk] *s.* Kri'tik *f,* kritische Besprechung *od.* Abhandlung.
croak [krəʊk] **I** *v/i.* **1.** quaken *(Frosch);* krächzen *(Rabe);* **2.** unken *(Unglück prophezeien);* **3.** *sl.* ,abkratzen' *(sterben);* **II** *v/t.* **4.** *et.* krächzen(d sagen); **5.** *sl.* abmurksen *(töten);* **III** *s.* **6.** Quaken *n;* Krächzen *n;* **7.** → **croaker** 1; **'croak·er** [-kə] *s.* **1.** Schwarzseher *m,* Miesmacher *m;* **2.** *Am. sl.* Quacksalber *m;* **'croak·y** [-kɪ] *adj.* □ krächzend.
Cro·at [ˈkrəʊæt] *s.* Kro'ate *m,* Kro'atin *f;* **Cro·a·tian** [krəʊˈeɪʃən] *adj.* kro'atisch.
cro·chet [ˈkrəʊʃeɪ] **I** *s. a.* **~work** Häkelarbeit *f,* Häke'lei *f:* **~ hook** Häkelnadel *f;* **II** *v/t. u. v/i. pret. u. p.p.* **'cro·cheted** [-ʃeɪd] häkeln.
crock¹ [krɒk] **I** *s.* **1.** Klepper *m,* alter Gaul; **2.** *sl.* a) ,altes Wrack' *(Person od. Sache),* b) *Am.* ,altes Ekel' *od.* ,alter Säufer'; **II** *v/i.* **3.** *mst* **~ up** zs.-brechen, -krachen; **III** *v/t.* **4.** ka'puttmachen.
crock² [krɒk] *s.* **1.** irdener Topf *od.* Krug; **2.** Topfscherbe *f;* **'crock·er·y** [-kərɪ] *s.* (irdenes) Geschirr, Steingut *n,* Töpferware *f.*
croc·o·dile [ˈkrɒkədaɪl] *s.* **1.** *zo.* Kroko-'dil *n;* **2.** Kroko'dilleder *n;* **3.** *Brit.* F Zweierreihe *f* von Schulmädchen; **~ tears** *s. pl.* Kroko'dilstränen *pl.*
cro·cus [ˈkrəʊkəs] *s.* ♀ 'Krokus *m.*
Croe·sus [ˈkriːsəs] *s.* 'Krösus *m.*
croft [krɒft] *s. Brit.* **1.** kleines (Acker-) Feld *(beim Haus);* **2.** kleiner Bauernhof *m;* **'croft·er** [-tə] *s. Brit.* Kleinbauer

m.
crois·sant [ˈkwæsɑːŋ] *s.* Crois'sant *n,* Hörnchen *n.*
crom·lech [ˈkrɒmlek] *s.* 'Kromlech *m,* dru'idischer Steinkreis.
crone [krəʊn] *s.* altes Weib.
cro·ny [ˈkrəʊnɪ] *s.* alter Freund, Kum'pan *m:* **old ~** Busenfreund, Intimus *m,* ,Spezi' *m.*
crook [krʊk] **I** *s.* **1.** Hirtenstab *m;* **2.** *eccl.* Bischofs-, Krummstab *m;* **3.** Krümmung *f,* Biegung *f;* **4.** Haken *m;* **5.** *(Schirm)*Krücke *f;* **6.** F Gauner *m,* Betrüger *m,* *fig.* Ga'nove *m:* **on the ~** unehrlich, hintenherum; **II** *v/t. u. v/i.* **7.** (sich) krümmen, (sich) biegen; **'~·back** *s.* Buck(e)lige(r *m*) *f;* **'~·backed** *adj.* buck(e)lig.
crooked¹ [krʊkt] *adj.* mit e-r Krücke: **~ stick** Krückstock *m.*
crook·ed² [ˈkrʊkɪd] *adj.* □ **1.** krumm, gekrümmt; gebeugt; **2.** buck(e)lig, verwachsen; **3.** *fig.* unehrlich, betrügerisch: **~ ways** ,krumme' Wege.
croon [kruːn] *v/i. u. v/t.* leise *od.* schmachtend singen *od.* summen; **'croon·er** [-nə] *s.* Schlager-, Schnulzensänger *m.*
crop [krɒp] **I** *s.* **1.** Feldfrucht *f, bsd.* Getreide *n* auf dem Halm, Saat *f:* **the ~s** a) die Saaten, b) die Gesamternte; **~ rotation** Fruchtfolge *f,* -wechsel *m;* **2.** Bebauung *f:* **in ~** bebaut; **3.** Ernte *f,* Ertrag *m:* **~ failure** Missernte *f;* **4.** *fig.* Ertrag *m,* Ausbeute *f (of* an *dat.);* **5.** Menge *f,* Haufen *m (Sachen od. Personen);* **6.** *zo.* Kropf *m (Vögel);* **7.** a) Peitschenstock *m,* b) Reitpeitsche *f;* **8.** kurzer Haarschnitt, kurz geschnittenes Haar; **II** *v/t.* **9.** abschneiden; *Haar* kurz scheren; *Ohren, Schwanz* stutzen; **10.** abbeißen, -fressen; **11.** ✓ bepflanzen, bebauen; **III** *v/i.* **12.** (Ernte) tragen; **13.** *geol.* **~ up, ~ out** zutage treten; **14.** **~ up** *fig.* plötzlich auftauchen, -treten, sich zeigen; **'crop-eared** *adj.* mit gestutzten Ohren; **'crop·per** [-pə] *s.* **1.** *a* **good ~** e-e gut tragende Pflanze; **2.** F Fall *m,* Sturz *m:* **come a ~** ,auf die Nase fallen' *(a. fig.);* **3.** *orn.* Kropftaube *f.*
cro·quet [ˈkrəʊkeɪ] *sport* **I** *s.* 'Krocket *n;* **II** *v/t. u. v/i.* krockieren.
cro·quette [krɒˈket] *s. Küche:* Kro'kette *f.*
cro·sier [ˈkrəʊʒə] *s. R.C.* Bischofs-, Krummstab *m.*
cross [krɒs] **I** *s.* **1.** Kreuz *n (zur Kreuzigung);* **2.** *the ♀* a) das Kreuz Christi, b) das Christentum, c) das Kruzi'fix *n;* **3.** Kreuz *n (Zeichen od. Gegenstand):* **make the sign of the ~** sich bekreuzigen; **sign with a ~** mit e-m Kreuz *(statt Unterschrift)* unterzeichnen; **mark with a ~** ankreuzen; **4.** (Ordens)Kreuz *n;* **5.** *fig.* Kreuz *n,* Leiden *n,* Not *f:* **bear one's ~** sein Kreuz tragen; **6.** Querstrich *m (des Buchstabens* t); **7.** Gaune-'rei *f,* ,krumme Tour': **on the ~** unehrlich; **8.** *biol.* Kreuzung *f,* Mischung *f;* *fig.* Mittelding *n;* **9.** Kreuzungspunkt *m;* **10.** *sport* Cross *m:* a) *Fußball etc.:* Schrägpass *m,* b) *Tennis:* diagonal geschlagener Ball, c) *Boxen:* Schlag über den Arm des Gegners; **II** *v/t.* **11.** kreuzen, über Kreuz legen: **~ one's legs** die Beine kreuzen *od.* überschlagen; **~ swords with s.o.** die Klingen mit j-m kreuzen *(a. fig.);* **~ s.o.'s hand** *(od.* **palm)** a) j-m (Trink)Geld geben, b) j-n ,schmieren'; **12.** e-n Querstrich ziehen durch: **~ one's t's** sehr sorgfältig sein; **~ a cheque** e-n Scheck ,kreuzen' *(als*

Verrechnungsscheck *kennzeichnen*); →
cheque; ~ **off** (*od.* **out**) ausstreichen; ~
off *fig. et.* ‚abschreiben'; **13.** durch-,
über'queren, *Grenze* über'schreiten,
Zimmer durch'schreiten, (hin'über)ge-
hen, (-)fahren über (*acc.*): ~ **the ocean**
über den Ozean fahren; ~ **the street**
über die Straße gehen; *it* ~**ed my mind**
es fiel mir ein, es kam mir in den Sinn;
~ **s.o.'s path** j-m in die Quere kommen; **14.** sich kreuzen mit: *your letter*
~**ed mine** Ihr Brief kreuzte sich mit
meinem; ~ **each other** sich kreuzen,
sich schneiden, sich treffen; **15.** *biol.*
kreuzen; **16.** *fig. Plan* durch'kreuzen,
vereiteln; entgegentreten (*dat.*): **be**
~**ed in love** Unglück in der Liebe haben; **17.** das Kreuzzeichen machen auf
(*acc.*) *od.* über (*dat.*): ~ **o.s.** sich bekreuzigen; **III** *v/i.* **18.** *a.* ~ **over** hi-
nübergehen, -fahren; 'übersetzen; **19.**
sich treffen; sich kreuzen (*Briefe*) **IV**
adj. □ **20.** quer (liegend, laufend),
Quer...; schräg; sich (über)'schneidend; **21.** (*to*) entgegengesetzt (*dat.*),
im 'Widerspruch (zu), Gegen...; **22.** F
ärgerlich, mürrisch, böse (**with** mit): *as*
~ *as two sticks* bitterböse; **23.** *sl.*
unehrlich.

cross| ac·tion *s.* ⚖ Gegen-, 'Widerkla-
ge *f*; ~ **ap·peal** *s.* ⚖ Anschlussberufung
f; '~**bar** *s.* **1.** Querholz *n*, -riegel *m*,
-stange *f*, -balken *m*; **2.** ⚙ Tra'verse *f*;
3. *a) Fußball:* Querlatte *f*, *b) Hoch-*
sprung: Latte *f*; '~**bench** *parl. Brit.* **I** *s.*
Querbank *f* der Par'teilosen (*im Ober-*
haus); **II** *adj.* par'teilos, unabhängig;
'~**bones** *s. pl.* zwei gekreuzte Knochen unter e-m Totenkopf; '~**bow**
[-bəʊ] *s.* Armbrust *f*; '~**bor·der** *adj.*
grenzüberschreitend; '~**bred** *adj. biol.*
durch Kreuzung erzeugt, gekreuzt;
'~**breed** *s.* **1.** Mischrasse *f*; **2.** Kreuzung *f*, Mischling *m*; **II** *v/t.* [*irr.* →
breed] **3.** kreuzen; ~'**Chan·nel** *adj.*
den ('Ärmel)Ka'nal über'querend: ~
steamer Kanaldampfer *m*; '~**check I**
v/t. **1.** (von verschiedenen Gesichtspunkten aus) über'prüfen; **2.** *Eisho-*
ckey: crosschecken; **II** *s.* **3.** mehrfache
Über'prüfung; **4.** *Eishockey:* 'Cross-
check *m*; ~'**coun·try I** *adj.* Querfeldein...; Gelände..., *mot. a.* geländegängig: ~ **skiing** Skilanglauf *m*; ~ **race** →
II *s. sport a)* Querfeld'ein-, Crosslauf
m, *b) Radsport:* Querfeld'einrennen *n*;
'~**cur·rent** *s.* Gegenströmung *f* (*a.*
fig.); '~**cut I** *v/t.* **1.** *a)* quer schneidend, Quer..., *b)* quer geschnitten: ~
file Doppelfeile *f*; ~ **saw** Ablängsäge *f*;
II *s.* **2.** Querweg *m*; **3.** ⚙ Kreuzhieb *m*.
crosse [krɒs] *s. sport* La'crosse-Schläger
m.

cross| en·try *s.* ✝ Gegenbuchung *f*; '~-
ex·am·i·na·tion *s.* ⚖ Kreuzverhör *n*;
‚~**ex·am·ine** → **I** ⚖ ins Kreuzverhör
nehmen; '~**eyed** *adj.* schielend; '~-
fade *v/t. Film etc.:* über'blenden; ‚~-
'**fer·ti·lize** *v/i. biol.* sich kreuzweise
(*fig. gegenseitig*) befruchten; '~**fire** *s.* ⚔
Kreuzfeuer *n* (*a. fig.*); '~**grained** *adj.*
1. quer gefasert; **2.** *fig.* 'widerspenstig,
eigensinnig; kratzbürstig; '~**hatch·ing**
s. Kreuzschraffierung *f*; ~ **head**, *a.*
head·ing *s. Zeitung:* 'Zwischen‚überschrift *f*.

cross·ing ['krɒsɪŋ] *s.* **1.** Kreuzen *n*,
Kreuzung *f* (*a. biol.*); **2.** Durch-, Über-
'querung *f*; **3.** 'Überfahrt *f*; ('Straßen
etc.),Übergang *m*; **4.** (Straßen-, Eisenbahn)Kreuzung *f*: **level** (*Am.* **grade**) ~
schienengleicher (*oft* unbeschrankter)
Bahnübergang; '~**o·ver** *s. biol.* Cros-

sing-'over *n*, Genaustausch *m* zwischen
Chromo'somenpaaren.

'**cross|-legged** *adj.* mit 'übergeschlage-
nen Beinen, *a.* im Schneidersitz;
'~**light** *s.* schräg einfallendes Licht.

cross·ness ['krɒsnɪs] *s.* Verdrießlichkeit *f*, schlechte Laune.

'**cross|·o·ver** *s.* **1.** → **crossing** 2–4; **2.**
biol. ausgetauschtes Gen; **3.** ♫ *a)* Über-
'kreuzung *f*, *b) opt.,* TV Bündelknoten
m; '~**patch** *s.* F ‚Kratzbürste' *f*; '~-
piece *s.* ⚙ Querstück *n*, -balken *m*,
-holz *n*; '~**pol·li·na·tion** *s. bot.* Fremd-
bestäubung *f*; ‚~'**pur·pos·es** *s. pl.* **1.**
'Widerspruch *m*: **be at** ~ *a)* einander
entgegenarbeiten, *b)* sich missverstehen; **talk at** ~ aneinander vorbeireden;
2. *sg. konstr. ein* Frage- u. Antwort-
Spiel *n*; ‚~'**ques·tion I** *s.* ⚖ Frage *f* im
Kreuzverhör; **II** *v/t.* → **cross-exam-**
ine; ~ **ref·er·ence** *s.* Kreuz-, Querverweis *m*; '~**road** *s.* **1.** Querstraße *f*; **2.**
pl. mst sg. konstr. Straßenkreuzung *f*:
at a ~**s** an e-r Kreuzung; **at the** ~**s** *fig.*
am Scheidewege; ~ **sec·tion** *s.* ⚓, ⚙ *u.*
fig. Querschnitt *m* (*of* durch); '~**stitch**
s. Kreuzstich *m*; ~ **sum** *s.* Quersumme
f; ~ **talk** *s.* **1.** *teleph. etc.* Nebenspre-
chen *n*; **2.** Ko'pieref‚fekt *m* (*Tonband*);
3. *Brit.* Wortgefecht *n*; '~**tie** *s.* Schie-
nenschwelle *f*; '~**town** *adj. Am.* quer
durch die Stadt (gehend *od.* fahrend
od. reichend); ~ **vot·ing** *s. Brit. pol.*
Abstimmung *f* über Kreuz (*wobei ein-*
zelne Abgeordnete mit der Gegenpartei
stimmen); '~**walk** *s. Am.* 'Fußgänger-
‚überweg *m*; '~**ways** → **crosswise**;
~ **wind** *s.* ✈, ⚓ Seitenwind *m*; '~**wise**
adv. quer, kreuzweise; kreuzförmig; '~-
word (**puz·zle**) *s.* Kreuzworträtsel *n*.

crotch [krɒtʃ] *s.* **1.** Gabelung *f*; **2.**
Schritt *m* (*der Hose od. des Körpers*).

crotch·et ['krɒtʃɪt] *s.* **1.** ♪ Viertelnote *f*;
2. Schrulle *f*, Ma'rotte *f*; '**crotch·et·y**
[-tɪ] *adj.* **1.** grillenhaft; **2.** F mürrisch,
schrullenhaft, verschroben.

cro·ton ['krəʊtən] *s.* ♥ 'Kroton *m*; ⚬ **bug**
s. zo. Am. Küchenschabe *f*.

crouch [kraʊtʃ] **I** *v/i.* **1.** hocken, sich
(nieder)ducken, (sich zs.-)kauern; **2.**
fig. kriechen, sich ducken (**to** vor); **II** *s.*
3. kauernde Stellung, geduckte Hal-
tung; Hockstellung *f*.

croup[1] [kru:p] *s.* ✚ Krupp *m*, Halsbräune *f*.

croup[2], **croupe** [kru:p] *s.* Kruppe *f* des
Pferdes.

crou·pi·er ['kru:pɪə] *s.* Croupi'er *m*.

crow[1] [krəʊ] *s.* **1.** *orn.* Krähe *f*: **as the** ~
flies *a)* schnurgerade, *b)* (in der) Luftlinie; **eat** ~ *Am.* F zu Kreuze kriechen,
‚klein und hässlich' sein *od.* werden;
have a ~ **to pluck** (*od.* **pick**) **with** *s.o.*
mit j-m ein Hühnchen zu rupfen haben;
2. rabenähnlicher Vogel; **3.** *Am. contp.*
Neger *m*.

crow[2] [krəʊ] **I** *v/i.* [*irr.*] **1.** krähen
(*Hahn, a. Kind*); **2.** (vor Freude) quietschen; **3.** (**over, about**) *a)* triumphieren (über *acc.*), *b)* protzen, prahlen
(mit); **II** *s.* **4.** Krähen *n* (*Hahn*); **5.**
(Freuden)Schrei(*e pl.*) *m*.

'**crow|-bar** *s.* ⚙ Brech-, Stemmeisen *n*;
'~**ber·ry** [-bərɪ] *s.* ♥ Krähenbeere *f*.

crowd [kraʊd] **I** *s.* **1.** (Menschen)Menge
f, Gedränge *n*: ~**s of people** Men-
schenmassen; ~ **scene** *Film:* Massen-
szene *f*; **he would pass in a** ~ er ist
nicht schlechter als andere; **2. the** ~ das
gemeine Volk; der Pöbel: **follow the** ~
mit der Masse gehen; **3.** F ‚Ver'ein' *m*,
Bande *f* (*Gesellschaft*): **a jolly** ~; **4.** Ansammlung *f*, Haufen *m*: **a** ~ **of books**;

II *v/i.* **5.** sich drängen, zs.-strömen; vorwärts drängen: ~ **in** sich drängen, sich
hin'eindrängen; ~ **in upon** *s.o.* auf j-n
einstürmen (*Gedanken etc.*); **III** *v/t.* **6.**
über'füllen, voll stopfen (**with** mit); →
crowded 1; ~ **in** 'einpressen, -stopfen
(**into** in *acc.*); **8.** (zs.-)drängen: ~ (**on**)
sail ⚓ alle Segel beisetzen; ~ **out** verdrängen; ausschalten; (*wegen Platz-*
mangels) aussperren; **9.** *Am. a)* (vorwärts *etc.*) drängen, *b) Auto etc.* abdrängen, *c)* j-m im Nacken sitzen, *d)* j-s
Geduld, Glück etc. strapazieren: ~**ing**
thirty an die dreißig; ~ **up** Preise in die
Höhe treiben; '**crowd·ed** [-dɪd] *adj.* **1.**
(**with**) über'füllt, voll gestopft (mit),
voll, wimmelnd (von): ~ **to overflow-**
ing zum Bersten voll; ~ **profession**
überlaufener Beruf; **2.** gedrängt, zs.-
gepfercht; **3.** bedrängt, beengt; **4.** voll
ausgefüllt, arbeits-, ereignisreich: ~
hours.

'**crow·foot** *pl.* **-foots** *s.* **1.** ♥ Hahnenfuß
m; **2.** → **crow's-feet.**

crown [kraʊn] **I** *s.* **1.** Siegerkranz *m*,
Ehrenkrone *f*; **2.** *a)* (Königs- *etc.*)Kro-
ne *f*, *b)* Herrschermacht *f*, Thron *m*:
succeed to the ~ den Thron besteigen;
c) **the** ♕ die Krone, der König *etc.*, *a.*
der Staat *od.* Fiskus: ~ **cases** *Brit.*
Strafsachen; **3.** Krone *f* (*Abzeichen*); **4.**
fig. Krone *f*, Palme *f*, *sport a.* (Meister)Titel *m*; **5.** Gipfel *m*: *a)* höchster
Punkt, *b) fig.* Krönung *f*, Höhepunkt
m; **6.** Krone *f* (*Währung*): *a) Brit. obs.*
Fünfschillingstück *n*: **half a** ~ 2 Schilling 6 Pence, *b) Währungseinheit von*
Dänemark, Norwegen, Schweden etc.;
7. *a)* Scheitel *m*, Wirbel *m* (*Kopf*), *b)*
Kopf *m*, Schädel *m*; **8.** ♥ (Baum)Krone
f; **9.** *a) anat.* (Zahn)Krone *f*, *b)* (künstliche) Krone *f*; **10.** *a)* Haarkrone *f*, *b)*
Schopf *m*, Kamm *m* (*Vogel*); **11.** Kopf
m e-s *Hutes*; **12.** △ Krone *f*, Schlussstein *m* (*a. fig.*); **II** *v/t.* **13.** krönen: **be**
~**ed king** zum König gekrönt werden;
~**ed heads** gekrönte Häupter; **14.** *fig.*
krönen, ehren, belohnen; zieren,
schmücken; **15.** *fig.* krönen, den Gipfel
od. Höhepunkt bilden von: ~**ed with**
success von Erfolg gekrönt; **16.** *fig.*
die Krone aufsetzen (*dat.*): ~ **all** allem
die Krone aufsetzen (*a. iro.*); **to** ~ **all**
(*Redew.*) *iro.* zu allem Überfluss; **17.**
fig. glücklich voll'enden; **18.** ✚ *Zahn*
über'kronen; **19.** *Damespiel:* zur Dame
machen; **20.** *sl.* j-m ‚eins aufs Dach'
geben'; ~ **cap** *s.* Kron(en)korken *m*; ♕
Col·o·ny *s. Brit.* 'Kronkolo‚nie *f*; ♕
Court *npr. Brit.* ⚖ Gericht für Strafsachen höherer Ordnung (*nur in England*
u. Wales); ~ **glass** *s.* **1.** Mondglas *n*,
Butzenscheibe *f*; **2.** Kronglas *n*.

crown·ing ['kraʊnɪŋ] *adj.* krönend, alles
über'bietend, höchst: ~ **achievement**
Glanzleistung *f*.

crown| jew·els *s. pl.* 'Kronju‚welen *pl.*,
'Reichsklein‚odien *pl.*; ~ **land** *s.* Kron-
Staatsgut *n*; ♕ **law** *s.* ⚖ *Brit.* Strafrecht
n; ~ **prince** *s.* Kronprinz *m*; ~ **prin-**
cess *s.* 'Kronprin‚zessin *f*; ~ **wheel** *s.*
⚙ Kronrad *n* (*Uhr etc.*); *mot.* Antriebs-
kegelrad *n*.

'**crow's|-feet** ['krəʊz-] *pl.* ‚Krähenfüße'
pl., Fältchen *pl.*; ~ **nest** *s.* ⚓ Ausguck
m, Krähennest *n*.

cru·cial ['kru:ʃl] *adj.* **1.** 'kritisch, entscheidend: ~ **moment**; ~ **point** springender Punkt; ~ **test** Feuerprobe *f*; **2.**
schwierig; **3.** kreuzförmig, Kreuz...

cru·ci·ble ['kru:sɪbl] *s.* **1.** ⚙ (Schmelz-)
Tiegel *m*: ~ **steel** Tiegelgussstahl *m*; **2.**
fig. Feuerprobe *f*.

C

cru·ci·fix ['kruːsɪfɪks] s. Kruzi'fix n; **cru·ci·fix·ion** [ˌkruːsɪ'fɪkʃn] s. Kreuzigung f; **'cru·ci·form** [-fɔːm] adj. kreuzförmig; **'cru·ci·fy** [-faɪ] v/t. **1.** kreuzigen (a. fig.); **2.** fig. a) martern, quälen, b) Begierden abtöten, c) j-n ‚fertig machen‘.

crud [krʌd] s. F Dreck m, ‚Mist‘ m.

crude [kruːd] adj. □ **1.** roh: a) ungekocht, b) unver-, unbearbeitet: ~ oil Rohöl n; **2.** primi'tiv: a) plump, grob, b) simpel, c) bar'barisch; **3.** roh, grob, ungehobelt, unfein; **4.** roh, unfertig, unreif; 'undurch‚dacht: ~ figures Statistik: rohe od. nicht aufgeschlüsselte Zahlen; **5.** grell, geschmacklos (Farbe); **6.** fig. ungeschminkt, nackt: ~ facts; **'crude·ness** [-nɪs] s. Rohheit f, Grobheit f, Unfertigkeit f, Unreife f (a. fig.); **'cru·di·ty** [-dɪtɪ] s. **1.** → crudeness; **2.** et. Unfertiges od. Unbearbeitetes; **3.** et. Geschmackloses.

cru·el ['kruəl] I adj. □ **1.** grausam (to gegen); **2.** hart, unbarmherzig, roh, gefühllos; **3.** schrecklich, mörderisch: ~ heat; II adv. **4.** F furchtbar, ‚grausam‘: ~ hot; '**cru·el·ty** [-tɪ] s. **1.** Grausamkeit f (to gegen['über]); → mental cruelty; **2.** Miss'handlung f, Quäle'rei f: ~ to animals Tierquälerei; **3.** Schwere f, Härte f.

cru·et ['kruːɪt] s. **1.** Essig-, Ölfläschchen n; **2.** R.C. Messkännchen n; **3.** a. ~ stand Me'nage f, Gewürzständer m.

cruise [kruːz] I v/i. **1.** ♣ a) kreuzen, e-e Kreuzfahrt od. Seereise machen, b) her'umfahren: cruising taxi Taxi n auf Fahrgastsuche; **2.** ✈, mot. mit Reisegeschwindigkeit fliegen od. fahren; II s. **3.** Seereise f, Kreuz-, Vergnügungsfahrt f; ~ con·trol s. mot. Temporegler m; ~ mis·sile s. ✕ Marschflugkörper m.

cruis·er ['kruːzə] s. **1.** ♣ a) Kreuzer m, b) Kreuzfahrtschiff n; **2.** Am. (Funk-)Streifenwagen m; **3.** Boxen: ~ weight Am. Halbschwergewicht n; '**cruis·ing** [-zɪŋ] adj. ✈, mot. Reise...: ~ speed; ~ gear mot. Schongang m; ~ radius Aktionsradius m; ~ level ✈ Reiseflughöhe f.

crumb [krʌm] I s. **1.** Krume f: a) Krümel m, Brösel m, Brosame m, b) weicher Teil des Brotes; **2.** fig. a) Brocken m, b) Krümchen n, ein bisschen; **3.** sl. ‚Blödmann‘ m; II v/t. **4.** Küche: panieren; **5.** zerkrümeln; '**crum·ble** [-mbl] I v/t. **1.** zerkrümeln, -bröckeln; II v/i. **2.** zerbröckeln, -fallen; **3.** fig. a) zerfallen, zu'grunde gehen, b) (langsam) zs.-brechen; **4.** ✝ abbröckeln (Kurse); '**crum·bling** [-mblɪŋ], '**crum·bly** [-mblɪ] adj. **1.** krüm(e)lig, bröck(e)lig; **2.** zerbröckelnd, -fallend; **crumb·y** ['krʌmɪ] adj. **1.** voller Krumen (f), weich, krüm(e)lig.

crum·my ['krʌmɪ] adj. F lausig, mies.

crum·pet ['krʌmpɪt] s. **1.** Brit. Sauerteigfladen m; **2.** sl. ‚Miezen‘ pl.: she's a nice piece of ~ sie ist sehr sexy.

crum·ple ['krʌmpl] I v/t. **1.** a. ~ up zerknittern, zer-, zs.-knüllen; **2.** fig. j-n 'umwerfen; II v/i. **3.** faltig zerdrückt werden, zs.-schrumpeln; **4.** oft ~ up zs.-brechen (a. fig.), einstürzen; ~ zone s. mot. Knautschzone f.

crunch [krʌntʃ] I v/t. **1.** knirschend (zer)kauen; **2.** zermalmen; II v/i. **3.** knirschend kauen; **4.** knirschen; III s. **5.** Knirschen n; **6.** F fig. a) Druck(ausübung f) m, b) böse Situati'on, c) 'kritischer Mo'ment, 'Krise f: when it comes to the ~ wenn es hart auf hart geht.

crup·per ['krʌpə] s. a) Schwanzriemen

---

m, b) Kruppe f (des Pferdes).

cru·sade [kruː'seɪd] I s. hist. Kreuzzug m (a. fig.); II v/i. e-n Kreuzzug unter'nehmen; fig. zu Felde ziehen, kämpfen; **cru'sad·er** [-də] s. hist. Kreuzfahrer m; fig. Kämpfer m.

cruse [kruːz] s. bibl. irdener Krug.

crush [krʌʃ] I s. **1.** (zermalmender) Druck; **2.** Gedränge n, Gewühl n; **3.** große Gesellschaft od. Party; **4.** sl. Schwarm m: have a ~ on s.o. in j-n ‚verknallt‘ sein; II v/t. **5.** a. ~ up od. down zerquetschen, -drücken, -malmen; **6.** zerstoßen, -kleinern, mahlen; ~ed stone Schotter m; **7.** a. ~ up zerknittern, -knüllen; **8.** drücken, drängen; **9.** a. ~ out ausquetschen, -drücken; **10.** a. ~ out od. down fig. er-, unter'drücken, über'wältigen, zerschmettern, zertreten, vernichten; III v/i. **11.** zerknittern, sich zerdrücken; **12.** zerbrechen; **13.** sich drängen; '**crush·a·ble** [-ʃəbl] adj. **1.** knitterfest; **2.** ~ zone (od. bin) mot. Knautschzone f; **crush bar·ri·er** s. Brit. Absperrung f; '**crush·er** [-ʃə] s. **1.** ⊕ a) Zer'kleinerungsma‚schine f, Brechwerk n, b) Presse f, Quetsche f; **2.** F a) vernichtender Schlag, b) ‚tolles Ding‘; '**crush·ing** [-ʃɪŋ] adj. □ fig. vernichtend, erdrückend; **crush room** s. thea. Foy'er n.

crust [krʌst] I s. **1.** Kruste f, Rinde f (Brot, Pastete); **2.** Knust m, Stück n hartes Brot; **3.** sl. Schorf m; **5.** ♥, zo. Schale f; **6.** Niederschlag m (in Weinflaschen), Ablagerung f; **7.** sl. Frechheit f; **8.** Harsch m; II v/t. **9.** a. ~ over mit e-r Kruste über'ziehen; III v/i. **10.** e-e Kruste bilden; verharschen (Schnee); → crusted.

crus·ta·cea [krʌ'steɪʃə] s. pl. zo. Krusten-, Krebstiere pl.; **crus'ta·cean** [-'steɪʃən] I adj. zu den Krusten- od. Krebstieren gehörig, Krebs...; II s. Krusten-, Krebstier n; **crus'ta·ceous** [-'steɪʃəs] → crustacean I.

crust·ed ['krʌstɪd] adj. **1.** mit e-r Kruste über'zogen: ~ snow Harsch(schnee) m; **2.** abgelagert (Wein); **3.** fig. a) alt'hergebracht, b) eingefleischt, ‚verkrustet‘; '**crust·y** [-tɪ] adj. □ **1.** krustig; **2.** mit e-r Kruste (versehen); **3.** fig. barsch.

crutch [krʌtʃ] s. **1.** Krücke f: go on ~es auf od. an Krücken gehen; **2.** fig. Krücke f, Stütze f.

crux [krʌks] s. **1.** springender Punkt; **2.** Schwierigkeit f: a) ‚Haken‘ m, b) harte Nuss, (schwieriges) Pro'blem; **3.** ♐ ast. Kreuz n des Südens.

cry [kraɪ] I s. **1.** Schrei m (a. Tier), Ruf m (for nach): within ~ (of) in Rufweite (von); a far ~ from fig. a) weit entfernt von, b) et. ganz anderes als; still a far ~ fig. noch in weiter Ferne; **2.** Geschrei n: much ~ and little wool viel Geschrei um nichts; the popular ~ die Stimme des Volkes; **3.** Weinen n, Klagen n: have a good ~ sich (ordentlich) ausweinen; **4.** Bitten n, Flehen n; **5.** (Schlacht)Ruf m; Schlag-, Losungswort n; **6.** hunt. Anschlagen n, Gebell n (Meute): in full ~ fig. in voller Jagd od. Verfolgung; **7.** hunt. Meute f; fig. Herde f, Menge f: follow in the ~ mit der Masse gehen; II v/i. **8.** schreien, laut (aus)rufen: ~ for help um Hilfe rufen; ~ for vengeance nach Rache schreien; **9.** weinen, heulen, jammern; **10.** hunt. anschlagen, bellen; III v/t. **11.** et. schreien, (aus)rufen; **12.** Waren etc. ausrufen; **13.** flehen um; **14.** weinen: ~ one's eyes out sich die Augen ausweinen; ~ o.s. to sleep sich in den Schlaf

---

weinen; ~ down v/t. her'untersetzen, -machen; ~ off v/t. u. v/i. (plötzlich) absagen, zu'rücktreten (von); ~ out I v/t. ausrufen; II v/i. aufschreien: ~ against heftig protestieren gegen; for crying out loud! F verdammt noch mal!; ~ up v/t. laut rühmen.

'cry‚ba·by s. kleiner Schreihals; fig. contp. Heulsuse f.

cry·ing ['kraɪɪŋ] adj. fig. a) (himmel-)schreiend: ~ shame, b) dringend: ~ need.

cryo- [kraɪəʊ] in Zssgn Kälte..., Kryo...: **cryogen** Kältemittel n; **cryogenic** a) ⊕ Kälte erzeugend, b) kryogenisch: ~ computer; **cryosurgery** ✚ Kryo-, Kältechirurgie f.

crypt [krɪpt] s. △ 'Krypta f, 'unterirdisches Gewölbe, Gruft f; '**cryp·tic** [-tɪk] adj. geheim, verborgen; rätselhaft, dunkel: ~ colo(u)ring zo. Schutzfärbung f; '**cryp·ti·cal** [-tɪkl] adj. → cryptic.

crypto- [krɪptəʊ] in Zssgn geheim, krypto...: ~-communist verkappter Kommunist; **cryp·to·gam** [-gæm] s. ♥ Krypto'game f, Sporenpflanze f; **cryp·to·gam·ic** [ˌkrɪptəʊ'gæmɪk], **cryp·tog·a·mous** [krɪp'tɒɡəməs] adj. ♥ krypto'gamisch; '**cryp·to·gram** [-græm] s. Text m in Geheimschrift, verschlüsselter Text; '**cryp·to·graph** [-ɡrɑːf] s. **1.** → cryptogram; **2.** Geheimschriftgerät n; **cryp·tog·ra·phy** [krɪp'tɒɡrəfɪ] s. Geheimschrift f; **cryp·tol·o·gist** [krɪp'tɒlədʒɪst] s. (Ver-, Ent)Schlüssler m.

crys·tal ['krɪstl] I s. **1.** Kri'stall m (a. 🔭, min., phys.): as clear as ~ od. ~ clear a) kristallklar, b) fig. sonnenklar; **2.** a. ~ glass a) Kri'stall(glas) n, b) coll. Kristall n, Glaswaren pl.; **3.** Uhrglas n; **4.** ⚡ a) (De'tektor)Kri‚stall m) b) (Kris'tall)De‚tektor m, c) (Schwing)Quarz m: ~ set Kristallempfänger m; II adj. **5.** Kristall..., kri'stallen; **5.** kri'stallklar; ~ de·tec·tor → crystal 4 b; ~ gaz·er s. Hellseher(in); ~ gaz·ing s. Hellsehen n.

crys·tal·line ['krɪstəlaɪn] adj. 🔭, min. kristal'linisch, kri'stallen, kri'stallartig, Kristall...: ~ lens anat. (Augen)Linse f; '**crys·tal·liz·a·ble** [-aɪzəbl] adj. kristallisierbar; **crys·tal·li·za·tion** [ˌkrɪstəlaɪ'zeɪʃn] s. Kristallisati'on f, Kristallisierung f, Kri'stallbildung f; '**crys·tal·lize** [-aɪz] I v/t. **1.** kristallisieren; **2.** fig. feste Form geben (dat.), klären; **3.** Früchte kandieren; II v/i. **4.** kristallisieren; **5.** fig. sich kristallisieren, kon'krete od. feste Form annehmen; **crys·tal·log·ra·phy** [ˌkrɪstə'lɒɡrəfɪ] s. Kristallogra'phie f.

cub [kʌb] I s. **1.** zo. das Junge (des Fuchses, Bären etc.); **2.** a. unlicked ~ grüner Junge; **3.** ,Küken‘ n, Anfänger m: ~ reporter (unerfahrener) junger Reporter; **4.** a. ~ scout Wölfling m, Jungpfadfinder m; II v/i. **5.** Junge werfen (Füchse etc.).

cub·age ['kjuːbɪdʒ] → cubature.

Cu·ban ['kjuːbən] I adj. ku'banisch; II s. Ku'baner(in).

cu·ba·ture ['kjuːbətʃə] s. △ **1.** Raum(inhalts)berechnung f; **2.** Rauminhalt m.

cub·by(·hole) ['kʌbɪ(həʊl)] s. **1.** gemütliches Plätzchen n; **2.** ‚Ka'buff‘ n, winziger Raum.

cube [kjuːb] I s. **1.** ♱ Würfel m, 'Kubus m; **2.** (a. Eis-, phot. Blitz)Würfel m: ~ sugar Würfelzucker m; **3.** ♱ Ku'bikzahl f, dritte Po'tenz: ~ root Kubikwurzel f; **4.** Pflasterstein m (in Würfel-

C

form); **II** *v/t.* **5.** ⅋ kubieren: a) zur dritten Po'tenz erheben: *two ~d* zwei hoch drei (2³), b) den Rauminhalt messen von (*od. gen.*); **6.** in Würfel schneiden *od.* pressen.

cu·bic ['kju:bɪk] *adj.* (□ *~ally*) **1.** Kubik..., Raum...: *~ capacity* mot. Hubraum *m*; *~ content* Rauminhalt *m*, Volumen *n*; *~ metre*, *Am.* *meter* Kubik-, Raum-, Festmeter *m*; **2.** kubisch, würfelförmig, Würfel...; **3.** ⅋ kubisch: *~ equation* kubische Gleichung, Gleichung dritten Grades.

cu·bi·cle ['kju:bɪkl] *s.* kleiner abgeteilter (Schlaf)Raum; Zelle *f*, Nische *f*, Kabine *f*; ♬ Schallzelle *f*.

cub·ism ['kju:bɪzəm] *s.* Ku'bismus *m*; **'cub·ist** [-ɪst] **I** *s.* Ku'bist *m*; **II** *adj.* ku'bistisch.

cu·bit ['kju:bɪt] *s.* hist. Elle *f* (*Längenmaß*); **'cu·bi·tus** [-təs] *s.* anat. a) 'Unterarm *m*, b) Ell(en)bogen *m*.

cuck·old ['kʌkəʊld] **I** *s.* Hahnrei *m*; **II** *v/t.* zum Hahnrei machen, j-m Hörner aufsetzen.

cuck·oo ['kʊku:] **I** *s.* **1.** *orn.* Kuckuck *m*; **2.** Kuckucksruf *m*; **3.** *sl.* ,Heini' *m*; **II** *v/i.* **4.** ,kuckuck' rufen; **III** *adj.* **5.** *sl.* ,bekloppt'; *~ clock s.* Kuckucksuhr *f*; '*~,flow·er s.* ♥ Wiesenschaumkraut *n*.

cu·cum·ber ['kju:kʌmbə] *s.* Gurke *f*; → *cool* 2; *~ tree s. e-e* amer. Ma'gnolie.

cu·cur·bit [kju:'kɜ:bɪt] *s.* ♥ Kürbisgewächs *n*.

cud [kʌd] *s.* Klumpen *m*, 'wiedergekäutes Futter: *chew the ~* a) wiederkäuen, b) *fig.* überlegen, nachdenken.

cud·dle ['kʌdl] **I** *v/t.* hätscheln, ,knuddeln', *a.* schmusen mit; **II** *v/i.* *~ up* a) sich kuscheln *od.* schmiegen (*to* an *acc.*), b) sich (wohlig) zs.-kuscheln: *~ up together* sich aneinander kuscheln; **III** *s.* enge Um'armung, Lieb'kosung *f*; **'cud·dle·some** [-səm], **'cud·dly** [-lɪ] *adj.* ,knudd(e)lig'.

cudg·el ['kʌdʒəl] **I** *s.* Knüppel *m*, Keule *f*: *take up the ~s for s.o.* für j-n eintreten, für j-n e-e Lanze brechen; **II** *v/t.* prügeln: *~ one's brains fig.* sich den Kopf zerbrechen (*for* wegen, *about* über *acc.*).

cue¹ [kju:] **I** *s.* **1.** *thea. etc.*, *a.* *fig.* Stichwort *n*; ♪ Einsatz *m*: *~ card TV* ,Neger' *m*; (*dead*) *on ~* (genau) aufs Stichwort, *fig.* wie gerufen; **2.** Wink *m*, Fingerzeig *m*: *give s.o. his ~* j-m die Worte in den Mund legen; *take the ~ from s.o.* sich nach j-m richten; **II** *v/t.* **3.** *j-m* das Stichwort *od.* (♪) den Einsatz geben: *~ s.o. in fig.* j-n ins Bild setzen.

cue² [kju:] *s.* **1.** Queue *n*, 'Billardstock *m*; **2.** → *queue* 2.

cuff¹ [kʌf] *s.* **1.** Man'schette *f* (*a.* ⊕), Stulpe *f*; Ärmel- (*Am. a.* Hosen)aufschlag *m*: *~ link* Manschettenknopf *m*; *off the ~* F aus dem Handgelenk *od.* Stegreif; *on the ~ Am.* F a) auf Pump, b) gratis; **2.** *pl.* Handschellen *pl.*

cuff² [kʌf] **I** *v/t.* schlagen, *a.* ohrfeigen; **II** *s.* Schlag *m*, Klaps *m.*

cui·rass [kwɪ'ræs] *s.* **1.** *hist.* 'Kürass *m*, Brustharnisch *m*; **2.** ⚕ a) Gipsverband *m* um Rumpf u. Hals, b) *ein* 'Sauerstoffapparat *m*; **3.** *zo.* Panzer *m*; **cui·ras·sier** [,kwɪrə'sɪə] *s.* ✕ Küras'sier *m.*

cui·sine [kwi:'zi:n] *s.* Küche *f* (*Kochkunst*): *French ~.*

cul-de-sac [,kʊldə'sæk, 'kʌldəsæk] *pl.* **-sacs** (*Fr.*) *s.* Sackgasse *f* (*a.* fig.).

cu·li·nar·y ['kʌlɪnərɪ] *adj.* Koch..., Küchen...: *~ art* Kochkunst *f*; *~ herbs* Küchenkräuter.

cull [kʌl] **I** *v/t.* **1.** pflücken; **2.** *fig.* ausle-

---

sen, -suchen; **II** *s.* **3.** *et.* (als minderwertig) Aussortiertes.

culm¹ [kʌlm] *s.* **1.** Kohlenstaub *m*, Grus *m*; **2.** *geol.* Kulm *m, n.*

culm² [kʌlm] *s.* (Gras)Halm *m.*

cul·mi·nate ['kʌlmɪneɪt] *v/i.* **1.** *ast.* kulminieren; **2.** *fig.* den Höhepunkt erreichen; gipfeln (*in* in *dat.*); **cul·mi·na·tion** [,kʌlmɪ'neɪʃn] *s.* **1.** *ast.* Kulmination *f*; **2.** *bsd. fig.* Gipfel *m*, Höhepunkt *m*, höchster Stand.

cu·lottes [kju:'lɒts] *s. pl.* Hosenrock *m.*

cul·pa·bil·i·ty [,kʌlpə'bɪlətɪ] *s.* Sträflichkeit *f*, Schuld *f*; **cul·pa·ble** ['kʌlpəbl] *adj.* □ sträflich, schuldhaft; strafbar: *~ negligence* ⅋⅋ grobe Fahrlässigkeit.

cul·prit ['kʌlprɪt] *s.* **1.** Schuldige(r *m*) *f*, *a. iro.* Missetäter(in); **2.** ⅋⅋ a) Angeklagte(r *m*) *f*, b) Täter(in).

cult [kʌlt] *s.* **1.** *eccl.* Kult(us) *m*; **2.** *fig.* Kult *m* (*Verehrung, a. dumme Mode*): *~ figure* a) Idol *n*, b) Kultfigur *f.*

cul·ti·va·ble ['kʌltɪvəbl] *adj.* kultivierbar (*a. fig.*).

cul·ti·vate ['kʌltɪveɪt] *v/t.* **1.** ✎ a) Boden bebauen, bestellen, kultivieren, b) Pflanzen züchten, ziehen, (an)bauen; **2.** *fig.* entwickeln, verfeinern, fort-, ausbilden, *Kunst etc.* fördern; **3.** zivilisieren; **4.** *Kunst etc.* pflegen, betreiben, sich widmen (*dat.*); **5.** sich befleißigen (*gen.*), Wert legen auf (*acc.*); **6.** a) *e-e Freundschaft etc.* pflegen, b) freundschaftlichen Verkehr suchen *od.* pflegen mit, sich *j-n* ,warm halten'; **'cul·ti·vat·ed** [-tɪd] *adj.* **1.** bebaut, kultiviert (*Land*); **2.** ✎ gezüchtet, Kultur...; **3.** kultiviert, gebildet; **cul·ti·va·tion** [,kʌltɪ'veɪʃn] *s.* **1.** Bearbeitung *f*, Bestellung *f*, Bebauung *f*, Urbarmachung *f*: *under ~* bebaut; **2.** Anbau *m*, Ackerbau *m*; **3.** Züchtung *f*; **4.** *fig.* (Aus)Bildung *f*, Pflege *f*; **5.** Kul'tur *f*, Kultiviertheit *f*; Bildung *f*; **'cul·ti·va·tor** [-tə] *s.* **1.** Landwirt *m*; **2.** Züchter *m*; **3.** ✎ Kulti'vator *m* (*Gerät*).

cul·tur·al ['kʌltʃərəl] *adj.* □ **1.** Kultur..., kultu'rell: *~ channel TV etc.*: Kul'turka,nal *m*; ♬ *Heritage of the World* Weltkul'turerbe *n*; **2.** → *cultivated* 2; **cul·ture** ['kʌltʃə] *s.* **1.** → *cultivation* 1, 2, 4; **2.** a) (*Obst- etc.*)Anbau *m*, (*Pflanzen*)Zucht *f*, b) (*Tier*)Zucht *f*, Züchtung *f* (*a. fig.*), c) (*Pflanzen-, a. Bakterien- etc.*)Kul'tur *f*: *~ medium* künstlicher Nährboden; *~ pearl* Zuchtperle *f*; **3.** Kul'tur *f*: a) (Geistes)Bildung *f*, b) Kultiviertheit *f*: *~ vulture* F Kul'turbeflissene(r *m*) *f*; **4.** Kul'tur *f*: a) Kul'turkreis *m*, b) Kul'turform *f od.* -stufe *f*: *~ lag* partielle Kulturrückständigkeit; *~ shock* Kulturschock *m*; **'cul·tured** [-tʃəd] *adj.* **1.** kultiviert, gepflegt, gebildet; **2.** gezüchtet: *~ pearl* Zuchtperle *f.*

cul·ver ['kʌlvə] *s.* Ringeltaube *f.*

cul·vert ['kʌlvət] *s.* ⊕ (über'wölbter) 'Abzugska,nal; 'unterirdische (Wasser-) Leitung; ('Bach,)Durchlass *m.*

cum [kʌm] (*Lat.*) *prp.* **1.** mit, samt; **2.** *Brit.* F und gleichzeitig, ... in 'einem: *garage-~-workshop.*

cum·ber·some ['kʌmbəsəm] *adj.* □ **1.** lästig, beschwerlich, hinderlich; **2.** schwerfällig, klobig.

Cum·bri·an ['kʌmbrɪən] **I** *adj.* Cumberland betreffend; **II** *s.* Bewohner(in) von Cumberland.

cum·brous ['kʌmbrəs] → *cumbersome.*

cum·in ['kʌmɪn] *s.* Kreuzkümmel *m.*

cum·mer·bund ['kʌməbʌnd] *s. Mode:* Kummerbund *m.*

---

cu·mu·la·tive ['kju:mjʊlətɪv] *adj.* □ **1.** *a.* ✝ kumula'tiv: *~ dividend*; **2.** sich (an)häufend *od.* steigernd *od.* summierend; anwachsend; **3.** zusätzlich, verstärkend; *~ ev·i·dence s.* ⅋⅋ verstärkender Beweis; *~ vot·ing s.* Kumulieren *n* (*bei Wahlen*).

cu·mu·lus ['kju:mjʊləs] *pl.* **-li** [-laɪ] *s.* 'Kumulus *m*, Haufenwolke *f.*

cu·ne·ate ['kju:nɪɪt] *adj. bsd.* ♥ keilförmig; **'cu·ne·i·form** [-ɪɪfɔ:m] **I** *adj.* **1.** keilförmig; **2.** Keilschrift *f*: *~ characters* → 3; **II** *s.* **3.** Keilschrift *f*; **'cu·ni·form** [-ɪfɔ:m] → *cuneiform.*

cun·ning ['kʌnɪŋ] **I** *adj.* □ **1.** listig, schlau; **2.** geschickt, klug; **3.** *Am.* F niedlich, ,süß'; **II** *s.* **4.** Schlauheit *f*, Gerissenheit *f*; **5.** Geschicktheit *f.*

cunt [kʌnt] *s.* V Fotze *f.*

cup [kʌp] **I** *s.* **1.** Tasse *f*, Schale *f*: *~ and saucer* Ober- und Untertasse; *that's not my ~ of tea Brit.* das ist nicht mein Fall; **2.** Kelch *m* (*a. eccl.*), Becher *m*; **3.** *sport* Cup *m*, Po'kal *m*: *~ final* Pokalendspiel *n*; *~ tie* Pokalspiel *n*, -paarung *f*; **4.** Weinbecher *m*: *be fond of the ~* gern (einen) trinken; *be in one's ~s* zu tief ins Glas geschaut haben; **5.** Bowle *f*; **6.** *et.* Schalenförmiges, *z.B.* Büstenhalterschale *f od. sport* 'Unterleibs-, Tiefschutz *m*; **7.** *fig.* Kelch *m* (*der Freude, des Leidens*): *drink the ~ of joy* den Becher der Freude leeren; *drain the ~ of sorrow to the dregs* den Kelch des Leidens bis auf die Neige leeren; *his ~ is full* das Maß s-r Leiden (*od.* Freuden) ist voll; **8.** → *cupful* 2; **II** *v/t.* **9.** Kinn in die (hohle) Hand legen; *Hand* wölben über (*acc.*): *cupped hand* hohle Hand; **10.** ⚕ schröpfen; '*~,bear·er s.* Mundschenk *m.*

cup·board ['kʌbəd] *s.* (*bsd.* Speise-, Geschirr)Schrank *m*; *~ bed s.* Schrankbett *n*; *~ love s.* berechnende Liebe.

cu·pel [kju:pəl] *s.* ⚗, ⊕ Ku'pelle *f.*

cup·ful ['kʌpfʊl] *pl.* **-fuls** *s.* **1.** *e-e* Tasse (voll); **2.** *Am. Küche:* ½ Pint *n* (*0,235 l*).

Cu·pid ['kju:pɪd] *s.* **1.** *antiq.* 'Kupido *m*, 'Amor *m* (*a. fig. Liebe*); **2.** ⚥ Amo'rette *f.*

cu·pid·i·ty [kju:'pɪdətɪ] *s.* (Hab)Gier *f*, Begierde *f*, Begehrlichkeit *f.*

cu·po·la ['kju:pələ] *s.* **1.** Kuppel(dach *n*) *f*; **2.** *a.* ⊕ *furnace* ⊕ Ku'polofen *m*; **3.** ✕, ⚓ Panzerturm *m.*

cu·pre·ous ['kju:prɪəs] *adj.* kupfern, kupferartig, -haltig; **'cu·pric** [-ɪk] *adj.* ⚗ Kupfer...; **,cu·pro·'nick·el** [,kju:prəʊ-] *s.* Kupfernickel *n*; **'cu·prous** [-rəs] → *cupric.*

cur [kɜ:] *s.* **1.** Köter *m*; **2.** *fig.* ,Hund' *m*, ,Schwein' *n.*

cur·a·bil·i·ty [,kjʊərə'bɪlətɪ] *s.* Heilbarkeit *f*; **cur·a·ble** ['kjʊərəbl] *adj.* heilbar (*a.* ⅋⅋ *Rechtsmangel*).

cu·ra·cy ['kjʊərəsɪ] *s. eccl.* Amt *n* e-s *curate.*

cu·rate **I** *s.* ['kjʊərət] *eccl.* Hilfsgeistliche(r) *m*, Vi'kar *m*, Ku'rat *m*; **II** *v/t. e-e Ausstellung etc.* organisieren (u. betreuen).

cur·a·tive ['kjʊərətɪv] **I** *adj.* heilend, Heil...; **II** *s.* Heilmittel *n.*

cu·ra·tor [,kjʊə'reɪtə] *s.* **1.** Mu'seumsdi,rektor *m*; **2.** *Brit. univ.* (*Oxford*) Mitglied *n* des Kura'toriums; **3.** ⅋⅋ *Scot.* Vormund *m*; **4.** ⅋⅋ Verwalter *m*, Pfleger *m*; **cu·ra·tor·ship** [-ʃɪp] *s.* Amt *n od.* Amtszeit *f* e-s *curator.*

curb [kɜ:b] **I** *s.* **1.** a) Kan'dare *f*, b) Kinnkette *f*; **2.** *fig.* Zaum *m*, Zügel(ung *f*) *m*: *put a ~ on s.th.* e-r Sache Zügel anlegen, et. zügeln; **3.** *Am.* → *kerb*; **4.** *vet.* Spat *m*, Hasenfuß *m*; **II** *v/t.* **5.** an

C

die Kan'dare nehmen; **6.** *fig.* zügeln, im Zaum halten; drosseln, einschränken; ~ **bit** *s.* Kan'darenstange *f*; ~ **mar·ket** *Am.* → **kerb** 3; '~**stone** *Am.* → **kerb-stone**.

curd [kɜːd] *s. oft pl.* geronnene *od.* dicke Milch, Quark *m*: ~ **cheese** Quark-, Weißkäse *m*; **cur·dle** ['kɜːdl] **I** *v/t. Milch* gerinnen lassen: ~ **one's blood** einem das Blut in den Adern erstarren lassen; **II** *v/i.* gerinnen, dick werden (*Milch*): **it made my blood** ~ das Blut erstarrte mir in den Adern; '**curd·y** [-dɪ] *adj.* geronnen; dick, flockig.

cure [kjʊə] **I** *s.* **1.** ✚ Heilmittel *n*; *fig.* Mittel *n* Re'zept *n* (**for** gegen); **2.** ✚ Kur *f*, Heilverfahren *n*, Behandlung *f*; **3.** ✚ Heilung *f*: **past** ~ a) unheilbar krank, b) unheilbar (*Krankheit*), c) *fig.* hoffnungslos; **4.** *eccl.* a). ~ **of souls** Seelsorge *f*, b) Pfar'rei *f*; **II** *v/t.* **5.** ✚ *j-n* (**of** von) *od. Krankheit od. fig. Übel* heilen (*a.* ⚖ *Rechtsmangel etc.*), kurieren: ~ **s.o. of lying** j-m das Lügen abgewöhnen; **6.** haltbar machen: ~ a) räuchern, b) einpökeln, -salzen, c) trocknen, d) beizen; **7.** ⊙ a) vulkanisieren, b) aushärten (*Kunststoffe*); '~**all** *s.* All'heilmittel *n*.

cu·ret·tage [kjʊə'retɪdʒ] *s.* ✚ Ausschabung *f*.

cur·few ['kɜːfjuː] *s.* **1.** *hist.* a) Abendläuten *n*, b) Abendglocke *f*; **2.** Sperrstunde *f*; **3.** ✕ a) Ausgehverbot *n*, b) Zapfenstreich *m*.

cu·ri·a ['kjʊərɪə] *s. R.C.* 'Kurie *f*.

cu·rie ['kjʊərɪ] *s. phys.* Cu'rie *n*.

cu·ri·o ['kjʊərɪəʊ] *pl.* **-os** *s.* → **curiosity** 2 a *u. c.*

cu·ri·os·i·ty [ˌkjʊərɪ'nsətɪ] *s.* **1.** Neugier *f*, Wissbegierde *f*; **2.** Kuriosi'tät *f*: a) Rari'tät *f*, *pl.* Antiqui'täten, b) Sehenswürdigkeit *f*, c) Kuri'osum *n* (*Sache od. Person*); ~ **shop** *s.* Antiqui'täten-, Rari'tätenladen *m*.

cu·ri·ous ['kjʊərɪəs] *adj.* □ **1.** neugierig; wissbegierig: **I am** ~ **to know if** ich möchte gern wissen, ob; **2.** kuri'os, seltsam, merkwürdig: ~**ly enough** merkwürdigerweise; **3.** F komisch, wunderlich.

curl [kɜːl] **I** *v/t.* **1.** *Haar* locken *od.* kräuseln; **2.** *Wasser* kräuseln; *Lippen* (ver-ächtlich) schürzen; **3.** ~ **up** zs.-rollen: ~ **o.s. up** → 6 a; **II** *v/i.* **4.** sich locken *od.* kräuseln (*Haar*); **5.** wogen, sich wellen *od.* winden; **6.** ~ **up** a) sich hochringeln (*Rauch*), b) sich zs.-rollen: ~ **up on the sofa** es sich auf dem Sofa gemütlich machen; **7.** *sport* Curling spielen; **III** *s.* **8.** Locke *f*: **in** ~**s** gelockt; **9.** (Rauch-) Ring *m*, Kringel *m*; **10.** Windung *f*; **11.** Kräuseln *n der Lippen*; **12.** ♀ Kräuselkrankheit *f*; **curled** [-ld] → **curly**; '**curl·er** [-lə] *s.* **1.** Lockenwickel *m*; **2.** *sport* Curlingspieler *m*.

cur·lew ['kɜːljuː] *s.* Brachvogel *m*.

curl·i·cue ['kɜːlɪkjuː] *s.* Schnörkel *m*.

curl·ing ['kɜːlɪŋ] *s.* **1.** *sport* Curling *n*, Ringeln *n*; **2.** *sport* Curling *n*: ~ **stone** Curlingstein *m*; **3.** ⊙ bördeln; ~ **i·rons**, ~ **tongs** *s. pl.* (Locken)Brennschere *f*.

'**curl·pa·per** *s.* Pa'pierhaarwickel *m*.

curl·y ['kɜːlɪ] *adj.* **1.** lockig, kraus, gekräuselt, **2.** wellig; gewunden; '~**-head**, '~**pate** *s.* F Locken- *od.* Krauskopf *m* (*Person*).

cur·mudg·eon [kɜː'mʌdʒən] *s.* Brummbär *m*.

cur·rant ['kʌrənt] *s.* **1.** Ko'rinthe *f*; **2.** **red** (**white**, **black**) ~ Rote (Weiße, Schwarze) Jo'hannisbeere.

cur·ren·cy ['kʌrənsɪ] *s.* **1.** 'Umlauf *m*,

Zirkulati'on *f*: **give** ~ **to** Gerücht *etc.* in Umlauf setzen; **2.** a) (allgemeine) Geltung, (Allge'mein)Gültigkeit *f*, b) Gebräuchlichkeit *f*, Geläufigkeit *f*, c) Verbreitung *f*; **3.** ✝ a) Währung *f*, Va'luta *f*; → **foreign** 1, **hard currency**, b) Zahlungsmittel *n od. pl.*, c) 'Geld,umlauf *m*, d) 'umlaufendes Geld, e) Laufzeit *f* (*Wechsel, Vertrag*): ~ **account** *s.* ✝ 'Währungs-, De'visen,konto *n*; ~ **bill** *s.* De'visenwechsel *m*; ~ **bond** *s.* Fremdwährungsschuldverschreibung *f*; ~ **cri·sis** *s.* Währungskrise *f*; ~ **re·a·lign·ment** *s.* Neuordnung der Währungsparitäten; ~ **re·form** *s.* 'Währungsre,form *f*; ~ **up·heav·als** *s. pl.* 'Währungsturbu,lenzen *pl.*

cur·rent ['kʌrənt] **I** *adj.* □ → **currently**; **1.** laufend (*Jahr, Konto, Unkosten etc.*); **2.** gegenwärtig, jetzig, aktu'ell: ~ **events** Tagesereignisse; ~ **price** ✝ Tagespreis *m*; **3.** 'umlaufend, kursierend (*Geld, Gerücht etc.*); **4.** a) allgemein bekannt *od.* verbreitet, b) üblich, geläufig, gebräuchlich: **not in** ~ **use** nicht allgemein üblich, c) allgemein gültig *od.* anerkannt; **5.** ✝ a) (markt)gängig (*Ware*), b) gültig (*Geld*), c) verkehrsfähig, d) → 3; **II** *s.* **6.** Strömung *f*, Strom *m* (*beide a. fig.*): **against the** ~ gegen den Strom; ~ **of air** Luftstrom; **7.** *fig.* a) Trend *m*, Ten'denz *f*, b) (Ver)Lauf *m*, Gang *m*; **8.** ⚡ Strom *m*; ~ **ac·count** *s.* ✝ laufendes Konto, Girokonto *n*; ~ **coin** *s.* gängige Münze (*a. fig.*); ~ **ex·change** *s.* (**at the** ~ zum) Tageskurs *m*. **cur·rent·ly** ['kʌrəntlɪ] *adv.* **1.** jetzt, zur Zeit, gegenwärtig; **2.** *fig.* fließend.

cur·rent| me·ter *s.* ⚡ Stromzähler *m*; ~ **mon·ey** *s.* ✝ 'umlaufendes Geld.

cur·ric·u·lum [kə'rɪkjʊləm] *pl.* **-lums**, **-la** [-lə] *s.* Lehr-, Studienplan *m*; ~ **vi·tae** ['vaɪtiː] *s.* Lebenslauf *m*.

cur·ri·er ['kʌrɪə] *s.* Lederzurichter *m*.

cur·ry[1] ['kʌrɪ] **I** *s.* Curry(gericht *n*) *m, n*: ~ **powder** Currypulver *n*; **II** *v/t.* mit Curry(soße) zubereiten: **curried chicken** Curryhuhn *n*.

cur·ry[2] ['kʌrɪ] *v/t.* **1.** *Pferd* striegeln; **2.** *Leder* zurichten; **3.** verprügeln; **4.** ~ **fa·vo(u)r with s.o.** sich bei j-m lieb Kind machen (wollen); '~**comb** *s.* Striegel *m*.

curse [kɜːs] **I** *s.* **1.** Fluch(wort *n*) *m*; Verwünschung *f*; **2.** *eccl.* Bann(fluch) *m*; Verdammnis *f*; **3.** Fluch *m*, Unglück *n* (**to** für); **4. the** ~ F die ‚Tage' (*der Frau*); **II** *v/t.* **5.** verfluchen, verwünschen, verdammen: ~ **him!** der Teufel soll ihn holen!; **6.** fluchen auf (*acc.*), beschimpfen; **7.** *pass.* **be** ~**d with s.th.** mit et. gestraft *od.* geplagt sein; **III** *v/i.* **8.** fluchen, Flüche ausstoßen; '**curs·ed** [-sɪd] *adj.* □ *a.* F verflucht, verdammt, verwünscht.

cur·sive ['kɜːsɪv] **I** *adj.* kur'siv: ~ **char·acters** → **II** *s. typ.* Schreibschrift *f*.

cur·sor ['kɜːsə] *s.* **1.** *Computer*: Cursor *m*; **2.** ⊙ Schieber *m*, ⚠ Zeiger *m*.

cur·so·ri·ness ['kɜːsərɪnɪs] *s.* Flüchtigkeit *f*, Oberflächlichkeit *f*; **cur·so·ry** ['kɜːsərɪ] *adj.* □ flüchtig, oberflächlich.

curst [kɜːst] *obs. pret. u. p.p. von* **curse**.

curt [kɜːt] *adj.* □ **1.** kurz (gefasst), knapp; **2.** (**with**) barsch, schroff (gegen), kurz angebunden (mit).

cur·tail [kɜː'teɪl] *v/t.* **1.** (ab-, ver)kürzen; **2.** *Ausgaben etc.* kürzen, *a. Rechte* be-, einschränken, beschneiden; *Preise etc.* her'absetzen; **cur'tail·ment** [-mənt] *s.* **1.** (Ab-, Ver)Kürzung *f*; **2.** Kürzung *f*, Beschneidung *f*; Beschränkung *f*.

cur·tain ['kɜːtn] **I** *s.* **1.** Vorhang *m* (*a. fig.*), Gar'dine *f*: **draw the** ~(**s**) den Vorhang (die Gardinen) zuziehen; **draw the** ~ **over s.th.** *fig.* et. begraben; **lift the** ~ *fig.* den Schleier lüften; **behind the** ~ hinter den Kulissen; ~ **of fire** ✕ Feuervorhang; ~ **of rain** Regenwand *f*; **2.** *thea.* a) Vorhang *m*, b) Aktschluss *m*: **the** ~ **rises** der Vorhang geht auf; **the** ~ **falls** der Vorhang fällt (*a. fig.*); **it's** ~**s for him** F es ist aus mit ihm; **now it's** ~**s!** F jetzt ist der Ofen aus!, aus ists!; **3.** *thea.* Her'vorruf *m*: **take ten** ~**s** zehn Vorhänge haben; **II** *v/t.* **4.** mit Vorhängen versehen; ~ **call** → **curtain** 3; ~ **fall** *s. thea.* Fallen *n* des Vorhanges; ~ **lec·ture** *s. thea.* **1.** kurzes Vorspiel; **2.** *fig.* Vorspiel *n*, Auftakt (**to** zu); ~ **wall** *s.* ⚠ **1.** Blendwand; **2.** Zwischenwand *f*.

curt·s(e)y ['kɜːtsɪ] **I** *s.* Knicks *m*: **drop a** ~ → **II** *v/i.* e-n Knicks machen, knicksen (**to** vor *dat.*).

cur·va·ceous [kɜː'veɪʃəs] *adj.* F ‚kurvenreich' (*Frau*); **cur·va·ture** ['kɜːvətʃə] *s.* Krümmung *f* (*a.* ♈, *geol.*): ~ **of the spine** ✚ Rückgratverkrümmung *f*.

curve [kɜːv] **I** *s.* **1.** Kurve *f* (*a.* ♈), Krümmung *f*, Biegung *f*, Bogen *m*; **2.** *pl.* F ‚Kurven' *pl.*, Rundungen *pl.*; **II** *v/t.* **3.** biegen, krümmen; **III** *v/i.* **4.** sich biegen *od.* wölben *od.* krümmen; **curved** [-vd] *adj.* gekrümmt, gebogen, krumm.

cur·vet [kɜː'vet] **I** *s.* Reitkunst: Kur'bette *f*, Bogensprung *m*; **II** *v/i.* kurbettieren.

cur·vi·lin·e·ar [ˌkɜːvɪ'lɪnɪə] *adj.* krummlinig (begrenzt).

cush·ion ['kʊʃɪ] **I** *s.* **1.** Kissen *n*, Polster *n* (*a. fig.*); **2.** Wulst *m* (*für die Frisur*); **3.** Bande *f* (*Billard*); **4.** *vet.* Strahl *m* (*Pferdehuf*); **5.** ⊙ Puffer *m*, Dämpfer *m*; **6.** *phys.* ⊙ Luftkissen *n*; **II** *v/t.* **7.** durch Kissen schützen, polstern (*a. fig.*); **8.** Stoß, Fall dämpfen *od.* auffangen; **9.** weich betten; **10.** ⊙ abfedern; '~**craft** *s.* Luftkissenfahrzeug(e *pl.*) *n*.

cush·ioned ['kʊʃənd] *adj.* **1.** gepolstert, Polster...; **2.** *fig.* bequem, behaglich; **3.** ⊙ stoßgedämpft.

cush·y ['kʊʃɪ] *adj. Brit. sl.* ‚gemütlich', bequem, angenehm: ~**job.**

cusp [kʌsp] *s.* **1.** Spitze *f*; ♈ Scheitelpunkt *m* (*Kurve*); **2.** *ast.* Horn *n* (*Halbmond*); **4.** ⚠ Nase *f* (*gotisches Maßwerk*); **cusped** [-pt], '**cus·pi·dal** [-pɪdl] *adj.* spitz (zulaufend).

cus·pi·dor ['kʌspɪdɔː] *s. Am.* **1.** Spucknapf *m*; **2.** ✗ Speitüte *f*.

cuss [kʌs] *s.* F **1.** Fluch *m*: ~ **word** Fluch *m*, Schimpfwort *n*; → **tinker** 1; **2.** Kerl *m*; '**cuss·ed** [-sɪd] *adj.* F **1.** verflucht, -flixt; **2.** boshaft, gemein; '**cuss·ed·ness** [-sɪdnɪs] *s.* F Bosheit *f*, Gemeinheit *f*, Tücke *f*.

cus·tard ['kʌstəd] *s.* Eiercreme *f*: (**running**) ~ Vanillesoße *f*; ~ **ap·ple** *s.* ♀ Zimtapfel *m*; ~ **pow·der** *s. ein* 'Pudding,pulver *n*; ~ **pie** *s.* **1.** Sahnetorte *f*; **2.** *thea.* F Kla'mauk(komödie *f*) *m*.

cus·to·di·an [kʌ'stəʊdjən] *s.* **1.** Aufseher *m*, Wächter *m*, Hüter *m*; **2.** (⚖ Vermögens)Verwalter *m*, ⚖ *a.* Verwahrer *m*, *Am. a.* Vormund *m*; **cus·to·dy** ['kʌstədɪ] *s.* **1.** Aufsicht *f* (**of** über *acc.*), (Ob)Hut *f*, Schutz *m*; **2.** Verwahrung *f*, Verwaltung *f*; **3.** ⚖ a) Gewahrsam *m*, Haft *f*: **protective** ~ Schutzhaft *f*; **take into** ~ verhaften, in Gewahrsam nehmen, b) Gewahrsam *m* (*tatsächlicher Besitz*), c) Sorgerecht *n*; **4.** ✝ *Am.*

De'pot *n.*

cus·tom ['kʌstəm] **I** *s.* **1.** Brauch *m*, Gewohnheit *f*, Sitte *f*; *coll.* Sitten u. Gebräuche *pl.*, *pl.* Brauchtum *n*; **2.** ᵵᵵ Gewohnheitsrecht *n*; **3.** ✝ Kundschaft *f*, Kunden(kreis *m*) *pl.*: *draw (od. get) a lot of ~ from* viel Geschäft machen mit; *take one's custom elsewhere* anderswo Kunde werden; *withdraw one's ~ from* s-e Kundschaft entziehen (*dat.*); **4.** *pl.* a) Zoll *m*, b) Zoll(behörde *f*) *m*, Zollamt *n*; **II** *adj.* **5.** *Am.* a) auf Bestellung od. nach Maß arbeitend: ~ *tailor* Maßschneider *m*, b) → *custom- -made*: *~built* einzeln (*od.* nach Kundenangaben) angefertigt; ~ *shoes* Maßschuhe; '**cus·tom·ar·i·ly** [-mərɪlɪ] *adv.* üblicherweise, herkömmlicherweise; '**cus·tom·ar·y** [-mərɪ] *adj.* □ **1.** gebräuchlich, herkömmlich, üblich, gewohnt, Gewohnheits...; **2.** ᵵᵵ gewohnheitsrechtlich; '**cus·tom·er** [-mə] *s.* **1.** Kunde *m*, Kundin *f*; Abnehmer(in), Käufer(in): ~ *country* Abnehmerland *n*; *~'s check am.* Barscheck *m*: *regular* ~ Stammkunde *m od.* -gast *m*; **2.** F Bursche *m*, ,Kunde' *m*: *queer* ~ komischer Kauz; *ugly* ~ übler Kunde; '**cus·tom·ize** [-maɪz] *v/t.* **1.** ✝ auf den Kundenbedarf zuschneiden; **2.** *Auto etc.* individu'ell herrichten.

'**cus·tom··house** *s.* Zollamt *n*; '**~-made** *adj.* nach Maß *od.* auf Bestellung *od.* spezi'ell angefertigt, Maß...

cus·tom·ize ['kʌstəmaɪz] *v/t.* kundengerecht anfertigen.

cus·toms| **clear·ance** *s.* Zollabfertigung *f*, ~ **dec·la·ra·tion** *s.* 'Zolldeklarati,on *f*, -erklärung *f*; ~ **ex·am·i·na·tion**, ~ **in·spec·tion** *s.* 'Zollkon,trolle *f*; ~ **of·fi·cer** *s.* Zollbeamte(r) *m*; ~ **un·ion** *s.* 'Zollverein *m*, -uni,on *f*; ~ **war·rant** *s.* Zollauslieferungsschein *m*; ~ **ware·house** *s.* Zolllager *n*.

cut [kʌt] **I** *s.* **1.** Schnitt *m*: *a ~ above* e-e Stufe besser als; → *haircut*; **2.** Schnittwunde *f*; **3.** Hieb *m*, Schlag *m*: ~ *and thrust* a) *Fechten:* Hieb u. Stoß *m* (*od.* Stich *m*), b) *fig.* (feindseliges) Hin u. Her, ,Schlagabtausch' *m*; **4.** Schnitte *f*, Stück *n* (*bsd. Fleisch*); Ab-, Anschnitt *m*; Schur *f* (*Wolle*); Schlag *m* (*Holzfällen*); ✗ Mahd *f* (*Gras*); **5.** F (An)Teil *m*: *my ~ is 10%*; **6.** (Zu)Schnitt *m*, Fas'son *f* (*bsd. Kleidung*); *fig.* Art *f*, Schlag *m*; **7.** *typ.* a) Druckstock *m*, b) Holzschnitt *m*, (Kupfer)Stich *m*, c) Kli-'schee *n*; **8.** Schnitt *m*, Schliff *m* (*Edelstein*); **9.** Gesichtsschnitt *m*; **10.** Beschneidung *f*, Kürzung *f*, Streichung *f*, Abzug *m*, Abstrich *m* (*Preis, Lohn, a. Text etc.*): *power ~ ⚡* Stromsperre *f*; → *short cut*; **11.** ⚙, 🐦 *etc.* Einschnitt *m*, Kerbe *f*, Graben *m*; **12.** a) Stich *m*, Bosheit *f*, b) Grußverweigerung *f*: *give s.o. the ~ direct* j-n ostentativ schneiden; **13.** *Kartenspiel:* Abheben *n*; **14.** *Tennis:* Schnitt *m*; **15.** *Film etc.:* Schnitt *m*, (scharfe) Über'blendung *f*; **II** *adj.* **16.** ge-, beschnitten, behauen: ~ *flowers* Schnittblumen; ~ *glass* geschliffenes Glas, Kristall *n*; ~ *prices* herabgesetzte Preise; *well-~ features* fein geschnittene Züge; *~ and dried* fix u. fertig, schablonenhaft; *badly ~ a- bout* arg zugerichtet; **III** *v/t.* [*irr.*] **17.** (ab-, be-, 'durch-, zer)schneiden; ~ *one's finger* sich in den Finger schneiden; ~ *one's nails* sich die Nägel schneiden; ~ *a book* ein Buch aufschneiden; ~ *a joint* e-n Braten vorschneiden, zerlegen; ~ *to pieces* zerstückeln; **18.** *Hecke* beschneiden, stut-

zen; **19.** *Gras, Korn* mähen; *Baum* fällen; **20.** schlagen; *Kohlen* hauen; *Weg* aushauen, -graben; *Holz* hacken; *Graben* stechen; *Tunnel* bohren: ~ *one's way* sich e-n Weg bahnen (*a. fig.*); **21.** *Tier* verschneiden, kastrieren: ~ *horse* Wallach *m*; **22.** *Kleid* zuschneiden; *et.* zu'rechtschneiden; *Stein* behauen; *Glas, Edelstein* schleifen: ~ *it fine fig.* a) es (zu) knapp bemessen, b) es gerade noch schaffen; ~ *a deal fig., bsd. Am.* F ein Abkommen treffen; **23.** einschneiden, -ritzen, schnitzen; **24.** *Tennis:* Ball schneiden; **25.** *Text etc., a. Betrag* beschneiden, kürzen, zs.-streichen; *sport Rekord* brechen; **26.** *Film:* a) schneiden, über'blenden: ~ *to* hinüberblenden zu, b) abbrechen; **27.** verdünnen, verwässern; **28.** *fig. j-n* schneiden, nicht grüßen: ~ *s.o. dead* j-n völlig ignorieren; **29.** *fig.* schneiden (*Wind*); verletzen, kränken (*Worte*); **30.** *Verbindung* abbrechen, aufgeben; fern bleiben von, *Vorlesung* ,schwänzen'; **31.** *Zahn* bekommen; **32.** *Schlüssel* anfertigen; **33.** *Spielkarten* abheben; **IV** *v/i.* [*irr.*] **34.** schneiden (*a. fig.*), hauen: *it ~s both ways* es ist ein zweischneidiges Schwert; ~ *and come again* greifen Sie tüchtig zu! (*beim Essen*); *it ~s into his time* es kostet ihn Zeit; ~ *into a conversation* in e-e Unterhaltung eingreifen; **35.** sich schneiden lassen; **36.** F ,abhauen': ~ *and run* Reißaus nehmen; **37.** (*in der Schule etc.*) ,schwänzen'; **38.** *Kartenspiel:* abheben; **39.** *sport* (den Ball) schneiden; **40.** ~ *across* a) quer durch *et.* gehen, b) *fig.* hin'ausgehen über (*acc.*), c) *fig.* wider'sprechen, d) *fig. Am.* einbeziehen;

Zssgn mit adv.:

cut| **a·long** *v/i.* F sich auf die Beine machen; ~ **back I** *v/t.* beschneiden, stutzen, *fig. a.* kürzen, zs.-streichen, verringern; **II** *v/i.* ,rückblenden (*to* auf *acc.*) (*Film, Roman etc.*); ~ **down I** *v/t.* **1.** zerschneiden; **2.** *Baum* fällen, *j-n a.* niederschlagen; **3.** *fig.* a) → *cut back* I, b) drosseln; **II** *v/i.* **4.** ~ *on s.th.* et. einschränken; ~ **in I** *v/t.* **1.** ⚙ einschalten (*a. Filmszene*); **2.** *j-n* beteiligen (*on* an *dat.*); **II** *v/i.* **3.** unter'brechen, sich einmengen *od.* einschalten (*a. teleph.*); **4.** einspringen; **5.** *mot.* einscheren; **6.** F (*beim Tanzen*) abklatschen; ~ **loose I** *v/t.* **1.** trennen, losmachen; **2.** *cut o.s. loose* sich trennen *od.* lossagen; **II** *v/i.* **3.** sich gehen lassen; **4.** sich lossagen; **5.** *sl.* a) loslegen (*with* mit), b) ,auf den Putz hauen'; ~ **off** *v/t.* **1.** abschneiden, -schlagen, -hauen: ~ *s.o.'s head* j-n köpfen; **2.** unter'brechen, trennen; **3.** *Strom etc.* absperren, abdrehen; **4.** *Debatte* beenden; **5.** niederschlagen, dal'niraffen; vernichten; **6.** *cut s.o. off with a shilling* j-n enterben; ~ **out I** *v/t.* **1.** aus-, zuschneiden: ~ *for a job* wie geschaffen für e-n Posten; → *work* 1; **2.** *j-n* ausstechen; verdrängen; **3.** *Am. sl.* unter'lassen: *cut it out!* lass den Quatsch!; **4.** aufgeben; entfernen; *Am. Tier* von der Herde absondern; **5.** ⚙ ausschalten; **II** *v/i.* **6.** ⚙ sich ausschalten, aussetzen; **7.** ausscheren (*Fahrzeug*); **8.** *Kartenspiel:* ausscheiden; ~ **short** *v/t.* **1.** unter'brechen; *j-m* ins Wort fallen; **2.** plötzlich beenden, kürzen; *es kurz machen*; ~ **un·der** ✝ *j-n* unter'bieten; ~ **up I** *v/t.* **1.** in Stücke schneiden, zerhauen; zerlegen; **2.** vernichten; **3.** F ,verreißen', ,heruntermachen'; **4.** tief betrüben, aufregen: *be badly ~* ganz ,kaputt' sein; **II** *v/i.*

Brit. F ~ *fat (od. rich)* reich sterben; **6.** F ,den wilden Mann' spielen: ~ *rough* ,massiv' werden; **7.** *Am. sl.* a) ,angeben', b) Unsinn treiben.

,**cut-and-'dried** *adj.* **1.** (fix und) fertig, fest(gelegt); **2.** scha'blonenhaft.

cu·ta·ne·ous [kjuː'teɪnjəs] *adj.* ✤ Haut...: ~ *eruption* Hautausschlag *m*.

'**cut·a·way I** *s.* Cut(away) *m*; **II** *adj.* ⚙ Schnitt...(*-modell etc.*): ~ *view* Ausschnitt(darstellung *f*) *m*.

'**cut·back** *s.* **1.** *Film:* Rückblende *f*; **2.** Kürzung *f*, Beschneidung *f*, Verringerung *f*.

cute [kjuːt] *adj.* □ F **1.** schlau, clever; **2.** *Am.* niedlich, ,süß'.

cu·ti·cle ['kjuːtɪkl] *s.* ✤, *anat.* Oberhaut *f*, Epi'dermis *f*; Nagelhaut *f*: ~ *scissors* Hautschere *f*.

cu·tie ['kjuːtɪ] *s. Am. sl.* ,dufte Biene' (*Mädchen*).

'**cut-in** *s. Film:* a) Einschnitt(szene *f*) *m*, b) *a. Zeitung:* Zwischentitel *m*.

cu·tis ['kjuːtɪs] *s. anat.* 'Kutis *f*, Lederhaut *f*.

cut·lass ['kʌtləs] *s.* **1.** ⚓ *hist.* Entermesser *n*; **2.** Ma'chete *f*.

cut·ler ['kʌtlə] *s.* Messerschmied *m*; '**cut·ler·y** [-ərɪ] *s.* **1.** Messerwaren *pl.*; **2.** *coll.* Essbesteck(e *pl.*) *n*.

cut·let ['kʌtlɪt] *s.* Schnitzel *n*.

'**cut|·off** *s.* **1.** ⚙ (Ab)Sperrung *f*; **2.** ⚙, ⚡ Ab-, Ausschaltung *f* (*a. Vorrichtung*); **3.** *Am.* Abkürzung(sweg *m*) *f*; '**~·out** *s.* **1.** Ausschnitt *m*; 'Ausschneidefi,gur *f*; **2.** ⚡ a) Ausschalter *m*, Sicherung *f*; **3.** *mot.* Auspuffklappe *f*; '**~·purse** *s.* Taschendieb(in); '**~·rate** *adj.* ✝ ermäßigt, her'abgesetzt, billig (*a. fig.*).

cut·ter ['kʌtə] *s.* **1.** Schneidende(r) *m*; (Blech-, Holz)Schneider *m* (Stein)Hauer *m* (Glas-, Dia'mant)Schleifer *m*; **2.** Zuschneider *m*; **3.** ⚙ Schneidewerkzeug *n*; **4.** *Film:* Cutter(in); **5.** *Küche:* Ausstechform *f*; **6.** ⚓ a) Kutter *m*, b) Beiboot *n*, c) *Am.* Küstenwachboot *n*.

'**cut·throat I** *s.* **1.** Mörder *m*; **2.** *fig.* Halsabschneider *m*; **II** *adj.* **3.** *fig.* mörderisch, halsabschneiderisch: ~ *competition*.

cut·ting ['kʌtɪŋ] **I** *s.* **1.** Schneiden *n*; Zuschneiden *n*; **2.** *bsd.* 🐦 Einschnitt *m* 'Durchstich *m*; **3.** ⚙ a) Fräsen *n*, spa[...] abhebende Bearbeitung, b) Kerb[...] Schlitz *m*, c) *pl.* Späne *pl.*, Schr[...] *pl.*; **4.** (Zeitungs)Ausschnitt *m*; [...] Schnitzel *pl.*, Abfälle *pl.*; **6.** ✤ [...] *m*, Steckling *m*; **7.** *Film:* Schn[...] *adj.* □ **8.** schneidend, Schn[...] *fig.* schneidend (*Wind*), sch[...] beißend (*Hohn*); ~ *die* [...] sen *n*, 'Stanzscha,blon[...] Schneide *f*: *be (at) th[...]* mitmischen, zur Spit[...] **pers** *s. pl.* Kneifza[...] Schneidbrenner *n*[...]

cut·tle ['kʌtl], '~[...] Tintenfisch.

cy·a·nate ['sa[...] **an·ic** [saɪ[...] Zyansäure[...] 'nid *n*: [...] Zyanka[...] *s.* Zy[...]

cy·b[...] ca[...]

virtu'eller Raum.

cy·borg ['saɪbɔːg] *s. Science-Fiction*: Cyborg *m* (*Wesen zwischen Mensch u. Roboter*).

cyc·la·men ['sɪkləmən] *s.* ♀ Alpenveilchen *n.*

cy·cle ['saɪkl] **I** *s.* **1.** 'Zyklus *m,* Kreis (-lauf) *m,* 'Umlauf *m*: *lunar ~* Mondzyklus; → *business cycle; come full ~* a) e-n ganzen Kreislauf beschreiben, b) *fig.* zum Anfangspunkt zurückkehren; **2.** *a.* ♀, *phys.* Peri'ode *f*: *in ~s* periodisch wiederkehrend; *~s per second* (*abbr.* **cps**) Hertz; **3.** (Gedicht-, Sagen)Kreis *m;* **4.** Folge *f,* Reihe *f,* 'Serie *f,* 'Zyklus *m;* **5.** ⊙ 'Kreispro,zess *m;* Arbeitsgang *m;* **6.** *mot.* Takt *m*: *four--stroke ~* Viertakt; *four-~ engine* Viertaktmotor *m;* **7.** a) Fahrrad *n*: *~ path* (*od.* **track**) Rad(fahr)weg *m,* b) Motorrad *n,* c) Dreirad *n;* **II** *v/i.* **8.** Rad fahren, radeln; **III** *v/t.* **9.** e-n Kreislauf 'durchmachen lassen; **10.** *a.* ⊙ peri'odisch wieder'holen; **'cy·cle·way** *s.* Rad(fahr)weg *m;* **'cy·clic, 'cy·clical** [-lɪk(l)] *adj.* □ **1.** zyklisch, peri'odisch, kreisläufig; **2.** ✝ konjunk'turbedingt, -po,litisch, Konjunktur...; **'cy·cling** [-lɪŋ] *s.* **1.** Radfahren *n*: *~ tour* Radtour *f;* **2.** Rad(renn)sport *m;* **'cy·clist** [-lɪst] *s.* Radfahrer(in).

cy·clo-cross [ˌsaɪkləˈkrɒs] *s. Radsport*: Querfeld'einfahren *n.*

cy·clom·e·ter [saɪˈklɒmɪtə] *s.* **1.** ⊙ Wegmesser *m;* **2.** ♀ Zyklo'meter *m.*

cy·cloid ['saɪklɔɪd] **I** *s.* ♀ Zyklo'ide *f;* **II** *adj. allg.* zyklo'id.

cy·clone ['saɪkləʊn] *s.* **1.** *meteor.* a) Zyklon *m,* Wirbelsturm *m,* b) Zy'klone *f,* Tief(druckgebiet) *n;* **2.** *fig.* Or'kan *m.*

cy·clop(a)e·di·a [ˌsaɪkləʊˈpiːdjə] → **encyclop(a)edia**.

Cy·clo·pe·an [saɪˈkləʊpjən] *adj.* zy'klopisch, riesig; **Cy·clops** ['saɪklɒps] *pl.* **Cy·clo·pes** [saɪˈkləʊpiːz] *s.* Zy'klop *m.*

cy·clo·tron ['saɪklətrɒn] *s. Kernphysik:* 'Zyklotron *n.*

cy·der → **cider**.

cyg·net ['sɪgnɪt] *s.* junger Schwan.

cyl·in·der ['sɪlɪndə] *s.* **1.** ♀, ⊙, *typ.* Zy'linder *m,* Walze *f*: *six-~ car* Sechszylinderwagen *m;* **2.** ⊙ Trommel *f,* Rolle *f;* 'Mess-, 'Dampfzy,linder *m;* Gas-, Stahlflasche *f;* Stiefel *m* (*Pumpe*); *~ block s. mot.* Zy'linderblock *m; ~ bore s.* Zy'linderbohrung *f; ~ es·cape·ment s.* Zy'linderhemmung *f* (*Uhr*); *~ head s.* Zy'linderkopf *m; ~ jack·et s.* Zy'lindermantel *m; ~ print·ing s. typ.* Walzendruck *m.*

cy·lin·dri·cal [sɪˈlɪndrɪkl] *adj.* zy'lindrisch, Zylinder...

cym·bal ['sɪmbl] *s.* ♪ **1.** Becken *n;* **2.** 'Zimbel *f;* **'cym·bal·ist** [-bəlɪst] *s.* Beckenschläger *m;* **'cym·ba·lo** [-bələʊ] *pl.* **-los** *s.* ♪ Hackbrett *n.*

Cym·ric ['kɪmrɪk] **I** *adj.* kymrisch, bsd. wa'lisisch; **II** *s. ling.* Kymrisch *n.*

cyn·ic ['sɪnɪk] *s.* **1.** Zyniker *m,* bissiger Spötter; **2.** ⚲ *antiq. phls.* Kyniker *m;*

'cyn·i·cal [-kl] *adj.* □ zynisch; **'cyn·i·cism** [-ɪsɪzəm] *s.* **1.** Zy'nismus *m;* **2.** zynische Bemerkung.

cy·no·sure ['sɪnəzjʊə] *s.* **1.** *fig.* Anziehungspunkt *m,* Gegenstand *m* der Bewunderung; **2.** *fig.* Leitstern *m;* **3.** ⚲ *ast.* a) Kleiner Bär, b) Po'larstern *m.*

cy·pher → **cipher**.

cy·press ['saɪprɪs] *s.* Zy'presse *f.*

Cyp·ri·ote ['sɪprɪəʊt], **'Cyp·ri·ot** [-ɪət] **I** *s.* Zypri'ot(in), Zyprer(in); **II** *adj.* zyprisch.

Cy·ril·lic [sɪˈrɪlɪk] *adj.* ky'rillisch.

cyst [sɪst] *s.* **1.** ♀ Zyste *f;* **2.** Kapsel *f,* Hülle *f;* **'cyst·ic** [-tɪk] *adj.* **1.** ♀ zystisch; **2.** *anat.* Blasen...; **cys·ti·tis** [sɪsˈtaɪtɪs] *s.* ♀ Blasenentzündung *f;* **'cys·to·scope** [-təskəʊp] *s.* ♀ Blasenspiegel *m;* **cys·tos·co·py** [sɪsˈtɒskəpɪ] *s.* ♀ Blasenspiegelung *f.*

cy·to·blast ['saɪtəʊblæst] *s. biol.* Zyto'blast *m,* Zellkern *m.*

cy·tol·o·gy [saɪˈtɒlədʒɪ] *s. biol.* Zytolo'gie *f,* Zellenlehre *f.*

czar [zɑː] *s.* Zar *m.*

czar·das ['tʃɑːdæʃ] *s.* 'Csárdás *m.*

czar·e·vitch ['zɑːrəvɪtʃ] *s.* Za'rewitsch *m;* **cza·ri·na** [zɑːˈriːnə] *s.* Zarin *f;* **'czar·ism** [-rɪzəm] *s.* Zarentum *n;* **'czar·ist** [-rɪst], **czar·is·tic** [zɑːˈrɪstɪk] *adj.* za'ristisch; **cza·rit·za** [zɑːˈrɪtsə] → **czarina**.

Czech [tʃek] **I** *s.* **1.** Tscheche *m,* Tschechin *f;* **2.** *ling.* Tschechisch *n;* **II** *adj.* **3.** tschechisch.

D, d [diː] *s.* **1.** D *n*, d *n* (*Buchstabe*); **2.** ♪ D *n*, d *n* (*Note*); **3.** *ped. Am.* Vier *f*, Ausreichend *n* (*Note*).

'd [-d] F *für* **had, should, would**: **you'd**.

dab¹ [dæb] **I** *v/t.* **1.** leicht klopfen, antippen; **2.** be-, abtupfen; **3.** bestreichen; **4.** *typ.* abklatschen, klischieren; **5.** *a.* ~ **on** *Farbe etc.* auftragen; **6.** *sl.* Fingerabdrücke machen von; **II** *v/i.* **7.** ~ **at** → 1, 2; **III** *s.* **8.** (leichter) Klaps, Tupfer *m*; **9.** Klecks *m*, Spritzer *m*; **10.** *Am. sl.* Fingerabdruck *m*.

dab² [dæb] *s.* F Könner *m*, ,Künstler' *m*, Ex'perte *m*: **be a** ~ **at s.th.** et. aus dem Effeff können.

dab·ber ['dæbə] *s. typ.* a) Farbballen *m*, b) Klopfbürste *f*.

dab·ble ['dæbl] **I** *v/t.* **1.** bespritzen, besprengen; **II** *v/i.* **2.** plantschen, plätschern; **3.** *fig.* ~ **in s.th.** sich aus Liebhaberei *od.* oberflächlich *od.* dilet'tantisch mit et. befassen, ein bisschen *malen etc.*; **'dab·bler** [-lə] *s.* Ama'teur *m*, *contp.* Dilet'tant(in), Stümper(in).

dab·ster ['dæbstə] *s.* **1.** → dab²; **2.** F *Am.* Stümper *m*.

dace [deɪs] *s. ichth.* Häsling *m*.

da·cha ['dætʃə] *s.* Datscha *f*.

dachs·hund ['dækshʊnd] *s. zo.* Dachshund *m*, Dackel *m*.

dac·tyl ['dæktɪl] *s.* Daktylus *m* (*Versfuß*); **dac·tyl·ic** [dæk'tɪlɪk] *adj. u. s.* dak'tylisch(er Vers).

dac·ty·lo·gram [dæk'tɪləʊɡræm] *s.* Fingerabdruck *m*.

dad [dæd] *s.* F ,Paps' *m*, Vati *m*.

Da·da·ism ['dɑːdəɪzəm] *s.* Dada'ismus *m*; **'Da·da·ist** [-ɪst] **I** *s.* Dada'ist *m*; **II** *adj.* dada'istisch.

dad·dy ['dædɪ] → dad; ~ **long·legs** [ˌdædɪ'lɒŋleɡz] *s. zo.* **1.** *Brit.* Schnake *f*; **2.** *Am.* Weberknecht *m*.

dae·mon → demon.

daf·fo·dil ['dæfədɪl] *s.* ♀ Gelbe Nar'zisse, Osterblume *f*, -glocke *f*.

daft [dɑːft] *adj.* □ F verrückt, blöde, ,doof', ,bekloppt'.

dag·ger ['dæɡə] *s.* **1.** Dolch *m*: **be at ~s drawn** (**with**) *fig.* auf (dem) Kriegsfuß stehen (mit); **look ~s at s.o.** j-n mit Blicken durchbohren; **2.** *typ.* Kreuz (-zeichen) *n* (†).

da·go ['deɪɡəʊ] *pl.* -gos *od.* -goes *s. sl. contp.* = Spanier, Portugiese *od.* Italiener; *weitS.* ,Ka'nake' *m*, (verdammter) Ausländer.

da·guerre·o·type [də'ɡerəʊtaɪp] *s. phot.* a) Daguerreoty'pie *f*, b) Daguerreo'typ *n* (*Bild*).

dahl·ia ['deɪljə] *s.* ♀ Dahlie *f*.

Dail Eir·eann [ˌdaɪl'eərən] *a.* **Dail** *s.* Abgeordnetenhaus *n von Eire*.

dai·ly ['deɪlɪ] **I** *adj.* **1.** täglich, Tage(s)...: **our ~ bread** unser täglich(es) Brot; ~ **wages** Tagelohn *m*; ~ **newspaper** → 5; **2.** alltäglich, häufig, ständig; **II** *adv.* **3.** täglich; **4.** immer, ständig; **III** *s.* **5.** Tageszeitung *f*; **6.** *Brit.* Zugeh-, Putzfrau *f*.

dain·ti·ness ['deɪntɪnɪs] *s.* **1.** Zierlichkeit *f*, Niedlichkeit *f*; **2.** wählerisches Wesen, Verwöhntheit *f*; **3.** Geziertheit *f*, Zimperlichkeit *f*; **4.** Schmackhaftigkeit *f*; **dain·ty** ['deɪntɪ] **I** *adj.* □ **1.** zierlich, niedlich, fein, reizend; **2.** köstlich, exqui'sit; **3.** wählerisch, verwöhnt (*bsd. im Essen*); **4.** geziert, zimperlich; **5.** lecker, schmackhaft; **II** *s.* **6.** *a. fig.* Leckerbissen *m*, Delika'tesse *f*.

dair·y ['deərɪ] *s.* **1.** Molke'rei *f*; **2.** Milchwirtschaft *f*, Molke'rei(betrieb *m*) *f*; **3.** Milchhandlung *f*, ~ **bar** *s. Am.* Milchbar *f*; ~ **cat·tle** *s. pl.* Milchvieh *n*; ~ **farm** *s.* auf Milchwirtschaft spezialisierter Bauernhof; ~ **lunch** → **dairy bar**; **'~·maid** *s.* **1.** Melkerin *f*; **2.** Molke'reiangestellte *f*; **'~·man** [-mən] *s.* [*irr.*] **1.** Milchmann *m*; **2.** Melker *m*, Schweizer *m*; ~ **prod·uce** *s.* Molke'reipro,dukte *pl.*

da·is ['deɪɪs] *pl.* -is·es *s.* **1.** Podium *n*, E'strade *f*; **2.** *obs.* Baldachin *m*.

dai·sy ['deɪzɪ] **I** *s.* **1.** ♀ Gänseblümchen *n*: (**double**) ~ Tausendschön(chen) *n*; **be pushing up the daisies** *sl.* ,sich die Radies-chen von unten betrachten' (*tot sein*); → **fresh** 4; **2.** *sl.* a) 'Prachtexem,plar *n*, b) Prachtkerl *m*, ,Perle' *f*; **II** *adj.* **3.** *sl.* erstklassig, prima; ~ **chain** *s.* **1.** Gänseblumenkränzchen *n*; **2.** *fig.* Reigen *m*, Kette *f*; **'~·cut·ter** *s.* **1.** Pferd *n* mit schleppendem Gang; **2.** *sport* Flachschuss *m*; ~ **wheel** *s. Schreibmaschine, Drucker:* 'Typenrad *n*: ~ **typewriter** 'Typenradschreibma,schine *f*.

dale [deɪl] *s. poet.* Tal *n*; **dales·man** ['deɪlzmən] *s.* [*irr.*] Talbewohner *m* (*bsd. in Nordengland*).

dal·li·ance ['dælɪəns] *s.* **1.** Tröde'lei *f*, Bumme'lei *f*; **2.** Tände'lei *f*: a) Spiele'rei *f*, b) Schäke'rei *f*, Liebe'lei *f*; **dal·ly** ['dælɪ] **I** *v/i.* **1.** trödeln, Zeit verständeln; **2.** tändeln, spielen, liebäugeln (**with** mit); **3.** scherzen, schäkern; **II** *v/t.* **4.** ~ **away** Zeit vertrödeln; *Gelegenheit* verpassen.

Dal·ma·tian [dæl'meɪʃjən] **I** *adj.* **1.** dalma'tinisch; **II** *s.* **2.** Dalma'tiner(in); **3.** Dalma'tiner *m* (*Hund*).

dal·ton·ism ['dɔːltənɪzəm] *s.* ஃ Farbenblindheit *f*.

dam¹ [dæm] **I** *s.* **1.** (Stau)Damm *m*, Wehr *n*, Talsperre *f*; **2.** Stausee *m*, *fig.* Damm *m*; **II** *v/t.* **4.** *a.* ~ **up** a) stauen, (ab-, ein-, zu'rück)dämmen (*a. fig.*), b) (ab)sperren, hemmen (*a. fig.*).

dam² [dæm] *s. zo.* Mutter(tier *n*) *f*.

dam·age ['dæmɪdʒ] **I** *s.* **1.** (**to**) Schaden *m* (an *dat.*), (Be)Schädigung *f* (*gen.*): **do** ~ Schaden anrichten; **do** ~ **to** → 6; ~ **by sea** ⚓ Seeschaden *m*, Havarie *f*; ~ **limitation** Schadensbegrenzung *f*; **3.** *pl.* ⚖ Schadensersatz *m*: **for** ~**s** auf Schadensersatz *klagen*; **sl.** Kosten *pl.*: **what's the** ~**?** was kostet es?; **II** *v/t.* **5.** beschädigen; **6.** *j-n, j-s Ruf etc.* schädigen,

Schaden zufügen, *j-m* schaden; **'dam·age·a·ble** [-dʒəbl] *adj.* leicht zu beschädigen(d); **'dam·aged** [-dʒd] *adj.* **1.** beschädigt, schadhaft, de'fekt; **2.** verletzt, (körper)geschädigt; **3.** verdorben; **'dam·ag·ing** [-dʒɪŋ] *adj.* □ schädlich, nachteilig (**to** für).

dam·a·scene(d) ['dæməsiːn(d)] *adj.* Damaszener..., damasziert.

dam·ask ['dæməsk] **I** *s.* **1.** Da'mast *m* (*Stoff*); **2.** *a.* ~ **rose** ஃ Damas'zenerrose *f*; **II** *adj.* **4.** Damast...; Damaszener...; **5.** rosarot; **III** *v/t.* **6.** *Stahl* damaszieren; **7.** da'mastartig weben; **8.** *fig.* verzieren.

dame [deɪm] *s.* **1.** *Brit.* a) Freifrau *f*, b) ♀ *der dem* **knight** *entsprechende Titel:* ♀ **Diana X**; **2.** alte Dame: ♀ **Nature** Mutter *f* Natur; **3.** *ped.* Schul- *od.* Heimleiterin *f*; **4.** *Am. sl.* ,Frau' *f*, Weibsbild *n*.

damn [dæm] **I** *v/t.* **1.** verdammen (*a. eccl.*); verwünschen, verfluchen: (**oh**) ~**!**, ~ **it** (**all**)**!** *sl.* verflucht!; ~ **you!** *sl.* hol dich der Teufel!; **well, I'll be ~ed!** nicht zu glauben!, das ist die Höhe!; **I'll be ~ed if** a) ich fress 'nen Besen, wenn..., b) es fällt mir nicht im Traum ein (*das zu tun*); **I'll be ~ed if I know!** ich habe keinen blassen Dunst; **2.** verurteilen, verwerfen, ablehnen; **3.** vernichten, ruinieren; **4.** ♀ Fluch *m*; **5.** **I don't care a** ~ *sl.* das kümmert mich einen Dreck; **not worth a** ~ keinen Pfifferling wert; **III** *adj. u. adv.* **6.** → **damned** 2, 3; **'dam·na·ble** [-nəbl] *adj.* □ **1.** verdammenswert; **2.** F ab'scheulich; **dam·na·tion** [dæm'neɪʃn] **I** *s.* **1.** Verdammung *f*; **2.** Ru'in *m*; **II** *int.* **3.** verflucht!; **damned** [dæmd] *adj.* **1.** verdammt: **the** ~ *eccl.* die Verdammten; **2.** *sl.* verflucht: ~ **fool** Idiot *m*, ,Blödmann' *m*; **do one's ~est** sein Möglichstes tun; **3.** *a. adv. Bekräftigung: sl.* verdammt: **a** ~ **sight better** viel besser; **every** ~ **one** jeder Einzelne; ~ **funny** urkomisch; **he** ~ **well ought to know** das müsste er wahrhaftig wissen; **II** *int.* **4.** verdammt!; **damn·ing** ['dæmɪŋ] *adj. fig.* erdrückend, vernichtend: ~ **evidence**.

Dam·o·cles ['dæməkliːz] *npr.* Damokles: **sword of** ~ Damoklesschwert *n*.

damp [dæmp] **I** *adj.* □ **1.** feucht; dunstig: ~ **course** △ Isolierschicht *f*; ~ **smell** modriger Geruch; **II** *s.* **2.** Feuchtigkeit *f*; **3.** Dunst *m*; **4.** → **fire-damp**; **5.** *fig.* Dämpfer *m*, Entmutigung *f*, Hemmnis *n*: **cast a** ~ **over s.th.** et. dämpfen *od.* lähmen, et. überschatten; **III** *v/t.* **6.** an-, befeuchten; **7.** *a.* ~ **down** *fig. Eifer etc.* dämpfen (*a.* ♪, ⚡, *phys.*); (ab)schwächen, drosseln (*a.* ⚙); ersticken; ~ **course** *s.* △ Sperrbahn *f* (*gegen Nässe*).

damp·en ['dæmpən] **I** *v/t.* **1.** an-, befeuchten; **2.** *fig.* dämpfen, ,niederdrücken'; entmutigen; **II** *v/i.* **3.** feucht werden; **'damp·er** [-pə] *s.* **1.** Dämpfer *m* (*bsd. fig.*): **cast a** ~ **on** et. dämpfen, lähmend wirken auf (*acc.*); **2.** ⊙ Ofen-, Zugklappe *f*, Schieber *m*; **3.** ♪ Dämpfer

D

m; **4.** ⚡ Dämpfung f; **5.** *Brit.* Stoß-dämpfer m; **'damp·ish** [-pɪʃ] *adj.* etwas feucht, klamm; **'damp·ness** [-nɪs] s. Feuchtigkeit f; **'damp·proof** *adj.* feuchtigkeitsbeständig.

dam·sel ['dæmzl] s. *obs. od. iro.* Maid f.

dam·son ['dæmzən] s. ♀ Damas'zenerpflaume f; **~ cheese** s. steifes Pflaumenmus.

dan [dæn] s. *Judo etc.:* Dan m.

dance [dɑːns] **I** *v/i.* **1.** tanzen: **~ to s.o.'s pipe** (*od.* **tune**) *fig.* nach j-s Pfeife tanzen; **2.** tanzen: a) (her'um)hüpfen, b) flattern, schaukeln (*Blätter etc.*); **II** *v/t.* **3.** e-n Tanz tanzen: **~ attendance on s.o.** *fig.* um j-n scharwenzeln; **4.** *Tier* tanzen lassen; *Kind* schaukeln; **III** s. **5.** Tanz m: **give a ~** e-n Ball geben; **lead s.o. a ~** a) j-n zum Narren halten, b) j-m das Leben sauer machen; *♀ of Death* Totentanz; **~ hall** s. 'Tanzlo,kal n.

danc·er ['dɑːnsə] s. Tänzer(in).

danc·ing ['dɑːnsɪŋ] s. Tanzen n, Tanzkunst f; **~ girl** s. (Tempel)Tänzerin f (*in Asien*); **~ les·son** s. Tanzstunde f; **~ mas·ter** s. Tanzlehrer m.

D and C [,diːənd'siː] *abbr.* (= *dilatation and curettage*) ✚ Dilatati'on f u. Ausschabung f.

dan·de·li·on ['dændɪlaɪən] s. ♀ Löwenzahn m.

dan·der ['dændə] s.: **get s.o.'s ~ up** F j-n ,auf die Palme' bringen.

dan·di·fied ['dændɪfaɪd] *adj.* stutzer-, geckenhaft, geschniegelt.

dan·dle ['dændl] *v/t.* **1.** *Kind* auf den Armen *od.* auf den Knien schaukeln; **2.** hätscheln; **3.** verhätscheln, verwöhnen.

dan·druff ['dændrəf] *a.* **'dan·driff** [-rɪf] s. (Kopf-, Haar)Schuppen *pl.*

dan·dy ['dændɪ] **I** s. **1.** Dandy m, Stutzer m; **2.** F *et.* Großartiges: **the ~** genau das Richtige; **3.** ⚓ Scha'luppe f; **4.** ⚓ a) Heckmaster m, b) Besansegel n; **II** *adj.* **5.** stutzerhaft; **6.** F erstklassig, prima, ,bestens'; **~ brush** s. Striegel m.

dan·dy·ish ['dændɪʃ] → *dandy* 5; **'dan·dy·ism** [-ɪzəm] s. stutzerhaftes Wesen.

Dane [deɪn] s. **1.** Däne m, Dänin f; **2.** → *Great Dane*.

dan·ger ['deɪndʒə] **I** s. **1.** Gefahr f (*to* für): **in ~ of one's life** in Lebensgefahr; **be in ~ of falling** Gefahr laufen zu fallen; **the signal is at ~** 🚆 das Signal steht auf Halt; **2.** Bedrohung f, Gefährdung f (*to gen.*); **II** *adj.* Gefahren...: **~ area** Gefahrenzone f; Sperrgebiet n; **be on** (**off**) **the ~ list** in (außer) Lebensgefahr; **~ money**, **~ pay** Gefahrenzulage f; **~ point** Gefahrenpunkt m; **~ signal** Not-, Warnsignal n; **'dan·ger·ous** [-dʒərəs] *adj.* □ **1.** gefährlich, gefahrvoll (**to** für); **2.** bedenklich.

dan·gle ['dæŋgl] **I** *v/i.* **1.** baumeln, (herab)hängen; **2.** **~ after s.o.** sich an j-n anhängen, j-m nachlaufen; **~ after girls**; **II** *v/t.* **3.** schlenkern, baumeln lassen; **~ s.th. before s.o.** *fig.* j-m et. verlockend in Aussicht stellen.

Dan·iel ['dænjəl] s. *bibl.* (das Buch) Daniel m.

Dan·ish ['deɪnɪʃ] **I** *adj.* **1.** dänisch; **II** s. **2. the ~** die Dänen; **3.** *ling.* Dänisch n, das Dänische; **~ pas·try** s. *ein* Blätterteiggebäck n.

dank [dæŋk] *adj.* feucht, nasskalt, dumpfig.

Da·nu·bi·an [dæ'njuːbjən] *adj.* Donau...

daph·ne ['dæfnɪ] s. ♀ Seidelbast m.

dap·per ['dæpə] *adj.* **1.** a'drett, ele'gant,

iro. geschniegelt; **2.** flink, gewandt.

dap·ple ['dæpl] *v/t.* tüpfeln, sprenkeln; **'dap·pled** [-ld] *adj.* **1.** gesprenkelt, gefleckt, scheckig; **2.** bunt.

,dap·ple-'grey (**horse**) s. Apfelschimmel m.

dar·bies ['dɑːbɪz] s. *pl. sl.* Handschellen *pl.*

Dar·by and Joan ['dɑːbɪ ən(d) 'dʒəʊn] glückliches älteres Ehepaar: **~ club** Seniorenklub m.

dare [deə] **I** *v/i.* [*irr.*] **1.** es wagen, sich (ge)trauen; sich erdreisten, sich unter-'stehen: **he ~n't do it** er wagt es nicht (zu tun); **how ~ you say that?** wie können Sie es wagen, das zu sagen?; **don't** (**you**) **~ to touch me!** untersteh dich nicht, mich anzurühren!; **how ~ you!** a) untersteh dich!, b) was fällt dir ein!; **I ~ say** a) ... wohl ..., ich könnte mir denken dass, b) allerdings (a. iro.); **II** *v/t.* [*irr.*] **2.** et. wagen, sich mutig begegnen (*dat.*), trotzen (*dat.*); **4.** j-n her'ausfordern: **I ~ you!** du traust dich ja nicht!; **I ~ you to deny it** wage nicht, es abzustreiten; **'~,dev·il I** s. Wag(e)hals m, Draufgänger m, Teufelskerl m; **II** *adj.* tollkühn, waghalsig; **'~,dev·il·(t)ry** *v/t.* Tollkühnheit f.

dar·ing ['deərɪŋ] **I** *adj.* □ **1.** wagemutig, kühn, verwegen; **2.** unverschämt, dreist; **3.** *fig.* gewagt, kühn; **II** s. **4.** Wagemut m.

dark [dɑːk] **I** *adj.* □ → *darkly*; **1.** dunkel, finster: **it is getting ~** es wird dunkel; **2.** dunkel (*Farbe*): **~ blue** dunkelblau; **~ hair** braunes *od.* dunkles Haar; → *hue* 1; **3.** geheim(nisvoll), dunkel, verborgen, unklar: **a ~ secret** ein tiefes Geheimnis; **keep s.th. ~** et. geheim halten; **4.** böse, finster, schwarz: **~ thoughts**; **5.** düster, trübe, freudlos: **~ future**; **the ~ side of things** die Schattenseite der Dinge; **6.** dunkel, unerforscht; kul'turlos; **II** s. **7.** Dunkel (-heit f) n, Finsternis f: **in the ~** im Dunkel(n); **at ~** bei Einbruch der Dunkelheit; **8.** *pl. paint.* Schatten m; **9.** *fig.* Dunkel n, Ungewissheit f, das Geheime, Unwissenheit f: **keep s.o. in the ~** j-n im Ungewissen lassen; **I am in the ~** ich tappe im Dunkeln; **a leap in the ~** ein Sprung ins Ungewisse; *♀ Ages* *pl.* das frühe Mittelalter; *♀ Con·ti·nent* s. *hist.* der dunkle Erdteil, Afrika n.

dark·en ['dɑːkən] **I** *v/t.* **1.** verdunkeln (a. fig.), verfinstern: **don't ~ my door again!** komm mir nie wieder ins Haus!; **2.** dunkel *od.* dunkler färben; **3.** *fig.* verdüstern, trüben; **II** *v/i.* **4.** dunkel werden, sich verdunkeln (*etc.* → I); **'dark·ish** [-kɪʃ] *adj.* **1.** etwas dunkel, schwärzlich; **2.** trübe; **3.** dämmerig.

dark lan·tern s. 'Blendla,terne f.

dark·ling ['dɑːklɪŋ] *adj.* sich verdunkelnd; **'dark·ly** [-lɪ] *adv. fig.* **1.** finster, böse; **2.** dunkel, geheimnisvoll; **3.** undeutlich; **he 'dark·ness** [-nɪs] s. **1.** *a. fig.* Dunkelheit f, Finsternis f; **2.** dunkle Färbung f; **3.** das Böse: **the powers of ~** die Mächte der Finsternis; **4.** Unwissenheit f; **5.** Unklarheit f; **6.** Heimlichkeit f.

'dark|·room [-rʊm] s. *phot.* Dunkelkammer f; **'~-skinned** *adj.* dunkelhäutig; **'~-slide** s. *phot.* Kas'sette f.

dark·y ['dɑːkɪ] s. *contp.* Neger(in).

dar·ling ['dɑːlɪŋ] **I** s. **1.** Liebling m, Schatz m: **~ of fortune** Glückskind n; **aren't you a ~** du bist doch ein Engel; **II** *adj.* **2.** lieb, geliebt; Herzens...; **3.** reizend, ,süß', entzückend.

darn¹ [dɑːn] **I** *v/t.* *Strümpfe etc.* stopfen,

ausbessern; **II** s. das Gestopfte.

darn² [dɑːn] *v/t. sl. für* **damn** 1; **darned** [-nd] *adj. u. adv. sl. für* **damned** 2, 3.

darn·er ['dɑːnə] s. **1.** Stopfer(in); **2.** Stopf-ei n, -pilz m.

darn·ing ['dɑːnɪŋ] s. Stopfen n; **~ egg** s. Stopf-ei n; **~ nee·dle** s. Stopfnadel f; **~ yarn** s. Stopfgarn n.

dart [dɑːt] **I** s. **1.** Wurfspeer m, -spieß m; **2.** (Wurf)Pfeil m; *fig.* Stachel m des Spotts; **3.** Satz m, Sprung m: **make a ~ for** losstürzen auf (*acc.*); **4.** *pl. sg. konstr.* Darts n (*Wurfpfeilspiel*): **~board** Zielscheibe f; **5.** Abnäher m (*in Kleidern*); **II** *v/t.* **6.** schleudern, schießen; *Blicke* zuwerfen; **III** *v/i.* **7.** sausen, flitzen: **~ at** s.o. auf j-n losstürzen; **~ off** davonstürzen; **8.** sich blitzschnell bewegen, zucken, schnellen (*Schlange, Zunge*), huschen (a. Auge).

Dart·moor ['dɑːt,mʊə] *a.* **~ pris·on** s. englische Strafanstalt.

Dar·win·ism ['dɑːwɪnɪzəm] s. Darwi'nismus m.

dash [dæʃ] **I** *v/t.* **1.** schleudern, (heftig) stoßen *od.* schlagen, schmettern: **~ to pieces** zerschmettern; **~ out s.o.'s brains** j-m den Schädel einschlagen; **2.** (be)spritzen; (über)'schütten, über-'gießen (a. fig.): **~ off** *od.* **down** *Schriftliches* hinwerfen, -hauen; **3.** *Hoffnung etc.* zunichte machen, vereiteln; **4.** *fig.* a) niederdrücken, deprimieren, b) aus der Fassung bringen, verwirren; **5.** (ver)mischen (a. fig.); **6.** F → **damn** 1: **~ it** (**all**)! verflixt!; **II** *v/i.* **7.** sausen, flitzen, stürmen; *sport* spurten: **~ off** davonjagen, -stürzen; **8.** heftig (auf)schlagen, prallen, klatschen; **III** s. **9.** Sprung m, (Vor)Stoß m; Anlauf m, Ansturm m: **at a** (*od.* **one**) **~** mit 'einem Schlag; **make a ~** (**for**, **at**) (los)stürmen, sich stürzen (auf *acc.*); **10.** (Auf)Schlagen n, Prallen n, Klatschen n; **11.** Zusatz m; Schuss m *Rum etc.*; Prise f *Salz etc.*; Anflug m, Stich m (**of red** ins Rote); Klecks m (*Farbe*): **add a ~ of colo(u)r** *fig.* e-n Farbtupfer aufsetzen; **12.** Federstrich m; *typ.* Gedankenstrich m; **♪**, **⚘**, **tel.** Strich m; **13.** Schneid m, Schwung m, Schmiss m; Ele'ganz f: **cut a ~** Aufsehen erregen, e-e gute Figur abgeben; **14.** *sport* a) Kurzstreckenlauf m, b) Spurt m; **15.** ⊕ F → **'~-board** s. ✈, *mot.* Arma'turen-, Instru'mentenbrett n.

dashed [dæʃt] *adj. u. adv.* F verflixt; **'dash·er** [-ʃə] s. **1.** Butterstößel m; **2.** F ele'gante Erscheinung, fescher Kerl; **'dash·ing** [-ʃɪŋ] *adj.* □ **1.** schneidig, forsch, kühn; **2.** ele'gant, flott, fesch.

das·tard ['dæstəd] s. (gemeiner) Feigling, Memme f; **'das·tard·li·ness** [-lɪnɪs] s. **1.** Feigheit f; **2.** Heimtücke f; **'das·tard·ly** [-lɪ] *adj.* **1.** feig(e); **2.** (heim)tückisch, gemein.

da·ta ['deɪtə] s. *pl. von* **datum** (*oft* [*fälschlich*] *sg. konstr.*) (a. *technische*) Daten *pl. od.* Angaben *pl. od.* Einzelheiten *pl. od.* 'Unterlagen *pl.*; Tatsachen *pl.*; ⊕ (Mess-, Versuchs)Werte *pl.*; *Computer:* Daten *pl.:* **personal ~** Personalangaben, Personalien, (*electronic*) **~ processing** (elektronische) Datenverarbeitung; **~ abuse** Datenmissbrauch m; **~ bank** Datenbank f; **~ carrier** Datenträger m; **~ collection** Datenerfassung f; **~ communication(s** *pl.*) 'Datenkommunikati,on f; **~ display device** Datensichtgerät n; **~ editing**

Datenaufbereitung f; ~ **exchange** Datenaustausch m; ~ **file** Datei f; ~ **input** Dateneingabe f; ~ **logger** Datenerfassungssystem n; ~ **medium** Datenträger m; ~ **output** Datenausgabe f; ~ **printer** Datendrucker m (Gerät); ~ **protection** Datenschutz m; ~ **protection officer** Datenschutzbeauftragte m; ~ **recall** Datenabruf m; ~ **transfer** (od. **transmission**) Datenübertragung f; ~ **typist** Datentypist(in).

da·ta·base ['deɪtəbeɪs] s. 'Datenbank f: **set up a** ~ e-e Datenbank aufbauen; **maintain a** ~ e-e Datenbank unter'halten.

date¹ [deɪt] s. ♀ **1.** Dattel f; **2.** a. ~ **tree** Dattelpalme f.

date² [deɪt] s. **1.** Datum n, Zeitangabe f, (Monats)Tag m: **what's the** ~ **to-day?** der Wievielte ist heute?; **2.** Datum n, Zeit(punkt m) f: **at an early** ~ (recht) bald; **of recent** ~ neu(eren Datums), modern; **fix a** ~ e-n Termin festsetzen; **3.** Zeit(raum m) f, E'poche f: **of Roman** ~ aus der Römerzeit; **4.** ♥ a) Ausstellungstag m (Wechsel), b) Frist f, Ziel n: ~ **of delivery** Liefertermin m; ~ **of maturity** Fälligkeitstag m; **at long** ~ auf lange Sicht; **5.** heutiger Tag: **of this** (od. **today's**) ~ heutig; **four weeks after** ≈ heute in vier Wochen; **to** ~ bis heute; **out of** ~ veraltet, überholt, unmodern; **go out of** ~ veralten; **up to** ~ zeitgemäß, modern, auf der Höhe (der Zeit), auf dem Laufenden; **bring up to** ~ auf den neuesten Stand bringen, modernisieren; → **up-to-date**; **6.** F Verabredung f, Rendez'vous n: **have a** ~ **with s.o.** mit j-m verabredet sein; **make a** ~ sich verabreden; **7.** F (Verabredungs)Partner(in): **who is your** ~**?** mit wem bist du verabredet?; **II** v/t. **8.** Brief etc. datieren: ~ **ahead** voraus-, vordatieren; **9.** a) ein Datum od. e-e Zeit festsetzen od. angeben für, b) e-r bestimmten Zeit zuordnen; **10.** herleiten (**from** aus); **11.** als über'holt od. veraltet kennzeichnen; **12.** a. ~ **up** F a) sich verabreden mit, b) (regelmäßig) ,gehen' mit: ~ **a girl**; **III** v/i. **13.** datieren, datiert sein (**from** von); **14.** ~ **from** (od. **back to**) stammen od. sich herleiten aus, entstanden sein in (dat.); **15.** ~ **back to** zu'rückreichen bis, zu-'rückgehen auf (e-e Zeit); **16.** veralten, sich über'leben.

date| block s. ('Abreiß)Ka,lender m; ~ **change** s. Datumswechsel m.

dat·ed ['deɪtɪd] adj. **1.** veraltet, über-'holt; **2.** ~ **up** F ,ausgebucht' (Person), voll besetzt (Tag); **'date·less** [-lɪs] adj. **1.** undatiert; **2.** endlos; **3.** zeitlos (Mode, Kunstwerk etc.).

'date|·line s. **1.** Datumszeile f (e-r Zeitung etc.); **2.** geogr. Datumsgrenze f; ~ **palm** → date¹ 2; ~ **rape** s. Vergewaltigung f nach e-m Rendezvous; ~ **stamp** s. Datums- od. Poststempel m.

da·ti·val [də'taɪvəl] adj. ling. Dativ...

da·tive ['deɪtɪv] **I** s. a. ~ **case** ling. Dativ m, dritter Fall; **II** v/t. da'tivisch, Dativ...

da·tum ['deɪtəm] pl. **-ta** [-tə] s. **1.** et. Gegebenes od. Bekanntes, Gegebenheit f; **2.** Vor'aussetzung f, Grundlage f; **3.** Å gegebene Größe; **4.** → **data**; ~ **line** s. surv. Bezugslinie f; ~ **point** s. **1.** Å, phys. Bezugspunkt m; **2.** surv. Nor-'malfixpunkt m.

daub [dɔːb] **I** v/t. **1.** be-, verschmieren, bestreichen; **2.** (on) schmieren, streichen (auf acc.); **3.** Wand bewerfen, verputzen; **4.** fig. besudeln; **II** v/i. **5.** paint.

klecksen, schmieren; **III** s. **6.** (Lehm-) Bewurf m; **7.** paint. Schmiere'rei f, Farbenkleckse'rei f, schlechtes Gemälde; **'daub·(st)er** [-b(st)ə] s. Schmierer(in); Farbenkleckser(in).

daugh·ter ['dɔːtə] s. **1.** Tochter f (a. fig.): ~ **language** Tochtersprache f; → **Eve¹; 2.** → ~ **com·pa·ny** s. ♥ Tochter (-gesellschaft) f; **~-in-law** ['dɔːtərɪnlɔː] pl. **~s-in-law** [-təz-] s. Schwiegertochter f; **'daugh·ter·ly** [-lɪ] adj. töchterlich.

daunt [dɔːnt] v/t. einschüchtern, (er-) schrecken; entmutigen: **nothing** ~**ed** unverzagt; **a** ~**ing task** e-e beängstigende Aufgabe; **'daunt·less** [-lɪs] adj. □ unerschrocken.

dav·en·port ['dævnpɔːt] s. **1.** kleiner Sekre'tär (Schreibtisch); **2.** Am. (bsd. Bett)Couch f.

Da·vy Jones's lock·er ['deɪvɪ'dʒəʊnzɪz] s. ♣ Meeresgrund m, nasses Grab: **go to** ~ ertrinken.

daw [dɔː] s. orn. obs. Dohle f.

daw·dle ['dɔːdl] **I** v/i. trödeln, bummeln; **II** v/t. a. ~ **away** Zeit vertrödeln; **'daw·dler** [-lə] s. Trödler(in), Bummler(in).

dawn [dɔːn] **I** v/i. **1.** tagen, dämmern, anbrechen (Morgen, Tag); **2.** fig. (her-auf)dämmern, erwachen, entstehen; **3.** ~ (**up**)**on** fig. j-m dämmern, klarwerden, zum Bewusstsein kommen; **II** s. **4.** Morgendämmerung f, Tagesanbruch m: **at** ~ beim Morgengrauen, bei Tagesanbruch; **5.** (An)Beginn m, Erwachen n, Anbruch m.

day [deɪ] s. **1.** Tag m (Ggs. Nacht): **by** ~ bei Tage; **before** ~ vor Tagesanbruch; ~ **and night** Tag u. Nacht, immer; **2.** Tag m (Zeitraum): ~**'s work** Tagesleistung f; **three** ~**s from London** drei Tage(reisen) von London; **she is 30 if a** ~ sie ist mindestens 30 Jahre alt; **3.** bestimmter Tag: **New Year's** ♀ Neujahrstag; **4.** festgesetzter Tag: ~ **of payment** ♥ Zahlungstermin m; **5.** pl. (Lebens)Zeit f, Zeit(en pl.) f, Tage pl.: **in my young** ~**s** in m-r Jugend; **student** ~**s** Studentenzeit f; **after** ~ Tag für Tag; **the** ~ **after** tags darauf; **the** ~ **after tomorrow** übermorgen; **all** ~ **long** den ganzen Tag, den lieben langen Tag; **the** ~ **before yesterday** vorgestern; ~ **by** ~ (tag)täglich, Tag für Tag; **for** ~**s** (**on end**) tagelang; **call it a** ~ F (für heute) Schluss machen; **have a nice** ~**!** F mach's gut!; **let's call it a** ~**!** F Feierabend!, Schluss für heute!; **carry** (od. **win**) **the** ~ den Sieg davontragen; **end one's** ~**s** s-e Tage beschließen; **every other** ~ alle zwei Tage, e-n Tag um den andern; **fall on evil** ~**s** ins Unglück geraten; **he** (od. **it**) **has had his** (od. **its**) ~ s-e beste Zeit ist vorüber; ~ **in,** ~ **out** tagaus, tagein; **in his** ~ zu s-r Zeit, einst; **late in the** ~ reichlich spät; **that's all in the** ~**'s work** fig. das gehört alles mit dazu; **that made my** ~ F damit war der Tag für mich gerettet; **what's the time of** ~**?** wie viel Uhr ist es?; **know the time of** ~ fig. wissen, was die Glocke geschlagen hat; **pass the time of** ~ **with s.o.** j-n grüßen; **one** ~ eines Tages, einmal; **the other** ~ neulich; **save the** ~ die Lage retten; **some** ~ (**or other**) e-s Tages, nächstens einmal; (**in**) **these** ~**s** heutzutage; **this** ~ heute; **this** ~ **week** heute vor e-r Woche; **in those** ~**s** damals; **those were the** ~**s!** das waren

noch Zeiten!; **to a** ~ auf den Tag genau; **what** ~ **of the month is it?** den Wievielten haben wir heute?; ~ **bed** s. Bettcouch f; **'~·book** s. **1.** Tagebuch n; **2.** ♥ a) Jour'nal n, b) Verkaufsbuch n, c) Kassenbuch n; **'~·boy** s. Brit. Ex'terne(r) m (e-s Internats); **'~·break** s. (**at** ~ bei) Tagesanbruch m; **,~-by-'day** adj. (tag)täglich; **'~-care cen·ter** s. Am. Kindertagesstätte f; **'~-care coach** s. ⚙ Am. Per'sonenwagen m; **'~·dream I** s. **1.** Wachtraum m, Träume'rei f; **2.** fig. Luftschloss n; **II** v/i. **3.** (mit offenen Augen) träumen; **'~·dream·er** s. Träumer(in); **'~·fly** s. zo. Eintagsfliege f; **'~·girl** s. Brit. Ex-'terne f (e-s Internats); ~ **la·bo·(u)r·er** s. Tagelöhner m; ~ **let·ter** s. Am. 'Brieftele,gramm n.

'day·light s. **1.** Tageslicht n: **by** od. **in** ~ bei Tag(eslicht); → **broad** 2; **let** ~ **into s.th.** fig. a) et. der Öffentlichkeit zugänglich machen, b) et. aufhellen; **beat the** ~**s out of s.o.** F j-n windelweich schlagen; **he saw** ~ **at last** fig. a) endlich ging ihm ein Licht auf, b) endlich sah er Land; **2.** (**at** ~ bei) Tagesanbruch m; **3.** (lichter) Zwischenraum m; ~ **rob·ber·y** s. F Wucher(ei f) m; ~ **sav·ing time** s. Sommerzeit f.

'day|·long adj. u. adv. den ganzen Tag (dauernd); ~ **nurs·er·y** s. **1.** Kindertagesstätte f, -krippe f; Spielzimmer n; ~ **pu·pil** s. ex'terner Schüler, ex'terne Schülerin (e-s Internats); ~ **re·lease** s. zur beruflichen Fortbildung freigegebene Zeit; ~ **re·turn** s. ⚙, Bus: Tagesrückfahrkarte f; **'~·room** s. Tagesraum m; ~ **school** s. **1.** Exter'nat n, Schule f ohne Inter'nat; **2.** Tagesschule f; ~ **shift** s. Tagschicht f; **be on** ~ Tagschicht haben; ~ **stu·dent** Ex'terne(r m) f e-s Internats; ~ **tick·et** s. ⚙ Tagesrückfahrkarte f; **'~·time** s. **1.** Tageszeit f, (heller) Tag: **in the** ~ bei Tage; **2.** ♥ Arbeitstag m; **,~-to-'** adj. (tag)täglich: ~ **money** ♥ Tagesgeld n; **'~·trad·er** s. Börse: 'Day,trader m, 'Tagesspeku,lant m.

daze [deɪz] **I** v/t. betäuben, lähmen (a. fig.); blenden; verwirren; **II** s. Betäubung f, Benommenheit f: **in a** ~ benommen, betäubt; **'daz·ed·ly** [-zɪdlɪ] adv. betäubt etc. (→ **daze I**).

daz·zle ['dæzl] **I** v/t. **1.** blenden (a. fig.); **2.** fig. verwirren, verblüffen; **3.** ✕ durch Anstrich tarnen; **II** s. **4.** Blenden n; Glanz m; **5.** a. ~ **paint** ✕ Tarnanstrich m; **'daz·zler** [-lə] s. F **1.** ,Blender' m; **2.** ,tolle Frau'; **'daz·zling** [-lɪŋ] adj. □ **1.** blendend, glänzend (a. fig.); fig. strahlend (schön); **2.** verwirrend.

D-Day ['diːdeɪ] s. Tag der alliierten Landung in der Normandie, 6. Juni 1944.

dea·con ['diːkən] s. eccl. Dia'kon m; **'dea·con·ess** [-kənɪs] s. eccl. **1.** Dia-'konin f; **2.** Diako'nisse f; **'dea·con·ry** [-rɪ] s. eccl. Diako'nat n.

de·ac·ti·vate [,diː'æktɪveɪt] v/t. **1.** ✕ a) Einheit auflösen, b) Munition entschärfen; **2.** außer Akti'on od. Betrieb setzen.

dead [ded] **I** adj. □ → **deadly** II; **1.** tot, gestorben, leblos: **as** ~ **as a doornail** (od. **as mutton**) mausetot; ~ **body** Leiche f, Leichnam m; **he is a** ~ **man** fig. er ist ein Kind des Todes; ~ **matter** tote Materie (→ 11); ~ **and gone** tot u. begraben (a. fig.); ~ **to the world** F ,total weg' (bewusstlos, volltrunken); **I'm** ~ F ich bin ,total fertig'!; **wait for a** ~ **man's shoes** a) auf e-e Erbschaft warten, b) nur darauf warten, dass je-

D

mand stirbt (*um seine Position einzu-nehmen*); **2.** *fig. allg.* tot: a) ausgestor-ben: ~ *languages* tote Sprachen, b) über'lebt, veraltet: ~ *customs*, c) matt, stumpf: ~ *colo(u)rs*; ~ *eyes*, d) nichts sagend, farb-, ausdruckslos, e) geistlos, f) leer, öde: ~ *streets*; ~ *land*, g) still, stehend: ~ *water*, h) *sport* nicht im Spiel: ~ *ball* ‚toter Ball'; **3.** unzugäng-lich, unempfänglich (*to* für), taub (*to* gegen *Ratschläge etc.*); **4.** gefühllos, ab-gestorben: ~ *fingers*; **5.** *fig.* gefühllos, abgestumpft (*to* gegen); **6.** erloschen: ~ *fire*; ~ *volcano*; ~ *passions*; **7.** 🏛 un-gültig; **8.** *bsd.* † still, ruhig, flau: ~ *season*; **9.** † tot, umsatzlos: ~ *assets* unproduktive (Kapital)Anlage; ~ *capi-tal* (*stock*) totes Kapital (Inventar); **10.** ⊙ a) tot, außer Betrieb, b) de'fekt: ~ *valve*; ~ *engine* ausgefallener *od.* ab-gestorbener Motor, c) leer, erschöpft: ~ *battery*, d) tot, starr: ~ *axle*, e) ⚡ tot, strom-, spannungslos; **11.** *typ.* abge-legt: ~ *matter* Ablegesatz *m*; **12.** *bsd.* ⚠ blind, Blend...: ~ *floor*; ~ *window* totes Fenster; **13.** Sack... (*ohne Aus-gang*): ~ *street* Sackgasse *f*; **14.** schal, abgestanden: ~ *drinks*; **15.** verwelkt, dürr, abgestorben: ~ *flowers*; **16.** völ-lig, to'tal: ~ *calm* Flaute *f*, (völlige) Windstille; ~ *certainty* absolute Ge-wissheit; *in* ~ *earnest* in vollem Ernst; ~ *loss* Totalverlust *m*, *fig.* totaler Aus-fall (*Person*); ~ *silence* Totenstille *f*; ~ *stop* völliger Stillstand; *come to a* ~ *stop* schlagartig stehen bleiben *od.* auf-hören; **17.** todsicher, unfehlbar: *he is a* ~ *shot*; **18.** äußerst: *a* ~ *strain*; *a* ~ *push* ein verzweifelter, aber vergebli-cher Stoß; **II** *s.* **19.** stillste Zeit: *at* ~ *of night* mitten in der Nacht; *the* ~ *of winter* der tiefste Winter; **20.** *the* ~ a) der (die, das) Tote, b) *coll.* die Toten: *several* ~ mehrere Tote; *rise from the* ~ von den Toten auferstehen; **III** *adv.* **21.** restlos, völlig, gänzlich, abso'lut, to'tal: ~ *asleep* in tiefstem Schlaf; ~ *drunk* sinnlos betrunken; ~ *slow!* *mot.* Schritt fahren; ~ *straight* schnurgera-de; ~ *tired* todmüde; *the facts are* ~ *against him* alles spricht gegen ihn; **22.** plötzlich, schlagartig, abrupt: *stop* ~; **23.** genau: ~ *against* genau gegenüber von (*od. dat.*); ~ (*set*) *against* ganz u. gar *od.* entschieden ge-gen (*et.* eingestellt); ~ *set on* scharf auf (*acc.*).

dead| **ac·count** *s.* † 'umsatzloses Kon-to; ,~-(and-)a'live *adj. fig.* (tod)lang-weilig; '~-beat *s.* F **1.** Schnorrer *m*; **2.** Gammler *m*; ,~-'beat *adj.* F todmüde, völlig ka'putt; ~ **cen·ter** *Am.*, ~ **cen-tre** *Brit. s.* ⊙ **1.** toter Punkt; **2.** genaue Mitte; **3.** tote Spitze (*der Drehbank*); ~ **drop** *s. Spionage:* toter Briefkasten; ~ **duck** *s.:* *be a* ~ F keine Chance mehr haben, passé sein.

dead·en ['dedn] *v/t.* **1.** *Gefühl etc.* (ab-)töten, abstumpfen (*to* gegen); betäu-ben; **2.** *Geräusch, Schlag etc.* dämpfen, (ab)schwächen; **3.** ⊙ mattieren.

dead| **end** *s.* **1.** Sackgasse *f* (*a. fig.*): *come to a* ~ in e-e Sackgasse geraten; **2.** ⊙ blindes Ende; '~-end *adj.* **1.** ohne Ausgang, Sack...: ~ *street* Sackgasse *f*; ~ *station* Kopfbahnhof *m*; **2.** *fig.* aus-weglos; **3.** ohne Aufstiegschancen: ~ *job*; **4.** verwahrlost, Slum...: ~ *kid* ver-wahrlostes Kind; '~-fall *s.* Baumfalle *f*; ~ *file s.* abgelegte Akte; ~ *fire s.* Elms-feuer *n*; ~ *freight s.* ⚓ Fehlfracht *f*; ~ *hand* → *mortmain*; '~-head *s.* F a) Freikarteninhaber(in), b) Schwarzfah-

rer(in), c) *Am. contp.* ‚Blindgänger' *m*, ‚Niete' *f*, d) *Am.* Mitläufer *m*; ~ *heat s. sport* totes Rennen; ~ **let·ter** *s.* **1.** *fig.* toter Buchstabe (*unwirksames Gesetz*); **2.** unzustellbarer Brief; '~-line *s.* **1.** letzter *od.* äußerster Termin, Frist(ab-lauf *m*) *f; Zeitung:* Redakti'onsschluss *m:* ~ *pressure* Termindruck *m*; *meet the* ~ den Termin *od.* die Frist ein-halten; **2.** Stichtag *m*; **3.** äußerste Grenze; **4.** *Am.* Todesstreifen *m* (*Straf-anstalt*).

dead·li·ness ['dedlɪnɪs] *s. das* Tödliche; tödliche Wirkung.

dead| **load** *s.* ⊙ totes Gewicht, tote Last, Eigengewicht *n*; '~-lock **I** *s. fig.* toter Punkt, 'Patt(situati,on *f*) *n:* *break the* ~ den toten Punkt überwinden; *come to a* ~ → **II** *v/i.* sich festfahren, stecken bleiben, an e-m toten Punkt an-langen: ~ed festgefahren.

dead·ly ['dedlɪ] **I** *adj.* **1.** tödlich, tod-bringend: ~ *poison*; ~ *precision* tödliche Genauigkeit; ~ *sin* Todsünde *f*; ~ *combat* Kampf *m* auf Leben u. Tod; **2.** *fig.* unversöhnlich, grausam: ~ *enemy* Todfeind *m*; ~ *fight* mör-derischer Kampf; **3.** totenähnlich: ~ *pallor* Leichenblässe *f*; **4.** F schrecklich, groß, äußerst: ~ *haste*; **II** *adv.* **5.** to-tenähnlich: ~ *pale* leichenblass; **6.** F schrecklich, tod...: ~ *dull* sterbens-langweilig.

dead| **march** *s.* ♪ Trauermarsch *m*; ~ **ma·rine** *s. sl.* leere ‚Pulle'.

dead·ness ['dednɪs] *s.* **1.** Leblosigkeit *f*, Erstarrung *f*; *fig. a.* Leere *f*, Öde *f*; **2.** Gefühllosigkeit *f*, Gleichgültigkeit *f*, Kälte *f*; **3.** *bsd.* † Flauheit *f*, Flaute *f*; **4.** Glanzlosigkeit *f*.

dead| **net·tle** *s.* ♣ Taubnessel *f*; ~ **pan** *s.* F ausdrucksloses Gesicht; '~-pan *adj.* **1.** ausdruckslos; **2.** mit ausdrucks-losem Gesicht; **3.** *fig.* trocken (*Hu-mor*); ~ *point s.* ⊙ toter Punkt; ~ **reck·on·ing** *s.* ⚓ gegisstes Besteck, Koppeln *n*; ~ *set s.* **1.** *hunt.* Stehen *n des Hundes*; **2.** verbissene Feind-schaft; **3.** hartnäckiges Bemühen *od.* Werben (*at* um): *make a* ~ *at* sich hartnäckig bemühen um; ~ **wa·ter** *s.* **1.** stehendes Wasser; **2.** ⚓ Kielwasser *n*, Sog *m*; ~ **weight** *s.* **1.** a) ganze Last, volles Gewicht, b) totes Gewicht, Eigengewicht *n*; **2.** *fig.* schwere Last; '~-weight ca·pac·i·ty *s.* Tragfähigkeit *f*; '~-wood *s.* **1.** totes Holz, *weitS.* Reisig *n*; **2.** *fig.* Plunder *m*; ~ Laden-hüter *m*; **3.** *fig. et.* Veraltetes *n:* Über'holtes; (nutzloser) 'Ballast.

de-aer·ate [diː'eɪəreɪt] *v/t.* entlüften.

deaf [def] *adj.* ☐ **1.** ♣ taub: *the* ~ die Tauben *pl.*; ~ *and dumb* taubstumm; ~-*and-dumb language* Taubstum-mensprache *f*; ~ *as a post* stock-taub; → *ear¹* 1; **2.** schwerhörig; **3.** *fig.* (*to*) taub (gegen), unzugänglich (für); ~ *aid s.* Hörgerät *n*; '~-en [-fn] *v/t.* **1.** taub machen; betäuben; **2.** *Schall* dämpfen; **3.** *Wände* schall-dicht machen; '~-en-ing [-fnɪŋ] *adj.* ohrenbetäubend; ,~-'mute **I** *adj.* taubstumm; **II** *s.* Taubstumme(r *m*) *f*; '~-ness [-nɪs] *s.* **1.** ♣ Taub-heit *f* (*a. fig. to* gegen); **2.** Schwerhörig-keit *f*.

deal¹ [diːl] **I** *v/i.* [*irr.*] **1.** (*with*) sich be-fassen *od.* beschäftigen *od.* abgeben (mit); **2.** (*with*) handeln (von), *et.* be-handeln *od.* zum Thema haben; **3.** ~ *with* sich mit e-m *Problem etc.* befassen *od.* ausein'ander setzen; *et.* in Angriff nehmen; **4.** ~ *with et.* erledigen, mit *et.*

od. j-m fertig werden; **5.** ~ *with od.* by behandeln (*acc.*), 'umgehen mit: ~ *fair-ly with s.o.* j-n anständig behandeln, sich fair gegen j-n verhalten; **6.** ~ *with* † Geschäfte machen *od.* Handel trei-ben mit, in Geschäftsverkehr stehen mit; **7.** † handeln, Handel treiben (*in* mit): ~ *in paper*; **8.** dealen (*mit Rauschgift handeln*); **9.** *Kartenspiel:* ge-ben; **II** *v/t.* [*irr.*] **10.** *oft* ~ *out et.* ver-, austeilen: ~ *out rations*; ~ *s.o.* (*s.th.*) *a blow,* ~ *a blow at s.o.* (*s.th.*) j-m (e-r Sache) e-n Schlag versetzen; **11.** *j-m et.* zuteilen; **12.** *Karten od. j-m e-e Karte* geben; **III** *s.* F **13.** Handlungsweise *f*, Verfahren *n*, Poli'tik *f*; → *New Deal*; **14.** Behandlung *f*; → *raw* 10, *square* 37; **15.** Geschäft *n*, Handel *m: it's a* ~! abgemacht!; (*a*) *good* ~! gutes Ge-schäft!, nicht schlecht!; *no* ~! F da läuft nichts!; *big* ~! *Am. sl.* na und?, pah!; *no big* ~ *Am. sl.* keine große Sache; **16.** Abkommen *n*, Über'einkunft *f:* *make* (*od. do*) *a* ~ ein Abkommen treffen, sich einigen; **17.** *Kartenspiel: it is my* ~ ich muss geben.

deal² [diːl] *s.* **1.** Menge *f*, Teil *m: a great* ~ (*of money*) sehr viel (Geld); *a good* ~ ziemlich viel, ein gut Teil; *think a great* ~ *of s.o.* sehr viel von j-m halten; **2.** e-e ganze Menge: *a* ~ *worse* F viel schlechter.

deal³ [diːl] *s.* **1.** Diele *f*, Brett *n*, Planke *f* (*bsd. aus Kiefernholz*); **2.** Tannen- *od.* Kiefernholz *n*.

deal·er ['diːlə] *s.* **1.** † Händler(in), Kaufmann *m:* ~ *in antiques* Antiquitä-tenhändler; *plain* ~ *fig.* ehrlicher Mensch; **2.** *Brit. Börse:* Dealer *m* (*der auf eigene Rechnung Geschäfte tätigt*); **3.** Dealer *m* (*Rauschgifthändler*); **4.** *Kartenspiel:* Geber(in); '**deal·ing** [-lɪŋ] *s.* **1.** *mst pl.* 'Umgang *m*, Verkehr *m*, Beziehungen *pl.:* *have* ~*s with s.o.* mit j-m zu tun haben; *there is no* ~ *with her* mit ihr ist nicht auszukommen; **2.** † a) Handel *m*, Geschäft *n* (*in* in *dat.*, mit), b) Geschäftsverkehr *m*, c) Ge-schäftsgebaren *n*; **3.** Verhalten *n*, Handlungsweise *f*; **4.** Austeilen *n*, Ge-ben *n* (*von Karten*).

dealt [delt] *pret. u. p.p. von* **deal¹**.

dean [diːn] *s.* **1.** *Brit. univ.* a) De'kan *m* (*Vorstand e-r Fakultät od. e-s College*); b) Fellow *m* mit besonderen Aufgaben (*Oxford, Cambridge*); **2.** *Am. univ.* a) Vorstand *m* e-r Fakul'tät, b) Hauptbe-rater(in) (*der Studen-ten*); **3.** *eccl.* De'kan *m*, De'chant *m*; **4.** Vorsitzende(r *m*) *f*, Präsi'dent(in): ⚑ *of the Diplomatic Corps* Doyen *m* des Diplomatischen Korps; '**dean·er·y** [-nərɪ] *s.* Deka'nat *n*.

dear [dɪə] **I** *adj.* ☐ → *dearly*; **1.** teuer, lieb (*to dat.*): ~ *mother* liebe Mutter; ⚑ *Sir,* (*in Briefen*) Sehr geehrter Herr (*Name*)!; *my* ~*est wish* mein Herzenswunsch; *for* ~ *life* als ob es ums Leben ginge; *hold* ~ (wert-) schätzen; **2.** teuer, kostspielig; ~ *money policy* Hochzinspolitik *f*; **II** *adv.* **3.** teuer: *it cost him* ~ es kam ihn teuer zu stehen; → *dearly* 2; **III** *s.* **4.** Liebs-te(r *m*) *f*, Liebling *m*, Schatz *m: isn't she a* ~? ist sie nicht ein Engel?; *there's a* ~! sei (so) lieb!; **IV** *int.* **5.** oh ~!, ~, ~!, ~ *me!* du liebe Zeit!, ach je!; **dear·ie** ['dɪərɪ] → *deary*; '**dear·ly** [-lɪ] *adv.* **1.** innig, herzlich; **2.** teuer; → *buy* 3; '**dear·ness** [-nɪs] *s.* **1.** Kostspielig-keit *f*, hoher Preis *od.* Wert (*a. fig.*); **2.** *das* Liebe(nswerte).

dearth [dɜːθ] *s.* **1.** Mangel *m* (*of* an

dat.); **2.** Hungersnot *f.*

dear·y ['dɪərɪ] *s.* F Liebling *m*, Schätzchen *n.*

death [deθ] *s.* **1.** Tod *m*: **⁓s** Todesfälle; *to (the)* ⁓ zu Tode, bis zum Äußersten; *at ᵴ's door* an der Schwelle des Todes; *bleed to* ⁓ (sich) verbluten; *do to* ⁓ a) j-n umbringen, b) *fig. et.* ‚kaputtmachen' *od.* ‚zu Tode reiten'; *done to* ⁓ F *Küche:* totgekocht; *frozen to* ⁓ erfroren; *sure as* ⁓ tod-, bombensicher; *tired to* ⁓ todmüde; *catch one's* ⁓ sich den Tod holen (*engS.* durch Erkältung); *be in at the* ⁓ *fig.* das Ende miterleben; *that will be his* ⁓ das wird ihm das Leben kosten; *he'll be the* ⁓ *of me* a) er bringt mich noch ins Grab, b) ich lach mich noch tot über ihn; *hold on like grim* ⁓ verbissen festhalten, sich festkrallen (*to* an *dat.*); *put to* ⁓ zu Tode bringen, *bsd.* hinrichten; **2.** Tod *m*, (Ab)Sterben *n*, Ende *n*, Vernichtung *f*: *united in* ⁓ im Tode vereint; **⁓ ag·o·ny** *s.* Todeskampf *m*; **'⁓-bed** *s.* Sterbebett *n*: **⁓ repentance** Reue *f* auf dem Sterbebett; **⁓ ben·e·fit** *s.* **1.** Sterbegeld *n*; **2.** bei Todesfall fällige Versicherungsleistung; **'⁓-blow** *s.* Todesstreich *m*; *fig.* Todesstoß *m* (*to* für); **⁓ cell** *s.* ⁜ Todeszelle *f*; **⁓ cer·tif·i·cate** *s.* Sterbeurkunde *f*, Totenschein *m*; **⁓ du·ty** *s. obs.* Erbschaftssteuer *f*; **⁓ grant** *s.* Sterbegeld *n*; **⁓ house** → ⁓ *row*; **⁓ in·stinct** *s. psych.* Todestrieb *m*; **⁓ knell** *s.* Totengeläut *n*, -glocke *f* (*a. fig.*).

death·less ['deθlɪs] *adj.* □ *bsd. fig.* unsterblich; **'death·like** *adj.*, **'death·ly** [-lɪ] *adj. u. adv.* totenähnlich, Todes..., Leichen..., toten...: ⁓ *pale* leichenblass.

death| mask *s.* Totenmaske *f*; **⁓ pen·al·ty** *s.* Todesstrafe *f*; **⁓ rate** *s.* Sterblichkeitsziffer *f*; **⁓ rat·tle** *s.* Todesröcheln *n*; **⁓ ray** *s.* Todesstrahl *m*; **⁓ roll** *s.* Zahl *f* der Todesopfer; ⁜ Gefallenen-, Verlustliste *f*; **⁓ row** *s. Am.* Todestrakt *m* (*e-r Strafanstalt*); **⁓'s head** *s.* **1.** Totenkopf *m* (*bsd. als Symbol*); **2.** *zo.* Totenkopf *m* (*Falter*); **⁓ throes** *s. pl.* Todeskampf *m*; **'⁓-trap** *s. fig.* ‚Mausefalle' *f*; **⁓ war·rant** *s.* **1.** ⚖ Hinrichtungsbefehl *m*; **2.** *fig.* Todesurteil *n*; **'⁓-watch** *s. Brit. a.* **⁓ beetle** *zo.* Klopfkäfer *m*; **⁓ wish** *s.* Todeswunsch *m.*

deb [deb] *s.* F *abbr. für* **débutante.**

dé·bâ·cle [deɪ'bɑːkl] (*Fr.*) *s.* **1.** De'bakel *n*, Zs.-bruch *m*, Kata'strophe *f*; **2.** Massenflucht *f*, wildes Durchein'ander; **3.** *geol.* Eisgang *m.*

de·bar [dɪ'bɑː] *v/t.* **1.** (*from*) j-n ausschließen (von), hindern (an *dat. od. zu inf.*); **2.** *s.o. s.th.* j-m et. versagen *od.* verhindern.

de·bark [dɪ'bɑːk] → *disembark.*

de·base [dɪ'beɪs] *v/t.* **1.** (cha'rakterlich) verderben, verschlechtern; **2.** (*o.s.* sich) entwürdigen, erniedrigen; **3.** entwerten; im Wert mindern; *Wert* mindern; **4.** *Münzen* verschlechtern; **5.** verfälschen; **de·based** [-st] *adj.* **1.** verderbt (*etc.*); **2.** minderwertig (*Geld*); **3.** abgegriffen (*Wort*).

de·bat·a·ble [dɪ'beɪtəbl] *adj.* **1.** disku'tabel; **2.** strittig, fraglich, um'stritten; **3.** bestreitbar, anfechtbar; **de·bate** [dɪ'beɪt] **I** *v/t.* **1.** debattieren, diskutieren; **2.** ⁓ *with o.s.* hin u. her über'legen; **II** *v/t.* **3.** *et.* debattieren, erörtern, diskutieren; **4.** erwägen, sich *et.* über'legen; **III** *s.* **5.** De'batte *f* (*a. parl.*), Erörterung *f*: *be under* ⁓ zur Debatte stehen; ⁓ *on request parl.* aktuelle Stunde; **de'bat·er** [-tə] *s.* **1.** Debat'tierer *m*,

Dispu'tant *m*; **2.** *parl.* Redner *m*; **de'bat·ing** [-tɪŋ] *adj.*: ⁓ *club od. society* Debattierklub *m.*

de·bauch [dɪ'bɔːtʃ] **I** *v/t.* **1.** sittlich verderben; **2.** verführen, verleiten; **II** *s.* **3.** Ausschweifung *f*, Orgie *f*; **4.** Schwelge'rei *f*; **de'bauched** [-tʃt] *adj.* ausschweifend, liederlich, zügellos; **deb·au·chee** [ˌdebɔː'tʃiː] *s.* Wüstling *m*; **de'bauch·er** [-tʃə] *s.* Verführer *m*; **de'bauch·er·y** [-tʃərɪ] *s.* Ausschweifung (-en *pl.*) *f*, Orgie(n *pl.*) *f*; Schwelge'rei *f.*

de·ben·ture [dɪ'bentʃə] *s.* **1.** Schuldschein *m*; **2.** ✝ a) *a.* ⁓ *bond,* ⁓ *certificate* Obligati'on *f*, Schuldverschreibung *f*, b) *Brit.* Pfandbrief *m*: ⁓ *holder* Obligationsinhaber *m*; *Brit.* Pfandbriefinhaber(in); ⁓ *stock Brit.* Obligationen *pl.*, Anleiheschuld *f*, *Am.* Vorzugsaktien erster Klasse; **3.** ✝ Rückzollschein *m.*

de·bil·i·tate [dɪ'bɪlɪteɪt] *v/t.* schwächen, entkräften; **de·bil·i·ta·tion** [dɪ,bɪlɪ-'teɪʃn] *s.* Schwächung *f*, Entkräftung *f*; **de·bil·i·ty** [-ətɪ] *s.* Schwäche *f*, Kraftlosigkeit *f*, Erschöpfung(szustand *m*) *f.*

deb·it ['debɪt] **I** *s.* ✝ **1.** Debet *n*, Soll *n*, Schuldposten *m*: ⁓ *and credit* Soll u. Haben *n*; **2.** Belastung *f*: *to the* ⁓ *of* zu Lasten von; **3.** *a.* ⁓ *side* Debetseite *f*: *charge (od. carry) a sum to s.o.'s* ⁓ j-s Konto mit e-r Summe belasten; **II** *v/t.* **4.** debitieren, belasten (*with* mit); **III** *adj.* **5.** Debet..., Schuld...: ⁓ *account*; ⁓ *balance* Debetsaldo *m*; *your* ⁓ *balance* Saldo *m* zu Ihren Lasten; ⁓ *entry* Lastschrift *f*; ⁓ *note* Lastschriftanzeige *f.*

de·block [ˌdiː'blɒk] *v/t.* ✝ *eingefrorene Konten* freigeben.

deb·o·nair(e) [ˌdebə'neə] *adj.* **1.** höflich, gefällig; **2.** heiter, fröhlich; **3.** 'lässig(-ele,gant).

de·bouch [dɪ'baʊtʃ] *v/i.* **1.** ⁜ her'vorbrechen; **2.** einmünden, sich ergießen (*Fluss*).

De·brett [də'bret] *npr.*: ⁓'s *peerage* englisches Adelsregister.

de·brief·ing [ˌdiː'briːfɪŋ] *s.* ⁜, ✈ Einsatzbesprechung *f* (*nach dem Flug*).

de·bris ['deɪbriː] *s.* Trümmer *pl.*, (Gesteins)Schutt *m* (*a. geol.*).

debt [det] *s.* Schuld *f* (*Geld od. fig.*); Verpflichtung *f*: ⁓-*collecting agency* Inkassobüro *n*; ⁓ *collector* Inkassobeauftragte(r) *m*; *collection of* ⁓ Inkasso *n*; ⁓ *restructuring* Umschuldung *f*; *bad* ⁓s zweifelhafte Forderungen *od.* Außenstände; ⁓ *of gratitude* Dankesschuld; ⁓ *of hono(u)r* Ehrenschuld; *pay one's* ⁓ *to nature* der Natur s-n Tribut entrichten, sterben; *run into* ⁓ in Schulden geraten; *run up* ⁓s Schulden machen; *be in* ⁓ verschuldet sein, Schulden haben; *be in s.o.'s* ⁓ *fig.* j-m verpflichtet sein, in j-s Schuld stehen; **'debt·or** [-tə] *s.* Schuldner(in), ✝ Debitor *m*: *common* ⁓ Gemeinschuldner *m.*

de·bug [ˌdiː'bʌɡ] *v/t.* **1.** ⊕ F (die) ‚Mucken' *e-r Maschine* beseitigen; ⁓ *program* Computer: Fehlersuchprogramm *n*; **2.** entwanzen (*a.* F *von Minispionen befreien*).

de·bunk [ˌdiː'bʌŋk] *v/t.* F entlarven.

de·bu·reau·cra·tize [ˌdiːbjʊə'rɒkrətaɪz] *v/t.* entbürokratisieren.

de·bus [ˌdiː'bʌs] *v/i.* aus dem *od.* e-m Bus aussteigen.

dé·but, *Am.* **de·but** ['deɪbuː] (*Fr.*) *s.* De'büt *n*: a) erstes Auftreten (*thea. od. in der Gesellschaft*), b) Anfang *m*, An-

tritt *m* (*e-r Karriere etc.*): *make one's* ⁓ sein Debüt geben; **déb·u·tant**, *Am.* **deb·u·tant** ['debjuːtɑː] (*Fr.*) *s.* Debü'tant *m*; **déb·u·tante**, *Am.* **deb·u·tante** ['debjuːtɑːnt] (*Fr.*) *s.* Debü'tantin *f.*

deca- [dekə] *in Zssgn* zehn(mal).

dec·ade ['dekeɪd] *s.* **1.** De'kade *f*: a) Jahr'zehnt *n*, b) Zehnergruppe *f*; **2.** ᵴ, ◉ De'kade *f.*

dec·a·dence ['dekədəns] *s.* Deka'denz *f*, Entartung *f*, Verfall *m*, Niedergang *m*; **'dec·a·dent** [-nt] **I** *adj.* deka'dent, entartet, verfallend; Dekadenz...; **II** *s.* deka'denter Mensch.

de·caf ['diːkæf] *s.* F koffe'infreier Kaffee.

de·caf·fein·ate [ˌdiː'kæfɪneɪt] *v/t. Kaffee* koffe'infrei machen.

dec·a·gon ['dekəɡən] *s.* Å Zehneck *n*; **dec·a·gram(me)** ['dekəɡræm] *s.* De'ka'gramm *n.*

de·cal [dɪ'kæl] → *decalcomania.*

de·cal·ci·fy [ˌdiː'kælsɪfaɪ] *v/t.* entkalken.

de·cal·co·ma·ni·a [dɪ,kælkəʊ'meɪnɪə] *s.* Abziehbild(verfahren) *n.*

dec·a|·li·ter *Am.*, **⁓·li·tre** *Brit.* ['dekəˌliːtə] *s.* Deka'liter *m*, *n*; **ᵴ·log(ue)** ['dekəlɒɡ] *s. bibl.* Deka'log *m*, die Zehn Gebote *pl.*; **⁓·me·ter** *Am.*, **⁓·me·tre** *Brit.* ['dekə,miːtə] *s.* Deka'meter *m*, *n.*

de·camp [dɪ'kæmp] *v/i.* **1.** ⁜ das Lager abbrechen; **2.** F sich aus dem Staube machen.

de·cant [dɪ'kænt] *v/t.* **1.** ab-, 'umfüllen; **2.** dekantieren, vorsichtig abgießen; **de'cant·er** [-tə] *s.* **1.** Ka'raffe *f*; **2.** Klärflasche *f.*

de·cap·i·tate [dɪ'kæpɪteɪt] *v/t.* **1.** enthaupten, köpfen; **2.** *Am.* F entlassen, ‚absägen'; **de·cap·i·ta·tion** [dɪ,kæpɪ-'teɪʃn] *s.* **1.** Enthauptung *f*; **2.** *Am.* F ‚Rausschmiss'.

de·car·bon·ate [ˌdiː'kɑːbəneɪt] *v/t.* Kohlensäure *od.* Kohlen'dioxid entziehen (*dat.*); **de·car·bon·ize** [ˌdiː'kɑːbə-naɪz] *v/t.* dekarbonisieren; **de·car·bu·rize** [ˌdiː'kɑːbjʊəraɪz] → *decarbonize.*

de·car·tel·i·za·tion ['diː,kɑːtəlaɪ'zeɪʃn] *s.* ✝ Entkartellisierung *f*, (Kon'zern-) Entflechtung *f*; **de·car·tel·ize** [ˌdiː'kɑː-təlaɪz] *v/t.* entflechten.

de·cath·lete [dɪ'kæθliːt] *s. sport* Zehnkämpfer *m*; **de·cath·lon** [dɪ'kæθlɒn] *s.* Zehnkampf *m.*

dec·a·tize ['dekətaɪz] *v/t.* Seide dekatieren.

de·cay [dɪ'keɪ] **I** *v/t.* **1.** verfallen, zerfallen (*a. phys.*), in Verfall geraten, zu-'grunde gehen; **2.** verderben, verkümmern, verblühen; **3.** (ver)faulen (*a.* Zahn), (ver)modern, verwesen; **4.** schwinden, abnehmen, schwach werden, (her'ab)sinken; ⁓ed *with age* altersschwach; **II** *s.* **5.** Verfall *m*, Zerfall *m* (*a. phys. von Radium etc.*): *fall into* ⁓ → 1; **6.** Nieder-, Rückgang *m*, Verblühen *n*; Ru'in *m*; **7.** ✲ Karies *f*, (Zahn)Fäule *f*; Schwund *m*; **8.** Fäulnis *f*, Vermodern *n*; **de'cayed** [-eɪd] *adj.* **1.** ver-, zerfallen; kraftlos; zerrüttet; **2.** her'untergekommen; **3.** verblüht; **4.** verfault, morsch; *geol.* verwittert; **5.** ✲ kari'ös, schlecht (*Zahn*).

de·cease [dɪ'siːs] **I** *v/i.* sterben, verscheiden; **II** *s.* Tod *m*, Ableben *n*; **de'ceased** [-st] **I** *adj.* verstorben; **II** *s. the* ⁓ a) der *od.* die Verstorbene, b) die Verstorbenen *pl.*

de·ce·dent [dɪ'siːdənt] *s.* ⚖ *Am.* **1.** → *deceased* II; **2.** Erb-lasser(in).

de·ceit [dɪ'siːt] *s.* **1.** Betrug *m*, (bewusste) Täuschung; Betrüge'rei *f*; **2.** Falschheit *f*, Tücke *f*; **de'ceit·ful** [-fʊl] *adj.* □

betrügerisch; falsch, 'hinterlistig; **de-'ceit·ful·ness** [-fʊlnɪs] s. Falschheit f, 'Hinterlist f, Arglist f.
de·ceiv·a·ble [dɪ'si:vəbl] adj. leicht zu täuschen(d); **de·ceive** [dɪ'si:v] **I** v/t. **1.** täuschen (Person od. Sache), trügen (Sache): **be ~d** sich täuschen lassen, sich irren (**in** in dat.); **~ o.s.** sich et. vormachen; **2.** mst pass. Hoffnung etc. enttäuschen; **II** v/i. **3.** trügen, täuschen (Sache); **de'ceiv·er** [-və] s. Betrüger (-in).
de·cel·er·ate [ˌdi:'seləreɪt] **I** v/t. verlangsamen; die Geschwindigkeit verringern von (od. gen.); **II** v/i. sich verlangsamen; s-e Geschwindigkeit verringern; **de·cel·er·a·tion** ['di:ˌselə'reɪʃn] s. Verlangsamung f; Geschwindigkeitsabnahme f: **~ lane** mot. Verzögerungsspur f.
De·cem·ber [dɪ'sembə] s. De'zember m: **in ~** im Dezember.
de·cen·cy ['di:snsɪ] s. **1.** Anstand m, Schicklichkeit f: **for ~'s sake** anstandshalber; **sense of ~** Anstandsgefühl n; **2.** Anständigkeit f; **3.** pl. Anstand m; **4.** pl. Annehmlichkeiten pl. des Lebens.
de·cen·ni·al [dɪ'senjəl] **I** adj. ☐ **1.** zehnjährig; **2.** alle zehn Jahre 'wiederkehrend; **II** s. **3.** Am. Zehn'jahrfeier f; **de-'cen·ni·al·ly** [-lɪ] adv. alle zehn Jahre; **de'cen·ni·um** [-jəm] pl. **-ni·ums, -ni·a** [-jə] s. Jahr'zehnt n, De'zennium n.
de·cent ['di:snt] adj. ☐ **1.** anständig: a) schicklich, b) sittsam, c) ehrbar; **2.** de'zent, unaufdringlich; **3.** F ,anständig': a) annehmbar: **a ~ meal**, b) nett: **that was ~ of him.**
de·cen·tral·i·za·tion [di:ˌsentrəlaɪ'zeɪʃn] s. Dezentralisierung f; **de·cen·tral·ize** [ˌdi:'sentrəlaɪz] v/t. dezentralisieren.
de·cep·tion [dɪ'sepʃn] s. **1.** Täuschung f, Irreführung f; **2.** Betrug m; **3.** Trugbild n; **de'cep·tive** [-ptɪv] adj. ☐ täuschend, irreführend, trügerisch: **appearances are ~** der Schein trügt.
deci- [desɪ] in Zssgn Dezi...
dec·i·bel ['desɪbel] s. phys. Dezi'bel n.
de·cide [dɪ'saɪd] **I** v/t. **1.** et. entscheiden; **2.** j-n bestimmen, veranlassen; et. bestimmen, festsetzen: **~ the right moment; that ~d me** das gab für mich den Ausschlag, das bestärkte mich in m-m Entschluss; **the weather ~d me against going** aufgrund des Wetters entschloss ich mich, nicht zu gehen; **II** v/i. **3.** entscheiden, bestimmen, den Ausschlag geben; **4.** beschließen; sich entscheiden od. entschließen (**in fa-vo[u]r of** für; **against doing** nicht zu tun; **to do** zu tun); **5.** zu dem Schluss od. der Über'zeugung kommen: **I ~d that it was worth trying; 6.** feststellen, finden: **we ~d that the weather was too bad; 7. ~ (up)on** sich entscheiden für od. über (acc.); festsetzen, -legen, bestimmen (acc.); **de'cid·ed** [-dɪd] adj. ☐ **1.** entschieden, unzweifelhaft, deutlich; **2.** entschieden, entschlossen, fest, bestimmt; **de'cid·ed·ly** [-dɪdlɪ] adv. entschieden, fraglos, bestimmt; **de-'cid·er** [-də] s. **1.** sport Entscheidungskampf m, Stechen n; **2.** das Entscheidende, die Entscheidung.
de·cid·u·ous [dɪ'sɪdjuəs] adj. ♀ jedes Jahr abfallend: **~ tree** Laubbaum m; **2.** zo. abfallend (Geweih etc.).
dec·i·gram(me) ['desɪgræm] s. Dezi'gramm n; **~·li·ter** Am., **~·li·tre** Brit. ['desɪˌli:tə] s. Dezi'liter m, n.
dec·i·mal ['desɪml] ♣ **I** adj. ☐ → **deci-**

mal·ly; dezi'mal, Dezimal...: **~ frac-tion**; **go ~** das Dezimalsystem einführen; **II** s. a) Dezi'malzahl f, b) Dezi'male f, Dezi'malstelle f: **circulating (re-curring) ~** periodische (unendliche) Dezimalzahl; **'dec·i·mal·ize** [-məlaɪz] v/t. auf das Dezi'malsy,stem 'umstellen; **'dec·i·mal·ly** [-məlɪ] adv. **1.** nach dem Dezi'malsy,stem; **2.** in Dezi'malzahlen (ausgedrückt).
dec·i·mal| place s. Dezi'malstelle f; **~ point** s. Komma n (im Englischen ein Punkt) vor der ersten Dezi'malstelle: **floating ~** Fließkomma (Taschenrechner etc.); **~ sys·tem** s. Dezi'malsy,stem n.
dec·i·mate ['desɪmeɪt] v/t. dezimieren, fig. a. stark schwächen od. vermindern; **dec·i·ma·tion** [desɪ'meɪʃn] s. Dezimierung f.
dec·i·me·ter Am., **dec·i·me·tre** Brit. ['desɪˌmi:tə] s. Dezi'meter m, n.
de·ci·pher [dɪ'saɪfə] v/t. **1.** entziffern; **2.** dechiffrieren; **3.** fig. enträtseln; **de'ci-pher·a·ble** [-fərəbl] adj. entzifferbar; fig. enträtselbar; **de'ci·pher·ment** [-mənt] s. Entzifferung f etc.
de·ci·sion [dɪ'sɪʒn] s. **1.** Entscheidung f (a. ♣); Entscheid m, Urteil n, Beschluss m: **make** (od. **take**) **a ~** e-e Entscheidung treffen; **2.** Entschluss m: **arrive at a ~, come to a ~, take a ~** zu e-m Entschluss kommen; **3.** Entschlusskraft f, Entschlossenheit f: **~ of char-acter** Charakterstärke f; **~·,mak·er** s. Entscheidungsträger m; **~·,mak·ing** adj. entscheidungstragend, entscheidend: **~ board.**
de·ci·sive [dɪ'saɪsɪv] adj. ☐ **1.** entscheidend, ausschlag-, maßgebend; endgültig, schlüssig: **be ~ in** entscheidend beitragen zu; **be ~ of** entscheiden (acc.); **~ battle** Entscheidungsschlacht f; **2.** entschlossen, entschieden (Person); **de'ci-sive·ness** [-nɪs] s. **1.** entscheidende Kraft; **2.** Maßgeblichkeit f; **3.** Endgültigkeit f; **4.** Entschiedenheit f.
deck [dek] **I** s. **1.** ♣ Deck n: **on ~** a) auf Deck, b) Am. F bereit, zur Hand; **all hands on ~!** alle Mann an Deck!; **be-low ~** unter Deck; **clear the ~s (for action)** a) das Schiff klar zum Gefecht machen, b) fig. sich bereitmachen; **2.** ✈ Tragdeck n, -fläche f; **3.** 🚃 (Wag-'gon)Dach n; **4.** (Ober)Deck n (Bus); **5.** a) Laufwerk n (e-s Plattenspielers), b) → **tape deck**; **6.** sl. ,Briefchen' n (Rauschgift); Spiel n, Pack m (Spiel-)Karten; **II** v/t. **7.** oft **~ out** a) (aus-) schmücken, b) j-n her'ausputzen; **'~·chair** s. Liegestuhl m.
-deck·er [dekə] s. in Zssgn ...decker m; → **three-decker.**
deck| game s. Bordspiel n; **~ hand** s. ♣ Ma'trose m.
deck·le-edged [ˌdekl'edʒd] adj. **1.** mit Büttenrand; **2.** unbeschnitten: **~ book.**
de·claim [dɪ'kleɪm] **I** v/i. **1.** reden, e-e Rede halten; **2. ~ against** eifern od. wettern gegen; **3.** Phrasen dreschen; **II** v/t. **4.** deklamieren, (contp. bom'bastisch) vortragen.
dec·la·ma·tion [ˌdeklə'meɪʃn] s. **1.** Deklamati'on f (a. ♪); **2.** bom'bastische Rede; **3.** Ti'rade f; **4.** Vortragsübung f; **de·clam·a·to·ry** [dɪ'klæmətərɪ] adj. ☐ **1.** Rede..., Vortrags...; **2.** deklama'torisch; **3.** eifernd; **4.** bom'bastisch, theatralisch.
de·clar·a·ble [dɪ'kleərəbl] adj. zollpflichtig; **de'clar·ant** [-rənt] s. **1.** ♣ Erschienene(r m) f; **2.** Am. Einbürgerungsanwärter(in).

dec·la·ra·tion [ˌdeklə'reɪʃn] s. **1.** Erklärung f, Aussage f: **make a ~** eine Erklärung abgeben; **~ of intent** Absichtserklärung; **~ of war** Kriegserklärung; **2.** Mani'fest n, Proklamati'on f; **3.** ♣ f a) Am. Klageschrift f, b) Beteuerung f (an Eides Statt); **4.** Anmeldung f, Angabe f: **~ of bankruptcy** ♣ Konkursanmeldung; **customs ~** Zolldeklaration f, -erklärung f; **5.** Bridge: Ansage f; **de-clar·a·tive** [dɪ'klærətɪv] adj.: **~ sen-tence** ling. Aussagesatz m; **de·clar·a-to·ry** [dɪ'klærətərɪ] adj. erklärend: **be ~ of** erklären, darlegen, feststellen; **~ judgment** ♣ Feststellungsurteil n.
de·clare [dɪ'kleə] **I** v/t. **1.** erklären, aussagen, verkünden, bekannt machen, proklamieren: **~ war (on)** (j-m) den Krieg erklären, fig. (j-m) den Kampf ansagen; **he was ~d winner** er wurde zum Sieger erklärt; **2.** erklären, behaupten; **3.** angeben, anmelden; erklären, deklarieren (Zoll); ♣ Dividende festsetzen; **4.** Kartenspiel: ansagen; **5. ~ o.s.** a) sich erklären (a. durch Heiratsantrag), sich offenbaren, s-e Meinung kundtun, b) sich im wahren Licht zeigen; **~ o.s. for s.th.** sich zu e-r Sache bekennen; **II** v/i. **6.** erklären, bestätigen: **well, I ~!** ich muss schon sagen!, nanu!; **7.** sich erklären od. entscheiden (**for** für; **against** gegen); **8. ~ off** a) absagen, b) sich lossagen (**from** von); Kricket: ein Spiel vorzeitig abbrechen; **de'clared** [-eəd] adj. ☐ fig. erklärt (Feind etc.); **de'clar·ed·ly** [-eərɪdlɪ] adv. erklärtermaßen, ausgesprochen.
de·clas·si·fy [dɪ'klæsɪfaɪ] v/t. die Geheimhaltung (gen.) aufheben, Dokumente etc. freigeben.
de·clen·sion [dɪ'klenʃn] s. **1.** Abweichung f, Abfall m (**from** von); **2.** Verfall m, Niedergang m; **3.** ling. Deklinati'on f; **de'clen·sion·al** [-ʃənl] adj. ling. Deklinations...
de·clin·a·ble [dɪ'klaɪnəbl] adj. ling. deklinierbar; **dec·li·na·tion** [ˌdeklɪ'neɪʃn] s. **1.** Neigung f, Abschüssigkeit f; **2.** Abweichung f; **3.** ast., phys. Deklinati'on f: **~ compass** ♣ Deklinationsbussole f; **compass ~** Missweisung f.
de·cline [dɪ'klaɪn] **I** v/i. **1.** sich neigen, sich senken; **2.** sich neigen, zur Neige od. zu Ende gehen: **declining years** Lebensabend m; **3.** abnehmen, nachlassen, zu'rückgehen; sich verschlechtern, schwächer werden; verfallen; **4.** sinken, fallen (Preise); **5.** (höflich) ablehnen; **II** v/t. **6.** neigen, senken; **7.** ablehnen, nicht annehmen, ausschlagen; es ablehnen (**doing** od. **to do** zu tun); **8.** ling. deklinieren, beugen; **III** s. **9.** Neigung f, Senkung f, Abhang m; **10.** Neige f, Ende n: **~ of life** Lebensabend m; **11.** Nieder-, Rückgang m, Abnahme f; Verschlechterung f: **be on the ~** a) zur Neige gehen, b) im Niedergang begriffen sein, sinken; **~ of strength** Kräfteverfall m; **~ of** (od. **in**) **prices** Preisrückgang; **~ in value** Wertminderung f; **12.** ♣ körperlicher od. geistiger Verfall, Siechtum n.
de·cliv·i·tous [dɪ'klɪvɪtəs] adj. abschüssig, steil; **de'cliv·i·ty** [-vətɪ] s. **1.** Abschüssigkeit f; **2.** Abhang m.
de·clutch [ˌdi:'klʌtʃ] v/i. mot. auskuppeln.
de·coct [dɪ'kɒkt] v/t. auskochen, absieden; **de'coc·tion** [-kʃn] s. **1.** Auskochen n, Absieden n; **2.** Absud m; pharm. De'kokt n.
de·code [ˌdi:'kəʊd] v/t. dekodieren (a. ling., Computer), dechiffrieren, ent-

D

schlüsseln, über'setzen; ,**de'cod·er** [-də] *s. a. Radio, Computer*: Dekoder *m.*

dé·col·le·té [deı'kɒlteı] (*Fr.*) *adj.* **1.** (tief) ausgeschnitten (*Kleid*); **2.** dekolletiert (*Dame*).

de·col·o·nize [,di:'kɒlənaız] *v/t.* dekolonisieren, in die Unabhängigkeit entlassen.

de·col·or·ant [di:'kʌlərənt] **I** *adj.* entfärbend, bleichend; **II** *s.* Bleichmittel *n*; **de'col·o(u)r·ize** [-raız] *v/t.* entfärben, bleichen.

de·com·mis·sion [,di:kə'mıʃn] *v/t.* **1.** *Atomkraftwerk etc.* stilllegen; **2.** *Schiff etc.* außer Dienst nehmen: *ʌing of arms* Außerdienstnahme *f* von Waffen.

de·com·pose [,di:kəm'pəʊz] **I** *v/t.* **1.** zerlegen, spalten; **2.** zersetzen; **3.** 🜨, *phys.* scheiden, abbauen; **II** *v/i.* **4.** sich auflösen, zerfallen; **5.** sich zersetzen, verwesen, verfaulen; ,**de·com'posed** [-zd] *adj.* verfault, verdorben; **de·com·po·si·tion** [,di:kɒmpə'zıʃn] *s.* **1.** 🜨, *phys.* Zerlegung *f*, Aufspaltung *f*, Scheidung *f*, Auflösung *f*, Abbau *m*; **2.** Zersetzung *f*, Zerfall *m*; **3.** Verwesung *f*, Fäulnis *f.*

de·com·press [,di:kəm'pres] *v/t.* dekomprimieren, den Druck vermindern in (*dat.*); ,**de·com'pres·sion** [-eʃn] *s.* Dekompressi'on *f*, Druckverminderung *f.*

de·con·tam·i·nate [,di:kən'tæmıneıt] *v/t.* entgiften, -seuchen, -strahlen; **de·con·tam·i·na·tion** ['di:kən,tæmı'neıʃn] *s.* Entgiftung *f*, -seuchung *f*, -gasung *f.*

de·con·trol [,di:kən'trəʊl] **I** *v/t.* die Zwangsbewirtschaftung aufheben von *od.* für; *Waren, Handel* freigeben; **II** *s.* Aufhebung *f* der Zwangsbewirtschaftung, Freigabe *f.*

dé·cor ['deıkɔː] (*Fr.*) *s.* △, *thea. etc.* De'kor *m, n*, Ausstattung *f.*

dec·o·rate ['dekəreıt] *v/t.* **1.** (aus)schmücken, (ver)zieren, dekorieren; **2.** *Wohnung* a) (neu) tapezieren *od.* streichen, b) einrichten, ausstatten; **3.** *mit e-m Orden* dekorieren, auszeichnen; **dec·o·ra·tion** [,dekə'reıʃn] *s.* **1.** Ausschmückung *f*, Verzierung *f*; **2.** Schmuck *m*, Zierrat *m*, Dekorati'on *f*; **3.** Orden *m*, Ehrenzeichen *n*; **4.** *a. interior ʌ* a) Innenausstattung *f*, b) 'Innenarchitek,tur *f.*

Dec·o·ra·tion Day → *Memorial Day.*

dec·o·ra·tive ['dekərətıv] *adj.* □ dekora'tiv, schmückend, ornamen'tal, Zier..., Schmuck...: ~ *plant* Zierpflanze *f*; **dec·o·ra·tor** ['dekəreıtə] *s.* **1.** De'kora'teur *m*; **2.** → *interior* 1; **3.** Maler *m* u. Tapezierer *m.*

dec·o·rous ['dekərəs] *adj.* □ schicklich, anständig.

de·cor·ti·cate [,di:'kɔːtıkeıt] *v/t.* **1.** entrinden; schälen; **2.** enthülsen.

de·co·rum [dı'kɔːrəm] *s.* **1.** Anstand *m*, Schicklichkeit *f*, De'korum *n*; **2.** Eti'kette *f*, Anstandsformen *pl.*

de·coy I *s.* ['di:kɔı] **1.** Köder *m*, Lockspeise *f*; **2.** *a.* ~ *duck* Lockvogel *m* (*a. fig.*); **3.** *hunt.* Entenfang *m*, -falle *f*; **4.** ✕ Scheinanlage *f*; **II** *v/t.* [dı'kɔı] **5.** ködern, locken; **6.** *fig.* (ver)locken, verleiten; ~ *ship s.* ⚓, ✕ U-Boot-Falle *f.*

de·crease [di:'kri:s] **I** *v/i.* abnehmen, sich vermindern, kleiner werden: ~ *in length* kürzer werden; **II** *v/t.* vermindern, verringern, reduzieren, her'absetzen; **III** *s.* ['di:kri:s] Abnahme *f*, Verminderung *f*, Verringerung *f*, Rückgang *m*: ~ *in prices* Preisrückgang; *be on the* ~ → I; **de'creas·ing·ly** [-sıŋlı]

adv. immer weniger: ~ *rare.*

de·cree [dı'kri:] **I** *s.* **1.** De'kret *n*, Erlass *m*, Verfügung *f*, Verordnung *f*: *issue a* ~ e-e Verfügung erlassen; *by* ~ auf dem Verordnungsweg; **2.** 🏛 Entscheid *m*, Urteil *n*: *absolute* rechtskräftiges (Scheidungs)Urteil; → *nisi*; **3.** *fig.* Ratschluss *m Gottes*, Fügung *f* des Schicksals; **II** *v/t.* **4.** verfügen, an-, verordnen.

dec·re·ment ['dekrımənt] *s.* Abnahme *f*, Verminderung *f.*

de·crep·it [dı'krepıt] *adj.* **1.** altersschwach, klapp(e)rig (*beide a. fig.*); **2.** verfallen, baufällig.

de·cres·cent [dı'kresnt] *adj.* abnehmend: ~ *moon.*

de·cry [dı'kraı] *v/t.* schlecht machen, her'untermachen, her'absetzen.

dec·u·ple ['dekjʊpl] **I** *adj.* zehnfach; **II** *s.* das Zehnfache; **III** *v/t.* verzehnfachen.

de·cus·sate [dı'kʌsət] *adj.* **1.** sich kreuzend *od.* schneidend; **2.** ⚕ kreuzgegenständig.

ded·i·cate ['dedıkeıt] *v/t.* (*to dat.*) **1.** weihen, widmen; **2.** *s-e Zeit etc.* widmen; **3.** ~ *o.s.* sich widmen *od.* hingeben; sich zuwenden; **4.** *Buch etc.* widmen, zueignen; **5.** *Am.* feierlich eröffnen *od.* einweihen; **6.** a) der Öffentlichkeit zugänglich machen, b) dem öffentlichen Verkehr über'geben: ~ *a road*; **7.** *dem Feuer, der Erde* über'antworten; '**ded·i·cat·ed** [-tıd] *adj.* **1.** pflichtbewusst, hingebungsvoll; **2.** engagiert; **3.** spezi'ell: ~ *line teleph.*, *Internet*: Standleitung *f*; **4.** zugehörig; **5.** *EDV* dezi'diert. **ded·i·ca·tion** [,dedı'keıʃn] *s.* **1.** Weihung *f*, Widmung *f*; feierliche Einweihung; **2.** 'Hingabe *f* (*to an acc.*), Engage'ment *n*; **3.** Widmung *f*, Zueignung *f*; **4.** *Am.* feierliche Einweihung *od.* Eröffnung; **5.** 'Übergabe *f* an den öffentlichen Verkehr; '**ded·i·ca·tor** [-tə] *s.* Widmende(r *m*) *f*; '**ded·i·ca·to·ry** [-kətərı] *adj.* (Ein)Weihungs...; Widmungs..., Zueignungs...

de·duce [dı'dju:s] *v/t.* **1.** folgern, schließen (*from* aus); **2.** ab-, 'herleiten (*from* von); **de'duc·i·ble** [-səbl] *adj.* **1.** zu folgern(d); **2.** ab-, 'herleitbar, 'herzuleiten(d).

de·duct [dı'dʌkt] *v/t. e-n Betrag* abziehen (*from* von), einbehalten; (*von der Steuer*) absetzen: *after ʌing* nach Abzug von *od. gen.*; *ʌing expenses* abzüglich (der) Unkosten; **de'duct·i·ble** [-təbl] *adj.* **1.** abzugsfähig; **2.** (*von der Steuer*) absetzbar; **de'duc·tion** [-kʃn] *s.* **1.** Abzug *m*, Abziehen *n*; **2.** ✝ Abzug *m*, Ra'batt *m*, (Preis)Nachlass *m*; ~ *at source* Quellenbesteuerung *f*; **3.** (Schluss)Folgerung *f*, Schluss *m*; **4.** 'Herleitung *f*; **de'duc·tive** [-tıv] *adj.* □ **1.** deduk'tiv, folgernd, schließend; **2.** → *deducible.*

deed [di:d] **I** *s.* **1.** Tat *f*, Handlung *f*: *in word and* ~ in Wort u. Tat; **2.** Helden-, Großtat *f*; **3.** 🏛 (Vertrags-, *bsd.* Über'tragungs)Urkunde *f*, Doku'ment *n*: ~ *of donation* Schenkungsurkunde; **II** *v/t.* **4.** *Am.* urkundlich über'tragen (*to* auf *j-n*); ~ *poll* 🏛 einseitige (gesiegelte) Erklärung (*e-r Vertragspartei*).

dee·jay ['di:dʒeı] *s.* F Diskjockey *m.*

deem [di:m] **I** *v/i.* denken, meinen; **II** *v/t.* halten für, erachten für, betrachten als: *I* ~ *it advisable.*

de·e·mo·tion·al·ize [,di:ı'məʊʃnəlaız] *v/t.* versachlichen.

de·em·pha·size [,di:'emfəsaız] *v/t.* bagatellisieren.

deem·ster ['di:mstə] *s.* Richter *m* (*auf*

der Insel Man).

deep [di:p] **I** *adj.* □ → *deeply*; **1.** tief (*vertikal*): ~ *hole*; ~ *snow*; ~ *sea* Tiefsee *f*; *in* ~ *water(s) fig.* in Schwierigkeiten; *go off the* ~ *end* a) *Brit.* in Rage kommen, b) *Am.* et. unüberlegt riskieren; **2.** tief (*horizontal*): ~ *cupboard*; ~ *forests*; ~ *border* breiter Rand; *they marched four* ~ sie marschierten in Viererreihen; *three men* ~ drei Mann hoch (*zu dritt*); **3.** tief, vertieft, versunken (*in* in *acc.*): ~ *in thought*; **4.** tief, gründlich, scharfsinnig: ~ *learning* gründliches Wissen; ~ *intellect* scharfer Verstand; *a* ~ *thinker* ein tiefer Denker; **5.** tief, heftig, stark, fest, schwer: ~ *sleep* tiefer Schlaf; ~ *mourning* tiefe Trauer; ~ *disappointment* tiefe *od.* bittere Enttäuschung; ~ *interest* großes Interesse; ~ *grief* schweres Leid; ~ *in debt* stark *od.* tief verschuldet; **6.** tief, innig, aufrichtig: ~ *love*; ~ *gratitude*; **7.** tief, dunkel; verborgen, geheim: ~ *night* tiefe Nacht; ~ *silence* tiefes *od.* völliges Schweigen; ~ *secret* tiefes Geheimnis; ~ *designs* dunkle Pläne; *he is a* ~ *one sl.* er hat es faustdick hinter den Ohren; **8.** schwierig: ~ *problem*; *that is too* ~ *for me* das ist mir zu hoch; **9.** tief, dunkel (*Farbe, Klang*); **10.** *psych.* un(ter)bewusst; **11.** ⚜ subku'tan; **II** *adv.* **12.** tief (*a. fig.*): ~ *into the flesh* ins Fleisch; *still waters run* ~ stille Wasser sind tief; ~ *into the night* (bis) tief in die Nacht (hinein); *drink* ~ unmäßig trinken; **III** *s.* **13.** Tiefe *f* (*a. fig.*); Abgrund *m*: *in the* ~ *of night* in tiefster Nacht; **14.** *the* ~ *poet.* das Meer.

'**deep-dish pie** *s.* 'Napfpa,stete *f*; ,~-'**draw** *v/t.* [*irr.*] ☉ tiefziehen; ,~-'**drawn** *adj.* **1.** ☉ tiefgezogen; **2.** ~ *sigh* tiefer Seufzer.

deep·en ['di:pən] **I** *v/t.* **1.** tiefer machen, vertiefen; verbreitern; **2.** *fig.* vertiefen (*a. Farben*), verstärken, steigern; **II** *v/i.* **3.** tiefer werden, sich vertiefen; **4.** *fig.* sich verstärken *od.* steigern, stärker werden; **5.** dunkler werden.

'**deep-felt** *adj.* tief empfunden; ,~-'**freeze I** *s.* Tiefkühlgerät *n*, -truhe *f*, -schrank *m*; **II** *adj.* Tiefkühl..., Gefrier...; **III** *v/t.* [*irr.*] tiefkühlen, einfrieren; ,~-'**fro·zen** *adj.* tiefgefroren, Tiefkühl...; '~-**fry** *v/t.* frittieren, in schwimmendem Fett braten; ~ *fry·er s.*, ,~-,**fry·ing pan** *s.* Frit'teuse *f*; ,~-'**laid** *adj.* schlau (*Plan*).

deep·ly ['di:plı] *adv.* tief (*a. fig.*): ~ *indebted* äußerst dankbar; ~ *hurt* tief *od.* schwer gekränkt; ~ *interested* höchst interessiert; ~ *read* sehr belesen; *drink* ~ unmäßig trinken; *go* ~ *into to s.th.* e-r Sache auf den Grund gehen.

deep·ness ['di:pnıs] *s.* **1.** Tiefe *f* (*a. fig.*); **2.** Dunkelheit *f*; **3.** Gründlichkeit *f*; **4.** Scharfsinn *m*; **5.** Durch'triebenheit *f.*

,**deep-'read** *adj.* sehr belesen; ,~-'**root·ed** *adj. bsd. fig.* tief eingewurzelt, fest verwurzelt; *fig. a.* eingefleischt; ,~-'**sea** *adj.* Tiefsee..., Hochsee...: ~ *fish* Tiefseefisch *m*; ~ *fishing* Hochseefischerei *f*; ,~-'**seat·ed** → *deep-rooted*; '~-**set** *adj.* tief liegend: ~ *eyes*; *the* ♀ *South s. Am.* der tiefe Süden (*südlichste Staaten der USA*).

deer [dıə] *pl.* **deer** *s.* **1.** *zo.* a) Hirsch *m*, b) Reh *n*: *red* ~ Rot-, Edelhirsch; **2.** Hoch-, Rotwild *n*; ~ *for·est s.* Hochwildgehege *n*; '~-**hound** *s.* Schottischer Jagdhund; ~ **lick** *s.* Salzlecke *f*; '~-**park** *s.* Wildpark *m*; '~-**shot** *s.* Rehpos-

D

ten *m* (*Schrot*); '~·**skin** *s.* Hirsch-, Rehleder *n*; '~,**stalk·er** *s.* **1.** Pirscher *m*; **2.** Jagdmütze *f*; '~,**stalk·ing** *s.* (Rotwild)Pirsch *f.*

de·es·ca·late [,diː'eskəleɪt] **I** *v/t.* **1.** *Krieg etc.* deeskalieren; **2.** *fig.* her'unterschrauben; **II** *v/i.* **3.** deeskalieren; **de·es·ca·la·tion** [,diːeskə'leɪʃn] *s. pol.* Deeskalati'on *f (a. fig.).*

de·face [dɪ'feɪs] *v/t.* **1.** entstellen, verunstalten, beschädigen; **2.** ausstreichen, unleserlich machen; **3.** *Briefmarken* entwerten; **de'face·ment** [-mənt] *s.* Entstellung *f (etc.).*

de fac·to [diː'fæktəʊ] (*Lat.*) **I** *adj.* De-facto-...; **II** *adv.* de 'facto, tatsächlich.

de·fal·ca·tion [,diːfæl'keɪʃn] *s.* **1.** Veruntreuung *f*, Unter'schlagung *f*; **2.** unter'schlagenes Geld.

def·a·ma·tion [,defə'meɪʃn] *s.* Verleumdung *f*, Beleidigung; **de·fam·a·to·ry** [dɪ'fæmətərɪ] *adj.* □ verleumderisch, Schmäh...: *be ~ of s.o.* j-n verleumden; **de·fame** [dɪ'feɪm] *v/t.* verleumden; **de·fam·er** [dɪ'feɪmə] *s.* Verleumder(in).

de·fat·ted [diː'fætɪd] *adj.* entfettet.

de·fault [dɪ'fɔːlt] **I** *s.* **1.** (Pflicht)Versäumnis *n*, Unter'lassung *f*; **2.** *bsd.* ✝ Nichterfüllung *f*, Verzug *m*, Versäumnis *n*, Säumnis *f*, Zahlungseinstellung *f*; *engS.* Zahlungsverzug *m*: *be in ~* im Verzug sein; **3.** ⚖ Nichterscheinen *n* vor Gericht: *judg(e)ment by ~* Versäumnisurteil *n*; **4.** *sport* Nichtantreten *n*; **5.** Fehlen *n*, Mangel *m*: *in ~ of* mangels, in Ermangelung (*gen.*); *in ~ of which* widrigenfalls; *go by ~* unterbleiben; **6.** *Computer*: Default *m*, Vor-, Grundeinstellung *f*; **II** *v/i.* **7.** s-n Verpflichtungen nicht nachkommen: *~ on s.th.* et. vernachlässigen, mit et. im Rückstand sein; **8.** ✝ s-n Verbindlichkeiten nicht nachkommen, im (Zahlungs)Verzug sein: *~ on a debt* s-e Schuld nicht bezahlen; **9.** ⚖ nicht vor Gericht erscheinen; **10.** *sport* nicht antreten; **III** *v/t.* **11.** e-r Verpflichtung nicht nachkommen, in Verzug geraten mit; **12.** ⚖ wegen Nichterscheinens (vor Gericht) verurteilen; **13.** *sport* nicht antreten (*zu e-m Kampf*); **de'fault·er** [-tə] *s.* **1.** Säumige(r *m*) *f*; **2.** ✝ a) säumiger Zahler *od.* Schuldner, b) Zahlungsunfähige(r *m*) *f*; **3.** ⚖ vor Gericht nicht Erscheinende(r *m*) *f*; **4.** ✕ *Brit.* Delin'quent *m.*

de·fea·sance [dɪ'fiːzns] *s.* ⚖ **1.** Aufhebung *f*, Annullierung *f*, Nichtigkeitserklärung *f*; **2.** Nichtigkeitsklausel *f*; **de'fea·si·ble** [-zəbl] *adj.* anfecht-, annullierbar.

de·feat [dɪ'fiːt] **I** *v/t.* **1.** besiegen, schlagen: *it ~s me to inf.* es geht über m-e Kraft zu *inf.*; **2.** *Angriff etc.* zu'rückschlagen, abwehren; **3.** *parl.* Antrag zu Fall bringen, ablehnen; **4.** vereiteln, zu-'nichte machen: *that ~s the purpose* das verfehlt den Zweck; **II** *s.* **5.** Niederwerfung *f*, Besiegung *f*; **6.** Niederlage *f* (*a. fig.*): *admit ~* sich geschlagen geben; **7.** *parl.* Ablehnung *f*; **8.** Vereitelung *f*, Vernichtung *f*; **9.** 'Misserfolg *m*, Fehlschlag *m*; **de'feat·ism** [-tɪzəm] *s.* Defä'tismus *m*, Miesmache'rei *f*; **de'feat·ist** [-tɪst] **I** *s.* Defä'tist *m*; **II** *adj.* defä'tistisch.

def·e·cate ['defɪkeɪt] **I** *v/t.* reinigen; *fig.* läutern; **II** *v/i.* ⚕ Stuhlgang haben; **def·e·ca·tion** [,defɪ'keɪʃn] *s.* ⚕ Stuhlgang *m.*

de·fect **I** *s.* ['diːfekt] **1.** De'fekt *m*, Fehler *m* (*in* an *dat.*, in *dat.*): *~ in title* ⚖

Fehler im Recht; **2.** Mangel *m*, Unvollkommenheit *f*, Schwäche *f*; **3.** (*geistiger od. psychischer*) De'fekt; ⚕ Gebrechen *n*: *~ in character* Charakterfehler *m*; *~ of vision* Sehfehler *m*; **II** *v/i.* [dɪ'fekt] **4.** abtrünnig werden; **5.** *zum Feind* 'übergehen; **de·fec·tion** [dɪ'fekʃn] *s.* **1.** Abfall *m*, Lossagung *f* (*from* von); **2.** Treubruch *m*; **3.** 'Übertritt *m* (*to* zu); **de·fec·tive** [dɪ'fektɪv] **I** *adj.* □ **1.** mangelhaft, unvollkommen: *mentally ~* schwachsinnig; *he is ~ in* es mangelt ihm an (*dat.*); **2.** schadhaft, de'fekt; **II** *s.* **3.** *mental ~* Schwachsinnige(r *m*) *f*; **de·fec·tive·ness** [dɪ'fektɪvnɪs] *s.* **1.** Mangelhaftigkeit *f*; **2.** Schadhaftigkeit *f*; **de·fec·tor** [dɪ'fektə] *s.* Abtrünnige(r *m*) *f*, 'Überläufer(in).

de·fence, *Am.* **de·fense** [dɪ'fens] *s.* **1.** Verteidigung *f*, Schutz *m*, Abwehr *f*: *come to s.o.'s ~* j-m zu Hilfe kommen; *~ mechanism* *biol., psych.* Abwehrmechanismus *m*; **2.** ⚖ *allg.* Verteidigung *f*, *a.* Einrede *f*: *in his ~* zu s-r Entlastung; *conduct one's own ~* sich selbst verteidigen; → *counsel* 4; *witness* 1; **3.** Verteidigung *f*, Rechtfertigung *f*: *in his ~* zu s-r Rechtfertigung; **4.** ✕ Verteidigung *f*, *sport a.* Abwehr *f* (*Spieler od. deren Spielweise*); *pl.* Verteidigungsanlagen *pl.*: *~ spending* Verteidigungsausgaben *pl.*; **de·fence·less** [-lɪs] *adj.* **1.** schutz-, wehr-, hilflos; **2.** ✕ unbefestigt; **de·fence·less·ness** [-lɪsnɪs] *s.* Schutz-, Wehrlosigkeit *f.*

de·fend [dɪ'fend] *v/t.* **1.** (*from*, *against*) verteidigen (gegen), schützen (vor *dat.*, gegen); **2.** *Meinung etc.* verteidigen, rechtfertigen; **3.** *Rechte* schützen, wahren; **4.** ⚖ a) j-n verteidigen, b) sich auf e-e *Klage* einlassen: *~ the suit* den Klageanspruch bestreiten; **de·fend·a·ble** [-dəbl] *adj.* zu verteidigen(d); **de·fend·ant** [-dənt] ⚖ **I** *s.* a) *Zivilrecht*: Beklagte(r *m*) *f*, b) *Strafrecht*: Angeklagte(r *m*) *f*; **II** *adj.* a) beklagt, b) angeklagt; **de·fend·er** [-də] *s.* **1.** Verteidiger *m*, *sport a.* Abwehrspieler *m*; **2.** Beschützer *m.*

de·fense *etc. Am.* → **defence** *etc.*

de·fen·si·ble [dɪ'fensəbl] *adj.* □ **1.** zu verteidigen(d), haltbar; **2.** zu rechtfertigen(d), vertretbar; **de·fen·sive** [-sɪv] **I** *adj.* □ **1.** defen'siv, verteidigend, schützend; abwehrend (*a. fig. Geste etc.*); **2.** Verteidigungs...; Schutz..., Abwehr... (*a. biol.*); **II** *s.* **3.** Defen'sive *f*, Verteidigung *f*: *on the ~* in der Defensive.

de·fer¹ [dɪ'fɜː] *v/t.* **1.** auf-, verschieben; **2.** hin'ausschieben; zu'rückstellen (*Am. a.* ✕).

de·fer² [dɪ'fɜː] *v/i.* (*to*) sich fügen, nachgeben (*dat.*), sich beugen (vor *dat.*); sich j-n Wunsche fügen; **def·er·ence** ['defərəns] *s.* **1.** Ehrerbietung *f*, Achtung *f*: *with all due ~ to* bei aller Hochachtung vor (*dat.*); **2.** Nachgiebigkeit *f*, Rücksicht(nahme) *f*: *in ~ to your wishes* wunschgemäß; **def·er·ent** ['defərənt] *adj.*, **def·er·en·tial** [,defə'renʃl] *adj.* □ **1.** ehrerbietig; **2.** rücksichtsvoll.

de·fer·ment [dɪ'fɜːmənt] *s.* **1.** Aufschub *m*; **2.** ✕ *Am.* Zu'rückstellung *f* (vom Wehrdienst); **de·fer·ra·ble** [-ɜːrəbl] *adj.* **1.** aufschiebbar; **2.** ✕ *Am.* zu-'rückstellbar.

de·ferred| an·nu·i·ty [dɪ'fɜːd] *s.* hin'ausgeschobene Rente; *~ bond* *s. Am.* Obligati'on *f* mit aufgeschobener Zinszahlung; *~ pay·ment* *s.* **1.** Zahlungsaufschub *m*, **2.** Ratenzahlung *f*; *~ shares*

s. pl. ✝ Nachzugsaktien *pl.*; *~ terms* *s. pl. Brit.* 'Abzahlungssy,stem *n*: *on ~* auf Abzahlung *od.* Raten.

de·fi·ance [dɪ'faɪəns] *s.* **1.** a) Trotz *m*, 'Widerstand *m*, b) Hohn *m*, offene Verachtung: *in ~ of* ungeachtet (*gen.*), trotz (*gen. od. dat.*), e-m *Gebot etc.* zuwider, j-m zum Trotz *od.* Hohn; *bid ~, set at ~* Trotz bieten, Hohn sprechen (*to dat.*); **2.** Her'ausforderung *f*; **de-'fi·ant** [-nt] *adj.* □ trotzig, her'ausfordernd.

de·fi·cien·cy [dɪ'fɪʃnsɪ] *s.* **1.** (*of*) Mangel *m* (an *dat.*), Fehlen *n* (von): *~ disease* ⚕ Mangelkrankheit *f*; **2.** Fehlbetrag *m*, Manko *n*, Ausfall *m*, Defizit *n*; **3.** Mangelhaftigkeit *f*, Schwäche *f*, Lücke *f*, Unzulänglichkeit *f*; **de·fi·cient** [-nt] *adj.* □ **1.** unzureichend, mangelhaft, ungenügend: *be ~ in* ermangeln (*gen.*), es fehlen lassen an (*dat.*), arm sein an (*dat.*); *he is ~ in courage* ihm fehlt es an Mut; **2.** fehlend: *~ amount* Fehlbetrag *m.*

def·i·cit ['defɪsɪt] *s.* ✝ Defizit *n*, Fehlbetrag *m*, 'Unterbi,lanz *f*; **2.** Mangel (*in* an *dat.*); *~ spend·ing* *s.* ✝ Deficit-spending *n*, Defizitfinanzierung *f.*

de·file¹ **I** *s.* ['diːfaɪl] **1.** Engpass *m*, Hohlweg *m*; **2.** ✕ Vor'beimarsch *m*; **II** *v/i.* [dɪ'faɪl] **3.** defilieren, vor'beimarschieren.

de·file² [dɪ'faɪl] *v/t.* **1.** beschmutzen, verunreinigen; **2.** *fig.* besudeln, beflecken, verunglimpfen; **3.** schänden; **4.** entweihen; **de·file·ment** [-mənt] *s.* Besudelung *f etc.*

de·fin·a·ble [dɪ'faɪnəbl] *adj.* □ definier-, erklär-, bestimmbar; **de·fine** [dɪ'faɪn] *v/t.* **1.** *Wort etc.* definieren, (genau) erklären; **2.** (genau) bezeichnen *od.* bestimmen; kennzeichnen, festlegen; klarmachen; **3.** scharf abzeichnen, (klar) um'reißen, be-, um'grenzen.

def·i·nite ['defɪnɪt] *adj.* □ **1.** bestimmt (*a. ling.*), präzis, klar, deutlich, eindeutig, genau; **2.** defini'tiv, endgültig; **def·i·nite·ly** [-lɪ] *adv.* **1.** bestimmt (*etc.*); **2.** zweifellos, abso'lut, entschieden; **def·i·nite·ness** [-nɪs] *s.* Bestimmtheit *f*; **def·i·ni·tion** [,defɪ'nɪʃn] *s.* **1.** Definiti'on *f*, (genaue) Erklärung; (Begriffs)Bestimmung *f*; **2.** Genauigkeit *f*, Ex'aktheit *f*; **3.** (*a.* Bild-, Ton-) Schärfe *f*, Präzisi'on *f*; *TV* Auflösung *f*; **de·fin·i·tive** [dɪ'fɪnɪtɪv] **I** *adj.* □ **1.** defini'tiv, endgültig; maßgeblich (*Buch*); **2.** → *definite* 1; **II** *s.* **3.** *ling.* Bestimmungswort *n.*

def·la·grate ['defləgreɪt] *v/i.* (*u. v/t.*) 🜍 rasch abbrennen (lassen); **def·la·gra·tion** [,deflə'greɪʃn] *s.* 🜍 Verpuffung *f.*

de·flate [dɪ'fleɪt] *v/t.* **1.** (die) Luft ablassen aus, entleeren; **2.** ✝ *Geldumlauf etc.* deflationieren, her'absetzen; **3.** *fig.* a) j-n 'klein u. hässlich machen', b) ernüchtern; **de·fla·tion** [-eɪʃn] *s.* **1.** Ablassen *n* von Luft *od.* Gas; **2.** ✝ Deflati'on *f*; **de·fla·tion·ar·y** [-eɪʃnərɪ] *adj.* ✝ deflatio'nistisch, Deflations...

de·flect [dɪ'flekt] **I** *v/t.* ablenken, *sport a. Schuss* abfälschen; **II** *v/i.* abweichen (*from* von); **de·flec·tion**, *Brit. a.* **de-'flex·ion** [-ekʃn] *s.* **1.** Ablenkung *f* (*a. phys.*); **2.** Abweichung *f* (*a. fig.*); **3.** Ausschlag *m* (*Zeiger etc.*); **de·flec·tor** [-tə] *s.* De'flektor *m*, Ablenkvorrichtung *f*: *~ coil* ⚡ Ablenkspule *f.*

de·flo·rate ['diːflɔːreɪt] → *deflower*; **def·lo·ra·tion** [,diːflɔː'reɪʃn] *s.* Deflorati'on *f*, Entjungferung *f.*

de·flow·er [,diː'flaʊə] *v/t.* **1.** deflorieren,

D

entjungfern; **2.** *fig.* e-r Sache den Reiz nehmen.
de·fo·li·ant [ˌdiːˈfəʊlɪənt] *s.* 🦠, ✗ Entlaubungsmittel *n*; **de·fo·li·ate** [ˌdiːˈfəʊlɪeɪt] *v/t.* entblättern, entlauben; **de·fo·li·a·tion** [ˌdiːfəʊlɪˈeɪʃn] *s.* Entblätterung *f.*
de·for·est·a·tion [diːˌfɒrɪˈsteɪʃn] *s.* Abforstung *f*, -holzung *f*; Entwaldung *f.*
de·form [dɪˈfɔːm] *v/t.* **1.** *a.* ⊙, *phys.* verformen; **2.** verunstalten, entstellen, deformieren; verzerren (*a. fig.*, 🅰, *phys.*); **3.** *Charakter* verderben, ‚verbiegen‘; **de·for·ma·tion** [ˌdiːfɔːˈmeɪʃn] *s.* **1.** *a.* ⊙, *phys.* Verformung *f*; **2.** Verunstaltung *f*, Entstellung *f*; ‚Missbildung *f*; **3.** 🅰, *phys.* —; **de'formed** [-md] *adj.* verformt (*etc.* → **deform**); **de'form·i·ty** [-mətɪ] *s.* **1.** Entstelltheit *f*, Hässlichkeit *f*; **2.** ‚Missbildung *f*, Auswuchs *m*; **3.** ‚missgestaltete Per'son *od.* Sache; Verderbtheit *f*, mo'ralischer De'fekt.
de·fraud [dɪˈfrɔːd] *v/t.* betrügen (*of* um): ~ *the revenue* Steuern hinterziehen; *with intent to* ~ in betrügerischer Absicht, arglistig; **de·frau·da·tion** [ˌdiːfrɔːˈdeɪʃn] *s.* Betrug *m*; Hinter'ziehung *f*, Unter'schlagung *f*; **de'fraud·er** [-də] *s.* ‘Steuerhinter‚zieher *m.*
de·fray [dɪˈfreɪ] *v/t. Kosten* tragen, bestreiten, bezahlen.
de·frock [ˌdiːˈfrɒk] → **unfrock.**
de·frost [ˌdiːˈfrɒst] *v/t.* von Eis befreien, *Windschutzscheibe etc.* entfrosten, *Kühlschrank etc.* abtauen, *Tiefkühlkost etc.* auftauen: ~*ing rear window mot.* heizbare Heckscheibe.
deft [deft] *adj.* □ geschickt, gewandt; **'deft·ness** [-nɪs] *s.* Geschicktheit *f*, Gewandtheit *f.*
de·funct [dɪˈfʌŋkt] **I** *adj.* **1.** verstorben; **2.** erloschen, nicht mehr existierend, ehemalig; **II** *s.* **3.** *the* ~ der *od.* die Verstorbene.
de·fuse [ˌdiːˈfjuːz] *v/t. Bombe etc.*, *fig. a. Lage etc.* entschärfen.
de·fy [dɪˈfaɪ] *v/t.* **1.** trotzen, Trotz *od.* die Stirn bieten (*dat.*); **2.** sich wider'setzen (*dat.*); **3.** sich hin'wegsetzen über (*acc.*), verstoßen gegen; **4.** standhalten, Schwierigkeiten machen (*dat.*): ~ *description* jeder Beschreibung spotten; ~ *translation* (fast) unübersetzbar sein; **5.** her'ausfordern: *I* ~ *anyone to do it* den möchte ich sehen, der das fertig bringt; *I* ~ *you to do it* ich weiß genau, dass du es nicht (tun) kannst.
de·gauss [ˌdiːˈgaʊs] *v/t. Schiff* entmagnetisieren.
de·gen·er·a·cy [dɪˈdʒenərəsɪ] *s.* Degenerati'on *f*, Entartung *f*, Verderbtheit *f*; **de·gen·er·ate I** *v/i.* [dɪˈdʒenəreɪt] (*into*) entarten: a) *biol. etc.* degenerieren (zu), b) *allg.* ausarten (zu, in *acc.*), herabsinken (zu, auf die Stufe *gen.*), a. verflachen, **II** *adj.* [-rət] degeneriert, entartet; verderbt; **III** *s.* [-rət] degenerierter Mensch; **de·gen·er·a·tion** [dɪˌdʒenəˈreɪʃn] *s.* Degenerati'on *f*, Entartung *f*; *biol. a.* Rückentwicklung *f.*
deg·ra·da·tion [ˌdegrəˈdeɪʃn] *s.* **1.** Degradierung *f* (*a.* ✗), Ab-, Entsetzung *f*; **2.** Verminderung *f*, Schwächung *f*, Verschlechterung *f*, Entartung *f*, Degenerati'on *f* (*a. biol.*); **3.** Entwürdigung *f*, Erniedrigung *f*, Her'absetzung *f*; **4.** 🦠 Abbau *m*; **5.** *phys.* Degradati'on *f*; **6.** *geol.* Verwitterung *f*; **de·grade** [dɪˈgreɪd] **I** *v/t.* **1.** degradieren (*a.* ✗), (her)'absetzen; **2.** vermindern, her'untersetzen, verschlechtern; **3.** erniedrigen, entwürdigen; **4.** 🦠 abbauen; **II** *v/i.*

5. (ab)sinken, her'unterkommen; **6.** entarten; **de·grad·ing** [dɪˈgreɪdɪŋ] *adj.* erniedrigend, entwürdigend; her'absetzend.
de·gree [dɪˈgriː] *s.* **1.** Grad *m*, Stufe *f*, Maß *n*: *by* ~*s* allmählich; *by slow* ~*s* ganz allmählich; *in some* ~ einigermaßen; *in no* ~ keineswegs; *in the highest* ~ im höchsten Maße *od.* Grad(e), aufs Höchste; *to what* ~ in welchem Maße, wie weit *od.* sehr; *to a* ~ a) in hohem Maße, b) einigermaßen, c) → *to a certain* ~ bis zu e-m gewissen Grade, ziemlich; **2.** 🅰, *geogr.*, *phys.* Grad *m*: ~ *of latitude* Breitengrad; *32* ~*s centigrade* 32 Grad Celsius; ~ *of hardness* Härtegrad; *of high* ~ hochgradig; **3.** *univ.* Grad *m*, Würde *f*: *doctor's* ~ Doktorwürde; *take one's* ~ e-n akademischen Grad erwerben, (*zum Doktor*) promovieren; ~ *day* Promotionstag *m*; **4.** (Verwandtschafts)Grad *m*; **5.** Rang *m*, Stand *m*: *of high* ~ von hohem Rang; **6.** *ling. a.* ~ *of comparison* Steigerungsstufe *f*; **7.** ♪ Tonstufe *f*, Inter'vall *n.*
de·gres·sion [dɪˈgreʃn] *s.* ✝ Degressi'on *f*; **de'gres·sive** [-esɪv] *adj.* ✝ degres'siv: ~ *depreciation* degressive Abschreibung.
de·hu·man·ize [ˌdiːˈhjuːmənaɪz] *v/t.* entmenschlichen.
de·hy·drate [ˌdiːˈhaɪdreɪt] *v/t.* 🦠 dehydrieren, das Wasser entziehen (*dat.*); dörren, trocknen: ~*d vegetables* Trocken-, Dörrgemüse *n*; **de·hy·dra·tion** [ˌdiːhaɪˈdreɪʃn] *s.* Dehy'drierung *f*, Wasserentzug *m*; Dörren *n*, Trocknen *n.*
de·ice [ˌdiːˈaɪs] *v/t.* enteisen; **de·ic·er** [-sə] *s.* Enteisungsmittel *n*, -anlage *f*, -gerät *n.*
de·i·de·ol·o·gize [ˈdiːˌaɪdɪˈɒlədʒaɪz] *v/t.* entideologisieren.
de·i·fi·ca·tion [ˌdiːɪfɪˈkeɪʃn] *s.* **1.** Apothe'ose *f*, Vergötterung *f*; **2.** *et.* Vergöttlichtes; **de·i·fy** [ˈdiːɪfaɪ] *v/t.* **1.** zum Gott erheben; **2.** als Gott verehren, anbeten (*a. fig.*).
deign [deɪn] **I** *v/i.* sich her'ablassen, geruhen, belieben (*to do* zu tun); **II** *v/t.* sich her'ablassen zu: *he* ~*ed no answer.*
de·in·stall [ˌdiːɪnˈstɔːl] *v/t. Computer:* ‚deinstal'lieren.
de·ism [ˈdiːɪzəm] *s.* De'ismus *m*; **de·ist** [ˈdiːɪst] *s.* De'ist(in); **de·is·tic**, **de·is·ti·cal** [diːˈɪstɪk(l)] *adj.* → de'istisch; **de·i·ty** [ˈdiːɪtɪ] *s.* **1.** Gottheit *f*; **2.** *the ⚲ eccl.* die Gottheit, Gott *m.*
de·ject·ed [dɪˈdʒektɪd] *adj.* □ niedergeschlagen, deprimiert; **de·jec·tion** [-kʃn] *s.* **1.** Niedergeschlagenheit *f*, Trübsinn *m*; **2.** 💊 a) Stuhlgang *m*, b) Stuhl *m*, Kot *m.*
de ju·re [ˌdiːˈdʒʊərɪ] (*Lat.*) **I** *adj.* De-jure-...; **II** *adv.* de 'jure, von Rechts wegen.
dek·ko [ˈdekəʊ] *s. sl.* (kurzer) Blick: *have a* ~ mal schauen.
de·lac·ta·tion [ˌdiːlækˈteɪʃn] *s.* 💊 Abstillen *n*, Entwöhnung *f.*
de·lay [dɪˈleɪ] *v/t.* **1.** ver-, auf-, hin'ausschieben, verzögern, verschleppen; **2.** auf-, hinhalten, hindern, hemmen; **II** *v/i.* **3.** zögern, zaudern; Zeit verlieren, sich aufhalten; **III** *s.* **4.** Aufschub *m*, Verzögerung *f*, Verzug *m*: *without* ~ unverzüglich; ~ *of payment* ✝ Zahlungsaufschub *m*; **de·layed** [dɪˈleɪd] *adj.* verzögert, verspätet, nachträglich, Spät-...: ~*-action bomb* Bombe *f* mit Verzögerungszünder; ~ *fuse* Verzöge-

rungszünder *m*; ~ *ignition* ⊙ Spätzündung *f*; **de·lay·ing** [dɪˈleɪɪŋ] *adj.* aufschiebend, verzögernd; 'hinhaltend: ~ *action* Verzögerung(saktion) *f*, Hinhaltung *f*; ✗ hinhaltendes Gefecht; ~ *tactics* Hinhaltetaktik *f.*
del cred·er·e [ˌdelˈkredərɪ] *s.* ✝ Del'kredere *n*, Bürgschaft *f.*
de·le [ˈdiːliː] (*Lat.*) *typ.* **I** *v/t.* tilgen, streichen; **II** *s.* Dele'atur(zeichen) *n.*
de·lec·ta·ble [dɪˈlektəbl] *adj.* □ köstlich; **de·lec·ta·tion** [ˌdiːlekˈteɪʃn] *s.* Ergötzen *n*, Vergnügen *n*, Genuss *m.*
del·e·ga·cy [ˈdelɪgəsɪ] *s.* Abordnung *f*, Delegati'on *f*; **del·e·gate I** *s.* [-gət] **1.** Delegierte(r *m*) *f*, Vertreter(in), Abgeordnete(r *m*) *f*; **2.** *parl. Am.* Kon'gressabgeordnete(r *m*) *f* (*e-s Einzelstaats*); **II** *v/t.* [-geɪt] **3.** abordnen, delegieren; bevollmächtigen; **4.** (*to*) Aufgabe, Vollmacht *etc.* über'tragen, delegieren (an *acc.*); **del·e·ga·tion** [ˌdelɪˈgeɪʃn] *s.* **1.** Abordnung *f*, Ernennung *f*; **2.** Über'tragung *f* (*Vollmacht etc.*), Delegieren *n*; Über'weisung *f*; **3.** Delegati'on *f*, Abordnung *f*; **4.** *pl. parl. Am.* die (Kon'gress)Abgeordneten *pl.* (*e-s Einzelstaats*).
de·lete [dɪˈliːt] *v/t.* tilgen, (aus)streichen, ausradieren; *Computer:* entfernen, löschen; ~ *key s.* Löschtaste *f.*
del·e·te·ri·ous [ˌdelɪˈtɪərɪəs] *adj.* □ schädlich, verderblich, nachteilig.
de·le·tion [dɪˈliːʃn] *s.* Streichung *f*: a) Tilgung *f*, b) *das* Ausgestrichene.
delft [delft], *a.* **delf** [delf] *s.* **1.** Delfter Fay'encen *pl.*; **2.** *allg.* glasiertes Steingut.
del·i [ˈdelɪ] *s.* F → **delicatessen.**
de·lib·er·ate I *adj.* □ [dɪˈlɪbərət] **1.** über'legt, wohlerwogen, bewusst, absichtlich, vorsätzlich: *a* ~ *lie* e-e bewusste Lüge; **2.** bedächtig: a) besonnen, vorsichtig, b) gemächlich, langsam; **II** *v/t.* [-bəreɪt] **3.** über'legen, erwägen; **II** *v/i.* [-bəreɪt] **4.** nachdenken, über'legen; **5.** beratschlagen, sich beraten (*on* über *acc.*); **de'lib·er·ate·ness** [-nɪs] *s.* **1.** Vorsätzlichkeit *f*; **2.** Bedächtigkeit *f*; **de·lib·er·a·tion** [dɪˌlɪbəˈreɪʃn] *s.* **1.** Über'legung *f*; **2.** Beratung *f*; **3.** Bedachtsam-, Behutsamkeit *f*, Vorsicht *f*; **de'lib·er·a·tive** [-rətɪv] *adj.* beratend: ~ *assembly.*
del·i·ca·cy [ˈdelɪkəsɪ] *s.* **1.** Zartheit *f*, Feinheit *f*; Zierlichkeit *f*; **2.** Zartheit *f*, Schwächlichkeit *f*, Empfindlichkeit *f*, Anfälligkeit *f*; **3.** Anstand *m*, Zartgefühl *n*, Takt *m*: ~ *of feeling* Feinfühligkeit *f*; **4.** Feinheit *f*, Genauigkeit *f*; **5.** *fig.* Kitzligkeit *f*: *negotiations of great* ~ sehr heikle Besprechungen; **6.** (*a. fig.*) Leckerbissen *m*, Delika'tesse *f*; **'del·i·cate** [-kət] *adj.* □ **1.** zart, fein, zierlich; **2.** zart (*a. Gesundheit, Farbe*), empfindlich, zerbrechlich, schwächlich: *she was in a* ~ *condition* sie war in anderen Umständen; **3.** fein, leicht, dünn; **4.** sanft, leise: ~ *hint* zarter Wink; **5.** fein, genau; **6.** fein, anständig; **7.** vornehm; verwöhnt; **8.** heikel, kitzlig, schwierig; **9.** zartfühlend, feinfühlig, taktvoll; **10.** lecker, schmackhaft, deli'kat; **del·i·ca·tes·sen** [ˌdelɪkəˈtesn] *s. pl.* **1.** Delika'tessen *pl.*, Feinkost *f*; **2.** *sg. konstr.* Feinkostgeschäft *n.*
de·li·cious [dɪˈlɪʃəs] *adj.* □ köstlich: a) wohlschmeckend, b) herrlich.
de·lict [ˈdiːlɪkt] *s.* ⚖ De'likt *n.*
de·light [dɪˈlaɪt] **I** *s.* Vergnügen *n*, Freude *f*, Wonne *f*, Entzücken *n*: *to my* ~ zu m-r Freude; *take* ~ *in* → III; **II** *v/t.*

erfreuen, entzücken; **III** v/i. ~ *in* (gro-ße) Freude haben an (*dat.*), Vergnügen finden an (*dat.*); sich ein Vergnügen machen aus; **de'light·ed** [-tɪd] *adj.* □ entzückt, (hoch)erfreut (*with* über *acc.*): *I am* (*od.* **shall be**) ~ *to come* ich komme mit dem größten Vergnügen; **de'light·ful** [-fʊl] *adj.* □ entzückend, reizend; herrlich, wunderbar.

de·lim·it [diːˈlɪmɪt], **de·lim·i·tate** [dɪˈlɪmɪteɪt] v/t. abgrenzen, die Grenze(n) festsetzen von (*od. gen.*); **de·lim·i·ta·tion** [dɪˌlɪmɪˈteɪʃn] s. Abgrenzung f.

de·lin·e·ate [dɪˈlɪnɪeɪt] v/t. **1.** skizzieren, entwerfen, zeichnen; **2.** beschreiben, schildern, darstellen; **de·lin·e·a·tion** [dɪˌlɪnɪˈeɪʃn] s. **1.** Skizze f, Entwurf m, Zeichnung f; **2.** Beschreibung f, Schilderung f, Darstellung f.

de·lin·quen·cy [dɪˈlɪŋkwənsɪ] s. **1.** Vergehen n; **2.** Pflichtvergessenheit f; ⚖ Kriminali'tät f, → **juvenile** 1; **de'lin·quent** [-nt] **I** *adj.* **1.** straffällig, krimi'nell; **2.** pflichtvergessen: ~ *taxes* Am. Steuerrückstände; **II** s. **3.** Delin'quent (-in), Straffällige(r m) f, (Straf)Täter (-in); → **juvenile** 1; **4.** Pflichtvergessene(r m) f.

del·i·quesce [ˌdelɪˈkwes] v/i. bsd. 🏵 zerfließen; wegschmelzen.

de·lir·i·ous [dɪˈlɪrɪəs] *adj.* □ **1.** 🌡 irreredend, fantasierend: *be* ~ irrereden, fantasieren; **2.** *fig.* rasend, wahnsinnig (*with* vor *dat.*): ~ (*with joy*) überglücklich.

de·lir·i·um [dɪˈlɪrɪəm] s. **1.** 🌡 De'lirium n, (Fieber)Wahn m; 🌡 Rase'rei f, Verzückung f; ~ **tre·mens** [ˈtriːmenz] s. De'lirium n 'tremens, Säuferwahnsinn m.

de·liv·er [dɪˈlɪvə] v/t. **1.** befreien, erlösen, retten (*from* von, aus); **2.** *Frau* entbinden (*of* von), *Kind* ‚holen' (*Arzt*): *be ~ed of a child* entbunden werden, entbinden; **3.** *Meinung* äußern; *Urteil* aussprechen; *Rede etc.* halten; **4.** ~ *o.s.* äußern (*of* acc.), sich äußern (*on* über acc.); **5.** *Waren* liefern: ~ (*the goods*) F Wort halten, die Sache ‚schaukeln', ,es schaffen'; **6.** ab-, ausliefern; über'geben, -'bringen, -'liefern; über'senden, (hin)befördern; **7.** *Briefe* zustellen; *Nachricht* bestellen; ⚖ zustellen; **8.** ~ *up* abgeben, -'treten, über'geben, -'liefern; ⚖ her'ausgeben: ~ *o.s. up* sich ergeben *od.* stellen (*to* dat.); **9.** *Schlag* versetzen; ✕ (ab)feuern; **de'liv·er·a·ble** [-vərəbl] *adj.* ✝ lieferbar, zu liefern(d); **de'liv·er·ance** [-vərəns] s. **1.** Befreiung f, Erlösung f, (Er)Rettung f (*from* aus, von); **2.** Äußerung f, Verkündung f; **de'liv·er·er** [-vərə] s. **1.** Befreier m, Erlöser m, (Er)Retter m; **2.** Über'bringer m.

de·liv·er·y [dɪˈlɪvərɪ] s. **1.** Lieferung f: *on* ~ bei Lieferung, bei Empfang; *take* ~ (*of*) abnehmen (acc.); **2.** ✉ Zustellung f; **3.** Ab-, Auslieferung f, Aushändigung f, 'Übergabe f (a. ⚖); **4.** Über-'bringung f, -'sendung f, Beförderung f; **5.** ⊙ (Zu)Leitung f, Zuführung f; Förderung f; Leistung f; **6.** *rhet.* Vortragsweise f; **7.** *Baseball, Kricket:* 'Wurf (-,technik) m; **8.** ✕ Abfeuern n; **9.** 🌡 Entbindung f; ~ **charge** s. ✉ Zustellgebühr f; **~·man** s. [*irr.*] Ausfahrer m; Verkaufsfahrer m; ~ **note** s. ✝ Lieferschein m; ~ **or·der** s. ✝ Auslieferungsschein m, Lieferschein m; ~ **pipe** s. Leitungsröhre f; ~ **room** s. ✝ Entbindungssaal m, -zimmer n, Kreißsaal m; ~ **ser·vice** s. ✉ Zustelldienst m; ~ **truck** s. mot. Am., ~ **van** s. Brit. Lieferwagen

m.

dell [del] s. kleines, enges Tal.
de·louse [ˌdiːˈlaʊs] v/t. entlausen.
Del·phic [ˈdelfɪk] *adj.* delphisch, *fig. a.* dunkel, zweideutig.
del·phin·i·um [delˈfɪnɪəm] s. 🌺 Rittersporn m.
del·ta [ˈdeltə] s. *allg.* (a. Fluss)Delta n; ~ **con·nec·tion** s. ⚡ Dreieckschaltung f; ~ **rays** s. pl. phys. Deltastrahlen pl.; ~ **wing** s. ✈ Deltaflügel m.
del·toid [ˈdeltɔɪd] **I** *adj.* deltaförmig; **II** s. anat. Deltamuskel m.
de·lude [dɪˈluːd] v/t. täuschen, irreführen; (be)trügen: ~ *o.s.* sich Illusionen hingeben, sich et. vormachen; **2.** verleiten (*into* zu).
del·uge [ˈdeljuːdʒ] **I** s. **1.** (große) Über-'schwemmung: *the* 🌊 *bibl.* die Sintflut; **2.** *fig.* Flut f, (Un)Menge f; **II** v/t. **3.** *a. fig.* über'schwemmen, -'fluten, -'schütten.
de·lu·sion [dɪˈluːʒn] s. **1.** (Selbst)Täuschung f, Verblendung f, Wahn m, Irrglauben m; 🌡 Wahnvorstellung f: *be* (*od. labo[u]r*) *under the* ~ *that* in dem Wahn leben, dass; → **grandeur** 3; **de'lu·sive** [-uːsɪv] *adj.* □ irreführend, trügerisch, Wahn...
de luxe [dəˈlʌks] *adj.* Luxus...
delve [delv] v/i. *fig.* (*into*) sich vertiefen (in *acc.*), erforschen, ergründen (*acc.*); graben (*for* nach): ~ *among* stöbern in (*dat.*).
de·mag·net·ize [ˌdiːˈmægnɪtaɪz] v/t. entmagnetisieren.
dem·a·gog [ˈdeməgɒg] *Am.* → **demagogue**; **dem·a·gog·ic**, **dem·a·gog·i·cal** [ˌdeməˈgɒgɪk(l)] *adj.* □ demagogisch, aufwieglerisch; **dem·a·gogue** [-gɒg] s. Dema'goge m; **dem·a·gog·y** [-gɪ] s. Demago'gie f.
de·mand [dɪˈmɑːnd] **I** v/t. **1.** *Person:* et. verlangen, fordern, begehren (*of, from* von, *a. that* dass, *to do* zu tun): ~ *payment*; **2.** *Sache:* erfordern, verlangen (*acc., that* dass), bedürfen (*gen.*): *the matter ~s great care* die Sache erfordert große Sorgfalt; **3.** *oft* ⚖ beanspruchen; **4.** wissen wollen, fragen nach: *the police ~ed his name*; **II** s. **5.** Verlangen n, Forderung f, Ersuchen n: *on* ~ auf Verlangen, b) ✝ bei Vorlage, bei Sicht; **6.** ✝ (*for*) Nachfrage f (nach), Bedarf m (an *dat.*) (*Ggs.* **supply**): *in* ~ *a. fig.* gefragt, begehrt, gesucht; **7.** (*on*) Anspruch m, Anforderung f (an *acc.*); Beanspruchung f (*gen.*): *make great ~s on* sehr in Anspruch nehmen (*acc.*), große Anforderungen stellen an (*acc.*); **8.** ⚖ (Rechts-)Anspruch m, Forderung f; ~ **bill** s. ✝ Am. Sichtwechsel m; ~ **de·pos·it** s. ✝ Sichteinlage f; ~ **draft** → **demand bill**.
de·mand·ing [dɪˈmɑːndɪŋ] *adj.* **1.** anspruchsvoll (*a. fig. Musik etc.*), schwierig; **2.** genau, streng; **3.** fordernd.
de·mand| man·age·ment s. Nachfragesteuerung f; ~ **note** s. **1.** Brit. Zahlungsaufforderung f; **2.** Sichtwechsel m; ~ **pull** s. 'Nachfrageinflati,on f.
de·mar·cate [ˈdiːmɑːkeɪt] v/t. a. fig. abgrenzen (*from* gegen, von); **de·mar·ca·tion** [ˌdiːmɑːˈkeɪʃn] s. Abgrenzung f, Grenzziehung f: *line of* ~ a) Grenzlinie f (a. fig.), b) pol. Demarkationslinie f, c) fig. Trennungslinie f, -strich m; ~ *dispute* Kompetenzstreit unter Gewerkschaften.
dé·marche [deɪˈmɑːʃ] (*Fr.*) s. De'marche f, diplo'matischer Schritt.
de·mean¹ [dɪˈmiːn] v/t.: ~ *o.s.* sich benehmen, sich verhalten.

de·mean² [dɪˈmiːn] v/t.: ~ *o.s.* sich erniedrigen; **de'mean·ing** [-nɪŋ] *adj.* erniedrigend.
de·mean·o(u)r [dɪˈmiːnə] s. Benehmen n, Verhalten n, Haltung f.
de·ment·ed [dɪˈmentɪd] *adj.* □ wahnsinnig, verrückt (F a. fig.); **de'men·ti·a** [-nʃɪə] s. 🌡 **1.** Schwachsinn m; **2.** Wahn-, Irrsinn m.
de·mer·it [diːˈmerɪt] s. **1.** Schuld(haftigkeit) f, Fehler m, Mangel m; **2.** Unwürdigkeit f; **3.** Nachteil m, schlechte Seite; **4.** *mst* ~ *mark* ped. Am. Tadel m, Minuspunkt m.
dem·e·ra·ra sug·ar [ˌdeməˈreərə] s. brauner (Rohr)Zucker.
de·mesne [dɪˈmeɪn] s. ⚖ Eigenbesitz m, freier Grundbesitz; Landgut n, Do'mäne f: *Royal* ~ Krongut n; **2.** fig. Do'mäne f, Gebiet n.
'dem·i|·god [ˈdemɪ-] s. Halbgott m; **'~·john** [-dʒɒn] s. Korbflasche f, 'Glasbal,lon m.
de·mil·i·ta·rize [ˌdiːˈmɪlɪtəraɪz] v/t. entmilitarisieren.
dem·i|·monde [ˌdemɪˈmɔ̃:nd] s. Halbwelt f; **~·'pen·sion** s. 'Halbpensi,on f; **~·rep** [ˈdemɪrep] s. Frau f von zweifelhaftem Ruf.
de·mise [dɪˈmaɪz] ⚖ **I** s. **1.** Be'sitzüber-,tragung f *od.* -verpachtung f: ~ *of the Crown* Übergehen n der Krone *an den Nachfolger*; **2.** Ableben n, Tod m; **II** v/t. **3.** *allg.* et. über'tragen, a. verpachten *od.* vermachen.
dem·i·sem·i·qua·ver [ˈdemɪsemɪˌkweɪvə] s. ♪ Zweiunddreißigstel(note f) n.
de·mis·sion [dɪˈmɪʃn] s. Rücktritt m, Abdankung f, Demissi'on f.
de·mo [ˈdeməʊ] s. F **1.** ‚Demo' f (*Demonstration*); **2.** a) Vorführband n, b) Vorführwagen m.
de·mob [ˌdiːˈmɒb] v/t. Brit. F → **demobilize** 1b.
de·mo·bi·li·za·tion [ˈdiːˌməʊbɪlaɪˈzeɪʃn] s. Demobilisierung f: a) Abrüstung f, b) Entlassung f aus dem Wehrdienst; **de·mo·bi·lize** [diːˈməʊbɪlaɪz] v/t. **1.** demobilisieren: a) abrüsten, b) *Truppen* entlassen, *Heer* auflösen; **2.** ✕ *Kriegsschiff* außer Dienst stellen.
de·moc·ra·cy [dɪˈmɒkrəsɪ] s. **1.** Demokra'tie f; **2.** 🏛 Am. die Demo'kratische Par'tei (*od. deren Grundsätze*); **dem·o·crat** [ˈdeməkræt] s. **1.** Demo-'krat(in); **2.** 🏛 Am. pol. Demo'krat(in), Mitglied n der Demo'kratischen Par'tei; **dem·o·crat·ic** [ˌdeməˈkrætɪk] *adj.* (□ ~*ally*) **1.** demo'kratisch; **2.** 🏛 pol. Am. demo'kratisch (*die Demokratische Partei betreffend*); **de·moc·ra·ti·za·tion** [dɪˌmɒkrətaɪˈzeɪʃn] s. Demokratisierung f; **de·moc·ra·tize** [dɪˈmɒkrətaɪz] v/t. demokratisieren.
dé·mo·dé [ˌdeɪməʊˈdeɪ] (*Fr.*), **de·mod·ed** [diːˈməʊdɪd] *adj.* altmodisch, außer Mode.
de·mog·ra·pher [diːˈmɒgrəfə] s. Demo'graph m; **de'mog·ra·phy** [-fɪ] s. Demogra'phie f.
de·mol·ish [dɪˈmɒlɪʃ] v/t. **1.** ab-, niederreißen; **2.** *Festung* schleifen; **3.** ✕ sprengen, *a. fig.* (a. j-n) vernichten, ka'puttmachen; **5.** *sport* F ‚über'fahren'; **dem·o·li·tion** [ˌdeməˈlɪʃn] s. **1.** Abbruch m, Niederreißen n; **2.** Schleifen n (*Festung*); **3.** ✕ Spreng...: ~ *bomb* Sprengbombe f; ~ *squad* Sprengkommando n; **4.** Vernichtung f.
de·mon (*myth. oft* *daemon*) [ˈdiːmən] **I** s. **1.** 'Dämon m, böser Geist, 'Satan m (a. fig.); **2.** fig. Teufelskerl m: ~ *for work* ‚Wühler' m, unermüdlicher Ar-

beiter; **II** *adj.* **3.** dä'monisch, *fig a.* wild, besessen.

de·mon·e·ti·za·tion [di:ˌmʌnɪtaɪ'zeɪʃn] *s.* Außer'kurssetzung *f*, Entwertung *f*; **de·mon·e·tize** [ˌdi:'mʌnɪtaɪz] *v/t.* außer Kurs setzen.

de·mo·ni·ac [dɪ'məʊnɪæk] **I** *adj.* **1.** dä'monisch, teuflisch; **2.** besessen, rasend, tobend; **II** *s.* **3.** Besessene(r *m*) *f*; **de·mo·ni·a·cal** [ˌdi:məʊ'naɪəkl] *adj.* □ → *demoniac* 1, 2; **de·mon·ic** [di:'mɒnɪk] *adj.* (□ ~*ally*) dä'monisch, teuflisch; **de·mon·ism** ['di:mənɪzəm] *s.* Dä'monenglaube *m*; **de·mon·ize** ['di:mənaɪz] *v/t.* dämonisieren, *fig. a.* verteufeln; **de·mon·ol·o·gy** [ˌdi:mə'nɒlədʒɪ] *s.* Dä'monenlehre *f*.

de·mon·stra·ble ['demənstrəbl] *adj.* □ beweisbar, nachweislich; **dem·on·strate** ['demənstreɪt] **I** *v/t.* **1.** demonstrieren: a) be-, nachweisen, b) veranschaulichen, darlegen; **2.** vorführen; **II** *v/i.* **3.** demonstrieren, e-e Demonstrati'on veranstalten; **dem·on·stra·tion** [ˌdemən'streɪʃn] *s.* **1.** Demon'strierung *f*, Veranschaulichung *f*, Darstellung *f*; **2.** a) Beweis *m* (*of* für), b) Beweisführung *f*; **3.** Vorführung *f*, Demonstrati'on *f* (*to* vor *j-m*): ~ *car* Vorführwagen *m*; **4.** (Gefühls)Äußerung *f*, Bekundung *f*; **5.** Demonstrati'on *f* (*a. pol. u.* ✕), Kundgebung *f*; **6.** ✕ 'Täuschungsma,növer *n*; **de·mon·stra·tive** [dɪ'mɒnstrətɪv] **I** *adj.* □ **1.** anschaulich (zeigend); über'zeugend, beweiskräftig: *be* ~ *of* → *demonstrate* 1; **2.** demonstra'tiv, ostenta'tiv, auffällig, betont; **3.** ausdrucks-, gefühlvoll; **4.** *ling.* Demonstrativ..., hinweisend: ~ *pronoun*; **II** *s.* **5.** *ling.* Demonstra'tivum *n*; **dem·on·stra·tive·ness** [dɪ'mɒnstrətɪvnɪs] *s.* das Demonstra'tive *od.* Ostenta'tive, Betontheit *f*; **dem·on·stra·tor** [-reɪtə] *s.* **1.** Beweisführer *m*, Erklärer *m*; **2.** ✝ a) Vorführer(in), b) 'Vorführmo,dell *n*; **3.** *pol.* Demon'strant(in); **4.** *univ.* a) Assi'stent *m*, b) ⚕ 'Prosektor *m*.

de·mor·al·i·za·tion [dɪˌmɒrəlaɪ'zeɪʃn] *s.* Demoralisati'on *f*: a) Sittenverfall *m*, Zuchtlosigkeit *f*, b) Entmutigung *f*, Demoralisierung *f*; **de·mor·al·ize** [dɪ'mɒrəlaɪz] *v/t.* demoralisieren: a) (sittlich) verderben, b) zersetzen, c) zermürben, entmutigen, d) die ('Kampf)Mo,ral *od.* die Diszi'plin *der Truppe* unter'graben; **de·mor·al·iz·ing** [dɪ'mɒrəlaɪzɪŋ] *adj.* demoralisierend.

de·mote [ˌdi:'məʊt] *v/t.* **1.** degradieren; **2.** *ped. Am.* zu'rückversetzen.

de·moth(·ball) [ˌdi:'mɒθ(bɔːl)] *v/t.* ✕ *Am. Flugzeuge etc.* ,entmotten', wieder in Dienst stellen.

de·mo·tion [ˌdi:'məʊʃn] *s.* **1.** Degradierung *f*; **2.** *ped. Am.* Zu'rückversetzung *f*.

de·mo·ti·vate [ˌdi:'məʊtɪveɪt] *v/t.* demotivieren.

de·mount [ˌdi:'maʊnt] *v/t.* abmontieren, abnehmen; zerlegen; **de·mount·a·ble** [-təbl] *adj.* abmontierbar; zerlegbar.

de·mur [dɪ'mɜː] **I** *v/i.* **1.** Einwendungen machen, Bedenken äußern (*to* gegen); zögern; **2.** ✝ e-n Rechtseinwand erheben; **II** *s.* **3.** Einwand *m*, Bedenken *n*, Zögern *n*: *without* ~ anstandslos, ohne Zögern.

de·mure [dɪ'mjʊə] *adj.* □ **1.** zimperlich, spröde; **2.** sittsam, prüde; **3.** zu'rückhaltend; **4.** gesetzt, ernst, nüchtern; **de·'mure·ness** [-nɪs] *s.* **1.** Zimperlichkeit *f*; **2.** Zu'rückhaltung *f*; **3.** Gesetztheit *f*.

de·mur·rage [dɪ'mʌrɪdʒ] *s.* ✝ **1.** a) ⚓

'Überliegezeit *f*, b) 🚂 zu langes Stehen (*bei der Entladung*); **2.** a) ⚓ ('Über-)Liegegeld *n*, b) 🚂 Wagenstandgeld *n*, c) Lagergeld *n*.

de·mur·rer [dɪ'mʌrə] *s.* ✝ Rechtseinwand *m*.

de·my [dɪ'maɪ] *pl.* -'mies [-aɪz] *s.* **1.** Sti-pendi'at *m* (*Magdalen College, Oxford*); **2.** *ein Papierformat.*

den [den] *s.* **1.** Lager *n*, Bau *m*, Höhle *f wilder Tiere:* *lion's* ~ Löwengrube *f*, *fig.* Höhle des Löwen; **2.** *fig.* Höhle *f*, Versteck *n*: *robber's* ~ Räuberhöhle; ~ *of vice* Lasterhöhle; **3.** a) (gemütliches) Zimmer, ,Bude' *f*, b) Arbeitszimmer *n*, c) *contp.* ,Loch' *n*, Höhle *f*.

de·na·tion·al·ize [ˌdi:'næʃnəlaɪz] *v/t.* **1.** entnationalisieren, den natio'nalen Cha'rakter nehmen (*dat.*); **2.** *j-m* die Staatsbürgerschaft aberkennen; **3.** ✝ entstaatlichen, reprivatisieren.

de·nat·u·ral·ize [ˌdi:'nætʃrəlaɪz] *v/t.* **1.** s-r wahren Na'tur entfremden; **2.** *j-n* denaturalisieren, ausbürgern.

de·na·ture [ˌdi:'neɪtʃə] *v/t.* 🔬 denaturieren.

de·na·zi·fi·ca·tion [di:ˌnɑːtsɪfɪ'keɪʃn] *s. pol.* Entnazifizierung *f*.

den·dri·form [dendrɪfɔːm] *adj.* baumförmig; **'den·droid** [-rɔɪd] *adj.* baumähnlich; **'den·dro·lite** [-rəlaɪt] *s.* Pflanzenversteinerung *f*; **den·drol·o·gy** [den'drɒlədʒɪ] *s.* Dendrolo'gie *f*, Baumkunde *f*.

dene¹ [di:n] *s. Brit.* (Sand)Düne *f*.

dene² [di:n] *s.* kleines Tal.

de·ni·a·ble [dɪ'naɪəbl] *adj.* abzuleugnen(d), zu verneinen(d); **de·ni·al** [dɪ'naɪəl] *s.* **1.** Ablehnung *f*, Verweigerung *f*, -sagung *f*; Absage *f*, abschlägige Antwort: *take no* ~ sich nicht abweisen lassen; **2.** Verneinung *f*, Leugnen *n*, Ab-, Verleugnung *f*: *official* ~ Dementi *n*.

de·nic·o·tin·ize [ˌdi:nɪ'kɒtɪnaɪz] *v/t.* ent-nikotisieren: ~*d* nikotinfrei, -arm.

de·ni·er¹ [dɪ'naɪə] *s.* **1.** Leugner(in); **2.** Verweigerer *m*.

de·nier² ['denɪə] *s.* ✝ Deni'er *m* (*Einheit für die Fadenstärke bei Seidengarn etc.*).

de·nier³ [dɪ'nɪə] *s. hist.* Deni'er *m* (*Münze*).

den·i·grate ['denɪgreɪt] *v/t.* anschwärzen, verunglimpfen; **den·i·gra·tion** [ˌdenɪ'greɪʃn] *s.* Anschwärzung *f*, Verunglimpfung *f*.

den·im ['denɪm] *s.* **1.** Köper *m*; **2.** *pl.* Overall *m od.* Jeans *pl.* aus Köper.

den·i·zen ['denɪzn] *s.* **1.** Ein-, Bewohner *m* (*a. fig.*); **2.** *hist. Brit.* (teilweise) eingebürgerter Ausländer; **3.** *et.* Eingebürgertes (*Tier, Pflanze, Wort*); **4.** Stammgast *m*.

de·nom·i·nate [dɪ'nɒmɪneɪt] *v/t.* (be-) nennen, bezeichnen; **de·nom·i·na·tion** [dɪˌnɒmɪ'neɪʃn] *s.* **1.** Benennung *f*, Bezeichnung *f*; Name *m*; **2.** Gruppe *f*, Klasse *f*; **3.** (*Maß- etc.*)Einheit *f*; Nennwert *m* (*Banknoten*): *shares in small* ~*s* Aktien kleiner Stückelung; **4.** a) Konfessi'on *f*, Bekenntnis *n*, b) Sekte *f*; **de·nom·i·na·tion·al** [dɪˌnɒmɪ'neɪʃənl] *adj.* konfessio'nell, Konfessions..., Bekenntnis...: ~ *school*; **de·nom·i·na·tion·al·ism** [dɪˌnɒmɪ'neɪʃnəlɪzəm] *s.* Prin'zip *n* des konfessio'nellen 'Unterrichts; **de·nom·i·na·tor** [dɪ'nɒmɪneɪtə] *s.* ⚹ Nenner *m*: *common* ~ gemeinsamer Nenner (*a. fig.*); → *reduce* 11.

de·no·ta·tion [ˌdi:nəʊ'teɪʃn] *s.* **1.** Bezeichnung *f*; **2.** Bedeutung *f*, Be'griffs,umfang *m*; **de·note** [dɪ'nəʊt] *v/t.* **1.** be-, kennzeichnen, anzeigen, andeu-

ten; **2.** bedeuten.

dé·noue·ment [deɪ'nu:mãːŋ] (*Fr.*) *s.* **1.** Lösung *f* (*des Knotens im Drama etc.*); **2.** Ausgang *m*.

de·nounce [dɪ'naʊns] *v/t.* **1.** öffentlich anprangern, brandmarken, verurteilen; **2.** anzeigen, *contp.* denunzieren (*to* bei); **3.** *Vertrag* kündigen; **de'nounce·ment** [-mənt] *s.* **1.** (öffentliche) Anprangerung *od.* Verurteilung; **2.** Anzeige *f*, *contp.* Denunziati'on *f*; **3.** Kündigung *f* (*of gen.*), Rücktritt *m* (*vom Vertrag*).

dense [dens] *adj.* □ **1.** dicht (*a. phys.*), dick (*Nebel etc.*); **2.** gedrängt, eng; **3.** *fig.* beschränkt, schwer von Begriff; **4.** *phot.* dicht, kräftig (*Negativ*); **'dense·ness** [-nɪs] *s.* **1.** Dichtheit *f*, Dichte *f*; **2.** *fig.* Beschränktheit *f*, Schwerfälligkeit *f*; **'den·si·ty** [-sətɪ] *s.* **1.** Dichte *f* (*a.* 📷, *phys.*), Dichtheit *f*: *traffic* ~ Verkehrsdichte; **2.** Gedrängtheit *f*, Enge *f*; **3.** *fig.* Beschränktheit *f*, Dummheit *f*; **4.** *phot.* Dichte *f*, Schwärzung *f*.

dent [dent] **I** *s.* Beule *f*, Einbeulung *f*: *make a* ~ *in* F a) ein Loch reißen in (*Ersparnisse etc.*), b) *j-s Stolz etc.* ,anknacksen'; **II** *v/t. u. v/i.* (sich) einbeulen: ~ *s.o.'s image fig.* j-s Image schaden.

den·tal ['dentl] **I** *adj.* **1.** 🦷 Zahn...; zahnärztlich: ~ *floss* Zahnseide *f*; ~ *plate* Platte *f*, Zahnersatz *m*; ~ *surgeon* Zahnarzt *m*; ~ *technician* Zahntechniker(in); **2.** *ling.* Dental..., Zahn...: ~ *sound* → 3; **II** *s.* **3.** *ling.* Den'tal(laut) *m*; **den·tate** ['denteɪt] *adj.* ⚘, *zo.* gezähnt; **den·ta·tion** [den-'teɪʃn] *s.* ⚘, *zo.* Zähnung *f*; **den·ti·cle** ['dentɪkl] *s.* Zähnchen *n*; **den·tic·u·lat·ed** [den'tɪkjʊleɪtɪd] *adj.* **1.** gezähnt; **2.** gezackt; **den·ti·form** ['dentɪfɔːm] *adj.* zahnförmig; **den·ti·frice** ['dentɪfrɪs] *s.* Zahnputzmittel *n*; **den·tils** ['dentɪlz] *s. pl.* 🏛 Zahnschnitt *m*; **den·tine** ['denti:n] *s.* 🦷 Den'tin *n*, Zahnbein *n*; **den·tist** ['dentɪst] *s.* Zahnarzt *m*, -ärztin *f*; **den·tist·ry** ['dentɪstrɪ] *s.* Zahnheilkunde *f*; **den·ti·tion** [den'tɪʃn] *s.* 🦷 **1.** Zahnnen *n* (*der Kinder*); **2.** 'Zahnformel *f*, -sy,stem *n*; **den·ture** ['dentʃə] *s.* **1.** *anat.* Gebiss *n*; **2.** a) künstliches Gebiss, ('Voll)Pro,these *f*, b) ('Teil)Pro,these *f*.

de·nu·cle·ar·ize [ˌdi:'nju:klɪəraɪz] *v/t.* a'tomwaffenfrei machen, e-e atomwaffenfreie Zone schaffen in (*dat.*).

de·nu·da·tion [ˌdi:nju:'deɪʃn] *s.* **1.** Entblößung *f*; **2.** *geol.* Abtragung *f*; **de·nude** [dɪ'nju:d] *v/t.* **1.** (*of*) entblößen (von), berauben (*gen.*) (*a. fig.*); **2.** *geol.* bloßlegen.

de·nun·ci·a·tion [dɪnʌnsɪ'eɪʃn] → *denouncement*; **de·nun·ci·a·tor** [dɪ'nʌnsɪeɪtə] *s.* Denunzi'ant(in); **de·nun·ci·a·to·ry** [dɪ'nʌnsɪətərɪ] *adj.* **1.** denunzierend; **2.** anprangernd, brandmarkend.

de·ny [dɪ'naɪ] *v/t.* **1.** ab-, bestreiten, in Abrede stellen, dementieren, (ab)leugnen, verneinen: *it cannot be denied that ...*, *there is no* ~*ing* (*the fact*) *that ...* es lässt sich nicht *od.* es ist nicht zu leugnen *od.* bestreiten, dass; *I* ~ *saying so* ich bestreite, dass ich das gesagt habe; ~ *a charge* e-e Beschuldigung zurückweisen; **2.** *Glauben, Freund* verleugnen; *Unterschrift* nicht anerkennen; **3.** *Bitte etc.* ablehnen; ✝ *Antrag* abweisen; *j-m et.* abschlagen, verweigern, versagen: ~ *o.s. the pleasure* sich das Vergnügen versagen; *he was denied the privilege* das Vorrecht wurde ihm versagt; *he was hard to* ~

es war schwer, ihn abzuweisen; ***she denied herself to him*** sie versagte sich ihm; **4.** ***~ o.s. to s.o.*** sich vor j-m verleugnen lassen.

de·o·dor·ant [diːˈəʊdərənt] **I** *s.* De(s)odo'rant *n*: ***roll-on ~*** 'Deoroller *m*; **II** *adj.* de(s)odorierend: ***~ spray*** 'Deospray *m od. n*; **de·o·dor·i·za·tion** [diːˌəʊdəraɪˈzeɪʃn] *s.* Desodorierung *f*; **de·o·dor·ize** [diːˈəʊdəraɪz] *v/t.* de(s)odorieren; **de'o·dor·iz·er** [-raɪzə] → ***deodorant*** I.

de·ox·i·dize [diːˈɒksɪdaɪz] *v/t.* ⚗ den Sauerstoff entziehen (*dat.*).

de·part [dɪˈpɑːt] *v/i.* **1.** (***for*** nach) weg-, fortgehen, *bsd.* abreisen, abfahren; **2.** 🚆 *etc.* abgehen, abfahren, ✈ abfliegen; **3.** *a.* ~ (***from***) ***this life*** 'hinscheiden, entschlafen, sterben; **4.** (***from***) abweichen (von *e-r Regel*, *der Wahrheit etc.*), *Plan etc.* ändern, aufgeben: ***~ from one's word*** sein Wort brechen; **de'part·ed** [-tɪd] *adj.* **1.** vergangen; **2.** verstorben: ***the ~*** der *od.* die Verstorbene, *coll.* die Verstorbenen; **de'part·ment** [-mənt] *s.* **1.** Fach *n*, Gebiet *n*, Res'sort *n*, Geschäftsbereich *m*: ***that's your ~!*** F das ist dein Ressort!; **2.** Abteilung *f*: ***~ of German*** *univ.* germanistische Abteilung; ***export ~*** ☤ Exportabteilung; ***~ store*** Waren-, Kaufhaus *n*; **3.** *pol.* Departe'ment *n* (*in Frankreich*); **4.** Dienst-, Geschäftsstelle *f*, Amt *n*: ***health ~*** Gesundheitsamt; **5.** *pol.* Ministerium *n*: ***℞ of Defense*** *Am.* Verteidigungsministerium; ***℞ of the Interior*** *Am.* Innenministerium; **6.** ⚔ Bereich *m*, Zone *f*; **de·part·men·tal** [ˌdiːpɑːtˈmentl] *adj.* **1.** Abteilungs...; Bezirks...; Fach...; **2.** Ministerial...; **de·part·men·tal·ize** [ˌdiːpɑːtˈmentəlaɪz] *v/t.* in (viele) Abteilungen gliedern.

de·par·ture [dɪˈpɑːtʃə] *s.* **1.** Weggang *m*, *bsd.* ⚔ Abzug *m*: ***take one's ~*** sich verabschieden, weg-, fortgehen; **2.** a) Abreise *f*, b) 🚆 *etc.* Abfahrt *f*, ✈ Abflug *m*: (***time of***) ~ Abfahrts- *od.* Abflugzeit *f*; ***~ gate*** Flugsteig *m*; ***~ lounge*** Abflughalle *f*; ***~ platform*** Abfahrtsbahnsteig *m*; **3.** Abweichen *n*, Abweichung *f* (***from*** von *e-m Plan*, *e-r Regel etc.*); **4.** *fig.* Anfang *m*, Beginn *m*: ***a new ~*** a) ein neuer Anfang, b) ein neuer Weg, ein neues Verfahren; ***point of ~*** Ausgangspunkt *m*; **5.** 'Hinscheiden *n*, Tod *m*.

de·pend [dɪˈpend] *v/i.* **1.** (***on***, ***upon***) abhängen (von), ankommen (auf *acc.*): ***it ~s on the weather***; ***it ~s on you***; ***~ing on the quantity used*** je nach (der zu verwendenden) Menge; ***~ing on whether*** je nachdem, ob; ***that ~s*** F das kommt (ganz) darauf an, je nachdem; **2.** (***on***, ***upon***) a) abhängig sein (von), b) angewiesen sein (auf *acc.*): ***he ~s on my help***; **3.** sich verlassen (***on***, ***upon*** auf *acc.*): ***you may ~ on that man***; ***~ upon it!*** verlass dich drauf!; **de·pend·a·bil·i·ty** [dɪˌpendəˈbɪlətɪ] *s.* Zuverlässigkeit *f*; **de'pend·a·ble** [-dəbl] *adj.* □ verlässlich, zuverlässig; **de·pend·ance** [-dəns] *Am.* → ***dependence***; **de·pend·ant** [-dənt] **I** *s.* Abhängige(r *m*) *f*, *bsd.* (Fa'milien)Angehörige(r *m*) *f*; **II** *adj. Am.* → ***dependent*** I; **de'pend·ence** [-dəns] *s.* **1.** (***on***, ***upon***) Abhängigkeit *f* (von), Angewiesensein *n* (auf *acc.*); Bedingtsein *n* (durch); **2.** Vertrauen *n*, Verlass *m* (***on***, ***upon*** auf *acc.*); **3.** ***in ~*** ⚖ in der Schwebe; **4.** Nebengebäude *n*, Depen'dance *f*; **de'pend·en·cy** [-dənsɪ] **1.** → ***dependence*** 1; **2.** *pol.* Schutzgebiet *n*, Kolo'nie *f*; **de'pend·ent** [-dənt] **I** *adj.* **1.** (***on***, ***upon***) abhängig (von): a) angewiesen (auf *acc.*), b) bedingt (durch); **2.** vertrauend, sich verlassend (***on***, ***upon*** auf *acc.*); **3.** (***on***) 'untergeordnet (*dat.*), abhängig (von), unselbstständig: ***~ clause*** *ling.* Nebensatz *m*; **4.** her'abhängend (***from*** von); **II** *s.* **5.** *Am.* → ***dependant*** I.

de·peo·ple [ˌdiːˈpiːpl] *v/t.* entvölkern.

de·per·son·al·ize [ˌdiːˈpɜːsnəlaɪz] *v/t.* **1.** *psych.* entper'sönlichen; **2.** 'unperˌsönlich machen.

de·pict [dɪˈpɪkt] *v/t.* **1.** (ab)malen, zeichnen, darstellen; **2.** schildern, beschreiben, veranschaulichen.

dep·i·late [ˈdepɪleɪt] *v/t.* enthaaren, depilieren; **dep·i·la·tion** [ˌdepɪˈleɪʃn] *s.* Enthaarung *f*; **de·pil·a·to·ry** [dɪˈpɪlətərɪ] **I** *adj.* enthaarend; **II** *s.* Enthaarungsmittel *n*.

de·plane [ˌdiːˈpleɪn] *v/t. u. v/i.* aus dem Flugzeug ausladen (aussteigen).

de·plen·ish [dɪˈplenɪʃ] *v/t.* entleeren.

de·plete [dɪˈpliːt] *v/t.* **1.** (ent)leeren; **2.** Raubbau treiben mit; *Vorräte*, *Kräfte etc.* erschöpfen; *Bestand etc.* dezimieren: ***~ a lake of fish*** e-n See abfischen; **de·ple·tion** [dɪˈpliːʃn] *s.* **1.** Entleerung *f*; **2.** Raubbau *m*; Erschöpfung *f*; ⚕ *a.* Erschöpfungszustand *m*; ☤ *a.* Sub'stanzverlust *m*; ***~ of the ozone layer*** Ozonabbau *m*.

de·plor·a·ble [dɪˈplɔːrəbl] *adj.* □ **1.** bedauerns-, beklagenswert; **2.** erbärmlich, kläglich; **de·plore** [dɪˈplɔː] *v/t.* beklagen: a) bedauern, b) miss'billigen, c) betrauern.

de·ploy [dɪˈplɔɪ] **I** *v/t.* **1.** ⚔ a) aufmarschieren lassen, entwickeln, entfalten, b) *a. allg.* verteilen, *Raketen etc.* aufstellen; **2.** *Arbeitskräfte etc.* einsetzen; **3.** *fig.* anwenden, einsetzen; **II** *v/i.* **4.** sich entwickeln, sich entfalten, ausschwärmen, Ge'fechtsformatiˌon annehmen; **III** *s.* **5.** → **de'ploy·ment** [-mənt] *s.* **1.** ⚔ Entfaltung *f*, -wicklung *f*, Aufmarsch *m*; Gliederung *f*, Aufstellung *f*; **2.** ☤ *etc.* Einsatz *m*, Verteilung *f*.

de·poi·son [ˌdiːˈpɔɪzn] *v/t.* entgiften.

de·po·lar·ize [ˌdiːˈpəʊləraɪz] *v/t.* **1.** ϟ, *phys.* depolarisieren; **2.** *fig.* *Überzeugung etc.* erschüttern.

de·po·lit·i·cize [ˌdiːpəˈlɪtɪsaɪz] *v/t.* entpolitisieren.

de·pone [dɪˈpəʊn] → ***depose*** II; **de'po·nent** [-nənt] **I** *adj.* **1.** ***~ verb*** *ling.* → 2; **II** *s.* **2.** *ling.* De'ponens *n*; **3.** ⚖ vereidigter Zeuge; *in Urkunden*: *der* (*die*) Erschienene.

de·pop·u·late [ˌdiːˈpɒpjʊleɪt] *v/t.* (*v/i.* sich) entvölkern; **de·pop·u·la·tion** [diːˌpɒpjʊˈleɪʃn] *s.* Entvölkerung *f*.

de·port [dɪˈpɔːt] *v/t.* **1.** (zwangsweise) fortschaffen; **2.** *pol.* a) deportieren, b) ausweisen, *Ausländer* abschieben, c) *hist.* verbannen; **3.** ***~ o.s.*** sich *gut etc.* betragen *od.* benehmen; **de·por·ta·tion** [ˌdiːpɔːˈteɪʃn] *s.* Deportati'on *f*, Zwangsverschickung *f*; Ausweisung *f*; *hist.* Verbannung *f*; **de·por·tee** [ˌdiːpɔːˈtiː] *s.* Deportierte(r *m*) *f*; **de'port·ment** [-mənt] *s.* **1.** Benehmen *n*, Betragen *n*, Verhalten *n*; **2.** (Körper)Haltung *f*.

de·pos·a·ble [dɪˈpəʊzəbl] *adj.* absetzbar; **de·pos·al** [dɪˈpəʊzl] *s.* Absetzung *f*; **de·pose** [dɪˈpəʊz] **I** *v/t.* **1.** absetzen, entheben (***from*** *gen.*); entthronen; **2.** ⚖ eidlich erklären, unter Eid zu Proto'koll geben; **II** *v/i.* (*bsd.* in Form e-r schriftlichen, beeideten Erklärung) aussagen *od.* bezeugen (***to s.th.*** et., ***that*** dass).

de·pos·it [dɪˈpɒzɪt] **I** *v/t.* **1.** ab-, niedersetzen, ab-, niederlegen; *Eier* (ab)legen; **2.** ⚗, ⊛, *geol.* ablagern, -setzen, anschwemmen; **3.** *Geld* a) einzahlen, *a. Sache* hinter'legen, deponieren; über'geben, b) anzahlen; **II** *v/i.* **4.** ⚗ sich absetzen *od.* ablagern *od.* niederschlagen; **III** *s.* **5.** ⚗, ⊛ Ablagerung *f*, (Boden)Satz *m*, Niederschlag *m*, Sedi'ment *n*; Schicht *f*, Belag *m*; **6.** ⚒, *geol.* Ablagerung *f*, Lager *n*, Flöz *n*; **7.** ☤ a) De'pot *n*: ***place on ~*** einzahlen, hinterlegen, b) Einzahlung *f*, Einlage *f*, Guthaben *n*: ***~s*** Depositen; ***~ account*** Termineinlagekonto *n*; **8.** Flaschenpfand *n*, *schweiz.* De'pot *n*.; **de'pos·i·tar·y** [-tərɪ] *s.* **1.** Deposi'tar(in), Verwahrer(in); **2.** → ***depot*** 1.

dep·o·si·tion [ˌdepəˈzɪʃn] *s.* **1.** Amtsenthebung *f*; Absetzung *f* (***from*** von); **2.** ⚗, ⊛, *geol.* Ablagerung *f*, Niederschlag *m*; **3.** ⚖ (Proto'koll *n od.* Abgabe *f* e-r beeideten) Erklärung *od.* Aussage; **4.** (Bild *n* der) Kreuzabnahme *f Christi*; **de·pos·i·tor** [dɪˈpɒzɪtə] *s.* ☤ a) Hinter'leger(in), b) Einzahler(in), c) Kontoinhaber(in); **de·pos·i·to·ry** [dɪˈpɒzɪtərɪ] *s.* **1.** a) Aufbewahrungsort *m*, b) → ***depot*** 1; **2.** *fig.* Fundgrube *f*.

de·pot [ˈdepəʊ] *s.* **1.** De'pot *n*, Lagerhaus *n*, -platz *m*, Niederlage *f*; **2.** *Am.* Bahnhof *m*; **3.** ⚔ De'pot *n*: a) Gerätepark *m*, b) (Nachschub)Lager *n*, c) Sammelplatz *m*, d) Ersatztruppenteil *m*; **4.** ⚕ De'pot *n*.

dep·ra·va·tion [ˌdeprəˈveɪʃn] → ***depravity***; **de·prave** [dɪˈpreɪv] *v/t. moralisch* verderben; **de·praved** [dɪˈpreɪvd] *adj.* verderbt, verkommen, verworfen, schlecht; **de·prav·i·ty** [dɪˈprævətɪ] *s.* **1.** Verderbtheit *f*, Verworfenheit *f*; Schlechtigkeit *f*; **2.** böse Tat.

dep·re·cate [ˈdeprɪkeɪt] *v/t.* miss'billigen, verurteilen, verwerfen; **'dep·re·cat·ing** [-tɪŋ] *adj.* □ **1.** miss'billigend, ablehnend; **2.** entschuldigend; **3.** wegwerfend, (bescheiden) abwehrend; **dep·re·ca·tion** [ˌdeprɪˈkeɪʃn] *s.* 'Missbilligung *f*; **'dep·re·ca·tor** [-tə] *s.* Gegner(in); **'dep·re·ca·to·ry** [-kətərɪ] → ***deprecating***.

de·pre·ci·ate [dɪˈpriːʃɪeɪt] **I** *v/t.* **1.** a) gering schätzen, b) her'absetzen, -würdigen; **2.** a) *im Preis od. Wert* her'absetzen, b) abschreiben; **3.** ☤ *Währung* abwerten; **II** *v/i.* **4.** im Preis *od.* Wert sinken; **de'pre·ci·at·ing** [-tɪŋ] → ***depreciatory***; **de·pre·ci·a·tion** [dɪˌpriːʃɪˈeɪʃn] *s.* **1.** a) Geringschätzung *f*, b) Her'absetzung *f*, -würdigung *f*; **2.** ☤ a) Wertminderung *f*, Kursverlust *m*, b) Abschreibung *f*, c) Abwertung *f*: ***~ fund*** Abschreibungsfond *m*; **de'pre·ci·a·to·ry** [-ʃjətərɪ] *adj.* geringschätzig, verächtlich, abschätzig.

dep·re·da·tion [ˌdeprɪˈdeɪʃn] *s. oft pl.* **1.** Plünderung *f*, Verwüstung *f*; **2.** *fig.* Raubzug *m*; **dep·re·da·tor** [ˈdeprɪdeɪtə] *s.* Plünderer *m*.

de·press [dɪˈpres] *v/t.* **1.** a) *j-n* deprimieren, bedrücken, b) *Stimmung* drücken; **2.** *Tätigkeit*, *Handel* niederdrücken; *Preis*, *Wert* (her'ab)drücken, senken: ***~ the market*** ☤ die Kurse drücken; **3.** *Leistung etc.* schwächen, her'absetzen; **4.** *Pedal*, *Taste etc.* (nieder)drücken; **de'pres·sant** [-snt] ⚕ **I** *adj.* dämpfend, beruhigend; **II** *s.* Depressi'onsmittel *n*.

de·pressed [dɪˈprest] *adj.* **1.** deprimiert, niedergeschlagen, bedrückt (*Person*), gedrückt (*Stimmung*, *a.* ☤

Börse); **2.** verringert, geschwächt (*Tätigkeit etc.*); **3.** † flau (*Markt*), gedrückt (*Preis*), Not leidend (*Industrie*); **~ a·re·a** *s.* Notstandsgebiet *n.*

de·press·ing [dɪ'presɪŋ] *adj.* □ **1.** deprimierend, bedrückend; **2.** kläglich; **de·'pres·sion** [-eʃn] *s.* **1.** Depressi'on *f*, Niedergeschlagenheit *f*, Ge-, Bedrücktheit *f*; Melancho'lie *f*; **2.** Senkung *f*, Vertiefung *f*; geol. Landsenke *f*; **3.** † Fallen *n* (*Preise*); Wirtschaftskrise *f*, Depressi'on *f*, Flaute *f*, Tiefstand *m*; **4.** ast., surv. Depressi'on *f*; **5.** meteor. Tief(druckgebiet) *n*; **6.** Abnahme *f*, Schwächung *f*; **7.** ✗ Schwäche *f*, Entkräftung *f*; **de'pres·sive** [-sɪv] *adj.* deprimiert, psych. depres'siv.

dep·ri·va·tion [ˌdeprɪ'veɪʃn] *s.* **1.** Beraubung *f*, Entziehung *f*, Entzug *m*; **2.** (schmerzlicher) Verlust; **3.** Entbehrung *f*, Mangel *m*; **4.** psych. Deprivati'on *f*, (Liebes- *etc.*)Entzug *m*; **de·prive** [dɪ'praɪv] *v/t.* **1.** (*of s.th.*) (*j-n od. et.* e-r Sache) berauben, (*j-m* et.) entziehen *od.* nehmen: *be ~d of s.th.* et. entbehren (müssen); **~d child** *psych.* an Liebesentzug leidendes Kind; **~d persons** benachteiligte *od.* unterprivilegierte Personen; **2.** (*of s.th.*) *j-n* ausschließen (von et.), (*j-m* et.) vorenthalten; **3.** eccl. *j-n* absetzen.

depth [depθ] *s.* **1.** Tiefe *f*: *eight feet in ~* acht Fuß tief; *get out of one's ~* den (sicheren) Grund unter den Füßen verlieren (*a. fig.*); *be out of one's ~* a) im *Wasser* nicht mehr stehen können, b) *fig.* ratlos *od.* unsicher sein, ,schwimmen'; *it is beyond my ~* es geht über m-n Horizont; **2.** Tiefe *f* (*als 3. Dimension*): **~ of a cupboard**; **3.** a) a. **~ of focus** *od.* **field** Schärfentiefe *f*, *bsd. phot.* Tiefenschärfe *f*, c) Tiefe *f* (*von Farben, Tönen*); **4.** *oft pl.* Tiefe *f*, Mitte *f*, (*das*) Innerste (*a. fig.*): *in the ~ of night* mitten in der Nacht; *in the ~ of winter* mitten im Winter; *from the ~ of misery* aus tiefstem Elend; **5.** *fig.* a) Tiefe *f*: *~ of meaning*, b) tiefer Sinn, c) Tiefe *f*, Intensi'tät *f*: *~ of grief*; *in ~* eingehend, tief schürfend, d) (Gedanken)Tiefe *f*, Tiefgründigkeit *f*, e) Scharfsinn *m*, f) Dunkelheit *f*, Unklarheit *f*; **6.** ✗ Teufe *f*; **7.** psych. 'Unterbewusstsein *n*: **~ analysis** tiefenpsychologische Analyse; **~ interview** Tiefeninterview *n*; **~ psychology** Tiefenpsychologie *f*; **~ bomb**, **~ charge** *s.* ✗ Wasserbombe *f*.

dep·u·rate ['depjʊreɪt] *v/t.* ✗, ✗, ✗ reinigen, läutern.

dep·u·ta·tion [ˌdepjʊ'teɪʃn] *s.* Deputati'on *f*, Abordnung *f*; **de·pute** [dɪ'pjuːt] *v/t.* **1.** abordnen, delegieren, deputieren; **2.** *Aufgabe etc.* über'tragen (**to** *dat.*); **dep·u·tize** ['depjʊtaɪz] **I** *v/t.* (als Vertreter) ernennen, abordnen; **II** *v/i.* **~ for s.o.** *j-n* vertreten; **dep·u·ty** ['depjʊtɪ] **I** *s.* **1.** (Stell)Vertreter(in), Beauftragte(r *m*) *f*; **2.** *pol.* Abgeordnete(r *m*) *f*; **II** *adj.* **3.** stellvertretend, Vize...: **~ chairman** stellvertretende(r) Vorsitzende(r), Vizepräsident(in).

de·rac·i·nate [dɪ'ræsɪneɪt] *v/t.* entwurzeln (*a. fig.*); ausrotten, vernichten.

de·rail [dɪ'reɪl] *v/i. u. v/t.* entgleisen (lassen); **de'rail·ment** [-mənt] *s.* Entgleisung *f*.

de·range [dɪ'reɪndʒ] *v/t.* **1.** in Unordnung bringen, durchein'ander bringen; **2.** stören; **3.** verrückt machen, (geistig) zerrütten; **de'ranged** [-dʒd] *adj.* **1.** in Unordnung, gestört: *a ~ stomach* e-e Magenverstimmung; **2.** ✗ *a. mentally*

~ geistesgestört; **de'range·ment** [-mənt] *s.* **1.** Unordnung *f*, Durcheinander *n*; **2.** Störung *f*; **3.** ✗ *a. mental ~* Geistesgestörtheit *f*.

de·ra·tion [ˌdiː'ræʃn] *v/t.* die Rationierung von ... aufheben, *Ware* freigeben.

Der·by ['dɑːbɪ] *s.* **1.** *Rennsport:* a) (*das*) englische Derby (*in Epsom*), b) *allg.* Derby *n* (*Pferderennen*); **2.** ♬ *sport* (*bsd.* Lo'kal)Derby *n*; **3.** ♬ *Am.* ,Me'lone' *f*.

de·reg·u·la·tion [ˌdiːregjʊ'leɪʃn] *s.* † Deregulierung *f*, Abbau *m* staatlicher Kontrollen.

der·e·lict ['derɪlɪkt] **I** *adj.* **1.** herrenlos, aufgegeben, verlassen; **2.** her'untergekommen, zerfallen, baufällig; **3.** nachlässig: **~ in duty** pflichtvergessen; **II** *s.* **4.** ✗ herrenloses Gut; **5.** ✗ a) aufgegebenes Schiff, b) treibendes Wrack; **6.** menschliches Wrack, *a.* Obdachlose(r *m*) *f*; **7.** Pflichtvergessene(r *m*) *f*; **der·e·lic·tion** [ˌderɪ'lɪkʃn] *s.* **1.** Aufgeben *n*, Preisgabe *f*; **2.** Verlassenheit *f*; **3.** Vernachlässigung *f*, Versäumnis *n*: **~ of duty** Pflichtversäumnis *f*; **4.** Versagen *n*; **5.** Ver-, Zerfall *m*; **6.** ✗ a) Besitzaufgabe *f*, b) Verlandung *f*, Landgewinn *m* in'folge Rückgangs des Wasserspiegels.

de·re·strict [ˌdiːrɪ'strɪkt] *v/t.* die Einschränkungsmaßnahmen aufheben für; **,de·re'stric·tion** [-kʃn] *s.* Aufhebung *f* der Einschränkungsmaßnahmen, *bsd.* der Geschwindigkeitsbegrenzung.

de·ride [dɪ'raɪd] *v/t.* verlachen, -höhnen; -spotten; **de'rid·er** [-də] *s.* Spötter *m*; **de'rid·ing·ly** [-dɪŋlɪ] *adv.* spöttisch.

de ri·gueur [dərɪ'gɜː] (*Fr.*) *pred. adj.* **1.** streng nach der Eti'kette; **2.** unerlässlich, ,ein Muss'.

de·ri·sion [dɪ'rɪʒn] *s.* Hohn *m*, Spott *m*: **hold in ~** verspotten; **bring into ~** zum Gespött machen; **be the ~ of s.o.** *j-s* Gespött sein; **de·ri·sive** [dɪ'raɪsɪv], **de·ri·so·ry** [dɪ'raɪsərɪ] *adj.* □ höhnisch, spöttisch.

de·riv·a·ble [dɪ'raɪvəbl] *adj.* **1.** ab-, herleitbar (**from** von); **2.** erreichbar, zu gewinnen(d) (**from** aus); **der·i·va·tion** [ˌderɪ'veɪʃn] *s.* **1.** Ab-, Herleitung *f* (*a. ling.*); **2.** Ursprung *m*, Herkunft *f*, Abstammung *f*; **de·riv·a·tive** [dɪ'rɪvətɪv] **I** *adj.* **1.** abgeleitet; **2.** sekun'där; **II** *s.* **3.** *et.* Ab- *od.* Hergeleitetes; **4.** *ling.* Ableitung *f*, abgeleitete Form (*od.* ✗ Funkti'on); **5.** ✗ Deri'vat *n*, Abkömmling *m*; **de·rive** [dɪ'raɪv] **I** *v/t.* **1.** (**from**) herleiten (von), zu'rückführen (auf *acc.*), verdanken (*dat.*): **be ~d from** → 4; **~d income** † abgeleitetes Einkommen; **2.** bekommen, erlangen, gewinnen: **~d from coffee** aus Kaffee gewonnen; **~ profit from** Nutzen ziehen aus; **~ pleasure from** Freude haben an (*dat.*); **3.** ✗, ✗, *ling.* ableiten; **II** *v/i.* **4.** (**from**) (ab)stammen *od.* herrühren *od.* abgeleitet sein *od.* sich ableiten von.

derm [dɜːm], **der·ma** ['dɜːmə] *s.* anat. Haut *f*; **der·mal** ['dɜːml] *adj.* anat. Haut...; **der·ma·ti·tis** [ˌdɜːmə'taɪtɪs] *s.* ✗ Derma'titis *f*, Hautentzündung *f*; **der·ma·tol·o·gist** [ˌdɜːmə'tɒlədʒɪst] *s.* Dermato'loge *m*, Hautarzt *m*; **der·ma·tol·o·gy** [ˌdɜːmə'tɒlədʒɪ] *s.* ✗ Dermatolo'gie *f*.

der·o·gate ['derəgeɪt] **I** *v/i.* (**from**) **1.** Abbruch tun, schaden (*dat.*), beeinträchtigen, schmälern (*acc.*); **2.** abweichen (von *e-r Norm etc.*); **II** *v/t.* **3.** herabsetzen; **der·o·ga·tion** [ˌderə'geɪʃn] *s.* **1.** Beeinträchtigung *f*, Schmälerung *f*, Nachteil *m*; **2.** Her'absetzung *f*; **de·rog·a·to·ry** [dɪ'rɒgətərɪ] *adj.* □ (**to**)

nachteilig (für), abträglich (*dat.*), schädlich (*dat. od.* für): **be ~** schaden, beeinträchtigen; **2.** abfällig, geringschätzig (*Worte*).

der·rick ['derɪk] *s.* **1.** ✗ a) Mastenkran *m*, b) Ausleger *m*; **2.** ✗ Bohrturm *m*; **3.** ✗ Ladebaum *m*.

der·ring-do [ˌderɪŋ'duː] *s.* Verwegenheit *f*, Tollkühnheit *f*.

der·vish ['dɜːvɪʃ] *s.* Derwisch *m*.

de·sal·i·nate [ˌdiː'sælɪneɪt] *v/t.* entsalzen.

des·cant **I** *s.* ['deskænt] **1.** *poet.* Lied *n*, Weise *f*; **2.** ♪ a) Dis'kant *m*, b) variierte Melo'die; **II** *v/i.* [dɪ'skænt] **3.** sich auslassen (**on** über *acc.*); **4.** ♪ diskantieren.

de·scend [dɪ'send] **I** *v/i.* **1.** her'unter-, hin'untersteigen, -gehen, -kommen, -fahren, -fallen, -sinken; ab-, aussteigen; ✗ einfahren; ✈ niedergehen, landen; **2.** sinken, fallen, sich senken (*Straße*), abfallen (*Gebirge*); **3.** *mst* **be ~ed** abstammen, herkommen (**from** von, aus); **4.** (**to**) zufallen (*dat.*), 'übergehen, sich vererben (auf *acc.*); **5.** (**to**) sich hergeben, sich erniedrigen (zu); **6.** (**to**) 'übergehen (zu), eingehen (auf *ein Thema etc.*); **7.** (**on, upon**) sich stürzen (auf *acc.*), herfallen (über *acc.*), einfallen (in *acc.*); her'einbrechen (über *acc.*); *fig. j-n* ,über'fallen' (*Besuch etc.*); **8.** ✗, *ast.* fallen, absteigen; **II** *v/t.* **9.** *Treppe etc.* her'unter-, hin'untersteigen, -gehen *etc.*; **de'scend·ant** [-dənt] *s.* **1.** Nachkomme *m*, Abkömmling *m*; **2.** *ast.* Deszen'dent *m*.

de·scent [dɪ'sent] *s.* **1.** Her'unter-, Hinuntersteigen *n*, Abstieg *m*; Talfahrt *f*; ✗ Einfahrt *f*; ✈ Landung *f*, (*Fallschirm*)Absprung *m*; **2.** Abhang *m*, Abfall *m*, Senkung *f*, Gefälle *n*; **3.** *fig.* Abstieg *m*, Niedergang *m*, Fallen *n*, Sinken *n*; **4.** Abstammung *f*, Herkunft *f*, Geburt *f*; **5.** ✗ Vererbung *f*, 'Übergang *m*, Über'tragung *f*; **6.** (**on, upon**) 'Überfall *m* (auf *acc.*), Einfall *m* (in *acc.*), Angriff *m* (auf *acc.*); **7.** bibl. Ausgießung *f* (*des Heiligen Geistes*); **8.** **~ from the cross** paint. Kreuzabnahme *f*.

de·scrib·a·ble [dɪ'skraɪbəbl] *adj.* zu beschreiben(d); **de·scribe** [dɪ'skraɪb] *v/t.* **1.** beschreiben, schildern; **2.** (**as**) bezeichnen (als), nennen (*acc.*); **3.** *bsd.* ✗ *Kreis, Kurve* beschreiben; **de·scrip·tion** [dɪ'skrɪpʃn] *s.* **1.** Beschreibung *f* (*a.* ✗ *etc.*), Darstellung *f*, Schilderung *f*: **beautiful beyond ~** unbeschreiblich *od.* unsagbar schön; **2.** Bezeichnung *f*; **3.** Art *f*, Sorte *f*: **of the worst ~** schlimmster Art; **de·scrip·tive** [dɪ'skrɪptɪv] *adj.* □ **1.** beschreibend, schildernd: **~ geometry** darstellende Geometrie; **be ~ of** beschreiben, bezeichnen; **2.** anschaulich (geschrieben *od.* schreibend).

de·scry [dɪ'skraɪ] *v/t.* gewahren, wahrnehmen, erspähen, entdecken.

des·e·crate ['desɪkreɪt] *v/t.* entweihen, -heiligen, schänden; **des·e·cra·tion** [ˌdesɪ'kreɪʃn] *s.* Entweihung *f*, -heiligung *f*, Schändung *f*.

de·seg·re·gate [ˌdiː'segrɪgeɪt] *v/t.* die Rassenschranken aufheben in (*dat.*); **de·seg·re·ga·tion** [ˌdiːsegrɪ'geɪʃn] *s.* Aufhebung *f* der Rassentrennung.

de·sen·si·tize [ˌdiː'sensɪtaɪz] *v/t.* **1.** ✗ desensibilisieren, unempfindlich machen; **2.** phot. lichtunempfindlich machen.

de·sert¹ [dɪ'zɜːt] *s. oft pl.* **1.** Verdienst *n*; **2.** verdienter Lohn (*a. iro.*), Strafe *f*:

get one's ~*s* s-n wohlverdienten Lohn empfangen.

des·ert² ['dezət] **I** *s.* **1.** Wüste *f;* **2.** Ödland *n;* **3.** *fig.* Öde *f;* Einöde *f;* **4.** *fig.* Öde *f,* Fadheit *f;* **II** *adj.* **5.** öde, wüst; verödet, verlassen: ~ *island* einsame Insel; **6.** Wüsten...

de·sert³ [dı'zɜːt] **I** *v/t.* **1.** verlassen; im Stich lassen; ᵗᵗ *Ehepartner* (böswillig) verlassen; **2.** untreu *od.* abtrünnig werden *(dat.):* ~ *the colo(u)rs* ✗ fahnenflüchtig werden; **II** *v/i.* **3.** ✗ desertieren, fahnenflüchtig werden; 'überlaufen, -gehen *(to* zu); **de'sert·ed** [-tıd] *adj.* **1.** verlassen, ausgestorben, menschenleer; **2.** verlassen, einsam; **de'sert·er** [-tə] *s.* ✗ a) Fahnenflüchtige(r) *m,* Deser'teur *m,* b) 'Überläufer *m;* **2.** *fig.* Abtrünnige(r *m) f;* **de'ser·tion** [-ɜːʃn] *s.* **1.** Verlassen *n,* Im-'Stich-Lassen *n;* **2.** Abtrünnigwerden *n,* Abfall *m (from* von); **3.** ᵗᵗ böswilliges Verlassen; **4.** ✗ Fahnenflucht *f.*

de·serve [dı'zɜːv] **I** *v/t.* verdienen, verdient haben *(acc.),* würdig *od.* wert sein *(gen.):* ~ *praise* Lob verdienen; **II** *v/i.* ~ *well of* sich verdient gemacht haben um; ~ *ill of* e-n schlechten Dienst erwiesen haben *(dat.);* **de'serv·ed·ly** [-vıdlı] *adv.* verdientermaßen, mit Recht; **de'serv·ing** [-vıŋ] *adj.* **1.** verdienstvoll, verdient *(Person);* **2.** verdienstlich, -voll *(Tat);* **3.** *be* ~ *of* → *deserve* I.

des·ha·bille ['dezæbiːl] → *dishabille.*

des·ic·cate ['desıkeıt] *v/t. u. v/i.* (aus-) trocknen, ausdörren: ~*d milk* Trockenmilch *f;* ~*d fruit* Dörrobst *n;* **des·ic·ca·tion** [,desı'keıʃn] *s.* (Aus)Trocknung *f,* Trockenwerden *n;* **'des·ic·ca·tor** [-tə] *s.* ⊕ 'Trockenappa,rat *m.*

de·sid·er·a·tum [dı,zıdə'reıtəm] *pl.* **-ta** [-tə] *s. et.* Erwünschtes, Erfordernis *n,* Bedürfnis *n.*

de·sign [dı'zaın] **I** *v/t.* **1.** entwerfen, (auf)zeichnen, skizzieren: ~ *a dress* ein Kleid entwerfen; **2.** gestalten, ausführen, anlegen; **3.** *fig.* entwerfen, ausdenken, ersinnen: ~*ed to do s.th.* dafür bestimmt *od.* darauf angelegt, et. zu tun *(Sache);* **4.** planen, beabsichtigen: ~ *doing (od. to do)* beabsichtigen zu tun; **5.** bestimmen: a) vorsehen *(for* für, *as* als), b) ausersehen: ~*ed to be a priest* zum Priester bestimmt; **II** *v/i.* **6.** Zeichner *od.* Konstruk'teur *od.* De'signer sein; **III** *s.* **7.** Entwurf *m,* Zeichnung *f,* Plan *m,* Skizze *f;* **8.** Muster *n,* Zeichnung *f,* Fi'gur *f,* Des'sin *n: floral* ~ Blumenmuster; *registered* ~ ᵗᵗ Gebrauchsmuster; *protection of* ~*s* ᵗᵗ Musterschutz *m;* **9.** a) Gestaltung *f,* Formgebung *f,* De'sign *n,* b) Bauart *f,* Konstrukti'on *f,* Ausführung *f,* Mo'dell *n;* → *industrial design;* **10.** Anlage *f,* Anordnung *f;* **11.** Absicht *f,* Plan *m;* Zweck *m,* Ziel *n: by* ~ mit Absicht; **12.** böse Absicht, Anschlag *m: have* ~*s on (od. against)* et. im Schilde führen gegen, a. *iro.* e-n Anschlag vorhaben auf *(acc.).*

des·ig·nate ['dezıgneıt] **I** *v/t.* **1.** bezeichnen, (be)nennen; **2.** kennzeichnen; **3.** berufen, ausersehen, bestimmen, ernennen *(for* zu); **II** *adj.* **4.** designiert, einstweilig ernannt: *bishop* ~; **des·ig·na·tion** [,dezıg'neıʃn] *s.* **1.** Bezeichnung *f,* Name *m;* **2.** Kennzeichnung *f;* **3.** Bestimmung *f;* **4.** einstweilige Ernennung *od.* Berufung.

de·signed [dı'zaınd] *adj.* □ **1.** *(for)* bestimmt *etc.* (für); → *design* 3, 4, 5; **2.** vorsätzlich, absichtlich; **de'sign·ed·ly** [-nıdlı] *adv.* → *designed* 2; **de'sign·er** [-nə] *s.* **1.** Entwerfer(in): a) (Muster-) Zeichner(in), b) De'signer(in), (Form-) Gestalter(in), Gebrauchsgrafiker(in), c) ⊕ Konstruk'teur *m;* **2.** Ränkeschmied *m,* Intri'gant(in); **de'sign·ing** [-nıŋ] *adj.* □ ränkevoll, intri'gant.

de·sir·a·bil·i·ty [dı,zaıərə'bılətı] *s.* Erwünschtheit *f;* **de·sir·a·ble** [dı'zaıərəbl] *adj.* □ **1.** wünschenswert, erwünscht; **2.** begehrenswert, reizvoll; **de·sire** [dı'zaıə] **I** *v/t.* **1.** wünschen, begehren, verlangen, wollen: *if* ~*d* auf Wunsch; *leaves much to be* ~*d* lässt viel zu wünschen übrig; **2.** j-n bitten, ersuchen; **II** *s.* **3.** Wunsch *m,* Verlangen *n,* Begehren *n (for* nach); **4.** Wunsch *m,* Bitte *f: at (od. by) s.o.'s* ~ auf (j-s) Wunsch; **5.** Lust *f,* Begierde *f;* **6.** *das* Gewünschte; **de·sir·ous** [dı'zaıərəs] *adj.* □ *(of)* begierig, verlangend (nach), wünschend *(acc.): I am* ~ *to know* ich möchte (sehr) gern wissen; *the parties are* ~ *to ...* (in Verträgen) die Parteien beabsichtigen, zu ...

de·sist [dı'zıst] *v/i.* abstehen, ablassen, Abstand nehmen *(from* von): ~ *from asking* aufhören zu fragen.

desk [desk] *s.* **1.** Schreibtisch *m;* **2.** (Lese-, Schreib-, Noten-, Kirchen-, ⊕ Schalt)Pult *n;* **3.** ✝ (Zahl)Kasse *f: pay at the* ~*!* zahlen Sie an der Kasse!; *first* ~ ♪ erstes Pult *(Orchester);* **4.** *eccl. kath. Am.* Kanzel *f;* **5.** *Am.* Redakti'on *f: city* ~ Lokalredaktion; **6.** Auskunft (-sschalter *m) f;* **7.** Empfang *m,* Rezepti'on *f (im Hotel):* ~ *clerk Am.* Empfangschef *m;* **II** *adj.* **8.** Schreibtisch..., Büro...: ~ *work;* ~ *calender* Tischkalender *m;* ~ *sergeant* Dienst habender (Polizei)Wachtmeister; ~ *set* Schreibzeug(garnitur *f) n.*

desk·top ['desktɒp] *s. a.* ~ *computer (od. calculator)* 'Desktop(-Com,puter) *m,* Tischrechner *m;* ~ *cop·i·er* ['kɒpıə] *s.* 'Tischko,pierer *m;* ~ *pub·lish·ing s. Computer:* Desktop-'Publishing *n.*

des·o·late I *adj.* □ ['desələt] **1.** wüst, unwirtlich, öde; verwüstet; **2.** verlassen, einsam; **3.** trostlos, *fig. a.* öde; **II** *v/t.* [-leıt] **4.** verwüsten; **5.** einsam zu-'rücklassen; **6.** betrüben, bekümmern; **'des·o·late·ness** [-nıs] → *desolation* 2, 3; **des·o·la·tion** [,desə'leıʃn] *s.* **1.** Verwüstung *f,* -ödung *f;* **2.** Verlassenheit *f,* Einsamkeit *f;* **3.** Trostlosigkeit *f,* Elend *n.*

de·spair [dı'speə] **I** *v/i.* *(of)* verzweifeln (an *dat.),* ohne Hoffnung sein, alle Hoffnung aufgeben *od.* verlieren (auf *acc.): the patient's life is* ~*d of* man bangt um das Leben des Kranken; **II** *s.* Verzweiflung *f (at* über *acc.),* Hoffnungslosigkeit *f: drive s.o. to* ~*, be s.o.'s* ~ j-n zur Verzweiflung bringen; **de'spair·ing** [-eərıŋ] *adj.* □ verzweifelt.

des·patch *etc.* → *dispatch etc.*

des·per·a·do [,despə'rɑːdəu] *pl.* **-does, -dos** *s.* Despe'rado *m.*

des·per·ate ['despərət] *adj.* □ **1.** verzweifelt: *she was* ~ sie war (völlig) verzweifelt; *a* ~ *deed* e-e Verzweiflungstat; ~ *efforts* verzweifelte *od.* krampfhafte Anstrengungen; ~ *remedy* äußerstes Mittel; *be* ~ *for s.th. od. to get s.th.* et. verzweifelt *od.* ganz dringend brauchen, et. unbedingt haben wollen; **2.** verzweifelt, hoffnungs-, ausweglos: ~ *situation;* **3.** verzweifelt, despa'rat, zu allem fähig, zum Äußersten entschlossen *(Person);* **4.** F schrecklich: *a* ~ *fool;* ~*ly in love* wahnsinnig verliebt;

not ~*ly* F a) nicht unbedingt, b) nicht übermäßig *(schön etc.);* **des·per·a·tion** [,despə'reıʃn] *s.* **1.** (höchste) Verzweiflung, Hoffnungslosigkeit *f;* **2.** Rase'rei *f,* Verzweiflung *f: drive to* ~ rasend machen, zur Verzweiflung bringen.

des·pi·ca·ble ['despıkəbl] *adj.* □ verächtlich, verachtenswert.

de·spise [dı'spaız] *v/t.* verachten, *Speise etc. a.* verschmähen: *not to be* ~*d* nicht zu verachten.

de·spite [dı'spaıt] **I** *prp.* trotz *(gen.),* ungeachtet *(gen.);* **II** *s.* Bosheit *f,* Tücke *f;* Trotz *m,* Verachtung *f: in* ~ *of* → I.

de·spoil [dı'spɔıl] *v/t.* plündern, berauben *(of gen.);* **de'spoil·ment** [-mənt], **de·spo·li·a·tion** [dı,spəulı'eıʃn] *s.* Plünderung *f,* Beraubung *f.*

de·spond [dı'spɒnd] **I** *v/i.* verzagen; verzweifeln *(of* an *dat.);* **II** *s. obs.* Verzweiflung *f;* **de'spond·en·cy** [-dənsı] *s.* Verzagtheit *f,* Mutlosigkeit *f;* **de·'spond·ent** [-dənt] *adj.* □, **de·'spond·ing** [-dıŋ] *adj.* □ verzagt, mutlos, kleinmütig.

des·pot ['despɒt] *s.* Des'pot *m,* Gewaltherrscher *m; fig.* Ty'rann *m;* **des·pot·ic, des·pot·i·cal** [de'spɒtık(l)] *adj.* □ des'potisch, herrisch, ty'rannisch; **'des·pot·ism** [-pətızəm] *s.* Despo'tismus *m,* Tyran'nei *f,* Gewaltherrschaft *f.*

des·qua·mate ['deskwəmeıt] *v/i.* **1.** ♣ sich abschuppen; **2.** sich häuten.

des·sert [dı'zɜːt] *s.* Des'sert *n,* Nachtisch *m:* ~ *spoon* Dessertlöffel *m.*

des·ti·na·tion [,destı'neıʃn] *s.* **1.** Bestimmungsort *m;* Reiseziel *n: country of* ~ ✝ Bestimmungsland *n;* **2.** Bestimmung *f,* Zweck *m,* Ziel *n.*

des·tine ['destın] *v/t.* bestimmen, vorsehen *(for* für, *to do* zu tun); **'des·tined** [-nd] *adj.* bestimmt: ~ *for* unterwegs nach *(Schiff etc.); he was* ~ *(to inf.)* es war ihm beschieden (zu *inf.),* er sollte *(inf.);* **'des·ti·ny** [-nı] *s.* **1.** Schicksal *n,* Geschick *n,* Los *n: he met his* ~ sein Schicksal ereilte ihn; **2.** Vorsehung *f;* **3.** Verhängnis *n,* zwingende Notwendigkeit; **4.** *the* Destinies die Parzen *(Schicksalsgöttinnen).*

des·ti·tute ['destıtjuːt] *adj.* **1.** verarmt, mittellos, Not leidend; **2.** *(of)* ermangelnd, entblößt *(gen.),* ohne *(acc.),* bar *(gen.);* **II** *s.* **3.** *the* ~ die Armen; **des·ti·tu·tion** [,destı'tjuːʃn] *s.* **1.** Armut *f,* (bittere) Not, Elend *n;* **2.** (völliger) Mangel *(of* an *dat.).*

de·stroy [dı'strɔı] *v/t.* **1.** zerstören, vernichten; **2.** zertrümmern, *Gebäude etc.* niederreißen; **3.** *et.* ruinieren, unbrauchbar machen; **3.** j-n, e-e *Armee etc.* vernichten, *Insekten etc. a.* vertilgen; **4.** töten; **5.** *fig.* j-n, j-s *Ruf, Gesundheit etc.* ruinieren, zu'grunde richten, *Hoffnungen etc.* zu'nichte machen, zerstören; **6.** F j-n ka'puttmachen *od.* fertig machen; **de'stroy·er** [-ɔıə] *s. a.* ✗, ⚓ Zerstörer *m.*

de·struct [dı'strʌkt] **I** *v/t.* **1.** ✗ (aus Sicherheitsgründen) zerstören; **II** *v/i.* **2.** zerstört werden; **3.** sich selbst zerstören; **de'struct·i·ble** [-təbl] *adj.* zerstörbar; **de'struc·tion** [-kʃn] *s.* **1.** Zerstörung *f,* Vernichtung *f;* **2.** Abriss *m (e-s Gebäudes);* **3.** Tötung *f;* **de'struc·tive** [-tıv] *adj.* □ **1.** zerstörend, vernichtend *(a. fig.): be* ~ *of* et. zerstören *od.* untergraben; **2.** zerstörerisch, destruk'tiv, schädlich, verderblich: ~ *to health* gesundheitsschädlich; **4.** rein negativ, destruk'tiv *(Kritik);* **de'struc·tive·ness** [-tıvnıs] *s.* **1.** zerstörende *od.* vernich-

D

tende Wirkung; **2.** *das* Destruk'tive, destruk'tive Eigenschaft; **de'struc·tor** [-tə] *s.* ☉ (Müll)Verbrennungsofen *m*.

des·ue·tude [dɪ'sjuːɪtjuːd] *s.* Ungebräuchlichkeit *f*: *fall into* ~ außer Gebrauch kommen.

de·sul·phu·rize [‚diː'sʌlfəraɪz] *v/t.* 🦚 entschwefeln.

des·ul·to·ri·ness ['desəltərɪnɪs] *s.* **1.** Zs.-hangs-, Plan-, Ziellosigkeit *f*; **2.** Flüchtigkeit *f*, Oberflächlichkeit *f*, Sprunghaftigkeit *f*; **des·ul·to·ry** ['desəltərɪ] *adj.* **1.** 'unzu,sammenhängend, planlos, ziellos, oberflächlich; **2.** abschweifend, sprunghaft; **3.** unruhig; **4.** vereinzelt, spo'radisch.

de·tach [dɪ'tætʃ] **I** *v/t.* **1.** ab-, loslösen, losmachen, abtrennen, *a.* ☉ abnehmen; **2.** absondern; befreien; **3.** ✕ abkommandieren; **II** *v/i.* **4.** sich (los)lösen; **de'tach·a·ble** [-tʃəbl] *adj.* abnehmbar (*a.* ☉); abtrennbar; lose; **de'tached** [-tʃt] *adj.*, **de'tached·ly** [-tʃtlɪ] *adv.* **1.** getrennt, gesondert; **2.** einzeln, frei-, al'lein stehend (*Haus*); **3.** *fig.* a) objek'tiv, unvoreingenommen, b) uninteressiert, c) distanziert; **4.** *fig.* losgelöst, entrückt; **de'tach·ment** [-mənt] *s.* **1.** Absonderung *f*, Abtrennung *f*, Loslösung *f*; **2.** *fig.* (innerer) Abstand, Di'stanz *f*, Losgelöstsein *n*, (innere) Freiheit; **3.** *fig.* Objektivi'tät *f*, Unvoreingenommenheit *f*; **4.** Gleichgültigkeit *f* (*from* gegen); **5.** ✕ → *detail* 5 a u. b.

de·tail ['diːteɪl] **I** *s.* **1.** De'tail *n*: a) Einzelheit *f*, b) *a. pl. coll.* (nähere) Einzelheiten *pl.*: *in* ~ im Einzelnen, ausführlich; *go* (*od. enter*) *into* ~(*s*) ins Einzelne gehen, es ausführlich behandeln; **2.** Einzelteil *m*; **3.** 'Nebensache *f*, -umstand *m*, Kleinigkeit *f*; **4.** *Kunst etc.*: De'tail(darstellung *f*) *n*, b) Ausschnitt *m*; **5.** ✕ a) Ab'teilung *f*, Trupp *m*, b) ('Sonder)Kom,mando *n*, c) ('Abkomman,dierung *f*, d) Sonderauftrag *m*; **II** *v/t.* **6.** ausführlich berichten über (*acc.*), genau schildern; einzeln aufzählen *od.* -führen; **7.** ✕ abkommandieren; **'de·tailed** [-ld] *adj.* ausführlich, genau, eingehend.

de·tain [dɪ'teɪn] *v/t.* **1.** *j-n* auf-, abhalten, zu'rück(halten, hindern; **2.** 🏛 *j-n* in (Unter'suchungs)Haft behalten; **3.** *et.* vorenthalten, einbehalten; **4.** *ped.* nachsitzen lassen; **de·tain·ee** [‚diːteɪ'niː] *s.* 🏛 Häftling *m*; **de'tain·er** [-nə] *s.* 🏛 **1.** 'widerrechtliche Vorenthaltung; **2.** Anordnung *f* der Haftfortdauer.

de·tect [dɪ'tekt] *v/t.* **1.** entdecken; (heraus)finden, ermitteln; **2.** feststellen, wahrnehmen; **3.** aufdecken, enthüllen; **4.** ertappen (*in* bei); **5.** *Radio*: gleichrichten; **de'tect·a·ble** [-təbl] *adj.* feststellbar; **de'tec·ta·phone** [-təfɒn] *s. teleph.* Abhörgerät *n*; **de'tec·tion** [-kʃn] *s.* **1.** Ent-, Aufdeckung *f*; Feststellung *f*; **2.** *Radio*: Gleichrichtung *f*; **3.** *coll.* Krimi'nalro,mane *pl.*; **de·tec·tive** [-tɪv] **I** *adj.* Detektiv..., Krimi nal...: ~ *force* Kriminalpolizei *f*; ~ *story* Kriminalroman *m*; *do* ~ *work bsd. fig.* Detektivarbeit leisten; **II** *s.* Detek'tiv *m*, Krimi'nalbeamte(r) *m*, Ge'heimpoli,zist *m*; **de'tec·tor** [-tə] *s.* **1.** Auf-, Entdecker *m*; **2.** ☉ a) Sucher *m*, b) Anzeigevorrichtung *f*; **3.** ⚡ a) De'tektor *m*, b) Gleichrichter *m*.

de·tent [dɪ'tent] *s.* ☉ Sperrhaken *m*, -klinke *f*, Sperre *f*; Auslösung *f*.

dé·tente [deɪ'tãːnt] (*Fr.*) *s. bsd. pol.* Entspannung *f*.

de·ten·tion [dɪ'tenʃn] *s.* **1.** Festnahme *f*;

2. (*a.* Unter'suchungs)Haft *f*, Gewahrsam *m*, Ar'rest *m*: ~ *barracks* Militärgefängnis *n*; ~ *center Am.*, ~ *home Brit.* Jugendstrafanstalt *f*; ~ *colony* Strafkolonie *f*; **3.** *ped.* Nachsitzen *n*, Arrest *m*; **4.** Ab-, Zu'rückhaltung *f*; **5.** Einbehaltung *f*, Vorenthaltung *f*.

de·ter [dɪ'tɜː] *v/t.* abschrecken, abhalten (*from* von).

de·ter·gent [dɪ'tɜːdʒənt] **I** *adj.* reinigend; **II** *s.* Reinigungs-, Wasch-, Geschirrspülmittel *n*.

de·te·ri·o·rate [dɪ'tɪərɪəreɪt] **I** *v/i.* **1.** sich verschlechtern *od.* verschlimmern, schlecht(er) werden, verderben; **2.** an Wert verlieren; **II** *v/t.* **3.** verschlechtern; **4.** beeinträchtigen; im Wert mindern; **de·te·ri·o·ra·tion** [dɪ‚tɪərɪə'reɪʃn] *s.* **1.** Verschlechterung *f*; Verfall *m*; **2.** Wertminderung *f*.

de·ter·ment [dɪ'tɜːmənt] *s.* **1.** Abschreckung *f*; **2.** → *deterrent* II.

de·ter·mi·na·ble [dɪ'tɜːmɪnəbl] *adj.* bestimmbar; **de'ter·mi·nant** [-nənt] **I** *adj.* **1.** bestimmend, entscheidend; **II** *s.* **2.** entscheidender Faktor; **3.** 🅰, *biol.* Determi'nante *f*; **de'ter·mi·nate** [-nət] *adj.* ☐ bestimmt, fest(gesetzt), entschieden; **de·ter·mi·na·tion** [dɪ‚tɜːmɪ'neɪʃn] *s.* **1.** Ent-, Beschluss *m*; **2.** Entscheidung *f*; Bestimmung *f*, Festsetzung *f*; **3.** Bestimmung *f*, Ermittlung *f*, Feststellung *f*; **4.** Bestimmtheit *f*, Entschlossenheit *f*, Zielstrebigkeit *f*; feste Absicht; **5.** Ziel *n*, Begrenzung *f*; Ablauf *m*, Ende *n*; **6.** Richtung *f*, Neigung *f*, Drang *m*; **de'ter·mi·na·tive** [-nətɪv] *adj.* ☐ **1.** (näher) bestimmend, einschränkend; **2.** entscheidend; **II** *s.* **3.** *et.* Entscheidendes *od.* Charakte'ristisches; *a. ling.* a) Determina'tiv *n*, b) Bestimmungswort *n*; **de·ter·mine** [dɪ-'tɜːmɪn] **I** *v/t.* **1.** entscheiden; regeln; **2.** *et.* bestimmen, festsetzen, beschließen (*a. to do* zu tun, *that* dass); **3.** feststellen, ermitteln, her'ausfinden; **4.** *j-n* bestimmen, veranlassen (*to do* zu tun); **5.** *bsd.* 🏛 beendigen, aufheben; **II** *v/i.* **6.** (*on*) sich entscheiden (für), sich entschließen (zu); beschließen (*on doing* zu tun); **7.** *bsd.* 🏛 enden, ablaufen; **de'ter·mined** [-mɪnd] *adj.* ☐ (fest) entschlossen, fest, entschieden, bestimmt; **de'ter·min·er** [-mɪnə] *s. ling.* Bestimmungswort *n*; **de'ter·min·ism** [-mɪnɪzəm] *s. phls.* Determi'nismus *m*.

de·ter·rence [dɪ'terəns] *s.* Abschreckung *f*; **de'ter·rent** [-nt] **I** *adj.* abschreckend; **II** *s.* Abschreckungsmittel *n*.

de·test [dɪ'test] *v/t.* verabscheuen, hassen; **de'test·a·ble** [-təbl] *adj.* ☐ abscheulich, hassenswert; **de·tes·ta·tion** [‚diːte'steɪʃn] *s.* (*of*) Verabscheuung *f* (*gen.*), Abscheu *m* (vor *dat.*): *hold in* ~ verabscheuen.

de·throne [dɪ'θrəʊn] *v/t.* entthronen (*a. fig.*); **de'throne·ment** [-mənt] *s.* Entthronung *f*.

det·o·nate ['detəneɪt] **I** *v/t.* explodieren lassen, zur Explosi'on bringen; **II** *v/i.* explodieren; *mot.* klopfen; **'det·o·nat·ing** [-tɪŋ] *adj.* ☉ Spreng..., Zünd..., Knall...; **det·o·na·tion** [‚detə'neɪʃn] *s.* Detonati'on *f*, Knall *m*; **'det·o·na·tor** [-tə] *s.* ☉ **1.** Bri'sanzsprengstoff *m*; **2.** Zünd-, Sprengkapsel *f*.

de·tour, dé·tour ['diː‚tʊə] **I** *s.* **1.** 'Umweg *m*; Abstecher *m*; **2.** a) 'Umleitung *f*, b) Um'gehungsstraße *f*; **3.** *fig.* 'Umschweif *m*; **4.** ~ e-n 'Umweg machen; **III** *v/t.* **5.** e-n 'Umweg machen um; **6.** *Verkehr* 'umleiten.

de·tox·i·fi·ca·tion ['diː‚tɒksɪfɪ'keɪʃn] *s.* **1.** Entgiftung *f*; **2.** 🎗 Entziehungskur *f*; **de·tox·i·fy** [‚diː'tɒksɪfaɪ] **I** *v/t.* **1.** entgiften, unschädlich machen; **2.** 🎗 *be detoxified* e-e Entziehungskur machen; **II** *v/i* **3.** sich entgiften; **4.** Giftstoffe abbauen (*durch freiwilligen Entzug*); **5.** giftfrei (*od.* unschädlich) werden.

de·tract [dɪ'trækt] **I** *v/t.* Aufmerksamkeit *etc.* ablenken; **II** *v/i.* (*from*) a) Abbruch tun (*dat.*), beeinträchtigen, schmälern (*acc.*), b) her'absetzen; deprecate; **de'trac·tion** [-kʃn] *s.* **1.** a) Beeinträchtigung *f*, Schmälerung *f*, b) Her'absetzung *f*; **2.** Verunglimpfung *f*; **de'trac·tor** [-tə] *s.* **1.** Kritiker *m*, Her'absetzer *m*; **2.** Verunglimpfer *m*.

de·train [‚diː'treɪn] 🚂, ✕ **I** *v/i.* aussteigen; **II** *v/t.* ausladen; **'de'train·ment** [-mənt] *s.* **1.** Aussteigen *n*; **2.** Ausladen *n*.

det·ri·ment ['detrɪmənt] *s.* Schaden *m*, Nachteil *m*: *to the* ~ *of* zum Schaden *od.* Nachteil (*gen.*); *without* ~ *to* ohne Schaden für; *be a* ~ *to health* gesundheitsschädlich sein; **det·ri·men·tal** [‚detrɪ'mentl] *adj.* ☐ (*to*) schädlich, nachteilig (für), abträglich (*dat.*).

de·tri·tal [dɪ'traɪtl] *adj. geol.* Geröll..., Schutt...; **de'trit·ed** [-tɪd] *adj.* **1.** abgenützt; abgegriffen (*Münze*); *fig.* abgedroschen; **2.** *geol.* verwittert; **de·tri·tion** [dɪ'trɪʃn] *s. geol.* Ab-, Zerreibung *f*; **de'tri·tus** [-təs] *s. geol.* Geröll *n*, Schutt *m*.

de trop [də'trəʊ] (*Fr.*) *pred. adj.* 'überflüssig, zu viel (des Guten).

deuce [djuːs] *s.* **1.** Würfeln, Kartenspiel: Zwei *f*; **2.** *Tennis*: Einstand *m*; **3.** F Teufel *m*: *who* (*what*) *the* ~? wer (was) zum Teufel?; *a* ~ *of a row* ein Mordskrach (*Lärm od. Streit*); *there's the* ~ *to pay* F das dicke Ende kommt noch; *play the* ~ *with* Schindluder treiben mit *j-m*; **deuced** [-st] *adj.*, **'deuced·ly** [-sɪdlɪ] *adv.* F verteufelt, verflixt.

deu·te·ri·um [djuː'tɪərɪəm] *s.* Deu'terium *n*, schwerer Wasserstoff.

Deu·ter·on·o·my [‚djuːtə'rɒnəmɪ] *s. bibl.* Deutero'nomium *n*, Fünftes Buch Mose.

Deutsch·mark ['dɔɪtʃmɑːk] *s.* Deutsche Mark *f*.

de·val·u·ate [‚diː'væljʊeɪt] 🏦 abwerten; **de·val·u·a·tion** [‚diːvæljʊ'eɪʃn] *s.* 🏦 Abwertung *f*; **de·val·ue** [‚diː'væljuː] → *devaluate*.

dev·as·tate ['devəsteɪt] *v/t.* verwüsten, vernichten (*beide a. fig.*): *be devastated fig.* am Boden zerstört sein; **'dev·as·tat·ing** [-tɪŋ] *adj.* ☐ **1.** verheerend, vernichtend (*a. Kritik etc.*); **2.** F e'norm, fan'tastisch, 'umwerfend; **dev·as·ta·tion** [‚devə'steɪʃn] *s.* Verwüstung *f*.

de·vel·op [dɪ'veləp] **I** *v/t.* **1.** *allg. Theorie, Kräfte, Tempo etc.* entwickeln (*a.* 🅰, 🎶, *phot.*), *Muskeln etc. a.* bilden, *Interesse etc. a.* zeigen, an den Tag legen, *Fähigkeiten etc. a.* entfalten, *Gedanken, Plan etc. a.* ausarbeiten, gestalten (*into* zu); **2.** entwickeln, ausbauen: ~ *an industry*; **3.** *Bodenschätze*, *Bauland* erschließen, nutzbar machen, *Altstadt* sanieren; **4.** sich *e-e Krankheit* zuziehen, *Fieber etc.* bekommen; **II** *v/i.* **5.** sich entwickeln (*from* aus); sich entfalten: ~ *into* sich entwickeln zu, zu *et.* werden; **6.** zu'tage treten, sich zeigen; **de'vel·op·er** [-pə] *s.* **1.** *phot.* Entwickler *m*; **2.** *late* ~ *psych.* Spätentwickler *m*; **3.** (Stadt)Planer *m*; **de'vel·op·ing**

D

[-pɪŋ] adj.: ~ **bath** phot. Entwicklungs-bad n; ~ **company** Bauträger m; ~ **country** pol. Entwicklungsland n; **de-'vel·op·ment** [-mənt] s. **1.** Entwicklung f (a. phot.); **2.** Entfaltung f, Entstehen n, Bildung f, Wachstum n; Schaffung f; **3.** Erschließung f, Nutzbarmachung f; Ausbau m, 'Umgestaltung f: ~ **area** Entwicklungs-, Notstandsgebiet n; **ripe for** ~ baureif; **4.** ℒ ♱ Entwicklung(sabteilung) f; **5.** Darlegung f, Ausarbeitung f; 'Durchführung f (a. ♪); **de·vel·op·ment·al** [dɪ,veləp-'mentl] adj. Entwicklungs...

de·vi·ate ['diːvɪeɪt] **I** v/i. abweichen, abgehen, abkommen (**from** von); **II** v/t. ablenken.

de·vi·a·tion [,diːvɪ'eɪʃn] s. **1.** Abweichung f, Abweichen n (**from** von); **2.** bsd. phys., opt. Ablenkung f; **3.** ✍, ♱ Abweichung f, Ablenkung f, Abtrieb m; **de·vi·a·tion·ism** [-ʃənɪzəm] s. pol. Abweichlertum n; **de·vi·a·tion·ist** [-ʃənɪst], **de·vi·a·tor** ['diːvɪeɪtə] s. pol. Abweichler(in).

de·vice [dɪ'vaɪs] s. **1.** Plan m, Einfall m, Erfindung f: **left to one's own** ~**s** sich selbst überlassen; **2.** Anschlag m, böse Absicht, Kniff m; **3.** ⊙ Vor-, Einrichtung f, Gerät n; fig. Behelf m, Kunstgriff m; **4.** Wahlspruch m, De'vise f; **5.** her. Sinn-, Wappenbild n; **6.** Muster n, Zeichnung f.

dev·il ['devl] **I** s. **1.** the ~, a. the ℒ der Teufel: **between the** ~ **and the deep sea** fig. zwischen zwei Feuern, in auswegloser Lage; **like the** ~, F wie der Teufel, wie wahnsinnig; **go to the** ~ sl. zum Teufel od. vor die Hunde gehen; **go to the** ~**!** scher dich zum Teufel!; **play the** ~ **with** F Schindluder treiben mit; **the** ~ **take the hindmost** den Letzten beißen die Hunde; **there's the** ~ **to pay** F das setzt was ab!; **the** ~**!** F a) (verärgert) zum Teufel!, zum Henker!, b) (erstaunt) Donnerwetter!; **2.** Teufel m, böser Geist, 'Satan m (a. fig.); → **due** 9; **tattoo**[1] 2; **3.** fig. Laster n, Übel n; **4.** poor ~ armer Teufel od. Schlucker; **5.** a. ~ **of a fellow** Teufelskerl m, toller Bursche; **6.** a (od. the) ~ F e-e verflixte Sache: ~ **of a job** Heiden-, Mordsarbeit f; **who (what, how) the** ~ ... wer (was, wie) zum Teufel ...; ~ **a one** kein Einziger; **7.** Handlanger m, Laufbursche m; → **printer** 1; **8.** ♱ As'sessor m (bei e-m **barrister**); **9.** scharf gewürztes Gericht; **10.** ⊙ Reißwolf m; **II** v/t. **11.** F schikanieren, piesacken; **12.** scharf gewürzt braten: **devil(l)ed eggs** gefüllte Eier; **13.** ⊙ zerfasern, wolfen; **III** v/i. **14.** als As'sessor (bei e-m **barrister**) arbeiten; '~-,**dodg·er** s. F Prediger m; '~-**fish** s. Seeteufel m.

dev·il·ish ['devlɪʃ] **I** adj. □ **1.** teuflisch; **2.** F fürchterlich, höllisch, verteufelt; **II** adv. **3.** → 2.

,dev·il-may-'care adj. **1.** leichtsinnig; **2.** verwegen.

dev·il·ment ['devlmənt] s. **1.** Unfug m; **2.** Schurkenstreich m; **dev·il·ry** ['devlrɪ] s. **1.** Teufe'lei f, Untat f; **2.** 'Übermut m; **3.** Teufelsbande f; **4.** Teufelskunst f.

dev·il's | **ad·vo·cate** ['devlz] s. R.C. Advo'catus m Di'aboli; '~-**bones** s. pl. Würfel(spiel n) pl.; ~ **book** s. (des Teufels) ,Gebetbuch' n (Spielkarten); ~ **darn·ing-nee·dle** s. zo. Li'belle f; ~ **food cake** s. Am. schwere Schoko'ladentorte.

de·vi·ous ['diːvjəs] adj. □ **1.** abwegig, irrig; **2.** gewunden (a. fig.): ~ **path**

Ab-, Umweg m; **3.** verschlagen, unredlich: **by** ~ **means** auf krummen Wegen, ,hintenherum'; ~ **step** Fehltritt m; **'de·vi·ous·ness** [-nɪs] s. **1.** Abwegigkeit f; **2.** Gewundenheit f; **3.** Unaufrichtigkeit f, Verschlagenheit f.

de·vis·a·ble [dɪ'vaɪzəbl] adj. **1.** erdenkbar, -lich; **2.** ♱ vermachbar; **de·vise** [dɪ'vaɪz] **I** v/t. **1.** ausdenken, ersinnen, erfinden, konstruieren; **2.** ♱ Grundbesitz vermachen, hinter'lassen (**to** dat.); **II** s. **3.** ♱ Vermächtnis n; **dev·i·see** [,devɪ'ziː] s. ♱ Vermächtnisnehmer (-in); **de·vis·er** [dɪ'vaɪzə] s. Erfinder (-in); Planer(in); **de·vi·sor** [,devɪ'zɔː] s. ♱ Erb-lasser(in).

de·vi·tal·ize [,diː'vaɪtəlaɪz] v/t. der Lebenskraft berauben, schwächen.

de·void [dɪ'vɔɪd] adj.: ~ **of** ohne (acc.), leer an (dat.), frei von, bar (gen.), ...los: ~ **of feeling** gefühllos.

de·voir [də'vwɑː] (Fr.) s. obs. **1.** Pflicht f; **2.** pl. Höflichkeitsbezeigungen pl., Artigkeiten pl.

dev·o·lu·tion [,diːvə'luːʃn] s. **1.** Ab-, Verlauf m; **2.** bsd. ♱ 'Übergang m, Über'tragung f; Heimfall m; parl. Über'weisung f; **3.** pol. ,Dezentralisati'on f, Regionalisierung f; **4.** biol. Entartung f.

de·volve [dɪ'vɒlv] **I** v/t. **1.** (**upon**) über-'tragen (dat.), abwälzen (auf acc.); **II** v/i. **2.** (**on**, **upon**) 'übergehen (auf acc.), zufallen (dat.); sich vererben auf (acc.); **3.** j-m obliegen.

De·vo·ni·an [de'vəʊnjən] **I** adj. **1.** Devonshire betreffend; **2.** geol. de'vonisch; **II** s. **3.** Bewohner(in) von Devonshire; **4.** geol. De'von n.

de·vote [dɪ'vəʊt] v/t. (**to** dat.) **1.** widmen, opfern, weihen, 'hingeben; **2.** ~ **o.s.** sich widmen od. 'hingeben; sich verschreiben; **de·vot·ed** [-tɪd] adj. □ **1.** 'hingebungsvoll: a) aufopfernd, treu, b) anhänglich, liebevoll, zärtlich, c) eifrig, begeistert; **2.** todgeweiht; **de·vo·tee** [,devəʊ'tiː] s. **1.** begeisterter Anhänger; **2.** Verehrer m; Verfechter m; **3.** Frömmler m; **4.** Fa'natiker m, Eiferer m; **de·vo·tion** [-əʊʃn] s. **1.** Widmung f; **2.** 'Hingabe f: a) Ergebenheit f, Treue f, b) (Auf)Opferung f, c) Eifer m, 'Hingebung f, d) Liebe f, Verehrung f, innige Zuneigung; **3.** eccl. a) Andacht f, Frömmigkeit f, b) pl. Gebet(e pl.) n; **de·vo·tion·al** [-əʊʃənl] adj. **1.** andächtig, fromm; **2.** Andachts..., Erbauungs...

de·vour [dɪ'vaʊə] v/t. **1.** verschlingen, fressen; **2.** wegraffen, verzehren, vernichten; **3.** fig. Buch verschlingen; mit Blicken verschlingen od. verzehren; **4.** j-n verzehren (Leidenschaft): **be** ~**ed by** sich verzehren vor (Gram etc.); **de·'vour·ing** [-ərɪŋ] adj. □ **1.** gierig; **2.** fig. verzehrend.

de·vout [dɪ'vaʊt] adj. □ **1.** fromm; **2.** a. fig. andächtig; **3.** innig, herzlich; **4.** sehnlich, eifrig; **de·'vout·ness** [-nɪs] s. **1.** Frömmigkeit f; **2.** Andacht f; 'Hingabe f; **3.** Eifer m, Inbrunst f.

dew [djuː] s. **1.** Tau m; **2.** fig. Tau m: a) Frische f, b) Feuchtigkeit f, Tränen pl.; '~-**ber·ry** s. ♀ e-e Brombeere; '~-**drop** s. Tautropfen m.

dew·i·ness ['djuːɪnɪs] s. Tauigkeit f, (Tau)Feuchtigkeit f.

'dew·|·lap s. **1.** zo. Wamme f; **2.** F (altersbedingte) Halsfalte; ~ **point** s. phys. Taupunkt m; ~ **worm** s. Angeln: Tauwurm m.

dew·y ['djuːɪ] adj. □ **1.** taufeucht; a. fig. taufrisch; **2.** feucht; poet. um'flort (Au-

---

gen); **3.** frisch, erfrischend; '~-**eyed** adj. iro. na'iv, ,blauäugig'.

dex·ter ['dekstə] adj. **1.** recht, rechts (-seitig); **2.** her. rechts (vom Beschauer aus links); **dex·ter·i·ty** [dek'sterətɪ] s. **1.** Geschicklichkeit f, Gewandtheit f; **2.** Rechtshändigkeit f; **'dex·ter·ous** [-tərəs] adj. □ **1.** gewandt, geschickt, behänd, flink; **2.** rechtshändig; **'dex·tral** [-trəl] adj. □ **1.** rechtsseitig; **2.** rechtshändig.

dextro- [dekstrəʊ] in Zssgn (nach) rechts.

dex·trose ['dekstrəʊs] s. ♠ Dex'trose f, Traubenzucker m.

dex·trous ['dekstrəs] → **dexterous**.

dhoo·ti ['duːtɪ], **dho·ti** ['dəʊtɪ] pl. **-tis** [-tɪz] s. (Indien) Lendentuch n.

di·a·be·tes [,daɪə'biːtiːz] s. ♠ Dia'betes m, Zuckerkrankheit f; **di·a·bet·ic** [,daɪə'betɪk] **I** adj. dia'betisch, zuckerkrank; **II** s. Dia'betiker(in), Zuckerkranke(r m) f.

di·a·ble·rie [dɪ'ɑːblərɪ] s. Zaube'rei f, Hexe'rei f, Teufe'lei f.

di·a·bol·ic, di·a·bol·i·cal [,daɪə'bɒlɪk(l)] adj. □ dia'bolisch, teuflisch; **di·ab·o·lism** [daɪ'æbəlɪzəm] s. **1.** Teufe'lei f; **2.** Teufelskult m.

di·ac·id [daɪ'æsɪd] adj. zweisäurig.

di·ac·o·nate [daɪ'ækəneɪt] s. eccl. Diako'nat n.

di·a·crit·ic [,daɪə'krɪtɪk] **I** adj. dia'kritisch, unter'scheidend; **II** s. ling. dia'kritisches Zeichen.

di·ac·tin·ic [,daɪæk'tɪnɪk] adj. phys. die ak'tinischen Strahlen 'durchlassend.

di·a·dem ['daɪədem] s. **1.** Dia'dem n, Stirnband n; **2.** Hoheit f, Herrscherwürde f, -gewalt f.

di·aer·e·sis [daɪ'ɪərɪsɪs] s. ling. a) Diä'rese f, b) Trema n.

di·ag·nose ['daɪəgnəʊz] v/t. ♠ diagnostizieren, fig. a. bestimmen, feststellen; **di·ag·no·sis** [,daɪəg'nəʊsɪs] pl. **-ses** [-siːz] s. ♠ Dia'gnose f, Befund m, fig. a. Beurteilung f, Bestimmung f; **di·ag·nos·tic** [,daɪəg'nɒstɪk] ♠ **I** adj. (□ ~**ally**) dia'gnostisch: ~ **of** fig. sympto'matisch für; **II** s. a) Sym'ptom n, b) pl. sg. konstr. Dia'gnostik f; **di·ag·nos·ti·cian** [,daɪ-əgnɒs'tɪʃn] s. ♠ Dia'gnostiker(in).

di·ag·o·nal [daɪ'ægənl] **I** adj. □ **1.** diago'nal; schräg (laufend), über Kreuz; **II** s. **2.** a. ~ **line** ⅄ Diago'nale f; **3.** a. ~ **cloth** Diago'nal m, schräg geripptes Gewebe.

di·a·gram ['daɪəgræm] s. Dia'gramm n, grafische Darstellung, Schaubild n, Plan m, Schema n: **wiring** ~ ⚡ Schaltbild n, -plan m: **you need a** ~**?** iro. brauchst du e-e Zeichnung (dazu)?; **di·a·gram·mat·ic** [,daɪəgrə'mætɪk] adj. (□ ~**ally**) diagram'matisch, grafisch, sche'matisch.

di·al ['daɪəl] **I** s. **1.** a. ~ **plate** Zifferblatt n (Uhr); **2.** a. ~ **plate** ⊙ Skala f, Skalen-, Zifferscheibe f; **3.** teleph. Wähl-, Nummernscheibe f; **4.** Radio: Skalenscheibe f, Skala f; ~ **light** Skalenbeleuchtung f; **5.** → **sundial**; **6.** sl. Vi'sage f (Gesicht); **II** v/t. **7.** teleph. wählen: ~**ing code** Brit. Vorwahl(nummer) f; ~ **tone** Am., ~**ing tone** Brit. Amtszeichen n.

di·a·lect ['daɪəlekt] s. Dia'lekt m, Mundart f; **di·a·lec·tal** [,daɪə'lektl] adj. □ dia'lektisch, mundartlich; **di·a·lec·tic** [,daɪə'lektɪk] **I** adj. □ **1.** phls. dia'lektisch; **2.** spitzfindig; **3.** ling. → **dialectal**; **II** s. **4.** oft pl. phls. Dia'lektik f; **5.** Spitzfindigkeit f; **di·a·lec·ti·cal** [,daɪə'lektɪkl] adj. □ **1.** → **dialectal**; **2.** → **dialectic**

D

1, 2; **di·a·lec·ti·cian** [ˌdaɪəlekˈtɪʃn] *s.* phls. Diaˈlektiker *m.*

di·a·logue, *Am. a.* **di·a·log** [ˈdaɪəlɒg] *s.* Diaˈlog *m,* (Zwie)Gespräch *n;* ~ **box** *s. Computer:* Diaˈlogfeld *n,* -ˌfenster *n;* ~ **track** *s. Film:* Sprechband *n.*

di·al·y·sis [daɪˈælɪsɪs] *s.* **1.** 🜛 Diaˈlyse *f;* **2.** ⚕ Diaˈlyse *f,* Blutwäsche *f.*

di·am·e·ter [daɪˈæmɪtə] *s.* **1.** Aͣ Diaˈmeter *m,* ˈDurchmesser *m;* **2.** ˈDurchmesser *m,* Dicke *f,* Stärke *f:* **inner** ~ lichte Weite; **di·a·met·ri·cal** [ˌdaɪəˈmetrɪkl] *adj.* □ **1.** diaˈmetrisch; **2.** *fig.* diametral, genau entgegengesetzt.

di·a·mond [ˈdaɪəmənd] I *s.* **1.** *min.* Diaˈmant *m:* **black** ~ a) schwarzer Diamant, b) *fig.* (Stein)Kohle *f;* **rough** ~ a) ungeschliffener Diamant, b) *fig.* Mensch *m* mit gutem Kern u. rauer Schale; **it was** ~ **cut** ~ es war Wurst wider Wurst, die beiden standen sich in nichts nach; **2.** ◉ (ˈGlaser)Diaˌmant *m;* **3.** Aͣ a) Raute *f,* ˈRhombus *m,* b) spitzgestelltes Viereck; **4.** *Kartenspiel:* Karo *n;* **5.** *Baseball:* a) Spielfeld *n,* b) Innenfeld *n;* **6.** *typ.* Diaˈmant *f (Schriftgrad);* II *adj.* **7.** diaˈmanten, Diamant...; **8.** rhombisch, rautenförmig; ~ **cut·ter** *s.* Diaˈmantschleifer *m;* ~ **drill** *s.* ◉ Diaˈmantbohrer *m;* ~ **field** *s.* Diaˈmantenfeld *n;* ~ **ju·bi·lee** *s.* diaˈmantenes Jubiˈläum; ~ **mine** *s.* Diaˈmantenmine *f;* ~ **pane** *s.* rautenförmige Fensterscheibe; **'~-shaped** *adj.* rautenförmig; ~ **wed·ding** *s.* diaˈmantene Hochzeit.

di·an·thus [daɪˈænθəs] *s.* ♣ Nelke *f.*

di·a·per [ˈdaɪəpə] I *s.* **1.** Diˈaper *m,* Gänseaugenstoff *m;* **2.** *a.* ~ **pattern** Rauten-, Karomuster *n;* **3.** *Am.* (Baby-) Windel *f;* **4.** Monatsbinde *f;* II *v/t.* **5.** mit Rautenmuster verzieren; ~ **rash** *s.* ⚕ Wundsein *n beim Säugling.*

di·aph·a·nous [daɪˈæfənəs] *adj.* ˈdurchsichtig, -scheinend.

di·a·pho·ret·ic [ˌdaɪəfəˈretɪk] *adj. u. s.* ⚕ schweißtreibend(es Mittel).

di·a·phragm [ˈdaɪəfræm] *s.* **1.** *anat.* Scheidewand *f, bsd.* Zwerchfell *n;* **2.** ⚕ Diaˈphragma *n (Verhütungsmittel);* **3.** *teleph. etc.* Memˈbran(e) *f;* **4.** *opt., phot.* Blende *f;* ~ **shut·ter** *s. phot.* Blendenverschluss *m;* ~ **valve** *s.* Membranventil *n.*

di·a·rist [ˈdaɪərɪst] *s.* Tagebuchschreiber(in); **'di·a·rize** [-raɪz] I *v/i.* Tagebuch führen; II *v/t.* ins Tagebuch eintragen.

di·ar·rh(o)e·a [ˌdaɪəˈrɪə] *s.* ⚕ Diarˈrhö(e) *f,* ˈDurchfall *m.*

di·a·ry [ˈdaɪərɪ] *s.* **1.** Tagebuch *n:* **keep a** ~ ein Tagebuch führen; **2.** Taschenkaˌlender *m,* (Vor)Merkbuch *n,* Terˈmin-, Noˈtizbuch *n.*

Di·as·po·ra [daɪˈæspərə] *s. allg.* Diˈaspora *f.*

di·as·to·le [daɪˈæstəlɪ] *s.* ⚕ *u. Metrik:* Diaˈstole *f.*

di·a·ther·my [ˈdaɪəθɜːmɪ] *s.* ⚕ Diatherˈmie *f.*

di·ath·e·sis [daɪˈæθɪsɪs] *pl.* **-ses** [-siːz] *s.* ⚕ *u. fig.* Neigung *f,* Anlage *f.*

di·a·to·ma·ceous earth [ˌdaɪətəˈmeɪʃəs] *s. geol.* Kieselgur *f.*

di·a·ton·ic [ˌdaɪəˈtɒnɪk] *adj.* ♪ diaˈtonisch.

di·a·tribe [ˈdaɪətraɪb] *s.* gehässiger Angriff, Hetze *f,* Hetzrede *f od.* -schrift *f.*

di·ba·sic [daɪˈbeɪsɪk] *adj.* 🜛 zweibasisch.

dib·ble¹ [ˈdɪbə] → **dibble** I.

dib·ble² [ˈdɪbl] I *s.* Dibbelstock *m,* Pflanz-, Setzholz *n;* II *v/t. a.* ~ **in** mit e-m Setzholz pflanzen; III *v/i.* mit e-m Setzholz Löcher machen, dibbeln.

dibs [dɪbz] *s.* **1.** *pl. sg. konstr. Brit.* Kinderspiel mit Steinchen etc.; **2.** F Recht *n* (**on** auf *acc.*); **3.** *Am. sl.* (ein paar) ˌKrötenʼ *pl.* (*Geld*).

dice [daɪs] I *s. pl. von* **die²** 1 Würfel *pl.,* Würfelspiel *n:* **play** (**at**) ~ → II; **no** ~! *Am. sl.* ˌda läuft nichtsʼ!; → **load** 10; II *v/i.* würfeln, knobeln; III *v/t. Küche:* in Würfel schneiden.

dic·ey [ˈdaɪsɪ] *adj.* F preˈkär, heikel.

di·chot·o·my [daɪˈkɒtəmɪ] *s.* Dichotoˈmie *f;* a) *bsd. Logik:* Zweiteilung *f e-s Begriffs,* b) ♣, *zo.* wiederˈholte Gabelung.

di·chro·mat·ic [ˌdaɪkrəʊˈmætɪk] *adj.* **1.** dichroˈmatisch, zweifarbig; **2.** ⚕ dichroˈmat.

dick [dɪk] *s.* **1.** *Brit. sl.* Kerl *m;* **2.** *Am. sl.* ˌSchnüfflerʼ *m:* **private** ~ Privatdetektiv *m;* **3.** V ˌSchwanzʼ *m.*

dick·ens [ˈdɪkɪnz] *s. sl.* Teufel *m:* **what the** ~! was zum Teufel!; **a** ~ **of a mess** ein böser Schlamassel.

dick·er¹ [ˈdɪkə] *v/i.* feilschen, schachern (**for** um).

dick·er² [ˈdɪkə] *s.* 🕀 zehn Stück.

dick·(e)y¹ [ˈdɪkɪ] *s.* F **1.** Hemdbrust *f;* **2.** Bluseneinsatz *m;* **3.** *a.* ~ **bow** ˌFliegeʼ *f,* Schleife *f;* **4.** *a.* ~ **bird** Vögelchen *n,* Piepmatz *m;* **5.** Rück-, Not-, Klappsitz *m;* **6.** *Brit.* F Esel *m.*

dick·(e)y² [ˈdɪkɪ] *adj.* F wack(e)lig, ˌmiesʼ: ~ **heart** schwaches Herz.

di·cot·y·le·don [ˌdaɪkɒtɪˈliːdən] *s.* ♣ Dikoˈtyle *f,* zweikeimblättrige Pflanze.

dic·ta [ˈdɪktə] *pl. von* **dictum.**

dic·tate [dɪkˈteɪt] I *v/t.* (**to** dat.) **1.** Brief etc. diktieren; **2.** diktieren, vorschreiben, gebieten (*a. fig.*); **3.** auferlegen; **4.** eingeben; II *v/i.* **5.** diktieren, ein Dikˈtat geben; **6.** diktieren, befehlen: **he will not be** ~**d to** er lässt sich keine Vorschriften machen; III *s.* [ˈdɪkteɪt] **7.** Gebot *n,* Befehl *m,* Dikˈtat *n:* **the** ~**s of reason** das Gebot der Vernunft; **dic·ˈta·tion** [-eɪʃn] *s.* **1.** Dikˈtat *n:* a) Diktieren *n,* b) Dikˈtatschreiben *n,* c) diktierter Text; **2.** Befehl(e *pl.*) *m,* Geheiß *n;* **dic·ˈta·tor** [-tə] *s.* Dikˈtator *m,* Gewalthaber *m;* **dic·ta·to·ri·al** [ˌdɪktəˈtɔːrɪəl] *adj.* □ diktaˈtorisch; **dic·ˈta·tor·ship** [-təʃɪp] *s.* Dikˈtatur *f;* **dic·ˈta·tress** [-trɪs] *s.* Dikˈtatorin *f.*

dic·tion [ˈdɪkʃn] *s.* **1.** Diktiˈon *f,* Ausdrucksweise *f,* Stil *m,* Sprache *f;* **2.** (deutliche) Aussprache.

dic·tion·ar·y [ˈdɪkʃnrɪ] *s.* **1.** Wörterbuch *n;* **2.** (*bsd.* einsprachiges) enzyklo-ˈpädisches Wörterbuch; **3.** Lexikon *n,* Enzyklopäˈdie *f:* **a walking** (*od.* **living**) ~ *fig.* ein wandelndes Lexikon.

dic·to·graph [ˈdɪktəgraːf] *s.* Abhörgerät *n (beim Telefon).*

dic·tum [ˈdɪktəm] *pl.* **-ta** [-tə], **-tums** *s.* **1.** Machtspruch *m;* **2.** 🜛 richterliches Diktum, (Aus)Spruch *m;* **3.** Spruch *m,* geflügeltes Wort.

did [dɪd] *pret. von* **do¹.**

di·dac·tic [dɪˈdæktɪk] *adj.* (□ ~**ally**) **1.** diˈdaktisch, lehrhaft, belehrend: ~ **play** *thea.* Lehrstück *n;* ~ **poem** Lehrgedicht *n;* **2.** schulmeisterlich.

did·dle¹ [ˈdɪdl] *v/t. sl.* beschwindeln, be-trügen, übers Ohr hauen.

did·dle² [ˈdɪdl] *v/i.* F zappeln.

did·n't [ˈdɪdnt] F *für* **did not.**

didst [dɪdst] *obs. 2. sg. pret. von* **do¹.**

die¹ [daɪ] I *v/i. pres. p.* **dy·ing** [ˈdaɪɪŋ] **1.** sterben (**of** an *acc.*): ~ **of hunger** hungers sterben, verhungern; ~ **from a wound** an e-r Verwundung sterben; ~ **a violent death** e-s gewaltsamen Todes sterben; ~ **of** (*od.* **with**) **laughter** *fig.* sich totlachen; ~ **of boredom** vor Lange(r)weile fast umkommen; ~ **a beggar** als Bettler sterben; ~ **hard** a) zählebig sein (*a. Sache*), ˌnicht totzukriegen seinʼ, b) nicht nachgeben (wollen); **never say** ~! nur nicht aufgeben!; → **bed** 1; **boot¹** 1; **ditch** 1; **harness** 1; **2.** eingehen (*Pflanze, Tier*), verenden (*Tier*); **3.** *fig.* ver-, ˌuntergehen, schwinden, aufhören, sich verlieren, verhallen, erlöschen, vergessen werden; **4.** *mst* **be dying** (**for, to** *inf.*) sich sehnen (nach; danach, zu *inf.*), brennen (auf *acc.;* darauf, zu *inf.*): **I am dying to ...** ich würde schrecklich gern; II *v/t.* **5.** e-s natürlichen *etc.* Todes sterben; *Zssgn mit adv.:*

die **a·way** *v/i.* **1.** schwächer werden, nachlassen, sich verlieren, schwinden; **2.** ohnmächtig werden; ~ **down** *v/i.* **1.** → **die away** 1; **2.** ♣ (von oben) absterben; ~ **off** *v/i.* ˈhin-, wegsterben; ~ **out** *v/i.* aussterben (*a. fig.*).

die² [daɪ] *s.* **1.** *pl.* **dice** Würfel *m:* **the** ~ **is cast** die Würfel sind gefallen; **straight as a** ~ a) pfeilgerade, b) *fig.* grundehrlich; → **dice; straight** 4; **2.** Würfelspiel *n;* **3.** *bsd. Küche:* Würfel *m;* **4.** *pl.* **dies** △ Würfel *m e-s Sockels;* **5.** *pl.* **dies** ◉ a) (Press-, Spritz)Form *f,* Gesenk *n:* **lower** ~ Matrize *f;* **upper** ~ Patrize *f,* b) (Münz)Prägestempel *m,* c) Schneideisen *n,* Stanze *f,* d) Gussform *f.*

'die|-a·way *adj.* schmachtend; **'~-cast** *v/t.* ◉ spritzgießen, spritzen; ~ **cast·ing** *s.* ◉ Spritzguss *m;* **'~-hard** I *s.* **1.** unnachgiebiger Mensch, Dickschädel *m;* **2.** *pol.* hartnäckiger Reaktioˈnär; **3.** zählebige Sache; II *adj.* **4.** hartnäckig, zäh u. unnachgiebig; **5.** zählebig; ~ **head** *s.* ◉ Schneidkopf *m.*

di·e·lec·tric [ˌdaɪɪˈlektrɪk] ⚡ I *s.* Di-eˈlektrikum *n;* II *adj.* (□ ~**ally**) dieˈlektrisch: ~ **strength** Spannungs-, Durchschlagfestigkeit *f.*

di·en·ceph·a·lon [ˌdaɪɪnˈsefələn] *s. anat.* Zwischenhirn *n.*

di·er·e·sis → **diaeresis.**

Die·sel [ˈdiːzl] I Diesel *m (Motor, Fahrzeug od. Kraftstoff);* II *adj.* Diesel...; **die·sel·ize** [ˈdiːzəlaɪz] *v/t.* ◉ auf Dieselbetrieb ˈumstellen.

'die·sink·er *s.* ◉ Werkzeugmacher *m.*

di·e·sis [ˈdaɪɪsɪs] *pl.* **-ses** [-siːz] *s.* **1.** *typ.* Doppelkreuz *n;* **2.** ♪ Kreuz *n.*

di·es non [ˌdaɪiːzˈnɒn] *s.* 🜛 gerichtsfreier Tag.

die stock *s.* ◉ Schneidkluppe *f.*

di·et¹ [ˈdaɪət] *s.* **1.** *parl.* a) ˈUnterhaus *n* (*in Japan etc.*), b) *hist.* Reichstag *m;* **2.** 🜛 *Scot.* Geˈrichtster,min *m.*

di·et² [ˈdaɪət] I *s.* **1.** Nahrung *f,* Ernährung *f,* (*a. fig.* geistige) Kost: **vegetable** ~ vegetarische Kost; **full** (**low**) ~ reichliche (magere) Kost; **2.** ⚕ Diˈät *f,* Schon-, Krankenkost *f:* **be** (**put**) **on a** ~ auf Diät gesetzt sein, Diät leben (müssen); II *v/t.* **3.** *j-n* auf Diˈät setzen: ~ **o.s.** → 4; III *v/i.* **4.** Diˈät halten; **'di·e·tar·y** [-tərɪ] ⚕ I *adj.* **1.** diäˈtetisch, Diät...; II *s.* **2.** Diˈätvorschrift *f;* **3.** ˈSpeise(rati,on) *f.*

di·e·tet·ic [ˌdaɪɪˈtetɪk] *adj.* (□ ~**ally**) → **dietary** 1; **di·e·ˈtet·ics** [-ks] *s. pl. sg. od. pl. konstr.* ⚕ Diäˈtetik *f;* **di·et·kunde** *f;* **di·e·ˈti·tian, di·e·ˈti·cian** [-ˈtɪʃn] *s.* **1.** Diˈätassis,tent(in); **2.** Diäˈtetiker(in).

dif·fer [ˈdɪfə] *v/i.* **1.** sich unterˈscheiden, verschieden sein, abweichen (**from** von); **2.** (*mst* **with**, *a.* **from**) nicht überˈeinstimmen (mit), anderer Meinung

D

sein (als): *I beg to* ~ ich bin (leider) anderer Meinung; **3.** uneinig sein (*on* über *acc.*); → *agree* 2; **dif·fer·ence** ['dıfrəns] *s.* **1.** 'Unterschied *m*, Verschiedenheit *f*: ~ *in price* Preisunterschied; ~ *of opinion* Meinungsverschiedenheit; *that makes a (great)* ~ a) das macht et. (*od.* viel) aus, b) das ändert die Sache; *it made all the* ~ das änderte die Sache vollkommen; *it makes no* ~ (*to me*) es ist (mir) gleich(gültig); *what's the* ~? was macht es schon aus?; **2.** 'Unterschied *m*, unter'scheidendes Merkmal: *the* ~ *between him and his brother*; **3.** 'Unterschied *m* (*in Menge*), Diffe'renz *f* (*a.* ✝, ♈): *split the* ~ a) sich in die Differenz teilen, b) e-n Kompromiß schließen; **4.** Besonderheit *f*: *a film with a* ~ ein Film (von) ganz besonderer Art *od.* ‚mit Pfiff'; *holidays with a* ~ Ferien ‚mal anders'; **5.** Meinungsverschiedenheit *f*, Diffe'renz *f*; **dif·fer·ent** ['dıfrənt] *adj.* □ **1.** (*from*, *a.* *to*) verschieden (von), abweichend (von); anders (*pred.* als), ander (*attr.* als): *in two* ~ *countries* in zwei verschiedenen Ländern; *that's a* ~ *matter* das ist etwas anderes; *at* ~ *times* verschiedentlich, mehrmals; **2.** außergewöhnlich, besonder. **dif·fer·en·tial** [,dıfə'renʃl] **I** *adj.* □ **1.** 'unterschiedlich, charakte'ristisch, Unterscheidungs...; **2.** ⊕, ⚷, ♈, *phys.* Differenzial...; **3.** ✝ gestaffelt, Differenzial..., Staffel...: ~ *tariff*; **II** *s.* **4.** ⊕, *mot.* Differenzi'al-, Ausgleichsgetriebe *n*; **5.** ♈ Differenzi'al *n*; ('Preis-, 'Lohn- *etc.*)Gefälle *n*, (-)Diffe,renz *f*; ~ *cal·cu·lus* *s.* ♈ Differenzi'alrechnung *f*; ~ *du·ty* *s.* ✝ Differenzi'alzoll *m*; ~ *gear* *s.* ⊕ Differenzi'al-, Ausgleichsgetriebe *n*; ~ *rate* *s.* ✝ 'Ausnahmeta,rif *m*. **dif·fer·en·ti·ate** [,dıfə'renʃıeıt] **I** *v/t.* **1.** einen 'Unterschied machen zwischen (*dat.*), unter'scheiden, vonein'ander abgrenzen; unter'scheiden, trennen (*from* von): *be* ~*d* → 4; **II** *v/i.* **3.** e-n 'Unterschied machen, unter'scheiden, differenzieren (*between* zwischen *dat.*); **4.** sich unter'scheiden *od.* entfernen; sich verschieden entwickeln; **dif·fer·en·ti·a·tion** [,dıfərenʃı'eıʃn] *s.* Differenzierung *f*: a) Unter'scheidung *f*, b) (Auf)Teilung *f*, c) Spezialisierung *f*, d) ♈ Ableitung *f*. **dif·fi·cult** ['dıfıkəlt] *adj.* **1.** schwierig, schwer; **2.** beschwerlich, mühsam; schwierig, schwer zu behandeln(d); **'dif·fi·cul·ty** [-tı] *s.* **1.** Schwierigkeit *f*: a) Mühe *f*: *with* ~ mit Mühe, schwer, mühsam; *have* (*od.* *find*) ~ *in doing s.th.* et. schwierig (zu tun) finden, b) schwierige Sache, c) Hindernis *n*, 'Widerstand *m*: *make difficulties* Schwierigkeiten bereiten; **2.** *oft pl.* (*a.* Geld)Schwierigkeiten *pl.*, (-)Verlegenheit *f*. **dif·fi·dence** ['dıfıdəns] *s.* Schüchternheit *f*, mangelndes Selbstvertrauen; **'dif·fi·dent** [-nt] *adj.* □ schüchtern, ohne Selbstvertrauen, scheu: *be* ~ *about doing* sich scheuen zu tun, et. nur zaghaft *od.* zögernd tun. **dif·fract** [dı'frækt] *v/t. phys.* beugen; **dif'frac·tion** [-kʃn] *s. phys.* Beugung *f*, Diffrakti'on *f*. **dif·fuse** [dı'fju:z] **I** *v/t.* **1.** ausgießen, -schütten; **2.** *bsd. fig.* verbreiten; **3.** ♒, *phys.*, *opt.* diffundieren: a) zerstreuen, b) vermischen, c) durch'dringen; **II** *v/i.* **4.** sich verbreiten; **5.** ♒, *phys.* diffundieren: a) sich zerstreuen, b) sich vermischen, c) eindringen; **III** *adj.*

[dı'fju:s] □ **6.** dif'fus: a) weitschweifig, langatmig, b) unklar (*Gedanken etc.*), c) ♒, *phys.* zerstreut: ~ *light* diffuses Licht; **7.** *fig.* verbreitet; **dif·fus·i·bil·i·ty** [dı,fju:zə'bılətı] *s. phys.* Diffusi'onsvermögen *n*; **dif'fus·i·ble** [-zəbl] *adj. phys.* diffusi'onsfähig; **dif·fu·sion** [dı'fju:ʒn] *s.* **1.** Ausgießen *n*; **2.** *fig.* Verbreitung *f*; **3.** Weitschweifigkeit *f*; **4.** ♒, *phys.*, *a.* sociol. Diffusi'on *f*; **dif·fu·sive** [dı'fju:sıv] *adj.* □ *bsd. fig.* **1.** sich verbreitend; **2.** *fig.* weitschweifig; **3.** ♒, *phys.* Diffusions...; **dif'fu·sive·ness** [dı'fju:sıvnıs] *s.* **1.** *phys.* Diffusi'onsfähigkeit *f*; **2.** *fig.* Weitschweifigkeit *f*. **dig** [dıg] **I** *s.* **1.** Grabung *f*; **2.** F (archäo-'logische) Ausgrabung(sstätte); **3.** F Puff *m*, Stoß *m*: ~ *in the ribs* Rippenstoß; **4.** F *fig.* (Seiten)Hieb *m* (*at* auf *j-n*); **5.** *Am.* F ‚Büffler' *m*; **6.** *pl. Brit.* ‚Bude', (*bsd.* Studenten)Zimmer *n*; **II** *v/t.* [*irr.*] **7.** *Loch etc.* graben; *Boden* 'umgraben; *Bodenfrüchte* ausgraben; **8.** *fig.* ‚ausgraben', ans Tageslicht bringen, her'ausfinden; **9.** F *j-m* e-n Stoß geben: ~ *spurs into a horse* e-m Pferd die Sporen geben; **10.** F a) ‚kapieren', b) ‚stehen auf', ein ‚Fan' sein von, c) sich ansehen *od.* anhören; **III** *v/i.* [*irr.*] **11.** graben (*for* nach); **12.** *fig.* a) forschen (*for* nach), b) sich gründlich beschäftigen (*into* mit); **13.** ~ *into* F a) ‚reinhauen' in *e-n Kuchen etc.*, b) sich einarbeiten in (*acc.*); **14.** *Am. sl.* ‚büffeln', ‚ochsen';
Zssgn mit adv.:
dig| in I *v/t.* **1.** eingraben (*a. fig.*); **2.** **dig o.s. in** sich eingraben, *fig. a.* sich verschanzen; **II** *v/i.* **3.** ✕ sich eingraben, sich verschanzen; ~ **out** *v/t.* **1.** ausgraben; **2.** → *dig* 8; ~ **up** *v/t.* **1.** 'um-, ausgraben; **2.** → *dig* 8. **di·gest** [dı'dʒest] **I** *v/t.* **1.** *Speisen* verdauen; **2.** *fig.* verdauen: a) (innerlich) verarbeiten, über'denken, in sich aufnehmen, b) ertragen, verwinden; **3.** ordnen, einteilen; **4.** ♒ digerieren, ausziehen, auflösen; **II** *v/i.* **5.** sich verdauen lassen: ~ *well* leicht verdaulich sein; **6.** ♒ sich auflösen; **III** *s.* ['daıdʒest] **7.** (*of*) a) Auslese *f* (*a. Zeitschrift*), Auswahl *f* (aus), b) Abriß *m* (*gen.*), 'Überblick *m* (über *acc.*); **8.** ⚖ systematisierte Sammlung von Gerichtsentscheidungen; **di'gest·i·ble** [-təbl] *adj.* □ verdaulich, bekömmlich; **di'ges·tion** [-tʃən] *s.* **1.** Verdauung *f*: *easy of* ~ leicht verdaulich; **2.** *fig.* (innerliche) Verarbeitung; **di'ges·tive** [-tıv] **I** *adj.* □ **1.** verdauungsfördernd; **2.** bekömmlich; **3.** Verdauungs... (*-apparat*, *-trakt etc.*); **II** *s.* **4.** verdauungsförderndes Mittel. **dig·ger** ['dıgə] *s.* **1.** Gräber(in); **2.** → *gold digger*; **3.** 'Grabgerät *n*, -ma,schine *f*; **4.** Erdarbeiter *m*; **5.** *a.* ~ *wasp* Grabwespe *f*; **6.** *sl.* Au'stralier *m od.* Neu'seeländer *m*; **dig·gings** ['gıŋz] *s. pl.* **1.** *sg. od. pl. konstr.* Goldbergwerk *n*; **2.** Aushub *m* (*Erde*); **3.** → *dig* 6. **dig·it** ['dıdʒıt] *s.* **1.** *anat.*, *zo.* Finger *m od.* Zehe *f*; **2.** Fingerbreite *f* (*Maß*); **3.** *ast.* astro'nomischer Zoll (*1/12 des Sonnen- od. Monddurchmessers*); **4.** ♈ a) eine der Ziffern von 0 bis 9, Einer *m*, b) Stelle *f*: *three-* ~ *number* dreistellige Zahl; **'dig·it·al** [-tl] **I** *adj.* **1.** Finger...; **2.** *EDV*, *Computer etc.* digi'tal, Digital...: ~ *clock*; ~ *display* Digitalanzeige *f*; ~ *recording* Digitalaufzeichnung *f*; ~ *technology* Digitaltechnik; ~*ly remastered* digital re'mastered; **II** *s.* **3.** ♪

Taste *f*; **dig·i·tal·is** [,dıdʒı'teılıs] *s.* **1.** ⚘ Fingerhut *m*; **2.** ♎ Digi'talis *n*; **'dig·i·tate**, **'dig·i·tat·ed** [-teıt(ıd)] *adj.* **1.** ⚘ gefingert, handförmig; **2.** *zo.* gefingert; **'dig·i·tize** *v/t. EDV etc.*: digitali'sieren. **dig·ni·fied** ['dıgnıfaıd] *adj.* würdevoll, würdig; **dig·ni·fy** ['dıgnıfaı] *v/t.* **1.** ehren, auszeichnen; Würde verleihen (*dat.*); **2.** zieren, schmücken; **3.** hochtrabend benennen. **dig·ni·tar·y** ['dıgnıtərı] *s.* **1.** Würdenträger *m*; **2.** *eccl.* Prä'lat *m*; **dig·ni·ty** ['dıgnıtı] *s.* **1.** Würde *f*, würdevolles Auftreten; **2.** Würde *f*, (hoher) Rang, *a.* Ansehen *n*: *beneath my* ~ unter m-r Würde; *stand on one's* ~ sich nichts vergeben wollen; **3.** *fig.* Größe *f*: ~ *of soul* Seelengröße, -adel *m*. **di·graph** ['daıgrɑ:f] *s. ling.* Di'graph *m* (*Verbindung von zwei Buchstaben zu einem Laut*). **di·gress** [daı'gres] *v/i.* abschweifen; **di'gres·sion** [-eʃn] *s.* Abschweifung *f*; **di'gres·sive** [-sıv] *adj.* □ **1.** abschweifend; **2.** abwegig. **digs** [dıgz] → *dig* 6. **di·he·dral** [daı'hi:drəl] **I** *adj.* **1.** di-'edrisch, zweiflächig: ~ *angle* ♈ Flächenwinkel *m*; **2.** ✈ V-förmig; **II** *s.* **3.** ♈ Di'eder *m*, Zweiflächner *m*; **4.** ✈ V-Form *f*, V-Stellung *f*. **dike¹** [daık] **I** *s.* **1.** Deich *m*, Damm *m*; **2.** Erdwall *m*, erhöhter Fahrdamm; **3.** *a. fig.* Schutzwall *m*, *fig.* Bollwerk *n*; **4.** a) Graben *m*, b) Wasserlauf *m*; **5.** *a.* ~ *rock geol.* Gangstock *m*; **II** *v/t.* **6.** eindämmen, -deichen. **dike²** [daık] *v/t. a.* ~ *out od.* *up Am.* F aufputzen. **dike³** [daık] *s. sl.* ‚Lesbe' *f*. **dik·tat** [dık'tɑ:t] *s.* (*Ger.*) *pol.* Dik'tat *n*. **di·lap·i·date** [dı'læpıdeıt] **I** *v/t.* **1.** *Haus etc.* verfallen lassen; **2.** vergeuden; **II** *v/i.* **3.** verfallen, baufällig werden; **di'lap·i·dat·ed** [-tıd] *adj.* **1.** verfallen, baufällig; **2.** klapp(e)rig (*Auto etc.*); **di·lap·i·da·tion** [dı,læpı'deıʃn] *s.* **1.** Verfall *m*, Baufälligkeit *f*; **2.** *geol.* Verwitterung *f*; **3.** *pl. Brit.* notwendige Repara'turen (*zu Lasten des Mieters*). **di·lat·a·bil·i·ty** [daı,leıtə'bılətı] *s. phys.* Dehnbarkeit *f*, (Aus)Dehnungsvermögen *n*; **di·lat·a·ble** [daı'leıtəbl] *adj. phys.* (aus)dehnbar. **dil·a·ta·tion** [,daıleı'teıʃn] *s. phys.* Ausdehnung *f*; ✈ Erweiterung *f*. **di·late** [daı'leıt] **I** *v/t.* **1.** (aus)dehnen, (aus)weiten, erweitern: *with* ~*d eyes* mit aufgerissenen Augen; **II** *v/i.* **2.** sich (aus)dehnen *od.* (aus)weiten *od.* erweitern; **3.** *fig.* sich (ausführlich) verbreiten *od.* auslassen ([*up*]*on* über *acc.*); **di'la·tion** [-eıʃn] → *dilatation*; **di·la·tor** [-tə] *s.* Di'lator: a) *anat.* Dehnmuskel *m*, b) ✈ Dehnsonde *f*. **dil·a·to·ri·ness** ['dılətərınıs] *s.* Saumseligkeit *f*, Verschleppung *f*; **dil·a·to·ry** ['dılətərı] *adj.* □ **1.** aufschiebend (*a. ⚖*), verzögernd, 'hinhaltend, Verzögerungs..., Verschleppungs..., Hinhalte...: ~ *tactics*; **2.** langsam, saumselig. **dil·do** ['dıldəʊ] *s.* Godemi'ché *m* (*künstlicher Penis*). **di·lem·ma** [dı'lemə] *s.* Di'lemma *n*, Zwangslage *f*, Klemme *f*: *on the horns of a* ~ in e-r Zwickmühle. **dil·et·tan·te** [,dılı'tæntı] **I** *pl.* **-ti** [-ti:], **-tes** [-tız] *s.* **1.** Dilet'tant(in): a) 'Nichtfachmann *m*, Ama'teur(in), b) *contp.* Stümper(in); **2.** Kunstliebhaber(in); **II** *adj.* **3.** → **dil·et'tant·ish** [-tıʃ] *adj.* □

D

dilet'tantisch; **,dil·et'tant·ism** [-tɪzəm] s. Dilettan'tismus m.

dil·i·gence¹ ['dɪlɪʒãːns] (Fr.) s. hist. Postkutsche f.

dil·i·gence² ['dɪlɪdʒəns] s. Fleiß m, Eifer m; a. ✿ Sorgfalt f; **'dil·i·gent** [-nt] adj. □ **1.** fleißig, emsig; **2.** sorgfältig, gewissenhaft.

dill [dɪl] s. ♀ Dill m, Gurkenkraut n.

dil·ly-dal·ly ['dɪlɪdælɪ] v/i. F **1.** die Zeit vertrödeln, (her'um)trödeln; **2.** zaudern, schwanken.

dil·u·ent ['dɪljʊənt] **I** adj. 🜄 verdünnend; **II** s. 🜍 Verdünnungsmittel n.

di·lute [daɪ'ljuːt] **I** v/t. **1.** verdünnen, bsd. wässern; **2.** Farben dämpfen; **3.** fig. (ab)schwächen, verwässern: ~ **la·bo(u)r** Facharbeit in Arbeitsgänge zerlegen, deren Ausführung nur geringe Fachkenntnisse erfordert; **II** adj. **4.** verdünnt; **3.** fig. (ab)geschwächt, verwässert; **di'lut·ed** [-tɪd] adj. → dilute II; **dil·u·tee** [,daɪlju'tiː] s. zwischen dem angelernten u. dem Facharbeiter stehender Beschäftigter; **di·lu·tion** [daɪ'luːʃn] s. **1.** Verdünnung f, Verwässerung f; **2.** verdünnte Lösung; **3.** fig. Abschwächung f, Verwässerung f: ~ **of labo(u)r** Zerlegung von Facharbeit in Arbeitsgänge, deren Ausführung nur geringe Fachkenntnisse erfordert.

di·lu·vi·al [daɪ'luːvjəl], **di·lu·vi·an** [-jən] adj. **1.** geol. dilluvi'al, Eiszeit...; **2.** Überschwemmungs...; **3.** (Sint)Flut...; **di·lu·vi·um** [-jəm] s. geol. Di'luvium n.

dim [dɪm] **I** adj. □ **1.** (halb)dunkel, düster, trübe (a. fig.); **2.** undeutlich, verschwommen, schwach; **3.** blass, matt (Farbe); **4.** F schwer von Begriff; **II** v/t. **5.** verdunkeln, verdüstern; trüben; **6.** a. ~ **out** Licht abblenden, dämpfen; **7.** mattieren; **III** v/i. **8.** sich verdunkeln; **9.** matt od. trübe werden; **10.** undeutlich werden; verblassen (a. fig.).

dime [daɪm] s. Am. Zehn'centstück n; fig. Groschen m: ~ **novel** Groschenroman m; ~ **store** billiges Warenhaus; **they are a ~ a dozen** a) sie sind spottbillig, b) es gibt jede Menge davon.

di·men·sion [dɪ'menʃn] **I** s. **1.** Dimensi'on f (a. A): a) Abmessung f, Maß n, Ausdehnung f, b) pl. oft fig. Ausmaß n, Größe f, 'Umfang m: **of vast ~s** riesengroß; **II** v/t. **2.** bemessen, dimensionieren: **amply ~ed**; **3.** mit Maßangaben versehen: **~ed sketch** Maßskizze f; **di·men·sion·al** [-ʃənl] adj. mst in Zssgn dimensio'nal.

di·min·ish [dɪ'mɪnɪʃ] **I** v/t. **1.** vermindern (a. ♪), verringern; **2.** verkleinern (a. A), her'absetzen (a. fig.); **3.** (ab)schwächen; **4.** △ verjüngen; **II** v/i. **5.** sich vermindern, abnehmen: ~ **in value** an Wert verlieren.

dim·i·nu·tion [,dɪmɪ'njuːʃn] s. **1.** Verminderung f, Verringerung f; Verkleinerung f (a. ♪); **2.** Abnahme f; **3.** △ Verjüngung f; **di·min·u·ti·val** [dɪ,mɪnju'taɪvl] adj. □ → diminutive 2; **di·min·u·tive** [dɪ'mɪnjʊtɪv] **I** adj. □ **1.** klein, winzig; **2.** ling. Diminutiv..., Verkleinerungs...; **II** s. **3.** ling. Diminu'tiv(um) n, Verkleinerungsform f od. -silbe f.

dim·i·ty ['dɪmɪtɪ] s. Dimity m, Barchentköper m.

dim·mer ['dɪmə] s. **1.** Dimmer m (Helligkeitseinsteller); **2.** pl. mot. a) Abblendlicht n, b) Standlicht n: ~ **switch** Abblendschalter m; **dim·ness** ['dɪmnɪs] s. **1.** Dunkelheit f, Düsterkeit f; **2.** Mattheit f; **3.** Undeutlichkeit f.

di·mor·phic [daɪ'mɔːfɪk], **di·mor·phous** [-fəs] adj. di'morph, zweigestaltig.

'dim-out s. ✕ Teilverdunkelung f.

dim·ple ['dɪmpl] **I** s. **1.** Grübchen n (Wange); **2.** Vertiefung f; **3.** Kräuselung f (Wasser); **II** v/t. **4.** Grübchen machen in (acc.); **5.** Wasser kräuseln; **III** v/i. **6.** Grübchen bekommen; **7.** sich kräuseln (Wasser); **'dim·pled** [-ld], **'dim·ply** [-lɪ] adj. **1.** mit Grübchen; **2.** gekräuselt (Wasser).

,dim-'wit·ted adj. sl. **1.** dämlich; **2.** (geistig) beschränkt.

din [dɪn] **I** s. **1.** Lärm m, Getöse n; **2.** Geklirr n (Waffen), Gerassel n; **II** v/t. **3.** durch Lärm betäuben; **4.** et. dauernd (vor)predigen: ~ **s.th. into s.o.('s ears)** j-m et. einhämmern; **III** v/i. **5.** lärmen; **6.** dröhnen (with von).

dine [daɪn] **I** v/i. **1.** speisen, essen: ~ **in (out)** zu Hause (auswärts) essen; ~ **off** (od. on) **roast beef** Rostbraten essen; **II** v/t. **2.** j-n bei sich zu Gast haben, bewirten; **3.** für ... Personen Platz zum Essen haben, fassen (Zimmer, Tisch); **'din·er** [-nə] s. **1.** Tischgast m; **2.** 🚆 Speisewagen m; **3.** Am. Imbissstube f, 'Esslo,kal n.

di·nette [daɪ'net] s. Essecke f.

ding [dɪŋ] **I** v/t. **1.** läuten; **2.** → din 4; **II** v/i. **3.** läuten.

ding·dong [,dɪŋ'dɒŋ] **I** s. Bimbam n; **II** adj.: **a ~ fight** ein hin u. her wogender Kampf.

din·ghy ['dɪŋgɪ] s. **1.** ⚓ a) Dingi n, b) Beiboot n; **2.** Schlauchboot n.

din·gi·ness ['dɪndʒɪnɪs] s. **1.** trübe od. schmutzige Farbe; **2.** Schmuddeligkeit f; **3.** Schäbigkeit f (a. fig.); **4.** fig. Anrüchigkeit f.

din·gle ['dɪŋgl] s. Waldschlucht f.

din·go ['dɪŋgəʊ] pl. **-goes** s. zo. Dingo m (Wildhund Australiens).

din·gus ['dɪŋgəs] s. Am. sl. **1.** Dingsda n; **2.** ,Ding' n (Penis).

din·gy ['dɪndʒɪ] adj. □ **1.** schmutzig, schmuddelig; **2.** schäbig (a. fig.); **3.** fig. anrüchig.

din·ing| car ['daɪnɪŋ] s. 🚆 Speisewagen m; ~ **hall** s. Speisesaal m; ~ **room** s. Speise-, Esszimmer n; ~ **ta·ble** s. Esstisch m.

dink [dɪŋk] s. **1. dinks** pl. → dinkies; **2.** Am. contp. Vietna'mese m, -'mesin f; **din·kies** ['dɪŋkiːz] s. pl. (double income no kids) kinderlose Doppelverdiener pl.

din·kum ['dɪŋkəm] adj. Austral. F re'ell: ~ **oil** die volle Wahrheit.

dink·y ['dɪŋkɪ] **I** adj. F **1.** Brit. zierlich, niedlich, nett; **2.** Am. klein; **II** s. F gut verdienende(r) Partner(in) in e-r kinderlosen Partnerschaft; → **dinkies**.

din·ner ['dɪnə] s. **1.** Hauptmahlzeit f, Mittag-, Abendessen n: **after ~** nach dem Essen, nach Tisch; **be at ~** bei Tisch sein; **stay for** (od. **to**) ~ zum Essen bleiben; ~ **is ready** es (od. das Essen) ist angerichtet; **what are we having for ~?** was gibt es zum Essen?; **2.** Di'ner n, Festessen n: **at a ~** bei od. auf e-m Diner; ~ **coat** s. bsd. Am. Smoking m; ~ **dance** s. Abendgesellschaft f mit Tanz; ~ **jack·et** s. Smoking m; ~ **pail** s. Am. Essgefäß n; ~ **par·ty** s. Tisch-, Abendgesellschaft f; ~ **serv·ice**, ~ **set** s. 'Speiser,vice n, Tafelgeschirr n; ~ **ta·ble** s. Esstisch m; ~ **time** s. Tischzeit f; ~ **wag·on** s. Servierwagen m.

di·no·saur ['daɪnəʊsɔː] s. zo. Dino'saurier m.

dint [dɪnt] **I** s. **1.** Beule f, Delle f; **2.** Strieme f; **3.** **by ~ of** kraft, vermöge, mittels (alle gen.); **II** v/t. **4.** einbeulen.

di·oc·e·san [daɪ'ɒsɪsn] eccl. **I** adj. Diöze-san...; **II** s. (Diöze'san)Bischof m; **di·o·cese** ['daɪəsɪs] s. Diö'zese f.

di·ode ['daɪəʊd] s. ⚡ **1.** Di'ode f, Zweipolröhre f; **2.** Kri'stalldi,ode f.

Di·o·nys·i·ac [,daɪə'nɪzɪæk], **Di·o·ny·sian** [-zɪən] adj. dio'nysisch.

di·op·ter Am., Brit. **di·op·tre** [daɪ'ɒptə] s. phys. Diop'trie f; **di·op·tric** [-trɪk] phys. **I** adj. **1.** di'optrisch, lichtbrechend; **II** s. **2.** → diopter; **3.** pl. sg. konstr. Di'optrik f, Brechungslehre f.

di·o·ra·ma [,daɪə'rɑːmə] s. Dio'rama n (plastisch wirkendes Schaubild).

Di·os·cu·ri [,daɪəʊ'skjʊəraɪ] s. pl. Dios-'kuren pl. (Castor u. Pollux).

di·ox·ide [daɪ'ɒksaɪd] s. 🜍 Di'o,xid n.

di·ox·in [daɪ'ɒksɪn] s. 🜍 Dio'xin n.

dip [dɪp] **I** v/t. **1.** (ein)tauchen (in, into in acc.): ~ **one's hand into one's pocket** in die Tasche greifen (a. fig. Geld ausgeben); **2.** färben; **3.** Schafe etc. dippen (Desinfektionsbad); **4.** Kerzen ziehen; **5.** ⚓ Flagge (zum Gruß) dippen, auf- u. niederholen; **6.** a. ~ **up** schöpfen (from, out of aus); **7.** mot. Scheinwerfer abblenden; **II** v/i. **8.** 'unter-, eintauchen; **9.** sich senken od. neigen (Gelände, Waage, Magnetnadel); **10.** ✕ ab-, einfallen; **11.** nieder- u. wieder auffliegen; **12.** ✈ vor dem Steigen tiefer gehen; **13.** fig. hin'eingreifen: ~ **into** a) e-n Blick werfen in (acc.), sich flüchtig befassen mit, b) Reserven angreifen; ~ **into one's purse** (od. **pocket**) (tief) in die Tasche greifen; ~ **deep into the past** die Vergangenheit erforschen; **III** s. **14.** Eintauchen n; **15.** kurzes Bad(en); **16.** ❂ Farbbad n; Tauchbad n: ~ **brazing** Tauchlöten n; **17.** Desinfekti'onsbad n (Schafe); **18.** geschöpfte Flüssigkeit; **19.** Am. F Tunke f, Soße f; **20.** (gezogene) Kerze; **21.** Neigung f, Senkung f, Gefälle n; Neigungswinkel m; **22.** geol. Abdachung f, Einfallen n, Versinken n; **23.** schnelles Hin'ab(- u. Hin'auf)Fliegen; **24.** ✈ plötzliches Tiefergehen vor dem Steigen; **25.** ⚓ Dippen n (kurzes Niederholen der Flagge); **26.** fig. flüchtiger Blick, ,Ausflug' m (in die Politik etc.); **27.** Angreifen n (into e-s Vorrats etc.); **28.** sl. Taschendieb m.

diph·the·ri·a [dɪf'θɪərɪə] s. 🜍 Diphthe-'rie f.

diph·thong ['dɪfθɒŋ] s. ling. **1.** Diph-'thong m, 'Doppelvo,kal m; **2.** die Ligatur æ od. œ; **diph·thon·gal** [dɪf'θɒŋgl] adj. ling. diph'thongisch; **diph·thong-i·za·tion** [,dɪfθɒŋgaɪ'zeɪʃn] s. ling. Diphthongierung f.

di·ple·gi·a [daɪ'pliːdʒɪə] s. 🜍 Diple'gie f, doppelseitige Lähmung.

di·plo·ma [dɪ'pləʊmə] s. Di'plom n, (a. Ehren-, Sieger)Urkunde f; **di·plo·ma·cy** [-əsɪ] s. pol., a. fig. Diploma'tie f; **di·plo·maed** [-məd] adj. diplomiert, Diplom...; **dip·lo·mat** ['dɪpləmæt] s. pol., a. fig. Diplo'mat m; **dip·lo·mat·ic** [,dɪplə'mætɪk] adj. (□ ~ally) **1.** pol. diplo'matisch (a. fig.): ~ **body** (od. **corps**) diplomatisches Korps; ~ **service** diplomatischer Dienst; **2.** urkundlich; **dip·lo·mat·ics** [,dɪplə'mætɪks] s. pl. sg. konstr. Diplo'matik f, Urkundenlehre f; **di·plo·ma·tist** [-ətɪst] → diplomat; **di·plo·ma·tize** [-ətaɪz] v/i. diplo'matisch vorgehen.

di·po·lar [daɪ'pəʊlə] adj. ⚡ zweipolig; **di·pole** ['daɪpəʊl] s. Di'pol m.

dip·per ['dɪpə] s. **1.** orn. Taucher m; **2.** Schöpflöffel m; **3.** ❂ a) Baggereimer m, b) Bagger m; **4.** ❂ Färber m, Beizer

D

m; **5.** *ast.* ♉, **Big** ♉ *Am.* Großer Bär; **Little** ♉ *Am.* Kleiner Bär; **6.** *s. eccl. obs.* 'Wiedertäufer *m*; ~ **dredg·er** *s.* Löffelbagger *m*.

dip·ping ['dɪpɪŋ] *s.* **1.** ◎ (Tauch)Bad *n*; **2.** *in Zssgn* Tauch...: ~ **electrode**; ~ **compass** Inklinationskompass *m*; ~ **rod** Wünschelrute *f*.

dip·py ['dɪpɪ] *adj.* □ F **1.** (ein bisschen) verrückt; **2.** 'übergeschnappt, me'schugge.

dip·so·ma·ni·a [ˌdɪpsəʊ'meɪnjə] *s.* 🎗 Dipsoma'nie *f* (*periodisch auftretende Trunksucht*); ˌdip·so'ma·ni·ac [-nɪæk] *s.* Dipso'mane *m*, Dipso'manin *f*.

'dip|·stick *s. mot.* (Öl- *etc.*)Messstab *m*; ~ **switch** *s. mot. Brit.* Abblendschalter *m*.

dip·ter·a ['dɪptərə] *s. pl. zo.* Zweiflügler *pl.*; 'dip·ter·al [-rəl], 'dip·ter·ous [-rəs] *adj.* zweiflügelig.

dip·tych ['dɪptɪk] *s.* Diptychon *n*.

dire ['daɪə] *adj.* **1.** grässlich, entsetzlich, schrecklich; **2.** unheilvoll; **3.** äußerst, höchst: **be in ~ need of** *et.* ganz dringend brauchen.

di·rect [dɪ'rekt] **I** *v/t.* **1.** lenken, leiten, führen; beaufsichtigen; ♪ dirigieren; *Film, TV:* Re'gie führen bei: **~ed by** unter der Regie von; **2.** *Aufmerksamkeit, Blicke* richten, lenken (**to, towards** auf *acc.*): **be ~ed to doing s.th.** darauf abzielen, et. zu tun (*Verfahren etc.*); **3.** *Worte etc.* richten, *Brief* richten, adressieren (**to** an *acc.*); **4.** anweisen, beauftragen; (An)Weisung geben (*dat.*): ~ **the jury as to the law** 🏛 den Geschworenen Rechtsbelehrung erteilen; **5.** anordnen, verfügen, bestimmen: ~ **s.th. to be done** anordnen, dass et. geschieht; **as ~ed** nach Vorschrift, laut Anordnung; **6.** befehlen; **7.** (**to**) den Weg zeigen (nach, zu), verweisen (an *acc.*); **II** *v/i.* **8.** befehlen, bestimmen; **9.** ♪ dirigieren; *Film, TV:* Re'gie führen; **III** *adj.* □ → *directly*; **10.** di'rekt, gerade; **11.** di'rekt, unmittelbar (*a.* ◎, ⚡, *phys., pol.*): ~ **action** *pol.* direkte Aktion; ~ **advertising** Werbung *f* beim Konsumenten; ~ **costing** ✝ *Am.* Grenzkostenrechnung *f*; ~ **current** ⚡ Gleichstrom *m*; ~ **dial(l)ing** *teleph.* Durchwahl *f*; ~ **debiting** Einzugsverfahren *n*; ~**-debit mandate** Einzugsermächtigung *f*; ~ **distance dialing** *teleph. Am.* Selbstwählfernverkehr *m*; ~ **evidence** unmittelbarer Beweis; ~ **flight** Di'rektflug *m*; ~ **hit** Volltreffer *m*; ~ **line** a) direkte (Abstammungs)Linie, b) *teleph.* 'Durchwahl *f*; ~ **method** direkte Methode (*Sprachunterricht*); **the ~ opposite** das genaue Gegenteil; ~ **responsibility** persönliche Verantwortung; ~ **selling** ✝ Direktverkauf *m*; ~ **taxes** direkte Steuern; ~ **train** durchgehender Zug; **12.** gerade, offen (deutlich: ~ **answer**; ~ **question**; **13.** *ling.* ~ **method** direkte Methode; ~ **object** direktes Objekt; ~ **speech** direkte Rede; **14.** *ast.* rechtläufig; **IV** *adv.* **15.** di'rekt, unmittelbar (**to** zu, an *acc.*).

di·rec·tion [dɪ'rekʃn] *s.* **1.** Richtung *f* (*a.* ◎, *phys., fig.*): **sense of ~** Orts-, Orientierungssinn *m*; **in the ~ of** in (der) Richtung nach *od.* auf (*acc.*); **in all ~s** nach allen Richtungen *od.* Seiten; **in many ~s** in vieler Hinsicht; **2.** Leitung *f*, Führung *f*, Lenkung *f*: **under his ~** unter s-r Leitung; **3.** Leitung *f*, Direkti'on *f*, Direk'torium *n*; **4.** *Film, TV:* Re'gie *f*; **5.** *mst pl.* (An)Weisung *f*, Anleitung *f*, Belehrung *f*, Anordnung *f*,

Vorschrift *f*, Richtlinie *f*: **by ~ of** auf Anordnung von; **give ~s** Anweisungen *od.* Vorschriften geben; **~s for use** Gebrauchsanweisung; **full ~s inside** genaue Anweisung(en) anbei; **6.** Anschrift *f*, A'dresse *f* (*Brief*).

di·rec·tion·al [dɪ'rekʃənl] *adj.* **1.** Richtungs...; **2.** ⚡ a) Richt..., b) Peil...; ~ **aer·i·al**, *bsd. Am.* ~ **an·ten·na** ⚡ 'Richtan,tenne *f*, -strahler *m*; ~ **beam** *s.* ⚡ Richtstrahl *m*; ~ **ra·di·o** ⚡ **1.** Richtfunk *m*; ~ **beacon** ♄ Richtfunkfeuer *n*; **2.** Peilfunk *m*; ~ **trans·mit·ter** *s.* ⚡ **1.** Richtfunksender *m*; **2.** Peilsender *m*.

di'rec·tion| find·er *s.* ⚡ (Funk)Peiler *m*, Peilempfänger *m*; ~ **find·ing** *s.* a) (Funk)Peilung *f*, Richtungsbestimmung *f*, b) Peilwesen *n*; ~ **set** Peilgerät *n*; ~ **in·di·ca·tor** *s.* **1.** *mot.* (Fahrt)Richtungsanzeiger *m*, Blinker *m*; **2.** ✈ Kursweiser *m*.

di·rec·tive [dɪ'rektɪv] **I** *adj.* lenkend, leitend, richtungweisend; **II** *s.* Direk'tive *f*, (An)Weisung *f*, Vorschrift *f*; **di'rect·ly** [dɪ'rektlɪ] **I** *adv.* **1.** gerade, di'rekt; **2.** unmittelbar, di'rekt (*a.* ◎): ~ **proportional** direkt proportional; ~ **opposed** genau entgegengesetzt; **3.** *bsd. Brit.* [*a.* 'drekli] so'fort, gleich, bald; **II** *cj.* **4.** *bsd. Brit.* [*F a.* 'dreklɪ] so'bald (als): ~ **he entered** sobald er eintrat; **di'rect·ness** [-tnɪs] *s.* **1.** Di'rekt-, Geradheit *f*, gerade Richtung; **2.** Unmittelbarkeit *f*; **3.** Offenheit *f*; **4.** Deutlichkeit *f*.

di·rec·tor [dɪ'rektə] *s.* **1.** Di'rektor *m*, Leiter *m*, Vorsteher *m*; **2.** ✝ a) Di'rektor *m*: ~**-general** Generaldirektor *m*, b) Mitglied *n* des Verwaltungsrats (*e-r AG*); → **board** 10; **3.** *Film etc.:* Regis'seur *m*; **4.** ♪ Diri'gent *m*; **5.** ✖ Kom'mandogerät *n*; **di'rec·to·rate** [-tərət] *s.* **1.** → *directorship*; **2.** Direk'torium *n*, Leitung *f*; **3.** ✝ a) Direk'torium *n*, b) Verwaltungsrat *m*; **di'rec·tor·ship** [-ʃɪp] *s.* Direk'torenposten *m*, -stelle *f*.

di·rec·to·ry [dɪ'rektərɪ] *s.* **1.** a) A'dressbuch *n*, b) Tele'fonbuch *n*, c) Branchenverzeichnis *n*: ~ **enquiries**, *Am.* ~ **assistance** Telefonauskunft *f*, d) *Computer:* Verzeichnis *n*; **2.** *eccl.* Gottesdienstordnung *f*; **3.** Leitfaden *m*; **4.** Direk'torium *n*; **5.** ♫ *hist.* Direk'torium *n* (*französische Revolution*).

di·rec·tress [dɪ'rektrɪs] *s.* Direk'torin *f*, Vorsteherin *f*, Leiterin *f*.

dire·ful ['daɪəfʊl] → *dire*.

dirge [dɜ:dʒ] *s.* Klage-, Trauerlied *n*, Totenklage *f*.

dir·i·gi·ble ['dɪrɪdʒəbl] **I** *adj.* lenkbar; **II** *s.* lenkbares Luftschiff.

dirk [dɜ:k] *s.* Dolch *m*.

dirn·dl ['dɜ:ndl] (*Ger.*) *s.* Dirndl(kleid) *n*.

dirt [dɜ:t] *s.* **1.** Schmutz *m* (*a. fig.*), Kot *m*, Dreck *m*; **2.** Staub *m*, Boden *m*, (lockere) Erde; **3.** *fig.* Plunder *m*, Schund *m*; **4.** *fig.* unflätige Reden *pl.*; Gemeinhei(en *pl.*) *f*: **eat ~** sich widerspruchslos demütigen; **fling** (*od.* **throw**) ~ **at s.o.** j-n in den Schmutz ziehen; **do s.o.** ~ *sl.* j-n ganz gemein reinlegen; **treat s.o. like** ~ j-n wie (den letzten) Dreck behandeln; ˌ~-'**cheap** *adj. u. adv.* spottbillig.

dirt·i·ness ['dɜ:tɪnɪs] *s.* **1.** Schmutz *m*, Schmutzigkeit *f* (*a. fig.*); **2.** Gemeinheit *f*, Niedertracht *f*.

dirt| road *s. Am.* unbefestigte Straße; ~ **track** *s. sport mot.* Aschenbahn *f*.

dirt·y ['dɜ:tɪ] *adj.* □ **1.** schmutzig, dreckig, Schmutz...: ~ **brown** schmutzig braun; ~ **work** a) Schmutzarbeit *f*, b)

fig. unsauberes Geschäft, Schurkerei *f*; **2.** *fig.* gemein, niederträchtig: **a ~ look** ein böser Blick; **a ~ lot** ein Lumpenpack; ~ **trick** Gemeinheit *f*; **do the ~ on s.o.** *Brit. sl.* j-n gemein behandeln; **3.** *fig.* schmutzig, unflätig, unanständig: **a ~ mind** schmutzige Gedanken *od.* Fantasie; **4.** schlecht, *bsd.* ⚓ stürmisch (*Wetter*); **II** *v/t.* **5.** beschmutzen, besudeln (*a. fig.*); **III** *v/i.* **6.** schmutzig werden; schmutzen.

dis·a·bil·i·ty [ˌdɪsə'bɪlətɪ] *s.* **1.** Unvermögen *n*, Unfähigkeit *f*; **2.** 🏛 Rechtsunfähigkeit *f*; **3.** Körperbeschädigung *f*, -behinderung *f*; Gebrechen *n*; Arbeits-, Erwerbsunfähigkeit *f*; Invalidi'tät *f*; ✖ → *disablement* 2; **4.** Unzulänglichkeit *f*; **5.** Benachteiligung *f*, Nachteil *m*; ~ **ben·e·fit** *s.* Invalidi'tätsrente *f*; ~ **in·sur·ance** *s.* Inva'lidenversicherung *f*; ~ **pen·sion** *s.* (Kriegs)Versehrtenrente *f*.

dis·a·ble [dɪs'eɪbl] *v/t.* **1.** unfähig machen, außer'stand setzen (**from doing s.th.** et. zu tun); **2.** unbrauchbar *od.* untauglich machen (**for** für, zu); **3.** ✖ a) dienstuntauglich machen, b) kampfunfähig machen; **4.** verkrüppeln; **5.** 🏛 geschäfts- *od.* rechtsunfähig machen; **dis'a·bled** [-ld] *adj.* **1.** 🏛 geschäfts- *od.* rechtsunfähig; **2.** arbeits-, erwerbsunfähig, inva'lide; **3.** ✖ a) dienstuntauglich, b) kriegsversehrt: **a ~ ex-soldier** ein Kriegsversehrter, c) kampfunfähig; **4.** ✖ manövrierunfähig, seeuntüchtig; **5.** *mot.* fahruntüchtig: ~ **car**; **6.** unbrauchbar; **7.** (körperlich *od.* geistig) behindert; **dis'a·ble·ment** [-mənt] *s.* **1.** → *disability* 2, 3; **2.** ✖ a) (Dienst-)Untauglichkeit *f*, b) Kampfunfähigkeit *f*.

dis·a·buse [ˌdɪsə'bju:z] *v/t.* aus dem Irrtum befreien, e-s Besseren belehren, aufklären (**of s.th.** über *acc.*): ~ **o.s.** (*od.* **one's mind**) **of s.th.** sich von et. (*Irrtümlichem*) befreien, sich et. aus dem Kopf schlagen.

dis·ac·cord [ˌdɪsə'kɔ:d] **I** *v/i.* nicht über'einstimmen; **II** *s.* Uneinigkeit *f*; 'Widerspruch *m*.

dis·ac·cus·tom [ˌdɪsə'kʌstəm] *v/t.* abgewöhnen (**s.o. to s.th.** j-m et.).

dis·ad·van·tage [ˌdɪsəd'vɑ:ntɪdʒ] *s.* Nachteil *m*, Schaden *m*: **be at a ~**, **la·bo(u)r under a ~** im Nachteil sein; **to s.o.'s ~** zu j-s Nachteil *od.* Schaden; **put s.o. at a ~** j-n benachteiligen; **take s.o. at a ~** j-s ungünstige Lage ausnutzen; **sell to** (*od.* **at a**) ~ mit Verlust verkaufen; **dis·ad·van·ta·geous** [ˌdɪsædvɑ:n'teɪdʒəs] *adj.* □ nachteilig, ungünstig, unvorteilhaft, schädlich (**to** für).

dis·af·fect·ed [ˌdɪsə'fektɪd] *adj.* □ **1.** (**to, towards**) unzufrieden (mit), abgeneigt (*dat.*); **2.** *pol.* unzuverlässig, untreu; **dis·af·fec·tion** [-kʃn] *s.* Unzufriedenheit *f* (**for** mit), (*a. pol.* Staats-)Verdrossenheit *f*.

dis·af·firm [ˌdɪsə'fɜ:m] *v/t.* **1.** (ab)leugnen; **2.** 🏛 aufheben, 'umstoßen.

dis·af·for·est [ˌdɪsə'fɒrɪst] *v/t.* **1.** 🏛 *e-m Wald* den Schutz durch das Forstrecht nehmen; **2.** abholzen.

dis·ag·i·o [dɪs'ædʒɪəʊ] *s.* ✝ Dis'agio *n*, Abschlag *m*.

dis·a·gree [ˌdɪsə'gri:] *v/i.* **1.** (**with**) nicht über'einstimmen (mit), im 'Widerspruch stehen (zu, mit); sich wider'sprechen; **2.** (**with**) anderer Meinung sein (als), nicht zustimmen (*dat.*); **3.** (**with**) nicht einverstanden sein (mit), gegen *et.* sein, ablehnen (*acc.*); **4.** (sich) streiten (**on** über *acc.*); **5.**

D

(**with** *j-m*) schlecht bekommen, nicht zuträglich sein (*Essen etc.*); ˌ**dis·a·'gree·a·ble** [-'grɪəbl] *adj.* □ **1.** unangenehm, widerlich, lästig; **2.** unliebenswürdig, eklig; ˌ**dis·a'gree·a·ble·ness** [-'grɪəblnɪs] *s.* **1.** Widerwärtigkeit *f*; **2.** Lästigkeit *f*; **3.** Unliebenswürdigkeit *f*; ˌ**dis·a'gree·ment** [-mənt] *s.* **1.** Unstimmigkeit *f*, Verschiedenheit *f*, 'Widerspruch *m*; **2.** Meinungsverschiedenheit *f*, 'Misshelligkeit *f*, Streit *m*.

dis·al·low [ˌdɪsə'laʊ] *v/t.* **1.** nicht zulassen (*a.* ⚖️) *od.* erlauben, verweigern; **2.** nicht anerkennen, nicht gelten lassen, *sport a.* annullieren, nicht geben; ˌ**dis·al'low·ance** [-'laʊəns] *s.* Nichtanerkennung *f*, *sport a.* Annullierung *f*.

dis·ap·pear [ˌdɪsə'pɪə] *v/i.* **1.** verschwinden (**from** von, aus); **2.** verloren gehen, aufhören; ˌ**dis·ap'pear·ance** [-'pɪərəns] *s.* **1.** Verschwinden *n*; **2.** ⊙ Schwund *m*; ˌ**dis·ap'pear·ing** [-'pɪərɪŋ] *adj.* **1.** verschwindend; **2.** versenkbar.

dis·ap·point [ˌdɪsə'pɔɪnt] *v/t.* **1.** enttäuschen: **be ˷ed** enttäuscht sein (**at** *od.* **with** *über acc.*, **in** von *dat.*); **be ˷ed of s.th.** um et. betrogen *od.* gebracht werden; **2.** *Hoffnung* (ent)täuschen, zu'nichte machen; ˌ**dis·ap'point·ed** [-tɪd] *adj.* enttäuscht; ˌ**dis·ap'point·ing** [-tɪŋ] *adj.* □ enttäuschend; ˌ**dis·ap'point·ment** [-mənt] *s.* **1.** Enttäuschung *f* (*a. von Hoffnungen etc.*): **to my ˷** zu m-r Enttäuschung; **2.** Enttäuschung *f* (*enttäuschende Person od. Sache*).

dis·ap·pro·ba·tion [ˌdɪsæprəʊ'beɪʃn] *s.* 'Missbilligung *f*.

dis·ap·prov·al [ˌdɪsə'pruːvl] *s.* (**of**) 'Missbilligung *f* (*gen.*), 'Missfallen *n* (über *acc.*); ˌ**dis·ap·prove** [ˌdɪsə'pruːv] **I** *v/t.* miss'billigen, ablehnen; **II** *v/i.* da'gegen sein: **˷ of** → I; ˌ**dis·ap'prov·ing·ly** [-vɪŋlɪ] *adv.* miss'billigend.

dis·arm [dɪs'ɑːm] **I** *v/t.* **1.** entwaffnen (*a. fig.*); **2.** *freimachen*; *Bomben etc.* entschärfen; **3.** besänftigen; **II** *v/i.* **4.** *pol.*, ✕ abrüsten; **dis'ar·ma·ment** [-məmənt] *s.* **1.** Entwaffnung *f*; **2.** *pol.*, ✕ Abrüstung *f*; **dis'arm·ing** [-mɪŋ] *adj.* □ *fig.* entwaffnend.

dis·ar·range [ˌdɪsə'reɪndʒ] *v/t.* in Unordnung bringen; ˌ**dis·ar'range·ment** [-mənt] *s.* Verwirrung *f*, Unordnung *f*.

dis·ar·ray [ˌdɪsə'reɪ] **I** *v/t.* in Unordnung bringen, durchein'ander bringen; **II** *s.* Unordnung *f*: **be in ˷** a) in Unordnung sein, b) ✕ in Auflösung begriffen sein; **throw into ˷** → I.

dis·as·sem·ble [ˌdɪsə'sembl] *v/t.* ⊙ ausein'ander nehmen, ausein'ander montieren, zerlegen; ˌ**dis·as'sem·bly** [-blɪ] *s.* Zerlegung *f*, Abbau *m*.

dis·as·ter [dɪ'zɑːstə] *s.* Unglück *n* (**to** für), Unheil *n*, Kata'strophe *f*: **˷ area** Katastrophengebiet *n*; **˷ relief** Katastrophenhilfe *f*; **dis'as·trous** [-trəs] *adj.* □ unglückselig, unheil-, verhängnisvoll, katastro'phal, verheerend.

dis·a·vow [ˌdɪsə'vaʊ] *v/t.* **1.** nicht anerkennen, abrücken *od.* sich lossagen von; **2.** in Abrede stellen, ableugnen; ˌ**dis·a'vow·al** [-'vaʊəl] *s.* **1.** Nichtanerkennung *f*; **2.** Ableugnung *f*.

dis·band [dɪs'bænd] **I** *v/t.* ✕ *Truppen etc.* entlassen, auflösen; **II** *v/i. bsd.* ✕ sich auflösen; **dis'band·ment** [-mənt] *s.* ✕ Auflösung *f*.

dis·bar [dɪs'bɑː] *v/t.* ⚖️ aus der Anwaltschaft ausschließen.

dis·be·lief [ˌdɪsbɪ'liːf] *s.* Unglaube *m*, Zweifel *m* (**in** an *dat.*); ˌ**dis·be'lieve**

[-'iːv] **I** *v/t. et.* nicht glauben, bezweifeln; *j-m* nicht glauben; **II** *v/i.* nicht glauben (**in** an *acc.*); ˌ**dis·be'liev·er** [-'iːvə] *s. a. eccl.* Ungläubige(r *m*) *f*, Zweifler(in).

dis·bur·den [dɪs'bɜːdn] *v/t. mst fig.* von e-r Bürde befreien, entlasten (**of**, **from** von): **˷ one's mind** sein Herz erleichtern.

dis·burse [dɪs'bɜːs] *v/t.* **1.** be-, auszahlen; **2.** *Geld* auslegen; **dis'burse·ment** [-mənt] *s.* **1.** Auszahlung *f*; **2.** Auslage *f*, Verauslagung *f*.

disc [dɪsk] → **disk**.

dis·card [dɪ'skɑːd] **I** *v/t.* **1.** *Gewohnheit, Vorurteil etc.* ablegen, aufgeben, *Kleider etc.* ausscheiden, ausrangieren; **2.** *Freund* fallen lassen; **3.** *Karten* ablegen *od.* abwerfen; **II** *v/i.* **4.** *Kartenspiel*: Karten ablegen *od.* abwerfen; **III** *s.* ['dɪskɑːd] **5.** *Kartenspiel*: a) Ablegen *n*, b) abgeworfene Karte(n *pl.*); **6.** *et.* Abgelegtes, ausrangierte Sache: **go into the ˷** *Am.* a) in Vergessenheit geraten, b) außer Gebrauch kommen.

dis·cern [dɪ'sɜːn] *v/t.* **1.** wahrnehmen, erkennen; **2.** feststellen; **3.** *obs.* unter'scheiden (können); **dis'cern·i·ble** [-nəbl] *adj.* □ erkennbar, sichtbar; **dis'cern·ing** [-nɪŋ] *adj.* scharf(sichtig), kritisch (urteilend), klug; **dis'cern·ment** [-mənt] *s.* **1.** Scharfblick *m*, Urteilskraft *f*; **2.** Einsicht *f* (**of** in *acc.*); **3.** Wahrnehmen *n*; **4.** Wahrnehmungsvermögen *n*.

dis·charge [dɪs'tʃɑːdʒ] **I** *v/t.* **1.** *Waren, Wagen* ab-, ausladen; *Schiff* aus-, entladen; *Personen* ausladen, absetzen; (*Schiffs*)*Ladung* löschen; **2.** ⚡ entladen; **3.** ausströmen (lassen), aussenden, -stoßen, ergießen; absondern: **˷ matter** ⚕️ eitern; **4.** ✕ *Geschütz etc.* abfeuern, abschießen; **5.** entlassen, verabschieden, fortschicken; **6.** *Gefangene etc.* freilassen; *Patienten* entlassen; **7.** *s-n Gefühlen* Luft machen, *s-n Zorn* auslassen (**on** an *dat.*); *Flüche* ausstoßen; **8.** freisprechen, entlasten (**of** von); **9.** befreien, entbinden (**of**, **from** von); **10.** *Schulden* bezahlen, tilgen; *Wechsel* einlösen; *Verpflichtungen, Aufgabe* erfüllen; *s-n Verbindlichkeiten* nachkommen; *obs. Gläubiger* befriedigen; ⚖️ *Urteil etc.* aufheben: **˷ed bankrupt** entlasteter Gemeinschuldner; **11.** *Amt* ausüben, versehen; *Rolle* spielen; **12.** ˷ **o.s.** sich ergießen, münden; **II** *v/i.* **13.** ⚡ sich entladen (*a. Gewehr*); **14.** sich ergießen, abfließen; **15.** ⚕️ eitern; **III** *s.* **16.** Ent-, Ausladung *f*, Löschen *n* (*Schiff, Waren*); **17.** ⚡ Entladung *f*: **˷ current** Entladestrom *m*; **18.** Ausfließen *n*, -strömen *n*, Abfluss *m*; Ausstoßen *n* (*Rauch*); **19.** Absonderung *f* (*Eiter*), Ausfluss *m*; **20.** Abfeuern *n* (*Geschütz etc.*); **21.** a) (Dienst)Entlassung *f*, b) (Entlassungs)Zeugnis *n*; **22.** Ent-, Freilassung *f*; **23.** ⚖️, ✕ Befreiung *f*, Entlastung *f*; Rehabilitati'on *f*: **˷ of a bankrupt** Aufhebung *f* des Konkursverfahrens; **24.** Erfüllung *f* (*Aufgabe*), Ausübung *f*, Ausführung *f*; **25.** Bezahlung *f*, Einlösung *f*; **26.** Quittung *f*: **˷ in full** vollständige Quittung; **dis'charg·er** [-dʒə] *s.* ⚡ Entlader *m*.

dis·ci·ple [dɪ'saɪpl] *s.* Jünger *m* (*bsd. bibl.*; *a. fig.*), Schüler *m*; **dis'ci·ple·ship** [-ʃɪp] *s.* Jünger-, Anhängerschaft *f*.

dis·ci·pli·nar·i·an [ˌdɪsɪplɪ'neərɪən] *s.* Zuchtmeister *m*, strenger Lehrer *od.* Vorgesetzter *m*; **dis·ci·pli·nar·y** ['dɪsɪplɪnərɪ] *adj.* **1.** erzieherisch, Zucht...; **2.**

disz̓ipli'narisch: **˷ action** Disziplinarverfahren *n*; **˷ punishment** Disziplinarstrafe *f*; **˷ transfer** Strafversetzung *f*; **dis·ci·pline** ['dɪsɪplɪn] **I** *s.* **1.** Schulung *f*, Erziehung *f*; **2.** Diszi'plin *f* (*a. eccl.*), Zucht *f*; 'Selbstdiszi‚plin *f*; **3.** Bestrafung *f*, Züchtigung *f*; **4.** Diszi'plin *f*, Wissenszweig *m*; **II** *v/t.* **5.** schulen, erziehen; **6.** disziplinieren: a) an Disziplin gewöhnen, b) bestrafen: **well ˷d** (wohl)diszipliniert; **badly ˷d** disziplinlos, undisziplinert.

dis·claim [dɪs'kleɪm] *v/t.* **1.** abstreiten, in Abrede stellen; **2.** a) *et.* nicht anerkennen, b) *e-e Verantwortung* ablehnen, c) jede Verantwortung ablehnen für; **3.** wider'rufen, dementieren; verzichten auf (*acc.*), keinen Anspruch erheben auf (*acc.*), ⚖️ *a. Erbschaft* ausschlagen; **dis'claim·er** [-mə] *s.* **1.** ⚖️ Verzicht(leistung *f*) *m*, Ausschlagung *f* (*e-r Erbschaft*); **2.** 'Widerruf *m*, De'menti *n*.

dis·close [dɪs'kləʊz] *v/t.* **1.** bekannt geben *od.* machen; **2.** aufdecken, ans Licht bringen, enthüllen; **3.** zeigen, verraten, offenbaren; **dis'clo·sure** [-əʊʒə] *s.* **1.** Enthüllung *f*; **2.** Bekanntgabe *f*, Verlautbarung *f*; **3.** *Patentrecht*: Offenbarung *f*.

dis·co ['dɪskəʊ] *pl.* **-cos** *s.* F ‚Disko' *f* (*Diskothek*).

dis·cog·ra·phy [dɪs'kɒɡrəfɪ] *s.* Schallplattenverzeichnis *n*.

dis·col·o(u)r [dɪs'kʌlə] **I** *v/t.* **1.** verfärben; entfärben; **2.** *fig.* entstellen; **II** *v/i.* **3.** sich verfärben; **4.** verschießen; **dis·col·o(u)r·a·tion** [dɪsˌkʌlə'reɪʃn] *s.* **1.** Verfärbung *f*; Entfärbung *f*; **2.** verschossene Stelle; **3.** Fleck *m*; **dis'col·o(u)red** [-əd] *adj.* verfärbt; verschossen.

dis·com·fit [dɪs'kʌmfɪt] *v/t.* **1.** aus der Fassung bringen, verwirren; **2.** *obs.* schlagen, besiegen; **3.** *j-s* Pläne durch'kreuzen; **dis'com·fi·ture** [-tʃə] *s.* *obs.* Niederlage *f*; **2.** Durch'kreuzung *f*; **3.** a) Verwirrung *f*, b) Verlegenheit *f*.

dis·com·fort [dɪs'kʌmfət] *s.* **1.** Unbehagen *n*; **2.** Verdruss *m*; **3.** *körperliche* Beschwerde.

dis·com·mode [ˌdɪskə'məʊd] *v/t.* belästigen, *j-m* zur Last fallen.

dis·com·pose [ˌdɪskəm'pəʊz] *v/t.* **1.** in Unordnung bringen; **2.** → **disconcert** 1; ˌ**dis·com'pos·ed·ly** [-zɪdlɪ] *adj.* verwirrt; ˌ**dis·com'po·sure** [-əʊʒə] *s.* Verwirrung *f*, Fassungslosigkeit *f*.

dis·con·cert [ˌdɪskən'sɜːt] *v/t.* **1.** aus der Fassung bringen, verwirren; **2.** beunruhigen; **3.** durchein'ander bringen; ˌ**dis·con'cert·ed** [-tɪd] *adj.* verwirrt; beunruhigt; ˌ**dis·con'cert·ing** [-tɪŋ] *adj.* beunruhigend, peinlich.

dis·con·nect [ˌdɪskə'nekt] *v/t.* **1.** trennen (**with**, **from** von); **2.** ⊙ auskuppeln, *Kupplung* ausrücken; **3.** ⚡ trennen; *Gerät* ausstecken; **4.** *Gas, Strom, Telefon* abstellen; *Telefongespräch* unter'brechen, *Teilnehmer* trennen; ˌ**dis·con'nect·ed** [-tɪd] *adj.* □ **1.** getrennt, losgelöst; **2.** zs.-hanglos; ˌ**dis·con'nect·ing** [-tɪŋ] *adj.* ⚡ Trenn..., Ausschalt...; ˌ**dis·con'nec·tion** [-kʃn] *s.* **1.** Trennung *f* (*a.* ⚡); **2.** ⊙ Abstellung *f*; *teleph.* Unter'brechung *f*.

dis·con·so·late [dɪs'kɒnsəlet] *adj.* □ untröstlich; trostlos (*a. fig.*).

dis·con·tent [ˌdɪskən'tent] *s.* **1.** Unzufriedenheit *f* (**at**, **with** mit); **2.** Unzufriedene(r *m*) *f*; ˌ**dis·con'tent·ed** [-tɪd] *adj.* □ unzufrieden (**with** mit); ˌ**dis-**

con'tent·ment [-mənt] → *discontent*
1.

dis·con·tin·u·ance [ˌdɪskən'tɪnjʊəns], **dis·con·tin·u'a·tion** [-njʊ'eɪʃn] s. **1.** Unter'brechung f; **2.** Einstellung f (a. ⚖ des Verfahrens); **3.** Aufgeben n; **dis·con·tin·ue** [ˌdɪskən'tɪnjuː] **I** v/t. **1.** unter'brechen, aussetzen; **2.** einstellen (a. ⚖); *Zeitung* abbestellen; **4.** aufhören (*doing* zu tun); **II** v/i. **5.** aufhören; **dis·con·ti'nu·i·ty** [-tɪ'njuːətɪ] s. Diskontinui'tät f, Zs.-hanglosigkeit f; **dis·con'tin·u·ous** [-jʊəs] adj. □ **1.** diskontinuierlich, unter'brochen, 'unzu,sammenhängend; **2.** sprunghaft.

dis·cord ['dɪskɔːd] s. **1.** Uneinigkeit f, Zwietracht f, Streit m; → *apple*; **2.** ♪ Disso'nanz f, 'Missklang m; **3.** Lärm m; **dis·cord·ance** [dɪ'skɔːdəns] s. **1.** Uneinigkeit f; **2.** 'Missklang m, Disso'nanz f; **dis·cord·ant** [dɪ'skɔːdənt] adj. □ **1.** uneinig, sich wider'sprechend; **2.** 'unhar,monisch; **3.** ♪ disso'nantisch, 'misstönend.

dis·co·theque ['dɪskəʊtek] s. Disko'thek f.

dis·count ['dɪskaʊnt] **I** s. **1.** ✝ Preisnachlass m, Abschlag m, Ra'batt m, Skonto m, n; *allow a ~* (e-n) Rabatt gewähren; **2.** ✝ a) Dis'kont m, Wechselzins m, b) → *discount rate*; **3.** ✝ Abzug m (*vom Nominalwert*): *at a ~* a) unter Pari, b) *fig.* unbeliebt, nicht geschätzt od. gefragt; *sell at a ~* mit Verlust verkaufen; **4.** *fig.* Abzug m, Vorbehalt m, Abstriche pl.; **II** v/t. [a. dɪ'skaʊnt] **5.** ✝ e-n Abzug gewähren auf (acc.); **6.** *Wechsel* diskontieren; **7.** im Wert vermindern, beeinträchtigen; **8.** unberücksichtigt lassen; **9.** mit Vorsicht aufnehmen, nur teilweise glauben; **dis·count·a·ble** [dɪ'skaʊntəbl] adj. ✝ diskontierbar, dis'kontfähig.

dis·count| bank s. ✝ Dis'kontbank f; **~ bill** s. Dis'kontwechsel m; **~ bro·ker** s. ✝ Dis'kont-, Wechselmakler m.

dis·coun·te·nance [dɪ'skaʊntɪnəns] v/t. **1.** → *discomfit* 1; **2.** (offen) miss'billigen, ablehnen.

dis·count| house s. ✝ **1.** *Am.* Dis'count-, Dis'kontgeschäft n; **2.** *Brit.* Dis'kontbank f; **~ rate** s. ✝ Dis'kontsatz m; **~ shop**, **~ store** → *discount house* 1.

dis·cour·age [dɪ'skʌrɪdʒ] v/t. **1.** entmutigen; **2.** abschrecken, abhalten, *j-m* abraten (*from* von; *from doing* et. zu tun); **3.** hemmen, beeinträchtigen; **4.** miss'billigen; **dis·cour·age·ment** [dɪ'skʌrɪdʒmənt] s. **1.** Entmutigung f; **2.** a) Abschreckung f, b) Abschreckungsmittel n; **3.** Hemmung f, Hindernis n, Schwierigkeit f (*to* für); **dis·cour·ag·ing** [dɪ'skʌrɪdʒɪŋ] adj. □ entmutigend.

dis·course **I** s. ['dɪskɔːs] **1.** Unter'haltung f, Gespräch n; **2.** Abhandlung f, bsd. Vortrag m, Dis'kurs m, Predigt f; Abhandlung f; **II** v/i. [dɪ'skɔːs] **3.** e-n Vortrag halten (*on* über acc.), mst. *fig.* predigen od. dozieren (*on* über acc.); **4.** sich unter'halten (*on* über acc.).

dis·cour·te·ous [dɪs'kɜːtjəs] adj. □ unhöflich; **dis'cour·te·sy** [-tɪsɪ] s. Unhöflichkeit f.

dis·cov·er [dɪ'skʌvə] v/t. **1.** *Land etc.* entdecken; **2.** entdecken, ausfindig machen, erspähen; **3.** entdecken, (heraus)finden, (plötzlich) erkennen; **4.** aufdecken, enthüllen; **dis·cov·er·a·ble** [dɪ'skʌvərəbl] adj. **1.** zu entdecken(d); **2.** wahrnehmbar, feststellbar; **dis·cov·er·er** [dɪ'skʌvərə] s. Ent-

dis·cov·er·y [dɪ'skʌvərɪ] s. **1.** Entdeckung f (a. fig.); **2.** Fund m; **3.** Feststellung f; **4.** Enthüllung f; **5.** ~ *of documents* ⚖ Offenlegung f prozesswichtiger Urkunden.

dis·cred·it [dɪs'kredɪt] **I** v/t. **1.** in Verruf od. 'Misskre,dit bringen (*with* bei); ein schlechtes Licht werfen auf (acc.), diskreditieren; **2.** anzweifeln; keinen Glauben schenken (dat.); **II** s. **3.** schlechter Ruf, 'Misskre,dit m, Schande f: *bring s.o. into ~*, *bring ~ on s.o.* → 1; **4.** Zweifel m: *throw ~ on* et. zweifelhaft erscheinen lassen; **dis'cred·it·a·ble** [-təbl] adj. □ schändlich; **dis'cred·it·ed** [-tɪd] adj. **1.** verrufen, diskreditiert; **2.** unglaubwürdig.

dis·creet [dɪ'skriːt] adj. □ **1.** 'um-, vorsichtig, besonnen, verständig; **2.** dis'kret, taktvoll, verschwiegen.

dis·crep·an·cy [dɪ'skrepənsɪ] s. **1.** Diskre'panz f, Unstimmigkeit f, Verschiedenheit f; **2.** 'Widerspruch m, Zwiespalt m.

dis·crete [dɪ'skriːt] adj. □ **1.** getrennt, einzeln; **2.** unstet, unbeständig; **3.** ⚓ unstetig, dis'kret.

dis·cre·tion [dɪ'skreʃn] s. **1.** 'Um-, Vorsicht f, Besonnenheit f, Klugheit f: *act with ~* vorsichtig handeln; **2.** Verfügungsfreiheit f, Machtbefugnis f: *age* (*od. years*) *of ~* Alter n der freien Willensbestimmung, Strafmündigkeit f (*14 Jahre*); **3.** Gutdünken n, Belieben n; (⚖ freies) Ermessen: *at* (*your*) *~* nach (Ihrem) Belieben; *it is within your ~* es steht Ihnen frei; *use your own ~* handle nach eigenem Gutdünken od. Ermessen; *surrender at ~* bedingungslos kapitulieren; **4.** Diskreti'on f: a) Takt (-gefühl n) m, b) Zu'rückhaltung f, c) Verschwiegenheit f; **5.** Nachsicht f: *ask for ~*; **dis·cre·tion·ar·y** [dɪ'skreʃnərɪ] adj. □ dem eigenen Gutdünken über'lassen, ins freie Ermessen gestellt, wahlfrei: *~ clause* ⚖ Kannvorschrift f; *~ income* frei verfügbares Einkommen; *~ powers* unumschränkte Vollmacht, Handlungsfreiheit f.

dis·crim·i·nate [dɪ'skrɪmɪneɪt] **I** v/i. (scharf) unter'scheiden, e-n 'Unterschied machen: *~ between* unterschiedlich behandeln (acc.); *~ against s.o.* j-n benachteiligen od. diskriminieren; *~ in favo(u)r of s.o.* j-n begünstigen od. bevorzugen; **II** v/t. (scharf) unter'scheiden; abheben, absondern (*from* von); **dis·crim·i·nat·ing** [dɪ'skrɪmɪneɪtɪŋ] adj. □ **1.** unter'scheidend, charakte'ristisch; **2.** scharfsinnig, klug, urteilsfähig; anspruchsvoll; **3.** diskriminierend, benachteiligend; **4.** ✝ Differenzial..., Sonder...: *~ duty* Differenzialzoll m; **5.** ⚡ Rückstrom...; Selektiv...; **dis·crim·i·na·tion** [dɪ,skrɪmɪ'neɪʃn] s. **1.** 'unterschiedliche Behandlung, Diskriminierung f: *~ against* (*in favo[u]r of*) *s.o.* Benachteiligung f (Begünstigung f) e-r Person; **2.** Scharfblick m, Urteilsfähigkeit f, Unter'scheidungsvermögen n; **dis·crim·i·na·tive** [dɪ'skrɪmɪnətɪv] adj. □, **dis·crim·i·na·to·ry** [dɪ'skrɪmɪnətərɪ] adj. **1.** charakte'ristisch, unter'scheidend; **2.** 'unterschiedlich (behandelnd); Sonder..., Ausnahme...

dis·cur·sive [dɪ'skɜːsɪv] adj. □ **1.** abschweifend, unbeständig; sprunghaft; **2.** weitschweifig, allgemein gehalten; **3.** phls. folgernd, diskur'siv.

dis·cus [dɪ'skʌs] s. *sport* Diskus m: *~ throw* Diskuswerfen n; *~ thrower* Diskuswerfer m.

dis·cuss [dɪ'skʌs] v/t. **1.** diskutieren, besprechen, erörtern; **2.** sprechen od. reden über (acc.); **3.** F sich *e-e Flasche Wein etc.* zu Gemüte führen; **dis·cus·sion** [dɪ'skʌʃn] s. **1.** Diskussi'on f, Erörterung f, Besprechung f: *be under ~* zur Debatte stehen, erörtert werden; *matter for ~* Diskussionsthema n; *~ group* Diskussionsgruppe f; **2.** Behandlung f (*e-s Themas*).

dis·dain [dɪs'deɪn] **I** v/t. **1.** verachten; a. *Essen etc.* verschmähen; **2.** es für unter s-r Würde halten (*doing*, *to do* zu tun); **II** s. **3.** Verachtung f, Geringschätzung f; **4.** Hochmut m; **dis'dain·ful** [-fʊl] adj. □ **1.** verachtungsvoll, geringschätzig: *be ~ of s.th.* et. verachten; **2.** hochmütig.

dis·ease [dɪ'ziːz] s. 🎗, *biol. u. fig.* Krankheit f, Leiden n: *sexually transmitted ~* Geschlechtskrankheit f; **diseased** [dɪ'ziːzd] adj. **1.** krank, erkrankt; **2.** krankhaft.

dis·em·bark [ˌdɪsɪm'bɑːk] **I** v/t. ausschiffen; **II** v/i. sich ausschiffen, von Bord od. an Land gehen; **dis·em·bar·ka·tion** [ˌdɪsembɑː'keɪʃn] s. Ausschiffung f.

dis·em·bar·rass [ˌdɪsɪm'bærəs] v/t. **1.** *j-m* aus e-r Verlegenheit helfen; **2.** (*o.s.* sich) befreien (*of* von).

dis·em·bod·i·ment [ˌdɪsɪm'bɒdɪmənt] s. **1.** Entkörperlichung f; **2.** Befreiung f von der körperlichen Hülle; **dis·em·bod·y** [ˌdɪsɪm'bɒdɪ] v/t. **1.** entkörperlichen: *disembodied voice* geisterhafte Stimme; **2.** *Seele* von der körperlichen Hülle befreien.

dis·em·bow·el [ˌdɪsɪm'baʊəl] v/t. **1.** ausnehmen, *erlegtes Wild a.* ausweiden; **2.** *j-m* den Bauch aufschlitzen.

dis·en·chant [ˌdɪsɪn'tʃɑːnt] v/t. desillusionieren, ernüchtern: *be ~ed with* sich keinen Illusionen mehr hingeben über (acc.), enttäuscht sein von; **dis·en'chant·ment** [-mənt] s. Ernüchterung f, Enttäuschung f: *~ with politics* Politikverdrossenheit f.

dis·en·cum·ber [ˌdɪsɪn'kʌmbə] v/t. **1.** befreien (*of* von e-r Last etc.) (a. fig.); **2.** ⚖ entschulden; *Grundstück etc.* hypo'thekenfrei machen.

dis·en·fran·chise [ˌdɪsɪn'fræntʃaɪz] → *disfranchise*

dis·en·gage [ˌdɪsɪn'geɪdʒ] **I** v/t. **1.** losmachen, freimachen, (los)lösen, befreien (*from* von); **2.** befreien, entbinden (*from* von); **3.** ⊙ loskuppeln, ausrücken, ausschalten: *~ the clutch* auskuppeln; **4.** 🛩 abscheiden, entbinden; **II** v/i. **5.** sich freimachen, loskommen (*from* von); **6.** ⚔ sich absetzen (*vom Feind*); **dis·en·gaged** [-dʒd] adj. frei, nicht besetzt; abkömmlich; **dis·en'gage·ment** [-mənt] s. **1.** Befreiung f, Loslösung f (a. ⚔), Entbindung f (a. 🛩); **2.** ⚔ Absetzen n; *pol.* Disen'gagement n; **dis·en'gag·ing** [-dʒɪŋ] adj.: ⊙ *~ gear* Ausrück-, Auskuppelungsvorrichtung f; *~ lever* Ausrückhebel m.

dis·en·tan·gle [ˌdɪsɪn'tæŋgl] **I** v/t. entwirren (a. fig.), lösen; fig. befreien; **II** v/i. sich loslösen; fig. sich befreien; **dis·en'tan·gle·ment** [-mənt] s. Loslösung f; Entwirrung f; Befreiung f.

dis·en·ti·tle [ˌdɪsɪn'taɪtl] v/t. *j-m* e-n Rechtsanspruch nehmen: *be ~d to* keinen Anspruch haben auf (acc.).

dis·e·qui·lib·ri·um [ˌdɪsekwɪ'lɪbrɪəm] s. bsd. fig. gestörtes Gleichgewicht, Ungleichgewicht n.

dis·es·tab·lish [ˌdɪsɪ'stæblɪʃ] v/t. **1.** abschaffen; **2.** *Kirche* vom Staat trennen; **dis·es·tab·lish·ment** [ˌdɪsɪ'stæblɪʃmənt] *s.*: ~ *of the Church* Trennung *f* von Kirche u. Staat.

dis·fa·vo(u)r [͵dɪsˈfeɪvə] **I** *s.* 'Missbilligung *f*, -fallen *n*; Ungnade *f*: *regard with* ~ mit Missfallen betrachten; *be in (fall into)* ~ in Ungnade gefallen sein (fallen); **II** *v/t.* ungnädig behandeln; ablehnen.

dis·fig·ure [dɪsˈfɪgə] *v/t.* **1.** entstellen, verunstalten; **2.** beeinträchtigen; Abbruch tun (*dat.*); **dis'fig·ure·ment** [-mənt] *s.* Entstellung *f*, Verunstaltung *f*.

dis·fran·chise [͵dɪsˈfræntʃaɪz] *v/t.* j-m die Bürgerrechte *od.* das Wahlrecht entziehen; **͵dis'fran·chise·ment** [-tʃɪzmənt] *s.* Entziehung *f* der Bürgerrechte *etc.*

dis·gorge [dɪsˈgɔːdʒ] **I** *v/t.* **1.** ausspeien, -werfen, -stoßen, ergießen; **2.** widerwillig wieder her'ausgeben; **II** *v/i.* **3.** sich ergießen, sich entladen.

dis·grace [dɪsˈgreɪs] **I** *s.* **1.** Schande *f*, Schmach *f*: *bring* ~ *on s.o.* → 4; **2.** Schande *f*, Schandfleck *m* (*to* für): *he is a* ~ *to the party*; **3.** Ungnade *f*: *be in* ~ *with* in Ungnade gefallen sein bei; **II** *v/t.* **4.** Schande bringen über (*acc.*), j-m Schande bereiten; **5.** j-m s-e Gunst entziehen; mit Schimpf entlassen: *be* ~*d* in Ungnade fallen; **6.** ~ *o.s.* a) sich blamieren, b) sich schändlich benehmen; **dis'grace·ful** [-fʊl] *adj.* □ schändlich, schimpflich, schmachvoll.

dis·grun·tle [dɪsˈgrʌntl] *v/t. Am.* verärgern, verstimmen; **dis'grun·tled** [-ld] *adj.* verärgert, verstimmt (*at* über *acc.*), unwirsch.

dis·guise [dɪsˈgaɪz] **I** *v/t.* **1.** verkleiden, maskieren; tarnen; **2.** *Handschrift, Stimme* verstellen; **3.** *Gefühle, Wahrheit* verhüllen, verbergen, verhehlen; tarnen; **II** *s.* **4.** Verkleidung *f, a. fig.* Maske *f*, Tarnung *f*: *in* ~ maskiert, verkleidet, *fig.* verkappt; → *blessing*; **5.** Verstellung *f*; **6.** Vorwand *m*, Schein *m*; **dis'guised** [-zd] *adj.* verkleidet, maskiert *etc.*; *fig.* verkappt.

dis·gust [dɪsˈgʌst] **I** *s.* **1.** (*at, for*) Ekel *m* (vor *dat.*), 'Widerwille *m* (gegen): *in* ~ mit Abscheu; **II** *v/t.* **2.** anekeln, anwidern; **3.** entrüsten, verärgern, empören; **dis'gust·ed** [-tɪd] *adj.* □ (*with, at*) angeekelt, angewidert (von): ~ *with life* lebensüberdrüssig; **2.** em'pört, entrüstet (über *acc.*); **dis'gust·ing** [-tɪŋ] *adj.* □ **1.** ekelhaft, widerlich, ab'scheulich; **2.** F schrecklich.

dish [dɪʃ] **I** *s.* **1.** Schüssel *f*, Platte *f*, Teller *m*; **2.** Gericht *n*, Speise *f*: *cold* ~*es* kalte Speisen; **3.** *pl.* Geschirr *n*: ~ *cloth, Brit.* Geschirrtuch *n*: → *wash* 16; **4.** F a) ͵dufte Puppe', b) ͵dufter Typ', c) ͵prima Sache'; **II** *v/t.* **5.** *mst* ~ *up* Speisen anrichten, auftragen; **6.** ~ *up* fig. auftischen; **7.** ~ *out* a) austeilen, b) *sl.* auftischen, von sich geben; **8.** *sl.* ͵anschmieren', her'einlegen; **9.** *sl.* a) j-n ͵erledigen', ͵fertig machen', b) *et.* restlos vermasseln; **10.** ◎ *schüsselartig* wölben; vertiefen.

dis·ha·bille [͵dɪsæˈbiːl] *s.* Negli'gee *n*, Morgenrock *m*: *in* ~ im Negligee.

dis·har·mo·ni·ous [͵dɪshɑːˈməʊnjəs] *adj.* □ dishar'monisch; **dis·har·mo·ny** [͵dɪsˈhɑːmənɪ] *s.* Disharmo'nie *f*, 'Missklang *m*.

dis·heart·en [dɪsˈhɑːtn] *v/t.* entmutigen, deprimieren; **dis'heart·en·ing** [-nɪŋ] *adj.* □ entmutigend, bedrückend.

dished [dɪʃt] *adj.* **1.** kon'kav gewölbt; ◎ gestürzt (*Räder*); **2.** F ͵erledigt', ͵ka'putt'.

di·shev·el(l)ed [dɪˈʃevld] *adj.* **1.** zerzaust, wirr, aufgelöst (*Haar*); **2.** unordentlich, ungepflegt, schlampig.

dis·hon·est [dɪsˈɒnɪst] *adj.* □ unehrlich, unredlich; unlauter, betrügerisch; **dis'hon·es·ty** [-tɪ] *s.* Unehrlichkeit *f*, Unredlichkeit *f*.

dis·hon·o·(u)r [dɪsˈɒnə] **I** *s.* **1.** Unehre *f*, Schmach *f*, Schande *f* (*to* für); **2.** Beschimpfung *f*; **II** *v/t.* **3.** entehren (*a. Frau*); Schande bringen über (*acc.*); **4.** schimpflich behandeln; **5.** *sein Wort* nicht einlösen; **6.** ✝ *Scheck etc.* nicht honorieren, nicht einlösen; **dis'hon-o(u)·ra·ble** [-nərəbl] *adj.* □ **1.** schimpflich, unehrenhaft: ~ *discharge* ✕ unehrenhafte Entlassung; **2.** ehrlos; **dis'hon·o(u)·ra·ble·ness** [-nərəblnɪs] *s.* **1.** Schändlichkeit *f*, Gemeinheit *f*; **2.** Ehrlosigkeit *f*.

dish| **rack** *s.* Geschirrständer *m*; ~ **tow·el** *s.* Geschirrtuch *m*; ~ **wash·er** *s.* **1.** Tellerwäscher(in); **2.** Ge'schirr͵spülma͵schine *f*; '~͵**wa·ter** *s.* Spülwasser *n*.

dish·y [ˈdɪʃɪ] *adj. sl.* schick, ͵toll': ~ *girl.*

dis·il·lu·sion [͵dɪsɪˈluːʒn] **I** *s.* Ernüchterung *f*, Enttäuschung *f*; **II** *v/t.* ernüchtern, desillusionieren, von Illusi'onen befreien; **͵dis·il'lu·sion·ment** [-mənt] → *disillusion* **I.**

dis·in·cen·tive [͵dɪsɪnˈsentɪv] **I** *s.* **1.** Abschreckungsmittel *n*: *be a* ~ *to* abschreckend wirken auf (*acc.*); **2.** ✝ leistungshemmender Faktor; **II** *adj.* **3.** abschreckend; **4.** ✝ leistungshemmend.

dis·in·cli·na·tion [͵dɪsɪnklɪˈneɪʃn] *s.* Abneigung *f* (*for, to* gegen): ~ *to buy* Kaufunlust *f*; **dis·in·cline** [͵dɪsɪnˈklaɪn] *v/t.* abgeneigt machen; **͵dis·in'clined** [-ˈklaɪnd] *adj.* abgeneigt (*to dat., to do* zu tun).

dis·in·fect [͵dɪsɪnˈfekt] *v/t.* desinfizieren, keimfrei machen; **͵dis·in'fect·ant** [-tənt] **I** *s.* Desinfekti'onsmittel *n*; **II** *adj.* desinfizierend, keimtötend; **͵dis·in'fec·tion** [-kʃn] *s.* Desinfekti'on *f*, **͵dis·in'fec·tor** [-tə] *s.* Desinfekti'onsgerät *n*.

dis·in·fest [͵dɪsɪnˈfest] *v/t.* von Ungeziefer *etc.* befreien, entwesen, entlausen.

dis·in·fla·tion [͵dɪsɪnˈfleɪʃn] → *deflation* **2.**

dis·in·gen·u·ous [͵dɪsɪnˈdʒenjʊəs] *adj.* □ **1.** unaufrichtig; **2.** 'hinterhältig, arglistig; **͵dis·in'gen·u·ous·ness** [-nɪs] *s.* **1.** Unredlichkeit *f*, Unaufrichtigkeit *f*; **2.** 'Hinterhältigkeit *f*.

dis·in·her·it [͵dɪsɪnˈherɪt] *v/t.* enterben; **͵dis·in'her·it·ance** [-təns] *s.* Enterbung *f*.

dis·in·hi·bi·tion [͵dɪsɪnhɪˈbɪʃn] *s. psych.* Enthemmung *f*.

dis·in·te·grate [dɪsˈɪntɪgreɪt] **I** *v/t.* **1.** (*a. phys.*) (in s-e Bestandteile) auflösen, aufspalten, zerkleinern; **2.** *fig.* auflösen, zersetzen, zertrümmern; **II** *v/i.* **3.** sich (in s-e Bestandteile, *fig. a.* in nichts) auflösen, sich aufspalten, sich zersetzen; **4.** ver-, zerfallen (*a. fig.*); **dis·in·te·gra·tion** [dɪs͵ɪntɪˈgreɪʃn] *s.* **1.** (*a. phys.*) Auflösung *f*, Aufspaltung *f*, Zerstückelung *f*, Zertrümmerung *f*, Zersetzung *f*; **2.** Zerfall *m* (*a. fig.*); **3.** *geol.* Verwitterung *f*.

dis·in·ter [͵dɪsɪnˈtɜː] *v/t. Leiche* exhumieren, ausgraben (*a. fig.*).

dis·in·ter·est·ed [dɪsˈɪntrəstɪd] *adj.* □ **1.** uneigennützig, selbstlos; **2.** objek'tiv, unvoreingenommen; **3.** unbeteiligt; **dis'in·ter·est·ed·ness** [-nɪs] *s.* **1.** Uneigennützigkeit *f*; **2.** Objektivi'tät *f*.

dis·in·ter·ment [͵dɪsɪnˈtɜːmənt] *s.* **1.** Exhumierung *f*; **2.** Ausgrabung *f* (*a.*

fig.).

dis·joint [dɪsˈdʒɔɪnt] *v/t.* **1.** ausein'ander nehmen, zerlegen, zerstückeln; **2.** ✗ ver-, ausrenken; **3.** (ab)trennen; **4.** *fig.* in Unordnung *od.* aus den Fugen bringen; **dis'joint·ed** [-tɪd] *adj.* □ *fig.* zu'sammenhanglos, wirr.

dis·junc·tion [dɪsˈdʒʌŋkʃn] *s.* Trennung *f*; **dis'junc·tive** [-ktɪv] *adj.* □ **1.** (ab-) trennend, ausschließend; **2.** *ling., phls.* disjunk'tiv.

disk [dɪsk] *s.* **1.** *allg.* Scheibe *f*; **2.** ◎ Scheibe *f*, La'melle *f*; Si'gnalscheibe *f*; **3.** ♀, *anat.*, *zo.* Scheibe *f*, *anat. a.* Bandscheibe *f*: *slipped* ~ Bandscheibenvorfall *m*; **4.** *teleph.* Wählscheibe *f*; **5.** *sport* a) Diskus *m*, b) *Eishockey*: Scheibe *f*, Puck *m*; **6.** (Schall)Platte *f*; **7.** *Computer*: Platte *f*: a) *floppy* ~ Dis'kette *f*, b) *a. hard* ~ Festplatte *f*; ~ **brake** *s.* ◎ Scheibenbremse *f*; ~ **clutch** *s. mot.* Scheibenkupplung *f*.

disk drive [ˈdɪskdraɪv] *s. Computer*: a) *a. floppy* ~ Dis'kettenlaufwerk *n*, b) *a. hard* ~ ('Fest)Plattenlaufwerk *n*.

disk·ette [dɪsˈket] *s.* Dis'kette *f*.

'disk| **jock·ey** *s.* Diskjockey *m*; ~ **pack** *s. Computer*: Plattenstapel *m*; ~ **valve** *s.* ◎ 'Tellerven͵til *n*.

dis·like [dɪsˈlaɪk] **I** *v/t.* nicht leiden können, nicht mögen; *et.* nicht gern *od.* (nur) ungern tun: *make o.s.* ~*d* sich unbeliebt machen; **II** *s.* Abneigung *f*, 'Widerwille *m* (*to, of, for* gegen): *take a* ~ *to* e-e Abneigung fassen gegen.

dis·lo·cate [ˈdɪsləʊkeɪt] *v/t.* **1.** verrücken; *a. Industrie, Truppen etc.* verlagern; **2.** ✗ ver-, ausrenken: ~ *one's arm* sich den Arm verrenken; **3.** *fig.* erschüttern; **4.** *geol.* verwerfen; **dis·lo·ca·tion** [͵dɪsləʊˈkeɪʃn] *s.* **1.** Verrückung *f*; Verlagerung *f* (*a.* ✗); **2.** ✗ Verrenkung *f*; **3.** *fig.* Erschütterung *f*; **4.** *geol.* Verwerfung *f*.

dis·lodge [dɪsˈlɒdʒ] *v/t.* **1.** entfernen, her'ausnehmen, losreißen; **2.** vertreiben, verjagen, verdrängen; **3.** ✕ *Feind* aus der Stellung werfen; **4.** ausquartieren.

dis·loy·al [͵dɪsˈlɔɪəl] *adj.* □ untreu, treulos, verräterisch; **͵dis'loy·al·ty** [-tɪ] *s.* Untreue *f*, Treulosigkeit *f*.

dis·mal [ˈdɪzməl] **I** *adj.* □ **1.** düster, trübe, bedrückend, trostlos; **2.** furchtbar, grässlich; **II** *s.* **3.** *the* ~*s* der Trübsinn: *be in the* ~*s* Trübsinn blasen; **'dis·mal·ly** [-məlɪ] *adv.* **1.** düster *etc.*; **2.** schmählich.

dis·man·tle [dɪsˈmæntl] *v/t.* **1.** ab-, demontieren; *Bau* abbrechen, niederreißen; **2.** ausein'ander nehmen, zerlegen; **3.** ♨ a) abwracken, b) abwracken; *Festung* schleifen; **5.** *Haus* (aus)räumen; **6.** unbrauchbar machen; **dis'man·tle·ment** [-mənt] *s.* **1.** Abbruch *m*, Demon'tage *f*, Zerlegung *f*; **2.** ♨ Abtakelung *f*; **3.** ✕ Schleifung *f*.

dis·may [dɪsˈmeɪ] **I** *v/t.* erschrecken, in Schrecken versetzen, bestürzen, entsetzen: *not* ~*ed* unbeirrt; **II** *s.* Schreck(en) *m*, Entsetzen *n*, Bestürzung *f*.

dis·mem·ber [dɪsˈmembə] *v/t.* zergliedern, zerstückeln, verstümmeln (*a. fig.*); **dis'mem·ber·ment** [-mənt] *s.* Zerstückelung *f etc.*

dis·miss [dɪsˈmɪs] *v/t.* **1.** entlassen, gehen lassen, verabschieden: ~*!* ✕ weg-(ge)treten!; **2.** entlassen (*from* aus *dem Dienst*), absetzen, abbauen; wegschicken: *be* ~*ed from the service* ✕ aus dem Heer *etc.* entlassen *od.* ausgestoßen werden; **3.** *Thema etc.* fallen lassen, aufgeben, hin'weggehen über (*acc.*),

D

Vorschlag ab-, zu'rückweisen, *Gedanken* verbannen, von sich weisen; ⚖ *Klage* abweisen: ~ *from one's mind et.* aus s-n Gedanken verbannen; ~ *as ...* als ... abtun, kurzerhand als ... betrachten; **dis'miss·al** [-sl] *s.* **1.** Entlassung *f* (*from* aus): ~ *pay* Abfindung *f*; **2.** Aufgabe *f*, Abtun *n*; **3.** ⚖ Abweisung *f*.

dis·mount [ˌdɪsˈmaʊnt] **I** *v/i.* **1.** absteigen, absitzen (*from* von); **II** *v/t.* **2.** aus dem Sattel heben; abwerfen (*Pferd*); **3.** (ab)steigen von; **4.** abmontieren, ausbauen, ausein'ander nehmen.

dis·o·be·di·ence [ˌdɪsəˈbiːdjəns] *s.* **1.** Ungehorsam *m* (*to* gegen), Gehorsamsverweigerung *f*: *civil* ~ *pol.* ziviler *od.* bürgerlicher Ungehorsam; **2.** Nichtbefolgung *f*; **,dis·o·be·di·ent** [-nt] *adj.* ☐ ungehorsam (*to* gegen); **dis·o·bey** [ˌdɪsəˈbeɪ] *v/t.* **1.** *j-m* nicht gehorchen, ungehorsam sein gegen *j-n*; **2.** *Gesetz etc.* nicht befolgen, miss'achten, *Befehl a.* verweigern: *I will not be ~ed* ich dulde keinen Ungehorsam.

dis·o·blige [ˌdɪsəˈblaɪdʒ] *v/t.* **1.** ungefällig sein gegen *j-n*; **2.** *j-n* kränken; **,dis·o'blig·ing** [-dʒɪŋ] *adj.* ☐ ungefällig, unfreundlich.

dis·or·der [dɪsˈɔːdə] **I** *s.* **1.** Unordnung *f*, Verwirrung *f*; **2.** (Ruhe)Störung *f*; Aufruhr *m*, Unruhe(n *pl.*) *f*; **3.** ungebührliches Betragen; **4.** ☆ Störung *f*, Erkrankung *f*: *mental* ~ Geistesstörung; **II** *v/t.* **5.** in Unordnung bringen, durchein'ander bringen, stören; **6.** *den Magen* verderben; **dis·or·dered** [-əd] *adj.* **1.** in Unordnung, durchein'ander (*beide a. fig.*); **2.** gestört, (*a.* geistes)krank: *my stomach is* ~ ich habe mir den Magen verdorben; **dis·or·der·li·ness** [-lɪnɪs] *s.* **1.** Unordentlichkeit *f*; **2.** Schlampigkeit *f*; **3.** Unbotmäßigkeit *f*; **4.** Liederlichkeit *f*; **dis·or·der·ly** [-lɪ] *adj.* **1.** unordentlich, schlampig; **2.** ordnungs-, gesetzwidrig, aufrührerisch; **3.** Ärgernis erregend: ~ *conduct* ⚖ ordnungswidriges Verhalten, grober Unfug; ~ *house* *mst* Bordell *n*, *a.* Spielhölle *f*; ~ *person* Ruhestörer *m*.

dis·or·gan·i·za·tion [dɪsˌɔːɡənaɪˈzeɪʃn] *s.* Desorganisati'on *f*, Auflösung *f*, Zerrüttung *f*, Unordnung *f*; **dis·or·gan·ize** [dɪsˈɔːɡənaɪz] *v/t.* auflösen, zerrütten, in Unordnung bringen, desorganisieren; **dis·or·gan·ized** [dɪsˈɔːɡənaɪzd] *adj.* in Unordnung, desorganisiert.

dis·o·ri·ent [dɪsˈɔːrɪent] *v/t. a. psych.* desorientieren: *~ed* desorientiert, *psych. a.* ,gestört', la'bil; **dis·o·ri·en·tate** [-teɪt] → *disorient*.

dis·own [dɪsˈəʊn] *v/t.* **1.** nicht (als sein eigen *od.* als gültig) anerkennen, nichts zu tun haben wollen mit; **2.** ableugnen; **3.** *Kind* verstoßen.

dis·par·age [dɪˈspærɪdʒ] *v/t.* **1.** in Verruf bringen; **2.** her'absetzen, verächtlich machen; **3.** verachten; **dis·par·age·ment** [dɪˈspærɪdʒmənt] *s.* Her'absetzung *f*, Verächtlichmachung *f*: *no* ~ (*intended*) ohne Ihnen nahe treten zu wollen; **dis·par·ag·ing** [dɪˈspærɪdʒɪŋ] *adj.* ☐ gering-, abschätzig, verächtlich.

dis·pa·rate [ˈdɪspərət] **I** *adj.* ☐ ungleich(artig), (grund)verschieden, unvereinbar, dispa'rat; **II** *s. pl.* unvereinbare Dinge *pl.*; **dis·par·i·ty** [dɪˈspærətɪ] *s.* Verschiedenheit *f*: ~ *in age* (*zu gro*ßer) Altersunterschied *m*.

dis·pas·sion·ate [dɪˈspæʃnət] *adj.* ☐ leidenschaftslos, ruhig, gelassen, sachlich, nüchtern.

dis·patch [dɪˈspætʃ] **I** *v/t.* **1.** *j-n od. et.*

(ab)senden, *et.* (ab)schicken, versenden, befördern, *Telegramm* aufgeben; **2.** abfertigen (*a.* 🐎); **3.** rasch *od.* prompt erledigen *od.* ausführen; **4.** ins Jenseits befördern, töten; **5.** F ,wegputzen', rasch aufessen; **II** *s.* **6.** Absendung *f*, Versand *m*, Abfertigung *f*, Beförderung *f*; **7.** rasche Erledigung; **8.** Eile *f*, Schnelligkeit *f*: *with* ~ eilends, prompt; **9.** (*oft* verschlüsselte) (Eil)Botschaft; **10.** Bericht *m* (*e-s Korrespondenten*); **11.** *pl.* Kriegsberichte *pl.*: *mentioned in ~es* ✗ im Kriegsbericht rühmend erwähnt; **12.** Tötung *f*: *happy* ~ Harakiri *n*; ~ *boat s.* Ku'rierboot *n*; ~ *box s.*, ~ *case s.* **1.** Ku'riertasche *f*; **2.** *Brit.* Aktenkoffer *m*.

dis·patch·er [dɪˈspætʃə] *s.* **1.** 🚂 Fahrdienstleiter *m*; **2.** ✝ *Am.* Abteilungsleiter *m* für Produkti'onsplanung.

dis·patch| goods *s. pl.* Eilgut *n*; ~ **note** *s.* Pa'ketkarte *f* für 'Auslandspa,ket; ~ **rid·er** *s.* ✗ Melderreiter *m*, -fahrer *m*.

dis·pel [dɪˈspel] *v/t. Menge etc., a. fig. Befürchtungen etc.* zerstreuen, *Nebel* zerteilen.

dis·pen·sa·ble [dɪˈspensəbl] *adj.* ☐ entbehrlich, verzichtbar; erlässlich; **dis·pen·sa·ry** [dɪˈspensərɪ] *s.* 'Werksod. 'Krankenhausapo,theke *f*; **2.** ✗ a) Laza'rettapo,theke *f*, b) ('Kranken)Re,vier *n*; **dis·pen·sa·tion** [ˌdɪspenˈseɪʃn] *s.* **1.** Aus-, Verteilung *f*; **2.** Gabe *f*; **3.** göttliche Fügung; Fügung *f* (*des Schicksals*), Walten *n* (*der Vorsehung*); **4.** religi'öses Sy'stem; **5.** Regelung *f*, Sy'stem *n*; **6.** ⚖, *eccl.* (*with, from*) Dis'pens *m*, Befreiung *f* (von,) Erlass *m* (*gen.*); **7.** Verzicht *m* (*with* auf *acc.*); **dis·pense** [dɪˈspens] **I** *v/t.* **1.** aus-, verteilen; *Sakrament* spenden: ~ *justice* Recht sprechen; **2.** *Arzneien* (nach Re'zept) zubereiten u. abgeben; **3.** dispensieren, entheben, befreien, entbinden (*from* von); **II** *v/i.* **4.** Dis'pens erteilen; **5.** ~ *with* a) verzichten auf (*acc.*), b) überflüssig machen, auskommen ohne: *it can be ~d with* man kann darauf verzichten, es ist entbehrlich; **dis·pens·er** [dɪˈspensə] *s.* **1.** Ver-, Austeiler *m*; **2.** ⊕ Spender *m* (*Gerät*); (*Briefmarken- etc.*)Auto'mat *m*; → **dis·pens·ing chem·ist** [dɪˈspensɪŋ] *s.* Apo'theker(in).

dis·per·sal [dɪˈspɜːsl] *s.* **1.** (Zer)Streuung *f*; Verbreitung *f*; Zersplitterung *f*; **2.** ✗, *a.* ✝ Auflockerung *f*; ~ **a·pron** *s.* ✈ (ausein'ander gezogener) Abstellplatz; ~ **a·re·a** *s.* ✈ → *dispersal apron*; **2.** ✗ Auflockerungsgebiet *n*.

dis·perse [dɪˈspɜːs] **I** *v/t.* **1.** verstreuen; **2.** → *dispel*; **3.** *Nachrichten etc.* verbreiten; **4.** 🔬, *phys.* dispergieren, zerstreuen; **5.** ✗ a) *Formation* auflockern, b) versprengen; **II** *v/i.* **6.** sich zerstreuen (*Menge*); **7.** sich auflösen; **8.** sich verteilen *od.* zersplittern; **dis·pers·ed·ly** [dɪˈspɜːsɪdlɪ] *adv.* verstreut, vereinzelt; **dis·per·sion** [dɪˈspɜːʃn] *s.* **1.** Zerstreuung *f* (*a. fig.*); Verteilung *f* (*von Nebel*); **2.** *a.* 📐, ✗ Streuung *f*; ~ *pattern* Trefferbild *n*, b) → *dispersal* 2; **3.** 🔬 Dispersi'on(sphase) *f*: ~ *agent* Dispersionsmittel *n*; **4.** 📐 Zerstreuung *f*, Di'aspora *f der Juden*.

dis·pir·it [dɪˈspɪrɪt] *v/t.* entmutigen, niederdrücken, deprimieren; **dis'pir·it·ed** [-tɪd] *adj.* ☐ niedergeschlagen, mutlos, deprimiert.

dis·place [dɪsˈpleɪs] *v/t.* **1.** versetzen, -rücken, -lagern, -schieben; **2.** verdrängen (*a.* ⚓); **3.** *j-n* ablösen, entlassen; **4.** ersetzen; **5.** verschleppen: *~d person hist.* Verschleppte(r *m*) *f*; **dis·place-**

ment [-mənt] *s.* **1.** Verlagerung *f*, Verschiebung *f*; **2.** Verdrängung *f* (*a.* ⚓, *phys.*); ⊕ Kolbenverdrängung *f*; **3.** Ersetzung *f*, Ersatz *m*; **4.** *psych.* Af'fektverlagerung *f*: ~ *activity* Übersprunghandlung *f*.

dis·play [dɪˈspleɪ] **I** *v/t.* **1.** entfalten: a) ausbreiten, b) *fig.* an den Tag legen, zeigen: ~ *activity* (*strength etc.*); **2.** (*contp.* protzig) zur Schau stellen, zeigen; **3.** ✝ ausstellen, -legen; **4.** *typ.* her'vorheben; **II** *s.* **5.** Entfaltung *f* (*a. fig. von Tatkraft, Macht etc.*); **6.** (*a.* protzige) Zur'schaustellung; **7.** ✝ Ausstellung *f*, (Waren)Auslage *f*, Dis'play *n*: *be on* ~ ausgestellt *od.* zu sehen sein; **8.** Aufwand *m*, Pomp *m*, Prunk *m*: *make a great* ~ a) großen Prunk entfalten, b) *of s.th.* et. (protzig) zur Schau stellen; **9.** *Computer*: Dis'play *n*: a) Sichtanzeige *f*, b) Sichtbildgerät *n*; **10.** *typ.* Her'vorhebung *f*; **III** *adj.* **11.** ✝ Ausstellungs..., Schau...: ~ *advertising* Displaywerbung *f*; ~ *artist*, *~man* (Werbe)Dekorateur *m*; ~ *box*, ~ *pack* Schaupackung *f*; ~ *case* Schaukasten *m*, Vitrine *f*; ~ *window* Auslagefenster *n*; **12.** *Computer*: Display..., Sicht(bild)...: ~ *unit* → 9 b; ~ **be'hav·i·o(u)r** *s. zo.* Imponiergehabe *n*.

dis·please [dɪsˈpliːz] *v/t.* **1.** *j-m* miss'fallen; **2.** *j-n* ärgern, verstimmen; **3.** *das Auge* beleidigen; **dis'pleased** [-zd] *adj.* (*at, with*) unzufrieden (mit), ungehalten (über *acc.*); **dis'pleas·ing** [-zɪŋ] *adj.* ☐ unangenehm; **dis·pleas·ure** [dɪsˈpleʒə] *s.* 'Missfallen *n* (*at* über *acc.*): *incur s.o.'s* ~ j-s Unwillen erregen.

dis·port [dɪsˈpɔːt] *v/t.*: ~ *o.s.* a) sich vergnügen *od.* amüsieren, b) her'umtollen, sich (ausgelassen) tummeln.

dis·pos·a·ble [dɪˈspəʊzəbl] **I** *adj.* **1.** (frei) verfügbar: ~ *income*; **2.** ✝ Einweg..., Wegwerf...: ~ *package*; **II** *s.* **3.** Einweg-, Wegwerfgegenstand *m*; **dis·pos·al** [dɪˈspəʊzl] *s.* **1.** Anordnung *f*, Aufstellung *f* (*a.* ✗); Verwendung *f*; **2.** Erledigung *f*: a) (endgültige) Regelung *e-r Sache*, b) Vernichtung *f e-s Gegners etc.*; **3.** Verfügung(srecht *n*) *f* (*of* über *acc.*): *be at s.o.'s* ~ j-m zur Verfügung stehen; *place s.th. at s.o.'s* ~ j-m et. zur Verfügung stellen; *have the* ~ *of* verfügen (können) über (*acc.*); **4.** ✝, ⚖ a) 'Übergabe *f*, Über'tragung *f*, b) Veräußerung *f*, Verkauf *m*: *for* ~ zum Verkauf; **5.** Beseitigung *f*, (Müll- *etc.*) Abfuhr *f*, (-)Entsorgung *f*; **dis·pose** [dɪsˈpəʊz] **I** *v/t.* **1.** anordnen, aufstellen (*a.* ✗); zu'rechtlegen, einrichten; ein-, verteilen; **2.** *j-n* bewegen, geneigt machen, veranlassen (*to* zu; *to do* zu tun); **II** *v/i.* **3.** verfügen, Verfügungen treffen; **4.** ~ *of* a) (frei) verfügen *od.* disponieren über (*acc.*), b) entscheiden über (*acc.*), lenken, c) (endgültig) erledigen: ~ *of an affair*, d) *j-n od. et.* abtun, abfertigen, e) loswerden, sich entledigen (*gen.*), f) wegschaffen, beseitigen: ~ *of trash*, g) *e-n Gegner etc.* erledigen, unschädlich machen, vernichten, h) ✗ *Bomben etc.* entschärfen, i) verzehren, trinken: ~ *of a bottle*, j) über'geben, -'tragen: ~ *of by will* testamentarisch vermachen, letztwillig verfügen oder (*acc.*); *disposing mind* ⚖ Testierfähigkeit *f*, k) verkaufen, veräußern, ✝ *a.* absetzen, abstoßen, l) *s-e Tochter* verheiraten (*to* an *acc.*); **dis·posed** [dɪsˈpəʊzd] *adj.* **1.** geneigt, bereit (*to* zu; *to do* zu tun); **2.** ☆ anfällig (*to* für); **3.** gelaunt, gesinnt: *well-~*

D

wohlgesinnt, *ill-~* übel gesinnt (*to-wards* dat.); **dis·po·si·tion** [ˌdɪspə-'zɪʃn] s. **1.** a) Veranlagung f, Dispositi'on f, b) (Wesens)Art f; **2.** a) Neigung f, Hang m (*to* zu), b) ✹ Anfälligkeit f (*to* für); **3.** Stimmung f; **4.** Anordnung f, Aufstellung f (a. ✕); **5.** (*of*) a) Erledigung f (gen.), b) bsd. ♈ Entscheidung f (über acc.); **6.** (bsd. göttliche) Lenkung; **7.** pl. Dispositi'onen pl., Vorkehrungen pl.: *make* (*one's*) *~s* (s-e) Vorkehrungen treffen, disponieren; **8.** → *disposal* 3.

dis·pos·sess [ˌdɪspə'zes] v/t. **1.** enteignen, aus dem Besitz (*of* gen.) setzen; *Mieter* zur Räumung zwingen; **2.** berauben (*of* gen.); **3.** sport j-m den Ball abnehmen; **dis·pos'ses·sion** [-eʃn] s. Enteignung f etc.

dis·praise [dɪs'preɪz] s. Her'absetzung f: *in ~* geringschätzig.

dis·proof [ˌdɪs'pruːf] s. Wider'legung f.

dis·pro·por·tion [ˌdɪsprə'pɔːʃn] s. 'Missverhältnis n; ˌdis·pro'por·tion·ate [-ʃnət] adj. □ **1.** unverhältnismäßig (groß od. klein), in keinem Verhältnis stehend (*to* zu); **2.** über'trieben, unangemessen; **3.** unproportioniert.

dis·prove [ˌdɪs'pruːv] v/t. wider'legen.

dis·pu·ta·ble [dɪ'spjuːtəbl] adj. □ strittig; **dis·pu·tant** [dɪ'spjuːtənt] s. Dispu'tant m, Gegner m.

dis·pu·ta·tion [ˌdɪspjuː'teɪʃn] **1.** Dis'put m, Streitgespräch n, Wortwechsel m; **2.** Disputati'on f, wissenschaftliches Streitgespräch; ˌdis·pu'ta·tious [-ʃəs] adj. □ streitsüchtig; **dis·pute** [dɪ'spjuːt] **I** v/i. **1.** streiten, *Wissenschaftler:* a. disputieren (*on, about* über acc.); **2.** (sich) streiten, zanken; **II** v/t. **3.** streiten od. disputieren über (acc.); **4.** in Zweifel ziehen, anzweifeln; **5.** kämpfen um, j-m streitig machen; **III** s. **6.** Dis'put m, Kontro'verse f: *in* (od. *under*) *~* umstritten, strittig; *beyond* (od. *without*) *~* unzweifelhaft, fraglos; **7.** (heftiger) Streit.

dis·qual·i·fi·ca·tion [dɪsˌkwɒlɪfɪ'keɪʃn] s. **1.** Disqualifikati'on f, Disqualifizierung f; **2.** Untauglichkeit f, mangelnde Eignung od. Befähigung (*for* für); **3.** disqualifizierender 'Umstand; **4.** sport Disqualifikati'on f, Ausschluss m; **dis·qual·i·fy** [dɪs'kwɒlɪfaɪ] v/t. **1.** ungeeignet od. unfähig od. untauglich machen (*for* für): *be disqualified for* ungeeignet (etc.) sein für; **2.** für unfähig od. untauglich von nur berechtigt erklären (*for* zu): *~ s.o. from* (*holding*) *public office* j-m die Fähigkeit zur Ausübung e-s öffentlichen Amtes absprechen od. nehmen; *~ s.o. from driving* j-m die Fahrerlaubnis entziehen; **3.** sport disqualifizieren, ausschließen.

dis·qui·et [dɪs'kwaɪət] **I** v/t. beunruhigen; **II** s. Unruhe f, Besorgnis f; **dis-'qui·et·ing** [-tɪŋ] adj. beunruhigend; **dis'qui·e·tude** [-aɪətjuːd] → *disquiet* II.

dis·qui·si·tion [ˌdɪskwɪ'zɪʃn] s. ausführliche Abhandlung od. Rede.

dis·rate [dɪs'reɪt] v/t. ♣ degradieren.

dis·re·gard [ˌdɪsrɪ'ɡɑːd] **I** v/t. **1.** a) nicht beachten, ignorieren, außer Acht lassen, b) absehen von, ausklammern; **2.** nicht befolgen, miss'achten; **II** s. **3.** Nichtbeachtung f, Ignorierung f (*of, for* gen.); **4.** 'Missachtung f (*of, for* gen.); **5.** Gleichgültigkeit f (*of, for* gegen'über); ˌdis·re'gard·ful [-fʊl] adj. □: *be ~ of* → *disregard* 1 a.

dis·rel·ish [ˌdɪs'relɪʃ] s. Abneigung f, 'Widerwille m (*for* gegen).

dis·re·mem·ber [ˌdɪsrɪ'membə] v/t. F et. vergessen (haben).

dis·re·pair [ˌdɪsrɪ'peə] s. Verfall m; Baufälligkeit f, schlechter (baulicher) Zustand: *in* (*a state of*) *~* baufällig; *fall into ~* baufällig werden.

dis·rep·u·ta·ble [dɪs'repjutəbl] adj. □ verrufen, anrüchig; **dis·re·pute** [ˌdɪsrɪ-'pjuːt] s. Verruf m, Verrufenheit f, schlechter Ruf: *bring into ~* in Verruf bringen.

dis·re·spect [ˌdɪsrɪ'spekt] **I** s. **1.** Respektlosigkeit f (*to, for* gegenüber); **2.** Unhöflichkeit f (*to* gegen); **II** v/t. **3.** sich re'spektlos benehmen gegen'über; **4.** unhöflich behandeln, ˌdis·re'spect-ful [-fʊl] adj. □ **1.** re'spektlos (*to* gegen); **2.** unhöflich (*to* zu).

dis·robe [ˌdɪs'rəʊb] **I** v/t. entkleiden (a. fig.) (*of* gen.); **II** v/i. s-e Kleidung od. Amtstracht ablegen.

dis·root [ˌdɪs'ruːt] v/t. **1.** entwurzeln, ausreißen; **2.** vertreiben.

dis·rupt [dɪs'rʌpt] **I** v/t. **1.** zerbrechen, sprengen, zertrümmern; **2.** zerreißen, (zer)spalten; **3.** unter'brechen, stören; **4.** zerrütten; **5.** *Versammlung, Koalition etc.* sprengen; **II** v/i. **6.** zerreißen; **7.** ⚡ 'durchschlagen; **dis'rup·tion** [-pʃn] s. **1.** Zerreißung f, Zerschlagung f; Unter'brechung f; **2.** Zerrissenheit f, Spaltung f; **3.** Bruch m; **4.** Zerrüttung f; **dis'rup·tive** [-tɪv] adj. **1.** zerbrechend, zertrümmernd, zerreißend; **2.** zerrüttend; **3.** ⚡ Durchschlags...(-*festigkeit etc.*): *~ discharge* Durchschlag m.

dis·sat·is·fac·tion [ˈdɪsˌsætɪs'fækʃn] s. Unzufriedenheit f (*at, with* mit); **'dis-ˌsat·is'fac·to·ry** [-ktərɪ] adj. unbefriedigend; **dis·sat·is·fied** [ˌdɪs'sætɪs-faɪd] adj. unzufrieden (*with, at* mit); **dis·sat·is·fy** [ˌdɪs'sætɪsfaɪ] v/t. nicht befriedigen, j-n verdrießen; j-m miss'fallen.

dis·sect [dɪ'sekt] v/t. **1.** zergliedern, zerlegen; **2.** a) ✹ sezieren, b) ✹, ⚕, zo. präparieren; **3.** fig. zergliedern, analysieren; **dis'sec·tion** [-kʃn] s. **1.** Zergliederung f, fig. a. Aufgliederung f, b) (genaue) Ana'lyse; **2.** ✹ Sezieren n; **3.** ✹, ⚕, zo. Präpa'rat n; **dis'sec·tor** [-tə] s. **1.** ✹ Sezierer m; **2.** ✹, ⚕, zo. Präpa'rator m.

dis·seise, dis·seize [ˌdɪ'siːz] v/t. ♈ j-m 'widerrechtlich den Besitz entziehen; ˌdis'sei·sin, ˌdis'sei·zin [-zɪn] s. ♈ 'widerrechtliche Besitzentziehung.

dis·sem·ble [dɪ'sembl] **I** v/t. **1.** verhehlen, verbergen, sich et. nicht anmerken lassen; **2.** vortäuschen, simulieren; **3.** obs. unbeachtet lassen; **II** v/i. **4.** sich verstellen, heucheln; **dis'sem·bler** [-lə] s. **1.** Heuchler(in); **2.** Simu'lant (-in).

dis·sem·i·nate [dɪ'semɪneɪt] v/t. **1.** Saat ausstreuen (a. fig.); **2.** fig. verbreiten: *~ ideas*; *~d sclerosis* ✹ multiple Sklerose; **dis·sem·i·na·tion** [dɪˌsemɪ'neɪʃn] s. Ausstreuung f; fig. a. Verbreitung f.

dis·sen·sion [dɪ'senʃn] s. Meinungsverschiedenheit(en pl.) f, Diffe'renz(en pl.) f.

dis·sent [dɪ'sent] **I** v/i. **1.** (*from*) anderer Meinung sein (als), nicht über'einstimmen (mit); **2.** eccl. von der Staatskirche abweichen; **II** s. **3.** Meinungsverschiedenheit f, andere Meinung; **4.** eccl. Abweichen n von der Staatskirche; **dis'sent·er** [-tə] s. **1.** Andersdenkende(r m) f; **2.** eccl. a) Dissi'dent m, b) oft ♉ Dis'senter m, Nonkonfor'mist (-in); **dis'sen·ti·ent** [-nʃɪənt] **I** adj. an-

ders denkend, abweichend: *without a ~ vote* ohne Gegenstimme; **II** s. a) Andersdenkende(r m) f, b) Gegenstimme f: *with no ~* ohne Gegenstimme.

dis·ser·ta·tion [ˌdɪsə'teɪʃn] s. **1.** (wissenschaftliche) Abhandlung; **2.** Dissertati'on f.

dis·serv·ice [ˌdɪs'sɜːvɪs] s. (*to*) schlechter Dienst (an dat.): *do a ~ j-m* e-n schlechten Dienst erweisen; *be of ~ to s.o.* j-m zum Nachteil gereichen.

dis·sev·er [dɪs'sevə] v/t. trennen, absondern, spalten.

dis·si·dence ['dɪsɪdəns] s. **1.** Meinungsverschiedenheit f; **2.** pol., eccl. Dissi-'dententum n; **'dis·si·dent** [-nt] **I** adj. **1.** anders denkend, nicht über'einstimmend, abweichend; **II** s. **2.** Andersdenkende(r m) f; **3.** eccl. Dissi'dent(in), pol. a. Re'gimekritiker(in).

dis·sim·i·lar [dɪ'sɪmɪlə] adj. □ (*to*) verschieden (von), unähnlich (dat.); **dis-sim·i·lar·i·ty** [ˌdɪsɪmɪ'lærətɪ] s. Verschiedenartigkeit f, Unähnlichkeit f; 'Unterschied m.

dis·sim·u·late [dɪ'sɪmjʊleɪt] **I** v/t. verbergen, verhehlen; **II** v/i. sich verstellen; heucheln; **dis·sim·u·la·tion** [dɪ-ˌsɪmjʊ'leɪʃn] s. **1.** Verheimlichung f; **2.** Verstellung f, Heuche'lei f; **3.** ✹ Dissimulati'on f.

dis·si·pate ['dɪsɪpeɪt] **I** v/t. **1.** zerstreuen (a. fig. u. phys.); *Nebel* zerteilen; **2.** a) verschwenden, vergeuden, verzetteln, b) *Geld* 'durchbringen, verprassen; **3.** fig. verscheuchen, vertreiben; **4.** phys. a) *Hitze* ableiten, b) in 'Wärmeener,gie 'umwandeln; **II** v/i. **5.** sich zerstreuen (a. fig.); sich zerteilen (*Nebel*); **6.** ein ausschweifendes Leben führen; **'dis·si-pat·ed** [-tɪd] adj. ausschweifend, zügellos; **dis·si·pa·tion** [ˌdɪsɪ'peɪʃn] s. **1.** Zerstreuung f (a. fig. u. phys.); **2.** Vergeudung f; **3.** Verprassen n, 'Durchbringen n; **4.** Ausschweifung(en pl.) f; zügelloses Leben; **5.** phys. a) Ableitung f, b) Dissipati'on f.

dis·so·ci·ate [dɪ'səʊʃɪeɪt] **I** v/t. **1.** trennen, loslösen, absondern (*from* von); **2.** ✹ dissoziieren; *~ o.s.* (*from*) sich lossagen od. distanzieren od. abrücken (von); **II** v/i. **4.** sich (ab)trennen od. loslösen; **5.** ✹ dissoziieren; **dis·so-ci·a·tion** [dɪˌsəʊsɪ'eɪʃn] s. **1.** (Ab-) Trennung f, Loslösung f; **2.** Abrücken n; **3.** ✹, psych. Dissoziati'on f.

dis·sol·u·bil·i·ty [dɪˌsɒljʊ'bɪlətɪ] s. **1.** Löslichkeit f; **2.** Auflösbarkeit f, Trennbarkeit f; **dis·sol·u·ble** [dɪ'sɒl-jʊbl] adj. **1.** löslich; **2.** ♈ auflösbar, trennbar.

dis·so·lute ['dɪsəluːt] adj. □ ausschweifend, zügellos; **'dis·so·lute·ness** [-nɪs] s. Ausschweifung f, Zügellosigkeit f.

dis·so·lu·tion [ˌdɪsə'luːʃn] s. **1.** Auflösung f (a. parl., ✝; a. Ehe); **2.** a. Aufhebung f; **3.** Zersetzung f; **4.** ✹ Lösung f.

dis·solv·a·ble [dɪ'zɒlvəbl] → *dissoluble*; **dis·solve** [dɪ'zɒlv] **I** v/t. **1.** auflösen (a. fig., ✝, Parlament, Firma etc.): *Ehe* a. scheiden; lösen (a. ✹): *~d in tears* in Tränen aufgelöst; **2.** ♈ aufheben; **3.** auflösen, zersetzen; **4.** vernichten; **5.** *Geheimnis etc.* lösen; **6.** *Film:* über'blenden; **II** v/i. **7.** sich auflösen (a. fig.), zergehen, schmelzen; **8.** zerfallen; **9.** sich (in nichts) auflösen, verschwinden; **10.** *Film:* über'blenden, inein'ander 'übergehen; **III** s. **11.** *Film:* Über'blendung f; **dis'sol·vent** [-vənt] **I** adj. (auf)lösend; zersetzend; **II** s. ✹ Lösungsmittel n.

D

dis·so·nance ['dɪsənəns] s. Disso'nanz f: a) ♪ 'Missklang m (a. fig.), b) fig. Unstimmigkeit f; **'dis·so·nant** [-nt] adj. □ **1.** ♪ disso'nant (a. fig.); **2.** 'misstönend; **3.** fig. unstimmig.

dis·suade [dɪ'sweɪd] v/t. **1.** j-m abraten (**from** von); **2.** j-n abbringen (**from** von); **dis'sua·sion** [-eɪʒn] s. **1.** Abraten n; **2.** Abbringen n; **dis'sua·sive** [-eɪsɪv] adj. □ abratend.

dis·syl·lab·ic, **dis·syl·la·ble** → **disyllabic, disyllable**.

dis·sym·met·ri·cal [ˌdɪsɪ'metrɪkl] adj. 'unsym,metrisch; **dis·sym·met·ry** [ˌdɪ'sɪmɪtrɪ] s. Asymme'trie f.

dis·taff ['dɪstɑːf] s. (Spinn)Rocken m; fig. das Reich der Frau: **~ side** weibliche Linie e-r Familie.

dis·tance ['dɪstəns] **I** s. **1.** a) Entfernung f, b) Ferne f: **at a ~** a) in einiger Entfernung, b) von weitem; **in the ~** in der Ferne; **from a ~** aus einiger Entfernung; **at an equal ~** gleich weit (entfernt); **a good ~ off** ziemlich weit entfernt; **braking ~** mot. Bremsweg m; **stopping ~** mot. Anhalteweg m; **within striking ~** handgreiflich nahe, in erreichbarer Nähe; → **hail** 7; **walking** II; **2.** Zwischenraum m, Abstand m (**between** zwischen); **3.** Entfernung f, Strecke f: **~ covered** zurückgelegte Strecke; **4.** zeitlicher Abstand, Zeitraum m; **5.** fig. Abstand m, Entfernung f, 'Unterschied m; **6.** fig. Di'stanz f, Abstand m, Re'serve f, Zu'rückhaltung f: **keep s.o. at a ~** j-m gegenüber reserviert sein, sich j-n vom Leib halten; **keep one's ~** den Abstand wahren, (die gebührende) Distanz halten; **7.** paint. etc. a) Perspek'tive f, b) a. pl. 'Hintergrund m, c) Ferne f; **8.** ♪ Inter'vall n; **9.** sport a) Di'stanz f, Strecke f, b) fenc., Boxen: Di'stanz f, c) Langstrecke f: **~ race** Langstreckenlauf m; **~ runner** Langstreckenläufer(in); **II** v/t. **10.** über'holen, hinter sich lassen, sport a. distanzieren: **~d** fig. distanziert; **11.** fig. über'flügeln; **'dis·tant** [-nt] adj. □ **1.** entfernt (a. fig.), weit (**from** von); fern (Ort od. Zeit): **~ relation** entfernte(r) od. weitläufige(r) Verwandte(r); **~ resemblance** entfernte od. schwache Ähnlichkeit; **~ dream** vager Traum, schwache Aussicht; **2.** weit vonein'ander entfernt; **3.** zu'rückhaltend, kühl, distanziert; **4.** ⊕ Fern...: **~ control** Fernsteuerung f; **~ reading instrument** Fernmessgerät n.

dis·taste [ˌdɪs'teɪst] s. (**for**) 'Widerwille m, Abneigung f (gegen), Ekel m, Abscheu m (vor dat.); **dis'taste·ful** [-fʊl] adj. □ **1.** Ekel erregend; **2.** fig. a) unangenehm, zu'wider (**to** dat.), b) ekelhaft, widerlich.

dis·tem·per¹ [dɪ'stempə] **I** s. **1.** Tempera- od. Leimfarbe f; **2.** 'Temperamale,rei f (a. Bild); **II** v/t. **3.** mit Temperafarbe(n) (an)malen.

dis·tem·per² [dɪ'stempə] s. **1.** vet. a) Staupe f (bei Hunden), b) Druse f (bei Pferden); **2.** obs. a) üble Laune, b) Unpässlichkeit f, c) po'litische Unruhe(n pl.).

dis·tend [dɪ'stend] **I** v/t. (aus)dehnen, weiten; aufblähen; **II** v/i. sich (aus)dehnen etc.; **dis·ten·si·ble** [dɪ'stensəbl] adj. (aus)dehnbar; **dis·ten·sion** [dɪ'stenʃn] s. (Aus)Dehnung f; Aufblähung f.

dis·tich ['dɪstɪk] s. **1.** Distichon n (Verspaar); **2.** gereimtes Verspaar.

dis·til, Am. **dis·till** [dɪ'stɪl] **I** v/t. **1.** 🝆 a) ('um)destillieren, abziehen, b) abdestil-

lieren (**from** aus), c) entgasen: **~(l)ing flask** Destillierkolben m; **2.** Branntwein brennen (**from** aus); **3.** her'abtropfen lassen: **be ~led** sich niederschlagen; **4.** fig. das Wesentliche he'rausdestil,lieren, -arbeiten (**from** aus); **II** v/i. **5.** 🝆 destillieren; **6.** (her'ab)tropfen; **7.** fig. sich her'auskristalli,sieren; **dis·til·late** ['dɪstɪlət] s. 🝆 Destil'lat n; **dis·til·la·tion** [ˌdɪstɪ'leɪʃn] s. **1.** 🝆 Destillati'on f; **2.** Brennen n (von Branntwein); **3.** Ex'trakt m, Auszug m; **4.** fig. 'Quintes,senz f, Kern m; **dis·til·ler** [dɪ'stɪlə] s. Branntweinbrenner m; **dis·til·ler·y** [dɪ'stɪlərɪ] s. **1.** 🝆 Destil'lierappa,rat m; **2.** Destilla'teur m, ('Branntwein)Brenne,rei f.

dis·tinct [dɪ'stɪŋkt] adj. □ → **distinctly**; **1.** ver-, unter'schieden: **as ~ from** im Unterschied zu, zum Unterschied von; **2.** einzeln, getrennt, (ab)gesondert; **3.** eigen, selbstständig; **4.** ausgeprägt, charakte'ristisch; **5.** klar, eindeutig, bestimmt, entschieden, ausgesprochen, deutlich; **dis·tinc·tion** [dɪ'stɪŋkʃn] s. **1.** Unter'scheidung f: **a ~ without a difference** e-e spitzfindige Unterscheidung; **2.** 'Unterschied m: **in ~ from** (od. **to**) im Unterschied zu, zum Unterschied von; **draw** (od. **make**) **a ~ between** e-n Unterschied machen zwischen (dat.); **3.** Unter'scheidungsmerkmal n, Kennzeichen n; **4.** her'vorragende Eigenschaft; **5.** Besonderheit f, Ehrung f; **6.** (hoher) Rang; **7.** Würde f; Vornehmheit f; **8.** Ruf m, Berühmtheit f; **dis·tinc·tive** [dɪ'stɪŋktɪv] adj. □ **1.** unter'scheidend, Unterscheidungs...; **2.** kenn-, bezeichnend, charakte'ristisch (**of** für), besonder; **3.** deutlich, ausgesprochen; **dis·tinc·tive·ness** [dɪ'stɪŋktɪvnɪs] s. **1.** Besonderheit f; **2.** → **distinctness** 1; **dis·tinct·ly** [dɪ'stɪŋktlɪ] adv. deutlich, fig. a. ausgesprochen; **dis·tinct·ness** [dɪ'stɪŋktnɪs] s. **1.** Deutlichkeit f, Klarheit f; **2.** Verschiedenheit f; **3.** Verschiedenartigkeit f.

dis·tin·gué [dɪ'stæŋɡeɪ] (Fr.) adj. distingu'iert, vornehm.

dis·tin·guish [dɪ'stɪŋɡwɪʃ] **I** v/t. **1.** (**between** unter'scheiden (zwischen), (zwei Dinge etc.) ausein'ander halten: **as ~ed from** zum Unterschied von, im Unterschied zu; **be ~ed by** sich durch et. unterscheiden od. weitS. auszeichnen; **2.** wahrnehmen, erkennen; **3.** kennzeichnen, charakterisieren: **~ing mark** Merkmal n, Kennzeichen n; **4.** auszeichnen, rühmend her'vorheben: **~ o.s.** sich auszeichnen (a. iro.); **II** v/i. **5.** unter'scheiden, e-n 'Unterschied machen; **dis·tin·guish·a·ble** [dɪ'stɪŋɡwɪʃəbl] adj. □ **1.** unter'scheidbar; **2.** wahrnehmbar, erkennbar; **3.** kenntlich (**by** an dat., durch); **dis·tin·guished** [dɪ'stɪŋɡwɪʃt] adj. □ **1.** → **distinguishable** 1, 2; **2.** bemerkenswert, berühmt (**for** wegen, **by** durch); **3.** vornehm; **4.** her'vorragend, ausgezeichnet.

dis·tort [dɪ'stɔːt] v/t. **1.** verdrehen (a. fig.); a. Gesicht verzerren (a. ⊕, 🝆 u. fig.); verrenken; ⊕ verformen: **~ing mirror** Vexier-, Zerrspiegel m; **2.** fig. Tatsachen etc. verdrehen, entstellen; **dis·tor·tion** [dɪ'stɔːʃn] s. **1.** Verdrehung f (a. phys.); Verrenkung f; Verzerrung f (a. 🝆, phot.); Verziehung f, Verwindung f (a. ⊕); **2.** fig. Entstellung f, Verzerrung f.

dis·tract [dɪ'strækt] v/t. **1.** Aufmerksamkeit, Person etc. ablenken; **2.** j-n zerstreuen; **3.** erregen, aufwühlen; **4.** beunruhigen, stören, quälen; **5.** rasend

machen; **dis·tract·ed** [dɪ'stræktɪd] adj. □ **1.** verwirrt; **2.** beunruhigt; **3.** außer sich, von Sinnen: **~ with** (od. **by**) **pain** wahnsinnig vor Schmerzen; **dis·trac·tion** [dɪ'strækʃn] s. **1.** Ablenkung f, a. Zerstreuung f; **2.** Zerstreutheit f; **3.** Verwirrung f; **4.** Wahnsinn m, Rase'rei f: **drive s.o. to ~** j-n zur Raserei bringen; **love to ~** bis zum Wahnsinn lieben; **5.** oft pl. Ablenkung f, Zerstreuung f, Unter'haltung f.

dis·train [dɪ'streɪn] 🜚 v/i.: **~ (up)on** a) j-n pfänden, b) et. mit Beschlag belegen; **dis·train·ee** [ˌdɪstreɪ'niː] s. Pfandschuldner(in); **dis·train·er** [dɪ'streɪnə], **dis·train·or** [ˌdɪstreɪ'nɔː] s. Pfandgläubiger(in); **dis·traint** [dɪ'streɪnt] s. Beschlagnahme f.

dis·traught [dɪ'strɔːt] → **distracted**.

dis·tress [dɪ'stres] **I** s. **1.** Qual f, Pein f, Schmerz m; **2.** Leid n, Kummer m, Sorge f; **3.** Elend n; Not(lage) f; **4.** ♄ Seenot f: **~ call** Notruf m, SOS-Ruf m; **~ rocket** Notrakete f; **~ signal** Notsignal n; **5.** 🜚 a) Beschlagnahme f, b) mit Beschlag belegte Sache; **II** v/t. **6.** quälen, peinigen, bedrücken; beunruhigen; betrüben: **~ o.s.** sich sorgen (**about** um); **7.** → **distrain**; **dis·tressed** [dɪ'strest] adj. **1.** (**about**) beunruhigt (über acc., wegen), besorgt (um); **2.** bekümmert, betrübt; unglücklich; **3.** bedrängt, in Not, Not leidend: **~ area** Brit. Notstandsgebiet n; **~ ships** Schiffe in Seenot; **4.** erschöpft; **dis·tress·ful** [dɪ'stresfʊl], **dis·tress·ing** [dɪ'stresɪŋ] adj. □ **1.** quälend; **2.** bedrückend.

dis·trib·ut·a·ble [dɪ'strɪbjutəbl] adj. **1.** verteilbar; **2.** zu verteilen(d); **dis·trib·u·tar·y** [dɪ'strɪbjutərɪ] s. geogr. abzweigender Flussarm, bsd. Deltaarm m; **dis·trib·ute** [dɪ'strɪbjuːt] v/t. **1.** ver-, austeilen (**among** unter acc., **to** an acc.). **2.** zuteilen (**to** dat.); **3.** ✝ a) Waren vertreiben, absetzen, b) Filme verleihen, c) Dividende, Gewinne ausschütten; **4.** Post zustellen; **5.** verbreiten, ausstreuen; Farbe etc. verteilen; **6.** auf-, einteilen; ✗ gliedern; **7.** typ. a) Satz ablegen, b) Farbe auftragen; **dis·trib·u·tee** [dɪˌstrɪbjuː'tiː] s. **1.** Empfänger(in); **2.** 🜚 Erbe m, Erbin f; **dis·trib·ut·er** → **distributor**.

dis·trib·ut·ing| a·gent [dɪ'strɪbjutɪŋ] s. ✝ (Großhandels)Vertreter m; **~ center** Am., Brit. **~ cen·tre** s. ✝ 'Absatz-, Ver'teilungs,zentrum n.

dis·tri·bu·tion [ˌdɪstrɪ'bjuːʃn] s. **1.** Ver-, Austeilung f; **2.** ⊕, 🜚 a) Verteilung f, b) Verzweigung f; **3.** Ver-, Ausbreitung f; **4.** Einteilung f, a. ✗ Gliederung f; **5.** a) Verteilung f, b) Gabe f, Spende f; **6.** ✝ a) Vertrieb m, Absatz m, b) Verleih m (von Filmen), c) Ausschüttung f (von Dividenden, Gewinnen); **7.** Ausstreuen n (von Samen); **8.** Verteilen n (von Farben etc.); **9.** typ. a) Ablegen n (des Satzes), b) Auftragen n (von Farbe); **dis·trib·u·tive** [dɪ'strɪbjutɪv] **I** adj. □ **1.** aus-, zu-, verteilend, Verteilungs...: **~ share** 🜚 gesetzlicher Erbteil; **~ justice** fig. ausgleichende Gerechtigkeit; **2.** jeden Einzelnen betreffend; **3.** ✗, ling. distribu'tiv, Distributiv...; **II** s. **4.** ling. Distribu'tivum n; **dis·trib·u·tor** [dɪ'strɪbjutə] s. **1.** Verteiler m (a. ⊕, 🜚); **2.** ✝ a) Großhändler m, Gene'ralvertreter m, b) pl. (Film)Verleih m; **3.** ⊕ Verteilerdüse f.

dis·trict ['dɪstrɪkt] s. **1.** Di'strikt m, (Verwaltungs)Bezirk m, Kreis m; **2.** (Stadt)Bezirk m, (-)Viertel n; **3.** Gegend f, Gebiet n, Landstrich m; **~ at-**

tor·ney *s. Am.* Staatsanwalt *m*; ♀
Coun·cil *s. Brit.* Bezirksamt *n*; ♀
Court *s.* ⚖ *Am.* (Bundes)Bezirksgericht *n*; **~ heat·ing** *s.* Fernheizung *f*; **~ judge** *s.* ⚖ *Am.* Richter *m* an e-m (Bundes)Bezirksgericht; **~ man·ag·er** *s.* Be'zirksleiter(in), Gebietsleiter(in); **~ nurse** *s.* Gemeindeschwester *f*.

dis·trust [dɪs'trʌst] **I** *s.* 'Misstrauen *n*, Argwohn *m* (*of* gegen): *have a ~ of s.o.* j-m misstrauen; **II** *v/t.* miss'trauen (*dat.*); **dis'trust·ful** [-fʊl] *adj.* □ 'misstrauisch, argwöhnisch (*of* gegen): **~ of o.s.** gehemmt, ohne Selbstvertrauen.

dis·turb [dɪ'stɜːb] **I** *v/t.* stören (*a.* ⚙, ♫, ⚕, *meteor. etc.*): a) behindern, b) belästigen, c) beunruhigen, d) aufschrecken, -scheuchen, e) durchein'ander bringen, in Unordnung bringen: *~ed at* beunruhigt über (*acc.*); *~ the peace* ⚖ die öffentliche Sicherheit u. Ordnung stören; **II** *v/i.* stören; **dis·turb·ance** [dɪ'stɜːbəns] *s.* **1.** Störung *f* (*a.* ⚙, ♫, ⚕, 📡); **2.** Belästigung *f*; Beunruhigung *f*; Aufregung *f*; **3.** Unruhe *f*, Tu'mult *m*, Aufruhr *m*: *~ of the peace* ⚖ öffentliche Ruhestörung; *cause* (*od.* *create*) *a ~* ⚖ die öffentliche Sicherheit u. Ordnung stören; **4.** Verwirrung *f*; **5.** *~ of possession* ⚖ Besitzstörung *f*; **dis·turb·er** [dɪ'stɜːbə] *s.* Störenfried *m*, Unruhestifter(in); **dis·turb·ing** [dɪ'stɜːbɪŋ] *adj.* □ beunruhigend.

dis·un·ion [ˌdɪs'juːnjən] *s.* **1.** Trennung *f*, Spaltung *f*; **2.** Uneinigkeit *f*, Zwietracht *f*; **dis·u·nite** [ˌdɪsjuː'naɪt] *v/t. u. v/i.* (sich) trennen; *fig.* (sich) entzweien; **dis·u·nit·ed** [ˌdɪsjuː'naɪtɪd] *adj.* entzweit, verfeindet; **dis·u·ni·ty** [ˌdɪs'juːnətɪ] → *disunion* 2.

dis·use I *s.* [ˌdɪs'juːs] Nichtgebrauch *m*; Aufhören *n e-s Brauchs*: *fall into ~* außer Gebrauch kommen; **II** *v/t.* [ˌdɪs'juːz] nicht mehr gebrauchen; **dis·used** [ˌdɪs'juːzd] *adj.* **1.** ausgedient, nicht mehr benützt; **2.** stillgelegt (*Bergwerk etc.*), außer Betrieb.

dis·yl·lab·ic [ˌdɪsɪ'læbɪk] *adj.* (□ *~ally*) zweisilbig; **di·syl·la·ble** [dɪ'sɪləbl] *s.* zweisilbiges Wort.

ditch [dɪtʃ] **I** *s.* **1.** (Straßen)Graben *m*: *last ~* verzweifelter Kampf, Not(lage) *f*; *die in the last ~* bis zum letzten Atemzug kämpfen (*a. fig.*); **2.** Abzugsgraben *m*; **3.** Bewässerungs-, Wassergraben *m*; **4.** ✈ *sl.* ‚Bach' *m* (*Meer, Gewässer*); **II** *v/t.* **5.** mit e-m Graben versehen, Gräben ziehen durch; **6.** durch Abzugsgräben entwässern; **7.** F *Wagen* in den Straßengraben fahren: *be ~ed* im Straßengraben landen; **8.** *sl.* a) *Wagen etc.* stehen lassen, b) j-m entwischen, c) j-m den ‚Laufpass' geben, j-n ‚sausen' lassen, d) *et.* ‚wegschmeißen', e) *Am.* Schule schwänzen; **9.** ✈ *sl. Maschine* im ‚Bach' landen; **III** *v/i.* **10.** Gräben ziehen *od.* ausbessern; **11.** ✈ *sl.* notlanden, notwassern; **'ditch·er** [-tʃə] *s.* **1.** Grabenbauer *m*; **2.** Grabbagger *m*; **'ditch·wa·ter** *s.* abgestandenes, fauliges Wasser; → *dull* 4.

dith·er ['dɪðə] **I** *v/i.* **1.** bibbern, zittern; **2.** *fig.* schwanken (*between* zwischen *dat.*); **3.** aufgeregt sein; **II** *s.* **4.** *fig.* Schwanken *n*; **5.** Aufregung *f*: *be all of* (*od. in*) *a ~* F aufgeregt sein, ‚bibbern'.

dith·y·ramb ['dɪθɪræmb] *s.* **1.** Dithy'rambus *m*; **2.** Lobeshymne *f*; **dith·y·ram·bic** [ˌdɪθɪ'ræmbɪk] *adj.* dithy'rambisch; enthusi'astisch.

dit·to ['dɪtəʊ] (*abbr. do.*) **I** *adv.* dito, des'gleichen: *~ marks* Ditozeichen *n*;

---

say ~ to s.o. j-m beipflichten; **II** *s.* F Dupli'kat *n*, Ebenbild *n*.

dit·ty ['dɪtɪ] *s.* Liedchen *n*.

di·u·ret·ic [ˌdaɪjʊə'retɪk] **I** *adj.* diu're-tisch, harntreibend; **II** *s.* harntreibendes Mittel, Diu'retikum *n*.

di·ur·nal [daɪ'ɜːnl] *adj.* □ **1.** täglich ('wiederkehrend), Tag(es)...; **2.** *zo.* 'tagak,tiv, bei Tag auftretend.

di·va ['diːvə] *s.* Diva *f*.

di·va·gate ['daɪvəgeɪt] *v/i.* abschweifen; **di·va·ga·tion** [ˌdaɪvə'geɪʃn] *s.* Abschweifung *f*, Ex'kurs *m*.

di·va·lent ['daɪ,veɪlənt] *adj.* 🜨 zweiwertig.

di·van [dɪ'væn] *s.* **1.** a) Diwan *m*, (Liege)Sofa *n*, b) *a.* **~ bed** Bettcouch *f*; **2.** Diwan *m*: a) *orientalischer Staatsrat*, b) *Regierungskanzlei*, c) *Gerichtssaal*, d) *öffentliches Gebäude*; **3.** Diwan *m* (*orientalische Gedichtsammlung*).

di·var·i·cate [daɪ'værɪkeɪt] *v/i.* sich gabeln, sich spalten; abzweigen.

dive [daɪv] **I** *v/i.* **1.** tauchen (*for* nach, *into* in *acc.*); **2.** 'untertauchen; **3.** e-n Kopf- *od.* Hechtsprung (*a. Torwart*) machen; **4.** *Wasserspringen:* springen; **5.** ✈ e-n Sturzflug machen; **6.** (hastig) hin'eingreifen *od.* -fahren (*into* in *acc.*); **7.** sich stürzen, verschwinden (*into* in *acc.*); **8.** (*into*) sich vertiefen (in *ein Buch etc.*); **9.** fallen (*Thermometer etc.*); **II** *s.* **10.** ('Unter)Tauchen *n*, ⚓ *a.* Tauchfahrt *f*; **11.** Kopfsprung *m*; Hechtsprung *m* (*a. des Torwarts*): *make a ~* → 3; *take a ~ sport sl.* a) *Fußball:* ‚e-e Schwalbe bauen', b) ‚sich (einfach) hinlegen' (*Boxer*); **12.** *Wasserspringen:* Sprung *m*; **13.** ✈ Sturzflug *m*; **14.** F Spe'lunke *f*, Kneipe *f*; **'~·bomb** *v/t. u. v/i.* im Sturzflug mit Bomben angreifen; **~ bomb·er** *s.* Sturzkampfflugzeug *n*, Sturzbomber *m*, Stuka *m*.

div·er ['daɪvə] *s.* **1.** Taucher(in); *sport* Wasserspringer(in); **2.** *orn. ein* Tauchvogel *m, bsd.* Pinguin *m*.

di·verge [daɪ'vɜːdʒ] *v/i.* **1.** divergieren (*a.* ⚕, *phys.*), ausein'ander gehen, *od.* laufen, sich trennen; abweichen; **2.** abzweigen (*from* von); **3.** verschiedener Meinung sein; **di·ver·gence** [-dʒəns], **di·ver·gen·cy** [-dʒənsɪ] *s.* **1.** ⚕, *phys.* etc. Diver'genz *f*; **2.** Ausein'anderlaufen *n*; **3.** Abzweigung *f*; Abweichung *f*; **5.** Meinungsverschiedenheit *f*; **di·'ver·gent** [-dʒənt] *adj.* □ **1.** divergierend (*a.* ⚕, *phys. etc.*); **2.** ausein'ander gehend *od.* laufend; **3.** abweichend.

di·vers ['daɪvɜːz] *adj. obs.* etliche.

di·verse [daɪ'vɜːs] *adj.* □ **1.** verschieden, ungleich; **2.** mannigfaltig; **di·ver·si·fi·ca·tion** [daɪˌvɜːsɪfɪ'keɪʃn] *s.* **1.** abwechslungsreiche Gestaltung; **2.** ✝ Diversifizierung *f*, Streuung *f*: *~* (*of products*) Verbreiterung *f* des Produktionsprogramms; **3.** Verschiedenartigkeit *f*; **di·'ver·si·fied** [-sɪfaɪd] *adj.* **1.** verschieden(artig); **2.** ✝ a) verteilt (*Risiko*), b) verteilt angelegt (*Kapital*), c) diversifiziert (*Produktion*); **di·'ver·si·fy** [-sɪfaɪ] *v/t.* **1.** verschieden(artig) *od.* abwechslungsreich gestalten, variieren; **2.** ✝ diversifizieren, streuen.

di·ver·sion [daɪ'vɜːʃn] *s.* **1.** Ablenkung *f*; **2.** ✕ 'Ablenkungsma,növer *n* (*a. fig.*); **3.** *Brit.* 'Umleitung *f* (*Verkehr*); **4.** *fig.* Zerstreuung *f*, Zeitvertreib *m*; **di·'ver·sion·a·ry** [-ʃnərɪ] *adj.* ✕ Ablenkungs...; **di·'ver·sion·ist** *pol.* **I** *s.* Diversio'nist(in), Sabo'teur(in); **II** *adj.* diversio'nistisch.

di·ver·si·ty [daɪ'vɜːsətɪ] *s.* **1.** Verschie-

---

denheit *f*, Ungleichheit *f*; **2.** Mannigfaltigkeit *f*.

di·vert [daɪ'vɜːt] *v/t.* **1.** ablenken, ableiten, abwenden (*from* von, *to* nach), lenken (*to* auf *acc.*); **2.** abbringen (*from* von); **3.** *Geld etc.* abzweigen (*to* für); **4.** *Brit. Verkehr* 'umleiten; **5.** zerstreuen, unter'halten; **di·'vert·ing** [-tɪŋ] *adj.* □ unter'haltsam, amü'sant.

di·vest [daɪ'vest] *v/t.* **1.** entkleiden (*of gen.*); **2.** *fig.* entblößen, berauben (*of gen.*): *~ s.o. of* j-m *ein Recht etc.* entziehen *od.* nehmen; *~ o.s. of et.* ablegen, *et.* ab- *od.* aufgeben, sich *e-s Rechts etc.* entäußern; **di·'vest·i·ture** [-tɪtʃə], **di·'vest·ment** [-stmənt] *s. fig.* Entblößung *f*, Beraubung *f*.

di·vide [dɪ'vaɪd] **I** *v/t.* **1.** (ein)teilen (*in, into* in *acc.*): *be ~d into* zerfallen in (*acc.*); **2.** ⚕ teilen, dividieren (*by* durch); **3.** verteilen (*between, among* unter *acc. od. dat.*): *~ s.th. with s.o.* et. mit j-m teilen; **4.** *a.* **~ up** zerteilen, zerlegen; zerstückeln, spalten; **5.** entzweien, ausein'ander bringen; **6.** trennen, absondern, scheiden (*from* von); *Haar scheiteln*; **7.** *Brit. parl.* (im Hammelsprung) abstimmen lassen; **II** *v/i.* **8.** sich teilen; zerfallen (*in, into* in *acc.*); **9.** ⚕ a) sich teilen lassen (*by* durch), b) aufgehen (*into* in *dat.*); **10.** sich trennen *od.* spalten; **11.** *parl.* im Hammelsprung abstimmen; **III** *s.* **12.** *Am.* Wasserscheide *f*; **13.** *fig.* Trennlinie *f*: *the Great* ♀ der Tod; **di·'vid·ed** [-dɪd] *adj.* geteilt (*a. fig.*): *~ opinions* geteilte Meinungen; *~ counsel* Uneinigkeit *f*; *his mind was ~* er war unentschlossen; *~ against themselves* unter sich uneins; *~ highway Am.* Schnellstraße *f*; *~ skirt* Hosenrock *m*.

div·i·dend ['dɪvɪdend] *s.* **1.** ⚕ Divi'dend *m*; **2.** ✝ Divi'dende *f*, Gewinnanteil *m*: *Brit. cum ~, Am. ~ on* einschließlich Dividende; *Brit. ex ~, Am. ~ off* ausschließlich Dividende; *pay ~s fig.* sich bezahlt machen; **3.** ✝ Rate *f*, (Kon'kurs)quote *f*; **~ cou·pon**, **~ war·rant** *s.* ✝ Divi'dendenschein *m*.

di·vid·er [dɪ'vaɪdə] *s.* **1.** (Ver)Teiler(in); **2.** *pl.* Stechzirkel *m*; **3.** Trennwand *f*; **di·'vid·ing** [-dɪŋ] *adj.* Trennungs..., Scheide...; ⚙ Teil...

div·i·na·tion [ˌdɪvɪ'neɪʃn] *s.* **1.** Weissagung *f*, Wahrsagung *f*; **2.** (Vor)Ahnung *f*.

di·vine [dɪ'vaɪn] **I** *adj.* □ **1.** Gottes..., göttlich, heilig: *~ service* Gottesdienst *m*; *~ right of kings* Königtum *n* von Gottes Gnaden, Gottesgnadentum *n*; **2.** *fig.* F göttlich, himmlisch; **II** *s.* **3.** Geistliche(r) *m*; **4.** Theo'loge *m*; **III** *v/t.* **5.** (vor'aus)ahnen; erraten; **6.** weissagen, prophe'zeien: *divining rod* Wünschelrute *f*; **di·'vin·er** [-nə] *s.* **1.** Wahrsager *m*; **2.** (Wünschel)Rutengänger *m*.

div·ing ['daɪvɪŋ] *s.* **1.** Tauchen *n*; **2.** *sport* Wasserspringen *n*; **~ bell** *s.* Taucherglocke *f*; **~ board** *s.* Sprungbrett *n*; **~ duck** *s.* Tauchente *f*; **~ dress** → *diving suit*; **~ hel·met** *s.* Taucherhelm *m*; **~ suit** *s.* Taucheranzug *m*; **~ tow·er** *s.* Sprungturm *m*.

di·vin·i·ty [dɪ'vɪnətɪ] *s.* **1.** Göttlichkeit *f*, göttliches Wesen; **2.** Gottheit *f*: *the* ♀ die Gottheit, Gott; **3.** Theolo'gie *f*; **4.** *a.* ~ *fudge Am. ein* Schaumgebäck; **div·i·nize** ['dɪvɪnaɪz] *v/t.* vergöttlichen.

di·vis·i·bil·i·ty [dɪˌvɪzɪ'bɪlətɪ] *s.* Teilbarkeit *f*; **di·vis·i·ble** [dɪ'vɪzəbl] *adj.* □ teilbar; **di·vi·sion** [dɪ'vɪʒn] *s.* **1.** (Auf-, Ein)Teilung *f* (*into* in *acc.*); Verteilung *f*, Gliederung *f*: *~ of labo(u)r* Arbeits-

teilung; ~ *into shares* ✝ Stückelung f;
2. Trennung f, Grenze f, Scheidelinie f,
-wand f; **3.** Teil m, Ab'teilung f (a. e-s
Amtes etc.), Abschnitt m; **4.** Gruppe f,
Klasse f; **5.** ✕ Divisi'on f; **6.** sport 'Liga
f, (Spiel-, Boxen etc.: Gewichts)Klasse
f; **7.** pol. Bezirk m; **8.** parl. (Abstimmung f durch) Hammelsprung m: *go
into* ~ zur Abstimmung schreiten;
upon a ~ nach Abstimmung; **9.** fig.
Spaltung f, Kluft f; Uneinigkeit f, Diffe'renz f; **10.** Ⓐ Divisi'on f, Dividieren
n; **di·vi·sion·al** [dɪ'vɪʒənl] adj. □ **1.**
Trenn..., Scheide...: ~ *line* [s. **2.** Abteilungs...; **3.** ✕ Divisions...; **di·vi·sive**
[dɪ'vaɪsɪv] adj. **1.** teilend; scheidend; **2.**
entzweiend; trennend; **di·vi·sor**
[dɪ'vaɪzə] s. Ⓐ Di'visor m, Teiler m.
di·vorce [dɪ'vɔːs] **I** s. **1.** 🏛 (Ehe)Schei-
dung f: ~ *action*, ~ *suit* Scheidungsklage f, -prozess m; *obtain a* ~ geschieden
werden; *seek a* ~ auf Scheidung klagen; **2.** fig. (völlige) Trennung f (*from*
von); **II** v/t. **3.** 🏛 Ehegatten scheiden;
4. ~ *one's husband* (*wife*) 🏛 sich von
s-m Mann (s-r Frau) scheiden lassen;
5. fig. (völlig) trennen, scheiden, (los-)
lösen (*from* von); **di·vor·cee** [dɪˌvɔː-
'siː] s. Geschiedene(r m) f.
div·ot ['dɪvət] s. **1.** Scot. Sode f, Rasenstück n; **2.** Golf: Divot n, Kote'lett n.
div·ul·ga·tion [ˌdaɪvʌl'geɪʃn] s. Enthüllung f, Preisgabe f.
di·vulge [daɪ'vʌldʒ] v/t. Geheimnis etc.
enthüllen, preisgeben; **di'vulge·ment**
[-mənt], **di'vul·gence** [-dʒəns] → *di-
vulgation*.
div·vy ['dɪvɪ] v/t. oft ~ *up* Am. F aufteilen.
dix·ie¹ ['dɪksɪ] s. ✕ sl. **1.** Kochgeschirr
n; **2.** ,'Gulaschka‚none' f.
Dix·ie² ['dɪksɪ] s. → *Dixieland*; 'Dix·ie-
crat [-kræt] s. Am. pol. Mitglied e-r
Splittergruppe der Demokratischen Partei in den Südstaaten; **'Dix·ie·land** s. **1.**
Bezeichnung für den Süden der USA; **2.**
♪ Dixieland m, Dixie m.
DIY cen·tre [ˌdiːaɪ'waɪ] s. bsd. Brit.
Heimwerkermarkt m, Baumarkt m.
diz·zi·ness ['dɪzɪnɪs] s. Schwindel(anfall) m; Benommenheit f; **diz·zy** ['dɪzɪ]
I adj. □ **1.** schwindlig: ~ *spell* Schwindelanfall m; **2.** schwindelnd, Schwindel
erregend: ~ *heights*; **3.** verwirrt, benommen; **4.** unbesonnen; **5.** F verrückt; **II** v/t. **6.** schwindlig machen; **7.**
verwirren.
D-mark ['diːmɑːk] s. Deutsche Mark.
DNA fin·ger·print [ˌdiːeneɪ'fɪŋgəprɪnt]
s. ge'netischer Fingerabdruck.
do¹ [duː; də] **I** v/t. [irr.] **1.** tun, machen:
what can I ~ *for you?* womit kann ich
dienen?; *what does he* ~ *for a living?*
womit verdient er sein Brot?; ~ *right*
recht tun; → *done* 1; **2.** tun, ausführen,
sich beschäftigen mit, verrichten, voll-
'bringen, erledigen: ~ *business* Geschäfte machen; ~ *one's duty* s-e
Pflicht tun; ~ *French* Französisch lernen; ~ *Shakespeare* Shakespeare
durchnehmen od. behandeln; ~ *it into
German* es ins Deutsche übersetzen; ~
lecturing Vorlesungen halten; *my
work is done* m-e Arbeit ist getan od.
fertig; *he had done working* er war
mit der Arbeit fertig; ~ *60 miles per
hour* 60 Meilen die Stunde fahren; *he
did all the talking* er führte das große
Wort; *it can't be done* es geht nicht; ~
one's best sein Bestes tun, sich alle
Mühe geben; ~ *better* a) (et.) Besseres
tun od. leisten, b) sich verbessern; →
done; **3.** herstellen, anfertigen: ~ *a*

translation e-e Übersetzung machen; ~
a portrait ein Porträt malen; **4.** j-m et.
tun, zufügen, erweisen, gewähren: ~
s.o. harm j-m schaden; ~ *s.o. an injustice* j-m ein Unrecht zufügen, j-m unrecht tun; *these pills* ~ *me* (*no*) *good*
diese Pillen helfen mir (nicht); **5.** bewirken, erreichen: *I did it* ich habe es
geschafft; *now you've done it!* b.s.
nun hast du es glücklich geschafft!; **6.**
herrichten, in Ordnung bringen, (zu-
'recht)machen, Speisen zubereiten: ~ *a
room* ein Zimmer aufräumen od. ,ma-
chen'; ~ *one's hair* das Haar machen, sich frisieren; *I'll* ~ *the flowers*
ich werde die Blumen gießen; **7.** Rolle
etc. spielen, ,machen': ~ *Hamlet* den
Hamlet spielen; ~ *the host* den Wirt
spielen; ~ *the polite* den höflichen
Mann markieren; **8.** genügen, passen,
recht sein (dat.): *will this glass* ~ *you?*
genügt Ihnen dieses Glas?; **9.** F erschöpfen, ermüden: *he was pretty
well done* er war ,erledigt' (am Ende
s-r Kräfte); **10.** F erledigen, abfertigen:
I'll ~ *you next* ich nehme Sie als Nächsten dran; ~ *a town* e-e Stadt besichtigen od. ,erledigen'; *that has done me*
das hat mich ,fertig gemacht' od. ruiniert; ~ *3 years in prison* sl. drei Jahre
,abbrummen'; **11.** F ,reinlegen', ,übers
Ohr hauen', ,einseifen': ~ *s.o. out of
s.th.* j-n um et. betrügen od. bringen;
you have been done (*brown*) du bist
schön angeschmiert worden; **12.** F behandeln, versorgen, bewirten: ~ *s.o.
well* j-n gut versorgen; ~ *o.s. well* es
sich gut gehen lassen, sich gütlich tun; **II**
v/i. [irr.] **13.** handeln, vorgehen,
sich verhalten: *he did well to come* er
tat gut daran zu kommen; *nothing
~ing!* a) es ist nichts los, b) F nichts zu
machen!, ausgeschlossen!; *it's* ~ *or die
now!* jetzt gehts ums Ganze!; *have
done!* hör auf!, genug davon!; →
Rome; **14.** vor'ankommen, Leistungen
voll'bringen: ~ *well* a) es gut machen,
Erfolg haben, b) gedeihen, gut verdienen (→ 15); ~ *badly* schlecht daran
sein, schlecht mit et. fahren; *he did
brilliantly at his examination* er hat
ein glänzendes Examen gemacht; **15.**
sich befinden: ~ *well* a) gesund sein, b)
in guten Verhältnissen leben, c) sich
gut erholen; *how* ~ *you* ~? a) guten
Tag!, b) obs. wie geht es Ihnen?, c) es
freut mich (, Sie kennen zu lernen); **16.**
genügen, ausreichen, passen, recht
sein: *will this quality* ~? reicht diese
Qualität aus?; *that will* ~ a) das genügt,
b) genug davon!; *it will* ~ *tomorrow* es
hat Zeit bis morgen; *that won't* ~ a)
das genügt nicht, b) das geht nicht (an);
that won't ~ *with me* das verfängt bei
mir nicht; *it won't* ~ *to be rude* mit
Grobheit kommt man nicht weit(er),
man darf nicht unhöflich sein; *I'll make
it* ~ ich werde damit (schon) auskommen od. reichen; **III** v/aux. **17.** Verstärkung: *I* ~ *like it* es gefällt mir sehr; ~ *be
quiet!* sei doch still!; *he did come* er ist
tatsächlich gekommen; *they did go,
but* sie sind zwar od. wohl gegangen,
aber; **18.** Umschreibung: a) in Fragesätzen: ~ *you know him? No, I don't*
kennst du ihn? Nein (, ich kenne ihn
nicht), b) in mit *not* verneinten Sätzen:
he did not (od. *didn't*) *come* er ist
nicht gekommen; **19.** bei Umstellung
nach *hardly*, *little* etc.: *rarely does
one see such things* solche Dinge
sieht man selten; **20.** statt Wiederholung des Verbs: *you know as well as I*

~ Sie wissen so gut wie ich; *did you buy
it? – I did!* hast du es gekauft? – jawohl!; *I take a bath – so* ~ *I* ich nehme
ein Bad – ich auch; **21.** *you learn German, don't you?* du lernst Deutsch,
nicht wahr?; *he doesn't work too
hard, does he?* er arbeitet sich nicht
tot, nicht wahr?;
Zssgn mit prp.:
do| by v/i. behandeln, handeln an
(dat.): *do well by s.o.* j-n gut od. anständig behandeln; *do* (*[un]to others*)
as you would be done by was du nicht
willst, dass man dir tu, das füg auch
keinem andern zu; ~ **for** v/i. **1.** passen
od. sich eignen für od. als; ausreichen
für; **2.** F j-m den Haushalt führen; **3.**
sorgen für; **4.** F zu'grunde richten, ruinieren: *he is done for* er ist ,erledigt';
~ **to** → *do by*; ~ **with** v/t. u. v/i. **1.** : *I
can't do anything with him* (*it*) ich
kann nichts mit ihm (damit) anfangen; *I
have nothing to* ~ *it* ich habe nichts
damit zu schaffen, es geht mich nichts
an, es betrifft mich nicht; *I won't have
anything to* ~ *you* ich will mit dir nichts
zu schaffen haben; **2.** auskommen od.
sich begnügen mit: *can you* ~ *bread
and cheese for supper?* genügen dir
Brot und Käse zum Abendessen?; **3.**
er-, vertragen: *I can't* ~ *him and his
cheek* ich kann ihn mit s-r Frechheit
nicht ertragen; **4.** mst *could* ~ (gut) gebrauchen können: *I could* ~ *the
money*; *he could* ~ *a haircut* er müsste
sich mal (wieder) die Haare schneiden
lassen; ~ **with·out** v/i. auskommen ohne, et. entbehren, verzichten auf (acc.):
we shall have to ~ wir müssen ohne
(es) auskommen;
Zssgn mit adv.:
do| a·way with v/i. **1.** beseitigen, ab-
schaffen, aufheben; **2.** Geld 'durchbringen; **3.** 'umbringen, töten; ~ **down** v/t.
F **1.** reinlegen, ,übers Ohr hauen', ,be-
scheißen'; **2.** j-n ,untermachen'; **3.** in
v/t. sl. **1.** j-n 'umbringen; **2.** → *do
down* 1; **3.** j-n ,erledigen', ,schaffen'; ~
out v/t. F Zimmer etc. säubern; ~ **up**
v/t. **1.** a) zs.-schnüren, b) Päckchen verschnüren, zu'rechtmachen, c) einpacken, d) Kleid etc. zumachen; **2.** das
Haar hoch stecken; **3.** herrichten, in
Ordnung bringen; **4.** → *do in* 3.
do² [duː] pl. dos, do's [-z] s. **1.** sl.
Schwindel m, ,Beschiss' m, fauler Zauber; **2.** Brit. F Fest n, ,Festivi'tät' f,
,große Sache'; **3.** *do's and don'ts* Gebote pl. u. Verbote pl., Regeln pl.
do³ [dəʊ] s. ♪ do n (Solmisationssilbe).
do·a·ble ['duːəbl] adj. 'durchführ-,
machbar; **'do-all** s. Fak'totum n.
doat [dəʊt] → *dote*.
do·ber·man ['dəʊbəmən] pl. **-mans**
[-mənz] s. Hund: 'Dobermann m.
doc [dɒk] F abbr. für doctor.
do·cent [dəʊ'sent] s. Am. Pri'vatdo‚zent
m.
do·cile ['dəʊsaɪl] adj. □ **1.** fügsam, gefügig; **2.** gelehrig; **3.** fromm (Pferd);
do·cil·i·ty [dəʊ'sɪlətɪ] s. **1.** Fügsamkeit
f; **2.** Gelehrigkeit f.
dock¹ [dɒk] **I** s. **1.** Dock n: dry ~, graving ~ Trockendock n; floating ~
Schwimmdock n; wet ~ Dockhafen m;
put in ~ → 6; **2.** Hafenbecken n, Anlegeplatz m: ~ authorities Hafenbehör-
de f; ~ dues → dockage¹ 1; ~ strike
Dockarbeiterstreik m; **3.** pl. Docks pl.,
Dock-, Hafenanlagen pl.; **4.** Am. Kai
m; **5.** 🚢 Am. Laderampe f; **II** v/t. **6.**
Schiff (ein)docken; **7.** Raumschiffe
koppeln; **III** v/i. **8.** ins Dock gehen,

docken; im Dock liegen; **9.** anlegen (*Schiff*); **10.** andocken (*Raumschiffe*).

dock² [dɒk] **I** s. **1.** Fleischteil m des Schwanzes; **2.** Schwanzstummel m; **3.** Schwanzriemen m; **4.** (Lohn- etc.)Kürzung f; **II** v/t. **5.** a) stutzen, b) den Schwanz stutzen od. kupieren (*dat.*); **6.** *fig.* beschneiden, kürzen.

dock³ [dɒk] s. ✠ Anklagebank f: *be in the* ~ auf der Anklagebank sitzen; *put in the* ~ *fig.* anklagen.

dock⁴ [dɒk] s. ♀ Ampfer m.

dock·age¹ ['dɒkɪdʒ] s. ⚓ **1.** Dock-, Hafengebühren pl., Kaigebühr f; **2.** Docken n; **3.** → *dock¹* 3.

dock·age² ['dɒkɪdʒ] s. Kürzung f.

dock·er ['dɒkə] s. Brit. Dock-, Hafenarbeiter m.

dock·et ['dɒkɪt] **I** s. **1.** ✠ a) Ge'richts-, Ter'minka‚lender m, b) Brit. 'Urteilsre-‚gister n, c) Am. Pro'zessliste f; **2.** Inhaltsangabe f, -vermerk m; **3.** Am. Tagesordnung f; **4.** ✝ a) A'dresszettel m, Eti'kett n, b) Brit. Zollquittung f, c) Brit. Bestell-, Lieferschein m; **II** v/t. **5.** in e-e Liste eintragen (→ 1 b u. c); **6.** mit Inhaltsangabe od. Eti'kett versehen; **7.** Am. auf die Tagesordnung setzen.

dock·ing ['dɒkɪŋ] s. *Raumfahrt:* Andocken n, Kopp(e)lung f.

'dock·land s. Hafenviertel n; **'~‚mas-ter** s. 'Hafenkapi‚tän m, Dockmeister m; **'~‚war·rant** s. ✝ Docklagerschein m; **~ work·er** → *docker*; **'~‚yard** s. ⚓ **1.** Werft f; **2.** Brit. Ma'rinewerft f.

doc·tor ['dɒktə] **I** s. **1.** Doktor m, Arzt m: ~*'s stuff* F Medizin f; *that's just what the* ~ *ordered* das ist genau das Richtige; *doll* ~ F Puppendoktor; **2.** univ. Doktor m: ☿ *of Divinity* (*Laws*) Doktor der Theologie (Rechte); *take one's* ~*'s degree* (zum Doktor) promovieren; *Dear* ~ Sehr geehrter Herr Doktor!; **3.** ☿ *of the Church* Kirchenvater m; **4.** ⚓ sl. Smutje m, Schiffskoch m; **5.** ⊕ Schaber m, Abstreichmesser n; **6.** *Angeln:* künstliche Fliege; **II** v/t. **7.** ‚verarzten', ärztlich behandeln; **8.** F *Tier* kastrieren; **9.** ‚ausbessern', zu-'rechtflicken'; **10.** a. ~ *up* a) *Wein etc.* (ver)pantschen, b) *Abrechnungen etc.* ‚frisieren', (ver)fälschen; **III** v/i. **11.** F (als Arzt) praktizieren; **'doc·tor·al** [-təral] adj. Doktor(s)...: ~ *candidate* Doktorand(in); ~ *cap* Doktorhut m; **'doc·tor·ate** [-tərit] s. Dokto'rat n, Doktorwürde f; **doc·tor's sur·ger·y** s. 'Arzt‚praxis f.

doc·tri·naire [‚dɒktrɪ'neə] **I** s. Doktri'när m, Prin'zipienreiter m; **II** adj. doktri'när.

doc·tri·nal [dɒk'traɪnl] adj. ☐ lehrmäßig, Lehr...; *weitS* dog'matisch: ~ *prop-osition* Lehrsatz m; ~ *theology* Dogmatik f; **doc·trine** ['dɒktrɪn] s. **1.** Doktrin f, Lehre f, Lehrmeinung f; **2.** bsd. pol. Dok'trin f, Grundsatz m: *party* ~ Parteiprogramm n.

doc·u·dra·ma ['dɒkju‚drɑ:mə] s. Film, TV: Dokumen'tarspiel n.

doc·u·ment ['dɒkjumənt] **I** s. **1.** Doku-'ment n, Urkunde f, Schrift-, Aktenstück n, 'Unterlage f, pl. a. Akten pl.; **2.** Beweisstück n; **3.** (*shipping*) ~s pl. ✝ Ver'lade-, 'Schiffspa‚piere pl.: ~s *against acceptance* (*payment*) Dokumente gegen Akzept (Bezahlung); **II** v/t. [-ment] **4.** dokumentieren (a. fig.), (urkundlich) belegen; **5.** *Buch etc.* mit (genauen) Beleghinweisen versehen; **6.** ✝ mit den notwendigen Pa'pieren versehen; **doc·u·men·ta·ry** [‚dɒkju'men-

---

tərɪ] **I** adj. **1.** dokumen'tarisch, urkundlich: ~ *bill* ✝ Dokumententratte f; ~ *evidence* Urkundenbeweis m; **2.** *Film etc.:* Dokumentar..., Tatsachen...: ~ *film*; ~ *novel*; **II** s. Dokumen'tar-, Tatsachenfilm m; **doc·u·men·ta·tion** [‚dɒkjumen'teɪʃn] s. Dokumentati'on f: a) Urkunden-, Quellenbenutzung f, b) dokumen'tarischer Nachweis od. Beleg.

dod·der¹ ['dɒdə] s. ♀ Teufelszwirn m, Flachsseide f.

dod·der² ['dɒdə] v/i. F **1.** zittern (*vor Schwäche*); **2.** wack(e)lig gehen, wackeln; **'dod·dered** [-əd] adj. **1.** astlos (*Baum*); **2.** altersschwach, tatterig; **'dod·der·ing** [-ərɪŋ], **'dod·der·y** [-ərɪ] adj. F se'nil, tatterig, vertrottelt.

dod·dle ['dɒdl] s. Brit. F Kinderspiel n, Kleinigkeit f: *it's a* ~ es ist kinder'leicht.

do·dec·a·gon [dəʊ'dekəgən] s. ▵ Zwölfeck n.

do·dec·a·he·dron [‚dəʊdekə'hedrən] pl. **-drons, dra** [-drə] s. ▵ Dodeka'eder n, Zwölfflächner m; **‚do·dec·a'syl·la·ble** [-'sɪləbl] s. zwölfsilbiger Vers.

dodge [dɒdʒ] **I** v/i. **1.** (rasch) zur Seite springen, ausweichen; **2.** a) schlüpfen, b) sich verstecken, c) flitzen; **3.** Ausflüchte gebrauchen, Winkelzüge machen; **4.** sich drücken; **II** v/t. **5.** ausweichen (*dat.*); **6.** F sich drücken vor, um-'gehen, aus dem Weg gehen (*dat.*), vermeiden; **III** s. **7.** Sprung m zur Seite, rasches Ausweichen; **8.** Kniff m, Trick m: *be up to all the* ~s mit allen Wassern gewaschen sein; **dodg·em** (**car**) ['dɒdʒəm] s. (Auto)Scooter m; **'dodg·er** [-dʒə] s. **1.** ‚Schlitzohr' n; **2.** Gauner m, Schwindler m; **3.** Drückeberger m; **4.** Am. Hand-, Re'klamezettel m; **'dodg·y** [-dʒɪ] adj. Brit. F **1.** vertrackt; **2.** ris'kant; **3.** nicht einwandfrei.

do·do ['dəʊdəʊ] s. **1.** 'Dodo m, 'Dronte f (*ausgestorbener Vogel*): *as dead as a* ~ mausetot; *fig* völlig ‚aus', ein ‚alter Hut'; **2.** F ‚Schnecke' f (*Person*), Trottel m; **3.** contp. Ewig'gestriger m, F ‚Grufti' m.

doe [dəʊ] s. zo. **1.** a) Damhirschkuh f, b) Rehgeiß f; **2.** *Weibchen der Hasen, Kaninchen etc.*

do·er ['du:ə] s. ‚Macher' m, Tatmensch m.

does [dʌz; dəz] 3. pres. sg. von *do¹*.

'doe·skin s. **1.** a) Rehfell n, b) Rehleder n; **2.** Doeskin n (*ein Wollstoff*).

doest [dʌst] obs. od. poet. 2. pres. sg. von *do¹*: *thou* ~ du tust.

doff [dɒf] v/t. **1.** *Kleider* ablegen, ausziehen; *Hut* lüften, ziehen; **2.** *fig.* Gewohnheit ablegen.

dog [dɒg] **I** s. **1.** zo. Hund m; **2.** engS. Rüde m (*männlicher Hund, Wolf* [a. *dog wolf*], *Fuchs* [a. *dog fox*] etc.); **3.** oft *dirty* ~ (gemeiner) Hund m, Schuft m; **4.** F Bursche m, Kerl m: *gay* ~ lustiger Vogel; *lucky* ~ Glückspilz m; *sly* ~ schlauer Fuchs; **5.** ast. a) *Greater* (*Lesser*) ☿ Großer (Kleiner) Hund, b) → *Dog Star*; **6.** *the* ~s Brit. F das Windhundrennen; **7.** ⊕ a) Klaue f, Knagge f, b) Anschlag(bolzen) m, c) Bock m, Gestell n; **8.** ⚒ ⚔ Hund m, Förderwagen m; **9.** → *firedog*; *Besondere Redewendungen:* *not a* ~*'s chance* nicht die geringste Chance; ~ *in the manger* Neidhammel m; ~s *of war* Kriegsfurien; ~*'s dinner* F Pfusch(arbeit f) m; ~ *does not eat* eine Krähe hackt der anderen kein Auge aus; *go to the* ~s vor die Hunde gehen; *every* ~ *has his day*

---

jeder hat einmal Glück im Leben; *help a lame* ~ *over a stile* j-m in der Not helfen; *lead a* ~*'s life* ein Hundeleben führen; *lead s.o. a* ~*'s life* j-m das Leben zur Hölle machen; *let sleeping* ~s *lie* a) schlafende Hunde soll man nicht wecken, lass die Finger davon, b) lass den Hund begraben sein, rühr nicht alte Geschichten auf; *put on* ~ F‚angeben', vornehm tun; *throw to the* ~s wegwerfen, vergeuden, *fig.* den Wölfen (zum Fraß) vorwerfen, opfern;

II v/t. **10.** j-m auf dem Fuße folgen, j-n verfolgen, jagen, j-m nachspüren: ~ *s.o.'s steps* j-m auf den Fersen bleiben; **11.** *fig.* verfolgen: ~*ged by bad luck.*

dog| **bis·cuit** s. Hundekuchen m; **'~·cart** s. Dogkart m (*Wagen*); **‚~-'cheap** adj. u. adv. F spottbillig; ~ **col·lar** s. **1.** Hundehalsband n; **2.** F Kol'lar n, (steifer) Kragen e-s Geistlichen; ~ **days** s. pl. Hundstage pl.

doge [dəʊdʒ] s. hist. Doge m.

'dog-ear s. Eselsohr m; **'~-eared** adj. mit Eselsohren (*Buch*); ~ **end** s. Brit. F (Ziga'retten)Kippe f; **'~-fight** s. Handgemenge n; ✗ Einzel-, Nahkampf m; ✈ Kurven-, Luftkampf m; **'~-fish** s. kleiner Hai, bsd. Hundshai m.

dog·ged ['dɒgɪd] adj. ☐ verbissen, hartnäckig, zäh; **'dog·ged·ness** [-nɪs] s. Verbissenheit f, Zähigkeit f.

dog·ger ['dɒgə] s. ⚓ Dogger m (*zweimastiges Fischerboot*).

dog·ger·el ['dɒgərəl] **I** s. Knittelvers m; **II** adj. holperig (*Vers etc.*).

dog·gie ['dɒgɪ] → *doggy* 1; ~ **bag** s. F Beutel m zum Mitnehmen von Essensresten (*im Restaurant*).

dog·gish ['dɒgɪʃ] adj. ☐ **1.** hundeartig, Hunde...; **2.** bissig, mürrisch.

dog·go ['dɒgəʊ] adv.: *lie* ~ a) sich nicht mucksen, b) sich versteckt halten.

dog·gone ['dɒgɒn] adj. u. int. Am. F verdammt.

dog·gy ['dɒgɪ] **I** s. **1.** Hündchen n, Wauwau m; **II** adj. **2.** hundeartig; **3.** hundeliebend; **4.** Am. F todschick.

'dog·house s. Hundehütte f: *in the* ~ Am. F in Ungnade; ~ **Lat·in** s. 'Küchenla‚tein n; ~ **lead** [li:d] s. Hundeleine f.

dog·ma ['dɒgmə] pl. **-mas, -ma·ta** [-mətə] s. **1.** eccl. Dogma n: a) Glaubenssatz m, b) 'Lehrsys‚tem n; **2.** Lehrsatz m; **3.** fig. Dogma m, Grundsatz m.

dog·mat·ic [dɒg'mætɪk] **I** adj. (☐ ~al-ly) eccl. u. fig. contp. dog'matisch; **II** s. pl. sg. konstr. Dog'matik f; **'dog·ma-tism** [-ətɪzəm] s. contp. Dogma'tismus m; **'dog·ma·tist** [-ətɪst] s. eccl. u. contp. Dog'matiker m; **'dog·ma·tize** [-ətaɪz] **I** v/i. bsd. contp. dogmatisieren, dog'matische Behauptungen aufstellen (*on* über *acc.*); **II** v/t. dogmatisieren, zum Dogma erheben.

‚do-'good·er s. F Weltverbesserer m, Humani'tätsa‚postel m.

'dog|-‚pad·dle v/i. (wie ein Hund) paddeln; ~ **rac·ing** s. Hunderennen n; ~ **rose** s. ♀ Heckenrose f.

'dogs‚bod·y [-dʒz-] s. F ‚Kuli' m (*der die Dreckarbeit machen muss*).

'dog's-ear etc. → *dog-ear* etc.

dog| **show** s. Hundeausstellung f; **'~·skin** s. Hundsleder n; ☿ **Star** s. ast. Sirius m, Hundsstern m; ~ **tag** s. **1.** Hundemarke f; **2.** ✗ Am. sl. ‚Hundemarke' f (*Erkennungsmarke*); ~ **tax** s. Hundesteuer f; **‚~-'tired** adj. hundemüde; **'~·tooth** s. [irr.] ⚓ 'Zahnorna-

D

,ment *n*; '**~·trot** *s.* leichter Trab; '**~·watch** *s.* ⚓ ,Plattfuß' *m* (*Wache*); '**~·wood** *s.* ♀ Hartriegel *m*.

doi·ly ['dɔɪlɪ] *s.* (Zier)Deckchen *n*.

do·ing ['duːɪŋ] *s.* **1.** Tun *n*: *that was your ~* a) das hast du getan, b) es war deine Schuld; *that will take some ~* das will erst getan sein; **2.** *pl.* a) Taten *pl.*, Tätigkeit *f*, b) Vorfälle *pl.*, Begebenheiten *pl.*, c) Treiben *n*, Betragen *n*: *fine ~s these!* das sind mir schöne Geschichten!; **3.** *pl. sg. konstr. Brit.* F ,Dingsbums' *n*.

doit [dɔɪt] *s.* Deut *m*: *not worth a ~* keinen Pfifferling wert.

,do-it-your'self I *s.* Heimwerken *n*; II *adj.* Do-it-yourself-..., Heimwerker...; **,do-it-your'self·er** [-fə] *s.* F Heimwerker *m*.

dol·drums ['dɒldrəmz] *s. pl.* **1.** *geogr.* a) Kalmengürtel *m*, -zone *f*, b) Kalmen *pl.*, äquatori'ale Windstillen *pl.*; **2.** Niedergeschlagenheit *f*, Trübsinn *m*: *in the ~* a) deprimiert, Trübsal blasend, b) e-e Flaute durchmachend (*Geschäft etc.*).

dole [dəʊl] I *s.* **1.** milde Gabe, Almosen *n*; **2.** a. *~ money bsd. Brit.* F ,Stütze' *f* (*Arbeitslosengeld*): *be* (*od.* *go*) *on the ~* stempeln gehen; II *v/t.* **3.** *mst ~ out* sparsam aus-, verteilen.

dole·ful ['dəʊlfʊl] *adj.* ☐ traurig; trübselig; **'dole·ful·ness** [-nɪs] *s.* Trübseligkeit *f*.

dol·i·cho·ce·phal·ic [,dɒlɪkəʊsɛ'fælɪk] *adj.* langköpfig, -schädelig.

'do-,lit·tle *s.* F Faulpelz *m*.

doll [dɒl] I *s.* **1.** Puppe *f*: *~'s house* Puppenstube *f*, -haus *n*; *~'s pram bsd. Brit.* Puppenwagen *m*; *~'s face fig.* Puppengesicht *n*; **2.** F ,Puppe' *f* (*Mädchen*); *Am. sl. allg.* Frau *f*; II *v/t. u. v/i.* *~ up* F (sich) fein machen: *all ~ed up* aufgedonnert.

dol·lar ['dɒlə] *s.* Dollar *m*: *the almighty ~* das Geld, der Mammon; *~ diplomacy* Dollardiplomatie *f*.

doll·ish ['dɒlɪʃ] *adj.* ☐ puppenhaft.

dol·lop ['dɒləp] *s.* F Klumpen *m*, ,Klacks' *m*; *Am.* ,Schuss' *m*: *~ of brandy*.

doll·y ['dɒlɪ] I *s.* **1.** Püppchen *n*; **2.** ⊙ a) niedriger Trans'portkarren, b) *Film*: Kamerawagen *m*, c) 'Schmalspurlokomo,tive *f* (*an Baustellen*); **3.** ⊙ Nietkolben *m*; **4.** Wäschestampfer *m*, -stößel *m*; **5.** *Am.* Anhängerbock *m* (*Sattelschlepper*); **6.** a. *~ bird* F ,Püppchen' *n* (*Mädchen*); II *adj.* **7.** puppenhaft; III *v/t.* **8.** *~ in* (*out*) *Film*: die Kamera vorfahren (zu'rückfahren); *~ shot s. Film*: Fahraufnahme *f*.

dol·man ['dɒlmən] *pl.* -**mans** *s.* **1.** Damenmantel *m* mit capeartigen Ärmeln; *~ sleeve* capeartiger Ärmel; **2.** Dolman *m* (*Husarenjacke*).

dol·men ['dɒlmen] *s.* Dolmen *m* (*vorgeschichtliches Steingrabmal*).

dol·o·mite ['dɒləmaɪt] *s. min.* Dolo'mit *m*: *the ~s geogr.* die Dolomiten.

do·lor *Am.* → *dolour*; **dol·or·ous** ['dɒlərəs] *adj.* ☐ traurig, schmerzlich; **do·lour** ['dɒlə] *s.* Leid *n*, Pein *f*, Qual *f*, Schmerz *m*.

dol·phin ['dɒlfɪn] *s.* **1.** *zo.* a) Del'phin *m*, b) Tümmler *m*; **2.** *ichth.* 'Goldmak,rele *f*; **3.** ⚓ a) Ankerboje *f*, b) Dalbe *f*.

dolt [dəʊlt] *s.* Dummkopf *m*, Tölpel *m*; **'dolt·ish** [-tɪʃ] *adj.* ☐ tölpelhaft, dumm.

do·main [dəʊ'meɪn] *s.* **1.** Do'mäne *f*, Staatsgut *n*; **2.** Landbesitz *m*; Herrengut *n*; **3.** (*power of*) *eminent ~ Am.* Enteignungsrecht *n des Staates*; **4.** *fig.*

Do'mäne *f*, Gebiet *n*, Bereich *m*, Sphäre *f*, Reich *n*.

dome [dəʊm] *s.* **1.** *allg.* Kuppel *f*; **2.** Wölbung *f*; **3.** *obs.* Dom *m*, *poet. a.* stolzer Bau; **4.** ⊙ Haube *f*, Deckel *m*; **5.** *Am.* ,Birne' *f* (*Kopf*); **domed** [-md] *adj.* gewölbt; kuppelförmig.

Domes·day Book ['duːmzdeɪ] *s. Reichsgrundbuch Englands* (*1086*).

'dome-shaped → *domed*.

do·mes·tic [dəʊ'mestɪk] I *adj.* (☐ *~ally*) **1.** häuslich, Haus..., Haushalts..., Familien..., Privat...: *~ affairs* häusliche Angelegenheiten (→ 4); *~ court Am.* Familiengericht *n*; *~ drama thea.* bürgerliches Drama; *~ economy od. science* Hauswirtschaft(slehre) *f*; *~ life* Familienleben *n*; *~ relations law ☆* *Am.* Familienrecht *n*; *~ servant* → 6; **2.** häuslich (veranlagt): *a ~ man*; **3.** inländisch, Inland(s)..., einheimisch, Landes...; Innen..., Binnen...: *~ bill ✝* Inlandswechsel *m*; *~ goods* Inlandswaren; *~ mail Am.* Inlandspost *f*; *~ trade* Binnenhandel *m*; **4.** *pol.* inner, Innen...: *~ affairs* innere *od.* innenpolitische Angelegenheiten (→ 1); *~ policy* Innenpolitik *f*; **5.** zahm, Haus...: *~ animal* Haustier *n*; II *s.* **6.** Hausangestellte(r *m*) *f*, Dienstbote *m*; **do'mes·ti·cate** [-keɪt] *v/t.* **1.** domestizieren: a) zähmen, zu Haustieren machen, b) zu Kulturpflanzen machen; **2.** an häusliches Leben gewöhnen: *not ~d* a) nichts vom Haushalt verstehend, b) nicht am Familienleben hängend, ,nicht gezähmt'; **3.** *Wilde* zivilisieren; **do·mes·ti·ca·tion** [dəʊ,mestɪ'keɪʃn] *s.* **1.** Domestizierung *f*: a) Zähmung *f*, b) ♀ Kultivierung *f*; **2.** Gewöhnung *f* an häusliches Leben; **3.** Einbürgerung *f*; **do·mes·tic·i·ty** [,dəʊme'stɪsətɪ] *s.* **1.** (Neigung *f* zur) Häuslichkeit *f*; **2.** häusliches Leben; **3.** *pl.* häusliche Angelegenheiten *pl.*

dom·i·cile ['dɒmɪsaɪl], *Am. a.* '**dom·i·cil** [-sɪl] I *s.* **1.** a) (ständiger *od.* bürgerlichrechtlicher) Wohnsitz, b) Wohnort *m*, c) Wohnung *f*; **2.** ✝ Sitz *m* e-r Gesellschaft; **3.** *a. legal ~* ☆ Gerichtsstand *m*; II *v/t.* **4.** ansässig *od.* wohnhaft machen, ansiedeln; **5.** ✝ *Wechsel* domizilieren; '**dom·i·ciled** [-ld] *adj.* **1.** ansässig, wohnhaft; **2.** *~ bill ✝* Domizilwechsel *m*; **dom·i·cil·i·ar·y** [,dɒmɪ'sɪljərɪ] *adj.* Haus..., Wohnungs...: *~ arrest* Hausarrest *m*; *~ visit* Haussuchung *f*; **dom·i·cil·i·ate** [,dɒmɪ'sɪljeɪt] *v/t.* ✝ *Wechsel* domizilieren.

dom·i·nance ['dɒmɪnəns] *s.* **1.** (Vor-)Herrschaft *f*, (Vor)Herrschen *n*; **2.** Macht *f*; **3.** *biol.* Domi'nanz *f*; '**dom·i·nant** [-nt] I *adj.* ☐ **1.** dominierend, vorherrschend; **2.** beherrschend: a) bestimmend, entscheidend: *~ factor*, b) em'porragend, weithin sichtbar; **3.** *biol.* domi'nant, überlagernd; II *s.* **5.** *biol.* vorherrschendes Merkmal; ♪, *a.* ♀ Domi'nante *f*; '**dom·i·nate** [-neɪt] I *v/t.* beherrschen (*a. fig.*): a) herrschen über (*acc.*), b) em'porragen über (*acc.*); II *v/i.* dominieren, (vor)herrschen: *~ over* herrschen über (*acc.*); **dom·i·na·tion** [,dɒmɪ'neɪʃn] *s.* (Vor-)Herrschaft *f*; **dom·i·neer** [-'nɪə] *v/i.* **1.** den Herrn spielen, anmaßend auftreten; **2.** (*over*) des'potisch herrschen (über *acc.*), tyrannisieren (*acc.*); '**dom·i·neer·ing** [-'nɪərɪŋ] *adj.* ☐ **1.** ty'rannisch, herrisch, gebieterisch; **2.** anmaßend.

do·min·i·cal [dəʊ'mɪnɪkl] *adj. eccl.* des Herrn (*Jesu*): *~ day* Tag *m* des Herrn

(*Sonntag*); *~ prayer* das Gebet des Herrn (*Vaterunser*); *~ year* Jahr *n* des Herrn.

Do·min·i·can [də'mɪnɪkən] *eccl.* I *adj.* **1.** *eccl.* Dominikaner..., domini'kanisch; **2.** *pol.* dominikanisch; II *s.* **3.** *a. ~ friar* Domini'kaner(mönch) *m*; **4.** *pol.* Domini'kaner(in).

dom·i·nie ['dɒmɪnɪ] *s.* **1.** *Scot.* Schulmeister *m*; **2.** (Herr) Pastor *m*.

do·min·ion [də'mɪnjən] *s.* **1.** (Ober-) Herrschaft *f*, (Regierungs)Gewalt *f*; **2.** ☆ a) Eigentumsrecht *n*, b) (tatsächliche) Gewalt (*über e-e Sache*); **3.** (Herrschafts)Gebiet *n*; **4.** a) *hist.* ☾ Do'minion *n* (*im Brit. Commonwealth*), b) *the* ☾ *Am.* Kanada *n*.

dom·i·no ['dɒmɪnəʊ] *pl.* -**noes** *s.* **1.** a) *pl. sg. konstr.* Domino(spiel) *n*, b) Dominostein *m*; **2.** Domino *m* (*Maskenkostüm od. Person*); *~ the·o·ry s. pol.* 'Dominotheo,rie *f*.

don[1] [dɒn] *s.* **1.** ☾ *span. Titel*; *weitS.* Spanier *m*; **2.** *Brit.* Universitätslehrer *m* (*Fellow od. Tutor*); **3.** Fachmann *m* (*at in dat., in*).

don[2] [dɒn] *v/t. et.* anziehen, *den Hut* aufsetzen.

do·nate [dəʊ'neɪt] *v/t.* schenken (*a. ☆*), stiften, *a. Blut etc.* spenden (*to s.o.* j-m); **do'na·tion** [-eɪʃn] *s.* Schenkung *f* (*a. ☆*), Stiftung *f*, Gabe *f*, Geschenk *n*, Spende *f*.

done [dʌn] I *p.p. von do*[1]; II *adj.* **1.** getan: *well ~!* gut gemacht!, bravo!; *it isn't ~* so et. tut man nicht, das gehört sich nicht; *what is to be ~?* was ist zu tun?, was soll geschehen?; *~ at ... in Urkunden*: gegeben in *der Stadt New York etc.*; **2.** erledigt (*a. fig.*): *get s.th. ~ et.* erledigen (lassen); *he gets things ~* er bringt et. zuwege; **3.** *gar: is the meat ~ yet?; well ~* durchgebraten; **4.** F fertig: *have ~ with* a) fertig sein mit (*a. fig.*), b) nicht mehr brauchen, c) nichts mehr zu tun haben wollen mit; **5.** *a. ~ up*, *~ in* erschöpft, ,erledigt', ,fertig'; **6.** *~!* abgemacht!

do·nee [dəʊ'niː] *s.* ☆ Beschenkte(r *m*) *f*, Schenkungsempfänger(in).

dong [dɒŋ] *s. Am.* F ,Pimmel' *m* (*Penis*).

don·gle ['dɒŋgl] *s. Computer*: Dongle *n od. m* (*Ansteckteil, ohne das geschützte Software nicht funktioniert*).

don·jon ['dɒndʒən] *s.* **1.** Don'jon *m*, Hauptturm *m*; **2.** Bergfried *m*, Burgturm *m*.

don·key ['dɒŋkɪ] I *s.* Esel *m* (*a. fig.*): *~'s years Brit.* F e-e ,Ewigkeit'; **2.** → *donkey engine*; II *adj.* **3.** ⊙ Hilfs...: *~ pump*, *~ en·gine s.* ⊙ kleine (*transportable*) 'Hilfsma,schine; '**~·work** *s.* F Dreckarbeit *f*.

don·nish ['dɒnɪʃ] *adj.* **1.** gelehrt; **2.** belehrend.

do·nor ['dəʊnə] *s.* Geber *m*; Schenker *m* (*a. ☆*); Spender *m* (*a. ♥*), Stifter *m*; *~ card s.* Or'ganspenderausweis *m*.

'do-,noth·ing I *s.* Faulenzer(in); II *adj.* faul, nichtstuerisch.

Don Quix·ote [,dɒn'kwɪksət] *s.* Don Qui'chotte *m* (*weltfremder Idealist*).

don't [dəʊnt] I *s.* F für *do not*, b) *sl. für does not*; II *s.* F Verbot *n*; → *do*[2] 3; *~ know s.* a) Unentschiedene(r *m*) *f*, b) j-d, der (*bei e-r Umfrage*) keine Meinung hat.

doo·dah ['duːdɑː] *s.* F Dingsbums; *all of a ~* durcheinander.

doo·dle ['duːdl] I *s.* gedankenlos hingezeichnete Fi'gur(en *pl.*), Gekritzel *n*; II *v/i. et.* (gedankenlos) 'hinkritzeln,

D

‚Männchen malen'.

doom [duːm] **I** s. **1.** Schicksal n; (bsd. böses) Geschick, Verhängnis n: **he met his ~** das Schicksal ereilte ihn; **2.** Verderben n, 'Untergang m, a. Tod m, fig. Todesurteil n; **3.** obs. Urteilsspruch m, Verdammung f; **4. the day of ~** das Jüngste Gericht; → **crack** 1; **II** v/t. **5.** verurteilen, verdammen (**to** zu): **~ to death**; **doomed** [-md] adj. a) verloren, dem 'Untergang geweiht, b) bsd. fig. verdammt, verurteilt (**to** zu, **to do** zu tun): **~ to failure** zum Scheitern verurteilt; **the ~ train** der Unglückszug m; **dooms·day** ['duːmzdeɪ] s. das Jüngste Gericht: **till ~** bis zum Jüngsten Tag; **Dooms·day Book** → **Domesday Book**; **dooms·day cult** (od. **group**) s. Weltuntergangssekte f; **doom·ster** ['duːmstə] s. 'Weltuntergangspro,phet m.

door [dɔː] s. **1.** Tür f: **out of ~s** draußen, im Freien; **within ~s** im Haus(e), drinnen; **from ~ to ~** von Haus zu Haus; **delivered to your ~** frei Haus (geliefert); **two ~s away** (od. **off**) zwei Häuser weiter; → **next** 1; **2.** Ein-, Zugang m, Tor n, Pforte f (alle a. fig.): **at death's ~** am Rande des Grabes; **lay s.th. at s.o.'s ~** j-m et. zur Last legen; **lay the blame at s.o.'s ~** j-m die Schuld zuschieben; **close** (od. **bang, shut**) **the ~ on** a) j-n abweisen, b) et. unmöglich machen; **open a ~ to s.th.** et. ermöglichen, b.s. e-r Sache Tür u. Tor öffnen; **see** (od. **show**) **s.o. to the ~** j-n zur Tür begleiten; **show s.o. the ~** j-m die Tür weisen; **turn out of ~s** j-n hinauswerfen; → **darken** 1; '**~·bell** s. Türklingel f; **~ han·dle** s. Türgriff m, -klinke f; '**~·keep·er** s. Pförtner m; '**~·key child** s. Schlüsselkind n; '**~·knob** s. Türgriff m; '**~·knock·er** s. Türklopfer m; '**~·man** [-mən] s. [irr.] (livrierter) Porti'er; '**~·mat** s. Fußmatte f, Fußabstreifer m (a. fig. contp.); '**~·nail** s. Türnagel m; → **dead** 1; '**~·plate** s. Türschild n; '**~·post** s. Türpfosten m; '**~·step** s. (Haus)Türstufe f: **on s.o.'s ~** vor j-s Tür (a. fig.); '**~-to-'~** adj.: **~ selling** Verkauf m an der Haustür; '**~·way** s. **1.** Torweg m; **2.** Türöffnung f; **3.** fig. Zugang m; '**~·yard** s. Am. Vorgarten m.

dope [dəʊp] **I** s. **1.** Schmiere f, dicke Flüssigkeit f; **2.** ✈ (Spann)Lack m, Firnis m; **3.** ⚙ Schmiermittel n; Zusatz (-stoff) m; Ben'zinzusatzmittel n; **4.** sl. ‚Stoff', Rauschgift n; **5.** sl. Reiz-, Aufputschmittel n; **6.** oft **inside ~** sl. Geheimtipp(s pl.) m, 'Insider-Informati,on(en pl.) f (**on** über); **7.** sl. Trottel m, Idi'ot m; **II** v/t. **8.** ✈ lackieren, firnissen; **9.** ⚙ dem Benzin ein Zusatzmittel beimischen; **10.** sl. j-m ‚Stoff' geben; **11.** sl. a) sport dopen, b) e-m Pferd ein leistungshemmendes Präpa'rat geben, c) ein Getränk etc. (mit e-m Betäubungsmittel) präpa'rieren, d) fig. einschläfern, -lullen; **12.** mst **~ out** sl. a) her'ausfinden, ausfindig machen, b) ausknobeln; **~ fiend** s. sl. Rauschgiftsüchtige(r m) f.

dop·ey ['dəʊpɪ] adj. sl. doof.

dop·ing ['dəʊpɪŋ] s. sport 'Doping n: **~ problem** 'Dopingprob,lem n; **~ test** Dopingtest m, -kon,trolle f; **take a firm anti~ line** sich entschieden gegen das Doping aussprechen.

dor [dɔː], **dor·bee·tle** ['dɔːˌbiːtl] s. zo. **1.** Mist-, Rosskäfer m; **2.** Maikäfer m.

Do·ri·an ['dɔːrɪən] **I** adj. dorisch; **II** s. Dorier m; **Dor·ic** ['dɔrɪk] **I** adj. **1.** do-

risch: **~ order** △ dorische (Säulen)Ordnung; **2.** breit, grob (Mundart); **II** s. **3.** Dorisch n, dorischer Dia'lekt; **4.** breiter od. grober Dia'lekt.

dorm [dɔːm] s. F für **dormitory**.

dor·man·cy ['dɔːmənsɪ] s. Schlafzustand m, Ruhe(zustand m) f (a. ♀); '**dor·mant** [-nt] adj. **1.** schlafend (a. her.), ruhend (a. ♀), untätig (a. Vulkan); **2.** zo. Winterschlaf haltend; **3.** fig. a) schlummernd, la'tent, verborgen, b) unbenutzt, brachliegend: **~ talent**; **~ capital** † totes Kapital; **~ partner** † stiller Teilhaber; **~ title** † ruhender od. nicht beanspruchter Titel; **lie ~** ruhen, brachliegen.

dor·mer ['dɔːmə] s. △ **1.** (Dach)Gaupe f; **2.** a. **~ window** stehendes Dachfenster.

dor·mi·to·ry ['dɔːmɪtrɪ] s. **1.** Schlafsaal m; **2.** (bsd. Stu'denten)Wohnheim n; **~ sub·urb** s. Schlafstadt f.

dor·mouse ['dɔːmaʊs] pl. **-mice** [-maɪs] s. zo. Haselmaus f; → **sleep** 1.

dor·my ['dɔːmɪ] adj. Golf: dormy (mit so viel Löchern führend, wie noch zu spielen sind): **be ~ two** dormy 2 stehen.

dor·sal ['dɔːsl] adj. □ dor'sal (♀, zo., anat., ling.), Rücken...

do·ry¹ ['dɔːrɪ] s. Dory n (Boot).

do·ry² ['dɔːrɪ] → **John Dory**.

dos·age ['dəʊsɪdʒ] s. **1.** Dosierung f; **2.** → **dose** 1, 2; **dose** [dəʊs] **I** s. **1.** ✚ Dosis f, (Arz'nei)Gabe f; **2.** fig. Dosis f, ‚Schuss' m, Porti'on f; **3.** a. **~ of clap** V Tripper m; **II** v/t. **4.** Arznei dosieren; **5.** j-m Arz'nei geben; **6.** Wein zuckern.

doss [dɒs] Brit. sl. **I** s. ‚Falle' f, ‚Klappe' f, Schlafplatz m; **II** v/i. ‚pennen'.

dos·ser¹ ['dɒsə] s. Rücken(trag)korb m.

dos·ser² ['dɒsə] s. sl. **1.** ‚Pennbruder' m; **2.** → **dosshouse**.

'**doss·house** s. sl. ‚Penne' f (billige Pension).

dos·si·er ['dɒsɪeɪ] s. Dossi'er n, Akten pl., Akte f.

dost [dʌst; dɒst] obs. od. poet. 2. pres. sg. von **do¹**.

dot¹ [dɒt] s. ⚏ Mitgift f.

dot² [dɒt] **I** s. **1.** Punkt m (a. ♪), Tüpfelchen n: **~s and dashes** Punkte u. Striche, tel. Morsezeichen; **come on the ~** F auf den Glockenschlag pünktlich kommen; **at seven-thirty on the ~** um Punkt sieben Uhr dreißig; **since the year ~** F seit e-r Ewigkeit; **2.** Tupfen m, Fleck m; **3.** et. Winziges, Knirps m; **II** v/t. **4.** punktieren (a. ♪): **~ted line; sign on the ~ted line** (fig. ohne weiteres) unterschreiben; **5.** mit dem i-Punkt versehen: **~ the** (od. **one's**) **i's** [and cross the (od. **one's**) **t's**] fig. peinlich genau od. penibel sein; **6.** tüpfeln; **7.** über-'säen, sprenkeln; **~ted with flowers**; **8.** sl. **~ s.o. one** j-m eine ‚knallen'.

dot·age ['dəʊtɪdʒ] s. **1.** Senili'tät f: **he is in his ~** er ist kindisch od. senil geworden; **2.** fig. Affenliebe f, Vernarrtheit f; '**do·tard** [-təd] s. se'niler Mensch; **dote** [dəʊt] v/i. **1.** kindisch od. senil sein; **2.** (**on**) vernarrt sein (in acc.), abgöttisch lieben (acc.).

doth [dʌθ; dəθ] obs. od. poet. 3. pres. sg. von **do¹**.

dot·ing ['dəʊtɪŋ] adj. □ **1.** vernarrt (**on** in acc.): **he is a doting husband** er liebt s-e Frau abgöttisch; **2.** se'nil, kindisch.

dot ma·trix print·er s. 'Matrix,drucker m (Gerät).

dot·ter·el, **dot·trel** ['dɒtrəl] s. orn. Mor'nell(regenpfeifer) m.

dot·ty ['dɒtɪ] adj. **1.** punktiert, getüpfelt;

2. F wackelig; **3.** F ‚bekloppt'.

dou·ble ['dʌbl] **I** adj. □ **1.** doppelt, Doppel..., zweifach, gepaart: **~ the amount** der doppelte od. zweifache Betrag; **~ bottom** doppelter Boden (Schiff, Koffer); **~ doors** Doppeltür f; **~ taxation** Doppelbesteuerung f; **~ width** doppelte Breite, doppelt breit; **~ pneumonia** ✚ doppelseitige Lungenentzündung; **~ standard of morals** fig. doppelte od. doppelbödige Moral; **(of) what it was** doppelt od. zweimal so viel wie vorher; **2.** Doppel..., verdoppelt, verstärkt: **~ ale** Starkbier n; **3.** Doppel..., für zwei bestimmt: **~ bed** Doppelbett n; **~ room** Doppel-, Zweibettzimmer n; **4.** ♀ gefüllt (Blume); **5.** ♪ eine Ok'tave tiefer, Kontra...; **6.** zwiespältig, zweideutig, doppelsinnig; **7.** unaufrichtig, falsch: **~ character**; **8.** gekrümmt, gebeugt; **II** adv. **9.** doppelt, noch einmal: **~ as long**; **10.** doppelt, zweifach: **see ~** doppelt sehen; **play** (**at**) **~ or quit(s)** alles aufs Spiel setzen; **11.** paarweise, zu zweit: **sleep ~**; **III** s. **12.** das Doppelte od. Zweifache; **13.** Doppel n, Dupli'kat n: **14.** a) Gegenstück n, Ebenbild n, b) Double n, Doppelgänger m; **15.** Windung f, Falte f; **16.** Haken m (bsd. Hase, a. Person), plötzliche Kehrtwendung; **17. at the ~** ✕ im Schnellschritt; **18.** mst pl. sg. konstr. sport Doppel n: **play a ~s** (**match**); **men's ~s** Herrendoppel; **19.** sport a) Doppelsieg m, b) Doppelniederlage f; **20.** Doppelwette f; **21.** Film: Double n, thea. zweite Besetzung; **22.** Bridge etc.: Doppel n; **IV** v/t. **23.** verdoppeln (a. ♪); **24.** um das Doppelte über'treffen; **25.** oft **~ up** ('um-, zs.-) falten, 'um-, zs.-legen, 'umschlagen; **26.** Beine 'übereinschlagen; Faust ballen; **27.** ⚓ um'segeln, -'schiffen; **28.** a) Film, TV als Double einspringen für, j-n doubeln, b) **~ the parts of A. and B.** thea. etc. A. u. B. in e-r Doppelrolle spielen; **29.** Spinnerei: doublieren; **30.** Karten: Gebot doppeln; **V** v/i. **31.** sich verdoppeln; **32.** sich falten (lassen); **33.** a) plötzlich kehrtmachen, b) e-n Haken schlagen; **34.** thea. a) e-e Doppelrolle spielen, b) **~ for** → 28a; **35.** ♪ zwei Instru'mente spielen; **36.** ✕ a) im Schnellschritt marschieren, b) F Tempo vorlegen; **37.** a) den Einsatz verdoppeln, b) Bridge: doppeln.

Zssgn mit adv.:

dou·ble| back I v/t. → **double** 25; **II** v/i. kehrtmachen; **~ in** v/t. nach innen falten, einbiegen, -schlagen; **~ up I** v/t. **1.** → **double** 25; **2.** (zs.-)krümmen; **II** v/i. **3.** → **double** 32; **4.** sich krümmen od. biegen (a. fig. **with** vor Schmerz, Lachen); **5.** das Zimmer etc. gemeinsam benutzen: **~ on s.th.** sich (in) et. teilen.

,**dou·ble|-'act·ing**, **,~-'ac·tion** adj. ⚙ doppelt wirkend; **~ a·gent** s. pol. 'Doppela,gent m; '**~-,bar·rel(l)ed** adj. **1.** doppelläufig: **~ gun** Doppelflinte f; **2.** zweideutig; **3.** zweifach: **~ name** Doppelname m; **~ bass** [beɪs] → **contrabass**; '**~-,bed·ded** adj.: **~ room** Zweibettzimmer n; **~ bend** s. S-Kurve f; **~ bill** s. Doppelveranstaltung f; ,**~-'breast·ed** adj. zweireihig (Anzug); ,**~-'check** v/t. genau nachprüfen; **~ chin** s. Doppelkinn n; **~ click** s. Computer: Doppelklick m; '**~-click I** v/i doppelklicken (**on** auf acc.); **II** v/t doppelklicken auf (acc.); **~ col·umn** s. Doppelspalte f (Zeitung): **in ~s** zweispaltig; ,**~-'cross** v/t. ein doppeltes od.

falsches Spiel treiben mit, *bsd. den Partner* ,anschmieren'; ~ **date** *s.* 'Doppelrendez‚vous *n* (*zweier Paare*); ,~-'**deal·er** *s.* falscher *od.* ‚linker' Kerl, Betrüger *m*; ,~-'**deal·ing I** *adj.* falsch, betrügerisch; **II** *s.* Betrug *m*, Gemeinheit *f*; ,~-'**decker** *s.* **1.** Doppeldecker *m* (*Schiff, Flugzeug, Omnibus*); **2.** a) zweistöckiges Haus *etc.*, b) E'tagenbett *n*, c) Ro'man *m* in zwei Bänden, d) *Am.* F Doppelsandwich *n*; ~ **Dutch** *s.* F Kauderwelsch *n*; ,~-'**dyed** *adj.* **1.** zweimal gefärbt; **2.** *fig.* eingefleischt, Erz...: ~ **villain** Erzgauner *m*; ~ **ea·gle** *s.* **1.** *her.* Doppeladler *m*; **2.** *Am.* goldenes 20-Dollar-Stück; ,~-'**edged** *adj.* zweischneidig (*a. fig.*): ~ **sword**; ~ **en·ten·dre** [ˌduːblɑ̃ːnˈtɑːndrə] (*Fr.*) *s. allg.* Zweideutigkeit *f*; ~ **en·try** ✝ **1.** doppelte Buchung; **2.** doppelte Buchführung; ~ **ex·po·sure** *s. phot.* Doppelbelichtung *f*; '~-**faced** *adj.* heuchlerisch, scheinheilig, unaufrichtig; ~ **fault** *s. Tennis:* Doppelfehler *m*; ~ **fea·ture** *s. Film:* 'Doppelpro‚gramm *n* (*zwei Spielfilme in jeder Vorstellung*); ~ **first** *s. univ. Brit.* mit Auszeichnung erworbener *honours degree* in zwei Fächern; '~-**gang·er** [-ˌgæŋə] *s. psych.* Doppelgänger *m*; ,~-'**glaze** *v/t* mit Doppelverglasung versehen; ~ **glaz·ing** *s.* **1.** Doppelverglasung *f*; **2.** Doppelfenster *pl.*; ~ **har·ness** *s. fig.* Ehestand *m*, -joch *n*; ~ **in·dem·ni·ty** *s. Am.* Verdoppelung *f* der Versicherungssumme (*bei Unfalltod*); ,~-'**jointed** *adj.* mit ‚Gummigelenken' (*Person*); ~ **life** *s.* Doppelleben *n*; ~ **meaning** *s.* Zweideutigkeit *f*; ,~-'**mind·ed** *adj.* **1.** wankelmütig, unentschlossen; **2.** unaufrichtig; ~ **mur·der** *s.* Doppelmord *m*.

dou·ble·ness [ˈdʌblnɪs] *s.* **1.** *das* Doppelte; **2.** Doppelzüngigkeit *f*, Falschheit *f*.

,**dou·ble|-'park** *v/t. u. v/i. mot.* in zweiter Reihe parken; ,~-'**quick** ✕ **I** *s.* → *double time*; **II** *adv.* F im Eiltempo; ,~-'**spaced** *adj.* zweizeilig, mit doppeltem Zeilenabstand; ~ **star** *s. ast.* Doppelstern *m*; ,~-'**stop** ♪ **I** *s.* Doppelgriff *m* (*Streichinstrument*); **II** *v/t.* Doppelgriffe spielen auf (*dat.*).

dou·blet [ˈdʌblɪt] *s.* **1.** *hist.* Wams *n*; **2.** Paar *n* (*Dinge*); **3.** Du'blette *f*: a) Dupli'kat *n*, b) *typ.* Doppelsatz *m*; **4.** *pl.* Pasch *m* (*beim Würfeln*).

dou·ble| take *s. sl.* ‚Spätzündung' *f* (*verzögerte Reaktion*): **I did a ~ when** ich stutzte zweimal, als; '~-**talk** *s.* F doppeldeutiges Gerede, ‚Augenauswische'rei' *f*; ~ **tax·a·tion** *s.* ✝ Doppelbesteuerung *f*; ,~-'**think** *s.* ‚Zwiedenken' *n*; ~ **time** *s.* ✕ a) Schnellschritt *m*, b) (langsamer) Laufschritt: **in ~** F im Eiltempo, fix; ,~-'**tongued** *adj.* doppelzüngig, falsch; ,~-'**tracked** *adj.* 🚄 zweigleisig; ~ **vi·son** *s.* ✝ Doppeltsehen *n*: **suffer from ~** doppelt sehen.

dou·bling [ˈdʌblɪŋ] *s.* **1.** Verdoppelung *f*; **2.** Faltung *f*; **3.** Haken(schlagen *n*) *m*; **4.** Trick *m*; **dou·bly** [ˈdʌblɪ] *adv.* doppelt.

doubt [daʊt] **I** *v/i.* **1.** zweifeln; schwanken, Bedenken haben; **2.** zweifeln (*of, about* an e-r Sache); (dar'an) zweifeln, (es) bezweifeln (*whether, if* ob; *that* dass; *neg. u. interrog. that, but that, but* dass): **I ~ whether he will come** ich zweifle, ob er kommen wird; **II** *v/t.* **3.** *et.* bezweifeln: **I ~ his honesty**; **I ~ it**; **4.** miss'trauen (*dat.*), keinen Glauben schenken (*dat.*): ~ **s.o.**; ~ **s.o's words**; **III** *s.* **5.** Zweifel *m* (*of* an

dat., about hinsichtlich *gen.*; *that* dass): **no ~, without ~, beyond ~** zweifellos, fraglos, gewiss; **I have no ~** ich zweifle nicht (daran), ich bezweifle es nicht; **be in ~ about** Zweifel haben an (*dat.*); **leave s.o. in no ~ about s.th.** j-n nicht im Ungewissen über et. lassen; → *benefit* 1; **6.** a) Bedenken *n*, Besorgnis *f*, (*about* wegen), b) Argwohn *m*: **raise ~s** Zweifel aufkommen lassen; **7.** Ungewissheit *f*: **be in ~** unschlüssig sein; '**doubt·er** [-tə] *s.* Zweifler(in); '**doubt·ful** [-fʊl] *adj.* □ **1.** zweifelnd, im Zweifel, unschlüssig: **be ~ of** (*od. about*) *s.th.* an e-r Sache zweifeln, im Zweifel über et. sein; **2.** zweifelhaft: a) unsicher, fraglich, unklar, b) fragwürdig, bedenklich, c) ungewiss, d) verdächtig, dubi'os; '**doubt·ful·ness** [-fʊlnɪs] *s.* **1.** Zweifelhaftigkeit *f*: a) Unsicherheit *f*, b) Fragwürdigkeit *f*, c) Ungewissheit *f*; **2.** Unschlüssigkeit *f*; '**doubt·ing** [-tɪŋ] *adj.* □ zweifelnd: a) schwankend, unschlüssig, b) 'misstrauisch: ⚋ **Thomas** ungläubiger Thomas; '**doubt·less** [-lɪs] *adv.* zweifellos, sicherlich.

dou·ceur [duːˈsɜː] (*Fr.*) *s.* **1.** (Geld)Geschenk *n*, Trinkgeld *n*; **2.** Bestechungsgeld *n*.

douche [duːʃ] **I** *s.* **1.** Dusche *f*, Brause *f*: **cold ~** *a. fig.* kalte Dusche; **2.** ☀ a) Spülung *f*, Dusche *f*, b) Irri'gator *m*; **II** *v/t. u. v/i.* **3.** (sich) (ab)duschen; **4.** ☀ (aus)spülen; **III** *v/i.* **5.** ☀ e-e Spülung machen.

dough [dəʊ] *s.* **1.** Teig *m* (*a. weitS.*); **2.** *bsd. Am. sl.* ‚Zaster' *m* (*Geld*); '~-**boy** *s.* **1.** Mehlkloß *m*; **2.** *a.* **~-foot** *Am. sl.* Landser *m* (*Infanterist*); '~-**nut** *s.* Krapfen *m*, Ber'liner (Pfannkuchen) *m*.

dough·ty [ˈdaʊtɪ] *adj.* □ *obs. od. poet.* mannhaft, tapfer.

dough·y [ˈdəʊɪ] *adj.* **1.** teigig (*a. fig.*); **2.** klitschig, nicht 'durchgebacken.

dour [dʊə] *adj.* □ **1.** mürrisch; **2.** streng, hart; **3.** halsstarrig, stur.

douse [daʊs] *v/t.* **1.** a) ins Wasser tauchen, b) begießen; **2.** F Licht auslöschen; **3.** ♆ a) *Segel* laufen lassen, b) *Tau* loswerfen.

dove [dʌv] *s.* **1.** *orn.* Taube *f*: ~ **of peace** Friedenstaube; **2.** Täubchen *n*, ‚Schatz' *m*; **3.** *eccl.* Taube *f* (*Symbol des Heiligen Geistes*); **4.** *pol.* ‚Taube' *f*: **~s and hawks** Tauben u. Falken; '~-**col·o(u)r** *s.* Taubengrau *n*; '~-**cot(e)** [ˈdʌvkɒt] *s.* Taubenschlag *m*; '~-**eyed** *adj.* sanftäugig; '~-**like** *adj.* sanft.

'**dove's-foot** [ˈdʌvz-] *s.* ♣ Storchschnabel *m*.

'**dove·tail I** *s.* **1.** ⊚ Schwalbenschwanz *m*, Zinke *f*; **II** *v/t.* **2.** verschwalben, verzinken; **3.** *fig.* fest zs.-fügen, (inein'ander) verzahnen, verquicken; **4.** einfügen, -passen, -gliedern (*into* in *acc.*); **5.** passend zs.-setzen; einpassen (*into* in *acc.*); **III** *v/i.* **6.** genau passen (*into* in *acc.*, zu; *with* mit); angepasst sein (*with dat.*); genau inein'ander greifen *od.* passen.

dow·a·ger [ˈdaʊədʒə] *s.* **1.** Witwe *f* (von Stande): **queen ~** Königinwitwe; ~ **duchess** Herzoginwitwe; **2.** Ma'trone *f*, würdevolle ältere Dame.

dow·di·ness [ˈdaʊdɪnɪs] *s.* Schäbigkeit *f*, Schlampigkeit *f*; **dow·dy** [ˈdaʊdɪ] **I** *adj.* □ **1.** schlecht gekleidet, ‚unele‚gant, schäbig, schlampig; **II** *s.* **2.** nachlässig gekleidete Frau; **3.** *Am.* (ein) Apfelauflauf *m*.

dow·el [ˈdaʊəl] ⊚ **I** *s.* (Holz-, *a.* Wand-)Dübel *m*, Holzpflock *m*; **II** *v/t.* (ver)dübeln.

dow·er [ˈdaʊə] **I** *s.* **1.** 🚄 Wittum *n*; **2.** *obs.* Mitgift *f*; **3.** Begabung *f*; **II** *v/t.* **4.** ausstatten (*a. fig.*).

Dow-Jones av·er·age *od.* **in·dex** [ˌdaʊˈdʒəʊnz] *s.* ✝ Dow-Jones-Index *m* (*Aktienindex der New Yorker Börse*).

down¹ [daʊn] *s.* **1.** a) Daunen *pl.*, flaumiges Gefieder, b) Daune *f*, Flaumfeder *f*: ~ **quilt** Daunendecke *f*; **2.** Flaum *m* (*a.* ♀), feine Härchen *pl.*

down² [daʊn] *s.* **1.** a) Hügel *m*, b) Düne *f*; **2.** *pl.* waldloses, *bsd.* grasbewachsenes Hügelland.

down³ [daʊn] **I** *adv.* **1.** (*Richtung*) nach unten, her-, hin'unter, her-, hin'ab, abwärts, zum Boden, nieder...: ~ **from** von ... herab, von ... an, fort von; ~ **to** bis (hinunter) zu; ~ **to the last man** bis zum letzten Mann; ~ **to our times** bis in unsere Zeit; **burn ~** niederbrennen; **~!** nieder!, *zum Hund:* leg dich!; ~ **with the capitalists!** nieder mit den Kapitalisten!; **2.** *Brit.* a) nicht in London, b) nicht an der Universi'tät: ~ **to the country** aufs Land, in die Provinz; **3.** *Am.* ins Geschäftsviertel, in die Stadt (-mitte); **4.** südwärts; **5.** angesetzt: ~ **for Friday** für Freitag angesetzt; ~ **for second reading** *parl.* zur zweiten Lesung angesetzt; **6.** (in) bar, so'fort: **pay ~** bar bezahlen; **one pound ~** ein Pfund sofort *od.* als Anzahlung; **7.** **be ~ on s.o.** F a) j-n ‚auf dem Kieker' haben, b) über j-n herfallen; **8.** (*Lage, Zustand*) unten; unten im Hause: ~ **below** unten; ~ **there** dort unten; ~ **under** F in *od.* nach Australien *od.* Neuseeland; ~ **in the country** auf dem Land(e); ~ **south** (unten) im Süden; **he is not ~ yet** er ist noch nicht unten *od.* (*morgens*) noch nicht aufgestanden; **9.** 'untergegangen (*Gestirne*); **10.** her'abgelassen (*Haare, Vorhänge*); **11.** gefallen (*Preise, Temperatur etc.*); billiger (*Ware*); **12.** **he was two points ~** *sport* er lag zwei Punkte zurück; **he is £10 ~** *fig.* er hat 10 £ verloren; **13.** a) niedergestreckt, am Boden (liegend), b) *Boxen:* am Boden, ‚unten': ~ **and out** k.o., *fig.* (a. *physisch u. psychisch*) ‚erledigt', ‚kaputt', ‚fix u. fertig'; ~ **with flu** mit Grippe im Bett; **14.** niedergeschlagen, deprimiert; **15.** her'untergekommen, in elenden Verhältnissen lebend: ~ **at heels** abgerissen; **II** *adj.* **16.** abwärts gerichtet, nach unten, Abwärts...: ~ **trend** fallende Tendenz; **17.** *Brit.* von London abfahrend *od.* kommend: ~ **train**; ~ **platform** Abfahrtsbahnsteig *m* (*in London*); **18.** *Am.* in Richtung Stadt(mitte), zum Geschäftsviertel (hin); **III** *prp.* **19.** her-, hin'unter, her-, hin'ab, entlang: ~ **the hill** den Hügel hinunter; ~ **the river** flussabwärts; **further ~ the river** weiter unten am Fluss; ~ **the road** die Straße entlang; ~ **the middle** durch die Mitte; ~ **(the) wind** ♆ mit dem Wind; → **downtown**; **20.** (*Zeit*) durch: ~ **the ages** durch alle Zeiten; **IV** *s.* **21.** Nieder-, Rückgang *m*; Tiefstand *m*; **22.** Depressi'on *f*, (seelischer) Tiefpunkt; **23.** F Groll *m*: **have a ~ on s.o.** j-n auf dem ‚Kieker' haben; **V** *v/t.* **24.** zu Fall bringen (*a. sport u. fig.*); niederschlagen; bezwingen; ruinieren; **25.** niederlegen: ~ **tools** die Arbeit niederlegen, in den Streik treten; **26.** ✓ abschießen, ‚runterholen'; **27.** F *ein Getränk* ‚runterkippen'.

,**down|-and-'out I** *adj.* völlig ‚erledigt', ‚restlos fertig'; ganz ‚auf den Hund' gekommen; **II** *s.* Pennbruder *m*; ,~-**at-(-the-)'heels** *adj. allg.* he'runterge-

kommen; '**~·beat I** s. **1.** ♪ erster Schlag (des Taktes); **2. on the ~** fig. im Rückgang (begriffen); **II** adj. **3.** F pessi'mistisch; '**~·cast I** adj. **1.** niedergeschlagen (a. Augen), deprimiert; **2.** ⊕ einziehend (Schacht); **II** s. **3.** ⊕ Wetterschacht m.
down·er ['daʊnə] s. **1.** Beruhigungsmittel n; **2.** a) ,Dämpfer' m, b) depres'sive Stimmung: **be on a ~** down sein, c) Pechsträhne f, depres'sive Phase.
'**down|·fall** s. **1.** fig. Sturz m; **2.** starker Regen- od. Schneefall; **3.** fig. Nieder-, 'Untergang m; '**~·grade** s. **1.** Gefälle n; **2.** fig. Niedergang m: **on the ~** im Niedergang begriffen; **II** v/t. **3.** im Rang her'absetzen, degradieren; **4.** niedriger einstufen; **5.** ✝ in der Quali'tät herabsetzen, verschlechtern; **,~-'heart·ed** adj. niedergeschlagen, entmutigt; **,~·'hill I** adv. abwärts, berg'ab (beide a. fig.): **he is going ~** fig. es geht bergab mit ihm; **II** adj. abschüssig: **~ race** Skisport: Abfahrtslauf m; '**~·hill·er** s. Skisport: Abfahrtsläufer(in).
Down·ing Street ['daʊnɪŋ] s. Downing Street f (Amtssitz des Premiers od. der brit. Regierung).
down·load ['daʊnləʊd] Computer: **I** v/t. Datei her'unterladen; **II** s. (Her'unter)Laden n (von Dateien, a. aus dem Internet).
,down|-'mar·ket adj. Billig-, Massen-; **~ pay·ment** s. Barzahlung f; **2.** Anzahlung f; '**~·pipe** s. ⊕ Fallrohr n; '**~·play** v/t. her'unterspielen, bagatelli'sieren; '**~·pour** s. Regenguss m, Platzregen m; '**~·right I** adj. **1.** völlig, absolut, to'tal: **a ~ lie** e-e glatte Lüge; **a ~ rogue** ein Erzschurke; **2.** offen(herzig), gerade, ehrlich, unverblümt, unzweideutig; **II** adv. **3.** völlig, ganz u. gar, durch u. durch, ausgesprochen, to'tal; **,~·'ri·ver** → **downstream**; '**~·side** s. Kehrseite f; **,~·'size I** v/t. verkleinern, redu'zieren, abbauen, F ,abspecken'; **II** v/i. sich verkleinern, F ,abspecken'; '**~·siz·ing** s. ✝ 'Downsizing n (Abbau von Arbeitskräften etc.); **,~·'stairs I** adv. **1.** (die Treppe) hin'unter od. hin'ab; nach unten; **2.** a) unten (im Haus), b) e-e Treppe tiefer; **II** adj. **3.** im unteren Stockwerk (gelegen), unter; **III** s. **4.** pl. a. sg. konstr. unteres Stockwerk, 'Untergeschoss n; **,~·'state** Am. **I** adv. in der od. die Pro'vinz; **II** s. (bsd. südliche) Pro'vinz (e-s Bundesstaates); **,~·'stream I** adv. **1.** strom'abwärts; **2.** mit dem Strom; **II** adj. stromabwärts gelegen od. gerichtet; '**~·stroke** s. **1.** Grundstrich m beim Schreiben; **2.** ⊕ Abwärts-, Leerhub m; '**~·swing** s. Abwärtstrend m, Rückgang m; '**~·time** s. Ausfallzeit f; **,~-to-'earth** adj. rein sachlich, nüchtern; **,~·town** Am. **I** adv. **1.** im od. ins Geschäftsviertel, in der od. die Innenstadt; **II** adj. [daʊntaʊn] **2.** zum Geschäftsviertel, im Geschäftsviertel (gelegen od. tätig): **~ Chicago** die Innenstadt od. City von Chicago; **3.** ins od. durchs Geschäftsviertel (fahrend etc.); **III** s. ['daʊntaʊn] **4.** Geschäftsviertel n, Innenstadt f, City f; '**~·trend** s. Abwärtstrend m; '**~·turn** → **downswing**.
down·ward ['daʊnwəd] **I** adv. **1.** abwärts, hin'ab, hin'unter, nach unten; **2.** fig. abwärts, berg'ab; **3.** zeitlich: abwärts: **from ... to** von... (herab) bis...; **II** adj. **4.** Abwärts... (a. ⊕, phys. u. fig.); fig. sinkend (Preise etc.); '**down·wards** [-wədz] → **downward** I.
down·y¹ ['daʊnɪ] adj. **1.** mit Daunen od.

Flaum bedeckt; **2.** flaumig, weich; **3.** sl. gerieben, ausgekocht.
down·y² ['daʊnɪ] adj. sanft gewellt (u. mit Gras bewachsen).
dow·ry ['daʊərɪ] s. **1.** Mitgift f, Aussteuer f; **2.** Gabe f, Ta'lent n.
dowse¹ [daʊz] → **douse**.
dowse² [daʊz] v/i. mit der Wünschelrute suchen; '**dows·er** [-zə] s. (Wünschel-)Rutengänger m; '**dows·ing rod** [-zɪŋ] s. Wünschelrute f.
doy·en ['dɔɪən] s. (Fr.) **1.** Rangälteste(r) m; **2.** Doy'en m eines diplomatischen Korps; **3.** fig. Nestor m, Altmeister m.
doze [dəʊz] **I** v/i. dösen, (halb) schlummern: **~ off** einnicken; **II** s. a) Dösen n, b) Nickerchen n.
doz·en ['dʌzn] s. **1.** sg. u. pl. (vor Haupt- u. nach Zahlwörtern etc. außer nach some) Dutzend n: **two ~ eggs** 2 Dutzend Eier; **2.** Dutzend n (a. weitS.): **~s of birds** Dutzende von Vögeln; **some ~s of children** einige Dutzend Kinder; **~s of people** F ein Haufen Leute; **~s of times** F x-mal, hundertmal; **by the ~,** in **~s** zu Dutzenden, dutzendweise; **cheaper by the ~** im Dutzend billiger; **do one's daily ~** Frühgymnastik machen; **talk nineteen to the ~** Brit. reden wie ein Wasserfall; → **baker** 1.
doz·y ['dəʊzɪ] adj. □ schläfrig, verschlafen, dösig.
drab¹ [dræb] **I** adj. gelbgrau, graubraun; fig. grau, trüb(e); düster (Farben etc.); freudlos (Dasein etc.); langweilig; **II** s. Gelbgrau n, Graubraun n.
drab² [dræb] **1.** Schlampe f; **2.** Dirne f, Hure f.
drab·ble ['dræbl] → **draggle** I.
drachm [dræm] s. **1.** → **drachma** 1; **2.** → **dram**.
drach·ma ['drækmə] pl. **-mas, -mae** [-miː] s. **1.** Drachme f; **2.** → **dram**.
Dra·co ['dreɪkəʊ] s. ast. Drache m; **Dra·co·ni·an** [drə'kəʊnjən], **Dra·con·ic** [drə'kɒnɪk] adj. dra'konisch, hart, äußerst streng.
draff [dræf] s. **1.** Bodensatz m; engS. Trester m; **2.** Vieh-, Schweinetrank m.
draft [drɑːft] **I** s. **1.** Skizze f, Zeichnung f; **2.** Entwurf m: a) Skizze f, b) ⊕, △ Riss m, c) Kon'zept n: **~ agreement** Vertragsentwurf m; **3.** ✕ a) ('Sonder-)Kom,mando n, Abteilung f, b) Ersatz (-truppe f) m, c) Aushebung f, Einberufung f, Einziehung f: **~ evader** Am. Drückeberger m; **~-exempt** Am. vom Wehrdienst befreit; **4.** ✝ a) Zahlungsanweisung f, b) Tratte f, (trassierter) Wechsel, c) Scheck m, d) Ziehung f, Trassierung f: **~ (payable) at sight** Sichttratte, -wechsel; **5.** ✝ Abhebung f, Entnahme f: **make a ~ on** Geld abheben von; **6.** fig. (starke) Beanspruchung: **make a ~ on** in Anspruch nehmen (acc.); **7.** → **draught** bsd. Am. → **draught** 1, 7, 8; **II** v/t. **8.** skizzieren, entwerfen; **9.** Schriftstück aufsetzen, abfassen; **10.** ✕ a) auswählen, abkommandieren, b) ✕ einziehen, -berufen (into zu); **draft·ee** [drɑːf'tiː] s. ✕ Am. Einberufene(r) m, Eingezogene(r) m; '**draft·er** [-tə] s. **1.** Urheber m, Verfasser m, Planer m; **2.** → **draftsman** 2.
draft·ing| board ['drɑːftɪŋ] s. Zeichenbrett n; **~ room** s. Am. ⊕ 'Zeichensaal, -bü,ro m.
drafts·man ['drɑːftsmən] s. [irr.] **1.** (Konstrukti'ons-, Muster)Zeichner m; **2.** Entwerfer m, Verfasser m.
draft·y ['drɑːftɪ] adj. zugig.
drag [dræg] **I** s. **1.** ♣ a) Schleppnetz n,

b) Dregganker m; **2.** ✔ a) schwere Egge, b) Mistharke f; **3.** ⊕ Baggerschaufel f; **4.** ⊕ a) Rollwagen m, b) Lastschlitten m, Schleife f; **5.** vierspännige Kutsche; **6.** Hemmschuh m (a. fig. on für); **7.** aer., phys. 'Luft,widerstand m; **8.** hunt. a) Fährte f, Witterung f, b) Schleppe f (künstliche Fährte), c) Schleppjagd f; **9.** fig. schleppendes Verfahren; **10.** F mühsame Sache, ,Schlauch' m; **11.** F a) fade Sache, unangenehme od. ,blöde' Sache: **what a ~!** so ein Mist!, c) fader od. ,mieser' Kerl; **12.** Am. F Einfluss m, Beziehungen pl.; **13.** F Zug m (at, on an e-r Zigarette); **14.** F (bsd. von Transvestiten getragene) Frauenkleidung: **~ queen** Homosexuelle(r) m in Frauenkleidung; **15.** Am. F Straße f; **16.** F für **drag race**; **II** v/t. **17.** schleppen, schleifen, zerren, ziehen: **~ one's feet** schlurfen, fig. ,langsam tun'; **~ the anchor** ♣ vor Anker treiben; **18.** mit e-m Schleppnetz absuchen (for nach) od. fangen od. finden; **19.** ausbaggern; **20.** fig. hi'neinziehen, schleppen (into in acc.); → **drag in**; **III** v/i. **21.** geschleppt werden; **22.** schleppen, schleifen, zerren; schlurfen (Füße); **23.** fig. zerren, ziehen (at an dat.); **24.** mit e-m Schleppnetz suchen, dreggen (for nach); **25.** → **drag on**; **26.** → **drag behind**; **27.** ✝ schleppend gehen; **28.** ♪ schleppen; **~ a·long I** v/t. (weg-)schleppen; **II** v/i. sich da'hinschleppen; **~ a·way** v/t. wegschleppen, -zerren: **drag o.s. away from** iro. sich losreißen von; **~ behind** v/i. a. fig. zu'rückbleiben, nachhinken; **~ down** v/t. herunterziehen; **2.** fig. j-n ,fertig machen', zermürben; **~ in** v/t. **1.** hin'einziehen; **2.** fig. a) j-n (mit) hin'einziehen, b) et. (krampfhaft) aufs Tapet bringen, bei den Haaren her'beiziehen; **~ on** v/i. fig. a) sich da'hinschleppen, b) sich in die Länge ziehen, sich hinziehen (Rede etc.); **~ out** v/t. **1.** in die Länge ziehen, hin'ausziehen; **2.** fig. et. aus j-m herausholen; **~ up** v/t. **1.** hochziehen; **2.** F Skandal etc. ausgraben; **3.** fig. Kind recht u. schlecht aufziehen.
drag| an·chor s. Treib-, Schleppanker m; **~ chain** s. Hemmkette f.
drag·gle ['drægl] **I** v/t. **1.** beschmutzen; **II** v/i. **2.** nachschleifen; **3.** nachhinken; '**drag·gle·tail** s. Schlampe f.
'**drag|·hound** s. hunt. Jagdhund m für Schleppjagden; **~ hunt** s. Schleppjagd f; '**~·lift** s. Schlepplift m; '**~·line** s. **1.** Schleppleine f, ✔ -seil n; **2.** Schürfkübelbagger m; '**~·net** s. **1.** a) ♣ Schleppnetz n, b) hunt. Streichnetz n; **2.** fig. (Fahndungs)Netz n (der Polizei): **~ operation** Großfahndung f.
drag·o·man ['drægəʊmən] pl. **-mans** od. **-men** s. hist. Dragoman m, Dolmetscher m.
drag·on ['drægən] s. **1.** Drache m, Lindwurm m, Schlange f: **the old ⚥** Satan m; **2.** F ,Drache(n)' m (zänkische Frau etc.); '**~·fly** s. zo. Li'belle m; '**~·'s teeth** pl. **1.** ✕ (Panzer)Höcker pl.; **2.** fig. Drachensaat f: **sow ~** Zwietracht säen.
drag·oon [drə'guːn] **I** s. ✕ Dra'goner m; **II** v/t. fig. zwingen (into zu).
drag| race s. mot. Dragsterrennen n; '**~·rope** s. **1.** Schleppseil n; **2.** ✔ a) Leitseil n, b) Vertauungsleine f; **~ show** s. F Transve'stitenshow f.
drag·ster ['drægstə] s. mot. Dragster m (formelfreier Spezialrennwagen).
drain [dreɪn] **I** v/t. **1.** Land entwässern, dränieren, trockenlegen; **2.** ✗ a) Wun-

de von Eiter säubern, b) Eiter abziehen; **3.** a. **~ off**, **~ away** (Ab)Wasser etc. ableiten, -führen, -ziehen; **4.** austrinken, leeren; → **dreg** 1; **5.** Ort etc. kanalisieren; **6.** fig. aufzehren, verschlucken; Vorräte etc. aufbrauchen, erschöpfen; **~ed** fig. erschöpft, Person: a. ausgelaugt; **7.** (of) berauben (gen.), arm machen (an dat.); **II** v/i. **8.** a. **~ off**, **~ away** (langsam) abfließen, -tropfen; versickern; **9.** a. **~ away** fig. da'hin-, verschwinden; **10.** (langsam) austrocknen; **11.** sich entwässern; **III** s. **12.** Ableitung f, Abfluss m, fig. a. Aderlass m: **foreign ~** ✝ Kapitalabwanderung f; → **brain drain**; **13.** Abflussrohr n, 'Abzugska,nal m, Entwässerungsgraben m; Gosse f: **down the ~** F ,futsch', ,im Eimer'; **go down the ~** vor die Hunde gehen; **pour down the ~** Geld zum Fenster hinauswerfen; **14.** pl. Kanalisati'on f; **15.** ✻ Drän m, Ka'nüle f; **16.** fig. (on) Belastung f, Beanspruchung f (gen.): **a great ~ on the purse** e-e schwere finanzielle Belastung.

drain·age ['dreɪnɪdʒ] s. **1.** Ableitung f, Abfluss m; Entleerung f; **2.** Entwässerung f, Trockenlegung f, a. ✻ Drai'nage f; **3.** Entwässerungsanlage f; **4.** Kanalisati'on f; **5.** Abwasser n; **~ a·re·a**, **~ ba·sin** s. Einzugsgebiet n e-s Flusses; **~ tube** s. ✻ 'Abflussa,nüle f.

drain cock s. ☉ Abflusshahn m.

drain·er ['dreɪnə] s. **1.** Abtropfgefäß n, Seiher m; **2.** → **draining board**.

drain·ing board ['dreɪnɪŋ] s. Abtropfbrett n.

'drain·pipe s. **1.** Abflussrohr n; **2.** pl. a. **~ trousers** F Röhrenhose(n pl.) f.

drake [dreɪk] s. orn. Enterich m.

dram [dræm] s. **1.** Drachme f (Gewicht); **2.** ,Schluck' m (Whisky etc.).

dra·ma ['drɑːmə] **I** s. **1.** Drama n: a) Schauspiel n, b) dra'matische Dichtung od. Litera'tur, Dra'matik f; **2.** Schauspielkunst f; **3.** fig. Drama n; **II** adj. **4.** Schauspiel...: **~ school**.

dra·mat·ic [drə'mætɪk] adj. (□ **~ally**) **1.** dra'matisch (a. ♪), Schauspiel..., Theater...: **~ rights** Aufführungsrechte; **~ school** Schauspielschule f; **~ tenor** ♪ Heldentenor m; **2.** fig. dramatisch, spannend, aufregend, erregend; **3.** fig. drastisch: **~ changes**; **dra'mat·ics** [-ks] s. pl. sg. od. pl. konstr. **1.** Dramatur'gie f; **2.** The'ater-, bsd. Liebhaberaufführungen pl.; **3.** contp. thea'tralisches Benehmen od. Getue.

dram·a·tis per·so·nae [,drɑːmətɪs pɜː'səʊnaɪ] s. pl. **1.** Per'sonen pl. der Handlung; **2.** Rollenverzeichnis n.

dram·a·tist ['dræmətɪst] s. Dra'matiker m; **dram·a·ti·za·tion** [,dræmətaɪ'zeɪʃn] s. Dramatisierung f (a. fig.), Bühnenbearbeitung f; **dram·a·tize** ['dræmətaɪz] **I** v/t. **1.** dramatisieren: a) für die Bühne bearbeiten, b) fig. aufbauschen: **~ o.s.** sich aufspielen; **II** v/i. **2.** sich für die Bühne etc. bearbeiten lassen; **3.** fig. über'treiben; **dram·a·tur·gic** [,dræmə'tɜːdʒɪk] adj. drama'turgisch; **dram·a·tur·gist** ['dræmə,tɜːdʒɪst] s. Drama'turg m; **dram·a·tur·gy** ['dræmə,tɜːdʒɪ] s. Dramatur'gie f.

drank [dræŋk] pret. von **drink**.

drape [dreɪp] **I** v/t. **1.** drapieren: a) (mit Stoff) behängen, b) in (schöne) Falten legen, c) et. hängen (over über acc.), (ein)hüllen (in in acc.); **II** v/i. **2.** schön fallen (Stoff etc.); **'drap·er** [-pə] s. Tuch-, Stoffhändler m: **~'s (shop)** Textilgeschäft n; **'dra·per·y** [-pərɪ] s. **1.** dekora'tiver Behang, Drapierung f; **2.**

Faltenwurf m; **3.** coll. Tex'tilien pl., Tex'til-, Webwaren pl., Stoffe pl.; **4.** Am. Vorhangstoffe pl., Vorhänge pl.

dras·tic ['dræstɪk] adj. (□ **~ally**) drastisch (a. ✻), 'durchgreifend, rigo'ros.

drat [dræt] int. F: **~ it (you)!** zum Teufel damit (mit dir)!; **'drat·ted** [-tɪd] adj. F verdammt.

draught [drɑːft] **I** s. **1.** Ziehen n, Zug m: **~ animal** Zugtier n; **2.** Fischzug m (Fischen od. Fang); **3.** Abziehen n (aus dem Fass): **beer on ~** Bier n vom Fass; **~ beer** Brit. Fassbier n; **4.** Zug m, Schluck m: **a ~ of beer** ein Schluck Bier; **at a** (od. **one**) **~** auf 'einen Zug, mit 'einem Mal; **5.** ✻ Arz'neitrank m; **6.** ⚓ Tiefgang m; **7.** (Luft)Zug m, Zugluft f: **there is a ~** es zieht; **~ excluder** Dichtungsstreifen m (für Türen etc.): **feel the ~** F ,den Wind im Gesicht spüren', in (finanzi'eller) Bedrängnis sein; **8.** ☉ Zug m (Schornstein etc.); **9.** pl. sg. konstr. Brit. Damespiel n; **10.** → **draft** I; **II** v/t. **11.** → **draft** II; **'~·board** s. Brit. Dame- od. Schachbrett n.

draughts·man s. [irr.] **1.** ['drɑːftsmæn] Brit. Damestein m; **2.** [-mən] → **draftsman**.

draught·y ['drɑːftɪ] adj. zugig.

draw [drɔː] **I** s. **1.** ☉ Ziehen n, Zug m: **quick on the ~** F a) schnell (mit der Pistole), b) fig. ,fix', schlagfertig; **2.** Ziehung f, Verlosung f; **3.** fig. Zugkraft f; **4.** a) Attrakti'on f, Glanznummer f (Person od. Sache), b) thea. Zugstück n, Schlager m; → **box office** 2; **5.** sport Unentschieden n: **end in a ~** unentschieden ausgehen; **II** v/t. [irr.] **6.** Wagen, Pistole, Schwert, Los, (Spiel)Karte, Zahn etc. ziehen; Gardine zuziehen od. aufziehen; Bier, Wein abziehen, -zapfen; Bogen(sehne) spannen: **~ s.o. into talk** j-n ins Gespräch ziehen; → **conclusion** 3, **bow²** 1, **parallel** 3; **7.** fig. anziehen, -locken, fesseln; her'vorrufen; j-n zu et. bewegen; sich et. zuziehen: **feel ~n to s.o.** sich zu j-m hingezogen fühlen; **~ attention** die Aufmerksamkeit lenken (**to** auf acc.); **~ an audience** Zuhörer anlocken; **~ ruin upon o.s.** sich selbst sein Grab graben; **~ tears from s.o.** j-n zu Tränen rühren; **8.** Gesicht verziehen; → **drawn** 2; **9.** holen, sich verschaffen; entnehmen: **~ water** Wasser holen od. schöpfen; **~ (a) breath** Atem holen, fig. aufatmen; **~ a sigh** (auf)seufzen; **~ consolation** Trost schöpfen (**from** aus); **~ inspiration** sich Anregung holen (**from** von, bei, durch); **10.** Mahlzeiten, ✗ Rationen in Empfang nehmen, a. Gehalt, Lohn beziehen; Geld holen, abheben, entnehmen; **11.** ziehen, auslosen: **~ a prize** e-n Preis gewinnen, fig. Erfolg haben; **~ bonds** ✝ Obligationen auslosen; **12.** fig. her'ausziehen, -bringen, her'aus-, entlocken: **~ applause** Beifall entlocken (**from** dat.); **~ information from s.o.** j-n aushorchen; **~ a reply from s.o.** e-e Antwort aus j-m herausholen; **13.** ausfragen, -horchen (**s.o. on s.th** j-n über et.); j-n aus s-r Reserve her'auslocken: **he refused to be ~n** er ließ sich nicht aushorchen; **14.** zeichnen: **~ a portrait**; **~ a line** e-e Linie ziehen; **~ it fine** fig. es zeitlich etc. gerade noch schaffen; → **line¹** 12; **15.** gestalten, darstellen, schildern; **16.** a. **~ up** Schriftstück entwerfen, aufsetzen: **~ a deed** e-e Urkunde aufsetzen; **~ a cheque** (Am. **check**) e-n Scheck ausstellen; **~ a bill** e-n Wechsel ziehen (**on** auf j-n); **17.** ⚓ e-n Tiefgang von ...

---

haben; **18.** Tee ziehen lassen; **19.** geschlachtetes Tier ausnehmen, Wild a. ausweiden; **20.** hunt. Wald, Gelände durch'stöbern, abpirschen; Teich ausfischen; **21.** ☉ Draht ziehen; strecken, dehnen; **22.** **~ the match** sport unentschieden spielen; **III** v/i. [irr.] **23.** ziehen (a. Tee, Schornstein); **24.** das Schwert, die Pistole etc. ziehen, zur Waffe greifen; **25.** sich (leicht etc.) ziehen lassen; **26.** zeichnen, malen; **27.** Lose ziehen, losen (**for** um); **28.** unentschieden spielen; **29.** sich (hin)begeben; sich nähern: **~ close** (**to s.o.** j-m) näher rücken; **~ round the table** sich um den Tisch versammeln; **~ into the station** ᴬ in den Bahnhof einfahren; → **draw near**, **level** 11; **30.** ✝ (e-n Wechsel) ziehen (**on** auf acc.); **31.** **~ on** in Anspruch nehmen (acc.), her'anziehen (acc.), Gebrauch machen von, zu'rückgreifen auf (acc.); Kapital, Vorräte angreifen: **~ on one's imagination** sich et. einfallen lassen;

Zssgn mit adv.:

draw a·part **I** v/i. **1.** sich lösen, abrücken (**from** von); **2.** sich ausein'ander leben; **II** v/t. **3.** → **~ a·side** v/t. j-n bei'seite nehmen, a. et. zur Seite ziehen; **~ a·way** **I** v/t. **1.** weg-, zu'rückziehen; **2.** ablenken; **3.** weglocken; **II** v/i. **4.** (**from**) sich entfernen (von); abrücken (von); **5.** (**from**) e-n Vorsprung gewinnen (vor dat.), sich lösen (von); **~ back** **I** v/t. **1.** Truppen, Vorhang etc. zu'rückziehen; **2.** ✝ Zoll zu'rückerhalten; **II** v/i. **3.** sich zu'rückziehen; **~ down** v/t. her'abziehen, Jalousien her'unterlassen; **~ in I** v/t. **1.** a. Luft einziehen; fig. j-n (mit) hin'einziehen; **3.** Ausgaben etc. einschränken; **II** v/i. **4.** einfahren (Zug); **5.** abnehmen, kürzer werden (Tage); **7.** sich einschränken; **~ near** v/i. sich nähern (**to** dat.), her'anrücken; **~ off I** v/t. **1.** ab-, zu'rückziehen; **2.** ✽ ausziehen; **3.** abzapfen; **4.** Handschuhe etc. ausziehen; **5.** fig. ablenken; **II** v/i. **6.** sich zurückziehen; **~ on I** v/t. **1.** anziehen: **~ gloves**; **2.** fig. a) anziehen, anlocken, b) verursachen; **II** v/i. **3.** sich nähern; **~ out I** v/t. **1.** her'ausziehen, -holen; **2.** fig. a) Aussage her'ausholen, -locken, b) j-n ausholen, -horchen; **3.** ✗ Truppen a) abkommandieren, b) aufstellen; **4.** fig. ausdehnen, hin'ausziehen, in die Länge ziehen; **II** v/i. **5.** länger werden (Tage); **6.** ausfahren (Zug); **~ up I** v/t. **1.** her'aufziehen, aufrichten: **draw o.s. up** sich aufrichten; **2.** Truppen etc. aufstellen; **3.** a) → **draw** 16, b) ✝ Bilanz aufstellen, c) Plan etc. entwerfen; **4.** anhalten lassen: **~ a horse** Pferd zum Stehen bringen; **II** v/i. **6.** (an)halten; **7.** vorfahren (Wagen); **8.** aufmarschieren; **9.** (**with**, **to**) her'ankommen (an acc.), einholen (acc.).

'draw·back s. **1.** Nachteil m, Hindernis n, ,Haken' m; **2.** ✝ Zollrückvergütung f; **'~·bridge** s. Zugbrücke f; **'~·card** → **drawing card**.

draw·ee [drɔː'iː] s. ✝ Bezogene(r) m.

draw·er ['drɔːə] s. **1.** Zeichner m; **2.** ✝ Aussteller m e-s Wechsels; **3.** [drɔː] a) Schublade f, -fach n, b) pl. Kom'mode f; **4.** pl. [drɔːz] a. **pair of ~s** 'Unterhose f, b) (Damen)Schlüpfer m.

draw·ing ['drɔːɪŋ] s. **1.** Ziehen n; **2.** Zeichnen n: **out of ~** verzeichnet; **3.** Zeichnung f, Skizze f; **4.** Ziehung f, Verlosung f; **5.** ✝ a) pl. Bezüge pl., Einnahmen pl., b) Abhebung f, c) Trassierung f, Ziehung f (Wechsel); **~**

ac·count s. ✝ **1.** Girokonto n; **2.** Spesenkonto n; **~ block** s. Zeichenblock m; **~ board** s. Reiß-, Zeichenbrett n; **back to the ~!** F wir müssen noch einmal von vorn anfangen!; **~ card** s. thea. Am. Zugnummer f (Stück od. Person); **~ com·pass·es** s. pl. (Reiß-, Zeichen-) Zirkel m; **~ ink** s. (Auszieh)Tusche f; **~ pen** s. Reißfeder f; **~ pen·cil** s. Zeichenstift m; **~ pin** s. Brit. Reiß-, Heftzwecke f; **~ pow·er** s. fig. Zugkraft f; **~ room** s. **1.** Gesellschaftszimmer n, Salon m: **not fit for a ~** nicht ‚salonfähig'; **~ comedy** Salonkomödie f; **2.** Empfang m (Brit. bsd. bei Hofe); **3.** 🔊 Am. Pri'vatabteil n: **~ car** Salonwagen m; **~ set** s. Reißzeug n.

drawl [drɔːl] **I** v/t. u. v/i. gedehnt od. schleppend sprechen; **II** s. gedehntes Sprechen.

drawn [drɔːn] **I** p.p. von **draw**; **II** adj. **1.** gezogen (a. 🌑 Draht); **2.** fig. a) abgespannt, b) verhärmt (Gesicht): **~ with pain** schmerzverzerrt; **3.** sport: unentschieden: **~ match** Unentschieden n; **~ but·ter** (sauce) Buttersoße f; **~ work** s. Hohlsaumarbeit f.

draw| po·ker s. Kartenspiel: Draw Poker n; '**~·string** s. Zug- od. Vorhangschnur f; **~ well** s. Ziehbrunnen m.

dray [dreɪ], a. **~ cart** s. Rollwagen m; **~ horse** s. Zugpferd n; '**~·man** [-mən] s. [irr.] Rollkutscher m.

dread [dred] **I** v/t. (sehr) fürchten, (große) Angst haben od. sich fürchten vor (dat.); **II** s. Furcht f, große Angst, Grauen n (of vor dat.); **III** adj. poet. → **dreadful** 1; '**dread·ed** [-dɪd] adj. gefürchtet; '**dread·ful** [-fʊl] adj. □ **1.** furchtbar, schrecklich (beide a. fig. F); → **penny dreadful**; **2.** F a) grässlich, scheußlich, b) furchtbar groß od. lang, kolos'sal; '**dread·locks** s. pl. Rastafrisur f; '**dread·nought** s. **1.** ✕ Dreadnought m, Schlachtschiff n; **2.** dicker, wetterfester Stoff od. Mantel.

dream [driːm] **I** s. **1.** Traum m: **pleasant ~s!** F träume süß!; **wet ~** ‚feuchter Traum' (Pollution); **2.** Traum(zustand) m, Träume'rei f; **3.** fig. (Wunsch-) Traum m, Sehnsucht f, Ide'al n: **~ fac·tory** ‚Traumfabrik' f; **~ job** Traumberuf m; **4.** fig. ‚Gedicht' n, Traum m: **a ~ of a hat** ein traumhaft schöner Hut; **a perfect ~** traumhaft schön; **II** v/i. [a. irr.] **5.** träumen (of von) (a. fig.); **6.** träumerisch od. verträumt sein; **7.** mst neg. ahnen: **I shouldn't ~ of such a thing** das würde mir nicht einmal im Traume einfallen; **I shouldn't ~ of doing that** ich würde nie daran denken, das zu tun; **he little dreamt that** er ahnte kaum, dass; **III** v/t. [a. irr.] **8.** träumen (a. fig.); **9. ~ away** verträumen; **10. ~ up** F sich et. einfallen lassen od. ausdenken; '**dream·boat** s. F sl. a) ‚Schatz' m, b) ‚dufter Typ', c) Schwarm m, Ide'al n; '**dream·er** [-mə] s. Träumer(in) (a. fig.); '**dream·i·ness** [-mɪnɪs] s. **1.** Verträumtheit f; **2.** Traumhaftigkeit f, Verschwommenheit f; '**dream·ing** [-mɪŋ] → **dreamy** 1.

'**dream·land** s. Traumland n; '**~·like** adj. traumhaft; '**~·sic·le** [-sɪkl] s. Traumgebilde n.

dreamt [dremt] pret. u. p.p. von **dream**.

dream world s. Traumwelt f.

dream·y ['driːmɪ] adj. □ **1.** verträumt, träumerisch; **2.** traumhaft, verschwommen; **3.** F traumhaft (schön).

drear [drɪə] adj. poet. → **dreary**; **drear·ie** ['drɪərɪ] s. F fader od. ‚mieser' Typ.

drear·i·ness ['drɪərɪnɪs] s. **1.** Tristheit f, Trostlosigkeit f; **2.** Langweiligkeit f; **drear·y** ['drɪərɪ] adj. □ **1.** allg. trist, trüb(selig); **2.** langweilig, fad(e); **3.** F ‚mies', ‚blöd'.

dredge¹ [dredʒ] **I** s. **1.** 🌑 Bagger m; **2.** Schleppnetz n; **II** v/t. **3.** ausbaggern; **4.** oft **~ up** mit dem Schleppnetz fangen od. her'aufholen; **5.** fig. a) **~ up** Tatsachen ausgraben, b) durch'forschen; **III** v/i. **6.** mit dem Schleppnetz fischen (for nach); **7. ~ for** suchen nach.

dredge² [dredʒ] v/t. (mit Mehl etc.) bestreuen.

dredg·er¹ ['dredʒə] s. **1.** 🌑 Bagger m; **2.** Schwimmbagger m; **3.** Schleppnetzfischer m.

dredg·er² ['dredʒə] s. (Mehl- etc.)Streuer m.

dreg [dreg] s. mst pl. (Boden)Satz m, Hefe f: **drain** (od. **drink**) **to the ~s** Glas bis zur Neige leeren; **not a ~** gar nichts; → **cup** 7; **2.** mst pl. fig. Abschaum m (der Menschheit), Hefe f (des Volkes): **the ~s of mankind**.

drench [drentʃ] **I** v/t. **1.** durch'nässen: **~ed in blood** blutgetränkt; **~ed with rain** vom Regen (völlig) durchnässt; **~ed in tears** in Tränen gebadet; **2.** vet. Tieren Arz'nei einflößen; **II** s. **3.** (Regen)Guss m; **4.** vet. Arz'neitrank m; '**drench·er** [-tʃə] s. **1.** Regenguss m; **2.** vet. Gerät n zum Einflößen von Arz-'neien.

Dres·den (**chi·na**) ['drezdən] s. Meißner Porzel'lan n.

dress [dres] **I** s. **1.** Kleidung f, Anzug m (a. ✕); **2.** (Damen)Kleid n; **3.** Abend-, Gesellschaftskleidung f: **full ~** Gesellschaftsanzug m, Gala f; **4.** fig. Gewand n, Kleid n, Gestalt f; **II** v/t. **5.** be-, ankleiden, anziehen: → **o.s.** → 11; **6.** einkleiden; **7.** thea. mit Ko'stümen ausstatten: **~ it** Kostümprobe abhalten; **8.** schmücken, Schaufenster etc. dekorieren: **~ ship** 🔊 über die Toppen flaggen; **9.** zu'rechtmachen, herrichten, zubereiten, behandeln, bearbeiten; Salat anmachen; Huhn etc. koch- od. bratfertig machen; Haare frisieren; Leder zurichten; Tuch glätten, appretieren; Erz etc. aufbereiten; Stein behauen; Flachs hecheln; Boden düngen; ⚕ Wunde behandeln, verbinden; **10.** ✕ (aus)richten; **III** v/i. **11.** sich ankleiden od. anziehen; **12.** Abend- od. Festkleidung anziehen, sich ,in Gala werfen'; **13.** sich (geschmackvoll etc.) kleiden: **~ well (badly)**; **14.** ✕ sich (aus)richten; **~ down** v/t. **1.** Pferd striegeln; **2.** F j-m ,eins auf den Deckel geben'; **~ up I** v/t. **1.** fein anziehen, herausputzen; **II** v/i. **2.** sich fein machen, sich auftakeln; **3.** sich kostümieren od. verkleiden.

dres·sage ['dresaːʒ] **I** s. sport Dres'sur (-reiten n) f; **II** adj. Dressur...

dress| cir·cle s. thea. erster Rang; **~ clothes** s. pl. Gesellschaftskleidung f; **~ coat** s. Frack m; **~ de·sign·er** s. Modezeichner(in).

dress·er¹ ['dresə] s. **1.** thea. a) Kostümi'er m, b) Garderobi'ere f; **2.** j-d, der sich sorgfältig etc. kleidet; **3.** ⚕ Operati'onsassi,stent m; **4.** ‚Schaufensterdekora,teur m; **5.** 🌑 a) Zurichter m, Aufbereiter m, b) Appretierer m.

dress·er² ['dresə] s. **1.** a) Küchen-, Geschirrschrank m, b) Anrichte f; **2.** → **dressing table**.

dress·ing ['dresɪŋ] s. **1.** Ankleiden n; **2.** 🌑 a) (Nach)Bearbeitung f, Aufbereitung f, Zurichtung f; **3.** 🌑 Appre'tur f; **4.** Zubereitung f von Speisen; **5.** a)

Dressing n (Salatsoße), b) Am. Füllung f; **6.** ⚕ a) Verbinden n (Wunde), b) Verband m; **7.** ✎ Dünger m; ⚕ Toi'lettentasche f, 'Reiseneces,saire n; ,**~-'down** s. F Standpauke f, Rüffel m; **~ gown** s. Schlaf-, Morgenrock m; **~ room** s. **1.** Ankleidezimmer n; **2.** (‚Künstler)Garde,robe f; **3.** sport (‚Umkleide)Ka,bine f; **~ sta·tion** s. ✕ (Feld)Verband(s)platz m; **~ ta·ble** s. Fri'sierkom,mode f.

'**dress| mak·er** s. (Damen)Schneider (-in); ,**~·mak·ing** s. Schneidern n; **~ pa·rade** s. **1.** Modevorführung f; **2.** Pa'rade f in 'Galauni,form; **~ pat·tern** s. Schnittmuster n; **~ re·hears·al** s. thea. Gene'ralprobe f (a. fig.), Kos-'tümprobe f; **~ shield** s. Schweißblatt n; **~ shirt** s. Frackhemd n; **~ suit** s. Frackanzug m; **~ u·ni·form** s. ✕ großer Dienstanzug m.

dress·y ['dresɪ] adj. □ **1.** ele'gant (gekleidet), weitS. modebewusst; **2.** geschniegelt; **3.** F schick, fesch (Kleid).

drew [druː] pret. von **draw**.

drib·ble ['drɪbl] **I** v/i. **1.** tröpfeln (a. fig.); **2.** sabbern, geifern; **3.** sport dribbeln; **II** v/t. **4.** (her'ab)tröpfeln lassen, träufeln; **5.** sport **~ the ball** (mit dem Ball) dribbeln.

drib·(b)let ['drɪblɪt] s. kleine Menge; **by ~s** fig. in kleinen Mengen, kleckerweise.

dribs and drabs [,drɪbzən'dræbz] s. pl.: **in ~** F kleckerweise.

dried [draɪd] adj. getrocknet: **~ cod** Stockfisch m; **~ fruit** Dörrobst n; **~ milk** Trockenmilch f.

dri·er¹ ['draɪə] s. **1.** Trockenmittel n, Sikka'tiv n; **2.** 'Trockenappa,rat m, Trockner m: **hair-~** Föhn m.

dri·er² ['draɪə] comp. von **dry**.

dri·est ['draɪɪst] sup. von **dry**.

drift [drɪft] **I** s. **1.** Treiben n; **2.** fig. Abwanderung f: **~ from the land** Landflucht f; **3.** ⚓, ⛵ Abtrift f, -trieb m; **4.** Ballistik: Seitenabweichung f; **5.** Drift(strömung) f (im Meer); (Strömungs)Richtung f; **6.** fig. a) Strömung f, Ten'denz f, Lauf m, Richtung f, b) Absicht f, c) Gedankengang m, d) Sinn m: **the ~ of what he said** was er meinte od. sagen wollte; **7.** a) Treibholz n, b) Treibeis n, c) Schneegestöber n; **8.** Treibgut n; **9.** (Schnee)Verwehung f, (Schnee-, Sand)Wehe f; **10.** geol. Geschiebe n; **11.** fig. Einfluss m, (treibende) Kraft; **12.** 'Treibenlassen n, Sich-'treiben-Lassen n, Ziellosigkeit f: **pol·icy of ~**; **II** v/i. **13.** treiben (a. fig. **into** in e-n Krieg etc.), getrieben werden: **let things ~** den Dingen ihren Lauf lassen; **~ away** v/t. abwandern, b) sich entfernen (**from** von); **~ apart** fig. sich auseinander leben; **14.** sich (willenlos) treiben lassen; **15.** auf et. zutreiben; **16.** gezogen werden, geraten od. (hinein)schlittern (**into** in acc.); **17.** sich häufen (Sand, Schnee); **III** v/t. **18.** (da'hin)treiben, (fort)tragen; **19.** aufhäufen, zs.-tragen; **~ an·chor** s. ⚓ Treibanker m.

drift·er ['drɪftə] s. **1.** zielloser Mensch, ‚Gammler' m; **2.** Treibnetzfischer(boot n) m.

drift| ice s. Treibeis n; **~ net** s. Treibnetz n; '**~·wood** s. Treibholz n.

drill¹ [drɪl] **I** s. **1.** 🌑 'Bohrgerät n, -ma,schine f, Bohrer m: → **chuck** Bohrfutter n; **2.** Drill m: a) ✕ Exerzieren n, b) (Luftschutz- etc.)Übung f, c) fig. strenge Schulung, d) 'Ausbildung(sme,thode) f; **II** v/t. **3.** Loch bohren; **4.** ✕ u. fig. drillen, einexerzieren: **~ him in**

D

Latin ihm Lateinisch einpauken; **5.** *fig.* drillen, gründlich ausbilden; **III** *v/i.* **6.** (⊛ *engS.* ins Volle) bohren: ~ **for oil** nach Öl bohren; **7.** ⚔ a) exerzieren (a. *fig.*), b) gedrillt *od.* ausgebildet werden.

drill² [drɪl] ⚐ I *s.* **1.** (Saat)Rille *f*, Furche *f*; **2.** 'Drill-, 'Säma,schine *f*; **II** *v/t.* **3.** *Saat* in Reihen säen; **4.** *Land* in Reihen besäen.

drill³ [drɪl] *s.* Drill(ich) *m*, Drell *m*.

drill¹ bit *s.* ⊛ **1.** Bohrspitze *f*; **2.** Einsatzbohrer *m*; ~ **ground** *s.* ⚔ Exerzierplatz *m*.

drill·ing ['drɪlɪŋ] *s.* **1.** Bohren *n*; **2.** Bohrung *f* (*for* nach *Öl etc.*); **3.** → **drill¹** 2; ~ **rig** *s.* Bohrinsel *f*.

'drill,mas·ter *s.* **1.** ⚔ Ausbilder *m*; **2.** *fig.* ,Einpauker' *m*; ~ **ser·geant** *s.* ⚔ 'Ausbildungs,unteroffi,zier *m*.

dri·ly ['draɪlɪ] *adv. von* **dry** (*mst fig.*).

drink [drɪŋk] I *s.* **1.** a) Getränk *n*, b) Drink *m*, alko'holisches Getränk, c) *coll.* Getränke *pl.*; ~**s machine** Getränkeautomat *m*; **have a ~** et. trinken, e-n Drink nehmen; **have a ~ with s.o.** mit j-m ein Glas trinken; **a ~ of water** ein Schluck Wasser; **food and ~** Essen *n* u. Getränke *pl.*; **2.** das Trinken, der Alkohol: **take to** ~ sich das Trinken angewöhnen; **3.** *sl. der* ,Große Teich' (*Meer*); **II** *v/t.* [*irr.*] **4.** *Tee etc.* trinken; *Suppe* essen: ~ **s.o. under the table** j-n unter den Tisch trinken; **5.** trinken, saufen (*Tier*); **6.** trinken *od.* anstoßen auf (*acc.*); → **health** 3; **7.** (aus)trinken, leeren; → **cup** 7; **8.** *fig.* → **drink in**; **III** *v/i.* [*irr.*] **9.** trinken; **10.** saufen (*Tier*); **11.** trinken, *weitS. a.* ein Trinker sein; **12.** trinken *od.* anstoßen (**to** auf *acc.*): ~ **to s.o.** a. j-m zuprosten; ~ **a·way** *v/t.* **1.** *sein Geld etc.* vertrinken; **2.** *s-e Sorgen* im Alkohol ersäufen; ~ **in** *v/t. fig.* **1.** *Luft etc.* einsaugen, (tief) einatmen; **2.** *fig.* (hingerissen) in sich aufnehmen, verschlingen: ~ **s.o.'s words**; ~ **off**, ~ **up** *v/t.* austrinken.

drink·a·ble ['drɪŋkəbl] *adj.* trinkbar, Trink...; **drink·er** ['drɪŋkə] *s.* **1.** Trinkende(r *m*) *f*: **beer** ~ Biertrinker *m*; **2.** Trinker(in): **a heavy** ~.

drink·ing ['drɪŋkɪŋ] *s.* **1.** *allg.* Trinken *n*; **2.** → ~ **bout** *s.* Trinkgelage *n*; ~ **cup** *s.* Trinkbecher *m*; ~ **foun·tain** *s.* Trinkbrunnen *m*; ~ **song** *s.* Trinklied *n*; ~ **straw** *s.* Trinkhalm *m*; ~ **wa·ter** *s.* Trinkwasser *n*.

drip [drɪp] I *v/i.* **1.** (her'ab)tropfen, (-)tröpfeln; **2.** tropfen (*Wasserhahn*); **3.** triefen (**with** von, vor *dat.*) (a. *fig.*); **II** *v/t.* **4.** (her'ab)tröpfeln *od.* (her'ab-) tropfen lassen; **III** *s.* **5.** → **dripping** 1, 2; **6.** △ Traufe *f*; **7.** ⊛ Tropfrohr *n*; **8.** ⚕ a) 'Tropfinfusi,on *f*, b) Tropf *m*: **be on the** ~ am Tropf hängen; **9.** F ,Nulpe' *f*, ,Blödmann' *m*; ~ **cof·fee** *s. Am.* Filterkaffee *m*; **,~-'dry I** *adj.* bügelfrei; **II** *v/t.* tropfnass aufhängen; **'~-feed** *v/t.* ⚕ parente'ral *od.* künstlich ernähren.

drip·ping ['drɪpɪŋ] *s.* **1.** Tröpfeln *n*, Tropfen *n*; **2.** *a. pl.* her'abtröpfelnde Flüssigkeit; **3.** (abtropfendes) Bratenfett: ~ **pan** Fettpfanne *f*; **II** *adj.* **4.** a. *fig.* triefend (**with** von); **5.** a. ~ **wet** triefend nass, tropfnass.

'drip·proof *adj.* ⊛ tropfwassergeschützt.

drip·py ['drɪpɪ] *adj. sl.* **1.** langweilig, lahm(arschig); **2.** rührselig, kitschig.

drive [draɪv] I *s.* **1.** Fahrt *f*, bsd. Aus-, Spa'zierfahrt *f*: **take** (*od.* **go for**) **a** ~ → **drive out** II; **an hour's** ~ e-e e-e Autostunde entfernt; **2.** a) Fahrweg *m*, -straße *f*, b) (pri'vate) Auf-, Einfahrt *f*,

---

c) Zufahrtsstraße *f*; **3.** a) (Zs.-)Treiben *n* (*von Vieh etc.*), b) zs.-getriebene Tiere; **4.** Treibjagd *f*; **5.** ⚔ a) Antrieb *m*: **rear(-wheel)** ~ Hinterradantrieb *m*, b) *mot. a.* Steuerung *f*: **left-hand** ~ Linkssteuerung *f*, c) *Computer*: Laufwerk *n*; **6.** ⚔ Vorstoß *m*; **7.** *sport* a) Schuss *m*, b) *Golf, Tennis*: Drive *m*, Treibschlag *m*; **8.** Tatkraft *f*, Schwung *m*, E'lan *m*, Dy'namik *f*; **9.** Trieb *m*, Drang *m*: **sexual** ~ Geschlechtstrieb; **10.** ('Sammel-, Ver'kaufs- *etc.*)Akti,on *f*, Kam'pagne *f*, (*bes.* Werbe)Feldzug *m*; **II** *v/t.* [*irr.*] **11.** *Vieh, Wild, Keil, etc.* treiben; *Ball* treiben, (weit) schlagen, schießen; *Nagel* einschlagen, treiben (**into** in *acc.*); *Pfahl* einrammen; *Schwert etc.* stoßen; *Tunnel* bohren, treiben: ~ **s.th. into s.o.** *fig.* j-m et. einbläuen; ~ **all before one** *fig.* jeden Widerstand überwinden, unaufhaltsam sein; → **home** 13; **12.** vertreiben, -jagen; **13.** *hunt.* jagen, treiben; **14.** (zur Arbeit) antreiben, hetzen: ~ **s.o. hard** a) j-n schinden, b) j-n in die Enge treiben; ~ **o.s.** (**hard**) sich abschinden *od.* überanstrengen; **15.** *fig.* j-n dazu bringen *od.* treiben *od.* veranlassen *od.* zwingen (**to** zu; **to do** zu tun): ~ **to despair** zur Verzweiflung treiben; ~ **s.o. mad** j-n verrückt machen; **driven by hunger** vom Hunger getrieben; **16.** *Wagen* fahren, lenken, steuern; **17.** *j-n od. et.* (im Auto) fahren, befördern; **18.** ⊛ (an-, be)treiben (*mst pass.*): **driven by steam** mit Dampf betrieben, mit Dampfantrieb; **19.** zielbewusst 'durchführen: ~ **a hard bargain** hart verhandeln; **he ~s a roaring trade** er treibt e-n schwunghaften Handel; **III** *v/i.* [*irr.*] **20.** (da'hin)treiben, getrieben werden: ~ **before the wind** ⚓ vor dem Wind treiben; **21.** eilen, stürmen, jagen; **22.** stoßen, schlagen; **23.** (e-n *od.* den Wagen) fahren: **can you ~?** können Sie Auto fahren?; **24.** ~ **at** *fig.* (ab)zielen auf (*acc.*): **what is he driving at?** was will *od.* meint er eigentlich?, worauf will er hinaus?; **25.** schwer arbeiten (**at** an *dat.*);

Zssgn mit adv.:

drive| a·way I *v/t. a. fig.* vertreiben; verjagen; **II** *v/i.* wegfahren; ~ **in** I *v/t.* **1.** *Pfahl* einrammen, *Nagel* einschlagen; **2.** *Vieh* eintreiben; **II** *v/i.* **3.** hin'einfahren; ~ **on** I *v/t.* vo'rantreiben (a. *fig.*); **II** *v/i.* weiterfahren; ~ **out** I *v/t.* aus-, vertreiben; **II** *v/i.* spazieren fahren, ausfahren; ~ **up** I *v/t. Preise* in die Höhe treiben; **II** *v/i.* vorfahren (**to** vor *dat.*).

'drive-in I *adj.* Auto..., Drive-in-...; **II** *s.* a) Auto-, Drive-in-Kino *n*, -rasthaus *n etc.*, b) Auto-, Drive-in-Schalter *m* e-r Bank.

driv·el ['drɪvl] I *v/i.* **1.** sabbern, geifern; **2.** dummes Zeug schwatzen, faseln; **II** *s.* **3.** Gesabber *n*, Gefasel *n*, Fase'lei *f*; **'driv·el·(l)er** [-lə] *s.* a) (blöder) Schwätzer.

driv·en ['drɪvn] *p.p. von* **drive**.

driv·er ['draɪvə] *s.* **1.** (An)Treiber *m*; **2.** Fahrer *m*, Lenker *m*, b) (*Kran- etc., Brit. Lokomotiv*)Führer *m*, c) Kutscher *m*; **3.** (Vieh)Treiber *m*; **4.** F Antreiber *m*, (Leute)Schinder *m*; **5.** ⊛ a) Treibrad *n*, Ritzel *n*, b) Mitnehmer *m*, c) Ramme *f*; **6.** *Computer*: Treiber *m*; **7.** *Golf*: Driver *m* (*Holzschläger 1*); **~'s cab** *s.* ⚙ Führerhaus *n*; **~'s li·cense** *s. mot. Am.* Führerschein *m*; **~'s seat** *s.* Fahrer-, Führersitz *m*: **in the** ~ *fig.* am Ruder.

drive| shaft → **driving shaft**; **'~·way** *s.* → **drive** 2; **'~·your,self** *adj. Am.*

Selbstfahrer...: ~ **car** Mietwagen *m*.

driv·ing ['draɪvɪŋ] I *adj.* **1.** (an)treibend: ~ **force** treibende Kraft; ~ **rain** stürmischer Regen; **2.** a) ⊛ Antriebs..., Treib..., Trieb..., b) *TV* Treiber...(-*impulse etc.*); **3.** *mot.* Fahr...: ~ **comfort**; ~ **instructor** Fahrlehrer *m*; ~ **lessons** Fahrstunden; **take** ~ **lessons** Fahrunterricht nehmen, den Führerschein machen; ~ **licence** *Brit.* Führerschein *m*; ~ **mirror** Rückspiegel *m*; ~ **school** Fahrschule *f*; ~ **test** Fahrprüfung *f*; **II** *s.* **4.** Treiben *n*; **5.** (Auto)Fahren *n*; ~ **ax·le** *s.* Antriebsachse *f*; ~ **belt** *s.* Treibriemen *m*; ~ **gear** *s.* Triebwerk *n*, Getriebe *n*; ~ **i·ron** *s. Golf*: Driving Iron *m* (*Eisenschläger Nr. 1*); ~ **pow·er** *s.* ⊛ Antriebskraft *f*, -leistung *f*; ~ **shaft** *s.* ⊛ Antriebswelle *f*; ~ **wheel** *s.* Triebrad *n*.

driz·zle ['drɪzl] I *v/i.* nieseln; **II** *s.* Nieselel-, Sprühregen *m*; **'driz·zly** [-lɪ] *adj.* Niesel-, Sprüh...: ~ **rain**; **it was a ~ day** es nieselte den ganzen Tag.

droll [drəʊl] *adj.* □ drollig, spaßig, komisch; **droll·er·y** ['drəʊlərɪ] *s.* **1.** Posse *f*, Schwank *m*; **2.** Spaß *m*; **3.** Komik *f*, Spaßigkeit *f*.

drome [drəʊm] F *für* **aerodrome**, **airdrome**.

drom·e·dar·y ['drɒmədərɪ] *s. zo.* Drome'dar *n*.

drone¹ [drəʊn] I *s.* **1.** *zo.* Drohne *f*; **2.** *fig.* Drohne *f*, Schma'rotzer *m*; **3.** ⚔ ferngesteuertes Flugzeug *n*; 'Fernlenkra,kete *f*; **II** *v/i.* **4.** faulenzen; **III** *v/t.* **5.** ~ **away** vertrödeln.

drone² [drəʊn] I *v/i.* **1.** brummen, summen, dröhnen; **2.** *fig.* leiern, eintönig reden; **II** *v/t.* **3.** herleiern; **III** *s.* **4.** ♪ a) Bor'dun *m*, b) Basspfeife *f* des Dudelsacks; **5.** Brummen *n*, Summen *n*; **6.** *fig.* a) Geleier *n*, b) einschläfernder Redner.

drool [druːl] I *v/i.* **1.** sabbern, geifern; **2.** (dummes Zeug) schwatzen; **3.** ~ **over** (*od.* **about**) sich begeistern für, vernarrt sein in (*acc.*); **II** *v/t.* **4.** et. salbungsvoll von sich geben *od.* versprechen; **III** *s.* **5.** ,Geschwätz' *n*, ,Gefasel' *n*.

droop [druːp] I *v/i.* **1.** (schlaff) her'abhängen *od.* -sinken; **2.** ermatten, erschlaffen; **3.** sinken, schwinden (*Mut etc.*), erlahmen (*Interesse etc.*); **4.** *fig.* den Kopf hängen lassen (a. *Blume*); **5.** ✝ abbröckeln (*Preise*); **II** *v/t.* **6.** (schlaff) her'abhängen lassen; **III** *s.* **7.** Her'abhängen *n*, Senken *n*; **8.** Erschlaffen *n*; **'droop·ing** [-pɪŋ] *adj.* □ **1.** (herunter)hängend, schlaff (a. *fig.*); **2.** matt; **3.** welk.

drop [drɒp] I *s.* **1.** Tropfen *m*: **in ~s** tropfenweise (a. *fig.*); **a ~ in the bucket** (*od.* **ocean**) *fig.* ein Tropfen auf e-n heißen Stein; **2.** ✝ *mst pl.* Tropfen *pl.*; **3.** a) Tropfen *m*, Tröpfchen *n*, b) Glas *n*, ,Gläs·chen' *n*: **he has had a ~ too much** er hat ein Glas *od.* eins über den Durst getrunken; **4.** Bon'bon *m*, *in*: **fruit ~s** Drops *pl.*; **5.** a) Fall *m*, Fallen *n*: **at the ~ of a hat** F beim geringsten Anlass; **get** *od.* **have the ~ on s.o.** F j-m (*beim Ziehen e-r Waffe*) zuvorkommen, b) Fall(tiefe *f*) *m*, 'Höhen,unterschied *m*, c) steiler Abfall, Gefälle *n*; **6.** *fig.* Fall *m*, Sturz *m*, Rückgang *m*: ~ **in prices** Preissturz, -rückgang; ~ **in the temperature** Temperaturabfall, -sturz; ~ **in the voltage** ⚡ Spannungsabfall; **7.** → **airdrop** I; **8.** ⊛ a) (Fall-) Klappe *f*, -vorrichtung *f*, b) Falltür *f*, c) Vorrichtung *f* zum Her'ablassen von

Lasten: (*letter*) ~ *Am.* (Brief)Einwurf *m*; **9.** *thea.* Vorhang *m*; **II** *v/i.* **10.** (herab)tropfen, (-)tröpfeln; **11.** (he'rab-, her'unter)fallen: *let s.th.* ~ a) et. fallen lassen, b) → 26; **12.** (nieder-)sinken, fallen: ~ *into a chair*; ~ *dead* tot umfallen; ~ *dead! sl.* geh zum Teufel!; *ready* (*od. fit*) *to* ~ zum Umfallen müde; **13.** *fig.* aufhören, ‚einschlafen': *our correspondence* ~*ped*; **14.** (ver)fallen: ~ *into a habit* in e-e Gewohnheit verfallen; ~ *asleep* einschlafen; **15.** a) (ab)sinken, sich senken, b) sinken, fallen, her'untergehen (*Preise, Thermometer etc.*); **16.** sich senken (*Stimme*); **17.** sich legen (*Wind*); **18.** zufällig *od.* unerwartet kommen: ~ *into the room*, ~ *across s.o.* (*s.th.*) zufällig auf j-n (et.) stoßen; **19.** *zo.* (Junge) werfen, *bsd.* a) lammen, b) kalben, c) fohlen; **III** *v/t.* **20.** (her'ab)tropfen *od.* (-)tröpfeln lassen; **21.** senken, her'ablassen; **22.** fallen lassen: ~ *a book*; **23.** (hin'ein)werfen (*into* in *acc.*); **24.** *Bomben etc.* (ab)werfen; **25.** ♻ den Anker auswerfen; **26.** *e-e Bemerkung* fallen lassen: ~ *a remark*; ~ *me a line!* schreibe mir ein paar Zeilen!; **27.** *ein Thema, e-e Gewohnheit etc.* fallen lassen: ~ *a subject* (*habit etc.*); **28.** *e-e Tätigkeit* aufgeben, aufhören mit: ~ *the correspondence* die Korrespondenz einstellen; ~ *it!* hör auf damit!, lass das!; **29.** *j-n* fallen lassen, nichts mehr zu tun haben wollen mit; **30.** *Am.* a) *j-n* entlassen, b) *sport Spieler* aus der Mannschaft nehmen; **31.** *zo. Junge, bsd. Lämmer* werfen; **32.** *e-e Last, a. Passagiere* absetzen; **33.** F *Geld* a) loswerden, b) verlieren; **34.** *Buchstaben etc.* auslassen: ~ *one's aitches* a) das ‚h' nicht sprechen, b) *fig.* e-e vulgäre Aussprache haben; **35.** a) zu Fall bringen, zu Boden schlagen, b) F *j-n* ‚abknallen'; **36.** ab-, her'unterschießen: ~ *a bird*; **37.** *die Augen od. die Stimme* senken; **38.** *sport e-n Punkt, ein Spiel* abgeben (*to* gegen);

Zssgn mit adv.:

drop ‖ **a·round** *v/i.* F vor'beikommen, (kurz) ‚her'einschauen'; ~ **a·way** *v/i.* **1.** abfallen; **2.** immer weniger werden; (e-r nach dem anderen) weggehen; ~ **back**, ~ **be·hind** *v/i.* **1.** zu'rückbleiben, -fallen; **2.** sich zu'rückfallen lassen; ~ **down** *v/i.* **1.** her'abtröpfeln; **2.** her'unterfallen; ~ **in** *v/i.* **1.** her'einkommen (*a. fig. Aufträge etc.*); **2.** (kurz) her'einschauen (*on* bei), ‚her'einschneien'; ~ **off I** *v/i.* **1.** abfallen (*a. ♻*); **2.** zu'rückgehen (*Umsatz etc.*), nachlassen (*Interesse etc.*); **3.** einschlafen, -nicken; **II** *v/t.* **4.** → *drop* 32; ~ **out** *v/i.* **1.** her'ausfallen (*of* aus); **2.** ‚aussteigen' (*of* aus *der Politik, s-m Beruf etc.*), *a.* die Schule, das Studium abbrechen.

drop ‖ **ball** *s. Fußball*: Schiedsrichterball *m*; ~ **cur·tain** *s. thea.* Vorhang *m*; '~**-down men·u** *s. Computer*: 'Drop-down-Me‚nü *n*; '~**-forge** *v/t.* ⊕ im Gesenk schmieden; ~ **forg·ing** *s.* ⊕ **1.** Gesenkschmieden *n*; **2.** Gesenkschmiedestück *n*; '~**·head** *s.* **1.** ⊕ Versenkvorrichtung *f*; **2.** *mot. Brit. a.* ~ **coupé** Kabrio'lett *n*; ~ **kick** *s. sport* Dropkick *m*.

drop·let ['drɒplɪt] *s.* Tröpfchen *n*.

drop ‖ **let·ter** *s.* **1.** *Am.* postlagernder Brief; **2.** Ortsbrief *m*; '~**·out** *s.* Drop-out *m*: a) ‚Aussteiger' *m* aus der Gesellschaft, b) (Schul-, Studien)Abbrecher *m*, c) *Computer*: Sig'nalausfall *m*, d) *Tonband*: Schadstelle *f*.

drop·per ['drɒpə] *s.* Tropfglas *n*, Tropfenzähler *m*: *eye* ~ Augentropfer *m*; '**drop·pings** [-pɪŋz] *s. pl.* **1.** Mist *m*, tierischer Kot; **2.** (Ab)Fallwolle *f*.

drop ‖ **scene** *s.* **1.** *thea.* (Zwischen)Vorhang *m*; **2.** *fig.* Fi'nale *n*, Schlussszene *f*; ~ **seat** *s.* Klappsitz *m*; ~ **shot** *s. Tennis etc.*: Stoppball *m*; ~ **shut·ter** *s. phot.* Fallverschluss *m*.

drop·si·cal ['drɒpsɪkl] *adj.* □ *🞂* **1.** wassersüchtig; **2.** ödema'tös.

'**drop-stitch** *s.* Fallmasche *f*.

drop·sy ['drɒpsɪ] *s. 🞂* Wassersucht *f*.

dross [drɒs] *s.* **1.** ⊕ Schlacke *f*; **2.** Abfall *m*, Unrat *m*; *fig.* wertloses Zeug.

drought [draʊt] *s.* Dürre *f* (*a. fig. Mangel of* an *dat.*); (Zeit *f* der) Trockenheit *f*; '**drought·y** [-tɪ] *adj.* **1.** trocken, dürr; **2.** regenlos.

drove[1] [drəʊv] *pret. von* **drive**.

drove[2] [drəʊv] *s.* **1.** (Vieh)Herde *f*; **2.** *fig.* Schar *f*: *in* ~*s* in hellen Scharen; '**dro·ver** [-və] *s.* Viehtreiber *m*.

drown [draʊn] **I** *v/i.* **1.** ertrinken; **II** *v/t.* **2.** ertränken, ersäufen: *be* ~*ed* → 1; ~ *one's sorrows* s-e Sorgen (im Alkohol) ertränken; **3.** über'schwemmen (*a. fig.*): ~*ed in tears* tränenüberströmt; **4.** *a.* ~ *out fig.* übertönen.

drowse [draʊz] **I** *v/i.* **1.** dösen: ~ *off* eindösen; **II** *v/t.* **2.** schläfrig machen; **3.** *mst* ~ *away Zeit etc.* verdösen; '**drow·si·ness** [-zɪnɪs] *s.* Schläfrigkeit *f*; '**drow·sy** [-zɪ] *adj.* □ **1.** a) schläfrig, b) verschlafen (*a. fig.*); **2.** einschläfernd.

drub [drʌb] *v/t.* F **1.** (ver)prügeln: ~ *s.th. into s.o.* j-m et. einbläuen; **2.** *sport* ‚über'fahren'; '**drub·bing** [-bɪŋ] *s.* F (Tracht *f*) Prügel *pl.*: *take a* ~ *a. sport* Prügel beziehen, ‚über'fahren werden'.

drudge [drʌdʒ] **I** *s.* **1.** *fig.* F Packesel *m*, Arbeitstier *n*, Kuli *m*; **2.** → *drudgery*; **II** *v/i.* **3.** sich (ab)placken, sich abschinden, schuften; '**drudg·er·y** [-dʒərɪ] *s.* Placke'rei *f*, Schinde'rei *f*; '**drudg·ing** [-dʒɪŋ] *adj.* □ **1.** mühsam; **2.** stumpfsinnig.

drug [drʌg] **I** *s.* **1.** Arz'nei(mittel *n*) *f*, Medika'ment *n*: *be on a* ~ ein Medikament (ständig) nehmen; **2.** Rauschgift *n*, Droge *f* (*a. fig.*): *be on* ~*s*, F *do* ~*s* → 8; *get off the drug* von den Drogen loskommen; *hard* ~*s pl.* harte Drogen *pl.*; *soft* ~*s* weiche Drogen *pl.*; **3.** ~ *on* (*Am. a.* in) *the market* 🞂 schwer verkäufliche Ware, *a.* Ladenhüter *m*; **II** *v/t.* **4.** j-m Medika'mente geben; **5.** *j-n* unter Drogen setzen; **6.** ein Betäubungsmittel beimischen (*dat.*); **7.** *j-n* betäuben (*a. fig.*): ~*ged with sleep* schlaftrunken; **III** *v/i.* **8.** Drogen *od.* Rauschgift nehmen; ~ **a·buse** *s.* **1.** 'Drogen‚missbrauch *m*; **2.** Arz'neimittel‚missbrauch *m*; ~ **ad·dict** *s.* Drogen- *od.* Rauschgiftsüchtige(r *m*) *f*; '~**-ad·dict·ed** *adj.* **1.** drogen- *od.* rauschgiftsüchtig; **2.** *fig.* süchtig; ~ **ad·dic·tion** *s.* **1.** Drogen- *od.* Rauschgiftsucht *f*; **2.** Arz'neimittelsucht *f*; ~ **com·pa·ny** *s.* 'Pharmaunter‚nehmen *n*; ~ **deal·er** *s.* Drogenhändler(in), -dealer *m*; ~ **de·pend·ence** *s.* Drogenabhängigkeit *f*.

drug·gie ['drʌgɪ] *s.* F 'Junkie *m*, Drogenabhängige(r *m*) *f*.

drug·gist ['drʌgɪst] *s. Am.* **1.** Apo'theker *m*; **2.** Inhaber(in) e-s Drugstores.

drug ‖ **ped·dler**, '~**·push·er** *s.* Rauschgifthändler *m*, ‚Pusher' *m*; ~ **scene** *s.* Drogenszene *f*; ~ **squad** *s. bsd. Brit.* 'Rauschgiftdezer‚nat *n*.

drug·ster ['drʌgstə] → *drug addict*.

'**drug·store** *s. Am.* **1.** Apo'theke *f*; **2.** Drugstore *m* (*Drogerie, Kaufladen u.*

Imbissstube).

'**drug** ‖**-‚tak·ing** *s.* Drogenkonsum *m*; ~ **traf·fick·ing** ['træfɪkɪŋ] *s.* Drogenhandel *m*.

Dru·id ['druːɪd] *s.* Dru'ide *m*; '**Dru·id·ess** [-dɪs] *s.* Dru'idin *f*.

drum [drʌm] **I** *s.* **1.** ♪ Trommel *f*: *beat the* ~ die Trommel schlagen *od.* (*a. fig.*) rühren, trommeln; **2.** *pl.* Schlagzeug *n*; **3.** Trommeln *n* (*a. fig. des Regens etc.*); **4.** ⊕ Trommel *f*, Walze *f*, Zy'linder *m*; **5.** ✗ Trommel *f* (*am Maschinengewehr etc.*); **6.** Trommel *f*, trommelförmiger Behälter; **7.** *anat. a.* Mittelohr *n*, b) Trommelfell *n*; **8.** △ Säulentrommel *f*; **II** *v/i.* **9.** *a. weitS.* trommeln (*on* auf *acc.*, *at* an *acc.*); **10.** (rhythmisch) dröhnen; **11.** *fig. Am.* die Trommel rühren (*for* für); **III** *v/t.* **12.** *Rhythmus* trommeln: ~ *s.th. into s.o.* j-m et. einhämmern; **13.** trommeln auf (*acc.*); ~ *out v/t.* j-n ausstoßen (*of* aus); ~ *up v/t.* a) zs.-trommeln, (an)werben, ‚auf die Beine stellen', b) *Am.* sich et. einfallen lassen.

drum ‖ **brake** *s.* Trommelbremse *f*; '~**·fire** *s.* ✗ Trommelfeuer *n* (*a. fig.*); '~**·head** *s.* **1.** ♪, *anat.* Trommelfell *n*; **2.** ~ **court martial** ✗ Standgericht *n*; **3.** ~ **service** ✗ Feldgottesdienst *m*; ~ **ma·jor** *s.* ✗ 'Tambourma‚jor *m*; ~ **ma·jor·ette** *s.* 'Tambourma‚jorin *f*.

drum·mer ['drʌmə] *s.* **1.** ♪ a) Trommler *m*, b) Schlagzeuger *m*; **2.** ✝ *Am.* F Handlungsreisende(r) *m*.

'**drum·stick** *s.* **1.** Trommelstock *m*, -schlägel *m*; **2.** 'Unterschenkel *m* (*von zubereitetem Geflügel*).

drunk [drʌŋk] **I** *adj. mst pred.* **1.** betrunken (*on* von): *get* ~ sich betrinken; ~ *as a lord* (*od. a fish od.* F *a skunk*) total blau, stockbetrunken, F-besoffen; ~ *and incapable* volltrunken; ~ *driving ⚖* Trunkenheit *f* am Steuer; **2.** *fig.* (be)trunken, berauscht (*with* vor, von): ~ *with joy* freudetrunken; **II** *s.* **3.** *sl.* a) Betrunkene(r *m*) *f*, b) Säufer(in); **4.** a) Saufe'rei *f*, Besäufnis *n*, b) ‚Affe' *m*, Rausch *m*; **III** *p.p. von* **drink**; '**drunk·ard** [-kəd] *s.* Säufer *m*, Trunkenbold *m*; '**drunk·en** [-kən] *adj.* □ betrunken; *fig.* → *drunk* 2: *a* ~ *man* ein Betrunkener; *a* ~ *brawl* ein im Rausch angefangener Streit; *a* ~ *party* ein Saufgelage *n*; '**drunk·en·ness** [-kənnɪs] *s.* Betrunkenheit *f*.

drupe [druːp] *s. 🞂* Steinfrucht *f*, -obst *n*.

dry [draɪ] **I** *adj.* □ **1.** trocken: *not yet* ~ *behind the ears* noch nicht trocken hinter den Ohren; ~ *cough* trockener Husten; *run* ~ austrocknen, versiegen; → *dock*[1] 1; **2.** trocken, regenarm, niederschlagsarm: ~ *country*; ~ *summer*; **3.** dürr, ausgedörrt; **4.** ausgetrocknet; **5.** F durstig; **6.** durstig machend: ~ *work*; **7.** trockenstehend (*Kuh*); **8.** F ‚trocken': a) mit Alkoholverbot: *a* ~ *State*, b) ohne Alkohol: *a* ~ *party*, c) weg vom Alkohol: *he is now* ~; **9.** antialko'holisch: ~ *law* Prohibitionsgesetz *n*; *go* ~ das Alkoholverbot einführen; **10.** 'unproduk‚tiv, ‚ausgeschrieben': ~ *writer*; **11.** herb, trocken (*Wein etc.*); **12.** *fig.* trocken, langweilig; nüchtern: ~ *as dust* strohtrocken, sterbenslangweilig; ~ *facts* nüchterne *od.* nackte Tatsachen; **13.** *fig.* trocken: ~ *humo(u)r*; **II** *v/t.* **14.** (ab)trocknen: ~ *one's hands* sich die Hände abtrocknen; **15.** *Obst* dörren; **16.** *a.* ~ *up* austrocknen; trockenlegen; **III** *v/i.* **17.** trocknen, trocken werden; **18.** ~ *up* a) ein-, ver-, austrocknen, b) F versiegen,

D

aufhören, c) F die ‚Klappe' halten: ~ *up!*; **IV** *s.* **19.** Trockenheit *f.*

dry·ad ['draɪəd] *s.* Dry'ade *f.*

dry·as·dust ['draɪəzdʌst] **I** *s.* Stubengelehrte(r) *m*; **II** *adj.* strohtrocken, sterbenslangweilig.

dry|bat·ter·y *s.* ⚡ 'Trockenbatte,rie *f*; ~ **cell** *s.* ⚡ 'Trockenele,ment *n*; ‚~-'**clean** *v/t.* chemisch reinigen; ‚~-'**clean·er('s)** *s.* chemische Reinigung(sanstalt); ‚~-'**clean·ing** *s.* chemische Reinigung; '~-**cure** *v/t.* Fleisch etc. dörren od. einsalzen; ‚~'**dock** *v/t.* ♻ ins Trockendock bringen.

dry·er ['draɪə] → **drier¹**.

'**dry|-farm** *s.* Trockenfarm *f*; ~ **fly** *s.* Angeln: Trockenfliege *f*; ~ **goods** *s. pl.* ✝ *Am.* Tex'tilien *pl.*; ~ **ice** *s.* Trockeneis *n.*

dry·ing ['draɪɪŋ] *adj.* Trocken...

dry·ly → **drily**.

dry meas·ure *s.* Trockenmaß *n.*

dry·ness ['draɪnɪs] *s.* Trockenheit *f*: a) trockener Zustand, b) Dürre *f*, c) Hu'morlosigkeit *f*, d) Langweiligkeit *f.*

'**dry|-nurse** **I** *s.* **1.** Säuglingsschwester *f*; **II** *v/t.* **2.** *Säuglinge* pflegen; **3.** F bemuttern (*a. fig.*); '~-**out farm** *s.* F Entziehungsheim *n*; ~ **rot** *s.* **1.** Trockenfäule *f*; **2.** ♀ Hausschwamm *m*; **3.** *fig.* Verfall *m*; ~ **run** *s.* **1.** ✕ *Am.* Übungsschießen *n* ohne scharfe Muniti'on; **2.** F Probe *f*, Test *m*; '~-**salt** *v/t.* dörren u. einsalzen; ‚~-'**shod** *adv.* trockenen Fußes.

du·al ['djuːəl] **I** *adj.* □ doppelt, Doppel..., Zwei..., ❂ *a.* Zwillings...: ~ **carriageway** *Brit.* Schnellstraße *f*; ~ **display** *EU* → **dual pricing**; ~-**income family** Doppelverdiener *pl.*; ~ **nationality** doppelte Staatsangehörigkeit; ~ **pricing** (*od. price display*) doppelte Preisauszeichnung *f od.* -angabe *f*; ~-**purpose** ❂ Doppel..., Zwei..., Mehrzweck...; **II** *s. ling. a.* ~ **number** 'Dual *m*, Du'alis *m*; '**du·al·ism** [-lɪzəm] *s.* Dua'lismus *m*; **du·al·i·ty** [djuː'ælətɪ] *s.* Duali'tät *f*, Zweiheit *f.*

dub [dʌb] *v/t.* **1.** ~ *s.o. a knight* j-n zum Ritter schlagen; **2.** *fig. humor.* titulieren, nennen: *they ~bed him Fatty*; **3.** ❂ zurichten; **4.** *Leder* einfetten; **5.** a) *Film* synchronisieren, b) (nach)synchronisieren, c) ~ *in* einsynchronisieren.

dub·bin ['dʌbɪn] *s.* Lederfett *n.*

dub·bing ['dʌbɪŋ] *s.* **1.** Ritterschlag *m*; **2.** *Film*: ('Nach)Synchronisati,on *f*; **3.** → **dubbin**.

du·bi·ous ['djuːbjəs] *adj.* □ **1.** zweifelhaft: a) unklar, zweideutig, b) ungewiss, unbestimmt, c) fragwürdig, dubi'os, d) unzuverlässig; **2.** a) im Zweifel (*of, about* über *acc.*), unsicher, b) unschlüssig; '**du·bi·ous·ness** [-nɪs] *s.* **1.** Zweifelhaftigkeit *f*; **2.** Ungewissheit *f*; **3.** Fragwürdigkeit *f.*

du·cal ['djuːkl] *adj.* herzoglich, Herzogs...

duc·at ['dʌkət] *s.* **1.** *hist.* Du'katen *m*; **2.** *pl. obs. sl.* ‚Mo'neten' *pl.*

duch·ess ['dʌtʃɪs] *s.* Herzogin *f*; **duch·y** ['dʌtʃɪ] *s.* Herzogtum *n.*

duck¹ [dʌk] *s.* **1.** *pl.* **ducks**, *coll.* **duck** *orn.* (*engS.* weibliche) Ente: *like a dying* ~ (*in a thunderstorm*) F völlig verdattert; *take to s.th. like a* ~ *takes to water* F sich in et. sofort in s-m Element fühlen; *it ran off him like water off a* ~*'s back* F es ließ ihn völlig kalt; *can a* ~ (*od. fish*) *swim?* F worauf du dich verlassen kannst!, da fragst du noch?; *play ~s and drakes* a) Steine (über das Wasser) hüpfen lassen, b)

(*with*) *fig.* aasen (mit); **2.** Ente *f*, Entenfleisch *n*: *roast* ~ Entenbraten *m*; **3.** F ,(Gold)Schatz' *m*, ,Süße(r' *m*) *f*; **4.** F a) ,Vogel' *m*, b) ,Tante' *f*: *a funny old* ~; **5.** ✕ Am'phibienlastkraftwagen *m*; **6.** *Kricket*: Null *f*, null Punkte *pl.*

duck² [dʌk] **I** *v/i.* **1.** (rasch) 'untertauchen; **2.** (*a. fig.*) sich ducken (*to* vor *dat.*); **3.** *a.* ~ *out* F ,verduften', verschwinden; ~ *out of* → 5 c; **II** *v/t.* **4.** ('unter)tauchen; **5.** a) *den Kopf* ducken *od.* einziehen, b) *e-n Schlag* abducken, ausweichen (*dat.*), c) F sich ,drücken' vor (*dat.*), ausweichen (*dat.*).

duck³ [dʌk] *s.* **1.** Segeltuch *n*; **2.** *pl.* Segeltuchhose *f.*

'**duck|·bill** *s.* **1.** *zo.* Schnabeltier *n*; **2.** ♀ *Brit.* roter Weizen; '~-**billed plat·y·pus** → **duckbill**; '~·**board** *s.* Laufbrett *n.*

duck·ie ['dʌkɪ] → **duck¹** 3.

duck·ing ['dʌkɪŋ] *s.*: *give s.o. a* ~ j-n untertauchen; *get a* ~ völlig durchnässt werden.

duck·ling ['dʌklɪŋ] *s.* Entchen *n.*

duck shot *s.* Entenschrot *m, n.*

duck·y ['dʌkɪ] F **I** *s.* → **duck¹** 3; **II** *adj.* ,goldig', ,süß'.

duct [dʌkt] *s.* **1.** ❂ Röhre *f*, Leitung *f*; (*a.* ⚡ *Kabel- etc.*)Ka'nal *m*; **2.** ♀, *anat., zo.* Gang *m*, Ka'nal *m*; '**duc·tile** [-taɪl] *adj.* **1.** ❂ dehn-, streck-, schmied-, hämmerbar; **2.** biegsam, geschmeidig; **3.** fügsam; **duc·til·i·ty** [dʌk'tɪlətɪ] *s.* Dehnbarkeit *f etc.*; '**duct·less** [-lɪs] *adj.*: ~ *gland anat.* endokrine Drüse, Hormondrüse *f.*

dud [dʌd] F **I** *s.* **1.** ✕ Blindgänger *m* (*a. fig. Person*); **2.** ,Niete' *f*: a) Versager *m*, b) Reinfall *m*; **3.** *pl. a.*) ,Kla'motten' *pl.* (*Kleider*), b) Krempel *m*; **4.** *a.* ~ *cheque* (*Am. check*) ungedeckter Scheck; **II** *adj.* **5.** ,mies', schlecht; **6.** gefälscht: ~ *note* ‚Blüte' *f.*

dude [djuːd] *s. Am.* **1.** F ,Typ' *m*, Kerl *m*; **2.** Dandy *m*, **3.** Stadtmensch *m*, ‚Stadtfrack' *m*: ~ *ranch* Ferienranch *f.*

dudg·eon ['dʌdʒən] *s.*: *in high* ~ sehr aufgebracht.

due [djuː] **I** *adj.* □ → **duly**; **1.** ✝ fällig, so'fort zahlbar: *fall* (*od. become*) ~ fällig werden; *when* ~ bei Verfall *od.* Fälligkeit; ~ *date* Fälligkeitstag *m*; *the balance* ~ *to us from A.* der uns von A. geschuldete Saldo; **2.** *zeitlich* fällig, erwartet: *the train is* ~ *at …* der Zug ist um … fällig *od.* soll um … ankommen; *he is* ~ *to return today* er wird heute zurückgewartet; **3.** gebührend, angemessen, geziemend, gehörig: *it is* ~ *to him* (*to do, to say*) es steht ihm zu (zu tun, zu sagen) (→ *a.* 5); *hono(u)r to whom hono(u)r is* ~ Ehre, wem Ehre gebührt; *with all* ~ *respect to you* bei aller dir schuldigen Achtung; *after* ~ *consideration* nach reiflicher Überlegung; *in* ~ *time* zur rechten *od.* gegebenen Zeit; → *care* 2, *course* 1, *form* 3; **4.** verpflichtet: *be* ~ *to go* gehen müssen *od.* sollen; **5.** ~ *to* zuzuschreiben(d) (*dat.*), verursacht durch: ~ *to an accident* auf einen Unfall *od.* Zufall zurückzuführen; *death was* ~ *to cancer* Krebs war die Todesursache; *it is* ~ *to him* es ist ihm zu verdanken; **6.** ~ *to* (*inkorrekt statt owing to*) wegen (*gen.*), auf Grund *od.* in'folge von (*od. gen.*): ~ *to his poverty*; **7.** *Am.* im Begriff *sein*; **II** *adv.* **8.** genau, gerade: ~ *east* genau nach Osten; **III** *s.* **9.** *das* Gebührende, (An-) Recht *n*, Anspruch *m*: *it is my* ~ es gebührt mir; *to give you your* ~ um dir nicht unrecht zu tun; *give the devil his*

~ *fig.* selbst dem Teufel *od.* s-m Feind Gerechtigkeit widerfahren lassen; *give him his* ~*!* das muss man ihm lassen!; **10.** *pl.* Gebühren *pl.*, Abgaben *pl.*, Beitrag *m.*

du·el ['djuːəl] **I** *s. a. fig.* Du'ell *n*, (Zwei)Kampf *m*: *students'* ~ Mensur *f*; **II** *v/i.* sich duellieren; '**du·el·ist** [-lɪst] *s.* Duel'lant *m.*

du·en·na [djuː'enə] *s.* Anstandsdame *f.*

du·et [djuː'et] *s.* **1.** ♪ Du'ett *n*, Duo *n*: *play a* ~ ein Duo *od.* (*am Klavier*) vierhändig spielen; **2.** *fig.* Duo *n*, Paar *n*, ‚Pärchen' *n.*

duf·fel ['dʌfl] *s.* **1.** Düffel *m* (*Baumwollgewebe*): ~ *coat* Dufflecoat *m*; **2.** *Am.* F Ausrüstung *f*; ~ *bag* Matchbeutel *m.*

duff·er ['dʌfə] *s.* Trottel *m.*

duf·fle → **duffel**.

dug¹ [dʌg] *pret. u. p.p. von* **dig**.

dug² [dʌg] *s.* **1.** Zitze *f*; **2.** Euter *n.*

du·gong ['duːgɒŋ] *s. zo.* Seekuh *f.*

'**dug·out** *s.* **1.** ✕ 'Unterstand *m*; **2.** Einbaum *m.*

duke [djuːk] *s.* Herzog *m*; '**duke·dom** [-dəm] *s.* **1.** Herzogswürde *f*; **2.** Herzogtum *n.*

dul·cet ['dʌlsɪt] *adj.* **1.** wohlklingend, einschmeichelnd: *in* ~ *tone* in süßem Ton; '**dul·ci·fy** [-sɪfaɪ] *v/t.* **1.** versüßen; **2.** *fig.* besänftigen; '**dul·ci·mer** [-sɪmə] *s.* ♪ **1.** Hackbrett *n*; **2.** Zimbal *n.*

dull [dʌl] **I** *adj.* □ **1.** dumm, schwer von Begriff; **2.** langsam, schwerfällig, träge; **3.** teilnahmslos, stumpf; **4.** langweilig, fade: *a* ~ *evening*; ~ *as ditchwater* F stinklangweilig; **5.** schwach (*Licht etc., a. Sehkraft, Gehör*); **6.** matt, trübe (*Farbe, Augen*); dumpf (*Klang, Schmerz*); glanz-, leblos; **7.** stumpf (*Klinge*); **8.** trübe (*Wetter*); blind (*Spiegel*); **9.** ge-, betrübt; **10.** ♻ windstill; ✝ flau, still; *Börse*: lustlos; **II** *v/t.* **11.** *Klinge* stumpf machen; **12.** mattieren, glanzlos machen; trüben; **13.** *fig.* a) abstumpfen; b) dämpfen, schwächen, mildern; *Schmerz* betäuben; **III** *v/i.* **14.** abstumpfen (*a. fig.*); **15.** sich trüben; **16.** abflauen; '**dull·ard** [-ləd] *s.* Dummkopf *m*; '**dull·ish** [-lɪʃ] *adj.* ziemlich dumm *etc.*; '**dul(l)·ness** [-nɪs] *s.* **1.** Dummheit *f*, Dumpfheit *f*; **2.** Langweiligkeit *f*; **3.** Trägheit *f*; **4.** Schwäche *f*; **5.** Mattheit *f*; Trübheit *f*; Stumpfheit *f*; **6.** ✝ Flaute *f.*

du·ly ['djuːlɪ] *adv.* **1.** ordnungsgemäß, vorschriftsmäßig, wie es sich gehört, richtig; **2.** gebührend, gehörig; **3.** rechtzeitig, pünktlich.

dumb [dʌm] *adj.* □ **1.** *allg.* stumm (*a. fig.*): ~ *animals* stumme Geschöpfe; *the* ~ *masses fig.* die stumme Masse; *strike s.o.* ~ j-m die Sprache verschlagen; *struck* ~ *with horror* sprachlos vor Entsetzen; → *deaf* 1; **2.** *bsd. Am.* F doof, blöd; '~-**bell** *s.* **1.** *sport* Hantel *f*; **2.** *Am. sl.* Trottel *m*; '~'**found** *v/t.* verblüffen; '~'**found·ed** *adj.* verblüfft, sprachlos; ~ **show** *s.* **1.** Gebärdenspiel *n*, stummes Spiel; **2.** Panto'mime *f*; **wait·er** *s.* **1.** stummer Diener, Ser'viertisch *m*; **2.** Speisenaufzug *m.*

dum·dum ['dʌmdʌm] *a.* ~ **bul·let** *s.* Dum'dum(geschoss) *n.*

dum·found *etc.* → **dumbfound** *etc.*

dum·my ['dʌmɪ] **I** *s.* **1.** *allg.* At'trappe *f*, ✝ *a.* Schau-, Leerpackung *f*; **2.** Kleider-, Schaufensterpuppe *f*; **3.** Puppe *f*, Fi'gur *f* (*als Zielscheibe od. für Crashtests*); **4.** ✝ *etc.* Strohmann *m*; **5.** (Karten-, *bsd.* Whist)spiel *n* mit) Strohmann *m*; **6.** *Am.* F ,Blödmann' *m*; **7.** *Am.* vierseitige (Verkehrs)Ampel; **8.** *Brit.* (Ba-by)Schnuller *m*; **9.** *typ.* Blindband *m*; **II** *adj.* **10.** Schein...: **~ candidates**; **~ cartridge** ✗ Exerzierpatrone *f*; **~ gun** Gewehr- *od.* Geschützattrappe *f*; **~ warhead** blinder Gefechtskopf.

dump [dʌmp] **I** *v/t.* **1.** ('hin)plumpsen *od.* ('hin)fallen lassen, 'hinwerfen; **2.** abladen, schütten, auskippen: **~ truck** *mot.* Kipper *m*; **3.** ✗ lagern, stapeln; **4.** ✝ zu Dumpingpreisen verkaufen, verschleudern; **5.** a) *et.* wegwerfen, ‚ab-laden', *Auto* loswerden, b) *j-n* abschieben, loswerden; **II** *s.* **6.** Plumps *m*, dumpfer Schlag; **7.** (Schutt-, Müll)Ab-ladeplatz *m*, Müllhalde *f*; **8.** ✗ Halde *f*; **9.** ✗ (*Munitions- etc.*)De'pot *n*, Stapel-platz *m*, (Nachschub)Lager *n*; **10.** *sl.* a) Bruchbude *f* (*Haus*); ‚Dreckloch' *n* (*Haus*, *Wohnung*), b) (elendes) Kaff; '**~-cart** *s.* Kippkarren *m*, -wagen *m*.

dump·er (**truck**) ['dʌmpə] *s. mot.* Kipper *m*.

dump·ing ['dʌmpɪŋ] *s.* **1.** Schuttabladen *n*; **2.** ✝ Dumping *n*, Ausfuhr *f* zu Schleuderpreisen; **~ ground** → *dump* 7; **~ price** *s.* 'Dumping-Preis *m*.

dump·ling ['dʌmplɪŋ] *s.* **1.** Kloß *m*, Knödel *m*; **2.** F ‚Dickerchen' *n* (*Person*).

dumps [dʌmps] *s. pl.*: **be** (**down**) **in the ~** F ‚down' *od.* deprimiert sein.

dump·y ['dʌmpɪ] *adj.* plump, unter'setzt.

dun[1] [dʌn] *v/t.* **1.** *Schuldner* mahnen, drängen: **~ning letter** Zahlungsaufforderung *f*; **2.** bedrängen, belästigen.

dun[2] [dʌn] **I** *adj.* grau-, schwärzlich braun; dunkel (*a. fig.*); **II** *s.* Braune(r) *m* (*Pferd*).

dunce [dʌns] *s.* **1.** Dummkopf *m*; **2.** *ped.* schlechter Schüler.

dun·der·head ['dʌndəhed] *s.* Schwach-kopf *m*; '**dun·der,head·ed** [-dɪd] *adj.* schwachköpfig.

dune [dju:n] *s.* Düne *f*: **~ buggy** *mot.* Strandbuggy *m*.

dung [dʌŋ] **I** *s.* Mist *m*, Dung *m*, Dünger *m*; (Tier)Kot *m*: **~ beetle** Mistkäfer *m*; **~ fork** Mistgabel *f*; **~ heap**, **~ hill** Mist-haufen *m*; **~ hill fowl** Hausgeflügel *n*; **II** *v/t.* düngen.

dun·ga·ree [,dʌŋgə'ri:] *s.* **1.** grober Baumwollstoff; **2.** *pl.* Arbeitsanzug *m*, -hose *f*.

dun·geon ['dʌndʒən] *s.* Burgverlies *n*; Kerker *m*.

dunk [dʌŋk] *v/i. u. v/t.* eintunken; *fig.* (ein)tauchen.

dun·no [də'nəʊ] F *für* (*I*) *don't know*.

du·o ['dju:əʊ] *pl.* **-os** → *duet*.

duo- [dju:əʊ] *in Zssgn* zwei.

du·o·dec·i·mal [,dju:əʊ'desɪml] *adj.* ☌ duodezi'mal; **,du·o'dec·i·mo** [-məʊ] *pl.* **-mos** *s. typ.* **1.** Duo'dezfor,mat *n*; **2.** Duo'dezband *m*.

du·o·de·nal [,dju:əʊ'di:nl] *adj.*: **~ ulcer** ✗ Zwölffingerdarmgeschwür *n*; **,du·o-'de·num** [-nəm] *s. anat.* Zwölf'finger-darm *m*.

du·o·logue ['dju:əlɒg] *s.* **1.** Zwiege-spräch *n*; **2.** Duo'drama *n*.

dupe [dju:p] **I** *s.* **1.** Betrogene(r *m*) *f*, ‚Lackierte(r' *m*) *f*: **be the ~ of s.o.** auf j-n hereinfallen; **2.** Gimpel *m*, Leicht-gläubige(r *m*) *f*; **II** *v/t.* **3.** j-n ‚reinlegen', ‚anschmieren', hinters Licht führen.

du·ple ['dju:pl] *adj.* zweifach: **~ ratio** ☌ doppeltes Verhältnis; **~ time** ♪ Zweier-takt *m*; '**du·plex** [-leks] **I** *adj. mst* ☉ doppelt, Doppel..., *a.* ♫ Duplex...: **~ apartment** → **II** b; **~ burner** Doppel-brenner *m*; **~ house** → **II** a; **~ telegra-phy** Gegensprech-, Duplextelegrafie *f*;

II *s. Am.* a) 'Zweifa,milien-, Doppel-haus *n*, b) Maiso'nette *f*.

du·pli·cate ['dju:plɪkət] **I** *adj.* **1.** dop-pelt, Doppel...: **~ proportion** ☌ dop-peltes Verhältnis; **2.** genau gleich *od.* entsprechend, Duplikat...: **~ key** Nach-schlüssel *m*; **~ part** Ersatzteil *n*; **~ pro-duction** Reihen-, Serienfertigung *f*; **II** *s.* **3.** Dupli'kat *n*, Doppel *n*, Zweit-schrift *f*; **4.** doppelte Ausfertigung: **in ~**; **5.** ✝ a) Se'kundawechsel *m*, b) Pfandschein *m*; **6.** Seitenstück *n*, Ko-'pie *f*; **III** *v/t.* [-keɪt] **7.** verdoppeln, im Dupli'kat herstellen; **8.** ein Dupli'kat anfertigen von; **9.** kopieren, abschrei-ben; **10.** ver'vielfältigen, 'umdrucken; **11.** *fig. et.* 'nachvollziehen; wieder'ho-len; **du·pli·ca·tion** [,dju:plɪ'keɪʃn] *s.* **1.** Verdoppelung *f*, Ver'vielfältigung *f*; 'Umdruck *m*; **2.** Wieder'holung *f*; '**du-pli·ca·tor** [-keɪtə] *s.* Ver'vielfältigungs-appa,rat *m*; **du·plic·i·ty** [dju:'plɪsətɪ] *s.* **1.** Doppelzüngigkeit *f*, Falschheit *f*; **2.** Duplizi'tät *f*.

du·ra·bil·i·ty [,djʊərə'bɪlətɪ] *s.* **1.** Dauer (-haftigkeit) *f*; **2.** Haltbarkeit *f*; **du·ra-ble** ['djʊərəbl] **I** *adj.* ☐ **1.** dauerhaft; **2.** haltbar, ✝ *a.* langlebig: **~ goods** → **II** *s. pl.* ✝ Gebrauchsgüter *pl.*

du·ral·u·min [djʊə'ræljʊmɪn] *s.* Du'ral *n*, 'Duralu,min *n*.

du·ra·tion [djʊə'reɪʃn] *s.* Dauer *f*: **for the ~** a) bis zum Ende, b) F für die Dau-er des Krieges.

dur·ing ['djʊərɪŋ] *prp.* während: **~ the night** während (*od.* in *od.* im Laufe) der Nacht.

durst [dɜːst] *pret. obs. von* **dare**.

dusk [dʌsk] **I** *s.* (Abend)Dämmerung *f*: **at ~** bei Einbruch der Dunkelheit; **II** *adj. poet.* düster; '**dusk·y** [-kɪ] *adj.* ☐ **1.** dunkel (*a. Hautfarbe*); **2.** dunkel-häutig.

dust [dʌst] **I** *s.* **1.** Staub *m*: **bite the ~** *fig.* ins Gras beißen; **raise a ~** a) e-e Staubwolke aufwirbeln, b) *fig.* viel Staub aufwirbeln; **the ~ has settled** *fig.* die Aufregung hat sich gelegt; **shake the ~ off one's feet** *fig.* a) den Staub von seinen Füßen schütteln, b) entrüstet weggehen; **throw ~ in s.o.'s eyes** *fig.* j-m Sand in die Augen streu-en; **in the ~** *fig.* a) im Staube, gedemü-tigt, b) tot; **lick the ~** *fig.* im Staube kriechen; → *dry* 12; **2.** Staub *m*, Asche *f*, sterbliche 'Überreste *pl.*: **turn to ~ and ashes** zu Staub u. Asche werden, zerfallen; **3.** *sl.* Müll *m*, b) Keh-richt *m*; **4.** ♀ Blütenstaub *m*; **5.** (Gold- *etc.*)Staub *m*; **6.** Bestäubungs-mittel *n*, Pulver *n*; **II** *v/t.* **7.** abstauben; **8.** *a.* **~ down** ausbürsten, -klopfen: **~ s.o.'s jacket** F j-n vermöbeln; **9.** be-streuen, (ein)pudern; **10.** *Pulver etc.* stäuben, streuen; '**~·bin** [-st-] *s. Brit.* **1.** Mülleimer *m*; **2.** Mülltonne *f*; **~ liner** Müllbeutel *m*; **~ bowl** *s. Am. geogr.* Trockengebiet *n*; '**~·cart** [-st-] *s. Brit.* Müllwagen *m*; **~ cloth** *s. Am.* Staub-tuch *n*; '**~·coat** [-st-] *s.* Staubmantel *m*; **~ cov·er** *s.* **1.** 'Schutz,umschlag *m* (*um Bücher*); **2.** Schonbezug *m*.

dust·er ['dʌstə] *s.* **1.** Staubtuch *n*, -we-del *m*; **2.** Streudose *f*; **3.** Staubmantel *m*.

dust·ing ['dʌstɪŋ] *s.* **1.** Abstauben *n*; **2.** (Ein)Pudern *n*: **~ powder** Körperpuder *m*; **3.** *sl.* Abreibung *f*, (Tracht *f*) Prügel *pl.*

---

dust **jack·et** → *dust cover* 1; '**~-man** [-tmən] *s.* [*irr.*] *Brit.* Müllmann *m*; '**~-pan** [-st-] *s.* Kehrichtschaufel *f*; '**~-proof** *adj.* staubdicht; **~ trap** *s.* ‚Staubfänger' *m*; '**~-up** *s.* F **1.** ‚Krach' *m*; **2.** (handgreifliche) Ausein'anderset-zung.

dust·y ['dʌstɪ] *adj.* ☐ **1.** staubig; **2.** sand-farben; **3.** *fig.* verstaubt, fade: **not so ~** F gar nicht so übel; **4.** vage, unklar.

Dutch [dʌtʃ] **I** *adj.* **1.** holländisch, nie-derländisch: **talk to s.o. like a ~ uncle** j-m e-e Standpauke halten; **2.** *sl.* deutsch; **II** *adv.* **3.** *go* **~** getrennte Kasse machen; **III** *s.* **4.** *ling.* Hollän-disch *n*, das Holländische: **that's all ~ to me** das sind für mich böhmische Dörfer; **5.** *sl.* Deutsch *n*; **6.** **the ~** *pl.* a) die Holländer *pl.*, b) *sl.* die Deutschen *pl.*: **that beats the ~!** F das ist ja die Höhe!; **7.** **be in ~ with s.o.** F bei j-m ‚unten durch' sein; **8.** **my old ~** *sl.* mei-ne ‚Alte' (*Ehefrau*); **~ cour·age** *s.* F angetrunkener Mut.

'**Dutch·man** [-mən] *s.* [*irr.*] **1.** Hollän-der *m*, Niederländer *m*: **I'm a ~ if** F ich lass mich hängen, wenn; **... or I'm a ~** ... oder ich will Hans heißen; **2.** *Am. sl.* Deutsche(r) *m*; **~ tile** *s.* glasierte Ofen-kachel *f*; **~ treat** *s.* F Essen *n etc.*, bei dem jeder für sich bezahlt; '**~,wom·an** *s.* [*irr.*] Holländerin *f*, Niederländerin *f*.

du·te·ous ['dju:tjəs] → **dutiful**; '**du·ti·a-ble** [-jəbl] *adj.* zoll- *od.* steuerpflichtig; '**du·ti·ful** [-tɪfʊl] *adj.* ☐ **1.** pflichtge-treu; **2.** gehorsam; **3.** pflichtgemäß.

du·ty ['dju:tɪ] *s.* **1.** Pflicht *f*, Schuldigkeit *f* (**to**, **towards** gegen['über]): **do one's ~** s-e Pflicht tun (**by s.o.** an j-m); (**as**) **in ~ bound** a) pflichtgemäß, b) *a.* **~-bound** verpflichtet (*et. zu tun*); **~ call** Pflichtbesuch *m*; **2.** Pflicht *f*, Aufgabe *f*, Amt *n*; **3.** (amtlicher) Dienst: **on ~** Dienst habend *od.* tuend, im Dienst; **be on ~** Dienst haben, im Dienst sein; **be off ~** dienstfrei haben; **~ chemist** dienstbereite Apotheke; **~ doctor** ✚ Bereitschaftsarzt *m*: **~ officer** ✗ Offi-zier *m* vom Dienst; **~ solicitor** ⚖ *Brit.* Offizialverteidiger *m*; **do ~ for** a) j-n vertreten, b) *fig.* dienen *od.* benutzt werden als; **4.** Ehrerbietung *f*; **5.** ☉ a) (Nutz)Leistung *f*, b) Arbeitsweise *f*, c) Funkti'on *f*; **6.** ✝ a) Abgabe *f*, b) Ge-bühr *f*, c) Zoll *m*: **~ on exports** Aus-fuhrzoll; **~-free** zollfrei; **~-free shop** Duty-free- Shop *m*; **~-paid** verzollt; **pay ~ on** *et.* verzollen *od.* versteuern.

du·um·vi·rate [dju:'ʌmvɪrət] *s.* Duumvi-'rat *n*.

du·vet ['du:veɪ] *s. bsd. Brit.* a) Federbett *n*, b) mit syn'thetischem *Material gefülltе* Bettdecke.

dwarf [dwɔ:f] **I** *pl. mst* **dwarv·es** [-vz] *s.* **1.** Zwerg(in) (*a. fig.*); **2.** ♀, *zo.* Zwerg-pflanze *f od.* -tier *n*; **II** *adj.* ☐ **3.** *bsd.* ♀, *zo.* Zwerg...; **III** *v/t.* **4.** verkümmern lassen, in der Entwicklung hindern *od.* hemmen (*beide a. fig.*); **5.** klein er-scheinen lassen: **be ~ed by** verblassen neben (*dat.*); **6.** *fig.* in den Schatten stellen; '**dwarf·ish** [-fɪʃ] *adj.* ☐ zwer-genhaft, winzig.

dwell [dwel] *v/i.* [*irr.*] **1.** wohnen, leben; **2.** *fig.* **~ on** verweilen bei, näher einge-hen auf (*acc.*), Nachdruck legen auf (*acc.*); **3.** **~ on** ♪ *Ton* (aus)halten; **4.** **~ in** begründet sein in (*dat.*); '**dwell·er** [-lə] *s. mst in Zssgn* Bewohner(in);

'**dwell·ing** [-lɪŋ] *s. a.* **~ place** Wohnung *f*, Wohnsitz *m*; Aufenthalt *m*: **~ house** Wohnhaus *n*; **~ unit** Wohneinheit *f*.

dwelt [dwelt] *pret. u. p.p. von* **dwell**.

dwin·dle ['dwɪndl] *v/i.* abnehmen, schwinden, (zs.-)schrumpfen: ~ *away* dahinschwinden.

dye [daɪ] **I** *s.* **1.** Farbstoff *m*, Farbe *f*; **2.** ⊙ Färbeflüssigkeit *f*; **3.** (Haar)Färbemittel *n*; **4.** Färbung *f* (*a. fig.*): *of the deepest* ~ übelster Sorte; **II** *v/t.* **5.** färben: ~*d-in-the-wool* in der Wolle gefärbt, *fig.* waschecht, *Politiker etc.* durch und durch; **III** *v/i.* **6.** sich färben (lassen); '**dye·house** *s.* Färbe'rei *f*.

dy·er ['daɪə] *s.* Färber *m*; ~'**s oak** *s.* ♀ Färbereiche *f*.

'**dye·stuff** *s.* Farbstoff *m*; '~·**works** *s. pl. oft sg. konstr.* Färbe'rei *f*.

dy·ing ['daɪɪŋ] *adj.* **1.** sterbend: *be* ~ im Sterben liegen; ~ *wish* letzter Wunsch; ~ *words* letzte Worte; *to my* ~ *day* bis an mein Lebensende; **2.** *a. fig.* aussterbend: ~ *tradition*; **3.** a) ersterbend (*Stimme*), b) verhallend; **4.** schmachtend (*Blick*).

dyke [daɪk] *s.* **1.** → *dike¹*; **2.** *sl.* ‚Lesbe' *f* (*Lesbierin*).

dy·nam·ic [daɪ'næmɪk] *adj.* (□ ~*ally*) dy'namisch (*a. allg. fig.*); **dy·nam·ics** [-ks] *s. pl. sg. konstr.* **1.** Dy'namik *f:* a) *phys.* Bewegungslehre, b) *fig.* Schwung *m*, Kraft *f*; **2.** *fig.* Triebkraft *f*, treibende Kraft; **dy·na·mism** ['daɪnəmɪzəm] *s.* **1.** *phls.* Dyna'mismus *m*; **2.** dy'namische Kraft, Dy'namik *f*.

dy·na·mite ['daɪnəmaɪt] **I** *s.* **1.** Dyna'mit *n*; **2.** F a) Zündstoff *m*, 'hochbri‚sante Sache, b) gefährliche Per'son *od.* Sache, c) ‚tolle' Person *od.* Sache, *e-e* ‚Wucht'; **II** *v/t.* **3.** (mit Dyna'mit) sprengen; '**dy·na·mit·er** [-tə] *s.* Sprengstoffattentäter *m*.

dy·na·mo ['daɪnəməʊ] *s.* **1.** ⚡ Dy'namo (-ma‚schine *f*) *m*, 'Gleichstrom-, 'Lichtma‚schine *f*; **2.** *fig.* ‚Ener'giebündel' *n*; ~·**e·lec·tric** [‚daɪnəməʊ'lektrɪk] *adj.* (□ ~*ally*) *phys.* e'lektrody‚namisch;

‚**dy·na'mom·e·ter** [-'mɒmɪtə] *s.* ⊙ Dy'namo'meter *n*, Kraftmesser *m*.

dy·nas·tic [dɪ'næstɪk] *adj.* (□ ~*ally*) dy'nastisch; **dy·nas·ty** ['dɪnəstɪ] *s.* Dynastie *f*, Herrscherhaus *n*.

dyne [daɪn] *s. phys.* Dyn *n* (*Krafteinheit*).

dys·en·ter·y ['dɪsntrɪ] *s.* Dysente'rie *f*, Ruhr *f*.

dys·func·tion [dɪs'fʌŋkʃn] *s.* ✚ Funkti'onsstörung *f*.

dys·lex·i·a [dɪs'leksɪə] *s.* ✚ Dysle'xie *f*, Legasthe'nie *f*; **dys'lex·ic I** *s.* Legas-'theniker(in) *f*; **II** *adj.* legas'thenisch: *be* ~ Legas'theniker(in) sein.

dys·pep·si·a [dɪs'pepsɪə] *s.* ✚ Dyspep-'sie *f*, Verdauungsstörung *f*; **dys'pep·tic** [-ptɪk] **I** *adj.* **1.** ✚ dys'peptisch; **2.** *fig.* missgestimmt; **II** *s.* **3.** Dys'peptiker (-in).

dys·tro·phy ['dɪstrəfɪ] *s.* ✚ Dystro'phie *f*, Ernährungsstörung *f*.

E, e [iː] *s.* **1.** E *n*, e *n* (*Buchstabe*); **2.** ♪ E *n*, e *n* (*Note*); **3.** *ped. Am.* Fünf *f*, Mangelhaft *n* (*Note*).

each [iːtʃ] **I** *adj.* jeder, jede, jedes: ~ **man** jeder (Mann); ~ **one** jede(r) Einzelne; ~ **and every one** jeder Einzelne, all u. jeder; **II** *pron.* (ein) jeder, (e-e) jede, (ein) jedes: ~ **of us** jede(r) von uns; ~ **has a car** jede(r) hat ein Auto; ~ **other** einander, sich (gegenseitig); **III** *adv.* je, pro Per'son *od.* Stück: *a penny* ~ je e-n Penny.

ea·ger [ˈiːgə] *adj.* □ **1.** eifrig: ~ **beaver** F Übereifrige(r) *m*, ‚Arbeitspferd' *n*; **2.** (*for*, *after*, *to inf.*) begierig (auf *acc.*, nach, zu *inf.*), erpicht (auf *acc.*); **3.** begierig, gespannt: *an* ~ *look*; **4.** heftig (*Begierde etc.*); **'ea·ger·ness** [-nɪs] *s.* Eifer *m*; Begierde *f*; Ungeduld *f*.

ea·gle [ˈiːgl] *s.* **1.** *orn.* Adler *m*; **2.** *Am.* goldenes Zehn'dollarstück; **3.** *pl.* ✕ Adler *m* (*Rangabzeichen e-s Obersten der US-Armee*); **4.** *Golf:* Eagle *n* (*zwei Schläge unter Par*); **'~-'eyed** *adj.* adleräugig, scharfsichtig; ~ **owl** *s. orn.* Uhu *m*.

ea·glet [ˈiːglɪt] *s. orn.* junger Adler.

ea·gre [ˈeɪgə] *s.* Flutwelle *f*.

ear¹ [ɪə] *s.* **1.** *anat.* Ohr *n*: *up to the* ~*s* F bis über die Ohren; *a word in your* ~ ein Wort im Vertrauen; *be all* ~*s* ganz Ohr sein; *bring s.th. about one's* ~*s* sich et. einbrocken *od.* auf den Hals laden; *not to believe one's* ~*s* s-n Ohren nicht trauen; *his* ~*s were burning* ihm klangen die Ohren; *have one's* ~ *to the ground* F die Ohren offen halten; *set by the* ~*s* gegeneinander aufhetzen; *fall on deaf* ~*s* auf taube Ohren stoßen; *turn a deaf* ~ *to* taub sein gegen; *it came to my* ~*s* es kam mir zu Ohren; **2.** *fig.* Gehör *n*, Ohr *n*: *by* ~ nach dem Gehör; *play by* ~ nach dem Gehör spielen, improvisieren; *play it by* ~ *fig.* (es) von Fall zu Fall entscheiden, es darauf ankommen lassen; *have a good* ~ ein feines Gehör haben; *an* ~ *for music* musikalisches Gehör, *weitS.* Sinn *m* für Musik; **3.** *fig.* Gehör *n*, Aufmerksamkeit *f*: *give* (*od.* *lend*) *one's* ~ *to s.o.* j-m Gehör schenken; *have s.o.'s* ~ j-s Vertrauen genießen; **4.** Henkel *m*; Öse *f*, Öhr *n*.

ear² [ɪə] *s.* (Getreide)Ähre *f*, (Mais-) Kolben *m*.

ear|·ache [ˈɪəreɪk] *s.* ✚ Ohrenschmerzen *pl.*; **'~-ˌcatch·er** *s.* eingängige Melo'die; **'~-drops** *s. pl.* **1.** Ohrgehänge *n*; **2.** ✚ Ohrentropfen *pl.*; **'~-drum** *s. anat.* Trommelfell *n*; **'~-ful** [-fʊl] *s.*: *get an* ~ F ‚et. zu hören bekommen'.

earl [ɜːl] *s.* (brit.) Graf *m*: ⚷ *Marshal* Großzeremonienmeister *m*; **'earl·dom** [-dəm] *s.* **1.** Grafenwürde *f*; **2.** *hist.* Grafschaft *f*.

ear·li·er [ˈɜːlɪə] *comp. von* early; **I** *adv.* früher, ‚vorher'; **II** *adj.* früher, vergangen; **'ear·li·est** [-ɪɪst] *sup. von* early; **I** *adv.* am frühesten, frühestens; **II** *adj.* frühest:

at the ~ frühestens; → *convenience* 1; **'ear·li·ness** [-ɪnɪs] *s.* **1.** Frühe *f*, Frühzeitigkeit *f*; **2.** Frühaufstehen *n*.

'ear·lobe *s.* Ohrläppchen *n*.

ear·ly [ˈɜːlɪ] **I** *adv.* **1.** früh(zeitig): ~ *in the day* früh am Tag; *as* ~ *as May* schon im Mai; ~ *on* a) schon früh(zeitig), b) bald; **2.** bald: *as* ~ *as possible* so bald wie möglich; **3.** am Anfang; **4.** zu früh: *he arrived five minutes* ~; **5.** früher: *he left five minutes* ~; **II** *adj.* **6.** früh(zeitig): *at an* ~ *hour* zu früher Stunde; *in his* ~ *days* in s-r Jugend; *it's* ~ *days yet fig.* es ist noch früh am Tage; ~ *fruit* Frühobst *n*; ~ *history* Frühgeschichte *f*; ~ *riser* Frühaufsteher(in); → *bird* 1; **7.** anfänglich, Früh...: *the* ~ *Christians* die ersten Christen; **8.** vorzeitig, zu früh: *an* ~ *death* you are ~ *today* du bist heute (et.) zu früh (dran); **9.** baldig, schnell: *an* ~ *reply*; ~ *morn·ing tea s.* e-e Tasse Tee(, die morgens ans Bett gebracht wird); ~ *re·tire·ment scheme s.* Vorruhestandsregelung *f*; ~ *warn·ing sys·tem s.* ✕ 'Frühwarnsyˌstem *n*.

'ear|·mark I *s.* **1.** Ohrmarke *f* (*Vieh*); **2.** Kennzeichen *n*, Merkmal *n*; **3.** Eselsohr *n*; **II** *v/t.* **4.** kenn-, bezeichnen; **5.** *Geld etc.* bestimmen, vorsehen, zu'rücklegen (*for* für): ~*ed* zweckgebunden (*Mittel etc.*); **'~-muff** *s.* Ohrenschützer *m*.

earn [ɜːn] *v/t.* **1.** *Geld etc.* verdienen (*a. fig.*): ~*ed income* Arbeitseinkommen *n*; ~*ing capacity* Ertragsfähigkeit *f*, ~*ing power* a) Erwerbsfähigkeit *f*, b) Ertragsfähigkeit *f*; ~*ing value* Ertragswert *m*; *a well-~ed rest* e-e wohlverdiente Ruhepause; **2.** *fig.* (sich) et. verdienen, *Lob etc.* ernten.

ear·nest¹ [ˈɜːnɪst] *s.* **1.** *a.* ~ *money* Handgeld *n*, Anzahlung *f* (*of* auf *acc.*): *in* ~ als Anzahlung; **2.** *fig.* Zeichen *n* (*des guten Willens etc.*); **3.** *fig.* Vorgeschmack *m*.

ear·nest² [ˈɜːnɪst] **I** *adj.* □ **1.** ernst; **2.** ernst-, gewissenhaft; **3.** ernstlich: a) ernst (gemeint), b) dringend, c) ehrlich, aufrichtig; **II** *s.* **4.** Ernst *m*: *in good* ~ in vollem Ernst; *are you in* ~? ist das Ihr Ernst?; *be in* ~ *about s.th.* es ernst meinen mit et.; **'ear·nest·ness** [-nɪs] *s.* Ernst(haftigkeit *f*) *m*.

earn·ings [ˈɜːnɪŋz] *s. pl.* Verdienst *m*: a) Einkommen *n*, Lohn *m*, Gehalt *n*, b) Einnahmen *pl.*, Gewinn *m*, ~*related pension* verdienstbezogene Rente.

'ear|·phone *s.* **1.** a) Ohrhörer *m od.* -muschel *f*, b) Kopfhörer *m*; **2.** a) Haarschnecke *f*, b) *pl.* 'Schneckenfriˌsur *f*; **'~·piece** *s.* **1.** Ohrenklappe *f*; **2.** a) *teleph.* Hörmuschel *f*, b) → *earphone* 1; **3.** (Brillen)Bügel *m*; **'~-ˌpierc·ing** *adj.* ohrenzerreißend; **'~·ring** *s.* Ohrring *m*; **'~-shot** *s.*: *within* (*out of*) ~ in (außer) Hörweite; **'~-ˌsplit·ting** *adj.* ohrenzerreißend.

earth [ɜːθ] **I** *s.* **1.** Erde *f*, Erdball *m*,

Welt *f*: *on* ~ auf Erden, auf der Erde; *why on* ~? F warum in aller Welt?; *cost the* ~ *fig.* ein Vermögen kosten; **2.** *das* (trockene) Land; Erde *f*, (Erd-) Boden *m*: *down to* ~ *fig.* nüchtern, prosaisch, rea'listisch; *come back to* ~ auf den Boden der Wirklichkeit zurückkehren; **3.** ♈ Erde *f*: *rare* ~*s* seltene Erden; **4.** (*Fuchs- etc.*)Bau *m*: *run to* ~ a) *hunt.* Fuchs *etc.* bis in s-n Bau verfolgen (*Hund*, *Frettchen*), b) *fig.* aufstöbern, herausfinden, a. j-n zur Strecke bringen; *gone to* ~ *fig.* untergetaucht; **5.** ⚡ *Brit.* a) Erdung *f*, Erde *f*, Masse *f*, b) Erdschluss *m*; **II** *v/t.* **6.** *mst* ~ *up* ✿ mit Erde bedecken, häufeln; **7.** ⚡ *Brit.* erden; **'~-born** *adj.* staubgeboren, irdisch, sterblich; **'~-bound** *adj.* erdgebunden.

earth·en [ˈɜːθn] *adj.* irden, tönern, Ton...; **'~ware I** *s.* Steingut(geschirr) *n*, Töpferware *f*; **II** *adj.* Steingut..., Ton...

earth·i·ness [ˈɜːθɪnɪs] *fig.* Derbheit *f*, Urigkeit *f*.

earth·ling [ˈɜːθlɪŋ] *s.* a) Erdenbürger (-in), b) *Science Fiction:* Erdbewohner (-in); **'earth·ly** [-lɪ] *adj.* **1.** irdisch, weltlich: ~ *joys*; **2.** F begreiflich: *no* ~ *reason* kein erfindlicher Grund; *of no* ~ *use* völlig unnütz; *you haven't an* ~ (*chance*) du hast nicht die geringste Chance.

earth| moth·er *s. fig.* Urweib *n*; **'~-ˌmov·ing** *adj.* ✿ Erdbewegungs...: ~ *equipment*; **'~-quake** *s.* **1.** Erdbeben *n*; **2.** *fig.* 'Umwälzung *f*, Erschütterung *f*; **'~-ˌshak·ing** *adj. fig.* welterschütternd; ~ **trem·or** *s.* leichtes Erdbeben; **'~-ward(s)** [-wəd(z)] *adv.* erdwärts; ~ **wave** *s.* **1.** Bodenwelle *f*; **2.** Erdbebenwelle *f*; **'~-worm** *s.* Regenwurm *m*.

earth·y [ˈɜːθɪ] *adj.* **1.** erdig, Erd...; **2.** weltlich *od.* materi'ell (gesinnt); **3.** *fig.* a) grob, b) derb, ro'bust, urig (*Person*, *Humor etc.*).

earl| trum·pet *s.* ✚ Hörrohr *n*; **'~-wax** *s.* Ohrenschmalz *n*; **'~-wig** *s. zo.* Ohrwurm *m*; **'~-ˌwit·ness** *s.* Ohrenzeuge *m*.

ease [iːz] **I** *s.* **1.** Bequemlichkeit *f*, Behagen *n*, Wohlgefühl *n*: *at* (*one's*) ~ a) ruhig, entspannt, gelöst, b) behaglich, c) gemächlich, d) ungeniert, ungezwungen, wie zu Hause; *take one's* ~ es sich bequem machen; *be* (*od.* *feel*) *at* ~ sich wohl *od.* wie zu Hause fühlen; **2.** Gemächlichkeit *f*, innere Ruhe, Sorglosigkeit *f*, Entspannung *f*: *ill at* ~ unbehaglich, unruhig; *put* (*od.* *set*) *s.o. at* ~ a) j-n beruhigen, b) j-m die Befangenheit nehmen; **3.** Ungezwungenheit *f*, Na'türlichkeit *f*, Zwanglosigkeit *f*, Freiheit *f*: *live at* ~ in guten Verhältnissen leben; *at* ~! ✕ rührt euch!; **4.** Linderung *f*, Erleichterung *f*; **5.** Spielraum *m*, Weite *f*; **6.** Leichtigkeit *f*: *with* ~ bequem, mühelos; **7.** ✚ a) Nachgeben *n*

E

(*Preise*), b) Flüssigkeit f (*Kapital*); **II** v/t. **8.** erleichtern, beruhigen: **~ one's mind** sich erleichtern *od.* beruhigen; **9.** *Schmerzen* lindern; **10.** lockern, entspannen (*beide a. fig.*); **11.** sacht *od.* vorsichtig bewegen *od.* manövrieren: **one's foot into the shoe** vorsichtig in den Schuh fahren; **12.** *mst* **~ down** die *Fahrt etc.* verlangsamen, vermindern; **III** v/i. **13.** erleichtern; **14.** *mst* **~ off** *od.* **up** a) nachlassen, sich abschwächen (*a.* ♥ *Preise*), b) sich entspannen (*Lage*); c) (*bei der Arbeit*) kürzer treten, d) weniger streng sein (**on** zu).

ea·sel ['iːzl] s. *paint.* Staffe'lei f.

ease·ment ['iːzmənt] s. ♊ Grunddienstbarkeit f.

eas·i·ly ['iːzɪlɪ] adv. **1.** leicht, mühelos, bequem, glatt; **2.** a) sicher, durchaus, b) bei weitem; **'eas·i·ness** [-ɪnɪs] s. **1.** Leichtigkeit f; **2.** Ungezwungenheit f, Zwanglosigkeit f; **3.** Leichtfertigkeit f; **4.** Bequemlichkeit f.

east [iːst] **I** s. **1.** Osten m: (**to the**) **~ of** östlich von; **~ by north** ♣ Ost zu Nord; **2.** *a.* ♀ Osten m: **the** ♀ *a.*) Brit. Ostengland m, b) *Am.* die Oststaaten pl., c) *pol.* der Osten, d) der Orient, e) *hist.* das Oströmische Reich; **3.** *poet.* Ost (-wind) m; **II** adj. **4.** Ost..., östlich; **III** adv. **5.** nach Osten, ostwärts; **6.** **~ of** östlich von (*od. gen.*); **'~·bound** adj. nach Osten fahrend *etc.*; ♀ **End** s. Eastend n (*Stadtteil Londons*); **♀--'End·er** s. Bewohner(in) des **East End**.

East·er ['iːstə] s. Ostern n *od.* pl., Osterfest n: **at ~** an *od.* zu Ostern; **~ Day** Oster(sonn)tag m; **~ egg** Osterei n.

east·er·ly ['iːstəlɪ] **I** adj. östlich, Ost...; **II** adv. von *od.* nach Osten.

east·ern ['iːstən] adj. **1.** östlich, Ost...; **2.** ostwärts, Ost...; ♀ **Church** s. die griechisch-ortho'doxe Kirche; ♀ **Em·pire** s. *hist. das* Oströmische Reich.

east·ern·er ['iːstənə] s. **1.** Bewohner (-in) des Ostens e-s Landes; **2.** ♀ *Am.* Oststaatler(in).

'East·er|·tide, ~ time s. Osterzeit f.

East In·di·a·man s. [*irr.*] *hist.* Ost'indienfahrer m (*Schiff*).

East Side s. *Am.* Ostteil von Manhattan.

east|·ward ['iːstwəd] adj. u. adv. ostwärts, nach Osten, östlich: **~ enlarge·ment** Osterweiterung f (*der Nato etc.*); **'~·wards** [-z] adv. → **eastward**.

eas·y ['iːzɪ] **I** adj. □ → **easily**; **1.** leicht, mühelos: **~ victory**; **~ of access** leicht zugänglich *od.* erreichbar; **2.** leicht, einfach: **an ~ language**; **an ~ task**; **~ money** leicht verdientes Geld (→ 11 c); **3.** *a.* **~ in one's mind** ruhig, unbesorgt (**about** um), unbeschwert, sorglos: **I'm ~** F ich bin mit allem einverstanden; **4.** bequem, leicht, angenehm: **an ~ life**; **live in ~ circumstances**, F **be on ~ street** in guten Verhältnissen leben; **be ~ on the ear** (**eye**) F hübsch anzuhören (anzusehen) sein; **5.** frei von Schmerzen *od.* Beschwerden: **feel eas·ier** sich besser fühlen; **6.** gemächlich, gemütlich: **an ~ walk**; **7.** nachsichtig (**on** mit); **8.** leicht, mäßig, erträglich: **an ~ penalty**; **on ~ terms** zu günstigen Bedingungen; **be ~ on** *et.* schonen *od.* nicht belasten; **9.** a) leichtfertig, b) locker, frei (*Moral etc.*); **10.** ungezwungen, zwanglos, natürlich, frei: **~ manners**; **~ style** leichter *od.* flüssiger Stil; **11.** ♥ a) flau, lustlos (*Markt*), b) wenig gefragt (*Ware*), c) billig (*Geld*); **II** adv. **12.** leicht, bequem: **~ to clean** leicht zu reinigen(d), pflegeleicht; **go ~, take it ~**

a) sich Zeit lassen, langsam tun, b) sich nicht aufregen; **take it ~!** a) immer mit der Ruhe!, b) keine Bange!; **go ~ on** a) j-n *od. et.* sachte anfassen, b) schonend *od.* sparsam umgehen mit; **~!**, F **~ does it!** sachte!, langsam!; **stand ~!** ✗ rührt euch!; **easier said than done** (das ist) leichter gesagt als getan; **~ come, ~ go** wie gewonnen, so zerronnen; **'~-care** adj. pflegeleicht; **~ chair** s. Sessel m; **'~,go·ing** adj. **1.** gelassen; **2.** unbeschwert; **3.** leichtlebig; **~--peas·y** [-'piːzɪ] adj. Brit. F ganz einfach, kinderleicht (*Frage etc.*).

eat [iːt] **I** s. **1.** pl. F ,Fres'salien' pl., ,Futter' n; **II** v/t. [*irr.*] **2.** essen (*Mensch*), fressen (*Tier*): **~ s.o. out of house and home** j-n arm (fr)essen; **~ one's words** alles(, was man gesagt hat,) zurücknehmen; **don't ~ me** F friss mich nur nicht (gleich) auf!; **what's ~ing him?** F was (für e-e Laus) ist ihm über die Leber gelaufen?, was hat er denn?; (*siehe auch die Verbindungen mit anderen Substantiven*); **3.** zerfressen, -nagen, nagen an (*dat.*): **~en by acid** von Säure zerfressen; **4.** fressen, nagen: **~ holes into s.th.**; **5.** → **eat up**; **III** v/i. **6.** essen: **~ well**; **7.** fressen (*Tier*); **8.** fressen, nagen (*a. fig.*): **~ into** a) sich (hin)einfressen in (*acc.*), b) *Reserven etc.* angreifen, ein Loch reißen in (*acc.*): **~ through s.th.** sich durch et. hindurchfressen; **9.** sich essen (lassen): **it ~s like beef**; *Zssgn mit adv.*:

eat| a·way I v/t. **1.** *geol.* a) erodieren, auswaschen, b) abtragen; **II** v/i. **2.** (tüchtig) zugreifen; **3.** **~ at →** 1; **~ out I** v/i. auswärts essen, essen gehen; **II** v/t. **~ one's heart out** Trübsal blasen, schrecklich leiden; **...**, **~ your heart out, ...** a) ..., da kannst du (können Sie) vor Neid platzen, ..., b) ..., da hast du (haben Sie) Pech gehabt, ...; **~ up** v/t. **1.** aufessen (*Mensch*), auffressen (*Tier*) (*beide a. v/i.*); **2.** *Reserven etc.* verschlingen, völlig aufbrauchen; **3.** j-n verzehren (*Gefühl*): **be eaten up with envy** vor Neid platzen; **4.** F a) ,fressen', ,schlucken' (*glauben*), b) j-s Worte verschlingen, c) *et.* mit den Augen verschlingen; **5.** F *Kilometer* ,fressen' (*Auto*).

eat·a·ble ['iːtəbl] **I** adj. ess-, genießbar; **II** s. *mst* pl. Esswaren pl.; **'eat-by date** s. (Mindest)Haltbarkeitsdatum n; **eat·en** ['iːtn] p.p. von **eat**; **eat·er** ['iːtə] s. Esser(in): **be a poor ~** ein schwacher Esser sein, sehr wenig essen.

eat·ing ['iːtɪŋ] **I** s. **1.** Essen n, Speise f; **II** adj. Ess...: **~ apple**; **3.** *fig.* nagend; zehrend; **~ house** s. 'Esslo,kal n.

eau de Co·logne [,əʊdəkə'ləʊn] (*Fr.*) s. Kölnischwasser n.

eaves [iːvz] s. pl. **1.** Dachgesims n, -vorsprung m; **2.** Traufe f; **'~·drop** v/i. (heimlich) lauschen *od.* horchen: **~ on** j-n, ein Gespräch belauschen; **'~,drop·per** s. Horcher(in), Lauscher(in): **~s hear what they deserve** der Lauscher an der Wand hört s-e eigne Schand.

ebb [eb] **I** s. **1.** Ebbe f: **~ and flow** Ebbe u. Flut, *fig. das* Hin u. Her *der Schlacht etc.*, *das* Auf u. Ab *der Wirtschaft etc.*; **2.** *fig.* Ebbe f, Tiefstand m: **at a low ~** *fig.* auf e-m Tiefstand; **II** v/i. **3.** zu'rückgehen (*a. fig.*): **~ and flow** steigen u. fallen, *fig. a.* kommen u. gehen; **4.** *a.* **~ away** *fig.* verebben, abnehmen; **~ tide →** ebb 1 u. 2.

eb·on ['ebən] *poet. für* ebony; **'eb·onite** [-naɪt] s. Ebo'nit n (*Hartkautschuk*);

'eb·on·ize [-naɪz] v/t. schwarz beizen; **'eb·on·y** [-nɪ] **I** s. Ebenholz(baum m) n; **II** adj. a) aus Ebenholz, b) (tief-) schwarz.

e·bul·li·ence [ɪ'bʌljəns], **e·bul·li·en·cy** [-sɪ] s. **1.** Aufwallen n (*a. fig.*); **2.** *fig.* 'Überschäumen n, -schwänglichkeit f; **e·bul·li·ent** [-nt] adj. □ *fig.* sprudelnd, 'überschäumend (**with** von), 'überschwänglich; **eb·ul·li·tion** [,ebə'lɪʃən] → **ebullience**.

e-cash ['iːkæʃ] s. 'E-Cash n, elektronische 'Geldüber,weisung f.

ec·cen·tric [ɪk'sentrɪk] **I** adj. (□ **~ally**) **1.** ⊙, ♏ ex'zentrisch; **2.** *ast.* nicht rund; **3.** *fig.* ex'zentrisch: a) wunderlich, über'spannt, verschroben, b) ausgefallen; **II** s. **4.** Ex'zentriker(in); **5.** ⊙ Ex-'zenter m: **~ wheel** Exzenterscheibe f; **ec·cen·tric·i·ty** [,eksen'trɪsətɪ] s. ⊙, ♏ u. *fig.* Exzentrizi'tät, *fig. a.* Über-'spanntheit f, Verschrobenheit f.

Ec·cle·si·as·tes [ɪ,kliːzɪ'æstiːz] s. *bibl.* Ekklesi'astes m, der Prediger Salomo; **ec,cle·si·as·ti·cal** [-tɪkl] adj. □ kirchlich, geistlich: **~ law** Kirchenrecht n; **ec,cle·si·as·ti·cism** [-tɪsɪzəm] s. Kirchentum n; Kirchlichkeit f.

ech·e·lon ['eʃəlɒn] **I** s. **1.** ✗ a) Staffel (-ung) f, (Angriffs)Welle f: **in ~** staffelförmig, b) ✈ 'Staffelflug m, -formati,on f, c) (Befehls)Ebene f; **2.** *fig.* Rang m, Stufe f: **the upper ~s** die höheren Ränge; **II** v/t. **3.** staffeln, (staffelförmig) gliedern.

e·chi·no·derm [e'kaɪnədɜːm] s. *zo.* Stachelhäuter m.

ech·o ['ekəʊ] **I** pl. **-oes** s. **1.** *a. fig.* Echo n, 'Widerhall m: (**sympathetic**) **~** Anklang m; **find an ~** ein (...) Echo finden, Anklang finden; **to the ~** laut, schallend; **2.** *fig.* Echo n (*Person*); **3.** ♪ Wieder'holung f; **4.** ⚡, *TV:* Echo n, *Radar: a.* Schattenbild n; **5.** (genaue) Nachahmung f; **II** v/i. **6.** 'widerhallen (**with** von); **7.** hallen; **III** v/t. **8.** Ton zu'rückwerfen, 'widerhallen lassen; **9.** *fig.* 'Widerhall erwecken; **10.** *Worte* echoen; (j-m) *et.* nachbeten; **11.** echoen, nachahmen; **~ sound·er** s. ♣ Echolot n; **~ sound·ing** s. ♣ Echolotung f.

é·clair [eɪ'kleə] (*Fr.*) s. E'clair n.

é·clat ['eɪklɑː] (*Fr.*) s. **1.** glänzender Erfolg, allgemeiner Beifall, öffentliches Aufsehen n; **2.** *fig.* Auszeichnung f, Geltung f.

ec·lec·tic [e'klektɪk] **I** adj. (□ **~ally**) ek'lektisch; **II** s. Ek'lektiker m; **ec·lec·ti·cism** [e'klektɪsɪzəm] s. *phls.* Eklekti'zismus m.

e·clipse [ɪ'klɪps] **I** s. **1.** *ast.* Verfinsterung f, Finsternis f: **~ of the moon** Mondfinsternis f; **partial ~** partielle Finsternis; **2.** Verdunkelung f; **3.** *fig.* Schwinden n, Niedergang m: **in ~** im Schwinden, *a.* in der Versenkung verschwunden; **II** v/t. **4.** *ast.* verfinstern; **5.** verdunkeln; **6.** *fig.* in den Schatten stellen, über'ragen.

ec·logue ['eklɒg] s. Ek'loge f, Hirtengedicht n.

eco- [iːkəʊ] *in Zssgn* öko'logisch, Umwelt..., Öko...; **,e·co·ca'tas·tro·phe** s. 'Umweltkata,strophe f; **e·co·cide** ['iːkəʊsaɪd] s. 'Umweltzerstörung f; **'e·co·,friend·ly** adj. 'umweltfreundlich; **'e·co·home** s. Ökohaus n.

ec·o·log·i·cal [,iːkə'lɒdʒɪkl] adj. □ *biol.* öko'logisch, Umwelt...: **~ system →** ecosystem; **,ec·o·log·i·cal·ly** [-kəlɪ] adv.: **~ harmful** (*od.* **noxious**) umweltfeindlich; **~ beneficial** umweltfreund-

lich; e·col·o·gist [iːˈkɒlədʒɪst] *s. biol.* Öko'loge *m;* **e·col·o·gy** [iːˈkɒlədʒɪ] *s. biol.* Ökolo'gie *f.*

e-com·merce [ˈiːˌkɒmɜːs] *s.* ✝ 'E-,Commerce *m,* elekt'ronischer Handel: ~ **business** a) Handel im 'Internet, 'E-,Commerce *m,* b) 'E-,Commerce-Firma *f.*

e·co·no·met·rics [ɪˌkɒnəˈmetrɪks] *s. pl. sg. konstr.* ✝ Ökonome'trie *f.*

e·co·nom·ic [ˌiːkəˈnɒmɪk] **I** *adj.* (□ ~al·ly) **1.** (natio'nal)öko,nomisch, (volks-) wirtschaftlich, Wirtschafts...: ~ **area** Wirtschaftsraum *m;* ~ **divide** Wirtschaftsgefälle *n;* ~ **geography** Wirtschaftsgeographie *f;* ~ **growth** Wirtschaftswachstum *n;* ~ **indicators** Konjunkturindikatoren *pl.;* ~ **migrant** Wirtschaftsflüchtling *m;* ~ **miracle** Wirtschaftswunder *n;* ~ **policy** Wirtschaftspolitik *f;* ~ **recovery** konjunktureller Aufschwung; ~ **refugee** Wirtschaftsflüchtling *m;* ~ **science** → 3; ~ **slowdown** Konjunkturrückgang *m;* ~ **summit** Wirtschaftsgipfel *m;* **2.** wirtschaftlich, ren'tabel; **II** *s. pl. sg. konstr.* **3.** a) Natio'nalökono,mie *f,* Volkswirtschaft(slehre) *f,* b) → **economy** 4; **,e·co·nom·i·cal** [-kl] *adj.* □ wirtschaftlich, sparsam, *Person a.* haushälterisch: **be** ~ **with s.th.** mit et. Haus halten od. sparsam umgehen.

e·con·o·mist [ɪˈkɒnəmɪst] *s.* **1.** *a.* **political** ~ Volkswirt(schaftler) *m,* Natio'nalöko,nom *m;* **2.** sparsamer Wirtschafter, guter Haushälter; **e'con·o·mize** [-maɪz] **I** *v/t.* **1.** sparsam 'umgehen mit, Haus halten mit, sparen; **2.** nutzbar machen; **II** *v/i.* **3.** sparen: a) sparsam wirtschaften, Einsparungen machen: ~ **on** → 1, b) sich einschränken (*in* in *dat.*); **e'con·o·miz·er** [-maɪzə] *s.* **1.** haushälterischer Mensch; **2.** ⊕ Sparanlage *f, bsd.* Wasser-, Luftvorwärmer *m;* **e·con·o·my** [ɪˈkɒnəmɪ] **I** *s.* **1.** Sparsamkeit *f,* Wirtschaftlichkeit *f;* **2.** *fig.* sparsame Anwendung, Sparsamkeit *f* in den (künstlerischen) Mitteln: ~ **of style** knapper Stil; **3.** a) Sparmaßnahme *f,* b) Einsparung *f,* c) Ersparnis *f;* **4.** ✝ 'Wirtschaft(ssy,stem *n od.* -lehre *f) f:* **political** ~ → **economic** 3a; **5.** Sy'stem *n,* Aufbau *m,* Gefüge *n;* **II** *adj.* **6.** Spar...: ~ **bottle;** ~ **class** ✈ Economyklasse *f;* ~ **drive** Sparmaßnahmen *pl.;* **~-priced** preisgünstig, billig, Billig...

'e·co|,pol·i·cy *s.* 'Umweltpoli,tik *f;* **e·co·sphere** [ˈiːkəʊsfɪə(r)] *s.* Ökosphäre *f;* **'~·sys·tem** *s.* 'Ökosy,stem *n;* **'~·type** *s. biol.* Öko'typus *m.*

ec·ru [ˈeɪkruː] *adj.* e'krü, na'turfarben, ungebleicht (*Stoff*).

ec·sta·size [ˈekstəsaɪz] *v/t. (u. v/i.)* in Ek'stase versetzen (geraten).

ec·sta·sy [ˈekstəsɪ] *s.* **1.** Ek'stase *f,* Verzückung *f,* Rausch *m,* (Taumel *m* der) Begeisterung *f:* **go into ecstasies over** in Verzückung geraten über (*acc.*), hingerissen sein von; **2.** Aufregung *f;* **3.** ✡ Ek'stase *f,* krankhafte Erregung; **4.** 'Ecstasy *n* (*Droge*); **ec·stat·ic** [ɪkˈstætɪk] *adj.* (□ ~ally) **1.** ek'statisch, verzückt, begeistert, hingerissen; **2.** entzückend, hinreißend.

ec·to·blast [ˈektəʊblɑːst], **'ec·to·derm** [-dɜːm] *s. biol.* Ekto'derm *n,* äußeres Keimblatt; **'ec·to·plasm** [-plæzəm] *s. biol. u. Spiritismus:* Ekto'plasma *n.*

ec·u·men·i·cal [ˌiːkjuːˈmenɪkl] *adj. bsd. eccl.* öku'menisch: ~ **council** a) *R.C.* ökumenisches Konzil, b) Weltkirchenrat *m.*

ec·ze·ma [ˈeksɪmə] *s.* ✡ Ek'zem *n.*

E-Day [ˈiːdeɪ] *s. pol. Tag des Beitritts Großbritanniens zur EWG.*

ed·dy [ˈedɪ] **I** *s. (Wasser-, Luft)*Wirbel *m,* Strudel *m (a. fig.);* **II** *v/i.* (um'her-)wirbeln.

e·del·weiss [ˈeɪdlvaɪs] *s.* Edelweiß *n.*

e·de·ma [iːˈdiːmə] → **oedema**

E·den [ˈiːdn] *s. bibl.* (der Garten) Eden *n,* das Para'dies *(a. fig.).*

edge [edʒ] **I** *s.* **1.** a) *a.* **cutting** ~ Schneide *f,* b) Schärfe *f (der Klinge):* **the knife has no** ~ das Messer schneidet nicht; **put an** ~ **on s.th.** et. schärfen *od.* schleifen; **take the** ~ **off** a) *Messer etc.* stumpf machen, b) *fig. e-r Sache* die Spitze abbrechen, die Schärfe nehmen; **2.** *fig.* Schärfe *f,* Spitze *f,* Heftigkeit *f:* **give an** ~ **to s.th.** et. verschärfen *od.* in Schwung bringen; **not to put too fine an** ~ **on it** kein Blatt vor den Mund nehmen; **he is** (*od.* **his nerves are**) **on** ~ er ist gereizt *od.* nervös; **3.** Ecke *f,* Zacke *f,* (scharfe) Kante; Grat *m:* ~ **of a chair** Stuhlkante; **set** (**up**) **on** ~ hochkant stellen; → **tooth** 1; **4.** Rand *m,* Saum *m,* Grenze *f:* **the** ~ **of the lake** der Rand *od.* das Ufer des Sees; ~ **of a page** Rand e-r (Buch)Seite; **on the** ~ **of** a) am Rande (*der Verzweiflung etc.*), an der Schwelle (*gen.*), kurz vor (*dat.*), b) im Begriff (**of doing** zu tun); **5.** Schnitt *m (Buch);* → **gilt-edged** 1; **6.** F Vorteil *m:* **have the** ~ **on** (*od.* **over**) *s.o.* e-n Vorteil gegenüber j-m haben, j-m ,voraus' *od.* ,über' sein; **II** *v/t.* **7.** schärfen, schleifen; **8.** um'säumen, um'randen; begrenzen, einfassen; **9.** ⊕ beschneiden, abkanten; **10.** *langsam* schieben, rücken, drängen: ~ **o.s. into s.th.** sich in et. (hinein)drängen; **III** *v/i.* **11.** sich *wohin* schieben *od.* drängen; *Zssgn mit adv.:*

edge| a·way *v/i.* **1.** (langsam) wegrücken; **2.** wegschleichen; ~ **in I** *v/t.* einschieben; **II** *v/i.* sich hin'eindrängen *od.* -schieben; ~ **off** → **edge away;** ~ **on** *v/t.* j-n antreiben; ~ **out** *v/t.* (*v/i.* sich) hin'ausdrängen.

edged [edʒd] *adj.* **1.** schneidend, scharf; **2.** *in Zssgn* ...schneidig; **3.** eingefasst, gesäumt; **4.** *in Zssgn* ...randig; ~ **tool** *s.* **1.** → **edge tool;** **2.** **play with edge**(d) **tools** *fig.* mit dem Feuer spielen.

edge| tool *s.* Schneidewerkzeug *n;* **'~·ways** [-weɪz], **'~·wise** [-waɪz] *adv.* a) seitlich, mit der Kante nach oben *od.* vorn, b) hochkant(ig): **I couldn't get a word in** ~ *fig.* ich bin kaum zu Wort gekommen.

edg·ing [ˈedʒɪŋ] *s.* Rand *m;* Besatz *m,* Einfassung *f,* Borte *f;* **edg·y** [ˈedʒɪ] *adj.* **1.** kantig, scharf; **2.** *fig.* ner'vös, gereizt; **3.** *paint.* scharflinig.

ed·i·bil·i·ty [ˌedɪˈbɪlətɪ] *s.* Ess-, Genießbarkeit *f;* **ed·i·ble** [ˈedɪbl] **I** *adj.* ess-, genießbar: ~ **oil** Speiseöl *n;* **II** *s. pl.* Esswaren *pl.*

e·dict [ˈiːdɪkt] *s.* Erlass *m, hist.* E'dikt *n.*

ed·i·fi·ca·tion [ˌedɪfɪˈkeɪʃn] *s. fig.* Erbauung *f.*

ed·i·fice [ˈedɪfɪs] *s. a. fig.* Gebäude *n,* Bau *m;* **'ed·i·fy** [-faɪ] *v/t. fig.* erbauen, aufrichten; **'ed·i·fy·ing** [-faɪɪŋ] *adj.* □ erbaulich (*a. iro.*).

ed·it [ˈedɪt] *v/t.* **1.** *Texte etc.* a) her'ausgeben, edieren, b) redigieren, druckfertig machen; **2.** *Zeitung* als Her'ausgeber leiten; **3.** *Buch etc.* bearbeiten, zur Veröffentlichung fertig machen; kürzen; *Film, Tonband* schneiden: ~ **out** a) herausstreichen, b) herausschneiden; **~ing table** *TV* Schneidetisch *m;* **4.** *Computer: Daten* edi'tieren; **5.** *fig.* zu-

'rechtstutzen; **e·di·tion** [ɪˈdɪʃn] *s.* **1.** Ausgabe *f:* **pocket** ~ Taschen(buch)ausgabe; **morning** ~ Morgenausgabe (*Zeitung*); **2.** Auflage *f:* **first** ~ erste Auflage, Erstdruck *m,* -ausgabe *f* (*Buch*); **run into 20** ~**s** 20 Auflagen erleben; **3.** *fig. (kleinere etc.)* Ausgabe *f;* **'ed·i·tor** [-tə] *s.* **1.** *a.* ~ **in chief** Herausgeber(in) (*e-s Buchs etc.*); **2.** Zeitung: a) *a.* ~ **in chief** 'Chefredak,teur (-in), b) Redak'teur(in): **the** ~**s** die Redaktion; **3.** *Film, TV:* Cutter(in); **ed·i·to·ri·al** [ˌedɪˈtɔːrɪəl] **I** *adj.* □ **1.** Herausgeber...; **2.** redakti'onell, Redaktions...: ~ **staff** Redaktion *f;* **II** *s.* **3.** 'Leitar,tikel *m;* **ed·i·to·ri·al·ize** [ˌedɪˈtɔːrɪəlaɪz] *v/i.* (e-n) 'Leitar,tikel schreiben; **'ed·i·tor·ship** [-təʃɪp] *s.* Positi'on *f* e-s Her'ausgebers *od.* ('Chef)Redak,teurs; **'ed·i·tress** [-trɪs] *s.* Her'ausgeberin *f etc.* (→ **editor**).

ed·u·cate [ˈedjuːkeɪt] *v/t.* erziehen (*a. weitS.* **to** zu), unter'richten, (aus)bilden: **he was** ~**d at ...** er besuchte die (Hoch)Schule in ...; **'ed·u·cat·ed** [-tɪd] *adj.* **1.** gebildet; **2.** **an** ~ **guess** e-e fundierte Annahme.

ed·u·ca·tion [ˌedjuːˈkeɪʃn] *s.* **1.** Erziehung *f (a. weitS.* **to** zu demokratischem *Denken etc.*), (Aus)Bildung *f;* **2.** (*erworbene*) Bildung, Bildungsstand *m:* **general** ~ Allgemeinbildung *f;* **3.** Bildungs-, Schulwesen *n;* **4.** (Aus)Bildungsgang *m;* **5.** Päda'gogik *f,* Erziehungswissenschaft *f;* **ed·u·ca·tion·al** [-ʃnəl] *adj.* □ **1.** erzieherisch, Erziehungs..., päda'gogisch, Unterrichts...: ~ **film** Lehrfilm *m;* ~ **psychology** Schulpsychologie *f;* ~ **television** Schulfernsehen *n;* ~ **toys** pädagogisch wertvolles Spielzeug; **2.** Bildungs...: ~ **leave** Bildungsurlaub *m;* ~ **level** Bildungsniveau *n;* ~ **misery** Bildungsnotstand *m;* **ed·u·ca·tion·al·ist** [-ʃnəlɪst], *a.* **ed·u·ca·tion·ist** [-ʃnɪst] *s.* Päda'goge *m,* Päda'gogin *f:* a) Erzieher(in), b) Erziehungswissenschaftler(in); **ed·u·ca·tive** [ˈedjuːkətɪv] *adj.* **1.** erzieherisch, Erziehungs...; **2.** bildend, Bildungs...; **'ed·u·ca·tor** [ˈedjuːkeɪtə] → **educationalist.**

e·duce [iːˈdjuːs] *v/t.* **1.** her'ausholen, entwickeln; **2.** *Begriff* ableiten; **3.** ✿ ausziehen, extrahieren.

ed·u·tain·ment [ˌedjuːˈteɪnmənt] *s. TV etc.:* Edu'tainment *n,* bildende Unter'haltung.

Ed·war·di·an [edˈwɔːdjən] *adj.* aus *od.* im Stil der Zeit König Eduards (*bsd.* Eduards VII.).

eel [iːl] *s.* Aal *m;* ~ **buck**, **'~·pot** *s.* Aalreuse *f;* **'~·spear** *s.* Aalgabel *f;* **'~·worm** *s. zo.* Älchen *n,* Fadenwurm *m.*

e'en [iːn] *poet.* → **even**[1], [3]

e'er [eə] *poet.* → **ever.**

ee·rie, **ee·ry** [ˈɪərɪ] *adj.* □ unheimlich, schaurig; **'ee·ri·ness** [-nɪs] *s.* Unheimlichkeit *f.*

eff [ef] *v/i.:* ~ **off** V ,abhauen'; → **effing.**

ef·face [ɪˈfeɪs] *v/t.* **1.** wegwischen, -reiben, löschen; **2.** *bsd. fig.* auslöschen, tilgen; **3.** in den Schatten stellen: ~ **o.s.** sich (bescheiden) zurückhalten, sich im Hintergrund halten; **ef'face·a·ble** [-səbl] *adj.* auslöschbar; **ef'face·ment** [-mənt] *s.* Auslöschung *f,* Tilgung *f,* Streichung *f.*

ef·fect [ɪˈfekt] **I** *s.* **1.** Wirkung *f* (**on** auf *acc.*): **take** ~ wirken (→ 4); **2.** (Ein-)Wirkung *f,* Einfluss *m,* Erfolg *m,* Folge *f:* **of no** ~ nutzlos, vergeblich; **3.** (gesuchte) Wirkung, Eindruck *m,* Ef'fekt *m:* **general** ~ Gesamteindruck *m;* **have an** ~

E

on wirken auf (acc.); *calculated* od. *meant for* ~ auf Effekt berechnet; *special* ~*s* pl. Spezi'alef,fekte pl.; *straining after* ~ Effekthascherei f; 4. Wirklichkeit f; ⅍ (Rechts)Wirksamkeit f, (-)Kraft f, Gültigkeit f: *in* ~ a) tatsächlich, eigentlich, im Wesentlichen, b) ⅍ etc. in Kraft, gültig; *with* ~ *from* mit Wirkung vom; *come into* (od. *take*) ~ wirksam werden, in Kraft treten; *carry into* ~ ausführen, verwirklichen; 5. Inhalt m, Sinn m, Absicht f; *to this* ~ diesbezüglich, in diesem Sinn; *words to this* ~ derartige Worte; 6. ⊚ Leistung f, 'Nutzef,fekt m; 7. pl. ✝ a) Ef'fekten pl., b) Vermögen(swerte pl.) n, Habe f, c) Barbestand m, d) (Bank)Guthaben n: *no* ~*s* ohne Deckung (*Scheck*); II v/t. 8. be-, erwirken, verursachen; 9. ausführen, erledigen, voll'ziehen, tätigen, bewerkstelligen: ~ *an insurance* ✝ e-e Versicherung abschließen; ~ *payment* Zahlung leisten; ef'fec·tive [-tɪv] I adj. □ 1. wirksam, erfolgreich, wirkungsvoll, kräftig: ~ *range* ✕ wirksame Schussweite; 2. eindrucks-, ef'fektvoll; 3. (rechts)wirksam, rechtskräftig, gültig, in Kraft: ~ *from* od. *as of* mit Wirkung vom; ~ *immediately* mit sofortiger Wirkung; ~ *date* Tag m des In-Kraft-Tretens; *become* ~ in Kraft treten; 4. tatsächlich, effek'tiv, wirklich; 5. ✕ dienstfähig, kampffähig, einsatzbereit: ~ *strength* → 7b; 6. ⊚ wirksam, nutzbar, Nutz...: ~ *capacity* od. *output* Nutzleistung f; II s. pl. ✕ a) einsatzfähige Sol'daten pl., b) Iststärke f; ef·'fec·tive·ness [-tɪvnɪs] s. Wirksamkeit f; ef'fec·tu·al [-tʃʊəl] adj. □ 1. wirksam; 2. → *effective* 3; 3. wirklich, tatsächlich; ef'fectu·ate [-tjʊeɪt] → *effect* 8, 9.

ef·fem·i·na·cy [ɪ'femɪnəsɪ] s. 1. Weichlichkeit f, Verweichlichung f; 2. unmännliches Wesen; ef'fem·i·nate [-nət] adj. □ 1. weichlich, verweichlicht; 2. unmännlich, weibisch.

ef·fer·vesce [,efə'ves] v/i. 1. (auf)brausen, moussieren, sprudeln, schäumen; 2. fig. ('über)sprudeln, 'überschäumen; ,ef·fer'ves·cence [-sns] s. 1. (Auf-) brausen n, Moussieren n; 2. fig. ('Über)Sprudeln n, 'Überschäumen n; ,ef·fer'ves·cent [-snt] adj. 1. sprudelnd, schäumend; moussierend: ~ *powder* Brausepulver n; 2. fig. ('über-)sprudelnd, 'überschäumend.

ef·fete [ɪ'fiːt] adj. erschöpft, entkräftet, kraftlos, verbraucht.

ef·fi·ca·cious [,efɪ'keɪʃəs] adj. □ wirksam; ef·fi·ca·cy ['efɪkəsɪ] s. Wirksamkeit f.

ef·fi·cien·cy [ɪ'fɪʃənsɪ] s. allg. Effizi'enz f: a) Tüchtigkeit f, Leistungsfähigkeit f (a. e-s Betriebs etc.), b) Wirksamkeit f, ⊚ (Nutz)Leistung f, Wirkungsgrad m, c) Tauglichkeit f, Brauchbarkeit f, d) ✝, ⊚ Wirtschaftlichkeit f: ~ *engineer*, ~ *expert* ✝ Rationalisierungsfachmann m; ~ *wages* leistungsbezogener Lohn; ~ *apartment* Am. (Einzimmer)Appartement n; ef'fi·cient [-nt] adj. □ 1. allg. effizi'ent: a) tüchtig, (a. ⊚ leistungs)fähig, b) wirksam, c) gründlich, d) zügig, rasch, e) ratio'nell, wirtschaftlich, f) tauglich, gut funktionierend, ⊚ a. leistungsstark; 2. ~ *cause* phls. wirkende Ursache.

ef·fi·gy ['efɪdʒɪ] s. Bild(nis) n: *burn s.o. in* ~ j-n in effigie od. symbolisch verbrennen.

ef·fing ['efɪŋ] adj. V verdammt, Scheiß...

ef·flo·resce [,eflɔː'res] v/i. 1. bsd. fig. aufblühen, sich entfalten; 2. ⚗ ausblühen, -wittern; ,ef·flo'res·cence [-sns] s. 1. bsd. fig. (Auf)Blühen n; 2. Effflores'zenz: a) ⚗ Ausblühen n, Beschlag m, b) ⚕ Ausschlag m; ,ef·flo'res·cent [-snt] adj. 1. bsd. fig. (auf)blühend; 2. ⚗ ausblühend.

ef·flu·ence ['eflʊəns] s. Ausfließen n, -strömen n; Ausfluss m; 'ef·flu·ent [-nt] I adj. 1. ausfließend, -strömend; II s. 2. Ausfluss m; 3. Abwasser n.

ef·flux ['eflʌks] s. 1. Ausfluss m, Ausströmen n; 2. fig. Ablauf m (der Zeit).

ef·fort ['efət] s. 1. Anstrengung f: a) Bemühung f, Versuch m, b) Mühe f: *make an* ~ sich bemühen, sich anstrengen; *make every* ~ sich alle Mühe geben; *put a lot of* ~ *into it* sich gewaltig anstrengen bei der Sache; *spare no* ~ keine Mühe scheuen; *with an* ~ mühsam; F Leistung f: *a good* ~; 'ef·fort·less [-lɪs] adj. mühelos, leicht.

ef·fron·ter·y [ɪ'frʌntərɪ] s. Frechheit f, Unverschämtheit f.

ef·fuse [ɪ'fjuːz] I v/t. 1. ausgießen, ausströmen (lassen); 2. Licht etc. verbreiten; II v/i. 3. ausströmen; III adj. [-s] 4. ⚘ ausgebreitet; ef·fu·sion [ɪ'fjuːʒn] s. 1. Ausströmen n; Ausgießung f; Erguss m (a. fig.): ~ *of blood* ⚔ Bluterguss; 2. phys. Effusi'on f; 3. 'Überschwänglichkeit f, ef'fu·sive [-sɪv] adj. □ 'überschwänglich; ef'fu·sive·ness [-sɪvnɪs] → *effusion* 3.

e·gad [ɪ'gæd] int. obs. F o Gott!

e·gal·i·tar·i·an [ɪ,gælɪ'teərɪən] I s. Verfechter(in) des Egalita'rismus; II adj. egali'tär; e,gal·i'tar·i·an·ism [-nɪzəm] s. Egalita'rismus m.

egg¹ [eg] s. 1. Ei n: *in the* ~ fig. im Anfangsstadium; *a bad* ~ fig. F ein übler Kerl; *as sure as* ~*s is* od. *are* ~*s* sl. todsicher; *have* (od. *put*) *all one's* ~*s in one basket* alles auf 'eine Karte setzen; *lay an* ~ thea. sl. durchfallen; *lay an* ~*! sl. ,leck mich'!; → *grandmother*; 2. biol. Eizelle f; 3. ✕ sl. ,Ei' n, ,Koffer' m (*Bombe etc.*).

egg² [eg] v/t. mst ~ *on* anstacheln.

'egg|,beat·er s. 1. Küche: Schneebesen m; 2. Am. F Hubschrauber m; ~ *coal* s. Nusskohle f; ~ *co·sy*, Am. ~ *co·zy* s. Eierwärmer m; '~·cup s. Eierbecher m; ~ *flip* s. Eierflip m; '~·head s. F ,Eierkopf' m (*Intellektueller*); '~·nog → *egg flip*; '~·plant s. ⚘ Eierfrucht f, Auber'gine f; ~ *roll* s. Frühlingsrolle f; '~·shaped adj. eiförmig; ~ *shell* I s. Eierschale f: ~ *china* Eierschalenporzellan n; II adj. zerbrechlich; ~ *spoon* s. Eierlöffel m; ~ *tim·er* s. Eieruhr f; ~ *whisk* s. Küche: Schneebesen m.

e·go ['egəʊ] pl. -os s. 1. psych. Ich n, Selbst n, Ego n; 2. Selbstgefühl n, -bewusstsein n, a. Stolz m, F Selbstsucht f, Selbstgefälligkeit f: ~ *trip* F ,Egotrip' m (*geistige Selbstbefriedigung, Angeberei etc.*); *that will boost his* ~ das wird ihm Auftrieb geben od. ,gut tun'; *it feeds his* ~ das stärkt sein Selbstbewusstsein; *his* ~ *was low* s-e Moral war auf null; *need one's* ~ *stroked* Streicheleinheiten für sein Ego brauchen.

e·go·cen·tric [,egəʊ'sentrɪk] adj. ego'zentrisch, ichbezogen; e·go·ism ['egəʊɪzəm] s. Ego'ismus m (a. phls.), Selbstsucht f; e·go·ist ['egəʊɪst] s. 1. Ego'ist(in); 2. → *egotist* 1; e·go·is·tic,

e·go·is·ti·cal [,egəʊ'ɪstɪk(l)] adj. □ ego'istisch; e·go·ma·ni·a [,egəʊ'meɪnjə] s. krankhafte Selbstsucht od. -gefälligkeit f; e·go·tism ['egəʊtɪzəm] s. 1. Ego'tismus m: a) 'Selbstüber,hebung f, b) Ichbezogenheit f, c) Geltungsbedürfnis n; 2. → *egoism*; e·go·tist ['egəʊtɪst] s. 1. Ego'tist(in), geltungsbedürftiger od. selbstgefälliger Mensch; 2. → *egoist* 1; e·go·tis·tic, e·go·tis·ti·cal [,egəʊ'tɪstɪk(l)] adj. □ 1. selbstgefällig, ego'tistisch, geltungsbedürftig; 2. → *egoistic*.

e·gre·gious [ɪ'griːdʒəs] adj. □ unerhört, ungeheuer(lich), krass, Erz...

e·gress ['iːgres] s. 1. Ausgang m; 2. Ausgangsrecht n; 3. fig. Ausweg m; 4. ast. Austritt m; e·gres·sion [iː'greʃn] s. Ausgang m, -tritt m.

e·gret ['iːgret] s. 1. orn. Silberreiher m; 2. Reiherfeder f; 3. ⚘ Federkrone f.

E·gyp·tian [ɪ'dʒɪpʃn] I adj. 1. ä'gyptisch: ~ *cotton* Mako f, m, n; II s. 2. Ä'gypter(-in); 3. ling. Ä'gyptisch n.

E·gyp·to·log·i·cal [ɪ,dʒɪptə'lɒdʒɪkl] adj. ägypto'logisch; E·gyp·tol·o·gist [ɪ:dʒɪp'tɒlədʒɪst] s. Ägypto'loge m; E·gyp·tol·o·gy [ɪ:dʒɪp'tɒlədʒɪ] s. Ägyptolo'gie f.

eh [eɪ] int. 1. eh?: a) wie (bitte)?, b) nicht wahr?; 2. ei!, sieh da!

ei·der ['aɪdə] s. orn. a. ~ *duck* Eiderente f; '~·down s. 1. coll. Eiderdaunen pl.; 2. Daunendecke f.

ei·det·ic [aɪ'detɪk] psych. I Ei'detiker(-in); II adj. ei'detisch.

eight [eɪt] I adj. 1. acht: ~*-hour day* Achtstundentag m; II s. 2. Acht f (Zahl, Spielkarte etc.): *have one over the* ~ sl. e-n ,in der Krone' haben; 3. Rudern: Achter m (Boot od. Mannschaft); eight·een [,eɪ'tiːn] I adj. achtzehn; II s. Achtzehn f; eight·eenth [,eɪ'tiːnθ] I adj. achtzehnt; II s. Achtzehntel n; 'eight·fold [eɪt] I adj. u. adv. achtfach; II s. Achtel n (a. ♪); eighth·ly ['eɪtθlɪ] adv. achtens; 'eight·i·eth [-tɪθ] I adj. achtzigst; II s. Achtzigstel n; 'eight·y [-tɪ] I adj. achtzig; II s. Achtzig f: *the eighties* die Achtzigerjahre (eines Jahrhunderts); *he is in his eighties* er ist in den Achtzigern.

Ein·stein·i·an [aɪn'staɪnjən] adj. einsteinsch(er, -e, -es).

ei·ther ['aɪðə] I adj. 1. jeder, jede, jedes (von zweien), beide: *on* ~ *side* auf beiden Seiten; *there is nothing in* ~ *bottle* beide Flaschen sind leer; 2. (irgend)ein (von zweien): ~ *way* auf die e-e od. andere Art; ~ *half of the cake* (irgend-) eine Hälfte des Kuchens; II pron. 3. (irgend)ein (von zweien): ~ *of you can come* (irgend)einer von euch (beiden) kann kommen; *I didn't see* ~ ich sah keinen (von beiden); 4. beides: ~ *is possible*; III cj. 5. ~ ... or entweder ... oder: ~ *be quiet or go!* entweder sei still oder geh!; 6. neg.: ~ ... *or* weder ... noch: *it isn't good* ~ *for parent or child* es ist weder für Eltern noch Kinder gut; IV adv. 7. neg.: nor ... ~ (und) auch nicht, noch: *he could not hear nor speak* ~ er konnte weder hören noch sprechen; *I shall not go* ~ ich werde auch nicht gehen; *she sings, and not badly* ~ sie singt, und gar nicht schlecht; 8. *without* ~ *good or bad intentions* ohne gute oder schlechte Absichten; ,~·'or s. Entweder-Oder n.

e·jac·u·late [ɪ'dʒækjʊleɪt] I v/t. 1. physiol. Samen ausstoßen; 2. Worte ausstoßen; II v/i. 3. physiol. ejakulieren; 4.

fig. aus-, her'vorstoßen; **III** *s.* **5.** *physiol.* Ejaku'lat *n*; **e·jac·u·la·tion** [ɪˌdʒækju-'leɪʃn] *s.* **1.** ✶ Ejakulati'on *f*, Samenerguss *m*; **2.** a) Ausruf *m*, b) Stoßseufzer *m*, -gebet *n*; **e'jac·u·la·to·ry** [-lətərɪ] *adj.* **1.** ✶ Ejakulations...; **2.** hastig (ausgestoßen): ~ *prayer* Stoßgebet *n*.

e·ject [ɪ'dʒekt] **I** *v/t.* **1.** (*from*) *j-n* hinauswerfen (aus), vertreiben (aus, von); entlassen (aus); **2.** ♃ exmittieren, ausweisen (*from* aus); **3.** ⊙ ausstoßen, -werfen; **II** *v/i.* **4.** ⤴ den Schleudersitz betätigen; **e'jec·tion** [-kʃn] *s.* **1.** (*from* aus) Vertreibung *f*, Entfernung *f*; Entlassung *f*; **2.** ⊙ Ausstoßung *f*, Auswerfen *n*: ~ *seat* ⤴ Schleudersitz *m*; **e'ject·ment** [-mənt] *s.* **1.** → *ejection* 1; **2.** ♃ a) Räumungsklage *f*, b) Her'ausgabeklage *f*; **e'jec·tor** [-tə] *s.* **1.** Vertreiber *m*; **2.** ⊙ a)'Auswurfappaˌrat *m*, Strahlpumpe *f*, b) ✗ (Pa'tronenhülsen)Auswerfer *m*: ~ *seat* ⤴ Schleudersitz *m*.

eke [iːk] *v/t.* ~ *out* a) *Flüssigkeit, Vorrat etc.* strecken, b) *Einkommen* aufbessern, c) ~ *out a living* sich (mühsam) durchschlagen.

el [el] *s.* **1.** L *n*, l *n* (*Buchstabe*); **2.** ⛟ F Hochbahn *f*.

e·lab·o·rate I *adj.* [ɪ'læbərət] □ **1.** sorgfältig *od.* kunstvoll ausgeführt *od.* (aus)gearbeitet; **2.** (wohl) durchdacht, (sorgfältig) ausgearbeitet: *an ~ report*; **3.** a) kunstvoll, kompliziert, b) 'umständlich; **II** *v/t.* [-brreɪt] **4.** sorgfältig aus- *od.* her'ausarbeiten, ver'vollkommnen; **5.** *Theorie* entwickeln; **6.** genau darlegen; **III** *v/i.* **7.** ~ (*up*)*on* ausführlich behandeln, sich verbreiten über (*acc.*); **e'lab·o·rate·ness** [-nɪs] *s.* **1.** sorgfältige *od.* kunstvolle Ausführung; **2.** a) Sorgfalt *f*, b) Kompliziertheit *f*, c) ausführliche Behandlung; **e·lab·o·ra·tion** [ɪˌlæbə'reɪʃn] *s.* **1.** → *elaborateness* 1; **2.** (Weiter)Entwicklung *f*.

é·lan [eɪ'lɑ̃ːŋ] (*Fr.*) *s.* E'lan *m*, Schwung *m*.

e·land ['iːlənd] *s.* 'Elenantiˌlope *f*.

e·lapse [ɪ'læps] *v/i.* vergehen, verstreichen (*Zeit*), ablaufen (*Frist*).

e·las·tic [ɪ'læstɪk] **I** *adj.* (□ ~*ally*) **1.** e'lastisch: a) federnd, spannkräftig (*alle a. fig.*), b) dehnbar, biegsam, geschmeidig (*a. fig.*): ~ *conscience* weites Gewissen; *an ~ word* ein dehnbarer Begriff; **2.** *phys.* a) elastisch, b) expansi'onsfähig (*Gas*), c) inkompres'sibel (*Flüssigkeit*): ~ *force* → *elasticity*; **3.** Gummi...: ~ *band*; ~ *stocking* Gummistrumpf *m*; **II** *s.* **4.** Gummiband *n*, -zug *m*; **5.** Gummigewebe *n*, -stoff *m*; **e'las·ti·cat·ed** [-keɪtɪd] *adj.* mit Gummizug; **e·las·tic·i·ty** [ˌelæ'stɪsətɪ] *s.* Elastizi'tät *f*: a) Spannkraft *f* (*a. fig.*), b) Dehnbarkeit *f*, Biegsamkeit *f*, Geschmeidigkeit *f* (*a. fig.*).

e·late [ɪ'leɪt] *v/t.* **1.** mit Hochstimmung erfüllen, begeistern, freudig erregen; **2.** *j-m* Mut machen; **3.** *j-n* stolz machen; **e'lat·ed** [-tɪd] *adj.* □ **1.** in Hochstimmung, freudig erregt (*at* über *acc.*, *with* durch); **2.** stolz; **e'la·tion** [-eɪʃn] *s.* **1.** Hochstimmung *f*, freudige Erregung; **2.** Stolz *m*.

el·bow ['elbəʊ] **I** *s.* **1.** Ell(en)bogen *m*: *at one's ~* a) in Reichweite, bei der Hand, b) *fig.* an s-r Seite; *out at ~s* a) schäbig (*Kleidung*), b) schäbig gekleidet, heruntergekommen (*Person*); *be up to the ~s in work* bis über die Ohren in der Arbeit stecken; *bend od. lift one's ~* F 'einen heben'; **2.** Biegung *f*, Krümmung *f*, Ecke *f*, Knie *n*; **3.** ⊙ Knie *n*; (Rohr)Krümmer *m*, Winkel

(-stück *n*) *m*; **II** *v/t.* **4.** mit dem Ellbogen stoßen, drängen (*a. fig.*): ~ *s.o. out* *j-n* hinausdrängen; ~ *o.s. through* sich durchdrängeln; ~ *one's way* → 5; **III** *v/i.* **5.** sich (mit den Ellbogen) e-n Weg bahnen (*through* durch); ~ *chair. s.* Arm-, Lehnstuhl *m*; ~ *grease* *s. humor.* **1.** ,Arm-, Knochenschmalz' *n* (*Kraft*); **2.** schwere Arbeit; '~·**room** [-rom] *s.* Bewegungsfreiheit *f*, Spielraum *m* (*a. fig.*).

eld [eld] *s. obs.* **1.** (Greisen)Alter *n*; **2.** alte Zeiten *pl.*

eld·er¹ ['eldə] *adj.* **1.** älter: *my ~ brother* mein älterer Bruder; **2.** rangälter: ⚲ *Statesman pol. u. fig.* ,großer alter Mann'; **II** *s.* **3.** (der, die) Ältere: *he is my ~ by two years* er ist zwei Jahre älter als ich; *my ~s* ältere Leute als ich; **4.** Re'spektsperˌson *f*; **5.** *oft pl.* (Kirchen-, Gemeinde- *etc.*)Älteste(r) *m*.

el·der² ['eldə] *s.* Ho'lunder *m*; **'el·der·ˌber·ry** *s.* Ho'lunderbeere *f*.

eld·er·ly ['eldəlɪ] *adj.* ältlich: *an ~ couple* ein älteres Ehepaar; **eld·est** ['eldɪst] *adj.* ältest: *my ~ brother* mein ältester Bruder.

El Do·ra·do [ˌeldə'rɑːdəʊ] *pl.* -dos *s.* (El)Do'rado *n*.

e·lect [ɪ'lekt] **I** *v/t.* **1.** *j-n* in ein Amt wählen: ~ *s.o. to an office*; **2.** *et.* wählen, sich entscheiden für: ~ *to do s.th.* sich (dazu) entschließen *od.* es vorziehen, et. zu tun; *he was ~ed president* er wurde zum Präsidenten gewählt; **3.** *eccl.* auserwählen; **II** *adj.* **4.** (*nachgestellt*) designiert, zukünftig: *bride ~* Zukünftige *f*, Braut *f*; *the president ~ der* designierte Präsident; **5.** erlesen; **6.** *eccl.* (*von Gott*) auserwählt; **III** *s.* **7.** *eccl. u. fig. the ~* die Auserwählten *pl.*; **e'lec·tion** [-kʃn] *s. mst pol.* Wahl *f*: ~ *campaign* Wahlkampf *m*, -feldzug *m*; ~ *pledge* Wahlversprechen *n*; ~ *returns* Wahlergebnisse; **e·lec·tion·eer** [ɪˌlekʃə'nɪə] *v/i. pol.* Wahlkampf betreiben: ~ *for s.o.* für *j-n* Wahlpropaganda machen *od.* Stimmen werben; **e·lec·tion·eer·ing** [ɪˌlekʃə'nɪərɪŋ] *s. pol.* 'Wahlpropaˌganda *f*, -kampf *m*, -feldzug *m*; **e'lec·tive** [-tɪv] **I** *adj.* □ **1.** gewählt, durch Wahl, Wahl...; **2.** wahlberechtigt, wählend; **3.** *ped. Am.* wahlfrei, fakulta'tiv → 4; **II** *s.* **4.** *ped. Am.* Wahlfach *n*; **e'lec·tor** [-tə] *s.* **1.** *pol.* a) Wähler(in), b) *Am.* Wahlmann *m*; **2.** ⚲ *hist.* Kurfürst *m*; **e'lec·tor·al** [-tərəl] *adj.* **1.** Wahl..., Wähler...: ~ *college Am.* Wahlmänner *pl.* (*e-s Staates*); **2.** *hist.* Kurfürsten...; **e'lec·tor·ate** [-tərət] *s.* **1.** *pol.* Wähler (-schaft *f*) *pl.*; **2.** *hist.* a) Kurwürde *f*, b) Kurfürstentum *n*; **e'lec·tress** [-trɪs] *s.* **1.** Wählerin *f*; **2.** ⚲ *hist.* Kurfürstin *f*.

e·lec·tric [ɪ'lektrɪk] *adj.* (□ ~*ally*) **1.** a) e'lektrisch: *cable* (*charge*, *current*, *light etc.*), b) Elektro...: ~ *motor*, c) Elektrizitäts...: ~ *works*, d) eˌlektro-'technisch; **2.** *fig.* a) elektrisierend: *an ~ effect*, b) spannungsgeladen: ~ *atmosphere*; **e'lec·tri·cal** [-kl] → *electric* 1: ~ *engineer* Elektroingenieur *m od.* -techniker *m*; ~ *engineering* Elektrotechnik *f*.

e·lec·tric| arc *s.* Lichtbogen *m*; ~ *art* *s.* Lichtkunst *f*; ~ *blan·ket s.* Heizdecke *f*; ~ *blue s.* Stahlblau *n*; ~ *chair s.* ♃ e'lektrischer Stuhl; ~ *cir·cuit s.* Stromkreis *m*; ~ *eel s. zo.* Zitteraal *m*; ~ *eye s.* **1.** Fotozelle *f*; **2.** magisches Auge; ~ *gui·tar s.* e'lektrische Gi'tarre, 'E-Gi,tarre *f*.

e·lec·tri·cian [ˌɪlek'trɪʃn] *s.* E'lektriker

m, Eˌlektro'techniker *m*.

e·lec·tric·i·ty [ˌɪlek'trɪsətɪ] *s.* Elektrizi'tät *f*; ~ *con·sump·tion s.* Stromverbrauch *m*; ~ *gen·er·a·tion s.* Stromerzeugung *f*.

e·lec·tric| plant *s.* e'lektrische Anlage; ~ *ray s. zo.* Zitterrochen *m*; ~ *shock s.* **1.** e'lektrischer Schlag; **2.** ♃ E'lektroschock *m*; ~ *steel s.* ⊙ E'lektrostahl *m*; ~ *storm s.* Gewittersturm *m*; ~ *torch s.* (e'lektrische) Taschenlampe.

e·lec·tri·fi·ca·tion [ɪˌlektrɪfɪ'keɪʃn] *s.* **1.** Elektrisierung *f* (*a. fig.*); **2.** Elektrifizierung *f*; **e·lec·tri·fy** [ɪ'lektrɪfaɪ] *v/t.* **1.** elektrisieren (*a. fig.*), e'lektrisch laden; **2.** elektrifizieren; **3.** *fig.* anfeuern, erregen, begeistern.

e·lec·tro [ɪ'lektrəʊ] *pl.* -tros *s. typ.* F Gal'vano *n*, Kli'schee *n*.

electro- [ɪlektrəʊ] *in Zssgn* Elektro..., elektro..., e'lektrisch.

e·lec·tro|·a·nal·y·sis [ɪˌlektrəʊ-] *s.* ⚡ Eˌlektroana'lyse *f*; ~·**'car·di·o·gram** ♥ Eˌlektrokardio'gramm *n*, EK'G *n*; ~·**'chem·is·try** *s.* Eˌlektroche'mie *f*.

e·lec·tro·cute [ɪ'lektrəkjuːt] *v/t.* **1.** auf dem e'lektrischen Stuhl hinrichten; **2.** durch elektrischen Strom töten; **e·lec·tro·cu·tion** [ɪˌlektrə'kjuːʃn] *s.* Hinrichtung *f od.* Tod *m* durch elektrischen Strom.

e·lec·trode [ɪ'lektrəʊd] *s.* ⚡ Elek'trode *f*.

e·lec·tro|·dy·nam·ics *s. pl. sg. konstr.* Eˌlektrody'namik *f*; ~·**en·gi'neer·ing** *s.* Eˌlektro'technik *f*; ~·**ki'net·ics** *s. pl. sg. konstr.* Eˌlektroki'netik *f*.

e·lec·trol·y·sis [ˌɪlek'trɒlɪsɪs] *s.* Elektro-'lyse *f*; **e·lec·tro·lyte** [ɪ'lektrəʊlaɪt] *s.* Elektro'lyt *m*.

e·lec·tro|·'mag·net *s.* Eˌlektroma'gnet *m*; ~·**mag'net·ic** (□ ~*ally*) eˌlektroma'gnetisch; ~·**me'chan·ics** *s. pl. sg. konstr.* Eˌlektrome'chanik *f*.

e·lec·trom·e·ter [ˌɪlek'trɒmɪtə] *s.* Eˌlektro'meter *n*.

e·lec·tro|·'mo·tive *adj.* eˌlektromo'torisch; ~·**'mo·tor** *s.* Eˌlektro'motor *m*.

e·lec·tron [ɪ'lektrɒn] *phys.* **I** *s.* Elektron *n*; **II** *adj.* Elektronen...: ~ *microscope*; **e·lec·tron·ic** [ˌɪlek'trɒnɪk] *adj.* (□ ~*ally*) elekt'ronisch, Elektronen...: ~ *banking* Elec'tronic 'Banking *n*; ~ *cash* 'E-cash *n*, e'lektronische 'Geldüber,weisung *f*; ~ *commerce* elekt'ronischer Handel, 'E-ˌCommerce *m*; ~ *flash phot.* Elektronenblitz *m*; ~ *funds transfer* EDV-'Überweisungsverkehr *m*; ~ *mail* elektronische Post; ~ *music* elektronische Musik; **e·lectron·ics** [ˌɪlek'trɒnɪks] *s. pl. sg. konstr.* Elekt'ronik *f* (*a. als Konstruktionsteil*).

e·lec·tro|·plate [ɪ'lektrəʊ-] **I** *v/t.* elektroplattieren, galvanisieren; **II** *s.* elektroplattierte Ware; ~·**scope** [-əskəʊp] *s. phys.* Eˌlektro'skop *n*; ~·**scop·ic** [ˌɪlektrə'skɒpɪk] *adj.* (□ ~*ally*) eˌlektro-'skopisch; ~·**'ther·a·py** [ˌɪlektrəʊ-] *s.* ✶ Eˌlektrothera'pie *f*; ~·**type** **I** *s.* **1.** Gal'vano *n*; **2.** galˌvano'plastischer Druck; **II** *v/t.* **3.** galˌvano'plastisch vervielfältigen.

el·e·gance ['elɪgəns] *s. allg.* Ele'ganz *f*; **'el·e·gant** [-nt] *adj.* □ **1.** ele'gant: a) fein, geschmackvoll, vornehm (*u. schön*), b) gewählt, gepflegt, c) anmutig, d) geschickt, gekonnt; **2.** F erstklassig, ,prima'.

el·e·gi·ac [ˌelɪ'dʒaɪək] **I** *adj.* e'legisch (*a. fig. schwermütig*), Klage...; **II** *s.* elegischer Vers; *pl.* elegisches Gedicht; **el·e·gize** ['elɪdʒaɪz] *v/i.* e-e Ele'gie schrei-

E

ben (**upon** auf *acc.*); **el·e·gy** ['elɪdʒɪ] *s.* Ele'gie *f*, Klagelied *n*.

el·e·ment ['elɪmənt] *s.* **1.** *allg.* Ele'ment *n*: a) *phls.* Urstoff *m*, b) Grundbestandteil *m*, c) 🜂 Grundstoff *m*, d) ⊕ Bauteil *n*, e) Grundlage *f*; **2.** Grundtatsache *f*, wesentlicher Faktor: **an ~ of risk** ein gewisses Risiko; **~ of surprise** Überraschungsmoment *n*; **~ of uncertainty** Unsicherheitsfaktor; **3.** ⚖ Tatbestandsmerkmal *n*; **4.** *pl.* Anfangsgründe *pl.*, Anfänge *pl.*, Grundlage(n *pl.*) *f*; **5.** *pl.* Na'turkräfte *pl.*, Ele'mente *pl.*; **6.** ('Lebens)Ele,ment *n*, gewohnte Um'gebung: **be in** (**out of**) **one's ~** (nicht) in s-m Element sein; **7.** *fig.* Körnchen *n*, Fünkchen *n*, Hauch *m*: **an ~ of truth** ein Körnchen Wahrheit; **8.** a) ✕ Truppenteil *m*, b) ✈ Rotte *f*; **9.** (Bevölkerungs-) Teil *m*, (*kriminelle etc.*) Ele'mente *pl.*; **el·e·men·tal** [,elɪ'mentl] *adj.* **1.** elemen'tar: a) ursprünglich, na'türlich, b) urgewaltig, c) wesentlich; **2.** Elementar..., Ur...

el·e·men·ta·ry [,elɪ'mentərɪ] *adj.* □ **1.** → *elemental* 1 *u.* 2; **2.** elemen'tar, Elementar..., Einführungs..., Anfangs..., grundlegend; **3.** elemen'tar, einfach; **4.** 🜂, ⚛, *phys.* elemen'tar, Elementar...: **~ particle** Elementarteilchen *n*; **5.** rudimen'tär, unentwickelt; **~ ed·u·ca·tion** *s.* **1.** Grundschul-, Volksschulbildung *f*; **2.** Volksschulwesen *n*; **~ school** *s.* Volks-, Grundschule *f*.

el·e·phant ['elɪfənt] *s.* **1.** *zo.* Ele'fant *m*: **~ seal** See-Elefant; **pink ~** F ,weiße Mäuse' *pl.*, Halluzinationen *pl.*; **white ~** *fig.* lästiger *od.* kostspieliger Besitz; **2.** ein Papierformat (711 × 584 mm); **el·e·phan·ti·a·sis** [,elɪfən'taɪəsɪs] *s.* 🜊 Elefan'tiasis *f*; **el·e·phan·tine** [,elɪ'fæntaɪn] *adj.* **1.** ele'fantenartig, Elefanten...; **2.** *fig.* riesenhaft; **3.** plump, schwerfällig.

El·eu·sin·i·an [,eljuː'sɪnɪən] *adj. antiq.* eleu'sinisch.

el·e·vate ['elɪveɪt] *v/t.* **1.** hoch-, em'porheben; aufrichten; erhöhen; **2.** *Blick* erheben; *Stimme* heben; **3.** (**to**) *j-n* erheben (in *den Adelsstand*), befördern (zu *e-m Posten*); **4.** *fig. j-n* (*seelisch*) erheben, erbauen; **5.** erheitern; **6.** *Niveau etc.* heben; **7.** ✕ *Geschützrohr* erhöhen; **'el·e·vat·ed** [-tɪd] **I** *adj.* **1.** erhöht; Hoch...: **~ railway**, *Am.* **~ railroad** Hochbahn *f*; **2.** gehoben (*Position, Stil etc.*), erhaben (*Gedanken*); **3.** a) erheitert, b) F beschwipst; **II** *s.* **4.** *Am.* F Hochbahn *f*; **'el·e·vat·ing** [-tɪŋ] *adj.* **1.** *bsd.* ⊕ hebend, Hebe..., Höhen...; **2.** *fig.* a) erhebend, erbaulich, b) erheiternd; **el·e·va·tion** [,elɪ'veɪʃn] *s.* **1.** Hoch-, Em'porheben *n*; **2.** (Boden)Erhebung *f*, (An)Höhe *f*; **3.** Höhe *f* (*a. ast.*), (Grad *m* der) Erhöhung *f*; **4.** *geogr.* Meereshöhe *f*; **5.** ✕ Richthöhe *f*; **6.** ⊕ Aufstellung *f*, Errichtung *f*; **7.** ⚖ Aufriss *m*: **front ~** Vorderansicht *f*; **8.** a) (**to**) Erhebung *f* (in *den Adelsstand*), Beförderung *f* (zu *e-m Posten etc.*), b) gehobene Positi'on; **9.** *fig.* (*seelische*) Erhebung, Erbauung *f*; **10.** *fig.* Hebung *f* (*des Niveaus etc.*); **11.** *fig.* Erhabenheit *f*, Gehobenheit *f* (*des Stils etc.*); **'el·e·va·tor** [-tə] *s.* **1.** ⊕ a) Hebe-, Förderwerk *n*, b) Hebewerk *n*, c) *Am.* Fahrstuhl *m*, Aufzug *m*; **2.** Getreidesilo *m*; **3.** ✈ Höhensteuer *n*, -ruder *n*; **4.** *anat.* Hebemuskel *m*.

el·ev·en [ɪ'levn] **I** *adj.* **1.** elf; **II** *s.* **2.** Elf *f*; **3.** *sport* Elf *f*; **e,lev·en-'plus** *s. ped. Brit. hist.* im Alter von 11–12 Jahren abgelegte Prüfung, die über die schulische Weiterbildung entschied; **e'lev·en-**

ses [-zɪz] *s. pl. Brit.* F zweites Frühstück; **e'lev·enth** [-nθ] **I** *adj.* □ **1.** elft; → *hour* 2; **II** *s.* **2.** (*der, die, das*) Elfte; **3.** Elftel *n*.

elf [elf] *pl.* **elves** [elvz] *s.* **1.** Elf *m*, Elfe *f*; **2.** Kobold *m*; **3.** *fig.* a) Knirps *m*, b) (kleiner) Racker; **elf·in** ['elfɪn] **I** *adj.* Elfen..., Zwergen...; **II** *s.* → *elf*; **elf·ish** ['elfɪʃ] *adj.* **1.** elfenartig; **2.** schelmisch, koboldhaft.

'elf-lock *s.* Weichselzopf *m*, verfilztes Haar.

e·lic·it [ɪ'lɪsɪt] *v/t.* **1.** (*from j-m, e-m Instrument etc.*) et. entlocken; **2.** (*from aus j-m*) *e-e Aussage etc.* her'auslocken, -holen; **3.** *e-e Reaktion* auslösen, her'vorrufen; **4.** *et.* ans Licht bringen.

e·lide [ɪ'laɪd] *v/t. ling. Vokal od. Silbe* elidieren, auslassen.

e·li·gi·bil·i·ty [,elɪdʒə'bɪlətɪ] *s.* **1.** Eignung *f*, Befähigung *f*: **his eligibilities** s-e Vorzüge; **2.** Berechtigung *f*; **3.** Wählbarkeit *f*; **4.** Teilnahmeberechtigung *f*, *sport a.* Startberechtigung *f*; **el·i·gi·ble** ['elɪdʒəbl] **I** *adj.* □ **1.** (**for**) infrage kommend (für): a) geeignet, akzep'tabel (für), b) berechtigt, befähigt (zu), qualifiziert (für): **~ for a pension** pensionsberechtigt, c) wählbar; **2.** wünschenswert, vorteilhaft; **3.** teilnahmeberechtigt, *sport a.* startberechtigt; **II** *s.* **4.** F infrage kommende Per'son *od.* Sache.

e·lim·i·nate [ɪ'lɪmɪneɪt] *v/t.* **1.** beseitigen, entfernen, ausmerzen, *a.* ⚕ eliminieren (**from** aus); **2.** ausscheiden (*a.* 🜂, *physiol.*), ausschließen, *a. Gegner* ausschalten: **be ~d** *sport* ausscheiden; **3.** *fig. et.* ausklammern, ignorieren; **e·lim·i·na·tion** [ɪ,lɪmɪ'neɪʃn] *s.* **1.** Beseitigung *f*, Entfernung *f*, Ausmerzung *f*, Eliminierung *f*, *a.* ⚕ Eliminati'on *f*; **3.** 🜂, *physiol., a. sport* Ausscheidung *f*: **~ contest** Ausscheidungs-, Qualifikationswettbewerb *m*; **4.** Ausschaltung *f* (*e-s Gegners*); **5.** *fig.* Ignorierung *f*; **e·'lim·i·na·tor** [-tə] *s. Radio:* Sieb-, Sperrkreis *m*.

e·li·sion [ɪ'lɪʒn] *s. ling.* Elisi'on *f*, Auslassung *f* (*e-s Vokals od. e-r Silbe*).

e·lite [eɪ'liːt] (*Fr.*) *s.* E'lite *f*: a) Auslese *f*, (*das*) Beste, (*die*) Besten *pl.*, b) Führungs-, Oberschicht *f*, c) ✕ E'lite-, Kerntruppe *f*; **e'lit·ism** [-tɪzəm] *s.* eli'täres Denken; **e'lit·ist** [-tɪst] *adj.* eli'tär.

e·lix·ir [ɪ'lɪksə] *s.* **1.** Eli'xier *n*, Zauber-, Heiltrank *m*: **~ of life** Lebenselixier; **2.** All'heilmittel *n*.

E·liz·a·be·than [ɪ,lɪzə'biːθn] **I** *adj.* elisabe'thanisch; **II** *s.* Zeitgenosse *m* E'lisabeths I. von England.

elk [elk] *s. zo.* **1.** Elch *m*, Elen *m, n*; **2.** *Am.* Elk *m*, Wa'piti *m*.

ell [el] *s.* Elle *f*; → *inch* 2.

el·lipse ['lɪps] *s.* **1.** ⚕ El'lipse *f*; **2.** → **el'lip·sis** [-sɪs] *pl.* **-ses** [-siːz] *s. ling.* El'lipse *f*, Auslassung *f* (*a. typ.*); **el·'lip·soid** [-sɔɪd] *s.* ⚕ Ellipso'id *n*; **el·'lip·tic, el·'lip·ti·cal** [-ptɪk(l)] *adj.* □ **1.** ⚕ el'liptisch; **2.** *ling.* elliptisch, unvollständig (*Satz*).

elm [elm] *s.* Ulme *f*, Rüster *f*.

el·o·cu·tion [,elə'kjuːʃn] *s.* **1.** Vortrag(sweise *f*) *m*, Dikti'on *f*; **2.** Vortragskunst *f*; **3.** Sprechtechnik *f*; **el·o·'cu·tion·ist** [-nɪst] *s.* **1.** Vortragskünstler(in); **2.** Sprecherzieher(in).

e·lon·gate [ɪ'lɒŋɡeɪt] **I** *v/t.* **1.** verlängern; *bsd.* ⊕ strecken, dehnen; **II** *v/i.* **2.** sich verlängern; **3.** ♀ spitz zulaufen; **III** *adj.* **4.** → **'e·lon·gat·ed** [-tɪd] *adj.* **1.** verlängert; **~ charge** ✕ gestreckte La-

dung; **2.** lang u. dünn; **e·lon·ga·tion** [,iːlɒŋ'ɡeɪʃn] *s.* **1.** Verlängerung *f*; **2.** ⊕ Streckung *f*, Dehnung *f*; **2.** *ast., phys.* Elongati'on *f*.

e·lope [ɪ'ləʊp] *v/i.* (mit e-m *od.* e-r Geliebten) ,durchbrennen': **~ with** *a.* die *Geliebte* entführen; **e'lope·ment** [-mənt] *s.* ,'Durchbrennen' *n*; Flucht *f*; Entführung *f*; **e'lop·er** [-pə] *s.* Ausreißer(in).

el·o·quence ['eləkwəns] *s.* Beredsamkeit *f*, Redegewandtheit *f*, -kunst *f*; **'el·o·quent** [-nt] *adj.* □ **1.** beredt, redegewandt; **2.** *fig.* a) sprechend, ausdrucksvoll, b) beredt, viel sagend (*Blick etc.*).

else [els] *adv.* **1.** (*neg. u. interrog.*) sonst, weiter, außerdem: **anything ~?** sonst noch etwas?; **what ~ can we do?**; was können wir sonst (noch) tun?; **no one ~** sonst *od.* weiter niemand; **where ~?** wo anders?, wo sonst (noch)?; **2.** anderer, andere, anderes: **that's something ~** das ist et. anderes; **everybody ~** alle anderen *od.* Übrigen; **somebody ~'s dog** der Hund e-s anderen; **3.** *oft* **or ~** oder, sonst, wenn nicht: **hurry, (or) ~ you will be late** beeile dich, oder du kommst zu spät *od.* sonst kommst du zu spät; **or ~!** (*drohend*) sonst passiert was!; **,~'where** *adv.* **1.** sonst wo, anderswo; **2.** 'anderswo'hin.

e·lu·ci·date [ɪ'luːsɪdeɪt] *v/t. Geheimnis etc.* aufhellen, aufklären; *Text, Gründe etc.* erklären; **e·lu·ci·da·tion** [ɪ,luːsɪ'deɪʃn] *s.* Erklärung *f*; Aufhellung *f*, -klärung *f*; **e'lu·ci·da·to·ry** [-tərɪ] *adj.* erklärend, aufhellend.

e·lude [ɪ'luːd] *v/t.* **1.** (geschickt) ausweichen, entgehen, sich entziehen (*dat.*): *Gesetz etc.* um'gehen; **2.** *fig. j-m* entgehen, *j-s* Aufmerksamkeit entgehen; **3.** sich nicht (er)fassen lassen von, sich entziehen (*dat.*): **it ~s definition** es lässt sich nicht definieren; **4.** *j-m* nicht einfallen; **e'lu·sion** [-uːʒn] *s.* **1.** (*of*) Ausweichen *n*, Entkommen *n* (vor *dat.*); Um'gehung *f* (*gen.*); **2.** Ausflucht *f*, List *f*; **e'lu·sive** [-uːsɪv] *adj.* □ **1.** ausweichend (*of dat.*, vor *dat.*); **2.** schwer zu fassen(d) (*Dieb etc.*); **3.** schwer fassbar, schwer zu definieren(d) *od.* zu übersetzen(d); **4.** um'gehend; **5.** unzuverlässig; **e'lu·sive·ness** [-uːsɪvnɪs] *s.* **1.** Ausweichen *n* (*of* vor *dat.*), ausweichendes Verhalten; **2.** Unbestimmbarkeit *f*, Undefinierbarkeit *f*; **e'lu·so·ry** [-uːsərɪ] *adj.* **1.** trügerisch; **2.** → *elusive*.

e·lu·tri·ate [ɪ'luːtrɪeɪt] *v/t.* 🜂 (aus-) schlämmen.

el·ver ['elvə] *s. ichth.* junger Aal.

elves [elvz] *pl. von* **elf**; **'elv·ish** [-vɪʃ] → **elfish**.

E·ly·sian [ɪ'lɪzɪən] *adj.* e'lysisch, *fig. a.* para'diesisch; **E'ly·si·um** [-əm] *s.* E'lysium *n*, *fig. a.* Para'dies *n*.

em [em] *s.* **1.** M *n*, m *n* (*Buchstabe*); **2.** *typ.* Geviert *n*.

'em [əm] F *für* **them**: **let 'em**.

e·ma·ci·ate [ɪ'meɪʃɪeɪt] *v/t.* **1.** auszehren, ausmergeln; **2.** *Boden* auslaugen; **e'ma·ci·at·ed** [-tɪd] *adj.* **1.** abgemagert, ausgezehrt, ausgemergelt; **2.** ausgelaugt (*Boden*); **e·ma·ci·a·tion** [ɪ,meɪsɪ'eɪʃn] *s.* **1.** Auszehrung *f*, Abmagerung *f*; **2.** Auslaugung *f*.

e-mail ['iːmeɪl] **I** *s.* E-Mail *f*; **II** *v/t* per *od.* als E-Mail schicken.

em·a·nate ['eməneɪt] *v/i.* **1.** ausströmen (*Gas etc.*), ausstrahlen (*Licht*) (**from** von); **2.** *fig.* herrühren, ausgehen (**from** von); **em·a·na·tion** [,emə'neɪʃn] *s.* **1.** Ausströmen *n*; **2.** Ausströmung *f*,

Ausstrahlung *f* (*a. fig.*); **3.** Auswirkung *f*; **4.** *phls., psych., eccl.* Emanati'on *f*.

e·man·ci·pate [ɪ'mænsɪpeɪt] *v/t.* **1.** (*o.s.* sich) emanzipieren, unabhängig machen, befreien (*from* von); **2.** *Sklaven* freilassen; **e'man·ci·pat·ed** [-tɪd] *adj.* **1.** *allg.* emanzipiert: *an ~ woman*; *an ~ citizen* ein mündiger Bürger; **2.** freigelassen (*Sklave*); **e·man·ci·pa·tion** [ɪ,mænsɪ'peɪʃn] *s.* **1.** Emanzipati'on *f*; **2.** Freilassung *f*, Befreiung *f* (*a. fig.*) (*from* von); **e·man·ci·pa·tion·ist** [ɪ,mænsɪ'peɪʃnɪst] *s.* Befürworter(in) der Emanzipati'on *od.* der Sklavenbefreiung; **e'man·ci·pa·to·ry** [-pətərɪ] *adj.* emanzipa'torisch.

e·mas·cu·late I *v/t.* [ɪ'mæskjʊleɪt] **1.** entmannen, kastrieren; **2.** *fig.* verweichlichen; **3.** entkräften, (ab)schwächen; verwässern; **4.** *Sprache* farb- *od.* kraftlos machen; II *adj.* [-lɪt] **5.** entmannt; **6.** verweichlicht; **7.** verwässert, kraftlos; **e·mas·cu·la·tion** [ɪ,mæskjʊ-'leɪʃn] *s.* **1.** Entmannung *f*; **2.** Verweichlichung *f*; **3.** Schwächung *f*; **4.** *fig.* Verwässerung *f* (*Text etc.*).

em·balm [ɪm'bɑːm] *v/t.* **1.** einbalsamieren; **2.** *fig. j-s Andenken* bewahren *od.* pflegen: *be ~ed in* fortleben in (*dat.*); **em'balm·ment** [-mənt] *s.* Einbalsamierung *f*.

em·bank [ɪm'bæŋk] *v/t.* eindämmen, -deichen; **em'bank·ment** [-mənt] *s.* **1.** Eindämmung *f*, -deichung *f*; **2.** (Erd-) Damm *m*; **3.** (Bahn-, Straßen)Damm *m*; **4.** gemauerte Uferstraße.

em·bar·go [em'bɑːgəʊ] I *s.* **1.** ♻ Em'bargo *n*: a) (Schiffs)Beschlagnahme *f* (*durch den Staat*), b) Hafensperre *f*; **2.** ♉ a) Handelssperre *f*, b) *a. allg.* Sperre *f*, Verbot *n*: ~ *on imports* Einfuhrsperre; II *v/t.* **3.** *Handel, Hafen* sperren, ein Em'bargo verhängen über (*acc.*); **4.** beschlagnahmen.

em·bark [ɪm'bɑːk] I *v/t.* **1.** ♻, ✈ Passagiere an Bord nehmen, ♻ *a.* einschiffen, *Waren a.* verladen (*for* nach); **2.** *Geld* investieren (*in* in *dat.*); II *v/i.* **3.** ♻ sich einschiffen (*for* nach), an Bord gehen; **4.** *fig.* (*on*) (*et.*) anfangen *od.* unter'nehmen; **em·bar·ka·tion** [,embɑː-'keɪʃn] *s.* ♻ Einschiffung *f*, (*von Waren*) *a.* Verladung *f* (*a.* ✈); ✈ Einsteigen *n*.

em·bar·ras de rich·esse(s) [ɑ̃:ˌrbɑ,rɑdəri:'ʃes] (*Fr.*) *s.* die Qual der Wahl.

em·bar·rass [ɪm'bærəs] *v/t.* **1.** *j-n* in Verlegenheit bringen *od.* in e-e peinliche Lage versetzen, verwirren; **2.** *j-n* behindern, *j-m* lästig sein; **3.** in Geldverlegenheit bringen; **4.** *et.* behindern, erschweren, komplizieren; **em'bar·rassed** [-st] *adj.* **1.** verlegen, peinlich berührt; **2.** ♉ in Geldverlegenheit; **em-'bar·rass·ing** [-sɪŋ] *adj.* □ unangenehm, peinlich (*to* dat.); **em'bar·rass·ment** [-mənt] *s.* **1.** Verlegenheit *f*; **2.** *bsd.* ♣ Behinderung *f*, Störung *f*; **3.** Geldverlegenheit *f*.

em·bas·sy ['embəsɪ] *s.* **1.** Botschaft *f*: a) Botschaftsgebäude *n*, b) 'Botschaftspersonal *n*; **2.** diplo'matische Missi'on.

em·bat·tle [ɪm'bætl] *v/t.* **1.** ✗ in Schlachtordnung aufstellen; **~d** kampfbereit (*a. fig.*); **2.** ⚔ mit Zinnen versehen.

em·bed [ɪm'bed] *v/t.* **1.** (ein)betten, (ein)lagern, eingraben; **2.** *im Gedächtnis etc.* verankern.

em·bel·lish [ɪm'belɪʃ] *v/t.* **1.** verschöne(r)n, schmücken, verzieren; **2.** *fig. Erzählung etc.* ausschmücken; *die*

Wahrheit beschönigen; **em'bel·lish·ment** [-mənt] *s.* **1.** Verschönerung *f*, Schmuck *m*; **2.** *fig.* a) Ausschmückung *f*, b) Beschönigung *f*.

em·ber¹ ['embə] *s.* **1.** *mst pl.* glühende Kohle *od.* Asche; **2.** *pl. fig.* letzte Funken *pl.*

em·ber² ['embə] *adj.*: **~ days** *eccl.* Quatember(fasten *n*) *pl.*

em·ber³ ['embə] *s. orn. a.* **~goose** Eistaucher *m*.

em·bez·zle [ɪm'bezl] *v/t.* veruntreuen, unter'schlagen; **em'bez·zle·ment** [-mənt] *s.* Veruntreuung *f*, Unter'schlagung *f*; **em'bez·zler** [-lə] *s.* Veruntreuer(in).

em·bit·ter [ɪm'bɪtə] *v/t.* **1.** *j-n* verbittern; **2.** *et.* (noch) verschlimmern; **em'bit·ter·ment** [-mənt] *s.* **1.** Verbitterung *f*; **2.** Verschlimmerung *f*.

em·bla·zon [ɪm'bleɪzn] *v/t.* **1.** he'raldisch schmücken *od.* ausschmücken; **2.** schmücken; **3.** *fig.* feiern, verherrlichen, groß her'ausstellen; **4.** 'auspo,saunen; **em-'bla·zon·ment** [-mənt] *s.* Wappenschmuck *m*; **em'bla·zon·ry** [-rɪ] *s.* **1.** Wappenmale'rei *f*; **2.** Wappenschmuck *m*.

em·blem ['embləm] *s.* **1.** Em'blem *n*, Sym'bol *n*: *national ~* Hoheitszeichen *n*; **2.** Kennzeichen *n*; *fig.* Verkörperung *f*; **em·blem·at·ic, em·blem·at·i·cal** [,emblɪ'mætɪk(l)] *adj.* □ sym'bolisch, sinnbildlich.

em·bod·i·ment [ɪm'bɒdɪmənt] *s.* **1.** Verkörperung *f*; **2.** Darstellung *f*; **3.** ⊕ Anwendungsform *f*; **4.** Einverleibung *f*; **em·bod·y** [ɪm'bɒdɪ] *v/t.* **1.** kon'krete Form geben (*dat.*); **2.** verkörpern, darstellen; **3.** aufnehmen (*in* in *acc.*); **4.** um'fassen, in sich schließen.

em·bold·en [ɪm'bəʊldən] *v/t.* ermutigen.

em·bo·lism ['embəlɪzəm] *s.* ♣ Embo'lie *f*.

em·bon·point [,ɔ̃:ˌmbɔ̃:m'pwæ:ŋ] (*Fr.*) *s.* Embon'point *m*, Beleibtheit *f*, ‚Bäuchlein' *n*.

em·bos·om [ɪm'bʊzəm] *v/t.* **1.** ans Herz drücken; **2.** *fig.* ins Herz schließen; **3.** *fig.* um'schließen.

em·boss [ɪm'bɒs] *v/t.* ⊕ **1.** a) bosseln, erhaben *od.* in Reli'ef ausarbeiten, prägen, b) (mit dem Hammer) treiben; **2.** mit erhabener Arbeit schmücken; **3.** *Stoffe* gaufrieren; **em'bossed** [-st] *adj.* ⊕ a) erhaben gearbeitet, Relief..., getrieben, b) geprägt, gepresst, c) gaufriert; **em'boss·ment** [-mənt] *s.* Reli'efarbeit *f*.

em·bou·chure [,ɒmbʊ'ʃʊə] (*Fr.*) *s.* **1.** Mündung *f* (*Fluss*); **2.** ♪ a) Mundstück *n* (*Blasinstrument*), b) Ansatz *m*.

em·brace [ɪm'breɪs] I *v/t.* **1.** um'armen, in die Arme schließen; **2.** um'schließen, um'geben, um'klammern; *a. fig.* einschließen, um'fassen; **3.** erfassen, (in sich) aufnehmen; **4.** *Religion, Angebot* annehmen; *Beruf, Gelegenheit* ergreifen; *Hoffnung* hegen; II *v/i.* **5.** sich um'armen; III *s.* **6.** Um'armung *f*.

em·bra·sure [ɪm'breɪʒə] *s.* **1.** △ Laibung *f*; **2.** ✗ Schießscharte *f*.

em·bro·ca·tion [,embrəʊ'keɪʃn] *s.* ♣ **1.** Einreibemittel *n*; **2.** Einreibung *f*.

em·broi·der [ɪm'brɔɪdə] *v/t.* **1.** *Muster* sticken; **2.** *Stoff* besticken, mit Sticke'rei verzieren; **3.** *fig. Bericht* ausschmücken, ‚garnieren'.

em·broi·der·y [ɪm'brɔɪdərɪ] *s.* **1.** Sticke'rei *f*: *do ~* sticken; **2.** *fig.* Ausschmückung *f*; ~ **cot·ton** *s.* Stickgarn *n*; ~ **frame** *s.* Stickrahmen *m*.

em·broil [ɪm'brɔɪl] *v/t.* **1.** *j-n* verwickeln,

hin'einziehen (*in* in *acc.*); **2.** *j-n* in Kon'flikt bringen (*with* mit); **3.** durchein'ander bringen, verwirren; **em'broil·ment** [-mənt] *s.* **1.** Verwicklung *f*; **2.** Verwirrung *f*.

em·bry·o ['embrɪəʊ] *pl.* **-os** *s. biol.* a) Embryo *m*, b) Fruchtkeim *m*: *in* ~ *fig.* im Keim, im Entstehen, im Werden; **em·bry·on·ic** [,embrɪ'ɒnɪk] *adj.* **1.** Embryo..., embryo'nal; **2.** *fig.* (noch) unentwickelt, keimend, rudimen'tär.

em·bus [ɪm'bʌs] ✗ I *v/t.* auf Kraftfahrzeuge verladen; II *v/i.* aufsitzen.

em·cee [em'siː] I *s.* Conférenci'er *m*; II *v/t.* (*u. v/i.*) als Conférencier leiten (fungieren).

e·mend [iː'mend] *v/t. Text* verbessern, korrigieren; **e·men·da·tion** [,iːmen-'deɪʃn] *s.* Verbesserung *f*, Korrek'tur *f*; **e·men·da·tor** ['iːmendeɪtə] *s.* (Text-) Verbesserer *m*; **e'mend·a·to·ry** [-dətərɪ] *adj.* (text)verbessernd.

em·er·ald ['emərəld] I *s.* **1.** Sma'ragd *m*; **2.** Sma'ragdgrün *n*; **3.** *typ.* In'sertie *f* (*e-e* 6½*-Punkt-Schrift*); II *adj.* **4.** sma'ragdgrün; **5.** mit Sma'ragden besetzt; **♀ Isle** *s.* die Grüne Insel (*Irland*).

e·merge [ɪ'mɜːdʒ] *v/i.* **1.** *allg.* auftauchen: a) an die (Wasser)Oberfläche kommen, b) *a. fig.* zum Vorschein kommen, sich zeigen: *signs are emerging that ...* es gibt Anzeichen dafür, dass ...; c) *fig.* sich erheben (*Frage, Problem*), d) *fig.* auftreten, in Erscheinung treten; **2.** her'vor-, herauskommen (*from* aus); **3.** sich herausstellen *od.* ergeben (*Tatsache*); **4.** (*als Sieger etc.*) her'vorgehen (*from* aus); **5.** *fig.* aufstreben; **e'mer·gence** [-dʒəns] *s.* Auftauchen *n*, *fig. a.* Auftreten *n*, Entstehen *n*.

e·mer·gen·cy [ɪ'mɜːdʒənsɪ] I *s.* Not(lage *f*, -fall *m*) *f*, kritische Lage, Krise *f*, unvorhergesehenes Ereignis, dringender Fall: *in an ~, in case of ~* im Notfall, notfalls; *state of ~* Notstand *m*, *pol. a.* Ausnahmezustand *m*; II *adj.* Not..., Behelfs..., (Aus)Hilfs...; *pol.* Notstands..., Soforthilfe..., **~ brake** *s.* Not-, *mot.* Handbremse *f*; **~ call** *s. teleph.* Notruf *m*; **~ de·cree** *s.* Notverordnung *f*; **~ doc·tor** *s.* Notarzt *m*, -ärztin *f*; **~ door, ~ ex·it** *s.* Notausgang *m*; **~ hos·pi·tal** *s.* A'kutkrankenhaus *n*; **~ land·ing** *s.* ✈ Notlandung *f*; **~ laws** *s. pl. pol.* Notstandsgesetze *pl.*; **~ meet·ing** *s.* Dringlichkeitssitzung *f*; **~ number** *s.* Notruf(nummer *f*) *m*; **~ pow·ers** *s. pl. pol.* Vollmachten *pl.* auf Grund e-s Notstandsgesetzes; **~ ra·tion** *s.* ✗ eiserne Rati'on; **~ ser·vice** *s.* Rettungsdienst *m*, Notdienst *m*; **~ tel·e·phone** *s.* 'Notruftele,fon *n*, *an Straßen*: Notrufsäule *f*; **~ ward** *s.* Notaufnahme *f*, 'Unfallstati,on *f*.

e·mer·gent [ɪ'mɜːdʒənt] *adj.* □ **1.** auftauchend (*a. fig.*); **2.** *fig.* (jung u.) aufstrebend (*Land*): **~ country** *a.* Schwellenland *n*.

e·mer·i·tus [iː'merɪtəs] *adj.* emeritiert: **~ professor**.

em·er·y ['emərɪ] I *s. min.* Schmirgel *m*; II *v/t.* (ab)schmirgeln; **~ board** *s.* Sandblattnagelfeile *f*; **~ cloth** *s.* Schmirgelleinen *n*; **~ pa·per** *s.* 'Schmirgelpa,pier *n*; **~ wheel** *s.* Schmirgelscheibe *f*.

e·met·ic [ɪ'metɪk] *pharm.* I *adj.* e'metisch, Brechreiz erregend; II *s.* E'metikum *n*, Brechmittel *n* (*a. fig.*).

em·i·grant ['emɪɡrənt] I *s.* Auswanderer *m*, Emi'grant(in); II *adj.* auswandernd, emigrierend, Auswanderungs...; **'em·i·grate** [-reɪt] *v/i.* emigrieren, auswandern; **em·i·gra·tion** [ˌemɪˈɡreɪʃn] s. Auswanderung f, Emigrati'on f.

em·i·nence [ˈemɪnəns] s. **1.** Erhöhung f, (An)Höhe f; **2.** hohe Stellung, (hoher) Rang, Würde f; **3.** Ansehen n, Berühmtheit f, Bedeutung f; **4.** bedeutende Per'sönlichkeit; **5.** ♫ R.C. Emi'nenz f (Kardinal).

é·mi·nence grise [ˌeɪmiːnãːˈnsˈɡriːz] (Fr.) s. pol. graue Emi'nenz.

em·i·nent [ˈemɪnənt] adj. □ **1.** her'vorragend, ausgezeichnet, berühmt; **2.** emi'nent, bedeutend, außergewöhnlich; **3.** → domain 3; 'em·i·nent·ly [-ntlɪ] adv. ganz besonders, in hohem Maße.

e·mir [eˈmɪə] s. Emir m; **e·mir·ate** [-ɪə-rɪt] s. Emi'rat n (Würde od. Land e-s Emirs).

em·is·sar·y [ˈemɪsərɪ] s. **1.** Abgesandte(r) m, Emis'sär m; **2.** Ge'heima,gent m.

e·mis·sion [ɪˈmɪʃn] s. **1.** Ausstrahlung f (von Licht etc.), Ausstoß m (von Rauch etc.), Aus-, Verströmen n, phys. Emissi'on f; **~-free** abgasfrei; **~ standards** Emissionsnormen pl.; **2.** physiol. Ausfluss m, (bsd. Samen)Erguss m; **3.** ♦ Ausgabe f (von Banknoten), von Wertpapieren: a. Emissi'on f; **e·mis·sive** [-ɪsɪv] adj. ausstrahlend; **e·mit** [ɪˈmɪt] v/t. **1.** Lava, Rauch ausstoßen, Licht etc. ausstrahlen, Gas etc. aus-, verströmen, phys. Elektronen etc. emittieren; **2.** a) e-n Ton, a. e-e Meinung von sich geben, b) e-n Schrei etc. ausstoßen; **3.** ♦ Banknoten ausgeben, Wertpapiere a. emittieren.

Em·my [ˈemɪ] pl. **-mys, -mies** s. Am. Emmy m (Fernsehpreis).

e·mol·li·ent [ɪˈmɒlɪənt] **I** adj. erweichend (a. fig.); **II** s. pharm. erweichendes Mittel, Weichmacher m.

e·mol·u·ment [ɪˈmɒljʊmənt] s. mst pl. Einkünfte pl.

e·mote [ɪˈməʊt] v/i. emotio'nal reagieren, e-n Gefühlsausbruch erleiden od. (thea.) mimen.

e·mo·tion [ɪˈməʊʃn] s. **1.** Emoti'on f, Gemütsbewegung f, (Gefühls)Regung f, Gefühl n; **2.** Gefühlswallung f, Erregung f, Leidenschaft f; **3.** Rührung f, Ergriffenheit f; **e·mo·tion·al** [-ʃənl] adj. □ → emotionally; **1.** emotio'nal, emotio'nell: a) gefühlsmäßig, -bedingt, b) Gefühls..., Gemüts..., seelisch, c) gefühlsbetont, empfindsam: **~ block** Affektstau m; **2.** gefühlvoll, rührselig; **3.** rührend, ergreifend; **e·mo·tion·al·ism** [-ʃnəlɪzəm] s. **1.** Gefühlsbetontheit f, Empfindsamkeit f; **2.** Gefühlsduse'lei; **3.** Gefühlsäußerung f; **e·mo·tion·al·ist** [-ʃnəlɪst] s. Gefühlsmensch m; **e·mo·tion·al·i·ty** [ɪˌməʊʃəˈnælɪtɪ] s. Emotionali'tät f, emotio'nale Verhaltensweise; **e·mo·tion·al·ize** [-ʃnəlaɪz] **I** v/t. j-n od. et. emotionalisieren; **II** v/i. in Gefühlen schwelgen; **e·mo·tion·al·ly** [-ʃnəlɪ] adv. gefühlsmäßig, seelisch, emotio'nal, emotio'nell: **~ disturbed** seelisch gestört; **e·mo·tion·less** [-lɪs] adj. ungerührt, gefühllos, kühl; **e·mo·tive** [-əʊtɪv] adj. □ **1.** gefühlsbedingt, emo'tiv; **2.** gefühlvoll; **3.** gefühlsbetont: **~ word** Reizwort n.

em·pale → impale.

em·pan·el [ɪmˈpænl] v/t. in die Liste (bsd. der Geschworenen) eintragen: **~ the jury** Am. die Geschworenenliste aufstellen.

em·pa·thize [ˈempəθaɪz] v/i. Einfühlungsvermögen haben od. zeigen; sich einfühlen können (with in acc.); 'em·pa·thy [-θɪ] s. Einfühlung(svermögen n) f, Empa'thie f.

em·pen·nage [ɪmˈpenɪdʒ] s. ✈ Leitwerk n.

em·per·or [ˈempərə] s. Kaiser m; **~ moth** s. zo. kleines Nachtpfauenauge.

em·pha·sis [ˈemfəsɪs] s. **1.** ling. Betonung f, Ton m, Ak'zent m; **2.** fig. Betonung f, Gewicht n, Nachdruck m, Schwerpunkt m: **lay ~ on s.th.** Gewicht od. Wert auf e-e Sache legen, et. hervorheben od. betonen; **give ~ to →** 'em·pha·size [-saɪz] v/t. (nachdrücklich) betonen (a. ling.), Nachdruck verleihen (dat.), hervorheben, unterstreichen; **em·phat·ic** [ɪmˈfætɪk] adj. (□ **~ally**) nachdrücklich: a) betont, em'phatisch, ausdrücklich, deutlich, b) bestimmt, (ganz) entschieden.

em·phy·se·ma [ˌemfɪˈsiːmə] s. ♣ Em-phy'sem n.

em·pire [ˈempaɪə] **I** s. **1.** (Kaiser)Reich n: **the British** ♫ das Brit. Weltreich; ♫ **Day** obs. brit. Staatsfeiertag (am 24. Mai, dem Geburtstag Königin Victo-rias); **~ produce** Erzeugnis n aus dem brit. Weltreich; **2.** ♦ u. fig. Im'perium n: **tobacco ~**; **3.** Herrschaft f (over über acc.); **II** adj. **4.** Reichs...: **~ building** a) Schaffung f e-s Weltreichs, b) fig. Schaffung e-s eigenen Imperiums od. e-r Hausmacht; **5.** Empire..., im Em-'pirestil: **~ furniture**.

em·pir·ic [emˈpɪrɪk] **I** s. **1.** Em'piriker (-in), **2.** obs. Kurpfuscher m; **II** adj. **3.** → em'pir·i·cal [-kl] adj. □ em'pirisch, erfahrungsmäßig, Erfahrungs...; **em·'pir·i·cism** [-ɪsɪzəm] s. **1.** Empi'rismus m; **2.** obs. Kurpfusche'rei f; **em'pir·i·cist** [-ɪsɪst] s. **1.** Em'piriker(in); **2.** phls. Empi'rist(in).

em·place [ɪmˈpleɪs] v/t. ✕ Geschütz in Stellung bringen; **em'place·ment** [-mənt] s. **1.** Aufstellung f; **2.** ✕ a) In-'Stellung-Bringen n, b) Geschützstellung f, c) Bettung f.

em·plane [ɪmˈpleɪn] ✈ **I** v/t. Passagiere an Bord nehmen, Waren a. verladen (for nach); **II** v/i. an Bord gehen.

em·ploy [ɪmˈplɔɪ] **I** v/t. **1.** j-n beschäftigen; an-, einstellen, einsetzen: **be ~ed in doing s.th.** damit beschäftigt sein, et. zu tun; **2.** an-, verwenden, gebrauchen; **II** s. **3.** a) → employment 1, b) Dienst(e pl.) m: **be in s.o.'s ~** in j-s Dienst(en) stehen, bei j-m angestellt od. beschäftigt sein; **em'ploy·a·ble** [-ɔɪəbl] adj. **1.** zu beschäftigen(d), anstellbar; **2.** arbeitsfähig; **3.** verwendbar; **em·ploy·é** [ɒmˈplɔɪeɪ] s., **em·ploy·ee** [ˌemplɔɪˈiː] s. Arbeitnehmer (-in), (engS. **salaried ~**) Angestellte(r m) f: **the ~s** a) die Belegschaft e-s Betriebs, b) die Arbeitnehmer(schaft f) pl; **em'ploy·er** [-ɔɪə] s. **1.** Arbeitgeber(in), Unter'nehmer(in), Chef(in), Dienstherr(in): **~'s contribution** Arbeitgeberanteil m; **~'s liability** Unternehmerhaftpflicht f; **~s' association** Arbeitgeberverband m; **2.** ♦ Auftraggeber(in).

em·ploy·ment [ɪmˈplɔɪmənt] s. **1.** Beschäftigung f (a. allg.), Arbeit f, (An-)Stellung f, Arbeitsverhältnis n: **in ~** beschäftigt; **out of ~** stellen-, arbeitslos; **full ~** Vollbeschäftigung f; **2.** Ein-, Anstellung f; **3.** Beruf m, Tätigkeit f, Geschäft n; **4.** Gebrauch m, Ver-, Anwendung f, Einsatz m; **~ a·gen·cy, ~ bu·reau** s. 'Stellenvermittlung(sbü,ro n) f; **~ ex·change** s. Brit. obs. Arbeitsamt n; **~ mar·ket** s. Stellen-, Arbeitsmarkt m; **~ serv·ice a·gen·cy** s. Brit. Arbeitsamt n.

em·poi·son [ɪmˈpɔɪzn] v/t. **1.** bsd. fig.

vergiften; **2.** verbittern.

em·po·ri·um [emˈpɔːrɪəm] s. **1.** a) Handelszentrum n, b) Markt m (Stadt); **2.** Warenhaus n.

em·pow·er [ɪmˈpaʊə] v/t. **1.** bevollmächtigen, ermächtigen (to zu): **be ~ed to** befugt sein zu; **2.** befähigen (to zu).

em·press [ˈempres] s. Kaiserin f.

emp·ti·ness [ˈemptɪnɪs] s. **1.** Leerheit f, Leere f; **2.** fig. Hohlheit f, Leere f.

emp·ty [ˈemptɪ] **I** adj. **1.** leer: **~ of** fig. bar (gen.), ohne; **~ of meaning** nichts sagend; **feel ~** F (Kohldampf haben); **on an ~ stomach** auf nüchternen Magen; **2.** leer (stehend), unbewohnt; **3.** leer, unbeladen; **4.** fig. leer, hohl, nichts sagend; **II** v/t. **5.** (aus-, ent)leeren; **6.** Glas etc. leeren, austrinken; **7.** Haus etc. räumen; **8.** leeren, gießen, schütten (into in acc.); **9.** berauben (of gen.); **10. ~ itself →** 12; **III** v/i. **11.** sich leeren; **12.** sich ergießen, münden (into the sea ins Meer); **IV** s. **13.** pl. ♦ Leergut n; **,~·'hand·ed** adj. mit leeren Händen; **,~·'head·ed** adj. hohlköpfig.

e·mu [ˈiːmjuː] s. orn. Emu m.

em·u·late [ˈemjʊleɪt] v/t. wetteifern mit; nacheifern (dat.), es gleichtun wollen (dat.); **em·u·la·tion** [ˌemjʊˈleɪʃn] s. Wetteifer m; Nacheifern n.

e·mul·si·fy [ɪˈmʌlsɪfaɪ] v/t. emulgieren; **e'mul·sion** [-ʃn] s. ♣, ♣, phot. Emulsi'on f.

en [en] s. typ. Halbgeviert n.

en·a·ble [ɪˈneɪbl] v/t. **1.** j-n befähigen, in den Stand setzen, es j-m ermöglichen od. möglich machen (to do zu tun); **2.** j-n berechtigen, ermächtigen: **Enabling Act** Ermächtigungsgesetz n; **3.** et. möglich machen, ermöglichen: **~ s.th. to be done** es ermöglichen, dass et. geschieht; **this ~s the housing to be detached** dadurch kann das Gehäuse abgenommen werden.

en·act [ɪˈnækt] v/t. **1.** ♫ a) Gesetz erlassen: **~ing clause** Einführungsklausel f, b) verfügen, verordnen, c) Gesetzeskraft verleihen (dat.); **2.** thea. a) Stück aufführen, inszenieren (a. fig.), b) Person, Rolle darstellen, spielen; **3.** be **~ed** fig. stattfinden, über die Bühne od. vor sich gehen; **en·act·ment** [ɪˈnækʃn] s. **1.** ♫ a) Erlassen n (Gesetz), b) Erhebung f zum Gesetz, c) Verfügung f, Verordnung f, Erlass m; **2.** thea. a) Inszenierung f (a. fig.), b) Darstellung f (e-r Rolle).

en·am·el [ɪˈnæml] **I** s. **1.** E'mail(le f) n, Schmelzglas n; **2.** Gla'sur f (auf Töpferwaren); **3.** a. **~ ware** E'mailgeschirr n; **4.** Lack m; **5.** Nagellack m; **6.** E'mailmale,rei f; **7.** anat. Zahnschmelz m; **II** v/t. **8.** emaillieren: **~(l)ing furnace** Emaillierofen m; **9.** glasieren; **10.** lackieren; **11.** in E'mail malen; **en·am·el·(l)er** [ɪˈnæmlə] s. Email'leur m, Schmelzarbeiter m.

en·am·o·(u)r [ɪˈnæmə] v/t. mst pass. verliebt machen: **be ~ed of** a) verliebt sein in (acc.), b) fig. sehr angetan sein von.

en bloc [ãːˈblɒk] (Fr.) en bloc, im Ganzen, als Ganzes.

en·cae·ni·a [enˈsiːnjə] s. Gründungs-, Stiftungsfest n.

en·cage [ɪnˈkeɪdʒ] v/t. (in e-n Käfig) einsperren, einschließen.

en·camp [ɪnˈkæmp] **I** v/i. sein Lager aufschlagen, bsd. ✕ lagern; **II** v/t. bsd. ✕ lagern lassen: **be ~ed** lagern; **en·'camp·ment** [-mənt] s. ✕ **1.** (Feld)Lager n; **2.** Lagern n.

en·cap·su·late [ɪnˈkæpsjʊleɪt] ein-, verkapseln; *fig.* kurz zs.-fassen.

en·case [ɪnˈkeɪs] *v/t.* **1.** einschließen; **2.** umˈschließen, umˈhüllen; **3.** ⊚ verkleiden, umˈmanteln.

en·cash [ɪnˈkæʃ] *v/t. Brit. Scheck etc.* einlösen; **en'cash·ment** [-mənt] *s.* Einlösung *f.*

en·caus·tic [enˈkɔːstɪk] *paint.* **I** *adj.* enˈkaustisch, eingebrannt; **II** *s.* Enˈkaustik *f;* **~ tile** *s.* bunt glasierte Kachel.

en·ce·phal·ic [ˌenkeˈfælɪk] *adj.* ✻ Gehirn…; **,en·ceph·a'li·tis** [-kefəˈlaɪtɪs] *s.* ✻ Gehirnentzündung *f,* Enzephaˈlitis *f.*

en·chant [ɪnˈtʃɑːnt] *v/t.* **1.** verzaubern: **~ed wood** Zauberwald *m;* **2.** *fig.* bezaubern, entzücken; **en'chant·er** [-tə] *s.* Zauberer *m;* **en'chant·ing** [-tɪŋ] *adj.* □ bezaubernd, entzückend; **en'chant·ment** [-mənt] *s.* **1.** Zauber *m,* Zaubeˈrei *f;* Verzauberung *f;* **2.** *fig.* a) Zauber *m,* b) Bezauberung *f,* c) Entzücken *n;* **en'chant·ress** [-trɪs] *s.* **1.** Zauberin *f;* **2.** *fig.* bezaubernde Frau.

en·chase [ɪnˈtʃeɪs] *v/t.* **1.** *Edelstein* fassen; **2.** ziselieren: **~d work** getriebene Arbeit; **3.** (ein)gravieren.

en·ci·pher [ɪnˈsaɪfə] → *encode.*

en·cir·cle [ɪnˈsɜːkl] *v/t.* **1.** umˈgeben, -ˈringen; **2.** umˈfassen, umˈschlingen; **3.** einkreisen (*a. pol.*), umˈzingeln, ✗ *a.* einkesseln; **en'cir·cle·ment** [-mənt] *s.* Einkreisung *f* (*a. pol.*), Umˈzingelung *f,* ✗ *a.* Einkesselung *f.*

en·clasp [ɪnˈklɑːsp] → *encircle* 2.

en·clave **I** *s.* [ˈenkleɪv] Enˈklave *f;* **II** *v/t.* [enˈkleɪv] *Gebiet* einschließen, umˈgeben.

en·clit·ic [ɪnˈklɪtɪk] *ling.* **I** *adj.* (□ **~ally**) enˈklitisch; **II** *s.* enklitisches Wort, Enˈklitikon *n.*

en·close [ɪnˈkləʊz] *v/t.* **1.** (*in*) einschließen, ⊚ *a.* einkapseln (in *dat. od. acc.*), umˈgeben (mit); **2.** umˈringen; **3.** umˈfassen; **4.** *Land* einfried(ig)en, umˈzäunen; **5.** beilegen, -fügen (*in a letter* e-m Brief); **en'closed** [-zd] *adj.* **1.** *a. adv.* anˈbei, beiliegend, in der Anlage: **~ please find** in der Anlage erhalten Sie; **2.** ⊚ geschlossen, gekapselt: **~ motor,** **en'clo·sure** [-əʊʒə] *s.* **1.** Einschließung *f;* **2.** Einfried(ig)ung *f,* Umˈzäunung *f;* **3.** eingehegtes Grundstück; **4.** Zaun *m,* Mauer *f;* **5.** Anlage *f* (*zu e-m Brief etc.*).

en·code [enˈkəʊd] *v/t. Text* verschlüsseln, chiffrieren, kodieren.

en·co·mi·um [enˈkəʊmjəm] *s.* Lobrede *f,* -lied *n,* Lobpreisung *f.*

en·com·pass [ɪnˈkʌmpəs] *v/t.* **1.** umˈgeben (*with* mit); **2.** *fig.* umˈfassen, einschließen; **3.** *fig. j-s Ruin etc.* herˈbeiführen.

en·core [ɒŋˈkɔː] (*Fr.*) **I** *int.* **1.** da ˈcapo!, noch einmal!; **II** *s.* **2.** Daˈkapo(ruf *m*) *n;* **3.** a) Wiederˈholung *f,* b) Zugabe *f:* **he got an ~** er musste e-e Zugabe geben; **III** *v/t.* **4.** (durch Daˈkaporufe) nochmals verlangen: **~ a song; 5.** *j-n* um e-e Zugabe bitten; **IV** *v/i.* da ˈcapo rufen.

en·coun·ter [ɪnˈkaʊntə] **I** *v/t.* **1.** *j-m od. e-r Sache* begegnen, *j-n od. et.* treffen, auf *j-n, a.* auf *Fehler, Widerstand, Schwierigkeiten etc.* stoßen; **2.** mit *j-m* (*feindlich*) zs.-stoßen *od.* aneinˈander geraten; **3.** entgegentreten (*dat.*); **II** *v/i.* **4.** sich begegnen; **III** *s.* **5.** Begegnung *f;* **6.** Zs.-stoß *m* (*a. fig.*), Gefecht *n;* **7.** *psych.* Trainingsgruppensitzung *f:* **~ group** Trainingsgruppe *f.*

en·cour·age [ɪnˈkʌrɪdʒ] *v/t.* **1.** *j-n* ermutigen, *j-m* Mut machen, *j-n* ermuntern (*to* zu); **2.** *j-n* anfeuern; **3.** *j-m* zureden;

4. *j-n* unterˈstützen, bestärken (*in* in *dat.*); **5.** *et.* fördern, unterˈstützen, begünstigen; **en'cour·age·ment** [-mənt] *s.* **1.** Ermutigung *f,* Ermunterung *f,* Ansporn *m* (*to* für); **2.** Anfeuerung *f;* **3.** Unterˈstützung *f,* Bestärkung *f;* **4.** Förderung *f,* Begünstigung *f;* **en'cour·ag·ing** [-dʒɪŋ] *adj.* □ **1.** ermutigend; **2.** hoffnungsvoll, viel versprechend.

en·croach [ɪnˈkrəʊtʃ] *v/i.* **1.** (*on, upon*) unbefugt eindringen *od.* -greifen (in *acc.*), sich ˈÜbergriffe leisten (in, auf *acc.*), (*j-s Recht*) verletzen; **2.** (*on, upon*) über Gebühr beanspruchen, missbrauchen; zu weit gehen; **3.** (*on, upon*) *et.* beeinträchtigen, schmälern; **en'croach·ment** [-mənt] *s.* **1.** (*on, upon*) Eingriff *m* (in *acc.*), ˈÜbergriff *m* (in, auf *acc.*), Verletzung *f* (*gen.*); **2.** Beeinträchtigung *f,* Schmälerung *f* (*on, upon gen.*); **3.** ˈÜbergreifen *n,* Vordringen *n.*

en·crust [ɪnˈkrʌst] **I** *v/t.* **1.** ver-, überˈkrusten; **2.** reich verzieren; **II** *v/i.* **3.** eine Kruste bilden; **,en·crus'ta·tion** *s.* **1.** Krustenbildung *f;* **2.** reiche Verzierung.

en·crypt [ɪnˈkrɪpt, en-] *v/t. Computer, TV etc.*: verschlüsseln; **en'cryp·tion** [-ʃn] *s.* Verschlüsselung *f:* **~ program** Ver'schlüsselungspro,gramm *n;* **~ system** Ver'schlüsselungssys,tem *n.*

en·cum·ber [ɪnˈkʌmbə] *v/t.* **1.** belasten (*a. Grundstück etc.*): **~ed with mortgages** hypothekarisch belastet; **~ed with debts** (völlig) verschuldet; **2.** (be)hindern; **3.** *Räume* voll stopfen, über'laden; **en'cum·brance** [-brəns] *s.* **1.** Last *f,* Belastung *f;* **2.** Hindernis *n,* Behinderung *f;* **3.** ✝ (Grundstücks)Belastung *f,* Hypo'theken-, Schuldenlast *f;* **4.** (Fa'milien)Anhang *m, bsd.* Kinder *pl.*: **without ~(s); en'cum·branc·er** [-brənsə] *s.* ✝ Hypo'thekengläubiger (-in).

en·cy·clic, en·cy·cli·cal [ɪnˈsɪklɪk(l)] **I** *adj.* □ en'zyklisch; **II** *s. eccl.* (päpstliche) En'zyklika.

en·cy·clo·p(a)e·di·a [en,saɪkləʊˈpiːdjə] *s.* Enzyklopäˈdie *f;* **en,cy·clo'p(a)edic, en,cy·clo'p(a)e·di·cal** [-dɪk(l)] *adj.* enzyklo'pädisch, um'fassend.

en·cyst [enˈsɪst] *v/t.* ✻, *zo.* ein-, verkapseln; **en'cyst·ment** [-mənt] *s.* ✻, *zo.* Ein-, Verkapselung *f.*

end [end] **I** *s.* **1.** (*örtlich*) Ende *n:* **begin at the wrong ~** falsch herum anfangen; **from one ~ to another, from ~ to ~** von Anfang bis (zum) Ende; **at the ~ of the letter** am Ende *od.* Schluss des Briefes; **no ~ of** a) unendlich, unzählig, b) sehr viel(e); **no ~ of trouble** endlose Mühe *od.* Scherereien; **no ~ of a fool** Vollidiot *m;* **no ~ disappointed** F maßlos enttäuscht; **he thinks no ~ of himself** er ist grenzenlos eingebildet; **on ~** a) ununterbrochen, b) aufrecht, hochkant; **for hours on ~** stundenlang; **stand s.th. on ~** et. hochkant stellen; **my hair stood on ~** mir standen die Haare zu Berge; **at our** (*od. this*) **~** F bei uns, hier; **be at an ~** a) zu Ende sein, aus sein, b) mit s-n Mitteln *od.* Kräften am Ende sein; **at a loose ~** a) müßig, b) ohne feste Bindung, c) verwirrt; **there's an ~ of it!** Schluss damit!, basta!; **there's an ~ to everything** alles hat mal ein Ende; **come to an ~** ein Ende nehmen, zu Ende gehen; **come to a bad ~** ein schlimmes Ende nehmen; **go** (*in*) **off the deep ~** F außer sich geraten, ˌhochgehen'; **keep one's ~ up** a) s-n Mann stehen, b) sich nicht unterkriegen lassen; **make both ~s**

meet finanziell über die Runden kommen; **make an ~ of** (*od.* **put an ~ to**) **s.th.** Schluss machen mit et., e-r Sache ein Ende setzen; **put an ~ to o.s.** s-m Leben ein Ende machen; **he is the** (*absolute*) **~!** F a) er ist das ˌLetzte'!, b) er ist ˌzum Brüllen'!; **it's the ~** F a) das ist das ˌLetzte', b) es ist ˌsagenhaft'; **2.** (*äußerstes*) Ende, *mst* entfernte Gegend: **the other ~ of the street** das andere Ende der Straße; **the ~ of the road** *fig.* das Ende; **to the ~s of the earth** bis ans Ende der Welt; **3.** ⊚ Spitze *f,* Kopf(ende *n*) *m,* Stirnseite *f:* **~ to ~** der Länge nach; **~ on** mit dem Ende *od.* der Spitze voran; **4.** (*zeitlich*) Ende *n,* Schluss *m:* **in the ~** am Ende, schließlich; **at the ~ of May** Ende Mai; **to the bitter ~** bis zum bitteren Ende; **to the ~ of time** bis in alle Ewigkeit; **without ~** unaufhörlich; **no ~ in sight** kein Ende abzusehen; **5.** Tod *m,* Ende *n,* 'Untergang *m:* **near one's ~** dem Tod(e) nahe; **the ~ of the world** das Ende der Welt; **you'll be the ~ of me!** du bringst mich noch ins Grab!; **6.** Rest *m,* Endchen *n,* Stück(chen) *n,* Stummel *m,* Stumpf *m:* **the ~ of a pencil; 7.** ⚓ Kabel-, Tauende *n;* **8.** Folge *f,* Ergebnis *n:* **the ~ of the matter was that** die Folge (davon) war, dass; **9.** Ziel *n,* (End)Zweck *m,* Absicht *f:* **to this ~** zu diesem Zweck; **to no ~** vergebens; **gain one's ~s** s-n Zweck erreichen, **for one's own ~** zum eigenen Nutzen; **private ~s** Privatinteressen; **the ~ justifies the means** der Zweck heiligt die Mittel; **II** *v/t.* **10.** *a.* **~ off** beend(ig)en, zu Ende führen; *e-r Sache* ein Ende machen: **~ it all** F ˌSchluss machen' (*sich umbringen*); **the dictionary to ~ all dictionaries** das beste Wörterbuch aller Zeiten; **11.** a) *a.* **~ up** *et.* ab-, beschließen, b) *den Rest s-r Tage* verbringen, *s-e Tage* beschließen; **III** *v/i.* **12.** *a.* **~ off** enden, aufhören, schließen: **all's well that ~s well** Ende gut, alles gut; **13.** *a.* **~ up** enden, ausgehen (*by, in, with* damit, dass): **~ happily** gut ausgehen; **he ~ed by boring me** schließlich langweilte er mich; **~ in disaster** mit e-m Fiasko enden; **14.** sterben; **15.** **~ up** a) enden, ˌlanden' (*in prison* im Gefängnis), b) enden (*as* als): **he ~ed up as an actor** er wurde schließlich Schauspieler.

'end-all → *be-all.*

en·dan·ger [ɪnˈdeɪndʒə] *v/t.* gefährden, in Gefahr bringen.

en·dear [ɪnˈdɪə] *v/t.* beliebt machen (**to** bei *j-m*): **~ o.s. to s.o.** a) j-s Zuneigung gewinnen, b) sich bei j-m lieb machen; **en'dear·ing** [-ɪərɪŋ] *adj.* □ lieb, gewinnend; liebenswert; **en'dearment** [-mənt] *s.*: (*term of*) **~** Kosewort *n,* -name *m;* **words of ~** liebe *od.* zärtliche Worte.

en·deav·o(u)r [ɪnˈdevə] **I** *v/i.* (*after*) sich bemühen (um), streben (nach); **II** *v/t.* (ver)suchen, bemüht *od.* bestrebt sein (**to do s.th.** et. zu tun); **III** *s.* Bemühung *f,* Bestreben *n,* Anstrengung *f:* **to make every ~** sich nach Kräften bemühen.

en·dem·ic [enˈdemɪk] **I** *adj.* (□ **~ally**) **1.** en'demisch: a) (ein)heimisch, b) ✻ örtlich begrenzt (auftretend), c) *zo.,* ♀ *in e-m bestimmten Gebiet verbreitet;* **II** *s.* **2.** ✻ en'demische Krankheit; **3.** a) *zo.* en'demisches Tier, b) en'demische Pflanze.

end game *s.* **1.** Schlussphase *f* (*e-s Spiels*); **2.** *Schach:* Endspiel *n.*

end·ing [ˈendɪŋ] *s.* **1.** Ende *n,* (Ab-)

Schluss *m*: **happy** ~ glückliches Ende, Happy End *n*; **2.** *ling.* Endung *f*; **3.** *fig.* Ende *n*, Tod *m*.

en·dive ['endɪv] *s.* ♀ ('Winter)En,divie *f*.

end·less ['endlɪs] *adj.* □ **1.** endlos, ohne Ende, un'endlich; **2.** ewig, unauf'hörlich; **3.** unendlich lang; **4.** ☉ endlos: ~ **belt** endloses Band; ~ **chain** endlose Kette, Raupenkette *f*, Paternosterwerk *n*; ~ **paper** Endlos-, Rollenpapier *n*; ~ **screw** Schraube *f* ohne Ende, Schnecke *f*; **'end·less·ness** [-nɪs] *s.* Un'endlichkeit *f*, Endlosigkeit *f*.

en·do·car·di·tis [,endəʊkɑː'daɪtɪs] *s.* ✚ Herzinnenhautentzündung *f*, Endokar-'ditis *f*; **en·do·car·di·um** [,endəʊ'kɑː-dɪəm] *s. anat.* innere Herzhaut, Endo-'kard *n*; **en·do·carp** ['endəʊkɑːp] *s.* ♀ Endo'karp *n* (*innere Fruchthaut*); **en·do·crane** ['endəʊkreɪn] *s. anat.* Schädelinnenfläche *f*, Endo'kranium *n*; **en·do·crine** ['endəʊkraɪn] *adj.* endo-'krin, mit innerer Sekreti'on: ~ **glands**; **en·dog·a·my** [en'dɒgəmɪ] *s. sociol.* Endoga'mie *f*; **en·dog·e·nous** [en'dɒdʒɪnəs] *adj. bsd.* ♀ endo'gen; **en·do·par·a·site** [,endəʊ'pærəsaɪt] *s. zo.* Endopara'sit *m*; **en·do·plasm** ['endəʊplæzəm] *s. biol.* innere Proto'plasmaschicht, Endo'plasma *n*.

en·dorse [ɪn'dɔːs] *v/t.* **1.** a) *Dokument* auf der Rückseite beschreiben, b) e-n Vermerk *od.* Zusatz machen auf (*dat.*), c) *bsd. Brit.* e-e Strafe vermerken auf (*e-m Führerschein*); **2.** ✝ a) *Scheck etc.* indossieren, girieren, b) *a.* ~ **over** über'tragen, -'weisen (**to** *j-m*), c) *e-e Zahlung* auf der Rückseite des Schecks *etc.* bestätigen; **3.** a) *e-n Plan etc.* billigen, gutheißen, b) sich *e-r Ansicht etc.* anschließen: ~ **s.o.'s opinion** *j-m* beipflichten; **en·dor·see** [,endɔː'siː] *s.* ✝ Indos'sat *m*, Indossa'tar *m*; Gi'rat *m*; **en'dorse·ment** [-mənt] *s.* **1.** Vermerk *m od.* Zusatz *m* (*auf der Rückseite von Dokumenten*); **2.** ✝ a) Indossa'ment *n*, Giro *n*, b) Über'tragung *f*: ~ **in blank** Blankogiro; ~ **in full** Vollgiro; **3.** *fig.* Billigung *f*, Unter'stützung *f*; **en'dors-er** [-sə] *s.* ✝ Indos'sant *m*, Gi'rant *m*: **preceding** ~ Vormann *m*.

en·dow [ɪn'daʊ] *v/t.* **1.** dotieren, e-e Stiftung machen (*dat.*); **2.** *et.* stiften: ~ **s.o. with s.th.** *j-m et.* stiften; **3.** *fig.* ausstatten (**with** mit *e-m Talent etc.*); **en-'dowed** [-aʊd] *adj.* **1.** gestiftet: **well-~** wohlhabend; ~ **school** aus Stiftungsgeldern finanzierte Schule; **2.** ~ **with** *dj.* ausgestattet mit: ~ **with many talents**; **she is well** ~ *humor.* sie ist von der Natur reichlich ausgestattet; **en'dow·ment** [-mənt] *s.* **1.** a) Stiftung *f*, b) *pl.* Stiftungsgeld *n*: ~ **insurance** (*Brit.* **as·surance**) ✝ Versicherung *f* auf den Todes- u. Erlebensfall; **2.** *fig.* Begabung *f*, Ta'lent *n*, *mst pl.* (körperliche *od.* geistige) Vorzüge *pl.*

end| pa·per *s.* Vorsatzblatt *n*; ~ **prod·uct** ✝ *u. fig.* 'Endpro,dukt *n*; ~ **rhyme** *s.* Endreim *m*.

en·dur·a·ble [ɪn'djʊərəbl] *adj.* □ erträglich, leidlich.

en·dur·ance [ɪn'djʊərəns] **I** *s.* **1.** Dauer *f*; **2.** Dauerhaftigkeit *f*; **3.** a) Ertragen *n*, Aushalten *n*, Erdulden *n*, b) Ausdauer *f*, Geduld *f*, Standhaftigkeit *f*: **beyond** (*od.* **past**) ~ unerträglich, nicht auszuhalten(d); **4.** ☉ Dauerleistung *f*; Lebensdauer *f*; **II** *adj.* **5.** Dauer...; ~ **flight** ✈ Dauerflug *m*; ~ **lim·it** *s.* ☉ Belastungsgrenze *f*; ~ **run** *s.* Dauerlauf *m*; ~ **test** *s.* ☉ Belastungs-,

Ermüdungsprobe *f*.

en·dure [ɪn'djʊə] **I** *v/i.* **1.** an-, fortdauern; **2.** 'durchhalten; **II** *v/t.* **3.** aushalten, ertragen, erdulden, 'durchmachen: **not to be** ~**d** unerträglich; **4.** *fig.* (*nur neg.*) ausstehen, leiden: **I cannot** ~ **him**; **en'dur·ing** [-ərɪŋ] *adj.* □ an-, fortdauernd, bleibend.

end us·er *s.* ✝ Endverbraucher *m*, End(be)nutzer *m*.

'end·ways [-weɪz], **'end·wise** [-waɪz] *adv.* **1.** mit dem Ende nach vorn *od.* oben; **2.** aufrecht; **3.** der Länge nach.

en·e·ma ['enɪmə] *s.* ✚ **1.** Kli'stier *n*, Einlauf *m*; **2.** Kli'stierspritze *f*.

en·e·my ['enəmɪ] **I** *s.* ✕ Feind *m*; **2.** Gegner *m*, Feind *m*: **the Old** ⚥ *bibl.* der Teufel, der böse Feind; **be one's own** (**worst**) ~ sich selbst (am meisten) schaden *od.* im Weg stehen; **make an** ~ **of s.o.** sich *j-n* zum Feind machen; **she made no enemies** sie machte sich keine Feinde; **II** *adj.* **3.** feindlich, Feind...: ~ **action** Feind-, Kriegseinwirkung *f*; ~ **alien** feindlicher Ausländer; ~ **country** Feindesland *n*; ~ **prop·erty** ✝ Feindvermögen *n*.

en·er·get·ic [,enə'dʒetɪk] **I** *adj.* (□ ~**al·ly**) **1.** e'nergisch: a) tatkräftig, b) nachdrücklich; **2.** (sehr) wirksam; **3.** *phys.* ener'getisch; **II** *s. pl. sg. konstr.* **4.** *phys.* Ener'getik *f*; **en·er·gize** ['enə-dʒaɪz] **I** *v/t.* **1.** *et.* kräftigen, Ener'gie verleihen (*dat.*); *j-n* anspornen; **2.** ⚡, ☉, *phys.* erregen: ~**d** ⚡ unter Spannung (stehend); **II** *v/i.* **3.** energisch handeln.

en·er·gu·men [,enɜː'gjuːmen] *s.* Enthusi'ast(in), Fa'natiker(in).

en·er·gy ['enədʒɪ] *s.* **1.** Ener'gie *f*: a) Kraft *f*, Nachdruck *m*, b) Tatkraft *f*; **2.** Wirksamkeit *f*, 'Durchschlagskraft *f*; **3.** ⚡, *phys.* Ener'gie *f*, Kraft *f*, Leistung *f*: ~ **crisis** Energiekrise *f*; ~**-efficient** energieeffizient; ~ **recovery** Energierückgewinnung *f*; ~**-saving** Energie sparend; ~ **squandering** Energieverschwendung *f*; ~ **tax** Energiesteuer *f*.

en·er·vate ['enɜːveɪt] *v/t.* a) entnerven, b) entkräften, schwächen (*alle a. fig.*); **en·er·va·tion** [,enɜː'veɪʃn] *s.* **1.** Entnervung *f*; **2.** Entkräftung *f*, Schwächung *f*; **3.** Schwäche *f*.

en·fee·ble [ɪn'fiːbl] *v/t.* schwächen.

en·feoff [ɪn'fef] *v/t. hist.* belehnen (**with** mit); **en'feoff·ment** [-mənt] *s.* **1.** Belehnung *f*; **2.** Lehnsbrief *m*; **3.** Lehen *n*.

en·fi·lade [,enfɪ'leɪd] ✕ **I** *s.* Flankenfeuer *n*; **II** *v/t.* (mit Flankenfeuer) bestreichen.

en·fold [ɪn'fəʊld] *v/t.* **1.** *a. fig.* einhüllen (**in** in *acc.*), um'hüllen (**with** mit); **2.** um'fassen, -'armen; **3.** falten.

en·force [ɪn'fɔːs] *v/t.* **1.** a) (mit Nachdruck) geltend machen: ~ **an argument**, b) Geltung verschaffen (*dat.*), *Gesetz etc.* 'durchführen; ✝ *Forderungen* (gerichtlich) geltend machen: *Schuld* beitreiben, d) ⚖ *Urteil* voll-'strecken: ~ **a contract** (s-e) Rechte aus e-m Vertrag geltend machen; **2.** (**on**, **upon**) *et.* 'durchsetzen (bei *j-m*); *Gehorsam etc.* erzwingen (von *j-m*); **3.** (**on**, **upon** *dat.*) aufzwingen, auferlegen; **en'force·a·ble** [-səbl] *adj.* 'durchsetz-, erzwingbar; ⚖ voll'streckbar, beitreibbar; (ein)klagbar; **en'forced** [-st] *adj.* erzwungen, aufgezwungen: ~ **sale** Zwangsverkauf *m*; **en'for·ced·ly** [-sɪdlɪ] *adv.* **1.** notgedrungen, zwangsweise, gezwungenermaßen; **en-'force·ment** [-mənt] *s.* **1.** Erzwingung *f*, 'Durchsetzung *f*; **2.** a) ✝ (gerichtliche) Geltendmachung, b) ⚖ Voll'stre-

ckung *f*, Voll'zug *m*: ~ **officer** Vollzugsbeamte(r) *m*.

en·frame [ɪn'freɪm] *v/t.* einrahmen.

en·fran·chise [ɪn'fræntʃaɪz] *v/t.* **1.** *j-m* die Bürgerrechte *od.* das Wahlrecht verleihen: **be** ~**d** das Wahlrecht erhalten; **2.** *e-r Stadt* po'litische Rechte gewähren; **3.** *Brit. e-m Ort* Vertretung im 'Unterhaus verleihen; **4.** *Sklaven* freilassen; **5.** befreien (**from** von); **en-'fran·chise·ment** [-tʃɪzmənt] *s.* **1.** Verleihung *f* der Bürgerrechte *od.* des Wahlrechts; **2.** Gewährung *f* po'litischer Rechte; **3.** Freilassung *f*, Befreiung *f*.

en·gage [ɪn'geɪdʒ] **I** *v/t.* **1.** (*o.s.* sich) (*vertraglich etc.*) verpflichten *od.* binden (**to do s.th.** et. zu tun); **2.** **become** (*od.* **get**) ~**d** sich verloben (**to** mit); **3.** *j-n* an-, einstellen, *Künstler etc.* engagieren; **4.** a) *et.* mieten, *Zimmer* belegen, nehmen, b) *Platz etc.* (vor)bestellen, belegen; **5.** *j-n*, *j-s Kräfte etc.* in Anspruch nehmen, *j-n* fesseln: ~ **s.o. in conversation** *j-n* ins Gespräch ziehen; ~ **s.o.'s attention** *j-s* Aufmerksamkeit auf sich lenken *od.* in Anspruch nehmen; **6.** ✕ a) *Truppen* einsetzen, b) *Feind* angreifen, *Feindkräfte* binden; **7.** ☉ einrasten lassen; *Kupplung etc.* einrücken, *e-n Gang* einlegen, -schalten; **II** *v/i.* **8.** sich verpflichten, es über'nehmen (**to do s.th.** et. zu tun); **9.** Gewähr leisten, garantieren, sich verbürgen (**that** dass); **10.** ✕ angreifen, den Kampf beginnen; ~ **in** sich beschäftigen *od.* befassen *od.* abgeben mit; **11.** ~ **in** sich beteiligen an (*dat.*), sich einlassen in *od.* auf (*acc.*); **12.** ☉ inein'ander greifen, einrasten; **en'gaged** [-dʒd] *adj.* **1.** verpflichtet; **2.** *a.* ~ **to be married** verlobt (**to** mit); **3.** beschäftigt, nicht abkömmlich, ,besetzt': **are you** ~? sind Sie frei?; **be** ~ **in** (*od.* **on**) beschäftigt sein mit, arbeiten an (*dat.*); **deeply** ~ **in conversation** in ein Gespräch vertieft; **my time is fully** ~ ich bin zeitlich völlig ausgelastet; **4.** *teleph. Brit.* besetzt: ~ **tone** *od.* **signal** Besetztzeichen *n*; **5.** ☉ eingerückt, im Eingriff (stehend); **en-'gage·ment** [-mənt] *s.* **1.** (*vertragliche etc.*) Verpflichtung *f*: **without** ~ unverbindlich, *a.* freibleibend; **be under an** ~ **to s.o.** *j-m* (gegenüber) verpflichtet sein; ~**s** ✝ Zahlungsverpflichtungen *pl.*; **2.** Verabredung *f*: ~ **diary** Terminkalender *m*; **3.** Verlobung *f* (**to** mit): ~ **ring** Verlobungsring *m*; **4.** (An)Stellung *f*, Stelle *f*, Posten *m*; **5.** *thea.* Enga-ge'ment *n*; **6.** Beschäftigung *f*, Tätigkeit *f*; **7.** ✕ Kampf(handlung *f*) *m*, Gefecht *n*; **8.** ☉ Eingriff *m*; **en'gag·ing** [-dʒɪŋ] *adj.* □ **1.** einnehmend, gewinnend; **2.** ☉ Ein- u. Ausrück...: ~ **gear**.

en·gen·der [ɪn'dʒendə] *v/t. fig.* erzeugen, her'vorbringen, -rufen.

en·gine ['endʒɪn] **I** *s.* **1.** *allg.* Ma'schine *f*, b) Motor *m*, c) 🚂 Lokomo'tive *f*; **2.** ☉ Holländer *m*, Stoffmühle *f*; **3.** Feuerspritze *f*; **II** *v/t.* **4.** mit Ma'schinen *od.* Mo'toren *od.* e-m Motor versehen; ~ **block** *s.* Motorblock *m*; ~ **build·er** *s.* Ma'schinenbauer *m*; ~ **driv·er** *s.* Loko-mo'tivführer *m*.

en·gi·neer [,endʒɪ'nɪə] **I** *s.* **1.** a) Ingeni'eur *m*, b) Techniker *m*, c) Me'chaniker *m*: ~**s** *teleph.* Stördienst *m*; **2.** *a.* **mechanical** ~ Ma'schinenbauer *m*, -ingeni,eur *m*; **3.** *a.* ⚓ Maschi'nist *m*; **4.** *Am.* Lokomo'tivführer *m*; **5.** ✕ Pio'nier *m*; **II** *v/t.* **6.** *Straßen*, *Brücken etc.* bauen, anlegen, konstruieren, errichten; **7.** *fig. geschickt* in die

Wege leiten, ‚organisieren‘, ‚einfädeln‘, ‚deichseln‘; **III** *v/i.* **8.** als Ingeni'eur tätig sein; **,engi'neer·ing** [-ɪərɪŋ] *s.* **1.** Technik *f, engS.* Ingeni'eurwesen *n;* (*a.* **mechanical** ∼) Ma'schinen- u. Gerätebau *m:* ∼ **department** technische Abteilung, Konstruktionsbüro *n;* ∼ **sciences** technische Wissenschaften; ∼ **standards committee** Fachnormenausschuss *m;* ∼ **works** Maschinenfabrik *f;* **2.** **social** ∼ angewandte Sozialwissenschaft; **3.** ✕ Pio'nierwesen *n.*

en·gine| fit·ter *s.* Ma'schinenschlosser *m,* Mon'teur *m;* ∼ **lathe** *s.* ⊙ Leitspindeldrehbank *f;* '∼**·man** [-mən] *s.* [*irr.*] **1.** Maschi'nist *m;* **2.** Lokomo'tivführer *m;* ∼ **oil** *s.* 'Motoröl *n;* ∼ **room** *s.* Ma'schinenraum *m.*

en·gird [ɪn'ɡɜːd], **en·gir·dle** [-dl] *v/t.* um'gürten, -'geben, -'schließen.

Eng·land·er ['ɪŋɡləndə] *s.* Engländer *m:* **Little** ∼ *pol. hist.* Gegner der imperialistischen Politik.

Eng·lish ['ɪŋɡlɪʃ] **I** *adj.* **1.** englisch: ∼ **disease,** ∼ **sickness** ✝ ‚englische Krankheit‘; ∼ **flute** ♩ Blockflöte *f;* ∼ **studies** *pl.* Anglistik *f;* **II** *s.* **2. the** ∼ die Engländer; **3.** *ling.* Englisch *n,* das Englische: ∼ ∼ britisches Englisch; **in** ∼ auf Englisch, im Englischen; **into** ∼ ins Englische; **from** (**the**) ∼ aus dem Englischen, **the King's** (*od.* **Queen's**) ∼ gutes, reines Englisch; **in plain** ∼ *fig.* ‚auf gut Deutsch‘, ‚im Klartext‘; **4.** *typ.* Mittel *f* (*Schriftgrad*); **Eng·lish·ism** ['ɪŋlɪʃɪzəm] *s. bsd. Am.* **1.** *ling.* Briti'zismus *m;* **2.** englische Eigenart; **3.** Anglophi'lie *f;* **'Eng·lish·man** [-mən] *s.* [*irr.*] Engländer *m;* **'Eng·lish,wom·an** *s.* [*irr.*] Engländerin *f.*

en·gorge [ɪn'ɡɔːdʒ] *v/t.* **1.** gierig verschlingen; **2.** ✻ *Gefäß etc.* anschoppen: ∼**d kidney** Stauungsniere *f.*

en·graft [ɪn'ɡrɑːft] *v/t.* **1.** (auf)pfropfen (**into** in *acc.,* **upon** auf *acc.*); **2.** *fig.* a) einfügen, b) verankern (**into** in *dat.*).

en·grained [ɪn'ɡreɪnd] *adj. fig.* **1.** eingefleischt, unverbesserlich; **2.** eingewurzelt.

en·gram [ɪn'ɡræm] *s. biol., psych.* En'gramm *n.*

en·grave [ɪn'ɡreɪv] *v/t.* **1.** (ein)gravieren, (ein)meißeln, *in Holz:* (ein)schnitzen, einschneiden (**on** in, auf *acc.*); **2. it is** ∼**d** (**up**)**on his memory** (*od.* **mind**) *fig.* es hat sich ihm tief eingeprägt; **en·'grav·er** [-və] *s.* Gra'veur *m,* (Kunst-) Stecher *m:* ∼ (**on copper**) Kupferstecher *m;* **en·'grav·ing** [-vɪŋ] *s.* **1.** Gravieren *n,* Gravierkunst *f;* **2.** (Kupfer-, Stahl)Stich *m;* Holzschnitt *m.*

en·gross [ɪn'ɡrəʊs] *v/t.* **1.** ✍ a) *Urkunde* ausfertigen, b) e-e Reinschrift anfertigen von, c) in gesetzlicher *od.* rechtsgültiger Form ausdrücken, d) *parl.* e-m *Gesetzentwurf* die endgültige Fassung geben; **2.** ✝ a) *Ware* spekula'tiv aufkaufen, b) *den Markt* monopolisieren; **3.** *fig. j-s Aufmerksamkeit etc.* (ganz) in Anspruch nehmen; *et.* an sich reißen; **en·'grossed** [-st] *adj.* vertieft, versunken (**in** in *acc.*); **en·'gross·ing** [-sɪŋ] *adj.* **1.** fesselnd, spannend; **2.** voll in Anspruch nehmend; **en·'gross·ment** [-mənt] *s.* **1.** ✍ Ausfertigung *f,* Reinschrift *f e-r Urkunde;* **2.** ✝ a) (spekula'tiver) Aufkauf, b) Monopolisierung *f;* **3.** Inanspruchnahme *f* (**of, with** durch).

en·gulf [ɪn'ɡʌlf] *v/t.* **1.** über'fluten; **2.** verschlingen (*a. fig.*).

en·hance [ɪn'hɑːns] *v/t.* **1.** erhöhen, vergrößern, steigern, heben; **2.** *et.* (vorteil-

haft) zur Geltung bringen; **en·'hance·ment** [-mənt] *s.* Steigerung *f,* Erhöhung *f,* Vergrößerung *f.*

e·nig·ma [ɪ'nɪɡmə] *s.* Rätsel *n* (*a. fig.*); **e·nig·mat·ic, e·nig·mat·i·cal** [,enɪɡ'mætɪk(l)] *adj.* ☐ rätselhaft, dunkel; **e'nig·ma·tize** [-ətaɪz] **I** *v/i.* in Rätseln sprechen; **II** *v/t. et.* in Dunkel hüllen, verschleiern.

en·join [ɪn'dʒɔɪn] *v/t.* **1.** *et.* auferlegen, vorschreiben (**on s.o.** j-m); **2.** *j-m* befehlen, einschärfen, *j-n* (eindringlich) mahnen (**to do** zu tun); **3.** bestimmen, Anweisung(en) erteilen (**that** dass); **4.** ✍ unter'sagen (**s.th. on s.o.** j-m et.: **s.o. from doing s.th.** j-m, et. zu tun).

en·joy [ɪn'dʒɔɪ] *v/t.* **1.** Vergnügen *od.* Gefallen finden *od.* Freude haben an (*dat.*), sich erfreuen an (*dat.*): **I** ∼ **dancing** ich tanze gern, Tanzen macht mir Spaß; **did you** ∼ **the play?** hat das (Theater)Stück gefallen?; ∼ **o.s.** sich amüsieren *od.* gut unterhalten; **did you** ∼ **yourself in London?** hat es dir in London gefallen?; ∼ **yourself!** viel Spaß!; **2.** genießen, sich *et.* schmecken lassen: **I** ∼ **my food** das Essen schmeckt mir; **3.** sich *e-s Besitzes* erfreuen, *et.* haben, besitzen, genießen; erleben: ∼ **good health** sich e-r guten Gesundheit erfreuen; ∼ **a right** ein Recht genießen *od.* haben; **en·'joy·a·ble** [-ɪəbl] *adj.* ☐ **1.** brauch-, genießbar; **2.** angenehm, erfreulich, schön; **en·'joy·ment** [-mənt] *s.* **1.** Genuss *m,* Vergnügen *n,* Gefallen *n,* Freude *f* (**of** an *dat.*); **2.** Genuss *m* (*e-s Besitzes od. Rechtes*), Besitz *m:* **quiet** ∼ ✍ ruhiger Besitz; **3.** ✍ Ausübung *f* (*e-s Rechts*).

en·kin·dle [ɪn'kɪndl] *v/t. fig.* entflammen, entzünden, entfachen.

en·lace [ɪn'leɪs] *v/t.* **1.** um'schlingen; **2.** verstricken.

en·large [ɪn'lɑːdʒ] **I** *v/t.* **1.** vergrößern (*a. gra.ʃt*), *Kenntnisse etc. a.* erweitern, *Einfluss etc. a.* ausdehnen: ∼**d and revised edition** erweiterte u. verbesserte Auflage; ∼ **the mind** den Gesichtskreis erweitern; **II** *v/i.* **2.** sich vergrößern *od.* ausdehnen *od.* erweitern, zunehmen; **3.** *phot.* sich vergrößern lassen; **4.** *fig.* sich verbreiten *od.* weitläufig auslassen (**upon** über *acc.*); **en·'large·ment** [-mənt] *s.* **1.** Vergrößerung *f* (*a. phot.*), Erweiterung *f,* Ausdehnung *f;* ✻ (Herz-) Erweiterung *f,* (*Mandel- etc.*) Schwellung *f;* **2.** Erweiterungs-, Anbau *m;* **en·'larg·er** [-dʒə] *s.* Vergrößerungsgerät *n.*

en·light·en [ɪn'laɪtn] *v/t. fig.* erleuchten, aufklären, belehren (**on, as to** über *acc.*); **en·'light·ened** [-nd] *adj.* **1.** erleuchtet, aufgeklärt; **2.** verständig; **en·'light·en·ing** [-nɪŋ] *adj.* aufschlussreich; **en·'light·en·ment** [-mənt] *s.* Aufklärung *f,* Erleuchtung *f:* (**Age of**) ♩ *hist.* (Zeitalter *n* der) Aufklärung.

en·list [ɪn'lɪst] **I** *v/t.* **1.** *Soldaten* anwerben, *Rekruten* einstellen: ∼**ed men** *Am.* Unteroffiziere und Mannschaften; **2.** *fig. j-n* her'anziehen, gewinnen, engagieren (**in** für): ∼ **s.o.'s services** j-s Dienste in Anspruch nehmen; **II** *v/i.* **3.** ✕ sich anwerben lassen, Sol'dat werden, sich (freiwillig) melden; **4.** (**in**) mitwirken (bei), sich beteiligen (an *dat.*); **en·'list·ment** [-mənt] *s.* **1.** ✕ (An)Werbung *f,* Einstellung *f;* **2.** ✕ *Am.* a) Eintritt *m* in den Wehrdienst, b) (Dauer *m* der) (Wehr)Dienstverpflichtung; **3.** *fig.* Gewinnung *f* (*zur Mitarbeit*), Her'an-, Hin'zuziehung *f* (*von Helfern*).

en·liv·en [ɪn'laɪvn] *v/t.* beleben, in

Schwung bringen, ‚ankurbeln‘.

en masse [ɑ̃:ŋ'mæs] (*Fr.*) *adv.* **1.** in Massen; **2.** im Großen; **3.** zu'sammen, als Ganzes.

en·mesh [ɪn'meʃ] *v/t.* **1.** in e-m Netz fangen; **2.** *fig.* verstricken.

en·mi·ty ['enmətɪ] *s.* Feindschaft *f,* -seligkeit *f,* Hass *m:* **at** ∼ **with** verfeindet *od.* in Feindschaft mit; **bear no** ∼ nichts nachtragen.

en·no·ble [ɪ'nəʊbl] *v/t.* adeln (*a. fig.*), in den Adelsstand erheben; *fig.* veredeln, erhöhen; **en·'no·ble·ment** [-mənt] *s.* **1.** Erhebung *f* in den Adelsstand; **2.** *fig.* Veredelung *f.*

en·nui [ɑ̃:'nwiː] (*Fr.*) *s.* Langeweile *f.*

e·nor·mi·ty [ɪ'nɔːmətɪ] *s.* Ungeheuerlichkeit *f:* a) Enormi'tät *f,* b) Untat *f,* Gräuel *m,* Frevel *m;* **e'nor·mous** [-məs] *adj.* ☐ e'norm, ungeheuer(lich), gewaltig, riesig; **e'nor·mous·ness** [-məsnɪs] *s.* Riesengröße *f.*

e·nough [ɪ'nʌf] **I** *adj.* genug, ausreichend: ∼ **bread, bread** ∼ genug Brot, Brot genug; **not** ∼ **sense** nicht genug Verstand; **this is** ∼ (**for us**) das genügt (uns); **I was fool** ∼ **to believe her** ich war so dumm u. glaubte ihr; **he was not man** ∼ (*od.* ∼ **of a man**) (**to** *inf.*) er war nicht Manns genug (zu *inf.*); **that's** ∼ **to drive me mad** das macht mich (noch) wahnsinnig; **II** *s.* Genüge *f,* genügende Menge: **have** (**quite**) ∼ (völlig) genug haben; **I've had** ∼, **thank you** danke, ich bin satt; **I have** ∼ **of it** ich bin (*od.* habe) es satt, ‚ich bin bedient‘; ∼ **of that!, said!** genug davon!, Schluss damit!; ∼ **and to spare** mehr als genug; ∼ **is as good as a feast** allzu viel ist ungesund; **III** *adv.* genug, genügend; ganz, recht, ziemlich: **it's a good** ∼ **story** die Geschichte ist nicht übel; **he does not sleep** ∼ er schläft nicht genug; **be kind** ∼ **to help me** sei so gut und hilf mir; **oddly** ∼ sonderbarerweise; **safe** ∼ durchaus sicher; **sure** ∼ tatsächlich, gewiss; **true** ∼ nur zu wahr; **well** ∼ recht *od.* ziemlich *od.* ganz gut; **he could do it well** ∼ (**but** ...) er könnte es (zwar) recht gut, (aber ...); **you know well** ∼ du weißt es (ganz) genau; **that's not good** ∼ das reicht nicht, das lasse ich nicht gelten.

en pas·sant [ɑ̃:m'pæsɑ̃:ŋ] (*Fr.*) *adv.* en pas'sant: a) im Vor'beigehen, b) beiläufig, neben'her, -'bei.

en·plane [ɪn'pleɪn] → **emplane**.

en·print ['enprɪnt] *s. Brit. phot.* Abzug vom Negativ in der Größe $5{,}0 \times 3{,}5$ Zoll.

en·quire *etc.* → **inquire** *etc.*

en·rage [ɪn'reɪdʒ] *v/t.* wütend machen; **en·'raged** [-dʒd] *adj.* wütend, aufgebracht (**at, by** über *acc.*).

en·rapt [ɪn'ræpt] *adj.* hingerissen, entzückt; **en·'rap·ture** [-tʃə] *v/t.* entzücken: ∼**d with** hingerissen von.

en·rich [ɪn'rɪtʃ] *v/t.* **1.** (*a. o.s.* sich) bereichern (*a. fig.*); wertvoll(er) machen; **2.** anreichern: a) ⊙, ✻ veredeln, b) ertragreich(er) machen, c) den Nährwert erhöhen; **3.** ausschmücken, verzieren; **4.** *fig.* a) *Geist* bereichern, b) *Wert* steigern; **en·'rich·ment** [-mənt] *s.* **1.** Bereicherung *f* (*a. fig.*); **2.** ⊙, ✻ Anreicherung *f;* **3.** *fig.* Befruchtung *f;* **4.** Ausschmückung *f.*

en·rol(l) [ɪn'rəʊl] **I** *v/t.* **1.** *j-s Namen* eintragen, -schreiben (**in** in *acc.*); *univ. j-n* immatrikulieren: ∼ **o.s.** → 5; **2.** a) *mst* ✕ (an)werben, b) ♣ anmustern, anheuern, c) *Arbeiter* einstellen: **be enrolled** eingestellt werden, in e-e Firma eintreten; **3.** als Mitglied aufnehmen: ∼

o.s. in a society e-r Gesellschaft beitreten; **4.** ⚖ registrieren, protokollieren; **II** *v/i.* **5.** sich einschreiben (lassen), *univ.* sich immatrikulieren: **~** *for a course* e-n Kurs belegen; **en'rol(l)ment** [-mənt] *s.* **1.** Eintragung *f*, -schreibung *f*; *univ.* Immatrikulati'on *f*; **2.** *bsd.* ✕ Anwerbung *f*, Einstellung *f*, Aufnahme *f*; **3.** Beitrittserklärung *f*; **4.** ⚖ Re'gister *n*.

en route [ã:n'ru:t] (*Fr.*) *adv.* unterwegs (*for* nach); auf der Reise (*from ... to* von ... nach).

ens [enz] *pl.* **entia** ['enʃɪə] (*Lat.*) *s. phls.* Ens *n*, Sein *n*, Wesen *n*.

en·sconce [ɪn'skɒns] *v/t.* **1.** (*mst* **~** *o.s.* sich) verstecken, verbergen; **2. ~** *o.s.* es sich bequem machen (*in* e-m *Sessel etc.*).

en·sem·ble [ã:n'sã:mbl] (*Fr.*) *s.* **1.** *das* Ganze, Gesamteindruck *m*; **2.** ♪, *thea.* En'semble *n*; **3.** *Mode:* En'semble *n*, Kom'plet *n*.

en·shrine [ɪn'ʃraɪn] *v/t.* **1.** *in* e-n Schrein einschließen; **2.** (als Heiligtum) bewahren; **3.** als Schrein dienen für.

en·shroud [ɪn'ʃraʊd] *v/t.* ein-, verhüllen (*a. fig.*).

en·sign ['ensaɪn; *bsd.* ✕ u. ♣ 'ensn] *s.* **1.** Fahne *f*, Stan'darte *f*, ♣ (Schiffs-)Flagge, *bsd.* (Natio'nal)Flagge *f*: *white* (*red*) **~** Flagge der brit. Kriegs- (Handels)marine; *blue* **~** Flagge der brit. Flottenreserve; **2.** ['ensaɪn] *hist. Brit.* Fähnrich *m*; **3.** ['ensn] ♣ *Am.* Leutnant *m* zur See; **4.** (Rang)Abzeichen *n*.

en·si·lage ['ensɪlɪdʒ] ✔ **I** *s.* **1.** Silierung *f*; **2.** Silo-, Gärfutter *n*; **II** *v/t.* **3.** → **en·sile** [ɪn'saɪl] *v/t.* ✔ *Futterpflanzen* silieren.

en·slave [ɪn'sleɪv] *v/t.* versklaven, zum Sklaven machen (*a. fig.*): *be* **~***d by* j-m *od.* e-r *Sache* verfallen sein; **en·'slave·ment** [-mənt] *s.* **1.** Versklavung *f*, Sklave'rei *f*; **2.** *fig.* (*to*) sklavische Abhängigkeit *f* (von) *od.* Bindung (an *acc.*), Hörigkeit *f*.

en·snare [ɪn'sneə] *v/t.* **1.** *in* e-r Schlinge fangen; **2.** *fig.* berücken, bestricken, um'garnen.

en·sue [ɪn'sju:] *v/i.* **1.** 'darauf folgen, (nach)folgen; **2.** folgen, sich ergeben (*from* aus); **en·'su·ing** [-ɪŋ] *adj.* (nach)folgend.

en·sure [ɪn'ʃʊə] *v/t.* **1.** (*against*, *from*) (*o.s.* sich) sichern, sicherstellen (gegen), schützen (vor); **2.** Gewähr bieten für, garantieren (*et.*, *that* dass, *s.o. being* dass j-d ist); **3.** für *et.* sorgen: **~** *that* dafür sorgen, dass.

en·tail [ɪn'teɪl] **I** *v/t.* **1.** ⚖ a) in ein Erbgut umwandeln, b) als Erbgut vererben (*on* auf *acc.*): **~***ed estate* Erb-, Familiengut *n*; **~***ed interest* beschränktes Eigentumsrecht; **2.** *fig.* a) mit sich bringen, zur Folge haben, nach sich ziehen, b) erforderlich machen, erfordern; **II** *s.* **3.** ⚖ a) (Über'tragung *f* als) unveräußerliches Erbgut, b) (festgelegte) Erbfolge.

en·tan·gle [ɪn'tæŋgl] *v/t.* **1.** *Haare, Garn etc.* verwirren, 'verfilzen; **2.** (*o.s.* sich) verwickeln, -heddern (*in in acc.*); **3.** *fig.* verwickeln, verstricken: **~** *o.s. in s.th.*, *become* **~***d in s.th.* in e-e Sache verwickelt werden; *become* **~***d with s.o.* sich mit j-m einlassen; **en·'tan·gle·ment** [-mənt] *s.* **1.** *a. fig.* Verwicklung *f*, Verwirrung *f*, Verstrickung *f*; **2.** *fig.* Kompliziertheit *f*; **3.** Liebschaft *f*, Liai-'son *f*; **4.** ✕ Drahtverhau *m*.

en·tente [ã:n'tã:nt] (*Fr.*) *s.* En'tente *f*, Bündnis *n*.

en·ter ['entə] **I** *v/t.* **1.** eintreten, -fahren, -steigen, (hin'ein)gehen, (-)kommen in (*acc.*), *Haus etc.* betreten; in *ein Land* einreisen; ✕ einrücken in (*acc.*); ♣, ✈ einlaufen in (*acc.*): **~** *the skull* in den Schädel eindringen (*Kugel etc.*); *the idea* **~***ed my head* (*od.* *mind*) mir kam der Gedanke, ich hatte die Idee; **2.** sich in *et.* begeben: **~** *a hospital* ein Krankenhaus aufsuchen; **3.** eintreten in (*acc.*), beitreten (*dat.*), Mitglied werden (*gen.*): **~** *s.o.'s service* in j-s Dienst treten; **~** *a club* e-m Klub beitreten; **~** *the university* sein Studium aufnehmen; **~** *the army* (*the Church*) Soldat (Geistlicher) werden; **~** *a profession* e-n Beruf ergreifen; **4.** eintragen, -schreiben; hin'einbringen; j-n aufnehmen, zulassen: **~** *one's name* sich einschreiben *od.* anmelden; **~** *s.o. at a school* j-n zur Schule anmelden; *be* **~***ed univ.* immatrikuliert werden; **5.** ✝ (ver)buchen, eintragen: **~** *to s.o.'s debit* j-m *et.* in Rechnung stellen; → *credit* 2; **~** *up Posten* regelrecht verbuchen; **6.** *sport* melden, nennen (*for* für); **7.** ♣, ✝ *Schiff* einklarieren; *Waren beim Zollamt* deklarieren; **8.** einreichen, -bringen, geltend machen: **~** *an action* ⚖ e-e Klage einreichen; **~** *a motion parl.* e-n Antrag einbringen; **~** *a protest* Protest erheben; **II** *v/i.* **9.** (ein)treten, her'ein-, hin'einkommen, -gehen; ✕ einrücken; eindringen: *I don't* **~** *in it fig.* ich habe damit nichts zu tun; **~***!* herein!; **10.** *sport* sich melden, nennen (*for* für, zu); **11.** *thea.* auftreten: **⚲** *Hamlet* Hamlet tritt auf; *Zssgn mit prp.:*

en·ter| in·to *v/i.* **1.** → *enter* 1, 2, 3; **2.** *Vertrag, Bündnis* eingehen, schließen: **~** *an obligation* e-e Verpflichtung eingehen; **~** *a partnership* sich assoziieren; **3.** *et.* beginnen, sich beteiligen an (*dat.*), eingehen auf (*acc.*), sich einlassen auf *od.* in (*acc.*): **~** *correspondence* in Briefwechsel treten; **~** *a joke* auf e-n Scherz eingehen; → *detail* 1; **4.** sich hin'einversetzen in (*acc.*): **~** *s.o.'s feelings* sich in j-n hineinversetzen, j-s Gefühle verstehen; **~** *the spirit* sich in den Geist e-r *Sache* einfühlen *od.* hineinversetzen; **~** *the spirit of the game* mitmachen; **5.** e-e Rolle spielen bei: *this did not* **~** *our plans* das war nicht eingeplant; **~** *on od.* **up·on** *v/i.* **1.** ⚖ *Besitz* ergreifen von: **~** *an inheritance* e-e Erbschaft antreten; **2.** a) *Thema* anschneiden, b) sich in *ein Gespräch* einlassen; **3.** a) beginnen, in *ein* (*neues*) *Stadium od. ein neues Lebensjahr* eintreten, b) *Amt* antreten, *Laufbahn* einschlagen; **4.** in *ein neues Stadium* treten.

en·ter·ic [en'terɪk] *adj.* **1.** *anat.* enterisch, Darm...: **~** *fever* (Unterleibs)Typhus *m*; **2.** ♯ darmlöslich: **~** *pill* darmlösliche Pille; **en·ter·i·tis** [,entə'raɪtɪs] *s.* ♯ 'Darmka-,tarr(h) *m*, Ente'ritis *f*.

en·ter key [en'təki:] *s. Computer:* Eingabetaste *f*, 'Enter-Taste *f*.

en·ter·o·gas·tri·tis [,entərəʊɡæ'straɪtɪs] *s.* Magen-'Darm-Ka,tarr(h) *m*; **en·ter·on** [en'terən] *pl.* **-ter·a** [-rə] *s.* Enteron *n*, (*bsd.* Dünn)Darm *m*.

en·ter·prise ['entəpraɪz] *s.* **1.** Unter-'nehmen *n*, -'nehmung *f*; **2.** ✝ Unter-'nehmen *n*, Betrieb *m*: *free* **~** *zone* Gewerbegebiet *n*; *free* **~** freies Unternehmertum, freie (Markt)Wirtschaft; *free* **~** *economist* Marktwirtschaftler *m*; **3.** Initia'tive *f*, Unter'nehmungsgeist *m*, -lust *f*; **'en·ter·pris·ing** [-zɪŋ] *adj.* □

1. unter'nehmend, unter'nehmungslustig, mit Unter'nehmungsgeist; **2.** kühn, wagemutig.

en·ter·tain [,entə'teɪn] **I** *v/t.* **1.** (angenehm) unter'halten, amüsieren (*a. iro.*); **2.** j-n gastlich aufnehmen, bewirten, einladen; **3.** *Furcht, Hoffnung etc.* hegen; **4.** *Vorschlag etc.* in Erwägung ziehen, eingehen auf (*acc.*), näher treten (*dat.*): **~** *an idea* sich mit e-m Gedanken tragen; **II** *v/i.* **5.** Gäste empfangen, ein gastliches Haus führen: *they* **~** *a great deal* sie haben oft Gäste; **en·ter'tain·er** [-nə] *s.* **1.** Gastgeber(in); **2.** Unter'halter(in), *engS.* Enter'tainer (-in), Unter'haltungskünstler(in); **en·ter'tain·ing** [-nɪŋ] *adj.* □ unter'haltend, -'haltsam, amü'sant; **en·ter'tain·ment** [-mənt] *s.* **1.** Unter'haltung *f*, Belustigung *f*: *place of* **~** Vergnügungsstätte *f*; **~** *tax* Vergnügungssteuer *f*; *much to his* **~** sehr zu s-r Belustigung; **2.** (öffentliche) Unterhaltung, *thea. etc.* a. Enter'tainment *n*: **~** *electronics* Unterhaltungselektronik *f*; **~** *expenses* Bewirtungskosten *pl.*; **~** *industry* Unterhaltungsindustrie *f*; **~***s officer* Animateur *m*; **3.** Gastfreundschaft *f*, Bewirtung *f*: **~** *allowance* ✝ Aufwandsentschädigung *f*; **4.** Fest *n*, Gesellschaft *f*.

en·thral(l) [ɪn'θrɔ:l] *v/t.* **1.** *fig.* bezaubern, fesseln, in s-n Bann schlagen; **2.** *obs.* unter'jochen; **en·'thrall·ing** [-lɪŋ] *adj.* fesselnd, bezaubernd; **en·'thral(l)·ment** [-mənt] *s.* **1.** Bezauberung *f*; **2.** *obs.* Unter'jochung *f*.

en·throne [ɪn'θrəʊn] *v/t.* auf den Thron setzen, *a. eccl. Bischof* inthronisieren: *be* **~***d fig.* thronen; **en·'throne·ment** [-mənt] *s.* Inthronisati'on *f*.

en·thuse [ɪn'θju:z] F **I** *v/t.* begeistern; **II** *v/i.* (*about*) begeistert sein (von), schwärmen (für, von); **en·'thu·si·asm** [-zɪæzəm] *s.* **1.** Enthusi'asmus *m*, Begeisterung *f* (*for* für, *about* über *acc.*); **2.** Schwärme'rei *f*; **en·'thu·si·ast** [-zɪæst] *s.* **1.** Enthusi'ast(in); **2.** Schwärmer(in); **en·thu·si·as·tic** [ɪn-,θju:zɪ'æstɪk] *adj.* (□ **~***ally*) enthusi'astisch, begeistert (*about*, *over* über *acc.*): *become* (*od.* *get*) **~** in Begeisterung geraten.

en·tice [ɪn'taɪs] *v/t.* **1.** locken: **~** *s.o. away* a) j-n weglocken (*from* von), b) ✝ j-n abwerben; **~** *s.o.'s wife away* j-m s-e Frau abspenstig machen; **2.** verlocken, -leiten, -führen (*into s.th.* zu et., *to do od. into doing* zu tun); **en·'tice·ment** [-mənt] *s.* **1.** (Ver-)Lockung *f*, (An)Reiz *m*; **2.** Verführung *f*, -leitung *f*; **en·'tic·ing** [-sɪŋ] *adj.* □ verlockend, verführerisch.

en·tire [ɪn'taɪə] **I** *adj.* □ → *entirely*; **1.** ganz, völlig, vollkommen, vollständig, vollzählig, kom'plett, Gesamt...; **2.** ganz, unversehrt, unbeschädigt; **3.** voll, ungeschmälert, uneingeschränkt: *he enjoys my* **~** *confidence*; **4.** nicht kastriert: **~** *horse* Hengst *m*; **II** *s.* **5.** *das* Ganze; **6.** nicht kastriertes Pferd, Hengst *m*; **7.** ♥ Ganzsache *f*; **en·'tire·ly** [-lɪ] *adv.* **1.** völlig, gänzlich, ganz u. gar; **2.** ausschließlich: *it is* **~** *his fault*; **en·'tire·ty** [-tɪ] *s. das* Ganze, Ganzheit *f*, Gesamtheit *f*: *in its* **~** in s-r Gesamtheit, als Ganzes.

en·ti·tle [ɪn'taɪtl] *v/t.* **1.** *Buch etc.* betiteln: **~***d Buch etc.* mit dem Titel ...; **2.** j-n anreden, titulieren; **3.** (*to*) j-n berechtigen (zu), j-m ein Anrecht geben (auf *acc.*): *be* **~***d to* berechtigt sein zu, e-n (Rechts)Anspruch haben auf (*acc.*); **~d to vote** stimm-, wahlberechtigt; **en·ti·tle·ment** [-mənt] *s.* (berechtigter) Anspruch; zustehender Betrag.

en·ti·ty ['entətɪ] *s.* **1.** Dasein *n*; **2.** Wesen *n*, Ding *n*; **3.** 🏚 'Rechtsper,sönlichkeit *f*; **legal ~** juristische Person; **4.** *EDV etc.*: Enti'tät *f*, (separate) Informationseinheit *f*.

en·tomb [ɪn'tuːm] *v/t.* **1.** begraben, beerdigen; **2.** verschütten, lebendig begraben; **en'tomb·ment** [-mənt] *s.* Begräbnis *n*.

en·to·mo·log·i·cal [ˌentəmə'lɒdʒɪk(l)] *adj.* ☐ entomo'logisch, Insekten...; **en·to·mol·o·gist** [ˌentəʊ'mɒlədʒɪst] *s.* Entomo'loge *m*; **en·to·mol·o·gy** [ˌentəʊ'mɒlədʒɪ] *s.* Entomolo'gie *f*, In'sektenkunde *f*.

en·tou·rage [ˌɒntʊ'rɑːʒ] (*Fr.*) *s.* Entou'rage *f*: a) Um'gebung *f*, b) Gefolge *n*.

en·to·zo·on [ˌentəʊ'zəʊɒn] *pl.* **-zo·a** [-ə] *s. zo.* Ento'zoon *n* (*Parasit*).

entr'acte ['ɒntrækt] (*Fr.*) *s. thea.* Zwischenakt *m*, -spiel *n*.

en·trails ['entreɪlz] *s. pl.* **1.** *anat.* Eingeweide *pl.*; **2.** *fig.* das Innere.

en·train [ɪn'treɪn] 🚂 **I** *v/i.* einsteigen; **II** *v/t.* verladen.

en·trance¹ ['entrəns] *s.* **1.** a) Eintreten *n*, Eintritt *m*, b) 🚢 Einlaufen *n*, Einfahrt *f*, c) ✈ Einflug *m*: **~ duty** 🛃 Eingangszoll *m*; **make one's ~** eintreten, erscheinen (→ 4); **2.** Ein-, Zugang *m*; Zufahrt *f*, (a. Hafen)Einfahrt *f*: **~ hall** (Eingangs-, Vor)Halle *f*, Hausflur *m*; **3.** Einlass *m*, Ein-, Zutritt *m*: **~ fee** a) Eintritt(sgeld *n*) *m*, b) Aufnahmegebühr *f*; **~ examination** Aufnahmeprüfung *f*; **no ~!** Zutritt verboten!; **4.** *thea.* Auftritt *m*: **make one's ~** auftreten; **5.** (**on**, **upon**) Antritt *m* (*e-s Amtes, e-r Erbschaft etc.*); **6.** *fig.* (**to**) Beginn *m* (*gen.*), Einstieg *m* (in *acc.*).

en·trance² [ɪn'trɑːns] *v/t.* in Verzückung versetzen, hinreißen; **~d** ver-, entzückt, hingerissen; **~d with joy** freudetrunken; **en'trance·ment** [-mənt] *s.* Verzückung *f*; **en'tranc·ing** [-sɪŋ] *adj.* hinreißend, bezaubernd.

en·trant ['entrənt] *s.* **1.** Eintretende(r *m*) *f*; **2.** neues Mitglied; **3.** Berufsanfänger(in) (**to** in *dat.*); **4.** *bsd. sport* Teilnehmer(in), Konkur'rent(in), *a.* Bewerber(in).

en·trap [ɪn'træp] *v/t.* **1.** (in e-r Falle) fangen; **2.** verführen, verleiten (**into doing** zu tun).

en·treat [ɪn'triːt] *v/t.* **1.** *j-n* dringend bitten *od.* ersuchen, anflehen; **2.** *et.* erflehen; **3.** *obs. od. bibl. j-n* behandeln; **en'treat·ing·ly** [-ɪŋlɪ] *adv.* flehentlich; **en'treat·y** [-tɪ] *s.* dringende Bitte, Flehen *n*.

en·trée ['ɒntreɪ] (*Fr.*) *s.* **1.** *bsd. fig.* Zutritt *m* (**into** zu); **2.** *Küche*: a) En'tree *n*, Zwischengericht *n*, b) *Am.* Hauptgericht *n*; **3.** ♪ En'tree *n*.

en·tre·mets ['ɒntrəmeɪ; *pl.* 'ɒntrəmeɪz] (*Fr.*) *s.* a) Zwischengericht *n*, b) Süßspeise *f*.

en·trench [ɪn'trentʃ] *v/t.* ✕ mit Schützengräben durch'ziehen, befestigen: **~ o.s.** sich verschanzen *od.* festsetzen (*beide a. fig.*); **~ed** *fig.* eingewurzelt, verwurzelt; **en'trench·ment** [-mənt] *s.* ✕ **1.** Verschanzung *f*; **2.** *pl.* Schützengräben *pl.*

en·tre·pôt ['ɒntrəpəʊ] (*Fr.*) ✝ **1.** Lager-, Stapelplatz *m*; **2.** (Waren-, Zoll-) Niederlage *f*.

en·tre·pre·neur [ˌɒntrəprə'nɜː] (*Fr.*) *s.* **1.** ✝ Unter'nehmer *m*; **2.** *Am.* Veran-

stalter *m*; **en·tre·pre'neur·i·al** [-ɜːrɪəl] *adj.* ✝ unter'nehmerisch, Unternehmer...

en·tre·sol ['ɒntrəsɒl] (*Fr.*) *s.* 🔺 Zwischen-, Halbgeschoss, *östr.* -geschoß *n*.

en·trust [ɪn'trʌst] *v/t.* **1.** anvertrauen (**to** *dat.*); **2.** *j-n* betrauen (**with s.th.** mit et.).

en·try ['entrɪ] *s.* **1.** Zugang *m*, Zutritt *m*, Einreise *f*, Einreisegenehmigung *f*; **~ visa** Einreisevisum *n*; **no ~!** Kein Zutritt!, *mot.* Keine Einfahrt!; **2.** Eintritt *m*, -gang *m*, -fahrt *f*, -zug *m*, -rücken *m*; **3.** Eingang(stür *f*) *m*, Einfahrt(stor *n*) *f*; (Eingangs)Halle *f*; **4.** *thea.* Auftritt *m*; **5.** (Amts-, Dienst)Antritt *m*: **~ into office** (**service**); **6.** 🏚 a) Besitzantritt *m*, -ergreifung *f* (**upon** gen.), b) Eindringen *n*, -bruch *m*; **7.** *fig.* Beitritt *m* (**to**, **into** zu); **8.** ✝, ⚓ Einklarierung *f*: **~ inwards** Einfuhrdeklaration *f*; **9.** Eintragung *f*, Vermerk *m*; **10.** ✝ a) Buchung *f*: **credit ~** Gutschrift *f*; **debit ~** Lastschrift *f*; **make an ~** (**of**) (*et.*) buchen, b) Posten *m*, c) Eingang *m* (*von Geldern*); **11.** Stichwort *n* (*Lexikon*); **12.** *bsd. sport* a) Meldung *f*, Nennung *f*, Teilnahme *f*: **~ form** (An)Meldeformular *n*; **~ fee** Nenngebühr *f*, Startgeld *n*, b) → **entrant** 4; '**~·phone** *s.* Sprechanlage *f*.

en·twine [ɪn'twaɪn] *v/t.* **1.** um'schlingen, um'winden, (ver)flechten (*a. fig.*); **~d letters** verschlungene Buchstaben; **2.** winden, schlingen (**about** um).

en·twist [ɪn'twɪst] *v/t.* (ver)flechten, um'winden, verknüpfen.

e·nu·cle·ate [ɪ'njuːklɪeɪt] *v/t.* **1.** 🗡 Tumor ausschälen; **2.** *fig.* erläutern, deutlich machen.

e·nu·mer·ate [ɪ'njuːməreɪt] *v/t.* **1.** aufzählen; **2.** spezifizieren; **e·nu·mer·a·tion** [ɪˌnjuːmə'reɪʃn] *s.* **1.** Aufzählung *f*; **2.** Liste *f*, Verzeichnis *n*; **e'nu·mer·a·tor** [-tə] *s.* Zähler *m* (*bei Volkszählungen*).

e·nun·ci·ate [ɪ'nʌnsɪeɪt] *v/t.* **1.** (deutlich) ausdrücken, -sprechen; **2.** behaupten, erklären, formulieren; *Grundsatz* aufstellen; **e·nun·ci·a·tion** [ɪˌnʌnsɪ'eɪʃn] *s.* **1.** Ausdruck *m*; Ausdrucks-, Vortragsweise *f*; **2.** Erklärung *f*, Verkündung *f*; Aufstellung *f* (*e-s Grundsatzes*); **e'nun·ci·a·tive** [-nʃɪətɪv] *adj.*: **be ~ of s.th.** et. ausdrücken.

en·ure → **inure**.

en·vel·op [ɪn'veləp] **I** *v/t.* **1.** einwickeln, -schlagen, (ein)hüllen (**in** in *acc.*); **2.** *oft fig.* um-, ver'hüllen, um'geben; **3.** ✕ um'fassen, um'klammern; **II** *s.* **4.** *Am.* → **en·ve·lope** *f* (*e-s Umschlags*); **en·ve·lope** ['envələʊp] *s.* **1.** Decke *f*, Hülle *f* (*a. anat.*), 'Umschlag *m*; **2.** 'Brief,umschlag *m*; **3.** ✈ (Bal'lon)Hülle *f*; **4.** ✿ Kelch *m*; **en'vel·op·ment** [-mənt] *s.* **1.** Um'hüllung *f*, Hülle *f*; **2.** ✕ Um'fassung(sangriff *m*) *f*, Um'klammerung *f*.

en·ven·om [ɪn'venəm] *v/t.* **1.** vergiften (*a. fig.*); **2.** *fig.* a) verschärfen, b) mit Hass erfüllen.

en·vi·a·ble ['envɪəbl] *adj.* ☐ beneidenswert, zu beneiden(d); '**en·vi·er** [-vɪə] *s.* Neider(in); '**en·vi·ous** [-vɪəs] *adj.* ☐ (**of**) neidisch (auf *acc.*), 'missgünstig (gegen): **be ~ of s.o. because of** *j-n* beneiden um.

en·vi·ron [ɪn'vaɪərən] *v/t.* um'geben (*a. fig.*); **en'vi·ron·ment** [-mənt] *s.* **1.** *a.* **~s** *pl.* Um'gebung *f* (*e-s Ortes*); **2.** *biol., sociol.* Um'gebung *f*, 'Umwelt *f*, Mili'eu *n* (*a.* 🧠): **~ policy** 'Umweltpolitik *f*; **en·vi·ron·men·tal** [ɪnˌvaɪərən'mentl] *adj.* ☐ *biol., psych.* Milieu..., Um-

welt(s)...: **~ awareness** Umweltbewusstsein *n*; **~ly aware** 'umweltbe,wusst; **~ compatibility** Umweltverträglichkeit *f*; **~ compatibility assessment** Umweltverträglichkeitsprüfung *f*; **~ crime** a) 'Umweltkriminali,tät *f*, b) 'Umweltverbrechen *n*, Verbrechen *n* an der 'Umwelt; **~ disaster** Umweltkatastrophe *f*; **~ engineering** Umwelttechnik *f*; **~ly friendly** umweltfreundlich; **~ impact** Umwelteinfluss *m*; **~ pollution** Umweltverschmutzung *f*; **~ protection** Umweltschutz *m*; **~ regulations** Umweltschutzbestimmungen *pl.*; **~ summit** 'Umweltgipfel(treffen *n*) *m*; **~ technology** Umwelttechnik *f*; **en·vi·ron·men·tal·ism** [ɪnˌvaɪərən'mentəlɪzəm] *s.* **1.** 'Umweltschutz(bewegung *f*) *m*; **2.** *sociol.* Environmenta'lismus *m*; **en·vi·ron·men·tal·ist** [ɪnˌvaɪərən'mentəlɪst] *s.* 'Umweltschützer(in); **en·vi·ron·men·tal·ly** [ɪnˌvaɪərən'mentəlɪ] *adv.* in Bezug auf *od.* durch die Umwelt: **~ beneficial** (**harmful**) umweltfreundlich (-belastend, -schädigend, -feindlich); **en·vi·rons** [ɪn'vaɪərənz] *s. pl.* Um'gebung *f*, 'Umgegend *f*.

en·vis·age [ɪn'vɪzɪdʒ] *v/t.* **1.** in Aussicht nehmen, ins Auge fassen, gedenken (**doing** *et.* zu tun); **2.** sich *et.* vorstellen; **3.** *j-n, et.* begreifen (**as** als).

en·vi·sion [ɪn'vɪʒn] *v/t.* sich *et.* vorstellen.

en·voy¹ ['envɔɪ] *s.* Zueignungs-, Schlussstrophe *f* (*e-s Gedichts*).

en·voy² ['envɔɪ] *s.* **1.** *pol.* Gesandte(r) *m*; **2.** Abgesandte(r) *m*, Be'vollmächtigte(r) *m*.

en·vy ['envɪ] **I** *s.* **1.** (**of**) Neid *m* (auf *acc.*), 'Missgunst *f* (gegen): **be eaten up with ~** vor Neid platzen; → **green** 1; **2.** Gegenstand *m* des Neides: **his car is the ~ of all** alle beneiden ihn um sein Auto; **II** *v/t.* **3.** *j-n* (um *et.*) beneiden: **I ~** (**him**) **his car** ich beneide ihn um sein Auto; **4.** *j-m et.* miss'gönnen.

en·wrap [ɪn'ræp] → **wrap** I.

en·zyme ['enzaɪm] *s.* 🧪 En'zym *n*, Fer'ment *n*.

e·o·cene ['iːəʊsiːn] *s. geol.* Eo'zän *n*;

e·o·lith·ic [ˌiːəʊ'lɪθɪk] *adj. geol.* eo'lithisch.

e·on → **aeon**.

ep·au·let(te) ['epəʊlet] *s.* ✕ Epau'lette *f*, Achselschnur *f*, -stück *n*.

é·pée ['epeɪ] (*Fr.*) *s. fenc.* Degen *m*; **é·pee·ist** ['epeɪɪst] *s.* Degenfechter *m*.

ep·en·the·sis [e'penθɪsɪs] *s. ling.* Epen'these *f*, Lauteinfügung *f*.

e·pergne [ɪ'pɜːn] (*Fr.*) *s.* Tafelaufsatz *m*.

e·phed·rin(e) [ɪ'fedrɪn; 🧪 'efɪdriːn] *s.* 🧪 Ephe'drin *n*.

e·phem·er·a [ɪ'femərə] *s.* **1.** *zo. u. fig.* Eintagsfliege *f*; **2.** *pl. von* **ephemeron**; **e'phem·er·al** [-rəl] *adj.* ephe'mer: a) eintägig, b) *fig.* flüchtig, kurzlebig; **e'phem·er·on** [-rɒn] *pl.* **-a** [-ə], **-ons** *s. zo. u. fig.* Eintagsfliege *f*.

E·phe·sian [ɪ'fiːʒjən] *s.* **1.** 'Epheser(in); **2.** *pl. bibl.* (Brief *m* des Paulus an die) 'Epheser *pl.*

ep·ic ['epɪk] **I** *adj.* (☐ **~ally**) **1.** episch: **~ poem** Epos *n*; **2.** *fig.* heldenhaft, he'roisch, Helden...: **~ laughter** homerisches Gelächter; **II** *s.* **3.** Epos *n*, Heldengedicht *n*; **4.** *allg.* episches Werk.

ep·i·cene ['episiːn] *adj. ling. u. fig.* beiderlei Geschlechts.

ep·i·cen·ter *Am.*, **ep·i·cen·tre** ['episentə] *Brit.*, **ep·i·cen·trum** ['episentrəm] *s.* **1.** Epi'zentrum *n* (*Gebiet über dem Erdbebenherd*); **2.** *fig.* Mittelpunkt

m.

ep·i·cure ['epɪˌkjuə] *s.* Genießer *m*, Genussmensch *m*; Feinschmecker *m*; **ep·i·cu·re·an** [ˌepɪkjuə'riːən] I *adj.* **1.** ♎ *phls.* epiku'reisch; **2.** a) genusssüchtig, schwelgerisch, b) feinschmeckerisch; II *s.* **3.** ♎ *phls.* Epiku'reer *m*; **4.** → *epicure*; **'ep·i·cur·ism** [-kjuərɪzəm] *s.* **1.** ♎ *phls.* Epikure'ismus *m*; **2.** Genusssucht *f.*

ep·i·cy·cle ['epɪsaɪkl] *s.* Ⓐ, *ast.* Epi'zykel *m*; **ep·i·cy·clic** [ˌepɪ'saɪklɪk] *adj.* epi'zyklisch: ~ *gear* ⊕ Planetengetriebe *n*; **ep·i·cy·cloid** [ˌepɪ'saɪklɔɪd] *s.* Ⓐ Epizyklo'ide *f.*

ep·i·dem·ic [ˌepɪ'demɪk] I *adj.* (□ ~*ally*) ⚕ epi'demisch, seuchenartig, *fig.* a. grassierend; II *s.* ⚕ Epide'mie *f*, Seuche *f* (*beide a. fig.*); **ˌep·i·dem·i·cal** [-kl] → *epidemic* I; **ep·i·de·mi·ol·o·gy** [ˌepɪdiːmɪ'ɒlədʒɪ] *s.* ⚕ Epidemiolo'gie *f.*

ep·i·der·mis [ˌepɪ'dɜːmɪs] *s. anat.* Epi'dermis *f*, Oberhaut *f.*

ep·i·gas·tri·um [ˌepɪ'ɡæstrɪəm] *s. anat.* Epi'gastrium *n*, Oberbauchgegend *f*, Magengrube *f.*

ep·i·glot·tis [ˌepɪ'ɡlɒtɪs] *s. anat.* Epi'glottis *f*, Kehldeckel *m.*

ep·i·gone ['epɪɡəʊn] *s.* Epi'gone *m.*

ep·i·gram ['epɪɡræm] *s.* Epi'gramm *n*, Sinngedicht *n*, -spruch *m*; **ep·i·gram·mat·ic** [ˌepɪɡrə'mætɪk] *adj.* (□ ~*ally*) **1.** epigram'matisch; **2.** kurz u. treffend, scharf pointiert; **ep·i·gram·ma·tist** [ˌepɪ'ɡræmətɪst] *s.* Epigram'matiker *m*; **ep·i·gram·ma·tize** [ˌepɪ'ɡræmətaɪz] I *v/t.* **1.** kurz u. treffend formulieren; **2.** ein Epi'gramm verfassen über *od.* auf (*acc.*); II *v/i.* **3.** Epi'gramme verfassen.

ep·i·graph ['epɪɡrɑːf] *s.* **1.** Epi'graph *n*, Inschrift *f*; **2.** Sinnspruch *m*, Motto *n*; **ep·i·graph·ic** [ˌepɪ'ɡræfɪk] *adj.* epi'graphisch; **e·pig·ra·phist** [e'pɪɡrəfɪst] *s.* Epi'graphiker *m*, Inschriftenforscher *m.*

ep·i·lep·sy ['epɪlepsɪ] *s.* ⚕ Epilep'sie *f*; **ep·i·lep·tic** [ˌepɪ'leptɪk] *adj.* epi'leptisch; II *s.* Epi'leptiker(in).

ep·i·logue, *Am. a.* **ep·i·log** ['epɪlɒɡ] *s.* **1.** Epi'log *m*: a) Nachwort *n*, b) *thea.* Schlussrede *f*, c) *fig.* Ausklang *m*, Nachspiel *n*, -lese *f*; **2.** *Radio, TV:* (Wort *n* zum) Tagesausklang *m.*

E·piph·a·ny [ɪ'pɪfənɪ] *s. eccl.* **1.** Epi'phanias *n*, Drei'königsfest *n*; **2.** ♎ Epipha'nie *f* (*göttliche Erscheinung*).

e·pis·co·pa·cy [ɪ'pɪskəpəsɪ] *s. eccl.* Episko'pat *m, n*: a) bischöfliche Verfassung, b) Gesamtheit *f* der Bischöfe, c) Amtstätigkeit *f* e-s Bischofs, d) Bischofsamt *n*, -würde *f*; **e·pis·co·pal** [-pl] *adj.* □ *eccl.* bischöflich: ♎ *Church* Episko'palkirche *f*; **e·pis·co·pa·li·an** [ɪˌpɪskəʊ'peɪljən] I *adj.* **1.** bischöflich; **2.** zu e-r Episko'palkirche gehörig; II *s.* **3.** Mitglied *n* e-r Episko'palkirche; **e·pis·co·pate** [-kəʊpət] *s. eccl.* Episko'pat *m, n*: a) → *episcopacy* b u. d, b) Bistum *n.*

ep·i·sode ['epɪsəʊd] *s. allg.* Epi'sode *f*: a) Neben-, Zwischenhandlung *f* (*im Drama etc.*), eingeflochtene Erzählung, b) (Neben)Ereignis *n*, Vorfall *m*, Erlebnis *n*, c) ♪ Zwischenspiel *n*; **ep·i·sod·ic, ep·i·sod·i·cal** [ˌepɪ'sɒdɪk(l)] *adj.* □ epi'sodisch.

e·pis·te·mol·o·gy [eˌpɪstɪ'mɒlədʒɪ] *s. phls.* Er'kenntnistheo,rie *f.*

e·pis·tle [ɪ'pɪsl] *s.* **1.** E'pistel *f*, Sendschreiben *n*; **2.** ♎ a) *bibl.* (Römer- *etc.*) Brief *m*, b) *eccl.* E'pistel *f* (*Auszug aus* a); **3.** E'pistel *f*, (*bsd.* langer) Brief; **e'pis·to·lar·y** [-stələrɪ] *adj.* ... Brief...

ep·i·style ['epɪstaɪl] *s.* 🏛 Epi'styl *n*,

Tragbalken *m.*

ep·i·taph ['epɪtɑːf] *s.* **1.** Epi'taph *n*, Grabschrift *f*; **2.** Totengedicht *n.*

ep·i·the·li·um [ˌepɪ'θiːljəm] *pl.* **-ums** *od.* **-a** [-ə] *s. anat.* Epi'thel *n.*

ep·i·thet ['epɪθet] *s.* **1.** E'pitheton *n*, Beiwort *n*, Attri'but *n*; **2.** Beiname *m.*

e·pit·o·me [ɪ'pɪtəmɪ] *s.* **1.** Auszug *m*, Abriss *m*, (kurze) Inhaltsangabe *od.* Darstellung: *in* → a) auszugsweise, b) in gedrängter Form; **2.** *fig.* (*of*) a) kleines Gegenstück (zu), Minia'tur *f* (*gen.*), b) Verkörperung *f* (*gen.*); **e'pit·o·mize** [-maɪz] *v/t.* e-n Auszug machen aus, *et.* kurz darstellen *od.* ausdrücken.

ep·i·zo·on [ˌepɪ'zəʊɒn] *pl.* **-a** [-ə] *s. zo.* Epi'zoon *n*; **ep·i·zo·ot·ic** [ˌepɪzəʊ'ɒtɪk] *s. vet.* Epizoo'tie *f* (*Tierseuche*).

e·poch ['iːpɒk] *s.* **1.** E'poche *f* (*a. geol. u. ast.*), Zeitalter *n*, -abschnitt *m*: *this marks an* → dies ist ein Markstein *od.* Wendepunkt (*in der Geschichte*); **ep·och·al** ['epɒkl] *adj.* epo'chal: a) Epochen..., b) → **'e·poch-ˌmak·ing** *adj.* E'poche machend, bahnbrechend.

ep·o·nym ['epəʊnɪm] *s.* Epo'nym *n* (*Gattungsbezeichnung, die auf e-n Personennamen zurückgeht*).

ep·o·pee ['epəʊpiː] *s.* **1.** → *epos*; **2.** epische Dichtung.

ep·os ['epɒs] *s.* **1.** Epos *n*, Heldengedicht *n*; **2.** (*mündlich überlieferte*) epische Dichtung.

Ep·som salt ['epsəm] *s.*, *oft pl. sg. konstr.* Epsomer Bittersalz *n.*

eq·ua·bil·i·ty [ˌekwə'bɪlətɪ] *s.* **1.** Gleichmäßigkeit *f*; **2.** Gleichmut *m*; **eq·ua·ble** ['ekwəbl] *adj.* □ **1.** gleichförmig, -mäßig; **2.** ausgeglichen, gleichmütig, gelassen.

e·qual ['iːkwəl] I *adj.* □ *equally*; **1.** gleich: *be* ~ *to* gleich sein, gleichen (*dat.*) (→ *a.* 2); *of* ~ *size*, ~ *in size* gleich groß; *with* ~ *courage* mit demselben Mut; *not* ~ *to* of geringer als; *other things being* ~ unter sonst gleichen Umständen; **2.** entsprechend: ~ *to the demand; be* ~ *to* gleichkommen (*dat.*); → 1; ~ *to new* wie neu; **3.** fähig, im'stande, gewachsen: ~ *to do* fähig zu tun; ~ *to a task* (*the occasion*) e-r Aufgabe (der Sache) gewachsen; **4.** aufgelegt, geneigt (*to dat. od.* zu): ~ *to a cup of tea* e-r Tasse Tee nicht abgeneigt; **5.** gleichmäßig; **6.** gleichberechtigt, -wertig, ebenbürtig: *on* ~ *terms* a) unter gleichen Bedingungen, b) auf gleicher Stufe stehend (*with* mit); ~ *opportunities* Chancengleichheit *f*; ~ *rights for women* Gleichberechtigung *f* der Frau; **7.** gleichmütig, gelassen: ~ *mind* Gleichmut *m*; II *s.* **8.** Gleichgestellte(r *m*) *f*, Ebenbürtige(r *m*) *f*: *your* ~s deinesgleichen; ~*s in age* Altersgenossen; *he has no* ~, *he is without* ~ er hat nicht *od.* sucht seinesgleichen; *be the* ~ *of s.o.* j-m ebenbürtig sein; III *v/t.* **9.** gleichen (*dat.*), gleichkommen (*in* an *dat.*): *not to be* ~(*l*)*ed* ohnegleichen (sein).

e·qual·i·tar·i·an [ɪˌkwɒlɪ'teərɪən] *etc.* → *egalitarian etc.*

e·qual·i·ty [iː'kwɒlətɪ] *s.* Gleichheit *f*: ~ (*of rights*) Gleichberechtigung *f*; ~ *of opportunity* Chancengleichheit *f*; ~ *of votes* Stimmengleichheit *f*; *be on an* ~ *with* a) auf gleicher Stufe stehen mit (*j-m*), b) gleichbedeutend sein mit (*et.*); ~ *sign, sign of* ~ Ⓐ Gleichheitszeichen *n*; **e·qual·i·za·tion** [ˌiːkwəlaɪ'zeɪʃn] *s.* **1.** Gleichstellung *f*, -machung *f*; **2.** *bsd.* ⚓ Ausgleich(ung *f*) *m*: ~ *fund* Ausgleichsfonds *m*; **3.** a) ⊕ Abgleich *m*, b) ⚡, *phot.* Entzerrung *f.*

e·qual·ize ['iːkwəlaɪz] I *v/t.* **1.** gleichmachen, -stellen, -setzen, angleichen; **2.** ausgleichen, kompensieren; **3.** a) ⊕ abgleichen, b) ⚡, *phot.* entzerren; II *v/i.* **4.** *sport* ausgleichen, den Ausgleich erzielen; **'e·qual·iz·er** [-zə] *s.* **1.** ⊕ Stabili'sator *m*; **2.** ⚡ Entzerrer *m*; **3.** *sport* Ausgleichstreffer *m od.* -punkt *m*; **4.** *sl.* Schießeisen *n*; **'e·qual·ly** [-əlɪ] *adv.* ebenso, gleich(ermaßen), in gleicher Weise; **'e·quals sign** [-lz] *s.* Ⓐ Gleichheitszeichen *n.*

e·qua·nim·i·ty [ˌekwə'nɪmətɪ] *s.* Gleichmut *m*, Gelassenheit *f.*

e·quate [ɪ'kweɪt] I *v/t.* **1.** ausgleichen; **2.** *j-n, et.* gleichstellen, -setzen (*to, with dat.*); **3.** Ⓐ in die Form e-r Gleichung bringen; **4.** als gleich(wertig) ansehen *od.* behandeln; II *v/i.* **5.** gleichen, entsprechen (*with dat.*); **e'quat·ed** [-tɪd] *adj.* ♏ Staffel...: ~ *calculation of interest* Staffelzinsrechnung *f*; **e'qua·tion** [-eɪʃn] *s.* **1.** Ausgleich *m*; **2.** Gleichheit *f*; **3.** Ⓐ, ♎, *ast.* Gleichung *f*: ~ *formula* Gleichungsformel *f*; **4.** *sociol.* Ge'samtkom,plex *m* der Fak'toren u. Mo'tive menschlichen Verhaltens; **e'qua·tor** [-tə] *s.* Ä'quator *m*; **e·qua·to·ri·al** [ˌekwə'tɔːrɪəl] *adj.* äquatori'al.

eq·uer·ry ['ekwərɪ; ɪ'kwerɪ] *s. Brit.* **1.** königlicher Stallmeister; **2.** per'sönlicher Diener (*e-s Mitglieds der königlichen Familie*).

e·ques·tri·an [ɪ'kwestrɪən] I *adj.* Reit(er)...: ~ *sports* Reitsport *m*; ~ *statue* Reiterstandbild *n*; II *s.* (Kunst)Reiter (-in).

equi- [iːkwɪ] *in Zssgn* gleich.

ˌequi'an·gu·lar *adj.* Ⓐ gleichwink(e)lig; **~'dis·tant** *adj.* □ gleich weit entfernt, in gleichem Abstand (*from* von); **ˌ~'lat·er·al** *bsd.* Ⓐ *adj.* gleichseitig: ~ *triangle*; II *s.* gleichseitige Fi'gur.

e·qui·li·brate [ˌiːkwɪ'laɪbreɪt] *v/t.* **1.** ins Gleichgewicht bringen (*a. fig.*); **2.** ⊕ auswuchten; **3.** ⚡ abgleichen; **e·qui·li·bra·tion** [ˌiːkwɪlaɪ'breɪʃn] *s.* **1.** Gleichgewicht *n*; **2.** Herstellung *f* des Gleichgewichts; **e·qui·li·brist** [iː'kwɪlɪbrɪst] *s.* Äquili'brist(in), *bsd.* Seiltänzer(in); **e·qui·lib·ri·um** [-'lɪbrɪəm] *s. phys.* Gleichgewicht *n* (*a. fig.*), Ba'lance *f.*

e·quine ['iːkwaɪn] *adj.* Pferde...

e·qui·noc·tial [ˌiːkwɪ'nɒkʃl] I *adj.* **1.** Äquinoktial..., die Tagund'nachtgleiche betreffend: ~ *point* → *equinox* 2; II *s.* **2.** a. ~ *circle od. line* 'Himmelsä,quator *m*; **3.** *pl.* → ~ *gale s.* Äquinokti'alsturm *m.*

e·qui·nox ['iːkwɪnɒks] *s.* **1.** Äqui'noktium *n*, Tagund'nachtgleiche *f*: *vernal* ~ Frühlingsäquinoktium; **2.** Äquinokti'alpunkt *m.*

e·quip [ɪ'kwɪp] *v/t.* **1.** ausrüsten, -statten (*with* mit) (*a.* ⚓, ✕, ⚒), *Klinik etc.* einrichten; **2.** *fig.* ausrüsten (*with* mit), *j-m das* (geistige) Rüstzeug geben (*for* für); **equ·i·page** ['ekwɪpɪdʒ] *s.* **1.** Ausrüstung *f* (*a.* ✕, ⚓); **2.** *obs.* Gebrauchsgegenstände *pl.*; **3.** Equi'page *f*, Kutsche *f*; **e'quip·ment** [-mənt] *s.* **1.** ✕, ⚓ Ausrüstung *f*; **2.** a) *a.* ⊕ Ausrüstung *f*, -stattung *f*, b) *mst pl.* Ausrüstung(sgegenstände *pl.*) *f*, Materi'al *n*, c) ⊕ Einrichtung *f*, (Betriebs)Anlage(n *pl.*) *f*, Ma'schine(n *pl.*) *f*, Gerät *n*, Appara'tur *f*, d) 🚂 *Am.* rollendes Materi'al; **3.** *fig.* (geistiges) Rüstzeug.

e·qui·poise ['ekwɪpɔɪz] I *s.* **1.** Gleichgewicht *n* (*a. fig.*); **2.** *fig.* Gegengewicht *n* (*to* zu); II *v/t.* **3.** im Gleichgewicht halten; **4.** ein Gegengewicht bilden zu.

eq·ui·ta·ble ['ekwɪtəbl] *adj.* □ **1.** ge-

201

equitableness – escape

recht, (recht u.) billig; **2.** 'unpar,teiisch; **3.** ⚖ a) auf dem Billigkeitsrecht beruhend, b) billigkeitsgerichtlich: ~ **mortgage** ✝ Hypothek *f* nach dem Billigkeitsrecht; **'eq·ui·ta·ble·ness** [-nɪs] → **equity** 1; **'eq·ui·ty** [-tɪ] *s.* **1.** Billigkeit *f*, Gerechtigkeit *f*, 'Unpar,teilichkeit *f*: *in* ~ billiger-, gerechterweise; **2.** ⚖ a) (*ungeschriebenes*) Billigkeitsrecht: *Court of* ⚖ Billigkeitsgericht *n*, b) Anspruch *m* nach dem Billigkeitsrecht; **3.** ⚖ Wert *m* nach Abzug aller Belastungen, reiner Wert (*e-s Hauses etc.*); **4.** ✝ a) *a.* ~ *capital* Eigenkapital *n* (*e-r Gesellschaft*), b) *a.* ~ *security* Dividendenpapier *n*; **5.** ⚖ *Brit.* Gewerkschaft *f* der Schauspieler.

e·quiv·a·lence [ɪ'kwɪvələns] *s.* Gleichwertigkeit *f* (*a.* 🜔); **e'quiv·a·lent** [-nt] **I** *adj.* □ **1.** gleichwertig, -bedeutend, entsprechend: *be* ~ *to* gleichkommen, entsprechen (*dat.*), den gleichen Wert haben wie; **2.** 🜔, 🜚 gleichwertig, äquiva'lent; **II** *s.* **3.** Gegenwert *m* (*of* von *od. gen.*); gleiche Menge; **4.** Gegen-, Seitenstück *n* (*of*, *to* zu); **5.** genaue Entsprechung, Äquiva'lent.

e·quiv·o·cal [ɪ'kwɪvəkl] *adj.* □ **1.** zweideutig, doppelsinnig; **2.** ungewiss, zweifelhaft; **3.** fragwürdig, verdächtig; **e'quiv·o·cal·ness** [-nɪs] *s.* Zweideutigkeit *f*; **e'quiv·o·cate** [-keɪt] *v/i.* zweideutig reden, Worte verdrehen; **e·quiv·o·ca·tion** [ɪ,kwɪvə'keɪʃn] *s.* Zweideutigkeit *f*; Ausflucht *f*; Wortverdrehung *f*; **e'quiv·o·ca·tor** [-keɪtə] *s.* Wortverdreher(in).

e·ra [ɪ'ɪərə] *s.* Ära *f*: a) Zeitrechnung *f*, b) E'poche *f*, Zeitalter *n*: *mark an* ~ e-e Epoche einleiten.

e·rad·i·ca·ble [ɪ'rædɪkəbl] *adj.* ausrottbar, auszurotten(d); **e'rad·i·cate** [-keɪt] *v/t. mst fig.* ausrotten; **e·rad·i·ca·tion** [ɪ,rædɪ'keɪʃn] *s.* Ausrottung *f*.

e·rase [ɪ'reɪz] *v/t.* **1.** a) *Farbe etc.* ab-, auskratzen, b) *Schrift etc.* ausstreichen, -radieren, *a. Tonbandaufnahme* löschen: *erasing head* Löschkopf *m*; **2.** *fig.* auslöschen, (aus)tilgen (*from* aus): ~ *from one's memory* aus dem Gedächtnis löschen; **3.** a) vernichten, auslöschen, b) *Am. sl.* ‚kaltmachen' (*töten*); **e'ras·er** [-zə] *s.* **1.** Radiermesser *n*; **2.** Radiergummi *m*; **e·ra·sion** [ɪ'reɪʒn] *s.* **1.** → *erasure*; **2.** 🜚 Auskratzung *f*; **e·ra·sure** [ɪ'reɪʒə] *s.* **1.** Ausradierung *f*, Tilgung *f*, Löschung *f*; **2.** ausradierte *od.* gelöschte Stelle.

ere [eə] *poet.* **I** *cj.* ehe, bevor; **II** *prp.* vor: ~ *long* bald; ~ *this* schon vorher; ~ *now* vordem, bislang.

e·rect [ɪ'rekt] **I** *v/t.* **1.** aufrichten, -stellen; **2.** *Gebäude etc.* errichten, bauen; **3.** 🜚 aufstellen, montieren; **4.** *fig. Theorie* aufstellen; **5.** ⚖ einrichten, gründen; **6.** 🜚 *das Lot, e-e Senkrechte* fällen, errichten; **II** *adj.* □ **7.** aufgerichtet, aufrecht: *with head* ~ erhobenen Hauptes; *stand* ~*(ly)* gerade stehen, *fig.* standhaft bleiben; **8.** *physiol.* erigiert (*Penis*); **9.** zu Berge stehend, sich sträubend (*Haare*); **e'rec·tile** [-taɪl] *adj.* **1.** aufrichtbar; **2.** aufgerichtet; *physiol.* erek'til, Schwell...: ~ *tissue*; **e'rect·ing** [-tɪŋ] *s.* **1.** 🜚 Aufbau *m*, Mon'tage *f*; **2.** *opt.* 'Bild,umkehrung *f*; **e'rec·tion** [-kʃn] *s.* **1.** Auf-, Errichtung *f*, Aufführung *f*; **2.** Bau *m*, Gebäude *n*; **3.** 🜚 Mon'tage *f*; **4.** *physiol.* Erekti'on *f*; **5.** ⚖ Gründung *f*; **e'rect·ness** [-nɪs] *s.* **1.** aufrechte Haltung (*a. fig.*); **2.** *a. fig.* Geradheit *f*; **e'rec·tor** [-tə] *s.* **1.**

Erbauer *m*; **2.** *anat.* E'rektor *m*, Aufrichtmuskel *m*.

er·e·mite ['erɪmaɪt] *s.* Ere'mit *m*, Einsiedler *m*.

e·re·tail·er ['iː,riːteɪlə] *s.* ✝ 'E-,Retailer *m*, elekt'ronischer Einzelhändler.

erg [ɜːɡ], **er·gon** ['ɜːɡɒn] *s. phys.* Erg *n*, Ener'gieeinheit *f*.

er·go·nom·ic [,ɜːɡəʊ'nɒmɪk] *adj.* (□ ~*ally*) ergo'nomisch; ,**er·go'nom·ics** *s. pl. sg. konstr. sociol.* Ergono'mie *f*, Ergo'nomik *f* (*Lehre von den Leistungsmöglichkeiten des Menschen*).

er·got ['ɜːɡət] *s.* 🜎 Mutterkorn *n*.

e·ri·ca ['erɪkə] *s.* 🜎 Erika *f*.

Er·in ['ɪərɪn] *npr. poet.* Erin *n*, Irland *n*.

er·mine ['ɜːmɪn] *s.* **1.** *zo.* Herme'lin *n* (*a. her.*); **2.** Herme'lin(pelz) *m*.

erne, *Am. a.* **ern** [ɜː] *s. orn.* Seeadler *m*.

e·rode [ɪ'rəʊd] *v/t.* **1.** an-, zer-, wegfressen; **2.** *geol.* erodieren, auswaschen; **3.** 🜚 *u. fig.* verschleißen; **4.** aushöhlen, unter'graben.

e·ro·gen·ic [,erəʊ'dʒenɪk], **e·rog·e·nous** [ɪ'rɒdʒɪnəs] *adj. physiol.* ero'gen: ~ *zone*.

e·ro·sion [ɪ'rəʊʒn] *s.* **1.** Zerfressen *n*; **2.** *geol.* Erosi'on *f*, Auswaschung *f*; Verwitterung *f*; **3.** 🜚 Verschleiß *m*, Abnützung *f*, Schwund *m*; **4.** *fig.* Aushöhlung *f*; **e'ro·sive** [-əʊsɪv] *adj.* ätzend, zerfressend.

e·rot·ic [ɪ'rɒtɪk] **I** *adj.* (□ ~*ally*) e'rotisch; **II** *s.* E'rotiker(in); **e'rot·i·ca** [-kə] *pl.* E'rotika *pl.*; **e'rot·i·cism** [-ɪsɪzəm] *s.* E'rotik *f*.

err [ɜː] *v/i.* **1.** (sich) irren: ~ *on the safe side*, ~ *on the side of caution* übervorsichtig sein; *to* ~ *is human* Irren ist menschlich; **2.** falsch sein, fehlgehen (*Urteil*); **3.** (mo'ralisch) auf Abwege geraten.

er·rand ['erənd] *s.* Botengang *m*, Auftrag *m*: *go on* (*od. run*) *an* ~ e-n (Boten)Gang *od.* e-e Besorgung machen, e-n Auftrag ausführen; '~**boy** *s.* Laufbursche *m*.

er·rant ['erənt] *adj.* **1.** um'herziehend, (-)wandernd, fahrend: ~ *knight*; **2.** *fig.* a) fehlgeleitet, auf Ab- *od.* Irrwegen, b) abtrünnig, fremdgehend (*Ehepartner*); '**er·rant·ry** [-trɪ] **1.** Um'herziehen *n*; **2.** *hist.* fahrendes Rittertum.

er·ra·ta [e'rɑːtə] → *erratum*.

er·rat·ic [ɪ'rætɪk] *adj.* (□ ~*ally*) **1.** (um-'her)wandernd, (-)ziehend; **2.** *geol.*, 🜎 er'ratisch: ~ *block*, ~ *boulder* erratischer Block, Findling *m*; **3.** ungleich-, unregelmäßig, regel-, ziellos; **4.** unstet, unberechenbar, sprunghaft.

er·ra·tum [e'rɑːtəm] *pl.* **-ta** [-tə] *s.* **1.** Druckfehler *m*; **2.** *pl.* Druckfehlerverzeichnis *n*, Er'rata *pl.*

err·ing ['ɜːrɪŋ] *adj.* □ **1.** → *erroneous*; **2.** a) irrend, sündig, b) → *errant* 2.

er·ro·ne·ous [ɪ'rəʊnjəs] *adj.* □ irrig, irrtümlich, unrichtig, falsch; **er'ro·ne·ous·ly** [-lɪ] *adv.* irrtümlicherweise, fälschlich, aus Versehen.

er·ror ['erə] *s.* **1.** Irrtum *m*, Fehler *m*, Versehen *n*: ~ *message* Computer: 'Fehlermeldung *f*, -,message *f*; *in* ~ irrtümlicherweise; *be in* ~ sich irren; ~*s (and omissions) excepted* ✝ Irrtümer (u. Auslassungen) vorbehalten; ~ *of omission* Unterlassungssünde *f*; ~ *of judg(e)ment* Trugschluss *m*, irrige Ansicht, falsche Beurteilung; **2.** 🜎, *ast.* Fehler *m*, Abweichung *f*; ~ *rate* Fehlerquote *f*; ~ *in range a.* ⚔ Längenabweichung; **3.** ⚖ *a.* Tatsachen- *od.* Rechtsirrtum *m*: ~ *in law* (*in fact*), b) Formfehler *m*, Verfahrensmangel *m*: *writ of*

~ Revisionsbefehl *m*; **4.** Fehltritt *m*, Vergehen *n*.

er·satz ['eəzæts] (*Ger.*) **I** *s.* Ersatz(stoff) *m*; **II** *adj.* Ersatz...

Erse [ɜːs] *ling.* **I** *adj.* **1.** gälisch; **2.** irisch; **II** *s.* **3.** Gälisch *n*; **4.** Irisch *n*.

erst·while ['ɜːstwaɪl] **I** *adv.* ehedem, früher; **II** *adj.* ehemalig, früher.

e·ruc·tate [ɪ'rʌkteɪt] *v/i.* aufstoßen, rülpsen; **e·ruc·ta·tion** [,iːrʌk'teɪʃn] *s.* Aufstoßen *n*, Rülpsen *n*.

er·u·dite ['eruːdaɪt] *adj.* □ gelehrt (*a. Abhandlung etc.*), belesen; **er·u·di·tion** [,eruː'dɪʃn] *s.* Gelehrsamkeit *f*, Belesenheit *f*.

e·rupt [ɪ'rʌpt] *v/i.* **1.** ausbrechen (*Vulkan, a. Ausschlag, Streit etc.*); **2.** *geol.* her'vorbrechen, eruptieren (*Lava etc.*); **3.** 'durchbrechen (*Zähne*); **4.** plötzlich auftauchen: ~ *into the room* ins Zimmer platzen; **5.** *fig.* (zornig) losbrechen, ‚explodieren'; **e'rup·tion** [-pʃn] *s.* **1.** Ausbruch *m* (*e-s Vulkans, Streits etc.*); **2.** Her'vorbrechen *n*, *geol.* Erupti'on *f*; **3.** 'Durchbruch *m* (*der Zähne*); **4.** 🜍 Erupti'on *f*: a) Ausbruch *m* *e-s Ausschlags*, b) Ausschlag *m*; **5.** (Wut- *etc.*)Ausbruch *m*; **e'rup·tive** [-tɪv] *adj.* □ **1.** *geol.* erup'tiv: ~ *rock* Eruptivgestein; **2.** 🜍 von Ausschlag begleitet.

er·y·sip·e·las [,erɪ'sɪpɪləs] *s.* 🜍 (Wund-)Rose *f*; **er·y'sip·e·loid** [-lɔɪd] *s.* 🜍 (Schweine)Rotlauf *m*.

es·ca·lade [,eskə'leɪd] ⚔ *hist.* **I** *s.* Eska-'lade *f*, Mauerersteigung *f* (*mit Leitern*), Erstürmung *f*; **II** *v/t.* mit Sturmleitern ersteigen.

es·ca·late ['eskəleɪt] **I** *v/t.* **1.** *Krieg etc.* eskalieren (*stufenweise verschärfen*); **2.** *Erwartungen, Preise etc.* höher schrauben; **II** *v/i.* **3.** eskalieren; **4.** steigen, in die Höhe gehen (*Preise etc.*); **es·ca·la·tion** [,eskə'leɪʃn] *s.* **1.** ⚔, *pol.* Eskalati'on *f*; **2.** ✝ *Am.* Anpassung *f* der Löhne *od.* Preise an gestiegene (Lebenshaltungs)Kosten; **'es·ca·la·tor** ['eskəleɪtə] *s.* **1.** Rolltreppe *f*; **2.** *a.* ~ *clause* ✝ (Preis-, Lohn)Gleitklausel *f*.

es·ca·lope ['eskələʊp] *s.* (*bsd.* Wiener) Schnitzel *n*.

es·ca·pade [,eskə'peɪd] *s.* Eska'pade *f*: a) toller Streich, b) ‚Seitensprung' *m*.

es·cape [ɪ'skeɪp] **I** *v/t.* **1.** *j-m* entfliehen, -kommen, -rinnen; **2.** *e-r Sache* entgehen, -rinnen, *et.* vermeiden: *he just* ~*d being killed* er entging knapp dem Tode; *I cannot* ~ *the impression* kann mich des Eindrucks nicht erwehren; **3.** *fig. j-m* entgehen, über'sehen *od.* nicht verstanden werden *von j-m*: *that fact* ~*d me* diese Tatsache entging mir; *the sense* ~*s me* der Sinn leuchtet mir nicht ein; *it* ~*d my notice* ich bemerkte es nicht; **4.** (*dem Gedächtnis*) entfallen: *his name* ~*s me* sein Name ist mir entfallen; **5.** entfahren, -schlüpfen: *an oath* ~*d him*; **II** *v/i.* **6.** (*from*) (ent)fliehen, entkommen, -rinnen, -laufen, -wischen, -weichen (aus, von), flüchten, ausbrechen (aus); **7.** (*oft from*) sich retten (vor *dat.*), (ungestraft *od.* mit dem Leben) da'vonkommen; **8.** a) ausfließen, b) entweichen, ausströmen (*Gas etc.*); **III** *s.* **9.** Entrinnen *n*, -weichen *n*, -kommen *n*, Flucht *f* (*from* aus, von): *have a narrow* ~ mit knapper Not davon- *od.* entkommen; *that was a narrow* ~*!* das war knapp!, das hätte ins Auge gehen können!; *make one's* ~ entkommen, sich aus dem Staub machen; **10.** Rettung *f* (*from* vor *dat.*): (*way of*) ~ Ausweg *m*; **11.**

Fluchtmittel *n*; → *fire escape*; **12.** Ausströmen *n*, Entweichen *n*; **13.** *fig.* (Mittel *n* der) Entspannung *f od.* Zerstreuung *f*, Unter'haltung *f*: ~ *reading* Unterhaltungslektüre *f*; ~ **art·ist** *s.* **1.** Entfesselungskünstler *m*; **2.** Ausbrecherkönig *m*; ~ *car s.* Fluchtwagen *m*; ~ **chute** *s.* ✓ Notrutsche *f*; ~ **clause** *s.* Befreiungsklausel *f*.

es·ca·pee [,eskeɪ'piː] *s.* entwichener Strafgefangener, Ausbrecher *m*.

es·cape| hatch *s.* **1.** a) ⚓ Notluke *f*, b) ✓ Notausstieg *m*; **2.** *fig.* 'Schlupfloch' *n*; ~ **key** *s. Computer:* Es'cape-Taste *f*; ~ **mech·a·nism** *s. psych.* 'Abwehrme,cha,nismus *m*.

es·cape·ment [ɪ'skeɪpmənt] *s.* **1.** Hemmung *f* (*der Uhr*); **2.** Vorschub *m* (*der Schreibmaschine*); ~ **wheel** *s.* **1.** Hemmungsrad *n* (*der Uhr*); **2.** Schaltrad *n* (*der Schreibmaschine*).

es·cape| pipe *s.* **1.** Abflussrohr *n*; **2.** Abzugsrohr *n* (*für Gase*); ~**-proof** *adj.* ausbruchssicher; ~ **route** *s.* Fluchtweg *m*; ~ **shaft** *s. geol.* Steilabbruch *m*.

es·cap·ism [ɪs'keɪpɪzəm] *s. psych.* Eska-'pismus *m*, Wirklichkeitsflucht *f*; **es·cap·ist** [ɪ'skeɪpɪst] I *s.* j-d, der vor der Reali'tät zu fliehen sucht; II *adj.* eska-'pistisch, *weitS.* Zerstreuungs.., Unterhaltungs...: ~ *literature*.

es·ca·pol·o·gist [,eskeɪ'pɒlədʒɪst] *s.* **1.** → *escape artist* 1; **2.** j-d, der sich immer wieder geschickt herauswindet.

es·carp·ment [ɪ'skɑːpmənt] *s.* **1.** ✕ Böschung *f*; **2.** *geol.* Steilabbruch *m*.

es·cha·to·log·i·cal [,eskətə'lɒdʒɪkl] *adj. eccl.* eschato'logisch; **es·cha·tol·o·gy** [,eskə'tɒlədʒɪ] *s.* Eschatolo'gie *f*.

es·cheat [ɪs'tʃiːt] ⚖ I *s.* **1.** Heimfall *m* (*an den Staat*); **2.** Heimfallsgut *n*; **3.** Heimfallsrecht *n*; II *v/i.* **4.** an'heim fallen; III *v/t.* **5.** (als Heimfallsgut) einziehen.

es·chew [ɪs'tʃuː] *v/t. et.* (ver)meiden, scheuen, sich enthalten (*gen.*).

es·cort I *s.* [ˈeskɔːt] **1.** ✕ Es'korte *f*, Bedeckung *f*, Begleitmannschaft *f*; **2.** a) ✓, ⚓ Geleit(schutz) *n*) *n*, b) a) ~ *vessel* ⚓ Geleitschiff *n*: ~ *fighter* ✓ Begleitjäger *m*; **3.** *fig.* a) Geleit *n*, Schutz *m*, b) Begleitung *f*, Gefolge *n*, Begleiter(in): ~ *agency* Begleitagentur *f*; II *v/t.* [ɪ'skɔːt] **4.** ✕ eskortieren; **5.** ✓, ⚓ Geleit(schutz) geben (*dat.*); **6.** *fig.* a) geleiten, b) begleiten.

es·cri·toire [,eskriːˈtwɑː] (*Fr.*) *s.* Schreibpult *n*.

es·crow [e'skrəʊ] *s.* ⚖ bei e-m Dritten (*als Treuhänder*) hinterlegte Vertragsurkunde, die erst bei Erfüllung e-r Bedingung in Kraft tritt.

es·cutch·eon [ɪ'skʌtʃ ən] *s.* **1.** Wappen (-schild *m*) *n*: *a blot on his* ~ *fig.* ein Fleck auf s-r (weißen) Weste; **2.** ⚓ a) (Deck)Schild *n* (*e-s Schlosses*), b) Abdeckung *f* (*e-s Schalters*); **3.** *zo.* Spiegel *m*, Schild *m*.

e-shop·per ['iː,ʃɒpə] *s.* ✝ 'E-,Shopper *m*, elekt'ronischer Kunde.

Es·ki·mo ['eskɪməʊ] *pl.* **-mos** *s.* **1.** Eskimo *m*; **2.** Eskimosprache *f*.

e·soph·a·gus [iː'sɒfəgəs] → *oesophagus*.

es·o·ter·ic [,esəʊ'terɪk] *adj.* (□ ~*ally*) eso'terisch: a) *phls.* nur für Eingeweihte bestimmt, b) geheim, pri'vat.

es·pal·ier [ɪ'spæljə] *s.* **1.** Spa'lier *n*; **2.** Spa'lierbaum *m*.

es·pe·cial [ɪ'speʃl] *adj.* □ besonder: a) her'vorragend, b) Haupt..., hauptsächlich, spezi'ell; **es·pe·cial·ly** [ɪ'speʃəlɪ]

adv. besonders, hauptsächlich: *more* ~ ganz besonders.

Es·pe·ran·tist [,espə'ræntɪst] *s. ling.* Espe-ran'tist(in); **Es·pe·ran·to** [,espə'ræntəʊ] *s.* Espe'ranto *n*.

es·pi·o·nage [,espɪə'nɑːʒ] *s.* Spio'nage *f*: *industrial* ~ Werkspionage.

es·pla·nade [,esplə'neɪd] *s.* **1.** Espla'na-de *f* (*a.* ✕ *hist.*), großer freier Platz; **2.** (*bsd.* 'Strand)Prome,nade *f*.

es·pous·al [ɪ'spaʊzl] *s.* **1.** (*of*) Eintreten *n*, Par'teinahme *f* (für); Annahme *f* (*gen.*); **2.** *pl. obs.* a) Vermählung *f*, b) Verlobung *f*; **es·pouse** [ɪ'spaʊz] *v/t.* **1.** Par'tei ergreifen für, eintreten für, sich *e-r Sache* verschreiben, *e-n Glauben* annehmen; **2.** *obs.* a) sich vermählen mit, zur Frau nehmen, b) (*to*) zur Frau geben (*dat.*), c) (*o.s.* sich) verloben (*to* mit).

es·pres·so [e'spresəʊ] (*Ital.*) *s.* **1.** Es'presso *m*; **2.** Es'pressoma,schine *f*; ~ **bar**, ~ **ca·fé** *s.* Es'presso(bar *f*) *n*.

es·prit ['espriː] (*Fr.*) *s.* Es'prit *m*, Geist *m*, Witz *m*; ~ **de corps** [,espriːdə'kɔː] (*Fr.*) *s.* Korpsgeist *m*.

es·py [ɪ'spaɪ] *v/t.* erspähen.

Es·qui·mau ['eskɪməʊ] *pl.* **-maux** [-məʊz] → *Eskimo*.

es·quire [ɪ'skwaɪə] *s.* **1.** *Brit. obs.* → *squire* 1; **2.** *abbr. Esq.* (*ohne Mr., Dr. etc. auf Briefen dem Namen nachgestellt*): *John Smith, Esq.* Herrn John Smith.

ess [es] *s.* **1.** S *n*, s *n*; **2.** S-Form *f*.

es·say I *s.* ['eseɪ] **1.** Essay *m, n*, Abhandlung *f*, Aufsatz *m*; **2.** Versuch *m*; II *v/t. u. v/i.* [e'seɪ] **3.** versuchen; '**es·say·ist** [-ɪst] *s.* Essay'ist(in).

es·sence ['esns] *s.* **1.** *phls.* a) Es'senz *f*, Wesen *n*, b) Sub'stanz *f*, abso'lutes Sein; **2.** *fig.* Es'senz *f*, *das* Wesentliche, Kern *m*: *of the* ~ von entscheidender Bedeutung; **3.** Es'senz *f*, Ex'trakt *m*.

es·sen·tial [ɪ'senʃl] I *adj.* □ → *essentially*; **1.** wesentlich; **2.** wichtig, unentbehrlich, erforderlich; lebenswichtig: ~ *goods*; **3.** 🜍 ä'therisch: ~ *oil*; II *s. mst pl.* **4.** *das* Wesentliche *od.* Wichtigste, Hauptsache *f*; wesentliche Punkte *pl.*; unentbehrliche Sache *od.* Per'son; **es·sen·ti·al·i·ty** [ɪ,senʃɪ'ælətɪ] → *essential* 4; **es'sen·tial·ly** [-lɪ] *adv.* im Wesentlichen, eigentlich, in der Hauptsache; in hohem Maße.

es·tab·lish [ɪ'stæblɪʃ] *v/t.* **1.** ein-, errichten, gründen; einführen; *Regierung* bilden; *Gesetz* aufstellen; *Rekord, Theorie* aufstellen; ✝ *Konto* eröffnen; **2.** j-n einsetzen, 'unterbringen; ✝ etablieren: ~ *o.s.* sich niederlassen *od.* einrichten, ✝ u. *fig.* sich etablieren; **3.** *Kirche* verstaatlichen; **4.** feststellen, festsetzen; *s-e Identität etc.* nachweisen; **5.** Geltung verschaffen (*dat.*); *Forderung, Ansicht* 'durchsetzen; *Ordnung* schaffen; **6.** Verbindung herstellen; **7.** begründen: ~ *one's reputation* sich e-n Namen machen; **es·tab·lished** [ɪ'stæblɪʃt] *adj.* **1.** bestehend; **2.** feststehend, fest begründet, unzweifelhaft; **3.** planmäßig (*Beamter*): *the* ~ *staff* das Stammpersonal; **4.** ⚖ *Church* Staatskirche *f*; **es·tab·lish·ment** [ɪ'stæblɪʃmənt] *s.* **1.** Er-, Einrichtung *f*; Einsetzung *f*; Gründung *f*, Einführung *f*, Schaffung *f*; **2.** Feststellung *f*, -setzung *f*; **3.** (*großer*) Haushalt; ✝ Unter'nehmen *n*, Firma *f*: *keep a large* ~ a) ein großes Haus führen, b) ein bedeutendes Unternehmen leiten; **4.** Anstalt *f*, Insti'tut *n*; **5.** organisierte Körperschaft: *civil* ~ Beamtenschaft *f*; *military* ~ stehendes Heer; *naval* ~ Flotte *f*; **6.** festes Perso'nal, Perso'nal-

od. ✕ Mannschaftsbestand *m*; Sollstärke *f*: *peace* ~ Friedensstärke; *war* ~ Kriegsstärke; **7.** Staatskirche *f*; **8.** *the* ⚎ das Establishment (*etablierte Macht, herrschende Schicht, konventionelle Gesellschaft*).

es·tate [ɪ'steɪt] *s.* **1.** Stand *m*, Klasse *f*, Rang *m*: *the Three* ⚎s (*of the Realm*) *Brit.* die drei (*gesetzgebenden*) Stände; *third* ~ *Fr. hist.* dritter Stand, Bürgertum *n*; *fourth* ~ *humor.* Presse *f*; **2.** *obs.* (Zu)Stand *m*: *man's* ~ *bibl.* Mannesalter; **3.** ⚖ a) Besitz *m*, Vermögen *n*; → *personal* 1, *real* 3, b) (Kon'kurs *etc.*)Masse *f*, Nachlass *m*; **4.** ⚖ Besitzrecht *n*, Nutznießung *f*; **5.** Grundbesitz *m*, Besitzung *f*, Gut *n*: *family* ~ Familienbesitz *m*; **6.** (Wohn)Siedlung *f*; **7.** → *estate car*; ~ **a·gent** *s. Brit.* **1.** Grundstücksmakler *m*; **2.** Grundstücksverwalter *m*; ~ **bot·tled** *adj.* auf dem (Wein)Gut abgefüllt; *als Aufschrift:* Gutsabfüllung!; ~ **car** *s. Brit.* Kombiwagen *m*; ~ **du·ty** *s. Brit. obs.*, ~ **tax** *s. Am.* Erbschaftssteuer *f*.

es·teem [ɪ'stiːm] I *v/t.* **1.** achten, (hoch) schätzen; **2.** erachten *od.* ansehen als, halten für; II *s.* **3.** Wertschätzung *f*, Achtung *f*: *to hold in* (*high*) ~ achten.

es·ter ['estə] *s.* 🜍 Ester *m*.

Es·ther ['estə] *npr. u. s. bibl.* (das Buch) Esther *f*.

es·thete *etc.* → *aesthete etc.*

Es·tho·ni·an [e'stəʊnjən] I *s.* **1.** Este *m*, Estin *f*; **2.** *ling.* Estnisch *n*; II *adj.* **3.** estnisch, estländisch.

es·ti·ma·ble ['estɪməbl] *adj.* □ achtens-, schätzenswert; **es·ti·mate** I *v/t.* ['estɪmeɪt] **1.** (ab-, ein)schätzen, taxieren, veranschlagen (*at auf acc.*): *an* ~*d 200 buyers* schätzungsweise 200 Käufer; *time of arrival* (*od. departure*) voraussichtliche Ankunftszeit (*od.* Abflug-, Abfahrtszeit); **2.** bewerten, beurteilen; II *s.* ['estɪmeɪt] **3.** (Ab-, Ein)Schätzung *f*, Veranschlagung *f*, (Kosten)Anschlag *m*: *rough* ~ grober Überschlag; *at a rough* ~ grob geschätzt; **4.** *the* ⚎s *pl. pol.* der (Staats)Haushaltsplan; **5.** Bewertung *f*, Beurteilung *f*: *form an* ~ *of et.* beurteilen *od.* einschätzen; **es·ti·ma·tion** [,estɪ'meɪʃn] *s.* **1.** Urteil *n*, Meinung *f*: *in my* ~ nach m-r Ansicht; **2.** Bewertung *f*, Schätzung *f*; **3.** Achtung *f*: *hold in* (*high*) ~ hoch schätzen.

es·ti·val → *aestival*.

es·top [ɪ'stɒp] *v/t.* ⚖ rechtshemmenden Einwand erheben gegen, hindern (*from* an *dat.*, *from doing* zu tun); **es·top·pel** [ɪ'stɒpl] *s.* ⚖ Ausschluss *m* e-r Klage *od.* Einrede.

es·trange [ɪ'streɪndʒ] *v/t.* j-n entfremden (*from dat.*): *become* ~*d* a) sich entfremden (*from dat.*), b) sich auseinander leben; **es·tranged** [ɪ'streɪndʒd] *adj.* **1.** *an* ~ *couple* ein Paar, das sich auseinander gelebt hat; **2.** ⚖ getrennt lebend: *his* ~ *wife* s-e von ihm getrennt lebende Frau; *she is* ~ *from her husband* sie lebt von ihrem Mann getrennt; **es·trange·ment** [ɪ'streɪndʒmənt] *s.* Entfremdung *f* (*from* von).

es·tro·gen ['estrədʒən] *s. biol.*, 🜍 Östro'gen *n*.

es·tu·ar·y ['estjʊərɪ] *s.* **1.** (den Gezeiten ausgesetzte) Flussmündung; **2.** Meeresarm *m*, -buch *f*.

et cet·er·a [ɪt'setərə] *abbr. etc., &c.* (*Lat.*) und so weiter; **et'cet·er·a** *s.* **1.** (*lange etc.*) Reihe; **2.** *pl.* allerlei Dinge.

etch [etʃ] *v/t. u. v/i.* **1.** ätzen; **2.** a) Kupfer stechen, b) radieren; **3.** schneiden, kratzen (*on* in *acc.*): *sharply* ~*ed fea-*

tures *fig.* scharf geschnittene Gesichtszüge; *the event was ~ed on* (*od.* **in**) *his memory* das Ereignis hatte sich s-m Gedächtnis (tief) eingeprägt; **4.** *fig.* (klar *etc.*) zeichnen, (gut *etc.*) her'ausarbeiten; **etch·er** ['etʃə] *s.* **1.** Kupferstecher *m*; **2.** Radierer *m*; **etch·ing** ['etʃɪŋ] *s.* **1.** Ätzen *etc.* (→ **etch** 1, 2); **2.** a) Radierung *f*, b) Kupferstich *m*: *come up and see my ~s humor.* wollen Sie sich m-e Briefmarkensammlung ansehen?

e·ter·nal [ɪ'tɜ:nl] **I** *adj.* □ **1.** ewig, immer während: *the ℰ City* die Ewige Stadt (*Rom*); **2.** unab'änderlich: *~ romantic* hoffnungsloser Romantiker; **3.** F ewig, unaufhörlich; **II** *s.* **4.** *the ℰ* Gott *m*; **5.** *pl.* ewige Dinge *pl.*; **e·ter·nal·ize** [-nəlaɪz] *v/t.* verewigen; **e·ter·ni·ty** [-nətɪ] *s.* **1.** Ewigkeit *f* (*a.* F *fig.* lange Zeit): *from here to ~, to all ~* bis in alle Ewigkeit; **2.** *eccl.* a) das Jenseits, b) *pl.* ewige Wahrheiten; **e·ter·nize** [-naɪz] → **eternalize**.

eth·ane ['eθeɪn] *s.* 🜛 Äthan *n*; **eth·ene** ['eθi:n] *s.* Ä'then *n*, Äthy'len *n*; **eth·e·nol** ['eθənɒl] *s.* Vi'nylalko,hol *m*; **eth·e·nyl** ['eθənɪl] *s.* Äthyli'den *n*.

e·ther ['i:θə] *s.* **1.** 🜛, *phys.* Äther *m*; **2.** *poet.* Äther *m*, Himmel *m*; **e·the·re·al** [i:'θɪərɪəl] *adj.* □ **1.** 🜛 a) ätherartig, b) ä'therisch; **2.** ä'therisch, himmlisch; vergeistigt; **e·the·re·al·ize** [i:'θɪərɪəlaɪz] *v/t.* **1.** 🜛 ätherisieren; **2.** vergeistigen, verklären; **'e·ther·ize** [-əraɪz] *v/t.* □ **1.** 🜛 in Äther verwandeln; **2.** 🜻 mit Äther narkotisieren.

eth·ic ['eθɪk] **I** *adj.* **1.** → **ethical**; **II** *s.* **2.** *pl. sg. konstr.* Sittenlehre *f*, Ethik *f*; **3.** *pl.* Sittlichkeit *f*, Mo'ral *f*, Ethos *n*: *professional ~s* Standesehre *f*, Berufsethos; **'eth·i·cal** [-kl] *adj.* □ **1.** *phls.*, *a. ling.* ethisch; **2.** ethisch, mo'ralisch, sittlich; **3.** von ethischen Grundsätzen (geleitet); **4.** dem Berufsethos entsprechend; **5.** *pharm.* re'zeptpflichtig; **'eth·i·cist** [-ɪsɪst] *s.* Ethiker *m*.

E·thi·o·pi·an [i:θɪ'əupjən] **I** *adj.* äthi'opisch; **II** *s.* Äthi'opier(in).

eth·nic ['eθnɪk] **I** *adj.* □ **1.** ethnisch, völkisch, Volks...: *~ cleansing* ethnische Säuberung; *~ group* Volksgruppe *f*; *~ German* Volksdeutsche(r *m*) *f*; *~ joke* Witz *m* auf Kosten e-r bestimmten Volksgruppe; **II** *s.* **2.** Angehörige(r *m*) *f* e-r (homo'genen) Volksgruppe; **3.** *pl.* sprachliche *od.* kultu'relle Zugehörigkeit; **'eth·ni·cal** [-kl] → **ethnic**; **eth·nog·ra·pher** [eθ'nɒgrəfə] *s.* Ethno'graph *m*; **eth·no·graph·ic** [,eθnəʊ'græfɪk] *adj.* □ ethno'graphisch, völkerkundlich; **eth·nog·ra·phy** [eθ'nɒgrəfɪ] *s.* Ethnogra'phie *f*, (beschreibende) Völkerkunde; **eth·no·log·i·cal** [,eθnəʊ'lɒdʒɪkl] *adj.* □ ethno'logisch; **eth·nol·o·gist** [eθ'nɒlədʒɪst] *s.* Ethno'loge *m*, Völkerkundler *m*; **eth·nol·o·gy** [eθ'nɒlədʒɪ] *s.* Ethnolo'gie *f*, (vergleichende) Völkerkunde.

e·thol·o·gist [i:'θɒlədʒɪst] *s.* Etho'loge *m*, (Tier)Verhaltensforscher *m*; **e'thol·o·gy** [-dʒɪ] *s.* Etholo'gie *f*, Verhaltensforschung *f*.

e·thos ['i:θɒs] *s.* **1.** Ethos *n*, Cha'rakter *m*, Wesensart *f*, Geist *m*, sittlicher Gehalt (*e-r Kultur*); **2.** ethischer Wert.

eth·yl ['eθɪl; 🜛 'i:θaɪl] *s.* 🜛 Ä'thyl *n*: *~ alcohol* Äthylalkohol *m*; **eth·yl·ene** ['eθɪli:n] *s.* Äthy'len *n*, Kohlenwasserstoffgas *n*.

e·ti·o·lat·ed ['i:tɪəleɪtɪd] *adj.* **1.** verkümmert (*Pflanze, Erinnerung etc.*); **2.** bleichsüchtig, blass u. ausgezehrt (Gesicht).

et·i·quette ['etɪket] *s.* Eti'kette *f*: a) Zeremoni'ell *n*, b) Anstandsregeln *pl.*, (gute) 'Umgangsformen *pl.*

E·ton| col·lar ['i:tn] *s.* breiter, steifer 'Umlegekragen; **~ Col·lege** *s.* berühmte englische Public School; **~ crop** *s.* Herrenschnitt *m* (*für Damen*).

E·to·ni·an [i:'təʊnjən] **I** *adj.* Eton...; **II** *s.* Schüler *m* des Eton College.

E·ton jack·et *s.* schwarze, kurze Jacke der Etonschüler.

E·trus·can [ɪ'trʌskən] **I** *adj.* **1.** e'truskisch; **II** *s.* **2.** E'trusker(in); **3.** *ling.* E'truskisch *n*.

et·y·mo·log·ic, et·y·mo·log·i·cal [,etɪməʊ'lɒdʒɪk(l)] *adj.* □ etymo'logisch; **et·y·mol·o·gist** [,etɪ'mɒlədʒɪst] *s.* Etymo'loge *m*; **et·y·mol·o·gy** [,etɪ'mɒlədʒɪ] *s.* allg. Etymolo'gie *f*; **et·y·mon** ['etɪmɒn] *s.* Etymon *n*, Stammwort *n*.

eu·ca·lyp·tus [,ju:kə'lɪptəs] *s.* ♣ Euka'lyptus *m*.

Eu·cha·rist ['ju:kərɪst] *s. eccl.* Eucharistie *f*: a) *die Feier des heiligen Abendmahls*, b) *die eucharistische Gabe* (*Brot u. Wein*).

eu·chre ['ju:kə] *v/t. Am.* F prellen, betrügen.

Eu·clid ['ju:klɪd] *s.* die (Eu'klidische) Geome'trie.

EU coun·try ['i:ju:] *s.* E'U-Land *n*.

eu·gen·ic [ju:'dʒenɪk] **I** *adj.* (□ *~ally*) eu'genisch; **II** *s. pl. sg. konstr.* Eu'genik *f* (*Erbhygiene*); **eu·ge·nist** ['ju:dʒɪnɪst] *s.* Eu'geniker *m*.

EU law ['i:ju:] *s.* E'U-Gesetz *n*.

eu·lo·gist ['ju:lədʒɪst] *s.* Lobredner(in); **eu·lo·gis·tic** [,ju:lə'dʒɪstɪk] *adj.* (□ *~ally*) preisend, lobend; **'eu·lo·gize** [-dʒaɪz] *v/t.* loben, preisen, rühmen; **'eu·lo·gy** [-dʒɪ] *s.* **1.** Lob(preisung *f*) *n*; **2.** Lobrede *f od.* -schrift *f*.

eu·nuch ['ju:nək] *s.* Eu'nuch *m, weitS. a.* Ka'strat *m*.

eu·pep·si·a [ju:'pepsɪə] *s.* 🜻 nor'male Verdauung; **eu'pep·tic** [-ptɪk] *adj.* **1.** 🜻 gut verdauend; **2.** *fig.* gut gelaunt.

eu·phe·mism ['ju:fɪmɪzəm] *s.* Euphe'mismus *m*, beschönigender Ausdruck, sprachliche Verhüllung; **eu·phe·mis·tic** [,ju:fɪ'mɪstɪk] *adj.* (□ *~ally*) euphe'mistisch, beschönigend, verhüllend.

eu·phon·ic [ju:'fɒnɪk] *adj.* (□ *~ally*) eu'phonisch, wohlklingend; **eu·pho·ny** ['ju:fənɪ] *s.* Eupho'nie *f*, Wohlklang *m*.

eu·phor·bi·a [ju:'fɔ:bjə] *s.* ♣ Wolfsmilch *f*.

eu·pho·ri·a [ju:'fɔ:rɪə] *s.* 🜻 *u. fig.* Eupho'rie *f*; **eu'phor·ic** [-'fɒrɪk] *adj.* (□ *~ally*) eu'phorisch; **eu·pho·ry** ['ju:fərɪ] → **euphoria**.

eu·phu·ism ['ju:fju:ɪzəm] *s.* Euphu'ismus *m* (*schwülstiger Stil od. Ausdruck*); **eu·phu·is·tic** [,ju:fju:'ɪstɪk] *adj.* (□ *~ally*) euphu'istisch, schwülstig.

Eu·rail·pass ['jʊəreɪlpɑ:s] *s.* 🚃 Eu'railpass *m*.

Eur·a·sian [juə'reɪʒjən] **I** *s.* Eu'rasier (-in); **II** *adj.* eu'rasisch.

EU reg·u·la·tion ['i:ju:] *s.* E'U-Bestimmung *f*.

Eu·ro ['jʊərəʊ] *s. Währung:* 'Euro *m*.

Euro- [jʊərəʊ] *in Zssgn* euro'päisch, Euro...

eu·ro·cent ['jʊərəʊsent] *s. Währung:* 'Eurocent *m*.

'Eu·ro|·cheque *s.* 🜻 Eurocheque *m*, -scheck *m*: *~ card* Eurochequekarte *f*; **,~'com·mun·ism** *s.* 'Eurokommu,nismus *m*; **~'crat** ['jʊərəʊkræt] *s.* Euro'krat *m*; **~'cur·ren·cy** *s.* Eurowährung *f*; **'~,dol·lar** *s.* 🜻 Eurodollar *m*.

Eu·ro·pe·an [,jʊərə'pi:ən] **I** *adj.* euro'pä-

isch: *~ Central Bank* Euro'päische Zent'ralbank; *~ Commission* Euro'päische Kommissi'on *f*; *~ Court of Justice* Euro'päischer Gerichtshof; *~ Cup sport* Europacup *m*; *~ Economic and Monetary Union* Europäische Wirtschafts- u. Währungsunion *f*; *~ (Economic) Community* Europäische (Wirtschafts)Gemeinschaft; *~ elections pl.* Eu'ropawahlen *pl.*; *~ Free Trade Area* Euro'päische Freihandelszone; *~ Investment Bank* Euro'päische Investiti'onsbank; *~ Monetary Institute* Europäisches Währungsinstitut; *~ Monetary System* Europäisches Währungssystem; *~ Monetary Union* Euro'päische Währungsunion *f*; *~ Parliament* Europaparlament *n*; *~ plan Am.* Hotelzimmervermietung *f* ohne Verpflegung; *~ single market* europäischer Binnenmarkt; *~ Union* Europäische Union; **II** *s.* Euro'päer(in), **,Eu·ro'pe·an·ism** [-nɪzəm] *s.* Euro'päertum *n*; **,Eu·ro'pean·ize** [-naɪz] *v/t.* europäisieren.

Eu·ro·pol ['jʊərəʊpɒl] *s.* 'Europol *f* (*Europäisches Polizeiamt*).

Eu·ro·scep·tic ['jʊərəʊskeptɪk] *s.* Euroskeptiker *m*.

Eu·ro sym·bol *s.* 'Euro-Sym,bol *n*.

Eu·ro·vi·sion ['jʊərəʊ,vɪʒn] *s. u. adj.* TV Eurovision(s...) *f*.

Eu·sta·chi·an tube [ju:'steɪʃən] *s. anat.* eu'stachische Röhre, 'Ohrtrom,pete *f*.

eu·tha·na·si·a [,ju:θə'neɪʒə] *s.* **1.** sanfter *od.* leichter Tod; **2.** Euthana'sie *f*: *active* (*passive*) *~* 🜻 aktive (passive) Sterbehilfe.

EU-wide [,i:'ju:waɪd] *adj.* E'U-weit.

e·vac·u·ant [ɪ'vækjʊənt] **I** *adj.* abführend; **II** *s.* Abführmittel *n*; **e·vac·u·ate** [ɪ'vækjʊeɪt] *v/t.* **1.** ent-, ausleeren: *~ the bowels* a) den Darm entleeren, b) abführen; **2.** a) *Luft etc.* her'auspumpen, b) *Gefäß* luftleer pumpen; **3.** a) *Personen* evakuieren, b) ✕ *Truppen* verlegen, *Verwundete etc.* abtransportieren, c) *Gebiet* evakuieren, *a. Haus* räumen; **e·vac·u·a·tion** [ɪ,vækjʊ'eɪʃn] *s.* **1.** Aus-, Entleerung *f*; **2.** 🜻 a) Stuhlgang *m*, b) Stuhl *m*, Kot *m*; **3.** a) Evakuierung *f*, b) ✕ Verlegung *f* (*von Truppen*), 'Abtrans,port *m*, c) Räumung *f*; **e·vac·u·ee** [ɪ,vækju:'i:] *s.* Evakuierte(r *m*) *f*.

e·vade [ɪ'veɪd] *v/t.* **1.** ausweichen (*dat.*); **2.** *j-m* entkommen; sich *e-r Sache* entziehen, *e-r Sache* entgehen, ausweichen, *et.* um'gehen, vermeiden; sich *e-r Pflicht etc.* entziehen, 🏛 *Steuern* hinter'ziehen: *~ a question* e-r Frage ausweichen; *~ definition* sich nicht definieren lassen; **e'vad·er** [-də] *s. j-d, der sich e-r Sache entzieht*; → **tax evader**.

e·val·u·ate [ɪ'væljʊeɪt] *v/t.* **1.** auswerten; **2.** bewerten, beurteilen; **3.** abschätzen; **4.** berechnen; **e·val·u·a·tion** [ɪ,væljʊ'eɪʃn] *s.* **1.** Auswertung *f*; **2.** Bewertung *f*, Beurteilung *f*; **3.** Schätzung *f*; **4.** Berechnung *f*.

ev·a·nesce [,i:və'nes] *v/i.* sich verflüchtigen; schwinden, **,ev·a'nes·cence** [-sns] *s.* (Da'hin)Schwinden *n*, Verflüchtigung *f*; **,ev·a'nes·cent** [-snt] *adj.* □ **1.** (ver-, da'hin)schwindend, flüchtig; **2.** vergänglich.

e·van·gel·ic [,i:væn'dʒelɪk] *adj.* (□ *~ally*) **1.** die Evan'gelien betreffend, Evan'gelien...; **2.** evan'gelisch; **,e·van'gel·i·cal** [-kl] *adj.* □ → **evangelic**.

e·van·ge·lism [ɪ'vændʒəlɪzəm] *s.* Verkündigung *f* des Evan'geliums; **e'van·ge·list** [-lɪst] *s.* **1.** Evange'list *m*; **2.**

Evange'list *m*, Erweckungs-, Wanderprediger *m*; **3.** Patri'arch *m der Mormonen*; **e'van·ge·lize** [-laɪz] **I** *v/i.* das Evan'gelium verkünden; **II** *v/t.* missio'nieren, (zum Christentum) bekehren.

e·vap·o·rate [ɪ'væpəreɪt] **I** *v/i.* **1.** verdampfen, -dunsten, sich verflüchtigen; **2.** *fig.* verfliegen, sich verflüchtigen (*a.* F *abhauen*); **II** *v/t.* **3.** verdampfen od. verdunsten lassen; **4.** ⊙ ab-, eindampfen, evaporieren: **∼d milk** Kondensmilch *f*; **e·vap·o·ra·tion** [ɪ,væpə'reɪʃn] *s.* **1.** Verdampfung *f*, -dunstung *f*; **2.** *fig.* Verflüchtigung *f*, Verfliegen *n*; **e'vap·o·ra·tor** [-tə] *s.* ⊙ Abdampfvorrichtung *f*, Verdampfer *m*.

e·va·sion [ɪ'veɪʒn] *s.* **1.** Entkommen *n*, -rinnen *n*; **2.** Ausweichen *n*, Um'gehung *f*, Vermeidung *f*; → *tax evasion*; **3.** Ausflucht *f*, Ausrede *f*.

e·va·sive [ɪ'veɪsɪv] *adj.* □ **1.** ausweichend: **∼ answer**, **∼ action** Ausweichmanöver *n*; **be ∼** *fig.* ausweichen; **2.** schwer fassbar *od.* feststellbar; **e'vasive·ness** [-nɪs] *s.* ausweichendes Verhalten.

Eve[1] [iːv] *npr. bibl.* Eva *f*: **daughter of ∼** Evastochter *f* (*typische Frau*).

eve[2] [iːv] *s.* **1.** *poet.* Abend *m*; **2.** *mst* 2 Vorabend *m*, -tag *m* (*e-s Festes*); **3.** *fig.* Vorabend *m*: **on the ∼ of** am Vorabend von (*od. gen.*); **be on the ∼ of** kurz vor (*dat.*) stehen.

e·ven[1] ['iːvn] *adv.* **1.** so'gar, selbst, auch: **∼ the king** sogar der König; **he ∼ kissed her** er küsste sie sogar; **∼ if**, **∼ though** selbst wenn, wenn auch; **∼ now** a) selbst jetzt, noch jetzt, b) eben *od.* gerade jetzt, c) schon jetzt; **not ∼ now** selbst jetzt noch nicht, nicht einmal jetzt; *or* **∼** oder auch (nur), oder gar; **without ∼ looking** ohne auch nur hinzusehen; **2.** *vor comp.* noch: **∼ better** (sogar) noch besser; **3.** *nach neg.:* **not ∼** nicht einmal; **I never ∼ saw it** ich habe es nicht einmal gesehen; **4.** gerade, eben: **∼ as I expected** gerade *od.* genau wie ich erwartete; **∼ as he spoke** gerade als er sprach; **∼ so** dennoch, trotzdem, immerhin, selbst dann.

e·ven[2] ['iːvn] **I** *adj.* □ **1.** eben, flach, gerade; **2.** waag(e)recht, horizon'tal; → *keel* 1; **3.** in gleicher Höhe (**with** mit): **∼ with the ground** dem Boden gleich; **4.** gleich: **∼ chances** gleiche Chancen; **stand an ∼ chance of winning** e-e echte Siegeschance haben; **∼ money** gleicher Einsatz (*Wette*); **∼ bet** Wette *f* mit gleichem Einsatz; **of ∼ date** ⸆ gleichen Datums; **5.** ⸆ a) ausgeglichen, schuldenfrei, b) ohne Gewinn od. Verlust: **be ∼ with s.o.** mit j-m quitt sein; **get ∼ with s.o.** mit j-m abrechnen *od.* quitt werden, *fig. a.* es j-m heimzahlen; → *break even*; **6.** gleich-, regelmäßig; im Gleichgewicht (*a. fig.*); **7.** ausgeglichen, ruhig (*Gemüt etc.*): **∼ voice** ruhige *od.* kühle Stimme; **8.** gerecht, 'unpar,teiisch; **9.** a) gerade (*Zahl*), b) geradzahlig (*Schwingungen etc.*), c) rund, voll (*Summe*): **∼ page** (Buch)Seite *f* mit gerader Zahl; **10.** genau, prä'zise: **an ∼ dozen** genau ein Dutzend; **II** *v/t.* **11.** (ein)ebnen, glätten; **12.** *a.* **∼ out** ausgleichen; **13.** **∼ up** ⸆ Rechnung aus-, Konten abstimmen; **III** *v/i.* **14.** *mst.* **∼ out** eben werden; **15.** *a.* **∼ out** sich ausgleichen; **16.** **∼ up on** mit *j-m* quitt werden.

e·ven[3] ['iːvn] *s. poet.* Abend *m*.

e·ven·'hand·ed *adj.* 'unpar,teiisch, objek'tiv.

eve·ning ['iːvnɪŋ] *s.* **1.** Abend *m*: **in the ∼** abends, am Abend; **on the ∼ of** am Abend (*gen.*); **this** (*tomorrow*) **∼** heute (morgen) Abend; **2.** 'Abend (-unter,haltung *f*) *m*, Gesellschaftsabend *m*; **3.** *fig.* Ende *n*, bsd. (*a.* **∼ of life**) Lebensabend *m*; **∼ class·es** *s. pl. ped.* 'Abendunter,richt *m*; **∼ dress** *s.* **1.** Abendkleid *n*; **2.** Gesellschaftsanzug *m*, bsd. a) Frack *m*, b) Smoking *m*; **∼ pa·per** *s.* Abendzeitung *f*; **∼ school** → *night-school*; **∼ shirt** *s.* Frackhemd *n*; **∼ star** *s.* Abendstern *m*.

e·ven·ness ['iːvnnɪs] *s.* **1.** Ebenheit *f*, Geradheit *f*; **2.** Gleichmäßigkeit *f*; **3.** Gleichheit *f*; **4.** Gelassenheit *f*, Seelenruhe *f*, Ausgeglichenheit *f*.

'e·ven·song *s.* Abendandacht *f*.

e·vent [ɪ'vent] *s.* **1.** Ereignis *n*, Vorfall *m*, Begebenheit *f*: (*quite*) **an ∼** ein großes Ereignis; **after the ∼** hinterher, im Nachhinein; **before the ∼** vorher, im Voraus; **2.** Ergebnis *n*, Ausgang *m*: **in the ∼** schließlich; **3.** Fall *m*, 'Umstand *m*: **in either ∼** in jedem Fall; **in any ∼** auf jeden Fall; **at all ∼s** auf alle Fälle, jedenfalls; **in the ∼ of** im Falle (*gen. od.* dass); **4.** *bsd. sport* a) Veranstaltung *f*, b) Diszi'plin *f* (*Sportart*), c) Wettbewerb *m*, -kampf *m*.

e·ven·'tem·pered *adj.* ausgeglichen, gelassen, ruhig.

e·vent·ful [ɪ'ventfʊl] *adj.* **1.** ereignisreich; **2.** denkwürdig, bedeutsam.

'e·ven·tide *s. poet.* (**at ∼** zur) Abendzeit *f*.

e·ven·tu·al [ɪ'ventʃʊəl] *adj.* □ → *eventually*; **1.** schließlich: **this led to his ∼ dismissal** dies führte schließlich *od.* letzten Endes zu s-r Entlassung; **2.** *obs.* eventu'ell, etwaig; **e·ven·tu·al·i·ty** [ɪ,ventʃʊ'ælətɪ] *s.* Möglichkeit *f*, Eventuali'tät *f*; **e'ven·tu·al·ly** [-lɪ] *adv.* schließlich, endlich; **e'ven·tu·ate** [-fʊeɪt] *v/i.* **1.** ausgehen, enden (*in* in *dat.*); **2.** die Folge sein (*from gen.*).

ev·er ['evə] *adv.* **1.** immer, ständig, unaufhörlich: **for ∼** (*and ∼*), **for ∼ and a day** für immer (u. ewig); **∼ and again** (*obs. anon*) dann u. wann, hin und wieder; **∼ since**, **∼ after** seit der Zeit, seitdem; **yours ∼ ...** Viele Grüße, dein(e) *od.* Ihr(e) ...; **2.** *vor comp.* immer: **∼ larger** immer größer; **∼ increasing** ständig zunehmend; **3.** *neg., interrog., konditional:* je(mals): **do you ∼ see him?** siehst du ihn jemals?; **if I ∼ meet him** falls ich ihn je treffe; **did you ∼?** F hast du Töne?, na, so was!; **the fastest ∼** F der (die, das) Schnellste aller Zeiten; **4.** nur, irgend, über'haupt: **as soon as ∼ I can** sobald ich nur kann; **what ∼ do you mean?** was (in aller Welt) meinst du denn (eigentlich)?; **how ∼ did he manage?** wie hat er es nur fertig gebracht?; **hardly ∼**, **seldom if ∼** fast niemals; **5.** **∼ so** sehr, noch so: **∼ so simple** ganz einfach; **∼ so long** e-e Ewigkeit; **∼ so many** sehr viele; **thank you ∼ so much!** tausend Dank!; **if I were ∼ so rich** wenn ich noch so reich wäre; **∼ such a nice man** wirklich ein netter Mann.

'ev·er|·glade *s. Am.* sumpfiges Flussgebiet; **'∼·green I** *adj.* **1.** immergrün; **2.** unverwüstlich, nie veraltend, immer wieder gern gehört: **∼ song** → 4; **II** *s.* **3.** ♀ a) immergrüne Pflanze, b) Immergrün *n*; **4.** Evergreen *m*, *n* (*Schlager*); **'∼·last·ing I** *adj.* □ **1.** immer während, ewig (*a. Gott, Schnee*): **∼ flower** → 5; **2.** *fig.* F unaufhörlich, endlos; **3.** dauer

haft, unbegrenzt haltbar, unverwüstlich; **II** *s.* **4.** Ewigkeit *f*; **5.** ♀ Immor'telle *f*, Strohblume *f*; **,∼'more** *adv.* **1.** immerfort: **for ∼** in Ewigkeit; **2.** je(mals) wieder.

ev·er·y ['evrɪ] *adj.* **1.** jeder, jede, jedes, all: **he has read ∼ book on this subject**; **∼ other** a) jeder andere, b) → *other* 6; **∼ day** jeden Tag, alle Tage, täglich; **∼ four days** alle vier Tage; **∼ fourth day** jeden vierten Tag; **∼ now and then** (*od. again*), **∼ so often** F gelegentlich, hin u. wieder; **∼ bit** (*of it*) ganz, völlig; **∼ bit as good** genauso gut; **∼ time** a) jedesmal(, wenn), sooft, b) jederzeit, F *a.* allemal; **2.** jeder, jede, jedes (*einzelne ... od.* erdenkliche ...), all: **her ∼ wish** jeder ihrer Wünsche, alle ihre Wünsche; **have ∼ reason** allen Grund haben; **their ∼ liberty** ihre ganze Freiheit; **'∼·body** *pron.* jeder(mann); **'∼·day** *adj.* **1.** (all)täglich; **2.** Alltags...; **3.** (mittel)mäßig; **'∼·one**, **∼ one** *pron.* jeder(mann): **in ∼'s mouth** in aller Munde; **'2·man** *s. bsd. thea.* Jedermann *m*; **'∼·thing** *pron.* **1.** alles: **∼ new** alles Neue; **2.** F die Hauptsache, alles: **speed is ∼**; **he** (*it*) **has ∼** F er (es) hat alles *od.* ist ,fantastisch'; **'∼·where** *adv.* 'überall, allenthalben.

e·vict [ɪ'vɪkt] *v/t.* ᴣᴵᴬ **1.** *j-n* zur Räumung zwingen; *fig. j-n* gewaltsam vertreiben; **2.** wieder in Besitz nehmen; **e'vic·tion** [-kʃn] *s.* ᴣᴵᴬ **1.** Zwangsräumung *f*, Heraussetzung *f*: **∼ order** Räumungsbefehl *m*; **2.** Wiederinbe'sitznahme *f*.

ev·i·dence ['evɪdəns] **I** *s.* **1.** ᴣᴵᴬ a) Be'weis(mittel *n*, -stück *n*, -materi,al *n*) *m*, Beweise *pl.*, Ergebnis *n* der Beweisaufnahme *f*, b) 'Unterlage *f*, Beleg *m*, c) (Zeugen)Aussage *f*, Zeugnis *n*: **a piece of ∼** ein Beweisstück; **medical ∼** Aussage *f od.* Gutachten *n* des medizinischen Sachverständigen; **for lack of ∼** mangels Beweises; **in ∼ of** zum Beweis (*gen.*); **offer in ∼** Beweisantritt *m*; **on the ∼** auf Grund des Beweismaterials; **admit in ∼** als Beweis zulassen; **call s.o. in ∼** j-n als Zeugen benennen; **give** *od.* **bear ∼** (**of**) (als Zeuge) aussagen (über *acc.*), *fig.* zeugen (von); **hear ∼** Zeugen vernehmen; **hearing** *od.* **taking of ∼** Beweisaufnahme *f*; **turn King's** (*od.* **Queen's**, *Am.* **State's**) **∼** als Kronzeuge auftreten; **2.** Augenscheinlichkeit *f*, Klarheit *f*: **in ∼** sichtbar, er-, offensichtlich; **be much in ∼** stark in Erscheinung treten, deutlich feststellbar sein; stark vertreten sein; **3.** (An)Zeichen *n*, Spur *f*: **there is no ∼** es ist nicht ersichtlich *od.* feststellbar, nichts deutet darauf hin; **II** *v/t.* **4.** dartun, be-, nachweisen, zeigen; **'ev·i·dent** [-nt] *adj.* □ → *evidently*; augenscheinlich, einleuchtend, offensichtlich, klar (ersichtlich); **ev·i·den·tial** [,evɪ'denʃl] *adj.* □, **ev·i·den·tia·ry** [,evɪ'denʃərɪ] *adj.* **1.** ᴣᴵᴬ beweiserheblich; Beweis... (-*kraft*, -*wert*); **2.** über'zeugend: **be ∼ of** et. (klar) beweisen; **'ev·i·dent·ly** [-ntlɪ] *adv.* offensichtlich, zweifellos.

e·vil ['iːvl] **I** *adj.* □ **1.** übel, böse, schlimm: **∼ eye** a) böser Blick, b) schlimmer Einfluss; **the 2 One** der Teufel; **∼ repute** schlechter Ruf; **∼ spirit** böser Geist; **2.** gottlos, boshaft, schlecht: **∼ tongue** Lästerzunge *f*; **3.** unglücklich: **∼ day** Unglückstag *m*; **fall on ∼ days** ins Unglück geraten; **II** *s.* **4.** Übel *n*, Unglück *n*: **the lesser of two ∼s**, **the lesser** das geringere Übel; **5.** *das* Böse, Sünde *f*, Verderbtheit *f*: **do ∼** Böses tun; **the powers of ∼** die Mächte der Finsternis; *the social* ~ die Prostitution; **,~-dis'posed** → *evil-minded*; **,~-'do·er** s. Übeltäter(in); **,~-'mind·ed** *adj.* übel gesinnt, bösartig; **,~-'speak·ing** *adj.* verleumderisch.

e·vince [ɪ'vɪns] *v/t.* dartun, be-, erweisen, bekunden, zeigen.

e·vis·cer·ate [ɪ'vɪsəreɪt] *v/t.* **1.** *Tier* ausnehmen, *hunt. a.* ausweiden; **2.** *fig. et.* inhalts- *od.* bedeutungslos machen; **e·vis·cer·a·tion** [ɪˌvɪsə'reɪʃn] *s.* Ausweidung *f.*

ev·o·ca·tion [ˌevəʊ'keɪʃn] *s.* **1.** (Geister)Beschwörung *f;* **2.** *fig.* (*of*) a) Wachrufen *n* (*gen.*), b) Erinnerung *f* (an *acc.*); **3.** plastische Schilderung; **e·voc·a·tive** [ɪ'vɒkətɪv] *adj.* **1.** *be ~ of* erinnern an (*acc.*); **2.** sinnträchtig, beziehungsreich.

e·voke [ɪ'vəʊk] *v/t.* **1.** *Geister* her'beirufen, beschwören; **2.** *fig.* her'vor-, wachrufen, wecken.

ev·o·lu·tion [ˌiːvə'luːʃn] *s.* **1.** Entwicklung *f*, Entfaltung *f*, (Her'aus)Bildung *f*; **2.** *biol.* Evoluti'on *f: theory of* ~ Evolutionstheorie *f*; **3.** Folge *f*, (Handlungs)Ablauf *m*; **4.** ✕ Ma'növer *n*, Bewegung *f*; **5.** *phys.* (*Gas- etc.*) Entwicklung *f*; **6.** ⚭ Wurzelziehen *n*; **ev·o'lu·tion·ar·y** [-nərɪ] *adj.* Entwicklungs..., *biol.* Evolutions...; **ev·o'lu·tion·ist** [-ʃənɪst] I *s.* Anhänger(in) der (*biologischen*) Entwicklungslehre; **II** *adj.* die Entwicklungslehre betreffend.

e·volve [ɪ'vɒlv] I *v/t.* **1.** entwickeln, entfalten, her'ausarbeiten; **2.** *Gas, Wärme* aus-, verströmen; **II** *v/i.* **3.** sich entwickeln *od.* entfalten (*into* zu); **4.** entstehen (*from* aus).

ewe [juː] *s. zo.* Mutterschaf *n;* ~ *lamb s. zo.* Schaflamm *m.*

ew·er ['juːə] *s.* Wasserkrug *m.*

ex¹ [eks] *prp.* **1.** ✝ a) aus, ab, von: ~ *factory* ab Fabrik; ~ *works* ab Werk; → *ex officio*, b) ohne, exklu'sive: ~ *all* ausschließlich aller Rechte; ~ *dividend* ohne Dividende; **2.** → *ex cathedra etc.*

ex² [eks] *s.* X *n*, x *n* (*Buchstabe*).

ex- [eks] *in Zssgn* Ex..., ehemalig; Alt...

ex·ac·er·bate [ek'sæsəbeɪt] *v/t.* **1.** *j-n* verärgern; **2.** *et.* verschlimmern; **ex·ac·er·ba·tion** [ek,sæsə'beɪʃn] *s.* **1.** Verärgerung *f;* **2.** Verschlimmerung *f.*

ex·act [ɪg'zækt] I *adj.* □ → *exactly*; **1.** ex'akt, genau, (genau) richtig: *the ~ time* die genaue Zeit; *the ~ sciences* die exakten Wissenschaften; **2.** streng, genau: ~ *rules*; **3.** me'thodisch, gewissenhaft, sorgfältig (*Person*); **4.** genau, tatsächlich: *his ~ words;* **II** *v/t.* **5.** *Gehorsam, Geld etc.* fordern, verlangen; **6.** *Zahlung* eintreiben, einfordern; **7.** *Geschick etc.* erfordern; **ex'act·ing** [-tɪŋ] *adj.* **1.** streng, genau; **2.** anspruchsvoll: *an ~ customer; be ~* hohe Anforderungen stellen; **3.** hart, aufreibend (*Aufgabe etc.*); **ex'ac·tion** [-kʃn] *s.* **1.** Fordern *n;* **2.** Eintreiben *n;* **3.** (unmäßige) Forderung; **ex'act·i·tude** [-tɪtjuːd] → *exactness;* **ex'act·ly** [-lɪ] *adv.* **1.** genau, ex'akt; **2.** sorgfältig; **3.** *als Antwort:* genau, ganz recht, du sagst (Sie sagen) es: *not ~* a) nicht ganz, b) *iro.* nicht gerade *od.* eben *schön etc.;* **4.** *wo, wann etc.* eigentlich; **ex'act·ness** [-nɪs] *s.* **1.** Ex'aktheit *f*, Genauigkeit *f*, Richtigkeit *f;* **2.** Sorgfalt *f.*

ex·ag·ger·ate [ɪg'zædʒəreɪt] I *v/t.* **1.** über'treiben; über'trieben darstellen; aufbauschen; **2.** 'überbewerten; **3.** 'übersteigern; **II** *v/i.* **4.** über'treiben; **ex'ag·ger·at·ed** [-tɪd] *adj.* □ über'trieben, -'zogen; **ex·ag·ger·a·tion** [ɪgˌzæ-

dʒə'reɪʃn] *s.* Über'treibung *f.*

ex·alt [ɪg'zɔːlt] *v/t.* **1.** *im Rang* erheben, erhöhen (*to* zu); **2.** (lob)preisen, verherrlichen: ~ *to the skies* in den Himmel heben; **3.** verstärken (*a. fig.*); **ex·al·ta·tion** [ˌegzɔːl'teɪʃn] *s.* **1.** Erhebung *f;* **2** *of the Cross eccl.* Kreuzeserhöhung *f;* **2.** Begeisterung *f*, Ek'stase *f*, Erregung *f;* **ex'alt·ed** [-tɪd] *adj.* **1.** gehoben: ~ *style;* **2.** hoch: ~ *rank;* ~ *ideal;* **3.** begeistert; **4.** über'trieben hoch: *have an ~ opinion of o.s.*

ex·am [ɪg'zæm] F *für examination* 2.

ex·am·i·na·tion [ɪgˌzæmɪ'neɪʃn] *s.* **1.** Unter'suchung *f* (*a.* ✚), Prüfung *f* (*of, into gen.*); Besichtigung *f*, 'Durchsicht *f:* (*up*)*on ~* bei näherer Prüfung; *be under ~* geprüft *od.* erwogen werden (→ *a.* 3); **2.** *ped.* Prüfung *f*, Ex'amen *n:* ~ *paper* Prüfungsarbeit *f*, -aufgabe(n *pl.*) *f; take* (*od. go in for*) *an ~* sich e-r Prüfung unterziehen; **3.** ✚ a) *Zivilprozess:* Vernehmung *f*, b) *Strafprozess:* Verhör *n: be under ~* vernommen werden (→ *a.* 1).

ex·am·ine [ɪg'zæmɪn] I *v/t.* **1.** unter'suchen (*a.* ✚), prüfen (*a. ped.*), examinieren, besichtigen, 'durchsehen, revidieren: ~ *one's conscience* sein Gewissen prüfen; **2.** ✚ vernehmen, *Straftäter* verhören; **II** *v/i.* **3.** ~ *into s.th.* et. untersuchen; **ex·am·i·nee** [ɪgˌzæmɪ'niː] *s.* Prüfling *m*, (Prüfungs)Kandi,dat(in); **ex'am·in·er** [-nə] *s.* **1.** *allg.* Prüfer(in); **2.** ✚ beauftragter Richter; **ex'am·in·ing bod·y** [-nɪŋ] *s.* Prüfungsausschuss *m.*

ex·am·ple [ɪg'zɑːmpl] *s.* **1.** Beispiel *n* (*of* für): *for ~* zum Beispiel; *without ~* beispiellos, ohnegleichen; **2.** Vorbild *n*, Beispiel *n: hold up an ~* als Beispiel hinstellen; *set a good ~* ein gutes Beispiel geben; *take an ~ by* sich ein Beispiel nehmen an (*dat.*); **3.** warnendes Beispiel: *let this be an ~ to you* lass dir das e-e Warnung sein; *make an ~ of s.o.* an j-m ein Exempel statuieren.

ex·as·per·ate [ɪg'zæspəreɪt] *v/t.* ärgern, wütend machen, aufbringen; **ex'as·per·at·ed** [-tɪd] *adj.* aufgebracht, erbost; **ex'as·per·at·ing** [-tɪŋ] *adj.* □ ärgerlich, zum Verzweifeln; **ex·as·per·a·tion** [ɪgˌzæspə'reɪʃn] *s.* Wut *f: in ~* wütend.

ex ca·the·dra [ˌekskə'θiːdrə] I *adj.* maßgeblich, autorita'tiv; **II** *adv.* ex 'cathedra; maßgeblich.

ex·ca·vate ['ekskəveɪt] *v/t.* **1.** ausgraben (*a. fig.*), ausschachten, -höhlen; **2.** *Zahnmedizin:* exkavieren; **ex·ca·va·tion** [ˌekskə'veɪʃn] *s.* **1.** Ausgrabung *f;* **2.** Ausschachtung *f*, Aushöhlung *f;* Aushub *m;* **3.** *geol.* Auskolkung *f;* **4.** *Zahnmedizin:* Exkavati'on *f;* 'ex·ca·va·tor [-tə] *s.* **1.** Ausgräber *m;* **2.** Erdarbeiter *m;* **3.** ⚙ (Trocken)Bagger *m.*

ex·ceed [ɪk'siːd] I *v/t.* **1.** über'schreiten, -'steigen (*a. fig.*); **2.** *fig.* a) hin'ausgehen über (*acc.*), b) *j-n, et.* über'treffen; **II** *v/i.* **3.** zu weit gehen, das Maß über-'schreiten; **4.** her'ausragen; **ex'ceed·ing** [-dɪŋ] *adj.* □ → *exceedingly;* **1.** außer'ordentlich, äußerst; **2.** mehr als, über: *not ~* (von) höchstens; **ex'ceed·ing·ly** [-dɪŋlɪ] *adv.* 'überaus, äußerst, aufs Äußerste.

ex·cel [ɪk'sel] I *v/t.* über'treffen (*o.s.* sich selbst); **II** *v/i.* sich auszeichnen, her'vorragen (*in od. at* in *dat.*).

ex·cel·lence ['eksələns] *s.* **1.** Vor'trefflichkeit *f;* **2.** her'vorragende Leistung; '**Ex·cel·len·cy** [-sɪ] *s.* Exzel'lenz *f* (*Titel*): *Your ~* Eure Exzellenz; 'ex·cel·lent

[-nt] *adj.* □ vor'züglich, ausgezeichnet, her'vorragend.

ex·cel·si·or [ek'selsɪɔː] *s.* **1.** *Am.* Holzwolle *f;* **2.** *typ.* Bril'lant *f* (*Schriftgrad*).

ex·cept [ɪk'sept] I *v/t.* **1.** ausnehmen, -schließen (*from* von, aus); **2.** sich *et.* vorbehalten; → *error* 1; **II** *v/i.* **3.** Einwendungen machen, Einspruch erheben (*against* gegen); **III** *prp.* **4.** ausgenommen, außer, mit Ausnahme von (*od. gen.*): ~ *for* abgesehen von, bis auf (*acc.*); **IV** *cj.* **5.** es sei denn, dass; außer, wenn: ~ *that* außer, dass; **ex'cept·ing** [-tɪŋ] *prp.* (*nach always od. neg.*) ausgenommen, außer; **ex'cep·tion** [-pʃn] *s.* **1.** Ausnahme *f: by way of ~* ausnahmsweise; *with the ~ of* mit Ausnahme von (*od. gen.*), außer, bis auf (*acc.*); *without ~* ohne Ausnahme, ausnahmslos; *make no ~(s)* keine Ausnahme machen; *an ~ to the rule* e-e Ausnahme von der Regel; **2.** Einwendung *f*, Einwand *m*, Einspruch *m* (*a.* ✚ *Rechtsmittelvorbehalt*): *take ~ to* a) Einwendungen machen *od.* protestieren gegen, b) Anstoß nehmen an (*dat.*); **ex'cep·tion·a·ble** [-pʃnəbl] *adj.* □ **1.** anfechtbar; **2.** anstößig; **ex'cep·tion·al** [-pʃnl] *adj.* □ → *exceptionally;* **1.** außergewöhnlich, Ausnahme..., Sonder...: ~ *case* Ausnahmefall *m;* **2.** ungewöhnlich (gut); **ex'cep·tion·al·ly** [-pʃnlɪ] *adv.* **1.** ausnahmsweise; **2.** außergewöhnlich.

ex·cerpt I *v/t.* [ek'sɜːpt] **1.** *Textstelle* exzerpieren, ausziehen; **II** *s.* ['eksɜːpt] **2.** Ex'zerpt *n*, Auszug *m;* **3.** Sonder(ab)-druck *m.*

ex·cess [ɪk'ses] *s.* **1.** 'Übermaß *n*, -fluss *m* (*of* an *dat.*): ~ *of ...* zu viel ...; *carry to ~* über'treiben, *et.* zu weit treiben; **2.** Ex'zess *m*, Unmäßigkeit *f*, Ausschweifung *f; mst pl.* Ausschreitungen *pl.:* *drink to ~* übermäßig trinken; **3.** 'Überschuss *m* (*a.* ⚭, ✚, ✈) Mehrsumme *f: in ~* mehr als, über ...; *be in ~ of* überschreiten, -steigen; ~ *of exports* Ausfuhrüberschuss *m;* ~ *bag·gage s.* ✈ *Am.* 'Übergepäck *n;* ~ *ca·pac·i·ty s.* Überkapazität *f;* ~ *cost s.* Mehrkosten *pl.;* ~ *cur·rent s.* ⚡ 'Überstrom *m;* ~ *fare s.* (Fahrpreis)Zuschlag *m;* ~ *freight s.* 'Überfracht *f.*

ex·ces·sive [ɪk'sesɪv] *adj.* □ 'übermäßig, über'trieben; unangemessen hoch (*Strafe etc.*).

ex·cess| lug·gage *s.* ✈ 'Übergepäck *n;* ~ *post·age s.* Nachporto *n*, -gebühr *f;* ~ *prof·its tax s. Am.* Mehrgewinnsteuer *f;* ~ *volt·age s.* ⚡ 'Überspannung *f;* ~ *weight s.* Mehrgewicht *n.*

ex·change [ɪks'tʃeɪndʒ] I *v/t.* **1.** (*for*) aus-, 'umtauschen (gegen), vertauschen (mit); **2.** *Geld* eintauschen, ('um)wechseln (*for* gegen); **3.** (*gegenseitig*) *Blicke, Küsse, Plätze* tauschen; *Grüße, Gedanken, Gefangene etc.* austauschen; *Worte, Schüsse etc.* wechseln: ~ *blows* sich prügeln; **4.** ersetzen (*for* durch); **5.** ⚙ auswechseln; **II** *v/i.* **6.** ~ *for* wert sein: *one Euro ~s for one dollar;* **III** *s.* **7.** Tausch *m* (*a. Schach*), Aus-, 'Umtausch *m*, Auswechselung *f*, Tauschhandel *m: in ~* als Ersatz, dafür; *in ~ for* gegen, als Entgelt für; ~ *of letters* Schriftwechsel *m;* ~ *of blows* Schlagwechsel *m*, *Boxen: a.* Schlagabtausch *m;* ~ *of shots* Schusswechsel *m;* ~ *of views* Meinungsaustausch; **8.** ✝ a) ('Um-) Wechsel *n*, Wechselverkehr *m: money* ~ Geldwechsel *m;* → *bill²* 3, c) → *rate¹* 2, d) *foreign* ~ Devisen *pl.*, Valuta *f*, e) Wechselstube *f;* **9.** ✝ Börse *f;*

E

10. (Fernsprech)Amt *n*, Vermittlung *f*; **ex·change·a·ble** [-dʒəbl] *adj.* **1.** (aus-)tausch-, auswechselbar (*for* gegen); **2.** Tausch...

ex·change| bro·ker *s.* **1.** Wechselmakler *m*; **2.** De'visenmakler *m*; **~ con·trol** *s.* De'visenbewirtschaftung *f*, -kon,trolle *f*; **~ list** *s.* ✝ Kurszettel *m*; **~ of·fice** *s.* Wechselstube *f*; **~ rate** *s.* ✝ 'Umrechnungs-, Wechselkurs *m*: **~ adjustment** Wechselkursberichtigung *f*; **~ fluctuation band** Bandbreite der Wechselkurse; **~ parity** Wechselkursparität *f*; **~ reg·ula·tions** *s. pl.* ✝ De'visenbestimmungen *pl.*; **~ re·stric·tions** *s. pl.* ✝ De'visenbeschränkungen *pl.*; **~ stu·dent** *s.* 'Austauschstu,dent(in).

ex·cheq·uer [ɪks'tʃekə] *s.* **1.** *Brit.* Schatzamt *n*, Staatskasse *f*, Fiskus *m*: **the ~** das Finanzministerium; **~ bill** *obs.* Schatzwechsel *m*; **~ bond** Schatzanweisung *f*; **2.** ✝ (Geschäfts)Kasse *f*.

ex·cis·a·ble [ek'saɪzəbl] *adj.* (verbrauchs)steuerpflichtig.

ex·cise¹ I *v/t.* [ek'saɪz] besteuern; II ['eksaɪz] *a.* **~ duty** Verbrauchssteuer *f*: **~man** Steuereinnehmer *m*.

ex·cise² [ek'saɪz] *v/t.* ✂ her'ausschneiden, entfernen; **ex·ci·sion** [ek'sɪʒn] *s.* **1.** ✂ Exzisi'on *f*, Ausschneidung *f*; **2.** Ausmerzung *f*.

ex·cit·a·bil·i·ty [ɪk,saɪtə'bɪlətɪ] *s.* Reizbar-, Erregbarkeit *f*, Nervosi'tät *f*; **ex·cit·a·ble** [ɪk'saɪtəbl] *adj.* reiz-, erregbar, ner'vös; **ex·cit·ant** ['eksɪtənt] *s.* ✂ Reizmittel *n*, 'Stimulans *n*; **ex·ci·ta·tion** [,eksɪ'teɪʃn] *s.* **1.** *a.* ✓, ⚚ Erregung *f*; **2.** ✂ Reiz *m*, 'Stimulus *m*.

ex·cite [ɪk'saɪt] *v/t.* **1.** *j-n* er-, aufregen: **get ~d** (*over*) sich aufregen (über *acc.*); **2.** *j-n* an-, aufreizen, aufstacheln; **3.** *j-n* (*sexuell*) erregen; **4.** *Interesse etc.* erregen, erwecken, her'vorrufen; **5.** ✂ *Nerv* reizen; **6.** ⚡ erregen; **7.** *phot.* lichtempfindlich machen; **ex·cit·ed** [-tɪd] *adj.* ☐ erregt; aufgeregt; **ex·cite·ment** [-mənt] *s.* **1.** Er-, Aufregung *f*; **2.** Reizung *f*; **ex·cit·er** [-tə] *s.* ⚡ Erreger *m*; **ex·cit·ing** [-tɪŋ] *adj.* **1.** erregend; aufregend; spannend, anregend, toll; **2.** ⚡ Erreger...

ex·claim [ɪk'skleɪm] I *v/i.* **1.** ausrufen, (auf)schreien; **2.** eifern, wettern (*against* gegen); II *v/t.* **3.** ausrufen.

ex·cla·ma·tion [,eksklə'meɪʃn] *s.* **1.** Ausruf *m*, (Auf)Schrei *m*; **2.** *a.* **~ mark**, *note of ~*, *Am.* **point of ~** Ausrufe-, Ausrufungszeichen *n*; **3.** heftiger Pro'test; **4.** *ling.* a) Ausrufesatz *m*, b) Interjekti'on *f*; **ex·clam·a·to·ry** [ek-'sklæmətərɪ] *adj.* **1.** exklama'torisch: **~ style**; **2.** Ausrufe...: **~ sentence**.

ex·clave ['eks'kleɪv] *s.* Ex'klave *f*.

ex·clude [ɪk'sklu:d] *v/t.* ausschließen (*from* von): **not excluding myself** mich selbst nicht ausgenommen; **ex·'clu·sion** [-u:ʒən] *s.* **1.** Ausschließung *f*, Ausschluss *m* (*from* von): **to the ~ of** unter Ausschluss von; **2.** ⊚ Absperrung *f*; **~ zone** *s. pol.* Schutzzone *f*.

ex·clu·sive [ɪk'sklu:sɪv] I *adj.* ☐ → **exclusively**; **1.** ausschließend: **~ of** aus schließlich (*gen.*), abgesehen von, ohne; **be ~ of** *et.* ausschließen; **2.** a) ausschließlich, al'leinig, Allein..., Sonder...: **~ agent** Alleinvertreter *m*; **~ rights** ausschließliche Rechte; **be ~ to** beschränkt sein auf (*acc.*), b) Exklusiv...: **~ contract** (*report etc.*); **3.** exklu'siv: a) vornehm, b) anspruchsvoll; **4.** unnahbar; II *s.* **5.** Exklu'sivbericht *m*; **ex·clu·sive·ly** [-lɪ] *adv.* ausschließlich, nur; **ex·clu·sive·ness** [-nɪs] *s.* Ex-

klusivi'tät *f*.

ex·cog·i·tate [eks'kɒdʒɪteɪt] *v/t.* (sich) *et.* ausdenken, ersinnen.

ex·com·mu·ni·cate [,ekskə'mju:nɪkeɪt] *v/t. R.C.* exkommunizieren; **ex·com·mu·ni·ca·tion** ['ekskə,mju:nɪ'keɪʃn] *s.* Exkommunikati'on *f*.

ex·co·ri·ate [eks'kɔ:rɪeɪt] *v/t.* **1.** die Haut abziehen von; *Baum* abrinden; **2.** *Haut* wund reiben, abschürfen; **3.** heftig angreifen, vernichtend kritisieren; **ex·co·ri·a·tion** [eks,kɔ:rɪ'eɪʃn] *s.* **1.** (Haut)Abschürfung *f*; **2.** Wundreiben *n*.

ex·cre·ment ['ekskrɪmənt] *s.* *oft pl.* Kot *m*, Exkre'mente *pl.*

ex·cres·cence [ɪk'skresns] *s.* **1.** Auswuchs *m* (*a. fig.*); **2.** ❀ Wucherung *f*; **ex·cres·cent** [-nt] *adj.* **1.** auswachsend; wuchernd; **2.** *fig.* 'überflüssig; **3.** *ling.* eingeschoben.

ex·cre·ta [ek'skri:tə] *s. pl.* Ex'krete *pl.*; **ex·crete** [ek'skri:t] *v/t.* absondern, ausscheiden; **ex·cre·tion** [-i:ʃn] *s.* **1.** Ausscheidung *f*; **2.** Ex'kret *n*.

ex·cru·ci·ate [ɪk'skru:ʃɪeɪt] *v/t. fig.* quälen; **ex·cru·ci·at·ing** [-tɪŋ] *adj.* ☐ **1.** qualvoll, heftig; **2.** F schauderhaft, unerträglich.

ex·cul·pate ['eksk^lpeɪt] *v/t.* rein waschen, rechtfertigen, freisprechen (*from* von); **ex·cul·pa·tion** [,eksk^l'peɪʃn] *s.* Entschuldigung *f*, Rechtfertigung *f*, Entlastung *f*.

ex·cur·sion [ɪk'skɜ:ʃn] *s.* **1.** (*a.* wissenschaftliche) Exkursi'on, Ausflug *m*, Abstecher *m*, Streifzug *m* (*alle a. fig.*): **~ train** Sonder-, Ausflugszug *m*; **2.** Abschweifung *f*; **3.** Abweichung *f* (*a. ast.*); **ex·cur·sion·ist** [-ʃnɪst] *s.* Ausflügler (-in); **ex·cur·sive** [-ɜ:sɪv] *adj.* ☐ **1.** abschweifend; **2.** weitschweifig; sprunghaft; **ex·cur·sus** [-ɜ:səs] *pl.* **-sus·es** *s.* Ex'kurs *m* (*Erörterung od. Abschweifung*).

ex·cus·a·ble [ɪk'skju:zəbl] *adj.* ☐ entschuldbar, verzeihlich.

ex·cuse I *v/t.* [ɪk'skju:z] **1.** *j-n od. et.* entschuldigen, *j-m et.* verzeihen: **~ me** a) entschuldigen Sie!, b) aber erlauben Sie mal!; **~ me for being late**, **~ my being late** verzeih, dass ich zu spät komme; **please ~ my mistake** bitte entschuldige m-n Irrtum; **2.** Nachsicht mit *j-m* haben; **3.** *et.* entschuldigen, über'sehen; **4.** *et.* entschuldigen, e-e Entschuldigung für *et.* sein, rechtfertigen: **that does not ~ your conduct**; **5.** (*from*) *j-n* befreien (von), *j-m et.* erlassen: **~ s.o. from attendance**; **~d from duty** vom Dienst befreit; **he begs to be ~d** er lässt sich entschuldigen; **I must be ~d from doing this** ich muss es leider ablehnen, dies zu tun; **6.** *j-m et.* erlassen; II *s.* [-kju:s] **7.** Entschuldigung *f*: **offer (od. make) an ~** sich entschuldigen; **please make my ~s to her** bitte entschuldige mich bei ihr; **8.** Rechtfertigung *f*: **there is no ~ for his conduct** sein Benehmen ist nicht zu entschuldigen; **9.** Vorwand *m*, Ausrede *f*, Ausflucht *f*; **10.** dürftiger Ersatz: **a poor ~ for a car** e-e armselige ‚Kutsche'; **ex'cuse-me** *s.* Tanz *m* mit Abklatschen.

ex·di·rec·to·ry *adj.*: **~ number** *teleph.* Geheimnummer *f*.

ex·e·at ['eksɪæt] (*Lat.*) *s. Brit.* (kurzer) Urlaub (*für Studenten*).

ex·e·cra·ble ['eksɪkrəbl] *adj.* ☐ abscheulich, scheußlich; **ex·e·crate** ['eksɪkreɪt] I *v/t.* **1.** verfluchen, verwünschen; **2.** verabscheuen; II *v/i.* **3.** fluchen; **ex·e·cra·tion** [,eksɪ'kreɪʃn] *s.* **1.**

Verwünschung *f*, Fluch *m*; **2.** Abscheu *m*: **hold in ~** verabscheuen.

ex·ec·u·tant [ɪg'zekjʊtənt] *s.* Ausführende(r *m*) *f*, *bsd.* ♪ Vortragende(r *m*) *f*; **ex·e·cute** ['eksɪkju:t] *v/t.* **1.** aus-, 'durchführen, verrichten, tätigen; **2.** *Amt* ausüben; **3.** ♪, *thea.* vortragen, spielen; **4.** ✝ a) *Urkunde* (rechtsgültig) ausfertigen, durch 'Unterschrift, Siegel *etc.* voll'ziehen, b) *Urteil* voll'strecken, *bsd. j-n* hinrichten, c) *j-n* pfänden; **ex·e·cu·tion** [,eksɪ'kju:ʃn] *s.* **1.** Aus-, 'Durchführung *f*, Verrichtung *f*: **carry into ~** ausführen; **2.** (*Art u. Weise der*) Ausführung: a) ♪ Vortrag *m*, Spiel *n*, Technik *f*, b) *Kunst, Literatur:* Darstellung *f*, Stil *m*; **3.** ✝ a) Ausfertigung *f*, b) Errichtung *f* (*e-s Testaments*), c) Voll'ziehung *f*, ('Urteils-, *a.* 'Zwangs-) Voll,streckung *f*, Pfändung *f*, d) Hinrichtung *f*: **sale under ~** Zwangsversteigerung *f*; **levy ~ against a company** die Zwangsvollstreckung in das Vermögen e-r Gesellschaft betreiben; **ex·e·cu·tion·er** [-ʃnə] *s.* **1.** Henker *m*, Scharfrichter *m*; **2.** *sport* Voll'strecker *m*; **ex·ec·u·tive** [-tɪv] I *adj.* ☐ **1.** ausübend, voll'ziehend, *pol.* Exekutiv...: **~ officer** Verwaltungsbeamte(r) *m*; **~ power** → 3; **2.** ✝ geschäftsführend, leitend: **~ board** Vorstand *m*; **~ committee** Exekutivausschuss *m*; **~ floor** Chefetage *f*; **~ functions** Führungsaufgaben; **~ post** leitende Stellung; **~ staff** leitende Angestellte *pl.*; II *s.* **3.** Exeku'tive *f*, voll'ziehende Gewalt (*im Staat*); **4.** *a.* **senior ~** ✝ leitender Angestellter; **5.** ✗ *Am.* stellvertretender Komman'deur; **ex·ec·u·tor** [-tə] *s.* ✝ Testa'mentsvoll,strecker *m*, Erbschaftsverwalter *m*: **literary ~** Nachlassverwalter e-s Autors; **ex·ec·u·to·ry** [-tərɪ] *adj.* **1.** ✝ bedingt, erfüllungsbedürftig: **~ contract**; **2.** Ausführungs...; **ex·ec·u·trix** [-trɪks] *s.* ✝ Testa'mentsvoll,streckerin *f*.

ex·e·ge·sis [,eksɪ'dʒi:sɪs] *s.* Exe'gese *f*, (Bibel)Auslegung *f*; **ex·e·gete** ['eksɪdʒi:t] *s.* Exe'get *m*; **ex·e·get·ic** [-'dʒetɪk] I *adj.* ☐ exe'getisch, auslegend; II *s. pl. sg. konstr.* Exe'getik *f*.

ex·em·plar [ɪg'zemplə] *s.* **1.** Muster(beispiel) *n*, Vorbild *n*; **2.** typisches Beispiel; **3.** *typ.* (Druck)Vorlage *f*; **ex'em·pla·ry** [-ərɪ] *adj.* ☐ **1.** exem'plarisch: a) beispiel-, musterhaft, b) warnend, abschreckend, dra'konisch (*Strafe etc.*); **2.** typisch, Muster...

ex·em·pli·fi·ca·tion [ɪg,zemplɪfɪ'keɪʃn] *s.* **1.** Erläuterung *f* durch Beispiele; Veranschaulichung *f*; **2.** Beleg *m*, Beispiel *n*, Muster *n*; **3.** ✝ beglaubigte Abschrift, Ausfertigung *f*; **ex·em·pli·fy** [ɪg'zemplɪfaɪ] *v/t.* veranschaulichen: a) durch Beispiele erläutern, b) als Beispiel dienen für; **2.** e-e beglaubigte Abschrift machen von.

ex·empt [ɪg'zempt] I *v/t.* **1.** *j-n* befreien, ausnehmen (*from* von *Steuern, Verpflichtungen etc.*): **~ed amount** ✝ (Steuer)Freibetrag *m*; **2.** ✗ (*vom Wehrdienst*) freistellen; II *adj.* befreit, ausgenommen, frei (*from* von): **~ from taxes** steuerfrei; **ex'emp·tion** [-pʃn] *s.* **1.** Befreiung *f*, Freisein *n* (*from* von): **~ from taxes** Steuerfreiheit *f*; **~ from liability** ✝ Haftungsausschluss *m*; **2.** ✗ Freistellung *f* (*vom Wehrdienst*); **3.** *pl.* ✝ unpfändbare Gegenstände *pl. od.* Beträge *pl.*; **4.** Sonderstellung *f*, Vorrechte *pl.*

ex·er·cise ['eksəsaɪz] I *s.* **1.** Ausübung *f* (*e-s Amtes, der Pflicht, e-r Kunst, e-s*

Rechts, der Macht etc.), Gebrauch *m*, Anwendung *f*; **2.** *oft pl.* (*körperliche od. geistige*) Übung, (*körperliche*) Bewegung, *sport* (Turn)Übung *f*: **do one's ~s** Gymnastik machen; **take ~** sich Bewegung machen; **~ therapy** Bewegungstherapie *f*; **physical ~** Leibesübungen *pl.*; (*military*) **~** a) Exerzieren *n*, b) Manöver *n*; (*religious*) **~** Gottesdienst *m*, Andacht *f*; **3.** Übungsarbeit *f*, Schulaufgabe *f*; **~ book** Schul-, Schreibheft *n*; **4.** ♪ Übung(sstück *n*) *f*; **5.** *pl. Am.* Feier(lichkeiten *pl.*) *f*; **II** *v/t.* **6.** *ein Amt, ein Recht, Macht, Einfluss* ausüben, *Einfluss, Recht, Macht* geltend machen, *et.* anwenden; *Geduld* üben; **7.** *Körper, Geist* üben, trainieren; **8.** *j-n* üben, ausbilden; **9.** *s-e Glieder, Tiere* bewegen; **10.** *j-n, j-s Geist* stark beschäftigen, plagen, beunruhigen: **be ~d** beunruhigt sein (*about* über *acc.*); **III** *v/i.* **11.** sich Bewegung machen; **12.** *sport* trainieren; **13.** ✕ exerzieren.

ex·ert [ɪgˈzɜːt] *v/t.* gebrauchen, anwenden; *Druck, Einfluss etc.* ausüben (**on** auf *acc.*); *Autorität* geltend machen: **~ o.s.** sich anstrengen; **ex·er·tion** [-ɜːʃn] *s.* **1.** Anwendung *f*, Ausübung *f*; **2.** Anstrengung *f*: a) Stra'paze *f*, b) Bemühung *f*.

ex·e·unt [ˈeksɪʌnt] (*Lat.*) *thea.* (sie gehen) ab: **~ omnes** alle ab.

ex·fo·li·ate [eksˈfəʊlɪeɪt] *v/i. mst* 🌿 abblättern, sich abschälen; **ex·fo·li·a·tion** [eks.fəʊlɪˈeɪʃn] *s.* Abblätterung *f*.

ex-gra·ti·a [eksˈgreɪʃə] *adj.* freiwillig; ✝ **~ payment** Kulanzzahlung *f*.

ex·ha·la·tion [ˌekshəˈleɪʃn] *s.* **1.** Ausatmen *n*; **2.** Verströmen *n*; **3.** a) Gas *n*, b) Rauch *m*, c) Geruch *m*, Ausdünstung *f*; **ex·hale** [eksˈheɪl] **I** *v/t.* **1.** ausatmen; **2.** *Gas, Geruch etc.* verströmen, *Rauch* ausstoßen; **II** *v/i.* **3.** ausströmen; **4.** ausatmen.

ex·haust [ɪgˈzɔːst] **I** *v/t.* **1.** *mst* 🔧 a) (ent)leeren, b) luftleer pumpen, c) *Luft, Wasser etc.* her'auspumpen, *Gas* auspuffen, d) absaugen; **2.** *allg.* erschöpfen: a) *Boden* ausmergeln, b) *Bergwerk etc.* völlig abbauen, c) *Vorräte* ver-, aufbrauchen, d) *j-n* ermüden, entkräften, e) *j-s Kräfte* strapazieren; **3.** *Thema* erschöpfend behandeln; *alle Möglichkeiten* ausschöpfen; **II** *v/i.* **4.** ausströmen; **5.** sich entleeren; **III** *s.* **6.** 🔧 a) Dampfaustritt *m*, b) *a.* **~ gas** Abgas *n*, c) Auspuffgase *pl.*; **7.** *mot.* Auspuff *m*: **~ box** Auspufftopf *m*; **~ brake** Motorbremse *f*; **~ emission test** Abgastest *m*; **~ fumes** Abgase; **8.** → **exhauster**; **ex·haust·ed** [-tɪd] *adj.* **1.** aufgebraucht, zu Ende, erschöpft (*Vorräte*), vergriffen (*Auflage*), abgelaufen (*Frist, Versicherung*); **2.** *fig.* erschöpft, ermattet; **ex·haust·er** [-tə] *s.* 🔧 (Ent-)Lüfter *m*, Absaugevorrichtung *f*, Ex-'haustor *m*; **ex·haust·ing** [-tɪŋ] *adj.* ermüdend, anstrengend, strapazi'ös; **ex·haus·tion** [-tʃn] *s.* **1.** 🔧 a) (Ent)Leerung *f*, b) Her'auspumpen *n*, c) Absaugung *f*; **2.** Ausströmen *n* (*von Dampf etc.*); **3.** Erschöpfung *f*, (völliger) Verbrauch; **4.** *fig.* Erschöpfung *f*, Ermüdung *f*, Entkräftung *f*; **5.** ♠ Approximati'on *f*; **ex·haus·tive** [-tɪv] *adj.* □ **1.** *fig.* erschöpfend; **2.** → **exhausting**.

ex·haust‖pipe *s.* 🔧 Auspuffrohr *n*; **~ pol·lu·tion** *s.* Luftverschmutzung *f* durch Abgase; **~ pol·lu·tion stand·ards** *s. pl.* Abgaswerte *pl.*; **~ steam** *s.* 🔧 Abdampf *m*; **~ stroke** *s.* 🔧 Auspuffhub *m*; **~ valve** *s.* 🔧 'Auslassven,til *n*.

---

ex·hib·it [ɪgˈzɪbɪt] **I** *v/t.* **1.** ausstellen, zur Schau stellen: **~ goods**; **2.** *fig.* zeigen, an den Tag legen, entfalten; **3.** 📖 vorlegen; **II** *v/i.* **4.** ausstellen; **III** *s.* **5.** Ausstellungstück *n*, Expo'nat *n*; **6.** 📖 a) Eingabe *f*, b) Beweisstück *n*, Beleg *m*, c) Anlage *f zu e-m Schriftsatz*.

ex·hi·bi·tion [ˌeksɪˈbɪʃn] *s.* **1.** a) Ausstellung *f*, Schau *f*: **be on ~** ausgestellt sein, zu sehen sein, b) Vorführung *f*: **~ contest** *sport* Schaukampf *m*; **make an ~ of o.s.** sich lächerlich *od.* zum Gespött machen, ‚auffalen'; **2.** *fig.* Zur'schaustellung *f*, Bekundung *f*; **3.** 📖 Vorlage *f*, Beibringung *f* (*von Beweisen etc.*); **4.** *Brit. univ.* Sti'pendium *n*; **ex·hi'bi·tion·er** [-ʃnə] *s. Brit. univ.* Stipendi'at *m*; **ex·hi'bi·tion·ism** [-ʃnɪzəm] *s. psych. u. fig.* Exhibitio'nismus *m*; **ex·hi'bi·tion·ist** [-ʃnɪst] *psych. u. fig.* **I** *s.* Exhibitio'nist *m*; **II** *adj.* exhibitio'nistisch; **ex·hib·i·tor** [ɪgˈzɪbɪtə] *s.* **1.** Aussteller *m*; **2.** Kinobesitzer *m*.

ex·hil·a·rant [ɪgˈzɪlərənt] → **exhilarating**; **ex·hil·a·rate** [ɪgˈzɪləreɪt] *v/t.* **1.** erheitern; **2.** beleben, erfrischen; **ex·hil·a·rat·ed** [-tɪd] *adj.* erheitert, heiter, amüsiert; **ex·hil·a·rat·ing** [-tɪŋ] *adj.* □ erheiternd, erfrischend, amü'sant; **ex·hil·a·ra·tion** [ɪgˌzɪləˈreɪʃn] *s.* **1.** Erheiterung *f*; **2.** Heiterkeit *f*.

ex·hort [ɪgˈzɔːt] *v/t.* ermahnen; **ex·hor·ta·tion** [ˌegzɔːˈteɪʃn] *s.* Ermahnung *f*.

ex·hu·ma·tion [ˌekshjuːˈmeɪʃn] *s.* Exhumierung *f*; **ex·hume** [eksˈhjuːm] *v/t.* **1.** *Leiche* exhumieren; **2.** *fig.* ausgraben.

ex·i·gence [ˈeksɪdʒəns], **ex·i·gen·cy** [-dʒənsɪ; ɪgˈzɪ-] *s.* **1.** Dringlichkeit *f*; **2.** Not(lage) *f*; **3.** *mst pl.* (An)Forderung *f*; **'ex·i·gent** [-nt] *adj.* **1.** dringend, kritisch; **2.** anspruchsvoll.

ex·i·gu·i·ty [ˌeksɪˈgjuːətɪ] *s.* Dürftigkeit *f*; **ex·ig·u·ous** [egˈzɪgjʊəs] *adj.* dürftig.

ex·ile [ˈeksaɪl] **I** *s.* **1.** a) Ex'il *n*, b) Verbannung *f*: **government in ~** Exilregierung *f*; **the** ♠ *bibl.* die Babylonische Gefangenschaft; **2.** a) im Ex'il Lebende(r *m*) *f*, b) Verbannte(r *m*) *f*; **II** *v/t.* **3.** a) exilieren, b) verbannen (**from** aus), in die Verbannung schicken.

ex·ist [ɪgˈzɪst] *v/i.* **1.** existieren, vor'handen sein, da sein: **do such things ~?** gibt es so etwas?; **2.** sich finden, vorkommen (**in** in *dat.*); **3.** (**on**) existieren, leben (von); **ex'ist·ence** [-təns] *s.* **1.** Exi'stenz *f*, Vor'handensein *n*, Vorkommen *n*: **call into ~** ins Leben rufen; **be in ~** bestehen, existieren; **remain in ~** weiter bestehen; **2.** Exi'stenz *f*, Leben *n*, Dasein *n*: **a wretched ~** ein kümmerliches Dasein; **3.** Exi'stenz *f*, (Fort-)Bestand *m*; **ex'ist·ent** [-tənt] *adj.* **1.** existierend, bestehend, vor'handen, lebend; **2.** gegenwärtig.

ex·is·ten·tial [ˌegzɪˈstenʃl] *adj.* **1.** Existenz...; **2.** *phls.* Existenzial...; **ex·is·'ten·tial·ism** [-ʃəlɪzəm] *s.* Existenzia'lismus *m*, Exi'stenzphiloso,phie *f*; **ex·is·'ten·tial·ist** [-ʃəlɪst] *s.* Existenzia'list (-in).

ex·ist·ing [ɪgˈzɪstɪŋ] → **existent**.

ex·it [ˈeksɪt] **I** *s.* **1.** Abgang *m*: a) *thea.* Abtreten *n* (*von der Bühne*), b) *fig.* Tod *m*: **make one's ~** → 6a, 7; **2.** (*a. Not*)Ausgang *m*; **3.** 🔧 Abzug *m*, -fluss *m*, Austritt *m*; **4.** Ausreise *f*: **~ permit** Ausreisegenehmigung *f*; **~ visa** Ausreisevisum *n*; **5.** (Autobahn)Ausfahrt *f*; **II** *v/i.* **6.** *thea.* a) abgehen, abtreten, b) *Bühnenanweisung*: (*er, sie geht*) ab: ♠ *Romeo*; **7.** *fig.* sterben; **III** 🔧 **8.** *v/t. Computer*: Programm beenden.

---

ex li·bris [eksˈlaɪbrɪs] (*Lat.*) *s.* Ex'libris *n*, Bücherzeichen *n*.

‚ex·o·bi·ol·o·gy [ˌeksəʊ-] *s.* Exo-, Ektobiolo'gie *f*.

ex·o·carp [ˈeksəʊkɑːp] *s.* 🌿 Exo'karp *n*, äußere Fruchthaut.

ex·o·crine [ˈeksəʊkraɪn] *physiol.* **I** *adj.* **1.** exo'krin; **II** *s.* **2.** äußere Sekreti'on; **3.** exo'krine Drüse.

ex·o·don·ti·a [ˌeksəʊˈdɒnʃɪə] *s.* ‚**ex·o'don·tics** [-ntɪks] *s. pl. sg. konstr.* 'Zahnchirur,gie *f*.

ex·o·dus [ˈeksədəs] *s.* **1.** a) *bibl. u. fig.* Auszug *m*, b) ♠ *bibl.* Exodus *m*, Zweites Buch Mose; **2.** *fig.* Ab-, Auswanderung *f*, Massenflucht *f*; Aufbruch *m*: **~ of capital** ✝ Kapitalabwanderung; **rural ~** Landflucht.

ex of·fi·ci·o [ˌeksəˈfɪʃɪəʊ] (*Lat.*) **I** *adv.* von Amts wegen; **II** *adj.* Amts..., amtlich.

ex·on·er·ate [ɪgˈzɒnəreɪt] *v/t.* **1.** *Angeklagten etc., a. Schuldner* entlasten (**from** von); **2.** *j-n* befreien, entbinden (**from** von); **ex·on·er·a·tion** [ɪgˌzɒnəˈreɪʃn] *s.* **1.** Entlastung *f*; **2.** Befreiung *f*.

ex·or·bi·tance [ɪgˈzɔːbɪtəns] *s.* Maßlosigkeit *f*; **ex'or·bi·tant** [-nt] *adj.* □ maßlos, über'trieben, unverschämt: **~ price** Wucherpreis *m*.

ex·or·cism [ˈeksɔːsɪzəm] *s.* Exor'zismus *m*, Teufelsaustreibung *f*, Geisterbeschwörung *f*; **'ex·or·cist** [-ɪst] *s.* Exor-'zist *m*, Teufelsaustreiber *m*, Geisterbeschwörer *m*; **'ex·or·cize** [-saɪz] *v/t. Teufel* austreiben, *Geister* beschwören, bannen.

ex·or·di·um [ekˈsɔːdjəm] *s.* Einleitung *f*, Anfang *m* (*e-r Rede*).

ex·o·ter·ic [ˌeksəʊˈterɪk] *adj.* (□ **~ally**) exo'terisch, für Außenstehende bestimmt, gemeinverständlich.

ex·ot·ic [ɪgˈzɒtɪk] *adj.* (□ **~ally**) ex'otisch: a) aus-, fremdländisch, b) fremdartig, bi'zarr; **ex'ot·i·ca** [-kə] *s. pl.* E'xotika *pl.* (*fremdländische Kunstwerke*).

ex·pand [ɪkˈspænd] **I** *v/t.* **1.** ausbreiten, -spannen, entfalten; **2.** ✝, *phys. u. fig.* ausdehnen, -weiten, erweitern: **~ed metal** Streckmetall *n*; **~ed plastics** Schaumkunststoffe; **~ed program(me)** erweitertes Programm; **3.** *Abkürzung* ausschreiben; **II** *v/i.* **4.** sich ausbreiten *od.* -dehnen; sich erweitern (*a. fig.*): **his heart ~ed with joy** sein Herz schwoll vor Freude; **5.** *fig.* sich entwickeln, aufblühen (**into** zu); größer werden; **6.** *fig.* a) *vor Stolz, Freude etc.* ‚aufblühen', b) aus sich her'ausgehen; **ex'pand·er** [-də] *s. sport* Ex'pander *m*; **ex'pand·ing** [-dɪŋ] *adj.* sich (aus)dehnend, dehnbar; **ex'panse** [-ns] *s.* weiter Raum, weite Fläche, Weite *f*, Ausdehnung *f*; *orn.* Spannweite *f*; **ex'pan·sion** [-nʃn] *s.* **1.** Ausbreitung *f*, Erweiterung *f*, Zunahme *f*; (✝ *Industrie-, Produktions-, a. Kredit*)Ausweitung *f*; *pol.* Expansi'on *f*; **2.** *a.* 🔧, phys. (Aus)Dehnung *f*, Expansi'on *f*: **~ engine** Expansionsmaschine *f*; **~ stroke** *mot.* Arbeitstakt *m*, Expansionshub *m*; **3.** 'Umfang *m*, Raum *m*, Weite *f*; **ex'pan·sion·ism** [-nʃ ənɪzəm] *s.* Expansi'onspoli,tik *f*; **ex'pan·sion·ist** [-nʃ ənɪst] **I** *s.* Anhänger(in) der Expansi'onspoli,tik; **II** *adj.* Expansions...; **ex'pan·sive** [-nsɪv] *adj.* □ **1.** ausdehnungsfähig, ausdehnend, (Aus)Dehnungs...; **2.** ausgedehnt, weit, um'fassend; **3.** *fig.* mitteilsam, aufgeschlossen; **4.** *fig.* 'überschwänglich; **ex'pan-sive·ness** [-nsɪvnɪs] *s.* **1.** Ausdehnungsvermögen *n*; **2.** *fig.* a) Mitteilsamkeit *f*, Aufgeschlossenheit *f*, b) 'Überschwänglichkeit *f*.

ex par·te [ˌeks'pɑːtɪ] (*Lat.*) *adj. u. adv.* 🏛 einseitig (*Prozesshandlung*).

ex·pa·ti·ate [ek'speɪʃɪeɪt] *v/i.* sich weitläufig auslassen *od.* verbreiten (**on** über *acc.*); **ex·pa·ti·a·tion** [ek,speɪʃɪ'eɪʃn] *s.* weitläufige Erörterung, Erguss *m*, ‚Salm' *m*.

ex·pa·tri·ate I *v/t.* [eks'pætrɪeɪt] **1.** ausbürgern, expatriieren, *j-m* die Staatsangehörigkeit aberkennen; **~ o.s.** auswandern, s-e Staatsangehörigkeit aufgeben; **II** *adj.* [-ɪət] **2.** verbannt, ausgebürgert; **3.** ständig im Ausland lebend; **III** *s.* [-ɪət] **4.** Ausgebürgerte(r *m*) *f*; **5.** (freiwillig) im Ex'il *od.* ständig im Ausland Lebende(r *m*) *f*; **ex·pa·tri·a·tion** [eks-,pætrɪ'eɪʃn] *s.* **1.** Ausbürgerung *f*, Aberkennung *f* der Staatsangehörigkeit; **2.** Auswanderung *f*; **3.** Aufgabe *f* s-r Staatsangehörigkeit.

ex·pect [ɪk'spekt] *v/t.* **1.** *j-n* erwarten: *I ~ him to dinner* ich erwarte ihn zum Essen; **2.** *et.* erwarten *od.* vor'hersehen; entgegensehen (*dat.*): *I did not ~ that question* auf diese Frage war ich nicht gefasst *od.* vorbereitet; **3.** erwarten, hoffen, rechnen auf (*acc.*): *I ~ you to come* ich erwarte, dass du kommst; *I ~ (that) he will come* ich erwarte, dass er kommt; **4.** *et. von j-m* erwarten, verlangen: *you ~ too much from him*; **5.** F annehmen, denken, vermuten: *that is hardly to be ~ed* das ist kaum anzunehmen; *I ~ so* ich denke ja (*od.* schon); **ex'pect·ance** [-təns], **ex'pect·an·cy** [-tənsɪ] *s.* (*of*) **1.** Erwartung *f* (*gen.*); Hoffnung *f*, Aussicht *f* (auf *acc.*); **2.** ⚓, 🏛 Anwartschaft *f* (auf *acc.*); **ex'pect·ant** [-tənt] **I** *adj.* □ **1.** erwartend: *be ~ of et.* erwarten; *~ heir* a) ⚓ Erb(schafts)anwärter(in), b) Thronanwärter *m*; **2.** erwartungsvoll; **3.** zu erwarten(d); **4.** schwanger: *~ mother* werdende Mutter, Schwangere *f*; **II** *s.* **5.** ⚓ Anwärter(in) (*of* auf *acc.*); **ex·pec·ta·tion** [ˌekspek'teɪʃn] *s.* **1.** Erwartung *f*, Erwarten *n*: *beyond* (*contrary to*) *~* über (wider) Erwarten; *according to ~* erwartungsgemäß; *come up to ~* den Erwartungen entsprechen; **2.** Gegenstand *m* der Erwartung; **3.** *oft pl.* Hoffnung *f*, Aussicht *f*: *~ of life* Lebenserwartung *f*; **ex'pect·ing** [-tɪŋ] *adj.*: *she is ~* F sie ist in anderen Umständen.

ex·pec·to·rant [ek'spektərənt] *adj. u. s. pharm.* schleimlösend(es Mittel); **ex·pec·to·rate** [ek'spektəreɪt] **I** *v/t.* ausspucken, -husten; **II** *v/i.* a) (aus-)spucken, b) Blut spucken; **ex·pec·to·ra·tion** [ek,spektə'reɪʃn] *s.* **1.** Auswerfen *n*, Aushusten *n*, -spucken *n*; **2.** Auswurf *m*.

ex·pe·di·ence [ɪk'spiːdjəns], **ex'pe·di·en·cy** [-sɪ] *s.* **1.** Ratsamkeit *f*, Zweckmäßigkeit *f*; **2.** Nützlichkeit *f*, Zweckdienlichkeit *f*; **3.** Eigennutz *m*; **ex'pe·di·ent** [-nt] **I** *adj.* □ **1.** ratsam, angebracht; **2.** zweckmäßig, -dienlich, praktisch, nützlich, vorteilhaft; **3.** eigennützig; **II** *s.* **4.** (Hilfs)Mittel *n*, (Not)Behelf *m*.

ex·pe·dite ['ekspɪdaɪt] *v/t.* **1.** beschleunigen, fördern; **2.** schnell ausführen; **3.** befördern, expedieren.

ex·pe·di·tion [ˌekspɪ'dɪʃn] *s.* **1.** Eile *f*, Schnelligkeit *f*; **2.** (Forschungs)Reise *f*, Expediti'on *f*; **3.** ✗ Feldzug *m*; **ex·pe-'di·tion·ar·y** [-ʃnərɪ] *adj.* Expeditions...: *~ force* Expeditionskorps *n*; **ex·pe'di·tious** [-ʃəs] *adj.* □ schnell, rasch, prompt.

ex·pel [ɪk'spel] *v/t.* (*from*) **1.** vertreiben, wegjagen (aus, von); **2.** ausstoßen, -schließen, hi'nauswerfen (aus); **3.** aus-, verweisen, verbannen (aus), *schweiz. pol.* ausschaffen (*des Landes verweisen*) (aus); **4.** *Rauch etc.* ausstoßen (aus); **ex·pel·lee** [ˌekspe'liː] *s.* (Heimat)Vertriebene(r *m*) *f*.

ex·pend [ɪk'spend] *v/t.* **1.** *Geld* ausgeben; **2.** *Mühe, Zeit etc.* ver-, aufwenden (**on** für); **3.** verbrauchen; **ex'pend·a·ble** [-dəbl] **I** *adj.* **1.** verbrauchbar, Verbrauchs...; **2.** entbehrlich; **3.** ✗ (*im Notfall*) zu opfern(d); **II** *s.* **4.** *mst pl. et.* Entbehrliches; **5.** ✗ verlorener Haufen; **ex'pend·i·ture** [-dɪtʃə] *s.* **1.** Aufwand *m*, Verbrauch *m* (*of* an *dat.*); **2.** (Geld)Ausgabe(n *pl.*) *f*, (Kosten-)Aufwand *m*, Auslage(n *pl.*) *f*, Kosten *pl.*: *cash ~* 🕆 Barauslagen.

ex·pense [ɪk'spens] *s.* **1.** → *expenditure* 2; **2.** *pl.* Unkosten *pl.*, Spesen *pl.*: *~ account* 🕆 Spesenkonto *n*; *~ allowance* 🕆 Aufwandsentschädigung *f*, Spesenvergütung *f*; *~ report* Spesenabrechnung *f*; *travel(l)ing ~s* Reisespesen; *and all ~s paid* und alle Unkosten *od.* Spesen (werden) vergütet; *at an ~ of* mit e-m Aufwand von; *at great ~* mit großen Kosten; *at my ~* auf m-e Kosten, für m-e Rechnung; *they laughed at my ~ fig.* sie lachten auf m-e Kosten; *at the ~ of his health* auf Kosten s-r Gesundheit; *go to great ~* sich in (große) (Un)Kosten stürzen; *put s.o. to great ~* j-n in große (Un-)Kosten stürzen; *spare no ~* keine Kosten scheuen; **ex'pen·sive** [-sɪv] *adj.* □ teuer, kostspielig, aufwändig.

ex·pe·ri·ence [ɪk'spɪərɪəns] **I** *s.* **1.** a) Erfahrung *f*, (Lebens)Praxis *f*, b) Erfahrenheit *f*, (praktische) Erfahrung, Praxis *f*, praktische Kenntnisse *pl.*, Fach-, Sachkenntnis *f*: *by* (*od. from*) *~* aus (eigener) Erfahrung; *in my ~* nach m-n Erfahrungen, m-s Wissens; *~ in cooking* Kochkenntnisse; *business ~* Geschäftserfahrung, -routine *f*; *driving ~* Fahrpraxis; *previous ~* Vorkenntnisse; **2.** Erlebnis *n*: *I had a strange ~*; **3.** Vorkommnis *n*, Geschehnis *n*; **4.** *Am. eccl.* religi'öse Erweckung; **II** *v/t.* **5.** erfahren: a) kennen lernen, b) erleben, c) erleiden, *Schlimmes* 'durchmachen, *Vergnügen etc.* empfinden: *~ kindness* Freundlichkeit erfahren; *~ difficulties* auf Schwierigkeiten stoßen; **ex'pe·ri·enced** [-st] *adj.* erfahren, routiniert, bewandert, (fach-, sach)kundig.

ex·pe·ri·en·tial·ism [ɪk,spɪərɪ'enʃəlɪzəm] *s. phls.* Empi'rismus *m*.

ex·per·i·ment **I** *s.* [ɪk'sperɪmənt] Versuch *m*, Experi'ment *n*; **II** *v/i.* [-ment] experimentieren, Versuche anstellen (**on, upon** an *dat.*; **with** mit): *~ with s.th. a.* et. erproben.

ex·per·i·men·tal [ek,sperɪ'mentl] *adj.* □ **1.** *phys.* Versuchs..., experimen'tell, Experimental...: *~ animal* Versuchstier *n*; *~ physics* Experimentalphysik *f*; *~ station* Versuchsanstalt *f*; **2.** experimentierfreudig; **3.** Erfahrungs...; **ex·per·i·men·tal·ist** [-təlɪst] *s.* Experimen'tator *m*; **ex·per·i·men·tal·ly** [-təlɪ] *adv.* experimen'tell, versuchsweise; **ex·per·i·men·ta·tion** [ek,sperɪmen'teɪʃn] *s.* Experimentieren *n*.

ex·pert ['eksp3ːt] **I** *adj* [*pred. a.* ɪk'sp3ːt] □ **1.** erfahren, kundig; **2.** geschickt, gewandt (**at, in** in *dat.*); **3.** fachmännisch, fach-, sachkundig; Fach...(-*ingenieur, -wissen etc.*); **4.** Sachverständigen...: *~ opinion* (Sachverständigen-)Gutachten *n*; *~ witness* 🏛 Sachverständige(r *m*) *f*; **II** *s.* **5.** a) Fachmann *m*, Ex'perte *m*, b) Sachverständige(r *m*) *f*, Gutachter(in) (**at, in** in *dat.*; **on** *s.th.* [auf dem Gebiet] e-r Sache); **ex·per·tise** [ˌeksp3ː'tiːz] *s.* **1.** Exper'tise *f*, (Sachverständigen)Gutachten *n*; **2.** Sach-, Fachkenntnis *f*, Know-how *n*; **3.** (fachmännisches) Können; **'ex·pert·ness** [-nɪs] *s.* **1.** Erfahrenheit *f*; **2.** Geschicklichkeit *f*; **ex·pert sys·tem** ['eksp3ːt] *s.* *Computer:* Ex'pertensys,tem *n*.

ex·pi·a·ble ['ekspɪəbl] *adj.* sühnbar; **'ex·pi·ate** [-ɪeɪt] *v/t.* sühnen, wieder gutmachen, (ab)büßen; **ex·pi·a·tion** [ˌekspɪ'eɪʃn] *s.* Sühne *f*, Buße *f*: *in ~ of s.th.* um et. zu sühnen, als Sühne für et.; **'ex·pi·a·to·ry** [-ɪətərɪ] *adj.* sühnend, Sühn(e)..., Buß...: *be ~ of et.* sühnen.

ex·pi·ra·tion [ˌekspɪ'reɪʃn] *s.* **1.** Ausatmen *n*; **2.** *fig.* Ablauf *m* (*e-r Frist, e-s Vertrags*), Ende *n*; **3.** 🕆 a) Fälligwerden *n*, b) Verfall *m* (*e-s Wechsels*): *~ date* Verfallsdatum *n*; **ex·pi·ra·to·ry** [ɪk'spaɪərətərɪ] *adj.* Ausatmungs...

ex·pire [ɪk'spaɪə] *v/i.* **1.** ausatmen, -hauchen (*a. v/t.*); **2.** sein Leben aushauchen, verscheiden; **3.** ablaufen (*Frist, Vertrag etc.*), erlöschen (*Patent, Recht etc.*), enden, ungültig werden, verfallen; **4.** 🕆 fällig werden; **ex'pired** [-əd] *adj.* ungültig, verfallen, erloschen; **ex'pi·ry** [-ərɪ] → *expiration* 2, 3.

ex·plain [ɪk'spleɪn] **I** *v/t.* **1.** erklären, erläutern, ausein'ander setzen (*s.th. to s.o.* j-m et.): *~ s.th. away* a) sich aus et. herausreden, b) e-e einleuchtende Erklärung für et. finden; **2.** erklären, begründen, rechtfertigen: *~ o.s.* a) sich erklären, b) sich rechtfertigen; **II** *v/i.* **3.** es erklären: *you have got a little ~ing to do* da müsstest du (mir, uns) schon einiges erklären; **ex'plain·a·ble** [-nəbl] *adj.* → *explicable*; **ex·pla·na·tion** [ˌeksplə'neɪʃn] *s.* **1.** Erklärung *f*, Erläuterung *f* (*for, of* für): *in ~ of* als Erklärung für; *make some ~* e-e Erklärung abgeben; **2.** Er-, Aufklärung *f*; **3.** Verständigung *f*; **ex·plan·a·to·ry** [ɪk'splænətərɪ] *adj.* □ erklärend, erläuternd.

ex·ple·tive [ek'spliːtɪv] **I** *adj.* **1.** ausfüllend, (Aus)Füll...; **II** *s.* **2.** *ling.* Füllwort *n*; **3.** Füllsel *n*, Lückenbüßer *m*; **4.** a) Fluch *m*, b) Kraftausdruck *m*.

ex·pli·ca·ble [ɪk'splɪkəbl] *adj.* erklärbar, erklärlich; **ex·pli·cate** ['eksplɪkeɪt] *v/t.* **1.** explizieren, erklären; **2.** *Theorie etc.* entwickeln; **ex·pli·ca·tion** [ˌeksplɪ'keɪʃn] *s.* **1.** Erklärung *f*, Erläuterung *f*; **2.** Entwicklung *f*.

ex·plic·it [ɪk'splɪsɪt] *adj.* □ **1.** deutlich, klar, ausdrücklich; **2.** offen, deutlich (*Person*) (**on** in Bezug auf *acc.*); **3.** ✶ expli'zit.

ex·plode [ɪk'spləʊd] **I** *v/t.* **1.** a) zur Explosi'on bringen, explodieren lassen, b) (in die Luft) sprengen; **2.** *fig.* a) *Plan etc.* über den Haufen werfen, zum Platzen bringen, zu'nichte machen: *~ a myth* e-e Illusion zerstören, b) *Theorie etc.* wider'legen, *e-m Gerücht etc.* den Boden entziehen; **II** *v/i.* **3.** a) explodieren, ✗ *a.* krepieren (*Granate etc.*), b) in die Luft fliegen; **4.** *fig.* ausbrechen (*into, with* in *acc.*), ‚platzen' (*with* vor *dat.*): *~ with fury* vor Wut platzen, ‚explodieren'; *~ with laughter* in schallendes Gelächter ausbrechen; **5.** *fig.*

sprunghaft ansteigen, sich explosi'ons-artig vermehren; **ex'plod·ed view** [-dɪd] s. ◉ Darstellung f e-r Maschine etc. in zerlegter Anordnung.

ex·ploit I v/t. [ɪk'splɔɪt] **1.** et. auswerten; *kommerziell* verwerten; ✗ etc. ausbeuten, abbauen; **2.** fig. b.s. et. od. j-n ausbeuten, -nutzen; et. ausschlachten, Kapi'tal schlagen aus; **II** s. ['eksplɔɪt] **3.** (Helden)Tat f; **4.** Großtat f, große Leistung; **ex·ploi·ta·tion** [ˌeksplɔɪ'teɪʃn] s. ♰ (*Patent- etc.*)Verwertung f; ◉ Ausnutzung f, -beutung f (*beide a. fig. b.s.*); ✗ Abbau m, Gewinnung f; **ex'ploi·ter** [-tə] s. Ausbeuter m (a. fig.).

ex·plo·ra·tion [ˌeksplə'reɪʃn] s. **1.** Erforschung f (*e-s Landes*); **2.** Unter'suchung f.

ex·plor·a·tive [ek'splɒrətɪv], **ex'plor·a·to·ry** [-tərɪ] adj. **1.** (er)forschend, Forschungs...; **2.** Erkundungs..., untersuchend, sondierend; ◉ etc. Versuchs..., Probe...: ~ **drilling**; ~ **talks** Sondierungsgespräche; **ex·plore** [ɪk'splɔː] v/t. *Land* erforschen; *et.* erforschen, erkunden, unter'suchen (*a. ✗*), sondieren; **ex·plor·er** [ɪk'splɔːrə] s. Forscher m, Forschungsreisende(r m) f.

ex·plo·sion [ɪk'spləʊʒn] s. **1.** a) Explosi'on f (*a. ling.*), Entladung f, b) Knall m, Detonati'on f; **2.** fig. Explosi'on f: **population** ~; **3.** fig. Zerstörung f, Widerlegung f; **4.** fig. (*Wut- etc.*)Ausbruch m.

ex·plo·sive [ɪk'spləʊsɪv] **I** adj. □ **1.** explo'siv, Knall..., Spreng..., Explosions...; **2.** fig. jähzornig, aufbrausend; **II** s. **3.** Explo'siv-, Sprengstoff m; **4.** ling. → **plosive** II; ~ **charge** s. Sprengladung f; ~ **cot·ton** s. Schießbaumwolle f; ~ **flame** s. Stichflamme f; ~ **force** s. Sprengkraft f.

ex·po·nent [ek'spəʊnənt] s. **1.** A Expo'nent m, Hochzahl f; **2.** fig. Expo'nent (-in) m, a) Repräsen'tant(in), Vertreter (-in), b) Verfechter(in); **3.** Inter'pret (-in); **ex·po·nen·tial** [ˌekspəʊ'nenʃl] A **I** adj. Exponential...; **II** s. Exponenti'algröße f.

ex·port I v/t. u. v/i. [ek'spɔːt] **1.** exportieren, ausführen; **II** s. ['ekspɔːt] **2.** Ex-'port m, Ausfuhr(handel m) f; **3.** Ex-'port-, 'Ausfuhrar,tikel m; **4.** pl. a) (Ge'samt)Ex,port m, (-)Ausfuhr f, b) Ex'portgüter pl.; **III** adj. ['ekspɔːt] **5.** Ausfuhr..., Export...: ~ **duty** Ausfuhrzoll m; ~ **license**, ~ **permit** Ausfuhrgenehmigung f; ~ **trade** Export-, Ausfuhr-, Außenhandel f; **ex'port·a·ble** [-təbl] adj. ex'portfähig, zur Ausfuhr geeignet; **ex·por·ta·tion** [ˌekspɔː'teɪʃən] s. Ausfuhr f, Ex'port m; **ex'porter** [-tə] s. Expor'teur m.

ex·pose [ɪk'spəʊz] **I** v/t. **1.** *Kind* aussetzen; *Waren* ausstellen (**for sale** zum Verkauf); **3.** fig. e-r Gefahr, e-m Übel aussetzen, preisgeben: ~ **o.s.** sich exponieren; ~ **o.s. to ridicule** sich lächerlich machen; **4.** fig. a) (**o.s.** sich) bloßstellen, b) j-n entlarven, c) et. aufdecken, enthüllen; **5.** et. darlegen, ausein'ander setzen; **6.** entblößen (a. ✗), enthüllen, zeigen; **7.** phot. belichten; **II** s. **8.** Am. → **exposé**.

ex·po·sé [ek'spəʊzeɪ] (Fr.) s. **1.** Expo'see n, Darlegung f; **2.** Enthüllung f, Entlarvung f.

ex·posed [ɪk'spəʊzd] adj. **1.** pred. ausgesetzt (**to** dat.); **2.** unverdeckt, offen (-liegend); **3.** ungeschützt, exponiert; **4.** phot. belichtet.

ex·po·si·tion [ˌekspəʊ'zɪʃn] s. **1.** Ausstellung f, Schau f; **2.** Darlegung(en pl.) f, Ausführung(en pl.) f; **3.** thea. u. ♪ Expositi'on f; **ex·pos·i·tor** [ek'spɒzɪtə] s. Erklärer m; **ex·pos·i·to·ry** [ek'spɒzɪtərɪ] adj. erklärend.

ex·pos·tu·late [ɪk'spɒstjʊleɪt] v/i. **1.** protestieren; **2.** ~ **with** j-m ernste Vorhaltungen machen, j-n zu'rechtweisen; **ex·pos·tu·la·tion** [ɪkˌspɒstjʊ'leɪʃn] s. **1.** Pro'test m; **2.** ernste Vorhaltung, Verweis m.

ex·po·sure [ɪk'spəʊʒə] s. **1.** (Kindes-)Aussetzung f; **2.** Aussetzen n, Preisgabe f; **3.** Ausgesetztsein n, Preisgebensein n (**to** dat.): **death from** ~ Tod m durch Erfrieren od. vor Entkräftung etc.; **4.** Entblößung f: **indecent** ~ unsittliche (Selbst)Entblößung; **5.** fig. a) Bloßstellung f, b) Entlarvung f, c) Enthüllung f, Aufdeckung f; **6.** phot. Belichtung f: ~ **meter** Belichtungsmesser m; **time** ~ Zeitaufnahme f; ~ **value** Lichtwert m (*e-s Films*); **7.** Lage f (*e-s Gebäudes*): **southern** ~ Südlage.

ex·pound [ɪk'spaʊnd] v/t. **1.** erklären, erläutern; *Theorie* entwickeln; **2.** auslegen.

ex·press [ɪk'spres] **I** v/t. **1.** obs. *Saft* auspressen, ausdrücken; **2.** fig. ausdrücken, äußern, zum Ausdruck bringen: **be** ~**ed o.s.** sich äußern, sich erklären; **be** ~**ed** zum Ausdruck kommen; **3.** bezeichnen, bedeuten, darstellen; **4.** *Gefühle etc.* offen'baren, zeigen, bekunden; **5.** a) Brit. durch Eilboten od. als Eilgut schicken, b) bsd. Am. durch ein ('Schnell)Trans,portunter,nehmen befördern lassen; **II** adj. □ → **expressly**; **6.** ausdrücklich, bestimmt, deutlich, eindeutig; **7.** besonder: **for the** ~ **pur·pose** eigens zu dem Zweck; **8.** Express..., Schnell..., Eil...; **III** adv. **9.** → **expressly**; **10.** Brit. durch Eilboten, per Ex'press, als Eilgut; **IV** s. **11.** Brit. a) Eilbote m, b) Eilbeförderung f, c) Eilbrief m, -gut n; **12.** D-Zug m; **13.** Am. → **express company**; **ex'press·age** [-sɪdʒ] s. Am. **1.** Beförderung f durch ein ('Schnell)Trans,portunter-,nehmen; **2.** Eilfracht(gebühr) f.

ex·press com·pa·ny s. Am. ('Schnell-)Trans,portunter,nehmen n; ~ **de·liv·er·y** s. a) Brit. Eilzustellung f, b) → **expressage** 1; ~ **goods** s. pl. Eilfracht f, -gut n.

ex·pres·sion [ɪk'spreʃn] s. **1.** Ausdruck m, Äußerung f: **find** ~ **in** sich äußern in (dat.); **give** ~ **to** Ausdruck verleihen (dat.); **beyond** ~ unsagbar; **2.** Redensart f, Ausdruck m; **3.** Ausdrucksweise f, Dikti'on f; **4.** Ausdruck(skraft f) m: **with** ~ mit Gefühl, ausdrucksvoll; **5.** (Gesichts)Ausdruck m; **6.** A Ausdruck m, Formel f; **ex'pres·sion·ism** [-ʃnɪzəm] s. Expressio'nismus m; **ex'pres·sion·ist** [-ʃnɪst] I s. Expressio'nist(in); **II** adj. expressio'nistisch; **ex'pres·sion·less** [-lɪs] adj. ausdruckslos.

ex·pres·sive [ɪk'spresɪv] adj. □ **1.** ausdrückend (**of** acc.): **be** ~ **of** et. ausdrücken; **2.** ausdrucksvoll; **3.** Ausdrucks...; **ex'pres·sive·ness** [-nɪs] s. **1.** Ausdruckskraft f; **2.** das Ausdrucksvolle; **ex'press·ly** [-slɪ] adv. **1.** ausdrücklich; **2.** eigens, besonders.

ex'press·man [-mæn] s. [irr.] Am. Angestellte(r) m e-s ('Schnell)Trans,portunter,nehmens; ~ **train** s. D-Zug m; ~**·way** s. bsd. Am. Schnellstraße f.

ex·pro·pri·ate [eks'prəʊprɪeɪt] v/t. ♰♰ j-n od. et. enteignen; **ex·pro·pri·a·tion** [eksˌprəʊprɪ'eɪʃn] s. ♰♰ Enteignung f.

ex·pul·sion [ɪk'spʌlʃn] s. (**from**) **1.** Vertreibung f (aus); **2.** pol. Ausweisung f, Verbannung f, Abschiebung f (aus); **3.** Ausstoßung f (aus), Ausschließung (aus, von): ~ **from school**; **4.** ✿ Austreibung f; **ex'pul·sive** [-lsɪv] adj. aus-, vertreibend.

ex·punge [ek'spʌndʒ] v/t. **1.** (aus)streichen; a. fig. löschen (**from** aus); **2.** fig. ausmerzen, vernichten.

ex·pur·gate ['ekspɜːgeɪt] v/t. *Buch etc.* (von anstößigen Stellen) reinigen: ~**d version** gereinigte Version; **ex·pur·ga·tion** [ˌekspɜː'geɪʃn] s. Reinigung f.

ex·quis·ite ['ekskwɪzɪt] adj. □ **1.** köstlich, (aus)erlesen, vor'züglich, ausgezeichnet, exqui'sit; **2.** gepflegt, fein: ~ **taste**; **3.** äußerst fein: **an** ~ **ear**; **4.** äußerst, höchst; **5.** heftig: ~ **pain**; ~ **pleasure** großes Vergnügen.

ex-serv·ice·man [ˌeks'sɜːvɪsmən] s. [irr.] ehemaliger Sol'dat, Vete'ran m.

ex·tant [ek'stænt] adj. (noch) vor'handen od. bestehende.

ex·tem·po·ra·ne·ous [ekˌstempə'reɪnɪəs], **ex·tem·po·rar·y** [ɪk'stempərərɪ] adj. □ improvisiert, extemporiert, unvorbereitet, aus dem Stegreif: ~ **trans·lation** Stegreifübersetzung f; **ex·tem·po·re** [ek'stempərɪ] **I** adj. u. adv. → **extemporaneous**; **II** s. Improvisati'on f, Stegreifgedicht n, unvorbereitete Rede; **ex·tem·po·rize** [ɪk'stempəraɪz] v/t. u. v/i. aus dem Stegreif od. unvorbereitet reden od. dichten od. spielen, improvisieren; **ex·tem·po·riz·er** [ɪk'stempəraɪzə] s. Improvi'sator m, Stegreifdichter m.

ex·tend [ɪk'stend] **I** v/t. **1.** (aus)dehnen, ausbreiten; **2.** verlängern; **3.** vergrößern, erweitern, ausbauen: ~ **a facto·ry**; **4.** *Seil etc.* spannen, ziehen; **5.** *Hand etc.* ausstrecken; **6.** *Nahrungsmittel* strecken; **7.** fig. e-n Besuch, s-e Macht etc. ausdehnen (**to** auf acc.), e-e Frist, s-n Pass, e-n Vertrag etc. verlängern, ✿ a. prolongieren; **8.** (**to**, **to·wards** dat.) a) Gunst, Hilfe etc. gewähren, Gutes erweisen, b) s-n Dank, Glückwunsch etc. aussprechen, e-e Einladung schicken, c) e-n Gruß entbieten; **9.** ✈ Fahrgestell ausfahren; **10.** ✗ ausschwärmen lassen; **11.** Abkürzungen voll ausschreiben; Kurzschrift in Normalschrift über'tragen; **12.** Sport das Letzte her'ausholen aus (e-m Pferd etc.): ~ **o.s.** sich völlig ausgeben; **II** v/i. **13.** sich ausdehnen od. erstrecken, reichen (**to** bis zu); hin'ausgehen (**beyond** über acc.); **14.** ✗ ausschwärmen; **ex·'tend·ed** [-dɪd] adj. **1.** ausgedehnt (a. Zeitraum); **2.** ausgestreckt: ~ **hands**; **3.** verlängert; **4.** ausgebreitet; typ. breit: ~ **formation** ✗ auseinander gezogene Formation; ~ **order** ✗ geöffnete Ordnung; **5.** groß, um'fassend: ~ **family** Großfamilie f.

ex·ten·si·bil·i·ty [ɪkˌstensə'bɪlətɪ] s. (Aus)Dehnbarkeit f; **ex·ten·si·ble** [ɪk'stensəbl] adj. (aus)dehnbar, (aus-)streckbar; ausziehbar (*Tisch*): ~ **table** Ausziehtisch m.

ex·ten·sion [ɪk'stenʃn] s. **1.** Ausdehnung f (a. fig.; **to** auf acc.); Ausbreitung f; (Frist- Kredit- etc.)Verlängerung f, ✿ a. Prolongati'on f: ~ **of leave** Nachurlaub m; **2.** ◉ Dehnung f, Streckung f (a. ✿); **3.** fig. Vergrößerung f, Erweiterung f, Ausbau m; Computer: Erweiterung f (Anhängsel hinter Dateinamen); **4.** Ausdehnung f, 'Umfang m; **5.** △ Anbau m (Gebäude); **6.** teleph. Nebenanschluss m, a. Appa'rat m; **7.** phot. (Kamera)Auszug m; ~ **band·age** s. ✿ Streckverband m; ~ **board** s.

E

teleph. 'Hauszent,rale *f*; ~ **cord** *s.*, ~ **flex** *s.* ⚡ Verlängerungskabel *n*; ~ **lad·der** *s.* Ausziehleiter *f*; ~ **ta·ble** *s. Am.* Ausziehtisch *m.*
ex·ten·sive [ɪk'stensɪv] *adj.* □ ausgedehnt (*a.* ⚕ *u. fig.*), um'fassend; eingehend; exten'siv (*a.* ✓); **ex'ten·sive·ness** [-nɪs] *s.* Ausdehnung *f*, 'Umfang *m*; **ex'ten·sor** [-sə] *s. anat.* Streckmuskel *m.*
ex·tent [ɪk'stent] *s.* **1.** Ausdehnung *f*, Länge *f*, Weite *f*, Höhe *f*, Größe *f*; **2.** ⚕ *u. fig.* Bereich *m*; **3.** Raum *m*, Strecke *f*; **4.** *fig.* 'Umfang *m*, (Aus)Maß *n*, Grad *m*: ***to the ~ of*** bis zum Betrag *od.* zur Höhe von; ***to some*** (*od.* ***a certain***) ~ in gewissem Grade, einigermaßen; ***to the full ~*** in vollem Umfang, völlig.
ex·ten·u·ate [ek'stenjʊeɪt] *v/t.* **1.** abschwächen, mildern: ***extenuating circumstances*** ⚖ mildernde Umstände; **2.** beschönigen, bemänteln; **ex·ten·u·a·tion** [ek,stenjʊ'eɪʃn] *s.* **1.** Abschwächung *f*, Milderung *f*; **2.** Beschönigung *f.*
ex·te·ri·or [ek'stɪərɪə] **I** *adj.* **1.** äußer, Außen...: ~ ***angle*** Außenwinkel *m*; ~ ***to*** abseits von, außerhalb (*gen.*); **2.** von außen (ein)wirkend *od.* kommend; **3.** *pol.* auswärtig: ~ ***possessions***; ~ ***policy***; **II.** *s.* **4.** *das* Äußere: a) Außenseite *f*, b) äußere Erscheinung *f* (*e-r Person*), c) *pol.* auswärtige Angelegenheiten *pl.*; **5.** *Film*: Außenaufnahme *f.*
ex·ter·mi·nant [ɪk'stɜːmɪnənt] *s.* Vertilgungsmittel *n*; **ex·ter·mi·nate** [ɪk'stɜːmɪneɪt] *v/t.* ausrotten (*a. fig.*), *Ungeziefer etc. a.* vertilgen; **ex·ter·mi·na·tion** [ɪk,stɜːmɪ'neɪʃn] *s.* Ausrottung *f*, Vertilgung *f*: ~ ***camp*** *hist.* Vernichtungslager *n*; **ex'ter·mi·na·tor** [-tə] *s.* **1.** Kammerjäger *m*; **2.** → ***exterminant.***
ex·tern [ek'stɜːn] *s.* **1.** Ex'terne(r *m*) *f* (*e-s Internats*); **2.** *Am.* ex'terner 'Krankenhausarzt *od.* -assi,stent; **ex'ter·nal** [-nl] **I** *adj.* □ → ***externally***; **1.** äußer, äußerlich, Außen...: ~ ***angle*** ⚕ Außenwinkel *m*; ~ ***ear*** äußeres Ohr; ***for ~ use*** ⚕ zum äußerlichen Gebrauch, äußerlich; ~ ***to*** außerhalb (*gen.*); ~ ***world*** Außenwelt *f*; **2.** von außen (ein)wirkend *od.* kommend; **3.** (äußerlich) wahrnehmbar; **4.** ✝, *pol.* auswärtig, Außen..., Auslands...: ~ ***affairs*** auswärtige Angelegenheiten; ~ ***frontiers*** *EU* Außengrenze *f*; ~ ***loan*** Auslandsanleihe *f*; ~ ***rate of duty*** *EU* Außenzollsatz *m*; ~ ***trade*** Außenhandel *m*; **5.** ✝ außerbetrieblich, Fremd...; **II.** *s.* **6.** *mst pl. das* Äußere; **7.** *pl.* Äußerlichkeiten *pl.*, Nebensächlichkeiten *pl.*; **ex'ter·nal·ize** [-nəlaɪz] *v/t. psych.* **1.** objektivieren; **2.** *Konflikte* nach außen verlagern; **ex'ter·nal·ly** [-nəlɪ] *adv.* äußerlich, von außen.
ex·ter·ri·to·ri·al ['eks,terɪ'tɔːrɪəl] *etc.* → ***extraterritorial*** *etc.*
ex·tinct [ɪk'stɪŋkt] *adj.* **1.** erloschen (*a. fig. Titel etc., geol. Vulkan*); **2.** ausgestorben (*Pflanze, Tier etc.*), 'untergegangen (*Rasse, Reich etc.*); nicht mehr existierend; **3.** abgeschafft, aufgehoben; **ex'tinc·tion** [-kʃn] *s.* **1.** Erlöschen *n*; **2.** Aussterben *n*, 'Untergang *m*; **3.** (Aus)Löschen *n*; **4.** Vernichtung *f*; **5.** Abschaffung *f*; **6.** Tilgung *f*; **7.** ⚡, *phys.* Löschung *f.*
ex·tin·guish [ɪk'stɪŋgwɪʃ] *v/t.* **1.** *Feuer, Lichter* (aus)löschen; **2.** *fig. Leben, Gefühl* auslöschen, ersticken, töten; **3.** vernichten; **4.** *fig.* in den Schatten stellen; **5.** *fig. j-n* zum Schweigen bringen; **6.** (*a.* ⚖) abschaffen, aufheben; **7.** *Schuld* tilgen; **ex'tin·guish·er** [-ʃə] *s.* **1.** Löschgerät *n*; **2.** Löschhütchen *n* (*für Kerzen*); **3.** Glut-, Ziga'rettentöter *m.*
ex·tir·pate ['ekstɜːpeɪt] *v/t.* **1.** (mit den Wurzeln) ausreißen; **2.** *fig.* ausmerzen, ausrotten; **3.** ⚕ exstirpieren, entfernen.
ex·tol, *Am. a.* **ex·toll** [ɪk'stəʊl] *v/t.* (lob)preisen, rühmen.
ex·tort [ɪk'stɔːt] *v/t.* (***from***) a) *et.* erpressen, erzwingen (von), b) *a. Bewunderung etc.* abringen, abnötigen (*dat.*).
ex·tor·tion [ɪk'stɔːʃn] *s.* **1.** Erpressung *f*; **2.** Wucher *m*; **ex'tor·tion·ate** [-nət] *adj.* **1.** erpresserisch; **2.** unmäßig, Wucher...; **ex'tor·tion·er** [-ʃnə], **ex'tor·tion·ist** [-nɪst] *s.* **1.** Erpresser *m*; **2.** Wucherer *m.*
ex·tra ['ekstrə] **I** *adj.* **1.** zusätzlich, Extra..., Sonder..., Neben...: ~ ***charge*** Zuschlag *m*; ~ ***charges*** Nebenkosten; ~ ***dividend*** Extra-, Zusatzdividende *f*; ~ ***pay*** Zulage *f*; ~ ***time*** *sport* (Spiel-) Verlängerung *f*; ***if you pay an ~ two pounds*** wenn Sie noch zwei Pfund zulegen; **2.** besonder, außergewöhnlich; besonders gut: ***it is nothing ~*** es ist nichts Besonderes; **II** *adv.* **3.** extra, besonders: ~ ***high***; ~ ***late***; ***be charged for ~*** gesondert berechnet werden; **III** *s.* **4.** *et.* Außergewöhnliches, *bsd.* a) Sonderarbeit *f*, -leistung *f*, b) *bsd. mot.* Extra *n*, c) Sonderberechnung *f*, Zuschlag *m*: ***heating and light are ~s*** Heizung u. Licht werden gesondert berechnet; **5.** *pl.* Nebenkosten *pl.*; **6.** Extrablatt *n* (*Zeitung*); **7.** Aushilfskraft *f*; **8.** *thea.*, *Film*: Sta'tist(in).
ex·tract I *v/t.* [ɪk'strækt] **1.** her'ausziehen, -holen (***from*** aus); **2.** extrahieren: a) ⚕ *Zahn*(*wurzel*) ziehen, b) ⚗ ausscheiden, -ziehen, c) *Metall etc.* gewinnen, d) ⚕ *Wurzel* ziehen; **3.** *Honig etc.* schleudern; **4.** *Beispiele etc.* ausziehen, exzerpieren (***from a text*** aus e-m Text); **5.** *fig.* (***from***) *et.* her'ausholen (aus), entlocken (*dat.*); **6.** *fig.* ab-, herleiten; **II** *s.* ['ekstrækt] **7.** *a.* ⚗ Auszug *m*, Ex'trakt *m*: ~ ***of beef*** Fleischextrakt; ~ ***of account*** Kontoauszug; **ex'trac·tion** [-kʃn] *s.* **1.** Her'ausziehen *n*; **2.** Extrakti'on *f*: a) ⚕ Ziehen *n* (*e-s Zahns*), b) ⚗ Ausziehen *n*, Ausscheidung *f*, Gewinnung *f*, c) ⚕ Ziehen *n* (*Wurzel*); **3.** *fig.* Entlockung *f*; **4.** Abstammung *f*, Herkunft *f*; **ex'trac·tive** [-tɪv] *adj.*: ~ ***industry*** Industrie *f* zur Gewinnung von Naturprodukten; **ex'trac·tor** [-tə] *s.* **1.** ⚙, ⚔ Auszieher *m*, -werfer *m*; **2.** ⚕ (Geburts-, Zahn-, Wurzel)Zange *f*; **3.** Trockenschleuder *f*; **4.** Ent'safter *m*; **5.** Dunstabzug(svorrichtung *f*) *m*: ~ ***hood*** Dunstabzugshaube *f.*
ex·tra·cur·ric·u·lar [,ekstrəkə'rɪkjʊlə] *adj.* **1.** *ped.*, *univ.* außerhalb des Stunden- *od.* Lehrplans; **2.** außerplanmäßig.
ex·tra·dit·a·ble ['ekstrədaɪtəbl] *adj.* **1.** auszuliefern(d): ~ ***criminal***; **2.** auslieferungsfähig: ~ ***offence***; **ex·tra·dite** ['ekstrədaɪt] *v/t.* ausliefern; **ex·tra·di·tion** [,ekstrə'dɪʃn] *s.* Auslieferung *f*: ***request for ~*** Auslieferungsantrag *m.*
,ex·tra|·ju'di·cial *adj.* ⚖ außergerichtlich; **,~'mar·i·tal** *adj.* außerehelich; **,~'mu·ral** *adj.* außerhalb der Mauern (*e-r Stadt od. Universität*): ~ ***courses*** Hochschulkurse außerhalb der Universität; ~ ***student*** Gasthörer(in).
ex·tra·ne·ous [ek'streɪnjəs] *adj.* □ **1.** fremd (***to*** *dat.*); **2.** unwesentlich; **3.** ***be ~ to*** nicht gehören zu.
ex·traor·di·nar·i·ly [ɪk'strɔːdnrəlɪ] *adv.*, **ex·traor·di·nar·y** [ɪk'strɔːdnrɪ] *adj.* **1.** außerordentlich: ***ambassador ~*** Sonderbotschafter *m*; **2.** ungewöhnlich, seltsam, merkwürdig.
ex·trap·o·late [ek'stræpəʊleɪt] *v/t.* extrapolieren.
,ex·tra|'sen·so·ry *adj. psych.* außersinnlich: ~ ***perception*** außersinnliche Wahrnehmung; **,~·ter'res·trial** *adj.* außerirdisch; **'~,ter·ri'to·ri·al** *adj.* ,exterritori'al; **'~,ter·ri·to·ri'al·i·ty** *s.* ,Exterritoriali'tät *f*; ~ **time** *s. sport* (Spiel)Verlängerung *f.*
ex·trav·a·gance [ɪk'strævəgəns] *s.* **1.** Verschwendung *f*; **2.** Ausschweifung *f*, Zügellosigkeit *f*, 'Übermut *m*; **3.** Extrava'ganz *f*, 'Übermaß *n*, Über'triebenheit *f*, Über'spanntheit *f*; **ex'trav·a·gant** [-nt] *adj.* □ **1.** verschwenderisch; **2.** ausschweifend, zügellos; **3.** extrava'gant, über'trieben, -'spannt; **ex·trav·a·gan·za** [ek,strævə'gænzə] *s.* **1.** fan'tastisches Werk (*Musik od. Literatur*); **2.** Ausstattungsstück *n.*
ex·treme [ɪk'striːm] **I** *adj.* □ → ***extremely***; **1.** äußerst, weitest, letzt: ~ ***border*** äußerster Rand; ~ ***value*** Extremwert *m*; → ***unction*** 3 c; **2.** äußerst, höchst; außergewöhnlich, über'trieben: ~ ***case*** äußerster (Not)Fall; ~ ***measure*** drastische *od.* radikale Maßnahme; ~ ***necessity*** zwingende Notwendigkeit; ~ ***old age*** hohes Greisenalter; ~ ***penalty*** höchste Strafe, *a.* Todesstrafe *f*; **3.** *pol.* ex'trem, radi'kal: ~ ***Left*** äußerste Linke; ~ ***views***; **II** *s.* **4.** äußerstes Ende: ***at the other ~*** am entgegengesetzten Ende; **5.** *das* Äußerste, höchster Grad, Ex'trem *n*: ***awkward in the ~*** äußerst peinlich; ***go to ~s*** vor nichts zurückschrecken; ***go to the other ~*** ins andere Extrem fallen; **6.** 'Übermaß *n*, Über'triebenheit *f*: ***carry s.th. to an ~*** et. zu weit treiben; **7.** Gegensatz *m*: ***~s meet*** Extreme berühren sich; **8.** *pl. obs.* äußerste Not; **ex'treme·ly** [-lɪ] *adv.* äußerst, höchst; **ex'trem·ism** [-mɪzəm] *s.* Extre'mismus *m*, Radika'lismus *m*; **ex'trem·ist** [-mɪst] *s.* **I** Extre'mist(in), Radi'kale(r *m*) *f*; **II** *adj.* extre'mistisch; **ex'trem·i·ty** [-remətɪ] *s.* **1.** *das* Äußerste, äußerstes Ende, äußerste Grenze: ***to the last ~*** bis zum Äußersten; ***drive s.o. to extremities*** j-n zum Äußersten treiben; ***resort to extremities*** zu drastischen Mitteln greifen; **2.** *fig.* a) höchster Grad: ~ ***of joy*** Übermaß der Freude, b) äußerste Not, verzweifelte Situation: ***reduced to extremities*** in größter Not, c) verzweifelter Gedanke; **3.** *pl.* Gliedmaßen *pl.*, Extremi'täten *pl.*
ex·tri·cate ['ekstrɪkeɪt] *v/t.* **1.** (***from***) her'auswinden, -ziehen (aus), befreien (aus, von): ~ ***o.s.*** sich befreien; **2.** ⚗ *Gas* frei machen; **ex·tri·ca·tion** [,ekstrɪ'keɪʃn] *s.* **1.** Befreiung *f*; **2.** ⚗ Freimachen *n.*
ex·trin·sic [ek'strɪnsɪk] *adj.* (□ ***~ally***) **1.** äußer; **2.** a) nicht zur Sache gehörig, b) unwesentlich: ***be ~ to s.th.*** nicht zu et. gehören.
ex·tro·ver·sion [,ekstrəʊ'vɜːʃn] *s. psych.* Extro- *od.* Extraversi'on *f*; **ex·tro·vert** ['ekstrəʊvɜːt] *psych.* **I** *s.* Extro- *od.* Extraver'tierte(r *m*) *f*; **II** *adj.* extro- *od.* extraver'tiert.
ex·trude [ek'struːd] **I** *v/t.* **1.** ausstoßen, (her)'auspressen; **2.** ⚙ strangpressen; **II** *v/i.* **3.** vorstehen; **ex'tru·sion** [-uːʒn] *s.* **1.** Ausstoßung *f*; **2.** ⚙ a) Strangpressen *n*, b) Strangpressling *m.*

ex·u·ber·ance [ɪgˈzjuːbərəns] *s.* **1.** (*of*) (ˈÜber)Fülle (von *od. gen.*), Reichtum *m* (an *dat.*); **2.** ˈÜberschwang *m*; Ausgelassenheit *f*; **3.** (Wort)Schwall *m*; **ex·ˈu·ber·ant** [-nt] *adj.* □ **1.** üppig, (ˈüber)reichlich; **2.** *fig.* a) (ˈüber)schwänglich, b) (ˈüber)sprudelnd, ausgelassen; **3.** *fig.* (äußerst) fruchtbar.

ex·ude [ɪgˈzjuːd] **I** *v/t.* **1.** ausschwitzen, absondern; **2.** *fig.* von sich geben, verströmen; **II** *v/i.* **3.** *a. fig.* ausströmen (*from* aus, von).

ex·ult [ɪgˈzʌlt] *v/i.* frohˈlocken, jubeln, triumphieren (*at, over, in* über *acc.*); **ex·ˈult·ant** [-tənt] *adj.* □ frohˈlockend, jubelnd, triumphierend; **ex·ul·ta·tion** [ˌegzʌlˈteɪʃn] *s.* Jubel *m*, Frohˈlocken *n*.

ex·urb [ˈeksɜːb] *s. Am.* (vornehmes) Einzugsgebiet (*e-r Großstadt*); **ex·ur·ban·ite** [ɪgˈzɜːbənaɪt] *s. Am.* Bewohner(in) e-s *exurb*; **ex·ur·bia** [ɪgˈzɜːbɪə] *s.* die (vornehmen) Außenbezirke *pl.*

eye [aɪ] **I** *s.* **1.** Auge *n*: *an ~ for an ~ bibl.* Auge um Auge; *under my ~s* vor m-n Augen; *up to the ~s in work* bis über die Ohren in Arbeit; *with one's ~s shut* mit geschlossenen Augen (*a. fig.*); *be all ~s* ganz Auge sein; *cry one's ~s out* sich die Augen ausweinen; **2.** *fig.* Blick *m*, Gesichtssinn *m*, Auge(nmerk) *n*: *with an ~ to* a) im Hinblick auf (*acc.*), b) mit der Absicht zu (*inf.*); *cast an ~ over* e-n Blick werfen auf (*acc.*); *catch* (*od.* *strike*) *the ~* ins Auge fallen; *she caught his ~* sie fiel ihm auf; *catch the Speaker's ~ parl.* das Wort erhalten; *do s.o. in the ~* F j-n ˈreinlegenˈ *od.* ˈübers Ohr hauenˈ; *give an ~ to s.th.* et. anblicken, ein

Auge auf et. haben; *give s.o. the* (*glad*) *~* j-m e-n einladenden Blick zuwerfen; *have an ~ for* e-n Sinn *od.* Blick *od.* ein (offenes) Auge haben für; *he has an ~ for beauty* er hat Sinn für Schönheit; *have an ~ to s.th.* a) ein Auge auf et. haben, b) auf et. achten; *keep an ~ on* ein (wachsames) Auge haben auf (*acc.*); *make ~s at* j-m verliebte Blicke zuwerfen; → *meet* 9; *open s.o.'s ~s* (*to s.th.*) j-m die Augen öffnen (für et.); *that made him open his ~s* das verschlug ihm die Sprache; *you can see that with half an ~* das sieht doch ein Blinder!; *set* (*od.* *clap*) *~s on* zu Gesicht bekommen; *close one's ~s to* die Augen verschließen vor (*dat.*); *my ~!* F denkste!, von wegen!, Quatsch!; **3.** Ansicht *f*: *in the ~s of* nach Ansicht von; *see ~ to ~ with s.o.* mit j-m übereinstimmen; **4.** Öhr *n* (*Nadel*); Öse *f*; **5.** ♀ Auge *n*, Knospe *f*; **6.** *zo.* Auge *n* (*Schmetterling, Pfauenschweif*); **7.** △ rundes Fenster; **8.** Auge *n*, windstilles Zentrum e-s Sturms; **II** *v/t.* **9.** ansehen, betrachten, (scharf) beobachten, ins Auge fassen: *~ s.o. from top to toe* j-n von oben bis unten mustern.

eye|ap·peal *s.* optische Wirkung, atˈtrakˈtive Gestaltung; **'~·ball** *s.* Augapfel *m*; **'~·black** *s.* Wimperntusche *f*; **'~·brow** *s.* Augenbraue *f*: *~ pencil* Augenbrauenstift *m*; *raise one's ~s fig.* die Stirn runzeln; *cause raised ~s* Aufsehen *od.* Missfallen erregen; **'~-·catch·er** *s.* Blickfang *m*; **'~-·catch·ing** *adj.* ins Auge fallend, auffallend.

eyed [aɪd] *adj. in Zssgn* ...äugig; mit (...) Ösen.

'eye|·ful *s.* F **1.** ˈtoller Anblickˈ; **2.** ˈtolle Frauˈ; **3.** *get an ~ of this!* sieh dir das mal an!; **'~·glass** *s.* **1.** Monˈokel *n*; **2.** *opt.* Okuˈlar *n*; **3.** *pl. a.* pair of *~es bsd. Am.* Brille *f*; **'~·hole** *s.* **1.** Augenhöhle *f*; **2.** Guckloch *n*; **'~·lash** *s. mst pl.* Augenwimper *f*; → *bat*³; *~ lens s.* Okuˈlarlinse *f*.

eye·let [ˈaɪlɪt] *s.* **1.** Öse *f*; **2.** Loch *n*.

eye|lev·el *s.* (*on ~* in) Augenhöhe *f*; **'~·lid** *s.* Augenlid *n*; → *bat*³; **'~·lin·er** *s.* Eyeliner *m*; **'~-·o·pen·er** *s.* **1.** *fig.* Überˈraschung *f*, Entdeckung *f*: *that was an ~ to me* das hat mir die Augen geöffnet; **2.** *Am.* F (*bsd. alkoholischer*) ˈMuntermacherˈ; **'~·piece** *s. opt.* Okuˈlar *n*; *~ rhyme s.* Augenreim *m*; **'~·shade** *s.* Sonnenschild *m*; **'~·shadow** *s.* Lidschatten *m*; **'~·shot** *s.*: (*with*)*in* (*beyond od. out of*) *~* in (außer) Sichtweite; **'~·sight** *s.* Augenlicht *n*, Sehkraft *f*: *poor ~* schwache Augen *pl.*; *~ sock·et s. anat.* Augenhöhle *f*; **'~·sore** *s. fig.* Schandfleck *m*, et. Hässliches; **'~·strain** *s.* Überˈanstrengung *f* der Augen; **'~·tooth** *s.* [*irr.*] *anat.* Augen-, Eckzahn *m*: *he'd give his eye-teeth for it* er würde alles darum geben; **'~·wash** *s.* **1.** *pharm.* Augenwasser *n*; **2.** *fig.* a) ˈQuatschˈ *m*, b) Augen(aus)wischeˈrei *f*; **'~·wit·ness I** *s.* Augenzeuge *m*; **II** *v/t.* Augenzeuge sein *od.* werden von (*od. gen.*).

ey·rie [ˈaɪərɪ] *s. orn.* Horst *m*.

E·ze·ki·el, E·ze·chi·el [ɪˈziːkjəl] *npr. u. s. bibl.* (das Buch) Heˈsekiel *m od.* Eˈzechiel *m*; **Ez·ra** [ˈezrə] *npr. u. s. bibl.* (das Buch) Esra *m od.* Esdras *m*.

E

F, f [ef] *s.* **1.** F *n*, f *n* (*Buchstabe*); **2.** ♪ F *n*, f *n* (*Note*); **3.** ♫ *ped.* Sechs *f*, Ungenügend *n* (*Note*).

fab [fæb] *adj. sl.* → **fabulous** 2.

Fa·bi·an ['feɪbjən] **I** *adj.* **1.** Hinhalte..., Verzögerungs...: ~ **tactics**; **2.** *pol.* die **Fabian Society** betreffend; **II** *s.* **3.** *pol.* Fabier(in); **'Fa·bi·an·ism** [-nɪzəm] *s.* Poli'tik *f* der → **Fa·bi·an So·ci·e·ty** *s.* (*sozialistische*) Gesellschaft der Fabier.

fa·ble ['feɪbl] *s.* **1.** Fabel *f* (*a. e-s Dramas*); Sage *f*, Märchen *n*; **2.** *coll.* a) Fabeln *pl.*, b) Sagen *pl.*; **3.** *fig.* ,Märchen' *n*; **'fa·bled** [-ld] *adj.* **1.** legen'där; **2.** (frei) erfunden.

fab·ric ['fæbrɪk] *s.* **1.** Bau *m* (*a. fig*); Gebilde *n*; **2.** *fig.* a) Gefüge *n*, Struk'tur *f*, b) Sy'stem *n*; **3.** Stoff *m*, Gewebe *n*; ☉ Leinwand *f*, Reifengewebe *n*: ~ **gloves** Stoffhandschuhe; **'fab·ri·cate** [-keɪt] *v/t.* **1.** fabrizieren, herstellen, (an)fertigen; **2.** *fig.* ,fabrizieren': a) erfinden, b) fälschen; **fab·ri·ca·tion** [‚fæbrɪˈkeɪʃn] *s.* **1.** Herstellung *f*, Fabrikati'on *f*; **2.** *fig.* Erfindung *f*, ,Märchen' *n*, Lüge *f*; **3.** Fälschung *f* **'fab·ri·ca·tor** [-keɪtə] *s.* **1.** Hersteller *m*; **2.** *fig. b.s.* Erfinder *m*, Urheber *m e-r Lüge etc.*, Lügner *m*; **3.** Fälscher *m*.

fab·u·list ['fæbjʊlɪst] *s.* **1.** Fabeldichter (-in); **2.** Schwindler(in); **'fab·u·lous** [-ləs] *adj.* □ **1.** legen'där, Sagen..., Fabel...; **2.** *fig.* F fabel-, sagenhaft, ,toll'.

fa·çade [fəˈsɑːd] (*Fr.*) *s.* △ Fas'sade *f* (*a. fig.*), Vorderseite *f*.

face [feɪs] **I** *s.* **1.** Gesicht *n*, Angesicht *n*, Antlitz *n* (*a. fig.*): **for s.o.'s fair ~** *iro.* um j-s schönen Augen willen; **in** (**the**) **~ of** a) angesichts (*gen.*), gegenüber (*dat.*), b) trotz (*gen. od. dat.*); **in the ~ of danger** angesichts der Gefahr; **to s.o.'s ~** j-m ins Gesicht *sagen etc.*; **~ to ~** von Angesicht zu Angesicht; **~ to with** Auge in Auge mit, gegenüber, vor (*dat.*); **fly in the ~ of** a) j-m ins Gesicht fahren, b) *fig.* sich offen widersetzen (*dat.*), trotzen (*dat.*); **I couldn't look him in the ~** ich konnte ihm (vor Scham) nicht in die Augen sehen; **do** (**up**) **one's ~**, F **put one's ~ on** sich ,anmalen' (*schminken*); **set one's ~ against s.th.** sich e-r Sache widersetzen, sich gegen et. wenden; **show one's ~** sich blicken lassen; **shut the door in s.o.'s ~** j-m die Tür vor der Nase zuschlagen; **2.** (Gesichts)Ausdruck *m*, Aussehen *n*, Miene *f*: **make** (*od. pull*) **a ~** (*od. ~s*) ein Gesicht (*od. e-e Grimasse*) machen *od.* schneiden; **make** (*od. pull*) **a long ~** *fig.* ein langes Gesicht machen; **put a bold ~ on** a) e-r Sache gelassen entgegensehen, b) sich et. Unangenehmes etc. nicht anmerken lassen; **put a good** (*od. brave*) **~ on the matter** gute Miene zum bösen Spiel machen; **3.** *fig.* Stirn *f*, Unverfrorenheit *f*, Frechheit *f*: **have the ~ to** *inf.* die Stirn haben zu *inf.*; **4.** Ansehen *n*: **save** (**one's**) **~** das Gesicht wahren;

lose ~ das Gesicht verlieren; **loss of ~** Prestigeverlust *m*; **5.** *das* Äußere, Gestalt *f*, Erscheinung *f*, Anschein *m*: **on the ~ of it** auf den ersten Blick, oberflächlich betrachtet, vordergründig; **put a new ~ on s.th.** et. in neuem *od.* anderem Licht erscheinen lassen; **6.** Ober-, Außenfläche *f*, Fläche *f* (*a. Ⓐ*), Seite *f*; ☉ Stirnfläche *f*; ☉ (Amboss-, Hammer)Bahn *f*: **the ~ of the earth** die Erdoberfläche, die Welt; **7.** Oberseite *f*; rechte Seite (*Stoff etc.*): **lying on its ~** nach unten gekehrt liegend; **8.** Fas'sade *f*, Vorderseite *f*; **9.** Bildseite *f* (*Spielkarte*); *typ.* Bild *n* (*Type*); Zifferblatt *n* (*Uhr*); **10.** Wand *f* (*Berg etc.*, ⚒ Kohlenflöz): **at the ~** ⚒ am (Abbau)Stoß, vor Ort; **II** *v/t.* **11.** ansehen, j-m ins Gesicht sehen *od.* das Gesicht zuwenden; **12.** gegen'überstehen, gegen- -sitzen, -treten (*dat.*); nach *Osten etc.* blicken *od.* liegen (*Raum*): **the man facing me** der Mann mir gegenüber; **the house ~s the sea** das Haus liegt nach dem Meer zu; **the window ~s the street** das Fenster geht auf die Straße; **the room ~s east** das Zimmer liegt nach Osten; **13.** (mutig) entgegentreten *od.* begegnen (*dat.*), ins Auge sehen (*dat.*), die Stirn bieten (*dat.*): **~ the enemy**; **~ death** dem Tod ins Auge blicken; **~ it out** die Sache durchstehen; **~ s.o. off** *Am.* es auf e-e Kraft- *od.* Machtprobe mit j-m ankommen lassen; → **music** 1; **14.** *oft* **be ~d with** sich e-r *Gefahr etc.* gegen'übersehen, gegen- 'überstehen (*dat.*): **he was ~d with ruin** er stand vor dem Nichts; **15.** et. hinnehmen, sich mit et. abfinden: **~ the facts**; **let's ~ it, ...!** seien wir ehrlich, ...!; **16.** 'umkehren, -wenden; *Spielkarten* aufdecken; **17.** *Schneiderei:* besetzen, einfassen, mit Aufschlägen versehen; **18.** ☉ verkleiden, verblenden, über'ziehen; **19.** ☉ Stirnflächen bearbeiten, (plan)schleifen, glätten; **III** *v/i.* **20.** *bsd.* ⚔ **~ about** kehrtmachen (*a. fig.*): **left ~!** *Am.* links um!; **right about ~!** rechts um kehrt!; **21.** **~ off** Eishockey: das Bully ausführen; **22.** **~ up to** → 13, 15.

'face|-a,bout → **about-face**; **~ brick** *s.* △ Verblendstein *m*; **~ card** *s.* Kartenspiel: Bild(karte *f*) *n*; **'~-cloth** *s.* Waschlappen *m*; **~ cream** *s.* Gesichtscreme *f*.

-faced [feɪst] *adj. in Zssgn* mit e-m ... Gesicht.

'face|-down *s. Am.* Kraft-, Machtprobe *f*; **~ flan·nel** → **facecloth**; **~ grind·ing** *s.* ☉ Planschleifen *n*; **~ guard** *s.* Schutzmaske *f*; **~ lathe** *s.* ☉ Plandrehbank *f*.

face·less ['feɪslɪs] *adj.* gesichtslos, *fig. a.* ano'nym.

'face|-lift I *s.* → **face-lifting**; **II** *v/t. fig.* verschönern; **'~-lift·ing** *s.* **1.** Gesichtsstraffung *f*, Facelifting *n*; **2.** *fig.* Verschönerung *f*, Renovierung *f*; **'~-off** *s.*

1. *Eishockey:* Bully *n*: **~ circle** Anspielkreis *m*; **2.** → **facedown**; **~ pack** *s.* Gesichtspackung *f*, -maske *f*.

fac·er ['feɪsə] *s.* **1.** Schlag *m* ins Gesicht (*a. fig.*); **2.** *fig.* Schlag *m* (ins Kon'tor); **3.** *Brit.* F ,harte Nuss'.

'face-,sav·ing *adj.*: **~ excuse** Ausrede *f*, um das Gesicht zu wahren.

fac·et ['fæsɪt] **I** *s.* **1.** a) Fa'cette *f* (*a. fig.*), b) Schliff-, Kri'stallfläche *f*; **2.** *fig.* Seite *f*, A'spekt *m*; **II** *v/t.* **3.** facettieren; **~ed eye** *zo.* Facettenauge *n*.

fa·ce·tious [fəˈsiːʃəs] *adj.* □ scherzhaft, witzig, drollig, spaßig; **fa·ce·tious·ness** [-nɪs] *s.* Scherzhaftigkeit *f etc.*

face-to-face *adj.* per'sönlich; **2.** di'rekt; **~ tow·el** *s.* (Gesichts)Handtuch *n*; **~ val·ue** *s.* **1.** ♦ Nenn-, Nomi'nalwert *m*; **2.** scheinbarer Wert, *das* Äußere: **take s.th. at its ~** et. für bare Münze nehmen *od.* unbesehen glauben.

fa·ci·a ['feɪʃə] *s. Brit.* **1.** Firmen-, Ladenschild *n*; **2.** *a.* **~ board, ~ panel** *mot.* Arma'turenbrett *n*.

fa·cial ['feɪʃl] **I** *adj.* □ a) Gesichts...: **~ pack** Gesichtspackung *f*, b) des Gesichts, im Gesicht; **II** *s.* *Kosmetik:* Gesichtsbehandlung *f*.

-fa·cient [feɪʃənt] *in Zssgn* verursachend, machend.

fac·ile ['fæsaɪl] *adj.* □ **1.** leicht (zu tun *od.* zu meistern *etc.*); **2.** *fig.* oberflächlich; **3.** flüssig (*Stil*).

fa·cil·i·tate [fəˈsɪlɪteɪt] *v/t.* erleichtern, fördern; **fa·cil·i·ta·tion** [fəsɪlɪˈteɪʃn] *s.* Erleichterung *f*, Förderung *f*; **fa·cil·i·ty** [-tɪ] *s.* **1.** Leichtigkeit *f* (*der Ausführung etc.*); **2.** Oberflächlichkeit *f*; **3.** Flüssigkeit *f* (*des Stils*); **4.** (günstige) Gelegenheit *f*, Möglichkeit *f* (*for* für, zu); **5.** *mst pl.* Einrichtung(en *pl.*) *f*, Anlage(n *pl.*) *f*; **6.** *mst pl.* Erleichterung(en *pl.*) *f*, Vorteil(e *pl.*) *m*, Vergünstigung(en *pl.*) *f*, Annehmlichkeit(en *pl.*) *f*.

fac·ing ['feɪsɪŋ] *s.* **1.** ⚔ Wendung *f*, Schwenkung *f*: **go through one's ~s** *fig.* zeigen (müssen), was man kann; **put s.o. through his ~s** *fig.* j-n auf Herz u. Nieren prüfen; **2.** Außen-, Oberschicht *f*, Belag *m*, 'Überzug *m*; **3.** ☉ Plandrehen *n*: **~ lathe** Plandrehbank *f*; **4.** △ a) Verkleidung *f*, -blendung *f*, b) Bewurf *m*: **~ brick** Verblendstein *m*; **5.** *a.* **~ sand** ☉ fein gesiebter Formsand; **6.** *Schneiderei:* a) Aufschlag *m*, b) Besatz *m*, Einfassung *f*: **~s** ⚔ (Uniform-)Aufschläge.

fac·sim·i·le [fækˈsɪmɪlɪ] **I** *s.* **1.** Fak'simile *n*, Reprodukti'on *f*; **2.** 'Telefax *n*, 'Telekopie *f*; **3.** *a.* **~ transmission** *od.* **broadcast(ing)** a) ⚡, *tel.* Bildfunk *m*: **~ apparatus** Bildfunkgerät *n*, b) Fak'simileübertragung *f*; **II** *v/t.* **4.** faksimilieren.

fact [fækt] *s.* **1.** Tatsache *f*, Wirklichkeit *f*, Wahrheit *f*: **~ and fancy** Dichtung u. Wahrheit; **~s and figures** genaue Daten; **naked** (*od. hard*) **~s** nackte Tatsachen; **in** (**point of**) **~** in der Tat, tatsächlich, genau gesagt; *it is a* ~ es stimmt, es ist e-e Tatsache; **founded on** ~ auf Tatsachen beruhend; **the** ~ (*of the matter*) *is* Tatsache ist od. die Sache ist die (*that* dass); **know s.th. for a** ~ et. (ganz) sicher wissen; **tell the** ~**s of life to a child** ein Kind (sexuell) aufklären; **2.** ♂ a) Tatsache f: *in* ~ *and law* in tatsächlicher u. rechtlicher Hinsicht; **the** ~**s** (*of the case*) der Tatbestand *m*, die Tatumstände *pl.*, der Sachverhalt *m*, b) Tat f: *before* (*after*) *the* ~ vor (nach) begangener Tat; → *accessory* 7; '~**·find·ing** *adj.* Untersuchungs...: ~ *committee*; ~ *tour* Informationsreise f.

fac·tion ['fækʃn] *s.* **1.** Fakti'on f, Splittergruppe f; **2.** Zwietracht f; '**fac·tion·al·ism** [-ʃnəlɪzəm] *s.* Par'teigeist *m*; '**fac·tion·ist** [-ʃənɪst] *s.* Par'teigänger *m*; '**fac·tious** [-ʃəs] *adj.* □ **1.** vom Par'teigeist beseelt, fakti'ös; **2.** aufruhrerisch.

fac·ti·tious [fæk'tɪʃəs] *adj.* □ gekünstelt, künstlich.

fac·ti·tive ['fæktɪtɪv] *adj.* *ling.* fakti'tiv, bewirkend: ~ *verb*.

fac·tor ['fæktə] *s.* **1.** *fig.* Faktor *m* (a. ♉, ♃, *phys.*), (mitwirkender) 'Umstand, Mo'ment *n*, Ele'ment *n*: *safety* ~ Sicherheitsfaktor; **2.** *biol.* Erbfaktor *m*; **3.** ♉ a) (Handels)Vertreter *m*, Kommissio'när *m*, b) *Am.* Finan'zierungskommissio‚när *m*; **4.** ♌ *Scot.* (Guts-)Verwalter *m*; '**fac·tor·ing** [-tərɪŋ] *s.* ♉ Factoring *n* (*Absatzfinanzierung u. Kreditrisikoabsicherung*); '**fac·to·ry** [-tərɪ] *s.* **1.** Fa'brik f: ♌ *Acts* Arbeiterschutzgesetze; ~ *cost* Herstellungskosten *pl.*; ~ *expenses* Gemeinkosten *pl.*; ~ *farming* Massentierhaltung f; ~ *hand* Fabrikarbeiter *m*; ~ *ship* Fabrikschiff *n*; ~**·made** fabrikmäßig hergestellt, Fabrik... (*-ware etc.*); **2.** ♉ Handelsniederlassung f, Fakto'rei f.

fac·to·tum [fæk'təʊtəm] *s.* Fak'totum *n*, ‚Mädchen *n* für alles'.

fac·tu·al ['fæktjʊəl] *adj.* □ **1.** tatsächlich: ~ *situation* Sachlage f, -verhalt *m*; **2.** Tatsachen...: ~ *report*; **3.** sachlich.

fac·ul·ta·tive ['fækltətɪv] *adj.* fakulta'tiv, wahlfrei: ~ *subject ped.* Wahlfach *n*; **fac·ul·ty** ['fæklti] *s.* **1.** Fähigkeit f, Vermögen *n*, Kraft f: ~ *of hearing* Hörvermögen; **2.** Gabe f, Anlage f, Ta'lent *n*, Fähigkeit f: (*mental*) *faculties* Geisteskräfte; **3.** *univ.* a) Fakul'tät f, Abteilung f, b) (Mitglieder *pl.* e-r) Fakul'tät, Lehrkörper *m*, c) (Ver'waltungs)Perso‚nal *n* (*a. e-r Schule*): *the medical* ~ die medizinische Fakultät, *weitS.* die Mediziner *pl.*; **4.** ♌ Ermächtigung f, Befugnis f (*for* zu, für).

fad [fæd] *s.* **1.** Mode(torheit) f; **2.** ‚Fimmel' *m*, Ma'rotte f; '**fad·dish** [-dɪʃ] **1.** Mode..., vor'übergehend; **2.** ex'zentrisch: ~ *woman* Frau, die jede Mode (-torheit) mitmacht.

fade [feɪd] **I** *v/i.* **1.** (ver)welken; **2.** verschießen, -blassen, ver-, ausbleichen (*Farbe etc.*); **3.** a. ~ *away* verklingen (*Lied, Stimme etc.*), abklingen (*Schmerzen etc.*), verblassen (*Erinnerung etc.*), schwinden, zerrinnen (*Hoffnungen etc.*), verrauchen (*Zorn etc.*), sich auflösen (*Menge*), (in der Ferne *etc.*) verschwinden, immer weniger werden (*Person*); **4.** *Radio*: schwinden (*Ton, Sender*); **5.** ♿ nachlassen (*Bremsen*); **6.** nachlassen, abbauen (*Sportler*); **7.** *bsd. Am.* F ‚verduften'; **8.** *Film, Radio*: über'blenden: ~ *in* (*od. up*) auf- *od.* eingeblendet werden; ~ (*out*) aus- *od.* abgeblendet werden; **II** *v/t.* **9.** (ver)welken lassen; **10.** *Farbe*

etc. ausbleichen; **11.** a. ~ *out Ton, Bild* aus- *od.* abblenden: ~ *in* (*od. up*) auf- *od.* einblenden; '**fad·ed** [-dɪd] *adj.* □ **1.** welk, verwelkt, -blüht (*alle a. fig. Schönheit etc.*); **2.** verblasst, verblichen, -schossen; '**fade-in** *s. Film, Radio, TV*: Auf-, Einblendung f; '**fade·less** [-lɪs] *adj.* □ **1.** licht-, farbecht; **2.** *fig.* unvergänglich; '**fade-out** *s.* **1.** *Film, Radio, TV*: Aus-, Abblendung f: *do a* ~ *sl.* ‚sich verziehen'; **2.** *phys.* Ausschwingen *n*; '**fad·er** [-də] *s. Radio, TV*: Auf- *od.* Abblendregler *m*; '**fad·ing** [-dɪŋ] **I** *adj.* **1.** (ver)welkend (*a. fig.*); **2.** ausbleichend (*Farbe*); **3.** matt, schwindend; **4.** *fig.* vergänglich; **II** *s.* **5.** (Ver)Welken *n*; **6.** Verblassen *n*, Ausbleichen *n*; **7.** *Radio*: Fading *n*, Schwund *m*: ~ *control* Schwundregelung f; **8.** ♿ Fading *n* (*Nachlassen der Bremswirkung*).

fae·cal ['fiːkl] *adj.* fä'kal, Kot...: ~ *matter* Kot *m*; **fae·ces** ['fiːsiːz] *s. pl.* Fä'kalien *pl.*, Kot *m*.

fa·er·ie, **fa·er·y** ['feəri] **I** *s. obs.* **1.** → *fairy* 1; **2.** Märchenland *n*; **II** *adj.* **3.** Feen..., Märchen...

fag¹ [fæg] *s. sl.* **1.** ‚Glimmstängel' *m*, Ziga'rette f; **2.** → **fag(g)ot** 5.

fag² [fæg] **I** *v/i.* **1.** *Brit.* sich (ab)schinden; **2.** ~ *for s.o. Brit. ped.* e-m älteren Schüler Dienste leisten; **II** *v/t.* **3.** a. ~ *out* F ermüden, erschöpfen; **4.** *Brit. ped.* sich von *e-m jüngeren Schüler* bedienen lassen; **III** *s.* **5.** Placke'rei f, Schinde'rei f; **6.** Erschöpfung f; **7.** *Brit. ped.* ‚Diener' *m* (→ 2).

fag³ [fæg] → **fag(g)ot** 5.

fag end *s.* **1.** Ende *n*, Schluss *m*; **2.** letzter *od.* schäbiger Rest; **3.** *Brit. sl.* (Ziga'retten)Kippe f.

fag·ging ['fægɪŋ] *s. a.* ~ *system Brit. ped.* die Sitte, dass jüngere Schüler den älteren Dienste leisten müssen.

fag·(g)ot ['fægət] *s.* **1.** Reisigbündel *n*; **2.** Fa'schine f; **3.** ♿ a) Bündel *n* Stahlstangen, b) 'Schweißpa‚ket *n*; **4.** *Brit. Küche*: Frika'delle f aus Inne'reien; **5.** *sl.* ‚Homo' *m*, Schwule(r) *m*.

Fahr·en·heit ['færənhaɪt] *s.*: *10°* ~ zehn Grad Fahrenheit, 10° F.

fa·ience [faɪ'ɑːns] (*Fr.*) *s.* Fay'ence f.

fail [feɪl] **I** *v/i.* **1.** versagen (*Stimme, Herz, Motor etc., a. fig. Person*); aufhören, zu Ende gehen, nicht (aus)reichen, versiegen (*Vorrat*); ~ *abysmally* kläglich versagen; **2.** miss'raten (*Ernte*), nicht aufgehen (*Saat*); **3.** nachlassen, schwächer werden, schwinden, abnehmen: *his health* ~*ed* s-e Gesundheit ließ nach; **4.** unter'lassen, versäumen, verfehlen; *he* ~*ed to come* er kam nicht; *he never* ~*s to come* er kommt immer; *don't* ~ *to come!* komm ja (*od.* bestimmt)!; *he cannot* ~ *to win* er muss (einfach) gewinnen; ~ *in one's duty* s-e Pflicht versäumen; *he* ~*s in perseverance* es fehlt ihm an Ausdauer; **5.** a) s-n Zweck verfehlen, miss'lingen, fehlschlagen, miss'glücken, b) es nicht fertig bringen *od.* schaffen (*zu inf.*): *the plan* ~*ed* der Plan scheiterte; *if everything else* ~*s* wenn alle Stränge reißen; *I* ~ *to see why* ich sehe nicht ein, warum; *he* ~*ed in his attempt* der Versuch misslang ihm; *it* ~*ed in its effect* die erhoffte Wirkung blieb aus; *a* ~*ed husband* als Ehemann ein Versager; *a* ~*ed artist* ein verkrachter Künstler; **6.** *ped.* 'durchfallen (*in* in *dat.*); **7.** ♉ Bank'rott machen, in Kon'kurs geraten; **II** *v/t.* **8.** im Stich lassen, enttäuschen: *I will never* ~ *you*; *my courage* ~*ed me* mir sank der Mut;

words ~ *me* mir fehlen die Worte; **9.** *j-m* fehlen; **10.** *ped.* a) *j-n* 'durchfallen lassen (*in der Prüfung*), b) 'durchfallen in (*der Prüfung*); **III** *s.* **11.** *he got a* ~ *in biology ped.* er ist in Biologie durchgefallen; **12.** *without* ~ ganz bestimmt, unbedingt; '**fail·ing** [-lɪŋ] **I** *adj.*: *never* ~ nie versagend, unfehlbar; **II** *prp.* in Ermangelung (*gen.*), ohne: ~ *this* andernfalls; ~ *which* widrigenfalls; **III** *s.* Mangel *m*, Schwäche f; Fehler *m*, De'fekt *m*.

'**fail-safe**, '**~-proof** *adj.* pannensicher (*a. fig.*).

fail·ure ['feɪljə] *s.* **1.** Fehlen *n*; **2.** Ausbleiben *n*, Versagen *n*; **3.** Unter'lassung f, Versäumnis *n*: ~ *to comply* Nichtbefolgung f; ~ *to pay* Nichtzahlung f; **4.** Fehlschlag(en *n*) *m*, Scheitern *n*, Miss'lingen *n*, 'Misserfolg *m*: *crop* ~ Missernte f; **5.** *fig.* Zs.-bruch *m*, Schiffbruch *m*; ♉ Bank'rott *m*, Kon'kurs *m*: *meet with* ~ → *fail* 5; **6.** ♂, ♿ (*Herz-, Nieren- etc.*)Versagen *n*, Störung f, De'fekt *m*, ♿ a. Panne f; **7.** Abnahme f, Versiegen *n*; **8.** *ped.* 'Durchfallen *n* (*in der Prüfung*); **9.** a) Versager *m*, ‚Niete' f (*Person od. Sache*), b) ‚Reinfall' *m*, ‚Pleite' f (*Sache*).

faint [feɪnt] **I** *adj.* □ **1.** schwach, matt, kraftlos: *feel* ~ sich matt *od.* e-r Ohnmacht nahe fühlen; **2.** schwach, matt (*Ton, Farbe, a. fig.*): *a* ~ *effort*; *I haven't got the* ~*est idea* ich habe nicht die leiseste Ahnung; ~ *hope* schwache Hoffnung; **3.** furchtsam; **II** *s.* **4.** (*dead* ~ tiefe) Ohnmacht; **III** *v/i.* **5.** schwach *od.* matt werden (*with* vor *dat.*); **6.** in Ohnmacht fallen (*with* vor *dat.*): ~*ing fit* Ohnmachtsanfall *m*; ~ *with happiness* vor Glück zerspringen; '~**-heart** *s.* Feigling *m*; '~**-heart·ed** *adj.* □ feig(e), furchtsam.

faint·ness ['feɪntnɪs] *s.* **1.** Schwäche f (*a. fig.*), Mattigkeit f: ~ *of heart* Feigheit f, Furchtsamkeit f; **2.** Ohnmachtsgefühl *n*.

fair¹ [feə] **I** *adj.* □ → *fairly*; **1.** schön, hübsch, lieblich: *the* ~ *sex* das schöne Geschlecht; **2.** a) hell (*Haut, Haar*), blond (*Haar*), zart (*Teint, Haut*), b) hellhäutig; **3.** rein, sauber, tadel-, makellos, *fig. a.* unbescholten: ~ *name* guter Ruf; **4.** *fig.* schön, gefällig: *give s.o.* ~ *words* *j-n* mit schönen Worten abspeisen; **5.** deutlich, leserlich: ~ *copy* Reinschrift f; **6.** klar, heiter (*Himmel*) schön, trocken (*Wetter, Tag*): *set* ~ beständig; **7.** frei, unbehindert: ~ *game* jagdbares Wild, *bsd. fig.* Freiwild *n* (*to* für); **8.** günstig (*Wind*), aussichtsreich, gut: ~ *chance* reelle Chance; *be in a* ~ *way to* auf dem besten Wege sein zu; **9.** anständig: a) *bsd. sport* fair, b) ehrlich, offen, aufrichtig, c) 'unpar‚teiisch, d) fair: ~ *price* angemessener Preis; ~ *and square* offen u. ehrlich, anständig; ~ *play* a) faires Spiel, b) *fig.* Anständigkeit f, Fairness f; *by* ~ *means or foul* so oder so; ~ *is* ~ Gerechtigkeit muss sein!; ~ *enough!* in Ordnung!; *all's* ~ *in love and war* im Krieg u. in der Liebe ist alles erlaubt; **10.** leidlich, ziemlich *od.* einigermaßen gut, nicht übel: *be a* ~ *judge* ein recht gutes Urteil haben (*of* über *acc.*); ~ *to middling* gut bis mittelmäßig, *iro.* ‚mittelprächtig'; ~ *average* guter Durchschnitt; **11.** ansehnlich, beträchtlich, ganz schön: *a* ~ *sum*; **II** *adv.* → *a. fairly*; **12.** schön, gut, freundlich, höflich; **13.** rein, sauber, leserlich; **14.** günstig: *bid* (*od.* *promise*) ~ a) sich gut anlassen, zu Hoffnungen berechtigen, b) Aussicht haben, versprechen (*to inf.*

zu *inf.*); **15.** anständig, fair: *play* ~ fair spielen, *a. fig.* sich an die Spielregeln halten; **16.** genau: ~ *in the face* mitten ins Gesicht; **17.** völlig; **III** *v/t.* **18.** ⊕ zurichten, glätten; **19.** *Flugzeug etc.* verkleiden.

fair² [feə] *s.* **1.** a) Jahrmarkt *m*, b) Volksfest *n*; **2.** Messe *f*, Ausstellung *f*: *at the industrial* ~ auf der Industriemesse; **3.** Ba'sar *m*.

'fair|-faced *adj.*: ~ *concrete* △ Sichtbeton *m*; **'~-ground** *s.* **1.** Messegelände *n*; **2.** Rummelplatz *m*; ,**~-'haired** *adj.* blond: ~ *boy fig. iro.* Liebling *m* (*des Chefs etc.*).

fair·ing¹ ['feərɪŋ] *s.* ✈ Verkleidung *f*.

fair·ing² ['feərɪŋ] *s. obs.* Jahrmarktsgeschenk *n*.

fair·ly ['feəlɪ] *adv.* **1.** ehrlich; **2.** anständig(erweise); **3.** gerecht(erweise); **4.** ziemlich; **5.** leidlich; **6.** völlig; **7.** geradezu; **8.** deutlich; **9.** genau.

,**fair-'mind·ed** *adj.* aufrichtig, gerecht (denkend).

fair·ness ['feənɪs] *s.* **1.** Schönheit *f*; **2.** a) Blondheit *f*, b) Hellhäutigkeit *f*; **3.** Klarheit *f* (*des Himmels*); **4.** Anständigkeit *f*: a) *bsd. sport* Fairness *f*, b) Ehrlichkeit *f*, c) Gerechtigkeit *f*: *in* ~ gerechterweise; *in* ~ *to him* um ihm Gerechtigkeit widerfahren zu lassen; **5.** ↯, ✝ Lauterkeit *f* (*des Wettbewerbs etc.*).

,**fair|-'spo·ken** *adj.* freundlich, höflich; **'~-way** *s.* **1.** ♨ Fahrwasser *n*, -rinne *f*; **2.** *Golf*: Fairway *n*; '**~-,weath·er** *adj.* Schönwetter...: ~ *friends fig.* Freunde nur in guten Zeiten.

fair·y ['feərɪ] **I** *s.* **1.** Fee *f*, Elf(e *f*) *m*; **2.** *sl.* ,Homo' *m*, Schwule(r) *m*; **II** *adj.* □ **3.** feenhaft (*a. fig.*): ~ *godmother fig.* gute Fee; '**~-land** *s.* Feen-, Märchenland *n*; ~ *tale s.* Märchen *n* (*a. fig.*).

faith [feɪθ] *s.* **1.** (*in*) Glaube(n) *m* (an *acc.*), Vertrauen *n* (auf *acc.*, zu): *have od. put* ~ *in* a) Glauben schenken (*dat.*), b) Vertrauen haben zu; *on the* ~ *of* im Vertrauen auf (*acc.*); **2.** *eccl.* (*überzeugter*) Glaube(n), b) Glaube(nsbekenntnis *n*) *m*: *the Christian* ~; **3.** Treue *f*, Redlichkeit *f*: *breach of* ~ Treu-, Vertrauensbruch *m*; *in good* ~ in gutem Glauben, gutgläubig (*a.* ↯); *in bad* ~ in böser Absicht, arglistig (*a.* ↯), ↯ bösgläubig; **4.** Versprechen *n*: *keep one's* ~ (sein) Wort halten; ~ *cure* → *faith healing.*

faith·ful ['feɪθfʊl] **I** *adj.* □ **1.** treu (*to dat.*); **2.** (pflicht)getreu; **3.** ehrlich, aufrichtig; **4.** gewissenhaft; **5.** (wahrheits- *od.* wort)getreu, genau; **6.** glaubwürdig, zuverlässig; **7.** *eccl.* gläubig; **II** *s.* **8.** *the* ~ *eccl.* die Gläubigen *pl.*; **9.** *pl.* treue Anhänger *pl.*; '**faith·ful·ly** [-fʊlɪ] *adv.* **1.** treu, ergeben: *Yours* ~ Mit freundlichen Grüßen (*Briefschluss*); **2.** → *faithful* 2–5; **3.** F nachdrücklich: *promise* ~ fest versprechen; '**faith·fulness** [-nɪs] *s.* **1.** (*a.* Pflicht)Treue *f*; **2.** Ehrlichkeit *f*; **3.** Gewissenhaftigkeit *f*; **4.** Genauigkeit *f*; **5.** Glaubwürdigkeit *f*.

faith| heal·er *s.* Gesundbeter(in); ~ **heal·ing** *s.* Gesundbeten *n*.

faith·less ['feɪθlɪs] *adj.* □ **1.** *eccl.* ungläubig; **2.** treulos; **3.** unehrlich.

fake [feɪk] F **I** *v/t.* **1.** nachmachen, fälschen; *Presse etc.*: Foto *etc.* ,türken'; **2.** *Bilanz etc.* ,frisieren'; **3.** vortäuschen; **4.** *sport* a) *Gegner* täuschen, b) *Schlag etc.* antäuschen; **II** *s.* **5.** Fälschung *f*, Nachahmung *f*; **6.** Schwindel *m*; **7.** Schwindler *m*, ,Schauspieler' *m*, j-d, der nicht ,echt' ist; **III** *adj.* **8.** nachge-

macht, gefälscht; **9.** falsch; **10.** vorgetäuscht; ~ *asylum seeker* 'Scheinasy-,lant(in) **'fak·er** *s.* **1.** Fälscher *m*; **2.** Simu'lant(in); **3.** → *fake* 7.

fa·kir ['feɪˌkɪə] *s.* **1.** Fakir *m*; **2.** *Am.* F → *fake* 7.

fal·con ['fɔːlkən] *s. orn.* Falke *m*; '**fal·con·er** [-nə] *s. hunt.* Falkner *m*; '**fal·con·ry** [-kənrɪ] *s.* **1.** Falkne'rei *f*; **2.** Falkenbeize *f*, -jagd *f*.

fall [fɔːl] **I** *s.* **1.** Fall(en *n*) *m*, Sturz *m*: *have a* (*bad*) ~ (schwer) stürzen; *ride for a* ~ a) verwegen reiten, b) *fig.* das Schicksal herausfordern; **2.** a) (Ab)Fallen *n* (*der Blätter etc.*), b) *Am.* Herbst *m*; **3.** Fallen *n* (*des Vorhangs*); **4.** Fall *m*, Faltenwurf *m* (*von Stoff*); **5.** *phys.* a) *a. free* ~ freier Fall, b) Fallhöhe *f*, -strecke *f*; **6.** a) (Regen-, Schnee)Fall *m*, b) Regen-, Schneemenge *f*; **7.** Zs.-fallen *n*, Einsturz *m* (*e-s Hauses*); **8.** Fallen *n*, Sinken *n*, Abnehmen *n* (*Temperatur, Flut, Preis*): *heavy* ~ *in prices* Kurs-, Preissturz *m*; *speculate on the* ~ auf Baisse spekulieren; **9.** Abfallen *n*, Gefälle *n*, Neigung *f* (*des Geländes*); **10.** Fall *m* (*a. e-r Festung etc.*), Sturz *m*, Nieder-, 'Untergang *m*, Abstieg *m*, Verfall *m*, Ende *n*; **11.** Fall *m*, Fehltritt: *the* ♀ (*of man*) der (erste) Sündenfall *m*; **12.** *mst pl.* Wasserfall *m*; **13.** Wurf *m* (*Lämmer etc.*); **14.** *Ringen*: Niederwurf *m*: *win by* ~ Schultersieg *m*; *try a* ~ *with s.o. fig.* sich mit j-m messen; **II** *v/i.* [*irr.*] **15.** fallen: *the curtain* ~*s* der Vorhang fällt; **16.** (ab)fallen (*Blätter etc.*); **17.** (he'run-ter)fallen, abstürzen: *he fell to his death* er stürzte tödlich ab; **18.** ('um-, hin-, nieder)fallen, zu Boden fallen, zu Fall kommen; **19.** 'umfallen, -stürzen (*Baum etc.*); **20.** (*in Falten od. Locken*) her'abfallen; **21.** *fig. allg.* fallen: a) (*im Kampf*) getötet werden, b) erobert werden (*Stadt etc.*), c) gestürzt werden (*Regierung*), d) e-n Fehltritt begehen (*Frau*); **22.** *fig.* fallen (*Preis, Temperatur, Flut*), abnehmen, sinken: *his courage fell* ihm sank der Mut; *his face fell* er machte ein langes Gesicht; **23.** abfallen, sich senken (*Gelände*); **24.** (*in Stücke*) zerfallen; **25.** (*zeitlich*) fallen: *Easter* ~*s late this year*; **26.** her'einbrechen (*Nacht*); **27.** *fig.* fallen (*Worte etc.*); **28.** *krank, fällig etc.* werden: ~ *ill* (*due*);

Zssgn mit prp.:

fall| a·mong *v/i.* unter ... (*acc.*) geraten *od.* fallen: ~ *the thieves bibl. u. fig.* unter die Räuber fallen; ~ **be·hind** *v/i.* zu'rückbleiben hinter (*acc.*) (*a. fig.*); ~ **for** *v/i.* F auf *et. od. j-n* reinfallen, *a.* sich in *j-n* ,verknallen'; ~ **from** *v/i.* abfallen von, abtrünnig *od.* untreu werden (*dat.*): ~ *grace* a) sündigen, b) in Ungnade fallen; ~ **in·to** *v/i.* **1.** kommen *od.* geraten *od.* verfallen in (*acc.*): ~ *disuse* außer Gebrauch kommen; ~ *a habit* in e-e Gewohnheit verfallen; → *line¹* 9; **2.** in *Teile* zerfallen; ~ *ruin* zerfallen; **3.** münden in (*acc.*) (*Fluss*) **4.** fallen in (*ein Gebiet od. Fach*); ~ **on** *v/i.* **1.** treffen, fallen auf (*acc.*) (*a. Blick etc.*); **2.** herfallen über (*acc.*), über'fallen (*acc.*); **3.** in *et.* geraten: ~ *evil days* e-e schlimme Zeit durchmachen müssen; ~ **o·ver** *v/i.* fallen über (*acc.*): *o.s. to do s.th.* F sich ,fast umbringen', *et.* zu tun; ~ **to** *v/i.* **1.** mit *et.* beginnen: ~ *work*; **2.** fallen an (*acc.*), j-m zufallen *od.* obliegen (*to do* zu tun); ~ **un·der** *v/i.* *fig.* **1.** unter *ein Gesetz etc.* fallen, zu *et.* gehören; **2.** *der Kritik etc.* unter-

'liegen; ~ **with·in** → *fall into* 4.

Zssgn mit adv.:

fall| a·stern *v/i.* ♨ zu'rückbleiben; ~ **a·way** *v/i.* **1.** → *fall* 23; **2.** → *fall off* 1; ~ **back** *v/i.* **1.** zu'rückweichen: ~ (*up*)*on fig.* zurückgreifen auf (*acc.*); **2.** → ~ **be·hind** *v/i. a. fig.* zu'rückbleiben, -fallen: ~ *with* in Rückstand *od.* Verzug geraten mit; ~ **down** *v/i.* **1.** hin-, hinunterfallen; **2.** 'umfallen, einstürzen; **3.** (*ehrfürchtig*) auf die Knie sinken, niederfallen; **4.** F (*on*) a) versagen (bei), b) Pech haben (mit); ~ **in** *v/i.* **1.** einfallen, -stürzen; **2.** ✕ antreten; **3.** *fig.* a) sich anschließen (*Person*), b) sich einfügen (*Sache*); **4.** ✝ ablaufen, fällig werden; **5.** ~ **with** (zufällig) treffen (*acc.*), stoßen auf (*acc.*); **6.** ~ **with** a) zustimmen (*dat.*), b) passen zu, entsprechen (*dat.*), c) sich anpassen (*dat.*); ~ **off** *v/i. fig.* **1.** zu'rückgehen, sinken, nachlassen, abnehmen; **2.** (*from*) abfallen (von), abtrünnig werden (*dat.*); **3.** ♨ (vom Strich) abfallen; **4.** ✈ abrutschen; ~ **out** *v/i.* **1.** her'ausfallen; **2.** *fig.* ausfallen, sich erweisen als; **3.** sich ereignen; **4.** ✕ wegtreten; **5.** sich streiten *od.* entzweien; ~ **o·ver** *v/i.* 'umfallen, -kippen: ~ *backwards* F sich ,fast umbringen' (*et. zu tun*); ~ **through** *v/i.* **1.** 'durchfallen (*a. fig.*); **2.** *fig.* a) miss'lingen, b) ins Wasser fallen; ~ **to** *v/i.* **1.** zufallen (*Tür*); **2.** ,reinhauen', (tüchtig) zugreifen (*beim Essen*); **3.** handgemein werden.

fal·la·cious [fə'leɪʃəs] *adj.* □ trügerisch: a) irreführend, b) irrig, falsch; **fal·la·cy** ['fæləsɪ] *s.* **1.** Trugschluss *m*, Irrtum *m*: *popular* ~ weit verbreiteter Irrtum; **2.** Unlogik *f*; **3.** Täuschung *f*.

fall·en ['fɔːlən] **I** *p.p. von fall*; **II** *adj. allg.* gefallen: a) gestürzt (*a. fig.*), b) entehrt (*Frau*), c) (*im Krieg*) getötet, d) erobert (*Stadt etc.*): ~ *angel* gefallener Engel; **III** *s. coll. the* ~ die Gefallenen *pl.*; ~ **arch·es** *s. pl.* Senkfüße *pl.*

fall guy *s. Am.* F **1.** a) Opfer *n* (*e-s Betrügers*), b) ,Gimpel' *m*; **2.** Sündenbock *m*.

fal·li·bil·i·ty [,fælə'bɪlətɪ] *s.* Fehlbarkeit *f*; **fal·li·ble** ['fæləbl] *adj.* □ fehlbar.

,**fall·ing|-a·way** , ~-'off ['fɔːlɪŋ] *s.* Rückgang *m*, Abnahme *f*, Sinken *n*; ~ **sickness** *s.* ☞ Fallsucht *f*; ~ **star** *s.* Sternschnuppe *f*.

Fal·lo·pi·an tubes [fə'ləʊpɪən] *s. pl. anat.* Eileiter *pl.*

'fall·out *s.* **1.** *phys.* radioak'tiver Niederschlag, Fall-'out *m*: ~ *shelter* 'Strahlenschutzraum *m*; **2.** *fig.* a) 'Nebenpro-,dukt *n*, b) (böse) Auswirkung(en *pl.*).

fal·low¹ ['fæləʊ] **I** *adj.* brach(liegend): *lie* ~ brachliegen; **II** *s.* Brache *f*: a) Brachfeld *n*, b) Brachliegen *n*.

fal·low² ['fæləʊ] *adj.* falb, fahl, braungelb; ~ **deer** [-ləʊd-] *s. zo.* Damhirsch *m*, -wild *n*.

false [fɔːls] **I** *adj.* □ *allg.* falsch: a) unrichtig, fehlerhaft, irrig, b) unwahr, c) (*to*) treulos (gegen), untreu (*dat.*), d) irreführend, vorgetäuscht, trügerisch, 'hinterhältig, e) gefälscht, unecht, künstlich, f) Schein..., fälschlich (so genannt), g) 'widerrechtlich, rechtswidrig: ~ *alarm* blinder Alarm (*a. fig.*); ~ *ceiling* △ Zwischendecke *f*; ~ *coin* Falschgeld *n*; ~ *hair* falsche Haare; ~ *imprisonment* ↯ Freiheitsberaubung *f*; ~ *key* Nachschlüssel *m*; ~ *pregnancy* ☞ Scheinschwangerschaft *f*; ~ *shame* falsche Scham; ~ *start* Fehlstart *m*; ~ *step* Fehltritt *m*; ~ *tears* Krokodilstränen; ~ *teeth* falsche Zähne; **II** *adv.*

falsch, unaufrichtig: *play s.o.* ~ ein falsches Spiel mit j-m treiben; **,false--'heart·ed** *adj.* falsch, treulos; **'false-hood** [-hʊd] *s.* **1.** Unwahrheit *f*, Lüge *f*; **2.** Falschheit *f*; **'false·ness** [-nɪs] *s. allg.* Falschheit *f.*

fal·set·to [fɔːl'setəʊ] *pl.* **-tos** *s.* Fistelstimme *f*, ♪ *a.* Fal'sett(stimme *f*) *n.*

fal·sies ['fɔːlsɪz] *s. pl.* F Schaumgummieinlagen *pl.* (*im Büstenhalter*).

fal·si·fi·ca·tion [,fɔːlsɪfɪ'keɪʃn] *s.* (Ver-)Fälschung *f*; **fal·si·fi·er** ['fɔːlsɪfaɪə] *s.* Fälscher(in); **fal·si·fy** ['fɔːlsɪfaɪ] *v/t.* **1.** fälschen; **2.** verfälschen, falsch *od.* irreführend darstellen; **3.** *Hoffnungen* enttäuschen; **fal·si·ty** ['fɔːlsɪtɪ] *s.* **1.** Irrtum *m*, Unrichtigkeit *f*; **2.** Lüge *f*, Unwahrheit *f.*

falt·boat ['fɔːltbəʊt] *s.* Faltboot *n.*

fal·ter ['fɔːltə] **I** *v/i.* schwanken: a) taumeln, b) zögern, zaudern, c) stocken (*a. Stimme*): *his courage ~ed* der Mut verließ ihn; **II** *v/t. et.* stammeln; **'fal·ter·ing** [-tərɪŋ] *adj.* □ *allg.* schwankend (→ *falter* I).

fame [feɪm] *s.* **1.** Ruhm *m*, (guter) Ruf, Berühmtheit *f*: *of ill ~* berüchtigt; *house of ill ~* Freudenhaus *n*; **2.** *obs.* Gerücht *n*; **famed** [-md] *adj.* berühmt, bekannt (*for wegen gen.*, für).

fa·mil·iar [fə'mɪljə] **I** *adj.* □ **1.** vertraut: a) gewohnt: *a ~ sight*, b) bekannt: *a ~ face*, c) geläufig: *a ~ expression*; *~ quotations* geflügelte Worte; **2.** vertraut, bekannt (*with* mit): *be ~ with a. et.* gut kennen; *make o.s. ~ with* a) sich mit j-m bekannt machen, b) sich mit *et.* vertraut machen; *the name is ~ to me* der Name ist mir vertraut; **3.** vertraut, in'tim, eng: *a ~ friend*; *be on ~ terms with s.o.* mit j-m gut bekannt sein; (*too*) *~ contp.* allzu familiär, plumpvertraulich; **4.** ungezwungen, famili'är; **II** *s.* **5.** Vertraute(r *m*) *f*; **6.** *a. ~ spirit* Schutzgeist *m*; **fa·mil·i·ar·i·ty** [fə,mɪlɪ'ærətɪ] *s.* **1.** Vertrautheit *f*, Bekanntschaft *f* (*with* mit); **2.** a) famili'ärer Ton, Ungezwungenheit *f*, Vertraulichkeit *f*, b) *contp.* plumpe Vertraulichkeit; **fa·mil·iar·i·za·tion** [fə,mɪljərar'zeɪʃn] *s.* (*with*) Vertrautmachen *n od.* -werden *n* (mit), Gewöhnung *f* (an *acc.*); **fa·mil·iar·ize** [-əraɪz] *v/t.* (*with*) vertraut *od.* bekannt machen (mit), gewöhnen (an *acc.*).

fam·i·ly ['fæməlɪ] **I** *s.* **1.** Fa'milie *f* (*a. biol. u. fig.*): *~ of nations* Völkerfamilie; *she was living as one of the ~* sie gehörte zur Familie, sie hatte Familienanschluss; **2.** Fa'milie *f*: a) Geschlecht *n*, Sippe *f*, *a.* Verwandtschaft *f*, b) Ab-, Herkunft *f*: *of (good) ~* aus gutem *od.* vornehmem Hause; **3.** *ling.* (Sprach-)Fa,milie *f*; **4.** ♣ Schar *f*; **II** *adj.* **5.** Familien...: *~ business* (*tradition etc.*); *~ doctor* Hausarzt *m*; *~ environment* häusliches Milieu; *~ warmth* Nestwärme *f*; *in a ~ way* zwanglos; *be in the ~ way* F in anderen Umständen sein; *~ al·low·ance s.* Kindergeld *n*; *~ cir·cle s.* **1.** Fa'milienkreis *m*; **2.** *thea. Am.* oberer Rang; *~ court s.* ♈ Fa'miliengericht *n*; *~ man s.* [*irr.*] **1.** Mann *m* mit Fa'milie, Fa'milienvater *m*; **2.** häuslicher Mensch; *~ plan·ning s.* Fa'milienplanung *f*; *'~,size pack·age s.* Haushaltspackung *f*; *~ skel·e·ton s.* streng gehütetes Fa'miliengeheimnis; *~ tree s.* Stammbaum *m.*

fam·ine ['fæmɪn] *s.* **1.** Hungersnot *f*; **2.** Mangel *m*, Knappheit *f* (*of an dat.*); **3.** Hunger *m* (*a. fig.*).

fam·ish ['fæmɪʃ] **I** *v/i.* **1.** *obs.* verhungern: *be ~ing* F am Verhungern sein; **2.** darben; **II** *v/t. obs.* verhungern lassen: *he ate as if ~ed* er aß, als ob er am Verhungern wäre.

fa·mous ['feɪməs] *adj.* □ **1.** berühmt (*for* wegen *gen.*, für); **2.** F fa'mos, ausgezeichnet, prima.

fan¹ [fæn] **I** *s.* **1.** Fächer *m*: *~ dance*; *~ aerial* ⚡ Fächerantenne *f*; *~-fold paper* Endlospapier, EDV-Papier *n*; **2.** ⚙ a) Venti'lator *m*, Lüfter *m*, b) *a. blower* (Flügelrad)Gebläse *n*, c) ⚡ (Worfel)Schwinge *f*, d) ⚓ Flügel *m*, Schraubenblatt *n*; **II** *v/t.* **3.** *Luft* fächeln; **4.** um'fächeln, *j-m* Luft zufächeln; **5.** *Feuer* anfachen: *~ the flame fig.* Öl ins Feuer gießen; **6.** *fig.* entfachen; (an)wedeln; **7.** ⚡ worfeln, schwingen; **III** *v/i.* **8.** *oft ~ out* a) sich (fächerförmig) ausbreiten, b) ✕ ausschwärmen.

fan² [fæn] *s.* F Fan *m*, begeisterter Anhänger: *~ club* Fanklub *m*; *~ mail* Verehrerpost *f.*

fa·nat·ic [fə'nætɪk] **I** *s.* Fa'natiker(in); **II** *adj.* → **fa'nat·i·cal** [-kl] *adj.* □ fa'natisch; **fa'nat·i·cism** [-ɪsɪzəm] *s.* Fana'tismus *m.*

fan·ci·er ['fænsɪə] *s.* (*Tier-, Blumenetc.*)Liebhaber(in) *od.* Züchter(in); **'fan·ci·ful** [-ɪfʊl] *adj.* □ **1.** (allzu) fanta'siereich, schrullig, wunderlich (*Person*); **2.** bi'zarr, ausgefallen (*Sache*); **3.** eingebildet, unwirklich; **4.** fan'tastisch, wirklichkeitsfremd.

fan·cy ['fænsɪ] **I** *s.* **1.** Fanta'sie *f*: a) Einbildungskraft *f*, b) Fanta'sievorstellung *f*, c) (bloße) Einbildung; **2.** I'dee *f*, plötzlicher Einfall *m*: *I have a ~ that* ich habe so e-e Idee, dass; **3.** Laune *f*, Grille *f*; **4.** (individu'eller) Geschmack; **5.** (*for*) Neigung *f* (zu), Vorliebe *f* (für), Gefallen *n* (an *dat.*): *have a ~ for* gern haben (wollen) (*acc.*), Lust haben zu *od.* auf (*acc.*); *take a ~ to* Gefallen finden an (*dat.*), sympathisch finden (*acc.*); *take (a fancy) catch) s.o.'s* j-m gefallen; *just as the ~ takes you* nach Lust u. Laune; **6.** *coll. the ~* die (*Sport-, Tier- etc.*)Liebhaberwelt; **II** *adj.* **7.** Fantasie..., fan'tastisch: *~ name* Fantasiename *m*; *~ price* Fantasie-, Liebhaberpreis *m*; **8.** Mode...: *~ article*; **9.** (reich) verziert, bunt, kunstvoll, ausgefallen, extrafein: *~ cakes* feines Gebäck; *~ car* schicker Wagen; *~ dog* Hund *m* aus e-r Liebhaberzucht; *~ foods* Delikatessen; *~ words contp.* geschwollene Ausdrücke; **III** *v/t.* **10.** sich *j-n od. et.* vorstellen: *~ (that)!* a) stell dir vor!, b) sieh mal einer an!, nanu!; *~ meeting you here!* nanu, du hier?; **11.** glauben, denken, annehmen; **12.** *~ o.s.* sich einbilden (*to be* zu sein), sich halten für: *~ o.s. (very important)* sehr wichtig vorkommen; **13.** gern haben *od.* mögen: *I don't ~ this suit* dieser Anzug gefällt mir nicht; **14.** Lust haben (auf *acc.*; *doing* zu tun): *I could ~ an ice cream* ich hätte Lust auf ein Eis; **15.** *~ up Am.* F aufputzen, ,Pfiff geben' (*dat.*); *~ ball s.* Ko'stümfest *n*, Maskenball *m*; *~ dress s.* ('Masken-)Ko,stüm *n*, Maskenanzug *m*: *~ fancy ball*; *,~-'free adj.* frei u. ungebunden; *~ goods s. pl.* **1.** 'Modear,tikel *pl.*; **2.** kleine Ge'schenkar,tikel *pl.*, *a.* Nippes *pl.*; *~ man s.* [*irr.*] *sl.* **1.** ,Louis' *m*, Zuhälter *m*; **2.** Liebhaber *m*; *~ pants s. Am. sl.* **1.** ,feiner Pinkel'; **2.** ,Waschlappen' *m*; *~ wom·an s.* [*irr.*] **1.** Geliebte *f*; **2.** Prostituierte *f*; *'~-work s.* feine (Hand-) Arbeit.

fan·dan·gle [fæn'dæŋl] *s.* F ,Firlefanz' *m.*

fane [feɪn] *s. poet.* Tempel *m.*

fan·fare ['fænfeə] *s.* ♪ Fan'fare *f*, Tusch *m*: *with much ~ fig.* mit großem Tamtam.

fang [fæŋ] *s.* **1.** *zo.* a) Fang(zahn) *m* (*Raubtier*), b) Hauer *m* (*Eber*), c) Giftzahn *m* (*Schlange*); **2.** *pl.* F Zähne *pl.*, ,Beißer' *pl.*; **3.** *anat.* Zahnwurzel *f*; **4.** ⚙ Dorn *m.*

fan| heat·er *s.* Heizlüfter *m*; **'~-light** *s.* △ (fächerförmiges) (Tür)Fenster, Oberlicht *n.*

fan·ner ['fænə] *s.* ⚙ Gebläse *n.*

fan·ny ['fænɪ] *s.* **1.** *Am. sl.* ,Arsch' *m*; **2.** *Brit.* V ,Möse' *f.*

fan ov·en ['ʌvn] *s.* Heißluftherd *m.*

fan·ta·sia [fæn'teɪzjə] *s.* ♪ Fanta'sia *f*; **fan·ta·size** ['fæntəsaɪz] *v/i.* **1.** fantasieren (*about* von); **2.** (mit offenen Augen) träumen; **fan·tas·tic** [-'tæstɪk] *adj.* (□ *~ally*) *allg.* fan'tastisch: a) unwirklich, b) verstiegen, über'spannt, c) ab'surd, aus der Luft gegriffen, d) F ,toll', sagenhaft; **fan·ta·sy** ['fæntəsɪ] *s.* **1.** Fanta'sie *f*: a) Einbildungskraft *f*, b) Fanta'sievorstellung *f*, c) (Tag-, Wach)Traum *m*, d) Hirngespinst *n*; **2.** ♪ Fanta'sia *f.*

fan| trac·er·y *s.* △ Fächermaßwerk *n*; *~ vault·ing s.* △ Fächergewölbe *n.*

fan·zine ['fænziːn] *s.* 'Fanmaga,zin *n* (*Zeitschrift*).

far [fɑː] **I** *adj.* **1.** fern, (weit) entfernt, weit; **2.** (*vom Sprecher aus*) entfernter: *at the ~ end* am anderen Ende; **3.** weit vorgerückt, fortgeschritten (*in* in *dat.*); **II** *adv.* **4.** weit, fern: *~ away*, *~ off* weit weg, weit entfernt; *from ~* von weit her; *~ and near* nah u. fern, überall; *~ and wide* weit und breit; *~ and away the best* a) bei weitem *od.* mit Abstand das Beste, b) bei weitem am besten; *as ~ as* a) so weit *od.* so viel (wie), insofern als, b) bis (nach); *as ~ as that goes* was das betrifft; *as ~ back as 1907* schon (im Jahre) 1907; *in as (od. so) as* insofern als; *so ~* bisher, bis jetzt; *so ~ so good* so weit, so gut; *~ from* weit entfernt von, keineswegs; *~ from completed* noch lange *od.* längst nicht fertig; *~ from rich* alles andere als reich; *~ from it!* keineswegs!, ganz u. gar nicht!; *I am ~ from believing it* ich bin weit davon entfernt, es zu glauben; *~ into* bis weit *od.* hoch *od.* tief in (*acc.*); *~ into the night* bis spät *od.* tief in die Nacht; *~ out* a) weit draußen *od.* hinaus, b) F ,toll'; *be ~ out* weit danebenliegen (*mit e-r Vermutung etc.*); *~ up* hoch oben; *~ be it from me (to inf.)* es liegt mir fern (zu *inf.*); *go ~* a) weit *od.* lange (aus)reichen, b) es weit bringen; *ten dollars don't go ~* mit 10 Dollar kommt man nicht weit; *go too ~ fig.* zu weit gehen; *that went ~ to convince me* das hat mich beinahe überzeugt; *I will go so ~ as to say* ich will sogar behaupten; **5.** *a. by ~* weit(aus), bei weitem, sehr viel, ganz: *~ better* viel besser; *(by) ~ the best* a) weitaus der (die, das) Beste, b) bei weitem am besten.

far·ad ['færəd] *s.* ⚡ Fa'rad *n.*

'far·a·way *adj.* **1.** → *far* 1; **2.** *fig.* verträumt, versonnen, (geistes)abwesend.

farce [fɑːs] *s.* **1.** *thea.* Posse *f*, Schwank *m*; **2.** *fig.* Farce *f*, ,The'ater' *n*; **'far·ci·cal** [-sɪkl] *adj.* □ **1.** possenhaft, Possen...; **2.** *fig.* ab'surd.

fare [feə] **I** *s.* **1.** a) Fahrpreis *m*, -geld *n*, b) Flugpreis *m*: *what's the ~?* was kostet die Fahrt *od.* der Flug?; *~ stage*

Brit. Fahrpreiszone *f*, Teilstrecke *f* (*Bus etc.*); *any more ~s?* noch jemand zugestiegen?; **2.** Fahrgast *m* (*bsd. e-s Taxis*); **3.** Kost *f* (*a. fig.*), Verpflegung *f*, Nahrung *f*: *slender ~* magere Kost; *literary ~* literarische Kost, geistiges ‚Menü‘; **II** *v/i.* **4.** sich befinden: (er)gehen: *how did you ~?* wie ist es dir ergangen?; *he ~d ill, it ~d ill with him* er war schlecht d(a)ran; *we ~d no better* uns ist es nicht besser ergangen; *~ alike* in der gleichen Lage sein; **5.** *poet.* reisen, sich aufmachen: *~ thee well!* leb wohl!

Far East *s.: the ~* der Ferne Osten.

ˌfareˈwell **I** *int.* lebe(n Sie) wohl!, lebt wohl!; **II** *s.* Lebeˈwohl *n*, Abschiedsgruß *m*: *bid s.o. ~* j-m Lebewohl sagen; *make one's ~s* sich verabschieden; *take one's ~ of* Abschied nehmen von (*a. fig.*); *~ to* adieu ..., nie wieder ...; **III** *adj.* Abschieds...

ˌfar-ˈfamed *adj.* ‘weithin berühmt; ˌ~-ˈfetched *adj. fig.* weit hergeholt, an den Haaren her'beigezogen; ˌ~-ˈflung *adj.* **1.** weit (ausgedehnt); **2.** *fig.* weit gespannt; **3.** weit entfernt; ˌ~-ˈgo·ing → *far-reaching*.

fa·ri·na [fəˈraɪnə] *s.* **1.** (feines) Mehl; **2.** 🌱 Stärke *f*; **3.** *Brit.* 🌱 Blütenstaub *m*; **4.** *zo.* Staub *m*; far·i·na·ceous [ˌfærɪˈneɪʃəs] *adj.* Mehl..., Stärke...

farm [fɑːm] **I** *s.* **1.** (Bauern)Hof *m*, landwirtschaftlicher Betrieb, Gut(shof *m*) *n*, Farm *f*; **2.** (*Geflügel- etc.*)Farm *f*; **3.** *obs.* Bauernhaus *n*; **4.** *bsd. Am.* a) Sa-na'torium *n*, b) Entziehungsanstalt *f*; **II** *v/t.* **5.** *Land* bebauen, bewirtschaften; **6.** *Geflügel etc.* züchten; **7.** pachten; **8.** *oft ~ out* verpachten, in Pacht geben (*to. s.o.* j-m *od.* an j-n); **9.** *mst ~ out* a) *Kinder* in Pflege geben, b) ♀ *Arbeit* vergeben (*to* an *acc.*); **III** *v/i.* **10.** Landwirt sein; **farm·er** [-mə] *s.* **1.** (Groß-) Bauer *m*, Landwirt *m*, Farmer *m*; **2.** Pächter *m*; **3.** (*Geflügel- etc.*)Züchter *m*.

farm⎪ hand *s.* Landarbeiter(in); '~-house *s.* Bauern-, Gutshaus *n*: *~ bread* Landbrot *n*; *~ butter* Landbutter *f*.

farm·ing [ˈfɑːmɪŋ] *s.* **1.** Landwirtschaft *f*; **2.** (*Geflügel- etc.*)Zucht *f*.

farm⎪ la·bo(u)r·er → *farm hand*; *~* land *s.* Ackerland *n*; '~-stead *s.* Bauernhof *m*, Gehöft *n*; *~ work·er* → *farm hand*; '~-yard *s.* Wirtschaftshof *m* (e-s Bauernhofs).

far·o [ˈfeərəʊ] *s.* Phar(a)o *n* (*Kartenglücksspiel*).

far-off [ˌfɑːrˈɒf] → *far* 1, *faraway* 2.

far-out [ˌfɑːrˈaʊt] *adj. sl.* **1.** ‚toll‘, ‚super‘; **2.** ‚verrückt‘.

far·ra·go [fəˈrɑːɡəʊ] *pl.* -gos, *Am.* -goes *s.* Kunterbunt *n* (*of* aus, von).

ˌfar-ˈreach·ing *adj.* **1.** *bsd. fig.* weit reichend; **2.** *fig.* folgenschwer, tief greifend.

far·ri·er [ˈfærɪə] *s.* Hufschmied *m*; ✗ Beschlagmeister *m*.

far·row [ˈfærəʊ] **I** *s.* Wurf *m* Ferkel: *with ~* trächtig (*Sau*) **II** *v/i.* ferkeln; **III** *v/t.* Ferkel werfen.

ˌfar-ˈsee·ing *adj. fig.* weit blickend; ˌ~-ˈsight·ed *adj.* **1.** *fig.* → *far-seeing*; **2.** 🌱 weitsichtig; ˌ~-ˈsight·ed·ness *s.* **1.** *fig.* Weitblick *m*, ‘Umsicht *f*; **2.** 🌱 Weitsichtigkeit *f*.

fart [fɑːt] V **I** *s.* Furz *m*; **II** *v/i.* furzen: *~ around fig.* herumalbern, -blödeln.

far·ther [ˈfɑːðə] **I** *adj.* **1.** *comp. von far*; **2.** → *further* 3, 4; **3.** entfernter (*vom Sprecher aus*): *the ~ shore* das gegenüberliegende Ufer; *at the ~ end* am

anderen Ende; **II** *adv.* **4.** weiter: *so far and no ~* bis hierher u. nicht weiter; **5.** → *further* 1, 2; 'far·ther·most → *farthest* 2; 'far·thest [-ðɪst] **I** *adj.* **1.** *sup.* von *far*; **2.** entferntest, weitest; **II** *adv.* **3.** am weitesten, am entferntesten.

far·thing [ˈfɑːðɪŋ] *s. Brit. hist.* Farthing *m* (¼ Penny): *not worth a* (*brass*) *~ fig.* keinen (roten) Heller wert; *it doesn't matter a ~* das macht gar nichts.

Far West *s. Am.* Gebiet der Rocky Mountains u. der pazifischen Küste.

fas·ci·a [ˈfeɪʃə] *pl.* -ae [-ʃiː] *s.* **1.** Binde *f*, (Quer)Band *n*; **2.** *zo.* Farbstreifen *m*; **3.** [ˈfæʃɪə] *anat.* Muskelhaut *f*; **4.** △ a) Gurtsims *m*, b) Bund *m* (*von Säulenschäften*); **5.** ⚙ (Bauch- *etc.*)Binde *f*; **6.** → *facia*.

fas·ci·cle [ˈfæsɪkl] *s.* **1.** a. 🌱 Bündel *n*, Büschel *n*; **2.** Fas'zikel *m*: a) (Teil)Lieferung *f*, Einzelheft *n* (*Buch*), b) Aktenbündel *n*; fas·cic·u·lar [fəˈsɪkjʊlə], fas·cic·u·late [fəˈsɪkjʊlət] *adj.* büschelförmig.

fas·ci·nate [ˈfæsɪneɪt] *v/t.* **1.** faszinieren: a) bezaubern, b) fesseln, packen, gefangen nehmen: *~d* fasziniert, (wie) gebannt; **2.** hypnotisieren; 'fas·ci·nat·ing [-tɪŋ] *adj.* ☐ faszinierend: a) hinreißend, b) fesselnd, spannend; fas·ci·na·tion [ˌfæsɪˈneɪʃn] *s.* **1.** Faszinati'on *f*, Bezauberung *f*; **2.** Zauber *m*, Reiz *m*.

Fas·cism [ˈfæʃɪzəm] *s. pol.* Fa'schismus *m*; 'Fas·cist [-ɪst] **I** *s.* Fa'schist *m*; **II** *adj.* fa'schistisch.

fash·ion [ˈfæʃn] **I** *s.* **1.** Mode *f*: *come into ~* in Mode kommen; *set the ~* die Mode diktieren, *fig.* den Ton angeben; *it is* (*all*) *the ~* es ist (große) Mode; *in the English ~* nach englischer Mode (*od.* Art, → 2); *out of ~* aus der Mode, unmodern; *~ designer* Modedesigner(in); **2.** Sitte *f*, Brauch *m*, Art *f* (u. Weise *f*), Stil *m*, Ma'nier *f*: *behave in a strange ~* sich sonderbar benehmen; *after their ~* nach ihrer Weise; *after* (*od. in*) *a ~* schlecht u. recht, ‚so lala‘; *an artist after a ~* so etwas wie ein Künstler; **3.** (feine) Lebensart, gute Ma'nieren *pl.: a man of ~;* **4.** Machart *f*, Form *f* (Zu)Schnitt *m*, Fas'son *f*; **II** *v/t.* **5.** herstellen, machen; **6.** bilden, formen, gestalten; **7.** anpassen; **III** *adv.* **8.** wie: *horse-~* nach Pferdeart, wie ein Pferd; fash·ion·a·ble [ˈfæʃnəbl] **I** *adj.* ☐ **1.** modisch, mo'dern; **2.** vornehm, ele'gant; **3.** in Mode, Mode...: *~ complaint* Modekrankheit *f*; **II** *s.* **4.** *the ~s* die elegante Welt, die Schickeria.

'fash·ion⎪ mag·a·zine *s.* 'Modejour,nal *n*; '~,mon·ger *s.* Modenarr *m*; *~* parade *s.* Mode(n)schau *f*; *~ plate s.* **1.** Modebild *n*, -blatt *n*; **2.** F ‚'superelegante‘ Per'son; *~ show s.* Mode(n)schau *f*.

fast¹ [fɑːst] **I** *adj.* **1.** schnell, geschwind, rasch: *~ train* Schnell-, D-Zug *m*; *my watch is ~* m-e Uhr geht vor: *pull a ~ one on s.o.* sl. j-n ‚reinlegen‘; **2.** ‚schnell‘ (*hohe Geschwindigkeit gestattend*): *~ road;* *~ tennis court;* *~ lane mot.* Überholspur *f*; **3.** *phot.* lichtstark; **4.** flott, leichtlebig; **II** *adv.* **5.** schnell: *~ and furious* Schlag auf Schlag; **6.** häufig, reichlich, stark; **7.** leichtsinnig: *live ~* ein flottes Leben führen.

fast² [fɑːst] **I** *adj.* **1.** fest(gemacht), befestigt, unbeweglich; fest zs.-haltend: *make ~* festmachen, befestigen, *Tür* (fest) verschließen; *~ friend* treuer Freund; **2.** beständig, haltbar: *~ col-o(u)r* (wasch)echte Farbe; *~ to light*

lichtecht; **II** *adv.* **3.** fest, sicher: *be ~ asleep* fest schlafen; *stuck ~* festgefahren; *play ~ and loose* Schindluder treiben (*with* mit).

fast³ [fɑːst] *bsd. eccl.* **I** *v/i.* **1.** fasten; **II** *s.* **2.** Fasten *n*: *break one's ~* das Fasten brechen, *a.* frühstücken; **3.** Fastenzeit *f*.

'fast⎪-back *s. mot.* (Wagen *m* mit) Fließheck *n*; *~* breed·er (re·ac·tor) *s. phys.* schneller Brüter.

fas·ten [ˈfɑːsn] **I** *v/t.* **1.** befestigen, festmachen, -binden (*to, on* an *dat.*); **2.** a. *~ up* (fest) zumachen, (ver-, ab)schließen, zuknöpfen, ver-, zuschnüren; zs.-fügen, verbinden: *~ with nails* zunageln; *~ down* a) befestigen, b) F j-n ‚festnageln‘ (*to* auf *acc.*); **3.** *Augen* heften, *a. s-e Aufmerksamkeit* richten (*on* auf *acc.*); **4.** *~* (*up*)*on fig.* a) j-m e-n *Spitznamen* ‚anhängen‘, geben, b) j-m *et.* ‚anhängen‘ *od.* ‚in die Schuhe schieben‘; **II** *v/i.* **5.** sich schließen *od.* festmachen lassen; **6.** *~* (*up*)*on* a) sich heften *od.* klammern an (*acc.*), b) *fig.* sich stürzen auf (*acc.*), ‚einhaken‘ bei, aufs Korn nehmen (*acc.*); 'fas·ten·er [-nə] *s.* Befestigung(smittel *n*, -vorrichtung *f*) *f*, Verschluss *m*, Halter *m*, Druckknopf *m*; 'fas·ten·ing [-nɪŋ] *s.* **1.** → *fastener;* **2.** Befestigung *f*, Sicherung *f*, Halterung *f*.

fast food [ˌfɑːstˈfuːd] *s.* Fast Food *f*; 'fast-food res·tau·rant *s.* Schnellimbiss *m*, -gaststätte *f*.

fas·tid·i·ous [fæsˈtɪdɪəs] *adj.* ☐ anspruchsvoll, heikel, wählerisch; fas·tid·i·ous·ness [-nɪs] *s.* anspruchsvolles Wesen.

fast·ing cure [ˈfɑːstɪŋ] *s.* Fasten-, Hungerkur *f*.

'fast-mov·ing *adj.* **1.** schnell; **2.** *fig.* tempogeladen, spannend.

fast·ness¹ [ˈfɑːstnɪs] *s.* **1.** *obs.* Schnelligkeit *f*; **2.** *fig.* Leichtlebigkeit *f*.

fast·ness² [ˈfɑːstnɪs] *s.* **1.** Feste *f*, Festung *f*; **2.** Zufluchtsort *m*; **3.** ‘Widerstandsfähigkeit *f*, Beständigkeit *f* (*to* gegen), Echtheit *f* (*von Farben*): *~ to light* Lichtechtheit *f*.

fast-sell·ing *adj.* gut gehend.

'fast-talk *v/t.* F j-n beschwatzen (*into doing s.th.* et. zu tun).

fat [fæt] **I** *adj.* ☐ → *fatly*; **1.** dick, beleibt, fett, feist: *~ stock* Mastvieh *n*; *~ type typ.* Fettdruck *m*; **2.** fett, fetthaltig, fettig, ölig: *~ coal* Fettkohle *f*; **3.** *fig.* ‚dick‘: *~ bank account;* *~ purse;* **4.** *fig.* fett, einträglich: *a ~ job* ein lukrativer Posten; *~ soil* fetter *od.* fruchtbarer Boden; *a ~ lot it helps! sl. iro.* das hilft mir (uns) herzlich wenig; *a ~ chance sl.* herzlich wenig Aussicht (-en); **II** *s.* **5.** a. 🐄, *biol.* Fett *n*: *run to ~* Fett ansetzen; *the ~ is in the fire* der Teufel ist los; **6.** *the ~* das Beste: *live on* (*od. off*) *the ~ of the land* in Saus u. Braus leben; **III** *v/t.* **7.** a. *~ up* mästen: *kill the ~ted calf* a) *bibl.* das gemästete Kalb schlachten, b) ein Willkommensfest geben.

fa·tal [ˈfeɪtl] *adj.* ☐ **1.** tödlich, todbringend, mit tödlichem Ausgang: *a ~ ac·cident* ein tödlicher Unfall; **2.** unheilvoll, verhängnisvoll (*to* für): *~ mistake;* **3.** schicksalhaft, entscheidend; **4.** Schicksals...: *~ thread* Lebensfaden *m*; 'fa·tal·ism [-təlɪzəm] *s.* Fata'lismus *m*; 'fa·tal·ist [-təlɪst] *s.* Fata'list *m*; fa·tal·is·tic [ˌfeɪtəˈlɪstɪk] *adj.* (☐ ~ally) fata'listisch.

fa·tal·i·ty [fəˈtælətɪ] *s.* **1.** Verhängnis *n*, Unglück *n*; **2.** Schicksalhaftigkeit *f*; **3.**

tödlicher Ausgang *od.* Verlauf; **4.** Todesfall *m*, -opfer *n*.

fa·ta mor·ga·na [ˌfɑːtəmɔːˈgɑːnə] *s.* Fata Morˈgana *f*.

fat cat [ˌfætˈkæt] *s. contp.* F ‚Geldsack‘ (*Reicher*); '**fat-cat** *adj. contp.* F ‚stinkreich‘.

fate [feɪt] *s.* **1.** Schicksal *n*, Geschick *n*, Los *n*: *he met his ~* das Schicksal ereilte ihn; *he met his ~ calmly* er sah s-m Schicksal ruhig entgegen; *seal s.o.'s ~* j-s Schicksal besiegeln; **2.** Verhängnis *n*, Verderben *n*, 'Untergang *m*: *go to one's ~* den Tod finden; **3.** Schicksalsgöttin *f*: *the ⚮s* die Parzen; '**fat·ed** [-tɪd] *adj.* **1.** vom Schicksal (dazu) bestimmt: *they were ~ to meet* es war ihnen bestimmt, sich zu begegnen; **2.** dem 'Untergang geweiht; '**fate·ful** [-fʊl] *adj.* □ **1.** schicksalhaft; **2.** verhängnisvoll; **3.** schicksalsschwer.

'**fat⎮·head** *s.* F ‚Blödmann‘ *m*; '**~-ˌhead·ed** *adj.* dämlich, doof.

fa·ther [ˈfɑːðə] I *s.* **1.** Vater *m*: *like ~ like son* der Apfel fällt nicht weit vom Stamm; *⚮ Time* Chronos *m*, die Zeit; *⚮* (Gott)Vater *m*; **3.** *eccl.* a) Pastor *m*, b) *R.C.* Pater *m*, c) *R.C.* Vater *m* (*Bischof, Abt*): *the Holy ⚮* der Heilige Vater; *~ confessor* Beichtvater; *⚮ of the Church* Kirchenvater; **4.** *mst pl.* Ahn *m*, Vorfahr *m*: *be gathered to one's ~s* zu s-n Vätern versammelt werden; **5.** *fig.* Vater *m*, Urheber *m*: *the ~ of chemistry*; *⚮ of the House Brit.* dienstältestes Parlamentsmitglied; *the wish was ~ to the thought* der Wunsch war der Vater des Gedankens; **6.** *pl.* Stadt-, Landesväter *pl.*: *the ⚮s of the Constitution* die Gründer der USA; **7.** väterlicher Freund (*to gen.*); II *v/t.* **8.** *Kind* zeugen; **9.** *et.* ins Leben rufen, her'vorbringen; **10.** wie ein Vater sein zu *j-m*; **11.** die Vaterschaft (*gen.*) anerkennen; **12.** *fig.* a) die Urheberschaft (*gen.*) anerkennen, b) die Urheberschaft (*gen.*) *od.* die Schuld für *et.* zuschreiben (*on, upon dat.*); *⚮ Christ·mas s. Brit.* Weihnachtsmann *m*; **~ fig·ure** *s. psych.* ˈVaterfiˌgur *f*.

fa·ther·hood [ˈfɑːðəhʊd] *s.* Vaterschaft *f*; '**fa·ther-in-law** [-ərɪn-] *s.* Schwiegervater *m*; '**fa·ther·land** *s.* Vaterland *n*: *the ⚮* Deutschland *n*; '**fa·ther·less** [-lɪs] *adj.* vaterlos; '**fa·ther·li·ness** [-lɪnɪs] *s.* Väterlichkeit *f*; '**fa·ther·ly** [-lɪ] *adj. u. adv.* väterlich.

fath·om [ˈfæðəm] *s.* **1.** a) ⚓ Faden *m* (*Tiefenmaß: 1,83 m*), b) *obs. u. fig.* Klafter *m*, *n*, c) ⚒ *Raummaß* (= 1,17 m³); II *v/t.* **2.** ⚓ (aus)loten (*a. fig.*); **3.** *fig.* ergründen; '**fath·om·less** [-lɪs] *adj.* □ unergründlich (*a. fig.*); '**fath·om line** *s.* ⚓ Lotleine *f*.

fa·tigue [fəˈtiːg] I *s.* **1.** Ermüdung *f* (*a.* ⚙), Erschöpfung *f* (*a.* ✦ *des Bodens*): *~ strength* ⚙ Dauerfestigkeit *f*; *~ test* ⚙ Ermüdungsprobe *f*; **2.** schwere Arbeit, Mühsal *f*, Straˈpaze *f*; **3.** ✕ a) *a. ~ duty* Arbeitsdienst *m*: *~ detail*, *~ party* Arbeitskommando *n*, b) *pl. a. ~ clothes*, *~ dress* Arbeits-, Drillichanzug *m*; II *v/t. u. v/i.* **4.** ermüden (*a.* ⚙); **fa·ti·guing** [-gɪŋ] *adj.* □ ermüdend, anstrengend.

fat·less [ˈfætlɪs] *adj.* ohne Fett, mager; '**fat·ling** [-lɪŋ] *s.* junges Masttier; '**fat·ly** [-lɪ] *adv. fig.* reichlich; '**fat·ness** [-nɪs] *s.* Fettheit *f*: a) Beleibtheit *f*, b) Fettigkeit *f*, Fetthaltigkeit *f*; '**fat·ten** [-tn] I *v/t.* **1.** fett *od.* dick machen: *~ing* dick machend; **2.** *Tier*, F *a. Person* mästen; **3.** *Land* düngen; II *v/i.* **4.** fett *od.* dick

werden; **5.** sich mästen (*on* von); '**fat·tish** [-tɪʃ] *adj.* etwas fett, dicklich; '**fat·ty** [-tɪ] I *adj. a.* 🐟, ⚛ fetthaltig, fettig, Fett...: *~ acid* Fettsäure *f*; *~ degeneration* Verfettung *f*; *~ heart* Herzverfettung; *~ tissue* Fettgewebe *n*; II *s.* F Dickerchen *n*.

fa·tu·i·ty [fəˈtjuːətɪ] *s.* Albernheit *f*; **fat·u·ous** [ˈfætjʊəs] *adj.* □ albern, dumm.

fau·cal [ˈfɔːkl] *adj.* Kehl..., Rachen...; **fau·ces** [ˈfɔːsiːz] *s. pl. mst sg. konstr. anat.* Rachen *m*.

fau·cet [ˈfɔːsɪt] *s.* ⊛ *Am.* a) (Wasser-)Hahn *m*, b) (Fass)Zapfen *m*.

faugh [fɔː] *int.* pfui!

fault [fɔːlt] I *s.* **1.** Schuld *f*, Verschulden *n*: *it is not his ~* er hat *od.* trägt *od.* ihn trifft keine Schuld, es ist nicht s-e Schuld; *be at ~* schuld(ig) sein, die Schuld tragen (→ 4a); **2.** Fehler *m*, (⚛ *a. Sach*)Mangel *m*: *find ~* nörgeln, kritteln; *find ~ with* et. auszusetzen haben an (*dat.*), herumnörgeln an (*dat.*); *to a ~* allzu(sehr), ein bisschen zu *ordnungsliebend etc.*; **3.** (Cha'rakter)Fehler *m*: *in spite of all his ~s*, et. a) Fehler *m*, Irrtum *m*: *be at ~* sich irren, *hunt. u. fig. a.* auf der falschen Fährte sein, b) Vergehen *n*, Fehltritt *m*; **5.** ⊛ De'fekt *m*: *a)* Fehler *m*, Störung *f*, b) ⚡ Erd-, Leitungsfehler *m*; **6.** *Tennis etc.*: Fehler *m*; **7.** *geol.* Verwerfung *f*; II *v/t.* **8.** et. was auszusetzen haben an (*dat.*): *he* (*it*) *can't be ~ed* an ihm (daran) ist nichts auszusetzen; **9.** *et.* ˌverpatzen‘; III *v/i.* **10.** e-n Fehler machen; '**~·find·er** *s.* Nörgler(in), Krittler(in); '**~·find·ing** I *s.* Kritte'lei *f*, Nörge'lei *f*; II *adj.* nörglerisch, kritt(e)lig.

fault·i·ness [ˈfɔːltɪnɪs] *s.* Fehlerhaftigkeit *f*; '**fault·less** [-tlɪs] *adj.* □ einwand-, fehlerfrei, untadelig; '**fault·less·ness** [-tlsnɪs] *s.* Fehler-, Tadellosigkeit *f*; '**fault·y** [-tɪ] *adj.* □ fehlerhaft, schlecht, ⊛ *a.* de'fekt: *~ design* Fehlkonstruktion *f*.

faun [fɔːn] *s. myth. u. fig.* Faun *m*.

fau·na [ˈfɔːnə] *s.* Fauna *f*, (*a.* Abhandlung *f* über e-e) Tierwelt *f*.

faux pas [ˌfəʊˈpɑː] *pl.* **pas** [pɑːz] *s.* Faux'pas *m*.

fa·vo(u)r [ˈfeɪvə] I *s.* **1.** Gunst *f*, Wohlwollen *n*: *be* (*od.* stand) *high in s.o.'s ~* bei j-m in besonderer Gunst stehen *od.* gut angeschrieben sein; *be in ~* (*with*) beliebt sein (bei), begehrt sein (von); *find ~* Gefallen *od.* Anklang finden; *find ~ with s.o.* (*od. in s.o.'s eyes*) Gnade vor j-s Augen finden, j-m gefallen; *grant s.o. a ~* j-m e-e Gunst gewähren; *grant s.o. one's ~s* j-m s-e Gunst gewähren (*Frau*); *by ~ of* a) mit gütiger Erlaubnis (*gen.*) von, b) überreicht von (*Brief*); *in ~ of* für, *a.* ✝ zugunsten von (*od. gen.*); *who is in ~ (of it)?* wer ist dafür?; *out of ~* a) in Ungnade (gefallen), b) nicht mehr gefragt *od.* beliebt; **2.** Gefallen *m*, Gefälligkeit *f*: *as a ~* aus Gefälligkeit; *by ~ of* mit gütiger Erlaubnis von, durch gütige Vermittlung von; *do me a ~* tu mir e-n Gefallen; *ask s.o. a ~* j-n um e-n Gefallen bitten; *we request the ~ of your company* wir laden Sie höflich ein; **3.** Begünstigung *f*, Bevorzugung *f*: *show ~ to s.o.* j-n bevorzugen; *under ~ of night* im Schutze der Nacht; **4.** ✝ *obs.* Schreiben *n*; **5.** a) kleines (*auf e-r Party etc. verteiltes*) Geschenk, b) 'Scherzarˌtikel *m*; **6.** (Par'tei- *etc.*)Abzeichen *n*; II *v/t.* **7.** günstig gesinnt sein (*dat.*), j-m wohl wollen *od.* gewogen sein; **8.** begünstigen: a) bevorzugen,

vorziehen, *a. sport* favorisieren, b) günstig sein für, fördern, c) eintreten für, für *et.* sein; **9.** einverstanden sein (*with* mit); **10.** j-n beehren *od.* erfreuen (*with* mit); **11.** j-m ähnlich sein; **12.** schonen: *~ one's leg*; '**fa·vo(u)r·a·ble** [-vərəbl] *adj.* □ **1.** wohlgesinnt, gewogen, geneigt (*to dat.*); **2.** *allg.* günstig: a) vorteilhaft (*to*, *for* für), b) befriedigend, gut, c) positiv, zustimmend: *~ answer*, d) viel versprechend; '**fa·vo(u)red** [-vəd] *adj.* begünstigt: *the ~ few* die Auserwählten; → *most-favo(u)red-nation clause*; '**fa·vo(u)r·ite** [-vərɪt] I *s.* **1.** Liebling *m* (*a. fig. Schriftsteller, Schallplatte etc.*), *contp.* Günstling *m*: *be s.o.'s* (*great*) *~* bei j-m (sehr) beliebt sein; *that book is a great ~ of mine* dieses Buch liebe ich sehr; **2.** *sport* Favoˈrit(in); **3.** *Computer, Internet*: Favoˈrit *m* (*Webseite*): *add favorites* zu Favoriten hinˈzufügen; *organize favorites* Favoriten verwalten; II *adj.* **4.** Lieblings...: *~ dish* Leibgericht *n*; '**favo(u)r·it·ism** [-vərɪtɪzəm] *s.* Günstlings-, Vetternwirtschaft *f*.

fawn[1] [fɔːn] I *s.* **1.** *zo.* Damkitz *n*, Rehkalb *n*; **2.** Rehbraun *n*; II *adj.* **3.** *a.* *~-colo(u)red* rehbraun; III *v/t.* **4.** *ein Kitz* setzen.

fawn[2] [fɔːn] *v/i.* **1.** schwänzeln, wedeln; **2.** *fig.* (*upon*) scharˈwenzeln (um), katzbuckeln (vor *j-m*); '**fawn·ing** [-nɪŋ] *adj.* □ *fig.* kriecherisch, schmeichlerisch.

fax [fæks] I *s.* **1.** Fax *n*, Faxkopie *f*; **2.** *~* (**ma·chine**) Fax *n*, Faxgerät *n*; II *v/t.* **3.** faxen: *~ s.o. s.th.*, *~ s.th. through to s.o.* j-m et. faxen; *~ num·ber s.* 'Faxnummer *f*.

fay [feɪ] *s. poet.* Fee *f*.

faze [feɪz] *v/t.* F j-n durchein'ander bringen: *not to ~ s.o.* j-n kalt lassen.

fe·al·ty [ˈfiːəltɪ] *s.* **1.** *hist.* Lehenstreue *f*; **2.** *fig.* Treue *f*.

fear [fɪə] I *s.* **1.** Furcht *f*, Angst *f* (*of* vor *dat.*, *that od. lest* dass ...): *be in ~ of* → 6; *in ~ of one's life* in Todesangst; *for ~* a) aus Furcht vor (*dat.*) *od.* dass, b) um nicht, damit nicht; *for ~ of losing it* um es nicht zu verlieren; *without ~ or favo(u)r* ganz objektiv *od.* unparteiisch; *no ~!* keine Bange!; **2.** *pl.* Befürchtung *f*, Bedenken *pl.*; **3.** Sorge *f*, Besorgnis *f* (*for* um); **4.** Gefahr *f*, Risiko *n*: *there is not much ~ of that* das ist kaum zu befürchten; **5.** Scheu *f*, Ehrfurcht *f* (*of* vor): *~ of God* Gottesfurcht; *put the ~ of God into s.o.* j-m e-n heiligen Schrecken einjagen; II *v/t.* **6.** fürchten, sich fürchten vor (*dat.*), Angst haben vor (*dat.*); **7.** *et.* befürchten: *~ the worst*; **8.** *Gott* fürchten; III *v/i.* **9.** sich fürchten, Angst haben; **10.** besorgt sein (*for* um): *never ~!* sei unbesorgt!; '**fear·ful** [-fʊl] *adj.* □ **1.** furchtbar, fürchterlich, schrecklich (*alle a. fig.* F); **2.** furchtsam, angsterfüllt, bange (*of* vor *dat.*); **3.** besorgt, in (großer) Sorge (*of* um, *that od. lest* dass); **4.** ehrfürchtig; '**fear·less** [-lɪs] *adj.* □ furchtlos, unerschrocken; '**fear·less·ness** [-lsnɪs] *s.* Furchtlosigkeit *f*; '**fear·some** [-səm] *adj.* □ *mst humor.* Furcht erregend, schrecklich, grässlich.

fea·si·bil·i·ty [ˌfiːzəˈbɪlətɪ] *s.* 'Durchführbarkeit *f*, Machbarkeit *f*; **fea·si·ble** [ˈfiːzəbl] *adj.* □ aus-, 'durchführbar, machbar, möglich.

feast [fiːst] I *s.* **1.** *eccl.* Fest(tag *m*) *n*, Feiertag *m*; **2.** Festmahl *n*, -essen *n*; → *enough* II; **3.** (Hoch)Genuss *m*: *a ~ for* *the eyes* e-e Augenweide; **II** *v/t.* **4.** (festlich) bewirten; **5.** ergötzen: ~ *one's eyes on* s-e Augen weiden an (*dat.*); **III** *v/i.* **6.** (*on*) schmausen (von), sich gütlich tun (an *dat.*); schwelgen (in *acc.*); **7.** (*on*) sich weiden (an *dat.*), schwelgen (in *dat.*).

feat [fiːt] *s.* **1.** Helden-, Großtat *f*: ~ *of arms* Waffentat; **2.** (*technische etc.*) Großtat, große Leistung; **3.** a) Kunst-, Meisterstück *n*, b) Kraftakt *m*.

feath·er ['feðə] **I** *s.* **1.** Feder *f*, *pl.* Gefieder *n*: *in fine* (*od. full*) ~ *f* a) (bei) bester Laune, b) in Hochform; *that is a* ~ *in his cap* darauf kann er stolz sein; *that will make the* ~*s fly* da werden die Fetzen fliegen; *you might have knocked me down with a* ~ ich war einfach ,platt' (*erstaunt*); → *bird* 1, *fur* 3, *white feather*; **2.** Pfeilfeder *f*; **3.** Schaumkrone *f* (*e-r Welle*); **II** *v/t.* **4.** mit Federn versehen *od.* schmücken; *Pfeil* fiedern; **5.** *Rudern:* Riemen flach drehen; ~ *bed* **I** *s.* **1.** Ma'tratze *f* mit Federfüllung; **2.** *fig.* ,gemütliche Sache'; **II** *v/t.* **3.** verhätscheln; **III** *v/i.* **4.** unnötige Arbeitskräfte einstellen; '~·**bed·ding** *s.* (*gewerkschaftlich geforderte*) 'Überbesetzung mit Arbeitskräften; '~**-brained** *adj.* **1.** schwachköpfig; **2.** leichtsinnig; ~ *dust·er* *s.* Staubwedel *m*.

feath·ered ['feðəd] *adj.* gefiedert: ~ *tribe(s)* Vogelwelt *f*.

feath·er·ing ['feðəriŋ] *s.* **1.** Gefieder *n*; **2.** Befiederung *f*; **3.** ✈ Segelstellung *f* (*Propeller*).

'**feath·er·weight** *s.* **1.** *sport* Federgewicht(ler *m*) *n*; **2.** ,Leichtgewicht' *n* (*Person*); **3.** *fig. contp.* a) ,Würstchen' *n* (*Person*), b) ,kleine Fische' *pl.* (*et. Belangloses*); **II** *adj.* **4.** Federgewichts...

feath·er·y ['feðəri] *adj.* feder(n)artig.

fea·ture ['fiːtʃə] **I** *s.* **1.** (Gesichts)Zug *m*; **2.** Merkmal *n*, Charakte'ristikum *n*, (Haupt)Eigenschaft *f*; Hauptpunkt *m*, -teil *m*, Besonderheit *f*; **3.** (Gesichts-)Punkt *m*, Seite *f*; **4.** ('Haupt)Attrakti,on *f*, Darbietung *f*; **5.** *a.* ~ *film* a) Spielfilm *m*, b) Hauptfilm *m*; **6.** *a.* ~ *pro·gram(me)* *Radio, TV:* Feature *n*, (aktu'eller) Dokumen'tarbericht; **7.** *a.* ~ *article*, ~ *story* Feature *n*, Spezi'alar,tikel *m* e-r Zeitung; **II** *v/t.* **8.** kennzeichnen, bezeichnend sein für; **9.** (als Besonderheit) haben *od.* aufweisen, sich auszeichnen durch; **10.** (groß her'aus-) bringen, her'ausstellen; (als Hauptschlager) zeigen *od.* bringen; *Film etc.:* in der Hauptrolle zeigen: *a film featuring X* ein Film mit X in der Hauptrolle; '**fea·ture-length** *adj.* mit Spielfilmlänge; '**fea·ture·less** [-lis] *adj.* nichts sagend.

feb·ri·fuge ['febrifjuːdʒ] *s.* ✒ Fiebermittel *n*; **fe·brile** ['fiːbrail] *adj.* fiebrig, Fieber...

Feb·ru·ar·y ['februəri] *s.* Februar *m*: *in* ~ im Februar.

fe·cal *etc.* → *faecal etc.*

feck·less ['feklis] *adj.* □ **1.** schwach, kraftlos; **2.** hilflos; **3.** zwecklos.

fe·cund ['fiːkənd] *adj.* fruchtbar, produk'tiv (*beide a. fig.*); '**fe·cun·date** [-deit] *v/t.* fruchtbar machen; befruchten (*a. biol.*); **fe·cun·da·tion** [,fiːkən'deiʃn] *s.* Befruchtung *f*; **fe·cun·di·ty** [fi'kʌndəti] *s.* Fruchtbarkeit *f*, Produkti'vi'tät *f*.

fed[1] [fed] *pret. u. p.p. von* **feed**.

fed[2] [fed] *s. Am.* **F 1.** FB'I-A,gent *m*; **2.** *mst* ⌾ (*die*) 'Bundes,gierung.

fed·er·al ['fedərəl] **I** *adj.* □ *pol.* **1.** födera'tiv; **2.** *mst* ⌾ Bundes...: a) bundesstaatlich, den Bund *od.* die 'Bundesre,gierung betreffend, b) *USA* Unions...: ~ *government* Bundesregierung *f*; ~ *jurisdiction* Bundesgerichtsbarkeit *f*; *the* ⌾ *Republic* (*of Germany*) die Bundesrepublik (Deutschland) ⌾ *State* *Am.* Bundesstaat *m*, (Einzel)Staat *m*; **3.** ⌾ *Am. hist.* födera'listisch; **II** *s.* **1.** (*Am. hist.* ⌾) Föde'ra'list *m*; ⌾ **Bu·reau of In·ves·ti·ga·tion** *s.* amer. Bundeskrimi'nalamt *n od.* -poli,zei *f* (*abbr.* FBI).

fed·er·al·ism ['fedərəlizəm] *s. pol.* Föde'ra'lismus *m*; '**fed·er·al·ist** [-ist] **I** *adj.* föde'ra'listisch; **II** *s.* Föde'ra'list *m*; '**fed·er·al·ize** [-laiz] *v/t.* → *federate* I.

fed·er·ate ['fedəreit] **I** *v/t. u. v/i.* (sich) föderalisieren, (sich) zu e-m (Staaten-) Bund vereinigen; **II** *adj.* [-rət] föderiert, verbündet; **fed·er·a·tion** [,fedə-'reiʃn] *s.* **1.** Födera'ti'on *f*: a) po'litischer Zs.-schluss, b) Staatenbund *m*; **2.** Bundesstaat *m*; **3.** ✝ (Zen'tral-, Dach-) Verband *m*; '**fed·er·a·tive** [-rətiv] *adj.* □ → *federal* 1.

fe·do·ra [fi'dɔːrə] *s. Am.* (weicher) Filzhut.

fee [fiː] **I** *s.* **1.** Gebühr: a) ('Anwalts-*etc.*)Hono,rar *n*, Vergütung *f*, b) amtliche Gebühr, Taxe *f*, c) (Mitglieds)Beitrag *m*, d) (*admission od. entrance*) ~ Eintrittsgeld *n*, e) Trinkgeld *n*: *doctor's* ~ Arztrechnung *f*; *school* ~(*s*) Schulgeld *n*; **2.** *Fußball:* Trans'fersumme *f*; **3.** *hist.* Lehn(s)gut *n*; **4.** ⚎ Eigentum(srecht) *n*: ~ *simple* (uneingeschränktes) Eigentumsrecht, Grundeigentum; ~ *tail* erbrechtlich gebundenes Grundeigentum; *hold land in* ~ Land zu Eigen haben; **II** *v/t.* **5.** *j-m* e-e Gebühr *etc.* bezahlen.

fee·ble ['fiːbl] *adj.* □ *allg.* schwach, *fig. a.* lahm, kläglich (*Versuch, Ausrede etc.*), matt (*Lächeln, Stimme*); '**fee·ble·-'mind·ed** *adj.* schwachsinnig; '**fee·ble·ness** [-nis] *s.* Schwäche *f*.

feed [fiːd] **I** *v/t.* [*irr.*] **1.** Nahrung zuführen (*dat.*), *Tier, Kind, Kranken* füttern (*on, with* mit), *e-m Menschen* zu essen geben, *e-m Tier* zu fressen geben, *Vieh* weiden lassen: ~ (*at the breast*) *Säugling* stillen; ~ *up* a) *Vieh* mästen, b) *j-n* ,hochpäppeln'; *be fed up with* F *et.* satt haben, ,die Nase voll haben' von; *I'm fed up to the teeth with him* (*it*) F er (es) ,steht mir bis hierher'; ~ *the fishes* a) ,die Fische füttern' (*bei Seekrankheit*), b) ertrinken; ~ *a cold* bei Erkältung tüchtig essen; **2.** *Familie etc.* ernähren (*on* von), erhalten; **3.** versorgen (*with* mit); **4.** ⚙ a) *Maschine* speisen, beschicken, b) *Material* zuführen, *Werkstück* vorschieben, *Daten in e-n Computer* eingeben; ~ *back* a) ⚡ rückkoppeln, b) *fig.* zu'rückleiten (*to* an *acc.*); **5.** *Feuer* unter'halten; **6.** *fig.* a) *Gefühl, Hoffnung etc.* nähren, Nahrung geben (*dat.*), b) befriedigen: ~ *one's vanity*; ~ *one's eyes on* s-e Augen weiden an (*dat.*); **7.** *thea.* F *j-m* Stichworte liefern; **8.** *sport* F *j-n* ,bedienen', mit Bällen ,füttern'; **9.** *oft* ~ *down*, ~ *close Wiese* abweiden lassen; **II** *v/i.* [*irr.*] **10.** a) fressen (*Tier*), b) F ,futtern' (*Mensch*); **11.** sich ernähren, leben (*on* von); **III** *s.* **12.** Fütterung *f*; F Mahlzeit *f*; **13.** Futter *n*, Nahrung *f*: *off one's* ~ ohne Appetit; *out at* ~ auf der Weide; **14.** ⚙ a) Speisung *f*, Beschickung *f*, (Materi'al)Zuführung *f*, b) (Werkzeug)Vorschub *m*; **15.** Zufuhr *f*, La-

dung *f*; Beschickungsgut *n*; '~**-back** *s.* ⚡ *u. fig.* Feed-back *n*; ~ *bag* *s. Am.* Futtersack *m*.

feed·er ['fiːdə] *s.* **1.** *a heavy* ~ ein starker Esser (*Mensch*) *od.* Fresser (*Tier*); **2.** ⚙ a) Beschickungsvorrichtung *f*, b) ⚡ Speiseleitung *f*, Feeder *m*; **3.** *Verkehr:* Zubringerlinie *f*, -strecke *f*: ~ (*road*) Zubringerstraße *f*; **4.** Bewässerungs-, Zuflussgraben *m*; Nebenfluss *m*; **5.** *Brit.* a) Lätzchen *n*, b) (Saug)Flasche *f*; **6.** *thea. Am.* F Stichwortgeber *m*; ~ *line* *s.* **1.** *Verkehr:* Zubringerlinie *f*; **2.** → *feeder* 2 b.

feed hop·per *s.* Fülltrichter *m*.

feed·ing ['fiːdiŋ] **I** *s.* **1.** Fütterung *f*; **2.** Ernährung *f*; **3.** ⚙ → *feed* 14 a; **II** *adj.* **4.** Zufuhr...; ~ *bottle* *s.* (Saug)Flasche *f*; ~ *cup* *s.* ⚕ Schnabeltasse *f*.

feed pipe *s.* Zuleitungsrohr *n*.

feel [fiːl] **I** *v/t.* [*irr.*] **1.** (an-, be)fühlen, betasten; *just* ~ *my hand* fühl mal m-e Hand (an); ~ *one's way* sich vortasten (*a. fig.*), *fig.* vorsichtig vorgehen, sondieren; ~ *s.o. up* *sl.* j-n ,abgrapschen' *od.* ,befummeln'; **2.** a) fühlen, spüren, wahrnehmen, merken, b) empfinden: ~ *the cold*; ~ *pleasure* Freude *od.* Lust empfinden; *he felt the loss deeply* der Verlust traf ihn schwer; *s.o.'s wrath* j-s Zorn zu spüren bekommen; *make itself felt* spürbar werden, zu spüren sein; *a (long-)felt want* ein dringendes Bedürfnis, ein (längst) spürbarer Mangel; **3.** a) ahnen, spüren, b) glauben, c) halten für: *I* ~ *it (to be) my duty* ich halte es für m-e Pflicht; **4.** *a.* ~ *out et.* sondieren, *j-m* ,auf den Zahn fühlen'; **II** *v/i.* **5.** fühlen: a) empfinden, b) durch Tasten feststellen *od.* festzustellen suchen (*whether, if* ob; *how* wie); **6.** ~ *for* a) tasten nach, b) suchen nach, c) *et.* herauszufinden suchen; **7.** sich fühlen, sich befinden, sich vorkommen wie, sein: ~ *cold* frieren; *I* ~ *cold* mir ist kalt; ~ *ill* sich krank fühlen; ~ *certain* sicher sein; ~ *quite o.s. again* wieder ,auf dem Posten' sein; ~ *like* (*doing*) *s.th.* Lust haben zu et. (*od.* et. zu tun); ~ *up to s.th.* a) sich e-r Sache gewachsen fühlen, b) sich in der Lage fühlen zu et., c) in (der) Stimmung sein zu et.; **8.** ~ *for* (*od. with*) *s.o.* Mitgefühl mit j-m haben; *we* ~ *with you* wir fühlen mit dir (*od.* euch); **9.** das Gefühl *od.* den Eindruck haben, finden, meinen, glauben (*that* dass): *I* ~ *that* ich finde, dass ...; *how do you* ~ *about it?* was meinst du dazu: *it is felt in London* in London ist man der Ansicht; ~ *strongly* a) entschiedene Ansichten haben, b) sich erregen (*about* über *acc.*); **10.** sich weich *etc.* anfühlen: *velvet* ~*s soft*; **11.** *impers. I know how it* ~*s to be hungry* ich weiß, was es heißt, hungrig zu sein; **III** *s.* **12.** Gefühl *n* (*wie sich et. anfühlt*): *a sticky* ~; **13.** (An-) Fühlen *n*: *soft to the* ~ weich anzufühlen; *let me have a* ~ lass mich mal fühlen; **14.** Gefühl *n*: a) Empfindung *f*, Eindruck *m*, b) Stimmung *f*, Atmo-'sphäre *f*, c) feiner In'stinkt, ,Riecher' *m* (*for* für): *clutch* ~ *mot.* Gefühl für richtiges Kuppeln.

feel·er ['fiːlə] *s.* *zo.* Fühler *m* (*a. fig.*): *put* (*od. throw*) *out a* ~ s-e Fühler ausstrecken, sondieren; **2.** ⚙ a) Dorn *m*, Fühler *m*, b) Taster *m*; '**feel·ing** [-liŋ] **I** *s.* **1.** Gefühl *n*, Gefühlssinn *m*; **2.** Gefühl(szustand *m*) *n*, Stimmung *f*: *bad* (*od. ill*) ~ Groll *m*, böses Blut, Feindseligkeit *f*; *good* ~ a) gutes Gefühl, b) Wohlwollen *n*; *no hard* ~*s!* F a) nicht böse sein!, b) (das) macht nichts!; **3.** *pl.* Gefühle *pl.*, Empfindlichkeit *f*: *hurt s.o.'s* ~*s* j-s Gefühle *od.* j-n verletzen; **4.** Feingefühl, Empfindsamkeit: *have a* ~ *for* Gefühl haben für; **5.** (Gefühls)Eindruck *m*: *I have a* ~ *that* ich habe (so) das Gefühl, dass; **6.** Gefühl *n*, Gesinnung *f*, Ansicht *f*: *strong* ~*s* a) starke Überzeugung, b) Erregung *f*; **7.** Auf-, Erregung *f*, Rührung *f*: *with* ~ a) mit Gefühl, gefühlvoll, b) mit Nachdruck, c) erbittert; ~*s ran high* die Gemüter erhitzten sich; **8.** (Vor)Gefühl *n*, Ahnung *f*; **II** *adj.* □ **9.** fühlend, Gefühls...; **10.** gefühlvoll: a) mitfühlend, b) voll Gefühl, lebhaft.

feel-good fac·tor ['fiːlɡʊd] *s.* subjek'tives Wohlbefinden.

feet [fiːt] *pl. von* **foot.**

feign [feɪn] **I** *v/t.* **1.** *et.* vortäuschen, *Krankheit a.* simulieren: ~ *death* sich tot stellen; **2.** *e-e Ausrede etc.* erfinden; **II** *v/i.* **3.** sich verstellen, so tun als ob, simulieren; **'feign·ed·ly** [-nɪdlɪ] *adv.* zum Schein.

feint¹ [feɪnt] **I** *s.* **1.** *sport* Finte *f* (*a. fig.*); **2.** ⚔ Scheinangriff *m*, 'Täuschungsma,növer *n* (*a. fig.*); **II** *v/i.* **3.** *sport* fintieren: ~ *at* (*od.* *upon*) *j-n* täuschen; **III** *v/t.* **4.** *sport Schlag etc.* antäuschen.

feint² [feɪnt] *adj. typ.* schwach: ~ *lines*.

feist·y ['faɪstɪ] *adj.* □ *bsd. Am.* **1.** lebhaft, munter; **2.** draufgängerisch, aggres'siv; **3.** reizbar, streitsüchtig; **4.** knifflig (*Problem etc.*).

feld·spar ['feldspɑː] *s. min.* Feldspat *m*.

fe·lic·i·tate [fɪ'lɪsɪteɪt] *v/t.* (*on*) beglückwünschen, *j-m* gratulieren (zu); **fe·lic·i·ta·tion** [fɪ,lɪsɪ'teɪʃn] *s.* Glückwunsch *m*; **fe'lic·i·tous** [-təs] *adj.* □ glücklich (gewählt), treffend (*Ausdruck etc.*); **fe·'lic·i·ty** [-tɪ] *s.* **1.** Glück(seligkeit *f*) *n*; **2.** a) glücklicher Einfall, b) glücklicher Griff, c) treffender Ausdruck.

fe·line ['fiːlaɪn] **I** *adj.* □ **1.** Katzen...; **2.** katzenartig, -haft: ~ *grace*; **3.** *fig.* falsch, tückisch; **II** *s.* **4.** Katze *f*.

fell¹ [fel] *pret. von* **fall.**

fell² [fel] *v/t. Baum* fällen, *Gegner a.* niederstrecken.

fell³ [fel] *adj. poet.* **1.** grausam, wild, mörderisch; **2.** tödlich.

fell⁴ [fel] *s.* **1.** Balg *m*, Tierfell *n*; Vlies *n*; **2.** struppiges Haar.

fell⁵ [fel] *s. Brit.* **1.** Hügel *m*, Berg *m*; **2.** Moorland *n*.

fel·lah ['felə] *pl.* **-lahs, fel·la·heen** [,felə'hiːn] (*Arab.*) *s.* Fel'lache *m*.

fell·er ['felə] F → **fellow** 4.

fel·loe ['feləʊ] *s.* (Rad)Felge *f*.

fel·low ['feləʊ] **I** *s.* **1.** Gefährte *m*, Gefährtin *f*, Genosse *m*, Genossin *f*, Kame'rad(in) *m*: ~*s in misery* Leidensgenossen; **2.** Mitmensch *m*, Zeitgenosse *m*; **3.** Ebenbürtige(r *m*) *f*: *he will never have his* ~ er wird nie seinesgleichen finden; **4.** F Kerl *m*, Bursche *m*, ,Mensch' *m*, ,Typ' *m*: *my dear* ~ mein lieber Freund!; *good* ~ guter Kerl; *old* ~*!* alter Knabe!; *a* ~ man, einer; **5.** *der* (*die, das*) Da'zugehörige, der (*die, das*) andere *e-s Paares*: *where is the* ~ *of this shoe?*; **6.** Fellow *m*: a) Mitglied *n* e-s College (*Dozent, der im College wohnt*), b) Inhaber(in) e-s 'Forschungssti,pendiums, c) *Am.* Stu'dent(in) höheren Se'mesters, c) Mitglied *n* e-r gelehrten *etc.* Gesellschaft; **II** *adj.* **7.** Mit...: ~ *being* Mitmensch *m*; ~ *citizen* Mitbürger *m*; ~ *countryman* Landsmann *m*; ~ *feeling* a) Zs.-gehörigkeitsgefühl *n*, b) Mitgefühl *n*; ~ *student* Studienkollege *m*, -kollegin *f*, Kommilitone *m*, Kom-

militonin *f*; ~ *travel(l)er* a) Mitreisende(r *m*) *f*, b) *pol.* Mitläufer(in), Sympathisant(in), *bsd.* Kommunistenfreund (-in).

fel·low·ship ['feləʊʃɪp] *s.* **1.** *oft good* ~ a) Kame'radschaft(lichkeit) *f*, b) Geselligkeit *f*; **2.** (*geistige etc.*) Gemeinschaft, Verbundenheit *f*; **3.** Gemein-, Gesellschaft *f*, Gruppe *f*; **4.** *univ.* a) die Fellows *pl.*, b) *Brit.* Stellung *f* e-s Fellow, c) Sti'pendienfonds *m*, d) 'Forschungssti,pendium *n*.

fel·on¹ ['felən] *s.* Nagelgeschwür *n*.

fel·on² ['felən] *s.* (Schwer)Verbrecher *m*; **fe·lo·ni·ous** [fə'ləʊnjəs] *adj.* □ 🏛 verbrecherisch; **'fel·o·ny** [-nɪ] *s.* 🏛 *Am.* Verbrechen *n*, *Brit. obs.* Schwerverbrechen *n*.

fel·spar ['felspɑː] → **feldspar.**

felt¹ [felt] *pret. u. p.p. von* **feel.**

felt² [felt] **I** *s.* Filz *m*; **II** *adj.* Filz...: ~ *-tip(ped) pen*, ~ *tip*, ~ *pen* Filzschreiber *m*, -stift *m*; **III** *v/t. u. v/i.* (sich) verfilzen; **'felt·ing** [-tɪŋ] *s.* Filzstoff *m*.

fe·male ['fiːmeɪl] **I** *adj.* **1.** weiblich (*a.* ♀): ~ *dog* Hündin *f*, ~ *student* Studentin *f*; **2.** weiblich, Frauen...: ~ *dress* Frauenkleidung *f*; **3.** ⚙ Hohl..., Steck...: ~ *screw* Schraubenmutter *f*; ~ *thread* Muttergewinde *n*; **II** *s.* **4.** a) Frau *f*, b) Mädchen *n*, c) *contp.* Weibsbild *n*, -stück *n*; **5.** *zo.* Weibchen *n*; **6.** ♀ weibliche Pflanze.

feme| cov·ert [fiːm] *s.* 🏛 verheiratete Frau; ~ *sole* *s.* 🏛 a) unverheiratete Frau, b) vermögensrechtlich selbstständige Ehefrau: ~ *trader* selbstständige Geschäftsfrau.

fem·i·nine ['femɪnɪn] **I** *adj.* □ **1.** weiblich (*a. ling.*); **2.** weiblich, Frauen...: ~ *voice*; **3.** fraulich, sanft, zart; **4.** weibisch, femi'nin; **II** *s.* **5.** *ling.* Femininum *n.*

fem·i·nin·i·ty [,femɪ'nɪnətɪ] *s.* **1.** Fraulich-, Weiblichkeit *f*; **2.** weibische *od.* femi'nine Art; **3.** *coll.* (*die*) (holde) Weiblichkeit; **fem·i·nism** ['femɪnɪzəm] *s.* Femi'nismus *m*; Frauenrechtsbewegung *f*; **fem·i·nist** ['femɪnɪst] *s.* Frauenrechtler(in), Femi'nist(in).

fem·o·ral ['femərəl] *adj. anat.* Oberschenkel(knochen)...; **fe·mur** ['fiːmə] *pl.* **-murs** *od.* **fem·o·ra** ['femərə] *s.* Oberschenkel(knochen) *m*.

fen [fen] *s.* Fenn *n*: a) Marschland *n*, b) (Flach)Moor *n*: *the* ~*s* die Niederungen in *East Anglia*.

fence [fens] **I** *s.* **1.** Zaun *m*, Einzäunung *f*, Gehege *n*: *mend one's* ~*s Am. pol.* s-e angeschlagene Position festigen; *sit on the* ~ a) sich abwartend *od.* neutral verhalten, b) unschlüssig sein; **2.** *Reitsport:* Hindernis *n*; **3.** *sport das* Fechten; **4.** *sl.* a) Hehler *m*, b) Hehlernest *n*; **II** *v/t.* **5.** *a.* ~ *in* einzäunen, einfrieden: ~ *in* (*od. round, off*) um'zäunen; ~ *off* abzäunen; **6.** ~ *in* einsperren; **7.** *fig.* schützen, sichern (*from* vor *dat.*): ~ *off Fragen etc.* abwehren, parieren; **8.** *sl. Diebesbeute* an e-n Hehler verkaufen; **III** *v/i.* **9.** fechten; **10.** *fig.* Ausflüchte machen, ausweichen; **11.** *sl.* Hehle'rei treiben; ~ *month* *s. hunt. Brit.* Schonzeit *f*.

fenc·er ['fensə] *s. sport* **1.** Fechter(in); **2.** Springpferd *n*.

fence sea·son → **fence month.**

fenc·ing ['fensɪŋ] *s.* **1.** *sport* Fechten *n*; **2.** *fig.* ausweichendes Verhalten, Ausflüchte *pl.*; **3.** a) Zaun *m*, b) Zäune *pl.*, c) 'Zaunmateri,al *n*.

fend [fend] **I** *v/t.* **1.** ~ *off* abwehren; **II** *v/i.* **2.** sich wehren; **3.** ~ *for* sorgen für:

~ *for o.s.* für sich selbst sorgen, sich ganz allein durchs Leben schlagen; **'fend·er** [-də] *s.* **1.** ⊙ Schutzvorrichtung *f*; **2.** *rail. etc.* Puffer *m*; **3.** *mot. Am.* Kotflügel *m*: ~ *bender* F (Unfall *m* mit) Blechschaden *m*; **4.** Schutzblech *n am Fahrrad*; **5.** ⚓ Fender *m*; **6.** Ka'minvorsetzer *m*, -gitter *n*.

fen·es·tra·tion [,fenɪ'streɪʃn] *s.* **1.** △ Fensteranordnung *f*; **2.** 🐛 'Fensterung(soperati,on) *f*.

fen fire *s.* Irrlicht *n*.

Fe·ni·an ['fiːnjən] *hist.* **I.** *s.* Fenier *m*; **II** *adj.* fenisch; **'Fe·ni·an·ism** [-nɪzəm] *s.* Feniertum *n*.

fen·nel ['fenl] *s.* ♀ Fenchel *m*.

feoff [fef] → **fief; feoff·ee** [fe'fiː] *s.* 🏛 Belehnte(r) *m*: ~ *in* (*od. of*) *trust* Treuhänder(in); **feoff·er** ['fefə], **feof·for** [fe'fɔː] *s.* 🏛 Lehnsherr *m*.

fe·ral ['fɪərəl] *adj.* **1.** wild (lebend); **2.** *fig.* wild, bar'barisch.

fer·e·to·ry ['ferɪtərɪ] *s.* Re'liquienschrein *m.*

fer·ment [fə'ment] **I** *v/t.* **1.** in Gärung bringen, *fig. a.* in Wallung bringen, erregen; **II** *v/i.* **2.** gären (*a. fig.*); **III** *s.* ['fɜːment] **3.** 🐛 Fer'ment *n*, Gärstoff *m*; **4.** 🐛 Gärung *f*, *fig. a.* (innere) Unruhe, Aufruhr *m*: *the country was in a state of* ~ es gärte im Land; **fer·men·ta·tion** [,fɜːmen'teɪʃn] *s.* **1.** 🐛 Fermentati'on *f*, Gärung *f* (*a. fig.*); **2.** *fig.* Aufruhr *m*, (innere) Unruhe.

fern [fɜːn] *s.* ♀ Farn(kraut *n*) *m*; **'fern·y** [-nɪ] *adj.* **1.** farnartig; **2.** voller Farnkraut.

fe·ro·cious [fə'rəʊʃəs] *adj.* □ **1.** wild, grausam, grimmig, heftig; **2.** *Am.* F a) ,toll', b) *contp.* ,grausam'; **fe·roc·i·ty** [fə'rɒsətɪ] *s.* Grausamkeit *f*, Wildheit *f*.

fer·re·ous ['ferɪəs] *adj.* eisenhaltig.

fer·ret ['ferɪt] **I** *s.* **1.** *zo.* Frettchen *n*; **2.** *fig.* ,Spürhund' *m* (*Person*); **II** *v/i.* **3.** *hunt.* mit Frettchen jagen; **4.** ~ *about* her'umsuchen (*for* nach); **III** *v/t.* **5.** ~ *out* *fig. et.* aufspüren, -stöbern, herausfinden.

fer·ric ['ferɪk] *adj.* 🐛 Eisen...; **fer·ri·cy·a·nide** [,ferɪ'saɪənaɪd] *s.* Zy'aneisenverbindung *f*; **fer·rif·er·ous** [fe'rɪfərəs] *adj.* 🐛 eisenhaltig.

Fer·ris wheel ['ferɪs] *s.* Riesenrad *n*.

fer·ro- [ferəʊ] *in Zssgn* Eisen...; ~*'con·crete* *s.* 'Eisenbe,ton *m*; '~*type* *s. phot.* Ferroty'pie *f*.

fer·rous ['ferəs] *adj.* eisenhaltig, Eisen...

fer·rule ['feruːl] *s.* **1.** ⊙ Stockzwinge *f*; **2.** Muffe *f*.

fer·ry ['ferɪ] **I** *s.* **1.** Fähre *f*, Fährschiff *n*, -boot *n*; **2.** *a.* ~ *service* Fährdienst *m*; **3.** ✈ Über'führungsdienst *m* (*von der Fabrik zum Flugplatz*); **4.** *Raumfahrt:* (Lande)Fähre *f*; **II** *v/t.* **5.** 'übersetzen; *bsd.* ✈ über'führen; befördern; **III** *v/i.* **6.** 'übersetzen; '~*boat* → **ferry** 1; ~ *bridge* *s.* **1.** Tra'jekt *m*, *n*, Eisenbahnfähre *f*; **2.** Landungsbrücke *f*; '~*man* [-mən] *s.* [*irr.*] Fährmann *m*.

fer·tile ['fɜːtaɪl] *adj.* □ **1.** *a. fig.* fruchtbar, produk'tiv, reich (*in, of* an *dat.*); **2.** *fig.* schöpferisch; **fer·til·i·ty** [fə'tɪlətɪ] *s. a. fig.* Fruchtbarkeit *f*, Reichtum *m*; **fer·ti·li·za·tion** [,fɜːtɪlaɪ'zeɪʃn] *s.* **1.** Fruchtbarmachen *n*; **2.** *biol. u. fig.* Befruchtung *f*; **3.** ✍ Düngung *f*; **'fer·ti·lize** [-tɪlaɪz] *v/t.* **1.** fruchtbar machen; **2.** *biol. u. fig.* befruchten; **3.** ✍ düngen; **'fer·ti·liz·er** [-tɪlaɪzə] *s.* (Kunst)Dünger *m*, Düngemittel *n.*

fer·ule ['feruːl] **I** *s.* (flaches) Line'al (*zur Züchtigung*), (Zucht)Rute *f* (*a. fig.*); **II**

F

v/t. züchtigen.

fer·ven·cy ['fɜ:vənsɪ] → *fervo(u)r* 1; **'fer·vent** [-nt] *adj.* □ **1.** *fig.* glühend, feurig, inbrünstig, leidenschaftlich; **2.** (glühend) heiß; **'fer·vid** [-vɪd] *adj.* □ → *fervent* 1; **'fer·vo(u)r** [-və] *s.* **1.** *fig.* Glut *f*, Feuer(eifer *m*) *n*, Leidenschaft *f*, Inbrunst *f*; **2.** Glut *f*, Hitze *f*.

fess(e) [fes] *s. her.* (Quer)Balken *m*.

fes·tal ['festl] *adj.* □ festlich, Fest...

fes·ter ['festə] **I** *v/i.* **1.** schwären, eitern: *~ing sore* Eiterbeule *f* (*a. fig.*); **2.** verwesen, verfaulen; **3.** *fig.* gären: *~ in s.o.'s mind* an j-m nagen *od.* fressen; **II** *s.* **4.** a) Schwäre *f*, eiternde Wunde, b) Geschwür *n*.

fes·ti·val ['festəvl] **I** *s.* **1.** Fest(tag *m*) *n*, Feier *f*; **2.** Festspiele *pl.*, 'Festival *n*; **II** *adj.* **3.** festlich, Fest...; **4.** Festspiel...; **'fes·tive** [-tɪv] *adj.* □ **1.** festlich, Fest...; **2.** fröhlich, gesellig; **fes·tiv·i·ty** [fe'stɪvətɪ] *s.* **1.** *oft pl.* Fest(lichkeit *f*) *n*; **2.** festliche Stimmung.

fes·toon [fe'stu:n] **I** *s.* Gir'lande *f*; **II** *v/t.* mit Gir'landen schmücken.

fe·tal ['fi:tl] *etc.* → *foetal etc.*

fetch [fetʃ] **I** *v/t.* **1.** (her'bei)holen, (her)bringen: *~ a doctor* e-n Arzt holen; *~ s.o. round* F j-n ‚rumkriegen‘; **2.** *et. od. j-n* abholen; **3.** *Atem* holen: *~ a sigh* (auf)seufzen; *~ tears* (ein paar) Tränen hervorlocken; **4.** *~ up et.* erbrechen; **5.** apportieren (*Hund*); **6.** *Preis etc.* (ein)bringen, erzielen; **7.** *fig.* fesseln, anziehen, für sich einnehmen; **8.** *j-m e-n Schlag* versetzen: *~ s.o. one* j-m ‚eine langen‘ *od.* ‚runterhauen‘; **9.** ⚓ erreichen; **II** *v/i.* **10.** *~ and carry for s.o.* j-s Handlanger sein, j-n bedienen; **11.** *~ up* F ‚landen‘ (*at, in* in *dat.*); **'fetch·ing** [-tʃɪŋ] *adj.* F reizend, bezaubernd.

fête [feɪt] **I** *s.* Fest(lichkeit *f*) *n*; **II** *v/t.* j-n *od. et.* feiern.

fet·id ['fetɪd] *adj.* □ stinkend.

fet·ish ['fetɪʃ] *s.* Fetisch *m*; **'fet·ish·ism** [-ʃɪzəm] *s.* Fetischkult *m*, *a. psych.* Feti'schismus *m*; **'fet·ish·ist** [-ʃɪst] *s.* Feti'schist *m*.

fet·lock ['fetlɒk] *s. zo.* **1.** Behang *m*; **2.** *a. ~ joint* Fesselgelenk *n* (*des Pferdes*).

fet·ter ['fetə] **I** *s.* **1.** (Fuß)Fessel *f*; **2.** *pl. fig.* Fesseln *pl.*; **II** *v/t.* **3.** fesseln, *fig. a.* hemmen, behindern.

fet·tle ['fetl] *s.* Verfassung *f*, Zustand *m*: *in good* (*od. fine*) *~* (gut) in Form.

fe·tus ['fi:təs] → *foetus.*

feu [fju:] *s.* ⚖ *Scot.* Lehen *n*.

feud¹ [fju:d] **I** *s.* Fehde *f*: *be at ~ with* mit *j-m* in Fehde liegen; **II** *v/i.* sich befehden.

feud² [fju:d] *s.* ⚖ Lehen *n*, Lehn(s)gut *n*; **'feu·dal** [-dl] *adj.* ⚖ Feudal..., Lehns..., feu'dal; **'feu·dal·ism** [-dəlɪzəm] *s.* Feuda'lismus *m*; **feu·dal·i·ty** [fju:'dælətɪ] *s.* **1.** Lehenswesen *n*; **2.** Lehnbarkeit *f*; **'feu·da·to·ry** [-dətərɪ] **I** *s.* Lehnsmann *m*, Va'sall *m*; **II** *adj.* Lehns...

feuil·le·ton ['fɜ:ɪtɔ̃:ŋ] (*Fr.*) *s.* Feuille'ton *n*, kultu'reller Teil (*e-r Zeitung*).

fe·ver ['fi:və] **I** *s.* **1.** ⚕ Fieber *n*: *~ heat* a) Fieberhitze *f*, b) *fig.* → 2; **2.** *fig.* Fieber *n*, fieberhafte Aufregung, a. Sucht *f*, Rausch *m*: *gold ~*; *in a ~ of excitement* in fieberhafter Aufregung; *reach ~ pitch* den Höhe- *od.* Siedepunkt erreichen; *work at ~ pitch* fieberhaft arbeiten; **II** *v/i.* **3.** fiebern (*a. fig. for* nach); **'fe·vered** [-əd] *adj.* **1.** fiebernd, fiebrig; **2.** *fig.* fieberhaft, aufgeregt; **'fe·ver·ish** [-vərɪʃ] *adj.* □ **1.** fieberkrank, fiebrig, Fieber...; **2.** *fig.*

fieberhaft; **'fe·ver·ish·ness** [-vərɪʃnɪs] *s.* Fieberhaftigkeit *f* (*a. fig.*).

few [fju:] *adj. u. s.* (*pl.*) **1.** (*Ggs.* **many**) wenige; *~ persons*; *some ~* einige wenige; *his friends are ~* er hat (nur) wenige Freunde; *no ~er than* nicht weniger als; *~ and far between* (sehr) dünn gesät; *the lucky ~* die wenigen Glücklichen; **2.** *a ~* (*Ggs.* **none**) einige, ein paar: *a ~ days* einige Tage; *not a ~* nicht wenige, viele; *a good ~* e-e ganze Menge; *only a ~* nur wenige; *every ~ days* alle paar Tage; *have a ~* F ein paar ‚kippen‘; **'few·ness** [-nɪs] *s.* geringe Anzahl.

fey [feɪ] *adj. Scot.* **1.** todgeweiht; **2.** 'übermütig; **3.** 'übersinnlich.

fez [fez] *s.* Fes *m*.

fi·an·cé [fɪ'ɑ̃:ŋseɪ] (*Fr.*) *s.* Verlobte(r) *m*; **fi·an·cée** [-seɪ] (*Fr.*) *s.* Verlobte *f*.

fi·at ['faɪæt] *s.* **1.** ⚖ *Brit.* Gerichtsbeschluss *m*; **2.** Befehl *m*, Erlass *m*; **3.** Ermächtigung *f*; *~ mon·ey s. Am.* Pa'piergeld *n* ohne Deckung.

fib [fɪb] *v/i.* **1.** kleine Lüge, Schwinde'lei *f*, Flunke'rei *f*: *tell a ~* → **II** *v/i.* schwindeln, flunkern; **'fib·ber** [-bə] *s.* F Flunkerer *m*, Schwindler *m*.

fi·ber *Am.*, **fi·bre** ['faɪbə] *Brit. s.* **1.** ◎, *biol.* Faser *f*, Na'turfaser (*a. Wolle, Fell*); **2.** Bal'laststoffe *pl.*; **3.** Faserstoff *m*, -gefüge *n*, Tex'tur *f*; **4.** *fig.* a) Struk'tur *f*, b) Schlag *m*, Cha'rakter *m*: *moral ~* ,Rückgrat *n*‘; *of coarse ~* grobschlächtig; **'~·board** *s.* ◎ Holzfaserplatte *f*; **'~·glass** *s.* ◎ Fiberglas *n*; **'~·op·tic ca·ble** *s.* ◎ Glasfaserkabel *n*.

fi·bril ['faɪbrɪl] *s.* **1.** Fäserchen *n*; **2.** ♀ Wurzelfaser *f*; **'fi·brin** [-brɪn] *s.* **1.** Fib'rin *n*, Blutfaserstoff *m*; **2.** *a. plant ~* Pflanzenfaserstoff *m*; **'fi·broid** [-brɔɪd] **I** *adj.* faserartig, Faser...; **II** *s.* → **fi·bro·ma** [faɪ'brəʊmə] *pl.* **-ma·ta** [-mətə] *s.* ✚ Fib'rom *n*; Fasergeschwulst *f*; **fi·bro·si·tis** [ˌfaɪbrəʊ'saɪtɪs] *s.* ✚ Bindegewebsentzündung *f*; **'fi·brous** [-brəs] *adj.* □ **1.** faserig, Faser...; **2.** ◎ sehnig (*Metall*).

fib·u·la ['fɪbjʊlə] *pl.* **-lae** [-li:] *s.* **1.** *anat.* Wadenbein *n*; **2.** *antiq.* Fibel *f*, Spange *f*.

fiche [fi:ʃ] *s.* Fiche *n*, *m* (*Mikrodatenkarte*).

fick·le ['fɪkl] *adj.* unbeständig, launisch, *Person a.* wankelmütig; **'fick·le·ness** [-nɪs] *s.* Unbeständigkeit *f*, Wankelmut *m*.

fic·tile ['fɪktaɪl] *adj.* **1.** formbar; **2.** tönern, irden: *~ art* Töpferkunst *f*; *~ ware* Steingut *n*.

fic·tion ['fɪkʃn] *s.* **1.** (freie) Erfindung, Dichtung *f*; *contp.* ‚Märchen‘ *n*; **2.** a) Belle'tristik *f*, 'Prosa-, Ro'manlitera,tur *f*: *work of ~*, b) *coll.* Ro'mane *pl.*, Prosa *f* (*e-s Autors*); **3.** ⚖ Fikti'on *f*; **'fic·tion·al** [-ʃənl] *adj.* **1.** erdichtet; **2.** Roman...

fic·ti·tious [fɪk'tɪʃəs] *adj.* □ **1.** (frei) erfunden, fik'tiv; **2.** unwirklich, Fantasie..., Roman...; **3.** ⚖ *etc.* fik'tiv: *~ name*, b) fingiert, falsch, Schein...: *~ bill* ✚ Kellerwechsel *m*; **fic'ti·tious·ness** [-nɪs] *s.* das Fik'tive; Unechtheit *f*.

fid·dle ['fɪdl] **I** *s.* **1.** ♪ Fiedel *f*, Geige *f*: *play first* (*second*) *~ fig.* die erste (zweite) Geige spielen; → *fit¹* 5; **2.** *Brit.* F a) Schwindel *m*, Betrug *m*, Schiebung *f*, b) Manipulati'on *f*; **II** *v/i.* **3.** F fiedeln, geigen; **4.** *a. ~ about* (*od. around*) her'umtrödeln; **5.** (*with*) spielen (mit), her'umfingern (an *dat.*),

contp. her'umpfuschen (an *dat.*); **III** *v/t.* **6.** F fiedeln; **7.** *~ away* F *Zeit* vertrödeln; **8.** *Brit.* F ,frisieren‘, manipulieren; **IV** *int.* **9.** Quatsch!; **,~·de·'dee** [-dɪ'di:] → *fiddle* 9; **'~·,fad·dle** [-,fædl] **I** *s.* **1.** Lap'palie *f*; **2.** Unsinn *m*; **II** *v/i.* **3.** dummes Zeug reden; **4.** die Zeit vertrödeln.

fid·dler ['fɪdlə] *s.* **1.** Geiger(in): *pay the ~* F ,blechen‘; **2.** *Brit.* F Schwindler *m*.

'fid·dle·stick I *s.* Geigenbogen *m*; **II** *int.* *~s!* F Quatsch!

fid·dling ['fɪdlɪŋ] *adj.* F läppisch, geringfügig, ,poplig‘.

fi·del·i·ty [fɪ'delətɪ] *s.* **1.** (*a.* eheliche) Treue (*to* gegenüber, zu); **2.** Genauigkeit *f*, genaue Über'einstimmung *od.* 'Wiedergabe: *with ~* wortgetreu; **3.** ♫ 'Wiedergabe(güte) *f*, Klangtreue *f*.

fidg·et ['fɪdʒɪt] **I** *s.* **1.** *oft pl.* ner'vöse Unruhe, Zappe'lei *f*; **2.** ,Zappelphilipp‘ *m*, Zapp(e)ler *m*; **II** *v/t.* **3.** ner'vös *od.* zapp(e)lig machen; **III** *v/i.* **4.** (her'rum)zappeln, zapp(e)lig sein; **5.** *~ with* (herum)fuchteln *od.* (-)hantieren mit; **'fidg·et·i·ness** [-tɪnɪs] *s.* Zapp(e)ligkeit *f*, Nervosi'tät *f*; **'fidg·et·y** [-tɪ] *adj.* ner'vös, zappelig: *~ Philipp* → *fidget* 2.

fi·du·ci·ar·y [fɪ'dju:ʃjərɪ] ⚖ **I** *s.* **1.** Treuhänder(in); **II** *adj.* **2.** treuhänderisch, Treuhand..., Treuhänder...; **3.** ✚ ungedeckt (*Noten*).

fie [faɪ] *int. oft ~ upon you!* pfui(, schäm dich)!

fief [fi:f] *s.* Lehen *n*, Lehn(s)gut *n*.

field [fi:ld] **I** *s.* **1.** ♪ Feld *n*; **2.** ✕ a) (*Gold-, Öl- etc.*)Feld *n*, b) (Gruben-) Feld *n*, (Kohlen)Flöz *n*: *coal ~*; **3.** *fig.* Bereich *m*, (Sach-, Fach)Gebiet *n*: *in the ~ of art* auf dem Gebiet der Kunst; *in his ~* auf s-m Gebiet, in s-m Fach; *~ of activity* Tätigkeitsbereich; *~ of application* Anwendungsbereich; **4.** a) (weite) Fläche, b) ♁, ♌, *phys., a. her.* Feld *n*: *~ of force* Kraftfeld; *~ of vision* Blick-, Gesichtsfeld, *fig.* Gesichtskreis *m*, Horizont *m*; **5.** *sport* a) Spielfeld *n*, (Sport)Platz *m*: *take the ~* einlaufen, auf den Platz kommen (→ 6), b) Feld *n* (*geschlossene Gruppe*), c) Teilnehmer(feld *n*) *pl.*, Besetzung *f*, *fig.* Wettbewerbsteilnehmer *pl.*: *fair ~ and no favo(u)r* gleiche Bedingungen für alle; *play the ~* F sich keine Chance entgehen lassen (*in der Liebe*), d) *Baseball, Kricket:* 'Fängerpar,tei *f*; **6.** ✕ a) *poet.* (Schlacht)Feld *n*, (Feld)Schlacht *f*, b) Feld *n*, Front *f*: *in the ~* an der Front, im Felde; *hold* (*od. keep*) *the ~* sich behaupten; *take the ~* ins Feld rücken, den Kampf eröffnen; *win the ~* den Sieg davontragen; **7.** ✕ Feld *n* (*im Geschützrohr*); **8.** ♪ (Operati'ons)Feld *n*; **9.** *TV* Feld *n*, Rasterbild *n*; **10.** a) *bsd. psych., sociol.* Praxis *f*, Wirklichkeit *f*, b) ✚ Außeneinsatz *m*, (praktischer) Einsatz; → *field service*, *field study*, *fieldwork* 2–4 *etc.*; **II** *v/t.* **11.** *sport* Mannschaft, Spieler aufs Feld schicken; **12.** *Baseball, Kricket:* a) den *Ball* auffangen u. zu'rückwerfen, b) *Spieler* im Feld aufstellen; **13.** *fig.* e-e *Frage etc.* kontern; **III** *v/i.* **14.** *Kricket etc.:* bei der 'Fängerpar,tei sein.

'field| am·bu·lance *s.* ✕ Sanka *m*, Sani'tätswagen *m*; *~ coil* *s.* ♫ Feldspule *f*; *~ day s.* **1.** ✕ a) Felddienstübung *f*, b) 'Truppenpa,rade *f*; **2.** *Am.* a) *ped.* Sportfest *n*, b) Exkursi'onstag *m*; **3.** *have a ~ fig.* a) s-n großen Tag haben, b) e-n Mordsspaß haben (*with* mit); *~ en·gi·neer s.* Außendiensttechniker

m.

field·er ['fiːldə] *s. Kricket etc.:* a) Fänger *m,* b) Feldspieler *m,* c) *pl.* 'Fängerpar-,tei *f.*

field| e·vent *s. sport* technische Diszip-lin, *pl. mst* 'Sprung- u. 'Wurfdiszi,pli-nen *pl.;* **~ glass(·es** *pl.*) *s.* Fernglas *n,* Feldstecher *m;* **~ goal** *s. Basketball:* Feldkorb *m;* **~ gun** *s.* ✕ Feldgeschütz *n;* **~ hos·pi·tal** *s.* ✕ Feldlaza,rett *n;* **~ kitch·en** *s.* ✕ Feldküche *f;* ♀ **Mar-shal** *s.* ✕ Feldmarschall *m;* **~ mouse** *s.* [*irr.*] Feldmaus *f;* **~ of·fi·cer** *s.* ✕ 'Stabsoffi,zier *m;* **~ pack** *s.* ✕ Marsch-gepäck *n,* Tor'nister *m;* **~ re·search** *s.* ✝ *etc.* Feldforschung *f;* **~ ser·vice** *s.* ✝ Außendienst *m.*

fields·man ['fiːldzmən] *s.* [*irr.*] → **field-er** a, b.

field| sports *s. pl.* Sport *m* im Freien (*bsd. Jagen, Fischen*); **~ stud·y** *s.* Feld-studie *f;* **~ test** *s.* praktischer Versuch; **~ train·ing** *s.* ✕ Geländeausbildung *f;* '**~·work** *s.* **1.** ✕ Feldschanze *f;* **2.** prak-tische (wissenschaftliche) Arbeit, *a.* Arbeit *f* im Gelände; **3.** ✝ Außendienst *m,* -einsatz *m;* **4.** *Markt-, Meinungsfor-schung:* Feldarbeit *f;* '**~·work·er** *s.* **1.** ✝ Außendienstmitarbeiter(in); **2.** Inter-'viewer(in), Befrager(in).

fiend [fiːnd] *s.* **1.** a) *a. fig.* Satan *m,* Teufel *m,* b) Dämon *m, fig. a.* Unhold *m;* **2.** *bsd. in Zssgn:* a) Süchtige(r *m*) *f:* **opium ~,** b) Fa'natiker(in), Narr *m,* Fex *m:* **~ fresh-air fiend,** c) *Am. sl.* ,Ka'none' *f* (**at** in *dat.*); '**fiend·ish** [-dɪʃ] *adj.* □ teuflisch, unmenschlich; *fig.* F verteufelt, ,gemein'; '**fiend·ish-ness** [-dɪʃnɪs] *s.* teuflische Bosheit; *fig.* Gemeinheit *f.*

fierce [fɪəs] *adj.* □ **1.** wild, grimmig, wütend (*alle a. fig.*); **2.** heftig, scharf; **3.** grell; '**fierce·ness** [-nɪs] *s.* Wildheit *f,* Grimmigkeit *f;* Schärfe *f,* Heftigkeit *f.*

fi·er·y ['faɪərɪ] *adj.* □ **1.** brennend, glü-hend (*a. fig.*); **2.** *fig.* feurig, hitzig, hef-tig; **3.** feuerrot; **4.** feuergefährlich; **5.** Feuer...

fife [faɪf] ♪ **I** *s.* **1.** (Quer)Pfeife *f;* **2.** → *fifer;* **II** *v/t. u. v/i.* **3.** (*auf der Querpfei-fe*) pfeifen; '**fif·er** [-fə] *s.* (Quer)Pfeifer *m.*

fif·teen [,fɪf'tiːn] **I** *adj.* **1.** fünfzehn; **II** *s.* **2.** Fünfzehn *f;* **3.** *Rugby:* Fünfzehn *f;* ,**fif'teenth** [-nθ] **I** *adj.* **1.** fünfzehnt; **II** *s.* **2.** der (*die, das*) Fünfzehnte; **3.** Fünf-zehntel *n.*

fifth [fɪfθ] **I** *adj.* □ **1.** fünft; **II** *s.* **2.** der (*die, das*) Fünfte; **3.** Fünftel *n;* **4.** ♪ Quinte *f;* **~ col·umn** *s. pol.* fünfte Ko-'lonne.

fifth·ly ['fɪfθlɪ] *adv.* fünftens.

fifth wheel *s.* **1.** *mot.* a) Ersatzrad *n,* b) Drehschemel(ring) *m* (*Sattelschlepper*); **2.** *fig.* fünftes Rad am Wagen.

fif·ti·eth ['fɪftɪɪθ] **I** *adj.* **1.** fünfzigst; **II** *s.* **2.** der (*die, das*) Fünfzigste; **3.** Fünfzigs-tel *n;* **fif·ty** ['fɪftɪ] **I** *adj.* fünfzig; **II** *s.* Fünfzig *f* (*in the fifties* in den Fünfziger-jahren (*e-s Jahrhunderts*); *he is in his fifties* er ist in den Fünfzigern); ,**fif·ty-**'**fif·ty** *adj. u. adv.* F fifty-fifty, ,halbe--halbe'.

fig¹ [fɪg] *s.* ♀ **1.** Feige *f: I don't care a ~ (for it)* F das ist mir schnuppe!; **2.** Fei-genbaum *m.*

fig² [fɪg] *s.* F **1.** Kleidung *f,* Gala *f: in full ~* in voller Gala; **2.** Zustand *m: in good ~* gut in Form; **II** *v/t.* **3. ~ out** her'ausputzen.

fight [faɪt] **I** *s.* **1.** Kampf *m* (*a. fig.*), Gefecht *n:* **~ against drugs** Drogen-

bekämpfung *f;* **make a ~ of it, put up a ~** kämpfen, sich wehren; *put up a good* **~** sich tapfer schlagen; **2.** a) Schläge'rei *f,* Raufe'rei *f,* b) *sport* (Box)Kampf *m:* *have a ~* → 12; *make a ~ for* kämpfen um; **3.** Kampf(es)lust *f,* -fähigkeit *f:* *show* **~** sich zur Wehr setzen; *there is no ~ left in him* er ist kampfmüde *od.* ,fertig'; **4.** Streit *m,* Kon'flikt *m;* **II** *v/t.* [*irr.*] **5.** *j-n od. et.* bekämpfen, bekrie-gen, ankämpfen mit *od.* gegen, sich schla-gen mit, *sport a.* boxen gegen; *fig.* an-kämpfen gegen (*e-e schlechte Gewohn-heit etc.*); **~ back** (*od. down*) *fig.* Trä-nen, Enttäuschung unterdrücken; **~ off** *j-n od. et.* abwehren, *a. e-e* Erkältung *etc.* bekämpfen; **6.** *e-n* Krieg, *e-n* Pro-zess führen, *e-e* Schlacht schlagen *od.* austragen, *e-e* Sache ausfechten: **~ a duel** sich duellieren; **~ an election** kandidieren; **~ it out** es (untereinan-der) ausfechten; **7.** *et.* verfechten, sich einsetzen für; **8.** *et.* erkämpfen: **~ one's way** sich durchschlagen; **9.** ✕ *Truppen etc.* kommandieren, (im Kampf) füh-ren; **III** *v/i.* **10.** kämpfen (*with od.* **against** mit *od.* gegen, *for* um): **~ against s.th.** gegen et. ankämpfen; **~ back** sich zur Wehr setzen; **11.** boxen; **12.** sich raufen *od.* prügeln *od.* schlagen.

fight·er ['faɪtə] *s.* **1.** Kämpfer *m,* Streiter *m;* **2.** Schläger *m,* Raufbold *m;* **3.** *sport* (*bsd.* Offen'siv)Boxer *m;* **4.** *a.* **~ plane** ✕, ✈ Jagdflugzeug *n,* Jäger *m:* **~- -bomber** Jagdbomber *m;* **~ group** *Brit.* Jagdgruppe *f, Am.* Jagdgeschwader *n;* **~-interceptor** Abfangjäger *m;* **~ pilot** Jagdflieger *m.*

fight·ing ['faɪtɪŋ] **I** *s.* Kampf *m,* Kämpfe *pl;* **II** *adj.* Kampf...; streitlustig; **~ chance** *e-e* re'elle Chance (*wenn man sich anstrengt*); **~ cock** *s.* Kampf-hahn *m* (*a. fig.*): *live like a ~* in Saus u. Braus leben; **~ dog** *s.* Kampfhund *m.*

fig leaf *s.* Feigenblatt *n* (*a. fig.*).

fig·ment ['fɪgmənt] *s.* **1.** *oft* **~ of the imagination** Fanta'siepro,dukt *n,* rei-ne Einbildung; **2.** ,Märchen' *n,* (pure) Erfindung.

fig tree *s.* Feigenbaum *m.*

fig·ur·a·tive ['fɪgjʊrətɪv] *adj.* □ **1.** *ling.* bildlich, über'tragen, fi'gürlich, meta-'phorisch; **2.** bilderreich (*Stil*); **3.** sym-'bolisch.

fig·ure ['fɪgə] **I** *s.* **1.** Fi'gur *f,* Form *f,* Gestalt *f,* Aussehen *n: keep one's ~* schlank bleiben; **2.** *fig.* Fi'gur *f,* Per'son *f,* Per'sönlichkeit *f* (bemerkenswerte) Erscheinung: *a public ~* e-e Persönlich-keit des öffentlichen Lebens; **~ of fun** komische Figur; *cut* (*od. make*) *a poor ~* e-e traurige Figur abgeben; **3.** Darstellung *f* (*bsd. des menschlichen Körpers*), Bild *n,* Statue *f;* **4.** *a.* ❍, ♫ Fi'gur *f, weitS. a.* Zeichnung *f,* Dia-'gramm *n; a.* Abbildung *f,* Illustrati'on *f* (*in e-m Buch etc.*); **5.** *Tanz, Eiskunst-lauf etc.:* Fi'gur *f;* **6.** (Stoff)Muster *n;* **7.** *a.* **~ of speech** a) ('Rede-, 'Sprach)Fi-,gur *f,* b) Me'tapher *f,* Bild *n;* **8.** ♪ a) Fi'gur *f,* b) (Bass)Bezifferung *f;* **9.** Zahl(zeichen *n*) *f,* Ziffer *f: run into three ~s* in die Hunderte gehen; *be good at ~s* ein guter Rechner sein; **10.** Preis *m,* Summe *f: at a low ~* billig; **II** *v/t.* **11.** gestalten, formen; **12.** bildlich darstellen, abbilden; **13.** *a.* **~ to o.s.** sich et. vorstellen; **14.** verzieren (*a. a.* ❍) mustern; **15. ~ out** F a) ausrechnen, b) ausknobeln, ,rauskriegen', c) ,kapie-ren': *I can't ~ him out* ich werde aus ihm nicht schlau; **III** *v/i.* **16. ~ out at**

sich belaufen auf (*acc.*); **17. ~ on** *Am.* F a) rechnen mit, b) sich verlassen auf (*acc.*); **18.** erscheinen, vorkommen, e-e Rolle spielen: **~ large** e-e große Rolle spielen; **~ on a list** auf e-r Liste stehen; **19.** F (genau) passen: *that ~s!* das ist klar!; **~ dance** *s.* Fi'gurentanz *m;* '**~·head** *s.* ⚓ Gali'onsfi,gur *f, fig. a.* ,Aushängeschild' *n;* **~ skat·er** *s. sport* (Eis)Kunstläufer(in); **~ skat·ing** *s. sport* Eiskunstlauf *m.*

fig·u·rine ['fɪgjʊriːn] *s.* Statu'ette *f,* Fi-gu'rine *f.*

fil·a·ment ['fɪləmənt] *s.* **1.** Faden *m* (*a. anat.*); Faser *f;* **2.** ♀ Staubfaden *m;* **3.** ⚡ (Glüh-, Heiz)Faden *m:* **~ battery** Heiz-batterie *f.*

fil·bert ['fɪlbət] *s.* ♀ **1.** Haselnussstrauch *m;* **2.** Haselnuss *f.*

filch [fɪltʃ] *v/t.* F ,klauen' (*stehlen*).

file¹ [faɪl] **I** *s.* **1.** Aufreihdraht *m,* -faden *m;* **2.** (Akten-, Brief-, Doku'menten-*etc.*)Ordner *m,* Sammelmappe *f, a.* Kar'tei(kasten *m*) *f;* **3.** a) Akte(nstück *n*) *f, a.* Dossi'er *n* (*der Polizei etc.*): **~ number** Aktenzeichen *n,* b) Akten (-bündel *n,* -stoß *m*) *pl.,* c) Ablage *f,* abgelegte Briefe *pl. od.* Pa'piere *pl.: on* **~** bei den Akten, d) *Computer:* Da'tei *f: activate a ~* e-e Datei aufrufen; *attach a ~* e-e Datei (*als Attachment*) anhän-gen; *close* (*od. open*) *a ~* e-e Datei öffnen (*od.* schließen); *insert a ~* e-e Datei einfügen, e) Liste *f,* Verzeichnis *n:* **~ management** Dateiverwaltung *f;* **4.** ✕ Reihe *f;* **5.** Reihe *f* (*Personen od. Sachen hintereinander*); **II** *v/t.* **6.** Briefe *etc.* ablegen, einordnen, ab-, einheften, zu den Akten nehmen, *Computer:* ab-speichern; **7.** Antrag, ♜ Klage einrei-chen; **III** *v/i.* **8.** hinterein'ander *od.* ✕ in Reihe (hi'nein-, hin'aus- *etc.*)mar-schieren.

file² [faɪl] **I** *s.* **1.** ❍ Feile *f;* **II** *v/t.* **2.** ❍ feilen; **3.** *Stil* feilen, glätten.

file| man·ag·er *s. Computer:* Da'tei-,manager *m;* **~ name** *s.* Dateiname *m.*

fi·let ['fɪlɪt] (*Fr.*) *s.* **1.** *Küche:* Fi'let *n;* **2.** *a.* **~ lace** Fi'let *n,* Netz(sticke'rei *f*) *n.*

fil·i·al ['fɪljəl] *adj.* □ kindlich, Kindes..., Sohnes..., Tochter...; **fil·i·a·tion** [,fɪli-'eɪʃn] *s.* **1.** Kindschaft(sverhältnis *n*) *f:* **~ proceeding** ♜ *Am.* Vaterschaftspro-zess *m;* **2.** Abstammung *f;* **3.** Herkunfts-feststellung *f;* **4.** Verzweigung *f.*

fil·i·bus·ter ['fɪlɪbʌstə] **I** *s.* **1.** *hist.* Frei-beuter *m;* **2.** *parl. Am.* a) Obstrukti'on *f,* Verschleppungstaktik *f,* b) Obstrukti'onspo,litiker *m;* **II** *v/i.* **3.** *parl. Am.* Obstrukti'on treiben; **III** *v/t.* **4.** Antrag *etc.* durch Obstrukti'on zu Fall bringen.

fil·i·gree ['fɪlɪgriː] *s.* Fili'gran(arbeit *f*) *n.*

fil·ing| cab·i·net ['faɪlɪŋ] *s.* Akten-schrank *m;* **~ card** *s.* Kar'teikarte *f.*

fil·ings ['faɪlɪŋz] *s. pl.* Feilspäne *pl.*

Fil·i·pi·no [,fɪlɪ'piːnəʊ] **I** *pl.* **-nos** *s.* Fili-'pino *m;* **II** *adj.* philip'pinisch.

fill [fɪl] **I** *s.* **1.** *eat one's ~* sich satt essen; *have one's ~ of s.th.* genug von et. haben; *weep one's ~* sich ausweinen; **2.** Füllung *f* (*Material od. Menge*): *a ~ of petrol mot.* e-e Tankfüllung; **II** *v/t.* **3.** (an-, aus)füllen, voll füllen: **~ s.o.'s glass** j-m einschenken; **~ the sails** die Segel (auf)blähen; **4.** ab-, einfüllen: **~ wine into bottles;** **5.** (*mit Nahrung*) sättigen; **6.** *Pfeife* stopfen; **7.** *Zahn* fül-len, plombieren; **8.** *die Straßen, ein Sta-dion etc.* füllen; **9.** *a. fig.* erfüllen: *smoke ~ed the room; grief ~ed his heart; ~ed with fear* angsterfüllt; **10.** *Amt, Posten* a) besetzen, b) ausfüllen, beklei-den: **~ s.o.'s place** j-s Stelle einneh-

fill in – fine

F

men, j-n ersetzen; **11.** *Auftrag* ausführen: **~ an order**; → *bill*[2] 4; **III** *v/i.* **12.** sich füllen, *(Segel)* sich (auf)blähen; **~ in I** *v/t.* **1.** Loch *etc.* auf-, ausfüllen; **2.** *Brit. Formular* ausfüllen; **3.** a) *Namen etc.* einsetzen, b) *Fehlendes* ergänzen; **4.** *fill s.o. in* F *(on* über *acc.)* j-n ins Bild setzen, j-n informieren; **II** *v/i.* **5.** einspringen **(for s.o.** für j-n); **~ out I** *v/t.* **1.** *bsd. Am. Formular* ausfüllen; **2.** *Bericht etc.* abrunden; **II** *v/i.* **3.** fülliger werden *(Figur), (Person a.)* zunehmen, *(Gesicht)* voller werden; **~ up I** *v/t.* **1.** auffüllen, voll füllen: **~ her up!** F voll tanken, bitte; **2.** → *fill in* 2; **II** *v/i.* **3.** sich füllen.

fill·er ['fɪlə] *s.* **1.** Füllvorrichtung *f, a.* 'Abfüllma,schine *f,* Trichter *m*: **~ cap** *mot.* Tankverschluss *m*; **2.** Füllstoff *m,* Zusatzmittel *n*; **3.** *paint.* Spachtel(masse *f) m,* Füller *m*; **4.** *fig.* Füllsel *n,* Füller *m*; **5.** *ling.* Füllwort *n*; **6.** Sprengladung *f.*

fil·let ['fɪlɪt] **I** *s.* **1.** Stirn-, Haarband *n*; **2.** Leiste *f,* Band *n*; **3.** Zierstreifen *m,* Fi'let *n (am Buch)*; **4.** △ Leiste *f,* Rippe *f*; **5.** *Küche:* Fi'let *n*; **6.** ⊕ a) Hohlkehle *f,* b) Schweißnaht *f*; **II** *v/t.* **7.** mit e-m Haarband *od.* e-r Leiste *etc.* schmücken; **8.** *Küche:* a) filetieren, b) als Fi'let zubereiten.

fill·ing ['fɪlɪŋ] **I** *s.* **1.** Füllung *f,* Füllmasse *f,* Einlage *f,* Füllsel *n*; **2.** (Zahn)Plombe *f,* (-)Füllung *f*; **3.** *das* 'Voll-, Aus-, Auffüllen, Füllung *f*: **~ machine** Abfüllmaschine *f*; **~ station** *Am.* Tankstelle *f*; **II** *adj.* **4.** sättigend.

fil·lip ['fɪlɪp] **I** *s.* **1.** Schnalzer *m (mit Finger u. Daumen)*; **2.** Klaps *m*; **3.** *fig.* Ansporn *m,* Auftrieb *m*: **give a ~ to** → 6; **II** *v/t.* **4.** schnippen, schnipsen; **5.** *j-m* e-n Klaps geben; **6.** *fig.* anspornen, in Schwung bringen.

fil·ly ['fɪlɪ] *s.* **1.** *zo.* Stutenfohlen *n*; **2.** *fig.* 'wilde Hummel' *(Mädchen).*

film [fɪlm] **I** *s.* **1.** Mem'bran(e) *f,* Häutchen *n,* Film *m*; **2.** *phot.* Film *m*; **3.** Film *m*: **the ~s** die Filmindustrie, der Film, das Kino; **be in ~s** beim Film sein; **shoot a ~** e-n Film drehen; **4.** (hauch)dünne Schicht, 'Überzug *m (Zellophan- etc.)*Haut *f*; **5.** (hauch)dünnes Gewebe, *a.* Faser *f*; **6.** Trübung *f (des Auges),* Schleier *f*; **II** *v/t.* **7.** (mit e-m Häutchen *etc.)* über'ziehen; **8.** a) *Szene etc.* filmen, **~ed report** Filmbericht *m,* b) *Roman etc.* verfilmen; **III** *v/i.* **9.** *a.* **~ over** sich mit e-m Häutchen über'ziehen; **10.** a) sich (gut) verfilmen lassen, b) e-n Film drehen, filmen; **~ li·brar·y** *s.* 'Filmar,chiv *n*; **~ mak·er** *s.* Filmemacher *m*; **~ pack** *s. phot.* Filmpack *m*; **~ reel** *s.* Filmspule *f*; **~·set** *v/t.* [*irr.*] *typ.* im Foto- *od.* Filmsatz herstellen; **~ star** *s.* Filmstar *m*; **~ strip** *s.* Bildstreifen *m*; **2.** Bildband *n*; **~ ver·sion** *s.* Verfilmung *f.*

film·y ['fɪlmɪ] *adj.* □ **1.** mit e-m Häutchen bedeckt; **2.** duftig, zart, hauchdünn; **3.** trübe, verschleiert *(Auge).*

Fi·lo·fax ['faɪləʊfæks] *npr. Warenzeichen:* Ter'minplaner *m.*

fi·lo pas·try ['faɪləʊ] *s.* Blätterteiggebäck *n.*

fil·ter ['fɪltə] **I** *s.* **1.** Filter *m,* Seihtuch *n,* Seiher *m*; **2.** ⚡, ⊕, ⚡, *phot., phys., tel.* Filter *n, m*; **3.** *mot. Brit.* grüner Pfeil *(für Abbieger)*; **II** *v/t.* **4.** filtern: a) ('durch)seihen, b) filtrieren: **~ off (out)** ab- (heraus)filtern; **III** *v/i.* **5.** 'durchsickern, *(Licht a.)* 'durchscheinen, -dringen; **6.** *fig.* **~ out** *od.* **through** 'durchsickern *(Nachrichten etc.)*; **~ into** ein-

sickern *od.* -dringen in *(acc.)*; **7. ~ out** langsam *od.* grüppchenweise herauskommen *(of* aus); **8.** *mot. Brit.* a) die Spur wechseln, b) sich einordnen **(to the left** links), c) abbiegen *(bei grünem Pfeil)*; **~ bag** *s.* Filtertüte *f*; **~ bed** *s.* **1.** Kläranlage *f,* -becken *n*; **2.** Filterschicht *f*; **~ char·coal** *s.* ⊕ Filterkohle *f*; **~ cir·cuit** *s.* ⚡ Siebkreis *m*; **~ lane** *s. mot.* Abbiegespur *f*; **~ pa·per** *s.* 'Filterpa,pier *n*; **~ tip** *s.* **1.** Filter(mundstück *n) m*; **2.** 'Filterziga,rette *f*; **'~-tipped** mit Filter, Filter...: **~ cigarette.**

filth [fɪlθ] *s.* **1.** Schmutz *m,* Dreck *m*; **2.** *fig.* Schmutz *m,* Schweine'rei(en *pl.) f*; **3.** a) unflätige Sprache, b) unflätige Ausdrücke *pl.,* Unflat *m*; **'filth·i·ness** [-θɪnɪs] *s.* Schmutzigkeit *f (a. fig.)*; **'filth·y** [-θɪ] **I** *adj.* □ **1.** schmutzig, dreckig, *fig. a.* schweinisch; **2.** *fig.* unflätig; **3.** F ekelhaft, scheußlich: **~ mood; ~ weather** *a.* 'Sauwetter' *n*; **II** *adv.* **4.** F ,unheimlich', ,furchtbar': **~ rich** stinkreich.

fil·trate ['fɪltreɪt] **I** *v/t.* filtrieren; **II** *s.* Fil'trat *n*; **fil'tra·tion** [fɪl'treɪʃn] *s.* Filtrati'on *f.*

fin¹ [fɪn] *s.* **1.** *zo.* Flosse *f,* Finne *f*; **2.** ⚓ Kielflosse *f*; **3.** ✈ a) (Seiten)Flosse *f,* b) ✗ Steuerschwanz *m (e-r Bombe)*; **4.** ⊕ a) Grat *m,* (Guss)Naht *f,* b) (Kühl)Rippe *f*; **5.** Schwimmflosse *f*; **6.** *sl.* ,Flosse' *f (Hand).*

fin² [fɪn] *s. Am. sl.* Fünf'dollarschein *m.*

fi·na·gle [fɪ'neɪgl] F **I** *v/t.* **1.** *et.* her'ausschinden; **2.** (sich) *et.* ergaunern; **3.** *j-n* betrügen, begaunern; **II** *v/i.* **4.** gaunern, mogeln.

fi·nal ['faɪnl] **I** *adj.* □ → **finally 1.** letzt, schließlich; **2.** endgültig, End..., Schluss...: **~ assembly** ⊕ Endmontage *f*; **~ date** Schlusstermin *m*; **~ disposal site** Endlager *n*; **~ examination** Abschlussprüfung *f*; **~ score** *sport* Endstand *m*; **~ speech** ⚖ Schlussplädoyer *n*; **~ storage** Endlagerung *f (von Atommüll etc.)*; **~ whistle** *sport* Schlusspfiff *m*; **3.** endgültig: a) 'unwider,ruflich, b) entscheidend, c) ⚖ rechtskräftig: **after ~ judg(e)ment** nach Rechtskraft des Urteils; **4.** per'fekt; **5.** *ling.* a) auslautend, End..., Schluss..., b) Absichts..., Final...: **~ clause**; **II** *s.* **6.** *a. pl.* Fi'nale *n,* Endkampf *m od.* -runde *f od.* -spiel *n od.* -lauf *m*; **7.** *mst pl. univ.* 'Schlusse,xamen *n,* -prüfung *f*; **8.** F Spätausgabe *f (e-r Zeitung)*; **fi·na·le** [fɪ'nɑːlɪ] *s.* Fi'nale *n*: a) *♪ (mst schneller)* Schlusssatz, b) *thea.* Schluss(szene *f) m (bsd. Oper)*, c) *fig.* (dra'matisches) Ende; **'fi·nal·ist** [-nəlɪst] *s.* **1.** *sport* Fina'list(in), Endspiel-, Endkampf-, Endrundenteilnehmer(in); **2.** *univ.* Ex'amenskandi,dat(in); **fi·nal·i·ty** [faɪ'nælətɪ] *s.* **1.** Endgültigkeit *f*; **2.** Entschiedenheit *f*; **'fi·nal·ize** [-nəlaɪz] *v/t.* **1.** be-, voll'enden, (endgültig) erledigen, abschließen; **2.** endgültige Form geben *(dat.)*; **'fi·nal·ly** [-nəlɪ] *adv.* **1.** endlich, schließlich, zu'letzt; **2.** zum (Ab)Schluss; **3.** endgültig, defini'tiv.

fi·nance [faɪ'næns] **I** *s.* **1.** Fi'nanz *f,* Fi'nanzwesen *n,* -wirtschaft *f,* -wissenschaft *f*; **2.** *pl.* Fi'nanzen *pl.,* Einkünfte *pl.,* Vermögenslage *f*; **II** *v/t.* **3.** finanzieren; **~ act** *s. pol.* Steuergesetz *n*; **~ bill** *s.* **1.** *pol.* Fi'nanzvorlage *f*; **2.** ✝ Fi'nanzwechsel *m*; **~ com·pa·ny** *s.* ✝ Fi'nanzierungsgesellschaft *f*; **~ house** *s.* ✝ *Brit.* 'Kundenkre,ditbank *f.*

fi·nan·cial [faɪ'nænʃl] *adj.* □ finanzi'ell, Finanz..., Geld..., Fiskal...: **~ aid** Finanzhilfe *f*; **~ backer** Geldgeber *m*; **~**

columns Handels-, Wirtschaftsteil *m*; **~ investment** Geldanlage *f*; **~ paper** Börsen-, Handelsblatt *n*; **~ plan** Finanzierungsplan *m*; **~ policy** Finanzpolitik *f*; **~ situation** *(od. condition)* Vermögenslage *f*; **~ standing** Kreditwürdigkeit *f*; **~ statement** ✝ Bilanz *f*; **~ year** a) ✝ Geschäftsjahr *n,* b) *parl.* Haushalts-, Rechnungsjahr *n*; **fi·nan·cier** [-nsɪə] **I** *s.* **1.** Finanzi'er *m*; **2.** Fi'nanz(fach)mann *m*; **II** *v/t.* **3.** finanzieren; **III** *v/i.* **4.** *(bsd.* skrupellose) Geldgeschäfte machen.

finch [fɪntʃ] *s. orn.* Fink *m.*

find [faɪnd] **I** *v/t.* [*irr.*] **1.** finden; **2.** finden, (an)treffen, stoßen auf *(acc.)*: *I found him in* ich traf ihn zu Hause an; **~ a good reception** e-e gute Aufnahme finden; **3.** entdecken, bemerken, sehen, feststellen, (her'aus)finden: **he found that ...** er stellte fest *od.* fand, dass; *I ~ it easy* ich finde es leicht; **~ one's way** den Weg finden **(to** nach, zu), sich zurechtfinden *(in* in *dat.)*; **~ its way into** *fig.* hineingeraten in *(acc.) (Sache)*; **~ o.s.** a) sich wo *od.* wie befinden, b) sich sehen: **~ o.s. surrounded,** c) sich finden, sich voll entfalten, s-e Fähigkeiten erkennen, d) zu sich selbst finden (→ 5); *I found myself telling a lie* ich ertappte mich bei e-r Lüge; **4.** finden: a) beschaffen, auftreiben, b) erlangen, sich verschaffen, c) *Zeit etc.* aufbringen; **5.** *j-n* versorgen, ausstatten *(in* mit): **be well found in clothes; all found** freie Station, freie Unterkunft u. Verpflegung; **~ o.s.** sich selbst versorgen; **6.** ⚖ (be)finden für, erklären (für): *he was found guilty*; **7. ~ out** a) *et.* herausfinden, -bekommen, b) *j-n* ertappen, entlarven, durch'schauen; **II** *v/i.* [*irr.*] **8.** ⚖ (be)finden, für (für Recht) erkennen *(that* dass): **~ for the defendant** a) die Klage abweisen, b) *Strafprozess:* den Angeklagten freisprechen; **~ against the defendant** a) der Klage stattgeben, b) *Strafprozess:* den Angeklagten verurteilen; **III** *s.* **9.** Fund *m,* Entdeckung *f*; **'find·er** [-də] *s.* **1.** Finder *m,* Entdecker *m*: **~s keepers** F wer etwas findet, darf es (auch) behalten; **~'s reward** Finderlohn *m*; **2.** *phot.* Sucher *m*; **'find·ing** [-dɪŋ] *s.* **1.** Fund *m,* Entdeckung *f*; **2.** *mst pl. phys. etc.* Befund *m (a. ⚕),* Feststellung(en *pl.) f,* Erkenntnis(se *pl.) f*; **3.** ⚖ Feststellung *f,* der Geschworenen: a) Spruch *m*: **~s of fact** Tatsachenfeststellungen; **4.** *pl.* Werkzeuge *pl. od.* Materi'al *n (von Handwerkern).*

fine¹ [faɪn] **I** *adj.* □ **1.** *allg.* fein: a) dünn, zart, zierlich: **~ china,** b) scharf: *a ~ edge,* c) rein: **~ silver** Feinsilber *n*; *gold 24 carats ~* 24-karätiges Gold, d) *aus kleinsten Teilchen bestehend:* **~ sand,** e) schön: *a ~ ship; ~ weather,* f) vornehm, edel: *a ~ man,* g) geschmackvoll, gepflegt, ele'gant, h) angenehm, lieblich: *a ~ scent,* i) feinsinnig: *a ~ distinction* in feiner Unterschied; **2.** prächtig, großartig: *a ~ view; a ~ musician; a ~ fellow* ein feiner *od.* prächtiger Kerl (→ 3); **3.** F, *a. iro.* fein, schön: *that's all very ~ but ...* das ist ja alles gut u. schön, aber ...; *a ~ fellow you are!* *contp.* du bist mir ein schöner Genosse!; *that's ~ with me!* in Ordnung!; **4.** F fein, genau, fino-...; **II** *adv.* **5.** F fein: a) vornehm *(a. contp.)*: *talk ~,* b) sehr gut, ,bestens': *that will suit me ~* das passt mir ausgezeichnet; **6.** knapp: *cut (od. run) it ~* ins Gedränge *(bsd.* in Zeitnot) kommen; **III** *v/t.* **7. ~**

away, **~ down** fein(er) machen, abschleifen, zuspitzen; **8.** *oft* **~ down** *Wein etc.* läutern, klären; **9.** *metall.* frischen; **IV** *v/i.* **10. ~ away, ~ down, ~ off** fein(er) werden, abnehmen, sich abschleifen; **11.** sich klären.

fine² [faɪn] **I** *s.* **1.** ⚖ Geldstrafe *f*, Bußgeld *n*; **2.** *in* **~** a) schließlich, b) kurzum; **II** *v/t.* **3.** mit e-r Geldstrafe *od.* e-m Bußgeld belegen: *he was* **~***d £2* er musste 2 Pfund (Strafe) bezahlen.

fine| **ad·just·ment** *s.* ⚙ Feineinstellung *f*; **~ arts** *s. pl. (die)* schönen Künste *pl.*; '**~·bore** *v/t.* ⚙ präzisi'onsbohren; **~ cut** *s.* Feinschnitt *m (Tabak);* ˌ**~-'draw** *v/t.* [*irr.* → *draw*] **1.** fein zs.-nähen, kunststopfen; **2.** ⚙ *Draht* fein ausziehen; ˌ**~-'drawn** → *fine-spun.*

fine·ness ['faɪnnɪs] *s. allg.* Feinheit *f*; '**fin·er·y** [-nərɪ] *s.* **1.** Putz *m*, Staat *m*; **2.** ⚙ a) Frischofen *m*, b) Frische'rei *f*; **fines** [faɪnz] *s. pl.* ⚙ Grus *m*, fein gesiebtes Materi'al; ˌ**fine-'spun** *adj.* fein gesponnen *(a. fig.).*

fi·nesse [fɪ'nes] **I** *s.* **1.** Fi'nesse *f*: a) Spitzfindigkeit *f*, b) (kleiner) Kunstgriff, Kniff *m*; **2.** Raffi'nesse *f*, Schlauheit *f*; **3.** *Kartenspiel:* Schneiden *n*; **II** *v/i.* **4.** *Kartenspiel:* schneiden; **5.** ˌtrick·sen', Kniffe anwenden.

ˌ**fine**|-'**tooth**(**ed**) *adj.* fein (gezahnt): **~ comb** Staubkamm *m*; *go over s.th. with a* **~ comb** a) et. genau durchsuchen, b) et. genau unter die Lupe nehmen; **~ tun·ing** *s. Radio:* Feinabstimmung *f*.

fin·ger ['fɪŋgə] **I** *s.* **1.** Finger *m*: *first, second, third* **~** Zeige-, Mittel-, Ringfinger; *fourth (od. little)* **~** kleiner Finger; *get (od. pull) one's* **~** *out Brit.* F ˌsich am Riemen reißen'; *have (od. keep) one's* **~** *in the pie* die Hand im Spiel haben; *keep one's* **~***s crossed for s.o.* j-m den Daumen drücken *od.* halten; *lay (od. put) one's* **~** *on s.th. fig.* den Finger auf et. legen; *not to lay a* **~** *on s.o.* j-m kein Härchen krümmen, j-n nicht anrühren; *not to lift (od. raise, stir) a* **~** keinen Finger rühren; *put the* **~** *on s.o.* → **10**; *twist (od. wrap, wind) s.o. (a)round one's little* **~** j-n um den (kleinen) Finger wickeln; *work one's* **~***s to the bone (for s.o.)* sich (für j-n) die Finger abarbeiten; → *a. Verbindungen mit anderen Verben u. Substantiven*; **2.** Finger(ling) *m (am Handschuh);* **3.** (Uhr)Zeiger *m*; **4.** Fingerbreit *m*; **5.** schmaler Streifen: schmales Stück; **6.** ⚙ Daumen *m*, Greifer *m*; **7.** *sl.* → *finger man*; **II** *v/t.* **8.** a) betasten, befühlen, b) her'umfingern an *(dat.)*, spielen mit; **9.** ♪ a) et. mit den Fingern spielen, b) *Noten* mit Fingersatz versehen; **10.** *Am.* F a) j-n verpfeifen, b) j-n beschatten, c) *Opfer* ausspähen; **III** *v/i.* **11.** her'umfingern (*at* an *dat.*), spielen (*with* mit); '**~·board** *s.* ♪ a) Griffbrett *n*, b) Klavia'tur *f*, c) Manu'al *n (der Orgel);* **~ bowl** *s.* Fingerschale *f*; '**~·breadth** *s.* Fingerbreit *m*.

-fin·gered [fɪŋgəd] *adj. in Zssgn* mit ... Fingern, ...fing(e)rig.

fin·ger·ing ['fɪŋgərɪŋ] *s.* ♪ Fingersatz *m*.

fin·ger| **man** *s.* Spitzel *m (e-r Bande);* '**~·mark** *s.* Fingerabdruck *m (Schmutzfleck);* '**~·nail** *s.* Fingernagel *m*; **~ nut** *s.* ⚙ Flügelmutter *f*; '**~·paint** *v/i.* Fingerfarbe *f*; **II** *v/t. u. v/i.* mit Fingerfarben malen; **~ post** *s.* **1.** Wegweiser *m*; **2.** *fig.* Fingerzeig *m*; '**~·print** *s.* Fingerabdruck *m*; **II** *v/t.* von j-m Fingerabdrücke machen; '**~·stall** *s.* Fingerling *m*; '**~·tip** *s. mst fig.* Fingerspitze *f*: *have*

---

at one's **~***s Kenntnisse* parat haben; *to one's* **~***s* durch u. durch.

fin·i·cal ['fɪnɪkl] *adj.* ☐, '**fin·ick·ing** [-kɪŋ], '**fin·ick·y** [-kɪ] *adj.* **1.** über'trieben genau, pe'dantisch; **2.** heikel, ˌpingelig'; **3.** affek'tiert, geziert; **4.** knifflig.

fi·nis ['fɪnɪs] *(Lat.) s.* Ende *n*.

fin·ish ['fɪnɪʃ] **I** *s.* **1.** Ende *n*, Schluss *m*; **2.** *sport* a) Endspurt *m*, Finish *n*, b) Ziel *n*, c) Endkampf *m*, Entscheidung *f*: *be in at the* **~** in die Endrunde kommen, *fig.* das Ende miterleben; **3.** Voll'endung *f*, letzter Schliff, Ele'ganz *f*; **4.** ⚙ a) (äußerliche) Ausführung, Bearbeitung(sgüte) *f*, Oberflächenbeschaffenheit *f*, b) ('Lack- *etc.*),Überzug *m*, c) Poli'tur *f*, d) Appre'tur *f*; **5.** gute Ausführung *od.* Verarbeitung; **6.** ⚐ a) Ausbau *m*, b) Verputz *m*; **II** *v/t.* **7.** a. **~ off** voll'enden, beendigen, fertig stellen, erledigen, zu Ende führen: **~** *a task;* **~** *a book* ein Buch auslesen *od.* zu Ende lesen; **8.** a. **~ off** *(od. up)* a) *Vorräte* auf-, verbrauchen, b) aufessen *od.* austrinken; **9.** a. **~ off** a) j-n ˌerledigen', j-m den Rest geben *(töten od. erschöpfen od. ruinieren),* b) bsd. e-m Tier den Gnadenschuss *od.* -stoß geben; **10.** a) a. **~ off** *(od. up)* et. vervollkommnen, e-r Sache den letzten Schliff geben, b) j-m feine Lebensart beibringen; **11.** ⚙ nachbearbeiten, fertig bearbeiten, *Papier* glätten, *Stoff* zurichten, appretieren, *Möbel etc.* polieren; **III** *v/i.* **12.** a. **~ off** *(od. up)* enden, schließen, aufhören *(with* mit): *have you* **~***ed?* bist du fertig?; *he* **~***ed by saying* abschließend *od.* zum Abschluss sagte er; **13.** a. **~ up** enden, *im Gefängnis etc.* ˌlanden'; **14.** enden, zu Ende gehen; **15. ~ with** mit j-m *od.* et. Schluss machen: *I'm* **~***ed with him!* mit ihm bin ich fertig!; *have* **~***ed with s.o. (od. s.th.)* j-n (et.) nicht mehr brauchen; *I haven't* **~***ed with you yet!* ich bin noch nicht fertig mit dir!; **16.** *sport* einlaufen, durchs Ziel gehen: **~** *third* a. Dritter werden, den dritten Platz belegen, *allg.* als Dritter fertig sein.

fin·ished ['fɪnɪʃt] *adj.* **1.** beendet, fertig: *half-***~** *products* Halbfabrikate; **~ goods** Fertigwaren; **~ part** Fertigteil *n*; **2.** *fig.* ˌerledigt' *(erschöpft od. todgeweiht): he is* **~** mit ihm ist es aus!; **3.** voll'endet, voll'kommen; '**fin·ish·er** [-ʃə] *s.* **1.** ⚙ a) Fertigbearbeiter *m*; Appretierer *m*, b) Ma'schine *f* zur Fertigbearbeitung, *z.B.* Fertigwalzwerk *n*; **2.** F vernichtender Schlag, ˌK.- 'o.-Schlag' *m*; **3.** *strong* **~** *sport* (starker) Spurtläufer.

fin·ish·ing ['fɪnɪʃɪŋ] **I** *s.* **1.** Voll'enden *n*, Fertigmachen *n*, -stellen *n*; **2.** ⚙ a) Fertigbearbeitung *f*, b) (abschließende) Oberflächenbehandlung *f*, *z.B.* Hochglanzpolieren *n od.* Veredelung, d) Appre'tur *f (von Stoffen);* **3.** *sport* Abschluss *m*; **II** *adj.* **4.** abschließend; → *touch* 3; **~ a·gent** *s.* ⚙ Appre'turmittel *n*; **~ in·dus·try** *s.* Ver'edelungsindustrie *f*, verarbeitende Indu'strie; **~ lathe** *s.* ⚙ Fertigdrehbank *f*; **~ line** *s. sport* Ziellinie *f*; **~ mill** *s.* ⚙ Fertigwalzwerk *n*; **2.** Schlichtfräser *m*; **~ post** *s. sport* Zielpfosten *m*; **~ school** *s.* 'Mädchenpensio,nat *n (zur Vorbereitung auf das gesellschaftliche Leben).*

fi·nite ['faɪnaɪt] *adj.* **1.** begrenzt, endlich *(a. ⚛);* **2.** *ling.* fi'nit: **~ form** a. Personalform *f*; **~ verb** Verbum *n* finitum.

fink [fɪŋk] *Am. sl.* **I** *s.* **1.** Streikbrecher *m*; **2.** Spitzel *m*; **3.** ˌDreckskerl' *m*; **II** *v/i.* **4. ~ on** j-n verpfeifen; **5. ~ out** sich

---

drücken, ˌaussteigen'.

Finn [fɪn] *s.* Finne *m*, Finnin *f*.

fin·nan had·dock ['fɪnən] *s.* geräucherter Schellfisch.

finned [fɪnd] *adj.* **1.** *ichth.* mit Flossen; **2.** ⚙ gerippt; **fin·ner** ['fɪnə] *s. zo.* Finnwal *m*.

Finn·ish ['fɪnɪʃ] **I** *adj.* finnisch; **II** *s. ling.* Finnisch *n*.

fin·ny ['fɪnɪ] *adj.* **1.** → *finned* 1; **2.** Flossen..., Fisch...

fiord [fɪ'ɔːd] *s. geogr.* Fjord *m*.

fir [fɜː] *s.* **1.** ♣ Tanne *f*, Fichte *f*; **2.** Tannen-, Fichtenholz *n*; **~ cone** *s.* Tannenzapfen *m*.

fire ['faɪə] **I** *s.* **1.** Feuer *n (a. Edelstein):* **~ and brimstone** a) *bibl.* Feuer u. Schwefel *n*, b) *eccl.* Hölle *f* u. Verdammnis *f*: *be on* **~** brennen, in Flammen stehen, *fig.* Feuer u. Flamme sein; *catch* **~** Feuer fangen, in Brand geraten, *fig.* in Hitze geraten; *go through* **~** *and water for s.o. fig.* für j-n durchs Feuer gehen; *play with* **~** *fig.* mit dem Feuer spielen; *pull s.th. out of the* **~** *fig.* et. aus dem Feuer reißen; *set on* **~**, *set* **~** *to* anzünden, in Brand stecken; **2.** Feuer *n (im Ofen etc.):* *on a slow* **~** bei schwachem Feuer *(kochen);* **3.** Brand *m*, Feuer(sbrunst *f*) *n:* *where's the* **~***?* F wo brennts?; **4.** *Brit.* Heizgerät *n*; **5.** *fig.* Feuer *n*, Glut *f*, Leidenschaft *f*, Begeisterung *f*; **6.** ✕ Feuer *n*, Beschuss *m*: *blank* **~** blindes Schießen; *come under* **~** unter Beschuss geraten *(a. fig.);* *come under* **~** *from s.o. fig.* in j-s Schusslinie geraten; *hang* **~** a) *Schusswaffe* Feuer loszgehen *(Schusswaffe), fig.* auf sich warten lassen *(Sache);* *hold one's* **~** *fig.* sich zurückhalten; *miss* **~** versagen *(Schusswaffe), fig.* fehlschlagen; **II** *v/t.* **7.** anzünden, in Brand stecken; **8.** *Kessel* heizen, *Ofen* (be)feuern, beheizen: **~** *up inflation fig.* die Inflation ˌanheizen'; **9.** *Ziegel* brennen; **10.** *Tee* feuern; **11.** *fig.* j-n, j-s *Gefühle* entflammen, j-n in Begeisterung versetzen, j-s *Fantasie* beflügeln; **12.** a. **~ off** a) *Schusswaffe* abfeuern, b) *Schuss* abfeuern, -geben, c) *Sprengladung, Rakete* zünden; **13.** a. **~ off** *fig.* a) *Fragen etc.* abschießen, b) j-n mit Fragen bombardieren; **14.** *Motor* anlassen *(fig.* ˌfeuern', ˌrausschmeißen'; **III** *v/i.* **16.** Feuer fangen, (an)brennen; **17.** ✕ feuern, schießen *(at, on* auf *acc.):* **~** *away!* F schieß los!; **18.** zünden *(Motor);* **19.** a. **~ up** ˌhochgehen', wütend werden.

fire| **a·larm** *s.* **1.** 'Feuera,larm *m*; **2.** Feuermelder *m*; '**~·arm** [-ərɑːm] *s.* Feuer-, Schusswaffe *f*; **~ certificate** *Brit.* Waffenschein *m*; '**~·ball** *s.* **1.** *hist.* ✕ *u. ast.* Feuerkugel *f*; **2.** Feuerball *m (Sonne, Explosion etc.);* **3.** Kugelblitz *m*; **~ bal·loon** *s.* 'Heißluftbal,lon *m*; '**~·brand** *s.* **1.** brennendes Holzscheit; **2.** *fig.* Unruhestifter *m*, Aufwiegler *m*; '**~·brick** *s.* feuerfester Ziegel, Scha'mottestein *m*; **~ bri·gade** *s. Brit.* Feuerwehr *f (a. fig. pol. etc.);* '**~·bug** *s. sl.* ˌFeuerteufel' *m*; **~ clay** *s.* feuerfester Ton, Scha'motte *f*; **~ com·pa·ny** *s.* **1.** *Am.* Feuerwehr *f*; **2.** → *fire-office;* **~ con·trol** *s.* **1.** ✕ Feuerleitung *f*; **2.** Brandbekämpfung *f*; '**~·crew** *s.* Löschmannschaft *f*; '**~·crack·er** *s.* Frosch *m (Knallkörper);* '**~·damp** *s.* ⚒ schlagende Wetter *pl.*, Grubengas *n*; **~ de·part·ment** *s. Am.* Feuerwehr *f*; '**~·dog** *s.* Ka'minbock *m*; **~ drag·on** *s.* Feuer speiender Drache; **~ drill** *s.* **1.** 'Feuera,larmübung *f*; **2.** Feuerwehrübung *f*; '**~·,eat·er** [-ər,iː-] *s.* **1.** Feuer-

F

schlucker *m*; **2.** *fig.* ‚Eisenfresser' *m*; **en·gine** *s.* **1.** Feuerspritze *f*; **2.** Löschfahrzeug *n*; ~ **es·cape** *s.* Feuerleiter *f*, -treppe *f*; ~ **ex·tin·guish·er** *s.* Feuerlöscher *m*; '~**fight·er** *s.* Feuerwehrmann *m*; *pl.* Löschmannschaft *f*; '~**fight·ing** **I** *s.* Brandbekämpfung *f*; **II** *adj.* Lösch..., Feuerwehr...; '~**fly** *s.* Glühwürmchen *n*; '~**guard** *s.* **1.** Ka'mingitter *n*; **2.** Brandwache *f* od. -wart *m*; **hose** *s.* Feuerwehrschlauch *m*; ~ **lane** *f* Feuerschneise *f*; '~**man** [-mən] *s.* [*irr.*] **1.** Feuerwehrmann *m*; *pl.* Löschmannschaft *f*; **2.** Heizer *m*; ~ **of·fice** [-ər,ɒ-] *s. Brit.* Feuerversicherung(sanstalt) *f*; '~**place** *s.* (offener) Ka'min; '~**plug** *s.* ◉ Hy'drant *m*; ~ **point** *s.* Flammpunkt *m*; ~ **pol·i·cy** *s. Brit.* 'Feuerversicherungspo,lice *f*; ~ **pow·er** *s.* ✕ Feuerkraft *f*; '~**proof I** *adj.* feuerfest, -sicher: ~ **curtain** *thea.* eiserner Vorhang; **II** *v/t.* feuerfest machen; ~ **rais·er** *s. Brit.* Brandstifter(in); ~ **serv·ice** *s. Brit.* Feuerwehr *f*; ~ **ship** *s.* ⚓ Brander *m*; '~**side** *s.* **1.** (offener) Ka'min *m*: ~ **chat** Plauderei *f* am Kamin; **2.** *fig.* häuslicher Herd, Da'heim *n*; ~ **sta·tion** *s.* Feuerwehrwache *f*; '~**storm** *s.* Feuersturm *m*; '~**trap** *s.* ‚Mausefalle' *f* (*Gebäude ohne genügende Notausgänge*); ~ **wall** *s.* Brandmauer *f*; '~**ward·en** *s. Am.* **1.** Brandmeister *m*; **2.** Brandwache *f*; '~**watch·er** *s. Brit.* Brandwache *f*, Luftschutzwart *m*; '~**wa·ter** *s.* F ‚Feuerwasser' *n* (*Schnaps etc.*); '~**wood** *s.* Brennholz *n*; '~**works** *s. pl.* Feuerwerk *n* (*a. fig.*): **a** ~ **of wit**; **there were** ~ da flogen die Fetzen.

fir·ing ['faɪərɪŋ] *s.* **1.** ✕ (Ab)Feuern *n*; **2.** ◉ Zünden *n*; **3.** a) Heizen *n*, b) Feuerung *f*, c) 'Brennmateri,al *n*; ~ **line** *s.* ✕ Feuerlinie *f*, -stellung *f*; Kampffront *f*: **be in** (*Am.* **on**) **the** ~ *fig.* in der Schusslinie stehen; ~ **or·der** *s.* **1.** ✕ Schießbefehl *m*; **2.** *mot.* Zündfolge *f*; ~ **par·ty**, ~ **squad** *s.* ✕ a) 'Ehrensa,lutkom,mando *n*, b) Exekuti'onskom,mando *n*.

fir·kin ['fɜːkɪn] *s.* **1.** (Holz)Fässchen *n*; **2.** Viertelfass *n* (*Hohlmaß = etwa 40 l*).

firm[1] [fɜːm] **I** *adj.* □ **1.** fest, stark, hart; **2.** ✝ fest: ~ **offer**; ~ **market**; **3.** fest, beständig; **4.** standhaft, fest, entschlossen, bestimmt: **be** ~ **with s.o.** j-m gegenüber hart sein; **II** *adv.* **5.** fest: **stand** ~ *fig.* festbleiben; **III** *v/t.* **6.** *a.* ~ **up** fest machen; **IV** *v/i.* **7.** *a.* ~ **up** fest werden; **8.** *a.* ~ **up** ✝ anziehen (*Preise*), sich erholen (*Markt*).

firm[2] [fɜːm] *s.* Firma *f*: a) Firmenname *m*, b) Unter'nehmen *n*, Geschäft *n*, Betrieb *m*.

fir·ma·ment ['fɜːməmənt] *s.* Firma'ment *n*, Himmelsgewölbe *n*.

firm·ness ['fɜːmnɪs] *s.* **1.** Festigkeit *f*, Entschlossenheit *f*, Beständigkeit *f*; **2.** ✝ Festigkeit *f*, Stabili'tät *f*.

fir nee·dle *s.* Tannennadel *f*.

first [fɜːst] **I** *adj.* → **firstly**; **1.** erst: **at** ~ **hand** aus erster Hand, direkt; **in the** ~ **place** zuerst, an erster Stelle; ~ **thing** (**in the morning**) (morgens) als Allererstes; ~ **things** ~**!** das Wichtigste zuerst!; **he doesn't know the** ~ **thing** er hat keine (blasse) Ahnung; → **cousin**; **2.** erst, best, bedeutendst, führend: ~ **officer** ⚓ Erster Offizier; ~ **quality** beste *od.* prima Qualität; **II** *adv.* **3.** zu'erst, voran: **head** ~ (mit dem) Kopf voraus; **4.** zum ersten Mal; **5.** eher, lieber; **6.** ~ **off** F (zu)'erst (einmal); **I must** ~ **do that**; **7.** zu'erst, als Erst(er, -e, -es), an erster Stelle: ~ **come,** ~ **served** wer

zuerst kommt, mahlt zuerst; ~ **or last** früher oder später; ~ **and last** a) vor allen Dingen, b) im großen Ganzen; ~ **of all** zuallerst, vor allen Dingen; → 8; **III** *s.* **8.** (*der, die, das*) Erste *od.* (*fig.*) Beste: ~ **among equals** Primus inter Pares sein; **at** ~ zuerst, anfangs, zunächst; **from the** ~ von Anfang an; **from** ~ **to last** durchweg, von A bis Z; **9.** ♪ erste Stimme; **10.** *mot.* (*der*) erste Gang; **11.** *der* (Monats)Erste; **12.** ⚙ F erste Klasse; **13.** *univ. Brit.* akademischer Grad erster Klasse; **14.** *pl.* ✝ Ware(*n pl.*) *f* erster Quali'tät, erste Wahl; **15.** ~ **of exchange** ✝ Primawechsel *m*; ~ **aid** *s.* erste Hilfe: **render** ~ erste Hilfe leisten; ,~'**aid** *adj.* Erste-Hilfe-...: ~ **kit** Verbandskasten *m*; ~ **post** *od.* **station** Sanitätswache *f*, Unfallstation *f*; ~ **bid** *s.* ✝ Erstgebot *n*; '~**born I** *adj.* erstgeboren; **II** *s.* (*der, die, das*) Erstgeborene; ~ **cause** *s. phls.* Urgrund *m* aller Dinge, Gott *m*; ~ **class** *s.* **1.** ⚙ *etc.* erste Klasse; **2.** *univ. Brit.* → **first** 13; ,~'**class I** *adj. u. adv.* **1.** erstklassig, ausgezeichnet; F prima; **2.** ⚙ *etc.* erster Klasse: ~ **mail** a) *Am.* Briefpost *f*, b) *Brit.* bevorzugt beförderte Inlandspost; ~ **cost** *s.* ✝ Selbstkosten(preis *m*) *pl.*, Gestehungskosten *pl.*, Einkaufspreis *m*; ~ **floor** *s.* **1.** *Brit.* erste(r) Stock, erste E'tage; **2.** *Am.* Erdgeschoss, östr. -geschoß *n*; ~ **fruits** *s. pl.* ⚘ Erstlinge *pl.*; **2.** *fig.* a) erste Erfolge *pl.*, b) Erstlingswerk(e *pl.*) *n*; ,~**gen·er'a·tion** *adj.* Computer etc. der ersten Generati'on; ,~'**hand** *adj. u. adv.* aus erster Hand, di'rekt; ~ **la·dy** *s.* First Lady *f*: a) *Gattin e-s Staatsoberhauptes*, b) *führende Persönlichkeit*: **the** ~ **of jazz**; ~ **lieu·ten·ant** *s.* ✕ Oberleutnant *m*.

first·ling ['fɜːstlɪŋ] *s.* Erstling *m*; **first·ly** ['fɜːstlɪ] *adv.* erstens, zu'erst (einmal).

first name *s.* Vorname *m*; ~ **night** *s. thea.* Erst-, Uraufführung *f*, Premi'ere *f*; ,~'**night·er** *s.* Premi'erenbesucher (-in); ~ **pa·pers** *s. pl. Am.* (erster) Antrag e-s Ausländers auf amer. Staatsangehörigkeit; ~ **per·son** *s.* **1.** *ling.* erste Per'son; **2.** Ichform *f* (*in Romanen etc.*); ~ **prin·ci·ples** *s. pl.* 'Grundprin,zipien *pl.*; ,~'**rate** → **first-class** 1; ~ **ser·geant** *s.* ✕ *Am.* Hauptfeldwebel *m*; ~ **strike** *s.* ✕ (ato'marer) Erstschlag; ,~'**time** *adj.:* ~ **voter** Erstwähler(in).

firth [fɜːθ] *s.* Meeresarm *m*, Förde *f*.

fir tree *s.* Tanne(nbaum *m*) *f*.

fis·cal ['fɪskl] *adj.* □ fis'kalisch, steuerlich, Finanz...: ~ **policy** Finanzpolitik *f*; ~ **stamp** Banderole *f*; ~ **year** a) *Am.* Geschäftsjahr *n*, b) *parl. Am.* Haushalts-, Rechnungsjahr *n*, c) *Brit.* Steuerjahr *n*.

fish [fɪʃ] **I** *pl.* **fish** *od.* (*Fischarten*) **fishes** *s.* **fried** ~ Bratfisch *m* u. Pommes 'frites; **drink like a** ~ saufen wie ein Loch; **like a** ~ **out of water** wie ein Fisch auf dem Trockenen; **I have other** ~ **to fry** ich habe Wichtigeres zu tun; **all is** ~ **that comes to his net** er nimmt unbesehen alles (mit); **a pretty kettle of** ~ F e-e schöne Bescherung; **neither** ~ **nor flesh** (**nor good red herring**), **neither** ~ **nor fowl** F weder Fisch noch Fleisch, nichts Halbes und nichts Ganzes; **there are plenty more** ~ **in the sea** F es gibt noch mehr davon auf der Welt; **loose** ~ F lockerer Vogel; **queer** ~ F komischer Kauz; **can a** ~ (*od.* **duck**) **swim**? worauf du dich verlassen kannst!, da fragst du noch?; ~ **feed** 1; **2.** *ast. the* ⨋(*es pl.*) *die* Fische *pl.*: **be** (a) ⨋**es** Fisch sein; **II** *v/t.* **3.** fischen, *Fische* fan

gen, angeln; **4.** a) fischen *od.* angeln in (*dat.*), b) *Fluss etc.* abfischen, absuchen: ~ **up** j-n auffischen; **5.** *fig. a.* ~ **out** her'vorkramen, -holen, -ziehen; **6.** ◉ verlaschen; **III** *v/i.* **7.** (**for**) fischen, angeln (auf *acc.*); **8.** ~ **for** *fig.* a) fischen nach: ~ **for compliments**, b) aus sein auf (*acc.*): ~ **for information**; **9.** *a.* ~ **around** kramen (**for** nach).

fish and chips *s. Brit.* Bratfisch *m* u. Pommes 'frites; ~ **ball** *s.* 'Fischfrika,delle *f*, -klops *m*; ~ **bas·ket** *s.* (Fisch-)Reuse *f*; ~ **bone** *s.* Gräte *f*; ~ **bowl** *s.* Goldfischglas *n*; ~ **cake** → **fish ball**; ~ **eat·ers** *s. pl.* Fischbesteck *n*.

fish·er ['fɪʃə] *s.* **1.** Fischer *m*, Angler *m*; **2.** *zo.* Fischfänger *m*; '**fish·er·man** [-mən] *s.* [*irr.*] **1.** (*a.* Sport)Fischer *m*; **2.** Fischdampfer *m*; '**fish·er·y** [-ərɪ] *s.* **1.** Fische'rei *f*, Fischfang *m*; **2.** Fischzuchtanlage *f*; **3.** Fischgründe *pl.*, Fanggebiet *n*.

'**fish·eye** (**lens**) *s. phot.* 'Fischauge(nobjek,tiv) *n*; ~ **fin·gers** *s. pl. Küche:* Fischstäbchen *pl.*; ~ **flour** *s.* Fischmehl *n*; ~ **glue** *s.* Fischleim *m*; '~**hook** *s.* Angelhaken *m*.

fish·ing ['fɪʃɪŋ] *s.* **1.** Fischen *n*, Angeln *n*; **2.** → **fishery** 1, 3; ~ **boat** *s.* Fischerboot *n*; ~ **grounds** *s. pl.* → **fishery** 3; ~ **in·dus·try** *s.* Fische'rei(gewerbe *n*) *f*; ~ **line** *s.* Angelschnur *f*; ~ **net** *s.* Fischnetz *n*; ~ **pole** *s.*, ~ **rod** *s.* Angelrute *f*; ~ **tack·le** *s.* Angel- *od.* Fische'reigeräte *pl.*; ~ **vil·lage** *s.* Fischerdorf *n*.

fish lad·der *s.* Fischleiter *f*, -treppe *f*; ~ **meal** *s.* Fischmehl *n*; ~ **mon·ger** *s. Brit.* Fischhändler *m*; '~**net** *adj.* Netz...: ~ **shirt**; ~ **stockings**; ~ **oil** *s.* Fischtran *m*; '~**plate** *s.* ⚙ Lasche *f*; '~**pond** *s.* Fischteich *m*; '~**pot** *s.* Fischreuse *f*; ~ **slice** *s.* Fischheber *m*; ~ **sto·ry** *s. Am.* F ‚Seemannsgarn' *n*; ~ **tank** *s.* A'quarium *n*; '~**wife** *s.* [*irr.*] Fischhändlerin *f*: **swear like a** ~ keifen wie ein Fischweib.

fish·y ['fɪʃɪ] *adj.* □ **1.** fischartig, Fisch...: ~ **eyes** *fig.* Fischaugen; **2.** fischreich; **3.** F ,faul', verdächtig: **there's s.th.** ~ **about it** daran ist irgendetwas faul.

fis·sile ['fɪsaɪl] *adj. bsd. phys.* spaltbar: ~ **material** 'Spaltmateri,al *n*; **fis·sion** ['fɪʃn] *s.* **1.** *phys.* Spaltung *f* (*a. fig.*): ~ **bomb** A'tombombe *f*; **2.** *biol.* (Zell-)Teilung *f*; **fis·sion·a·ble** ['fɪʃnəbl] → **fissile**.

fis·sip·a·rous [fɪ'sɪpərəs] *adj. biol.* sich durch Teilung vermehrend, fissi'par.

fis·sure ['fɪʃə] *s.* Spalt(e *f*) *m*, Riss *m* (*a.* ⚕), Ritz(e *f*) *m*, Sprung *m*; '**fis·sured** [-əd] *adj.* gespalten, rissig (*a.* ◉); ⚕ schrundig.

fist [fɪst] **I** *s.* **1.** Faust *f*: ~ **law** Faustrecht *n*; **2.** *humor.* a) ,Pfote' *f*, Hand *f*, b) ‚Klaue', Handschrift *f* (*a. fig.*); **3.** F Versuch *m* (**at** mit); **II** *v/t.* **4.** mit der Faust schlagen; **5.** packen.

-fist·ed [fɪstɪd] *adj. in Zssgn* mit e-r ... Faust *od.* Hand, mit ... Fäusten.

'**fist·ful** [-fʊl] *s.* (e-e) Hand *f* voll.

fist·ic, **fist·i·cal** ['fɪstɪk(l)] *adj. sport* Box...; '**fist·i·cuffs** [-kʌfs] *s. pl.* Faustschläge *pl.*, Schläge'rei *f*.

fis·tu·la ['fɪstjʊlə] *s.* ⚕ Fistel *f*.

fit[1] [fɪt] **I** *adj.* □ **1.** a) passend, geeignet, b) fähig, tauglich: ~ **to drink** trinkbar; ~ **to drive** fahrtüchtig; ~ **to eat** ess-, genießbar; **laugh** ~ **to burst** F vor Lachen beinahe platzen; **he was** ~ **to be tied** *Am.* F er hatte eine Stinkwut; **he is not** ~ **for the**

F

job er ist für den Posten nicht geeignet; → *drop* 12; **2.** wert, würdig: *not to be* ~ *to* inf. es nicht verdienen zu *inf.*; *not* ~ *to be seen* nicht präsentabel *od.* vorzeigbar; **3.** angemessen, angebracht: *more than* ~ über Gebühr; *see* (*od.* *think*) ~ es für richtig *od.* angebracht halten (*to do* zu tun); **4.** schicklich, geziemend: *it is not* ~ *for us to do so* es gehört sich *od.* ziemt sich nicht, dass wir das tun; **5.** a) gesund, b) fit, (gut) in Form: *keep* ~ sich in Form *od.* fit halten; *as* ~ *as a fiddle* a) kerngesund, b) quietschvergnügt; **II** *s.* **6.** Passform *f*, Sitz *m* (*Kleid*): *it is a bad* (*perfect*) ~ es sitzt schlecht (tadellos); *it is a tight* ~ es sitzt stramm, *fig.* es ist sehr knapp bemessen; **7.** ⊚ Passung *f*; **III** *v/t.* **8.** passend *od.* geeignet machen (*for* für), anpassen (*to* an *acc.*); **9.** passen für *od.* auf (*j-n*), e-r Sache angemessen *od.* angepasst sein: *the key* ~*s the lock* der Schlüssel passt (ins Schloss); *the description* ~*s him* die Beschreibung trifft auf ihn zu; *the name* ~*s him* der Name passt zu ihm; ~ *the facts* (mit den Tatsachen überein)stimmen; *to* ~ *the occasion* (*Redew.*) dem Anlass entsprechend; **10.** *j-m* passen (*Kleid* etc.); **11.** sich eignen für; **12.** *j-n* befähigen (*for* für; *to do* zu tun); **13.** *j-n* vorbereiten, ausbilden (*for* für); **14.** *a.* ⊚ ausrüsten, -statten, einrichten, versehen (*with* mit); **15.** ⊚ a) einpassen, -bauen (*into* in *acc.*), b) anbringen (*to* an *dat.*), c) → *fit up* 2; **16.** a) an *j-m* Maß nehmen, b) *Kleid* etc. anprobieren; **IV** *v/i.* **17.** passen: a) sitzen (*Kleid*), b) angemessen sein, c) sich eignen; **18.** ~ *into* passen in (*acc.*), sich einfügen in (*acc.*); ~ *in* **I** *v/t.* einfügen, -passen, *a. fig. j-n* *od.* et. einschieben; **II** *v/i.* (*with*) passen (in *acc.*), über'einstimmen (mit); ~ *on* *v/t.* **1.** *Kleid* etc. anprobieren; **2.** anbringen, (an)montieren (*to* an *acc.*); ~ *out* → *fit*¹ 14; ~ *up* *v/t.* **1.** → *fit*¹ 14; **2.** ⊚ aufstellen, montieren.

fit² [fɪt] *s.* **1.** ⚕ *u. fig.* Anfall *m*, Ausbruch *m*: ~ *of coughing* Hustenanfall; ~ *of anger* Wutanfall; ~ *of laughter* Lachkrampf *m*; *have a* ~ F „Zustände‘ *od.* e-n Lachkrampf kriegen; *give s.o. a* ~ F j-n e-n Schrecken einjagen, b) j-n ‚auf die Palme bringen‘; **2.** (plötzliche) Anwandlung, Laune *f*: ~ *of generosity* Anwandlung von Großzügigkeit, Spendierlaune; *by* ~*s* (*and starts*) a) stoß-, ruckweise, b) spo'radisch.

fitch [fɪtʃ], **fitch·ew** ['fɪtʃuː] *s. zo.* Iltis *m*.

fit·ful ['fɪtfʊl] *adj.* □ unstet, unbeständig, veränderlich; sprung-, launenhaft; **fit·ment** ['fɪtmənt] *s.* **1.** Einrichtungsgegenstand *m*; *pl.* Ausstattung *f*, Einrichtung *f*; **2.** *Am.* (Tropf- *etc.*) Vorrichtung *f*; **fit·ness** ['fɪtnɪs] *s.* **1.** Eignung *f*, Fähig-, Tauglichkeit *f*: ~ *test* Eignungsprüfung *f* (→ 5); **2.** Zweckmäßigkeit *f*; **3.** Angemessenheit *f*; **4.** Schicklichkeit *f*; **5.** a) Gesundheit *f*, b) (gute) Form, Fitness *f*: ~ *room* Fitnessraum *m*; ~ *test* *sport* Fitnesstest *m*; ~ *trail* *Am.* Trimmpfad *m*; **fit·ted** ['fɪtɪd] *adj.* **1.** passend, geeignet; **2.** nach Maß (gearbeitet), zugeschnitten: ~ *carpet* Teppichboden *m*; ~ *coat* taillierter Mantel; **3.** Einbau...: ~ *kitchen*; **fit·ter** ['fɪtə] *s.* **1.** Ausrüster *m*, Einrichter *m*; **2.** Schneider(in) *f*; **3.** ⊚ Mon'teur *m*, Me'chaniker *m*; Installa'teur *m*; (Ma'schinen)Schlosser *m*; **fit·ting** ['fɪtɪŋ] **I** *adj.* □ **1.** a)

passend, geeignet, b) angemessen, c) schicklich; **II** *s.* **2.** Anprobe *f*: ~ *room* 'Anproberaum *m*, -ka,bine *f*; **3.** ⊚ Einpassen *n*, -bauen *n*; **4.** ⊚ Mon'tage *f*, Installieren *n*, Aufstellung *f*: ~ *shop* Montagehalle *f*; **5.** *pl.* ⊚ Beschläge *pl.*, Zubehör *n*, Arma'turen *pl.*, Ausstattungsgegenstände *pl.*; **6.** ⊚ a) Passarbeit *f*, b) Passteil *n*, c) Bau-, Zubehörteil *n*, d) (Rohr)Verbindung *f*, e) Einrichtung *f*, Ausrüstung *f*, -stattung *f*; **'fit·up** *s. thea. Brit.* F **1.** provi'sorische Bühne; **2.** *a.* ~ *company* (kleine) Wanderbühne.

five [faɪv] **I** *adj.* fünf; ~-*and-ten* *Am.* billiges Kaufhaus; ~*day week* Fünftagewoche *f*; ~*finger exercise* ♪ Fünffingerübung *f*, *fig.* Kinderspiel *n*; ~-*o'clock shadow* Anflug *m* von Bartstoppeln am Nachmittag; ~*year plan* Fünfjahresplan *m*; **II** *s.* Fünf *f*: *the* ~ *of hearts* die Herzfünf (*Spielkarte*); *'five·fold* *adj. u. adv.* fünffach; *'fiv·er* [-və] *s.* F *Brit.* Fünf'pfund-, *Am.* Fünf'dollarschein *m*; **fives** [-vz] *s. pl. sg. konstr. sport Brit.* ein Wandballspiel *n*.

fix [fɪks] **I** *v/t.* **1.** befestigen, festmachen, anheften, anbringen (*to* an *acc.*); → *bayonet* I; **2.** *fig.* verankern: ~ *s.th. in s.o.'s mind* j-m et. einprägen; **3.** *Termin, Preis etc.* festsetzen, -legen (*at* auf *acc.*), bestimmen, verabreden; **4.** *Blick, s-e Aufmerksamkeit etc.* richten, heften, *Hoffnung* setzen (*on* auf *acc.*); **5.** *j-s Aufmerksamkeit* fesseln; **6.** *j-n, et.* fixieren, anstarren; **7.** *die Schuld etc.* zuschreiben (*on dat.*); **8.** ✈, ⚓ die Posi'ti'on bestimmen von (*od. gen.*); **9.** *phot.* fixieren; **10.** (zur mikro'skopischen Unter'suchung) präparieren; **11.** ⊚ *Werkstücke* feststellen; **12.** reparieren, instand setzen; **13.** *bsd. Am. et.* zu'rechtmachen, *Essen* zubereiten: ~ *s.o. a drink* j-m e-n Drink mixen; ~ *one's face* sich schminken; ~ *one's hair* sich frisieren; **14.** *a.* ~ *up et.* arrangieren, regeln, *a.* in Ordnung bringen, *Streit* beilegen; **15.** F a) *e-n Wahlkampf etc.* (vorher) ‚arrangieren‘, manipulieren, b) *j-n* ‚schmieren‘, bestechen; **16.** F *es j-m* ‚besorgen‘ *od.* ‚geben‘; **17.** *mst* ~ *up* a) *j-n* 'unterbringen, b) *with j-m et.* besorgen; **18.** *mst* ~ *up Vertrag* (ab)schließen; **II** *v/i.* **19.** 🔥 fest werden, erstarren; **20.** sich festsetzen; **21.** ~ (*up*)*on* a) sich entscheiden *od.* entschließen für *od.* zu, et. wählen, b) → 3; **22.** *Am.* F vorhaben, planen: *it's* ~*ing to rain* es wird gleich regnen; **23.** *sl.* ‚fixen‘ (*Drogensüchtiger*); **III** *s.* **24.** F üble Lage, ‚Klemme‘ *f*, ‚Patsche‘ *f*; **25.** F a) Schiebung *f*, b) Bestechung *f*; **26.** ✈, ⚓ a) Standort *m*, Positi'on *f*; Ortung *f*; **27.** *sl.* ‚Fix‘ *m*, ‚Schuss‘ *m* (*Drogeninjektion*): *give o.s. a* ~ sich ,e-n Schuss setzen‘; **28.** F (rasche, pro-vi'sorische) Lösung: *quick* ~ (rasche) Notlösung, Provi'sorium *n*; **fix·ate** ['fɪkseɪt] *v/t.* **1.** → *fix* 1; **2.** *Am. j-n, et.* fixieren; **3.** *fig.* erstarren *od.* stagnieren lassen; **4.** *be* ~*d on psych.* fixiert sein auf (*acc.*); **fix·a·tion** [fɪk'seɪʃn] *s.* **1.** Fi'xierung *f*, Befestigung *f*; **2.** Festlegung *f*; **3.** *psych.* a) 🔥 *fixed idea*, b) (*Mutter- etc.*)Bindung *f*, (-)Fi'xierung *f*; **'fix·a·tive** [-sətɪv] **I** *s.* Fixa'tiv *n*, Fi'xiermittel *n*; **II** *adj.* Fixier...

fixed [fɪkst] *adj.* □ → *fixedly*; **1.** fest (angebracht), befestigt, (orts)fest, Fest-...(*antenne etc.*); starr (*Geschütz, Kupplung etc.*); **2.** 🔥 gebunden: ~ *oil* 🔥 starr (*Blick*), unverwandt (*Aufmerksam-*

keit); **4.** *bsd.* ⚓ fest(gelegt, -stehend): ~ *assets* feste Anlagen, Anlagevermögen *n*; ~ *capital* ⚓ Anlagekapital *n*; ~ *conversion rates Geld:* feste Umrechnungskurse *pl.*; ~ *cost* feste Kosten, Fixkosten *pl.*; ~ *income* festes Einkommen; ~ *price* fester Preis, Festpreis *m*, *a.* gebundener Preis; **5.** F abgekartet, manipuliert; **6.** F (*gut etc.*) versorgt *od.* versehen (*for* mit); ~ *i·de·a* *s. psych.* fixe I'dee, Zwangsvorstellung *f*; ~-'*in·ter·est*(-,bear·ing) *adj.* ⚓ festverzinslich.

fix·ed·ly ['fɪksɪdlɪ] *adv.* starr, unverwandt.

fixed‖ point *s.* A Fixpunkt *m*; ~ *sight* *s.* ✕ 'Standvi,sier *n*; ~ *star* *s.* Fixstern *m*; ~-'*wing air·craft* *s.* ✈ Starrflügler *m*.

fix·er ['fɪksə] *s.* **1.** *phot.* Fi'xiermittel *n*; **2.** F ,Organi'sator‘ *m*, Manipu'lator *m*; **3.** *sl.* ,Dealer‘ *m*; **'fix·ing** [-ksɪŋ] *s.* **1.** Befestigen *n*, Anbringen *n*: ~ *bolt* Haltebolzen *m*; ~ *screw* Stellschraube *f*; **2.** Repara'tur *f*; **3.** *phot.* Fixieren *n*; **4.** Festlegung *f*, 'Fixing *n* (*von Wechsel- od. Börsenkursen*); **5.** *pl. bsd. Am.* a) Geräte *pl.*, b) Zubehör *n, c)* Zutaten *pl.*, *fig. a.* Drum u. Dran *n*; **'fix·i·ty** [-ksətɪ] *s.* Festigkeit *f*, Beständigkeit *f*: ~ *of purpose* Zielstrebigkeit *f*; **'fix·ture** [-kstʃə] *s.* **1.** feste Anlage, Installati'onsteil *m*: *lighting* ~ Beleuchtungskörper *m*; **2.** Inven'tarstück *n*, 🔥 festes Inven'tar *od.* Zubehör: *be a* ~ *humor.* zum (lebenden) Inventar gehören; ~*s and fittings* bewegliche u. unbewegliche Einrichtungsgegenstände; **3.** Spannvorrichtung *f*, -futter *m*; **4.** *bsd.* *sport Brit.* (Ter'min *m* für e-e) Veranstaltung *f*.

fizz [fɪz] **I** *v/i.* **1.** zischen; **2.** moussieren, sprudeln; **3.** *fig.* sprühen (*with vor dat.*); **II** *s.* **4.** Zischen *n*; **5.** Sprudeln *n*; **6.** a) Sprudel *m*, b) Fizz *m* (*Mischgetränk*), c) F ,Schampus‘ *m* (*Sekt*); **'fiz·zle** [-zl] **I** *s.* **1.** → *fizz* 4; **2.** F ‚Pleite‘ *f*, Misserfolg *m*; **II** *v/i.* **3.** → *fizz* 1; **4.** *a.* ~ *out* *fig.* verpuffen, im Sand verlaufen; **'fiz·zy** [-zɪ] *adj.* **1.** zischend; **2.** sprudelnd, moussierend.

fjord [fjɔːd] → *fiord*.

flab·ber·gast ['flæbəgɑːst] *v/t.* F verblüffen: *I was* ~*ed* ich war ‚platt‘.

flab·bi·ness ['flæbɪnɪs] *s.* **1.** Schlaffheit *f* (*a. fig.*); **2.** Schwammigkeit *f*; **flab·by** ['flæbɪ] *adj.* □ **1.** schlaff; **2.** schwammig; **3.** *fig.* ‚schlapp‘, ‚schlaff‘, schwach.

flac·cid ['flæksɪd] *adj.* → *flabby*; **flac·cid·i·ty** [flæk'sɪdətɪ] → *flabbiness*.

flack¹ [flæk] → *flak*.

flack² [flæk] *s. Am. sl.* 'Pressea,gent *m*.

flag¹ [flæg] **I** *s.* **1.** Fahne *f*, Flagge *f*: ~ *of convenience* ⚓ Billigflagge *f*; *hoist* (*od. fly*) *one's* ~ a) die Fahne aufziehen, b) das Kommando übernehmen (*Admiral*); *strike one's* ~ a) die Flagge streichen, *fig. a.* kapitulieren, b) das Kommando abgeben (*Admiral*); *keep the* ~ *flying fig.* die Fahne hochhalten; **2.** → *flagship*; **3.** *sport* (Markierungs-)Fähnchen *n*; **4.** a) (Kar'tei)Reiter *m*, b) Lesezeichen *n*; **5.** *hunt.* Fahne *f* (*Schwanz*); **6.** *typ.* Im'pressum *n* (*e-r Zeitung*); **II** *v/t.* **7.** beflaggen; **8.** *sport Strecke* ausflaggen; **9.** *et.* signalisieren; ~ *offside Fußball:* Abseits winken; **10.** ~ *down Fahrzeug* anhalten, *Taxi* herbeiwinken, *sport Rennen, Fahrer* abwinken.

flag² [flæg] *s.* ♀ Gelbe *od.* Blaue Schwertlilie.

flag³ [flæg] *v/i.* **1.** schlaff her'abhängen;

flag – flat

226

2. *fig.* nachlassen, erlahmen, ermatten; **3.** langweilig werden.

flag⁴ [flæg] **I** *s.* (Stein)Platte *f*, Fliese *f*; **II** *v/t.* mit (Stein)Platten *od.* Fliesen belegen.

flag| cap·tain *s.* Komman'dant *m* des Flaggschiffs; **~ day** *s.* **1.** *Brit.* Opfertag *m* (Straßensammlung); **2.** ♀ *Am.* Jahrestag *m* der Natio'nalflagge (*14. Juni*).

flag·el·lant ['flædʒələnt] **I** *s. eccl.* Geißler *m*, Flagel'lant *m* (*a. psych.*); **II** *adj.* geißelnd (*a. fig.*); **'flag·el·late** [-leıt] **I** *v/t.* geißeln (*a. fig.*); **II** *s. zo.* Geißeltierchen *n*; **flag·el·la·tion** [ˌflædʒə'leıʃn] *s.* Geißelung *f* (*a. fig.*).

flag·eo·let [ˌflædʒəʊ'let] *s.* ♪ Flageo'lett *n.*

flag·ging¹ ['flægıŋ] *adj.* erlahmend.

flag·ging² ['flægıŋ] *s. collect.* a) (Stein-)Platten *pl.*, b) Fliesen *pl.*, c) gefliester Boden.

flag| lieu·ten·ant *s.* ♣ *Brit.* Flaggleutnant *m*; **~ of·fi·cer** *s.* ♣ 'Flaggoffi,zier *m.*

flag·on ['flægən] *s.* **1.** bauchige (Wein-)Flasche, **2.** (Deckel)Krug *m.*

fla·gran·cy ['fleıgrənsı] *s.* **1.** Schamlosigkeit *f*, Ungeheuerlichkeit *f*; **2.** Krassheit *f*; **'fla·grant** [-nt] *adj.* □ **1.** schamlos, schändlich, ungeheuerlich; **2.** krass, ekla'tant, schreiend.

'flag·ship *s.* ♣ Flaggschiff *n* (*a. fig.*); *fig.* Aushängeschild *n*; **'~·staff**, **'~·stick** *s.* Fahnenstange *f*, -mast *m*, Flaggenmast, ♣ Flaggenstock *m*; **~ sta·tion** *s.* 🚂 *Am.* Bedarfshaltestelle *f*; **'~·stone** → **flag⁴** I; **~ stop** → **flag station**; **'~-·wav·er** *s.* ♣ Hur'rapatri,ot *m*; **'~-·wav·ing** *s.* Hur'rapatri,tismus *m*; **II** *adj.* hur'rapatri,otisch.

flail [fleıl] **I** *s.* **1.** ✗ Dreschflegel *m*; **II** *v/t.* **2.** dreschen; **3.** wild einschlagen auf j-n; **4.** **~ one's arms** mit den Armen fuchteln.

flair [fleə] *s.* **1.** (besondere) Begabung, Ta'lent *n*; **2.** (feines) Gespür (*for* für).

flak [flæk] (*Ger.*) *s.* **1.** ✗ Flak *f*: a) 'Fliegerabwehr(ka,none *od.* -truppe) *f*, b) Flakfeuer *n*; **2.** *fig.* F (heftiger) ‚Beschuss‘, ‚Zunder‘ *m* (*Kritik etc.*).

flake [fleık] **I** *s.* **1.** (*Schnee-, Seifen-, Hafer- etc.*)Flocke *f*; **2.** dünne Schicht, Schuppe *f*, Blättchen *n*; **3.** Fetzen *m*, Splitter *m*; **4.** *Am. sl.* ‚Spinner‘ *m*; **II** *v/t.* **5.** abblättern; **6.** flockig machen; **III** *v/i.* **7.** in Flocken fallen; **8. ~ off** abblättern, sich abschälen; **9. ~ out** F a) ‚umkippen‘ (*ohnmächtig werden*), b) ‚einpennen‘, c) ‚sich verziehen‘; **flaked** [-kt] *adj.* flockig, Blättchen..., Flocken...; **'flak·y** [-kı] *adj.* **1.** flockig; **2.** blätterig: **~ pastry** Blätterteig *m*; **3.** *Am. sl.* verrückt.

flam·beau ['flæmbəʊ] *pl.* **-x** [-z] *od.* **-s** *s.* **1.** Fackel *f*; **2.** Leuchter *m.*

flam·boy·ance [flæm'bɔıəns] *s.* **1.** Extrava'ganz *f*; **2.** über'ladener Schmuck; **3.** Grellheit *f*; **4.** *fig.* a) Bom'bast *m*, b) Großartigkeit *f*; **flam'boy·ant** [-nt] *adj.* □ **1.** extrava'gant; **2.** grell, leuchtend; **3.** farbenprächtig; **4.** *fig.* flammend; **5.** auffallend; **6.** über'laden (*a. Stil*); **7.** bom'bastisch, pom'pös; **8.** △ wellig: **~ style** Flammenstil *m.*

flame [fleım] **I** *s.* **1.** Flamme *f*: **be in ~s** in Flammen stehen; **2.** *fig.* Feuer *n*, Flamme *f*, Glut *f*, Leidenschaft *f*, Heftigkeit *f*: **fan the ~** Öl ins Feuer gießen; **3.** Leuchten *n*, Glanz *m*; **4.** F ‚Flamme‘ *f*, ‚Angebetete‘ *f*: **an old ~ of mine**; **5.** *Computer*, *E-Mail*: Flame *n*, beleidigende E-Mail; **II** *v/i.* **6.** lodern: **~ up** a) auflodern, b) in Flammen aufgehen,

c) *fig.* aufbrausen; **7.** leuchten, (rot) glühen: **her eyes ~d with anger** ihre Augen flammten vor Wut; **her cheeks ~d red** ihr Gesicht flammte; **~ cut·ter** *s.* ☺ Schneidbrenner *m*; **~ mail** *s.* → **flame** 5; **'~-proof** *adj. tech.* **1.** feuerfest; **2.** explosi'onsgeschützt; **'~-·throw·er** *s.* ✗ Flammenwerfer *m.*

flam·ing ['fleımıŋ] *adj.* **1.** lodernd (*a. Farben etc.*), brennend; **2.** *fig.* glühend, leidenschaftlich; **3.** *Brit.* F a) verdammt: **you ~ idiot!**, b) gewaltig, Mords...: **a ~ row** ein ‚Mordskrach‘.

flam·ma·ble ['flæməbl] → **inflammable**.

flan [flæn] *s.* Obst-, Käsekuchen *m.*

flange [flændʒ] ☺ **I** *s.* **1.** Flansch *m*; **2.** Rad-, Spurkranz *m*; **II** *v/t.* **3.** (an)flanschen: **~d motor** Flanschmotor *m*; **~d rim** umbördelter Rand.

flank [flæŋk] **I** *s.* **1.** Flanke *f*, Weiche *f* (*der Tiere*); **2.** Seite *f*, Flanke *f* (*e-r Person*); **3.** Seite *f* (*e-s Gebäudes etc.*): **~ clearance** ☺ Flankenspiel *n*; **4.** ✗ Flanke *f*, Flügel *m* (*beide a. fig.*): **turn the ~ (of)** die Flanke (*gen.*) aufrollen; **II** *v/t.* **5.** flankieren, seitlich stehen von, säumen, um'geben; **6.** ✗ flankieren, die Flanke (*gen.*) decken *od.* angreifen; **7.** flankieren, (seitwärts) um'gehen; **III** *v/i.* **8.** angrenzen, -stoßen; seitlich liegen; **'flank·ing** [-kıŋ] *adj.* seitlich; angrenzend; ✗ Flanken..., Flankierungs...: **~ fire**; **~ march** Flankenmarsch *m.*

flan·nel ['flænl] **I** *s.* **1.** Fla'nell *m*: **~-mouthed** *Am. fig.* (aal)glatt; **2.** *pl.* Fla'nellkleidung *f*, *bsd.* Fla'nellhose *f*; **3.** *bsd.* Fla'nell,unterwäsche *f od.* -unterhose *f*; **4.** *Brit.* Waschlappen *m*; **5.** *Brit.* F ‚Schmus‘ *m*; **II** *v/t.* **6.** mit Fla'nell bekleiden; **7.** mit Fla'nell abreiben; **III** *v/i.* **8.** *Brit.* F ‚Schmus‘ reden.

flan·nel·et(te) [ˌflænl'et] *s.* 'Baumwoll-fla,nell *m.*

flap [flæp] **I** *s.* **1.** Schlag *m*, Klaps *m*; **2.** Flügelschlag *m*; **3.** (*Verschluss*)Klappe *f* (*Tasche, Briefkasten, Buchumschlag etc.*); **4.** (*Tisch-, Fliegen-, ✈ Lande-*)Klappe *f*; Falltür *f*; **5.** Lasche *f* (*Schuh, Karton*); **6.** weiche Krempe; **7.** ✈ Hautlappen *m*; **8.** F Aufregung *f*: **be (all) in a ~** (ganz) aus dem Häuschen sein; **don't get into a ~!** reg dich nicht auf!; **II** *v/t.* **9.** e-n Klaps *od.* Schlag geben (*dat.*); **10.** auf u. ab (*od.* hin u. her) bewegen, mit *den Flügeln etc.* schlagen; **III** *v/i.* **11.** flattern; **12.** flattern, mit den Flügeln schlagen: **~ off** davonflattern; **13.** klatschen, schlagen (*against* gegen); **14.** F sich aufregen; **15.** *Am.* F ‚quasseln‘; **'~-·doo·dle** *s.* F Quatsch *m*; **'~-·eared** *adj.* schlappohrig; **'~-·jack** *s. bsd. Am.* Pfannkuchen *m.*

flap·per ['flæpə] *s.* **1.** Fliegenklappe *f*; **2.** Klappe *f*, her'abhängendes Stück; **3.** *zo.* (breite) Flosse *f*; **4.** *sl.* ‚Flosse‘ *f* (*Hand*); **5.** *sl. hist.* ‚irre Type‘ (*Mädchen in den 20er Jahren*).

flare [fleə] **I** *s.* **1.** (auf)flackerndes Licht; Aufflackern *n*, -leuchten *n*, Lodern *n*; **2.** a) Leuchtfeuer *n*, b) 'Licht-, 'Feuersi,gnal *n*, c) ✗ Leuchtkugel *f od.* -bombe *f*; **3.** *fig.* → **flare-up** 2; **4.** *Mode*: Schlag *m*: **with a ~** ausgestellt (*Rock*), *Hose a.* mit Schlag; **II** *v/i.* **5.** flackern, lodern, leuchten: **~ up** a) aufflammen, -flackern, -lodern (*alle a. fig.*), b) *a.* **~ out** *fig.* aufbrausen; **6.** ausgestellt sein (*Rock etc.*); **III** *v/t.* **7.** flackern lassen; **8.** aufflammen lassen; **9.** mit Licht *od.* Feuer signalisieren; **10.** flattern lassen; **11.** *Mode*: ausstellen (*Rock etc.*), bau-

schen (→ *a.* 4); **~ pis·tol** *s.* ✗ 'Leucht-pi,stole *f*; **'~-up** [-ərap] *s.* **1.** Aufflackern *n*, -lodern *n* (*a. fig.*); **2.** *fig.* a) Aufbrausen *n*, Wutausbruch *m*, b) ,Krach‘ *m*, (plötzlicher) Streit.

flash [flæʃ] **I** *s.* **1.** Aufblitzen *n*, Blitz *m*, Strahl *m*: **~ of fire** Feuergarbe *f*; **~ of hope** *fig.* Hoffnungsstrahl; **~ of wit** Geistesblitz; **like a ~** *fig.* wie der Blitz; **catch a ~ of** *fig.* e-n Blick erhaschen von; **give s.o. a ~** *mot.* j-n anblinken; **2.** Stichflamme *f*: **a ~ in the pan** *fig.* a) e-e ,Eintagsfliege‘ *f*, b) ein ,Strohfeuer‘; **3.** Augenblick *m*: **in a ~** im Nu, blitzartig, -schnell; **for a ~** e-n Augenblick lang; **4.** *Radio etc.*: 'Durchsage *f*, Kurzmeldung *f*; **5.** ✗ *Brit.* (Uni'form-)Abzeichen *n*; **6.** *phot.* F Blitz(licht *n*) *m*; **7.** *bsd. Am.* F Taschenlampe *f*; **8.** *sl.* ,Flash‘ *m* (*Drogenwirkung*); **II** *v/t.* **9.** *a.* **~ on** aufleuchten *od.* (auf)blitzen lassen: **he ~ed a light in my face** er leuchtete mir (plötzlich) ins Gesicht; **~ one's lights** *mot.* die Lichthupe betätigen; **his eyes ~ed fire** s-e Augen sprühten Feuer *od.* Blitze (*an* *~ s.o. a glance* j-m e-n Blick zuwerfen); **10.** (*mit Licht*) signalisieren; **11.** F *et.* zücken *od.* kurz zeigen (*at s.o.* j-m): **~ a badge**; **12.** F zur Schau tragen, protzen mit; **13.** Nachricht (*per Funk etc.*) 'durchgeben; **III** *v/i.* **14.** aufflammen, (auf)blitzen; zucken (*Blitz, Lichtschein*); **15.** blinken; **16.** sich blitzartig bewegen, rasen, flitzen: **~ by** vorbeirasen, *fig.* wie im Flug(e) vergehen; **it ~ed across** (*od.* **through**) **his mind that** plötzlich schoss es ihm durch den Kopf, dass; **~ out** *fig.* aufbrausen; **17. ~ back** zurückblenden (*im Film etc.*) (**to** auf *acc.*); **IV** *adj.* **18.** F → **flashy**; **19.** F a) geschniegelt, ,aufgedonnert‘ (*Person*), b) protzig; **20.** F falsch, gefälscht; **21.** *in Zssgn* Schnell...; **'~-back** *s.* **1.** Rückblende *f* (*Film, Roman etc.*); **2.** ☺ (Flammen)Rückschlag *m*; **~ bomb** *s.* ✗, *phot.* Blitzlichtbombe *f*; **~ bulb** *s.* *phot.* Blitzlicht(lampe *f*) *n*; **~ card** *s.* **1.** Illustrati'onstafel *f*; **2.** *sport* Wertungstafel *f*; **~ cube** *s. phot.* Blitzwürfel *m.*

flash·er ['flæʃə] *s.* **1.** *mot.* Lichthupe *f*; **2.** *Brit.* F Exhibitio'nist *m.*

flash| flood *s.* plötzliche Überschwemmung; **~ gun** *s. phot.* Blitzleuchte *f*, Elek'tronenblitzgerät *n*; **~ lamp** → **flash bulb**; **'~-light** *s.* **1.** ♣ Leuchtfeuer *n*; **2.** *phot.* Blitzlicht *n*; **3.** *Am.* Taschenlampe *f*; **4.** blinkendes Re'klamelicht; **'~-·o·ver** *s.* ⚡ 'Überschlag *m*; **~ point** *s. phys.* Flammpunkt *m*; **~ weld·ing** *s.* ☺ Abschmelzschweißen *n.*

flash·y ['flæʃı] *adj.* □ protzig, auffällig, grell, ,knallig‘.

flask [flɑːsk] *s.* **1.** (Taschen-, Reise-, Feld)Flasche *f*; **2.** ☺ Kolben *m*, Flasche *f*; **3.** ☺ Formkasten *m.*

flat¹ [flæt] **I** *s.* **1.** Fläche *f*, Ebene *f*; **2.** flache Seite: **~ of the hand** Handfläche *f*; **3.** Flachland *n*, Niederung *f*; **4.** Untiefe *f*, Flach *n*; **5.** *thea.* Ku'lisse *f*; **7.** *mot.* ,Plattfuß‘ *m*, Reifenpanne *f*; **8.** → **flatcar**; **9.** **the ~** *Pferdesport*: die Flachrennen *pl.*; **10.** *pl.* flache Schuhe; *sl.* **11.** flach, eben; platt (*a. Reifen*); ra'sant (*Flugbahn*): **~ feet** Plattfüße; **the ~ hand** die flache *od.* offene Hand; **~ nose** platte Nase; **as ~ as a pancake** F flach wie ein Brett (*Mädchen*); **12.** hingestreckt, flach am Boden liegend: **knock ~** umhauen; **lay ~** dem Erdboden gleichmachen; **13.** entschieden, glatt: **a ~ refusal**; **and that's ~** und damit basta!; **14.** fade, schal (*Bier* etc.); **15.** *a.* ✝ lustlos, flau; **16.** a) langweilig, fad(e), ,lahm', b) flach, oberflächlich; **17.** a) einheitlich: **~ price** (*od.* *rate*) Einheitspreis *m*, b) pau'schal: **~ fee** Pauschalgebühr *f*; → *flat price, flat rate*; **18.** *paint., phot.* a) matt, b) kon'trastlos; **19.** klanglos (*Stimme*); **20.** ♪ a) erniedrigt (*Note*), b) mit B-Vorzeichen (*Tonart*); **21.** leer (*Batterie*); **III** *adv.* **22.** flach: *fall* **~** a) der Länge nach hinfallen, b) *fig.* F ,danebengehen' (*missglücken od. s-e Wirkung verfehlen*), *thea. etc.* ,durchfallen'; **23.** genau: *in 10 seconds* **~**; *in nothing* **~** blitzschnell; **24.** eindeutig; **25.** entschieden, kate'gorisch; **26.** ♪ a) um e-n halben Ton niedriger, b) zu tief: *sing* **~**; **27.** ohne Zinsen; **28.** F völlig: **~ broke** ,total pleite'; **29. ~ out** F auf Hochtouren, ,volle Pulle' (*fahren, arbeiten etc.*); **30. ~ out** F ,to'tal erledigt'.

flat² [flæt] *s. Brit.* (E'tagen)Wohnung *f*.

'flat|-bed trail·er *s. mot.* Tiefladeanhänger *m*; **'~·boat** *s.* ⚓ Prahm *m*; **'~·car** *s.* ❀ Am. Plattformwagen *m*; **cost** *s.* ✝ Selbstkosten(preis *m*) *pl.*; **'~·fish** *s.* Plattfisch *m*; **'~·foot** *s.* [*irr.*] **1.** ♣ Platt-, Senkfuß *m*; **2.** *pl. a.* **~s** *sl.* ,Bulle' *m* (*Polizist*); **'~-'foot·ed** *adj.* **1.** ♣ plattfüßig: *be* **~** Plattfüße haben; **2.** ◉ standfest; **3.** F ,eisern', entschieden; **4.** *Brit.* F linkisch, unbeholfen; **'~-hunt** *v/i.* *go* **~***ing* *Brit.* auf Wohnungssuche gehen; **'~·i·ron** *s.* **1.** Bügeleisen *n*; **2.** ◉ Flacheisen *n*.

flat·let ['flætlɪt] *s. Brit.* Kleinwohnung *f*.

flat·ly ['flætlɪ] *adv.* kate'gorisch, rundweg.

'flat·mate *s. Brit.* Mitbewohner(in).

flat·ness ['flætnɪs] *s.* **1.** Flachheit *f*; **2.** Plattheit *f*, Eintönigkeit *f*; **3.** Entschiedenheit *f*; **4.** ✝ Flauheit *f*.

'flat|-nosed pli·ers *s. pl.* ◉ Flachzange *f*; **'~·pack fur·ni·ture** *s.* Möbel für Selbstabholer; **~ price** *s.* ✝ Pau'schalpreis *m*; **~ race** *s.* Flachrennen *n*; **~ rate** *s.* Einheits-, Pau'schalsatz *m*; **~ screen** *s. Computer, TV:* Flachbildschirm *m*; **~ sea·son** *s.* 'Flachrennsaison *f*.

flat·ten ['flætn] **I** *v/t.* **1.** flach *od.* eben *od.* glatt machen, (ein)ebnen, planieren: **~ o.s. against s.th.** sich (platt) an et. drücken; **2.** ◉ a) abflachen (*a.* ♣), b) ausbeulen, flach hämmern; **3.** dem Erdboden gleichmachen; **4.** F *Gegner* ,flachlegen', *weitS.* ,fertig machen'; **5.** ♪ *Note* um e-n halben Ton erniedrigen; **6.** *paint.* Farben dämpfen, *a.* ◉ grundieren; **II** *v/i.* **7.** flach *od.* eben werden; **~ out I** *v/t.* **1.** → *flatten* 2; **2.** ✈ *das Flugzeug* (*vor der Landung*) aufrichten; **II** *v/i.* **3.** → *flatten* 7; **4.** ✈ ausschweben.

flat·ter ['flætə] *v/t.* **1.** *j-m* schmeicheln: *be* **~ed** sich geschmeichelt fühlen (*at, by* durch); **~ s.o. into doing s.th.** j-n so lange umschmeicheln, bis er et. tut; **2.** *fig.* *j-m* schmeicheln (*Bild etc.*): *the picture* **~s** *him* das Bild ist geschmeichelt; **3.** *fig.* dem Ohr, *j-s* Eitelkeit *etc.* schmeicheln, wohl tun; **4. ~ o.s.** sich schmeicheln *od.* einbilden (*that* dass), b) sich beglückwünschen (*on* zu); **'flat·ter·er** [-ərə] *s.* Schmeichler(in); **'flat·ter·ing** [-ərɪŋ] *adj.* □ schmeichelhaft: a) schmeichlerisch, b) geschmeichelt (*Bild etc.*); **'flat·ter·y** [-ərɪ] *s.* Schmeiche'lei *f*.

flat·tie ['flætɪ] → *flatfoot* 2.

'flat·top *s.* ✈ Am. F Flugzeugträger *m*.

flat·u·lence ['flætjʊləns], **'flat·u·len·cy** [-sɪ] *s.* **1.** ♣ Blähung(en *pl.*) *f*; **2.** *fig.* a)

Hohlheit *f*, b) Schwülstigkeit *f*; **'flat·u·lent** [-nt] *adj.* □ **1.** blähend; **2.** *fig.* a) hohl, b) schwülstig.

'flat·ware *s. Am.* **1.** (Tisch-, Ess)Besteck *n*; **2.** flaches (Ess)Geschirr.

flaunt [flɔːnt] **I** *v/t.* **1.** zur Schau stellen, protzen mit: **~ o.s.** → 3; **2.** *Am.* e-n *Befehl etc.* miss'achten; **II** *v/i.* **3.** (herum)stolzieren, paradieren; **4.** a) stolz wehen, b) prangen.

flau·tist ['flɔːtɪst] *s.* ♪ Flötenspieler(in).

fla·vo(u)r ['fleɪvə] **I** *s.* **1.** (Wohl)Geschmack *m*, A'roma *n*, *a.* Geschmacksrichtung *f*: **~ enhancer** Aromazusatz *m*; **~-enhancing** geschmacksverbessernd; **2.** Würze *f*, A'roma *n*, aro'matischer Geschmackstoff, ('Würz)Es,senz *f*; **3.** *fig.* Beigeschmack *m*, Anflug *m*; **II** *v/t.* **4.** würzen (*a. fig.*), Geschmack geben (*dat.*); **III** *v/i.* **5. ~ of** schmecken *od.* riechen nach (*a. fig. contp.*); **'fla·vo(u)red** [-əd] *adj.* würzig, schmackhaft; *in Zssgn* mit ... Geschmack; **'fla·vo(u)r·ing** [-vərɪŋ] *s.* → *flavo(u)r* 2; **'fla·vo(u)r·less** [-lɪs] *adj.* ohne Geschmack, fad(e), schal.

flaw [flɔː] **I** *s.* **1.** Fehler *m*: a) Mangel *m*, Makel *m*, b) ◉, ✝ fehlerhafte Stelle, De'fekt *m* (*a. fig.*), Fabrikati'onsfehler *m*; **2.** Sprung *m*, Riss *m*, Bruch *m*; **3.** Blase *f*, Wolke *f* (*im Edelstein*); **4.** ♁ a) Formfehler *m*, b) Fehler *m* im Recht; **5.** *fig.* schwacher Punkt, Mangel *m*; **II** *v/t.* **6.** brüchig *od.* rissig machen; **7.** *fig.* Fehler aufzeigen in (*dat.*); **8.** verunstalten; **'flaw·less** [-lɪs] *adj.* □ fehler-, einwandfrei, tadellos; lupenrein (*Edelstein*).

flax [flæks] *s.* ♀ **1.** Flachs *m*, Lein *m*; **2.** Flachs(faser *f*) *m*; **flax·en** ['flæksən] *adj.* **1.** Flachs...; **2.** flachsartig; **3.** flachsen, flachsfarben: **~-haired** flachsblond; **'flax·seed** *s.* ♀ Leinsamen *m*.

flay [fleɪ] *v/t.* **1.** *Tier* abhäuten, *hunt.* abbalgen: **~ s.o. alive** F a) kein gutes Haar an j-m lassen, b) j-n ,zur Schnecke' machen; **2.** et. schälen; **3.** *j-n* auspeitschen; **4.** F *j-n* ausplündern *od.* ,ausnehmen'.

flea [fliː] *s. zo.* Floh *m*: *send s.o. away with a* **~** *in his ear* j-m ,heimleuchten'; **'~·bag** *s. sl.* **1.** a) ,Flohkiste' *f* (*Bett*), b) Schlafsack *m*; **2.** ,Schlampe' *f*; **~ bite** *s.* **1.** Flohbiss *m*; **2.** Baga'telle *f*; **'~-,bit·ten** *adj.* **1.** von Flöhen zerbissen; **2.** rötlich gesprenkelt (*Pferd etc.*); **~ mar·ket** *s.* Flohmarkt *m*.

fleck [flek] **I** *s.* **1.** Licht-, Farbfleck *m*; **2.** a) (Haut)Fleck *m*, b) Sommersprosse *f*; **3.** (Staub- *etc.*)Teilchen *n*: **~ of dust**; **~ of mud** Dreckspritzer *m*; **~ of snow** Schneeflocke *f*; **II** *v/t.* **4.** → **'fleck·er**; **'fleck·er** [-kə] *v/t.* sprenkeln.

flec·tion ['flekʃn] *etc. Am.* → *flexion etc.*

fledge [fledʒ] **I** *v/t.* *Pfeil etc.* befiedern, mit Federn versehen; **II** *v/i. orn.* flügge werden: **~d** flügge; **'fledg(e)·ling** [-dʒlɪŋ] *s.* **1.** eben flügge gewordener Vogel; **2.** *fig.* Grünschnabel *m*, Anfänger *m*.

flee [fliː] **I** *v/i.* [*irr.*] **1.** fliehen, flüchten (*before, from* vor *dat.*; *from* aus, von): **~ from justice** sich der Strafverfolgung entziehen; **2.** eilen; **3. ~ from** → 5; **II** *v/t.* [*irr.*] **4.** fliehen aus: **~ the country**; **5.** aus dem Weg gehen (*dat.*), meiden.

fleece [fliːs] **I** *s.* **1.** Vlies *n*, Schaffell *n*; **2.** *a.* **~ wool** Schur(wolle) *f*; **3.** *fig.* dickes Gewebe, Flausch *m*; **4.** (Haar)Pelz *m*; **5.** Schnee- *od.* Wolkendecke *f*; **II** *v/t.* **6.** *fig.* schröpfen (*of* um), ,rupfen';

7. bedecken; **'fleec·y** [-sɪ] *adj.* wollig, weich: **~ cloud** Schäfchenwolke *f*.

fleet¹ [fliːt] *s.* **1.** (*bsd.* Kriegs)Flotte *f*: ✎ *Admiral Am.* Großadmiral *m*; *merchant* **~** Handelsflotte; **2.** ✈ Gruppe *f*, Geschwader *n*; **3. ~** (*of cars*) Wagenpark *m*.

fleet² [fliːt] *adj.* □ **1.** schnell, flink: **~ of foot**, **~-footed** schnellfüßig; **2.** *poet.* → *fleeting*.

fleet·ing ['fliːtɪŋ] *adj.* □ (schnell) dahineilend, flüchtig, vergänglich: **~ time**; **~ glimpse** flüchtiger (An)Blick *od.* Eindruck; **'fleet·ness** [-nɪs] *s.* **1.** Schnelligkeit *f*; **2.** Flüchtigkeit *f*.

Fleet Street *npr.* Fleet Street *f*: a) *das frühere Londoner Presseviertel*, b) *fig. die (Londoner) Presse.*

Flem·ing ['flemɪŋ] *s.* Flame *m*, Flamin *f*, Flämin *f*; **Flem·ish** [-mɪʃ] **I** *s.* **1.** *the* **~** die Flamen *pl.*; **2.** *ling.* Flämisch *n*; **II** *adj.* **3.** flämisch.

flench [flenʃ], **flense** [flenz] *v/t.* **1.** a) *den Wal* flensen, b) *den Walspeck* abziehen; **2.** *Seehund* häuten.

flesh [fleʃ] **I** *s.* **1.** Fleisch *n*: *my own* **~** *and blood* mein eigen Fleisch u. Blut; *more than* **~** *and blood can bear* einfach unerträglich; *in* **~** *obs.* korpulent, dick; *lose* **~** abmagern, abnehmen; *put on* **~** Fett ansetzen, zunehmen; *press (the)* **~** *Am.* F Hände schütteln; (*bare*) **~** *iro.* (nacktes) Fleisch, ,Fleischbeschau' *f*; → *creep* 4; **2.** Körper *m*, Leib *m*: *in the* **~** leibhaftig, (höchst)persönlich, *weitS.* in natura; *become one* **~** ,ein Leib u. 'eine Seele werden'; **3.** a) sündiges Fleisch, b) *fig.* Fleischeslust *f*: *pleasures of the* **~** Freuden des Fleisches; **4.** Menschheit *f*: *go the way of all* **~** den Weg allen Fleisches gehen; **5.** (Frucht)Fleisch *n*; **II** *v/t.* **6.** *Jagdhund* Fleisch kosten lassen; **7.** *Tierhaut* ausfleischen; **8.** *mst* **~ out** *fig. Gesetz etc.* ,mit Fleisch versehen', Sub'stanz verleihen (*dat.*); **~ col·o(u)r** *s.* Fleischfarbe *f*; **'~-,col·o(u)red** *adj.* fleischfarben.

flesh·ings ['fleʃɪŋz] *s. pl.* fleischfarbene Strumpfhose *f*; **flesh·ly** ['fleʃlɪ] *adj.* **1.** fleischlich: a) leiblich, b) sinnlich; **2.** irdisch, menschlich.

'flesh|·pot *s.*: *the* **~s** *of Egypt fig.* die Fleischtöpfe Ägyptens; **~ tights** → *fleshings*; **~ tints** *s. pl. paint.* Fleischtöne *pl.*; **~ wound** *s.* Fleischwunde *f*.

flesh·y ['fleʃɪ] *adj.* **1.** fleischig (*a. Früchte etc.*), dick; **2.** fleischartig.

fleur-de-lis [ˌflɜːdəˈliː] *pl.* **fleurs-de-lis** [ˌflɜːdəˈliːz] (*Fr.*) *s.* **1.** *her.* Lilie *f*; **2.** *königliches Wappen Frankreichs.*

flew [fluː] *pret. von* **fly¹**.

flews [fluːz] *s. pl.* Lefzen *pl.*

flex [fleks] **I** *v/t. anat.* beugen, biegen: **~ one's knees**; **~ one's muscles** die Muskeln anspannen, *a.* die Muskeln spielen lassen (*a. fig.*); **II** *s.* ⚡ *bsd. Brit.* (Anschluss-, Verlängerungs)Kabel *n*; **flex·i·bil·i·ty** [ˌfleksəˈbɪlətɪ] *s.* **1.** Biegsamkeit *f*, Elastizi'tät *f*; **2.** *fig.* Flexibili'tät *f*, Wendigkeit *f*, Beweglichkeit *f*; **flex·i·ble** ['fleksəbl] *adj.* □ **1.** fle'xibel: a) biegsam, e'lastisch, b) *fig.* wendig, anpassungsfähig, geschmeidig: **~ car** *mot.* wendiger Wagen; **~ drive shaft** ◉ Kardanwelle *f*; **~ gun** schwenkbares Geschütz; **~ metal tube** Metallschlauch *m*; **~ policy** flexible Politik; **~ working hours** Gleitzeit(regelung) *f*; **2.** lenkbar, folg-, fügsam; **'flex·ile** [-ksɪl] → *flexible*; **'flex·ion** [-kʃn] *s.* **1.** *bsd. anat.* Biegen *n*, Beugung *f*; **2.** *ling.* Flexi'on (*n*), Beugung *f*; **'flex·ion·al** [-kʃənl] *adj.*

F

ling. flektiert, Flexions..., Beugungs...; **'flex·i·time** *s.* gleitende Arbeitszeit, Gleitzeit *f*; **'flexor** [-ksə] *s. anat.* Beuger *m*, Beugemuskel *m*; **'flex·time** *s. Am.* → *flexitime.*

flib·ber·ti·gib·bet [,flɪbətɪ'dʒɪbɪt] *s.* a) Klatschbase *f*, b) ,verrückte Nudel'.

flick[1] [flɪk] **I** *s.* **1.** leichter, schneller Schlag, Klaps *m*; **2.** a) Schnipser *m*, (Finger)Schnalzen *n*, b) (Peitschen-) Schnalzen *n*, (-)Knall *m*: **a ~ of the wrist** schnelle Drehung des Handgelenks; **II** *v/t.* **3.** schnippen, schnipsen; e-n Klaps geben (*dat.*); *Schalter* an- *od.* ausknipsen; *Messer* (auf)schnappen lassen; **III** *v/i.* **4.** schnellen; **5. ~ through** *Buch etc.* 'durchblättern.

flick[2] [flɪk] *s.* F a) Film *m*, b) *pl.* ,Kintopp' *m*, Kino *n*.

flick·er ['flɪkə] **I** *s.* **1.** Flackern *n*: **a ~ of hope** ein Hoffnungsfunke; **2.** Zucken *n*; **3.** *Bildschirm:* Flimmern *n*: **~-free** flimmerfrei; **4.** Flattern *n*; **II** *v/i.* **5.** *a. fig.* (auf)flackern; **6.** zucken; **7.** *TV* flimmern; **8.** huschen (**over** über *acc.*) (*Augen*).

flick knife *s.* [*irr.*] *Brit.* Schnappmesser *n.*

fli·er ['flaɪə] *s.* **1.** etwas, das fliegt (*Vogel, Insekt, etc.*); **2.** ✈ Flieger *m*: a) Pi'lot *m*, b) ,Vogel' *m* (*Flugzeug*); **3.** Flieger *m* (*Trapezkünstler*); **4.** *Am.* a) Ex'press(zug) *m*, b) Schnell(auto)bus *m*; **5.** ⊙ Schwungrad *n*; **6. take a ~** F a) e-n Riesensatz machen, b) *Am.* sich auf e-e gewagte Sache einlassen; **7.** *Am.* Flugblatt *n*, Re'klamezettel *m*; **8.** F für *flying start.*

flight[1] [flaɪt] *s.* Flucht *f*: **put to ~** in die Flucht schlagen; **take** (**to**) **~** die Flucht ergreifen; **~ of capital** ✝ Kapitalflucht; **~ capital** Fluchtkapital *n.*

flight[2] [flaɪt] *s.* **1.** Flug *m*, Fliegen *n*: **in ~** im Flug; **2.** ✈ a) Flug *m*, b) Flug(strecke *f*) *m*; **3.** Schwarm *m* (*Vögel od. Insekten*), Flug *m*, Schar *f* (*Vögel*): **in the first ~** *fig.* an der Spitze; **4.** ✈, ✕ a) Schwarm *m* (*4 Flugzeuge*), b) Kette *f* (*3 Flugzeuge*); **5.** (*Geschoss-, Pfeil- etc.*) Hagel *m*; **6.** (*Gedanken- etc.*)Flug *m*, Schwung *m*; **7. ~ of stairs** (*od.* **steps**) Treppe *f*; **~ at·tend·ant** *s.* Flugbegleiter(in); **~ con·trol** *s.* ✈ **1.** Flugsicherung *f*; **2.** Steuerfläche *f* (*z. B. Seitenruder, Klappen*), **~ con·trol·ler** *s.* Fluglotse *m*, -lotsin *f*; **~ deck** *s.* **1.** ⚓ Flugdeck *n*; **2.** ✈ Cockpit *n*; **~ en·gi·neer** *s.* 'Bordingeni,eur *m*; **~ feath·er** *s. orn.* Schwungfeder *f.*

flight·i·ness ['flaɪtɪnɪs] *s.* **1.** Flatterhaftigkeit *f*; **2.** Leichtsinn *m.*

flight| in·struc·tor *s.* ✈ Fluglehrer *m*; **~ lane** *s.* ✈ Flugschneise *f*; **~ lieu·ten·ant** *s. Brit.* (Flieger)Hauptmann *m*; **~ me·chan·ic** *s.* 'Bordme,chaniker *m*; **~ path** *s.* **1.** ✈ Flugroute *f*; **2.** *Ballistik:* Flugbahn *f*; **~ re·cord·er** *s.* ✈ Flugschreiber *m*; **'~-test** *v/t.* im Flug erproben: **~ed** flugerprobt; **~ tick·et** *s.* Flugticket *n*; **'~-,worth·y** *adj.* flugtauglich (*Person*); fluggeeignet (*Maschine*).

flight·y ['flaɪtɪ] *adj.* □ **1.** flatterhaft, launisch, fahrig; **2.** leichtsinnig.

flim·flam ['flɪmflæm] **I** *s.* **1.** Quatsch *m*; **2.** ,fauler Zauber', Trick(s *pl.*) *m*; **II** *v/t.* j-n ,reinlegen'.

flim·si·ness ['flɪmzɪnɪs] *s.* **1.** Dünnheit *f*; **2.** *fig.* Fadenscheinigkeit *f*; **3.** Dürftigkeit *f*; **flim·sy** ['flɪmzɪ] **I** *adj.* □ **1.** (hauch)dünn, zart, leicht, schwach; **2.** *fig.* dürftig, 'durchsichtig, schwach, fadenscheinig: **a ~ excuse**; **II** *s.* **3.** a) 'Durchschlag-, 'Kohlepa,pier *n*, b)

'Durchschlag *m*; **4.** *pl.* F ,Reizwäsche' *f.*

flinch[1] [flɪntʃ] *v/i.* **1.** zu'rückschrecken (**from**, **at** vor *dat.*); **2.** (zu'rück)zucken, zs.-fahren (*vor Schmerz etc.*): **without ~ing** ohne mit der Wimper zu zucken.

flinch[2] [flɪntʃ] → *flench.*

fling [flɪŋ] **I** *s.* **1.** Wurf *m*: (**at**) **full ~** mit voller Wucht; **2.** Ausschlagen *n* (*des Pferdes*); **3.** *fig.* F Versuch *m*: **have a ~ at s.th.** es mit et. probieren; **have a ~ at s.o.** über j-n herfallen, gegen j-n sticheln; **4. have one's** (*od.* **a**) **~** sich austoben; **5.** *ein schottischer Tanz*; **II** *v/t.* [*irr.*] **6.** schleudern, werfen: **~ open** *Tür* aufreißen; **~ s.th. in s.o.'s teeth** *fig.* j-m et. ins Gesicht schleudern; **~ o.s. at s.o.** a) sich auf j-n stürzen, b) *fig.* sich j-m an den Hals werfen; **~ o.s. into s.th.** *fig.* sich in *od.* auf e-e Sache stürzen; **III** *v/i.* [*irr.*] **7.** eilen, stürzen (**out of the room** aus dem Zimmer); **8. ~ out** (**at**) ausschlagen (nach) (*Pferd*); *Zssgn mit adv.*:

fling| a·way *v/t.* **1.** wegwerfen; **2.** *fig. Zeit, Geld* vergeuden, verschwenden (**on** für *et.*, **an** *j-n*); **~ back** *v/t. Kopf* zu'rückwerfen; **~ down** *v/t.* zu Boden werfen; **~ off I** *v/t.* **1.** *Kleider, a. Joch, Skrupel* abwerfen; **2.** *Verfolger* abschütteln; **3.** *Gedicht etc.* ,hinhauen'; **4.** *Bemerkung* fallen lassen; **II** *v/i.* **5.** da'vonstürzen; **~ on** *v/t.* (sich) *Kleider* 'überwerfen; **~ out I** *v/t.* **1.** *j-n* hin'auswerfen; **2.** *et.* wegwerfen; **3.** *Worte* her'vorstoßen; **4.** *Arme* (plötzlich) ausstrecken; **II** *v/i.* **5.** → *fling* 7, 8.

flint [flɪnt] *s.* **1.** *min.* Flint *m*, Feuerstein *m* (*a. des Feuerzeugs*); **2.** → **~ glass** *s.* ⊙ Flintglas *n*; **'~-lock** *s.* ✕ *hist.* Steinschloss(gewehr) *n.*

flint·y ['flɪntɪ] *adj.* □ **1.** aus Feuerstein; **2.** kieselhart; **3.** *fig.* hart(herzig).

flip[1] [flɪp] **I** *v/t.* **1.** schnipsen, schnellen: **~ off** wegschnipsen; **~** (**over**) *Buchseiten, Schallplatte etc.* wenden, *a. Spion* 'umdrehen; **~ a coin** e-e Münze hochwerfen (*zum Losen*); **2. ~ one's lid** (*od.* **top**) → 5; **II** *v/i.* **3.** schnipsen; **4. ~ through** *Buch etc.* 'durchblättern; **5.** a **~ out** *sl.* ,ausflippen', ,durchdrehen'; **III** *s.* **6.** Schnipser *m*; **7.** *sport* Salto *m*; **8.** ✈ *Brit.* F kurzer Rundflug; **IV** *adj.* **9.** (→ *flippant*, b) gut aufgelegt.

flip[2] [flɪp] *s.* Flip *m* (*alkoholisches Mischgetränk mit Ei*).

flip chart ['flɪptʃɑːt] *s.* 'Flipchart *f* (*für Präsentationen*).

flip-flap ['flɪpflæp] → **'flip-flop** [-flɒp] *s.* **1.** Klappern *n*; **2.** *sport* Flickflack *m*, 'Handstand,überschlag *m*; **3.** *a.* **~ circuit** ⚡ Flipflopschaltung *f*; **4.** 'Zehensan,dale *f*; **II** *v/i.* **5.** klappern; **6.** *sport* e-n Flic(k)flac(k) machen.

flip·pan·cy ['flɪpənsɪ] *s.* **1.** ,Schnoddrigkeit' *f*, vorlaute Art; **2.** Leichtfertigkeit *f*, Frivoli'tät *f*; **'flip·pant** [-nt] *adj.* □ **1.** ,schnodd(e)rig', vorlaut, frech; **2.** fri'vol, leichtfertig.

flip·per ['flɪpə] *s.* **1.** *zo.* (Schwimm)Flosse *f*; **2.** *sport* Schwimmflosse *f*; **3.** *sl.* ,Flosse' *f* (*Hand*).

flirt [flɜːt] **I** *v/t.* **1.** schnipsen; **2.** wedeln mit: **~ a fan**; **II** *v/i.* **3.** her'umflattern; **4.** flirten (**with** mit) (*a. fig. pol. etc.*): **~ with death** mit dem Leben spielen; **5.** *mit e-r Idee* spielen, liebäugeln; **III** *s.* **6.** a) ko'kette Frau, b) Schäker *m*; **7.** → **flir·ta·tion** [flɜː'teɪʃn] *s.* **1.** Flirten *n*; **2.** Flirt *m*; **3.** Liebäugeln *n*; **flir·ta·tious** [flɜː'teɪʃəs] *adj.* (gern) flirtend, ko'kett.

flit [flɪt] *v/i.* **1.** flitzen, huschen, sausen; **2.** (um'her)flattern; **3.** *fig.* verfliegen (*Zeit*); **4.** *Brit.* F heimlich ausziehen; **II**

s. **5.** *a.* **moonlight ~** *Brit.* F Auszug *m* bei Nacht u. Nebel.

flitch [flɪtʃ] *s.* **1.** *a.* **~ of bacon** gesalzene *od.* geräucherte Speckseite; **2.** Heilbuttschnitte *f*; **3.** Walspeckstück *n.*

fliv·ver ['flɪvə] *s. Am. sl.* **1.** kleine ,Blechkiste' (*Auto, Flugzeug*); **2.** ,Pleite' *f* (*Misserfolg*).

float [fləʊt] **I** *v/i.* **1.** (im Wasser) treiben, schwimmen; **2.** ⚓ flott sein *od.* werden; **3.** schweben, treiben, gleiten; **4.** *a.* ✝ 'umlaufen, in 'Umlauf sein; ✝ gegründet werden; **5.** (ziellos) her'umwandern; **6.** *Am.* häufig den Wohnsitz *od.* Arbeitsplatz wechseln; **II** *v/t.* **7.** schwimmen *od.* treiben lassen; *Baumstämme* flößen; **8.** ⚓ flottmachen; **9.** schwemmen, tragen (*Wasser*) (*a. fig.*); **10.** über'schwemmen (*a. fig.*); **11.** *fig. Verhandlungen etc.* in Gang bringen, lancieren; *Gerücht etc.* in 'Umlauf setzen; **12.** ✝ a) *Gesellschaft* gründen, c) *Anleihe* auflegen, c) *Wertpapiere* in 'Umlauf bringen; **13.** ✝ floaten, den Wechselkurs (*gen.*) freigeben; **III** *s.* **14.** Floß *n*; **15.** schwimmende Landebrücke; **16.** *Angeln:* (Kork)Schwimmer *m*; **17.** *ichth.* Schwimmblase *f*; **18.** ⊙, ✈ Schwimmer *m*; **19.** *a.* **~ board** (Rad-)Schaufel *f*; **20.** a) niedriger Plattformwagen (*für Güter*), b) Festwagen *m* (*bei Umzügen etc.*); **21.** ⊙ a) Raspel *f*, b) Pflasterkelle *f*; **22.** *pl. thea.* Rampenlicht *n*; **23.** *Brit.* Notgroschen *m*; **'float·a·ble** [-təbl] *adj.* **1.** schwimmfähig; **2.** flößbar (*Fluss*); **'float·age, float·a·tion** → *flotage, flotation.*

float bridge *s.* Floßbrücke *f.*

float·er ['fləʊtə] *s.* **1.** ✝ Gründer *m* e-r Firma; **2.** ✝ *Brit.* erstklassiges 'Wertpa,pier; **3.** *Am.* F ,Zugvogel' *m* (*j-d, der ständig Wohnsitz od. Arbeitsplatz wechselt*); **4.** Springer *m* (*im Betrieb*); **5.** *pol.* a) Wechselwähler *m*, b) *Wähler, der s-e Stimme illegal in mehreren Wahlbezirken abgibt*; **6.** *Am. sl.* Wasserleiche *f.*

float·ing ['fləʊtɪŋ] **I** *adj.* □ **1.** schwimmend, treibend, Schwimm..., Treib...; **2.** schwebend (*a. fig.*); **3.** lose, beweglich; **4.** schwankend; **5.** ohne festen Wohnsitz, wandernd; **6.** ✝ a) 'umlaufend (*Geld etc.*), b) schwebend (*Schuld*), c) flüssig (*Kapital*), d) fle'xibel (*Wechselkurs*), e) frei konvertierbar (*Währung*); **II** *s.* **7.** ✝ Floating *n*, Freigabe *f* des Wechselkurses; **~ an·chor** *s.* ⚓ Treibanker *m*; **~ as·sets** *s. pl.* ✝ flüssige Ak'tiva *pl.*; **~ ax·le** *s.* ⊙ Schwingachse *f*; **~ bridge** *s.* Tonnen-, Floßbrücke *f*; **~ cap·i·tal** *s.* ✝ 'Umlaufvermögen *n*; **~ crane** *s.* ⊙ Schwimmkran *m*; **~ dec·i·mal point** → *floating point*; **~ dock** *s.* ⚓ Schwimmdock *n*; **~ ice** *s.* Treibeis *n*; **~ kid·ney** *s.* ✚ Wanderniere *f*; **~ light** *s.* ⚓ Leuchtboje *f od.* -schiff *n*; **~ mine** *s.* ✕ Treibmine *f*; **~ point** *s. Computer etc.:* Fließkomma *n*; **~ pol·i·cy** *s.* ✝ Pau'schalpo,lice *f*; **~ rib** *s. anat.* falsche Rippe; **~ trade** *s.* ✝ Seefrachthandel *m*; **~ vote** *od.* **vot·ers** *pl.*) *s. pol.* Wechselwähler *pl.*

'float|-plane *s.* ✈ Schwimmerflugzeug *n*; **~ switch** *s.* ⚡ Schwimmerschalter *m*; **~ valve** *s.* ⊙ 'Schwimmerven,til *n.*

floc·cose ['flɒkəʊs], **'floc·cu·lent** [-kjʊlənt] *adj.* flockig, wollig; **'floc·cus** [-kəs] *pl.* **-ci** [-ksaɪ] *s.* **1.** Flocke *f*; **2.** Büschel *n*; **3.** *orn.* Flaum *m.*

flock[1] [flɒk] **I** *s.* **1.** Herde *f* (*bsd. Schafe*); **2.** Schwarm *m*, *hunt.* Flug *m* (*Vögel*); **3.** Menge *f*, Schar *f* (*Personen*): **come in ~s** (in Scharen) herbeiströmen; **4.** *eccl.* Herde *f*, Gemeinde *f*; **II**

v/i. **5.** *fig.* strömen: ~ *to a place* zu e-m Ort (hin)strömen; ~ *to s.o.* j-m zuströmen, in Scharen zu j-m kommen; ~ *together* zs.-strömen.

flock² [flɒk] *s.* **1.** (Woll)Flocke *f*; **2.** *sg. od. pl.* a) Wollabfall *m*, b) Wollpulver *n* (*für Tapeten etc.*): ~ (*wall*)*paper* Velourstapete *f.*

floe [fləʊ] *s.* Treibeis *n*, Eisscholle *f.*

flog [flɒg] *v/t.* **1.** prügeln, schlagen: ~ *a dead horse* a) s-e Zeit verschwenden, b) offene Türen einrennen; ~ *s.th. to death fig.* et. zu Tode reiten; **2.** auspeitschen; **3.** ~ *s.th. into s.o.* j-m et. einbläuen; ~ *s.th. out of s.o.* j-m et. austreiben; **4.** *Brit.* F et. ‚verscheuern‘, ‚verkloppen‘; **'flog·ging** [-gɪŋ] *s.* **1.** Tracht *f* Prügel; **2.** Prügelstrafe *f.*

flood [flʌd] **I** *s.* **1.** Flut *f* (*a. Ggs. Ebbe*): *on the* ~ mit der (*od.* bei) Flut; **2.** Überschwemmung *f* (*a. fig.*), Hochwasser *n*: *the ⌀ bibl.* die Sintflut; **3.** *fig.* Flut *f*, Strom *m*, Schwall *m* (*von Briefen, Worten etc.*): *a* ~ *of tears* ein Tränenstrom; **II** *v/t.* **4.** über'schwemmen, -'fluten (*a. fig.*): ~ *the market* ⊤ den Markt überschwemmen; **5.** unter Wasser setzen; **6.** ♻ fluten; **7.** *mot. den Motor* ‚absaufen‘ lassen; **8.** *Fluss* anschwellen lassen; **9.** *fig.* strömen in (*acc.*), sich ergießen über (*acc.*); **III** *v/i.* **10.** *a. fig.* fluten, strömen, sich ergießen: ~ *in* hereinströmen; **11.** a) anschwellen (*Fluss*), b) über die Ufer treten; **12.** 'überlaufen (*Bad etc.*); **13.** über'schwemmt werden; ~ **con·trol** *s.* Hochwasserschutz *m*; ~ **dis·as·ter** *s.* 'Hochwasserkata‚strophe *f*; '~**·gate** *s.* Schleusentor *n*, *fig.* Schleuse *f*: *open the* ~*s to fig.* Tür u. Tor öffnen (*dat.*).

flood·ing [flʌdɪŋ] *s.* **1.** Über'schwemmung *f*; **2.** ♣ Gebärmutterblutung *f.*

'flood|·light I *s.* **1.** Scheinwerfer-, Flutlicht *n*; **2.** *a.* ~ *projector* Scheinwerfer *m*: *under* ~*s* bei Flutlicht; **II** *v/t.* [*irr.* → **light¹**] (mit Scheinwerfern) beleuchten *od.* anstrahlen: *floodlit* in Flutlicht getaucht; *floodlit match sport* Flutlichtspiel *n*; '~**·mark** *s.* Hochwasserstandszeichen *n*; '~ **tide** *s.* Flut(zeit) *f.*

floor [flɔː] **I** *s.* **1.** (Fuß)Boden *m*: *mop* (*od.* *wipe*) *the* ~ *with s.o.* j-n ‚fertig machen‘, mit j-m ‚Schlitten fahren‘; **2.** Tanzfläche *f*: *take the* ~ auf die Tanzfläche gehen (→ 3); **3.** *parl.* Sitzungs-, Ple'narsaal *m*: *cross the* ~ zur Gegenpartei übergehen; *admit to the* ~ j-m das Wort erteilen; *get* (*have od.* *hold*) *the* ~ das Wort erhalten (haben); *take the* ~ das Wort ergreifen (→ 2); **4.** ⊤ Börsensaal *m*; **5.** Stock(werk *n*) *m*, Geschoss, *östr.* Geschoß *n*; → *first floor etc.*; **6.** (Meeres- *etc.*)Boden *m*, Grund *m*, (Fluss-, Tal- *etc.* ⚒ Strecken)Sohle *f*; **7.** Minimum *n*: *price* ~; *cost* ~ Mindestkosten *pl.*; **II** *v/t.* **8.** e-n (Fuß)Boden legen in (*dat.*); **9.** zu Boden strecken, niederschlagen; **10.** F a) *j-n* ‚umhauen‘: ~*ed* sprachlos, ‚platt‘, b) *j-n* ‚schaffen‘; **11.** *Am. das Gaspedal etc.* voll ‚durchtreten‘; '~**·cloth** *s.* Scheuertuch *n*; ~ **cov·er·ing** *s.* Fußbodenbelag *m.*

floor·er [flɔːrə] *s.* F **1.** vernichtender Schlag, *fig. a.* ‚Schlag *m* ins Kon'tor‘; **2.** ‚harte Nuss‘, knifflige Frage.

floor ex·er·cis·es *s. pl.* Bodenturnen *n.*

floor·ing [flɔːrɪŋ] *s.* **1.** (Fuß)Boden *m*; **2.** Bodenbelag *m.*

floor| lamp *s.* Stehlampe *f*; ~ **lead·er** *s. pol. Am.* Frakti'onsvorsitzende(r) *m*; ~ **man·ag·er** *s.* **1.** ⊤ Ab'teilungsleiter *m* (*in e-m Kaufhaus*); **2.** *pol. Am.* Geschäftsführer *m* (*e-r Partei*); **3.** *TV* Auf-

---

nahmeleiter *m*; ~ **plan** *s.* **1.** Grundriss *m* (*e-s Stockwerks*); **2.** Raumverteilungsplan *m* (*auf e-r Messe etc.*); ~ **show** *s.* Varie'teevorstellung *f* (*in e-m Nachtklub etc.*); ~ **space** *s.* Bodenfläche *f*; ~ **tile** *s.* Fußbodenfliese *f*; ~ **trad·er** *s. Börse:* Par'ketthändler(in); '~**·walk·er** *s.* (Aufsicht führender) Ab'teilungsleiter (*in e-m Kaufhaus*).

floo·zie [fluːzɪ] *s. Am. sl.* ‚Flittchen‘ *n.*

flop [flɒp] **I** *v/i.* **1.** ('hin)plumpsen; **2.** (*into*) sich (in e-n *Sessel etc.*) plumpsen lassen; **3.** a) zappeln, b) flattern; **4.** F a) *ped., thea. etc.* ‚durchfallen‘, b) *allg.* e-e ‚Pleite‘ sein, ‚da'nebengehen‘; **II** *v/t.* **5.** ('hin)plumpsen lassen; **III** *s.* **6.** Plumps *m*; **7.** F a) *thea. etc.* ‚Durchfall‘ *m*, ‚Flop‘ *m*, b) ‚Pleite‘ *f*, ‚Reinfall‘ *m*, c) Versager *m*, ‚Niete‘ *f* (*Person*) **IV** *adv. u. int.* **8.** plumps; **'flop·house** *s. Am. sl.* ‚Penne‘ *f*, (billige) ‚Absteige‘; **'flop·py** [-pɪ] *adj.* **1.** schlaff, schlotterig: ~ *ears* Schlappohren; ~ *hat* Schlapphut *m*; ~ *disk Computer:* Diskette *f*; ~ (*disk*) *drive* Dis'ketten‚laufwerk *n.*

flo·ra [flɔːrə] *pl.* **-ras**, *a.* **-rae** [-riː] *s.* **1.** Flora *f*, (*a.* Abhandlung *f* über e-e) Pflanzenwelt *f*; **2.** *physiol.* (*Darm- etc.*) Flora *f*; **'flo·ral** [-rəl] *adj.* □ Blumen..., Blüten..., *a.* geblümt: ~ *design* Blumenmuster *n*; ~ *emblem* Wappenblume *f.*

Flor·en·tine [flɒrəntaɪn] **I** *adj.* floren'tinisch, Florentiner...; **II** *s.* Floren'tiner(in).

flo·res·cence [flɔːresns] *s.* ♣ Blüte (-zeit) *f* (*a. fig.*); **flo·ret** [flɔːrɪt] *s.* Blümchen *n.*

flo·ri·cul·ture [flɔːrɪkʌltʃə] *s.* Blumenzucht *f.*

flor·id [flɒrɪd] *adj.* □ **1.** rot, gerötet: ~ *complexion*; **2.** blühend (*Gesundheit*); **3.** über'laden: a) blumig (*Stil*), b) 'übermäßig verziert; **4.** ♪ figuriert; **5.** ♫ stark ausgeprägt (*Krankheit*).

Flo·rid·i·an [flɒrɪdɪən] **I** *adj.* Florida...; **II** *s.* Bewohner(in) von Florida.

flor·in [flɒrɪn] *s.* **1.** *Brit. hist.* Zwei'schillingstück *n*; **2.** *obs.* (*bsd.* niederländischer) Gulden.

flo·rist [flɒrɪst] *s.* Blumenhändler(in), -züchter(in).

floss¹ [flɒs] *s.* **1.** Ko'kon-, Seidenwolle *f*; **2.** Flo'rettgarn *n*; **3.** *a.* ~ *silk* Schappe-, Flo'rettseide *f*; **4.** ♣ Seidenbaumwolle *f*; **5.** Flaum *m*, seidige Sub'stanz; **6.** *a. dental* ~ Zahnseide *f.*

floss² [flɒs] *s.* ⊙ **1.** Glasschlacke *f*; **2.** *a.* ~ *hole* Schlackenloch *n.*

floss·y [flɒsɪ] *adj.* **1.** flo'rettseiden, -seidig; **3.** *Am. sl.* ‚schick‘.

flo·tage [fləʊtɪdʒ] *s.* **1.** Schwimmen *n*; **2.** Schwimmfähigkeit *f*; **3.** *et.* Schwimmendes *n*, Treibendes, Treibgut *n.*

flo·ta·tion [fləʊteɪʃn] *s.* **1.** → *flotage* 1; **2.** Schweben *n*; **3.** ⊤ a) Gründung *f* (*e-r Gesellschaft*), b) In'umlaufbringung *f* (*von Wertpapieren etc.*), c) Auflegung *f* (*e-r Anleihe*); **4.** ⊙ Flotati'on *f.*

flo·til·la [fləʊtɪlə] *s.* ♣ Flot'tille *f.*

flot·sam [flɒtsəm] *s.*, *a.* ~ *and jet·sam s.* **1.** ♣ Strand-, Treibgut *n*; **2.** *fig.* Strandgut *n* des Lebens; **3.** *fig.* 'Überbleibsel *pl.*, Krimskrams *m.*

flounce¹ [flaʊns] *v/i.* **1.** erregt stürmen *od.* stürzen; **2.** stolzieren; **3.** sich herumwerfen, zappeln.

flounce² [flaʊns] **I** *s.* Vo'lant *m*, Besatz *m*; Falbel *f*; **II** *v/t.* mit Vo'lants besetzen.

floun·der¹ [flaʊndə] *v/i.* **1.** zappeln, strampeln, *fig. a.* sich (ab)quälen; **2.**

---

taumeln, stolpern, um'hertappen; **3.** *fig.* sich verhaspeln, nicht weiterwissen, *a. sport* ins ‚Schwimmen‘ kommen.

floun·der² [flaʊndə] *s. ichth.* Flunder *f.*

flour [flaʊə] *s.* **1.** Mehl *n*; **2.** feines Pulver, Mehl *n*; **II** *v/t.* **3.** *Am.* (zu Mehl) mahlen; **4.** mit Mehl bestreuen.

flour·ish [flʌrɪʃ] **I** *v/i.* **1.** gedeihen, *fig. a.* blühen, florieren; **2.** auf der Höhe s-r Macht *od.* s-s Ruhmes stehen; **3.** wirken, erfolgreich sein (*Künstler etc.*); **4.** prahlen; **5.** sich geschraubt ausdrücken; **6.** sich auffällig benehmen; **7.** Schnörkel *od.* Floskeln machen; **8.** ♪ a) fantasieren, b) e-n Tusch spielen; **II** *v/t.* **9.** schwingen, schwenken; **10.** zur Schau stellen, protzen mit; **11.** (aus)schmücken; **III** *s.* **12.** Schwingen *n*, Schwenken *n*; **13.** Schwung *m*, schwungvolle Gebärde; **14.** Schnörkel *m*; **15.** Floskel *f*; **16.** ♪ a) bravou'röse Pas'sage, b) Tusch *m*: ~ *of trumpets* Trompetenstoß *m*, Fanfare *f*, *fig.* (großes) Trara; **'flour·ish·ing** [-ʃɪŋ] *adj.* □ blühend, gedeihend, florierend: ~ *trade* schwunghafter Handel.

floury [flaʊərɪ] *adj.* mehlig.

flout [flaʊt] **I** *v/t.* **1.** verspotten, -höhnen; **2.** *Befehl, Ratschlag etc.* miss'achten, *Angebot etc.* ausschlagen; **II** *v/i.* **3.** spotten (*at* über *acc.*), höhnen.

flow [fləʊ] **I** *v/i.* **1.** fließen, strömen, fluten, rinnen, laufen (*alle a. fig.*): ~ *freely* in Strömen fließen (*Sekt etc.*); **2.** *fig.* da'hinfließen, gleiten; **3.** ♣ steigen (*Flut*); **4.** wallen (*Haar, Kleid etc.*), lose he'rabhängen; **5.** *fig.* (*from*) herrühren (von), entspringen (*dat.*); **6.** *fig.* (*with*) reich sein (an *dat.*), 'überfließen (vor *dat.*), voll sein (von); **II** *v/t.* **7.** über'fluten, -'schwemmen; **III** *s.* **8.** Fließen *n*, Strömen *n* (*beide a. fig.*), Rinnen *n*: ~ *characteristics phys.* Strömungsbild *n*; ~ *chart* (*od.* *sheet*) *Computer,* ⊤ Flussdiagramm *n*; ~ *pattern phys.* Stromlinienbild *n*; ~ *production,* ~ *system* ⊤ Fließbandfertigung *f*; **9.** Fluss *m*, Strom *m* (*beide a. fig.*): ~ *of traffic* Verkehrsfluss, -strom; **10.** Zu*od.* Abfluss *m*; **11.** Wallen *n*; **12.** *fig.* (*Wort- etc.*)Schwall *m*, Erguss *m* (*a. von Gefühlen*); **13.** *physiol.* F Peri'ode *f.*

flow·er [flaʊə] **I** *s.* **1.** Blume *f*: *say it with* ~*s!* lasst Blumen sprechen!; **2.** ♣ a) Blüte *f*, b) Blütenpflanze *f*, c) Blüte (-zeit) *f* (*a. fig.*): *be in* ~ in Blüte stehen, blühen; *in the* ~ *of his life* in der Blüte s-r Jahre; **3.** *fig. das* Beste *od.* Feinste, Auslese *f*, E'lite *f*; **4.** *fig.* Blüte *f*, Zierde *f*; **5.** ('Blumen)Orna‚ment *n*, (-)Verzierung *f*: ~*s of speech* Floskeln; **6.** *typ.* Vi'gnette *f*; **7.** *pl.* 🜍 Blumen *pl.*: ~*s of sulphur* Schwefelblumen *pl.*, -blüte *f*; **II** *v/i.* **8.** blühen, *fig. a.* in höchster Blüte stehen; **III** *v/t.* **9.** mit Blumen(mustern) verzieren, blüme(l)n; ~ *bed s.* Blumenbeet *n*; ~ *child s.* [*irr.*] ‚Blumenkind‘ *n* (*Hippie*).

flow·ered [flaʊəd] *adj.* **1.** mit Blumen geschmückt; **2.** geblümt; **3.** *in Zssgn* ...blütig.

flow·er girl *s.* **1.** Blumenmädchen *n*; **2.** *Am.* Blumen streuendes Mädchen (*bei e-r Hochzeit*).

flow·er·ing [flaʊərɪŋ] **I** *adj.* blühend, Blüten...: ~ *plant* Blütenpflanze *f*; **II** *s.* Blüte(zeit) *f.*

flow·er| peo·ple *s.* ‚Blumenkinder‘ *pl.* (*Hippies*); ~ **piece** *s. paint.* Blumenstück *n*; '~**·pot** *s.* Blumentopf *m*; ~ **show** *s.* Blumenausstellung *f.*

flow·er·y [flaʊərɪ] *adj.* **1.** blumen-, blütenreich; **2.** geblümt; **3.** *fig.* blumig.

flowing – flyblow 230

flow·ing ['fləʊɪŋ] *adj.* □ **1.** fließend, strömend; **2.** *fig.* flüssig (*Stil etc.*); **3.** wallend (*Bart, Kleid*); **4.** wehend, flatternd (*Haar etc.*).

'flow,me·ter *s.* ☉ 'Durchflussmesser *m.*

flown [fləʊn] *p.p. von* fly¹.

flu [fluː] *s.* ✻ F Grippe *f.*

flub [flʌb] *Am. sl.* **I** *s.* (grober) Schnitzer; **II** *v/i.* (e-n groben) Schnitzer machen, patzen.

flub·dub ['flʌbdʌb] *s. Am. sl.* Geschwafel *n*, ,Quatsch' *m.*

fluc·tu·ate ['flʌktjʊeɪt] *v/i.* schwanken: a) fluktuieren (*a.* ✝), sich (ständig) verändern, b) *fig.* unschlüssig sein; 'fluc·tu·at·ing [-tɪŋ] *adj.* schwankend: a) fluktuierend, b) unschlüssig: ~ ex·change rate frei schwankender Wechselkurs; fluc·tu·a·tion [,flʌktjʊ'eɪʃn] *s.* **1.** Schwankung *f*, Fluktuati'on *f* (*beide a.* ✝, ⚡, *phys.*): ~ margin Bandbreite *f*; Schwankungsbreite *f*; cyclical ~ ✝ Konjunkturschwankung; **2.** *fig.* Schwanken *n.*

flue¹ [fluː] *s.* **1.** ☉ a) Rauchfang *m*, Esse *f*, b) Abzugsrohr *n*, (Feuerungs)Zug *m*: ~ gas Rauch-, Abgas *n*, c) Heizröhre *f*, d) Flammrohr *n*, 'Feuerka,nal *m*; **2.** ♪ a) a. ~ pipe Lippenpfeife *f*, b) Kernspalt *m der Orgelpfeife.*

flue² [fluː] *s.* Flusen *pl.*, Staubflocken *pl.*

flue³ [fluː] *s.* ⚓ Schleppnetz *n.*

flu·en·cy ['fluːənsɪ] *s.* Fluss *m* (*der Rede etc.*), Flüssigkeit *f* (*des Stils etc.*); Gewandtheit *f*; 'flu·ent [-nt] *adj.* □ **1.** fließend, geläufig: speak ~ German, be ~ in German fließend Deutsch sprechen; **2.** flüssig, ele'gant (*Stil etc.*), gewandt (*Redner etc.*).

fluff [flʌf] **I** *s.* **1.** Staubflocke *f*, Fussel(n *pl.*) *f*; **2.** Flaum *m* (*a. erster Bartwuchs*); **3.** F *sport, thea. etc.* ,Patzer' *m*; **4.** *Am.* Schaumspeise *f*; **5.** *thea. Am.* F ,leichte Kost'; **6.** *oft* bit of ~ F ,Betthäschen' *n*, ,Mieze' *f*; **II** *v/t.* **7.** ~ out, ~ up a) *Federn* aufplustern, b) *Kissen etc.* aufschütteln; **8.** F *bsd. thea., sport* ,verpatzen'; **III** *v/i.* **9.** F *thea., sport* ,patzen'; 'fluf·fy [-fɪ] *adj.* **1.** flaumig; **2.** *thea. Am.* F leicht, anspruchslos.

flu·id ['fluːɪd] **I** *s.* **1.** Flüssigkeit *f*; **II** *adj.* **2.** flüssig; **3.** *fig.* → fluent; **4.** *fig.* fließend, veränderlich; ~ cou·pling, ~ clutch *s.* ☉ hy'draulische Kupplung; ~ drive *s.* ☉ Flüssigkeitsgetriebe *n.*

flu·id·i·ty [fluː'ɪdətɪ] *s.* **1.** *phys.* a) flüssiger Zustand, Flüssigkeit(sgrad *m*) *f*, b) Gasförmigkeit *f*; **2.** *fig.* Veränderlichkeit *f*; **3.** Flüssigkeit *f des Stils etc.*

flu·id| me·chan·ics *s. pl. sg. konstr. phys.* 'Strömungsme,chanik *f*; ~ ounce *s. Hohlmaß*: a) *Brit.* = 28,4 ccm, b) *Am.* = 29,6 ccm; ~ pres·sure *s.* ☉, *phys.* hy'draulischer Druck.

fluke¹ [fluːk] *s.* **1.** ⚓ Ankerflügel *m*; **2.** ☉ Bohrlöffel *m*; **3.** 'Widerhaken *m*; **4.** Schwanzflosse *f* (*des Wals*); **5.** *zo.* Leberegel *m.*

fluke² [fluːk] *s.* **1.** ,Dusel' *m*, ,Schwein' *n*: ~ hit Zufallstreffer *m*; **2.** *Billard*: glücklicher Stoß; 'fluk·(e)y [-kɪ] *adj. sl.* **1.** Glücks..., Zufalls...; **2.** unsicher.

flume [fluːm] **I** *s.* **1.** Klamm *f*; **2.** künstlicher Wasserlauf, Ka'nal *m*; **II** *v/t.* **3.** durch e-n Kanal flößen.

flum·mer·y ['flʌmərɪ] *s.* **1.** *Küche*: (Hafer)Mehl *n*, b) Flammeri *m* (*Süßspeise*); **2.** F a) *fig.* leere Schmeiche'lei, b) ,Quatsch' *m.*

flum·mox ['flʌməks] *v/t. sl.* verblüffen, aus der Fassung bringen.

flung [flʌŋ] *pret. u. p.p. von* fling.

flunk [flʌŋk] *ped. Am. sl.* **I** *v/t.* **1.**

,'durchrauschen' *od.* ,'durchrasseln' lassen; **2.** *oft* ~ out von der Schule ,werfen'; **3.** ,'durchrasseln' in (*e-r Prüfung, e-m Fach*); **II** *v/i.* **4.** ,'durchrasseln', ,'durchrauschen'; **III** *s.* **5.** 'Durchfallen *n.*

flunk·(e)y ['flʌŋkɪ] *s.* **1.** *oft contp.* La'kai *m*; **2.** *contp.* Kriecher *m*, Speichellecker *m*; **3.** *Am.* Handlanger *m*; 'flunk·(e)y·ism [-ɪɪzəm] *s.* Speichelle'cke'rei *f.*

flu·or ['fluːɔː] → fluorspar.

flu·o·resce [,fluə'res] *v/i.* ☢, *phys.* fluoreszieren; flu·o·res·cence [-sns] *s.* ☢, *phys.* Fluores'zenz *f*; flu·o·res·cent [-snt] *adj.* fluoreszierend: ~ lamp Leuchtstofflampe *f*; ~ screen Leuchtschirm *m*; ~ tube Leucht(stoff)röhre *f.*

flu·or·ic [fluː'ɒrɪk] *adj.* ☢ Fluor...: ~ acid Flusssäure *f*; flu·o·ri·date ['fluərɪdeɪt] *v/t. Trinkwasser* fluorieren; flu·o·ride ['fluəraɪd] *s.* ☢ Fluo'rid *n*; flu·o·rine ['fluəriːn] *s.* ☢ Fluor *n*; flu·o·rite ['fluəraɪt] *s.* → fluorspar; flu·o·ro·scope ['fluərəskəʊp] *s.* ✻ Fluoro'skop *n*, Röntgenbildschirm *m*; flu·o·ro·scop·ic [,fluərə'skɒpɪk] *adj.*: ~ screen → fluoroscope; 'flu·or·spar *s. min.* Flussspat *m*, Fluo'rit *n.*

flur·ry ['flʌrɪ] **I** *s.* **1.** a) Windstoß *m*, b) (Regen-, Schnee)Schauer *m*; **2.** *fig.* Hagel *m*, Wirbel *m von Schlägen etc.*; **3.** *fig.* Aufregung *f*, Unruhe *f*: in a ~ aufgeregt; **4.** Hast *f*; **5.** kurze, plötzliche Belebung (*an der Börse*); **II** *v/t.* **6.** beunruhigen.

flush¹ [flʌʃ] **I** *v/i.* (aufgeregt) auffliegen; **II** *v/t. Vögel* aufscheuchen.

flush² [flʌʃ] **I** *s.* **1.** a) Erröten *n*, b) Röte *f*; **2.** (Wasser)Schwall *m*, Strom *m*; **3.** a) (Aus)Spülung *f*, b) (Wasser)Spülung *f* (*im WC*); **4.** (Gefühls)Aufwallung *f*, Hochgefühl *n*, Erregung *f*: ~ of anger Wutanfall *m*; ~ of success Triumphgefühl *n*; ~ of victory Siegestaumel *m*; **5.** Glanz *m*, Blüte *f* (*der Jugend etc.*); **6.** ✻ Wallung *f*, (Fieber)Hitze *f*; → hot flushes; **II** *v/t.* **7.** *j-n* erröten lassen; **8.** a. ~ out (aus)spülen: ~ down hinunterspülen; ~ the toilet spülen; **9.** unter Wasser setzen; **10.** erregen, erhitzen: ~ed with anger wutentbrannt; ~ed with joy außer sich vor Freude; **III** *v/i.* **11.** erröten, rot werden (with *vor dat.*); **12.** strömen, schießen (a. Blut); **13.** spülen (*WC etc.*).

flush³ [flʌʃ] **I** *adj.* **1.** eben, auf gleicher Höhe; **2.** ☉ fluchtgerecht, glatt (anliegend), *typ.* bündig (abschließend) (with mit) (alle a. adv.): ~ left linksbündig; ~ right rechtsbündig; **3.** a) ☉ versenkt, Senk...: ~ screw, b) ⚡ Unterputz...: ~ socket; **4.** ('über)voll (with von); **5.** blühend, frisch; **6.** ~ (with money) F gut bei Kasse; ~ with one's money verschwenderisch; **II** *v/t.* **7.** ebnen, bündig machen; **8.** ☉ Fugen ausstreichen.

flush⁴ [flʌʃ] *Poker*: Flush *m*; → royal 1, straight flush.

flus·ter ['flʌstə] **I** *v/t.* durchein'ander bringen, aufregen, ner'vös machen; **II** *v/i.* a) ner'vös werden, durchein'ander kommen, b) sich aufregen; **III** *s.* → flutter 8.

flute [fluːt] **I** *s.* **1.** ♪ a) Flöte *f*, b) → flutist, c) a. ~ stop 'Flötenre,gister *n* (*Orgel*); **2.** △, ☉ Rille *f*, Riefe *f*, Hohlkehle *f*; **3.** ☉ (Span-)Nut *f*; **4.** Rüsche *f*; **II** *v/i.* **5.** Flöte spielen, flöten (a. fig.); **III** *v/t.* **6.** et. auf der Flöte spielen, flöten (a. fig.); **7.** △, ☉ riefen, riffeln, auskehlen, kannelieren; *Stoff* kräuseln; 'flut·ed [-tɪd] *adj.* **1.** flötenartig, sanft; **2.** gerieft, gerillt; 'flut·ing [-tɪŋ] *s.* **1.** △

Riffelung *f*; **2.** Falten *pl.*, Rüschen *pl.*; **3.** Flöten *n* (a. fig.); 'flut·ist [-tɪst] *s.* Flö'tist(in).

flut·ter ['flʌtə] **I** *v/i.* **1.** flattern (a. ✻ Herz), wehen; **2.** a) aufgeregt hin- und herrennen, b) aufgeregt sein; **3.** zittern; **4.** flackern; **II** *v/t.* **5.** schwenken, flattern lassen, wedeln mit, mit den Flügeln schlagen, mit den Augendeckeln ,klimpern'; **6.** → fluster I; **III** *s.* **7.** Flattern *n* (a. ✻ Puls etc.); **8.** Aufregung *f*, Tu'mult *m*: all in a ~ ganz durcheinander; **9.** Brit. F kleine Spekulati'on od. Wette; **10.** Schwimmen: Kraulbeinschlag *m.*

flu·vi·al ['fluːvjəl] *adj.* fluvi'al, Fluss..., in Flüssen vorkommend.

flux [flʌks] *s.* **1.** Fließen *n*, Fluss *m* (a. ⚡, *phys.*); **2.** Ausfluss *m* (a. ✻); **3.** Strom *m* (a. fig.), Flut *f* (a. fig.): ~ and reflux Flut u. Ebbe (a. fig.); ~ of words Wortschwall *m*; **4.** ständige Bewegung, Wandel *m*: in (a state of) ~ im Fluss; **5.** ☉ Fluss-, Schmelzmittel *n*, Zuschlag *m*; 'flux·ion·al [-kʃənl] *adj.* **1.** fließend, veränderlich; **2.** A Fluxions...

fly¹ [flaɪ] **I** *s.* **1.** Fliegen *n*, Flug *m* (a. ⚡): on the ~ a) im Fluge, schnell, prompt, b) in Bewegung; **2.** Brit. hist. Einspänner *m*, Droschke *f*; **3.** a) Knopfleiste *f*, b) Hosenklappe *f*, -schlitz *m*; **4.** Zelttür *f*; **5.** ☉ → flywheel; **6.** Unruh *f* (Uhr); **7.** typ. thea. Sof'fitten pl.; **II** *v/i.* [irr.] **8.** fliegen: ~ blind (od. on instruments) ⚡ blind fliegen; ~ high (od. at high game) fig. hoch hinauswollen; → let¹ Redew.; **9.** flattern, wehen; **10.** verfliegen (Zeit), zerrinnen (Geld); **11.** stieben, fliegen (Funken etc.): ~ to pieces zerspringen, bersten, reißen; **12.** stürmen, stürzen, sausen: ~ to arms zu den Waffen eilen; he flew into her arms er flog in ihre Arme; send s.o. ~ing a) j-n fortjagen, b) j-n zu Boden schleudern; send things ~ing Sachen umherwerfen; ~ at s.o. auf j-n losgehen; I must ~! F ich muss schleunigst weiter!; → temper 3; **13.** (nur pres., inf. u. p.pr.) fliehen; **III** *v/t.* [irr.] **14.** fliegen lassen: ~ hawks hunt. mit Falken jagen; → kite 1; **15.** ⚡ a) Flugzeug fliegen, führen, b) j-n, et. (hin)fliegen, im Flugzeug befördern, c) Strecke fliegen, d) Ozean etc. über'fliegen; **16.** Fahne, Flagge a) führen, b) hissen, wehen lassen; **17.** Zaun etc. im Sprung nehmen; **18.** (nur pres., inf. u. p.pr.) a) fliehen aus, b) fliehen vor (dat.), meiden; ~ in ⚡ v/t. u. v/i. einfliegen; ~ off v/i. **1.** fortfliegen; **2.** fortstürmen; **3.** abspringen (Knopf); ~ o·pen v/i. auffliegen (Tür etc.); ~ out v/i. **1.** ausfliegen; **2.** hin'ausstürzen; **3.** wütend werden: ~ at s.o. auf j-n losgehen.

fly² [flaɪ] *s.* **1.** zo. Fliege *f*: a ~ in the ointment ein Haar in der Suppe; break a ~ on the wheel mit Kanonen nach Spatzen schießen; no flies on him (od. it) F ,den legt man nicht so schnell aufs Kreuz'; they died (od. dropped) like flies sie starben wie die Fliegen; he wouldn't hurt (od. harm) a ~ er tut keiner Fliege was zuleide; I would like to be a ~ on the wall da würde ich gern ,Mäuschen spielen'; **2.** Angeln: (künstliche) (Angel)Fliege: cast a ~ e-e Angel auswerfen.

fly³ [flaɪ] *adj. sl.* gerissen, raffiniert.

fly·a·ble ['flaɪəbl] *adj.* ⚡ **1.** flugtüchtig; **2.** ~ weather Flugwetter *n.*

fly| a·gar·ic *s.* ✿ Fliegenpilz *m*; '~·a·way *adj.* **1.** flatternd; **2.** flatterhaft; **3.** Am. flugbereit; '~·blow *s.* Fliegenei *n*,

-dreck *m*; '**~·blown** *adj.* **1.** von Fliegen beschmutzt; **2.** *fig.* besudelt; '**~·by** *s.* **1.** ✈ Vorbeiflug *m*; **2.** *Raumfahrt:* Flyby *n* (*Navigationstechnik*); '**~·by-night** F **I** *s.* **1.** *zo.* Nachtschwärmer *m*; **2.** a) Schuldner, der sich heimlich *od.* bei Nacht aus dem Staub macht, b) ✝ zweifelhafter Kunde; **II** *adj.* **3.** ✝ zweifelhaft, anrüchig; '**~·catch·er** *s.* **1.** Fliegenfänger *m*; **2.** *orn.* Fliegenschnäpper *m*.

fly·er → **flier**.

'**fly-fish** *v/i.* mit (künstlichen) Fliegen angeln.

fly·ing ['flaiıŋ] **I** *adj.* **1.** fliegend, Flug...; **2.** flatternd, fliegend, wehend; → **colour** 10; **3.** kurz, flüchtig: **~** *visit* Stippvisite *f*; **4.** *sport* a) fliegend: **~** *flying start*, b) mit Anlauf: **~** *jump*; **5.** schnell; **6.** fliehend, flüchtig; **II** *s.* **7.** a) Fliegen *n*, Flug *m*, b) Fliege'rei *f*, Flugwesen *n*; **~** *boat* s. ✈ Flugboot *n*; **~** *bomb* s. ⚔ fliegende Bombe, Ra'ketenbombe *f*; **~** *bridge* s. **1.** Rollfähre *f*; **2.** ⚓ Laufbrücke *f*; **~** *but·tress* s. △ Strebebogen *m*; **~** *cir·cus* s. ✈ **1.** ⚔ rotierende 'Staffelformati,on (*im Einsatz*); **2.** Schaufliegergruppe *f*; **~** *col·umn* s. ⚔ fliegende *od.* schnelle Ko'lonne; **~** *ex·hi·bi·tion* s. Wanderausstellung *f*; **~** *field* s. (*kleiner*) Flugplatz; **~** *fish* s. Fliegender Fisch; **~** *fox* s. *zo.* Flughund *m*; **~** *lane* s. ✈ (Ein-)Flugschneise *f*; ⚥ *Of·fi·cer* s. ✈ *Brit.* Oberleutnant *m der RAF*; **~** *range* s. ✈ Akti'onsradius *m*; **~** *sau·cer* s. fliegende 'Untertasse; **~** *school* s. Fliegerschule *f*; **~** *speed* s. Fluggeschwindigkeit *f*; **~** *squad* s. *Brit.* 'Überfallkom,mando *n* (*Polizei*); **~** *squad·ron* s. ✈ (Flieger)Staffel *f*; **2.** *Am.* a) fliegende Ko'lonne, b) 'Rollkom,mando *n*; **~** *start* s. *sport* fliegender Start: *get off to a ~* glänzend wegkommen, *a. fig.* e-n glänzenden Start haben; **~** *u·nit* s. ✈ fliegender Verband; **~** *weight* s. ✈ Fluggewicht *n*; **~** *wing* s. Nurflügelflugzeug *n*.

'**fly·|·leaf** s. *typ.* Vorsatz-, Deckblatt *n*; '**~·o·ver** s. **1.** → *fly-past*; **2.** *Brit.* ('Straßen-, 'Eisenbahn)Über,führung *f*; '**~·pa·per** s. Fliegenfänger *m*; '**~·past** s. ✈ 'Luftpa,rade *f*; **~·rod** s. Angelrute *f* (*für künstliche Fliegen*); **~** *sheet* s. **1.** Flug-, Re'klameblatt *n*; **2.** ('Zelt)Überdach *n*; '**fly,swat·ter** s. Fliegenklappe *f*, -klatsche *f*; '**~·weight** *sport* **I** s. Fliegengewicht(ler *m*) *n*; **II** *adj.* Fliegengewichts...; '**~·wheel** s. ⚙ Schwungrad *n*.

'**f-,num·ber** s. *phot.* **1.** Blende *f* (*Einstellung*); **2.** Lichtstärke *f* (*vom Objektiv*).

foal [fəʊl] *zo.* **I** s. Fohlen *n*, Füllen *n*: *in* (*od. with*) **~** trächtig (*Stute*); **II** *v/t.* Fohlen werfen; **III** *v/i.* fohlen, werfen; '**~·foot** *pl.* '**~·foots** s. ♣ Huflattich *m*.

foam [fəʊm] **I** s. Schaum *m*; **II** *v/i.* schäumen (*with rage fig.* vor Wut): *he ~ed at the mouth* der Schaum stand ihm vor dem Mund, *fig. a.* er schäumte vor Wut; **III** *v/t.* schäumen: *~ed concrete* Schaumbeton *m*; *~ed plastic* Schaumstoff *m*; **~** *ex·tin·guish·er* Schaum(feuer)löscher *m*; **~** *rub·ber* Schaumgummi *n*, *m*.

foam·y ['fəʊmı] *adj.* schäumend.

fob¹ [fɒb] s. **1.** Uhrtasche *f* (*im Hosenbund*); **2.** a. **~** *chain* Chate'laine *f* (*Uhrband*, *-kette*).

fob² [fɒb] *v/t.* **1.** **~** *off s.th. on s.o.* j-m et. ,andrehen' *od.* ,aufhängen'; **2.** **~** *s.o. off* j-n abspeisen, *j-n* abwimmeln (*with mit*).

fob³, **f.o.b.**, **F.O.B.** *abbr. für free on board* (→ *free* 13).

fo·cal ['fəʊkl] *adj.* **1.** A, *phys.*, *opt.* im Brennpunkt stehend (*a. fig.*), fo'kal, Brenn(punkt)...: **~** *distance*, **~** *length* Brennweite *f*; **~** *plane* Brennebene *f*; **~** *point* Brennpunkt *m* (*a. fig.*); **2.** ☞ fo'kal, Herd...; '**fo·cal·ize** [-kəlaız] → **focus** 4, 5.

fo'c's'le ['fəʊksl] → **forecastle**.

fo·cus ['fəʊkəs] *pl.* **-cus·es**, **-ci** [-saı] **I** s. **1.** a) A, ⊙, *phys.* Brennpunkt *m*, Fokus *m*, b) *TV* Lichtpunkt *m*, c) *phys.* Brennweite *f*, d) *opt.* Scharfeinstellung *f*: *in ~* scharf eingestellt, *fig.* klar und richtig; *out of ~* unscharf, verschwommen (*a. fig.*); *bring into ~* → 4, 5; **~** *control* Scharfeinstellung *f* (*Vorrichtung*); **2.** *fig.* Brenn-, Mittelpunkt *m*: *be the ~ of attention* im Mittelpunkt des Interesses stehen; *bring (in)to ~* in den Brennpunkt rücken; **3.** Herd *m* (*e-s Erdbebens, Aufruhrs etc.*), ☞ *a.* Fokus *m*; **II** *v/t.* **4.** *opt.*, *phot.* fokussieren, (*v/i.* sich) scharf einstellen; **5.** *phys.* (*v/i.* sich) im Brennpunkt vereinigen, (sich) sammeln; **6.** **~** *on fig.* (*v/i.* sich) konzentrieren *od.* richten auf (*acc.*).

fo·cus·(s)ing *lens* ['fəʊkəsıŋ] s. Sammellinse *f*; **~** *scale* s. *phot.* Entfernungsskala *f*; **~** *screen* s. *phot.* Mattscheibe *f*.

fod·der ['fɒdə] **I** s. (Trocken)Futter *n*; *humor.* ,Futter' *n*; **II** *v/t.* Vieh füttern.

foe [fəʊ] s. Feind *m* (*a. fig.*); *a. sport u. fig.* Gegner *m*, 'Widersacher *m* (*to gen.*).

foe·tal ['fi:tl] *adj.* ☞ fö'tal; **foe·tus** ['fi:təs] s. ☞ Fötus *m*.

fog [fɒg] **I** s. **1.** (dichter) Nebel; **2.** a) Dunst *m*, b) Dunkelheit *f*; **3.** *fig.* a) Nebel *m*, Verschwommenheit *f*, b) Verwirrung *f*: *in a ~* (völlig) ratlos; **4.** ☞ (abgesprühter) Nebel; **5.** *phot.* Schleier *m*; **II** *v/t.* **6.** in Nebel hüllen, einnebeln; **7.** *fig.* verdunkeln, verwirren; **8.** *phot.* verschleiern; **III** *v/i.* **9.** neb(e)lig werden; (sich) beschlagen (*Scheibe etc.*); **~** *bank* s. Nebelbank *f*; '**~·bound** *adj.* **1.** in dichten Nebel eingehüllt; **2.** *be ~* ⚓, ✈ wegen Nebels festsitzen.

fo·gey → **fogy**.

fog·gi·ness ['fɒgınıs] s. **1.** Nebligkeit *f*; **2.** Verschwommenheit *f*, Unklarheit *f*; '**fog·gy** [-gı] *adj.* □ **1.** neb(e)lig; **2.** trüb, dunstig; **3.** *fig.* a) nebelhaft, verschwommen, unklar, b) benebelt (*with* vor *dat.*): *I haven't got the foggiest (idea)* F ,ich habe keinen blassen Schimmer'; **4.** *phot.* verschleiert.

'**fog·horn** s. Nebelhorn *n*; '**~·light** s. *mot.* Nebelscheinwerfer *m*: *rear ~ mot.* Nebelschlussleuchte *f*.

fo·gy ['fəʊgı] s. *mst old ~* ,alter Knacker'; '**fo·gy·ish** [-ıʃ] *adj.* verknöchert, verkalkt, altmodisch.

foi·ble ['fɔıbl] s. *fig.* Faible *n*, (kleine) Schwäche *f*.

foil¹ [fɔıl] *v/t.* **1.** a) vereiteln, durch'kreuzen, zu'nichte machen, b) *j-m* e-n Strich durch die Rechnung machen; **2.** *hunt.* Spur verwischen.

foil² [fɔıl] **I** s. ⊙ (Me'tall- *od.* Kunststoff)Folie *f*, 'Blattme,tall *n*; **2.** ⊙ (Spiegel)Belag *m*; **3.** Folie *f*, 'Unterlage *f* (*für Edelsteine*); **4.** *fig.* Folie *f*, 'Hintergrund *m*: *serve as a ~ to* als Folie dienen (*dat.*); **5.** △ Blattverzierung *f*; **II** *v/t.* **6.** ⊙ mit Me'tallfolie belegen; **7.** △ mit Blätterwerk verzieren.

foil³ [fɔıl] s. *fenc.* **1.** Flo'rett *n*; **2.** *pl.* Flo'rettfechten *n*.

foils·man ['fɔılzmən] s. [*irr.*] *fenc.* Flo'rettfechter *m*.

foist [fɔıst] *v/t.* **1.** **~** *s.th. on s.o.* a) j-m

et. ,andrehen', b) j-m et. aufhalsen; **2.** einschmuggeln.

fold¹ [fəʊld] **I** *v/t.* **1.** falten: **~** *cloth* (*one's hands*); **~ed mountains** *geol.* Faltengebirge *n*; **~** *one's arms* die Arme verschränken; **2.** *oft* **~** *up* zs.-falten, -legen, -klappen; **3.** *a.* **~** *down* a) 'umbiegen, kniffen, b) her'unterklappen: **~** *back* Bettdecke etc. zurückschlagen, Stuhllehne etc. zurückklappen; **4.** ⊙ falzen; **5.** einhüllen, um'schließen: **~** *in one's arms* in die Arme schließen; **6.** *Küche:* **~** *in Ei* etc. einrühren, 'unterziehen; **II** *v/i.* **7.** sich falten *od.* zs.-legen *od.* zs.-klappen (lassen); **8.** *mst* **~** *up* F a) zs.-brechen (*a. fig.*), b) ✝ ,zumachen' (müssen), ,eingehen' (*Firma etc.*): **~** *up with laughter* sich biegen vor Lachen; **III** *s.* **9.** Falte *f*; Windung *f*; 'Umschlag *m*; **10.** ⊙ Falz *m*, Kniff *m*; **11.** *typ.* Bogen *m*; **12.** *geol.* Bodenfalte *f*.

fold² [fəʊld] **I** s. **1.** (Schaf)Hürde *f*, Pferch *m*; **2.** Schafherde *f*; **3.** *eccl.* a) (Schoß *m* der) Kirche, b) Herde *f*, Gemeinde *f*; **4.** *fig.* Schoß *m* der Fa'milie *od.* Par'tei: *return to the ~*; **II** *v/t.* **5.** Schafe einpferchen.

-fold [-fəʊld] *in Zssgn* ...fach, ...fältig.

'**fold·|·a·way** *adj.* zs.-klappbar, Klapp...: **~** *bed*; '**~·boat** s. Faltboot *n*.

fold·er ['fəʊldə] s. **1.** 'Faltpro,spekt *m*, -blatt *n*, Bro'schüre *f*, Heft *n*; **2.** Aktendeckel *m*, Mappe *f*, Schnellhefter *m*; **3.** ⊙ 'Falzma,schine *f*, -bein *n*; **4.** Falzer *m* (*Person*).

fold·ing ['fəʊldıŋ] *adj.* zs.-legbar, zs.-klappbar, aufklappbar, Falt..., Klapp...; **~** *bed* s. Klappbett *n*; **~** *bi·cy·cle* s. Klapp(fahr)rad *n*; **~** *boat* s. Faltboot *n*; **~** *cam·er·a* s. 'Klapp,kamera *f*; **~** *car·ton* s. Faltschachtel *f*; **~** *chair* s. Klappstuhl *m*; **~** *doors* s. *pl.* Flügeltür *f*; **~** *gate* s. zweiflügeliges Tor; **~** *hat* s. Klapphut *m*; **~** *lad·der* s. Klappleiter *f*; **~** *rule* s. zs.-legbarer Zollstock; **~** *screen* s. spanische Wand; **~** *ta·ble* s. Klapptisch *m*; **~** *top* s. *mot.* Rolldach *n*.

fo·li·a·ceous [,fəʊlı'eıʃəs] *adj.* blattartig; blätt(e)rig, Blätter...; **fo·li·age** ['fəʊlııdʒ] s. **1.** Laub(werk) *n*, Blätter *pl.*: **~** *plant* Blattpflanze *f*; **2.** △ Blattverzierung *f*; **fo·li·aged** ['fəʊlııdʒd] *adj.* **1.** *in Zssgn* ...blätt(e)rig; **2.** △ mit Blätterwerk verziert.

fo·li·ate ['fəʊlıeıt] **I** *v/t.* **1.** △ mit Blätterwerk verzieren: **~d capital** Blätterkapitell *n*; **2.** ⊙ mit Folie belegen; **II** *v/i.* **3.** ♣ Blätter treiben; **4.** sich in Blätter spalten; **III** *adj.* [-ıət] **5.** belaubt; **6.** blattartig; **fo·li·a·tion** [,fəʊlı'eıʃn] s. **1.** ♣ Blattbildung *f*, -wuchs *m*, Belaubung *f*; **2.** △ (Verzierung *f* mit) Blätterwerk *n*; **3.** ⊙ Foliierung *f*; Folie *f*; **4.** Paginierung *f* (*Buch*); **5.** *geol.* Schieferung *f*.

fo·li·o ['fəʊlıəʊ] *pl.* **-os** s. **1.** (Folio-)Blatt *n*; **2.** 'Folio(for,mat) *n*; **3.** *a.* **~** *volume* Foli'ant *m*; **4.** nur vorderseitig nummeriertes Blatt; **5.** Seitenzahl *f* (*Buch*); **6.** ✝ Kontobuchseite *f*; **II** *v/t.* **7.** Buch etc. paginieren.

folk [fəʊk] **I** *pl.* **folk**, **folks** s. **1.** *pl.* (die) Leute *pl.*; **~s** *pl.* (*nur* **~s**) F m-e etc. ,Leute' *pl.* (*Familie*); **2.** *pl.* (*nur* **~s**) F m-e etc. ,Leute' *pl.* (*Familie*); **3.** *obs.* Volk *n*, Nati'on *f*; **4.** F ,Folk' *m* (*Volksmusik*); **II** *adj.* **5.** Volks...: **~** *dance*.

folk·lore ['fəʊklɔ:] s. Folk'lore *f* (a) Volkskunde *f*, b) Volkstum *n* (*Bräuche etc.*); '**folk,lor·ism** [-,lɔ:rızəm] → **folklore**; a; '**folk,lor·ist** [-,lɔ:rıst] s. Folk'lorist *m*, Volkskundler *m*; '**folk,lor·is·tic** [-lɔ:'rıstık] *adj.* folklo'ristisch.

F

folk song s. **1.** Volkslied n; **2.** Folksong m (bsd. sozialkritisches Lied).

folk·sy ['fəʊksɪ] adj. **1.** F gesellig, 'umgänglich; **2.** volkstümlich, contp. a. volkstümelnd.

fol·li·cle ['fɒlɪkl] s. **1.** ♣ Fruchtbalg m; **2.** anat. a) Fol'likel n, Drüsenbalg m, b) Haarbalg m.

fol·low ['fɒləʊ] **I** s. **1.** Billard: Nachläufer m; **II** v/t. **2.** allg. folgen (dat.): a) (zeitlich u. räumlich) nachfolgen (dat.), sich anschließen (dat.): ~ s.o. close j-m auf dem Fuß folgen; a dinner ~ed by a dance ein Essen mit anschließendem Tanz, b) verfolgen (acc.), entlanggehen, -führen (acc.) (Straße), c) (zeitlich) folgen auf (acc.), nachfolgen (dat.): ~ one's father as manager s-m Vater als Direktor (nach)folgen, d) nachgehen (dat.), verfolgen (acc.), sich widmen (dat.), betreiben (acc.), Beruf ausüben: ~ one's pleasure s-m Vergnügen nachgehen; ~ the sea (the law) Seemann (Jurist) sein, e) befolgen, beachten, die Mode mitmachen; sich richten nach (Sache): ~ my advice, f) j-m als Führer od. Vorbild folgen, sich bekennen zu, zustimmen (dat.): **I cannot ~ your view** Ihren Ansichten kann ich nicht zustimmen, g) folgen können (dat.), verstehen (acc.): do you ~ me? können Sie mir folgen?, h) (mit dem Auge od. geistig) verfolgen, beobachten (acc.): ~ a tennis match; ~ events; **3.** verfolgen (acc.), ✕ a. nachstoßen (dat.): ~ the enemy; **III** v/i. **4.** (räumlich od. zeitlich) (nach)folgen, sich anschließen; ~ (up)on folgen auf (acc.); **I ~ed after him** ich folgte ihm nach; as ~s wie folgt, folgendermaßen; letter to ~ Brief folgt; **5.** mst impers. folgen, sich ergeben (from aus): it ~s from this hieraus folgt; it does not ~ that dies besagt nicht, dass; so what ~s? und was folgt daraus?; it doesn't ~! das ist nicht unbedingt so!
Zssgn mit adv.:

fol·low|a·bout v/t. überall('hin) folgen (dat.); ~ **on** v/i. gleich weitermachen od. -gehen; ~ **out** v/t. Plan etc. 'durchziehen; ~ **through** **I** v/t. → follow out; **II** v/i. bsd. Golf: 'durchschwingen; ~ **up** **I** v/t. **1.** (eifrig od. energisch weiter-) verfolgen, e-r Sache nachgehen; auf e-n Brief, Schlag etc. e-n anderen folgen lassen, nachstoßen mit; **2.** fig. e-n Vorteil ausnutzen; **II** v/i. **3.** ✕ nachstoßen (a. fig. with mit); **4.** ✝ nachfassen.

fol·low·er ['fɒləʊə] s. **1.** obs. Verfolger (-in); **2.** a) Anhänger m (pol., sport etc.), Jünger m, Schüler m, b) pl. → following 1; **3.** hist. Gefolgsmann m; **4.** Begleiter m; **5.** pol. Mitläufer(in); '**fol·low·ing** [-əʊɪŋ] **I** s. **1.** a) Gefolge n, Anhang m, b) Gefolgschaft f, Anhänger pl.; **2.** the ~ das Folgende, b) die Folgenden pl.; **II** adj. **3.** folgend; **III** prp. **4.** im Anschluss an (acc.).

,**fol·low·my·'lead·er** [-əʊmɪ-] s. Kinderspiel, bei dem jede Aktion des Anführers nachgemacht werden muss; ,~-'through s. **1.** bsd. Golf: 'Durchschwung m; **2.** fig. 'Durchführung f; '~-up **I** s. **1.** Weiterverfolgen n e-r Sache; **2.** Ausnutzung f e-s Vorteils; **3.** ✕ Nachstoßen n (a. fig.); **4.** bsd. ✝ Nachfassen n; **5.** Radio, TV etc.: Fortsetzung f (to gen.); **6.** ♣ Nachbehandlung f; **II** adj. **7.** weiter, Nach...: ~ advertising Nachfasswerbung f; ~ conference Nachfolgekonferenz f; ~ costs Folgekosten pl.; ~ file Wiedervorlagemappe f; ~ letter Nachfassschreiben n; ~ order

Anschlussauftrag m; ~ question Zusatzfrage f.

fol·ly ['fɒlɪ] s. **1.** Narr-, Torheit f, Narre'tei f; **2.** Follies pl. (sg. konstr.) thea. Re'vue f.

fo·ment [fəʊ'ment] v/t. **1.** ✍ bähen, mit warmen 'Umschlägen behandeln; **2.** fig. anfachen, schüren, aufhetzen (zu); **fo·men·ta·tion** [,fəʊmen'teɪʃn] s. **1.** ✍ Bähung f; heißer 'Umschlag; **2.** fig. Aufhetzung f, -wiegelung f; **fo'ment·er** [-tə] s. Aufwiegler(in), Schürer(in).

fond [fɒnd] adj. □ → fondly; **1.** zärtlich, liebevoll; **2.** töricht, (allzu) kühn, über'trieben: ~ hope; it went beyond my ~est dreams es übertraf m-e kühnsten Träume; **3.** be ~ of j-n od et. lieben, mögen, gern haben: be ~ of smoking gern rauchen.

fon·dant ['fɒndənt] s. Fon'dant m.

fon·dle ['fɒndl] v/t. (liebevoll) streicheln, hätscheln; '**fond·ly** [-lɪ] adv. **1.** → fond 1; **2.** I ~ hoped that ... ich war so töricht zu hoffen, dass ...; '**fond·ness** [-dnɪs] s. **1.** Zärtlichkeit f; **2.** Liebe f, Zuneigung f (of zu); **3.** Vorliebe (for für).

font [fɒnt] s. **1.** eccl. Taufstein m, -becken n: ~ name Taufname m; **2.** Ölbehälter m (Lampe); **3.** poet. Quelle f, Brunnen m; **4.** typ. Schrift f, Font m: ~ size Schriftgrad m.

fon·ta·nel(le) [,fɒntə'nel] s. anat. Fonta'nelle f.

food [fu:d] s. **1.** Essen n, Kost f, Nahrung f, Verpflegung f: ~ and drink Essen u. Trinken; ~ plant Nahrungspflanze f; **2.** Nahrungs-, Lebensmittel pl.: ~ analyst Lebensmittelchemiker(in); ~ chain Nahrungskette f; ~ poisoning Lebensmittelvergiftung f; ~ processor 'Küchenma,schine f; ~ slicer Allesschneider m (Küchengerät); **3.** Futter n; **4.** fig. Nahrung f, Stoff m: ~ for thought Stoff zum Nachdenken; '~-stuff → food 2.

food·ie ['fu:dɪ] s. F Feinschmecker m.

fool¹ [fu:l] **I** s. **1.** Narr m, Närrin f, Dummkopf m, ,Idi'ot(in)': he is no ~ er ist nicht dumm; he is nobody's ~ er lässt sich nichts vormachen; he is a ~ for Fer ist ganz verrückt auf (acc.); I am a ~ to him ich bin ein Waisenknabe gegen ihn; make a ~ of → 4; make a ~ of o.s. sich lächerlich machen, sich blamieren; **2.** (Hof)Narr m, Hans'wurst m: play the ~ → 8; **II** adj. **3.** Am. F blöd, ,doof': a ~ question; **III** v/t. **4.** j-n zum Narren od. zum Besten haben: you could have ~ed me! iro. was du nicht sagst!, ach nee!; **5.** betrügen (out of um), täuschen; verleiten (into doing zu tun); **6.** ~ away Zeit etc. vergeuden; **IV** v/i. **7.** Spaß machen, spaßen: he was only ~ing Am. er tat ja nur so (als ob); **8.** ~ about, ~ around her'umalbern, Unsinn od. Faxen machen; **9.** (her'um)spielen (with mit, an dat.).

fool² [fu:l] s. bsd. Brit. Süßspeise aus Obstpüree u. Sahne.

fool·er·y ['fu:lərɪ] s. → folly 1.

'**fool|,har·di·ness** s. Tollkühnheit f; '~,har·dy adj. tollkühn, verwegen.

fool·ing ['fu:lɪŋ] s. Dummheit(en pl.) f, Unfug m, Spiele'rei f; '**fool·ish** [-lɪʃ] adj. □ dumm, töricht: a) albern, läppisch, b) unklug; '**fool·ish·ness** [-ʃnɪs] s. Dumm-, Tor-, Albernheit f; '**fool·proof** adj. **1.** kinderleicht, idi'otensicher; **2.** ☺ betriebssicher; **3.** todsicher.

fools·cap ['fu:lskæp] s. Schreib- u. Druckpapierformat (34,2×43,1 cm).

fool's| er·rand [fu:lz] s. ,Metzgergang' m; ~ **par·a·dise** s. Wolken'kuckucksheim n: live in a ~ sich Illusionen hingeben.

foos·ball ['fu:sbɔ:l] s. bsd. Am. Tischfußball m, F Kicker m.

foot [fʊt] **I** pl. **feet** [fi:t] s. **1.** Fuß m: on ~ a) zu Fuß, b) fig. im Gange; on one's feet auf den Beinen (a. fig.); my ~ (od. feet)! F von wegen!, Quatsch!; it is wet under ~ der Boden ist nass; carry (od. sweep) s.o. off his feet a) j-n begeistern, b) j-s Herz im Sturm erobern; fall on one's feet fig. immer auf die Füße fallen; get on (od. to) one's feet aufstehen; find one's feet a) gehen lernen od. können, b) sich ,finden', sich ,freischwimmen', c) wissen, was man tun soll od. kann, d) festen Boden unter den Füßen haben; have one ~ in the grave mit einem Fuß im Grabe stehen; put one's ~ down a) energisch werden, ein Machtwort sprechen, b) mot. Gas geben; put one's ~ in it, Am. a. put one's ~ in one's mouth F ins Fettnäpfchen treten, sich danebenbenehmen; put one's best ~ forward a) sein Bestes geben, sich mächtig anstrengen, b) sich von der besten Seite zeigen; put s.o. (od. s.th.) on his (its) feet fig. j-n (od. et.) wieder auf die Beine bringen; put od. set a (od. one's) ~ wrong et. Falsches tun od. sagen; set on ~ et. in Gang bringen od. in die Wege leiten; set ~ on od. in betreten; tread under ~ mit Füßen treten (mst fig.); → cold 3; **2.** Fuß m (0,3048 m): 3 feet long 3 Fuß lang; **3.** fig. Fuß m (Berg, Glas, Säule, Seite, Strumpf, Treppe): at the ~ of the page unten auf od. am Fuß der Seite; **4.** Fußende n (Bett, Tisch etc.); **5.** ✕ a) hist. Fußvolk n: 500 ~ 500 Fußsoldaten, b) Infante'rie f: the 4th ~ Infanterieregiment Nr. 4; **6.** Versfuß m; **7.** Schritt m, Tritt m: a heavy ~; **8.** pl. ~s Bodensatz m; **II** v/t. **9.** ~ it F a) ,tippeln', zu Fuß gehen, b) tanzen; **10.** e-n Fuß anstricken an (acc.); **11.** bezahlen, begleichen: ~ the bill; **12.** mst ~ up zs.-zählen, addieren.

foot·age ['fʊtɪdʒ] s. **1.** Gesamtlänge f, -maß n (in Fuß); **2.** Filmmeter pl.

,**foot|-and-'mouth dis·ease** s. vet. Maul- u. Klauenseuche f; '~·ball s. sport a) Fußball(spiel n) m: ~ fan 'Fußball,fan m, -,anhänger(in), b) Am. Football(spiel n) m: ~ match (team) Fußballspiel n (-mannschaft f); ~ pools pl. Fußballtoto n; '~,ball·er s. Fußballspieler m, Fußballer m; '~·bath s. Fußbad n; '~·boy s. **1.** Laufbursche m; **2.** Page m; ~ brake s. Fußbremse f; '~·bridge s. 'Fußgängerüber,führung f, -brücke f, (Lauf)Steg m; ~ can·dle s. phys. Foot-Candle f (Lichteinheit); ~ con·trol s. ☺ Fußsteuerung f, -schaltung f; ~ drop s. ✍ Spitzfuß m.

foot·ed ['fʊtɪd] adj. mst in Zssgn mit ... Füßen, ...füßig; '**foot·er** [-tə] s. **1.** in Zssgn ... Fuß od. lang: a six-~ ein sechs Fuß großer Mensch; **2.** Brit. sl. Fußball(spiel n) m; **3.** Computer: Fußzeile f (in Textverarbeitung).

'**foot|·fall** s. Schritt m, Tritt m (Geräusch); ~ **fault** s. Tennis: Fußfehler m; '~·gear s. Schuhwerk n; ~ **guard** s. Fußschutz m; '~·hill s. **1.** Vorberg m; **2.** pl. Ausläufer pl. e-s Gebirges; '~·hold s. Stand m, Raum m zum Stehen; fig. Halt m, Stütze f; ('Ausgangs)Basis f, (-)Positi,on f: gain a ~ (festen) Fuß fassen.

foot·ing ['fʊtɪŋ] s. **1.** → foothold: lose

(*od. **miss*) **one's** ~ ausgleiten, den Halt verlieren; **2.** Aufsetzen *n* der Füße.

foo·tle ['fuːtl] **F I** *v/i.* **1.** *oft* ~ *around* her'umtrödeln; **2.** a) her'umalbern, b) ‚Stuss' reden; **II** *v/t.* **3.** ~ *away Zeit, Geld etc.* vergeuden, *Chance* vertun; **III** *s.* **4.** ‚Stuss' *m.*

'foot·lights *s. pl. thea.* **1.** Rampenlicht (-er *pl.*) *n*; **2.** Bühne *f* (a. *Schauspielerberuf*).

foo·tling ['fuːtlɪŋ] *adj. sl.* albern, läppisch.

'foot|·loose *adj.* (völlig) ungebunden *od.* frei; '~·**man** [-mən] *s.* [*irr.*] La'kai *m*, Diener *m*; '~·**mark** *s.* Fußspur *f*; '~·**note** *s.* Fußnote *f*; ‚~·**'op·er·at·ed** *adj.* mit Fußantrieb, Tret..., Fuß...; '~·**pad** *s. obs.* Straßenräuber *m*; ~ **pas·sen·ger** *s.* Fußgänger(in); '~·**path** *s.* **1.** (Fuß)Pfad *m*; **2.** Bürgersteig *m*; '~·**pound** *s.* Foot-Pound *n* (*Arbeits- u. Energie-Einheit*); '~·‚**pound·al** [-‚paʊndl] *n* Foot-Poundal *n* (¹/₃₂ *Foot-pound*); '~·**print** *s.* Fußabdruck *m, pl. a.* Fußspur(en *pl.*) *f*; '~·**race** *s.* Wettlauf *m*; '~·**rest** *s.* Fußstütze *f*, -raste *f*; ~ **rule** *s.* Zollstock *m*; '~·**scrap·er** *s.* Fußabtreter *m* (*aus Metall*).

foot·sie ['futsɪ] *s.* **F 1.** ‚Füßeln' *n*: **play** ~ **with s.o.** mit j-m ‚füßeln'; **2.** heimliches Flirten.

Foot·sie ['futsɪ] *npr.* F Börse: 'Footsie-‚Index *m* (*FTSE-100 Index*).

'foot|·sore *adj.* fußkrank; '~·**step** *s.* **1.** Tritt *m*, Schritt *m*; **2.** Fuß(s)tapfe *f*: **follow in s.o.'s** ~**s** in j-s Fußstapfen treten, j-s Beispiel folgen; '~·**stool** *s.* Schemel *m*, Fußbank *f*; ~ **switch** *s.* ⊙ Fußschalter *m*; '~·**way** *s.* Fußweg *m*; '~·**wear** → *footgear*; '~·**work** *s. sport* Beinarbeit *f*.

fooz·ball ['fuːzbɔːl] *s. bsd. Am.* Tischfußball *n*, F Kicker *n*.

foo·zle ['fuːzl] *sl.* **I** *v/t.* ‚verpatzen'; **II** *v/i.* ‚patzen', ‚Mist bauen'; **III** *s.* Murks *m*; ‚Patzer' *m.*

fop [fɒp] *s.* Stutzer *m*, Geck *m*, ‚Fatzke' *m*; '**fop·per·y** [-pərɪ] *s.* Affigkeit *f*; '**fop·pish** [-pɪʃ] *adj.* □ geckenhaft, affig.

for [fɔː; fə] **I** *prp.* **1.** *allg.* für: *a gift* ~ *him*; *it is good* ~ *you*; *I am* ~ *the plan*; *an eye* ~ *beauty* Sinn für das Schöne; *it was very awkward* ~ *her* es war sehr peinlich für sie, es war ihr sehr unangenehm; *he spoilt their weekend* ~ *them* er verdarb ihnen das ganze Wochenende; ~ *and against* für u. wider; **2.** für, (mit der Absicht) zu, um (...willen): *apply* ~ *the post* sich um die Stellung bewerben; *die* ~ *a cause* für e-e Sache sterben; *go* ~ *a walk* spazieren gehen; *come* ~ *dinner* zum Essen kommen; *what* ~? wozu?, wofür?; **3.** (*Wunsch, Ziel*) nach, auf (*acc.*): *a claim* ~ *s.th.* ein Anspruch auf e-e Sache; *the desire* ~ *s.th.* der Wunsch *od.* das Verlangen nach et.; *call* ~ *s.o.* nach j-m rufen; *wait* ~ *s.th.* auf etwas warten; *oh,* ~ *a car!* ach, hätte ich doch e-n Wagen!; **4.** a) (*passend od. geeignet*) für, b) (*bestimmt*) für *od.* zu: *tools* ~ *cutting* Werkzeuge zum Schneiden, Schneidewerkzeuge; *the right man* ~ *the job* der richtige Mann für diesen Posten; **5.** (*Mittel*) gegen: *a remedy* ~ *influenza*; *treat s.o.* ~ *cancer* j-n gegen *od.* auf Krebs behandeln; *there is nothing* ~ *it but to give in* es bleibt nichts (anderes) übrig, als nachzugeben; **6.** (*als Belohnung*) für: *a medal* ~ *bravery*; **7.** (*als Entgelt*) für, gegen,

um: *I sold it* ~ *£10* ich verkaufte es für 10 Pfund; **8.** (*im Tausch*) für, gegen: *I exchanged the knife* ~ *a pencil*; **9.** (*Betrag, Menge*) über (*acc.*): *a postal order* ~ *£20*; **10.** (*Grund*) aus, vor (*dat.*), wegen (*gen. od. dat.*): ~ *this reason* aus diesem Grund; ~ *fun od.* zum Spaß; *die* ~ *grief* aus *od.* vor Gram sterben; *weep* ~ *joy* vor Freude weinen; *I can't see* ~ *the fog* ich kann nichts sehen wegen des Nebels *od.* vor lauter Nebel; **11.** (*als Strafe etc.*) für, wegen: *punished* ~ *theft*; **12.** dank, wegen: *were it not* ~ *his energy* wenn er nicht so energisch wäre, dank s-r Energie; **13.** für, in Anbetracht (*gen.*), im Verhältnis zu: *he is tall* ~ *his age* er ist groß für sein Alter; *it is rather cold* ~ *July* es ist ziemlich kalt für Juli; ~ *a foreigner he speaks rather well* für e-n Ausländer spricht er recht gut; **14.** (*zeitlich*) für, während (*gen.*), auf (*acc.*), für die Dauer von, seit: ~ *a week* e-e Woche (lang); *come* ~ *a week* kommen auf *od.* für e-e Woche; ~ *hours* stundenlang; ~ *some time past* seit längerer Zeit; *the first picture* ~ *two months* der erste Film in *od.* seit zwei Monaten; **15.** (*Strecke*) weit, lang: *run* ~ *a mile* e-e Meile (weit) laufen; **16.** nach, auf (*acc.*), in Richtung auf (*acc.*): *the train* ~ *London* der Zug nach London; *the passengers* ~ *Rome* die nach Rom reisenden Passagiere; *start* ~ *Paris* nach Paris abreisen; *now* ~ *it!* Brit. F jetzt (nichts wie) los *od.* drauf!, ran!; **17.** für, an Stelle von (*od. gen.*), (an)'statt: *he appeared* ~ *his brother*; **18.** für, in Vertretung *od.* im Auftrage *od.* im Namen von (*od. gen.*): *act* ~ *s.o.*; **19.** für, als: *example* als *od.* zum Beispiel; *books* ~ *presents* Bücher als Geschenk; *take that* ~ *an answer* nimm das als Antwort; **20.** trotz (*gen. od. dat.*): ~ *all that* trotz alledem; ~ *all his wealth* trotz s-s ganzen Reichtums, bei allem Reichtum; ~ *all you may say* sage, was du willst; **21.** was ... betrifft: *as* ~ *me* was mich betrifft *od.* an(be)langt; *as* ~ *that matter* was das betrifft; ~ *all I know* soviel ich weiß; **22.** *nach adj. u. vor inf.*: *it is too heavy* ~ *me to lift* es ist so schwer, dass ich es nicht heben kann; es ist zu schwer für mich; *he ran too fast* ~ *me to catch him* er rannte zu schnell, als dass ich ihn hätte einholen können; *it is impossible* ~ *me to come* es ist mir unmöglich zu kommen, ich kann unmöglich kommen; *it seemed useless* ~ *him to continue* es erschien sinnlos, dass er noch weitermachen sollte; **23.** *mit s. od. pron. u. inf.*: *it is time* ~ *you to go home* es ist Zeit, dass du heimgehst; *it is* ~ *you to decide* die Entscheidung liegt bei Ihnen; *he called* ~ *the girl to bring him tea* er rief nach dem Mädchen, damit es ihm Tee bringe; *don't wait* ~ *him to turn up yet* wartet nicht darauf, dass er noch auftaucht; *wait* ~ *the rain to stop!* warte, bis der Regen aufhört!; *there is no need* ~ *anyone to know* es braucht niemand zu wissen; *I should be sorry* ~ *you to think that* es täte mir Leid, wenn du das dächtest; *he brought some papers* ~ *me to sign* er brachte mir einige Papiere zur Unterschrift; **24.** (*ethischer Dativ*): *that's a wine* ~ *you* das ist vielleicht ein Weinchen, das nenne ich e-n Wein; *that's gratitude* ~ *you!* a) das ist (wahre) Dankbarkeit!, b) *iro.* von wegen Dankbarkeit!; **25.** *Am.*

nach: *he was named* ~ *his father*; **II** *cj.* **26.** a) denn, weil, b) nämlich; **III** *s.* **27.** Für *n.*

for·age ['fɒrɪdʒ] **I** *s.* **1.** (Vieh)Futter *n*; **2.** Nahrungssuche *f*; **3.** ✕ 'Überfall *m*; **II** *v/i.* **4.** (nach) Nahrung *od.* Futter suchen; **5.** *fig.* her'umstöbern, -kramen (*for* nach); **6.** ✕ e-n 'Überfall machen; **III** *v/t.* **7.** mit Nahrung *od.* Futter versorgen; **8.** *obs.* (aus)plündern; ~ **cap** *s.* ✕ Feldmütze *f.*

for·ay ['fɒreɪ] **I** *s.* **1.** a) Beute-, Raubzug *m*, b) ✕ Ein-, 'Überfall *m*; **2.** *fig.* ‚Ausflug' *m* (*into* in *acc.*); **II** *v/i.* **3.** plündern; **4.** einfallen (*into* in *acc.*).

for·bade [fə'bæd], *a.* **for·bad** [-'bæd] *pret. von forbid.*

for·bear¹ ['fɔːbeə] *s.* Vorfahr *m.*

for·bear² [fɔː'beə] **I** *v/t.* [*irr.*] **1.** unter'lassen, Abstand nehmen von, sich enthalten (*gen.*): *I cannot* ~ *laughing* ich muss (einfach) lachen; **II** *v/i.* [*irr.*] **2.** Abstand nehmen (*from* von); es unterlassen; **3.** nachsichtig sein (*with* mit); **for'bear·ance** [-eərəns] *s.* **1.** Unter'lassung *f*; **2.** Geduld *f*, Nachsicht *f*; **for'bear·ing** [-eərɪŋ] *adj.* □ nachsichtig, geduldig.

for·bid [fə'bɪd] *v/t.* [*irr.*] **1.** verbieten, unter'sagen (*j-m et. od.* zu tun); **2.** unmöglich machen, ausschließen; **II** *v/i.* **3.** *God* ~*!* Gott behüte!; **for'bid·den** [-dn] *p.p. von forbid u. adj.* verboten: ~ *fruit fig.* verbotene Frucht; ℨ *City hist.* die Verbotene Stadt (*in Peking*); **for'bid·ding** [-dɪŋ] *adj.* □ **1.** abschreckend, abstoßend, scheußlich; **2.** bedrohlich, gefährlich; **3.** ‚unmöglich', unerträglich.

for·bore [fɔː'bɔː] *pret. von forbear²*. **for'borne** [-ɔːn] *p.p. von forbear².*

force [fɔːs] **I** *s.* **1.** (*a. fig.* geistige, politische etc.) Kraft (*a. phys.*), Stärke *f* (*a. Charakter*), Wucht *f*: *join* ~*s* a) sich zs.-tun, b) ✕ s-e Streitkräfte vereinigen; **2.** Gewalt *f*, Macht *f*: *by* ~ a) gewaltsam, b) zwangsweise; *by* ~ *of arms* mit Waffengewalt; **3.** Zwang *m* (*a.* ⚖), Druck *m*: ~ *of circumstances* Zwang der Verhältnisse; Einfluss *m*, Wirkung *f*, Wert *m*; Nachdruck *m*, Über-'zeugungskraft *f*: *by* ~ *of* vermittels; ~ *of habit* Macht *f* der Gewohnheit; *lend* ~ *to* Nachdruck verleihen (*dat.*); **5.** ⚖ (Rechts)Gültigkeit *f*, (-)Kraft *f*: *in* ~ in Kraft, geltend; *come* (*put*) *into* ~ in Kraft treten (setzen); **6.** *ling.* Bedeutung *f*, Gehalt *m*; **7.** ✕ Streit-, Kriegsmacht *f*, Truppe(n *pl.*) *f*, Verband *m*: *the* (*armed*) ~*s* die Streitkräfte; *la-bo(u)r* ~ Arbeitskräfte *pl.*, Belegschaft *f*; *a strong* ~ *of police* ein starkes Polizeiaufgebot *f*; **8.** *the* ℨ *Brit.* die Poli'zei; **9.** F Menge *f*: *in* ~ in großer Zahl *od.* Menge; *the police came out in* ~ die Polizei rückte in voller Stärke aus; **II** *v/t.* **10.** zwingen, nötigen: ~ *s.o.'s hand* j-n (zum Handeln) zwingen; ~ *one's way* sich durchzwängen; ~ *s.th. from s.o.* j-m et. entreißen; **11.** erzwingen, forcieren, 'durchsetzen: *a smile* gezwungen lächeln; **12.** treiben, drängen; *Preise* hochtreiben: ~ *s.th. on s.o.* j-m et. aufdrängen *od.* -zwingen; **13.** ⚘ treiben, hochzüchten; **14.** forcieren, beschleunigen: ~ *the pace*; **15.** j-m, *a.* e-r Frau, *a. fig.* dem Sinn etc. Gewalt antun; *Ausdruck* zu Tode hetzen; **16.** *Tür etc.* aufbrechen, (-)sprengen; **17.** ✕ erstürmen, über'wältigen; **18.** ~ *down* a) ✈ zur Landung zwingen, b) *Essen* hin'unterwürgen.

forced [fɔːst] *adj.* □ **1.** erzwungen, forciert, Zwangs...: ~ *lubrication* →

F

force feed; *~ labo(u)r* Zwangsarbeit *f*; *~ landing* ✈ Notlandung *f*; *~ loan* ✝ Zwangsanleihe *f*; *~ march* ✗ Eil-, Gewaltmarsch *m*; *~ sale* ⚖ Zwangsverkauf *m*, -versteigerung *f*; **2.** forciert, gekünstelt, gezwungen (*Lächeln etc.*); manieriert (*Stil etc.*); **'forc·ed·ly** [-sɪdlɪ] *adv.* → *forced.*

force| *feed*; ☉ Druckschmierung *f*; **'~-feed** *v/t.* [*irr.* → *feed*] *j-n* zwangsernähren; *~ field s. phys.* Kräftefeld *n*.

force·ful ['fɔːsfʊl] *adj.* □ **1.** kräftig, wuchtig (*a. fig.*); **2.** eindringlich, -druckvoll; zwingend, über'zeugend (*Argumente etc.*); **'force·ful·ness** [-nɪs] *s.* Eindringlichkeit *f*, Wucht *f*.

'force-land I *v/t.* ✈ zur Notlandung zwingen; **II** *v/i.* notlanden.

force ma·jeure [ˌfɔːsmæˈʒɜː] (*Fr.*) *s.* ⚖ höhere Gewalt.

'force-meat *s. Küche:* Farce *f*, (Fleisch-) Füllung *f*.

for·ceps ['fɔːseps] *s. sg. u. pl.* 🜨 a) Zange *f*, b) Pin'zette *f*: *~ delivery* 🜨 Zangengeburt *f*.

force pump *s.* ☉ Druckpumpe *f*.

for·ci·ble ['fɔːsəbl] *adj.* □ **1.** gewaltsam: *~ feeding* Zwangsernährung *f*; **2.** → *forceful.*

forc·ing| *bed* ['fɔːsɪŋ], *~ frame s.* ✎ Früh-, Mistbeet *n*; *~ house s.* Treibhaus *n*.

ford [fɔːd] **I** *s.* Furt *f*; **II** *v/i.* 'durchwaten; **III** *v/t.* durch'waten; **'ford·a·ble** [-dəbl] *adj.* seicht.

fore [fɔː] **I** *adj.* vorder, Vorder..., Vor..., früher; **II** *s.* Vorderteil *m*, *n*, -seite *f*, Front *f*: *to the ~* a) bei der *od.* zur Hand, zur Stelle, b) am Leben, c) im Vordergrund: *come to the ~* a) hervortreten, in den Vordergrund treten, b) sich hervortun; **III** *int. Golf:* Achtung!

ˌfore-and-'aft [-ɔːrə-] *adj.* ⚓ längsschiffs: *~ sail* Stagsegel *n*.

fore·arm¹ ['fɔːrɑːm] *s.* 'Unterarm *m*.

fore·arm² [fɔːrˈɑːm] *v/t.*: *~ o.s.* sich wappnen; → *forewarn.*

'fore|·bear → *forbear*¹; **'~·bode** [-'bəʊd] *v/t.* **1.** vor'hersagen, prophe'zeien; **2.** ahnen lassen, deuten auf (*acc.*); **3.** ein böses Omen sein für; **4.** *Schlimmes* ahnen, vor'aussehen; **~·bod·ing** [-'bəʊdɪŋ] *s.* **1.** (böses) Vorzeichen *od.* Omen; **2.** (böse) Ahnung; **3.** Prophe'zeiung *f*; **'~·cast I** *v/t.* [*irr.* → *cast*] **1.** vor'aussagen, vor'hersehen; **2.** vor'ausberechnen, im Vor'aus schätzen *od.* planen; **3.** *Wetter etc.* vor'hersagen; **II** *s.* **4.** Vor'her-, Vor'aussage *f*: *weather ~* Wetterbericht *m*, -vorhersage; **~·cas·tle** ['fəʊksl] *s.* ⚓ Back *f*, Vorderdeck *n*; **'~·check·ing** *s. sport* Forechecking *n*, frühes Stören; **~·close** *v/t.* **1.** ⚖ ausschließen (*of* von *-m Rechtsanspruch*); **2.** *~ a mortgage* a) e-e Hypothekenforderung geltend machen, b) e-e Hypothek (gerichtlich) für verfallen erklären, *c*) *Am.* aus e-r Hypothek die Zwangsvollstreckung betreiben; für verfallen erklären; **3.** (ver)hindern; **4.** *Frage etc.* vor'wegnehmen; **~·clo·sure** *s.* ⚖ a) (gerichtliche) Verfallserklärung (*e-r Hypothek*), b) *Am.* Zwangsvollstreckung *f*: *~ action* Ausschlussklage *f*; *~ sale Am.* Zwangsversteigerung *f*; **'~·deck** *s.* ⚓ Vorderdeck *n*; **'~·doom** *v/t.*: *~ed* (*to failure*) *fig.* von vornherein zum Scheitern verurteilt, tot geboren; **'~·fa·ther** *s.* Ahn *m*, Vorfahr *m*; **'~·fin·ger** *s.* Zeigefinger *m*; **'~·foot** *s.* [*irr.*] **1.** *zo.* Vorderfuß *m*; **2.** ⚓ Stevenanlauf *m*; **'~·front** *s.* vorderste Reihe

(*a. fig.*): *in the ~ of the battle* ✗ in vorderster Linie; *be in the ~ of s.o.'s mind j-n* (*geistig*) sehr beschäftigen; **~·'gath·er** → *forgather*; **~·'go** *v/t. u. v/i.* [*irr.* → *go*] **1.** vor'hergehen (*dat.*), zeitlich *a.* vor'hergehen (*dat.*): *~ing* vor'hergehend, vorerwähnt, vorig; **2.** → *forgo*; **'~·gone** *adj.*: *~ conclusion* ausgemachte Sache, Selbstverständlichkeit *f*: *his success was a ~ conclusion* sein Erfolg stand von vornherein fest *od.* war ‚vorprogrammiert'; **'~·ground** *s.* Vordergrund *m* (*a. fig.*); **'~·hand I** *s.* ✗ Vorderhand *f* (*Pferd*); **2.** *sport* Vorhand(schlag *m*) *f*; **II** *adj.* **3.** *sport* Vorhand...

fore·head ['fɒrɪd] *s.* Stirn *f*.

'fore·hold *s.* ⚓ vorderer Laderaum.

for·eign ['fɒrən] *adj.* **1.** fremd, ausländisch, auswärtig, Auslands..., Außen...: *~ affairs pol.* auswärtige Angelegenheiten; *~ aid* Auslandshilfe *f*; *~-born* im Ausland geboren, *~ bill* (*of exchange*) ✝ Auslandswechsel *m*; *~ control* Überfremdung *f*; *~ correspondent* 'Auslandskorrespon,dent(in); *~ country*, *~ countries* Ausland *n*; *~ currency* a) ausländische Währung, b) ✝ Devisen *pl.*; *~ department* Auslandsabteilung *f*; *~ exchange* ✝ De'visen *pl.*: *~ exchange market* ✝ De'visenmarkt *m*, -börse *f*; *~ exchange reserves* ✝ De'visenreserven *pl.*; *~ language* Fremdsprache *f*; *~-language* a) fremdsprachig, b) fremdsprachlich, Fremdsprachen...; 🜨 *Legion* ✗ Fremdenlegion *f*; *~ minister pol.* Außenminister *m*; 🜨 *Office Brit.* Außenministerium *n*; *~-owned* in ausländischem Besitz (befindlich); *~ policy* Außenpolitik *f*; 🜨 *Secretary Brit.* Außenminister *m*; *~ trade* ✝ Außenhandel *m*; *~ word* a) Fremdwort *n*, b) Lehnwort *n*; *~ worker* Gastarbeiter(in); **2.** fremd (*to dat.*): *~ body* (*od. matter*) Fremdkörper *m*; *that is ~ to his nature* das ist ihm wesensfremd; **3.** *~ to* nicht gehörig *od.* passend zu.

for·eign·er ['fɒrənə] *s.* **1.** Ausländer (-in); **2.** Ausländisches (*z. B. Schiff, Produkt etc.*).

fore·|judge *v/t.* im Vor'aus *od.* voreilig entscheiden *od.* beurteilen; **~·'know** *v/t.* [*irr.* → *know*] vor'herwissen, vor'ausahnen; **~·'knowl·edge** *s.* Vor'herwissen *n*, vor'herige Kenntnis; **'~·la·dy** *Am.* → *forewoman*; **'~·land** [-lənd] *s.* Vorland *n*, Vorgebirge *n*, Landspitze *f*; **'~·leg** *s.* Vorderbein *n*; **'~·lock** *s.* Stirnlocke *f*, -haar *n*: *take time by the ~* die Gelegenheit beim Schopfe fassen; **'~·man** [-mən] *s.* [*irr.*] **1.** Werkmeister *m*, Vorarbeiter *m*, ⚒ Po'lier *m*; Aufseher *m*; **2.** ⚖ Obmann *m der Geschworenen*; **'~·mast** [-mɑːst, ⚓ -məst] *s.* ⚓ Fockmast *m*; **'~·most I** *adj.* vorderst, erst, best, vornehmst; **II** *adv.* zu'erst: *first and ~* zuallererst; *feet ~* mit den Füßen voran; **'~·name** *s.* Vorname *m*; **'~·noon** *s.* Vormittag *m*.

fo·ren·sic [fəˈrensɪk] *adj.* (□ *~ally*) fo'rensisch, Gerichts...: *~ medicine.*

ˌfore·or'dain [-ɔːˈ-] *v/t.* vor'herbestimmen; **~·or·di'na·tion** [-ɔːˈ-] *s. eccl.* Vor'herbestimmung *f*; **'~·part** *s.* **1.** Vorderteil *m*; **2.** Anfang *m*; **'~·play** *s.* (*sexuelles*) Vorspiel; **'~·run·ner** *s. fig.* **1.** Vorläufer *m*; **2.** Vorbote *m*, Anzeichen *n*; **'~·sail** [-seɪl, ⚓ -sl] *s.* ⚓ Focksegel *n*; **~·see** *v/t.* [*irr.* → *see*¹] vor'aussehen *od.* -wissen; **'~·see·a·ble** [-ˈsiːəbl] *adj.* vor'auszusehen(d), absehbar: *in the ~ future* in absehbarer Zeit; **'~·shad·ow** *v/t.* ahnen lassen, (*drohend*) ankündi-

gen; **'~·sheet** *s.* ⚓ **1.** Fockschot *f*; **2.** *pl.* Vorderboot *n*; **3.** ⚓ Uferland *n*, (Küsten)Vorland *n*; **~·'short·en** *v/t.* Figuren in Verkürzung *od.* perspek'tivisch zeichnen; **'~·sight** *s.* **1.** a) Weitblick *m*, b) (*weise*) Vor'aussicht; → *hindsight* **1**; **2.** Blick *m* in die Zukunft; **3.** ✗ (Vi-'sier)Korn *n*; **'~·skin** *s. anat.* Vorhaut *f*.

for·est ['fɒrɪst] **I** *s.* Wald *m* (*a. fig. von Masten etc.*), Forst *m*: *~ fire* Waldbrand *m*; **II** *v/t.* aufforsten.

fore·|stall *v/t.* **1.** *j-m* zu'vorkommen; **2.** *e-r Sache* vorbeugen, *et.* vereiteln; **3.** *Einwand etc.* vor'wegnehmen; **4.** ✝ (*spekula'tiv*) aufkaufen; **'~·stay** *s.* ⚓ Fockstag *n*.

for·est deaths ['fɒrɪst] *pl.* Waldsterben *n*; **for·est·ed** ['fɒrɪstɪd] *adj.* bewaldet; **'for·est·er** [-tə] *s.* **1.** Förster *m*; **2.** Waldbewohner *m* (*a. Tier*); **'for·est·ry** [-trɪ] *s.* **1.** Forstwirtschaft *f*, -wesen *n*; **2.** Wälder *pl.*

'fore·|taste *s.* Vorgeschmack *m*; **~·'tell** *v/t.* [*irr.* → *tell*] **1.** vor'her-, vor'aussagen; **2.** andeuten, ahnen lassen; **'~·thought** → *foresight* **1**; **'~·top** [-tɒp, ⚓ -təp] *s.* ⚓ Fock-, Vormars *m*; **ˌ~·top'gal·lant** *s.* ⚓ Vorbramsegel *n*: *~ mast* Vorbramstenge *f*; **'~·top·mast** [-mɑːst, ⚓ -məst] *s.* ⚓ Fock-, Vormarssstenge *f*; **'~·top·sail** [-seɪl, ⚓ -sl] *s.* ⚓ Vormarssegel *n*.

for ev·er, **for·ev·er** [fəˈrevə] *adv.* **1.** a. *~ and ever* für od. auf immer, für alle Zeit; **2.** andauernd, ständig, unaufhörlich; **3.** F ‚ewig' (lang); **for ev·er·more**, **for·ev·er·more** *adv.* für immer u. ewig.

fore·|'warn *v/t.* vorher warnen (*of* vor *dat.*): *~ed is forearmed* gewarnt sein heißt gewappnet sein; **'~·wom·an** *s.* [*irr.*] **1.** Vorarbeiterin *f*, Aufseherin *f*; **2.** ⚖ Obmännin *f der Geschworenen*; **'~·word** *s.* Vorwort *n*; **'~·yard** *s.* ⚓ Fockrahe *f*.

for·feit ['fɔːfɪt] **I** *s.* **1.** (Geld-, *a.* Vertrags)Strafe *f*, Buße *f*: *pay the ~ of one's life* mit s-m Leben bezahlen; **2.** Verlust *m*, Einbuße *f*; **3.** verwirktes Pfand: *pay a ~* ein Pfand geben; **4.** *pl.* Pfänderspiel *n*; **II** *v/t.* **5.** verwirken, verlieren, *fig.* einbüßen, verscherzen; **III** *adj.* **6.** verwirkt, verfallen; **'for·fei·ture** [-tʃə] *s.* Verlust *m*, Verwirkung *f*, Verfallen *n*, Einziehung *f*, Entzug *m*.

for·fend [fɔːˈfend] *v/t.* **1.** *obs.* verhüten: *God ~!* Gott behüte!; **2.** *Am.* schützen, sichern (*from* vor *dat.*).

for·gath·er [fɔːˈgæðə] *v/i.* zs.-kommen, sich treffen; verkehren (*with* mit).

for·gave [fəˈgeɪv] *pret. von forgive.*

forge¹ [fɔːdʒ] *v/i.*: *~ ahead* a) sich (mühsam) vor'ankämpfen, sich Bahn brechen, b) *fig.* (allmählich) Fortschritte machen, c) (sich) nach vorn drängen, *a. sport* sich an die Spitze setzen.

forge² [fɔːdʒ] **I** *s.* **1.** Schmiede *f* (*a. fig.*); **2.** ☉ a) Schmiedefeuer *n*, -esse *f*, b) Glühofen *m*, c) Hammerwerk *n*: *~ lathe* Schmiededrehbank *f*; **II** *v/t.* **3.** schmieden (*a. fig.*); **4.** *fig.* a) formen, schaffen, b) erfinden, sich ausdenken; **5.** fälschen: *~ a document*; **'forge·a·ble** [-dʒəbl] *adj.* schmiedbar; **'forg·er** [-dʒə] *s.* **1.** Schmied *m*; **2.** Erfinder *m*, Erschaffer *m*; **3.** Fälscher *m*: *~* (*of coin*) Falschmünzer *m*; **'forg·er·y** [-dʒərɪ] *s.* **1.** Fälschen *n*: *~ of a document* ⚖ Urkundenfälschung *f*; **~·proof** fälschungssicher; **2.** Fälschung *f*, Falsi'fikat *n*.

for·get [fəˈget] **I** *v/t.* [*irr.*] **1.** vergessen, nicht denken an (*acc.*), nicht bedenken, sich nicht erinnern an (*acc.*): *I ~ his*

name sein Name ist mir entfallen; **2.** vergessen, verlernen: *I have forgotten my French*; **3.** vergessen, unter'lassen: **~ it!** F a) vergiss es!, schon gut!, b) *iro.* das kannst du vergessen!; *don't you ~ it* merk dir das!; **4. ~ o.s.** a) (nur) an andere denken, b) sich vergessen, ,aus der Rolle fallen'; **II** *v/i. [irr.]* **5.** vergessen: **~ about it!** denk nicht mehr daran!; *I ~!* das ist mir entfallen!; **for'get·ful** [-fʊl] *adj.* □ **1.** vergesslich; **2.** achtlos, nachlässig (*of* gegenüber): **~ of one's duties** pflichtvergessen; **for'get·ful·ness** [-fʊlnɪs] *s.* **1.** Vergesslichkeit *f*; **2.** Achtlosigkeit *f*.

for'get-me-not *s.* ♀ Ver'gissmeinnicht *n*.

for·giv·a·ble [fə'ɡɪvəbl] *adj.* verzeihlich, entschuldbar; **for·give** [fə'ɡɪv] *v/t. [irr.]* **1.** verzeihen, vergeben; **2.** *j-m e-e Schuld etc.* erlassen; **for'giv·en** [-vn] *p.p. von* **forgive**; **for'give·ness** [-vnɪs] *s.* **1.** Verzeihung *f*, -gebung *f*; **2.** Versöhnlichkeit *f*; **for'giv·ing** [-vɪŋ] *adj.* □ **1.** versöhnlich, nachsichtig; **2.** verzeihend.

for·go [fɔː'ɡəʊ] *v/t. [irr. → go]* verzichten auf (*acc.*).

for·got [fə'ɡɒt] *pret.* [*u. p.p. obs.*] *von* **forget**; **for'got·ten** [-tn] *p.p. von* **forget**.

fork [fɔːk] **I** *s.* **1.** (*Ess-, Heu-, Mist- etc.*) Gabel *f* (*a.* ✪); **2.** ♪ (Stimm)Gabel *f*; **3.** Gabelung *f*, Abzweigung *f*; **4.** *Am.* a) Zs.-fluss *m*, b) *oft pl.* Gebiet *n* an e-r Flussgabelung; **II** *v/t.* **5.** gabelförmig machen, gabeln; **6.** mit e-r Gabel aufladen *od.* 'umgraben *od.* wenden; **7.** *Schach: zwei Figuren* gleichzeitig angreifen; **III** *v/i.* **8.** sich gabeln *od.* spalten; **~ out, ~ over, ~ up** *v/t. u. v/i.* ,blechen' (*zahlen*); **forked** [-kt] *adj.* gabelförmig, gegabelt, gespalten; zickzackförmig (*Blitz*); **'fork-lift (truck)** *s.* ✪ Gabelstapler *m*.

for·lorn [fə'lɔːn] *adj.* **1.** verlassen, einsam; **2.** verzweifelt, hilflos; unglücklich, elend; **~ hope** *s.* **1.** aussichtsloses Unter'nehmen; **2.** letzte (verzweifelte) Hoffnung; **3.** ✕ a) verlorener Haufen *od.* Posten, b) 'Himmelfahrtskom,mando *n*.

form [fɔːm] *s.* **1.** Form *f*, Gestalt *f*, Fi'gur *f*; **2.** ✪ Form *f*, Fas'son *f*, Mo'dell *n*, Scha'blone *f*; △ Schalung *f*; **3.** Form *f*, Art *f*, Me'thode *f*, (An)Ordnung *f*, Schema *n*: *in due ~* vorschriftsmäßig; **4.** Form *f*, Fassung *f* (*Wort, Text, a. ling.*), Formel *f* (*Gebet etc.*); **5.** *phls.* Wesen *n*, Na'tur *f*; **6.** 'Umgangsform *f*, Ma'nieren *pl.*, Benehmen *n*: *good (bad) ~* guter (schlechter) Ton; *it is good (bad) ~* es gehört *od.* schickt sich (nicht); **7.** Formblatt *n*, Formu'lar *n*: *printed ~* Vordruck *m*; **~ letter** Schemabrief *m*; **8.** Formali'tät *f*, Äußerlichkeit *f*: *matter of ~* Formsache *f*; *mere ~* bloße Förmlichkeit; **9.** Form *f*, (körperliche *od.* geistige) Verfassung: *in (od. on) ~* (gut) in Form; *off (od. out of) ~* nicht in Form; **10.** *Brit.* a) (Schul-)Bank *f*, b) (Schul)Klasse *f*: **~ master (mistress)** Klassenlehrer(in) *m*; **11.** *typ.* → **forme**; **II** *v/t.* **12.** formen, bilden (*a. ling.*); schaffen, gestalten (*into* zu, *after* nach); *Regierung* bilden, *Gesellschaft etc.* gründen; **13.** *den Charakter etc.* formen, bilden; **14.** a) *e-n Teil etc.* bilden, ausmachen, b) dienen als; **15.** anordnen, zs.-stellen; **16.** ✕ formieren, aufstellen; **17.** *e-n Plan* fassen, entwerfen; **18.** sich *e-e Meinung* bilden; **19.** *e-e Freundschaft etc.* schließen; **20.**

e-e Gewohnheit annehmen; **21.** ✪ formen; **III** *v/i.* **22.** sich formen *od.* bilden *od.* gestalten, Form annehmen, entstehen; **23.** a. **~ up** ✕ sich formieren *od.* aufstellen, antreten.

-form [-fɔːm] *in Zssgn* ...förmig.

for·mal ['fɔːml] **I** *adj.* □ → **formally**; **1.** förmlich, for'mell: a) offizi'ell: **~ call** Höflichkeitsbesuch *m*, b) feierlich: **~ event** → 5; **~ dress** → 6, c) steif, 'unper,sönlich, d) (peinlich) genau, pe'dantisch (die Form wahrend), e) formgerecht, vorschriftsmäßig: **~ contract** förmlicher Vertrag; **2.** for'mal, for'mell: a) rein äußerlich, b) rein gewohnheitsmäßig, c) scheinbar, Schein...; **3.** for'mal: a) herkömmlich, konventio'nell: **~ style**, b) schulmäßig, streng me'thodisch, c) Form...: **~ defect** ✪ Formfehler *m*; **4.** regelmäßig: **~ garden** architektonischer Garten; **II** *s. Am.* **5.** Veranstaltung, für die Gesellschaftskleidung vorgeschrieben ist; **6.** Gesellschafts-, Abendanzug *m od.* -kleid *n*.

form·al·de·hyde [fɔː'mældɪhaɪd] *s.* ✿ Formalde'hyd *m*; **for·ma·lin** ['fɔːməlɪn] *s.* ✿ Forma'lin *n*.

form·al·ism ['fɔːməlɪzəm] *s. allg.* Forma'lismus *m*; **'form·al·ist** [-lɪst] *s.* Forma'list *m*; **for·mal·is·tic** [,fɔːmə'lɪstɪk] *adj.* forma'listisch; **for·mal·i·ty** [fɔː'mælətɪ] *s.* **1.** Förmlichkeit: a) Herkömmlichkeit *f*, b) Zeremo'nie *f*, c) *das* Offizi'elle, d) Steifheit *f*, e) Umständlichkeit *f*: *without ~* ohne viel Umstände (zu machen); **2.** Formali'tät *f*: a) Formsache *f*, b) Formvorschrift *f*: *for the sake of ~* aus formellen Gründen; **3.** Äußerlichkeit *f*, leere Geste; **'for·mal·ize** [-laɪz] *v/t.* **1.** zur bloßen Formsache machen, b) formalisieren, feste Form geben (*dat.*); **'for·mal·ly** [-əlɪ] *adv.* **1.** for'mell, in aller Form; **2.** → **formal**.

for·mat ['fɔːmæt] **I** *s.* **1.** *typ.* a) Aufmachung *f*, b) For'mat *n*; **2.** *Computer:* For'matvorlage *f*; **3.** Ein-, Ausrichtung *f*; **II** *v/t.* **4.** *Computer:* formatieren: **~ a disk** e-e Dis'kette formatieren.

for·ma·tion [fɔː'meɪʃn] *s.* **1.** Bildung *f*: a) Formung *f*, Gestaltung *f*, b) Entstehung *f*, Entwicklung *f*: **~ of gas** Gasbildung *f*, c) Gründung *f*: **~ of a company**; d) Gebilde *n*: *word ~s* Wortbildungen; **2.** Anordnung *f*, Zs.-setzung *f*, Struk'tur *f*; **3.** ✈, ✕, *sport* Formati'on *f*, Aufstellung *f*: **~ flight** Formations-, Verbandsflug *m*; **4.** *geol.* Formati'on *f*; **form·a·tive** ['fɔːmətɪv] **I** *adj.* **1.** formend, gestaltend, bildend; **2.** prägend, Entwicklungs...: **~ years of a person**; **3.** *ling.* formbildend: **~ element** → 5; **4.** ♀, *zo.* morpho'gen; **II** *s.* **5.** *ling.* Forma'tiv *n*.

for·mat·ting ['fɔːmætɪŋ] *s. Computer:* Forma'tierung *f*.

forme [fɔːm] *s. typ.* (Druck)Form *f*.

form·er¹ ['fɔːmə] *s.* **1.** Former *m* (*a.* ✪), Gestalter *m*; **2.** *ped. Brit. in Zssgn* Schüler(in) der ... Klasse; **3.** ✈ Spant *m*.

for·mer² ['fɔːmə] *adj.* □ **1.** früher, vorig, ehe-, vormalig, vergangen: *in ~ times* vormals, einst; *he is his ~ self again* er ist wieder (ganz) der Alte; *the ~ Mrs. A.* die frühere Frau A.; **2.** *the ~ sg. u. pl. der etc.* (die *pl.*) Ersterwähnte(n *pl.*), -genannte(n *pl.*), Erste(n *pl.*): *the ~ ..., the latter ...* der Erstere ..., der Letztere ...; **'for·mer·ly** [-lɪ] *adv.* früher, vor-, ehemals: *Mrs. A., ~ B.* a) Frau A., geborene B., b) Frau A., ehemalige Frau B.

'form,fit·ting *adj.* **1.** eng anliegend: **~ dress**; **2.** körpergerecht: **~ chair**.

For·mi·ca [fɔː'maɪkə] *TM npr.* Reso'pal *TM n*.

for·mic ac·id ['fɔːmɪk] *s.* ✿ Ameisensäure *f*.

for·mi·da·ble ['fɔːmɪdəbl] *adj.* □ **1.** schrecklich, Furcht erregend; **2.** gewaltig, ungeheuer, e'norm; **3.** beachtlich, ernst zu nehmend: **~ opponent**; **4.** äußerst schwierig: **~ problem**.

form·ing ['fɔːmɪŋ] *s.* **1.** Formen *n*; **2.** ✪ (Ver)Formen *n*, Fassonieren *n*; **form·less** ['fɔːmlɪs] *adj.* □ formlos.

for·mu·la ['fɔːmjʊlə] *pl.* **-las, -lae** [-liː] *s.* **1.** ✿, ⚕ *etc., a. mot.* Formel *f*, *pharm. u. fig. a.* Re'zept *n*; **2.** Formel *f*, fester Wortlaut; **3.** *contp.* a) ,Schema F', b) (leere) Phrase; **'for·mu·lar·y** [-ərɪ] *s.* **1.** Formelsammlung *f*, -buch *n* (*bsd. eccl.*); **2.** *pharm.* Re'zeptbuch *n*; **'for·mu·late** [-leɪt] *v/t.* formulieren; **for·mu·la·tion** [,fɔːmjʊ'leɪʃn] *s.* Formulierung *f*, Fassung *f*.

'form·work *s.* △ (Ver)Schalung *f*, Schalungen *pl.*

for·ni·cate ['fɔːnɪkeɪt] *v/i.* unerlaubten außerehelichen Geschlechtsverkehr haben; *bibl. u. weitS.* Unzucht treiben, huren; **for·ni·ca·tion** [,fɔːnɪ'keɪʃn] *s.* ✪ unerlaubter außerehelicher Geschlechtsverkehr; *weitS.* Unzucht *f*, Hure'rei *f*; **'for·ni·ca·tor** [-tə] *s.* j-d, der unerlaubten außerehelichen Geschlechtsverkehr hat; *weitS.* Wüstling *m*.

for·rad·er ['fɒrədə] *adv.: get no ~ Brit.* F nicht vom Fleck kommen.

for·sake [fə'seɪk] *v/t. [irr.]* **1.** *j-n* verlassen, im Stich lassen; **2.** *et.* aufgeben; **for'sak·en** [-kən] **I** *p.p. von* **forsake**; **II** *adj.* (gott)verlassen, einsam; **for'sook** [-'sʊk] *pret. von* **forsake**.

for·sooth [fə'suːθ] *adv. iro.* wahrlich, für'wahr.

for·swear [fɔː'sweə] *v/t. [irr. → swear]* **1.** eidlich bestreiten; **2.** unter Pro'test zu'rückweisen; **3.** abschwören (*dat.*), feierlich entsagen (*dat.*); feierlich geloben (*es nie wieder zu tun etc.*); **4. ~ o.s.** e-n Meineid leisten; **for'sworn** [-'swɔːn] **I** *p.p. von* **forswear**; **II** *adj.* meineidig.

for·syth·i·a [fɔː'saɪθjə] *s.* ♀ For'sythie *f*.

fort [fɔːt] *s.* ✕ Fort *n*, Feste *f*, Festungswerk *n*: *hold the ~ fig.* ,die Stellung halten'.

forte¹ ['fɔːteɪ] *s. fig.* j-s Stärke *f*, starke Seite.

for·te² ['fɔːtɪ] *adv.* ♪ forte, laut.

forth [fɔːθ] *adv.* **1.** her, vor, her; → *bring forth etc.*; **2.** her'aus, hinaus; **3.** (dr)außen; **4.** vo'ran, vorwärts; **5.** weiter: *and so ~* und so weiter; *from that day ~* von diesem Tag an; **6.** weg, fort.

Forth Bridge [,fɔːθ'brɪdʒ] *npr.: it's like painting the ~ Brit. fig.* das nimmt ja nie ein Ende.

forth'com·ing *adj.* **1.** bevorstehend, kommend; **2.** erscheinend, unter'wegs: *be ~* erfolgen, sich einstellen; **3.** in Kürze erscheinend (*Buch*) *od.* anlaufend (*Film*); **4.** bereitstehend, verfügbar; **5.** zu'vor-, entgegenkommend (*Person*); **6.** mitteilsam; **'~-right** *adj. u. adv.* offen (und ehrlich), gerade(her'aus); **,~'with** [-'wɪθ] *adv.* so'fort, (so)'gleich, unverzüglich.

for·ti·eth ['fɔːtɪɪθ] **I** *adj.* **1.** vierzigst; **II** *s.* **2.** Vierzigste(r *m*) *f*, *n*; **3.** Vierzigstel *n*.

for·ti·fi·a·ble ['fɔːtɪfaɪəbl] *adj.* zu befestigen(d); **for·ti·fi·ca·tion** [,fɔːtɪfɪ'keɪʃn] *s.* **1.** ✕ a) Befestigung *f*, b)

F

Befestigung(sanlage) f, c) Festung f; **2.** (a. geistige od. mo'ralische) Stärkung; **3.** a) Verstärkung f (a. ⊕), b) Anreicherung f; **4.** fig. Unter'mauerung f; **'for·ti·fi·er** [-faɪə] s. Stärkungsmittel n; **for·ti·fy** ['fɔːtɪfaɪ] v/t. **1.** (a. geistig od. mo'ralisch) kräftigen, **2.** ⊕ verstärken; Nahrungsmittel anreichern; Wein etc. verstärken; **3.** ✕ befestigen; **4.** bekräftigen, stützen, unter'mauern; **5.** bestärken, ermutigen.

for·tis·si·mo [fɔː'tɪsɪməʊ] adv. ♪ sehr stark od. laut, for'tissimo.

for·ti·tude ['fɔːtɪtjuːd] s. (seelische) Kraft: bear s.th. with ~ et. mit Fassung od. tapfer ertragen.

fort·night ['fɔːtnaɪt] s. bsd. Brit. vierzehn Tage: this day ~ a) heute in 14 Tagen, b) heute vor 14 Tagen; a ~'s holiday ein vierzehntägiger Urlaub; **'fort·night·ly** [-lɪ] bsd. Brit. **I** adj. vierzehntägig, halbmonatlich, Halbmonats...; **II** adv. alle 14 Tage; **III** s. Halbmonatsschrift f.

For·tran ['fɔːtræn] s. FORTRAN n (Computersprache).

for·tress ['fɔːtrɪs] s. ✕ Festung f, fig. a. Bollwerk n.

for·tu·i·tous [fɔː'tjuːɪtəs] adj. □ zufällig; **for'tu·i·ty** [-tɪ] s. Zufall m, Zufälligkeit f.

for·tu·nate ['fɔːtʃnət] adj. □ **1.** glücklich: be ~ a) Glück haben (Person), b) ein (wahres) Glück sein (Sache); how ~! welch ein Glück!, wie gut!; **2.** Glück verheißend; günstig; vom Glück begünstigt (Leben); **'for·tu·nate·ly** [-lɪ] adv. glücklicherweise, zum Glück.

for·tune ['fɔːtʃuːn] s. **1.** Glück(sfall m) n, (glücklicher) Zufall: good ~ Gück; ill ~ Unglück; try one's ~ sein Glück versuchen; make one's ~ sein Glück machen; **2.** a. ♀ myth. For'tuna f, Glücksgöttin f: ~ favo(u)red him das Glück war ihm hold; **3.** Schicksal n, Geschick n, Los n: tell (od. read) ~s wahrsagen; read s.o.'s ~ j-m die Karten legen od. aus der Hand lesen; have one's ~ told sich wahrsagen lassen; **4.** Vermögen n: make a ~ ein Vermögen verdienen; come into a ~ ein Vermögen erben; marry a ~ e-e gute Partie machen; a small ~ F ein kleines Vermögen (viel Geld); ~ hunt·er ['fɔːtʃən-] s. Mitgiftjäger m; ~ tell·er ['fɔːtʃən-] s. Wahrsager(in); ~ tell·ing ['fɔːtʃən-] s. Wahrsage'rei f.

for·ty ['fɔːtɪ] **I** adj. **1.** vierzig: the ♀ Thieves die 40 Räuber (1001 Nacht); → wink 4; **II** s. **2.** Vierzig: he is in his forties er ist in den Vierzigern; in the forties in den Vierzigerjahren (e-s Jahrhunderts); **3.** the Forties die See zwischen Schottlands Nord'ost- u. Norwegens Süd'westküste; **4.** the roaring forties stürmischer Teil des Ozeans (zwischen dem 39. u. 50. Breitengrad).

fo·rum ['fɔːrəm] s. **1.** antiq. u. fig. Forum n; **2.** Gericht n, Tribu'nal n (a. fig.); engS. ♊ Gerichtsort m, örtliche Zuständigkeit; **3.** Forum n, (öffentliche) Diskussi'on(sveranstaltung).

for·ward ['fɔːwəd] **I** adv. **1.** vor, nach vorn, vorwärts, vor'an, vor'aus, weiter: from this day ~ von heute an; freight ~ ♀ Fracht gegen Nachnahme; buy ~ ♀ auf Termin kaufen; go ~ fig. Fortschritte machen, vorankommen; help ~ weiterhelfen (dat.); → bring (carry, come, etc.) forward; **II** adj. □ **2.** vorwärts od. nach vorn gerichtet, Vorwärts...: a ~ motion; ~ defence ✕ Vorwärtsverteidigung f; ~ planning

Vorausplanung f; ~ speed mot. Vorwärtsgang m; ~ strategy ✕ Vorwärtsstrategie f; **3.** vorder; **4.** a) ♀ frühreif (a. fig. Kind), b) zeitig (Frühling etc.); **5.** zo. a) hochträchtig, b) gut entwickelt; **6.** fig. a) fortgeschritten, b) fortschrittlich; **7.** fig. vorlaut, dreist; **8.** fig. a) vorschnell, -eilig, b) schnell bereit (to do s.th. et. zu tun); **9.** ♀ auf Ziel od. Zeit, Termin...: ~ business (market, sale, etc.); ~ rate Terminkurs m, Kurs m für Termingeschäfte; **III** s. **10.** sport Stürmer m: ~ line Sturm(reihe f) m; **IV** v/t. **11.** a) fördern, begünstigen, b) beschleunigen; **12.** befördern, schicken, verladen; **13.** Brief etc. nachsenden, weiterbefördern.

for·ward·er ['fɔːwədə] s. Spedi'teur; **'for·ward·ing** [-dɪŋ] **I** s. Versand m; **II** adj. Versand...: ~ charges; ~ instructions; ~ agent Spediteur m; ~ note Frachtbrief m; ~ address Nachsendeadresse f; **'for·ward-look·ing** adj. vorausschauend, fortschrittlich; **'forward·ness** [-dnɪs] s. **1.** Frühzeitigkeit f, Frühreife f (a. ♀); **2.** Dreistigkeit f, vorlaute Art; **3.** Voreiligkeit f.

for·wards ['fɔːwədz] → forward I.

fosse [fɒs] s. **1.** (Burg-, Wall)Graben m; **2.** anat. Grube f.

fos·sil ['fɒsl] **I** s. **1.** geol. Fos'sil n; Versteinerung f; **2.** F ‚Fos'sil‘ n: a) verkalkter, verknöcherter Mensch, b) et. ‚Vorsintflutliches‘; **II** adj. **3.** fos'sil, versteinert: ~ fuel fossiler Brennstoff; ~ oil Erd-, Steinöl n; **4.** F a) verknöchert, verkalkt (Person), b) vorsintflutlich (Sache); **fos·sil·if·er·ous** [ˌfɒsɪ'lɪfərəs] adj. fos'silienhaltig; **fos·sil·i·za·tion** [ˌfɒsɪlaɪ'zeɪʃn] s. **1.** Versteinerung f; **2.** F Verknöcherung f; **'fos·sil·ize** [-sɪlaɪz] **I** v/t. geol. versteinern; **II** v/i. versteinern; fig. verknöchern, verkalken.

fos·so·ri·al [fɒ'sɔːrɪəl] adj. zo. grabend, Grab...

fos·ter ['fɒstə] **I** v/t. **1.** Kind etc. a) aufziehen, b) in Pflege haben od. geben; **2.** et. fördern; begünstigen, protegieren; **3.** Wunsch etc. hegen, nähren; **II** adj. **4.** Pflege...: ~ child (father, mother etc.).

fos·ter·ling ['fɒstəlɪŋ] s. Pflegekind n.

fought [fɔːt] pret. u. p.p. von fight.

foul [faʊl] **I** adj. □ **1.** a) stinkend, widerlich, übel riechend (a. Atem), b) verpestet, schlecht (Luft), c) faul, verdorben (Lebensmittel etc.); **2.** schmutzig, verschmutzt; **3.** verstopft; **4.** voll Unkraut, überwachsen; **5.** schlecht, stürmisch (Wetter etc.), widrig (Wind); **6.** ♭ a) unklar (Taue etc.), b) in Kollisi'on (geratend) (of mit); **7.** fig. a) widerlich, ekelhaft, b) abscheulich, gemein: ~ deed ruchlose Tat, c) schädlich, gefährlich: ~ tongue böse Zunge, d) schmutzig, zotig, unflätig: ~ language; **8.** F scheußlich; **9.** unehrlich, betrügerisch; **10.** sport unfair, regelwidrig; **11.** typ. unsauber (Druck etc.), b) voller Fehler od. Änderungen; **II** adv. **12.** auf gemeine Art, gemein (etc. → 7–10): play ~ sport foul spielen; play s.o. ~ j-m übel mitspielen; **13.** fall ~ of ♭ zs.-stoßen mit (a. fig.); **III** s. **14.** through fair and ~ durch dick u. dünn; **15.** ♭ Zs.-stoß m; **16.** sport a) Foul n, Regelverstoß m, b) → foul shot; **IV** v/t. **17.** a. ♭ up a) beschmutzen (a. fig.), verschmutzen, verunreinigen, b) verstopfen; **18.** sport foulen; **19.** ♭ zs.-stoßen mit; **20.** a. ~ up sich verwickeln in (dat.) od. mit; **21.** ~ up F a) ‚vermasseln‘, ‚versauen‘, b) durchein'ander

bringen; **V** v/i. **22.** schmutzig werden; **23.** ♭ zs.-stoßen (with mit); **24.** sich verwickeln; **25.** sport foulen, ein Foul begehen; **26.** ~ up F a) ‚Mist bauen‘, ‚patzen‘, b) durchein'ander kommen.

'foul-mouthed adj. unflätig; ~ play s. **1.** sport unfaires Spiel, Unsportlichkeit f; **2.** (Gewalt)Verbrechen n, bsd. Mord m; ~ shot s. Basketball: Freiwurf m; '~-,spo·ken → foul-mouthed.

found¹ [faʊnd] pret. u. p.p. von find.

found² [faʊnd] v/t. ⊕ schmelzen; gießen.

found³ [faʊnd] fig. **I** v/t. **1.** gründen, errichten; **2.** begründen, einrichten, ins Leben rufen, Schule etc. stiften: ♀ing Fathers Am. Staatsmänner aus der Zeit der Unabhängigkeitserklärung; **3.** fig. gründen, stützen (on auf acc.): be ~ed on → 4; well-~ed wohl begründet, fundiert; **II** v/i. **4.** (on) sich stützen (auf acc.), beruhen, sich gründen (auf dat.).

foun·da·tion [faʊn'deɪʃn] s. **1.** oft pl. △ Grundmauer f, Funda'ment n (a. fig.); 'Unterbau m, -lage f, Bettung f (Straße etc.); **2.** Grund(lage f) m, Basis f: without (any) ~ (völlig) unbegründet; shaken to the ~s in den Grundfesten erschüttert; lay the ~s of den Grund(stock) legen zu; **3.** Gründung f, Errichtung f; **4.** (gemeinnützige) Stiftung: be on the ~ Geld aus der Stiftung erhalten; **5.** Ursprung m, Beginn m; **6.** steifes (Zwischen)Futter: ~ muslin Steifleinen n; **7.** a. ~ garment a) Mieder n, b) Kor'sett n, c) pl. Mieder (-waren) pl.; **8.** a. ~ cream Kosmetik: Grundierung f; ~ stone s. Grundstein m (a. fig.); → lay¹ 5.

found·er¹ ['faʊndə] s. Gründer m, Stifter m: ~'s shares ♀ Gründeraktien.

found·er² ['faʊndə] s. ⊕ Gießer m.

found·er³ ['faʊndə] **I** v/i. **1.** ♭ sinken, 'untergehen; **2.** einstürzen, -fallen; **3.** fig. scheitern; **4.** vet. a) lahmen, b) zs.-brechen (Pferd); **5.** stecken bleiben; **II** v/t. **6.** Pferd lahm reiten; **7.** Schiff zum Sinken bringen.

found·ing mem·ber ['faʊndɪŋ] s. Gründungsmitglied n.

found·ling ['faʊndlɪŋ] s. Findling m, Findelkind n: ~ hospital Findelhaus n.

found·ress ['faʊndrɪs] s. Gründerin f, Stifterin f.

found·ry ['faʊndrɪ] s. ⊕ Gieße'rei f.

fount¹ [faʊnt] s. typ. (Setzkasten m mit) Schriftsatz m.

fount² [faʊnt] → fountain 2, 4a.

foun·tain ['faʊntɪn] s. **1.** Fon'täne f: a) Springbrunnen m, b) (Wasser)Strahl m; **2.** Quelle f, fig. a. Born m: ♀ of Youth Jungbrunnen m; **3.** a) (Trink-) Brunnen m, b) → soda fountain; **4.** ⊕ a) (Öl-, Tinten- etc.)Behälter m, b) Reser'voir n; '~-head s. Quelle f (a. fig.); fig. Urquell m; ~ pen s. Füll(feder)-halter m.

four [fɔː] **I** adj. **1.** vier; **II** s. **2.** Vier f (Zahl, Spielkarte etc.): the ~ of hearts die Herzvier; by ~s immer vier (auf einmal); on all ~s a) auf allen vieren, b) fig. stimmend, richtig; be on all ~s with übereinstimmen mit, genau entsprechen (dat.); **3.** Rudern: Vierer m (Boot od. Mannschaft); '~-'cor·nered adj. viereckig, mit vier Ecken; '~-,cy·cle adj.: ~ engine ⊕ Viertaktmotor m; '~-eyes s. pl. sg. konstr. F ‚Brillenschlange‘ f; ~ flush s. Poker: unvollständige Hand; '~,flush·er s. Am. Bluffer m, ‚falscher Fuffziger‘; '~-fold adj. u. adv. vierfach; ,~-'four (time) s.

♩ Vier'vierteltakt *m*; ,~-'**hand·ed** *adj.*
♩, *zo.* vierhändig; ⚹ **Hun·dred** *s.*: *the ~
Am.* die Hautevolee (*e-r Gemeinde*);
,~-**in-'hand** [-ɔːrɪn-] *s.* **1.** Vierspänner
m; **2.** Viergespann *n*; '~-,**leaf(ed) clover** *s.* ♣ vierblätt(e)riges Kleeblatt; '~-
-**legged** *adj.* vierbeinig; '~-,**let·ter
word** *s.* unanständiges Wort; ,~-'**oar**
[-ɔːrɔ:] *s.* Vierer *m* (*Boot*); '~-**part** *adj.*
♩ vierstimmig (*Satz*); '~-**pence** [-pəns]
s. Brit. hist. Vierpencestück *n*; '~-**plex**
[-pleks] *s. Am.* 'Vierfamilienhaus *n*; ,~-
-'**post·er** *s.* **1.** Himmelbett *n*; **2.** ⚓ *sl.*
Viermaster *m*; ,~-'**score** *adj. obs.* achtzig; '~-,**seat·er** *s. mot.* Viersitzer *m*;
'~-**some** [-səm] *s. Golf:* Vierer *m*; *fig.
humor.* ,Quar'tett' *n*; ,~-'**speed gear**
s. ⚙ Vierganggetriebe *m*; ,~-'**square**
adj. u. adv. **1.** qua'dratisch; **2.** *fig.* a)
fest, unerschütterlich, b) grob, barsch;
'~-**star** *I s. Brit.* 'Super(ben,zin) *n*; **II**
adj. Viersterne...: ~ *general*; ~ *hotel*;
~ *petrol Brit.* → I; '~-**stroke** *adj.*: ~
engine ⚙ Viertaktmotor *m*.

four·teen [,fɔː'tiːn] **I** *adj.* vierzehn; **II** *s.*
Vierzehn *f*; ,**four'teenth** [-nθ] **I** *adj.*
vierzehnt; **II** *s.* a) (*der, die, das*) Vierzehnte, b) Vierzehntel *n*.

fourth [fɔːθ] **I** *adj.* □ **1.** viert; **2.** viertel;
II *s.* **3.** (*der, die, das*) Vierte; **4.** Viertel
n; **5.** ♩ Quarte *f*; **6.** *the* ⚹ (*of July*) *Am.*
der Vierte (Juli), der Unabhängigkeits-
tag; '**fourth·ly** [-lɪ] *adv.* viertens.

,**four·'way** *adj.*: ~ *switch* ⚡ Vier-
fach-, Vierwegeschalter *m*; ,~-'**wheel**
adj. vierräd(e)rig; Vierrad...(-*antrieb*,
-*bremse*): ~ *drive* a) Vierradantrieb *m*,
b) Geländefahrzeug *n*.

fowl [faʊl] **I** *pl.* **fowls**, *coll. mst* **fowl** *s.*
1. Haushuhn *n od.* -ente *f*, *a.* Truthahn
m; *coll.* Geflügel *n* (*a. Fleisch*), Hühner
pl.: ~ *house* Hühnerstall *m*; ~ *pest* Hüh-
nerpest *f*; ~ *pox* Geflügelpocken *pl*; ~
run Hühnerhof *m*, Auslauf *m*; **2.** *selten*
Vogel *m*, Vögel *pl.*: *the* ~(*s*) *of the air
bibl.* die Vögel unter dem Himmel; **II** *v/i.*
3. Vögel fangen *od.* schießen; '**fowl·er**
[-lə] *s.* Vogelfänger *m*; '**fowl·ing** [-lɪŋ]
s. Vogelfang *m*, -jagd *f*: ~ *piece* Vogel-
flinte *f*; ~ *shot* Hühnerschrot *n*.

fox [fɒks] **I** *s.* **1.** *zo.* Fuchs *m*: *set the* ~
to keep the geese den Bock zum
Gärtner machen; ~ *and geese* Wolf u.
Schafe (*ein Brettspiel*); **2.** (*sly old*) ~
fig. (schlauer) Fuchs; **3.** Fuchspelz(kragen) *m*; **II** *v/t.* **4.** *sl.* über'listen, ,reinle-
gen'; **III** *v/i.* **5.** stockfleckig werden
(*Papier*); ~ *brush s. hunt.* Lunte *f*,
Fuchsschwanz *m*; '~-**glove** *s.* ♣ Fingerhut *m*; '~-**hole** *s.* **1.** Fuchsbau *m*; **2.** ✕
Schützenloch *n*; ~ *hunt*, '~-,**hunt·ing**
s. Fuchsjagd *f*; ~ *mark s.* Stockfleck *m*;
'~-**tail** *s.* **1.** Fuchsschwanz *m*; **2.** ♣
Fuchsschwanzgras *m*; ~ *ter·ri·er s. zo.*
Foxterrier *m*; '~-**trot** *s. u. v/i.* Foxtrott
m (tanzen).

fox·y ['fɒksɪ] *adj.* **1.** gerissen, listig; **2.**
fuchsrot; **3.** stockfleckig (*Papier*).

foy·er ['fɒɪeɪ] (*Fr.*) *s. allg.* Fo'yer *n*.

fra·cas ['fræːkɑː] *pl.* ~ [-kɑːz] *s.* Aufruhr
m, Spek'takel *m*.

frac·tion ['frækʃn] *s.* **1.** ♣ Bruch *m*: ~
bar, ~ *line*, ~ *stroke* Bruchstrich *m*; **2.**
Bruchteil *m*, Frag'ment *n*; Stückchen *n*,
ein bisschen: *not by a* ~ nicht im Geringsten; *by a* ~ *of an inch* um ein Haar; ~
of a share ✝ Teilaktie *f*; **3.** *eccl.*
Brechen *m* des Brotes; '**frac·tion·al**
[-ʃnl] *adj.* **1.** a. ♣ Bruch..., gebrochen: ~ *amount* Teilbetrag *m*; ~ *currency* Scheidemünze *f*; ~ *part* Bruchteil *m*; **2.** *fig.* unbedeutend, mini'mal;
3. 🜂 fraktioniert, teilweise; '**frac·tion-**

ar·y [-ʃnərɪ] *adj.* Bruch(stück)...,
Teil...; '**frac·tion·ate** [-ʃəneɪt] *v/t.* 🜂
fraktionieren.

frac·tious ['frækʃəs] *adj.* □ **1.** mürrisch,
zänkisch, reizbar; **2.** störrisch; '**frac-
tious·ness** [-nɪs] *s.* **1.** Reizbarkeit *f*; **2.**
'Widerspenstigkeit *f*.

frac·ture ['fræktʃə] **I** *s.* **1.** ♣ Frak'tur *f*,
Bruch *m* (*a. fig.*); **2.** *min.* Bruchfläche
f; **3.** *ling.* Brechung *f*; **II** *v/t.* **4.** (zer)bre-
chen: ~ *one's arm* sich den Arm bre-
chen; ~*d skull* Schädelbruch *m*; **III** *v/i.*
5. (zer)brechen.

frag·ile ['frædʒaɪl] *adj.* **1.** zerbrechlich
(*a. fig.*); **2.** ⚙ brüchig; **3.** *fig.* schwach,
zart (*Gesundheit etc.*), gebrechlich
(*Person*); **fra·gil·i·ty** [frə'dʒɪlətɪ] *s.* **1.**
Zerbrechlichkeit *f*; **2.** Brüchigkeit *f*; **3.**
fig. Ge-, Zerbrechlichkeit *f*, Zartheit *f*.

frag·ment ['frægmənt] *s.* **1.** Bruchstück
n (*a.* ⚙), -teil *m*; **2.** Stück *n*, Brocken
m, Splitter *m* (*a.* ✕), Fetzen *m*; 'Überrest *m*; **3.** (lite'rarisches *etc.*) Frag-
'ment; **frag·men·tal** [fræg'mentl] *adj.*
1. *geol.* Trümmer...; **2.** → '**frag·men-
tar·y** [-tərɪ] *adj.* **1.** zerstückelt, aus
Stücken bestehend; **2.** fragmen'tarisch,
unvollständig, bruchstückhaft; **frag-
men·ta·tion** [,frægmen'teɪʃn] *s.* Zerstückelung *f*, -splitterung *f*: ~ *bomb* ✕
Splitterbombe *f*.

fra·grance ['freɪgrəns] *s.* Wohlgeruch
m, Duft *m*, A'roma *n*; '**fra·grant** [-nt]
adj. □ **1.** wohlriechend, duftend: *be* ~
with a) duften nach, b) *fig.* angenehm,
köstlich.

frail [freɪl] *adj.* □ **1.** zerbrechlich; **2.** a)
zart, schwach, b) gebrechlich, c) (*charakterlich*) schwach, d) schwach, seicht
(*Buch etc.*); '**frail·ty** [-tɪ] *s.* **1.** Zerbrechlichkeit *f*; **2.** a) Zartheit *f*, b) Gebrechlichkeit *f*; **3.** a) Schwachheit *f*,
(mo'ralische) Schwäche, b) Fehltritt *m*.

fraise [freɪz] *s.* **1.** ✕ Pali'sade *f*; **2.** ⚙
Bohrfräse *f*.

fram·b(o)e·si·a [fræm'biːzɪə] *s.* ♣
Frambö'sie *f* (*tropische Hautkrankheit*).

frame [freɪm] **I** *s.* **1.** (*Bilder-, Fenster-
etc.*)Rahmen *m* (*a.* ⚙, *mot.*): ~ *aerial*
Rahmenantenne *f*; **2.** (*a. Brillen-,
Schirm-, Wagen*)Gestell *n*, Gerüst *n*; **3.**
Einfassung *f*; **4.** △ a) Balkenwerk *n*: ~
house Holz- *od.* Fachwerkhaus *n*, b)
Geripe *n*, Ske'lett *n*: *steel* ~; **5.** *typ.*
('Setz)Re,gal *n*; **6.** ⚡ Stator *m*; **7.** ⚓, ⚓
a) Spant *n*, *m*, b) Gerippe *n*; **8.** *TV* a)
Abtastfeld *n*, b) Raster(bild *n*) *m*; **9.**
Film: Einzelbild *n*; **10.** *Comic strips:*
Bild *n*; **11.** ♪ verglaster Treibbeetkas-
ten; **12.** *Weberei:* ('Spinn-, 'Web)Ma-
,schine *f*; **13.** a) Rahmen(erzählung *f*)
m, b) 'Hintergrund *m*; **14.** Körper(bau)
m, Fi'gur *f*: *the mortal* ~ die sterbliche
Hülle; **15.** *fig.* Rahmen *m*, Sy'stem *n*:
within the ~ *of* im Rahmen (*gen.*); **16.**
bsd. ~ *of mind* (Gemüts)Verfassung *f*,
(-)Zustand *m*, Stimmung *f*; **17.** →
frame-up; **II** *v/t.* **18.** zs.-fügen, -set-
zen; **19.** a) *Bild etc.* (ein)rahmen,
(-)fassen, b) *fig.* um'rahmen; **20.** *et.* ersinnen, entwerfen, *Plan* schmieden,
Gedicht etc. machen, verfertigen, *Politik etc.* abstecken; **21.** *Worte, a. Entschuldigung etc.* formulieren; **22.** gestalten, formen, bilden; **23.** anpassen
(*to dat.*); **24.** *a.* ~ *up sl.* a) *et.* ,drehen',
,schaukeln', b) *j-m et.* ,anhängen',
,reinhängen': *a match* ein Spiel (vorher) absprechen; **framed** [-md] *adj.* **1.**
gerahmt; **2.** △ Fachwerk...; **3.** ⚓, ⚓ in
Spanten; '**fram·er** [-mə] *s.* **1.** (Bilder-)
Rahmer *m*; **2.** *fig.* Gestalter *m*, Entwerfer *m*.

frame| saw *s.* ⚙ Spannsäge *f*; ~ **sto·ry**,
~ **tale** *s.* Rahmenerzählung *f*; ~ **tent** *s.*
Steilwandzelt *n*; '~-**up** *s.* **F 1.** Kom'plott
n, In'trige *f*, Falle *f*; **2.** abgekartetes
Spiel, Schwindel *m*; '~-**work** *s.* **1.** ⚙, *a.*
♪ *u. biol.* Gerüst *n*, Gerippe *n*; **2.** △
Fachwerk *n*, Gebälk *n*; **3.** 🪑 Gestell *n*;
4. *fig.* Rahmen *m*, Gefüge *n*, Sy'stem *n*:
within the ~ *of* im Rahmen (*gen.*).

franc [fræŋk] *s.* **1.** Franc *m* (*Währungseinheit Frankreichs etc.*); **2.** Franken *m*
(*Währungseinheit der Schweiz*).

fran·chise ['fræntʃaɪz] *s.* **1.** *pol.* a)
Wahl-, Stimmrecht *n*, b) Bürgerrecht(e
pl.) *n*; **2.** *Am.* Privi'leg *n*; **3.** *hist.* Ge-
rechtsame *f*; **4.** ✝ *bsd. Am.* a) *a. sport*
Konzessi'on *f*, b) Al'leinverkaufsrecht
n, c) 'Rechtsper,sönlichkeit *f*, d) Fran-
chise *n*, Franchising *n* (*Vertriebsart*); **5.**
Versicherung: Fran'chise *f*.

Fran·cis·can [fræn'sɪskən] **I** *s.* Franzis-
'kaner(mönch) *m*; **II** *adj.* Franziskaner...

Fran·co-Ger·man [,fræŋkəʊ'dʒɜːmən]
adj.: the ~ *War* der Deutsch-Französische Krieg (*1870/71*).

Fran·co·ni·an [fræŋ'kəʊnjən] *adj.* fränkisch.

Fran·co|·phile ['fræŋkəʊfaɪl], '~-**phil**
[-fɪl] **I** *s.* Franko'phile *m*, Fran'zosenfreund *m*; **II** *adj.* franko'phil; '~-**phobe**
[-fəʊb] **I** *s.* Fran'zosenhasser *m*, -feind
m; **II** *adj.* fran'zosenfeindlich.

fran·gi·ble ['frændʒɪbl] *adj.* zerbrechlich.

fran·gi·pane ['frændʒɪpeɪn] *s. Art* Man-
delcreme *f*.

Fran·glais ['frɑ̃ːŋgleɪ] (*Fr.*) *s.* stark ang-
lisiertes Französisch.

Frank[1] [fræŋk] *s. hist.* Franke *m*.

frank[2] [fræŋk] **I** *adj.* □ → **frankly**; **1.**
offen, aufrichtig, frei(mütig); **II** *s.* **2.** ♺
hist. a) Freivermerk *m*, b) Portofreiheit
f; **III** *v/t.* **3.** *Brief* (*a.* mit der Ma'schine)
frankieren; *~ing machine* Frankierma-
schine *f*; **4.** *j-m* (freien) Zutritt verschaffen; **5.** *et.* amtlich freigeben.

frank[3] [fræŋk] *Am.* **F** *für* **frank·furt·er**
['fræŋkfɜːtə] *s.* Frankfurter (Würstchen
n) *f*.

frank·in·cense ['fræŋkɪn,sens] *s.* Weihrauch *m*.

Frank·ish ['fræŋkɪʃ] *adj. hist.* fränkisch.

frank·lin ['fræŋklɪn] *s. hist.* **1.** Freisasse
m; **2.** kleiner Landbesitzer.

frank·ly ['fræŋklɪ] *adv.* **1.** → **frank**[2]; **2.**
frei her'aus, frank u. frei; **3.** *a.* ~
speaking offen gestanden *od.* gesagt;
'**frank·ness** [-nɪs] *s.* Offenheit *f*, Freimütigkeit *f*.

fran·tic ['fræntɪk] *adj.* □ (*mst* ~*ally*) **1.**
wild, außer sich, rasend (*with* vor *dat.*);
wütend; **2.** verzweifelt: ~ *efforts*; **3.**
hektisch: *a* ~ *search*.

frap·pé ['fræpeɪ] (*Fr.*) *adj.* eisgekühlt;
II *s.* Frap'pee *m* (*Getränk*).

frat [fræt] *sl.* → **fraternity** 3.

fra·ter·nal [frə'tɜːnl] **I** *adj.* □ **1.** brüderlich, Bruder...; **2.** *biol.* zweieiig: ~
twins; **II** *s.* **3.** *a.* ~ *association*, ~ *society Am.* Verein *m* zur Förderung gemeinsamer Interessen; **fra'ter·ni·ty**
[-nətɪ] *s.* **1.** Brüderlichkeit *f*; **2.** Vereinigung *f*, Zunft *f*, Gilde *f*: *the angling* ~
die Zunft der Angler; *the legal* ~ die
Juristen *pl.*; **3.** *Am.* Stu'dentenverbin-
dung *f*; **frat·er·ni·za·tion** [,frætənaɪ-
'zeɪʃn] *s.* Verbrüderung *f*; '**frat·er·nize**
['frætənaɪz] *v/i.* sich verbrüdern, *bsd.*
✕ fraternisieren.

frat·ri·cid·al [,frætrɪ'saɪdl] *adj.* bruder-
mörderisch: ~ *war* Bruderkrieg *m*; '**frat-
ri·cide** ['frætrɪsaɪd] *s.* **1.** Bruder-, Ge-

F

schwistermord *m*; **2.** Bruder-, Geschwistermörder *m*.

fraud [frɔːd] *s.* **1.** ⚖ Betrug *m*, arglistige Täuschung: *by ~* arglistig; *obtain by ~* sich *et.* erschleichen; **~ department** Betrugsdezernat *n*; **2.** Schwindel *m*; **3.** F a) Schwindler *m*, ‚falscher Fuffziger', b) ‚Schauspieler' *m*, j-d, der nicht ‚echt' ist; **'fraud·u·lence** [-djʊləns] *s.* Betrüge'rei *f*; **'fraud·u·lent** [-djʊlənt] *adj.* □ betrügerisch, arglistig: **~ bankruptcy** betrügerischer Bankrott; **~ conversion** Unterschlagung *f*; **~ preference** Gläubigerbegünstigung *f*; **~ representation** Vorspiegelung *f* falscher Tatsachen; **~ transaction** Schwindelgeschäft *n*.

fraught [frɔːt] *adj. mst fig.* (**with**) voll (von), beladen (mit): **~ with danger** gefahrvoll; **~ with meaning** bedeutungsschwer, -schwanger; **~ with sorrow** kummerbeladen; **2.** F a) schlimm, b) ‚schwer im Druck'.

fray¹ [freɪ] *s.* **1.** (lauter) Streit; **2.** a) Schläge'rei *f*, b) ✗ *u. fig.* Kampf *m*: *eager for the ~* kampflustig.

fray² [freɪ] **I** *v/t.* **1.** a. **~ out** Stoff *etc.* abtragen, 'durchscheuern, ausfransen, *a. fig.* abnutzen: **~ed nerves** strapazierte Nerven; **~ed at the edges** *fig.* sehr mitgenommen; **~ed temper** *fig.* gereizte Stimmung; **2.** Geweih fegen; **II** *v/i.* **3.** *a.* **~ out** sich abnutzen (*a. fig.*), sich ausfransen *od.* 'durchscheuern; **4.** *fig.* sich ereifern: **tempers began to ~** die Stimmung wurde gereizt.

fraz·zle ['fræzl] **I** *v/t.* **1.** ausfransen; **2.** *oft* **~ out** F *j-n* fix u. fertig' machen; **II** *v/i.* **3.** sich ausfransen *od.* 'durchscheuern; **III** *s.* **4.** Franse *f*: **worn to a ~** F ‚fix u. fertig'; **work o.s. to a ~** F sich ‚kaputtmachen' (vor Arbeit); **burnt to a ~** total verkohlt.

freak [friːk] **I** *s.* **1.** 'Missbildung *f*, (*Mensch, Tier*) *a.* 'Missgeburt *f*, Monstrosi'tät *f*: **~ of nature** Laune *f* der Natur, *contp.* Monstrum *n*; **~ show** Monstrositätenkabinett *n*; **2.** Grille *f*, Laune *f*; **3.** ‚verrückte' *od.* ‚irre' Sache; **4.** *sl.* ‚Freak' *m*: a) ‚irrer Typ', *contp.* ‚Ausgeflippte(r' *m*) *f*, ‚Spinner' *m*, b) (*Jazz-, Computer- etc.*) Narr *m*, c) Süchtige(r *m*) *f*: **pill ~**; **II** *adj.* **5.** → **freakish**; **III** *v/i.* **6.** *a.* **~ out** *sl.* ‚ausflippen' (*Süchtiger, a. allg. fig.*); **IV** *v/t.* **7.** *sl. j-n* ‚ausflippen' lassen; **'freak·ish** [-kɪʃ] *adj.* □ **1.** launisch, unberechenbar (*Wetter etc.*); **2.** ‚verrückt', ‚irr'; **'freak·out** *s. sl.* **1.** ‚Horrortrip' *m*; **2.** ‚Ausflippen' *n*; **'freak·y** *adj.* F **1.** unheimlich; **2.** ‚schräg', irre.

freck·le ['frekl] **I** *s.* **1.** Sommersprosse *f*; **2.** Fleck(chen *n*) *m*; **II** *v/t.* **3.** tüpfeln, sprenkeln; **III** *v/i.* **4.** Sommersprossen bekommen; **'freck·led** [-ld] *adj.* sommersprossig.

free [friː] **I** *adj.* □ (→ *a.* 18) **1.** frei: a) unabhängig, b) selbstständig, c) ungebunden, d) ungehindert, e) uneingeschränkt, f) in Freiheit (befindlich): *a ~ man*; *the ☾ World*; **~ elections**; *you are ~ to go* es steht dir frei zu gehen; *it's* (*od. this is*) *a ~ country* F hier kann jeder tun u. lassen, was er will: *'Mind if I sit here?' – 'It's a ~ country'* ‚Darf ich mich hierher setzen?' – ‚Ich kann Sie *od.* dich nicht daran hindern'; **2.** frei: a) *unbeschäftigt*: *I am ~ after 5 o'clock*, b) ohne Verpflichtungen: *a ~ evening*, c) nicht besetzt: *this room is ~*; **3.** frei: a) *nicht wörtlich*: *a ~ translation*, b) nicht an Regeln gebunden: *a ~ verse*; **~ skating** *sport* Kür(laufen *n*) *f*, c) frei gestaltet: *a ~ version*; **4.** (**from**,

of) frei (von), ohne (*acc.*): **~ from error** fehlerfrei; **~ from infection** frei von ansteckenden Krankheiten; **~ from pain** schmerzfrei; **~ of debt** schuldenfrei; **~ and unencumbered** ⚖ unbelastet, hypothekenfrei; **~ of taxes** steuerfrei; **5.** 🏦 frei, nicht gebunden; **6.** frei, los(e); **7.** frei, unbefangen, ungezwungen: **~ manners**; **8.** a) offen(herzig), freimütig, b) unverblümt, c) unverschämt: *make ~ with* sich Freiheiten herausnehmen gegen *j-n*; **9.** allzu frei, unanständig: **~ talk**; **10.** freigebig, großzügig: *be ~ with s.th.*; **11.** leicht, flott, zügig; **12.** (kosten-, gebühren-) frei, kostenlos, unentgeltlich, gratis, zum Nulltarif: **~ copy** Freiexemplar *n*; **~ fares** Nulltarif *m*; **~ gift** ✝ Zugabe *f*, Gratisprobe *f*; **~ ticket** a) Freikarte *f*, b) Freifahrschein *m*; **13.** ✝ frei (*Klausel*): **~ on board** frei an Bord; **~ on rail** frei Waggon; **~ domicile** frei Haus; **14.** ✝ frei verfügbar: **~ assets**; **15.** öffentlich: **~ library** Volksbibliothek *f*; *be* (*made*) **~ of s.th.** freien Zutritt zu et. haben; **16.** willig, bereit; **17.** *Turnen:* ohne Geräte: **~ gymnastics** Freiübungen; **II** *adv.* **18.** *allg.* frei (→ I): *go ~* frei ausgehen; *run ~* ⊖ leer laufen (*Maschine*); **III** *v/t.* **19.** *a. fig.* befreien (*from* von, aus); **20.** freilassen; **21.** entlasten (*from, of* von).

free| **ar·e·a** *s. fig.* Freiraum *m*; **~ back** *s. sport* Libero *m*; **'~·bee, '~·bie** [-biː] *s.* F ('Gratis)Geschenk *n*: *get s.th. as a ~* et. gratis bekommen; **'~·board** *s.* ⚓ Freibord *m*; **'~·boot·er** *s.* Freibeuter *m*; **☾ Church** *s.* Freikirche *f*; **'~·cut·ting** *adj.*: **~ steel** ⊖ Automatenstahl *m*.

freed·man ['friːdmæn] *s.* [*irr.*] Freigelassene(r) *m*.

free·dom ['friːdəm] *s.* **1.** a) Freiheit *f*, b) Unabhängigkeit *f*: **~ of the press** Pressefreiheit; **~ of the seas** Freiheit der Meere; **~ of the city** (*od. town*) Ehrenbürgerrecht *n*; **~ from taxation** Steuerfreiheit; **~ fighter** Freiheitskämpfer (-in); **2.** freier Zutritt, freie Benutzung; **3.** Freimütigkeit *f*, Offenheit *f*; **4.** Zwanglosigkeit *f*; **5.** Aufdringlichkeit *f*, (plumpe) Vertraulichkeit; **6.** *phls.* Willensfreiheit *f*, Selbstbestimmung *f*.

free| **en·er·gy** *s. phys.* freie *od.* ungebundene Ener'gie; **~ en·ter·prise** *s.* freies Unter'nehmertum *f*; **~ fall** *s.* ✈ *phys.* freier Fall; **~ fight** *s.* ('Massen-) Schläge'rei *f*; **'~·fone** *s.* gebührenfreies Telefo'nieren: *call us on ~ ...* rufen Sie uns gebührenfrei unter ... an; **~ number** gebührenfreie Tele'fonnummer; **'~·for·all** [-ər,ɔːl] F **1.** → *free fight*; **2.** wildes ‚Gerangel'; **~ hand** *s.*: *give s.o. a ~* j-m freie Hand lassen; **'~·hand** *adj.* **1.** Freihand..., freihändig: **~ drawing**; **2.** *fig.* a) frei, b) ausschweifend; **'~·hand·ed** *adj.* **1.** freigebig, großzügig; **2.** → **freehand**; **'~·heart·ed** *adj.* **1.** freimütig, offen (-herzig); **2.** → **freehanded**; **'~·hold** *s.* (volles) Eigentumsrecht an Grundbesitz; **~ flat** *Brit.* Eigentumswohnung *f*; **'~·hold·er** *s.* Grund- u. Hauseigentümer *m*; **~ kick** *s. Fußball:* Freistoß *m*: (**in**)**direct ~**; **la·bo(u)r** *s.* nicht organisierte Arbeiter(schaft *f*) *pl.*; **'~·lance I** *s.* **1.** a) freier Schriftsteller *od.* Journa'list (*etc.*), Freiberufler *m*; freischaffender Künstler, b) freier Mitarbeiter; **2.** *pol.* Unabhängige(r) *m*, Par'teilose(r) *m*; **II** *adj.* **3.** freiberuflich (tätig), freischaffend; **III** *v/i.* **4.** freiberuflich tätig sein; **'~·lanc·er** → **freelance** 1; **~ list** *s.* **1.** Liste *f* zollfreier Ar'tikel; **2.** Liste *f* der

Empfänger von 'Freikarten *od.* -exem,plaren; **~ liv·er** *s.* Schlemmer *m*, Genießer *m*; **'~·load·er** *s.* F ‚Schnorrer(in)', Schmarotzer(in) *m*; **~ love** *s.* freie Liebe; **~ man** *s.* [*irr.*] *Fußball:* freier Mann, Libero *m*; **'~·man** *s.* [*irr.*] **1.** [-mæn] freier Mann; **2.** [-mən] (Ehren)Bürger *m* (*Stadt*); **~ mar·ket** *s.* ✝ **1.** freier Markt; **2.** *Börse:* Freiverkehr *m*; **'☾·ma·son** *s.* Freimaurer *m*: **~s' lodge** Freimaurerloge *f*; **'☾·ma·son·ry** *s.* **1.** Freimaure'rei *f*; **2.** *fig.* Zs.-gehörigkeitsgefühl *n*; **'~·phone** *s.* → **freefone**; **~ play** *s.* **1.** ⊖ Spiel *n*; **2.** *fig.* freie Hand; **~ port** *s.* Freihafen *m*; **'~·post** *s. Brit. Teil e-r Adresse:* etwa Gebühr zahlt Empfänger; **'~·range** *adj.*: **~ hens** Freilandhühner; **~ rid·er** → **freeloader**; **~ share** *s.* ✝ Freiaktie *f*.

free·si·a ['friːzjə] *s.* ⚘ Freesie *f*.

free| **speech** *s.* Redefreiheit *f*; **'~·spoken** *adj.* offen, freimütig; **'~·standing** *adj.*: **~ exercises** Freiübungen *pl.*; **~ sculpture** Freiplastik *f*; **~ state** *s.* Freistaat *m*; **'~·style** *sport* **I** *s.* Freistil (-schwimmen *n etc.*) *m*; **II** *adj.* Freistil..., Kür...: **~ skating** Kür(laufen *n*) *f*; **'~·think·er** *s.* Freidenker *m*, Freigeist *m*; **'~·think·ing** *adj.* **~ thought** *s.* Freidenke'rei *f*, -geiste'rei *f*; **~ throw** *s. Basketball:* Freiwurf *m*; **'~·trade a·re·a** *s.* Freihandelszone *f*; **'~·trad·er** *s.* Anhänger *m* des Freihandels; **~ vote** *s. parl.* Abstimmung *f* ohne Frakti'onszwang; **'~·ware** *s. Computer:* 'Freeware *f* (*kostenlos erhältliche*[*s*] *Computerprogramm*[*e pl.*]); **'~·way** *s. Am.* gebührenfreie Schnellstraße; **'~·wheel** ⊖ **I** *s.* Freilauf *m*; **II** *v/i.* im Freilauf fahren; **'~·wheel·ing** *adj.* F **1.** sorglos; **2.** frei u. ungebunden; **~ will** *s.* freier Wille, Willensfreiheit *f*.

freeze [friːz] **I** *v/i.* [*irr.*] → **frozen**; **1.** frieren (*a. impers.*): *it is freezing hard* es friert stark; *I am freezing* mir ist eiskalt; **~ to death** erfrieren; **2.** gefrieren; **3.** *a.* **~ up** (*od. over*) ein-, zufrieren, vereisen; **4.** an-, festfrieren: **~ on to** *sl.* sich wie eine Klette an *j-n* heften; **5.** (*vor Kälte, fig. vor Schreck etc.*) erstarren, eisig werden (*Person, Gesicht*): *it made my blood ~* es ließ mir das Blut in den Adern erstarren; **~!** *sl.* keine Bewegung!; **6.** **~ up** *Computer:* ‚abstürzen'; **II** *v/t.* [*irr.*] **7.** zum Gefrieren bringen: *I was frozen* mir war eiskalt; **8.** erfrieren lassen; **9.** *Fleisch etc.* einfrieren, tiefkühlen; ✚ vereisen; **10.** *a. fig.* erstarren lassen, *fig. a.* lähmen: **~ out** F *j-n* hinausekeln, kaltstellen; **11.** ✝ *Guthaben etc.* sperren, *a. Preise etc., pol.* diplomatische Beziehungen einfrieren: **~ prices** (**wages**) *a.* e-n Preis- (Lohn)stopp einführen; **12.** **~ up** *Computer:* zum Absturz bringen; **III** *s.* **13.** Gefrieren *n*; **14.** Erstarrung *f*; **15.** 'Frost(peri,ode *f*) *m*, Kälte(welle) *f*; **16.** ✝ *pol.* Einfrieren *n*, ✝ *a.* (Preis-, Lohn)Stopp *m*: **~ on wages**; *put a ~ on* → 10; **'~·dry** *v/t.* gefriertrocknen; **~ dry·er** *s.* Gefriertrockner *m*.

freez·er ['friːzə] *s.* **1.** Ge'frierma,schine *f od.* -kammer *f*; **2.** Tiefkühlgerät *n*; **3.** Gefrierfach *n* (*Kühlschrank*); **'freeze-up** *s.* **1.** starker Frost; **2.** Com'puterabsturz *m*, F -crash *m*; **'freez·ing** [-zɪŋ] **I** *adj.* □ **1.** ⊖ Gefrier..., Kälte...: **~ compartment** → *freezer* 3; **below ~ point** unter dem Gefrierpunkt, unter null; **2.** eisig; **3.** kalt, unnahbar; **II** *s.* **4.** Einfrieren *n* (*a.* ✝, *pol.*); **5.** *a.* ✚ Vereisung *f*; **6.** Erstarrung *f*.

freight [freɪt] **I** s. **1.** Fracht f, Beförderung f; **2.** ♺ (Am. a. ✈, 🚂, mot.) Fracht(gut n) f, Ladung f: ~ **and carriage** Brit. See- und Landfracht; **3.** Fracht(gebühr) f: ~ **forward** Fracht gegen Nachnahme; **4.** Am. → **freight train**; **II** v/t. **5.** Schiff, Am. a. Güterwagen etc. befrachten, beladen; **6.** Güter verfrachten; **'freight·age** [-tɪdʒ] s. **1.** Trans'port m; **2.** → freight 2, 3.

freight| bill s. ✝ Am. Frachtbrief m; ~ **car** s. Am. Güterwagen m.

freight·er [freɪt-] s. **1.** a) Frachtschiff n, Frachter m, b) Trans'portflugzeug n; **2.** a) Befrachter m, Reeder m, b) Ab-, Verlader m.

'freight|·lin·er s. Brit. Con'tainerzug m; ~ **rate** s. ✝ Frachtsatz m; ~ **sta·tion** s. Am. Güterbahnhof m; ~ **train** s. Am. Güterzug m.

French [frentʃ] **I** adj. **1.** fran'zösisch: ~ **master** Französischlehrer; **II** s. **2.** the ~ die Franzosen pl.; **3.** ling. Fran'zösisch n: in ~ a) auf Französisch, b) im Französischen; ~ **beans** grüne Bohnen pl.; ~ **Ca·na·di·an I** s. **1.** 'Frankoka,nadier(in); **2.** ling. ka'nadisches Fran'zösisch; **II** adj. **3.** 'frankoka-,nadisch; ~ **chalk** s. Schneiderkreide f; ~ **doors** Am. → French windows; ~ **dress·ing** s. French Dressing n (Salatsoße aus Öl, Essig, Senf u. Gewürzen); ~ **fried po·ta·toes**, F ~ **fries** [fraɪz] s. pl. Am. Pommes 'frites pl.; ~ **horn** s. ♪ (Wald)Horn n; ~ **kiss** Zungenkuss m; ~ **leave** s.: take ~ sich auf Französisch empfehlen, sich französisch empfehlen; ~ **let·ter** s. F 'Pa'riser' m (Kondom); ~ **loaf** s. [irr.] Ba'guette f; '~·man [-mən] s. [irr.] Fran'zose m; ~ **mar·i·gold** s. ♀ Stu'dentenblume f; ~ **pol·ish** s. Schellackpoli,tur f; ~ **roof** s. △ Man'sardendach n; ~ **win·dows** s. pl. Ter'rassen-, Bal'kontür f; '~·wom·an s. [irr.] Fran'zösin f.

fre·net·ic [frə'netɪk] adj. (□ ~ally) → frenzied.

fren·zied ['frenzɪd] adj. **1.** fre'netisch (Geschrei etc.), rasend: ~ applause; **2.** a) außer sich, rasend (with vor dat.), b) wild, hektisch; **fren·zy** ['frenzɪ] **I** s. **1.** Wahnsinn m, Rase'rei f: in a ~ of hate rasend vor Hass; **2.** wilde Aufregung; **3.** Verzückung f, Ek'stase f; **4.** Wirbel m, Hektik f; **II** v/t. **5.** rasend machen.

fre·quen·cy ['fri:kwənsɪ] s. **1.** Häufigkeit f (a. ♻, biol.); **2.** phys. Fre'quenz f, Schwingungszahl f: high ~ Hochfrequenz; ~ **band** s. ⚡ Fre'quenzband n; ~ **chang·er** s. ⚡ con·vert·er s. ⚡, phys. Fre'quenzwandler m; ~ **curve** s. ♻, biol. Häufigkeitskurve f; ~ **mod·u·la·tion** s. phys. Fre'quenzmodulati,on f; ~ **range** s. phys. Frequenzbereich m.

fre·quent I adj. ['fri:kwənt] □ → frequently; **1.** häufig, (häufig) wieder-'holt: be ~ häufig vorkommen; he is a ~ visitor er kommt häufig zu Besuch; **2.** ⚕ beschleunigt (Puls); **II** v/t. [frɪ'kwent] **3.** häufig od. oft be-, aufsuchen, frequentieren; **fre·quen·ta·tive** [frɪ'kwentətɪv] ling. **I** adj. frequenta'tiv; **II** s. Frequenta'tiv(um) n; **fre·quent·er** [frɪ'kwentə] s. (fleißiger) Besucher, Stammgast m; **'fre·quent·ly** [-lɪ] adv. oft, häufig.

fres·co ['freskəʊ] **I** pl. **-cos, -coes** s. a) 'Freskomale,rei f, b) Fresko(gemälde n) n; **II** v/t. in Fresko (be)malen.

fresh [freʃ] **I** adj. □ (→ a. 8); **1.** allg. frisch; **2.** neu: ~ evidence; ~ news; ~

arrival Neuankömmling m; make a ~ start neu anfangen; take a ~ look at et. noch einmal od. von e-r anderen Seite betrachten; **3.** frisch: a) zusätzlich: ~ supplies, b) nicht alt: ~ eggs, c) nicht eingemacht: ~ vegetables a. Frischgemüse n; ~ meat Frischfleisch n; ~ herrings grüne Heringe, d) sauber, rein: ~ shirt; **4.** frisch: a) blühend, gesund: ~ complexion, b) ausgeruht, erholt: (as) ~ as a daisy quicklebendig; **5.** frisch: a) unverbraucht, b) erfrischend, c) kräftig: ~ wind, d) kühl; **6.** fig. ,grün', unerfahren; **7.** F frech, ,pampig': don't get ~ with me! werd (mir) ja nicht frech!; **II** adv. **8.** frisch: ~ from frisch od. direkt von od. aus; **III** s. **9.** Frische f, Kühle f: ~ of the day der Tagesanfang; **10.** → freshet.

fresh-'air fiend s. F 'Frischluftfa,natiker(in), -,postel m.

fresh·en ['freʃn] **I** v/t. a. ~ up **1.** j-n erfrischen: ~ o.s. up → 4; **2.** fig. et. auffrischen, ,aufpolieren'; **II** v/i. mst ~ up **3.** frisch werden, aufleben; **4.** sich frisch machen; **5.** auffrischen (Wind); **'fresh·er** [-ʃə] Brit. F → freshman; **'fresh·et** [-ʃɪt] s. Hochwasser n, Flut f (a. fig.); **'fresh·man** [-mən] s. [irr.] Stu'dent m im ersten Se'mester; **'fresh·ness** [-ʃnɪs] s. Frische f; Neuheit f; Unerfahrenheit f.

fresh| wa·ter s. Süßwasser n; '~·,wa·ter adj. **1.** Süßwasser...: ~ fish; **2.** Am. Provinz...: ~ college.

fret¹ [fret] s. ♪ Bund m, Griffleiste f.

fret² [fret] **I** s. △ etc. **1.** durch'brochene Verzierung; **2.** Gitterwerk n; **II** v/t. **3.** durch'brochen od. gitterförmig verzieren.

fret³ [fret] **I** v/t. **1.** ◈, 🐀 an-, zerfressen, angreifen; **2.** abnutzen, -scheuern; **3.** j-n ärgern, reizen; **II** v/i. **4.** a) sich ärgern: ~ and fume vor Wut schäumen, b) sich Sorgen machen; **III** s. **5.** Ärger m, Verärgerung f; **'fret·ful** [-fʊl] adj. □ ärgerlich, gereizt.

fret| saw s. ◈ Laubsäge f; '~·work s. **1.** △ etc. Gitterwerk n; **2.** Laubsägearbeit f.

Freud·i·an ['frɔɪdɪən] **I** s. Freudi'aner (-in); **II** adj. freudi'anisch, freudsch: ~ slip psych. freudsche Fehlleistung.

fri·a·ble ['fraɪəbl] adj. bröck(e)lig, krümelig.

fri·ar ['fraɪə] s. eccl. (bsd. Bettel-) Mönch m: Black 2 Dominikaner m; Grey 2 Franziskaner m; White 2 Karmeliter m; **'fri·ar·y** [-ərɪ] s. Mönchskloster n.

fric·as·see ['frɪkəsiː] (Fr.) **I** s. Frikas'see n; **II** v/t. [,frɪkə'siː] frikassieren.

fric·a·tive ['frɪkətɪv] ling. **I** adj. Reibe...; **II** s. Reibelaut m.

fric·tion ['frɪkʃn] **I** s. **1.** ◈, phys. Reibung f, Frikti'on f; **2.** bsd. ⚕ Einreibung f; **3.** fig. Reibungen pl., Reibe'rei f, Spannungen pl., 'Misshelligkeit f; **II** adj. **4.** ◈, phys. Reibungs...: ~ brake; ~ clutch; ~ drive Friktionsantrieb m; ~ gear(ing) Friktionsgetriebe n; ~ match Streichholz n; ~ surface Lauffläche f; ~ tape Am. Isolierband n; **'fric·tion·al** [-ʃənl] adj. **1.** Reibungs..., Friktions...; **2.** ~ unemployment temporäre Arbeitslosigkeit; **'fric·tion·less** [-lɪs] adj. ◈ reibungsfrei, -arm.

Fri·day ['fraɪdɪ] s. Freitag m: on ~ am Freitag; on ~s freitags; → Good Friday, girl Friday.

fridge [frɪdʒ] s. F Kühlschrank m.

fried [fraɪd] adj. **1.** gebraten; → fry² 1; **2.** Am. sl. ,blau', besoffen; '~·cake s. Am. Krapfen m.

friend [frend] s. **1.** Freund(in): ~ at court ,Vetter' (einflussreicher Freund); ~ of the court ⚖ sachverständiger Beistand (des Gerichts); → next 1; be ~s with s.o. mit j-m befreundet sein; make ~s with mit j-m Freundschaft schließen; a ~ in need is a ~ indeed der wahre Freund zeigt sich erst in der Not; **2.** Bekannte(r m) f; **3.** Helfer(in), Förderer m; **4.** Hilfe f, Freund(in); **5.** Brit. a) my honourable ~ parl. mein Herr Kollege od. Vorredner (Anrede), b) my learned ~ ⚖ mein verehrter Herr Kollege; **6.** Society of 2s Gesellschaft der Freunde, die Quäker; **'friend·less** [-lɪs] adj. ohne Freunde; **'friend·li·ness** [-lɪnɪs] s. Freund-(schaft)lichkeit f; freundschaftliche Gesinnung; **'friend·ly** [-lɪ] adj. **1.** freundlich; **2.** freundschaftlich, Freundschafts...: ~ match sport Freundschaftsspiel n; a ~ nation e-e befreundete Nation; **3.** wohlwollend, -gesinnt: ~ neutrality pol. wohlwollende Neutralität; 2 Society Versicherungsverein m auf Gegenseitigkeit; ~ troops ⚔ eigene Truppen; **4.** günstig; **II** s. **5.** sport F Freundschaftsspiel n; **'friend·ship** [-ʃɪp] s. **1.** Freundschaft f; **2.** → friendliness.

fri·er → fryer.

fries [fraɪz] s. pl. bsd. Am. Pommes 'frites pl.

Frie·sian ['friːzjən] → Frisian.

frieze¹ [friːz] **I** s. **1.** △ Fries m; **2.** Zierstreifen m (Tapete etc.); **II** v/t. **3.** mit e-m Fries versehen.

frieze² [friːz] s. Fries m (Wollzeug).

frig [frɪg] V **I** v/t. ,ficken'; **II** v/i. ,wichsen'.

frig·ate ['frɪgɪt] s. ♣ Fre'gatte f.

frige [frɪdʒ] → fridge.

fright [fraɪt] **I** s. Schreck(en) m, Entsetzen n: get (od. have) a ~ erschrecken; give s.o. a ~ j-n erschrecken; take ~ a) erschrecken, b) scheuen (Pferd); get off with a ~ mit dem Schrecken davonkommen; he looked a ~ F er sah ,verboten' aus; **II** v/t. poet. → frighten; **'fright·en** [-tn] **I** v/t. **1.** a) j-n erschrecken (s.o. to death j-n zu Tode), j-m e-n Schrecken einjagen, b) j-m Angst einjagen: ~ s.o. into doing s.th. j-n so einschüchtern, dass er et. tut; I was ~ed ich erschrak od. bekam Angst (of vor dat.); **2.** ~ away vertreiben, -scheuchen; **II** v/i. **3.** he ~s easily a) er ist sehr schreckhaft, b) dem kann man leicht Angst einjagen; **'fright·ened** [-tnd] adj. erschreckt, erschrocken, verängstigt; **'fright·en·ing** [-tnɪŋ] adj. □ erschreckend; **'fright·ful** [-fʊl] adj. □ **1.** furchtbar, schrecklich, entsetzlich, grässlich, scheußlich (alle a. F fig.); **'fright·ful·ly** [-flɪ] adv. furchtbar (etc.); **'fright·ful·ness** [-fʊlnɪs] s. **1.** Schrecklichkeit f; **2.** Schreckensherrschaft f, Terror m.

frig·id ['frɪdʒɪd] adj. □ **1.** kalt, frostig, eisig (alle a. fig.): ~ zone geogr. kalte Zone; **2.** fig. kühl, steif; **3.** fri-'gid, gefühlskalt; **fri·gid·i·ty** [frɪ'dʒɪdətɪ] s. Kälte f, Frostigkeit f (a. fig.); psych. Frigidi'tät f.

frill [frɪl] **I** s. **1.** (Hals-, Hand)Krause f, Rüsche f; **2.** Pa'pierkrause f, Man'schette f; **3.** zo., orn. Kragen m; **4.** mst pl. contp. ,Verzierungen' pl., Kinkerlitzchen pl., ,Mätzchen' f, Firlefanz m: put on ~s fig. ,auf vornehm machen', sich aufplustern; without ~s ,ohne Kinkerlitzchen', schlicht; **II** v/t. **5.** mit e-r Krause besetzen; **6.** kräuseln; **III** v/i. **7.** phot. sich kräuseln; **'frill·ies**

F

[-lız] *s. pl. Brit.* F ‚Reizwäsche‘ *f,* ‚Spitzen‚unterwäsche *f.*

fringe [frɪndʒ] **I** *s.* **1.** Franse *f,* Besatz *m;* **2.** Rand *m,* Einfassung *f,* Um'randung *f;* **3.** ‚Ponyfri‚sur *f;* **4.** a) Randbezirk *m,* -gebiet *n (a. fig.),* b) *fig.* Rand(zone *f) m,* Grenze *f:* **~s of civilization,** c) → **fringe group;** → **lunatic** I; **5. the ℐ** *thea.* der ‚Fringe‘ *(avantgardistisches Gegen-Festival zum Edinburgh Festival);* **II** *v/t.* **6.** mit Fransen besetzen; **7.** (um)'säumen; **~ ben·e·fits** *s. pl.* (Gehalts-, Lohn)Nebenleistungen *pl.*

fringed [frɪndʒd] *adj.* gefranst.

fringe| group *s. sociol.* Randgruppe *f;* **~ the·a·ter** *Am.,* **~ the·a·tre** *Brit.* Experimen'tierthe‚ater *m.*

frip·per·y [ˈfrɪpərɪ] *s.* **1.** Putz *m,* Flitterkram *m;* **2.** Tand *m,* Plunder *m;* **3.** *fig.* → **frill** 4.

fris·bee [ˈfrɪzbiː] *TM s.* ‚Frisbee *TM s.*

Fri·sian [ˈfrɪzɪən] **I** *s.* **1.** Friese *m,* Friesin *f;* **2.** *ling.* Friesisch *n;* **II** *adj.* **3.** friesisch.

frisk [frɪsk] **I** *v/i.* **1.** her'umtollen, -hüpfen; **II** *v/t.* **2.** wedeln mit; **3.** *j-n* ‚filzen‘, *a. et.* durch'suchen; **III** *s.* **4.** a) Ausgelassenheit *f,* b) Freudensprung *m;* **5.** F ‚Filzen‘ *n;* **'frisk·i·ness** [-kɪnɪs] *s.* Lustigkeit *f,* Ausgelassenheit *f;* **'frisk·y** [-kɪ] *adj.* ☐ lebhaft, munter, ausgelassen.

fris·son [ˈfrɪsɔ̃ː] *(Fr.) s.* (leichter) Schauer.

frit [frɪt] *v/t.* ⊕ fritten, schmelzen.

frith [frɪθ] → **firth.**

frit·ter¹ [ˈfrɪtə] *s.* Bei'gnet *m (Gebäck).*

frit·ter² [ˈfrɪtə] *v/t.* **1.** *mst* **~ away** verplempern, vergeuden; **2.** a) zerfetzen, b) in Streifen schneiden, *Küche:* schnetzeln.

fritz [frɪts] *s. Am. sl.:* **on the ~** kaputt, ‚im Eimer‘.

friv·ol [ˈfrɪvl] **I** *v/i.* (he'rum)tändeln; **II** *v/t.* **~ away** → **fritter²** 1; **fri·vol·i·ty** [frɪˈvɒlətɪ] *s.* Frivoli'tät *f:* a) Leichtsinn(igkeit *f) m,* Oberflächlichkeit *f,* b) Leichtfertigkeit *f (Rede od. Handlung);* **'friv·o·lous** [-vələs] *adj.* ☐ **1.** fri'vol, leichtsinnig, -fertig; **2.** nicht ernst zu nehmen(d); **3.** ⚖ schika'nös.

frizz¹ [frɪz] **I** *v/t. u. v/i.* (sich) kräuseln; **II** *s.* gekräuseltes Haar.

frizz² [frɪz] → **frizzle¹** I.

friz·zle¹ [ˈfrɪzl] **I** *v/i.* brutzeln; **II** *v/t.* (braun) rösten.

friz·zle² [ˈfrɪzl] → **frizz¹;** **'friz·zly** [-lɪ], **'friz·zy** [-zɪ] *adj.* kraus, gekräuselt.

fro [frəʊ] *adv.:* **to and ~** hin u. her, auf u. ab.

frock [frɒk] **I** *s.* **1.** (Mönchs)Kutte *f;* **2.** (Damen)Kleid *n;* **3.** ♣ Wolljacke *f;* **4.** Kinderkleid *n,* Kittel *m;* **5.** Gehrock *m;* **6.** (Arbeits)Kittel *m;* **II** *v/t.* **7.** mit e-m geistlichen Amt bekleiden; **8.** mit e-m Kittel bekleiden; **~ coat** *s.* Gehrock *m.*

frog [frɒg] *s.* **1.** *zo.* Frosch *m:* **have a ~ in the throat** e-n Frosch im Hals haben, heiser sein; **2.** Schnurbesatz *m,* -verschluss *m (Rock);* **3.** ✕ Quaste *f,* Säbeltasche *f;* **4.** ❦ Herz-, Kreuzungsstück *n;* **5.** ⚡ Oberleitungsweiche *f;* **6.** *zo.* Strahl *m (Pferdehuf);* **7.** *Am. sl.* Bizeps *m;* **8.** ⚘ *sl. contp.* ‚Scheißfran‚zose‘ *m;* **~ kick** *s. Schwimmen:* Grätschstoß *m;* **'~-man** [-mən] *s. [irr.]* Froschmann *m,* ✕ *a.* Kampfschwimmer *m;* **'~-march** *v/t. j-n* (mit dem Gesicht nach unten) fortschleppen; **~'s legs** *s. pl.* Froschschenkel *pl.;* **~ spawn** *s.* **1.** *zo.* Froschlaich *m;* **2.** ⚘ Froschlaichalge *f.*

frol·ic [ˈfrɒlɪk] **I** *s.* **1.** Her'umtollen *n,* Ausgelassenheit *f;* **2.** Jux *m,* Spaß *m,* Streich *m;* **II** *v/i. pret. u. p.p.* **'frol·icked** [-kt] **3.** her'umtollen, -toben; **'frol·ic·some** [-səm] *adj.* 'übermütig, ausgelassen.

from [frɒm; frəm] *prp.* von, von ... her, aus, aus ... her'aus: a) *Ort, Herkunft:* **a gift ~ his son** ein Geschenk von s-m Sohn; **~ outside** (*od.* **without**) von (dr)außen; **the train ~ X** der Zug von *od.* aus X; **he is ~ Kent** er ist *od.* stammt aus Kent; *auf Sendungen:* **~ ...** Absender ..., b) *Zeit:* **~ 2 to 4 o'clock** von 2 bis 4 Uhr; **~ now** von jetzt an; **a child** von Kindheit an, c) *Entfernung:* **6 miles ~ Rome** 6 Meilen von Rom (entfernt); **far ~ the truth** weit von der Wahrheit entfernt, d) *Fortnehmen:* **stolen ~ the shop** (**the table**) aus dem Laden (vom Tisch) gestohlen; **take it ~ him!** nimm es ihm weg!, e) *Anzahl:* **~ six to eight boats** sechs bis acht Boote, f) *Wandlung:* **~ bad to worse** immer schlimmer, g) *Unterscheidung:* **he does not know black ~ white** er kann Schwarz u. Weiß nicht unterscheiden, h) *Quelle, Grund:* **~ my point of view** von meinem Standpunkt (aus), **~ what he said** nach dem, was er sagte; **painted ~ life** nach dem Leben gemalt; **he died ~ hunger** er verhungerte; **~ a·bove** *adv.* von oben; **~ a·cross** *adv. u. prp.* von jenseits *(gen.),* von der anderen Seite *(gen.);* **~ a·mong** *prp.* aus ... her'aus; **~ be·fore** *prp.* aus der Zeit vor *(dat.);* **~ be·neath** *adv.* von unten; *prp.* unter *(dat.)* ... her'vor *od.* her'aus; **~ be·tween** *prp.* zwischen *(dat.)* ... her'vor; **~ be·yond** *adv. u. prp.* von jenseits *(gen.);* **~ in·side** *adv.* von innen; *prp.* aus ... her'aus: **~ the house** aus dem Inneren des Hauses (heraus); **~ out of** *prp.* aus ... her'aus; **~ un·der** → **from beneath.**

frond [frɒnd] *s.* 🌿 (Farn)Wedel *m.*

front [frʌnt] **I** *s.* **1.** *allg.* Vorder-, Stirnseite *f,* Front *f;* **2.** △ (Vorder)Front *f,* Fas'sade *f;* **3.** Vorderteil *n;* **4.** ✕ a) Front *f,* Kampflinie *f,* -gebiet *n,* b) Frontbreite *f:* **at the ~** an der Front; **on all ~s** an allen Fronten *(a. fig.);* **5.** Vordergrund *f,* Spitze *f:* **in ~** an der *od.* die Spitze, vorn, davor; **in ~ of** vor *(dat.);* **to the ~** nach vorn; **come to the ~** *fig.* in den Vordergrund treten; **up ~** a) vorn, *fig. a.* an der Spitze, b) nach vorn, *fig. a.* an die Spitze; **6.** (Straßen-, Wasser)Front *f:* **the ~** *Brit.* die Strandpromenade *f;* **7.** *fig.* Front *f:* a) *(bsd. politische)* Organisati'on, b) Sektor *m:* **on the economic ~** an der wirtschaftlichen Front; **8.** a) ‚Strohmann‘ *m,* b) ‚Aushängeschild‘ *n (e-r Interessengruppe od. Geheimorganisation etc.);* **9.** F ‚Fas'sade‘ *f:* **put up a ~** a) sich Allüren geben, b) ‚Theater spielen‘; **show a bold ~** kühn auftreten; **maintain a ~** den Schein wahren; **10.** *poet.* a) Stirn *f,* b) Antlitz *n;* **11.** *fig.* Frechheit *f:* **have the ~ to** *(inf.)* die Stirn haben zu *(inf.);* **12.** Hemdbrust *f;* **13.** (falsche) Stirnlocken *pl.;* **14.** *meteor.* Front *f:* **cold ~;** **II** *adj.* **15.** Front..., Vorder...: **~ en·trance,** **~ row** vorder(st)e Reihe; **~ tooth** Vorderzahn *m;* **16. ~ man** ‚Strohmann‘ *m;* **17.** *ling.* Vorderzungen...; **III** *v/t.* **18.** gegen'überstehen, -liegen *(dat.):* **the house ~s the sea** das Haus liegt (nach) dem Meer zu; **the windows ~ the street** die Fenster gehen auf die Straße; **19.** *j-m* entgegen-, gegen'übertreten, *j-m* die Stirn bieten; **20.** mit e-r Front *od.* Vorderseite versehen; **21.** als Front *od.* Vorderseite

dienen für; **22.** *ling.* palatalisieren; **23.** *TV Brit.* Programm moderieren; **IV** *v/i.* **24. ~ on** (*od.* **to[wards]**) → 18; **25. ~ for** als ‚Strohmann‘ *od.* ‚Aushängeschild‘ fungieren für.

front·age [ˈfrʌntɪdʒ] *s.* **1.** (Vorder)Front *f (e-s Hauses):* **~ line** Bau(flucht)linie *f;* **~ road** *Am.* Parallelstraße *zu e-r Schnellstraße (mit Wohnhäusern, Geschäften etc.);* **have a ~ on** → **front** 18; **2.** Land *n* an der Straßen- *od.* Wasserfront; **3.** Grundstück *n* zwischen der Vorderfront *u.* Haus *u.* der Straße; **4.** ✕ Front- *od.* Angriffsbreite *f.*

fron·tal [ˈfrʌntl] **I** *adj.* **1.** fron'tal, Vorder..., Front...: **~ attack (collision)** Frontalangriff *m (-zs-stoß m);* **~ axle** ⊕ Vorderachse *f;* **2.** ⊕, *anat.* Stirn...; **II** *s.* **3.** *eccl.* Ante'pendium *n;* **4.** △ Ziergiebel *m;* **~ bone** *s.* Stirnbein *n;* **~ si·nus** *s.* Stirn(bein)höhle *f.*

front| bench *s. parl.* vordere Sitzreihe *(für Regierung u. Oppositionsführer);* **'bench·er** *s. parl.* führendes Frakti'onsmitglied; **~ door** *s.* Haus-, Vordertür *f;* **~ drive** *s. mot.* Frontantrieb *m;* **'~-end col·li·sion** *s. mot.* Auffahrunfall *m;* **~ en·gine** *s.* Frontmotor *m.*

fron·tier [ˈfrʌntɪə] **I** *s.* **1.** (Landes)Grenze *f;* **2.** *Am.* Grenzgebiet *n,* Grenze *f (zum Wilden Westen):* **new ~s** *fig.* neue Ziele; **3.** *fig. oft pl.* Grenze *f,* Grenzbereich *m;* Neuland *n;* **II** *adj.* **4.** Grenz...: **~ town;** **'fron·tiers·man** [-ɪəzmən] *s. [irr.] Am. hist.* Grenzbewohner *m.*

fron·tis·piece [ˈfrʌntɪspiːs] *s.* Fronti'spiz *n:* a) Titelbild *n (Buch),* b) △ Giebelseite *f od.* -feld *n.*

front·let [ˈfrʌntlɪt] *s.* **1.** *zo.* Stirn *f;* **2.** Stirnband *n.*

front| line *s.* ✕ Kampffront *f,* Front(linie) *f;* **'~-line** *adj.:* **~ officer** Frontoffizier *m;* **~ mo·ney** *s. Am.* **1.** Vorschuss *m;* **2.** ‚Startkapi‚tal *n;* **~ page** *s.* Titelseite *f (Zeitung);* **'~-page** *adj.:* **~ news** wichtige *od.* aktuelle Nachricht(en); **~ pas·sen·ger** *s. mot.* Beifahrer(in); **'~-run·ner** *s.* **1.** *sport* a) Spitzenreiter *m (a. fig.),* b) Favo'rit(in); **2.** *pol.* ‚Spitzenkandi‚dat(in); **3.** Tempoläufer *m;* **~ seat** *s.* Vordersitz *m;* **~ sight** *s.* ✕ Korn *n;* **~ view** *s.* Vorderansicht *f;* **'~-wheel** *adj.:* **~ drive** ⊕ Vorderradantrieb *m.*

frosh [frɒʃ] *s. sg. u. pl. Am.* → **freshman.**

frost [frɒst] **I** *s.* **1.** Frost *m:* **10 degrees of ~** *Brit.* 10 Grad Kälte; **2.** Eisblumen *pl.,* Reif *m;* **3.** *fig.* Kühle *f,* Kälte *f,* Frostigkeit *f;* **4.** *sl.* ‚Reinfall‘ *m;* ‚Pleite‘ *f;* **II** *v/t.* **5.** mit Reif *od.* Eis über'ziehen; **6.** ⊕ Glas mattieren; **7.** *Küche:* a) glasieren, mit Zuckerguss über'ziehen, b) mit (Puder)Zucker bestreuen; **8.** Frostschäden verursachen bei; **9.** *j-n* sehr kühl behandeln; **'~-bite** *s.* ✚ Erfrierung *f;* **'~-bit·ten** *adj.* ✚ erfroren.

frost·ed [ˈfrɒstɪd] *adj.* **1.** bereift, über'froren; **2.** ⊕ mattiert: **~ glass** Matt-, Milchglas *n;* **3.** ✚ erfroren; **4.** mit Zuckerguss, glasiert; **'frost·i·ness** [-tɪnɪs] *s.* Frost *m,* eisige Kälte *(a. fig.);* **'frost·ing** [-tɪŋ] *s.* **1.** Zuckerguss *m,* Gla'sur *f;* **2.** ⊕ Mattierung *f;* **'frost·work** *s.* Eisblumen *pl.;* **'frost·y** [-tɪ] *adj.* ☐ **1.** eisig, frostig *(a. fig.);* **2.** mit Reif *od.* Eis bedeckt; **3.** *fig.* eisig: **~ hair.**

froth [frɒθ] **I** *s.* **1.** Schaum *m;* **2.** ✚ (Blasen)Schaum *m;* **3.** *fig.* ‚Firlefanz‘ *m;* **II** *v/t.* **4.** a) zum Schäumen bringen, b) zu Schaum schlagen; **III** *v/i.* **5.** schäumen *(a. fig. vor Wut);* **'froth·i·ness** [-θɪnɪs] *s.* **1.** Schäumen *n,* Schaum *m;* **2.** *fig.*

Seicht-, Hohlheit *f*; **'froth·y** [-θɪ] *adj.* □ **1.** schaumig, schäumend; **2.** *fig.* seicht, hohl.

frou-frou ['fru:fru:] (*Fr.*) *s.* **1.** Knistern *n*, Rascheln *n* (*von Seide*); **2.** Flitter *m*.

fro·ward ['frəʊəd] *adj.* □ *obs.* eigensinnig.

frown [fraʊn] **I** *v/i.* a) die Stirn runzeln (**at** über *acc.*; *a. fig.*), b) finster dreinschauen: **~ (up)on** stirnrunzelnd *od.* finster betrachten, *fig.* missbilligen (*acc.*); **II** *v/t.* **~ down** j-n durch finstere Blicke einschüchtern; **III** *s.* Stirnrunzeln *n*; finsterer Blick; **'frown·ing** [-nɪŋ] *adj.* □ **1.** stirnrunzelnd; **2.** a) miss'billigend, b) finster (*Blick*); **3.** bedrohlich.

frowst [fraʊst] F **I** *s.* ‚Mief‘ *m*; **II** *v/i.* im ‚Mief‘ hocken; **'frowst·y** [-tɪ] *adj.* muffig, ‚miefig‘.

frowz·i·ness ['fraʊzɪnɪs] *s.* **1.** Schlampigkeit *f*; Ungepflegtheit *f*; **2.** muffiger Geruch; **frowz·y** ['fraʊzɪ] *adj.* **1.** schlampig, ungepflegt; **2.** muffig.

froze [frəʊz] *pret. von* **freeze**; **'fro·zen** [-zn] **I** *p.p. von* **freeze**; **II** *adj.* **1.** (ein-, zu)gefroren; **2.** erfroren; **3.** gefroren, Gefrier...: **~ food** Tiefkühlkost *f*; **~ meat** Gefrierfleisch *n*; **4.** eisig, frostig (*a. fig.*); **5.** kalt, teilnahms-, gefühllos; **6.** ✝ eingefroren: a) festliegend: **~ capital**, b) gestoppt: **~ prices**; **~ wages**; **7.** **~ facts** *Am.* unumstößliche Tatsachen.

fruc·ti·fi·ca·tion [ˌfrʌktɪfɪ'keɪʃn] *s.* ✿ **1.** Fruchtbildung *f*; **2.** Befruchtung *f*; **fruc·ti·fy** ['frʌktɪfaɪ] ✿ **I** *v/i.* Früchte tragen (*a. fig.*); **II** *v/t.* befruchten (*a. fig.*); **fruc·tose** ['frʌktəʊs] *s.* Fruchtzucker *m*.

fru·gal ['fru:gl] *adj.* □ **1.** sparsam, haushälterisch (**of** mit); **2.** genügsam, bescheiden; **3.** einfach, spärlich, fru'gal: **a ~ meal**; **fru·gal·i·ty** [fru:'gælətɪ] *s.* Sparsamkeit *f*; Genügsamkeit *f*; Einfachheit *f*.

fru·giv·o·rous [fru:'dʒɪvərəs] *adj. zo.* fruchtfressend.

fruit [fru:t] **I** *s.* **1.** ✿ a) Frucht *f*, b) Samenkapsel *f*; **2.** *coll.* ✿ Früchte *pl.*: **bear ~** Früchte tragen (*a. fig.*), b) Obst *n*; **3.** *bibl.* Nachkommen(schaft *f*) *pl.*: **~ of the body** Leibesfrucht *f*; **4.** *mst pl. fig.* Frucht *f*, Früchte *pl.*, Ergebnis *n*, Erfolg *m*, Gewinn *m*; **5.** *sl.* ‚Spinner‘ *m*; **6.** *Am. sl.* ‚Homo‘ *m*; **II** *v/i.* **7.** ✿ (Früchte) tragen; **fruit·ar·i·an** [fru:'teərɪən] *s.* Obstesser(in), Rohköstler(in).

'fruit·cake *s.* **1.** englischer Kuchen; **2.** *Brit. sl.* ‚Spinner‘ *m*; **~ cock·tail** *s.* Früchtecocktail *m*; **~ cup** *s.* Früchtebecher *m*.

fruit·er·er ['fru:tərə] *s.* Obsthändler *m*; **'fruit·ful** [-tfʊl] *adj.* □ **1.** fruchtbar (*a. fig.*); **2.** *fig.* erfolgreich; **'fruit·ful·ness** [-tfʊlnɪs] *s.* Fruchtbarkeit *f*.

fru·i·tion [fru:'ɪʃn] *s.* Erfüllung *f*, Verwirklichung *f*: **come to ~** sich verwirklichen, Früchte tragen.

fruit| jar *s.* Einweckglas *n*; **~ juice** *s.* Obstsaft *m*; **~ knife** *s.* [*irr.*] Obstmesser *n*.

fruit·less ['fru:tlɪs] *adj.* □ **1.** unfruchtbar; **2.** *fig.* frucht-, erfolglos, vergeblich.

fruit| ma·chine *s. Brit.* F ‚Spielauto,mat‘ *m*; **~ pulp** *s.* Fruchtfleisch *n*; **~ sal·ad** *s.* **1.** 'Obstsa,lat *m*; **2.** *fig. humor.* ‚La-'metta‘ *n*, Ordenspracht *f*; **~ tree** *s.* Obstbaum *m*.

fruit·y ['fru:tɪ] *adj.* **1.** fruchtartig; **2.** fruchtig (*Wein*); **3.** so'nor (*Stimme*); **4.** *Brit. sl.* ‚saftig‘, ‚gepfeffert‘ (*Witz*); **5.** *Am.* F ‚schmalzig‘.

---

fru·men·ta·ceous [ˌfru:mən'teɪʃəs] *adj.* getreideartig, Getreide...

frump [frʌmp] *s. a.* **old ~** ‚alte Schachtel‘, ‚Spi'natwachtel‘ *f*; **'frump·ish** [-pɪʃ], **'frump·y** [-pɪ] *adj.* **1.** altmodisch; **2.** schlampig, ungepflegt.

frus·trate [frʌ'streɪt] *v/t.* **1.** *et.* vereiteln, durch'kreuzen, zu'nichte machen; **2.** *j-n od. et.* hemmen, (be)hindern, *j-n* einengen, *j-n* am Fortkommen hindern; **3.** *j-m* die *od.* jede Hoffnung *od.* Aussicht nehmen, *j-n* zu'rückwerfen: **I was ~d in my efforts** meine Bemühungen wurden vereitelt; **4.** frustrieren: a) *j-n* entmutigen, b) *j-n* enttäuschen, c) mit Minderwertigkeitsgefühlen erfüllen; **frus'trat·ed** [-tɪd] *adj.* **1.** vereitelt, gescheitert: **~ plans**; **2.** gescheitert (*Person*), ‚verhindert‘ (*Maler etc.*); **3.** frustriert: a) entmutigt, b) enttäuscht, c) voller Minderwertigkeitsgefühle; **frus'trat·ing** [-tɪŋ] *adj.* frustrierend, entäuschend, entmutigend; **frus'tra·tion** [-eɪʃn] *s.* **1.** Vereitelung *f*; **2.** Behinderung *f*, Hemmung *f*; **3.** Enttäuschung *f*, 'Misserfolg *m*, Rückschlag *m*; **4.** *psych. u. allg.* Frustrati'on *f*: a) Enttäuschung *f*, b) *a.* **sense of ~** das Gefühl, ein Versager zu sein, Minderwertigkeitsgefühle *pl.*, Niedergeschlagenheit *f*; **5.** aussichtslose Sache (**to** für).

frus·tum ['frʌstəm] *pl.* **-tums** *od.* **-ta** [-tə] *s.* 𝒜 Stumpf *m*: **~ of a cone** Kegelstumpf.

fry[1] [fraɪ] *s. pl.* **1.** a) junge Fische *pl.*, b) Fischrogen *m*; **2.** **small ~** a) ‚junges Gemüse‘, Kinder *pl.*, b) kleine (*unbedeutende*) Leute *pl.*, c) ‚kleine Fische‘ *pl.*, Lappalien *pl.*

fry[2] [fraɪ] **I** *v/t.* **1.** braten: **fried potatoes** Bratkartoffeln; **2.** *Am. sl.* auf dem e'lektrischen Stuhl hinrichten; **II** *v/i.* **3.** braten, schmoren; **4.** *Am. sl.* auf dem e'lektrischen Stuhl hingerichtet werden; **III** *s.* **5.** Gebratenes *n*, *bsd.* gebratene Inne'reien *pl.*; **6.** *Am. bsd. in Zssgn:* Brat-, Grillfest *n*: **fish ~**; **fry·er** ['fraɪə] *s.* **1.** j-d, der et. brät: **he is a fish ~** er hat ein Fischrestaurant; **2.** (*Fisch- etc.*)Bratpfanne *f*; **3.** *et.* zum Braten Geeignetes, *bsd.* Brathühnchen *n*; **fry·ing pan** ['fraɪɪŋ] *s.* Bratpfanne *f*: **jump out of the ~ into the fire** vom Regen in die Traufe kommen.

fuch·sia ['fju:ʃə] *s.* ✿ Fuchsie *f*.

fuch·sine ['fu:ksiːn] *s.* 🜿 Fuch'sin *n*.

fuck [fʌk] V **I** *v/t.* **1.** ‚ficken‘, ‚vögeln‘: **~ it!** ‚Scheiße‘!; **~ you!**, **get ~ed!** a) du Scheißkerl!, b) leck mich am Arsch!; **2.** **~ up** *et.* ‚versauen‘ *od.* ‚vermasseln‘: (**all**) **~ed up** (total) ‚im Arsch‘; **II** *v/i.* **3.** ‚ficken‘, ‚vögeln‘; **4.** **~ around** *fig.* herumgammeln; **~ off!** verpiss dich!; **III** *s.* **5.** ‚Fick‘ *m*: **I don't give a ~** *fig.* das ist mir ‚scheißegal‘; **~!** ‚Scheiße‘!; **'fuck·er** [-kə] *s.* V **1.** ‚Ficker‘ *m*; **2.** ‚(Scheiß-)Kerl‘ *m*: **poor ~** ‚armes Schwein‘; **'fuck·ing** [-kɪŋ] V **I** *adj.* verdammt, Scheiß... (*oft nur verstärkend*); **II** *adv.* verdammt: **~ cold** ‚saukalt‘; **~ good** ‚unheimlich‘ gut, ‚sagenhaft‘.

fud·dle ['fʌdl] F **I** *v/t.* **1.** berauschen: **~ o.s.** → 3; **2.** verwirren; **II** *v/i.* **3.** saufen, sich ‚voll laufen lassen‘; **III** *s.* **4.** Verwirrung *f*: **get in a ~** durcheinander kommen; **'fud·dled** [-ld] *adj.* F **1.** ‚benebelt‘; **2.** verwirrt.

fud·dy-dud·dy ['fʌdɪˌdʌdɪ] F **I** *s.* ‚verkalkter Trottel‘; **II** *adj.* ‚verkalkt‘.

fudge [fʌdʒ] F **I** *v/t.* **1.** *oft* **~ up** zu'rechtpfuschen, zs.-stoppeln; **2.** ‚frisieren‘, fälschen; **II** *v/i.* **3.** ‚blöd da'herreden‘; **4.** **~ on** *e-m Problem etc.* ausweichen;

III *s.* **5.** ‚Quatsch‘ *m*, Blödsinn *m*; **6.** *Zeitung:* (Ma'schine *f od.* Spalte *f* für) letzte Meldungen *pl.*; **7.** *Küche:* (*Art*) Fon'dant *m*.

fu·el ['fjʊəl] **I** *s.* Brennstoff *m*: a) 'Brenn-, 'Heizmateri,al *n*, b) Betriebs-, Treib-, Kraftstoff *m*: **add ~ to the flames** (*od.* **fire**) *fig.* Öl ins Feuer gießen; **add ~ to** *fig. et.* schüren; **II** *v/i.* Brennstoff nehmen; *a.* **~ up** (auf)tanken, ⚓ bunkern; **III** *v/t.* mit Brennstoff versehen, ✈ *a.* betanken; ⚓ Öl bunkern: **fuelled with** be- *od.* getrieben mit; **~-'air mix·ture** *s. mot.* Kraftstoff-Luft-Gemisch *n*; **~ cap** *s.* Tankdeckel *m*; **~ e·con·o·my** *s.* sparsamer Kraftstoffverbrauch; **~ el·e·ment** *s. Reaktor:* 'Brennele,ment *n*; **~ feed** *s.* Brennstoffzuleitung *f*; **~ gas** *s.* Heizgas *n*; **~ ga(u)ge** *s. mot.* Kraftstoffmesser *m*, Ben'zinuhr *f*; **~-ˌguzz·ling** *adj.* F ‚Ben'zin fressend‘ (*Motor etc.*); **~ in·jec·tion en·gine** *s.* Einspritzmotor *m*; **~ jet** *s.* Kraftstoffdüse *f*; **~ oil** *s.* Heizöl *n*; **~ pump** *s. mot.* Kraftstoff-, Ben'zinpumpe *f*; **~ rod** *s. Reaktor:* Brennstab *m*.

fug [fʌg] *s.* F ‚Mief‘ *m*.

fu·ga·cious [fju:'geɪʃəs] *adj.* kurzlebig (*a.* ✿), flüchtig, vergänglich.

fug·gy ['fʌgɪ] *adj.* F ‚miefig‘.

fu·gi·tive ['fju:dʒɪtɪv] **I** *s.* a) Flüchtige(r *m*) *f*, b) *pol. etc.* Flüchtling *m*, c) Ausreißer *m*: **~ from justice** flüchtiger Rechtsbrecher; **II** *adj.* flüchtig, *fig. a.* vergänglich, kurzlebig.

fu·gle·man ['fju:glmæn] *s.* [*irr.*] (An-, Wort)Führer *m*.

fugue [fju:g] *s.* **1.** ♪ Fuge *f*; **2.** *psych.* Fu'gue *f*; **II** *v/t. u. v/i.* **3.** ♪ fugieren.

ful·crum ['fʌlkrəm] *pl.* **-cra** [-krə] *s.* **1.** *phys.* Dreh-, Hebe-, Stützpunkt *m*; **2.** *fig.* Angelpunkt *m*.

ful·fil(l) [fʊl'fɪl] *v/t.* **1.** *allg.* erfüllen; **2.** voll'bringen, -'ziehen, ausführen; **ful'fil(l)·ment** [-mənt] *s.* Erfüllung *f*.

ful·gent ['fʌldʒənt] *adj.* □ *poet.* strahlend, glänzend; **ful·gu·rant** ['fʌlgjʊərənt] *adj.* (auf)blitzend.

full[1] [fʊl] **I** *adj.* □ → **fully**; **1.** *allg.* voll: **~ of** voll von, voller *Fische etc.*, *fig. a.* a) reich an (*dat.*), b) (ganz) erfüllt von: **~ of plans** voller Pläne; **~ of o.s.** (ganz) von sich eingenommen; **a ~ heart** ein (über)volles Herz; **2.** voll, ganz: **a ~ mile**; **a ~ hour** e-e volle *od.* ‚geschlagene‘ Stunde; **3.** voll, rund, vollschlank; **4.** weit (geschnitten): **a ~ skirt**; **5.** voll, kräftig: **~ colo(u)r**; **~ voice**; **6.** schwer, vollmundig: **~ wine**; **7.** voll besetzt: **~ up** (voll) besetzt (*Bus etc.*); **house ~!** *thea.* ausverkauft!; **8.** ausführlich, genau, voll(ständig): **~ details**; **9.** reichlich: **a ~ meal**; **10.** a) voll, unbeschränkt: **~ power** Vollmacht *f*, b) voll (-berechtigt): **~ member**; **11.** echt, rein: **a ~ sister** e-e leibliche Schwester; **12.** F ‚voll‘: a) *a.* **~ up** satt, b) betrunken; **II** *adv.* **13.** völlig, gänzlich, ganz: **know ~ well that** ganz genau wissen, dass; **14.** gerade, genau, di'rekt: **~ in the face**; **15.** **~ out** mit Vollgas *fahren*, auf Hochtouren *arbeiten*; **III** *s.* **16.** **in ~** voll(ständig): **write in ~** *et.* ausschreiben; **to the ~** vollständig, bis ins Kleinste, total; **at the ~** auf dem Höhepunkt *od.* Höchststand.

full[2] [fʊl] *v/t.* □ → ⊕ *Tuch* walken.

full| age *s.:* **of ~** 🜚 mündig, volljährig; **~-back** *s.* a) *Fußball, Hockey:* Verteidiger *m*, b) *Rugby:* Schlussspieler *m*; **~ blood** *s. biol.* Vollblut *n*; **~-'blood·ed** *adj.* **1.** reinrassig, Vollblut...; **2.** *fig.*

F

Vollblut...: ~ **socialist**; ,~-'**blown** adj.
1. ♀ ganz aufgeblüht; **2.** fig. a) voll
entwickelt, ausgereift, b) F → **fully
fledged** 2, 3; ~ **board** s. 'Vollpensi‚on
f; ,~-'**bod·ied** adj. **1.** schwer, üppig; **2.**
schwer, vollmundig: ~ **wine**; ,~-'**bottomed** adj. **1.** breit, mit großem Boden: ~ **wig** Allongeperücke f; **2.** ⚓ mit
großem Laderaum; '~-**bound** adj.
Ganzleder..., Ganzleinen...: ~ **book**; ~
dress s. **1.** Gesellschaftsanzug m; **2.**
✗ 'Galauni‚form f; ,~-'**dress** adj. **1.**
Gala...: ~ **uniform**; **2.** ~ **rehearsal** →
dress rehearsal; **3.** fig. groß angelegt,
um'fassend.
ful·ler ['fulə] s. ⊛ **1.** (Tuch)Walker m;
2. (halb)runder Setzhammer; ~'s
earth s. min. Fullererde f.
,**full**|'**face** I s. **1.** En-'face-Bild n, Vor-
deransicht f; **2.** typ. (halb)fette Schrift;
II adj. **3.** en face; **4.** typ. (halb)fett;
,~-'**faced** adj. **1.** mit vollem Gesicht,
pausbäckig; **2.** typ. fett; ,~-'**fash·ioned**
Am. → **fully fashioned**; ,~-'**fledged**
→ **fully fledged**; ~ **gal·lop** s.: at ~ in
vollem od. gestrecktem Galopp; ,~-
-'**grown** adj. ausgewachsen; ~ **hand** s.
full house 2; ,~-'**heart·ed** adj. rückhaltlos, voll; ~ **house** s. **1.** thea. etc.
volles Haus; **2.** Poker: Full'house n;
,~-'**length** adj. **1.** in voller Größe, lebensgroß: ~ **portrait**; **2.** bodenlang
(Kleid); **3.** abendfüllend (Film); ~ **load**
s. **1.** ⊛, ✈ Gesamtgewicht n; **2.** ⚡ Voll-
last f; ~ **nel·son** s. Ringen: Doppelnel-
son m.
full·ness ['fulnɪs] s. **1.** Fülle f: in the ~
of time zur gegebenen Zeit; **2.** fig.
('Über)Fülle f (des Herzens); **3.** Körperfülle f; **4.** Sattheit f (a. Farben); **5.** ♪
Klangfülle f; **6.** Weite f (Kleid).
,**full**|-'**page** adj. ganzseitig; ~ **pro·fes-
sor** s. Am. univ. Ordi'narius m; ,~-
-'**rigged** adj. **1.** ⚓ voll getakelt; **2.** voll
ausgerüstet; ~ **scale** s. ⊛ na'türliche
Größe; ,~-'**scale** adj. **1.** in na'türlicher
Größe; **2.** fig. groß angelegt, um'fassend: ~ **attack** ✗ Großangriff m; ~
test Großversuch m; ~ **war** regelrech-
ter Krieg; ~ **stop** s. **1.** (Schluss)Punkt
m; **2.** fig. Schluss m, Ende n, Stillstand
m; '~-**text search** s. Computer: 'Voll-
textsuche f; ,~-'**time** I adj. ✝ hauptberuflich (tätig): ~ **job** Ganztagsstellung
f, -beschäftigung f; II adv. ganztags;
'~-,**tim·er** s. ganztägig Beschäftigte(r
m) f; ,~-'**track** adj.: ~ **vehicle** ⊛ Voll-
ketten-, Raupenfahrzeug n; ,~-'**view**
adj. ✓ Vollsicht...
ful·ly ['fulɪ] adv. voll, völlig, gänzlich;
ausführlich: ~ **ten minutes** volle zehn
Minuten; ~ **automatic** vollautomatisch; ~ **entitled** voll berechtigt; ~ **fashioned** adj. mit (voller) Passform
(Strümpfe etc.); ~ **fledged** adj. **1.** flügge (Vogel); **2.** fig. richtig(gehend): **a** ~
pilot; **3.** fig. ,ausgewachsen': **a** ~
scandal.
ful·mar ['fulmə] s. orn. Fulmar m, Eis-
sturmvogel m.
ful·mi·nant ['fʌlmɪnənt] adj. **1.** krachend; **2.** ✲ plötzlich ausbrechend; **ful-
mi·nate** ['fʌlmɪneɪt] I v/i. **1.** donnern,
explodieren (a. fig.); **2.** fig. (los)don-
nern, wettern; II v/t. **3.** zur Explosi'on
bringen; **4.** fig. Befehle etc. donnern;
III s. **5.** 🜍 Fulmi'nat n: ~ **of mercury**
Knallquecksilber n; '**ful·mi·nat·ing**
[-neɪtɪŋ] adj. **1.** 🜍 explodierend,
Knall...: ~ **powder** Knallpulver n; **2.**
fig. donnernd, wetternd; **3.** → **fulminant** 2; **ful·mi·na·tion** [,fʌlmɪ'neɪʃn] s.
1. Explosi'on f, Knall m; **2.** fig. Don-

nern n, Wettern n.
ful·ness bsd. Am. → **fullness**.
ful·some ['fulsəm] adj. □ **1.** über'trieben: ~ **flattery**; **2.** obs. widerlich.
ful·vous ['fʌlvəs] adj. rötlich gelb.
fum·ble ['fʌmbl] I v/i. **1.** a. ~ **around** a)
um'hertappen, -tasten (for nach): ~ for
tappen od. suchen nach, b) (her'um-)
fummeln (at an dat.); **2.** (with) ungeschickt 'umgehen (mit), sich ungeschickt anstellen (bei); **3.** sport ,pat-
zen'; II v/t. **4.** ,verpatzen'; **5.** ~ **out** et.
mühsam (her'vor)stammeln; III s. **6.**
(Her'um)Tappen n, (-)Fummeln n; **7.**
sport ,Patzer' m; '**fum·bler** [-lə] s.
Stümper m, ,Patzer' m; '**fum·bling**
[-lɪŋ] adj. □ tappend; täppisch, ungeschickt.
fume [fjuːm] I s. **1.** oft pl. a) (unangenehmer) Dampf, Rauch(gas n) m,
Schwade f, b) Dunst m, Nebel m; **2.** fig.
Koller m, Erregung f, Wut f; **3.** fig.
Schall m u. Rauch m; II v/t. **4.** Holz
räuchern, dunkler machen, beizen: ~d
oak dunkles Eichenholz; III v/i. **5.** rauchen, dunsten, dampfen; **6.** fig. wüten
(at gegen), (vor Wut) schäumen: **fuming with anger** kochend vor Wut.
fu·mi·gant ['fjuːmɪgənt] s. Ausräuche-
rungsmittel n; **fu·mi·gate** ['fjuːmɪgeɪt]
v/t. ausräuchern; **fu·mi·ga·tion** [,fjuː-
mɪ'geɪʃn] s. Ausräucherung f; '**fu·mi-
ga·tor** [-geɪtə] s. 'Ausräucherappa‚rat
m.
fun [fʌn] I s. Scherz m, Spaß m, Ulk m:
for (od. **in**) ~ aus od. zum Spaß; **for the**
~ **of it** spaßeshalber, zum Spaß; **it's not
all** ~ **and games** es ist gar nicht so
rosig; **it is** ~ es macht Spaß; **he** (**it**) **is
great** ~ F er (es) ist sehr amüsant od.
lustig; **have** ~! viel Spaß!; **make** ~ **of
s.o.** sich über j-n lustig machen; **I don't
see the** ~ **of it** ich finde das (gar) nicht
komisch; II adj. lustig, spaßig: ~ **man** →
funster.
func·tion ['fʌŋkʃn] I s. **1.** Funkti'on f
(a. ♣, ⊛, biol., ling., phys.): a) Aufgabe f, b) Zweck m, c) Tätigkeit f, d)
Arbeits-, Wirkungsweise f, e) Amt n, f)
(Amts)Pflicht f, Obliegenheit f: **out of**
~ ⊛ außer Betrieb, kaputt; **2.** a) feierlicher od. festlicher Anlass, Feier f,
Zeremo'nie f, b) Veranstaltung f,
(gesellschaftliches) Fest; II v/i. **3.** fungieren, tätig sein; **4.** ⊛ etc. funktionieren, arbeiten.
func·tion·al ['fʌŋkʃənl] adj. □ → **func-
tionally**; **1.** amtlich, dienstlich; **2.** a) ✲,
♣, ⊛ funktio'nell, Funktions...: ~ **disorder** ✲ Funktionsstörung f, b) funkti'onsfähig, -tüchtig; **3.** sachlich, praktisch, zweckbetont, -mäßig: ~ **building**
Zweckbau m; '**func·tion·al·ism** [-ʃnə-
lɪzəm] s. **1.** △, psych. Funktiona'lismus
m; **2.** Zweckmäßigkeit f; '**func·tion-
al·ize** [-ʃnəlaɪz] v/t. funktionstüchtig
machen, wirksam gestalten; '**func·tion-
al·ly** [-ʃnəlɪ] adv. in funktioneller Hinsicht; '**func·tion·ar·y** [-ʃnərɪ] s. Funktio'när m.
func·tion key ['fʌŋkʃniː] s. Computer:
Funkti'onstaste f.
fund [fʌnd] I s. **1.** a) Kapi'tal n, Geldsumme f, b) zweckgebunden: Fonds m:
relief ~ Hilfsfonds f; **strike** ~ Streik-
fonds; **2.** pl. (Bar-, Geld)Mittel pl.,
Gelder pl.: **be in** ~**s** (gut) bei Kasse
sein; **no** ~**s** ✝ kein Guthaben, keine
Deckung; **public** ~**s** öffentliche Gelder; **3.** ⚡**s** pl. a) Brit. fundierte 'Staats-
pa‚piere pl., Kon'sols pl., b) Am. Ef-
'fekten pl.; **4.** fig. Vorrat m, Schatz m,
Fülle f, Grundstock m (of von, an dat.);

II v/t. **5.** ✝ a) in 'Staatspa‚pieren anlegen, b) fundieren, konsolidieren: ~**ed
debt** fundierte Schuld; ~ **rais·er** s. Veranstaltung zum Aufbringen von Geldmitteln, bsd. Wohltätigkeitsveranstaltung f; ~ **rais·ing** s. Geld-, Kapitalbe-
schaffung f.
fun·da·ment ['fʌndəmənt] s. **1.** ⚓ u.
fig. Funda'ment n; **2.** humor. die ,vier
Buchstaben' pl., Gesäß n.
fun·da·men·tal [,fʌndə'mentl] I adj. □
→ **fundamentally**; **1.** fundamen'tal,
grundlegend, wesentlich (**to** für),
Haupt...; **2.** grundsätzlich, Grund...,
elemen'tar: ~ **colo**(**u**)**r** Grund-, Primär-
farbe f; ~ **particle** phys. Elementarteilchen n; ~ **research** Grundlagenforschung f; ~ **tone** ♪ Grundton m; ~
truth(**s**) Grundwahrheit(en) f; II s. **3.**
oft pl. 'Grundlage f, -prin‚zip n, -begriff
m; **4.** ♪ Grundton m; **fun·da·men·tal-
ism** [-təlɪzəm] s. eccl. Fundamenta'lismus m, streng wörtliche Bibelgläubig-
keit; ,**fun·da·men·tal·ist** s. eccl. Fundamenta'list(in); ,**fun·da·men·tal·ly**
[-təlɪ] adv. im Grunde, im Wesentlichen.
fu·ner·al ['fjuːnərəl] I s. **1.** Begräbnis n,
Beerdigung f, Bestattung f: **that's your**
~! sl. das ist deine Sache!; **2.** a. ~ **procession** Leichenzug m; **3.** Am. Trauerfeier f; II adj. **4.** Begräbnis..., Leichen..., Trauer..., Grab...: ~ **director**
Bestattungsunternehmer m; ~ **home**
(od. **parlor**) Am. Leichenhalle f; ~
march ♪ Trauermarsch m; ~ **pile**, ~
pyre Scheiterhaufen m; ~ **service**
Trauergottesdienst m; ~ **urn** Totenurne
f; '**fu·ner·ar·y** [-nərərɪ], **fu·ne·re·al**
[fjuː'nɪərɪəl] adj. □ **1.** Begräbnis...,
Leichen... Trauer...; **2.** fig. düster, wie
be-i-em Begräbnis.
'**fun·fair** s. Brit. Vergnügungspark m,
Rummelplatz m.
fun·gal ['fʌŋgl] adj. Pilz...; **fun·gi**
['fʌŋgaɪ] pl. von **fungus**.
fun·gi·ble ['fʌndʒɪbl] adj. ⚖ vertretbar
(Sache): ~ **goods** Fungibilien.
fun·gi·cid·al [,fʌndʒɪ'saɪdl] adj. pilztö-
tend; **fun·gi·cide** ['fʌndʒɪsaɪd] s. pilz-
tötendes Mittel; **fun·goid** ['fʌŋgɔɪd]
adj., **fun·gous** ['fʌŋgəs] adj. pilz-,
schwammartig, a. ✲ schwammig; **fungus** ['fʌŋgəs] pl. **fun·gi** ['fʌŋgaɪ] od.
-**gus·es** s. **1.** ♀ Pilz m, Schwamm m; **2.**
✲ Fungus m, schwammige Geschwulst;
3. humor. Bart m.
fu·nic·u·lar [fjuː'nɪkjulə] I adj. Seil...,
Ketten...; II s. a. ~ **railway** (Draht-)
Seilbahn f.
funk [fʌŋk] F I s. **1.** ,Schiss' m, ,Bammel'
m, Angst f: **be in a blue** ~ a) ,schwer
Schiss haben' (of vor dat.), b) völlig
,down' sein; ~ **hole** ✗ a) ,Helden-
keller' m, Unterstand m, b) fig.
Druckposten m; **2.** feiger Kerl; **3.**
Drückeberger m; II v/i. **4.** ,Schiss'
haben od. bekommen; **5.** ,kneifen', sich
drücken; III v/t. **6.** ,Schiss' haben vor
(dat.); **7.** ,kneifen' vor (dat.), sich
drücken vor (dat.) od. um; '**funk·y** [-kɪ]
adj. feig(e).
fun·nel ['fʌnl] I s. **1.** Trichter m; **2.** ⚓, 🕭
Schornstein m; **3.** ⊛ Luftschacht m; **4.**
Vul'kanschlot m; II v/t. **5.** eintrichtern,
-füllen; **6.** fig. schleusen.
fun·nies ['fʌnɪz] s. pl. F **1.** Comic Strips
pl., Comics pl.; **2.** Witzseite f.
fun·ny ['fʌnɪ] adj. □ **1.** a. **haha** komisch, drollig, lustig, ulkig; **2.** ,ko-
misch': a) a. ~ **peculiar** sonderbar,
merkwürdig, b) F unwohl, c) F zweifelhaft, faul: **the** ~ **thing is that** das Merk-

würdige ist, dass; *funnily enough* merkwürdigerweise; **~** *business* F ‚faule Sache‘, ‚krumme Tour‘; **~** **bone** *s.* Musi'kantenknochen *m*; **~** *farm s. sl.* ‚Klapsmühle‘ *f*; '**~-man** [-mən] *s.* [*irr.*] Komiker *m*; **~** **pa·per** *s. Am.* Comicteil *m e-r Zeitung*.

fun·ster ['fʌnstə] *s.* F Spaßvogel *m*.

fur [fɜː] **I** *s.* **1.** Pelz *m*, Fell *n*: *make the* **~** *fly* ‚Stunk‘ machen; **2.** a) Pelzbesatz *m*, b) *a.* **~** *coat* Pelzmantel *m*, c) *pl.* Pelzwerk *n*, -kleidung *f*, Rauchwaren *pl.*; **3.** *coll.* Pelztiere *pl.*: **~** *and feather* Haarwild u. Federwild *n*; **4.** ✗ (Zungen)Belag *m*; **5.** ☉ Kesselstein *m*; **6.** mit Pelz besetzen *od.* füttern; **7.** ☉ mit Kesselstein über'ziehen; **III** *v/i.* **8.** ☉ Kesselstein ansetzen.

fur·be·low ['fɜːbɪləʊ] *s.* **1.** Falbel *f*, Faltensaum *m*; **2.** *pl. contp.* ‚Firlefanz‘ *m*.

fur·bish ['fɜːbɪʃ] *v/t.* **1.** polieren; **2.** *oft* **~** *up* herrichten, renovieren; **3.** *mst* **~** *up fig.* ‚aufpolieren‘, auffrischen.

fur·cate ['fɜːkeɪt] **I** *adj.* gabelförmig, gegabelt, gespalten; **II** *v/i.* sich gabeln *od.* teilen; **fur·ca·tion** [fɜː'keɪʃn] *s.* Gabelung *f*.

fu·ri·ous ['fjʊərɪəs] *adj.* □ **1.** wütend; **2.** wild, aufbrausend: **~** *temper*; **3.** wild, heftig, furi'os: *a* **~** *attack*.

furl [fɜːl] *v/t. Fahne, Segel* aufrollen, *Schirm* zs.-rollen.

fur·long ['fɜːlɒŋ] *s.* Achtelmeile *f* (*201,17 m*).

fur·lough ['fɜːləʊ] *bsd.* ✗ **I** *s.* (Heimat-)Urlaub *m*; **II** *v/t.* beurlauben.

fur·nace ['fɜːnɪs] *s.* **1.** ☉ (Schmelz-, Brenn-, Hoch)Ofen *m*: *enamel(l)ing* **~** Farbenschmelzofen; **2.** ☉ (Heiz)Kessel *m*, Feuerung *f*; **3.** *fig.* ‚Backofen‘ *m*, glühend heißer Raum *od.* Ort; **4.** *fig.* Feuerprobe *f*, harte Prüfung: *tried in the* **~** gründlich erprobt.

fur·nish ['fɜːnɪʃ] *v/t.* **1.** ausstatten, -rüsten, versehen, -sorgen (*with* mit); **2.** *Wohnung* einrichten, ausstatten, möblieren: **~** *ed room* möbliertes Zimmer; **3.** *allg. a. Beweise etc.* liefern, beschaffen, er- *od.* beibringen; '**fur·nish·er** [-ʃə] *s.* **1.** Liefe'rant *m*; **2.** *Am.* Herrenausstatter *m*; '**fur·nish·ing** [-ʃɪŋ] *s.* **1.** Ausrüstung *f*, -stattung *f*; **2.** *pl.* Einrichtung *f*, Mobili'ar *n*: *soft* **~** *s* Möbelstoffe; **3.** *pl. Am.* ('Herren)Be,kleidungsar,tikel *pl.*; **4.** ☉ a) Zubehör *n*, *m*, b) Beschläge *pl.*

fur·ni·ture ['fɜːnɪtʃə] *s.* **1.** Möbel *pl.*, Einrichtung *f*, Mobili'ar *n*: *piece of* **~** Möbel(stück) *n*; **~** *remover* Möbelspediteur *m od.* -packer *m*; **~** *van* Möbelwagen *m*; **2.** Ausrüstung *f*, -stattung *f*; **3.** Inhalt *m*, Bestand *m*; **4.** *geistiges* Rüstzeug, Wissen *n*; **5.** ☉ Zubehör *n*, *m*.

fu·ror ['fjʊərɔː] *s. Am.*, **fu·ro·re** [fjʊə'rɔːrɪ] *s.* **1.** Ek'stase *f*, Begeisterungstaumel *m*; **2.** Wut *f*; **3.** Fu'rore *n*, Aufsehen: *create a* **~** Furore machen.

furred [fɜːd] *adj.* **1.** mit Pelz besetzt *od.* bekleidet; **2.** ✗ belegt (*Zunge*); **3.** ☉ mit Kesselstein belegt.

fur·ri·er ['fʌrɪə] *s.* Kürschner *m*, Pelzhändler *m*; '**fur·ri·er·y** [-ərɪ] *s.* **1.** Pelzwerk *n*; **2.** Kürschne'rei *f*.

fur·row ['fʌrəʊ] **I** *s.* **1.** ✓ Furche *f*; **2.**

Bodenfalte *f*; **3.** ☉ Rille *f*; **4.** Runzel *f*, Furche *f* (*a. anat.*); **II** *v/t.* **5.** pflügen; **6.** ☉ riefen, auskehlen; **7.** *Wasser* durch'furchen; **8.** runzeln; **III** *v/i.* **9.** sich furchen (*Stirn etc.*).

fur·ry ['fɜːrɪ] *adj.* **1.** pelzartig, Pelz...; **2.** → *furred* 2.

fur seal *s. zo.* Bärenrobbe *f*.

fur·ther ['fɜːðə] **I** *adv.* **1.** *comp. von far* weiter, ferner, entfernter: *no* **~** nicht weiter; *I'll see you* **~** *first* F ich werde dir was husten!; **2.** ferner, weiterhin, über'dies, außerdem; **II** *adj.* **3.** weiter, ferner, entfernter: *the* **~** *end* das andere Ende; **4.** *fig.* weiter: **~** *education Brit.* Fort-, Weiterbildung *f*; **~** *particulars* weitere Einzelheiten, Näheres; *until* **~** *notice* bis auf weiteres; *anything* **~**? (sonst) noch etwas?; **III** *v/t.* **5.** fördern, unter'stützen; '**fur·ther·ance** [-ðərəns] *s.* Förderung *f*, Unter'stützung *f*; '**fur·ther·more** *adv.* ferner, über'dies, außerdem; '**fur·ther·most** *adj.* **1.** fernst, weitest; **2.** äußerst; '**fur·thest** ['fɜːðɪst] *adj. u. adv.* **1.** *sup. von far*; **2.** *fig.* weitest, meist: *at the* **~** höchstens; **II** *adv.* **3.** am weitesten.

fur·tive ['fɜːtɪv] *adj.* □ **1.** heimlich, verstohlen; **2.** heimlichtuerisch; '**fur·tive·ness** [-nɪs] *s.* Heimlichkeit *f*, Verstohlenheit *f*.

fu·run·cle ['fjʊərʌŋkl] *s.* ✗ Fu'runkel *m*; **fu·run·cu·lo·sis** [fjʊ,rʌŋkjʊ'ləʊsɪs] *s.* ✗ Furunku'lose *f*.

fu·ry ['fjʊərɪ] *s.* **1.** (wilder) Zorn *m*, Wut *f*; **2.** Wildheit *f*, Heftigkeit *f*: *like* **~** wie toll; **3.** ⚘ *antiq.* Furie *f*; **4.** *fig.* Furie *f* (*böses Weib etc.*).

furze [fɜːz] *s.* ♀ Stechginster *m*.

fuse [fjuːz] **I** *s.* **1.** ✗ Zünder *m*: **~** *cord* Abreißschnur *f*; **2.** ⚡ (Schmelz)Sicherung *f*: **~** *box* Sicherungsdose *f*, -kasten *m*; **~** *wire* Sicherungsdraht *m*; *he blew a* **~** ihm ist die Sicherung durchgebrannt (*a. fig.* F); *he has a short* **~** *Am.* F bei ihm brennt leicht die Sicherung durch; **II** *v/t.* **3.** ✗ Zünder anbringen an (*dat.*); **4.** ☉ (ab)sichern; **5.** *phys.*, ☉ (ver)schmelzen; **6.** *fig.* verschmelzen, vereinigen, ✦ *a.* fusionieren; **III** *v/i.* **7.** ⚡ 'durchbrennen; **8.** ☉ schmelzen; **9.** *fig.* verschmelzen, ✦ *a.* fusionieren.

fu·se·lage ['fjuːzɪlɑːʒ] *s.* ✈ (Flugzeug-)Rumpf *m*.

fu·sel (oil) ['fjuːzl] *s.* Fuselöl *n*.

fu·si·ble ['fjuːzəbl] *adj.* schmelzbar, -flüssig: **~** *cut-out* ⚡ Schmelzsicherung *f*.

fu·sil ['fjuːzɪl] *s.* ✗ *hist.* Steinschlossflinte *f*, Mus'kete *f*; **fu·sil·ier**, *Am. a.* **fu·sil·eer** [,fjuːzɪ'lɪə] *s.* ✗ Füsi'lier *m*; **fu·sil·lade** [,fjuːzɪ'leɪd] **I** *s.* **1.** ✗ Salve *f*; **2.** Exekuti'onskom,mando *n*; **3.** *fig.* Hagel *m*; **II** *v/t.* **4.** ✗ unter Salvenfeuer nehmen; **5.** (standrechtlich) erschießen, füsilieren.

fus·ing ['fjuːzɪŋ] *s.* ☉ Schmelzen *n*: **~** *burner* Schneidbrenner *m*; **~** *point* Schmelzpunkt *m*; **fu·sion** ['fjuːʒn] *s.* **1.** ☉ Schmelzen *n*: **~** *welding* Schmelzschweißen *n*; **2.** Schmelzmasse *f*; **3.** *biol., opt., Kernphysik*: Fusi'on *f* (*Verschmelzung*): **~** *bomb* Wasserstoffbombe *f*; **~** *reactor* Fusionsreaktor *m*; **4.** *fig.* Verschmelzung *f*, Vereinigung *f*;

Zs.-schluss *m*, Fusi'on *f* (*a.* ✦, *pol.*).

fuss [fʌs] **I** *s.* **1.** a) (unnötige) Aufregung, b) Hektik *f*; **2.** ‚Wirbel‘ *m*, ‚The'ater‘ *n*, Getue *n*: *make a* **~** a) → 5, b) *a. kick up a* **~** ‚Krach schlagen‘; *a lot of* **~** *about nothing* viel Lärm um nichts; **3.** Ärger *m*, Unannehmlichkeiten *pl.*; **II** *v/i.* **4.** sich (unnötig) aufregen (*about* über *acc.*): *don't* **~**! nur keine Aufregung!, schon gut!; **5.** viel ‚Wirbel‘ *od.* ‚Wind‘ machen (*about*, *of*, *over* um *j-n od. et.*); **6.** sich (viel) Umstände machen (*over* mit *e-m Gast etc.*): **~** *over s.o.* a) *j-n* bemuttern; **~** *about* (*od. around*) ‚herumfuhrwerken‘; **7.** heikel sein; **III** *v/t.* **8.** *j-n* ner'vös machen; '**fuss,budg·et** *Am.* → *fusspot*; '**fuss·i·ness** ['fʌsɪnɪs] *s.* **1.** (unnötige) Aufregung *f*; **2.** Hektik *f*; **3.** Kleinlichkeit *f*; **4.** heikle Art; '**fusspot** *s.* F Umstands-, Kleinigkeitskrämer *m*, ‚pingeliger‘ Kerl; **fuss·y** ['fʌsɪ] *adj.* □ **1.** a) aufgeregt, b) hektisch; **2.** kleinlich, ‚pingelig‘; **3.** heikel, wählerisch, ‚eigen‘ (*about* hinsichtlich *gen.*, mit).

fus·tian ['fʌstɪən] **I** *s.* **1.** Barchent *m*; **2.** *fig.* Schwulst *m*; **II** *adj.* **3.** Barchent...; **4.** *fig.* schwülstig.

fus·ti·ga·tion [,fʌstɪ'geɪʃn] *s. humor.* Tracht *f* Prügel.

fust·i·ness ['fʌstɪnɪs] *s.* **1.** Moder(geruch) *m*; **2.** *fig.* Rückständigkeit *f*; **fust·y** ['fʌstɪ] *adj.* **1.** mod(e)rig, muffig; **2.** a) verstaubt, antiquiert, b) rückständig.

fu·tile ['fjuːtaɪl] *adj.* □ nutz-, sinn-, zweck-, aussichtslos, vergeblich; **fu·til·i·ty** [fjuː'tɪlətɪ] *s.* Zweck-, Nutz-, Wert-, Sinnlosigkeit *f*.

fu·ton ['fuːtɒn] *s.* 'Futon *m*.

fu·ture ['fjuːtʃə] **I** *s.* **1.** Zukunft *f*: *in* **~** in Zukunft, künftig; *in the near* **~** in der nahen Zukunft, bald; *for the* **~** für die Zukunft, künftig; *have no* **~** keine Zukunft haben; *there is no* **~** *in that!* das hat keine Zukunft!; **2.** *ling.* Fu'tur(um) *n*, Zukunft *f*: **~** *perfect* Futurum exactum, zweite Zukunft; **3.** *pl.* ✦ a) Ter'mingeschäfte *pl.*, b) Ter'minwaren *pl.*; **II** *adj.* **4.** (zu)künftig, Zukunfts...; **5.** *ling.* fu'turisch: **~** *tense* → 2; **6.** ✦ Termin...; **~** *life s.* Leben *n* nach dem Tode.

fu·tur·ism ['fjuːtʃərɪzəm] *s. Kunst:* Futu'rismus *m*; '**fu·tur·ist** [-ɪst] **I.** *adj.* **1.** futu'ristisch; **II.** *s.* **2.** Futu'rist *m*; **3.** → *futurologist*; **fu·tu·ri·ty** [fjuː'tjʊərətɪ] *s.* **1.** Zukunft *f*; **2.** zukünftiges Ereignis; **3.** Zukünftigkeit *f*.

fu·tur·ol·o·gist [,fjuːtʃə'rɒlədʒɪst] *s.* Futuro'loge *m*, Zukunftsforscher *m*; '**fu·tur·ol·o·gy** [-dʒɪ] *s.* Futurolo'gie *f*, Zukunftsforschung *f*.

fuze *Am.* → *fuse*.

fuzz [fʌz] **I** *s.* **1.** (feiner) Flaum *m*; **2.** Fusseln *pl.*, Fäserchen *pl.*; **3.** F a) Wuschelhaar(e *pl.*) *n*, b) ‚Zottelbart‘ *m*; **4.** *sl.* a) ‚Bulle‘ *m* (*Polizist*), b) *the* **~** *coll.* die Bullen (*die Polizei*); **II** *v/t.* **5.** zerfasern; **6.** *fig.* ‚benebeln‘; **III** *v/i.* **7.** zerfasern; '**fuzz·y** [-zɪ] *adj.* □ **1.** flaumig; **2.** faserig, fusselig; **3.** kraus, struppig (*Haar*); **4.** verschwommen; **5.** benommen.

fyl·fot ['fɪlfɒt] *s.* Hakenkreuz *n*.

G, g [dʒiː] *s.* **1.** G *n*, g *n* (*Buchstabe*); **2.** ♩ G *n*, g *n* (*Note*): **G flat** Ges *n*, ges *n*; **G sharp** Gis *n*, gis *n*; **3.** **G** *Am. sl.* ‚Riese‘ *m* (*1000 Dollar*).

gab [gæb] F **I** *s.* ‚Gequassel‘ *n*, Geschwätz *n*: **stop your ∼!** halt den Mund!; **the gift of the ∼** ein gutes Mundwerk; **II** *v/i.* ‚quasseln‘.

gab·ar·dine ['gæbədiːn] *s.* Gabardine *m* (*feiner Wollstoff*).

gab·ble ['gæbl] **I** *v/i.* **1.** plappern; **2.** schnattern; **4.** *et.* **3.** *et.* plappern; **4.** *et.* ‚her'unterleiern‘; **III** *s.* **5.** ‚Gebrabbel‘ *n*; **6.** Geschnatter *n*; **'gab·bler** [-lə] *s.* Schwätzer(in); **'gab·by** [-bɪ] *adj.* F geschwätzig.

gab·er·dine → **gabardine**.

gab·fest ['gæbfest] *s. Am.* F ‚Quasse'lei‘ *f*.

ga·bi·on ['geɪbjən] *s.* ✕ Schanzkorb *m*.

ga·ble ['geɪbl] *s.* △ **1.** Giebel *m*; **2.** *a.* **∼ end** Giebelwand *f*; **'ga·bled** [-ld] *adj.* giebelig, Giebel...; **'ga·blet** [-lɪt] *s.* giebelförmiger Aufsatz (*über Fenstern*), Ziergiebel *m*.

gad¹ [gæd] **I** *v/i. mst* **∼ about** sich herumtreiben, ‚rumsausen‘; **II** *s.* **be on the ∼** → I.

gad² [gæd] *int.*: (**by**) **∼!** *obs.* bei Gott!

'gad|·a·bout *s.* Her'umtreiber(in); **'∼·fly** *s.* **1.** *zo.* Viehbremse *f*; **2.** *fig.* Störenfried *m*, lästiger Mensch.

gadg·et ['gædʒɪt] *s.* F **1.** *a.* Appa'rat *m*, Ge'rät *n*, Vorrichtung *f*, b) *iro.* ‚Apparätchen‘ *n*, ‚Kinkerlitzchen‘ *n*, technische Spiele'rei; **2.** ‚Dingsbums‘ *n*; **3.** *fig.* ‚Dreh‘ *m*, Kniff *m*; **gadg·e·teer** [ˌgædʒɪ'tɪə] *s.* F Liebhaber *m* von technischen Spiele'reien *od.* Neuerungen; **'gadg·et·ry** [-trɪ] *s.* **1.** a) Appa'rate *pl.*, b) *iro.* technische Spiele'reien *pl.*; **2.** Beschäftigung *f* mit technischen Spiele'reien; **'gadg·et·y** [-tɪ] *adj.* F **1.** raffiniert (konstruiert); **2.** Apparate...; **3.** versessen auf technische Spiele'reien.

Ga·dhel·ic [gæ'delɪk] → **Gaelic**.

gad·wall ['gædwɔːl] *s. orn.* Schnatterente *f*.

Gael [geɪl] *s.* Gäle *m*; **'Gael·ic** [-lɪk] **I** *s. ling.* Gälisch *n*, das Gälische; **II** *adj.* gälisch.

gaff¹ [gæf] *s.* **1.** *Fischen:* Landungshaken *m*; **2.** ⚓ Gaffel *f*; **3.** Stahlsporn *m*; **4.** *Am. sl.* ‚Schlauch‘ *m*: **stand the ∼** durchhalten; **5.** *Am. sl.* Schwindel *m*; **6.** *sl.* ‚Quatsch‘ *m*: **blow the ∼** alles verraten, allg. ‚plaudern‘.

gaff² [gæf] *s. Brit. sl. a.* **penny ∼** Varie'tee *n*, ‚Schmiere‘ *f*.

gaffe [gæf] *s.* Faux'pas *m*, (grobe) Taktlosigkeit.

gaf·fer ['gæfə] *s.* **1.** *humor.* ‚Opa‘ *m*; **2.** *Brit.* F a) Chef *m*, b) Vorarbeiter *m*.

gag [gæg] **I** *v/t.* **1.** knebeln, *fig. a.* mundtot machen; **2.** *zum* Würgen reizen; **3.** *a.* **∼ up** *thea.* mit Gags spicken; **II** *v/i.* **4.** würgen (**on** an *dat.*); **5.** *thea. etc.* F Gags anbringen, *allg.* witzeln; **III** *s.* **6.** Knebel *m*, *fig. a.* Knebelung *f*; **7.** ✽ Mundsperrer *m*; **8.** *parl.* Schluss *m* der

De'batte; **9.** *thea. u. allg.* F Gag *m*: a) witziger Einfall, komische Po'inte, ‚Knüller‘ *m*, b) Jux *m*, Ulk *m*, c) Trick *m*.

ga·ga ['gɑːgɑː] *adj. sl.* a) vertrottelt, b) ‚plem'plem‘: **go ∼ over** in Verzückung geraten über (*acc.*).

gag bit *s.* Zaumgebiss *n*.

gage¹ [geɪdʒ] **I** *s.* **1.** *hist. u. fig.* Fehdehandschuh *m*; **2.** ('Unter)Pfand *n*; **II** *v/t.* **3.** *obs.* zum Pfand geben.

gage² [geɪdʒ] → **gauge**.

gage³ [geɪdʒ] → **greengage**.

gag·gle ['gægl] **I** *v/i.* **1.** schnattern; **II** *s.* **2.** Geschnatter *n*; **3.** a) Gänseherde *f*, b) F schnatternde Schar: **a ∼ of girls**.

gag·man ['gægmən] *s.* [*irr.*] *thea. etc.* Gagman *m* (*Pointenerfinder etc.*).

gai·e·ty ['geɪtɪ] *s.* **1.** Frohsinn *m*, Fröhlich-, Lustigkeit *f*; **2.** *oft pl.* Lustbarkeit *f*, Fest *n*; **3.** *fig.* (Farben)Pracht *f*.

gai·ly ['geɪlɪ] *adv.* **1.** → **gay** 1, 2; **2.** unbekümmert, sorglos.

gain [geɪn] **I** *v/t.* **1.** *s-n Lebensunterhalt etc.* verdienen; **2.** gewinnen: **∼ time**; **3.** *das Ufer etc.* erreichen; **4.** *fig.* erreichen, erlangen, erringen: **∼ wealth** Reichtümer erwerben; **∼ experience** Erfahrung(en) sammeln; **∼ admission** Einlass finden; **5.** *j-m et.* einbringen, -tragen; **6.** zunehmen an (*dat.*): **∼ strength** (**speed**) kräftiger (schneller) werden; **he ∼ed 10 pounds** (**in weight**) er nahm 10 Pfund zu; **7.** **∼ over** *j-n* für sich gewinnen; **8.** vorgehen um *2 Minuten etc.* (*Uhr*); **II** *v/i.* **9.** besser *od.* kräftiger werden; **10.** ✝ Gewinn *od.* Pro'fit machen; **11.** (an Wert) gewinnen, im Ansehen steigen, besser zur Geltung kommen; **12.** zunehmen (**in** an *dat.*): **∼** (**in weight**) (an Gewicht) zunehmen; **13.** (**on, upon**) a) näher her'ankommen (an *dat.*), (an) Boden gewinnen, aufholen (gegen'über), b) *s-n* Vorsprung vergrößern (vor *dat.*, gegen'über); **14.** (**on, upon**) 'übergreifen (auf *acc.*); **15.** vorgehen (*Uhr*); **III** *s.* **16.** Gewinn *m*, Vorteil *m*, Nutzen *m* (**to** für); **17.** Zunahme *f*, Steigerung *f*: **∼ in weight** Gewichtszunahme; **18.** ✝ a) Gewinn *m*, Pro'fit *m*: **for ∼** ⚖ gewerbsmäßig, in gewinnsüchtiger Absicht, b) Wertzuwachs *m*; **19.** ⚡, *phys.* Verstärkung *f*: **∼ control** Lautstärkeregelung *f*; **'gain·er** [-nə] *s.* **1.** Gewinner *m*; **2.** *sport* Auerbach(sprung) *m*: **full ∼** Auerbachsalto *m*; **half ∼** Auerbachkopfsprung *m*; **'gain·ful** [-fʊl] *adj.* □ einträglich, Gewinn bringend: **∼ occupation** Erwerbstätigkeit *f*; **∼ly employed** erwerbstätig; **'gain·ings** [-nɪŋz] *s. pl.* Gewinn(e *pl.*) *m*, Einkünfte *pl.*, Pro'fit *m*; **'gain·less** [-lɪs] *adj.* **1.** unvorteilhaft, ohne Gewinn; **2.** nutzlos.

gain·say [ˌgeɪn'seɪ] *v/t.* [*irr.* → **say**] *obs.* **1.** *et.* bestreiten, leugnen: **there is no ∼ing that** das lässt sich nicht leugnen; **2.** *j-m* wider'sprechen.

gainst, 'gainst [geɪnst] *poet. abbr. für*

against.

gait [geɪt] *s.* Gangart *f* (*a. fig. Tempo*), Gang *m*.

gai·ter ['geɪtə] *s.* **1.** Ga'masche *f*; **2.** *Am.* Zugstiefel *m*.

gal¹ [gæl] *s.* F Mädchen *n*.

gal² [gæl] *s. phys.* Gal *n* (*Einheit der Beschleunigung*).

ga·la ['gɑːlə] **I** *adj.* **1.** festlich, Gala...; **II** *s.* **2.** *a.* **∼ occasion** festlicher Anlass, Fest *n*; **3.** Galaveranstaltung *f*; **4.** *sport Brit.* (Schwimm- *etc.*)Fest *n*.

ga·lac·tic [gə'læktɪk] *adj.* **1.** *ast.* Milchstraßen...; **2.** *physiol.* Milch...

Ga·la·tians [gə'leɪʃjənz] *s. pl. bibl.* (Brief *m* des Paulus an die) Galater *pl.*

gal·ax·y ['gæləksɪ] *s.* **1.** *ast.* Milchstraße *f*, Gala'xie *f*: **the ℒ** die Milchstraße, die Galaxis; **2.** *fig.* Schar *f* (*prominenter etc. Personen*).

gale¹ [geɪl] *s.* Sturm *m*; steife Brise: **∼ force** Sturmstärke *f*; **∼ of laughter** Lachsalve *f*.

gale² [geɪl] *s.* ♣ Heidemyrthe *f*.

ga·le·na [gə'liːnə] *s. min.* Gale'nit *m*, Bleiglanz *m*.

Ga·li·cian [gə'lɪʃɪən] **I** *adj.* ga'lizisch; **II** *s.* Ga'lizier(in).

Gal·i·le·an¹ [ˌgælɪ'liːən] **I** *adj.* **1.** galiläisch; **II** *s.* Gali'läer(in); **3.** **the ∼** der Gali'läer (*Christus*); **4.** Christ(in).

Gal·i·le·an² [ˌgælɪ'liːən] *adj.* gali'leisch: **∼ telescope**.

gal·i·lee ['gælɪliː] *s.* △ Vorhalle *f*.

gal·i·pot ['gælɪpɒt] *s.* Gali'pot-, Fichtenharz *n*.

gall¹ [gɔːl] *s.* **1.** *obs.* a) *anat.* Gallenblase *f*, b) *physiol.* Galle(nflüssigkeit) *f*; **2.** *fig.* Galle *f*: a) Bitterkeit *f*, Erbitterung *f*, b) Bosheit *f*; **3.** F Frechheit *f*.

gall² [gɔːl] **I** *s.* **1.** wund geriebene Stelle; **2.** *fig.* a) Ärger *m*, b) Ärgernis *n*; **II** *v/t.* **3.** wund reiben; **4.** (ver)ärgern; **III** *v/i.* **5.** reiben, scheuern; **6.** sich wund reiben; **7.** sich ärgern.

gall³ [gɔːl] *s.* ♣ Galle *f*.

gal·lant ['gælənt] **I** *adj.* □ **1.** tapfer, heldenhaft; **2.** prächtig, stattlich; **3.** ga'lant: a) höflich, ritterlich, b) amou'rös, Liebes...; **II** *s.* **4.** Kava'lier *m*; **5.** Verehrer *m*; **6.** Geliebte(r) *m*; **'gal·lant·ry** [-trɪ] *s.* **1.** Tapferkeit *f*; **2.** Galante'rie *f*, Ritterlichkeit *f*; **3.** heldenhafte Tat; **4.** Liebe'lei *f*.

gall| blad·der *s. anat.* Gallenblase *f*; **∼ duct** *s. anat.* Gallengang *m*.

gal·le·on ['gælɪən] *s.* ⚓ *hist.* Gale'one *f*.

gal·ler·y ['gælərɪ] *s.* **1.** △ a) Gale'rie *f*, b) Em'pore *f* (*in Kirchen*); **2.** *thea.* dritter Rang, *a. weitS.* Gale'rie *f*: **play to the ∼** für die Galerie spielen, *fig. a.* nach Effekt haschen; **3.** ('Kunst-, Ge'mälde)Gale,rie *f*; **4.** a) ✼ Laufgang *m*, b) ✪ Laufsteg *m*, c) ✕ *u.* ✕ Stollen *m*, d) → **shooting gallery**; **5.** *fig.* Gale'rie *f*, Schar *f* (*Personen*).

gal·ley ['gælɪ] *s.* **1.** ⚓ a) Ga'leere *f*, b) Langboot *n*; **2.** ⚓ Kom'büse *f*, Küche *f*;

3. *typ.* Setzschiff *n*; **4.** *a.* ~ *proof typ.* Fahne *f*; ~ **slave** *s.* **1.** Ga'leerensklave *m*; **2.** *fig.* Sklave *m*, ‚Kuli‘ *m*; ‚~'**west** *adv.*: **knock** ~ *Am.* F a) j-n zs.-schlagen, b) *fig.* j-n ‚umhauen‘, c) *et.* (total) ‚kaputtmachen‘.

'**gall·fly** *s. zo.* Gallwespe *f*.

gal·lic¹ ['gælɪk] *adj.*: ~ **acid** 🜊 Gallussäure *f*.

Gal·lic² ['gælɪk] *adj.* **1.** gallisch; **2.** fran-'zösisch; '**Gal·li·cism** [-ɪsɪzəm] *s. ling.* Galli'zismus *m*, französische Spracheigenheit; '**Gal·li·cize** [-ɪsaɪz] *v/t.* französi(si)eren.

gal·li·na·ceous [ˌgælɪ'neɪʃəs] *adj. orn.* hühnerartig.

gall·ing ['gɔːlɪŋ] *adj.* ärgerlich (*Sache*).

gal·li·pot¹ → *galipot*.

gal·li·pot² ['gælɪpɒt] *s.* Salbentopf *m*, Medika'mentenbehälter *m*.

gal·li·vant [ˌgælɪ'vænt] *v/i.* **1.** sich amüsieren; **2.** ~ *around* sich her'umtreiben.

'**gall·nut** *s.* ♀ Gallapfel *m*.

gal·lon ['gælən] *s.* Gal'lone *f* (*Hohlmaß*; *Brit.* 4,5459 l, *Am.* 3,7853 l).

gal·loon [gə'luːn] *s.* Tresse *f*.

gal·lop ['gæləp] **I** *v/i.* **1.** galoppieren; **2.** F ‚sausen‘: ~ *through s.th.* *et.* ‚im Galopp‘ erledigen; ~ *through a book* ein Buch durchfliegen; ~*ing consumption* (*inflation*) galoppierende Schwindsucht (Inflation); **II** *v/t.* **3.** galoppieren lassen; **III** *s.* **4.** Ga'lopp *m* (*a. fig.*): *at full* ~ in gestrecktem Galopp; **gal·lo·pade** [ˌgælə'peɪd] → *galop*.

Gal·lo·phile ['gæləʊfaɪl], '**Gal·lo·phil** [-fɪl] *s.* Fran'zosenfreund *m*; '**Gal·lo·phobe** [-fəʊb] *s.* Fran'zosenhasser *m*.

gal·lows ['gæləʊz] *s. pl. mst sg. konstr.* **1.** Galgen *m*; **2.** galgenähnliches Gestell, Galgen *m*; ~ *bird s.* F Galgenvogel *m*; ~ *hu·mo(u)r s.* 'Galgenhu,mor *m*; ~ *tree s.* *gallows* 1.

'**gall·stone** *s.* 🜊 Gallenstein *m*.

Gal·lup poll ['gæləp] *s.* 'Meinungs,umfrage *f*.

gal·lus·es ['gæləsɪz] *s. pl. Am.* F Hosenträger *pl.*

gal·op ['gæləp] **I** *s.* Ga'lopp *m* (*Tanz*); **II** *v/i.* e-n Ga'lopp tanzen.

ga·lore [gə'lɔː] *adv.* F ‚in rauen Mengen‘: *whisk(e)y* ~ *a.* jede Menge Whisky.

ga·losh [gə'lɒʃ] *s. mst pl.* 'Über-, Gummischuh *m*, Ga'losche *f*.

ga·lumph [gə'lʌmf] *v/i.* F stapfen, trapsen.

gal·van·ic [gæl'vænɪk] *adj.* (□ *ally*) ⚡, *phys.* gal'vanisch; *fig.* F elektrisierend; **gal·va·nism** ['gælvənɪzəm] *s.* **1.** *phys.* Galva'nismus *m*; **2.** 🜊 Galvanisati'on *f*; **gal·va·ni·za·tion** [ˌgælvənaɪ'zeɪʃn] *s.* ⚡, 🜊 Galvanisierung *f*; **gal·va·nize** ['gælvənaɪz] *v/t.* **1.** ⚙ galvanisieren, (feuer)verzinken; **2.** 🜊 mit Gleichstrom behandeln; *fig.* F j-n elektrisieren: ~ *into action* j-n schlagartig aktiv werden lassen; **gal·va·nom·e·ter** [ˌgælvə'nɒmɪtə] *s. phys.* Galvano'meter *n*; **gal·va·no·plas·tic** [ˌgælvənəʊ'plæstɪk] *adj.* ⚙ galvano'plastisch; **gal·va·no·plas·tics** [ˌgælvənəʊ'plæstɪks] *s. pl. sg. konstr.*, **gal·va·no·plas·ty** [ˌgælvənəʊ'plæstɪ] *s.* Galvano'plastik *f*, E,lektroty'pie *f*; **gal·va·no·scope** ['gælvənəʊskəʊp] *s. phys.* Galvano'skop *n*.

gam·bit ['gæmbɪt] *s.* **1.** *Schach:* Gam'bit *n*, Eröffnung *f*; **2.** *fig.* a) erster Schritt, Einleitung *f*, b) (raffinierter) Trick.

gam·ble ['gæmbl] **I** *v/i.* **1.** (um Geld) spielen: ~ *with s.th.* *fig.* *et.* aufs Spiel setzen; *you can* ~ *on that* darauf kannst du wetten; *she* ~*d on his com-*

---

ing sie verließ sich darauf, dass er kommen würde; **2.** *Börse:* spekulieren; **II** *v/t.* **3.** ~ *away* verspielen (*a. fig.*); **4.** (als Einsatz) setzen (*on* auf *acc.*), *fig.* aufs Spiel setzen; **III** *s.* **5.** Glücksspiel *n*, Ha'sardspiel *n* (*a. fig.*); **6.** *fig.* Wagnis *n*, Risiko *n*; '**gam·bler** [-lə] *s.* Spieler(in); *fig.* Hasar'deur *m*; '**gam·bling** [-blɪŋ] *s.* Spielen *n*: ~ *den* Spielhölle *f*; ~ *debt* Spielschuld *f*.

gam·boge [gæm'buːʒ] *s.* ♀ Gummigutt *n*.

gam·bol ['gæmbl] **I** *v/i.* her'umtanzen, Luftsprünge machen; **II** *s.* Freuden-, Luftsprung *m*.

game¹ [geɪm] **I** *s.* **1.** Spiel *n*, Zeitvertreib *m*, Sport *m*: ~*s pl.* (*Olympische etc.*) Spiele, *ped.* Sport; ~ *of golf* Golfspiel; ~ *of skill* Geschicklichkeitsspiel; *play the* ~ *fig.* sich an die Spielregeln halten; *play a good* ~ gut spielen; *play* ~*s with s.o.* *fig.* mit j-m sein Spiel treiben; *play a losing* ~ auf der Verliererstraße sein; *be on* (*off*) *one's* ~ gut (nicht) in Form sein; *the* ~ *is yours* du hast gewonnen; *2.* Spiel *n* (*einzelnes*) Spiel, Par'tie *f* (*Schach etc.*); *Tennis:* Spiel *n* (*in e-m Satz*): ~, *set and match Tennis:* Spiel, Satz u. Sieg; **3.** Scherz *m*, Ulk *m*: *make* ~ *of* sich lustig machen über (*acc.*); **4.** Spiel *n*, Unter'nehmen *n*, Plan *m*: *the* ~ *is up* das Spiel ist aus *od.* verloren; *give the* ~ *away* F sich *od.* alles verraten; *play a double* ~ ein doppeltes Spiel treiben; *play a waiting* ~ e-e abwartende Haltung einnehmen; *I know his* (*little*) ~ ich weiß, was er im Schilde führt; *see through s.o.'s* ~ j-s Spiel *od.* j-n durchschauen; *beat s.o. at his own* ~ j-n mit s-n eigenen Waffen schlagen; *two can play at this* ~! das kann ich auch!; **5.** *pl. fig.* Schliche *pl.*, Tricks *pl.*; **6.** Spiel *n* (*Geräte etc.*); **7.** F Branche *f*, Geschäft *n*: *he is in the advertising* ~ er macht in Werbung; *she's on the* ~ ‚sie geht auf den Strich‘; **8.** *hunt.* Wild *n*: *big* ~ Großwild; *fly at higher* ~ höher hinauswollen; **9.** Wildbret *n*: ~ *pie* Wildpastete *f*; **II** *adj.* □ **10.** Jagd..., Wild...; **11.** schneidig, mutig; **12.** a) aufgelegt (*for* zu), b) bereit (*for* zu, *to do* zu tun): *I am* ~! ich bin dabei!, ich mache mit!; **III** *v/i.* **13.** (um Geld) spielen; **IV** *v/t.* **14.** ~ *away* verspielen.

game² [geɪm] *adj.* F lahm: *a* ~ *leg.*

game| bag *s.* Jagdtasche *f*; ~ *bird s.* Jagdvogel *m*; '~,**cock** *s.* Kampfhahn *m* (*a. fig.*); ~ *fish s.* Sportfisch *m*; ~ *fowl s.* **1.** Federwild *n*; **2.** Kampfhahn *m*; '~,**keep·er** *s. Brit.* Wildhüter *m*; ~ *li·cence s. Brit.* Jagdschein *m*.

game·ness ['geɪmnɪs] *s.* Mut *m*, Schneid *m*.

game| park *s.* Wildpark *m*; ~ *plan s. Am. fig.* ‚Schlachtplan‘ *m*; ~ *point s.* *sport* a) entscheidender Punkt, b) *Tennis:* Spielball *m*, c) *Tischtennis:* Satzball *m*; ~ *pre·serve s.* Wildgehege *n*.

games·man·ship ['geɪmzmənʃɪp] *s. bsd. sport* die Kunst, mit allen (gerade noch erlaubten) Tricks zu gewinnen.

games| mas·ter [geɪmz] *s. ped. Brit.* Sportlehrer *m*; ~ *mis·tress s. ped. Brit.* Sportlehrerin *f*.

game·some ['geɪmsəm] *adj.* □ lustig, ausgelassen.

game·ster ['geɪmstə] *s.* Spieler(in) (*um Geld*).

gam·ete [gæ'miːt] *s. biol.* Ga'met *m* (*Keimzelle*).

game ward·en *s.* Jagdaufseher *m*.

gam·in ['gæmɪn] *s.* Gassenjunge *m*.

---

gam·ing ['geɪmɪŋ] *s.* Spielen *n* (*um Geld*): ~ *laws* Gesetze über Glücksspiele u. Wetten; ~ *house s.* Spielhölle *f*, 'Spielka,sino *n*; ~ *ta·ble s.* Spieltisch *m*.

gam·ma ['gæmə] *s.* **1.** Gamma *n* (*griech. Buchstabe*): ~ *rays phys.* Gammastrahlen; **2.** *phot.* Kon'trastgrad *m*; **3.** *ped. Brit.* Drei *f*, Befriedigend *n*.

gam·mer ['gæmə] *s. Brit.* F ‚Oma‘ *f*.

gam·mon¹ ['gæmən] *s.* **1.** (schwach) geräucherter Schinken; **2.** unteres Stück e-r Speckseite.

gam·mon² ['gæmən] *s.* ⚓ Bugsprietzurring *f*.

gam·mon³ ['gæmən] F **I** *s.* **1.** Humbug *m*: a) Schwindel *m*, b) ‚Quatsch‘ *m*; **II** *v/i.* **2.** ‚quatschen‘, Unsinn reden; **3.** sich verstellen, so tun als ob; **III** *v/t.* **4.** j-n ‚reinlegen‘.

gamp [gæmp] *s. Brit.* F (großer) Regenschirm, ‚Fa'miliendach‘ *n*.

gam·ut ['gæmət] *s.* ♪ Tonleiter *f*; *fig.* Skala *f*: *run the whole* ~ *of emotion* von e-m Gefühl ins andere taumeln.

gam·y ['geɪmɪ] *adj.* **1.** nach Wild riechend *od.* schmeckend: ~ *taste* a) Wildgeschmack *m*, b) Hautgout *m*; **2.** F schneidig, mutig.

gan·der ['gændə] *s.* **1.** Gänserich *m*; → *sauce* 1; **2.** *fig.* F ‚Esel‘ *m*, Dussel *m*; **3.** *sl.* Blick *m*: *take a* ~ *at* sich (rasch) *et.* angucken.

gang [gæŋ] **I** *s.* **1.** ('Arbeiter)Ko,lonne *f*, (-)Trupp *m*; **2.** Gang *f*, (Verbrecher-)Bande *f*; **3.** *contp.* Bande *f*, Horde *f*, Clique *f*; **4.** ⊗ Satz *m* (*Werkzeuge*): ~ *of tools*; **II** *v/i.* **5.** *mst* ~ *up* sich zs.-tun, sich zs.-rotten (*on*, *against* gegen).

'**gang·bang I** *s. bsd. Am.* F **1.** a) als Bande um'herziehen, Bandenaktivitäten *pl.* betreiben, b) Bandenüberfälle *pl.* machen; **II** *v/t.* **2.** *bsd. Am.* F herfallen über (*acc.*), anpöbeln, über'fallen; **3.** a) e-e Frau als Gruppe von Männern vergewaltigen, b) e-e Frau als Gruppe von Männern nacheinander ‚bumsen‘; **III** *s.* **4.** a) Vergewaltigung e-r Frau durch mehrere Männer, b) Geschlechtsverkehr mehrerer Männer mit e-r Frau; **5.** *bsd. Am.* F von e-r Straßenbande begangenes Verbrechen; '~,**bang·er** *s.* **1.** *bsd. Am.* F Mitglied *n* e-r Straßenbande; **2.** a) Mitglied e-r Straßenbande, das e-e Frau od. Frauen nacheinander vergewaltigt, b) Mitglied e-r Gruppe von Männern, die mit e-r Frau od. Frauen nacheinander Geschlechtsverkehr haben; '~,**bang·ing** *s.* **1.** *bsd. Am.* F das Auftreten od. die Aktivitäten von Straßenbanden, Bandenaktivitäten *pl.*; **2.** a) Vergewaltigung(en *pl.*) e-r Frau od. von Frauen durch mehrere Männer nacheinander; b) Geschlechtsverkehr mehrerer Männer nacheinander mit e-r Frau; '~·**board** *s.* ⚓ Laufplanke *f*; ~ *boss* → *ganger*; ~ *cut·ter s.* ⊗ Satz-, Mehrfachfräser *m*.

gang·er ['gæŋə] *s.* Vorarbeiter *m*, Kapo *m*.

'**gang·land** *s.* ‚Unterwelt‘ *f*.

gan·gling ['gæŋglɪŋ] *adj.* schlaksig.

gan·gli·on ['gæŋglɪən] *pl.* -**a** [-ə] *s.* **1.** *anat.* Ganglion *n*, Nervenknoten *m*: ~ *cell* Ganglienzelle *f*; **2.** 🜊 'Überbein *n*; **3.** *fig.* Knoten-, Mittelpunkt *m*, Zentrum *n*.

'**gang·plank** → *gangway* 2b; ~ *rape* → *gangbang* b.

gan·grene ['gæŋgriːn] **I** *s.* **1.** 🜊 Brand *m*, Gan'grän *n*; **2.** *fig.* Fäulnis *f*, sittlicher Verfall; **II** *v/t. u. v/i.* **3.** 🜊 brandig machen (werden); '**gan·gre·nous** [-rɪ-**

G

nəs] *adj.* ⚓ brandig.
gang saw *s.* ⊛ Gattersäge *f.*
gang·ster ['gæŋstə] *s.* Gangster *m.*
'gang·way I *s.* **1.** 'Durchgang *m*, Pas'sage *f*; **2.** a) ⚓ Fallreep *n*, b) ⚓ Gangway *f*, Landungsbrücke *f*, c) ✈ Gangway *f*; **3.** *Brit. thea. etc.* (Zwischen)Gang *m*; **4.** ✗ Strecke *f*; **5.** ⊛ a) Schräge *f*, Rutsche *f*, b) Laufbühne *f*; **II** *int.* **6.** Platz (machen) (, bitte)!
gan·net ['gænɪt] *s. orn.* Tölpel *m.*
gant·let ['gæntlɪt] → **gauntlet**[1].
gan·try ['gæntrɪ] *s.* **1.** ⊛ Fasslager *n*; **2.** *a.* ~ **bridge** *a.* ✆ Kranbrücke *f*: ~ **crane** Portalkran *m*; **3.** a) 🚂 Si'gnalbrücke *f*, b) *mot.* Schilderbrücke *f*; **4.** *a.* ~ **scaffold** *Raumfahrt:* Mon'tageturm *m.*
Gan·y·mede ['gænɪmiːd] *s.* **1.** *a.* ♎ Mundschenk *m*; **2.** *ast.* Gany'med *m.*
gaol [dʒeɪl] *bsd. Brit.* → **jail** *etc.*
gap [gæp] *s.* **1.** Lücke *f*, Spalt *m*, Öffnung *f*; **2.** ✗ Bresche *f*, Gasse *f*; **3.** (Berg)Schlucht *f*; **4.** *fig.* a) Lücke *f*, b) Zwischenraum *m*, -zeit *f*, c) Unter'brechung *f*, d) Kluft *f*, 'Unterschied *m*: **close the** ~ **die Lücke schließen**; **fill** (*od.* **stop**) *a* ~ e-e Lücke ausfüllen (*od.* schließen); **leave a** ~ e-e Lücke hinterlassen; **find** (*od.* **spot**) *a* ~ **in the market** e-e Marktlücke finden (*od.* erkennen, ausfindig machen); **dollar** ~ ✝ Dollarlücke; **rocket** ~ Raketenlücke; ~ **in one's education** Bildungslücke; **5.** ⚡ Funkenstrecke *f*.
gape [geɪp] **I** *v/i.* **1.** den Mund aufreißen (*vor Staunen etc.*), staunen: **stand gaping** Maulaffen feilhalten; **2.** starren, glotzen, gaffen: ~ **at s.o.** j-n anstarren; **3.** gähnen; **4.** *fig.* klaffen, gähnen, sich öffnen *od.* auftun; **II** *s.* **5.** Gaffen *n*, Glotzen *n*; **6.** Staunen *n*; **7.** Gähnen *n*; **8.** *the* ~*s pl. sg. konstr. a) vet.* Schnabelsperre *f*, b) *humor.* Gähnkrampf *m*; **'gap·ing** [-pɪŋ] *adj.* □ **1.** gaffend, glotzend; **2.** klaffend (*Wunde*), gähnend (*Abgrund*).
gap·py ['gæpɪ] *adj.* lückenhaft (*a. fig.*).
ga·rage ['gærɑːdʒ] **I** *s.* **1.** Ga'rage *f*; **2.** Repara'turwerkstätte *f* u. Tankstelle *f*; **II** *v/t.* **3.** *Auto* a) in e-r Ga'rage ab- *od.* 'unterstellen, b) in die Ga'rage fahren.
garb [gɑːb] **I** *s.* Tracht *f*, Gewand *n* (*a. fig.*); **II** *v/t.* kleiden.
gar·bage ['gɑːbɪdʒ] *s.* **1.** *Am.* Abfall *m*, Müll *m*; ~ **bag** Müllbeutel *m*; ~ **can** Mülleimer *m*, -tonne *f*; ~ **chute** Müllschlucker *m*; **2.** *fig.* a) Schund *m*, b) 'Abschaum' *m*; **3.** *Computer:* wertlose Daten *pl.*
gar·ble ['gɑːbl] *v/t. Text etc.* a) durcheinander bringen, b) verstümmeln, entstellen, 'frisieren'.
gar·den ['gɑːdn] **I** *s.* **1.** Garten *m*; **2.** *fig.* Garten *m*, fruchtbare Gegend: **the** ~ **of England** die Grafschaft Kent; **3.** *mst pl.* Gartenanlagen *pl.*, Park *m*: **botanical** ~**(s)** botanischer Garten; **II** *v/i.* **4.** gärtnern, im Garten arbeiten; **5.** Gartenbau treiben; **III** *adj.* **6.** Garten...: ~ **plants**; ~ **cit·y** *s. Brit.* Gartenstadt *f*; ~ **cress** *s.* ⚘ Gartenkresse *f.*
gar·den·er ['gɑːdnə] *s.* Gärtner(in).
gar·den| **frame** *s.* glasgedeckter Pflanzenkasten; ~ **gnome** *s.* Gartenzwerg *m.*
gar·de·ni·a [gɑː'diːnjə] *s.* ⚘ Gar'denie *f.*
gar·den·ing ['gɑːdnɪŋ] *s.* **1.** Gartenbau *m*; **2.** Gartenarbeit *f.*
gar·den| **mo(u)ld** *s.* ⚘ Blumen(topf)erde *f*; ~ **par·ty** *s.* Gartenfest *n*, -party *f*; ~ **path** *s.*: **lead s.o. up the** ~ *fig.* j-n hinters Licht führen; ♎ **State** *s. Am.* (*Beiname für*) New Jersey *n*; ~ **stuff** *s.* Gartenerzeugnisse *pl.*; ~ **sub·urb** *s.*

Brit. Gartenvorstadt *f*; ~ **truck** *Am.* → **garden stuff**; ~ **white** *s. zo.* Weißling *m.*
gar·gan·tu·an [gɑː'gæntjʊən] *adj.* riesig, gewaltig, ungeheuer.
gar·gle ['gɑːgl] **I** *v/t.* **1.** a) gurgeln mit: ~ **salt water**, b) ~ **one's throat** → **3.** *Worte* (her'vor)gurgeln; **II** *v/i.* **3.** gurgeln; **III** *s.* **4.** Gurgeln *n*; **5.** Gurgelmittel *n.*
gar·goyle ['gɑːgɔɪl] *s.* **1.** △ Wasserspeier *m*; **2.** *fig.* Scheusal *n.*
gar·ish ['geərɪʃ] *adj.* □ grell, schreiend, aufdringlich, protzig.
gar·land ['gɑːlənd] **I** *s.* **1.** Gir'lande *f* (*a.* △), Blumengewinde *n*, -gehänge *n*; (*a. fig.* Sieges)Kranz *m*; **2.** *fig.* (*bsd.* Gedicht)Sammlung *f*; **II** *v/t.* **3.** bekränzen.
gar·lic ['gɑːlɪk] *s.* ⚘ Knoblauch *m*; **'gar·lick·y** [-kɪ] *adj.* **1.** knoblauchartig; **2.** nach Knoblauch schmeckend *od.* riechend.
gar·ment ['gɑːmənt] *s.* **1.** Kleidungsstück *n*, *pl. a.* Kleider *pl.*; **2.** *fig.* Gewand *n*, Hülle *f.*
gar·ner ['gɑːnə] **I** *s.* **1.** *obs.* Getreidespeicher *m*; **2.** *fig.* Speicher *m*, Vorrat *m* (*of* an *dat.*); **II** *v/t.* **3.** a) speichern (*a. fig.*), b) aufbewahren, c) sammeln (*a. fig.*), d) erlangen, erwerben.
gar·net ['gɑːnɪt] **I** *s. min.* Gra'nat *m*; **II** *adj.* gra'natrot.
gar·nish ['gɑːnɪʃ] **I** *v/t.* **1.** schmücken, verzieren, *bsd.* Küche: garnieren (*a. fig. iro.*); **3.** ⚖ a) *Forderung beim Drittschuldner* pfänden, b) *dem Drittschuldner* ein Zahlungsverbot zustellen; **II** *s.* **4.** Orna'ment *n*, Verzierung *f*; **5.** Küche: Garnierung *f* (*a. fig. iro.*); **gar·nish·ee** [ˌgɑːnɪ'ʃiː] ⚖ **I** *s.* Drittschuldner *m*; **II** *v/t.* → **garnish** 3; **'gar·nish·ment** [-mənt] *s.* **1.** → **garnish** 4; **2.** ⚖ a) (Forderungs)Pfändung *f*, b) Zahlungsverbot *n* an den Drittschuldner, c) *Brit.* Mitteilung *f* an den Pro'zessgegner; **'gar·ni·ture** [-ɪtʃə] *s.* **1.** → **garnish** 4; **2.** Zubehör *n*, Ausstattung *f.*
ga·rotte → **garrot(t)e**.
gar·ret ['gærət] *s.* a) Dachstube *f*, Man'sarde *f*, b) Dachgeschoss, *östr.* -geschoß *n.*
gar·ri·son ['gærɪsn] ✗ **I** *s.* **1.** Garni'son *f* (*Standort od. stationierte Truppen*); **II** *v/t.* **2.** Ort mit e-r Garni'son belegen; **3.** *Truppen* in Garni'son legen: **be** ~**ed in** Garnison liegen; ~ **cap** *s.* Feldmütze *f*; ~ **com·mand·er** *s.* 'Standortkomman,dant *m*; ~ **town** *s.* Garni'sonsstadt *f.*
gar·rot(t)e [gə'rɒt] **I** *s.* **1.** ('Hinrichtung *f* durch die) Ga(r)'rotte *f*; **2.** Erdrosselung *f*; **II** *v/t.* **3.** ga(r)rottieren; **4.** erdrosseln.
gar·ru·li·ty [gæ'ruːlətɪ] *s.* Geschwätzigkeit *f*; **gar·ru·lous** ['gærʊləs] *adj.* □ geschwätzig.
gar·ter ['gɑːtə] *s.* **1.** a) Strumpfband *n*, b) Sockenhalter *m*, c) *Am.* Strumpfhalter *m*, Straps *m*: ~ **belt** Hüfthalter *m*, -gürtel *m*; **2.** *the* ♎ a) *a.* **the Order of the** ♎ der Hosenbandorden (*der höchste brit. Orden*), b) der Hosenbandorden (*Abzeichen*), c) die Mitgliedschaft des Hosenbandordens; **II** *v/t.* **3.** mit e-m Strumpfband *etc.* befestigen *od.* versehen.
gas [gæs] **I** *s.* **1.** 🔥 Gas *n*; **2.** (Leucht-) Gas *n*; **3.** ✗ Grubengas *n*; **4.** ⚓ Lachgas *n*; **5.** ✗ (Gift)Gas *n*, (Gas)Kampfstoff *m*: ~ **shell** Gasgranate *f*; **6.** *mot.* F a) *Am.* Ben'zin *n*, 'Sprit' *m*, b) 'Gas(pe,dal) *n*: **step on the** ~ Gas geben, 'auf die Tube drücken' (*beide a. fig.*); **7.** *sl.* a) 'Gequatsche' *n*, b) 'Gaudi' *f*, Mords-

spaß *m*: **it's a** (**real**) ~*!* (das ist) zum Brüllen!, *weitS.* große Klasse!; **II** *v/t.* **8.** mit Gas versorgen *od.* füllen; **9.** ⊛ begasen; **10.** vergasen, mit Gas töten *od.* vernichten; **11.** ~ **up** *mot. Auto* voll tanken; **III** *v/i.* **12.** *mst* ~ **up** *Am.* F (auf-) tanken; **13.** F 'quatschen'; **'~·bag** *s.* **1.** ⊛ Gassack *m*, -zelle *f*; **2.** F 'Quatscher' *m*; ~ **bomb** *s.* ✗ Kampfstoffbombe *f*; ~ **bot·tle** *s.* ⊛ Gas-, Stahlflasche *f*; ~ **burn·er** *s.* Gasbrenner *m*; ~ **cham·ber** *s.* **1.** Gaskammer *f* (*zur Hinrichtung*); **2.** ✗ Gasprüfraum *m*; ~ **coal** *s.* Gaskohle *f*; ~ **coke** *s.* (Gas)Koks *m*; ~ **cook·er** *s.* Gasherd *m*; ~ **cyl·in·der** *s.* Gasflasche *f*; ~ **en·gine** *s.* 'Gasmotor *m*, -ma,schine *f.*
gas·e·ous ['gæsjəs] *adj.* **1.** 🔥 a) gasartig, -förmig, b) Gas...; **2.** *fig.* leer.
gas| **field** *s.* (Erd)Gasfeld *n*; **'~·,fired** *adj.* mit Gasfeuerung, gasbeheizt; ~ **fit·ter** *s.* 'Gasinstalla,teur *m*; ~ **fit·ting** *s.* **1.** 'Gasinstallati,on *f*; **2.** *pl.* 'Gasarma,turen *pl.*; ~ **gan·grene** *s.* ⚕ Gasbrand *m*; ~ **guz·zler** *s. mot. bsd. Am.* F Ben'zinschlucker *m*, -fresser *m.*
gash [gæʃ] **I** *s.* **1.** klaffende Wunde, tiefer Schnitt *od.* Riss; **2.** Spalte *f*; **II** *v/t.* **3.** *j-m* e-e klaffende Wunde beibringen.
gas| **heat·er** *s.* Gasofen *m*; ~ **heat·ing** *s.* Gasheizung *f.*
gas·i·fi·ca·tion [ˌgæsɪfɪ'keɪʃn] *s.* ⊛ Vergasung *f*; **gas·i·fy** ['gæsɪfaɪ] **I** *v/t.* vergasen, in Gas verwandeln; **II** *v/i.* zu Gas werden.
gas jet *s.* Gasflamme *f*, -brenner *m.*
gas·ket ['gæskɪt] *s.* ⊛ 'Dichtung(sman,schette *f*, -sring *m*) *f*: **blow a** ~ *fig.* F 'durchdrehen'.
'gas·light *s.* Gaslicht *n*, -lampe *f*; ~ **light·er** *s.* **1.** Gasfeuerzeug *n*; **2.** Gasanzünder *m*; ~ **main** *s.* (Haupt-) Gasleitung *f*; '~·**man** [-mæn] *s.* [*irr.*] **1.** 'Gasinstalla,teur *m*; **2.** Gasmann *m*, -ableser *m*; ~ **man·tle** *s.* (Gas)Glühstrumpf *m*; ~ **mask** *s.* ✗ Gasmaske *f*; ~ **me·ter** *s.* ⊛ Gasuhr *f*, -zähler *m*; ~ **mo·tor** → **gas engine**.
gas·o·lene, gas·o·line ['gæsəʊliːn] *s.* **1.** 🔥 Gaso'lin *n*, Gasäther *m*; **2.** *Am.* Ben'zin *n*: ~ **ga(u)ge** Kraftstoffmesser *m*, Benzinuhr *f.*
gas·om·e·ter [gæ'sɒmɪtə] *s.* Gaso'meter *m*, Gasbehälter *m.*
gas ov·en *s.* Gasherd *m.*
gasp [gɑːsp] **I** *v/i.* keuchen (*a. Maschine etc.*): ~ **for breath** nach Luft schnappen; **it made me** ~ mir stockte der Atem (*vor Erstaunen*); ~ **for s.th.** *fig.* nach et. lechzen; **II** *v/t.* a. ~ **out** *Worte* (her'vor)keuchen: ~ **one's life out** sein Leben aushauchen; **III** *s.* a) Keuchen *n*, b) Laut *m* des Erstaunens *od.* Erschreckens: **at one's last** ~ in den letzten Zügen (liegend), *fig.* 'am Eingehen'; **'gasp·er** [-pə] *s. Brit. sl.* 'Stäbchen' *n* (*Zigarette*).
gas| **pipe** *s.* Gasrohr *n*; '~·**proof** *adj.* gasdicht; ~ **pump** *s. mot. Am.* Zapfsäule *f*; ~ **range** *s. Am.* Gasherd *m*; ~ **ring** *s.* Gasbrenner *m*, -kocher *m.*
gassed [gæst] *adj.* vergast, gaskrank, -vergiftet; **gas·ser** ['gæsə] *s.* **1.** Gas freigebende Ölquelle; **2.** F 'Quatscher' *m*; **gas·sing** ['gæsɪŋ] *s.* **1.** ⊛ Behandlung *f* mit Gas; **2.** Vergasung *f*; **3.** F 'Quatschen' *n.*
gas| **sta·tion** *s. Am.* Tankstelle *f*; ~ **stove** *s.* Gasherd *m od.* -ofen *m*; ~ **tank** *s.* Gas- *od. Am.* F Ben'zinbehälter *m*; ~ **tar** *s.* Steinkohlenteer *m.*
gas·ter·o·pod ['gæstərəpɒd] → **gastropod**.

G

'**gas·tight** *adj.* gasdicht.

gas·tric ['gæstrɪk] *adj.* ✚ gastrisch, Magen...: **~ acid** Magensäure *f*; **~ flu** Darmgrippe *f*; **~ juice** Magensaft *m*; **~ ulcer** Magengeschwür *n*; **gas·tri·tis** [gæ'straɪtɪs] *s.* ✚ Ga'stritis *f*, Magenschleimhautentzündung *f*; **gas·tro·en·ter·i·tis** [ˌgæstrəʊentə'raɪtɪs] *s.* ✚ Gastroente'ritis *f*, 'Magen-'Darm-Ka-,tarr(h) *m*; **gas·tro·in·tes·ti·nal** [ˌgæstrəʊɪn'testɪnl] *adj.* ✚ gastrointesti'nal.

gas·trol·o·gist [gæ'strɒlədʒɪst] *s.* **1.** ✚ Facharzt *m* für Magenkrankheiten; **2.** *humor.* Gastronomen *m*.

gas·tro·nome ['gæstrənəʊm], **gas·tron·o·mer** [gæ'strɒnəmə] *s.* Feinschmecker *m*; **gas·tro·nom·ic, gas·tro·nom·i·cal** [ˌgæstrə'nɒmɪk(l)] *adj.* □ feinschmeckerisch; **gas·tron·o·mist** [gæ'strɒnəmɪst] → **gastronome**; **gas·tron·o·my** [gæ'strɒnəmɪ] *s.* **1.** Gastrono'mie *f*, höhere Kochkunst; **2.** *fig.* Küche *f*: **the Italian ~.**

gas·tro·pod ['gæstrəpɒd] *s. zo.* Gastro-'pode *m*, Schnecke *f*.

gas·tro·scope ['gæstrəʊskəʊp] *s.* ✚ Magenspiegel *m*.

gas| weld·ing *s.* ⊕ Gasschweißen *n*; '**~·works** *s. pl. sg. konstr.* Gaswerk *n*.

gat [gæt] *s. Am. sl.* ,Ka'none' *f*, ,Ballermann' *m*, ,Schießeisen' *n*.

gate [geɪt] **I** *s.* **1.** Tor *n*, Pforte *f*, *fig. a.* Zugang *m*, Weg *m* (**to** zu): **crash the ~** → **gatecrash**; **2.** a) ✚ Sperre *f*, Schranke *f*, b) ✈ Flugsteig *m*; **3.** (enger) Eingang, (schmale) 'Durchfahrt; **4.** (Gebirgs)Pass *m*; **5.** ⊕ (Schleusen-)Tor *n*; **6.** *sport:* a) *Slalom:* Tor *n*, b) → **starting gate**; **7.** *sport* a) Besucherzahl *f*, b) (Gesamt)Einnahmen *pl.*, Kasse *f*; **8.** ⊕ Schieber *m*, Ven'til *n*; **9.** Gießerei: (Einguss)Trichter *m*, Anschnitt *m*; **10.** *phot.* Bild-, Filmfenster *n*; **11.** ↯ 'Tor-im,puls *m*; **12.** *TV* Ausblendstufe *f*; **13.** *Am.* F a) ,Rausschmiss' *m*, b) ,Laufpass' *m*: **get the ~** ,gefeuert' werden; **give s.o. the ~** a) j-n ,feuern', b) j-m den Laufpass geben; **II** *v/t.* **14.** *ped., univ. Brit.* j-m den Ausgang sperren: **he was ~d** er erhielt Ausgangsverbot; '**~·crash** *v/i.* (*u. v/t.*) F a) uneingeladen kommen *od.* gehen (zu *e-r Party etc.*), b) sich (ohne zu bezahlen) einschmuggeln (in *e-e Veranstaltung*); '**~,crash·er** *s.* F Eindringling *m*: a) uneingeladener Gast, b) *j-d, der sich in e-e Veranstaltung einschmuggelt*; '**~,keep·er** *s.* **1.** Pförtner *m*; **2.** ✚ Bahn-, Schrankenwärter *m*; '**~·leg(ged) ta·ble** *s.* Klapptisch *m*; **~ mon·ey** → **gate** 7b; '**~·post** *s.* Tor-, Türpfosten *m*: **between you and me and the ~** im Vertrauen *od.* unter uns (gesagt); '**~·way** *s.* **1.** Torweg *m*, Einfahrt *f*; **2.** *fig.* Tor *n*, Zugang *m*: **~ drug** Einstiegsdroge *f*.

gath·er ['gæðə] **I** *v/t.* **1.** Personen versammeln; → **father** 4; **2.** Dinge (an)sammeln, anhäufen: **~ wealth; ~ experience** Erfahrung(en) sammeln; **~ facts** Fakten zs.-tragen, Material sammeln; **~ strength** Kräfte sammeln; **3.** a) ernten, sammeln, b) *Blumen, Obst etc.* pflücken; **4.** a. **~ up** aufsammeln, -lesen, -heben: **~ o.s. together** zs.-raffen; **~ s.o. in one's arms** j-n in s-e Arme schließen; **5.** erwerben, gewinnen, ansetzen: **~ dust** verstauben; **~ speed** Geschwindigkeit aufnehmen, schneller werden; **~ way** ♎ in Fahrt kommen (*a. fig.*), *fig.* sich durchsetzen; **6.** *fig.* folgern (*a. ⚕*), schließen (**from** aus); **7.** *Näherei:* raffen, kräuseln, zs.-ziehen; → **brow** 1; **8.**

~ up a) *Kleid etc.* aufnehmen, zs.-raffen, b) *die Beine* einziehen; **II** *v/i.* **9.** sich versammeln *od.* scharen (**round s.o.** um j-n); **10.** sich (an)sammeln, sich häufen; **11.** sich zs.-ziehen *od.* -ballen (*Wolken, Gewitter*); **12.** anwachsen, sich entwickeln, zunehmen; **13.** ⚕ a) reifen (*Abszess*), b) eitern (*Wunde*); '**gath·er·er** [-ərə] *s.* **1.** Erntearbeiter(in), Schnitter(in), Winzer *m*; **2.** (Ein)Sammler *m*; Geldeinnehmer *m*; '**gath·er·ing** [-ðərɪŋ] *s.* **1.** Sammeln *n*; **2.** Sammlung *f*; **3.** a) (Menschen)Ansammlung *f*, b) Versammlung *f*, Zs.-kunft *f*; **4.** ⚕ a) Reifen *n*, b) Eitern *n*; **5.** Kräuseln *n*; **6.** *Buchbinderei:* Lage *f*.

gat·ing ['geɪtɪŋ] *s.* **1.** ↯ a) Austastung *f*, b) (Sig'nal)Auswertung *f*; **2.** *ped., univ. Brit.* Ausgangsverbot *n*.

gauche [gəʊʃ] *adj.* **1.** linkisch; **2.** taktlos; **gau·che·rie** ['gəʊʃərɪ:] *s.* **1.** linkische Art; **2.** Taktlosigkeit *f*.

Gau·cho ['gaʊtʃəʊ] *pl.* **-chos** *s.* Gaucho *m*.

gaud [gɔːd] *s.* **1.** billiger Schmuck, Flitterkram *m*; **2.** *oft pl.* (über'triebener) Prunk; '**gaud·i·ness** [-dɪnɪs] *s.* **1.** → **gaud**; **2.** Protzigkeit *f*, Geschmacklosigkeit *f*; '**gaud·y** [-dɪ] **I** *adj.* □ (farben-) prächtig, auffällig (bunt), *Farben:* grell, schreiend, *Einrichtung etc.:* protzig; **II** *s. ped., univ. Brit.* jährliches Festessen.

gauf·fer → **goffer**.

gauge [geɪdʒ] **I** *s.* **1.** Nor'mal-, Eichmaß *n*; **2.** ⊕ Messgerät *n*, Messer *m*, Anzeiger *m*: *bsd.* a) Pegel *m*, Wasserstandsanzeiger *m*, b) Mano'meter *n*, Druckmesser *m*, c) Lehre *f*, d) Maß-, Zollstock *m*, e) *typ.* Zeilenmaß *n*; **3.** ⊕ (Blech-, Draht)Stärke *f*; **4.** *Strumpfherstellung:* Gauge *n* (*Maschenzahl*); **5.** ✗ Ka'liber *n*; **6.** ✚ Spur(weite) *f*; **7.** ♎ *oft* **gage** Abstand *m*, Lage *f*: **have the lee** (**weather**) **~** zu Lee (Luv) liegen (*Schiff*); **8.** 'Umfang *m*, Inhalt *m*: **take the ~ of** → 12; **9.** *fig.* Maßstab *m*, Norm *f*; **II** *v/t.* **10.** (ab)lehren, (ab-, aus)messen; **11.** eichen, justieren; **12.** *fig.* (ab)schätzen, beurteilen; **~ lathe** *s.* Präzisi'onsdrehbank *f*.

gaug·er ['geɪdʒə] *s.* Eichmeister *m*.

gaug·ing ['geɪdʒɪŋ] *s.* ⊕ Eichung *f*, Messung *f*: **~ office** Eichamt *n*.

Gaul [gɔːl] *s.* **1.** Gallier *m*; **2.** Fran'zose *m*; '**Gaul·ish** [-lɪʃ] **I** *adj.* gallisch; **II** *s. ling.* Gallisch *n*.

Gaull·ism ['gəʊlɪzəm] *s. pol.* Gaul'lismus *m*.

gaunt [gɔːnt] *adj.* □ **1.** a) hager, mager, b) ausgemergelt; **2.** verlassen, öde; **3.** kahl.

gaunt·let¹ ['gɔːntlɪt] *s.* ✗ *hist.* Panzerhandschuh *m*; **2.** *fig.* Fehdehandschuh *m*: **fling** (*od.* **throw**) **down the ~** (**to s.o.**) (j-m) den Fehdehandschuh hinwerfen, (j-m) herausfordern; **pick** (*od.* **take**) **up the ~** die Herausforderung annehmen; **3.** Schutzhandschuh *m*.

gaunt·let² ['gɔːntlɪt] *s.*: **run the ~** Spießruten laufen (*a. fig.*); **run the ~ of s.th.** et. durchstehen müssen.

gaun·try ['gɔːntrɪ] → **gantry**.

gauss [gaʊs] *s. phys.* Gauß *n*.

gauze [gɔːz] *s.* **1.** Gaze *f*, ✚ *a.* (Verbands)Mull *m*: **~ bandage** Mull-, Gazebinde *f*; **2.** *fig.* Dunst *m*, Schleier *m*; '**gauz·y** [-zɪ] *adj.* gazeartig, hauchdünn.

ga·vage [gævɑːʒ] *s.* ✚ künstliche Sonderernährung.

gave [geɪv] *pret. von* **give**.

gav·el ['gævl] *s.* **1.** Hammer *m* e-s *Auktionators, Vorsitzenden etc.*; **2.** (Maurer)Schlägel *m*.

ga·vot(te) [gə'vɒt] *s.* ♪ Ga'votte *f*.

gawk [gɔːk] **I** *s. contp.* (Bauern)Lackel *m*; **II** *v/i.* → **gawp**; '**gawk·y** [-kɪ] *adj. contp.* ,blöd(e)', trottelhaft.

gawp [gɔːp] *v/i.* glotzen: **~ at** anglotzen.

gay [geɪ] *adj.* □ → **gaily**; **1.** lustig, fröhlich; **2.** a) bunt, (farben)prächtig, b) **~ with** belebt von, geschmückt mit, b) fröhlich, lebhaft (*Farben*); **3.** flott, *Person:* a. lebenslustig: **a ~ dog** ein ,lockerer Vogel'; **4.** liederlich; **5.** *Am. sl.* ,pampig', frech; **6.** F homosexu'ell, ,schwul', Schwulen...: **⚥ Lib**(**eration**) *die* Schwulenbewegung.

gaze [geɪz] **I** *v/i.* starren: **~ at** anstarren; **~** (**up**)**on** ansichtig werden (*gen.*); **II** *s.* (starrer) Blick, Starren *n*.

ga·ze·bo [gə'ziːbəʊ] *s.* Gebäude *n* mit schönem Ausblick, Aussichtspunkt *m*.

ga·zelle [gə'zel] *s. zo.* Ga'zelle *f*.

gaz·er ['geɪzə] *s.* Gaffer *m*.

ga·zette [gə'zet] **I** *s.* **1.** Zeitung *f*; **2.** *Brit.* Amtsblatt *n*, Staatsanzeiger *m*; **II** *v/t.* **3.** *Brit.* im Amtsblatt bekannt geben *od.* veröffentlichen; **gaz·et·teer** [ˌgæzə'tɪə] *s.* alpha'betisches Ortsverzeichnis (mit Ortsbeschreibung).

gear [gɪə] **I** *s.* **1.** ⊕ a) Zahnrad *n*, b) *a. pl.* Getriebe *n*, Triebwerk *n*; **2.** ⊕ a) Über'setzung *f*, b) *mot. etc.* Gang *m*: **first** (**second**, *etc.*) **~; in high ~** in hohen *od.* schnellen Gang; **get into** (**high**) **~** *fig.* in Fahrt *od.* Schwung kommen; **in low** (*od.* **bottom**) **~** im ersten Gang; (**in**) **top ~** im höchsten Gang; **change** (*Am.* **shift**) **~**(**s**) schalten; **change into second ~** den zweiten Gang einlegen, c) *pl.* Gangschaltung *f* (*e-s Fahrrads*); **3.** ⊕ Eingriff *m*: **in ~** a) eingerückt, eingeschaltet, b) *fig.* funktionierend, in Ordnung; **in ~ with** im Eingriff stehend mit; **out of ~** a) ausgerückt, ausgeschaltet, b) *fig.* in Unordnung, nicht funktionierend; **throw out of ~** ausrücken, -schalten, *fig.* durcheinander bringen; **4.** ✈, ♎ *etc. mst in Zssgn* Vorrichtung *f*, Gerät *n*; → **landing gear** *etc.*; **5.** Ausrüstung *f*, Gerät *n*, Werkzeug(e *pl.*) *n*, Zubehör *n*: **fishing ~** Angelgerät *n*, -zeug *n*; **6.** F a) Hausrat *m*, b) Habseligkeiten *pl.*, Sachen *pl.*, c) Aufzug *m*, Kleidung *f*; **7.** (Pferde- *etc.*)Geschirr *n*; **II** *v/t.* **8.** ⊕ a) mit e-m Getriebe versehen, b) über'setzen, c) in Gang setzen (*a. fig.*): **~ up** ins Schnelle übersetzen, *fig.* steigern, verstärken; **9.** *fig.* (**to, for**) einstellen *od.* abstimmen (auf *acc.*), anpassen (*dat. od.* an *acc.*); **10.** ausrüsten; **11.** *a.* **~ up** *Tiere* anschirren; **III** *v/i.* **12.** ⊕ a) eingreifen (**into, with** in *acc.*), b) inein'ander greifen; **13.** **~ up** (**down**) *mot.* hinauf- (her'unter)schalten; **14.** *fig.* (**with**) passen (zu), eingerichtet *od.* abgestimmt sein (auf *acc.*).

'**gear| box** *s.* ⊕ Getriebe(gehäuse) *n*; **~ change** *s. Brit. mot.* (Gang)Schaltung *f*; **~ cut·ter** *s.* Zahnradfräser *m*; **~ drive** → **gearing** 1.

gear·ed [gɪəd] *adj.* ⊕ verzahnt; Getriebe...; **gear·ing** ['gɪərɪŋ] *s.* ⊕ **1.** (Zahnrad)Getriebe *n*, Vorgelege *n*; **2.** Über'setzung *f* (*e-s Getriebes*); Transmissi'on *f*; **3.** Verzahnung *f*.

'**gear| le·ver** *s.* Schalthebel *m*; **~ ra·tio** *s.* Über'setzung(sverhältnis *n*) *f*; **~ rim** *s.* Zahnkranz *m*; **~ shaft** *s.* Getriebe-, Schaltwelle *f*; **~ shift** *s. Am.* a) → **gear change**, b) → **gear lever**; '**~·wheel** *s.* Getriebe-, Zahnrad *n*.

geck·o ['gekəʊ] *pl.* **-os, -oes** *s. zo.* Gecko *m* (*Echse*).

gee¹ [dʒiː] *s.* G *n*, g *n* (*Buchstabe*).

gee² [dʒi:] **I** s. **1.** *Kindersprache*: ‚Hotte-'hü' n (*Pferd*); **II** int. **2.** a. ~ *up!* a) hott! (*nach rechts*), b) hü(h), hott! (*schneller*); **3.** Am. F na so was!, Mann!

geek [gi:k] s. **1.** komischer Typ; **2.** (Computer- *etc.*)Freak m; **3.** Langweiler m.

geese [gi:s] pl. *von* **goose.**

gee| whiz [ˌdʒi:ˈwɪz] → **gee²** 3; '~**-whiz** adj. Am. F **1.** ‚toll', Super...; **2.** Sensations...

gee·zer [ˈgi:zə] s. F komischer (alter) Kauz, ‚Opa' m.

Gei·ger count·er [ˈgaɪgə] s. phys. Geigerzähler m.

gei·sha [ˈgeɪʃə] s. Geisha f.

gel [dʒel] **I** s. **1.** Gel n; **II** v/i. **2.** gelieren; **3.** → *jell* 3.

gel·a·tin(e) [ˌdʒeləˈti:n] s. **1.** Gelatine f; **2.** Gal'lerte f; **3.** a. *blasting* ~ 'Sprenggela,tine f; **ge·lat·i·nize** [dʒəˈlætɪnaɪz] v/i. u. v/t. gelatinieren (lassen); **ge·lat·i·nous** [dʒəˈlætɪnəs] adj. gallertartig.

geld [geld] v/t. *Tier* kastrieren, verschneiden; '**geld·ing** [-dɪŋ] s. kastriertes Tier, bsd. Wallach m.

gel·id [ˈdʒelɪd] adj. □ eisig.

gel·ig·nite [ˈdʒelɪgnaɪt] s. ☉ Gela'tinedyna,mit n.

gem [dʒem] **I** s. **1.** Edelstein m; **2.** Gemme f; **3.** fig. Perle f, Ju'wel n, Glanz-, Prachtstück n: ~ *role* thea. Glanzrolle f; **4.** Am. Brötchen n; **5.** typ. e-e 3¹/₂-Punkt-Schrift; **II** v/t. **6.** mit Edelsteinen schmücken.

gem·i·nate I adj. [ˈdʒemɪnət] paarweise, Doppel...; **II** v/t. u. v/i. [-neɪt] (sich) verdoppeln (a. ling.); **gem·i·na·tion** [ˌdʒemɪˈneɪʃn] s. Verdoppelung f (a. ling.).

Gem·i·ni [ˈdʒemɪnaɪ] s. pl. ast. Zwillinge pl.

gem·ma [ˈdʒemə] pl. **-mae** [-mi:] s. **1.** ♀ a) Gemme f, Brutkörper m, b) Blattknospe f; **2.** biol. Gemme f; '**gem·mate** [-meɪt] adj. biol. sich durch Knospung fortpflanzend; **gem·ma·tion** [dʒeˈmeɪʃn] s. **1.** ♀ Knospenbildung f; **2.** biol. Fortpflanzung f durch Knospen; **gem·mif·er·ous** [dʒeˈmɪfərəs] adj. **1.** edelsteinhaltig; **2.** biol. → *gemmate.*

gems·bok [ˈgemzbɒk] s. zo. 'Gämsan,ti,lope f.

gen [dʒen] Brit. sl. **I** s. Informati'on(en pl.) f; **II** v/t. u. v/i.: ~ *up* (sich) informieren.

gen·der [ˈdʒendə] s. ling. Genus n, Geschlecht n (a. humor. von Personen); ~ **ben·der** s. F jemand vom anderen Ufer.

gene [dʒi:n] s. biol. Gen n, Erbfaktor m: ~ *bank* 'Genbank f; ~ *pool* Erbmasse f; ~ *technology* Gentechnologie f.

gen·e·a·log·i·cal [ˌdʒi:njəˈlɒdʒɪkl] adj. □ genea'logisch: ~ *tree* Stammbaum m.

gen·e·al·o·gist [ˌdʒi:nɪˈælədʒɪst] s. Genea'loge m, Ahnenforscher m; ¸**gen·e'al·o·gize** [-dʒaɪz] v/i. Stammbaumforschung treiben; ¸**gen·e'al·o·gy** [-dʒɪ] s. Genealo'gie f: a) Ahnenforschung f, b) Ahnentafel f, c) Abstammung f.

gen·er·a [ˈdʒenərə] pl. *von* **genus.**

gen·er·al [ˈdʒenərəl] **I** adj. □ → *generally*; **1.** allgemein, um'fassend: ~ *knowledge* (*medicine*) Allgemeinbildung f (-medizin f); ~ *outlook* allgemeine Aussichten; *the* ~ *public* die breite Öffentlichkeit; **2.** allgemein (*nicht speziell*): ~ *dealer* Brit. Gemischtwarenhändler m; *the* ~ *reader* der Durchschnittsleser; ~ *store* Ge-

mischtwarenhandlung f; ~ *term* Allgemeinbegriff m; *in* ~ *terms* allgemein (ausgedrückt); **3.** allgemein (üblich), gängig, verbreitet: ~ *practice; as a* ~ *rule* meistens; **4.** allgemein gehalten, ungefähr: *a* ~ *idea* e-e ungefähre Vorstellung; ~ *resemblance* vage Ähnlichkeit; *in a* ~ *way* in großen Zügen, in gewisser Weise; **5.** allgemein, General..., Haupt...: ~ *agent* ✝ Generalvertreter m; ~ *manager* ✝ Generaldirektor m; ~ *meeting* ✝ General-, Hauptversammlung f; **6.** (*Amtstiteln nachgestellt*) mst General ~ *consul* Generalkonsul m; **II** s. **7.** ✗ a) Gene'ral m, b) Heerführer m, Feldherr m, Stra'tege m; **8.** ✗ Am. a) (Vier'sterne)Gene,ral m (*zweithöchster Offiziersrang*), b) ~ *of the army* Fünf'sternegene,ral m (*höchster Offiziersrang*); **9.** eccl. ('Ordens)Gene,ral m; **10.** the ~ das Allgemeine: ☙ (*Überschrift*) Allgemeines; *in* ~ im Allgemeinen.

gen·er·al| ac·cept·ance s. ✝ uneingeschränktes Ak'zept; ☙ **As·sem·bly** s. **1.** pol. Voll-, Gene'ralversammlung f (*der UNO*); **2.** pol. Am. Parla'ment n (*einiger Einzelstaaten*); **3.** eccl. oberstes Gericht der schottischen Kirche; ~ **car·go** s. ✝, ♣ Stückgut(ladung f) n; ☙ **Cer·tif·i·cate of Ed·u·ca·tion** s. ped. Brit.: ~ *O level etwa*: mittlere Reife; ~ *A level etwa*: Abitur n; ~ **de·liv·er·y** ☙ Am. **1.** (Ausgabestelle f für) postlagernde Sendungen pl.; **2.** ‚postlagernd'; **e·lec·tion** s. pol. allgemeine Wahlen pl.; ~ **head·quar·ters** s. pl. mst sg. konstr. ✗ Großes Hauptquartier; **hos·pi·tal** s. allgemeines Krankenhaus.

gen·er·al·is·si·mo [ˌdʒenərəˈlɪsɪməʊ] pl. **-mos** s. ✗ Genera'lissimus m, Oberbefehlshaber m.

gen·er·al·ist [ˈdʒenərəlɪst] s. Genera'list m (*Ggs.* Spezialist).

gen·er·al·i·ty [ˌdʒenəˈrælətɪ] s. **1.** pl. allgemeine Redensarten pl., Gemeinplätze pl.; **2.** Allgemeingültigkeit f; **3.** allgemeine Regel; **4.** Unbestimmtheit f; **5.** obs. Mehrzahl f, große Masse; **gen·er·al·i·za·tion** [ˌdʒenərəlaɪˈzeɪʃn] s. Verallgemeinerung f; **gen·er·al·ize** [ˈdʒenərəlaɪz] **I** v/t. **1.** verallgemeinern; **2.** auf e-e allgemeine Formel bringen; **3.** paint. in großen Zügen darstellen; **II** v/i. **4.** verallgemeinern; **gen·er·al·ly** [ˈdʒenərəlɪ] adv. **1.** oft ~ *speaking* allgemein, im Allgemeinen, im Großen u. Ganzen; **2.** allgemein; **3.** gewöhnlich, meistens.

gen·er·al| med·i·cine s. Allge'meinmedi,zin f; ~ **meet·ing** s. General-, Hauptversammlung f; ~ **of·fi·cer** ✗ Gene'ral m, Offi'zier m im Gene'ralsrang; ~ **par·don** s. (Gene'ral)Amnes,tie f; ☙ **Post Of·fice** s. Hauptpostamt n; ~ **prac·ti·tion·er** s. Arzt m für Allge'meinmedi,zin, praktischer Arzt; ¸~ '**pur·pose** adj. ☉ Mehrzweck..., Universal...; ~ *road* vom Individu'alverkehr genutzte Straße; ~ *road vehicle* Allzweckfahrzeug n.

gen·er·al·ship [ˈdʒenərəlʃɪp] s. **1.** ✗ Gene'ralsrang m; **2.** Strate'gie f: a) Feldherrnkunst f, b) a. allg. geschickte Taktik.

gen·er·al| staff s. ✗ Gene'ralstab m: ~ *chief of* ~ Generalstabschef m; ~ **strike** s. ✝ Gene'ralstreik m.

gen·er·ate [ˈdʒenəreɪt] v/t. **1.** bsd. ✿, phys. erzeugen (a. ⚡), Gas, Rauch entwickeln, a. ⚛ bilden; **2.** biol. zeugen; **3.** fig. erzeugen, her'vorrufen, bewir-

ken, verursachen.

gen·er·at·ing sta·tion [ˈdʒenəreɪtɪŋ] s. ⚡ Kraftwerk n.

gen·er·a·tion [ˌdʒenəˈreɪʃn] s. **1.** Generati'on f: *the rising* ~ die junge (*od.* heranwachsende) Generation; ~ *gap* Generationsunterschied m, Generationenkonflikt m; **2.** Generati'on f, Menschenalter n (*etwa 33 Jahre*): ~s F e-e Ewigkeit; **3.** ⊙, ⚡ Generati'on f: *a new* ~ *of cars*; **4.** biol. Entwicklungsstufe f; **5.** Zeugung f, Fortpflanzung f; **6.** bsd. ✿, ⚡, phys. Erzeugung f (a. ⚛), Entwicklung f; **7.** Entstehung f; ¸**gen·er'a·tion·al** [-ʃənl] adj. Generations...: ~ *conflict*; **gen·er·a·tive** [ˈdʒenərətɪv] adj. **1.** biol. Zeugungs..., Fortpflanzungs..., Geschlechts...; **2.** biol. fruchtbar; **3.** ling. genera'tiv: ~ *grammar*; **gen·er·a·tor** [ˈdʒenəreɪtə] s. **1.** ⚡ Gene'rator m, Stromerzeuger m, Dy'namoma,schine f; **2.** ⊙ a) Gaserzeuger m: ~ *gas* Generatorgas n, b) Dampferzeuger m, -kessel m; **3.** ⊙ (Ab)Wälzfräser m; **4.** 🔬 Entwickler m; **5.** ♪ Grundton m.

ge·ner·ic [dʒɪˈnerɪk] adj. (□ ~*ally*) **1.** allgemein, gene'rell; **2.** ge'nerisch, Gattungs...: ~ *term od. name* Gattungsname m, Oberbegriff m.

gen·er·os·i·ty [ˌdʒenəˈrɒsətɪ] s. **1.** Großzügigkeit f: a) Freigebigkeit f, b) Edelmut m, Hochherzigkeit f; **2.** edle Tat; **3.** Fülle f; **gen·er·ous** [ˈdʒenərəs] adj. □ **1.** großzügig: a) freigebig, b) edel, hochherzig; **2.** reichlich, üppig: ~ *mouth* volle Lippen pl.; **3.** vollmundig, gehaltvoll (*Wein*); fruchtbar (*Boden*).

gen·e·sis [ˈdʒenɪsɪs] s. **1.** Genesis f, Ge'nese f, Entstehung f; **2.** ☙ bibl. Genesis f, Erstes Buch Mose; **3.** Ursprung m.

gen·et [ˈdʒenɪt] s. zo. **1.** Ge'nette f, Ginsterkatze f; **2.** Ge'nettepelz m.

ge·net·ic [dʒɪˈnetɪk] **I** adj. (□ ~*ally*) **1.** bsd. biol. ge'netisch: a) entwicklungsgeschichtlich, b) Vererbungs..., Erb..., c) 'gentechnisch: ~ *code* genetischer Kode; ~ *engineering* Genmanipulation f, -technik f; ~*ally manipulated, changed, modified* genetisch (*od.* gentechnisch) manipuliert, verändert; ~ *fingerprint* genetischer Fingerabdruck; ~ *information* Erbinformation f; **II** s. pl. biol. **2.** sg. konstr. Ge'netik f, Vererbungslehre f; **3.** ge'netische Formen pl. u. Erscheinungen pl.; **ge'net·i·cist** [-ɪsɪst] s. biol. Ge'netiker m.

ge·nette [dʒɪˈnet] → *genet.*

ge·ne·va¹ [dʒɪˈni:və] s. Ge'never m, Wa'cholderschnaps m.

Ge·ne·va² [dʒɪˈni:və] **I** npr. Genf n; **II** adj. Genfer(...); ~ **bands** s. pl. eccl. Beffchen n; ~ **Con·ven·tion** s. pol., ✗ Genfer Konventi'on f; ~ **cross** → *red 1*; ~ **drive** s. ⊙ Mal'teserkreuzantrieb m; ~ **gown** s. eccl. Ta'lar m.

ge·ni·al [ˈdʒi:njəl] adj. □ **1.** freundlich (a. fig. Klima etc.), herzlich: *in* ~ *company* in angenehmer Gesellschaft; **2.** belebend, anregend; **ge·ni·al·i·ty** [ˌdʒi:nɪˈælətɪ] s. **1.** Freundlichkeit f, Herzlichkeit f; **2.** Milde f (*Klima*).

ge·nie [ˈdʒi:nɪ] s. dienstbarer Geist, Dschinn m.

ge·ni·i [ˈdʒi:nɪaɪ] pl. *von* **genie** u. **genius** 4.

gen·i·tal [ˈdʒenɪtl] adj. Zeugungs..., Geschlechts..., geni'tal: ~ *gland* Keimdrüse f; '**gen·i·tals** [-lz] s. pl. Geni'talien pl., Geschlechtsteile pl.

gen·i·ti·val [ˌdʒenɪˈtaɪvl] adj. Genitiv..., genitivisch; **gen·i·tive** [ˈdʒenɪtɪv] s. a. ~ *case* ling. Genitiv m, zweiter Fall.

G

gen·i·to-u·ri·nar·y [ˌdʒenɪtəʊˈjʊərɪnərɪ] *adj.* ♂ urogeni'tal.

ge·ni·us [ˈdʒiːnjəs] *pl.* **'ge·ni·us·es** *s.* **1.** Ge'nie *n:* a) geni'aler Mensch, b) (*ohne pl.*) Geniali'tät *f,* geni'ale Schöpferkraft; **2.** Begabung *f,* Gabe *f;* **3.** Genius *m,* Geist *m,* Seele *f, das* Eigentümliche (*e-r Nation etc.*): *~ of a period* Zeitgeist; **4.** *pl.* **'ge·ni·i** [-nɪaɪ] *antiq.* Genius *m,* Schutzgeist *m: good (evil) ~* guter (böser) Geist (*a. fig.*); *~* **lo·ci** [ˈləʊsaɪ] (*Lat.*) *s.* a) Genius *m* Loci, Schutzgeist *m* e-s Ortes, b) Atmo'sphäre *f* e-s Ortes.

gen·o·blast [ˈdʒenəʊblɑːst] *s. biol.* reife Geschlechtszelle.

gen·o·cide [ˈdʒenəʊsaɪd] *s.* Geno'zid *m, n,* Völker-, Gruppenmord *m.*

Gen·o·ese [ˌdʒenəʊˈiːz] **I** *s.* Genu'eser (-in); **II** *adj.* genu'esisch, Genueser...

ge·nome [ˈdʒiːnəʊm] *s. biol.* Ge'nom *n.*

gen·o·type [ˈdʒenəʊtaɪp] *s. biol.* Geno'typ(us) *m.*

gen·re [ˈʒɑ̃ːŋrə] (*Fr.*) *s.* **1.** Genre *n,* (*a.* Litera'tur)Gattung *f: ~ painting* Genremalerei *f;* **2.** Form *f,* Stil *m.*

gent [dʒent] *s.* **1.** F *für* **gentleman; 2.** *pl. sg. konstr.* F ,Herrenklo' *n;* **3.** *Am.* F ,Knabe', Kerl *m.*

gen·teel [dʒenˈtiːl] *adj.* □ **1.** *obs.* vornehm; **2.** vornehm tuend, geziert, affek'tiert; **3.** ele'gant, fein.

gen·tian [ˈdʒenʃɪən] *s.* ♀ Enzian *m; ~* **bit·ter** *s. pharm.* 'Enziantink,tur *f.*

gen·tile [ˈdʒentaɪl] **I** *s.* Nichtjude *m,* -jüdin *f, bsd.* Christ(in); **2.** Heide *m,* Heidin *f;* **3.** 'Nichtmor,mone *m,* -mor,monin *f;* **II** *adj.* **4.** nichtjüdisch, *bsd.* christlich; **5.** heidnisch; **6.** 'nichtmor,monisch.

gen·til·i·ty [dʒenˈtɪlətɪ] *s.* **1.** *obs.* vornehme Herkunft; **2.** Vornehmheit *f;* **3.** Vornehmtue'rei *f.*

gen·tle [ˈdʒentl] *adj.* □ **1.** freundlich, sanft, gütig, liebenswürdig: *~ reader* geneigter Leser; **2.** milde, ruhig, mäßig, leicht, sanft, zart: *~ blow* leichter Schlag; *~ craft* Angelsport *m; ~ hint* zarter Wink; *~ rebuke* sanfter Tadel; *the ~ sex* das zarte Geschlecht; *~ slope* sanfter Abhang; **3.** zahm, fromm (*Tier*); **4.** edel, vornehm: *of ~ birth* von vornehmer Geburt; '*~*folk(s) *s. pl.* vornehme Leute *pl.*

gen·tle·man [ˈdʒentlmən] *s.* [*irr.*] **1.** Gentleman *m:* a) Ehrenmann *m,* b) Mann *m* von Lebensart u. Cha'rakter: *~'s* od. *gentlemen's*) *agreement* Gentleman's *od.* Gentlemen's) Agreement *n,* ♀ *etc.* Vereinbarung *f* auf Treu u. Glauben; *~'s ~* (Kammer)Diener *m;* **2.** Herr *m: gentlemen* a) (*Anrede*) m-e Herren!, b) *in Briefen:* Sehr geehrte Herren (*oft unübersetzt*); *~ farmer* Gutsbesitzer *m* e-r Dame; *~ rider* Herrenreiter *m;* **gentlemen('s)** Herren(toilette *f*) *pl.;* **3.** Titel von Hofbeamten: *~ in waiting* Kämmerer *m; ~-at-arms* Leibgardist *m;* **4.** *obs.* Privati'er *m;* **5.** *hist.* a) Mann *m* von Stand, b) Edelmann *m;* '*~*-like → *gentlemanly;* 'gen·tle·man·li·ness [-lɪnɪs] *s.* **1.** vornehmes *od.* feines Wesen, Vornehmheit *f;* **2.** feines Benehmen; 'gen·tle·man·ly [-lɪ] *adj.* ,gentlemanlike', vornehm, fein.

gen·tle·ness [ˈdʒentlnɪs] *s.* **1.** Freundlichkeit *f,* Güte *f,* Milde *f,* Sanftheit *f;* **2.** *obs.* Vornehmheit *f.*

'gen·tle,wom·an *s.* [*irr.*] Dame *f* (von Lebensart u. Cha'rakter; von Stand *od.* Bildung); 'gen·tle,wom·an·like, 'gen·tle,wom·an·ly [-lɪ] *adj.* damenhaft,

vornehm.

gen·tly [ˈdʒentlɪ] *adv. von* **gentle.**

gen·try [ˈdʒentrɪ] *s.* **1.** Oberschicht *f;* **2.** *Brit.* Gentry *f,* niederer Adel; **3.** *a. pl. konstr.* F Leute *pl.*, Sippschaft *f.*

gen·u·flect [ˈdʒenjuːflekt] *v/i.* (*bsd. eccl.*) knien, die Knie beugen, *contp.* e-n Kniefall machen (*before* vor *dat.*); **gen·u·flec·tion, *Brit. a.* gen·u·flex·ion** [ˌdʒenjuːˈflekʃn] *s.* Kniebeugung *f, fig.* Kniefall *m.*

gen·u·ine [ˈdʒenjʊɪn] *adj.* □ echt a) au'thentisch, b) ernsthaft (*Angebot etc.*), c) aufrichtig (*Mitgefühl etc.*), d) ungekünstelt (*Lachen etc.*); '**gen·u·ine·ness** [-nɪs] *s.* Echtheit *f.*

ge·nus [ˈdʒiːnəs] *pl.* **gen·er·a** [ˈdʒenərə] *s.* **1.** ♀, *zo.*, *phls.* Gattung *f;* **2.** *fig.* Art *f,* Klasse *f.*

ge·o·cen·tric [ˌdʒiːəʊˈsentrɪk] *adj. ast.* geo'zentrisch; '**ge·o'chem·is·try** [-ˈkemɪstrɪ] *s.* Geoche'mie *f;* '**ge·o'cy·clic** [-ˈsaɪklɪk] *adj. ast.* geo'zyklisch.

ge·ode [ˈdʒiːəʊd] *s. min. allg.* Ge'ode *f.*

ge·o·des·ic, ge·o·des·i·cal [ˌdʒiːəʊˈdes·ɪk(l)] *adj.* □ geo'dätisch; **ge·od·e·sist** [dʒiːˈɒdɪsɪst] *s.* Geo'dät *m;* **ge·od·e·sy** [dʒiːˈɒdɪsɪ] *s.* Geodä'sie *f* (*Erdvermessung*); **ge·o'det·ic, ge·o'det·i·cal** [-etɪk(l)] *adj.* geo'dätisch.

ge·og·ra·pher [dʒɪˈɒɡrəfə] *s.* Geo'graph (-in); **ge·o·graph·ic, ge·o·graph·i·cal** [dʒɪəˈɡræfɪk(l)] *adj.* □ geo'graphisch: *geographical mile;* **ge·o'gra·phy** [-fɪ] *s.* **1.** Geogra'phie *f,* Erdkunde *f;* **2.** geo'graphische Abhandlung; **3.** geo'graphische Beschaffenheit.

ge·o·log·ic, ge·o·log·i·cal [ˌdʒɪəʊˈlɒdʒɪk(l)] *adj.* □ geo'logisch; **ge·ol·o·gist** [dʒɪˈɒlədʒɪst] *s.* Geo'loge *m,* Geo'login *f;* **ge·ol·o·gize** [dʒɪˈɒlədʒaɪz] *v/i.* geo'logische Studien betreiben; **II** *v/t.* geo'logisch unter'suchen; **ge·ol·o·gy** [dʒɪˈɒlədʒɪ] *s.* **1.** Geolo'gie *f;* **2.** geo'logische Abhandlung; **3.** geo'logische Beschaffenheit.

ge·o·mag·net·ism [ˌdʒɪəʊˈmæɡnɪtɪzəm] *s. phys.* 'Erdmagne,tismus *m.*

ge·o·man·cy [ˈdʒɪəʊmænsɪ] *s.* Geoman'tie *f,* Geo'mantik *f* (*Art Wahrsagerei*).

ge·om·e·ter [dʒɪˈɒmɪtə] *s.* **1.** *obs.* Geo'meter *m;* **2.** Ex'perte *m* auf dem Gebiet der Geome'trie; **3.** *zo.* Spannerraupe *f;* **ge·o·met·ric, ge·o·met·ri·cal** [ˌdʒɪəʊˈmetrɪk(l)] *adj.* □ geo'metrisch; **ge·om·e·tri·cian** [ˌdʒɪəʊmeˈtrɪʃn] → *geometer* 1, 2; **ge'om·e·try** [-mətrɪ] *s.* **1.** Geome'trie *f;* **2.** geo'metrische Abhandlung.

ge·o·phys·i·cal [ˌdʒɪəʊˈfɪzɪkl] *adj.* geophysi'kalisch; '**ge·o'phys·ics** [-ks] *s. pl., oft sg. konstr.* Geophy'sik *f.*

ge·o·pol·i·tics [ˌdʒɪəʊˈpɒlɪtɪks] *s. pl., oft sg. konstr.* Geopoli'tik *f.*

George [dʒɔːdʒ] *s.: St ~* der heilige Georg (*Schutzpatron Englands*): *St ~'s Cross* Georgskreuz *n; ~ Cross od. Medal* ✕ *Brit.* Georgskreuz *n* (*Orden*); *by ~!* a) beim Zeus!, b) Mann!; *let ~ do it! Am. sl.* solls machen, wer Lust hat!

geor·gette [dʒɔːˈdʒet] *Am.* ♀ *s.* Geor'gette *m* (*Seidenkrepp*).

Geor·gi·an [ˈdʒɔːdʒjən] **I** *adj.* **1.** geor·gi'anisch: a) *aus der Zeit der Könige Georg I.–IV. (1714–1830),* b) *aus der Zeit der Könige Georg V. u. VI. (1910–52);* **2.** geor'ginisch (*den Staat Georgia, USA, betreffend*); **3.** ge'orgisch (*die Sowjetrepublik Georgien betreffend*); **II** *s.* **4.** Ge'orgier(in).

ge·o·sci·ence [ˌdʒiːəʊˈsaɪəns] *s.* Geo-

wissenschaft *f.*

ge·o·ther·mal [ˌdʒiːəʊˈθɜːml] *adj.* geothermisch; *~ energy* Erdwärme *f.*

ge·ra·ni·um [dʒɪˈreɪnjəm] *s.* ♀ **1.** Storchschnabel *m;* **2.** Ge'ranie *f.*

ger·fal·con [ˈdʒɜːˌfɔːlkən] *s. orn.* G(i)erfalke *m.*

ger·i·at·ric [ˌdʒerɪˈætrɪk] **I** *adj.* ♂ geri'atrisch; **II** *s. humor.* Greis *m;* **ger·i·a·tri·cian** [ˌdʒerɪəˈtrɪʃn] *s.* Geri'ater *m,* Facharzt *m* für Alterskrankheiten); ,**ger·i'at·rics** [-ks] *s. pl., oft sg. konstr.* Geria'trie *f.*

germ [dʒɜːm] **I** *s.* **1.** ♀, *biol.* Keim *m* (*a. fig.* Ansatz, *Ursprung*); **2.** a) *biol.* Mikrobe *f,* b) ♂ Keim *m,* Ba'zillus *m,* Bak'terie *f,* Krankheitserreger *m;* **II** *v/i. u. v/t.* keimen (lassen).

ger·man[1] [ˈdʒɜːmən] *adj.* leiblich: *brother ~* leiblicher Bruder.

Ger·man[2] [ˈdʒɜːmən] **I** *adj.* **1.** deutsch; **II** *s.* **2.** Deutsche(r *m*) *f;* **3.** *ling.* Deutsch *n, das* Deutsche: *in ~* a) auf Deutsch, b) im Deutschen; *into ~* ins Deutsche; *from (the) ~* aus dem Deutschen.

,**Ger·man-A'mer·i·can I** *adj.* 'deutsch-ameri,kanisch; **II** *s.* 'Deutschameri,kaner(in).

ger·man·der [dʒɜːˈmændə] *s.* ♀ **1.** Ga'mander *m; 2. a. ~ speedwell* Ga'manderehrenpreis *m.*

ger·mane [dʒɜːˈmeɪn] *adj.* (*to*) gehörig (zu), zs.-hängend (mit), betreffend (*acc.*), passend (zu).

Ger·man·ic[1] [dʒɜːˈmænɪk] **I** *adj.* **1.** ger'manisch; **2.** deutsch; **II** *s.* **3.** *ling. das* Ger'manische.

ger·man·ic[2] [dʒɜːˈmænɪk] *adj.* ♠ Germanium...: *~ acid.*

Ger·man·ism [ˈdʒɜːmənɪzəm] *s.* **1.** *ling.* Germa'nismus *m,* deutsche Spracheigenheit; **2.** (*typisch*) deutsche Art; **3.** *et.* typisch Deutsches; **4.** Deutschfreundlichkeit *f;* '**Ger·man·ist** [-ɪst] *s.* Germa'nist(in); '**Ger·man·i·ty** [dʒɜːˈmænətɪ] → *Germanism* 2.

ger·ma·ni·um [dʒɜːˈmeɪnjəm] *s.* ♠ Ger'manium *n.*

Ger·man·i·za·tion [ˌdʒɜːmənaɪˈzeɪʃn] *s.* Germanisierung *f,* Eindeutschung *f;* **Ger·man·ize** [ˈdʒɜːmənaɪz] **I** *v/t.* germanisieren, eindeutschen; **II** *v/i.* deutsch werden.

Ger·man mea·sles *s. pl. sg. konstr.* ♂ Röteln *pl.*

Ger·man·o·phil [dʒɜːˈmænəfɪl], **Ger·'man·o·phile** [-faɪl] **I** *adj.* deutschfreundlich; **II** *s.* Deutschfreundliche(r *m*) *f;* **Ger'man·o·phobe** [-fəʊb] *s.* Deutschenhasser(in); **Ger·man·o·pho·bi·a** [dʒɜːˌmænəˈfəʊbjə] *s.* Deutschfeindlichkeit *f.*

Ger·man| po·lice dog, ~ shep·herd (dog) *s. Am.* Deutscher Schäferhund; *~ sil·ver s.* Neusilber *n; ~ steel s.* ⊕ Schmelzstahl *m; ~ text, ~ type s. typ.* Frak'tur(schrift) *f.*

germ| car·ri·er *s.* ♂ Keim-, Ba'zillenträger *m; ~ cell s. biol.* Keimzelle *f.*

ger·men [ˈdʒɜːmɪn] *s.* ♀ Fruchtknoten *m.*

ger·mi·cid·al [ˌdʒɜːmɪˈsaɪdl] *adj.* keimtötend; **ger·mi·cide** [ˈdʒɜːmɪsaɪd] *adj. u. s.* keimtötend(es Mittel).

ger·mi·nal [ˈdʒɜːmɪnl] *adj.* □ **1.** *biol.* Keim(zellen)...; **2.** ♂ Keim..., Bakterien...; **3.** *fig.* keimend, im Keim befindlich: *~ ideas;* '**ger·mi·nant** [-nənt] *adj.* keimend (*a. fig.*); '**ger·mi·nate** [-neɪt] ♀ **I** *v/i.* keimen (*a. fig. sich entwickeln*); **II** *v/t.* zum Keimen bringen, keimen lassen (*a. fig.*); **ger·mi·na·tion**

G

[ˌdʒɜːmɪˈneɪʃn] s. ♣ Keimen n (a. fig.); **'ger·mi·na·tive** [-nətɪv] adj. ♣ **1.** Keim...; **2.** (keim)entwicklungsfähig. **'germ·proof** adj. keimsicher, -frei; ~ **war·fare** s. ✗ Bak'terienkrieg m, bio'logische Kriegführung.

ge·ron·toc·ra·cy [ˌdʒerɒnˈtɒkrəsɪ] s. Gerontokra'tie f, Altenherrschaft f. **ger·on·tol·o·gist** [ˌdʒerɒnˈtɒlədʒɪst] Geronto'loge m; **ger·on'tol·o·gy** [-dʒɪ] → **geriatrics.**

ger·ry·man·der ['dʒerɪmændə] I v/t. **1.** pol. die Wahlbezirksgrenzen in e-m Gebiet manipulieren; **2.** Fakten manipulieren, verfälschen; II s. **3.** pol. manipulierte Wahlbezirksabgrenzung.

ger·und ['dʒerənd] s. ling. Ge'rundium n; **ge·run·di·al** [dʒɪˈrʌndjəl] adj. ling. Gerundial...; **ger·un·di·val** [ˌdʒerən'daɪvl] adj. ling. Gerundiv..., gerun'divisch; **ge·run·dive** [dʒɪˈrʌndɪv] s. ling. Gerun'div n.

ges·ta·tion [dʒesˈteɪʃn] s. **1.** a) Schwangerschaft f, b) zo. Trächtigkeit f; **2.** fig. Reifen n.

ges·ta·to·ri·al chair [ˌdʒestəˈtɔːrɪəl] s. Tragsessel m des Papstes.

ges·tic·u·late [dʒeˈstɪkjʊleɪt] v/i. gestikulieren, (her'um)fuchteln; **ges·tic·u·la·tion** [dʒeˌstɪkjuˈleɪʃn] s. **1.** Gestikulati'on f, Gestik f, Gebärdenspiel n, Gesten pl.; **2.** lebhafte Geste; **ges·tic·u·la·to·ry** [-lətərɪ] adj. gestikulierend.

ges·ture ['dʒestʃə] I s. **1.** Gebärde f, Geste f: ~ **of friendship** fig. freundschaftliche Geste; **2.** Gebärdenspiel n; II v/i. **3.** → **gesticulate.**

get [get] I v/t. [irr.] **1.** bekommen, erhalten, ‚kriegen'; ~ **it** F ‚sein Fett kriegen', etwas ‚erleben'; ~ **a** (**radio**) **station** e-n Sender (rein)bekommen od. (-)kriegen; **2.** a) ~ **s.th.** (**for o.s.**), **get o.s. s.th.** sich et. verschaffen od. besorgen, et. erwerben od. kaufen od. finden: ~ (**o.s.**) **a car**, b) ~ **s.o. s.th.**, ~ **s.th. for s.o.** j-m et. besorgen od. verschaffen; **3.** Ruhm etc. erlangen, erringen, erwerben, Sieg erringen, erzielen, Reichtum erwerben, kommen zu, Wissen, Erfahrung erwerben, sich aneignen; **4.** Kohle etc. gewinnen, fördern; **5.** erwischen: a) (zu fassen) kriegen, packen, fangen, b) ertappen, c) treffen, d) sl. ‚kriegen', ‚erledigen' (abschießen, töten): (**I've**) **got him!** (ich) hab ihn!; **he'll ~ you yet!** er kriegt dich doch (noch)!; **he's got it bad**(**ly**) F allg. ‚ihn hats bös erwischt'; **you've got me there!** F da bin ich überfragt!, da muss ich passen!; **that ~s me!** F a) das kapier ich nicht!, b) das geht mir auf die Nerven!, c) das geht mir unter die Haut od. an die Nieren!; **6.** a) holen: ~ **help** (**a doctor**, etc.), b) bringen, holen: ~ **me the book**, c) ('hin)bringen, wohin schaffen: ~ **me to the hospital!**; **7.** (a. telefonisch etc.) erreichen; **8.** have got s. haben: **I've got enough money**, b) (mit inf.) müssen: **we have got to do it**; **it's got to be wrong** es muss falsch sein; **9.** machen, werden lassen: ~ **o.s. dirty** sich schmutzig machen; ~ **one's feet wet** nasse Füße bekommen; ~ **s.o. nervous** j-n nervös machen; **10.** (mit p.p.) lassen: ~ **one's hair cut** sich die Haare schneiden lassen; ~ **the door shut** die Tür zubekommen; ~ **things done** etwas zuwege bringen; **11.** (mit inf. od. pres. p.) dazu bringen od. bewegen: **s.o. to talk** j-n zum Sprechen bringen; ~ **the machine to work**, ~ **the machine working** die Maschine in Gang bringen; → **go** 21; **12.** a) machen, zu-

bereiten: ~ **dinner**, b) Brit. F essen, zu sich nehmen: ~ **breakfast** frühstücken; **13.** F ‚kapieren', verstehen (a. hören): **I didn't ~ that!**; **I don't ~ him** ich versteh nicht, was er will; **don't ~ me wrong!** versteh mich nicht falsch!; **got it?** kapiert?; ~ **that!** iron. a) was sagst du dazu?, b) sieh (od. hör) dir das (bloß mal) an!; II v/i. **14.** kommen, gelangen: ~ **home** nach Hause kommen, zu Hause ankommen; ~ **into debt** (**into a rage**) in Schulden (in Wut) geraten; ~ **somewhere** F weiterkommen, Erfolg haben; **now we are ~ting somewhere!** jetzt kommen wir der Sache schon näher!; ~ **nowhere, not to ~ anywhere** nicht weiterkommen; **that will ~ us nowhere!** so kommen wir nicht weiter!; **15.** (mit adj. od. p.p.) werden: ~ **old**; ~ **better** a) besser werden, sich (ver)bessern, b) sich erholen; ~ **caught** gefangen od. erwischt werden; ~ **tired** müde werden, ermüden; **16.** (mit inf.) dahin kommen: ~ **to like it** daran Gefallen finden, es allmählich mögen; ~ **to know** kennen lernen; **how did you ~ to know that?** wie hast du das erfahren?; ~ **to be friends** Freunde werden; **17.** (mit pres. p.) anfangen, beginnen: **they got quarrel**(**l**)**ing**; ~ **talking** a) ins Gespräch kommen, b) zu reden anfangen; → **go** 21; **18.** sl. ‚abhauen': ~**!** hau ab!;

Zssgn mit prp.:

get| a·round v/i. F **1.** et. um'gehen; **2.** a) j-n ‚her'umkriegen', b) j-n ‚reinlegen'; ~ **at** v/i. **1.** (her'an)kommen an (acc.), erreichen: **I can't ~ my books**; **2.** an j-n ‚rankommen', j-m beikommen; **3.** et. ‚kriegen', ‚auftreiben'; **4.** et. her'ausbekommen, e-r Sache auf den Grund kommen; **5.** sagen wollen: **what is he getting at?** worauf will er hinaus?; **6.** j-n ‚schmieren', bestechen; ~ **be·hind** v/i. **1.** sich stellen hinter (acc.), fig. a. j-n unterstützen; **2.** zu'rückbleiben hinter (dat.); ~ **off** v/i. **1.** a) absteigen von, b) aussteigen aus; **2.** freikommen von; ~ **on** v/i. a) Pferd, Wagen etc. besteigen, b) steigen in (acc.): ~ **to one's feet** sich erheben; ~ **to** F hinter et. od. hinter j-s Schliche kommen; ~ **out of** v/i. **1.** her'aussteigen, -kommen, -gelangen aus; **2.** e-e Gewohnheit ablegen: ~ **smoking** das Rauchen abgewöhnen; **3.** fig. aus e-r Sache ‚aussteigen'; sich her'auswinden aus: ~ **from under** F sich herauswinden; **4.** sich drücken vor (dat.); **5.** Geld etc. aus j-m ‚herausholen'; **6.** et. bei e-r Sache ‚kriegen'; ~ **o·ver** v/i. **1.** (hinüber)kommen über (acc.); **2.** fig. hin'wegkommen über (acc.); **3.** et. überstehen; ~ **round** → **get around**; ~ **through** v/i. **1.** kommen durch (e-e Prüfung, den Winter etc.); **2.** Geld ‚durchbringen; **3.** et. erledigen; ~ **to** v/i. **1.** kommen nach, erreichen; **2.** a) sich machen an (acc.), b) (zufällig) dazu kommen: **we got to talking about it** wir kamen darauf zu sprechen;

Zssgn mit adv.:

get| a·bout v/i. **1.** her'umgehen; **2.** he'rumkommen; **3.** (wieder) auf den Beinen sein (nach Krankheit); **4.** sich her'umsprechen od. verbreiten (Gerücht); ~ **a·cross** I v/i. **1.** fig. ‚ankommen': a) ‚einschlagen', Anklang finden: **the play got across**; b) sich verständlich machen; **2.** (to j-m) klar werden; II v/t. **3.** e-r Sache Wirkung od. Erfolg verschaffen, et. an den Mann bringen: **get an idea across**; **4.** et. klarmachen;

~ **a·head** v/i. F vorankommen, Fortschritte machen: ~ **of s.o.** j-n überholen od. überflügeln; ~ **a·long** v/i. **1.** auskommen (**with** mit j-m); **2.** zu'recht, auskommen (**with** mit et.); **3.** → **get on** 1; **4.** weitergehen: ~**!** verschwinde!; ~ **with you!** F a) verschwinde!, b) jetzt hör aber auf!; **5.** älter werden; ~ **a·way** v/i. **1.** loskommen, sich losmachen: **you can't ~ from that** a) darüber kannst du dich nicht hinwegsetzen, b) das musst du doch einsehen; **you can't ~ from the fact that** man kommt um die Tatsache nicht herum, dass; **2.** bsd. sport ‚wegkommen': a) starten, b) sich lösen; **3.** → **get along** 4; **4.** entkommen, entwischen: **he won't ~ with that** damit kommt er nicht durch; **he gets away with everything** (od. **with murder**) er kann sich alles erlauben; ~ **back** I v/t. **1.** zu'rückbekommen: **get one's own back** b) sich rächen; **get one's own back on s.o.** → 3; II v/i. **2.** zu'rückkommen; **3.** ~ **at s.o.** F sich an j-m rächen; ~ **be·hind** v/i. zu'rückbleiben; in Rückstand kommen; ~ **by** v/i. **1.** vor'bei-, 'durchkommen; **2.** aus-, zu'recht, kommen, ‚es schaffen'; ~ **down** I v/i. **1.** her'unterkommen, -steigen; **2.** aus-, absteigen; **3.** ~ **to s.th.** sich an et. (her'an)machen; ~ **business** 5; II v/t. **4.** herunterholen, -schaffen; **5.** aufschreiben; **6.** Essen etc. runterkriegen; **7.** fig. j-n ‚fertig machen'; ~ **in** I v/t. **1.** hin'einbringen, -schaffen, -bekommen; **2.** Ernte einbringen; **3.** einfügen; **4.** Bemerkung, Schlag etc. anbringen; **5.** Arzt etc. (hin)'zuziehen; II v/i. **6.** hin'ein- od. her'eingelangen, -kommen; **7.** einsteigen; **8.** pol. (ins Parla'ment etc.) gewählt werden; **9.** ~ **on** F mitmachen bei; **10.** ~ **with s.o.** sich mit j-m anfreunden; ~ **off** I v/t. **1.** Kleid etc. ausziehen; **2.** losbekommen, -kriegen; **3.** Brief etc. ‚loslassen'; II v/i. **4.** abreisen; **5.** ✈ abheben; **6.** (**from**) absteigen (von), aussteigen (aus): **tell s.o. where to ~** F j-m ‚Bescheid stoßen'; **7.** da'vonkommen: ~ **cheaply** a) billig wegkommen, b) mit e-m blauen Auge davonkommen; **8.** entkommen; **9.** (von der Arbeit) wegkommen; ~ **on** I v/i. **1.** vor'ankommen (a. fig.): ~ **in life** a) es zu et. bringen, b) a. ~ (**in years**) älter werden; **be getting on for sixty** auf die sechzig zugehen; ~ **without** ohne et. auskommen; **let's ~ with it!** machen wir weiter!; **it was getting on** es wurde spät; **2.** → **get along** 1, 2; **3.** ~ **to** F a) Brit. sich in Verbindung setzen mit, teleph. j-n anrufen, b) et. ‚spitzkriegen', c) j-m auf die Schliche kommen; II v/t. **4.** et. vor'antreiben; **5. get it on** a) anfangen, loslegen (mit), b) bsd. Am. F ‚bumsen' (**with** mit); ~ **out** I v/t. **1.** her'ausbekommen, -kriegen (a. fig.); **2.** a) her'ausholen, b) hin'ausschaffen; **3.** Worte her'ausbringen; II v/i. **4.** aussteigen, b) herauskommen, c) hin'ausgehen: ~**!** raus!; ~ **from under** Am. F mit heiler Haut davonkommen; **5.** fig. F ‚aussteigen'; **6.** → **get out of** (*Zssgn mit prp.*); ~ **round** v/i. dazu kommen (**to doing s.th.** et. zu tun); ~ **through** I v/t. **1.** 'durchbringen, -bekommen (a. fig.); **2.** (**to** j-m) et. klarmachen; II v/i. **4.** a. fig., a. ped., teleph. 'durchkommen. **5.** (**with**) fertig werden mit, (et.) ‚schaffen'; **6.** (**to** j-m) klar werden; ~ **to·geth·er** I v/t. **1.** zs.-bringen; **2.** zs.-tragen; **3. get it together** F ‚es bringen'; II v/i. **4.** zs.-kommen; **5.** sich einig werden; ~ **up** I v/t. **1.** hin'aufbringen, -schaffen; **2.** ins Werk setzen; **3.** veranstalten, organisieren; **4.**

(ein)richten, vorbereiten; **5.** konstruieren, zs.-basteln; **6.** (*o.s.* sich) her'ausputzen; **7.** *Buch etc.* ausstatten; *Waren* (hübsch) aufmachen; **8.** *thea.* einstudieren; **9.** F ,büffeln'; **II** *v/i.* **10.** aufstehen.

get|-at-a-ble [get'ætəbl] *adj.* **1.** erreichbar (*Ort od. Sache*); **2.** zugänglich (*Ort od. Person*); '**~-a-way** *s.* **1.** F Flucht *f*, Entkommen *n*: **~** *car* Fluchtwagen *m*; *make one's* **~** entkommen, entwischen, sich aus dem Staub machen; **2.** ✈, *sport* Start *m*; **3.** *mot.* Anzugsvermögen *n*; '**~-off** *s.* Abheben *n.*

get·ter ['getə] *s.* ⚒ Hauer *m*.

'get|-to,geth·er *s.* Zs.-kunft *f*, zwangloses Bei'sammensein; '**~-'tough** *adj. Am.* F hart, aggres'siv: **~** *policy*; '**~-up** *s.* **1.** Aufbau *m*, Anordnung *f*; **2.** Aufmachung *f*: a) Ausstattung *f*, b) ,Aufzug' *m*, Kleidung *f*; **3.** *thea.* Inszenierung *f*.

gew·gaw ['gju:gɔ:] *s.* **1.** → *gimcrack* I; **2.** *fig.* Lap'palie *f*, Kleinigkeit *f*.

gey·ser *s.* **1.** ['gaɪzə] Geysir *m*, heiße Quelle; **2.** ['gi:zə] *Brit.* ('Gas-) ,Durchlauferhitzer *m*.

ghast·li·ness ['gɑ:stlɪnɪs] *s.* **1.** Grausigkeit *f*, schreckliches Aussehen; **2.** Totenblässe *f*; **ghast·ly** ['gɑ:stlɪ] **I** *adj.* **1.** grässlich, gräulich, entsetzlich (*alle a. fig.* F); **2.** gespenstisch; **3.** totenbleich; **4.** verzerrt (*Lächeln*); **II** *adv.* **5.** grässlich *etc.*: **~** *pale* totenblass.

gher·kin ['gɜ:kɪn] *s.* Essig-, Gewürzgurke *f*.

ghet·to ['getəʊ] *pl.* **-tos** *s. hist. u. sociol.* G(h)etto *n*; '**~,blast·er** *s.* F Dröhne *f*; Heuler *m*.

ghost [gəʊst] **I** *s.* **1.** Geist *m*, Gespenst *n*: *lay a* **~** e-n Geist beschwören; *lay the* **~s** *of the past fig.* Vergangenheitsbewältigung betreiben; *the* **~** *walks thea. sl.* es gibt Geld; **2.** Geist *m*, Seele *f* (*nur noch in*): *give* (*od.* *yield*) *up the* **~** den Geist aufgeben (*a. fig.* F); **3.** *fig.* Spur *f*, Schatten *m*: *not the* **~** *of a chance* F nicht die geringste Chance; *the* **~** *of a smile* der Anflug e-s Lächelns; **4.** → *ghost writer*; **5.** *opt. TV* Doppelbild *n*; **II** *v/t.* **6.** *j-n* verfolgen (*Erinnerungen etc.*); **7.** *Buch etc.* als Ghostwriter schreiben; **III** *v/i.* **8.** Ghostwriter sein (*for* für); '**~-like** → *ghostly*.

ghost·li·ness ['gəʊstlɪnɪs] *s.* Geisterhaftigkeit *f*; **ghost·ly** ['gəʊstlɪ] *adj.* geisterhaft, gespenstisch.

ghost| sto·ry *s.* Geister-, Gespenstergeschichte *f*; **~** *town* *s. Am.* Geisterstadt *f*, verödete Stadt; **~** *train* *s.* Geisterbahn *f*; **~** *word* *s.* Ghostword *n* (*falsche Wortbildung*); '**~-write** → *ghost* 7, 8; **~** *writ·er* *s.* Ghostwriter *m*.

ghoul [gu:l] *s.* **1.** Ghul *m* (*Leichen fressender Dämon*); **2.** *fig.* Unhold *m* (*Person mit makabren Gelüsten*), *z.B.* Grabschänder *m*; '**ghoul·ish** [-lɪʃ] *adj.* □ **1.** ghulenhaft; **2.** gräulich, ma'kaber.

G.I. [,dʒi:'aɪ] (*von Government Issue*) ✗ *Am.* F **I** *s.* ,G'I' *m* (*US-Soldat*); **II** *adj.* GI-..., Kommiss...; *weitS.* vorschriftsmäßig.

gi·ant ['dʒaɪənt] **I** *s.* Riese *m*, *fig. a.* Gi'gant *m*, Ko'loss *m*; **II** *adj.* riesenhaft, riesig; *a.* ♀, *zo.* Riesen...: **~** *slalom* Riesenslalom *m*; **~** *stride* Riesenschritt *m*; **~('s) stride** Rundlauf *m* (*Turngerät*); **~** *wheel* Riesenrad *n*; '**gi·ant·ess** [-tes] *s.* Riesin *f*.

gib [gɪb] *s.* ☉ **1.** Keil *m*, Bolzen *m*; **2.** 'Führungsline,al *n* (*e-r Werkzeugmaschine*); **3.** Ausleger *m* (*e-s Krans*).

gib·ber ['dʒɪbə] *v/i.* schnattern, quatschen; '**gib·ber·ish** [-ərɪʃ] *s.* Ge-

---

schnatter *n*; Geschwätz, ,Geschwafel' *n*.

gib·bet ['dʒɪbɪt] **I** *s.* **1.** Galgen *m*; **2.** ☉ Kran- *od.* Querbalken *m*; **II** *v/t.* **3.** *j-n* hängen; **4.** *fig.* anprangern, bloßstellen.

gib·bon ['gɪbən] *s. zo.* Gibbon *m*.

gib·bous ['gɪbəs] *adj.* **1.** gewölbt; **2.** buck(e)lig.

gibe [dʒaɪb] **I** *v/t.* verhöhnen, verspotten; **II** *v/i.* spotten (*at* über *acc.*); **III** *s.* höhnische Bemerkung, Stiche'lei *f*, Seitenhieb *m*.

gib·lets ['dʒɪblɪts] *s. pl.* Inne'reien *pl.*, *bsd.* Hühner-, Gänseklein *n*.

gid·di·ness ['gɪdɪnɪs] *s.* **1.** Schwindel (-gefühl *n*) *m*; **2.** *fig.* a) Leichtsinn *m*, Flatterhaftigkeit *f*, b) Wankelmütigkeit *f*; **gid·dy** ['gɪdɪ] *adj.* □ **1.** schwind(e)lig: *I am* (*od.* *feel*) **~** mir ist schwind(e)lig; **2.** *a. fig.* Schwindel erregend, schwindelnd; **3.** *fig.* a) leichtsinnig, flatterhaft, b) ,verrückt', ,wild'.

gie [gi:] *Scot. für give.*

gift [gɪft] **I** *s.* **1.** Geschenk *n*, Gabe *f*: *make a* **~** *of et.* schenken; *I wouldn't have it as a* **~** das nähme ich nicht (mal) geschenkt; *it's a* **~**! das ist ja geschenkt (*billig*)!; **2.** ⚖ Schenkung *f*; **3.** ⚖ Verleihungsrecht *n*: *the office is in his* **~** er kann dieses Amt verleihen; **4.** *fig.* Begabung *f*, Gabe *f*, Ta'lent *n* (*for, of* für): **~** *for languages* Sprachbegabung; *of many* **~s** vielseitig begabt; → *gab* I; **II** *v/t.* **5.** (be)schenken; '**gift·ed** [-tɪd] *adj.* begabt, talen'tiert.

gift| horse *s.*: *don't look a* **~** *in the mouth* e-m geschenkten Gaul schaut man nicht ins Maul; **~** *shop* *s.* Ge-'schenkar,tikelladen *m*; **~** *tax* Schenkungssteuer *f*; **~** *to·ken*, **~** *vouch·er* *s.* Geschenkgutschein *m*; '**~-wrap** *v/t.* geschenkmäßig verpacken; **~** *wrap·ping* *s.* Ge'schenkpa,pier *m*.

gig¹ [gɪg] *s.* **1.** ⚓ Gig(boot *n*) *f*; **2.** Gig *f* (*Ruderboot*); **3.** Gig *n* (*zweirädriger, offener Einspänner*); **4.** Fischspeer *m*; **5.** ☉ ('Tuch),Rauma,schine *f*.

gig² [gɪg] *s.* ♪ F a) Engage'ment *n*, b) Auftritt *m*.

gig·a·byte ['gɪgəbaɪt] *s. Computer*: 'Gigabyte *n*.

gi·gan·tic [dʒaɪ'gæntɪk] *adj.* (□ **~ally**) gi'gantisch: a) riesenhaft, Riesen..., b) riesig, ungeheuer (groß).

gig·gle ['gɪgl] **I** *v/i. u. v/t.* kichern; **II** *s.* Gekicher *n*, Kichern *n*; '**gig·gly** [-lɪ] *adj.* ständig kichernd.

gig·o·lo ['ʒɪgələʊ] *pl.* **-los** *s.* Gigolo *m*.

Gil·ber·ti·an [gɪl'bɜ:tjən] *adj.* in der Art (*des Humors*) von W. S. Gilbert; *fig.* komisch, possenhaft.

gild¹ [gɪld] → *guild.*

gild² [gɪld] *v/t.* [*irr.*] **1.** vergolden; **2.** *fig.* a) verschöne(r)n, (aus)schmücken, b) über'tünchen, verbrämen, c) versüßen: **~** *the pill* die bittere Pille versüßen; '**gild·ed** [-dɪd] *adj.* vergoldet, golden (*a. fig.*): **~** *cage* *fig.* goldener Käfig; **~** *youth* Jeunesse dorée *f*; '**gild·er** [-də] *s.* Vergolder *m*; '**gild·ing** [-dɪŋ] *s.* **1.** Vergoldung *f*; **2.** *fig.* Verschönerung *f etc.* (→ *gild²* 2).

gill¹ [gɪl] *s.* **1.** *ichth.* Kieme *f*; **2.** *pl.* Doppelkinn *n*: *rosy* (*green*) *about the* **~s** rosig, frisch aussehend (grün im Gesicht); **3.** *orn.* Kehllappen *m*; **4.** ♀ La'melle *f*: **~** *fungus* Blätterpilz *m*; **5.** ☉ (Heiz-, Kühl)Rippe *f*.

gill² [gɪl] *s. Scot.* **1.** waldige Schlucht; **2.** Gebirgsbach *m*.

gill³ [dʒɪl] *s.* Viertelpinte *f* (*Brit.* 0,14, *Am.* 0,12 Liter).

Gill⁴ [dʒɪl] *s. obs.* Liebste *f*.

---

gil·ly·flow·er ['dʒɪlɪ,flaʊə] *s.* ♀ **1.** Gartennelke *f*; **2.** Lev'koje *f*; **3.** Goldlack *m*.

gilt [gɪlt] **I** *pret. u. p.p. von gild²*; **II** *adj.* **1.** → *gilded*; **III** *s.* **2.** Vergoldung *f*; **3.** *fig.* Reiz *m*: *take the* **~** *off the gingerbread* der Sache den Reiz nehmen; '**~-edged** *adj.* **1.** mit Goldschnitt; **2.** **~** *securities* ✝ mündelsichere (Wert)Papiere *pl.*

gim·bals ['dʒɪmbəlz] *s. pl.* ☉ Kar'danringe *pl.*, -aufhängung *f*.

gim·crack ['dʒɪmkræk] **I** *s.* **1.** wertloser *od.* kitschiger Gegenstand *od.* Schmuck, (*a. technische*) Spiele'rei, ,Mätzchen' *n*; **2.** *pl.* → *gimcrackery*; **II** *adj.* **3.** wertlos, kitschig; '**gim,cracker·y** [-kərɪ] *s.* Plunder *m*, ,Kinkerlitzchen' *pl.*

gim·let ['gɪmlɪt] *s.* **1.** ☉ Handbohrer *m*: **~** *eyes fig.* stechende Augen; **2.** *Am.* ein Cocktail.

gim·mick ['gɪmɪk] *s.* F **1.** → *gadget*; **2.** *fig.* ,Dreh' *m*, (Re'klame- *etc.*)Masche *f*; ,Aufhänger' *m*, ,Knüller' *m*, *a.* Gimmick *m*, *n*; '**gim·mick·ry** [-krɪ] *s.* F (technische) Mätzchen *pl.*

gimp [gɪmp] *s. Schneiderei*: Gimpe *f*.

gin¹ [dʒɪn] *s.* Gin *m*, Wa'cholderschnaps *m*: **~** *and it* Gin u. Wermut *m*; **~** *and tonic* Gin Tonic *m*.

gin² [dʒɪn] **I** *s.* **1.** *a. cotton* **~** Ent'körnungsma,schine *f*; **2.** ☉ Hebezeug *n*, Winde *f*; ⚓ Spill *n*; **3.** ☉ Göpel *m*, 'Förderma,schine *f*; **4.** *hunt.* Falle *f*, Schlinge *f*; **II** *v/t.* **5.** Baumwolle entkörnen; **6.** mit e-r Schlinge fangen.

gin·ger ['dʒɪndʒə] **I** *s.* **1.** ♀ Ingwer *m*; **2.** Rötlich(gelb) *n*, Ingwerfarbe *f*; **3.** F a) ,Mumm' *m*, Schneid *m* (*e-r Person*), b) Schwung *m*, ,Schmiss' *m* (*a. e-r Sache*), c) ,Pfeffer', ,Pfiff' *m* (*e-r Geschichte etc.*); **II** *adj.* **4.** rötlich (gelb); **5.** F schwungvoll, ,schmissig'; **III** *v/t.* **6.** mit Ingwer würzen; **7.** *a.* **~** *up fig.* a) *et.* ,ankurbeln', b) *j-n* aufmöbeln, c) *j-n* ,scharfmachen', d) *e-m Film etc.* ,Pfiff' geben; **~** *ale*, **~** *beer* *s.* Ginger-ale *n*, 'Ingwerlimo,nade *f*; '**~-bread I** *s.* **1.** Ingwer-, Pfefferkuchen *m*; → *gilt* 3; **2.** *fig. contp.* über'ladene Verzierung, Kitsch *m*; **II** *adj.* **3.** kitschig, über'laden; **~** *group* *s. pol. Brit.* Gruppe *f* von Scharfmachern.

gin·ger·ly ['dʒɪndʒəlɪ] *adv. u. adj.* sachte, behutsam; zimperlich.

'**gin·ger|-nut** *s.* Ingwerkeks *m*; **~** *pop* *s.* F *für ginger ale*; '**~-snap** *s.* Ingwerwaffel *f*; **~** *wine* *s.* Ingwerwein *m*.

gin·ger·y ['dʒɪndʒərɪ] *adj.* **1.** Ingwer...; **2.** → *ginger* 4; **3.** *fig.* a) → *ginger* 5, b) beißend.

ging·ham ['gɪŋəm] *s.* Gingham *m*, Gingan *m* (*Baumwollstoff*).

gin·gi·vi·tis [,dʒɪndʒɪ'vaɪtɪs] *s.* ⚕ Zahnfleischentzündung *f*.

gink·go ['gɪŋkəʊ] *pl.* **-gos** *od.* **-goes** *s.* ♀ Gingko *m* (*Baum*).

gin mill *s. Am.* F Kneipe *f*.

gin·ner·y ['dʒɪnərɪ] *s.* Entkörnungswerk *n* (*für Baumwolle*).

gin| pal·ace *s.* auffällig dekoriertes Wirtshaus; **~** *rum·my* *s. Form des Rommees*; **~** *sling* *s. Am.* Mischgetränk *n* mit Gin.

gip·sy ['dʒɪpsɪ] **I** *s.* **1.** Zi'geuner(in) (*a. fig.*); **2.** Zi'geunersprache *f*; **II** *adj.* **3.** zi'geunerhaft, Zigeuner...; **III** *v/i.* **4.** ein Zi'geunerleben führen; '**gip·sy·dom** [-dəm] *s.* **1.** Zi'geunertum *n*; **2.** *coll.* Zi'geuner *pl.*

gi·raffe [dʒɪ'rɑ:f] *s. zo.* Gi'raffe *f*.

gird [gɜ:d] *v/t.* [*irr.*] **1.** *obs. j-n* (um)'gürten; **2.** *Kleid etc.* gürten, mit e-m Gürtel

G

halten; **3.** *oft* ~ *on Schwert etc.* 'umgürten, an-, 'umlegen: ~ *s.th. on s.o.* j-m et. umgürten; **4.** *j-m, sich ein Schwert* 'umgürten: ~ *o.s.* (*up*), ~ (*up*) *one's loins fig.* sich rüsten *od.* wappnen; **5.** binden (*to* an *acc.*); **6.** um'geben, -'schließen: *sea-girt* meerumschlungen; **7.** *fig.* ausstatten, -rüsten.

gird·er ['gɜːdə] *s.* ⊛ (Längs)Träger *m*: ~ *bridge* Balken-, Trägerbrücke *f*.

gir·dle ['gɜːdl] **I** *s.* **1.** Gürtel *m*, Gurt *m*; **2.** Hüfthalter *m*, -gürtel *m*; **3.** *anat. in Zssgn* (Knochen)Gürtel *m*; **4.** *fig.* Gürtel *m* (*Umkreis, Umgebung*); **II** *v/t.* **5.** um'gürten; **6.** um'geben, einschließen; **7.** *Baum* ringeln.

girl [gɜːl] *s.* **1.** Mädchen *n*: *a German* ~ e-e junge Deutsche; ~*'s name* weiblicher Vorname; *my eldest* ~ m-e älteste Tochter; *the* ~*s* F a) die Töchter *pl.* des Hauses, b) die Damen *pl.*; **2.** (Dienst-) Mädchen *n*; **3.** F ,Mädchen' n (*es jungen Mannes*); ~ *Fri·day s.* (unentbehrliche) Gehilfin, ,rechte Hand' (*des Chefs, bsd. Sekretärin*); '~*friend s.* Freundin *f*; ~ *guide s. Brit.* Pfadfinderin *f*.

girl·hood ['gɜːlhʊd] *s.* Mädchenzeit *f*, -jahre *pl.*, Jugend(zeit) *f*; **'girl·ie** [-lɪ] *s.* F Mädchen *n*: ~ *mag(azine)* ,Titten-u.-Po'-Magazin *n*; **'girl·ish** [-lɪʃ] *adj.* □ mädchenhaft; **'girl·ish·ness** [-lɪʃnɪs] *s.* das Mädchenhafte; **girl scout** *s. Am.* Pfadfinderin *f*.

gi·ro ['dʒaɪrəʊ] *s.* (*der*) Postscheckdienst (*in England*): ~ *account* Postscheckkonto *n*.

girt[1] [gɜːt] *pret. u. p.p. von* **gird.**

girt[2] [gɜːt] **I** *s.* 'Umfang *m*; **II** *v/t.* den 'Umfang messen von; **III** *v/i.* messen (*an Umfang*).

girth [gɜːθ] **I** *s.* **1.** 'Umfang *m*; **2.** 'Körper,umfang *m*; **3.** (Sattel-, Pack)Gurt *m*; **4.** ⊛ Tragriemen *m*, Gurt *m*; **II** *v/t.* **5.** *Pferd* gürten; **6.** an-, aufschnallen; **7.** a) → *gird* 6, b) → *girt*[2] II.

gis·mo → **gizmo.**

gist [dʒɪst] *s.* **1.** das Wesentliche, Hauptpunkt *m*, -inhalt *m*, Kern *m* der Sache; **2.** ⚖ Grundlage *f*: ~ *of action* Klagegrund *m*.

git [gɪt] *s. Brit.* F *contp.* Kerl *m*: *that stupid* ~ dieser blöde Hund.

give [gɪv] **I** *s.* **1.** *fig.* a) Nachgiebigkeit *f*, b) Elastizi'tät *f*; → *give and take*; **2.** Elastizi'tät *f* (*des Fußbodens etc.*); **II** *v/t.* [*irr.*] **3.** he geben, (über)'reichen; schenken: *he gave me a book*; ~ *a present* ein Geschenk machen; ~ *s.o. a blow* j-m e-n Schlag versetzen; ~ *it to him!* F gibs ihm!, gib ihm Saures (*Strafe, Schelte*)!; ~ *me Mozart any time* a) Mozart geht mir über alles, b) da lobe ich mir (doch) Mozart; ~ *as good as one gets* (*od.* takes) mit gleicher Münze zurückzahlen; ~ *or take* plus/ minus; **4.** geben, zahlen: *how much did you* ~ *for that hat?*; **5.** (ab-, weiter)geben, über'tragen; (zu)erteilen, an-, zuweisen; verleihen: *she gave me her bag to carry* sie gab mir ihre Tasche zu tragen; ~ *s.o. a part in a play* j-m e-e Rolle in e-m Stück geben; ~ *s.o. a title* j-m e-n Titel verleihen; **6.** hingeben, widmen, schenken: ~ *one's attention to* s-e Aufmerksamkeit widmen (*dat.*); ~ *one's mind to s.th.* sich e-r Sache widmen; ~ *one's life* sein Leben hingeben *od.* opfern (*for* für); **7.** geben, (dar)bieten, reichen: *he gave me his hand*; *do* ~ *us a song* singen Sie uns doch bitte ein Lied; **8.** gewähren, liefern, geben: *cows* ~ *milk* Kühe

geben *od.* liefern Milch; ~ *no result* kein Ergebnis zeitigen; *it was not* ~*n him to inf.* es war ihm nicht gegeben *od.* vergönnt, zu *inf.*; **9.** verursachen: ~ *pleasure* Vergnügen bereiten *od.* machen; ~ *pain* Schmerzen bereiten, wehtun; **10.** zugeben, -gestehen, erlauben: *just* ~ *me 24 hours* gib mir nur 24 Stunden (Zeit); *I* ~ *you till tomorrow!* ich gebe dir noch bis morgen Zeit!; *I* ~ *you that point* in diesem Punkt gebe ich dir Recht; **11.** ausführen, äußern, vortragen: ~ *a cry* e-n Schrei ausstoßen, aufschreien; ~ *a loud laugh* laut auflachen; ~ *s.o. a look* j-m e-n Blick zuwerfen, j-n anblicken; ~ *a party* e-e Party geben; ~ *a play* ein Stück geben *od.* aufführen; ~ *a lecture* e-n Vortrag halten; ~ *one's name* s-n Namen nennen *od.* angeben; **12.** beschreiben, mitteilen, geben: ~ *us the facts*; (*come on*,) ~! *Am.* F sag schon!, raus mit der Sprache!; **III** *v/i.* [*irr.*] **13.** geben, schenken, spenden (*to dat.*): ~ *generously*; ~ *and take fig.* geben u. nehmen, einander entgegenkommen; **14.** nachgeben (*a.* ⚓ *Preise*), -lassen, weichen, versagen: ~ *under pressure* unter Druck nachgeben; *his knees gave under him* s-e Knie versagten; *what* ~*s?* *sl.* was ist los?; *s.th.'s got to* ~ *sl.* es muss (doch) was passieren; **15.** a) nachgeben, (*Fußboden etc.*) *a.* federn, b) sich dehnen (*Schuhe etc.*): ~ *but not to break* sich biegen, aber nicht brechen; *the chair* ~*s comfortably* der Stuhl federt angenehm; *the foundations are giving* das Fundament senkt sich; **16.** a) führen (*into* in *acc.*; *on* auf *acc.*, nach) (*Straße etc.*), b) gehen (*on* [-*to*] nach) (*Fenster etc.*);

Zssgn mit adv.:

give| **a·way** *v/t.* **1.** weg-, hergeben, verschenken (*a. fig. u. sport den Sieg etc.*); → *bride*; **2.** *Preise* verteilen; **3.** aufgeben, opfern, preisgeben; **4.** verraten: *his accent gives him away*; *give o.s. away* sich verraten *od.* verplappern; → *show* 14; ~ *back v/t.* **1.** zu-'rückgeben; **2.** *Blick* erwidern; ~ *forth v/t.* **1.** → *give off*; **2.** Ansicht etc. äußern; **3.** veröffentlichen, bekannt geben; ~ *in* **I** *v/t.* **1.** *Gesuch etc.* einreichen, abgeben; **II** *v/i.* **2.** (*to dat.*) nachgeben (*dat.*), b) sich anschließen (*dat.*); **3.** aufgeben, sich geschlagen geben; ~ *off v/t. Dampf etc.* abgeben, *Gas, Wärme etc.* aus-, verströmen, *Rauch etc.* ausstoßen, *Geruch* verbreiten, ausströmen; ~ *out* **I** *v/t.* **1.** ausgeben, aus-, verteilen; **2.** bekannt geben: *give it out that*) verkünden, dass, b) behaupten, dass; **3.** → *give off*; **II** *v/i.* **4.** zu Ende gehen (*Kräfte, Vorrat*): *his strength gave out* die Kräfte verließen ihn; **5.** versagen (*Kräfte, Maschine etc.*); ~ *o·ver* **I** *v/t.* **1.** über'geben (*to dat.*); **2.** *et.* aufgeben: ~ *doing s.th.* aufhören, et. zu tun; **3.** *give o.s. over to sich der Verzweiflung etc.* hingeben, verfallen (*dat.*): *give o.s. over to drink*; **II** *v/i.* **4.** aufhören; ~ *up* **I** *v/t.* **1.** aufgeben, aufhören mit, et. sein lassen: ~ *smoking* das Rauchen aufgeben; **2.** (*als aussichtslos*) aufgeben: ~ *a plan*; *he was given up by the doctors*; **3.** *j-n* ausliefern: *give o.s. up* sich (freiwillig) stellen (*to the police* der Polizei); **4.** *et.* abgeben, abtreten (*to* an *acc.*); **5.** *give o.s. up to* a) → *give over* 3, b) sich e-r *Sache* widmen; **II** *v/i.* **6.** (es) aufgeben, sich geschlagen geben, *weitS.* a. resignieren.

give| **and take** *s.* **1.** (*ein*) Geben u. Nehmen, beiderseitiges Nachgeben, Kompro'miss(bereitschaft *f*) *m*; **2.** Meinungsaustausch *m*; ,~*-and-'take* [-vənt-] *adj.* Kompromiss..., Ausgleichs...; '~*·a·way* **I** *s.* **1.** (ungewolltes) Verraten, Verplappern *n*; **2.** ⚓ a) Werbegeschenk *n*, b) kostenlos verteilte Zeitung; **3.** *a.* ~ *show* TV Quiz(sendung *f*) *n*, Preisraten *n*; **II** *adj.* **4.** ~ *price* Schleuderpreis *m*.

giv·en ['gɪvn] **I** *p.p. von* **give**; **II** *adj.* **1.** gegeben, bestimmt: *at a* ~ *time* zur festgesetzten Zeit; *under the* ~ *conditions* unter den gegebenen Umständen; **2.** ~ *to* a) ergeben, verfallen (*dat.*): ~ *to drinking*, b) neigend zu: ~ *to boasting*; **3.** ⚕, *phls.* gegeben, bekannt; **4.** vor'ausgesetzt: ~ *health* Gesundheit vorausgesetzt; **5.** in Anbetracht (*gen.*): ~ *his temperament*; **6.** *auf Dokumenten*: gegeben, ausgefertigt (*am*): ~ *this 10th day of May*; ~ *name* *s. Am.* Vorname *m*.

giv·er ['gɪvə] *s.* **1.** Geber(in), Spender (-in); **2.** ⚓ (*Wechsel*)Ausstellerm.

giz·mo ['gɪzməʊ] *s. Am.* F ,Dingsbums' *n*.

giz·zard ['gɪzəd] *s.* **1.** *ichth., orn.* Muskelmagen *m*; **2.** F Magen *m*: *that sticks in my* ~.

gla·brous ['gleɪbrəs] *adj.* ⚘, *zo.* kahl.

gla·cé ['glæseɪ] (*Fr.*) *adj.* **1.** glasiert, mit Zuckerguss; **2.** kandiert; **3.** Glacee..., Glanz... (*Leder, Stoff*).

gla·cial ['gleɪsjəl] *adj.* **1.** *geol.* Eis..., Gletscher...: ~ *epoch od. period* Eiszeit *f*; ~ *man* Eiszeitmensch *m*; **2.** 🜨 Eis...: ~ *acetic acid* Eisessig *m*; **3.** eisig (*a. fig.*); **gla·ci·a·tion** [‚glæsɪ'eɪʃn] *s.* **1.** Vereisung *f*; **2.** Vergletscherung *f*.

gla·cier ['glæsjə] *s.* Gletscher *m*.

glac·i·ol·o·gy [‚glæsɪ'ɒlədʒɪ] *s.* Glaziolo-'gie *f*, Gletscherkunde *f*.

gla·cis ['glæsɪs; *pl.* -sɪz] *s.* **1.** Abdachung *f*; **2.** ✕ Gla'cis *n*.

glad [glæd] *adj.* □ → *gladly*; **1.** (*pred.*) froh, erfreut (*of, at* über *acc.*): *I am* ~ *of it* ich freue mich darüber, es freut mich; *I am* ~ *to hear* (*to say*) es freut mich zu hören (sagen zu können); *I am* ~ *to come* ich komme gern; *I should be* ~ *to know* ich möchte gern wissen; **2.** freudig, froh, fröhlich, erfreulich: *give s.o. the* ~ *eye sl.* j-m e-n einladenden Blick zuwerfen, j-m schöne Augen machen; *give s.o. the* ~ *hand* → *glad*-*hand*; ~ *rags sl.* ,Sonntagsstaat' *m*; ~ *news* frohe Kunde; **'glad·den** [-dn] *v/t.* erfreuen.

glade [gleɪd] *s.* Lichtung *f*, Schneise *f*.

'glad-hand *v/t.* F *j-n* herzlich *od.* 'überschwänglich begrüßen.

glad·i·a·tor ['glædɪeɪtə] *s.* Gladi'ator *m*; *fig.* Streiter *m*, Kämpfer *m*; **glad·i·a·to·ri·al** [‚glædɪə'tɔːrɪəl] *adj.* Gladiatoren...

glad·i·o·lus [‚glædɪ'əʊləs] *pl.* -**li** [-laɪ] *od.* -**lus·es** *s.* ⚘ Gladi'ole *f*.

glad·ly ['glædlɪ] *adv.* mit Freuden, gern(e); **glad·ness** ['glædnɪs] *s.* Freude *f*, Fröhlichkeit *f*; **glad·some** ['glædsəm] *adj.* □ *obs.* **1.** erfreulich; **2.** freudig, fröhlich.

Glad·stone (**bag**) ['glædstən] *s.* zweiteilige leichte Reisetasche.

glair [gleə] **I** *s.* **1.** Eiweiß *n*; **2.** Eiweißleim *m*; **3.** eiweißartige Sub'stanz; **II** *v/t.* **4.** mit Eiweiß(leim) bestreichen.

glaive [gleɪv] *s. poet.* (Breit)Schwert *n*.

glam·or *Am.* → **glamour.**

glam·or·ize ['glæməraɪz] *v/t.* **1.** (mit viel Re'klame *etc.*) verherrlichen; **2.** e-n besonderen Zauber verleihen (*dat.*);

'glam·or·ous [-rəs] *adj.* bezaubernd (schön), zauberhaft; **glam·our** ['glæmə] **I** *s.* **1.** Zauber *m*, Glanz *m*, bezaubernde Schönheit: **~ boy** a) Schönling *m*, b) ,toller Kerl'; **~ girl** Glamourgirl *n*, (Re'klame-, Film)Schönheit *f*; **cast a ~ over** bezaubern, *j-n* in s-n Bann schlagen; **2.** falscher Glanz; **II** *v/t.* **3.** bezaubern.

glance¹ [glɑːns] **I** *v/i.* **1.** e-n Blick werfen, (rasch *od.* flüchtig) blicken (**at** auf *acc.*): **~ over** (*od.* **through**) **a letter** e-n Brief überfliegen; **2.** (auf)blitzen, (auf-)leuchten; **3. ~ off** abgleiten (von) (*Messer etc.*), abprallen (von) (*Kugel etc.*): **hit** (*od.* **strike**) **s.o. a glancing blow** j-n (mit einem Schlag) streifen; **4.** (**at**) *Thema* flüchtig berühren *od.* streifen, *bsd.* anspielen (auf *acc.*); **II** *v/t.* **5. ~ one's eye over** (*od.* **through**) → 1; **III** *s.* **6.** flüchtiger Blick (**at** auf *acc.*): **at a ~** mit 'einem Blick; **at first ~** auf den ersten Blick; **take a ~ at** → 1; **7.** (Auf-)Blitzen *n*, (Auf)Leuchten *n*; **8.** Abprallen *n*, Abgleiten *n*; **9.** (**at**) flüchtige Erwähnung (*gen.*), Anspielung *f* (auf *acc.*).

glance² [glɑːns] *s. min.* Blende *f*, Glanz *m*: **lead ~** Bleiglanz.

gland¹ [glænd] *s. biol.* Drüse *f*.

gland² [glænd] *s.* ⊗ **1.** Dichtungsstutzen *m*; **2.** Stopfbuchse *f*.

glan·dered ['glændəd] *adj. vet.* rotzkrank; **'glan·der·ous** [-dərəs] *adj.* **1.** Rotz...; **2.** rotzkrank; **glan·ders** ['glændəz] *s. pl. sg. konstr.* Rotz(krankheit *f*) *m* (*der Pferde*).

glan·du·lar ['glændjʊlə] *adj. biol.* drüsig, Drüsen...: **~ fever** (pfeiffersches) Drüsenfieber; **'glan·du·lous** [-əs] → **glandular**.

glans [glænz] *pl.* **'glan·des** [-diːz] *s. anat.* Eichel *f*.

glare¹ [gleə] **I** *v/i.* **1.** grell leuchten *od.* sein, *Farben:* a. schreiend sein; → **glaring**; **2.** wütend starren: **~ at s.o.** j-n wütend anstarren; **II** *s.* **3.** blendendes Licht, greller Schein, grelles Leuchten: **be in the full ~ of publicity** im Scheinwerferlicht der Öffentlichkeit stehen; **4.** *fig.* das Grelle *od.* Schreiende; **5.** wütender Blick.

glare² [gleə] *Am.* **I** *s.* spiegelglatte Fläche: **a ~ of ice**; **II** *adj.* spiegelglatt: **~ ice** Glatteis *n*.

glar·ing ['gleərɪŋ] *adj.* □ **1.** grell (*Sonne etc.*), *Farben:* a. schreiend; **2.** *fig.* krass, ekla'tant (*Fehler etc.*), (himmel)schreiend (*Unrecht etc.*); **3.** wütend, funkelnd (*Blick*).

glass [glɑːs] **I** *s.* **1.** Glas *n*: **broken ~** Glasscherben *pl.*; **2.** → **glassware**; **3.** a) (Trink)Glas *n*, b) Glas(gefäß) *n*; **4.** Glas *n* (voll): **a ~ too much** ein Gläschen zu viel; **5.** Glas(scheibe *f*) *n*; **6.** Spiegel *m*; **7.** *opt.* a) Lupe *f*, Vergrößerungsglas *n*, b) *pl. a.* **pair of ~es** Brille *f*, c) Linse *f*, Augenglas *n*, d) (Fern- *od.* Opern)Glas *n*, e) Mikro'skop *n*; **8.** Uhrglas *n*; **9.** a) Thermo'meter *n*, b) Baro'meter *n*; **10.** Sanduhr *f*; **II** *v/t.* **11.** verglasen: **~ in** einglasen; **~ bead** Glasperle *f*; **~ block** *s.* △ Glasziegel *m*; **~ blow·er** *s.* Glasbläser *m*; **~ blow·ing** *s.* Glasbläse'rei *f*; **~ brick** → **glass block**; **~ case** *s.* Glasschrank *m*, Vi'trine *f*; **~ cloth** *s.* **1.** ⊗ Glas(faser)gewebe *n*; **2.** Gläsertuch *n*; **~ cul·ture** *s.* 'Treibhauskul,tur *f*; **~ cut·ter** *s.* **1.** Glasschleifer *m*; **2.** ⊗ Glasschneider *m* (*Werkzeug*); **~ eye** *s.* Glasauge *n*; **~ fi·bre** *s.* Glasfaser *f*, -fiber *f*.

glass·ful ['glɑːsfʊl] *pl.* **-fuls** *s. ein* Glas *n*

voll.

'glass|·house *s.* **1.** → **glasswork** 2; **2.** Treibhaus *n*: **people who live in ~s should not throw stones** wer im Glashaus sitzt, soll nicht mit Steinen werfen; **3.** ✕ *Brit. sl.* ,Bau' *m* (*Gefängnis*); **~ jaw** *s.* Boxen: F ,Glaskinn' *n*; **~ pa·per** *s.* 'Glaspa,pier *n*; **'~·ware** *s.* Glas(waren *pl.*) *n*, Glasgeschirr *n*, -sachen *pl.*; **~ wool** *s.* ⊗ Glaswolle *f*; **'~·work** *s.* ⊗ **1.** Glas(waren)herstellung *f*; **2.** *pl. mst sg. konstr.* 'Glashütte *f*, -fa,brik *f*.

glass·y ['glɑːsɪ] *adj.* □ **1.** gläsern, glasartig, glasig; **2.** glasig (*Auge*).

Glas·we·gian [glæs'wiːdʒən] **I** *adj.* aus Glasgow; **II** *s.* Glasgower(in).

Glau·ber('s) salt ['glɔːbə(z)] *s.* Glaubersalz *n*.

glau·co·ma [glɔː'kəʊmə] *s.* ✚ Glau'kom *n*, grüner Star; **glau·cous** ['glɔːkəs] *adj.* graugrün.

glaze [gleɪz] **I** *v/t.* **1.** verglasen, mit Glasscheiben versehen: **~ in** einglasen; **2.** polieren, glätten; **3.** ⊗, *a. Küche:* glasieren, mit Gla'sur über'ziehen; **4.** *paint.* lasieren; **5.** ⊗ *Papier* satinieren; **6.** *Augen* glasig machen; **II** *v/i.* **7.** e-e Gla'sur *od.* Poli'tur annehmen, blank werden; **8.** glasig werden (*Augen*); **III** *s.* **9.** Poli'tur *f*, Glätte *f*, Glanz *m*; **10.** a) Gla'sur *f* (*a. auf Kuchen etc.*), b) Gla-'surmasse *f*; **11.** La'sur *f*; **12.** ⊗ Satinierung *f*; **13.** Glasigkeit *f*; **14.** a) Eisschicht *f*, b) ✗ Vereisung *f*, c) *Am.* Glatteis *n*; **glazed** [-zd] *adj.* **1.** verglast, Glas...: **~ veranda**; **2.** ⊗ glatt, blank, poliert, Glanz...: **~ paper** Glanzpapier *n*; **~ tile** Kachel *f*; **3.** glasiert; **4.** lasiert; **5.** satiniert; **6.** poliert; **7.** glasig (*Augen*); **8.** vereist: **~ frost** *Brit.* Glatteis *n*; **'glaz·er** [-zə] *s.* ⊗ **1.** Glasierer *m*; **2.** Polierer *m*; **3.** Satinierer *m*; **4.** Polier-, Schmirgelscheibe *f*; **'gla·zier** [-zjə] *s.* Glaser *m*; **'glaz·ing** [-zɪŋ] *s.* **1.** a) Verglasen *n*, b) Glaserarbeit *f*; **2.** Fenster(scheiben) *pl.*; **3.** ⊗ *u. Küche:* a) Gla'sur *f*, b) Glasieren *n*; **4.** a) Poli'tur *f*, b) Polieren *n*; **5.** Satinieren *n*; **6.** *paint.* a) La'sur *f*, b) Lasieren *n*; **'glaz·y** [-zɪ] *adj.* **1.** glasig, glasiert; **2.** glanzlos, glasig (*Auge*).

gleam [gliːm] **I** *s.* schwacher Schein, Schimmer *m* (*a. fig.*): **~ of hope** Hoffnungsschimmer; **the ~ in his eye** das Funkeln s-r Augen; **II** *v/i.* glänzen, leuchten, schimmern, *Augen a.* funkeln.

glean [gliːn] **I** *v/t.* **1.** *Ähren* (auf-, nach-)lesen, *Feld* sauber lesen; **2.** *fig.* sammeln, zs.-tragen, a. her'ausfinden: **~ from** schließen *od.* entnehmen aus; **II** *v/i.* **3.** Ähren lesen; **'glean·er** [-nə] *s.* Ährenleser *m*; *fig.* Sammler *m*; **'glean·ings** [-nɪŋz] *s. pl.* **1.** ⚘ Nachlese *f*; **2.** *fig.* das Gesammelte.

glebe [gliːb] *s.* **1.** ⚖, *eccl.* Pfarrland *n*; **2.** *poet.* (Erd)Scholle *f*, Feld *n*.

glede [gliːd] *s. orn.* Gabelweihe *f*.

glee [gliː] *s.* **1.** Fröhlichkeit *f*, Ausgelassenheit *f*; **2.** (*a.* Schaden)Freude *f*, Froh'locken *n*; **3.** ♪ *hist.* Glee *m* (*geselliges Lied*): **~ club** *bsd. Am.* Gesangverein *m*; **'glee·ful** [-fʊl] *adj.* □ **1.** ausgelassen, fröhlich; **2.** schadenfroh, froh'lockend; **'glee·man** [-mən] *s.* [*irr.*] *hist.* fahrender Sänger.

glen [glen] *s.* enges Tal, Bergschlucht *f*, Klamm *f*.

glen·gar·ry [glen'gærɪ] *s.* Mütze *f* der Hochlandschotten.

glib [glɪb] *adj.* □ **1.** a) zungen-, schlagfertig, b) gewandt, ,fix': **a ~ tongue** e-e glatte Zunge; **2.** oberflächlich; **'glib·ness** [-nɪs] *s.* **1.** Zungen-, Schlagfertig-

keit *f*; Gewandtheit *f*; **2.** Glätte *f*, Oberflächlichkeit *f*.

glide [glaɪd] **I** *v/i.* **1.** gleiten (*a. fig.*): **~ along** dahingleiten, -fliegen (*a. Zeit*); **~ out** hinausgleiten, -schweben (*Person*); **2.** ✈ a) gleiten, e-n Gleitflug machen, b) segeln; **II** *s.* **3.** (Da'hin)Gleiten *n*; **4.** ✈ a) Gleitflug *m*, b) Segelflug *m*: **~ path** Gleitweg *m*; **5.** → **glissade** 2; **6.** *ling.* Gleitlaut *m*; **'glid·er** [-də] *s.* ⚓ Gleitboot *n*; **2.** ✈ a) Segelflugzeug *n*, b) *a.* **~ pilot** Segelflieger(in); **3.** Skisport: Gleiter(in); **'glid·ing** [-dɪŋ] *s.* **1.** Gleiten *n*; **2.** ✈ a) → **glide** 3, b) das Segelfliegen.

glim·mer ['glɪmə] **I** *v/i.* **1.** glimmen, schimmern; **II** *s.* **2.** a) Glimmen *n*, b) *a. fig.* Schimmer *m*, (schwacher) Schein: **a ~ of hope** ein Hoffnungsschimmer; **3.** *min.* Glimmer *m*.

glimpse [glɪmps] **I** *s.* **1.** flüchtiger (An-)Blick: **catch a ~ of** → 4; **2.** (*of*) flüchtiger Eindruck (von), kurzer Einblick (in *acc.*); **3.** *fig.* Schimmer *m*, schwache Ahnung; **II** *v/t.* **4.** *j-n, et.* (nur) flüchtig zu sehen bekommen, e-n flüchtigen Blick erhaschen von; **III** *v/i.* **5.** flüchtig blicken (**at** auf *acc.*).

glint [glɪnt] **I** *s.* Schimmer *m*, Schein *m*, Glitzern *n*; **II** *v/i.* schimmern, glitzern, blinken.

glis·sade [glɪ'saːd] **I** *s.* **1.** *mount.* Abfahrt *f*; **2.** *Tanz:* Glis'sade *f*, Gleitschritt *m*; **II** *v/i.* **3.** *mount.* abfahren; **4.** *Tanz:* Gleitschritte machen.

glis·ten ['glɪsn] **I** *v/i.* glitzern, glänzen; **II** *s.* Glitzern *n*, Glanz *m*.

glitch [glɪtʃ] *s.* ⊗ F **1.** (Funkti'ons)Störung *f*, ,Macke' *f*, ,Problem' *n*; **2.** *fig.* Rückschlag *m*.

glit·ter ['glɪtə] **I** *v/i.* **1.** glitzern, funkeln, *a. fig.* strahlen, glänzen; → **gold** 1; **II** *s.* **2.** Glitzern *n* (*etc.*), Glanz *m*; **3.** *fig.* Pracht *f*, Prunk *m*, Glanz *m*; **glit·ter·a·ti** [ˌglɪtə'raːtɪ] *s. pl.* Schickimickis *pl.*; **'glit·ter·ing** [-tərɪŋ] *adj.* □ **1.** glitzernd (*etc.*); **2.** glanzvoll, prächtig.

glitz [glɪts] *s.* F Pomp *m*, 'Glamour *m*; **'glitz·y** *adj.* **1.** pom'pös, glanzvoll; **2.** prunkvoll, schick (*Kleidung*).

gloat [gləʊt] *v/i.:* **~ over** sich weiden an (*dat.*): a) verzückt betrachten (*acc.*), b) sich hämisch *od.* diebisch freuen über (*acc.*); **'gloat·ing** [-tɪŋ] *adj.* □ schadenfroh, hämisch.

glob [glɒb] *s.* F ,Klacks' *m*, ,Klecks' *m*.

glob·al ['gləʊbl] *adj.* glo'bal: a) 'weltum,fassend, Welt...; **~ economy** Weltwirtschaft *f*; **~ warming** Erwärmung *f* der 'Erdatmo,sphäre, b) um'fassend, pau'schal, Gesamt...; **,glo·bal·i'za·tion** *s. bsd.* ✝ Globali'sierung *f*; **glo·bal·ize** *bsd.* ✝ **I** *v/i.* **1.** weltweit tätig werden; **II** *v/t.* **2.** globali'sieren; **3.** die Globali'sierung *gen.* ermöglichen; **'glo·bate** [-beɪt] *adj.* kugelförmig.

globe [gləʊb] **I** *s.* **1.** Kugel *f*: **~ of the eye** Augapfel *m*; **2.** Pla'net *m*: **the ~** der Erdball, die Erdkugel, die Erde; **3.** *geogr.* Globus *m*; **4.** a) Lampenglocke *f*, b) Goldfischglas *n*; **5.** *hist.* Reichsapfel *m*; **II** *v/t. u. v/i.* **6.** kugelförmig machen (werden); **~ ar·ti·choke** *s.* ⚘ Arti'schocke *f*; **'~·fish** *s.* Kugelfisch *m*; **'~,trot·ter** *s.* Weltenbummler(in), Globetrotter(in); **'~,trot·ting** **I** *s.* Globetrotten *n*; **II** *adj.* Weltenbummler..., Globetrotter...

glo·bose ['gləʊbəʊs] → **globular** 1; **glo·bos·i·ty** [gləʊ'bɒsətɪ] *s.* Kugelform *f*, -gestalt *f*; **glob·u·lar** ['glɒbjʊlə] *adj.* □ **1.** kugelförmig: **~ lightning** Kugelblitz *m*; **2.** aus Kügelchen (bestehend); **glob-**

ule ['glɒbjuːl] s. Kügelchen n.

glom·er·ate ['glɒmərət] adj. (zs.-)geballt, knäuelförmig; **glom·er·a·tion** [,glɒmə'reɪʃn] s. Zs.-ballung f, Knäuel m, n.

gloom [gluːm] I s. **1.** a. fig. Dunkel n, Düsterkeit f; **2.** fig. düstere Stimmung, Schwermut f, Trübsinn m: *cast a ~ over* e-n Schatten werfen über (acc.); II v/i. **3.** traurig od. verdrießlich od. düster blicken od. aussehen; **4.** sich verdüstern; **'gloom·i·ness** [-mɪnɪs] s. **1.** → gloom 1, 2; **2.** fig. Hoffnungslosigkeit f; **'gloom·y** [-mɪ] adj. □ **1.** a. fig. düster, trübe; **2.** schwermütig, trübsinnig, düster, traurig; **3.** hoffnungslos.

glo·ri·fi·ca·tion [,glɔːrɪfɪ'keɪʃn] s. **1.** Verherrlichung f; **2.** eccl. a) Verklärung f, b) Lobpreisung f; **3.** Brit. F lautes Fest; **glo·ri·fied** ['glɔːrɪfaɪd] adj. F ,besser': *a ~ barn*; *a ~ office boy*; **glo·ri·fy** ['glɔːrɪfaɪ] v/t. **1.** verherrlichen; **2.** eccl. a) lobpreisen, b) verklären; **3.** erstrahlen lassen, e-e Zierde sein (gen.); **4.** F ,aufmotzen', ,hochjubeln'; → glorified.

glo·ri·ole ['glɔːrɪəʊl] s. Glori'ole f, Heiligenschein m.

glo·ri·ous ['glɔːrɪəs] adj. □ **1.** ruhmvoll, -reich, glorreich; **2.** herrlich, prächtig, wunderbar (alle a. F fig.): *a ~ mess* iro. ein schönes Chaos.

glo·ry ['glɔːrɪ] I s. **1.** Ruhm m, Ehre f: *covered in ~* ruhmbedeckt; *~ be!* F a) juchhu!, b) Donnerwetter!; → Old Glory; **2.** Stolz m, Zierde f, Glanz (-punkt) m; **3.** eccl. Verehrung f, Lobpreisung f; **4.** Herrlichkeit f, Glanz m, Pracht f, Glorie f; höchste Blüte; **5.** eccl. a) himmlische Herrlichkeit, b) Himmel m: *gone to ~* F in die ewigen Jagdgründe eingegangen (tot); *send to ~* F j-n ins Jenseits befördern; **6.** → gloriole; II v/i. **7.** sich freuen, triumphieren, froh'locken (in über acc.); **8.** (in) sich sonnen (in dat.), sich rühmen (gen.); *~ hole* s. F a) Rumpelkammer f od. -kiste f; b) Kramschublade f.

gloss¹ [glɒs] I s. **1.** Glanz m: *~ paint* Glanzlack m; **2.** fig. äußerer Glanz; II v/t. **3.** glänzend machen; **4.** mst *~ over* fig. a) beschönigen, b) vertuschen.

gloss² [glɒs] I s. **1.** (Rand)Glosse f, Erläuterung f, Anmerkung f; **2.** Kommen'tar m, Auslegung f; II v/t. **3.** glossieren; **4.** oft *~ over* (absichtlich) irreführend deuten; **'glos·sa·ry** [-sərɪ] s. Glos'sar n.

gloss·eme [glɒ'siːm] s. ling. Glos'sem n.

gloss·i·ness ['glɒsɪnɪs] s. Glanz m; **gloss·y** ['glɒsɪ] I adj. □ **1.** glänzend: *~ paper* (Hoch)Glanzpapier n; **2.** auf ('Hoch)Glanzpa,pier gedruckt, Hochglanz...: *~ magazine*; **3.** fig. a) raffiniert, b) prächtig (aufgemacht); II s. **4.** 'Hochglanzmaga,zin n.

glot·tal ['glɒtl] adj. **1.** anat. Stimmritzen...: *~ chink* → glottis; **2.** ling. glot'tal: *~ stop* Knacklaut m; **glot·tis** ['glɒtɪs] s. anat. Stimmritze f.

glove [glʌv] I s. **1.** Handschuh m: *fit (s.o.) like a ~* a) (j-m) wie angegossen sitzen, b) fig. (auf j-n) haargenau passen; *take the ~s off* Ernst machen, ,massiv werden'; *with the ~s off, without ~s* unsanft, rücksichts-, schonungslos; **2.** sport (Box-, Fecht-, Reit- etc.) Handschuh m; **3.** *fling* (od. *throw*) *down the ~* (to s.o.) fig. (j-m) den Fehdehandschuh hinwerfen, (j-n) herausfordern; *pick* (od. *take*) *up the ~* die Herausforderung annehmen; II v/t. **4.** mit Handschuhen bekleiden: *~d* be-

handschuht; *~ box, ~ com·part·ment* s. mot. Handschuhfach n; *~ pup·pet* s. Handpuppe f.

glow [gləʊ] I v/i. **1.** glühen; **2.** fig. glühen: a) leuchten, strahlen, b) brennen (Gesicht); **3.** fig. (er)glühen, brennen (with vor dat.): *~ with anger* vor Zorn glühen; II s. **4.** Glühen n, Glut f: *in a ~* glühend; **5.** fig. Glut f: a) Glühen n, Leuchten n, b) Hitze f, Röte f (im Gesicht etc.): *in a ~, all of a ~* glühend, ganz gerötet, c) Feuer n, Leidenschaft f.

glow·er ['glaʊə] v/i. finster (drein)blicken: *~ at* finster anblicken.

glow·ing ['gləʊɪŋ] adj. □ **1.** glühend; **2.** fig. glühend: a) leuchtend, strahlend, b) brennend, c) 'überschwänglich, begeistert: *a ~ account*; *in ~ colo(u)rs* in glühenden od. leuchtenden Farben schildern etc.

glow| plug s. mot. Glühkerze f; **'~·worm** s. Glühwürmchen n.

gloze [gləʊz] → gloss¹ 4.

glu·cose ['gluːkəʊs] s. 🜊 Glu'kose f, Glu'cose f, Traubenzucker m.

glue [gluː] I s. **1.** Leim m; **2.** Klebstoff m; *~ sniffing* Klebstoffschnüffeln n; *~ stick* Klebestift m; II v/t. **3.** leimen, kleben (on auf acc., to an acc.): *~ (to-gether)* zs.-kleben; **4.** fig. (to) heften (auf acc.), drücken (an acc., gegen): *she remained ~d to her mother* sie ,klebte' an ihrer Mutter; *~d to his TV set* er saß wie angewachsen vor dem Bildschirm; **glue·y** ['gluːɪ] adj. klebrig.

glum [glʌm] adj. □ **1.** verdrossen; **2.** bedrückt, niedergeschlagen.

glume [gluːm] s. ♀ Spelze f.

glut [glʌt] I v/t. **1.** den Hunger stillen; **2.** über'sättigen (a. fig.): *~ o.s. on* (od. with) sich überessen mit od. an (dat.); **3.** † Markt über'schwemmen; II s. **5.** Über'sättigung f; **6.** † 'Überangebot n, Schwemme f: *~ of eggs*; *a ~ in the market* e-e Marktschwemme.

glu·tam·ic ac·id [gluː'tæmɪk] s. 🜊 Gluta'minsäure f.

glu·ten ['gluːtən] s. 🜊 Kleber m, Glu'ten n; **'glu·ti·nous** [-tɪnəs] adj. □ klebrig.

glut·ton ['glʌtn] s. **1.** Vielfraß m (a. zo.); **2.** fig. ein Unersättlicher: *a ~ for books* ein Bücherwurm, e-e Leseratte; *a ~ for punishment* ein Maso'chist; *a ~ for work* ein Arbeitstier; **'glut·tonous** [-nəs] adj. □ gefräßig, unersättlich (a. fig.); **'glut·ton·y** [-nɪ] s. Gefräßigkeit f, Unersättlichkeit f (a. fig.).

glyc·er·in(e) ['glɪsəriːn], **'glyc·er·ol** [-rɒl] s. 🜊 Glyze'rin n.

glyph [glɪf] s. 🜊 Glypte f, Glyphe f: a) (verti'kale) Furche od. Rille, b) Skulp-'tur f.

glyp·tic ['glɪptɪk] I adj. Steinschneide...; II s. zo. pl. sg. konstr. Glyptik f, Steinschneidekunst f; **glyp·tog·ra·phy** [glɪp-'tɒgrəfɪ] s. Glyptogra'phie f: a) Steinschneidekunst f, b) Gemmenkunde f.

G-man ['dʒiːmæn] s. [irr.] F G-Mann m, FB'I-A,gent m.

GM| crops ['dʒiːem] pl. 'gentechnisch verändertes Getreide (od. Gemüse); *~ foods* pl. 'gentechnisch veränderte Lebensmittel pl.; *~ maize* s. 'gentechnisch veränderter Mais; *~ po·ta·toes* (to·ma·toes pl. etc.) pl. 'gentechnisch veränderte Kartoffeln (Tomaten etc.).

gnarled [nɑːld] adj. **1.** knorrig (Baum, a. Hand, Person etc.); **2.** fig. mürrisch, ruppig.

gnash [næʃ] v/t. **1.** et. knirschend bei-

ßen; **2.** *~ one's teeth* mit den Zähnen knirschen (vor Wut etc.): *wailing and ~ing of teeth* Heulen u. Zähneklappern n; **'gnash·ers** [-ʃəz] s. pl. F ,dritte Zähne' pl.

gnat [næt] s. zo. **1.** (Stech)Mücke f: *strain at a ~* fig. Haarspalterei betreiben; **2.** Am. Kriebelmücke f.

gnaw [nɔː] I v/t. **1.** nagen an (dat.) (a. fig.), ab-, zernagen; **2.** zerfressen (Säure etc.); **3.** fig. quälen, zermürben; II v/i. **4.** nagen: *~ at* → 1; **5.** *~ into* sich einfressen in (acc.); **6.** fig. nagen, zermürben; **gnaw·er** ['nɔːə] s. zo. Nagetier n; **gnaw·ing** ['nɔːɪŋ] I adj. nagend (a. fig.); II s. Nagen n (a. fig.): Qual f.

gneiss [naɪs] s. geol. Gneis m.

gnome¹ [nəʊm] s. **1.** Gnom m, Zwerg m (beide a. contp. Person), Kobold m; **2.** Gartenzwerg m.

gnome² ['nəʊmiː] s. Gnome f, Sinnspruch m.

gnom·ish ['nəʊmɪʃ] adj. gnomenhaft, zwergenhaft.

gno·sis ['nəʊsɪs] s. phls. Gnosis f; **Gnos·tic** ['nɒstɪk] I adj. gnostisch; II s. Gnostiker m; **Gnos·ti·cism** ['nɒstɪsɪzəm] s. Gnosti'zismus m.

gnu [nuː] s. zo. Gnu n.

go [gəʊ] I pl. **goes** [gəʊz] s. **1.** Gehen n: *on the ~* F ständig in Bewegung, immer ,auf Achse'; *from the word ~* F von Anfang an; *it's a ~!* abgemacht!; **2.** Schwung m, ,Schmiss' m: *he is full of ~* er hat Schwung, er ist voller Leben od. sehr unternehmungslustig; **3.** F Mode f: *be all the ~* große Mode sein; **4.** F Erfolg m: *make a ~ of it* es zu e-m Erfolg machen, bei od. mit et. Erfolg haben; *it's no ~!* es geht nicht!, nichts zu tun!; **5.** F Versuch m: *have a ~ at it!* probiers doch mal!; *at one ~* auf 'einen Schlag, auf Anhieb; *at the first ~* gleich beim ersten Versuch; *it's your ~!* du bist an der Reihe od. dran!; **6.** F ,Geschichte' f: *what a ~!* ,ne schöne Geschichte od. Bescherung!; *it was a near ~!* es ging gerade noch (mal) gut!; **7.** F a) Porti'on f (e-r Speise), b) Glas n: *his third ~ of brandy* sein dritter Kognak; **8.** Anfall m (e-r Krankheit): *my second ~ of influenza* m-e zweite Grippe; II adj. **9.** ⊙ F: *you are ~* (for take-off)! alles klar (zum Start)!; III v/i. [irr.] **10.** gehen, fahren, reisen, sich begeben (to nach): *~ on foot* zu Fuß gehen; *~ by train* mit dem Zug fahren; *~ by plane* (od. air) mit dem Flugzeug reisen, fliegen; *~ to Paris* nach Paris reisen od. gehen; *there he goes!* da ist er (ja)!; *who goes there?* ✕ wer da?; **11.** verkehren, fahren (Bus, Zug etc.); **12.** (fort)gehen, abfahren, abreisen (to nach): *don't ~ yet* geh noch nicht (fort)!; *let me ~!* a) lass mich gehen!, b) lass mich los!; *~ here you ~ again!* F jetzt fängst du schon wieder an!; *here we ~ again* F jetzt geht das schon wieder los!; *just ~ and try it!* versuchs doch mal!; *here goes!* also los!, jetzt gehts los!; **14.** gehen, führen: *this road goes to York*; **15.** sich erstrecken, reichen, gehen (to bis): *the belt doesn't ~ round her waist* der Gürtel geht od. reicht nicht um ihre Taille; *it goes a long way* es reicht lange (aus); *as far as it goes* bis zu e-m gewissen Grade, soweit man das sagen kann; **16.** fig. gehen: *~ as far as to say* so weit gehen zu sagen; *let it ~ at that!* lass es dabei bewenden!; **~ all out** F sich ins Zeug legen (**for** für); *s. die Verbindungen mit anderen Stichwörtern;* **17.** ⚓ (**into**) gehen (in *acc.*), enthalten sein (in *dat.*): **5 into 10 goes twice;** **18.** gehen, passen (**in, into** in *acc.*): **it does not ~ into my pocket;** **19.** gehören (**in, into** in *acc.*, **on** auf *acc.*): **the books ~ on this shelf** die Bücher gehören *od.* kommen auf dieses Regal; **20. ~ to** gehen an (*acc.*) (*Siegerpreis etc.*), zufallen (*dat.*) (*Erbe*); **21.** ⊙ *u. fig.* gehen, laufen, funktionieren: **get ~ing** ⊙ in Gang kommen, *fig. a.* in Schwung od.Fahrt kommen (*Person, Party etc.*), *Person: a.* loslegen; **get s.th.** (*od. s.o.*) **~ing** et. (*Maschine, Projekt etc.*) in Gang bringen, et. (*Party etc.*) (*od.* j-n) in Schwung *od.* Fahrt bringen; **keep ~ing** ⊙ weiterlaufen, *fig.* weitermachen (*Person*); **that hope kept her ~ing** diese Hoffnung hielt sie aufrecht; **this sum will keep you ~ing** diese Summe wird dir (fürs Erste) weiterhelfen; **22.** *kalt, schlecht, verrückt etc.* werden: **~ blind** erblinden; **~ Conservative** zu den Konservativen übergehen; **~ decimal** das Dezimalsystem einführen; **23.** (*gewöhnlich*) *in e-m Zustand* sein, sich befinden: **~ armed** bewaffnet sein; **~ in rags** (ständig) in Lumpen herumlaufen; **~ hungry** hungern; **24. ~ by** (*od.* [**up**]**on**) sich halten an (*acc.*), gehen *od.* sich richten nach: **have nothing to ~** (**up**)**on** keine Anhaltspunkte haben; **~ing by her clothes** ihrer Kleidung nach (zu urteilen); **25.** 'umgehen, im 'Umlauf sein, kursieren (*Gerüchte etc.*): **the story goes** es heißt, man erzählt sich; **26.** gelten (**for** für): **what he says goes** F was er sagt, gilt; **that goes for you too!** das gilt auch für dich!; **it goes without saying** das versteht sich von selbst; **27. ~ by the name of** a) unter dem Namen ... laufen, b) auf den Namen ... hören (*Hund*); **28.** im Allgemeinen sein: **as men ~** wie Männer eben *od.* (nun einmal) sind; **29.** vergehen, verstreichen: **how time goes!; one minute to ~** noch e-e Minute; **30.** ✝ (weg)gehen, verkauft werden: **the coats went for £ 60;** **31.** (**on, in**) ausgegeben werden (für), aufgehen (in *dat.*) (*Geld*): **all his money went in drink;** **32.** dazu beitragen, dienen (**to** zu): **it goes to show** dies zeigt, daran erkennt man; **this only goes to show you the truth** dies dient nur dazu, Ihnen die Wahrheit zu zeigen; **33.** (aus)gehen, verlaufen, sich entwickeln *od.* gestalten: **it went well** es ging gut (aus), es lief (alles) gut; **things have gone badly with me** es ist mir schlecht ergangen; **the decision went against him** die Entscheidung fiel zu s-n Ungunsten aus; **~ big** F ein Riesenerfolg sein; **34. ~ with** gehen *od.* sich vertragen mit, passen zu: **black goes well with yellow;** **35.** ertönen, läuten (*Glocke*), schlagen (*Uhr*): **the door bell went** es klingelte; **bang went the gun** die Kanone machte bumm; **36.** lauten (*Worte etc.*), gehen: **this is how the tune goes** so geht die Melodie; **37.** gehen, verschwinden, abgeschafft werden: **my hat is gone!** mein Hut ist weg!; **he must ~** er muss weg; **these laws must ~** diese Gesetze müssen weg; **warmongering must ~!** Schluss mit der Kriegshetze!; **38.** (da'hin)schwinden: **his strength is ~ing; my eyesight is ~ing** m-e Augen werden immer schlechter; **trade is ~ing**

der Handel kommt zum Erliegen; **the shoes are ~ing** die Schuhe gehen (langsam) kaputt; **39.** sterben: **he is (dead and) gone** er ist tot; **40.** (*pres. p. mit inf.*) *zum Ausdruck e-r Zukunft, e-r Absicht od. et. Unabänderlichem:* **it is ~ing to rain** es wird (gleich *od.* bald) regnen; **he is ~ing to read it** er wird *od.* will es (bald) lesen; **she is ~ing to have a baby** sie bekommt ein Kind; **I was (just) ~ing to do it** ich wollte es eben tun, ich war gerade dabei *od.* im Begriff, es zu tun; **41.** (*mit nachfolgendem Gerundium*) *mst* gehen: **~ swimming** schwimmen gehen; **he goes frightening people** er erschreckt immer die Leute; **42.** (da'ran)gehen, sich anschicken: **he went to find him** er ging ihn suchen; **he went and sold it** F er hat es doch tatsächlich verkauft; **43.** erlaubt sein: **everything goes here** hier ist alles erlaubt; **anything goes!** F alles ist ,drin‘ (*möglich*); **44. pizzas to ~!** *Am.* Pizzas zum Mitnehmen!; **IV** *v/t.* [*irr.*] **45.** *e-n Betrag* wetten, setzen (**on** auf *acc.*); **46. ~ it** F a) (mächtig) rangehen, sich dahinterklemmen, b) es toll treiben, ,auf den Putz hauen‘: **~ it alone** es ganz allein(e) machen; **~ it!** ran!, feste!, drauf!;

Zssgn mit prp.:

go| a·bout *v/i.* in Angriff nehmen, sich machen an (*acc.*), anpacken (*acc.*); **~ af·ter** *v/i.* **1.** nachlaufen (*dat.*); **2.** → **go for** 4; **~ a·gainst** *v/i.* wider'streben (*dat.*), *j-s Prinzipien* zu'widerlaufen; **~ at** *v/i.* **1.** losgehen auf (*acc.*); **2.** → **go about;** **~ be·hind** *v/i.* unter'suchen, auf den Grund gehen (*dat.*); **~ be·tween** *v/i.* vermitteln zwischen (*dat.*); **~ beyond** *v/i. fig.* über'schreiten, *Erwartungen etc.* über'treffen; **~ by** *v/i.* **1.** sich richten nach, sich halten an (*acc.*), urteilen nach; **2.** auf *e-n Namen* hören; **~ for** *v/i.* **1.** holen (gehen); **2.** *e-n Spaziergang etc.* machen; **3.** gelten als *od.* für; **4.** streben nach, sich bemühen um; **5.** F losgehen auf (*acc.*), sich stürzen auf (*acc.*), *fig.* herziehen über (*acc.*); **6.** *sl.* ,stehen‘ auf (*dat.*); **~ in·to** *v/i.* **1.** hin'eingehen in (*acc.*); **2.** eintreten in (*ein Geschäft etc.*): **~ business** Kaufmann werden; **3.** (genau) unter'suchen *od.* prüfen; eingehen auf (*acc.*); **4.** geraten in (*acc.*): **~ a faint** in Ohnmacht fallen; **~ off** *v/i.* **1.** abgehen von; **2.** *j-n, et.* nicht mehr mögen *od.* wollen; **~ on** *v/i.* **1.** sich stützen auf (*acc.*); **2.** sich richten nach, sich halten an (*acc.*), urteilen nach: **I have nothing to ~** ich habe keine Anhaltspunkte; **~ o·ver** → **go through** 1, 2, 3; **~ through** *v/i.* **2.** 'durchgehen, -nehmen, -sprechen; **2.** (gründlich) über'prüfen *od.* unter'suchen; **3.** 'durchsehen, -gehen, -lesen; **4.** durch'suchen; **5.** a) 'durchmachen, erleiden, b) erleben; **6.** *Vermögen* 'durchbringen; **~ with** *v/i.* **1.** begleiten; **2.** gehören zu; **3.** über'einstimmen mit; **4.** passen zu; **5.** mit *j-m* ,gehen‘; **~ without** *v/i.* **1.** auskommen ohne, sich behelfen ohne; **2.** verzichten auf (*acc.*);

Zssgn mit adv.:

go| a·bout *v/i.* **1.** um'hergehen, -fahren, -reisen; **2.** a) kursieren, im 'Umlauf sein (*Gerüchte etc.*), b) 'umgehen (*Grippe etc.*); **3.** ⚓ wenden; **~ a·head** *v/i.* **1.** vorwärts gehen, vor'angehen: **~!** *fig.* los!, nur zu!; **~ with** a) weitermachen mit, b) Ernst machen mit, durchführen; **2.** (*erfolgreich*) vor'ankommen; **3.** *bsd. sport* sich an die Spitze setzen; **~ a·long** *v/i.* **1.** weitergehen; **2.** *fig.*

weitermachen; **3.** mitgehen, -kommen (**with** mit); **4. ~ with** einverstanden sein mit, mitmachen bei; **~ a·round** *v/i.* **1.** → **go about** 1, 2; **2.** → **go round**; **~ back** *v/i.* **1.** zu'rückgehen: **~ to** *fig.* zurückgehen auf (*acc.*), zurückreichen bis; **2. ~ on** *fig.* a) *j-n* im Stich lassen, b) *sein Wort etc.* nicht halten, c) *Entscheidung* rückgängig machen; **~ by** *v/i.* **1.** vor'beigehen (*a. Chance etc.*), -fahren; **2.** vergehen (*Zeit*): **in days gone by** in längst vergangenen Tagen; **~ down** *v/i.* **1.** hin'untergehen: **~ in history** *fig.* in die Geschichte eingehen; **2.** 'untergehen (*Schiff, Sonne etc.*); **3.** zu Boden gehen (*Boxer etc.*); **4.** *thea.* fallen (*Vorhang*); **5.** zu'rückgehen, sinken, fallen (*Fieber, Preise etc.*); **6.** a) sich im Niedergang befinden, b) zugrunde gehen; **7.** *sport* absteigen; **8.** ,(runter)rutschen‘ (*Essen*); **9.** *fig.* (**with**) a) Anklang finden, ,ankommen‘ (bei): **it went down well with him,** b) ,geschluckt‘ werden: **that won't ~ with me** das nehme ich dir nicht ab; **10.** *Brit.* London verlassen; **11.** *univ. Brit.* a) die Universi'tät verlassen, b) in die Ferien gehen; **~ in** *v/i.* **1.** hin'eingehen: **~ and win!** auf in den Kampf!; **2. ~ for** a) sich befassen mit, betreiben, *Sport etc.* treiben, b) mitmachen bei, c) *ein Examen* machen, d) hinarbeiten auf (*acc.*), e) sich einsetzen für, f) sich begeistern für; **~ off** *v/i.* **1.** fort-, weggehen, -laufen; (*Zug etc.*) abfahren; *thea.* abgehen; **2.** losgehen (*Gewehr, Sprengladung etc.*); **3.** (**into**) los-, her'ausplatzen (mit), ausbrechen (in *Gelächter etc.*); **4.** nachlassen, sich verschlechtern; **5.** (*gut etc.*) von'statten gehen; **6.** a) einschlafen, b) ohnmächtig werden; **7.** verderben, schlecht werden (*Essen etc.*), sauer werden (*Milch*); **8.** ausgehen (*Licht etc.*); **~ on** *v/i.* **1.** weitergehen *od.* -fahren; **2.** weitermachen, fortfahren (**with** mit; **doing** zu tun): **~!** a) (mach) weiter!, b) *iro.* hör auf!, ach komm!; **~ reading** weiterlesen; **3.** fortdauern, weitergehen; **4.** vor sich gehen, vorgehen, passieren; **5.** sich ,aufführen‘: **don't ~ like that!** hör schon auf damit!; **6.** F a) unaufhörlich reden (**about** über *acc.*, von), b) ständig herumnörgeln (**at** an *dat.*); **7.** angehen (*Licht etc.*); **8. ~ for** gehen auf (*acc.*), bald sein: **it's going on for five o'clock; ~ out** *v/i.* **1.** ausgehen: a) spazieren gehen, b) zu Veranstaltungen *od.* Gesellschaften gehen, c) erlöschen (*Feuer, Licht*): **~ fishing** fischen (*od.* zum Fischen) gehen; **2.** in den Streik treten; **3.** aus der Mode kommen; **4.** *pol.* abgelöst werden; **5.** *sport* ausscheiden; **6.** zu'rückgehen (*Flut*); **7. ~ to** *j-m* entgegenschlagen (*Herz*), sich *j-m* zuwenden (*Sympathie*); **~ o·ver** *v/i.* **1.** hin'übergehen (**to** zu); **2.** 'übertreten, -gehen (**to** zu *e-r anderen Partei etc.*); **3.** vertagt werden; **4. ~ big** F ein Bombenerfolg sein; **~ round** *v/i.* **1.** her'umgehen (*a. fig. j-m im Kopf*); **2.** (für alle) (aus)reichen: **there is enough (of it) to ~; ~ through** *v/i.* **1.** 'durchgehen, angenommen werden (*Antrag*); **2. ~ with** 'durchführen; **~ to·geth·er** *v/i.* **1.** zs.-passen (*Farben etc.*); **2.** F mitein'ander ,gehen‘ (*Liebespaar*); **~ un·der** *v/i.* **1.** 'untergehen (*a. fig.*); **2.** *fig.* ,eingehen‘ (*Firma etc.*), ,ka'puttgehen‘; **~ up** *v/i.* **1.** hin'aufgehen (*a. fig.*); **2.** *fig.* steigen (*Fieber, Preise etc.*); **3.** *thea.* hochgehen (*Vorhang*); **4.** gebaut werden; **5.** *Brit.* nach London fahren; **6.** *Brit.* (zum Se'mesteranfang)

G

G

zur Universi'tät gehen; **7.** *sport* aufsteigen.

goad [gəʊd] **I** *s.* **1.** Stachelstock *m des
Viehtreibers*; **2.** *fig.* Stachel *m*; Ansporn
m; **II** *v/t.* **3.** antreiben; **4.** *mst* ~ **on** *fig.*
j-n an-, aufstacheln, (an)treiben (*into
doing s.th.* dazu, et. zu tun).

'go-a-head I *adj.* **1.** voller Unter'nehmungsgeist *od.* Initia'tive, zielstrebig;
II *s.* **2.** (Mensch *m* mit) Unter'nehmungsgeist *od.* Initia'tive; **3. get the** ~
(on) ,grünes Licht' bekommen (für);
give s.o. the ~ j-m ,grünes Licht'
geben.

goal [gəʊl] *s.* **1.** Ziel *n* (*a. fig.*); **2.** *sport*
a) Ziel *n*, b) (*Fußball- etc.*)Tor *n*, c)
Tor(erfolg *m*, -schuss *m*) *n*: **score a** ~
ein Tor schießen; **'~a·re·a** *s. sport* Torraum *m*; **'~,get·ter** *s.* Torjäger *m*.

goal·ie ['gəʊlɪ] F → **goalkeeper**.

'goal|,keep·er *s. sport* Tormann *m*,
-wart *m*, -hüter(in); ~ **kick** *s.* (Tor-)
Abstoß *m*; ~ **line** *s.* a) Torlinie *f*, b)
Torauslinie *f*, c) *Rugby:* Mallinie *f*;
'~mouth *s.* Torraum *m*; **'~post** *s.* Torpfosten *m*: **move** (*od. shift*) **the** ~**s** F
fig. (plötzlich *od.* unerwartet) die Spielregeln ändern, sich nicht an die verein-
barten Bedingungen halten.

,go-as-you-'please *adj.* ungebunden.

goat [gəʊt] *s.* **1.** a) Ziege *f*, b) *a.* **he-~**
Ziegenbock *m*: **play the** (**giddy**) ~ *fig.*
herumkaspern; **get s.o.'s** ~ *sl.* j-n ,auf
die Palme bringen'; **2.** *fig.* (geiler)
Bock; **3.** F Sündenbock *m*; **4.** ♌ *ast.* →
Capricorn; **goat·ee** [gəʊ'tiː] *s.* Spitzbart *m*; **'goat·herd** *s.* Ziegenhirt *m*;
'goat·ish [-tɪʃ] *adj.* □ **1.** bockig; **2.** *fig.*
geil.

goat|'s beard *s.* ♀ Bocks- *od.* Geiß-
od. Ziegenbart *m*; **'~skin** *s.* Ziegenle-
der(flasche *f*) *n*; **'~,suck·er** *s. orn.* Zie-
genmelker *m*.

gob¹ [gɒb] *s.* F **1.** (*a.* Schleim)Klumpen
m; **2.** *oft pl.* ,Haufen' *m*, Menge *f*.

gob² [gɒb] *s.* ♟ *Am. sl.* ,Blaujacke' *f*,
Ma'trose *m* (*US-Kriegsmarine*).

gob·bet ['gɒbɪt] *s.* Brocken *m*.

gob·ble¹ ['gɒbl] **I** *v/t. mst* ~ **up** verschlingen (*a. fig.*); **II** *v/i.* gierig essen.

gob·ble² ['gɒbl] **I** *v/i.* kollern (*Truthahn*); **II** *s.* Kollern *n*.

gob·ble·dy·gook ['gɒbldɪguːk] *s.* F **1.**
,Be'amtenchi,nesisch' *n*; **2.** (Be'rufs-)
Jar,gon *m*; **3.** ,Geschwafel' *n*.

gob·bler¹ ['gɒblə] *s.* Fresser(in).

gob·bler² ['gɒblə] *s.* Truthahn *m*, Puter *m*.

Gob·e·lin ['gəʊbəlɪn] **I** *adj.* Gobelin...;
II *s.* Gobe'lin *m*.

'go-be,tween *s.* **1.** Mittelsmann *m*, Ver-
mittler(in); **2.** Makler(in); **3.** Kupp-
ler(in).

gob·let ['gɒblɪt] *s.* **1.** *obs.* Po'kal *m*; **2.**
Kelchglas *n*.

gob·lin ['gɒblɪn] *s.* Kobold *m*.

gob·smacked ['gɒbsmækt] *adj. Brit.* F
to'tal verblüfft, ,platt': **I was** ~ mir
,blieb die Spucke weg'.

go-by ['gəʊbɪ] *s. ichth.* Meergrundel *f*.

go-by ['gəʊbaɪ] *s.*: **give s.o. the** ~ F j-n
,schneiden' *od.* ignorieren; **give s.th.
the** ~ F die Finger von et. lassen.

'go-cart *s.* **1.** Laufstuhl *m* (*Gehhilfe für
Kinder*); **2.** Sportwagen *m* (*für Kinder*);
3. Handwagen *m*; **4.** → **go-kart**.

god [gɒd] *s.* **1.** Gott(heit *f*) *m*; Götze *m*,
Abgott *m*: ~ **of love** Liebesgott, Amor
m; **ye** ~**s!** F heiliger Strohsack!; **a sight
for the** ~**s** ein Bild für (die) Götter; **2.**
♌ Gott *m*: ♌**'s acre** Gottesacker *m*;
house of ♌ Gotteshaus *n*; **play** ~ den
lieben Gott spielen; ♌ **forbid!** Gott behüte!; ♌ **help him** Gott sei ihm gnädig;

so help me ♌ so wahr mir Gott helfe;
♌ **knows** a) weiß Gott, b) wer weiß(,
ob etc.); ♌ **willing** so Gott will; **thank**
♌ Gott sei Dank; **for** ♌**'s sake** a) um
Gottes willen, b) verdammt noch
mal!; **the good** ♌ der liebe Gott;
good ♌**!, my** ~**!,** (**oh**) ~**!** du lieber
Gott!, lieber Himmel!; → **act** 1 *etc.*;
3. *fig.* (Ab)Gott *m*; **4.** *pl. thea.* (Publikum *n* auf der) Gale'rie *f*, ,O'lymp' *m*;
,~'aw·ful *adj.* F scheußlich, ,beschis-
sen'; **'~child** *s.* [*irr.*] Patenkind *n*;
,~'dam·mit *int. bsd. Am.* F verdammt
noch mal; **'~,damn(ed)** *adj., adv. u.
int.* (gott)verdammt; **,~'damn·it** *int.* →
goddammit.

god·dess ['gɒdɪs] *s.* Göttin *f* (*a. fig.*).

'god|,fa·ther I *s.* Patin *m* (*a. fig.*), Paten-
onkel *m*, Taufzeuge *m*: **stand** ~ **to** → **II**
v/t. a. fig. Pate stehen bei, aus der Taufe heben; **'~,fear·ing** *adj.* gottesfürchtig; **'~,for,sak·en** *adj. contp.* gottver-
lassen.

god·head ['gɒdhed] *s.* Gottheit *f*; **'godless** [-lɪs] *adj.* ohne Gott; *fig.* gottlos;
'god·like *adj.* **1.** gottähnlich, göttlich;
2. göttergleich; **'god·li·ness** [-lɪnɪs] *s.*
Frömmigkeit *f*; Gottesfurcht *f*; **'god·ly**
[-lɪ] *adj.* fromm.

'god|,moth·er *s.* Patin *f*, Patentante *f*;
'~,par·ent *s.* Pate *m*, Patin *f*; **'~send** *s.*
fig. Geschenk *n* des Himmels, Glücks-
fall *m*, Segen *m*; **'~son** *s.* Patensohn *m*;
,~'speed *s.*: **bid s.o.** ~ j-m viel Glück
od. glückliche Reise wünschen.

go·er ['gəʊə] *s.* **1. be a good** ~ gut laufen (*bsd. Pferd*); **2. in Zssgn** *mst* ...besu-
cher(in), ...gänger(in).

gof·fer ['gəʊfə] **I** *v/t.* kräuseln, plissieren; **II** *s.* Plis'see *n*.

'go-,get·ter *s.* F j-d, der weiß, was er
will; Draufgänger *m*.

gog·gle ['gɒgl] **I** *v/i.* **1.** stieren, glotzen;
II *s.* **2.** stierer Blick; **3.** *pl.* Schutzbrille
f; **'~box** *s. bsd. Brit.* F ,Glotze' *f* (*Fernseher*).

go-go ['gəʊgəʊ] *adj.* **1.** ~ **girl** Go-go-
Girl *n*; **2.** *fig.* a) schwungvoll, b) schick.

Goid·el·ic [gɔɪ'delɪk] → **Gaelic**.

go-in ['gəʊ'ɪn] *s.* Go-'in *n*.

go·ing ['gəʊɪŋ] **I** *s.* **1.** (Weg)Gehen *n*,
Abreise *f*; **2.** Straßenzustand *m*, (*Pferdesport*) Geläuf *n*; **3.** Tempo *n*: **good** ~
ein flottes Tempo; **rough** (*od.* **heavy**) ~
e-e Schinderei; **while the** ~ **is good** a)
solange noch Zeit ist, b) solange es
noch gut läuft; **II** *adj.* **4.** in Betrieb,
arbeitend: **a** ~ **concern** ein gut gehendes Geschäft; **5.** vor'handen: **still** ~
noch zu haben; **the best beer** ~ das
beste Bier, das es gibt; ~**,** ~**,** **gone!**
(*Auktion*) zum Ersten, zum Zweiten,
zum Dritten!; **6.** geltend: ~ **price**
Marktpreis *m*; ~ **rate** geltender Satz;
,go·ing-'o·ver *s.* F **1.** Über'prüfung *f*;
2. a) Tracht *f* Prügel, b) Standpauke *f*;
,go·ings-'on *s. pl.* F *mst* b.S. Vorgänge
pl., Treiben *n*: **strange** ~ merkwürdige
Dinge.

goi·ter *Am.*, **goi·tre** *Brit.* ['gɔɪtə] *s.* ♟
Kropf *m*; **'goi·trous** [-trəs] *adj.* **1.**
kropfartig; **2.** mit e-m Kropf (behaftet).

go-kart ['gəʊkɑːt] *s. mot.* Gokart *m*.

gold [gəʊld] **I** *s.* **1.** Gold *n*: **all is not** ~
that glitters es ist nicht alles Gold, was
glänzt; **a heart of** ~ *fig.* ein goldenes
Herz; **worth one's weight in** ~ unbezahlbar, mit Gold aufzuwiegen;
→ **good** 8; **2.** Gold(münzen *pl.*) *n*; **3.**
Geld *n*, Reichtum *m*; **4.** Goldfarbe *f*; **II**
adj. **5.** aus Gold, golden, Gold...: ~
dollar Golddollar *m*; ~ **watch** goldene
Uhr; ~ **back·ing** *s.* ♟ Golddeckung *f*; ~

bar *s.* ♟ Goldbarren *m*; ~ **bloc** *s.* ♟
Goldblock(länder *pl.*) *m*; ~ **brick** *Am.*
F **I** *s.* **1.** falscher Goldbarren; **2.** *fig.* a)
wertlose Sache, b) Schwindel *m*, ,Be-
schiss' *m*: **sell s.o. a** ~ → 4; **3.** Drückeberger *m*; **II** *v/t.* **4.** j-n ,übers Ohr hau-
en'; ~ **bul·lion** *s.* Gold *n* in Barren; **'~-
,dig·ger** *s.* **1.** Goldgräber *m*; **2.** *sl.*
*Frau, die nur hinter dem Geld der Män-
ner her ist*; ~ **dust** *s.* Goldstaub *m*.

gold·en ['gəʊldən] *adj.* **1.** *mst fig.* golden: ~ **days**; ~ **disc** goldene Schallplatte; ~ **opportunity** einmalige Gelegenheit; **2.** goldgelb, golden (*Haar etc.*); ~
age *s.* das goldene Zeitalter; ~ **calf** *s.
bibl. u. fig.* das Goldene Kalb; ~ **ea·gle**
s. orn. Gold-, Steinadler *m*; ♌ **Fleece**
s. myth. das Goldene Vlies; ~ **handshake** *s.* F **1.** Abfindung *f* bei Entlassung; **2.** ,'Umschlag' *m* (*mit e-m Geldgeschenk der Firma*); ~ **mean** *s.* die
goldene Mitte; *das* goldene Mittelweg;
~ **o·ri·ole** *s. orn.* Pi'rol *m*; ~ **pheas·ant**
s. orn. 'Goldfa,san *m*; ~ **rule** *s.* **1.** *bibl.*
goldene Sittenregel; **2.** *fig.* goldene Regel; ~ **sec·tion** *s.* Goldener Schnitt; ~
wed·ding *s.* goldene Hochzeit.

gold| fe·ver *s.* Goldfieber *n*, -rausch *m*;
'~field *s.* Goldfeld *n*; **'~finch** *s. orn.*
Stieglitz *m*, Distelfink *m*; **'~fish** *s.*
Goldfisch *m*; **'~foil** *s.* Blattgold *n*;
'~,ham·mer *s. orn.* Goldammer *f*; ~
lace *s.* Goldtresse *f*, -borte *f*; ~ **leaf** *s.*
Blattgold *n*; ~ **med·al** *s.* 'Goldme,daille
f; ~ **med·al·(l)ist** *s. sport* 'Goldme,dail-
lengewinner(in); ~ **mine** *s.* Goldberg-
werk *n*; Goldgrube *f* (*a. fig.*); ~ **plate** *s.*
goldenes Tafelgeschirr; **'~,plat·ed** *adj.*
vergoldet; ~ **point** *s.* ♟ Goldpunkt *m*;
~ **rush** → **gold fever**; **'~smith** *s.*
Goldschmied *m*; ~ **stand·ard** *s.* Gold-
währung *f*; ♌ **Stick** *s. Brit.* Oberst *m*
der königlichen Leibgarde.

golf [gɒlf] *sport* **I** *s.* Golf(spiel) *n*; **II** *v/i.*
Golf spielen; ~ **ball** *s.* **1.** Golfball *m*; **2.**
Kugelkopf *m* (*der Schreibmaschine*); ~
club *s.* **1.** Golfschläger *m*; **2.** Golfklub
m.

golf·er ['gɒlfə] *s.* Golfspieler(in).

golf links *s. pl., a. sg. konstr.* Golfplatz
m.

Go·li·ath [gə'laɪəθ] *s. fig.* Goliath *m*,
Riese *m*, Hüne *m*.

gol·li·wog(g) ['gɒlɪwɒg] *s.* **1.** gro'teske
schwarze Puppe; **2.** *fig.* ,Vogelscheu-
che' *f* (*Person*).

gol·ly ['gɒlɪ] *int. a.* **by** ~**!** F Menschenskind!, Mann!

go·losh [gə'lɒʃ] → **galosh**.

Go·mor·rah, Go·mor·rha [gə'mɒrə] *s.*
fig. Go'morr(h)a *n*, Sündenpfuhl *m*.

go·nad ['gəʊnæd] *s.* ♟ Keim-, Ge-
schlechtsdrüse *f*.

gon·do·la ['gɒndələ] *s.* **1.** Gondel *f* (*a.
e-s Ballons, e-r Seilbahn etc.*); **2.** *Am.*
flaches Flussboot; **3.** *a.* ~ **car** ♟ *Am.*
offener Güterwagen; **gon·do·lier**
[,gɒndə'lɪə] *s.* Gondoli'ere *m*.

gone [gɒn] **I** *p.p. von* **go**; **II** *adj.* **1.**
weg(gegangen), fort: **he is** ~; **be** ~**!** fort
mit dir!; **I must be** ~ ich muss weg; **2.**
verloren, verschwunden, weg, da'hin;
3. ,hin', ,futsch': a) weg, verbraucht, b)
ka'putt, c) ruiniert, d) tot; **a** ~ **case** ein
hoffnungsloser Fall; **a** ~ **man** → **goner**;
a ~ **feeling** ein Schwächegefühl; **all his
money is** ~ sein ganzes Geld ist weg
od. ,futsch'; **4.** mehr als, älter als, über:
he is ~ **forty**; **5.** F (**on**) ganz ,weg'
(von): a) begeistert (von), b) ,verknallt'
(in *acc.*); **6.** *sl.* ,high', ,weg'; **7.** **she's
four months** ~ F sie ist im 4. Monat;
gon·er ['gɒnə] *s.* 'Todeskandi,dat *m*:

he is a ~ F er ist ‚erledigt‘ (*a. weitS.*).
gon·fa·lon [ˈɡɒnfələn] *s.* Banner *n.*
gong [ɡɒŋ] I *s.* **1.** Gong *m*; **2.** ✗ *Brit. sl.* Orden *m*; II *v/t.* **3.** *Brit. Auto* durch 'Gongsi‚gnal stoppen (*Polizei*).
go·ni·om·e·ter [ˌɡəʊnɪˈɒmɪtə] *s.* ✠ *u. Radio*: Winkelmesser *m.*
gon·o·coc·cus [ˌɡɒnəʊˈkɒkəs] *pl.* **-coc-ci** [-ˈkɒkaɪ] *s.* ⚕ Gono'kokkus *m.*
gon·or·rhoe·a, *Am. mst* **gon·or·rhe·a** [ˌɡɒnəˈriːə] *s.* ⚕ Gonor'rhö(e) *f*, Tripper *m.*
goo [ɡuː] *s. sl.* **1.** Schmiere *f*, klebriges Zeug; **2.** *fig.* sentimen'taler Kitsch, ‚Schmalz‘ *m.*
good [ɡʊd] I *adj.* **1.** gut, angenehm, erfreulich: ~ **news**; **it is** ~ **to be rich** es ist angenehm, reich zu sein; ~ **morning** (**evening**)! guten Morgen (Abend)!; ~ **afternoon!** guten Tag! (*nachmittags*); ~ **night!** a) gute Nacht! (*a.* F *fig.*), b) guten Abend!; (**it's a**) ~ **time** sich amüsieren; (**it's a**) ~ **thing that** es ist gut, dass; **be** ~ **eating** gut schmecken; **2.** gut, geeignet, nützlich, günstig, zuträglich: **is this** ~ **to eat?** kann man das essen?; **milk is** ~ **for children** Milch ist gut für Kinder; ~ **for gout** gut für *od.* gegen Gicht; **that's** ~ **for you!** *a. iro.* das tut dir gut!; **get in** ~ **with s.o.** sich mit j-m gut stellen; **what is it** ~ **for?** wofür ist es gut?, wozu dient es?; **3.** befriedigend, reichlich, beträchtlich: **a** ~ **hour** e-e gute Stunde; **a** ~ **day's journey** e-e gute Tagereise; **a** ~ **many** ziemlich viele; **a** ~ **threshing** e-e ordentliche Tracht Prügel; ~ **money** *sl.* hoher Lohn; **4.** (*vor adj.*) verstärkend: **a** ~ **long time** sehr lange (Zeit); ~ **old age** hohes Alter; ~ **and angry** F äußerst erbost; **5.** gut, tugendhaft: **lead a** ~ **life** ein rechtschaffenes Leben führen; **a** ~ **deed** e-e gute Tat; **6.** gut, gewissenhaft: **a** ~ **father and husband** ein guter Vater und Gatte; **7.** gut, gütig, lieb: ~ **to the poor** gut zu den Armen; **it is** ~ **of you to help me** es ist nett (von Ihnen), dass Sie mir helfen; **be** ~ **enough** (*od.* **so** ~ **as**) **to fetch it** sei so gut und hole es; **be** ~ **enough to hold your tongue!** halt gefälligst deinen Mund!; **my** ~ **man** F mein Lieber!; **8.** artig, lieb, brav (*Kind*): **be a** ~ **boy**; **as** ~ **as gold** a) kreuzbrav, b) goldrichtig; **9.** gut, geschickt, tüchtig (**at** *in dat.*): **a** ~ **rider** ein guter Reiter; **he is** ~ **at golf** er spielt gut Golf; **10.** gut, geachtet: **of** ~ **family** aus guter Familie; **11.** gültig (*a.* ✝), echt: **a** ~ **reason** ein triftiger Grund; **tell false money from** ~ falsches Geld von echtem unterscheiden; **a** ~ **Republican** ein guter *od.* überzeugter Republikaner; **be as** ~ **as** auf dasselbe hinauslaufen; **as** ~ **as finished** so gut wie fertig; **he has as** ~ **as promised** er hat es so gut wie versprochen; **12.** gut, genießbar, frisch: **a** ~ **egg**; **is this fish still** ~?; **13.** gut, gesund, kräftig: **in** ~ **health** bei guter Gesundheit, gesund; **be** ~ **for** ‚gut‘ sein für, fähig zu *od.* geeignet sein zu; **I am** ~ **for another mile** ich schaffe noch eine Meile; **he is always** ~ **for a surprise** er ist immer für e-e Überraschung gut; **I am** ~ **for a walk** ich habe Lust zu e-m Spaziergang; **14.** *bsd.* ✝ gut, sicher, zuverlässig: **a** ~ **firm** e-e gute *od.* zahlungsfähige Firma; ~ **debts** sichere Schulden; **be** ~ **for any amount** für jeden Betrag gut sein; II *s.* **15.** das Gute, Gutes *n*, Wohl *n*: **the common** ~ das Gemeinwohl; **do s.o.** ~ a) j-m Gutes tun, b) j-m gut *od.* wohl tun; **he is up**

to no ~ er führt nichts Gutes im Schilde; **it comes to no** ~ es führt zu nichts Gutem; **16.** Nutzen *m*, Vorteil *m*: **for his** ~ zu s-m Nutzen; **he is too nice for his own** ~ er ist viel zu nett; **what is the** ~ **of it?**, **what** ~ **is it?** was nützt es?, wozu soll das gut sein?; **it's no** ~ a) es taugt nichts, b) es ist zwecklos; **it is no** ~ **trying** es hat keinen Wert *od.* Sinn, es zu versuchen; **much** ~ **may it do you** *iro.* wohl bekomms!; **for** ~ (**and all**) für immer, endgültig, ein für alle Mal; **to the** ~ obendrein, extra, ✝ als Gewinn *od.* Kreditsaldo; **it's all to the** ~ es ist nur zu s-m *etc.* Besten; **17. the** ~ *pl.* die Guten *pl. od.* Rechtschaffenen *pl.*; **18.** *pl.* (bewegliche) Habe: ~**s and chattels** Hab u. Gut *n*; F *j-s* ‚Siebensachen‘ *pl.*; **19.** *pl.* Güter *pl.*, Waren *pl.*, Gegenstände *pl.*: **by** ~**s** ✝ *Brit.* als Frachtgut; → **deliver** 5.
Good| Book *s.* die Bibel; ‚~'**by(e)** [-'baɪ] I *s.* **1.** Abschiedsgruß *m*: **say** ~ **to** *j-m* auf (*od.* Auf) Wiedersehen sagen, sich von *j-m* verabschieden; **you may say** ~ **to that!** F das kannst du vergessen!; **2.** Abschied *m*; II *adj.* Abschieds...: ~ **kiss**; III *int.* [ˌɡʊdˈbaɪ] **3.** auf Wiedersehen!, adi'eu!, a'de!: **then** ~ **democracy!** *fig. iron.* dann ade Demokratie!; ‚~'**fel-low·ship** *s.* gute Kame'radschaft, Kame'radschaftlichkeit *f*; ~**-for-noth·ing** I [ˈɡʊdfəˌnʌθɪŋ] *adj.* nichtsnutzig; II [ˌɡʊdfəˈn-] *s.* Taugenichts *m*, Nichtsnutz *m*; ⚹ **Fri·day** *s. eccl.* Kar'freitag *m*; ~ **hu·mo(u)r** *s.* gute Laune; ‚~'**hu·mo(u)red** *adj.* □ **1.** bei guter Laune, gut aufgelegt; **2.** gutmütig.
good·ish [ˈɡʊdɪʃ] *adj.* **1.** ziemlich gut; **2.** ziemlich (*Menge*); **good·li·ness** [ˈɡʊdlɪnɪs] *s.* **1.** Güte *f*, Wert *m*; **2.** Anmut *f*; **3.** Schönheit *f*.
‚**good|**-'**look·ing** *adj.* gut aussehend, hübsch, schön; ~ **looks** *s. pl.* gutes Aussehen, Schönheit *f*.
good·ly [ˈɡʊdlɪ] *adj.* **1.** schön, anmutig; **2.** beträchtlich, ansehnlich; **3.** *oft iro.* glänzend, prächtig.
'**good|·man** [-mæn] *s.* [*irr.*] *obs.* Hausvater *m*, Ehemann *m*; ⚹ **Death** Freund Hein *m*; ‚~'**na·tured** *adj.* □ gutmütig, gefällig; ‚~'**neigh·bo(u)r·li·ness** *s.* gutnachbarliches Verhältnis; ⚹ **Neighbo(u)r pol·i·cy** *s.* Poli'tik *f* der guten Nachbarschaft.
good·ness [ˈɡʊdnɪs] *s.* **1.** Tugend *f*, Frömmigkeit *f*; **2.** Güte *f*, Freundlichkeit *f*; **3.** Wert *m*, Güte *f*; *engS.* das Wertvolle *od.* Nahrhafte; **4.** ~ **gra-cious!**, **my** ~! du meine Güte!, du lieber Gott!; ~ **knows** weiß der Himmel; **for** ~' **sake** um Himmels willen; **thank** ~! Gott sei Dank!; **I wish to** ~ wollte Gott.
goods| a·gent *s.* ✝ ('Bahn)Spedi‚teur *m*; ~ **en·gine** *s.* Güterzugloko‚mo‚tive *f*; ~ **lift** *s. Brit.* Lastenaufzug *m.*
good speed *Am.* → **godspeed**.
goods| sta·tion *s. Brit.* Güterbahnhof *m*; ~ **train** *s. Brit.* Güterzug *m*; ~ **van** *s. mot. Brit.* Lieferwagen *m*; ~ **wag·on** *s. Brit.* Güterwagen *m*; ~ **yard** *s. Brit.* Güter(bahn)hof *m.*
‚**good|**-'**tem·pered** *adj.* □ gutartig, -mütig, ausgeglichen; '~**-time Charlie** [ˈtʃɑːlɪ] *s. Am.* F lebenslustiger *od.* vergnügungssüchtiger Mensch; ‚~'**will** *s.* **1.** Wohlwollen *n*, guter Wille, Verständigungsbereitschaft *f*: ~ **tour** *pol.* Goodwillreise *f*; ~ **visit** Freundschaftsbesuch *m*; **2.** *mst* **good will** ✝ a) Goodwill *m*, (ide'eller) Firmen- *od.* Geschäftswert (*guter Ruf, Kundenstamm etc.*).

good·y [ˈɡʊdɪ] F I *s.* **1.** Bon'bon *m, n, pl.* Süßigkeiten *pl.*, gute Sachen; **2.** *fig.* ‚klasse Ding‘; **3.** *Film etc.*: Gute(r *m*) *f* (*Ggs Schurke*); **4.** Tugendbold *m*, Mucker *m*; II *adj.* **5.** frömmelnd, ‚mora'linsauer‘; III *int.* **6.** prima!, ‚Klasse‘!; '~-‚**good·y** → **goody** 4, 5, 6.
goo·ey [ˈɡuːɪ] *adj. sl.* klebrig, schmierig.
goof [ɡuːf] F I *s.* **1.** ‚Pfeife‘ *f*, Idi'ot *m*; **2.** ‚Schnitzer‘ *m*, ‚Patzer‘ *m*; II *v/t.* **3.** *oft* ~ **up** ‚vermasseln‘; III *v/i.* **4.** ‚Mist bauen‘; **5.** *oft* ~ **around** ‚her'umspinnen‘.
'**go-off** *s.* Start *m*: **at the first** ~ (gleich) beim ersten Mal, auf Anhieb.
'**goof·y** [ˈɡuːfɪ] *adj.* □ *sl.* ‚doof‘, ‚bekloppt‘.
gook [ɡʊk] *s. Am. sl. contp.* ‚Schlitzauge‘ *n* (*Asiate*).
goon [ɡuːn] *s. sl.* **1.** *Am.* angeheuerter Schläger; **2.** → **goof** 1.
goose [ɡuːs] I *pl.* **geese** [ɡiːs] *s.* **1.** *orn.* Gans *f*: **cook s.o.'s** ~ F es j-m ‚besorgen‘, j-n ‚fertig machen‘; **he's cooked his** ~ **with me** F bei mir ist er ‚unten durch‘; **all his geese are swans** bei ihm ist immer alles besser als bei andern; **kill the** ~ **that lays the golden eggs** das Huhn schlachten, das goldene Eier legt; → **sauce** 1; **2.** Gans *f*, Gänsebraten *m*; **3.** *fig.* a) Dummkopf *m*, b) (dumme) Gans; **4.** (*pl.* **goos·es**) Schneiderbügeleisen *n*; II *v/t.* **5.** F *j-n* (in den ‚Po‘) zwicken.
goose·ber·ry [ˈɡʊzbərɪ] *s.* **1.** ♀ Stachelbeere *f*: **play** ~ F den Anstandswauwau spielen; **2.** *a.* ~ **wine** Stachelbeerwein *m*; ~ **fool** *s.* Stachelbeercreme *f* (*Speise*).
goose| bumps *s. pl.*, ~ **flesh** *s. fig.* Gänsehaut *f*; '~**-neck** *s.* ⊕ Schwanenhals *m*; ~ **pim·ples** *s. pl.* → **goose bumps**; ~ **quill** *s.* Gänsekiel *m*; '~**-skin** → **goose bumps**; ~ **step** *s.* ✗ Pa'rade-, Stechschritt *m.*
goos·ey [ˈɡuːsɪ] *s. fig.* Gäns·chen *n.*
go·pher[1] [ˈɡəʊfə] *s. Am. zo.* a) Taschenratte *f*, b) Ziesel *m*, c) Gopherschildkröte *f*, d) *a.* ~ **snake** Schildkrötenschlange *f.*
go·pher[2] → **goffer**.
go·pher[3] [ˈɡəʊfə] *s. bibl.* Baum, aus dessen Holz Noah die Arche baute; '~**-wood** *s. Am.* ♀ Gelbholz *n.*
Gor·di·an [ˈɡɔːdjən] *adj.*: **cut the** ~ **knot** den gordischen Knoten durch'hauen.
gore[1] [ɡɔː] *s.* (*bsd.* geronnenes) Blut.
gore[2] [ɡɔː] I *s.* **1.** Zwickel *m*, Keil(stück *n*) *m*; II *v/t.* **2.** keilförmig zuschneiden; **3.** e-n Zwickel einsetzen in (*acc.*).
gore[3] [ɡɔː] *v/t.* (mit den Hörnern) durch'bohren, aufspießen.
gorge [ɡɔːdʒ] I *s.* **1.** enge (Fels-)Schlucht *f*; **2.** *rhet.* Kehle *f*, Schlund *m*: **my** ~ **rises at it** *fig.* mir wird übel davon *od.* dabei; **3.** Schlemme'rei *f*, Völle'rei *f*; **4.** △ Hohlkehle *f*; II *v/i.* **5.** schlemmen: ~ **on** (*od.* **with**) → 7; III *v/t.* **6.** gierig verschlingen; **7.** ~ **o.s. on** (*od.* **with**) sich voll fressen mit, *et.* in sich hineinschlingen.
gor·geous [ˈɡɔːdʒəs] *adj.* □ **1.** prächtig, prachtvoll (*beide a. fig.* F); **2.** F großartig, wunderbar, ‚toll‘.
Gor·gon [ˈɡɔːɡən] *s.* **1.** *myth.* Gorgo *f*; **2.** a) hässliches *od.* abstoßendes Weib, b) ‚Drachen‘ *m*; **gor·go·ni·an** [ɡɔːˈɡəʊnjən] *adj.* **1.** Gorgonen...; **2.** schauerlich.
go·ril·la [ɡəˈrɪlə] *s.* **1.** *zo.* Go'rilla *m*; **2.** *Am. sl.* ‚Gorilla‘ *m*: a) Leibwächter *m* e-s Gangsters *etc.*, b) Scheusal *n.*
gor·mand·ize [ˈɡɔːməndaɪz] I *v/t. et.* gierig verschlingen; II *v/i.* schlemmen;

'gor·mand·iz·er [-zə] *s.* Schlemmer (-in).

gorse [gɔːs] *s.* ♀ *Brit.* Stechginster *m.*

gor·y ['gɔːrɪ] *adj.* **1.** *poet.* a) blutbefleckt, voll Blut, b) blutig: ~ *battle;* **2.** *fig.* blutrünstig.

gosh [gɒʃ] *int.* F Mensch!, Mann!

gos·hawk ['gɒshɔːk] *s. orn.* Hühnerhabicht *m.*

gos·ling ['gɒzlɪŋ] *s.* **1.** junge Gans, Gäns·chen *n;* **2.** *fig.* Grünschnabel *m.*

,go-'slow *s.* ♣ *Brit.* Bummelstreik *m.*

gos·pel ['gɒspl] *s. eccl. a.* ₤ Evan'gelium *n* (*a. fig.*): **take s.th. for ~** et. für bare Münze nehmen; ~ *song* Gospelsong *m;* ~ *truth fig.* absolute Wahrheit; **'gospel·(l)er** [-pələ] *s.* Vorleser *m* des Evan'geliums: *hot* ~ a) religiöser Eiferer, b) fa'natischer Befürworter.

gos·sa·mer ['gɒsəmə] **I** *s.* **1.** Alt'weibersommer *m,* Spinnfäden *pl.;* **2.** a) feine Gaze, b) hauchdünner Stoff; **3.** *et.* sehr Zartes u. Dünnes; **II** *adj.* **4.** leicht u. zart, hauchdünn.

gos·sip ['gɒsɪp] **I** *s.* **1.** Klatsch *m,* Tratsch *m:* ~ *column* Klatschspalte *f;* ~ *columnist* Klatschkolumnist(in); **2.** Plaude'rei *f,* Schwatz *m,* Plausch *m;* **3.** Klatschbase *f;* **II** *v/i.* **4.** klatschen, tratschen; **5.** plaudern; **'gos·sip·y** [-pɪ] *adj.* **1.** klatschhaft, -süchtig; **2.** schwatzhaft; **3.** im Plauderton (geschrieben).

got [gɒt] *pret. u. p.p. von* **get**.

Goth [gɒθ] *s.* **1.** Gote *m;* **2.** *fig.* Bar'bar *m.*

Go·tham ['gəʊθəm, 'gɒ-] *s. Am.* (*Spitzname für*) New York; **'Go·tham·ite** *s.* [-maɪt] *humor.* New Yorker(in).

Goth·ic ['gɒθɪk] **I** *adj.* **1.** gotisch; **2.** *fig.* bar'barisch, roh; **3.** *typ.* a) *Brit.* gotisch, b) *Am.* Grotesk...; **4.** *Literatur:* a) ba'rock, ro'mantisch, b) Schauer...: ~ *novel;* **II** *s.* **5.** *ling.* Gotisch *n;* **6.** ₳ Gotik *f,* gotischer (Bau)Stil; **7.** *typ.* a) *Brit.* Frak'tur *f,* gotische Schrift, b) *Am.* Gro'tesk *f;* **Goth·i·cism** ['gɒθɪsɪzəm] *s.* **1.** Gotik *f;* **2.** *fig.* Barba'rei *f,* 'Unkul,tur *f.*

,go-to-'meet·ing *adj.* F Sonntags..., Ausgeh...: ~ *suit.*

got·ten ['gɒtn] *obs. od. Am. p.p. von* **get**.

gou·ache [gʊ'ɑːʃ] (*Fr.*) *s. paint.* Gou-'ache *f.*

gouge [gaʊdʒ] **I** *s.* **1.** ☉ Hohlmeißel *m;* **2.** Rille *f,* Furche *f;* **3.** *Am.* F a) Gaune'rei *f,* b) Erpressung *f;* **II** *v/t.* **4.** a) ~ *out* ☉ ausmeißeln, -höhlen, -stechen; **5.** ~ *out s.o.'s eye* a) j-m den Finger ins Auge stoßen, b) j-m ein Auge ausdrücken *od.* -stechen; **6.** *Am.* F a) j-n über'vorteilen, b) e-e Summe erpressen.

gou·lash ['guːlæʃ] *s.* Gulasch *n:* ~ *communism pol. contp.* Gulaschkommunismus *m.*

gourd [gʊəd] *s.* **1.** ♀ Flaschenkürbis *m;* **2.** Kürbisflasche *f.*

gour·mand ['gʊəmənd] **I** *s.* **1.** Schlemmer *m,* Gour'mand *m;* **2.** → *gourmet;* **II** *adj.* schlemmerisch.

gour·met ['gʊəmeɪ] *s.* Feinschmecker *m,* Gour'met *m.*

gout [gaʊt] *s.* **1.** ✿ Gicht *f;* **2.** ✐ Gicht *f* (*Weizenkrankheit*): ~ *fly zo.* Gelbe Halmfliege; **'gout·y** [-tɪ] *adj.* ☐ **1.** gichtkrank; **2.** zur Gicht neigend; **3.** gichtisch, Gicht...: ~ *concretion* Gichtknoten *m.*

gov·ern ['gʌvn] **I** *v/t.* **1.** regieren (*a. ling.*); beherrschen (*a. fig.*); **2.** leiten, führen, verwalten, lenken; **3.** *fig.* regeln, bestimmen, maßgebend sein für, leiten: ~*ed by circumstances* durch

die Umstände bestimmt; *I was* ~*ed by* ich ließ mich leiten von ...; **4.** beherrschen, zügeln; **5.** ☉ regeln, steuern; **II** *v/i.* **6.** regieren, herrschen (*a. fig.*); **'gov·ern·ance** [-nəns] *s.* **1.** Regierungsgewalt *f od.* -form *f;* **2.** *fig.* Herrschaft *f,* Gewalt *f,* Kon'trolle *f* (*of* über *acc.*); **'gov·ern·ess** [-nɪs] **I** *s.* Erzieherin *f,* Gouver'nante *f;* **II** *v/i.* Erzieherin sein; **'gov·ern·ing** [-nɪŋ] *adj.* **1.** regierend, Regierungs...; **2.** leitend, Vorstands...: ~ *body* Vorstand *m,* Leitung *f;* **3.** *fig.* leitend, Leit...: ~ *idea* Leitgedanke *m;* **gov·ern·ment** ['gʌvnmənt] *s.* **1.** a) Regierung *f,* Herrschaft *f,* Kon'trolle *f* (*of, over* über *acc.*), b) Regierungsgewalt *f,* c) Leitung *f,* Verwaltung *f;* **2.** Re'gierung(sform *f,* -ssy,stem *n*) *f;* **3.** (*e-s bestimmten Landes*) *mst* ₤ die Regierung: *the British* ₤; ~ *agency* Regierungsstelle *f,* (-)Behörde *f;* ~ *bill parl.* Regierungsvorlage *f;* ~ *spokesman* Regierungssprecher *m;* **4.** Staat *m:* ~ *bonds,* ~ *securities* a) Staatsanleihen, -papiere, b) *Am.* Bundesanleihen; ~ *employee* Angestellte(r *m*) *f* des öffentlichen Dienstes; ~ *grant* staatlicher Zuschuss; ~ *indebtedness* Staatsverschuldung *f;* ~ *issue Am.* von der Regierung gestellte Ausrüstung; ~ *monopoly* Staatsmonopol *n;* **5.** *univ.* Politolo'gie *f;* **6.** *ling.* Rekti'on *f;* **gov·ern·men·tal** [,gʌvn'mentl] *adj.* ☐ Regierungs..., Staats..., staatlich; **gov·ern·men·tal·ize** [,gʌvn'mentəlaɪz] *v/t.* unter staatliche Kon'trolle bringen.

,gov·ern·ment|-in-'ex·ile *pl.* **,~s-in-'ex·ile** *s. pol.* E'xilregierung *f;* '~-owned *adj.* staatseigen; '~-run *adj.* staatlich (*Rundfunk etc.*).

gov·er·nor ['gʌvənə] *s.* **1.** Gouver'neur *m* (*a. e-s Staates der USA*): ~ *general* Generalgouverneur; **2.** ✖ Komman-'dant *m;* **3.** a) *allg.* Di'rektor *m,* Leiter *m,* Vorsitzende(r) *m,* b) Präsi'dent *m* (*e-r Bank*), c) *Brit.* Ge'fängnisdi,rektor *m,* d) *pl.* Vorstand *m,* Direk'torium *n;* **4.** F *der* 'Alte': a) 'Alter Herr' (*Vater*), b) Chef *m* (*a. als Anrede*); **5.** ☉ Regler *m:* ~ *valve* Reglerventil *n;* **'gov·er·nor·ship** [-ʃɪp] *s.* **1.** Gouver'neursamt *n;* **2.** Amtszeit *f* e-s Gouver'neurs.

gown [gaʊn] **I** *s.* **1.** Kleid *n;* **2.** *bsd.* ♂✝ *u. univ.* Ta'lar *m,* Robe *f;* **3.** *coll.* Stu'denten(schaft *f*) *pl. u.* Hochschullehrer *pl.* (*e-r Universitätsstadt*): *town and* ~ Stadt u. Universität; **II** *v/t.* **4.** mit e-m Ta'lar *etc.* bekleiden; **gowns·man** ['gaʊnzmən] *s.* [*irr.*] Robenträger *m* (*Anwalt, Richter, Geistlicher etc.*).

goy [gɔɪ] *s.* ,Goi' *m* (*jiddisch für Nichtjude*).

grab [græb] **I** *v/t.* **1.** (hastig *od.* gierig) ergreifen, an sich reißen, fassen, packen, (sich) ,schnappen'; **2.** *fig.* a) sich ,schnappen', an sich reißen, b) *e-e Gelegenheit* beim Schopf ergreifen; **3.** *fig.* *Publikum* packen, fesseln; **II** *v/i.* **4.** ~ *at* (hastig *od.* gierig) greifen *od.* ,schnappen' nach; **III** *s.* **5.** (hastiger *od.* gieriger) Griff (*for* nach): *make a* ~ *at* → 1 u. 4; *be up for* ~*s* F für jeden zu haben *od.* zu gewinnen sein; **6.** *fig.* Griff (*for* nach *der Macht etc.*); **7.** ☉ (Bagger-, Kran)Greifer *m:* ~ *crane* Greiferkran *m;* ~ *dredge(r)* Greiferbagger *m;* ~ *handle* Haltegriff *m;* ~ *bag s. Am.* **1.** ,Grabbelsack' *m;* **2.** *fig.* Sammel'surium *n.*

grab·ber ['græbə] *s.* Habgierige(r *m*) *f,* ,Raffke' *m.*

grab·ble ['græbl] *v/i.* tasten, tappen, suchen (*for* nach).

grab raid *s.* 'Raub,überfall *m.*

grace [greɪs] **I** *s.* **1.** Anmut *f,* Grazie *f,* Liebreiz *m,* Charme *m:* *the three* ₤*s myth.* die drei Grazien; **2.** Anstand *m,* Takt *m,* Schicklichkeit *f:* *have the* ~ *to do* den Anstand haben zu tun; *with* ~ mit Anstand *od.* Würde *od.* ,Grazie' (→ *a.* 3); **3.** Bereitwilligkeit *f:* *with a good* ~ bereitwillig, gern; *with a bad* ~ widerwillig, (nur) ungern; **4.** *mst pl.* gute Eigenschaften, schöner Zug: *social* ~*s* feine Lebensart; **5.** Gunst *f,* Wohlwollen *n,* Huld *f,* Gnade *f:* *be in s.o.'s good* ~*s* in j-s Gunst stehen, bei j-m gut angeschrieben sein; *be in s.o.'s bad* ~*s* bei j-m in Ungnade sein; *fall from* ~ in Ungnade fallen; *by way of* ~ ✝ auf dem Gnadenwege; *act of* ~ Gnadenakt *m;* **6.** *by the* ~ *of God* von Gottes Gnaden; *in the year of* ~ im Jahre des Heils; **7.** *eccl.* a) *a.* *state of* ~ Stand *m* der Gnade, b) Tugend *f:* ~ *of charity* (Tugend der) Nächstenliebe *f,* c) *say* ~ das Tischgebet sprechen; **8.** ✝, ✝✝ Aufschub *m,* (Zahlungs-, Nach)Frist *f: days of* ~ Respekttage (*pl.*); *grant s.o. a week's* ~ j-m e-e Woche Aufschub gewähren; **9.** ₤ (*Eure, Seine, Ihre*) Gnaden *pl.* (*Titel*): *Your* ₤ a) Eure Hoheit (*Herzogin*), b) Eure Exzellenz (*Erzbischof*); **10.** *a.* ~ *note* ♪ Verzierung *f;* **II** *v/t.* **11.** zieren, schmücken; **12.** *fig.* a) zieren, b) (be)ehren, auszeichnen; **'grace·ful** [-fʊl] *adj.* ☐ **1.** anmutig, grazi'ös, reizend, ele'gant; **2.** geziemend, takt-, würdevoll; ~*ly fig.* mit Anstand *od.* Würde *alt werden etc.*; **'grace·ful·ness** [-fʊlnɪs] *s.* Anmut *f,* Grazie *f;* **grace·less** [-lɪs] *adj.* ☐ **1.** 'ungrazi,ös, reizlos, 'unele,gant; **2.** *obs.* verworfen.

grac·ile ['græsaɪl] *adj.* zierlich, gra'zil, zart(gliedrig).

gra·cious ['greɪʃəs] **I** *adj.* ☐ **1.** gnädig, huldvoll, wohlwollend; **2.** *poet.* gütig, freundlich; **3.** *eccl.* gnädig, barmherzig (*Gott*); **4.** *obs.* für **graceful** 1; **5.** a) angenehm, b) geschmackvoll, schön: ~ *living* elegantes Leben, kultivierter Luxus; **II** *int.* **6.** ~ *me!,* ~ *goodness!,* *good* ~*!* du meine Güte!, lieber Himmel!; **'gra·cious·ness** [-nɪs] *s.* **1.** Gnade *f, eccl. a.* Barm'herzigkeit *f;* **2.** *poet.* Güte *f,* Freundlichkeit *f.*

grad [græd] *s.* F Stu'dent(in).

gra·date [grə'deɪt] **I** *v/t. Farben* abstufen, inein'ander 'übergehen lassen, abtönen; **II** *v/i.* stufenweise (inein'ander) 'übergehen; **gra·da·tion** [grə'deɪʃn] *s.* **1.** Abstufung *f:* a) Abtönung *f,* b) Staffelung *f;* **2.** Stufenleiter *f,* -folge *f;* **3.** *ling.* Ablaut *m.*

grade [greɪd] **I** *s.* **1.** Grad *m,* Stufe *f,* Klasse *f;* **2.** ✖ *Am.* Dienstgrad *m;* **3.** (*höherer etc.*) (Be'amten)Dienst; **4.** Art *f,* Gattung *f,* Sorte *f,* Quali'tät *f,* Güte *f,* Klasse *f:* ₤ *A* ✝ (Güte)Klasse A (→ 6); **5.** Steigung *f,* Gefälle *n,* Neigung *f,* Ni'veau *n* (*a. fig.*): ~ *crossing* (schienengleicher) Bahnübergang; *at* ~ *Am.* auf gleicher Höhe; *on the up* ~ aufwärts (gehend), im Aufstieg; *make the* ~ ,es schaffen'; **6.** *ped. Am.* a) (Schüler *pl.* e-r) Klasse *f,* b) Note *f,* Zen'sur *f,* c) *pl.* (Grund)Schule *f:* ~ *A* (Note *f*) „sehr gut" *n* (→ 4); **II** *v/t.* **7.** sortieren, einteilen, -reihen, -stufen, staffeln; **8.** *ped.* benoten, zensieren; **9.** ~ *up* verbessern, veredeln; ~ (*up*) *Vieh* (auf)kreuzen; **10.** *Gelände* planieren; **11.** *ling.* ablauten; **12.** → *gradate* I; **'grad·er** [-də] *s.* **1.** a) Sortierer(in), b) Sor'tierma,schine *f;* **2.** ☉ Pla'nierma,schine *f;* **3.** *Am. ped.*

in Zssgn ...klässler *m*: *fourth* ~ Viert-klässler.

grade school *s. Am.* Grundschule *f.*

gra·di·ent ['greɪdjənt] **I** *s.* **1.** Neigung *f*, Steigung *f*, Gefälle *n* (*des Geländes etc.*); **2.** ⚓ Gradi'ent *m* (*a. meteor.*), Gefälle *n*; **II** *adj.* **3.** gehend, schreitend; **4.** *zo.* Geh..., Lauf...

grad·u·al ['grædjʊəl] **I** *adj.* □ all'mählich, schritt-, stufenweise, langsam (fortschreitend), gradu'ell; **II** *s. eccl.* Gradu'ale *n*; **'grad·u·al·ly** [-əlɪ] *adv.* a) nach u. nach, b) → **gradual** I.

grad·u·ate ['grædʒʊət] **I** *s.* **1.** *univ.* a) 'Hochschulabsol,vent(in), Aka'demiker (-in), b) Graduierte(r *m*) *f* (*bsd. Inhaber[in] des niedrigsten akademischen Grades*), c) *Am.* Stu'dent(in) an e-r *graduate school*; **2.** *ped. Am.* ('Schul-)Absol,vent(in): *high-school* ~ *etwa* Abiturient(in); **3.** *fig. Am.* ‚Pro'dukt' *n* (*e-r Anstalt etc.*); **4.** *Am.* Messgefäß *n*; **II** *adj.* **5.** *univ.* a) Akademiker..., b) graduiert: ~ *student* → 1, c) für Graduierte: ~ *course* (Fach)Kurs *m* an e-r *graduate school*; **6.** *Am.* staatlich geprüft, Diplom...: ~ *nurse*; **7.** → *graduated* 1; **III** *v/t.* [-djʊeɪt] **8.** ⚙ mit e-r Maßeinteilung versehen, in Grade einteilen, *a.* ⚓ gradieren; **9.** abstufen, staffeln; **10.** *univ.* graduieren, *j-m* en (*bsd. den niedrigsten*) aka'demischen Grad verleihen; **11.** *ped. Am.* a) *oft be~d from* die Abschlussprüfung bestehen an (*e-r Schule*), absolvieren, her'vorgehen aus, b) *j-n* (*in die nächste Klasse*) versetzen; **IV** *v/i.* [-djʊeɪt] **12.** *univ.* graduieren, e-n (*bsd. den niedrigsten*) aka'demischen Grad erwerben (*from* an *dat.*); **13.** *ped. Am.* die Abschlussprüfung bestehen: ~ *from* → 11a; **14.** sich staffeln, sich abstufen: ~ *into* a) sich entwickeln zu, b) allmählich übergehen in (*acc.*); **'grad·u·at·ed** [-jʊetɪd] *adj.* **1.** abgestuft, gestaffelt; **2.** ⚙ graduiert, mit e-r Gradeinteilung: ~ *dial* Skalenscheibe *f*; **grad·u·ate school** *s. univ. Am.* a) höhere 'Fachse,mester *pl.* (*mit Studienziel ‚Magister'*), b) Universi'tät(seinrichtung) *zur Erlangung höherer akademischer Grade*; **grad·u·a·tion** [,grædjʊ'eɪʃn] *s.* **1.** Abstufung *f*, Staffelung *f*; **2.** ⚙ a) Gradeinteilung *f*, b) Grad-, Teilstrich(e *pl.*) *m*; **3.** ⚓ Gradierung *f*; **4.** *univ.* Graduierung *f*, Erteilung *f od.* Erlangung *f* e-s aka'demischen Grades; **5.** *ped. Am.* a) Absolvieren *n* (*from e-r Schule*), b) Schluss-, Verleihungsfeier *f.*

Graeco- [gri:kəʊ] *in Zssgn* griechisch, gräko...

graf·fi·to [grə'fi:təʊ] *pl.* **-ti** [-tɪ] *s.* **1.** (S)Graf'fito *m, n*, Kratzmale'rei *f*; **2.** *pl.* Wandkritze'leien *pl.*, Graf'fiti *pl.*

graft [grɑ:ft] **I** *s.* **1.** ♀ a) Pfropfreis *n*, b) veredelte Pflanze, c) Pfropfstelle *f*; **2.** ☤ a) Transplan'tat *n*, b) Transplantati'on *f*; **3.** *bsd. Am.* F a) Korrupti'on *f*, b) Bestechungs-, Schmiergelder *pl.*; **II** *v/t.* **4.** ♀ a) *Zweig* pfropfen, b) *Pflanze* okulieren, veredeln; **5.** ☤ *Gewebe* transplantieren, verpflanzen; **6.** *fig.* (*in*, [*up*]*on*) a) *et.* aufpfropfen (*dat.*), b) *Ideen etc.* einimpfen (*dat.*), c) über-'tragen (auf *acc.*); **III** *v/i.* **7.** *bsd. Am.* F a) sich (durch 'Amts,missbrauch) bereichern, b) Schmiergelder zahlen; **'graft·er** [-ə] *s.* **1.** ♀ Pfropfer *m*, b) Pfropfmesser *n*; **2.** *bsd. Am.* F kor'rupter Be-'amter *od.* Po'litiker *etc.*

Grail [greɪl] *s. eccl.* Gral *m.*

grain [greɪn] **I** *s.* **1.** ♀ (Samen-, *bsd.* Getreide)Korn *n*; **2.** *coll.* Getreide *n*,

Korn *n*; **3.** Körnchen *n*, (*Sand- etc.*) Korn *n*: *of fine* ~ feinkörnig; → *salt* 1; **4.** *fig.* Spur *f*, *ein bisschen*: *a* ~ *of truth* ein Körnchen Wahrheit; *not a* ~ *of hope* kein Funke Hoffnung; **5.** ⚖ Gran *n* (*Gewicht*); **6.** a) Faser(ung) *f*, Maserung *f* (*Holz*), b) Narbe *f* (*Leder*), d) *metall.* Korn *n*, Körnung *f*, e) Strich *m* (*Tuch*), f) *min.* Korn *n*, Gefüge *n*: ~ (*side*) Narbenseite (*Leder*); *it goes against the* ~ (*with me*) *fig.* es geht mir gegen den Strich; **7.** *hist.* Coche'nille *f* (*Farbstoff*): *dyed in* ~ a) *im* Rohzustand gefärbt, b) *a. fig.* waschecht; **8.** *phot.* a) Korn *n*, b) Körnigkeit *f* (*Film*); **II** *v/t.* **9.** körnen, granulieren; **10.** ⚙ *Leder:* a) enthaaren, b) körnen, narben; **11.** ⚙ *Holz etc.* (*künstlich*) masern, ädern; **12.** ⚙ a) *Papier* narben, b) in der Wolle färben; ~ *al·co·hol* *s.* ⚗ Ä'thylalkohol *m*; ~ *leath·er* *s.* genarbtes Leder.

gram¹ [græm] *s.* → *chickpea.*

gram² [græm] *Am.* → *gramme.*

gram·i·na·ceous [,græmɪ'neɪʃəs], **gra·min·e·ous** [grə'mɪnɪəs] *adj.* ♀ grasartig, Gras...; **gram·i·niv·o·rous** [,græmɪ'nɪvərəs] *adj.* Gras fressend.

gram·mar ['græmə] *s.* **1.** Gram'matik *f* (*a. Lehrbuch*): *bad* ~ ungrammatisch; **2.** *fig.* Grundbegriffe *pl.*; **gram·mar·i·an** [grə'meərɪən] *s.* **1.** Gram'matiker (-in); **2.** Verfasser(in) e-r Gram'matik; **gram·mar school** *s.* **1.** *Brit.* höhere Schule, *etwa* Gym'nasium *n*; **2.** *Am. etwa* Grundschule *f*; **gram·mat·i·cal** [grə'mætɪkl] *adj.* □ gram'matisch, grammati'kalisch: *not* ~ grammatisch falsch.

gramme [græm] *s.* Gramm *n.*

gram mol·e·cule *s. phys.* 'Grammmole,kül *n.*

Gram·my ['græmɪ] *s.* Grammy *m* (*amer. Schallplattenpreis*).

gram·o·phone ['græməfəʊn] *s.* a) Grammo'phon *n*, b) Plattenspieler *m*; ~ *rec·ord* *s.* Schallplatte *f.*

gram·pus ['græmpəs] *s. zo.* Schwertwal *m*: *blow like a* ~ *fig.* wie ein Nilpferd schnaufen.

gran·a·ry ['grænərɪ] *s.* Kornkammer *f* (*a. fig.*), Kornspeicher *m.*

grand [grænd] **I** *adj.* □ **1.** großartig, gewaltig, grandi'os, eindrucksvoll, prächtig: *in* ~ *style* großartig; **2.** (*geistig etc.*) groß, bedeutend, über'ragend; **3.** erhaben (*Stil etc.*); **4.** (*gesellschaftlich*) groß, hoch stehend, vornehm, distinguiert: ~ *air* Vornehmheit *f*, Würde *f*, *iro.* Gran'dezza *f*; *do the* ~ den vornehmen Herrn spielen; *..., he said ~ly ...,* sagte er großartig; **5.** Haupt...: ~ *question:* ~ *staircase* Haupttreppe *f*; ~ *total* Gesamtsumme *f*; **6.** F großartig, prächtig: *a* ~ *idea*; *have a* ~ *time* sich glänzend amüsieren; **II** *s.* **7.** ♪ Flügel *m*; **8.** *pl.* **grand** *Am. sl.* ‚Riese' *m* (*1000 Dollar*).

gran·dad → *granddad.*

gran·dam ['grændæm] *s.* **1.** Großmutter *f*; **2.** alte Dame.

'grand|·aunt *s.* Großtante *f*; **'~·child** [-ntʃ-] *s.* [*irr.*] Enkel(in); **'~·dad** [-ndæd] *s.* ‚Opa' *m* (*a. alter Mann*); **'~·daugh·ter** [-n,dɔ:-] *s.* Enkelin *f*; ♀-'Du·cal** [-n dʒ-] *adj.* großherzoglich; ♀ **Duch·ess** [-ndʒ-] *s.* Großherzogin *f*; ♀ **Duch·y** *s.* Großherzogtum *n*; ♀ **Duke** *s.* **1.** Großherzog *m*; **2.** *hist.* (*russischer*) Großfürst.

gran·dee [græn'di:] *s.* Grande *m.*

gran·deur ['grændʒə] *s.* **1.** Großartigkeit *f* (*a. iro.*); **2.** Größe *f*, Erhabenheit

f; **3.** Vornehmheit *f*, Hoheit *f*, Würde *f*: *delusions of* ~ Größenwahnsinn *m*; **4.** Herrlichkeit *f*, Pracht *f.*

'grand,fa·ther ['grænd,f-] *s.* Großvater *m*: ~('s) *clock* Standuhr *f*; ~('s) *chair* Ohrensessel *m*; **'grand,fa·ther·ly** [-lɪ] *adj.* großväterlich (*a. fig.*).

gran·dil·o·quence [græn'dɪləkwəns] *s.* **1.** (Rede)Schwulst *m*, Bom'bast *m*; **2.** Großspreche'rei *f*; **gran'dil·o·quent** [-nt] *adj.* □ **1.** schwülstig, hochtrabend, ‚geschwollen'; **2.** großsprecherisch.

gran·di·ose ['grændɪəʊs] *adj.* □ **1.** großartig, grandi'os; **2.** pom'pös, prunkvoll; **3.** schwülstig, hochtrabend, bom'bastisch.

grand| ju·ry *s.* ⚖ *Am.* Anklagejury *f* (*Geschworene, die die Eröffnung des Hauptverfahrens beschließen od. ablehnen*); ~ *lar·ce·ny* *s.* ⚖ *Am.* schwerer Diebstahl; **~·ma** ['grænmɑ:], **~·mam·ma** ['grænmə,mɑ:] *s.* F 'Großma,ma *f*, ‚Oma' *f*; ~ *mas·ter* *s.* **1.** Schach: Großmeister *m*; **2.** *Grand Master* Großmeister *m* (*der Freimaurer etc.*); **'~,moth·er** [-n,m-] *s.* Großmutter *f*: *teach your* ~ *to suck eggs!* das Ei will klüger sein als die Henne!; **'~,moth·er·ly** [-lɪ] *adj.* großmütterlich (*a. fig.*); ♀ **Na·tion·al** *s.* *Pferderennen:* Grand National *n* (*Hindernisrennen auf der Aintree-Rennbahn bei Liverpool*); **'~,neph·ew** [-n,n-] *s.* Großneffe *m.*

grand·ness ['grændnɪs] → *grandeur.*

'grand|·niece [-nni:s] *s.* Großnichte *f*; ~ *old man* *s.* ,großer alter Mann' (*e-r Berufsgruppe etc.*); ♀ **Old Par·ty**, *abbr.* **GOP** *s. pol. Am.* die Republi'kanische Par'tei *der USA*; ~ *op·er·a* *s.* ♪ große Oper; **~·pa** ['grænpɑ:], **~·pa·pa** ['grænpə,pɑ:] *s.* ‚Opa' *m*, 'Großpa,pa *m*; **'~,par·ent** [-n,p-] *s.* **1.** Großvater *m od.* -mutter *f*; **2.** *pl.* Großeltern *pl.*; ~ *pi·an·o* *s.* ♪ (Kon'zert)Flügel *m*; **'~,sire** [-n,s-] *s. obs.* **1.** alter Herr; **2.** Großvater *m*; **'~·son** [-ns-] *s.* Enkel *m*; ~ *slam* *s.* **1.** *Tennis:* Grand Slam *m*; **2.** → *slam²*; **'~·stand** [-ndʃ-] **I** *s. sport* 'Haupttri,büne *f*: *play to the* ~ → III; **II** *adj.* Haupttribünen...: ~ *seat*; ~ *play* F Effekthascherei *f*; ~ *finish* packendes Finish; **III** *v/i. Am.* F sich in Szene setzen, ‚e-e Schau abziehen'; ~ *tour* *s. hist.* Bildungs-, Kava'liersreise *f*; **'~,un·cle** *s.* Großonkel *m.*

grange [greɪndʒ] *s.* **1.** Farm *f*; **2.** kleiner Gutshof *od.* Landsitz.

gra·nif·er·ous [grə'nɪfərəs] *adj.* ♀ Körner tragend.

gran·ite ['grænɪt] **I** *s. min.* Gra'nit *m* (*a. fig.*): *bite on* ~ *fig.* auf Granit beißen; **II** *adj.* Granit...; *fig.* hart, eisern, unbeugsam; **gra·nit·ic** [græ'nɪtɪk] → *granite* II.

gra·niv·o·rous [grə'nɪvərəs] *adj.* Körner fressend.

gran·nie, gran·ny ['grænɪ] *s.* F **1.** ‚Oma' *f*: ~ *glasses* Nickelbrille *f*; ~ *annexe* Einliegerwohnung *f*; **2.** *a.* ~('s) *knot* ⚓ Alt'weiberknoten *m.*

grant [grɑ:nt] **I** *v/t.* **1.** bewilligen, gewähren (*s.o. a credit etc.*): *j-m e-n* Kredit *etc.*): *it was not ~ed to her* es war ihr nicht vergönnt; *God* ~ *that* gebe Gott, dass; **2.** *e-e Erlaubnis etc.* geben, erteilen; **3.** *e-e Bitte etc.* erfüllen, (*a.* ⚖ *e-m Antrag etc.*) stattgeben; **4.** ⚖ über-'tragen, ‚eignen, verleihen, *Patent* erteilen; **5.** zugeben, zugestehen, einräumen: *I* ~ *you that ...* ich gebe zu, dass ...; ~*ed, but* zugegeben, aber; ~*ed that ...* a) zugegeben, dass, b) angenommen, dass; *take for* ~*ed* a) *et.* als erwiesen annehmen, b) *et.* als selbstverständlich betrachten, c) gar nicht mehr wissen, was man an *j-m* hat; **II** *s.* **6.** a) Bewilligung *f*, Gewährung *f*, b) Zuschuss *m*, Unter'stützung *f*, Subventi'on *f*; **7.** (Ausbildungs-, Studien)Beihilfe *f*, Sti'pendium *n*; **8.** ❊ a) Verleihung *f e-s Rechts*, Erteilung *f e-s Patents etc.*, b) (urkundliche) Über'tragung (**to** auf *acc.*); **9.** *Am.* zugewiesenes Amt; **gran·tee** [grɑːnˈtiː] *s.* **1.** Begünstigte(r *m*) *f*; **2.** ❊ a) Zessio'nar(in), Rechtsnachfolger(in), b) Privile'gierte(r *m*) *f*; **,grant-in-'aid** *pl.* **,grants-in-'aid** *s.* a) *Brit.* Re'gierungszuschuss *m* an Kom'munen, b) *Am.* Bundeszuschuss *m* an Einzelstaaten; **gran·tor** [grɑːnˈtɔː] *s.* ❊ a) Ze'dent(in), b) Li'zenzgeber(in).

gran·u·lar [ˈgrænjʊlə] *adj.* **1.** gekörnt, körnig; **2.** granuliert; **'gran·u·late** [-leɪt] **I** *v/t.* **1.** körnen, granulieren; **2.** *Leder* rauen, narben; **II** *v/i.* körnig werden; **'gran·u·lat·ed** [-leɪtɪd] *adj.* **1.** gekörnt, körnig, granuliert (*a.* ❧): ~ **sugar** Kristallzucker *m*; **2.** geraut; **gran·u·la·tion** [ˌgrænjuˈleɪʃn] *s.* **1.** Körnen *n*, Granulieren *n*; **2.** Körnigkeit *f*; **3.** ❧ Granulati'on *f*; **'gran·ule** [-juːl] *s.* Körnchen *n*; **'gran·u·lous** [-ləs] → **granular.**

grape [greɪp] *s.* **1.** Weintraube *f*, -beere *f*: **the (juice of the)** ~ der Saft der Reben (*Wein*); **but that's just sour** ~**s** *fig.* aber ihm (*etc.*) hängen die Trauben zu hoch; → **bunch** 1; **2.** → **grapevine** 1; **3.** *pl. vet.* a) Mauke *f*, b) 'Rindertuberku,lose *f*; **~ cure** *s.* ❧ Traubenkur *f*; **'~·fruit** *s.* ❀ Grapefruit *f*, Pampelmuse *f*; **~ juice** *s.* Traubensaft *m*; **'~·louse** [*irr.*] *zo.* Reblaus *f*; **'~·shot** *s.* ✗ Kar'tätsche *f*; **'~·stone** *s.* (Wein)Traubenkern *m*; **~ sug·ar** *s.* Traubenzucker *m*; **'~·vine** *s.* **1.** ❀ Weinstock *m*; **2.** F a) Gerücht *n*, b) *a.* ~ **telegraph** ,Buschtrommel' *f*, 'Nachrichtensy,stem *n*: **hear s.th. on the** ~ *et.* gerüchteweise hören.

graph [græf] *s.* **1.** Schaubild *n*, Dia'gramm *n*, grafische Darstellung, Kurvenblatt *n*; **2.** *bsd.* ✏ Kurve *f*: ~ **paper** Millimeterpapier *n*; **3.** *ling.* Graph *m*; **'graph·ic** [-fɪk] **I** *adj.* (□ ~*ally*) **1.** anschaulich, plastisch, lebendig (*geschildert od.* schildernd); **2.** grafisch, zeichnerisch: ~ **arts** → 4; ~ **artist** Grafiker(in); **3.** Schrift..., Schreib...; **II** *s. pl. sg. konstr.* **4.** Grafik, grafische Kunst; **5.** technisches Zeichnen; **6.** grafische Darstellung (*als Fach*); **'graph·i·cal** [-fɪkl] *adj.* □ → **graphic** I; **'graph·ics card** *s. Computer:* 'Grafikkarte *f*.

graph·ite [ˈgræfaɪt] *s. min.* Gra'phit *m*, Reißblei *n*; **gra·phit·ic** [grəˈfɪtɪk] *adj.* Graphit...

graph·o·log·i·cal [ˌgræfəˈlɒdʒɪkl] *adj.* □ grapho'logisch; **graph·ol·o·gist** [græˈfɒlədʒɪst] *s.* Grapho'loge *m*; **graph·ol·o·gy** [græˈfɒlədʒɪ] *s.* Grapholo'gie *f*, Handschriftendeutung *f*.

grap·nel [ˈgræpnl] *s.* **1.** ⚓ a) Enterhaken *m*, b) Dregganker *m*, Dregge *f*; **2.** ❊ a) Ankereisen *n*, b) (Greif)Haken *m*, Greifer *m*.

grap·ple [ˈgræpl] **I** *s.* **1.** → **grapnel** 1 a u. 2 b; **2.** a) Griff *m* (*a. beim Ringen etc.*), b) Handgemenge *n*, Kampf *m*; **II** *v/t.* **3.** ❊ entern; **4.** ❊ verankern, festklammern; **5.** packen, fassen; **III** *v/i.* **6.** e-n Enterhaken *od.* Greifer gebrauchen; **7.** ringen, kämpfen (*a. fig.*): ~ **with s.th.** *fig.* sich mit et. herumschlagen.

grap·pling| hook, ~ **i·ron** [ˈgræplɪŋ] → **grapnel** 1 a u. 2 b.

grasp [grɑːsp] **I** *v/t.* **1.** packen, fassen, (er)greifen; → **nettle** 1; **2.** an sich reißen; **3.** *fig.* verstehen, begreifen, (er-)fassen; **II** *v/i.* **4.** zugreifen, zupacken; **5.** ~ **at** greifen nach; → **shadow** 2, **straw** 1; **6.** ~ **at** *fig.* streben nach; **III** *s.* **7.** Griff *m*; **8.** a) Reichweite *f*, b) *fig.* Macht *f*, Gewalt *f*, Zugriff *m*: **within one's** ~ in Reichweite, *fig. a.* greifbar nahe; **within the** ~ **of** in der Gewalt von (*od. gen.*); **9.** *fig.* Verständnis *n*, Auffassungsgabe *f*: **it is within his** ~ das kann er begreifen; **it is beyond his** ~ es geht über seinen Verstand; **have a good** ~ **of s.th.** *et.* gut beherrschen; **'grasp·ing** [-pɪŋ] *adj.* □ habgierig.

grass [grɑːs] **I** *s.* **1.** ❀ Gras *n*: **hear the** ~ **grow** *fig.* das Gras wachsen hören; **not to let the** ~ **grow under one's feet** nicht lange zaudern, keine Zeit verschwenden; **2.** Gras *n*, Rasen *m*: **keep off the** ~ Betreten des Rasens verboten!; **3.** Grasland *n*, Weide *f*: **be (out) at** ~ auf der Weide sein, b) F im Ruhestand sein; **put** (*od.* **turn**) **out to** ~ a) *Vieh* auf die Weide treiben, b) *bsd. e-m Rennpferd* das Gnadenbrot geben, c) F *j-n* in Rente schicken; **4.** *sl.* ,Grass' *n*, Mariju'ana *n*; **II** *v/t.* **5.** a) *a.* ~ **down** mit Gras besäen, b) *a.* ~ **over** mit Rasen bedecken; **6.** *Vieh* weiden (lassen); **7.** *Wäsche* auf dem Rasen bleichen; **8.** *Vogel* abschießen; **9.** *sport Gegner* zu Fall bringen; **III** *v/i.* **10.** grasen, weiden; **11.** *Brit. sl.* ,singen': ~ **on s.o.** j-n ,verpfeifen'; **~ blade** *s. zo.* Grashalm *m*; ~ **court** *s. Tennis:* Rasenplatz *m*; **,~·green** *adj.* grasgrün; **'~·grown** *adj.* mit Gras bewachsen; **'~,hop·per** *s.* **1.** *zo.* (Feld)Heuschrecke *f*, Grashüpfer *m*; **2.** ✈, ✗ Leichtflugzeug *n*; **'~·land** *s.* Weide(land *n*) *f*; **'~·plot** *s.* Rasenplatz *m*; ~ **roots** *s. pl.* **1.** *fig.* Wurzel *f*; **2.** *pol.* a) Basis *f* (*e-r Partei*), b) länd-liche Bezirke *od.* Landbevölkerung *f*; **'~·roots** *adj. pol.* a) (an) der Basis (*e-r Partei*), b) bodenständig: ~ **democracy**; ~ **snake** *s. zo.* Ringelnatter *f*; ~ **wid·ow** *s.* **1.** Strohwitwe *f*; **2.** *Am.* geschiedene *od.* getrennt lebende Frau; ~ **wid·ow·er** *s.* **1.** Strohwitwer *m*; **2.** *Am.* geschiedener *od.* getrennt lebender Mann.

grass·y [ˈgrɑːsɪ] *adj.* grasbedeckt, grasig, Gras...

grate¹ [greɪt] **I** *v/t.* **1.** *Käse etc.* reiben, *Gemüse etc. a.* raspeln; **2.** a) knirschen mit: ~ **one's teeth**, b) kratzen mit, c) quietschen mit; **3.** *et.* krächzen(d sagen); **II** *v/i.* **4.** knirschen *od.* kratzen *od.* quietschen; **5.** wehtun (*[up]on s.o.* j-m): ~ **on s.o.'s nerves** an j-s Nerven zerren; ~ **on the ear** dem Ohr wehtun; ~ **on s.o.'s ears** j-m in den Ohren wehtun.

grate² [greɪt] *s.* **1.** Gitter *n*; **2.** (Feuer-, ❊ Kessel)Rost *m*; **3.** Ka'min *m*; **4.** *Wasserbau:* Fangrechen *m*; **'grat·ed** [-tɪd] *adj.* vergittert.

grate·ful [ˈgreɪtfʊl] *adj.* □ **1.** dankbar (**to s.o. for s.th.** j-m für et.): **a letter** ein Dank(es)brief; **2.** *fig.* dankbar (*Aufgabe etc.*); **3.** angenehm, wohltuend, will'kommen (**to s.o.** j-m); **'grate·ful·ness** [-nɪs] *s.* Dankbarkeit *f*.

grat·er [ˈgreɪtə] *s.* Reibe *f*, Reibeisen *n*, Raspel *f*.

grat·i·cule [ˈgrætɪkjuːl] *s.* ❊ **1.** a) (Grad)Netz *n*, Koordi'natensy,stem *n*, b) mit e-m Netz versehene Zeichnung; **2.** Fadenkreuz *n*.

grat·i·fi·ca·tion [ˌgrætɪfɪˈkeɪʃn] *s.* **1.** Be-

friedigung *f*: a) Zu'friedenstellung *f*, b) Genugtuung *f* (**at** über *acc.*); **2.** Freude *f*, Vergnügen *n*, Genuss *m*; **3.** *obs.* Gratifikati'on *f*; **grat·i·fy** [ˈgrætɪfaɪ] *v/t.* **1.** befriedigen: ~ **one's thirst for knowledge** s-n Wissensdurst stillen; **2.** *j-m* gefällig sein; **3.** erfreuen: **be gratified** sich freuen; **I am gratified to hear** ich höre mit Genugtuung *od.* Befriedigung; **grat·i·fy·ing** [ˈgrætɪfaɪɪŋ] *adj.* □ erfreulich, befriedigend (**to** für).

gra·tin [ˈgrætæŋ] (*Fr.*) *s.* **1.** Bratkruste *f*: **au** ~ gratiniert, überbacken; **2.** Gra'tin *n*, gratinierte Speise.

grat·ing¹ [ˈgreɪtɪŋ] *adj.* □ **1.** kratzend, knirschend; **2.** krächzend, heiser; **3.** unangenehm.

grat·ing² [ˈgreɪtɪŋ] *s.* **1.** Gitter *n* (*a. phys.*), Gitterwerk *n*; **2.** ❊ (Balken-, Lauf)Rost *m*; **3.** ⚓ Gräting *f*.

gra·tis [ˈgreɪtɪs] **I** *adv.* gratis, unentgeltlich, um'sonst; **II** *adj.* unentgeltlich, frei, Gratis...

grat·i·tude [ˈgrætɪtjuːd] *s.* Dankbarkeit *f*: **in** ~ **for** aus Dankbarkeit für.

gra·tu·i·tous [grəˈtjuːɪtəs] *adj.* □ **1.** → **gratis** II; **2.** ❊ ohne Gegenleistung; **3.** freiwillig, unverlangt; **4.** grundlos, unberechtigt, unverdient; **gra·tu·i·ty** [-tɪ] *s.* **1.** (Geld)Geschenk *n*, Gratifikati'on *f*, Sondervergütung *f*, Zuwendung *f*; **2.** Trinkgeld *n*.

gra·va·men [grəˈveɪmen] *s.* **1.** ❊ a) (Haupt)Beschwerdegrund *m*, b) *das* Belastende *e-r Anklage*; **2.** *bsd. eccl.* Beschwerde *f*.

grave¹ [greɪv] *s.* **1.** Grab *n*: **dig one's own** ~ sein eigenes Grab schaufeln; **have one foot in the** ~ mit einem Bein im Grab stehen; **rise from the** ~ (von den Toten) auferstehen; **turn in one's** ~ sich im Grabe umdrehen; **2.** *fig.* Grab *n*, Tod *m*, Ende *n*.

grave² [greɪv] **I** *adj.* □ **1.** ernst: a) feierlich, b) bedenklich: ~ **illness** (**voice**, *etc.*), c) gewichtig, schwerwiegend, d) gesetzt, würdevoll, e) schwer, tief: ~ **thoughts**; **2.** dunkel, gedämpft (*Farbe*); **3.** *ling.* fallend: ~ **accent** → 5; **4.** tief (*Ton*); **II** *s.* **5.** *ling.* Gravis *m*, Ac'cent *m* grave.

grave³ [greɪv] *v/t.* [*irr.*] *obs.* **1.** *Figur* (ein)schnitzen, (-)meißeln; **2.** *fig.* eingraben, -prägen.

grave⁴ [greɪv] *v/t.* ⚓ *Schiffsboden* reinigen u. teeren.

'grave,dig·ger *s.* Totengräber *m* (*a. zo. u. fig.*).

grav·el [ˈgrævl] **I** *s.* **1.** Kies *m*: ~ **pit** Kiesgrube *f*; **2.** Schotter *m*; **3.** *geol.* Geröll *n*; **4.** ❧ Harngrieß *m*; **II** *v/t.* **5.** a) mit Kies bestreuen, b) beschottern; **6.** *fig.* verwirren, verblüffen.

grav·en [ˈgreɪvn] *p.p. von* **grave³** *u. adj.* geschnitzt: ~ **image** Götzenbild *n*.

grav·er [ˈgreɪvə] → **graving tool.**

Graves' dis·ease [greɪvz] *s.* ❧ base'dowsche Krankheit.

'grave|·side *s.*: **at the** ~ am Grab; **'~·stone** *s.* Grabstein *m*; **'~·yard** *s.* Fried-, Kirchhof *m*.

grav·id [ˈgrævɪd] *adj.* a) schwanger, b) trächtig (*Tier*).

gra·vim·e·ter [grəˈvɪmɪtə] *s. phys.* Gravi'meter *n*: a) Dichtemesser *m*, b) Schweremesser *m*.

grav·ing| dock [ˈgreɪvɪŋ] *s.* ⚓ Trockendock *n*; ~ **tool** *s.* ❊ Grabstichel *m*.

grav·i·tate [ˈgrævɪteɪt] *v/i.* **1.** sich (durch Schwerkraft) fortbewegen; **2.** *a. fig.* gravieren, (hin)streben (**towards** zu, nach); **3.** *fig.* sich hingezogen fühlen, tendieren, (hin)neigen (**to, towards**

zu); **4.** sinken, fallen; **grav·i·ta·tion** [ˌgrævɪ'teɪʃn] s. **1.** phys. Gravitati'on f: a) Schwerkraft f, b) Gravitieren n; **2.** fig. Neigung f, Hang m, Ten'denz f; **grav·i·ta·tion·al** [ˌgrævɪ'teɪʃənl] adj. phys. Gravitations...: ~ **force** Schwerkraft f; ~ **field** Schwerefeld n; ~ **pull** Anziehungskraft f.

grav·i·ty ['grævətɪ] I s. **1.** Ernst m: a) Feierlichkeit f, b) Bedenklichkeit f, c) Gesetztheit f, d) Schwere f; **2.** ♪ Tiefe f (Ton); **3.** phys. a) a. **force of** ~ Gravitati'on f, Schwerkraft f, b) (Erd)Schwere f, c) Erdbeschleunigung; → **centre** 1, **specific** 8; II adj. **4.** phys., ◎ Schwerkraft...: ~ **drive**; ~ **feed** Gefällezuführung f; ~ **tank** Falltank m.

gra·vure [grə'vjʊə] s. Gra'vüre f.

gra·vy ['greɪvɪ] s. **1.** Braten-, Fleischsaft m; **2.** (Fleisch-, Braten)Soße f; **3.** sl. a) lukra'tive Sache, b) (unverhoffter) Gewinn: *that's pure* ~! das ist ja fantastisch!; ~ **beef** s. Saftbraten m; ~ **boat** s. Sauci'ere f, Soßenschüssel f; ~ **train** s.: *get on the* ~ sl. a) leicht ans große Geld kommen, b) ein Stück vom ‚Kuchen' abkriegen.

gray etc. bsd. Am. → **grey** etc.

graze¹ [greɪz] I v/t. **1.** Vieh weiden (lassen); **2.** abweiden, -grasen; II v/i. **3.** weiden, grasen (Vieh): **grazing ground** Weideland n.

graze² [greɪz] I v/t. **1.** streifen: a) leicht berühren, b) schrammen; **2.** ⚕ (ab-)schürfen, (auf)schrammen; II v/i. **3.** streifen; III s. **4.** Streifen n; **5.** ⚕ Abschürfung f, Schramme f; **6.** a. **grazing shot** Streifschuss m.

gra·zier ['greɪzjə] s. Viehzüchter m.

grease I s. [gri:s] **1.** (zerlassenes) Fett, Schmalz n; **2.** ◎ Schmierfett n, -mittel n, Schmiere f; **3.** a) Wollfett n, b) Schweißwolle f; **4.** vet. (Flechten)Mauke f (Pferd); **5.** hunt. Feist n: *in* ~ *of pride* (od. *prime*) fett (Wild); II v/t. [gri:z] **6.** ◎ (ein)fetten, (ab)schmieren; → **lightning** I; **7.** beschmieren; **8.** F j-n ‚schmieren', bestechen; ~ **cup** s. Stauferbüchse f; ~ **gun** s. ◎ (Ab-)Schmierpresse f; ~ **mon·key** s. F ✈, mot. (bsd. ‚Auto-, ‚Flugzeug)Me,chaniker m; ~ **paint** s. thea. (Fett)Schminke f; '~**proof** adj. Fett abstoßend.

greas·er ['gri:zə] s. **1.** Schmierer m, Öler m; **2.** ◎ Schmiervorrichtung f; **3.** Brit. F 'Autome,chaniker m; **4.** Brit. F contp. ‚Schleimscheißer' m; **5.** Am. contp. Mexi'kaner m.

greas·i·ness ['gri:zɪnɪs] s. **1.** Fettig-, Öligkeit f; **2.** Schmierigkeit f; **3.** Schlüpfrigkeit f; **4.** fig. Aalglätte f; **greas·y** ['gri:zɪ] adj. □ **1.** fettig, schmierig, ölig; **2.** fettig, schmierig, beschmiert; **3.** glitschig, schlüpfrig; **4.** ungewaschen (Wolle); **5.** fig. a) aalglatt, b) ölig, c) schmierig.

great [greɪt] I adj. □ → **greatly**; **1.** groß, beträchtlich: *a* ~ **number** e-e große Anzahl; *a* ~ **many** sehr viele; *the* ~ **majority** die große Mehrheit; *live to a* ~ **age** ein hohes Alter erreichen; **2.** groß, Haupt...: *to a* ~ **extent** in hohem Maße; ~ **friends** dicke Freunde; **3.** groß, bedeutend, berühmt: *a* ~ **poet**; *a* ~ **city** e-e bedeutende Stadt; ~ **issues** wichtige Probleme; **4.** hoch stehend, vornehm, berühmt: *a* ~ **family**; *the* ~ **world** die gute Gesellschaft; **5.** großartig, vor'züglich, wertvoll: *a* ~ **opportunity** e-e vorzügliche Gelegenheit; *it is a* ~ **thing to be healthy** es ist viel wert, gesund zu sein; **6.** erhaben, hoch: ~ **thoughts**; **7.** eifrig: *a* ~ **reader**; **8.**

---

groß(geschrieben); **9.** nur pred. a) gut: *he is* ~ *at golf* er spielt (sehr) gut Golf, er ist ,ganz groß' im Golfspielen, b) interes'siert: *he is* ~ *on dogs* er ist ein großer Hundeliebhaber; **10.** F großartig, wunderbar, prima: *we had a* ~ **time** wir haben uns herrlich amüsiert, es war sagenhaft (schön); *the* ~ **thing is that ...** das Großartige (daran) ist, dass; **11.** *in Verwandtschaftsbezeichnungen*: a) Groß..., b) (vor **grand...**) Ur...; **12.** *als Beiname*: **the 2 Elector** der Große Kurfürst; **Frederick the 2** Friedrich der Große; II s. **13.** the ~ pl. die Großen pl., die Promi'nenten pl.; **14.** pl. Brit. univ. 'Schlussex,amen n für den Grad des B.A. (Oxford).

,great|-'aunt s. Großtante f; **2 Char·ter** → **Magna C(h)arta**; ~ **cir·cle** s. & Großkreis m (e-r Kugel); '~**coat** s. (Herren)Mantel m; **2 Dane** s. zo. Dänische Dogge; ~ **di·vide** s. **1.** geogr. Hauptwasserscheide f: *the* **Great Divide** die Rocky Mountains; *cross the* ~ fig. die Schwelle des Todes überschreiten; **2.** fig. Krise f, entscheidende Phase.

Great·er Lon·don ['greɪtə] s. Groß-London n.

,great|-'grand,child s. Urenkel(in); '~**-'grand,daugh·ter** s. Urenkelin f; '~**-'grand,fa·ther** s. Urgroßvater m; '~**-'grand,moth·er** s. Urgroßmutter f; '~**-'grand,par·ents** s. pl. Urgroßeltern pl.; '~**-'grand,son** s. Urenkel m; ~ **gross** s. zwölf Gros pl.; '~**-'heart·ed** adj. **1.** beherzt; **2.** hochherzig; **2 Lakes** s. pl. die Großen Seen pl. (USA).

great·ly ['greɪtlɪ] adv. sehr, höchst, außerordentlich, 'überaus.

Great Mo·gul ['məʊgʌl] s. hist. Großmogul m; **2·'neph·ew** s. Großneffe m. **great·ness** ['greɪtnɪs] s. **1.** Größe f, Erhabenheit f: ~ **of mind** Geistesgröße f; **2.** Größe f, Bedeutung f, Wichtigkeit f, Rang m; **3.** Ausmaß n.

,great|-'niece s. Großnichte f; **2 Plains** s. pl. Am. Präriegebiete im Westen der USA; **2 Pow·ers** s. pl. pol. Großmächte pl.; **2 Seal** s. hist. Großsiegel n; ~ **tit** s. orn. Kohlmeise f; '~**-'un·cle** s. Großonkel m; **2 Wall (of Chi·na)** s. die Chi'nesische Mauer; **2 War** s. (bsd. der Erste) Weltkrieg.

greave [gri:v] s. hist. Beinschiene f. **greaves** [gri:vz] s. pl. Grieben pl. **grebe** [gri:b] s. orn. (See)Taucher m. **Gre·cian** ['gri:ʃn] I adj. **1.** bsd. klassisch) griechisch; II s. **2.** Grieche m, Griechin f; **3.** Grä'zist m.

greed [gri:d] s. Gier f (**for** nach); Habgier f, -sucht f: ~ **for power** Machtgier; '**greed·i·ness** [-dɪnɪs] s. **1.** Gierigkeit f; **2.** Gefräßigkeit f; '**greed·y** [-dɪ] adj. □ **1.** gierig (**for** auf acc., nach): ~ **for power** machtgierig; **2.** habgierig; **3.** gefräßig, gierig.

Greek [gri:k] I s. **1.** Grieche m, Griechin f: *when* ~ *meets* ~ fig. wenn zwei Ebenbürtige sich miteinander messen; **2.** ling. Griechisch n, das Griechische: *that's* ~ *to me* das sind für mich böhmische Dörfer; II adj. **3.** griechisch: ~ **Church** s. ,griechisch-ortho'doxe od. -ka'tholische Kirche; ~ **cross** s. griechisches Kreuz; ~ **gift** s. fig. Danaergeschenk n; ~ **Or·tho·dox Church** → **Greek Church**.

green [gri:n] I adj. □ **1.** allg. grün (a. weitS. grünend, schneefrei, unreif): ~ **apples** (fields); ~ **food**, ~ **vegetables** → 13; ~ **with envy** grün od. gelb vor

---

Neid; ~ **with fear** schreckensbleich; **2.** grün, frisch: ~ **fish**; ~ **wine** neuer Wein; **3.** roh, frisch, Frisch...: ~ **meat**; ~ **coffee** Rohkaffee m; **4.** ◎ nicht fertig verarbeitet: ~ **ceramics** ungebrannte Töpferwaren; ~ **hide** ungegerbtes Fell; ~ **ore** Roherz m; **5.** ◎ fa'brikneu: ~ **assembly** Erstmontage f; ~ **run** Einfahren n, erster Lauf; **6.** fig. frisch: a) neu, b) lebendig: ~ **memories**; **7.** fig. grün, unerfahren, na'iv: *a* ~ **youth**; ~ *in* **years** jung an Jahren; **8.** jugendlich: ~ **old age** rüstiges Alter; II s. **9.** Grün n, grüne Farbe: *the* **Greens** pl. pol. die Grünen: *the lights are at* ~ mot. die Ampel steht auf Grün; *at* ~ bei Grün; **10.** Grünfläche f, Rasen(platz) m: *village* ~ Dorfanger m, -wiese f; **11.** Golfplatz m; **12.** fig. Grün n, grünes Laub; **13.** *mst* pl. grünes Gemüse, Blattgemüse n; **14.** fig. Jugendfrische f; **15.** sl. ‚Kies' m (Geld); III v/t. **16.** grün machen od. färben; IV v/i. **17.** grün werden, grünen.

'green|-back s. **1.** Am. F Dollarschein m; **2.** zo. Laubfrosch m; ~ **belt** s. Grüngürtel m (um e-e Stadt); ~ **card** s. **1.** Am. grüne Karte f (Aufenthaltsgenehmigung); **2.** Brit. mot. grüne Versicherungskarte f; ~ **cheese** s. **1.** unreifer Käse; **2.** Molkenkäse m; **3.** Kräuterkäse m; ~ **cloth** s. bsd. Am. **1.** Spieltisch m; **2.** Billardtisch m; ~ **crop** s. ✗ Grünfutter n.

green·er·y ['gri:nərɪ] s. **1.** Grün n, Laub n; **2.** → **greenhouse** 1.

'green|-eyed adj. fig. eifersüchtig, neidisch: *the* ~ **monster** die Eifersucht; '~**finch** s. orn. Grünfink m; ~ **fin·gers** s. pl. F gärtnerische Begabung: *he has* ~ bei ihm gedeihen alle Pflanzen, ‚er hat einen grünen Daumen'; '~**fly** s. zo. Brit. grüne Blattlaus; '~**gage** s. Reine-'claude f; '~**,gro·cer** s. Obst- u. Gemüsehändler m; '~**,gro·cer·y** s. **1.** Obst- u. Gemüsehandlung f; **2.** pl. Obst n u. Gemüse n; '~**horn** s. F **1.** ‚Greenhorn' n, Grünschnabel m, (unerfahrener) Neuling; **2.** Gimpel m; '~**house** s. **1.** Treib-, Gewächshaus n: ~ **effect** Treibhauseffekt m; ~ **gases** Treibhausgase pl.; **2.** ✈ F Vollsichtkanzel f.

green·ish ['gri:nɪʃ] adj. grünlich.

Green·land·er ['gri:nləndə] s. Grönländer(in).

green light s. grünes Licht (bsd. der Verkehrsampel; a. fig. Genehmigung): *give s.o. the* ~ fig. j-m grünes Licht geben; ~ **lung** s. Brit. ‚grüne Lunge', Grünflächen pl.; '~**man** [-mən] s. [irr.] Platzmeister m (Golfplatz).

green·ness ['gri:nnɪs] s. **1.** Grün n, das Grüne; **2.** fig. Frische f, Munterkeit f, Kraft f; **3.** fig. Unreife f, Unerfahrenheit f.

green| pound s. ✝ grünes Pfund (EG-Verrechnungseinheit); '~**room** [-rʊm] s. thea. 'Künstlerzimmer n, -garde,robe f; '~**,sick·ness** s. ⚕ Bleichsucht f; '~**stick (frac·ture)** s. ⚕ Knickbruch m; '~**stuff** s. **1.** Grünfutter n; **2.** grünes Gemüse; '~**sward** s. Rasen m; ~ **ta·ble** s. Konfe'renztisch m; ~ **tea** s. grüner Tee; ~ **thumb** Am. → **green fingers**.

Green·wich (Mean) Time ['grenɪdʒ] s. Greenwicher Zeit.

greet [gri:t] v/t. **1.** grüßen; **2.** begrüßen, empfangen; **3.** fig. dem Auge begegnen, ans Ohr dringen, sich j-m bieten (Anblick); **4.** e-e Nachricht etc. freudig etc. aufnehmen; '**greet·ing** [-tɪŋ] s. **1.** Gruß m, Begrüßung f; **2.** pl. a) Grüße pl., b) Glückwünsche pl.: ~**s card**

Glückwunschkarte f.

gre·gar·i·ous [grɪ'geərɪəs] adj. □ **1.** gesellig; **2.** zo. in Herden od. Scharen lebend, Herden...; **3.** ⚘ traubenartig wachsend; **gre'gar·i·ous·ness** [-nɪs] s. **1.** Geselligkeit f; **2.** zo. Zs.-leben n in Herden.

Gre·go·ri·an [grɪ'gɔːrɪən] adj. gregori'anisch: ~ **calendar**; ~ **chant** ♪ gregorianischer Gesang.

greige [greɪʒ] adj. u. s. ⊙ na'turfarben(e Stoffe pl.).

grem·lin ['gremlɪn] s. sl. böser Geist, Kobold m (der Maschinenschaden etc. anrichtet).

gre·nade [grɪ'neɪd] s. **1.** ✕ Ge'wehr-, 'Handgra,nate f; **2.** 'Tränengaspa,trone f; **gren·a·dier** [,grenə'dɪə] s. ✕ Grena-'dier m.

gres·so·ri·al [gre'sɔːrɪəl] adj. orn., zo. Schreit..., Stelz...: ~ **birds**.

Gret·na Green mar·riage ['gretnə] s. Heirat f in Gretna Green (Schottland).

grew [gruː] pret. von **grow**.

grey [greɪ] **I** adj. □ **1.** grau; **2.** grau (-haarig), ergraut: **grow** → 8; **3.** farblos, blass; **4.** trübe, düster, grau: **a** ~ **day**; ~ **prospects** trübe Aussichten; **5.** ⊙ neu'tral, farblos, na'turfarben: ~ **cloth** ungebleichter Baumwollstoff; **II** s. **6.** Grau n, graue Farbe: **dressed in** ~ grau od. in Grau gekleidet; **7.** zo. Grauschimmel m; **III** v/i. **8.** grau werden, ergrauen: ~**ing** angegraut (Haare); ~ **a·re·a** s. **1.** Statistik: Grauzone f; **2.** Brit. Gebiet n mit hoher Arbeitslosigkeit; '~**·back** s. **1.** zo. Grauwal m; **2.** Am. F ,Graurock' m (Soldat der Südstaaten im Bürgerkrieg); ~ **crow** s. orn. Nebelkrähe f; '~**·fish** s. ein Hai(fisch) m; ~ **goose** → **greylag**; ,~'**head·ed** adj. **1.** grauköpfig; **2.** fig. alterfahren; '~**·hen** s. orn. Birk-, Haselhuhn n; '~**·hound** s. Windhund m; ~ **racing** Windhundrennen n.

grey·ish ['greɪɪʃ] adj. gräulich, Grau...

grey·lag ['greɪlæg] s. orn. Grau-, Wildgans f.

grey| mar·ket s. ⊛ grauer Markt; ~ **mat·ter** s. **1.** ⚘ graue ('Hirnrinden-) Sub,stanz; F ,Grips' m, ,Grütze' f (Verstand); ~ **mul·let** s. ichth. Meeräsche f.

grey·ness ['greɪnɪs] s. **1.** Grau n; **2.** fig. Trübheit f, Düsterkeit f.

grey squir·rel s. zo. Grauhörnchen n.

grid [grɪd] s. **1.** Gitter n, Rost m; **2.** ⚡ a) Bleiplatte f, b) Gitter n (in Elektronenröhre); **3.** ⚡ etc. Versorgungsnetz n; **4.** Gitternetz n auf Landkarten: ~**ded map** Gitternetzkarte f; **5.** → **gridiron** 1, 4, 6; ~ **bi·as** s. ⚡ Gittervorspannung f; ~ **cir·cuit** s. ⚡ Gitterkreis m.

grid·dle ['grɪdl] s. **1.** Kuchen-, Backblech n: ~ **cake** Pfannkuchen m; **be on the** ~ F ,in die Mangel genommen werden'; **2.** ⊙ Drahtsieb n.

'**grid,i·ron** s. **1.** Bratrost m; **2.** ⊙ Gitterrost m; **3.** Netz(werk) n (Leitungen, Bahnlinien etc.); **4.** ⚓ Balkenrost m; **5.** thea. Schnürboden m; **6.** American Football: F Spielfeld n.

grid| leak s. ⚡ 'Gitter(ableit),widerstand m; ~ **line** s. Gitternetzlinie f (auf Landkarten); '~**·lock** s. **1.** mot. Verkehrsstau m, Verkehrsinfarkt m; **2.** fig. festgefahrene Situation; '~**·locked** adj. **1.** mot. a) verstopft (Straßen), b) stehend, zum Stillstand gekommen (Verkehr); **2.** fig. festgefahren (Situation etc.); ~ **plate** s. ⚡ Gitterplatte f; ~ **square** s. 'Planqua,drat n.

grief [griːf] s. Gram m, Kummer m,

Leid n, Schmerz m: **bring to** ~ zu Fall bringen, zugrunde richten; **come to** ~ a) zu Schaden kommen, verunglücken, b) zugrunde gehen, c) fehlschlagen, scheitern: **good** ~! F meine Güte!; '~ -,**strick·en** adj. kummervoll.

griev·ance ['griːvns] s. **1.** Beschwerde (-grund m) f, (Grund m zur) Klage f: ~ **committee** Schlichtungsausschuss m; **2.** Missstand m; **3.** Groll m; **4.** Unzufriedenheit f; **grieve** [griːv] **I** v/t. betrüben, bekümmern, j-m wehtun; **II** v/i. bekümmert sein, sich grämen (**at**, **a-bout** über acc., wegen; **for** um); '**griev-ous** [-vəs] adj. □ **1.** schmerzlich, bitter, quälend; **2.** schwer, schlimm: ~ **error**; ~ **bodily harm** ⚖ schwere Körperverletzung; **3.** bedauerlich; '**griev·ous-ness** [-vəsnɪs] s. das Schmerzliche etc.

grif·fin¹ ['grɪfɪn] s. **1.** myth., her. Greif m; **2.** → **griffon¹**.

grif·fin² ['grɪfɪn] s. Neuankömmling m (im Orient).

grif·fon¹ ['grɪfən] s., a. ~ **vul·ture** s. orn. Weißköpfiger Geier.

grif·fon² ['grɪfən] s. **1.** → **griffin¹** 1; **2.** Grif'fon m (ein Vorstehhund).

grift·er ['grɪftə] s. Am. sl. Gauner m.

grill¹ [grɪl] **I** s. **1.** Grill m, (Brat)Rost m; **2.** Grillen n; **3.** Gegrillte(s) n; **4.** → **grillroom**; **II** v/t. **5.** Fleisch etc. grillen; **6.** ~ **o.s.** sich (in der Sonne) grillen; **7.** a. **give a** ~**ing** F j-n ,in die Mangel nehmen', ,ausquetschen' (bsd. Polizei); **III** v/i. **8.** gegrillt werden.

grill² [grɪl] → **grille**.

grille [grɪl] s. **1.** Tür-, Fenster-, Schaltergitter n; **2.** Gitterfenster n, Sprechgitter n; **3.** mot. (Kühler)Grill m; **grilled** [-ld] adj. vergittert.

grill·er ['grɪlə] → **grill¹** 1; '**grill·room** s. Grill(room) m.

grilse [grɪls] s., a. pl. ichth. junger Lachs.

grim [grɪm] adj. □ **1.** grimmig: a) zornig, wütend, b) erbittert, verbissen: ~ **struggle**, c) hart, schlimm, grausam; **2.** schrecklich, grausig: ~ **accident**.

gri·mace [grɪ'meɪs] **I** s. Gri'masse f, Fratze f: **make a** ~, **make** ~**s** → **II** v/i. e-e Gri'masse od. Gri'massen schneiden, das Gesicht verzerren od. verziehen.

gri·mal·kin [grɪ'mælkɪn] s. **1.** (alte) Katze; **2.** alte Hexe (Frau).

grime [graɪm] **I** s. (zäher) Schmutz od. Ruß; **II** v/t. beschmutzen; '**grim·i·ness** [-mɪnɪs] s. Schmutzigkeit f.

Grimm's law [grɪmz] s. ling. (Gesetz n der) Lautverschiebung f.

grim·ness ['grɪmnɪs] s. Grimmigkeit f, Schreckichkeit f; Grausamkeit f, Härte f; Verbissenheit f.

grim·y ['graɪmɪ] adj. □ schmutzig, rußig.

grin [grɪn] **I** v/i. grinsen, feixen, oft nur (verschmitzt) lächeln: ~ **at s.o.** j-n angrinsen od. anlächeln; ~ **to o.s.** in sich hineingrinsen; ~ **and bear it** a) gute Miene zum bösen Spiel machen, b) die Zähne zs.-beißen; **II** v/t. et. grinsend sagen; **III** s. Grinsen n, (verschmitztes) Lächeln.

grind [graɪnd] **I** v/t. [irr.] **1.** Messer etc. schleifen, wetzen, schärfen; Glas schleifen: ~ **in** Ventile einschleifen; → **ax** 1; **2.** a. ~ **down** (zer)mahlen, zerreiben, -kleinern, -stoßen, -stampfen, schroten; **3.** Kaffee, Korn, Mehl etc. mahlen; **4.** ⊙ schmirgeln, glätten, polieren; **5.** ~ **down** abwetzen; → 2 u. 11; **6.** ~ **one's teeth** mit den Zähnen knirschen; **7.** knirschend (hinein)bohren; **8.**

Leierkasten etc. drehen; **9.** ~ **out** a) Zeitungsartikel etc. her'unterschreiben, b) ♪ her'unterspielen; **10.** ~ **out** et. mühsam her'vorbringen; **11.** a. ~ **down** fig. (unter)'drücken, schinden, quälen: ~ **the faces of the poor** die Armen (gnadenlos) ausbeuten; **12.** ~ **s.th. into s.o.** F j-m et. ,einpauken'; **II** v/i. [irr.] **13.** mahlen; **14.** knirschen; **15.** F sich plagen od. abschinden; **16.** ped. F ,pauken', ,ochsen', ,büffeln'; **III** s. **17.** F Schinde'rei f: **the daily** ~; **18.** ped. F a) ,Pauken' n, ,Büffeln' n, b) Streber(in), ,Büffler(in)'; **19.** Brit. sl. ,Nummer' f (Koitus); '**grind·er** [-də] s. **1.** (Messer-, Scheren-, Glas)Schleifer m; **2.** Schleifstein m; **3.** oberer Mühlstein; **4.** ⊙ a) 'Schleifma,schine f, b) Mahlwerk n, Mühle f, c) Quetschwerk n; **5.** a) (Kaffee)Mühle f, b) a. **meat** ~ Fleischwolf m; **6.** anat. a) Backenzahn m, b) pl. sl. Zähne pl.; '**grind·ing** [-dɪŋ] **I** s. **1.** Mahlen n; **2.** Schleifen n; **3.** Knirschen n; **II** adj. **4.** mahlend (etc. → **grind** I u. II); **5.** Mahl..., Schleif...: ~ **mill** a) Mahlwerk n, Mühle f, b) Schleif-, Reibmühle f; ~ **paste** Schleifpaste f; **6.** ~ **work** ,Schinderei' f.

'**grind·stone** [-nds-] s. Schleifstein m: **keep s.o.'s nose to the** ~ fig. j-n hart od. schwer arbeiten lassen; **keep one's nose to the** ~ schwer arbeiten, sich ranhalten; **get back to the** ~ sich wieder an die Arbeit machen.

grin·go ['grɪŋgəʊ] pl. -**gos** s. Gringo m (lateinamer. Spottname für Ausländer, bsd. Angelsachsen).

grip [grɪp] **I** s. **1.** Griff m (a. die Art, et. zu packen): **come to** ~**s with** a) aneinander geraten mit, b) fig. sich auseinander setzen mit, et. in Angriff nehmen; **be at** ~**s with** a) in e-n Kampf verwickelt sein mit, b) fig. sich auseinander setzen od. ernsthaft beschäftigen mit e-r Sache; **2.** fig. a) Griff m, Halt m, b) Herrschaft f, Gewalt f, Zugriff m, c) Verständnis n, 'Durchblick' m: **in the** ~ **of** in den Klauen od. in der Gewalt (gen.); **get a** ~ **on** in s-e Gewalt od. (geistig) in den Griff bekommen; **have a** ~ **on** et. in der Gewalt haben, fig. Zuhörer etc. fesseln, gepackt halten; **have a (good)** ~ **on** die Lage, e-e Materie etc. (sicher) beherrschen, die Situation etc. (klar) erfassen; **lose one's** ~ a) die Herrschaft verlieren (**of** über acc.), b) (bsd. geistig) nachlassen; **3.** (bestimmter) Händedruck m (z.B. der Freimaurer); **4.** (Hand)Griff m (Koffer etc.); **5.** Haarspange f; **6.** ⊙ Greifer m, Klemme f; **7.** ⊙ Griffigkeit f (a. von Autoreifen); **8.** thea. Ku'lissenschieber m; **9.** Reisetasche f; **II** v/t. **10.** packen, ergreifen; **11.** fig. j-n packen: a) ergreifen (Furcht, Spannung), b) Leser, Zuhörer etc. fesseln; **12.** fig. begreifen, verstehen; **13.** festklemmen; **III** v/i. **14.** Halt finden; **15.** fig. packen, fesseln; ~ **brake** s. ⊙ Handbremse f.

gripe [graɪp] **I** v/t. **1.** zwicken: **be** ~**d** Bauchschmerzen od. e-e Kolik haben; **2.** ⚓ Boot etc. sichern; **II** v/i. **3.** F nörgeln, ,meckern'; **III** s. **4.** pl. ⚕ Bauchweh n, Kolik f; **5.** F (Grund m zur) ,Mecke'rei' f; **6.** pl. ⚓ Seile pl. zum Festmachen.

grip·per ['grɪpə] s. ⊙ Greifer m, Halter m; '**grip·ping** [-pɪŋ] adj. **1.** fig. fesselnd, packend, spannend; **2.** ⊙ Greif..., Klemm...: ~ **lever** Spannhebel m; ~ **tool** Spannwerkzeug n.

'**grip·sack** s. Am. Reisetasche f.

gris·kin ['grɪskɪn] s. Brit. Küche: Rippenstück *n.*

gris·ly ['grɪzlɪ] *adj.* grässlich.

grist [grɪst] *s.* **1.** Mahlgut *n*, -korn *n*: *that's ~ to his mill* das ist Wasser auf s-e Mühle; *bring ~ to the mill* Gewinn bringen; *all is ~ to his mill* er weiß aus allem Kapital zu schlagen; **2.** Malzschrot *m, n*; **3.** *Am.* ('Grundlagen)Materi,al *n*; **4.** Stärke *f*, Dicke *f* (*Garn od. Tau*).

gris·tle ['grɪsl] *s.* Knorpel *m*; **'gris·tly** [-lɪ] *adj.* knorpelig.

grit [grɪt] **I** *s.* **1.** *geol.* a) grober Sand, Kies *m*, b) *a.* ~ *stone* grober Sandstein; **2.** *fig.* Mut *m*, ,Mumm' *m*; **3.** *pl.* Haferschrot *m, n*, -grütze *f*; **II** *v/i.* **4.** knirschen, mahlen; **III** *v/t.* **5.** ~ *one's teeth* a) die Zähne zs.-beißen, b) mit den Zähnen knirschen; **'grit·ty** [-tɪ] *adj.* **1.** sandig, kiesig; **2.** *fig.* F mutig.

griz·zle¹ ['grɪzl] *v/i. Brit.* F **1.** quengeln; **2.** sich beklagen.

griz·zle² ['grɪzl] *s.* **1.** graue Farbe, Grau *n*; **2.** graues Haar; **'griz·zled** [-ld] *adj.* grau(haarig); **'griz·zly** [-lɪ] **I** *adj.* → *grizzled*; **II** *s. a.* ~ *bear* Grisli(bär) *m*, Graubär *m*.

groan [grəʊn] **I** *v/i.* **1.** stöhnen, ächzen (*with* vor; *a. fig. leiden* ***beneath***, ***under*** unter *dat.*); **2.** ächzen, knarren (*Tür etc.*): ~ *ing board* (*od.* ***table***) ein überladener Tisch; **II** *v/t.* **3.** ächzen, unter Stöhnen äußern; **4.** ~ *down* durch Laute des Unmuts zum Schweigen bringen; **III** *s.* **5.** Stöhnen *n*, Ächzen *n*: *give a* ~ → 1; **6.** Laut *m* des Unmuts.

groats [grəʊts] *s. pl.* Hafergrütze *f*.

gro·cer ['grəʊsə] *s.* Lebensmittelhändler *m*; **'gro·cer·y** [-sərɪ] *s.* **1.** Lebensmittelgeschäft *n*; **2.** *mst pl.* Lebensmittel *pl.*; **3.** Lebensmittelhandel *m*; **gro·ce·te·ri·a** [,grəʊsə'tɪərɪə] *s. Am.* Lebensmittelgeschäft *n* mit Selbstbedienung.

grog [grɒg] **I** *s.* Grog *m*; **II** *v/i.* Grog trinken.

grog·gi·ness ['grɒgɪnɪs] *s.* **1.** F Betrunkenheit *f*, ,Schwips' *m*; **2.** Wack(e)ligkeit *f*; **3.** *a. Boxen:* Benommenheit *f*, (halbe) Betäubung; **'grog·gy** [-gɪ] *adj.* **1.** groggy: a) *Boxen:* angeschlagen, b) F erschöpft, ,ka'putt', c) F wacklig (auf den Beinen); **2.** wacklig; **3.** morsch.

groin [grɔɪn] *s.* **1.** *anat.* Leiste *f*, Leistengegend *f*; **2.** ∆ Grat(bogen) *m*, Rippe *f*; **3.** ⊕ Buhne *f*; **groined** [-nd] *adj.* gerippt: ~ *vault* Kreuzgewölbe *n*.

grom·met ['grɒmɪt] → *grummet*.

groom [gru:m] **I** *s.* **1.** Pferdepfleger *m*, Stallbursche *m*; **2.** Bräutigam *m*; **3.** *Brit.* Diener *m*, königlicher Be'amter; → *bedchamber*; **II** *v/t.* **4.** *Pferd* striegeln, pflegen; **5.** *Person, Kleidung* pflegen: *well-~ed* gepflegt; **6.** *fig.* a) *j-n* aufbauen (*for presidency* als zukünftigen Präsidenten), lancieren, b) *j-n als Nachfolger etc.* ,her'anziehen'; **grooms·man** ['gru:mzmən] *s.* [*irr.*] *Am.* → *best man*.

groove [gru:v] **I** *s.* **1.** Rinne *f*, Furche *f* (*a. anat.*): *in the* ~ *sl. obs.* a) ,groß in Form', b) *Am.* in Mode; **2.** ⊕ a) Rinne *f*, Furche *f*, b) Nut *f*, Hohlkehle *f*, Rille *f*, c) Kerbe *f*; **3.** Rille *f* (*e-r Schallplatte*); **4.** ⊕ Zug *m* (*in Gewehren etc.*); **5.** *fig.* a) gewohntes Geleise, b) altes Geleise, alter Trott, Scha'blone *f*, Rou'tine *f*: *get into a* ~ in e-e Gewohnheit od. in e-n (immer gleichen) Trott verfallen; *run* (*od.* ***work***) *in a* ~ sich in e-m ausgefahrenen Geleise bewegen, stagnieren; **6.** *sl.* ,klasse Sache'; *it's a ~!* das ist klasse!; **II** *v/t.* **7.** ⊕ a) auskehlen, rillen, falzen, nuten, kerben, b) *Gewehrlauf etc.* ziehen; **III** *v/i. sl.* **8.** Spaß haben (*with* bei *od.* mit); **9.** Spaß machen, ,(große) Klasse sein'; **grooved** [-vd] *adj.* gerillt; genutet; **'groov·y** [-vɪ] *adj.* **1.** scha'blonenhaft; **2.** *sl.* ,toll', ,klasse'.

grope [grəʊp] **I** *v/i.* **1.** tasten (*for* nach): ~ *about* herumtasten, -tappen, -suchen; ~ *in the dark bsd. fig.* im Dunkeln tappen; ~ *for* (*od.* ***after***) *a solution* nach e-r Lösung suchen; **II** *v/t.* **2.** tastend suchen: ~ *one's way* sich vorwärts tasten; **3.** F *Mädchen* ,befummeln'; **grop·er** *s.* F Grapscher *m*; **'grop·ing·ly** [-pɪŋlɪ] *adv.* tastend: a) tappend, b) *fig.* vorsichtig, unsicher.

gros·beak ['grəʊsbiːk] *s. orn.* Kernbeißer *m*.

gros·grain ['grəʊgreɪn] *adj. u. s.* grob gerippt(es Seidentuch).

gross [grəʊs] **I** *adj.* □ → *grossly*; **1.** dick, feist, plump; **2.** grob(körnig); **3.** roh, grob, derb; **4.** schwer, grob (*Fehler, Pflichtverletzung etc.*): ~ *negligence* ⚖ grobe Fahrlässigkeit; **5.** schwerfällig; **6.** dicht, stark, üppig: ~ *vegetation*; **7.** a) derb, grob, unfein, b) unanständig; **8.** brutto, Brutto..., Roh..., Gesamt...: ~ *amount* Gesamtbetrag *m*; ~ *domestic product* Brutto'inlandspro,dukt *n*; ~ *margin* ✝ 'Brutto,marge *f*; ~ *national product* Brutto-sozi'alpro,dukt *n*; ~ *profit* Rohgewinn *m*; ~ *register(ed) ton* Bruttoregistertonne *f*; ~ *tonnage* Bruttotonnengehalt *m*; ~ *weight* Bruttogewicht *n*; **II** *s.* **9.** das Ganze, die Masse: *in* (*the*) ~ im Ganzen, in Bausch u. Bogen; **10.** *pl.* gross Gros *n* (*12 Dutzend*); **III** *v/t.* **11.** brutto verdienen od. einnehmen od. (*Film etc.*) einspielen; **'gross·ly** [-lɪ] *adv.* äußerst, maßlos, ungeheuerlich; ⚖ *etc.* grob: ~ *negligent*; **'gross·ness** [-nɪs] *s.* **1.** Schwere *f*, Ungeheuerlichkeit *f*; **2.** Rohheit *f*, Derbheit *f*, Grobheit *f*; **3.** Anstößigkeit *f*, Unanständigkeit *f*; **4.** Dicke *f*; **5.** Plumpheit *f*.

gro·tesque [grəʊ'tesk] **I** *adj.* □ **1.** gro'tesk (*a. Kunst*); **II** *s.* **2.** das Gro'teske; **3.** *Kunst:* Gro'teske *f*, gro'teske Fi'gur; **gro'tesque·ness** [-nɪs] *s.* das Gro'teske.

grot·to ['grɒtəʊ] *pl.* **-toes** *od.* **-tos** *s.* Höhle *f*, Grotte *f*.

grot·ty ['grɒtɪ] *adj. Brit. sl.* **1.** ,mies'; **2.** grässlich, eklig.

grouch [graʊtʃ] F **I** *v/i.* **1.** nörgeln, ,meckern', **II** *s.* **2.** a) ,miese' Laune, b) *have a* ~ → 1; **3.** a) ,Meckerfritze' *m*, b) ,Miesepeter' *m*; **'grouch·y** [-tʃɪ] *adj.* □ F a) ,sauer', ,grantig', b) nörglerisch.

ground¹ [graʊnd] **I** *s.* **1.** (Erd)Boden *m*, Erde *f*, Grund *m*: *above* ~ a) oberirdisch, ⚒ über Tage, b) am Leben; *below* ~ a) ⚒ unter Tage, b) unter der Erde, tot; *down to the* ~ *fig.* völlig, total, restlos; *from the* ~ *up Am.* von Grund auf; *break new* (*od.* ***fresh***) ~ Land urbar machen, *a. fig.* Neuland erschließen; *cut the* ~ *from under s.o.'s feet* j-m den Boden unter den Füßen wegziehen; *fall to the* ~ zu Boden fallen, *fig.* sich zerschlagen, ins Wasser fallen; *fall on stony* ~ *fig.* auf taube Ohren stoßen; *get off the* ~ a) *v/t. fig.* et. in Gang bringen, et. verwirklichen, b) *v/i.* ✈ abheben, c) *v/i. fig.* in Gang kommen, verwirklicht werden; *go to* ~ im Bau verschwinden (*Fuchs*), *fig.* ,untertauchen' (*Verbrecher*); *play s.o. into the* ~ *sport* F j-n in Grund u. Boden spielen; **2.** Boden *m*, Grund *m*, Gebiet *n* (*a. fig.*), Strecke *f*, Gelände *n*: *on German* ~ auf deutschem Boden; *be on safe* ~ sich auf sicherem Boden bewegen; *be forbidden* ~ *fig.* tabu sein; *cover much* ~ e-e große Strecke zurücklegen, *fig.* viel umfassen, weit reichen; *cover the* ~ *well fig.* nichts außer Acht lassen, alles in Betracht ziehen; *gain* ~ (an) Boden gewinnen, *fig. a.* um sich greifen, Fuß fassen; *give* (*od.* ***lose***) ~ (an) Boden verlieren (*a. fig.*); *go over the* ~ *fig.* die Sache durchsprechen, alles gründlich prüfen; *hold* (*od.* ***stand***) *one's* ~ standhalten, nicht weichen, sich od. s-n Standpunkt behaupten; *shift one's* ~ seinen Standpunkt ändern, umschwenken; **3.** Grundbesitz *m*, Grund *m* u. Boden *m*, Lände'reien *pl.*; **4.** Gebiet *n*, Grund *m*, *bsd. sport* Platz *m*: *cricket* ~; **5.** *hunting* ~ Jagd(-gebiet *n*) *f*; **6.** *pl.* (Garten)Anlagen *pl.*: *standing in its own ~s* von Anlagen umgeben (*Haus*); **7.** Meeresboden *m*, (Meeres)Grund *m*: *take* ~ auflaufen, stranden; **8.** *pl.* Bodensatz *m* (*Kaffee etc.*); **9.** Grundierung *f*, Grund(farbe *f*) *m*, Grund(fläche *f*) *m*; **10.** *a. pl.* Grundlage *f* (*a. fig.*); **11.** *fig.* (Beweg-)Grund *m*: ~ *for divorce* Scheidungsgrund; *on the ~(s) of* aufgrund (*gen.*), wegen (*gen.*); *on the ~(s) that* mit der Begründung, dass; *on medical ~s* aus gesundheitlichen Gründen; *have no ~(s) for* keinen Grund haben für (*od.* zu *inf.*); **12.** ⚡ Erde *f*, Erdung *f*, Erdschluss *m*: ~ *cable* Massekabel *n*; **13.** *thea.* Par'terre *n*; **II** *v/t.* **14.** niederlegen, -setzen; → *arm²* 1; **15.** ⚓ *Schiff* auf Grund setzen; **16.** ⚡ erden; **17.** ⊕, *paint.* grundieren; **18.** a) e-m Flugzeug od. Piloten Startverbot erteilen, b) *mot. Am.* j-m die Fahrerlaubnis entziehen: *be ~ed* nicht (ab)fliegen od. starten können od. dürfen, (*Passagiere*) *a.* festsitzen; **19.** *fig.* (*on, in*) gründen, stützen (auf *acc.*), begründen (in *dat.*): *~ed in fact* auf Tatsachen beruhend; *be ~ed in* → 22; **20.** (*in*) j-n einführen (in *acc.*), j-m die Anfangsgründe beibringen (*gen.*): *well ~ed in* mit guten (Vor-)Kenntnissen in (*od. gen.*); **III** *v/i.* **21.** ⚓ stranden, auflaufen; **22.** (*on, upon*) beruhen (auf *dat.*), sich gründen (auf *acc.*).

ground² [graʊnd] **I** *pret. u. p.p. von grind*; **II** *adj.* **1.** gemahlen: ~ *coffee*; **2.** matt (geschliffen); → *ground glass*.

ground·age ['graʊndɪdʒ] *s.* ⚓ *Brit.* Hafengebühr *f*, Ankergeld *n*.

,ground|·'air *adj.* ✈ Boden-Bord-...; ~ **a·lert** *s.* ✈, ✗ A'larm-, Startbereitschaft *f*; ~ **an·gling** *s.* Grundangeln *n*; ~ **at·tack** *s.* ✈ Angriff *m* mit Erdziele, Tiefangriff *m*; ~ **bass** *s.* ♪ Grundbass *m*; ~ **box** *s.* ♀ Zwergbuchsbaum *m*; ~ **clear·ance** *s. mot.* Bodenfreiheit *f*; ~ **col·o(u)r** *s.* Grundfarbe *f*; ~ **con·nec·tion** → *ground¹* 12; ~ **-con,trolled ap·proach** *s.* ✈ GC'A-Anflug *m* (*per Bodenradar*); ~ **crew** *s.* ✈ 'Bodenper-so,nal *n*; ~ **fish** *s. ichth.* Grundfisch *m*; ~ **fish·ing** *s.* Grundangeln *n*; ~ **floor** *s. Brit.* Erdgeschoss, *östr.* -geschoß *n*: *get in on the* ~ F a) ✝ sich zu den Gründerbedingungen beteiligen, b) von Anfang an mit dabei sein, c) ganz unten anfangen (*in e-r Firma etc.*); ~ **fog** *s.* Bodennebel *m*; ~ **forc·es** *s. pl.* ✗ Bodentruppen *pl.*, Landstreitkräfte *pl.*; ~ **form** *s. ling.* a) Grundform *f*, b) Wurzel *f*, c) Stamm *m*; ~ **frost** *s.* Bodenfrost *m*; ~ **glass** *s.* **1.** Mattglas *n*; **2.** *phot.* Mattscheibe *f*; ~ **game** *s. hunt. Brit.* Niederwild *n*; ~ **hog** *s. zo. Amer.* Murmeltier

G

n; ~ **host·ess** *s.* ✈ Ground-Hostess *f;* ~ **ice** *s. geol.* Grundeis *n.*

ground·ing ['graʊndɪŋ] *s.* **1.** Funda'ment *n,* 'Unterbau *m;* **2.** a) Grundierung *f,* b) Grundfarbe *f;* **3.** ⚓ Stranden *n;* **4.** ⚡ Erdung *f;* **5.** a) 'Anfangs͵unterricht *m,* Einführung *f,* b) (Vor)Kenntnisse *pl.*

ground·less ['graʊndlɪs] *adj.* □ grundlos, unbegründet.

ground| lev·el *s. phys.* Bodennähe *f;* ~ **line** *s.* ᴀ Grundlinie *f;* '~·**man** [-n(d)mæn] *s. [irr.] sport* Platzwart *m;* ~ **note** *s.* ♪ Grundton *m;* '~·**nut** [-n(d)n-] *s.* Erdnuss *f;* ~ **plan** *s.* **1.** △ Grundriss *m;* **2.** *fig.* (erster) Entwurf, Kon'zept *n;* ~ **plane** *s.* Horizon'talebene *f;* ~ **plate** *s.* **1.** △ Grundplatte *f;* **2.** ⚡ Erdplatte *f;* ~ **rule** *s.* Grundregel *f;* ~ **sea** *s.* ⚓ Grundsee *f;* ~ **sheet** *s.* **1.** Zeltboden *m;* **2.** *sport* Regenplane *f* (*für das Spielfeld*); '~·**s·man** [-n(d)mən] → *ground·man;* ~ **speed** *s.* ✈ Geschwindigkeit *f* über Grund; ~ **staff** → *ground crew;* ~ **sta·tion** *s.* 'Bodenstati͵on *f;* ~ **swell** *s.* **1.** (Grund)Dünung *f;* **2.** *fig.* Anschwellen *n;* ͵~·**to-'air** *adj.* a) ✈ Boden-Bord-...: ~ *communication,* b) ✕ Boden-Luft-...: ~ *weapon;* '~·͵**wa·ter lev·el** *s. geol.* Grundwasserspiegel *m;* ~ **wave** *s.* ⚡, *phys.* Bodenwelle *f;* '~·**work** *s.* **1.** △ a) Erdarbeit *f,* b) 'Unterbau *m,* Funda'ment *n* (*a. fig.*); **2.** *fig.* Grundlage(n *pl.*) *f;* **3.** *paint. etc.* Grund *m.*

group [gruːp] **I** *s.* **1.** *allg., a.* 🐾, ᴀ, ♪, *biol., sociol. etc.* Gruppe *f;* **2.** *fig.* Gruppe *f,* Kreis *m:* **the Group of Eight** ✈, *pol.* die G-8(-Staaten *pl.*) *f;* **3.** *parl.* a) Gruppe *f* (*Partei mit zu wenig Abgeordneten für e-e Fraktion,* b) Frakti'on *f;* **4.** ✈ Gruppe *f,* Kon'zern *m;* **5.** ✕ a) Gruppe *f,* b) Kampfgruppe *f* (*2 od. mehr Bataillone*); **6.** ✈ a) *Brit.* Geschwader *n:* ~ *captain* Oberst *m* (*der RAF*), b) *Am.* Gruppe *f;* **7.** ♪ a) Instru'menten- od. Stimmgruppe *f,* b) Notengruppe *f;* **II** *v/t.* **8.** gruppieren, anordnen; **9.** klassifizieren, einordnen; **III** *v/i.* **10.** sich gruppieren; ~ **drive** *s.* ⊙ Gruppenantrieb *m;* ~ **dynam·ics** *s. pl. sg. konstr. sociol., psych.* 'Gruppendy͵namik *f.*

group·ie ['gruːpɪ] *s.* ͵Groupie' *n* (*weiblicher Fan*).

group| sex *s.* Gruppensex *m;* ~ **ther·a·py** *s. psych.* 'Gruppenthera͵pie *f;* ~ **work** *s. sociol.* Gruppenarbeit *f.*

grouse[1] [graʊs] *s. sg. u. pl. orn.* **1.** Waldhuhn *n;* **2.** Schottisches Moorhuhn.

grouse[2] [graʊs] **I** *v/i.* meckern (über *acc.*), nörgeln (an *dat.,* über *acc.*); **II** *s.* Nörge'lei *f,* Gemecker *n;* '**grous·er** [-sə] *s.* ͵Meckerfritze' *m.*

grout [graʊt] **I** *s.* **1.** ⊙ Vergussmörtel *m;* **2.** Schrotmehl *n;* **3.** *pl.* Hafergrütze *f;* **II** *v/t.* **4.** *Fugen* ausstreichen.

grove [grəʊv] *s.* Hain *m,* Gehölz *n.*

grov·el ['grɒvl] *v/i.* **1.** am Boden kriechen; **2.** ~ *before* (*od.* **to**) *s.o. fig.* vor j-m kriechen, vor j-m zu Kreuze kriechen; **3.** ~ *in* schwelgen in (*dat.*), frönen (*dat.*); '**grov·el·(l)er** [-lə] *s.* Kriecher *m,* Speichellecker *m;* '**grov·el·(l)ing** [-lɪŋ] *adj.* □ *fig.* kriecherisch, unter'würfig.

grow [grəʊ] **I** *v/i. [irr.]* **1.** wachsen; **2.** ♀ wachsen, vorkommen; **3.** wachsen: a) größer *od.* stärker werden, sich entwickeln, b) *fig.* anwachsen, zunehmen (*in* an *dat.*); **4.** (all'mählich) werden: ~ *rich;* ~ *less* sich vermindern; ~ *light*

hell(er) werden, sich aufklären; **II** *v/t. [irr.]* **5.** (an)bauen, züchten, ziehen: ~ *apples;* **6.** (sich) wachsen lassen: ~ *one's hair long;* ~ *a beard* sich e-n Bart stehen lassen;

Zssgn mit adv. u. prp.:

grow|a·way *v/i.:* ~ *from* sich j-m entfremden; ~ *from* → *grow out of;* ~ **in·to** *v/i.* **1.** hin'einwachsen in (*acc.*) (*a. fig.*); **2.** werden zu, sich entwickeln zu; ~ **on** *v/i.* **1.** Einfluss *od.* Macht gewinnen über (*acc.*): *the habit grows on one* man gewöhnt sich immer mehr daran; **2.** *j-m* lieb werden *od.* ans Herz wachsen; ~ **out of** *v/i.* **1.** her'auswachsen aus: ~ *one's clothes;* **2.** *fig.* entwachsen (*dat.*), über'winden (*acc.*), ablegen: ~ *a habit;* **3.** erwachsen *od.* entstehen aus, e-e Folge sein (*gen.*); ~ **up** *v/i.* **1.** auf-, her'anwachsen: ~ (*into*) *a beauty* sich zu e-r Schönheit entwickeln; **2.** erwachsen werden: ~! sei kein Kindskopf!; **3.** sich einbürgern (*Brauch etc.*); **4.** sich entwickeln, entstehen; ~ **up·on** → *grow on.*

grow·er ['grəʊə] *s.* **1.** (*schnell etc.*) wachsende Pflanze: *a fast* ~; **2.** Züchter *m,* Pflanzer *m,* Erzeuger *m,* in *Zssgn* ...bauer *m;* **grow·ing** ['grəʊɪŋ] **I** *adj.* □ **1.** wachsend (*a. fig. zunehmend*); **II** *s.* **2.** Anbau *m;* **3.** Wachstum *n:* ~ *pains* a) Wachstumsschmerzen, b) *fig.* Anfangsschwierigkeiten, ͵Kinderkrankheiten'.

growl [graʊl] **I** *v/i.* **1.** knurren (*Hund etc.*), brummen (*Bär*) (*beide a. fig. Person*): ~ *at j-n* anknurren; **2.** (g)rollen (*Donner*); **II** *v/t.* **3.** *Worte* knurren; **III** *s.* **4.** Knurren *n,* Brummen *n;* **5.** (G)Rollen *n;* '**growl·er** [-lə] *s.* **1.** knurriger Hund; **2.** *fig.* ͵Brummbär' *m;* **3.** *ichth.* Knurrfisch *m;* **4.** ⚡ Prüfspule *f;* **5.** kleiner Eisberg.

grown [grəʊn] **I** *p.p. von* **grow;** **II** *adj.* **1.** gewachsen; → *full-grown;* **2.** erwachsen: ~ *man* Erwachsene(r) *m;* **3.** *a.* ~ *over* be-, über'wachsen; ~·**up** **I** *adj.* [͵grəʊn'ʌp] **1.** erwachsen; **2.** a) für Erwachsene: ~ *books,* b) Erwachsenen...: ~ *clothes;* **II** *s.* ['grəʊnʌp] **3.** Erwachsene(r *m*) *f.*

growth [grəʊθ] *s.* **1.** Wachsen *n,* Wachstum *n* (*a. fig. u.* ✈); **2.** Wuchs *m,* Größe *f;* **3.** Anwachsen *n,* Zunahme *f,* Zuwachs *m;* **4.** *fig.* Entwicklung *f;* **5.** a) Anbau *m,* b) Pro'dukt *n,* Erzeugnis *n: of one's own* ~ selbst gezogen; **6.** ♀ Schössling *m,* Trieb *m;* **7.** ✗ Gewächs *n,* Wucherung *f;* ~ **in·dus·try** *s.* ✈ 'Wachstumsindu͵strie *f;* ~ **rate** *s.* ✈ Wachstumsrate *f.*

groyne [grɔɪn] *s. Brit.* ⊙ Buhne *f.*

grub [grʌb] **I** *v/i.* **1.** a) graben, wühlen, b) jäten, c) roden; **2.** ͵wühlen', schwer arbeiten; **3.** *fig.* stöbern, wühlen, kramen; **4.** *sl.* ͵futtern', essen; **II** *v/t.* **5.** a) aufwühlen, b) 'umgraben, c) roden; **6.** *oft* ~ *up* a) ausjäten, b) (mit den Wurzeln) ausgraben, c) *fig.* ausgraben, aufstöbern; **III** *s.* **7.** *zo.* Made *f,* Larve *f;* **8.** *fig.* Arbeitstier *n;* **9.** *sl.* ͵Futter' *n* (*Essen*).

grub·ber ['grʌbə] *s.* **1.** ✗ a) Rodehacke *f,* -werkzeug *n,* b) Eggenpflug *m;* **2.** → *grub* 8; '**grub·by** [-bɪ] *adj.* **1.** schmudelig; **2.** madig.

'**grub·stake** *s. Am.* ✗ e-m Schürfer gegen Gewinnbeteiligung gegebene Ausrüstung u. Verpflegung; ♀ **Street I** *s. fig.* armselige Lite'raten *pl.;* **II** *adj.* (lite'rarisch) minderwertig, ͵dritter Garni'tur'.

grudge [grʌdʒ] **I** *v/t.* **1.** (*s.o. s.th. od. s.th. to s.o.*) (j-m et.) miss'gönnen *od.* nicht gönnen, (j-n um et.) beneiden; **2.** ~ *doing s.th.* et. nur widerwillig *od.*

ungern tun; **II** *s.* **3.** Groll *m: bear s.o. a* ~, *have a* ~ *against s.o.* e-n Groll gegen j-n hegen; '**grudg·er** [-dʒə] *s.* Neider *m;* '**grudg·ing** [-dʒɪŋ] *adj.* □ **1.** neidisch, 'missgünstig; **2.** 'widerwillig, ungern (getan *od.* gegeben): *she was very* ~ *in her thanks* sie bedankte sich nur sehr widerwillig.

gru·el ['grʊəl] *s.* Haferschleim *m;* Schleimsuppe *f;* '**gru·el·(l)ing** [-lɪŋ] **I** *adj. fig.* mörderisch, aufreibend, zermürbend; **II** *s. Brit.* F a) harte Strafe *od.* Behandlung, b) Stra'paze *f,* ͵Schlauch' *m.*

grue·some ['gruːsəm] *adj.* □ grausig, grauenhaft, schauerlich.

gruff [grʌf] *adj.* □ **1.** schroff, barsch, ruppig; **2.** rau (*Stimme*); '**gruff·ness** [-nɪs] *s.* **1.** Barsch-, Schroffheit *f;* **2.** Rauheit *f.*

grum·ble ['grʌmbl] **I** *v/i.* **1.** a) murren, schimpfen (*at, about, over* über *acc.,* wegen), b) knurren, brummen; **2.** (g)rollen (*Donner*); **II** *s.* **3.** Murren *n,* Knurren *n;* **4.** (G)Rollen *n;* '**grum·bler** [-lə] *s.* Brummbär *m,* Nörgler *m;* '**grum·bling** [-lɪŋ] *adj.* □ **1.** brummig; **2.** murrend.

grume [gruːm] *s.* (*bsd.* Blut)Klümpchen *n.*

grum·met ['grʌmɪt] *s. Brit.* **1.** ⚓ Seilschlinge *f;* **2.** ⊙ (Me'tall)Öse *f.*

gru·mous ['gruːməs] *adj.* geronnen, dick, klumpig (*Blut etc.*).

grump [grʌmp] *s. Am.* F **1.** → *grumbler;* **2.** *pl.* Missmut *m: have the* ~s missmutig sein; '**grump·y** ['grʌmpɪ] *adj.* □ mürrisch, missmutig.

Grun·dy ['grʌndɪ] *s.* engstirnige, sittenstrenge Per'son: *Mrs.* ~ *a.* ͵die Leute' *pl.* (*die gefürchtete öffentliche Meinung*): *what will Mrs.* ~ *say?*

grunge [grʌndʒ] *s. bsd. Am.* **1.** F Schmutz *m;* **2.** *a.* ~ *rock* ♪ Grunge *m;* **3.** Grunge *m* (*Modestil der frühen 90er-Jahre, der schmuddelige Kleidung propagierte*); '**grun·gy** *adj. bsd. Am.* **1.** hässlich, her'untergekommen (*Gebäude etc.*); **2.** schmutzig, schmuddelig (*Kleidung*).

grunt [grʌnt] **I** *v/i. u. v/t.* **1.** grunzen; **2.** *fig.* murren, brummen; **3.** ächzen, stöhnen (*with* vor *dat.*); **II** *s.* **4.** Grunzen *n;* **5.** → *growler* 3.

gryph·on ['grɪfən] → *griffin*[1] 1.

'**G-string** *s.* **1.** ♪ G-Saite *f;* **2.** a) ͵letzte Hülle' (*e-r Stripteasetänzerin*), b) Tanga *m* (*Mini-Bikini*).

gua·na ['gwɑːnə] → *iguana.*

gua·no ['gwɑːnəʊ] *s.* Gu'ano *m.*

guar·an·tee [͵gærən'tiː] **I** *s.* **1.** Garan'tie *f:* a) Bürgschaft *f,* Sicherheit *f,* b) Gewähr *f,* Zusicherung *f,* c) Garan'tiefrist *f:* ~ (*card*) Garantieschein *m;* **there is a one-year** ~ **on this camera** die Kamera hat ein Jahr Garantie; **2.** Kauti'on *f,* Sicherheit(sleistung) *f,* Pfand(summe *f*) *n;* **3.** Bürge *m,* Bürgin *f;* **4.** Sicherheitsempfänger(in); **II** *v/t.* **5.** (sich ver-) bürgen für, Garan'tie leisten für; **6.** *et.* garantieren, gewährleisten, sicherstellen, verbürgen; **7.** schützen, sichern (*from, against* vor *dat.,* gegen); '**guar·an'tor** [-'tɔː] *s. bsd.* ⚖ Bürge *m,* Bürgin *f,* Ga'rant(in); **guar·an·ty** ['gærəntɪ] → *guarantee* 1, 2, 3.

guard [gɑːd] **I** *v/t.* **1.** (*against, from*) (be)hüten, (be)schützen, bewahren (vor *dat.*), sichern (gegen): ~ *one's interests fig.* s-e Interessen wahren; ~ *your tongue!* hüte deine Zunge!; **2.** bewachen, beaufsichtigen; **3.** ⊙ (ab)sichern; **4.** *Schach:* Figur decken; **II** *v/i.*

guard boat – gum arabic

5. (*against*) auf der Hut sein, sich hüten *od.* schützen *od.* in Acht nehmen (vor *dat.*), vorbeugen (*dat.*); **III** *s.* **6.** a) ✕ *etc.* Wache *f*, (Wach)Posten *m*, b) Wächter *m*, c) Aufseher *m*, Wärter *m*, d) Bewacher *m*, Sicherheitsbeamter *m*; **7.** ✕ a) Wachmannschaft *f*, Wache *f*, b) Garde *f*, Leibwache *f*: *~ of hono(u)r* Ehrenwache *f*, c) *⸚s pl. Brit.* 'Garde (-korps *n*, -regi,ment *n*) *f*; **8.** 🔊 a) *Brit.* Schaffner *m*, b) *Am.* Bahnwärter *m*; **9.** Bewachung *f*, Aufsicht *f*: *keep under close ~* scharf bewachen; *be on ~* auf Wache sein; *stand* (*mount, relieve, keep*) *~* Wache stehen (beziehen, ablösen, halten); **10.** *fenc., Boxen etc.,* a. *Schach:* Deckung *f*: *lower one's ~* die Deckung herunternehmen, *fig.* sich e-e Blöße geben, nicht aufpassen; **11.** *fig.* Wachsamkeit *f*: *on one's ~* auf der Hut, vorsichtig; *off one's ~* nicht auf der Hut, unachtsam; *put s.o. on his ~* j-n warnen; *throw s.o. off his ~* j-n überrumpeln; **12.** ⊙ Schutzvorrichtung *f*, -gitter *n*, -blech *n*; **13.** a) Stichblatt *n* (am Degen), b) Bügel *m* (am Gewehr); **14.** *fig.* Vorsichtsmaßnahme *f*, Sicherung *f*; *~ boat s.* ⚓ Wachboot *n*; *~ book s.* **1.** *Brit.* Sammelalbum *n*; **2.** ✕ Wachbuch *n*; *~ chain s.* Sicherheitskette *f*; *~ dog s.* Wachhund *m*; *~ du-ty s.* Wachdienst *m*: *be on ~* Wache haben.

guard·ed ['gɑːdɪd] *adj.* □ *fig.* vorsichtig, zu'rückhaltend: *~ hope* gewisse Hoffnung; *~ optimism* gedämpfter Optimismus; **'guard·ed·ness** [-nɪs] *s.* Vorsicht *f*, Zu'rückhaltung *f*.

'guard·house *s.* ✕ **1.** 'Wachlo,kal *n*, -haus *n*; **2.** Ar'restlo,kal *n*.

guard·i·an ['gɑːdjən] *s.* **1.** Hüter *m*, Wächter *m*: *~ angel* Schutzengel *m*; *~ of the law* Gesetzeshüter; **2.** ♯ Vormund *m*: *~ ad litem* Prozessvertreter *m* (*für Minderjährige od. Geschäftsunfähige*); **'guard·i·an·ship** [-ʃɪp] *s.* **1.** ♯ Vormundschaft *f*: *be* (*place*) *under ~* unter Vormundschaft stehen (stellen); **2.** *fig.* Schutz *m*, Obhut *f*.

'guard| rail *s.* **1.** Handlauf *m*; **2.** *mot.* Leitplanke *f*; **'~·man** [-dzmən] *s.* [*irr.*] ✕ **1.** → *guard* 6a; **2.** Gar'dist *m*; **3.** *Am.* Natio'nalgar,dist *m*.

Gua·te·ma·lan [ˌgwætɪ'mɑːlən] **I** *adj.* guatemal'tekisch; **II** *s.* Guatemal'teke *m*, -'tekin *f*.

gua·va ['gwɑːvə] *s.* ♀ Gua'jave *f*.

gu·ber·na·to·ri·al [ˌgjuːbənə'tɔːrɪəl] *adj. bsd. Am.* Gouverneurs...

gudg·eon¹ ['gʌdʒən] *s.* **1.** *ichth.* Gründling *m*; **2.** *fig.* Gimpel *m*.

gudg·eon² ['gʌdʒən] *s.* **1.** ⊙ Zapfen *m*, Bolzen *m*: *~ pin* Kolbenbolzen; **2.** ⚓ Ruderöse *f*.

guel·der rose ['geldə] *s.* ♀ Schneeball *m*.

Guelph, Guelf [gwelf] *s.* Welfe *m*, Welfin *f*; **'Guelph·ic, 'Guelf·ic** [-fɪk] *adj.* welfisch.

guer·don ['gɜːdən] *poet.* **I** *s.* Sold *m*, Lohn *m*; **II** *v/t.* belohnen.

gue·ril·la → *guerrilla*.

Guern·sey ['gɜːnzɪ] *s.* **1.** Guernsey (-rind) *n*; **2.** *a.* ⸚ ⚓ 'Wollpul,lover *m*.

guer·ril·la [gə'rɪlə] *s.* ✕ **1.** Gue'rilla *m*, Parti'san *m*; **2.** *mst* **~ war(fare)** Gue'rillakrieg *m*, *fig.* Kleinkrieg *m*.

guess [ges] **I** *v/t.* **1.** erraten: *~ a riddle*; *~ s.o.'s thoughts*; *~ who!* rate mal, wer!; **2.** (ab)schätzen (*at* auf): *~ s.o.'s age*; **3.** ahnen, vermuten; **4.** *bsd. Am.* F glauben, denken, meinen, ahnen; **II** *v/i.* **5.** schätzen (*at s.th.* et.); **6.** a) raten, b) her'umraten (*at, about* an *dat.*): *keep s.o. ~ing* j-n im Unklaren *od.* Un-

gewissen lassen; *~ing game* Ratespiel *n*; **III** *s.* **7.** Schätzung *f*, Vermutung *f*, Annahme *f*: *my ~ is that* ich schätze *od.* vermute, dass; *that's anybody's ~* das weiß niemand; *your ~ is as good as mine* ich kann auch nur raten; *a good ~!* gut geraten *od.* geschätzt; *at a ~* bei bloßer Schätzung; *at a rough ~* grob geschätzt; *by ~* schätzungsweise; *by ~ and by god* F ,nach Gefühl u. Wellenschlag'; *make* (*od. take*) *a ~* raten, schätzen; *miss one's ~* ,danebenhauen', falsch raten; *~ rope* → *guest rope*; *~ stick s. Am. sl.* **1.** Rechenschieber *m*; **2.** Maßstab *m*.

guess·ti·mate F **I** *s.* ['gestɪmət] grobe Schätzung, bloße Rate'rei; **II** *v/t.* [-meɪt] ,über den Daumen peilen'.

'guess·work *s.* (bloße) Rate'rei, (reine) Vermutung(en *pl.*).

guest [gest] **I** *s.* **1.** Gast *m*: *paying ~* (Pensions)Gast; *~ of hono(u)r* Ehrengast; *be my ~!* aber bitte(, ja!; **2.** ♀, *zo.* Einmieter *m* (*Parasit*); **II** *v/i.* **3.** *bsd. Am. thea.* gastieren, als Gast mitwirken (*on* bei); *~ book s.* Gästebuch *n*; *~·duc·tor s.* ♪ 'Gastdiri,gent *m*; *'~·house s.* Pensi'on *f*; Gästehaus *n*; *~ room* [rum] *s.* Gästezimmer *n*; *~ rope*, *~ warp* ['ges-] *s.* ⚓ **1.** Schlepptrosse *f*; **2.** Bootstau *n*.

guf·faw [gʌ'fɔː] **I** *s.* schallendes Gelächter; **II** *v/i.* laut lachen.

guid·a·ble ['gaɪdəbl] *adj.* lenkbar, lenksam; **'guid·ance** [-dns] *s.* **1.** Leitung *f*, Führung *f*; **2.** Anleitung *f*, Belehrung *f*, Unter'weisung *f*: *for your ~* zu Ihrer Orientierung; **3.** (*Berufs-, Ehe- etc.*)Beratung *f*, Führung *f*: *~ counsel(l)or* a) Berufs-, Studienberater *m*, b) Heilpädagoge *m*.

guide [gaɪd] **I** *v/t.* **1.** j-n führen, geleiten, j-m den Weg zeigen; **2.** ⊙ *u. fig.* lenken, leiten, führen, steuern; **3.** *et., a.* j-n bestimmen: *~ s.o.'s actions* (*life, etc.*); *be ~d by* sich leiten lassen von, folgen (*dat.*), bestimmt sein von; **4.** anleiten, belehren, beraten(d zur Seite stehen *dat.*); **II** *s.* **5.** Führer(in), Leiter (-in); **6.** (*Reise-, Fremden-, Berg- etc.*) Führer *m*; **7.** (*Reise- etc.*)Führer *m* (*to* durch, von) (*Buch*); **8.** (*to*) Leitfaden *m*, Handbuch *n* (*gen.*); **9.** Berater (-in); **10.** *fig.* Richtschnur *f*, Anhaltspunkt *m*: *if that* (*he*) *is any ~* wenn man sich danach (nach ihm) überhaupt richten kann; **11.** → *girl guide*; **12.** a) Wegweiser *m*, b) 'Wegmar,kierung(szeichen *n*) *f*; **13.** ⊙ Führung *f*; *~ bar s.* ⊙ Führungsschiene *f*; *~ beam s.* ✈ (Funk)Leitstrahl *m*; *~ blade s.* ⊙ Leitschaufel *f* (*Turbine*); *~ block s.* ⊙ Führungsschlitten *m*; *'~·book* → *guide* 7.

guid·ed ['gaɪdɪd] *adj.* **1.** (fern)gelenkt: *~ missile* ✕ Fernlenkgeschoss *n*, Fernlenkkörper *m*; **2.** geführt: *~ tour* Führung *f*.

guide| dog *s.* Blindenhund *m*; *'~·line s.* **1.** ✈ Schleppseil *n*; **2.** (*on gen.*) Richtlinie *f*, -schnur *f*; *'~·post s.* Wegweiser *m*; *~ pul·ley s.* ⊙ Leit-, 'Umlenkrolle *f*; *~ rail s.* → *guide bar*; *~ rod s.* ⊙ Führungsstange *f*; *~ rope s.* ✈ Schlepptau *n*; *'~·way s.* ⊙ Führungsbahn *f*.

guid·ing ['gaɪdɪŋ] *adj.* führend, leitend, Lenk...: *~ principle* Leitprinzip *n*; *~ rule s.* Richtlinie *f*; *~ star s.* Leitstern *m*.

gui·don ['gaɪdən] *s.* **1.** Wimpel *m*, Fähnchen *n*, Stan'darte *f*; **2.** Stan'dartenträger *m*.

guild [gɪld] *s.* **1.** Gilde *f*, Zunft *f*, Innung *f*; **2.** Vereinigung *f*.

guil·der ['gɪldə] *s.* Gulden *m*.

'guild·hall *s.* **1.** *hist.* Gilden-, Zunfthaus *n*; **2.** Rathaus *n*: *the ⸚ das Rathaus der City von London.

guile [gaɪl] *s.* (Arg)List *f*, Tücke *f*; **'guile·ful** [-fʊl] *adj.* □ arglistig, tückisch; **'guile·less** [-lɪs] *adj.* □ arglos, ohne Falsch, treuherzig, harmlos; **'guile·less·ness** [-lɪsnɪs] *s.* Harm-, Arglosigkeit *f*.

guil·lo·tine [ˌgɪlə'tiːn] **I** *s.* **1.** Guillo'tine *f*, Fallbeil *n*; **2.** ⊙ Pa'pier,schneidema,schine *f*; **3.** *Brit. parl.* Befristung *f* der De'batte; **II** *v/t.* **4.** guillotinieren, durch die Guillo'tine hinrichten.

guilt [gɪlt] *s.* Schuld *f* (*a.* ♯): *joint ~* Mitschuld; *~ complex* Schuldkomplex *m*; **'guilt·i·ness** [-tɪnɪs] *s.* **1.** Schuld *f*; **2.** Schuldbewusstsein *n*, -gefühl *n*; **'guilt·less** [-lɪs] *adj.* □ **1.** schuldlos, unschuldig (*of* an *dat.*); **2.** *fig.* (*of*) a) unwissend, unerfahren (in *dat.*): *be ~ of s.th.* et. nicht kennen (*a. fig.*), b) frei *od.* unberührt (von), ohne (*acc.*); **'guilt·y** [-tɪ] *adj.* □ schuldig (*of gen.*): *find* (*not*) *~* für (un)schuldig erklären (*on a charge* e-r Anklage); **2.** schuldbewusst, -beladen: *a ~ conscience* ein schlechtes Gewissen.

guin·ea ['gɪnɪ] *s.* **1.** *Brit.* Gui'nee *f* (*£1.05*); **2.** → *~ fowl s.*, *~ hen s.* Perlhuhn *n*; *~ pig s.* **1.** Meerschweinchen *n*; **2.** *fig.* Ver'suchska,ninchen *n*.

guise [gaɪz] *s.* **1.** Gestalt *f*, Erscheinung *f*, Aufmachung *f*: *in the ~ of* als ... (verkleidet); **2.** *fig.* Maske *f*, (Deck-)Mantel *m*: *under the ~ of* in der Maske (*gen.*), unter dem Deckmantel (*gen.*).

gui·tar [gɪ'tɑː] *s.* ♪ Gi'tarre *f*; **gui'tar·ist** [-rɪst] *s.* Gitar'rist(in), Gi'tarrenspieler(in).

gulch [gʌlʃ] *s. Am.* (Berg)Schlucht *f*.

gulf [gʌlf] **I** *s.* **1.** Golf *m*, Meerbusen *m*, Bucht *f*; **2.** *a. fig.* Abgrund *m*, Schlund *m*; **3.** *fig.* Kluft *f*; **4.** Strudel *m*; **II** *v/t.* **5.** *fig.* verschlingen.

gull¹ [gʌl] *s. orn.* Möwe *f*.

gull² [gʌl] **I** *v/t.* über'tölpeln; **II** *s.* Gimpel *m*, Trottel *m*.

gul·let ['gʌlɪt] *s.* **1.** *anat.* Schlund *m*, Speiseröhre *f*; **2.** Gurgel *f*, Kehle *f*; **3.** Wasserrinne *f*; **4.** ⊙ 'Förderka,nal *m*.

gul·li·bil·i·ty [ˌgʌlɪ'bɪlətɪ] *s.* Leichtgläubigkeit *f*, Einfalt *f*; **gul·li·ble** ['gʌləbl] *adj.* leichtgläubig, na'iv.

gul·ly ['gʌlɪ] *s.* **1.** (Wasser)Rinne *f*; **2.** ⊙ a) Gully, Sinkkasten *m*, Senkloch *n*, b) *a.* **~ drain** 'Abzugska,nal *m*: *~ hole* Abflussloch *n*.

gulp [gʌlp] **I** *v/t. mst* **~ down 1.** Speise hin'unterschlingen, *Getränk* hin'unterstürzen; **2.** Tränen, *et.* hin'unterschlucken, unter'drücken; **II** *v/i.* **3.** (*a. vor Rührung etc.*) schlucken; **4.** würgen; **III** *s.* **5.** (großer) Schluck: *at one ~* auf 'einen Zug.

gum¹ [gʌm] *s. mst pl. anat.* Zahnfleisch *n.*

gum² [gʌm] **I** *s.* **1.** ♀, ⊙ a) Gummi *n, m,* b) Gummiharz *n,* c) Kautschuk *m*; **2.** Klebstoff *m, bsd.* Gummilösung *f*; **3.** → a) *chewing gum,* b) *gum arabic,* c) *gum elastic,* d) *gum tree*; **4.** ♀ Gummifluss *m* (*Baumkrankheit*); **5.** 'Gummi (-bon,bon) *m, n*; **6.** *pl. Am.* Gummischuhe *pl.*; **II** *v/t.* **7.** gummieren; **8.** (an-, ver)kleben; **9.** *~ up* zukleben, b) F *et.* ,vermasseln'; **III** *v/i.* **10.** ♀ Gummi absondern (*Baum*).

gum³ [gʌm] *a.* ⸚ *s.*: *my ~!, by ~!* heiliger Strohsack!

gum| am·mo·ni·ac *s.* 🌿, ♣ Ammoni'akgummi *n, m*; *~ ar·a·bic s.* Gum-

G

mia'rabikum *n*; '**~·boil** *s.* ⚕ Zahnge-
schwür *n*; '**~·drop** → **gum²** 5; **~ e·las·**
tic *s.* Gummie'lastikum *n*, Kautschuk
m.
gum·my ['gʌmɪ] *adj.* **1.** gummiartig,
klebrig; **2.** Gummi...; **3.** gummihaltig.
gump·tion ['gʌmpʃn] *s.* F **1.** ‚Köpfchen'
n, ‚Grütze' *f*, ‚Grips' *m*; **2.** ‚Mumm' *m*,
Schneid *m.*
gum| res·in *s.* ⚕ Schleim-, Gummiharz
n; '**~·shield** *s.* Boxen: Zahnschutz *m*;
'**~·shoe** *s. Am.* **1.** F a) 'Gummi,über-
schuh *m*, b) Tennis-, Turnschuh *m*; **2.**
sl. ‚Schnüffler' *m* (*Detektiv, Polizist*); **~**
tree *s.* ⚕ **1.** Gummibaum *m*: *be up a ~*
sl. in der Klemme sein *od.* sitzen; **2.**
Euka'lyptus(baum) *m*; **3.** Tu'pelobaum
m; **4.** Amberbaum; '**~·wood** *s.* Holz
n des Gummibaums (*etc.* → **gum tree**).
gun [gʌn] I *s.* **1.** ✕ Geschütz *n*, Ka'none
f (*a. fig.*): *bring up one's big ~s*
schweres Geschütz auffahren (*a. fig.*);
go great ~s F ‚schwer in Fahrt sein';
stick to one's ~s fig. festbleiben, nicht
weichen *od.* nachgeben; *a big ~ sl.* ‚e-e
große Kanone', ‚ein großes Tier'; **2.**
(*engS.* Jagd)Gewehr *n*, Flinte *f*, Büchse
f; **3.** ‚Ka'none' *f*, Pi'stole *f*, Re'volver
m; **4.** *sport:* a) ‚Startpis,tole *f*, b) Start-
schuss *m*: *jump the ~* e-n Fehlstart verursachen, *fig.* voreilig handeln; **5.** Ka-
'nonen-, Sa'lutschuss *m*; **6.** Schütze *m*,
Jäger *m*; **7.** ✈, ⚙ a) Drosselklappe *f*,
b) Drosselhebel *m*: *give the engine*
the ~ Vollgas geben; II *v/i.* **8.** auf die
Jagd gehen; schießen; **9. ~ for** es abgesehen haben auf *j-n od. et.*; III *v/t.* **10.**
a) schießen auf (*acc.*), b) erschießen, c)
mst ~ down niederschießen; **11.** *oft ~*
up mot. F ‚auf Touren bringen': *~ the*
car up (Voll)Gas geben.
gun| bar·rel *s.* ✕ **1.** Geschützrohr *n*; **2.**
Gewehrlauf *m*; **~ bat·tle** *s.* Feuerge-
fecht *n*, Schieße'rei *f*; '**~·boat** *s.* Ka'no-
nenboot *n*: **~ diplomacy**; **~ cam·er·a**
s. ✈, ✕ 'Foto-M,G *n*; **~ car·riage** *s.*
✕ La'fette *f*; **~ cot·ton** *s.* Schießbaumwolle *f*; **~ dog** *s.* Jagdhund *m*; '**~·fight**
→ **gun battle**; '**~·fire** *s.* ✕ Geschütz-
feuer *n.*
gunge [gʌndʒ] *Brit.* F I *s.* klebrige Masse, klebriges (*od.* schmieriges) Zeug; II
v/t. a. **~ up** verkleben.
gung-ho [,gʌŋ'həʊ] *adj.* F **1.** allzu enthusi'astisch, voller Begeisterung; **2.**
'übereifrig.
gung·y ['gʌndʒɪ] *adj. Brit.* F **1.** klebrig,
schmierig; **2.** eklig, widerlich.
'**gun|-,hap·py** *adj.* schießwütig; **~ har·**
poon *s.* ⚓ Ge'schützhar,pune *f.*
gunk [gʌŋk] *bsd. Am.* F I *s.* klebriges
Zeug; II *v/t. a.* **~ up** verkleben.
gun| li·cence, *Am.* **~ li·cense** *s.* Waf-
fenschein *m*; '**~·lock** *s.* Gewehrschloss
n; '**~·man** [-mən] *s.* [*irr.*] Bewaffnete(r)
m; Re'volverheld *m*; '**~,met·al** *s.* Rotguss *m*; **~ moll** *s. Am. sl.* Gangsterbraut
f; **~ mount** *s.* ✕ La'fette *f.*
gun·ner ['gʌnə] *s.* **1.** ✕ a) Kano'nier *m*,
Artille'rist *m*, b) Richtschütze *m* (*Panzer etc.*), c) M'G-Schütze *m*, Gewehr-
führer *m*; **2.** ✈ Bordschütze *m*; **gun·**
ner·y ['gʌnərɪ] *s.* ✕ Schieß-, Geschütz-
wesen *n*: **~ officer** Artillerieoffizier
m.
gun·ny ['gʌnɪ] *s.* Juteleinwand *f*: **~ (bag)**
Jutesack *m.*
gun| pit *s.* ✕ **1.** Geschützstand *m*; **2.** ✈
Kanzel *f*; '**~·play** → **gun battle**; '**~·**
point *s.*: *at ~* mit vorgehaltener
(Schuss)Waffe; '**~·pow·der** *s.* ✕ Schießpulver *n*: ⚙ **Plot** *hist.* Pulververschwörung *f* (*in London* 1605); '**~·room**

[-rʊm] *s. Brit.* ⚓, ✕ Ka'dettenmesse *f*;
'**~·run·ner** *s.* Waffenschmuggler *m*;
'**~·run·ning** *s.* Waffenschmuggel *m.*
gun·sel ['gʌnsl] *Am. sl.* **1.** → **gunman**;
2. ‚Fiesling' *m*; **3.** Trottel *m.*
'**gun|·ship** *s.* ✈, ✕ Kampfhubschrauber
m; '**~·shot** *s.* (Ka'nonen-, Gewehr-)
Schuss *m*: **~ wound** Schusswunde *f*; **2.**
within (*out of*) **~** in (außer) Schussweite
(*a. fig.*); '**~·shy** *adj.* **1.** *hunt.* schuss-
scheu (*Hund etc.*); **2.** *Am.* F 'misstrauisch; '**~,sling·er** *s. Am.* F → **gunman**;
'**~·smith** *s.* Büchsenmacher *m*; **~ tur·**
ret *s.* ✕ **1.** Geschützturm *m*; **2.** ✈
Waffendrehstand *m.*
gun·wale ['gʌnl] *s.* ⚓ Schandeckel *m*;
2. Dollbord *n* (*am Ruderboot*).
gur·gi·ta·tion [,gɜːdʒɪ'teɪʃn] *s.* (Auf-)
Wallen *n*, Strudeln *n.*
gur·gle ['gɜːgl] *v/i.* gurgeln: a) gluckern
(*Wasser*), b) glucksen (*Stimme, Person,*
Wasser etc.).
Gur·kha ['gɜːkə] *s.* Gurkha *m, f* (*Mitglied e-s indischen Volksstamms*).
gu·ru ['gʊruː] *s.* Guru *m* (*a. fig.*).
gush [gʌʃ] I *v/i.* **1.** her'vorströmen,
-schießen, sich ergießen (*from* aus); **2.**
'überströmen (*with* von); **3.** (*over*) *fig.*
F schwärmen (von), sich 'überschwänglich *od.* verzückt äußern (über *acc.*); II
s. **4.** Schwall *m*, Strom *m*, Erguss *m* (*alle*
a. fig.); **5.** F Schwärme'rei *f*, 'Überschwänglichkeit *f*, (Gefühls)Erguss *m*;
'**gush·er** [-ʃə] *s.* **1.** Springquelle *f* (*Erd-*
öl); **2.** F Schwärmer(in); '**gush·ing**
[-ʃɪŋ] *adj.* □ **1.** ('über)strömend; **2.** →
'**gush·y** [-ʃɪ] *adj.* überschwänglich,
schwärmerisch.
gus·set ['gʌsɪt] I *s.* **1.** *Näherei etc.*:
Zwickel *m*, Keil *m*; **2.** ⚙ Winkelstück *n*,
Eckblech *n*; II *v/t.* **3.** e-n Zwickel *etc.*
einsetzen in (*acc.*).
gust [gʌst] *s.* **1.** Windstoß *m*, Bö *f*; **2.**
fig. (Gefühls)Ausbruch *m*, Sturm *m*
(*der Leidenschaft etc.*).
gus·ta·tion [gʌ'steɪʃn] *s.* **1.** Geschmack
m, Geschmackssinn *m*; **2.** Schmecken
n; **gus·ta·to·ry** ['gʌstətərɪ] *adj.* Geschmacks...
gus·to ['gʌstəʊ] *s.* Begeisterung *f*, Genuss *m*, Gusto *m.*
gust·y ['gʌstɪ] *adj.* □ **1.** böig, stürmisch;
2. *fig.* ungestüm.
gut [gʌt] I *s.* **1.** *pl.* Eingeweide *pl.*, Gedärme *pl.*: *I hate his ~s* F ich hasse ihn
wie die Pest; *I'll have his ~s for*
garters F den mach ich zur Schnecke
(*od.* fertig); **2.** *anat.* a) 'Darm(ka,nal)
m, b) (*bestimmter*) Darm; **3.** *a. pl.* F
Bauch *m*: *know s.th. at ~ level* et. instinktiv (genau) wissen; **4.** (*präparierter*)
Darm; **5.** a) Engpass *m*, b) enge
'Durchfahrt, Meerenge *f*; **6.** *pl.* F a) *das*
Innere: *the ~s of a machine*, b) Kern
m, *das* Wesentliche, c) Gehalt *m*, Sub-
'stanz *f*: *it has no ~s in it* es steckt
nichts dahinter; **7.** *pl.* ‚Mumm' *m*,
Schneid *m*; II *v/t.* **8.** Fisch *etc.* ausnehmen, -weiden; **9.** *Haus etc.* a) ausrauben, b) ausbrennen: *~ted by fire* völlig
ausgebrannt; **10.** *fig. Buch etc.* ‚ausschlachten'; III *adj.* **11.** F instink'tiv,
von innen her'aus, *a.* leidenschaftlich:
a ~ reaction; **12.** von entscheidender
Bedeutung: *a ~ problem*; '**gut·less**
[-lɪs] *adj.* ‚schlaff': a) ohne Schneid, b)
‚müde': *a ~ enterprise*; '**gut·sy** [-tsɪ]
adj. mutig, schneidig.
gut·ta-per·cha [,gʌtə'pɜːtʃə] *s.* **1.** 🌿
Gutta *n*; **2.** ⚕, ⚙ Gutta'percha *n.*
gut·ter ['gʌtə] I *s.* **1.** Dachrinne *f*; **2.**
Gosse *f*, Rinnstein *m*; *fig. contp.*
Gosse *f*: *language of the ~*; *take s.o.*

out of the ~ j-n aus der Gosse auflesen;
4. (Abfluss-, Wasser)Rinne *f*; **5.** ⚙ Rille *f*, Hohlkehlfuge *f*, Furche *f*; **6.** Ku-
gelfangrinne *f* (*der Bowlingbahn*); II
v/t. **7.** furchen, aushöhlen; III *v/i.* **8.**
rinnen, strömen; **9.** tropfen (*Kerze*); IV
adj. **10.** vul'gär, schmutzig, Schmutz...;
~ press *s.* Skan'dal-, Sensati'onspresse
f; '**~·snipe** *s.* Gassenkind *n.*
gut·tur·al ['gʌtərəl] *adj.* □ **1.** Kehl...,
guttu'ral (*beide a. ling.*), kehlig; **2.**
rau, heiser; II *s.* **3.** *ling.* Kehllaut *m*,
Guttu'ral *m.*
guv [gʌv], **guv·nor**, **guv'nor** ['gʌvnə] *sl.*
→ **governor** 4.
guy¹ [gaɪ] I *s.* **1.** F ‚Typ' *m*, Kerl *m*,
‚Bursche' *m*, **~s** *pl.* Leute *pl*; **2.** ‚Vogelscheuche' *f*, ‚Schießbudenfi,gur' *f*; **3.**
Zielscheibe *f* des Spotts; **4.** *Brit.* Spott-
figur *des* Guy Fawkes (*die am* **Guy**
Fawkes Day *verbrannt wird*); II *v/t.* **5.**
F *j-n* lächerlich machen, verulken.
guy² [gaɪ] I *s.* **1.** *a.* **~ rope** Halteseil *n*,
-tau *n*; **2.** a) ⚙ (Ab)Spannseil *n* (*e-s*
Mastes): **~ wire** Spanndraht *m*, b) ⚓
Gei(tau *n*) *f*; **3.** Spannschnur *f* (*Zelt*); II
v/t. **4.** mit e-m Tau *etc.* sichern, verspannen.
Guy Fawkes Day [,gaɪ'fɔːks] *s. Brit. der*
Jahrestag des **Gunpowder Plot** („*Pulververschwörung"* *katholischer Extremisten am 5. November 1605*).
guz·zle ['gʌzl] *v/t.* **1.** *a. v/i.* a) ‚saufen',
b) ,fressen'; **2.** *oft* **~ away** Geld verprassen, *bsd.* ,versaufen'; '**guz·zler** *s.* F
1. Säufer(in); **2.** Fresssack *m.*
gybe [dʒaɪb] *v/t. u. v/i.* ⚓ *Brit.* (sich)
'umlegen (*Segel beim Kreuzen*).
gym [dʒɪm] *s.* F **1.** *abbr. für* **gymnasium**
u. **gymnastics**: **~ shoe** Turnschuh *m*;
~ teacher Turnlehrer(in); **2.** 'Fitness-
,studio *n*, -club *m.*
gym·kha·na [dʒɪm'kɑːnə] *s.* Gym'khana
f (*Geschicklichkeitswettbewerb für Reiter, a. Austragungsort*).
gym·na·si·um [dʒɪm'neɪzjəm] *pl.* **-si·**
ums, **-si·a** [-zjə] *s.* **1.** Turnhalle *f*, *a.*
ped. (*nur das deutsche*) Gym'nasium;
gym·nast ['dʒɪmnæst] *s.* Turner(in); Tur-
ner(in); **gym·nas·tic** [-'næstɪk] I *adj.*
1. (□ **~ally**) gym'nastisch, turnerisch,
Turn..., Gymnastik...; II *s.* **2.** *pl. sg.*
konstr. Turnen *n*, Gym'nastik *f*: **mental**
~s ‚Gehirnakrobatik' *f*; **3.** *mst pl.*
Turn-, Gym'nastikübung *f.*
gyn·ae·co·log·ic, **gyn·ae·co·log·i·cal**
[,gaɪnɪkə'lɒdʒɪk(l)] *adj.* ⚕ gynäko'logisch; **gyn·ae·col·o·gist** [,gaɪnɪ'kɒlə-
dʒɪst] *s.* ⚕ Gynäko'loge *m*, -'login *f*,
Frauenarzt *m*, -ärztin *f*; **gyn·ae·col·o·gy**
[,gaɪnɪ'kɒlədʒɪ] *s.* ⚕ Gynäkolo'gie *f.*
gyp [dʒɪp] *sl.* I *v/i. u. v/t.* **1.** ‚bescheißen', ‚neppen'; II *s.* **2.** a) ‚Beschiss'
m, b) ‚Nepp' *m*; **3.** *give s.o.* **~** *j-n*
‚fertig machen'; **~ joint** *s. sl.* 'Nepplo-
,kal *n.*
gyp·se·ous ['dʒɪpsɪəs] *adj. min.* gipsar-
tig, Gips...; **gyp·sum** ['dʒɪpsəm] *s.*
min. Gips *m.*
gyp·sy ['dʒɪpsɪ] *etc. bsd. Am.* → **gipsy**
etc.
gy·rate I *v/i.* [,dʒaɪə'reɪt] kreisen, sich
(im Kreis) drehen, wirbeln; II *adj.*
['dʒaɪəreɪt] gewunden; **gy'ra·tion** [-eɪ-
ʃən] *s.* **1.** Kreisbewegung *f*, Drehung *f*;
2. *anat.*, *zo.* Windung *f*; **gy·ra·to·ry**
['dʒaɪərətərɪ] *adj.* kreisend, sich (im
Kreis) drehend.
gyr·fal·con ['dʒɜː,fɔːlkən] → **gerfalcon**.
gy·ro·com·pass ['dʒaɪrəʊ,kʌmpəs] *s.*
⚓, *phys.* Kreiselkompass *m*; '**gy·ro-**
graph [-əʊgrɑːf] *s.* ⚙ Um'drehungs-
zähler *m.*

gy·ro ho·ri·zon ['dʒaɪərəʊ] *s. ast.*, ✈ künstlicher Hori'zont.
gy·ro·pi·lot ['dʒaɪərəʊ,paɪlət] *s.* ✈ Auto-pi'lot *m*; **'gy·ro·plane** [-rəpleɪn] *s.* ✈ Tragschrauber *m*; **'gy·ro·scope** [-rə-skəʊp] *s.* **1.** *phys.* Gyro'skop *n*, Krei-sel *m*; **2.** ⚓, ✕ Ge'radlaufappa,rat *m* (*Torpedo*); **gy·ro·scop·ic** [,dʒaɪərə-'skɒpɪk] *adj.* (□ ~ally) Kreisel..., gyro-'skopisch; **gy·ro·sta·bi·liz·er** [,dʒaɪə-rəʊ'steɪbɪlaɪzə] *s.* ⚓, ✈ (Stabilisier-, Lage)Kreisel *m*; **'gy·ro·stat** [-rəʊstæt] *s.* Gyro'stat *m*.
gyve [dʒaɪv] *obs. od. poet.* **I** *s. mst pl.* (*bsd.* Fuß)Fessel *f*; **II** *v/t.* fesseln.

G

H, h [eɪtʃ] *s.* H *n*, h *n* (*Buchstabe*).
ha [hɑː] *int.* ha!, ah!
ha·be·as cor·pus [ˌheɪbjəsˈkɔːpəs] (*Lat.*) *s. a.* **writ of ~** ☆ Vorführungsbefehl *m* zur Haftprüfung: ☆ **Act** Habeas-Corpus-Akte *f* (*1679*).
hab·er·dash·er [ˈhæbədæʃə] *s.* **1.** Kurzwarenhändler(in); **2.** *Am.* Herrenausstatter *m*; **'hab·er·dash·er·y** [-ərɪ] *s.* **1.** a) Kurzwaren *pl.*, b) Kurzwarengeschäft *n*; **2.** *Am.* a) 'Herrenbeˌkleidungsarˌtikel *pl.*, b) Herrenmodengeschäft *n*.
ha·bil·i·ments [həˈbɪlɪmənts] *s. pl.* (Amts)Kleidung *f*, Kleider *pl.*
hab·it [ˈhæbɪt] *s.* **1.** (An)Gewohnheit *f*: **out of ~** aus Gewohnheit; **the force of ~** die Macht der Gewohnheit; **be in the ~ of doing s.th.** pflegen *od.* die (An-)Gewohnheit haben, et. zu tun; **get** (*od.* **fall**) **into a ~** sich et. angewöhnen; **break o.s. of a ~** sich et. abgewöhnen; **make a ~ of s.th.** et. zur Gewohnheit werden lassen; **2.** *oft* **~ of mind** Geistesverfassung *f*; **3.** *psych.* Habit *n*, *a. m*; **4.** ☞ Sucht *f*; **5.** (Amts-, Berufs-)Kleidung *f*, Tracht *f*; **6.** ♀ Habitus *m*, Wachstumsart *f*; **7.** *zo.* Lebensweise *f*.
hab·it·a·ble [ˈhæbɪtəbl] *adj.* □ bewohnbar; **hab·i·tant** *s.* **1.** [ˈhæbɪtənt] Einwohner(in); **2.** [ˈhæbɪtɔ̃ː] a) 'Franko-kaˌnadier *m*, b) Einwohner *m* fran'zösischer Abkunft (*in Louisiana*); **hab·i·tat** [ˈhæbɪtæt] *s.* ♀, *zo.* Habi'tat *n*, Heimat *f*, Stand-, Fundort *m*; **hab·i·ta·tion** [ˌhæbɪˈteɪʃn] *s.* Wohnen *n*; Wohnung *f*, Behausung *f*, Aufenthalt *m*: **unfit for human ~** unbewohnbar.
'hab·itˌform·ing *adj.* **1.** zur Gewohnheit werdend; **2.** ☞ Sucht erzeugend: **~ drug** Suchtmittel *n*.
ha·bit·u·al [həˈbɪtjʊəl] *adj.* □ **1.** gewohnt, üblich, ständig; **2.** gewohnheitsmäßig, Gewohnheits..., *contp. a.* no'torisch: **~ criminal** Gewohnheitsverbrecher *m*; **~ drinker** Gewohnheitstrinker (-in); **ha'bit·u·ate** [-jʊeɪt] *v/t.* **1.** (*o.s.* sich) gewöhnen (**to** an *acc.*; **to doing s.th.** daran, et. zu tun); **2.** *Am.* F frequentieren, häufig besuchen; **ha'bit·u·é** [-jʊeɪ] *s.* ständiger Besucher, Stammgast *m*.
ha·chures [hæˈʃjʊəz] *s. pl.* Schraffierung *f*, Schraf'fur *f*.
hack¹ [hæk] **I** *v/t.* **1.** (zer)hacken: **~ off** abhacken (**von**); **~ out** *fig.* grob darstellen, ‚hinhauen'; **~ to pieces** (*od.* **bits**) in Stücke hacken, *fig.* ‚kaputtmachen'; **2.** (ein)kerben; **3.** ✗ Boden (auf-, los-)hacken; **4.** ❂ Steine behauen; **5.** *sport* *j-n* (gegen das Schienbein) treten; **6.** *Computer:* sich et. als *Hacker* holen (**from** aus); **II** *v/i.* **7.** hacken: **~ at** a) hacken nach, b) einhauen auf (*acc.*); **8.** trocken u. stoßweise husten: **~ing cough** → 14; **9.** *sport* treten, ‚holzen'; **10.** *Computer:* hacken: **~ into a computer system** als *Hacker* in ein Computersystem eindringen; **III** *s.* **11.** Hieb *m*; **12.** Kerbe *f*; **13.** *sport* a) Tritt *m* (gegen das Schienbein), b) Trittwunde *f*; **14.** trockener, stoßweiser Husten.
hack² [hæk] **I** *s.* **1.** a) Reit- *od.* Kutschpferd *n*, b) Mietpferd *n*, Gaul *m*, Klepper *m*; **2.** *Am.* a) (Miets)Droschke *f*, b) F Taxi *n*, c) → **hackie**; **3.** a) Lohnschreiber *m*, Schriftsteller, der auf Bestellung arbeitet, b) Schreiberling *m*; **II** *adj.* **4.** **~ writer** → 3; **5.** einfallslos, mittelmäßig; **6.** → **hackneyed**; **III** *v/i.* **7.** *Brit.* ausreiten; **8.** *Am.* F a) in e-m Taxi fahren, b) ein Taxi fahren; **9.** auf Bestellung arbeiten (*Schriftsteller*).
hack·er [ˈhækə] *s. Computer:* Hacker *m*.
hack·ie [ˈhækɪ] *s. Am.* F Taxifahrer *m*.
hack·le [ˈhækl] **I** *s.* **1.** ❂ Hechel *f*; **2.** a) *orn.* (lange) Nackenfeder(n *pl.*), b) *pl.* (aufstellbare) Rücken- u. Halshaare *pl.* (*Hund*): **have one's ~s up** *fig.* wütend sein; **this got his ~s up**, **his ~s rose** (**at this**) das brachte ihn in Wut; **II** *v/t.* **3.** ❂ hecheln.
hack·ney [ˈhæknɪ] *s.* **1.** → **hack²** 1; **2.** *a.* **~ carriage** Droschke *f*; **'hack·neyed** [-ɪd] *adj. fig.* abgenutzt, abgedroschen.
'hack·saw *s.* ❂ Bügelsäge *f*.
had [hæd; həd] *pret. u. p.p. von* **have**.
had·dock [ˈhædək] *s.* Schellfisch *m*.
Ha·des [ˈheɪdiːz] *s.* **1.** *antiq.* Hades *m*, 'Unterwelt *f*; **2.** F Hölle *f*.
hae·mal [ˈhiːml] *adj. anat.* Blut(gefäß)...; **hae·mat·ic** [hiːˈmætɪk] **I** *adj.* a) blutgefüllt, b) Blut..., c) Blut bildend; **II** *s.* ☞ Hä'matikum *n*, Blut bildendes Mittel; **haem·a·tite** [ˈhemətaɪt] *s. min.* Häma'tit *m*; **hae·ma·tol·o·gy** [ˌhemə-ˈtɒlədʒɪ] *s.* ☞ Hämatolo'gie *f*; **hae·mo·glo·bin** [ˌhiːməʊˈɡləʊbɪn] *s.* Hämoglo-'bin *n*, roter Blutfarbstoff; **hae·mo·phile** [ˈhiːməʊfaɪl] *s.* ☞ Bluter *m*; **hae·mo·phil·i·a** [ˌhiːməʊˈfɪlɪə] *s.* ☞ Bluterkrankheit *f*, Hämophi'lie *f*; **hae·mo·phil·i·ac** [ˌhiːməʊˈfɪlɪæk] → **haemophile**; **haem·or·rhage** [ˈhemərɪdʒ] *s.* (**cerebral ~** Gehirn)Blutung *f*; **haem·or·rhoids** [ˈheməˌrɔɪdz] *s. pl.* ☞ Hämor-r(ho)'iden *pl.*
haft [hɑːft] *s.* Griff *m*, Heft *n*, Stiel *m*.
hag [hæg] *s.* ‚alte Vettel', Hexe *f*.
hag·gard [ˈhæɡəd] **I** *adj.* □ **1.** wild, verstört: **~ look**; **2.** a) abgehärmt, b) sorgenvoll, gequält, c) abgespannt, d) abgezehrt, hager; **3.** **~ falcon** → 4; **II** *s.* **4.** Falke, der ausgewachsen gefangen wurde.
hag·gle [ˈhæɡl] *v/i.* (**about**, **over**) schachern, feilschen, handeln (um); **'hag·gler** [-lə] *s.* Feilscher(in).
hag·i·og·ra·phy [ˌhæɡɪˈɒɡrəfɪ] *s.* Hagiogra'phie *f* (*Erforschung u. Beschreibung von Heiligenleben*); **ˌhag·iˈol·a·try** [-ˈɒlətrɪ] *s.* Heiligenverehrung *f*.
'hagˌrid·den *adj.* **1.** gepeinigt, gequält; **2.** *be* ~ *humor.* von Frauen schikaniert werden.
Hague Con·ven·tions [heɪɡ] *s. pl. pol.* die Haager Abkommen *pl*; **~ Tri·bu·nal** *s. pol.* der Haager Schiedshof.
hail¹ [heɪl] **I** *s.* **1.** Hagel *m* (*a. fig. von* Geschossen, Flüchen etc.*); **II** *v/i.* **2.** *impers.* hageln: **it is ~ing** es hagelt; **3.** *a.* **~ down** *fig.* (**on** auf *acc.*) (nieder)hageln, (nieder)prasseln; **III** *v/t.* **4.** *a.* **~ down** *fig.* (nieder)hageln *od.* (-)prasseln lassen (**on** auf *acc.*).
hail² [heɪl] **I** *v/t.* **1.** freudig *od.* mit Beifall begrüßen, zujubeln (*dat.*); **2.** *j-n, a.* Taxi her'beirufen *od.* -winken; **3.** *fig. et.* begrüßen, begeistert aufnehmen; **II** *v/i.* **4.** *bsd.* ⚓ rufen, sich melden; **5.** (her)stammen, (-)kommen (**from** *od.* aus); **III** *int.* **6.** heil!; **IV** *s.* **7.** Gruß *m*, Zuruf *m*: **within ~** (*od.* **~ing distance**) in Ruf- *od.* Hörweite, *fig.* greifbar nahe; **'hail·er** *s. Am.* Mega'phon *n*.
'hailˌfel·lowˌwell·'met [-ləʊ-] **I** *s.* a) umgänglicher Mensch, b) *contp.* plumpvertraulicher Kerl; **II** *adj.* a) umgänglich, b) *contp.* plumpvertraulich, c) **~ with** (sehr) vertraut *od.* auf Du u. Du mit; **'~stone** *s.* Hagelkorn *n*, -schloße *f*; **'~storm** *s.* Hagelschauer *m*.
hair [heə] *s.* **1.** *ein* Haar *n*: **by a ~** *fig.* ganz knapp *gewinnen etc.*; **to a ~** haargenau; **it turned on a ~** es hing an e-m Faden; **without turning a ~** ohne mit der Wimper zu zucken, kaltblütig; **split ~s** Haarspalterei treiben; **not to harm** (*od.* **hurt**) **a ~ on s.o.'s head** j-m kein Haar krümmen; **2.** *coll.* Haar *n*, Haare *pl.*: **comb s.o.'s ~ for him** (*od.* **her**) F *fig.* j-m gehörig den Kopf waschen; **do one's ~** sich die Haare machen; **get in s.o.'s ~** F j-m auf die Nerven fallen; **have s.o. by the short ~s** F j-n in der Hand haben; **have one's ~ cut** sich die Haare schneiden lassen; **have a ~ of the dog** (**that bit you**) F e-n Schluck Alkohol trinken, um s-n ‚Kater' zu vertreiben; **let one's ~ down** a) sein Haar aufmachen, b) *fig.* sich ungeniert benehmen, c) aus sich herausgehen, d) sein Herz ausschütten; **my ~ stood on end** mir sträubten sich die Haare; **keep s.o. out of one's ~** F sich j-n vom Leib halten; **keep your ~ on!** F nur keine Aufregung; **tear one's ~** sich die Haare raufen; **3.** ♀ Haar *n*; **4.** Härchen *n*, Fäserchen *n*; **'~breadth** *s.*: **by a ~** um Haaresbreite; **escape by a ~** mit knapper Not davonkommen; **'~brush** *s.* **1.** Haarbürste *f*; **2.** Haarpinsel *m*; **~ clippers** *s. pl.* 'Haarschneideˌmaˌschine *f*; **'~cloth** *s.* Haartuch *n*; **~ com·pass·es** *s. pl. a.* **pair of ~** Haar(strich)zirkel *m*; **'~ˌcurl·ing** *adj.* F **1.** grausig; **2.** haarsträubend; **'~cut** *s.* Haarschnitt *m*, *weitS.* Fri'sur *f*: **have a ~** sich die Haare schneiden lassen; **'~do** *pl.* **'~dos** *s.* F Fri'sur *f*; **'~ˌdress·er** *s.* Fri'seur *m*, Fri'seuse *f*; **'~ˌdress·ing** *s.* Frisieren *n*: **~ salon** Friseursalon *m*; **'~ˌdri·er** *s.* Haartrockner *m*: a) Föhn *m*, b) Trockenhaube *f*.
haired [heəd] *adj.* **1.** behaart; **2.** *in Zssgn* ...haarig.
hair fol·li·cle *s. anat.* Haarbalg *m*; **'~grip** *s.* Haarklammer *f*.
hair·i·ness [ˈheərɪnɪs] *s.* Behaartheit *f*;

hair·less ['heəlɪs] *adj.* unbehaart, haarlos, kahl.

'**hair**|·**line** *s.* **1.** Haaransatz *m*; **2.** a) feiner Streifen (*Stoffmuster*), b) fein gestreifter Stoff; **3.** Haarseil *n*; **4.** *a.* ~ **crack** ⊗ Haarriss *m*; **5.** *opt.* Fadenkreuz *n*; **6.** → *hair stroke*; ~ **mat·tress** *s.* 'Rosshaarma,tratze *f*; ~ **net** *s.* Haarnetz *n*; ~ **oil** *s.* Haaröl *n*; '~·**piece** *s.* Haarteil *n*, *für Männer*: Tou'pet *n*; '~·**pin** *s.* **1.** Haarnadel *f*; **2.** *a.* ~ **bend** Haarnadelkurve *f*; '~·,**rais·er** *s.* F *et.* Haarsträubendes, *z.B.* Horrorfilm *m*; '~·,**rais·ing** *adj.* F haarsträubend; ~ **re·stor·er** *s.* Haarwuchsmittel *n*.

hair's breadth → *hairbreadth*.

hair| **shirt** *s.* härenes Hemd; ~ **sieve** *s.* Haarsieb *n*; ~ **slide** *s.* Haarspange *f*; '~·**split·ter** *s. fig.* Haarspalter(in); '~·**split·ting** I *s.* Haarspalte'rei *f*; II *adj.* haarspalterisch; '~·**spring** ⊗ Haar-, Unruhfeder *f*; ~ **stroke** *s.* Haarstrich *m* (*Schrift*); '~·**style** *s.* Fri'sur *f*; ~ **styl·ist** *s.* Hair-Stylist *m*, 'Damenfri,seur *m*; '~·-,**trig·ger** I *s.* Stecher *m* (*am Gewehr*); II *adj.* F **2.** äußerst reizbar (*Person*); **3.** la'bil; **4.** prompt.

hair·y ['heərɪ] *adj.* **1.** haarig, behaart; **2.** Haar...; **3.** F ,haarig', schwierig.

hake [heɪk] *s. ichth.* Seehecht *m*.

ha·la·tion [həˈleɪʃn] *s. phot.* Halo-, Lichthofbildung *f*.

hal·berd ['hælbɜːd] *s.* ✗ *hist.* Helle'barde *f*; **hal·berd·ier** [,hælbəˈdɪə] *s.* Hellebar'dier *m*.

hal·cy·on ['hælsɪən] I *s. orn.* Eisvogel *m*; II *adj.* halky'onisch, friedlich; ~ **days** *s. pl.* **1.** halky'onische Tage *pl.*: a) Tage *pl.* der Ruhe (*auf dem Meer*), b) *fig.* Tage glücklicher Ruhe; **2.** *fig.* glückliche Zeit.

hale [heɪl] *adj.* gesund, kräftig: ~ *and hearty* gesund u. munter.

half [hɑːf] I *pl.* **halves** *s.* **1.** Hälfte *f*: *an hour and a* ~ anderthalb Stunden; ~ (*of*) *the girls* die Hälfte der Mädchen; ~ *the amount* die halbe Menge *od.* Summe; *cut in halves* (*od.* ~) in zwei Hälften *od.* Teile schneiden, halbieren; *do s.th. by halves* et. nur halb tun; *do things by halves* halbe Sachen machen; *not to do things by halves* Nägel mit Köpfen machen; *go halves with s.o.* (gleichmäßig) mit j-m teilen, mit j-m (bei et.) halbpart machen; *too clever by* ~ überschlau; *a game and a* ~ F ein ,Bombenspiel'; *not good enough by* ~ lange nicht gut genug; *torn in* ~ *fig.* hin- u. hergerissen; → *better*[1]; **2.** *sport*: a) Halbzeit *f*, (Spiel)Hälfte *f*, b) (Spielfeld)Hälfte *f*, c) *Golf*: Gleichstand *m*, d) → *halfback*; **3.** Fahrkarte *f* zum halben Preis; **4.** kleines Bier (*halbes Pint*); II *adj.* **5.** halb: *a* ~ *mile*, *mst* ~ *a mile* e-e halbe Meile; ~ *an hour*, *a* ~ *hour* e-e halbe Stunde; *two pounds and a* ~ zweieinhalb Pfund; *a* ~ *share* ein halber Anteil, e-e Hälfte; ~ *knowledge* Halbwissen *n*; *at* ~ *the price* zum halben Preis; *that's* ~ *the battle* damit ist es halb gewonnen; → *mind* 5, *eye* 2; III *adv.* **6.** halb, zur Hälfte: ~ *full*; *my work is* ~ *done*; ~ *as much* halb so viel; ~ *as much again* anderthalbmal so viel; ~ *past ten* halb elf (Uhr); ~ *one* (*two etc.*) F (= *half past one etc.*) halb zwei (drei *etc.*); **7.** halb(wegs), nahezu, fast: ~ *dead* halb tot; *not* ~ *bad* F gar nicht übel; *be* ~ *inclined* beinahe geneigt sein; *he* ~ *wished* (*suspected*) er wünschte (vermutete) fast.

,**half**|-**and**-'**half** [-fən(d)'hɑ-] I *s.* Halb-u.-

halb-Mischung *f*; II *adj.* halb u. 'halb; III *adv.* halb u. halb; '~·**back** *s.* **1.** *obs. Fußball etc.*: Läufer *m*; **2.** *Rugby*: Halbspieler *m*; ,~·'**baked** *adj. fig.* F **1.** ,grün', unreif, unerfahren; **2.** unausgegoren, nicht durch'dacht (*Plan etc.*); **3.** blöd; ~ **bind·ing** *s.* Halb(leder)band *m*; '~·**blood** *s.* **1.** Halbbürtigkeit *f*: *brother of the* ~ Halbbruder *m*; **2.** → *halfbreed* 1; ,~·'**blood·ed** → *half-bred* I; ~ **board** *s. Hotel*: 'Halbpensi,on *f*; ,~·'**bound** *adj.* im Halbband (*Buch*); '~-**bred** I *adj.* halbblütig, Halbblut...; II *s.* Halbblut(tier) *n*; '~·**breed** *s.* **1.** Mischling *m*, Halbblut *n* (*a. Tier*); **2.** *Am.* Me'stize *m*; **3.** ♀ Kreuzung *f*; II *adj.* **4.** → *half-bred*; '~·**broth·er** *s.* Halbbruder *m*; '~·**caste** → *half-breed* 1 *u.* half-bred; '~·**cloth** *adj.* in Halbleinen gebunden, Halbleinen...; ~ **cock** *s.*: *go off at a* ~ F a) vorzeitig ,hochgehen', wütend werden, b) ,da'nebengehen'; ~ **crown** *s. Brit. obs.* Halbkronenstück *n* (*Wert*: 2s.6d.); ~ **deck** *s.* ⚓ Halbdeck *n*; ~ **face** *s. paint.* Pro'fil *n*; ,~·'**heart·ed** *adj.* □ halbherzig; ~ **hol·i·day** *s.* halber Feier- *od.* Urlaubstag; ~ **hose** *s. coll., pl. konstr.* a) Halb-, Kniestrümpfe *pl.*, b) Socken *pl.*; ,~·'**hour** I *s.* halbe Stunde; II *adj.* a) halbstündig, b) halbstündlich; III *adv.* → ,~·'**hour·ly** *adv.* jede *od.* alle halbe Stunde, halbstündlich; ,~·'**length** *s. a.* ~ *portrait* Brustbild *n*; '~·**life** (**pe·ri·od**) *s.* 🔬, *phys.* Halbwertzeit *f*; ~ **mast** *s.*: *fly at* ~ auf halbmast *od.* ⚓ halbstock(s) setzen (*v/i.* wehen); ~ **meas·ure** *s.* Halbheit *f*, halbe Sache; ~ **moon** *s.* **1.** Halbmond *m*; **2.** (Nagel)Möndchen *n*; ~ **mourn·ing** *s.* Halbtrauer *f*; ~ **nel·son** *s. Ringen*: Halbnelson *m*; ,~·'**or·phan** *s.* Halbwaise *f*; ~ **pay** *s.* **1.** halbes Gehalt; **2.** ✗ Halbsold *m*; Ruhegeld *n*: *on* ~ außer Dienst; ~·**pen·ny** ['heɪpnɪ] *s.* **1.** *pl.* **half·pence** ['heɪpəns] halber Penny: *three halfpence, a penny* ~ eineinhalb Pennies; *turn up again like a bad* ~ immer wieder auftauchen; **2.** *pl.* **half·pen·nies** ['heɪpnɪz] Halbpennystück *n*; '~·**pint** *s.* **1.** halbes Pint (*bsd. Bier*); **2.** F ,halbe Porti'on'; '~·**pipe** *s. Skate-, Snowboarden etc.*: 'Halfpipe *f*; ,~·**seas**-'**o·ver** *adj.* ,angesäuselt'; '~·-,**sis·ter** *s.* Halbschwester *f*; ,~·'**staff** → *halfmast*; ~ **term** *s. univ. Brit.* kurze Ferien in der Mitte e-s Trimesters; ,~·'**tide** *s.* ⚓ Gezeitenmitte *f*; ,~·'**tim·bered** *adj.* △ Fachwerk...; ~ **time** *s.* **1.** halbe Arbeitszeit; **2.** *sport* Halbzeit *f*; ,~·'**time** I *adj.* **1.** Halbtags...: ~ *job*; **2.** *sport* Halbzeit...: ~ *score* Halbzeitstand *m*; II *adv.* **3.** halbtags; ,~·'**tim·er** *s.* Halbtagsbeschäftigte(r *m*) *f*; ~ **ti·tle** *s.* Schmutztitel *m*; '~·**tone** *s.* ♪, *paint.*, *typ.* Halbton *m*: ~ *process* Halbtonverfahren *n*; ~ -**track** I *s.* ⊗ Halbkettenantrieb *m*; **2.** Halbkettenfahrzeug *n*; II *adj.* **3.** Halbketten...; '~·**truth** *s.* Halbwahrheit *f*; ,~·'**vol·ley** *s. sport* Halbvolley *m*, Halbflugball *m*; ,~·'**way** I *adj.* **1.** auf halbem Weg *od.* in der Mitte (liegend): ~ *measures* halbe Maßnahmen; II *adv.* **2.** auf halbem Weg, in der Mitte; → *meet* 4; **3.** teilweise, halb(wegs); ,~·**way** '**house** *s.* **1.** auf halbem Weg gelegenes Gasthaus; **2.** *fig.* a) 'Zwischenstufe *f*, -,stati,on *f*, b) Kompro'miss *m*, *n*; **3.** Rehabilitati'onszentrum *n*; '~·**wit** *s.* Schwachkopf *m*, -sinnige(r *m*) *f*, Trottel *m*; ,~·'**wit·ted** *adj.* schwachsinnig, blöd; ,~·'**year·ly** *adv.* halbjährlich.

hal·i·but ['hælɪbət] *s.* Heilbutt *m*.

hal·ide ['hælaɪd] *s.* 🔬 Haloge'nid *n*.

hal·i·to·sis [,hælɪ'təʊsɪs] *s.* Hali'tose *f*, (übler) Mundgeruch.

hall [hɔːl] *s.* **1.** Halle *f*, Saal *m*; **2.** a) Diele *f*, Flur *m*, b) (Empfangs-, Vor-) Halle *f*, Vesti'bül *n*; **3.** a) (Versammlungs)Halle *f*, b) großes (öffentliches) Gebäude: ♫ *of Fame* Ruhmeshalle; **4.** *hist.* Gilden-, Zunfthaus *n*; **5.** *Brit.* Herrenhaus *n* (*e-s Landguts*); **6.** *univ.* a) *a.* ~ *of residence* Stu'dentenheim *n*, b) *Brit.* (Essen *o .im*) Speisesaal *m*, *a. Inst.*: Insti'tut *n*: *Science* ♁; **7.** *hist.* a) Schloss *n*, Stammsitz *m*, b) Fürsten-, Königssaal *m*, c) Festsaal *m*; ~ **clock** *s.* Standuhr *f*.

hal·le·lu·jah, hal·le·lu·iah [,hælɪ'luːjə] I *s.* Halle'luja *n*; II *int.* halle'luja!

hal·liard ['hæljəd] → *halyard*.

'**hall·mark** I *s.* **1.** Feingehaltsstempel *m* (*der Londoner Goldschmiedeinnung*); **2.** *fig.* (Güte)Stempel *m*, Gepräge *n*, (Kenn)Zeichen *n*; II *v/t.* **3.** Gold *od.* Silber stempeln; **4.** *fig.* kennzeichnen, stempeln.

hal·lo [hə'ləʊ] *bsd. Brit. für* **hello**.

hal·loo [hə'luː] I *int.* hallo!, he!; II *s.* Hallo *n*; III *v/i.* (hallo) rufen *od.* schreien: *don't* ~ *till you are out of the wood!* freu dich nicht zu früh!

hal·low[1] ['hæləʊ] *v/t.* heiligen: a) weihen, b) als heilig verehren: ~*ed be Thy name* geheiligt werde Dein Name.

hal·low[2] ['hæləʊ] → *halloo*.

Hal·low·e·en [,hæləʊ'iːn] *s.* Abend *m* vor Aller'heiligen; **Hal·low·mas** ['hæləʊmæs] *s. obs.* Aller'heiligen(fest) *n*.

hall| **por·ter** *s. bsd. Brit.* Ho'tel-, Hausdiener *m*; '~·**stand** *s.* a) *Am. a.* ~ *tree* Garde'robenständer *m*, b) 'Flurgarde,robe *f*.

hal·lu·ci·nate [hə'luːsɪneɪt] *v/i.* halluzinieren; **hal·lu·ci·na·tion** [hə,luːsɪ'neɪʃn] *s.* Halluzinati'on *f*; **hal·lu·ci·na·to·ry** [hə'luːsɪnətərɪ] *adj.* halluzina'torisch; **hal·lu·ci·no·gen** [hə'luːsɪnədʒen] *s.* 🔬 Halluzino'gen *n*.

'**hall·way** *s. Am.* **1.** (Eingangs)Halle *f*, Diele *f*; **2.** Korridor *m*.

halm [hɑːm] → *haulm*.

hal·ma ['hælmə] *s.* Halma(spiel) *n*.

ha·lo ['heɪləʊ] *pl.* **ha·loes, ha·los** *s.* **1.** Heiligen-, Glorienschein *m*, Nimbus *m* (*a. fig.*); **2.** *ast.* Halo *m*, Ring *m*, Hof *m*; **3.** *allg.* Ring *m*, (*phot.* Licht)Hof *m*; '**ha·loed** [-əʊd] *adj.* mit e-m Heiligenschein *etc.* um'geben.

hal·o·gen ['hælədʒen] *s.* 🔬 Halo'gen *n*, Salzbildner *m*: ~ *lamp* Halogenlampe *f*, *mot.* -scheinwerfer *m*.

halt[1] [hɔːlt] I *s.* **1.** a) Halt *m*, Pause *f*, Rast *f*, Aufenthalt *m*, b) *a. fig.* Stillstand *m*: *call a* ~ (*to*) (*fig.* Ein)Halt gebieten (*dat.*); *bring to a* ~ → 4; **2.** 🚆 *Brit.* (Bedarfs-)Haltestelle *f*, Haltepunkt *m*; II *v/t.* **3.** a) Halt machen lassen, anhalten (lassen), *a. fig.* zum Halten *od.* Stehen bringen; **III** *v/i.* **4.** a) anhalten, Halt machen, b) *fig.* zum Stehen *od.* Stillstand kommen: ~*!* halt!

halt[2] [hɔːlt] *v/i.* **1.** *obs.* hinken; **2.** *fig.* ,hinken' (*Vergleich etc.*), (*Vers etc.*) *a.* holpern; **3.** zögern, schwanken, stocken.

hal·ter ['hɔːltə] I *s.* **1.** Halfter *f, m, n*; **2.** Strick *m* (*zum Hängen*); **3.** rückenfreies Oberteil *od.* Kleid mit Nackenband; II *v/t.* **4.** *Pferd* (an)halftern; **5.** *j-n* hängen; '~·**neck** → *halter* 3.

halt·ing ['hɔːltɪŋ] *adj.* □ **1.** *obs.* hinkend; **2.** *fig.* a) hinkend, b) holp(e)rig;

3. stockend; **4.** zögernd, schwankend.
halve [hɑːv] v/t. **1.** halbieren: a) zu gleichen Hälften teilen, b) auf die Hälfte reduzieren; **2.** ⊙ verblatten.
halves [hɑːvz] pl. von **half**.
hal·yard ['hæljəd] s. ♣ Fall n.
ham [hæm] **I** s. **1.** Schinken m: ~ and eggs Schinken mit (Spiegel)Ei; **2.** anat. (hinterer) Oberschenkel, Gesäßbacke f, pl. Gesäß n; **3.** F a) a. ~ actor über'trieben od. mise'rabel spielender Schauspieler, 'Schmierenkomödi,ant (-in), b) fig. contp. ,Schauspieler(in)', c) Stümper(in); **4.** F Ama'teurfunker m; **II** v/t. **5.** F a) e-e Rolle über'trieben od. mise'rabel spielen: ~ it up → 6, b) et. verkitschen; **III** v/i. **6.** über'trieben od. mise'rabel spielen, wie ein 'Schmierenkomödi,ant auftreten.
ham·burg·er ['hæmbɜːgə] s. **1.** Am. Rinderhack n; **2.** a) a. ⚌ steak Fri'delle f, pl. Hamburger m.
Ham·burg steak ['hæmbɜːg] → **hamburger** 2a.
hames [heɪmz] s. pl. Kummet n.
'ham|-,fist·ed, '~-,hand·ed adj. F ungeschickt, tollpatschig.
ha·mite[1] ['heɪmaɪt] s. zo. Ammo'nit m.
Ham·ite[2] ['hæmaɪt] s. Ha'mit(in).
ham·let ['hæmlɪt] s. Weiler m, Flecken m, Dörfchen n.
ham·mer ['hæmə] **I** s. **1.** Hammer m (a. anat.): come (od. go) under the ~ unter den Hammer kommen, versteigert werden; go at it ~ and tongs F a) ,mächtig rangehen', b) (sich) streiten, dass die Fetzen fliegen; ~ and divider pol. Hammer u. Zirkel (Symbol der DDR); ~ and sickle pol. Hammer u. Sichel (Symbol der UdSSR); **2.** Hammer m (Klavier etc.); **3.** sport Hammer m; **4.** ⊙ a) Hammer(werk n) m, b) Hahn m (e-r Feuerwaffe); **II** v/t. **5.** (ein)hämmern, (ein)schlagen: ~ an idea into s.o.'s head fig. j-m e-e Idee einhämmern od. -bläuen; **6.** a. ~ out a) Metall hämmern, bearbeiten, formen, b) fig. ausarbeiten, schmieden, c) Differenzen ,ausbügeln'; **7.** a. ~ together zs.-hämmern, -zimmern; **8.** F a) vernichtend schlagen, sport a. ,über'fahren', b) besiegen; **9.** Börse: Brit. für zahlungsunfähig erklären; **III** v/i. **10.** hämmern (a. Puls etc.): ~ at einhämmern auf (acc.): ~ away draufloshämmern, -arbeiten; ~ away (at) fig. sich abmühen (mit); ~ blow s. Hammerschlag m; ~ drill s. ⊙ Schlagbohrer m.
ham·mered ['hæməd] adj. ⊙ gehämmert, getrieben, Treib...
ham·mer| face s. ⊙ Hammerbahn f; ~ forg·ing s. ⊙ Reckschmieden n; '~-,hard·en v/t. ⊙ kalthämmern; '~-head s. **1.** ichth. Hammerhai m; **2.** ⊙ (Hammer)Kopf m; ~·less ['hæməlɪs] adj. mit verdecktem Schlaghammer (Gewehr); '~-lock s. Ringen: Hammerlock m (Griff); ~ scale s. ⊙ (Eisen)Hammerschlag m, Zunder m; '~-smith s. ⊙ Hammerschmied m; ~ throw s. sport Hammerwerfen n; ~ throw·er s. sport Hammerwerfer m; '~-toe s. ⚕ Hammerzehe f.
ham·mock ['hæmək] s. Hängematte f.
ham·per[1] ['hæmpə] v/t. **1.** (be)hindern, hemmen; **2.** stören.
ham·per[2] ['hæmpə] s. **1.** (Pack-, Trag-) Korb m; **2.** Geschenkkorb m, ,Fresskorb' m.
ham·ster ['hæmstə] s. zo. Hamster m.
'ham·string I s. **1.** anat. Kniesehne f; **2.** zo. A'chillessehne f; **II** v/t. [irr. → string] **3.** (durch Zerschneiden der

Kniesehnen) lähmen; **4.** fig. lähmen.
hand [hænd] **I** s. **1.** Hand f (a. fig.): ~s off! Hände weg!; ~s up! Hände hoch!; be in good ~s fig. in guten Händen sein; fall into s.o.'s ~s j-m in die Hände fallen; give (od. lend) a (helping) ~ (j-m) helfen; give s.o. a ~ up j-m auf die Beine helfen; I am entirely in your ~s ich bin ganz in Ihrer Hand; I have his fate in my ~s sein Schicksal liegt in m-r Hand; he asked for her ~ er hielt um ihre Hand an; get a big ~ F starken Applaus bekommen; → Bes. Redew.; **2.** zo. a) Hand f (Affe), b) Vorderfuß m (Pferd), c) Schere f (Krebs); **3.** pl. Hände pl., Besitz m: change ~s → Bes. Redew.; **4.** (gute od. glückliche) Hand, Geschick n: he has a ~ for horses er versteht es, mit Pferden umzugehen; **5.** oft in Zssgn Arbeiter m, Mann (a. pl.), pl. Leute pl., ♣ Ma'trose: all ~s on deck! alle Mann an Deck!; **6.** Fachmann m, Routini'er m: an old ~ a. ein alter ,Hase' od. Praktikus; a good ~ at sehr geschickt in (dat.), ein guter Golfspieler etc.; **7.** Handschrift f: a legible ~; **8.** Unterschrift f: set one's ~ to a document; **9.** Handbreit f (4 engl. Zoll) (nur für die Größe e-s Pferdes); **10.** Kartenspiel: a) Spieler m, b) Blatt n, Karten pl.: show one's ~ → Bes. Redew., c) Runde f, Spiel n; **11.** (Uhr-) Zeiger m; **12.** Seite f (a. fig.): on the right ~ rechter Hand, rechts; on every ~ überall, ringsum; on all ~s a) überall, b) von allen Seiten; on the one ~, on the other ~ einerseits ... andererseits; **13.** Büschel m, n, Bündel n (Früchte), Hand f (Bananen); **14.** Fußball: Handspiel n: ~s! Hand!;
Besondere Redewendungen:
~ and foot a) an Händen u. Füßen (fesseln), b) fig. hinten u. vorn (bedienen); be ~ in glove (with) a) ein Herz u. 'eine Seele sein (mit), b) b.s. unter 'einer Decke stecken (mit); ~s down mühelos, spielend (gewinnen etc.); ~ in ~ Hand in Hand (a. fig.); ~ over fist a) Hand über Hand (klettern etc.), b) schnell, spielend, c) zusehends; ~ to ~ Mann gegen Mann (kämpfen); at ~ a) nahe, bei der Hand, b) nahe (bevorstehend), c) zur Hand, bereit, d) vorliegend; at first (second) ~ aus erster (zweiter) Hand od. Quelle; at the ~s of s.o. schlechte Behandlung etc. seitens j-s, durch j-n; by ~ a) mit der Hand, b) durch Boten, c) mit der Flasche (ein Kind ernähren); made by ~ handgefertigt, Handarbeit; take s.o. by the ~ a) j-n bei der Hand nehmen, b) F j-n unter s-e Fittiche nehmen; from ~ to mouth von der Hand in den Mund (leben); in ~ a) in der Hand, b) zur Verfügung, c) vorrätig, vorhanden, d) in Bearbeitung, e) fig. in der Hand od. Gewalt, f) im Gange; the matter in ~ die vorliegende Sache; the stock in ~ der Warenbestand; have the situation well in ~ die Lage gut im Griff haben; take in ~ a) et. in die Hand od. in Angriff nehmen, b) F j-n unter s-e Fittiche nehmen; on ~ a) verfügbar, vorrätig, b) vorliegend, c) bevorstehend, d) Am. zur Stelle; have s.th. on one's ~s et. auf dem Hals haben; out of ~ a) kurzerhand, ohne weiteres, b) außer Kontrolle, nicht mehr zu bändigen; get out of ~ a) außer Rand u. Band geraten, Party etc.: a. ausarten, b) außer Kontrolle geraten (Lage etc.); to ~ zur Hand; come to ~ eingehen, eintreffen (Brief etc.); under ~ a) unter Kontrolle, b) unter der

Hand, heimlich; with a heavy ~ mit harter Hand, streng; with a high ~ selbstherrlich, willkürlich; change ~s in andere Hände übergehen, den Besitzer wechseln; force s.o.'s ~ j-n zum Handeln zwingen; get s.th. off one's ~s et. loswerden; have a ~ in s.th. beteiligt sein an e-r Sache, b.s. a. die Hand im Spiel haben bei e-r Sache; have one's ~ in in Übung sein; hold ~s Händchen halten; hold (od. stay) one's ~ sich zurückhalten; join ~s sich die Hände reichen, fig. a. sich verbünden od. zs.-tun; keep one's ~ in in sich in Übung halten; keep a firm ~ on unter strenger Zucht halten; lay (one's) ~s on a) anfassen, b) ergreifen, habhaft werden (gen.), erwischen, c) gewaltsam Hand an j-n legen, d) eccl. ordinieren; I can't lay my ~s on it ich kann es nicht finden; play into s.o.'s ~s j-m in die Hände arbeiten; put one's ~ on a) finden, b) sich erinnern an (acc.); shake ~s sich die Hände schütteln; shake ~s with s.o., shake s.o. by the ~ j-m die Hand schütteln od. geben; show one's ~ fig. s-e Karten aufdecken; take a ~ at a game bei e-m Spiel mitmachen; try one's ~ at s.th. et. versuchen, sich mit et. probieren; wash one's ~s of it a) (in dieser Sache) s-e Hände in Unschuld waschen, b) nichts mit der Sache zu tun haben wollen; I wash my ~s of him mit ihm will ich nichts mehr zu tun haben; → off hand;
II v/t. **15.** ein-, aushändigen, (über')geben, (-)'reichen (s.o. s.th., s.th. to s.o. j-m et.): you have got to ~ it to him F das muss man ihm lassen (anerkennend); **16.** j-m helfen: ~ s.o. into (out of) the car;
Zssgn mit adv.:
hand| a·round v/t. her'umreichen; ~ back v/t. zu'rückgeben; ~ down v/t. **2.** et. her'unter- od. hin'unterreichen; **3.** j-n hin'untergeleiten; **3.** vererben, hinter'lassen (to dat.); **4.** (to) fig. weitergeben (an acc.), über'liefern (dat.); **5.** ⚖ a) Urteil etc. verkünden, b) Entscheidung e-s höheren Gerichts e-m 'untergeordneten Gericht über'mitteln; ~ in v/t. **1.** et. hin'ein- od. her'einreichen; **2.** abgeben, Bericht, Gesuch etc. einreichen; ~ on v/t. **1.** weiterreichen, -geben; **2.** → hand down 3; ~ out v/t. **1.** ausgeben, -teilen, verteilen (to an acc.); **2.** Ratschläge etc. verteilen; **3.** verschenken; ~ o·ver v/t. (to dat.) **1.** über'geben; **2.** über'lassen; **3.** (her)geben, aushändigen; **4.** j-n der Polizei etc. über'geben; ~ up v/t. hin'auf- od. her'aufreichen (to dat.).
'hand|·bag [-ndb-] s. **1.** (Damen)Handtasche f; **2.** Handtasche f, -koffer m; '~·ball [-ndb-] s. sport Handball(spiel n) m; '~·bar·row [-nd,b-] s. **1.** handcart; **2.** Trage f; '~·bell [-ndb-] s. Tisch-, Handglocke f; '~·bill [-ndb-] s. Hand-, Re'klamezettel m, Flugblatt n; '~·book [-ndb-] s. **1.** Handbuch n; **2.** Reiseführer m (of durch, von); '~·brake s. ⊙ Handbremse f; '~·breadth [-ndb-] s. Handbreit f; '~·cart [-ndk-] s. Handkarre(n m) f; '~·clasp [-ndk-] Am. → handshake; '~·craft [-ndk-] → handicraft; '~·cuff [-ndk-] **I** s. mst pl. Handschellen pl.; **II** v/t. j-m Handschellen anlegen: ~ed in Handschellen; ~ drill s. ⊙ Handbohrer m.
-handed [hændɪd] in Zssgn ...händig, mit ... Händen.
'hand|·ful [-ndful] s. **1.** Hand f voll (a. fig.

Personen); **2.** F Plage f (Person od. Sache), 'Nervensäge' f: **he is a ~** er macht einem ganz schön zu schaffen; **'~·glass** [-ndɡ-] s. **1.** Handspiegel m; **2.** (Lese-) Lupe f; **~ gre·nade** s. ✕ 'Handgra,nate f; **'~·grip** [-ndɡ-] s. **1.** Händedruck m; **2.** a. ⊕ Griff m; **3. come to ~s** handgemein werden; **'~·held I** adj. Film: tragbar (Kamera); **II** s. Computer: 'Handheld m, n; **'~·hold** s. **1.** Halt m, Griff m.

hand·i·cap ['hændɪkæp] **I** s. Handikap n: a) sport Vorgabe f, b) Vorgaberennen n od. -spiel n, c) fig. Behinderung f, Hindernis n, Nachteil m, Erschwerung f (**to** für); **II** v/t. sport (a. körperlich od. geistig) (be)hindern, benachteiligen, belasten: **~ped** behindert (etc.), gehandikapt.

hand·i·craft ['hændɪkrɑːft] s. **1.** Handfertigkeit f; **2.** (bsd. Kunst)Handwerk n.

hand·i·ness ['hændɪnɪs] s. **1.** Geschick (-lichkeit f) n; **2.** Handlichkeit f; **3.** Nützlichkeit f.

hand·i·work ['hændɪwɜːk] s. **1.** Handarbeit f; **2.** Werk n.

hand·ker·chief ['hæŋkətʃɪf] s. Taschentuch n.

'hand-,knit(·ted) adj. handgestrickt.

han·dle ['hændl] **I** s. **1.** Griff m, Stiel m; Henkel m (Topf); Klinke f (Tür); Schwengel m (Pumpe); ⊕ Kurbel f: **a ~ to one's name** F ein Titel; **fly off the ~** ,hochgehen', wütend werden; **2.** fig. a) Handhabe f, b) Vorwand m; **II** v/t. **3.** anfassen, berühren; **4.** handhaben, hantieren mit, Maschine bedienen: **~ with care! glass!** Vorsicht, Glas!; **5.** a) ein Thema etc. behandeln, e-e Sache a. handhaben, b) et. erledigen, 'durchführen, abwickeln, c) mit et. od. j-m fertig werden, et. deichseln: **I can ~ it (him)** damit (mit ihm) werde ich fertig; **6.** j-n behandeln, 'umgehen mit; **7.** a) e-n Boxer betreuen, trainieren, b) Tier dressieren (u. vorführen); **8.** sich beschäftigen mit; **9.** Güter befördern, weiterleiten; **10.** ✝ Handel treiben mit; **III** v/i. **11.** sich leicht etc. handhaben lassen; **12.** sich weich etc. anfühlen; **'~·bar** s. Lenkstange f.

hand·ler ['hændlə] s. **1.** Dres'seur m, Abrichter m; **2.** Boxen: a) Trainer m, b) Betreuer m, Sekun'dant m.

han·dling ['hændlɪŋ] s. **1.** Berühren n; **2.** Handhabung f; **3.** Führung f; **4.** a. weitS. Behandlung f; **5.** ✝ Beförderung f; **~ charg·es** s. pl. ✝ 'Umschlagspesen pl.

'hand|·loom s. Handwebstuhl m; **~ lug·gage** s. Handgepäck n; **,~·'made** [-nd'm-] adj. von Hand gemacht, handgefertigt, Hand...; handgeschöpft (Papier): **~ paper** Büttenpapier n; **'~,maid** (**-en**) [-nd,m-] s. **1.** obs. u. fig. Dienerin f, Magd f; **2.** fig. Gehilfe m, Handlanger(in); **,~·me-,down I** adj. **1.** fertig od. von der Stange (gekauft), Konfektions...; **2.** abgelegt, getragen; **II** s. **3.** Konfekti'onsanzug m, Kleid n von der Stange, pl. Konfekti'onskleidung f; **4.** abgelegtes Kleidungsstück; **,~·'op·er·at·ed** adj. ⊕ mit Handantrieb, handbedient, Hand...; **~ or·gan** s. ♪ Drehorgel f; **'~·out** s. **1.** Almosen n (a. fig.), (milde) Gabe, weitS. (Wahl- etc.) Geschenk n; **2.** Pro'spekt m, Hand-, Werbezettel m; **3.** Hand-out n (Informationsunterlage); **'~·pick** v/t. **1.** mit der Hand pflücken od. auslesen: **~ed** handverlesen; **2.** F sorgsam auswählen; **'~·rail** s. Handlauf m; Handleiste f; **'~·saw** s. Handsäge f; **~'s breadth** s. Handbreit f.

hand·sel ['hænsl] s. obs. **1.** Neujahrs-, od. Einstandsgeschenk n; **2.** Morgengabe f; Hand-, Angeld n.

'hand|·set s. teleph. Hörer m; **'~·shake** s. Händedruck m; **'~·signed** adj. handsigniert.

hand·some ['hænsəm] adj. □ **1.** hübsch, schön, gut aussehend, stattlich; **2.** beträchtlich, ansehnlich, stattlich: **a ~ sum**; **3.** großzügig, nobel, ,anständig': **~ is that ~ does** edel ist, wer edel handelt; **come down ~ly** sich großzügig zeigen; **4.** Am. geschickt; **'hand·some·ness** [-nɪs] s. **1.** Schönheit f, Stattlichkeit f, gutes Aussehen; **2.** Beträchtlichkeit f; **3.** Großzügigkeit f.

'hand|·spike s. ♣, ⊕ Handspake f, Hebestange f; **'~·spring** s. sport 'Handstand,überschlag m; **'~·stand** s. sport Handstand m; **,~-to-'hand** adj. Mann gegen Mann: **~ combat** Nahkampf m; **,~-to-'mouth** adj. kümmerlich: **lead a ~ existence** von der Hand in den Mund leben; **'~·wheel** s. ⊕ Hand-, Stellrad n; **'~,writ·ing** s. **1.** (Hand)Schrift f: **~ expert** ᴣ Schriftsachverständige(r m) f; **2.** et. Handgeschriebenes.

hand·y ['hændɪ] adj. □ **1.** zur Hand, bei der Hand, greifbar, leicht erreichbar; **2.** geschickt, gewandt; **3.** handlich, praktisch; **4.** nützlich: **come in ~** (sehr) gelegen kommen; **'~·man** s. [irr.] Mädchen in für alles, Fak'totum n.

hang [hæŋ] **I** s. **1.** Hängen n, Fall m, Sitz m (Kleid etc.); **2.** F a) Sinn m, Bedeutung f, b) (richtige) Handhabung: **get the ~ of s.th.** et. ka'pieren, den ,Dreh' rauskriegen; **3. I don't care a ~** F das ist mir völlig ,schnuppe'; **II** v/t. pret. u. p.p. **hung** [hʌŋ] nur 9 mst **hanged**; **4.** (**on**) aufhängen (an dat.), hängen (an acc.): **~ s.th. on a hook; ~ the head** den Kopf hängen lassen od. senken; **5.** (zum Trocknen etc.) aufhängen: **hung beef** gedörrtes Rindfleisch; **6.** Tür einhängen; **7.** Tapete ankleben; **8.** behängen: **hung with flags; 9.** (auf-) hängen: **~ o.s.** sich erhängen; **I'll be ~ed first** F eher lasse ich mich hängen!; **I'll be ~ed if** F ,ich will mich hängen lassen', wenn; **~ it (all)!** F zum Henker damit!; **10.** → **fire** 6; **III** v/i. **11.** hängen, baumeln (**by**, **on** an dat.); **~** → **bal·ance** 2, **thread** 1; **12.** (her'ab)hängen, fallen (Kleid etc.); **13.** hängen, gehängt werden: **he deserves to ~**; **let s.th. go ~** F sich den Teufel um et. scheren; **let it go ~!** F zum Henker damit!; **14.** (**on**) sich hängen (an dat.), sich klammern (an acc.): **~ on s.o.'s lips** (**words**) fig. an j-s Lippen (Worten) hängen; **15.** (**on**) hängen (an dat.), abhängen (von); **16.** sich senken od. neigen;

Zssgn mit prp.:

hang| a·bout, **~ a·round** v/i. her'umlungern od. sich her'umtreiben in (dat.) od. bei; **~ on** → **hang** 14, 15; **~ o·ver** v/i. **1.** fig. hängen od. schweben über (dat.), drohen (dat.); **2.** sich neigen über (acc.); **3.** aufragen über (acc.);

Zssgn mit adv.:

hang| a·bout, **~ a·round** v/i. **1.** herumlungern, sich her'umtreiben; **2.** trödeln; **3.** warten; **~ back** v/i. **1.** zögern; **2.** → **~ be·hind** v/i. zu'rückbleiben, -hängen; **~ down** v/i. her'unterhängen; **~ on** v/i. **1.** (**to**) a. fig. sich festhalten (an dat.), festhalten (acc.), nicht loslassen od. aufgeben; **2.** teleph. am Appa'rat bleiben; **3.** nicht nachlassen, ,dranbleiben'; **4.** warten; **~ out I** v/t. **1.** (hin- od. her)'aushängen; **II** v/i. **2.** her'aushängen; **3.** ausgehängt sein; **4.** F

a) hausen, sich aufhalten, b) sich her'umtreiben; **~ o·ver I** v/i. **1.** andauern; **II** v/t. **~ be hung over** F e-n ,Kater' haben; **~ to·geth·er** v/i. **1.** zs.-halten (Personen); **2.** zs.-hängen, verknüpft sein; **~ up I** v/t. **1.** aufhängen; **2.** aufschieben, hin'ausziehen: **be hung up** aufgehalten werden; **3. be hung up on** F a) e-n Komplex haben wegen, ,es haben' mit, b) besessen sein von; **II** v/i. **4.** teleph. (den Hörer) auflegen, einhängen: **she hung up on me!** sie legte einfach auf!

hang·ar ['hæŋə] s. Hangar m, Flugzeughalle f, -schuppen m.

'hang·dog I s. **1.** Galgenvogel m, -strick m; **II** adj. **2.** gemein; **3.** jämmerlich: **~ look** Armesündermiene f.

hang·er ['hæŋə] s. **1.** a) (Auf)Hänger m, b) Ankleber m, c) Tapezierer m; **2.** a) Kleiderbügel m, b) Aufhänger m (a. ⊕), Schlaufe f; **3.** a) Hirschfänger m, b) kurzer Säbel.

,hang·er-'on [-ər'ɒn] pl. **,hang·ers-'on** s. contp. **1.** Anhänger m, pl. a. Anhang m; **2.** ,Klette' f.

'hang|·glid·er s. sport **1.** Hängegleiter m, (Flug)Drachen m; **2.** Drachenflieger(in); **'~·glid·ing** s. sport Drachenfliegen n.

hang·ing ['hæŋɪŋ] **I** s. **1.** (Auf)Hängen n; **2.** (Er)Hängen n: **execution by ~** Hinrichtung f durch den Strang; **3.** mst pl. Wandbehang m, Ta'pete f, Vorhang m; **II** adj. **4.** a) (her'ab)hängend, Hänge..., b) hängend, abschüssig, ter'rassenförmig: **~ gardens; 5. a ~ matter** e-e Sache, die e-n an den Galgen bringt; **a ~ judge** ein Richter, der mit der Todesstrafe rasch bei der Hand ist; **~ com·mit·tee** s. Hängeausschuss m (bei Gemäldeausstellungen).

'hang|·man [-mən] s. [irr.] Henker m; **'~·nail** s. ✿ Niednagel m; **'~·out** s. F **1.** ,Bude' f, Wohnung f; **2.** Treffpunkt m, 'Stammlo,kal n; **'~,o·ver** s. **1.** 'Überbleibsel n; **2.** F ,Katzenjammer' m (a. fig.), ,Kater' m; **'~·up** s. F **1.** a) Kom'plex m, b) Fimmel m: **have a ~ about** → **hang** up 3; **2.** Pro'blem n.

hank [hæŋk] s. **1.** Strang m, Docke f (Garn etc.); **2.** Hank n (ein Garnmaß); **3.** ♣ Legel m.

han·ker ['hæŋkə] v/i. sich sehnen (**after**, **for** nach); **'han·ker·ing** [-ərɪŋ] s. Sehnsucht f, Verlangen n (**after**, **for** nach).

han·ky, a. **han·kie** ['hæŋkɪ] F → **handkerchief**.

han·ky-pan·ky [,hæŋkɪ'pæŋkɪ] s. sl. **1.** Hokus'pokus m; **2.** ,fauler Zauber', ,Mätzchen' n od. pl., Trick(s pl.) m; **3.** ,Techtelmechtel' n.

Han·o·ve·ri·an [,hænəʊ'vɪərɪən] **I** adj. han'nover(i)sch; pol. hist. hannove'ranisch; **II** s. Hannove'raner(in).

Han·sard ['hænsəd] s. parl. Brit. Parla'mentsproto,koll n.

hanse [hæns] s. hist. **1.** Kaufmannsgilde f; **2.** ⌾ Hanse f, Hansa f; **Han·se·at·ic** [,hænsɪ'ætɪk] adj. hanse'atisch, Hanse...: **~ the ~ League** die Hanse.

han·sel → **handsel**.

han·som (**cab**) ['hænsəm] s. Hansom m (zweirädrige Kutsche).

hap [hæp] obs. **I** s. a) Zufall m, b) Glücksfall m; **II** v/i. → **happen**; **,hap-'haz·ard** [-'hæzəd] **I** adj. u. adv. plan-, wahllos, willkürlich; **II** s.: **at ~** aufs Geratewohl; **'hap·less** [-lɪs] adj. □ glücklos, unglücklich.

hap·pen ['hæpən] v/i. **1.** geschehen, sich ereignen, vorkommen, -fallen, passieren, stattfinden, vor sich gehen: **what has ~ed?** was ist geschehen od. pas-

H

siert?; *... and nothing ~ed ...* u. nichts geschah; **2.** *impers.* zufällig geschehen, sich zufällig ergeben, sich (gerade) treffen: *it ~ed that* es traf *od.* ergab sich, dass; *as it ~s* a) wie es sich gerade trifft, b) wie es nun einmal so ist; **3.** *~ to inf.*: *we ~ed to hear it* wir hörten es zufällig; *it ~ed to be hot* zufällig war es heiß; **4.** *~ to* geschehen mit (*od. dat.*), passieren (*dat.*), zustoßen (*dat.*), werden aus: *what is going to ~ to his plan?* was wird aus s-m Plan?; *if anything should ~ to me* sollte mir et. zustoßen; **5.** *~ (up)on* a) zufällig begegnen (*dat.*) *od.* treffen (*acc.*), b) zufällig stoßen (auf *acc.*) *od.* finden (*acc.*); **6.** *~ along* F zufällig kommen; *~ in* F ,hereinschneien'; **hap·pen·ing** ['hæpnɪŋ] *s.* **1.** a) Ereignis *n*, b) Eintreten *n e-s* Ereignisses; **2.** *thea. u. humor.* Happening *n*: *~ artist* Happenist *m*; **hap·pen·stance** ['hæpənstæns] *s. Am.* F Zufall *m*.

hap·pi·ly ['hæpɪlɪ] *adv.* **1.** glücklich; **2.** glücklicherweise, zum Glück; **'hap·pi·ness** [-ɪnɪs] *s.* **1.** Glück *n* (*Gefühl*); **2.** glückliche Wahl (*e-s Ausdrucks etc.*), glückliche Formulierung; **hap·py** ['hæpɪ] *adj.* □ → *happily*; **1.** *allg.* glücklich: a) glückselig, b) beglückt, erfreut (*at, about* über *acc.*): *I am ~ to see you* es freut mich, Sie zu sehen; *I would be ~ to do that* ich würde das sehr *od.* liebend gern tun; *I am quite ~* (, *thank you*)*!* (danke,) ich bin wunschlos glücklich!, c) voller Glück: *~ days*, d) erfreulich: *~ event* freudiges Ereignis, e) Glück verheißend: *~ news*, f) gut, trefflich: *~ idea*, g) geglückt, treffend, passend: *a ~ phrase*; **2.** *in Glückwünschen*: *~ new year!* gutes neues Jahr!; **3.** F beschwipst, ,angesäuselt'; **4.** *in Zssgn* a) F wirr (im Kopf), benommen: → *slaphappy*, b) begeistert, ,verrückt', -freudig, -lustig → *trigger·happy*.

hap·py| dis·patch *s. euphem.* Hara'kiri *n*; **,~-go-'luck·y** [-gəʊ-] *adj. u. adv.* unbekümmert, sorglos, leichtfertig, lässig.

hap·tic ['hæptɪk] *adj.* haptisch.

har·a·ki·ri [,hærə'kɪrɪ] *s.* Hara'kiri *n* (*a. fig.*).

ha·rangue [hə'ræŋ] **I** *s.* **1.** Ansprache *f*, (flammende) Rede; **2.** Ti'rade *f*; **3.** Strafpredigt *f*; **II** *v/i.* **4.** e-e (bom'bastische *od.* flammende) Rede halten (*v/t.* vor *dat.*); **5.** e-e Strafpredigt halten (*v/t.* j-m).

har·ass ['hærəs] *v/t.* **1.** a) (ständig) belästigen, schikanieren, quälen, b) aufreiben, zermürben: *~ed* mitgenommen, (von Sorgen) gequält, (viel) geplagt; **2.** ✕ stören: *~ing fire* Störfeuer *n*; **'har·ass·ment** [-mənt] *s.* **1.** Belästigung *f*; **2.** Schikanieren *n*, Schi'kane(n *pl.*) *f*: *~ at work* 'Mobbing *n*; **3.** ✕ 'Störma,növer *pl.*

har·bin·ger ['hɑːbɪndʒə] **I** *s. fig.* a) Vorläufer *m*, b) Vorbote *m*: *the ~ of spring*; **II** *v/t. fig.* ankündigen.

har·bo(u)r ['hɑːbə] **I** *s.* **1.** Hafen *m*; **2.** *fig.* Zufluchtsort *m*, 'Unterschlupf *m*; **II** *v/t.* **3.** beherbergen, Schutz *od.* Zuflucht gewähren (*dat.*); **4.** verbergen, verstecken: *~ criminals*; **5.** *Gedanken, Groll etc.* hegen: *~ thoughts of revenge*; **III** *v/i.* **6.** ♴ (im Hafen) vor Anker gehen; *~ bar* Sandbank *f* vor dem Hafen; *~ dues* *s. pl.* Hafengebühren *pl.*; *~ mas·ter* *s.* Hafenmeister *m*; *~ seal* *s. zo.* Gemeiner Seehund.

hard [hɑːd] **I** *adj.* **1.** *allg.* hart (*a. Farbe, Stimme etc.*); **2.** fest: *~ knot*; **3.** schwer,

schwierig: a) mühsam, anstrengend, hart: *~ work*, b) schwer zu bewältigen(d): *~ problems* schwierige Probleme; *~ to believe* kaum zu glauben; *~ to imagine* schwer vorstellbar; *~ to please* schwer zufrieden zu stellen(d), ,schwierig' (*Kunde etc.*); **4.** hart, zäh, 'widerstandsfähig: *in ~ condition* sport konditionsstark, fit; *a ~ customer* F ein schwieriger ,Kunde', ein zäher Bursche; → *nail* Bes. Redew.; **5.** hart, angestrengt: *~ studies*; **6.** hart arbeitend, fleißig: *a ~ worker*; *try one's ~est* sich alle Mühe geben; **7.** heftig, stark: *a ~ rain*; *a ~ blow* ein harter *od.* schwerer Schlag (*a. fig.* *to* für); *be ~ on Kleidung etc.* (sehr) strapazieren (→ 8); **8.** hart: a) streng, rau: *~ climate* (*winter*), b) *fig.* hartherzig, gefühllos, streng, c) nüchtern, kühl (überlegend): *a ~ businessman*, d) drückend: *be ~ on s.o.* j-n hart anfassen *od.* behandeln; *it is ~ on him* es ist hart für ihn; *the ~ facts* die harten *od.* nackten Tatsachen; *~ sell*(ing) aggressive Verkaufstaktik; *~ times* schwere Zeiten; *have a ~ time* Schlimmes durchmachen (müssen); *he had a ~ time doing it* es fiel ihm schwer, dies zu tun; *give s.o. a ~ time* j-m hart zusetzen, j-m das Leben sauer machen; **9.** a) sauer, herb (*Getränk*), b) hart (*Droge*), *Getränk*: *a.* stark, 'hochpro,zentig; **10.** *phys.* hart: *~ water*; *~ X rays*; *~ wheat* ✏ Hartweizen *m*; **11.** ♴ hart (*Währung etc.*): *~ dollars*; *~ prices* harte *od.* starre Preise; **12.** *Phonetik*: a) hart, stimmlos, b) nicht palatalisiert; **13.** *~ up* a) schlecht bei Kasse, in (Geld)Schwierigkeiten, b) in Verlegenheit (*for* um); **II** *adv.* **14.** hart, fest; **15.** *fig.* hart, schwer: *work ~*; *think ~*; *drink ~* ein starker Trinker sein; *it will go ~ with him* es wird unangenehm für ihn sein; *hit s.o. ~* a) j-n hart Schlag versetzen, b) *fig.* ein harter Schlag für j-n sein; *~ hit* schwer betroffen; *be ~ pressed, be ~ put to it* in schwerer Bedrängnis sein; *look ~ at* scharf ansehen; *try ~* sich alle Mühe geben; → *die¹* 1; **16.** nah(e), dicht: *~ by* ganz in der Nähe; *~ on* (*od. after*) gleich nach; *~ aport* ♴ hart Backbord; **II** *v/i.* **17.** *get* (*have*) *a ~ on* V e-n ,Ständer' kriegen (haben).

,hard-and-'fast *adj.* fest, bindend, 'unumstößlich: *a ~ rule*; '*~-back* → *hardcover* II; '*~-ball* *s. Am.* Baseball(spiel *n*) *m*; **,~-'bit·ten** *adj.* **1.** verbissen, hartnäckig; **2.** → *hard-boiled* 2a; '*~-board* *s.* Hartfaserplatte *f*; **,~-'boiled** *adj.* **1.** hart (gekocht): *a ~ egg*; **2.** F ,knallhart': a) ,abgebrüht', ,hartgesotten', b) ,ausgekocht', gerissen, c) von hartem Rea'lismus: *~ fiction*; *~ case* *s.* **1.** Härtefall *m*; **2.** schwieriger Mensch; **3.** ,schwerer Junge' (*Verbrecher*); *~ cash* *s.* ♴ **1.** a) Hartgeld *n*, b) Bargeld *n*: *pay in ~* (in) bar (be)zahlen; **2.** klingende Münze; *~ coal* *s.* Anthra'zit *m*, Steinkohle *f*; *~ cop·y* *s. Computer*: Hard Copy *f*, Ausdruck *m*; *~ core* *s.* **1.** *Brit.* Schotter *m*; **2.** *fig.* harter Kern (*e-r Bande etc.*); **,~-'core** *adj. fig.* **1.** zum harten Kern gehörend; **2.** hart: *~ pornography*; *~ court* *s. Tennis*: Hartplatz *m*; '*~,cov·er* **I** *adj.* gebunden: *~ edition*; **II** *s.* Hard cover *n*, gebundene Ausgabe; *~ cur·ren·cy* *s.* ♴ harte Währung; *~ disk* *s. Computer*: Festplatte *f*; *~ drive* Festplattenlaufwerk *n*.

hard·en ['hɑːdn] **I** *v/t.* **1.** härten (*a.* ⊛), hart *od.* härter machen; **2.** *fig.* hart *od.*

gefühllos machen, verhärten: *~ed* verstockt, ,abgebrüht'; *a ~ed sinner* ein verstockter Sünder; **3.** bestärken; **4.** abhärten (*to* gegen); **II** *v/i.* **5.** hart werden, erhärten; **6.** *fig.* hart *od.* gefühllos werden, sich verhärten; **7.** *fig.* sich abhärten (*to* gegen); **8.** a) ♴ *u. fig.* sich festigen, b) ♴ anziehen, steigen (*Preise*); **'hard·en·er** [-nə] *s.* Härtemittel *n*, Härter *m*; **'hard·en·ing** [-nɪŋ] **I** *s.* Härten *n*, Härtung *f* (*a.* ⊛): *~ of the arteries* Arterienverkalkung *f*; **2.** → *hardener*; **II** *adj.* **3.** Härte...

,hard-'fea·tured *adj.* mit harten *od.* groben Gesichtszügen; *~ fi·ber*, *Brit.* **fi·bre** *s.* ⊛ Hartfaser *f*; *~ goods* *s. pl.* ♴ *Am.* Gebrauchsgüter *pl.*; *~ hat* *s.* **1.** *Brit.* Me'lone *f* (*Hut*); **2.** a) Schutzhelm *m*, b) F Bauarbeiter *m*; **3.** *Brit.* 'Erzreaktio,när *m*; **,~-'head·ed** *adj.* **1.** praktisch, nüchtern, rea'listisch; **2.** *Am.* starrköpfig, stur; **,~-'heart·ed** *adj.* □ hart(herzig), **,~-'hit·ting** *adj. fig.* hart, aggres'siv.

har·di·hood ['hɑːdɪhʊd], **'har·di·ness** [-ɪnɪs] *s.* **1.** Ausdauer *f*, Zähigkeit *f*; **2.** ♀ Winterfestigkeit *f*; **3.** Kühnheit *f*: a) Tapferkeit *f*, b) Verwegenheit *f*, c) Dreistigkeit *f*.

hard| la·bo(u)r *s.* ♴ Zwangsarbeit *f*; *~ line* *s.* **1.** *bsd. pol.* harte Linie, harter Kurs: *follow od. adopt a ~* e-n harten Kurs einschlagen; **2.** *pl.* Brit. ,Pech' (*on* für); **,~-'line** *adj. bsd. pol.* hart, kompro'misslos; **,~-'lin·er** *s. bsd. pol.* j-d, der e-n harten Kurs einschlägt; **,~-'luck sto·ry** *s. contp.*, ,Jammergeschichte'.

hard·ly ['hɑːdlɪ] *adv.* **1.** kaum, fast nicht: *~ ever* fast nie; *I ~ know her* ich kenne sie kaum; **2.** (wohl) kaum, schwerlich; **3.** mühsam, mit Mühe; **4.** hart, streng.

hard| mon·ey → *hard cash*; **,~-'mouthed** *adj.* **1.** hartmäulig (*Pferd*); **2.** *fig.* starrköpfig.

hard·ness ['hɑːdnɪs] *s.* **1.** Härte *f* (*a. fig.*); **2.** Schwierigkeit *f*; **3.** Hartherzigkeit *f*; **4.** 'Widerstandsfähigkeit *f*; **5.** Strenge *f*, Härte *f*.

,hard-'nosed F → a) *hard-boiled* 2a, b) *hard-headed* 2; *~ pan* *s.* **1.** *geol.* Ortstein *m*; **2.** harter Boden; **3.** *fig.* a) Grund(lage *f*) *m*, b) Kern *m* (der Sache); **,~-'press·ed** *adj.* (hart) bedrängt, unter Druck stehend; *~ re·turn* *s. Computer*: ,harte' Zeilenschaltung (*per Absatzmarke*); *~ rock* *s.* ♪ Hardrock *m*; *~ rub·ber* *s.* Hartgummi *m*; *~ sci·ence* *s.* (e-e) ex'akte Wissenschaft; *~ sell* *s.* aggressive Verkaufsmethode *f*; **,~-'set** *adj.* **1.** hart bedrängt; **2.** streng, starr; **3.** angebrütet (*Ei*); **'~-shell** *adj.* **1.** *zo.* hartschalig; **2.** *Am.* F ,eisern'.

hard·ship ['hɑːdʃɪp] *s.* **1.** Not *f*, Elend *n*; **2.** *a.* ♴ Härte *f*: *work ~ on s.o.* e-e Härte bedeuten für j-n; *~ case* Härtefall *m*.

hard| shoul·der *s. mot. Brit.* Standspur *f*; *~ sol·der* *s.* ⊛ Hartlot *n*; **'~-,sol·der** *v/t. u. v/i.* hartlöten; *~ tack* *s.* Schiffszwieback *m*; '*~-top* *s. mot.* Hardtop *n*, *m*: a) *festes, abnehmbares Autodach*, b) Auto mit *a*; '*~-ware* *s.* a) Me'tall-, Eisenwaren (*pl.*), b) Haushaltswaren *pl.*; **2.** *Computer, a. Sprachlabor*: Hardware *f*; **3.** *a. military ~* Waffen *pl.* u. mili'tärische Ausrüstung; **4.** *Am. sl.* Schießeisen *n od. pl.*; '*~-wood* *s.* Hartholz *n*, *bsd.* Laubbaumholz *n*; **,~-'work·ing** *adj.* fleißig, hart arbeitend.

har·dy ['hɑːdɪ] *adj.* □ **1.** a) zäh, ro'bust, b) abgehärtet; **2.** ♀ winterfest: *~ annual* a) winterfeste Pflanze, b) *humor.*

Frage, die jedes Jahr wieder aktuell wird; **3.** kühn: a) tapfer, b) verwegen, c) dreist.

hare [heə] **I** *s. zo.* Hase *m*: **run with the ~ and hunt with the hounds** *fig.* es mit beiden Seiten halten; **start a ~** *fig.* vom Thema ablenken; **~ and hounds** Schnitzeljagd *f*; **II** *v/i* F flitzen, sausen: **~ off** da'vonsausen; '**~·bell** *s.* ♣ Glockenblume *f*; '**~·brained** *adj.* ,verrückt'; '**~·foot** *s.* [*irr.*] ♥ **1.** Balsabaum *m*; **2.** Ackerklee *m*; ,**~·lip** ♪ Hasenscharte *f*.

ha·rem ['hɑːriːm] *s.* Harem *m*.

'**hare's-foot** → **harefoot**.

har·i·cot ['hærɪkəʊ] *s.* **1.** a. **~ bean** Gartenbohne *f*; **2.** 'Hammelra,gout *n*.

hark [hɑːk] *v/i.* **1.** *obs. u. poet.* horchen: **~ at him!** *Brit.* F hör dir ihn (*od.* den) an!; **2. ~ back** a) *hunt.* auf der Fährte zu'rückgehen (*Hund*), b) *fig.* zu'rückgreifen, -kommen, (*a. zeitlich*) zu'rückgehen (**to** auf *acc.*); '**hark·en** ['hɑːkən] → **hearken**.

har·le·quin ['hɑːlɪkwɪn] **I** *s.* Harlekin *m*, Hans'wurst *m*; **II** *adj.* bunt, scheckig; **har·le·quin·ade** [,hɑːlɪkwɪ'neɪd] *s.* Harleki'nade *f*, Possenspiel *n*.

har·lot ['hɑːlət] *obs.* Hure *f*, Metze *f*; '**har·lot·ry** [-rɪ] *s.* Hure'rei *f*.

harm [hɑːm] **I** *s.* **1.** Schaden *m*: **bodily ~** körperlicher Schaden, ✝ Körperverletzung *f*; **come to ~** zu Schaden kommen; **do ~ to s.o.** j-m schaden, j-m et. antun; (**there is**) **no ~ done!** es ist nichts (Schlimmes) passiert!; **it does more ~ than good** es schadet mehr, als dass es nützt; **there is no ~ in doing (s.th.)** es kann *od.* könnte nicht schaden, (et.) zu tun; **mean no ~** es nicht böse meinen; **keep out of ~'s way** die Gefahr meiden; **out of ~'s way** a) in Sicherheit, b) in sicherer Entfernung; **2.** Unrecht *n*, Übel *n*; **II** *v/t.* **3.** schaden (*dat.*), j-n verletzen (*a. fig.*); '**harm·ful** [-fʊl] *adj.* □ nachteilig, schädlich (**to** für): **~ publications** ✝ jugendgefährdende Schriften; '**harm·ful·ness** [-fʊl-nɪs] *s.* Schädlichkeit *f*; '**harm·less** [-lɪs] *adj.* □ **1.** harmlos: a) unschädlich, b) unschuldig, arglos, c) unverfänglich; **2. keep** (*od.* **save**) **s.o. ~** ✝ j-n schadlos halten; '**harm·less·ness** [-lɪsnɪs] *s.* Harmlosigkeit *f*.

har·mon·ic [hɑː'mɒnɪk] **I** *adj.* (□ **~ally**) **1.** ♪, ℛ, *phys.* har'monisch (*a. fig.*); **II** *s.* **2.** ♪, *phys.* Har'monische *f*: a) Oberton *m*, b) Oberwelle *f*; **3.** *pl. oft sg. konstr.* ♪ Harmo'nielehre *f*; **har·mon·i·ca** [-kə] *s.* **1.** *hist.* 'Glashar,monika *f*; **2.** 'Mundhar,monika *f*; **har·mo·ni·ous** [-'məʊnjəs] *adj.* □ har'monisch: a) ebenmäßig, b) wohlklingend, c) über'einstimmend, d) einträchtig; **har·mo·ni·ous·ness** [-'məʊnjəsnɪs] *s.* Harmo'nie *f*; **har·mo·ni·um** [-'məʊnjəm] *s.* ♪ Har'monium *n*; **har·mo·nize** ['hɑːmə-naɪz] **I** *v/i.* **1.** harmonieren (*a.* ♪), zs.-passen, in Einklang sein (**with** mit); **II** *v/t.* **2.** (**with**) harmonisieren, in Einklang bringen (mit); **3.** versöhnen; **4.** ♪ harmonisieren, mehrstimmig setzen; **har·mo·ny** ['hɑːmənɪ] *s.* **1.** Harmo'nie *f*: a) Wohlklang *m*, b) Eben-, Gleichmaß *n*, c) Einklang *m*, Eintracht *f*; **2.** ♪ Harmo'nie *f*.

har·ness ['hɑːnɪs] **I** *s.* **1.** (Pferde- *etc.*) Geschirr *n*: **in ~** *fig.* in der (täglichen) Tretmühle; **die in ~** in den Sielen sterben; **~ horse** *Am.* Traber(pferd *n*) *m*; **~ race** *Am.* Trabrennen *n*; **2.** a) *mot. etc.* (Sicherheits)Gurt *m* (*für Kinder*), b) (Fallschirm)Gurtwerk *n*; **3.** Laufge-

schirr *n für Kinder*; **4.** *Am. sl.* (Arbeits-) Kluft *f*, Uni'form *f* (*e-s Polizisten etc.*); **5.** ✗ *hist.* Harnisch *m*; **II** *v/t.* **6.** *Pferd etc.* a) anschirren, b) anspannen (**to an** *acc.*); **7.** *fig. Naturkräfte etc.* nutzbar machen.

harp [hɑːp] **I** *s.* **1.** ♪ Harfe *f*; **II** *v/i.* **2.** (die) Harfe spielen; **3.** *fig.* (**on**, **upon**) her'umreiten (auf *dat.*), dauernd reden (von); → **string** 5; '**harp·er** [-pə], '**harp·ist** [-pɪst] *s.* Harfe'nist(in).

har·poon [hɑː'puːn] **I** *s.* Har'pune *f*: **~ gun** Harpunengeschütz *n*; **II** *v/t.* harpunieren.

harp·si·chord ['hɑːpsɪkɔːd] *s.* ♪ Cembalo *n*.

har·py ['hɑːpɪ] *s.* **1.** *antiq.* Har'pyie *f*; **2.** *fig.* a) ,Geier' *m*, Blutsauger *m*, b) Hexe *f* (*Frau*).

har·que·bus ['hɑːkwɪbəs] *s.* ✗ *hist.* Hakenbüchse *f*, Arke'buse *f*.

har·ri·dan ['hærɪdən] *s.* alte Vettel.

har·ri·er[1] ['hærɪə] *s.* **1.** Verwüster *m*; Plünderer *m*; **2.** *orn.* Weihe *f*.

har·ri·er[2] ['hærɪə] *s.* **1.** *hunt.* Hund *m* für die Hasenjagd; **2.** *sport* Querfeld'einläufer(in).

Har·ro·vi·an [hə'rəʊvjən] *s.* Schüler *m* (*der Public School*) von Harrow.

har·row ['hærəʊ] **I** *s.* **1.** ✗ Egge *f*: **under the ~** *fig.* in großer Not; **II** *v/t.* **2.** ✗ eggen; **3.** *fig.* quälen, peinigen; *Gefühl* verletzen; '**har·row·ing** [-əʊɪŋ] *adj.* □ quälend, qualvoll, schrecklich.

har·rumph [hə'rʌmpf] *v/i.* **1.** sich (gewichtig) räuspern; **2.** missbilligend schnauben.

har·ry[1] ['hærɪ] *v/t.* **1.** verwüsten; **2.** plündern; **3.** quälen, peinigen.

Har·ry[2] ['hærɪ] *s.* **old ~** der Teufel; **play old ~ with** Schindluder treiben mit, ,zur Sau' machen.

harsh [hɑːʃ] *adj.* □ **1.** *allg.* hart: a) rau: **~ cloth**, b) rau, scharf: **~ voice**, **~ note**, c) grell: **~ colo(u)r**, d) barsch, schroff: **~ words**, e) streng: **~ penalty**; **2.** herb, scharf, sauer: **~ taste**; '**harsh·ness** [-nɪs] *s.* Härte *f*.

hart [hɑːt] *s.* Hirsch *m* (*nach dem 5. Jahr*): **~ of ten** Zehnender *m*.

har·te·beest ['hɑːtɪbiːst] *s. zo.* 'Kuhanti,lope *f*.

'**harts·horn** *s.* ℛ Hirschhorn *n*: **salt of ~** Hirschhornsalz *n*.

har·um-scar·um [,heərəm'skeərəm] **I** *adj.* F **1.** leichtsinnig, ,verrückt'; **2.** flatterhaft; **II** *s.* **3.** leichtsinniger *etc.* Mensch.

har·vest ['hɑːvɪst] **I** *s.* **1.** Ernte *f*: a) Ernten *n*, b) Erntezeit *f*, c) (Ernte)Ertrag *m*; **2.** *fig.* Ertrag *m*, Früchte *pl.*; **II** *v/t.* **3.** ernten, *fig. a.* einheimsen; **4.** *Ernte* einbringen; **5.** *fig.* sammeln; **III** *v/i.* **6.** die Ernte einbringen; '**har·vest·er** [-tə] *s.* **1.** Erntearbeiter(in); **2.** a) 'Mäh-, 'Erntema,schine *f*, b) Mähbinder *m*: **combine ~** Mähdrescher *m*.

har·vest· fes·ti·val *s.* Ernte'dankfest *n*; **~ home** *s.* **1.** Ernte(zeit) *f*; **2.** Erntefest *n*; **3.** Erntelied *n*; **~ moon** *s.* Vollmond *m* (*im September*).

has [hæz; həz] *3. sg. pres. von* **have**; '**~-been** *s.* F **1.** ,Über'holtes; **2.** ,ausrangierte' Per'son, j-d, der s-e Glanzzeit hinter sich hat.

hash[1] [hæʃ] **I** *v/t.* **1.** *Fleisch* (zer)hacken; **2.** *a.* **~ up** *fig.* et. ,vermasseln', verpatzen; **II** *s.* **3.** *Küche:* Ha'schee *n*; **4.** *fig. et.* Aufgewärmtes, ,Aufguss' *m*: **old ~** ,ein alter Hut'; **5.** *fig.* Kuddelmuddel *n*: **make a ~ of** → 2; **settle s.o.'s ~** F es j-m ,besorgen'.

hash[2] [hæʃ] *s.* F ,Hasch' *n* (*Haschisch*).

hash·eesh, **hash·ish** ['hæʃiːʃ] *s.* Haschisch *n*.

has·n't ['hæznt] F *für* **has not**.

hasp [hɑːsp] **I** *s.* **1.** ⊕ a) Haspe *f*, Spange *f*, b) Schließband *n*; **2.** Haspel *f*, Spule *f* (*für Garn*); **II** *v/t.* **3.** mit e-r Haspe *etc.* verschließen, zuhaken.

has·sle ['hæsl] *s.* F **I** *s.* **1.** Mühe *f*: **no ~** kein Problem; **2.** ,The'ater' *n*, ,Zirkus', 'Umständlichkeit (*en pl.*) *f*; **3.** Ärger *m*, ,Krach' *m*, (*a.* handgreifliche) Auseinandersetzung *f*; **II** *v/i.* **4.** ,Krach' haben *od.* sich prügeln; **III** *v/t.* **5.** *Am.* drangsalieren.

has·sock ['hæsək] *s.* **1.** Knie-, Betkissen *n*; **2.** Grasbüschel *n*.

hast [hæst] *obs. 2. sg. pres. von* **have**.

haste [heɪst] *s.* **1.** Eile *f*, Schnelligkeit *f*; **2.** Hast *f*, Eile *f*: **make ~** sich beeilen; **in ~** in Eile, hastig; **more ~, less speed** eile mit Weile; **~ makes waste** in der Eile geht alles schief; '**has·ten** [-sn] **I** *v/t.* a) j-n antreiben, b) *et.* beschleunigen; **II** *v/i.* sich beeilen, eilen, hasten: **I ~ to add that ...** ich muss gleich hinzufügen, dass; '**hast·i·ness** [-tɪnɪs] *s.* **1.** Eile *f*, Hastigkeit *f*, Über'eilung *f*, Voreiligkeit *f*; **2.** Heftigkeit *f*, Hitze *f*, ('Über-) Eifer *m*; '**hast·y** [-tɪ] *adj.* □ **1.** eilig, hastig, über'stürzt; **2.** voreilig, -schnell, über'eilt; **3.** heftig, hitzig.

hat [hæt] *s.* Hut *m*: **my ~!** *sl.* von wegen!, dass ich nicht lache; **a bad ~** *Brit.* F ein übler Kunde; **~ in hand** demütig, unterwürfig; **keep it under your ~!** behalte es für dich!, sprich nicht darüber!; **pass** (*od.* **send**) **the ~ round** den Hut herumgehen lassen, e-e Sammlung veranstalten; **take one's ~ off to s.o.** s-n Hut vor j-m ziehen (*a. fig.*); **~s off (to him)!** Hut ab (vor ihm)!; **I'll eat my ~ if** F ich fress e-n Besen, wenn; **produce out of a ~** hervorzaubern; **talk through one's ~** F dummes Zeug reden; **throw** (*od.* **toss**) **one's ~ in the ring** F ,s-n Hut in den Ring werfen' (*sich zum Kampf stellen od. kandidieren*); → **drop** 5.

hat·a·ble ['heɪtəbl] → **hateful**.

hatch[1] [hætʃ] *s.* **1.** ⏚, ✈ Luke *f*: **down the ~es!** *sl.* ,runter damit'!, prost!; **2.** ⏚ Lukendeckel *m*; **3.** Bodenluke *f*, -tür *f*; **4.** Halbtür *f*; **5.** 'Durchreiche *f* (*für Speisen*).

hatch[2] [hætʃ] **I** *v/t.* **1.** *a.* **~ out** *Eier, Junge* ausbrüten: **the ~ed, matched and dispatched** → 7; **2.** *a.* **~ out** *fig.* aushecken, -brüten, -denken; **II** *v/i.* **3.** *Junge* ausbrüten; **4.** *a.* **~ out** aus dem Ei ausschlüpfen; **5.** *fig.* sich entwickeln; **III** *s.* **6.** Brut *f*; **7.** **~es, matches, and dispatches** F Familienanzeigen *pl.*

hatch[3] [hætʃ] **I** *v/t.* schraffieren; **II** *s.* Schraf'fur *f*.

'**hatch·back** *s. mot.* (Wagen *m* mit) Hecktür *f*.

'**hat-check girl** *s. Am.* Garde'robenfräulein *n*.

hatch·el ['hætʃl] **I** *s.* **1.** (Flachs- *etc.*)Hechel *f*; **II** *v/t.* **2.** hecheln; **3.** *fig.* quälen, piesacken.

hatch·er ['hætʃə] *s.* **1.** Bruthenne *f*; **2.** 'Brutappa,rat *m*; **3.** *fig.* Aushecker(in), Planer(in); '**hatch·er·y** [-ərɪ] *s.* Brutplatz *m*.

hatch·et ['hætʃɪt] *s.* (*a.* Kriegs)Beil *n*: **bury** (**take up**) **the ~** *fig.* das Kriegsbeil begraben (ausgraben); **~ face** *s.* scharf geschnittenes Gesicht; **~ job** *s.* F **1.** ,Hinrichtung' *f*, ,Abschuss' *m*; **2.** ,Verriss' *m* (*Kritik*); **~ man** *s.* F **1.** ,Henker' *m*, Killer *m*; **2.** ,Zuchtmeister' *m*.

hatch·ing[1] ['hætʃɪŋ] *s.* **1.** Ausbrüten *n*; **2.** Ausschlüpfen *n*; **3.** Brut *f*; **4.** *fig.* Aushecken *n*.

hatch·ing[2] ['hætʃɪŋ] *s.* Schraffierung *f*. '**hatch·way** → **hatch**[1] 1–3.

hate [heɪt] I *v/t.* **1.** hassen (*like poison* wie die Pest): ~*d* verhasst; **2.** verabscheuen, hassen, nicht ausstehen können; **3.** nicht mögen *od.* wollen, sehr ungern tun: *I* ~ *to do it* ich tue es (nur) sehr ungern, es ist mir äußerst peinlich; *I* ~ *to think of it* bei dem (bloßen) Gedanken wird mir schlecht; II *s.* **4.** Hass *m* (*of, for* auf *acc.*, gegen): *full of* ~, *with* ~ hasserfüllt; ~ *object* Hassobjekt *n*; ~ *tunes fig.* Hassgesänge *pl.*; **5.** *et.* Verhasstes: *that's my pet* ~ F das ist mir ein Gräuel *od.* in tiefster Seele verhasst; **6.** Abscheu *m* (*of, for* vor *dat.*, gegen); '**hate·a·ble** [-təbl], '**hate·ful** [-fʊl] *adj.* □ hassenswert, verhasst, abscheulich; '**hat·er** [-tə] *s.* Hasser(in); '**hate,mong·er** *s.* (Auf)Hetzer *m*.

hath [hæθ; həθ] *obs.* 3. *sg. pres. von* **have**.

hat·less ['hætlɪs] *adj.* ohne Hut, barhäuptig.

'**hat|pin** *s.* Hutnadel *f*; '~**rack** *s.* Hutablage *f*.

ha·tred ['heɪtrɪd] *s.* (*of, for, against*) a) Hass *m* (gegen, auf *acc.*), b) Abscheu *m* (vor *dat.*).

hat stand *s.* Hutständer *m*.

hat·ter ['hætə] *s.* Hutmacher *m*, -händler *m*: *as mad as a* ~ total verrückt.

hat| tree *s. Am.* Hutständer *m*; ~ **trick** *s. sport* Hattrick *m*: *score a* ~ e-n Hattrick erzielen.

haugh·ti·ness ['hɔːtɪnɪs] *s.* Hochmut *m*, Über'heblichkeit *f*, Arro'ganz *f*; **haugh·ty** ['hɔːtɪ] *adj.* □ hochmütig, -näsig, über'heblich, arro'gant.

haul [hɔːl] I *s.* **1.** Ziehen *n*, Zerren *n*, Schleppen *n*; **2.** kräftiger Zug, Ruck *m*; **3.** Fischzug *m*, *fig. a.* Fang *m*, Beute *f*: *make a big* ~ e-n guten Fang *od.* reiche Beute machen; **4.** a) Beförderung *f*, Trans'port *m*, b) (Trans'port)Strecke *f*: *it was quite a* ~ *home* der Heimweg zog sich ganz schön hin; in (*od. over*) *the long* ~ auf lange Sicht, c) Ladung *f*: *a* ~ *of coal*; II *v/t.* **5.** ziehen, zerren, schleppen; → **coal** 2; **6.** befördern, transportieren; **7.** ⚒ fördern; **8.** heraufholen, (mit e-m Netz) fangen; **9.** ⚓ a) *Brassen* anholen, b) her'umholen, anluven: ~ *the wind* an den Wind gehen, *fig.* sich zurückziehen; III *v/i.* **10.** ziehen, zerren (*on, at* an *dat.*); **11.** mit dem Schleppnetz fischen; **12.** 'umspringen (*Wind*); **13.** ⚓ a) abdrehen, b) an den Wind gehen, c) *fig.* s-e Meinung ändern; ~ *down v/t.* **1.** *Flagge* ein- *od.* niederholen; **2.** *et.* her'unterschleppen *od.* -ziehen; ~ *in v/t.* ⚓ *Tau* einholen; ~ *off v/i.* **1.** ⚓ abdrehen; **2.** *Am.* F ausholen; ~ *round* → **haul** 12; ~ *up v/t.* **1.** → *haul* 9b; **2.** F sich j-n ,vorknöpfen'; **3.** F a) j-n vor den ,Kadi' schleppen, b) j-n ,schleppen' (*before* vor *e-n Vorgesetzten etc.*).

haul·age ['hɔːlɪdʒ] *s.* **1.** Ziehen *n*, Schleppen *n*; **2.** a) Trans'port *m*, Beförderung *f*: ~ *contractor* → *hauler* 2, b) Trans'portkosten *pl.*; **3.** ⚒ Förderung *f*; '**haul·er** [-lə], *Brit.* '**haul·ier** [-ljə] *s.* **1.** ⚒ Schlepper *m*; **2.** Trans'portunter,nehmer *m*, Spedi'teur *m*.

haulm [hɔːm] *s.* ♀ **1.** Halm *m*, Stängel *m*; **2.** *coll. Brit.* Halme *pl.*, Stängel *pl.*, (*Bohnen- etc.*)Stroh *n*.

haunch [hɔːntʃ] *s.* **1.** Hüfte *f*; **2.** *pl.* Gesäß *n*; **3.** *zo.* Keule *f*; **4.** *Küche*: Len-

denstück *n*, Keule *f*.

haunt [hɔːnt] I *v/t.* **1.** 'umgehen *od.* spuken in (*dat.*): *this place is* ~*ed* hier spukt es; **2.** *fig.* a) verfolgen, quälen, b) *j-m* nicht mehr aus dem Kopf gehen; **3.** frequentieren, häufig besuchen; II *v/i.* **4.** ständig verkehren (*with* mit); III *s.* **5.** häufig besuchter Ort, *bsd.* Lieblingsplatz *m*: *holiday* ~ beliebter Ferienort; **6.** a) Treffpunkt *m*, b) Schlupfwinkel *m*; **7.** *zo.* a) Lager *n*, b) Futterplatz *m*; '**haunt·ed** [-tɪd] *adj.*: *a* ~ *house* ein Haus, in dem es spukt; *he was a* ~ *man* er fand keine Ruhe mehr; ~*ed eyes* gehetzter Blick; '**haunt·ing** [-tɪŋ] *adj.* □ **1.** quälend, beklemmend; **2.** unvergesslich: ~ *beauty* betörende Schönheit; *a* ~ *melody* e-e Melodie, die einen verfolgt.

haut·boy ['əʊbɔɪ] *obs.* → **oboe**.

hau·teur [əʊ'tɜː] *s.* Hochmut *m*, Arro'ganz *f*.

Ha·van·a [hə'vænə] *s.* Ha'vanna(zi,garre) *f*.

have [hæv; həv] I *v/t.* [*irr.*] **1.** *allg.* haben, besitzen: *he has a house* (*a friend, a good memory*); *you* ~ *my word for it* ich gebe Ihnen mein Wort darauf; *let me* ~ *a sample* gib *od.* schicke *od.* besorge mir ein Muster; ~ *got* → *get* 8; **2.** haben, erleben: *we had a nice time* wir hatten es schön; **3.** a) *ein Kind* bekommen: *she had a baby in March*, b) *zo. Junge* werfen; **4.** *Gefühle, e-n Verdacht etc.* haben, hegen; **5.** behalten, haben: *may I* ~ *it?*; **6.** erhalten, bekommen: *we had no news from her*; (*not*) *to be had* (nicht) zu haben, (nicht) erhältlich; **7.** (erfahren) haben, wissen: *I* ~ *it from my friend*; *I* ~ *it from a reliable source* ich habe es aus verlässlicher Quelle (erfahren); *I* ~ *it!* ich habs!; → *rumo(u)r* I; **8.** *Speisen etc.* zu sich nehmen, einnehmen, essen *od.* trinken: *what will you* ~? was nehmen Sie?; *I had a glass of wine* ich trank ein Glas Wein; ~ *another sandwich!* nehmen Sie noch ein Sandwich!; ~ *a cigar* e-e Zigarre rauchen; ~ *a smoke?* wollen Sie (eine) rauchen?; ~ *breakfast* I, *dinner* 1, *etc.*; **9.** haben, ausführen, (mit)machen: ~ *a discussion* e-e Diskussion haben *od.* abhalten; ~ *a walk* e-n Spaziergang machen; **10.** können, beherrschen: *she has no French* sie kann kein Französisch; **11.** (be)sagen, behaupten: *as Mr. B has it* wie Herr B. sagt; *he will* ~ *it that* er behauptet steif und fest, dass; **12.** sagen, ausdrücken: *as Byron has it* wie Byron sagt, wie es bei Byron heißt; **13.** haben, dulden, zulassen: *I won't* ~ *it!*, *I am not having that!* ich dulde es nicht!, ich will es nicht (haben); *I won't* ~ *it mentioned* ich will nicht, dass es erwähnt wird; *he wasn't having any* F er ließ sich auf nichts ein; **14.** haben, erleiden: ~ *an accident*; **15.** *Brit.* F *j-n* ,reinlegen', ,übers Ohr hauen': *you've been had!* man hat dich reingelegt; **16.** (*vor inf.*) müssen: *I* ~ *to go now*; *I will* ~ *to do it*; *we* ~ *to obey* wir haben zu *od.* müssen gehorchen; *it has to be done* es muss getan werden; *it has to be* F *j-n* vor den ,Kadi' schleppen, b) *j-n* ,schleppen' (*before* vor *e-n Vorgesetzten etc.*) **17.** (*mit Objekt u. p.p.*) lassen: *I had a suit made* ich ließ mir e-n Anzug machen; *they had him shot* sie ließen ihn erschießen; **18.** (*mit Objekt u. p.p. zum Ausdruck des Passivs*): *I had my arm broken* ich brach mir den Arm; *he had a son born to him* ihm wurde ein Sohn geboren; ~ *a tooth out* sich e-n Zahn ziehen lassen; **19.** (*mit Objekt u. inf.*)

(veran)lassen: ~ *them come here at once!* lass sie sofort hierherkommen!; *I had him sit down* ich ließ ihn Platz nehmen; **20.** (*mit Objekt u. inf.*) es erleben (müssen), dass: *I had all my friends turn against me*; **21.** *in Wendungen wie*: *he has had it* F er ist ,erledigt' (*a. tot*) *od.* ,fertig'; *the car has had it* F das Auto ist ,hin' *od.* ,im Eimer'; *he had me there* da hatte er mich (an m-r schwachen Stelle *etc.*) erwischt; *I would* ~ *you to know it* ich möchte, dass Sie es wissen; *let s.o.* ~ *it* ,es j-m besorgen *od.* geben', j-n ,fertig machen'; ~ *it in for s.o.* F j-n ,auf dem Kieker haben'; *I did'nt know he had it in him* ich wusste gar nicht, dass er das Zeug dazu hat; ~ *it off (with s.o.) Brit. sl.* (mit j-m) ,bumsen'; *you are having me on!* F du nimmst mich (doch) auf den Arm!; ~ *it out with s.o.* die Sache mit j-m endgültig bereinigen; ~ *nothing on s.o.* F a) j-m nichts anhaben können, nichts gegen j-n in der Hand haben, b) j-m in keiner Weise überlegen sein; *I* ~ *nothing on tonight* ich habe heute Abend nichts vor; ~ *it (all) over s.o.* F j-m (haushoch) überlegen sein; ~ *what it takes* das Zeug dazu haben; II *v/i.* **22.** würde, täte (*mit as well, rather, better, best etc.*): *you had better go!* es wäre besser, du gingest!; *you had best go!* du tätest am besten daran zu gehen; III *v/aux.* **23.** haben: *I* ~ *seen* ich habe gesehen; **24.** (*bei vielen v/i.*) sein: *I* ~ *been* ich bin gewesen; IV *s.* **25.** *the* ~*s and the* ~ *-nots* die Begüterten u. die Habenichtse; **26.** *Brit.* F Trick *m*.

have·lock ['hævlɒk] *s. Am.* über den Nacken her'abhängender 'Mützen,überzug (*Sonnenschutz*).

ha·ven ['heɪvn] *s.* **1.** *mst fig.* (sicherer) Hafen *m*; **2.** Zufluchtsort *m*, A'syl *n*, O'ase *f*.

'**have-not** → **have** 25.

hav·er·sack ['hævəsæk] *s. bsd.* ✕ Provi'anttasche *f*.

hav·ings ['hævɪŋz] *s. pl.* Habe *f*.

hav·oc ['hævək] *s.* Verwüstung *f*, Zerstörung *f*: *cause* ~ große Zerstörungen anrichten *od.* (*a. fig.*) ein Chaos verursachen, schrecklich wüten; *play* (*od. cause, wreak*) ~ *with, make* ~ *of* verwüsten *od.* zerstören, *fig.* verheerend wirken auf (*acc.*), übel zurichten.

haw[1] [hɔː] *s.* ♀ **1.** Mehlbeere *f* (*Weißdornfrucht*); **2.** → **hawthorn**.

haw[2] [hɔː] I *int.* hm!, äh; II *v/i.* hm machen, sich räuspern; stockend sprechen.

Ha·wai·ian [hə'waɪən] I *adj.* ha'waiisch: ~ *guitar* Hawaiigitarre *f*; II *s.* Hawai'ianer(in).

'**haw·finch** *s. orn.* Kernbeißer *m*.

haw-haw I *int.* [,hɔː'hɔː] ha'ha!; II *s.* ['hɔːhɔː] (lautes) Ha'ha *n*.

hawk[1] [hɔːk] I *s.* **1.** *orn.* a) Falke *m*, b) Habicht *m*; **2.** *fig.* Halsabschneider *m*, Wucherer *m*; **3.** *pol.* ,Falke' *m*: *the* ~*s and the doves* die Falken u. die Tauben; II *v/i.* **4.** (*mit Falken*) Jagd machen (*at* auf *acc.*); III *v/t.* **5.** jagen.

hawk[2] [hɔːk] *v/t.* **1.** a) hausieren (gehen) mit (*a. fig.*), b) auf der Straße verkaufen; **2.** *a.* ~ *about* *Gerücht etc.* verbreiten.

hawk[3] [hɔːk] I *v/i.* sich räuspern; II *v/t.* *oft* ~ *up* aushusten; III *s.* Räuspern *n*.

hawk[4] [hɔːk] *s.* Mörtelbrett *n*.

hawk·er[1] ['hɔːkə] → **falconer**.

hawk·er[2] ['hɔːkə] *s.* **1.** Hausierer(in); **2.** Straßenhändler(in).

'**hawk-eyed** *adj.* mit Falkenaugen, scharfsichtig.

hawk·ing ['hɔːkɪŋ] → *falconry*.

hawk| **moth** *s. zo.* Schwärmer *m*; ~ **nose** *s.* Adlernase *f*.

hawse [hɔːz] *s.* ⚓ (Anker)Klüse *f*; '**haw·ser** [-zə] *s.* Trosse *f*.

'**haw·thorn** *s.* ♀ Weiß- *od.* Rot- *od.* Hagedorn *m*.

hay [heɪ] *s.* **1.** Heu *n*: *make* ~ Heu machen; *make* ~ *of s.th.* fig. et. durcheinander bringen *od.* zunichte machen; *make* ~ *while the sun shines* fig. das Eisen schmieden, solange es heiß ist; *hit the* ~ *sl.* ‚sich in die Falle hauen'; **2.** *sl.* Marihu'ana *n*; '~**·cock** *s.* Heuschober *m*; ~ **fe·ver** *s.* ✵ Heufieber *n*, -schnupfen *m*; ~ **field** *s.* Wiese *f* (*zum Mähen*); '~**·fork** *s.* Heugabel *f*; ~**·loft** *s.* Heuboden *m*; '~**·mak·er** *s.* **1.** Heumacher *m*; **2.** ✗, ☉ Heuwender *m*; **3.** *sl.* Boxen: ‚Heumacher' *m*, wilder Schwinger; '~**·rick** *s.* Heumiete *f*; '~**·seed** *s.* **1.** Grassamen *m*; **2.** *Am.* F ‚Bauer' *m*; '~**·stack** → *hayrick*; '~**·wire** *adj. sl.* a) ka'putt, b) (hoffnungslos) durchein'ander, c) verrückt (*Person*): *go* ~ a) kaputtgehen (*Sache*), b) ‚schief gehen', durcheinander geraten (*Sache*), c) überschnappen.

haz·ard ['hæzəd] **I** *s.* **1.** Gefahr *f*, Wagnis *n*, Risiko *n* (*a. Versicherung*): *health* ~ Gesundheitsrisiko; ~ *bonus* Gefahrenzulage *f*; *at all* ~*s* unter allen Umständen; *at the* ~ *of one's life* unter Lebensgefahr; **2.** Zufall *m*: *by* ~ zufällig; **3.** (*game of*) ~ Glücks-, Ha'sardspiel *n*; **4.** *Golf*: Hindernis *n*; **5.** *Brit. Billard*: *losing* ~ Verläufer *m*; *winning* ~ Treffer *m*; **6.** *pl.* Launen *pl.* (*des Wetters*); **II** *v/t.* **7.** riskieren, wagen, aufs Spiel setzen; **8.** zu sagen wagen, riskieren: ~ *a remark*; **9.** sich e-r Gefahr etc. aussetzen; '**haz·ard·ous** [-dəs] *adj.* ☐ a) gewagt, ris'kant, gefährlich, unsicher: ~ *waste* Sondermüll *m*.

haze[1] [heɪz] *s.* **1.** Dunst(schleier) *m*, feiner Nebel; **2.** *fig.* Nebel *m*, Schleier *m*: *his mind was in a* ~ a) er war wie betäubt, b) er ‚blickte nicht mehr durch'.

haze[2] [heɪz] *v/t. Am.* **1.** piesacken, schikanieren; **2.** beschimpfen.

ha·zel ['heɪzl] **I** *s.* **1.** ♀ Hasel(nuss)strauch *m*; **2.** (Hasel)Nussbraun *n*; **II** *adj.* (hasel)nussbraun; '~**·nut** *s.* ♀ Haselnuss *f*.

ha·zi·ness ['heɪzɪnɪs] *s.* **1.** Dunstigkeit *f*; **2.** *fig.* Unklarheit *f*, Verschwommenheit *f*; **ha·zy** ['heɪzɪ] *adj.* ☐ **1.** dunstig, diesig, leicht nebelig; **2.** *fig.* verschwommen, nebelhaft: *a* ~ *idea*; *be* ~ *about* nur e-e vage Vorstellung haben von; **3.** benommen.

H-bomb ['eɪtʃbɒm] *s.* ✗ H-Bombe *f* (*Wasserstoffbombe*).

he [hiː; hɪ] **I** *pron.* **1.** er; **2.** ~ *who* wer; derjenige, welcher; **II** *s.* **3.** ‚Er' *m*: a) Junge *m od.* Mann *m*, b) *zo.* Männchen *n*; **III** *adj.* **4.** *in Zssgn* männlich, ...männchen: ~**·goat** Ziegenbock *m*.

head [hed] **I** *v/t.* **1.** die Spitze bilden von (*od. gen.*), an der Spitze *od.* an erster Stelle stehen von (*od. gen.*): ~ *a list*; **2.** vor'an-, vor'ausgehen (*dat.*); **3.** (an)führen, leiten; ~*ed by* unter der Leitung von; **4.** lenken, steuern: ~ *off* a) 'um-, ablenken, b) abfangen, c) *fig.* abwenden, verhindern; **5.** betiteln; **6.** *bsd. Pflanzen* köpfen, *Bäume* kappen; **7.** *Fußball*: (~ *in* ein)köpfen; **II** *v/i.* **8.** a) gehen, fahren, b) (*for*) zu-, losgehen, -steuern (auf *acc.*): *he is* ~*ing for*

trouble er wird noch Ärger kriegen; **9.** ⚓ Kurs halten, zusteuern (*for* auf *acc.*); **10.** sich entwickeln: ~ (*up*) (e-n Kopf) ansetzen (*Kohl etc.*); **11.** entspringen (*Fluss*); **III** *s.* **12.** Kopf *m*: *back of the* ~ Hinterkopf *m*; *have a* ~ F e-n ‚Brummschädel' haben; *win by a* ~ um e-e Kopflänge *od.* (*a. fig.*) um e-e Nasenlänge gewinnen; → *Bes. Redew.*; **13.** *poet. u. fig.* Haupt *n*: ~ *of the family* Haupt der Familie, Familienoberhaupt; ~*s of state* Staatsoberhäupter *pl.*; **14.** Kopf *m*, Verstand *m*, *a.* Begabung *f* (*for* für): *he has a* (*good*) ~ *for languages* er ist (sehr) sprachbegabt; *two* ~*s are better than one* zwei Köpfe wissen mehr als einer; **15.** Spitze *f*, führende Stellung: *at the* ~ *of* an der Spitze (*gen.*); **16.** a) (An)Führer *m*, Leiter *m*, b) Chef *m*, c) Vorstand *m*, Vorsteher *m*, d) Di'rektor *m*, Direk'torin *f* (*e-r Schule*); **17.** Kopf(ende *n*) *m*, oberes Ende, oberer Teil *od.* Rand, Spitze *f*, *a.* oberer Absatz (*e-r Treppe*), Kopf *m* (*e-r Buchseite*, *e-s Briefes*, *e-r Münze*, *e-s Nagels*, *e-s Hammers etc.*): ~*s or tails?* Kopf oder Wappen?; **18.** Kopf *m* (*e-r Brücke od. Mole*); oberes *od.* unteres Ende (*e-s Sees*); Boden *m* (*e-s Fasses*); **19.** Kopf *m*, Spitze *f*, vorderes Ende, Vorderteil *m*, *n*, ⚓ Bug *m*; **20.** Kopf *m*, (einzelne) Per'son: *a pound a* ~ ein Pfund pro Person *od.* pro Kopf; **21.** a) (*pl.* ~) Stück *n* (*Vieh*): *50* ~ *of cattle*, b) *Brit.* Anzahl *f*, Herde *f*; **22.** (Haupt)Haar *n*: *a fine* ~ *of hair* schönes, volles Haar; **23.** ♀ a) (*Salat- etc.*)Kopf *m*, b) (*Baum*)Krone *f*, Wipfel *m*; **24.** *anat.* Kopf *m* (*e-s Knochens etc.*); **25.** ✵ 'Durchbruchsstelle *f* (*e-s Geschwürs*); **26.** Vorgebirge *n*, Landspitze *f*, Kap *n*; **27.** *hunt.* Geweih *n*; **28.** Schaum(krone *f*) *m* (*vom Bier etc.*); **29.** *Brit.* Rahm *m*, Sahne *f*; **30.** Quelle *f* (*e-s Flusses*); **31.** a) 'Überschrift *f*, Titelkopf *m*, b) Abschnitt *m*, Ka'pitel *n*, c) (Haupt)Punkt *m* (*e-r Rede etc.*), d) Ru'brik *f*, Katego'rie *f*, e) *typ.* (Titel-)Kopf *m*; **32.** *ling.* Oberbegriff *m*; **33.** ☉ a) Stauwasser *n*, b) Staudamm *m*; **34.** *phys.*, ☉ a) Gefälle *n*, b) Druckhöhe *f*, c) (Dampf- *etc.*)Druck *m*, d) Säule(nhöhe) *f*: ~ *of water* Wassersäule; **35.** ☉ a) Spindelkopf *m*, b) Spindelbank *f*, c) Sup'port *m* (*e-r Bohrbank*), d) (Gewinde)Schneidkopf *m*, e) Kopf-, Deckplatte *f*; **36.** (Wagen-, Kutschen-)Dach *n*; **37.** → *heading*; **IV** *adj.* **38.** Kopf...; **39.** Spitzen..., Vorder...; **40.** Chef..., Haupt..., Ober..., Spitzen..., führend, oberst: ~ *cook* Chefkoch *m*; *Besondere Redewendungen:* *that is* (*od. goes*) *above* (*od. over*) *my* ~ das ist zu hoch für mich, das geht über m-n Horizont; *talk above s.o.'s* ~ über j-s Kopf hinwegreden; *by* ~ *and shoulders* an den Haaren (*herbeiziehen*); (*by*) ~ *and shoulders* um Hauptteslänge (*größer etc.*), weitaus; ~ *and shoulders above s.o.* j-m haushoch überlegen; *from* ~ *to foot* von Kopf bis Fuß; *off* (*od. out of*) *one's* ~ F ‚übergeschnappt'; *I can do that* (*standing*) *on my* ~ F das kann ich im Schlaf, das mach ich ‚mit links'; *on this* ~ in diesem Punkt; *out of one's own* ~ von sich aus; *over s.o.'s* ~ *fig.* über j-s Kopf hinweg; ~ *over heels* a) kopfüber (*stürzen*), b) bis über beide Ohren (*verliebt*), c) *in debt* bis über die Ohren in Schulden (*stecken*); ~ *first* (*od. foremost*) → *headlong*; *bite s.o.'s* ~ *off* F j-m ‚den Kopf abreißen'; *bring to a* ~

zum Ausbruch *od.* zur Entscheidung *od.* ‚zum Klappen' bringen; *come to a* ~ a) ✵ aufbrechen, eitern, b) sich zuspitzen, zur Entscheidung *od.* ‚zum Klappen' kommen; *it entered my* ~ es fiel mir ein; *gather* ~ überhand nehmen, immer stärker werden; *give a horse his* ~ e-m Pferd die Zügel schießen lassen; *give s.o. his* ~ j-m s-n Willen lassen, j-n gewähren *od.* machen lassen; *give* (*s.o.*) ~ *Am.* V (j-m e-n) ‚blasen'; *go to the* ~ zu Kopfe steigen; *have* (*od. be*) *an old* ~ *on young shoulders* für sein Alter (schon) sehr reif sein; *keep one's* ~ kühlen Kopf bewahren; *keep one's* ~ *above water* sich über Wasser halten (*a. fig.*); *knock s.th. on the* ~ F et. (*e-n Plan etc.*) ‚über den Haufen werfen'; *laugh* (*shout*) *one's* ~ *off* sich halb totlachen (sich die Lunge aus dem Hals schreien); *lose one's* ~ *fig.* den Kopf verlieren; *make* ~ gut vorankommen; *make* ~ *against* sich entgegenstemmen (*dat.*); *I cannot make* ~ *or tail of it* ich kann daraus nicht schlau werden; *put s.th. into s.o.'s* ~ j-m et. in den Kopf setzen; *put that out of your* ~ schlag dir das aus dem Kopf; *they put their* ~*s together* sie steckten ihre Köpfe zusammen; *take s.th. into one's* ~ sich et. in den Kopf setzen; *talk one's* ~ *off* reden wie ein Wasserfall; *talk s.o.'s* ~ *off* j-m ein Loch in den Bauch reden'; *turn s.o.'s* ~ j-m den Kopf verdrehen.

'**head**|**·ache** *s.* **1.** Kopfschmerzen *pl.*, -weh *n*: *have a* ~ Kopfweh haben; **2.** F et., was Kopfzerbrechen *od.* Sorgen macht, schwieriges Problem, Sorge *f*; '~**·ach·y** *adj.* F **1.** an Kopfschmerzen leidend; **2.** Kopfschmerzen verursachend; '~**·band** *s.* Stirnband *n*; '~**·board** *s.* Kopfbrett *n* (*Bett*); ~ **boy** *s. Brit. ped.* Schulsprecher *m*; '~**·cheese** *s. Am.* Presskopf *m* (*Sülzwurst*); ~ **clerk** *s.* Bü'rochef *m*; '~**·dress** *s.* **1.** Kopfschmuck *m*; **2.** Fri'sur *f*.

-**headed** [hedɪd] *in Zssgn* ...köpfig.

head·ed ['hedɪd] *adj.* **1.** mit e-m Kopf *etc.* (versehen); **2.** mit e-r 'Überschrift (versehen), betitelt.

head·er ['hedə] *s.* **1.** △, ☉ a) Schlussstein *m*, b) Binder *m*; **2.** *take a* ~ a) *sport* e-n Kopfsprung machen, b) kopfüber *die Treppe etc.* hinunterstürzen; **3.** *Fußball*: Kopfball *m*, -stoß *m*; **4.** *Computer*: Kopfzeile *f* (*in Textverarbeitung*).

'**head**|**·first**, '~**·fore·most** → *headlong*; '~**·gear** *s.* **1.** Kopfbedeckung *f*; **2.** Kopfgestell *n*, Zaumzeug *n* (*vom Pferd*); **3.** ⚒ Fördergerüst *n*; ~ **girl** *s. Brit. ped.* Schulsprecherin *f*; '~**·hunt·er** *s.* **1.** Kopfjäger *m*; **2.** ✝ 'Headhunter *m*.

head·i·ness ['hedɪnɪs] *s.* **1.** Unbesonnenheit *f*, Ungestüm *n*; **2.** *das* Berauschende (*a. fig.*).

head·ing ['hedɪŋ] *s.* **1.** a) Kopfstück *n*, -ende *n*, b) Vorderende *n*, -teil *n*; **2.** 'Überschrift *f*, Titel(zeile *f*) *m*; **3.** Briefkopf *m*; **4.** (Rechnungs)Posten *m*; **5.** Thema *n*, Punkt *m*; **6.** ✗ Stollen *m*; **7.** a) ✈ Steuerkurs *m*, b) ⚓ Kompasskurs *m*; **8.** *Fußball*: Kopfballspiel *n*; ~ **stone** *s.* △ Schlussstein *m*.

'**head**|**·lamp** → *headlight*; '~**·land** *s.* **1.** ✈ Rain *m*; **2.** [-lənd] Landspitze *f*, -zunge *f*.

head·less ['hedlɪs] *adj.* **1.** kopflos (*a. fig.*), ohne Kopf; **2.** *fig.* führerlos.

'**head**|**·light** *s.* **1.** *mot. etc.* Scheinwerfer *m*: ~ *flasher* Lichthupe *f*; **2.** ⚓ Mast-,

Topplicht *n*; '**~·line** I *s.* **1.** a) 'Überschrift *f*, b) *Zeitung:* Schlagzeile *f*, c) *pl. a.* **~ news** *Radio, TV:* (*das*) Wichtigste in Schlagzeilen: *hit* (*od.* *make*) *the* **~s** Schlagzeilen machen; **II** *v/t.* **2.** e-e Schlagzeile widmen (*dat.*); **3.** *fig.* groß her'ausstellen; '**~·lin·er** *s. Am.* F **1.** *thea. etc.* Star *m*; **2.** promi'nente Per'sönlichkeit; '**~·lock** *s. Ringen:* Kopfzange *f*; '**~·long** I *adv.* **1.** kopf'über, mit dem Kopf vor'an; **2.** *fig.* Hals über Kopf, blindlings; **II** *adj.* **3.** mit dem Kopf vor'an: *a* **~** *fall*; **4.** *fig.* über'stürzt, unbesonnen, ungestüm; **~ louse** *s.* Kopflaus *f*; '**~·man** *s.* [*irr.*] **1.** ['hedmæn] Führer *m*; **2.** Häuptling *m*; **3.** [ˌhed'mæn] Vorarbeiter *m*; ˌ**~'mas·ter** *s.* Schulleiter *m*, Di'rektor *m*; ˌ**~'mis·tress** *s.* Schulleiterin *f*, Direk'torin *f*; **~ mon·ey** *s.* Kopfgeld *n*; **~ of·fice** *s.* 'Hauptbü,ro *n*, -geschäftsstelle *f*, -sitz *m*, Zen'trale *f*; ˌ**~·'on** *adj. u. adv.* **1.** fron'tal: **~ collision** Frontalzusammenstoß *m*; **2.** di'rekt; '**~·phone** *s. mst pl.* Kopfhörer *m*; '**~·piece** *s.* **1.** Kopfbedeckung *f*; **2.** Oberteil *n, bsd.* a) Türsturz *m*, b) Kopfbrett *n* (*Bett*); **3.** *typ.* 'Titelvi,gnette *f*; ˌ**~'quar·ters** *s. pl. oft sg. konstr.* **1.** ⚔ a) 'Hauptquar,tier *n*, b) Stab *m*, c) Kom'mandostelle *f*, d) 'Oberkom,mando *n*; **2.** *allg.* (*Feuerwehr-, Partei- etc.*)Zen'trale *f*, (Poli'zei-) Prä,sidium *n*; **3.** → *head office*; '**~·rest, ~ re·straint** *s.* Kopfstütze *f*; '**~·room** [-rʊm] *s.* lichte Höhe; '**~·sail** *s.* ⚓ Fockmastsegel *n*; '**~·scarf,** *pl.* **-scarfs, -scarves** [-vz] *s.* Kopftuch *n*; '**~·set** *s.* Kopfhörer *m*.

head·ship ['hedʃɪp] *s.* (oberste) Leitung, Führung *f*.

head|·shrink·er ['hedˌʃrɪŋkə] *s.* F Psychoana'lytiker(in); '**~·spring** *s.* **1.** Hauptquelle *f*; **2.** *fig.* Quelle *f*, Ursprung *m*; **3.** *sport* Kopfkippe *f*; '**~·stall** → *headgear* 2; '**~·stand** *s.* Kopfstand *m*; **~ start** *s.* **1.** *sport* a) Vorgabe *f*, b) Vorsprung *m* (*a. fig.*); **2.** *fig.* guter Start; '**~·stock** *s.* ⊙ **1.** Spindelstock *m*; **2.** Triebwerkgestell *n*; '**~·stone** *s.* **1.** △ a) Eck-, Grundstein *m* (*a. fig.*), b) Schlussstein *m*; **2.** Grabstein *m*; '**~·strong** *adj.* eigensinnig, halsstarrig; **~ tax** *s. Am., bsd.* Einwanderungssteuer *f* (*USA*); ˌ**~·to-'head** *adj. Am.* **1.** Mann gegen Mann; **2.** Kopf-anKopf-...: **~ race; ~ voice** *s.* Kopfstimme *f*; **~ wait·er** *s.* Oberkellner *m*; '**~·wa·ter** *s. mst pl.* Oberlauf *m*, Quellgebiet *n* (*Fluss*); '**~·way** *s.* **1.** ⚓ a) Fahrt *f* vor'aus, b) Fahrt *f*, Geschwindigkeit *f*; **2.** *fig.* Fortschritt(e *pl.*) *m: make* **~** vorankommen, Fortschritte machen; **3.** △ lichte Höhe; **4.** ⚒ *Brit.* Hauptstollen *m*; **5.** 🚋 Zugfolge *f*, -abstand *m*; **~ wind** *s.* Gegenwind *m*; '**~·word** *s.* Stichwort *n* (*im Wörterbuch*); '**~·work** *s.* geistige Arbeit; '**~·work·er** *s.* Geistes-, Kopfarbeiter *m*.

head·y ['hedɪ] *adj.* □ **1.** unbesonnen, ungestüm; **2.** a) berauschend (*Getränk; a. fig.*), b) berauscht (*with* von); **3.** *Am.* F schlau.

heal [hiːl] I *v/t.* **1.** *a. fig.* heilen, kurieren (*of* von); **2.** *fig.* versöhnen, *Streit etc.* beilegen; **II** *v/i.* **3.** *oft* **~ up, ~ over** (zu)heilen; '**heal·er** [-lə] *s.* **1.** Heil(end)er *m*; **2.** Gesundbeter(in); **2.** Heilmittel *n: time is a great* **~** die Zeit heilt alle Wunden; '**heal·ing** [-lɪŋ] I *s.* Heilung *f*; **II** *adj.* □ heilsam, heilend, Heil(ungs)...

health [helθ] *s.* **1.** Gesundheit *f*: **~ care** Gesundheitsfürsorge *f*; **~ centre** (*Am.*

center) Ärztezentrum *n*; **~ certificate** ärztliches Attest; **~ club** Fitnessklub *m*; **~ farm** Gesundheitsform *f*; **~ food** Reformkost *f*; **~ food shop** (*od.* *store*) Reformhaus *n*; **~ freak** Gesundheitsfanatiker(in); **~ insurance** Krankenversicherung *f*; **~ officer** *Am.* a) Beamte(r) *m* des Gesundheitsamtes, b) ⚓ Hafen-, Quarantänearzt *m*; **~ resort** Kurort *m*; **~ service** Gesundheitsdienst *m*; **~ visitor** Gesundheitsfürsorger(in); **2.** *a. state of* **~** Gesundheitszustand *m: ill* **~**; *in good* **~** gesund, bei guter Gesundheit; **3.** Gesundheit *f*, Wohl *n: drink* (*to*) *s.o.'s* **~** auf j-s Wohl trinken; *your* **~**! auf Ihr Wohl!; *here is to the* **~** *of the host* ein Prosit dem Gastgeber!; '**~-,con·scious** *adj.* gesundheitsbewusst; '**health·ful** [-fʊl] *adj.* □ → *healthy* 1, 2; '**health·y** [-θɪ] *adj.* □ **1.** *allg.* gesund (*a. fig.*): **~ body** (*climate, economy, etc.*); **2.** gesund(heitsfördernd), heilsam, bekömmlich; **3.** F gesund, kräftig: **~ appetite**; **4.** *not* **~** F ‚nicht gesund', schlecht, gefährlich.

heap [hiːp] I *s.* **1.** Haufe(n) *m: in* **~s** haufenweise; *be struck all of a* **~** F ‚platt' *od.* sprachlos sein; *fall in a* **~** (in sich) zs.-sacken; **2.** F Haufen *m*, Menge *f:* **~s of time** e-e *od.* jede Menge Zeit; **~s of times** unzählige Male; **~s better** sehr viel besser; **3.** *sl.* ‚Schlitten' *m* (*Auto*); **II** *v/t.* **4.** häufen: *a* **~ed spoonful** ein gehäufter Löffel (voll); **~ up** anhäufen, *fig. a.* aufhäufen; **~ insults** (*praises*) (*up*)*on s.o.* j-n mit Beschimpfung (Lob) überschütten; → *coal* 2; **5.** beladen, anfüllen.

hear [hɪə] [*irr.*] I *v/t.* **1.** hören: *I* **~** *him laugh*(*ing*) ich höre ihn lachen; *make o.s.* **~** sich Gehör verschaffen; *let's* **~** *it for him! Am.* F Beifall für ihn!; **2.** (an)hören: **~ a concert** sich ein Konzert anhören; **3.** *j-m* zuhören, *j-n* anhören: **~ s.o. out** j-n ausreden lassen; **4.** hören *od.* achten auf (*acc.*), *j-s* Rat folgen: *do you* **~** *me?* hast du (mich) verstanden?; **5.** *Bitte etc.* erhören; **6.** *ped. Aufgabe od. Schüler* abhören; **7.** *et.* hören, erfahren (*about, of* über *acc.*); **8.** ⚖ a) verhören, vernehmen, b) *Sachverständige etc.* anhören, c) (über) e-n Fall verhandeln: **~ and decide a case** über e-n Fall befinden; → *evidence* 1; **II** *v/i.* **9.** hören: **~!** **~!** *parl.* hört! hört! (*a. iro.*), bravo!, sehr richtig!; **10.** hören, erfahren, Nachricht erhalten (*from* von; *of, about* von, über [*acc.*]; *that* dass): *you'll* **~** *of this!* F das wirst du mir büßen!; *I won't* **~** *of it* ich erlaube *od.* dulde es nicht; *he would not* **~** *of it* er wollte davon nichts hören *od.* wissen; **heard** [hɜːd] *pret. u. p.p. von hear*; '**hear·er** [-ərə] *s.* (Zu)Hörer(in); '**hear·ing** [-ərɪŋ] *s.* **1.** Hören *n:* within (*out of*) **~** in (außer) Hörweite; *in his* **~** in s-r Gegenwart, solange er noch in Hörweite ist; **2.** Gehör(sinn *m*) *n:* **~ aid** Hörhilfe *f*, -gerät *n*; **~ spectacles** *pl.* Hörbrille *f*; *hard of* **~** schwerhörig; a) Anhören *n*, b) Gehör *n*, c) Audi'enz *f: gain a* **~** sich Gehör verschaffen; *give s.o. a* **~** j-n anhören; **4.** *thea. etc.* Hörprobe *f*; **5.** ⚖ a) Vernehmung *f*, b) *a. preliminary* **~** 'Vorunter,suchung *f*, c) (mündliche) Verhandlung, Ter'min *m*; **6.** *bsd. pol.* Hearing *n*, Anhörung *f*.

heark·en ['hɑːkən] *v/i. poet.* (*to*) a) horchen (auf *acc.*), b) Beachtung schenken (*dat.*).

'**hear·say** *s.* **1.** (*by* **~** vom) Hörensagen *n*; **2.** *a.* **~ evidence** ⚖ Beweis(e *pl.*) *m* vom Hörensagen, mittelbarer Beweis: **~**

rule Regel über den grundsätzlichen Ausschluss aller Beweise vom Hörensagen.

hearse [hɜːs] *s.* Leichenwagen *m*.

heart [hɑːt] *s.* **1.** *anat.* a) Herz *n*, b) Herzhälfte *f*; **2.** *fig.* Herz *n:* a) Seele *f*, Gemüt *n*, b) Liebe *f*, Zuneigung *f*, c) (Mit)Gefühl *n*, d) Mut *m*, e) Gewissen *n: change of* **~** Gesinnungswandel *m; affairs of the* **~** Herzensangelegenheiten; → *Bes. Redew.*; **3.** Herz *n*, (*das*) Innere, Kern *m*, Mitte *f: in the* **~** *of* inmitten (*gen.*), mitten in (*dat.*), im Herzen (*des Landes etc.*); **4.** Kern *m*, (*das*) Wesentliche: *go to the* **~** *of s.th.* zum Kern e-r Sache vorstoßen, e-r Sache auf den Grund gehen; *the* **~** *of the matter* der Kern der Sache, des Pudels Kern; **5.** Liebling *m*, Schatz *m*, mein Herz; **6.** *Kartenspiel:* a) Herz *n*, Cœur *n*, b) *pl.* Herz *n*, Cœur *n* (*Farbe*): *king of* **~s** Herzkönig *n*; **7.** ♣ Herz *n* (*Salat, Kohl*): **~ of oak** a) Kernholz *n* der Eiche, b) *fig.* Standhaftigkeit *f; Besondere Redewendungen:* **~ and soul** mit Leib u. Seele; **~'s desire** Herzenswunsch *m; after my* (*own*) **~** ganz nach m-m Herzen *od.* Geschmack *od.* Wunsch; *at* **~** im Innersten, im Grunde (m-s *etc.* Herzens); (*have, learn*) *by* **~** auswendig (wissen, lernen); *from one's* **~** von Herzen; *in one's* **~** (*of* **~s**) a) im Grunde s-s Herzens, b) insgeheim; *in good* **~** a) in gutem Zustand (*Boden*), *fig. a.* in guter Verfassung, gesund, *a.* guten Mutes; *to one's* **~'s content** nach Herzenslust; *with all my* **~** von *od.* mit ganzem Herzen; *with a heavy* **~** schweren Herzens; *bless my* **~**! du meine Güte!; *it breaks my* **~** es bricht mir das Herz; *you are breaking my* **~**! *iro.* ich fang gleich an zu weinen!; *cross my* **~**! Hand aufs Herz!; *eat one's* **~** *out* sich vor Gram verzehren; *not to have the* **~** *to do s.th.* es nicht übers Herz bringen, et. zu tun; *go to s.o.'s* **~** j-m zu Herzen gehen; *my* **~** *goes out to* ich empfinde tiefes Mitleid mit; *have a* **~**! hab Erbarmen!; *have no* **~** kein Herz *od.* Mitgefühl haben; *I have your health at* **~** deine Gesundheit liegt mir am Herzen; *I had my* **~** *in my mouth* das Herz schlug mir bis zum Halse, ich war zu Tode erschrocken; *have one's* **~** *in the right place* das Herz auf dem rechten Fleck haben; *his* **~** *is not in his work* er ist nicht mit ganzem Herzen dabei; *lose* **~** den Mut verlieren; *lose one's* **~** *to s.o.* sein Herz an j-n verlieren; *open one's* **~** a) (*of* **~s**) sein Herz ausschütten, b) großmütig sein; *clasp s.o. to one's* **~** j-n ans Herz *od.* an die Brust drücken; *put one's* **~** *into s.th.* mit Leib u. Seele bei et. sein; *set one's* **~** *on* sein Herz hängen an (*acc.*); *my* **~** *sank into my boots* das Herz rutschte mir in die Hose(n); *take* **~** Mut fassen; *I took* **~** *from that* das machte mir Mut; *take s.th. to* **~** sich et. zu Herzen nehmen; *wear one's* **~** *on one's sleeve* das Herz auf der Zunge tragen.

'**heart|·ache** *s.* Kummer *m*; **~ ac·tion** *s. physiol.* Herztätigkeit *f*; **~ at·tack** *s.* ⚕ Herzanfall *m*; '**~·beat** *s.* **1.** *physiol.* Herzschlag *m* (*Pulsieren*); **2.** *fig. Am.* Herzstück *n*; '**~·break** *s.* (Herze)Leid *n*, Gram *m*; '**~,break·ing** *adj.* herzzerreißend; '**~,bro·ken** *adj.* (ganz) gebrochen, todunglücklich, untröstlich; '**~·burn** *s.* ⚕ Sodbrennen *n*; **~ con·di·tion** *s.* ⚕ Herzleiden *n*.

-hearted [hɑːtɪd] *in Zssgn* ...herzig,

...mütig.

heart·en ['hɑːtn] v/t. ermutigen, aufmuntern; **'heart·en·ing** [-nɪŋ] adj. ermutigend.

heart‖ fail·ure s. ⚕ a) Herzversagen n, b) 'Herzinsuffizi,enz f; '**~·felt** adj. tiefempfunden, herzlich, aufrichtig, innig.

hearth [hɑːθ] s. **1.** Ka'min(platte f, -sohle f) m; **2.** Herd m, Feuerstelle f; **3.** ⊗ a) Schmiedeherd m, Esse f, b) Herd m, Hochofengestell n; **4.** fig. a. **~ and home** häuslicher Herd, Heim n; '**~·stone** s. **1.** → **hearth** 1 u. 4; **2.** Scheuerstein m.

heart·i·ly ['hɑːtɪlɪ] adv. **1.** herzlich: a) von Herzen, innig, b) iro. äußerst, gründlich: **dislike s.o. ~;** **2.** herzhaft, kräftig, tüchtig: **eat ~;** '**heart·i·ness** [-nɪs] s. **1.** Herzlichkeit f: a) Innigkeit f, b) Aufrichtigkeit f; **2.** Herzhaftigkeit f, Kräftigkeit f.

'**heart·land** s. Herz-, Kernland n.

heart·less ['hɑːtlɪs] adj. □ herzlos, grausam, gefühllos; '**heart·less·ness** [-nɪs] s. Herzlosigkeit f.

,**heart‖-'lung ma·chine** s. ⚕ 'Herz-'Lungen-Ma,schine f: **put on the ~** an die Herz-Lungen-Maschine anschließen; **~ pace·mak·er** s. ⚕ Herzschrittmacher m; **~ rate** s. physiol. 'Herzfre,quenz f; '**~·rend·ing** adj. herzzerreißend; **~ rot** s. Kernfäule f (Baum); '**~'s-blood** s. Herzblut n; '**~-,search·ing** s. Gewissenserforschung f; **~ shake** s. Kernriss m (Baum); '**~-shaped** adj. herzförmig; '**~·sick**, '**~·sore** adj. tief betrübt, todunglücklich; '**~·strings** s. pl. fig. Herz n, innerste Gefühle pl.: **pull at s.o.'s ~** j-m das Herz zerreißen, j-n tief rühren; **play on s.o.'s ~** mit j-s Gefühlen spielen; **~ sur·ger·y** s. ⚕ 'Herzchirur,gie f; '**~·throb** s. **1.** physiol. Herzschlag m; **2.** F Schatz m, Schwarm m; ,**~-to-'~** adj. offen, aufrichtig: **~ talk; ~ trans·plant** s. ⚕ Herzverpflanzung f; '**~-,warm·ing** adj. **1.** herzerfrischend; **2.** bewegend; '**~-whole** adj. **1.** (noch) ungebunden, frei; **2.** aufrichtig, rückhaltlos.

heart·y ['hɑːtɪ] **I** adj. □ → **heartily; 1.** herzlich: a) von Herzen kommend, warm, innig, b) aufrichtig, tief empfunden, c) iro. ,gründlich': **~ dislike; 2.** a) munter, b) e'nergisch, c) begeistert, d) herzlich, jovi'al; **3.** herzhaft, kräftig: **~ appetite (meal, kick); 4.** gesund, kräftig; **5.** fruchtbar (Boden); **II** s. **6.** sport Brit. dy'namischer Spieler; **7.** F Mat'rose m: **my hearties** meine Jungs.

heat [hiːt] **I** s. **1.** Hitze f: a) große Wärme, b) heißes Wetter; **2.** Wärme f (a. phys.); **3.** a) Erhitztheit f (des Körpers), b) (bsd. Fieber)Hitze f; **4.** (Glüh-)Hitze f, Glut f; **5.** Schärfe f (von Gewürzen etc.); **6.** fig. a) Ungestüm n, b) Zorn m, Wut f, c) Leidenschaft(lichkeit) f, Erregtheit f, d) Eifer m: **in the ~ of the moment** im Eifer des Gefechts; **in the ~ of passion** ⚖ im Affekt; **at one ~** in 'einem Zug, auf 'einen Schlag; **7.** sport a) (Einzel)Lauf m, b) a. **pre·liminary ~** Vorlauf m, c) 'Durchgang m, Runde f; **8.** zo. Brunst f, bsd. a) Läufigkeit f (e-r Hündin), b) Rolligkeit f (e-r Katze), c) Rossen n (e-r Stute), d) Stieren n (e-r Kuh): **in (od. on) ~** brünstig; **a bitch in ~** e-e läufige Hündin; **9.** metall. a) Schmelzgang m, b) Charge f; **10.** F Druck m: **turn on the ~** Druck machen; **turn (od. put) the ~ on s.o.** j-n unter Druck setzen; **the ~ is on** es herrscht ,dicke Luft'; **the ~ is off** es hat sich wieder beruhigt; **11. the ~** Am. F

die ,Bullen' pl. (Polizei); **II** v/t. **12.** a. **~ up** erhitzen (a. fig.), heiß machen, Speisen a. aufwärmen; **13.** Haus etc. heizen; **14. ~ up** fig. Diskussion, Konjunktur etc. anheizen; **III** v/i. **15.** sich erhitzen (a. fig.).

heat·a·ble ['hiːtəbl] adj. **1.** erhitzbar; **2.** heizbar.

heat‖ ap·o·plex·y → **heatstroke; ~ bar·ri·er** s. ✈ Hitzemauer f, -schwelle f.

heat·ed ['hiːtɪd] adj. □ erhitzt: a) heiß geworden, b) fig. erhitzt od. erregt (**with** von), aufgeregt: **~ debate.**

heat·er ['hiːtə] s. **1.** Heizgerät n, -körper m, (Heiz)Ofen m; **2.** ⚡ Heizfaden m; **3.** (Plätt)Bolzen m; **4.** sl. ,Ka'none' f, ,Ballermann' m (Pistole etc.); **~ plug** s. mot. Brit. Glühkerze f.

heath [hiːθ] s. **1.** bsd. Brit. Heide(land n) f; **2.** ♀ a) Erika f, b) Heidekraut n; '**~·bell** s. ♀ Heide(blüte) f.

hea·then ['hiːðn] **I** s. **1.** Heide m, Heidin f; **2.** fig. Bar'bar m; **II** adj. **3.** heidnisch, Heiden...; **4.** bar'barisch, unzivilisiert; '**hea·then·dom** [-dəm] s. **1.** Heidentum n; **2.** die Heiden pl.; '**hea·then·ish** [-ðənɪʃ] → **heathen** 3 u. 4; '**hea·then·ism** [-ðənɪzəm] s. **1.** Heidentum n; **2.** Barba'rei f.

heath·er ['heðə] → **heath** 2; '**~·bell** s. ♀ Glockenheide f; '**~·mix·ture** s. gesprenkelter Wollstoff.

heat·ing ['hiːtɪŋ] **I** s. **1.** Heizung f; **2.** ⊗ a) Beheizung f, b) Heißwerden n, -laufen n; **3.** phys. Erwärmung f; **4.** Erhitzung f (a. fig.); **II** adj. **5.** heizend, phys. erwärmend; **6.** Heiz...: **~ battery (costs, oil, etc.); ~ system** Heizung f; **~ jack·et** s. ⊗ Heizmantel m; **~ pad** s. Heizkissen n; **~ sur·face** s. ⊗ Heizfläche f.

heat‖ in·su·la·tion s. ⊗ Wärmedämmung f; '**~·proof** adj. hitzebeständig; **~ pro·stra·tion** s. ⚕ Hitzschlag m; **~ pump** s. ⊗ Wärmepumpe f; **~ rash** s. ⚕ Hitzeausschlag m; '**~-re,sist·ing** → **heatproof**; '**~·seal** v/t. Kunststoffe heißsiegeln; **~ shield** s. Raumfahrt: Hitzeschild m; '**~ spot** s. Hitzebläschen n; '**~·stroke** s. ⚕ Hitzschlag m; '**~-treat** v/t. ⊗ wärmebehandeln (a. ⚕); **~ u·nit** s. phys. Wärmeeinheit f; **~ wave** s. Hitzewelle f.

heave [hiːv] **I** v/t. (⚓ [irr.] pret. u. p.p. **hove** [həʊv]) **1.** (hoch)heben, (-)wuchten, (-)stemmen, (-)hieven: **~ coal** Kohlen schleppen; **~ s.o. into a post** fig. j-n auf e-n Posten ,hieven'; **2.** hochziehen, -winden; **3.** F schmeißen, schleudern; **4.** ⚓ hieven; **den Anker lichten**: **~ the lead (log)** loten (loggen); **~ to** beidrehen; **5.** ausstoßen: **~ a sigh; 6.** F ,(aus)kotzen', erbrechen; **7.** aufschwellen, dehnen; **8.** heben u. senken; **II** v/i. (⚓ [irr.] pret. u. p.p. **hove** [həʊv]) **9.** sich heben u. senken, wogen (a. Busen): **~ and set** ⚓ stampfen (Schiff); **10.** keuchen; **11.** F a) ,kotzen', sich heftig übergeben, b) würgen, Brechreiz haben: **his stomach ~d** ihm hob sich der Magen; **12.** ⚓ a) hieven, ziehen (at an dat.): **~ ho!** holt auf!, allg. hau ruck!, b) treiben: **~ in(to) sight** in Sicht kommen, fig. humor. ,aufkreuzen'; **~ to** beidrehen; **III** s. **13.** Heben n, Hub m, (mächtiger) Ruck; **14.** Hochziehen n, -winden n; **15.** Wurf m; **16.** Ringen: Hebegriff m; **17.** Wogen n: **~ of the sea** ⚓ Seegang m; **18.** geol. Verwerfung f; **19.** pl. sg. konstr. vet. Dämpfigkeit f; ,**~-'ho** ['-'həʊ] s.: **give s.o. the (old) ~** F j-n ,rausschmei-

ßen', b) j-m ,den Laufpass geben'.

heav·en ['hevn] s. **1.** Himmel(reich n) m: **go to ~** in den Himmel kommen; **move ~ and earth** fig. Himmel u. Hölle in Bewegung setzen; **to ~, to high ~s** F zum Himmel stinken (etc.); **in the seventh ~ (of delight)** fig. im siebten Himmel; **2.** fig. Himmel m, Para'dies n: **a ~ on earth; it was ~** es war himmlisch; **3.** ⚷ Himmel m, Gott m, Vorsehung f: **the ⚷s** die himmlischen Mächte; **4. by ~!, (good) ~s!** du lieber Himmel!; **for ~'s sake** um Himmels willen!; **~ forbid!** Gott behüte!; **thank ~!** Gott sei Dank!; **~ knows what ...** weiß der Himmel, was ...; **5.** mst pl. Himmel m, Firma'ment n: **the northern ~s** der nördliche (Sternen)Himmel; **6.** Himmel m, Klima n, Zone f.

heav·en·ly ['hevnlɪ] adj. himmlisch: a) Himmels...: **~ body** Himmelskörper m, b) göttlich, 'überirdisch: **~ hosts** himmlische Heerscharen, c) F himmlisch, wunderbar.

'**heav·en|-sent** adj. (wie) vom Himmel gesandt: **it was a ~ opportunity** es kam wie gerufen; '**~·ward** [-wəd] **I** adv. himmelwärts; **II** adj. gen Himmel gerichtet; '**~·wards** [-wədz] → **heavenward** I.

,**heav·i·er-than-'air** [,hevɪə-] adj. schwerer als Luft (Flugzeug).

heav·i·ly ['hevɪlɪ] adv. **1.** schwer (etc. → **heavy**): **suffer ~** schwere (finanzielle) Verluste erleiden; **~ polluted area** Belastungsgebiet n; **2.** mit schwerer Stimme; '**heav·i·ness** [-ɪnɪs] s. **1.** Schwere f (a. fig.); **2.** Gewicht n, Last f; **3.** Massigkeit f; **4.** Bedrückung f, Schwermut f; **5.** Schwerfälligkeit f; **6.** Schläfrigkeit f; **7.** Langweiligkeit f.

heav·y ['hevɪ] **I** adj. □ → **heavily; 1.** allg. schwer (a. ⚛, phys.): **~ load; ~ steps; ~ benzene** Schwerbenzin n; **~ industry** Schwerindustrie f; **with a ~ heart** schweren Herzens; **2.** ✕ schwer: **~ artillery (bomber, cruiser); bring up one's (od. the) ~ guns** F schweres Geschütz auffahren; **3.** schwer: a) heftig, stark: **~ fall** schwerer Sturz; **~ losses** schwere Verluste; **~ rain** starker Regen; **~ traffic** starker Verkehr, a. schwere Fahrzeuge pl., b) massig: **~ body**, c) wuchtig: **~ blow**, d) hart: **~ fine** hohe Geldstrafe; **4.** groß, beträchtlich: **~ buyer** Großabnehmer m; **~ orders** große Aufträge; **5.** schwer, stark, 'übermäßig: **~ drinker (eater)** starker Trinker (Esser); **6.** schwer: a) stark, 'hochpro,zentig: **~ beer** Starkbier n, b) stark, betäubend: **~ perfume**, c) schwer verdaulich: **~ food; 7.** drückend, lastend: **~ silence; 8.** meteor. a) schwer: **~ clouds**, b) finster, trüb: **~ sky**, c) drückend: **~ air; 9.** schwer: a) schwierig, mühsam: **a ~ task**, b) schwer verständlich: **a ~ book; 10. (with)** a) (schwer) beladen (mit), b) fig. über'laden (mit), voll (von); **11.** schwerfällig: **~ style; 12.** langweilig, stumpfsinnig; **13.** begriffsstutzig (Person); **14.** schläfrig, benommen (**with** von): **~ with sleep** schlaftrunken; **15.** ernst, düster; **16.** thea. etc. würdevoll od. (ge)streng: **a ~ husband; 17.** ✈ flau, schleppend; **18.** unwegsam, lehmig: **~ road; 19.** grob: **~ features; 20.** a) a. **~ with child** (hoch)schwanger, b) a. **~ with young** zo. trächtig; **21.** typ. fett (gedruckt); **II** adv. **22.** schwer (etc.): **hang ~** dahinschleichen (Zeit); **time was hanging ~ on my hands** die Zeit wurde mir lang; **lie ~ on s.o.** schwer auf j-m lasten; **III** s. **23.** thea. etc. a) Schurke m, b) würdiger älterer Herr; **24.** *sport* F Schwerge-wichtler *m*; **25.** *pl. Am.* F warme 'Un-terwäsche *f*; **26.** *Am.* F ‚schwerer Jun-ge' (*Verbrecher*); **27.** ✗ schwere Artil-le'rie; ‚~-'**armed** *adj.* ✗ schwer bewaff-net; ~ **chem·i·cals** *s. pl.* 'Schwerche-mi‚kalien *pl.*; ~ **con·crete** *s.* 'Schwer-be‚ton *m*; ~ **cur·rent** *s.* ⚡ Starkstrom *m*; ‚~-'**du·ty** *adj.* **1.** ⊚ Hochleistungs...; **2.** strapazierfähig; ‚~-'**hand·ed** *adj.* **1.** *a. fig.* plump, unbeholfen; **2.** drückend; ‚~-'**heart·ed** *adj.* niedergeschlagen, be-drückt; ~ **hy·dro·gen** *s.* 🜊 schwerer Wasserstoff; ~ **met·al** *s.* 'Schwerme‚tall *n*; ~ **oil** *s.* ⊚ Schweröl *n*; ~ **plate** *s.* Grobblech *n*; ~ **spar** *s. min.* Schwer-spat *m*; ~ **type** *s. typ.* Fettdruck *m*; ~ **wa·ter** *s.* 🜊 schweres Wasser; '~-**weight I** *s.* **1.** *sport* Schwergewicht (-ler *m*) *n*; **2.** ‚Schwergewicht' *n* (*Per-son od. Sache*); **3.** F Promi'nente(r) *m*, ‚großes Tier' *adj.* **4.** *sport* Schwerge-wichts...; **5.** schwer (*a. fig.*).

heb·dom·a·dal [heb'dɒmədl] *adj.* wö-chentlich; ⚄ *Council wöchentlich zs.-tretender Rat der Universität Oxford.*

He·bra·ic [hiː'breɪɪk] *adj.* (□ *~ally*) heb-räisch; **He·bra·ism** ['hiːbreɪɪzəm] *s.* **1.** *ling.* Hebra'ismus *m*; **2.** *das Jüdi-sche*; **He·bra·ist** ['hiːbreɪɪst] *s.* Hebra-'ist(in).

He·brew ['hiːbruː] **I** *s.* **1.** He'bräer(in), Jude *m*, Jüdin *f*; **2.** *ling.* He'bräisch *n*; **3.** F Kauderwelsch *n*; **4.** *pl. sg. konstr. bibl.* (Brief *m* an die) He'bräer *pl.*; **II** *adj.* **5.** he'bräisch.

Heb·ri·de·an [‚hebrɪ'diːən] **I** *adj.* he'bri-disch; **II** *s.* Bewohner(in) der Heb-riden.

hec·a·tomb ['hekətuːm] *s.* Heka'tombe *f* (*bsd. fig. gewaltige Menschenverluste*).

heck [hek] *s.* F Hölle *f*: *a ~ of a row* ein Höllenlärm; *what the ~?* was zum Teu-fel?; → *a. hell* 2.

heck·le ['hekl] *v/t.* **1.** Flachs hecheln; **2.** a) *j-n* ‚piesacken', b) *e-m* Redner durch Zwischenfragen zusetzen, ‚in die Zange nehmen'; '**heck·ler** [-lə] *s.* Zwischenru-fer *m*.

hec·tare ['hektɑː] *s.* Hektar *n*, *m*.

hec·tic ['hektɪk] *adj.* **1.** hektisch, schwindsüchtig: ~ *fever* Schwindsucht *f*; ~ *flush* hektische Röte; **2.** F fieber-haft, aufgeregt, hektisch: *have a ~ time* keinen Augenblick Ruhe haben.

hec·to·gram(me) ['hektəgræm] *s.* Hekto'gramm *n*; '**hec·to·graph** [-grɑːf] **I** *s.* Hekto'graph *m*; **II** *v/t.* hek-tographieren; '**hec·to‚li·ter** *Am.*, '**hec-to‚li·tre** *Brit.* [-‚liːtə] *s.* Hektoliter *m*, *n*.

hec·tor ['hektə] **I** *s.* Ty'rann *m*; **II** *v/t.* tyrannisieren, schikanieren: ~ *about* (*od. around*) *j-n* herumkommandieren; einhacken auf (*acc.*); **III** *v/i.* her'um-kommandieren.

he'd [hiːd] F *für* a) *he would*, b) *he had*.

hedge [hedʒ] **I** *s.* **1.** Hecke *f*, *bsd.* Hecken-zaun *m*; **2.** *fig.* Kette *f*, Absperrung *f*: *a ~ of police*; **3.** *fig.* (Ab)Sicherung *f* (*against* gegen); **4.** ⊤ Hedge-, De-ckungsgeschäft *n*; **II** *adj.* **5.** *fig.* drittran-gig, schlecht; **III** *v/t.* **6.** a. ~ *in* (*od. round*) a) *e-r* Hecke um'geben, ein-zäunen, b) *a.* ~ *about* (*od. around*) *fig. et.* behindern, c) *fig. j-n* einengen: ~ *off a. fig.* abgrenzen (*against* gegen); **7.** a) (ab)sichern (*against* gegen), b) sich ge-gen den Verlust *e-r* Wette *etc.* sichern: ~ *a bet*; ~ *one's bets fig.* auf Nummer sicher gehen; **IV** *v/i.* **8.** *fig.* ausweichen, sich nicht festlegen (wollen), sich winden, ‚kneifen'; **9.** sich vorsichtig äu-

ßern; **10.** sich (ab)sichern (*against* ge-gen); ~ *cut·ter s.* Heckenschere *f*; ~·**hog** ['hedʒhɒg] *s.* **1.** *zo.* a) Igel *m*, b) *Am.* Stachelschwein *n*; **2.** ♀ stachelige Samenkapsel; **3.** ✗ a) Igelstellung *f*, b) Drahtigel *m*, c) ⚓ Wasserbombenwerfer *m*; '~·**hop** *v/i.* ✈ dicht über dem Boden fliegen; '~·**hop·per** *s.* ✈ *sl.* Tiefflieger *m*; ~ *law·yer s.* 'Winkeladvo‚kat *m*.

hedg·er ['hedʒə] **1.** Heckengärtner *m*; **2.** *j-d, der sich nicht festlegen will.*

'**hedge·row** *s.* Hecke *f*; ~ *school s. Brit.* Klippschule *f*; ~ *shears s. pl. a. pair of* ~ Heckenschere *f*.

he·don·ic [hiː'dɒnɪk] *adj.* hedo'nistisch; **he·don·ism** ['hiːdəʊnɪzəm] *s. phls.* He-do'nismus *m*; **he·don·ist** ['hiːdəʊnɪst] *s.* Hedo'nist *m*; **he·do·nis·tic** [‚hiːdə-'nɪstɪk] *adj.* hedo'nistisch.

hee·bie-jee·bies [‚hiːbɪ'dʒiːbɪz] *s. pl.* F: *it gives me the* ~, *I get the* ~ dabei wirds mir ganz ‚anders', da krieg ich ‚Zustände'.

heed [hiːd] **I** *v/t.* beachten, Acht geben auf (*acc.*); **II** *v/i.* Acht geben; **III** *s.* Be-achtung *f*: *give* (*od. pay*) ~ *to*, *take* ~ *of* → **I**; *take* ~ **II**; '**heed·ful** [-fʊl] *adj.* □ achtsam: *be* ~ *of* → *heed* **I**; '**heed·less** [-lɪs] *adj.* □ achtlos, unachtsam: *be* ~ *of* keine Beachtung schenken (*dat.*); '**heed·less·ness** [-lɪs-nɪs] *s.* Achtlosigkeit *f*, Unachtsamkeit *f*.

hee-haw [‚hiː'hɔː] **I** *s.* **1.** 'I'ah *n* (*Esels-schrei*); **2.** *fig.* wieherndes Gelächter; **II** *v/i.* **3.** 'i'ahen; **4.** *fig.* wiehern(d lachen).

heel¹ [hiːl] **I** *v/t.* **1.** Absätze machen auf (*acc.*); **2.** Fersen anstricken an (*acc.*); **3.** *Fußball:* den Ball mit dem Absatz kicken; **II** *s.* **4.** Ferse *f*: ~ *of the hand Am.* Handballen *m*; **5.** Absatz *m*, Ha-cken *m* (*vom Schuh*); **6.** Ferse *f* (*Strumpf, Golfschläger*); **7.** Fuß *m*, En-de *n*, Rest *m*, *bsd.* (Brot)Kanten *m*; **8.** vorspringender Teil, Sporn *m*; **9.** *Am. sl.* ‚Scheißkerl' *m*;

Besondere Redewendungen:

~ *of Achilles* Achillesferse *f*; *at* (*od. on*) *s.o.'s* ~*s* j-m auf den Fersen, dicht hinter j-m; *on the* ~*s of s.th. fig.* un-mittelbar auf et. folgend, gleich nach et.; *down at* ~ a) mit schiefen Absät-zen, b) *a. out at* ~*s fig.* herunter-gekommen (*Person, Hotel etc.*); abgeris-sen, schäbig; *under the* ~ *of fig.* unter j-s Knute; *bring to* ~ *j-n* gefügig *od.* ‚kirre' machen; *come to* ~ a) bei Fuß gehen (*Hund*), b) gefügig werden, ‚spu-ren' (*od. kick*) *one's* ~*s* ungedul-dig warten; *dig* (*od. stick*) *one's* ~*s in* F ‚sich auf die Hinterbeine stellen'; *drag one's* ~*s fig.* sich Zeit lassen; *kick up one's* ~*s* F ‚auf den Putz hauen'; *lay s.o. by the* ~*s* j-n zur Strecke bringen, j-n dingfest machen; *show a clean pair of* ~*s*, *take to one's* ~*s* Fersengeld geben, die Beine in die Hand nehmen; *tread on s.o.'s* ~*s* j-m auf die Hacken treten; *turn on one's* ~*s* (auf dem Absatz) kehrtma-chen.

heel² [hiːl] *v/t. u. v/i. a.* ~ *over* (sich) auf die Seite legen (*Schiff*), krängen.

‚**heel-and-'toe walk·ing** *s. sport* Ge-hen *n*; '~·**ball** *s.* Polierwachs *n*; ~ **bone** *s. anat.* Fersenbein *n*.

heeled [hiːld] *adj.* **1.** mit *e-r* Ferse *od. e-m* Absatz (versehen); **2.** → *well-heeled*; '**heel·er** [-lə] *s. pol. Am.* Handlanger *m*, ‚La'kai' *m*.

'**heel·tap** *s.* **1.** Absatzfleck *m*; **2.** letzter Rest, Neige *f* (*im Glas*): *no* ~*s!* ex!

heft [heft] *v/t.* **1.** hochheben; **2.** in der Hand wiegen; '**heft·y** [-tɪ] *adj.* F **1.**

schwer; **2.** kräftig, stämmig; **3.** ‚mäch-tig', ‚saftig', gewaltig: ~ *blow* (*prices*).

He·ge·li·an [heɪ'giːljən] *s. phls.* Hege-li'aner *m*.

he·gem·o·ny [hɪ'gemənɪ] *s. pol.* Hege-mo'nie *f*.

heif·er ['hefə] *s.* Färse *f*, junge Kuh.

heigh [heɪ] *int.* hei!; he(da)!; ‚~-'**ho** [-'həʊ] *int.* ach jeh!; oh!

height [haɪt] *s.* **1.** Höhe *f* (*a. ast.*): *10 feet in* ~ 10 Fuß hoch; ~ *of fall* Fallhöhe *f*; **2.** (Körper)Größe *f*: *what is your* ~? wie groß sind Sie?; **3.** Anhöhe *f*; Erhe-bung *f*; **4.** *fig.* Höhe(punkt *m*) *f*, Gipfel *m*: *at its* ~ auf s-m (ihrem) *od.* dem Höhepunkt; *at the* ~ *of summer* (*of the season*) im Hochsommer (in der Hochsaison); *the* ~ *of folly* der Gipfel der Torheit; *dressed in the* ~ *of fash-ion* nach der neuesten Mode gekleidet; '**height·en** [-tn] **I** *v/t.* **1.** erhöhen (*a. fig.*); **2.** *fig.* vergrößern, -stärken, stei-gern, heben, vertiefen; **3.** her'vorhe-ben; **II** *v/i.* **4.** wachsen, (an)steigen.

height find·er, ~ **ga(u)ge** *s.* ✈ Höh-enmesser *m*.

hei·nous ['heɪnəs] *adj.* □ ab'scheulich, grässlich; '**hei·nous·ness** [-nɪs] *s.* Ab-'scheulichkeit *f*.

Heinz [haɪnz] *npr.:* ~ *57* F Prome'naden-mischung *f* (*Hund*).

heir [eə] *s.* **1.** ⚖ *u. fig.* Erbe *m* (*to od. of s.o.* j-s): ~ *to the throne* Thronfolger *m*; ~-*at-law*, ~ *general*, ~ *apparent* gesetzlicher Erbe; ~ *presumptive* mut-maßlicher Erbe; ~ *of the body* leibli-cher Erbe; **heir·dom** ['eədəm] → *heirship*; **heir·ess** ['eərɪs] *s.* (*bsd.* rei-che) Erbin; **heir·loom** ['eəluːm] *s.* (Fa-'milien)Erbstück *n*; **heir·ship** ['eəʃɪp] *s.* **1.** Erbrecht *n*; **2.** Erbschaft *f*, Erbe *n*.

heist [haɪst] *sl.* **I** *s.* a) ,Ding' *n* (*Raubüberfall od. Diebstahl*), b) Beute *f*; **II** *v/t.* über'fallen, ‚klauen'; erbeuten.

held [held] *pret. u. p.p. von hold²*.

he·li·an·thus [‚hiːlɪ'ænθəs] *s.* ♀ Sonnen-blume *f*.

hel·i·borne ['helɪbɔːn] *adj.* im Hub-schrauber befördert.

hel·i·bus ['helɪbʌs] *s.* ✈ Hubschrauber *m* für Per'sonenbeförderung, Lufttaxi *n*.

hel·i·cal ['helɪkl] *adj.* □ spi'ralen-, schrauben-, schneckenförmig: ~ *gear* ⊚ Schrägstirnrad *n*; ~ *spring* Schrau-benfeder *f*; ~ *staircase* Wendeltreppe *f*.

hel·i·ces ['helɪsiːz] *pl. von helix*.

hel·i·cop·ter ['helɪkɒptə] ✈ **I** *s.* Hub-schrauber *m*, Heli'kopter *m*: ~ *gunship* Kampfhubschrauber; **II** *v/i. u. v/t.* mit dem Hubschrauber fliegen *od.* beför-dern.

helio- [-hiːliəʊ-] *in Zssgn* Sonnen...

he·li·o·cen·tric [‚hiːlɪəʊ'sentrɪk] *adj. ast.* helio'zentrisch; **he·li·o·chro·my** ['hiː-lɪəʊ‚krəʊmɪ] *s.* 'Farbfotogra‚fie *f*; **he-li·o·gram** ['hiːlɪəʊgræm] *s.* Helio-'gramm *n*; **he·li·o·graph** ['hiːlɪəʊgrɑːf] **I** *s.* Helio'graph *m*; **II** *v/t.* heliographie-ren; **he·li·o·gra·vure** [‚hiːlɪəʊgrə'vjʊə] *s. typ.* Heliogra'vüre *f*.

he·li·o·trope ['heljətrəʊp] *s.* ♀, *min.* He-lio'trop *n*.

he·li·o·type ['hiːlɪətaɪp] *s. typ.* Licht-druck *m*.

hel·i·pad ['helɪpæd], '**hel·i·port** [-pɔːt] *s.* Heli'port *m*, Hubschrauberlandeplatz *m*; '**hel·i‚ski·ing** *s sport* 'Heli‚skiing *n* (*Skilaufen im Hochgebirge mit Hub-schraubertransport*).

he·li·um ['hiːljəm] *s.* 🜊 Helium *n*.

he·lix ['hiːlɪks] *pl.* **hel·i·ces** ['helɪsiːz] *s.* **1.** Spi'rale *f*; **2.** ⅄ Schneckenlinie *f*; **3.** *anat.* Helix *f*, Ohrleiste *f*; **4.** △ Schnecke *f*; **5.** *zo.* Helix *f* (*Schnecke*); **6.** 🐍 Helix *f* (*Molekülstruktur*).

hell [hel] **I** *s.* **1.** Hölle *f* (*a. fig.*): *it was* ~ es war die reinste Hölle; *catch* (*od. get*) ~ F 'eins aufs Dach kriegen'; *come* ~ *or high water* F (ganz) egal, was passiert, unter allen Umständen; *give s.o.* ~ F j-m 'die Hölle heiß machen'; ~ *for leather* F was das Zeug hält, wie verrückt; *there will be* ~ *to pay* F das werden wir schwer büßen müssen; *raise* ~ F 'e-n Mordskrach schlagen'; *suffer* ~ (*on earth*) die Hölle auf Erden haben; **2.** F (*verstärkend*) Hölle *f*, Teufel *m*: *a* ~ *of a noise* ein Höllenlärm; *be in a* ~ *of a temper* e-e 'Mordswut' *od.* e-e 'Stinklaune' haben; *a* (*od. one*) ~ *of a* (*good*) *car* ein 'verdammt' guter Wagen; *a* ~ *of a guy* ein prima Kerl; *go to* ~! 'scher dich zum Teufel'!, *a.* 'du kannst mich mal!'; *get the* ~ *out of here!* mach, dass du rauskommst!; *like* ~ wie verrückt (*arbeiten etc.*); *like* (*od. the*) ~ *you did!* 'e-n Dreck' hast du (getan)!; *what the* ~ ...? was zum Teufel ...?; *what the* ~! ach, was!; ~*'s bells* → 6; **3.** F Spaß *m*: *for the* ~ *of it* aus Spaß an der Freud; *the* ~ *of it is that ...* das Komische *od.* Tolle daran ist, dass; **4.** Spielhölle *f*; **5.** *typ.* De'fektenkasten *m*; **II** *int.* **6.** F a) *Brit. sl. a.* *bloody* ~! verdammt!, b) (*überrascht*) Teufel, Teufel!, Mann!; ~*, I didn't know* (*that*)*!* Mann, das hab ich nicht gewusst!

he'll [hi:l] F *für he will.*

'hell|,bend·er s. **1.** *zo.* Schlammteufel *m*; **2.** *Am.* F 'wilder Bursche'; ~**'bent** *adj.* F **1.** *be* ~ *on* (*doing*) *s.th.* ganz versessen sein auf et. (darauf, et. zu tun); **2.** 'verrückt', wild, leichtsinnig; '~**·broth** *s.* Hexen-, Zaubertrank *m*; '~**·cat** *s.* (wilde) Hexe, Xan'thippe *f*.

hel·le·bore ['helɪbɔː] *s.* ♣ Nieswurz *f*.

Hel·lene ['heli:n] *s.* Hel'lene *m*, Grieche *m*; **Hel·len·ic** [he'li:nɪk] *adj.* hel'lenisch, griechisch; **Hel·len·ism** ['helɪnɪzəm] *s.* Helle'nismus *m*, Griechentum *n*; **Hel·len·ist** ['helɪnɪst] *s.* Helle'nist *m*; **Hel·len·is·tic** [ˌhelɪ'nɪstɪk] *adj.* helle'nistisch; **Hel·len·ize** ['helɪnaɪz] *v/t. u. v/i.* (sich) hellenisieren.

hell|fire s. Höllenfeuer *n*; **2.** *fig.*Höllenqualen *pl.*; '~**·hound** *s.* **1.** Höllenhund *m*; **2.** *fig.* Teufel *m*.

hell·ion ['heljən] *s.* F Range *f, m*, Bengel *m*.

hell·ish ['helɪʃ] *adj.* ☐ **1.** höllisch (*a. fig.* F); **2.** F 'verteufelt', 'scheußlich'.

hel·lo [hə'ləʊ] **I** *int.* **1.** hal'lo!, *überrascht: a.* na'nu!; **II** *pl.* **-los** *s.* **2.** Hal'lo *n*; **3.** Gruß *m*: *say* ~ (*to s.o.*) (j-m) guten (*od.* Guten) Tag sagen; **III** *v/i.* **4.** hal'lo rufen.

hell·uv·a ['heləvə] *adj. u. adv.* F 'mordsmäßig', 'toll': *a* ~ *noise* ein Höllenlärm; *a* ~ *guy* a) ein prima Kerl, b) ein toller Kerl.

helm¹ [helm] *s.* **1.** ⚓ a) Ruder *n*, Steuer *n*, b) Ruderpinne *f*: *the ship answers the* ~ das Schiff gehorcht dem Ruder; **2.** *fig.* Ruder *n*, Führung *f*: ~ *of State* Staatsruder; *at the* ~ am Ruder *od.* an der Macht; *take the* ~ das Ruder übernehmen.

helm² [helm] *s. obs.* Helm *m*; **helmed** [-md] *adj. obs.* behelmt.

hel·met ['helmɪt] *s.* **1.** ✗ Helm *m*; **2.** (Schutz-, Sturz-, Tropen-, Taucher-) Helm *m*; **3.** ♣ Kelch *m*; **'hel·met·ed** [-tɪd] *adj.* behelmt.

helms·man ['helmzmən] *s.* [*irr.*] ⚓

Steuermann *m* (*a. fig.*).

Hel·ot ['helət] *s. hist.* He'lot(e) *m, fig.* (*mst* ⚓) *a.* Sklave *m*; **'hel·ot·ry** [-trɪ] *s.* **1.** He'lotentum *n*; **2.** *coll.* He'loten *pl.*

help [help] **I** *s.* **1.** Hilfe *f* (*a. Hilfedatei e-r Software*), Beistand *m*, Mit-, Beihilfe *f*: *by* (*od. with*) *the* ~ *of* mithilfe von; *he came to my* ~ er kam mir zu Hilfe; *it* (*she*) *is a great* ~ es (sie) ist e-e große Hilfe; *can I be of any* ~ (*to you*)*?* kann ich Ihnen (irgendwie) helfen *od.* behilflich sein?; **2.** Abhilfe *f*: *there is no* ~ *for it* da kann man nichts machen, es lässt sich nicht ändern; **3.** Hilfsmittel *n*; **4.** a) Gehilfe *m*, Gehilfin *f*, (*bsd.* Haus)Angestellte(r *m*) *f*, (*bsd.* Land)Arbeiter(in): *domestic* ~ Hausgehilfin, b) *coll.* ('Dienst)Perso,nal *n*, (Hilfs)Kräfte *pl.*; **II** *v/t.* **5.** j-m helfen *od.* beistehen *od.* behilflich sein, j-n unter'stützen (*in od. with s.th.* bei et.): *can I* ~ *you?* a) kann ich Ihnen behilflich sein?, b) werden Sie schon bedient?; *so* ~ *me* (*I did, etc.*)*!* Ehrenwort!; *be* ~*ing the police* *euphem.* (zurzeit) von der Polizei vernommen werden; → *god* 2; **6.** fördern, beitragen zu; **7.** lindern, helfen *od.* Abhilfe schaffen bei; **8.** ~ *s.o. to s.th.* a) j-m zu et. verhelfen, b) (*bsd. bei Tisch*) j-m et. reichen *od.* geben; ~ *o.s.* sich bedienen, zugreifen; ~ *o.s. to* a) sich bedienen mit, sich et. nehmen, b) sich et. aneignen *od.* nehmen (*a. iro. stehlen*); **9.** *mit can:* abhelfen (*dat.*), et. verhindern, vermeiden, ändern: *I can't* ~ *it* a) ich kanns nicht ändern, b) ich kann nichts dafür; *it can't be* ~*ed* da kann man nichts machen, es lässt sich nicht ändern; (*not*) *if I can* ~ *it* (nicht,) wenn ich es vermeiden kann; *how could I* ~ *it?* a) was konnte ich dagegen tun?, b) was konnte ich dafür?; *I can't* ~ *it* a) ich kann es nicht ändern, b) ich kann nichts dafür; *she can't* ~ *her freckles* für ihre Sommersprossen kann sie nichts; *don't be late if you can* ~ *it* komme möglichst nicht zu spät!; *I could not* ~ *laughing* ich musste einfach lachen; *I can't* ~ *feeling* ich werde das Gefühl nicht los; *I can't* ~ *myself* ich kann nicht anders; **III** *v/i.* **10.** helfen: *every little* ~*s* jede Kleinigkeit hilft; **11.** *don't stay longer than you can* ~! bleib nicht länger als nötig!;

Zssgn mit adv.:

help|down *v/t.* **1.** j-m her'unter-, hinunterhelfen; **2.** *j-m* 'Untergang (*gen.*) beitragen; ~ *in* *v/t.* j-m hin'einhelfen; ~ *off* *v/t.* **1.** → *help on* 1; **2.** *help s.o. off with his coat* j-m aus dem Mantel helfen; ~ *on* *v/t.* **1.** weiter-, forthelfen (*dat.*); **2.** *help s.o. on with his coat* j-m in den Mantel helfen; ~ *out* **I** *v/t.* **1.** j-m her'aus-, hin'aushelfen (*of* aus); **2.** *fig.* j-m aus der Not helfen; **3.** *fig.* j-m aushelfen, j-n unter'stützen; **II** *v/i.* **4.** aushelfen (*with* bei, mit); **5.** helfen, nützlich sein; ~ *through* *v/t.* j-m (hin)'durch-, hin'weghelfen; ~ *up* *v/t.* j-m her'auf-, hin'aufhelfen.

help·er ['helpə] *s.* **1.** Helfer(in); **2.** Gehilfe *m*, Gehilfin *f*; → *help* 4; **help·ful** ['helpfʊl] *adj.* ☐ **1.** hilfsbereit, behilflich (*to dat.*); **2.** hilfreich, nützlich (*to dat.*); **help·ful·ness** ['helpfʊlnɪs] *s.* **1.** Hilfsbereitschaft *f*; **2.** Nützlichkeit *f*; **help·ing** ['helpɪŋ] **I** *adj.* helfend, hilfreich: *lend* (*s.o.*) *a* ~ *hand* (j-m) helfen *od.* behilflich sein; **II** *s.* Porti'on *f* (*e-r Speise*): *have* (*od.* *take*) *a second* ~ sich noch mal (davon) nehmen; **help·less** ['helplɪs] *adj.* ☐ *allg.* hilflos: *be* ~

with laughter sich totlachen; **help·less·ness** ['helplɪsnɪs] *s.* Hilflosigkeit *f*; **help·line** ['helplaɪn] *s.* 'Helpline *f*: a) tele'fonische Beratung, b) Informati'onsdienst *m*, c) Notruf *m*.

'help·mate, **'help·meet** *s. obs.* Gehilfe *m*, Gehilfin *f*; (Ehe)Gefährte *m*, (Ehe-) Gefährtin *f*, Gattin *f*.

hel·ter-skel·ter [ˌheltə'skeltə] **I** *adv.* Hals über Kopf, in wilder Hast; **II** *adj.* hastig, über'stürzt; **III** *s.* Durchein'ander *n*, wilde Hast.

helve [helv] *s.* Griff *m*, Stiel *m*: *throw the* ~ *after the hatchet* *fig.* das Kind mit dem Bade ausschütten.

Hel·ve·tian [hel'vi:ʃjən] **I** *adj.* hel'vetisch, schweizerisch; **II** *s.* Hel'vetier (-in), Schweizer(in).

hem¹ [hem] **I** *s.* **1.** (Kleider-, Rock- *etc.*) Saum *m*; **2.** Rand *m*; **3.** Einfassung *f*; **II** *v/t.* **4.** *Kleid etc.* säumen; **5.** ~ *in*, ~ *about*, ~ *around* um'randen, einfassen; **6.** ~ *in* a) ✗ einschließen, b) *fig.* einengen.

hem² [hm] **I** *int.* hm!, hem!; **II** *s.* H(e)m *n*, Räuspern *n*; **III** *v/i.* 'hm', sich räuspern; stocken (*im Reden*): ~ *and haw* herumstottern, -drucksen.

he·mal *etc.* → *haemal etc.*

'he-man *s.* [*irr.*] F 'He-Man' *m*, 'richtiger' Mann, sehr männlicher Typ.

he·mat·ic *etc.* → *haematic etc.*

hem·i·ple·gi·a [ˌhemɪ'pli:dʒɪə] *s.* 🩺 einseitige Lähmung, Hemiple'gie *f*.

hem·i·sphere ['hemɪ,sfɪə] *s. bsd. geogr.* Halbkugel *f*, Hemi'sphäre *f* (*a. anat. des Großhirns*); **hem·i·spher·i·cal** [ˌhemɪ'sferɪkl], *a.* **hem·i·spher·ic** [ˌhemɪ'sferɪk] *adj.* hemi'sphärisch, halbkugelig.

'hem·line *s.* (Kleider)Saum *m*: ~*s are going up again* die Kleider werden wieder kürzer.

hem·lock ['hemlɒk] *s.* **1.** ♣ Schierling *m*; **2.** *fig.* Schierlings-, Giftbecher *m*; **3.** *a.* ~ *fir*, ~ *spruce* Hemlock-, Schierlingstanne *f*.

he·mo·glo·bin, **he·mo·phil·i·a**, **hem·or·rhage**, **hem·or·rhoids** *etc.* → *haemo...*

hemp [hemp] *s.* **1.** ♣ Hanf *m*; **2.** Hanf (-faser *f*) *m*; **3.** 'Hanfnar,kotikum *n*, *bsd.* Haschisch *n*; **'hemp·en** [-pən] *adj.* hanfen, Hanf...

'hem·stitch **I** *s.* Hohlsaum(stich) *m*; **II** *v/t.* mit Hohlsaum nähen.

hen [hen] *s.* **1.** *orn.* Henne *f*, Huhn *n*: ~*'s egg* Hühnerei *n*; **2.** Weibchen *n* (*von Vögeln, a. Krebs u. Hummer*); **3.** F a) (aufgeregte) 'Wachtel', b) Klatschbase *f*; '~**·bane** *s.* ♣, *pharm.* 'Bilsenkraut(ex,trakt *m*) *n*.

hence [hens] *adv.* **1.** *a. from* ~ (*räumlich*) von hier, von hinnen, fort: ~ *with it!* weg damit!; *go* ~ von hinnen gehen (*sterben*); **2.** *zeitlich:* von jetzt an, binnen: *a week* ~ in *od.* nach einer Woche; **3.** folglich, daher, deshalb; **4.** hieraus, daraus: ~ *it follows that* daraus folgt, dass; ~**'forth**, ~**'for·ward(s)** *adv.* von nun an, fort'an, künftig.

hench·man ['hentʃmən] *s.* [*irr.*] *bsd. pol.* a) Gefolgsmann *m*, b) *contp.* Handlanger *m*, j-s 'Krea'tur' *f*.

'hen|coop *s.* Hühnerstall *m*; ~ *har·ri·er* *s. orn.* Kornweihe *f*; ~ *hawk* *s. orn. Am.* Hühnerbussard *m*; ~**-'heart·ed** *adj.* feig(e).

hen·na ['henə] *s.* **1.** ♣ Hennastrauch *m*; **2.** Henna *f* (*Färbemittel*); **'hen·naed** [-nəd] *adj.* mit Henna gefärbt.

hen|par·ty *s.* F Kaffeeklatsch *m*; '~**·pecked** [-pekt] *adj.* F unter dem

H

Pan'toffel stehend: ~ **husband** Pantoffelheld *m*; '~·**roost** *s*. Hühnerstange *f od.* -stall *m.*

hen·ry ['henrɪ] *pl.* **-rys, -ries** *s. ₰, phys.* Henry *n* (*Einheit der Induktivität*).

hep [hep] → *hip*⁴.

he·pat·ic [hɪ'pætɪk] *adj. ⚕* he'patisch, Leber...; **hep·a·ti·tis** [ˌhepə'taɪtɪs] *s. ⚕* Leberentzündung *f*, Hepa'titis *f*; **hep·a·tol·o·gist** [ˌhepə'tɒlədʒɪst] *s. ⚕* He'pato'loge *m.*

'**hep·cat** *s. sl. obs.* Jazz-, *bsd.* Swingmusiker *m od.* -freund *m.*

hep·ta·gon ['heptəɡən] *s. A* Siebeneck *n*, Hepta'gon *n*; **hep·tag·o·nal** [hep-'tæɡənl] *adj. A* siebeneckig; **hep·ta·he·dron** [ˌheptə'hedrən] *pl.* **-drons** *od.* **-dra** [-drə] *s. A* Hepta'eder *n.*

hep·tath·lete [hep'tæθliːt] *s. sport* Siebenkämpferin *f*; **hep·tath·lon** [hep-'tæθlɒn] *s.* Siebenkampf *m.*

her [hɜː; hə] **I** *pron.* **1.** a) sie (*acc. von* **she**), b) ihr (*dat. von* **she**); **2.** F sie (*nom.*): *it's* ~ sie ist es; **II** *poss. adj.* **3.** ihr, ihre; **III** *refl. pron.* **4.** sich: *she looked about* ~ sie sah um sich.

her·ald ['herəld] **I** *s.* **1.** *hist.* a) Herold *m*, b) Wappenherold *m*; **2.** *fig.* Verkünder *m*; **3.** *fig.* (Vor)Bote *m*; **II** *v/t.* **4.** verkünden, ankündigen (*a. fig.*); **5.** *a.* ~ *in* a) einführen, b) einleiten.

he·ral·dic [he'rældɪk] *adj.* he'raldisch, Wappen...; **her·ald·ry** ['herəldrɪ] *s.* **1.** He'raldik *f*, Wappenkunde *f*; **2.** a) Wappen *n*, b) he'raldische Sym'bole *pl.*

herb [hɜːb] *s. ♀* a) Kraut *n*, b) Heilkraut *n*, c) Küchenkraut *n*: ~ **tea** Kräutertee *m*; **her·ba·ceous** [hɜː'beɪʃəs] *adj. ♀* krautartig, Kraut...: ~ **border** (Stauden)Rabatte *f*; '**herb·age** [-bɪdʒ] *s.* **1.** *coll.* Kräuter *pl.*, Gras *n*; **2.** ⚖ *Brit.* Weiderecht *n*; '**herb·al** [-bl] **I** *adj.* Kräuter..., Pflanzen...; **II** *s.* Pflanzenbuch *n*; '**herb·al·ist** [-bəlɪst] *s.* **1.** Kräuter-, Pflanzenkenner(in); **2.** Kräutersammler(in), -händler(in); **3.** Herba'list(in), Kräuterheilkundige(r *m*) *f*; **her·bar·i·um** [hɜː'beərɪəm] *s.* Her'barium *n.*

her·bi·vore ['hɜːbɪvɔː] *s. zo.* Pflanzenfresser *m*; **her·biv·o·rous** [hɜː'bɪvərəs] *adj.* Pflanzen fressend.

Her·cu·le·an [ˌhɜːkjʊ'liːən] *adj.* her'kulisch (*a. fig. riesenstark*), Herkules...: *the* ~ *labo(u)rs* die Arbeiten des Herkules; *a* ~ *labo(u)r fig.* e-e Herkulesarbeit; **Her·cu·les** ['hɜːkjʊliːz] *s. myth., ast. u. fig.* Herkules *m.*

herd [hɜːd] **I** *s.* **1.** Herde *f*, (*wild lebender Tiere a.*) Rudel *n*; **2.** *contp.* Herde *f*, Masse *f* (*Menschen*): *the common* (*od.* *vulgar*) ~ die Masse (Mensch), die große Masse; **3.** *in Zssgn* Hirt(in); **II** *v/t.* **4.** Vieh hüten; **5.** (~ *together* zs.-)treiben; **III** *v/i.* **6.** *a.* ~ *together* a) in Herden gehen *od.* leben, b) sich zs.-drängen; **7.** sich zs.-tun (*among, with* mit); '~·**book** *s. ✍* Herdbuch *n*; ~ *in·stinct s.* 'Herden, stinkt *m*, -trieb *m* (*a. fig.*); '~s·**man** [-dzmən] *s.* [*irr.*] **1.** *Brit.* Hirt *m*; **2.** Herdenbesitzer *m.*

here [hɪə] **I** *adv.* **1.** hier: *I am* ~ a) ich bin hier, b) ich bin da (*anwesend*); ~ *and there* a) hier u. da, da u. dort, b) hierhin u. dorthin, c) hin u. wieder, hie u. da; ~ *and now* hier u. jetzt *od.* heute; ~, *there and everywhere* (all)überall; *that's neither* ~ *nor there* a) das gehört nicht zur Sache, b) das besagt nichts; *we are leaving* ~ *today* wir reisen heute von hier ab; ~ *goes* F also los!; ~'*s to you!* auf dein Wohl!; ~ *you are!* hier (bitte)! (*da hast du es*); *this* ~ *man sl.* dieser Mann hier; **2.** (hier)her,

hierhin: *bring it* ~*!* bring es hierher!; *come* ~*!* komm her!; *this belongs* ~ das gehört hierher *od.* hierhin; **II** *s.* **3.** *the* ~ *and now* a) das Hier u. Heute, b) das Diesseits; '~·**a,bout(s)** [-ərə-] *adv.* hier her'um, in dieser Gegend; ,~'**af·ter** [-ɑːr'ɑː-] **I** *adv.* **1.** her'nach, nachher; **2.** in Zukunft; **II** *s.* **3.** Zukunft *f*; **4.** (*das*) Jenseits; ,~'**by** *adv.* 'hierdurch, hiermit.

he·red·i·ta·ble [hɪ'redɪtəbl] → *heritable*; **her·e·dit·a·ment** [ˌherɪ'dɪtəmənt] *s.* ⚖ a) *Brit.* Grundstück *n* (als Bemessungsgrundlage für die Kommu'nalabgaben), b) *Am.* vererblicher Vermögensgegenstand; **he'red·i·tar·y** [-tərɪ] *adj.* □ **1.** erblich, er-, vererbt, Erb...: ~ *disease ⚕* Erbkrankheit *f*, ~ *portion* ⚖ Pflichtteil *m*, ~ *succession Am.* Erbfolge *f*, ~ *taint ⚕* erbliche Belastung; **2.** *fig.* Erb..., alt'hergebracht: ~ *enemy* Erbfeind *m*; **he'red·i·ty** [-tɪ] *s. biol.* **1.** Vererbbarkeit *f*, Erblichkeit *f*; **2.** ererbte Anlagen *pl.*, Erbmasse *f.*

,**here**|'**from** *adv.* hieraus; ,~'**in** [-ər'ɪ-] *adv.* hierin; ,~·**in·a'bove** *adv.* im Vorstehenden, oben (*erwähnt*); ,~·**in'af·ter** *adv.* nachstehend, im Folgenden; ,~'**of** *adv.* hiervon, dessen.

her·e·sy ['herəsɪ] *s.* Ketze'rei *f*, Häre'sie *f*; '**her·e·tic** [-ɒtɪk] **I** *s.* Ketzer(in); **II** *adj.* → **he·ret·i·cal** [hɪ'retɪkl] *adj.* □ ketzerisch.

,**here**|'**to** [-'tuː] *adv.* **1.** hierzu; **2.** bis'her; ,~·**to'fore** [-tʊ-] *adv.* vordem, ehemals; ,~'**un·der** [-ər'ʌ-] **1.** → *hereinafter*; **2.** ⚖ kraft dieses (*Vertrags etc.*); ,~'**un·to** [-ər'ʌ-] → *hereto*; ,~·**up'on** [-ərə-] *adv.* hierauf, darauf('hin); ,~'**with** → *hereby.*

her·it·a·ble ['herɪtəbl] *adj.* □ **1.** erblich, vererbbar; **2.** erbfähig; '**her·it·age** [-ɪtɪdʒ] *s.* **1.** Erbe *n*: a) Erbschaft *f*, Erbgut *n*, b) *ererbtes Recht etc.*; **2.** *bibl.* (*das*) Volk Israel; '**her·i·tor** [-ɪtə] *s.* ⚖ Erbe *m.*

her·maph·ro·dite [hɜː'mæfrədaɪt] *s. biol.* Hermaphro'dit *m*, Zwitter *m*; **her'maph·ro·dit·ism** [-daɪtɪzəm] *s. biol.* Hermaphrodi'tismus *m*, Zwittertum *n od.* -bildung *f.*

her·met·ic [hɜː'metɪk] *adj.* (□ ~*ally*) her'metisch (*a. fig.*), luftdicht: ~ *seal* luftdichter Verschluss.

her·mit ['hɜːmɪt] *s.* Einsiedler *m* (*a. fig.*), Ere'mit *m*; '**her·mit·age** [-tɪdʒ] *s.* Einsiede'lei *f*, Klause *f.*

hermit crab *s. zo.* Einsiedlerkrebs *m.*

her·ni·a ['hɜːnjə] *s. ⚕* Bruch *m*, Hernie *f*; '**her·ni·al** [-jəl] *adj.*: ~ *truss ⚕* Bruchband *n.*

he·ro ['hɪərəʊ] *pl.* **-roes** *s.* **1.** Held *m*; **2.** *thea. etc.* Held *m*, 'Hauptper,son *f*; **3.** *antiq.* Heros *m*, Halbgott *m.*

he·ro·ic [hɪ'rəʊɪk] **I** *adj.* (□ ~*ally*) **1.** he'roisch (*a. paint. etc.*), heldenmütig, -haft, Helden...: ~ *age* Heldenzeitalter *n*; ~ *couplet* heroisches Reimpaar; ~ *poem* → 4b; ~ *tenor ♪* Heldentenor *m*; ~ *verse* → 4a; **2.** a) erhaben, b) hochtrabend (*Stil*); **3.** ⚒ drastisch, Radikal...; **II** *s.* **4.** a) he'roisches Versmaß, b) he'roisches Gedicht; **5.** *pl.* bom'bastische Worte *pl.*

her·o·in ['herəʊɪn] *s.* Hero'in *n.*

her·o·ine ['herəʊɪn] *s.* **1.** Heldin *f* (*a. thea. etc.*); **2.** *antiq.* Halbgöttin *f*; '**her·o·ism** [-ɪzəm] *s.* Heldentum *n*, Hero'ismus *m*; **he·ro·ize** ['hɪərəʊaɪz] **I** *v/t.* heroisieren, zum Helden machen; **II** *v/i.* den Helden spielen.

her·on ['herən] *s. orn.* Reiher *m*; '**her·on·ry** [-rɪ] *s.* Reiherhorst *m.*

he·ro| **wor·ship** *s.* **1.** Heldenverehrung

f; **2.** Schwärme'rei *f*; '~·,**wor·ship** *v/t.* **1.** als Helden verehren; **2.** schwärmen für.

her·pes ['hɜːpiːz] *s. ⚕* Herpes *m*, Bläschenausschlag *m.*

her·pe·tol·o·gy [ˌhɜːpɪ'tɒlədʒɪ] *s.* Herpetolo'gie *f*, Rep'tilienkunde *f.*

her·ring ['herɪŋ] *s. ichth.* Hering *m*; '~·**bone I** *s.* **1.** *a.* ~ *design*, ~ *pattern* Fischgrätenmuster *n*; **2.** fischgrätenartige Anordnung; **3.** *Stickerei:* ~ (*stitch*) Fischgrätenstich *m*; **4.** *Skilauf:* Grätenschritt *m*; **II** *v/t.* **5.** mit e-m Fischgrätenmuster säumen; **III** *v/i.* **6.** *Skilauf:* im Grätenschritt steigen; ~ *pond s.* humor. der 'Große Teich' (*Atlantik*).

hers [hɜːz] *poss. pron.* ihrer (ihre, ihres), der (die, das) Ihre (*od.* Ihrige): *my mother and* ~ meine u. ihre Mutter; *it is* ~ es gehört ihr; *a friend of* ~ e-e Freundin von ihr.

her·self [hɜː'self; hə-] *pron.* **1.** *refl.* sich: *she hurt* ~; **2.** sich (selbst): *she wants it for* ~; **3.** *verstärkend:* sie (*nom. od. acc.*) *od.* ihr (*dat.*) selbst: *she* ~ *did it*, *she did it* ~ sie selbst hat es getan, sie hat es selbst getan; *by* ~ allein, ohne Hilfe, von selbst; **4.** *she is not quite* ~ a) sie ist nicht ganz normal, b) sie ist nicht auf der Höhe; *she is* ~ *again* sie ist wieder die Alte.

hertz [hɜːts] *s. phys.* Hertz *n*; **Hertz·i·an** ['hɜːtsɪən] *adj. phys.* hertzsch: ~ *waves* hertzsche Wellen.

he's [hiːz; hɪz] F *für* a) *he is*, b) *he has.*

hes·i·tance ['hezɪtəns], '**hes·i·tan·cy** [-sɪ] *s.* Zögern *n*, Unschlüssigkeit *f*; '**hes·i·tant** [-nt] *adj.* **1.** zögernd, unschlüssig; **2.** *beim Sprechen:* stockend; '**hes·i·tate** [-teɪt] *v/i.* **1.** zögern, zaudern, unschlüssig sein, Bedenken haben (*to inf. zu inf.*): *not to* ~ *at* nicht zurückschrecken vor (*dat.*); **2.** (*beim Sprechen*) stocken; '**hes·i·tat·ing·ly** [-teɪtɪŋlɪ] *adv.* zögernd; **hes·i·ta·tion** [ˌhezɪ'teɪʃən] *s.* **1.** Zögern *n*, Zaudern *n*, Unschlüssigkeit *f*: *without any* ~ ohne (auch nur) zu zögern, bedenkenlos; **2.** Stocken *n.*

Hes·si·an ['hesɪən] **I** *adj.* **1.** hessisch; **II** *s.* **2.** Hesse *m*, Hessin *f*; **3.** ⚙ Juteleinen *n* (*für Säcke etc.*); ~ *boots s. pl.* Schaftstiefel *pl.*

het [het] *adj.*: ~ *up* F ganz 'aus dem Häus·chen'.

he·tae·ra [hɪ'tɪərə] *pl.* **-rae** [-riː], **he·tai·ra** [-'taɪərə] *pl.* **-rai** [-raɪ] *s. antiq.* He'täre *f.*

hetero- [hetərəʊ] *in Zssgn* anders, verschieden, fremd.

het·er·o ['hetərəʊ] *pl.* **-os** *s.* F 'Hetero' *m* (*Heterosexuelle[r]*).

het·er·o·clite ['hetərəʊklaɪt] *ling.* **I** *adj.* hetero'klitisch; **II** *s.* Hete'rokliton *n*; **het·er·o·dox** ['hetərəʊdɒks] *adj.* **1.** *eccl.* hetero'dox, anders-, irrgläubig; **2.** *fig.* 'unkonventio,nell; **het·er·o·dox·y** ['hetərəʊdɒksɪ] *s.* Andersgläubigkeit *f*, Irrglaube *m*; '**het·er·o·dyne** [-əʊdaɪn] *adj. Radio:* ~ *receiver* Überlagerungsempfänger *m*, Super(het) *m*; **het·er·o·ge·ne·i·ty** [ˌhetərəʊdʒɪ'niːɪtɪ] *s.* Verschiedenartigkeit *f*; **het·er·o·ge·ne·ous** [ˌhetərəʊ'dʒiːnjəs] *adj.* □ hetero-'gen, ungleichartig, verschiedenartig: ~ *number A* gemischte Zahl; **het·er·on·o·mous** [ˌhetə'rɒnəməs] *adj.* hetero-'nom: a) unselbstständig, b) *biol.* ungleichartig; **het·er·on·o·my** [ˌhetə'rɒnəmɪ] *s.* Heterono'mie *f*; **het·er·o·sex·u·al** [ˌhetərəʊ'seksjʊəl] **I** *adj.* heterosexu'ell; **II** *s.* Heterosexu'elle (*r m*) *f.*

hew [hju:] *v/t.* [*irr.*] hauen, hacken; *Steine* behauen; *Bäume* fällen; **~ down** *v/t.* 'um-, niederhauen, fällen; **~ out** *v/t.* **1.** aushauen; **2.** *fig.* (mühsam) schaffen: **~ a path for o.s.** sich s-n Weg bahnen.

hew·er ['hju:ə] *s.* **1.** (Holz-, Stein)Hauer *m*: **~s of wood and drawers of water** a) *bibl.* Holzhauer u. Wasserträger, b) einfache Leute; **2.** ✗ Hauer *m*;

hewn [hju:n] *p.p. von* **hew.**

hex [heks] *Am.* F I *s.* **1.** Hexe *f*; **2.** Zauber *m*: **put the ~ on →** II *v/t.* **3.** j-n behexen; *et.* ¸verhexen'.

hexa- [heksə] *in Zssgn* sechs; **¸hex·a-'dec·i·mal** [-'desıml] *adj.* □ ↗, *EDV* ¸hexadezi'mal; **hex·a·gon** ['heksəgən] *s.* ↗ Hexa'gon *n*, Sechseck *n*: **~ voltage** ⚡ Sechsspannung *f*; **hex·ag·o·nal** [hek'sægənl] *adj.* sechseckig; **'hex·a·gram** [-græm] *s.* Hexa'gramm *n* (*Sechsstern*); **hex·a·he·dral** [¸heksə'hedrəl] *adj.* ↗ sechsflächig; **hex·a·he·dron** [¸heksə'hedrən] *pl.* **-drons** *od.* **-dra** [-drə] *s.* ↗ Hexa'eder *n*; **hex·am·e·ter** [hek'sæmıtə] I *s.* He'xameter *m*; II *adj.* hexa'metrisch.

hey [heı] *int.* **1.** he!, heda!; **2.** erstaunt: he!, Mann!; **3.** hei; **→ presto** I.

hey·day ['heıdeı] *s.* Höhepunkt *m*, Blüte(zeit) *f*, Gipfel *m*: **in the ~ of his power** auf dem Gipfel s-r Macht.

Hez·bol·lah [¸hezbə'la:] *npr. coll.* His'bollah *f*.

H-hour ['eıtʃ¸auə] *s.* ✗ die Stunde X (*Zeitpunkt für den Beginn e-r militärischen Aktion*).

hi [haı] *int.* **1.** he!, heda!; **2.** hal'lo!, F *als Begrüßung: a.* ¸Tag'!

hi·a·tus [haı'eıtəs] *s.* **1.** Lücke *f*, Spalt *m*, Kluft *f*; **2.** *anat., ling.* Hi'atus *m*.

hi·ber·nate ['haıbəneıt] *v/i.* über'wintern: a) *zo.* Winterschlaf halten, b) den Winter verbringen; **hi·ber·na·tion** [¸haıbə'neıʃn] *s.* Winterschlaf *m*, Über'winterung *f*.

Hi·ber·ni·an [haı'bɜ:njən] *poet.* I *adj.* irisch; II *s.* Irländer(in).

hi·bis·cus [hı'bıskəs] *s.* ♀ Eibisch *m*.

hic·cough, hic·cup ['hıkʌp] I *s.* Schlucken *m*, Schluckauf *m*: **have the ~s →** II *v/i.* den Schluckauf haben.

hick [hık] *s. Am.* F ¸Bauer' *m*, 'Hinterwäldler *m*: **~ girl** Bauerntrampel *m*, *n*; **~ town** ¸(Provinz)Nest' *n*, Kaff *n*.

hick·o·ry ['hıkərı] *s.* ♀ **1.** Hickory (-baum) *m*; **2.** Hickoryholz *n od.* -stock *m*.

hid [hıd] *pret. u. p.p. von* **hide[1]**; **hid·den** ['hıdn] I *p.p. von* **hide[1]**; II *adj.* □ verborgen, versteckt, geheim; **~ persuaders** heimliche Verführer.

hide[1] [haıd] I *v/t.* [*irr.*] (**from**) verbergen (*dat. od.* vor *dat.*): a) verstecken (vor *dat.*), b) verheimlichen (*dat. od.* vor *dat.*), c) ver'hüllen: **~ from view** den Blicken entziehen, *od. Computer:* ausblenden; II *v/i.* [*irr.*] *a.* **~ out** sich verstecken (*a. fig.* **behind** hinter *dat.*).

hide[2] [haıd] I *s.* **1.** Haut *f*, Fell *n* (*beide a. fig.*): **save one's ~** die eigene Haut retten; **tan s.o.'s ~** F j-m das Fell gerben; **I'll have his ~ for this!** F das soll er mir bitter büßen!; II *v/t.* **2.** abhäuten; **3.** F j-n ¸verdreschen'.

hide[3] [haıd] *s.* Hufe *f* (*altes engl. Feldmaß, 60–120 acres*).

¸hide|-and-'seek *s.* Versteckspiel *n*: **play ~** Versteck spielen (*a. fig.*); **'~·a·way →** *hideout*; **'~·bound** *adj. fig.* engstirnig, beschränkt, borniert.

hid·e·ous ['hıdıəs] *adj.* □ ab'scheulich, scheußlich, schrecklich (*alle a.* F *fig.*); **'hid·e·ous·ness** [-nıs] *s.* Scheußlich-

keit *f etc.*

'hide·out *s.* **1.** Versteck *n*; **2.** Zufluchtsort *m*.

hid·ing[1] ['haıdıŋ] *s.* Versteck *n*: **be in ~** sich versteckt halten.

hid·ing[2] ['haıdıŋ] *s.* F Tracht *f* Prügel, ¸Dresche' *f*.

hie [haı] *v/i. obs. od. humor.* eilen.

hi·er·arch ['haıəra:k] *s. eccl.* Hier'arch *m*, Oberpriester *m*; **hi·er·ar·chic,** **hi·er·ar·chi·cal** [¸haıə'ra:kık(l)] *adj.* □ hier'archisch; **'hi·er·arch·y** [-kı] *s.* Hierar'chie *f*.

hi·er·o·glyph ['haıərəʊglıf] *s.* **1.** Hiero'glyphe *f*; **2.** *pl. mst sg. konstr.* Hiero'glyphenschrift *f*; **3.** *pl. humor.* Hiero'glyphen *pl.*, unleserliches Gekritzel; **hi·er·o·glyph·ic** [¸haıərəʊ'glıfık] I *adj.* (□ **~ally**) **1.** hiero'glyphisch; **2.** rätselhaft; **3.** unleserlich; II *s.* **4.** → *hieroglyph* 1–3; **hi·er·o·glyph·i·cal** [¸haıərəʊ'glıfıkl] *adj.* □ → *hieroglyphic* 1–3.

hi-fi [¸haı'faı] F I *s.* **1.** → *high fidelity*; **2.** Hi-Fi-Anlage *f*; II *adj.* **3.** Hi-Fi-...

hig·gle ['hıgl] *v/i.* → *haggle*.

hig·gle·dy-pig·gle·dy [¸hıgldı'pıgldı] F I *adv.* drunter u. drüber, (wie Kraut u. Rüben) durchein'ander; II *s.* Durcheinander *n*, Tohuwa'bohu *n*.

high [haı] I *adj.* (□ → *highly*) (→ *higher, highest*) **1.** hoch: **ten feet ~**; **a ~ tower**; **2.** hoch (gelegen): *↯* **Asia** Hochasien *n*; **~ latitude** *geogr.* hohe Breite; **the ~est floor** das oberste Stockwerk; **3.** hoch (*Grad*): **~ prices** (*temperature*); **~ favo(u)r** hohe Gunst; **~ praise** großes Lob; **~ speed** hohe Geschwindigkeit, ↯ hohe Fahrt, äußerste Kraft; **→ gear** 2a; **4.** stark, heftig: **~ wind**; **~ words** heftige Worte; **5.** hoch (im Rang), Hoch..., Ober..., Haupt...: **~ commissioner** Hoher Kommissar; **the Most** *↯* der Allerhöchste (*Gott*); **6.** hoch, bedeutend, wichtig: **~ aims** hohe Ziele; **~ politics** hohe Politik; **7.** hoch (*Stellung*), vornehm, edel: **of ~ birth**; **~ society** High Society *f*, die vornehme Welt; **~ and low** hoch u. niedrig; **8.** hoch, erhaben, edel; **9.** hoch, gut, erstklassig: **~ quality**; **~ performance** Hochleistung *f*; **10.** hoch, Hoch... (*auf dem Höhepunkt*): *↯* **Middle Ages** Hochmittelalter *n*; **~ period** Glanzzeit *f*; **11.** hoch, fortgeschritten (*Zeit*): **~ summer** Hochsommer *m*; **~ antiquity** fernes *od.* tiefes Altertum; **it is ~ time** es ist höchste Zeit; **~ noon**; **12.** *ling.* a) Hoch... (*Sprache*), b) hoch (*Laut*); **13.** a) hoch, b) schrill: **~ voice**; **14.** hoch (*im Kurs*), teuer; **15. → high and mighty**; **16.** ex'trem, eifrig: **a ~ Tory**; **17.** lebhaft (*Farbe*): **~ complexion** a) rosiger Teint, b) gerötetes Gesicht; **18.** erregend, spannend: **~ adventure**; **19.** a) heiter: **in ~ spirits** (in) gehobener Stimmung, b) F ¸blau' (*betrunken*), c) F ¸high' (*im Drogenrausch od. fig. in* euphorischer Stimmung); **20.** F ¸scharf', erpicht (**on** auf *acc.*); **21.** *Küche:* angegangen, mit Haut'gout; II *adv.* **22.** hoch: **aim ~** *fig.* sich hohe Ziele setzen; **run ~** a) hochgehen (*Wellen*), b) toben (*Gefühle*); **feelings ran ~** die Gemüter erhitzten sich; **play ~** hoch *od.* mit hohem Einsatz spielen; **pay ~** teuer bezahlen; **search ~ and low** überall suchen; **23.** üppig: **live ~**; III *s.* **24.** (An-)Höhe *f*: **on ~** a) hoch oben, droben, b) hoch (hinauf), c) im *od.* zum Himmel; **from on ~** a) von oben, b) vom Himmel; **25.** *meteor.* Hoch(druckgebiet) *n*; **26.** ⚙ a) höchster Gang, b) Gelände-

gang *m*: **shift into ~** den höchsten Gang einlegen; **27.** *fig.* Höchststand *m*: **reach a new ~**; **28.** F *für* **high school**; **29. he's still got his ~** F er ist immer noch ¸high'.

high| al·tar *s. eccl.* 'Hochaltar *m*; ¸**~-'al·ti·tude** *adj.* ✈ Höhen...: **~ flight**; **~ nausea** Höhenkrankheit *f*; **~ and dry** *adj.* hoch u. trocken, auf dem Trockenen: **leave s.o. ~** *fig.* j-n im Stich lassen; **~ and might·y** *adj.* F anmaßend, arro'gant; **'~-ball** *Am.* I *s.* **1.** Highball *m* (*Whisky-Cocktail*); **2.** a) Freie-'Fahrt-Si¸gnal *n*, b) Schnellzug *m*; II *v/i. u. v/t.* **3.** F mit vollem Tempo fahren; **~ beam** *s. mot. Am.* Fernlicht *n*; **'~¸bind·er** *s. Am.* F **1.** Gangster *m*; **2.** Gauner *m*; **3.** Rowdy *m*; **'~-blown** *adj. fig.* großspurig, aufgeblasen; **'~-born** *adj.* hochgeboren; **'~-boy** *s. Am.* Kom'mode *f* mit Aufsatz; **'~-bred** *adj.* vornehm, wohlerzogen; **'~-brow** *oft contp.* I *s.* Intellektu'elle(r *m*) *f*; II *adj. a.* **'~-browed** (betont) intellektu'ell, (geistig) anspruchsvoll, ¸hochgestochen'; *↯* **Church** *s.* High-Church *f*, angli'kanische Hochkirche; II *adj.* hochkirchlich, der High-Church; **'~-cir·cu·'la·tion** *adj.* auflagenstark; **'~-'class** *adj.* **1.** erstklassig; **2.** der High Society; **~ com·mand** *s.* ✗ 'Oberkom¸mando *n*; *↯* **Court (of Jus·tice)** *s. Brit.* oberstes (*erstinstanzliches*) Zi'vilgericht; **~ day** *s.*: **~s and holidays** Fest- u. Feiertage; **~ div·ing** *s. sport* Turmspringen *n*; **'~-'du·ty** *adj.* ⊛ Hochleistungs...

high·er ['haıə] I *comp. von* **high**; II *adj.* höher (*a. fig. Bildung, Rang etc.*), Ober...: **the ~ mammals** die höheren Säugetiere; **~ mathematics** höhere Mathematik; III *adv.* höher, mehr: **bid ~**; **'~-up** [-ərʌ-] *s.* F ¸höheres Tier'.

high·est ['haııst] I *sup. von* **high**; II *adj.* höchst (*a. fig.*), Höchst...: **~ bidder** Meistbietende(r *m*) *f*; III *adj.* am höchsten: **~ possible** höchstmöglich; IV *s.* (*das*) Höchste: **at its ~** auf dem Höhepunkt.

high| ex·plo·sive *s.* 'hochexplo¸siver *od.* 'hochbri¸santer Sprengstoff; **'~-ex'plo·sive** *adj.* 'hochexplo¸siv: **~ bomb** Sprengbombe *f*; **'~-fa'lu·tin** [-fə'lu:tın], **'~-fa'lu·ting** [-tıŋ] *adj. u. s.* hochtrabend(es Geschwätz); **~ farm·ing** *s.* ↗ inten'sive Bodenbewirtschaftung; **~ fi·del·i·ty** *s. Radio:* 'High Fi'delity *f* (*hohe Wiedergabequalität*), Hi-Fi *n*; **'~-fi'del·i·ty** *adj.* High-Fidelity-..., Hi-Fi-...; **fi·nance** *s.* 'Hochfi¸nanz *f*; **'~'fli·er →** **highflyer**; **'~-flown** *adj.* **1.** bom'bastisch, hochtrabend; **2.** hoch gesteckt (*Ziele etc.*), hochfliegend (*Pläne*); **'~'fly·er** *s.* **1.** Erfolgsmensch *m*; **2.** Ehrgeizling *m*, ¸Aufsteiger' *m*; **3.** schnell steigende Aktie; **'~-'fly·ing** *adj.* **1.** hoch fliegend; **2. →** **high-flown**; **~ fre·quen·cy** *s.* ⚡ 'Hochfre¸quenz *f*; **'~-'fre·quen·cy** *adj.* Hochfrequenz...; *↯* **Ger·man** *s. ling.* Hochdeutsch *n*; **'~-'grade** *adj.* erstklassig, hochwertig; **~ hand** *s.*: **with a ~ →** **'~'hand·ed** *adj.* □ anmaßend, selbstherrlich, eigenmächtig; **~ hat** *s.* Zy'linder *m* (*Hut*); **'~-'hat** I *s.* Snob *m*, hochnäsiger Mensch; II *adj.* hochnäsig; III *v/t.* j-n von oben her'ab behandeln; **'~-'heeled** *adj.* hochhackig (*Schuhe*); **~ jump** *s. sport* Hochsprung *m*: **be for the ~** *Brit.* F ¸dran' sein; **'~-land** [-lənd] I *s.* Hoch-, Bergland *n*: **the ↯s of Scotland** das schottische Hochland; II *adj.* hochländisch, Hochland...; **'~-land·er** [-ləndə] *s.* (*bsd. schottische[r]*) Hochländer(in);

,~-'lev·el *adj.* **1.** hoch: ~ *railway* Hochbahn *f;* **2.** *fig.* auf hoher Ebene, Spitzen...: ~ *talks;* ~ *officials* hohe Beamte; ~ *life* s. Highlife *n* (*exklusives Leben der vornehmen Welt*); '~·light I s. **1.** *paint., phot.* (Schlag)Licht *n;* **2.** *fig.* Höhe-, Glanzpunkt *m;* **3.** *pl.* (*Opern- etc.*)Querschnitt *m* (*Schallplatte etc.*); II *v/t.* **4.** *fig.* ein Schlaglicht werfen auf (*acc.*), her'vorheben, groß her'ausstellen; **5.** *Text* her'vorheben, mar'kieren; **6.** *Computer: Text* markieren; **7.** *Haare:* Strähnchen *pl.* machen in (*acc.*); **8.** *fig.* den Höhepunkt (*gen.*) bilden; '~·light·er s. **1.** Leuchtstift *m;* **2.** *Kosmetik:* Aufheller *m,* Töner *m;* '~·lights *pl.* Strähnchen *pl.* (*im Haar*).

high·ly ['haɪlɪ] *adv.* hoch, höchst, äußerst, sehr: ~ *gifted* hoch begabt; ~ *placed fig.* hoch gestellt; ~ *strung* → **high-strung;** ~ *paid* a) hoch bezahlt, b) teuer bezahlt; *think ~ of* viel halten von.

High| Mass s. *eccl.* Hochamt *n;* ,~- -'mind·ed *adj.* hochgesinnt; ,~-'mind·ed·ness s. hohe Gesinnung; ,~- -'necked *adj.* hochgeschlossen (*Kleid*).

high·ness ['haɪnɪs] s. **1.** *mst fig.* Höhe *f;* **2.** ♀ Hoheit *f* (*in Titeln*); **3.** Haut'gout *m* (*von Fleisch etc.*).

,high|-'pitched *adj.* **1.** hoch (*Ton etc.*); **2.** △ steil; **3.** exaltiert: a) über'spannt, b) über'dreht, aufgeregt; ~ *Höhepunkt m;* ,~-'pow·er(ed) *adj.* **1.** ⊛ Hochleistungs..., Groß..., stark; **2.** *fig.* dy'namisch; ,~-'pres·sure I *adj.* **1.** ⊛ u. *meteor.* Hochdruck...: ~ *area* Hoch(-druckgebiet) *n;* ~ *engine* Hochdruckmaschine *f;* **2.** F a) aufdringlich, aggressiv, b) dy'namisch: ~ *salesman;* II *v/t.* **3.** F *Kunden* ,beknien', ,bearbeiten'; ,~-'priced *adj.* teuer; ~ *priest* s. Hohe'priester *m* (*a. fig.*); ,~-'prin·ci·pled *adj.* von hohen Grundsätzen; ,~-'pro·file *adj. attr.* **1.** *Politiker etc.*: a) überall in den Medien prä'sent, b) publicitysüchtig; **2.** *it was a* ~ *campaign* e-e Kam'pagne, die in den Medien starke Beachtung fand; ,~-'proof *adj.* stark alko'holisch; ,~-,rank·ing *adj.*: ~ *officer* hoher Offizier; ~ *re·lief* s. 'Hochreli,ef *n;* ,~-,res·o·'lu·tion *adj.* TV hochauflösend; '~·rise I *adj.* Hoch(haus)...: ~ *building* → II s. Hochhaus *n;* '~·road s. Hauptstraße *f: the ~ to success fig.* der sicherste Weg zum Erfolg; ~ *school* s. *Am.* High School *f* (*weiterführende Schule*); ,~-'sea *adj.* Hochsee...; ~ *sea·son* s. 'Hochsai,son *f;* ~ *sign* s. *Am.* (*bsd.* warnendes) Zeichen; '~- -,sound·ing *adj.* hochtönend, -trabend; ,~-'speed *adj.* **1.** ⊛ a) schnell laufend: ~ *motor,* b) Schnell..., Hochleistungs...: ~ *regulator;* ~ *steel* Schnellarbeitsstahl *m,* c) Hochgeschwindigkeits...: ~ *train;* **2.** *phot.* a) hoch empfindlich: ~ *film,* b) lichtstark: ~ *lens;* ,~-'spir·it·ed *adj.* lebhaft, tempera'mentvoll; ~ *spir·its pl.* fröhliche Laune, gehobene Stimmung; ~ *spot* F → highlight 2; **street** s. Hauptstraße *f;* ,~-'strung *adj.* reizbar, (äußerst) ner'vös; ~ *ta·ble* s. *Brit. univ.* erhöhte Speisetafel (*für Dozenten etc.*); '~·tail *v/i.* a. ~ *it Am.* F (da'hin-, da'von)rasen, (-)flitzen; ~ *tea* s. *bsd. Brit.* frühes Abendessen; ~ *tech* [tek] s. *Am.,* High'tech *m, f;* ,~-'tech *adj.* ,High'tech..., 'hochtechno,logisch: ~ *medicine* Apparatemedizin *f;* ~ *tech·nol·o·gy* s. 'Hochtechnolo,gie *f;* ~ *ten·sion* s. ↯ Hochspannung *f;* ,~- -'ten·sion *adj.* ↯ Hochspannungs...; ~ *tide* s. **1.** Hochwasser *n* (*höchster Flut-*

wasserstand); **2.** *fig.* Höhepunkt *m;* ,~-'toned *adj.* **1.** *fig.* erhaben; **2.** vornehm; ~ *trea·son* s. Hochverrat *m;* '~-up s. F ,hohes Tier'; ~ *volt·age* → *high tension;* ~ *wa·ter* → *high tide* 1; ,~-'wa·ter mark s. a) Hochwasserstandsmarke *f,* b) *fig.* Höchststand *m;* '~·way s. Haupt(verkehrs)straße *f,* Highway *m: Federal* ~ *Am.* Bundesstraße *f;* ↯ *Code Brit.* Straßenverkehrsordnung *f;* ~ *robbery* a) Straßenraub *m,* b) F der ,reinste Nepp'; *the* ~ *to success* der sicherste Weg zum Erfolg; *all the* ~*s and byways* a) alle Wege, b) sämtliche Spielarten; '~·way·man [-mən] s. [*irr.*] Straßenräuber *m.*

hi·jack ['haɪdʒæk] I *v/t.* **1.** *Flugzeug* entführen; **2.** *Geldtransport etc.* über'fallen u. ausrauben; II s. **3.** Flugzeugentführung *f;* **4.** 'Überfall *m* (*auf Geldtransport etc.*); '**hi,jack·er** [-kə] s. **1.** Flugzeugentführer *m,* 'Luftpi,rat *m;* **2.** Räuber *m;* '**hi,jack·ing** [-kɪŋ] → *hijack* II.

hike [haɪk] I *v/i.* **1.** wandern; **2.** marschieren; **3.** hochrutschen (*Kleidungsstück*); II *v/t.* **4.** *mst* ~ *up* hochziehen; **5.** *Am.* *Preise etc.* (drastisch) erhöhen; III s. **6.** a) Wanderung *f,* b) ✕ Geländemarsch *m;* **7.** *Am.* (drastische) Erhöhung: *a* ~ *in prices;* '**hik·er** [-kə] s. Wanderer *m.*

hi·lar·i·ous [hɪ'leərɪəs] *adj.* □ vergnügt, 'übermütig, ausgelassen; **hi·lar·i·ty** [hɪ'lærətɪ] s. Ausgelassenheit *f,* 'Übermütigkeit *f.*

Hil·a·ry term ['hɪlərɪ] s. *Brit.* **1.** ♗ Gerichtstermine in der Zeit vom 11. Januar bis Mittwoch vor Ostern; **2.** *univ.* 'Frühjahrsse,mester *n.*

hill [hɪl] I s. **1.** Hügel *m,* Anhöhe *f,* kleiner Berg: *up* ~ *and down dale* bergauf u. bergab; *be over the* ~ a) s-e besten Jahre hinter sich haben, b) *bsd.* ☞ über den Berg sein; → *old* 3; **2.** (Erd- *etc.*)Haufen *m;* II *v/t.* **3.** a. ~ *up ✓ Pflanzen* häufeln; '~·bil·ly s. *Am.* F *contp.* Hinterwäldler *m:* ~ *music* 'Hillbillymusik *f;* ~ *climb* s. *mot., Radsport:* Bergrennen *n;* '~-,climb·ing a·bil·i·ty s. *mot.* Steigfähigkeit *f.*

hill·i·ness ['hɪlɪnɪs] s. Hügeligkeit *f.*

hill·ock ['hɪlək] s. kleiner Hügel.

,**hill|'side** s. Hang *m,* (Berg)Abhang *m;* ,~'top s. Bergspitze *f.*

hill·y ['hɪlɪ] *adj.* hügelig.

hilt [hɪlt] s. Heft *n,* Griff *m* (*Schwert etc.*): *up to the* ~ a) bis ans Heft, b) *fig.* total; *armed to the* ~ bis an die Zähne bewaffnet; *back s.o. up to the* ~ j-n voll (u. ganz) unterstützen; *prove up to the* ~ unwiderleglich beweisen.

him [hɪm] *pron.* **1.** a) ihn (*acc.*), b) ihm (*dat.*); **2.** F er (*nom.*): *it's* ~ er ist es; **3.** den(jenigen), wer: *I saw* ~ *who did it;* **4.** *refl.* sich: *he looked about* ~ er sah um sich.

Hi·ma·la·yan [,hɪmə'leɪən] *adj.* Himalaja...

him'self *pron.* **1.** *refl.* sich: *he cut* ~; **2.** sich (selbst): *he needs it for* ~; **3.** verstärkend: (er od. ihn od. ihm) selbst: *he* ~ *said it, he said it* ~ er selbst sagte es, er sagte es selbst; *by* ~ allein, ohne Hilfe, von selbst; **4.** *he is not quite* ~ a) er ist nicht ganz normal, b) er ist nicht auf der Höhe; *he is* ~ *again* er ist wieder (ganz) der Alte.

hind¹ [haɪnd] s. *zo.* Hindin *f,* Hirschkuh *f.*

hind² [haɪnd] *adj.* hinter, Hinter...: ~ *leg* Hinterbein *n; talk the* ~ *legs off a donkey* F unaufhörlich reden; ~ *wheel* Hinterrad *n.*

hind·er¹ ['haɪndə] *comp. von hind².*

hind·er² ['hɪndə] I *v/t.* **1.** aufhalten; **2.** (*from*) hindern (an *dat.*), abhalten (von): ~*ed in one's work* bei der Arbeit behindert *od.* gestört; II *v/i.* **3.** im Wege *od.* hinderlich sein, hindern.

Hin·di ['hɪndiː] s. *ling.* Hindi *n.*

'**hind·most** [-ndm-] *sup. von hind².*

,**hind'quar·ter** s. **1.** 'Hinterviertel *n* (*vom Schlachttier*); **2.** *pl.* a) 'Hinterteil *n,* Gesäß *n,* b) 'Hinterhand *f* (*vom Pferd*).

hin·drance ['hɪndrəns] s. **1.** Hinderung *f;* **2.** Hindernis *n* (*to* für).

'**hind·sight** s. **1.** ✕ Vi'sier *n;* **2.** *fig.* späte Einsicht: *by* ~, *with the wisdom of* ~ ,im Nachhinein', hinterher; *foresight is better than* ~ Vorsicht ist besser als Nachsicht; ~ *is easier than foresight* hinterher ist man immer klüger (als vorher), *contp. a.* hinterher kann man leicht klüger sein (als vorher).

Hin·du [,hɪn'duː] I s. **1.** Hindu *m;* **2.** Inder *m;* II *adj.* **3.** Hindu...; **Hin·du·ism** ['hɪnduːɪzəm] s. Hindu'ismus *m;* **Hin·du·sta·ni** [,hɪndu'stɑːnɪ] I s. *ling.* Hindu'stani *n;* II *adj.* hindu'stanisch.

hinge [hɪndʒ] I s. **1.** ⊛ Schar'nier *n,* Gelenk *n,* (Tür)Angel *f: off its* ~*s* aus den Angeln, *fig. a.* aus den Fugen; **2.** *fig.* Angelpunkt *m;* II *v/t.* **3.** mit Scharnieren *etc.* versehen; **4.** *Tür etc.* einhängen; III *v/i.* **5.** *fig.:* ~ *on* a) sich drehen um, b) abhängen von, ankommen auf (*acc.*); **hinged** [-dʒd] *adj.* (um ein Gelenk) drehbar, auf-, her'unter-, zs.-klappbar, Scharnier...; **hinge joint** s. **1.** → *hinge* 1; **2.** *anat.* Schar'niergelenk *n.*

hin·ny ['hɪnɪ] s. *zo.* Maulesel *m.*

hint [hɪnt] I s. **1.** Wink *m:* a) Andeutung *f,* b) Tipp *m,* Hinweis *m,* Fingerzeig *m: broad* ~ Wink mit dem Zaunpfahl; *take a* (*od. the* ~) den Wink verstehen; *drop a* ~ e-e Andeutung machen; **2.** Anspielung *f* (*at* auf *acc.*); **3.** Anflug *m,* Spur *f* (*of* von); II *v/t.* **4.** andeuten, *et.* zu verstehen geben; III *v/i.* **5.** (*at*) e-e Andeutung machen (von), anspielen (auf *acc.*).

hin·ter·land ['hɪntəlænd] s. **1.** 'Hinterland *n;* **2.** Einzugsgebiet *n.*

hip¹ [hɪp] s. **1.** *anat.* Hüfte *f: have s.o. on the* ~ *fig.* j-n in der Hand haben; **2.** → *hip joint;* **3.** △ a) Walm *m,* b) Walmsparren *m.*

hip² [hɪp] s. ♀ Hagebutte *f.*

hip³ [hɪp] *int.:* ~, ~, *hurrah!* hipp, hipp, hurra!

hip⁴ [hɪp] *adj. sl.* **1.** *be* ~ ,voll dabei' sein (*in der Mode etc.*); **2.** *be* ~ *to* im Bilde *od.* auf dem Laufenden sein über (*acc.*); *get* ~ *to et.* ,spitzkriegen'.

'**hip|·bath** s. Sitzbad *n;* '~·bone s. *anat.* Hüftbein *n;* ~ *flask* s. Taschenflasche *f,* ,Flachmann' *m;* ~ *joint* s. *anat.* Hüftgelenk *n.*

hipped¹ [hɪpt] *adj.* **1.** *in Zssgn* mit ... Hüften; **2.** △ Walm...: ~ *roof.*

hipped² [hɪpt] *adj. Am. sl.* versessen, ,scharf' (*on* auf *acc.*).

hip·pie ['hɪpɪ] s. Hippie *m.*

hip·po ['hɪpəʊ] *pl.* -pos s. F für *hippopotamus.*

hip·po·cam·pus [,hɪpəʊ'kæmpəs] *pl.* -pi [-paɪ] s. **1.** *myth.* Hippo'kamp *m;* **2.** *ichth.* Seepferdchen *n;* **3.** *anat.* Ammonshorn *n* (*des Gehirns*).

hip pock·et s. Gesäßtasche *f.*

Hip·po·crat·ic [,hɪpəʊ'krætɪk] s. hippo'kratisch: ~ *face;* ~ *oath.*

hip·po·drome ['hɪpədrəʊm] s. **1.** Hippo-

'drom n, Reitbahn f; **2.** a) Zirkus m, b) Varie'tee(the,ater) n; **3.** sport Am. sl. ‚Schiebung' f.

hip·po·griff, hip·po·gryph ['hɪpəgrɪf] s. Hippo'gryph m (Fabeltier).

hip·po·pot·a·mus [,hɪpə'pɒtəməs] pl. **-mus·es, -mi** [-maɪ] s. zo. Fluss-, Nilpferd n.

hip·py ['hɪpɪ] → **hippie**.

'**hip·shot** adj. **1.** mit verrenkter Hüfte; **2.** fig. (lenden)lahm.

hip·ster ['hɪpstə] s. sl. **1.** ‚cooler Typ'; **2.** pl. a. ~ **trousers** Brit. Hüfthose f.

hir·a·ble ['haɪərəbl] adj. mietbar.

hire ['haɪə] **I** v/t. **1.** et. mieten, Flugzeug chartern: ~**d car** Leih-, Mietwagen m; ~**d airplane** Charterflugzeug n; **2.** a. ~ **on** a) j-n ein-, anstellen, b) bsd. ⚓ anheuern, c) j-n engagieren: ~**d killer** bezahlter od. gekaufter Mörder, Killer m; **3.** mst ~ **out** vermieten; **4.** ~ **o.s. out** e-e Beschäftigung annehmen (**to** bei); **II** s. **5.** Miete f: **on** (od. **for**) ~ a) mietweise, b) zu vermieten(d); **for** ~ frei (Taxi); **take** (**let**) **a car on** ~ ein Auto (ver)mieten; ~ **car** Leih-, Mietwagen m; **6.** Entgelt n, Lohn m.

hire·ling ['haɪəlɪŋ] mst contp. **I** s. Mietling m; **II** adj. a) käuflich, b) b.s. angeheuert.

hire pur·chase s. bsd. Brit. ✞ Abzahlungs-, Teilzahlungs-, Ratenkauf m: **buy on** ~ auf Abzahlung kaufen; ~**-'pur·chase** adj.: ~ **agreement** Abzahlungsvertrag m; ~ **system** Teilzahlungssystem n.

hir·er ['haɪərə] s. **1.** Mieter(in); **2.** Vermieter(in).

hir·sute ['hɜːsjuːt] adj. **1.** haarig, zottig, struppig; **2.** ♀, zo. rauhaarig, borstig.

his [hɪz] poss. pron. **1.** sein, seine: ~ **family**; **2.** seiner (seine, seines), der (die, das) Seine (od. Seinige); **my father and** ~ mein u. sein Vater; **this hat is** ~ das ist sein Hut, dieser Hut gehört ihm; **a book of** ~ eines seiner Bücher, ein Buch von ihm.

hiss [hɪs] **I** v/i. **1.** zischen; **II** v/t. **2.** auszischen, -pfeifen; **3.** zischeln; **III** s. **4.** Zischen n.

hist [sɪt] int. sch!, pst!

his·tol·o·gist [hɪ'stɒlədʒɪst] s. ✚ Histo'loge m; **his·tol·o·gy** [-dʒɪ] s. ✚ Histo'logie f, Gewebelehre f; **his'tol·y·sis** [-lɪsɪs] s. ✚, biol. Histo'lyse f, Gewebszerfall m.

his·to·ri·an [hɪ'stɔːrɪən] s. Hi'storiker (-in), Geschichtsforscher(in); **his·tor·ic** [hɪ'stɒrɪk] adj. (□ ~ally) **1.** hi'storisch, geschichtlich (berühmt od. bedeutsam): ~ **buildings**; **a** ~ **speech**; **2.** → **his·tor·i·cal** [hɪ'stɒrɪkl] adj. □ **1.** hi'storisch: a) geschichtlich (belegt od. über'liefert): **a(n)** ~ **event**, b) Geschichts...: ~ **science**, c) geschichtlich orientiert: ~ **materialism** historischer Materialismus, d) geschichtlich(en Inhalts): ~ **novel** historischer Roman; **2.** → **historic** 1; **3.** ling. hi'storisch: ~ **present**; **his·to·ric·i·ty** [,hɪstə'rɪsɪtɪ] s. Geschichtlichkeit f; **his·to·ried** ['hɪstərɪd] → **historic** 1; **his·to·ri·og·ra·pher** [,hɪstɔːrɪ'ɒgrəfə] s. Historio'graph m, Geschichtsschreiber m; **his·to·ri·og·ra·phy** [,hɪstɔːrɪ'ɒgrəfɪ] s. Geschichtsschreibung f.

his·to·ry ['hɪstərɪ] s. **1.** Geschichte f: a) geschichtliche Vergangenheit od. Entwicklung, b) (ohne art.) Geschichtswissenschaft f: ~ **book** Geschichtsbuch n; **ancient** (**modern**) ~ alte (neuere) Geschichte; ~ **of art** Kunstgeschichte, **go**

down in ~ **as** als ... in die Geschichte eingehen; **make** ~ Geschichte machen; → **natural history**; **2.** Werdegang m (a. ☺), Entwicklung f, (Entwicklungs-) Geschichte f; **3.** allg., a. ✚ Vorgeschichte f, Vergangenheit f: (**case**) ~ Krankengeschichte f, Anamnese f; **have a** ~; **4.** (a. Lebens)Beschreibung f, Darstellung f; **5.** paint. Hi'storienbild n; **6.** hi'storisches Drama.

his·tri·on·ic [,hɪstrɪ'ɒnɪk] **I** adj. (□ ~**al·ly**) **1.** Schauspiel(er)..., schauspielerisch; **2.** thea'tralisch; **II** s. **3.** pl. a. sg. konstr. a) Schauspielkunst f, b) contp. Schauspiele'rei f, thea'tralisches Getue.

hit [hɪt] **I** s. **1.** Schlag m, Hieb m (a. fig.); **2.** a. sport u. fig. Treffer m, Internet: Zugriff m (auf e-e Homepage): **make a** ~ a) e-n Treffer erzielen, b) fig. gut ankommen (**with** bei); **3.** Glücksfall m, Erfolg m; **4.** thea., Buch etc.: Schlager m, ‚Knüller', Hit m: **song** ~ Schlager, Hit; **he** (**it**) **was a great** ~ (**with**) er (es) war ein großer Erfolg (bei); **5.** (Seiten)Hieb m, Spitze f (**at** gegen); **6.** bsd. Am. sl. ‚Abschuss' m, Ermordung f; **II** v/t. (irr.) **7.** schlagen, stoßen; Auto etc. rammen: ~ **one's head against s.th.** mit dem Kopf gegen et. stoßen; **8.** treffen (a. fig.): **be** ~ **by a bullet**; **when it** ~**s you** fig. wenn es dich packt; **you've** ~ **it** fig. du hast es getroffen (ganz recht); **9.** (seelisch) treffen: **be hard** (od. **badly**) ~ schwer getroffen sein (**by** durch); **10.** stoßen od. kommen auf (acc.), treffen, finden: ~ **the right road**; ~ **a mine** ⚓, ✗ auf e-e Mine laufen; ~ **the solution** die Lösung finden; **11.** fig. geißeln, scharf kritisieren; **12.** erreichen, et. ‚schaffen': **the car** ~**s 100 mph**; **prices** ~ **an all-time high** die Preise erreichten e-e Rekordhöhe; ~ **town** in der Stadt ankommen; **III** v/i. (irr.) **13.** treffen; **14.** schlagen (**at** nach); **15.** stoßen, schlagen (**against** gegen); **16.** ~ (**up**)**on** → 10; ~ **back** v/i. zu'rückschlagen (a. fig.): ~ **at s.o.** j-m Kontra geben; ~ **off** v/t. **1.** treffend od. über'zeugend darstellen od. schildern; **die Ähnlichkeit** genau treffen; **2.** hit it off with s.o. sich bestens vertragen od. glänzend auskommen mit j-m; ~ **out** v/i. um sich schlagen: ~ **at** auf j-n einschlagen, fig. über j-n od. et. losziehen.

,**hit|-and-'miss** adj. **1.** mit wechselndem Erfolg; **2.** → **hit-or-miss**; ~**-and-'run I** adj. **1.** ~ **accident** → 3; ~ **driver** (unfall)flüchtiger Fahrer; **2.** kurz(lebig); **II** s. **3.** Unfall m mit Fahrerflucht.

hitch [hɪtʃ] **I** s. **1.** Ruck m, Zug m; **2.** ⚓ Stich m, Knoten m; **3.** ‚Haken' m: **there is a** ~ (**somewhere**) die Sache hat (irgendwo) e-n Haken; **without a** ~ reibungslos, glatt; **II** v/t. **4.** (ruckartig) ziehen: ~ **up one's trousers** s-e Hosen hochziehen; **5.** befestigen, festhaken, ankoppeln, Pferd anspannen: **get** ~**ed** → 8; **III** v/i. **6.** hinken; **7.** sich festhaken; **8.** a. ~ **up** F heiraten; **9.** → '**-hike** v/i. F ‚per Anhalter' fahren, trampen; '**~,hik·er** s. F Anhalter(in), Tramper (-in).

hi-tech [,haɪ'tek] **I** s. ,Hi'tech n, f; **II** adj. ,Hi'tech...

hith·er ['hɪðə] **I** adv. hierher: ~ **and thither** hierhin u. dorthin, hin und her; **II** adj. diesseitig: **the** ~ **side** die nähere Seite; ♀ **India** Vorderindien n; ~**'to** [-'tuː] adv. bis'her, bis jetzt.

Hit·ler·ism ['hɪtlərɪzəm] s. Na'zismus m; '**Hit·ler·ite** [-raɪt] **I** s. Nazi m; **II** adj. na'zistisch.

hit| **list** s. sl. Abschussliste f (a. fig.); ~ **man** s. [irr.] Am. sl. Killer m; '**~-off** s. treffende Nachahmung, über'zeugende Darstellung; ~ **or miss** adv. aufs Gerate'wohl; ,**~-or-'miss** adj. **1.** sorglos, unbekümmert; **2.** aufs Gerate'wohl getan; ~ **pa·rade** s. 'Hitpa,rade f.

Hit-tite ['hɪtaɪt] s. hist. He'thiter m.

hive [haɪv] **I** s. **1.** Bienenkorb m, -stock m; **2.** Bienenvolk n, -schwarm m; **3.** fig. a) a. ~ **of activity** das reinste Bienenhaus, b) Sammelpunkt m, c) Schwarm m (von Menschen); **II** v/t. **4.** Bienen in e-n Stock bringen; **5.** Honig im Bienenstock sammeln; **6.** a. ~ **up** fig. a) sammeln, b) auf die Seite legen; **7.** ~ **off** a) Amt etc. abtrennen (**from** von), b) reprivatisieren; **III** v/i. **8.** in den Stock fliegen (Bienen): ~ **off** fig. a) abschwenken, b) sich selbstständig machen; **9.** sich zs.-drängen.

hives [haɪvz] s. pl. sg. od. pl. konstr. ✚ Nesselausschlag m.

HIV-neg·a·tive [,eɪtʃaɪviː'negətɪv] adj. ✚ HIV-'negativ; **HIV-'pos·i·tive** adj. ✚ HIV-'positiv.

Hiz·bol·lah [,hɪzbə'lɑː], **Hiz·bul·lah** [,hɪzbʊ'lɑː] npr. coll. His'bollah f.

ho [həʊ] int. **1.** halt!, holla!, heda!; **2.** na'nu!; **3.** contp. ha'ha!, pah!; **4.** westward ~! auf nach Westen!; ⚓ **land** ~! Land in Sicht!

hoar [hɔː] adj. obs. **1.** → **hoary**; **2.** (vom Frost) bereift, weiß.

hoard [hɔːd] **I** s. a) Hort m, Schatz m, b) Vorrat m (**of** an dat.); **II** v/t. u. v/i. a. ~ **up** horten, hamstern; '**hoard·er** [-də] s. Hamsterer m.

hoard·ing ['hɔːdɪŋ] s. **1.** Bau-, Bretterzaun m; **2.** Brit. Re'klamewand f.

,**hoar'frost** s. (Rau)Reif m.

hoarse [hɔːs] adj. □ **1.** heiser; '**hoarse·ness** [-nɪs] s. Heiserkeit f.

hoar·y ['hɔːrɪ] adj. □ **1.** weißlich; **2.** a) (alters)grau, ergraut, b) fig. altersgrau, (ur)alt, ehrwürdig.

hoax [həʊks] **I** s. **1.** Falschmeldung f, (Zeitungs)Ente f; **2.** Schabernack m, Streich m; **II** v/t. **3.** j-n zum Besten haben, j-m e-n Bären aufbinden od. et. weismachen.

hob[1] [hɒb] **I** s. **1.** Ka'mineinsatz m, -vorsprung m (für Kessel etc.); **2.** Kochfeld n (auf Herd); **3.** → **hobnail 2**; **4.** ☺ a) (Ab)Wälzfräser m, b) Strehlbohrer m; **II** v/t. **5.** ☺ abwälzen, verzahnen: ~**bing machine** → 4 a.

hob[2] [hɒb] s. Kobold m: **play** (od. **raise**) ~ **with** Schindluder treiben mit.

hob·ble ['hɒbl] **I** v/i. **1.** humpeln, hoppeln, a. fig. hinken, holpern; **II** v/t. **2.** e-m Pferd etc. die Vorderbeine fesseln; **3.** hindern; **III** s. **4.** Humpeln n.

hob·ble·de·hoy [,hɒbldɪ'hɔɪ] s. F (junger) Tollpatsch od. Flegel.

hob·by ['hɒbɪ] s. **1.** Steckenpferd n, Liebhabe'rei f, Hobby n; '**~-horse** s. **1.** Steckenpferd n (a. fig.); **2.** Schaukelpferd n; **3.** Karus'sellpferd n; '**hob·by·ist** [-ɪɪst] s. Hobby'ist m, engS. a. Bastler m, Heimwerker m.

'**hob·nail** s. grober Schuhnagel; '**hob·nailed** adj. **1.** genagelt; **2.** fig. ungehobelt; '**hob·nail(ed) liv·er** s. ✚ Säuferleber f.

'**hob·nob** v/i. **1.** in'tim od. ‚auf Du u. Du' sein, freundschaftlich verkehren (**with** mit); **2.** plaudern (**with** mit).

ho·bo ['həʊbəʊ] pl. **-bos, -boes** s. Am. **1.** Wanderarbeiter m; **2.** Landstreicher m, Tippelbruder m.

Hob·son's choice ['hɒbsnz] s.: *it's ~* man hat keine andere Wahl.

hock¹ [hɒk] **I** s. **1.** zo. Sprung-, Fesselgelenk n (*der Huftiere*); **2.** Hachse f (*beim Schlachttier*); **II** v/t. **3.** → **hamstring** 3.

hock² [hɒk] s. **1.** weißer Rheinwein; **2.** trockener Weißwein.

hock³ [hɒk] F **I** s.: *in ~* a) verschuldet, b) versetzt, verpfändet, c) *Am.* im ‚Knast'; **II** v/t. versetzen, verpfänden.

hock·ey ['hɒkı] s. a) Hockey n, b) *bsd. Am.* Eishockey n: ~ *stick* Hockeyschläger m.

'hock·shop s. *sl.* Pfandhaus n.

ho·cus ['həʊkəs] v/t. **1.** betrügen; **2.** j-n betäuben; **3.** *e-m Getränk* ein Betäubungsmittel beimischen; **,~·'po·cus** [-'pəʊkəs] s. Hokus'pokus m: a) *Zauberformel*, b) Schwindel m, fauler Zauber.

hod [hɒd] s. **1.** ⚒ Mörteltrog m, Steinbrett n (*zum Tragen*): ~ *carrier* → **hodman** 1; **2.** Kohleneimer m.

hodge·podge ['hɒdʒpɒdʒ] *bsd. Am.* → **hotchpotch**.

'hod·man [-mən] s. [*irr.*] **1.** ⚒ Mörtel-, Ziegelträger m; **2.** Handlanger m.

ho·dom·e·ter [hɒ'dɒmıtə] s. Hodo'meter n, Wegmesser m, Schrittzähler m.

hoe [həʊ] ⚵ **I** s. Hacke f; **II** v/t. Boden hacken; *Unkraut aushacken*: *a long row to ~* e-e schwere Aufgabe.

hog [hɒg] **I** s. **1.** (Haus-, Schlacht-) Schwein n, *Am. allg.* (a. Wild)Schwein n: *go the whole ~* F aufs Ganze gehen, ganze Arbeit leisten; **2.** F a) Vielfraß m, b) Flegel m, c) Schmutzfink m, Ferkel n; **3.** ⚒ Scheuerbesen m; **4.** ⚙ *Am.* (Reiß)Wolf m; **5.** → **hogget**; **II** v/t. **6.** *den Rücken* krümmen; **7.** scheren, stutzen; **8.** (gierig) verschlingen, ‚fressen', *fig.* a. an sich reißen, mit Beschlag belegen: ~ *the road* → 10; **III** v/i. **9.** den Rücken krümmen; **10.** F rücksichtslos in der (Fahrbahn)Mitte fahren; **'~·back** s. langer u. scharfer Gebirgskamm; ~ **chol·er·a** s. *vet. Am.* Schweinepest f.

hog·get ['hɒgıt] s. *Brit.* noch ungeschorenes einjähriges Schaf.

hog·gish ['hɒgıʃ] *adj.* □ a) schweinisch, b) rücksichtslos, c) gierig, gefräßig.

hog·ma·nay ['hɒgmənei] s. *Scot.* Sil'vester m, n.

hog| mane s. gestutzte Pferdemähne; **~'s back** → **hogback**.

hogs·head ['hɒgzhed] s. **1.** Hohlmaß, etwa 240 l; **2.** großes Faß.

'hog|·skin s. Schweinsleder n; **'~·tie** v/t. **1.** *e-m Tier* alle vier Füße zs.-binden; **2.** *fig.* lähmen, (be)hindern; **'~·wash** s. **1.** Schweinefutter n; **2.** *contp.* ‚Spülwasser' n (*Getränk*); **3.** Quatsch m, ‚Mist' m.

hoi(c)k [hɔık] v/t. ✈ hochreißen.

hoicks [hɔıks] *int. hunt.* hussa! (*Hetzruf an Hunde*).

hoi pol·loi [,hɔı'pɒlɔı] (*Greek*) s. **1.** *the ~* die (breite) Masse, der Pöbel; **2.** *Am. sl.* ‚Tam'tam' n (*about* um).

hoist¹ [hɔıst] *obs. p.p.*: ~ *with one's own petard fig.* in der eigenen Falle gefangen.

hoist² [hɔıst] **I** v/t. **1.** hochziehen, -winden, hieven, heben; **2.** *Flagge, Segel* hissen; **3.** *Am. sl.* ‚klauen'; **4.** ~ *a few Am. sl.* ein paar ‚heben'; **II** s. **5.** (Lasten)Aufzug m, Hebezeug n, Kran m, Winde f.

hoist·ing| cage ['hɔıstıŋ] s. ⚒ Förderkorb m; ~ **crane** s. ⚙ Hebekran m; **~·en·gine** s. **1.** ⚙ Hebewerk n; **2.** ⚒

'Förderma,schine f.

hoi·ty-toi·ty [,hɔıtı'tɔıtı] **I** *adj.* **1.** hochnäsig; **2.** leichtsinnig; **II** s. **3.** Hochnäsigkeit f.

ho·k(e)y-po·k(e)y [,həʊkı'pəʊkı] s. **1.** *sl.* →**hocus-pocus**; **2.** Speiseeis n.

ho·kum ['həʊkəm] s. *sl.* **1.** *thea.* ‚Mätzchen' *pl.*, Kitsch m; **2.** ‚Krampf' m, Quatsch m.

hold¹ [həʊld] s. ⚓, ✈ Lade-, Frachtraum m.

hold² [həʊld] **I** s. **1.** Halt m, Griff m: *catch* (*od. get, lay, seize, take*) ~ *of s.th.* et. ergreifen *od.* in die Hand bekommen *od.* zu fassen bekommen *od.* erwischen; *get ~ of s.o.* j-n erwischen; *get ~ of o.s. fig.* sich in die Gewalt bekommen; *keep ~ of* festhalten; *let go one's ~ of* loslassen; *miss one's ~* danebengreifen; *take ~ fig.* sich festsetzen, Wurzel fassen; **2.** Halt m, Stütze f: *afford no ~* keinen Halt bieten; **3.** *Ringen*: Griff m: (*with*) *no ~s barred fig.* mit harten Bandagen (*kämpfen*); **4.** (*on, over, of*) Gewalt f, Macht f (über *acc.*), Einfluss (auf *acc.*): *get a ~ on s.o.* j-n unter s-n Einfluss *od.* in s-e Macht bekommen; *have a* (*firm*) ~ *on s.o.* j-n in s-r Gewalt haben, j-n beherrschen; **5.** Einhalt m: *put a ~ on s.th.* et. stoppen; **6.** *Raumfahrt*: Unter'brechung f des Count-down; **II** v/t. [*irr.*] **7.** (fest)halten; **8.** sich *die Nase, die Ohren* zuhalten: ~ *one's nose* (*ears*); **9.** *Gewicht, Last etc.* tragen, (aus)halten; **10.** *in e-m Zustand* halten: ~ *o.s. erect* sich gerade halten; ~ (*o.s.*) *ready* (sich) bereithalten; **11.** (zu'rück-, ein-) behalten: ~ *the shipment* die Sendung zurück(be)halten; ~ *everything!* sofort aufhören!; **12.** zu'rück-, abhalten (*from* von et., *from doing s.th.* davon, et. zu tun); **13.** an-, aufhalten, im Zaume halten: *there is no ~ing him* er ist nicht zu halten *od.* zu bändigen; ~ *the enemy* den Feind aufhalten; **14.** *Am.* a) j-n festnehmen: *12 persons were held*, b) in Haft halten; **15.** *sport* sich erfolgreich verteidigen gegen *den Gegner*; **16.** j-n festlegen (*to* auf *acc.*): ~ *s.o. to his word* j-n beim Wort nehmen; **17.** a) *Versammlung, Wahl etc.* abhalten, b) *Fest etc.* veranstalten, c) *sport Meisterschaft etc.* austragen; **18.** (beibe)halten: ~ *the course*; **19.** *Alkohol* vertragen: ~ *one's liquor well* e-e ganze Menge vertragen; **20.** ✕ *u. fig. Stellung* halten, behaupten: ~ *one's own* sich behaupten (*with* gegen); ~ *the stage* a) sich halten (*Theaterstück*), b) *fig.* die Szene beherrschen, im Mittelpunkt stehen; ~ *fort*; **21.** innehaben: a) besitzen: ~ *land* (*shares, etc.*), b) *Amt* bekleiden, c) *Titel* führen, d) *Platz etc.* einnehmen, e) *Rekord* halten; **22.** a) enthalten: *the tank ~s 10 gallons*, b) Platz bieten für, 'unterbringen (können): *the hotel ~s 500 guests; the place ~s many memories* der Ort ist voll von Erinnerungen; *life ~s many surprises* das Leben ist voller Überraschungen; *what the future ~s* was die Zukunft bringt; **23.** *Bewunderung etc.* hegen, a. *Vorurteile etc.* haben (*for* für); **24.** behaupten, meinen: ~ (*the view*) *that* die Ansicht vertreten *od.* der Ansicht sein, dass; **25.** halten für: ~ *him to be a fool; it is held to be true* man hält es für wahr; **26.** ⚖ entscheiden (*that* dass); **27.** *fig.* fesseln: ~ *the audience*; ~ *s.o.'s attention*; **28.** ~ *to Am.* beschränken auf (*acc.*); **29.** ~ *against* j-m et. vorwerfen

od. verübeln; **30.** ♪ *Ton* (aus)halten; **III** v/i. [*irr.*] **31.** (stand)halten: *will the bridge ~?*; **32.** (sich) festhalten (*by, to* an *dat.*); **33.** sich verhalten: ~ *still* stillhalten; **34.** a. ~ *good* (weiterhin) gelten, gültig sein *od.* bleiben: *the promise still ~s* das Versprechen gilt noch; **35.** anhalten, andauern: *the fine weather held; my luck held* das Glück blieb mir treu; **36.** einhalten: ~*! halt!*; **37.** ~ *by* (*od.* *to*) j-m *od.* e-r Sache treu bleiben; **38.** ~ *with* es halten mit *j-m*, für *j-n od. et.* sein;

Zssgn mit adv.:

hold| back I v/t. **1.** zu'rückhalten; **2.** → *hold in*; **3.** zu'rückhalten mit, verschweigen; **II** v/i. **4.** sich zu'rückhalten (*a. fig.*); **5.** nicht mit der Sprache herausrücken; ~ **down** v/t. **1.** niederhalten, *fig.* a. unter'drücken; **2.** F a) *e-n Posten* (inne)haben, b) sich *in e-r Stellung* halten; ~ **forth I** v/t. **1.** (an)bieten; **2.** in Aussicht stellen; **II** v/i. **3.** sich auslassen *od.* verbreiten (*on* über *acc.*); **4.** *Am.* stattfinden; ~ **in I** v/t. im Zaum halten, zu'rückhalten: *hold o.s. in* a) II, b) den Bauch einziehen; **II** v/i. sich zu'rückhalten; ~ **off I** v/t. **1.** a) abhalten, fern halten, b) abwehren; **2.** *et.* aufschieben, j-n hinhalten; **II** v/i. **3.** sich fern halten (*from* von); **4.** a) zögern, b) warten; **5.** ausbleiben; ~ **on** v/i. **1.** a. *fig.* (a. sich) festhalten (*to* an *dat.*); **2.** aus-, 'durchhalten; **3.** andauern, -halten; **4.** *teleph.* am Appa'rat bleiben; **5.** ~*! immer langsam!, halt!*; **6.** ~ *to et.* behalten; ~ **out I** v/t. **1.** *die Hand etc.* ausstrecken: *hold s.th. out to s.o.* j-m et. hinhalten; **2.** in Aussicht stellen: *little hope wenig Hoffnung äußern od. haben*; **3.** *hold o.s. out as Am.* sich ausgeben für *od.* als; **II** v/i. **4.** reichen (*Vorräte*); **5.** aus-, 'durchhalten; **6.** sich behaupten (*against* gegen); **7.** ~ *on s.o.* j-m et. vorenthalten *od.* verheimlichen; **8.** ~ *for* F festen auf (*dat.*); ~ **o·ver** v/t. **1.** et. vertagen, -schieben (*until* auf *acc.*); **2.** ⚖ prolongieren; **3.** *Amt etc.* (weiter) behalten; **4.** *thea. etc. j-s* Engage'ment verlängern (*for* um); ~ **to·geth·er** v/t. u. v/i. zs.-halten (*a. fig.*); ~ **up I** v/t. **1.** (hoch)heben; **2.** hochhalten: ~ *to view* den Blicken darbieten; **3.** halten, stützen, tragen; **4.** aufrechterhalten; **5.** ~ *as* als *Beispiel etc.* hinstellen; **6.** j-n *od.* et. aufhalten, et. verzögern; **7.** j-n, *e-e Bank etc.* über'fallen; **II** v/i. **8.** → *hold out* 5, 6; **9.** sich halten (*Preise, Wetter*); **10.** sich bewahrheiten.

'hold|·all s. Reisetasche f; **'~·back** s. Hindernis n.

hold·er ['həʊldə] s. **1.** *oft in Zssgn* Halter m, Behälter m; **2.** ⚙ a) Halter (-ung f) m, b) Zwinge f; **3.** ✏ (Lampen)Fassung f; **4.** Pächter m; **5.** ♦ Inhaber(in) (*e-s Patents, Schecks etc.*), Besitzer(in): *previous ~* Vorbesitzer m; **6.** *sport* Inhaber(in) (*e-s Rekords, Titels etc.*).

'hold·fast s. **1.** ⚙ Klammer f, Zwinge f, Haken m, Kluppe f; **2.** ⚘ Haftscheibe f.

hold·ing ['həʊldıŋ] s. **1.** (Fest)Halten n; **2.** a) Pachtgut n, b) Pacht f, c) Grundbesitz m; **3.** *oft pl.* a) Besitz m, Bestand m (*an Effekten etc.*), b) (Aktien)Anteil m, (-)Beteiligung f: *large steel ~s* großer Besitz von Stahl(werks)aktien; **4.** ♦ a) Vorrat m, b) Guthaben n; **5.** ⚖ (gerichtliche) Entscheidung; ~ **at·tack** s. ✕ Fesselungsangriff m; ~ **com·pa·ny** s. ♦ Dach-, Holdinggesellschaft f; ~ **pat·tern** s. ✈

Warteschleife *f*.

'hold|,o·ver *s.* **1.** ,'Überbleibsel' *n* (*Amtsträger etc.*); **2.** *Film etc.*: a) Verlängerung *f*, b) *Künstler etc., dessen Engagement verlängert worden ist;* **'~-up** *s.* **1.** Verzögerung *f*, (*a.* Verkehrs)Stockung *f*; **2.** (bewaffneter) ('Raub),Überfall.

hole [həʊl] **I** *s.* **1.** Loch *n*: *be in a ~ fig.* in der Klemme sitzen; *make a ~ in fig.* ein Loch reißen in (*Vorräte*); *pick ~s in fig.* a) an *e-r Sache* herumkritteln, b) *Argument etc.* zerpflücken, c) *j-m* am Zeug flicken; *full of ~s fig.* fehlerhaft, ,wack(e)lig' (*Theorie etc.*); *like a ~ in the head* F unnötig wie ein Kropf; **2.** Loch *n*, Grube *f*; **3.** Höhle *f*, Bau *m* (*Tier*); **4.** *fig.* ,Loch' *n*: a) (Bruch)Bude *f*, b) ,Kaff' *n*, c) Schlupfwinkel *m*; **5.** *Golf*: a) Hole *n*, Loch *n*, b) (Spiel)Bahn *f*: *~ in one* As *n*; **II** *v/t.* **6.** ein Loch machen in (*acc.*), durch'löchern; **7.** ✕ schrämen; **8.** *Tier* in s-e Höhle treiben; **9.** *Golf: Ball* einlochen; **III** *v/i.* **10.** *mst ~ up* a) sich in die Höhle verkriechen (*Tier*), b) *Am.* F sich verstecken *od.* -kriechen; **11.** *a. ~ out Golf:* einlochen.

,hole-and-'cor·ner [-nd'k-] *adj.* **1.** heimlich, versteckt; **2.** anrüchig; **3.** armselig; **,hole-in-the-'wall** *s.* **1.** *Brit.* F 'Geldauto,mat *m*; **2.** (kleine) Spe'lunke, kleiner düsterer Laden.

hol·i·day ['hɒlədɪ] **I** *s.* **1.** (*public ~* gesetzlicher) Feiertag; **2.** freier Tag, Ruhetag *m*: *have a ~* e-n freien Tag haben (→ 3); *have a ~ from* sich von *et.* erholen können; **3.** *mst pl. bsd. Brit.* Ferien *pl.*, Urlaub *m*: *the Easter ~s* die Osterferien; *be on ~* im Urlaub sein; *go on ~* in Urlaub gehen; *have a ~* Urlaub haben (→ 2); *take a ~* Urlaub nehmen *od.* machen; *~s with pay* bezahlter Urlaub; **II** *adj.* **4.** Feiertags...: *~ clothes* Festtagskleidung *f*; **5.** *bsd. Brit.* Ferien..., Urlaubs...: *~ apartment* Ferienwohnung *f*; *~ camp* Feriendorf *n*; *~ course* Ferienkurs *m*; *~ home* a) Ferienhaus *n*, b) Ferienwohnung *f*; *~ trip* Urlaubsreise *f*; **III** *v/i.* **6.** *bsd. Brit.* Ferien *od.* Urlaub machen; **'~,mak·er** *s. bsd. Brit.* Urlauber(in).

,ho·li·er-than-'thou [,həʊlɪə-] *Am.* F **I** *s.* ,Phari'säer' *m*; **II** *adj.* phari'säisch.

ho·li·ness ['həʊlɪnɪs] *s.* Heiligkeit *f*: *His ☨ Seine Heiligkeit* (*Papst*).

ho·lism ['həʊlɪzəm] *s. phls.* Ho'lismus *m* (*Ganzheitstheorie*); **ho·lis·tic** [həʊ'lɪstɪk] *adj.* ho'listisch.

Hol·lands ['hɒləndz], *a.* **Hol·land gin** *s.* Ge'never *m*.

hol·ler ['hɒlə] *v/i. u. v/t.* F brüllen.

hol·low ['hɒləʊ] **I** *s.* **1.** Höhle *f*, (Aus-)Höhlung *f*, Hohlraum *m*: *~ of the hand* hohle Hand; *~ of the knee* Kniekehle *f*; *have s.o. in the ~ of one's hand fig.* j-n völlig in der Hand haben; **2.** Vertiefung *f*, Mulde *f*, Senke *f*; **3.** ⊙ a) Hohlkehle *f*, b) (Guss)Blase *f*; **II** *adj.* □ → *a.* III; **4.** hohl, Hohl...; **5.** hohl, dumpf (*Ton, Stimme*); **6.** *fig.* a) hohl, leer: *feel ~* Hunger haben, b) falsch: *~ promises*; *~ victory* wertloser Sieg; **7.** hohl: a) eingefallen (*Wangen*), b) tief liegend (*Augen*); **III** *adv.* **8.** hohl: *ring ~* hohl *od.* unglaubwürdig klingen; *beat s.o. ~* F j-n vernichtend schlagen; **IV** *v/t.* **9.** *oft ~ out* aushöhlen, -kehlen; *~ bit* ⊙ Hohlmeißel *m*, -bohrer *m*; *~ charge s.* ✕ Haft-Hohlladung *f*; **,~-'cheeked** *adj.* hohlwangig; **'~-eyed** *adj.* hohläugig; **,~-'ground** *adj.* ⊙ hohlgeschliffen.

hol·low·ness ['hɒləʊnɪs] *s.* **1.** Hohlheit *f*; **2.** Dumpfheit *f*; **3.** *fig.* a) Hohlheit *f*, Leere *f*, b) Falschheit *f*.

hol·low| square *s.* ✕ Kar'ree *n*; *~ tile s.* ⊙ Hohlziegel *m*; **'~-ware** *s.* tiefes (Küchen)Geschirr (*Töpfe etc.*).

hol·ly ['hɒlɪ] *s.* **1.** ♦ Stechpalme *f*; **2.** Stechpalmenzweige *pl.*

'hol·ly·hock *s.* ♦ Stockrose *f*.

hol·o·caust ['hɒləkɔːst] *s.* **1.** Massenvernichtung *f*, (*engS.* 'Brand)Kata,strophe *f*: *the ☨ pol. hist.* der Holocaust; **2.** Brandopfer *n*.

hol·o|·cene ['hɒləusiːn] *s. geol.* Holo-'zän *n*, Al'luvium *n*; **'~-gram** [-əʊgræm] *s. phys.* Holo'gramm *n*; **'~-graph** [-əʊgrɑːf; -əʊgræf] *adj. u. s.* ☆ eigenhändig geschrieben(e Urkunde).

ho·log·ra·phy [hɒ'lɒgrəfɪ] *s. phys.* Holo-gra'phie *f*.

hols [hɒlz] *s. pl. Brit.* F *für* **holiday** 3.

hol·ster ['həʊlstə] *s.* (Pi'stolen)Halfter *f, n*.

ho·ly ['həʊlɪ] **I** *adj.* □ **1.** heilig, (*Hostie etc.*) geweiht: *~ cow* (*od.* **smoke**)! F ,heiliger Bimbam'! **2.** fromm; **3.** gottgefällig; **II** *s.* **4.** *the ~ of holies bibl.* das Allerheiligste; **☨ Al·li·ance** *s. hist.* die Heilige Alli'anz; *~ bread s.* Abendmahlsbrot *n*, Hostie *f*; **☨ City** *s.* die Heilige Stadt; *~ day s.* kirchlicher Feiertag; **☨ Fa·ther** *s.* der Heilige Vater; **☨ Ghost** *s.* der Heilige Geist; **☨ Land** *s.* das Heilige Land; **☨ Of·fice** *s. R.C.* a) *hist.* die Inquisiti'on, b) *das Heilige Of-*'fizium; **☨ Ro·man Em·pire** *s. hist.* das Heilige Römische Reich; **☨ Sat·ur·day** *s.* Kar'samstag *m*; **☨ Scrip·ture** *s.* die Heilige Schrift; **☨ See** *s.* der Heilige Stuhl; **☨ Spir·it** → **Holy Ghost**; *~ ter·ror s.* F ,Nervensäge' *f*; **☨ Thurs·day** *s.* **1.** *R.C.* Grün'donnerstag *m*; **2.** (anglikanische Kirche) Himmelfahrtstag *m*; **☨ Trin·i·ty** *s.* die Heilige Drei'einigkeit *od.* Drei'faltigkeit; *~ wa·ter s. R.C.* Weihwasser *n*; **☨ Week** *s.* Karwoche *f*; **☨ Writ** → **Holy Scripture**.

hom·age ['hɒmɪdʒ] *s.* **1.** *hist. u. fig.* Huldigung *f*: *do* (*od.* **render**) *~* huldigen (*to dat.*); **2.** *fig.* Reve'renz *f*: *pay ~ to* Anerkennung zollen (*dat.*), (s-e) Hochachtung bezeigen (*dat.*).

Hom·burg (**hat**) ['hɒmbɜːg] *s.* Homburg *m* (*Herrenfilzhut*).

home [həʊm] **I** *s.* **1.** Heim *n*: a) Haus *n*, (*eigene*) Wohnung, b) Zu'hause *n*, Da-'heim *n*, c) Elternhaus *n*: *at ~* zu Hause, *östr., schweiz.* zu'hause, daheim (*a. sport*) (→ 2); *at ~ in* (*od.* **on**, **with**) *fig.* bewandert in (*dat.*), vertraut mit (*e-m Fachgebiet etc.*); *not at ~* (*to s.o.*) nicht zu sprechen (für j-n); *feel at ~* sich wie zu Hause fühlen; *make o.s. at ~* es sich bequem machen; tun, als ob man zu Hause wäre; *make one's ~ at* sich niederlassen in (*dat.*); *away from ~ bsd. sport* auswärts; **2.** Heimat *f* (*a.* ♦, *zo. u. fig.*), Geburts-Heimatland *n*: *at ~* a) im Lande, in der Heimat, b) im Inland, daheim; *at ~ and abroad* im In- u. Ausland; *a letter from ~* ein Brief von Zuhause; **3.** (ständiger *od.* jetziger) Wohnort, Heimatort *m*: *last ~* letzte Ruhestätte; Heim *n*, Anstalt *f*: *~ for the aged* Altenheim *n*; *~ for the blind* Blindenheim, -anstalt; **5.** *sport* a) Ziel *n*, b) → **home plate**, c) Heimspiel *n*; **II** *adj.* **6.** Heim..., Haus...: a) häuslich, Familien..., b) zu Hause ausgeübt: *~ life* häusliches Leben, Familienleben *n*; *~ remedy* Hausmittel *n*; *~-baked* selbst gebacken; **7.** Heimat...: *~ address* (*city*, *port etc.*); *~*

fleet ⚓ Flotte *f* in Heimatgewässern; **8.** einheimisch, inländisch, Inland(s)..., Binnen...: *~ affairs pol.* innere Angelegenheiten; *~ market* Inlands-, Binnenhandel *m*; **9.** *sport* a) Heim...: *~ advantage* (**match**, **win**, *etc.*): *~ strength* Heimstärke *f*, b) Ziel...; **10.** a) (wohl)gezielt, wirkungsvoll (*Schlag etc.*), b) *fig.* treffend, beißend (*Bemerkung etc.*); → **home thrust**, **home truth**; **III** *adv.* **11.** heim, nach Hause, *östr., schweiz.* nach'hause: *the way ~* der Heimweg; *go ~* nach Hause gehen (→ 13); → **write** 10; **12.** zu Hause, *östr., schweiz.* zu'hause (wieder) da'heim; **13.** a) ins Ziel, b) im Ziel, c) bis zum Ausgangspunkt, d) ganz, so weit wie möglich: *drive a nail ~* e-n Nagel fest einschlagen; *drive* (*od.* **bring**) *s.th. ~ to s.o.* j-m et. klarmachen *od.* beibringen *od.* vor Augen führen; *drive a charge ~ to s.o.* j-n überführen; *go* (*od.* **get**, **strike**) *~* ,sitzen', s-e Wirkung tun; *the thrust went ~* der Hieb saß; **IV** *v/i.* **14.** zu'rückkehren; **15.** ✈ a) (*per Leitstrahl*) das Ziel anfliegen, b) *mst ~ in on* ein Ziel auto'matisch ansteuern (*Rakete*); **V** *v/t.* **16.** *Flugzeug* (*per Radar*) einweisen, ,herunterholen'.

,home|-and-'home *adj. sport Am.* im Vor- u. Rückspiel ausgetragen: *~ match*; *~ bank·ing s.* 'Homebanking *n*; **'~,bod·y** *s.* häuslicher Mensch, *contp.* Stubenhocker(in); **'~-bound** *adj.* ans Haus gefesselt: *~ invalid*; **'~-bred** *adj.* **1.** einheimisch; **2.** *obs.* hausbacken; **'~-brew** *s.* selbst gebrautes Getränk (*bsd.* Bier); **'~,coming** *s.* Heimkehr *f*; **~ con·tents** *s. pl.* Hausrat *m*; **☨ Coun·ties** *s. pl.* die um London liegenden Grafschaften; **~ e·co·nom·ics** *s. pl. sg. konstr.* Hauswirtschaft(slehre) *f*; **~ front** *s.* Heimatfront *f*; **~ ground** *s. sport* eigener Platz; *fig.* vertrautes Gelände; **☨ Guard** *s.* Bürgerwehr *f*; **'~-,keep·ing** *adj.* häuslich, *contp.* stubenhockerisch; **'~-land** *s.* **1.** Heimat-, Vater-, Mutterland *n*; **2.** *pol.* Homeland *n*, Heimstatt *f* (*in Südafrika*).

home·less ['həʊmlɪs] *adj.* **1.** heimatlos; **2.** obdachlos; **'home·like** *adj.* wie zu Hause (*östr., schweiz.* zuhause), gemütlich; **home·li·ness** ['həʊmlɪnɪs] *s.* **1.** Einfachheit *f*, Schlichtheit *f*; **2.** Gemütlichkeit *f*; **3.** *Am.* Reizlosigkeit *f*; **home·ly** ['həʊmlɪ] *adj.* **1.** → **homelike**; **2.** freundlich; **3.** einfach, hausbacken; **4.** *Am.* reizlos: *a ~ girl*.

,home|'made *adj.* **1.** selbst gemacht, Hausmacher...; **2.** selbst gebastelt: *~ bomb*; **3.** ✟ a) einheimisch, im Inland hergestellt: *~ goods*, b) hausgemacht: *~ inflation*; **'~,mak·er** *s. Am.* **1.** Hausfrau *f*; **2.** Fa'milienpflegerin *f*; **'~,mak·ing** *s. Am.* Haushaltsführung *f*; **~ mar·ket** *s.* ✟ Inlandsmarkt *m*; **~ me·chan·ic** *s.* Heimwerker *m*; **~ mov·ie** *s.* Heimkino *n*.

homeo- *etc.* → **homoeo-** *etc.*

home| of·fice *s.* **1.** ☨ *Brit.* 'Innenministerium *n*; **2.** *bsd.* ✟ *Am.* Hauptsitz *m*; **~ page** *s. Internet:* 'Homepage *f* (*Startseite e-s Anbieters*); **~ perm** *s.* F Heim-Dauerwelle *f*; **~ plate** *s. Baseball:* Heimbase *n*.

hom·er ['həʊmə] *s.* F *für* **home run**.

Ho·mer·ic [həʊ'merɪk] *adj.* ho'merisch: *~ laughter*.

home| rule *s. pol.* a) 'Selbstre,gierung *f*, b) ☨ *hist.* Homerule *f* (*in Irland*); **~ run** *s. Baseball:* Homerun *m* (*Lauf über alle 4 Male*); **☨ Sec·re·tar·y** *s. Brit.* 'Innenmi,nister *m*; **~ shop·ping** *s.* Teleshopping *n*; '~·sick *adj.*: *be ~* Heimweh haben; '~,sick·ness *s.* Heimweh *n*; '~·spun I *adj.* **1.** a) zu Hause gesponnen, b) Homespun...: ~ *clothing*; **2.** *fig.* schlicht, einfach; II *s.* **3.** Homespun *n* (*Streichgarn[gewebe]*); '~·stead *s.* **1.** Heimstätte *f*, Gehöft *n*; **2.** ⚖ *Am.* Heimstätte *f* (*Grundparzelle od. gegen Zugriff von Gläubigern geschützter Grundbesitz*); ~ *straight*, ~ *stretch s.* *sport* Zielgerade *f*: *be on the ~ fig.* kurz vor dem Ziel stehen; ~ *thrust s. fig.* wohlgezielter Hieb; ~ *truth s.* harte Wahrheit, unbequeme Tatsache; '~·ward [-wəd] I *adv.* heimwärts, nach Hause, *östr.*, *schweiz.* nachhause; II *adj.* Heim..., Rück...; → *bound²*; '~·wards [-wədz] → *homeward* I; '~·work *s.* **1.** *ped.* Hausaufgabe(n *pl.*) *f*, Schularbeiten *pl.*: *do one's ~* s-e Hausaufgaben machen (*a. fig. sich gründlich vorbereiten*); **2.** ✝ Heimarbeit *f*; '~,work·er *s.* ✝ Heimarbeiter (-in); '~,wreck·er *s. j-d, der e-e Ehe zerstört.*

home·y *Am. für* **homy.**

hom·i·cid·al [ˌhɒmɪˈsaɪdl] *adj.* **1.** mörderisch, mordlustig; **2.** Mord..., Totschlags...; **hom·i·cide** [ˈhɒmɪsaɪd] *s.* **1.** *allg.* Tötung *f*, *engS.* a) Mord *m*, b) Totschlag *m*: ~ *by misadventure Am.* Unfall *m* mit Todesfolge; ~ (*squad*) Mordkommission *f*; **2.** Mörder(in), Totschläger(in).

hom·i·ly [ˈhɒmɪlɪ] *s.* **1.** Homi'lie *f*, Predigt *f*; **2.** *fig.* Mo'ralpredigt *f*.

hom·ing [ˈhəʊmɪŋ] I *adj.* **1.** heimkehrend: ~ *pigeon* Brieftaube *f*; ~ *instinct zo.* Heimkehrvermögen *n*; **2.** ✕ zielansteuernd (*Rakete etc.*); II *s.* ✔ **3.** a) Zielflug *m*, b) Zielpeilung *f*, c) Rückflug *m*: ~ *beacon* Zielflugfunkfeuer *n*; ~ *device* Zielfluggerät *n*.

hom·i·nid [ˈhɒmɪnɪd] *zo.* I *adj.* menschenartig; II *s.* Homi'nide *m*, menschenartiges Wesen; **'hom·i·noid** [-nɔɪd] *adj. u. s.* menschenähnlich(es Tier).

hom·i·ny [ˈhɒmɪnɪ] *s. Am.* **1.** Maismehl *n*; **2.** Maisbrei *m*.

ho·mo [ˈhəʊməʊ] *s.* F 'Homo' *m*.

homo- [həʊməʊ, hɒməʊ], **homoeo-** [həʊmjəʊ] *in Zssgn* gleich(artig).

ho·moe·o·path [ˈhəʊmjəʊpæθ] *s.* ⚕ Homöo'path(in); **ho·moe·o·path·ic** [ˌhəʊmjəʊˈpæθɪk] *adj.* (□ ~*ally*) ⚕ homöo'pathisch; **ho·moe·op·a·thist** [ˌhəʊmɪˈɒpəθɪst] → *homoeopath*; **ho·moe·op·a·thy** [ˌhəʊmɪˈɒpəθɪ] *s.* ⚕ Homöopa'thie *f*.

ho·mo·e·rot·ic [ˌhəʊməʊˈrɒtɪk] *adj.* homoe'rotisch.

ho·mo·ge·ne·i·ty [ˌhɒməʊdʒeˈniːətɪ] *s.* Homogeni'tät *f*, Gleichartigkeit *f*; **ho·mo·ge·ne·ous** [ˌhɒməʊˈdʒiːnjəs] *adj.* □ homo'gen: a) gleichartig, b) einheitlich; **ho·mo·gen·e·sis** [ˌhɒməʊˈdʒenɪsɪs] *s. biol.* Homoge'nese *f*; **ho·mog·e·nize** [hɒˈmɒdʒənaɪz] *v/t.* homogenisieren.

ho·mol·o·gate [hɒˈmɒləɡeɪt] *v/t.* **1.** ⚖ a) genehmigen, b) beglaubigen, bestätigen; **2.** *Ski- u. Motorsport*: homologieren; **ho'mol·o·gous** [-ɡəs] *adj.* ⚔, ⚕, *biol.* homo'log.

hom·o·nym [ˈhɒməʊnɪm] *s. ling.* Homo'nym *n* (*a. biol.*), gleich lautendes Wort; **ho·mo·nym·ic** [ˌhɒməʊˈnɪmɪk], **ho·mon·y·mous** [hɒˈmɒnɪməs] *adj.* homo'nym.

ho·mo·phile [ˈhɒməʊfaɪl] I *s.* Homo'phile(r *m*) *f*; II *adj.* homo'phil.

hom·o·phone [ˈhɒməʊfəʊn] *s. ling.* Homo'phon *n*; **hom·o·phon·ic** [ˌhɒməʊˈfɒnɪk] *adj.* ♪, *ling.* homo'phon.

ho·mop·ter·a [həʊˈmɒptərə] *s. pl. zo.* Gleichflügler *pl.* (*Insekten*).

ho·mo·sex·u·al [ˌhɒməʊˈseksjʊəl] I *s.* Homosexu'elle(r *m*) *f*; II *adj.* homosexu'ell; **ho·mo·sex·u·al·i·ty** [ˌhɒməʊˌseksjʊˈælətɪ] *s.* Homosexuali'tät *f*.

ho·mun·cu·lar [hɒˈmʌŋkjʊlə] *adj.* ho'munkulusähnlich; **ho'mun·cule** [-kjuːl], **ho'mun·cu·lus** [-kjʊləs] *pl.* **-li** [-laɪ] *s.* **1.** Ho'munkulus *m* (*künstlich erzeugter Mensch*); **2.** Menschlein *n*, Knirps *m*.

hom·y [ˈhəʊmɪ] *adj.* F gemütlich.

hon·cho [ˈhɒntʃəʊ] *s. Am.* F Boss *m*: *head ~* Big Boss *m*, 'Oberboss *m*.

hone [həʊn] I *s.* **1.** (feiner) Schleifstein; II *v/t.* **2.** honen, fein-, ziehschleifen; **3.** *fig.* a) schärfen, b) (aus)feilen.

hon·est [ˈɒnɪst] *adj.* □ **1.** ehrlich: a) redlich, rechtschaffen, anständig, b) offen, aufrichtig; **2.** *humor.* wacker, bieder; **3.** ehrlich verdient; **4.** *obs.* ehrbar (*Frau*); '**hon·est·ly** [-lɪ] I *adv.* → *honest*; II *int.* F a) offen gesagt, b) ehrlich!, c) *empört*: nein (*od.* also) wirklich!; ˌ**hon·est-to-'God,** ˌ**hon·est-to-**-'**good·ness** *adj.* F echt, wirklich, 'richtig'; '**hon·es·ty** [-tɪ] *s.* **1.** Ehrlichkeit *f*: a) Rechtschaffenheit *f*: ~ *is the best policy* ehrlich währt am längsten, b) Aufrichtigkeit *f*; **2.** *obs.* Ehrbarkeit *f*; **3.** ♀ 'Mondvi,ole *f*.

hon·ey [ˈhʌnɪ] *s.* **1.** Honig *m* (*a. fig.*); **2.** ♀ Nektar *m*; **3.** *bsd. Am.* a) 'Schatz' *m*, Süße(r *m*) *f*, b) *Am.* ˌsüßes' *od.* ˌschickes' Ding: *a ~ of a car* ein ˌklasse' Wagen; '**~·bag** *s. zo.* Honigmagen *m der Bienen*; '**~·bee** *s. zo.* Honigbiene *f*; '**~·bun(ch)** [-bʌn(tʃ)] → *honey* 3 a.

'**hon·ey·comb** [-kəʊm] I *s.* **1.** Bienen-, Honigwabe *f*; **2.** Waffelmuster *n* (*Gewebe*): ~ (*quilt*) Waffeldecke *f*; **3.** ⚙ Lunker *m*, (Guss)Blase *f*; **4.** *in Zssgn* ⚙ Waben... (*-kühler, -spule etc.*): ~ *stomach zo.* Netzmagen *m*; II *v/t.* **5.** (wabenartig) durch'löchern; **6.** *fig.* durch'setzen (*with* mit); '**hon·ey·combed** [-kəʊmd] *adj.* **1.** durch'löchert, löcherig, zellig; **2.** ⚙ blasig; **3.** *fig.* a) durch'setzt (mit), b) unter'graben (durch).

'**hon·ey|·dew** *s.* **1.** ♀ Honigtau *m*, Blatthonig *m*; ~ *melon* Honigmelone *f*; **2.** gesüßter Tabak; ~ **eat·er** *s. orn.* Honigfresser *m*.

hon·eyed [ˈhʌnɪd] *adj.* **1.** voller Honig; **2.** *a. fig.* honig'süß.

hon·ey| ex·trac·tor *s.* Honigschleuder *f*; ~ *flow s.* (Bienen)Tracht *f*; '**~·moon** I *s.* **1.** Flitterwochen *pl.*, Honigmond *m* (*a. iro. fig.*); **2.** Hochzeitsreise *f*; II *v/i.* **3.** a) die Flitterwochen verbringen, b) s-e Hochzeitsreise machen; '**~,moon·er** *s.* a) ˌFlitterwöchner' *m*, b) Hochzeitsreisende(r *m*) *f*; ~ *sac s. zo.* Honigmagen *m*; '**~,suck·le** *s.* ♀ Geißblatt *n*.

hon·ied [ˈhʌnɪd] → *honeyed.*

honk [hɒŋk] I *s.* **1.** Schrei *m* (*der Wildgans*); **2.** 'Hupensi,gnal *n*; II *v/i.* **3.** schreien; **4.** hupen.

honk·y-tonk [ˈhɒŋkɪtɒŋk] *s. Am. sl.* ˌSpe'lunke' *f*.

hon·or *etc. Am.* → *honour etc.*

hon·o·rar·i·um [ˌɒnəˈreərɪəm] *pl.* **-rar·i·a** [-ˈreərɪə], **-rar·i·ums** *s.* (*freiwillig gezahltes*) Hono'rar; **hon·or·ar·y** [ˈɒnərərɪ] *adj.* **1.** ehrend; **2.** Ehren...: ~ *doctor* (*member, etc.*); ~ *debt* Ehrenschuld *f*; ~ *degree* ehrenhalber verliehener akademischer Grad; **3.** ehrenamtlich: ~ *secretary*; **hon·or·if·ic** [ˌɒnəˈrɪfɪk] I *adj.* (□ ~*ally*) ehrend, Ehren...; II *s.* Ehrung *f*, Ehrentitel *m*.

hon·our [ˈɒnə] I *s.* **1.** Ehre *f*: (*sense of*) ~ Ehrgefühl *n*; (*up*)*on my ~!*, *Brit.* F ~ *bright!* Ehrenwort!; *man of ~* Ehrenmann *m*; *point of ~* Ehrensache *f*; *do s.o. ~* j-m zur Ehre gereichen, j-m Ehre machen; *do s.o. the ~ of doing s.th.* j-m die Ehre erweisen, et. zu tun; *he is an ~ to his parents* (*to his school*) er macht s-n Eltern Ehre (er ist e-e Zierde s-r Schule); *put s.o. on his ~* j-n bei s-r Ehre packen; (*in*) ~ *bound*, *on one's ~* moralisch verpflichtet; *to his ~ it must be said* zu s-r Ehre muss gesagt werden; (*there is*) ~ *among thieves* (es gibt so etwas wie) Ganovenehre *f*; *may I have the ~* (*of the next dance*) bitten?; **2.** Ehrung *f*, Ehre(n *pl.*) *f*: a) Ehrerbietung *f*, Ehrenbezeigung *f*, b) Hochachtung *f*, c) Auszeichnung *f*, (Ehren)Titel *m*, Ehrenamt *n*, -zeichen *n*: *in s.o.'s ~* zu j-s *od.* j-m zu Ehren; *hold* (*od.* *have*) *in ~* in Ehren halten; *pay s.o. the last* (*od. funeral*) ~*s* j-m die letzte Ehre erweisen; *military* ~*s* militärische Ehren; ~*s list Brit.* Liste *f* der Titelverleihungen (*zum Geburtstag des Herrschers etc.*) (→ 3); → *due* 3; **3.** *pl.* besondere Auszeichnung: ~*s degree* akademischer Grad mit Prüfung in e-m Spezialfach; ~*s list* Liste *f* der Studenten, die auf e-n *hon·ours degree* hinarbeiten; ~*s man Brit.*, ~*s student Am.* Student, der e-n *honours degree* anstrebt *od.* innehat; **4.** *pl.* Hon'neurs *pl.*: *do the* ~*s* die Honneurs machen, als Gastgeber(in) fungieren; **5.** *Kartenspiel*: Bild *n*; **6.** *Golf*: Ehre *f* (*Berechtigung zum 1. Schlag*): *it is his ~* er hat die Ehre; **7.** *Your* (*His*) ~ *obs.* Euer (Seine) Gnaden; II *v/t.* **8.** ehren; **9.** ehren, auszeichnen (*with* mit); **10.** beehren (*with* mit); **11.** j-m zur Ehre gereichen *od.* Ehre machen; **12.** e-r *Einladung etc.* Folge leisten; **13.** ✝ a) *Scheck etc.* honorieren, einlösen, b) *Schuld* begleichen, c) *Vertrag* erfüllen; **hon·our·a·ble** [ˈɒnərəbl] *adj.* □ **1.** achtbar, ehrenwert; **2.** rechtschaffen: *an ~ man* ein Ehrenmann; **3.** ehrenhaft, ehrlich (*Absicht etc.*); **4.** ehrenvoll, rühmlich; **5.** ⚌ (*der od. die*) Ehrenwerte (*in Großbritannien: Adelstitel od. Titel der Ehrendamen des Hofes, der Mitglieder des Unterhauses, der Bürgermeister; in USA: Titel der Mitglieder des Kongresses, hoher Beamter, der Richter u. Bürgermeister*): *Right* ⚌ (*der*) Sehr Ehrenwerte; → *friend* 5.

hooch [huːtʃ] *s. Am.* F 'Fusel' *m*.

hood [hʊd] I *s.* **1.** Ka'puze *f* (*a. univ. am Talar*); **2.** ♀ Helm *m*; **3.** *orn., zo.* Haube *f*, Schopf *m*; Brillenzeichnung *f* der Kobra; **4.** *mot.* a) *Brit.* Verdeck *n*, b) *Am.* (Motor)Haube *f*; **5.** ⚙ a) Kappe *f*, (Schutz)Haube *f*, b) Abzug(shaube *f*) *m* (*für Gas etc.*); **6.** → *hoodlum*; II *v/t.* **7.** j-m e-e Ka'puze aufsetzen; **8.** be-, verdecken.

hood·ed [ˈhʊdɪd] *adj.* **1.** mit e-r Ka'puze bekleidet; **2.** ver-, bedeckt, verhüllt (*a. Augen*); **3.** *orn.* mit e-r Haube; ~ *crow s. orn.* Nebelkrähe *f*; ~ *seal s. zo.* Mützenrobbe *f*; ~ *snake s. zo.* Kobra *f*.

hood·lum [ˈhuːdləm] *s.* F **1.** Rowdy *m*, ˌSchläger' *m*; **2.** Ga'nove *m*, Gangster *m*.

hoo·doo [ˈhuːduː] I *s. Am.* **1.** → *voodoo* I; **2.** a) Unglücksbringer *m*, b) Unglück *n*, Pech *n*; II *v/t.* **3.** a) verhexen, b) j-m Unglück bringen; III *adj.* **4.** Unglücks...

'**hood·wink** v/t. **1.** obs. die Augen verbinden (dat.); **2.** fig. hinters Licht führen, reinlegen.

hoo·ey ['huːɪ] s. sl. Quatsch m, Blödsinn m.

hoof [huːf] pl. **hoofs, hooves** [huːvz] **I** s. **1.** zo. a) Huf m, b) Fuß m: **on the ~** lebend (Schlachtvieh); **2.** humor. ,Pe-'dal' n, Fuß m; **3.** Huftier n; **II** v/t. **4.** F Strecke ,tippeln': **~ it** → 6, 7; **5. ~ out** j-n ,rausschmeißen'; **III** v/i. **6.** F ,tippeln', marschieren; **7.** F tanzen; ,**~- -and-'mouth dis·ease** s. vet. Maul- u. Klauenseuche f.

hoofed [huːft] adj. gehuft, Huf...; '**hoof·er** [-fə] s. Am. sl. Berufstänzer (-in), bsd. Re'vuegirl n.

hoo·ha ['huːhɑː] s. F ,Tam'tam' n.

hook [hʊk] **I** s. **1.** Haken m (a. 🦯): **~ and eye** Haken u. Öse; **~ and ladder** Am. Gerätewagen m der Feuerwehr; **by ~ or (by) crook** mit allen Mitteln, so oder so; **on one's own ~** F auf eigene Faust; **2.** ⊕ a) (Klammer-, Dreh)Haken m, b) (Tür)Angel f, Haspe f; **3.** Angelhaken m: **be off the ~** F ,aus dem Schneider' sein; **get s.o. off the ~** F j-m ,aus der Patsche' helfen, j-n ,herauspauken'; **get o.s. off the ~** sich aus der ,Schlinge' ziehen; **have s.o. on the ~** F j-n ,zappeln' lassen; **that lets him off the ~** damit ist er raus aus der Sache; **fall for s.o. (s.th.) ~, line and sinker** voll auf j-n (et.) ,abfahren'; **swallow s.th. ~, line and sinker** et. voll u. ganz ,schlucken'; **4.** ✍ Sichel f; **5.** a) scharfe Krümmung, b) gekrümmte Landspitze; **6.** pl. sl. ,Griffel' pl. (Finger); **7.** ♪ Notenfähnchen n; **8.** sport: a) Boxen: Haken m: **~ to the body** Körperhaken, b) Golf: Hook m (Kurvschlag); **II** v/t. **9.** an-, ein-, fest-, zuhaken; **10.** fangen, (sich) angeln (a. fig. F): **~ a husband** sich e-n Mann angeln; **he is ~ed** F a) er zappelt im Netz, er ist ,dran' od. ,geliefert', b) → hooked 3; **11.** sl. ,klauen', stehlen; **12.** krümmen; **13.** aufspießen; **14.** a) Boxen: j-m e-n Haken versetzen, b) Golf: Ball mit (e-m) Hook schlagen, c) (Eis)Hockey: Gegner haken; **15. ~ it** F ,verduften'; **III** v/i. **16.** sich zuhaken lassen; **17.** sich festhaken (**to** an dat.); **~ on I** v/t. **1.** ein-, anhaken; **II** v/i. **2.** → **hook** [bild]: **3.** sich einhängen (**to** s.o. bei j-m); **~ up** v/t. **1.** → **hook on** 1; **2.** zuhaken; **3.** ⊕ a) Gerät zs.-bauen, b) anschließen; **4.** Radio, TV: a) zs.-schalten, b) zuschalten (**with** dat.); **5.** bsd. Am. F a) sich zs.-tun (**with** mit), b) gehen zu (**with** dat.) (e-r Firma etc.).

hook·a(h) ['hʊkə] s. Huka f (orientalische Wasserpfeife).

hooked [hʊkt] adj. **1.** krumm, hakenförmig, Haken...; **2.** mit (e-m) Haken (versehen); **3.** F a) (**on**) süchtig (nach); fig. a. ,scharf' (auf acc.), ,verrückt' (nach): **~ on heroin** (**television**) heroin- (fernseh)süchtig, b) → **hook** 10.

hook·er ['hʊkə] s. **1.** ♣ a) Huker m, Fischerboot n, b) contp. ,alter Kahn'; **2.** sl. ,Nutte' f.

hook·ey → **hooky**.

'**hook|-nosed** adj. mit e-r Hakennase; '**~-up** s. **1.** Radio, TV: a) Zs.-, Konfe-'renzschaltung f, b) Zuschaltung f; **2.** ⚡ a) Schaltbild n, -schema n, b) Blockschaltung f; **3.** ⊕ Zs.-bau m; **4.** F a) Zs.-schluss m, Bündnis n, b) Absprache f; '**~-worm** s. zo. Hakenwurm m.

hook·y ['hʊkɪ] s.: **play ~** Am. F (bsd. die Schule) schwänzen.

hoo·li·gan ['huːlɪgən] s. 'Hooligan m, Rowdy m; '**hoo·li·gan·ism** [-nɪzəm] s.

Rowdytum n.

hoop¹ [huːp] **I** s. **1.** allg. Reif(en) m (a. als Schmuck, bei Kinderspielen, im Zirkus etc.): **~ (skirt)** Reifrock m; **go through the ~(s)** ,durch die Mangel gedreht werden'; **2.** ⊕ a) (Fass)Reif(en) m, b) (Stahl)Band n, Ring m: **~ iron** Bandeisen n, c) Öse f, d) Bügel m; **3.** (Finger)Ring m; **4.** Basketball: Korbring m; **5.** Krocket: Tor n; **II** v/t. **6.** Fass binden; **7.** um'geben, -'fassen; **8.** Basketball: Punkte erzielen.

hoop² [huːp] → **whoop**.

hoop·er¹ ['huːpə] s. Böttcher m, Küfer m, Fassbinder m.

hoop·er² ['huːpə] **~ swan** s. orn. Singschwan m.

hoo·poe ['huːpuː] s. orn. Wiedehopf m.

hoo·ray [hʊ'reɪ] → **hurrah**.

hoos(e)·gow ['huːsgaʊ] s. Am. sl. ,Kittchen' n, ,Knast' m.

hoot [huːt] **I** v/i. **1.** (höhnisch) johlen: **~ at s.o.** j-n verhöhnen; **2.** schreien (Eule); **3.** Brit. a) hupen (Auto), b) pfeifen (Zug etc.), c) heulen (Sirene etc.); **II** v/t. **4.** et. johlen; **5.** a. **~ down** niederschreien, auspfeifen; **6. ~ out, ~ off** durch Gejohle vertreiben; **III** s. **7.** (johlender) Schrei (a. der Eule), pl. Johlen n: **it's not worth a ~** F es ist keinen Pfifferling wert; **I don't care two ~s** F das ist mir völlig ,piepe'; **8.** Hupen n (Auto); Heulen n (Sirene); '**hoot·er** [-tə] s. **1.** Johler(in); **2.** a) mot. Hupe f, b) Si'rene f, Pfeife f.

Hoo·ver ['huːvə] (Fabrikmarke) **I** s. Staubsauger m; **II** v/t. mst 2 (ab)saugen; **III** v/i. (staub)saugen.

hooves [huːvz] pl. von **hoof**.

hop¹ [hɒp] **I** v/i. **1.** hüpfen, hopsen: **~ on** → 5; **~ off** F ,abschwirren'; **~ to it** Am. F sich (an die Arbeit) ,ranmachen'; **2.** F ,schwofen', tanzen; **3.** F a) ,flitzen', sausen, b) rasch wohin fahren od. fliegen; **II** v/t. **4.** hüpfen od. springen über (acc.): **~ it** ,abschwirren'; **5.** F a) (auf-) springen auf (acc.), b) einsteigen in (acc.): **~ a train**; **6.** ✍ über'fliegen, -'queren; **7.** Am. Ball hüpfen lassen; **8.** Am. F bedienen in (dat.); **III** s. **9.** Sprung m, Hops(er) m: **~, step, and jump** sport Dreisprung m; **be on the ~** F ,auf Trab' sein; **keep s.o. on the ~** F j-n ,in Trab halten'; **catch s.o. on the ~** F j-n erwischen od. überraschen; **10.** F ,Schwof', Tanz m; **11.** bsd. ✍ F ,Sprung', Abstecher m: **only a short ~** nur ein Katzensprung.

hop² [hɒp] **I** s. **1.** ♀ a) Hopfen m, b) pl. Hopfen(blüten pl.) m: **pick ~s** → 4; **2.** sl. Rauschgift n, engS. Opium n; **II** v/t. **3.** Bier hopfen; **4. ~ up** sl. a) (durch e-e Droge) ,high' machen, b) aufputschen (a. fig.), c) Am. Auto etc. ,frisieren'; **III** v/i. **5.** Hopfen zupfen; **~ bind, ~ bine** s. Hopfenranke f; **~ dri·er** s. Hopfendarre f.

hope [həʊp] **I** s. **1.** Hoffnung f (**of** auf acc.): **live in ~(s)** (immer noch) hoffen, die Hoffnung nicht aufgeben; **in the ~ of** ger. in der Hoffnung zu inf.; **past ~** hoffnungs-, aussichtslos; **he is past all ~** für ihn gibt es keine Hoffnung mehr; **2.** Hoffnung f) Zuversicht f, b) no **of success** keine Aussicht auf Erfolg; **not a ~** F keine Chance; **3.** Hoffnung f (Person od. Sache): **she is our only ~**; → **white hope**; **2. ~ forlorn hope** [bild]; **II** v/i. **5.** hoffen (**for** auf acc.): **~ against ~** die Hoffnung nicht aufgeben, verzweifelt hoffen; **~ for the best** das Beste hoffen; **I ~ so** hoffentlich, ich hoffe (es); **the ~d-for result** das erhoffte Er-

gebnis; **III** v/t. **6.** et. hoffen; **~ chest** s. Am. F Aussteuertruhe f.

hope·ful ['həʊpfʊl] **I** adj. □ **1.** hoffnungs-, erwartungsvoll: **be ~ of** et. hoffen; **be ~ about** optimistisch sein hinsichtlich (gen.); **2.** (a. iro.) viel versprechend; **II** s. **3.** a. iro. a) hoffnungsvoller od. viel versprechender (junger) Mensch, b) ,Opti-'mist' m; '**hope·ful·ly** [-fʊli] adv. **1.** → **hopeful** 1; **2.** hoffentlich; '**hope·ful·ness** [-nɪs] s. Opti'mismus m.

hope·less ['həʊplɪs] adj. □ hoffnungslos: a) verzweifelt, b) aussichtslos, c) unheilbar, d) mise'rabel, e) F unverbesserlich: **a ~ drunkard**; '**hope·less·ly** [-lɪ] adv. **1.** → **hopeless**; **2.** F heillos, to'tal; '**hope·less·ness** [-nɪs] s. Hoffnungslosigkeit f.

hop-o'-my-thumb [ˌhɒpəmɪ'θʌm] s. Knirps m, Zwerg m.

hop·per ['hɒpə] s. **1.** Hüpfende(r m) f; **2.** F Tänzer(in); **3.** zo. hüpfendes In-'sekt, bsd. Käsemade f; **4.** ⊕ a) Fülltrichter m, b) (Schüttgut-, Vorrats)Behälter m, c) a. **~(-bottom) car** 🚃 Fallboden-, Selbstentladewagen m, d) Spülkasten m, e) Computer: Karteneingabefach n.

hop·ping mad ['hɒpɪŋ] adj.: **be ~** F e-e ,Stinkwut' (im Bauch) haben.

'**hop|·scotch** s. Himmel-und-Hölle-Spiel n; **~ vine** → **hop bind**.

Ho·rae ['hɔːriː] s. pl. myth. Horen pl.

Ho·ra·tian [hə'reɪʃən] adj. ho'razisch: **~ ode**.

horde [hɔːd] **I** s. Horde f, (wilder) Haufen; **II** v/i. e-e Horde bilden; in Horden zs.-leben.

ho·ri·zon [hə'raɪzn] s. (a. fig. geistiger) Hori'zont, Gesichtskreis m: **apparent** (od. **sensible, visible**) **~** scheinbarer Horizont; **celestial** (od. **rational, true**) **~** wahrer Horizont; **on the ~** am Horizont (auftauchend od. sichtbar).

hor·i·zon·tal [ˌhɒrɪ'zɒntl] **I** adj. □ horizon'tal, waag(e)recht, a. liegend (Motor, Ventil etc.), a. Seiten... (bsd. Steuerung); **~ line** → **II** s. ☼ Horizon'tale f, Waag(e)rechte f; **~ bar** s. Turnen: Reck n; **~ com·bi·na·tion** s. ✝ Horizon'talverflechtung f, -kon,zern m; **~ plane** s. ☼ Horizon'talebene f; **~ pro·jec·tion** s. ☼ Horizon'talprojekti,on f: **~ plane** Grundrissebene f; **~ rud·der** s. ♣ Horizon'tal(steuer)ruder n, Tiefenruder n; **~ sec·tion** s. ⊕ Horizon'talschnitt m.

hor·mo·nal [hɔː'məʊnl] adj. biol. hor'mo'nal, Hormon...; **hor·mone** ['hɔː-məʊn] s. Hor'mon n; **~ bal·ance** s. Hormonspiegel m.

horn [hɔːn] **I** s. **1.** zo. a) Horn n, b) pl. Geweih n; **~ of dilemma**; **2.** zo. a) Horn n (Nashorn), b) Fühler m (Insekt), c) Fühlhorn n (Schnecke): **draw** (od. **pull**) **in one's ~s** fig. die Hörner einziehen, ,zurückstecken'; **3.** pl. fig. Hörner (des betrogenen Ehemanns): **put ~s on s.o.** j-m Hörner aufsetzen; **4.** (Pulver-, Trink)Horn n: **~ of plenty** Füllhorn; **5.** ♪ a) Horn n, b) F ,Blasinstru,ment n: **blow one's own ~** fig. ins eigene Horn stoßen; **6.** a) mot. Hupe f, b) ⊕ Si'gnalhorn n; **7.** a) (Schall)Trichter m, b) ⚡ Hornstrahler m; **8.** 'Horn(sub,stanz f) n: **~ handle** Horngriff m; **9.** Horn n (hornförmige Sache), bsd. a) Bergspitze f, b) Spitze f (der Mondsichel), c) Schuhlöffel m: **the 2** (das) Kap Horn; **10.** Sattelknopf m; **11.** V ,Ständer' m: **~ pill** Aphrodisiakum n; **II** v/t. **12.** a) mit den Hörnern stoßen, b) auf die Hörner nehmen; **III** v/i. **13. ~ in** sl. sich einmischen od. -drängen (**on** in acc.);

'**~·beam** s. ⚘ Hain-, Weißbuche f; '**~·blende** [-blend] s. min. Hornblende f.
horned [hɔːnd; poet. 'hɔːnɪd] adj. gehörnt, Horn...: **~ cattle** Hornvieh n; **~ owl** s. Ohreule f.
hor·net ['hɔːnɪt] s. zo. Hor'nisse f: **bring a ~'s nest about one's ears**, **stir up a ~'s nest** fig. in ein Wespennest stechen.
'**horn|·fly** s. zo. Hornfliege f; '**~·less** [-lɪs] adj. hornlos, ohne Hörner; '**~·pipe** s. ♪ Hornpipe f (Blasinstrument od. alter Tanz); '**~·rimmed** adj. mit Hornfassung: **~ spectacles** Hornbrille f; '**~·swog·gle** [-ˌswɒgl] v/t. sl. j-n ‚reinlegen'.
horn·y ['hɔːnɪ] adj. 1. hornig, schwielig: **~-handed** mit schwieligen Händen; 2. aus Horn, Horn...; 3. V geil, ‚scharf'.
hor·o·loge ['hɒrəlɒdʒ] s. Zeitmesser m, (Sonnen- od.)Uhr f.
hor·o·scope ['hɒrəskəʊp] s. Horo'skop n: **cast a ~** ein Horoskop stellen; '**hor·o·scop·er** [-pə] s. Horo'skopsteller(in).
hor·ren·dous [hɒ'rendəs] □ → **horrific**.
hor·ri·ble ['hɒrəbl] adj. □, **hor·rid** ['hɒrɪd] adj. □ schrecklich, fürchterlich, entsetzlich, grässlich, scheußlich, ab'scheulich; '**hor·ri·ble·ness** [-nɪs] s., **hor·rid·ness** ['hɒrɪdnɪs] s. Schrecklichkeit etc.
hor·rif·ic [hɒ'rɪfɪk] adj. (□ **~ally**) 1. schrecklich, entsetzlich; 2. hor'rend; **hor·ri·fy** ['hɒrɪfaɪ] v/t. entsetzen.
hor·ror ['hɒrə] I s. 1. Grau(s)en n, Entsetzen n: **seized with ~** von Grauen gepackt; **have the ~s** F a) ‚weiße Mäuse' sehen, b) ‚am Boden zerstört' sein; 2. (**of**) 'Widerwille m (gegen), Abscheu m (vor dat.): **have a ~ of** e-n Horror haben vor (dat.); 3. a) Schrecken m, Gräuel m, b) Gräueltat f: **the ~s of war** die Schrecken des Krieges; **scene of ~** Schreckensszene f; 4. Entsetzlichkeit f, (das) Schauerliche; 5. F Gräuel m (Person od. Sache), Scheusal n, Ekel n (Person); II adj. 6. Grusel..., Horror...: **~ film**; '**~·strick·en**, '**~·struck** adj. von Schrecken od. Grauen gepackt.
hors d'oeu·vre [ɔː'dɜːvrə] pl. **hors d'oeu·vres** [ɔː'dɜːvrəz] s. Hors'd'œuvre n, Vorspeise f.
horse [hɔːs] I s. 1. zo. Pferd n, Ross n, Gaul m: **to ~!** ✕ aufgesessen!; **a dark ~** fig. ein unbeschriebenes Blatt; **that's a ~ of another colo(u)r** fig. das ist etwas ganz anderes; **straight from the ~'s mouth** a) aus erster Hand, b) aus berufenem Mund; **back the wrong ~** aufs falsche Pferd setzen; **wild ~s will not drag me there!** keine zehn Pferde kriegen mich dorthin!; **flog a dead ~** a) offene Türen einrennen, b) sich unnötig mühen; **give the ~ its head** die Zügel schießen lassen; **hold your ~s!** F immer mit der Ruhe!; **get on** (od. **mount**) **one's high ~** sich aufs hohe Ross setzen; **ride** (od. **be on**) **one's high ~** auf dem od. s-m hohen Ross sitzen; **spur a willing ~** j-n unnötig antreiben; **work like a ~** wie ein Pferd arbeiten od. schuften; **you can lead a ~ to the water but you can't make it drink** man kann niemanden zu s-m Glück zwingen; 2. a) Hengst m, b) Wallach m; 3. coll. ✕ Kavalle'rie f, Reite'rei f: **1000 ~** 1000 Reiter; **~ and foot** Kavallerie u. Infanterie, die ganze Armee; 4. ⚙ (Säge- etc.)Bock m, Ständer m, Gestell n; 5. Turnen: Pferd n; 6.

Schach: F Pferd n, Springer m; 7. sl. Hero'in n; II v/t. 8. mit Pferden versehen: a) Truppen beritten machen, b) Wagen bespannen; 9. auf ein Pferd setzen od. laden; III v/i. 10. aufsitzen, aufs Pferd steigen; 11. rossen (Stute); 12. **~ around** F Blödsinn treiben; '**~-and-'bug·gy** adj. Am. ‚vorsintflutlich'; **~ ar·til·ler·y** ✕ berittene Artille'rie; '**~·back** s.: **on ~** zu Pferd(e); **go on ~** reiten; **~ bean** s. Saubohne f; **~ chest·nut** s. ⚘ 'Rosska,stanie f; **~ cop·er** s. Brit. Pferdehändler m.
horsed [hɔːst] adj. 1. beritten (Person); 2. (mit Pferden) bespannt.
horse| deal·er s. Pferdehändler m; **~ doc·tor** s. 1. Tierarzt m; 2. F ‚Viehdoktor' m (schlechter Arzt); '**~-drawn** adj. von Pferden gezogen, Pferde...; '**~-flesh** s. 1. Pferdefleisch n; 2. coll. Pferde pl.; '**~-fly** s. zo. (Pferde)Bremse f; ⚔ **Guards** s. pl. Brit. 'Gardekavalle,riebri,gade f; '**~-hair** s. Ross-, Pferdehaar n; **~ lat·i·tudes** s. pl. geogr. Rossbreiten pl.; **~ laugh** s. wieherndes Gelächter; **~ mack·er·el** s. Thunfisch m; 2. 'Rossma,krele f; '**~-man** [-mən] s. [irr.] 1. (geübter) Reiter; 2. Pferdezüchter m; '**~-man·ship** [-mənʃɪp] s. Reitkunst f; **~ op·er·a** s. F Western m (Film); '**~·play** s. ‚Blödsinn' m, Unfug m; '**~·pond** s. Pferdeschwemme f; '**~·pow·er** s. pl. (abbr. **h.p.**) phys. Pferdestärke f (= 1,01 PS); **~ race** s. Pferderennen n; **~ rac·ing** s. Pferderennen n od. pl.; '**~·rad·ish** s. ⚘ Meerrettich m; **~ sense** s. F gesunder Menschenverstand; '**~·shit** s. V ‚Scheiß (-dreck)' m; '**~·shoe** ['hɔːʃʃuː] I s. 1. Hufeisen n; 2. pl. sg. konstr. Am. Hufeisenwerfen n; II adj. 3. Hufeisen..., hufeisenförmig: **~ bend** (Straßen- etc.) Schleife f; **~ magnet** Hufeisenmagnet m; **~ table** in Hufeisenform aufgestellte Tische; **~ show** s. Reit- u. Springturnier m; '**~·tail** s. 1. Pferdeschwanz m (a. fig. Mädchenfrisur), Rossschweif m (a. hist. als türkisches Rangabzeichen od. Feldzeichen); 2. ⚘ Schachtelhalm m; **~ trad·ing** s. 1. Pferdehandel m; 2. pol. F ‚Kuhhandel' m; '**~·whip** I s. Reitpeitsche f; II v/t. (aus)peitschen; '**~·wom·an** s. [irr.] (geübte) Reiterin.
hors·y ['hɔːsɪ] adj. □ 1. pferdenärrisch; 2. Pferde...: **~ face**; **~ smell**; **~ talk** Gespräch n über Pferde.
hor·ta·tive ['hɔːtətɪv], '**hor·ta·to·ry** [-tərɪ] adj. 1. mahnend; 2. anspornend.
hor·ti·cul·tur·al [ˌhɔːtɪ'kʌltʃərəl] adj. Gartenbau...: **~ show** Gartenschau f; **hor·ti·cul·ture** ['hɔːtɪkʌltʃə] s. Gartenbau m; '**hor·ti·cul·tur·ist** [-ərɪst] s. 'Gartenbaux,perte m.
ho·san·na [həʊ'zænə] I int. hosi'anna!; II s. Hosi'anna n.
hose [həʊz] I s. 1. coll., pl. konstr. Strümpfe pl.; 2. hist. (Knie)Hose f; 3. pl. a. hoses Schlauch m: **garden ~** Gartenschlauch; 4. ⚙ Tülle f; II v/t. 5. (mit e-m Schlauch) spritzen: **~ down** abspritzen.
Ho·se·a [həʊ'zɪə] npr. u. s. bibl. (das Buch) Ho'sea m od. n. O'see m.
hose| pipe s. Schlauch(leitung f) m; '**~-proof** adj. ⊚ schwallwassergeschützt.
ho·sier ['həʊzɪə] s. Strumpfwarenhändler (-in); '**ho·sier·y** [-rɪ] s. coll. Strumpfwaren pl.
hos·pice ['hɒspɪs] s. 1. hist. Hos'piz n, Herberge f; 2. Sterbeklinik f.
hos·pi·ta·ble ['hɒspɪtəbl] adj. □ 1. gastfreundlich, (a. Haus etc.) gastlich; 2. fig.

freundlich: **~ climate**; 3. (**to**) empfänglich (für), aufgeschlossen (dat.).
hos·pi·tal ['hɒspɪtl] s. 1. Krankenhaus n, Klinik f, östr., schweiz. Spi'tal n: **~ fever** klassisches Fleckfieber; **~ nurse** Kranken(haus)schwester f; **~ social worker** Krankenhausfürsorgerin f; **~ tent** Sanitätszelt n; 2. ✕ Laza'rett n: **~ ship** (**train**) Lazarettschiff n (-zug m); 3. Tierklinik f; 4. hist. Spi'tal n: a) Armenhaus n, b) Altersheim n, c) Erziehungsheim n; 5. hist. Herberge f, Hos'piz n; 6. humor. Repara'turwerkstatt f: **dolls' ~** Puppenklinik f.
hos·pi·tal·i·ty [ˌhɒspɪ'tælətɪ] s. Gastfreundschaft f, Gastlichkeit f.
hos·pi·tal·i·za·tion [ˌhɒspɪtəlaɪ'zeɪʃn] s. 1. Aufnahme f od. Einweisung f in ein Krankenhaus; 2. Krankenhausaufenthalt m, -behandlung f; **hos·pi·tal·ize** ['hɒspɪtəlaɪz] v/t. 1. ins Krankenhaus einliefern od. einweisen; 2. im Krankenhaus behandeln.
Hos·pi·tal·(l)er ['hɒspɪtlə] s. 1. hist. Hospita'liter m, Johan'niter m; 2. Barm'herziger Bruder.
host¹ [həʊst] s. 1. (Un)Menge f, Masse f: **a ~ of questions** e-e Unmenge Fragen; 2. poet. (Kriegs)Heer n: **the ~ of heaven** a) die Gestirne, b) die himmlischen Heerscharen; **the Lord of ⚕s** bibl. der Herr der Heerscharen.
host² [həʊst] I s. 1. Gastgeber m, Hausherr m: **~ country** Gastland n, sport etc. Gastgeberland n; 2. (Gast)Wirt m: **reckon without one's ~** fig. die Rechnung ohne den Wirt machen; 3. TV etc.: a) Talk-, Showmaster m, b) Mode'rator m: **your ~ was ...** durch die Sendung führte (Sie) ...; 4. biol. Wirt m, Wirtstier n od. -pflanze f; II v/t. 5. a) TV etc.: Sendung moderieren, b) Veranstaltung ausrichten.
host³, oft ⚕ [həʊst] s. eccl. Hostie f.
hos·tage ['hɒstɪdʒ] s. 1. Geisel f: **take** (**hold**) **s.o. ~** j-n als Geisel nehmen (behalten); **taking of ~s** Geiselnahme f; 2. fig. ('Unter)Pfand n.
hos·tel ['hɒstl] s. 1. mst **youth ~** Jugendherberge f; 2. (Studenten-, Arbeiteretc.)Wohnheim n; 3. → '**hos·tel·ry** [-rɪ] s. obs. Wirtshaus n.
host·ess ['həʊstɪs] s. 1. Gastgeberin f; 2. (Gast)Wirtin f; 3. ✈ Ho'stess f, Stewar'dess f; 4. Ho'stess f (Betreuerin, Führerin); 5. Animier-, Tischdame f.
hos·tile ['hɒstaɪl] adj. □ 1. feindlich, Feind(es)...; 2. (**to**) fig. a) feindselig (gegen), feindlich gesinnt (dat.), b) stark abgeneigt (dat.); **hos·til·i·ty** [hɒ'stɪlətɪ] s. 1. Feindschaft f, Feindseligkeit f (**to** gegen); 2. Feindseligkeit f (Handlung); 3. pl. ✕ Feindseligkeiten pl., Krieg(shandlungen pl.) m.
hos·tler ['ɒslə] s. → **ostler**.
hot [hɒt] I adj. □ 1. heiß (a. fig.): **~ climate**; **~ tears**; **I am ~** mir ist heiß, ich bin erhitzt; **get ~** sich erhitzen (a. fig. u. ⊚); **~ under the collar** F wütend; **I went ~ and cold** es überlief mich heiß u. kalt; **~ scent** hunt. warme od. frische Fährte (a. fig.); 2. warm, heiß: **~ meal**; **~ and ~** ganz heiß, direkt vom Feuer; 3. a) scharf (Gewürz), b) scharf (gewürzt): **a ~ dish**; 4. fig. heiß, hitzig, heftig: **a ~ fight**; **~ words** heftige Worte; **grow ~** sich erhitzen (**over** über acc.); 5. leidenschaftlich, feurig: **a ~ temper** ein hitziges Temperament; **be ~ for** (od. **on**) F ‚scharf' sein auf (acc.); 6. wütend, erbost: **all ~ and bothered** ganz ‚aus dem Häuschen'; 7. ‚heiß': a) zo. brünstig, b) F geil, ‚scharf'

(*Person, Film etc.*); **8.** ‚heiß‘ (*im Such-spiel*): *you are getting ~ter!* a) (es wird) schon heißer!, b) *fig.* du kommst der Sache schon näher!; **9.** ganz neu *od.* frisch, ‚noch warm‘: ~ *from the press* frisch aus der Presse (*Nachrichten*), soeben erschienen (*Buch*); **10.** F a) ‚toll‘ (*großartig*): *he* (*it*) *is not so ~!* er (es) ist nicht so toll!; ~ *stuff* a) ‚dolles Ding‘, b) toller Kerl; *be ~ at* (*od. on*) ‚ganz groß‘ sein in (*e-m Fach*); **11.** ‚heiß‘ (*viel versprechend*): *a ~ tip*; *~ favo(u)rite bsd. sport* großer heißer *od.* hoher Favorit; **12.** ‚heiß‘ (*Jazz etc.*): ~ *music*; **13.** gefährlich: *make it ~ for s.o.* j-m die Hölle heiß machen, j-m ‚einheizen‘; *the place was getting too ~ for him* ihm wurde der Boden zu heiß (unter den Füßen); *be in ~ water* in ‚Schwulitäten‘ sein; *get into ~ water* a) j-n in ‚Schwulitäten‘ bringen, b) in ‚Schwulitäten‘ geraten, ‚Ärger kriegen‘; **14.** F a) ‚heiß‘ (*gestohlen, geschmuggelt etc.*): ~ *goods* ‚heiße Ware‘, b) (von der Polizei) gesucht; **15.** a) ⚡ Strom führend: → *hot line, hot wire*, b) *phys.* F ‚heiß‘ (*radioaktiv*); **16.** ⊙, ⚡ Heiß..., Warm..., Glüh...; **II** *adv.* **17.** heiß: *the sun shines ~*; *get it ~* (*and strong*) ‚eins aufs Dach kriegen‘, sein ‚Fett‘ bekommen; *give it s.o. ~* (*and strong*) F j-m die Hölle heiß machen, j-m ‚einheizen‘; → *blow¹* 4; **III** *v/t.* **18.** *mst ~ up* heiß machen; **19.** *~ up* F a) *Auto, Motor* ‚frisieren‘, ‚aufmotzen‘, b) ‚anheizen‘, c) Schwung bringen in (*acc.*), et. ‚aufmöbeln‘; **IV** *v/i.* **20.** *mst ~ up* heiß werden; **21.** *~ up* F a) sich verschärfen, b) schwungvoller werden.

hot| air *s.* **1.** ⊙ Heißluft *f*; **2.** *sl.* ‚heiße Luft‘, (leeres) Geschwätz; ‚~-'air *adj.* ⊙ Heißluft...: ~ *artist* ‚Windmacher‘ *m*; '~-bed *s.* **1.** 🌿 Mist-, Frühbeet *n*; *fig.* Brutstätte *f*; ‚~-'blood·ed *adj.* heißblütig; ~ *cath·ode s.* ⚡ 'Glühka-‚t(h)ode *f*.

hotch·pot ['hɒtʃpɒt] *s.* ⚖ Vereinigung *f* des Nachlasses zwecks gleicher Verteilung.

hotch·potch ['hɒtʃpɒtʃ] *s.* **1.** Eintopf (-gericht *n*) *m, bsd.* Gemüse(suppe *f*) *n* mit Hammelfleisch; **2.** *fig.* Mischmasch *m*.

hot dog *s.* Hot Dog *n, a. m.*

ho·tel [həʊˈtel] *s.* Ho'tel *n*: ~ *register* Fremdenbuch *n*; **ho·tel·ier** [həʊˈtelɪeɪ], **ho·tel keep·er** *s.* Hoteli'er *m*, Ho'telbesitzer(in) *od.* -di‚rektor *m*, -direk‚torin *f*.

hot| flush·es *s. pl.* ✽ fliegende Hitze; '~-foot F I *adv.* schleunigst; **II** *v/i. a.* ~ *it* rennen, flitzen; '~-gal·va·nize *v/t.* ⊙ feuerverzinken; '~-gos·pel·(l)er *s.* F Erweckungsprediger *m*; '~-head *s.* Hitzkopf *m*; ‚~-'head·ed *adj.* hitzköpfig; '~-house *s.* Treib-, Gewächshaus *n*; '~-key *s. Computer:* 'Hotkey *m*, Abkürzungstaste *f*; '~-line *s.* **1.** *bsd. pol.* ‚heißer Draht‘; **2.** *Computer etc.:* 'Hotline *f*; ~ *mon·ey s.* ✝ Hot Money *n*, ‚heißes Geld‘.

hot·ness ['hɒtnɪs] *s.* Hitze *f*.

'**hot|·plate** *s.* **1.** Koch-, Heizplatte *f*; **2.** Warmhalteplatte *f*; ~ *pot s.* Eintopf *m*; '~-press ⊙ **I** *s.* **1.** Heißpresse *f*; **2.** Dekatierpresse *f*; **II** *v/t.* **3.** heiß pressen; **4.** *Tuch* dekatieren; **5.** *Papier* satinieren; ~ *rod s. Am. sl.* ‚frisierter‘ Wagen; ~ *rod·der* ['rɒdə] *s. Am. sl.* **1.** Fahrer *m* e-s *hot rod*; **2.** a) ‚Raser‘ *m*, b) Verkehrsrowdy *m*; ~ *seat s. sl.* **1.** ✓ Schleudersitz *m* (*a. fig.*); **2.** *Am.* e'lektrischer Stuhl; '~-shot **I** *s. Am. sl.* **1.**

‚großes Tier‘; **2.** *bsd. sport* ‚Ka'none‘ *f*, ‚As‘ *n*; **3.** ✓, *mot.* ‚Ra'kete‘ *f*; **II** *adj.* **4.** ‚groß‘, ‚toll‘; ~ *spot s.* **1.** *pol.* Krisenherd *m*; **2.** F ‚heißes Ding‘ (*Nachtklub etc.*); ~ *spring s.* heiße Quelle, Ther'malquelle *f*; '~-spur *s.* Heißsporn *m*; ~ *tube s.* ⊙ Heiz-, Glührohr *n*; ~ *war s.* heißer Krieg; ‚~-'wa·ter *adj.* Heißwasser...: ~ *heating*; ~ *bottle* Wärmflasche *f*; ~ *wire s.* **1.** ⚡ a) Strom führender Draht, b) Hitzdraht *m*; **2.** *bsd. pol.* ‚heißer Draht‘; ‚~-'wire *v/t* F *ein Fahrzeug mit e-m Stück Draht* kurzschließen.

hound¹ [haʊnd] **I** *s.* **1.** Jagdhund *m*: *ride to* (*od. follow the*) ~*s* an e-r Parforcejagd (*bsd. Fuchsjagd*) teilnehmen; **2.** *sl.* ‚Hund‘ *m*, Schurke *m*; **3.** *Am. sl.* Fa'natiker(in): *movie ~* Kinonarr *m*; **4.** Verfolger *m* (*Schnitzeljagd*); **II** *v/t.* **5.** *mst fig.* jagen, hetzen, drängen, verfolgen: ~ *down* zur Strecke bringen; **6.** *a.* ~ *on* (auf)hetzen, antreiben.

hound² [haʊnd] *s.* **1.** ⚓ Mastbacke *f*; **2.** *pl.* ⊙ Seiten-, Diago'nalstreben *pl.* (*an Fahrzeugen*).

hour ['aʊə] *s.* **1.** Stunde *f*: *by the ~* stundenweise; *for ~s* (*and ~s*) stundenlang; *on the ~* (jeweils) zur vollen Stunde; *an ~'s work* e-e Stunde Arbeit; *10 minutes past the ~* 10 Minuten nach voll; **2.** (*Tages*)Zeit *f*: *at 14.20 ~s* um 14 Uhr 20; *at all ~s* zu jeder Zeit; *at an early ~* früh, zu früher Stunde; *at the eleventh ~ fig.* in letzter Minute, fünf Minuten vor zwölf; *keep early ~s* früh schlafen gehen (u. früh aufstehen); *sleep till all ~s* ‚bis in die Puppen‘ schlafen; *the small ~s* die frühen Morgenstunden; **3.** Zeitpunkt *m*, Stunde *f*: ~ *of death* Todesstunde; *his ~ has come* a) s-e Stunde ist gekommen, b) *a. his* (*last*) ~ *has struck* s-e letzte Stunde *od.* sein letztes Stündlein ist gekommen *od.* hat geschlagen; *question of the ~* aktuelle Frage; **4.** *pl.* (Arbeits-)Zeit *f*, (Arbeits-, Geschäfts-, Dienst-)Stunden *pl.*: *after ~s* a) nach Geschäftsschluss, b) nach der Arbeit, c) *fig.* zu spät; **5.** *pl. eccl.* a) Stundenbuch *n*, b) *R.C.* Stundengebete *pl.*; **6.** *⚶s pl. myth.* Horen *pl.*; ~ *cir·cle s. ast.* Stundenkreis *m*; '~-glass *s.* Stundenglas *n, bsd.* Sanduhr *f*; ~ *hand s.* Stundenzeiger *m*.

hou·ri ['hʊərɪ] *s.* **1.** Huri *f* (*mohammedanische Paradiesjungfrau*); **2.** *fig.* üppige Schönheit (*Frau*).

hour·ly ['aʊəlɪ] *adv. u. adj.* **1.** stündlich: ~ *wage* Stundenlohn *m*; **2.** ständig, dauernd: *in ~ fear*.

house [haʊs] **I** *pl.* **hous·es** ['haʊzɪz] *s.* **1.** Haus *n* (*Gebäude u. Hausbewohner*): *like a ~ on fire* ganz ‚toll‘, ‚prima‘; → *safe* 3; **2.** Wohnhaus *n*, Wohnung *f*, Heim *n*; Haushalt *m*: ~ *and home* Haus u. Hof; *keep ~* a) das Haus hüten, b) (*for s.o.* j-m) den Haushalt führen; *put* (*od. set*) *one's ~ in order* s-e Angelegenheiten ordnen, sein Haus bestellen; → *open* 10; **3.** Fa'milie *f*, Geschlecht *n*, (*bsd. Fürsten*)Haus *n*: *the ~ of Hanover*; **4.** *univ. Brit.* Haus *n*: a) Wohngebäude *n* (*e-s College, a. ped. e-s Internats*), b) College *n*; **5.** *thea.* a) (Schauspiel)Haus *n*: *full ~* volles Haus, b) Zuhörer *pl.*; → *bring down* 8, c) Vorstellung *f*: *the second ~* die zweite Vorstellung (*des Tages*); **6.** *mst ⚶ parl.* Haus *n*, Kammer *f*, Parla'ment *n*: *the ⚶ a*) → *House of Commons* (*Lords, Representatives*), b) *coll.* das Haus (*die Abgeordneten*):

enter the ⚶ Parlamentsmitglied werden; *there is a ⚶* es ist Parlamentssitzung; *no ⚶* das Haus ist nicht beschlussfähig; **7.** ✝ Haus *n*, Firma *f*: *the ⚶* die Londoner Börse; *on the ~* auf Kosten des Hauses (*a. weitS. des Wirts od. Gastgebers*); **8.** *ast.* a) Haus *n*, b) Tierkreiszeichen *n*; **II** *v/t.* [haʊz] **9.** 'unterbringen (*a.* ⊙); **10.** aufnehmen, beherbergen; **11.** Platz haben für; **III** *v/i.* [haʊz] **12.** hausen, wohnen.

house|a·gent *s. Brit.* Häusermakler *m*; ~ *ar·rest s.* 'Hausar‚rest *m*; '~-boat *s.* Hausboot *n*; '~-bod·y → **homebody**; '~-bound *adj.* ans Haus gefesselt; '~-break *v/t.* **1.** Hund etc. stubenrein machen; **2.** F *fig.* a) j-m Manieren beibringen, b) j-n ‚kirre‘ machen; '~-break·er *s.* **1.** ⚖ Einbrecher *m*; **2.** 'Abbruchunter‚nehmer *m*; '~-break·ing *s.* **1.** ⚖ Einbruch(sdiebstahl) *m*; **2.** Abbruch(arbeiten *pl.*) *m*; '~-bro·ken *adj.* stubenrein (*Hund etc.*); '~-clean *v/i.* **1.** Hausputz machen; **2.** (*a. v/t.*) *Am.* F gründlich aufräumen (*in dat.*); '~-‚clean·ing *s.* **1.** Hausputz *m*; **2.** *Am.* F 'Säuberungsakti‚on *f*; '~-coat *s.* Hauskleid *n*, Morgenrock *m*; '~-craft *s. Brit.* Hauswirtschaftslehre *f*; ~ *de·tec·tive s.* 'Hausdetek‚tiv *m* (*Hotel etc.*); ~ *dog s.* Haushund *m*; ~ *dust mite* Hausstaubmilbe *f*; ~ *allergy* 'Hausstaubmilbenaller‚gie *f*; '~-fly *s. zo.* Stubenfliege *f*.

house·hold ['haʊshəʊld] **I** *s.* **1.** Haushalt *m*; **2.** *the ⚶ Brit.* die königliche Hofhaltung: *⚶ Brigade, ⚶ Troops* Gardetruppen *pl.*; **II** *adj.* **3.** Haushalts..., häuslich: ~ *appliance* Haushaltsgerät *n*; ~ *commodities pl.* Haushaltswaren *pl.*; ~ *gods a*) *antiq.* Hausgötter *pl.*, b) *fig.* heilig gehaltene Dinge *pl.*; ~ *goods pl.* Haushaltswaren *pl*; ~ *remedy* ✽ Hausmittel *n*; ~ *soap* Haushaltsseife *f*; ~ *spending* Ausgaben der privaten Haushalte; **4.** all'täglich: *a ~ word* (*od. name*) ein (fester *od.* geläufiger) Begriff; '**house,hold·er** *s.* **1.** Haushaltsvorstand *m*; **2.** Haus- *od.* Wohnungsinhaber *m*.

'**house|-,hunt·ing** *s.* F Wohnungssuche *f*; '~-hus·band *s.* Hausmann *m*; '~-keep *v/i.* den Haushalt führen (*for s.o.* j-m); '~-keep·er *s.* **1.** Haushälterin *f*, Wirtschafterin *f*; **2.** Hausmeister(in); '~-keep·ing *s.* Haushaltung *f*, -wirtschaft *f*: ~ (*money*) Wirtschaftsgeld *n*; '~-maid *s.* Hausgehilfin *f*: ~*'s knee* ✽ Knieschleimbeutelentzündung *f*; '~-,mas·ter *s. ped. Brit.* Heimleiter *m* (*Lehrer, der für ein Wohngebäude e-s Internats zuständig ist*); '~-mate *s.* Hausgenosse *m*, -genossin *f*; '~,mis·tress *s. ped. Brit.* Heimleiterin *f* (*in e-m Internat*); ⚶ *of Com·mons s. parl. Brit.* 'Unterhaus *n*; ⚶ *of Lords s. parl. Brit.* Oberhaus *n*; ⚶ *of Rep·re·sent·a·tives s. parl. Am.* Repräsen'tantenhaus *n* (*Unterhaus des US-Kongresses*); ~ *or·gan s.* ✝ Hauszeitung *f*; ~ *paint·er s.* Maler *m*, Anstreicher *m*; ~ *par·ty s.* mehrtägige Party (*bsd. in e-m Landhaus*); '~-phone *s. Am.* 'Haustele‚fon *n*; ~ *phy·si·cian s.* **1.** Hausarzt *m* (*im Hotel etc.*); **2.** *im Krankenhaus* wohnender Arzt; ~ *plant s.* 🌱 Zimmerpflanze *f*; '~-proud *adj.* über'trieben ordentlich, pe'nibel; '~-room [-rʊm] *s.*: *give s.o.* ~ j-n (in sein Haus) aufnehmen; *he wouldn't give it* ~ *fig.* er nähme es nicht einmal geschenkt; ~ *search*

H

s. ⚓ Haussuchung f; **,~-to-'house** adj. von Haus zu Haus: **~ collection** Haussammlung f; **~ selling** Verkauf m an der Haustür; **'~-top** s. Dach n: **proclaim** (od. **shout**) **from the ~s** öffentlich verkünden, et. ,an die große Glocke hängen'; **'~-trained** adj. stubenrein (Hund etc.); **'~,warm·ing** (**par·ty**) s. Einzugsparty f (im neuen Haus).

'house·wife s. [irr.] **1.** Hausfrau f; **2.** ['hʌzɪf] Brit. 'Nähe,tui n, Nähzeug n; **'house,wife·ly** [-,waɪflɪ] adj. hausfraulich; **'house·wif·er·y** [-wɪfərɪ] → housekeeping; **'house·work** s. Haus(halts)arbeit f.

hous·ing¹ ['haʊzɪŋ] s. **1.** 'Unterbringung f; **2.** 'Unterkunft f, Obdach n; **3.** Wohnung f, coll. Häuser pl.: **~ development**, **~ estate** Wohnsiedlung f; **~ development scheme** Wohnungsbauprojekt n; **~ shortage** Wohnungsnot f; **~ situation** Lage f auf dem Wohnungsmarkt; **~ unit** Wohneinheit f; **4.** Wohnungsbau m od. -beschaffung f, ⚙ a) Gehäuse n, b) Gerüst n, c) Nut f.

hous·ing² ['haʊzɪŋ] s. Satteldecke f.

hove [həʊv] pret. u. p.p. von **heave**.

hov·el ['hɒvl] s. **1.** Schuppen m; **2.** contp. ,Bruchbude' f, ,Loch' n.

hov·el·(l)er ['hɒvlə] s. ⚓ **1.** Bergungsboot n; **2.** Berger m.

hov·er ['hɒvə] v/i. **1.** schweben (a. fig.); **2.** sich her'umtreiben od. aufhalten (**about** in der Nähe gen.); **3.** zögern, schwanken; **'~-craft** s. sg. u. pl. Hovercraft n, Luftkissenfahrzeug n; **'~-train** s. Hovertrain m, Schwebezug m.

how [haʊ] **I** adv. **1.** (fragend) wie: **~ are you?** wie geht es Ihnen?; **~ do you do?** (bei der Vorstellung) guten Tag!; **~ about ...?** wie stehts mit ...?; **~ about a cup of tea?** wie wäre es mit e-r Tasse Tee?; **~ about it?** (na), wie wärs?; **~ is it that ...?** wie kommt es, dass ...?; **~ now?** was soll das bedeuten?; **~ much?** wie viel?; **~ many?** wie viele?, wie viel?; **~ much is it?** was kostet es?; **~ do you know?** woher wissen Sie das?; **~ ever do you do it?** wie machen Sie das nur?; **2.** (ausrufend) wie: **~ absurd!**; **and ~!** F und wie!; **here's ~!** F auf Ihr Wohl!; **3.** (relativ) wie: **I know ~ far it is** ich weiß, wie weit es ist; **he knows ~ to ride** er kann reiten; **I know ~ to do it** ich weiß, wie man es macht; **II** s. **4.** Wie n: **the ~ and the why** das Wie u. Warum.

how·be·it [,haʊ'biːɪt] obs. **I** adv. nichtsdesto'weniger; **II** cj. ob'gleich, ob'schon.

how·dah ['haʊdə] s. (mst gedeckter) Sitz auf dem Rücken e-s Ele'fanten.

how-do-you-do [,haʊdjʊ'duː], **,how--d'ye-'do** [-djə'duː] s. F: **a nice ~** e-e schöne ,Bescherung'.

how·ev·er [haʊ'evə] **I** adv. **1.** wie auch (immer), wenn auch noch so: **~ good**; **~ it (may) be** wie dem auch sei; **~ you do it** wie du es auch machst; **2.** F wie ... bloß od. denn nur: **~ did you do it?**; **II** cj. **3.** je'doch, dennoch, doch, aber, in'des.

how·itz·er ['haʊɪtsə] s. Hau'bitze f.

howl [haʊl] **I** v/i. **1.** heulen (Wölfe, Wind etc.); **2.** brüllen, schreien (**with** vor dat.); **3.** F ,heulen', weinen; **4.** pfeifen (Wind, Radio etc.); **II** v/t. **5.** brüllen, schreien; **~ down** j-n niederschreien; **III** s. **6.** Heulen n, Geheul n; **7.** a) Schrei m: **~s of laughter** brüllendes Gelächter, b) Gebrüll n, Geschrei n: **be a ~** F ,zum Brüllen' sein; **'howl·er** [-lə]

s. **1.** Heuler(in); **2.** zo. Brüllaffe m; **3.** F grober Schnitzer, ,Heuler' m; **'howl·ing** [-lɪŋ] adj. **1.** heulend, brüllend; **2.** F ,toll', Mords...

how·so·ev·er [,haʊsəʊ'evə] → however 1.

,how-to-'do-it book s. Bastelbuch n.

hoy¹ [hɔɪ] s. ⚓ Leichter m.

hoy² [hɔɪ] **I** int. **1.** he!, hoi!; **2.** ⚓ a'hoi!; **II** s. **3.** He(ruf m) n.

hoy·den ['hɔɪdn] s. Range f, Wildfang m (Mädchen); **'hoy·den·ish** [-nɪʃ] adj. wild, ausgelassen.

hub [hʌb] s. **1.** (Rad)Nabe f: **~cap mot.** Radkappe f; **2.** fig. Mittel-, Angelpunkt m, Zentrum n: **~ of the universe** Mittelpunkt der Welt (bsd. fig.); **3. the ⚒** Am. (Spitzname für) Boston n.

hub·bub ['hʌbʌb] s. **1.** Stimmengewirr n; **2.** Lärm m, Tu'mult m.

hub·by ['hʌbɪ] s. F ,Männe' m, (Ehe-) Mann m.

hu·bris ['hjuːbrɪs] (Greek) s. Hybris f, freche 'Selbstüber,hebung.

huck·le ['hʌkl] s. **1.** anat. Hüfte f; **2.** Buckel m; **'~-ber·ry** s. ♥ Heidelbeere f; **'~-bone** s. anat. **1.** Hüftknochen m; **2.** Fußknöchel m.

huck·ster ['hʌkstə] **I** s. **1.** → hawker²; **2.** contp. Krämer(seele f) m, Feilscher m; **3.** Am. sl. 'Re'klamefritze' m (Werbefachmann); **II** v/i. **4.** hökern; hausieren; **5.** feilschen (**over** um).

hud·dle ['hʌdl] **I** v/t. **1.** a) mst **~ together** (od. **up**) zs.-werfen, auf e-n Haufen werfen, b) wohin stopfen; **2. ~ o.s.** (**up**) → 6; **~d up** zs.-gekauert; **3.** mst **~ together** (od. **up**) Brit. Bericht etc. a) ,hinhauen', b) zs.-stoppeln; **4. ~ on** sich ein Kleid etc. 'überwerfen, schlüpfen in (acc.); **5.** fig. vertuschen; **II** v/i. **6.** (**~ up** sich zs.-)kauern; **7.** a. **~ together** (od. **up**) sich zs.-drängen; **8. ~ (up) against** (od. **to**) sich kuscheln od. schmiegen an (acc.); **III** s. **9.** a) (wirrer) Haufen, b) Wirrwarr m; **10. go into a ~** F a) die Köpfe zs.-stecken, ,Kriegsrat halten', b) **with o.s.** ,mal nachdenken', mit sich zu Rate gehen.

hue¹ [hjuː] s.: **~ and cry** a. fig. (Zeter-) Geschrei n, Gezeter n; **raise a ~ and cry** ein Zetergeschrei erheben, lautstark protestieren (**against** gegen).

hue² [hjuː] s. Farbe f, (Farb)Ton m; Färbung f (a. fig.); **hued** [hjuːd] adj. in Zssgn ...farbig, ...farben.

huff [hʌf] **I** v/t. **1.** a) ärgern, verstimmen, b) ängstigen, c) ,piesacken': **~ into s.th.** j-n zu et. zwingen; **easily ~ed** leicht ,eingeschnappt', sehr übelnehmerisch; **2.** Damespiel: Stein wegnehmen; **II** v/i. **3.** a) sich ärgern, b) ,einschnappen'; **4.** a. **~ and puff** a) schnaufen, pusten, b) (vor Wut) schnauben; **III** s. **5.** Ärger m, Verstimmung f: **be in a ~** verstimmt od. ,eingeschnappt' sein; **huff·i·ness** ['hʌfɪnɪs] s. **1.** übelnehmerisches Wesen; **2.** Verärgerung f, Verstimmung f; **huff·ish** ['hʌfɪʃ], **huff·y** ['hʌfɪ] adj. □ **1.** übelnehmerisch; **2.** verärgert, ,eingeschnappt'.

hug [hʌg] **I** v/t. **1.** um'armen, an sich drücken: **~ o.s.** sich beglückwünschen (**on**, **over** zu); **2.** fig. (zäh) festhalten an (e-r Meinung etc.); **3.** sich dicht halten an (acc.): **~ the coast** sich dicht an die Küste (an den Straßenrand) halten; **the car ~s the road well** mot. der Wagen hat e-e gute Straßenlage; **II** v/i. **4.** ein'ander od. sich um'armen; **III** s. **5.** Um'armung f: **give s.o. a ~** j-n umarmen.

huge [hjuːdʒ] adj. □ riesig, ungeheuer, e'norm, gewaltig, mächtig (alle a. fig.); **'huge·ly** [-lɪ] adv. gewaltig, ungeheuer, ungemein; **'huge·ness** [-nɪs] s. ungeheure Größe.

hug·ger-mug·ger ['hʌgə,mʌgə] **I** s. **1.** ,Kuddelmuddel' m, n; **2.** Heimlichtue'rei f; **II** adj. u. adv. **3.** unordentlich; **4.** heimlich, verstohlen; **III** v/t. **5.** vertuschen, verbergen.

Hu·gue·not ['hjuːgənɒt] s. Huge'notte m, Huge'nottin f.

huh [hʌ] int. **1.** wie?, was?; **2.** ha(ha)!

hu·la ['huːlə], **hu·la-'hu·la** s. Hula f, n (Tanz der Eingeborenen auf Hawaii).

hulk [hʌlk] s. **1.** ⚓ Hulk f, m; **2.** Ko'loss m (Sache od. Person): **a ~ of a man** a. ein Riesenkerl, ein ungeschlachter Kerl; **'hulk·ing** [-kɪŋ], **'hulk·y** adj. **1.** ungeschlacht; **2.** sperrig, klotzig.

hull¹ [hʌl] **I** s. ♥ Schale f, Hülle f (beide a. weitS.), Hülse f; **II** v/t. schälen, enthülsen: **~ed barley** Graupen pl.

hull² [hʌl] **I** s. ⚓, ✈ Rumpf m: **~ down** weit entfernt (Schiff); **II** v/t. ⚓ den Rumpf treffen od. durch'schießen.

hul·la·ba·loo [,hʌləbə'luː] s. Lärm m, Tu'mult m, Trubel m.

hul·lo [hə'ləʊ] → hello.

hum [hʌm] **I** v/i. **1.** summen (Bienen, Draht, Person etc.); **2.** ⚡ brummen; **3. ~ and ha(w)** a) ,herumdrucksen', b) (hin u. her) schwanken; **4.** a. **~ with activity** F voller Leben od. Aktivi'tät sein: **make things ~** die Sache in Schwung bringen; **5.** ,muffeln', stinken; **II** v/t. **6.** summen; **III** s. **7.** Summen n; **8.** ⚡ Brummen m; **9.** [a. mm] Hm n: **~s and ha(w)s** verlegenes Geräusper.

hu·man ['hjuːmən] **I** adj. □ → humanly; **1.** menschlich (a. weitS. Person, Charakter etc.), Menschen..., Human... (-medizin etc.): **~ chain** Menschenkette f; **~ nature** menschliche Natur; **~ engineering** a) angewandte Betriebspsychologie, Arbeitsplatzgestaltung f, b) menschengerechte Gestaltung (von Maschinen etc.) zwecks optimaler Leistung; **~ interest** das menschlich Ansprechende; **~-interest story** ergreifende od. ein menschliches Schicksal schildernde Geschichte; **~ relations** zwischenmenschliche Beziehungen, (✝ innerbetriebliche) Kontaktpflege; **~ resources** pl. ✝ etc. 'Arbeitskräftepotenzi,al n; **department of ~ resources** in Firma: Perso'nalabteilung f; **the ~ race** das Menschengeschlecht; **~ rights** Menschenrechte; **~ rights abuse** Menschenrechtsverletzung f; **~ rights activist** Menschenrechtler m; **~ touch** menschliche Note; **that's only ~** das ist doch menschlich; **I am only ~** iro. ich bin auch nur ein Mensch; → err 1; **2.** → humane 1; **II** s. **3.** Mensch m; **hu·mane** [hjuː'meɪn] adj. □ **1.** hu'man, menschlich; **⚒ Society** Gesellschaft f zur Verhinderung von Grausamkeiten an Tieren; **2.** → humanistic 1; **hu·mane·ness** [hjuː'meɪnnɪs] s. Humani'tät f, Menschlichkeit f.

hu·man·ism ['hjuːmənɪzm] s. **1.** oft ⚒ Huma'nismus m; **2.** a) → humaneness, b) → humanitarianism; **'hu·man·ist** [-ɪst] **I** s. **1.** Huma'nist(in); **2.** → humanitarian II; **II** adj. → humanistic; **hu·man·is·tic** [,hjuːmə'nɪstɪk] adj. (□ **~ally**) **1.** huma'nistisch; **~ education**; **2.** a) → humane 1, b) → humanitarian; **hu·man·i·tar·i·an** [hjuː,mænɪ'teərɪən] **I** adj. humani'tär, menschenfreundlich, Humanitäts...; **II** s. Menschenfreund m; **hu·man·i·tar·i·an·ism** [hjuː,mænɪ'teərɪənızəm] *s.* Menschenfreundlichkeit *f*, humani'täre Gesinnung; **hu·man·i·ty** [hjuː'mænətɪ] *s.* **1.** die Menschheit; **2.** Menschsein *n*, menschliche Na'tur; **3.** Humani'tät *f*, Menschlichkeit *f*; **4.** *pl.* a) klassische Litera'tur, b) 'Altphilolo‚gie *f*, c) Geisteswissenschaften *pl.*

hu·man·i·za·tion [‚hjuːmənaɪ'zeɪʃn] *s.* **1.** Humanisierung *f*; **2.** Vermenschlichung *f*, Personifizierung *f*; **hu·man·ize** ['hjuːmənaɪz] *v/t.* **1.** humanisieren, hu'maner gestalten; **2.** vermenschlichen, personifizieren.

‚**hu·man'kind** *s.* die Menschheit, das Menschengeschlecht; '**hu·man·ly** [-lɪ] *adv.* **1.** menschlich; **2.** nach menschlichen Begriffen: ∼ *possible* menschenmöglich; ∼ *speaking* menschlich gesehen; **3.** hu'man, menschlich.

hum·ble ['hʌmbl] **I** *adj.* □ bescheiden: a) demütig: *in my* ∼ *opinion* nach m-r unmaßgeblichen Meinung; *my* ∼ *self* meine Wenigkeit; *Your* ∼ *servant obs.* Ihr ergebener Diener; *eat* ∼ *pie fig.* klein beigeben, zu Kreuze kriechen, b) anspruchslos, einfach, c) niedrig, dürftig, ärmlich: *of* ∼ *birth* von niedriger Geburt; **II** *v/t.* demütigen, erniedrigen; '**hum·ble·ness** [-nɪs] *s.* Demut *f*, Bescheidenheit *f*.

hum·bug ['hʌmbʌɡ] **I** *s.* **1.** ‚Humbug' *m*: a) Schwindel *m*, Betrug *m*, b) Unsinn *m*, ‚Mumpitz' *m*; **2.** Schwindler *m*, *bsd.* Hochstapler *m*, *a.* Scharlatan *m*; **3.** *a. mint* ∼ *Brit.* 'Pfefferminzbon‚bon *m*, *n*; **II** *v/t.* **4.** betrügen, ‚reinlegen'.

hum·ding·er [hʌm'dɪŋə] *s. sl.* **1.** ‚toller Bursche'; **2.** ‚tolles Ding'.

hum·drum ['hʌmdrʌm] **I** *adj.* **1.** eintönig, langweilig, fad; **II** *s.* **2.** Eintönigkeit *f*, Langweiligkeit *f*; **3.** langweilige Sache *f*. Per'son.

hu·mec·tant [hjuː'mektənt] *s.* 🛆 Feuchthaltemittel *n*.

hu·mer·al ['hjuːmərəl] *adj. anat.* **1.** Oberarmknochen...; **2.** Schulter...; **hu·mer·us** ['hjuːmərəs] *pl.* **-i** [-aɪ] *s.* Oberarm(knochen) *m*.

hu·mid ['hjuːmɪd] *adj.* feucht; **hu·mid·i·fi·er** [hjuː'mɪdɪfaɪə] *s.* Befeuchter *m*; **hu·mid·i·fy** [hjuː'mɪdɪfaɪ] *v/t.* befeuchten; **hu·mid·i·ty** [hjuː'mɪdətɪ] *s.* Feuchtigkeit(sgehalt *m*) *f*.

hu·mi·dor ['hjuːmɪdɔː] *s.* Feuchthaltebehälter *m*.

hu·mil·i·ate [hjuː'mɪlɪeɪt] *v/t.* erniedrigen, demütigen; **hu'mil·i·at·ing** [-tɪŋ] *adj.* demütigend, erniedrigend; **hu·mil·i·a·tion** [hjuː‚mɪlɪ'eɪʃn] *s.* Erniedrigung *f*, Demütigung *f*; **hu'mil·i·ty** [-ətɪ] → *humbleness.*

hum·ming ['hʌmɪŋ] *adj.* **1.** summend; **2.** 🎵 brummend; **3.** F a) lebhaft, schwungvoll, b) geschäftig; '∼·**bird** *s. orn.* Kolibri *m*; '∼·**top** *s.* Brummkreisel *m*.

hum·mock ['hʌmək] *s.* **1.** Hügel *m*; **2.** Eishügel *m*.

hu·mor *etc. Am.* → *humour etc.*

hu·mor·esque [‚hjuːmə'resk] *s.* 🎵 Humo'reske *f*; **hu·mor·ist** ['hjuːmərɪst] *s.* **1.** Humo'rist(in); **2.** Spaßvogel *m*; ‚**hu·mor'is·tic** [-'rɪstɪk] *adj.* (□ ∼*ally*) humo'ristisch; **hu·mor·ous** ['hjuːmərəs] *adj.* hu'morvoll, hu'morig, lustig; **hu·mor·ous·ness** ['hjuːmərəsnɪs] *s.* hu'morvolle Art, *(das)* Hu'morvolle, Komik *f*.

hu·mour ['hjuːmə] **I** *s.* **1.** Gemütsart *f*, Tempera'ment *n*; **2.** Stimmung *f*, Laune *f*: *in the* ∼ *for* aufgelegt zu; *in a good (bad)* ∼ (bei) guter (schlechter) Laune; *out of* ∼ schlecht gelaunt; **3.** Hu'mor *m*, Spaß *m*; Komik *f*, *das* Komische (e-r

Situation *etc.*); **4.** *a.* **sense of** ∼ (Sinn *m* für) Humor *m*; **5.** Spaß *m*; **6.** *physiol.* a) Körperflüssigkeit *f*, b) *obs.* Körpersaft *m*; **II** *v/t.* **7.** a) j-m s-n Willen tun *od.* lassen, b) j-n *od. et.* hinnehmen, mit Geduld ertragen; '**hu·mo(u)r·less** [-lɪs] *adj.* hu'morlos.

hump [hʌmp] **I** *s.* **1.** Buckel *m*, *bsd. des Kamels:* Höcker *m*; **2.** kleiner Hügel: *be over the* ∼ *fig.* über den Berg sein; **3.** *Brit.* F a) Trübsinn *m*, b) Stinklaune *f*: *give s.o. the* ∼ → 6; **II** *v/t.* **4.** *oft* ∼ *up* (zu e-m Buckel) krümmen: ∼ *one's back* e-n Buckel machen; **5.** a) sich *et.* aufladen, b) schleppen, tragen: ∼ *o.s.* (*od. it*) *Am. sl.* sich ‚ranhalten' (anstrengen); **6.** *Brit.* F a) j-n trübsinnig machen, b) *j-m* ‚auf den Wecker fallen'; **7.** V ‚bumsen' (*a. v/i.*); '∼·**back** *s.* **1.** Buckel *m*; **2.** Bucklige(r *m*) *f*; **3.** *zo.* Buckelwal *m*; '∼·**backed** *adj.* bucklig.

humped [hʌmpt] *adj.* **1.** bucklig, höckerig; **2.** holp(e)rig.

humph [mm; hʌmf] *int.* hm!, *contp.* pff!

hump·ty-dump·ty [‚hʌmptɪ'dʌmptɪ] *s.* ‚Dickerchen' *n*.

hump·y ['hʌmpɪ] → *humped.*

hu·mus ['hjuːməs] *s.* Humus *m*.

Hun [hʌn] *s.* **1.** Hunne *m*, Hunnin *f*; **2.** *fig.* Wan'dale *m*, Bar'bar *m*; **3.** F *contp.* Deutsche(r) *m*.

hunch [hʌntʃ] **I** *s.* **1.** → *hump* 1; **2.** Klumpen *m*; **3.** *a.* ∼ F das *od.* so ein Gefühl, e-n *od.* den Verdacht (*that* dass): *play a* ∼ e-r Intuition folgen; **II** *v/t.* **4.** *a.* ∼ *up* → *hump* 4: ∼ *one's shoulders* die Schultern hochziehen; **5.** *a.* ∼ *up* (sich) kauern; '∼·**back** → *humpback* 1 *u.* 2; '∼·**backed** → *humpbacked.*

hun·dred ['hʌndrəd] **I** *adj.* **1.** hundert: *a* (*od.* one) ∼ (ein)hundert; *several* ∼ *men* mehrere Hundert Mann; *a* ∼ *and one* hundert(erlei), zahllose; **II** *s.* **2.** Hundert *n* (*a. Zahl*): *by the* ∼ hundertweise; *several* ∼ mehrere Hundert; ∼*s of times* hundertmal; ∼*s of thousands* Hunderttausende; ∼*s and* ∼*s* Hunderte u. Aberhunderte; **3.** ✚ Hundert *n*; **4.** *hist. Brit.* Bezirk *m*, Hundertschaft *f*; **5.** ∼*s and thousands* Liebesperlen *pl.* (*auf Gebäck etc.*); '∼·**fold I** *adj. u. adv.* hundertfach, -fältig; **II** *s. das* Hundertfache; '∼·**per‚cent** *adj.* 'hundertpro‚zentig; ‚∼·**per'cent·er** *s. pol. Am.* 'Hurrapatri‚ot *m*.

hun·dredth ['hʌndrədθ] **I** *adj.* **1.** hundertst; **II** *s.* **2.** Hundertste(r *m*) *f*; **3.** Hundertstel *n*.

'**hun·dred·weight** *s.* a) *in England 112 lbs.*, b) *in USA 100 lbs.*, c) *a.* **metric** ∼ Zentner *m*.

hung [hʌŋ] *pret. u. p.p. von* **hang**.

Hun·gar·i·an [hʌŋ'ɡeərɪən] **I** *adj.* **1.** ungarisch; **II** *s.* **2.** Ungar(in); **3.** *ling.* Ungarisch *n*.

hun·ger ['hʌŋɡə] **I** *s.* **1.** Hunger *m*: ∼ *is the best sauce* Hunger ist der beste Koch; **2.** *fig.* Hunger *m*, Verlangen *n*, Durst *m* (*for, after* nach); **II** *v/i.* **3.** hungern, Hunger haben; **4.** *fig.* hungern (*for, after* nach); **III** *v/t.* **5.** aushungern; durch Hunger zwingen (*into* zu); ∼ **march** *s.* Hungermarsch *m*; ∼ **strike** *s.* Hungerstreik *m*.

hun·gry ['hʌŋɡrɪ] *adj.* □ **1.** hungrig: *be* (*od. feel*) ∼ hungrig sein, Hunger haben: *go* ∼ hungern; ∼ *as a hunter* (*od. bear*) hungrig wie ein Wolf; **2.** *fig.* hungrig (*for* nach): ∼ *for knowledge* wissensdurstig; **3.** ✓ karg, mager (*Boden*).

hunk [hʌŋk] *s.* F großes Stück, (dicker) Brocken.

hunk·y-do·ry [‚hʌŋkɪ'dɔːrɪ] *adj. Am. sl.* **1.** ‚klasse', prima; **2.** bestens, ‚in Butter'.

hunt [hʌnt] **I** *s.* **1.** Jagd *f*, Jagen *n*: *the* ∼ *is up* die Jagd hat begonnen; **2.** 'Jagd (-re‚vier *n*) *f*; **3.** Jagd(gesellschaft) *f*; **4.** *fig.* Jagd *f*: a) Verfolgung *f*, b) Suche *f* (*for* nach); **II** *v/t.* **5.** (*a. fig. j-n*) jagen, Jagd machen auf (*acc.*), hetzen: ∼*ed look fig.* gehetzter Blick; ∼ *down* erlegen, *a. fig.* zur Strecke bringen; ∼ *out* a) hinausjagen, b) *a.* ∼ *up* aufstöbern, -spüren, -treiben, *weitS.* forschen nach; **6.** *Revier* durch'jagen, -'stöbern, -'suchen (*a. fig.*) (*for* nach); **7.** jagen mit (*Hunden, Pferden etc.*); **8.** *Radar, TV:* abtasten; **III** *v/i.* **9.** jagen: ∼ *for* Jagd machen auf (*acc.*) (*a. fig.*); **10.** ∼ *after* (*od. for*) a) suchen nach, b) jagen *od.* streben nach; **11.** ☉ flattern; '∼·**killer satellite** ✕ Killersatellit *m*; **2.** Jagdhund *m od.* -pferd *n*; **3.** Sprungdeckeluhr *f*.

hunt·ing ['hʌntɪŋ] **I** *s.* **1.** Jagd *f*, Jagen *n*; **2.** → *hunt* 4; **3.** *Radar, TV:* Abtastvorrichtung *f*; **II** *adj.* **4.** Jagd...; ∼ **box** → *hunting lodge*; ∼ **cat** → *cheetah*; ∼ **crop** *s.* Jagdpeitsche *f*; ∼ **ground** *s.* 'Jagdre‚vier *n*, -gebiet *n* (*a. fig.*): *the happy* ∼*s* die ewigen Jagdgründe; ∼ **horn** *s.* Hift-, Jagdhorn *n*; ∼ **leop·ard** → *cheetah*; ∼ **li·cence**, *Am.* ∼ **li·cense** *s.* Jagdschein *m*; ∼ **lodge** *s.* Jagdhütte *f*; ∼ **sea·son** *s.* Jagdzeit *f*.

hunt·ress ['hʌntrɪs] *s.* Jägerin *f*.

hunts·man ['hʌntsmən] *s.* [*irr.*] **1.** Jäger *m*, Weidmann *m*; **2.** Rüdemeister *m*; '**hunts·man·ship** [-ʃɪp] *s.* Jäge'rei *f*, Weidwerk *n*.

hur·dle ['hɜːdl] **I** *s.* **1.** *sport u. fig.* a) Hürde *f*, b) *Hindernislauf, Pferdesport:* Hindernis *n* (*a. fig.*): *take* (*od. pass*) *the* ∼ *a. fig.* die Hürde nehmen; **2.** Hürde *f* (Weiden-, Draht)Geflecht *n*; **3.** ☉ Fa'schine *f*, Gitter *n*; **II** *v/t.* **4.** mit Hürden um'geben, um'zäunen; **5.** *ein Hindernis* über'springen; **6.** *fig. e-e Schwierigkeit* über'winden; **III** *v/i.* **7.** *sport:* e-n Hürden- *od.* Hindernislauf *od.* (*Pferdesport*) ein Hindernisrennen bestreiten; '**hur·dler** [-lə] *s. sport* a) Hürdenläufer (-in), b) Hindernisläufer *m*; **hur·dle race** *s. sport* a) Hürdenlauf *m*, b) Hindernislauf *m*, c) *Pferdesport:* Hindernisrennen *n*.

hur·dy-gur·dy ['hɜːdɪˌɡɜːdɪ] *s.* 🎵 a) Drehleier *f*, b) Leierkasten *m*.

hurl [hɜːl] **I** *v/t.* **1.** schleudern (*a. fig.*): ∼ *abuse at s.o.* j-m Beleidigungen ins Gesicht schleudern; ∼ *o.s.* sich stürzen (*on* auf *acc.*); **II** *v/i.* **2.** *sport* Hurling spielen; **III** *s.* **3.** Schleudern *n*; '**hurl·er** [-lə] *s. sport* Hurlingspieler *m*; '**hurl·ey** [-lɪ] *s. sport* **1.** → *hurling*; **2.** Hurlingstock *m*; '**hurl·ing** [-lɪŋ] *s. sport* Hurling (-spiel) *n* (*Art Hockey*).

hurl·y-burl·y ['hɜːlɪˌbɜːlɪ] **I** *s.* Tu'mult *m*, Aufruhr *m*; Wirrwarr *m*; **II** *adj.* turbu'lent.

hur·rah [hʊ'rɑː] **I** *int.* hur'ra!: ∼ *for ...!* hoch *od.* es lebe ...!; **II** *s.* Hur'ra(ruf *m*) *n*.

hur·ray [hʊ'reɪ] → *hurrah.*

hur·ri·cane ['hʌrɪkən] *s.* a) Hurrikan *m*, Wirbelsturm *m*, b) Or'kan *m*, *fig. a.* Sturm *m*; ∼ **deck** *s.* ⚓ Sturmdeck *n*; ∼ **lamp** *s.* 'Sturmla‚terne *f*.

hur·ried ['hʌrɪd] *adj.* □ eilig, hastig, schnell, über'eilt; '**hur·ri·er** [-ɪə] *s. Brit.*

H

⚒ Fördermann *m*.

hur·ry ['hʌrɪ] **I** *s*. **1.** Hast *f*, Eile *f*: *in a* ~ eilig, hastig; *be in a* ~ es eilig haben (*to do s.th.* et. zu tun); *there is no* ~ es eilt nicht, es hat keine Eile; *in my* ~ *I forgot* ... vor lauter Eile vergaß ich ...; *you will not beat that in a* ~ F das machst du nicht so bald *od*. leicht nach; *the* ~ *of daily life* die Hetze des Alltags; *in the* ~ *of business* im Drang der Geschäfte; **II** *v/t*. **2.** schnell *od*. eilig befördern *od*. bringen: ~ *through fig. Gesetzesvorlage etc*. durchpeitschen; **3.** *oft* ~ *up* (*od*. *on*) a) *j-n* antreiben, b) *et*. beschleunigen; **4.** *et*. über'eilen; **III** *v/i*. **5.** eilen, hasten: ~ *over s.th*. et. hastig *od*. flüchtig erledigen; **6.** *oft* ~ *up* sich beeilen: ~ *up!* beeil dich!, (mach) schnell!; ‚~'**scur·ry** [-'skʌrɪ] → *helter-skelter*; '~**-up** *adj*. *Am*. **1.** eilig, Eil...: ~ *job*; **2.** hastig: ~ *breakfast*.

hurst [hɜːst] *s*. **1.** (*obs. außer in Ortsnamen*) Forst *m*; **2.** *obs*. bewaldeter Hügel; **3.** *obs*. Sandbank *f*.

hurt [hɜːt] **I** *v/t*. [*irr*.] **1.** verletzen, verwunden (*beide a. fig*.): ~ *s.o.'s feelings; feel* ~ gekränkt *od*. verletzt sein; → *fly²* 1; **2.** schmerzen, wehtun (*dat*.) (*beide a. fig*.): drücken (*Schuh*); **3.** *j-m* schaden *od*. Schaden zufügen: *it won't* ~ *you to* *inf*. F du stirbst nicht gleich, wenn du; **4.** *et*. beschädigen; **II** *v/i*. [*irr*.] **5.** schmerzen, wehtun (*a. fig*.); **6.** schaden: *that won't* ~ das schadet nichts; **7.** F Schmerzen haben, *a. fig*. leiden (*from* an *dat*.); **III** *s*. **8.** Schmerz *m* (*a. fig*.); **9.** Verletzung *f*; **10.** Kränkung *f*; **11.** Schaden *m*, Nachteil *m*; '**hurt·ful** [-fʊl] *adj*. □ **1.** verletzend; **2.** schmerzlich; **3.** schädlich, nachteilig (*to* für).

hur·tle ['hɜːtl] **I** *v/i*. **1.** *obs*. zs.-prallen (mit), prallen, krachen (gegen); **2.** sausen, rasen; **3.** rasseln, poltern; **II** *v/t*. **4.** → *hurl* 1.

'**hur·tle·ber·ry** *s*. ♀ Heidelbeere *f*.

hus·band ['hʌzbənd] **I** *s*. (Ehe)Mann *m*, Gatte *m*, Gemahl *m*; **II** *v/t*. haushälterisch *od*. sparsam 'umgehen mit, Haus halten mit; '**hus·band·man** [-ndmən] *s*. [*irr*.] *obs*. Bauer *m*; '**hus·band·ry** [-rɪ] *s*. **1.** Landwirtschaft *f*; **2.** Haushalten *n*.

hush [hʌʃ] **I** *int*. **1.** still!, pst!; **II** *v/t*. **2.** zum Schweigen *od*. zur Ruhe bringen; **3.** *fig*. besänftigen, beruhigen; **4.** *mst* ~ *up* vertuschen; **III** *v/i*. **5.** still werden; **IV** *s*. **6.** Stille *f*, Ruhe *f*; '**hush·a·by** [-ʃəbaɪ] *int*. eiapo'peia!; **hushed** [-ʃt] *adj*. lautlos, still.

‚**hush|-'hush** *adj*. geheim (gehalten), Geheim..., heimlich; ~ **mon·ey** *s*. Schweigegeld *n*.

husk [hʌsk] **I** *s*. **1.** ♀ Hülse *f*, Schale *f*, Schote *f*, *Am. mst* Maishülse *f*; **2.** *fig*. (leere) Hülle, Schale *f*; **II** *v/t*. **3.** enthülsen, schälen; '**husk·er** [-kə] *s*. **1.** Enthülser(in); **2.** 'Schälma‚schine *f*; '**husk·i·ly** [-kɪlɪ] *adv*. mit rauer *od*. heiserer Stimme; '**husk·i·ness** [-kɪnɪs] *s*. Heiserkeit *f*, Rauheit *f*; '**husk·ing** [-kɪŋ] *s*. **1.** Enthülsen *n*, Schälen *n*; **2.** *a*. ~ *bee Am*. geselliges Maisschälen.

husk·y¹ ['hʌskɪ] **I** *adj*. □ **1.** hülsig; **2.** ausgedörrt; **3.** rau, heiser; **4.** F stämmig, kräftig; **II** *s*. **5.** F stämmiger Kerl.

hus·ky² ['hʌskɪ] *s*. *zo*. Husky *m*, Eskimohund *m*.

hus·sar [hʊ'zɑː] *s*. ✕ Hu'sar *m*.

Huss·ite ['hʌsaɪt] *s*. *hist*. Hus'sit *m*.

hus·sy ['hʌsɪ] *s*. **1.** Range *f*, ‚Fratz' *m*; **2.** ‚leichtes Mädchen', 'Flittchen' *n*.

hus·tings ['hʌstɪŋz] *s. pl. mst sg. konstr. pol*. a) Wahlkampf *m*, b) Wahl(en *pl*.)

f.

hus·tle ['hʌsl] **I** *v/t*. **1.** a) stoßen, drängen, b) (an)rempeln; **2.** a) hetzen, (an-) treiben, b) drängen (*into doing s.th*. dazu, et. zu tun); **3.** rasch *wohin* schaffen *od*. ‚verfrachten'; **4.** sich beeilen mit; **5.** ~ *up Am*. F ‚herzaubern'; **6.** *Am*. F a) *et*. ergattern, b) sich *et*. ergaunern; **II** *v/i*. **7.** sich drängen, hasten, hetzen, sich beeilen; **8.** *Am*. F a) mit Hochdruck arbeiten, b) ‚rangehen', Dampf da'hinter machen; **9.** *Am. sl*. a) ‚klauen', b) Betrüge'reien begehen, c) betteln, d) auf Kundschaft ausgehen (*a. Prostituierte*), e) ‚schwer hinterm Geld her sein'; **III** *s*. **10.** *mst* ~ *and bustle* a) Gedränge *n*, b) Gehetze *n*, c) ‚Betrieb' *m*; **11.** *Am*. F Gaune'rei *f*; '**hus·tler** [-lə] *s*. **1.** F rühriger Mensch, ‚Wühler' *m*; **2.** *bsd. Am*. F a) ‚Nutte' *f*, Prostitu'ierte *f*, b) (kleiner) Gauner.

hut [hʌt] **I** *s*. **1.** Hütte *f*; **2.** ✕ Ba'racke *f*; **II** *v/t. u. v/i*. **3.** in Ba'racken *od*. Hütten 'unterbringen (wohnen): ~*ted camp* Barackenlager *n*.

hutch [hʌtʃ] *s*. **1.** Kiste *f*, Kasten *m*; **2.** Trog *m*; **3.** (kleiner) Stall, Käfig *m*, Verschlag *m*; **4.** ⚒ Hund *m*; **5.** F Hütte *f*.

hut·ment ['hʌtmənt] *s*. ✕ **1.** 'Unterbringung *f* in Ba'racken; **2.** Ba'rackenlager *n*.

huz·za [hʊ'zɑː] *obs*. → *hurrah*.

hy·a·cinth ['haɪəsɪnθ] *s*. **1.** ♀ Hya'zinthe *f*; **2.** *min*. Hya'zinth *m*.

hy·ae·na → *hyena*.

hy·brid ['haɪbrɪd] **I** *s*. **1.** *biol*. Hy'bride *f*, *m*, Mischling *m*, Bastard *m*, Kreuzung *f*; **2.** *ling*. Mischwort *n*; **II** *adj*. **3.** hybrid: a) *biol*. Misch..., Bastard..., Zwitter..., b) *fig*. ungleichartig, gemischt; '**hy·brid·ism** [-dɪzəm], **hy·brid·i·ty** [haɪ'brɪdətɪ] *s*. *biol*. Mischbildung *f*, Kreuzung *f*; **hy·brid·i·za·tion** [‚haɪbrɪdaɪ'zeɪʃn] *s*. Kreuzung *f*; '**hy·brid·ize** [-daɪz] *v/t*. (*v/i*. sich) kreuzen.

Hy·dra ['haɪdrə] *s*. **1.** Hydra *f*: a) *myth*. vielköpfige Schlange, b) *ast*. Wasserschlange *f*; **2.** ♌ *fig*. Hydra *f* (*kaum auszurottendes Übel*); **3.** ♌ *zo*. 'Süßwasserpo,lyp *m*.

hy·dran·ge·a [haɪ'dreɪndʒə] *s*. ♀ Hor'tensie *f*.

hy·drant ['haɪdrənt] *s*. Hy'drant *m*.

hy·drate ['haɪdreɪt] ♞ **I** *s*. Hy'drat *n*; **II** *v/t*. hydratisieren; '**hy·drat·ed** [-tɪd] *adj*. ♞, *min*. hy'drathaltig; **hy·dra·tion** [haɪ'dreɪʃn] *s*. ♞ Hydra(ta)ti'on *f*.

hy·drau·lic [haɪ'drɔːlɪk] *adj*. (□ ~*ally*) ☉, *phys*. hy'draulisch: a) (Druck-) Wasser...: ~ *clutch* (*jack*, *press*) hydraulische Kupplung (Winde, Presse); ~ *power* (*pressure*) Wasserkraft *f* (-druck *m*), b) unter Wasser erhärtend: ~ *cement* hydraulischer Mörtel, Wassermörtel *m*; **II** *s. pl. sg. konstr. phys*. Hy'draulik *f* (*Wissenschaft*); ~ *brake* *s*. *mot*. hy'draulische Bremse, Flüssigkeitsbremse *f*; ~ *dock* *s*. ⚓ Schwimmdock *n*; ~ *en·gi·neer* *s*. 'Wasserbauingeni‚eur *m*; ~ *en·gi·neer·ing* *s*. Wasserbau *m*.

hy·dric ['haɪdrɪk] *adj*. ♞ Wasserstoff...: ~ *oxide* Wasser *n*; '**hy·dride** [-raɪd] *s*. ♞ Hy'drid *n*.

hy·dro ['haɪdrəʊ] *pl*. **-dros** *s*. F **1.** ✈ → *hydroplane* 1; **2.** ♌ *Brit*. F Ho'tel *n* mit hydro'pathischen Einrichtungen.

hydro- [haɪdrəʊ] *in Zssgn* a) Wasser..., b) ...wasserstoff *m*.

'**hy·dro|·bomb** *s*. ✕ 'Lufttor‚pedo *m*; ‚~'**car·bon** *s*. ♞ Kohlenwasserstoff *m*; ‚~'**cel·lu·lose** *s*. ♞ 'Hydrozellu‚lose *f*; ‚~'**ce'phal·ic** [-əʊse'fælɪk], ‚~'**ceph·a-**

lous [-əʊ'sefələs] *adj*. ♌ mit e-m Wasserkopf; [-əʊ'sefələs] *s*. ♌ Wasserkopf *m*; ‚~'**chlo·ric** *adj*. ♞ salzsauer: ~ *acid* Salzsäure *f*, Chlorwasserstoff *m*; ‚~'**chlo·ride** *s*. ♞ 'Chlorhy‚drat *n*; ‚~'**cy'an·ic ac·id** *s*. ♞ Blausäure *f*, Zy'anwasserstoffsäure *f*; ‚~**dy'nam·ic** *adj*. *phys*. hydrody'namisch; ‚~**dy'nam·ics** *s. pl. mst sg. konstr. phys*. Hydrody'namik *f*; ‚~**e'lec·tric** *adj*. ☉ hydroe'lektrisch: ~ *power station* (*od*. *plant*) Wasserkraftwerk *n*; ‚~**ex'tract** *v/t*. ☉ zentrifugieren, entwässern; ‚~**flu'or·ic ac·id** *s*. ♞ Flusssäure *f*; '~**foil** *s*. ⚓ Tragflügel(boot *n*) *m*.

hy·dro·gen ['haɪdrədʒən] *s*. ♞ Wasserstoff *m*: ~ *bomb* s. ♞ *cylinder* Wasserstoffflasche *f*, ~ *peroxide* Wasserstoffsuperoxid *n*; ~ *sulphide* Schwefelwasserstoff; '**hy·dro·gen·ate** [-ədʒɪneɪt] *v/t*. ♞ **1.** hydrieren; **2.** Öl härten; **hy·dro·gen·a·tion** [‚haɪdrədʒɪ'neɪʃn] *s*. ♞ **1.** Hydrierung *f*; **2.** (Öl)Härtung *f*; '**hy·dro·gen·ize** [-ədʒɪnaɪz] → *hydrogenate*; **hy·drog·e·nous** [haɪ'drɒdʒɪnəs] *adj*. ♞ wasserstoffhaltig, Wasserstoff...

hy·dro·graph·ic [‚haɪdrəʊ'græfɪk] *adj*. (□ ~*ally*) hydro'graphisch: ~ *map* ⚓ Seekarte *f*; ~ *office* (*od*. *department*) ⚓ Seewarte *f*; **hy·drog·ra·phy** [haɪ'drɒgrəfɪ] *s*. **1.** Hydrogra'phie *f*, Gewässerkunde *f*; **2.** Gewässer *pl*. (*e-r Landkarte*).

hy·dro·log·ic, **hy·dro·log·i·cal** [‚haɪdrəʊ'lɒdʒɪk(l)] *adj*. □ hydro'logisch; **hy·drol·o·gy** [haɪ'drɒlədʒɪ] *s*. Hydrolo'gie *f*.

hy·drol·y·sis [haɪ'drɒlɪsɪs] *pl*. **-ses** [-siːz] *s*. ♞ Hydro'lyse *f*; **hy·dro·lyt·ic** [‚haɪdrəʊ'lɪtɪk] *adj*. hydro'lytisch; **hydro·lyze** ['haɪdrəlaɪz] *v/t*. hydrolysieren.

hy·drom·e·ter [haɪ'drɒmɪtə] *s*. *phys*. Hydro'meter *n*.

hy·dro·path ['haɪdrəʊpæθ] → *hydropathist*; **hy·dro·path·ic** [‚haɪdrəʊ'pæθɪk] ♌ *adj*. hydro'pathisch, Wasserkur...; **hy·drop·a·thist** [haɪ'drɒpəθɪst] *s*. ♌ Hydro'path *m*, Kneipparzt *m*; **hy·drop·a·thy** [haɪ'drɒpəθɪ] *s*. ♌ Hydrothera'pie *f*.

hy·dro|·pho·bi·a [‚haɪdrəʊ'fəʊbjə] *s*. ♌ Hydropho'bie *f*: a) *a. psych*. Wasserscheu *f*, b) Tollwut *f*; ~**phyte** ['haɪdrəʊfaɪt] *s*. ♀ Wasserpflanze *f*; ~**plane** ['haɪdrəʊpleɪn] **I** *s*. **1.** ✈ Wasserflugzeug *n*; **2.** ✈ Gleitfläche *f* (*e-s Wasserflugzeugs*); **3.** ⚓ Tragflügelboot *n*; **4.** ⚓ Tiefenruder *n* (*e-s U-Boots*); **II** *v/i*. **5.** *Am*. → *aquaplane* 1; ~**pon·ics** [-'pɒnɪks] *s. pl. sg. konstr*. 'Hydro-, 'Wasserkul‚tur *f*; ‚~**qui'none** [-kwɪ'nəʊn] *s*. *phot*. Hydrochi'non *n*; ~**scope** [haɪ'drəskəʊp] *s*. ☉ Unter'wassersichtgerät *n*; ~**sphere** ['haɪdrəsfɪə] *s*. Hydro-'sphäre *f* (*die Wasserhülle der Erde*); ‚~**stat·ic** [-'stætɪk] *adj*. hydro'statisch; ‚~**stat·ics** [-'stætɪks] *s. pl. sg. konstr*. Hydro'statik *f*; ‚~**ther·a·py** [-'θerəpɪ] *s*. ♌ Hydrothera'pie *f*.

hy·drous ['haɪdrəs] *adj*. ♞ wasserhaltig.

hy·drox·ide [haɪ'drɒksaɪd] *s*. ♞ Hydro-'xid *n*; ~ *of sodium* Ätznatron *n*.

hy·e·na [haɪ'iːnə] *s*. *zo*. Hy'äne *f*: *laugh like a* ~ F sich schieflachen.

hy·giene ['haɪdʒiːn] *s*. **1.** Hygi'ene *f*, Gesundheitspflege *f*: *personal* ~ Körperpflege; *dental* (*food*, *sex*) ~ Zahn-(Nahrungs-, Sexual)hygiene; **2.** → *hygienic* II; **hy·gi·en·ic** [haɪ'dʒiːnɪk] **I** *adj*. (□ ~*ally*) hygi'enisch; sani'tär; **II** *s. pl. sg. konstr*. Hygi'ene *f*, Gesundheitslehre *f*; '**hy·gi·en·ist** [-nɪst] *s*. Hygi'eniker(in).

hy·gro·graph [ˈhaɪgrəgrɑːf] *s. meteor.* Hygroˈgraph *m*, selbstregistrierender Luftfeuchtigkeitsmesser; **hy·grom·e·ter** [haɪˈgrɒmɪtə] *s. meteor.* Hygroˈmeter *n*, Luftfeuchtigkeitsmesser *m*; **hy·gro·met·ric** [ˌhaɪgrəʊˈmetrɪk] *adj.* hygroˈmetrisch; **hy·grom·e·try** [haɪˈgrɒmɪtrɪ] *s.* Hygromeˈtrie *f*, Luftfeuchtigkeitsmessung *f*; **ˈhy·gro·scope** [-əskəʊp] *s. meteor.* Hygroˈskop *n*, Feuchtigkeitsanzeiger *m*; **hy·gro·scop·ic** [ˌhaɪgrəʊˈskɒpɪk] *adj.* hygroˈskopisch, Feuchtigkeit anzeigend *od. a.* anziehend.

hy·ing [ˈhaɪɪŋ] *pres.p. von* **hie.**

hy·men [ˈhaɪmen] *s.* **1.** *anat.* Hymen *n*, Jungfernhäutchen *n*; **2.** *poet.* Ehe *f*, Hochzeit *f*; **3.** ♂ *myth.* Hymen *m*, Gott *m* der Ehe.

hy·me·nop·ter·a [ˌhaɪməˈnɒptərə] *s. pl. zo.* Hautflügler *pl.*

hymn [hɪm] **I** *s.* Hymne *f (a. fig. Loblied, -gesang)*, Kirchenlied *n*, Choˈral *m*; **II** *v/t.* (lob)preisen; **III** *v/i.* Hymnen singen; **hym·nal** [ˈhɪmnəl] **I** *adj.* hymnisch, Hymnen...; **II** *s.* → **hymn book** *s.* Gesangbuch *n*; **hym·nic** [ˈhɪmnɪk] *adj.* hymnenartig; **ˈhym·no·dy** [-nəʊdɪ] *s.* **1.** Hymnensingen *n*; **2.** Hymnendichtung *f*; **3.** *coll.* Hymnen *pl.*

hy·oid (bone) [ˈhaɪɔɪd] *s. anat.* Zungenbein *n.*

hype[1] [haɪp] *sl.* **I** *s.* **1.** Pubˈlicity-, Werbe-, Reklamerummel *m*; **2.** ‚Spritze‘ *f*, ‚Schuss‘ *m (Rauschgift)*; **3.** ‚Fixer(in)‘; **II** *v/i.* **4.** *mst* ~ *up* ‚sich e-n Schuss setzen‘; **III** *v/t.* **5.** hochjubeln; **6.** *be* ~*d up* ‚high‘ sein *(a. fig.).*

hype[2] [haɪp] *sl.* **I** *s.* Trick *m*, ‚Beschiss‘ *m*; **II** *v/t.* j-n austricksen, ‚bescheißen‘.

ˌhy·per·a·cid·i·ty [ˌhaɪpərə-] *s.* ♂ Überˈsäuerung *f (des Magens).*

hy·per·bo·la [haɪˈpɜːbələ] *s.* ♂ Hyˈperbel *f (Kegelschnitt);* **hyˈper·bo·le** [-lɪ] *s. rhet.* Hyˈperbel *f*, Überˈtreibung *f*; **hy·per·bol·ic, hy·per·bol·i·cal** [ˌhaɪpəˈbɒlɪk(l)] *adj.* □ ♂, *rhet.* hyperˈbolisch.

hy·per·bo·re·an [ˌhaɪpəbɔːˈriːən] **I** *s. myth.* Hyperboˈreer *m*; **II** *adj.* hyperboˈreisch; **ˌhy·per·corˈrect** [ˌhaɪpə-] *adj.* ‚hyperkorˌrekt *(a. ling.);* **ˌhy·perˈcrit·i·cal** *adj.* □ hyperkritisch, allzu kritisch; **ˈhy·per·link** *s. bsd. Internet:* ˈHyperlink *m (anklickbare Textstelle für weitere Informationen);* **ˈhy·per·mar·ket** *s.* Groß-, Verbrauchermarkt *m*; **hy·per·me·tro·pi·a** [ˌhaɪpəmɪˈtrəʊpɪə], **hy·per·o·pi·a** [ˌhaɪpəˈrəʊpɪə] *s.* ♂ ˈÜbersichtigkeit *f*; **ˌhy·perˈsen·si·tive** *adj.* ˈüberempfindlich; **ˌhy·perˈson·ic** *adj. phys.* hyper-ˈsonisch *(etwas über fünffache Schallgeschwindigkeit);* **ˌhy·perˈten·sion** *s.* ♂ Hypertoˈnie *f*, erhöhter Blutdruck; **ˈhyper·text** *s. bsd. Internet:* ˈHypertext *m (über Hyperlinks verbundene Texte).*

hy·per·troph·ic [ˌhaɪpəˈtrɒfɪk], **hy·per·tro·phied** [haɪˈpɜːtrəʊfɪd] *adj.* ♂, *biol. u. fig.* hyperˈtroph; **hy·per·tro·phy** [haɪˈpɜːtrəʊfɪ] ♂, *biol. u. fig.* **I** *s.* Hypertroˈphie *f*; **II** *v/t. (v/i.* sich) ˈübermäßig vergrößern.

hy·phen [ˈhaɪfn] **I** *s.* **1.** Bindestrich *m*; **2.** Trennungszeichen *n*; **II** *v/t.* **3.** → **ˈhyphen·ate** [-fəneɪt] *v/t.* mit Bindestrich schreiben: ~*d American* ‚Bindestrichamerikaner‘ *m*; **hy·phen·a·tion** [ˌhaɪfəˈneɪʃn] *s.* a) Schreibung *f* mit Bindestrich, b) (Silben)Trennung *f.*

hyp·noid [ˈhɪpnɔɪd] *adj.* hypnoˈid, hypˈnose- *od.* schlafähnlich.

hyp·no·sis [hɪpˈnəʊsɪs] *pl.* **-ses** [-siːz] *s.* ♂ Hypˈnose *f*, **ˌhyp·noˈther·a·py** [ˌhɪpnəʊ-] *s. psych.* Hypnotheraˈpie *f*; **hyp·not·ic** [-ˈnɒtɪk] **I** *adj.* (□ ~*ally*) **1.** hypˈnotisch; **2.** einschläfernd; **3.** hypnotisierbar; **II** *s.* **4.** Hypˈnotikum *n*, Schlafmittel *n*; **5.** a) Hypnotisierte(r *m*) *f*, b) j-d, *der hypnotisierbar ist;* **ˈhyp·no·tism** [ˈhɪpnətɪzəm] *s.* ♂ **1.** Hypnoˈtismus *m*; **2.** a) Hypˈnose *f*, b) Hypnotisierung *f*; **hyp·no·tist** [ˈhɪpnətɪst] *s.* Hypnotiˈseur *m*; **hyp·no·ti·za·tion** [ˌhɪpnətaɪˈzeɪʃn] *s.* Hypnotisierung *f*; **ˈhyp·no·tize** [ˈhɪpnətaɪz] *v/t.* ♂ hypnotisieren *(a. fig.).*

hy·po[1] [ˈhaɪpəʊ] *s.* ♂, *phot.* Fixiersalz *n*, ˈNatriumthiosulˌfat *n.*

hy·po[2] [ˈhaɪpəʊ] *pl.* **-pos** *s.* F → a) *hypodermic injection*, b) *hypodermic syringe.*

hy·po·chon·dri·a [ˌhaɪpəʊˈkɒndrɪə] *s.* ♂ Hypochonˈdrie *f*, **ˌhy·poˈchon·dri·ac** [-ɪæk] ♂ **I** *adj.* (□ ~*ally*) hypoˈchondrisch; **II** *s.* Hypoˈchonder *m.*

hy·poc·ri·sy [hɪˈpɒkrəsɪ] *s.* Heucheˈlei *f*, Scheinheiligkeit *f*; **hyp·o·crite** [ˈhɪpəkrɪt] *s.* Hypoˈkrit *m*, Heuchler(in), Scheinheilige(r *m*) *f*; **hyp·o·crit·i·cal** [ˌhɪpəʊˈkrɪtɪkl] *adj.* □ heuchlerisch, scheinheilig.

hy·po·der·mic [ˌhaɪpəʊˈdɜːmɪk] ♂ **I** *adj.* (□ ~*ally*) **1.** subkuˈtan, hypoderˈmal, unter der *od.* die Haut; **II** *s.* **2.** → *hypodermic injection*; **3.** → *hypodermic syringe*; **4.** subkuˈtan angewandtes Mittel; ~ **in·jec·tion** *s.* ♂ subkuˈtane Injektiˈon; ~ **nee·dle** *s.* ♂ Nadel *f* für e-e subkuˈtane Spritze; ~ **syr·inge** *s.* ♂ Spritze *f* zur subkuˈtanen Injektiˈon.

hy·po·phos·phate [ˌhaɪpəʊˈfɒsfeɪt] *s.* ♋ ˈHypophosˌphat *n*; ~**phos·phor·ic ac·id** [ˌhaɪpəʊfɒsˈfɒrɪk] *s.* ♋ Hypo-, ˈUnterphosphorsäure *f.*

hy·poph·y·sis [haɪˈpɒfɪsɪs] *pl.* **-ses** [-siːz] *s. anat.* Hirnanhangdrüse *f*, Hyˈpophyse *f.*

hy·pos·ta·sis [haɪˈpɒstəsɪs] *pl.* **-ses** [-siːz] *s.* **1.** *phls.* Hypoˈstase *f*: a) Grundlage *f*, Subˈstanz *f*, b) Vergegenständlichung *f (e-s Begriffs);* **2.** ♂, *biol.* Hypoˈstase *f.*

hy·po·sul·fite, *bsd. Brit.* ~**sul·phite** [ˌhaɪpəʊˈsʌlfaɪt] *s.* ♋ **1.** Hyposulˈfit *n*, ˈunterschwefligsaures Salz; **2.** → *hypo*[1]; ~**sul·fu·rous**, *bsd. Brit.* ~**sul·phu·rous** [ˌhaɪpəʊˈsʌlfərəs] *adj.* ♋ ˈunterschweflig.

hy·po·tac·tic [ˌhaɪpəʊˈtæktɪk] *adj. ling.* hypoˈtaktisch, unterordnend.

hy·po·ten·sion [ˌhaɪpəʊˈtenʃn] *s.* ♂ zu niedriger Blutdruck, Hypotoˈnie *f.*

hy·pot·e·nuse [haɪˈpɒtənjuːz] *s.* Å Hypoteˈnuse *f.*

hy·poth·ec [ˈhaɪpəθɪk] *s.* ♊ *Scot.* Hypoˈthek *f*; **hy·poth·e·car·y** [haɪˈpɒθɪkərɪ] *adj.* ♊ hypotheˈkarisch: ~ *debts* Hypothekenschulden; ~ *value* Beleihungswert *m*; **hy·poth·e·cate** [haɪˈpɒθɪkeɪt] *v/t.* **1.** ♊ *Grundstück etc.* hypotheˈkarisch belasten; **2.** *Schiff* verbodmen; **3.** ♱ *Effekten* lombardieren; **hy·poth·e·ca·tion** [haɪˌpɒθɪˈkeɪʃn] *s.* **1.** ♊ hypotheˈkarische Belastung *(Grundstück etc.);* **2.** Verbodmung *f (Schiff);* **3.** ♱ Lombardierung *f (Effekten).*

hy·poth·e·sis [haɪˈpɒθɪsɪs] *pl.* **-ses** [-siːz] *s.* Hypoˈthese *f*: a) Annahme *f*, Vorˈaussetzung *f*: *working* ~ Arbeitshypothese, b) (bloße) Vermutung; **hy·poth·e·size** [-saɪz] **I** *v/i.* e-e Hypoˈthese aufstellen; **II** *v/t.* vorˈaussetzen, annehmen, vermuten; **hy·po·thet·ic, hy·po·thet·i·cal** [ˌhaɪpəʊˈθetɪk(l)] *adj.* □ hypoˈthetisch.

hyp·som·e·try [hɪpˈsɒmɪtrɪ] *s. geogr.* Höhenmessung *f.*

hys·sop [ˈhɪsəp] *s.* **1.** ⚘ Ysop *m*; **2.** *R.C.* Weihwedel *m.*

hys·ter·ec·to·my [ˌhɪstəˈrektəmɪ] *s.* ♂ ‚Hysterektoˈmie *f*, F ‚Toˈtaloperatiˌon‘ *(der Gebärmutter).*

hys·te·ri·a [hɪˈstɪərɪə] *s.* ♂ *u. fig.* Hysteˈrie *f*; **hys·ter·ic** [hɪˈsterɪk] ♂ **I** *s.* **1.** Hyˈsteriker(in); **2.** *pl. mst sg. konstr.* Hysteˈrie *f*, hyˈsterischer Anfall: *go (off) into* ~*s* a) e-n hysterischen Anfall bekommen, hysterisch werden, b) F e-n Lachkrampf bekommen; **II** *adj.* (□ ~*ally*) **3.** → **hys·ter·i·cal** [hɪˈsterɪkl] *adj.* □ ♂ *u. fig.* hysterisch.

I i

I¹, i [aɪ] *s.* I *n*, i *n* (*Buchstabe*).

I² [aɪ] **I** *pron.* ich; **II** *pl.* **I's** *s. das* Ich.

i·am·bic [aɪˈæmbɪk] **I** *adj.* jambisch; **II** *s.* a) Jambus *m* (*Versfuß*), b) jambischer Vers; **i'am·bus** [-bəs] *pl.* **-bi** [-baɪ], **-bus·es** *s.* Jambus *m*.

'I-beam *s.* ⊗ Doppel-T-Träger *m*; I-Formstahl *m*; ~ **section** I-Profil *n*.

I·be·ri·an [aɪˈbɪərɪən] **I** *s.* **1.** I'berer(in); **2.** *ling.* I'berisch *n*; **II** *adj.* **3.** i'berisch; **4.** die i'berische Halbinsel betreffend; **I·be·ro-** [-rəʊ] *in Zssgn* Ibero...; *~* **America** Lateinamerika *n*.

i·bex [ˈaɪbeks] *s. zo.* Steinbock *m*.

i·bi·dem [ɪˈbaɪdem], *a.* **ib·id** [ˈɪbɪd] (*Lat.*) *adv.* ebenda (*bsd. für Textstelle etc.*).

i·bis [ˈaɪbɪs] *s. zo.* Ibis *m*.

ice [aɪs] **I** *s.* **1.** Eis *n*: *broken* **~** Eisstücke *pl.*; *dry* **~** Trockeneis (*feste Kohlensäure*); *break the* **~** *fig.* das Eis brechen; *skate on* (*od.* **over**) *thin* **~** *fig.* a) ein gefährliches Spiel treiben, b) ein heikles Thema berühren; *cut no* **~** F keinen Eindruck machen, ‚nicht ziehen'; *that cuts no* **~** *with me* F das zieht bei mir nicht; *keep* (*od.* **put**) *on* **~** F et. *od.* j-n ‚auf Eis legen'; **2.** a) *Am.* Gefrorenes *n* aus Fruchtsaft *u.* Zuckerwasser, b) *Brit.* (Speise)Eis *n*, c) → *icing* 2; **3.** *sl.* Dia'manten *pl.*, ‚Klunkern' *pl.*; **II** *v/t.* **4.** mit Eis bedecken; **5.** in Eis verwandeln, vereisen; **6.** mit *od.* in Eis kühlen; **7.** überzuckern, glasieren; **8.** *sl.* j-n ‚umlegen'; **III** *v/i.* **9.** gefrieren: **~** *up* (*od.* **over**) zufrieren, vereisen.

ice| age *s. geol.* Eiszeit *f*; **~ ax(e)** *s. mount.* Eispickel *m*; **~ bag** *s. Am.* Eisbeutel *m*; **'~·berg** [-bɜːg] *s.* Eisberg *m* (*a. fig. sl. Person*): *the tip of the* **~** die Spitze des Eisbergs (*a. fig. sl.*); **~ blink** *s.* Eisblink *m*; **'~·boat** *s.* **1.** Eissegler *m*, Segelschlitten *m*; **2.** Eisbrecher *m*; **'~·bound** *adj.* eingefroren (*Schiff*); zugefroren (*Hafen*); vereist (*Straße*); **'~·box** *s.* **1.** *bsd. Am.* Eis-, Kühlschrank *m*; **2.** *Brit.* Eisfach *n*; **3.** Eisbox *f*; **4.** F ‚Eiskeller' *m* (*Raum*); **'~·break·er** *s.* ⚓ Eisbrecher *m* (*a. an Brücken*); **'~·cap** *s.* (*bsd. arktische*) Eisdecke; **~ cream** *s.* (Speise)Eis *n*, Eiscreme *f*: *vanilla* **~** Vanilleeis; **'~·cream** *adj.* Eis...: **~** *bar od.* **parlo(u)r** *s.* Eisdiele *f*; **~ cone** Eistüte *f*; **~ soda** Eis *n* in Sodawasser (*mit Sirup etc.*); **~ cube** *s.* Eiswürfel *m*.

iced [aɪst] *adj.* **1.** mit Eis bedeckt, vereist; **2.** eisgekühlt: **~** *tea* Eistee *f*; **3.** gefroren; **4.** glasiert, mit 'Zuckergla,sur *od.* -guss.

'ice|·fall *s.* gefrorener Wasserfall; **~ fern** *s.* Eisblume(n *pl.*) *f*; **~ floe** *s.* Eisscholle *f*; **~ foot** *s.* [*irr.*] (arktischer) Eisgürtel; **~ fox** *s. zo.* Po'larfuchs *m*; **'~·free** *adj.* eis-, vereisungsfrei; **~ hock·ey** *s.* Eishockey *n*; **~ house** *s.* Kühlhaus *n*.

Ice·land·er [ˈaɪsləndə] *s.* Isländer(in); **Ice·lan·dic** [aɪsˈlændɪk] **I** *adj.* isländisch; **II** *s. ling.* Isländisch *n*.

ice| lol·ly *s. Brit.* Eis *n* am Stiel; **~ ma-**

---

chine *s.* 'Eis-, 'Kältema,schine *f*; **'~·man** [-mæn] *s.* [*irr.*] *Am.* Eismann *m*, Eisverkäufer *m*; **~ pack** *s.* **1.** Packeis *n*; **2.** ✚ 'Eis,umschlag *m*, -beutel *m*; **3.** Kühlbeutel *m* (*in Kühltaschen etc.*); **~ pick** *s.* Eishacke *f*; **~ plant** *s.* ♀ Eiskraut *n*; **~ rink** *s.* (Kunst)Eisbahn *f*; **~ run** *s.* Eis-, Rodelbahn *f*; **~ show** *s.* 'Eisre,vue *f*; **'~·skate** **I** *s.* Schlittschuh *m*; **II** *v/i.* Schlittschuh laufen; **~ tea** Eistee *f*; **~ wa·ter** *s.* **1.** Eiswasser *n*; **2.** Schmelzwasser *n*; **~ yacht** → *iceboat* 1.

ich·thy·o·log·i·cal [ˌɪkθɪəˈlɒdʒɪkl] *adj.* ichthyo'logisch; **ich·thy·ol·o·gy** [ˌɪkθɪˈɒlədʒɪ] *s.* Ichthyolo'gie *f*, Fischkunde *f*; **ich·thy·oph·a·gous** [ˌɪkθɪˈɒfəgəs] *adj.* Fisch (fr)essend; **ˌich·thy·oˈsau·rus** [-ˈsɔːrəs] *pl.* **-ri** [-raɪ] *s. zo.* Ichthyo'saurier *m*.

i·ci·cle [ˈaɪsɪkl] *s.* Eiszapfen *m*.

i·ci·ly [ˈaɪsɪlɪ] *adv.* eisig (*a. fig.*); **'i·ci·ness** [-nɪs] *s.* **1.** Eiseskälte *f* (*a. fig.*), eisige Kälte; **2.** Vereisung *f* (*Straße etc.*).

ic·ing [ˈaɪsɪŋ] *s.* **1.** Eisschicht *f*; Vereisung *f*; **2.** Zuckerguss *m*: **~** *sugar Brit.* Puder-, Staubzucker *m*; **3.** *Eishockey*: unerlaubter Weitschuss.

i·com·merce [ˈaɪˌkɒmɜːs] *s.* 'I-,Commerce *m*, Handel *m* über das Internet.

i·con [ˈaɪkɒn] *s.* **1.** I'kone *f*, Heiligenbild *n*; **2.** *Computer*: 'Icon *n*. **i·con·o·clasm** [aɪˈkɒnəʊklæzəm] *s.* Bilderstürme'rei *f* (*a. fig.*); **i·con·o·clast** [aɪˈkɒnəʊklæst] *s.* Bilderstürmer *m* (*a. fig.*); **i·con·o·clas·tic** [aɪˌkɒnəʊˈklæstɪk] *adj.* bilderstürmend; *fig.* bilderstürmerisch; **i·co·nog·ra·phy** [ˌaɪkɒˈnɒgrəfɪ] *s.* Ikonogra'phie *f*; **i·co·nol·a·try** [ˌaɪkɒˈnɒlətrɪ] *s.* Bilderverehrung *f*; **i·co·nol·o·gy** [ˌaɪkɒˈnɒlədʒɪ] *s.* Ikonolo'gie *f*; **i·con·o·scope** [aɪˈkɒnəskəʊp] *s. TV* Ikono'skop *n*, Bildwandlerröhre *f*.

ic·tus [ˈɪktəs] *s.* 'Versak,zent *m*.

i·cy [ˈaɪsɪ] *adj.* □ **1.** eisig (*a. fig.*): **~** *cold* eiskalt; **2.** vereist, eisig, gefroren.

ID [ˌaɪˈdiː] F *abbr. für* **identity**, **identification** 'Ausweis *m*: **~** *card* (Perso'nal-) Ausweis.

id [ɪd] *s.* **1.** *psych.* Es *n*; **2.** *biol.* Id *n* (*Erbeinheit*).

I'd [aɪd] F *für* a) **I would**, **I should**, b) **I had**.

i·de·a [aɪˈdɪə] *s.* **1.** I'dee *f* (*a. phls.*, ♪): a) Vorstellung *f*, Begriff *m*, Ahnung *f*, b) Gedanke *m*: *form an* **~** *of* sich e-n Begriff machen von, sich et. vorstellen; *I have an* **~** *that* ich habe so das Gefühl, dass; (*I've*) *no* **~**! (ich habe) keine Ahnung!; *he hasn't the faintest* **~** er hat nicht die leiseste Ahnung; *the very* **~**!, *what an* **~**! *contp.* was für e-e Idee!, (na,) so was!, unmöglich!; *the very* **~** *makes me sick!* bei dem bloßen Gedanken (daran) wird mir schlecht!; *you have no* **~** *how ...* du kannst dir nicht vorstellen, wie ...; *could you give me an* **~** *of where* (*etc.*) *...*? können Sie mir ungefähr sagen, wo (*etc.*) ...?; *that's*

---

not my **~** *of fun* unter Spass stell ich mir was andres vor; *it is my* **~** *that* ich bin der Ansicht, dass; *the* **~** *entered my mind* mir kam der Gedanke; **2.** I'dee *f*: a) Einfall *m*, Gedanke *m*, b) Absicht *f*, Zweck *m*: *not a bad* **~** keine schlechte Idee; *the* **~** *is* der Zweck der Sache ist ...; *that's the* **~**! genau (darum dreht sichs)!; *what's the big* **~**? F was soll denn das?; *whose bright* **~** *was that?* wer hat sich denn das ausgedacht?; *put* **~s** *into s.o.'s head* j-m e-n Floh ins Ohr setzen; *have* **~s** F ‚Rosinen' im Kopf haben; *don't get* **~s** *about ...* mach dir keine Hoffnungen auf (*acc.*); **~s** *man* Ideenentwickler *m*; **i·de·aed**, **i·de·a'd** [-əd] *adj.* i'deenreich, voller I'deen.

i·de·al [aɪˈdɪəl] **I** *adj.* □ → *ideally*; **1.** ide'al (*a. phls.*), voll'kommen, vorbildlich, Muster...; **2.** ide'ell: a) Ideen..., b) auf Ide'alen beruhend, c) (nur) eingebildet; **3.** ↗ ide'al, uneigentlich: **~** *number*; **II** *s.* **4.** Ide'al *n*, Wunsch-, Vorbild *n*; **5.** *das* Ide'elle (*Ggs. das Wirkliche*); **i'de·al·ism** [-lɪzəm] *s.* Idea'lismus *m*; **i'de·al·ist** [-lɪst] *s.* Idea'list(in); **i·de·al·is·tic** [aɪˌdɪəˈlɪstɪk] *adj.* (□ **~ally**) idea'listisch; **i·de·al·i·za·tion** [aɪˌdɪəlaɪˈzeɪʃn] *s.* Idealisierung *f*; **i'de·al·ize** [-laɪz] *v/t. u. v/i.* idealisieren; **i'de·al·ly** [-lɪ] *adv.* **1.** ide'al(erweise), am besten; **2.** ide'ell, geistig; **3.** im Geiste.

i·dée fixe [ˌiːdeɪˈfiːks] (*Fr.*) *s.* fixe I'dee.

i·dem [ˈaɪdem] **I** *s.* der'selbe (Verfasser), das'selbe (Buch *etc.*); **II** *adv.* beim selben Verfasser.

i·den·tic [aɪˈdentɪk] *adj.* → *identical*; **~** *note pol.* gleich lautende Note; **i'den·ti·cal** [-kl] *adj.* □ (*with*) a) i'dentisch (mit), (genau) gleich (*dat.*): **~** *twins* eineiige Zwillinge, b) (der-, die-, das-) 'selbe (wie), c) gleichbedeutend (mit), gleich lautend (wie).

i·den·ti·fi·a·ble [aɪˈdentɪfaɪəbl] *adj.* identifizier-, feststell-, erkennbar; **i·den·ti·fi·ca·tion** [aɪˌdentɪfɪˈkeɪʃn] *s.* **1.** Identifizierung *f*: a) Gleichsetzung *f* (*with* mit), b) Feststellung *f* der Identi'tät, Erkennung *f*: **~** *mark* Kennzeichen *n*; **~** *papers*, **~** *card* → *identity card*; **~** *disk*, *Am.* **~** *tag* ✕ Erkennungsmarke *f*; **~** *parade* ✚ Gegenüberstellung *f* (zur Identifizierung e-s Verdächtigen); **2.** Legitimati'on *f*, Ausweis *m*; **3.** *Funk, Radar*: Kennung *f*; **i·den·ti·fy** [aɪˈdentɪfaɪ] **I** *v/t.* **1.** identifizieren, gleichsetzen, als i'dentisch betrachten (*with* mit): **~** *o.s. with* → 5; **2.** identifizieren, erkennen, die Identi'tät feststellen von (*od. gen.*); **3.** *biol.* die Art feststellen von (*od. gen.*); **4.** ausweisen, legitimieren; **II** *v/i.* **5.** **~** *with od.* **to** sich identifizieren.

i·den·ti·kit [aɪˈdentɪkɪt] *TM s. Brit.* ✚ *a.* **~** *picture* Phan'tombild *n*.

i·den·ti·ty [aɪˈdentətɪ] *s.* Identi'tät *f*: a) Gleichheit *f*, b) Per'sönlichkeit *f*: *loss of* **~** Identitätsverlust *m*; *mistaken* **~**

Personenverwechslung *f*; **establish s.o.'s ~** → **identify** 2; **prove one's ~** sich ausweisen; **reveal one's ~** sich zu erkennen geben; **~ card** *s.* (Perso'nal-) Ausweis *m*, Kenn-, Ausweiskarte *f*; **~ cri·sis** *s. psych.* Identi'tätskrise *f*.

id·e·o·gram ['ɪdɪəʊɡræm], **'id·e·o·graph** [-grɑːf] *s.* Ideo'gramm *n*, Begriffszeichen *n*.

id·e·o·log·ic, id·e·o·log·i·cal [ˌaɪdɪə'lɒdʒɪk(l)] *adj.* ideo'logisch; **id·e·ol·o·gist** [ˌaɪdɪ'plədʒɪst] *s.* **1.** Ideo'loge *m*; **2.** Theo'retiker *m*; **id·e·o·lo·gize** [ˌaɪdɪ-'plədʒaɪz] *v/t.* ideologisieren; **id·e·ol·o·gy** [ˌaɪdɪ'plədʒɪ] *s.* **1.** Ideolo'gie *f*, Denkweise *f*; **2.** Begriffslehre *f*; **3.** reine Theo'rie.

ides [aɪdz] *s. pl. antiq.* Iden *pl.*

id·i·o·cy ['ɪdɪəsɪ] *s.* Idio'tie *f*: a) (♂ hochgradiger) Schwachsinn, b) F Dummheit *f*, Blödsinn *m*.

id·i·om ['ɪdɪəm] *s. ling.* **1.** Idi'om *n*, Sondersprache *f*, Mundart *f*; **2.** Ausdrucksweise *f*, Sprache *f*; **3.** Sprachgebrauch *m*, -eigentümlichkeit *f*; **4.** idio'matische Wendung, Redewendung *f*; **id·i·o·mat·ic** [ˌɪdɪə'mætɪk] *adj.* (□ **~ally**) *ling.* **1.** idio'matisch, spracheigentümlich; **2.** sprachrichtig, -üblich.

id·i·o·plasm ['ɪdɪəplæzəm] *s. biol.* Idio-'plasma *n*, Erbmasse *f*.

id·i·o·syn·cra·sy [ˌɪdɪə'sɪŋkrəsɪ] *s.* Idiosynkra'sie *f*: a) per'sönliche Eigenart *od.* Veranlagung *od.* Neigung, b) ♂ krankhafte Abneigung.

id·i·ot ['ɪdɪət] *s.* Idi'ot *m*: a) ♂ Schwachsinnige(r *m*) *f*), b) F Dummkopf *m*: **~ card** TV ,Neger' *m*; **id·i·ot·ic** [ˌɪdɪ'ɒtɪk] *adj.* (□ **~ally**) idi'otisch: a) F dumm, blödsinnig, b) ♂ geistesschwach, schwachsinnig.

i·dle ['aɪdl] **I** *adj.* (□ **idly**) **1.** untätig, müßig: **the ~ rich** die reichen Müßiggänger; **2.** unbeschäftigt, arbeitslos; **3.** ⊕ a) außer Betrieb, stillstehend, b) im Leerlauf, Leerlauf...: **~ current** a) Leerlaufstrom *m*, b) Blindstrom *m*; **~ motion** Leergang *m*; **~ pulley** → **idler** 2 b; **~ wheel** → **idler** 2 a; **lie ~** stillliegen; **run ~** 9; **4.** ⚡ 'unproduk,tiv, brachliegend (*a.* ⚹), tot (*Kapital*); **~ capacity** ungenützte Kapazität; **~ time** Stillstandszeit *f*; **5.** ruhig, still, ungenutzt: **~ hours** Mußestunden; **6.** faul, träge: **~ fellow** Faulenzer *m*; **7.** a) nutz-, zweck-, sinnlos, vergeblich, b) leer (*Worte etc.*), c) müßig (*Mutmaßungen etc.*): **~ talk** leeres *od.* müßiges Gerede; **it would be ~ to** *inf.* es wäre müßig *od.* sinnlos zu *inf.*; **II** *v/i.* **8.** faulenzen: **~ about** herumtrödeln; **9.** ⊕ leer laufen, im Leerlauf sein; **III** *v/t.* **10.** *mst* **~ away** vertrödeln, verbummeln, müßig zubringen; **'i·dled** [-ld] *adj.* → **idle** 2; **'i·dle·ness** [-nɪs] *s.* **1.** Untätigkeit *f*, Muße *f*; **2.** Faulheit *f*, Müßiggang *m*; **3.** a) Leere *f*, Hohlheit *f*, b) Müßigkeit *f*, Nutz-, Zwecklosigkeit *f*, Vergeblichkeit *f*; **'i·dler** [-lə] *s.* **1.** Faulenzer(in), Müßiggänger(in); **2.** a) Zwischenrad *n*, b) Leerlaufrolle *f*; **'i·dling** [-lɪŋ] *s.* **1.** Nichtstun *n*, Müßiggang *m*; **2.** ⊕ Leerlauf *m*; **'i·dly** [-lɪ] *adv.* → **idle**.

i·dol ['aɪdl] *s.* I'dol *n*, Abgott *m* (*beide a.* fig.); Götze *m*, Götzenbild *n*: **make an ~ of** → **idolize**.

i·dol·a·ter [aɪ'dɒlətə] *s.* **1.** Götzendiener *m*; **2.** *fig.* Anbeter *m*, Verehrer *m*; **i'dol·a·tress** [-trɪs] *s.* Götzendienerin *f*; **i'dol·a·trous** [-trəs] *adj.* □ **1.** *fig.* abgöttisch; **2.** Götzen...; **i'dol·a·try** [-trɪ] *s.* **1.** Abgötte'rei *f*, Götzendienst

m; **2.** *fig.* Vergötterung *f*; **i·dol·i·za·tion** [ˌaɪdəlaɪ'zeɪʃn] *s.* **1.** Abgötte'rei *f*; **2.** *fig.* Vergötterung *f*; **i·dol·ize** ['aɪdəlaɪz] *v/t. fig.* abgöttisch verehren, vergöttern, anbeten.

i·dyl(l) ['ɪdɪl] *s.* **1.** I'dylle *f*, Hirtengedicht *n*; **2.** *fig.* I'dyll *n*; **i·dyl·lic** [aɪ'dɪlɪk] *adj.* (□ **~ally**) i'dyllisch.

if [ɪf] **I** *cj.* **1.** wenn, falls: **~ I were you** wenn ich Sie wäre, (ich) an Ihrer Stelle; **~ and when** *bsd.* ⚖ falls, im Falle (, dass); **~ any** wenn überhaupt einer (*od.* eine *od.* eines *od.* etwas), falls etwa *od.* je; **~ anything** a) wenn überhaupt etwas, b) wenn überhaupt (, *dann ist das Buch dicker etc.*); **~ not** wenn *od.* falls nicht; **~ so** wenn ja, *bsd.* in Formularen: *a.* zutreffendenfalls; **~ only to prove** und wäre es auch nur, um zu beweisen; **~ I know Jim** so wie ich Jim kenne; → **as if**; **2.** wenn auch: **he is nice ~ a bit silly**; **3.** ob: **try ~ you can do it!**; **I don't know ~ he will agree**; **4.** *ausrufend:* **~ I had only known!** hätte ich (das) nur gewusst!; **II** *s.* **5.** Wenn *n*: **without ~s or buts** ohne Wenn u. Aber.

ig·loo, a. i·glu ['ɪɡluː] *s.* Iglu *m*.

ig·ne·ous ['ɪɡnɪəs] *adj.* glühend: **~ rock** Erstarrungsgestein *n*, magmatisches Gestein.

ig·nis fat·u·us [ˌɪɡnɪs'fætjʊəs] (*Lat.*) *s.* **1.** Irrlicht *n*; **2.** *fig.* Trugbild *n*.

ig·nite [ɪɡ'naɪt] **I** *v/t.* **1.** an-, entzünden; **2.** ⚡, *mot.* zünden; **II** *v/i.* **3.** sich entzünden, Feuer fangen; **4.** ⚡, *mot.* zünden; **ig'nit·er** [-tə] *s.* Zündvorrichtung *f*, Zünder *m*.

ig·ni·tion [ɪɡ'nɪʃn] *s.* **1.** An-, Entzünden *n*; **2.** ⚡, *mot.* Zündung *f*; **3.** 🜨 Erhitzung *f*; **~ charge** *s.* ⊕ Zündladung *f*; **~ coil** *s.* ⚡ Zündspule *f*; **~ de·lay** *s.* ⊕ Zündverzögerung *f*; **~ key** *s. mot.* Zündschlüssel *m*; **~ lock** *s.* ⊕ Zündschloss *n*; **~ point** *s.* Zünd-, Flammpunkt *m*; **~ spark** *s.* ⚡ Zündfunke *m*; **~ tim·ing** *s.* Zündeinstellung *f*; **~ tube** *s.* 🜨 Glührohr *n*.

ig·no·ble [ɪɡ'nəʊbl] *adj.* □ **1.** gemein, unedel, niedrig; **2.** schandvoll, schändlich; **3.** von niedriger Geburt.

ig·no·min·i·ous [ˌɪɡnəʊ'mɪnɪəs] *adj.* □ schändlich, schimpflich; **ig·no·min·y** ['ɪɡnəmɪnɪ] *s.* **1.** Schmach *f*, Schande *f*; **2.** Schändlichkeit *f*.

ig·no·ra·mus [ˌɪɡnə'reɪməs] *pl.* **-mus·es** *s.* Igno'rant(in), Nichtswisser(in).

ig·no·rance ['ɪɡnərəns] *s.* Unwissenheit *f*: a) Unkenntnis *f* (*of gen.*), b) *contp.* Igno'ranz *f*, Beschränktheit *f*: **~ of the law is no excuse** Unkenntnis schützt vor Strafe nicht; **ig·no·rant** [-nt] *adj.* □ **1.** unkundig, nicht kennend *od.* wissend: **be ~ of et.** nicht wissen *od.* kennen, nichts wissen von; **2.** unwissend, ungebildet; **ig·no·rant·ly** [-ntlɪ] *adv.* unwissentlich; **ig·nore** [ɪɡ'nɔː] *v/t.* **1.** ignorieren, nicht beachten *od.* berücksichtigen, keine No'tiz nehmen von; **2.** ⚖ *Am. Klage* verwerfen, abweisen.

i·gua·na [ɪ'ɡwɑːnə] *s. zo.* Legu'an *m*.

i·kon ['aɪkɒn] → **icon**.

il·e·um ['ɪlɪəm] *s. anat.* Ileum *n*, Krummdarm *m*; **il·e·us** [-əs] *s.* ♂ Darmverschluss *m*.

i·lex ['aɪleks] *s.* ♣ **1.** Stechpalme *f*; **2.** Stecheiche *f*.

il·i·ac ['ɪlɪæk] *adj.* Darmbein...

il·i·ad ['ɪlɪəd] *s.* Ilias *f*, Ili'ade *f*: **an ~ of woes** *fig.* e-e endlose Leidensgeschichte.

il·i·um ['ɪlɪəm] *pl.* **'il·i·a** [-ə] *s. anat.* a) Darmbein *n*, b) Hüfte *f*.

ilk [ɪlk] *s.* **1. of that ~** *Scot.* gleichnamigen Ortes: **Kinloch of that ~ = Kinloch of Kinloch**; **2.** Art *f*, Sorte *f*: **people of that ~** solche Leute.

ill [ɪl] **I** *adj.* **1.** (*nur pred.*) krank: **be taken ~, fall ~ od. take ~** erkranken (*with, of* an *dat.*); **be ~ with a cold** e-e Erkältung haben; **~ with fear** krank vor Angst; **2.** (*moralisch*) schlecht, böse, übel; → **fame** 1; **3.** böse, feindlich: **~ blood** böses Blut; **with an ~ grace** widerwillig, ungern; **~ humo(u)r** *od.* **temper** üble Laune; **~ treatment** schlechte Behandlung, Misshandlung *f*; **~ will** Feindschaft *f*, Groll *m*; **I bear him no ~ will** ich trage ihm nichts nach; → **feeling** 2; **4.** nachteilig; ungünstig, schlecht, übel; **~ effect** üble Folge *od.* Wirkung; **it's an ~ wind (that blows nobody good)** et. Gutes ist an allem; → **health** 2, **luck** 1, **omen** I, **weed** 1; **5.** schlecht, unbefriedigend, fehlerhaft: **~ breeding** a) schlechte Erziehung, b) Ungezogenheit *f*; **~ management** Misswirtschaft *f*; **~ success** Misserfolg *m*, Fehlschlag *m*; **II** *adv.* **6.** schlecht, übel: **~ at ease** unruhig, unbehaglich, verlegen; **7.** böse, feindlich; **take s.th. ~** et. übel nehmen; **speak (think) ~ of s.o.** schlecht von j-m sprechen (denken); **8.** ungünstig: **it went ~ with him** es erging ihm schlecht; **it ~ becomes you** es steht dir schlecht an; **9.** ungenügend, schlecht: **~-equipped**; **10.** schwerlich, kaum: **I can ~ afford it** ich kann es mir kaum leisten; **III** *s.* **11.** Übel *n*, 'Missgeschick *n*, Ungemach *n*; **12.** *a. fig.* Leiden *n*, Krankheit *f*; **13.** das Böse, Übel *n*.

I'll [aɪl] **F** *für* **I shall, I will**.

,ill-'ad·vised *adj.* □ **1.** schlecht beraten; **2.** unbesonnen, unklug; **,~-af'fect·ed** → **ill-disposed**; **,~-as'sort·ed** *adj.* schlecht zs.-passend, zs.-gewürfelt; **,~--'bred** *adj.* schlecht erzogen, ungezogen; **,~-con'sid·ered** *adj.* unüberlegt, unbedacht, unklug; **,~-dis'posed** *adj.* übel gesinnt (**towards** *dat.*).

il·le·gal [ɪ'liːɡl] *adj.* □ 'ille,gal, ungesetzlich, gesetzwidrig, 'widerrechtlich, unerlaubt, verboten; **il·le·gal·i·ty** [ˌɪlɪ'ɡælətɪ] *s.* Gesetzwidrigkeit *f*: a) Ungesetzlichkeit *f*, Illegali'tät *f*, b) gesetzwidrige Handlung.

il·leg·i·bil·i·ty [ɪˌledʒɪ'bɪlətɪ] *s.* Unleserlichkeit *f*; **il·leg·i·ble** [ɪ'ledʒəbl] *adj.* □ unleserlich.

il·le·git·i·ma·cy [ˌɪlɪ'dʒɪtɪməsɪ] *s.* **1.** Unrechtmäßigkeit *f*; **2.** uneheliche Geburt (*an pl.*); **,il·le'git·i·mate** [-mət] *adj.* □ **1.** unrechtmäßig, rechtswidrig; **2.** außer-, unehelich; **3.** 'inkor,rekt, falsch; **4.** unzulässig, illegi'tim; **5.** unlogisch.

,ill-'fat·ed *adj.* unselig: a) unglücklich, Unglücks..., b) verhängnisvoll, unglückselig; **,~-'fa·vo(u)red** *adj.* □ unschön; **,~-'found·ed** *adj.* unbegründet, fragwürdig; **,~-'got·ten** *adj.* unrechtmäßig (erworben); **,~-'hu·mo(u)red** *adj.* übel gelaunt.

il·lib·er·al [ɪ'lɪbərəl] *adj.* □ **1.** knauserig; **2.** engherzig, -stirnig; **3.** *pol.* 'illibe,ral; **il·lib·er·al·ism** [-rəlɪzəm] *s. pol.* 'illibe,raler Standpunkt; **il·lib·er·al·i·ty** [ɪ,lɪbə'rælətɪ] *s.* **1.** Knause'rei *f*; **2.** Engherzigkeit *f*.

il·lic·it [ɪ'lɪsɪt] *adj.* □ = **illegal**: **~ trade** Schleich-, Schwarzhandel *m*; **~ work** Schwarzarbeit *f*.

il·lim·it·a·ble [ɪ'lɪmɪtəbl] *adj.* □ grenzenlos, unbegrenzt, unendlich weit.

il·lit·er·a·cy [ɪ'lɪtərəsɪ] *s.* **1.** Unbildung *f*; **2.** Analpha'betentum *n*; **il'lit·er·ate**

[-rət] **I** *adj.* **1.** ungebildet, unwissend; **2.** analpha'betisch, des Lesens u. Schreibens unkundig: *he is ~* er ist Analphabet; **3.** primi'tiv, unkultiviert: *~ style*; **4.** fehlerhaft, voller Fehler; **II** *s.* **5.** Ungebildete(r *m*) *f*; **6.** Analpha'bet(in).

‚ill·|·'judged *adj.* unbedacht, unklug; **‚~-'man·nered** *adj.* ungehobelt, ungezogen, mit schlechten 'Umgangsformen; **‚~-'matched** *adj.* schlecht zs.-passend; **‚~-'na·tured** *adj.* □ **1.** unfreundlich, boshaft; **2.** verärgert.

ill·ness ['ılnıs] *s.* Krankheit *f*.

il·log·i·cal [ı'lɒdʒıkl] *adj.* □ unlogisch; **il·log·i·cal·i·ty** [‚ılɒdʒı'kælətı] *s.* Unlogik *f*.

‚ill·|·'o·mened → *ill-fated*; **‚~-'starred** *adj.* unglücklich, unselig, vom Unglück verfolgt, unter e-m ungünstigen Stern (stehend); **‚~-'tem·pered** *adj.* schlecht gelaunt, übellaunig, mürrisch; **‚~-'timed** *adj.* ungelegen, unpassend, 'inoppor‚tun; zeitlich schlecht gewählt; **‚~-'treat** *v/t.* miss'handeln; schlecht behandeln.

il·lu·mi·nant [ı'ljuːmınənt] **I** *adj.* (er-) leuchtend, aufhellend; **II** *s.* Beleuchtungskörper *m*.

il·lu·mi·nate [ı'ljuːmıneıt] **I** *v/t.* **1.** be-, erleuchten, erhellen; **2.** illuminieren, festlich beleuchten; **3.** *fig.* a) erläutern, erhellen, erklären, aufhellen, b) *j*-n erleuchten; **4.** *Bücher etc.* ausmalen, illuminieren; **5.** *fig.* Glanz verleihen (*dat.*); **II** *v/i.* **6.** sich erhellen; **il·lu·mi·nat·ed** [-tıd] *adj.* beleuchtet, leuchtend, Leucht..., Licht...: *~ advertising* Leuchtreklame *f*; **il·lu·mi·nat·ing** [-tıŋ] *adj.* **1.** leuchtend, Leucht..., Beleuchtungs...: *~ gas* Leuchtgas *n*; *~ power* Leuchtkraft *f*; **2.** *fig.* aufschlussreich, erhellend; **il·lu·mi·na·tion** [ı‚ljuːmı'neıʃn] *s.* **1.** Be-, Erleuchtung *f*; **2.** *oft pl.* Illuminati'on *f*, Festbeleuchtung *f*; **3.** *fig.* a) Erläuterung *f*, Erhellung *f*, b) Erleuchtung *f*; **4.** *a. fig.* Licht *n* u. Glanz *m*; **5.** Illuminati'on *f*, Kolorierung *f*, Verzierung *f* (*von Büchern etc.*); **il·lu·mi·na·tive** [-nətıv] → *illuminating*.

il·lu·mine [ı'ljuːmın] *v/t.* → *illuminate* 1–3.

‚ill·'use [-'juːz] → *ill-treat*.

il·lu·sion [ı'luːʒn] *s.* Illusi'on *f*: a) (Sinnes)Täuschung *f*, → *optical*, b) Wahn *m*, Einbildung *f*, falsche Vorstellung, trügerische Hoffnung, c) Trugbild *n*, d) Blendwerk *n*: *be under an ~* e-r Täuschung unterliegen, sich Illusionen machen; *be under the ~ that* sich einbilden, dass; **il·lu·sion·ism** [-ʒnızəm] *s. bsd. phls.* Illusio'nismus *m*; **il·lu·sion·ist** [-ʒnıst] *s.* Illusio'nist *m* (*a. phls.*): a) Schwärmer(in), Träumer(in), b) Zauberkünstler *m*.

il·lu·sive [ı'luːsıv] *adj.* □ illu'sorisch, trügerisch; **il·lu·sive·ness** [-nıs] *s.* **1.** das Illu'sorische, Schein *m*; **2.** Täuschung *f*; **il·lu·so·ry** [-sərı] *adj.* □ → *illusive*.

il·lus·trate ['ıləstreıt] *v/t.* **1.** erläutern, erklären, veranschaulichen; **2.** illustrieren, bebildern; **il·lus·tra·tion** [‚ılə'streıʃn] *s.* Illustrati'on *f*: a) Erläuterung *f*, Erklärung *f*, Veranschaulichung *f*: *in ~ of* zur Veranschaulichung (*gen.*), b) Beispiel *n*, c) Bebildern *n*, Illustrieren *n*, d) Abbildung *f*, Bild *n*; **'il·lus·tra·tive** [-rətıv] *adj.* □ erläuternd, veranschaulichend, Anschauungs..., Beispiel...: *be ~ of* → *illustrate* 1; **'il·lus·tra·tor** [-tə] *s. allg.* Illu'strator *m*.

il·lus·tri·ous [ı'lʌstrıəs] *adj.* □ il'luster, berühmt, erhaben, erlaucht, glänzend.

I'm [aım] F *für I am*.

im·age ['ımıdʒ] *s.* **1.** Bild(nis) *n*; **2.** a) Standbild *n*, Bildsäule *f*, b) Heiligenbild *n*, c) Götzenbild *n*: *~ worship* Bilderanbetung *f*, *fig.* Götzendienst *m*; → *graven*; **3.** A, *opt.*, *phys.* Bild *n*: *~ converter tube* TV Bildwandlerröhre *f*; **4.** Ab-, Ebenbild *n*: *the (very) ~ of his father* ganz der Vater; **5.** bildlicher Ausdruck, Vergleich *m*, Me'tapher *f*: *speak in ~s* in Bildern reden; **6.** a) Vorstellung *f*, I'dee *f*, (geistiges) Bild, b) Image *n* (*Persönlichkeitsbild*): *the ~ of a politician*; *~ building* Imagepflege *f*; **7.** Verkörperung *f*; **'im·age·ry** [-dʒərı] *s.* **1.** Bilder *pl.*, Bildwerk(e *pl.*) *n*; **2.** Bilder(sprache *f*) *pl.*, Meta'phorik *f*; **3.** geistige Bilder *pl.*, Vorstellungen *pl.*

im·ag·i·na·ble [ı'mædʒınəbl] *adj.* □ vorstellbar, erdenklich, denkbar: *the finest weather ~* das denkbar schönste Wetter; **im·ag·i·nar·y** [-dʒınərı] *adj.* □ **1.** imagi'när (*a. A*), nur in der Vorstellung vor'handen, eingebildet, (nur) gedacht, Schein..., Fantasie...; **2.** (frei) erfunden, imagi'när; **3.** ✝ fingiert.

im·ag·i·na·tion [ı‚mædʒı'neıʃn] *s.* **1.** Fanta'sie *f*, Vorstellungs-, Einbildungskraft *f*, Einfallsreichtum *m*: *a man of ~* ein fantasievoller *od.* ideenreicher Mann; *he has no ~* er ist fantasielos; *use your ~!* lass dir was einfallen!; **2.** Einfälle *pl.*, I'deenreichtum *m*; **3.** Vorstellung *f*, Einbildung *f*: *in (my etc.) ~* in der Vorstellung, im Geiste; *pure ~* reine Einbildung; **im·ag·i·na·tive** [ı'mædʒınətıv] *adj.* □ **1.** fanta'siereich, erfinderisch, einfallsreich: *~ faculty* → *imagination* 1; **2.** fan'tastisch, fanta'sievoll: *~ story*; **3.** *contp.* ‚erdichtet‘; **im·ag·i·na·tive·ness** [ı'mædʒmətıvnıs] → *imagination* 1; **im·ag·ine** [ı'mædʒın] **I** *v/t.* **1.** sich *j*-n *od. et.* vorstellen *od.* denken: *I ~ him as a tall man*; *you can't ~ my joy*; *you can't ~ how ...* du kannst dir nicht vorstellen *od.* du machst dir kein Bild, wie ...; **2.** sich *et.* (*Unwirkliches*) einbilden: *you are imagining things!* du bildest dir das (alles) nur ein!; **3.** F glauben, denken, sich einbilden: *don't ~ that I am satisfied*; *~ to be* halten für; **II** *v/i.* **4.** sich vorstellen *od.* denken: *just ~!* F stell dir vor!, denk (dir) nur!

i·ma·go [ı'meıgəʊ] *pl.* -goes *od.* i·mag·i·nes** [ı'meıdʒınıːz] *s.* **1.** *zo.* voll entwickeltes Insekt; **2.** *psych.* I'mago *n*.

im·bal·ance [‚ım'bæləns] *s.* **1.** Unausgewogenheit *f*, Unausgeglichenheit *f*; **2.** *bsd. ✿* gestörtes Gleichgewicht (*im Körperhaushalt etc.*); **3.** *bsd. pol.* Ungleichgewicht *n*.

im·be·cile ['ımbısıl] **I** *adj.* □ **1.** ✿ geistesschwach; **2.** *contp.* dumm, idi'otisch; **II** *s.* **3.** ✿ Schwachsinnige(r *m*) *f*; **4.** *contp.* Idi'ot *m*, ‚Blödmann‘ *m*; **im·be·cil·i·ty** [‚ımbı'sılətı] *s.* **1.** ✿ Schwachsinn *m*; **2.** *contp.* Idio'tie *f*, Blödheit *f*.

im·bibe [ım'baıb] **I** *v/t.* **1.** *humor.* trinken; **2.** *fig.* Ideen etc. in sich aufnehmen, aufsaugen; **II** *v/i.* **3.** *humor.* trinken, bechern.

im·bro·glio [ım'brəʊlıəʊ] *pl.* -glios *s.* **1.** Verwicklung *f*, Verwirrung *f*, Komplikati'on *f*, verzwickte Lage; **2.** a) ernstes 'Missverständnis, b) heftige Ausein'andersetzung.

im·brue [ım'bruː] *v/t. mst fig.* (*with*, *in*) baden (in *dat.*), tränken, *a.* beflecken (mit).

im·bue [ım'bjuː] *v/t. fig.* erfüllen (*with* mit): *~d with* erfüllt *od.* durchdrungen von.

im·i·ta·ble ['ımıtəbl] *adj.* nachahmbar; **im·i·tate** ['ımıteıt] *v/t.* **1.** *j*-n, *j*-s Stimme, *Benehmen etc. od. et.* nachahmen, -machen, imitieren; **2.** *et.* imitieren, nachmachen, kopieren, *a.* fälschen; **3.** ähneln (*dat.*); **'im·i·tat·ed** [-teıtıd] *adj.* imitiert, unecht, künstlich; **im·i·ta·tion** [‚ımı'teıʃn] **I** *s.* **1.** Nachahmung *f*, Imitati'on *f*: *do an ~ of* → *imitate* 1; **2.** Nachbildung *f*, -ahmung *f*, das Nachgeahmte, Imitati'on *f*, Ko'pie *f*; **3.** Fälschung *f*; **II** *adj.* **4.** unecht, künstlich, Kunst..., Imitations...: *~ leather* Kunstleder *n*; **im·i·ta·tive** [-tətıv] *adj.* □ **1.** nachahmend, -bildend; auf Nachahmung *fremder Vorbilder* beruhend: *be ~ of* → *imitate* 1; **2.** nachgemacht, -geahmt (*of*); **3.** *ling.* lautmalend: *an ~ word*; **'im·i·ta·tor** [-teıtə] *s.* Nachahmer *m*, Imi'tator *m*.

im·mac·u·late [ı'mækjʊlıt] *adj.* □ **1.** *fig.* unbefleckt, makellos, rein: *2 Conception* R.C. Unbefleckte Empfängnis; **2.** untadelig, tadellos, einwandfrei; **3.** fleckenlos, sauber.

im·ma·nence ['ımənəns], **'im·ma·nen·cy** [-sı] *s. phls.*, *eccl.* Imma'nenz *f*, Innewohnen *n*; **'im·ma·nent** [-nt] *adj.* imma'nent, innewohnend.

im·ma·te·ri·al [‚ımə'tıərıəl] *adj.* **1.** unkörperlich, unstofflich; **2.** unwesentlich, (*a. ɬ*) unerheblich, belanglos; **‚im·ma·te·ri·al·ism** [-lızəm] *s.* Immateri'alismus *m*.

im·ma·ture [‚ımə'tjʊə] *adj.* □ unreif, unentwickelt (*a. fig.*); **‚im·ma·tu·ri·ty** [-'tjʊərətı] *s.* Unreife *f*.

im·meas·ur·a·ble [ı'meʒərəbl] *adj.* □ unermesslich, grenzenlos, riesig.

im·me·di·a·cy [ı'miːdjəsı] *s.* **1.** Unmittelbarkeit *f*, Di'rektheit *f*; **2.** Unverzüglichkeit *f*; **im·me·di·ate** [ı'miːdjət] *adj.* □ **1.** *Raum:* unmittelbar, nächst(gelegen): *~ contact* unmittelbare Berührung; *~ vicinity* nächste Umgebung; **2.** *Zeit:* unverzüglich, so'fortig, 'umgehend: *~ answer*, *~ steps* Sofortmaßnahmen; *~ objective* Nahziel *n*; *~ future* nächste Zukunft; **3.** augenblicklich, derzeitig: *~ plans*; **4.** di'rekt, unmittelbar; **5.** nächst (*Verwandtschaft*): *my ~ family* m-e nächsten Angehörigen; **im·me·di·ate·ly** [-jətlı] **I** *adv.* **1.** unmittelbar, di'rekt; **2.** so'fort, 'umgehend, unverzüglich, gleich, unmittelbar; **II** *cj.* **3.** *bsd. Brit.* so'bald (als).

im·me·mo·ri·al [‚ımı'mɔːrıəl] *adj.* □ un(vor)denklich, uralt: *from time ~* seit un(vor)denklichen Zeiten.

im·mense [ı'mens] *adj.* □ **1.** unermesslich, ungeheuer, riesig, im'mens; **2.** F gewaltig, e'norm, ‚riesig‘: *enjoy o.s. ~ly*; **im'men·si·ty** [-sətı] *s.* Unermesslichkeit *f*.

im·merse [ı'mɜːs] *v/t.* **1.** (ein)tauchen (*a. ☉*), versenken; **2.** *fig.* (*o.s.* sich) vertiefen *od.* versenken (*in* in *acc.*); **3.** *fig.* verwickeln, verstricken (*in* in *acc.*); **im'mersed** [-st] *adj. fig.* (*in*) versunken, vertieft (in *acc.*); **im·mer·sion** [ı'mɜːʃn] *s.* **1.** Ein-, 'Untertauchen *n*: *~ heater* a) Tauchsieder *m*, b) Boiler *m*; **2.** *fig.* Versunkenheit *f*, Vertieftsein *n*; **3.** *eccl.* Immersi'onstaufe *f*; **4.** *ast.* Immersi'on *f*.

im·mi·grant ['ımıgrənt] **I** *s.* Einwanderer *m*, Einwanderin *f*, Immi'grant(in); **II** *adj.* a) einwandernd, b) ausländisch, Fremd...: *~ workers*; **'im·mi·grate** *v/i.*

[-greɪt] **I** v/i. einwandern, immi'grieren (*into, to* in *acc.*, nach); **II** v/t. ansiedeln (*into* in *dat.*); **im·mi·gra·tion** [ˌɪmɪ-'greɪʃn] s. Einwanderung f, Immigrati'on f: ~ *officer* Beamte(r) m der Einwanderungsbehörde.

im·mi·nence ['ɪmɪnəns] s. **1.** nahes Bevorstehen; **2.** drohende Gefahr, Drohen n; **'im·mi·nent** [-nt] adj. ☐ nahe bevorstehend, a. drohend.

im·mis·ci·ble [ɪ'mɪsəbl] adj. ☐ unvermischbar.

im·mo·bile [ɪ'məʊbaɪl] adj. unbeweglich: a) bewegungslos, b) starr, fest; **im·mo·bil·i·ty** [ˌɪməʊ'bɪlətɪ] s. Unbeweglichkeit f; **im·mo·bi·li·za·tion** [ɪˌməʊbɪlaɪ'zeɪʃn] s. **1.** Unbeweglichmachen n; ✚ Ruhigstellung f, Immobilisierung f; **2.** ✝ a) Einziehung f (*von Münzen*), b) Festlegung f (*von Kapital*); **im·'mo·bi·lize** [-bɪlaɪz] v/t. **1.** unbeweglich machen; ✗ ruhig stellen; ✗ außer Gefecht setzen; ~*d* bewegungsunfähig (a. *Auto etc.*); **2.** ✝ a) *Münzen* aus dem Verkehr ziehen, b) *Kapital* festlegen; **im·'mo·bi·liz·er** [-bɪlaɪzə] s. mot. Wegfahrsperre f.

im·mod·er·ate [ɪ'mɒdərət] adj. ☐ unmäßig, maßlos, über'trieben, -'zogen.

im·mod·est [ɪ'mɒdɪst] adj. ☐ **1.** unbescheiden, anmaßend; **2.** schamlos, unanständig; **im'mod·es·ty** [-tɪ] s. **1.** Unbescheidenheit f, Frechheit f; **2.** Unanständigkeit f.

im·mo·late ['ɪməʊleɪt] v/t. **1.** opfern, zum Opfer bringen (a. fig.); **2.** schlachten (a. fig.); **im·mo·la·tion** [ˌɪməʊ-'leɪʃn] s. a. fig. Opferung f, Opfer n.

im·mor·al [ɪ'mɒrəl] adj. ☐ **1.** 'unmo,ralisch, unsittlich; **2.** ✝ sittenwidrig, unsittlich; **im·mo·ral·i·ty** [ˌɪmə'rælətɪ] s. 'Unmo,ral f, Sittenlosigkeit f, Unsittlichkeit f (a. *Handlung*).

im·mor·tal [ɪ'mɔːtl] **I** adj. ☐ **1.** unsterblich (a. fig.); **2.** ewig, unvergänglich; **II** s. **3.** Unsterbliche(r m) f (a. fig.); **im·mor·tal·i·ty** [ˌɪmɔː'tælətɪ] s. **1.** Unsterblichkeit f (a. fig.); **2.** Unvergänglichkeit f; **im·'mor·tal·ize** [-təlaɪz] v/t. unsterblich machen, verewigen.

im·mor·telle [ˌɪmɔː'tel] s. ✿ Immor'telle f, Strohblume f.

im·mov·a·bil·i·ty [ɪˌmuːvə'bɪlətɪ] s. **1.** Unbeweglichkeit f; **2.** fig. Unerschütterlichkeit f; **im·mov·a·ble** [ɪ'muːvəbl] **I** adj. ☐ **1.** unbeweglich: a) ortsfest: ~ *property* → 4, b) unbewegt, bewegungslos; **2.** zeitlich unveränderlich: ~ *feast* unbeweglicher Feiertag; **3.** fig. fest, unerschütterlich, unnachgiebig; **II** s. **4.** pl. ✝ unbewegliches Eigentum, Immo'bilien pl., Liegenschaften pl.

im·mune [ɪ'mjuːn] **I** adj. **1.** ✚ u. fig. (*from, against, to*) im'mun (gegen), unempfänglich (für); **2.** (*from, against, to*) geschützt, gefeit (gegen), frei (von); **II** s. **3.** im'mune Per'son; **im·mune de·fi·cien·cy syn·drome** s. ✚ Im'munschwäche,krankheit f; **im·mune sys·tem** s. ✚ Im'munsys,tem n; **im·mu·ni·ty** [-nətɪ] s. **1.** allg. Immuni'tät f: a) ✚ u. fig. Unempfänglichkeit f, b) ✝ Freiheit f, Befreiung f (*from* von *Strafe, Steuer*); **2.** ✝ Privi'leg n, Sonderrecht n; **3.** Freisein n (*from* von); **im·mu·ni·za·tion** [ˌɪmjuːnaɪ'zeɪʃn] s. ✚ Immunisierung f; **im·mu·nize** ['ɪmjuːnaɪz] v/t. ✚ immunisieren; im'mun machen (*against* gegen), schützen (vor *dat.*); **im·mu·no·gen** [ɪ'mjuːnəʊdʒen] s. ✚ Anti'gen n; **im·mu·nol·o·gy** [ˌɪmjuː'nɒlədʒɪ] s. ✚ Immuni'tätsforschung f, -lehre f.

im·mure [ɪ'mjʊə] v/t. **1.** einsperren, -schließen, -kerkern: ~ *o.s.* sich abschließen; **2.** einmauern.

im·mu·ta·bil·i·ty [ɪˌmjuːtə'bɪlətɪ] s. a. biol. Unveränderlichkeit f; **im·mu·ta·ble** [ɪ'mjuːtəbl] adj. ☐ unveränderlich, unwandelbar.

imp [ɪmp] s. **1.** Teufelchen n, Kobold m; **2.** humor. Schlingel m, Racker m.

im·pact I s. ['ɪmpækt] **1.** An-, Zs.-prall m, Auftreffen n; **2.** bsd. ✗ Auf-, Einschlag m: ~ *fuse* Aufschlagzünder m; **3.** ⊙, phys. a) Stoß m, Schlag m, b) Wucht f: ~ *extrusion* Schlagstrangpressen n; ~ *strength* ⊙ (Kerb)Schlagfestigkeit f; **4.** fig. a) (heftige) (Ein)Wirkung, Auswirkungen pl., (starker) Einfluss (*on* auf *acc.*), b) (starker) Eindruck (*on* auf *acc.*), c) Wucht f, Gewalt f, d) (*on*) Belastung f (*gen.*), Druck m (auf *acc.*): *make an* ~ (*on*) ,einschlagen' od. e-n starken Eindruck hinterlassen (bei), sich mächtig auswirken (auf *acc.*); **II** v/t. [ɪm'pækt] **5.** zs.-pressen; a. ✚ einkeilen, -klemmen.

im·pair [ɪm'peə] v/t. **1.** verschlechtern; **2.** beeinträchtigen: a) nachteilig beeinflussen, schwächen, b) (ver)mindern, schmälern; **im'pair·ment** [-mənt] s. Verschlechterung f, Beeinträchtigung f, Verminderung f, Schädigung f, Schmälerung f.

im·pale [ɪm'peɪl] v/t. **1.** hist. pfählen; **2.** aufspießen, durch'bohren; **3.** her. zwei Wappen durch e-n senkrechten Pfahl verbinden.

im·pal·pa·ble [ɪm'pælpəbl] adj. ☐ **1.** unfühlbar; **2.** äußerst fein; **3.** kaum (er)fassbar, nicht greifbar.

im·pan·el [ɪm'pænl] → *empanel*.

im·par·i·syl·lab·ic [ˌɪmˌpærɪsɪ'læbɪk] adj. u. s. ling. ungleichsilbig(es Wort).

im·par·i·ty [ɪm'pærətɪ] s. Ungleichheit f.

im·part [ɪm'pɑːt] v/t. **1.** (*to dat.*) geben: a) gewähren, zukommen lassen, b) e-e *Eigenschaft* geben; **2.** mitteilen: a) kundtun (*to dat.*): ~ *news*, b) vermitteln (*to dat.*): ~ *knowledge*, c) a. phys. übertragen (*to* auf *acc.*): *a motion*.

im·par·tial [ɪm'pɑːʃl] adj. ☐ 'unpar,teiisch, unvoreingenommen, unbefangen; **im·par·ti·al·i·ty** ['ɪmˌpɑːʃɪ'ælətɪ] s. 'Unpar,teilichkeit f, Unvoreingenommenheit f.

im·pass·a·ble [ɪm'pɑːsəbl] adj. ☐ unpassierbar.

im·passe [æm'pɑːs] (Fr.) s. Sackgasse f, fig. a. ausweglose Situati'on: *reach an* ~ fig. in e-e Sackgasse geraten, e-n toten Punkt erreichen; *break the* ~ aus der Sackgasse herauskommen.

im·pas·si·ble [ɪm'pæsɪbl] adj. ☐ (*to*) gefühllos (gegen), unempfindlich (für).

im·pas·sioned [ɪm'pæʃnd] adj. leidenschaftlich.

im·pas·sive [ɪm'pæsɪv] adj. ☐ **1.** teilnahms-, leidenschaftslos, ungerührt; **2.** gelassen; **3.** unbewegt: ~ *face*.

im·paste [ɪm'peɪst] v/t. **1.** zu e-m Teig kneten; **2.** paint. Farben dick auftragen, pa'stos malen; **im·pas·to** [ɪm'pæstəʊ] s. paint. Im'pasto n.

im·pa·tience [ɪm'peɪʃns] s. **1.** Ungeduld f; **2.** (*of*) Unduldsamkeit f, Abneigung f (gegen['über]), Unwille m (über *acc.*); **im·pa·tient** [-nt] adj. ☐ **1.** ungeduldig; **2.** (*of*) unduldsam (gegen), ungehalten (über *acc.*), unzufrieden (mit): *be* ~ *of* nicht (v)ertragen können (*acc.*), nichts übrig haben für; **3.** begierig (*for* nach, *to do* zu tun): *be* ~ *for et.* nicht erwarten können; *be* ~ *to do it* darauf brennen, es zu tun.

im·peach [ɪm'piːtʃ] v/t. **1.** j-n anklagen, beschuldigen (*of, with gen.*); **2.** ✝ Beamten etc. (wegen e-s Amtsvergehens) anklagen; **3.** anzweifeln, anfechten, infrage stellen: ~ *a witness* die Glaubwürdigkeit e-s Zeugen anzweifeln; **4.** angreifen, her'absetzen, tadeln, bemängeln; **im'peach·a·ble** [-tʃəbl] adj. anklag-, anfecht-, bestreitbar; **im·'peach·ment** [-mənt] s. **1.** Anklage f, Beschuldigung f; **2.** (öffentliche) Anklage e-s Ministers etc. wegen Amtsmissbrauchs, Hochverrats etc.; **3.** Anfechtung f, Bestreitung f der Glaubwürdigkeit od. Gültigkeit; **4.** In'fragestellung f; **5.** Vorwurf m, Tadel m.

im·pec·ca·bil·i·ty [ɪmˌpekə'bɪlətɪ] s. **1.** Sündlosigkeit f; **2.** Fehler-, Tadellosigkeit f; **im·pec·ca·ble** [ɪm'pekəbl] adj. ☐ **1.** sünd(en)los, rein; **2.** tadellos, untadelig, einwandfrei.

im·pe·cu·ni·os·i·ty ['ɪmpɪˌkjuːnɪ'ɒsətɪ] s. Mittellosigkeit f, Armut f; **im·pe·cu·ni·ous** [ˌɪmpɪ'kjuːnjəs] adj. mittellos, arm.

im·ped·ance [ɪm'piːdəns] s. ⚡ Impe-'danz f, 'Schein,widerstand m.

im·pede [ɪm'piːd] v/t. **1.** j-n (be)hindern; **2.** et. erschweren, verhindern; **im·ped·i·ment** [ɪm'pedɪmənt] s. **1.** Be-, Verhinderung f; **2.** Hindernis n (*to* für), ✚ Behinderung f: ~ *in one's speech* Sprachfehler m; **3.** ✝ (bsd. Ehe)Hindernis n, Hinderungsgrund m; **im·ped·i·men·ta** [ɪmˌpedɪ'mentə] s. pl. **1.** ✗ Gepäck n, Tross m; **2.** fig. Last f, (hinderliches) Gepäck, j-s ,Siebensachen' pl.

im·pel [ɪm'pel] v/t. **1.** (an)treiben, vorwärts treiben, drängen; **2.** zwingen, nötigen: *I felt* ~*led* ich war dazu gezwungen od. veranlasst, ich fühlte mich genötigt; **im·'pel·lent** [-lənt] **I** adj. (an)treibend, Trieb...; **II** s. Triebkraft f, Antrieb m; **im·'pel·ler** [-lə] s. ⊙ a) Flügel-, Laufrad n, b) Kreisel m (*e-r Pumpe*), c) ⚓ Laderlaufrad n.

im·pend [ɪm'pend] v/i. **1.** hängen, schweben (*over* über *dat.*); **2.** fig. a) unmittelbar bevorstehen, b) (*over*) drohend schweben (über *dat.*), drohen (*dat.*); **im·'pend·ing** [-dɪŋ] adj. nahe bevorstehend, drohend.

im·pen·e·tra·bil·i·ty [ɪmˌpenɪtrə'bɪlətɪ] s. **1.** 'Undurch,dringlichkeit f; **2.** fig. Unerforschlichkeit f, Unergründlichkeit f; **im·pen·e·tra·ble** [ɪm'penɪtrəbl] adj. ☐ **1.** 'undurch,dringlich (*by* für); **2.** fig. unergründlich, unerforschlich; **3.** fig. (*to, by*) unempfänglich (für), unzugänglich (*dat.*).

im·pen·i·tence [ɪm'penɪtəns] s., **im·pen·i·ten·cy** [-sɪ] s. Unbußfertigkeit f, Verstocktheit f; **im·pen·i·tent** [-nt] adj. ☐ unbußfertig, verstockt, reuelos.

im·per·a·ti·val [ɪmˌperə'taɪvl] → *imperative* 3; **im·per·a·tive** [ɪm'perətɪv] **I** adj. ☐ **1.** befehlend, gebieterisch, herrisch; **2.** 'unum,gänglich, dringend (nötig), unbedingt erforderlich; **3.** ling. impera'tivisch, Imperativ..., Befehls...: ~ *mood* → 5; **II** s. **4.** ling. Imperativ m, Gebot n; **5.** ling. Imperativ m, Befehlsform f.

im·per·cep·ti·bil·i·ty ['ɪmpəˌseptə'bɪlətɪ] s. Unwahrnehmbarkeit f; Unmerklichkeit f; **im·per·cep·ti·ble** [ˌɪmpə'septəbl] adj. ☐ **1.** nicht wahrnehmbar, unbemerkbar, unsichtbar, unhörbar; **2.** unmerklich; **3.** verschwindend klein.

im·per·fect [ɪm'pɜːfɪkt] **I** adj. ☐ **1.** 'unvoll,ständig, 'unvoll,endet; **2.** 'unvoll-,kommen (a. ✿, ♪): ~ *rhyme* unreiner

Reim; **3.** mangel-, fehlerhaft; **4.** *ling.* ~ **tense** → 5; **II** *s.* **5.** *ling.* Imperfekt *n*, 'unvoll,endete Vergangenheit; **im·per·fec·tion** [,ımpə'fekʃn] *s.* **1.** 'Unvoll- ,kommenheit *f*, Mangelhaftigkeit *f*; **2.** Mangel *m*, Fehler *m*.

im·per·fo·rate [ım'pɜːfərət] *adj.* **1.** *bsd. anat.* ohne Öffnung; **2.** nicht perforiert, ungezähnt (*Briefmarke*).

im·pe·ri·al [ım'pıərıəl] **I** *adj.* □ **1.** kaiserlich, Kaiser...; **2.** Reichs...; **3.** das brit. Weltreich betreffend, Empire...: ♀ **Conference** Empire-Konferenz *f*; **4.** *Brit.* gesetzlich (*Maße u. Gewichte*): ~ **gallon** (= *4,55 Liter*); **5.** großartig, herrlich; **II** *s.* **6.** Kaiserliche(r) *m* (*Soldat, Anhänger*); **7.** Knebelbart *m*; **8.** Imperi'al(pa,pier) *n* (*Format*: *brit.* 22×30 *in.*, *amer.* 23×31 *in.*); **im·pe·ri·al·ism** [-lızəm] *s. pol.* Imperia'lismus *m*; **im·pe·ri·al·ist** [-lıst] **I** *s.* **1.** *pol.* Imperia'list *m*; **2.** Kaiserliche(r) *m*; **II** *adj.* **3.** imperia'listisch; **4.** kaiserlich, kaisertreu; **im·pe·ri·al·is·tic** [ım,pıərıə'lıstık] *adj.* (□ ~**ally**) → *imperialist* 3, 4.

im·per·il [ım'perıl] *v/t.* gefährden.

im·pe·ri·ous [ım'pıərıəs] *adj.* □ **1.** herrisch, anmaßend, gebieterisch; **2.** dringend, zwingend; **im·pe·ri·ous·ness** [-nıs] *s.* **1.** Herrschsucht *f*, Anmaßung *f*, herrisches Wesen; **2.** Dringlichkeit *f*.

im·per·ish·a·ble [ım'perıʃəbl] *adj.* □ unvergänglich, ewig.

im·per·ma·nence [ım'pɜːmənəns], **im·'per·ma·nen·cy** [-sı] *s.* Unbeständigkeit *f*, Vergänglichkeit *f*; **im·'per·ma·nent** [-nt] *adj.* unbeständig, vor'übergehend, nicht von Dauer.

im·per·me·a·bil·i·ty [ım,pɜːmjə'bılətı] *s.* 'Un,durchlässigkeit *f*; **im·per·me·a·ble** [ım'pɜːmjəbl] *adj.* □ 'un,durchlässig (**to** für): ~ (**to water**) wasserdicht.

im·per·mis·si·ble [,ımpə'mısəbl] *adj.* unzulässig, unerlaubt.

im·per·son·al [ım'pɜːsnl] *adj. a. ling.* 'unper,sönlich: ~ **account** *✻* Sachkonto *n*; **im·per·son·al·i·ty** [ım,pɜːsə'nælətı] *s.* 'Unper,sönlichkeit *f*.

im·per·son·ate [ım'pɜːsəneıt] *v/t.* **1.** personifizieren, verkörpern; **2.** imitieren, nachahmen; **3.** sich ausgeben als *od.* für; **im·per·son·a·tion** [ım,pɜːsə-'neıʃn] *s.* **1.** Personifikati'on *f*, Verkörperung *f*; **2.** Nachahmung *f*, Imitati'on *f*; **3.** (betrügerisches *od.* scherzhaftes) Auftreten (**of** als); **im·'per·son·a·tor** [-tə] *s.* **1.** *thea.* a) Imi'tator *m*, b) Darsteller(in); **2.** Betrüger(in), Hochstapler(in).

im·per·ti·nence [ım'pɜːtınəns] *s.* Unverschämtheit *f*, Frechheit *f*; **im·'per·ti·nent** [-nt] *adj.* □ **1.** unverschämt, frech; **2.** *✻* nicht zur Sache gehörig, unerheblich; **3.** nebensächlich; **4.** unangebracht.

im·per·turb·a·bil·i·ty ['ımpə,tɜːbə'bılətı] *s.* Unerschütterlichkeit *f*, Gelassenheit *f*, Gleichmut *m*; **im·per·turb·a·ble** [,ımpə'tɜːbəbl] *adj.* □ unerschütterlich, gelassen.

im·per·vi·ous [ım'pɜːvjəs] *adj.* □ **1.** 'undurch,dringlich (**to** für), 'un,durchlässig: ~ **to rain** regendicht; **2.** *fig.* (**to**) unzugänglich (für *od. dat.*), unempfindlich (gegen); taub (gegen); **im·'per·vi·ous·ness** [-nıs] *s.* **1.** 'Undurch- ,dringlichkeit *f*, -lässigkeit *f*; **2.** *fig.* Unzugänglichkeit *f*, Unempfindlichkeit *f*.

im·pe·tig·i·nous [,ımpı'tıdʒınəs] *adj.* pustelartig; **im·pe·ti·go** [-'taıgəʊ] *s.* *✻* Impe'tigo *m*.

im·pet·u·os·i·ty [ım,petjʊ'ɒsətı] *s.* **1.** Heftigkeit *f*, Ungestüm *n*; **2.** impul'sive

Handlung; **im·pet·u·ous** [ım'petjʊəs] *adj.* □ heftig, ungestüm; hitzig, über- 'eilt, impul'siv; **im·pet·u·ous·ness** [ım'petjʊəsnıs] → *impetuosity*.

im·pe·tus ['ımpıtəs] *s.* **1.** *phys.* Stoß-, Triebkraft *f*, Schwung *m*; **2.** *fig.* Antrieb *m*, Anstoß *m*, Schwung *m*: **give a fresh ~ to** Auftrieb *od.* neuen Schwung verleihen (*dat.*).

im·pi·e·ty [ım'paıətı] *s.* **1.** Gottlosigkeit *f*; **2.** Pie'tätlosigkeit *f*.

im·pinge [ım'pındʒ] *v/i.* **1.** (**on, upon**) stoßen (an *acc.*, gegen), zs.-stoßen (mit), auftreffen (auf *acc.*); **2.** fallen, einwirken (**on** auf *acc.*): ~ **on the eye**, ~ **on the ear** ans Ohr dringen; **3.** (**on**) sich auswirken (auf *acc.*), beeinflussen (*acc.*); **4.** (**on**) ('widerrechtlich) eingreifen (in *acc.*) (verstoßen (gegen *Rechte etc.*).

im·pi·ous ['ımpıəs] *adj.* □ **1.** gottlos, ruchlos; **2.** pie'tätlos; **3.** re'spektlos.

imp·ish ['ımpıʃ] *adj.* □ schelmisch, spitzbübisch, verschmitzt.

im·plac·a·bil·i·ty [ım,plækə'bılətı] *s.* Unversöhnlichkeit *f*, Unerbittlichkeit *f*; **im·plac·a·ble** [ım'plækəbl] *adj.* □ unversöhnlich, unerbittlich.

im·plant [ım'plɑːnt] *v/t. fig.* einimpfen, a. *✻* einpflanzen (**in** *dat.*); **im·plan·ta·tion** [,ımplɑːn'teıʃn] *s.* **1.** *fig.* Einimpfung *f*; **2.** *mst fig. od.* *✻* Einpflanzung *f*.

im·plau·si·ble [ım'plɔːzəbl] *adj.* nicht plau'sibel, unwahrscheinlich, unglaubwürdig, -haft, wenig über'zeugend.

im·ple·ment I *s.* ['ımplımənt] **1.** Werkzeug *n* (*a. fig.*), Gerät *n*; **2.** *✻* *Scot.* Erfüllung *f* (*e-s Vertrages*); **II** *v/t.* [-ment] **3.** aus-, 'durchführen; **4.** in Kraft setzen; **5.** ergänzen; **6.** *✻* *Scot. Vertrag* erfüllen; **im·ple·men·tal** [,ımplı'mentl], **im·ple·men·ta·ry** [,ımplı-'mentərı] *adj.* Ausführungs...: ~ **orders** Ausführungsbestimmungen; **im·ple·men·ta·tion** [,ımplımen'teıʃn] *s.* Erfüllung *f*, Aus-, 'Durchführung *f*.

im·pli·cate ['ımplıkeıt] *v/t.* **1.** *fig.* verwickeln, hin'einziehen (**in** *acc.*), in Zs.-hang *od.* Verbindung bringen (**with** mit): ~**d in** verwickelt in (*acc.*), betroffen von (*acc.*); **2.** *fig.* a) → *imply* 1, b) zur Folge haben; **im·pli·ca·tion** [,ımplı-'keıʃn] *s.* **1.** Verwicklung *f*, Verflechtung *f*, (enge) Verbindung, Zs.-hang *m*; **2.** (eigentliche) Bedeutung, Andeutung *f*; **3.** Konse'quenz *f*, Folge *f*, Folgerung *f*, Auswirkung *f*: **by ~** a) als (natürliche) Folgerung *od.* Folge, b) implizite, durch sinngemäße Auslegung, ohne weiteres.

im·plic·it [ım'plısıt] *adj.* □ **1.** (mit *od.* stillschweigend) inbegriffen, stillschweigend, unausgesprochen; **2.** abso- 'lut, vorbehalt-, bedingungslos: ~ **faith** (**obedience**) blinder Glaube (Gehorsam); **im·plic·it·ly** [-lı] *adv.* **1.** im'plizite, stillschweigend, ohne weiteres; **2.** unbedingt; **im·plic·it·ness** [-nıs] *s.* **1.** Mit'inbegriffensein *n*; Selbstverständlichkeit *f*; **2.** Unbedingtheit *f*.

im·plied [ım'plaıd] *adj.* (stillschweigend *od.* mit) inbegriffen, einbezogen, sinngemäß (darin) enthalten, impliziert: ~ **condition**.

im·plode [ım'pləʊd] *v/i. phys.* implodieren.

im·plore [ım'plɔː] *v/t.* **1.** j-n anflehen, beschwören; **2.** *et.* erflehen, erbitten; **im·plor·ing** [-ɔːrıŋ] *adj.* □ flehentlich, inständig.

im·plo·sion [ım'pləʊʒn] *s. phys.* Implo- si'on *f*.

im·ply [ım'plaı] *v/t.* **1.** einbeziehen, in

sich schließen, (*stillschweigend*) be'inhalten; **2.** mit sich bringen, dar'auf hinauslaufen: *that implies* daraus ergibt sich, das bedeutet; **3.** besagen, bedeuten, schließen lassen auf (*acc.*); **4.** andeuten, 'durchblicken lassen, implizieren.

im·po·lite [,ımpə'laıt] *adj.* □ unhöflich, grob.

im·pol·i·tic [ım'pɒlətık] *adj.* □ 'undiplo- ,matisch, unklug.

im·pon·der·a·ble [ım'pɒndərəbl] **I** *adj.* unwägbar (*a. phys.*), unberechenbar; **II** *s. pl.* Impondera'bilien *pl.*, Unwägbarkeiten *pl.*

im·port I *v/t.* [ım'pɔːt] **1.** *✻* importieren, einführen: ~**ing country** Einfuhrland *n*; **2.** *Computer*: *Daten* importieren; **3.** *fig.* einführen, hin'einbringen; **4.** bedeuten, besagen; **II** *s.* ['ımpɔːt] **5.** *✻* Einfuhr *f*, Im'port *m*; *pl.* 'Einfuhrwaren *pl.*, -ar,tikel *pl.*; ~ **bounty** Einfuhrprämie *f*; ~ **duty** Einfuhrzoll *m*; ~ **licence** (*Am.* **license**), ~ **permit** Einfuhrgenehmigung *f*; ~ **quota** Einfuhrkontingent *n*; ~ **tariff** Einfuhrzoll *m*; **6.** Bedeutung *f*, Sinn *m*; **7.** Wichtigkeit *f*, Bedeutung *f*, Tragweite *f*; **im·port·a·ble** [-təbl] *adj.* *✻* einführbar, importierbar.

im·por·tance [ım'pɔːtns] *s.* **1.** Wichtigkeit *f*, Bedeutung *f*: **attach ~ to** Bedeutung beimessen (*dat.*); **conscious** (*od.* **full**) **of one's own ~ → important** 3; **it is of no ~** es ist unwichtig, es hat keine Bedeutung; **2.** Einfluss *m*, Ansehen *n*, Gewicht *n*: **a person of ~** e-e gewichtige Persönlichkeit; **im·por·tant** [-nt] *adj.* □ **1.** wichtig, wesentlich, bedeutend (**to** für); **2.** her'vorragend, bedeutend, angesehen, einflussreich; **3.** wichtigtuerisch, eingebildet, von s-r eigenen Wichtigkeit erfüllt.

im·por·ta·tion [,ımpɔː'teıʃn] *s.* *✻* **1.** Im'port *m*, Einfuhr *f*; **2.** Einfuhrware(n *pl.*) *f*; **im·port·er** [ım'pɔːtə] *s.* *✻* Im-por'teur *m*.

im·por·tu·nate [ım'pɔːtjʊnət] *adj.* □ lästig, zu-, aufdringlich; **im·por·tune** [,ımpɔː'tjuːn] *v/t.* dauernd (mit Bitten) belästigen, behelligen; **im·por·tu·ni·ty** [,ımpɔː'tjuːnətı] *s.* Aufdringlichkeit *f*, Hartnäckigkeit *f*.

im·pose [ım'pəʊz] **I** *v/t.* **1.** *Pflicht, Steuer etc.* auferlegen, aufbürden (**on**, **upon** *dat.*): ~ **a tax on s.th.** et. besteuern, et. mit e-r Steuer belegen; ~ **a penalty on s.o.** e-e Strafe verhängen gegen j-n, j-n mit e-r Strafe belegen; ~ **law and order** Recht u. Ordnung schaffen; **2.** ~ **s.th. on s.o.** a) j-m et. aufdrängen, b) j-m et. ,andrehen'; ~ **o.s. on s.o.** → 7; **3.** *typ. Kolumnen* ausschließen; **4.** *eccl. die Hände* (segnend) auflegen; **II** *v/i.* **5.** (**upon**) beeindrucken (*acc.*), imponieren (*dat.*); **6.** ausnutzen, miss'brauchen (**on** *acc.*): ~ **on s.o.'s kindness**; **7.** ~ **on s.o.** sich j-m aufdrängen, j-m zur Last fallen; **8.** betrügen, hinter'gehen (**on s.o.** j-n); **im·pos·ing** [-zıŋ] *adj.* □ eindrucksvoll, imponierend, impo'sant; **im·po·si·tion** [,ımpə'zıʃn] *s.* **1.** Auferlegung *f*, Aufbürdung *f* (*von Steuern, Pflichten etc.*), Verhängung *f* (*e-r Strafe*): ~ **of taxes** Besteuerung *f*; **2.** Last *f*, Belastung *f*; Auflage *f*, Pflicht *f*; **3.** Abgabe *f*, Steuer *f*; **4.** *ped. Brit.* Strafarbeit *f*; **5.** (schamlose) Ausnutzung (**on** *gen.*), Zumutung *f*; **6.** Über'vorteilung *f*, Schwindel *m*; **7.** *eccl.* (*Hand*)Auflegen *n*; **8.** *typ.* a) Ausschießen *n*, b) For'matmachen *n*.

im·pos·si·bil·i·ty [ım,pɒsə'bılətı] *s.* Unmöglichkeit f; **im·pos·si·ble** [ɪm'pɒ-səbl] adj. □ **1.** allg. unmöglich: a) unausführbar, b) ausgeschlossen, c) unglaublich: *it is ~ for me to do that* ich kann das unmöglich tun; **2.** F ‚unmöglich': *you are ~!*; **im·pos·si·bly** [ɪm'pɒsəblɪ] adv. **1.** unmöglich; **2.** unglaublich: *~ young*.

im·post ['ɪmpəʊst] I s. **1.** ✝ Auflage f, Abgabe f, Steuer f, bsd. Einfuhrzoll m; **2.** sl. Pferderennen: Handicap-Ausgleichsgewicht n; II v/t. **3.** Am. Importwaren zwecks Zollfestsetzung klassifizieren.

im·pos·tor [ɪm'pɒstə] s. Betrüger(in), Schwindler(in), Hochstapler(in); **im·pos·ture** [-tʃə] s. Betrug m, Schwindel m, Hochstape'lei f.

im·po·tence ['ɪmpətəns], **'im·po·ten·cy** [-sɪ] s. **1.** a) Unvermögen n, Unfähigkeit f, b) Hilf-, Machtlosigkeit f, Ohnmacht f; **2.** Schwäche f, Kraftlosigkeit f; **3.** ✒ Impotenz f; **'im·po·tent** [-nt] adj. □ **1.** a) unfähig, b) macht-, hilflos, ohnmächtig; **2.** schwach, kraftlos; **3.** ✒ impotent.

im·pound [ɪm'paʊnd] v/t. **1.** bsd. Vieh einpferchen, einsperren; **2.** Wasser sammeln, stauen; **3.** ⟨ꜩ⟩ a) beschlagnahmen, b) sicherstellen, in (gerichtliche od. behördliche) Verwahrung nehmen.

im·pov·er·ish [ɪm'pɒvərɪʃ] v/t. **1.** arm od. ärmer machen: *be ~ed* verarmen, verarmt sein; **2.** Land etc. auspowern, Boden etc. auslaugen; **3.** fig. a) ärmer machen, kulturell etc. verarmen lassen, b) e-r Sache den Reiz nehmen; **im'pov·er·ish·ment** [-mənt] s. a. fig. Verarmung f; Auslaugung f.

im·prac·ti·ca·bil·i·ty [ɪm,præktɪkə'bɪlətɪ] s. **1.** 'Undurch,führbarkeit f, Unmöglichkeit f; **2.** Unbrauchbarkeit f; **3.** Unpassierbarkeit f (e-r Straße etc.); **im·prac·ti·ca·ble** [ɪm'præktɪkəbl] adj. □ **1.** 'undurch,führbar, unmöglich; **2.** unbrauchbar; **3.** unpassierbar, unbefahrbar (Straße); **4.** unlenksam, störrisch (Person).

im·prac·ti·cal [ɪm'præktɪkl] adj. **1.** unpraktisch; **2.** (rein) theo'retisch, sinnlos; **3.** → impracticable.

im·pre·cate ['ɪmprɪkeɪt] v/t. Schlimmes her'abwünschen (on, upon auf acc.): *~ curses on s.o.* j-n verfluchen; **im·pre·ca·tion** [,ɪmprɪ'keɪʃn] s. Verwünschung f, Fluch m; **'im·pre·ca·to·ry** [-tərɪ] adj. Verwünschungs...

im·preg·na·bil·i·ty [ɪm,pregnə'bɪlətɪ] s. 'Unüber,windlichkeit f etc. (→ impregnable); **im·preg·na·ble** [ɪm'pregnəbl] adj. □ **1.** 'unüber,windlich, unbezwinglich, uneinnehmbar (Festung); **2.** unerschütterlich (to gegenüber); **im·preg·nate** I v/t. ['ɪmpregneɪt] **1.** biol. a) schwängern (a. fig.), b) befruchten (a. fig.); **2.** sättigen, durch'dringen; ⚙ tränken, imprägnieren; **3.** fig. et. od. j-n durch'dringen, erfüllen; **4.** paint. grundieren; II adj. [ɪm'pregnɪt] **5.** biol. a) geschwängert, schwanger, b) befruchtet; **6.** fig. (with) voll (von), durch'drungen (von); **im·preg·na·tion** [,ɪmpreg'neɪʃn] s. **1.** biol. a) Schwängerung f, b) Befruchtung f; **2.** Imprägnierung f, (Durch')Tränkung f, Sättigung f; **3.** fig. Befruchtung f, Durch'dringung f, Erfüllung f.

im·pre·sa·ri·o [,ɪmprɪ'sɑːrɪəʊ] pl. **-os** s. **1.** Impre'sario m; **2.** (The'ater- etc.)Di,rektor m.

im·pre·scrip·ti·ble [,ɪmprɪ'skrɪptəbl] adj. ꜩ a) unverjährbar, b) a. fig. unveräußerlich: *~ rights*.

im·press¹ v/t. [ɪm'pres] **1.** beeindrucken, Eindruck machen auf (acc.), imponieren (dat.): *be favo(u)rably ~ed by* e-n guten Eindruck erhalten od. haben von; *I am not ~ed* das imponiert mir gar nicht; *he is not easily ~ed* er lässt sich nicht so leicht beeindrucken; **2.** j-n erfüllen, durch'dringen (with mit); **3.** einprägen, -schärfen, klarmachen (on, upon dat.); **4.** (auf)drücken (on auf acc.), eindrücken; **5.** aufprägen, -drucken; **6.** fig. verleihen, erteilen (upon dat.); II v/i. **7.** Eindruck machen, imponieren; III s. ['ɪmpres] **8.** Prägung f; **9.** Abdruck m, Stempel m; **10.** fig. Gepräge n.

im·press² [ɪm'pres] v/t. **1.** requirieren, beschlagnahmen; **2.** bsd. ⚓ (zum Dienst) pressen.

im·press·i·ble [ɪm'presəbl] → **impressionable**.

im·pres·sion [ɪm'preʃn] s. **1.** Eindruck m: *make a (good) ~ (on s.o.)* (auf j-n) (e-n guten) Eindruck machen; *give s.o. a wrong ~* bei j-m e-n falschen Eindruck erwecken; *leave s.o. with an ~* bei j-m e-n Eindruck hinterlassen; *first ~s are often wrong* der erste Eindruck täuscht oft; **2.** Eindruck m, Vermutung f, Ahnung f: *I have an ~ (od. I am under the ~) that* ich habe den Eindruck, dass; **3.** Abdruck m (a. ✒), Prägung f; **4.** Ab-, Aufdruck m; **5.** typ. a) Abzug m, b) (bsd. unveränderte) Auflage (Buch): *new ~* Neudruck m, -auflage f; **6.** fig. Nachahmung f: *do (od. give) an ~ of s.o.* j-n imitieren; **im·'pres·sion·a·ble** [-ʃnəbl] **1.** für Eindrücke empfänglich; **2.** leicht zu beeindrucken(d), beeinflussbar, empfänglich; **im'pres·sion·ism** [-ʃnɪzm] s. Impressio'nismus m; **im'pres·sion·ist** [-ʃnɪst] I s. Impressio'nist(in); II adj. → **im·pres·sion·is·tic** [ɪm,preʃə'nɪstɪk] adj. (□ ~ally) impressio'nistisch.

im·pres·sive [ɪm'presɪv] adj. □ eindrucksvoll, impo'sant; **im'pres·sive·ness** [-nɪs] s. das Eindrucksvolle etc.

im·pri·ma·tur [,ɪmprɪ'meɪtə] s. **1.** Impri'matur n, Druckerlaubnis f; **2.** fig. Zustimmung f, Billigung f.

im·print I s. ['ɪmprɪnt] **1.** Ab-, Aufdruck m; **2.** Aufdruck m, Stempel m; **3.** typ. Im'pressum n, Erscheinungs-, Druckvermerk m; **4.** fig. Stempel m, Gepräge n; psych. Prägung f; II v/t. [ɪm'prɪnt] ([up]on) **5.** typ. aufdrucken (auf acc.); **6.** prägen (auf acc.); **7.** fig. einprägen (dat.); **8.** Kuss (auf)drücken (auf acc.).

im·pris·on [ɪm'prɪzn] v/t. **1.** ins Gefängnis werfen, einsperren, inhaftieren; **2.** fig. a) einsperren, -schließen, gefangenhalten, b) beschränken; **im'pris·on·ment** [-mənt] s. **1.** Einkerkerung f, Haft f, Gefangenschaft f (a. fig.); **2.** (sentence of) ~ ꜩ Freiheitsstrafe f; → false I.

im·prob·a·bil·i·ty [ɪm,prɒbə'bɪlətɪ] s. Unwahrscheinlichkeit f; **im·prob·a·ble** [ɪm'prɒbəbl] adj. □ **1.** unwahrscheinlich; **2.** unglaubwürdig.

im·pro·bi·ty [ɪm'prəʊbətɪ] s. Unredlichkeit f, Unehrlichkeit f.

im·promp·tu [ɪm'prɒmptjuː] I s. Impromp'tu n (a. ♪), Improvisati'on f; II adj. u. adv. improvisiert, aus dem Stegreif, Stegreif...

im·prop·er [ɪm'prɒpə] adj. □ **1.** ungeeignet, unpassend, untauglich (to für); **2.** unschicklich, ungehörig (Benehmen); **3.** a) unrichtig, falsch, b) unsachgemäß, c) unvorschriftsmäßig, d) 'miss-

bräuchlich: *~ use* Missbrauch m; **4.** ⚆ unecht: *~ fraction*; *~ integral* uneigentliches Integral; **im·pro·pri·e·ty** [,ɪmprə'praɪətɪ] s. **1.** Ungeeignetheit f, Untauglichkeit f; **2.** Unschicklichkeit f, Ungehörigkeit f; **3.** Unrichtigkeit f, a. ling. falscher Gebrauch.

im·prov·a·ble [ɪm'pruːvəbl] adj. **1.** verbesserungsfähig; **2.** ✔ anbaufähig, kultivierbar; **im·prove** [ɪm'pruːv] I v/t. **1.** allg., a. ⚆ verbessern; **2.** verfeinern; **3.** verschönern; **4.** Wert etc. erhöhen, steigern; **5.** vor'anbringen, ausbauen; **6.** Kenntnisse erweitern: *~ one's mind* sich weiterbilden; **7.** Gehalt aufbessern; **8.** Am. Land a) erschließen, im Wert steigern, b) kultivieren, meliorieren; **9.** ausnützen; → occasion 3; II v/i. **10.** sich (ver)bessern, besser werden, Fortschritte machen, sich erholen (gesundheitlich od. ✝ Preise): *~ in strength* kräftiger werden; *~ on acquaintance* bei näherer Bekanntschaft gewinnen; *the patient is improving* dem Patienten geht es besser; **11.** *~ on od. upon* a) verbessern, b) über'treffen: *not to be ~d upon* nicht zu übertreffen(d); **im'prove·ment** [-mənt] s. **1.** (Ver-)Besserung f, Ver'vollkommnung f, Verschönerung f: *~ in health* Besserung der Gesundheit; *~ of one's mind* (Weiter)Bildung f; *~ of one's knowledge* Erweiterung f des Wissens; **2.** Verfeinerung f, Veredelung f: *~ industry* Veredelungsindustrie f; **3.** Erhöhung f, Steigerung f, ✝ a. Erholung f, Steigen n; **4.** Meliorati'on f: a) ✔ Bodenverbesserung f, b) Erschließung f, c) Am. Wertverbesserung f (Grundstück etc.); **5.** Verbesserung f (a. Patent), Fortschritt(e pl.) m, Neuerung f, Gewinn m: *an ~ on od. upon* e-e Verbesserung gegenüber; **im'prov·er** [-və] s. **1.** Verbesserer m; **2.** ⚆ Verbesserungsmittel n; **3.** ✝ Volon'tär m.

im·prov·i·dence [ɪm'prɒvɪdəns] s. **1.** Unbedachtsamkeit f; **2.** Unvorsichtigkeit f, Leichtsinn m; **im'prov·i·dent** [-nt] adj. □ **1.** unbedacht; **2.** unvorsichtig, leichtsinnig (of mit).

im·prov·ing [ɪm'pruːvɪŋ] adj. □ **1.** (sich) bessernd; **2.** förderlich.

im·pro·vi·sa·tion [,ɪmprəvaɪ'zeɪʃn] s. Improvisati'on f (a. ♪): a) unvorbereitete Veranstaltung, 'Stegreifrede f, Kompositi,on f etc., b) Behelfsmaßnahme f, c) behelfsmäßige Vorrichtung; **im·prov·i·sa·tor** [ɪm'prɒvɪzeɪtə] s. Improvi'sator m; **im·pro·vise** [ɪm'prəvaɪz] v/t. u. v/i. allg. improvisieren: a) aus dem Stegreif od. unvorbereitet tun, b) rasch od. behelfsmäßig herstellen, aus dem Boden stampfen; **im·pro·vised** ['ɪmprəvaɪzd] adj. improvisiert: a) unvorbereitet, Stegreif..., b) behelfsmäßig; **im·pro·vis·er** ['ɪmprəvaɪzə] s. Improvi'sator m.

im·pru·dence [ɪm'pruːdəns] s. Unklugheit f, Unvorsichtigkeit f; **im'pru·dent** [-nt] adj. □ unklug.

im·pu·dence ['ɪmpjʊdəns] s. Unverschämtheit f, Frechheit f; **'im·pu·dent** [-nt] adj. □ unverschämt.

im·pugn [ɪm'pjuːn] v/t. bestreiten, anfechten, angreifen; **im·pugn·a·ble** [-nəbl] adj. bestreit-, anfechtbar; **im'pugn·ment** [-mənt] s. Anfechtung f, Einwand m.

im·pulse ['ɪmpʌls] s. **1.** Antrieb m, Stoß m, Triebkraft f; **2.** fig. Im'puls m: a) Anstoß m, Anreiz m, b) Anregung f, c) plötzliche Regung od. Eingebung: *act on ~* spontan od. impulsiv handeln; *on the ~ of the moment* e-r plötzlichen

Regung folgend; **~ buying** ♱ Impulskauf *m*; **~ goods** ♱ Waren, die impulsiv gekauft werden; **3.** ⚕, ⚡, ♄, *phys.* Im'puls *m*: **~ relay** ♱ Stromstoßrelais *n*.

im·pul·sion [ɪmˈpʌlʃn] *s.* **1.** Stoß *m*, Antrieb *m*; Triebkraft *f*; **2.** *fig.* Im'puls *m*, Antrieb *m*; **im'pul·sive** [-lsɪv] *adj.* □ **1.** (an)treibend, Trieb...; **2.** *fig.* impul'siv, leidenschaftlich; **im'pul·sive·ness** [-lsɪvnɪs] *s.* impul'sive Art, Leidenschaftlichkeit *f*.

im·pu·ni·ty [ɪmˈpjuːnətɪ] *s.* Straflosigkeit *f*: **with ~** straflos, ungestraft.

im·pure [ɪmˈpjʊə] *adj.* □ **1.** unrein: a) schmutzig, unsauber, b) verfälscht, mit Beimischungen, c) *fig.* gemischt, nicht einheitlich (*Stil*), d) *fig.* fehlerhaft; **2.** *fig.* unrein (*a. eccl.*), schmutzig, unanständig; **im·pu·ri·ty** [ɪmˈpjʊərətɪ] *s.* **1.** Unreinheit *f*, Unsauberkeit *f*; **2.** Unanständigkeit *f*; **3.** ⊚ Verunreinigung *f*, Schmutz(teilchen *n*) *m*, Fremdkörper *m*.

im·put·a·ble [ɪmˈpjuːtəbl] *adj.* zuzuschreiben(d), beizumessen(d) (**to** *dat.*); **im·pu·ta·tion** [ˌɪmpjuːˈteɪʃn] *s.* **1.** Zuschreibung *f*, Unter'stellung *f*; **2.** Be-, Anschuldigung *f*, Bezichtigung *f*; **3.** Makel *m*, (Schand)Fleck *m*; **im'put·a·tive** [-ətɪv] *adj.* □ **1.** zuschreibend; **2.** beschuldigend; **3.** unter'stellt; **im·pute** [ɪmˈpjuːt] *v/t.* (**to**) zuschreiben, zur Last legen, anlasten (*dat.*).

in [ɪn] **I** *prp.* **1.** *räumlich:* a) *auf die Frage wo?* in (*dat.*), an (*dat.*), auf (*dat.*): **~ London** in London; **~ here** hier drin (-nen); **~ the** (*od.* **one's**) **head** im Kopf; **~ the dark** im Dunkeln; **~ the sky** am Himmel; **~ the street** auf der Straße; **~ the country** (**field**) auf dem Land (Feld), b) *auf die Frage wohin?* in (*acc.*): **put it ~ your pocket!** steck(e) es in deine Tasche!; **2.** *zeitlich:* in (*dat.*), an (*dat.*), unter (*dat.*), bei, während, zu: **~ May** im Mai; **~ the evening** am Abend; **~ the beginning** am *od.* im Anfang; **~ a week('s time)** in *od.* binnen einer Woche; **~ 1960** (im Jahre) 1960; **~ his sleep** während er schlief, im Schlaf; **~ life** zu Lebzeiten; **not ~ years** seit Jahren nicht (mehr); **~ between meals** zwischen den Mahlzeiten; **3.** *Zustand, Beschaffenheit, Art u. Weise:* in (*dat.*), auf (*acc.*), mit: **~ a rage** in Wut; **~ trouble** in Not; **~ tears** in Tränen (aufgelöst), unter Tränen; **~ good health** bei guter Gesundheit; **~ (the) rain** im *od.* bei Regen; **~ German** auf Deutsch; **~ a loud voice** mit lauter Stimme; **~ order** der Reihe nach; **~ a whisper** flüsternd; **~ a word** mit 'einem Wort; **~ this way** in dieser *od.* auf diese Weise; **4.** *im Besitz, in der Macht:* in (*dat.*), bei, an (*dat.*): **it is not ~ him** es liegt ihm nicht; **he has** (**not**) **got it ~ him** er hat (nicht) das Zeug dazu; **~ Zahl, Maß:** in (*dat.*), aus, von, zu: **~ twos** zu zweien; **~ dozens** zu Dutzenden, dutzendweise; **one ~ ten** eine(r) *od.* ein(e)s von *od.* unter zehn, jede(r) *od.* jedes Zehnte; **6.** *Beteiligung:* in (*dat.*), an (*dat.*), bei: **~ the army** beim Militär; **~ society** in der Gesellschaft; **shares ~ a company** Aktien e-r Gesellschaft; **~ the university** an der Universität; **be ~ it** beteiligt sein; **he isn't ~ it** er gehört nicht dazu; **there is something** (**nothing**) **~ it** a) es ist et. (nichts) d(a)ran, b) es lohnt sich (nicht); **he is ~ there too** er ist auch mit dabei, er ‚mischt auch mit'; **7.** *Richtung:* in (*acc.*), auf (*acc.*): **trust ~ s.o.** auf j-n

vertrauen; **8.** *Zweck:* in (*dat.*), zu, als: **~ my defence** zu m-r Verteidigung; **~ reply to** in Beantwortung (*gen.*), als Antwort auf (*acc.*); **9.** *Grund:* in (*dat.*), aus, wegen, zu: **~ despair** in *od.* aus Verzweiflung; **~ his hono(u)r** ihm zu Ehren; **10.** *Tätigkeit:* in (*dat.*), bei, auf (*dat.*): **~ reading** beim Lesen; **~ saying this** indem ich dies sage; **~ search of** auf der Suche nach; **11.** *Material, Kleidung:* in (*dat.*), mit, aus, durch: **~ bronze** aus Bronze; **written ~ pencil** mit Bleistift geschrieben; **12.** *Hinsicht, Beziehung:* in (*dat.*), an (*dat.*), in Bezug auf (*acc.*): **~ size** an Größe; **a foot ~ length** einen Fuß lang; **~ that** weil, insofern als; **13.** *Bücher etc.:* in (*dat.*), bei: **~ Shakespeare** bei Shakespeare; **14.** *nach, gemäß:* **~ my opinion** m-r Meinung nach; **II** *adv.* **15.** innen, drinnen: **~ among** mitten unter; **~ between** dazwischen, zwischendurch; **be ~ for s.th.** et. zu erwarten *od.* gewärtigen haben; **he is ~ for a shock** er wird nicht schlecht erschrecken; **I am ~ for an examination** mir steht e-e Prüfung bevor; **now you're ~ for it** jetzt bist du ‚dran', jetzt kannst du dich auf et. gefasst machen; **have it ~ for s.o.** es auf j-n abgesehen haben, j-n auf dem ‚Kieker' haben; **be well ~ with s.o.** mit j-m gut stehen; **breed ~ and ~** Inzucht treiben; **~-and-~ breeding** Inzucht *f*; **~ and out** a) bald drinnen, bald draußen, b) hin u. her; **16.** hin'ein, her'ein, nach innen: **walk ~** hineingehen; **come ~!** herein!; **the way ~** der Eingang; **~ with you!** hinein mir dir!; **17.** da'zu, als Zugabe: **throw ~** zusätzlich geben; **III** *adj.* **18.** zu Hause, *östr., schweiz.* zu'hause; im Zimmer: **Mr. B. is not ~** Herr B. ist nicht zu Hause; **19.** da, angekommen: **the post is ~**; **the harvest is ~** die Ernte ist eingebracht; **20.** a) drin, b) F ‚in', in Mode, c) *sport* am Spiel, ‚dran', d) *pol.* an der Macht, im Amt, am Ruder: **~ party** *pol.* Regierungspartei *f*; **an ~ restaurant** ein Restaurant, das gerade ‚in' ist; **the ~ thing is to wear a wig** es ist ‚in' *od.* gerade Mode, e-e Perücke zu tragen; **~ side** Kricket: Schlägerpartei *f*; **be ~ on it** F eingeweiht sein; **IV** *s.* **21.** *pl.* Re'gierungspar,tei *f*; **22. know the ~s and outs of s.th.** genau Bescheid wissen bei e-r Sache.

in-¹ [ɪn] *in Zssgn* in..., innen, hinein..., Hin..., ein...

in-² [ɪn] *in Zssgn* un..., Un..., nicht.

in·a·bil·i·ty [ˌɪnəˈbɪlətɪ] *s.* Unfähigkeit *f*: **~ to pay** ♱ Zahlungsunfähigkeit, Insolvenz *f*.

in·ac·ces·si·bil·i·ty [ˈɪnækˌsesəˈbɪlətɪ] *s.* Unzugänglichkeit *f etc.*; **in·ac·ces·si·ble** [ˌɪnækˈsesəbl] *adj.* □ unzugänglich: a) unerreichbar, b) un'nahbar (**to** für *od. dat.*) (Person).

in·ac·cu·ra·cy [ɪnˈækjʊrəsɪ] *s.* **1.** Ungenauigkeit *f*; **2.** Fehler *m*, Irrtum *m*; **in'ac·cu·rate** [-rət] *adj.* □ **1.** ungenau; **2.** irrig, falsch.

in·ac·tion [ɪnˈækʃn] *s.* **1.** Untätigkeit *f*, Passivi'tät *f*; **2.** Trägheit *f*; **3.** Ruhe *f*; **in'ac·tive** [-ktɪv] *adj.* □ **1.** untätig; **2.** träge (*a. phys.*), müßig; **3.** ♱ flau, lustlos: **~ market**, **~ account** umsatzloses Konto; **~ capital** brachliegendes Kapital; **4.** ⚗ unwirksam, neu'tral; **5.** ✕ nicht ak'tiv, außer Dienst; **in·ac·tiv·i·ty** [ˌɪnækˈtɪvətɪ] *s.* **1.** Untätigkeit *f*; **2.** Trägheit *f* (*a. phys.*); **3.** ♱ Unbelebtheit *f*, Lustlosigkeit *f*; **4.** ⚗ Unwirksamkeit *f*.

in·a·dapt·a·bil·i·ty [ˈɪnəˌdæptəˈbɪlətɪ] *s.*

1. Mangel *m* an Anpassungsfähigkeit; **2.** Unanwendbarkeit *f* (**to** auf *acc.*, für); **in·a·dapt·a·ble** [ˌɪnəˈdæptəbl] *adj.* □ **1.** nicht anpassungsfähig; **2.** (**to**) unanwendbar (auf *acc.*), untauglich (für).

in·ad·e·qua·cy [ɪnˈædɪkwəsɪ] *s.* Unzulänglichkeit *f etc.*; **in'ad·e·quate** [-kwət] *adj.* □ unzulänglich, mangelhaft; unangemessen.

in·ad·mis·si·bil·i·ty [ˈɪnədˌmɪsəˈbɪlətɪ] *s.* Unzulässigkeit *f*; **in·ad·mis·si·ble** [ˌɪnədˈmɪsəbl] *adj.* □ unzulässig, nicht statthaft.

in·ad·vert·ence [ˌɪnədˈvɜːtəns], **in·ad·'vert·en·cy** [-sɪ] *s.* **1.** Unachtsamkeit *f*; **2.** Unabsichtlichkeit *f*; Versehen *n*; **in·ad'vert·ent** [-nt] *adj.* □ **1.** unachtsam; nachlässig; **2.** unabsichtlich, versehentlich.

in·ad·vis·a·bil·i·ty [ˈɪnədˌvaɪzəˈbɪlətɪ] *s.* Unratsamkeit *f*; **in·ad·vis·a·ble** [ˌɪnədˈvaɪzəbl] *adj.* □ nicht ratsam.

in·al·ien·a·ble [ɪnˈeɪljənəbl] *adj.* □ unveräußerlich: **~ rights**.

in·al·ter·a·ble [ɪnˈɔːltərəbl] *adj.* □ unveränderlich, unabänderlich.

in·am·o·ra·ta [ɪnˌæməˈrɑːtə] *s.* Geliebte *f*; **in·am·o·ra·to** [-təʊ] *pl.* **-tos** *s.* Geliebte(r) *m*.

in|-and-'in → in 15; **~-and-'out** *adj.* wechselhaft, schwankend.

in·ane [ɪˈneɪn] *adj.* □ hohl, geistlos, albern.

in·an·i·mate [ɪnˈænɪmət] *adj.* □ **1.** leblos, unbelebt; **2.** unbeseelt; **3.** *fig.* langweilig, fad(e); **4.** ♱ flau, matt; **in·an·i·ma·tion** [ɪnˌænɪˈmeɪʃn] *s.* Leblosigkeit *f*, Unbelebtheit *f*.

in·a·ni·tion [ˌɪnəˈnɪʃn] *s.* **1.** ⚕ Entkräftung *f*; **2.** (mo'ralische) Schwäche, Leere *f*.

in·an·i·ty [ɪˈnænətɪ] *s.* Geistlosigkeit *f*, Albernheit *f*: a) geistige Leere, Hohl-, Seichtheit *f*, b) dumme Bemerkung, *pl.* dummes Geschwätz.

in·ap·pli·ca·bil·i·ty [ˈɪnˌæplɪkəˈbɪlətɪ] *s.* Unanwendbarkeit *f*; **in·ap·pli·ca·ble** [ɪnˈæplɪkəbl] *adj.* □ (**to**) unanwendbar, nicht anwendbar *od.* zutreffend (auf *acc.*); ungeeignet (für).

in·ap·po·site [ɪnˈæpəzɪt] *adj.* □ unangebracht, unpassend.

in·ap·pre·ci·a·ble [ˌɪnəˈpriːʃəbl] *adj.* □ unmerklich, unbedeutend.

in·ap·pro·pri·ate [ˌɪnəˈprəʊprɪət] *adj.* □ **1.** unpassend: a) ungeeignet (**to, for** für), b) unangebracht, ungehörig; **2.** unangemessen (**to** *dat.*); **in·ap·pro·pri·ate·ness** [-nɪs] *s.* **1.** Ungeeignetheit *f*; **2.** Ungehörigkeit *f*; **3.** Unangemessenheit *f*.

in·apt [ɪnˈæpt] *adj.* □ **1.** unpassend, ungeeignet; **2.** ungeschickt, untauglich; **3.** unfähig; **in'ap·ti·tude** [-tɪtjuːd], **in'apt·ness** [-nɪs] *s.* **1.** Ungeeignetheit *f*; **2.** Ungeschicktheit *f*, Untauglichkeit *f*; **3.** Unfähigkeit *f*.

in·ar·tic·u·late [ˌɪnɑːˈtɪkjʊlət] *adj.* □ **1.** unartikuliert, undeutlich, unklar, schwer zu verstehen(d), unverständlich; **2.** undeutlich sprechend; **3.** unfähig, sich (deutlich) auszudrücken, wenig wortgewandt: **he is ~** a) er kann sich nicht ausdrücken, b) er ‚kriegt den Mund nicht auf'; **~ with rage** sprachlos vor Wut; **4.** *zo.* ungegliedert.

in·ar·tis·tic [ˌɪnɑːˈtɪstɪk] *adj.* (□ **~ally**) unkünstlerisch.

in·as·much [ˌɪnəzˈmʌtʃ] *cj.:* **~ as 1.** da (ja), weil; **2.** *obs.* in'sofern als.

in·at·ten·tion [ˌɪnəˈtenʃn] *s.* **1.** Unaufmerksamkeit *f*, Unachtsamkeit *f* (**to** gegenüber); **2.** Gleichgültigkeit *f* (**to** gegen); **in·at'ten·tive** [-ntɪv] *adj.* □ **1.** unaufmerksam (**to** gegenüber); **2.** gleichgültig (**to** gegen), nachlässig.

in·au·di·bil·i·ty [ɪn,ɔːdə'bɪlətɪ] *s.* Unhörbarkeit *f*; **in·au·di·ble** [ɪn'ɔːdəbl] *adj.* □ unhörbar.

in·au·gu·ral [ɪ'nɔːgjʊrəl] **I** *adj.* Einführungs..., Einweihungs..., Antritts..., Eröffnungs...: ~ *speech* → **II** *s.* Eröffnungs- *od.* Antrittsrede *f*; **in·au·gu·rate** [ɪ'nɔːgjʊreɪt] *v/t.* **1.** (feierlich) einführen *od.* einsetzen; **2.** einweihen, eröffnen; **3.** beginnen, einleiten: ~ *a new era*; **in·au·gu·ra·tion** [ɪ,nɔːgjʊ-'reɪʃn] *s.* **1.** (feierliche) Amtseinsetzung, -einführung *f*; **ℐ *Day** Am.* Tag *m* des Amtsantritts des Präsidenten; **2.** Einweihung *f*, Eröffnung *f*; **3.** Beginn *m*.

in·aus·pi·cious [,ɪnɔː'spɪʃəs] *adj.* □ **1.** ungünstig, unheilvoll, -drohend; **2.** unglücklich; **,in·aus'pi·cious·ness** [-nɪs] *s.* üble Vorbedeutung, Ungünstigkeit *f*.

,in-be'tween I *s.* **1.** Mittel-, Zwischending; **2.** a) Mittelsmann *m*, b) ✝ Zwischenhändler *m*; **II** *adj.* **3.** Zwischen...

in·board ['ɪnbɔːd] ✤ **I** *adj.* Innenbord...: ~ *engine* → III; **II** *adv.* (b)innenbords; **III** *s.* Innenbordmotor *m*.

in·born [,ɪn'bɔːn] *adj.* angeboren.

in·bred [,ɪn'bred] *adj.* **1.** angeboren, ererbt; **2.** durch Inzucht erzeugt, Inzucht...

in·breed [,ɪn'briːd] *v/t.* [*irr.* → *breed*] durch Inzucht züchten; **'in,breed·ing** [-dɪŋ] *s.* Inzucht *f*.

in·cal·cu·la·bil·i·ty [ɪn,kælkjʊlə'bɪlətɪ] *s.* Unberechenbarkeit *f*; **in·cal·cu·la·ble** [ɪn'kælkjʊləbl] *adj.* □ **1.** unberechenbar (*a. fig. Person etc.*); **2.** unermesslich.

in·can·des·cence [,ɪnkæn'desns] *s.* **1.** Weißglühen *n*, -glut *f*; **2.** Erglühen *n* (*a. fig.*); **,in·can'des·cent** [-nt] *adj.* **1.** weiß glühend; **2.** ◉ Glüh...: ~ *bulb* ⚡ Glühbirne *f*; ~ *burner* *phys.* Glühlichtbrenner *m*; ~ *filament* ⚡ Glühfaden *m*; ~ *lamp* ⚡ Glühlampe *f*; ~ *light* *phys.* Glühlicht *n*; **3.** *fig.* leuchtend, strahlend.

in·can·ta·tion [,ɪnkæn'teɪʃn] *s.* **1.** Beschwörung *f*; **2.** Zauber(spruch) *m*, Zauberformel *f*.

in·ca·pa·bil·i·ty [ɪn,keɪpə'bɪlətɪ] *s.* Unfähigkeit *f*, Unvermögen *n*; **in·ca·pa·ble** [ɪn'keɪpəbl] *adj.* □ **1.** unfähig: a) untüchtig, b) unbegabt; **2.** nicht fähig (*of gen., of doing* zu tun), nicht im'stande (*of doing* zu tun): ~ *of a crime* e-s Verbrechens nicht fähig; ~ *of working* arbeitsunfähig; **3.** (*physisch*) hilflos: *drunk and* ~ volltrunken; **4.** ungeeignet (*of* für): ~ *of improvement* nicht verbesserungsfähig; ~ *of solution* unlösbar.

in·ca·pac·i·tate [,ɪnkə'pæsɪteɪt] *v/t.* **1.** unfähig *od.* untauglich machen (*for s.th.* für et., *from doing* zu tun); *Gegner* außer Gefecht setzen; hindern (*from doing* an *dat.*, zu tun); **2.** ⚖ für (geschäfts)unfähig erklären; **,in·ca·'pac·i·tat·ed** [-tɪd] *adj.* **1.** erwerbs-, arbeitsunfähig; **2.** (körperlich *od.* geistig) behindert; **3.** (*legally*) ⚖ geschäftsunfähig; **,in·ca'pac·i·ty** [-tɪ] *s.* **1.** Unfähigkeit *f*, Untauglichkeit *f* (*for* für, zu; *for doing* zu tun): ~ (*for work*) Arbeits-, Erwerbs-, Berufsunfähigkeit *f*; **2.** *a. legal* ⚖ Geschäftsunfähigkeit *f*: ~ *to sue* *Am.* mangelnde Prozessfähigkeit.

in·cap·su·late [ɪn'kæpsjʊleɪt] → *encapsulate*.

in·car·cer·ate [ɪn'kɑːsəreɪt] *v/t.* **1.** einkerkern, einsperren (*a. fig.*); **2.** ⚕ *Bruch* einklemmen; **in·car·cer·a·tion** [ɪn,kɑːsə'reɪʃn] *s.* **1.** Einkerkerung *f*, Einsperrung *f* (*a. fig.*); **2.** ⚕ Einklemmung *f*.

in·car·nate I *v/t.* ['ɪnkɑːneɪt] **1.** verkörpern; **2.** feste Form *od.* Gestalt geben (*dat.*); **II** *adj.* [ɪn'kɑːneɪt] **3.** *eccl.* Fleisch geworden, in Menschengestalt; **4.** *fig.* leib'haftig: *a devil* ~ ein Teufel in Menschengestalt; *innocence* ~ die personifizierte Unschuld, die Unschuld in Person; **in·car·na·tion** [,ɪnkɑː'neɪʃn] *s.* Inkarnati'on *f*: a) ℐ *eccl.* Menschwerdung *f*, b) Inbegriff *m*, Verkörperung *f*.

in·case → *encase*.

in·cau·tious [ɪn'kɔːʃəs] *adj.* □ unvorsichtig, unbedacht.

in·cen·di·a·rism [ɪn'sendjərɪzəm] *s.* **1.** Brandstiftung *f*; **2.** *fig.* Aufwiegelung *f*, Aufhetzung *f*; **in·cen·di·ar·y** [ɪn'sendjərɪ] **I** *adj.* **1.** Feuer..., Brand...: ~ *bomb* → 5 a; ~ *bullet* → 5 b; **2.** ⚖ Brandstiftungs...: ~ *action* Brandstiftung *f*; **3.** *fig.* aufwiegelnd, -hetzend: ~ *speech* Hetzrede *f*; **II** *s.* **4.** Brandstifter(in); **5.** ✕ a) Brandbombe *f*, b) Brandgeschoss, *östr.* -geschoß *n*; **6.** *fig.* Unruhestifter *m*, Hetzer *m*.

in·cense¹ [ɪn'sens] *v/t.* erzürnen: ~*d* zornig, aufgebracht.

in·cense² ['ɪnsens] **I** *s.* **1.** Weihrauch *m*: ~ *burner* *eccl.* Räucherfass *n*, -vase *f*; **2.** Duft *m*; **3.** *fig.* ,Weihrauch' *m*, Lobhude'lei *f*; **II** *v/t.* **4.** (mit Weihrauch) beräuchern; **5.** durch'duften; **6.** *fig.* j-n beweihräuchern.

in·cen·so·ry ['ɪnsensərɪ] *s. eccl.* Weihrauchfass *n*.

in·cen·tive [ɪn'sentɪv] **I** *adj.* anspornend, antreibend, anreizend: ~ *bonus* (*pay*) ✝ Leistungsprämie *f* (-lohn *m*); **II** *s.* Ansporn *m*, (✝ Leistungs)Anreiz *m*: *buying* ~ Kaufanreiz.

in·cep·tion [ɪn'sepʃn] *s.* Beginn *m*, Anfang *m*; **in'cep·tive** [-ptɪv] *adj.* beginnend, anfangend, anfänglich, Anfangs...: ~ *verb ling.* inchoatives Verb.

in·cer·ti·tude [ɪn'sɜːtɪtjuːd] *s.* Ungewissheit *f*, Unsicherheit *f*.

in·ces·sant [ɪn'sesnt] *adj.* □ unaufhörlich, unablässig, ständig.

in·cest ['ɪnsest] *s.* Blutschande *f*, In'zest *m*; **in·ces·tu·ous** [ɪn'sestjʊəs] *adj.* □ blutschänderisch, inzestu'ös.

inch [ɪntʃ] **I** *s.* Zoll *m* (= 2,54 cm), *fig. a.* Zenti'meter *m od.* Milli'meter *m*: *every* ~ *a soldier* jeder Zoll ein Soldat; ~ *by* ~, *by* ~*es* Zentimeter um Zentimeter, zentimeterweise, langsam; *not to yield an* ~ nicht einen Zoll weichen *od.* nachgeben; *he came within an* ~ *of winning* er hätte um ein Haar gewonnen; *I came within an* ~ *of being killed* ich wurde um ein Haar getötet, ich bin dem Tod um Haaresbreite entgangen; *thrashed within an* ~ *of his life* fast zu Tode geprügelt; *give him an* ~ *and he'll take a yard* (*od. ell*) gibt man ihm den kleinen Finger, so nimmt er die ganze Hand; **II** *adj.* ...zöllig: *a two-*~ *rope*; **III** *v/i.* langsam *od.* zenti'meterweise schieben *od.* manövrieren; **IV** *v/i.* sich ganz langsam *od.* zentimeterweise (vorwärts- *etc.*)schieben *od.* -bewegen; **inched** [ɪntʃt] *adj. in Zssgn* ...zöllig.

in·cho·ate ['ɪnkəʊeɪt] *adj.* **1.** angefangen, anfangend, Anfangs...; **2.** 'unvollständig, rudimen'tär; **'in·cho·a·tive** [-tɪv] **I** *adj.* **1.** → *inchoate* 1; **2.** *ling.* inchoa'tiv; **II** *s.* **3.** *ling.* inchoa'tives Verb.

in·ci·dence ['ɪnsɪdəns] *s.* **1.** Ein-, Auftreten *n*, Vorkommen *n*; **2.** Häufigkeit *f*, Verbreitung *f*: ~ *of divorces* Scheidungsquote *f*, -rate *f*; **3.** a) Auftreffen *n* (*upon* auf *acc.*) (*a. phys.*), b) *phys.* Einfall(en *n*) *m* (*von Strahlen*); → *angle¹* 1; **4.** ✝ Anfall *m* (*e-r Steuer*): ~ *of taxation* Verteilung *f* der Steuerlast, Steuerbelastung *f*; **in·ci·dent** [-nt] **I** *adj.* **1.** (*to*) a) vorkommend (bei *od.* in *dat.*), b) → *incidental* 4; **2.** *bsd. phys.* ein-, auffallend, auftreffend (*Strahlen etc.*); **II** *s.* **3.** Vorfall *m*, Ereignis *n*, Vorkommnis *n*, *a. pol.* Zwischenfall *m*: *full of* ~ ereignisreich; **4.** 'Neben,umstand *m*, -sache *f*; **5.** Epi'sode *f*, Zwischenhandlung *f* (*im Drama etc.*); **6.** ⚖ a) (Neben)Folge *f* (*of* aus), b) 'Nebensache *f*, -,umstand *m*.

in·ci·den·tal [,ɪnsɪ'dentl] **I** *adj.* □ **1.** beiläufig, nebensächlich, Neben...: ~ *earnings* Nebenverdienst *m*; ~ *expenses* → 7; ~ *music* Begleit-, Bühnen-, Filmmusik *f*, musikalischer Hintergrund; **2.** gelegentlich; **3.** zufällig; **4.** (*to*) gehörig (zu), verbunden *od.* zs.-hängend (mit): *be* ~ *to* gehören zu, verbunden sein mit; *the expenses* ~ *thereto* die dabei entstehenden *od.* damit verbundenen Unkosten; **5.** folgend (*upon* auf *acc.*), nachher auftretend: ~ *images psych.* Nachbilder; **II** *s.* **6.** 'Neben,umstand *m*, -sächlichkeit *f*; **7.** *pl.* ✝ Nebenausgaben *pl.*, -spesen *pl.*; **,in·ci·'den·tal·ly** [-tlɪ] *adv.* **1.** beiläufig, neben'bei; **2.** zufällig; **3.** gelegentlich; **4.** neben'bei bemerkt, übrigens.

in·cin·er·ate [ɪn'sɪnəreɪt] *v/t.* verbrennen, *bsd. Leiche* einäschern; **in·cin·er·a·tion** [ɪn,sɪnə'reɪʃn] *s.* Verbrennung *f*, Einäscherung *f*; **in'cin·er·a·tor** [-tə] *s.* Verbrennungsofen *m*, -anlage *f*.

in·cip·i·ence [ɪn'sɪpɪəns], **in'cip·i·en·cy** [-sɪ] *s.* Anfang *m*; Anfangsstadium *n*; **in'cip·i·ent** [-nt] *adj.* □ beginnend, einleitend, Anfangs...; **in'cip·i·ent·ly** [-ntlɪ] *adv.* anfänglich, anfangs.

in·cise [ɪn'saɪz] *v/t.* **1.** einschneiden in (*acc.*), aufschneiden (*a. ⚕*): ~*d wound* Schnittwunde *f*; **2.** einritzen, -schnitzen, -kerben, -gravieren; **in·ci·sion** [ɪn'sɪʒn] *s.* (Ein)Schnitt *m* (*a. ⚕*), Kerbe *f*; **in'ci·sive** [-aɪsɪv] *adj.* □ *fig.* **1.** scharf: a) 'durchdringend: ~ *intellect*, b) beißend: ~ *irony*, c) prä'gnant: ~ *style*; **2.** *anat.* Schneide(zahn)...; **in'ci·sive·ness** [-aɪsɪvnɪs] *s. fig.* Schärfe *f*, Prä'gnanz *f*; **in'ci·sor** [-zə] *s. anat.* Schneidezahn *m*.

in·ci·ta·tion [,ɪnsaɪ'teɪʃn] *s.* **1.** Anregung *f*, Ansporn *m*, Antrieb *m*; **2.** → *incitement* 2; **in·cite** [ɪn'saɪt] *v/t.* **1.** anregen (*a. ⚕*), anspornen, anstacheln; **2.** aufhetzen, -wiegeln, ⚖ *a.* anstiften (*to* zu); **in'cite·ment** [ɪn'saɪtmənt] *s.* **1.** → *incitation* 1; **2.** Aufhetzung *f*, -wiegelung *f*, ⚖ *a.* Anstiftung *f* (*to commit a crime* zu e-m Verbrechen).

in·ci·vil·i·ty [,ɪnsɪ'vɪlətɪ] *s.* Unhöflichkeit *f*, Grobheit *f*.

in·ci·vism ['ɪnsɪvɪzəm] *s.* Mangel *m* an staatsbürgerlicher Gesinnung.

'in-,clear·ing *s.* ✝ *Brit.* Gesamtbetrag *m* der auf e-e Bank laufenden Schecks; Abrechnungsbetrag *m*.

in·clem·en·cy [ɪn'klemənsɪ] *s.* Rauheit *f*, Unfreundlichkeit *f*: ~ *of the weather* *a.* Unbilden *pl.* der Witterung; **in'clem·ent** [-nt] *adj.* □ **1.** rau, unfreundlich, streng (*Klima etc.*); **2.** hart, grausam.

in·clin·a·ble [ɪn'klaɪnəbl] *adj.* **1.** (hin-) neigend, tendierend (**to** zu); **2.** ◉

schräg stellbar.

in·cli·na·tion [ˌɪnklɪˈneɪʃn] s. **1.** fig. Neigung f, Vorliebe f, Hang m (**to**, **for** zu): **~ to buy** ✝ Kauflust f; **~ to stoutness** Neigung od. Anlage f zur Korpulenz; **2.** fig. Zuneigung f (**for** zu); **3.** ♣, phys. a) Neigung f, Schrägstellung f, Senkung f, b) Abhang m, c) Neigungswinkel m, Gefälle n; **4.** ast., phys. Inklinati'on f; **in·cline** [ɪnˈklaɪn] **I** v/i. **1.** sich neigen (**to**, **towards** nach), (schräg) abfallen; **2.** sich neigen (Tag); **3.** fig. neigen (**to**, **toward** zu): **~ to an opinion**; **~ to do s.th.** dazu neigen, et. zu tun; **4.** Anlage haben, neigen (**to** zu): **~ to corpulence**; **~ to red** ins Rötliche spielen; **5.** fig. (**to**) sich hingezogen fühlen (zu), gewogen sein (dat.); **II** v/t. **6.** Kopf etc. neigen: **~ one's ear to s.o.** fig. j-m sein Ohr leihen; **7.** fig. j-n bewegen, (dazu) veranlassen (**to** zu; **to do** zu tun): **this ~s me to doubt** dies lässt mich zweifeln; **this ~s me to go** im Hinblick darauf möchte ich lieber gehen; **III** s. **8.** Neigung f, Schräge f, Abhang m, Gefälle n; **in·clined** [ɪnˈklaɪnd] adj. **1.** geneigt, aufgelegt (**to** zu): **be ~** dazu neigen, (dazu) aufgelegt sein (**to do** zu tun); **2.** (dazu) neigend od. veranlagt (**to** zu); **3.** geneigt, gewogen, wohlgesinnt (**to** dat.); **4.** geneigt, schräg, schief, abschüssig: **~ plane** phys. schiefe Ebene; **in·cli·nom·e·ter** [ˌɪnklɪˈnɒmɪtə] s. **1.** Inklinati'onskompass m, -nadel f; **2.** ✈ Neigungsmesser m.

in·close [ɪnˈkləʊz] → **enclose**.

in·clude [ɪnˈkluːd] v/t. **1.** (in sich od. mit) einschließen, um'fassen, enthalten, be'inhalten: **all ~d** alles inbegriffen od. inklusive; **tax ~d** einschließlich od. inklusive Steuer; **2.** einschließen, betreffen, gelten für: **that ~s you, too!**; **~ me out!** humor. ohne mich!; **3.** einbeziehen, -schließen (**in** acc.), rechnen (**among** unter acc., zu); **4.** aufnehmen (**in** in e-e Gruppe, Liste etc.), erfassen; **5.** j-n (**in** s-m Testament) bedenken; **in·'cluding** [-dɪŋ] prp. einschließlich (gen.), bsd. ✝ inklu'sive (Verpackung etc.), (mit) inbegriffen, mit: **not ~** ausschließlich (gen.), bsd. ✝ exklusive; **up to and ~** bis einschließlich; **in·'clu·sion** [-uːʒn] s. **1.** Einbeziehung f, Einschluss m (**in** acc.): **with the ~ of** → **including**; **2.** Aufnahme f (**in** in acc.); **in·'clu·sive** [-uːsɪv] adj. □ **1.** einschließlich, inklu'sive (**of** gen.): **be ~ of** einschließen; (**to**) **Friday ~** (bis) einschließlich Freitag; **2.** alles einschließend od. enthaltend, ✝ Inklusiv..., Pauschal...: **~ price**.

in·cog·ni·to [ɪnˈkɒɡnɪtəʊ] **I** adv. **1.** in-'kognito, unter fremdem Namen: **travel ~**; **2.** ano'nym: **do good ~**; **II** pl. **-tos** s. **3.** In'kognito n; **4.** j-d, der in'kognito auftritt.

in·co·her·ence [ˌɪnkəʊˈhɪərəns] s. Zs.-hang(s)losigkeit f, Wirr-, Verwirrtheit f; **in·co'her·ent** [-nt] adj. □ zs.-hanglos, wirr (a. Person).

in·com·bus·ti·ble [ˌɪnkəmˈbʌstəbl] adj. □ unverbrennbar.

in·come [ˈɪŋkʌm] s. ✝ Einkommen n, Einkünfte pl. (**from** aus): **~ bond** Schuldverschreibung f mit gewinnabhängiger Verzinsung f; **~ bracket** od. **group** Einkommensstufe f; **~ return** Am. Rendite f; **~ statement** Am. Gewinn- u. Verlustrechnung f; **~ tax** Einkommensteuer f; **~ tax return** Einkommensteuererklärung f; **live within** (**beyond**) **one's ~** s-n Verhältnissen entsprechend (über s-e Verhältnisse)

leben.

in·com·er [ˈɪn.kʌmə] s. **1.** (Neu)Ankömmling m; **2.** ✝ (Rechts)Nachfolger(in).

in·com·ing [ˈɪn.kʌmɪŋ] **I** adj. **1.** her'einkommend: **the ~ tide** die Flut; **2.** ankommend (Telefongespräch, Zug etc.); **3.** nachfolgend, neu (Regierung, Präsident, Mieter etc.); **4.** ✝ eingehend (Post etc.): **~ goods** od. **stocks** Wareneingang m, -eingänge pl.; **~ orders** Auftragseingang m; **II** s. **5.** Ankommen n, Ankunft f; Eingang m; **6.** pl. ✝ Eingänge pl., Einkünfte pl.

in·com·men·su·ra·ble [ˌɪnkəˈmenʃərəbl] **I** adj. □ **1.** ♣ a) inkommensu'rabel, b) 'irratio,nal; **2.** nicht vergleichbar; **3.** völlig unverhältnismäßig, in keinem Verhältnis stehend (**with** zu); **II** s. **4.** ♣ inkommensu'rable Größe; **in·com·men·su·rate** [ˌɪnkəˈmenʃərət] adj. □ **1.** (**to**) unangemessen (dat.), unvereinbar (mit); **2.** → **incommensurable** I.

in·com·mode [ˌɪnkəˈməʊd] v/t. j-m lästig fallen, um'lassen, stören; **in·com'mo·di·ous** [-djəs] adj. □ unbequem: a) lästig (**to** dat. od. für), b) beengt.

in·com·mu·ni·ca·ble [ˌɪnkəˈmjuːnɪkəbl] adj. □ nicht mitteilbar, nicht auszudrücken(d); **in·com·mu·ni·ca·do** [ˌɪnkəmjuːnɪˈkɑːdəʊ] adj. vom Verkehr mit der Außenwelt abgeschnitten, ⚖ a. in Einzel- od. Isolierhaft; **in·com'mu·ni·ca·tive** [-ətɪv] adj. □ nicht mitteilsam, zu'rückhaltend, reserviert.

in·com·pa·ra·ble [ɪnˈkɒmpərəbl] adj. □ **1.** nicht zu vergleichen(d) (**with**, **to** mit); **2.** unvergleichlich, einzigartig; **in·'com·pa·ra·bly** [-blɪ] adv. unvergleichlich.

in·com·pat·i·bil·i·ty [ˈɪnkəmˌpætəˈbɪlətɪ] s. Unverträglichkeit f (a. ✿): a) Unvereinbarkeit f, 'Widersprüchlichkeit f, b) (charakterliche) Gegensätzlichkeit f; **in·com·pat·i·ble** [ˌɪnkəmˈpætəbl] adj. □ **1.** unver'einbar, 'widersprüchlich, einander wider'sprechend; **2.** unverträglich: a) nicht zs.-passend (a. Personen), b) ⊘, ✿, Computer: inkompa'tibel (Geräte, Medikamente etc.).

in·com·pe·tence [ɪnˈkɒmpɪtəns], **in·'com·pe·ten·cy** [-sɪ] s. **1.** Unfähigkeit f, Untüchtigkeit f; **2.** bsd. ⚖ a) Unzuständigkeit f, b) Unbefugtheit f, c) Unzulässigkeit f (e-r Aussage etc.), d) Am. Unzurechnungsfähigkeit f; **3.** Unzulänglichkeit f; **in·'com·pe·tent** [-nt] adj. □ **1.** unfähig, untauglich, ungeeignet; **2.** ⚖ a) unbefugt, b) unzuständig, 'inkompe,tent, c) Am. unzurechnungsfähig, geschäftsunfähig, d) unzulässig (a. Beweis, Zeuge); **3.** unzulänglich, mangelhaft.

in·com·plete [ˌɪnkəmˈpliːt] adj. □ **1.** 'unvoll,ständig, 'unvoll,endet; **2.** 'unvoll,kommen, lücken-, mangelhaft.

in·com·pre·hen·si·bil·i·ty [ɪnˌkɒmprɪhensəˈbɪlətɪ] s. Unbegreiflichkeit f; **in·com·pre·hen·si·ble** [ɪnˌkɒmprɪˈhensəbl] adj. □ unbegreiflich.

in·con·ceiv·a·ble [ˌɪnkənˈsiːvəbl] adj. □ **1.** unbegreiflich, unfassbar; **2.** undenkbar, unvorstellbar.

in·con·clu·sive [ˌɪnkənˈkluːsɪv] adj. □ **1.** nicht über'zeugend od. schlüssig, ohne Beweiskraft; **2.** ergebnislos; **in·con'clu·sive·ness** [-nɪs] s. **1.** Mangel m an Beweiskraft; **2.** Ergebnislosigkeit f.

in·con·dite [ɪnˈkɒndaɪt] adj. schlecht gemacht, mangelhaft; roh, grob.

in·con·gru·i·ty [ˌɪnkɒŋˈɡruːətɪ] s. **1.** Nichtüber'einstimmung f: a) 'Missverhältnis n, b) Unver'einbarkeit f; **2.** 'Widersinnigkeit f; **3.** Unangemessenheit f; **4.** ♣ 'Inkongru,enz f; **in·con·gru·ous** [ɪnˈkɒŋɡrʊəs] adj. □ **1.** nicht zuein'ander passend, nicht über'einstimmend, unver'einbar (**to**, **with** mit); **2.** 'widersinnig, ungereimt; **3.** unangemessen, ungehörig; **4.** ♣ 'inkongru,ent, nicht deckungsgleich.

in·con·se·quence [ɪnˈkɒnsɪkwəns] s. **1.** 'Inkonse,quenz f, Unlogik f, Folgewidrigkeit f; **2.** Belanglosigkeit f; **in·con·se·quent** [-nt] adj. □ **1.** 'inkonse-,quent, folgewidrig, unlogisch; **2.** nicht zur Sache gehörig, 'irrele,vant; **3.** belanglos, unwichtig; **in·con·se·quen·tial** [ˌɪnkɒnsɪˈkwenʃl] → **inconsequent**.

in·con·sid·er·a·ble [ˌɪnkənˈsɪdərəbl] adj. □ unbedeutend, unerheblich, belanglos, gering(fügig).

in·con·sid·er·ate [ˌɪnkənˈsɪdərət] adj. □ **1.** rücksichtslos, taktlos (**towards** gegen); **2.** 'unüber,legt; **in·con'sid·er·ate·ness** [-nɪs] s. **1.** Rücksichtslosigkeit f; **2.** Unbesonnenheit f.

in·con·sist·en·cy [ˌɪnkənˈsɪstənsɪ] s. **1.** (innerer) 'Widerspruch, Unver'einbarkeit f; **2.** 'Inkonse,quenz f, Folgewidrigkeit f; **3.** Unbeständigkeit f, Wankelmut m; **in·con'sist·ent** [-nt] adj. □ **1.** unver'einbar, (ein'ander) wider'sprechend, gegensätzlich; **2.** 'inkonse-,quent, folgewidrig, ungereimt; **3.** unbeständig, Person: a. 'inkonse,quent.

in·con·sol·a·ble [ˌɪnkənˈsəʊləbl] adj. □ untröstlich.

in·con·spic·u·ous [ˌɪnkənˈspɪkjʊəs] adj. □ unauffällig: **make o.s. ~** sich möglichst unauffällig verhalten.

in·con·stan·cy [ɪnˈkɒnstənsɪ] s. **1.** Unbeständigkeit f, Veränderlichkeit f; **2.** Wankelmut m, Treulosigkeit f; **3.** Ungleichförmigkeit f; **in'con·stant** [-nt] adj. □ **1.** unbeständig, unstet; **2.** wankelmütig; **3.** ungleichförmig.

in·con·test·a·ble [ˌɪnkənˈtestəbl] adj. □ **1.** unbestreitbar, unanfechtbar; **2.** 'un.um,stößlich, 'unwider,leglich.

in·con·ti·nence [ɪnˈkɒntɪnəns] s. **1.** (bsd. sexu'elle) Unmäßigkeit, Zügellosigkeit f, Unkeuschheit f; **2.** Nicht'haltenkönnen n, ✿ a. 'Inkonti,nenz f: **~ of speech** Geschwätzigkeit f; **~ of urine** ✿ Harnfluss m; **in'con·ti·nent** [-nt] adj. □ **1.** ausschweifend, zügellos, unkeusch; **2.** unauf'hörlich; **3.** nicht im'stande, et. zu'rückzuhalten od. bei sich zu behalten (a. ✿).

in·con·tro·vert·i·ble [ˌɪnkɒntrəˈvɜːtəbl] adj. □ unbestreitbar, unstrittig, unbestritten.

in·con·ven·ience [ˌɪnkənˈviːnjəns] **I** s. Unbequemlichkeit f, Lästigkeit f, Unannehmlichkeit f, Schwierigkeit f: **put s.o. to great ~** j-m große Ungelegenheiten bereiten; **II** v/t. belästigen, stören, j-m lästig sein, j-m Unannehmlichkeiten bereiten; **in·con'ven·ient** [-nt] adj. □ **1.** unbequem, lästig, störend, beschwerlich; **2.** Zeit, Lage etc.: ungünstig, 'ungeschickt'.

in·con·vert·i·bil·i·ty [ˈɪnkənˌvɜːtəˈbɪlətɪ] s. **1.** Unverwandelbarkeit f; **2.** ✝ a) Nichtkonver'tierbarkeit f, Nicht'umwandelbarkeit f (Guthaben), b) Nicht'einlösbarkeit f (Papiergeld), c) Nicht'umsetzbarkeit f (Waren); **in·con·vert·i·ble** [ˌɪnkənˈvɜːtəbl] adj. □ **1.** unverwandelbar; **2.** ✝ a) nicht 'umwandelbar, nicht konvertierbar, b) nicht einlösbar, c) nicht 'umsetzbar.

in·cor·po·rate [ɪn'kɔːpəreɪt] **I** v/t. **1.** vereinigen, verbinden, zs.-schließen; **2.** (*in*, *into*) einverleiben (*dat.*), *Staatsgebiet a.* eingliedern; einbauen, integrieren (in *acc.*); **3.** *Stadt* eingemeinden; **4.** (*in*, *into*) als Mitglied aufnehmen (in *acc.*); **5.** 🕮 als Körperschaft *od. Am.* als Aktiengesellschaft (amtlich) eintragen; 'Rechtsper,sönlichkeit verleihen (*dat.*); gründen, inkorporieren lassen; **6.** aufnehmen, enthalten, einschließen; **7.** ⊙, 🕮 (ver)mischen; **II** v/i. **8.** sich verbinden *od.* vereinigen; **9.** 🕮 e-e Körperschaft *etc.* bilden; **10.** ⊙, 🕮 sich vermischen; **III** adj. [-pərət] **11.** → in-'cor·po·rat·ed [-tɪd] adj. **1.** 🕆, 🕮 a) (als Körperschaft) (amtlich) eingetragen, inkorporiert, b) *Am.* als Aktiengesellschaft eingetragen: ~ **bank** *Am.* Aktienbank f; ~ **company** *Brit.* rechtsfähige (Handels)Gesellschaft, *Am.* Aktiengesellschaft f; **2.** (*in*, *into*) a) verbunden, zs.-geschlossen (mit), b) einverleibt (*dat.*); **3.** eingemeindet; **in·cor·po·ra·tion** [ɪn,kɔːpə'reɪʃn] s. **1.** Vereinigung f, Verbindung f; **2.** Einverleibung f, Eingliederung f, Aufnahme f (*into* in *acc.*); **3.** Eingemeindung f; **4.** 🕮 a) Bildung f *od.* Gründung f e-r Körperschaft *od.* (*Am.*) e-r Aktiengesellschaft: **articles of** ~ *Am.* Satzung f (e-r AG); **certificate of** ~ Korporationsurkunde f, *Am.* Gründungsurkunde f (e-r AG), b) amtliche Eintragung; **in'cor·po·ra·tor** [-tə] s. *Am.* Gründungsmitglied n.

in·cor·po·re·al [,ɪnkɔː'pɔːrɪəl] adj. □ **1.** unkörperlich, immateri'ell, geistig; **2.** 🕮 nicht greifbar: ~ **hereditaments** vererbliche Rechte; ~ **rights** Immaterialgüterrechte (*z. B. Patente*).

in·cor·rect [,ɪnkə'rekt] adj. □ **1.** unrichtig, ungenau, irrig, falsch; **2.** 'inkor-,rekt, ungehörig (*Betragen*); ,in·cor-'rect·ness [-nɪs] s. **1.** Unrichtigkeit f; **2.** Unschicklichkeit f.

in·cor·ri·gi·bil·i·ty [ɪn,kɒrɪdʒə'bɪlətɪ] s. Unverbesserlichkeit f; **in·cor·ri·gi·ble** [ɪn'kɒrɪdʒəbl] adj. □ unverbesserlich.

in·cor·rupt·i·bil·i·ty ['ɪnkə,rʌptə'bɪlətɪ] s. **1.** Unbestechlichkeit f; **2.** Unverderblichkeit f; **in·cor·rupt·i·ble** [,ɪnkə-'rʌptəbl] adj. □ **1.** unbestechlich, redlich; **2.** unverderblich, unvergänglich; **in·cor·rup·tion** ['ɪnkə,rʌpʃn] s. **1.** Unbestechlichkeit f; **2.** Unverdorbenheit f; **3.** *bibl.* Unvergänglichkeit f.

in·crease [ɪn'kriːs] **I** v/i. **1.** zunehmen, sich vermehren, größer werden, (an-)wachsen: ~ **in size** an Größe zunehmen; ~**d demand** Mehrbedarf m; **2.** steigen (*Preise*): sich steigern *od.* vergrößern *od.* verstärken *od.* erhöhen; **II** v/t. **3.** vergrößern, verstärken, vermehren, erhöhen, steigern: ~ **tenfold** verzehnfachen; **III** s. ['ɪnkriːs] **4.** Vergrößerung f, Vermehrung f, Verstärkung f, Erhöhung f, Zunahme f, (An)Wachsen n, Zuwachs m, Wachstum n, Steigen n, Steigerung f, Erhöhung f: **be on the** ~ zunehmen, wachsen; ~ **in wages** 🕆 Lohnerhöhung f, -steigerung f; ~ **of trade** Zunahme *od.* Aufschwung m des Handels; **5.** Ertrag m, Gewinn m; **in-'creas·ing·ly** [-sɪŋlɪ] adv. immer mehr: ~ **clear** immer klarer.

in·cred·i·bil·i·ty [ɪn,kredɪ'bɪlətɪ] s. **1.** Unglaubhaftigkeit f; **2.** Un'glaublichkeit f; **in·cred·i·ble** [ɪn'kredəbl] adj. □ **1.** unglaublich, unvor'stellbar (*a. fig.* unerhört, äußerst); **2.** unglaubhaft.

in·cre·du·li·ty [,ɪnkrɪ'djuːlətɪ] s. Ungläubigkeit f; **in·cred·u·lous** [ɪn'kredjʊləs] adj. □ ungläubig.

in·cre·ment ['ɪnkrɪmənt] s. **1.** Zuwachs m, Zunahme f; **2.** 🕆 (Gewinn-, Wert-)Zuwachs m, Mehrertrag m, -einnahme f; **3.** ⚕ Zuwachs m, Inkre'ment n, *bsd.* positives Differenti'al.

in·crim·i·nate [ɪn'krɪmɪneɪt] v/t. beschuldigen, belasten: ~ **o.s.** sich (selbst) belasten; **in·crim·i·nat·ing** [-tɪŋ] adj. belastend; **in·crim·i·na·tion** [ɪn,krɪmɪ-'neɪʃn] s. Beschuldigung f, Belastung f; **in'crim·i·na·to·ry** [-nətərɪ] → *incriminating*.

in·crust [ɪn'krʌst] → *encrust*.

in·crus·ta·tion [,ɪnkrʌs'teɪʃn] s. **1.** Verkrustung f (*a. fig.*); **2.** ⊙ a) Inkrustati'on f, Kruste f, b) Kesselstein(bildung f) m; **3.** Verkleidung f, Belag m (*Wand*); **4.** Einlegearbeit f.

in·cu·bate ['ɪnkjʊbeɪt] **I** v/t. **1.** *Ei* ausbrüten (*a. künstlich*); **2.** *Bakterien* im Brutschrank züchten; **3.** *fig.* ausbrüten, aushecken; **II** v/i. **4.** brüten; **in·cu·ba·tion** [,ɪnkjʊ'beɪʃn] s. **1.** Ausbrütung f, Brüten n; **2.** ⚕ Inkubati'on f: ~ **period** Inkubationszeit f; **'in·cu·ba·tor** [-tə] s. a) ⚕ Brutkasten m, Inku'bator m (*für Babys*), b) Brutschrank m (*für Bakterien*), c) 'Brutappa,rat m (*für Küken, Eier*).

in·cu·bus ['ɪŋkjʊbəs] s. **1.** ⚕ Alb(drücken n) m; **2.** *fig.* a) Albdruck m, b) Schreckgespenst n.

in·cul·cate ['ɪnkʌlkeɪt] v/t. einprägen, einschärfen, einimpfen (*on, in s.o.* j-m); **in·cul·ca·tion** [,ɪnkʌl'keɪʃn] s. Einschärfung f.

in·cul·pate ['ɪnkʌlpeɪt] v/t. **1.** an-, beschuldigen, anklagen; **2.** belasten; **in·cul·pa·tion** [,ɪnkʌl'peɪʃn] s. **1.** An-, Beschuldigung f; **2.** Vorwurf m.

in·cult [ɪn'kʌlt] adj. 'unkulti,viert, roh, grob.

in·cum·ben·cy [ɪn'kʌmbənsɪ] s. **1.** a) Innehaben n e-s Amtes, b) Amtszeit f, c) Amt(sbereich m) n; **2.** *eccl. Brit.* (Besitz m e-r) Pfründe f; **3.** *fig.* Obliegenheit f; **in'cum·bent** [-nt] **I** adj. □ **1.** obliegend: *it is* ~ **upon him** es ist s-e Pflicht; **2.** amtierend: *the* ~ **mayor**; **II** s. **3.** Amtsinhaber(in); **4.** *eccl. Brit.* Pfründeninhaber m.

in·cu·nab·u·la [,ɪnkjuː'næbjʊlə] s. *pl.* Inku'nabeln *pl.*, Wiegendrucke *pl.*

in·cur [ɪn'kɜː] v/t. sich *et.* zuziehen; auf sich laden *od.* ziehen, geraten in (*acc.*): ~ **displeasure** Missfallen erregen; ~ **debts** Schulden machen; ~ **losses** Verluste erleiden; ~ **liabilities** Verpflichtungen eingehen.

in·cur·a·bil·i·ty [ɪn,kjʊərə'bɪlətɪ] s. Unheilbarkeit f; **in·cur·a·ble** [ɪn'kjʊərəbl] **I** adj. □ unheilbar; **II** s. unheilbar Kranke(r m) f.

in·cu·ri·ous [ɪn'kjʊərɪəs] adj. □ **1.** nicht neugierig, gleichgültig, uninteressiert; **2.** 'unintres,sant.

in·cur·sion [ɪn'kɜːʃn] s. **1.** (feindlicher) Einfall, Raubzug m; Eindringen n (*a. fig.*); **3.** *fig.* Einbruch m, -griff m.

in·curve [,ɪn'kɜːv] v/t. (nach innen) krümmen, (ein)biegen.

in·debt·ed [ɪn'detɪd] adj. **1.** verschuldet; **2.** zu Dank verpflichtet: *I am* ~ **to you** *for* ich habe Ihnen zu danken für; **in-'debt·ed·ness** [-nɪs] s. **1.** Verschuldung f, Schulden pl.; **2.** Dankesschuld f, Verpflichtung f.

in·de·cen·cy [ɪn'diːsnsɪ] s. Unanständigkeit f, Anstößigkeit f; **2.** Zote f; **in-'de·cent** [-nt] adj. □ **1.** unanständig,

anstößig; a. 🕮 unsittlich, unzüchtig; **2.** ungebührlich: ~ **haste** unziemliche Hast.

in·de·ci·pher·a·ble [,ɪndɪ'saɪfərəbl] adj. nicht zu entziffern(d).

in·de·ci·sion [,ɪndɪ'sɪʒn] s. Unentschlossenheit f, Unschlüssigkeit f; ,**in·de·ci·sive** [-'saɪsɪv] adj. □ **1.** nicht entscheidend: *an* ~ **battle**; **2.** unentschlossen, unschlüssig, schwankend; **3.** unbestimmt.

in·de·clin·a·ble [,ɪndɪ'klaɪnəbl] adj. *ling.* undeklinierbar.

in·dec·o·rous [ɪn'dekərəs] adj. □ unschicklich, unanständig, ungehörig; **in·de·co·rum** [,ɪndɪ'kɔːrəm] s. Unschicklichkeit f.

in·deed [ɪn'diːd] adv. **1.** in der Tat, tatsächlich, wirklich: *it is very lovely* ~ es ist wirklich (sehr) hübsch; *if* ~ wenn überhaupt; *if* ~ *he were right* falls er wirklich Recht haben sollte; *we think,* ~ *we know this is wrong* wir glauben, ja wir wissen (sogar), dass dies falsch ist; ~ *I am quite sure* ich bin (mir) sogar ganz sicher; *yes,* ~*!* ja tatsächlich! (→ 3); *did you* ~*?* tatsächlich?, ach wirklich?; *you,* ~*!* iro. ausgerechnet du!, Du? dass ich nicht lache!; *what* ~*!* iro. na, was wohl?; *thank you very much* ~*!* reine herzlichen Dank!; *this is* ~ *an exception* das ist allerdings *od.* freilich e-e Ausnahme; **2.** zwar, wohl: *it is* ~ *a good plan, but ...*; **3.** (*in Antworten*) a. *yes* ~ a) allerdings(!), aber sicher(!), und ob(!), b) aber gern!, ja doch!, c) ach wirklich?, was Sie nicht sagen; ~ *you may not!* aber ja nicht!, kommt nicht infrage!

in·de·fat·i·ga·ble [,ɪndɪ'fætɪgəbl] adj. □ unermüdlich.

in·de·fea·si·ble [,ɪndɪ'fiːzəbl] adj. □ 🕮 unverletzlich, unantastbar.

in·de·fen·si·ble [,ɪndɪ'fensəbl] adj. □ unhaltbar: a) ✗ nicht zu verteidigen(d), b) *fig.* nicht zu rechtfertigen(d), unentschuldbar.

in·de·fin·a·ble [,ɪndɪ'faɪnəbl] adj. □ undefinierbar: a) unbestimmbar, b) unbestimmt.

in·def·i·nite [ɪn'defɪnət] adj. □ **1.** unbestimmt (*a. ling.*); **2.** unbegrenzt, unbeschränkt; **3.** unklar, undeutlich, ungenau; **in'def·i·nite·ly** [-lɪ] adv. **1.** auf unbestimmte Zeit; **2.** unbegrenzt; **in'def·i·nite·ness** [-nɪs] s. **1.** Unbestimmtheit f; **2.** Unbegrenztheit f.

in·del·i·ble [ɪn'deləbl] adj. □ unauslöschlich (*a. fig.*); untilgbar: ~ **ink** Zeichen-, Kopiertinte f; ~ **pencil** Tintenstift m.

in·del·i·ca·cy [ɪn'delɪkəsɪ] s. **1.** Unanständigkeit f, Unfeinheit f; **2.** Taktlosigkeit f; **in'del·i·cate** [-kət] adj. □ **1.** unanständig, unfein, derb; **2.** taktlos.

in·dem·ni·fi·ca·tion [ɪn,demnɪfɪ'keɪʃn] s. **1.** 🕆 a) → *indemnity* 1 a, b) Entschädigung f, Schadloshaltung f, Ersatzleistung f, c) → *indemnity* 1 c; **2.** 🕮 Sicherstellung f (*gegen Strafe*); **in·dem·ni·fy** [ɪn'demnɪfaɪ] v/t. **1.** entschädigen, schadlos halten (*for* für); **2.** sicherstellen, sichern (*from, against* gegen); **3.** 🕮 *parl.* a) j-m Entlassung erteilen, b) j-m Straflosigkeit zusichern; **in·dem·ni·ty** [ɪn'demnətɪ] s. **1.** 🕆 a) Sicherstellung f (*gegen Verlust od. Schaden*), Garan'tie(versprechen n) f, b) → *indemnification* 1 b, c) Entschädigung(sbetrag m) f, Abfindung f: ~ **against liability** Haftungsausschluss m; ~ **bond**, **letter of** ~ Ausfallbürgschaft f; ~ **insur-**

ance Schadensversicherung *f*; → **dou-ble indemnity**; **2.** ⚖, *parl.* Indemni'tät *f*.

in·dent¹ [ɪn'dent] **I** *v/t.* **1.** (ein-, aus-)kerben, auszacken: *~ed coastline* zerklüftete Küste; **2.** ⊕ (ver)zahnen; **3.** *typ. Zeile* einrücken; **4.** ⚖ *Vertrag* mit Doppel ausfertigen; **5.** ✝ *Waren* bestellen; **II** *v/i.* **6.** (*upon s.o. for s.th.*) (et. bei j-m) bestellen, (et. von j-m) anfordern; **III** *s.* ['ɪndent] **7.** Kerbe *f*, Einschnitt *m*, Auszackung *f*; **8.** *typ.* Einzug *m*; **9.** ⚖ Vertragsurkunde *f*; **10.** ✝ (Auslands)Auftrag *m*; **11.** ✗ *Brit.* Anforderung *f* (*von Vorräten*).

in·dent² *v/t.* [ɪn'dent] eindrücken, einprägen; **II** *s.* ['ɪndent] Delle *f*, Vertiefung *f*.

in·den·ta·tion [ˌɪnden'teɪʃn] *s.* **1.** Einschnitt *m*, Einkerbung *f*; Auszackung *f*, Zickzacklinie *f*; **2.** ⊕ Zahnung *f*; **3.** Einbuchtung *f*; Bucht *f*; **4.** *typ.* a) Einzug *m*, b) Absatz *m*; **5.** Vertiefung *f*, Delle *f*; **in·dent·ed** [ɪn'dentɪd] *adj.* **1.** (aus)gezackt; **2.** ✝ vertraglich verpflichtet; **in·den·tion** [ɪn'denʃn] → **indentation** 1, 2, 4; **in·den·ture** [ɪn'dentʃə] **I** *s.* **1.** Vertrag *m* od. Urkunde *f* (im Dupli'kat); **2.** ✝, ⚖ Lehrvertrag *m*, -brief *m*: *take up one's ~s* ausgelernt haben; **3.** amtliche Liste; **4.** → **indentation** 1, 2; **II** *v/t.* **5.** ✝, ⚖ durch (*bsd. Lehr*)Vertrag binden, vertraglich verpflichten.

in·de·pend·ence [ˌɪndɪ'pendəns] *s.* **1.** Unabhängigkeit *f* (*on, of* von): ℒ *Day Am.* Unabhängigkeitstag *m* (*4. Juli*); **2.** Selbstständigkeit *f*; **3.** hinreichendes Aus- *od.* Einkommen; **in·de·pend·en·cy** [-sɪ] *s.* **1.** → **independence**; **2.** unabhängiger Staat; **3.** ℒ → **Congregationalism**; **in·de·pend·ent** [-nt] *adj.* □ **1.** unabhängig (*of* von) (*a.* ♈, *ling.*), selbstständig (*a. Person*): *~ clause ling.* Hauptsatz *m*; **2.** a) selbstständig, -sicher, -bewusst, b) eigenmächtig, -ständig; **3.** *pol.* unabhängig (*Staat*), *Abgeordneter*: *a.* par'teilos, *parl.* frakti'onslos; **4.** vonein'ander unabhängig: *the various decisions were ~; we arrived ~ly at the same results* wir kamen unabhängig voneinander zu denselben Ergebnissen; **5.** finanzi'ell unabhängig: *~ gentleman, man of ~ means* Mann *m* mit Privateinkommen, Privatier *m*; **6.** eigen, Einzel...: *~ axle* ⊕ Schwingachse *f*; *~ fire* ✗ Einzel-, Schützenfeuer *n*; *~ suspension mot.* Einzelaufhängung *f*; **II** *s.* **7.** ℒ *pol.* Unabhängige(r *m*) *f*, Par'teilose(r *m*) *f*, *parl.* frakti'onsloser Abgeordneter; **8.** ℒ → **Congregationalist**.

in-'depth *adj.* tief schürfend, eingehend: *~ interview* Tiefeninterview *n*, Intensivbefragung *f*.

in·de·scrib·a·ble [ˌɪndɪ'skraɪbəbl] *adj.* □ **1.** unbeschreiblich; **2.** unbestimmt, undefinierbar.

in·de·struct·i·bil·i·ty ['ɪndɪˌstrʌktə'bɪlətɪ] *s.* Unzerstörbarkeit *f*; **in·de·struct·i·ble** [ˌɪndɪ'strʌktəbl] *adj.* □ unzerstörbar, (*a.* ✝) unverwüstlich.

in·de·ter·mi·na·ble [ˌɪndɪ't3:mɪnəbl] *adj.* **1.** unbestimmbar, nicht bestimmbar; **in·de·ter·mi·nate** [-nət] *adj.* □ **1.** unbestimmt (*a.* ♈), unentschieden, ungewiss, nicht festgelegt; unklar, vage; **2.** → **indeterminable**: *of ~ sex*; *~ sentence* ⚖ (Freiheits)Strafe *f* von unbestimmter Dauer; **in·de·ter·mi·na·tion** ['ɪndɪˌt3:mɪ'neɪʃn] *s.* **1.** Unbestimmtheit *f*; **2.** Ungewissheit *f*; **3.** Unentschlossenheit *f*; **in·de·ter·min·ism** [-mɪnɪzəm] *s.*

phls. Indetermi'nismus *m*, Lehre *f* von der Willensfreiheit *f*.

in·dex ['ɪndeks] **I** *pl.* **'in·dex·es, in·di·ces** ['ɪndɪsiːz] *s.* **1.** Inhalts-, Stichwortverzeichnis *n*, Ta'belle *f*, ('Sach)Re,gister *n*, Index *m*; **2.** *a.* ~ *file* Kar'tei *f*: ~ *card* Karteikarte *f*; **3.** ⊕ a) (An)Zeiger *m*, b) (Einstell)Marke *f*, Strich *m*, c) Zunge *f* (*Waage*); **4.** *typ.* Hand(zeichen *n*) *f*; **5.** *fig.* a) (An)Zeichen *n* (*of* für, von *od.* gen.), b) (*to*) Fingerzeig *m* (für), Hinweis *m* (auf *acc.*); **6.** *Statistik*: Indexziffer *f*, Vergleichs-, Messzahl *f*, ✝ Index *m*: *cost of living* ~ Lebenskosten-, Lebenshaltungsindex; *share price* ~ Aktienindex; **7.** ♈ a) Index *m*, Kennziffer *f*, b) Expo'nent *m*: ~ *of refraction phys.* Brechungsindex *od.* -exponent; **8.** *bsd. eccl.* Index *m* (*verbotener Bücher*); **9.** → **index finger**; **II** *v/t.* **10.** mit e-m Inhaltsverzeichnis versehen; **11.** in ein Verzeichnis aufnehmen; **12.** *eccl.* auf den Index setzen; **13.** ⊕ a) *Revolverkopf etc.* schalten: *~ing disc* Schaltscheibe *f*, b) *in Maßeinheiten* einteilen; ~ **fin·ger** *s.* Zeigefinger *m*; '~-**linked** *adj.* indexgebunden: ~ *pen·sion*; ~ *wage* Indexlohn *m*; ~ **num·ber** → **index** 6.

In·di·a | **ink** ['ɪndjə] → **Indian ink**; '~**man** [-mən] *s.* [*irr.*] (Ost)'Indienfahrer *m* (*Schiff*).

In·di·an ['ɪndjən] **I** *adj.* **1.** (ost)'indisch; **2.** *bsd. Am.* indi'anisch; **3.** *Am.* Mais...; **II** *s.* **4.** a) Inder(in), b) Ost'indier(in); **5.** *bsd. Am.* Indi'aner(in); ~ *club s. sport* (Schwing)Keule *f*; ~ **corn** *s.* Mais *m*; ~ *file s.: in* ~ im Gänsemarsch; ~ *giv·er s. Am.* F *j-d, der s-e Geschenke zurückverlangt*; ~ *ink s.* chi'nesische Tusche; ~ *meal s.* Maismehl *n*; ~ *pa·per* → *India paper*; ~ *summer s.* Alt'weiber-, Spät-, Nachsommer *m*.

In·di·a | **pa·per** *s.* 'Dünndruckpa,pier *n*; ~ **rub·ber** *s.* **1.** Kautschuk *m*, Gummi *n*, *m*: ~ *ball* Gummiball *m*; ~ *tree*; **2.** Radiergummi *m*.

In·dic ['ɪndɪk] *adj. ling.* indisch (*den indischen Zweig der indoiranischen Sprachen betreffend*).

in·di·cate ['ɪndɪkeɪt] *v/t.* **1.** anzeigen, angeben, bezeichnen, kennzeichnen; **2.** a) *Person*: andeuten, (an)zeigen, zu verstehen geben, b) *Sache*: hindeuten *od.* hinweisen auf (*acc.*), erkennen lassen (*acc.*), *a.* ⊕ anzeigen; **3.** ✈ indizieren, erfordern: *be ~d* indiziert sein, *fig.* angezeigt *od.* angebracht sein; **in·di·ca·tion** [ˌɪndɪ'keɪʃn] *s.* **1.** Anzeige *f*, Angabe *f*, Bezeichnung *f*; **2.** (*of*) a) (An-)Zeichen *n* (für), b) Hinweis *m* (auf *acc.*), c) (kurze) Andeutung: *give ~ of et.* ahnen lassen; *there is every ~* alles deutet darauf hin (*that* dass); **3.** ✈ a) Indikati'on *f*, b) Sym'ptom *n* (*a. fig.*); **4.** ⊕ a) Anzeige *f*, b) Grad *m*, Stand *m*; **in·dic·a·tive** [ɪn'dɪkətɪv] **I** *adj.* □ **1.** anzeigend, andeutend, hinweisend: *be ~ of* → *indicate* 2; **2.** *ling.* 'indika,tivisch: ~ *mood* → 3; **II** *s.* **3.** *ling.* Indikativ *m*, Wirklichkeitsform *f*; **in·di·ca·tor** [-tə] *s.* **1.** Anzeiger *m*; **2.** ⊕ a) Zeiger *m*, b) Anzeiger *m*, Anzeige- *od.* Ablesegerät *n*, Zähler *m*, (Leistungs)Messer *m*, c) Schauzeichen *n*, d) *mot.* Richtungsanzeiger *m*, e) *a.* ~ *telegraph* 'Zeigertele,graf *m*; **3.** ✈ Indi'kator *m*; **4.** *fig.* → *index* 5 *u.* 6; **in·dic·a·to·ry** [ɪn'dɪkətərɪ] → **indicative** 1.

in·di·ces ['ɪndɪsiːz] *pl. von* **index**.

in·di·ci·um [ɪn'dɪʃɪəm] *pl.* -**ci·a** [-ʃɪə] *s.* ⚘ *Am.* aufgedruckter Freimachungsvermerk.

in·dict [ɪn'daɪt] *v/t.* ⚖ anklagen (*for wegen*); **in'dict·a·ble** [-təbl] *adj.* ⚖ strafrechtlich verfolgbar: ~ *offence* schwurgerichtlich abzuurteilende Straftat, Verbrechen *n*; **in'dict·ment** [-mənt] **1.** (for'melle) Anklage (*vor e-m Geschworenengericht*); **2.** a) Anklagebeschluss *m* (*der grand jury*), b) (*Am. a.* **bill of** ~) Anklageschrift *f*.

in·dif·fer·ence [ɪn'dɪfrəns] *s.* **1.** (*to*) Gleichgültigkeit *f* (gegen), Inter'esselosigkeit *f* (gegen'über); **2.** Unwichtigkeit *f*: *it is a matter of complete ~ to me* das ist mir völlig gleichgültig; **3.** Mittelmäßigkeit *f*; **4.** Unwichtigkeit *f*; **in'dif·fer·ent** [-nt] *adj.* □ **1.** (*to*) gleichgültig (gegen), inter'esselos (gegen'über); **2.** 'unpar,teiisch; **3.** mittelmäßig, leidlich: ~ *quality*; **4.** mäßig, nicht besonders gut: *a very ~ cook*; **5.** unwichtig; **6.** ⚛, ✈, *phys.* neu'tral, indiffe'rent; **in'dif·fer·ent·ism** [-ntɪzəm] *s.* (Neigung *f* zur) Gleichgültigkeit *f*.

in·di·gence ['ɪndɪdʒəns] *s.* Armut *f*, Mittellosigkeit *f*.

in·di·gene ['ɪndɪdʒiːn] *s.* **1.** Eingeborene(r *m*) *f*; **2.** a) einheimisches Tier, b) einheimische Pflanze; **in·dig·e·nize** [ɪn'dɪdʒɪnaɪz] *v/t. Am.* **1.** a) *fig.* heimisch machen, einbürgern; **2.** (nur) mit einheimischem Perso'nal besetzen; **in·dig·e·nous** [ɪn'dɪdʒɪnəs] *adj.* □ **1.** a) ♀, *zo.* einheimisch (*to* in *dat.*); **2.** *fig.* angeboren (*to dat.*).

in·di·gent ['ɪndɪdʒənt] *adj.* □ arm, bedürftig, mittellos.

in·di·gest·ed [ˌɪndɪ'dʒestɪd] *adj. mst fig.* unverdaut; wirr; 'undurch,dacht; **in·di·gest·i·bil·i·ty** ['ɪndɪˌdʒestə'bɪlətɪ] *s.* Unverdaulichkeit *f*; **in·di·gest·i·ble** [-təbl] *adj.* □ unverdaulich (*a. fig.*); **in·di·ges·tion** [-tʃn] *s.* ✈ Magenverstimmung *f*, verdorbener Magen.

in·dig·nant [ɪn'dɪgnənt] *adj.* □ (*at, with*) entrüstet, ungehalten, empört (über *acc.*), peinlich berührt (von): *be-come* ~ sich entrüsten; **in·dig·na·tion** [ˌɪndɪg'neɪʃn] *s.* Entrüstung *f*, Unwille *m*, Empörung *f* (*at* über *acc.*): ~ *meeting* Protestkundgebung *f*; *fill s.o. with* ~ j-n ,aufbringen', empören.

in·dig·ni·ty [ɪn'dɪgnətɪ] *s.* Schmach *f*, Demütigung *f*, Kränkung *f*.

in·di·go ['ɪndɪgəʊ] *pl.* -**gos** *s.* Indigo *m*: ~-**blue** indigoblau; **in·di·got·ic** [ˌɪndɪ'gɒtɪk] *adj.* Indigo...

in·di·rect [ˌɪndɪ'rekt] *adj.* □ **1.** 'indi,rekt: ~ *lighting*; ~ *tax*; ~ *cost* ✝ Gemeinkosten *pl.*; **2.** nicht di'rekt *od.* gerade: ~ *route* Umweg *m*; ~ *means* Umwege, Umschweife *pl.*; **3.** *fig.* krumm, unredlich; **4.** *ling.* 'indi,rekt, abhängig: ~ *object* indirektes Objekt, Dativobjekt *n*; ~ *question* indirekte Frage; ~ *speech* indirekte Rede; **in·di·rec·tion** [ˌɪndɪ'rekʃn] *s.* **1.** 'Umweg *m* (*a. fig. b.s.* unlautere Methode): *by* ~ a) indirekt, auf Umwegen, b) *fig.* hinten herum, unehrlich; **2.** Unehrlichkeit *f*; **3.** Anspielung *f*, **in·di·rect·ness** [-nɪs] *s.* **1.** 'indi,rekte Art u. Weise; **2.** → **indirection**.

in·dis·cern·i·ble [ˌɪndɪ's3:nəbl] *adj.* nicht wahrnehmbar, unmerklich.

in·dis·ci·pline [ɪn'dɪsɪplɪn] *s.* Diszi'plin-, Zuchtlosigkeit *f*.

in·dis·cov·er·a·ble [ˌɪndɪ'skʌvərəbl] *adj.* □ nicht zu entdecken(d).

in·dis·creet [ˌɪndɪ'skriːt] *adj.* □ **1.** 'indis,kret; **2.** taktlos; **3.** 'unüber,legt.

in·dis·crete [ˌɪndɪ'skriːt] *adj.* homo'gen, kom'pakt, zs.-hängend.

in·dis·cre·tion [ˌɪndɪ'skreʃn] *s.* **1.** Indiskreti'on *f*; **2.** Taktlosigkeit *f*; **3.** 'Unüber,legtheit *f*.

in·dis·crim·i·nate [,ɪndɪ'skrɪmɪnət] *adj.* □ **1.** wahllos, blind, 'unterschiedslos; **2.** kri'tiklos, unkritisch; **3.** willkürlich; **in·dis·crim·i·na·tion** ['ɪndɪ,skrɪmɪ'neɪʃn] *s.* **1.** Wahl-, Kri'tiklosigkeit *f*, Mangel *m* an Urteilskraft; **2.** 'Unterschiedslosigkeit *f*.

in·dis·pen·sa·bil·i·ty ['ɪndɪ,spensə'bɪlətɪ] *s.* Unerlässlichkeit *f*, Unentbehrlichkeit *f*; **in·dis·pen·sa·ble** [,ɪndɪ'spensəbl] *adj.* □ **1.** unerlässlich, unentbehrlich (**for**, **to** für); **2.** ✕ unabkömmlich; **3.** unbedingt einzuhalten(d) *od.* zu erfüllen(d) (*Pflicht etc.*).

in·dis·pose [,ɪndɪ'spəʊz] *v/t.* **1.** untauglich machen (**for** zu); **2.** unpässlich machen, indisponieren; **3.** abgeneigt machen (**to do** zu tun), einnehmen (**towards** gegen); **in·dis'posed** [-zd] *adj.* **1.** indisponiert, unpässlich; **2.** (**towards**, **from**) a) nicht aufgelegt (zu), abgeneigt (*dat.*), b) eingenommen (gegen), abgeneigt (*dat.*); **in·dis·po·si·tion** [,ɪndɪspə'zɪʃn] *s.* **1.** Unpässlichkeit *f*; **2.** Abneigung *f*, 'Widerwille *m* (**to**, **towards** gegen).

in·dis·pu·ta·bil·i·ty ['ɪndɪ,spjuːtə'bɪlətɪ] *s.* Unbestreitbarkeit *f*, Unstrittigkeit *f*; **in·dis·pu·ta·ble** [,ɪndɪ'spjuːtəbl] *adj.* □ **1.** unbestreitbar, unstrittig, nicht zu bestreiten(d); **2.** unbestritten.

in·dis·sol·u·bil·i·ty ['ɪndɪ,sɒljʊ'bɪlətɪ] *s.* Unauflösbarkeit *f*; **in·dis·sol·u·ble** [,ɪndɪ'sɒljʊbl] *adj.* □ **1.** unauflösbar, -lich; **2.** unzertrennlich; **3.** 🛠 unlöslich.

in·dis·tinct [,ɪndɪ'stɪŋkt] *adj.* □ **1.** undeutlich, unklar, verworren, verschwommen; **in·dis'tinc·tive** [-tɪv] *adj.* □ ausdruckslos, nichts sagend; **in·dis'tinct·ness** [-nɪs] *s.* Undeutlichkeit *f etc.*

in·dis·tin·guish·a·ble [,ɪndɪ'stɪŋgwɪʃəbl] *adj.* □ **1.** nicht zu unter'scheiden(d) (**from** von); **2.** nicht wahrnehmbar *od.* erkennbar; **3.** unmerklich.

in·dite [ɪn'daɪt] *v/t.* ver-, abfassen.

in·di·vid·u·al [,ɪndɪ'vɪdjʊəl] **I** *adj.* □ → **individually**; **1.** einzeln, Einzel...: **each ~ word**; **~ case** Einzelfall *m*; **~ consumer** Einzelverbraucher *m*; **~ drive** ⊙ Einzelantrieb *m*; **2.** für 'eine Per'son bestimmt, eigen, per'sönlich, einzel: **~ credit** Personalkredit *m*; **~ property** Privatvermögen *n*; **~ psychology** Individualpsychologie *n*; **~ traffic** Individualverkehr *m*; **give ~ attention to** individuell behandeln, s-e persönliche Aufmerksamkeit schenken (*dat.*); **3.** individu'ell, per'sönlich, eigen(tümlich), charakte'ristisch: **an ~ style**; **4.** verschieden: **five ~ cups**; **II** *s.* **5.** 'Einzelper,son *f*, Indi'viduum *n*, Einzelne(r) *m*; **6.** *mst contp.* Per'son *f*, Indi'viduum *n*; **7.** ⚖ na'türliche Per'son *f*; **,in·di'vid·u·al·ism** [-lɪzəm] *s.* **1.** Individua'lismus *m*; **2.** Ego'ismus *m*; **,in·di'vid·u·al·ist** [-lɪst] **I** *s.* Individua'list(in); **II** *adj.* → **in·di·vid·u·al·is·tic** ['ɪndɪ,vɪdjʊə'lɪstɪk] *adj.* (□ *~ally*) individua'listisch; **in·di·vid·u·al·i·ty** ['ɪndɪ,vɪdju'ælətɪ] *s.* **1.** Individuali'tät *f*, (per'sönliche) Eigenart; **2.** *phls.* indi'vidu'elle Exi'stenz; **3.** → **individual** 5; **in·di·vid·u·al·i·za·tion** ['ɪndɪ,vɪdjʊəlaɪ'zeɪʃn] *s.* **1.** Individualisierung *f*; **2.** Einzelbetrachtung *f*; **,in·di'vid·u·al·ize** [-laɪz] *v/t.* **1.** individualisieren, individu'ell gestalten *od.* behandeln, e-e individu'elle *od.* eigene Note verleihen (*dat.*); **2.** einzeln betrachten; **,in·di'vid·u·al·ly** [-ələ] *adv.* **1.** ein-

zeln, (jeder, jede, jedes) für sich; **2.** einzeln betrachtet, für sich genommen; **3.** per'sönlich; **,in·di'vid·u·ate** [-jʊeɪt] *v/t.* **1.** → **individualize** 1; **2.** charakterisieren; **3.** unter'scheiden (**from** von).

in·di·vis·i·bil·i·ty ['ɪndɪ,vɪzɪ'bɪlətɪ] *s.* Unteilbarkeit *f*; **in·di·vis·i·ble** [,ɪndɪ'vɪzəbl] **I** *adj.* □ unteilbar; **II** *s.* ⚖ unteilbare Größe.

In·do-Chi·nese [,ɪndəʊtʃaɪ'niːz] *adj.* indochi'nesisch, 'hinterindisch.

in·doc·ile [ɪn'dəʊsaɪl] *adj.* **1.** ungelehrig; **2.** störrisch, unlenksam; **in·do·cil·i·ty** [,ɪndəʊ'sɪlətɪ] *s.* **1.** Ungelehrigkeit *f*; **2.** Unlenksamkeit *f*.

in·doc·tri·nate [ɪn'dɒktrɪneɪt] *v/t.* **1.** unter'weisen, schulen (**in** *dat.*); *pol.* indoktrinieren; **2.** *j-m et.* einprägen, -bleuen, -impfen; **3.** durch'dringen (**with** mit); **in·doc·tri·na·tion** [ɪn,dɒktrɪ'neɪʃn] *s.* Unter'weisung *f*, Belehrung *f*, Schulung *f*; *pol.* Indoktrinati'on *f*, po'litische Schulung, ideo'logischer Drill; **in'doc·tri·na·tor** [-tə] *s.* Lehrer *m*, Instruk'teur *m*.

'In·do|-,Eu·ro·pe·an [,ɪndəʊ-] *ling.* **I** *adj.* **1.** 'indoger'manisch; **II** *s.* **2.** *ling.* 'Indoger'manisch *n*; **3.** 'Indoger'mane *m*, -ger'manin *f*; **,~-Ger'man·ic** → **Indo-European** 1 *u.* 2; **,~-I'ra·ni·an** *ling.* **I** *adj.* 'indoi'ranisch, arisch; **II** *s.* 'Indoi'ranisch *n*, Arisch *n*.

in·do·lence ['ɪndələns] *s.* Indo'lenz *f*: a) Trägheit *f*, b) Lässigkeit *f*, c) 🛠 Schmerzlosigkeit *f*; **in·do·lent** [-nt] *adj.* □ indo'lent: a) träge, b) lässig, c) 🛠 schmerzlos.

in·dom·i·ta·ble [ɪn'dɒmɪtəbl] *adj.* □ **1.** unbezähmbar, nicht 'unterzukriegen(d); **2.** unbeugsam.

In·do·ne·sian [,ɪndəʊ'niːzjən] **I** *adj.* indo'nesisch; **II** *s.* Indo'nesier(in).

in·door ['ɪndɔː] *adj.* im *od.* zu Hause, östr., schweiz. zu'hause, Haus..., Zimmer..., Innen..., sport Hallen...: **~ aerial** ⚡ Zimmer-, Innenantenne *f*; **~ dress** Hauskleid(ung *f*) *n*; **~ games** a) Spiele fürs Haus, b) *sport* Hallenspiele; **~ swimming pool** Hallenbad *n*; **~ tournament** *sport* Hallenturnier *n*; **~ doors** [,ɪn'dɔːz] *adv.* **1.** im *od.* zu Hause, östr., schweiz. zuhause, drin(nen); **2.** ins Haus.

in·dorse [ɪn'dɔːs] *etc.* → **endorse** *etc.*

in·du·bi·ta·ble [ɪn'djuːbɪtəbl] *adj.* □ unzweifelhaft, zweifellos.

in·duce [ɪn'djuːs] *v/t.* **1.** *j-n* veranlassen, bewegen, (dazu) bringen, über'reden (**to do** zu tun); **2.** her'beiführen, verursachen, bewirken, her'vorrufen, führen zu: **~ a birth** 🩺 e-e Geburt einleiten; **~d sleep** künstlicher Schlaf; **3.** ⚡ Kernphysik, a. Logik: induzieren: **~ current** Induktionsstrom *m*; **in'duce·ment** [-mənt] *s.* **1.** a) Veranlassung *f*, Über'redung *f*, b) Verleitung (**to** zu); **2.** Anlass *m*, Beweggrund *m*; **3.** a) 🎯 Anreiz *m* (**to** zu); **4.** Her'beiführung *f*.

in·duct [ɪn'dʌkt] *v/t.* **1.** *in* ein Amt *etc.* einführen, -setzen; **2.** *j-n* einweihen (**to** *in acc.*); **3.** ✕ *Am.* zum Militär einberufen; **in'duct·ance** [-təns] *s.* ⚡ **1.** Induk'tanz *f*, induk'tiver ('Schein),Widerstand; **2.** 'Selbstindukti,on *f*; **~ coil** Drosselspule *f*; **in·duc·tee** [,ɪndʌk'tiː] *s.* ✕ *Am.* Einberufene(r) *m*, Re'krut *m*; **in'duc·tion** [-kʃn] *s.* **1.** Einführung, -setzung *f* (*in* ein Amt); **2.** ⊙ Zuführung *f*, Einlass *m*: **~ pipe** Einlassrohr *n*; **3.** Her'beiführung *f*, Auslösung *f*; **4.** Einleitung *f*, Beginn *m*; **5.** ✕ *Am.* Einberufung *f*: **~ order** Einberufungsbefehl

m; **6.** Anführung *f* (*Beweise etc.*); **7.** ⚡ Indukti'on *f*, sekun'däre Erregung: **~ coil** (**current**) Induktionsspule *f* (-strom *m*); **~ motor** Induktions-, Drehstrommotor *m*; **8.** ⚛, *phys.*, *phls.* Indukti'on *f*: **~ accelerator** Elektronenbeschleuniger *m*; **in'duc·tive** [-tɪv] *adj.* □ **1.** ⚡, *phys.*, *phls.* induk'tiv, Induktions...; **2.** ⚡ e-e Reakti'on her'vorrufend; **in'duc·tor** [-tə] *s.* ⚡, *biol.* In'duktor *m*.

in·dulge [ɪn'dʌldʒ] **I** *v/t.* **1.** e-r Neigung *etc.* nachgeben, frönen, sich hingeben, freien Lauf lassen; **2.** nachsichtig sein gegen: **~ s.o. in s.th.** *j-m et.* nachsehen; **3.** *j-m* nachgeben (**in** *in dat.*): **~ o.s. in** → 7; **4.** *j-m* gefällig sein; **5.** *j-n* verwöhnen; **II** *v/i.* **6.** sich hingeben, frönen (**in** *dat.*); **7.** **~ in** sich *et.* gönnen *od.* genehmigen *od.* leisten, *a.* sich gütlich tun an (*dat.*), *et.* essen *od.* trinken; **8.** F a) sich ,einen genehmigen', b) sich e-e Zigarette *etc.* gönnen *od.* ,genehmigen'; **in'dul·gence** [-dʒəns] *s.* **1.** Nachsicht *f*, Milde *f* (**to**, **of** gegenüber); **2.** Nachgiebigkeit *f*; **3.** Gefälligkeit *f*; **4.** Verwöhnung *f*; **5.** Befriedigung *f* (*e-r Begierde etc.*); **6.** (*in*) Frönen *n* (*dat.*), Schwelgen *n* (*in dat.*), Genießen *n* (*gen.*): (**excessive**) **~ in drink** übermäßiger Alkoholgenuss; **7.** Wohlleben *n*, Genusssucht *f*; **8.** Schwäche *f*, Leidenschaft *f* (**of** für); **9.** *R.C.* Ablass *m*: **sale of ~s** Ablasshandel *m*; **in'dul·genced** [-dʒənst] *adj.*: **~ prayer** *R.C.* Ablassgebet *n*; **in'dul·gent** [-dʒənt] *adj.* □ (**to**) nachsichtig, mild (gegen); schonend, sanft (mit).

in·du·rate ['ɪndjʊəreɪt] **I** *v/t.* **1.** (ver)härten, hart machen; **2.** *fig. a.*) abstumpfen, b) abhärten (**against**, **to** gegen); **II** *v/i.* **3.** sich verhärten: a) hart werden, b) *fig.* gefühllos werden, abstumpfen, **4.** abgehärtet werden; **in·du·ra·tion** [,ɪndjʊə'reɪʃn] *s.* **1.** (Ver)Härtung *f*; **2.** *fig.* Abstumpfung *f*; **3.** Verstocktheit *f*.

in·dus·tri·al [ɪn'dʌstrɪəl] *adj.* □ **1.** industri'ell, gewerblich, Industrie..., Fabrik..., Gewerbe..., Wirtschafts..., Betriebs..., Werks...: **~ accident** Betriebsunfall *m*; **~ decline** industrieller Niedergang; **~ effluent** Industrieabwässer *pl.*; **~ emissions** Industrieabgase *pl.*; **~ waste** Industrieabfälle *pl.*; **II** *s.* **2.** Industri'elle(r) *m*; **3.** *pl.* Indu'strieaktien *pl.*, -pa,piere *pl.*; **~ action** *s.* Arbeitskampf(maßnahmen *pl.*) *m*; **~ a·re·a** *s.* Indu'striegebiet *n*, -gelände *n*; **~ de·sign** *s.* Indu'striede,sign *n*; **~ de·sign·er** *s.* Indu'striede,signer *m*; **~ dis·pute** *s.* Arbeitsstreitigkeit *f*; **~ en·gi·neer·ing** *s.* In'dustrial Engi'neering *n* (*Rationalisierung von Arbeitsprozessen*); **~ es·pi·o·nage** *s.* 'Werk-, Indust'riespio,nage *f*; **~ es·tate** *s.* Brit. Indu'striegebiet *n*; **~ goods** *s. pl.* Indust'riepro,dukte *pl.*, Investiti'onsgüter *pl.*; **~ in·ju·ry** *s.* a) Berufsschaden *m*, b) Arbeitsunfall *m*.

in·dus·tri·al·ism [ɪn'dʌstrɪəlɪzəm] *s.* Indu'strialismus *m*; **in·dus·tri·al·ist** [-ɪst] → **industrial** 2; **in·dus·tri·al·i·za·tion** [ɪn,dʌstrɪəlaɪ'zeɪʃn] *s.* Industrialisierung *f*; **in·dus·tri·al·ize** [-aɪz] *v/t.* industrialisieren.

in·dus·tri·al| man·age·ment *s.* Betriebsführung *f*; **~ med·i·cine** *s.* Be'triebsmedi,zin *f*; **~ na·tion** *s.* Industriestaat *m*; **~ park** *s. Am.* Indu'striegebiet *n* (*e-r Stadt*); **~ part·ner·ship** *s.* ✝ *Am.* Gewinnbeteiligung *f* der Arbeitnehmer; **~ prop·er·ty** *s.* gewerbliches Eigentum; **~ psy·chol·o·gy** *s.* Be-

'triebspsycholo,gie f; **~ re·la·tions** s. pl. Beziehungen pl. zwischen Arbeitgeber u. Arbeitnehmern od. Gewerkschaften; **~ re·la·tions court** s. Am. Arbeitsgericht n; ⚥ **Rev·o·lu·tion** s. die industri'elle Revoluti'on; **~ school** s. Brit. Gewerbeschule f; **~ stocks** s. pl. Indu'striepa,piere pl.; **~ town** s. Industriestadt f; **~ tri·bu·nal** s. Arbeitsgericht n.

in·dus·tri·ous [ɪn'dʌstrɪəs] adj. □ fleißig, arbeitsam, emsig.

in·dus·try ['ɪndəstrɪ] s. **1.** a) Indu'strie f (e-s Landes etc.), b) Indu'strie (zweig m) f, Gewerbe(zweig m) n, Branche f: **the steel ~** die Stahlindustrie; **tourist ~** Tou'ristik f, Fremdenverkehrswesen n; **2.** Unter'nehmer (-schaft f) pl., Arbeitgeber pl.; **3.** Fleiß m, Arbeitseifer m.

in·dwell [,ɪn'dwel] [irr. → **dwell**] **I** v/t. **1.** bewohnen; **II** v/i. (**in**) **2.** wohnen (in dat.); **3.** fig. innewohnen (dat.); **in·dwell·er** ['ɪn,dwelə] s. poet. Bewohner(in).

in·e·bri·ate I v/t. [ɪ'niːbrɪeɪt] **1.** betrunken machen; **2.** fig. berauschen, trunken machen: **~d by success** vom Erfolg berauscht; **II** s. [-ɪət] **3.** Betrunkene(r) m; **4.** Alko'holiker(in); **III** adj. [-ɪət] **5.** betrunken; **6.** fig. berauscht; **in·e·bri·a·tion** [ɪ,niːbrɪ'eɪʃn], **in·e·bri·e·ty** [,ɪniː'braɪətɪ] s. Trunkenheit f (a. fig.), betrunkener Zustand.

in·ed·i·bil·i·ty [ɪn,edɪ'bɪlətɪ] s. Ungenießbarkeit f; **in·ed·i·ble** [ɪn'edɪbl] adj. ungenießbar, nicht essbar.

in·ed·it·ed [ɪn'edɪtɪd] adj. **1.** unveröffentlicht; **2.** ohne Veränderungen he'rausgegeben, nicht redigiert.

in·ef·fa·ble [ɪn'efəbl] adj. □ **1.** unaussprechlich, unbeschreiblich; **2.** (unsagbar) erhaben.

in·ef·face·a·ble [,ɪnɪ'feɪsəbl] adj. unauslöschlich.

in·ef·fec·tive [,ɪnɪ'fektɪv] adj. □ **1.** unwirksam (a. ⚕), wirkungslos; **2.** frucht-, erfolglos; **3.** unfähig, untauglich; **4.** (bsd. künstlerisch) nicht wirkungsvoll; **in·ef'fec·tive·ness** [-nɪs] s. **1.** Wirkungslosigkeit f; **2.** Erfolglosigkeit f.

in·ef·fec·tu·al [,ɪnɪ'fektjuəl] adj. □ **1.** → **ineffective** 1 u. 2; **2.** kraftlos; **,in·ef'fec·tu·al·ness** [-nɪs] s. **1.** → **ineffectiveness**; **2.** Nutzlosigkeit f; **3.** Schwäche f.

in·ef·fi·ca·cious [,ɪnefɪ'keɪʃəs] → **ineffective** 1, 2; **in·ef·fi·ca·cy** [ɪn'efɪkəsɪ] → **ineffectiveness**.

in·ef·fi·cien·cy [,ɪnɪ'fɪʃnsɪ] s. **1.** Wirkungslosigkeit f, 'Ineffizi,enz f: **~ of a remedy**; **2.** Unfähigkeit f, Inkompe'tenz f, Leistungsschwäche f (e-r Person); **3.** 'unratio,nelles Arbeiten etc., Unwirtschaftlichkeit f, 'Unproduktivi,tät f, 'Ineffizi,enz f: **~ of a method**; **in·ef'fi·cient** [-nt] adj. □ **1.** unwirksam, wirkungslos, 'ineffizi,ent; **2.** unfähig, untauglich, untüchtig, 'inkompe,tent; **3.** 'ineffizi,ent: a) leistungsschwach, b) 'unratio,nell, 'unproduk,tiv.

in·e·las·tic [,ɪnɪ'læstɪk] adj. **1.** 'une,lastisch (a. fig.); **2.** fig. starr, nicht fle'xibel; **in·e·las·tic·i·ty** [,ɪnɪlæs'tɪsɪtɪ] s. **1.** Mangel m an Elastizi'tät; **2.** fig. Starrheit f, Mangel m an Flexibili'tät.

in·el·e·gance [ɪn'elɪgəns] s. **1.** 'Unele,ganz f, Mangel m an Ele'ganz (a. fig.); **2.** fig. a) Derbheit f, Geschmacklosigkeit f, b) Unbeholfenheit f; **in'el·e·gant** [-nt] adj. □ **1.** 'unele,gant, ohne Ele'ganz (a. fig.); **2.** fig. a) derb, ge-

schmacklos, b) unbeholfen, plump.

in·el·i·gi·bil·i·ty [ɪn,elɪdʒə'bɪlətɪ] s. **1.** Untauglichkeit f, mangelnde Eignung; **2.** Unwählbarkeit f, Unfähigkeit f (in ein Amt gewählt zu werden etc.); **3.** mangelnde Berechtigung; **in·el·i·gi·ble** [ɪn'elɪdʒəbl] **I** adj. □ **1.** ungeeignet, nicht infrage kommend (for für): **~ for military service** (wehr)untauglich; **2.** unwählbar; **3.** ⚕ unfähig, nicht qualifiziert: **~ to hold an office**; **4.** (for) nicht berechtigt (zu), keinen Anspruch habend (auf acc.): **~ for a grant**; **~ to vote** nicht wahlberechtigt; **5.** a) unerwünscht, b) unpassend; **II** s. **6.** ungeeignete od. nicht infrage kommende Per'son.

in·e·luc·ta·ble [,ɪnɪ'lʌktəbl] adj. unvermeidlich, unentrinnbar.

in·ept [ɪ'nept] adj. □ **1.** unpassend; **2.** ungeschickt; **3.** albern, dumm; **in'ept·i·tude** [-tɪtjuːd], **in'ept·ness** [-nɪs] s. **1.** Ungeeignetheit f; **2.** Ungeschicktheit f; **3.** Albernheit f, Dummheit f.

in·e·qual·i·ty [,ɪnɪ'kwɒlətɪ] s. **1.** Ungleichheit f (a. Ⓐ, sociol.), Verschiedenheit f; **2.** Ungleichmäßigkeit f, Unregelmäßigkeit f; **3.** Unebenheit f (a. fig.); **4.** ast. Abweichung f.

in·eq·ui·ta·ble [ɪn'ekwɪtəbl] adj. □ ungerecht, unbillig; **in'eq·ui·ty** [-kwətɪ] s. Ungerechtigkeit f, Unbilligkeit f.

in·e·rad·i·ca·ble [,ɪnɪ'rædɪkəbl] adj. □ fig. unausrottbar; tief sitzend, tief eingewurzelt.

in·e·ras·a·ble [,ɪnɪ'reɪzəbl] adj. □ unauslöschbar, unauslöschlich.

in·ert [ɪ'nɜːt] adj. □ **1.** phys. träge: **~ mass**; **⚗** 'inak,tiv: **~ gas** Inert-, Edelgas n; **3.** unwirksam; **4.** fig. träge, untätig, schwerfällig, schlaff; **in·er·tia** [ɪ'nɜːʃjə] s. **1.** phys. (Massen)Trägheit f, Beharrungsvermögen n: **~ starter** mot. Schwungkraftanlasser m; **2.** fig. Träg-, Faulheit f; **3.** ⚗ Iner'tie f, Reakti'onsträgheit f; **in·er·tial** [ɪ'nɜːʃjəl] adj. phys. Trägheits...; **in'ert·ness** [-nɪs] s. Trägheit f.

in·es·cap·a·ble [,ɪnɪ'skeɪpəbl] adj. □ unvermeidlich: a) unentrinnbar, unabwendbar, b) unweigerlich.

in·es·sen·tial [,ɪnɪ'senʃl] **I** adj. unwesentlich, nebensächlich; **II** s. et. Unwesentliches, Nebensache f.

in·es·ti·ma·ble [ɪn'estɪməbl] adj. □ unschätzbar, unbezahlbar.

in·ev·i·ta·bil·i·ty [ɪn,evɪtə'bɪlətɪ] s. Unvermeidlichkeit f; **in·ev·i·ta·ble** [ɪn'evɪtəbl] **I** adj. □ unvermeidlich: a) unentrinnbar, b) zwangsläufig, unweigerlich, c) iro. obli'gat; **II** s. **the ~** das Unvermeidliche; **in·ev·i·ta·ble·ness** [ɪn'evɪtəblnɪs] → **inevitability**.

in·ex·act [,ɪnɪg'zækt] adj. □ ungenau; **,in·ex'act·i·tude** [-tɪtjuːd] s., **,in·ex·'act·ness** [-nɪs] s. Ungenauigkeit f.

in·ex·cus·a·ble [,ɪnɪk'skjuːzəbl] adj. □ **1.** unverzeihlich; **2.** unverantwortlich; **,in·ex·cus·a·bly** [-blɪ] adv. unverzeihlich(erweise).

in·ex·haust·i·bil·i·ty ['ɪnɪg,zɔːstə'bɪlətɪ] s. **1.** Unerschöpflichkeit f; **2.** Unermüdlichkeit f; **in·ex·haust·i·ble** [,ɪnɪg'zɔːstəbl] adj. □ **1.** unerschöpflich; **2.** unermüdlich.

in·ex·o·ra·bil·i·ty [ɪn,eksərə'bɪlətɪ] s. Unerbittlichkeit f; **in·ex·o·ra·ble** [ɪn'eksərəbl] adj. □ unerbittlich.

in·ex·pe·di·en·cy [,ɪnɪk'spiːdjənsɪ] s. **1.** Unzweckmäßigkeit f; **2.** Unklugheit f; **,in·ex·pe·di·ent** [-nt] adj. □ **1.** ungeeignet, unzweckmäßig, nicht ratsam; **2.** unklug.

in·ex·pen·sive [,ɪnɪk'spensɪv] adj. nicht teuer, preiswert, billig.

in·ex·pe·ri·ence [,ɪnɪk'spɪərɪəns] s. Unerfahrenheit f; **,in·ex'pe·ri·enced** [-st] adj. unerfahren: **~ hand** Nichtfachmann m.

in·ex·pert [ɪn'ekspɜːt] adj. □ **1.** ungeübt, unerfahren (in in dat.); **2.** ungeschickt; **3.** unsachgemäß.

in·ex·pi·a·ble [ɪn'ekspɪəbl] adj. □ **1.** unsühnbar; **2.** unversöhnlich.

in·ex·pli·ca·ble [,ɪnɪk'splɪkəbl] adj. □ unerklärlich, unverständlich; **,in·ex'pli·ca·bly** [-blɪ] adv. unerklärlich(erweise).

in·ex·plic·it [,ɪnɪk'splɪsɪt] adj. □ nicht deutlich ausgedrückt, nur angedeutet; unklar.

in·ex·plo·sive [,ɪnɪk'spləusɪv] adj. nicht explo'siv, explosi'onssicher.

in·ex·press·i·ble [,ɪnɪk'spresəbl] adj. □ unaussprechlich, unsäglich.

in·ex·pres·sive [,ɪnɪk'spresɪv] adj. □ **1.** ausdruckslos, nichts sagend; **2.** inhaltlos.

in ex·ten·so [,ɪnɪk'stensəu] (Lat.) adv. vollständig, ungekürzt; ausführlich.

in·ex·tin·guish·a·ble [,ɪnɪk'stɪŋgwɪʃəbl] adj. □ **1.** un(aus)löschbar; **2.** fig. unauslöschlich.

in·ex·tri·ca·ble [ɪn'ekstrɪkəbl] adj. □ **1.** unentwirrbar, un(auf)lösbar; **2.** gänzlich verworren.

in·fal·li·bil·i·ty [ɪn,fælə'bɪlətɪ] s. Unfehlbarkeit f (a. eccl.); **in·fal·li·ble** [ɪn'fæləbl] adj. □ unfehlbar.

in·fa·mous ['ɪnfəməs] adj. □ **1.** verrufen, berüchtigt (for wegen); **2.** schändlich, niederträchtig, gemein, in'fam; **3.** F mise'rabel, 'saumäßig'; **4.** ehrlos: a) ⚕ der bürgerlichen Ehrenrechte verlustig, b) entehrend, ehrenrührig: **~ conduct**; **in·fa·mous·ness** [-nɪs] → **infamy** 2; **'in·fa·my** [-mɪ] s. **1.** Ehrlosigkeit f, Schande f; **2.** Verrufenheit f; Schändlichkeit f, Niedertracht f; **3.** ⚕ Verlust m der bürgerlichen Ehrenrechte.

in·fan·cy ['ɪnfənsɪ] s. **1.** frühe Kindheit, Säuglingsalter n; **2.** ⚕ Minderjährigkeit f; **3.** fig. Anfangsstadium n: **in its ~** in den Anfängen od. 'Kinderschuhen' (steckend); **'in·fant** [-nt] **I** s. **1.** Säugling m, Baby n, kleines Kind; **2.** ⚕ Minderjährige(r m) f; **II** adj. **3.** Säuglings..., Kleinkinder...: **~ mortality** Säuglingssterblichkeit f; **~ prodigy** Wunderkind n; **~ school** Brit. etwa Vorschule f; **~ welfare** Säuglingsfürsorge f; **~ Jesus** das Jesuskind; **his ~ son** sein kleiner Sohn; **4.** ⚕ minderjährig; **5.** fig. jung, in den Anfängen (befindlich).

in·fan·ta [ɪn'fæntə] s. In'fantin f; **in'fan·te** [-tɪ] s. In'fant m.

in·fan·ti·cide [ɪn'fæntɪsaɪd] s. **1.** Kindestötung f; **2.** Kindesmörder(in).

in·fan·tile ['ɪnfəntaɪl] adj. **1.** kindlich, Kinder..., Kindes...; **2.** jugendlich; **3.** infan'til, kindisch; **~ (spi·nal) pa·ral·y·sis** s. ⚕ (spi'nale) Kinderlähmung.

in·fan·try ['ɪnfəntrɪ] s. ✗ Infante'rie f, Fußtruppen pl.; **'~·man** [-mən] s. [irr.] ✗ Infante'rist m.

in·farct [ɪn'fɑːkt] s. ☞ In'farkt m: **cardiac ~** Herzinfarkt; **in'farc·tion** [-kʃn] s. In'farkt(bildung f) m.

in·fat·u·ate [ɪn'fætjʊeɪt] v/t. betören, verblenden (with durch); **in'fat·u·at·ed** [-tɪd] adj. □ **1.** betört, verblendet (with durch); **2.** vernarrt (with in acc.); **in·fat·u·a·tion** [ɪn,fætjʊ'eɪʃn] s. Verblendung f; Verliebt-, Vernarrtheit f.

in·fect [ɪnˈfekt] *v/t.* 1. ✚ infizieren, anstecken (**with** mit, **by** durch): *become* ~*ed* sich anstecken; 2. *Sitten* verderben; *Luft* verpesten; 3. *fig. j-n* anstecken, beeinflussen; 4. einflößen (**s.o. with s.th.** j-m et.); **in·fec·tion** [-kʃn] *s.* 1. ✚ Infekti'on *f*, Ansteckung *f*: *catch an* ~ angesteckt werden, sich anstecken; 2. ✚ Ansteckungskeim *m*, Gift *n*; 3. *fig.* Ansteckung *f*: a) Vergiftung *f*, b) (*a.* schlechter) Einfluss, Einwirkung *f*; **in·fec·tious** [-kʃəs] *adj.* □ ✚ ansteckend (*a. fig. Lachen, Optimismus etc.*), infekti'ös, über'tragbar; **in·fec·tious·ness** [-kʃəsnɪs] *s. das* Ansteckende: a) ✚ Über'tragbarkeit *f*, b) *fig.* Einfluss *m*.

in·fe·lic·i·tous [ˌɪnfɪˈlɪsɪtəs] *adj.* 1. unglücklich; 2. unglücklich (gewählt), ungeschickt (*Worte, Stil*); **in·fe·lic·i·ty** [-tɪ] *s.* 1. Unglücklichkeit *f*; 2. Unglück *n*, Elend *n*; 3. unglücklicher *od.* ungeschickter Ausdruck *etc.*

in·fer [ɪnˈfɜː] *v/t.* 1. schließen, folgern, ableiten (**from** aus); 2. schließen lassen auf (*acc.*), an-, bedeuten; **in·fer·a·ble** [-ɜːrəbl] *adj.* zu schließen(d), zu folgern(d), ableitbar (**from** aus); **in·fer·ence** [ˈɪnfərəns] *s.* (Schluss)Folgerung *f*, (Rück)Schluss *m*: *make* ~*s* Schlüsse ziehen; **in·fer·en·tial** [ˌɪnfəˈrenʃl] *adj.* □ 1. zu folgern(d); 2. folgernd; 3. gefolgert; **in·fer·en·tial·ly** [ˌɪnfəˈrenʃəlɪ] *adv.* durch Schlussfolgerung.

in·fe·ri·or [ɪnˈfɪərɪə] I *adj.* 1. (**to**) 'untergeordnet (*dat.*); niedriger, geringer, geringwertiger (als): *be* ~ *to s.o.* j-m nachstehen; *he is* ~ *to none* er nimmt es mit jedem auf; 2. geringer, schwächer (**to** als); 3. 'untergeordnet, unter, nieder, zweitrangig: *the* ~ *classes* die unteren Klassen; ~ *court* ⚖ niederer Gerichtshof; 4. minderwertig, gering (mittel)mäßig: ~ *quality* usw. ⚖; 5. unter, tiefer gelegen, Unter...; 6. *typ.* tief stehend (*z. B. H₂*); 7. ~ *planet ast.* unterer Planet (*zwischen Erde u. Sonne*); II *s.* 8. 'Untergeordnete(r *m*) *f*, Unter'gebene(r *m*) *f*; 9. Geringere(r *m*) *f*, Schwächere(r *m*) *f*.

in·fe·ri·or·i·ty [ɪnˌfɪərɪˈɒrətɪ] *s.* 1. Minderwertigkeit *f*: ~ *complex* (*feeling*) *psych.* Minderwertigkeitskomplex *m* (-gefühl *n*); 2. (*a.* zahlen- *od.* mengenmäßige) Unter'legenheit *f*; 3. geringerer Stand *od.* Wert.

in·fer·nal [ɪnˈfɜːnl] *adj.* □ 1. höllisch, Höllen...: ~ *machine* Höllenmaschine *f*; ~ *regions* Unterwelt *f*; 2. *fig.* teuflisch; 3. F grässlich, höllisch; **in·fer·no** [-nəʊ] *pl.* **-nos** *s.* In'ferno *n*, Hölle *f*.

in·fer·tile [ɪnˈfɜːtaɪl] *adj.* unfruchtbar; **in·fer·til·i·ty** [ˌɪnfəˈtɪlətɪ] *s.* Unfruchtbarkeit *f*.

in·fest [ɪnˈfest] *v/t.* 1. heimsuchen, *Ort* unsicher machen; 2. plagen, verseuchen: ~*ed with* geplagt von, verseucht durch; 3. *fig.* über'laufen, -'schwemmen, -'fallen, sich festsetzen in (*dat.*): *be* ~*ed with* wimmeln von; **in·fes·ta·tion** [ˌɪnfeˈsteɪʃn] *s.* 1. Heimsuchung *f*, (Land)Plage *f*; Belästigung *f*; 2. *fig.* Über'schwemmung *f*.

in·feu·da·tion [ˌɪnfjuˈdeɪʃn] *s.* ⚖, *hist.* 1. Belehnung *f*; 2. ~ *of tithes* Zehntverleihung *f* an Laien.

in·fi·del [ˈɪnfɪdəl] *eccl.* I *s.* Ungläubige(r *m*) *f*; II *adj.* ungläubig; **in·fi·del·i·ty** [ˌɪnfɪˈdelətɪ] *s.* 1. Ungläubigkeit *f*; 2. (*bsd.* eheliche) Untreue.

in·field [ˈɪnfiːld] *s.* 1. ✐ a) dem Hof nahes Feld, b) Ackerland *n*; 2. *Kricket:* a) inneres Spielfeld, b) die dort stehenden Fänger; 3. *Baseball:* (Spieler *pl.*

im) Innenfeld *n*.

in·fight·ing [ˈɪnˌfaɪtɪŋ] *s.* 1. *Boxen:* Nahkampf *m*, Infight *m*; 2. *fig.* Gerangel *n*, Hickhack *n*.

in·fil·trate [ˈɪnfɪltreɪt] I *v/t.* 1. (*a.* ✖) einsickern in (*acc.*), 'durchsickern durch; 2. durch'setzen, -'tränken; 3. eindringen lassen, einschmuggeln (*into* in *acc.*); 4. *pol.* a) unter'wandern (*acc.*), b) *Agenten etc.* einschleusen (*into* in *acc.*); II *v/i.* 5. *a. fig.* einsickern, eindringen; 6. *pol.* (*into*) sich einschleusen (in *acc.*), unter'wandern (*acc.*); **in·fil·tra·tion** [ˌɪnfɪlˈtreɪʃn] *s.* 1. Einsickern *n* (*a.* ✖); Eindringen *n*; 2. Durch'tränkung *f*; 3. *pol.* Unter'wanderung *f*: ~ *of agents* Einschleusen *n* von Agenten; '**in·fil·tra·tor** [-tə] *s. pol.* Unter'wanderer *m*.

in·fi·nite [ˈɪnfɪnət] I *adj.* □ 1. un'endlich, endlos, unbegrenzt: ~ *loop Computer:* Endlosschleife *f*; 2. ungeheuer, 'allum,fassend; 3. *mit s. pl.* unzählige *pl.*; 4. ~ *verb ling.* Verbum *n* infinitum; II *s.* 5. *das* Un'endliche, un'endlicher Raum; 6. *the* ☌ Gott *m*; '**in·fi·nite·ly** [-lɪ] *adv.* 1. un'endlich; ungeheuer; 2. ~ *variable* ⊛ stufenlos (regelbar).

in·fin·i·tes·i·mal [ˌɪnfɪnɪˈtesɪml] I *adj.* □ winzig, un'endlich klein; II *s.* un'endlich kleine Menge; ~ *cal·cu·lus s.* ꓕ Infinitesi'malrechnung *f*.

in·fin·i·ti·val [ɪnˌfɪnɪˈtaɪvl] *adj. ling.* infinitivisch; **in·fin·i·tive** [ɪnˈfɪnətɪv] *ling.* I *s.* Infinitiv *m*, Nennform *f*; II *adj.* infinitivisch: ~ *mood* Infinitiv *m*.

in·fin·i·tude [ɪnˈfɪnɪtjuːd] → **infinity** 1 u. 2; **in·fin·i·ty** [-ətɪ] *s.* 1. Un'endlichkeit *f*, Unbegrenztheit *f*, Unermesslichkeit *f*; 2. un'endliche Größe *od.* Zahl; 3. ꓕ un'endliche Menge *od.* Größe, das Un'endliche: *to* ~ ad infinitum.

in·firm [ɪnˈfɜːm] *adj.* □ 1. schwach, gebrechlich; 2. *a.* ~ *of purpose* wankelmütig, unentschlossen, willensschwach; **in·fir·ma·ry** [-mərɪ] *s.* 1. Krankenhaus *n*; 2. Krankenzimmer *n* (*in Internaten etc.*); ✖ ('Kranken)Re,vier *n*; **in·fir·mi·ty** [-mɪtɪ] *s.* 1. Gebrechlichkeit *f*, (Alters)Schwäche *f*; Krankheit *f*; 2. *a.* ~ *of purpose* Cha'rakterschwäche *f*, Unentschlossenheit *f*.

in·fix I *v/t.* [ɪnˈfɪks] 1. eintreiben, befestigen; 2. *fig.* einprägen (*in dat.*); 3. *ling.* einfügen; II *s.* [ˈɪnfɪks] 4. *ling.* In'fix *n*, Einfügung *f*.

in·flame [ɪnˈfleɪm] I *v/t.* 1. *mst* ✚ entzünden; 2. *fig.* erregen, entflammen, reizen: ~*d with rage* wutentbrannt; II *v/i.* 3. sich entzünden (*a.* ✚), Feuer fangen; 4. *fig.* entbrennen (**with** vor *dat.*, von); sich erhitzen, in Wut geraten; **in·flamed** [-md] *adj.* entzündet; **in·flam·ma·bil·i·ty** [ɪnˌflæməˈbɪlətɪ] *s.* 1. Brennbarkeit *f*, Entzündlichkeit *f*; 2. *fig.* Erregbarkeit *f*, Jähzorn *m*; **in·flam·ma·ble** [ɪnˈflæməbl] I *adj.* 1. brennbar, leicht entzündlich; 2. feuergefährlich; 3. *fig.* reizbar, jähzornig, hitzig; II *s.* 4. *pl.* Zündstoffe *pl.*; **in·flam·ma·tion** [ˌɪnfləˈmeɪʃn] *s.* 1. ✚ Entzündung *f*; 2. Aufflammen *n*; 3. *fig.* Erregung *f*, Aufregung *f*; **in·flam·ma·to·ry** [ɪnˈflæmətərɪ] *adj.* 1. ✚ Entzündungs...; 2. *fig.* aufrührerisch, Hetz...: ~ *speech*.

in·flat·a·ble [ɪnˈfleɪtəbl] *adj.* aufblasbar: ~ *boat* Schlauchboot *n*; **in·flate** [ɪnˈfleɪt] *v/t.* 1. aufblasen, aufblähen (*beide a. fig.*), mit Luft *etc.* füllen, *Reifen etc.* aufpumpen; 2. ✚ *Preise* hoch-

treiben, 'übermäßig steigern; **in·flat·ed** [-tɪd] *adj.* 1. aufgebläht, aufgeblasen (*beide a. fig. Person*): ~ *with pride* stolzgeschwellt; 2. *fig.* geschwollen (*Stil*); 3. über'höht (*Preise*); **in·fla·tion** [-eɪʃn] *s.* 1. ✚ Inflati'on *f*: *creeping* (*galloping*) ~ schleichende (galoppierende) Inflation; *rate of* ~ Inflationsrate *f*; 2. *fig.* Dünkel *m*, Aufgeblasenheit *f*; 3. *fig.* Schwülstigkeit *f*; **in·fla·tion·ar·y** [-eɪʃnərɪ] *adj.* ✚ inflatio'när, inflatio'nistisch, Inflations...: ~ *period* Inflationszeit *f*; **in·fla·tion·ism** [-eɪʃnɪzəm] *s.* ✚ Inflatio'nismus *m*; **in·fla·tion·ist** [-eɪʃnɪst] *s.* Anhänger *m* des Inflatio'nismus.

in·flect [ɪnˈflekt] *v/t.* 1. (nach innen) biegen; 2. *ling.* flektieren, beugen, abwandeln; **in·flec·tion** [-kʃn] *etc.* → **inflexion** *etc.*

in·flex·i·bil·i·ty [ɪnˌfleksəˈbɪlətɪ] *s.* 1. Unbiegsamkeit *f*; 2. Unbeugsamkeit *f*; **in·flex·i·ble** [ɪnˈfleksəbl] *adj.* □ 1. 'une,lastisch, unbiegsam; 2. *fig.* a) unbeugsam, starr, b) unerbittlich.

in·flex·ion [ɪnˈflekʃn] *n* *s.* 1. Biegung *f*, Krümmung *f*; 2. (me'lodische) Modulati'on; 3. (Ton)Veränderung *f* der Stimme, weitS. feine Nu'ance; 4. *ling.* Flexi'on *f*, Beugung *f*, Abwandlung *f*; **in·'flex·ion·al** [-ʃənl] *adj. ling.* flektierend, Flexions...

in·flict [ɪnˈflɪkt] *v/t.* 1. *Leid etc.* zufügen; *Wunde, Niederlage* beibringen, *Schlag* versetzen, *Strafe* auferlegen, zudiktieren (**on, upon** *dat.*); 2. aufbürden (**on, upon** *dat.*): ~ *o.s. on s.o.* sich j-m aufdrängen; **in·flic·tion** [-kʃn] *s.* 1. Zufügung *f*, Auferlegung *f*, Verhängung *f* (*Strafe*); 2. Last *f*, Plage *f*; 3. Heimsuchung *f*, Strafe *f*.

in·flo·res·cence [ˌɪnflɔːˈresns] *s.* 1. ♀ a) Blütenstand *m*, b) *coll.* Blüten *pl.*; 2. *a. fig.* Aufblühen *n*, Blüte *f*.

in·flow [ˈɪnfləʊ] → **influx** 1.

in·flu·ence [ˈɪnfluəns] I *s.* 1. Einfluss *m*, (Ein)Wirkung *f* (**on, upon, over** auf *acc.*, **with** bei); ⚖ Beeinflussung *f*: *be under s.o.'s* ~ unter j-s Einfluss stehen; *under the* ~ *of drink* unter Alkoholeinfluss; *under the* ~ F ,blau'; 2. Einfluss *m*, Macht *f*: *bring one's* ~ *to bear* s-n Einfluss geltend machen; II *v/t.* 3. beeinflussen, (ein)wirken *od.* Einfluss ausüben auf (*acc.*); 4. bewegen, bestimmen; **in·flu·en·tial** [ˌɪnfluˈenʃl] *adj.* □ 1. einflussreich; maßgeblich; 2. von (großem) Einfluss (**on** auf *acc.*; **in** in *dat.*).

in·flu·en·za [ˌɪnfluˈenzə] *s.* ✚ Influ'enza *f*, Grippe *f*.

in·flux [ˈɪnflʌks] *s.* 1. Einfließen *n*, Zustrom *m*, Zufluss *m*; 2. ✚ (*Kapital- etc.*) Zufluss *m*, (Waren)Zufuhr *f*; 3. Mündung *f* (*Fluss*); 4. *fig.* Zustrom *m*: ~ *of visitors* Besucherstrom *m*.

in·fo [ˈɪnfəʊ] *s.* F Informati'on *f*.

in·fold [ɪnˈfəʊld] → **enfold**.

in·form [ɪnˈfɔːm] I *v/t.* (*of*) informieren (über *acc.*), verständigen, benachrichtigen, in Kenntnis setzen, unter'richten (von), j-m mitteilen (*acc.*): ~ *o.s. of s.th.* sich über et. informieren; *keep s.o.* ~*ed* j-n auf dem Laufenden halten; ~ *s.o. that* j-n davon in Kenntnis setzen, dass; II *v/i.* ~ *against s.o.* j-n anzeigen *od.* denunzieren.

in·for·mal [ɪnˈfɔːml] *adj.* □ 1. zwanglos, ungezwungen, nicht for'mell *od.* förmlich; 2. 'inoffizi,ell: ~ *visit* (*talks*); 3. *ling.* Umgangs...: ~ *speech*; 4. ⚖ formlos: a) formfrei: ~ *contract*, b) formwidrig; **in·for·mal·i·ty** [ˌɪnfɔːˈmælətɪ] *s.* **1.** Zwanglosigkeit *f*, Ungezwungenheit *f*; **2.** ⚖ a) Formlosigkeit *f*, b) Formfehler *m*.

in·form·ant [ɪn'fɔːmənt] *s.* **1.** Gewährsmann *m*, Infor'mant(in), (Informati'ons)Quelle *f*; **2.** → *informer*.

in·for·ma·tics [ˌɪnfə'mætɪks] *s. pl. oft sg. konstr.* Infor'matik *f*.

in·for·ma·tion [ˌɪnfə'meɪʃn] *s.* **1.** Nachricht *f*, Mitteilung *f*, Meldung *f*, Informati'on *f* (*a. Computer*): **~** *bureau*, **~** *office* Auskunftsstelle *f*, Auskunftei *f*; **~** *desk* Auskunft(sschalter *m*) *f*; **~** *fatigue syndrome* Ermüdungserscheinungen *pl.* durch Informationsüberfrachtung, durch Informationsflut bedingtes Ermüdungssyndrom *n*; **~** *flow* Informationsfluss *m*; **~** *highway* Datenautobahn *f*; **~** *retrieval* Informationsabruf *m*; **~** *science* Informatik *f*; **~** *scientist* Informatiker(in); **~** *superhighway* Datenautobahn *f*; **~** *technology* Informationstechnologie *f*, -technik *f*; **2.** Auskunft *f*, Bescheid *m*, Kenntnis *f*: *give* **~** Auskunft geben; *we have no* **~** wir sind nicht unterrichtet (*as to* über *acc.*); **3.** Erkundigungen *pl.*: *gather* **~** sich erkundigen, Auskünfte einholen; **4.** Unter'weisung *f*: *for your* **~** zu Ihrer Kenntnisnahme; **5.** Einzelheiten *pl.*, Angaben *pl.*; **6.** ⚖ Anklage *f*, Anzeige *f*: *lodge* **~** *against s.o.* Anklage erheben gegen j-n, j-n anzeigen; **in·for·'ma·tion·al** [-ʃənl] *adj.* informa'torisch, Informations...

in·form·a·tive [ɪn'fɔːmətɪv] *adj.* **1.** informa'tiv, lehr-, aufschlussreich; **2.** mitteilsam; **in·'form·a·to·ry** [-tərɪ] *adj.* → a) *informational*, b) *informative* 1; **in·'formed** [-md] *adj.* **1.** infor'miert, (gut) unter'richtet: **~** *quarters* unterrichtete Kreise; **2.** a) sachkundig, b) sachlich begründet *od.* einwandfrei, fun'diert; **3.** gebildet; **in·'form·er** [-mə] *s.* **1.** Infor'mant(in), Denunzi'ant(in): (*common*) **~**, (*police*) **~** Spitzel *m*; **2.** ⚖ Anzeigerstatter(in).

in·fo·tain·ment [ˌɪnfəʊ'teɪnmənt] *s. TV etc.* Info'tainment *n*.

in·fra ['ɪnfrə] *adv.* unten: *vide* (*od. see*) **~** siehe unten (*in Büchern*).

infra- [ɪnfrə] *in Zssgn* unter(halb).

in·frac·tion [ɪn'frækʃn] → *infringement*.

in·fra dig [ˌɪnfrə'dɪg] (*Lat. abbr.*) *adv. u. adj.* F unter m-r (*etc.*) Würde, unwürdig.

in·fran·gi·ble [ɪn'frændʒɪbl] *adj.* unzerbrechlich; *fig.* unverletzlich.

in·fra·'red *adj. phys.* infrarot; **~'son·ic** *adj.* Infraschall..., unter der Schallgrenze liegend.

in·fra·struc·ture *s. allg.* 'Infrastruk,tur *f*.

in·fre·quen·cy [ɪn'friːkwənsɪ] *s.* Seltenheit *f*; **in·'fre·quent** [-nt] *adj.* □ **1.** selten; **2.** spärlich, dünn gesät.

in·fringe [ɪn'frɪndʒ] **I** *v/t. Gesetz, Eid etc.* brechen, verletzen, verstoßen gegen; **II** *v/i.* (*on, upon*) *Rechte etc.* verletzen, eingreifen (in *acc.*); **in·'fringe·ment** [-mənt] *s.* (*on, upon*) (*Rechts- etc., a. Patent*)Verletzung *f*, (*Rechts-, Vertrags*)Bruch *m*, Über'tretung *f* (*gen.*); Verstoß *m* (gegen).

in·fu·ri·ate [ɪn'fjʊərɪeɪt] *v/t.* wütend *od.* rasend machen; **in·'fu·ri·at·ing** [-tɪŋ] *adj.* aufreizend, rasend machend.

in·fuse [ɪn'fjuːz] *v/t.* **1.** aufgießen, -brühen, ziehen lassen: **~** *tea* Tee aufgießen; **2.** *fig.* einflößen (*into dat.*); **3.** erfüllen (*with* mit); **~** *Tee-Ei n*; **in·'fu·si·ble** [-zəbl] *adj.* 🜌 unschmelzbar; **in·'fu·sion** [-ʒn]

s. **1.** Aufgießen *n*, -brühen *n*; **2.** Aufguss *m*, (Kräuter- *etc.*)Tee *m*; **3.** ✿ Infusi'on *f*; **4.** *fig.* Einflößung *f*; **5.** *fig.* a) Beimischung *f*, b) Zufluss *m*.

in·fu·so·ri·a [ˌɪnfjuː'zɔːrɪə] *s. pl. zo.* Infu'sorien *pl.*, Wimpertierchen *pl.*; **in·fu·so·ri·al** [-əl] *adj. zo.* Infusorien...: **~** *earth min.* Infusorienerde *f*, Kieselgur *f*; **in·fu·so·ri·an** [-ən] *zo.* **I** *s.* Wimpertierchen *n*, Infu'sorium *n*; **II** *adj.* → *infusorial*.

in·gen·ious [ɪn'dʒiːnjəs] *adj.* □ geni'al: a) erfinderisch, findig, b) geistreich, klug, c) sinn-, kunstvoll, raffiniert: **~** *design*; **in·'gen·ious·ness** [-nɪs] → *ingenuity*.

in·gé·nue ['ænʒeɪnjuː] *s.* **1.** na'ives Mädchen, ,Unschuld' *f*; **2.** *thea.* Na'ive *f*.

in·ge·nu·i·ty [ˌɪndʒɪ'njuːətɪ] *s.* **1.** Geniali'tät *f*, Erfindungsgabe *f*, Einfallsreichtum *m*, Findigkeit *f*, Geschicklichkeit *f*, Bril'lanz *f*; **2.** Raffi'nesse *f*, geni'ale Ausführung *etc.*

in·gen·u·ous [ɪn'dʒenjʊəs] *adj.* □ **1.** offen(herzig), treuherzig, unbefangen, aufrichtig; **2.** na'iv, einfältig, unschuldig; **in·'gen·u·ous·ness** [-nɪs] *s.* **1.** Offenheit *f*, Treuherzigkeit *f*; **2.** Naivi'tät *f*.

in·gest [ɪn'dʒest] *v/t. Nahrung* aufnehmen; **in·'ges·tion** [-tʃn] *s.* Nahrungsaufnahme *f*.

in·glo·ri·ous [ɪn'glɔːrɪəs] *adj.* □ **1.** unrühmlich, schimpflich; **2.** *obs.* ruhmlos.

in·go·ing ['ɪnˌgəʊɪŋ] *adj.* **1.** eintretend; **2.** neu (*Beamter, Mieter etc.*).

in·got ['ɪŋgət] *s.* ⊚ Barren *m*, Stange *f*, Block *m*: **~** *of gold* Goldbarren *m*; **~** *of steel* Stahlblock *m*; **~** *iron* Flussstahl *m*, -eisen *n*.

in·graft [ɪn'grɑːft] → *engraft*.

in·grain I *v/t.* [ˌɪn'greɪn] **1.** *obs.* in der Wolle *od.* Faser (*farbecht*) färben; **2.** *fig.* tief verwurzeln; **II** *adj.* [*attr.* 'ɪngreɪn; *pred.* ˌɪn'greɪn] **3.** → ,**in·'grained** [-nd] *adj. fig.* **1.** tief verwurzelt: **~** *prejudice*; **2.** eingefleischt: **~** *habit*; **3.** unverbesserlich.

in·grate [ɪn'greɪt] *obs.* **I** *adj.* undankbar; **II** *s.* Undankbare(r *m*) *f*.

in·gra·ti·ate [ɪn'greɪʃɪeɪt] *v/t.*: **~** *o.s. with s.o.* sich bei j-m einschmeicheln; **in·'gra·ti·at·ing** [-tɪŋ] *adj.* □ schmeichlerisch.

in·grat·i·tude [ɪn'grætɪtjuːd] *s.* Undank (-barkeit *f*) *m*.

in·gre·di·ent [ɪn'griːdjənt] *s.* 🜌, *Küche u. fig.*: Bestandteil *m*, Zutat *f*; *fig. a.* (*Charakter- etc.*)Merkmal *n*.

in·gress ['ɪngres] *s.* **1.** Eintritt *m* (*a. ast.*), Eintreten *n* (*into* in *acc.*); **2.** Zutritt *m*, Zugang (*into* zu); **3.** Zustrom *m*: **~** *of visitors*.

'in-group *s. sociol.* Ingroup *f*.

in·grow·ing ['ɪnˌgrəʊɪŋ] *adj.*, **'in·grown** *adj.* ✿ eingewachsen: *an* **~** *nail*.

in·gui·nal ['ɪŋgwɪnl] *adj.* ✿ Leisten...

in·gur·gi·tate [ɪn'gɜːdʒɪteɪt] *v/t. bsd. fig.* verschlingen, schlucken.

in·hab·it [ɪn'hæbɪt] *v/t.* bewohnen, wohnen *od.* (*a. zo.*) leben in (*dat.*); **in·'hab·it·a·ble** [-təbl] *adj.* bewohnbar; **in·'hab·it·ant** [-tənt] *s.* **1.** Bewohner (-in) (*e-s Hauses etc.*); **2.** Einwohner (-in) (*e-s Orts, e-s Landes*).

in·ha·la·tion [ˌɪnhə'leɪʃn] *s.* **1.** Einatmung *f*; **2.** ✿ Inhalati'on *f*; **in·hale** [ɪn'heɪl] **I** *v/t.* ✿ einatmen, inhalieren; **II** *v/i.* inhalieren, *beim Rauchen*: a. Lungenzüge machen; **in·hal·er** [ɪn'heɪlə] *s.* **1.** ✿ Inhalati'onsappa,rat *m*; **2.** j-d, der inhaliert.

in·har·mo·ni·ous [ˌɪnhɑː'məʊnjəs] *adj.*

□ 'unhar,monisch: a) 'misstönend, b) *fig.* uneinig.

in·here [ɪn'hɪə] *v/i.* **1.** innewohnen: a) anhaften (*in s.o.* j-m), b) eigen sein (*in s.th.* e-r Sache); **2.** enthalten sein (*in* in *dat.*); **in·'her·ence** [-ərəns] *s.* Innewohnen *n*, Anhaften *n*; *phls.* Inhä'renz *f*; **in·'her·ent** [-ərənt] *adj.* □ **1.** innewohnend, eigen, anhaftend (*alle: in dat.*): **~** *defect* (*od. vice*) ⚖ innerer Fehler; **2.** eingewurzelt; **3.** *phls.* inhä'rent; **in·'her·ent·ly** [-ərəntlɪ] *adv.* von Na'tur aus, schon an sich.

in·her·it [ɪn'herɪt] **I** *v/t.* **1.** ⚖, *biol., fig.* erben; **2.** *biol., fig.* ererben; **II** *v/i.* **3.** ⚖ erben, Erbe sein; **in·'her·it·a·ble** [-təbl] *adj.* **1.** ⚖, *biol., fig.* vererbbar, erblich (*Sache*); **2.** erbfähig, -berechtigt (*Person*); **in·'her·it·ance** [-təns] *s.* **1.** ⚖, *fig.* Erbe *n*, Erbschaft *f*, Erbteil *n*: **~** *tax Am.* Erbschaftssteuer *f*; **2.** ⚖, *biol.* Vererbung *f*: *by* ⚖ durch Vererbung, erblich; **in·'her·it·ed** [-tɪd] *adj.* ererbt, Erb... (*a. ling.*); **in·'her·i·tor** [-tə] *s.* Erbe *m* (*a. fig.*); **in·'her·i·tress** [-trɪs], **in·'her·i·trix** [-trɪks] *s.* Erbin *f*.

in·hib·it [ɪn'hɪbɪt] *v/t.* **1.** *et., psych.* j-n hemmen: **~ed** gehemmt; **2.** (*from*) j-n abhalten (von), hindern (an *dat.*): **~** *s.o. from doing s.th.* j-n daran hindern, et. zu tun; **in·hi·bi·tion** [ˌɪnhɪ'bɪʃn] *s.* **1.** Hemmung *f* (*a.* ⚙ *u. psych.*): **~** *threshold* 'Hemmschwelle *f*; **2.** Unter'sagung *f*, Verbot *n*; **3.** ⚖ Unter'sagungsbefehl *m* (*e-e Sache weiterzuverfolgen*); **in·'hib·i·tor** [-tə] *s.* 🜌, ⚙ Hemmstoff *m*, (*Korrosions- etc.*) Schutzmittel *n*; **in·'hib·i·to·ry** [-tərɪ] **1.** hemmend, Hemmungs... (*a.* ⚙ *u. psych.*), hindernd; **2.** unter'sagend, verbietend.

in·hos·pi·ta·ble [ɪn'hɒspɪtəbl] *adj.* □ ungastlich: a) nicht gastfreundlich, b) unwirtlich: **~** *climate*; **in·hos·pi·tal·i·ty** [ɪnˌhɒspɪ'tælətɪ] *s.* Ungastlichkeit *f*: a) mangelnde Gastfreundschaft *f*, b) Unwirtlichkeit *f*.

'in-,house *adj.* innerbetrieblich, betriebsintern

in·hu·man [ɪn'hjuːmən] *adj.* □, **in·hu·mane** [ˌɪnhjuː'meɪn] *adj.* □ unmenschlich, 'inhu,man; **in·hu·man·i·ty** [ˌɪnhjuː'mænətɪ] *s.* Unmenschlichkeit *f*.

in·hume [ɪn'hjuːm] *v/t.* beerdigen, bestatten.

in·im·i·cal [ɪ'nɪmɪkl] *adj.* □ (*to*) **1.** feindlich (gegen); **2.** schädlich, nachteilig (für).

in·im·i·ta·ble [ɪ'nɪmɪtəbl] *adj.* □ unnachahmlich, einzigartig.

in·iq·ui·tous [ɪ'nɪkwɪtəs] *adj.* □ **1.** ungerecht; **2.** frevelhaft; **3.** böse, lasterhaft, schlecht; **4.** gemein, niederträchtig; **in·'iq·ui·ty** [-tɪ] *s.* **1.** Ungerechtigkeit *f*; **2.** Niederträchtigkeit *f*; **3.** Schandtat *f*, Frevel *m*; **4.** Sünde *f*, Laster *n*.

in·i·tial [ɪ'nɪʃl] **I** *adj.* □ **1.** anfänglich, Anfangs..., Ausgangs..., erst, ursprünglich: **~** *advertising* ♦ Einführungswerbung *f*; **~** *capital expenditure* ♦ Anlagekosten *pl.*; **~** *cost* ♦ Anfangskosten *pl.*; **~** *material* ♦ Ausgangsmaterial *n*; **~** *position* ⊚, ✕ *etc.* Ausgangsstellung *f*; **~** *salary* Anfangsgehalt *n*; **~** *stages* Anfangsstadium *n*; **2.** *ling.* anlautend; **II** *s.* **3.** (großer) Anfangsbuchstabe, Initi'ale *f*; **4.** *pl.* Mono'gramm *n*; **5.** *ling.* Anlaut *m*; **III** *v/t.* **6.** mit Initi'alen versehen *od.* unter'zeichnen, paraphieren; **7.** mit e-m Mono'gramm versehen; **in·'i·tial·ly** [-ʃəlɪ] *adv.* am *od.* zu Anfang, anfänglich, zu'erst.

in·i·ti·ate I *v/t.* [ɪ'nɪʃɪeɪt] **1.** beginnen, einleiten, -führen, ins Leben rufen; **2.** *j-n* einweihen, -arbeiten, -führen (***into, in*** in *acc.*); **3.** *j-n* einführen, aufnehmen (***into*** in *acc.*); **4.** *pol.* als Erster beantragen; *Gesetzesvorlage* einbringen; II *adj.* [-ɪət] **5.** → ***initiated***; III *s.* [-ɪət] **6.** Eingeweihte(r *m*) *f*, Kenner(in); **7.** Eingeführte(r *m*) *f*; **8.** Neuling *m*, Anfänger (-in); **in'i·ti·at·ed** [-tɪd] *adj.* eingeführt, eingeweiht: ***the ~*** die Eingeweihten *pl.*; **in·i·ti·a·tion** [ɪˌnɪʃɪ'eɪʃn] *s.* **1.** Einleitung *f*, Beginn *m*; **2.** (feierliche) Einführung, -setzung *f*, Aufnahme *f* (***into*** in *acc.*); **3.** Einweihung *f*, Weihe *f*.

in·i·ti·a·tive [ɪ'nɪʃɪətɪv] I *s.* **1.** Initia'tive *f*: a) erster Schritt *od.* Anstoß, Anregung *f*: ***take the ~*** die Initiative ergreifen, den ersten Schritt tun; ***on s.o.'s ~*** auf j-s Anregung hin; ***on one's own ~*** aus eigenem Antrieb, b) Unter'nehmungsgeist *m*; **2.** *pol.* (Ge'setzes)Initiaˌtive *f*; II *adj.* **3.** einleitend; **4.** beginnend.

in·i·ti·a·tor [ɪ'nɪʃɪeɪtə] *s.* **1.** Initi'ator *m*, Urheber *m*, Anreger *m*; **2.** ⚔ (Initi'al-) Zündladung *f*; **3.** ⚗ reakti'onsauslösende Sub'stanz; **in'i·ti·a·to·ry** [-ɪətərɪ] *adj.* **1.** einleitend; **2.** einweihend, Einweihungs...

in·ject [ɪn'dʒekt] *v/t.* **1.** ⚕ a) (*a.* ⚙) einspritzen, b) ausspritzen (***with*** mit), c) e-e Einspritzung machen in (*acc.*); **2.** *fig.* einflößen, einimpfen (***into*** *dat.*); **3.** *Bemerkung* einwerfen.

in·jec·tion [ɪn'dʒekʃn] *s.* ⚕ Injekti'on *f*: a) Einspritzung *f* (*a.* ⚙), Spritze *f*, b) *das Eingespritzte*, c) Einlauf *m*, d) Ausspritzung *f* (*e-r Wunde etc.*): ***~ of money*** *fig.* ‚Spritze' *f*, Geldzuschuss *m*; **~ cock** *s.* Einspritzhahn *m*; **~ die** *s.* ⚙ Spritzform *f*; **~ mo(u)ld·ing** *s.* Spritzguss(verfahren *n*) *m*; **~ noz·zle** *s.* Einspritzdüse *f*; **~ syr·inge** *s.* ⚕ Injekti'onsspritze *f*.

in·jec·tor [ɪn'dʒektə] *s.* ⚙ In'jektor *m*, Dampfstrahlpumpe *f*.

in·ju·di·cious [ˌɪndʒuː'dɪʃəs] *adj.* □ unklug, 'unüberˌlegt.

In·jun ['ɪndʒən] *s. Am. humor.* Indi'aner *m*: ***honest ~!*** Ehrenwort!

in·junc·tion [ɪn'dʒʌŋkʃn] *s.* **1.** ⚖ gerichtliche Verfügung, *bsd.* (gerichtlicher) Unter'lassungsbefehl: ***interim ~*** einstweilige Verfügung; **2.** ausdrücklicher Befehl.

in·jure ['ɪndʒə] *v/t.* **1.** verletzen, beschädigen, verwunden: ***~ one's leg*** sich am Bein verletzen; **2.** *fig. j-n, j-s Stolz etc.* kränken, verletzen; **3.** schaden (*dat.*), schädigen, beeinträchtigen; **'in·jured** [-əd] *adj.* **1.** verletzt: ***the ~*** die Verletzten; **2.** geschädigt: ***the ~ party*** der Geschädigte; **3.** gekränkt, verletzt: ***~ innocence*** gekränkte Unschuld; **in·ju·ri·ous** [ɪn'dʒʊərɪəs] *adj.* □ **1.** schädlich, nachteilig (***to*** für): ***be ~ (to)*** schaden (*dat.*); **2.** beleidigend, verletzend (*Worte*); **3.** un(ge)recht; **in·ju·ry** ['ɪndʒərɪ] *s.* **1.** Verletzung *f*, Wunde *f* (***to*** an *dat.*): ***~ to the head*** Kopfverletzung, -wunde; **~ time** *sport* Nachspielzeit *f*; **2.** (Be)Schädigung *f* (***to*** *gen.*), Schaden *m* (*a.* ⚖): ***~ to person (property)*** Personen-(Sach)schaden; **3.** *fig.* Verletzung *f*, Kränkung *f* (***to*** *gen.*); **4.** Unrecht *n*.

in·jus·tice [ɪn'dʒʌstɪs] *s.* Unrecht *n*, Ungerechtigkeit *f*: ***do s.o. an ~*** j-m ein Unrecht antun.

ink [ɪŋk] I *s.* **1.** Tinte *f*: ***copying ~*** Kopiertinte *f*; **2.** Tusche *f*: ***~ drawing*** Tuschzeichnung *f*; → ***Indian ink***; **3.** *typ.* (Druck)Farbe *f*; → ***printer*** 1; **4.** *zo.* Tinte *f*, Sepia *f*; II *v/t.* **5.** mit Tinte schwärzen *od.* beschmieren; **6.** *typ. Druckwalzen* einfärben; **7.** ***~ in*** *mit Tusche* ausziehen, tuschieren; **8.** ***~ out*** *mit Tinte* unleserlich machen, ausstreichen; **~ bag** → ***ink sac***; **~ blot** *s.* Tintenklecks *m*.

ink·er ['ɪŋkə] *s.* **1.** → ***inking roller***; **2.** *typ.* Tuscher(in).

ink·ing ['ɪŋkɪŋ] *s. typ.* Einfärben *n*; **~ pad** *s.* Einschwärzballen *m*; **~ roll·er** *s.* Auftrag-, Farbwalze *f*.

ink-jet print·er ['ɪŋkdʒet] *s. Computer*: Tintenstrahldrucker *m*.

ink·ling ['ɪŋklɪŋ] *s.* **1.** Andeutung *f*, Wink *m*; **2.** dunkle Ahnung: ***get an ~ of s.th.*** et. merken, ‚Wind von et. bekommen'; ***not the least ~*** nicht die leiseste Ahnung.

ink| pad *s.* Farb-, Stempelkissen *n*; **~ pot** *s.* Tintenfass *n*; **~ rib·bon** *s.* Farbband *n*; **~ sac** *s. zo.* Tintenbeutel *m*; **'~·stand** *s.* **1.** Tintenfass *n*; **2.** Schreibzeug *n*; **'~·well** *s.* (eingelassenes) Tintenfass.

ink·y ['ɪŋkɪ] *adj.* **1.** tiefschwarz; **2.** voll Tinte, tintig.

in·laid [ˌɪn'leɪd; *attr.* 'ɪnleɪd] *adj.* eingelegt, Einlege..., Mosaik...: ***~ floor*** Parkett(fußboden *m*) *n*; ***~ table*** Tisch *m* mit Einlegearbeit; ***~ work*** Einlegearbeit *f*.

in·land ['ɪnlənd] I *s.* **1.** In-, Binnenland *n*; II *adj.* **2.** binnenländisch, Binnen...: ***~ town*** Stadt im Binnenland; **3.** inländisch, einheimisch, Inland..., Landes...; III *adv.* [ɪn'lænd] **4.** im Innern des Landes; **5.** ins Innere des Landes, landeinwärts; **~ bill (of ex·change)** ['ɪnlənd] *s.* ✝ Inlandwechsel *m*; **~ du·ty** *s.* ✝ Binnenzoll *m*.

in·land·er ['ɪnləndə] *s.* Binnenländer(in).

'in·land| mail *s. Brit.* Inlandspost *f*; **~ nav·i·ga·tion** *s.* Binnenschifffahrt *f*; **~ prod·uce** *s.* ✝ 'Landesproˌdukte *pl.*; **~ rev·e·nue** *s.* ✝ *Brit.* a) Steueraufkommen *n*, b) ≈ Steuerbehörde *f*; **~ trade** *s.* ✝ Binnenhandel *m*; **~ wa·ters**, **~ wa·ter·ways** *s. pl.* Binnengewässer *pl.*

in-laws ['ɪnlɔːz] *s. pl.* **1.** angeheiratete Verwandte *pl.*; **2.** Schwiegereltern *pl.*

in·lay I *v/t.* [*irr.* → ***lay***] [ˌɪn'leɪ] **1.** einlegen: ***~ with ivory***; **2.** furnieren; **3.** täfeln, parkettieren, auslegen; II *s.* ['ɪnleɪ] **4.** Einlegearbeit *f*, In'tarsia *f*; **5.** ⚕ (Zahn)Füllung *f*, Plombe *f*.

in·let ['ɪnlet] *s.* **1.** Meeresarm *m*, schmale Bucht; **2.** Eingang *m* (*a.* ⚕), Einlass *m* (*a.* ⚙): ***~ valve*** ⚙ Einlassventil *n*; **3.** Einsatz(stück *n*) *m*.

'in-line en·gine *s.* Reihenmotor *m*.

in·lin·er ['ɪnlaɪnə] *s. sport* **1.** Inlineskater *m*; **2.** Inline Skate *m*, Inliner *m*.

'in-line| skat·er *s. sport* 'Inlineˌskater(in); **~ skates** *s. pl. sport* Inline Skates *pl.*, 'Inliner *pl.*; **~ skat·ing** *s. sport* Inline Skating *n*.

in·ly·ing ['ɪnˌlaɪɪŋ] *adj.* innen liegend, Innen..., inner.

in·mate ['ɪnmeɪt] *s.* **1.** Insasse *m*, Insassin *f* (*bsd. e-r Anstalt etc.*); **2.** *obs.* Hausgenosse *m*, -genossin *f*; **3.** Bewohner(in) (*a. fig.*).

in·most ['ɪnməʊst] *adj.* **1.** (*a. fig.*) innerst; **2.** *fig.* tiefst, geheimst.

inn [ɪn] *s.* **1.** Gasthaus *n*, -hof *m*; **2.** Wirtshaus *n*; **3.** ***Inns*** *pl.* ***of Court*** ⚖ *die* (Gebäude *pl.* der) vier Rechtsschulen in London.

in·nards ['ɪnədz] *s. pl.* F *das Innere*, *bsd.* a) *die* Eingeweide *pl.* (*a. fig.*), b) *Küche*: *die* Inne'reien *pl.*

in·nate [ˌɪ'neɪt] *adj.* □ angeboren, eigen (*in dat.*); **ˌin'nate·ly** [-lɪ] *adv.* von Na'tur (aus).

in·ner ['ɪnə] I *adj.* **1.** inner, inwendig, Innen...: ***~ door*** Innentür *f*; **2.** *fig.* inner, vertraut: ***the ~ circle*** der engere Kreis (*von Freunden etc.*); **3.** geistig, seelisch, inner(lich): ***~ life*** *das* Innen- *od.* Seelenleben; **4.** verborgen, geheim; II *s.* **5.** (Treffer *m* in das) Schwarze (*e-r Schießscheibe*); **~ man** *s.* [*irr.*] innerer Mensch: a) Seele *f*, Geist *m*, b) *humor. der* Magen *m*: ***refresh the ~*** sich stärken.

'in·ner·most → ***inmost***.

in·ner| span *s.* △ lichte Weite; **~ surface** *s.* Innenfläche *f*, -seite *f*; **~ tube** *s.* ⚙ (Luft)Schlauch *m e-s Reifens*.

in·ner·vate ['ɪnɜːveɪt] *v/t.* **1.** ⚕ innervieren, mit Nerven versorgen; **2.** anregen, beleben.

in·ning ['ɪnɪŋ] *s.* **1.** *Brit.* **~s** *pl. sg. konstr.*, *Am.* **~** *sg.*: ***have one's ~(s)*** a) *Kricket, Baseball*: dran *od.* am Spiel *od.* am Schlagen sein, b) *fig.* an der Reihe sein, *pol.* an der Macht *od.* am Ruder sein; **2.** *pl. Brit.* Gelegenheit *f*, Glück *n*, Chance *f*.

'innˌkeep·er *s.* Gastwirt(in).

in·no·cence ['ɪnəsəns] *s.* **1.** *allg.* Unschuld *f*: a) ⚖ *etc.* Schuldlosigkeit *f* (***of*** an *dat.*), b) Keuschheit *f*, c) Harmlosigkeit *f*, d) Arglosigkeit *f*, Naivi'tät *f*, Einfalt *f*; **2.** Unwissenheit *f*; **'in·no·cent** [-snt] I *adj.* □ **1.** unschuldig: a) schuldlos (***of*** an *dat.*): ***~ air*** Unschuldsmiene *f*, b) keusch, rein, c) harmlos, d) arglos, na'iv, einfältig; **2.** harmlos: ***an ~ sport***; **3.** unbeabsichtigt: ***an ~ deception***; **4.** unwissend: ***he is ~ of such things*** er hat noch nichts von solchen Dingen gehört; **5.** ⚖ a) → 1 a, b) gutgläubig, c) le'gal; **6.** (***of***) frei (von), bar (*gen.*), ohne (*acc.*): ***~ of conceit*** frei von (jedem) Dünkel; ***~ of reason*** bar aller Vernunft; ***he is ~ of Latin*** er kann kein Wort Latein; II *s.* **7.** Unschuldige(r *m*) *f*: ***the slaughter of the ≈s*** a) *bibl.* der bethlehemitische Kindermord, b) *parl. sl.* das Über'bordwerfen von Vorlagen am Sessi'onsende; **8.** ‚Unschuld' *f*, na'iver Mensch, Einfaltspinsel *m*; **9.** Igno'rant(in), Nichtswisser(in).

in·noc·u·ous [ɪ'nɒkjʊəs] *adj.* □ unschädlich, harmlos.

in·no·vate ['ɪnəʊveɪt] *v/i.* Neuerungen einführen *od.* vornehmen; **in·no·va·tion** [ˌɪnəʊ'veɪʃn] *s.* Neuerung *f*, *a.* ✝ Innovati'on *f*; **'in·no·va·tive** [-tɪv] *adj.* innovationsfreudig: ***~ advance*** Innovationsschub *m*; **'in·no·va·tor** [-tə] *s.* Neuerer *m*.

in·nox·ious [ɪ'nɒkʃəs] *adj.* □ unschädlich.

in·nu·en·do [ˌɪnjuː'endəʊ] *pl.* **-does** *s.* **1.** (versteckte) Andeutung *od.* (boshafte) Anspielung, Anzüglichkeit *f*; **2.** Unter'stellung *f*.

in·nu·mer·a·ble [ɪ'njuːmərəbl] *adj.* □ unzählig, zahllos.

in·ob·serv·ance [ˌɪnəb'zɜːvəns] *s.* **1.** Unaufmerksamkeit *f*, Unachtsamkeit *f*; **2.** Nichteinhaltung *f*, -beachtung *f*.

in·oc·u·late [ɪ'nɒkjʊleɪt] *v/t.* **1.** ⚕ a) *Serum* einimpfen (***on, into s.o.*** j-m), b) *j-n* impfen (***against*** gegen); **2.** ***~ with*** *fig.* j-m et. einimpfen, *j-n* erfüllen mit; **3.** ⚘ okulieren; **in·oc·u·la·tion** [ɪˌnɒkjʊ'leɪʃn] *s.* **1.** ⚕ a) Impfung *f*: ***~ gun*** Impfpistole *f*; ***preventive ~*** Schutzimpfung, b) Einimpfung *f* (*a. fig.*); **2.** ⚘ Okulierung *f*.

in·o·dor·ous [ɪn'əʊdərəs] *adj.* □ geruchlos.

in·of·fen·sive [ˌɪnəˈfensɪv] *adj.* □ harmlos.

in·of·fi·cious [ˌɪnəˈfɪʃəs] *adj.* ♯ pflichtwidrig.

in·op·er·a·ble [ɪnˈɒpərəbl] *adj.* ✶ inoperabel, nicht operierbar.

in·op·er·a·tive [ɪnˈɒpərətɪv] *adj.* **1.** unwirksam: a) wirkungslos, b) ♯ ungültig, nicht in Kraft; **2.** a) außer Betrieb, b) nicht einsatzfähig.

in·op·por·tune [ɪnˈɒpətjuːn] *adj.* □ 'inoppor,tun, unangebracht, zur Unzeit (geschehen *etc.*), ungelegen.

in·or·di·nate [ɪˈnɔːdɪnət] *adj.* □ **1.** 'übermäßig, über'trieben, maßlos; **2.** ungeordnet; **3.** unbeherrscht.

in·or·gan·ic [ˌɪnɔːˈɡænɪk] *adj.* (□ ~*ally*) 'un-, ♬ 'anor,ganisch.

in·os·cu·late [ɪˈnɒskjʊleɪt] *mst* ✶ **I** *v/t.* vereinigen (*with* mit), einmünden lassen (*into* in *acc.*); **II** *v/i.* sich vereinigen; eng verbunden sein.

in·pa·tient [ˈɪnˌpeɪʃnt] *s.* 'Anstaltspati,ent(in), statio'närer Pati'ent: ~ *treatment* stationäre Behandlung.

in·pay·ment [ˈɪnˌpeɪmənt] *s.* ✝ Einzahlung *f.*

in·phase [ˈɪnfeɪz] *adj.* ⚡ gleichphasig.

in·plant [ˈɪnplɑːnt] *adj.* ✝ innerbetrieblich, (be'triebs)in,tern.

in·pour·ing [ˈɪnˌpɔːrɪŋ] **I** *adj.* (her-) 'einströmend; **II** *s.* (Her)'Einströmen *n.*

in·put [ˈɪnpʊt] *s.* Input *m:* a) ✝ eingesetzte Produkti'onsmittel *pl.:* ~-*output analysis* Input-Output-Analyse *f,* b) ⊕ eingespeiste Menge, c) ⚡ zugeführte Spannung *od.* Leistung, (Leistungs-) Aufnahme *f,* 'Eingangsener,gie *f:* ~ *amplifier Radio:* Eingangsverstärker *m;* ~ *circuit* ⚡ Eingangsstromkreis *m;* ~ *impedance* ⚡ Eingangswiderstand *m,* d) *Computer:* (Daten-, Pro'gramm)Eingabe *f.*

in·quest [ˈɪnkwest] *s.* **1.** ♯ a) gerichtliche Unter'suchung, b) *a.* **coroner's** ~ Gerichtsverhandlung *f* zur Feststellung der Todesursache (*bei ungeklärten Todesfällen*), c) Unter'suchungsergebnis *n,* Befund *m;* **2.** genaue Prüfung, Nachforschung *f.*

in·qui·e·tude [ɪnˈkwaɪətjuːd] *s.* Unruhe *f,* Besorgnis *f.*

in·quire [ɪnˈkwaɪə] **I** *v/t.* **1.** sich erkundigen nach, fragen nach, erfragen: ~ *the price;* ~ *one's way* sich nach dem Weg erkundigen; **II** *v/i.* **2.** fragen, sich erkundigen (*of s.o.* bei j-m; *for* nach; *about* über *acc.*, wegen): ~ *after s.o.* sich nach j-m *od.* nach j-s Befinden erkundigen; ~ *within!* Näheres im Hause (zu erfragen)!; **3.** ~ *into* unter'suchen, erforschen; **in'quir·er** [-ərə] *s.* **1.** Fragesteller(in), Nachfragende(r *m*) *f;* **2.** Unter'suchende(r *m*) *f;* **in'quir·ing** [-ərɪŋ] *adj.* □ forschend, fragend; neugierig.

in·quir·y [ɪnˈkwaɪərɪ] *s.* **1.** Erkundigung *f,* (An-, Nach)Frage *f:* *on* ~ auf Nachfrage *od.* Anfrage; *make inquiries* Erkundigungen einziehen (*of s.o.* bei j-m; *about* über *acc.*, wegen); *Inquiries pl.* Auskunft(sstelle) *f;* **2.** Unter'suchung *f,* Prüfung *f* (*into gen.*); (Nach)Forschung *f:* *board of* ~ Untersuchungsausschuss *m;* ~ *of·fice s.* 'Auskunft(sbü,ro *n*) *f.*

in·qui·si·tion [ˌɪnkwɪˈzɪʃn] *s.* **1.** (gerichtliche *od.* amtliche) Unter'suchung; **2.** *R.C.* a) *hist.* Inquisiti'on *f,* Ketzergericht *n,* b) Kongregati'on *f* des heiligen Of'fiziums; **3.** *fig.* strenges Verhör; ˌ**in·qui'si·tion·al** [-ʃənl] *adj.* **1.** Untersu-

chungs...; **2.** *R.C.* Inquisitions...; **3.** → **inquisitorial** 3.

in·quis·i·tive [ɪnˈkwɪzətɪv] *adj.* □ **1.** wissbegierig; **2.** neugierig, naseweis; **in'quis·i·tive·ness** [-nɪs] *s.* **1.** Wissbegierde *f;* **2.** Neugier(de) *f;* **in'quis·i·tor** [-tə] *s. R.C.* Inqui'sitor *m: Grand ₴* Großinquisitor; **in·quis·i·to·ri·al** [ɪnˌkwɪzɪˈtɔːrɪəl] *adj.* □ **1.** ♯ Untersuchungs...; **2.** *R.C.* Inquisitions...; **3.** inquisi'torisch, streng (verhörend); **4.** aufdringlich fragend, neugierig.

in| re [ˌɪnˈreɪ] (*Lat.*) *prp.* ♯ in Sachen, betrifft; ~ **rem** [ˌɪnˈrem] (*Lat.*) *adj.* ♯ dinglich: ~ *action.*

in·road [ˈɪnrəʊd] *s.* **1.** Angriff *m,* 'Überfall *m* (*on* auf *acc.*), Einfall *m* (*in, on* in *acc.*); **2.** *fig.* (*on, into*) Eingriff *m* (in *acc.*), 'Übergriff *m* (auf *acc.*), 'übermäßige In'anspruchnahme (*gen.*); **3.** Eindringen *n: make an* ~ *into fig.* e-n Einbruch erzielen in (*dat.*).

in·rush [ˈɪnrʌʃ] *s.* (Her)'Einströmen *n,* Zustrom *m.*

in·sa·lu·bri·ous [ˌɪnsəˈluːbrɪəs] *adj.* ungesund; ˌ**in·sa'lu·bri·ty** [-ətɪ] *s.* Gesundheitsschädlichkeit *f.*

in·sane [ɪnˈseɪn] *adj.* □ wahn-, irrsinnig: a) ✶ geisteskrank; → *asylum* 1, b) *fig.* verrückt, toll.

in·san·i·tar·y [ɪnˈsænɪtərɪ] *adj.* 'unhygi,enisch, gesundheitsschädlich.

in·san·i·ty [ɪnˈsænətɪ] *s.* Irr-, Wahnsinn *m:* a) ✶ Geisteskrankheit *f,* b) *fig.* Verrücktheit *f.*

in·sa·ti·a·bil·i·ty [ɪnˌseɪʃəˈbɪlətɪ] *s.* Unersättlichkeit *f;* **in·sa·ti·a·ble** [ɪnˈseɪʃəbl], **in·sa·ti·ate** [ɪnˈseɪʃɪət] *adj.* unersättlich (*a. fig.*).

in·scribe [ɪnˈskraɪb] *v/t.* **1.** (ein-, auf-) schreiben; **2.** beschriften, mit e-r Inschrift versehen; **3.** *bsd.* ✝ eintragen: ~*d stock Brit.* Namensaktien *pl.;* **4.** *Buch etc.* widmen (*to dat.*); **5.** ⚹ einbeschreiben; **6.** *fig.* (fest) einprägen (*in dat.*).

in·scrip·tion [ɪnˈskrɪpʃn] *s.* **1.** Beschriftung *f,* In-, Aufschrift *f;* **2.** Eintragung *f,* Registrierung *f* (*bsd. von Aktien*); **3.** Zueignung *f,* Widmung *f* (*Buch etc.*); **4.** △ Zeichnung *f;* **5.** ✝ *Brit.* (Ausgabe *f* von) Namensaktien *pl.;* **in'scrip·tion·al** [-ʃənl], **in'scrip·tive** [-ptɪv] *adj.* Inschriften...

in·scru·ta·bil·i·ty [ɪnˌskruːtəˈbɪlətɪ] *s.* Unergründlichkeit *f;* **in·scru·ta·ble** [ɪnˈskruːtəbl] *adj.* □ unergründlich: ~ *face* undurchdringliches Gesicht.

in·sect [ˈɪnsekt] *s.* **1.** *zo.* In'sekt *n,* Kerbtier *n;* **2.** *contp.* 'Wurm' *m,* 'Giftzwerg' *m* (*Person*); **in·sec·ti·cide** [ɪnˈsektɪsaɪd] *s.* In'sektengift *n,* Insekti'zid *n;* **in·sec·ti·vore** [ɪnˈsektɪvɔː] *s.* In'sektenfresser *m;* **in·sec·tiv·o·rous** [ˌɪnsekˈtɪvərəs] *adj. zo.* In'sekten fressend.

'in·sect| pow·der *s.* In'sektenpulver *n;* ~ **re·pel·lent** *s.* In'sektenschutzmittel *n.*

in·se·cure [ˌɪnsɪˈkjʊə] *adj.* □ **1.** unsicher: a) ungesichert, pre'kär, b) ungewiss, zweifelhaft; **2.** *psych.* unsicher, verunsichert: *make s.o. feel* ~ j-n verunsichern; ˌ**in·se'cu·ri·ty** [-ʊərətɪ] *s.* **1.** Unsicherheit *f;* **2.** Ungewissheit *f.*

in·sem·i·nate [ɪnˈsemɪneɪt] *v/t.* **1.** (ein-, aus)säen; **2.** *biol.* (*bsd.* künstlich) befruchten; **3.** *fig.* einimpfen; **in·sem·i·na·tion** [ɪnˌsemɪˈneɪʃn] *s.* **1.** (Ein)Säen *n;* **2.** *biol.* Befruchtung *f:* *artificial* ~ künstliche Befruchtung.

in·sen·sate [ɪnˈsenseɪt] *adj.* □ **1.** leb-, empfindungs-, gefühllos; **2.** unsinnig,

unvernünftig; **3.** → *insensible* 3.

in·sen·si·bil·i·ty [ɪnˌsensəˈbɪlətɪ] *s.* (*to*) **1.** (*a. fig.*) Gefühllosigkeit *f* (gegen), Unempfindlichkeit *f* (für); **2.** Bewusstlosigkeit *f;* **3.** Gleichgültigkeit *f* (gegen), Unempfänglichkeit *f* (für); Stumpfheit *f;* **in·sen·si·ble** [ɪnˈsensəbl] *adj.* □ **1.** unempfindlich, gefühllos (*to* gegen): ~ *from cold* vor Kälte gefühllos; **2.** bewusstlos; **3.** (*of, to*) unempfänglich (für); gleichgültig (gegen); **4.** *be* ~ *of* nicht (an)erkennen (*acc.*); **5.** unmerklich; **in·sen·si·bly** [ɪnˈsensəblɪ] *adv.* unmerklich.

in·sen·si·tive [ɪnˈsensətɪv] *adj.* (*to*) **1.** *a. phys.*, ⊕ unempfindlich (gegen); **2.** unempfänglich (für); gefühllos (gegen); **in·sen·si·tive·ness** [-nɪs] *s.* Unempfindlichkeit *f;* Unempfänglichkeit *f.*

in·sen·ti·ent [ɪnˈsenʃnt] → *insensible* 1.

in·sep·a·ra·bil·i·ty [ɪnˌsepərəˈbɪlətɪ] *s.* **1.** Untrennbarkeit *f;* **2.** Unzertrennlichkeit *f;* **in·sep·a·ra·ble** [ɪnˈsepərəbl] **I** *adj.* □ **1.** untrennbar (*a. ling.*); **2.** unzertrennlich; **II** *s.* **3.** *pl.* die Unzertrennlichen *pl.*

in·sert **I** *v/t.* [ɪnˈsɜːt] **1.** einfügen, -setzen, -schieben, *Diskette, CD(-ROM)* einlegen, *Worte a.* einschalten, *Instrument etc.* einführen, *Schlüssel etc.* (hi'nein)stecken (*in, into* in *acc.*); **2.** ⚡ ein-, zwischenschalten; **3.** *Münze* einwerfen; **4.** *Anzeige (in e-e Zeitung)* setzen, *ein Inserat* aufgeben; **II** *s.* [ˈɪnsɜːt] **1.** Einfügen *n* 2–4; **in'ser·tion** [-ɜːʃn] *s.* **1.** a) Einfügen *n* (*etc.* → *insert*), b) Einfügung *f,* Ein-, Zusatz *m,* Einschaltung *f* (*a.* ⚡); Einwurf *m* (*Münze*); **2.** (Zeitungs)Beilage *f;* **3.** (Spitzen- *etc.*) Einsatz *m;* **4.** Inse'rat *n,* Anzeige *f;* **in·sert key** [ɪnˈsɜːt] *s. Computer:* Einfügetaste *f;* **in·sert mode** [ɪnˈsɜːt] *s. Computer:* 'Einfüge,modus *m.*

'in-ˌser·vice *adj.* während der Dienstzeit: ~ *training* betriebliche Berufsförderung.

in·set **I** *s.* [ˈɪnset] **1.** → *insertion* 1 b, 2, 3; **2.** Eckeinsatz *m,* Nebenbild *n,* -karte *f;* **II** *v/t.* [irr. → *set*] [ˌɪnˈset] *pret. u. p.p. Brit. a.* **in·set·ted** [ˌɪnˈsetɪd] **1.** einfügen, -setzen.

in·shore [ˌɪnˈʃɔː] **I** *adj.* **1.** an *od.* nahe der Küste: ~ *fishing* Küstenfischerei *f;* **II** *adv.* **2.** a) küstenwärts, b) nahe der Küste; **3.** ~ *of* näher der Küste als: ~ *of a ship* zwischen Schiff und Küste.

in·side [ˌɪnˈsaɪd] **I** *s.* **1.** Innenseite *f,* -fläche *f,* innere Seite: *on the* ~ innen; *s.o. on the* ~ *fig.* → *insider* 1; **2.** *das* Innere: *from the* ~ von innen; ~ *out* das Innere nach außen, umgestülpt, *Kleidung:* verkehrt herum, links; *turn* ~ *out* (völlig) umkrempeln, durcheinander bringen, 'auf den Kopf stellen'; *know* ~ *out* in- u. auswendig kennen; **3.** F 'Eingeweide': ~ *pain in one's* ~ Bauch- *od.* Leibschmerzen; **II** *adj.* **4.** inner, inwendig, Innen...: ~ *diameter* lichter Durchmesser, lichte Weite; ~ *information* interne Informationen *pl.,* Informationen *pl.* aus erster Quelle; ~ *job* F Tat *f* e-s Eingeweihten *od.* Insiders; ~ *lane sport* Innenbahn *f;* ~ *story* Inside-Story *f* (*Bericht aus interner Sicht*); **III** *adv.* **5.** im Innern, innen, drin(nen); **6.** nach innen, hin'ein, her'ein: *go* ~; *put s.o.* ~ F j-n ,einlochen'; **7.** ~ *of* a) innerhalb (*gen.*), binnen: ~ *of a week,* b) *Am.* → 8; **IV** *prp.* **8.** innerhalb (*gen.*), im Innern (*gen.*), in (*dat.*): *be* ~ *the house;* **9.** in (*acc.*) ... (hin'ein *od.* he-rein): *go* ~ *the house;* **in·sid·er**

[ˌɪnˈsaɪdə] s. **1.** Eingeweihte(r m) f, Insider m; ~ **trading** (od. **dealing**) Börse: Insidergeschäfte pl.; **2.** Zugehörige(r m) f, Mitglied n.

in·sid·i·ous [ɪnˈsɪdɪəs] adj. □ **1.** heimtückisch, 'hinterhältig, tückisch; **2.** ✸ tückisch, schleichend; **in'sid·i·ous·ness** [-nɪs] s. 'Hinterlist f, Tücke f.

in·sight [ˈɪnsaɪt] s. (**into**) **1.** Einblick m (in acc.); **2.** Verständnis n (für), Kenntnis (gen.).

in·sig·ni·a [ɪnˈsɪɡnɪə] s. pl. In'signien pl., Ab-, Ehrenzeichen pl.

in·sig·nif·i·cance [ˌɪnsɪɡˈnɪfɪkəns] s., **in·sig'nif·i·can·cy** [-sɪ] s. Bedeutungslosigkeit f, Unwichtigkeit f, Belanglosigkeit f, Geringfügigkeit f; **in·sig'nif·i·cant** [-nt] adj. □ **1.** bedeutungs-, belanglos, unwichtig, geringfügig, unbedeutend; nichts sagend; **2.** verächtlich.

in·sin·cere [ˌɪnsɪnˈsɪə] adj. □ unaufrichtig, falsch; **in·sin'cer·i·ty** [-ˈserətɪ] s. Unaufrichtigkeit f.

in·sin·u·ate [ɪnˈsɪnjʊeɪt] v/t. **1.** andeuten, anspielen auf (acc.): **what are you insinuating?** was wollen Sie damit sagen?; **2.** j-m et. zu verstehen geben, et. vorsichtig beibringen; **3.** ~ **o.s. into s.o.'s favo(u)r** sich bei j-m einschmeicheln; **in'sin·u·at·ing** [-tɪŋ] adj. □ **1.** anzüglich; **2.** schmeichlerisch; **in·sin·u·a·tion** [ɪnˌsɪnjʊˈeɪʃn] s. **1.** Anspielung f, (versteckte) Andeutung f; **2.** Schmeiche'leien pl.

in·sip·id [ɪnˈsɪpɪd] adj. □ **1.** fade, geschmacklos, schal; **2.** fig. fade, abgeschmackt, geistlos; **in·si·pid·i·ty** [ˌɪnsɪˈpɪdətɪ] s. Geschmacklosigkeit f, Fadheit f, fig. a. Abgeschmacktheit f.

in·sist [ɪnˈsɪst] v/i. **1.** (**on**) bestehen (auf dat.), dringen (auf acc.), verlangen (acc.), insis'tieren (auf dat.): **I ~ on do·ing it** ich bestehe darauf, es zu tun; **if you ~!** wenn Sie darauf bestehen!; **2.** (**on**) beharren (auf dat., bei), bleiben (bei); **3.** beteuern (**on** acc.); **4.** (**on**) her'vorheben, nachdrücklich betonen (acc.); **5.** es sich nicht nehmen lassen (**on doing** zu tun); **6.** ~ **on doing** immer wieder umfallen etc. (Sache); **in'sist·ence** [-təns], **in'sist·en·cy** [-tənsɪ] s. **1.** Bestehen n, Beharren n (**on**, **upon** auf dat.); **2.** (**on**) Beteuerung f (gen.), Beharren (auf dat.); **3.** (**on**, **upon**) Betonung f (gen.); Nachdruck m (auf dat.); **4.** Beharrlichkeit f, Hartnäckigkeit f; **in'sist·ent** [-tənt] adj. □ **1.** beharrlich, dauernd, hartnäckig, drängend; **2.** be ~ **on** → **insist** 1–3; **3.** eindringlich, nachdrücklich, dringend; **4.** aufdringlich, grell (Farbe, Ton).

in·so·bri·e·ty [ˌɪnsəʊˈbraɪətɪ] s. Unmäßigkeit f (engS. im Trinken).

in·so·far → **far** 4.

in·so·la·tion [ˌɪnsəʊˈleɪʃn] s. Sonnenbestrahlung f, Sonnenbad n.

in·sole [ˈɪnsəʊl] s. **1.** Brandsohle f; **2.** Einlegesohle f.

in·so·lence [ˈɪnsələns] s. **1.** Über'heblichkeit f; **2.** Unverschämtheit f, Frechheit f; **'in·so·lent** [-nt] adj. □ **1.** anmaßend; **2.** unverschämt.

in·sol·u·bil·i·ty [ɪnˌsɒljʊˈbɪlətɪ] s. **1.** Un(auf)löslichkeit f; **2.** fig. Unlösbarkeit f; **in·sol·u·ble** [ɪnˈsɒljʊbl] I adj. □ **1.** un(auf)löslich; **2.** unlösbar, unerklärlich; **II** s. ✿ unlösliche Sub'stanz.

in·sol·ven·cy [ɪnˈsɒlvənsɪ] s. ✝ **1.** Zahlungsunfähigkeit f, Insol'venz f; **2.** Kon'kurs m; **in'sol·vent** [-nt] I adj. ✝ **1.** zahlungsunfähig, insol'vent; **2.** bsd. fig.

(moralisch etc.) bank'rott; **3.** Konkurs...: ~ **estate** konkursreifer Nachlass; **II** s. **4.** zahlungsunfähiger Schuldner.

in·som·ni·a [ɪnˈsɒmnɪə] s. ✸ Schlaflosigkeit f; **in'som·ni·ac** [-ɪæk] s. ✸ an Schlaflosigkeit Leidende(r m) f.

in·so·much [ˌɪnsəʊˈmʌtʃ] adv. **1.** so (sehr), dermaßen (**that** dass); **2.** → **inasmuch.**

in·sou·ci·ance [ɪnˈsuːsjəns] s. Sorglosigkeit f (etc. →) **in·sou·ci·ant** [-nt] adj. sorglos, unbekümmert, gleichgültig, lässig.

in·spect [ɪnˈspekt] v/t. **1.** unter'suchen, prüfen, nachsehen; **2.** besichtigen, sich (genau) ansehen, inspizieren; **3.** beaufsichtigen; **in'spec·tion** [-kʃn] s. **1.** Besichtigung f, An-, 'Durchsicht f; Einsicht(nahme) f (von Akten etc.): **for your ~** zur Ansicht; **free ~** Besichtigung ohne Kaufzwang; **be** (**laid**) **open to ~** zur Einsicht ausliegen; **2.** Unter'suchung f, Prüfung f, Kon'trolle f: ~ **hole** ✿ Schauloch n; ~ **lamp** ✿ Ableuchtlampe f; **3.** Besichtigung f, Inspekti'on f; **4.** Aufsicht f; **5.** ✕ Ap'pell m; **in'spec·tor** [-tə] s. **1.** In'spektor m, Kontrol'leur m (Bus etc.), Aufseher m, Aufsichtsbeamte(r) m: **customs ~** Zollinspektor m; ~ **of schools** Schulinspektor m; ~ **of weights and meas·ures** Eichmeister m; **2.** (Poli'zei)Inspektor m, (-)Kommis,sar m; **3.** ✕ Inspek'teur m; **in'spec·to·ral** [-tərəl] adj. Inspektor..., Aufsichts...; **in'spec·tor·ate** [-tərət] s. Inspekto'rat n: a) Aufsichtsbezirk m, b) Aufsichtsbehörde f, c) Aufseheramt n; **in'spec·to·ri·al** [ˌɪnspekˈtɔːrɪəl] adj. inspectoral; **in'spec·tor·ship** [-təʃɪp] s. In'spektoramt n; **2.** Aufsicht f.

in·spi·ra·tion [ˌɪnspəˈreɪʃn] s. **1.** eccl. göttliche Eingebung, Erleuchtung f; **2.** Inspirati'on f, Eingebung f, (plötzlicher) Einfall m; **3.** et. Inspirierendes; **4.** Anregung f: **at the ~ of** auf j-s Veranlassung; **5.** Begeisterung f; **in·spi·ra·tor** [ˈɪnspəreɪtə] s. ✸ Inha'lator m; **in·spir·a·to·ry** [ɪnˈspaɪərətərɪ] adj. (Ein-)Atmungs...

in·spire [ɪnˈspaɪə] v/t. **1.** begeistern, anfeuern; **2.** anregen, veranlassen; **3.** (**in s.o.**) Gefühl etc. einflößen, eingeben (j-m); erwecken, erregen (in j-m); **4.** fig. a) erleuchten, b) inspirieren, erfüllen (**with** mit), c) inspirieren; **5.** einatmen; **in'spired** [-əd] adj. **1.** bsd. eccl. erleuchtet; eingegeben; **2.** schöpferisch, einfallsreich; **3.** begeistert; **4.** a) glänzend, her'vorragend, b) schwungvoll; **5.** von ‚oben‘ (von der Regierung etc.) veranlasst; **in'spir·er** [-ərə] s. Anreger (-in); **in'spir·ing** [-ərɪŋ] adj. □ anregend, begeisternd, inspirierend.

in·spir·it [ɪnˈspɪrɪt] v/t. beleben, beseelen, anfeuern, ermutigen.

in·sta·bil·i·ty [ˌɪnstəˈbɪlətɪ] s. mst fig. **1.** Instabili'tät f, Unsicherheit f; **2.** Labili'tät f, Unbeständigkeit f.

in·stall [ɪnˈstɔːl] v/t. ✿ **1.** a) installieren, montieren, aufstellen, einbauen, b) einrichten, (an)legen, anbringen; **2.** j-n bestallen, in ein Amt einsetzen, -führen; **3.** ~ **o.s.** F sich niederlassen; **in·stal·la·tion** [ˌɪnstəˈleɪʃn] s. **1.** ✿ a) Installierung f, Einrichtung f, Einbau m, b) (fertige) Anlage od. Einrichtung; **2.** (Amts)Einsetzung f, Bestallung f.

in·stal(l)·ment¹ [ɪnˈstɔːlmənt] → **instal·lation.**

in·stal(l)·ment² [ɪnˈstɔːlmənt] s. **1.** ✝

Rate f, Teil-, Ab-, Abschlags-, Ratenzahlung f: **by ~s** in Raten; **first ~** Anzahlung f; ~ **credit** Teilzahlungskredit m; ~ **plan** Teilzahlungssystem n; **buy on the ~ plan** auf Raten kaufen, ‚abstottern‘; **2.** (Teil)Lieferung f (Buch etc.); **3.** Fortsetzung f (Roman etc.), Radio, TV: a. (Sende)Folge f.

in·stance [ˈɪnstəns] I s. **1.** (einzelner) Fall, Beispiel n: **in this ~** in diesem (besonderen) Fall; **for ~** zum Beispiel: **as an ~ of s.th.** als Beispiel für et.; **2.** Bitte f, Ersuchen n: **at his ~** auf sein Drängen od. Betreiben od. s-e Veranlassung; **3.** ✝ In'stanz f: **court of the first ~** Gericht n erster Instanz; **in the last ~** in letzter Instanz, fig. letztlich; **in the first ~** fig. in erster Linie, zuerst; **II** v/t. **4.** als Beispiel anführen; **5.** mit Beispielen belegen; **'in·stan·cy** [-sɪ] s. Dringlichkeit f.

in·stant [ˈɪnstənt] I s. **1.** Mo'ment m: a) (kurzer) Augenblick m, b) (genauer) Zeitpunkt m: **in an ~, on the ~** sofort, augenblicklich, im Nu; **at this ~** in diesem Augenblick; **this ~** sofort, augenblicklich; **II** adj. □ **1.** → **instantly; 2.** so'fortig, augenblicklich: ~ **camera** phot. Instant-, Sofortbildkamera f; ~ **coffee** Pulverkaffee m; ~ **glue** Sekundenkleber m; ~ **meal** Fertig-, Schnellgericht n; **3.** abbr. **inst.: the 10th** ~ der 10. dieses Monats; **4.** dringend.

in·stan·ta·ne·ous [ˌɪnstənˈteɪnjəs] adj. □ **1.** so'fortig, unverzüglich, augenblicklich: **death was ~** der Tod trat auf der Stelle ein; **2.** gleichzeitig (Ereignisse); **3.** phys., ✿ momen'tan, Augenblicks...: ~ **photo** Momentaufnahme f; ~ **shutter** phot. Momentverschluss m; **in·stan'ta·ne·ous·ly** [-lɪ] adv. so'fort, unverzüglich; auf der Stelle; **in·stan'ta·ne·ous·ness** [-nɪs] s. Augenblicklichkeit f; Blitzesschnelle f.

in·stan·ter [ɪnˈstæntə] adv. so'fort.

in·stant·ly [ˈɪnstəntlɪ] adv. so'fort, unverzüglich, augenblicklich.

in·state [ɪnˈsteɪt] v/t. in ein Amt einsetzen.

in·stead [ɪnˈsted] adv. **1.** ~ **of** (an)statt (gen.), an Stelle von: ~ **of me** statt meiner, an meiner statt od. Stelle; ~ **of going** (an)statt zu gehen; ~ **of at work** statt bei der Arbeit; **2.** stattdessen: **she sent the boy ~.**

in·step [ˈɪnstep] s. Rist m, Spann m (Fuß): ~ **raiser** Plattfußeinlage f; **high in the ~** F hochnäsig.

in·sti·gate [ˈɪnstɪgeɪt] v/t. **1.** an-, aufreizen, aufhetzen, anstiften (**to** tun, **to do** zu tun); **2.** et. (Böses) anstiften, anfachen; **in·sti·ga·tion** [ˌɪnstɪˈgeɪʃn] s. **1.** Anstiftung f, Aufhetzung f, -reizung f; **2.** Anregung f: **at the ~ of** auf Betreiben od. Veranlassung von (od. gen.); **'in·sti·ga·tor** [-tə] s. Anstifter(in), (Auf)Hetzer(in).

in·still [ɪnˈstɪl] v/t. **1.** einträufeln, -tröpfeln; **2.** fig. (**into**) a) j-m einflößen, -impfen, beibringen, b) et. durch'dringen (mit), einfließen lassen (in acc.); **in·stil·la·tion** [ˌɪnstɪˈleɪʃn], **in'stil(l)·ment** [-mənt] s. **1.** Einträufelung f; **2.** fig. Einflößung f, Einimpfung f.

in·stinct I s. [ˈɪnstɪŋkt] **1.** In'stinkt m, (Na'tur)Trieb m: **by ~, on ~, from ~** instinktiv; **2.** a) instink'tives Gefühl, (sicherer) In'stinkt, b) Begabung f (**for** für); **II** adj. [ɪnˈstɪŋkt] **3.** belebt, durch'drungen, erfüllt (**with** von); **in·stinc·tive** [ɪnˈstɪŋktɪv] adj. □ instink'tiv: a) in'stinkt-, triebmäßig, Instinkt..., b) unwillkürlich, c) angeboren.

in·sti·tute ['ɪnstɪtjuːt] **I** s. **1.** Insti'tut n, Anstalt f; **2.** (gelehrte etc.) Gesellschaft; **3.** Insti'tut n (Gebäude); **4.** pl. bsd. ✝ Grundgesetze pl., -lehren pl.; **II** v/t. **5.** ein-, errichten, gründen; einführen; **6.** einleiten, in Gang setzen: ~ an inquiry e-e Untersuchung einleiten; ~ legal proceedings Klage erheben, das Verfahren einleiten (against gegen); **7.** bsd. eccl. j-n einsetzen, einführen.

in·sti·tu·tion [ˌɪnstɪ'tjuːʃn] s. **1.** Insti'tut n, Anstalt f, Einrichtung f, Stiftung f, Gesellschaft f; **2.** Insti'tut n (Gebäude); **3.** Instituti'on f, Einrichtung f, (über'kommene) Sitte, Brauch m; **4.** Ordnung f, Recht n, Satzung f; **5.** F a) alte Gewohnheit, b) vertraute Sache, feste Einrichtung, c) allbekannte Per'son; **6.** Ein-, Errichtung f, Gründung f; **7.** eccl. Einsetzung f, **in·sti'tu·tion·al** [-ʃənl] adj. **1.** Institutions..., Instituts..., Anstalts...; **2.** ✝ Am. ~ advertising Repräsentationswerbung f; **in·sti'tu·tion·al·ize** [-ʃənlaɪz] v/t. **1.** et. institutionalisieren; **2.** j-n in e-e Anstalt einweisen.

in·struct [ɪn'strʌkt] v/t. **1.** (be)lehren, unter'weisen, -'richten, schulen, ausbilden (in in dat.); **2.** informieren, unter'richten; **3.** instruieren (a. ✝), anweisen, beauftragen; **in'struc·tion** [-kʃn] s. **1.** Belehrung f, Schulung f, Ausbildung f, 'Unterricht m: private ~ Privatunterricht; course of ~ Lehrgang m, Kursus m; **2.** pl. Auftrag m, Vorschrift (-en pl.) f, (An)Weisung(en pl.) f, Verhaltungsmaßregeln pl., Richtlinien pl., (a. Betriebs)Anleitung f: according to ~s auftrags-, weisungsgemäß, vorschriftsmäßig, ~s for use Gebrauchsanweisung; **3.** Am. ✝ mst pl. Rechtsbelehrung f; **4.** ✕ mst pl. Dienstanweisung f, Instrukti'on f; **in'struc·tion·al** [-kʃənl] adj. Unterrichts..., Erziehungs..., Ausbildungs..., Lehr...: ~ film Lehrfilm m; ~ staff Lehrkörper m; **in'struc·tive** [-tɪv] adj. □ belehrend; lehr-, aufschlussreich; **in'struc·tive·ness** [-tɪvnɪs] s. das Belehrende; **in'struc·tor** [-tə] s. **1.** Lehrer m; **2.** Ausbilder m (a. ✕); **3.** univ. Am. Do'zent m; **in'struc·tress** [-trɪs] s. Lehrerin f.

in·stru·ment ['ɪnstrʊmənt] **I** s. **1.** Instru'ment n (a. ♪): a) (feines) Werkzeug n, b) Appa'rat m, (bsd. Mess)Gerät n; **2.** pl. ✝ Besteck n; **3.** ✝, ✝☆ a) Doku'ment n, Urkunde f: 'Wertpa,pier m: ~ of payment Zahlungsmittel n; ~ payable to bearer ✝ Inhaberpapier; ~ to order Orderpapier, b) pl. Instrumen'tarium n: the ~s of credit policy; **4.** fig. Werkzeug n: a) (Hilfs)Mittel n, b) Handlanger(in); **II** v/t. **5.** ♪ instrumentieren; **III** adj. **6.** ☺ Instrumenten...: ~ board, ~ panel a) Schalt-, Armaturenbrett n, b) ➣ Instrumentenbrett n; ~ maker Apparatebauer m, Feinmechaniker m; **7.** ➣ Blind..., Instrumenten...: ~ flying; ~ landing; **in·stru·men·tal** [ˌɪnstrʊ'mentl] adj. □ → instrumentally; **1.** behilflich, dienlich, förderlich: be ~ in ger. behilflich sein od. wesentlich dazu beitragen, dass; e-e gewichtige Rolle spielen bei; **2.** ♪ Instrumental...; **3.** mit Instrumenten ausgeführt: ~ operation; ~ error ☺ Instrumentenfehler m; **4.** ~ case ling. Instrumental(is) m; **in·stru·men·tal·ist** [ˌɪnstrʊ'mentəlɪst] s. ♪ Instrumenta'list(in); **in·stru·men·tal·i·ty** [ˌɪnstrʊmen'tælətɪ] s. **1.** Mitwirkung f, Mithilfe f: through

his ~; **2.** (Hilfs)Mittel n; Einrichtung f; **in·stru·men·tal·ly** [ˌɪnstrʊ'mentəlɪ] adv. durch Instrumente; **in·stru·men·ta·tion** [ˌɪnstrʊmen'teɪʃn] s. ♪ Instrumentati'on f.

in·sub·or·di·nate [ˌɪnsə'bɔːdnət] adj. unbotmäßig, wider'setzlich, aufsässig; **in·sub·or·di·na·tion** ['ɪnsəˌbɔːdɪ'neɪʃn] s. Unbotmäßigkeit f etc.; Gehorsamsverweigerung f, Auflehnung f.

in·sub·stan·tial [ˌɪnsəb'stænʃl] adj. **1.** sub'stanzlos, unkörperlich; **2.** unwirklich; **3.** wenig nahrhaft.

in·suf·fer·a·ble [ɪn'sʌfərəbl] adj. □ unerträglich, unausstehlich.

in·suf·fi·cien·cy [ˌɪnsə'fɪʃnsɪ] s. **1.** Unzulänglichkeit f, Mangel(haftigkeit f) m; Untauglichkeit f; **2.** ✱ Insuffizi'enz f; **in·suf'fi·cient** [-nt] adj. □ **1.** unzulänglich, unzureichend, ungenügend; **2.** untauglich, mangelhaft, unfähig.

in·suf·flate ['ɪnsʌfleɪt] v/t. **1.** a. ✱, ☺ (hin)'einblasen; **2.** R.C. anhauchen; **'in·suf·fla·tor** [-tə] s. ☺, ✱ 'Einblaseappa,rat m.

in·su·lant ['ɪnsjʊlənt] s. ☺ Iso'lierstoff m, -materi,al n.

in·su·lar ['ɪnsjʊlə] adj. □ **1.** inselartig, insu'lar, Insel...; **2.** fig. isoliert, abgeschlossen; **3.** fig. engstirnig, beschränkt; **in·su·lar·i·ty** [ˌɪnsjʊ'lærɪtɪ] s. **1.** insu'lare Lage; **2.** fig. Abgeschlossenheit f; **3.** fig. Engstirnigkeit f, Beschränktheit f.

in·su·late ['ɪnsjʊleɪt] v/t. ♭, ☺ isolieren (a. fig. absondern); **'in·su·lat·ing** [-tɪŋ] adj. isolierend, Isolier...: ~ compound ♭ Isoliermasse f; ~ joint ♭ Isolierkupplung f; ~ switch Trennschalter m; ~ tape ♭ Isolierband n; **in·su·la·tion** [ˌɪnsjʊ'leɪʃn] s. Isolierung f; **'in·su·la·tor** [-tə] s. **1.** ♭ Iso'lator m; **2.** Isolierer m (Arbeiter).

in·su·lin ['ɪnsjʊlɪn] s. ✱ Insu'lin n.

in·sult **I** v/t. [ɪn'sʌlt] beleidigen, beschimpfen; **II** s. ['ɪnsʌlt] (to) Beleidigung f (für) (durch Wort od. Tat), Beschimpfung f (gen.): offer an ~ to → I; **in'sult·ing** [-tɪŋ] adj. □ **1.** beleidigend, beschimpfend: ~ language Schimpfworte pl.; **2.** unverschämt, frech.

in·su·per·a·ble [ɪn'sjuːpərəbl] adj. □ 'unüber,windlich.

in·sup·port·a·ble [ˌɪnsə'pɔːtəbl] adj. □ unerträglich, unaus'stehlich.

in·sur·a·bil·i·ty [ɪnˌʃʊərə'bɪlətɪ] s. ✝ Versicherungsfähigkeit f; **in·sur·a·ble** [ɪn'ʃʊərəbl] adj. □ ✝ **1.** versicherungsfähig, versicherbar: ~ value Versicherungswert m; **2.** versicherungspflichtig.

in·sur·ance [ɪn'ʃʊərəns] **I** s. **1.** ✝ Versicherung f: buy ~ sich versichern (lassen); ~ ✝ versichert sein; effect (od. take out) an ~ e-e Versicherung abschließen; **2.** ✝ a) Ver'sicherungspo,lice f, b) Versicherungsprämie f; **II** adj. Versicherungs...: ~ agent (broker, company, premium, value); ~ benefit Versicherungsleistung f; ~ certificate Versicherungsschein m; ~ claim Versicherungsanspruch m; ~ coverage Versicherungsschutz m; ~ fraud Versicherungsbetrug m; ~ office Versicherungsanstalt f; ~ policy Versicherungspolice f, -schein m; take out an ~ policy e-e Versicherung abschließen, sich versichern (lassen); **in'sur·ant** [-nt] → insured II.

in·sure [ɪn'ʃʊə] v/t. **1.** ✝ versichern (against gegen; for mit e-r Summe): ~ oneself (one's life, one's house); **2.** → ensure; **in'sured** [-ʊəd] ✝ **I** adj.: the ~ party → II; **II** s. the ~ der od. die

Versicherte, Versicherungsnehmer(in); **in'sur·er** [-ʊərə] s. ✝ Versicherer m, Versicherungsträger(in): the ~s die Versicherungsgesellschaft f.

in·sur·gent [ɪn'sɜːdʒənt] **I** adj. aufrührerisch, aufständisch; re'bellisch (a. fig.); **II** s. Aufrührer m, Aufständische(r) m; Re'bell m (a. pol. gegen die Partei).

in·sur·mount·a·ble [ˌɪnsə'maʊntəbl] adj. □ 'unüber,steigbar; fig. 'unüber,windlich.

in·sur·rec·tion [ˌɪnsə'rekʃn] s. Aufruhr m, Aufstand m, Erhebung f, Empörung f; **in·sur·rec·tion·al** [-ʃənl], **in·sur·'rec·tion·ar·y** [-ʃnərɪ] → insurgent I; **in·sur·rec·tion·ist** [-ʃnɪst] → insurgent II.

in·sus·cep·ti·bil·i·ty ['ɪnsəˌseptə'bɪlətɪ] s. Unempfänglichkeit f, Unzugänglichkeit f (to für); **in·sus·cep·ti·ble** [ˌɪnsə'septəbl] adj. **1.** (of) nicht fähig (zu), ungeeignet (für, zu); **2.** (of, to) unempfänglich (für), unzugänglich (dat.).

in·tact [ɪn'tækt] adj. **1.** in'takt, heil, unversehrt; **2.** unberührt, unangetastet.

in·tagl·io [ɪn'tɑːlɪəʊ] pl. -ios s. **1.** In'taglio n (Gemme mit eingeschnittenem Bild); **2.** eingraviertes Bild; **3.** In'taglioverfahren n, -arbeit f; **4.** typ. Am. Tiefdruck m.

in·take ['ɪnteɪk] s. **1.** ☺ a) Einlass(öffnung f) m: ~ valve Einlassventil n; ~ stroke mot. Saughub m, b) aufgenommene Ener'gie; **2.** Einnehmen n, Ein-, Ansaugen n; **3.** (Neu)Aufnahme f, Zustrom m, aufgenommene Menge: ~ of food Nahrungsaufnahme.

in·tan·gi·bil·i·ty [ɪnˌtændʒə'bɪlətɪ] s. Nichtgreifbarkeit f, Unkörperlichkeit f; **in·tan·gi·ble** [ɪn'tændʒəbl] **I** adj. □ **1.** nicht greifbar, immateri'ell (a. ✝), unkörperlich; **2.** fig. vage, unklar, unbestimmt; **3.** fig. unfassbar; **II** s. **4.** pl. ✝ immateri'elle Werte.

in·tar·si·a [ɪn'tɑːsɪə] s. Am. In'tarsia f, Einlegearbeit f.

in·te·ger ['ɪntɪdʒə] s. **A** ganze Zahl; **2.** → integral 5; **'in·te·gral** [-ɪgrəl] **I** adj. □ **1.** (zur Vollständigkeit) unerlässlich, integrierend, wesentlich, ☺ (fest) eingebaut, e-e Einheit bildend (with mit), integriert: an ~ part; **2.** ganz, vollständig: an ~ whole → 5; **3.** → intact 2; **4.** **A** a) ganz(zahlig), b) Integral...: ~ calculus Integralrechnung f; **II** s. **5.** ein vollständiges od. einheitliches Ganzes; **6.** **A** Inte'gral n; **'in·te·grand** [-ɪgrænd] s. **A** Inte'grand m; **'in·te·grant** [-ɪgrənt] → integral 1.

in·te·grate ['ɪntɪgreɪt] v/t. **1.** integrieren (a. **A**, ☺), zu e-m Ganzen zs.-fassen, zs.-schließen, vereinigen, vereinheitlichen; **2.** vervollständigen; **3.** eingliedern, integrieren (within in acc.); **4.** ♭ zählen (Messgerät); **5.** Am. Schule etc. für Farbige zugänglich machen; **'in·te·grat·ed** [-tɪd] adj. **1.** einheitlich, geschlossen, zs.-gefasst, integriert; ✝ Verbund...: ~ economy; **2.** zs.-hängend; **3.** ☺ eingebaut, integriert (Schaltung, Datenverarbeitung etc.): ~ circuit ♭ integrierter Schaltkreis; **4.** Am. ohne Rassentrennung: ~ school; **in·te·gra·tion** [ˌɪntɪ'greɪʃn] s. **1.** Zs.-schluss m, Vereinigung f, Integrati'on f, Vereinheitlichung f; **2.** Vervollständigung f; **3.** Eingliederung f; **4.** **A** Integrati'on f; **5.** Am. Aufhebung f der Rassenschranken; **in·te·gra·tion·ist** [ˌɪntɪ'greɪʃnɪst] s. Am. Verfechter(in) rassischer Gleichberechtigung.

in·teg·ri·ty [ɪn'tegrətɪ] s. **1.** Rechtschaffenheit f, (cha'rakterliche) Sauberkeit, (mo'ralische) Integri'tät; **2.** Vollständigkeit f, Unversehrtheit f; **3.** Reinheit f; **4.** ☈ Integri'tät f, Ganzzahligkeit f.

in·teg·u·ment [ɪnˈtegjʊmənt] s. anat. biol. Hülle f, Decke f, Haut f, Integu'ment n.

in·tel·lect [ˈɪntəlekt] s. **1.** Verstand m, Intel'lekt m, Denkvermögen n; **2.** kluger Kopf; coll. große Geister pl., Intelli'genz f; **in·tel·lec·tu·al** [ˌɪntəˈlektjʊəl] **I** adj. □ → **intellectually**; **1.** intellektu'ell: a) verstandesmäßig, Verstandes..., geistig, Geistes..., b) verstandesbetont, (geistig) anspruchsvoll: **~ power** Geisteskraft f; **~ property** geistiges Eigentum; **2.** intelli'gent; **II** s. **3.** Intellektu'elle(r m) f, Verstandesmensch m; **in·tel·lec·tu·al·ist** [ˌɪntəˈlektjʊəlɪst] → **intellectual** 3; **in·tel·lec·tu·al·i·ty** [ˈɪntəˌlektjʊˈælətɪ] s. Intellektuali'tät f, Verstandesmäßigkeit f; Geisteskraft f; **in·tel·lec·tu·al·ly** [ˌɪntəˈlektjʊəlɪ] adv. verstandesmäßig, mit dem Verstand.

in·tel·li·gence [ɪnˈtelɪdʒəns] s. **1.** Intelli'genz f: a) Klugheit f, Verstand m, b) scharfer Verstand, rasche Auffassungsgabe, c) → **intellect** 2: **~ quotient (test)** Intelligenzquotient m (-test m); **2.** Einsicht f, Verständnis m; **3.** Nachricht f, Mitteilung f, Informati'on f, Auskunft f; ✕ 'Nachrichtenmateri‚al n; **4.** a. **~ office**, **~ service**, ☈ **Department** ✕ (geheimer) Nachrichtendienst: **~ officer** Abwehr-, Nachrichtenoffizier m; **5. ~ with the enemy** (verräterische) Beziehungen pl. zum Feind; **in·tel·li·genc·er** [-sə] s. **1.** Berichterstatter (-in); **2.** A'gent(in), Spi'on(in); **in·tel·li·gent** [-nt] adj. □ **1.** intelli'gent, klug, gescheit; **2.** vernünftig: a) verständig, einsichtsvoll, b) vernunftbegabt; **in·tel·li·gent·si·a**, **in·tel·li·gent·zi·a** [ɪnˌtelɪˈdʒentsɪə] s. pl. konstr. coll. die Intelli'genz, die Intellektu'ellen pl.; **in·tel·li·gi·bil·i·ty** [ɪnˌtelɪdʒəˈbɪlətɪ] s. Verständlichkeit f; **in·tel·li·gi·ble** [-dʒəbl] □ verständlich, klar (**to** für od. dat.).

in·tem·per·ance [ɪnˈtempərəns] s. Unmäßigkeit f, Zügellosigkeit f, bsd. Trunksucht f; **in·tem·per·ate** [-rət] adj. □ **1.** unmäßig, maßlos; **2.** ausschweifend, zügellos; unbeherrscht; **3.** trunksüchtig.

in·tend [ɪnˈtend] v/t. **1.** beabsichtigen, vorhaben, planen, im Sinne haben (**s.th.** et.; **to do** od. **doing** zu tun); bestimmen (**for** für, zu): **our son is ~ed for the navy** unser Sohn soll (einmal) zur Marine gehen; **what is it ~ed for?** was ist der Sinn (od. Zweck) der Sache?, was soll das?; **3.** sagen wollen, meinen: **what do you ~ by this?**; **4.** bedeuten, sein sollen: **it was ~ed for a compliment** es sollte ein Kompliment sein; **5.** wollen, wünschen; **in·tend·ant** [-dənt] s. Verwalter m; **in·tend·ed** [-dɪd] **I** adj. □ **1.** beabsichtigt, gewünscht; **2.** absichtlich; **3.** F zukünftig: **my ~ wife**; **II** s. **4.** F Verlobte(r m) f: **her ~** ihr Zukünftiger; **in·tend·ing** [-dɪŋ] adj. angehend, zukünftig; ...lustig, ... willig: **~ buyer** ☈ (Kauf)Interessent (-in), Kaufwillige(r).

in·tense [ɪnˈtens] adj. □ **1.** inten'siv: a) stark, heftig: **~ heat** (**longing** etc.), b) hell, grell: **~ light**, c) tief, satt: **~ col·o(u)rs**, d) angespannt: **~ study**, e) (an-)gespannt, konzentriert: **~ look**, f) sehnlich, dringend, b) eindringlich: **~ style**; **2.** leidenschaftlich, stark gefühlsbetont; **in·tense·ly** [-lɪ] adv. **1.** äußerst, höchst; **2.** → **intense**; **in·tense·ness** [-nɪs] s. Intensi'tät f: a) Stärke f, Heftig-

keit f, b) Anspannung f, Angestrengtheit f, c) Feuereifer m, d) Leidenschaftlichkeit f, e) Eindringlichkeit f; **in·ten·si·fi·ca·tion** [ɪnˌtensɪfɪˈkeɪʃn] s. Verstärkung f (a. phot.); **in·ten·si·fi·er** [-sɪfaɪə] s. a. ⊙, phot. Verstärker m; **in·ten·si·fy** [-sɪfaɪ] **I** v/t. verstärken (a. phot.), steigern; **II** v/i. sich verstärken.

in·ten·sion [ɪnˈtenʃn] s. **1.** Verstärkung f; **2.** → **intenseness** a u. b; **3.** (Begriffs)Inhalt m.

in·ten·si·ty [ɪnˈtensətɪ] s. Intensi'tät f: a) (hoher) Grad, Stärke f, Heftigkeit f, b) ↯, ⊙, phys. (Laut-, Licht-, Strom- etc.)Stärke f, Grad m, c) → **intenseness**; **in·ten·sive** [-sɪv] **I** adj. □ **1.** inten'siv: a) stark, heftig, b) gründlich, erschöpfend: **~ study**; **~ course** ped. Intensivkurs m; **2.** verstärkend (a. ling.); **3.** ✍ a) stark wirkend, b) **~ care unit** Intensivstation f; **4.** ✝ inten'siv: a) ertragssteigernd, b) (arbeits-, lohn-, kosten- etc.)inten'siv; **II** s. **5.** bsd. ling. verstärkendes Ele'ment.

in·tent [ɪnˈtent] **I** s. **1.** Absicht f, Vorsatz m, Zweck m: **criminal ~** ⚖ Vorsatz, (verbrecherische) Absicht; **with ~ to defraud** in betrügerischer Absicht; **to all ~s and purposes** a) in jeder Hinsicht, durchaus, b) im Grunde, eigentlich, c) praktisch, sozusagen; **declaration of ~** Absichtserklärung f; **II** adj. □ **2.** erpicht, versessen (**on** auf acc.); **3.** (**on**) bedacht (auf acc.), eifrig beschäftigt (mit); **4.** aufmerksam, gespannt, eifrig.

in·ten·tion [ɪnˈtenʃn] s. **1.** Absicht f, Vorhaben n, Vorsatz m, Plan m (**to do** od. **of doing** zu tun): **with the best (of) ~s** in bester Absicht; **2.** pl. F (Heirats)Absichten pl.; **3.** Zweck m (a. eccl.), Ziel n; ✍ Sinn m, Bedeutung f; **in·ten·tion·al** [-ʃənl] adj. □ **1.** absichtlich, vorsätzlich; **2.** beabsichtigt; **in·ten·tioned** [-nd] adj. in Zssgn ...gesinnt: **well-~** gut gesinnt, wohlmeinend.

in·tent·ness [ɪnˈtentnɪs] s. gespannte Aufmerksamkeit, Eifer m: **~ of purpose** Zielstrebigkeit f.

in·ter [ɪnˈtɜː] v/t. beerdigen.

inter- [ɪntə] in Zssgn zwischen, Zwischen...; unter; gegen-, wechselseitig, ein'ander, Wechsel...

'in·ter·act¹ [-ækt] s. thea. Zwischenakt m, -spiel n.

in·ter'act² [-əˈrækt] v/i. aufein'ander wirken, sich gegenseitig beeinflussen; **in·ter'ac·tion** [-əˈrækʃn] s. Wechselwirkung f, Interakti'on f; **in·ter'ac·tive** [-tɪv] adj. interak'tiv: **~ application** interaktive Anwendung; **~ program** interaktives Programm; **~ software** interaktive Software.

in·ter'breed biol. **I** v/t. [irr. → **breed**] durch Kreuzung züchten, kreuzen; **II** v/i. [irr. → **breed**] a) sich kreuzen, b) Inzucht betreiben.

in·ter·ca·lar·y [ɪnˈtɜːkələrɪ] adj. eingeschaltet, eingeschoben; Schalt...: **~ day** Schalttag m; **in·ter·ca·late** [ɪnˈtɜːkəleɪt] v/t. einschieben, einschalten; **in·ter·ca·la·tion** [ɪnˌtɜːkəˈleɪʃn] s. **1.** Einschiebung f, Einschaltung f; **2.** Einlage f.

in·ter·cede [ˌɪntəˈsiːd] v/i. sich verwenden, sich ins Mittel legen, Fürsprache einlegen, intervenieren (**with** bei, **for** für); bitten (**with** bei j-m, **for** um et.); **in·ter'ced·er** [-də] s. Fürsprecher(in).

in·ter·cept I v/t. [ˌɪntəˈsept] **1.** Brief, Meldung, Flugzeug, Boten etc. abfan-

gen; **2.** Meldung auffangen, mit-, abhören; **3.** unter'brechen, abschneiden; **4.** den Weg abschneiden (dat.); **5.** Sicht versperren; **6.** ☈ a) abschneiden, b) einschließen; **II** s. [ˈɪntəsept] **7.** ☈ Abschnitt m; **8.** aufgefangene Meldung; **in·ter'cep·tion** [-pʃn] s. **1.** Ab-, Auffangen n (Meldung etc.); **2.** Ab-, Mithören n (Meldung): **~ service** Abhör-, Horchdienst m; **3.** Abfangen n (Flugzeug, Boten): **~ flight** Sperrflug m; **~ plane → interceptor** 2; **4.** Unter'brechung f, Abschneiden n; **5.** Aufhalten n, Hinderung f; **in·ter'cep·tor** [-tə] s. **1.** Auffänger m; **2.** a. **~ plane** ✈ ✕ Abfangjäger m.

in·ter·ces·sion [ˌɪntəˈseʃn] s. Fürbitte f (a. eccl.), Fürsprache f: **make ~ to s.o. for** bei j-m Fürsprache einlegen für, sich bei j-m verwenden für; (**service of**) **~** Bittgottesdienst m; **in·ter'ces·sor** [-esə] s. Fürsprecher(in), Vermittler(in) (**with** bei); **in·ter'ces·so·ry** [-esərɪ] adj. fürsprechend.

in·ter·change [ˌɪntəˈtʃeɪndʒ] **I** v/t. **1.** unterein'ander austauschen, auswechseln; **2.** vertauschen, auswechseln (a. ⊙); einander abwechseln lassen; **II** v/i. **3.** abwechseln (**with** mit), aufein'ander folgen; **III** s. **4.** Austausch m; Aus-, Abwechslung f; Wechsel m, Aufein'anderfolge f; **5.** ✝ Tauschhandel m; **6.** Am. (Straßen)Kreuzung f; (Autobahn-) Kreuz n; **in·ter·change·a·bil·i·ty** [ˈɪntəˌtʃeɪndʒəˈbɪlətɪ] s. Auswechselbarkeit f; **in·ter·change·a·ble** [-dʒəbl] adj. □ **1.** austauschbar, auswechselbar (a. ⊙, ✝); **2.** (mitein'ander) abwechselnd.

in·ter·cit·y adj. Inter'city...: **~ train** Inter'cityzug m.

in·ter·col·le·gi·ate adj. zwischen verschiedenen Colleges (bestehend).

in·ter·com [ˈɪntəkɒm] s. **1.** ✈, ⚓ Bordsprechanlage f; **2.** (Gegen-, Haus)Sprechanlage f; **3.** a) (Werk- etc.)Rufanlage f, b) Lautsprecheranlage f.

in·ter·com'mu·ni·cate v/i. **1.** miteinander verkehren od. in Verbindung stehen; **2.** → **communicate** 4; **in·ter·com‚mu·ni'ca·tion** s. gegenseitige Verbindung, gegenseitiger Verkehr: **~ system → intercom**.

in·ter'com·pa·ny adj. zwischenbetrieblich.

in·ter·con'nect I v/t. mitein'ander verbinden, ↯ a. zs.-schalten; **II** v/i. miteinander verbunden werden od. sein, fig. a. in Zs.-hang (miteinander) stehen; **in·ter·con'nec·tion 1.** (gegenseitige) Verbindung, fig. a. Zs.-hang m; **2.** ↯ a) Zs.-Schaltung f, b) verkettete Schaltung.

'in·ter‚con·ti'nen·tal adj. interkontinen'tal, Interkontinental...

'in·ter·course s. **1.** 'Umgang m, Verkehr m (**with** mit); **2.** ✝ Geschäftsverkehr m; **3.** a. **sexual ~** (Geschlechts-) Verkehr m.

in·ter'cross I v/t. **1.** ein'ander kreuzen lassen, a. zo. kreuzen; **II** v/i. **3.** sich kreuzen (a. ♀, zo.).

'in·ter·cut s. Film etc.: Einblendung f.

'in·ter·de‚nom·i'na·tion·al adj. interkonfessio'nell.

in·ter·de'pend v/i. vonein'ander abhängen; **in·ter·de'pend·ence**, **in·ter·de'pend·en·cy** s. gegenseitige Abhängigkeit; **in·ter·de'pend·ent** adj. □ vonein'ander abhängig, eng zs.-hängend od. verflochten, inein'ander greifend.

in·ter·dict I s. [ˈɪntədɪkt] **1.** Verbot n; **2.**

eccl. Inter'dikt *n*; **II** *v/t.* [ˌɪntə'dɪkt] **3.** (amtlich) unter'sagen, verbieten (*to s.o.* j-m): **~ *s.o. from s.th.*** j-n von et. ausschließen, j-m et. entziehen *od.* verbieten; **4.** *eccl.* mit dem Inter'dikt belegen; **in·ter'dic·tion** → *interdict* 1, 2.

in·ter·est ['ɪntrɪst] **I** *s.* **1.** (*in*) Inter'esse *n* (an *dat.*, für), (An)Teilnahme *f* (an *dat.*): *take an* **~** *in s.th.* sich für et. interessieren; **2.** Reiz *m*, Inter'esse *n*: *be of* **~** (*to*) interessant *od.* reizvoll sein (für), interessieren (*acc.*); **3.** Wichtigkeit *f*, Bedeutung *f*: *be of little* **~** von geringer Bedeutung sein; *of great* **~** von großem Interesse; **4.** *bsd.* ✝ Beteiligung *f*, Anteil *m* (*in* an *dat.*): *have an* **~** *in s.th.* an *od.* bei et. (*bsd.* finanziell) beteiligt sein; **5.** ✝ Interes'senten *pl.*, Kreise *pl.*: *the banking* **~** die Bankkreise *pl.*; *the landed* **~** die Grundbesitzer *pl.*; **6.** Inter'esse *n*, Vorteil *m*, Nutzen *m*, Gewinn *m*: *be in* (*od.* *to*) *the* **~(*s*)** *of* im Interesse von ... liegen; *in your* **~** zu Ihrem Vorteil; *look after one's* **~s** s-e Interessen wahren; *study s.o.'s* **~(*s*)** j-s Vorteil im Auge haben; **7.** Einfluss *m*, Macht *f*: *have* **~** *with* Einfluss haben bei; **8.** (An)Recht *n*, Anspruch *m* (*in* auf *acc.*); **9.** Gesichtspunkt *m*, Seite *f* (*in e-r Geschichte etc.*): → *human* I; **10.** (*nie pl.*) ✝ Zins(en *pl.*) *m*: *and* (*od.* *plus*) **~** züzüglich Zinsen; *ex* **~** ohne Zinsen; *free of* **~** zinslos; *bear* (*od.* *yield*) **~** Zinsen tragen, sich verzinsen; **~** *rate* ✝ Zinsfuß *m*, -satz *m*; **~** *rate policy* 'Zinspoli,tik *f*; **~** *account* a) Zinsrechnung *f*, b) Zinsenkonto *n*; **~** *certificate* Zinsenvergütungsschein *m*; **~** *pro and contra* Soll- u. Habenzinsen *pl.*; **~** *coupon* (*od.* *ticket, warrant*) Zinskupon *m*, -schein *m*; **11.** *fig.* Zinsen *pl.*: *return a blow with* **~** e-n Schlag mit Zins u. Zinseszinsen zurückgeben; **II** *v/t.* **12.** interessieren (*in* für), j-s Inter'esse *od.* Teilnahme erwecken (*in s.th.* an e-r Sache; *for s.o.* für j-n): ~ *o.s. in s.th.* sich interessieren für, Anteil nehmen an (*dat.*); **13.** interessieren, anziehen, reizen, fesseln; **14.** angehen, betreffen: *everyone is* **~*ed* *in this*** dies geht jeden an; **15.** *bsd.* ✝ beteiligen (*in* an *dat.*); **16.** gewinnen (*in* für).

in·ter·est·ed ['ɪntrɪstɪd] *adj.* □ **1.** interessiert, Anteil nehmend (*in* an *dat.*); aufmerksam: *be* **~** *in* sich interessieren für; *I was* **~** *to know* es interessierte mich zu wissen; **2.** *bsd.* ✝ beteiligt (*in* an *dat.*, bei): *the parties* **~** die Beteiligten; **3.** voreingenommen, par'teiisch; **4.** eigennützig: **~** *motives*; **'in·ter·est·ed·ly** [-lɪ] *adv.* mit Inter'esse, aufmerksam; **'in·ter·est·ing** [-tɪŋ] *adj.* □ interes'sant, fesselnd, bedeutsam: *in an* **~** *condition* *obs.* in anderen Umständen (*schwanger*); **'in·ter·est·ing·ly** [-tɪŋlɪ] *adv.* interes'santerweise.

'in·ter·face *s.* **1.** *allg. u. phys.* Zwischen-, Grenzfläche *f*; **2.** *Computer:* a) Interface *n*, Schnittstelle *f*, b) a. *user* **~** Benutzeroberfläche *f*.

in·ter·fere [ˌɪntə'fɪə] *v/i.* **1.** sich einmischen, da'zwischentreten, -kommen; dreinreden; sich Freiheiten her'ausnehmen; **2.** eingreifen, -schreiten: *it is time to* **~** s. *a.* ⊙ stören, hindern; **4.** zs.-stoßen (*a. fig.*), aufein'ander prallen; **5.** *phys.* aufein'ander treffen, sich kreuzen *od.* über'lagern; ⚡ stören; **6.** **~** *with* a) j-n stören, unter'brechen, (be)hindern, belästigen, b) et. stören, beeinträchtigen, sich einmischen in (*acc.*), störend einwirken auf (*acc.*); **7.** **~** *in* eingreifen in (*acc.*), sich befassen mit

od. kümmern um; **in·ter'fer·ence** [-ɪərəns] *s.* **1.** Einmischung *f* (*in* in *acc.*), Eingreifen *n* (*with* in *acc.*); **2.** Störung *f*, Hinderung *f*, Beeinträchtigung *f* (*with gen.*); **3.** Zs.-stoß(en *n*) *m* (*a. fig.*); **4.** *Am. sport* Abschirmen *n*: *run* **~** a) den balltragenden Stürmer abschirmen, b) (*for s.o.*) *fig.* (j-m) Schützenhilfe leisten; **5.** ⚡, *phys.* a) Interfe'renz *f*, Über'lagerung *f*, b) Störung *f*: *reception* **~** Empfangsstörung *f*; **~** *suppression* Entstörung *f*; **in·ter·fer·en·tial** [ˌɪntəfə'renʃl] *adj. phys.* Interferenz...; **in·ter'fer·ing** [-ɪərɪŋ] *adj.* □ **1.** störend, lästig: *be always* **~** F sich ständig einmischen; **2.** kollidierend, entgegenstehend: **~** *claim*.

in·ter'gla·cial *adj. geol.* zwischeneiszeitlich, interglazi'al.

in·ter·im ['ɪntərɪm] **I** *s.* **1.** Zwischenzeit *f*: *in the* **~** in der Zwischenzeit, einstweilen, vorläufig; **2.** Interim *n*, einstweilige Regelung *f*; **3.** ⚷ *hist.* Interim *n*; **II** *adj.* **4.** einstweilig, vorläufig, Übergangs..., Interims..., Zwischen...: **~** *report* Zwischenbericht *m*; → *injunction* 1; **~** *aid* *s.* Über'brückungshilfe *f*; **~** *bal·ance* (*sheet*) *s.* ✝ 'Zwischenbi,lanz *f*, -abschluss *m*; **~** *cer·tif·i·cate* *s.* ✝ Interimsschein *m*; **~** *cred·it* *s.* ✝ 'Interimskre,dit *m*; **~** *div·i·dend* *s.* ✝ 'Interimsdivi,dende *f*.

in·te·ri·or [ɪn'tɪərɪə] **I** *adj.* **1.** inner, innen gelegen; Innen... (*a.* ♔): **~** *decoration*, **~** *design* a) Innenausstattung *f*, b) Innenarchitektur *f*; **~** *decorator*, **~** *designer* a) Innenausstatter(in), b) Innenarchitekt(in); **2.** binnenländisch, Binnen...; **3.** inländisch, Inlands...; **4.** innerlich, geistig: **~** *monologue* *Literatur:* innerer Monolog; **II** *s.* **5.** *das* Innere (*a.* ♔), Innenraum *m*; **6.** *das* Innere, Binnenland *n*; **7.** *phot.* Innenaufnahme *f*; **8.** *das* Innere, wahres Wesen; **9.** *pol.* innere Angelegenheiten *pl.*: *Department of the* ⚷ *Am.* Innenministerium *n*.

in·ter·ject [ˌɪntə'dʒekt] *v/t.* **1.** Bemerkung da'zwischen-, einwerfen; da'zwischenrufen; **2.** einschieben, einschalten; **in·ter'jec·tion** [-kʃn] *s.* **1.** Aus-, Zwischenruf *m*; **2.** *ling.* Interjekti'on *f*; **in·ter'jec·tion·al** [-kʃənl] *adj.* □, **in·ter'jec·to·ry** [-tərɪ] *adj.* da'zwischengeworfen, eingeschoben, Zwischen...

in·ter'lace **I** *v/t.* **1.** inein'ander flechten, verflechten, verschlingen; **2.** durch'flechten, verweben (*a. fig.*); **3.** (ver)mischen; **4.** *Computer:* verschachteln; **II** *v/i.* **5.** sich verflechten *od.* kreuzen: *interlacing arches* ⚠ verschränkte Bogen; **III** *s.* **6.** *TV* Zwischenzeile *f*.

'in·ter·lan·guage *s.* Verkehrssprache *f*.

in·ter'lard *v/t. fig.* spicken, durch'setzen (*with* mit).

'in·ter·leaf *s.* [*irr.*] leeres Zwischenblatt; **in·ter'leave** *v/t.* **1.** Bücher durch'schießen; **2.** *Computer:* verschachteln.

in·ter'line *v/t.* **1.** zwischen die Zeilen schreiben *od.* setzen, einfügen; **2.** *typ.* Zeilen durch'schießen; **3.** *Kleidungsstück* mit e-m Zwischenfutter versehen; **in·ter'lin·e·ar** *adj.* **1.** da'zwischengeschrieben, zwischenzeilig, Interlinear...; **2.** *space typ.* Durchschuss *m*; **'in·ter·lin·e·a·tion** *s.* das Da'zwischengeschriebene.

in·ter'link **I** *v/t.* verketten (*a.* ⚡); **II** *s.* ['ɪntəlɪŋk] Binde-, Zwischenglied *n*.

in·ter'lock **I** *v/i.* **1.** inein'ander greifen (*a. fig.*): **~*ing directorate*** ✝ Schachtelaufsichtsrat *m*; **2.** 🔒 verblockt sein: **~*ing signals*** Blocksignale; **II** *v/t.* **3.**

zs.-schließen, inein'ander schachteln; **4.** inein'ander haken, verzahnen; **5.** ⊙, 🔒 verblocken: **~*ing plant*** Stellwerk *n*.

in·ter·lo·cu·tion [ˌɪntələʊ'kju:ʃn] *s.* Gespräch *n*, Unter'redung *f*; **in·ter·loc·u·tor** [ˌɪntə'lɒkjutə] *s.* Gesprächspartner (-in); **in·ter·loc·u·to·ry** [ˌɪntə'lɒkjutərɪ] *adj.* **1.** in Gesprächsform; Gesprächs...; **2.** ⚷ vorläufig, Zwischen...: **~** *injunction* einstweilige Verfügung.

in·ter·lop·er ['ɪntələʊpə] *s.* **1.** Eindringling *m*; **2.** ✝ Schleichhändler *m*.

in·ter·lude ['ɪntəlu:d] *s.* **1.** Zwischenspiel *n* (*a.* ♪ *u. fig.*); **2.** Pause *f*; **3.** Zwischenzeit *f*; **4.** Epi'sode *f*.

in·ter'mar·riage *s.* **1.** Mischehe *f* (*zwischen verschiedenen Konfessionen, Rassen etc.*); **2.** Heirat *f* unterein'ander *od.* zwischen nahen Blutsverwandten; **in·ter'mar·ry** *v/i.* **1.** unterein'ander heiraten (*Stämme etc.*), Mischehen eingehen; **2.** innerhalb der Fa'milie heiraten.

in·ter'med·dle *v/i.* sich einmischen (*with, in* in *acc.*).

in·ter·me·di·ar·y [ˌɪntə'mi:djərɪ] **I** *adj.* **1.** → *intermediate* 1; **2.** vermittelnd; **II** *s.* **3.** Vermittler(in); **4.** ✝ Zwischenhändler *m*; **in·ter'me·di·ate** [-jət] **I** *adj.* □ **1.** da'zwischenliegend, Zwischen..., Mittel...: **~** *between* liegend zwischen; **~** *colo(u)r* (*credit, product, stage, trade*) Zwischenfarbe *f* (-kredit *m*, -produkt *n*, -stadium *n*, -handel *m*); **~** *examination* → 4; **II** *s.* **2.** Zwischenglied *n*, -form *f*, -stück *n*; **3.** ♞ 'Zwischenpro,dukt *n*; **4.** Zwischenprüfung *f*; **5.** Vermittler(in), Mittelsmann *m*.

in·ter·ment [ɪn'tɜ:mənt] *s.* Beerdigung *f*, Beisetzung *f*.

in·ter·mez·zo [ˌɪntə'metsəʊ] *pl.* **-mez·zi** [-tsi:] *od.* **-mez·zos** *s.* Inter'mezzo *n*, Zwischenspiel *n*.

in·ter·mi·na·ble [ɪn'tɜ:mməbl] *adj.* □ **1.** grenzenlos, endlos; **2.** langwierig.

in·ter'min·gle → *intermix*.

in·ter'mis·sion *s.* Unter'brechung *f*, Aussetzen *n*; Pause *f*: *without* **~** pausenlos, unaufhörlich, ständig.

in·ter·mit [ˌɪntə'mɪt] **I** *v/t.* unter'brechen, aussetzen mit; **II** *v/i.* aussetzen, nachlassen; **in·ter'mit·tence** [-təns] *s.* Aussetzen *n*, Unter'brechung *f*; **in·ter'mit·tent** [-tənt] *adj.* □ mit Unter'brechungen, stoßweise; (zeitweilig) aussetzend, peri'odisch, intermittierend: *be* **~** aussetzen; **~** *fever* 🦟 Wechselfieber *n*; **~** *light* ⚓ Blinkfeuer *n*.

in·ter'mix **I** *v/t.* vermischen; **II** *v/i.* sich vermischen; **in·ter'mix·ture** *s.* **1.** Mischung *f*; **2.** Beimischung *f*, Zusatz *m*.

in·tern[1] **I** *v/t.* [ɪn'tɜ:n] internieren; **II** *s.* ['ɪntɜ:n] *Am.* Internierte(r *m*) *f*.

in·tern[2] ['ɪntɜ:n] *Am.* **I** *s.* 🩺 Assi'stenzarzt *m*, a. *med.* Prakti'kant(in); **II** *v/i.* als Assi'stenzarzt (*in Klinik*) tätig sein.

in·ter·nal [ɪn'tɜ:nl] **I** *adj.* □ **1.** inner, inwendig: **~** *organs anat.* innere Organe; **~** *diameter* Innendurchmesser *m*; **2.** 🩺 innerlich *od.* in'tern anzuwenden(d), einzunehmen(d): **~** *remedy*; **3.** inner(lich), geistig; **4.** einheimisch, in-, binnenländisch, Inlands..., Innen..., Binnen...: **~** *loan* ✝ Inlandsanleihe *f*; **~** *market* Binnenmarkt *m*; **~** *trade* Binnenhandel *m*; **5.** *pol.* inner, Innen...: **~** *affairs* innere Angelegenheiten; **6.** *ped.* in'tern, im College *etc.* wohnend; **7.** **~** *etc.* (be'triebs)in,tern, innerbetrieblich; **8.** *Computer:* in'tern (*Befehl etc.*); **II** *s.* **9.** *pl. anat.* innere Or'gane *pl.*; **10.** innere Na'tur; **~·com'bus·tion en·gine** *s.* ⊙ Verbrennungs-, Explo-

315

internalize – intimate

si'onsmotor *m*.

in·ter·na·lize [ɪn'tɜːnəlaɪz] *v/t. psych. et.* verinnerlichen, in sich aufnehmen.

in·ter·nal| med·i·cine *s.* ⚕ innere Medi'zin; ~ **rev·e·nue** *s. Am.* Steueraufkommen *n*; ⚖ **Office** Finanzamt *n*; ~ **rhyme** *s.* Binnenreim *m*; ~ **spe·cial·ist** *s.* ⚕ Inter'nist *m*, Facharzt *m* für innere Krankheiten; ~ **thread** *s.* ⊕ Innengewinde *n*.

in·ter·na·tion·al I *adj.* □ **1.** internatio'nal, zwischenstaatlich; ~ **candle** *phys.* Internationale Kerze (*Lichtstärke*); **2.** Welt..., Völker...; II *s.* **3.** *sport* a) Internatio'nale(r *m*) *f*, Natio'nalspieler (-in), b) F internatio'nales Länderspiel *n*; **4.** ⚖ *pol.* Internatio'nale *f*; **5.** *pl.* ✝ internatio'nal gehandelte 'Wertpa,piere *pl.*; **In·ter·na·tio·nale** [ˌɪntənæʃə'nɑːl] *s.* Internatio'nale *f* (*Kampflied*); **in·ter·na·tion·al·ism** *s.* **1.** Internationa'lismus *m*; **2.** internatio'nale Zs.-arbeit; **in·ter·na·tion·al·ist** *s.* **1.** Internatio'nalist *m*, Anhänger *m* des Internatio'nalismus; **2.** ⚕ Völkerrechtler *m*; **3.** → *international* 3 a; 'in·ter,na·tion·al·i·ty *s.* internatio'naler Cha'rakter; ,in·ter'na·tion·al·ize *v/t.* **1.** internationalisieren; **2.** internatio'naler Kon'trolle unter'werfen.

in·ter·na·tion·al| law *s.* Völkerrecht *n*; ⚖ **Mon·e·tar·y Fund** *s.* Internatio'naler Währungsfonds; ~ **mon·ey or·der** *s.* Auslandspostanweisung *f*; ~ **re·ply coupon** *s.* internatio'naler Antwortschein.

in·terne ['ɪntɜːn] → *intern²*.

in·ter·ne·cine [ˌɪntə'niːsaɪn] *adj.* **1.** gegenseitige Tötung bewirkend: ~ *duel*; ~ *war* gegenseitiger Vernichtungskrieg; **2.** mörderisch, vernichtend.

in·tern·ee [ˌɪntɜː'niː] *s.* Internierte(r *m*) *f*.

In·ter·net ['ɪntənet] *s.* *the* ~ das Internet; ~ *access* Internetanschluss *m*, -zugriff *m*; ~ *commerce* 'Internethandel *m*, Handel *m* über das Internet; ~ *connection* Internetanschluss, -verbindung *f*; ~ *service provider* Internetprovider *m*, -anbieter *m*; ~ *site* Internetseite *f*; → *surf* III.

in·tern·ment [ɪn'tɜːnmənt] *s.* Internierung *f*; ~ *camp* Internierungslager *n*; **in·tern·ship** ['ɪntɜːnʃɪp] *s. Am.* **1.** ⚕ Assis'tenzarzttätigkeit *f*; **2.** 'Praktikum *n*, Prakti'kantenzeit *f*.

'**in·ter,o·ce·an·ic** [-ər,əʊ-] *adj.* interoze'anisch, zwischen (zwei) Weltmeeren liegend, (zwei) Weltmeere verbindend.

in·ter·pel·late [ɪn'tɜːpeleɪt] *v/t. pol.* e-e Anfrage richten an (*acc.*); **in·ter·pel·la·tion** [ɪn,tɜːpe'leɪʃn] *s. pol.* Interpellati'on *f*.

,**in·ter'pen·e·trate** I *v/t.* völlig durch'dringen; II *v/i.* sich gegenseitig durch'dringen.

in·ter·phone ['ɪntəfəʊn] → *intercom*.

,**in·ter'plan·e·tar·y** *adj.* interplane'tarisch.

,**in·ter'play** *s.* Wechselwirkung *f*, -spiel *n*.

In·ter·pol ['ɪntəpɒl] *s.* Interpol *f* (*Internationale kriminalpolizeiliche Organisation*).

in·ter·po·late [ɪn'tɜːpəʊleɪt] *v/t.* **1.** interpolieren; *et.* einschalten, -fügen; **2.** (durch Einschiebung) ändern, *bsd.* verfälschen; **3.** A interpolieren; **in·ter·po·la·tion** [ɪn,tɜːpəʊ'leɪʃn] *s.* Interpolati'on *f* (*a.* A), Einschaltung *f*, Einschiebung *f* (*in e-n Text*).

,**in·ter'pose** I *v/t.* **1.** da'zwischenstellen, -legen, -bringen; ⊕ zwischenschalten; **2.** *et.* in den Weg legen; **3.** *Bemerkung*

einwerfen, einflechten; *Einwand etc.* vorbringen, *Veto* einlegen; II *v/i.* **4.** da'zwischenkommen, -treten; **5.** vermitteln, intervenieren; **6.** (sich) unter'brechen (*im Reden*); **in·ter·po·si·tion** [ɪn,tɜːpə'zɪʃn] *s.* **1.** Eingreifen *n*; **2.** Vermittlung *f*, Einfügung *f*, Einschaltung *f* (*a.* ⊕).

in·ter·pret [ɪn'tɜːprɪt] I *v/t.* **1.** interpretieren, auslegen, deuten; ansehen (*as* als); *bsd.* ✗ auswerten; **2.** dolmetschen; **3.** ♪, *thea. etc.* interpretieren, 'wiedergeben, darstellen; II *v/i.* **4.** dolmetschen, als Dolmetscher fungieren; **in·ter·pre·ta·tion** [ɪn,tɜːprɪ'teɪʃn] *s.* **1.** Erklärung *f*, Auslegung *f*, Deutung *f*; Auswertung *f*; **2.** (mündliche) 'Wiedergabe, Über'setzung *f*; **3.** ♪, *thea. etc.* Darstellung *f*, 'Wiedergabe *f*; Auffassung *f*, Interpretati'on *f* (*e-r Rolle etc.*); **in·ter·pret·er** [-tə] *s.* **1.** Erklärer(in), Ausleger(in), Inter'pret(in); **2.** Dolmetscher(in); **3.** *Computer:* Interpre'tierpro,gramm *n*; **in·ter·pret·er·ship** [-təʃɪp] *s.* Dolmetscherstellung *f*.

,**in·ter'ra·cial** *adj.* **1.** verschiedenen Rassen gemeinsam, inter'rassisch; **2.** zwischenrassisch: ~ *tension(s)* Rassenspannungen.

In·ter·rail tick·et ['ɪntəreɪl] *s.* 🚄 Interrailkarte *f*.

in·ter·reg·num [ˌɪntə'regnəm] *pl.* **-na** [-nə], **-nums** *s.* **1.** Inter'regnum *n*: a) herrscherlose Zeit, b) Zwischenregierung *f*; **2.** Pause *f*, Unter'brechung *f*.

,**in·ter·re'late** I *v/t.* zuein'ander in Beziehung bringen; II *v/i.* zuein'ander in Beziehung stehen, zs.-hängen; ,**in·ter·re'lat·ed** *adj.* in Wechselbeziehung stehend, (untereinan'der) zs.-hängend; ,**in·ter·re'la·tion** *s.* Wechselbeziehung *f*.

in·ter·ro·gate [ɪn'terəʊgeɪt] *v/t.* **1.** (be-) fragen; **2.** ausfragen, vernehmen, verhören; **in·ter·ro·ga·tion** [ɪn,terəʊ'geɪʃn] *s.* **1.** Frage *f* (*a. ling.*), Befragung *f*: ~ *mark, point of* ~ *ling.* Fragezeichen *n*; **2.** Vernehmung *f*, Verhör *n*: ~ *officer* Vernehmungsoffizier *m*, -beamter *m*; **in·ter·rog·a·tive** [ˌɪntə'rɒgətɪv] I *adj.* □ fragend, Frage...: ~ *pronoun* → II; II *s. ling.* Fragefürwort *n*; **in·ter·ro·ga·tor** [-tə] *s.* **1.** Fragesteller (-in); **2.** Vernehmungsbeamte(r) *m*; **3.** *pol.* Interpel'lant *m*; **in·ter·rog·a·to·ry** [ˌɪntə'rɒgətərɪ] I *adj.* **1.** fragend, Frage...; II *s.* **2.** Frage(stellung) *f*; **3.** ⚖ Beweisfrage *f* (*vor der Verhandlung*).

in·ter·rupt [ˌɪntə'rʌpt] *v/t.* **1.** *allg.*, *a.* ⚡ unter'brechen, *a. j-m* ins Wort fallen; **2.** aufhalten, stören, hindern; **in·ter·'rupt·ed** [-tɪd] *adj.* □ unter'brochen (*a.* ⚡, ⊕, ⚕); **in·ter'rupt·ed·ly** [-tɪdlɪ] *adv.* mit Unter'brechungen; **in·ter'rupt·er** [-tə] *s.* **1.** Unter'brecher *m* (*a.* ⚡, ⊕); **2.** Zwischenrufer(in), Störer(in), **in·ter·'rup·tion** [-pʃn] *s.* **1.** Unter'brechung *f* (*a.* ⚡), Stockung *f*: *without* ~ ununterbrochen; **2.** (⊕ Betriebs)Störung *f*.

in·ter·sect [ˌɪntə'sekt] I *v/t.* (durch-) 'schneiden; II *v/i.* sich schneiden *od.* kreuzen (*a.* A); ,**in·ter'sec·tion** [-kʃn] *s.* **1.** Durch'schneiden *n*; **2.** Schnitt-, Kreuzungspunkt *m*; **3.** A a) Schnitt *m*, b) *a.* *point of* ~ Schnittpunkt *m*, c) *a.* *line of* ~ Schnittlinie *f*; **4.** *Am.* (Straßen- *etc.*)Kreuzung *f*; **5.** ▲ Vierung *f*.

'**in·ter·sex** *s. biol.* Inter'sex *n* (*geschlechtliche Zwischenform*); ,**in·ter·'sex·u·al** *adj.* zwischengeschlechtlich.

,**in·ter'space** I *s.* Zwischenraum *m*, -zeit *f*; II *v/t.* Raum lassen zwischen (*dat.*); trennen.

in·ter·sperse [ˌɪntə'spɜːs] *v/t.* **1.** ein-

streuen, hier und da einfügen (*among* zwischen *acc.*); **2.** durch'setzen (*with* mit).

'**in·ter·state** *adj. Am.* zwischenstaatlich, zwischen den US-Bundesstaaten (bestehend *etc.*).

,**in·ter'stel·lar** *adj.* interstel'lar.

in·ter·stice [ɪn'tɜːstɪs] *s.* **1.** Zwischenraum *m*; **2.** Lücke *f*, Spalte *f*; **in·ter·sti·tial** [ˌɪntə'stɪʃl] *adj.* in Zwischenräumen (gelegen), zwischenräumlich, Zwischen...

,**in·ter'trib·al** *adj.* zwischen verschiedenen Stämmen (vorkommend).

,**in·ter'twine** *v/t. u. v/i.* (sich) verflechten *od.* verschlingen.

,**in·ter'ur·ban** [-ər'ɜː-] *adj.* Überland...: ~ *bus*.

in·ter·val ['ɪntəvl] *s.* **1.** Zwischenraum *m*, -zeit *f*, Abstand *m*: *at* ~*s* dann und wann, periodisch; → *lucid* 1; **2.** Pause *f* (*a. thea. etc.*): ~ *signal Radio:* Pausenzeichen *n*; **3.** ♪ Inter'vall *n*, Tonabstand *m*; ~ *train·ing s. sport* Inter'valltraining *n*.

in·ter·vene [ˌɪntə'viːn] *v/i.* **1.** (*zeitlich*) da'zwischenliegen, liegen zwischen (*dat.*); **2.** sich (in'zwischen) ereignen, (plötzlich) eintreten; **3.** (*unerwartet*) da'zwischenkommen: *if nothing* ~*s*; **4.** sich einmischen (*in* in *acc.*), einschreiten; **5.** (*helfend*) eingreifen, vermitteln; sich verwenden (*with s.o.* bei j-m); **6.** *bsd.* ✝, ⚖ intervenieren; ,**in·ter'ven·tion** [-'venʃn] *s.* **1.** Da'zwischenliegen *n*, -kommen *n*; **2.** Vermittlung *f*; **3.** Eingreifen *n*, -schreiten *n*, -mischung *f*; **4.** ✝, *pol.* (⚖ 'Neben)Interventi,on *f*; **5.** Einspruch *m*; ,**in·ter'ven·tion·ist** [-'venʃnɪst] *s. pol.* Befür'worter *m* e-r Interventi'on, Interventio'nist *m*.

in·ter·view ['ɪntəvjuː] I *s.* **1.** Inter'view *n*; **2.** Unter'redung *f*, (✝ *a.* Vorstellungs)Gespräch *n*: *hours for* ~*s* Sprechzeiten, -stunden *pl.*; II *v/t.* **3.** inter'viewen, ein Inter'view *od.* e-e Unter'redung haben mit, ein Gespräch führen mit; **in·ter·view·ee** [ˌɪntəvjuː'iː] *s.* Inter'viewte(r *m*) *f*; *a.* Kandi'dat(in) (*für e-e Stelle*); '**in·ter·view·er** [-juːə] *s.* Inter'viewer(in); Leiter(in) e-s Vorstellungsgesprächs.

'**in·ter·war** *adj.*: *the* ~ *period* die Zeit zwischen den (Welt)Kriegen.

,**in·ter'weave** *v/t.* (*irr.* → *weave*) **1.** verweben, verflechten (*a. fig.*); **2.** vermengen; **3.** durch'weben, -'flechten, -'wirken.

,**in·ter'zon·al** *adj.* Interzonen...

in·tes·ta·cy [ɪn'testəsɪ] *s.* ⚖ Fehlen *n* e-s Testa'ments; **in·tes·tate** [-teɪt] I *adj.* **1.** ohne Hinter'lassung e-s Testa'ments: *die* ~; **2.** nicht testamen'tarisch geregelt: ~ *estate*; ~ *succession* gesetzliche Erbfolge; II *s.* **3.** Erb-lasser(in), der (*od.* die) kein Testa'ment hinter'lassen hat.

in·tes·ti·nal [ɪn'testɪnl] *adj.* ⚕ Darm...: ~ *flora* Darmflora *f*; **in·tes·tine** [ɪn'testɪn] I *s. anat.* Darm *m*; *pl.* Gedärme *pl.*, Eingeweide *pl.*: *large* ~ Dickdarm; *small* ~ Dünndarm; II *adj.* inner, einheimisch: ~ *war* Bürgerkrieg *m*.

in·thral(l) [ɪn'θrɔːl] *Am.* → *enthral(l)*.

in·throne [ɪn'θrəʊn] *Am.* → *enthrone*.

in·ti·ma·cy ['ɪntɪməsɪ] *s.* **1.** Intimi'tät *f*: a) Vertrautheit *f*, vertrauter 'Umgang, b) (*contp. plumpe*) Vertraulichkeit; **2.** in'time (*sexuelle*) Beziehungen *pl.*

in·ti·mate¹ ['ɪntɪmət] I *adj.* □ **1.** vertraut, innig, in'tim: *on* ~ *terms* auf vertrautem Fuß; **2.** eng, nah; **3.** per'sönlich; **4.** in'tim, in geschlechtlichen Beziehungen (stehend) (*with* mit); **5.** gründlich: ~ *knowledge*; **6.** ⊙, ⚥ innig: ~ *contact*; ~ *mixture*; **II** *s.* **7.** Vertraute(r *m*) *f*, Intimus *m*.

in·ti·mate² ['ɪntɪmeɪt] *v/t.* **1.** andeuten, zu verstehen geben; **2.** nahe legen; **3.** ankündigen, mitteilen; **in·ti·ma·tion** [,ɪntɪ'meɪʃn] *s.* **1.** Andeutung *f*, Wink *m*; **2.** Mitteilung *f*.

in·tim·i·date [ɪn'tɪmɪdeɪt] *v/t.* einschüchtern, abschrecken, Bange machen; **in·tim·i·da·tion** [ɪn,tɪmɪ'deɪʃn] *s.* Einschüchterung *f*; ⚖ Nötigung *f*.

in·ti·tle [ɪn'taɪtl] *Am.* → **entitle**.

in·to ['ɪntʊ; 'ɪntə] *prp.* **1.** in (*acc.*), in (*acc.*) ... hin'ein: *go ~ the house*; *get ~ debt* in Schulden geraten; *flog ~ obedience* durch Prügel zum Gehorsam bringen; *translate ~ English* ins Englische übersetzen; *far ~ the night* tief in die Nacht; *she is ~ her thirties* sie ist Anfang dreißig; *Socialist ~ Conservative* die Verwandlung e-s Sozialisten in einen Konservativen; **2.** *Zustandsänderung*: zu: *make water ~ ice* Wasser zu Eis machen; *turn ~ cash* zu Geld machen; *grow ~ a man* ein Mann werden; **3.** 🅰 in: *divide ~ 10 parts* in 10 Teile teilen; *4 ~ 20 goes five times* 4 geht in 20 fünfmal; **4.** *be ~ s.th.* F a) auf (*acc.*) et. ,stehen', b) et. ,am Wickel' haben: *he is ~ modern art now* F er ,hat es' jetzt (*beschäftigt sich*) mit moderner Kunst.

in·tol·er·a·ble [ɪn'tɒlərəbl] *adj.* □ unerträglich; **in'tol·er·a·ble·ness** [-nɪs] *s.* Unerträglichkeit *f*; **in'tol·er·ance** [-lərəns] *s.* **1.** 'Intole,ranz *f*, Unduldsamkeit *f* (*of* gegen); **2.** 🕭 'Überempfindlichkeit *f* (*of* gegen); **in'tol·er·ant** [-lərənt] *adj.* □ **1.** unduldsam, 'intole,rant (*of* gegen); **2.** *be ~ of* nicht (v)ertragen können.

in·tomb [ɪn'tuːm] *Am.* → **entomb**.

in·to·nate ['ɪntəʊneɪt] *v/t.* → **intone**; **in·to·na·tion** [,ɪntəʊ'neɪʃn] *s.* **1.** *ling.* Intonati'on *f*, Tonfall *m*; **2.** ♪ Intonati'on *f*: a) Anstimmen *n*, b) Psalmodieren *n*, c) Tonansatz *m*; **in·tone** [ɪn'təʊn] *v/t.* **1.** ♪ anstimmen, intonieren; **2.** ♪ psalmodieren; **3.** (mit *e-m bestimmten Ton-fall*) (aus)sprechen.

in to·to [,ɪn'təʊtəʊ] (*Lat.*) *adv.* **1.** im Ganzen, insgesamt; **2.** vollständig.

in·tox·i·cant [ɪn'tɒksɪkənt] **I** *adj.* berauschend; **II** *s.* berauschendes Getränk, Rauschmittel *n*; **in'tox·i·cate** [-keɪt] *v/t.* (a. *fig.*) berauschen, (be)trunken machen; *~d with* berauscht od. trunken von *Wein*, *Liebe etc.*; **in·tox·i·ca·tion** [ɪn,tɒksɪ'keɪʃn] *s. a. fig.* Rausch *m*, Trunkenheit *f*.

intra- [ɪntrə] *in Zssgn* innerhalb.

,in·tra'car·di·ac *adj.* 🕭 im Herz'innern, intrakardi'al.

in·trac·ta·bil·i·ty [ɪn,træktə'bɪlətɪ] *s.* Unlenksamkeit *f*, 'Widerspenstigkeit *f*; **in·trac·ta·ble** [ɪn'træktəbl] *adj.* □ **1.** unlenksam, störrisch, halsstarrig; **2.** schwer zu bearbeiten(d) *od.* zu handhaben(d), ,widerspenstig'.

in·tra·dos [ɪn'treɪdɒs] *s.* 🔺 Laibung *f*.

in·tra·mu·ral [,ɪntrə'mjʊərəl] *adj.* **1.** innerhalb der Mauern (*e-r Stadt, e-s Hauses etc.*) befindlich; **2.** innerhalb der Universi'tät.

,in·tra'mus·cu·lar *adj.* 🕭 intramusku'lär.

In·tra·net ['ɪntrənet] *s. Computer:* Intranet *n* (*privates Netz*).

in·tran·si·gence [ɪn'trænsɪdʒəns] *s.* Unnachgiebigkeit *f*, Intransi'genz *f*; **in-**

'tran·si·gent [-nt] *adj. bsd. pol.* unnachgiebig, starr, intransi'gent.

in·tran·si·tive [ɪn'trænsɪtɪv] **I** *adj.* □ *ling.* intransitiv (*a.* 🅰); **II** *s. ling.* Intransitiv *n*.

in·trant ['ɪntrənt] *s.* Neueintretende(r *m*) *f*, (*ein Amt*) Antretende(r *m*) *f*.

,in·tra'state *adj.* innerstaatlich, *Am.* innerhalb e-s Bundesstaates.

in·tra·u·ter·ine de·vice ['ɪntrəjuːtəraɪn, -rɪn] *s.* 🕭 Spi'rale *f*, ,Intraute'rinpes,sar *n*.

,in·tra've·nous *adj.* 🕭 intrave'nös.

'in tray *s.* Ablagekorb *m* für eingehende Post.

in·trench [ɪn'trentʃ] → **entrench**.

in·trep·id [ɪn'trepɪd] *adj.* □ unerschrocken; **in·tre·pid·i·ty** [,ɪntrɪ'pɪdətɪ] *s.* Unerschrockenheit *f*.

in·tri·ca·cy ['ɪntrɪkəsɪ] *s.* **1.** Kompliziertheit *f*, Kniffligkeit *f*; **2.** Komplikati'on *f*, Schwierigkeit *f*; **in'tri·cate** [-kət] *adj.* □ verwickelt, kompliziert, knifflig, schwierig.

in·trigue [ɪn'triːg] **I** *v/i.* **1.** intrigieren, Ränke schmieden; **2.** ein Verhältnis haben (*with* mit); **II** *v/t.* **3.** fesseln, faszinieren; **4.** neugierig machen; **5.** verblüffen; **III** *s.* **6.** In'trige *f*: a) Ränkespiel *n*, *pl.* Ränke *pl.*, Machenschaften *pl.*, b) Verwicklung *f* (*im Drama etc.*); **in'tri·guer** [-gə] *s.* Intri'gant(in); **in'tri·guing** [-gɪŋ] *adj.* □ **1.** fesselnd, faszinierend; **2.** verblüffend; **3.** intrigierend, ränkevoll.

in·trin·sic [ɪn'trɪnsɪk] *adj.* (□ *~ally*) inner, wahr, eigentlich, wirklich, wesentlich, imma'nent: ~ *value* innerer Wert; **in'trin·si·cal·ly** [-kəlɪ] *adv.* wirklich, eigentlich; an sich: ~ *safe* ⚡ eigensicher.

in·tro·duce [,ɪntrə'djuːs] *v/t.* **1.** einführen: ~ *a new method*; **2.** einleiten, eröffnen, anfangen; **3.** (*into* in *acc.*) et. (her'ein)bringen; *Instrument etc.* einführen, -setzen; *Seuche* einschleppen; *parl. Gesetzesvorlage* einbringen; **4.** *Thema, Frage* anschneiden, aufwerfen; **5.** *j-n* (hin'ein)führen, (-)geleiten (*into* in *acc.*); **6.** (*to*) *j-n* einführen (in *acc.*), bekannt machen (mit *et.*); **7.** (*to*) *j-n* bekannt machen (mit *j-m*), vorstellen (*dat.*); **,in·tro'duc·tion** [-'dʌkʃn] *s.* **1.** Einführung *f*; **2.** Einleitung *f*, Anbahnung *f*; **3.** Einleitung *f*, Vorrede *f*, -wort *n*; **4.** Leitfaden *m*, Anleitung *f*; **5.** Einführung *f* (*Instrument*); Einschleppung *f* (*Seuche*); *pol.* Einbringung *f* (*Gesetz*); **6.** Vorstellung *f*: *letter of ~* Empfehlungsbrief *m*; **,in·tro'duc·to·ry** [-'dʌktərɪ] *adj.* einleitend, Einleitungs..., Vor...

in·tro·mis·sion [,ɪntrəʊ'mɪʃn] *s.* **1.** Einführung *f*; **2.** Zulassung *f*.

in·tro·spect [,ɪntrəʊ'spekt] *v/t.* sich (innerlich) prüfen; **,in·tro'spec·tion** [-kʃn] *s.* Selbstbeobachtung *f*, Innenschau *f*, Introspekti'on *f*; **,in·tro'spec·tive** [-tɪv] *adj.* □ introspek'tiv, selbstprüfend, nach innen gewandt.

in·tro·ver·sion [,ɪntrəʊ'vɜːʃn] *s.* **1.** Einwärtskehren *n*; **2.** *psych.* Introversi'on *f*, Introvertiertheit *f*; **in·tro·vert I** *s.* ['ɪntrəʊvɜːt] *psych.* introvertierter Mensch; **II** *v/t.* [,ɪntrəʊ'vɜːt] nach innen richten, einwärts kehren; *psych.* introvertieren.

in·trude [ɪn'truːd] **I** *v/t.* **1.** *fig.* (unnötigerweise) hi'neinbringen: ~ *one's own ideas into the argument*; **2.** *j-m* et. aufdrängen: ~ *s.o.* *upon s.o.* j-m et. aufdrängen; ~ *o.s.* *upon s.o.* sich j-m aufdrängen; **II** *v/i.* **3.** sich eindrängen *od.* einmischen (*into*

acc.), sich aufdrängen (*upon dat.*); **4.** (*upon*) *j-n* stören, belästigen: *am I intruding?* störe ich?; **in'trud·er** [-də] *s.* **1.** Eindringling *m*; **2.** Zudringliche(r *m*) *f*, Störenfried *m*; **3.** ✈ Störflugzeug *n*; **in'tru·sion** [-uːʒn] *s.* **1.** Eindrängen *n*, Eindringen *n*; **2.** Einmischung *f*; **3.** Zu-, Aufdringlichkeit *f*; **4.** Belästigung *f* (*upon gen.*); **5.** ⚖ Besitzstörung *f*; **in'tru·sive** [-uːsɪv] *adj.* □ **1.** auf-, zudringlich, lästig; **2.** *geol.* eingedrungen; **3.** *ling.* 'unetymo,logisch (eingedrungen); **in'tru·sive·ness** [-uːsɪvnɪs] → *intrusion* 3.

in·tu·it [ɪn'tjuːɪt] *v/t. u. v/i.* intui'tiv erfassen *od.* wissen; **in·tu·i·tion** [,ɪntjuː'ɪʃn] *s.* Intuiti'on *f*: a) unmittelbare Erkenntnis, b) Eingebung *f*, Ahnung *f*; **in·tu·i·tive** [ɪn'tjuːɪtɪv] *adj.* □ intui'tiv.

in·tu·mes·cence [,ɪntjuː'mesns] *s.* **1.** Anschwellen *n*; **2.** 🕭 Anschwellung *f*, Geschwulst *f*; **,in·tu'mes·cent** [-nt] *adj.* (an)schwellend.

in·twine [ɪn'twaɪn] *Am.* → **entwine**.

in·un·date ['ɪnʌndeɪt] *v/t.* über'schwemmen (*a. fig.*); **in·un·da·tion** [,ɪnʌn'deɪʃn] *s.* Über'schwemmung *f*, Flut *f* (*a. fig.*).

in·ure [ɪ'njʊə] **I** *v/t. mst pass.* (*to*) abhärten (gegen), gewöhnen (an *acc.*); **II** *v/i. bsd.* ⚖ wirksam *od.* gültig *od.* angewendet werden.

in·vade [ɪn'veɪd] *v/t.* **1.** einfallen *od.* eindringen *od.* einbrechen in (*acc.*); **2.** über'laufen, angreifen; **3.** *fig.* über'laufen, -'schwemmen, sich ausbreiten über (*acc.*); **4.** eindringen in (*acc.*), 'übergreifen auf (*acc.*); **5.** *fig.* erfüllen, ergreifen, befallen: *fear ~d all*; **6.** *fig.* verstoßen gegen, verletzen, antasten, eingreifen in (*acc.*); **in'vad·er** [-də] *s.* Eindringling *m*, Angreifer(in); *pl.* ⚔ Inva'soren *pl.*

in·va·lid¹ ['ɪnvəlɪd] **I** *adj.* **1.** a) krank, leidend, b) inva'lide, c) ⚔ dienstunfähig; **2.** Kranken...: ~ *chair* Rollstuhl *m*; ~ *diet* Krankenkost *f*; **3.** Kranke(r *m*) *f*; **4.** Inva'lide *m*; **III** *v/t.* [,ɪnvə'liːd] **5.** zum Inva'liden machen; **6.** *a.* ~ *out* ⚔ dienstuntauglich erklären *od.* als dienstuntauglich entlassen: *be ~ed out* als Invalide (aus dem Heer) entlassen werden.

in·val·id² [ɪn'vælɪd] *adj.* □ **1.** (rechts)ungültig, null u. nichtig; **2.** nichtig, nicht stichhaltig (*Argumente*); **in'val·i·date** [-deɪt] *v/t.* **1.** außer Kraft setzen: a) (für) ungültig erklären, 'umstoßen, b) ungültig *od.* unwirksam machen; **2.** *Argument etc.* entkräften; **in·val·i·da·tion** [ɪn,vælɪ'deɪʃn] *s.* **1.** Ungültigkeitserklärung *f*; **2.** Entkräftung *f*.

in·va·lid·ism ['ɪnvəlɪdɪzəm] *s.* 🕭 Invali-di'tät *f*.

in·va·lid·i·ty [,ɪnvə'lɪdətɪ] *s.* **1.** *bsd.* ⚖ Ungültigkeit *f*, Nichtigkeit *f*; **2.** 🕭 *Am.* Invalidi'tät *f*.

in·val·u·a·ble [ɪn'væljʊəbl] *adj.* □ unschätzbar, unbezahlbar, von unschätzbarem Wert.

in·var·i·a·bil·i·ty [ɪn,veərɪə'bɪlətɪ] *s.* Unveränderlichkeit *f*; **in·var·i·a·ble** [ɪn'veərɪəbl] **I** *adj.* □ unveränderlich, gleich bleibend; kon'stant (*a.* 🅰); **II** *s.* 🅰 Kon'stante *f*; **in·var·i·a·bly** [ɪn'veərɪəblɪ] *adv.* stets, ausnahmslos.

in·va·sion [ɪn'veɪʒn] *s.* **1.** (*of*) Invasi'on *f* (*gen.*): a) ⚔ *u. fig.* Einfall *m* (in *acc.*), 'Überfall *m* (auf *acc.*), b) Eindringen *n*, Einbruch *m* (in *acc.*); **2.** Andrang *m* (*of* zu); **3.** *fig.* (*of*) Eingriff *m* (in *acc.*), Verletzung *f* (*gen.*); **4.** 🕭 Anfall *m*; **in-**

'va·sive [-eɪsɪv] *adj.* **1.** ⚔ Invasions..., angreifend; **2.** (gewaltsam) eingreifend (*of* in *acc.*); **3.** zudringlich.

in·vec·tive [ɪn'vektɪv] *s.* Schmähung(en *pl.*) *f*, Beschimpfung *f*; *pl.* Schimpfworte *pl.*

in·veigh [ɪn'veɪ] *v/i.* (*against*) schimpfen (über, auf *acc.*), herziehen (über *acc.*).

in·vei·gle [ɪn'veɪgl] *v/t.* (*into*) **1.** verleiten, verführen (zu): ~ *s.o. into doing s.th.* j-n dazu verleiten, *et.* zu tun; **2.** locken (in *acc.*); **in'vei·gle·ment** [-mənt] *s.* Verleitung *f etc.*

in·vent [ɪn'vent] *v/t.* **1.** erfinden, ersinnen; **2.** *fig.* erfinden, erdichten; **in'ven·tion** [-nʃn] *s.* **1.** Erfindung *f* (*a. fig.*); **2.** (Gegenstand *m etc.* der) Erfindung *f*; **3.** Erfindungsgabe *f*; **4.** *contp.* Märchen *n*; **in'ven·tive** [-tɪv] *adj.* □ **1.** erfinderisch (*of* in *dat.*); Erfindungs...; **2.** schöpferisch, einfallsreich, origi'nell; **in'ven·tive·ness** [-tɪvnɪs] → *invention* 3; **in'ven·tor** [-tə] *s.* Erfinder(in).

in·ven·to·ry ['ɪnvəntrɪ] *a.* ⊕ **I** *s.* **1.** a) Inven'tar *n*, Bestandsverzeichnis, (-)Liste *f*, b) *Am.* Bestandsaufnahme *f*, Inven'tur *f*; **2.** Inven'tar *n*, Lagerbestand *m*, Vorräte *pl.*: *take* ~ Inventur machen; **II** *v/t.* **3.** inventarisieren: a) e-e Bestandsaufnahme machen von, b) im Inven'tar verzeichnen.

in·verse [ɪn'vɜːs] **I** *adj.* □ 'umgekehrt, entgegengesetzt; ⅍ in'vers, rezi'prok: ~*ly proportional* umgekehrt proportional; **II** *s.* 'Umkehrung *f*, Gegenteil *n*; **in'ver·sion** [ɪn'vɜːʃn] *s.* **1.** 'Umkehrung *f* (*a.* ♪); **2.** 🌡, ⅍, *ling., meteor.* Inversi'on *f*, *psych. a.* Homosexuali'tät *f*.

in·vert **I** *v/t.* [ɪn'vɜːt] **1.** 'umkehren (*a.* ♪), 'umdrehen, 'umwenden (*a.* ♪); **2.** *ling.* 'umstellen; **3.** 🌡 invertieren; **II** *s.* ['ɪnvɜːt] **4.** △ 'umgekehrter Bogen; **5.** ⊕ Sohle *f* (*Schleuse etc.*); **6.** *psych.* Invertierte(r *m*) *f*: a) Homosexu'elle(r *m*), b) Lesbierin *f*, c) Transsexu'elle(r *m*) *f*.

in·ver·te·brate [ɪn'vɜːtɪbrət] **I** *adj.* **1.** *zo.* wirbellos; **2.** *fig.* rückgratlos; **II** *s.* **3.** *zo.* wirbelloses Tier: *the* ~*s* die Wirbellosen.

in·vert·ed [ɪn'vɜːtɪd] *adj.* **1.** 'umgekehrt; 'umgestellt; **2.** *psych.* invertiert, homosexu'ell; **3.** ⊕ hängend: ~ *cylinders*, ~ *engine* Hängemotor *m*; ~ *com·mas s. pl.* Anführungszeichen *pl.*, 'Gänsefüßchen' *pl.*; ~ *flight s.* ✈ Rückenflug *m*; ~ *im·age s. phys.* Kehrbild *n*.

in·vest [ɪn'vest] **I** *v/t.* **1.** ✝ investieren, anlegen (*in* in *dat.*); **2.** (*with, in* mit) bekleiden (*a. fig.*); bedecken, um'hüllen; **3.** (*with*) kleiden (in *acc.*), ausstatten (mit *Befugnissen etc.*); um'geben (mit); **4.** (in Amt u. Würden) einsetzen; ⚔ einschließen, belagern; **II** *v/i.* **6.** investieren (*in* in *dat.*); **7.** ~ *in* F ,sein Geld investieren' in (*dat.*).

in·ves·ti·gate [ɪn'vestɪgeɪt] **I** *v/t.* unter'suchen, erforschen; ermitteln; **II** *v/i.* (*into*) nachforschen (nach), Ermittlungen anstellen (über *acc.*); **in·ves·ti·ga·tion** [ɪn,vestɪ'geɪʃn] *s.* **1.** Unter'suchung *f*, Nachforschung *f*; *pl.* Ermittlung(en *pl.*) *f*, Re'cherchen *pl.*; **2.** *wissenschaftliche* (Er)Forschung; **in'ves·ti·ga·tive** [-tɪv] *adj.* recherchierend, Untersuchungs...: ~ *journalism* Enthüllungsjournalismus *m*; ~ *reporter* recherchierender Reporter; **in'ves·ti·ga·tor** [-tə] *s.* **1.** Unter'suchende(r) *m*, (Er-, Nach)Forscher(in); **2.** Ermittler *m*, Unter'suchungsbeamte(r) *m*: *private* ~ (Pri'vat)Detek,tiv(in); **3.** Prüfer(in).

in·ves·ti·ture [ɪn'vestɪtʃə] *s.* **1.** Investi'tur *f*, (feierliche) Amtseinsetzung *f*; **2.** Belehnung *f*; **3.** *fig.* Ausstattung *f*.

in·vest·ment [ɪn'vestmənt] *s.* **1.** ✝ a) Investierung *f*, b) Investiti'on(en *pl.*) *f*, (Kapi'tal-, Geld)Anlage *f*, Anlagewerte *pl.*: *that's a good* ~ das ist e-e gute Geldanlage, *fig.* das lohnt sich *od.* macht sich bezahlt; **2.** ✝ Einlage *f*, Beteiligung *f* (*e-s Gesellschafters*); **3.** Ausstattung *f* (*with* mit); **4.** *biol.* (Außen-, Schutz)Haut *f*; **5.** ⚔ *obs.* Belagerung *f*; **6.** → *investiture* 1; ~ *ad·vis·er s.* Anlageberater *m*; ~ *bank s.* Investiti'ons-, In'vestmentbank *f*; ~ *bank·ing s.* Ef-'fektenbankgeschäft *n*; ~ *bonds s. pl.* festverzinsliche 'Anlagepa,piere *pl.*; ~ *cap·i·tal s.* 'Anlagekapi,tal *n*; ~ *com·pan·y s.* Kapi'talanlage-, In'vestmentgesellschaft *f*; ~ *cred·it s.* Investiti'onskre,dit *m*; ~ *fund s.* 'Anlagefonds *m*, *pl.* Investiti'onsmittel *pl.*; ~ *goods s. pl.* Investiti'onsgüter *pl.*; ~ *grant s.* Investitionsbeihilfe *f*; ~ *shares s. pl.* ✝ *stocks s. pl.* 'Anlagepa,piere *pl.*, -werte *pl.*; ~ *trust* → *investment company*: ~ *certificate* Anteilschein *m*, Investmentzertifikat *n*.

in·ves·tor [ɪn'vestə] *s.* ✝ In'vestor *m*, Geld-, Kapi'talanleger *m*.

in·vet·er·a·cy [ɪn'vetərəsɪ] *s.* Unausrottbarkeit *f*, ✚ Hartnäckigkeit *f*; **in'vet·er·ate** [-rɪt] *adj.* □ **1.** eingewurzelt; ✚ hartnäckig; **3.** eingefleischt, unverbesserlich.

in·vid·i·ous [ɪn'vɪdɪəs] *adj.* □ **1.** verhasst, ärgerlich; **2.** gehässig, boshaft, gemein; **in'vid·i·ous·ness** [-nɪs] *s.* **1.** das Ärgerliche; **2.** Gehässigkeit *f*, Bosheit *f*, Gemeinheit *f*.

in·vig·i·late [ɪn'vɪdʒɪleɪt] *ped. Brit.* **I** *v/i.* Aufsicht führen; **II** *v/t.* Aufsicht führen bei; **in,vig·i'la·tion** *s. ped. Brit.* Aufsicht *f*; **in'vig·i·la·tor** [-tə] *s. ped. Brit.* 'Aufsicht(sper,son) *f*, Aufsichtsführende(r *m*) *f*.

in·vig·or·ate [ɪn'vɪgəreɪt] *v/t.* stärken, kräftigen, beleben, *bsd. fig.* erfrischen: *invigorating* stärkend *etc.*; **in·vig·or·a·tion** [ɪn,vɪgə'reɪʃn] *s.* Kräftigung *f*, Belebung *f*.

in·vin·ci·bil·i·ty [ɪn,vɪnsɪ'bɪlətɪ] *s.* Unbesiegbarkeit *f etc.*; **in'vin·ci·ble** [ɪn'vɪnsəbl] *adj.* □ unbesiegbar, 'unüber,windlich.

in·vi·o·la·bil·i·ty [ɪn,vaɪələ'bɪlətɪ] *s.* Unverletzlichkeit *f*, Unantastbarkeit *f*; **in·vi·o·la·ble** [ɪn'vaɪələbl] *adj.* □ unverletzlich, unantastbar, heilig; **in·vi·o·late** [ɪn'vaɪələt] *adj.* □ **1.** unverletzt, unversehrt, nicht gebrochen (*Gesetz etc.*); **2.** unangetastet.

in·vis·i·bil·i·ty [ɪn,vɪzə'bɪlətɪ] *s.* Unsichtbarkeit *f*; **in'vis·i·ble** [ɪn'vɪzəbl] *adj.* □ unsichtbar (*to* für): ~ *ink* ~ *exports: pl.*; ~ *mending* Kunststopfen *n*; *he was* ~ *fig.* er ließ sich nicht sehen.

in·vi·ta·tion [,ɪnvɪ'teɪʃn] *s.* **1.** Einladung *f* (*to s.o.* an j-n): ~ *to tea* Einladung zum Tee; **2.** Aufforderung *f*, Ersuchen *n*; **3.** ~ *to bid* ✝ Ausschreibung *f*; **in·vite** [ɪn'vaɪt] *v/t.* **1.** einladen; ~ *s.o. in* j-n hereinbitten: ~*d lecture* Gastvorlesung *f*; **2.** *j-n* auffordern, bitten (*to do* zu tun); **3.** *et.* erbitten, ersuchen um, auffordern zu (*dat.*); ✝ ausschreiben; **4.** *Kritik, Gefahr etc.* herausfordern, sich aussetzen (*dat.*); **5.** a) einladen zu, ermutigen zu, b) (ver)locken (*to do* zu tun); **in'vit·ing** [ɪn'vaɪtɪŋ] *adj.* □ einladend, (ver)lockend.

in·vo·ca·tion [,ɪnvəʊ'keɪʃn] *s.* **1.** Anru-

fung *f*; **2.** *eccl.* Bittgebet *n*.

in·voice ['ɪnvɔɪs] ✝ **I** *s.* Fak'tura *f*, (Waren-, Begleit)Rechnung *f*: *as per* ~ laut Rechnung; ~ *amount* Rechnungsbetrag *m*; ~ *clerk* Fakturist(in); **II** *v/t.* fakturieren, in Rechnung stellen; **'in·voic·ing** *s.* ✝ Faktu'rierung *f*, In'rechnungstellung *f*: ~ *currency* Fakturierungswährung *f*.

in·voke [ɪn'vəʊk] *v/t.* **1.** anrufen, anflehen, flehen zu; **2.** flehen um, erflehen; **3.** *fig.* zu Hilfe rufen, sich berufen auf (*acc.*), anführen, zitieren; **4.** *Geist* beschwören.

in·vol·un·tar·i·ness [ɪn'vɒləntərɪnɪs] *s.* **1.** Unfreiwilligkeit *f*; **2.** 'Unwill,kürlichkeit *f*; **in·vol·un·tar·y** [ɪn'vɒləntərɪ] *adj.* □ **1.** unfreiwillig; **2.** 'unwill,kürlich; **3.** unabsichtlich.

in·vo·lute ['ɪnvəluːt] **I** *adj.* **1.** ♦ eingerollt; **2.** *zo.* mit engen Windungen; **3.** *fig.* verwickelt; **II** *s.* ⅍ Evol'vente *f*; **in·vo·lu·tion** [,ɪnvə'luːʃn] *s.* **1.** ♦ Einrollung *f*; **2.** Involuti'on *f*: a) *biol.* Rückbildung *f*, b) ⅍ Potenzierung *f*; **3.** Verwicklung *f*, Verwirrung *f*.

in·volve [ɪn'vɒlv] (→ *a. involved*) *v/t.* **1.** um'fassen, einschließen, involvieren; **2.** nach sich ziehen, zur Folge haben, mit sich bringen, verbunden sein mit, bedeuten: ~ *great expense; this would* ~ *(our) living abroad* das würde bedeuten, dass wir im Ausland leben müssten; **3.** nötig machen, erfordern: ~ *hard work*; **4.** betreffen: a) angehen: *the plan* ~*s all employees*, b) beteiligen (*in, with* an *dat.*): *the number of persons* ~*d*, c) sich handeln *od.* drehen um, gehen um, zum Gegenstand haben: *the case* ~*d some grave offences*, d) in Mitleidenschaft ziehen: *diseases that* ~ *the nervous system*; *it wouldn't* ~ *you* du hättest nichts damit zu tun; **5.** verwickeln, -stricken, hin'einziehen (*in* in *acc.*): ~*d in a lawsuit* in e-n Rechtsstreit verwickelt; ~*d in an accident* in e-n Unfall verwickelt, an e-m Unfall beteiligt; *I am not getting* ~*d in this!* ich lasse mich da nicht hineinziehen!; **6.** *j-n* (*seelisch, persönlich*) engagieren (*in* in *dat.*): ~ *o.s. with s.o.* sich mit j-m einlassen; *be* ~*d with s.o.* a) mit j-m zu tun haben, b) zu j-m e-e (enge) Beziehung haben, *erotisch*: a. mit j-m ein Verhältnis haben, es mit j-m ,haben'; *she was* ~*d with several men*; **7.** *j-n* in Schwierigkeiten bringen (*with* mit); **8.** *et.* verwickeln, verwirren; **in'volved** [-vd] *adj.* (→ *a. involve*) **1.** a) kompliziert, b) verworren: *an* ~ *sentence*; **2.** betroffen, beteiligt: *the persons* ~; **3.** *be* ~ a) → *involve* 4 c, b) mitspielen (*in* bei e-r *Sache*), c) auf dem Spiel stehen, gehen um: *the national prestige was* ~; **4.** (*in*) verwickelt, verstrickt (in *acc.*), beteiligt (an *dat.*); **5.** eingebegriffen; **6.** (*in, with*) a) stark beschäftigt (mit), versunken (in *acc.*), b) (stark) interessiert (an *dat.*); **7.** (*seelisch, innerlich*) engagiert: *emotionally* ~; *be deeply* ~ *with a girl* e-e enge Beziehung zu e-m Mädchen haben, stark empfinden für ein Mädchen; **in'volve·ment** [-mənt] *s.* **1.** Verwicklung *f*, -strickung *f* (*in* in *acc.*); **2.** Beteiligung *f* (*in* an *dat.*); **3.** Betroffensein *n*; **4.** (*seelisches od. persönliches*) Engagement; **5.** (*with*) a) (*innere*) Beziehung (zu), b) (*sexuelles*) Verhältnis (mit), c) Umgang (mit); **6.** Kompliziertheit *f*; **7.** komplizierte Sache, Schwierigkeit *f*.

in·vul·ner·a·bil·i·ty [ɪn,vʌlnərə'bɪlətɪ] *s.* **1.** Unverwundbarkeit *f*; **2.** *fig.* Unanfechtbarkeit f; **in·vul·ner·a·ble** [ɪn'vʌl-nərəbl] adj. □ **1.** unverwundbar, ungefährdet, gefeit (**to** gegen); **2.** fig. unanfechtbar.

in·ward ['ɪnwəd] **I** adj. □ **1.** inner(lich), Innen...; nach innen gehend: **~ parts** anat. innere Organe; **the ~ nature** der Kern, das eigentliche Wesen; **2.** fig. seelisch, geistig, inner(lich); **3. ~ duty** ✝ Eingangszoll m; **~ journey** ⚓ Heimfahrt f, -reise f; **~ mail** eingehende Post; **II** s. **4.** das Innere (a. fig.); **5.** pl. ['ɪnədz] F a) innere Organe pl., Eingeweide pl., b) Küche: Inne'reien pl.; **III** adv. **6.** nach innen; **7.** im Innern (a. fig.); **'in·ward·ly** [-lɪ] adv. **1.** innerlich, im Innern (a. fig.); nach innen; **2.** im Stillen, insgeheim, für sich, leise; **'inward·ness** [-nɪs] s. **1.** Innerlichkeit f; **2.** innere Na'tur, wahre Bedeutung; **'in·wards** [-dz] → inward 6, 7.

in·weave [,ɪn'wiːv] v/t. [irr. → weave] **1.** einweben (**into** in acc.); **2.** fig. ein-, verflechten.

in·wrought [,ɪn'rɔːt] adj. **1.** eingewoben, eingearbeitet; **2.** verziert; **3.** fig. (eng) verflochten.

i·o·date ['aɪəʊdeɪt] s. 🜍 Jo'dat n; **i·od·ic** [aɪ'ɒdɪk] adj. 🜍 jodhaltig, Jod...; **'i·o·dide** [-daɪd] s. 🜍 Jo'did n; **'i·o·dine** [-diːn] s. Jod n: **tincture of ~** Jodtinktur f; **'i·o·dism** [-dɪzəm] s. Jodvergiftung f; **'i·o·dize** [-daɪz] v/t. jodieren, mit Jod behandeln.

i·on ['aɪən] s. phys. I'on n.

I·o·ni·an [aɪ'əʊnjən] **I** adj. i'onisch; **II** s. I'onier(in).

I·on·ic¹ [aɪ'ɒnɪk] adj. i'onisch: **~ order** ionische Säulenordnung.

i·on·ic² [aɪ'ɒnɪk] adj. phys. i'onisch: **~ centrifuge** Ionenschleuder f; **~ migration** Ionenwanderung f.

i·o·ni·um [aɪ'əʊnɪəm] s. 🜍 I'onium n.

i·on·i·za·tion [,aɪənaɪ'zeɪʃn] s. phys. Ionisierung f; **i·on·ize** ['aɪənaɪz] phys. **I** v/t. ionisieren; **II** v/i. in I'onen zerfallen; **i·on·o·sphere** [aɪ'ɒnə,sfɪə] s. phys. Iono'sphäre f.

i·o·ta [aɪ'əʊtə] s. Jota n (griech. Buchstabe): **not an ~** fig. kein Jota od. bisschen.

IOU [,aɪəʊ'juː] s. Schuldschein m (= **I owe you**).

ip·so fac·to [,ɪpsəʊ'fæktəʊ] (Lat.) gerade (od. al'lein) durch diese Tatsache, eo ipso.

I·ra·ni·an [ɪ'reɪnjən] **I** adj. **1.** i'ranisch, persisch; **II** s. **2.** I'raner(in), Perser (-in); **3.** ling. I'ranisch n, Persisch n.

I·ra·qi [ɪ'rɑːkɪ] **I** s. **1.** I'raker(in); **2.** ling. I'rakisch n; **II** adj. **3.** i'rakisch.

i·ras·ci·bil·i·ty [ɪ,ræsɪ'bɪlətɪ] s. Jähzorn m, Reizbarkeit f; **i·ras·ci·ble** [ɪ'ræsəbl] adj. □ jähzornig, reizbar.

i·rate [aɪ'reɪt] adj. zornig, wütend.

ire ['aɪə] s. poet. Zorn m, Wut f; **'ire·ful** [-fʊl] adj. □ poet. zornig.

ir·i·des·cence [,ɪrɪ'desns] s. Schillern n; **ir·i·des·cent** [-nt] adj. schillernd, irisierend.

i·rid·i·um [aɪ'rɪdɪəm] s. 🜍 I'ridium n.

i·ris ['aɪərɪs] s. **1.** anat. Regenbogenhaut f, Iris f; **2.** ♀ Schwertlilie f.

I·rish ['aɪərɪʃ] **I** adj. **1.** irisch: **the ~ Free State** obs. der Irische Freistaat; → **bull³**; **II** s. **2.** ling. Irisch n; **3. the ~** pl. die Iren pl., die Irländer pl.; **'I·rish·ism** [-ʃɪzəm] s. irische (Sprach)Eigentümlichkeit f.

'I·rish·man [-mən] s. [irr.] Ire m, Irländer m; **~ stew** Küche: Irish Stew n; **~ ter·ri·er** s. Irischer Terrier;

'~wom·an s. [irr.] Irin f, Irländerin f.

irk [ɜːk] v/t. ärgern, verdrießen; **'irk·some** [-səm] adj. □ **1.** ärgerlich, verdrießlich; **2.** lästig.

i·ron ['aɪən] **I** s. **1.** Eisen n: **have (too) many ~s in the fire** (zu) viele Eisen im Feuer haben; **rule with a rod of ~** od. **with an ~ hand** mit eiserner Faust regieren; **strike while the ~ is hot** das Eisen schmieden, solange es heiß ist; **a man of ~** ein harter Mann; **he is made of ~** er hat e-e eiserne Gesundheit; **2.** Brandeisen n, -stempel m; **3.** (Bügel-, Plätt)Eisen n; **4.** Steigbügel m; **5.** Golf: Eisen n (Schläger); **6.** ⚙ 'Eisen (-präpa,rat) n: **take ~** Eisen einnehmen; **7.** pl. Hand-, Fußschellen pl., Eisen pl.: **put in ~s** → 14; **8.** pl. ⚙ Beinschiene f (Stützapparat): **put s.o.'s leg in ~s** j-m das Bein schienen; **II** adj. **9.** eisern, Eisen...: **~ bar** Eisenstange f; **10.** fig. eisern: a) hart, kräftig: **~ constitution** eiserne Gesundheit; **~ frame** kräftiger Körper(bau), b) ehern, hart, grausam: **~ fist** od. **hand** eiserne Faust (→ 1); **there was an ~ fist in a velvet glove** bei all s-r Freundlichkeit war mit ihm doch nicht zu spaßen, c) unbeugsam, unerschütterlich: **~ discipline** eiserne Zucht; **~ will** eiserner Wille; **III** v/t. **11.** bügeln, plätten; **12. ~ out** a) glätten, einebnen, glatt walzen, b) fig. ,ausbügeln', in Ordnung bringen; **13.** ⊕ mit Eisen beschlagen; **14.** fesseln, in Eisen legen.

I·ron| Age s. Eisenzeit f; **~ Chan·cel·lor** s.: **the ~** der Eiserne Kanzler (Bismarck); **'2-clad I** adj. **1.** gepanzert (Schiff), eisenverkleidet, -bewehrt, mit Eisenmantel; **2.** fig. eisern, starr, streng; **3.** fig. unangreifbar, abso'lut stichhaltig: **~ argument**; **II** s. **4.** hist. Panzerschiff n; **2 con·crete** s. ⊕ 'Eisenbe,ton m; **~ Cross** s. ✠ Eisernes Kreuz (Auszeichnung); **~ Cur·tain** s. pol. ,Eiserner Vorhang': **~ countries** die Länder pl. hinter dem Eisernen Vorhang; **~ Duke** s.: **the ~** der Eiserne Herzog (Wellington); **2 found·ry** s. Eisengieße'rei f; **2 horse** s. F obs. ,Dampfross' n (Lokomotive).

i·ron·ic, i·ron·i·cal [aɪ'rɒnɪk(l)] adj. **1.** i'ronisch, spöttisch (spöttisch); **2.** Situation etc.: seltsam, ,komisch', paradox; **i'ron·i·cal·ly** [-kəlɪ] adv. **1.** i'ronisch(erweise); **2.** komischerweise; **i·ro·nize** ['aɪərənaɪz] **I** v/t. et. ironisieren; **II** v/i. i'ronisch sein, spötteln.

i·ron·ing board ['aɪənɪŋ] s. Bügel-, Plättbrett n.

i·ron| lung s. ⚕ eiserne Lunge; **'~,mas·ter** s. Brit. 'Eisenfabri,kant m, obs. Eisenhüttenbesitzer m; **'~,mon·ger** s. bsd. Brit. Eisenwaren-, Me'tallwarenhändler(in); **'~,mon·ger·y** s. bsd. Brit. **1.** Eisen-, Me'tallwaren pl.; **2.** Eisenwaren-, Me'tallwarenhandlung f; **~ ore** s. metall. Eisenerz n; **~ ox·ide** s. 🜍 'Eiseno,xid n; **~ ra·tion** s. ✠ eiserne Rati'on; **'~sides** s. **1.** sg. Mann m von großer Tapferkeit; **2.** 2 pl. hist. Cromwells Reite'rei f od. Heer n; **3.** → **iron·clad** 4; **'~ware** s. Eisen-, Me'tallwaren pl.; **'~work** s. ⊕ 'Eisenbeschlag m, -konstrukti,on f; **'~works** s. pl. sg. konstr. Eisenhütte f.

i·ron·y¹ ['aɪənɪ] adj. **1.** eisern; **2.** eisenhaltig (Erde); **3.** eisenartig.

i·ro·ny² ['aɪərənɪ] s. **1.** Iro'nie f: **~ of fate** fig. Ironie des Schicksals; **tragic ~** tragische Ironie; **the ~ of it!** fig. welche Ironie (des Schicksals)!; **2.** i'ronische Bemerkung, Spötte'lei f.

Ir·o·quois ['ɪrəkwɔɪ] pl. **-quois** [-kwɔɪz] s. Iro'kese m, Iro'kesin f.

ir·ra·di·ance [ɪ'reɪdjəns] s. **1.** (An-, Aus-, Be)Strahlen n; **2.** Strahlenglanz m; **ir·ra·di·ant** [-nt] adj. a. fig. strahlend (**with** vor dat.); **ir·ra·di·ate** [-dɪeɪt] v/t. **1.** bestrahlen (a. ⚕), erleuchten; **2.** ausstrahlen; **3.** fig. Gesicht etc. aufheitern, verklären; **4.** fig. etc. erhellen, Licht werfen auf (acc.); **ir·ra·di·a·tion** [ɪ,reɪdɪ'eɪʃn] s. **1.** (Aus)Strahlen n, Leuchten n; **2.** phys. a) 'Strahlungsintensi,tät f, b) spe'zifische Strahlungsener,gie; **3.** Irradiati'on f: a) phot. Belichtung f, b) ⚕ Bestrahlung f, Durch'leuchtung f; **4.** fig. Erhellung f.

ir·ra·tion·al [ɪ'ræʃənl] **I** adj. □ **1.** unvernünftig: a) vernunftlos: **~ animal**, b) 'irratio,nal (a. ⚕, phls.), vernunftwidrig, unsinnig; **II** s. **2.** ⚕ 'Irratio,nalzahl f; **3. the ~** → **ir·ra·tion·al·i·ty** [ɪ,ræʃə'nælətɪ] s. Irrationali'tät f (a. ⚕, phls.), das 'Irratio,nale, Unvernunft f, Unsinnigkeit f.

ir·re·but·ta·ble [,ɪrɪ'bʌtəbl] adj. 'unwider,legbar.

ir·re·claim·a·ble [,ɪrɪ'kleɪməbl] adj. □ **1.** unverbesserlich; **2.** ✓ unbebaubar; **3.** 'unwieder,bringlich.

ir·rec·og·niz·a·ble [ɪ'rekəgnaɪzəbl] adj. □ nicht wieder zu erkennen(d), unkenntlich.

ir·rec·on·cil·a·bil·i·ty [ɪ,rekənsaɪlə'bɪlətɪ] s. **1.** Unvereinbarkeit f (**to, with** mit); **2.** Unversöhnlichkeit f; **ir·rec·on·cil·a·ble** [ɪ'rekənsaɪləbl] **I** adj. □ **1.** unvereinbar (**to, with** mit); **2.** unversöhnlich; **II** s. **3.** pol. unversöhnlicher Gegner.

ir·re·cov·er·a·ble [,ɪrɪ'kʌvərəbl] adj. □ **1.** unrettbar (verloren), 'unwieder,bringlich, unersetzlich: **~ debt** nicht beitreibbare (Schuld)Forderung; **2.** unheilbar, nicht wieder 'gutzumachen(d).

ir·re·deem·a·ble [,ɪrɪ'diːməbl] adj. □ **1.** nicht rückkaufbar; **2.** ✝ nicht (in Gold) einlösbar (Papiergeld); **3.** ✝ a) untilgbar: **~ loan**, b) unkündbar (Schuldverschreibung etc.); **4.** unrettbar (verloren), unverbesserlich, hoffnungslos.

ir·re·den·tism [,ɪrɪ'dentɪzəm] s. pol. Irreden'tismus m; **ir·re·den·tist** [-ɪst] pol. **I** s. Irreden'tist m; **II** adj. irreden'tistisch.

ir·re·duc·i·ble [,ɪrɪ'djuːsəbl] adj. □ **1.** nicht zu vereinfachen(d); **2.** nicht reduzierbar, nicht zu vermindern(d): **the ~ minimum** das äußerste Mindestmaß.

ir·re·fran·gi·ble [,ɪrɪ'frændʒəbl] adj. □ **1.** unverletzlich, nicht zu über'treten(d); **2.** opt. unbrechbar.

ir·ref·u·ta·ble [,ɪrɪ'fjuːtəbl] adj. □ 'unwider,legbar, nicht zu wid"er'legen(d).

ir·re·gard·less [,ɪrɪ'gɑːdlɪs] adj. Am. F: **~ of** ohne sich zu kümmern um.

ir·reg·u·lar [ɪ'regjʊlə] **I** adj. □ **1.** unregelmäßig (a. ♀, ling, a. Zähne etc.), ungleichmäßig, uneinheitlich; **2.** ungeordnet, unordentlich; **3.** ungehörig, ungebührlich; **4.** regel-, vorschriftswidrig; **5.** uneigentlich, ungültig; **6.** uneben, 'unsyste,matisch; **7.** ✠ 'irregu,lär; **II** s. **8.** pl. Parti'sanen pl., Freischärler pl.; **ir·reg·u·lar·i·ty** [ɪ,regjʊ'lærətɪ] s. **1.** Unregelmäßigkeit f (a. ling.), Ungleichmäßigkeit f; **2.** Regelwidrigkeit f; ⚖ Formfehler m, Verfahrensmangel m; **3.** Ungehörigkeit f; **4.** Ungebührlichkeit f; **5.** Unordnung f; **6.** Vergehen n, Verstoß m; **7.** pl. ✝ Am. Ausschussware(n pl.) f.

ir·rel·e·vance [ɪˈreləvəns], **ir'rel·e·van·cy** [-sɪ] s. 'Irrele,vanz f, Unerheblichkeit f, Belanglosigkeit f, Unwesentlichkeit f; **ir'rel·e·vant** [-nt] adj. □ 'irrele,vant, belanglos, unerheblich (**to** für) (alle a. ᵗᵗ), nicht zur Sache gehörig.

ir·re·li·gion [ˌɪrɪˈlɪdʒən] s. Religi'onslosigkeit f, Unglaube m; Gottlosigkeit f; ˌir·re'li·gious [-dʒəs] adj. □ 1. 'irreligi,ös, ungläubig, gottlos; 2. religi'onsfeindlich.

ir·re·me·di·a·ble [ˌɪrɪˈmiːdjəbl] adj. □ 1. unheilbar; 2. unabänderlich; 3. → irreparable.

ir·re·mis·si·ble [ˌɪrɪˈmɪsəbl] adj. □ 1. unverzeihlich; 2. unerlässlich.

ir·re·mov·a·ble [ˌɪrɪˈmuːvəbl] adj. □ 1. nicht zu entfernen(d); unbeweglich (a. fig.); 2. unabsetzbar.

ir·rep·a·ra·ble [ɪˈrepərəbl] adj. □ 1. 'irrepa,rabel, nicht wieder 'gutzumachen(d); 2. unersetzlich; 3. unheilbar (a. ✴).

ir·re·place·a·ble [ˌɪrɪˈpleɪsəbl] adj. unersetzlich, unersetzbar; **~ resources** nicht erneuerbare Ressourcen.

ir·re·press·i·ble [ˌɪrɪˈpresəbl] adj. □ 1. unbezähmbar, unbändig; 2. Person: a) nicht 'unterzukriegen(d), unverwüstlich, b) tempera'mentvoll.

ir·re·proach·a·ble [ˌɪrɪˈprəʊtʃəbl] adj. □ untadelig, einwandfrei, tadellos.

ir·re·sist·i·bil·i·ty [ˈɪrɪˌzɪstəˈbɪlətɪ] s. 'Unwider,stehlichkeit f; **ir·re·sist·i·ble** [ˌɪrɪˈzɪstəbl] adj. □ 1. 'unwider,stehlich (a. fig. Charme etc.); 2. unaufhaltsam.

ir·res·o·lute [ɪˈrezəluːt] adj. □ unentschlossen, schwankend; **ir'res·o·lute·ness** [-nɪs], **ir·res·o·lu·tion** [ˈɪˌrezəˈluːʃn] s. Unentschlossenheit f.

ir·re·spec·tive [ˌɪrɪˈspektɪv] adj. □: **~ of** ohne Rücksicht auf (acc.), ungeachtet (gen.), abgesehen von.

ir·re·spon·si·bil·i·ty [ˈɪrɪˌspɒnsəˈbɪlətɪ] s. 1. Unverantwortlichkeit f; 2. Verantwortungslosigkeit f; **ir·re·spon·si·ble** [ˌɪrɪˈspɒnsəbl] adj. □ 1. unverantwortlich (Handlung); 2. verantwortungslos (Person); 3. ᵗᵗ unzurechnungsfähig.

ir·re·spon·sive [ˌɪrɪˈspɒnsɪv] adj. 1. teilnahms-, verständnislos, gleichgültig (**to** gegenüber); 2. unempfänglich (**to** für); **be ~ to** a. nicht reagieren auf (acc.).

ir·re·triev·a·ble [ˌɪrɪˈtriːvəbl] adj. □ 1. 'unwieder,bringlich, unrettbar (verloren): **~ breakdown of marriage** ᵗᵗ unheilbare Zerrüttung der Ehe; 2. unersetzlich; 3. nicht wieder 'gutzumachen(d); ˌir·re'triev·a·bly [-əblɪ] adv.: **~ broken down** ᵗᵗ unheilbar zerrüttet (Ehe).

ir·rev·er·ence [ɪˈrevərəns] s. 1. Unehrerbietigkeit f, Re'spekt-, Pie'tätlosigkeit f; 2. 'Missachtung f; **ir'rev·er·ent** [-nt] adj. □ re'spektlos, ehrfurchtslos, pie'tätlos.

ir·re·vers·i·bil·i·ty [ˈɪrɪˌvɜːsəˈbɪlətɪ] s. 1. Nicht'umkehrbarkeit f; 2. 'Unwider,ruflichkeit f; **ir·re·vers·i·ble** [ˌɪrɪˈvɜːsəbl] adj. □ 1. nicht 'umkehrbar; 2. ⊙ nur in 'einer Richtung (laufend); 3. ⚕, ⚗, phys. irrever'sibel; 4. 'unwider,ruflich.

ir·rev·o·ca·bil·i·ty [ɪˌrevəkəˈbɪlətɪ] s. 'Unwider,ruflichkeit f; **ir·rev·o·ca·ble** [ɪˈrevəkəbl] adj. □ 'unwider,ruflich (a. ♱), endgültig.

ir·ri·ga·ble [ˈɪrɪgəbl] adj. ✓ bewässerungsfähig; **ir·ri·gate** [ˈɪrɪgeɪt] v/t. 1. ✓ bewässern, berieseln; 2. ✴ spülen; **ir·ri·ga·tion** [ˌɪrɪˈgeɪʃn] s. 1. ✓ Bewässe-rung f, Berieselung f; 2. ✴ Spülung f.

ir·ri·ta·bil·i·ty [ˌɪrɪtəˈbɪlətɪ] s. Reizbarkeit f (a. ✴); **ir·ri·ta·ble** [ˈɪrɪtəbl] adj. □ 1. reizbar; 2. gereizt, ✴ a. empfindlich.

ir·ri·tant [ˈɪrɪtənt] I adj. Reiz erzeugend, Reiz...; II s. a) Reizmittel n (a. fig.), b) ✕ Reiz(kampf)stoff m.

ir·ri·tate¹ [ˈɪrɪteɪt] v/t. reizen (a. ✴), (ver)ärgern, irritieren; **~d at** (od. **by** od. **with**) ärgerlich über (acc.).

ir·ri·tate² [ˈɪrɪteɪt] v/t. Scot. ᵗᵗ für nichtig erklären.

ir·ri·tat·ing [ˈɪrɪteɪtɪŋ] adj. □ irritierend, aufreizend; ärgerlich, lästig; **ir·ri·ta·tion** [ˌɪrɪˈteɪʃn] s. 1. Reizung f, Ärger m; 2. ✴ Reizung f, Reizzustand m.

ir·rupt [ɪˈrʌpt] v/i. eindringen, her'einbrechen; **ir'rup·tion** [-pʃn] s. Einbruch m: a) Eindringen n, (plötzliches) Hereinbrechen, b) (feindlicher) Einfall, 'Überfall m; **ir'rup·tive** [-tɪv] adj. hereinbrechend.

is [ɪz] 3. sg. pres. von **be**.

I·sa·iah [aɪˈzaɪə], a. **I·sa·ias** [-əs] npr. u. s. bibl. (das Buch) Je'saja m od. I'saias m.

is·chi·ad·ic [ˌɪskɪˈædɪk], mst ˌis·chi'at·ic [-ˈætɪk] adj. 1. anat. Hüft-, Sitzbein...; 2. ✴ ischi'atisch.

i·sin·glass [ˈaɪzɪŋglɑːs] s. Hausenblase f, Fischleim m.

Is·lam [ˈɪzlɑːm] s. Is'lam m; **Is·lam·ic** [ɪzˈlæmɪk] adj. is'lamisch; **Is·lam·ize** [ˈɪzləmaɪz] v/t. islamisieren.

is·land [ˈaɪlənd] s. 1. Insel f (a. fig. u. ✴); 2. Verkehrsinsel f; **'is·land·er** [-də] s. Inselbewohner(in), Insu'laner (-in).

isle [aɪl] s. poet. u. in npr. (kleine) Insel, poet. Eiland n.

ism [ˈɪzəm] s. Ismus m (bloße Theorie).

is·n't [ˈɪznt] F für **is not**.

i·so·bar [ˈaɪsəʊbɑː] s. 1. meteor. Iso'bare f; 2. phys. Iso'bar n.

i·so·chro·mat·ic [ˌaɪsəʊkrəʊˈmætɪk] adj. phys. isochro'matisch, gleichfarbig.

i·so·late [ˈaɪsəleɪt] v/t. 1. isolieren, absondern, abschließen (**from** von); 2. ⚗, ✴, ⚡, phys. isolieren; 3. fig. genau bestimmen; **'i·so·lat·ed** [-tɪd] adj. 1. isoliert (a. ⊙), (ab)gesondert, al'lein stehend, vereinzelt: **~ case** Einzelfall m; 2. einsam, abgeschieden; **i·so·la·tion** [ˌaɪsəˈleɪʃn] s. ⊙, pol., fig. Isolierung f, Isolati'on f: **~ ward** Isolierstation f; **in ~** fig. einzeln, für sich (betrachtet); **i·so·la·tion·ism** [ˌaɪsə'leɪʃnɪzəm] s. pol. Isolatio'nismus m; **i·so·la·tion·ist** [ˌaɪsə'leɪʃnɪst] s. pol. Isolatio'nist m.

i·so·mer [ˈaɪsəʊmɜː] s. ⚗ Iso'mer n; **i·so·mer·ic** [ˌaɪsəʊˈmerɪk] adj. ⚗ iso'mer.

i·so·met·ric [ˌaɪsəʊˈmetrɪk] ⚕ I adj. iso'metrisch; II s. pl. sg. konstr. Isome'trie f (a. Muskeltraining).

i·sos·ce·les [aɪˈsɒsɪliːz] adj. ⚕ gleichschenk(e)lig (Dreieck).

i·so·therm [ˈaɪsəʊθɜːm] s. Iso'therme f; **i·so·ther·mal** [ˌaɪsəʊ'θɜːml] adj. iso'thermisch, gleich warm: **~ line** → isotherm.

i·so·tope [ˈaɪsəʊtəʊp] s. ⚕, phys. Iso'top n.

Is·ra·el [ˈɪzreɪəl] s. bibl. (das Volk) Israel n; **Is·rae·li** [ɪzˈreɪlɪ] I adj. isra'elisch; II s. Isra'eli m; **Is·ra·el·ite** [ˈɪzrɪəlaɪt] I s. Israe'lit(in); II adj. israe'litisch, jüdisch.

is·su·a·ble [ˈɪʃuːəbl] adj. 1. auszugeben(d); 2. ♱ emittierbar; 3. ᵗᵗ zu veröffentlichen(d); **'is·su·ance** [-əns] s. (Her)'ausgabe f; Ver-, Erteilung f.

is·sue [ˈɪʃuː] I s. 1. Ausgabe f, Aus-, Erteilung f, Erlass m (Befehl); 2. Aus-, Her'ausgabe f; 3. ♱ a) (Ef'fekten-)Emissi,on f, (Aktien)Ausgabe f, Auflegen n (Anleihe); Ausstellung f (Dokument): **date of ~** Ausstellungsdatum n, Ausgabetag m; **bank of ~** Emissionsbank f, b) 'Wertpa,piere pl. der'selben Emissi'on; 4. bsd. ✕ Lieferung f, Ausgabe f, Zu-, Verteilung f; 5. Ausgabe f: a) Veröffentlichung f, Auflage f (Buch), b) Nummer f (Zeitung); 6. Streitfall m, (Streit)Frage f, Pro'blem n: **at ~** a) strittig, zur Debatte stehend, b) uneinig; **point at ~** strittige Frage; **evade the ~** ausweichen; **join** od. **take ~ with s.o.** sich mit j-m auf e-n Streit od. e-e Auseinandersetzung einlassen; 7. (Kern)Punkt m, Fall m, Sachverhalt m: **~ of fact** (law) ᵗᵗ Tatsachen-(Rechts)frage f; **side ~** Nebenpunkt m; **the whole ~** F das Ganze; **raise an ~** e-n Fall od. Sachverhalt anschneiden; 8. Ergebnis n, Ausgang m, (Ab)Schluss m: **in the ~** schließlich; **bring to an ~** entscheiden; **force an ~** e-e Entscheidung erzwingen; 9. Abkömmling pl., leibliche Nachkommenschaft: **die without ~** ohne direkte Nachkommen sterben; 10. bsd. ✴ Ab-, Ausfluss m; 11. Öffnung f, Mündung f; fig. Ausweg m; II v/t. 12. Befehle etc. ausgeben, erteilen; 13. ♱ Banknoten ausgeben, in 'Umlauf setzen; Anleihe auflegen; Dokumente ausstellen: **~d capital** effektiv ausgegebenes (Aktien)Kapital; 14. Bücher her'ausgeben, publizieren; 15. ✕ a) ausgeben, liefern, ver-, zuteilen, b) ausrüsten, beliefern (**with** mit); III v/i. 16. her'auskommen, -strömen; her'vorbrechen; 17. (**from**) herrühren (von), entspringen (dat.); 18. her'auskommen, her'ausgegeben werden (Schriften etc.); 19. ergehen, erteilt werden (Befehl etc.); 20. enden (**in** in dat.).

is·sue·less [ˈɪʃuːlɪs] adj. ohne Nachkommen.

is·su·er [ˈɪʃuːə] s. ♱ 1. Aussteller(in); 2. Ausgeber(in).

isth·mus [ˈɪsməs] s. 1. geogr. Isthmus m, Landenge f; 2. ✴ Verengung f.

it¹ [ɪt] I pron. 1. es (nom. od. acc.): **do you believe it?** glaubst du es?; 2. auf deutsches s. bezogen (nom., dat., acc.) m er, ihm, ihn; f sie, ihr, sie; n es, ihm, es; refl. (dat., acc.) sich; 3. unpersönliches od. grammatisches Subjekt: **it rains** es regnet; **what time is it?** wie viel Uhr ist es?; **it is I** (F **me**) ich bin es; **it was my parents** es waren m-e Eltern; 4. unbestimmtes Objekt (oft unübersetzt): **foot it** zu Fuß gehen; **I take it that** ich nehme an, dass; 5. verstärkend: **it is for this reason that** gerade aus diesem Grunde ...; 6. nach prp.: **at it** daran; **with it** damit etc.; **please see to it that** bitte sorge dafür, dass; II s. 7. F ,das Nonplus-'ultra', ,ganz große Klasse': **he thinks he's it**; 8. F a) das gewisse Etwas, bsd. 'Sex-Ap,peal m, b) Sex m, Geschlechtsverkehr m; 9. F **that's it!** a) das ist es (ja)!, b) das wärs (gewesen)!; F **this is it!** gleich gehts los!

it² [ɪt], a. ⚹ abbr. für **Italian**: **gin and it** Gin mit (italienischem) Wermut.

I·tal·ian [ɪˈtæljən] I adj. 1. itali'enisch: **~ handwriting** lateinische Schreibschrift; II s. 2. Itali'ener(in); 3. ling. Itali'enisch n; **I·tal·ian·ate** [-neɪt] adj. italianisiert, nach itali'enischer Art; **I·tal·ian·ism** [-nɪzəm] s. itali'enische (Sprachetc.)Eigenheit.

i·tal·ic [ɪˈtælɪk] **I** *adj.* **1.** *typ.* kur'siv; **2.** *ß*
ling. i'talisch; **II** *s. pl.* **3.** *typ.* Kur'siv-
schrift *f*; **i'tal·i·cize** [-ɪsaɪz] *typ. v/t.* **1.**
in Kur'siv drucken; **2.** durch Kur'siv-
schrift her'vorheben.
itch [ɪtʃ] **I** *s.* **1.** Jucken *n*; **2.** ☞ Krätze *f*;
3. *fig.* brennendes Verlangen, Sucht *f*
(*for* nach): *I have an ~ to do s.th.* es
,juckt' mich, et. zu tun; **II** *v/i.* **4.** jucken; **5.** *fig.* (*for*) brennen (auf *acc.*): *I*
am ~ing to do s.th. es ,juckt' mich, et.
zu tun; *my fingers ~ to do it* es juckt
mir (*od.* mich) in den Fingern, es zu
tun; **itch·ing** [ˈɪtʃɪŋ] **I** *s.* **1.** → *itch* 1, 3;
II *adj.* **2.** juckend; **3.** F a) ,scharf',
begierig, *a.* geil, b) ner'vös; **itch·y** [ˈɪtʃɪ]
adj. **1.** juckend; **2.** ☞ krätzig; **3.** →
itching 3.
i·tem [ˈaɪtəm] **I** *s.* **1.** Punkt *m* (*der Tages-*
ordnung etc.); Gegenstand *m*, Stück *n*;
Einzelheit *f*, De'tail *n*; ✝ (Buchungs-,
Rechnungs)Posten *m*; ('Waren)Ar,tikel
m; **2.** ('Presse)No,tiz *f*, (kurzer) Ar'tikel; **3.** *be an ~* F *von Personen:* ein

Paar sein, zusammen sein; **II** *adv. obs.*
4. des'gleichen, ferner; **'i·tem·ize**
[-maɪz] *v/t.* (einzeln) aufführen, spezifizieren.
it·er·ate [ˈɪtəreɪt] *v/t.* wieder'holen; **it·er-**
a·tion [ˌɪtəˈreɪʃn] *s.* Wieder'holung *f*;
'it·er·a·tive [-rətɪv] *adj.* (sich) wieder-
'holend; *ling.* itera'tiv.
i·tin·er·a·cy [ɪˈtɪnərəsɪ], **i'tin·er·an·cy**
[-ənsɪ] *s.* Um'herreisen *n*, -ziehen *n*;
i'tin·er·ant [-ənt] *adj.* ☐ (beruflich)
reisend *od.* um'herziehend, Reise...,
Wander...: *~ trade* Wandergewerbe *n*;
i'tin·er·ar·y [aɪˈtɪnərərɪ] **I** *s.* **1.** Reise-
route *f*, -plan *m*; **2.** Reisebericht *m*;
3. Reiseführer *m* (*Buch*); **4.** Straßen-
karte *f*; **II** *adj.* **5.** Reise...; **i·tin·er·ate**
[ɪˈtɪnəreɪt] *v/i.* (um'her)reisen.
its [ɪts] *pron.* sein, ihr, dessen, deren:
the house and ~ roof das Haus u. sein
(*od.* dessen) Dach.
it's [ɪts] F für a) *it is*, b) *it has*.
it·self [ɪtˈself] *pron.* **1.** *refl.* sich: *the dog*
hides ~; **2.** sich (selbst): *the kitten*

wants it for ~; **3.** *verstärkend:* selbst:
like innocence ~ wie die Unschuld
selbst; *by ~* (für sich) allein, von selbst;
in ~ an sich (betrachtet); **4.** al'lein
(schon), schon: *the garden ~ meas-*
ures two acres.
I've [aɪv] F *für I have.*
i·vied [ˈaɪvɪd] *adj.* 'efeuum,rankt, mit
Efeu bewachsen.
i·vo·ry [ˈaɪvərɪ] **I** *s.* **1.** Elfenbein *n*; **2.**
Stoßzahn *m* (*des Elefanten*); **3.** 'Elfen-
beinschnitze,rei *f*; **4.** *pl. sl.* a) *obs.* ,Bei-
ßer' *pl.*, Gebiss *n*, b) (*Spiel*)Würfel *pl.*,
c) Billardkugeln *pl.*, d) (Kla'vier)Tas-
ten *pl.*: *tickle the ivories* (auf dem
Klavier) klimpern; **II** *adj.* **5.** elfenbeinern, Elfenbein...; **6.** elfenbeinfarben;
~ nut *s.* ✿ Steinnuss *f*; *~ tow·er* *s. fig.*
Elfenbeinturm *m*: *live in an ~* im Elfenbeinturm sitzen.
i·vy [ˈaɪvɪ] *s.* ✿ Efeu *m*; *≎ League* *s.* die
acht Eliteuniversitäten im Osten der USA.
iz·zard [ˈɪzəd] *s.*: *from A to ~* von A bis
Z.

J, j [dʒeɪ] s. J n, j n, Jot n (Buchstabe).

jab [dʒæb] **I** v/t. **1.** (hin'ein)stechen, (-)stoßen; **II** s. **2.** Stich m, Stoß m; **3.** Boxen: Jab m, (kurze) Gerade; **4.** ✈ F Spritze f.

jab·ber ['dʒæbə] **I** v/t. u. v/i. **1.** schnattern, quasseln, schwatzen; **2.** nuscheln, undeutlich sprechen; **II** s. **3.** Geplapper n, Geschnatter n.

jack [dʒæk] **I** s. **1.** Mann m, Bursche m: *every man ~* F jeder Einzelne, alle (ohne Ausnahme); **2.** Kartenspiel: Bube m; **3.** ⊙ Hebevorrichtung f, Winde f: *car ~* Wagenheber m; **4.** Brit. Bowlsspiel: Zielkugel f; **5.** zo. a) Männchen n einiger Tiere, b) → jackass 1; **6.** ⚓ Gösch f, Bugflagge f; **7.** ⚡ a) Klinke f, b) Steckdose f; **8.** Am. sl. 'Zaster' m (Geld); **II** v/t. **9.** mst ~ up hochheben, -winden; Auto aufbocken; fig. F Preise hochtreiben; **10.** ~ in F et. 'aufstecken', 'hinschmeißen'; **III** v/i. **11.** ~ off Am. V 'wichsen'.

jack·al ['dʒækɔːl] s. **1.** zo. Scha'kal m; **2.** contp. Handlanger m.

jack·a·napes ['dʒækəneɪps] s. **1.** Geck m, Laffe m; **2.** Frechdachs m, (kleiner) Schlingel.

jack·ass ['dʒækæs] s. **1.** (männlicher) Esel; **2.** fig. contp. 'Esel' m.

'jack|·boot s. Schaftstiefel m; **'~·daw** s. orn. Dohle f.

jack·et ['dʒækɪt] **I** s. **1.** Jacke f, Jac'kett n; → *dust* 8; **2.** ⊙ Mantel m, Um'mantelung f, Hülle f, Um'wicklung f; **3.** ✕ (Geschoss-, östr. Geschoß-, a. Rohr)Mantel m; **4.** Buchhülle f, 'Schutz,umschlag m; Am. a. (Schallplatten)Hülle f; **5.** Haut f, Schale f: *potatoes (boiled) in their ~s*, a. ~ *potatoes* Pellkartoffeln; **II** v/t. **6.** ⊙ um'manteln, verkleiden, verschalen; ~ *crown* s. ✈ Jacketkrone f.

Jack| Frost s. Väterchen n Frost; **'2-·ham·mer** s. Presslufthammer m; **'2--in-·of·fice** wichtigtuerischer Beamter; **'2-in-the-·box** pl. **'2-in-the-,box·es** s. Schachtelmännchen n (Kinderspielzeug): *like a ~* fig. wie ein Hampelmann; **~ Ketch** [ketʃ] s. Brit. obs. der Henker; **'2-·knife I** s. [irr.] **1.** Klappmesser n; **2.** a. ~ *dive* sport Hechtbeuge f (Kopfsprung); **II** v/t. **3.** a. v/i. wie ein Taschenmesser zs.-klappen; **III** v/i. **4.** sport hechten; **5.** mot. sich quer stellen (Anhänger e-s Lastzugs); **2-of-·'all-trades** s. Aller'weltskerl m, Hans-'dampf m in allen Gassen; Fak'totum n; **'2-o'-,lan·tern** pl. **'2-o'-,lan·terns** [,dʒækəʊ-] **1.** Irrlicht n (a. fig.); **2.** 'Kürbis,la,terne f; **2 plane** s. ⊙ Schrupphobel m; **'2-·plug** s. Ba'nanenstecker m; Klinkenstecker m; **'2-·pot** s. Poker, Glücksspiel: Jackpot m, weitS. u. fig. Haupttreffer m, das große Los, fig. a. 'Schlager' m, Bombenerfolg m: *hit the ~* F fig. a) den Jackpot gewinnen, b) den Haupttreffer machen, c) großen Erfolg haben, den Vogel abschießen,

d) 'schwer absahnen'; ~ **Ro·bin·son** s.: *before you could say* ~ F im Nu, im Handumdrehen; **'2-·straw** s. a) Mi'kadostäbchen n, b) pl. Mi'kadospiel n; **2 tar** s. ⚓ F Ma'trose m; **2 tow·el** s. Rollhandtuch n.

Jac·o·be·an [,dʒækəʊ'biːən] adj. aus der Zeit Jakobs I.: ~ *furniture*.

Jac·o·bin ['dʒækəʊbɪn] s. **1.** hist. Jako-'biner m, fig. pol. a. radi'kaler 'Umstürzler, Revolutio'när m; **2.** orn. Jako-'binertaube f; **'Jac·o·bite** [-baɪt] s. hist. Jako'bit m.

Ja·cob's lad·der ['dʒeɪkəbz] s. **1.** bibl., a. ✿ Jakobs-, Himmelsleiter f; **2.** ⚓ Lotsentreppe f.

ja·cuz·zi [dʒə'kuːzi] TM s. Whirlpool m (Unterwassermassagebecken).

jade¹ [dʒeɪd] s. **1.** min. Jade m; **2.** Jadegrün n.

jade² [dʒeɪd] s. **1.** Schindmähre f, Klepper m; **2.** Weibsstück n; **'jad·ed** [-dɪd] adj. **1.** erschöpft, abgespannt; **2.** über-'sättigt, abgestumpft; **3.** schal (geworden): ~ *pleasures*.

jag [dʒæg] **I** s. **1.** Zacke f, Kerbe f; Zahn m; Auszackung f; Schlitz m, Riss m; **2.** sl. a) Schwips m, Rausch m: *have a ~ on* ,e-n im Krone haben', b) Sauftour f, Saufe'rei f, c) bsd. fig. Orgie f: *go on a ~* ,einen draufmachen'; *crying* ~ ,heulendes Elend'; **II** v/t. **3.** auszacken, einkerben; **4.** zackig schneiden od. reißen; **'jag·ged** [-gɪd] adj. □ **1.** zackig; schartig; **2.** schroff, zerklüftet; **3.** rau, grob (a. fig.); **4.** Am. sl. ,blau', besoffen.

jag·ger·y ['dʒægərɪ] s. coll. brauner Zucker (aus Palmensaft).

jag·uar ['dʒægjʊə] s. zo. Jaguar m.

Jah [dʒɑː], **Jah·ve(h)** ['jɑːveɪ] s. Je'hova m.

jail [dʒeɪl] **I** s. **1.** Gefängnis n, Strafanstalt f; **2.** Gefängnis(haft f) n; **II** v/t. **3.** ins Gefängnis werfen, einsperren, inhaftieren; **'~·bird** s. F ,Zuchthäusler' m, engS. ,Knastbruder' m; **'~·break** s. Ausbruch m (aus dem Gefängnis); **'~·break·er** s. Ausbrecher m.

jail·er ['dʒeɪlə] s. (Gefängnis)Aufseher m, (-)Wärter m, obs. u. fig. Kerkermeister m.

jake [dʒeɪk] Am. F s. **1.** Bauernlackel m, weitS. ,Knülch' m; **2.** ,Pinke' f (Geld); **II** adj. **3.** ,bestens', in Ordnung: *everything's ~*.

ja·lop·(p)y [dʒə'lɒpɪ] s. F ,alte Kiste' (Auto, Flugzeug).

jal·ou·sie ['ʒæluːzi] s. Jalou'sie f.

jam¹ [dʒæm] **I** v/t. **1.** a. ~ *in* a) et. (hinein)zwängen, -stopfen, -quetschen, Menschen a. (-)pferchen, b) einklemmen, -keilen; **2.** (zs.-, zer)quetschen; Finger etc. einklemmen, sich et. quetschen; **3.** et. pressen, (heftig) drücken; Knie etc. rammen (into in acc.): ~ (one's foot) on the brakes heftig auf die Bremse treten; **4.** verstopfen, -sperren, blockieren: a road ~med with

cars; ~med with people von Menschen verstopft, gedrängt voll; **5.** ⊙ verklemmen, blockieren; **6.** Funk: (durch Störsender) stören; **II** v/i. **7.** eingeklemmt sein, festsitzen; **8.** a. ~ in sich (hin'ein)quetschen, (-)zwängen, (-)drängen; **9.** ⊙ (sich ver)klemmen; ✕ Ladehemmung haben; **10.** Jazz: (frei) improvisieren; **III** s. **11.** Gedränge n, Gewühl n; **12.** Verstopfung f, Stauung f; (Verkehrs)Stockung f, (-)Stau m: *traffic ~*; **13.** ⊙ Blockierung f, Klemmen n; ✕ Ladehemmung f; **14.** F ,Klemme' f: *be in a ~* in der Klemme od. Patsche sitzen; *get s.o. out of a ~* j-m aus der Klemme od. Patsche helfen.

jam² [dʒæm] s. **1.** Marme'lade f: ~ *jar* Marmeladeglas n; **2.** Brit. F ,schicke Sache': *money for ~* leicht verdientes Geld; ~ *tomorrow* iro. schöne Versprechungen od. Aussichten; *that's ~ for him* das ist ein Kinderspiel für ihn.

Ja·mai·can [dʒə'meɪkən] **I** adj. jamai-'kanisch; **II** s. Jamai'kaner(in); **Ja·mai·ca rum** [dʒə'meɪkə] s. Ja'maikarum m.

jamb [dʒæm] s. (Tür-, Fenster)Pfosten m.

jam·bo·ree [,dʒæmbə'riː] s. **1.** Pfadfindertreffen n; **2.** F ,rauschendes Fest', ,tolle Party'.

jam·mer ['dʒæmə] s. Radio: Störsender m; **'jam·ming** [-mɪŋ] s. **1.** ⊙ Klemmung f; Hemmung f; **2.** Radio: Störung f: ~ *station* Störsender m; **'jam·my** [-mɪ] adj. Brit. sl. **1.** prima, ,Klasse'; **2.** glücklich, Glücks...: ~ *fellow* Glückspilz m.

,jam|-'packed adj. F voll gestopft, Bus etc. ,knallvoll'; ~ **roll** s. Bis'kuitrolle f; ~ **ses·sion** s. Jam-Session f (Jazzimprovisation).

Jane [dʒeɪn] **I** npr. Johanna f; **II** s. a. **2** sl. ,Weib' n.

jan·gle ['dʒæŋgl] **I** v/i. **1.** a) klirren, klimpern, b) bimmeln (Glocken); **2.** schimpfen; **II** v/t. **3.** a) klirren od. klimpern mit, b) bimmeln lassen; **4.** ~ s.o.'s nerves j-m auf die Nerven gehen; **III** s. **5.** a) Klirren n, Klimpern n, b) Bimmeln n; **6.** Gekreisch n, laute Streite'rei.

jan·i·tor ['dʒænɪtə] s. **1.** Pförtner m; **2.** bsd. Am. Hausmeister m.

Jan·u·ar·y ['dʒænjʊərɪ] s. Januar m: in ~ im Januar.

Ja·nus ['dʒeɪnəs] s. myth. Janus m; **'~-faced** adj. janusköpfig.

Jap [dʒæp] F contp. **I** s. ,Japs' m (Japaner); **II** adj. ja'panisch.

ja·pan [dʒə'pæn] **I** s. **1.** Japanlack m; **2.** lackierte Arbeit (in japanischer Art); **II** v/t. **3.** mit Japanlack über'ziehen, lackieren.

Jap·a·nese [,dʒæpə'niːz] **I** adj. **1.** ja'panisch; **II** s. **2.** Ja'paner(in); **3.** the ~ pl. die Japaner; **4.** ling. Ja'panisch n, das Ja'panische.

jar¹ [dʒɑ:] *s.* **1.** a) (*irdenes od. gläsernes*) Gefäß, Topf *m* (*ohne Henkel*), b) (Einmach)Glas *n*; **2.** *Brit.* F ‚Bierchen' *n*.

jar² [dʒɑ:] **I** *v/i.* **1.** kreischen, quietschen, kratzen (*Metall etc.*), durch Mark u. Bein gehen; **2.** ♪ dissonieren; **3.** (*on, upon*) *das Ohr, ein Gefühl* beleidigen, verletzen, wehtun (*dat.*): ~ *on the ear*; ~ *on the nerves* auf die Nerven gehen; **4.** sich ‚beißen', nicht harmonieren (*Farben etc.*); **5.** *fig.* sich nicht vertragen (*Ideen etc.*), im 'Widerspruch stehen (*with* zu), sich wider-'sprechen: **~ring opinions** widerstreitende Meinungen; **6.** schwirren, vibrieren; **II** *v/t.* **7.** kreischen *od.* quietschen lassen, ein unangenehmes Geräusch erzeugen mit; **8.** a) erschüttern, e-n Stoß versetzen (*dat.*), b) sich *das Knie etc.* anstoßen *od.* stauchen; **9.** *fig.* a) erschüttern, e-n Schock versetzen (*dat.*), b) → 3; **III** *s.* **10.** Kreischen *n*, Quietschen *n*, unangenehmes Geräusch; **11.** Ruck *m*, Stoß *m*, Erschütterung *f* (*a. fig.*); *fig.* Schock *m*, Schlag *m*; **12.** ♪ *u. fig.* 'Misston *m*; **13.** *fig.* 'Widerstreit *m*.

jar·di·nière [ˌʒɑ:di'njeə] (*Fr.*) *s.* **1.** Jardini'ere *f:* a) Blumenständer *m*, b) Blumenschale *f*; **2.** *Küche:* a) Gar'nierung *f*, b) (Fleisch)Gericht *n* à la jardinière.

jar·gon [ˈdʒɑ:gən] *s. allg.* Jar'gon *m:* a) Kauderwelsch *n*, b) Fach-, Berufssprache *f*, c) Mischsprache *f*, d) ungepflegte Ausdrucksweise.

jar·ring [ˈdʒɑ:rɪŋ] *adj.* □ **1.** 'misstönend, kreischend, schrill, unangenehm, ‚nerv-tötend': *a ~ note* ein Misston *od.* -klang (*a. fig.*); **2.** nicht harmonierend, *Farben:* a. sich beißend; → *a. jar²* 5.

jas·min(e) [ˈdʒæsmɪn] *s.* ♥ Jas'min *m*.

jas·per [ˈdʒæspə] *s. min.* Jaspis *m*.

jaun·dice [ˈdʒɔ:ndɪs] *s.* **1.** ♣ Gelbsucht *f*; **2.** *fig.* a) Neid *m*, Eifersucht *f*, b) Feindseligkeit *f*; **'jaun·diced** [-st] *adj.* **1.** ♣ gelbsüchtig; **2.** *fig.* voreingenommen, neidisch, eifersüchtig, scheel.

jaunt [dʒɔ:nt] **I** *s.* Ausflug *m*, Spritztour *f:* **go for** (*od.* **on**) *a* ~ → **II** *v/i.* e-e Spritztour *od.* e-n Ausflug machen; **'jaun·ti·ness** [-tɪnɪs] *s.* Flottheit *f*, ‚Feschheit' *f:* a) Munterkeit *f*, ‚Spritzigkeit' *f*, Schwung *m*, b) flotte Ele'ganz; **'jaunt·ing car** [-tɪŋ] *s.* leichter, zweirädriger Wagen; **'jaun·ty** [-tɪ] *adj.* □ fesch, flott: a) munter, ‚spritzig', b) keck, ele'gant: *with one's hat at a ~ angle* den Hut keck über dem Ohr.

Ja·va [ˈdʒɑ:və] *s. min.* F Kaffee *m*; **Java·nese** [ˌdʒɑ:vəˈni:z] **I** *adj.* **1.** ja'vanisch; **II** *s.* **2.** Ja'vaner(in): *the ~* die Javaner; **3.** *ling.* Ja'vanisch *n*, das Ja'vanische.

jave·lin [ˈdʒævlɪn] *s.* **1.** *a. sport* Speer *m*; **2.** *the ~* → ~ **throw(·ing)** *s. sport* Speerwerfen *n*; ~ **throw·er** *s.* Speerwerfer(in).

jaw [dʒɔ:] **I** *s.* **1.** *anat., zo.* Kiefer *m*, Kinnbacken *m*, -lade *f:* **lower** ~ Unterkiefer; **upper** ~ Oberkiefer; **2.** *mst pl.* Mund *m*, Maul *n*: **hold your** ~*! F* halts Maul!; **3.** *mst pl.* Schlund *m*, Rachen *m* (*a. fig.*): ~*s of death* der Rachen des Todes; **4.** ⊙ (Klemm)Backe *f*, Backen *m*; Klaue *f:* ~ *clutch* Klauenkupplung *f*; **5.** *sl.* a) (freches) Geschwätz, Frechheit *f*, b) Schwatz *m*, ‚Tratsch' *m*, c) Mo'ralpredigt *f*; **II** *v/i.* **6.** *sl.* a) ‚quatschen', ‚tratschen', b) schimpfen; **III** *v/t.* **7.** ~ *out sl.* j-n ‚anschnauzen'; **'~·bone** *s.* **1.** *anat., zo.* Kiefer(knochen) *m*, Kinnlade *f*; **2.** *Am. sl.* (**on** ~ auf) Kre'dit *m*;

'~·break·er *s.* F Zungenbrecher *m* (*Wort*); **'~·break·ing** *adj.* F zungenbrecherisch; ~ **chuck** *s.* ⊙ Backenfutter *n*.

jay [dʒeɪ] *s.* **1.** *orn.* Eichelhäher *m*; **2.** *fig.* ‚Trottel' *m*; **'~·walk** *v/i.* verkehrswidrig über die Straße gehen; **'~·walk·er** *s.* unachtsamer Fußgänger.

jazz [dʒæz] **I** *s.* **1.** 'Jazz(mu,sik *f*) *m:* ~ *band* Jazzkapelle *f*; **2.** *sl.* a) ‚Gequatsche' *n*, ‚blödes Zeug', b) ‚Quatsch' *m*, ‚Krampf' *m: and all that* ~ und all der Mist; **II** *v/t.* **3.** *mst* ~ *up* F a) verjazzen, b) *fig. et.* ‚aufmöbeln'; **III** *v/i.* **4.** jazzen; **5.** *Am. sl.* ‚vögeln'; **'jazz·er** [-zə] *s.* F Jazzmusiker *m*; **'jazz·y** [-zɪ] *adj.* F **1.** Jazz...; **2.** *fig.* a) ‚knallig', b) ‚toll', todschick.

jeal·ous [ˈdʒeləs] *adj.* □ **1.** eifersüchtig (*of* auf *acc.*): *a ~ wife*; **2.** (*of*) neidisch (auf *acc.*), 'missgünstig (gegen): *she is ~ of his fortune* sie beneidet ihn um *od.* missgönnt ihm s-n Reichtum; **3.** 'misstrauisch (*of* gegen); **4.** (*of*) besorgt (um), bedacht (auf *acc.*); **5.** *bibl.* eifernd (*Gott*); **'jeal·ous·y** [-sɪ] *s.* **1.** Eifersucht *f* (*of* auf *acc.*); *pl.* Eifersüchte-'leien; **2.** (*of*) Neid *m* (auf *acc.*), 'Missgunst *f* (gegen); **3.** Achtsamkeit *f* (*of* auf *acc.*).

jean *s.* **1.** [dʒeɪn] *Art* Baumwollköper *m*; **2.** *pl.* [dʒi:nz] Jeans *pl.: a pair of* ~*s* (e-e *od.* ein Paar) Jeans.

jeep [dʒi:p] (*Fabrikmarke*) *s.* Jeep *m:* a) ✕ *Art* Kübelwagen *m*, b) kleines geländegängiges Mehrzweckfahrzeug.

jeer [dʒɪə] **I** *v/i.* spotten, höhnen (*at* über *acc.*); **II** *s.* Hohn *m*, Stiche'lei *f*; **'jeer·ing** [-ɪərɪŋ] **I** *s.* Verhöhnung *f*; **II** *adj.* □ höhnisch.

Je·ho·vah [dʒɪˈhəʊvə] *s. bibl.* Je'hovah *m*; ~'*s* **Wit·ness·es** *s. pl.* Zeugen *pl.* Jehovas.

je·june [dʒɪˈdʒu:n] *adj.* □ **1.** mager, ohne Nährwert: ~ *food*; **2.** trocken: a) dürr (*Boden*), b) *fig.* fade, nüchtern; **3.** *fig.* simpel, na'iv.

jell [dʒel] *Am.* **I** *s.* **1.** → *jelly* 1–3; **II** *v/i.* **2.** → *jelly* II; **3.** *fig.* sich (her'aus-) kristallisieren, Gestalt annehmen; **4.** ‚zum Klappen kommen' (*Geschäft etc.*).

jel·lied [ˈdʒelɪd] *adj.* **1.** gallertartig, eingedickt; **2.** in Ge'lee *od.* As'pik: ~ *eel.*

jel·lo [ˈdʒeləʊ] *s. Am.* → *jelly* 2.

jel·ly [ˈdʒelɪ] **I** *s.* **1.** Gallert *n*, Gal'lerte *f*, *Küche:* a. Ge'lee *n*, Sülze *f*, As'pik *n*; **2.** a) Ge'lee *n* (*Marmelade*), b) Götterspeise *f*, ‚Wackelpeter' *m*, c) (rote *etc.*) Grütze (*Süßspeise*); **3.** gallertartige *od.* ‚schwabbelige' Masse, Brei *m:* **beat s.o. into a** ~ F j-n ‚zu Brei schlagen'; **4.** *Brit. sl.* Dyna'mit *n*; **II** *v/t.* **5.** zum Gelieren *od.* Erstarren bringen, eindicken; **6.** *Küche:* in Sülze *od.* As'pik *od.* Ge'lee (ein)legen; **III** *v/i.* **7.** gelieren, Ge'lee bilden; **8.** erstarren; ~ **ba·by** *s.* Gummibärchen *n*; **'~·bean** *s.* Weingummi(bon,bon) *n*; **'~·fish** *s.* **1.** Qualle *f*; **2.** *fig.* ‚Waschlappen' *m*; ~ **shoe** *s.* Badeschuh *m*.

jem·my [ˈdʒemɪ] **I** *s.* Brecheisen *n*; **II** *v/t.* mit dem Brecheisen öffnen, aufstemmen.

jen·ny [ˈdʒenɪ] *s.* **1.** → *spinning jenny*; **2.** ⊙ Laufkran *m*; **3.** *zo.* Weibchen *n*; ~ **ass** *s.* Eselin *f*; ~ **wren** *s. orn.* (weiblicher) Zaunkönig.

jeop·ard·ize [ˈdʒepədaɪz] *v/t.* gefährden, aufs Spiel setzen; **'jeop·ard·y** [-dɪ] *s.* Gefahr *f*, Gefährdung *f*, Risiko *n:* *put in* ~ → *jeopardize*; *no one shall be put twice in* ~ *for the same offence* **が** niemand darf wegen dersel-

ben Straftat zweimal vor Gericht gestellt werden.

jer·e·mi·ad [ˌdʒerɪˈmaɪəd] *s.* Jeremi'ade *f*, Klagelied *n*; **Jer·e·mi·ah** [ˌdʒerɪˈmaɪə] *npr. u. s.* **1.** *bibl.* (das Buch) Jere'mia(s) *m*; **2.** *fig.* 'Unglückspro,phet *m*, Schwarzseher *m*; ,**Jer·e'mi·as** [-əs] → **Jeremiah** 1.

jerk¹ [dʒɜ:k] **I** *s.* **1.** a) Ruck *m*, plötzlicher Stoß *od.* Schlag *od.* Zug, b) Satz *m*, Sprung *m*, Auffahren *n:* **by** ~*s* ruck-, sprung-, stoßweise; *with a* ~ plötzlich, mit e-m Ruck; *give s.th. a* ~ → 5; *put a* ~ *in it sl.* tüchtig rangehen; **2.** ♣ Zuckung *f*, Zucken *n*, (*bsd.* 'Knie-) Re,flex *m*; **3.** *pl. Brit. mst physical* ~*s sl.* Freiübungen; Gym'nastik *f*; **4.** *Am. sl.* a) ‚Blödmann' *m*, ‚Knülch' *m*, b) → **soda jerker**; **II** *v/t.* **5.** schnellen, ruckweise *od.* ruckartig *od.* plötzlich ziehen *od.* reißen *od.* stoßen *etc.:* ~ *o.s. free* sich losreißen; **III** *v/i.* **6.** (zs.-)zucken; **7.** (hoch- *etc.*)schnellen; **8.** sich ruckweise bewegen: ~ *to a stop* ruckartig anhalten; **9.** ~ *off Am. sl.* ‚wichsen'.

jerk² [dʒɜ:k] *v/t. Fleisch* in Streifen schneiden u. dörren.

jer·kin [ˈdʒɜ:kɪn] *s.* **1.** ärmellose Jacke; **2.** *hist.* (Leder)Wams *n*.

'jerk,wa·ter *Am.* F **I** *s.* **1.** *a.* ~ *town* kleines ‚Kaff'; **2.** *a.* ~ *train* Bummelzug *m*; **II** *adj.* **3.** unbedeutend, armselig.

jerk·y [ˈdʒɜ:kɪ] *adj.* □ **1.** ruckartig, stoß-, ruckweise; krampfhaft; **2.** *Am.* F ‚blöd'.

jer·o·bo·am [ˌdʒerəˈbəʊəm] *s. Brit.* Riesenweinflasche *f*.

jer·ry [ˈdʒerɪ] *s. Brit.* F **1.** Nachttopf *m*; **2.** *a.* J♪ Deutsche(r) *m*, deutscher Sol'dat, b) die Deutschen *pl.*; **'~·build·er** *s.* F Bauschwindler *m*; **'~·built** *adj.* F unsolide gebaut: ~ *house* ‚Bruchbude' *f*; ~ **can** *s. Brit.* F Ben'zinka,nister *m*.

jer·sey [ˈdʒɜ:zɪ] *s.* **1.** a) wollene Strickjacke, b) 'Unterjacke *f*; **2.** Jersey *m* (*Stoffart*); **3.** ♀ *zo.* Jerseyrind *n*.

jes·sa·mine [ˈdʒesəmɪn] → *jasmin(e)*.

jest [dʒest] **I** *s.* **1.** Scherz *m*, Spaß *m*, Witz *m:* *in* ~ im Spaß; *make a* ~ *of* witzeln über (*acc.*); **2.** Zielscheibe *f* des Witzes *od.* Spotts: *standing* ~ Zielscheibe ständigen Gelächters; **II** *v/i.* **3.** scherzen, spaßen, ulken; **'jest·er** [-tə] *s.* **1.** Spaßmacher *m*, -vogel *m*; **2.** *hist.* (Hof)Narr *m*; **'jest·ing** [-tɪŋ] *adj.* □ scherzend, spaßhaft: *no* ~ *matter* nicht zum Spaßen; **'jest·ing·ly** [-tɪŋlɪ] *adv.* im *od.* zum Spaß.

Jes·u·it [ˈdʒezjʊɪt] *s. eccl.* Jesu'it *m*; **Jes·u·it·i·cal** [ˌdʒezjʊˈɪtɪkl] *adj.* □ *eccl.* jesu'itisch, Jesuiten...; **'Jes·u·it·ry** [-rɪ] *s.* a) Jesui'tismus *m*, b) *contp.* Spitzfindigkeit *f*.

jet¹ [dʒet] **I** *s. min.* Ga'gat *m*, Pechkohle *f*, Jett *m, n*; **II** *adj. a.* ~**·black** tief-, pech-, kohlschwarz.

jet² [dʒet] **I** *s.* **1.** (*Feuer-, Wasser- etc.*) Strahl *m*, Strom *m*; ~ *of flame* Stichflamme *f*; **2.** ⊙ Strahlrohr *n*, Düse *f*; **3.** → a) *jet engine*, b) *jet plane*; **II** *v/t.* **4.** ausspritzen, -strahlen, her'vorstoßen; **III** *v/i.* **5.** her'vorschießen, ausströmen; **6.** mit Düsenflugzeug reisen, ‚jetten'; ~ **age** *s.* Düsenzeitalter *n*; ~ **bomb·er** *s.* ✈ Düsenbomber *m*; ~ **en·gine** *s.* ⊙ Düsen-, Strahltriebwerk *n*; ~ **fight·er** *s.* ✈ Düsenjäger *m*; ~ **lag** *s.* (physische) Prob'leme *pl.* durch die Zeitumstellung (*nach langen Flugreisen*); ~ **lin·er** *s.* ✈ Düsenverkehrsflugzeug *n*; ~ **plane** *s.* ✈ Düsenflugzeug *n*, F ‚Düse' *f*, Jet *m*; **'~·pro'pelled** *abbr.* ‚**~·'prop** *adj.* ✈ mit Düsenantrieb; ~ **pro·pul-**

sion *s.* ⊕, ✈ Düsen-, Rückstoß-, Strahlantrieb *m*.

jet·sam ['dʒetsəm] *s.* ♔ **1.** Seewurfgut *n*, über Bord geworfene Ladung; **2.** Strandgut *n*; → **flotsam**.

jet| set *s.* Jet-set *m*; '**~-**,**set·ter** *s.* Angehörige(r *m*) *f* des Jet-Set.

jet·ti·son ['dʒetɪsn] I *s.* **1.** ♔ Über'bordwerfen *n von Ladung*, Seewurf *m*; **2.** ✈ Notwurf *m*; II *v/t.* **3.** ♔ über Bord werfen; **4.** ✈ im Notwurf abwerfen; **5.** *fig. Pläne etc.* über Bord werfen; *alte Kleider etc.* wegwerfen, *Personen fallen lassen*; **6.** *Raketenstufe* absprengen; '**jet·ti·son·a·ble** [-nəbl] *adj.* ✈ abwerfbar, Abwurf...(-*behälter etc.*): **~ seat** Schleudersitz *m*.

jet·ton ['dʒetn] *s.* Je'ton *m*.

jet tur·bine *s.* 'Strahltur,bine *f*.

jet·ty ['dʒetɪ] *s.* ♔ **1.** Landungsbrücke *f*, -steg *m*; **2.** Hafendamm *m*, Mole *f*; **3.** Strömungsbrecher *m* (*Brücke*).

Jew [dʒu:] *s.* Jude *m*, Jüdin *f*; '**~-**,**bait·er** *s.* Judenhetzer *m*; '**~-**,**bait·ing** *s.* Judenverfolgung *f*, -hetze *f*.

jew·el ['dʒu:əl] I *s.* **1.** Ju'wel *n*, Edelstein *m*, *weitS.* Schmuckstück *n*: **~ box**, **~ case** Schmuckkästchen *n*; **2.** *fig.* Ju'wel *n*, Perle *f*; **3.** Stein *m* (*e-r Uhr*); II *v/t.* **4.** mit Ju'welen schmücken *od.* versehen, mit Edelsteinen besetzen; **5.** *Uhr* mit Steinen versehen; '**jew·el·(l)er** [-lə] *s.* Juwe'lier *m*; '**jew·el·ler·y**, *bsd. Am.* '**jew·el·ry** [-lrɪ] *s.* **1.** Ju'welen *pl.*; **2.** Schmuck(sachen *pl.*) *m*.

Jew·ess ['dʒu:ɪs] *s.* Jüdin *f*; '**Jew·ish** [-ɪʃ] *adj.* □ jüdisch, Juden...; **Jew·ry** ['dʒʊərɪ] *s.* **1.** *die* Juden *pl.*, (**world ~** das Welt)Judentum *n*; **2.** *hist.* Judenviertel *n*, G(h)etto *n*.

Jew's| ear *s.* ♣ Judasohr *n*; **~ harp** *s.* ♪ Maultrommel *f*.

jib¹ [dʒɪb] *s.* **1.** ♔ Klüver *m*: **~ boom** Klüverbaum *m*; **the cut of his ~** F seäußere Erscheinung *od.* sein Auftreten; **2.** ⊕ Ausleger *m* (*e-s Krans*).

jib² [dʒɪb] *v/i.* **1.** scheuen, bocken (**at** vor *dat.*) (*Pferd*); **2.** *Brit. fig.* (**at**) a) scheuen, zu'rückweichen (vor *dat.*), b) sich sträuben (gegen), c) störrisch *od.* bockig sein.

jibe¹ [dʒaɪb] *Am.* → **gybe**.

jibe² [dʒaɪb] → **gibe**.

jibe³ [dʒaɪb] *v/i. Am.* F über'einstimmen, sich entsprechen.

jif·fy [dʒɪfɪ], *a.* **jiff** [dʒɪf] *s.* F Augenblick *m*: **in a ~** im Nu; **wait a ~!** (einen) Moment!

jig¹ [dʒɪg] I *s.* **1.** ⊕ Spann-, Bohrvorrichtung *f*; **2.** ⚒ a) Kohlenwippe *f*, b) 'Setzma,schine *f*; II *v/t.* **3.** ⊕ mit e-r Einstellvorrichtung *od.* Schab'lone herstellen; **4.** ⚒ *Erze* setzen, scheiden.

jig² [dʒɪg] I *s.* **1.** ♪ Gigue *f* (*a. Tanz*); **2.** *Am. sl.* Schwof' *m*, Tanzparty *f*: **the ~ is up** *fig.* das Spiel ist aus; **3.** *fig.* Freudentanz *m*; II *v/t.* **4.** schütteln; III *v/i.* **5.** e-e Gigue tanzen; **6.** hopsen, tanzen.

jig·ger ['dʒɪgə] I *s.* **1.** Giguetänzer *m*; **2.** ♔ a) Be'san(mast) *m*, b) Handtalje *f*; **3.** *Golf:* Jigger *m* (*Schläger, mst Nr. 4*); **4.** a) Schnapsglas *n*, b) 'Schnäps-chen' *n*; **5.** *Am.* F Dings(bums) *n*, Appa'rat *m*; **6.** *a.* **~ flea** Sandfloh *m*; II *v/t. a.* **~ up** F **7.** sich einmischen (in *acc.*), herumpfuschen (an *dat.*), durchein'ander bringen; **8.** 'fri'sieren', manipu'lieren; **jig·gered** ['dʒɪgəd] *adj.* **1.** beschädigt, ka'putt; **2.** F 'fertig', 'ka'putt' (*Person*): **well, I'm ~** (*if*) hol mich der Teufel(, wenn).

jig·ger·y-pok·er·y [,dʒɪgərɪ'pəʊkərɪ] *s. Brit.* F fauler Zauber, 'Schmu' *m*.

jig·gle ['dʒɪgl] I *v/t.* (leicht) rütteln; II *v/i.* wippen, hüpfen, wackeln.

'**jig·saw** *s.* ⊕ **1.** Laubsäge *f*; **2.** 'Schweifsäge(ma,schine) *f*; **3.** → **~ puz·zle** *s.* Puzzle(spiel) *n*.

Jill [dʒɪl] → **Gill⁴**.

jilt [dʒɪlt] *v/t.* a) *e-m Liebhaber* den Laufpass geben, b) *ein Mädchen* sitzen lassen.

Jim Crow [,dʒɪm'krəʊ] *s. Am.* F **1.** *contp.* ,Nigger' *m*; **2.** 'Rassendiskrimi-,nierung *f*: **~ car** 🚃 Wagen *m* für Farbige.

jim-jams ['dʒɪmdʒæmz] *s. pl. sl.* **1.** De'lirium *n* tremens; **2.** a) Nervenflattern *n*, b) Gänsehaut *f*.

jim·my ['dʒɪmɪ] → **jemmy**.

jin·gle ['dʒɪŋgl] I *v/i.* **1.** klimpern, klirren, klingeln; II *v/t.* **2.** klingeln lassen, klimpern (mit), bimmeln (mit); III *s.* **3.** Geklingel *n*, Klimpern *n*; **4.** (eingängiges) Liedchen *od.* Vers-chen, *a.* Werbesong *m od.* -spruch *m*.

jin·go ['dʒɪŋgəʊ] I *pl.* **-goes** *s.* **1.** *pol.* Chauvi'nist(in); **2.** → **jingoism** II *int.* **3.** **by ~!** beim Zeus!; '**jin·go·ism** [-əʊɪzəm] *s. pol.* Chauvi'nismus *m*, Hur'rapatrio,tismus *m*; **jin·go·is·tic** [,dʒɪŋgəʊ'ɪstɪk] *adj.* chauvi'nistisch.

jink [dʒɪŋk] I *s.* **1.** 'Ausweich,növer *n*; **2.** **high ~s** ,Highlife' *n*, ,tolle Party'; II **3.** *v/i. u. v/t.* geschickt ausweichen.

jin·rik·i·sha, *a.* **jin·rick·sha** [dʒɪn'rɪkʃə] *s.* Rikscha *f*.

jinn [dʒɪn] *pl. von* **jin·nee** [dʒɪ'ni:] *s.* Dschinn *m* (*islamischer Geist*).

jinx [dʒɪŋks] *sl.* I *s.* **1.** Unheilbringer *m*; *weitS.* Unglück *n*, Pech *n* (**for** für): **there is a ~ on it!** das ist wie verhext!; **put a ~ on** → 3 b; **2.** Unheil *n*; II *v/t.* **3.** a) Unglück bringen (*dat.*), b) *et.* ,verhexen'.

jit·ter ['dʒɪtə] F I *v/i.* ner'vös sein, ,Bammel' haben, ,bibbern'; II *s.:* **the ~s** a) ,Bammel' *m* (*Angst*), b) ,Zustände' *pl.*, ,Tatterich' *m* (*Nervosität*); '**jit·ter·bug** [-bʌg] *s.* **1.** Jitterbug *m* (*Tanz*); **2.** *fig.* Nervenbündel *n*; '**jit·ter·y** [-ərɪ] *adj.* F nervös, ,bibbernd'.

jiu-jit·su [dʒu:'dʒɪtsu:] → **jujitsu**.

jive [dʒaɪv] I *s.* ♪ Jive *m*, (*Art*) 'Swingmu,sik *f od.* -tanz *m*; **2.** *Am. sl.* Gequassel *n*; II *v/i.* **3.** Jive *od.* Swing tanzen *od.* spielen.

job [dʒɒb] I *s.* **1.** *ein Stück Arbeit f:* **a ~ of work** e-e Arbeit; **a good ~ of work** e-e saubere Arbeit; **be paid by the ~** pro Auftrag bezahlt werden; **odd ~s** Gelegenheitsarbeiten; **make a good ~ of it** gute Arbeit leisten, s-e Sache gut machen; **it was quite a ~** es war (gar) nicht so einfach, es war e-e Mordsarbeit; **I had a ~ to do it** das war ganz schön schwer (für mich); **on the ~** a) an der Arbeit, ,dran', b) in Aktion, c) ,auf Draht'; **2.** Stück-, Ak'kordarbeit *f:* **by the ~** im Akkord; **3.** Stellung *f*, Tätigkeit *f*, Arbeit *f*, Job *m:* **a ~ as a typist**, **out of a ~** stellungslos; **know one's ~** s-e Sache verstehen; **on the ~ training** Ausbildung *f* am Arbeitsplatz; **create new ~s** neue Arbeitsplätze schaffen; **~s for the boys** *pol.* F Vetternwirtschaft *f;* **this is not everybody's ~** dies liegt nicht jedem; **4.** Aufgabe *f*, Pflicht *f*, Sache *f:* **it is your ~ to do it** es ist deine Sache; **5.** F Sache *f*, Angelegenheit *f*, Lage *f:* **a good ~ (too)!** ein (wahres) Glück!; **make the best of a bad ~** a) das Beste daraus machen, es retten, was zu retten ist, b) gute Miene zum bösen Spiel machen; **I gave it up as a bad ~** ich steckte es (*als aussichtslos*) auf; **I gave him up as a bad ~** ich ließ ihn fallen (*weil er nichts taugte etc.*); **just the ~!** genau das Richtige!; **6.** *sl.* a) Pro'fitgeschäft *n*, Schiebung *f*, ,krumme Tour', b) ,Ding' *n* (*Verbrechen*): **pull a ~** ein Ding drehen; **do his ~ for him** ihn ,fertig machen'; **7.** *bsd. Am.* F a) ,Dings' *n*, ,Appa'rat' *m* (*a. Auto etc.*), b) ,Nummer' *f*, ,Type' *f* (*Person*): **he's a tough ~** er ist ein unangenehmer Kerl; II *v/i.* **8.** Gelegenheitsarbeiten machen, ,jobben'; **9.** im Ak'kord arbeiten; **10.** Zwischenhandel treiben; **11.** Maklergeschäfte treiben, mit Aktien handeln; **12.** ,schieben', in die eigene Tasche arbeiten; III *v/t.* **13.** *a.* **~ out** ♔ a) *Arbeit* im Ak'kord vergeben, b) *Auftrag* (weiter)vergeben; **14.** spekulieren mit; **15.** als Zwischenhändler verkaufen; **16.** veruntreuen; *Amt* miss'brauchen: **~ s.o. into a post** j-m e-n Posten zuschanzen.

Job [dʒəʊb] *npr. bibl.* Hiob *m*, Job *m:* (**the Book of**) **~** (das Buch) Hiob *od.* Job; **patience of ~** *e-e* Engelsgeduld; **that would try the patience of ~** das würde selbst e-n Engel zur Verzweiflung treiben; **~'s comforter** schlechter Tröster (*der alles noch verschlimmert*); **~'s news**, **~'s post** Hiobsbotschaft *f*.

job a·nal·y·sis *s.* 'Arbeitsplatzana,lyse *f*.

job·ber ['dʒɒbə] *s.* **1.** Gelegenheitsarbeiter *m*; **2.** Ak'kordarbeiter *m*: **3.** ♔ Zwischen-, *Am.* Großhändler *m*; **4.** *Brit. Börse:* Jobber *m* (*der auf eigene Rechnung Geschäfte tätigt*); **5.** *Am.* 'Börsenspeku,lant *m*; **6.** Geschäftemacher *m*, ,Schieber' *m*, *a.* kor'rupter Beamter; '**job·ber·y** [-ərɪ] *s. b.s.* ,Schiebung' *f*, Korrupti'on *f*; **2.** 'Amts,missbrauch *m*; '**job·bing** [-bɪŋ] *s.* **1.** Gelegenheitsarbeit *f*; **2.** Ak'kordarbeit *f*; *Börse: Brit.* Ef'fektenhandel *m*, *a.* Spekulati'on(sgeschäfte *pl.*) *f*, **4.** Zwischen-, *Am.* Großhandel *m*; **5.** ,Schiebung' *f*.

job| cen·tre *s. Brit.* Arbeitsamt *n*; '**~-cre,at·ing** *adj.* arbeitsplatz(be)schaffend: **~ measures** *pl.* Arbeitsbeschaffungsprogramm *f.*; **~ cre·a·tion** *s.* Schaffung *f* von Arbeitsplätzen: **~ scheme** (*od.* **program[me]**) Arbeitsbeschaffungsprogramm *n*; **~ cuts** *s. pl.* Stellenabbau *m*; **~ de·scrip·tion** *s.* Arbeits(platz)-, Tätigkeitsbeschreibung *f*; **~ e·val·u·a·tion** *s.* Arbeits(platz)bewertung *f*; **~ hop·ping** *s.* häufiger Stellenwechsel (*zur Verbesserung des Einkommens*); **~ hunt·er** *s.* Stellungssuchende(r *m*) *f*; **~ kill·er** *s.* Jobkiller *m* (*arbeitsplatzvernichtende Maschine etc.*); '**~-less** [-lɪs] I *adj.* arbeitslos; II *s.: the ~ pl.* die Arbeitslosen *pl.*; **~ rate** Arbeitslosenquote *f*; **~ line**, **~ lot** *s.* ♔ **1.** Gelegenheitskauf *m*; **2.** Ramsch-, Par'tieware(n *pl.*) *f*; **~ mar·ket** *s.* Arbeitsmarkt *m*; **~ op·por·tu·ni·ties** *s. pl.* Stellenmarkt *m*, Stellenangebote *pl.*, Arbeitsmöglichkeiten *pl.*; **~ place·ment** *s.* Stellenvermittlung *f*; **~ print·ing** *s.* Akzi'denzdruck *m*; **~ pro·file** *s.* 'Anforderungspro,fil *n*; **~ ro·ta·tion** *s.* turnusmäßiger Arbeitsplatztausch; **~ sat·is·fac·tion** *s.* Zufriedenheit *f* am Arbeitsplatz; **~ se·cu·ri·ty** *s.* Sicherheit *f* des Arbeitsplatzes; **~ seek·er** *s.* Arbeitssuchende(r *m*) *f*; '**~-,seek·er's al·low·ance** 'Arbeitslosenunter,stützung *f* (*Geld*); **~ shar·ing** *s.* Jobsharing *n*, Arbeitsplatzteilung *f*; **~ work** *s.* **1.** Ak'kordarbeit *f*; **2.** → **job printing**.

jock·ey ['dʒɒkɪ] I *s.* Jockey *m*, Jockei *m*; II *v/t.* a) manipulieren, b) betrügen (**out of** um): **~ into s.th.** in et. hinein-

J

manövrieren, zu et. verleiten; ~ ***s.o. into a position*** j-m durch Protektion e-e Stellung verschaffen, ‚j-n lancieren'; **III** *v/i.* ~ ***for*** ‚rangeln' um (*a. fig.*): ~ ***for position*** *sport u. fig.* sich e-e gute (Ausgangs)Position zu schaffen suchen.

'jock·strap ['dʒɒk-] *s. bsd. sport* Suspen'sorium *n.*

jo·cose [dʒəʊ'kəʊs] *adj.* □ **1.** scherzhaft, komisch, drollig; **2.** heiter, ausgelassen.

joc·u·lar ['dʒɒkjʊlə] *adj.* □ **1.** scherzhaft, witzig; **2.** lustig, heiter; **joc·u·lar·i·ty** [ˌdʒɒkjʊ'lærətɪ] *s.* **1.** Scherzhaftigkeit *f*; **2.** Heiterkeit *f.*

joc·und ['dʒɒkənd] *adj.* □ lustig, fröhlich, heiter; **jo·cun·di·ty** [dʒəʊ'kʌndətɪ] *s.* Lustigkeit *f.*

jodh·purs ['dʒɒdpəz] *s. pl.* Reithose(n *pl.*) *f.*

jog [dʒɒg] **I** *v/t.* **1.** (an)stoßen, rütteln, ‚stupsen'; **2.** *fig.* aufrütteln: ~ ***s.o.'s memory*** j-s Gedächtnis nachhelfen; **II** *v/i.* **3.** *a.* ~ ***on***, ~ ***along*** (da'hin)trotten, (-)zuckeln; **4.** sich auf den Weg machen, ‚loszuckeln'; **5.** *fig. a.* ~ ***on*** a) weiterwursteln, b) s-n Lauf nehmen; **6.** *sport* ‚joggen', im Trimmtrab laufen; **III** *s.* **7.** (leichter) Stoß; **8.** Rütteln *n*; **9.** → ***jogtrot*** 1; **'jog·ging** [-gɪŋ] *s.* ‚Jogging' *n*, Trimmtrab *m*: ~ ***suit*** Jogginganzug *m.*

jog·gle ['dʒɒgl] **I** *v/t.* **1.** leicht schütteln *od.* rütteln; **2.** ⚙ verschränken, verzahnen; **II** *v/i.* **3.** sich schütteln, wackeln; **III** *s.* **4.** Stoß *m*, Rütteln *n*; **5.** ⚙ Verzahnung *f*, Nut *f* u. Feder *f.*

'jog·trot I *s.* **1.** gemächlicher Trab, Trott *m*; **2.** *fig.* Trott *m*: a) Schlendrian *m*, b) Eintönigkeit *f*; **II** *v/i.* **3.** → ***jog*** 3.

john [dʒɒn] *s. Am. sl.* Klo *n.*

John [dʒɒn] *npr. u. s. bibl.* Jo'hannes (-evanˌgelium *n*) *m*: ~ ***the Baptist*** Johannes der Täufer; (***the Epistles of***) ~ die Johannesbriefe; ~ **Bull** *s.* John Bull: a) *England*, b) *der* (*typische*) *Engländer*; ~ **Doe** [dəʊ] *s.*: ~ ***and Richard Roe*** ⚖ A. und B. (*fiktive Parteien*); ~ **Do·ry** ['dɔːrɪ] *s. ichth.* Heringskönig *m*; ~ **Han·cock** ['hænkɒk] *s. Am.* F *j-s* ‚Friedrich Wilhelm' *m* (*Unterschrift*).

john·ny ['dʒɒnɪ] *s. Brit.* F Bursche *m*, Typ *m*, ‚Knülch' *m*; ˌ**≗-come-'late·ly** *s. Am.* F **1.** Neuankömmling *m*, Neuling *m*; **2.** *fig.* ‚Spätzünder' *m*; ˌ**≗-on-the-'spot** *s. Am.* F a) j-d, der ‚auf Draht' ist, b) Retter *m* in der Not.

John·so·ni·an [dʒɒn'səʊnjən] *adj.* **1.** johnsonsch (*Samuel Johnson od. s-n Stil betreffend*); **2.** pom'pös, hochtrabend.

join [dʒɔɪn] **I** *v/t.* **1.** *et.* verbinden, -einigen, zs.-fügen (***to, on to*** mit): ~ ***hands*** a) die Hände falten, b) sich die Hand reichen (*a. fig.*), c) *fig.* sich zs.-tun; **2.** *Personen* vereinigen, zs.-bringen (***with, to*** mit): ~ ***in marriage*** verheiraten; ~ ***in friendship*** freundschaftlich verbinden; **3.** *fig.* verbinden, -ein(ig)en: ~ ***prayers*** gemeinsam beten; → ***battle*** 2, ***force*** 1, ***issue*** 6; **4.** sich anschließen (*dat. od.* an *acc.*), stoßen *od.* sich gesellen zu, sich einfinden bei: ~ ***s.o. in*** (***doing***) ***s.th.*** et. zusammen mit j-m tun; ~ ***s.o. in a walk*** (gemeinsam) mit j-m e-n Spaziergang machen, sich j-m auf e-m Spaziergang anschließen; ~ ***one's regiment*** zu s-m Regiment stoßen; ~ ***one's ship*** an Bord s-s Schiffes gehen; ***may I*** ~ ***you?*** a) darf ich mich Ihnen anschließen *od.* Ihnen Gesellschaft leisten, b) darf ich mitmachen?; ***I'll*** ~ ***you soon!*** ich komme bald (nach)!; ***will you*** ~ ***me in a drink?*** trinken Sie ein Glas mit mir?; → ***majority*** 1; **5.** *e-m Klub, e-r Partei etc.* beitreten, eintreten in (*acc.*): ~ ***the army*** ins Heer eintreten, Soldat werden; ~ ***a firm as a partner*** in e-e Firma als Teilhaber eintreten; **6.** a) teilnehmen *od.* sich beteiligen an (*dat.*), mitmachen bei, b) sich einlassen auf (*acc.*), *den Kampf* aufnehmen: ~ ***an action*** *jur.* e-m Prozess beitreten; ~ ***a treaty*** e-m (Staats)Vertrag beitreten; **7.** sich vereinigen mit, zs.-kommen mit, (ein-) münden in (*acc.*) (*Fluss, Straße*); **8.** *math. Punkte* verbinden; **9.** (an)grenzen an (*acc.*); **II** *v/i.* **10.** sich vereinigen *od.* verbinden, zs.-kommen, sich treffen (***with*** mit); **11.** a) ~ ***in*** (*s.th.*) → 6 a, b) ~ ***with s.o. in s.th.*** sich j-m bei et. anschließen, et. gemeinsam tun mit j-m: ~ ***in everybody!*** alle mitmachen!; **12.** anein'ander grenzen, sich berühren; **13.** ~ ***up*** Sol'dat werden, zum Mili'tär gehen; **III** *s.* **14.** Verbindungsstelle *f*, -linie *f*, Naht *f*, Fuge *f.*

join·der ['dʒɔɪndə] *s.* **1.** Verbindung *f*; **2.** ⚖ a) *a.* ~ ***of actions*** (objek'tive) Klagehäufung, b) *a.* ~ ***of parties*** Streitgenossenschaft *f*, c) ~ ***of issue*** Einlassung *f* (auf die Klage).

join·er ['dʒɔɪnə] *s.* Tischler *m*, Schreiner *m*: ~***'s bench*** Hobelbank *f*; **'join·er·y** [-ərɪ] *s.* **1.** Tischlerhandwerk *n*, Schreine'rei *f*; **2.** Tischlerarbeit *f.*

joint [dʒɔɪnt] **I** *s.* **1.** Verbindung(sstelle) *f*, *bsd.* a) *Tischlerei etc.*: Fuge *f*, Stoß *m*, b) (Löt)Naht *f*, Nahtstelle *f*, c) Falz *m* (*der Buchdecke*), d) *anat., biol.*, ♀, ⚙ Gelenk *n*: ***out of*** ~ ausgerenkt, *bsd. fig.* aus den Fugen; → ***nose*** *Bes. Redew.*; **2.** Verbindungsstück *n*, Bindeglied *n*; **3.** Hauptstück *n* (*e-s Schlachttiers*), Braten(stück *n*) *m*; **4.** *sl.* ‚Bude' *f*, ‚Laden' *m*: a) Lo'kal *n*, ‚Schuppen' *m*, *contp.* ‚'Bumsloˌkal' *n*, Spe'lunke *f*, b) Gebäude; **5.** *sl.* Joint *m* (*Marihuanazigarette*); **II** *adj.* (□ → ***jointly***) **6.** gemeinsam, gemeinschaftlich (*a.* ⚖): ~ ***invention***; ~ ***liability***; ~ ***effort***; ~ ***efforts*** vereinte Kräfte *od.* Anstrengungen; ~ ***and several*** ⚖ gesamtschuldnerisch, solidarisch, zur gesamten Hand (→ ***jointly***); ~ ***and several creditor*** (***debtor***) Gesamtgläubiger *m* (-schuldner *m*); ***take*** ~ ***action*** gemeinsam vorgehen, zs.-wirken; **7.** *bsd.* ⚖ Mit..., Neben...: ~ ***heir*** Miterbe *m*; ~ ***offender*** Mittäter *m*; ~ ***plaintiff*** Mitkläger *m*; **8.** vereint, zs.-hängend; **III** *v/t.* **9.** verbinden, zs.-fügen; **10.** ⚙ a) fugen, stoßen, verbinden, -zapfen, b) *Fugen* verstreichen; ~ **ac·count** *s.* ✝ Gemeinschaftskonto *n*: ***on*** (*od.* ***for***) ~ auf *od.* für gemeinsame Rechnung; ~ **ad·ven·ture** → ***joint venture***; ~ **cap·i·tal** *s.* ✝ Ge'sellschaftskapiˌtal *n*; ~ **com·mit·tee** *s. pol.* gemischter Ausschuss; ~ **cred·it** *s.* ✝ Konsorti'alkreˌdit *m*; ~ **cred·i·tor** *s.* ⚖ Gesamthandgläubiger *m*; ~ **debt** *s.* ⚖ gemeinsame Verbindlichkeit(en *pl.*) *f*, Gesamthandschuld *f*; ~ **debt·or** *s.* ⚖ Mitschuldner *m*, Gesamthandschuldner *m.*

joint·ed ['dʒɔɪntɪd] *adj.* **1.** verbunden; **2.** gegliedert, mit Gelenken (versehen): ~ ***doll*** Gliederpuppe *f.*

joint·ly ['dʒɔɪntlɪ] *adv.* gemeinschaftlich: ~ ***and severally*** a) gemeinsam u. jeder für sich, b) solidarisch, zur gesamten Hand, gesamtschuldnerisch.

joint| own·er *s.* ✝ Miteigentümer(in), Mitinhaber(in); ~ **own·er·ship** *s.* Miteigentum *n*; ~ **res·o·lu·tion** *s. pol.* gemeinsame Resoluti'on; ~ **stock** *s.* ✝ Ge'sellschafts-, 'Aktienkapiˌtal *n*; ˌ~**-'stock bank** *s.* Genossenschafts-, Aktienbank *f*; ˌ~**-'stock com·pa·ny** *s.* ✝ **1.** *Brit.* Aktiengesellschaft *f*; **2.** *Am.* offene Handelsgesellschaft auf Aktien; ˌ~**-'stock cor·po·ra·tion** *s. Am.* Aktiengesellschaft *f*; ~ **ten·an·cy** *s.* ✝ Mitbesitz *m*, -pacht *f*; ~ **un·der·tak·ing**, ~ **ven·ture** *s.* ✝ **1.** Ge'meinschaftsunterˌnehmen *n*; **2.** Gelegenheitsgesellschaft *f.*

joist [dʒɔɪst] ⚠ **I** *s.* (Quer)Balken *m*; (Quer-, Pro'fil)Träger *m*; **II** *v/t.* mit Pro'filträgern belegen.

joke [dʒəʊk] **I** *s.* **1.** Witz *m*: ***practical*** ~ Schabernack *m*, Streich *m*; ***play a practical*** ~ ***on s.o.*** j-m einen Streich spielen; ***crack*** ~***s*** Witze reißen; **2.** Scherz *m*, Spaß *m*: ***in*** ~ zum Scherz; ***he cannot take*** (*od.* ***see***) ***a*** ~ er versteht keinen Spaß; ***I don't see the*** ~***!*** was soll daran so witzig sein?; ***it's no*** ~***!*** a) (das ist) kein Witz!, b) das ist keine Kleinigkeit *od.* kein Spaß!; ***the*** ~ ***was on me*** der Spaß ging auf m-e Kosten; **II** *v/i.* **3.** Witze *od.* Spaß machen, scherzen, flachsen: ***I'm not joking!*** ich meine das ernst; ***you must be joking!*** soll das ein Witz sein?; **'jok·er** [-kə] *s.* **1.** Spaßvogel *m*, Witzbold *m*; **2.** *sl.* Kerl *m*, ‚Heini' *m*; **3.** *in Quiz etc.*: Joker *m* (*a. Spielkarte*) (*a. fig.*); **4.** *Am. sl. mst pol.* ‚'Hintertürklausel' *f*; **'jok·ing** [-kɪŋ] *s.* Scherzen *n*: ~ ***apart!*** Scherz beiseite!

jol·li·fi·ca·tion [ˌdʒɒlɪfɪ'keɪʃn] *s.* F (feucht)fröhliches Fest, Festivi'tät *f*; **jol·li·ness** ['dʒɒlɪnɪs], *mst* **jol·li·ty** ['dʒɒlətɪ] *s.* **1.** Fröhlichkeit *f*; **2.** Fest *n.*

jol·ly ['dʒɒlɪ] **I** *adj.* □ **1.** lustig, fi'del, vergnügt; **2.** F angeheitert, beschwipst; **3.** *Brit.* F a) nett, hübsch: ***a*** ~ ***room***, b) *iro.* ‚schön', ‚furchtbar': ***he must be a*** ~ ***fool*** er muss (ja) ganz schön blöd sein; **II** *adv.* **4.** *Brit.* F ziemlich, ‚mächtig', ‚furchtbar': ~ ***late***; ~ ***nice*** ‚unheimlich' nett; ~ ***good*** *a. iro.* (ist ja) Klasse!; ***a*** ~ ***good fellow*** ein ‚prima' Kerl; ***I*** ~ ***well told him*** ich hab es ihm (doch) ganz deutlich gesagt; ***you'll*** ~ ***well*** (***have to***) ***do it!*** du musst (es tun), ob du willst oder nicht; ***you*** ~ ***well know*** du weißt das ganz genau; **III** *v/t.* F **5.** *mst* ~ ***along*** *od.* ***up*** *j-n* bei Laune halten *od.* aufmuntern; ~ ***s.o. into doing s.th.*** j-n zu e-r Sache ‚bequatschen'; **6.** *j-n* ‚veräppeln'.

jol·ly boat ['dʒɒlɪ] *s.* ⚓ Jolle *f.*

Jol·ly Rog·er ['rɒdʒə] *s.* Totenkopf-, Pi'ratenflagge *f.*

jolt [dʒəʊlt] **I** *v/t.* **1.** ('durch)rütteln, stoßen; **2.** *Am. Boxen*: (*Gegner*) erschüttern (*a. fig.*); **3.** *fig. j-m* e-n Schock versetzen; **4.** *j-n* aufrütteln; **II** *v/i.* **5.** rütteln, holpern (*Fahrzeug*); **III** *s.* **6.** Ruck *m*, Stoß *m*, Rütteln *n*; **7.** Schock *m*; **8.** (harter) Schlag; **9.** F a) Wirkung *f* (*e-r Droge etc.*), b) ‚Schuss' *m* (*Kognak, Droge*).

Jo·nah ['dʒəʊnə] *npr. u. s.* **1.** *bibl.* (das Buch) Jonas *m*; **2.** *fig.* Unheilbringer *m*; **'Jo·nas** [-əs] → ***Jonah*** 1.

josh [dʒɒʃ] *sl.* **I** *v/t.* ‚aufziehen', veräppeln; **II** *s.* Hänse'lei *f.*

Josh·u·a ['dʒɒʃwə] *npr. u. s. bibl.* (das Buch) Josua *m od.* Josue *m.*

joss| house [dʒɒs] *s.* chi'nesischer Tempel; ~ **stick** *s.* Räucherstäbchen *n.*

jos·tle ['dʒɒsl] **I** *v/i.* drängeln: ~ ***against*** → **II** *v/t.* anrempeln, schubsen; **III** *s.* a) Gedränge *n*, Dränge'lei *f*, b) Rempe'lei *f.*

Jos·u·e ['dʒɒzjʊiː] → ***Joshua***.

jot [dʒɒt] **I** *s.*: ***not a*** ~ nicht ein bisschen; ***there's not a*** ~ ***of truth in it*** da ist

überhaupt nichts Wahres dran; **II** v/t.
mst **~ down** schnell hinschreiben od.
notieren od. hinwerfen; '**jot·ter** [-tə] s.
No'tizbuch n; '**jot·ting** [-tɪŋ] s. (kurze)
No'tiz.

joule [dʒuːl] s. phys. Joule n.
jounce [dʒaʊns] → **jolt** 1, 6, 7.
jour·nal ['dʒɜːnl] s. **1.** Jour'nal n, Zeitschrift f, Zeitung f; **2.** Tagebuch n; **3.** ✝
Jour'nal n, Memori'al n; **4.** Fax: Sende-
bericht m; **5.** **⚓s** pl. parl. Brit. Proto-
'kollbuch n; **6.** ⚓ Logbuch n; **7.** ☉
(Achs-, Lager)Zapfen m: **~ bearing** od.
box Achs-, Zapfenlager n; **jour·nal·ese**
[ˌdʒɜːnəˈliːz] s. contp. Zeitungsstil m;
'**jour·nal·ism** [-nəlɪzəm] s. Journa'lismus m; '**jour·nal·ist** [-nəlɪst] s. Journa-
'list(in) f; **jour·nal·is·tic** [ˌdʒɜːnəˈlɪstɪk]
adj. journa'listisch.
jour·ney ['dʒɜːnɪ] **I** s. **1.** Reise f: **go on a**
~ verreisen; **bus ~** Busfahrt f; **~'s end**
Ende n der Reise, fig. 'Endstation' f, a.
Tod m; **2.** Reise f, Strecke f, Route f,
Weg m, Fahrt f, Gang m: **it's a day's ~**
from here es ist e-e Tagereise von hier,
man braucht e-n Tag, um von hier dorthin zu kommen; **II** v/i. **3.** reisen; wandern; '**~·man** [-mən] s. [irr.] (Handwerks)Geselle m: **~ baker** Bäckerge-
selle.
joust [dʒaʊst] hist. **I** s. Turnier n; **II** v/i.
im Turnier kämpfen; fig. e-n Strauß
ausfechten.
Jove [dʒəʊv] npr. Jupiter m: **by ~!** a)
Donnerwetter!, b) beim Zeus!
jo·vi·al ['dʒəʊvjəl] adj. □ **1.** jovi'al (a.
contp.), freundlich, aufgeräumt, gemütlich: **a ~ fellow**; **2.** freundlich, nett:
a ~ welcome; **3.** heiter, vergnügt, lustig; **jo·vi·al·i·ty** [ˌdʒəʊvɪˈælətɪ] s. Joviali'tät f, Freundlichkeit f, Fröhlichkeit f.
jowl [dʒaʊl] s. **1.** ('Unter)Kiefer m; **2.**
(mst feiste od. Hänge)Backe f; →
cheek 1; **3.** zo. Wamme f.
joy [dʒɔɪ] s. **1.** Freude f (**at** über acc., **in**,
of an dat.): **to my (great) ~** zu m-r
(großen) Freude; **leap for ~** vor Freude
hüpfen; **tears of ~** Freudentränen; **it**
gives me great ~ es macht mir große
Freude; **my children are a great ~ to**
me m-e Kinder machen mir viel Freude; **wish s.o. ~ (of)** j-m Glück wünschen (zu); **I wish you ~!** iro. (na,
dann) viel Spaß!; **2.** Brit. F Erfolg m: **I**
didn't have any ~! ich hatte keinen
Erfolg!, es hat nicht geklappt!; '**joy·ful**
[-fʊl] adj. □ **1.** freudig, erfreut, froh:
be ~ sich freuen; **2.** erfreulich, froh;
'**joyful·ness** [-fʊlnɪs] s. Freude f, Fröhlichkeit f; '**joy·less** [-lɪs] adj. □ freudlos; **joy·ous** ['dʒɔɪəs] adj. □ → **joyful**.
joy| **ride** s. F Vergnügungsfahrt f, (wil-
de) Spritztour (bsd. in e-m gestohlenen
Auto); '**~·stick** s. **1.** ✈ F Steuerknüppel m; **2.** Computer: Joystick m.
ju·bi·lant ['dʒuːbɪlənt] adj. □ jubelnd,
froh'lockend, (glück)strahlend (a. Gesicht): **be ~ over** od. **at** → **jubilate**;
ju·bi·late **I** v/i. ['dʒuːbɪleɪt] **1.** jubeln, jubilieren,
überglücklich sein, triumphieren; **II** **⚓**
[ˌdʒuːbɪˈlɑːtɪ] (Lat.) s. eccl. **2.** (Sonntag
m) Jubi'late m (3. Sonntag nach
Ostern); **3.** Jubi'latepsalm m; **ju·bi·la·**
tion [ˌdʒuːbɪˈleɪʃn] s. Jubel m.
ju·bi·lee ['dʒuːbɪliː] s. **1.** (bsd. fünfzig-
jähriges) Jubi'läum: **silver ~** fünfund-
zwanzigjähriges Jubiläum; **2.** R.C. Ju-
bel-, Ablassjahr n.
Ju·da·ic [dʒuːˈdeɪɪk] adj. ju'daisch, jüdisch; '**Ju·da·ism** [dʒuːˈdeɪɪzəm] s. **1.**
Juda'ismus m; **2.** das Judentum; **Ju-**
da·ize ['dʒuːdeɪaɪz] v/t. judaisieren, jüdisch machen.

Ju·das ['dʒuːdəs] **I** npr. bibl. Judas m
(a. fig. Verräter): **~ kiss** Judaskuss m; **II**
⚓ s. Guckloch n, 'Spi'on' m.
Jude [dʒuːd] npr. u. s. bibl. Judas m:
(**the Epistle of**) **~** der Judasbrief.
jud·der ['dʒʌdə] v/i. **1.** rütteln, wackeln;
2. vibrieren.
judge [dʒʌdʒ] **I** s. **1.** **⚖** Richter m; **2.** mst
Preis-, sport a. Kampfrichter m; **3.** Ken-
ner m: **a (good) ~ of wine** ein Weinkenner; **I am no ~ of it** ich kann es nicht
beurteilen; **I am no ~ of music, but** ich
verstehe (zwar) nicht viel von Musik,
aber; **I'll be the ~ of that** das müssen Sie
mich schon selbst beurteilen lassen; **4.**
bibl. a) Richter m, b) **⚓s** pl. sg. konstr.
(das Buch der) Richter pl.; **II** v/t. **5.** **⚖** ein
Urteil fällen od. Recht sprechen über
(acc.), e-n Fall verhandeln; **6.** entscheiden (**s.th.** et.; **that** dass); **7.** beurteilen,
bewerten, einschätzen (**by** nach); **8.** a)
Preis-, sport Kampfrichter sein bei, b)
Leistungen etc. (als Preisrichter etc.) bewerten; **9.** betrachten als, halten für; **III**
v/i. **10.** **⚖** urteilen, Recht sprechen; **11.**
fig. richten; **12.** urteilen (**by, from** nach;
of über acc.): **~ for yourself!** urteilen Sie
selbst!; **judging by his words** s-n Worten nach zu urteilen; **how can I ~?** wie
soll 'ich das beurteilen?; **13.** schließen
(**from, by** aus); **14.** Preis-, sport Kampfrichter sein; **15.** a) denken, vermuten, b)
~ of sich et. vorstellen; **~ ad·vo·cate** s.
⚔ Kriegsgerichtsrat m; '**~-made law** s.
auf richterlicher Entscheidung beruhen-
des Recht, geschöpftes Recht.
judg(e)·ment ['dʒʌdʒmənt] s. **1.** **⚖** (Gerichts)Urteil n, gerichtliche Entscheidung: **~ by default** Versäumnisurteil;
give (od. **deliver, render, pronounce**)
~ ein Urteil erlassen od. verkünden (**on**
über acc.); **pass ~** ein Urteil fällen (**on**
über acc.); **sit in ~ on a case** Richter sein
in e-m Fall; **sit in ~ upon** über j-n zu
Gericht sitzen; → **error** 1; **2.** Beurteilung
f, Bewertung f (a. sport etc.), Urteil n; **3.**
Urteilsvermögen n: **man of ~** urteilsfähi-
ger Mann; **use your best ~!** handeln Sie
nach Ihrem besten Ermessen; **4.** Urteil
n, Ansicht f, Meinung f: **form a ~** sich
ein Urteil bilden; **against my better ~**
wider besseres Wissen; **give one's ~ on**
s.th. sein Urteil über et. abgeben; **in**
my ~ meines Erachtens; **5.** Schätzung f:
~ of distance; **6.** göttliches (Straf)Ge-
richt, Strafe f (Gottes): **the Last ⚓**, **the**
Day of ⚓, **⚓ Day** das Jüngste Gericht; **~**
cred·i·tor s. **⚖** Voll'streckungsgläubi-
ger(in); **~ debt** s. **⚖** voll'streckbare
Forderung, durch Urteil festgestellte
Schuld; **~ debt·or** s. **⚖** Vollstreckungs-
schuldner(in); '**~-proof** adj. Am. **⚖** unpfändbar.
judge·ship ['dʒʌdʒʃɪp] s. Richteramt n.
ju·di·ca·ture ['dʒuːdɪkətʃə] s. **⚖** **1.**
Rechtsprechung f, Rechtspflege f; **2.**
Gerichtswesen n, Ju'stiz(verwaltung) f;
→ **supreme** 1; **3.** coll. Richter(stand
m, -schaft f) pl.; **ju·di·cial** [dʒuːˈdɪʃl]
adj. □ **1.** **⚖** gerichtlich, Justiz..., Gerichts...: **~ error** Justizirrtum m; **~**
murder Justizmord m; **~ proceedings**
Gerichtsverfahren n; **~ office** Richteramt n, richterliches Amt; **~ power**
richterliche Gewalt; **~ separation**
gerichtliche Trennung der Ehe; **~**
system Gerichtswesen n; **2.** **⚖** Richter...,
richterlich; **3.** klar urteilend,
kritisch; **ju·di·ci·ar·y** [dʒuːˈdɪʃɪərɪ] **⚖**
I s. **1.** → **judicature** 2, 3; **2.** Am.
richterliche Gewalt; **II** adj. **3.** richterlich, Recht sprechend, gerichtlich: **⚓**
Committee Am. parl. Rechtsaus-

schuss m.
ju·di·cious [dʒuːˈdɪʃəs] adj. □ **1.** vernünftig, klug; **2.** wohl überlegt, verständnisvoll; **ju'di·cious·ness** [-nɪs] s.
Klugheit f, Einsicht f.
ju·do ['dʒuːdəʊ] s. sport Judo n; '**ju·do-**
ka [-əʊkɑː] s. Ju'doka m.
Ju·dy ['dʒuːdɪ] → **Punch**[2].
jug[1] [dʒʌg] s. **1.** Krug m, Kanne f,
Kännchen n; **2.** sl. 'Kittchen' n, 'Knast'
m; **II** v/t. **3.** schmoren od. dämpfen:
~ged hare Hasenpfeffer m; **4.** sl. 'einlochen'.
jug[2] [dʒʌg] **I** v/i. schlagen (Nachtigall);
II s. Nachtigallenschlag m.
'**jug·ful** [-fʊl] pl. **-fuls** ein Krug m (voll).
jug·ger·naut ['dʒʌgənɔːt] s. **1.** Moloch
m: **the ~ of war**; **2.** Brit. schwerer
'Brummi', Schwerlastwagen m, Lastzug m.
jug·gins ['dʒʌgɪnz] s. sl. Trottel m.
jug·gle ['dʒʌgl] **I** v/i. **1.** jonglieren; **2.** **~**
with fig. (mit) et. jonglieren, et. manipulieren: **~ with facts**; **~ with one's**
accounts s-e Konten 'frisieren'; **~ with**
words mit Worten spielen od. 'jonglieren', Worte verdrehen; **II** v/t. **3.** jonglieren mit; **4.** → 2; '**jug·gler** [-lə] s. **1.**
Jon'gleur m; **2.** Schwindler m; '**jug-**
gler·y [-lərɪ] s. **1.** Jonglieren n; **2.** Taschenspiele'rei f; **3.** Schwindel m, Hokus'pokus m.
Ju·go·slav ['juːgəʊslɑːv] **I** s. Jugo'slawe
m, Jugo'slawin f; **II** adj. jugo'slawisch.
jug·u·lar ['dʒʌgjʊlə] anat. **I** adj. Kehl...,
Gurgel...; **II** s. a. **~ vein** Hals-, Drossel-
ader f; '**ju·gu·late** [-leɪt] v/t. fig. abwürgen.
juice [dʒuːs] s. **1.** Saft m (a. fig.): **or-**
ange ~; **~ extractor** Entsafter m; **body**
~s Körpersäfte; **stew in one's own ~** F
im eigenen Saft schmoren; **2.** sl. a) ⚡
'Saft' m, Strom m, b) mot. Sprit m, c)
Am. 'Zeug' n, Whisky m; **3.** fig. Kern
m, Sub'stanz f, Es'senz f; '**juic·i·ness**
[-sɪnɪs] s. Saftigkeit f; '**juic·y** [-sɪ] adj. **1.**
saftig (a. fig.); **2.** F a) 'saftig', 'gepfeffert': **~ scandal**, b) pi'kant, 'schlüpfrig:
~ story, c) interessant, 'mit Pfiff';
Am. F lukra'tiv: **~ contract**; **4.** sl.
'scharf', 'dufte': **~ girl**.
ju·jit·su [dʒuːˈdʒɪtsuː] s. sport Jiu-Jitsu
n.
ju·jube ['dʒuːdʒuːb] s. **1.** ♀ Ju'jube f,
Brustbeere f; **2.** pharm. 'Brustbon,bon
m, n.
ju·jut·su [dʒuːˈdʒʊtsuː] → **jujitsu**.
'**juke**|**·box** ['dʒuːk-] s. Jukebox f (Musik-
automat); '**~-joint** s. Am. sl. 'Bumslo-
,kal' n, 'Jukeboxbude' f.
ju·lep ['dʒuːlep] s. **1.** süßliches (Arz'nei-)
Getränk; **2.** Am. Julep m (alkoholisches Eisgetränk).
Jul·ian ['dʒuːljən] adj. juli'anisch: **the ~**
calendar der julianische Kalender.
Ju·ly [dʒuːˈlaɪ] s. Juli m: **in ~** im Juli.
jum·ble ['dʒʌmbl] **I** v/t. **1.** a. **~ togeth-**
er, **~ up** zs.-werfen, in Unordnung
bringen, (wahllos) vermischen, durch-
ein'ander würfeln; **II** v/i. **2.** a. **~ togeth-**
er, **~ up** durchein'ander geraten, durchein'ander gerüttelt werden; **III** s. **3.**
Durchein'ander n, Wirrwarr m; **4.**
Ramsch m: **~ sale** Brit. Wohltätigkeits-
basar m; **~ shop** Ramschladen m.
jum·bo ['dʒʌmbəʊ] s. **1.** ✈ Ko'loss m: **~**
-sized riesig; **2.** → **jum·bo jet** s. ✈
Jumbo(-Jet) m.
jump [dʒʌmp] **I** s. **1.** Sprung m (a. fig.),
Satz m: **make** (od. **take**) **a ~** e-n
Sprung machen; **by ~s** sprungweise; (**always**) **on the ~** F (immer) auf
den Beinen od. in Eile; **keep s.o. on**

the ~ j-n in Trab halten; *get the* ~ *on s.o.* F j-m zuvorkommen, j-m den Rang ablaufen; *have the* ~ *on s.o.* F j-m gegenüber im Vorteil sein; *be* (*stay*) *one* ~ *ahead* fig. (immer) e-n Schritt voraus sein (*of* dat.); *give a* ~ → 15; *give s.o. a* ~ F j-n erschrecken; **2.** (Fallschirm)Absprung m: ~ *area* Absprunggebiet n; **3.** sport (Hoch- od. Weit)Sprung m: high (long od. Am. broad) ~; **4.** bsd. Reitsport: Hindernis n: *take the* ~; **5.** sprunghaftes Anwachsen, Em'porschnellen n (*in prices* der Preise etc.): ~ *in production* rapider Produktionsanstieg; **6.** (plötzlicher) Ruck; **7.** fig. Sprung m: a) abrupter 'Übergang, b) Über'springen n, -'gehen n, Auslassen n (*von Buchseiten etc.*); **8.** a) *Film*: Sprung m (*Überblenden etc.*), b) *Computer*: (Pro'gramm)Sprung m; **9.** *Damespiel*: Schlagen n; **10.** a) Rückstoß m (e-r *Feuerwaffe*), b) ✕ Abgangsfehler m; **11.** V ,Nummer' f (*Koitus*); **II** v/i. **12.** springen: ~ *at* (*od.* *to*) fig. sich stürzen auf (*acc.*), sofort zugreifen bei e-m *Angebot, Vorschlag etc.*, (*sofort*) aufgreifen, einhaken bei e-r *Frage etc.*; ~ *at the chance* die Gelegenheit beim Schopf ergreifen, mit beiden Händen zugreifen; → *conclusion* 3; ~ *down s.o.'s throat* F j-n ,anschnauzen'; ~ *off* a) abspringen (*von s-m Fahrrad etc.*), b) Am. F losgelen; ~ *on s.o.* F a) über j-n herfallen, b) j-m ,aufs Dach' steigen; ~ *out of one's skin* aus der Haut fahren; ~ *to it* F ,(d)rangehen', zupacken; ~ *to it!* ran!, mach schon!; ~ *up* aufspringen (*onto* auf *acc.*); **13.** (*mit dem Fallschirm*) (ab)springen; **14.** hopsen, hüpfen: ~ *up and down*; ~ *for joy* e-n Freudensprung *od.* Freudensprünge machen; *his heart* ~*ed for joy* das Herz hüpfte ihm im Leibe; **15.** zs.-zucken, -fahren, aufschrecken, hochfahren (*at* bei): *the noise made him* ~ der Lärm schreckte ihn auf *od.* ließ ihn zs.-zucken; **16.** fig. ab'rupt 'übergehen, -wechseln (*to* zu): ~ *from one topic to another*; **17.** a) rütteln (*Wagen etc.*), b) gerüttelt werden, schaukeln, wackeln; **18.** fig. sprunghaft ansteigen, em'porschnellen (*Preise etc.*); **19.** ◎ springen (*Filmstreifen, Schreibmaschine etc.*); **20.** *Damespiel*: schlagen; **21.** *Bridge*: (unvermittelt) hoch reizen; **22.** pochen, pulsieren; **23.** F voller Leben sein: *the place is* ~*ing* dort ist ,schwer was los'; *the party was* ~*ing* die Party war ,schwer in Fahrt'; **III** v/t. **24.** (hin'weg)springen über (*acc.*): ~ *the fence*; ~ *the rails* entgleisen (*Zug*); **25.** fig. über'springen, auslassen: ~ *a few lines*; ~ *the lights* F bei Rot über die Kreuzung fahren; ~ *the queue* Brit. sich vordrängeln, aus der Reihe tanzen (*a. fig.*); → *gun* 4; **26.** springen lassen: *he* ~*ed his horse over the ditch* er setzte mit dem Pferd über den Graben; **27.** *Damespiel*: schlagen; **28.** *Bridge*: (zu) hoch reizen; **29.** sl. ,abhauen' von: ~ *ship* (*town*); → *bail*¹ 1; **30.** a) aufspringen auf (*acc.*), b) abspringen von (*e-m fahrenden Zug*); **31.** schaukeln: ~ *a baby on one's knee*; **32.** F j-n überfallen, über j-n herfallen; **33.** em'porschnellen lassen, hoch treiben: ~ *prices*; **34.** Am. F j-n (*plötzlich*) *im Rang* befördern; **35.** V *Frau* ,bumsen'; **36.** → *jump-start*.

jump ball s. *Basketball*: Sprungball m.
jumped-up [ˌdʒʌmptˈʌp] adj. F **1.** (parveˈnühaft) hochnäsig, ,hochgestochen'; **2.** improvisiert.

jump·er¹ [ˈdʒʌmpə] s. **1.** Springer(in): *high* ~ *sport* Hochspringer(in); **2.** Springpferd n; **3.** ◎ Steinbohrer m; Bohrmeißel m; **4.** ⚡ Kurzschlussbrücke f.
jump·er² [ˈdʒʌmpə] s. **1.** (Am. ärmelloser) Pullover m; **2.** bsd. Am. Trägerkleid n, -rock m; **3.** (Kinder)Spielhose f.
jump·i·ness [ˈdʒʌmpɪnɪs] s. Nervosi'tät f.
jump·ing [ˈdʒʌmpɪŋ] s. **1.** Springen n: ~ *pole* Sprungstab m, -stange f; ~ *test* Reitsport: (Jagd)Springen n; **2.** Skisport: Sprunglauf m, Springen n; ~ *bean* s. ♥ Springende Bohne; ~ *jack* s. Hampelmann m; ~-*off place* s. **1.** fig. Sprungbrett n, Ausgangspunkt m; **2.** Am. F Ende n der Welt.
jump| *jet* s. ✈ (Düsen)Senkrechtstarter m; ~ *leads* s. pl. mot. Starthilfekabel n; '~-*off* s. Reitsport: Stechen n; ~ *seat* s. Not-, Klappsitz m; '~-*start* v/t. Auto mittels Starthilfekabel anlassen; 'jump-,start·er s. fig. Starthilfe f; ~ *suit* s. Overall m; ~ *turn* s. Skisport: 'Umsprung m.
jump·y [ˈdʒʌmpɪ] adj. ner'vös.
junc·tion [ˈdʒʌŋkʃn] s. **1.** Verbindung(spunkt m) f, Vereinigung f, Zs.-treffen n; Treffpunkt m; Anschluss m (a. ◎); (Straßen)Kreuzung f, (-)Einmündung f; **2.** ⬛ a) Knotenpunkt m, b) 'Anschlussstatiˌon f; **3.** Berührung f; ~ *box* s. ⚡ Abzweig-, Anschlussdose f; ~ *line* s. ⬛ Verbindungs-, Nebenbahn f.
junc·ture [ˈdʒʌŋktʃə] s. (kritischer) Augenblick *od.* Zeitpunkt: *at this* ~ in diesem Augenblick, an dieser Stelle.
June [dʒuːn] s. Juni m: *in* ~ im Juni.
jun·gle [ˈdʒʌŋɡl] s. **1.** Dschungel m, a. n (a. fig.): ~ *fever* Dschungelfieber n; *law of the* ~ Faustrecht n; **2.** (undurchdringliches) Dickicht (a. fig.); fig. Gewirr n: ~ *gym* Klettergerüst n (*für Kinder*); 'jun·gled [-ld] adj. mit Dschungel(n) bedeckt, verdschungelt.
jun·ior [ˈdʒuːnjə] **I** adj. **1.** junior (*nur nach Familiennamen u. abgekürzt zu Jr., jr., Jun., jun.*): *George Smith jr.*; *Smith* ~ Smith II (*von Schülern*); **2.** jünger (*im Amt*), 'untergeordnet, zweiter: ~ *clerk* a) untere(r) Büroangestellte(r), b) zweiter Buchhalter, c) jur. Brit. Anwaltspraktikant m, d) kleiner Angestellter; ~ *counsel* (*od.* *barrister*) jur. Brit. → *barrister* (*als Vorstufe zum King's Counsel*); ~ *partner* jüngerer Teilhaber, fig. der kleinere Partner; ~ *staff* untere Angestellte pl.; **3.** später, jünger, nachfolgend: ~ *forms* ped. Brit. die Unterklassen, *die* Unterstufe; ~ *school* Brit. Grundschule f; **4.** jur. rangjünger, (im Rang) nachstehend: ~ *mortgage*; **5.** sport Junioren..., Jugend...: ~ *championship*; **6.** Am. Kinder..., Jugend...: ~ *books*; **7.** jugendlich, jung: ~ *citizens* Jungbürger pl.; ~ *skin*; **8.** Am. F kleiner(er, e, es): *a* ~ *hurricane*; **II** s. **9.** Jüngere(r m) f: *he is my* ~ *by 2 years*, *he is 2 years my* ~ er ist (um) 2 Jahre jünger als ich; *my* ~*s* Leute, die jünger sind als ich; **10.** univ. Am. Stu'dent m a) im vorletzten Jahr vor s-r Graduierung, b) im 3. Jahr an e-m senior college, c) im 1. Jahr an e-m *junior college*; **11.** a. ⚄ (*ohne art*) a) Junior m (*Sohn mit dem Vornamen des Vaters*), b) allg. der Sohn, der Junge, c) Am. F Kleine(r) m; **12.** Jugendliche(r m) f; Her'anwachsende(r m) f: ~ *miss* Am. ,junge Dame' (*Mädchen*); **13.** 'Untergeordnete(r m) f

(im Amt), jüngere(r) Angestellte(r): *he is my* ~ *in this office* a) er untersteht mir in diesem Amt, b) er ist in dieses Amt nach mir eingetreten; **14.** Bridge: Junior m (*Spieler, der rechts vom Alleinspieler sitzt*); ~ *col·lege* s. Am. Juni'orencollege n (*umfasst die untersten Hochschuljahrgänge, etwa 16- bis 18-jährige Studenten*); ~ *high* (*school*) s. Am. (Art) Aufbauschule f (*für die high school*) (*dritt- u. viertletzte Klasse der Grundschule u. erste Klasse der high school*).
jun·ior·i·ty [ˌdʒuːnɪˈɒrətɪ] s. **1.** geringeres Alter *od.* Dienstalter; **2.** 'untergeordnete Stellung, niedrigerer Rang.
ju·ni·per [ˈdʒuːnɪpə] s. Wa'cholder m.
junk¹ [dʒʌŋk] **I** s. **1.** Trödel m, alter Kram, Plunder m: ~ *food* bsd. Am. Nahrung f mit geringem Nährwert; ~ *market* Trödel-, Flohmarkt m; ~ *dealer* Trödler m, Altwarenhändler m; ~ *mail* Papierkorb – Post f; ~ *shop* Trödelladen m; ~ *yard* Schrottplatz m; **2.** contp. Schund m, ,Mist', ,Schrott' m; **3.** sl. ,Stoff' m (*Rauschgift*); **II** v/t. Am. F a) wegwerfen, b) verschrotten, c) fig. zum alten Eisen *od.* über Bord werfen.
junk² [dʒʌŋk] s. Dschunke f.
jun·ket [ˈdʒʌŋkɪt] **I** s. **1.** a) Sahnequark m, b) Quarkspeise f mit Sahne; **2.** Festivi'tät f, Fete f; **3.** Am. F so genannte Dienstreise, Vergnügungsreise f auf öffentliche Kosten; **II** v/i. **4.** feiern, es sich wohl sein lassen.
junk·ie [ˈdʒʌŋkɪ] s. sl. ,Fixer' m, Rauschgiftsüchtige(r m) f.
Ju·no·esque [ˌdʒuːnəʊˈesk] adj. ju'nonisch.
jun·ta [ˈdʒʌntə] s. (Span.) **1.** pol. (bsd. Mili'tär)Junta f; **2.** → '*jun·to* [-təʊ] pl. -*tos* s. Clique f.
Ju·pi·ter [ˈdʒuːpɪtə] s. myth. u. ast. Jupiter m.
Ju·ras·sic [ˌdʒʊəˈræsɪk] geol. **I** adj. Jura..., ju'rassisch: ~ *period*; **II** s. 'Juraformatiˌon f.
ju·rat [ˈdʒʊəræt] s. Brit. **1.** hist. Stadtrat m (*Person*) in den **Cinque Ports**; **2.** Richter m auf den Kanalinseln; **3.** ⚖ Bekräftigungsformel f unter eidesstattlichen Erklärungen.
ju·rid·i·cal [ˌdʒʊəˈrɪdɪkl] adj. □ **1.** gerichtlich, Gerichts...; **2.** ju'ristisch, Rechts...: ~ *person* Am. juristische Person.
ju·ris·dic·tion [ˌdʒʊərɪsˈdɪkʃn] s. **1.** Rechtsprechung f; **2.** a) Gerichtsbarkeit f, b) (*örtliche u. sachliche*) Zuständigkeit (*of, over* für): *come under the* ~ *of* unter die Zuständigkeit fallen (*gen.*); *have* ~ *over* zuständig sein für; **3.** a) Gerichtsbezirk m, b) Zuständigkeitsbereich m; **ju·ris'dic·tion·al** [-ʃənl] adj. Gerichtsbarkeits..., Zuständigkeits...; **ju·ris·pru·dence** [ˌdʒʊərɪsˈpruːdəns] s. Rechtswissenschaft f, Jurispru'denz f; **ju·rist** [ˈdʒʊərɪst] s. **1.** Jurist(in); **2.** Brit. Stu'dent m der Rechte; **3.** Am. Rechtsanwalt m; **ju·ris·tic, ju·ris·ti·cal** [ˌdʒʊəˈrɪstɪk(l)] adj. □ ju'ristisch, Rechts...
ju·ror [ˈdʒʊərə] s. **1.** ⚖ Geschworene(r m) f; **2.** Preisrichter(in).
ju·ry¹ [ˈdʒʊərɪ] s. **1.** ⚖ die Geschworenen pl., Ju'ry f: *trial by* ~, ~ *trial* Schwurgerichtsverfahren n; *sit on the* ~ Geschworene(r) sein; **2.** Ju'ry f, Preisrichterausschuss m, sport a. Kampfgericht n; **3.** Sachverständigenausschuss m.
ju·ry² [ˈdʒʊərɪ] adj. ⚓, ✈ Ersatz...,

Hilfs..., Not...

ju·ry box s. ⚖ Geschworenenbank f;
'~·man [-mən] s. [*irr.*] ⚖ Geschwore-
ne(r) m; **~ pan·el** s. ⚖ Geschworenenliste f.

jus [dʒʌs] pl. **ju·ra** ['dʒʊərə] (*Lat.*) s.
Recht n.

jus·sive ['dʒʌsɪv] adj. *ling.* Befehls...,
impera'tivisch.

just [dʒʌst] **I** adj. □ → **II** u. **justly**; **1.**
gerecht (**to** gegen): **be ~ to** s.o. j-n
gerecht behandeln; **2.** gerecht, richtig,
angemessen, gehörig: **it was only ~** es
war nur recht u. billig; **~ reward** gerechter od. (wohl)verdienter Lohn; **3.**
rechtmäßig, wohl begründet: **a ~ claim**;
4. berechtigt, gerechtfertigt, (wohl) begründet: **~ indignation**; **5.** a) genau,
kor'rekt, b) wahr, richtig; **6.** *bibl.* gerecht, rechtschaffen: **the ~** die Gerechten pl.; **7.** ♪ rein; **II** adv. **8.** zeitlich: a)
gerade, (so)'eben: **they have ~ left; ~**
before I came kurz od. knapp bevor
ich kam; **~ after breakfast** kurz od.
gleich nach dem Frühstück; **~ now**
eben erst, soeben (→ b), b) genau, gerade (*zu diesem Zeitpunkt*): **~ as** gerade als, genau in dem Augenblick, als (→
9); **I was ~ going to say** ich wollte
gerade sagen; **~ now** a) gerade jetzt, b)
jetzt gleich (→ a); **~ then** a) gerade
damals, b) gerade in diesem Augen-
blick; **~ five o'clock** genau fünf Uhr; **9.**
örtlich u. fig.: genau: **~ there; ~ round**
the corner gleich um die Ecke; **~ as**
ebenso wie; **~ as good** genauso gut; **~**
about a) (so od. in) etwa, b) so ziemlich, c) so gerade, eben (noch); **~ about**
here ungefähr hier, hier herum; **~ so!**
ganz recht!; **that's ~ it!** das ist es ja
gerade od. eben!; **that's ~ like you!** das
sieht dir (ganz) ähnlich!; **that's ~ what**
I thought! (genau) das hab ich mir
(doch) gedacht!; **~ what do you mean**
(by that)? was (genau) wollen Sie damit sagen?; **~ how many are they?** wie
viele sind es genau?; **it's ~ as well** (es
ist) vielleicht besser od. ganz gut so;
we might ~ as well go! da können
wir genauso gut auch gehen!; **10.**
gerade (noch), ganz knapp, mit knap-

per Not: **we ~ managed**; **the bullet**
~ missed him die Kugel ging ganz
knapp an ihm vorbei; **~ possible**
immerhin möglich, nicht unmöglich;
~ too late gerade zu spät; **11.** nur,
lediglich, bloß: **~ in case** nur für den
Fall; **~ the two of us** nur wir beide;
~ for the fun of it nur zum Spaß;
~ a moment! (nur) e-n Augenblick!,
a. iro. Moment (mal)!; **~ give her a**
book schenk ihr doch einfach ein
Buch; **12.** vor imp. a) doch, mal,
b) nur: **~ tell me** sag (mir) mal, sag
mir nur od. bloß; **~ sit down, please!**
setzen Sie sich doch bitte; **~ think!**
denk mal!; **~ try!** versuchs doch (mal)!;
13. F einfach, wirklich: **~ wonderful.**

jus·tice ['dʒʌstɪs] s. **1.** Gerechtigkeit f
(**to** gegen); **2.** Rechtmäßigkeit f, Berechtigung f, Recht n: **with ~** mit od. zu
Recht; **3.** Gerechtigkeit f, gerechter
Lohn: **do ~ to** a) j-m od. e-r Sache
Gerechtigkeit widerfahren lassen, gerecht werden (dat.), b) et. (recht) zu
würdigen wissen, a. e-r Speise, dem
Wein tüchtig zusprechen; **the picture**
did ~ to her beauty das Bild wurde
ihrer Schönheit gerecht; **do o.s. ~** a)
sein wahres Können zeigen, b) sich
selbst gerecht werden; **~ was done** der
Gerechtigkeit wurde Genüge getan; **in**
~ to him um ihm gerecht zu werden,
fairerweise; **4.** ⚖ Gerechtigkeit f,
Recht n, Ju'stiz f: **administer ~** Recht
sprechen; **flee from ~** sich der verdienten Strafe (durch die Flucht) entziehen;
bring to ~ vor Gericht bringen; **in ~**
von Rechts wegen; **5.** Richter m:
Mr. ♀ X. (*Anrede in England*); **~ of**
the peace Friedensrichter (*Laien-*
richter); **'jus·tice·ship** [-ʃɪp] s. Richteramt n.

jus·ti·ci·a·ble [dʒʌ'stɪʃɪəbl] adj. ⚖ justizi'abel, gerichtlicher Entscheidung unter'worfen; **jus'ti·ci·ar·y** [-ɪərɪ] ⚖ **I** s.
Richter m; **II** adj. Justiz..., gerichtlich.

jus·ti·fi·a·ble ['dʒʌstɪfaɪəbl] adj. □ zu
rechtfertigen(d), berechtigt, vertretbar,
entschuldbar; **'jus·ti·fi·a·bly** [-lɪ] adv.
berechtigterweise.

jus·ti·fi·ca·tion [ˌdʒʌstɪfɪ'keɪʃn] s. **1.**

Rechtfertigung f: **in ~ of** zur Rechtfertigung von (od. gen.); **2.** Berechtigung f:
with ~ berechtigterweise, mit Recht; **3.**
typ. Justierung f, Ausschluss m; **jus·ti·**
fi·ca·to·ry ['dʒʌstɪfɪkeɪtərɪ] adj. rechtfertigend, Rechtfertigungs...; **jus·ti·fy**
['dʒʌstɪfaɪ] v/t. **1.** rechtfertigen (**before**
od. **to** s.o. vor j-m, j-m gegenüber); **be**
justified in doing s.th. et. mit gutem
Recht tun; ein Recht haben, et. zu tun;
berechtigt sein, et. zu tun; **2.** a) gutheißen, b) entschuldigen, c) j-m Recht
geben; **3.** eccl. rechtfertigen, von Sün-
denschuld freisprechen; **4.** ⊛ richtig
stellen, richten, justieren; **5.** typ. justieren, ausschließen, *Computer:* ausrichten.

just·ly ['dʒʌstlɪ] adv. **1.** richtig; **2.** mit
od. zu Recht, gerechterweise; **3.** verdientermaßen; **'just·ness** [-tnɪs] s. **1.**
Gerechtigkeit f; **2.** Rechtmäßigkeit f;
3. Richtigkeit f; **4.** Genauigkeit f.

jut [dʒʌt] **I** v/i. a. **~ out** vorspringen,
her'ausragen; **~ into s.th.** in et. hinein-
ragen; **II** s. Vorsprung m.

jute¹ [dʒuːt] ♀ Jute f.

Jute² [dʒuːt] s. Jüte m; **Jut·land**
['dʒʌtlənd] npr. Jütland n: **the Battle**
of ~ hist. die Skagerrakschlacht.

ju·ve·nes·cence [ˌdʒuːvə'nesns] s. **1.**
Verjüngung f: **well of ~** Jungbrunnen
m; **2.** Jugend f.

ju·ve·nile ['dʒuːvənaɪl] **I** adj. **1.** jugendlich, jung, Jugend...: **~ book** Jugendbuch n; **~ court** Jugendgericht n; **~ de-**
linquency Jugendkriminalität f; **~ de-**
linquent od. **offender** jugendlicher Täter; **~ stage** Entwicklungsstadium n; **II**
s. **2.** Jugendliche(r m) f; **3.** thea. jugendlicher Liebhaber, **4.** Jugendbuch
n; **ju·ve·nil·i·a** [ˌdʒuːvə'nɪlɪə] pl. **1.** Ju-
gendwerke pl. (*e-s Autors etc.*); **2.** Werke pl. für die Jugend; **ju·ve·nil·i·ty**
[ˌdʒuːvə'nɪlətɪ] s. **1.** Jugendlichkeit f; **2.**
jugendlicher Leichtsinn; **3.** pl. Kinde-
'reien pl.; **4.** coll. (die) Jugend.

jux·ta·pose [ˌdʒʌkstə'pəʊz] v/t. nebenein'ander stellen: **~d to** angrenzend an
(acc.); **jux·ta·po·si·tion** [ˌdʒʌkstəpə-
'zɪʃn] s. Nebenein'anderstellung f, -lie-
gen n.

J

K k

K, k [keɪ] s. K n, k n (Buchstabe).
kab·(b)a·la [kə'bɑːlə] → *ca(b)bala*.
ka·di ['kɑːdɪ] → *cadi*.
ka·ke·mo·no [ˌkækɪ'məʊnəʊ] pl. **-nos** s. Kake'mono n (*japanisches Rollbild*).
kale [keɪl] s. **1.** ♥ Kohl m, bsd. Grün-, Blattkohl m: (**curly**) ~ Krauskohl m; **2.** Kohlsuppe f; **3.** Am. sl. ,Zaster' m.
ka·lei·do·scope [kə'laɪdəskəʊp] s. Ka-leido'skop n (a. fig.); **ka·lei·do·scop-ic**, **ka·lei·do·scop·i·cal** [kəˌlaɪdə-'skɒpɪk(l)] adj. □ kaleido'skopisch.
'kale·yard s. Scot. Gemüsegarten m; ~ **school** s. schottische Heimatdichtung.
Kan·a·ka ['kænəkə, kə'nækə] s. Ka'nake m (*Südseeinsulaner, a. contp.*).
kan·ga·roo [ˌkæŋgə'ruː] pl. **-roos** s. zo. Känguru n; ~ **court** s. Am. sl. **1.** ,ille-,gales Gericht (z. B. unter Sträflingen); **2.** kor'ruptes Gericht.
Kant·i·an ['kæntɪən] phls. **I** adj. kan-tisch; **II** s. Kanti'aner(in).
ka·o·lin(e) ['keɪəlɪn] s. min. Kao'lin n.
kar·a·o·ke [ˌkærɪ'əʊkɪ] s Kara'oke n.
ka·ra·te [kə'rɑːtɪ] s. Ka'rate n; ~ **chop** s. Ka'rateschlag m.
kar·ma ['kɑːmə] s. **1.** *Buddhismus etc.:* Karma n; **2.** allg. Schicksal n.
Kar·ri·mat ['kærɪmæt] *TM Markenbe-zeichnung für Isomatten.*
kat·a·bat·ic wind [ˌkætæ'bætɪk] s. Fall-wind m, kata'batischer Wind.
kay·ak ['kaɪæk] s. Kajak m, n: **two-seat-er** ~ **sport** Kajakzweier m.
kay·o [ˌkeɪ'əʊ] F für *knock out* od. *knockout*.
ke·bab [kə'bæb] s. Ke'bab n (*orientali-sches Fleischspießgericht*).
keck [kek] v/i. würgen, (sich) erbrechen (müssen).
kedge [kedʒ] ♨ **I** v/t. warpen, verholen; **II** s. a. ~ **anchor** Wurf-, Warpanker m.
kedg·er·ee [ˌkedʒə'riː] s. Brit. Ind. Ked-ge'ree n (*Reisgericht mit Fisch, Eiern, Zwiebeln etc.*).
keel [kiːl] **I** s. **1.** ♨ Kiel m: **on an even** ~ im Gleichgewicht, fig. a. gleichmäßig, ruhig: **be on an even** ~ **again** fig. wie-der im Lot sein; **2.** poet. Schiff n; **3.** Kiel m: a) ✈ Längsträger m, b) ♥ Längsrippe f; **II** v/t. **4.** ~ **over** a) (,um-) kippen, kentern lassen, b) kiel'oben le-gen; **III** v/i. **5.** ~ **over** ,umschlagen, -kippen (a. fig.), kentern; kiel'oben lie-gen; **6.** F ,umkippen' (*Person etc.*);
'keel·age [-lɪdʒ] s. ♨ Kielgeld n, Ha-fengebühren pl.; **'keel·haul** v/t. **1.** j-n kielholen; **2.** fig. j-n ,zs.-stauchen';
keel·son ['kelsn] → *kelson*.
keen¹ [kiːn] adj. □ → *keenly*; **1.** scharf (geschliffen): ~ **edge** scharfe Schneide; **2.** scharf (*Wind*), schneidend (*Kälte*); **3.** beißend (*Spott*); **4.** scharf, 'durch-dringend: ~ **glance** (**smell**); **5.** grell (*Licht*), schrill (*Ton*); **6.** heftig, stark (*Schmerzen*); **7.** scharf (*Augen*), fein (*Sinne*): **be** ~**-eyed** (~**-eared**) scharfe Augen (ein feines Gehör) haben; **8.** fein, ausgeprägt (*Gefühl*; **of** für): a ~

sense of literature; **9.** heftig, stark, groß (*Freude etc.*): ~ **desire** heftiges Verlangen, heißer Wunsch; ~ **interest** starkes od. lebhaftes Interesse; ~ **com-petition** scharfe Konkurrenz; **10.** a. ~ **-witted** scharfsinnig; **a** ~ **mind** ein scharfer Verstand; **11.** eifrig, begeis-tert, leidenschaftlich: **a** ~ **swimmer**; ~ **on** begeistert von, sehr interessiert an (*dat.*); **he is** ~ **on dancing** er ist ein begeisterter Tänzer; **he is very** ~ F er ist ,schwer auf Draht'; **you shouldn't be too** ~! du solltest dich etwas zurück-halten!; (→ a. 13); **12.** (stark) inte-ressiert (*Bewerber etc.*); **13.** F erpicht, versessen, ,scharf' (**on**, **about** auf *acc.*): **he is** ~ **on doing** (od. **to do**) **it** er ist sehr darauf erpicht od. scharf da-rauf, es zu tun, es liegt ihm (sehr) viel daran, es zu tun; **I am not** ~ **on it** ich habe wenig Lust dazu, ich mache mir nichts daraus, es liegt mir nichts daran, ich lege keinen (gesteigerten) Wert da-rauf; **I am not** ~ **on sweets** ich mag keine Süßigkeiten; **I am not** ~ **on that idea** ich bin nicht gerade begeistert von dieser Idee; **as** ~ **as mustard** (**on**) F ganz versessen (auf *acc.*), Feuer u. Flamme (für); **14.** Brit. F niedrig, gut: ~ **prices**; **15.** Am. F ,prima', ,prächtig'.
keen² [kiːn] Ir. **I** s. Totenklage f; **II** v/i. wehklagen; **III** v/t. beklagen.
'keen-'edged adj. **1.** → *keen¹* 1; **2.** fig. messerscharf.
keen·ly ['kiːnlɪ] adv. **1.** scharf (etc. → **keen¹**); **2.** ungemein, äußerst, sehr; **'keen·ness** [-nnɪs] s. **1.** Schärfe f (a. fig.); **2.** Heftigkeit f; **3.** Eifer m, starkes Inter'esse, Begeisterung f; **4.** Scharf-sinn m; **5.** Feinheit f; **6.** fig. Bitterkeit f.
keep [kiːp] **I** s. **1.** a) Burgverlies n, b) Bergfried m; **2.** a) ('Lebens)Unterhalt m, b) 'Unterkunft f u. Verpflegung f: **earn one's** ~ s-n Lebensunterhalt ver-dienen; **3.** 'Unterhaltskosten pl.: **the** ~ **of a horse**; **4.** Obhut f, Verwahrung f; **5. for** ~**s** F auf od. für immer, endgül-tig; **II** v/t. [*irr.*] **6.** (be)halten, haben: ~ **the ticket in your hand** behalte die Karte in der Hand!; **he kept his hands in his pockets** er hatte die Hände in den Taschen; **7.** j-n od. et. lassen, (in *e-m gewissen Zustand*) (er)halten: ~ **apart** getrennt od. auseinander halten; ~ **a door closed** e-e Tür geschlossen halten; ~ **s.th. dry** et. trocken halten od. vor Nässe schützen; ~ **s.o. from doing s.th.** j-n davon abhalten, et. zu tun; ~ **s.th. to o.s.** et. für sich behalten; ~ **s.o. informed** j-n auf dem Laufenden halten; ~ **s.o. waiting** j-n warten las-sen; ~ **s.th. going** et. in Gang halten; ~ **s.o. going** a) j-n finanziell unterstüt-zen, b) j-n am Leben erhalten; ~ **a secret** et. geheim halten (**from s.o.** vor j-m); **8.** fig. (er)halten, (be)wahren: ~ **one's balance** das od. sein Gleichge-wicht (be)halten od. wahren; ~ **one's**

distance Abstand halten od. bewah-ren; **9.** (*im Besitz*) behalten: **you may** ~ **the book**; ~ **the change!** behalten Sie den Rest (*des Geldes*)!; ~ **your seat!** bleiben Sie (doch) sitzen!; **10.** fig. hal-ten, sich halten od. behaupten in od. auf (*dat.*): ~ **the stage** sich auf der Bühne behaupten; **11.** j-n auf-, 'hinhal-ten: **don't let me** ~ **you!** lass dich nicht aufhalten!; **12.** (fest)halten, bewachen: ~ **s.o.** (**a**) **prisoner** (od. **in prison**) j-n gefangen halten; ~ **s.o. for lunch** j-n zum Mittagessen dabehalten; **she** ~**s him here** sie hält ihn hier fest, er bleibt ihretwegen hier; ~ (**the**) **goal** sport das Tor hüten, im Tor stehen; **13.** aufhe-ben, (auf)halten: **I** ~ **all my old let-ters**; ~ **a secret** ein Geheimnis bewah-ren; ~ **for a later date** für später od. für e-n späteren Zeitpunkt aufheben; **14.** (aufrechter)halten, 'unterhalten: ~ **an eye on s.o.** j-n im Auge behalten; ~ **good relations with s.o.** zu j-m gute Beziehungen unterhalten; **15.** pflegen, (er)halten: ~ **in** (**good**) **repair** in gutem Zustand erhalten; **a well-kept garden** ein gut gepflegter Garten; **16.** e-e Ware führen, auf Lager haben: **we don't** ~ **this article**; **17.** Schriftstücke führen, halten: ~ **a diary**; ~ (**the**) **books** Buch führen; ~ **a record of s.th.** über (*acc.*) et. Buch führen od. Aufzeichnungen machen; **18.** ein Geschäft etc. führen, verwalten, vorstehen (*dat.*): ~ **a shop** ein (Laden)Geschäft führen od. betrei-ben; **19.** ein Amt etc. innehaben: ~ **a post**; **20.** Am. e-e Versammlung etc. (ab)halten: ~ **an assembly**; **21.** ein Versprechen etc. (ein)halten, einlösen: ~ **a promise**; ~ **an appointment** e-e Verabredung einhalten; **22.** das Bett, Haus, Zimmer hüten, bleiben in (*dat.*): ~ **one's bed** (**house, room**); **23.** Vor-schriften etc. be(ob)achten, (ein)halten, befolgen: ~ **the rules**; **24.** ein Fest bege-hen, feiern: ~ **Christmas**; **25.** ernäh-ren, er-, unter'halten, sorgen für: **have a family to** ~; **26.** (*bei sich*) haben, halten, beherbergen: ~ **boarders**; **27.** sich halten od. zulegen: ~ **a maid** ein Hausmädchen haben od. (sich) halten; **a kept woman** e-e Mätresse; ~ **a car** sich e-n Wagen halten, ein Auto haben; **28.** (be)schützen: **God** ~ **you!** **III** v/i. [*irr.*] **29.** bleiben: ~ **in bed**; ~ **at home**; ~ **in sight** in Sicht(weite) bleiben; ~ **out of danger** sich außer Gefahr halten; ~ (**to the**) **left** sich links halten, links fah-ren od. gehen; ~ **straight on** (immer) geradeaus gehen; → **clear** 6; **30.** sich halten, (in *e-m gewissen Zustand*) blei-ben: ~ **cool** kühl bleiben (a. fig.); ~ **quiet!** sei still!; ~ **to o.s.** für sich blei-ben, sich zurückhalten; ~ **friends** (wei-terhin) Freunde bleiben; ~ **in good health** gesund bleiben; **the milk** (**weather**) **will** ~ die Milch (das Wet-ter) wird sich halten; **the weather** ~**s fine** das Wetter bleibt schön; **that** (*matter*) *will* ~ F diese Sache hat Zeit *od.* eilt nicht; *how are you ~ing?* wie geht es dir?; **31.** *mit ger.* weiter...: ~ *going* a) weitergehen, b) weitermachen; ~ (*on*) *laughing* weiterlachen, nicht aufhören zu lachen, dauernd *od.* unaufhörlich lachen; ~ *smiling!* immer nur lächeln!, Kopf hoch!

Zssgn mit prp. u. adv.:

keep| a·head *v/i.* an der Spitze *od.* vorn(e) bleiben; ~ *of j-m* vorausbleiben; ~ **at** *v/i.* **1.** weitermachen mit: ~ *it!* bleib dran!, weiter so!; **2.** ~ *s.o.* j-n nicht in Ruhe lassen, j-m ständig zusetzen, j-n dauernd ‚bearbeiten‘; ~ **a·way** **I** *v/i.* wegbleiben, sich fern halten (*from* von); im Hintergrund bleiben; **II** *v/t.* fern halten (*from* von); ~ **back** **I** *v/t.* **1.** *allg.* zurückhalten: a) fern halten, b) *fig. Geld etc.* einbehalten, c) *et.* verschweigen (*from s.o.* j-m); **2.** *j-n, et.* aufhalten; *et.* verzögern; *Schüler* dabehalten; **II** *v/i.* **3.** im Hintergrund bleiben; ~ **down** **I** *v/t.* **1.** unten halten, *Kopf a.* ducken; **2.** *fig. Preise etc.* niedrig halten, be-, einschränken; **3.** *fig.* nicht aufod. hochkommen lassen, unter'drücken; **4.** *Essen etc.* bei sich behalten; *Schüler* (eine Klasse) wiederholen lassen; **II** *v/i.* **6.** unten bleiben; **7.** sich geduckt halten; ~ **from** **I** *v/t.* **1.** ab-, zu'rück-, fern halten von, hindern an (*dat.*), bewahren vor (*dat.*): *he kept me from work* er hielt mich von m-r Arbeit ab; *he kept me from danger* er bewahrte mich vor Gefahr; *I kept him from knowing too much* ich verhinderte, dass er zu viel erfuhr; **2.** vorenthalten, verschweigen: *you are keeping s.th. from me* du verschweigst mir et.; **II** *v/i.* **3.** sich fern halten von, sich enthalten (*gen.*), *et.* unterlassen *od.* nicht tun: *I couldn't* ~ *laughing* ich musste einfach lachen; ~ **in** **I** *v/t.* **1.** nicht außer Haus lassen, *bsd. Schüler* nachsitzen lassen; **2.** *Gefühle etc.* im Zaume halten; **3.** *Feuer* nicht ausgehen lassen; **4.** *Bauch* einziehen; **II** *v/i.* **5.** (dr)innen bleiben; **6.** anbleiben (*Feuer*); **7.** ~ *with* gut Freund bleiben mit, sich gut stellen mit; ~ **off** **I** *v/t.* fern halten (von); *die Hände* weglassen (von); **II** *v/i.* sich fern halten (von), *a. Getränk etc.* meiden: *if the rain keeps off* wenn es nicht regnet; ~ *the grass!* Betreten des Rasens verboten!; ~ **on** **I** *v/t.* **1.** *Kleider* anbehalten; *Hut* aufbehalten; **2.** *Angestellte etc.* behalten, weiterbeschäftigen; **II** *v/i.* **3.** *mit ger.* weiter...: ~ *doing s.th.* a) *et.* weiter tun, b) *et.* immer wieder tun, c) *et.* dauernd tun; → *keep* 31; **4.** ~ *at s.o.* an j-m her'umnörgeln, auf j-n ‚einhacken‘; **5.** weitergehen *od.* -fahren: *keep straight on!* immer geradeaus!; ~ **out** **I** *v/t.* **1.** nicht her'einlassen, abhalten: ~ *s.o.* (*the light etc.*); **2.** schützen *od.* bewahren vor (*dat.*), j-n *a.* her'aushalten aus (*e-r Sache*); **II** *v/i.* **3.** draußen bleiben, nicht her'einkommen, *Zimmer etc.* nicht betreten: ~*! a)* bleib draußen!, b) „Zutritt verboten“; **4.** ~ *of* sich her'aushalten aus, *et.* meiden: ~ *of debt* keine Schulden machen; ~ *of sight* sich nicht sehen lassen; ~ *of mischief!* mach keine Dummheiten!; *you* ~ *of this!* halten Sie sich da raus!; ~ **to I** *v/t.* **1.** *keep s.o. to his promise* j-n auf sein Versprechen festnageln; *keep s.th. to a minimum et.* auf ein Minimum beschränken; **2.** *keep o.s. to o.s.* für sich bleiben, Gesellschaft meiden; **II** *v/i.* **3.** festhalten an (*dat.*), bleiben bei: ~ *one's word*; ~ *the rules* an den

Regeln festhalten, die Vorschriften einhalten; ~ *the subject* (*od.* *point*) bleiben Sie beim Thema!; **4.** bleiben in (*dat.*) *od.* auf (*acc.*) *etc.*: ~ *one's bed* (*od.* *room*) im Bett (in s-m Zimmer) bleiben; ~ *the left!* halten Sie sich links!; ~ *o.s.* → 2; ~ **to·geth·er** **I** *v/t.* zu'sammenhalten; **II** *v/i.* a) zu'sammenbleiben, b) zu'sammenhalten (*Freunde etc.*); ~ **un·der** *v/t.* **1.** *j-n* unter'drücken, unten halten: *you won't keep him under* den kriegst du nicht klein; **2.** *j-n* unter Nar'kose halten; **3.** *Gefühle* unter'drücken, zügeln; **4.** *Feuer* unter Kon'trolle halten; ~ **up** **I** *v/t.* **1.** aufrecht (*a.* über Wasser) halten, hochhalten; **2.** *fig. Freundschaft, Moral etc.* aufrechterhalten, *Preise etc. a.* hoch halten, *et.* beibehalten, *Sitte etc.* weiterpflegen, *Tempo etc.* halten: ~ *a correspondence* in Briefwechsel bleiben; ~ *it up!* (nur) weiter so!; **3.** *Haus etc.* unter'halten, in'stand halten; **4.** *j-n am* Schlafen (-gehen) hindern; **II** *v/i.* **5.** andauern, -halten, nicht nachlassen; **6.** *lange etc.* aufbleiben: *we* ~ *late*; **7.** ~ *with* a) mit *j-m od. et.* Schritt halten, *fig. a.* mithalten (können), b) *j-m, e-r Sache* folgen können, c) sich auf dem Laufenden halten über (*acc.*), d) in Kon'takt bleiben mit *j-m*: ~ *with the times* mit der Zeit gehen; ~ *with the Joneses* den Nachbarn nicht nachstehen wollen.

keep·er ['kiːpə] *s.* **1.** Wächter(in), Aufseher(in) *m*, (Gefangenen-, Irren-, Tier-, Park-, Leuchtturm)Wärter(in) *m*, (Tier)Pfleger(in), Betreuer(in): *am I my brother's ~? bibl.* soll ich m-s Bruders Hüter sein?; **2.** Verwahrer *m*, Verwalter *m*: *Lord ⅃ of the Great Seal* Großsiegelbewahrer *m*; **3.** *mst in Zssgn:* a) Inhaber(in), Besitzer (-in): → *inn-keeper etc.*, b) Halter(in), Züchter(in): → *beekeeper*, c) j-d, der et. besorgt, betreut *od.* verteidigt: (*goal*) ~ *sport* Torwart *m*; **4.** ⊚ a) Schutzring *m*, b) Verschluss *m*, Schieber *m*, c) ⚷ Mag-'netanker *m*; **5.** *be a good* ~ sich gut halten (*Obst, Fisch etc.*); **6.** *sport abbr.* für *wicket*~.

keep-'fresh bag *s.* Frischhaltebeutel *m*.

keep·ing ['kiːpɪŋ] **I** *s.* **1.** Verwahrung *f*, Aufsicht *f*, Pflege *f*, (Ob)Hut *f*: *in safe* ~ in guter Obhut, sicher verwahrt; *have in one's* ~ in Verwahrung *od.* unter s-r Obhut haben; *put s.th. in s.o.'s* ~ j-m et. zur Aufbewahrung geben; **2.** 'Unterhalt *m*; **3.** *be in* (*out of*) ~ *with* mit et. (nicht) in Einklang stehen *od.* (nicht) übereinstimmen, *e-r Sache* (nicht) entsprechen; *in* ~ *with the times* zeitgemäß; **4.** Gewahrsam *m*, Haft *f*; **II** *adj.* **5.** haltbar: ~ *apples* Winteräpfel.

keep·sake ['kiːpseɪk] *s.* Andenken *n* (*Geschenk etc.*): *as* (*od.* for) *a* ~ zum Andenken.

kef·ir ['kefɪə] *s.* Kefir *m* (*Getränk aus gegorener Milch*).

keg [keg] *s.* **1.** kleines Fass, Fässchen *n*; **2.** *Brit.* (Alu'minium)Behälter *m* für Bier: ~ (*beer*) Bier *n* vom Fass; **3.** *Am.* Gewichtseinheit für Nägel = 45,3 kg.

kelp [kelp] *s.* ⚘ **1.** ein Seetang *m*; **2.** Kelp *n*, Seetangasche *f*.

kel·pie ['kelpɪ] *s. Scot.* Nix *m*, Wassergeist *m* in Pferdegestalt.

kel·son ['kelsən] *s.* ⚓ Kielschwein *n*.

kel·vin ['kelvɪn] *s. phys.* Kelvin *n*: ~ *temperature* Kelvintemperatur *f*, thermody'namische Temperatur.

Kelt·ic ['keltɪk] → *Celtic*.

ken [ken] **I** *s.* **1.** Gesichtskreis *m*, *fig. a.* Hori'zont *m*: *that is beyond* (*od.* *outside*) *my* ~ das entzieht sich m-r Kenntnis; **2.** (Wissens)Gebiet *n*; **II** *v/t.* **3.** *bsd. Scot.* kennen, verstehen, wissen.

ken·nel ['kenl] **I** *s.* **1.** Hundehütte *f*; **2.** *pl. mst sg. konstr.* a) Hundezwinger *m*, b) Hunde-, Tierheim *n*; **3.** *a. fig.* Meute *f*, Pack *n* (*Hunde*); **4.** *fig.* ‚Loch‘ *n*, armselige Behausung; **II** *v/t.* **5.** in e-r Hundehütte *od.* in e-m (Hunde)Zwinger halten.

Ken·tuck·y Der·by [ken'tʌkɪ] *s. sport* das wichtigste amer. Pferderennen (*für Dreijährige*).

Ken·yan ['kenjən] **I** *adj.* keni'anisch; **II** *s.* Keni'aner(in).

kep·i ['keɪpiː] *s.* ✕ Käppi *n*.

kept [kept] **I** *pret. u. p.p. von keep*; **II** *adj.:* ~ *woman* Mä'tresse *f*; *she is a* ~ *woman a.* sie lässt sich aushalten.

kerb [kɜːb] *s.* **1.** Bord-, Randstein *m*, Bord-, Straßenkante *f*: ~ *drill* Verkehrserziehung *f* für Fußgänger; **2.** *on the* ~ ✝ im Freiverkehr; ~ *mar·ket* ✝ Freiverkehrsmarkt *m*, Nachbörse *f*: ~ *price* Freiverkehrskurs *m*; '~·*stone* → *kerb* 1: ~ *broker* Freiverkehrsmakler *m*.

ker·chief ['kɜːtʃɪf] *s.* Hals-, Kopftuch *n*.

ker·fuf·fle [kə'fʌfl] *s. Brit.* F **1.** Lärm *m*, Krach *m*; **2.** *a. fuss and* ~ ‚The'ater‘ *n*, ‚Gedöns‘ *n*.

ker·mess ['kɜːmɪs], '**ker·mis** [-mɪs] *s.* **1.** Kirmes *f*, Kirchweih *f*; **2.** *Am.* 'Wohltätigkeitsba,sar *m*.

ker·nel ['kɜːnl] *s.* **1.** (Nuss- *etc.*)Kern *m*; **2.** (Hafer-, Mais- *etc.*)Korn *n*; **3.** *fig.* Kern *m*, das Innerste, Wesen *n*; **4.** ⚙ (*Guss- etc.*)Kern *m*.

ker·o·sene, **ker·o·sine** ['kerəsiːn] *s.* 🜊 Kero'sin *n*.

kes·trel ['kestrəl] *s.* Turmfalke *m*.

ketch [ketʃ] *s.* ⚓ Ketsch *f* (*zweimastiger Segler*).

ketch·up ['ketʃəp] *s.* Ket(s)chup *m, n*.

ket·tle ['ketl] *s.* (*Koch*)Kessel *m*: *put the* ~ *on* (Tee- *etc.*)Wasser aufstellen; *a pretty* (*od. nice*) ~ *of fish* F e-e schöne Bescherung; '~·*drum s.* ♪ (Kessel)Pauke *f*; '~·*drum·mer s.* ♪ (Kessel)Pauker *m*.

key [kiː] **I** *s.* **1.** Schlüssel *m*: *false* ~ Nachschlüssel *m*, Dietrich *m*; *power of the* ~ R.C. Schlüsselgewalt *f*; *turn the* ~ abschließen; **2.** *fig.* Schlüssel *m*, Lösung *f* (*to zu*): *the* ~ *to a problem* (*riddle etc.*); *the* ~ *to success* der Schlüssel zum Erfolg; **3.** *fig.* Schlüssel *m*: a) *Buch mit Lösungen* b) Zeichenerklärung *f* (*auf e-r Landkarte etc.*), c) Übersetzung(sschlüssel *m*) *f*, d) Kode (-schlüssel) *m*; **4.** Kennwort *n*, Chiffre *f* (*in Inseraten etc.*); **5.** ♪ a) Taste *f*, b) Klappe *f* (*an Blasinstrumenten*), c) Tonart *f*: *major* (*minor*) ~ Dur *n* (Moll *n*); *in the* ~ *of C minor* in C-Moll; *sing off* ~ falsch singen; *in* ~ *with fig.* in Einklang mit, d) → *key signature*; **6.** *fig.* Ton(art *f*) *m*: *in a high* (*low*) ~ laut (leise); *all in the same* ~ alles im selben Ton(fall), monoton; *in a low* ~ a) *paint. phot.* matt (getönt), in matten Farben (gehalten), b) *fig.* ‚lahm‘, ‚müde‘; **7.** ⊚ a) Keil *m*, Splint *m*, Bolzen *m*, b) Schraubenschlüssel *m*, c) Taste *f* (*der Schreibmaschine etc.*); **8.** ⚷ a) Taste *f*, Druckknopf *m*, b) Taster *m*, 'Tastkon,takt *m*; **9.** *tel.* Taster *m*, Geber *m*; **10.** *typ.* Setz-, Schließkeil *m*; **11.** ⚠ Keil *m*, Schlussstein *m*; **12.** ✕ Schlüsselstellung *f*, Macht *f* (*to* über *acc.*); **II** *adj.* **13.** *fig.* Schlüssel...: ~ *position*

Schlüsselstellung f, -position f; **~ offi-cial** Beamter in e-r Schlüsselstellung; **III** v/t. **14.** a. ~ **in**, ~ **on** ver-, festkeilen; **15.** a) tel. tasten, geben, b) Computer etc.: tasten: ~ **in** eintasten, -geben; **16.** ♪ stimmen: ~ **the strings**; **17.** (**to**, **for**) anpassen (an acc.), abstimmen (auf acc.); **18.** fig.: ~ **up** a) j-n in nervöse Spannung versetzen, b) allg. et. stei-gern: **~ed up** (an)gespannt, überreizt, 'überdreht'; **19.** mit e-m Kennwort ver-sehen; '**~·board I** s. **1.** a) ♪ Klavia'tur f, Tasta'tur f (Klavier), 'Keyboard n, b) Manu'al n (Orgel): ~ **instruments**, **~s** pl. Tasteninstrumente, c) Computer: Tasta'tur f; **2.** Tasten pl., Tasta'tur f (Schreibmaschine etc.); **II** v/t. **3.** Com-puter etc.: eintasten, -geben; '**~·board-er** s. a) Texterfasser(in), Datentypist(in), b) Setzer(in) m; '**~·board·ing** s. Com-puter: Eingabe f; ~ **bu·gle** s. ♪ Klap-penhorn n; ~ **card** s. Schlüsselkarte f (zum Türöffnen); ~ **cur·ren·cy** s. ✝, pol. Leitwährung m; ~ **date** s. Stichtag m; ~ **fos·sil** s. geol. 'Leitfos,sil n; '**~·hole** s. **1.** Schlüsselloch n: ~ **report** fig. Bericht m mit intimen Einzelheiten; ~ **surgery** med. F Schlüssellochchirur-gie f, endoskopische Chirurgie; **2.** Am. F Basketball: Freiwurfraum m; ~ **in·dus·try** s. 'Schlüsselindu,strie f; ~ **in·ter·est rate** s. ✝, pol. Leitzins m; ~ **man**, a. '**~·man** [-mæn] s. [irr.] 'Schlüs-selfi,gur f, Mann m in e-r 'Schlüsselposi-ti,on; ~ **map** s. 'Übersichtskarte f; ~ **mon·ey** s. **1.** Provisi'on f; **2.** ('Miet-) Kauti,on f; '**~·move** s. Schach: Schlüs-selzug m; '**~·note** s. **1.** ♪ Grundton m; **2.** fig. Grundton m, -gedanke m, Leit-gedanke m, Hauptthema n; **3.** pol. Am. Par'teilinie f, -pro,gramm n: ~ **address** programmatische Rede; ~ **speaker** = **keynoter**; **II** v/t. **4.** pol. Am. a) e-e program'matische Rede halten auf (e-m Parteitag etc.), b) program'matisch ver-künden, c) als Grundgedanken enthal-ten; **5.** kennzeichnen; '**~·not·er** s. pol. Am. Hauptsprecher m, po'litischer Pro-'grammredner m; ~ **punch** s. ⊙ (Kar-ten-, Tasta'tur)Locher m; '**~·punch op·er·a·tor** s. Locher(in); ~ **ring** s. Schlüsselring m; ~ **sig·na·ture** s. ♪ Vorzeichen n od. pl.; '**~·stone** s. **1.** △ Schlussstein m; **2.** fig. Grundpfeiler m, Funda'ment n; '**~·stroke** s. Anschlag m; '**~·way** s. ⊙ Keilnut f; ~ **wit·ness** s. ⚖ Hauptzeuge m; '**~·word** s. Schlüs-sel-, Stichwort n.

kha·ki ['kɑːkɪ] **I** s. **1.** Khaki n; **2.** a) Khakistoff m, b) 'Khakiuni,form f; **II** adj. **3.** khaki, staubfarben.

khan¹ [kɑːn] → **caravansary**.

khan² [kɑːn] s. Khan m (orientalischer Fürstentitel); '**khan·ate** [-neɪt] s. Kha-'nat n (Land e-s Khans).

khe·dive [kɪ'diːv] s. Khe'dive m.

kib·butz [kɪ'buːts] pl. **kib'butz·im** [-tsɪm] s. Kib'buz m.

khi [kaɪ] s. ♣ Chi n (griech. Buchstabe).

kibe [kaɪb] s. ♣ offene Frostbeule.

kib·itz ['kɪbɪts] v/i. ,kiebitzen'; '**kib-itz·er** [-tsə] s. F **1.** Kiebitz m (Zuschauer, bsd. beim Kartenspiel); **2.** fig. Besserwisser m.

ki·bosh ['kaɪbɒʃ] s.: **put the ~ on** sl. et. ,ka'puttmachen' od. ,vermasseln'.

kick [kɪk] **I** s. **1.** (Fuß)Tritt m (a. fig.), Stoß m: **give** s.o. od. s.th. **a ~** → 9; **get the ~** ,(raus)fliegen' (entlassen werden): **what he needs is a ~ in the pants** er braucht mal e-n kräftigen Tritt in den Hintern; **2.** Rückstoß m (Schusswaffe); **3.** Fußball: Schuss m; **4.** Schwimmen:

Beinschlag m; **5.** F (Stoß)Kraft f, Ener-'gie f, E'lan m: **give a ~ to** et. in Schwung bringen, e-r Sache ,Pfiff' ver-leihen; **he has no ~ left** er hat keinen Schwung mehr; **a novel with a ~** ein Roman mit ,Pfiff'; **6.** F (Nerven)Kitzel m: **get a ~ out of s.th.** an et. mächtig Spaß haben; **just for ~s** nur zum Spaß; **7.** (berauschende) Wirkung: **this cock-tail has got a ~** der Cocktail ,hat es aber in sich'; **8.** Am. F a) Groll m, b) (Grund m zur) Beschwerde f; **II** v/t. **9.** (mit dem Fuß) stoßen od. treten, e-n Fußtritt versetzen (dat.): ~ **s.o.'s be-hind** j-m in den Hintern treten; ~ **s.o. downstairs** j-n die Treppe hinunter-werfen; ~ **upstairs** fig. j-n durch Beför-derung kaltstellen; **I felt like ~ing my-self** ich hätte mich ohrfeigen können; **10.** sport a) Ball treten, kicken, b) Tor, Freistoß etc. schießen: ~ **a goal**; **11.** sl. ,runterkommen' von (e-m Rauschgift, e-r Gewohnheit); **III** v/i. **12.** (mit dem Fuß) stoßen od. treten: ~ **at** treten nach; **13.** um sich treten; **14.** strampeln (bsd. Baby); **15.** das Bein hochwerfen (Tänzer); **16.** ausschlagen (Pferd); **17.** zu'rückstoßen, -prallen (Schusswaffe); **18.** mot. ,stottern'; **19.** F a) ,meutern', sich mit Händen u. Füßen wehren, (**against**, **at** gegen), b) ,meckern', nör-geln (**about** über acc.); **20.** → **kick off** 3; ~ **a·bout** od. ~ **a·round I** v/t. **1.** Ball he'rumkicken; **2.** F j-n he'rumstoßen, schikanieren; **3.** F a) Idee etc. ,be-schwatzen', diskutieren, b) ,spielen' od. sich befassen mit; **II** v/i. **4.** F he-'rumreisen; **5.** F ,rumliegen' (Sache); ~ **in I** v/t. **1.** Tür etc. eintreten; **2.** sl. beisteuern; **II** v/i. **3.** sl. beisteuern; ~ **off I** v/i. **1.** Fußball: anstoßen, den An-stoß ausführen; **2.** F loslegen (**with** mit); **3.** Am. sl. ,abkratzen' (sterben); **II** v/t. **4.** wegschleudern; **5.** F et. star-ten, in Gang setzen; ~ **out** v/t. **1.** Fuß-ball: ins Aus schießen; **2.** sl. ,raus-schmeißen'; ~ **up** v/t. hochschleudern, Staub aufwirbeln; → **heel¹** Redew., **row³** I.

'**kick·back** s. **1.** F heftige Reakti'on; **2.** Am. sl. a) allg. Provisi'on f, Anteil m, b) (geheime) Rückvergütung f, c) Schmiergeld n.

'**kick·down** s. mot. Kickdown m (Durchtreten des Gaspedals).

kick·er ['kɪkə] s. **1.** (Aus)Schläger m (Pferd); **2.** Brit. a) Kicker m, Fußball-spieler m, b) Rugby: Kicker m (Spezia-list für Frei- und Strafstöße); **3.** ,Mecke-rer' m, Queru'lant(in).

'**kick·off** s. **1.** Fußball: Anstoß m; **2.** F Start m, Anfang m; '**~·start** v/t. mot. anlassen; '**~·start·er** s. mot. Kickstar-ter m, Tretanlasser m; ~ **turn** s. Ski-sport: Spitzkehre f.

kid¹ [kɪd] **I** s. **1.** zo. Zicklein n, Kitz(e f) n; **2.** a. **leather** Ziegen-, Gla'ceeleder n; → **kid glove**; **3.** F a) ,Kleine(r⁶ m) f, Kind n, Junge m, Mädchen n: **my ~ brother** mein kleiner Bruder; **that's ~ stuff!** das ist was für (kleine) Kinder!, b) Kid n (Jugendlicher); **II** v/i. **4.** zi-ckeln.

kid² [kɪd] F **I** v/t. j-n a) ,verkohlen', b) ,aufziehen', ,auf den Arm nehmen': **don't ~ me** erzähl mir doch keine Mär-chen; **don't ~ yourself** mach dir doch nichts vor; **II** v/i. a) albern, Jux ma-chen, b) schwindeln: **he was only ~ding** er hat (ja) nur Spaß gemacht; **no ~ding!** im Ernst!, ehrlich!; **you are ~ding!** das sagst du doch nur so!

kid·dy ['kɪdɪ] → **kid¹** 3.

kid| glove s. Gla'ceehandschuh m (a. fig.): **handle with ~s** fig. mit Samt- od. Glaceehandschuhen anfassen; '**~-glove** adj. fig. **1.** anspruchsvoll, wählerisch; **2.** sanft, diplo'matisch.

kid·nap ['kɪdnæp] v/t. kidnappen, ent-führen; '**kid·nap·(p)er** [-pə] s. Kidnap-per(in), Entführer(in); '**kid·nap·(p)ing** [-pɪŋ] s. Kidnapping n, Entführung f, Menschenraub m.

kid·ney ['kɪdnɪ] s. **1.** anat. Niere f (a. als Speise); **2.** fig. Art f, Schlag m, Sorte f: **a man of the same ~** ein Mann vom gleichen Schlag; ~ **bean** s. ♣ Weiße Bohne; ~ **ma·chine** s. ☣ künstliche Niere; '**~-shaped** adj. nierenförmig; ~ **stone** s. ☣ Nierenstein m.

kill [kɪl] **I** v/t. **1.** (o.s. sich) töten, 'um-bringen; ~ **off** abschlachten, ausrotten, vertilgen, beseitigen, ,abmurksen'; **two birds with one stone** fig. zwei Fliegen mit e-r Klappe schlagen; **be ~ed** getötet werden, ums Leben kom-men, umkommen, sterben; **be ~ed in action** ✕ (im Krieg od. im Kampf) fallen; **2.** Tiere schlachten; **3.** hunt. er-legen, schießen; **4.** ✕ abschießen, zer-stören, vernichten, Schiff versenken; **5.** töten, j-s Tod verursachen: **his reck-less driving will ~ him one day** sein leichtsinniges Fahren wird ihn noch das Leben kosten; **the job** (etc.) **is ~ing me** die Arbeit (etc.) bringt mich (noch) um; **the sight nearly ~ed me** der Anblick war zum Totlachen; **6.** a) zu'grunde richten, ruinieren, ka'puttmachen, b) Knospen etc. vernichten, zerstören; **7.** fig. wider'rufen, ungültig machen, strei-chen; **8.** fig. Gefühle (ab)töten, ersti-cken; **9.** Schmerzen stillen; **10.** unwirk-sam machen, Wirkung etc. aufheben, Farben übertönen, ,erschlagen'; **11.** Geräusche schlucken; **12.** fig. ein Ge-setz etc. zu Fall bringen, e-n Plan durch-'kreuzen; **13.** durch Kri'tik vernichten; **14.** sport den Ball töten; **15.** Zeit tot-schlagen: ~ **time**; **16.** a) e-e Maschine etc. abstellen, abschalten, den Motor a. ,abwürgen', b) Lichter ausschalten; **17.** F a) e-e Flasche etc. austrinken, b) e-e Zigarette ausdrücken; **II** v/i. **18.** töten: a) den Tod verursachen od. her'beifüh-ren, b) morden; **19.** F unwider'stehlich od. hinreißend sein, e-n tollen Ein-druck machen: **dressed to ~** todschick gekleidet, contp. aufgedonnert; **III** s. **20.** bsd. hunt. a) Tötung f (des Wildes), Abschuss m, b) erlegtes Wild, Strecke f: **be in at the ~** bei der Schluss dabei sein; **21.** a) ✕ Zerstörung f, b) ✈ Ab-schuss m, c) ⚓ Versenkung f.

kill·er ['kɪlə] s. **1.** Mörder m, Killer m; **2.** a. fig. Schlächter m; **3.** 'tödliche Krank-heit etc.; et., das e-n umbringt; **4.** bsd. in Zssgn Vertilgungsmittel n; **5.** Am. F a) schicke od. ,tolle' Frau, b) ,toller' Bursche, c) ,tolle' Sache, d) mörderi-scher Schlag; ~ **bee** s. 'Killerbiene f; ~ **in·stinct** s. 'Killerins,tinkt m; ~ **whale** s. zo. Schwertwal m.

kill·ing ['kɪlɪŋ] **I** s. **1.** a) Tötung f, Mor-den n, b) Mord(fall) m: **three more ~s in London**; **2.** Schlachten n; **3.** hunt. Erlegen n; **4.** make a ~ e-n Riesenge-winn machen; **II** adj. □ **5.** tödlich, ver-nichtend, mörderisch (a. fig.): **a glance** ein vernichtender Blick; **a pace** ein mörderisches Tempo; **6.** a. **~ly funny** F urkomisch, zum Brüllen.

'**kill·joy** s. Spielverderber(in), Stören-fried m, Miesmacher(in); '**~-time** adj. zum Zeitvertreib getan etc.

kiln [kɪln] s. Brenn-, Trocken-, Röst-,

Darrofen *m*, Darre *f*; '**~-dry** *v/t.* (*im Ofen*) dörren, darren, brennen, rösten.
ki·lo ['ki:ləʊ] *s.* Kilo *n.*
kil·o|·byte ['kɪləʊbaɪt] *s. Computer:* 'Kilobyte *n*; '**~·gram(me)** ['kɪləʊgræm] *s.* Kilo'gramm *n*, Kilo *n*; **~·gram·me·ter** *Am.*, **~·gram·me·tre** *Brit.* [,kɪləʊgræm'mi:tə] *s.* 'Meterkilo,gramm *n*; **~·hertz** ['kɪləʊhɜːts] *s.* ♩ Kilo'hertz *n*; **~·li·ter** *Am.*, **~·li·tre** *Brit.* ['kɪləʊ,li:tə] *s.* Kilo'liter *m*, *n*; **~·me·ter** *Am.*, **~·me·tre** *Brit.* ['kɪləʊ,mi:tə] *s.* Kilo'meter *m*; **~·met·ric**, **~·met·ri·cal** [,kɪləʊ'metrɪk(l)] *adj.* kilo'metrisch; **~·ton** ['kɪləʊtʌn] *s.* **1.** 1000 Tonnen *pl.*; **2.** *phys. Sprengkraft, die 1000 Tonnen TNT entspricht*; **~·volt** ['kɪləʊvəʊlt] *s.* ♩ Kilo'volt *n*; **~·watt** ['kɪləʊwɒt] *s.* ♩ Kilo'watt *n*: **~ hour** Kilowattstunde *f*.
kilt [kɪlt] **I** *s.* **1.** Kilt *m*, Schottenrock *m*; **II** *v/t.* **2.** aufschürzen; **3.** fälteln, plissieren; '**kilt·ed** [-tɪd] *adj.* mit e-m Kilt (bekleidet).
ki·mo·no [kɪ'məʊnəʊ] *pl.* **-nos** *s.* Kimono *m.*
kin [kɪn] **I** *s.* **1.** Fa'milie *f*, Sippe *f*; **2.** *coll. pl. konstr.* (Bluts)Verwandtschaft *f*, Verwandte *pl.*; → **kith**, **next** 1; **II** *adj.* **3.** (**to**) verwandt (mit), ähnlich (*dat.*).
kind¹ [kaɪnd] *s.* **1.** Art *f*: a) Typ *m*, Gattung *f*, b) Sorte *f*, c) Beschaffenheit *f*: *all* **~***s of* alle möglichen ..., alle Arten von; *all of a ~* (*with*) von der gleichen Art (wie); *the only one of its ~* das Einzige s-r Art; *two of a ~* zwei von derselben Sorte; *what ~ of ...?* was für ein ...?; *nothing of the ~* a) keineswegs, b) nichts dergleichen; *you'll do nothing of the ~* a. das wirst du schön bleiben lassen; *these ~* (*of people*) F diese Art Menschen; *he is not that ~ of person* F er ist nicht so (einer); *your ~* Leute wie Sie; *I know your ~* Ihre Sorte *od.* Ihren Typ kenne ich; *s.th. of the ~* etwas Derartiges, so etwas; *that ~ of* (*a*) *book* so ein Buch; *I haven't got that ~ of money* F so viel Geld hab ich nicht; *he felt a ~ of compunction* er empfand so etwas wie Reue; *I ~ of expected it* F ich hatte es halb *od.* irgendwie erwartet; *I ~ of promised it* F ich habe es so halb u. halb versprochen; *he is ~ of funny* F er ist etwas *od.* ein bisschen komisch; *I was a ~ of disappointed* F ich war schon ein bisschen enttäuscht; *I had ~ of thought that ...* F ich hatte eigentlich *od.* fast gedacht, dass; *that's not my ~ of film* F solche Filme sind nicht mein Fall; **2.** Natu'ralien *pl.*, Waren *pl.*: *pay in* **~**; *I shall pay him in* **~** *a. fig.* dem werd ich es in gleicher Münze zurückzahlen; **3.** *eccl.* Gestalt *f* (*von Brot u. Wein beim Abendmahl*).
kind² [kaɪnd] *adj.* □ → **kindly** II; **1.** gütig, freundlich, liebenswürdig, nett, lieb, gut (**to s.o.** zu j-m): *be so ~ as to* (*inf.*) seien Sie bitte so gut *od.* freundlich, zu (*inf.*); *would you be ~ enough to* wären Sie (vielleicht) so nett *od.* gut, zu *inf.*; *that was very ~ of you* das war wirklich nett *od.* lieb von dir; **2.** gutartig, fromm (*Pferd*).
kin·der·gar·ten ['kɪndə,gɑːtn] *s.* a) Kindergarten *m*, b) Vorschule *f.*
kind·heart·ed [,kaɪnd'hɑːtɪd] *adj.* gütig, gutherzig; ,**kind'heart·ed·ness** [-nɪs] *s.* (Herzens)Güte *f.*
kin·dle ['kɪndl] **I** *v/t.* **1.** an-, entzünden; **2.** *fig.* entflammen, -zünden, -fachen, *Interesse etc.* wecken; **3.** erleuchten; **II** *v/i.* **4.** a. *fig.* Feuer fangen, aufflammen; **5.** *fig.* (*at*) a) sich erregen (über

acc.), b) sich begeistern (für).
kind·li·ness ['kaɪndlɪnɪs] → **kindness**.
kin·dling ['kɪndlɪŋ] *s.* Anmach-, Anzündholz *n.*
kind·ly ['kaɪndlɪ] **I** *adj.* **1.** → **kind²**; **II** *adv.* **2.** gütig, freundlich; **3.** F freundlicherweise, liebenswürdig(erweise), gütig(st), freundlich(st): **~ tell me** sagen Sie mir bitte; **take ~ to** sich befreunden mit, sich hingezogen fühlen zu, lieb gewinnen; *he didn't take ~ to that* das hat ihm gar nicht gefallen, das passte ihm gar nicht; *will you ~ shut up!* *iro.* willst du gefälligst den Mund halten!; '**kind·ness** [-dnɪs] *s.* **1.** Güte *f*, Freundlichkeit *f*, Liebenswürdigkeit *f*: *out of the ~ of one's heart* aus reiner (Herzens)Güte; *please, have the ~ to* bitte, seien Sie so freundlich, zu *inf.*; **2.** Gefälligkeit *f*: *do s.o. a ~* j-m e-n Gefallen tun.
kin·dred ['kɪndrɪd] **I** *s.* **1.** (Bluts)Verwandtschaft *f*; **2.** *coll. pl. konstr.* Verwandte *pl.*, Verwandtschaft *f*, Fa'milie *f*; **II** *adj.* **3.** (bluts)verwandt; **4.** *fig.* verwandt, ähnlich, gleichartig: **~ languages**; **~ spirit** Gleichgesinnte(r *m*) *f*; *he and I are ~ spirits* er u. ich sind geistesverwandt *od.* verwandte Seelen.
kin·e·mat·ic, **kin·e·mat·i·cal** [,kɪnɪ'mætɪk(l)] *adj. phys.* kine'matisch; ,**kin·e'mat·ics** [-ks] *s. pl. sg. konstr. phys.* Kine'matik *f*, Bewegungslehre *f.*
ki·net·ic [kaɪ'netɪk] *adj. phys.* ki'netisch: **~ energy**; **ki'net·ics** [-ks] *s. pl. sg. konstr. phys.* Ki'netik *f*, Bewegungslehre *f.*
king [kɪŋ] **I** *s.* **1.** König *m*: **~ of beasts** König der Tiere (*Löwe*); → **King's Counsel** *etc.*; **2.** a) ♘ *of* ♘*s eccl. der* König der Könige (*Gott, Christus*), b) (**Book of**) ♘*s bibl.* (*das* Buch der) Könige *pl.*; **3.** a) *Kartenspiel, Schach:* König *m*, b) *Damespiel:* Dame *f*; **4.** *fig.* König *m*, Ma'gnat *m*: *oil ~*; **II** *v/i.* **5.** *~ it* König sein, den König spielen, herrschen (**over** über *acc.*).
king·dom ['kɪŋdəm] *s.* **1.** Königreich *n*; **2.** a. ♘ *of heaven* Himmelreich *n*, das Reich Gottes; *send s.o. to ~ come* F j-n ins Jenseits befördern; *till ~ come* F bis in alle Ewigkeit; **3.** *fig.* (Na'tur-) Reich *n*: *animal* (*vegetable, mineral*) **~** Tier- (Pflanzen-, Mineral)reich *n.*
'**king|,fish·er** *s. orn.* Eisvogel *m*; ♘ **James Bi·ble** *od.* **Ver·sion** *s.* autorisierte englische Bibelübersetzung *f.*
king·let ['kɪŋlɪt] *s.* unbedeutender König, Duo'dezfürst *m.*
'**king·ly** [-lɪ] *adj. u. adv.* königlich, majestätisch.
'**king|,mak·er** *s. bsd. fig.* Königsmacher *m*; '**~·pin** *s.* **1.** ⚙ Achsschenkelbolzen *m*; **2.** *Kegelspiel:* König *m*; **3.** F a) *der* ,Hauptmacher', *der* wichtigste Mann, b) *die* Hauptsache, *der* Dreh- u. Angelpunkt; **~ prawn** *s.* 'Hummerkrabbe *f*; ♘**'s Bench** (**Di·vi·sion**) *s.* ⚖ *Brit.* Abteilung des **High Court of Justice**, zuständig für a) *Zivilsachen* (*Obligations- und Deliktsrecht, Handels-, Steuer- u. Seesachen*), b) *Strafsachen* (*als oberste Instanz für summary offences*); ♘**'s Coun·sel** *s.* ⚖ *Brit.* Anwalt *m* der Krone; ♘**'s Eng·lish** → **English** 3; **~'s ev·i·dence** → **evidence** 1.
king·ship ['kɪŋʃɪp] *s.* Königtum *n.*
'**king-size(d)** *adj.* 'über,durchschnittlich groß, Riesen..., *fig.* F a. Mords...: **~ cigarettes** King-Size-Zigaretten.
King's Speech *s. Brit.* Thronrede *f.*
kink [kɪŋk] **I** *s.* **1.** *bsd.* ⚓ Kink *f*, Knick *m*, Schleife *f* (*Draht, Tau*); **2.** (Muskel-)

Zerrung *f od.* (-)Krampf *m*; **3.** *fig.* a) Schrulle *f*, Tick *m*, b) ,Macke' *f*, De'fekt *m*; **4.** *Brit.* F Abartigkeit *f*; **II** *v/i.* **5.** e-e Kink *etc.* haben (→ 1); **III** *v/t.* **6.** knicken, knoten, verknäueln; '**kink·y** [-kɪ] *adj.* **1.** voller Kinken, verdreht (*Tau etc.*); **2.** wirr, kraus (*Haar*); **3.** F a) spleenig, ,irre', ausgefallen, ,verrückt', b) *Brit.* per'vers, abartig.
kins·folk ['kɪnzfəʊk] *s. pl.* Verwandtschaft *f*, (Bluts)Verwandte *pl.*
kin·ship ['kɪnʃɪp] *s.* **1.** (Bluts)Verwandtschaft *f*; **2.** *fig.* Verwandtschaft *f.*
kins|·man ['kɪnzmən] *s.* [*irr.*] (Bluts-)Verwandte(r) *m*, Angehörige(r) *m*; **~·wom·an** ['kɪnz,wʊmən] *s.* [*irr.*] (Bluts)Verwandte *f*, Angehörige *f.*
ki·osk ['ki:ɒsk] *s.* **1.** Kiosk *m*, Verkaufsstand *m*; **2.** *Brit.* Tele'fonzelle *f.*
kip [kɪp] *sl.* **I** *s.* **1.** Schläfchen *n*; **2.** ,Falle' *f*, ,Klappe' *f* (*Bett*); **II** *v/i.* **3.** a) ,pennen' (*schlafen*), b) *mst* **~ down** sich ,hinhauen'.
kip·per ['kɪpə] **I** *s.* **1.** Räucherhering *m*, Bückling *m*; **2.** Lachs *m* (*während der Laichzeit*); **II** *v/t.* **3.** Heringe einsalzen u. räuchern: **~ed herring** → 1.
Kir·ghiz ['kɜːgɪz] *s.* Kir'gise *m.*
kirk [kɜːk] *s. Scot.* Kirche *f.*
Kirsch [kɪəʃ] *s.* Kirsch(wasser *n*) *m.*
kiss [kɪs] **I** *s.* **1.** Kuss *m*: **~ of death** *fig.* Todesstoß *m*; **~ of life** Mund-zu-Mund-Beatmung *f*; **blow** (*od.* **throw**) **a ~ to s.o.** j-m e-e Kusshand zuwerfen; **2.** leichte Berührung (*zweier Billardbälle etc.*); **3.** *Am.* Bai'ser *n* (*Zuckergebäck*); **4.** Zuckerplätzchen *n*; **II** *v/t.* **5.** küssen: **~ away** Tränen fortküssen; **~ s.o. good night** j-m e-n Gutenachtkuss geben: **~ s.o. goodbye** j-m e-n Abschiedskuss geben; *you can ~ your money goodbye!* F dein Geld hast du gesehen!; **~ one's hand to s.o.** j-m e-e Kusshand zuwerfen; **~ s.o.'s hand** j-m die Hand küssen; → **book** 1, **rod** 2; **6.** *fig.* leicht berühren; **III** *v/i.* **7.** sich küssen: **~ and make up** sich mit e-m Kuss versöhnen; **8.** *fig.* sich leicht berühren; '**kiss·a·ble** *adj.* küssenswert; **kiss curl** *s. Brit.* Schmachtlocke *f*; '**kiss·er** [-sə] *s. sl.* ,Fresse' *f* (*Mund od. Gesicht*).
kiss·ing gate ['kɪsɪŋ] *s.* Schwinggatter *n* (*das immer nur eine Person durchlässt*).
'**kiss|-off** *s. Am. sl.* **1.** Ende *n* (*a. Tod*); **2.** ,Rausschmiss' *m*; '**~-proof** *adj.* kussecht, -fest.
kit [kɪt] **I** *s.* **1.** (Angel-, Reit- *etc.*) Ausrüstung *f*: *gym ~* Sportsachen *pl.*, -zeug *n*; **2.** ✕ a) Mon'tur *f*, b) Gepäck *n*; **3.** a) Arbeitsgerät *n*, Werkzeug(e *pl.*) *n*, b) Werkzeugkasten *m*, -tasche *f*, Flickzeug *n*, c) Baukasten *m*, d) Bastelsatz *m*, e) *allg.* Behälter *m*: **first-aid ~** Verbandskasten *m*; **4.** *Zeitungswesen:* Pressemappe *f*; **5.** F a) Kram *m*, Zeug *n*, ,Sachen' *pl.*, b) Sippe *f*, ,Blase': *the whole ~* (*and caboodle*) der ganze Kram *od.* der ganze ,Verein'; **II** *v/t.* **6.** **~ out** *od.* **up** ausstatten (**with** mit); '**~-bag** *s.* **1.** Reisetasche *f*; **2.** ✕ Kleider-, Seesack *m.*
kitch·en ['kɪtʃɪn] **I** *s.* Küche *f*; **II** *adj.* Küchen..., Haushalts...; **kitch·en·et(te)** [,kɪtʃɪ'net] *s.* Kleinküche *f*, Kochnische *f.*
kitch·en| foil *s.* Haushalts- *od.* Alufolie *f*; **~ gar·den** *s.* Gemüsegarten *m*; '**~-maid** *s.* Küchenmädchen *n*; **~ mid·den** *s.* vorgeschichtlicher (Küchen-) Abfallhaufen *m*; **~ po·lice** *s.* ✕ *Am.* Küchendienst *m*; **~ range** *s.* Küchen-, Kochherd *m*; **~ scales** *s. pl.* Küchenwaage *f*; **~ sink** *s.* Ausguss *m*, Spülstein

m, ‚Spüle' *f*: **everything but the ~** *humor.* alles, der ganze Krempel; **~ drama** *thea.* realistisches Sozialdrama; **~ environment** Kleineleutemilieu *n*; **'~ware** *s.* Küchengeschirr *n od.* -geräte *pl.*

kite [kaɪt] *s.* **1.** (Pa'pier-, Stoff)Drachen *m*: **fly a ~** a) e-n Drachen steigen lassen, b) *fig.* e-n Versuchsballon loslassen, c) → 3; **2.** *orn.* Gabelweihe *f*; **3.** ✝ F Gefälligkeits-, Kellerwechsel *m*: **fly a ~** Wechselreiterei betreiben; → 1; **4.** ✈ *sl.* ‚Kiste' *f*, ‚Mühle' *f* (*Flugzeug*); **~ bal·loon** *s.* ✕ 'Fessel-, 'Drachenbal,lon *m*; **'~-,fly·ing** *s.* **1.** Steigenlassen *n* e-s Drachens; **2.** *fig.* Loslassen *n* e-s Versuchsbal,lons, Sondieren *n*; **3.** ✝ F Wechselreite'rei *f*; **'2·mark** *TM s.* *Brit.* *offizielles rautenförmiges Gütezeichen der British Standards Institution, das die Übereinstimmung mit der betreffenden Norm attestiert.*

kith [kɪθ] *s.*: **~ and kin** (Bekannte u.) Verwandte *pl.*; **with ~ and kin** mit Kind u. Kegel.

kitsch [kɪtʃ] *s.* Kitsch *m*.

kit·ten ['kɪtn] I *s.* Kätzchen *n*, junge Katze: **have ~s** F ‚Zustände' kriegen; II *v/i.* Junge werfen (*Katze*); **'kit·ten·ish** [-nɪʃ] *adj.* **1.** wie ein Kätzchen (geartet); **2.** (kindlich) verspielt *od.* ausgelassen.

kit·ty¹ ['kɪtɪ] *s.* Mieze *f*, Kätzchen *n*.

kit·ty² ['kɪtɪ] *s.* **1.** *Kartenspiel:* (Spiel-)Kasse *f*; **2.** (gemeinsame) Kasse.

ki·wi ['kiːwiː] *s.* **1.** *orn.* Kiwi *m*; **2.** ♀ Kiwi *f*.

klax·on ['klæksn] *s.* (Auto)Hupe *f*.

Kleen·ex ['kliːneks] *TM s.* *Warenname für Papiertaschentücher etc.*, F Pa'piertaschentuch *n.*

klep·to·ma·ni·a [ˌkleptəʊ'meɪnjə] *s.* *psych.* Kleptoma'nie *f*; **ˌklep·to'ma·ni·ac** [-niæk] I Klepto'mane *m*, Klepto'manin *f*; II *adj.* klepto'manisch.

klieg light [kliːg] *s.* *Film:* Jupiterlampe *f.*

klutz [klʌts] *s.* *Am. sl.* ‚Trottel' *m.*

knack [næk] *s.* **1.** Trick *m*, Kniff *m*, ‚Dreh' *m*; **2.** Geschick(lichkeit *f*) *n*, Kunst *f*, Ta'lent *n*: **the ~ of writing** die Kunst des Schreibens; **have the ~ of s.th.** den Dreh von et. heraushaben, wissen, wie man et. macht; **I've lost the ~** ich krieg es nicht mehr hin.

knack·er ['nækə] *s.* **1.** *Brit.* Abdecker *m*, Schinder *m*; **2.** ‚Abbruchunter,nehmer *m*; **'knack·ered** *adj.* *Brit.* *sl.* (ganz) ‚ka'putt', ‚to'tal geschafft'.

knag [næg] *s.* Knorren *m*, Ast *m* (*im Holz*).

knap·sack ['næpsæk] *s.* **1.** ✕ Tor'nister *m*; **2.** Rucksack *m*, Ranzen *m.*

knave [neɪv] *s.* **1.** *obs.* Schurke *m*, Schuft *m*, Spitzbube *m*; **2.** *Kartenspiel:* Bube *m*, Unter *m*; **'knav·er·y** [-vərɪ] *s.* *obs.* **1.** Schurke'rei *f*; **2.** Gaune'rei *f*; **'knav·ish** [-vɪʃ] *adj.* □ *obs.* schurkisch.

knead [niːd] *v/t.* **1.** kneten; **2.** (durch-)kneten, massieren; **3.** *fig.* formen (*into* zu); **knead·ing trough** [-dɪŋ] *s.* Backtrog *m.*

knee [niː] I *s.* **1.** Knie *n*: **on one's** (**bended**) **~s** auf Knien, kniefällig; **bend** (*od.* **bow**) **the ~ to** niederknien vor (*dat.*); **bring s.o. to his ~s** j-n auf *od.* in die Knie zwingen; **go on one's ~s to** a) niederknien vor (*dat.*), b) *fig.* j-n kniefällig bitten; **2.** ☉ a) Knie(stück) *n*, Winkel *m*, b) Knie(rohr) *n*, (Rohr-)Krümmer *m*; II *v/t.* **3.** mit dem Knie stoßen; **4.** F *Hose an den Knien ausbeu-*

len; **~ bend**(·**ing**) *s.* Kniebeuge *f*; **~ breech·es** *s. pl.* Kniehose(n *pl.*) *f*; **'~·cap** *s.* **1.** *anat.* Kniescheibe *f*; **2.** Knieleder *n*, -schützer *m*; **ˌ~'deep** *adj.* knietief, bis an die Knie (reichend); **ˌ~-'high 1.** → **knee-deep**; **2.** kniehoch; **'~-hole desk** *s.* Schreibtisch *m* mit Öffnung für die Knie; **~ jerk** *s.* ✚ 'Knie(sehnen)re,flex *m*; **~ joint** *s. anat.*, ☉ Kniegelenk *n.*

kneel [niːl] *v/i.* [*irr.*] a. **~ down** (nieder)knien (**to** vor *dat.*).

'knee|-length *adj.* knielang: **~ skirt** kniefreier Rock; **~ pad** *s.* Knieschützer *m*; **'~·pan** → **kneecap** 1; **~ pipe** *s.* ☉ Knierohr *n*; **~ shot** *s.* *Film:* 'Halbto,tale *f.*

knell [nel] I *s.* **1.** Totenglocke *f*, Grabgeläute *n* (*a. fig.*): **sound the ~** → 3; **2.** *fig.* Vorbote *m*, Ankündigung *f*; II *v/i.* **3.** läuten; III *v/t.* **4.** (*bsd. durch Läuten*) a) bekannt geben, b) zs.-rufen.

knelt [nelt] *pret. u. p.p. von* **kneel.**

knew [njuː] *pret von* **know.**

Knick·er·bock·er ['nɪkəbɒkə] *s.* **1.** (*Spitzname für den*) New Yorker; **2.** **2s** *pl.* Knickerbocker *pl.* (*Hose*).

knick·ers ['nɪkəz] *s. pl.* *Brit.* (Damen-)Schlüpfer *m*: **get one's ~ in a twist** *humor.* sich ‚ins Hemd machen'; **~!** Quatsch!, ‚Mist'!

knick-knack ['nɪknæk] *s.* **1.** a) Nippsache *f*, b) billiger Schmuck; **2.** Spiele'rei *f*, Schnickschnack *m.*

knife [naɪf] I *pl.* **knives** [naɪvz] *s.* **1.** Messer *n* (*a.* ☉, ✚): **play a good ~ and fork** ein starker Esser sein; **before you can say "~"** ehe man sichs versieht; **have** (**got**) **one's ~ into s.o.** j-n ‚gefressen' haben, es auf j-n abgesehen haben; **war to the ~** Krieg bis aufs Messer; **be** (**go**) **under the ~** F unterm Messer (*des Chirurgen*) sein (unters Messer kommen); **turn the ~** (**in the wound**) *fig.* Salz in die Wunde streuen; **watch s.o. like a ~** F j-n scharf beobachten; II *v/t.* **2.** mit e-m Messer bearbeiten; **3.** a) einstechen auf (*acc.*), mit e-m Messer stechen, b) erstechen, erdolchen; **4.** *Am. sl. bsd. pol.* j-m in den Rücken fallen, j-n ‚abschießen'; **~ edge** *s.* **1.** (Messer)Schneide *f*: **on a ~** *fig.* sehr aufgeregt (*about* wegen); **be balanced on a ~** *fig.* auf des Messers Schneide stehen; **2.** ☉ Waageschneide *f*; **'~-edged** *adj.* messerscharf; **~ grind·er** *s.* **1.** Scheren-, Messerschleifer *m*; **2.** Schleifrad *n*, -stein *m*; **~ rest** *s.* Messerbänkchen *n.*

knif·ing ['naɪfɪŋ] *s.* **1.** *hist.* Ritter *m*, Edelmann *m*; **2.** *Brit.* Ritter *m* (*niederster, nicht erblicher Adelstitel; Anrede:* **Sir** *u. Vorname*); **3.** Ritter *m* e-s Ordens: **2 of the Bath** Ritter des Bathordens; **2 of the Garter** Ritter des Hosenbandordens; **~ of the pen** *humor.* Ritter der Feder (*Schriftsteller*); → **Hospital(l)er** 1; **4.** *fig.* Ritter *m*, Kava'lier *m*; **5.** *Schach:* Springer *m*, Pferd *n*; II *v/t.* a) zum Ritter schlagen, b) adeln, in den Ritterstand erheben; **'knight·age** [-tɪdʒ] *s.* **1.** *coll.* Ritterschaft *f*; **2.** Ritterstand *m od.* -würde; **3.** Ritterliste *f.*

knight|bach·e·lor *pl.* **~s bach·e·lor** *s.* Ritter *m* (*Mitglied des niedersten englischen Ritterordens*); **~ er·rant** *pl.* **ˌ~·'er·rant·s** *s.* **1.** fahrender Ritter; **2.** *fig.* ‚Don Qui'xote' *m*; **ˌ~·'er·rant·ry** *s.* **1.** fahrendes Rittertum; **2.** *fig.* a) Abenteuerlust *f*, unstetes Leben, b) Donquichotte'rie *f.*

knight·hood ['naɪthʊd] *s.* **1.** Rittertum

n, -würde *f*, -stand *m*: **receive a ~** in den Ritterstand erhoben werden; **2.** *coll.* Ritterschaft *f.*

knight·ly ['naɪtlɪ] *adj. u. adv.* ritterlich.

Knight Tem·plar → **Templar** 1 *u.* 2.

knit [nɪt] I *v/t.* [*irr.*] **1.** a) stricken, b) ☉ wirken: **~ two, purl two** zwei rechts, zwei links (stricken); **2.** *a.* **~ together** zs.-fügen, verbinden, verknüpfen, vereinigen (*alle a. fig.*); → **close-knit**, **well-knit**; **3.** **~ up** a) fest verbinden, b) ab-, beschließen; **4.** Stirn runzeln, Augenbrauen zs.-ziehen; II *v/i.* [*irr.*] **5.** a) stricken, b) ☉ wirken; **6.** *a.* **~ up** sich (eng) verbinden *od.* zs.-fügen (*a. fig.*), zs.-wachsen (*Knochen etc.*); III *s.* **7.** Strickart *f*; [-tɪd] *adj.* gestrickt, Strick..., Wirk...; **'knit·ter** [-tə] *s.* **1.** Stricker(in); **2.** ☉ 'Strick-, 'Wirkma,schine *f.*

knit·ting ['nɪtɪŋ] *s.* **1.** a) Stricken *n*, b) ☉ Wirken *n*; **2.** Strickzeug *n*, -arbeit *f*; **~ ma·chine** *s.* 'Strickma,schine *f*; **~ nee·dle** *s.* Stricknadel *f.*

'knit·wear *s.* Strick-, Wirkwaren *pl.*

knives [naɪvz] *pl. von* **knife.**

knob [nɒb] *s.* **1.** (runder) Griff, Knopf *m*, Knauf *m*: **with ~s on** *sl.* (na) und ob!, und wie!; **and the same to you with** (**brass**) **~s on!** *sl.* das kann man erst recht von dir behaupten!; **2.** Knorren *m*, Ast *m* (*im Holz*); **3.** Buckel *m*, Beule *f*, Höcker *m*; **4.** Stück(chen) *n* (*Zucker etc.*); **5.** △ Knauf *m*; **6.** *Am. sl.* ‚Birne' *f* (*Kopf*); **7.** *Brit.* V ‚Schwanz' *m* (*Penis*); **'knob·bly** [-blɪ] *adj.* ‚knubbelig': **~ knees** ‚Knubbelknie' *pl.*; **'knob·by** [-bɪ] *adj.* **1.** knorrig; **2.** knoten-, knopf-, knaufartig.

knock [nɒk] I *s.* **1.** Schlag *m*, Stoß *m*: **he has had** (*od.* **taken**) **a few ~s** *fig.* F er hat ein paar Nackenschläge eingesteckt; **take the ~** *sl.* ‚schwer bluten müssen'; **the table has had a few ~s** F der Tisch hat ein paar Schrammen abgekriegt; **2.** Klopfen *n*, Pochen *n*: **there is a ~** (**at the door**) es klopft; **I'll give you a ~ at six** *Brit.* F ich klopfe um sechs (an Ihre Tür) (*zum Wecken*); II *v/t.* **3.** schlagen, stoßen: **~ s.o. cold** → **knock out** 2; **~ the bottom out of s.th.**, **~ s.th. on the head** *fig.* F et. zunichte machen, *Pläne* über den Haufen werfen; **~ s.o. sideways** (*od.* **for a loop**) F j-n ‚glatt umhauen'; **~ one's head against** a) mit dem Kopf stoßen gegen, b) die Stirn bieten (*dat.*); **~ s.th. into s.o.** j-m et. einhämmern *od.* einbläuen; **~ spots off s.o.** (**s.th.**) F j-m (e-r Sache) haushoch überlegen sein; **4.** klopfen, schlagen; **5.** F her'untermachen, herziehen über (*acc.*), kritisieren: **don't ~ him** (**so hard**)! mach ihn nicht (allzu) schlecht!; **6.** F j-n ‚umhauen', ‚umwerfen, sprachlos machen'; III *v/i.* **7.** schlagen, klopfen, pochen (**at the door** an die Tür): **~ before entering!** bitte anklopfen!; **8.** stoßen, schlagen, prallen (**against**, **into** gegen *od.* an *acc.*); **9.** ☉ a) rattern, rütteln (*Maschine*), b) klopfen (*Motor*, *Brennstoff*);

Zssgn mit adv.:

knock| a·bout, *bsd. Am.* **~ a·round** I *v/t.* **1.** her'umstoßen (*a. fig.* schikanieren); **2.** verprügeln; **3.** übel zurichten; II *v/i.* **4.** F sich her'umtreiben (**with** mit); **5.** her'umziehen, ‚rumliegen' (*Sache*); **~ back** *v/t.* *Brit.* F **1.** *Whisky etc.*,hinter die Binde gießen', ‚kippen'; **2.** j-n et. kosten: **that has ~ed me back a few pounds**; **3.** *fig.* j-n ,'umhauen', 'umwerfen; **~ down** *v/t.* **1.** niederschlagen, zu Boden schlagen (*a.*

fig.); **2.** → **knock over** 2; **3.** *Haus* abreißen; **4.** ◎ zerlegen, ausein'andernehmen; **5.** ♯ a) *bei Auktionen:* (**to s.o.** j-m) *et.* zuschlagen, b) F mit *dem Preis* 'runtergehen', c) F *j-n* her'unterhandeln (**to** auf *acc.*); **~ off** I *v/t.* **1.** her'unter-, abschlagen, weghauen; **2.** F aufhören mit: **~ work** → 7; **knock it off!** *sl.* hör doch auf damit!; **3.** F a) *et.* rasch erledigen, b) *et.* 'hinhauen', aus dem Ärmel schütteln; **4.** ♯ *vom Preis* abziehen: *he knocked £10 off the bill* er hat £10 (von der Rechnung) nachgelassen; **5.** F a) *Brit.* 'klauen', stehlen, b) *Bank etc.* ausrauben, c) *j-n* 'umlegen' (*töten*), d) V *Mädchen* 'bumsen'; **7.** F Feierabend machen; **~ out** *v/t.* **1.** (her)'ausschlagen, -klopfen; **2.** *sport* a) *Boxen:* k.o. schlagen, niederschlagen, b) *Gegner* ausschalten; **3.** F *j-n* 'umhauen': a) verblüffen, b) erschöpfen, c) 'ins Land der Träume schicken' (*Droge etc.*); **4.** ✕ abschießen; **5.** F *Melodie* 'runterspielen, -hacken'; **~ o·ver** *v/t.* **1.** 'umwerfen (*a. fig.*), 'umstoßen; **2.** über'fahren; **~ to·geth·er** *v/t.* **1.** schnell zs.-bauen *od.* -basteln, *Essen etc.* rasch zu'rechtmachen; **2.** anein'ander stoßen: *knock people's heads together fig.* die Leute zur Vernunft bringen; **~ up** I *v/t.* **1.** (*durch Klopfen*) wecken; **2.** F *Essen etc.* rasch 'auf die Beine stellen' *od.* zu'rechtmachen; **3.** F *Haus etc.* rasch 'hinstellen'; **4.** *Brit.* F *Geld* 'machen' (*verdienen*); **5.** *j-n* 'fertig machen' *od.* 'schaffen' (*erschöpfen*); **6.** V *Am. e-r Frau* ein Kind machen, *e-e Frau* 'anbumsen'; II *v/i.* **7.** *Tennis etc.:* sich warm spielen *od.* einspielen.

'knock|·a·bout *adj.* **1.** *thea.* F Radau..., Klamauk...; **2.** Alltags..., strapa'zierfähig: **~ clothes**; **~ car** Gebrauchswagen *m*; **'~·down** I *adj.* **1.** niederschmetternd (*a. fig.*): **~ blow** a) Schlag *m*, der j-n umwirft, b) *Boxen:* Niederschlag *m*, c) *fig.* Nackenschlag *m*, schwerer Schlag; **2.** ◎ zerlegbar, zs.-legbar; **3.** ♯ äußerst, niedrigst: **~ price** Schleuderpreis *m*; II *s.* **4.** ♯ Preissenkung *f*; **5.** F zerlegbares Möbelstück *od.* Gerät; **6.** *give s.o. a ~ to s.o. Am.* F j-n j-m vorstellen.

knock·er ['nɒkə] *s.* **1.** (Tür)Klopfer *m*; **2.** *sl.* Nörgler *m*, Krittler *m*; **3.** *pl.* V 'Titten' *pl.*; **'knock·ing** ['nɒkɪŋ] *s.* **1.** Klopfen *n* (*a. mot.*); **2.** F Kri'tik *f* (*of* an *dat.*): *he has taken a bad ~* er wurde schwer in die Pfanne gehauen.

knock|·'kneed *adj.* x-beinig; **~ knees** *s. pl.* X-Beine *pl.*; **'~·out** I *s.* **1.** *Boxen:* Knock-out *m*, K. 'o. *m*, Niederschlag *m*; **2.** *fig.* vernichtende Niederlage, tödlicher Schlag, das 'Aus' (**for** für j-n); **3.** F großartige *od.* 'tolle' Sache *od.* Per'son: *she's a real ~* sie sieht toll aus; II *adj.* **4.** *Boxen:* K.-o.-...: **~ blow** K.-o.-Schlag *m*; **~ system** K.-o.-System *n*; **~ match** Ausscheidungskampf *m*; **5.** *fig.* vernichtend; **6.** *Am. sl.* Betäubungs...: **~ pill**; **'~·proof** *adj. mot.* klopffest; **~ rat·ing** *s. mot.* Ok'tanzahl *f*; **'~·up** *s. sport* Einspielen *n*.

knoll [nəʊl] *s.* Hügel *m*, Kuppe *f*.

knot [nɒt] I *s.* **1.** Knoten *m*: *tie s.o. (up) into ~s fig.* F j-n 'fertig machen'; *his stomach was in a ~* sein Magen krampfte sich zusammen; **2.** Schleife *f*, Schlinge *f*, ✕ *a.* Achselstück *n*; **3.** Knorren *m*, Ast *m* (*im Holz*); **4.** ♀ Knoten *m*, Knospe *f*, Auge *n*; **5.** ♣ Knoten *m*: a) Stich *m* (*im Tau*), b) Seemeile *f* (*1,853 km/h*); **6.** *fig.* Knoten *m*, Schwierigkeit *f*, Pro'blem *n*: *cut the ~*

den Knoten 'durchhauen; **7.** *fig.* Band *n der Ehe etc.*: *tie the ~* den Bund fürs Leben schließen; **8.** Knäuel *m, n*, Haufen *m* (*Menschen etc.*); **9.** ☞ (*Gichtetc.*)Knoten *m*; II *v/t.* **10.** (ver)knoten, (ver)knüpfen; **11.** *fig.* verwickeln, verwirren; III *v/i.* **12.** (e-n) Knoten bilden; **13.** *fig.* sich verwickeln; **'~·hole** *s.* Astloch *n*.

knot·ted ['nɒtɪd] *adj.* **1.** ver-, geknotet; **2.** → **'knot·ty** [-tɪ] *adj.* **1.** knorrig (*Holz*); **2.** knotig, *fig.* verzwickt, schwierig, kompliziert.

knout [naʊt] *s.* Knute *f*.

know [nəʊ] I *v/t.* [*irr.*] **1.** *allg.* wissen: *come to ~* erfahren, hören; *he ~s what to do* er weiß, was zu tun ist; *~ what's what*, *~ all about it* genau Bescheid wissen; (**and**) *don't I ~ it!* und ob ich das weiß!; *he wouldn't ~ (that)* er kann das nicht *od.* kaum wissen; *I wouldn't ~!* das kann ich leider nicht sagen!; *iro.* weiß ich doch nicht!; *for all I ~* a) soviel ich weiß, b) was weiß ich?; *I would have you ~ that* ich möchte betonen *od.* Ihnen klarmachen, dass; *I have never ~n him to lie* m-s Wissens hat er nie gelogen; *what do you ~!* na, so was!; **2.** (es) können *od.* verstehen (*how to do* zu tun): *do you ~ how to do it?* wissen Sie, wie man das macht?, können Sie das?; *he ~s how to treat children* er versteht mit Kindern umzugehen; *do you ~ how to drive a car?* können Sie Auto fahren?; *he ~s (some) German* er kann (etwas) Deutsch; **3.** kennen, vertraut sein mit: *I have ~n him for years* ich kenne ihn (schon) seit Jahren; *he ~s a thing or two* F 'er ist nicht von gestern', er weiß (ganz gut) Bescheid; *get to ~* a) j-n, *et.* kennen lernen, b) *et.* erfahren, herausfinden; *after I first knew him* nachdem ich s-e Bekanntschaft gemacht hatte; **4.** erfahren, erleben: *he has ~n better days* er hat bessere Tage gesehen; *I have ~n it to happen* ich habe das schon erlebt; → *known* II, *mind* 4; **5.** ('wieder)erkennen, unter'scheiden: *I should ~ him anywhere* ich würde ihn überall erkennen; *~ one from the other* e-n vom anderen unterscheiden (können), die beiden auseinander halten können; *before you ~ where you are* im Handumdrehen; *I don't ~ whether I shall ~ him again* ich weiß nicht, ob ich ihn wieder erkennen werde; **6.** *Bibl.* (*geschlechtlich*) erkennen; II *v/i.* [*irr.*] **7.** wissen (**of** von, um), im Bilde sein: *do you ~?* Bescheid wissen (**about** über *acc.*), sich auskennen (**about** in *dat.*), *et.* verstehen (**about** von); *I ~ of s.o. who* ich weiß *od.* kenne j-n, der; *let me ~ (about it)* lass es mich wissen, sag mir Bescheid (darüber); *I ~ better!* so dumm bin ich nicht!; *I ~ better than to say that* ich werde mich hüten, das zu sagen; *you ought to ~ better (than that)* das sollten Sie besser wissen, so dumm werden Sie doch nicht sein; *he ought to ~ better than to go swimming after a big meal* er sollte so viel Verstand haben zu wissen, dass man nach e-m reichlichen Mahl nicht baden geht; *they don't ~ any better* sie kennens nicht anders; *not that I ~ of* ich nicht dass ich wüsste; *do (od. don't) you ~?* F nicht wahr?; *you ~* (*oft unübersetzt*) a) weißt du, wissen Sie, b) nämlich, c) schon, na ja; III *s.* **8.** *be in the ~* Bescheid wissen, im Bilde *od.* eingeweiht sein.

know·a·ble ['nəʊəbl] *adj.* was man wis

sen kann.

'know|·(it-)all *s.* Besserwisser *m*, 'Klugscheißer' *m*; **'~·how** *s.* Know-'how *n*: a) Sachkenntnis *f*, Fachwissen *n*, (praktische, *bsd.* technische) Kenntnis(se *pl.*) *od.* Erfahrung, Fertigkeiten *pl.*, b) ◎ Herstellungsverfahren *pl.*

know·ing ['nəʊɪŋ] I *adj.* □ **1.** intelli'gent, geschickt; **2.** verständnisvoll, wissend: **~ smile**; **with a ~ hand** mit kundiger Hand; **3.** schlau, raffiniert: **a ~ one** ein Schlauberger; II *s.* **4.** Wissen *n*: **there is no ~** man kann nie wissen; **'know·ing·ly** [-lɪ] *adv.* **1.** schlau, klug; **2.** verständnisvoll, wissend; **3.** wissentlich, bewusst, absichtlich.

knowl·edge ['nɒlɪdʒ] *s. nur sg.* **1.** Kenntnis *f*, Wissen *n*: *have ~ of* Kenntnis haben von, wissen (*acc.*); *have no ~ of* nichts wissen von *od.* über (*acc.*); *without my ~* ohne mein Wissen; *the ~ of the victory* die Kunde *od.* Nachricht vom Siege; *it has come to my ~* es ist mir zu Ohren gekommen, ich habe erfahren; *to (the best of) my ~* m-s Wissens, soviel ich weiß; *to the best of my ~ and belief* nach bestem Wissen u. Gewissen; *not to my ~* nicht dass ich wüsste; *~ of life* Lebenserfahrung *f*; → *carnal*; **2.** Wissen *n*, Kenntnisse *pl.*: *a good ~ of German* gute Deutschkenntnisse; *my ~ of Dickens* was ich von Dickens kenne; **'knowl·edge·a·ble** [-dʒəbl] *adj.* kenntnisreich, (gut) unter'richtet: *he is very ~ about wines* er weiß gut Bescheid über Weine, er ist ein Weinkenner.

known [nəʊn] I *p.p. von* **know**; II *adj.* bekannt: **~ quantity** & bekannte Größe; **make ~** bekannt machen; **make o.s. ~ to s.o.** F sich j-m vorstellen; **~ to all** allbekannt; **the ~ facts** die anerkannten Tatsachen.

knuck·le ['nʌkl] I *s.* **1.** Fingergelenk *n*, -knöchel *m*: **a rap over the ~s** *fig.* ein Verweis, e-e Rüge; **2.** (Kalbs- *od.* Schweins)Haxe (*od.* Hachse) *f*: **near the ~** *fig.* F reichlich 'gewagt' (*Witz etc.*); II *v/i.* **3.** **~ down**, **~ under** sich beugen, sich unter'werfen (**to** *dat.*), klein beigeben; **4.** **~ down to s.th.** sich an *et.* 'ranmachen', sich hinter *et.* 'klemmen': **~ down to work** sich an die Arbeit machen; **'~·bone** *s. anat., zo.* Knöchelbein *n*; **'~·dust·er** *s.* Schlagring *m*; **~ joint** *s.* **1.** *anat.* Knöchel-, Fingergelenk *n*; **2.** ◎ Kar'dan-, Kreuzgelenk *n*.

knurl [nɜːl] I *s.* **1.** Knoten *m*, Ast *m*, Buckel *m*; **2.** ◎ Rändelrad *n*; II *v/t.* **3.** rändeln, kordeln: **~ed screw** Rändelschraube *f*.

KO [ˌkeɪ'əʊ] → **knockout** 1 *u.* **knock out**.

ko·a·la [kəʊ'ɑːlə] *s. zo.* Ko'ala(bär) *m*.

kohl·ra·bi [ˌkəʊl'rɑːbɪ] *s.* ♀ Kohl'rabi *m*.

kol·khoz, **kol·khos** [kɒl'hɔːz] *s.* Kolchos *m, n*, Kol'chose *f*.

kook [kuk] *s. Am.* F 'komischer Typ', 'Spinner' *m*; **kook·y** ['kukɪ] *adj. Am.* F 'irr', verrückt.

ko·pe(c)k ['kəʊpek] → **copeck**.

Ko·ran [kɒ'rɑːn] *s.* Ko'ran *m*.

Ko·re·an [kə'rɪən] I *s.* Kore'aner(in); II *adj.* kore'anisch.

ko·sher ['kəʊʃə] *adj.* koscher: **~ food**; **~ restaurant**; **not quite ~** *fig.* F nicht ganz koscher.

Kos·o·var ['kɒsəvɑː] I *adj.* koso'varisch, 'Kosovo...; II *s.* Koso'var(in).

ko·tow [ˌkəʊ'taʊ], **kow·tow** [ˌkaʊ'taʊ] I *s.* Ko'tau *m*, unter'würfige Ehrenbezeigung; II *v/i.* a. *fig.* e-n Ko'tau machen: **~ to s.o.** e-n Kotau machen (*fig. a.*

kriechen) vor j-m.

kraal [krɑːl; *in Südafrika mst* krɔːl] *s.* *S.Afr.* Kral *m.*

kraft [krɑːft], *a.* **~ pa·per** *s. Am.* braunes 'Packpa,pier.

kraut [kraʊt] *sl. contp.* **I** *s.* Deutsche(r *m*) *f*; **II** *adj.* deutsch.

Krem·lin ['kremlɪn] *npr.* Kreml *m*; **Krem·lin·ol·o·gist** [ˌkremlɪ'nɒlədʒɪst]

s. Sowjeto'loge *m*, Kremlforscher(in).

ku·dos ['kjuːdɒs] *s.* F Ruhm *m*, Ehre *f*.

Ku Klux Klan [ˌkjuːklʌks'klæn] *s. Am. pol.* 'Ku-Klux-'Klan *m* (*rassistischer amer. Geheimbund*).

ku·lak ['kuːlæk] (*Russ.*) *s.* Ku'lak *m*, Großbauer *m*.

kum·quat ['kʌmkwɒt] *s.* ♀ Kumquat *f*.

kung fu [ˌkʌŋ'fuː; ˌkʊŋ-] *s.* Kung'fu *n*

(*chines. Kampfsport*).

Kurd [kɜːd] *s.* Kurde *m*, Kurdin *f*; **'Kurd·ish** [-ɪʃ] *adj.* kurdisch.

kur·saal ['kʊəzɑːl] *s.* (*Ger.*) Kursaal *m*, -haus *n*.

Ku·wait·i [kʊ'weɪtɪ] *s.* **I** *adj.* ku'waitisch; **II** *s.* Ku'waiter(in).

Kyr·i·e ['kɪɔriːeɪ], **~ e·le·i·son** [ə'leɪsɒn] *s. eccl.* Kyrie (e'leison) *n*.

K

L, l [el] *s.* L *n*, l *n* (*Buchstabe*).
laa·ger ['lɑːɡə] *s. S.Afr.* Lager *n*, *bsd.* Wagenburg *f.*
lab [læb] *s.* F La'bor *n.*
la·bel ['leɪbl] **I** *s.* **1.** Eti'kett *n* (*a. fig.*), (Klebe-, Anhänge)Zettel *m od.* (-) Schild(chen) *n*, Anhänger *m*, Aufkleber *m*; **2.** *fig.* a) Bezeichnung *f*, b) (Kenn)Zeichen *n*, Signa'tur *f*; **3.** Aufschrift *f*, Beschriftung *f*; **4.** Label *n*, 'Schallplatteneti,kett *n od.* F -firma *f*; **5.** *Computer:* Label *n* (*Markierung in e-m Programm*); **6.** ⚙ Kranzleiste *f*; **II** *v/t.* **7.** etikettieren, mit e-m Zettel *od.* Schild(chen) versehen; **8.** beschriften, mit e-r Aufschrift versehen: ⁓(l)ed *"poison"* mit der Aufschrift „Gift"; **9.** *a.* ⁓ *as fig.* als ... bezeichnen, zu ... stempeln, abstempeln als; **'la·bel·(l)er** [-lə] *s.* Etiket'tierma,schine *f.*
la·bi·a ['leɪbɪə] *pl. von* **labium.**
la·bi·al ['leɪbjəl] **I** *adj. anat., ling.* Lippen..., labi'al; **II** *s.* Lippenlaut *m*, La·bi'al *m.*
la·bile ['leɪbaɪl] *adj. allg.* la'bil.
la·bi·o·den·tal [,leɪbɪəʊ'dentl] *ling.* **I** *adj.* labioden'tal; **II** *s.* Labioden'tal *m*, Lippenzahnlaut *m.*
la·bi·um ['leɪbɪəm] *pl.* **-bi·a** [-bɪə] *s. anat.* Labium *n*, (*bsd.* Scham)Lippe *f.*
la·bor *etc. Am.* → **labour** *etc.*
la·bor·a·to·ry [*Brit.* lə'brɒtərɪ; *Am.* 'læbrə,tɔːrɪ] *s.* **1.** Labora'torium *n*: ⁓ *assistant* Laborant(in); ⁓ *technician* Chemotechniker(in); ⁓ *stage* Versuchsstadium *n*; **2.** *fig.* Werkstätte *f.*
la·bo·ri·ous [lə'bɔːrɪəs] *adj.* □ mühsam: a) anstrengend, schwierig, b) 'umständlich, schwerfällig (*Stil etc.*).
la·bor un·ion *s. Am.* Gewerkschaft *f.*
la·bour ['leɪbə] *Brit.* **I** *s.* **1.** a) (*bsd.* schwere) Arbeit, b) Anstrengung *f*, Mühe *f*: ⁓ *of Hercules* Herkulesarbeit *f*; ⁓ *of love* Liebesdienst *m*, gern *od.* unentgeltlich getane Arbeit; → *hard labo(u)r*; **2.** a) Arbeiterschaft *f*, Arbeiter(klasse *f*) *pl.*, b) Arbeiter *pl.*, Arbeitskräfte *pl.*: *cheap* ⁓; *shortage of* ⁓ Arbeitskräftemangel *m*; → *skilled* 2; **3.** ⁓ (*ohne Artikel*) → *Labour Party*; **4.** ✶ Wehen *pl.*: *be in* ⁓ in den Wehen liegen; **II** *v/i.* **5.** arbeiten (*at an dat.*); **6.** sich anstrengen (*to inf.* zu *inf.*), sich abmühen (*at, with* mit; *for* um *acc.*); **7.** *a.* ⁓ *along* sich mühsam fortbewegen *od.* da'hinschleppen, sich (da'hin)quälen; **8.** stampfen, schlingern (*Schiff*); **9.** (*under*) zu leiden haben (unter *dat.*), zu kämpfen haben (mit *Schwierigkeiten etc.*), kranken (an *dat.*); → *delusion* 2; **10.** ✶ in den Wehen liegen; **III** *v/t.* **11.** ausführlich eingehen auf (*acc.*), eingehend behandeln, *iro.* ,breittreten', herumreiten auf (*dat.*): *I need not* ⁓ *the point*; ⁓ *camp s.* Arbeitslager *n*; ⁂ **Day** *s.* Tag *m* der Arbeit; ⁓ *costs s.* Arbeitskosten *pl.*; ⁓ *dis·pute s.* ✶ Arbeitskampf *m.*
la·bo(u)red ['leɪbəd] *adj.* **1.** → **labo-**

rious; **2.** → **labo(u)ring** 2; **'la·bo(u)r·er** [-ərə] *s.* (*bsd. ungelernter*) Arbeiter.
La·bour Ex·change *s. Brit. obs.* Arbeitsamt *n.*
la·bo(u)r force *s.* Arbeitskräfte *pl.*, Belegschaft *f* (*e-s Betriebs*).
la·bo(u)r·ing ['leɪbərɪŋ] *adj.* **1.** arbeitend, werktätig: *the* ⁓ *classes*; **2.** mühsam, schwer (*Atem*).
'la·bo(u)r·in,ten·sive *adj.* ✶ 'arbeitsinten,siv.
la·bour·ite ['leɪbəraɪt] *s. Brit.* Anhänger (-in) *od.* Mitglied *n* der *Labour Party.*
la·bo(u)r| lead·er *s.* Arbeiterführer *m*; ⁓ *mar·ket* *s.* Arbeitsmarkt *m*; ⁓ *pains* *s. pl.* ✶ Wehen *pl.*
La·bour Par·ty *s. Brit. pol.* die Labour Party.
la·bo(u)r| re·la·tions *s. pl.* Beziehungen *pl.* zwischen Arbeitgeber(n) u. Arbeitnehmern; '⁓-,sav·ing *adj.* arbeitssparend; ⁓ *short·age s.* Arbeitskräftemangel *m*; ⁓ *turn·o·ver s.* Personalfluktuation *f.*
Lab·ra·dor (dog) ['læbrədɔː] *s. zo.* Neu'fundländer *m* (*Hund*).
la·bur·num [lə'bɜːnəm] *s.* ♣ Goldregen *m.*
lab·y·rinth ['læbərɪnθ] *s.* **1.** Laby'rinth *n*, Irrgarten *m* (*beide a. fig.*); **2.** *fig.* Wirrwarr *m*, Durchein'ander *n*; **3.** *anat.* Laby'rinth *n*, inneres Ohr; **lab·y·rin·thine** [,læbə'rɪnθaɪn] *adj.* laby'rinthisch (*a. fig.*).
lac¹ [læk] *s.* Gummilack *m*, Lackharz *n.*
lac² [læk] *s. Brit. Ind.* Lak *n* (*100 000, mst Rupien*).
lace [leɪs] *s.* **1.** Spitze *f* (*Stoff*); **2.** Litze *f*, Borte *f*, Tresse *f*, Schnur *f*: *gold* ⁓; **3.** Schnürband *n*, -senkel *m*; → *laced* 1; **4.** Schnur *f*, Band *n*; **II** *v/t.* **5.** *a.* ⁓ *up* (zu-, zs.-)schnüren; **6.** *j-n*, *j-s* Taille schnüren; **7.** ⁓ *s.o.* F → 14; **8.** *Finger etc.* ineinander schlingen; **9.** mit Spitzen *od.* Litzen besetzen; Schnürsenkel einziehen in; **10.** mit Streifenmuster verzieren; **11.** *fig.* durch'setzen (*with* mit): *a story* ⁓*d with jokes*; **12.** e-n Schuss Alkohol zugeben (*dat.*); **III** *v/i.* **13.** *a.* ⁓ *up* sich schnüren (lassen); **14.** ⁓ *into* F a) auf *j-n* einprügeln, b) *j-n* anbrüllen; **laced** [-st] *adj.* **1.** geschnürt, Schnür...; **2.** mit e-m Schuss Alkohol, ,mit Schuss': ⁓ *coffee.*
lace| pa·per *s.* Pa'pierspitzen *pl.*; ⁓ *pil·low* *s.* Klöppelkissen *n.*
lac·er·ate ['læsəreɪt] *v/t.* **1.** a) aufreißen, -schlitzen, zerfetzen, -kratzen, b) zerfleischen, zerreißen; **2.** *fig. j-n*, *j-s* Gefühle zutiefst verletzen; **lac·er·a·tion** [,læsə'reɪʃn] *s.* **1.** Zerreißung *f*, Zerfleischung *f* (*a. fig.*); **2.** ✶ Schnitt-, Risswunde *f*, Riss *m.*
'lace|-up (shoe) *s.* Schnürschuh *m*; '⁓-work *s.* Spitzenarbeit *f*, -muster *n*; **2.** *weitS.* Fili'gran(muster) *n.*
lach·ry·mal ['lækrɪml] **I** *adj.* **1.** Tränen...: ⁓ *gland*; **II** *s.* **2.** *pl. anat.* 'Trä-

nenappa,rat *m*; **3.** *hist.* Tränenkrug *m*; **'lach·ry·mose** [-məʊs] *adj.* □ **1.** weinerlich; **2.** *fig.* rührselig: ⁓ *story.*
lac·ing ['leɪsɪŋ] *s.* **1.** Litzen *pl.*, Tressen *pl.*; **2.** → **lace** 3; **3.** ,Schuss' *m* (Alkohol); **4.** Tracht *f* Prügel.
lack [læk] **I** *s.* (*of*) Mangel *m* (an *dat.*), Fehlen *n* (von): *for* ⁓ *of time* aus Zeitmangel; *there was no* ⁓ *of* es fehlte nicht *od.* da war kein Mangel an (*dat.*); **II** *v/t.* Mangel haben an (*dat.*), *et.* nicht haben *od.* besitzen: *he* ⁓*s time* ihm fehlt es an (der nötigen) Zeit, er hat keine Zeit; **III** *v/i.*: *be* ⁓*ing* fehlen, nicht vorhanden sein; *wine was not* ⁓*ing* an Wein fehlte es nicht; *he* ⁓*ed for nothing* es fehlte ihm an nichts; *be* ⁓*ing in* → II.
lack·a·dai·si·cal [,lækə'deɪzɪkl] *adj.* □ **1.** lustlos, gelangweilt, gleichgültig; **2.** schlaff, lasch.
lack·ey ['lækɪ] *s. bsd. fig. contp.* La'kai *m.*
'lack|,lus·ter *Am.*, '⁓,lus·tre *Brit. adj.* glanzlos, matt, *fig. a.* farblos.
la·con·ic [lə'kɒnɪk] *adj.* (□ ⁓*ally*) **1.** la'konisch, kurz u. treffend; **2.** wortkarg; **lac·o·nism** ['lækənɪzəm] *s.* Lako'nismus *m*: a) La'konik *f*, la'konische Kürze, b) la'konischer Ausspruch.
lac·quer ['lækə] **I** *s.* **1.** (Farb)Lack *m*, (Lack)Firnis *m*; **2.** a) (Nagel)Lack *m*, b) Haarspray *m*; **3.** *a.* ⁓*ware* Lackarbeit *f*, -waren *pl.*; **II** *v/t.* **4.** lackieren.
la·crosse [lə'krɒs] *s.* La'crosse *n* (*Ballspiel*): ⁓ *stick* La'crosseschläger *m.*
lac·tate ['lækteɪt] **I** *v/t. physiol.* Milch absondern; **II** *s.* 🜋 Lak'tat *n*; **lac·ta·tion** [læk'teɪʃn] *s.* Laktati'on *f*: a) Milchabsonderung *f*, b) Stillen *n*, c) Stillzeit *f*; **'lac·te·al** [-tɪəl] **I** *adj.* Milch..., milchähnlich; **II** *s. pl.* Milch-, Lymphgefäße *pl.*; **'lac·tic** [-tɪk] *adj.* Milch...: ⁓ *acid* Milchsäure *f*; **lac·tifer·ous** [læk'tɪfərəs] *adj.* Milch führend: ⁓ *duct* Milchgang *m*; **lac·tom·e·ter** [læk'tɒmɪtə] *s.* Lakto'meter *n*, Milchwaage *f*; **'lac·tose** [-təʊs] *s.* Lak'tose *f*, Milchzucker *m.*
la·cu·na [lə'kjuːnə] *pl.* **-nae** [-niː] *od.* **-nas** *s.* Lücke *f*, La'kune *f*: a) *anat.* Spalt *m*, Hohlraum *m*, b) (Text- *etc.*) Lücke *f*; **la'cu·nar** [-nə] *s.* ⚙ Kas'settendecke *f.*
la·cus·trine [lə'kʌstraɪn] *adj.* See...: ⁓ *dwellings* Pfahlbauten.
lac·y [leɪsɪ] *adj.* spitzenartig, Spitzen...
lad [læd] *s.* **1.** (junger) Kerl *od.* Bursche, Junge *m*: *he's just a* ⁓! er ist (doch) noch ein Junge!; *come on,* ⁓*s!* los, Jungs!; *he's a bit of a* ⁓ F *Brit.* er ist ein ziemlicher Draufgänger *od.* Schwerenöter; **2.** *Brit.* Stallbursche *m.*
lad·der ['lædə] **I** *s.* **1.** Leiter *f* (*a. fig.*): *the social* ⁓ *fig.* die gesellschaftliche Stufenleiter; *the* ⁓ *of fame* die (Stufen)Leiter des Ruhms; *kick down the* ⁓ die Leute loswerden wollen, die e-m beim Aufstieg geholfen haben; **2.** *Brit.* Lauf-

masche f; **3.** *Tischtennis etc.*: Ta'belle f;
II v/i. **4.** *Brit.* Laufmaschen bekommen
(*Strumpf*); **III** v/t. **5.** *Brit.* zerreißen: ~
one's stockings sich e-e Laufmasche
holen; '**~·proof** adj. *Brit.* (lauf)ma-
schenfest (*Strumpf*).

lad·die ['lædɪ] s. *bsd. Scot.* F Bürschchen
n.

lade [leɪd] p.p. a. '**lad·en** [-dn] v/t. **1.**
(be)laden, befrachten; **2.** *Waren* ver-,
aufladen; '**lad·en** [-dn] **I** p.p. *von* **lade**;
II adj. (**with**) a. fig. beladen od. befrachtet (mit), voll (von), voller: ~ **with
fruit** (schwer) beladen mit Obst.

la·di·da(h) [ˌlɑːdɪ'dɑː] adj. *Brit.* F affektiert, vornehmtuerisch, ,affig'.

la·dies'| choice s. Damenwahl f (*beim
Tanz*); ~ **man** s. [*irr.*] Frauenheld m,
Char'meur m; ~ **room** → **lady** 6.

lad·ing ['leɪdɪŋ] s. **1.** (Ver)Laden n; **2.**
Ladung f; → *bill*² 3.

la·dle ['leɪdl] **I** s. **1.** Schöpflöffel m,
(Schöpf-, Suppen)Kelle f; **2.** ⊛ Gieß-
kelle f, -löffel m; **3.** Schaufel f (*am Wasserrad*); **II** v/t. **4.** a. ~ **out** (aus)schöp-
fen, a. F fig. *Lob etc.* austeilen.

la·dy ['leɪdɪ] **I** s. **1.** Dame f: **she is no**
(od. **not a**) ~ sie ist keine Dame; **an
English** ~ e-e Engländerin; **young** ~
junge Dame, junges Mädchen; **young
~!** iro. (mein) liebes Fräulein!; **his
young** ~ F s-e (kleine) Freundin; **my**
(**dear**) ~ (verehrte) gnädige Frau; *ladies and gentlemen* m-e (sehr verehr-
ten) Damen u. Herren; **2.** **Lady** f
(*Titel*): **my** ~! Mylady!, gnädige Frau;
3. obs. od. F (*außer wenn auf e-e
Lady angewandt*) Gattin f, Gemahlin f:
the old ~ F a) die alte Dame (*Mutter*),
b) m-e etc. ,Alte' (*Frau*); **4.** Herrin f,
Gebieterin f: ~ **of the house** Hausherrin, Dame f des Hauses; **our sovereign** ~ *Brit.* die Königin; **5. Our** 2 Unsere Liebe Frau, die Mutter Gottes:
Church of Our 2 Marien-, (Lieb)Frau-
enkirche f; **6. Ladies** pl. sg. konstr. 'Da-
mentoi,lette f, ,Damen' n; **II** adj. **7.**
weiblich: ~ **doctor** Ärztin f; ~ **friend**
Freundin f; ~ **mayoress** Frau f
(Ober)Bürgermeister; ~ **dog** humor.
,Hundedame' f.

'**la·dy·bird** s. zo. Ma'rienkäfer(chen n)
m; 2 **Boun·ti·ful** s. fig. gute Fee;
'**~·bug** Am. → **ladybird**; 2 **Day** s. eccl.
Ma'riä Verkündigung f; '**~·fin·ger** s.
Löffelbiskuit n; ,**~·in-'wait·ing** s. Hofdame f; '**~·kill·er** s. F Herzensbrecher
m, Ladykiller m; '**~·like** adj. damenhaft, vornehm; '**~·love** s. obs. Geliebte
f; 2 **of the Bed-cham·ber** s. *Brit.* königliche Kammerfrau, Hofdame f.

la·dy·ship ['leɪdɪʃɪp] s. Ladyschaft f
(*Stand u. Anrede*): **her** (**your**) ~ ihre
(Eure) Ladyschaft.

la·dy's| maid s. Kammerzofe f; ~ **slip-
per** s. ♀ Frauenschuh m.

lag¹ [læg] **I** v/i. **1.** mst ~ **behind** a. fig.
zu'rückbleiben, nicht mitkommen,
nach-, hinter'herhinken; **2.** mst ~ **behind** a) sich verzögern, b) zögern, c) ⚡
nacheilen; **II** s. **3.** Zu'rückbleiben n,
Rückstand m, Verzögerung f (a. ⊛,
phys.): **cultural** ~ kultureller Rückstand; **4.** 'Zeitabstand m, -,unterschied
m; **5.** ⚡ negative Phasenverschiebung,
(Phasen)Nacheiling f.

lag² [læg] s. *Brit. sl.* **1.** ,Knastschieber'
m, ,Knacki' m; **2. do a** ~ ,(im Knast)
sitzen'.

lag³ [læg] **I** s. **1.** (Fass)Daube f; **2.** ⊛
Verschalungsbrett n; **II** v/t. **3.** mit Dauben versehen; **4.** ⊛ *Rohre etc.* isolieren,
um'wickeln.

lag·an ['lægən] s. ♆, ♒ versenktes
(Wrack)Gut.

la·ger (**beer**) ['lɑːgə] s. Lagerbier n (*ein
helles Bier*); **la·ger lout** s. *Brit.* F betrunkener Randa'lierer.

lag·gard ['lægəd] **I** adj. □ **1.** langsam,
bummelig, faul; **II** s. **2.** ,Trödler(in)',
Bummler(in); **3.** Nachzügler(in).

lag·ging ['lægɪŋ] s. ⊛ **1.** Verkleidung f,
Verschalung f; **2.** a) Isolierung f, Wärmeschutz m, b) Iso'liermateri,al n.

la·goon [lə'guːn] s. La'gune f.

la·ic, la·i·cal ['leɪɪk(l)] adj. weltlich, Lai-
en...; '**la·i·cize** [-ɪsaɪz] v/t. säkularisieren.

laid [leɪd] pret. u. p.p. von **lay**¹: ~ **up** →
lay up 4; ,**~-'back** adj. F **1.** cool, gelassen, entspannt, ruhig; **2.** stressfrei,
ruhig (*Lebensweise*).

lain [leɪn] p.p. von **lie**².

lair [leə] s. **1.** zo. a) Lager n, b) Höhle f,
Bau m (*des Wildes*); **2.** allg. Lager(statt
f) n; **3.** F fig. a) Versteck n, b) Zu-
flucht(sort m) f.

laird [leəd] s. *Scot.* Gutsherr m.

lais·sez-faire [ˌleɪseɪ'feə] (*Fr.*) s. Lais-
ser-'faire n (*Gewährenlassen, Nichteinmischung*).

la·i·ty ['leɪɪtɪ] s. **1.** (*bsd. rote*) Laienstand m, Laien
pl. (*Ggs. Geistlichkeit*); **2.** Laien pl.,
Nichtfachleute pl.

lake¹ [leɪk] s. **1.** (*bsd. rote*) Pig'mentfar-
be, Farblack m; **2.** Beizenfarbstoff m.

lake² [leɪk] s. (Binnen)See m: **the Great**
2 der Große Teich (*der Atlantische Ozean*); **the Great** 2s die Großen Seen (*an
der Grenze zwischen USA u. Kanada*);
the ~**s** → 2 **Dis·trict** s. das Seengebiet
(*im Nordwesten Englands*); ~ **dwell·er**
s. Pfahlbauer m; '**~·land** → **Lake District**; 2 **poet** s. Seendichter m (*e-r der 3 Dichter
der Lake school*); 2 **school** s. See-
schule f (*die Dichter Southey, Coleridge
u. Wordsworth*).

lam¹ [læm] sl. **I** v/t. verdreschen, ,ver-
möbeln'; **II** v/i.: ~ **into** a) → **I**, b) fig.
auf j-n einhauen'.

lam² [læm] Am. sl. **I** s.: **on the** ~ im
,Abhauen' (begriffen), auf der Flucht
(*vor der Polizei*); **take it on the** ~ → **II**
v/i. ,türmen', ,Leine ziehen'.

la·ma ['lɑːmə] s. eccl. Lama m; '**la·ma-
ism** [-ɪzəm] s. eccl. Lama'ismus m; '**la-
ma·ser·y** [-əsərɪ] s. Lamakloster n.

lamb [læm] **I** s. **1.** Lamm n: **in** (od. **with**)
~ trächtig (*Schaf*); **like a** ~ fig. wie ein
Lamm, lammfromm; **like a** ~ **to the
slaughter** fig. wie ein Lamm zur
Schlachtbank; **2.** Lamm(fleisch) n; **3.**
the 2 (**of God**) eccl. das Lamm (Gottes); **4.** F Schätzchen n; **II** v/i. **5.** lammen: ~**ing time** Lammzeit f.

lam·baste [læm'beɪst] v/t. sl. **1.** ,vermö-
beln' (*verprügeln*); **2.** fig. ,her'unter-
putzen', ,zs.-stauchen'.

lam·ben·cy ['læmbənsɪ] s. **1.** Züngeln n
(*e-r Flamme*); **2.** fig. (*geistreiches*)
Funkeln, Sprühen n; '**lam·bent** [-nt]
adj. □ **1.** züngelnd, flackernd; **2.** sanft
strahlend; **3.** fig. sprühend, funkelnd
(*Witz*).

lamb·kin ['læmkɪn] s. **1.** Lämmchen n;
2. fig. ,Schätzchen' n.

'**lamb·skin** s. **1.** Lammfell n; **2.** Schafleder n.

lamb's| tails s. pl. ♀ **1.** *Brit.* Haselkätz-
chen pl.; **2.** Am. Weiden-, Palmkätz-
chen pl.; ~ **wool** s. Lammwolle f.

lame [leɪm] **I** adj. □ **1.** lahm, hinkend: ~
in (od. **of**) **one leg** auf 'einem Bein
lahm; **2.** fig. ,lahm', ,müde': ~ **efforts**;
~ **story**; ~ **excuse** faule Ausrede; ~

verses holprige od. hinkende Verse; **II**
v/t. **3.** lahm machen, lähmen (a. fig.); ~
duck s. F **1.** Körperbehinderte(r m) f;
2. ,Versager' m, ,Niete' f; **3.** ✝ ruinier-
ter ('Börsen)Speku,lant; **4.** Am. pol.
nicht wieder gewählter Amtsinhaber,
bsd. Kongressmitglied od. Präsident, bis
zum Ende s-r Amtsperiode.

la·mel·la [lə'melə] pl. **-lae** [-liː] s. allg.
La'melle f, Plättchen n; **la·mel·lar** [-lə],
lam·el·late ['læməleɪt] adj. la'mellen-
artig, Lamellen...

lame·ness ['leɪmnɪs] s. **1.** Lahmheit f (a.
fig., contp.); **2.** fig. Schwäche f; **3.** Hinken n (*von Versen*).

la·ment [lə'ment] **I** v/i. **1.** jammern,
(weh)klagen, lamentieren (**for** od. **over**
um); **2.** trauern (**for** od. **over** um); **II**
v/t. **3.** bejammern, beklagen, bedau-
ern, betrauern; **III** s. **4.** Jammer m,
Wehklage f, Klage(lied n) f; **lam·en-
ta·ble** ['læməntəbl] adj. □ **1.** beklagenswert, bedauerlich; **2.** contp. erbärmlich, kläglich, jämmerlich (schlecht);
lam·en·ta·tion [ˌlæmən'teɪʃn] s. **1.**
Jammern n, Lamentieren n, (Weh)Kla-
ge f, iro. a. La'mento n; **2.** 2s (**of Jeremiah**) pl. mst sg. konstr. bibl. Klagelieder pl. Jere'miae.

lam·i·na ['læmɪnə] pl. **-nae** [-niː] s. **1.**
Plättchen n, Blättchen n; **2.** (dünne)
Schicht; **3.** ♀ Blattspreite f; '**lam·i·nal**
[-nl], '**lam·i·nar** [-nə] adj. **1.** blätterig;
2. (blättchenartig) geschichtet; **3.** phys.
lami'nar: ~ **flow** Laminarströmung f;
'**lam·i·nate** [-neɪt] v/t. **1.** ⊛ a) auswalzen, strecken, b) in Blättchen aufspalten, c) schichten; **2.** mit Plättchen belegen, mit Folie über'ziehen; **II** v/i. **3.**
sich in Plättchen od. Schichten spalten;
III s. **4.** ⊛ (Plastik-, Verbund)Folie f;
IV adj. **5.** → **laminar**.

lam·i·nat·ed ['læmɪneɪtɪd] adj. la'mel-
lenartig, Lamellen...; ⊛ a. blättrig od.
geschichtet: ~ **glass** Verbundglas n; ~
material Schichtstoff m; ~ **paper** Hart-
papier n; ~ **sheet** Schichtplatte f; ~
spring Blattfeder f; ~ **wood** Sperr-,
Pressholz n; **lam·i·na·tion** [ˌlæmɪ'neɪʃn]
s. **1.** ⊛ a) Lamellierung f, b) Streckung
f, c) Schichtung f; **2.** 'Blätterstruk,tur f.

lam·mer·gei·er, lam·mer·gey·er ['læ-
məgaɪə] s. orn. Lämmergeier m.

lamp [læmp] s. **1.** Lampe f, (Straßen-
etc.)La'terne f: **smell of the** ~ nach
,saurem Schweiß riechen', mehr Fleiß
als Talent verraten; **2.** ⚡ Lampe f: a)
Glühbirne f, b) Leuchte f; **3.** fig.
Leuchte f, Licht n; '**~·black** s. Lampen-
ruß m, -schwarz n; '**~·chim·ney** s.
'Lampenzy,linder m; '**~·light** s. (**by** od.
bei) Lampenlicht n.

lam·poon [læm'puːn] **I** s. Spott- od.
Schmähschrift f, Pam'phlet n, Sa'tire f;
II v/t. (*schriftlich*) verspotten, -höhnen;
lam'poon·er [-nə], **lam'poon·ist**
[-nɪst] s. Pamphle'tist(in).

'**lamp·post** s. La'ternenpfahl m: **between you and me and the** ~ F (ganz)
unter uns (gesagt).

lam·prey ['læmprɪ] s. ichth. Lam'prete f,
Neunauge n.

'**lamp·shade** s. Lampenschirm m.

Lan·cas·tri·an [læŋ'kæstrɪən] *Brit.* **I** s.
1. Bewohner(in) der Stadt od. Grafschaft Lancaster; **2.** hist. Angehörige(r
m) f od. Anhänger(in) des Hauses Lancaster; **II** adj. **3.** Lancaster...

lance [lɑːns] **I** s. **1.** Lanze f, Speer m:
break a ~ **for** (od. **on behalf of**) s.o.
e-e Lanze für j-n brechen; **2.** → **lancer**
1; **3.** → **lancet** 1; **II** v/t. **4.** mit e-r Lanze
durch'bohren; **5.** ✻ mit e-r Lan'zette

öffnen: **~** *a boil* ein Geschwür (*fig.* e-e Eiterbeule) aufstechen; **~ cor·po·ral** *s.* ✕ *Brit.* Ober-, Hauptgefreite(r) *m.*

lanc·er ['lɑːnsə] *s.* **1.** ✕ *hist.* U'lan *m*; **2.** *pl. sg. konstr.* Lanci'er *m* (*Tanz*).

lan·cet ['lɑːnsɪt] *s.* **1.** ✇ Lan'zette *f*; **2.** △ a) *a.* **~** *arch* Spitzbogen *m*, b) *a.* **~** *window* Spitzbogenfenster *n.*

land [lænd] **I** *s.* **1.** Land *n* (*Ggs. Meer, Wasser*): *by* **~** auf dem Landweg; *by* **~** *and by sea* zu Wasser u. zu Lande; *make* **~** ♩ Land sichten; *see how the* **~** *lies* sehen, wie der Hase läuft, die Lage ‚peilen‘; **2.** Land *n*, Boden *m*: *live off the* **~** a) von den Früchten des Landes leben, b) sich aus der Natur ernähren (*Soldaten etc.*); **3.** Land *n*, Grund *m* u. Boden *m*, Grundbesitz *m*, Lände'reien *pl.*; **~** *set-aside* *EU* Flächenstilllegung *f*; **4.** Land *n* (*Staat, Region*): *far-off* **~***s* ferne Länder; **5.** *fig.* Land *n*, Reich *n*: **~** *of the living* Diesseits *n*; **~** *of dreams* Reich der Träume; **II** *v/i.* **6.** ♩, ⚓ landen; **~** anlegen; **7.** landen, an Land gehen, aussteigen; **8.** landen, (an-) kommen: *he* **~***ed in a ditch* er landete in e-m Graben; **~** *on one's feet* auf die Füße fallen (*a. fig.*); **~** (*up*) *in prison* im Gefängnis landen; **9.** *sport* durchs Ziel gehen; **III** *v/t.* **10.** *Personen, Waren, Flugzeug* landen; *Schiffsgüter* landen, löschen, ausladen; *Fisch(fang)* an Land bringen; **11.** *bsd. Fahrgäste* absetzen; **12.** *j-n in Schwierigkeiten etc.* bringen, verwickeln: **~** *s.o. in difficulties*; **~** *s.o. with s.th.* j-m et. aufhalsen *od.* einbrocken; **~** *o.s.* (*od. be* **~***ed*) *in* (hinein)geraten in (*acc.*); **13.** F a) e-n *Schlag od. Treffer* landen: *I* **~***ed him one* ich hab ihm eine geknallt *od.* ‚verpasst‘; **14.** F *j-n od. et.* ‚erwischen‘, (sich) ‚schnappen‘, ‚kriegen‘: **~** *a prize* sich e-n Preis ‚holen‘; **~** *a good contract* e-n guten Vertrag ‚an Land ziehen‘.

land a·gent *s.* **1.** Grundstücksmakler *m*; **2.** *Brit.* Gutsverwalter *m.*

lan·dau ['lændɔː] *s.* Landauer *m* (*Kutsche*).

land bank *s.* 'Bodenkre,dit-, Hypo'thekenbank *f*; **~** *car·riage* *s.* 'Landtrans,port *m*, -fracht *f*; **~** *crab* *s. zo.* Landkrabbe *f.*

land·ed ['lændɪd] *adj.* Land..., Grund...: **~** *estate*, **~** *property* Grundbesitz *m*, -eigentum *n*; **~** *gentry* Landadel *m*; **~** *proprietor* Grundbesitzer (-in); *the* **~** *interest* *coll.* die Grundbesitzer.

'land·fall *s.* ♩ Landkennung *f*, Sichten *n* von Land; **~** *forc·es* *s. pl.* ✕ Landstreitkräfte *pl.*; **'~·grave** [-ndg-] *s. hist.* (deutscher) Landgraf; **'~·hold·er** *s.* Grundbesitzer *m od.* -pächter *m.*

land·ing ['lændɪŋ] *s.* **1.** ♩ Landen *n*, Landung *f*: a) Anlegen *n* (*e-s Schiffs*), b) Ausschiffung *f* (*von Personen*), c) Ausladen *n*, Löschen *n* (*der Fracht*); **2.** ⚓ Lande-, Anlegeplatz *m*; **3.** ✈ Landung *f*; **4.** △ Treppenabsatz *m*; **~** *beam* *s.* ✈ Landeleitstrahl *m*; **~** *card* *s.* Einreisekarte *f*; **~** *craft* *s.* ✕ Landungsboot *n*; **~** *field* *s.* ✈ Landeplatz *m*, -bahn *f*; **~** *flap* *s.* ✈ Landeklappe *f*; **~** *gear* *s.* ✈ Fahrgestell *n*, -werk *n*; **~** *net* *s.* Hamen *m*, Kescher *m*; **~** *par·ty* *s.* ✕ 'Landungstrupp *m*, -kom,mando *n*; **~** *place* → *landing* 2; **~** *stage* *s.* ⚓ Landungsbrücke *f*, -steg *m*; **~** *strip*, **~** *track* → *air strip.*

'land,la·dy ['læn,l-] *s.* (Haus-, Gast-, Pensi'ons)Wirtin *f.*

land·less ['lændlɪs] *adj.* ohne Grundbe-

sitz.

'land·|·locked *adj.* 'landum,schlossen, ohne Zugang zum Meer: **~** *country* Binnenstaat *m*; **'~·lop·er** [-,ləʊpə] *s.* Landstreicher *m*; **'~·lord** ['lænl-] *s.* **1.** Grundbesitzer *m*; **2.** Hauseigentümer *m*; **3.** Hauswirt *m*, ⚭ *a.* Hauswirtin *f*; **4.** (Gast)Wirt *m*; **'~·lub·ber** *s.* ⚓ ‚Landratte‘ *f*; **'~·mark** [-ndm-] *s.* **1.** Grenzstein *m*; **2.** ⚓ Seezeichen *n*; **3.** ✕ Gelände-, Orientierungspunkt *m*; **4.** Wahrzeichen *n* (*e-r Stadt etc.*); **5.** *fig.* Meilen-, Markstein *m*, Wendepunkt *m*: *a* **~** *in history*; **'~·mine** [-ndm-] *s.* ✕ Landmine *f*; **~** *of·fice* *s. Am.* Grundbuchamt *n*; **'~·,of·fice busi·ness** *s. Am.* F ‚Bombengeschäft‘ *n*; **'~·,own·er** *s.* Land-, Grundbesitzer(in); **~** *re·form* *s.* 'Bodenre,form *f*; **~** *reg·is·ter* *s.* Grundbuch *n.*

land·scape ['lænskeɪp] **I** *s.* **1.** Landschaft *f* (*a. paint.*); **2.** Landschaftsmale'rei *f*; **II** *v/i.* **3.** landschaftlich *od.* gärtnerisch gestalten, anlegen; **~** *ar·chi·tect* *s.* **1.** 'Landschaftsarchi,tekt(in); **2.** → **~** *gar·den·er* *s.* Landschaftsgärtner (-in), 'Gartenarchi,tekt(in); **~** *gar·den·ing* *s.* Landschaftsgärtne'rei *f*; **~** *paint·er* → **land·scap·ist** ['læn,skeɪpɪst] *s.* Landschaftsmaler(in).

'land·|·slide [-nds-] *s.* **1.** Erdrutsch *m*; **2.** *a.* **~** *victory* *pol. fig.* ‚Erdrutsch‘ *m*, über'wältigender (Wahl)Sieg; **'~·slip** [-nds-] *Brit.* → *landslide* 1; **~** *sur·vey·or* *s.* Geo'meter *m*, Land(ver)messer *m*; **~** *swell* [-nds-] *s.* ♩ einlaufende Dünung; **~** *tax* *s. obs.* Grundsteuer *f*; **~** *tor·toise* *s. zo.* Landschildkröte *f*; **'~·,wait·er** *s. Brit.* 'Zolin,spektor *m.*

land·ward ['lændwəd] **I** *adj.* land('ein)wärts (gelegen); **II** *adv. a.* **'land·wards** [-dz] land(ein)wärts.

lane [leɪn] *s.* **1.** (Feld)Weg *m*, (Hecken-) Pfad *m*; **2.** Gasse *f* a) Gässchen *n*, Sträßchen *n*, b) 'Durchgang *m*: *form a* **~** Spalier stehen, e-e Gasse bilden; **3.** Schneise *f*; **4.** ♩ Fahrrinne *f*, (Fahrt-) Route *f*; **5.** ✈ (Flug)Schneise *f*; **6.** *mot.* (Fahr)Spur *f*: *get in* **~***!* bitte einordnen!; **7.** *sport* (*einzelne*) Bahn (*e-s Läufers, Schwimmers etc.*).

lang syne [,læŋ'saɪn] *Scot.* **I** *adv.* vor langer Zeit; **II** *s.* längst vergangene Zeit; → *auld lang syne.*

lan·guage ['læŋgwɪdʒ] *s.* **1.** Sprache *f*: *foreign* **~***s* Fremdsprachen; **~** *of flowers* *fig.* Blumensprache; *talk the same* **~** *a. fig.* dieselbe Sprache sprechen; **2.** Sprache *f*, Ausdrucks-, Redeweise *f*, Worte *pl.*: *bad* **~** ordinäre Ausdrücke, Schimpfworte; *strong* **~** a) Kraftausdrücke, b) harte Worte *od.* Sprache; **3.** Sprache *f*, Stil *m*; **4.** (Fach)Sprache *f*: *medical* **~**; **5.** *sl.* ordi'näre Sprache: **~**, *Sir!* ich verbitte mir solche (gemeinen) Ausdrücke!; **~** *bar·ri·er* *s.* Sprachschranke *f*; **~** *la·bor·a·to·ry* *s. ped.* 'Sprachla,bor *n.*

lan·guid ['læŋgwɪd] *adj.* □ **1.** schwach, matt, schlaff; **2.** schleppend, träge; **3.** gelangweilt, lustlos, lau; **4.** lässig, träge; **5.** ♣ flau, lustlos (*Markt*).

lan·guish ['læŋgwɪʃ] *v/i.* **1.** ermatten, erschlaffen, erlahmen (*a. fig. Interesse, Konversation*); **2.** (ver)schmachten, da'hinsiechen, -welken: **~** *in prison* im Gefängnis schmachten; **3.** da'niederliegen (*Handel, Industrie etc.*); **4.** schmachtend blicken; **5.** schmachten (*for* nach); **6.** Sehnsucht haben, sich härmen (*for* nach); **'lan·guish·ing** [-ʃɪŋ] *adj.* □ **1.** ermattend, erlahmend (*a. fig.*); **2.** (ver)schmachtend, (da'hin-)

siechend, leidend; **3.** sehnsuchtsvoll, schmachtend (*Blick*); **4.** lustlos, träge (*a.* ♣), langsam; **5.** langsam (*Tod*), schleichend (*Krankheit*).

lan·guor ['læŋgə] *s.* **1.** Mattigkeit *f*, Schlaffheit *f*; **2.** Trägheit *f*, Schläfrigkeit *f*; **3.** Stumpfheit *f*, Gleichgültigkeit *f*, Lauheit *f*; **4.** Stille *f*, Schwüle *f*; **'lan·guor·ous** [-ərəs] *adj.* □ **1.** matt; **2.** schlaff, träge; **3.** stumpf, gleichgültig; **4.** schläfrig, wohlig; **5.** schmelzend (*Musik etc.*); **6.** (*a. sinnlich*) schwül.

lank [læŋk] *adj.* □ **1.** lang u. dünn, schlank, mager; **2.** glatt, strähnig (*Haar*); **'lank·i·ness** [-kɪnɪs] *s.* Schlaksigkeit *f*; **'lank·y** [-kɪ] *adj.* hoch aufgeschossen, schlaksig.

lan·o·lin(e) ['lænəʊlɪn (-liːn)] *s.* ⚕ Lano'lin *n*, Wollfett *n.*

lan·tern ['læntən] *s.* **1.** La'terne *f*; **2.** Leuchtkammer *f* (*e-s Leuchtturms*); **3.** △ La'terne *f* (*durchbrochener Dachaufsatz*); **'~·jawed** *adj.* hohlwangig; **~** *jaws* *s. pl.* eingefallene Wangen *pl.*; **~** *slide* *s. obs.* Dia(posi'tiv) *n*, Lichtbild *n*: **~** *lecture* Lichtbildervortrag *m.*

lan·yard ['lænjəd] *s.* **1.** ♩ Taljereep *n*; **2.** ✕ a) *obs.* Abzugsleine *f* (*Kanone*), b) Traggurt *m* (*Pistole*), c) (Achsel-) Schnur *f*; **3.** Schleife *f.*

lap[1] [læp] *s.* **1.** Schoß *m* (*e-s Kleides od. des Körpers*; *a. fig.*): *sit on s.o.'s* **~**; *in the* **~** *of the church*; *drop into s.o.'s* **~** j-m in den Schoß fallen; *in Fortune's* **~** im Schoß des Glücks; *it is in the* **~** *of the gods* es liegt im Schoß der Götter; *live in the* **~** *of luxury* ein Luxusleben führen; **2.** (Kleider- *etc.*)Zipfel *m.*

lap[2] [læp] **I** *v/t.* **1.** falten, wickeln (*round*, *about* um); **2.** einwickeln, -schlagen, -hüllen; **3.** *a. fig.* um'hüllen, (ein)betten, (-)hüllen: **~***ped in luxury* von Luxus umgeben; **4.** über'ein'ander legen, über'lappt anordnen; **5.** *sport* a) *Gegner* über'runden, b) *e-e Strecke* zu'rücklegen (*in 1 Minute etc.*); **II** *v/i.* **6.** sich winden *od.* legen (*round* um); **7.** hin'ausragen, -gehen (*a. fig.*; *over* über *acc.*); **8.** über'lappen; **9.** *sport* die *od.* s-e Runde drehen *od.* laufen (*at* in e-r Zeit von); **III** *s.* **10.** ⊙ Wickelung *f*, Windung *f*, Lage *f*; **11.** Über'lappung *f*, 'Überstand *m*; **12.** 'überstehender Teil, Vorstoß *m*; **13.** *Buchbinderei*: Falz *m*; **14.** *sport* Runde *f*; **15.** E'tappe *f* (*e-r Reise, a. fig.*).

lap[3] [læp] **I** *v/t.* **1.** *a.* **~** *up* auflecken; **2.** **~** *up* a) *Suppe etc.* gierig (hin'unter-) schlürfen, b) F et. ‚fressen‘ (*glauben*), c) F et. gierig (in sich) aufnehmen, et. liebend gern hören *etc.*: *they* **~***ped it up* es ging ihnen ‚runter wie Öl‘; **3.** plätschern gegen; **II** *v/i.* **4.** lecken, schlecken, schlürfen; **5.** plätschern; **III** *s.* **6.** Lecken *n*; **7.** Plätschern *n.*

'lap·dog *s.* Schoßhund *m.*

la·pel [lə'pel] *s.* (Rock)Aufschlag *m*, Re'vers *n, m.*

lap·i·dar·y ['læpɪdərɪ] **I** *s.* **1.** Edelsteinschneider *m*; **II** *adj.* **2.** Stein...; **3.** Steinschleiferei...; **4.** (Stein)Inschriften...; **5.** in Stein gehauen; **6.** *fig.* wuchtig, lapi'dar.

lap·is laz·u·li [,læpɪs'læzjʊlaɪ] *s. min.* Lapis'lazuli *m.*

Lap·land·er ['læplændə] → *Lapp* I.

Lapp [læp] **I** *s.* Lappe *m*, Lappin *f*, Lappländer(in); **II** *adj.* lappisch.

lap·pet ['læpɪt] *s.* **1.** Zipfel *m*; **2.** *anat., zo.* Hautlappen *m.*

Lap·pish ['læpɪʃ] → *Lapp* II.

lapse [læps] **I** *s.* **1.** Lapsus *m*, Fehler *m*, Versehen *n*: **~** *of the pen* Schreibfehler m; **~ of justice** Justizirrtum m; **~ of taste** Geschmacksverirrung f; **2.** Fehltritt m, Vergehen n, Entgleisung f: **~ from duty** Pflichtversäumnis n; **~ from faith** Abfall m vom Glauben; **3.** Absinken n, Abgleiten n, Verfall(en n) m (**into** in acc.); **4.** a) Ablauf m, Vergehen n (e-r Zeit), b) ⚖ (Frist)Ablauf m, c) Zeitspanne f; **5.** ⚖ a) Verfall m, Erlöschen n e-s Anspruchs etc., b) Heimfall m (von Erbteilen etc.); **6.** Aufhören, Verschwinden n, Aussterben n; **II** v/i. **7.** a) verstreichen (Zeit), b) ablaufen (Frist); **8.** verfallen (**into** in acc.): **~ into silence**; **9.** absinken, abgleiten, verfallen (**into** in Barbarei etc.); **10.** e-n Fehltritt tun, (mo'ralisch) entgleisen, sündigen; **11.** abfallen (**from faith** vom Glauben); **~ from duty** s-e Pflicht versäumen; **12.** ‚einschlafen', aufhören (Beziehung, Unterhaltung etc.); **13.** ⚖ a) verfallen, erlöschen (Recht etc.), b) heimfallen (**to** an acc.).

lap·top [ˈlæptɒp] s. Computer: Laptop m.

lap·wing [ˈlæpwɪŋ] s. orn. Kiebitz m.

lar·board [ˈlɑːbɔd] ⚓ obs. **I** s. Backbord n; **II** adj. Backbord...

lar·ce·ner [ˈlɑːsənə], **lar·ce·nist** [-nɪst] s. ⚖ Dieb m; **lar·ce·ny** [-nɪ] s. ⚖ Diebstahl m.

larch [lɑːtʃ] s. ♣ Lärche f.

lard [lɑːd] **I** s. **1.** Schweinefett n, -schmalz n; **II** v/t. **2.** Fleisch spicken: **~ing needle** (od. **pin**) Spicknadel f; **3.** fig. spicken (**with** mit); **'lard·er** [-də] s. Speisekammer f, -schrank m.

large [lɑːdʒ] **I** adj. □ → **largely**; **1.** groß: **a ~ room** (**horse**, **rock**, etc.); **~ screen** Großbildschirm m; (**as**) **~ as life** in (voller) Lebensgröße (a. humor.); **~r than life** a) Person: außergewöhnlich, 'extrava,gant, auffallend, b) Sache: 'übermäßig od. außergewöhnlich wichtig (od. bedeutend); **2.** groß (beträchtlich): **a ~ business** (**family**, **sum**, etc.); **a ~ meal** e reichliche Mahlzeit; **~ farmer** Großbauer m; **~ producer** Großerzeuger m; **3.** um'fassend, ausgedehnt, weit(gehend): **~ powers** umfassende Vollmachten; **4.** obs. großzügig; → a. **large-minded**; **II** adv. **5.** groß: **write ~; it was written ~ all over his face** fig. es stand ihm (deutlich) im Gesicht geschrieben; **6.** großspurig: **talk ~** ‚große Töne spucken'; **III** s. **7.** **at ~** a) auf freiem Fuß, in Freiheit: **set s.o. at ~** j-n auf freien Fuß setzen, b) (sehr) ausführlich: **discuss s.th. at ~**, c) ganz allgemein, d) in der Gesamtheit: **the nation at ~; talk at ~** ins Blaue hineinreden; **8.** **in** (**the**) **~** a) im Großen, in großem Maßstab, b) im Ganzen; **,~-ˈhand·ed** adj. fig. freigebig; **,~-ˈhearted** adj. fig. großherzig.

large·ly [ˈlɑːdʒlɪ] adv. **1.** in hohem Maße, großen-, größtenteils; **2.** weitgehend, im Wesentlichen; **3.** reichlich; **4.** allgemein.

,large-ˈmind·ed adj. vorurteilslos, tole'rant, aufgeschlossen.

large·ness [ˈlɑːdʒnɪs] s. **1.** Größe f; **2.** Größe f, Weite f, 'Umfang m; **3.** Großzügigkeit f, Freigebigkeit f; **4.** Großmütigkeit f.

'large-scale adj. groß (angelegt), 'umfangreich, ausgedehnt, Groß...: **~ attack** ✗ Großangriff m; **~ experiment** Großversuch m; **~ manufacture** Serienherstellung f; **a ~ map** e-e Karte in großem Maßstab.

lar·gess(e) [lɑːˈdʒes] s. **1.** Freigebigkeit f; **2.** a) Gabe f, reiches Geschenk, b)

reiche Geschenke pl.

larg·ish [ˈlɑːdʒɪʃ] adj. ziemlich groß.

lar·i·at [ˈlærɪət] s. Lasso m, n.

lark¹ [lɑːk] s. orn. Lerche f: **rise with the ~** mit den Hühnern aufstehen.

lark² [lɑːk] F **I** s. **1.** Jux m, Ulk m, Spaß m: **for a ~** zum Spaß, aus Jux; **have a ~** s-n Spaß haben od. treiben; **what a ~!** ist ja lustig od. ‚zum Brüllen'!; **2.** a) ‚Ding' n, Sache f, b) Quatsch m; **II** v/i. **3.** a. **~ about** od. **around** her'umalbern, -blödeln.

lark·spur [ˈlɑːkspɜː] s. ♣ Rittersporn m.

lar·ri·kin [ˈlærɪkɪn] s. bsd. Austral. (jugendlicher) Rowdy.

lar·va [ˈlɑːvə] pl. **-vae** [-viː] s. zo. Larve f; **'lar·val** [-vl] adj. zo. Larven...; **'lar·vi·cide** [-vɪsaɪd] s. Raupenvertilgungsmittel n.

la·ryn·ge·al [ˌlærɪnˈdʒiːəl] adj. Kehlkopf...; **,lar·yn·gi·tis** [-ˈdʒaɪtɪs] s. ✚ Kehlkopfentzündung f.

la·ryn·go·scope [ləˈrɪŋɡəskəʊp] s. ✚ Kehlkopfspiegel m.

lar·ynx [ˈlærɪŋks] s. anat. Kehlkopf m.

las·civ·i·ous [ləˈsɪvɪəs] adj. □ las'ziv: a) geil, lüstern, b) schlüpfrig: **~ story**.

la·ser [ˈleɪzə] s. phys. Laser m: **~ beam** s. phys. Laserstrahl m; **~ gun** s. 'Laserpis,tole f, -ka,none f; **~ med·i·cine** s. 'Lasermedi,zin f; **~ print·er** s. Laserdrucker m; **~ weap·ons** s. pl. Laserwaffen pl.

lash¹ [læʃ] **I** s. **1.** a) Peitschenschnur f, b) Peitsche(nende n) f; **2.** Peitschen-, Rutenhieb m: **the ~ of her tongue** fig. ihre scharfe Zunge; **3.** Peitschen n (a. fig. des Regens, des Sturms etc.); **4.** fig. (Peitschen)Hieb m; **5.** (Augen)Wimper f; **II** v/t. **6.** j-n peitschen, schlagen, auspeitschen: **~ the tail** mit dem Schwanz um sich schlagen; **~ the sea** das Meer peitschen (Sturm); **7.** peitschen od. schlagen an (acc.) od. gegen (Regen etc.); **8.** fig. geißeln, abkanzeln; **9.** heftig (an)treiben: **~ the audience into a fury** das Publikum aufpeitschen; **~ o.s. into a fury** sich in e-e Wut hineinsteigern; **III** v/i. **10.** a. fig. peitschen, schlagen: **~ about** (wild) um sich schlagen; **~ into s.o.** a) auf j-n einschlagen, b) fig. j-n wild attackieren; **11.** fig. peitschen, (Regen) a. prasseln: **~ down** niederprasseln; **12.** **~ out** a) (wild) um sich schlagen, b) ausschlagen (Pferd) (**at**) vom Leder ziehen, ‚einhauen' (auf j-n); **13.** **~ out on** F a) (mit Geld) ‚auf den Putz hauen' bei et., b) sich j-m gegenüber spendabel zeigen.

lash² [læʃ] v/t. a. **~ down** festbinden, -zurren (**to**, **on** an dat.).

lash·ing¹ [ˈlæʃɪŋ] s. **1.** a) Auspeitschung f, b) Prügel pl.; **2.** pl. Brit. F Masse(n pl.) f (Speise etc.).

lash·ing² [ˈlæʃɪŋ] s. **1.** Anbinden n; **2.** ⚓ Laschung f, Tau(werk) n.

lass [læs] s. bsd. Brit. **1.** Mädchen n; **2.** ‚Schatz' m; **las·sie** [ˈlæsɪ] → **lass**.

las·si·tude [ˈlæsɪtjuːd] s. Mattigkeit f.

las·so [læˈsuː] **I** pl. **-so(e)s** s. Lasso m, n; **II** v/t. mit e-m Lasso fangen.

last¹ [lɑːst] **I** adj. □ → **lastly**; **1.** letzt: **~ but one** vorletzt; **~ but two** drittletzt; **for the ~ time** zum letzten Mal(e); **to the ~ man** bis auf den letzten Mann; **2.** letzt, vorig: **~ Monday**, **Monday** (am) letzten od. vorigen Montag; **~ night** a) gestern Abend, b) in der vergangenen Nacht; **~ week** letzte od. vorige Woche; **the week before ~** (die) vorletzte Woche; **this day ~ week** heute vor e-r Woche; **on May 6th ~** am vergangenen 6. Mai; **3.** neu-

est, letzt: **the ~ news**; **the ~ thing in jazz** das Neueste im Jazz; **4.** letzt, al'lein übrig bleibend: **the ~ hope** die letzte (verbleibende) Hoffnung; **my ~ pound** mein letztes Pfund; **5.** letzt, endgültig, entscheidend; → **word** 1; **6.** äußerst: **of the ~ importance** von höchster Bedeutung; **this is my ~ price** dies ist mein äußerster od. niedrigster Preis; **7.** letzt, am wenigsten erwartet od. geeignet, unwahrscheinlich: **the ~ man I would choose** der Letzte, den ich wählen würde; **he is the ~ person I expected to see** mit ihm hatte ich am wenigsten gerechnet; **this is the ~ thing to happen** das ist völlig unwahrscheinlich; **8.** contp. ‚letzt', mise'rabelst; **II** adv. **9.** zu'letzt, als Letzter, -e, -es, an letzter Stelle: **~ of all** ganz zuletzt, zuallerletzt; **~ but not least** nicht zuletzt, nicht zu vergessen; **10.** zu'letzt, das letzte Mal, zum letzten Mal(e): **I ~ met him in Berlin**; **11.** zu guter Letzt; **12.** in Zssgn: **~-mentioned** letzterwähnt, -genannt; **III** s. **13.** **at ~** a) endlich, b) schließlich, zuletzt; **at long ~** schließlich (doch noch); **14.** der (die, das) Letzte: **the ~ of the Mohicans** der letzte Mohikaner; **he was the ~ to arrive** er traf als Letzter ein; **he would be the ~ to do that** er wäre der Letzte, der so etwas täte; **15.** der (die, das) Letztgenannte od. Letzte; **16.** F a) letzte Erwähnung, b) letzter (An)Blick, c) letztes Mal: **breathe one's ~** s-n letzten Atemzug tun; **hear the ~ of** zum letzten Mal(e) (od. nichts mehr) hören von et. od. j-m; **we shall never hear the ~ of this** das werden wir noch lang zu hören kriegen; **look one's ~ on s.th.** e-n (aller)letzten Blick auf et. werfen; **we shall never see the ~ of that man** den (Mann) werden wir nie mehr los; **17.** Ende n: **to the ~** a) bis zum Äußersten, b) bis zum Ende (od. Tod).

last² [lɑːst] **I** v/i. **1.** (an-, fort)dauern, währen: **too good to ~** zu schön, um lange zu währen od. um wahr zu sein; **it won't ~** es wird nicht lange anhalten od. so bleiben; **2.** bestehen: **as long as the world ~s**; **3.** 'durch-, aushalten: **he won't ~ much longer** er wird's nicht mehr lange machen; **4.** (sich) halten: **the paint will ~; ~ well** haltbar sein; **5.** (aus)reichen, genügen: **while the money ~s** solange das Geld reicht; **I must make my money ~** ich muss mit m-m Geld auskommen; **II** v/t. **6.** a. **~ out** j-m reichen: **it will ~ us a week**; **7.** mst **~ out** a) über'dauern, b) 'durchhalten, c) (es mindestens) ebenso lange aushalten wie.

last³ [lɑːst] s. Leisten m: **put on the ~** über den Leisten schlagen; **stick to your ~!** fig. (Schuster,) bleib bei deinem Leisten!

,last-ˈditch adj.: **~ stand** ein letzter (verzweifelter) Widerstand od. Versuch.

last·ing [ˈlɑːstɪŋ] **I** adj. □ dauerhaft, dauernd, anhaltend, Material etc. a. haltbar: **~ impression** nachhaltiger Eindruck; **II** s. Lasting n (fester Kammgarnstoff); **'last·ing·ness** [-nɪs] s. Dauer(haftigkeit) f, Haltbarkeit f.

last·ly [ˈlɑːstlɪ] adv. zu'letzt, schließlich, am Ende, zum Schluss.

last-min·ute [ˌlɑːstˈmɪnɪt] adj. in letzter Mi'nute: **~ flight** Last-Minute-Flug m.

latch [lætʃ] s. **1.** Klinke f, (Schnapp-) Riegel m: **on the ~** nur eingeklinkt (Tür); **2.** Schnappschloss n; **II** v/t. **3.** ein-, zuklinken; **III** v/i. **4.** sich einklinken, einschnappen; **5.** ~ **on to** F a) sich (wie e-e Klette) an *j-n* hängen, b) *e-e Idee* (gierig) aufgreifen, c) *et.* kapieren *od.* ‚spitzkriegen‘.

'**latch·key** *s.* **1.** Drücker *m*, Schlüssel *m* (*für ein Schnappschloss*); **2.** Haus- *od.* Wohnungsschlüssel *m*: ~ *child* Schlüsselkind *n*.

late [leɪt] **I** *adj.* □ → *lately*; **1.** spät: *at a* ~ *hour* zu später Stunde, spät (*beide a. fig.*); **on Monday at the** ~*st* spätestens am Montag; *it is* (*getting*) ~ es ist (schon) spät; *at a* ~*r time* später, zu e-m späteren Zeitpunkt; → *latest* I; **2.** vorgerückt, spät, Spät...: ~ *edition* (*programme, summer*) Spätausgabe *f* (-programm *n*, -sommer *m*); ♀ *Latin* Spätlatein *n*; *the* ~ *18th century* das späte 18. Jahrhundert; *in the* ~ *eighties* gegen Ende der Achtzigerjahre; *a man in his* ~ *eighties* ein Endachtziger; *in* ~ *May* Ende Mai; **3.** verspätet, zu spät: *be* ~ zu spät kommen (*for s.th.* zu et.), sich verspäten, spät dran sein, 🚆 *etc.* Verspätung haben: *be* ~ *for dinner* zu spät zum Essen kommen; *he was* ~ *with the rent* er bezahlte s-e Miete mit Verspätung *od.* zu spät; **4.** letzt, jüngst, neu: *the* ~ *war* der letzte Krieg; *of* ~ *years* in den letzten Jahren; **5.** a) letzt, früher, ehemalig, b) verstorben: *the* ~ *headmaster* der letzte *od.* der verstorbene Schuldirektor; *the* ~ *government* die letzte *od.* vorige Regierung; *my* ~ *residence* m-e frühere Wohnung; ~ *of Oxford* früher in Oxford (wohnhaft); **II** *adv.* **6.** spät: *of* ~ in letzter Zeit, neuerdings; *as* ~ *as last year* erst *od.* noch letztes Jahr; *until as* ~ *as 1984* noch bis 1984; *better* ~ *than never* lieber spät als gar nicht; ~ *into the night* bis spät in die Nacht; *sit* (*od. stay*) *up* ~ bis spät in die Nacht *od.* lange aufbleiben; *it's a bit* ~ F es ist schon ein bisschen spät dafür; (*even*) ~ *in life* (auch noch) in hohem Alter; *not* ~*r than* spätestens, nicht später als; ~*r on* später, nachher; *see you* ~*r!* bis später!, bis bald!; ~ *in the day* F reichlich spät, ‚ein bisschen‘ spät; **7.** zu spät: *come* ~; *the train arrived 20 minutes* ~ der Zug hatte 20 Minuten Verspätung; '~**·com·er** *s.* Zu'spätgekommene(r *m*) *f*, Nachzügler(in), *fig. a.* e-e Neuerscheinung, *et.* Neues: *he is a* ~ *in this field fig.* er ist neu in diesem (Fach)Gebiet.

late·ly ['leɪtlɪ] *adv.* **1.** vor kurzem, kürzlich; **2.** in letzter Zeit, seit einiger Zeit, neuerdings.

la·ten·cy ['leɪtənsɪ] *s.* La'tenz *f*, Verborgenheit *f*.

late·ness ['leɪtnɪs] *s.* **1.** späte Zeit, spätes Stadium: *the* ~ *of the hour* die vorgerückte Stunde; **2.** Verspätung *f*, Zu'spätkommen *n*.

la·tent ['leɪtənt] *adj.* □ la'tent (*a.* 🐟, *phys., psych.*), verborgen: ~ *abilities*; ~ *buds* unentwickelte Knospen; ~ *heat phys.* latente *od.* gebundene Wärme; ~ *period* Latenzstadium *n od.* -zeit *f*.

lat·er ['leɪtə] *comp. von* late.

lat·er·al ['lætərəl] **I** *adj.* □ **1.** seitlich, Seiten..., Neben..., Quer...: ~ *angle* (*view, wind*) Seitenwinkel *m* (-ansicht *f*, -wind *m*); ~ *branch* Seitenlinie *f* (*e-s Stammbaums*) *f*; **2.** *anat., ling.* late'ral; **II** *s.* **3.** Seitenteil *m*, -stück *n*; **4.** *ling.* Late'ral *m*; '**lat·er·al·ly** [-rəlɪ] *adv.* seitlich, seitwärts; von der Seite.

Lat·er·an ['lætərən] *s.* Late'ran *m*.

lat·est ['leɪtɪst] **I** *sup. von* late; **II** *adj.* **1.**

spätest; **2.** neuest: *the* ~ *fashion* (*news, etc.*); **3.** letzt: *he was the* ~ *to come* er kam als Letzter; **III** *adv.* **4.** am spätesten: *he came* ~ er kam als Letzter; **IV** *s.* **5.** (*der, die, das*) Neueste; **6.** *at the* ~ spätestens.

la·tex ['leɪteks] *s.* ♀ Milchsaft *m*, Latex *m*.

lath [lɑːθ] *s.* **1.** Latte *f*, Leiste *f*: → *thin* 2; **2.** *coll.* Latten(werk *n*) *pl.*

lathe [leɪð] *s.* ⚙ **1.** Drehbank *f*: ~ *tool* Drehstahl *m*; ~ *tooling* Bearbeitung *f* auf der Drehbank; **2.** Töpferscheibe *f*.

lath·er ['lɑːðə] **I** *s.* **1.** (Seifen)Schaum *m*; **2.** Schweiß *m* (*bsd. e-s Pferdes*): *in a* ~ schweißgebadet; *be in a* ~ *about s.th.* F sich über et. aufregen; **II** *v/t.* **3.** einseifen; **III** *v/i.* **4.** schäumen.

Lat·in ['lætɪn] **I** *s.* **1.** *ling.* La'tein(isch) *n*, das Lateinische; **2.** *antiq.* a) La'tiner *m*, b) Römer *m*; **3.** Ro'mane *m*, Ro'manin *f*, Südländer(in); **II** *adj.* **4.** *ling.* la'teinisch, Latein...; **3.** a) ro'manisch: *the* ~ *peoples*, b) südländisch: ~ *temperament*; **6.** *eccl.* römisch-ka'tholisch: ~ *Church*; **7.** la'tinisch; ,~**-A'mer·i·can I** *adj.* la'teinameri,kanisch; **II** *s.* La'teinameri,kaner(in).

Lat·in·ism ['lætɪnɪzəm] *s.* Lati'nismus *m*; '**Lat·in·ist** [-nɪst] *s.* Lati'nist(in), ,La'teiner' *m*; **Lat·in·i·za·tion** [,lætɪnaɪ'zeɪʃn] *s.* Latinisierung *f*; '**Lat·in·ize** [-naɪz] *v/t.* latinisieren; **La·ti·no** [lə'tiːnəʊ] *pl.* **-nos** *s. Am.* F (*US-*)Einwohner (*-in*) *lateinamerikanischer Abkunft.*

lat·ish ['leɪtɪʃ] *adj.* etwas spät.

lat·i·tude ['lætɪtjuːd] *s.* **1.** *ast., geogr.* Breite *f*: *degree of* ~ Breitengrad *m*; *in* ~ *40° N.* auf dem 40. Grad nördlicher Breite; **2.** *pl. geogr.* Breiten *pl.*, Gegenden *pl.*: *low* ~*s* niedere Breiten; *cold* ~*s* kalte Gegenden; **3.** *fig.* a) Spielraum *m*, Freiheit *f*, *allow s.o. great* ~ j-m große Freiheit gewähren, b) großzügige Auslegung (*e-s Begriffs etc.*); **4.** *phot.* Belichtungsspielraum *m*; **lat·i·tu·di·nal** [,lætɪ'tjuːdɪnl] *adj. geogr.* Breiten...

lat·i·tu·di·nar·i·an [,lætɪtjuːdɪ'neərɪən] **I** *adj.* libe'ral, tole'rant, *eccl. a.* freisinnig; **II** *s. bsd. eccl.* Freigeist *m*; ,**lat·i·tu·di'nar·i·an·ism** [-nɪzəm] *s. eccl.* Libe'ralität *f*, Tole'ranz *f*.

la·trine [lə'triːn] *s.* La'trine *f*.

lat·ter ['lætə] **I** *adj.* □ → *latterly*; **1.** *von zweien:* letzter: *the* ~ *name* der letztere *od.* letztgenannte Name; **2.** neuer, jünger: *in these* ~ *days* in der jüngsten Zeit; **3.** letzt, später: *the* ~ *years of one's life*; *the* ~ *half of June* die zweite Junihälfte; *the* ~ *part of the book* die zweite Hälfte des Buches; **II** *s.* **4.** *the* ~ a) der (die, das) Letztere, b) die Letzteren *pl.*; '~**-day** *adj.* aus neuester Zeit, mo'dern; '~**-day saints** *s. pl. eccl.* die Heiligen *pl.* der letzten Tage (*Mormonen*).

lat·ter·ly ['lætəlɪ] *adv.* **1.** in letzter Zeit, neuerdings; **2.** am Ende.

lat·tice ['lætɪs] **I** *s.* **1.** Gitter(werk) *n*; **2.** Gitterfenster *n od.* -tür *f*; **3.** Gitter(muster *n*) *n*; **II** *v/t.* **4.** vergittern; ~ *bridge s.* ⊘ Gitterbrücke *f*; ~ *frame*, ~ *gird·er s.* ⊘ Gitter-, Fachwerkträger *m*; ~ *win·dow s.* Gitter-, Rautenfenster *n*; '~**·work** → *lattice*.

Lat·vi·an ['lætvɪən] **I** *adj.* **1.** lettisch; **II** *s.* **2.** Lette *m*, Lettin *f*; **3.** *ling.* Lettisch *n*.

laud [lɔːd] **I** *s.* Lobgesang *m*; **II** *v/t.* loben, preisen, rühmen; '**laud·a·ble** [-dəbl] *adj.* □ löblich, lobenswert.

lau·da·num ['lɒdnəm] *s. pharm.* Lau'danum *n*, 'Opiumtink,tur *f*.

lau·da·tion [lɔː'deɪʃn] *s.* Lob *m*; **lauda·-**

to·ry ['lɔːdətərɪ] *adj.* lobend, Belobigungs..., Lob...

laugh [lɑːf] **I** *s.* **1.** Lachen *n*, Gelächter *n*, *thea. etc. a.* ‚Lacher‘ *m*, *contp.* (*böse etc.*) Lache: *with a* ~ lachend; *have a good* ~ *at s.th.* herzlich über e-e Sache lachen; *have the* ~ *of s.o.* über j-n (am Ende) triumphieren; *have the* ~ *on one's side* die Lacher auf s-r Seite haben; *the* ~ *was on me* der Scherz ging auf m-e Kosten; *raise a* ~ Gelächter erregen, e-n Lacherfolg erzielen; *what a* ~*!* (das) ist ja zum Brüllen!; *he* (*it*) *is a* ~ F er (es) ist doch zum Lachen; *just for* ~*s* nur zum Spaß; **II** *v/i.* **2.** lachen (*a. fig.*): *to make s.o.* ~ j-n zum Lachen bringen; *don't make me* ~*!* *iro.* dass ich nicht lache!; *he* ~*s best who* ~*s last* wer zuletzt lacht, lacht am besten; → *wrong* 2; **3.** *fig.* lachen, strahlen (*Himmel etc.*); **III** *v/t.* **4.** lachend äußern: ~ *a bitter* ~ bitter lachen; → *court* 9;

Zssgn mit adv. u. prp.:

~ *at v/i.* lachen *od.* sich lustig machen über *j-n od. e-e Sache*, *j-n* auslachen; ~ *a·way I v/t.* **1.** → *laugh off*; **2.** *Sorgen etc.* durch Lachen verscheuchen; **3.** *Zeit* mit Scherzen verbringen; **II** *v/i.* **4.** drauf'loslachen, lachen u. lachen; ~ *down v/t.* j-n durch Gelächter zum Schweigen bringen; ~ mit Lachen über'tönen, auslachen; ~ *off v/t. et.* lachend *od.* mit e-m Scherz abtun.

laugh·a·ble ['lɑːfəbl] *adj.* □ lachhaft, lächerlich, komisch.

laugh·ing ['lɑːfɪŋ] **I** *s.* **1.** Lachen *n*, Gelächter *n*; **II** *adj.* □ **2.** lachend; **3.** lustig: *it is no* ~ *matter* das ist nicht zum Lachen; **4.** *fig.* lachend, strahlend: *a* ~ *sky*; ~ *gas s.* 🜔 Lachgas *n*; ~ *gull s. orn.* Lachmöwe *f*; ~ *hy·e·na s. zo.* 'Fleckenhy,äne *f*; ~ *jack·ass s. orn.* Rieseneisvogel *m*; ~ *stock s.* Gegenstand *m* des Gelächters, Zielscheibe *f* des Spottes: *make a* ~ *of o.s.* sich lächerlich machen.

laugh·ter ['lɑːftə] *s.* Lachen *n*, Gelächter *n*.

launch [lɔːntʃ] **I** *v/t.* **1.** *Boot* aussetzen, ins Wasser lassen; **2.** *Schiff* a) vom Stapel lassen, b) taufen: *be* ~*ed* vom Stapel laufen *od.* getauft werden; **3.** ✈ katapultieren, abschießen; **4.** *Torpedo, Geschoss* abschießen, *Rakete a.* starten; **5.** *et.* schleudern, werfen: ~ *o.s into* → 12; **6.** *Rede, Kritik, Protest etc., a.* e-n *Schlag* vom Stapel lassen, loslassen; **7.** *et.* in Gang bringen, einleiten, starten, lancieren; **8.** *et.* lancieren: a) *Produkt, Buch, Film etc.* her'ausbringen, b) *Anleihe* auflegen, *Aktien* ausgeben; **9.** *j-n* lancieren, (gut) einführen, j-m ‚Starthilfe‘ geben; **10.** ✗ *Truppen* einsetzen, *an e-e Front etc.* schicken *od.* werfen; **II** *v/i.* **11.** *mst* ~ *out*, ~ *forth* losfahren, starten: ~ *out on a journey* sich auf e-e Reise begeben; **12.** ~ *out* (*into*) *fig.* a) sich (in *die Arbeit, e-e Debatte etc.*) stürzen, b) loslegen (mit e-r *Rede, e-r Tätigkeit etc.*), c) (*et.*) anpacken, (*e-e Karriere, ein Projekt etc.*) starten: ~ *out into* → *a.* 6; **13.** ~ *out* a) e-n Wortschwall von sich geben, b) F viel Geld springen lassen; **III** *s.* **14.** ⚓ Bar'kasse *f*; **15.** → *launching*. '**launch·er** [-tʃə] *s.* **1.** ✗ a) (Ra'keten)Werfer *m*, b) Abschussvorrichtung *f* (*Fernlenkgeschosse*); **2.** ✈ Kata'pult *m*, *n*, Startschleuder *f*.

launch·ing ['lɔːntʃɪŋ] *s.* **1.** ⚓ a) Stapellauf *m*, b) Aussetzen *n* (*von Booten*); **2.** Abschuss *m*, *e-r Rakete: a.* Start *m*; **3.**

✕ Kata'pultstart *m*; **4.** *fig.* a) Starten *n*, In-'Gang-Setzen *n*, b) Start *m*, c) Einsatz *m*; **5.** Lancierung *f*, Einführung *f* (*e-s Produkts etc.*), Herausgabe *f* (*e-s Buches etc.*); **~ pad**, **~ plat·form** *s*. Abschussrampe *f* (*e-r Rakete*); **~ rope** *s*. ✔ Startseil *n*; **~ site** *s*. ✕ (Ra'keten-) ,Abschuss,basis *f*; **~ ve·hi·cle** *s*. 'Startra-,kete *f*.

laun·der ['lɔːndə] **I** *v/t.* Wäsche waschen (u. bügeln); F *fig. illegal erworbenes Geld* ,waschen'; **II** *v/i.* sich (*leicht etc.*) waschen lassen; **laun·der·ette** [,lɔːndə-'ret] *s.* 'Waschsa,lon *m*; **'laun·dress** [-drɪs] *s.* Wäscherin *f*.

laun·dry ['lɔːndrɪ] *s.* **1.** Wäsche'rei *f*; **2.** F (schmutzige *od.* frisch gereinigte) Wäsche; **~ list 1.** Wäschezettel *m*; **2.** *Am.* F lange Liste.

lau·re·ate ['lɔːrɪət] **I** *adj.* **1.** lorbeergekrönt, -geschmückt; -bekränzt; **II** *s.* **2.** *mst* **poet ~** Hofdichter *m*; **3.** Preisträger *m*.

lau·rel ['lɔrəl] *s.* **1.** ♀ Lorbeer(baum) *m*; **2.** *mst pl. fig.* Lorbeeren *pl.*, Ehren *pl.*, Ruhm *m*: **look to one's ~s** sich behaupten wollen; **reap** (*od.* **win** *od.* **gain**) **~s** Lorbeeren ernten; **rest on one's ~s** sich auf s-n Lorbeeren ausruhen; **'lau·rel(l)ed** [-ld] *adj.* **1.** lorbeergekrönt; **2.** preisgekrönt.

lav [læv] *s. Brit.* F ,Klo' *n*.

la·va ['lɑːvə] *s. geol.* Lava *f*.

lav·a·to·ry ['lævətərɪ] *s.* Toi'lette *f*: **pub·lic ~** *a.* (öffentliche) Bedürfnisanstalt.

lav·en·der ['lævəndə] **I** *s.* **1.** ♀ La'vendel *m* (*a. Farbe*); **2.** La'vendel(wasser) *n*; **II** *adj.* **3.** la'vendelfarben.

lav·ish ['lævɪʃ] **I** *adj.* □ a) großzügig, reich, fürstlich, üppig (*Geschenke etc.*), b) reich, 'überschwänglich (*Lob etc.*), c) großzügig, verschwenderisch (*of mit, in* in *dat.*) (*Person*): **be ~ of** (*od.* **with**) um sich werfen mit, nicht geizen mit, verschwenderisch umgehen mit; **II** *v/t.* verschwenden, verschwenderisch (aus-) geben: **~ s.th. on s.o.** j-n mit et. überhäufen; **'lav·ish·ness** [-nɪs] *s.* Großzügigkeit *f* (*etc.*); Verschwendung(ssucht) *f*.

law [lɔː] *s.* **1.** (*objektives*) Recht, (*das*) Gesetz *n od.* (*die*) Gesetze *pl.*: **by** (*od.* **in**, **under the**) **~** nach dem Gesetz, von Rechts wegen, gesetzlich; **under German ~** nach deutschem Recht; **contra·ry to ~** gesetz-, rechtswidrig; **~ and order** Recht (*od.* Ruhe) u. Ordnung, *contp.* ,Law and order'; **become** (*od.* **pass into**) **~** Gesetz *od.* rechtskräftig werden; **lay down the ~** (*alles*) bestimmen, das Sagen haben; **take the ~ into one's own hands** zur Selbsthilfe greifen; **his word is the ~** was er sagt, gilt; **2.** Recht *n*: a) 'Rechtssy,stem *n*: **the English ~**, b) (*einzelnes*) Rechtsgebiet: **~ of nations** Völkerrecht; **3.** (*einzelnes*) Gesetz: **Election** ♀; **he is a ~ unto himself** er tut, was er will; **is there a ~ against it?** *iro.* ist das (etwa) verboten?; **4.** Rechtswissenschaft *f*, Jura *pl.*: **read** (*od.* **study**, **take**) **~** Jura studieren; **be in the ~** Jurist sein; **practise ~** e-e Anwaltspraxis ausüben; **5.** Gericht *n*, Rechtsweg *m*: **go to ~** vor Gericht gehen, den Rechtsweg beschreiten, prozessieren; **go to ~ with s.o.** j-n verklagen, gegen j-n prozessieren; **6.** *the ~* F die Polizei: **call in the ~**; **7.** (*künstlerisches etc.*) Gesetz: **the ~s of poetry**; **8.** (*Spiel*)Regel *f*: **the ~s of the game**; **9.** a) (Na'tur)Gesetz *n*, b) (wissenschaftliches) Gesetz: **the ~ of gravity**, c) (Lehr)Satz *m*: **~ of sines** Sinussatz; **10.** *eccl.* a) (göttliches) Gesetz, *coll.* die

Gebote (Gottes), b) *the ♀ (of Moses)* das Gesetz (des Moses), c) *the ♀* das Alte Testament; **11.** *hunt.*, *sport* Vorgabe *f*; **'~·a,bid·ing** *adj.* gesetzestreu, ordnungsliebend; **~ citizen**; **'~·break·er** *s.* Ge'setzesüber,treter(in); **~ court** *s.* Gericht(shof *m*) *n*.

law·ful ['lɔːfʊl] *adj.* □ **1.** gesetzlich, le-'gal; **2.** rechtmäßig, legi'tim: **~ son** ehelicher *od.* legitimer Sohn; **3.** rechtsgültig, gesetzlich anerkannt: **~ marriage** gültige Ehe; **'law·ful·ness** [-nɪs] *s.* Gesetzlichkeit *f*, Legali'tät *f*; Rechtsgültigkeit *f*.

'law,giv·er *s.* Gesetzgeber *m*.

law·less ['lɔːlɪs] *adj.* □ **1.** gesetzlos (*Land*, *Person*); **2.** gesetzwidrig, unrechtmäßig; **'law·less·ness** [-nɪs] *s.* **1.** Gesetzlosigkeit *f*; **2.** Gesetzwidrigkeit *f*.

Law Lord *s.* Mitglied *n* des brit. Oberhauses mit richterlicher Funkti'on.

lawn¹ [lɔːn] *s.* Rasen *m*.

lawn² [lɔːn] *s.* Li'non *m*, Ba'tist *m*.

lawn| mow·er *s.* Rasenmäher *m*; **~ sprin·kler** *s.* Rasensprenger *m*; **~ ten·nis** *s.* Rasentennis *n*.

law| of·fice *s.* 'Anwaltskanz,lei *f*, -praxis *f*; **~ of·fi·cer** *s.* ⚖ **1.** Ju'stizbeamte(r) *m*; **2.** *Brit. für* a) **Attorney General**, b) **Solicitor General**; **~ re·ports** *s. pl.* Urteilssammlung *f*, Sammlung *f* von richterlichen Entscheidungen; **~ school** *s.* **1.** 'Rechtsakade,mie *f*; **2.** *univ. Am.* ju'ristische Fakul'tät; **~ stu·dent** *s.* 'Jurastu,dent(in); **'~·suit** *s.* a) Pro'zess *m*, Verfahren *n*, b) Klage *f*: **bring a ~** e-n Prozess anstrengen, Klage einreichen (**against** gegen).

law·yer ['lɔːjə] *s.* **1.** (Rechts)Anwalt *m*, (-)Anwältin *f*; **2.** Rechtsberater(in); **3.** Ju'rist(in).

lax [læks] *adj.* □ **1.** lax, locker, (nach-) lässig (**about** hinsichtlich *gen.*, mit): **~ morals** lockere Sitten; **2.** lose, schlaff, locker; **3.** unklar, verschwommen; **4.** *Phonetik:* schlaff artikuliert; **5. ~ bowels** a) offener Leib, b) 'Durchfall *m*; **lax·a·tive** ['læksətɪv] ✚ **I** *s.* Abführmittel *n*; **II** *adj.* abführend; **lax·i·ty** ['læksətɪ], **'lax·ness** [-nɪs] *s.* **1.** Laxheit *f*, Lässigkeit *f*; **2.** Schlaffheit *f*, Lockerheit *f* (*a. fig.*); **3.** Verschwommenheit *f*.

lay¹ [leɪ] **I** *s.* **1.** *bsd. geogr.* Lage *f*: **the ~ of the land** die Lage; **2.** Schicht *f*, Lage *f*; **3.** Schlag *m* (*Tauwerk*); **4.** V a) ,Nummer' *f* (*Koitus*), b) **she is an easy ~** die ist gleich ,dabei'; **she is a good ~** sie ,bumst' gut; **II** *v/t.* [*irr.*] **5.** *allg.* legen: **~ it on the table**; **~ a cable** ein Kabel (ver)legen; **~ a bridge** e-e Brücke schlagen; **~ eggs** Eier legen; **~ the foundation(s) of** *fig.* den Grund (-stock) legen zu; **~ the foundation stone** den Grundstein legen; → *die Verbindungen mit den entsprechenden Substantiven etc.*; **6.** *fig.* legen, setzen: **~ stress on** Nachdruck legen auf (*acc.*), betonen; **~ an ambush** e-n Hinterhalt legen; **~ the ax(e) to a tree** die Axt an ein Baum legen; **the scene is laid in Rome** der Schauplatz *od.* Ort der Handlung ist Rom, *thea.* das Stück etc. spielt in Rom; **7.** anordnen, herrichten: **~ the table** (*od.* **the cloth**) den Tisch decken; **~ the fire** das Feuer (*im Kamin*) anlegen; **8.** belegen, bedecken: **~ the floor with a carpet**; **9.** (*before*) vorlegen (*dat.*), bringen (*vor acc.*): **~ one's case before a commission**; **10.** geltend machen, erheben: **~ an information against s.o.** Klage erheben *od.* (Straf)Anzeige erstatten gegen; **11.**

a) *Strafe etc.* verhängen, b) *Steuern* auferlegen; **12.** *Schuld etc.* zuschreiben, zur Last legen: **~ a mistake to s.o.('s charge)** j-m e-n Fehler zur Last legen; **13.** *Schaden* festsetzen (**at** auf *acc.*); **14.** a) *et.* wetten, b) setzen auf (*acc.*); **15.** *e-n Plan* schmieden; **16.** 'umlegen, niederwerfen: **~ s.o. low** (*od.* **in the dust**) j-n zu Boden strecken; **17.** *Getreide etc.* zu Boden drücken; **18.** *Wind, Wogen etc.* beruhigen, besänftigen: **the wind is laid** der Wind hat sich gelegt; **19.** *Staub* löschen; **20.** *Geist* bannen, beschwören; → **ghost** 1; **21.** ⚓ *Kurs* nehmen auf (*acc.*), ansteuern; **22.** ✕ *Geschütz* richten; **23.** V ,umlegen', ,bumsen'; **III** *v/i.* [*irr.*] **24.** (Eier) legen; **25.** wetten; **26.** zuschlagen: **~ about one** um sich schlagen; **~ into s.o.** *sl.* auf j-n einschlagen; **~ to** (mächtig) ,rangehen' an *e-e Sache*; **27.** (*fälschlich für lie²* II) liegen; *Zssgn mit adv.*:

lay| a·bout *v/i.* (heftig) um sich schlagen; **~ a·side**, **~ by** *v/t.* **1.** bei'seite legen; **2.** *fig.* a) aufgeben, b) ,ausklammern'; **3.** *Geld etc.* beiseite *od.* auf die ,hohe Kante' legen, zu'rücklegen; **~ down I** *v/t.* **1.** hinlegen; **2.** *Amt, Waffen etc.* niederlegen; **3.** *sein Leben* hingeben, opfern; **4.** *Geld* hinter'legen; **5.** *Grundsatz, Regeln etc.* aufstellen, festlegen, -setzen, vorschreiben, *Bedingung in e-m Vertrag* niederlegen, verankern; → **law** 1; **6.** a) die Grundlagen legen für, b) planen, entwerfen; **7.** ✚ besäen *od.* bepflanzen (**in**, **to**, **under**, **with** mit); **8.** *Wein etc.* (ein)lagern; **II** *v/i.* **9.** *fälschlich für lie down* 1; **~ in** *v/t.* sich eindecken mit, einlagern, *Vorrat* anlegen; **~ off I** *v/t.* **1.** *Arbeiter* (vorübergehend) entlassen; **2.** *die Arbeit* einstellen; **3.** *das Rauchen etc.* aufgeben: **~ smoking**; **4.** in Ruhe lassen: **~ (it)!** hör auf (damit)!; **II** *v/i.* **5.** aufhören; **~ on I** *v/t.* **1.** *Steuer etc.* auferlegen; **2.** *Peitsche* gebrauchen; **3.** *Farbe etc.* auftragen: **lay it on** a) (**thick**) *fig.* ,dick auftragen', übertreiben, b) e-e ,saftige' Rechnung stellen, c) draufschlagen; **4.** a) *Gas etc.* installieren, b) *Haus* ans (*Gas- etc.*)Netz anschließen; **5.** F a) auftischen, b) bieten, sorgen für, c) veranstalten, arrangieren; **II** *v/i.* **6.** zuschlagen, angreifen; **~ o·pen** *v/t.* **1.** bloßlegen; **2.** *fig.* a) aufdecken, b) offen legen; **~ out** *v/t.* **1.** ausbreiten; **2.** *Toten* aufbahren; **3.** *Geld* ausgeben; **4.** *allg.* gestalten, *Garten etc.* anlegen, et. entwerfen, planen, anordnen, *typ.* aufmachen, das Lay-out *e-r Zeitschrift etc.* machen; **5.** *sl.* a) j-n zs.-schlagen, b) j-n ,umlegen', ,kaltmachen'; **~ o·ver I** *v/t. et.* zu'rückstellen; **II** *v/i.* Aufenthalt haben, 'Zwischenstati,on machen; **~ to** *v/i.* ⚓ beidrehen; **~ up** *v/t.* **1.** → **lay in** 2. ansammeln, anhäufen; **3.** a) ⚓ *Schiff* auflegen, außer Dienst stellen, b) *mot.* stilllegen; **4. be laid up** (**with**) bettlägerig sein (wegen), im Bett liegen (mit *Grippe etc.*).

lay² [leɪ] *pret. von* **lie²**.

lay³ [leɪ] *adj.* Laien...: a) *eccl.* weltlich; b) laienhaft, nicht fachmännisch: **to the ~ mind** für den Laien(verstand).

lay⁴ [leɪ] *s. obs.* **1.** Bal'lade *f*; **2.** Lied *n*.

'lay·a·bout *s. bsd. Brit.* F Faulenzer *m*; **~ broth·er** *s. eccl.* Laienbruder *m*; **'~-by** *s. mot. Brit.* a) Rastplatz *m*, Parkplatz *m*, b) Parkbucht *f* (*Landstraße*); **~ days** *s. pl.* ⚓ Liegetage *pl.*, -zeit *f*; **'~-down** → **lie-down**.

lay·er I s. ['leɪə] **1.** Schicht f, Lage f: *in* ~*s* schicht-, lagenweise; **2.** Leger m, *in Zssgn* ...leger m; **3.** Leg(e)henne f: *this hen is a good* ~ diese Henne legt gut; **4.** ✔ Ableger m; **5.** ✗ 'Höhenrichtkano‚nier m; **II** v/t. **6.** ✔ durch Ableger vermehren; **7.** über‚lagern, schichtweise legen; ~ *cake* s. Schichttorte f.
lay·ette [leɪ'et] s. Babyausstattung f.
lay fig·ure s. **1.** Gliederpuppe f (*als Modell*); **2.** *fig.* Mario'nette f, Null f.
lay·ing ['leɪɪŋ] s. **1.** Legen n (*etc.* → *lay¹* II u. III): ~ *on of hands* Handauflegen n; **2.** Gelege n (*Eier*); **3.** ⚘ Bewurf m, Putz m.
lay‖ judge s. Laienrichter(in); '~·man [-mən] s. [*irr.*] **1.** Laie m (*Ggs. Geistlicher*); **2.** Laie m, Nichtfachmann m; '~·off s. **1.** (vor'übergehende) Entlassung; **2.** Feierschicht f; '~·out s. **1.** Planung f, Anordnung f, Anlage f; **2.** Plan m, Entwurf m; **3.** *typ.*, *a.* Elektronik: Lay-out n: ~ *man* Layouter m; **4.** Aufmachung f (*e-r Zeitschrift etc.*); ~ *sis·ter* s. Laienschwester f; '~·wom·an s. [*irr.*] Laiin f.
laze [leɪz] **I** v/i. *a.* ~ *around* faulenzen, bummeln, auf die faulen Haut liegen; **II** v/t. ~ *away* Zeit verbummeln; **III** s.: *have a* ~ → I; **la·zi·ness** ['leɪzɪnɪs] s. Faulheit f, Trägheit f.
la·zy ['leɪzɪ] adj. □ träg(e): a) faul, b) langsam, sich langsam bewegend; '~·bones s. F Faulpelz m.
'ld [d] F *für* would *od.* should.
lea [liː] s. *poet.* Flur f, Aue f.
leach [liːtʃ] **I** v/t. **1.** 'durchsickern lassen; **2.** (aus)laugen; **II** v/i. **3.** 'durchsickern.
lead¹ [liːd] s. **1.** Führung f, Leitung f: *under s.o.'s* ~; **2.** Führung f, Spitze f: *be in the* ~, *have the* ~ an der Spitze stehen, führen(d sein), *sport etc.* in Führung *od.* vorn liegen; *take the* ~ a) *a. sport* die Führung übernehmen, sich an die Spitze setzen, b) die Initiative ergreifen, c) vorangehen, neue Wege weisen; **3.** *bsd. sport* a) Führung f: *have a two-goal* ~ mit zwei Toren führen, b) Vorsprung m: *one minute's* ~ 'eine Minute Vorsprung (*over s.o.* vor j-m); **4.** Vorbild n, Beispiel n: *give s.o. a* ~ j-m mit gutem Beispiel vorangehen; *follow s.o.'s* ~ j-s Beispiel folgen; **5.** Hinweis m, Fingerzeig m, Anhaltspunkt m, Spur f: *the police have several* ~*s*; **6.** *Kartenspiel:* a) Vorhand f, b) zu'erst ausgespielte Karte: *your* ~! Sie spielen aus!, b) zu'erst ausgespielte Karte; **7.** *thea.* a) Hauptrolle f, b) Hauptdarsteller(in); **8.** ♪ a) Eröffnung f, Auftakt m, b) *Jazz etc.:* Lead n, Führungsstimme f (*Trompete etc.*); **9.** *Zeitung:* a) → *lead story*, b) (zs.-fassende) Einleitung; **10.** (Hunde)Leine f; **11.** ⚡ a) Leiter m, b) (Zu)Leitung f, c) *a.* **phase** ~ Voreilung f; **12.** ⚙ Steigung f (*e-s Gewindes*); **13.** ✗ Vorhalt m; **II** v/t. [*irr.*] **14.** führen: ~ *the way* vorangehen; *this is* ~*ing us nowhere* das bringt uns nicht weiter; → *nose Redew.*; **15.** j-n führen, bringen (*to* nach, zu) (*a. Straße etc.*); → *temptation*; **16.** (an)führen, an der Spitze stehen von, *a. Orchester etc.* leiten, *Armee* führen *od.* befehligen; ~ *the field sport* das Feld anführen, vorn liegen; **17.** j-n dazu bringen, bewegen, verleiten (*to do s.th.* et. zu tun): *this led me to believe* das machte mich glauben(, *dass*); **18.** a) *ein behagliches etc.* Leben führen, b) *j-m ein elendes etc.* Leben bereiten: ~ *s.o. a dog's life* j-m das Leben zur Hölle machen; **19.** *Karte, Farbe etc.* aus-, anspielen; **20.** *Kabel etc.* führen,

legen; **III** v/i. [*irr.*] **21.** führen: a) vorangehen, den Weg weisen (*a. fig.*), b) die erste Stelle einnehmen, c) *sport* in Führung liegen (*by* mit 7 *Metern etc.*): ~ *by points* nach Punkten führen; **22.** ~ *to* a) führen *od.* gehen zu *od.* nach (*Straße etc.*), b) *fig.* führen zu: *this is* ~*ing nowhere* das führt zu nichts; **23.** *Kartenspiel:* ausspielen (*with s.th.* et.): *who* ~*s?*; **24.** *Boxen:* angreifen (mit der Linken *od.* Rechten): *he* ~*s with his right* a. s-e Führungshand ist die Rechte, er ist Rechtsausleger; ~ *with one's chin fig.* das Schicksal herausfordern;
Zssgn mit adv.:
lead‖ a·stray v/t. in die Irre führen, *fig. a.* irre-, verführen; ~ **a·way** I v/t. **1.** a) j-n wegführen, b) → *lead off* 1; **2.** *fig.* j-n abbringen (*from* von e-m *Thema etc.*); **3.** *be led away* sich verleiten lassen; **II** v/i. **4.** ~ *from* von e-m *Thema etc.* wegführen; ~ **off** I v/t. **1.** j-n abführen; **2.** *fig.* einleiten, eröffnen; **II** v/i. **3.** den Anfang machen; ~ **on** I v/i. vor'angehen; **II** v/t. *fig.* a) j-n hinters Licht führen, b) j-n auf den Arm nehmen, c) j-n an der Nase herumführen; ~ **up** I v/t. (*to*) a) (hin'auf)führen (auf *acc.*), b) (hin'über)führen (zu); **II** v/i. ~ *to fig.* a) (all'mählich) führen zu, 'überleiten zu, *et.* einleiten: *what is he leading up to?* worauf will er hinaus?
lead² [led] **I** s. **1.** ⚗ Blei n; **2.** ⚓ Senkblei n, Lot n: *cast* (*od.* heave) *the* ~ loten; **3.** Blei n, Kugeln pl. (*Geschosse*); **4.** Gra'phit m, Reißblei n; **5.** (Blei)stift)Mine f; **6.** *typ.* 'Durchschuss m; **7.** Bleifassung f (*Fenster*); **8.** *pl. Brit.* a) bleierne Dachplatten pl., b) Bleidach n; **II** v/t. **9.** verbleien; **10.** mit Blei beschweren; **11.** *typ.* durch'schießen; ~ **con·tent** s. ⚗ Bleigehalt m (*im Benzin*).
lead·en ['ledn] adj. bleiern (*a. fig. Glieder, Schlaf etc.*; *a.* bleigrau), Blei...
lead·er ['liːdə] s. **1.** Führer(in), Erste(r m) f, *sport a.* Ta'bellenführer m; **2.** (An)Führer(in), (*pol.* Partei-, Fraktions-, Oppositions-, ✗ *bsd.* Zug-, Gruppen)Führer m: ⚒ *of the House parl.* Vorsitzende(r) m des Unterhauses; **3.** ♪ a) Kon'zertmeister m, erster Violi'nist, b) Führungsstimme f (*erster Sopran od. Bläser etc.*), c) *Am.* (Or'chester-, Chor)Leiter m, Diri'gent m; **4.** Leiter(in) (*e-s Projekts etc.*); **5.** Leitpferd n *od.* -hund n; **6.** ⚖ *Brit.* erster Anwalt (*mst Kronanwalt*): ~ *for the defence* Hauptverteidiger m; **7.** *bsd. Brit.* 'Leitar‚tikel m (*Zeitung*): ~ *writer* Leitartikler m; **8.** *allg. fig.* 'Spitzenrei‚ter' m, *pl. a.* Spitzengruppe f; **9.** ♠ a) 'Lockar‚tikel m, b) 'Spitzenar‚tikel m, führendes Pro'dukt, c) *pl. Börse:* führende Werte pl., d) *Statistik:* Index m; **10.** ✿ Haupttrieb m; **11.** *anat.* Sehne f; **12.** Startband n (*e-s Films etc.*); **13.** *typ.* Leit-, Ta'bellenpunkt m.
lead·er·ship ['liːdəʃɪp] s. **1.** Führung f, Leitung f; **2.** 'Führungsquali‚täten pl.
lead-free ['ledfriː] adj. bleifrei: ~ *petrol* bleifreies Benzin.
'lead-in ['liːd-] **I** s. ⚡ Zuleitung..., *a. fig.* Einführung...; **II** s. **2.** (An'tennen- *etc.*)Zuleitung f; **3.** *fig.* Einleitung f.
lead·ing ['liːdɪŋ] führend: a) erst, vorderst: *the* ~ *car*, b) *fig.* Haupt...: ~ *part thea.* Hauptrolle f; ~ *product* Spitzenprodukt n, c) tonangebend, maßgeblich: ~ *citizen* prominenter Bürger; ~ *ar·ti·cle* → *leader* 7, 9 a, b; ~ *case* s. ⚖ Präze'denzfall m; ~ *edge* s. ✈ Flü-

gelvorderkante f; '~·edge adj. Spitzen...: ~ *technology* Spitzentechnik f; ~ **la·dy** s. Hauptdarstellerin f; ~ **light** s. F *fig.* ‚Leuchte' f (*Person*); ~ **man** s. [*irr.*] Hauptdarsteller m; ~ **note** s. ♪ Leitton m; ~ **ques·tion** s. ⚖ Sugge'stivfrage f; ~ **reins**, *Am.* ~ **strings** s. pl. **1.** Leitzügel m; **2.** Gängelband n (*a. fig.*): *in* ~ *fig.* a) in den Kinderschuhen (steckend), b) am Gängelband.
lead‖ pen·cil [led] s. Bleistift m; ~ **poi·son·ing** s. 𝄪 Bleivergiftung f.
lead sto·ry [liːd] s. *Zeitung:* 'Hauptar‚tikel m, 'Aufmacher' m.
leaf [liːf] **I** pl. **leaves** [liːvz] s. **1.** ✿ (a. Blumen)Blatt n, pl. a. Laub n: *in* ~ belaubt, grün; *come into* ~ ausschlagen, grün werden; **2.** *coll.* a) Teeblätter pl., b) Tabakblätter pl.; **3.** Blatt n (*im Buch*): *take a* ~ *out of s.o.'s book fig.* sich an j-m ein Beispiel nehmen; *turn over a new* ~ *fig.* ein neues Leben beginnen; **4.** ⚙ a) Flügel m (*Tür, Fenster etc.*), b) Klappe *od.* Ausziehplatte f (*Tisch*), c) ✗ (*Visier*)Klappe f; **5.** ⚙ Blatt n, (dünne) Folie: *gold* ~ Blattgold n; **6.** ⚙ Blatt n (*Feder*); **II** v/t. u. v/i. **7.** ~ *through* 'durchblättern.
leaf·age ['liːfɪdʒ] s. Laub(werk) n.
leaf‖ bud s. Blattknospe f; ~ **green** s. ✿ Blattgrün n (*a. Farbe*).
leaf·less ['liːflɪs] adj. blätterlos, entblättert, kahl.
leaf·let ['liːflɪt] s. **1.** ✿ Blättchen n; **2.** a) Flugblatt n, b) Hand-, Re'klamezettel m, c) Merkblatt n, d) Pro'spekt m, Bro'schüre f.
leaf spring s. ⚙ Blattfeder f.
leaf·y ['liːfɪ] adj. **1.** belaubt, grün; **2.** Laub...; **3.** blattartig, Blatt...
league¹ [liːg] s. **1.** Liga f, Bund m: ⚒ *of Nations hist.* Völkerbund; **2.** Bündnis n, Bund m: *be in* ~ *with* im Bunde sein mit, unter 'einer Decke stecken mit; *be in* ~ *against s.o.* sich gegen j-n verbündet haben; **3.** *sport* Liga f: *he is not in the same* ~ (*with me*) *fig.* da (an mich) kommt er nicht ran.
league² [liːg] s. *obs.* Wegstunde f, Meile f (*etwa 4 km*).
leak [liːk] **I** s. **1.** a) ⚓ Leck n, b) undichte Stelle, Loch n: *spring a* ~ ein Leck *etc.* bekommen; *take a* ~ *sl.* ‚pinkeln' (gehen), c) → *leakage* 1; **2.** *fig.* a) ‚undichte Stelle' (*in e-m Amt etc.*), b) 'Durchsickern n (*von Informationen*), c) gezielte Indiskreti'on: *a* ~ *to the press* a. e-e der Presse zugespielte Information *etc.*; **3.** ⚡ a) Streuung(sverluste pl.) f, b) Fehlerstelle f; **II** v/i. **4.** lecken (*a.* ⚡ streuen), leck *od.* undicht sein, *Eimer etc. a.* (aus)laufen, tropfen; **5.** *a.* ~ *out* ausströmen, entweichen (*Gas*), b) auslaufen, sickern, tropfen (*Flüssigkeit*), c) 'durchsickern (*a. fig. Nachricht etc.*); **III** v/t. *a.* ~ *out* **6.** 'durchlassen: *the container* ~*ed* (*out*) *oil* aus dem Behälter lief Öl aus; **7.** *fig. Nachricht etc.* 'durchsickern lassen: ~ *s.th.* (*out*) *to* j-m et. zuspielen.
leak·age ['liːkɪdʒ] s. **1.** a) Lecken n, Auslaufen n, -strömen n, -treten n, b) → *leak* 1 a u. 2; **2.** *a. fig.* Schwund m, Verlust m; **3.** ⚡ Lec'kage f: ~ *cur·rent* s. ⚡ Leck-, Ableitstrom m.
leak·y ['liːkɪ] adj. leck, undicht.
lean¹ [liːn] adj. **1.** a) mager (*a. fig. Ernte, Fleisch, Jahre, Lohn etc.*), schmal, hager, b) schlank (*a. Management, Produktion*); **2.** ⚙ Mager... (-kohle *etc.*), Spar... (-beton, -gemisch *etc.*): '~·burn engine Magermotor m; ~ *production* schlanke Produktion f.

L

lean² [li:n] **I** v/i. [irr.] **1.** sich neigen (**to** nach), *Person a.* sich beugen (**over** über *acc.*), (sich) lehnen (**against** gegen, an *acc.*), sich stützen (**on** auf *acc.*); ~ **back** sich zurücklehnen; ~ **over** sich (vor)neigen *od.* (vor)beugen; ~ **over backward(s)** F sich ,fast umbringen' (*et. zu tun*); ~ **to(ward) s.th.** *fig.* zu et. (hin)neigen *od.* tendieren; **2.** ~ **on** *fig.* a) sich auf *j-n* verlassen, b) F *j-n* unter Druck setzen; **II** v/t. [irr.] **3.** neigen, beugen; **4.** lehnen (**against** gegen, an *acc.*), (auf)stützen (**on**, **upon** auf *acc.*); **III** s. **5.** Hang *m*, Neigung *f* (**to** nach); '**lean·ing** [-nɪŋ] **I** adj. sich neigend, geneigt, schief: ~ **tower** schiefer Turm; **II** s. Neigung *f*, Ten'denz *f* (*a. fig.* **towards** zu).

lean·ness ['li:nnɪs] s. Magerkeit *f* (*a. fig. der Ernte, Jahre etc.*).

leant [lent] *bsd. Brit.* pret. u. p.p. von **lean²**.

'**lean-to** [-tu:] **I** pl. **-tos** s. Anbau *m od.* Schuppen (*mit Pultdach*); **II** adj. angebaut, Anbau..., sich anlehnend.

leap [li:p] **I** v/i. [irr.] **1.** springen: **look before you** ~ erst wägen, dann wagen; **ready to** ~ **and strike** sprungbereit; ~ **for joy** vor Freude hüpfen (*a. Herz*); **2.** *fig.* a) springen, b) sich stürzen, c) *a.* ~ **up** (auf)lodern (*Flammen*), d) *a.* ~ **up** hochschnellen (*Preise etc.*): ~ **into view** plötzlich sichtbar werden *od.* auftauchen; ~ **at** sich (förmlich) auf *e-e* Gelegenheit *etc.* stürzen; ~ **into fame** mit 'einem Schlag berühmt werden; ~ **to a conclusion** voreilig e-n Schluss ziehen; ~ **to the eye**, ~ **out** ins Auge springen; **II** v/t. [irr.] **3.** über'springen (*a. fig.*), springen über (*acc.*); **4.** *Pferd etc.* springen lassen (**over** über *acc.*); **III** s. **5.** Sprung *m* (*a. fig.*): **a** ~ **in the dark** *fig.* ein Sprung ins Ungewisse; **a great** ~ **forward** *fig.* ein großer Sprung *od.* Schritt nach vorn; **by** ~**s** (**and bounds**) *fig.* sprunghaft; ~ **day** s. Schalttag *m*; '~·**frog I** s. Bockspringen *n*; **II** v/i. Bock springen; **III** v/t. Bock springen über (*acc.*), e-n Bocksprung machen über (*acc.*).

leapt [lept] pret. u. p.p. von **leap**.

leap year s. Schaltjahr *n*.

learn [lɜːn] **I** v/t. [irr.] **1.** (er)lernen; **2.** (**from**) a) erfahren, hören (von), b) ersehen, entnehmen (aus *e-m Brief etc.*); **3.** *sl.* ,lernen' (*lehren*); **II** v/i. [irr.] **4.** lernen: **he will never** ~**!** er lernt es nie!; **5.** erfahren, hören (**of**, **about** von); '**learn·ed** [-nɪd] adj. □ **1.** gelehrt, *Buch etc.*: *a.* wissenschaftlich, *Beruf etc.*: aka'demisch; '**learn·er** [-nə] s. **1.** Anfänger(in); **2.** Schüler(in), Lernende(r *m*) *f*: **slow** ~ Lernschwache(r *m*) *f*; **3.** *mot. a.* ~ **driver** Fahrschüler(in); '**learn·ing** [-nɪŋ] s. **1.** Gelehrsamkeit *f*, Gelehrtheit *f*, Wissen *n*: **man of** ~ Gelehrte(r *m*); **2.** (Er)Lernen *n*; **learnt** [-nt] pret. u. p.p. von **learn**.

lease [li:s] **I** s. **1.** Pacht-, Mietvertrag *m*; **2.** a) Verpachtung *f* (**to** an *acc.*), b) Pacht *f*, Miete *f*, c) → **leasing**: **a new** ~ **of life** *fig.* ein neues Leben, noch e-e (Lebens)Frist (*nach Krankheit etc.*); **put out to** (*od.* **to let out on**) ~ → 5; **take s.th. on** ~, **take a** ~ **of s.th.** → 6; **by** (*od.* **on**) ~ auf Pacht; **3.** Pachtbesitz *m*, -grundstück *n*; **4.** Pacht- *od.* Mietzeit *f od.* -verhältnis *n*; **II** v/t. **5.** ~ **out** verpachten *od.* vermieten (**to** an *acc.*); **6.** pachten *od.* mieten, *Investitionsgüter a.* leasen.

'**lease|·hold** [-shəʊ-] **I** s. **1.** Pacht- *od.* Mietbesitz *m*, Pacht- *od.* Mietgrundstück *n*, Pachtland *n*; **II** adj. **2.** gepach-

tet, Pacht...; '~,**hold·er** s. Pächter(in), Mieter(in).

leas·er ['li:sə] s. Pächter(in), Mieter(in), *von Investitionsgütern etc.*: *a.* Leasingnehmer(in).

leash [li:ʃ] **I** s. **1.** (Koppel-, Hunde)Leine *f*: **hold in** ~ a) → 4, b) *fig.* im Zaum halten; **strain at the** ~ a) an der Leine zerren, b) *fig.* vor Ungeduld platzen; **2.** *hunt.* Koppel *f* (*drei Hunde, Füchse etc.*); **II** v/t. **3.** (zs.-)koppeln; **4.** an der Leine halten.

leas·ing ['li:sɪŋ] s. **1.** Pachten *n*, Mieten *n*; **2.** Verpachten *n od.* Vermieten *n*, *von Investitionsgütern etc.*: *a.* Leasing *n*.

least [li:st] **I** adj. (*sup. von* **little**) geringst: a) kleinst, wenigst, mindest, b) unbedeutendst; **II** s. *das Mindeste, das wenigste*: **at** (**the**) ~ mindestens, wenigstens, zum Mindesten; **at the very** ~ allermindestens; **not in the** ~ nicht im Geringsten *od.* Mindesten; **say the** ~ (**of it**) gelinde gesagt; ~ **said soonest mended** je weniger Worte (darüber) desto besser; **that's the** ~ **of my worries** das ist m-e geringste Sorge; **III** adv. am wenigsten: ~ **of all** am allerwenigsten; **not** ~ nicht zuletzt; **the** ~ **complicated solution** die unkomplizierteste Lösung; **with the** ~ **possible effort** mit möglichst geringer Anstrengung.

leath·er ['leðə] **I** s. **1.** Leder *n* (*a. fig. humor. Haut; sport sl. Ball*): ~ **belt** Ledergürtel *m*; ~ **goods** Lederwaren *pl.*; ~ **jacket** Lederjacke *f*; **2.** Lederball *m*, -lappen *m*, -riemen *m etc.*; **3.** *pl.* a) Lederhose(n *pl.*) *f*, b) 'Lederga,maschen *pl.*; **II** v/t. **4.** mit Leder über'ziehen; **5.** F ,versohlen'; '~**·neck** s. ✕ *Am.* F ,Ledernacken', Ma'rineinfante,rist *m* (*des U.S. Marine Corps*).

leath·er·y ['leðərɪ] adj. ledern, zäh.

leave¹ [li:v] **I** v/t. [irr.] **1.** *allg.* verlassen: a) von *j-m od. e-m Ort* weggehen, b) abreisen *od.* abfahren *od.* abfliegen von (**for** nach), c) von *der Schule* abgehen, d) *j-n od. et.* im Stich lassen, *et.* aufgeben; **2.** lassen: ~ **open** offen lassen; **it** ~**s me cold** F es lässt mich kalt; ~ **it at that** F es dabei belassen *od.* (bewenden) lassen; ~ **things as they are** die Dinge so lassen, wie sie sind; → **leave alone**; **3.** (übrig) lassen: **6 from 8** ~**s 2** 8 minus 6 ist 2; **be left** übrig sein, (übrig) bleiben; **there's nothing left for us but to go** uns bleibt nichts übrig, als zu gehen; **to be left till called for** postlagernd; **4.** *Narbe etc.* zu'rücklassen, *Eindruck, Nachricht, Spur etc.* hinter'lassen: ~ **s.o. wondering whether** *j-n* im Zweifel darüber lassen, ob; ~ **s.o. to himself** *j-n* sich selbst überlassen; **5.** *s-n Schirm etc.* stehen *od.* liegen lassen, vergessen; **6.** über'lassen, an'heim stellen (**to** dat.): **I** ~ **it to you** (**to decide**) das *od.* nur machen; ~ **nothing to accident** nichts dem Zufall überlassen; **7.** (*nach dem Tode*) hinter'lassen, zu'rücklassen: **he** ~**s a wife and five children**; **8.** vermachen, vererben (**to s.o.** *j-m*); **9.** (*auf der Fahrt*) links *od.* rechts liegen lassen: ~ **the mill on the left**; **10.** aufhören mit, (unter)'lassen, *Arbeit etc.* einstellen; **II** v/i. [irr.] **11.** (fort-, weg-)gehen, (ab)reisen *od.* (ab)fahren *od.* (ab)fliegen (**for** nach); **12.** gehen, die Stellung aufgeben; *Zssgn mit adv.:*

leave|a·bout v/t. her'umliegen lassen; ~ **a·lone** v/t. **1.** al'lein lassen; **2.** *j-n od. et.* in Ruhe lassen; *et.* auf sich beruhen

lassen: **leave well alone** die Finger davon lassen; ~ **a·side** v/t. bei'seite lassen; ~ **be·hind** v/t. **1.** da- zu'rücklassen; **2.** → **leave¹** 4, 5; **3.** *Gegner etc.* hinter sich lassen; ~ **off I** v/t. **1.** weglassen; **2.** *Kleid etc.* a) nicht anziehen, b) ablegen, nicht mehr tragen; **3.** aufhören mit, *die Arbeit* einstellen; **4.** *Gewohnheit etc.* aufgeben; **II** v/i. **5.** aufhören; ~ **on** v/t. *Kleid etc.* anbehalten, *a. Licht etc.* anlassen; ~ **out** v/t. **1.** aus-, weglassen; **2.** draußen lassen; **3.** *j-n* ausschließen (**of** von): **leave her out of this!** lass sie aus dem Spiel!; ~ **o·ver** v/t. (*als Rest*) übrig lassen: **be left over** übrig (geblieben) sein.

leave² [li:v] s. **1.** Erlaubnis *f*, Genehmigung *f*: **ask** ~ **of s.o.** *j-n* um Erlaubnis bitten; **take** ~ **to say** sich zu sagen erlauben; **by your** ~**!** mit Verlaub!; **without so much as a by your** ~ *iro.* mir nichts, dir nichts; **2.** *a.* ~ **of absence** Urlaub *m*: **(go on)** ~ auf Urlaub (gehen); **a man on** ~ ein Urlauber; **3.** Abschied *m*: **take** (**one's**) ~ sich verabschieden, Abschied nehmen (**of s.o.** von *j-m*); **have taken** ~ **of one's senses** nicht (mehr) ganz bei Trost sein.

leav·en ['levn] **I** s. **1.** a) Sauerteig *m* (*a. fig.*), b) Hefe *f*, c) → **leavening**; **II** v/t. **2.** *Teig* a) säuern b) (auf)gehen lassen; **3.** *fig.* durch'setzen, -'dringen; '**leav·en·ing** [-nɪŋ] s. Treibmittel *n*, Gärungsstoff *m*.

leaves [li:vz] pl. von **leaf**.

'**leave-,tak·ing** s. Abschied(nehmen *n*) *m*.

leav·ing | **cer·tif·i·cate** ['li:vɪŋ] s. Abgangszeugnis *n*; ~ **do** s. F *bsd. Brit.* Abschiedsfeier *f*, -fete *f*, Ausstand *m*.

leav·ings ['li:vɪŋz] s./pl. **1.** 'Überbleibsel pl., Reste pl.; **2.** Abfall *m*.

Leb·a·nese [ˌlebə'ni:z] **I** adj. liba-'nesisch; **II** s. a) Liba'nese *m*, Liba'nesin *f*, b) pl. Liba'nesen pl.

lech·er ['letʃə] s. Wüstling *m*, *humor.* ,Lustmolch' *m*; **lech·er·ous** ['letʃərəs] adj. □ lüstern, geil; '**lech·er·y** [-ərɪ] s. Lüsternheit *f*, Geilheit *f*.

lec·tern ['lektɜːn] s. *eccl.* (Lese- *od.* Chor)Pult *n*.

lec·ture ['lektʃə] **I** s. **1.** Vortrag *m*; *univ.* Vorlesung *f*, Kol'leg *n* (**on** über *acc.*, **to** vor dat.): ~ **hall** (*od.* **room** *od.* **theatre**) Vortrags-, *univ.* Hörsaal *m*; ~ **tour** Vortragsreise *f*; **2.** Strafpredigt *f*: **give** (*od.* **read**) **s.o. a** ~ → 5; **II** v/i. **3.** e-n Vortrag *od.* Vorträge halten (**to s.o. on s.th.** vor *j-m* über e-e Sache); **4.** *univ.* e-e Vorlesung *od.* Vorlesungen halten, lesen (**on** über *acc.*); **III** v/t. **5.** *j-m* e-e Strafpredigt *od.* Standpauke halten; '**lec·tur·er** [-tʃərə] s. **1.** Vortragende(r *m*) *f*; **2.** *univ.* Do'zent(in), Hochschullehrer(in); **3.** *Church of England*: Hilfsprediger *m*; '**lec·ture·ship** [-ʃɪp] s. *univ.* Dozen'tur *f*, Lehrauftrag *m*.

led [led] pret. u. p.p. von **lead¹**.

ledge [ledʒ] s. **1.** Leiste *f*, Kante *f*; **2.** a) (Fenster)Sims *m od.* n, b) (Fenster-) Brett *n*; **3.** (Fels)Gesims *n*, (-)Vorsprung *m*; **4.** Felsbank *f*, Riff *n*.

ledg·er ['ledʒə] s. **1.** ✝ Hauptbuch *n*; **2.** △ Querbalken *m*, Sturz *m* (*e-s Gerüsts*); **3.** große Steinplatte; ~ **line** s. **1.** Angelleine *f* mit festliegendem Köder; **2.** ♪ Hilfslinie *f*.

lee [li:] s. **1.** (wind)geschützte Stelle; **2.** Windschattenseite *f*; **3.** ⚓ Lee(seite) *f*.

leech [li:tʃ] s. **1.** *zo.* Blutegel *m*: **stick like a** ~ **to s.o.** *fig.* wie e-e Klette an *j-m* hängen; **2.** *fig.* Blutsauger *m*,

Schma'rotzer *m*.

leek [liːk] *s*. ♀ (Breit)Lauch *m*, Porree *m*.

leer [lɪə] **I** *s*. (lüsterner *od*. gehässiger *od*. boshafter) (Seiten)Blick, anzügliches Grinsen; **II** *v/i*. (lüstern *etc*.) schielen (*at* nach); anzüglich grinsen; **leer·y** ['lɪərɪ] *adj. sl*. **1.** schlau; **2.** argwöhnisch (*of* gegenüber).

lees [liːz] *s. pl*. Bodensatz *m*: a) Hefe *f* (*a. fig*.): *drink* (*od. drain*) *to the* ~ *bsd. fig*. bis zur Neige leeren, b) Weinstein *m*.

lee‖ shore *s*. ♣ Leeküste *f*; ~ *side* *s*. ♣ Leeseite *f*.

lee·ward ['liːwəd; ♣ 'luːəd] **I** *adj*. Lee...; **II** *s*. Lee(seite) *f*: *to* ~ → **III** *adv*. leewärts.

'lee·way *s*. **1.** ♣, *a*. ✈ Abtrift *f*: *make* ~ abtreiben; **2.** *fig*. Rückstand *m*: *make up* ~ (den Rückstand) aufholen, (das Versäumte) nachholen; **3.** *fig*. Spielraum *m*.

left¹ [left] *pret. u. p.p. von* **leave¹**.

left² [left] **I** *adj*. **1.** link (*a. pol*.); **II** *adv*. **2.** links: *move* ~ nach links rücken; *turn* ~ links abbiegen; ~ *turn*! ✕ links um!; **III** *s*. **3.** Linke *f* (*a. pol*.), linke Seite: *on* (*od. to*) *the* ~ (*of*) links (von), linker Hand (von); *on our* ~ zu unserer Linken, links von uns; *to the* ~ nach links; *keep to the* ~ sich links halten, links fahren; *the* ~ *of the party* *pol*. der linke Flügel der Partei; **4.** *Boxen*: a) Linke *f* (*Faust*), b) Linke(r *m*) *f* (*Schlag*); **'~-hand** *adj*. **1.** link; **2.** → **left-handed** 1–4; **,~-'hand·ed** *adj*. □ **1.** linkshändig: *a* ~ *person* → **left-hander** 1; **2.** linkshändig, link (*Schlag etc*.); **3.** link, linksseitig; **4.** ⊕ linksgängig, -läufig, Links...: ~ *drive* Linkssteuerung *f*, ~ *screw* linksgängige Schraube; **5.** zweifelhaft, fragwürdig: ~ *compliments*; **6.** linkisch, ungeschickt; **7.** *hist*. morga'natisch, zur linken Hand (*Ehe*); **,~-'hand·er** *s*. **1.** Linkshänder(in); **2.** *Boxen*: Linke *f*.

left·ist ['leftɪst] *pol*. **I** *s*. Linke(r *m*) *f*, 'Linkspo,litiker(-in), -stehende(r *m*) *f* **II** *adj*. linksgerichtet, links stehend, Links...

,left‖-'lug·gage lock·er *s*. *Brit*. (Gepäck)Schließfach *m*; **,~-'lug·gage (of·fice)** *s*. *Brit*. Gepäckaufbewahrung(sstelle) *f*; **'~·o·ver I** *adj*. übrig (geblieben); **II** *s*. 'Überbleibsel *n*, (*bsd*. Speise)Rest *m*.

'left‖-wing *adj. pol*. dem linken Flügel angehörend, Links..., *Person*: a) linksgerichtet, links stehend: ~ *extremism* 'Linksextre,mismus *m*; ~ *extremist* 'Linksextre,mist(in); **,~-'wing·er** *s*. **1.** → **leftist** I; **2.** *sport* Linksaußen *m*.

leg [leg] **I** *s*. **1.** a) Bein *n*, b) 'Unterschenkel *m*; → *Bes. Redew*.; **2.** (*Hammel- etc*.)Keule *f*: ~ *of mutton*; **3.** a) Bein *n* (*Hose, Strumpf*), b) Schaft *m* (*Stiefel*); **4.** a) Bein *n* (*Tisch etc*.), b) Stütze *f*, c) Schenkel *m* (*Zirkel etc*., a. ⚔ Dreieck); **5.** E'tappe *f*, Abschnitt *m*, Teilstrecke *f*; **6.** *sport* a) E'tappe *f*, Teilstrecke *f*, b) Runde *f*, c) 'Durchgang *m*, Lauf *m*; **II** *v/i*. **7.** *mst* ~ *it* F a) tippeln, marschieren, b) rennen; *Besondere Redewendungen*: *on one's* ~*s* a) stehend (*bsd. um e-e Rede zu halten*), b) auf den Beinen (*Ggs. bettlägerig*): *be on one's last* ~*s* es nicht mehr lange machen, ‚am Eingehen' sein, auf dem letzten Loch pfeifen; *find one's* ~*s* s-e Beine gebrauchen lernen, *fig*. sich finden; *give s.o. a* ~ *up* j-m (hin)aufhelfen, *fig*. j-m unter die Arme greifen; *have not a* ~ *to stand on fig*. keinerlei Beweise *od*. kei-

---

ne Chance haben; *pull s.o.'s* ~ F j-n ‚auf den Arm nehmen' *od*. aufziehen; *shake a* ~ a) F das Tanzbein schwingen, b) *sl*. ‚Tempo machen'; *stand on one's own* ~*s* auf eigenen Füßen stehen; *stretch one's* ~*s* sich die Beine vertreten.

leg·a·cy ['legəsɪ] *s*. ⚖ Le'gat *n*, Vermächtnis *n* (*a. fig*.), *fig. a*. Erbe *n*, *contp*. Hinter'lassenschaft *f*.

le·gal ['liːgl] *adj*. □ **1.** gesetzlich, rechtlich: ~ *holiday* gesetzlicher Feiertag; ~ *reserves* ✝ gesetzliche Rücklagen; **2.** le'gal: a) (rechtlich *od*. gesetzlich) zulässig, gesetzmäßig, b) rechtsgültig: ~ *claim*; *not* ~ gesetzlich verboten *od*. nicht zulässig; *make* ~ legalisieren; **3.** Rechts..., ju'ristisch: ~ *adviser* Rechtsberater(in); ~ *aid* Prozesskostenhilfe *f*; ~ *capacity* Geschäftsfähigkeit *f*; ~ *entity* juristische Person; ~ *force* Rechtskraft *f*; ~ *position* Rechtslage *f*; ~ *remedy* Rechtsmittel *n*; **4.** gerichtlich: *a* ~ *decision*; *take* ~ *action* (*od*. *steps*) *against s.o*. gegen j-n gerichtlich vorgehen; **le·gal·ese** [,liːgə'liːz] *s*. Ju'ristensprache *f*, -jar,gon *m*; **le·gal·i·ty** [liːˈgælətɪ] *s*. Legali'tät *f*, Gesetzlichkeit *f*, Rechtmäßigkeit *f*, Zulässigkeit *f*.

le·gal·i·za·tion [,liːgəlaɪˈzeɪʃn] *s*. Legalisierung *f*; **le·gal·ize** ['liːgəlaɪz] *v/t*. legalisieren, rechtskräftig machen, *a*. amtlich beglaubigen, beurkunden.

leg·ate¹ ['legɪt] *s*. (päpstlicher) Le'gat.

le·gate² [lɪ'geɪt] *v/t*. (testamen'tarisch) vermachen.

leg·a·tee [,legə'tiː] *s*. ⚖ Lega'tar(in), Vermächtnisnehmer(in).

le·ga·tion [lɪ'geɪʃn] *s. pol*. Gesandtschaft *f*, Vertretung *f*.

leg·a·tor [,legə'tɔː; *Am*. lɪ'geɪtə] *s*. ⚖ Vermächtnisgeber(in), Erb-lasser(in).

leg·end ['ledʒənd] *s*. **1.** Sage *f*, (*a*. 'Heiligen)Le,gende *f*; **2.** Le'gende *f*: a) erläuternder Text, Beschriftung *f*, 'Bild,unterschrift *f*, b) Zeichenerklärung *f* (*auf Karten etc*.), c) Inschrift *f*; **3.** *fig*. legen'däre Gestalt *od*. Sache, Mythus *m*; **'leg·end·ar·y** [-dərɪ] *adj*. legen'där: a) sagenhaft, Sagen..., b) berühmt.

leg·er·de·main [,ledʒədə'meɪn] *s*. Taschenspiele'rei *f*, *a. fig*. (Taschenspieler)Trick *m*.

-legged [legd] *adj. bsd. in Zssgn mit* (...) Beinen, ...beinig; **leg·gings** ['legɪŋz] *s. pl*. **1.** Leggings *pl*.; **2.** 'Überhose *f*; **leg·gy** ['legɪ] *adj*. langbeinig.

leg·i·bil·i·ty [,ledʒɪ'bɪlətɪ] *s*. Leserlichkeit *f*; **leg·i·ble** ['ledʒəbl] *adj*. □ (gut) leserlich.

le·gion ['liːdʒən] *s*. **1.** *antiq*. ✕ Legi'on *f* (*a. fig. Unzahl*): *their name is* ~ *fig*. ihre Zahl ist Legion; **2.** Lᴇgi'on *f*, (*bsd*. Frontkämpfer)Verband *m*: *the American* (*British*) **⚷**; **⚷** *of Hono(u)r* französische Ehrenlegion; *the* (*Foreign*) **⚷** die (französische) Fremdenlegion; **legion·ar·y** [-dʒənərɪ] **I** *adj*. Legions...; **II** *s*. Legio'när *m*; **le·gion·naire** [,liːdʒə'neə] *s*. 'Fremden- *etc*.)Legio,när *m*.

leg·is·late ['ledʒɪsleɪt] **I** *v/i*. Gesetze erlassen; **II** *v/t*. durch Gesetze bewirken *od*. schaffen: ~ *away* durch Gesetze abschaffen; **leg·is·la·tion** [,ledʒɪs'leɪʃn] *s*. Gesetzgebung *f* (*a. weitS*. [erlassene] Gesetze *pl*.); **'leg·is·la·tive** [-lətɪv] **I** *adj*. □ **1.** gesetzgebend, legisla'tiv; **2.** Legislatur..., Gesetzgebungs...; **II** *s*. **3.** → **legislature**; **'leg·is·la·tor** [-leɪtə] *s*. Gesetzgeber *m*; **'leg·is·la·ture** [-leɪtʃə] *s*. Legisla'tive *f*, gesetzgebende Körperschaft.

le·git [lɪ'dʒɪt] *sl. für* **legitimate** I, **legiti-**

---

mate drama.

le·git·i·ma·cy [lɪ'dʒɪtɪməsɪ] *s*. **1.** Legitimi'tät *f*: a) Rechtmäßigkeit *f*, b) Ehelichkeit *f*: ~ *of birth*, c) Berechtigung *f*, Gültigkeit *f*; **2.** (Folge)Richtigkeit *f*.

le·git·i·mate [lɪ'dʒɪtɪmət] **I** *adj*. □ **1.** legi'tim: a) gesetzmäßig, gesetzlich, b) rechtmäßig, berechtigt (*Forderung etc*.), c) ehelich: ~ *birth*; ~ *son*; **2.** (folge)richtig, begründet, einwandfrei; **II** *v/t*. [-meɪt] **3.** legitimieren: a) für gesetzmäßig erklären, b) ehelich machen; **4.** als (rechts)gültig anerkennen; **5.** rechtfertigen; ~ *dra·ma* **s**. **1.** lite'rarisch wertvolles Drama; **2.** echtes Drama (*Ggs. Film etc*.).

le·git·i·ma·tion [lɪ,dʒɪtɪ'meɪʃn] *s*. Legitimati'on *f*: a) Legitimierung *f*, *a*. Ehelichkeitserklärung *f*, b) 'Ausweis(pa,piere *pl*.) *m*; **le·git·i·ma·tize** [lɪ'dʒɪtɪmətaɪz], **le·git·i·mize** [lɪ'dʒɪtɪmaɪz] → **legitimate** 3, 4, 5.

leg·less ['leglɪs] *adj*. ohne Beine, beinlos.

'leg·man *s*. [*irr*.] *bsd. Am*. **1.** Re'porter *m* (im Außendienst); **2.** ‚Laufbursche' *m*; **'~·pull** *s*. F Veräppelung *f*, Scherz *m*; **'~·room** [-rʊm] *s. mot*. Beinfreiheit *f*; **'~·show** *s*. F ‚Beinchenschau' *f*, Re-'vue *f*.

leg·ume ['legjuːm] *s*. **1.** ♀ a) Hülsenfrucht *f*, b) Hülse *f* (*Frucht*); **2.** *mst pl*. a) Hülsenfrüchte *pl*. (*als Gemüse*), b) Gemüse *n*; **le·gu·mi·nous** [le'gjuːmɪnəs] *adj*. Hülsen...; Hülsen tragend.

'leg·work *s*. F Laufe'rei *f*.

lei·sure ['leʒə] **I** *s*. **1.** Muße *f*, Freizeit *f*: *at* ~ → **leisurely**; *be at* ~ Zeit *od*. Muße haben; *at your* ~ wenn es Ihnen (gerade) passt; **2.** → **leisureliness**; **II** *adj*. Muße..., frei: ~ *hours*; ~ *activities* Freizeitbeschäftigungen *pl*., -gestaltung *f*; ~ *industry* Freizeitindustrie *f*; ~ *park* Freizeitpark *m*; ~ *time* Freizeit *f*; '~·*wear* Freizeit(be)kleidung *f*; **'lei·sured** [-əd] *adj*. frei, unbeschäftigt, müßig: *the* ~ *classes* die begüterten Klassen; **'lei·sure·li·ness** [-lɪnɪs] *s*. Gemächlichkeit *f*, Gemütlichkeit *f*; **'lei·sure·ly** [-lɪ] *adj. u. adv*. gemächlich, gemütlich.

leit·mo·tiv, a. leit·mo·tif ['laɪtməʊˌtiːf] *s. bsd. ♩* 'Leitmo,tiv *n*.

lem·ming ['lemɪŋ] *s. zo*. Lemming *m*.

lem·on ['lemən] **I** *s*. **1.** Zi'trone *f*; **2.** Zi'tronenbaum *m*; **3.** Zi'tronengelb *n*; **4.** *sl*. ‚Niete' *f*: a) ‚Flasche' *f* (*Person*), b) ‚Gurke' *f* (*Sache*): *hand s.o. a* ~ j-n schwer drankriegen; **II** *adj*. **5.** zi'tronengelb; **lem·on·ade** [,lemə'neɪd] *s*. Zi'tronenlimo,nade *f*.

lem·on‖ dab *s. ichth*. Rotzunge *f*; ~ *sole* *s. ichth*. Seezunge *f*; ~ *squash* *s. Brit*. Zi'tronenlimo,nade *f*; ~ *squeez·er* *s*. Zi'tronenpresse *f*.

le·mur ['liːmə] *s. zo*. Le'mur(e) *m*, Maki *m*.

lem·u·res ['lemjʊriːz] *s. pl. myth*. Le-'muren *pl*. (*Gespenster*).

lend [lend] *v/t*. [*irr*.] **1.** (aus-, ver)leihen: ~ *s.o. money* (*od. money to s.o*.) j-m Geld leihen, an j-n Geld verleihen; **2.** *fig*. Würde *etc*. verleihen (*to dat*.); **3.** *Hilfe etc*. leisten, gewähren: ~ *itself to* sich eignen zu *od*. für (*Sache*); → *ear¹* 3, *hand* 1; **4.** *s-n Namen* hergeben (*to* zu): ~ *o.s. to* sich hergeben zu; **lend·er** ['lendə] *s*. Aus-, Verleiher(in), Geld-, Kre'ditgeber(in); **lend·ing li·brar·y** ['lendɪŋ] *s*. 'Leihbüche,rei *f*; **lend·ing rate** *s*. Kre'ditzins *m*.

,Lend-'Lease Act *s. hist*. Leih-Pacht-Gesetz *n* (*1941*).

length [leŋθ] *s*. **1.** *allg*. Länge *f*: a) als

Maß, a. Stück n (Stoff etc.): **two feet in ~ 2 Fuß lang**, b) (a. lange) Strecke, c) 'Umfang m (Buch, Liste etc.), d) (a. lange) Dauer (a. Phonetik); **2.** sport Länge f (Vorsprung): **win by a ~** mit e-r Länge (Vorsprung) siegen; Besondere Redewendungen: **at ~** a) lang, ausführlich, b) endlich, schließlich; **at full ~** a) in allen Einzelheiten, ganz ausführlich, b) der Länge nach (hinfallen); **at great** (some) **~** sehr (ziemlich) ausführlich; **for any ~ of time** für längere Zeit; (over all) **the ~ and breadth of France** in ganz Frankreich (herum); **go** (to) **great ~s** a) sehr weit gehen, b) sich sehr bemühen; **he went** (to) **the ~ of asserting** er ging so weit zu behaupten; **go** (to) **all ~s** aufs Ganze gehen, vor nichts zurückschrecken; **go any ~** alles (Erdenkliche) tun.

length·en ['leŋθən] **I** v/t. **1.** verlängern, länger machen; **2.** ausdehnen; **3.** Wein etc. strecken; **II** v/i. **4.** sich verlängern, länger werden; **5. ~ out** sich in die Länge ziehen; **'length·en·ing** [-θənɪŋ] s. Verlängerung f.

length·i·ness ['leŋθɪnɪs] s. Langatmigkeit f, Weitschweifigkeit f.

'length·ways [-weɪz], Am. **'length·wise** adv. der Länge nach, längs.

length·y ['leŋθɪ] adj. □ **1.** (sehr) lang; **2.** fig. ermüdend od. 'übermäßig lang, langatmig.

le·ni·en·cy ['liːnjənsɪ], a. **le·ni·ence** ['liːnjəns] s. Milde f, Nachsicht f; **'le·ni·ent** [-nt] adj. □ mild(e), nachsichtig (to[wards] gegen'über).

lens [lenz] s. **1.** anat. Linse f (a. phys., ◉); **2.** opt. a) Linse f, b) Lupe f, (Vergrößerungs)Glas n; **3.** phot. Objek'tiv n, ‚Linse' f: **~ aperture** Blende f; **~ screen** Gegenlichtblende f.

lent¹ [lent] pret. u. p.p. von **lend**.

Lent² [lent] s. Fasten(zeit f) pl.

len·tic·u·lar [len'tɪkjʊlə] adj. □ **1.** linsenförmig, bsd. anat. Linsen...; **2.** phys. bikon'vex.

len·til ['lentɪl] s. ♀ Linse f.

Lent·lil·y s. ♀ Nar'zisse f; **~ term** s. Brit. 'Frühjahrstri,mester n.

Le·o ['liːəʊ] s. ast. Löwe m.

le·o·nine ['liːəʊnaɪn] adj. Löwen...

leop·ard ['lepəd] s. zo. Leo'pard m: **black ~** Schwarzer Panther; **the ~ can't change its spots** fig. die Katze lässt das Mausen nicht; **~ cat** s. zo. Ben-'galkatze f.

le·o·tard ['liːəʊtɑːd] s. Tri'kot(anzug m) n, sport Gym'nastikanzug m.

lep·er ['lepə] s. **1.** Leprakranke(r m) f; **2.** fig. Aussätzige(r m) f.

lep·i·dop·ter·ous [ˌlepɪ'dɒptərəs] adj. Schmetterlings...

lep·re·chaun ['leprəkɔːn] s. Ir. Kobold m.

lep·ro·sy ['leprəsɪ] s. ♣ Lepra f; **'lep·rous** [-əs] adj. a) leprakrank, b) leprös, Lepra...

les·bi·an ['lezbɪən] **I** adj. lesbisch; **II** s. Lesbierin f; **'les·bi·an·ism** [-nɪzəm] s. lesbische Liebe, Lesbia'nismus m.

lese-maj·es·ty [ˌliːz'mædʒɪstɪ] s. **1.** a. fig. Maje'stätsbeleidigung f; **2.** Hochverrat m.

le·sion ['liːʒn] s. **1.** Verletzung f, Wunde f; **2.** krankhafte Veränderung (e-s Organs).

less [les] **I** adv. (comp. von **little**) weniger (than als): **a ~ known** (od. **~--known**) **author** ein weniger bekannter Autor; **~ and ~** immer weniger od. seltener; **still** (od. **much**) **~** noch viel

weniger, geschweige denn; **the ~ so as** (dies) umso weniger, als; **II** adj. (comp. von **little**) geringer, kleiner, weniger: **in ~ time** in kürzerer Zeit; **of ~ importance** (value) von geringerer Bedeutung (von geringerem Wert); **no ~ a person than Churchill**; a. **Churchill, no ~** kein Geringerer als Churchill; **III** s. weniger, e-e kleinere Menge od. Zahl, ein geringeres (Aus)Maß: **for ~** billiger; **do with ~** mit weniger auskommen; **little ~ than robbery** so gut wie od. schon fast Raub; **nothing ~ than** zumindest; **nothing ~ than a disaster** e-e echte Katastrophe; **~ of that!** hör auf damit!; **IV** prp. weniger, minus, ♥ abzüglich.

les·see [le'siː] s. Pächter(in) od. Mieter (-in), von Investitionsgütern etc.: a. Leasingnehmer(in).

less·en ['lesn] **I** v/i. sich vermindern od. verringern, abnehmen, geringer werden, nachlassen; **II** v/t. vermindern, -ringern, -kleinern; fig. her'absetzen, schmälern; **'less·en·ing** [-nɪŋ] s. Nachlassen n, Abnahme f, Verringerung f, -minderung f.

less·er ['lesə] adj. (nur attr.) kleiner, geringer; unbedeutender.

les·son ['lesn] s. **1.** Lekti'on f (a. fig. Denkzettel, Strafe), Übungsstück n, (a. Haus)Aufgabe f; **2.** (Lehr-, 'Unterrichts)Stunde f; pl. 'Unterricht m, Stunden pl.: **give ~s** Unterricht erteilen; **take ~s from s.o.** Stunden od. Unterricht bei j-m nehmen; **3.** fig. Lehre f: **this was a ~ to me** das war mir e-e Lehre; **let this be a ~ to you** lass dir das zur Lehre od. Warnung dienen; **he has learnt his ~** er hat s-e Lektion gelernt; **4.** eccl. Lesung f.

les·sor [le'sɔː] s. Verpächter(in) od. Vermieter(in), von Investitionsgütern etc.: a. Leasinggeber(in).

lest [lest] cj. **1.** (mst mit folgendem **should** konstr.) dass od. da'mit nicht; aus Furcht, dass; **2.** (nach Ausdrücken des Befürchtens) dass: **fear ~...**.

let¹ [let] **I** s. **1.** Brit. ♥ a) Vermietung f, b) Mietwohnung f, Miethaus n: **get a ~ for** e-n Mieter finden für; **II** v/t. **2.** lassen, j-m erlauben: **~ him talk!** lass ihn reden!; **~ me help you** lassen Sie mich Ihnen helfen; **~ s.o. know** j-n wissen lassen od. Bescheid sagen; **~ into** a) (her)einlassen in (acc.), b) j-n einweihen in ein Geheimnis, c) Stück Stoff etc. einsetzen in (acc.); **~ s.o. off a penalty** j-m e-e Strafe erlassen; **~ s.o. off a promise** j-n von e-m Versprechen entbinden; **3.** vermieten (**to** an acc., **for** auf ein Jahr etc.): **"to ~"** „zu vermieten"; **~ Arbeit** etc. vergeben (**to** an j-n); **III** v/aux. [irr.] **5.** lassen, mögen, sollen (zur Umschreibung des Imperativs der 1. u. 2. Person): **~ us go! Yes, ~'s!** gehen wir! Ja, gehen wir! (od. Ja, einverstanden!); **~ him go there at once!** er soll sofort hingehen!; **~'s not** (F **don't let's**) **quarrel!** wir wollen doch nicht streiten!; (just) **~ them try** das sollen sie nur versuchen!; **~ me see!** Moment mal!; **~ A be equal to B** nehmen wir an, A ist gleich B; **~ it be known that** man soll od. alle sollen wissen, dass; **IV** v/i. [irr.] **6.** sich vermieten (lassen) (**at, for** für); Besondere Redewendungen: **~ alone** a) geschweige denn, ganz zu schweigen von, b) → **let alone**; **~ loose** loslassen; **~ be** a) et. sein lassen, die Finger lassen von, b) et. od. j-n in Ruhe lassen; **~ fall** a) (a. fig. Bemerkung)

fallen lassen, b) ♠ Senkrechte fällen (**on, upon** auf acc.); **~ fly** a) et. abschießen, fig. et. vom Stapel lassen, b) (v/i.) schießen (**at** auf acc.), c) fig. vom Leder ziehen, grob werden; **~ go** a) loslassen, fahren lassen, b) es sausen lassen, c) drauf'losrasen od. -schießen etc., d) loslegen; **~ o.s. go** a) sich gehen lassen, b) aus sich herausgehen; **~ go of s.th.** et. loslassen; **~ it go at that** lass es dabei bewenden; Zssgn mit adv.:

let| a·lone v/t. **1.** al'lein lassen, verlassen; **2.** j-n od. et. in Ruhe lassen; et. sein lassen, die Finger von et. lassen (a. fig.): **let well alone** lieber die Finger davonlassen; **~ down** v/t. **1.** hin'unter- od. her'unterlassen: **let s.o. down gently** mit j-m glimpflich verfahren; **2.** a) j-n im Stich lassen (**on** bei), b) j-n enttäuschen, c) j-n blamieren; **3.** die Luft aus e-m Reifen lassen; **~ in** v/t. **1.** (her)'einlassen; **2.** Stück etc. einlassen, -setzen; **3.** einweihen (**on** in acc.); **4.** **let s.o. in for** j-m et. aufhalsen od. einbrocken; **let o.s. in for** sich et. einbrocken od. einhandeln, sich auf et. einlassen; **~ off** v/t. **1.** Sprengladung etc. loslassen, Gewehr etc. abfeuern; Gas etc. ablassen; → **steam** 1; **2.** Witz etc. vom Stapel lassen; **3.** j-n laufen od. gehen lassen, mit e-r Geldstrafe etc. da'vonkommen lassen; **~ on** F **I** v/i. **1.** ‚plaudern' (Geheimnis verraten); **2.** vorgeben, so tun als ob; **II** v/t. **3.** ‚ausplaudern', verraten; **4.** sich et. anmerken lassen; **~ out** v/t. **1.** hin'aus- od. herauslassen; **2.** Kleid auslassen; **3.** Geheimnis ausplaudern; **4.** → **let¹** 3, 4; **~ up** v/i. F **1.** a) nachlassen, b) aufhören; **2.** **~ on** ablassen von, j-n in Ruhe lassen.

let² [let] s. **1.** Tennis: Netzaufschlag m, Netz(ball m) m; **2.** without **~ or hindrance** völlig unbehindert.

'let-down s. **1.** Nachlassen n; **2.** F Enttäuschung f; ✈ Her'untergehen n.

le·thal ['liːθl] adj. **1.** tödlich, todbringend; **2.** Todes...

le·thar·gic, le·thar·gi·cal [lɪ'θɑːdʒɪk(l)] adj. □ le'thargisch: a) ♣ schlafsüchtig, b) teilnahmslos, stumpf, träg(e); **leth·ar·gy** ['leθədʒɪ] s. Lethar'gie f: a) Teilnahmslosigkeit f, Stumpfheit f, b) ♣ Schlafsucht f.

Le·the ['liːθiː] s. **1.** Lethe f (Fluss des Vergessens im Hades); **2.** poet. Vergessen(heit f) n.

Lett [let] s. Latvian.

let·ter ['letə] **I** s. **1.** Buchstabe m (a. fig. buchstäblicher Sinn): **to the ~** fig. buchstabengetreu, (ganz) exakt; **the ~ of the law** der Buchstabe des Gesetzes; **in ~ and in spirit** dem Buchstaben u. dem Sinne nach; **2.** Brief m, Schreiben n (**to** an acc.): **by ~** brieflich, schriftlich; **~ of application** Bewerbungsschreiben; **~ of attorney** ♣ Vollmacht f; **~ of credit** ♥ Akkreditiv n; **~ of intent** schriftliche Absichtserklärung; **3.** pl. Urkunde f: **~s of administration** ♣ Nachlassverwalterzeugnis n; **~s testamentary** Testamentsvollstreckerzeugnis n; **~s** (od. **~**) **of credence**, **~s credential** pol. Beglaubigungsschreiben n; **~s patent** ♣ (sg. od. pl. konstr.) Patent(urkunde f) n; **4.** typ. a) Letter f, Type f, b) coll. Lettern pl., Typen pl., c) Schrift(art) f; **5.** pl. a) (schöne) Litera'tur, b) Bildung f, c) Wissenschaft f: **man of ~s** a) Literat m, b) Gelehrter m; **II** v/t. **6.** beschriften; mit Buchstaben bezeichnen; Buch betiteln.

let·ter| bomb s. Briefbombe f; '**~·box** s. bsd. Brit. Briefkasten m; **~ card** s. Briefkarte f.

let·tered ['letəd] adj. **1.** a) (lite'rarisch) gebildet, b) gelehrt; **2.** beschriftet, bedruckt.

let·ter| file s. Briefordner m; **~ found·er** s. typ. Schriftgießer m.

'**let·ter·head** s. **1.** (gedruckter) Briefkopf; **2.** 'Kopfpa,pier n.

let·ter·ing ['letərɪŋ] s. Aufdruck m, Beschriftung f.

,**let·ter·'per·fect** adj. **1.** thea. rollensicher; **2.** allg. buchstabengetreu.

'**let·ter|·press** s. typ. **1.** (Druck)Text m; **2.** Hoch-, Buchdruck m; **~ scales** s. pl. Briefwaage f; '**~·weight** s. Briefbeschwerer m.

Let·tish ['letɪʃ] → Latvian.

let·tuce ['letɪs] s. ♀ (bsd. 'Kopf)Sa‚lat m.

'**let-up** s. F Nachlassen n, Aufhören n, Unter'brechung f: without ~ unaufhörlich.

leu·co·cyte ['ljuːkəʊsaɪt] s. ⸱ physiol. Leuko'zyte f, weißes Blutkörperchen.

leu·co·ma [ljuːˈkəʊmə] s. ⚕ Leu'kom n (Hornhauttrübung).

leu·k(a)e·mi·a [ljuːˈkiːmɪə] s. ⚕ Leukä'mie f.

Le·van·tine ['levəntaɪn] I s. Levan'tiner (-in); II adj. levan'tinisch.

lev·ee¹ ['levɪ] s. (Ufer-, Schutz)Damm m, (Fluss)Deich m.

lev·ee² ['levɪ] s. **1.** hist. Le'ver n, Morgenempfang m (e-s Fürsten); **2.** Brit. Nachmittagsempfang m; **3.** allg. Empfang m.

lev·el ['levl] I s. **1.** Ebene f (a. geogr.), ebene Fläche; **2.** Horizon'tale f, Waagrechte f; **3.** Höhe f (a. geogr.), (Meeres-, Wasser-, physiol. Alkohol-, Blutzucker- etc.)Spiegel m, (Geräusch-, Wasser)Pegel m: on a ~ (with) auf gleicher Höhe (mit); he's on the ~ F a) er ist ‚in Ordnung', b) er meint es ehrlich; **4.** fig. (a. geistiges) Ni'veau, Stand m, Grad m, Stufe f: high ~ of education; the ~ of prices das Preisniveau; low production ~ niedriger Produktionsstand; come down to the ~ of others sich auf das Niveau anderer begeben; sink to the ~ of cut-throat practices auf das Niveau von Halsabschneidern absinken; find one's ~ fig. den Platz einnehmen, der e-m zukommt; **5.** (politische etc.) Ebene: a conference at (od. on) the highest ~ e-e Konferenz auf höchster Ebene; **6.** ⊕ a) Li'belle f, b) Wasserwaage f; **7.** ⊕, surv. Nivel'lierinstru,ment n; **8.** ⚒ a) Sohle f, b) Sohlenstrecke f; II adj. **9.** eben: a ~ road; **10.** horizon'tal, waag(e)recht; **11.** gleich (a. fig.): ~ crossing schienengleicher Übergang; a ~ teaspoon(ful) ein gestrichener Teelöffel (voll); ~ (with) a) auf gleicher Höhe (mit), b) gleich hoch (wie); draw ~ with j-n einholen, mit j-m gleichziehen; ~ with the ground a) zu ebener Erde, b) in Bodenhöhe; make ~ with the ground dem Erdboden gleichmachen; **12.** ausgeglichen: ~ race a. Kopf-an-Kopf-Rennen n; ~ stress ling. schwebende Betonung; ~ temperature gleich bleibende Temperatur; **13.** a) vernünftig, b) ausgeglichen (Person), c) kühl, ruhig (a. Stimme), d) ausgewogen (Urteil); **14.** F anständig, ehrlich, fair: a ~ playing field 'Chancengleichheit f, gleiche Bedingungen pl. für alle; III v/t. **15.** (ein)ebnen, planieren: ~ (with the ground) dem Erdboden gleichmachen; **16.** j-n zu Boden schlagen; **17.** fig. a)

gleichmachen, nivellieren, ‚einebnen', b) Unterschiede aufheben, c) ausgleichen; **18.** in horizon'tale Lage bringen; **19.** (at, against) a) Waffe, Blick, a. Kritik etc. richten (auf acc.), b) Anklage erheben (gegen); IV v/i. **20.** zielen (at auf acc.); **21.** ~ with s.o. F j-m gegenüber ehrlich sein; ~ down v/t. **1.** Löhne, Preise etc. nach unten angleichen; **2.** auf ein tieferes Ni'veau her'abdrücken; ~ off od. out I v/t. (v/i. das Flugzeug) abfangen od. aufrichten; II v/i. fig. sich einpendeln (at bei); ~ up v/t. **1.** (nach oben) angleichen; **2.** auf ein höheres Ni'veau heben.

,**lev·el·'head·ed** adj. vernünftig, nüchtern, klar.

lev·el·(l)er ['levlə] s. sociol. ‚Gleichmacher' m (Faktor).

le·ver ['liːvə] I s. **1.** ⊕, phys. a) Hebel m, b) Brechstange f; **2.** ⊕ Anker m (der Uhr): ~ escapement Ankerhemmung f; ~ watch Ankeruhr f; **3.** fig. Druckmittel n; II v/t. **4.** hebeln, mit e-m Hebel bewegen, (hoch- etc.)stemmen: ~ up; '**le·ver·age** [-vərɪdʒ] s. **1.** ⊕ Hebelkraft f, -wirkung f; **2.** fig. a) Einfluss m, b) Druckmittel n: put ~ on s.o. j-n unter Druck setzen.

lev·er·et ['levərɪt] s. Junghase m, Häschen n.

le·vi·a·than [lɪˈvaɪəθn] s. bibl. Levi'athan m, (See)Ungeheuer n; fig. Ungetüm n, Gi'gant m.

lev·i·tate ['levɪteɪt] v/i. u. v/t. (frei) schweben (lassen); **lev·i·ta·tion** [,levɪˈteɪʃn] s. Levitati'on f, (freies) Schweben.

lev·i·ty ['levətɪ] s. Leichtfertigkeit f, Frivoli'tät f.

lev·y ['levɪ] I s. ♦ a) Erhebung f (von Steuern etc.), b) Abgabe f: capital ~ Kapitalabgabe, c) Beitrag m, 'Umlage f; **2.** ⚖ Voll'streckungsvoll,zug m; **3.** ⚔ a) Aushebung f, b) a. pl. ausgehobene Truppen pl., Aufgebot n; II v/t. **4.** Steuern etc. erheben, a. Geldstrafe auferlegen (on dat.); **5.** a) beschlagnahmen, b) Beschlagnahme 'durchführen; **6.** ⚔ a) Truppen ausheben, b) Krieg anfangen od. führen ([up]on gegen).

lewd [luːd] adj. □ **1.** lüstern, geil; **2.** unanständig, schmutzig; '**lewd·ness** [-nɪs] s. **1.** Lüsternheit f; **2.** Unanständigkeit f.

lex·i·cal ['leksɪkl] adj. □ lexi'kalisch; **lex·i·cog·ra·pher** [,leksɪˈkɒɡrəfə] s. Lexiko'graph(in), Wörterbuchverfasser (-in); **lex·i·co·graph·ic, lex·i·co·graph·i·cal** [,leksɪkəʊˈɡræfɪk(l)] adj. □ lexiko'graphisch; **lex·i·cog·ra·phy** [,leksɪˈkɒɡrəfɪ] s. Lexikogra'phie f; **lex·i·col·o·gy** [,leksɪˈkɒlədʒɪ] s. Lexikolo'gie f; '**lex·i·con** [-kən] s. Lexikon n.

li·a·bil·i·ty [,laɪəˈbɪlətɪ] s. **1.** ♦, ⚖ a) Verpflichtung f, Verbindlichkeit f, Schuld f, Bilanz f: Passivposten m, pl. Pas'siva pl., b) Haftung f, Haftpflicht f, Haftbarkeit f: ~ insurance Haftpflichtversicherung f; → limited I, c) (Beitrags-, Schadenersatz- etc.)Pflicht f: ~ for damages; **2.** Verantwortlichkeit f: criminal ~ strafrechtliche Verantwortung; **3.** Ausgesetztsein n, Unter'worfensein n (to s.th. e-r Sache): ~ to penalty Strafbarkeit f; **4.** (to) Hang m (zu), Anfälligkeit f (für).

li·a·ble ['laɪəbl] adj. **1.** ♦, ⚖ verantwortlich, haftbar, -pflichtig (for für): be ~ for haften für; hold s.o. ~ j-n haftbar machen; **2.** verpflichtet (for zu); (steuer- etc.)pflichtig: ~ to od. for military service wehrpflichtig; **3.** (to)

neigend (zu), ausgesetzt (dat.), unter'worfen (dat.): be ~ to a) e-r Sache ausgesetzt sein od. unterliegen, b) (mit inf.) leicht et. tun (können), in Gefahr sein vergessen etc. zu werden, c) (mit inf.) et. wahrscheinlich tun: be ~ to a fine e-r Geldstrafe unterliegen; ~ to prosecution strafbar.

li·aise [lɪˈeɪz] v/i. (with) als Verbindungsmann fungieren (zu), die Verbindung aufrechterhalten (mit).

li·ai·son [liːˈeɪzɔːŋ, ⚔ -zən] (Fr.) s. **1.** Zs.-arbeit f, Verbindung f: ~ officer a) ⚔ Verbindungsoffizier m, b) Verbindungsmann m; **2.** Liai'son f: a) (Liebes-) Verhältnis n, b) ling. Bindung f.

li·a·na [lɪˈɑːnə] s. ♀ Li'ane f.

li·ar ['laɪə] s. Lügner(in).

Li·as ['laɪəs] s. geol. Lias m, f, schwarzer Jura.

li·ba·tion [laɪˈbeɪʃn] s. **1.** Trankopfer n; **2.** humor. Zeche'rei f.

li·bel ['laɪbl] I s. **1.** ⚖ a) Verleumdung f, üble Nachrede, Beleidigung f (durch e-e Veröffentlichung) (of, on gen.), b) Klageschrift f; **2.** ⚖ (on) Verleumdung f (gen.), Beleidigung f (gen.), Hohn m (auf acc.); II v/t. **3.** ⚖ (schriftlich etc.) verleumden; **4.** allg. verunglimpfen; '**li·bel·(l)ant** [-lənt] s. ⚖ Kläger(in); **li·bel·(l)ee** [,laɪbəˈliː] s. ⚖ Beklagte(r m) f; '**li·bel·(l)ous** [-bləs] adj. □ verleumderisch.

lib·er·al ['lɪbərəl] I adj. □ **1.** libe'ral, frei(sinnig), vorurteilsfrei, aufgeschlossen; **2.** großzügig: a) freigebig (of mit), b) reichlich (bemessen): a ~ gift ein großzügiges Geschenk; a ~ quantity e-e reichliche Menge, c) frei, weitherzig: ~ interpretation, d) allgemein (bildend): ~ education allgemein bildende Erziehung od. (gute) Allgemeinbildung; ~ profession freier Beruf; **3.** mst ⚘ pol. libe'ral: ⚘ Party; II s. **4.** oft ⚘ pol. Libe'rale(r m) f; ~ arts s. pl. Geisteswissenschaften pl. (Philosophie, Literatur, Sprachen, Soziologie etc.).

lib·er·al·ism ['lɪbərəlɪzəm] s. **1.** → liberality b; **2.** ⚘ pol. Libera'lismus m; **lib·er·al·i·ty** [,lɪbəˈrælətɪ] s. Großzügigkeit f: a) Freigebigkeit f, b) libe'rale Einstellung, Liberali'tät f; **lib·er·al·i·za·tion** [,lɪbərəlaɪˈzeɪʃn] s. ✝, pol. Liberalisierung f; '**lib·er·al·ize** [-laɪz] v/t. ✝, pol. liberalisieren.

lib·er·ate ['lɪbəreɪt] v/t. **1.** befreien (from von) (a. fig.); **2.** ♞ freisetzen; **lib·er·a·tion** [,lɪbəˈreɪʃn] s. **1.** Befreiung f; **2.** ♞ Freisetzen n od. -werden n; '**lib·er·a·tor** [-tə] s. Befreier m.

Li·be·ri·an [laɪˈbɪərɪən] I s. Li'berier(in); II adj li'berisch.

lib·er·tin·age ['lɪbətɪnɪdʒ] s. → libertinism; '**lib·er·tine** [-ətiːn] s. Wüstling m; '**lib·er·tin·ism** [-tɪnɪzəm] s. Sittenlosigkeit f, Liberti'nismus m.

lib·er·ty ['lɪbətɪ] s. **1.** Freiheit f: a) per'sönliche etc. Freiheit: religious ~ Religionsfreiheit, b) freie Wahl, Erlaubnis f: large ~ of action weitgehende Handlungsfreiheit, c) mst pl. Privi'leg n, (Vor)Recht n, d) b.s. Ungehörigkeit f, Frechheit f; **2.** hist. Brit. Freibezirk m (e-r Stadt);

Besondere Redewendungen:

at ~ a) in Freiheit, frei, b) berechtigt, c) unbenützt; be at ~ to do s.th. et. tun dürfen; you are at ~ to go es steht Ihnen frei zu gehen, Sie können gehen; set at ~ in Freiheit setzen, freilassen; take the ~ to do (od. of doing) s.th. sich die Freiheit nehmen, et. zu tun; take liberties with a) sich Freiheiten gegen *j-n* herausnehmen, b) willkürlich mit *et.* umgehen.

li·bid·i·nous [lɪˈbɪdɪnəs] *adj.* □ lüstern, triebhaft, *psych.* libidiˈnös, wollüstig; **li·bi·do** [lɪˈbiːdəʊ] *s. psych.* Liˈbido *f.*

Li·bra [ˈlaɪbrə] *s. ast.* Waage *f;* **'Li·bran** [-rən] *s.* Waage(mensch *m*) *f.*

li·brar·i·an [laɪˈbreərɪən] *s.* Biblioˈthekar (-in); **liˈbrar·i·an·ship** [-ʃɪp] *s.* **1.** Bibliotheˈkarsstelle *f;* **2.** Biblioˈthekswissenschaft *f.*

li·brar·y [ˈlaɪbrərɪ] *s.* **1.** Biblioˈthek *f:* a) *öffentliche* Bücheˈrei, b) *private* Büchersammlung, c) Studierzimmer *n,* d) Buchreihe *f;* **2.** Schallplattensammlung *f;* ~ **sci·ence** → *librarianship* 2.

li·bret·to [lɪˈbretəʊ] *s.* ♪ Liˈbretto *n,* Text(buch *n*) *m.*

Lib·y·an [ˈlɪbɪən] **I** *adj.* libysch; **II** *s.* Libyer(in).

lice [laɪs] *pl. von* **louse.**

li·cence [ˈlaɪsəns] **I** *s.* **1.** Erlaubnis *f,* Genehmigung *f;* **2.** (*a.* ♥ *Export-, Herstellungs-, Patent-, Verkaufs*)Liˈzenz *f,* Konzessiˈon *f,* behördliche Genehmigung, *z. B.* Schankerlaubnis *f;* amtlicher Zulassungsschein, Zulassung *f,* (*Führer-, Jagd-, Waffen- etc.*)Schein *m:* ~ **dodger** TV Schwarzseher *m,* Radio: Schwarzhörer *m;* ~ **fee** Liˈzenz- *od.* Konzessionsgebühr *f;* ~ **holder** Führerscheininhaber *m;* ~ **number** *mot.* Kraftfahrzeug- *od.* Kfz-Nummer *f;* ~ **plate** *mot.* amtliches *od.* polizeiliches Kennzeichen, Nummernschild *n;* ~ **to practise medicine** (ärztliche) Approbation; **3.** Heiratserlaubnis *f;* **4.** (*künstlerische, dichterische*) Freiheit; **5.** Zügellosigkeit *f;* **II** *v/t.* **6.** → *license* I; **'li·cense** [-ns] **I** *v/t.* **1.** *j-m* e-e (behördliche) Genehmigung *od.* e-e Liˈzenz *od.* e-e Konzessiˈon erteilen; **2.** *et.* lizenzieren, konzessionieren, (amtlich) genehmigen *od.* zulassen; **3.** *Buch* zur Veröffentlichung *od. Theaterstück* zur Aufführung freigeben; **4.** *j-n* ermächtigen; **II** *s.* **5.** *Am.* → *licence* I; **'li·censed** [-st] *adj.* **1.** konzessioniert, lizenziert, amtlich zugelassen: ~ **house** (*od.* **premises**) Lokal *n* mit Schankkonzession; **2.** Lizenz...: ~ **construction** Lizenzbau *m;* **3.** privilegiert; **li·cen·see** [ˌlaɪsənˈsiː] *s.* **1.** Liˈzenznehmer(in); **2.** Konzessiˈonsinhaber(in); **'li·cens·er** [-sə] *s.* Liˈzenzgeber *m,* Konzessiˈonserteiler *m;* **li·cen·ti·ate** [laɪˈsenʃɪət] *s. univ.* **1.** Lizenziˈat *m;* **2.** (*Grad*) Lizenziˈat *n.*

li·cen·tious [laɪˈsenʃəs] *adj.* □ unzüchtig, ausschweifend, lasterhaft.

li·chen [ˈlaɪkən] *s.* ♥, ♣ Flechte *f.*

lich gate [lɪtʃ] *s. überdachtes* Friedhofstor.

lick [lɪk] **I** *v/t.* **1.** (be-, ab)lecken, lecken an (*dat.*): ~ **off** ablecken; ~ **up** auflecken; ~ **one's lips** sich die Lippen lecken; ~ **s.o.'s boots** *fig.* vor *j-m* kriechen; ~ **into shape** *fig.* in die richtige Form bringen, zurechtbiegen, -stutzen; → *dust* 1; **2.** F a) *j-n* ˈverdreschen', b) schlagen, besiegen, c) über'treffen, ˈschlagen': **this ~s everything!,** d) *et.* ˈschaffen', fertig werden mit *e-m Problem:* **we have got it ~ed!;** **3.** lecken (*at an dat.*), *fig. a.* a) plätschern (*Welle*), b) züngeln (*Flamme*); **III** *s.* **4.** Lecken *n:* **give s.th. a ~** an *et.* lecken; **a ~ and a promise** e-e flüchtige Arbeit *etc.,* *bsd.* e-e ˌKatzenwäsche'; **5.** (*ein*) bisschen: **a ~ of paint; he didn't do a ~ of work** *Am.* F er hat keinen Strich getan; **6.** F a) Schlag *m,* b) ˌTempo' *n:* (**at**) **full ~** mit größter Geschwindigkeit;

7. Salzlecke *f.*

ˌlick·e·ty-ˈsplit [ˌlɪkətɪ-] *adv. Am.* F wie der Blitz.

lick·ing [ˈlɪkɪŋ] *s.* **1.** Lecken *n;* **2.** F (Tracht *f*) Prügel *pl.,* Abreibung *f* (*a. fig. Niederlage*).

'lick·spit·tle *s.* Speichellecker *m.*

lic·o·rice [ˈlɪkərɪs] → *liquorice.*

lid [lɪd] *s.* **1.** Deckel *m* (*a.* F Hut): **put the ~ on s.th.** *Brit.* F a) e-r Sache die Krone aufsetzen, b) *et.* endgültig ˌerledigen'; **clamp** (*od.* **put**) **the ~ on s.th.** *Am.* a) *et.* verbieten, b) scharf vorgehen gegen *et.,* c) *et.* (*Nachricht etc.*) sperren; **2.** (Augen)Lid *n.*

li·do [ˈliːdəʊ] *s. Brit.* Frei- *od.* Strandbad *n.*

lie¹ [laɪ] **I** *s.* Lüge *f,* Schwindel *m:* **tell a ~** (*od.* **lies**) lügen; → *white lie;* **give s.o. the ~** *j-n* der Lüge bezichtigen; **give the ~ to et. od. j-n** Lügen strafen; **he lived a ~** sein Leben war e-e einzige Lüge; **II** *v/i.* lügen: ~ **to s.o.** a) *j-n* belügen, *j-n* anlügen, b) *j-m* vorlügen (**that** dass).

lie² [laɪ] **I** *s.* **1.** Lage *f* (*a. fig.*): **the ~ of the land** *Brit. fig.* die Lage (der Dinge); **II** *v/i.* [*irr.*] **2.** *allg.* liegen: a) im Bett, im Hinterhalt, in Trümmern *etc.* liegen, b) *ausgebreitet, tot etc.* daliegen, c) begraben sein, ruhen, d) gelegen sein, sich befinden, e) lasten (**on** auf *der Seele, im Magen etc.*), f) begründet liegen, bestehen (**in** in *dat.*): ~ **dying** im Sterben liegen; ~ **behind** *fig.* a) hinter *j-m* liegen (*Erlebnis etc.*), b) dahinter stecken (*Motiv etc.*); ~ **in s.o.'s way** *j-m* zur Hand *od.* möglich sein, *a.* in *j-s* Fach schlagen; **his talents do not ~ that way** dazu hat er kein Talent; ~ **on s.o.** ƫ *j-m* obliegen; ~ **under a suspicion** unter e-m Verdacht stehen; ~ **under a sentence of death** zum Tode verurteilt sein; ~ **with s.o.** *obs. od. bibl.* *j-m* beischlafen, mit *j-m* schlafen; **as far as ~s with me** soweit es in m-n Kräften steht; **it ~s with you to do it** es liegt an dir, es zu tun; **3.** sich (hin)legen: ~ **on your back!** leg dich auf den Rücken!; **4.** führen, verlaufen (*Straße etc.*); **5.** ƫ zulässig sein (*Klage etc.*): **appeal ~s to the Supreme Court** Rechtsmittel können beim Obersten Gericht eingelegt werden;

Zssgn mit adv.:

lie| back *v/i.* sich zu'rücklegen; *fig.* die Hände in den Schoß legen; ~ **down** *v/i.* **1.** sich hinlegen; **2.** ~ **under, take lying down** Beleidigung *etc.* widerspruchslos hinnehmen, sich *et.* gefallen lassen: **we won't take that lying down!** das lassen wir uns nicht (so einfach) bieten!; ~ **in** *v/i.* **1.** im Bett bleiben; **2.** im Wochenbett liegen; ~ **off** *v/i.* **1.** ♣ vom Land *etc.* abhalten; **2.** *fig.* pausieren; ~ **low** *v/i.* sich versteckt halten; ~ **o·ver** *v/i.* liegen bleiben, aufgeschoben werden; ~ **to** *v/i.* ♣ beiliegen; ~ **up** *v/i.* **1.** ruhen (*a. fig.*); **2.** das Bett *od.* das Zimmer hüten (müssen); **3.** außer Betrieb sein.

lied [liːd] *pl.* **lie·der** [ˈliːdə] (*Ger.*) *s.* ♪ (*deutsches* Kunst)Lied.

lie de·tec·tor *s.* ˈLügen₍₎tektor *m.*

'lie-down *s.* F Schläfchen *n.*

lief [liːf] *adv. obs.* gern: ~**er than** lieber als; **I had** (*od.* **would**) **as ~ ...** ich würde eher *sterben etc.,* ich *ginge etc.* ebenso gern.

liege [liːdʒ] **I** *s.* **1.** *a.* ~ **lord** Leh(e)nsherr *m;* **2.** *a.* ~**man** Leh(e)nsmann *m;* **II** *adj.* **3.** Leh(e)ns...

lien [lɪən] *s.* ƫ (**on**) Pfandrecht *n* (**an** *dat.*), Zu'rückbehaltungsrecht *n* (auf

acc.).

lieu [ljuː] *s.:* **in ~ of** anstelle von (*od. gen.*), anstatt (*gen.*); **in ~ (of that)** stattdessen.

lieu·ten·an·cy [*Brit.* lefˈtenənsɪ; ♣ leˈt-; *Am.* luːˈt-] *s.* ✕, ♣ Leutnantsrang *m.*

lieu·ten·ant [*Brit.* lefˈtenənt; ♣ leˈt-; *Am.* luːˈt-] *s.* **1.** ✕, ♣ a) *allg.* Leutnant *m,* b) *Brit.* (*Am.* **first ~**) Oberleutnant *m,* c) ♣ (*Am. a.* ~ **senior grade**) Kapiˈtänleutnant *m;* ~ **junior grade** *Am.* Oberleutnant zur See; **2.** Statthalter *m;* **3.** *fig.* rechte Hand, ˌAdjuˈtant'; ~ **colo·nel** *s.* ✕ Oberst'leutnant *m;* ~ **gen·er·al** *s.* ✕ Geneˈralleutnant *m;* ~ **gov·er·nor** *s.* ˈVizegouverˌneur *m* (*im brit. Commonwealth od. e-s amer. Bundesstaates*).

life [laɪf] *pl.* **lives** [laɪvz] *s.* **1.** (*organisches*) Leben; → *large* 1; **2.** Leben *n:* a) Lebenserscheinung *pl.,* b) Lebewesen *pl.:* **there is no ~ on the moon; plant ~** Pflanzen(welt *f*) *pl.;* **3.** (Menschen)Leben *n:* **they lost their lives** sie kamen ums Leben; **three lives were lost** drei Menschenleben sind zu beklagen; ~ **and limb** Leib u. Leben; **4.** Leben *n* (*e-s Einzelwesens*): **it is a matter of ~ and death** es geht um Leben oder Tod; **early in ~** in jungen Jahren, (schon) früh; **5.** Leben *n,* Lebenszeit *f,* *a.* ◉ Lebensdauer *f:* **all his ~** sein ganzes Leben (lang); **6.** Leben(skraft *f*) *n:* **there is still ~ in the old dog yet!** *humor.* so alt u. klapprig bin ich (*od.* ist er) noch gar nicht!; **7.** a) Bestehen *n,* b) ƫƫ, ♥ Gültigkeitsdauer *f,* Laufzeit *f:* **the ~ of a contract** (**an insurance, patent,** *etc.*), c) *parl.* Legisla'turperiˌode *f;* **8.** Lebensweise *f,* -führung *f,* -wandel *m;* Leben *n:* **lead an honest ~** ein ehrbares Leben führen; **lead the ~ of Riley** F leben wie Gott in Frankreich; **9.** Leben *n,* Welt *f* (*menschliches Tun u. Treiben*): ~ **in Canada** das Leben in Kanada; **see ~** das Leben kennen lernen *od.* genießen, die Welt sehen; **10.** Leben *n,* Lebhaftigkeit *f,* Lebendigkeit *f:* **put ~ into s.th.** e-e Sache beleben, Leben in et. bringen; **he was the ~ and soul of** er war die Seele *des Unternehmens etc.,* er brachte Leben in die Party *etc.;* **11.** Leben(sbeschreibung *f*) *n,* Biogra'phie *f:* **the ~ of Churchill; 12.** *Versicherungswesen:* Lebensversicherung(en *pl.*) *f;*

Besondere Redewendungen:

for ~ a) fürs (ganze) Leben, b) *bsd.* ƫƫ *u. pol.* lebenslänglich, auf Lebenszeit, c) *a.* **for one's ~, for dear ~** ums (liebe) Leben **rennen** *etc.;* **not for the ~ of me** F nicht um alles in der Welt; **not on your ~!** nie(mals)!; **never in my ~** meiner Lebtag (noch) nicht; **to the ~** lebensecht, naturgetreu; **bring to ~** *fig.* lebendig werden lassen; **bring s.o. back to ~** *j-n* wieder beleben *od.* ins Leben zurückrufen; **come to ~** *fig.* lebendig werden, *Person:* a. munter werden; **seek s.o.'s ~** *j-m* nach dem Leben trachten; **save s.o.'s ~** *j-m* das Leben retten, *fig. humor.* *j-n* ˌretten'; **sell one's ~ dearly** *fig.* sein Leben teuer verkaufen; **such is ~** so ist das Leben; **take s.o.'s** (**one's own**) ~ *j-m* (sich [selbst]) das Leben nehmen; **this is the ~!** F Mann, ist das ein Leben!

ˌlife-and-ˈdeath [-fən'd-] *adj.* Kampf *etc.* auf Leben u. Tod; ~ **an·nu·i·ty** *s.* Leibrente *f;* ~ **as·sur·ance** *s. Brit.* Lebensversicherung *f;* **ˈ~-belt** *s.* **1.** *Brit.* Rettungsring *m;* **2.** *Am.* Rettungsgürtel *m*; '**~·blood** *s.* Herzblut *n* (*a. fig.*); '**~·boat** *s.* ⚓ Rettungsboot *n*; ~ **buoy** *s.* Rettungsring *m* (*od. Ähnliches*); ~ **cy·cle** *s.* **1.** Lebenszyklus *m*; **2.** Lebensphase *f*; ~ **ex·pect·an·cy** *s.* Lebenserwartung *f*; ~ **force** *s.* Lebenskraft *f*, Leben spendende Kraft; '**~-,giv·ing** *adj.* Leben spendend, belebend; '**~-guard** *s.* ✕ Leibgarde *f*; **2.** Rettungsschwimmer *m*, Bademeister *m*; ♀ **Guards** *s. pl.* ✕ Leibgarde *f* (zu Pferde), 'Gardekavalle,rie *f*; ~ **in·sur·ance** *s.* Lebensversicherung *f*; ~ **in·ter·est** *s.* ⚖ lebenslänglicher Nießbrauch; ~ **jack·et** *s.* Schwimmweste *f*.

life·less ['laɪflɪs] *adj.* ☐ leblos: a) tot, b) unbelebt, c) *fig.* matt, schwunglos, ,lahm', ♥ lustlos (*Börse*).

'**life|·like** *adj.* lebenswahr, -echt, na'turgetreu; '**~·line** *s.* **1.** ⚓ Rettungsleine *f*; **2.** Sig'nalleine *f* (*für Taucher*); **3.** *fig.* a) Lebensader *f* (*Versorgungsweg*), b) lebenswichtige Sache, ,Rettungsanker' *m*; **4.** Lebenslinie *f* (*in der Hand*); '**~·long** *adj.* lebenslänglich; ~ **mem·ber** *s.* Mitglied *n* auf Lebenszeit; ~ **of·fice** *s. Brit.* Lebensversicherungsgesellschaft *f*; ~ **pre·serv·er** *s.* **1.** *Am.* ⚓ Schwimmweste *f*, Rettungsgürtel *m*; **2.** Totschläger *m* (*Waffe*).

lif·er ['laɪfə] *s. sl.* **1.** Lebenslängliche(r *m*) *f* (*Strafgefangene[r]*); **2.** → *life sentence*; **3.** *Am.* Be'rufssol,dat *m*.

life| raft *s.* Rettungsfloß *n*; '**~·sav·er** *s.* **1.** Lebensretter(in); **2.** → *lifeguard* 2; **3.** *fig.* a) ,rettender Engel', b) *die* ,Rettung' (*Sache*); ~ **sen·tence** *s.* ⚖ lebenslängliche Freiheitsstrafe; '**~·size(d)** *adj.* lebensgroß, in Lebensgröße; '**~·span** *s.* Leben(sspanne *f*, -zeit *f*) *n*; '**~·style** *s.* Lebensstil *m*; '**~-sup,port sy·stem** *n* ⚕, ⚙ 'Lebenserhaltungssys,tem *n*; ~ **ta·ble** *s.* 'Sterblichkeitsta,belle *f*; '**~·time I** *s.* Lebenszeit *f*, Leben *n*, *a.* ⚙ Lebensdauer *f*: *the chance of a* ~ e-e einmalige Chance; **II** *adj.* lebenslänglich, Lebens...; ~ **vest** *s.* Rettungs-, Schwimmweste *f*; '**~·work** *s.* Lebenswerk *n*.

lift [lɪft] **I** *s.* **1.** (Auf-, Hoch)Heben *n*; **2.** stolze *etc.* Kopfhaltung; **3.** ⚙ a) Hub (-höhe *f*) *m*, b) Hubkraft *f*; **4.** ✈ a) Auftrieb *m*, b) Luftbrücke *f*; **5.** *fig.* a) Hilfe *f*, b) (innerer) Auftrieb *m*: *give s.o. a* ~ j-m helfen, b) j-m Auftrieb geben, j-n aufmuntern, c) j-n (im Auto) mitnehmen; **6.** a) *Brit.* Lift *m*, Aufzug *m*, Fahrstuhl *m*, b) (Ski-, Sessel)Lift *m*; **II** *v/t.* **7.** *a.* ~ *up* (auf-, em'por-, hoch-) heben; *Augen, Stimme etc.* erheben: ~ *s.th. down* et. herunterheben; *not to* ~ *a finger* keinen Finger rühren; **8.** *fig.* a) (*geistig od. sittlich*) heben, b) *aus der Armut etc.* em'porheben, c) *a.* ~ *up* (*innerlich*) erheben, aufmuntern; **9.** *Preise* erhöhen; **10.** *Kartoffeln* ausgraben, ernten; **11.** ,mitgehen lassen', ,klauen', stehlen (*a. fig. plagiieren*); **12.** *Gesicht etc.* liften, straffen: *have one's face ~ed* sich das Gesicht liften lassen; **13.** *Blockade, Verbot, Zensur etc.* aufheben; **III** *v/i.* **14.** sich heben (*a. Nebel*); sich (hoch)heben lassen; ~ *off* ✈ abheben, starten; '**lift·er** [-tə] *s.* **1.** (*sport* Gewicht)Heber *m*; **2.** ⚙ a) Hebegerät *n*, b) Nocken *m*, c) Stößel *m*; **3.** ,Langfinger' *m* (*Dieb*).

lift·ing ['lɪftɪŋ] *adj.* Hebe..., Hub...; ~ **jack** *s.* ⚙ Hebewinde *f*, *mot.* Wagenheber *m*.

'**lift-off** *s.* **1.** Start *m* (*Rakete*); **2.** Abheben *n* (*Flugzeug*).

lig·a·ment ['lɪgəmənt] *s. anat.* Liga'ment *n*, Band *n*.

---

lig·a·ture ['lɪgə,tʃʊə] **I** *s.* **1.** Binde *f*, Band *n*; **2.** *typ. u.* ♪ Liga'tur *f*; **3.** ☞ Abbindungsschnur *f*, Bindung *f*; **II** *v/t.* **4.** ver-, ☞ abbinden.

light¹ [laɪt] **I** *s.* **1.** *allg.* Licht *n* (*Helligkeit, Schein, Beleuchtung, Lichtquelle, Lampe, Tageslicht, fig. Aspekt, Erleuchtung*): *by the* ~ *of a candle* beim Schein e-r Kerze, bei Kerzenlicht; *bring* (*come*) *to* ~ *fig.* ans Licht *od.* an den Tag bringen (kommen); *cast* (*od. shed, throw*) *a* ~ *on s.th. fig.* Licht auf et. werfen; *place* (*od. put*) *in a favo(u)rable* ~ *fig.* in ein günstiges Licht stellen *od.* rücken; *see the* ~ *eccl.* erleuchtet werden; *see the* ~ (*of day*) *fig.* bekannt *od.* veröffentlicht werden; *I see the* ~! mir geht ein Licht auf!; (*seen*) *in the* ~ *of these facts* im Lichte *od.* angesichts dieser Tatsachen; *show s.th. in a different* ~ et. in e-m anderen Licht erscheinen lassen; *hide one's* ~ *under a bushel fig.* sein Licht unter den Scheffel stellen; *let there be* ~! *Bibl.* es werde Licht; *he went out like a* ~ F er war sofort ,weg' (*eingeschlafen*); **2.** Licht *n*: a) Lampe *f*, *a. pl.* Beleuchtung *f* (*beide a. mot. etc.*): ~*s out* ✕ Zapfenstreich *m*; ~*s out*! Lichter aus!, b) (*Verkehrs*)Ampel *f*: ~ *green light, red* 1; **3.** ⚓ a) Leuchtfeuer *n*, b) Leuchtturm *m*; **4.** Feuer *n* (*zum Anzünden*), *a.* Streichholz *n*: *put a* ~ *to s.th.* et. anzünden; *strike a* ~ ein Streichholz anzünden; *will you give me a* ~? darf ich Sie um Feuer bitten?; **5.** *fig.* Leuchte *f* (*Person*): *a shining* ~ e-e Leuchte, ein großes Licht; **6.** Lichtöffnung *f*, *bsd.* Fenster *n*, Oberlicht *n*; **7.** *paint.* a) Licht *n*, heller Teil (*e-s Gemäldes*); **8.** *fig.* Verstand *m*, geistige Fähigkeiten *pl.*: *according to his* ~*s* so gut er es eben versteht; **9.** *pl. sl.* Augen *pl.*; **II** *adj.* **10.** hell: ~*red* hellrot; **III** *v/t.* [*irr.*] **11.** *a.* ~ *up* anzünden; **12.** *oft* ~ *up* beleuchten (*a. das Gesicht*); ~ *up Augen etc.* aufleuchten lassen; **13.** j-m leuchten; **IV** *v/i.* [*irr.*] **14.** *a.* ~ *up* sich entzünden, angehen (*Feuer, Licht*); **15.** *mst* ~ *up fig.* sich erhellen, strahlen (*Gesicht*), aufleuchten (*Augen etc.*); **16.** ~ *up* a) die Pfeife *etc.* anzünden, sich e-e Zigarette anstecken, b) Licht machen.

light² [laɪt] **I** *adj.* ☐ → *lightly*; **1.** *allg.* leicht (*z. B. Last, Kleidung; Mahlzeit, Wein, Zigarre;* ✕ *Infanterie,* ⚓ *Kreuzer etc.; Hand, Schritt, Schlaf, Regen, Wind, Arbeit, Fehler, Strafe; Charakter; Musik, Roman*): ~ *of foot* leichtfüßig; *a* ~ *girl* ein ,leichtes' Mädchen; ~ *current* ⚡ Schwachstrom *m*; ~ *metal* Leichtmetall *n*; ~ *literature* (*od. reading*) Unterhaltungsliteratur *f*; ~ *railway* Kleinbahn *f*; ~ *in the head* benommen; ~ *on one's feet* leichtfüßig; *with a* ~ *heart* leichten Herzens; *no* ~ *matter* keine Kleinigkeit; *make* ~ *of* a) et. auf die leichte Schulter nehmen, b) bagatellisieren; **2.** zu leicht: ~ *weights* Untergewichte; **3.** locker (*Brot, Erde, Schnee*); **4.** sorglos, unbeschwert, heiter; **5.** a) leicht beladen, b) unbeladen; **II** *adv.* **6.** leicht: *travel* ~ mit leichtem Gepäck reisen.

light³ [laɪt] *v/i.* [*irr.*] **1.** fallen (*on auf acc.*); **2.** sich niederlassen (*on auf dat.*) (*Vogel etc.*); **3.** ~ (*up*)*on fig.* (zufällig) stoßen auf (*acc.*); **4.** ~ *out sl.* ,verduften'; **5.** ~ *into* F herfallen über j-n.

light| bar·ri·er *s.* ⚡ Lichtschranke *f*; '**~--e,mit·ting di·ode** *s.* ⚙ 'Leuchtdi,ode *f*. **light·en¹** ['laɪtn] **I** *v/i.* **1.** hell werden,

---

sich erhellen; **2.** blitzen; **II** *v/t.* **3.** erhellen.

light·en² ['laɪtn] **I** *v/t.* **1.** leichter machen, erleichtern (*beide a. fig.*); **2.** *Schiff* (ab)leichtern; **3.** aufheitern; **II** *v/i.* **4.** leichter werden (*a. fig. Herz etc.*).

light·er¹ ['laɪtə] *s.* Anzünder *m* (*a. Gerät*); (Taschen)Feuerzeug *n*.

light·er² ['laɪtə] *s.* ⚓ Leichter(schiff *n*) *m*, Prahm *m*; '**light·er·age** [-ərɪdʒ] *s.* Leichtergeld *n*.

,**light·er·than-'air** *adj.*: ~ *craft* Luftfahrzeug *n* leichter als Luft.

'**light|-,fin·gered** *adj.* **1.** geschickt; **2.** langfingerig, diebisch; '**~-,foot·ed** *adj.* leicht-, schnellfüßig; ,**~-'head·ed** *adj.* **1.** leichtsinnig, -fertig; **2.** 'übermütig, ausgelassen; **3.** a) wirr, leicht verrückt, b) schwind(e)lig; ,**~-'heart·ed** *adj.* ☐ fröhlich, heiter, unbeschwert; ~ **heavy·weight** *s. sport* Halbschwergewicht (-ler *m*) *n*; '**~·house** *s.* Leuchtturm *m*.

light·ing ['laɪtɪŋ] *s.* **1.** Beleuchtung *f*; ~ **effects** Lichteffekte; ~ **point** ⚡ Brennstelle *f*; **2.** Anzünden *n*; ,**~-'up time** *s.* Zeit *f* des Einschaltens der Straßenbeleuchtung *od.* (*mot.*) der Scheinwerfer.

light·ly ['laɪtlɪ] *adv.* **1.** *allg.* leicht: ~ *come* ~ *go* wie gewonnen, so zerronnen; **2.** gelassen, leicht; **3.** leichtfertig; **4.** leichthin; **5.** geringschätzig.

light·ness ['laɪtnɪs] *s.* **1.** Leichtheit *f*, Leichtigkeit *f* (*a. fig.*); **2.** Leichtverdaulichkeit *f*; **3.** Milde *f*; **4.** Behendigkeit *f*; **5.** Heiterkeit *f*; **6.** Leichtfertigkeit *f*, Leichtsinn *m*, Oberflächlichkeit *f*.

light·ning ['laɪtnɪŋ] **I** *s.* Blitz *m*: *struck by* ~ vom Blitz getroffen; *like* (*greased*) ~ *fig.* wie der *od.* ein geölter Blitz; **II** *adj.* blitzschnell, Schnell...: ~ *artist* Schnellzeichner *m*; *with* ~ *speed* mit Blitzesschnelle; ~ **ar·rest·er** *s.* ⚡ Blitzschutzsicherung *f*; ~ **bug** *s. Am.* Leuchtkäfer *m*; ~ **con·duc·tor**, ~ **rod** *s.* Blitzableiter *m*; ~ **strike** *s.* Blitzstreik *m*.

light| oil *s.* ⚙ Leichtöl *n*; ~ **pen** *s. Computer:* Lichtgriffel *m*.

lights [laɪts] *s. pl.* (Tier)Lunge *f*.

'**light|·ship** *s.* ⚓ Feuer-, Leuchtschiff *n*; ~ **source** *s.* ⚡, *phys.* Lichtquelle *f*; '**~·weight I** *adj.* leicht; **II** *s. sport* Leichtgewicht(ler *m*) *n*; F *fig.* a) ,kein großes Licht', b) unbedeutender Mensch; ~ **year** *s. ast.* Lichtjahr *n*.

lig·ne·ous ['lɪgnɪəs] *adj.* holzig, holzartig, Holz...; '**lig·ni·fy** [-nɪfaɪ] **I** *v/t.* in Holz verwandeln; **II** *v/i.* verholzen; '**lig·nin** [-nɪn] *s.* 🌿 Li'gnin *n*, Holzstoff *m*; '**lig·nite** [-naɪt] *s.* Braunkohle *f*, *bsd.* Li'gnit *m*.

lik·a·ble ['laɪkəbl] *adj.* liebenswert, sym'pathisch, nett.

like¹ [laɪk] **I** *adj. u. prp.* **1.** gleich (*dat.*), wie (*a. adv.*): *a man* ~ *you* ein Mann wie du; ~ *a man* wie ein Mann; *what is he* ~? a) wie sieht er aus?, b) wie ist er?; *he is* ~ *that* er ist nun mal so; *he is just* ~ *his brother* er ist genau (so) wie sein Bruder; *that's just* ~ *him!* das sieht ihm ähnlich!; *that's just* ~ *a woman!* typisch Frau!; *what does it look* ~? wie sieht es aus?; *it looks* ~ *rain* es sieht nach Regen aus; *feel* ~ (*doing*) *s.th.* zu et. aufgelegt sein, Lust haben, et. zu tun, et. gern tun wollen; *a fool* ~ *that* ein derartiger *od.* so ein Dummkopf; *a thing* ~ *that* so etwas; *I saw one* ~ *it* ich sah ein ähnliches (*Auto etc.*); *there is nothing* ~ es geht nichts über (*acc.*); *it is nothing* ~ *as bad as that* es ist bei weitem nicht so schlimm; *something ~ 100 tons* so etwa 100 Tonnen; *this is something ~!* F das lässt sich hören!; *that's more ~ it!* das lässt sich (schon) eher hören!; *~ master, ~ man* wie der Herr, sos Gescherr; **2.** gleich: *a ~ amount* ein gleicher Betrag; *in ~ manner* a) auf gleiche Weise, b) gleichermaßen; **3.** ähnlich; *the portrait is not ~* das Porträt ist nicht ähnlich; *as ~ as two eggs* ähnlich wie ein Ei dem anderen; **4.** ähnlich, gleich-, derartig: *... and other ~ problems* ... und andere derartige Probleme; **5.** F *od. obs.* (*a. adv.*) wahr'scheinlich: *he is ~ to pass his exam* er wird sein Examen wahrscheinlich bestehen; *~ enough*, *as ~ as not* höchstwahrscheinlich; **6.** *sl.* ,oder so': *let's go to the cinema ~*; **II** *cj.* **7.** *sl.* (*fälschlich für as*) wie: *~ I said*; *~ who?* wie wer, zum Beispiel?; **8.** *dial.* als ob; **III** *s.* **9.** der (*die, das*) Gleiche: *his ~* seinesgleichen; *the ~* der-, desgleichen; *and the ~* und dergleichen; *the ~(s) of* so etwas wie, solche wie; *the ~(s) of that* so etwas, etwas Derartiges; *the ~s of you* F Leute wie Sie.

like² [laɪk] **I** *v/t.* (gern) mögen: a) gern haben, (gut) leiden können, lieben, b) gern essen, trinken *etc.*: *~ doing* (*od. to do*) gern tun; *much ~d* gern beliebt; *I ~ it* es gefällt mir; *I ~ him* ich hab ihn gern, ich mag ihn (gern), ich kann ihn gut leiden; *I ~ fast cars* mir gefallen *od.* ich habe Spaß an schnellen Autos; *how do you ~ it?* wie gefällt es dir?, wie findest du es?; *we ~ it here* es gefällt uns hier; *I ~ that!* *iro.* so was hab ich gern!; *what do you ~ better?* was hast du lieber?, was gefällt dir besser?; *I should ~ to know* ich möchte gerne wissen; *I should ~ you to be here* ich hätte gern, dass du hier wär(e)st; *~ it or not* ob du willst oder nicht; *~ it or lump it!* F wenn du nicht willst, dann lass es eben bleiben!; *I ~ steak, but it doesn't ~ me* humor. ich esse Beefsteak gern, aber es bekommt mir nicht; **II** *v/i.* wollen: (*just*) *as you ~* (ganz) wie du willst; *if you ~* wenn du willst; **III** *s.* Neigung *f*, Vorliebe *f*: *~s and dislikes* Neigungen u. Abneigungen.

-like [laɪk] *in Zssgn* wie, ...artig, ...ähnlich, ...mäßig.

like·a·ble → *likable*.

like·li·hood ['laɪklɪhʊd] *s.* Wahr'scheinlichkeit *f*: *in all ~* aller Wahrscheinlichkeit nach; *there is a strong ~ of his succeeding* es ist sehr wahrscheinlich, dass es ihm gelingt; **like·ly** ['laɪklɪ] **I** *adj.* **1.** wahr'scheinlich, vor'aussichtlich: *not ~* schwerlich, kaum; *it is not ~* (*that*) *he will come*, *he is not ~ to come* es ist nicht wahrscheinlich, dass er kommen wird; *which is his most ~ route?* welchen Weg wird er voraussichtlich *od.* am ehesten einschlagen?; *this is not ~ to happen* das wird wahrscheinlich nicht *od.* wohl kaum geschehen; *not ~!* *iro.* glaubhaft!; **2.** glaubhaft: *a ~ story!* *iro.* wers glaubt, wird selig!; **3.** a) möglich, b) geeignet, infrage kommend, c) aussichtsreich, d) viel versprechend: *a ~ candidate*; *a ~ explanation* e-e mögliche Erklärung; *a ~ place* ein möglicher Ort (*wo sich et. befindet etc.*); **II** *adv.* **4.** wahr'scheinlich: *as ~ as not*, *very ~* höchstwahrscheinlich.

,like-'mind·ed *adj.* gleich gesinnt: *be ~ with s.o.* mit j-m übereinstimmen.

lik·en ['laɪkən] *v/t.* vergleichen (*to* mit).

like·ness ['laɪknɪs] *s.* **1.** Ähnlichkeit *f* (*to* mit); **2.** Gleichheit *f*; **3.** Gestalt *f*, Form *f*; **4.** Bild *n*, Por'trät *n*: *have one's ~ taken* sich malen *od.* fotografieren lassen; **5.** Abbild *n* (*of gen.*).

'like·wise *adv. u. cj.* eben-, gleichfalls, des'gleichen, ebenso.

lik·ing ['laɪkɪŋ] *s.* **1.** Zuneigung *f*: *have* (*take*) *a ~ for* (*od. to*) *s.o.* zu j-m eine Zuneigung haben (fassen), an j-m Gefallen haben (finden); **2.** (*for*) Gefallen *n* (an *dat.*), Neigung *f* (zu), Geschmack *m* (an *dat.*): *be greatly to s.o.'s ~* j-m sehr zusagen; *this is not to my ~* das ist nicht nach meinem Geschmack; *it's too big for my ~* es ist mir (einfach) zu groß.

li·lac ['laɪlək] **I** *s.* **1.** ♀ Spanischer Flieder; **2.** Lila *n* (*Farbe*); **II** *adj.* **3.** lila (-farben).

Lil·li·pu·tian [,lɪlɪ'pjuːʃjən] **I** *adj.* **1.** a) winzig, zwergenhaft, b) Liliput..., Klein(st)...; **II** *s.* **2.** Lilipu'taner(in); **3.** Zwerg *m*.

lilt [lɪlt] **I** *s.* **1.** fröhliches Lied; **2.** rhythmischer Schwung; **3.** a) singender Tonfall, b) fröhlicher Klang: *a ~ in her voice*; **II** *v/t. u. v/i.* **4.** trällern.

lil·y [lɪlɪ] *s.* ♀ Lilie *f*: *~ of the valley* Maiglöckchen *n*; *paint the ~* *fig.* schönfärben; ,~·'liv·ered *adj.* feig(e).

limb [lɪm] *s.* **1.** *anat.* Glied *n*, *pl.* Glieder *pl.*, Gliedmaßen *pl.*; **2.** Ast *m*: *out on a ~* F in e-r gefährlichen Lage; **3.** *fig.* a) Glied *n*, Teil *m*, b) Arm *m*, c) *ling.* (Satz)Glied *n*, d) ♃ Absatz *m*; **4.** F ,Satansbraten' *m*.

lim·ber¹ ['lɪmbə] **I** *adj.* geschmeidig (*a. fig.*), gelenkig; **II** *v/t. u. v/i. ~ up* geschmeidig machen, (sich) lockern, *v/i.* a. Lockerungsübungen machen, sich warm machen *od.* spielen.

lim·ber² ['lɪmbə] **I** *s.* ✗ Protze *f*; **II** *v/t. u. v/i. mst ~ up* ✗ aufprotzen.

lim·bo ['lɪmbəʊ] *s.* **1.** *eccl.* Vorhölle *f*; **2.** Gefängnis *n*; **3.** *fig.* a) ,Rumpelkammer' *f*, b) Vergessenheit *f*, c) Schwebe (-zustand *m*) *f*: *be in a ~* ,in der Luft hängen' (*Person od. Sache*).

lime¹ [laɪm] **I** *s.* **1.** ♦ Kalk *m*; **2.** ♪ Kalkdünger *m*; **3.** Vogelleim *m*; **II** *v/t.* **4.** kalken, mit Kalk düngen.

lime² [laɪm] *s.* ♀ Linde *f*.

lime³ [laɪm] *s.* ♀ Li'mone *f*, Limo'nelle *f*.

'lime|·kiln *s.* Kalkofen *m*; '~·light *s.* **1.** ⚙ Kalklicht *n*; **2.** *fig.* (*be in the ~* im) Rampenlicht *n od.* (im) Licht *n* der Öffentlichkeit *od.* (im) Mittelpunkt *m* des (öffentlichen) Inter'esses (stehen).

li·men ['laɪmen] *s. psych.* (Bewusstseins- *od.* Reiz)Schwelle *f*.

lime pit *s.* **1.** Kalkbruch *m*; **2.** Kalkgrube *f*; **3.** *Gerberei*: Äscher *m*.

Lim·er·ick ['lɪmərɪk] *s.* Limerick *m* (5- -zeiliger Nonsensvers).

'lime|·stone *s. min.* Kalkstein *m*; *~ tree s.* ♀ Linde(nbaum *m*) *f*.

lim·ey ['laɪmɪ] *s. Am. sl.* ,Tommy' *m* (*Brite*).

lim·it ['lɪmɪt] **I** *s.* **1.** *bsd. fig.* a) Grenze *f*, Schranke *f*, b) Beschränkung *f* (*on gen.*): *within ~s* in Grenzen, bis zu e-m gewissen Grade; *without ~* ohne Grenzen, grenzen-, schrankenlos; *there is a ~ to everything* alles hat seine Grenzen; *there is no ~ to his ambition* sein Ehrgeiz kennt keine Grenzen; *off ~s Am.* Zutritt verboten (*to* für); *that's my ~!* a) mehr schaffe ich nicht!, b) höher kann ich nicht gehen!; *that's the ~!* F das ist (doch) die Höhe!; *he is the ~!* F er ist unglaublich *od.* unmöglich!; *go to the ~* F bis zum

Äußersten gehen, *sport* über die Runden kommen; → *speed limit*; **2.** ✈, ⚙ Grenze *f*, Grenzwert *m*; **3.** zeitliche Begrenzung, Frist *f*: *extreme ~* ♃ äußerster Termin; **4.** ♃ a) Höchstbetrag *m*, b) Limit *n*, Preisgrenze *f*: *lowest ~* äußerster *od.* letzter Preis; **II** *v/t.* **5.** begrenzen, beschränken, einschränken (*to* auf *acc.*); *Preise* limitieren: *~ o.s. to* sich beschränken auf (*acc.*); **lim·i·ta·tion** [,lɪmɪ'teɪʃn] *s.* **1.** *fig.* Grenze *f*: *know one's ~s* s-e Grenzen kennen; **2.** Begrenzung *f*, Ein-, Beschränkung *f*; **3.** (*statutory period of*) *~* ♃ Verjährung(sfrist) *f*: *be barred by the statute of ~* verjähren *od.* verjährt sein; '**lim·it·ed** [-tɪd] **I** *adj.* beschränkt, begrenzt (*to* auf *acc.*): *~* (*express*) *train* → II; *~ in time* zeitlich begrenzt; *~* (*liability*) *company* ♃ *Brit.* Aktiengesellschaft *f*; *~ monarchy* konstitutionelle Monarchie; *~ parking zone* 'Kurzpark,zone *f*; *~ partner* ♃ Kommanditist(in); *~ partnership* ♃ Kommanditgesellschaft; **II** *s.* Schnellzug *m od.* Bus *m* mit Platzkarten; '**lim·it·less** [-lɪs] *adj.* grenzenlos.

lim·net·ic [lɪm'netɪk] *adj.* Süßwasser...

lim·ou·sine ['lɪmuːziːn] *s. mot.* **1.** *Brit.* Wagen *m* mit Glastrennscheibe; **2.** *Am.* Kleinbus *m*.

limp¹ [lɪmp] *adj.* □ **1.** schlaff, schlapp (*a. fig. kraftlos, schwach*): *go ~* erschlaffen, *Person*: a. ,abschlaffen'; **2.** biegsam, weich: *~ book cover*.

limp² [lɪmp] **I** *v/i.* **1.** hinken (*a. fig. Vers etc.*), humpeln; **2.** sich schleppen (*a. Schiff etc.*); **II** *s.* **3.** Hinken *n*: *walk with a ~* → 1.

lim·pet ['lɪmpɪt] *zo.* Napfschnecke *f*: *like a ~* *fig.* wie e-e Klette; *~ mine s.* ✗ Haftmine *f*.

lim·pid ['lɪmpɪd] *adj.* □ 'durchsichtig, klar (*a. fig. Stil etc.*), hell, rein; **lim·pid·i·ty** [lɪm'pɪdətɪ], '**lim·pid·ness** [-nɪs] *s.* 'Durchsichtigkeit *f*, Klarheit *f*.

limp·ness ['lɪmpnɪs] *s.* Schlaff-, Schlappheit *f*.

lim·y ['laɪmɪ] *adj.* **1.** Kalk..., kalkig: a) kalkhaltig, b) kalkartig; **2.** gekalkt.

lin·age ['laɪnɪdʒ] *s.* **1.** → *alignment*; **2.** a) Zeilenzahl *f*, b) 'Zeilenhono,rar *n*.

linch·pin ['lɪntʃpɪn] *s.* ⚙ Lünse *f*, Vorstecker *m*, Achsnagel *m*.

lin·den ['lɪndən] *s.* ♀ Linde *f*.

line¹ [laɪn] **I** *s.* **1.** Linie *f*, Strich *m*; **2.** a) (*Hand- etc.*)Linie *f*: *~ of fate* Schicksalslinie, b) Falte *f*, Runzel *f*, c) Zug *m* (*im Gesicht*); **3.** Zeile *f*: *drop s.o. a ~* j-m ein paar Zeilen schreiben; *read between the ~s* zwischen den Zeilen lesen; **4.** *TV* (Bild)Zeile *f*; **5.** a) Vers *m*, b) *pl. thea. ped.* Strafarbeit *f*, c) *thea. etc.* Rolle *f*, Text *m*; **6.** *pl.* F Trauschein *m*; **7.** F a) Informati'on *f*, Hinweis *m*: *get a ~ on* e-e Information erhalten über (*acc.*); **8.** *Am.* F a) ,Platte' *f* (*Geschwätz*), b) ,Tour' *f*, ,Masche' *f* (*Trick*); **9.** Linie *f*, Richtung *f*: *~ of attack* Angriffsrichtung, *fig.* Taktik *f*; *~ of fire* ✗ Schusslinie *f*; *~ of sight* a) Blickrichtung *f*, b) a. *~ of vision* Gesichtslinie, -achse *f*; *he said s.th. along these ~s* er sagte etwas in dieser Richtung; → *resistance* 1; **10.** *pl. fig.* Grundsätze *pl.*, Richtlinie(n *pl.*) *f*, Grundzüge *f*: *along these ~s* a) nach diesen Grundsätzen, b) folgendermaßen; *along general ~s* ganz allgemein, in großen Zügen; **11.** Art *f* (u. Weise), Me'thode *f*: *~ of approach* Art, et. anzupacken, Methode *f*; *~ of argument* (Art der) Argumentation *f*, -weise *f*; *take a strong ~* energisch auftreten *od.* werden (**with s.o.** j-m gegenüber); *take the ~ that* den Standpunkt vertreten, dass; *don't take that ~ with me!* komm mir ja nicht so! → *hard line* 1; **12.** Grenze *f*, Grenzlinie *f*: *draw the ~* (*at*) *fig.* die Grenze ziehen (bei); *I draw the ~ at that!* da hört es bei mir auf; *lay* (*od.* *put*) *on the ~ fig. sein Leben, s-n Ruf etc.* aufs Spiel setzen; *be on the ~* auf dem Spiel stehen; *your job is on the ~* es geht um deinen Job; *I'll lay it on the ~ for you!* F das kann ich Ihnen genau sagen!; **13.** *pl.* a) Linien(führung *f*) *pl.*, Kon'turen *pl.*, Form *f*, b) Riss *m*, Entwurf *m*; **14.** a) Reihe *f*, Kette *f*, b) *bsd. Am.* (Menschen-, *a.* Auto)Schlange *f*: *stand in ~* (**for**) anstehen *od.* Schlange stehen (nach); *drive in ~ mot.* Kolonne fahren; *be in ~ for fig.* Aussichten haben auf (*acc.*) *od.* Anwärter sein für; **15.** Übereinstimmung *f*: *be in* (**out of**) *~* (nicht) übereinstimmen *od.* im Einklang sein (**with** mit); *bring* (*od.* *get*) *into ~* a) in Einklang bringen (**with** mit), b) j-n ‚auf Vordermann' bringen, c) *pol.* gleichschalten; *fall into ~* sich einordnen, sich anschließen (**with** j-m); *toe the ~* ‚spuren', sich der (*Partei- etc.*)Disziplin beugen; *in ~ of duty bsd.* ✕ in Ausübung des Dienstes; **16.** a) (Abstammungs)Linie *f*, b) Fa'milie *f*, Geschlecht *n*: *the male ~* die männliche Linie; *in the direct ~* in direkter Linie; **17.** *pl.* Los *n*, Geschick *n*: *hard ~s* F Pech *n*; **18.** Fach *n*, Gebiet *n*, Sparte *f*: *~* (**of business**) Branche *f*, Geschäftszweig *m*; *that's not in my ~* das schlägt nicht in mein Fach, das liegt mir nicht; *that's more in my ~* das liegt mir schon eher; **19.** (*Verkehrs-, Eisenbahn- etc.*)Linie *f*, Strecke *f*, Route *f*, *engS.* Gleis *n*: *ship of the ~* Linienschiff *n*; *~s of communications* ✕ rückwärtige Verbindungen; *he was at the end of the ~ fig.* er war am Ende; *that's the end of the ~! fig.* Endstation!; **20.** (*Eisenbahn-, Luftverkehrs-, Autobus*)Gesellschaft *f*; **21.** a) ✂, ☉ Leitung *f*, *bsd.* Tele'fon- *od.* Tele'grafenleitung *f*: *the ~ is engaged* (*Am.* busy) die Leitung ist besetzt; *hold the ~!* bleiben Sie am Apparat!; *three ~s* 3 Anschlüsse; → *hot line*; **22.** ☉ (Fertigungs)Straße *f*; **23.** ✝ a) Sorte *f*, Warengattung *f*, b) Posten *m*, Par'tie *f*, c) Ar'tikel(,serie *f*) *m od. pl.*; **24.** ✕ a) Linie *f*: *behind the enemy's ~s* hinter den feindlichen Linien; *~ of battle* vorderste Linie, Kampflinie, b) Front *f*: *go up the ~* an die Front gehen; *all along the ~*, (**all**) *down the ~ fig.* auf der ganzen Linie, voll (u. ganz); *go down the ~ for Am.* F sich voll einsetzen für, c) Linie *f* (*Formation beim Antreten*), d) Fronttruppe *f*: *the ~s* die Linienregimenter; **25.** *geogr.* Längen- *od.* Breitenkreis *m*: *the ≈* der Äquator; **26.** ⚓ Linie *f*: *~ abreast* Dwarslinie; *~ ahead* Kiellinie; **27.** (Wäsche)Leine *f*, (starke) Schnur, Seil *n*, Tau *n*; **28.** *teleph.* a) Draht *m*, b) Kabel *n*; **29.** Angelschnur *f*; **II** *v/i.* **30.** → *line up* 1, 2; **III** *v/t.* **31.** linieren; **32.** zeichnen, skizzieren; **33.** *Gesicht* (durch) 'furchen; **34.** *Straße etc.* säumen: *soldiers ~d the street* Soldaten bildeten an der Straße Spalier; *~ in v/t.* einzeichnen; *~ off v/t.* abgrenzen; *~ through v/t.* 'durchstreichen; *~ up I v/i.* **1.** sich in e-r Linie *od.* Reihe aufstellen; **2.** Schlange stehen; **3.** *fig.* sich zs.-schließen; **II** *v/t.* **4.** in Linie *od.* in e-r Reihe aufstellen; **5.** aufstellen; **6.** *fig.* F *et.* ‚auf die Beine stellen', organi-

sieren, arrangieren.

line² [laɪn] *v/t.* **1.** *Kleid etc.* füttern; **2.** ☉ ausfüttern, -gießen, -kleiden, -schlagen, (innen) über'ziehen: *~ one's* (**own**) *pockets* in die eigene Tasche arbeiten, sich bereichern.

lin·e·age [ˈlɪnɪɪdʒ] *s.* **1.** (geradlinige) Abstammung; **2.** Stammbaum *m*; **3.** Geschlecht *n*, Fa'milie *f*.

lin·e·al [ˈlɪnɪəl] *adj.* □ geradlinig, in di'rekter Linie, di'rekt (*Abstammung, Nachkomme*).

lin·e·a·ment [ˈlɪnɪəmənt] *s.* (Gesichts-, *fig.* Cha'rakter)Zug *m*.

lin·e·ar [ˈlɪnɪə] *adj.* □ **1.** Linien..., geradlinig, *bsd.* ⚛, ☉, *phys.* line'ar (*Gleichung, Elektrode, Perspektive etc.*), Li-near...; **2.** Längen...(-ausdehnung, -maß *etc.*); **3.** Linien..., Strich..., strichförmig.

line| block *s.* → *line etching*; *~ break s. Computer:* Zeilenumbruch *m*; *~ draw·ing s.* Strichzeichnung *f*; *~ etch·ing s. Kunst:* Strichätzung *f*; *~ feed s. Computer:* Zeilenvorschub *m*; '*~·man* [-mən] *s.* [*irr.*] *Am.* **1.** 🚂 Streckenarbeiter *m*; **2.** → *linesman* 1.

lin·en [ˈlɪnɪn] **I** *s.* **1.** Leinen *n*, Leinwand *f*, Linnen *n*; **2.** (Bett-, 'Unter- *etc.*)Wäsche *f*: *wash one's dirty ~ in public fig.* s-e schmutzige Wäsche vor allen Leuten waschen; **II** *adj.* **3.** leinen, Leinen...: *~ closet* (*od.* *cupboard*) Wäscheschrank *m*.

lin·er¹ [ˈlaɪnə] *s.* **1.** ☉ Futter *n*, Buchse *f*; **2.** Einsatz(stück *n*) *m*.

lin·er² [ˈlaɪnə] *s.* **1.** ⚓ Linienschiff *n*; **2.** → *air liner*.

lines·man [ˈlaɪnzmən] *s.* [*irr.*] **1.** ✂ (Fernmelde)Techniker *m*, *engS.* Störungssucher *m*; **2.** 🚂 Streckenwärter *m*; **3.** *sport* Linienrichter *m*.

'**line-up** *s.* **1.** *sport* (Mannschafts)Aufstellung *f*, Aufgebot *n*; **2.** Gruppierung *f*; **3.** *Am.* ‚Schlange' *f*.

lin·ger [ˈlɪŋɡə] *v/i.* **1.** (*a. fig.*) (noch) verweilen, (zu'rück)bleiben (*beide a. Gefühl, Geschmack, Erinnerung etc.*), sich aufhalten; *fig. a.* nachklingen (*Töne, Gefühl etc.*): *~ on fig.* (noch) fortleben *od.* -bestehen (*Brauch etc.*); *~ on a subject* bei e-m Thema verweilen; **2.** a) zögern, b) trödeln; **3.** da'hinsiechen (*Kranker*); **4.** sich hinziehen *od.* -schleppen.

lin·ge·rie [ˈlæːnʒɔriː] (*Fr.*) *s.* ('Damen-) ‚Unterwäsche *f*.

lin·ger·ing [ˈlɪŋɡərɪŋ] *adj.* □ **1.** a) verweilend, b) langsam, zögernd; **2.** (zu-'rück)bleibend, nachklingend (*Ton, Gefühl etc.*); **3.** schleppend; **4.** schleichend (*Krankheit*); **5.** lang: a) sehnsüchtig, b) innig, c) prüfend (*Blick*): *a ~ look*.

lin·go [ˈlɪŋɡəʊ] *pl.* **-goes** [-gəʊz] *s.* Kauderwelsch *n*, *engS. a.* ('Fach)Jar,gon *m*.

lin·gua fran·ca [ˌlɪŋɡwəˈfræŋkə] *s.* Verkehrssprache *f*.

lin·gual [ˈlɪŋɡwəl] **I** *adj.* Zungen...; **II** *s.* Zungenlaut *m*.

lin·guist [ˈlɪŋɡwɪst] *s.* **1.** Sprachforscher (-in), Lingu'ist(in); **2.** Fremdsprachler (-in), Sprachkundige(r *m*) *f*: *he is a good ~* er ist sehr sprachbegabt; **lin·guis·tic** [lɪŋˈɡwɪstɪk] *adj.* (□ *~ally*) **1.** sprachwissenschaftlich, lingu'istisch; **2.** Sprach(en)...; **lin·guis·tics** [lɪŋˈɡwɪstɪks] *s. pl.* (*mst sg. konstr.*) Sprachwissenschaft *f*, Lingu'istik *f*.

lin·i·ment [ˈlɪnɪmənt] *s.* 💊 Einreibemittel *n*.

lin·ing [ˈlaɪnɪŋ] *s.* **1.** Futter(stoff *m*) *n*, (Aus)Fütterung *f* (*von Kleidern etc.*); **2.**

☉ Futter *n*, Ver-, Auskleidung *f*; Ausmauerung *f*; (*Brems- etc.*)Belag *m*; → *silver lining*.

link [lɪŋk] **I** *s.* **1.** (Ketten)Glied *n*; **2.** *fig.* a) Glied *n* (*in e-r Kette von Ereignissen etc.*), b) Bindeglied *n*; → *missing* 1, c) *Computer:* Link *m*; **3.** *freundschaftliche etc.* Bande *pl.*; **4.** Verbindung *f*, -knüpfung *f*, Zs.-hang *m* (**between** zwischen); **5.** Man'schettenknopf *m*; **6.** ☉ Glied *n* (*a.* ⚡), Verbindungsstück *n*, Gelenk *n*; **7.** *tel.* a) Streckenabschnitt *m*, b) Über'tragungsweg *m*; **8.** *TV* a) Verbindungsstrecke *f*, b) *~up* 3; **9.** *surv.* Messkettenglied *n*; **10.** → *links*; **II** *v/t.* **11.** *a. ~ up od.* *together* (**with**) a) verbinden, -knüpfen (mit): *~ arms* (**with**) sich einhaken (bei j-m), b) mitein'ander in Verbindung *od.* Zs.-hang bringen, c) anein'ander koppeln: *be ~ed* (**with**) zs.-hängen *od.* in Zs.-hang stehen (mit); *~ed* 🧬 gekoppelt (*a. biol. Gene*); **III** *v/i.* **12.** (**with**) a) sich verbinden (lassen) (mit), b) verknüpft sein (mit).

link·age [ˈlɪŋkɪdʒ] *s.* **1.** Verkettung *f*, *Computer: a.* Pro'grammverbindung *f*; **2.** ☉ Gestänge *n*, Gelenkviereck *n*; **3.** 🔗, *biol.* Koppelung *f*, (*a. phys. Atometc.*)Bindung *f*.

links [lɪŋks] *s. pl.* **1.** *bsd. Scot.* Dünen *pl.*; **2.** (*a. sg. konstr.*) Golfplatz *m*.

'**link-up** *s.* **1.** → *link* 4; **2.** (Anein'ander-) Koppeln *n*; **3.** *Radio, TV:* Zs.-schaltung *f*.

linn [lɪn] *s. bsd. Scot.* **1.** Teich *m*; **2.** Wasserfall *m*.

lin·net [ˈlɪnɪt] *s. orn.* Hänfling *m*.

li·no [ˈlaɪnəʊ] *abbr. für linoleum;* **li·no-cut** [ˈlaɪnəʊkʌt] *s.* Lin'olschnitt *m*.

li·no·le·um [lɪˈnəʊljəm] *s.* Lin'oleum *n*.

li·no·type [ˈlaɪnəʊtaɪp] *s. typ.* **1.** *a.* ≈ Linotype *f* (*Markenname für e-e Zeilensetz- u. -gießmaschine*); **2.** ('Setzma,schinen)Zeile *f*.

lin·seed [ˈlɪnsiːd] *s.* 🌱 Leinsamen *m*; *~ cake s.* Leinkuchen *m*; *~ oil s.* Leinöl *n*.

lint [lɪnt] **I** *s.* **1.** 💊 Schar'pie *f*, Zupflinnen *n*; **2.** *Am.* Fussel *f*; **II** *v/i.* **3.** *Am.* Fusseln bilden, fusseln.

lin·tel [ˈlɪntl] *s.* 🏛 (Tür-, Fenster)Sturz *m*.

li·on [ˈlaɪən] *s.* **1.** *zo.* Löwe *m* (*a. fig. Held; a. ast.* ≈): *the ~'s share fig.* Löwenanteil; *go into the ~'s den fig.* sich in die Höhle des Löwen wagen; **2.** ‚Größe' *f*, Berühmtheit *f* (*Person*); **3.** *pl.* Sehenswürdigkeiten *pl.* (*e-s Ortes*); '**li·on·ess** [-nes] *s.* Löwin *f*; '**li·on-,heart·ed** *adj.* furchtlos, mutig; **li·on·ize** [ˈlaɪənaɪz] *v/t.* j-n feiern, zum Helden des Tages machen.

lip [lɪp] *s.* **1.** Lippe *f*: *hang on s.o.'s ~s* an j-s Lippen hängen; *keep a stiff upper ~* Haltung bewahren; *lick* (*od.* *smack*) *one's ~s* die Lippen lecken; → *bite* 7; **2.** F Unverschämtheit *f*: *none of your ~!* keine Frechheiten!; **3.** Rand *m* (*Wunde, Schale, Krater etc.*); **4.** Tülle *f*, Schnauze *f* (*Krug etc.*).

lip·o·suc·tion [ˈlɪpəʊˌsʌkʃn] *s.* 💊 Fettabsaugung *f*.

'**lip|-read** *v/t. u. v/i.* [*irr.* → *read*] von den Lippen ablesen; '*~-,read·ing s.* Lippenlesen *n*; *~ salve* [sæ(l)v] *s.* Lippenbalsam *m*, -pflegestift *m*; *~ ser·vice s.* Lippendienst *m*: *pay ~ to* ein Lippenbekenntnis ablegen zu e-r Idee etc.; '*~·stick s.* Lippenstift *m*.

li·quate [ˈlaɪkweɪt] *v/t. metall.* (aus)seigern.

liq·ue·fa·cient [ˌlɪkwɪˈfeɪʃnt] **I** *s.* Verflüssigungsmittel *n*; **II** *adj.* verflüssi-

L

gend; **ˌliq·ue'fac·tion** [-'fækʃn] s. Verflüssigung f; **liq·ue·fi·a·ble** ['lıkwıfaıəbl] adj. schmelzbar; **liq·ue·fy** ['lıkwıfaı] v/t. u. v/i. (sich) verflüssigen; schmelzen; **li·ques·cent** [lı'kwesnt] adj. sich (leicht) verflüssigend, schmelzend.
li·queur [lı'kjʊə] s. Li'kör m.
liq·uid ['lıkwıd] I adj. □ **1.** flüssig; Flüssigkeits...: ~ **measure** Flüssigkeitsmaß n; ~ **crystal** Flüssigkristall m; ~ **crystal display** Flüssigkristallanzeige f; **2.** a) klar, hell u. glänzend, b) feucht (schimmernd): ~ **eyes**; ~ **sky**; **3.** perlend, wohltönend; **4.** ling. li'quid, fließend: ~ **sound** → 7; **5.** ⚓ li'quid, flüssig: ~ **assets**; II s. **6.** Flüssigkeit f; **7.** Phonetik: Liquida f, Fließlaut m.
liq·ui·date ['lıkwıdeıt] v/t. **1.** a) Schulden etc. tilgen, b) Schuldbetrag feststellen; **2.** Konten abrechnen, saldieren; **3.** ✝ Unternehmen liquidieren; **4.** ✝ Wertpapier flüssig machen, realisieren; **5.** j-n liquidieren (umbringen); **liq·ui·da·tion** [ˌlıkwı'deıʃn] s. **1.** ✝ a) Liquidati'on f, Abwicklung f (Unternehmen): **go into** ~ in Liquidation treten, b) Tilgung f (von Schulden), c) Abrechnung f, d) Realisierung f; **2.** fig. Liquidierung f, Beseitigung f; **'liq·ui·da·tor** [-tə] s. ✝ Liqui'dator m, Abwickler m.
li·quid·i·ty [lı'kwıdətı] s. **1.** flüssiger Zustand; **2.** ✝ Liquidi'tät f, (Geld)Flüssigkeit f.
liq·uor ['lıkə] I s. alko'holisches Getränk, coll. Spiritu'osen pl., Alkohol m (bsd. Branntwein u. Whisky): **in** ~, **the worse for** ~ betrunken; **2.** Flüssigkeit f; pharm. Arz'neilösung f; **3.** ⊛ a) Lauge f, b) Flotte f (Färbebad); II v/i. **4.** mst ~ **up** sl. 'einen heben'; III v/t. **5.** **get** ~**ed up** sich 'voll laufen' lassen; ~ **cab·i·net** s. Hausbar f.
liq·uo·rice ['lıkərıs] s. La'kritze f.
lisp [lısp] I v/i. **1.** (a. v/t. et.) lispeln, mit der Zunge anstoßen; **2.** stammeln; II s. **3.** Lispeln n, Anstoßen n (mit der Zunge).
lis·some, a. **lis·som** ['lısəm] adj. **1.** geschmeidig; **2.** wendig, a'gil.
list¹ [lıst] I s. Liste f, Verzeichnis n: **on the** ~ auf der Liste; ~ **price** ✝ Listenpreis m; II v/t. a) verzeichnen, aufführen, erfassen, katalogisieren; in e-e Liste eintragen, b) aufzählen: ~**ed** ✝ amtlich notiert, börsenfähig (Wertpapier); ~**ed option** börsengehandelte Option f.
list² [lıst] s. **1.** Saum m, Rand m; **2.** Weberei: Salband n, Webekante f; **3.** (Sal)Leiste f; **4.** pl. hist. a) Schranken pl. (e-s Turnierplatzes), b) Kampfplatz m (a. fig.): **enter the** ~**s** fig. in die Schranken treten, zum Kampf antreten.
list³ [lıst] ⚓ I s. Schlagseite f; II v/i. Schlagseite haben.
lis·ten ['lısn] v/i. **1.** horchen, hören, lauschen (**to** auf acc.): ~ **to** a) j-m zuhören, j-n anhören, b) auf j-n od. j-s Rat hören, j-m Gehör schenken, c) e-m Rat etc. folgen: ~**!** hör mal (zu)!; ~ **for** auf et. od. j-n horchen (warten); → **reason** 1; **2.** ~ **in** a) Radio hören, b) (am Telefon etc.) mithören od. mit anhören (**on s.th.** et.): ~ **in to** et. im Radio hören; **'lis·ten·er** [-nə] s. **1.** Horcher(in), Lauscher(in); **2.** Zuhörer(in); **3.** Radio: Hörer(in).
lis·ten·ing post ['lısnıŋ] s. ✕ **1.** Horchposten m (a. fig.); **2.** Abhörstelle f.
list·ing ['lıstıŋ] s. **1.** Auflistung f: a) Liste f, b) Eintrag m in e-r Liste; **2.** a. ~**s** Verzeichnis n.
list·less ['lıstlıs] adj. □ lustlos, teil-

nahmslos, matt, a'pathisch.
lists [lısts] → **list²** 4.
lit [lıt] I pret. u. p.p. von **light¹** u. **light³**; II adj. mst ~ **up** sl. ‚blau' (betrunken).
lit·a·ny ['lıtənı] s. eccl. u. fig. Lita'nei f.
li·tchi ['laı'tʃi; 'lıtʃı] s. Obst: 'Litschi f.
li·ter ['liːtə] Am. → **litre**.
lit·er·a·cy ['lıtərəsı] s. **1.** Fähigkeit f zu lesen u. zu schreiben; **2.** (lite'rarische) Bildung, Belesenheit f; **'lit·er·al** [-rəl] I adj. □ **1.** wörtlich, wortgetreu: ~ **translation**; **2.** wörtlich, buchstäblich, eigentlich: ~ **sense**; **3.** nüchtern, wahrheitsgemäu: ~ **account**; **the** ~ **truth** die reine Wahrheit; **4.** fig. buchstäblich: ~ **annihilation**; **a** ~ **disaster** e-e wahre od. echte Katastrophe; **5.** pe'dantisch, pro'saisch (Person); **6.** Buchstaben..., Schreib...: ~ **error** → 7; II s. **7.** Schreibod. Druckfehler m; **'lit·er·al·ism** [-əlızəm], **'lit·er·al·ness** [-rəlnıs] s. **1.** Festhalten n am Buchstaben, bsd. strenge od. allzu wörtliche Über'setzung etc. Auslegung, Buchstabenglaube m; **2.** Kunst: Rea'lismus m.
lit·er·ar·y ['lıtərərı] adj. □ **1.** lite'rarisch, Literatur...: ~ **historian** Literaturhistoriker(in); ~ **history** Literaturgeschichte f; ~ **language** Schriftsprache f; **2.** schriftstellerisch: **a** ~ **man** ein Literat; ~ **property** geistiges Eigentum; **3.** lite'rarisch gebildet; **4.** gewählt: **a** ~ **expression**; **lit·er·ate** ['lıtərət] I adj. **1.** des Lesens u. Schreibens kundig; **2.** (lite'rarisch) gebildet; **3.** lite'rarisch; II s. **4.** j-d, der Lesen u. Schreiben kann; **5.** Gebildete(r m) f; **lit·e·ra·ti** [ˌlıtə'rɑːtiː] s. pl. **1.** Lite'raten pl.; **2.** die Gelehrten pl.; **lit·e·ra·tim** [ˌlıtə'rɑːtım] (Lat.) adv. buchstäblich, (wort)wörtlich; **lit·er·a·ture** ['lıtərətʃə] s. **1.** Litera'tur f; **2.** Schriftstelle'rei f; **3.** Druckschriften pl., bsd. Pro'spekte pl., 'Unterlagen pl.
lithe [laıð] adj. □ geschmeidig; **'litheness** [-nıs] s. Geschmeidigkeit f.
lith·o·chro·mat·ic [ˌlıθəʊkrəʊ'mætık] adj. Farben-, Buntdruck...
lith·o·graph ['lıθəʊgrɑːf] I s. Lithogra'phie f, Steindruck m (Erzeugnis); II v/t. u. v/i. lithographieren; **li·thog·ra·pher** [lı'θɒgrəfə] s. Litho'graph m; **lith·o·graph·ic** [ˌlıθəʊ'græfık] adj. (□ ~**ally**) litho'graphisch, Steindruck...; **li·thog·ra·phy** [lı'θɒgrəfı] s. Lithogra'phie f, Steindruck m.
Lith·u·a·ni·an [ˌlıθjuː'eınjən] I s. **1.** Litauer(in); **2.** ling. Litauisch n; II adj. **3.** litauisch.
lit·i·gant ['lıtıgənt] ⚖ I s. Pro'zessführende(r m) f, (streitende) Par'tei; II adj. streitend, pro'zessführend; **lit·i·gate** ['lıtıgeıt] v/i. (u. v/t.) prozessieren (um), streiten (um); **lit·i·ga·tion** [ˌlıtı'geıʃn] s. Rechtsstreit m, Pro'zess m; **li·ti·gious** [lı'tıdʒəs] adj. □ **1.** ⚖ a) Prozess..., b) strittig, streitig; **2.** pro'zess-, streitsüchtig.
lit·mus ['lıtməs] s. 🜍 Lackmus n; ~ **pa·per** s. Lackmuspa,pier n.
li·tre ['liːtə] s. Brit. Liter m, n.
lit·ter ['lıtə] I s. **1.** Sänfte f; **2.** Trage f; **3.** Streu f; **4.** her'umliegende Sachen pl., bsd. her'umliegendes) Pa'pier u. Abfälle pl.; **5.** Wust m, Unordnung f; **6.** zo. Wurf m Ferkel etc.; II v/t. **7.** mst ~ **down** a) Streu legen für Tiere, b) Stall, Boden einstreuen, c) Pflanzen abdecken; **8.** a) verunreinigen, b) unordentlich verstreuen, her'umliegen lassen, c) Zimmer in Unordnung bringen, d) oft ~ **up** (unordentlich) her'umliegen in (dat.) od. auf (dat.): **be** ~**ed with** über-

sät sein mit (a. fig.); **9.** zo. Junge werfen; III v/i. **10.** (Junge) werfen.
lit·tle ['lıtl] I adj. **1.** klein: **a** ~ **house** ein kleines Haus, ein Häuschen; **a** ~ **one** ein Kleines (Kind); **our** ~ **ones** unsere Kleinen; **the** ~ **people** die Elfen; ~ **things** Kleinigkeiten pl.; **2.** kurz (Strecke od. Zeit); **3.** wenig: ~ **hope**; **a** ~ **honey** ein wenig od. ein bisschen od. etwas Honig; **4.** klein, gering(fügig), unbedeutend: **of** ~ **interest** von geringem Interesse; **5.** klein(lich), beschränkt, engstirnig: ~ **minds** Kleingeister pl.; **6.** gemein, erbärmlich; **7.** iro. klein: **her poor** ~ **efforts**; **his** ~ **ways** s-e kleinen Eigenarten od. Schliche; II adv. **8.** wenig, kaum, nicht sehr: **he** ~ **knows** er ahnt ja nicht (**that** dass); **we see** ~ **of her** wir sehen sie nur sehr selten; **make** ~ **of** et. bagatellisieren; **think** ~ **of** wenig halten von; III s. **9.** Kleinigkeit f, das wenige, ein bisschen: **a** ~ ein wenig, ein bisschen; **not a** ~ nicht wenig; **after a** ~ nach e-m Weilchen; **for a** ~ für ein Weilchen; **a** ~ **rash** ein bisschen voreilig; ~ **by** ~ nach und nach; ~ **or nothing** so gut wie nichts; **what** ~ **I have seen** das wenige, das ich gesehen habe; **every** ~ **helps** auch der kleinste Beitrag hilft; **'lit·tle·ness** [-nıs] s. **1.** Kleinheit f; **2.** Geringfügigkeit f, Bedeutungslosigkeit f; **3.** Kleinlichkeit f; **4.** Beschränktheit f.
lit·to·ral ['lıtərəl] I adj. a) Küsten..., b) Ufer...; II s. Küstenland n, -strich m.
li·tur·gic, li·tur·gi·cal [lı'tɜːdʒık(l)] adj. □ li'turgisch; **lit·ur·gy** ['lıtədʒı] s. eccl. Litur'gie f.
liv·a·ble ['lıvəbl] adj. **1.** a. ~**-in** wohnlich; **2.** mst ~**-with** 'umgänglich (Person); **3.** erträglich.
live¹ [lıv] v/i. **1.** allg. leben: ~ **to a great age** ein hohes Alter erreichen; ~ **to be eighty** achtzig Jahre alt werden; ~ **to see** et. erreichen; ~ **off** leben von, sich ernähren von; b.s. auf j-s Kosten leben; ~ **on** a) weiter-, fortleben, b) a. ~ **by** leben od. sich ernähren von; ~ **through s.th.** et. mit- od. durchmachen, et. miterleben; ~ **with** a) a. iro. mit der Atombombe etc. leben, b) bsd. sport F mit e-m Gegner etc. mithalten; **we** ~ **and learn!** man lernt nie aus!; ~ **and let** ~ leben und leben lassen; **he will** ~ **to regret it!** das wird er noch bereuen!; **2.** (über)'leben, am Leben bleiben: **the patient will** ~**!**; **3.** leben, wohnen: ~ **in a town**; **4.** leben, ein ehrliches etc. Leben führen: ~ **well** gut leben; ~ **to o.s.** (ganz) für sich leben; **5.** leben, das Leben genießen: **she wanted to** ~ sie wollte (et. er)leben; (**then**) **you haven't** ~**d!** humor. du weißt ja gar nicht, was du versäumt hast!; II v/t. **6.** ein anständiges etc. Leben führen od. leben: ~ **one's own life** sein eigenes Leben leben; **7.** (vor)leben, im Leben verwirklichen: **he** ~**d a lie** sein Leben war e-e einzige Lüge;
Zssgn mit adv.:
live down v/t. et. (durch tadellosen Lebenswandel) vergessen machen, sich reinwaschen od. rehabilitieren von: **I will never live it down** man wird das mir nie vergessen; ~ **in** v/i. im Haus od. Heim etc. wohnen, nicht außerhalb wohnen; ~ **out** v/i. außerhalb wohnen; ~ **to·geth·er** v/i. zu'sammen leben od. wohnen; ~ **up** I v/i.: ~ **to** den Anforderungen, Erwartungen etc. entsprechen, a. s-m Ruf gerecht werden; sein Versprechen halten; II v/t.: **live it up** ‚auf den Putz hauen', ‚toll leben'.

live² [laɪv] **I** *adj.* (*nur attr.*) **1.** le'bendig: a) lebend: **~ animals**, b) *fig.* lebhaft (*a. Debatte etc.*); rührig, tätig, e'nergisch (*Person*); **2.** aktu'ell: **a ~ question**; **3.** glühend (*Kohle etc.*) (*a. fig.*); ✕ scharf (*Munition*); ungebraucht (*Streichholz*); ⚡ Strom führend, geladen: **~ wire** *fig.* ‚Energiebündel' *n*; **~ load** ⊙ Nutzlast *f*; **~ steam** ⊙ Frischdampf *m*; **4.** *Radio, TV:* di'rekt, live, Direkt...; Live-...: **~ broadcast** Live-Sendung *f*, Direktübertragung *f*; **5.** ⊙ a) Trieb..., b) angetrieben; **II** *adv.* **6.** *Radio, TV:* di'rekt, live: **the game will be broadcast ~.**

-lived [lɪvd] *in Zssgn* ...lebig.

live·li·hood ['laɪvlihʊd] *s.* 'Lebens,unterhalt *m*, Auskommen *n*: **earn** (*od.* **make**) **a** (*od.* **one's**) **~** sein Brot *od.* s-n Lebensunterhalt verdienen.

live·li·ness ['laɪvlɪnɪs] *s.* **1.** Lebhaftigkeit *f*; **2.** Le'bendigkeit *f*.

live·long ['lɪvlɒŋ] *adj. poet.*: **all the ~ day** den lieben langen Tag.

live·ly ['laɪvlɪ] *adj.* □ **1.** *allg.* lebhaft, le'bendig (*Person, Geist, Gespräch, Rhythmus, Gefühl, Erinnerung, Farbe, Beschreibung etc.*): **~ hope** starke Hoffnung; **2.** kräftig, vi'tal; **3.** lebhaft, aufregend (*Zeit*): **make it** (*od.* **things**) **~ for** *j-m* (tüchtig) einheizen; **we had a ~ time** es war ‚schwer was los'; **4.** flott (*Tempo*).

liv·en ['laɪvn] *mst* **~ up** **I** *v/t.* beleben, Leben *od.* Schwung bringen in (*acc.*); **II** *v/i.* sich beleben, in Schwung kommen.

liv·er¹ ['lɪvə] *s. anat.* Leber *f*.

liv·er² ['lɪvə] *s.*: **be a fast ~** ein flottes Leben führen; **be a good ~** ‚gut leben'.

liv·er·ied ['lɪvərɪd] *adj.* livriert.

liv·er·ish ['lɪvərɪʃ] *adj.* F **1. be ~** es an der Leber haben; **2.** reizbar, mürrisch.

Liv·er·pud·li·an [,lɪvə'pʌdlɪən] **I** *adj.* aus *od.* von Liverpool; **II** *s.* Liverpooler(in).

'**liv·er·wort** *s.* ♣ Leberblümchen *n*.

liv·er·y ['lɪvərɪ] *s.* **1.** Li'vree *f*; **2.** (*bsd. Amts- od.* Gilden)Tracht *f*; *fig.* (*a. zo. Winter- etc.*)Kleid *n*; **3. → livery company**; **4.** Pflege *f* u. 'Unterbringung *f* (*von Pferden*) gegen Bezahlung: **at ~** in Futter stehen etc.; **5.** *Am.* **→ livery stable**; **6.** a) 'Übergabe *f*, Über'tragung *f*, b) *Brit.* 'Übergabe *f* von vom Vormundschaftsgericht freigegebenem Eigentum; **~ com·pa·ny** *s.* (Handels-) Zunft *f* der *City of London*; '**~·man** [-mən] *s.* [*irr.*] Zunftmitglied *n*; **~ serv·ant** *s.* livrierter Diener; **~ sta·ble** *s.* Mietstall *m*.

lives [laɪvz] *pl. von* **life**.

'**live·stock** ['laɪv-] *s.* Vieh(bestand *m*) *n*, lebendes Inven'tar.

liv·id ['lɪvɪd] *adj.* □ **1.** bläulich; bleifarben, graublau; **2.** fahl, aschgrau, blass (**with** *vor dat.*); **3.** *Brit.* F ‚fuchsteufelswild'; **li·vid·i·ty** [lɪ'vɪdətɪ], '**liv·id·ness** [-nɪs] *s.* Fahlheit *f*, Blässe *f*.

liv·ing ['lɪvɪŋ] **I** *adj.* □ **1.** lebend (*a. Sprachen*), le'bendig (*a. fig. Glaube, Gott etc.*): **no man ~** kein Sterblicher; **not a ~ soul** keine Menschenseele; **while ~** zu Lebzeiten; **the greatest of ~ statesmen** der größte lebende Staatsmann; **~ death** trostloses Dasein; **within ~ memory** seit Menschengedenken; **2.** glühend (*Kohle*); **3.** gewachsen (*Fels*); **4.** Lebens...: **~ conditions**; **II** *s.* **5. the ~** die Lebenden; **6.** (das) Leben; **7.** Leben *n*, Lebensweise *f*, -führung *f*: **good ~** üppiges Leben; **8.** 'Lebens,unterhalt *m*: **make a ~** s-n Lebensunter-

---

halt verdienen (**as** als, **out of** durch); **9.** Leben *n*, Wohnen *n*; **10.** *eccl. Brit.* Pfründe *f*; **~ room** [rʊm] *s.* Wohnzimmer *n*; **~ space** *s.* **1.** Wohnraum *m*, -fläche *f*; **2.** *pol.* Lebensraum *m*; **~ wage** *s.* ausreichender Lohn.

lix·iv·i·ate [lɪk'sɪvɪeɪt] *v/t.* auslaugen.

liz·ard ['lɪzəd] *s.* **1.** *zo.* a) Eidechse *f*, b) Echse *f*; **2.** Eidechsenleder *n*.

'**ll** [l; əl] F *für* **will** 1, 2, 4 *od.* **shall**.

lla·ma ['lɑ:mə] *s. zo.* Lama(wolle *f*) *n*.

lo [ləʊ] *int. obs.* siehe!, seht!: **~ and behold!** *oft humor.* sieh(e) da!

loach [ləʊtʃ] *s. ichth.* Schmerle *f*.

load [ləʊd] **I** *s.* **1.** Last *f* (*a. phys.*); **2.** *fig.* Last *f*, Bürde *f*: **take a ~ off s.o.'s mind** j-m e-e Last von der Seele nehmen; **that takes a ~ off my mind!** da fällt mir ein Stein vom Herzen!; **3.** Ladung *f* (*a. e-r Schusswaffe; a. Am. sl.* Menge Alkohol), Fracht *f*, Fuhre *f*: **a bus~ of tourists** ein Bus voll(er) Touristen; **have a ~ on** *Am. sl.* ‚schwer geladen' haben; **get a ~ of this!** F hör mal gut zu!; **~s of** F e-e Unmasse *f*, massenhaft *od.* jede Menge *Geld, Fehler etc.*; **4.** *fig.* Belastung *f*: (**work**) **~** (Arbeits)Pensum *n*; **5.** ⊙, ⚡ a) Last *f*, (Arbeits)Belastung *f*, b) Leistung *f*: **~ capacity** a) Ladefähigkeit *f*, b) Tragfähigkeit *f*, c) ⚡ Belastbarkeit *f*; **II** *v/t.* **6.** beladen; **7.** *Güter, Schusswaffe etc.* laden, aufladen, *Datei, Software* laden: **~ the camera** *phot.* e-n Film einlegen; **8.** *fig.* j-n über'häufen (**with** mit *Arbeit, Geschenken, Vorwürfen etc.*): **he's ~ed** *sl.* a) er hat Geld wie Heu, b) er hat ‚schwer geladen' *od.* ist ‚blau'; **9.** *den Magen* über'laden; **10.** beschweren: **~ dice** Würfel präparieren: **~ the dice** *fig.* die Karten zinken; **the dice are ~ed against him** *fig.* er hat kaum e-e Chance; **~ed question** Fangfrage *f*; **11.** *Wein* verfälschen; **III** *v/i.* **12.** *a.* **~ up** (auf-, ein)laden.

load·er ['ləʊdə] *s.* **1.** (Ver)Lader *m*; **2.** Verladevorrichtung *f*; **3.** *hunt.* Lader *m*; **4.** ✕ Ladeschütze *m*.

load·ing ['ləʊdɪŋ] *s.* **1.** (Be-, Auf)Laden *n*; **2.** a) Laden *n* (*e-r Schusswaffe*), b) Einlegen *n* e-s Films (*in die Kamera*); **3.** Ladung *f*, Fracht *f*; **4.** ⊙, ⚡, ✈ Belastung *f*; **5.** *Versicherung:* Verwaltungskostenanteil *m* (*der Prämie*); **~ bridge** *s.* Verlade-, ✈ Fluggastbrücke *f*; **~ coil** *s.* ⚡ Belastungsspule *f*.

load| line *s.* ⚓ Lade(wasser)linie *f*; '**~·star → lodestar**; '**~·stone → lodestone**.

loaf¹ [ləʊf] *pl.* **loaves** [ləʊvz] *s.* **1.** Laib *m* (*Brot*), *weitS.* Brot *n*: **half a ~ is better than no bread** (etwas ist) besser als gar nichts; **2.** Zuckerhut *m*: **~ sugar** Hutzucker *m*; **3.** *a.* **meat ~** Hackbraten *m*; **4.** *Brit. sl.* ‚Birne' *f*: **use your ~** denk mal ein bisschen (nach)!

loaf² [ləʊf] **I** *v/i. a.* **~ about** (*od.* **around**) her'umlungern, bummeln, faulenzen; **II** *v/t. a.* **~ away** *Zeit* verbummeln; '**loaf·er** [-fə] *s.* **1.** Faulenzer *m*, Nichtstuer *m*; Her'umtreiber(in); **2.** *Am.* Mokas'sin *m* (*Schuh*).

loam [ləʊm] *s.* Lehm(boden *m*) *m*; '**loam·y** [-mɪ] *adj.* lehmig, Lehm...

loan [ləʊn] **I** *s.* **1.** (Ver)Leihen *n*, Ausleihung *f*: **as a ~**, **on ~** leihweise; **it's on ~**, **it's a ~** ist geliehen; **ask for the ~ of s.th.** et. leihweise erbitten; **put out to ~** verleihen; **2.** Anleihe *f* (*a. fig.*): **take up a ~ on** e-e Anleihe aufnehmen auf *e-e Sache*; **government ~** Staatsanleihe *f*; **3.** Darlehen *n*, Kre'dit *m*: **~ on securities** Lombarddarlehen;

---

bankrate for ~s Lombardsatz *m*; **4.** Leihgabe *f* (*für e-e Ausstellung*); **II** *v/t. u. v/i.* **5.** (ver-, aus)leihen (**to** *dat.*); **~ bank** *s.* Darlehensbank *f*; **~ of·fice** *s.* Darlehenskasse *f*; **~ shark** *s.* F ‚Kre'dithai' *m*; **~ trans·la·tion** *s. ling.* 'Lehnübersetzung *f*; '**~·word** *s. ling.* Lehnwort *n*.

loath [ləʊθ] *adj.* (*nur pred.*) abgeneigt, nicht willens: **be ~ to do s.th.** et. nur sehr ungern tun; **nothing ~** durchaus nicht abgeneigt.

loathe [ləʊð] *v/t. et. od. j-n* verabscheuen, hassen, nicht ausstehen können; '**loath·ing** [-ðɪŋ] *s.* Abscheu *m*, Ekel *m*; '**loath·ing·ly** [-ðɪŋlɪ] *adv.* mit Abscheu *od.* Ekel; '**loath·some** [-səm] *adj.* □ widerlich, ab'scheulich, verhasst; ekelhaft, eklig.

loaves [ləʊvz] *pl. von* **loaf¹**.

lob [lɒb] **I** *s.* **1.** *Tennis:* Lob *m*; **II** *v/t.* **2.** den Ball lobben; **3.** (*engS. et.* von unten her) werfen.

lob·by ['lɒbɪ] **I** *s.* **1.** a) Vor-, Eingangshalle *f*, Vesti'bül *n*, *bsd. thea., Hotel:* Foy'er *n*, b) Wandelgang *m*, -halle *f*, Korridor *m*, *parl. a.* Lobby *f*; **2.** *pol.* Lobby *f*, (Vertreter *pl.* e-r) Inter'essengruppe *f*; **II** *v/t. u. v/i.* **3.** (auf Abgeordnete) Einfluss nehmen: **~ for** (mit Hilfe e-r Lobby) für die Annahme *e-s Antrags etc.* arbeiten; **~** (**through**) *Gesetzantrag* mit Hilfe e-r Lobby durchbringen; '**lob·by·ist** [-ɪɪst] *s. pol.* Lobby'ist(in).

lobe [ləʊb] *s.* ♣, *anat.* Lappen *m*: **~ of the ear** Ohrläppchen *n*; **lobed** [-bd] *adj.* gelappt, lappig.

lob·ster ['lɒbstə] *s. zo.* **1.** Hummer *m*: **as red as a ~** *fig.* krebsrot; **2.** (**spiny**) **~** Languste *f*.

lob·ule ['lɒbju:l] *s.* ♣, *anat.* Läppchen *n*.

lo·cal ['ləʊkl] **I** *adj.* □ **1.** lo'kal, örtlich, Lokal..., Orts...: **~ authorities** *pl.*, **~ government** Gemeinde-, Stadt-, Kommunalverwaltung *f*; **~ call** *teleph.* Ortsgespräch *n*; **~ news** Lokalnachrichten *pl.*; **~ politics** Lokalpolitik *f*; **~ time** Ortszeit *f*; **~ traffic** Lokal-, Orts-, Nahverkehr *m*; **~ train** → **5**; **2.** Orts..., ortsansässig: a) hiesig, b) dortig: **the ~ doctor**; **3.** lo'kal, örtlich, Lokal...: **~ an(a)esthesia** → **10**; **~ colo(u)r** *fig.* Lokalkolorit *n*; **a ~ custom** ein ortsüblicher Brauch; **~ expression** ortsgebundener Ausdruck; **~ radio** Lo'kalradio *n*; **~ TV** Lo'kalfernsehen *n*; **4.** *Brit.* (*als Postvermerk*) Ortsdienst!; **II** *s.* **5.** Vororts-, Nahverkehrszug *m*; **6.** *Am.* Zeitung: Lo'kalnachricht *f*; **7.** *Am.* Ortsgruppe *f* (*e-r Gewerkschaft etc.*); **8.** *pl.* Ortsansässige *pl.*; **9.** *Brit.* F Ortsgasthaus *n*, *a.* Stammkneipe *f*; **10.** ♣ Lo'kalanästhe,sie *f*, örtliche Betäubung.

lo·cale [ləʊ'kɑ:l] *s.* Schauplatz *m*, Ort *m* (*e-s Ereignisses etc.*).

lo·cal·ism ['ləʊkəlɪzəm] *s.* Provinzia'lismus *m*: a) *ling.* örtliche (Sprach)Eigentümlichkeit, b) provinzi'elle Borniertheit, c) Lo'kalpatrio,tismus *m*.

lo·cal·i·ty [ləʊ'kælətɪ] *s.* **1.** a) Ort *m*: **sense of ~** Ortssinn *m*, b) Gegend *f*; **2.** (örtliche) Lage.

lo·cal·i·za·tion [,ləʊkəlaɪ'zeɪʃn] *s.* Lokalisierung *f*, örtliche Bestimmung *od.* Festlegung *od.* Begrenzung; **lo·cal·ize** ['ləʊkəlaɪz] *v/t.* **1.** lokalisieren: a) örtlich festlegen *od.* fixieren, b) (örtlich) begrenzen (**to** auf *acc.*); **2.** Lo'kalkolo,rit geben (*dat.*).

lo·cate [ləʊ'keɪt] **I** *v/t.* **1.** ausfindig machen, ausfindig machen, die örtliche Lage *od.* den Aufenthalt ermitteln von (*od. gen.*); **2.** a) ⚓ *etc.* orten, b) ✕ *Ziel etc.* ausmachen; **3.**

Büro etc. errichten, einrichten; **4.** a) *(an e-m bestimmten Ort)* an- *od.* 'unterbringen, b) *an e-n Ort* verlegen: **be** ~**d** gelegen sein, *wo liegen od.* sich befinden; **II** *v/i.* **5.** *Am.* F sich niederlassen; **lo'ca·tion** [-eɪʃn] *s.* **1.** Lage *f:* a) Platz *m*, Stelle *f*, b) Standort *m*, Ort *m*, Örtlichkeit *f;* **2.** Ausfindigmachen *n*, Lokalisierung *f*, ♣ Ortung *f;* **3.** *Am.* a) Grundstück *n*, b) angewiesenes Land; **4.** *Film:* Gelände *n* für Außenaufnahmen, Drehort *m:* **on** ~ auf Außenaufnahme; ~ **shots** Außenaufnahmen *pl.;* **5.** Niederlassung *f*, Siedlung *f;* **6.** *Computer:* 'Speicherstelle *f*, -a,dresse *f*.

loc·a·tive ['lɒkətɪv] *ling.* **I** *adj.* Lokativ...: ~ **case** → **II** *s.* Lokativ *m*, Ortsfall *m*.

loch [lɒk; lɒx] *s. Scot.* **1.** See *m;* **2.** Bucht *f*.

lo·ci ['ləʊsaɪ] *pl. u. gen. von* **locus.**

lock¹ [lɒk] **I** *s.* **1.** *(Tür- etc.)*Schloss *n:* **under** ~ **and key** a) hinter Schloss u. Riegel *(Person)*, b) unter Verschluss *(Sache);* **2.** Verschluss *m*, Schließe *f;* **3.** Sperrvorrichtung *f;* **4.** *(Gewehr- etc.)* Schloss *n:* ~**, stock, and barrel** a) ganz u. gar, voll und ganz, mit Stumpf u. Stiel, b) mit allem Drum u. Dran, c) mit Sack u. Pack; **5.** a) Schleuse(nkammer) *f*, b) Luft-, Druckschleuse *f;* **6.** Knäuel *m*, *n*, Stau *m (von Fahrzeugen);* **7.** *mot. bsd. Brit.* Einschlag *m (der Vorderräder);* **8.** *Ringen:* Fessel(griff *m*) *f;* **II** *v/t.* **9.** (ab-, zu-, ver)schließen, zusperren, verriegeln; **10.** a. ~ **up** a) *j-n* einschließen, (ein)sperren, **(in, into** *in acc.),* b) → **lock up** 2; **11.** *(in die Arme)* schließen, *a. Ringen:* um'fassen, -'klammern; ~**ed** a) eng umschlungen, b) festgekeilt, *fig.* festsitzend, c) ineinander verkrallt: ~**ed in conflict; 12.** inein'ander schlingen, *die Arme* verschränken; → **horn; 13.** ⊚ sperren, sichern, arretieren, festklemmen; **14.** *mot.* Räder blockieren; **15.** *Schiff* ('durch)schleusen; **16.** *Kanal* mit Schleusen versehen; **17.** ✝ *Geld* festlegen, fest anlegen; **III** *v/i.* **18.** (ab-) schließen; **19.** sich schließen lassen; **20.** ⊚ inein'ander greifen, einrasten; **21.** *mot.* a) sich einschlagen lassen, b) blockieren *(Räder);* **22.** geschleust werden *(Schiff);*
Zssgn mit adv.:

lock| a·way *v/t.* weg-, einschließen; ~ **down** *v/t. Schiff* hin'abschleusen; ~ **in** *v/t.* einschließen, -sperren; ~ **on** *v/i.* **(to)** **1.** *Radar: (Ziel)* erfassen u. verfolgen; **2.** *Raumfahrt:* (an)koppeln (an *acc.);* **3.** *fig.* a) einhaken (bei), b) sich ,verbeißen' (in *acc.);* ~ **out** *v/t.* (a. *Arbeiter)* aussperren; ~ **up** *v/t.* **1.** → **lock¹** 9, 10; **2.** ver-, ein-, wegschließen; **4.** *Kapital* festlegen, fest anlegen; **4.** *Schiff* hin'aufschleusen.

lock² [lɒk] *s.* **1.** Locke *f; pl. poet.* Haar *n;* **2.** (Woll)Flocke *f;* **3.** Strähne *f*, Büschel *n*.

lock·age ['lɒkɪdʒ] *s.* **1.** Schleusen(anlage *f) pl.;* **2.** Schleusengeld *n;* **3.** ('Durch)Schleusen *n*.

lock·er ['lɒkə] *s.* **1.** (verschließbarer) Kasten *od.* Schrank, Spind *m*, *n:* ~ **room** Umkleideraum *m*, *sport* (Umkleide)Kabine *f;* → **shot²** 4; **2.** Schließfach *n*.

lock·et ['lɒkɪt] *s.* Medail'lon *n*.

lock| gate *s.* Schleusentor *n;* '~**jaw** ✦ Kaumuskelkrampf *m;* '~**nut** *s.* ⊚ Gegenmutter *f;* '~**out** *s.* Aussperrung *f (von Arbeitern);* ~ **smith** *s.* Schlosser *m;* ~ **stitch** *s.* Kettenstich *m;* '~**up** *s.* **1.** a) Gefängnis *n*, b) (Haft)Zelle(n *pl.)*

f; **2.** *Brit.* (kleiner) Laden; **3.** *mot.* 'Einzelga,rage *f;* **4.** Schließen *n*, (Tor)Schluss *m;* **5.** feste Anlage *(von Kapital).*

lo·co¹ ['ləʊkəʊ] *adj. Am. sl.* ,bekloppt', verrückt.

lo·co² ['ləʊkəʊ] *s.* Lok *f (Lokomotive).*

lo·co·mo·tion [,ləʊkə'məʊʃn] *s.* **1.** Fortbewegung *f;* **2.** Fortbewegungsfähigkeit *f;* '**lo·co,mo·tive** [-əʊtɪv] **I** *adj.* sich fortbewegend, fortbewegungsfähig, Fortbewegungs...: ~ **engine** → **II** *s.* Lokomo'tive *f*.

lo·cum ['ləʊkəm] F *für* ~ **te·nens** [,ləʊkəm'ti:nenz] *pl.* ~ **te·nen·tes** [-tɪ'nenti:z] *s.* Vertreter(in) *(z. B. e-s Arztes).*

lo·cus ['ləʊkəs] *pl. u. gen.* **lo·ci** ['ləʊsaɪ] *s.* (✦ geo'metrischer) Ort.

lo·cust ['ləʊkəst] *s.* **1.** *zo.* Heuschrecke *f;* **2.** a. ~ **tree** ♣ a) Ro'binie *f*, b) Jo'hannisbrotbaum *m;* **3.** ♣ Jo'hannisbrot *n*, Ka'rube *f*.

lo·cu·tion [ləʊ'kju:ʃn] *s.* **1.** Ausdrucksweise *f*, Redestil *m;* **2.** Redewendung *f*, Ausdruck *m*.

lode [ləʊd] *s.* ⚒ (Erz)Gang *m*, Ader *f;* '~**star** *s.* Leitstern *m* (a. *fig.), bsd.* Po'larstern *m;* '~**stone** *s.* **1.** Ma'gneteisen(stein *m) n;* **2.** *fig.* Ma'gnet *m*.

lodge [lɒdʒ] **I** *s.* **1.** *allg.* Häus·chen *n:* a) (Jagd-, Ski- *etc.)*Hütte *f*, b) Pförtnerhaus *n*, c) Parkwächter-, Forsthaus *n;* **2.** Pförtner-, Porti'erloge *f; Am.* Zen'tralgebäude *n (in e-m Park etc.);* **4.** *(bsd.* Freimaurer)Loge *f;* **5.** *(Indianer-)* Wigwam *m;* **II** *v/i.* **6. (with)** a) logieren, *(bsd.* in 'Untermiete) wohnen (bei), b) über'nachten (bei); **7.** stecken (bleiben) *(Kugel etc.);* **III** *v/t.* **8.** *j-n* a) 'unterbringen, aufnehmen, b) in 'Untermiete nehmen; **9.** *Geld* deponieren, hinter'legen; **10.** ✝ *Kredit* eröffnen; **11.** *Antrag, Beschwerde etc.* einreichen, *Anzeige* erstatten, *Berufung, Protest* einlegen **(with** bei); **12.** *Kugel, Messer etc.* (hin'ein)jagen, *Schlag* landen; '**lodge·ment** [-mənt] → **lodgment;** '**lodg·er** [-dʒə] *s.* ('Unter)Mieter(in).

lodg·ing ['lɒdʒɪŋ] *s.* **1.** 'Unterkunft *f*, ('Nacht)Quar,tier *n;* **2.** *pl.* a) *(bsd.* möbliertes) Zimmer, b) (möblierte) Zimmer *pl.*, c) Mietwohnung *f;* ~ **house** *s.* Fremdenheim *n*, Pensi'on *f*.

lodg·ment ['lɒdʒmənt] *s.* **1.** ⚖ Einreichung *f (Klage, Antrag etc.);* Erhebung *f (Beschwerde, Protest etc.);* Einlegung *f (Berufung);* **2.** Hinter'legung *f*, Deponierung *f*.

lo·ess ['ləʊɪs] *s. geol.* Löß *m*, Löss *m*.

loft [lɒft] **I** *s.* **1.** (Dach-, *a.* ✈ Heu)Boden *m*, Speicher *m:* **in the** ~ auf dem Dachboden; **2.** ⚓ Em'pore *f (für Kirchenchor, Orgel);* **3.** Taubenschlag *m;* **II** *v/t. u. v/i. Golf:* (den Ball) hoch schlagen; '**loft·er** [-tə] *s. Golf:* Schläger *m* für Hochbälle.

loft·i·ness ['lɒftɪnɪs] *s.* **1.** Höhe *f;* **2.** Erhabenheit *f (a. fig.);* **3.** Hochmut *m;* **loft·y** ['lɒftɪ] *adj.* □ **1.** hoch(ragend); **2.** *fig.* a) erhaben, b) hochfliegend, c) *contp.* hochtrabend; **3.** stolz, hochmütig.

log¹ [lɒg] **I** *s.* **1.** a) (Holz)Klotz *m*, (-)Block *m*, b) *(Feuer)*Scheit *n*, c) *(gefällter)* (Baum)Stamm: **in the** ~ unbehauen; **roll a** ~ **for s.o.** *Am.* j-m e-n Dienst erweisen, *bsd.* j-m et. zuschanzen; **sleep like a** ~ schlafen wie ein Klotz *od.* Bär; **2.** ⚓ Log *n;* **3.** ⚓ *etc.* → **logbook: keep a** ~ (**of)** Buch führen (über *acc.);* **4.** *Computer:* Proto'koll *n;* **II** *v/t.* **5.** ⚓ loggen: a) *Entfernung* zu-

'rücklegen, b) *Geschwindigkeit etc.* in das Logbuch eintragen; **II** *v/i.* **6.** ~ **in** *(od.* **on)** *Computer:* (sich) einloggen; **7.** ~ **out** *(od.* **off)** *Computer:* (sich) ausloggen.

log² [lɒg] → **logarithm.**

lo·gan·ber·ry ['ləʊgənbərɪ] *s.* ♣ Loganbeere *f (Kreuzung zwischen Bärenbrombeere u. Himbeere).*

log·a·rithm ['lɒgərɪðəm] *s.* Ⓐ Loga'rithmus *m;* **log·a·rith·mic, log·a·rith·mi·cal** [,lɒgə'rɪðmɪk(l)] *adj.* □ loga'rithmisch.

'**log| book** *s.* **1.** ⚓ Log-, ✈ Bord-, *mot.* Fahrtenbuch *n;* **2.** *mot. Brit.* Kraftfahrzeugbrief *m;* **3.** Reisetagebuch *n;* ~ **cab·in** *s.* Blockhaus *n*.

log·ger ['lɒgə] *s.* **1.** Holzfäller *m;* **2.** *Computer:* Regis'triergerät *n;* **3.** Maschine zum Be- u. Entladen von Holzstämmen; **4.** Traktor, *der in der Holzwirtschaft verwendet wird;* **II** *adj. Scot.* **5.** schwer; **6.** dick; **7.** dickköpfig; **8.** dumm.

log·ger·head ['lɒgəhed] *s.:* **be at** ~**s (with s.o.)** sich (mit j-m) in den Haaren liegen.

log·gia ['ləʊdʒə] *s.* ⚖ Loggia *f*.

logh [lɒx] *s. Ir.* See *m*.

log·ic ['lɒdʒɪk] *s. phls. u. fig.* Logik *f;* '**log·i·cal** [-kl] *adj.* □ **1.** logisch *(a. fig.* folgerichtig *od.* natürlich); **2.** *Computer:* logisch, Logik...; **lo·gi·cian** [ləʊ'dʒɪʃn] *s.* Logiker *m;* **lo·gis·tic** [ləʊ'dʒɪstɪk] **I** *adj.* **1.** *phls. u.* ✕ lo'gistisch; **II** *s.* **2.** *phls.* Lo'gistik *f;* **3.** *pl. mst sg. konstr. bsd.* ✕ Lo'gistik *f*.

log·o ['lɒgəʊ] → **logotype.** ⚓ F 'Logo *n*.

log·o·gram ['lɒgəʊgræm] *s.* Logo'gramm *n*, Wortzeichen *n*.

log·o·type ['lɒgəʊtaɪp] *s.* ✝ Firmen- *od.* Markenzeichen *n*.

'**log| roll** *pol. Am.* **I** *v/t. Gesetz* durch gegenseitige ,Schützenhilfe' 'durchbringen; **II** *v/i.* sich gegenseitig in die Hände arbeiten; ~**roll·ing** *s. pol.* ,Kuhhandel' *m*, gegenseitige Unter'stützung *(zur Durchsetzung von Gruppeninteressen etc.).*

loin [lɔɪn] *s.* **1.** *(mst pl.) anat.* Lende *f:* **gird up one's** ~**s** *fig.* sich rüsten *od* wappnen; **2.** *pl. bibl. u. poet.* a) Lenden *pl. (Fortpflanzungsorgane),* b) Schoß *m (der Frau);* **3.** *Küche:* Lende(nstück *n) f;* '~**cloth** *s.* Lendentuch *n*.

loi·ter ['lɔɪtə] **I** *v/i.* **1.** bummeln, trödeln; **2.** her'umlungern, -stehen, sich her'umtreiben; **II** *v/t.* **3.** ~ **away** *Zeit* vertrödeln; '**loi·ter·er** [-ərə] *s.* **1.** Bummler (-in), Faulenzer(in); **2.** Her'umtreiber(in).

loll [lɒl] **I** *v/i.* **1.** sich rekeln *od.* (her'um)lümmeln; **2.** sich lässig lehnen **(against** gegen); **3.** ~ **out** her'aushängen, baumeln *(Zunge);* **II** *v/t.* **4.** a. ~ **out** die *Zunge* her'aushängen lassen.

lol·li·pop ['lɒlɪpɒp] *s.* **1.** Lutscher *m (Stielbonbon);* **2.** *Brit.* Eis *n* am Stiel.

lol·lop ['lɒləp] *v/i.* F a) ,latschen', b) hoppeln.

lol·ly ['lɒlɪ] *s.* **1.** F für **lollipop; 2.** *Brit. sl.* ,Kies' *m (Geld).*

Lon·don·er ['lʌndənə] *s.* Londoner(in).

lone [ləʊn] *adj.* einsam: **play a** ~ **hand** *fig.* e-n Alleingang machen; → **wolf** 1; '**lone·li·ness** [-lɪnɪs] *s.* Einsamkeit *f;* '**lone·ly** [-lɪ] *adj. allg.* einsam: **be** ~ **for** *Am.* F Sehnsucht haben nach *j-m;* '**lon·er** ['ləʊnə] *s.* F Einzelgänger(in); '**lonesome** [-səm] *adj.* □ → **lonely.**

long¹ [lɒŋ] **I** *adj.* **1.** *allg.* lang *(a. fig.* langwierig, *a. ling.):* **two miles (weeks)** ~; ~ **journey** (**list, syllable);**

~ years of misery; **~ measure** Längenmaß n; **~ wave** ⚡ Langwelle f; **~er** comp. länger; **a ~ chance**, **~ odds** fig. geringe Aussichten; **a ~ dozen** 13 Stück; **~ drink** Longdrink m; **a ~ guess** e-e vage Schätzung; **~ time no see** F lange nicht gesehen!; **2.** lang, hoch (gewachsen): **a ~ fellow**; **3.** groß, zahlreich: **a ~ family**; **a ~ figure** eine vielstellige Zahl; **a ~ price** ein hoher Preis; **4.** weit reichend: **a ~ memory**; **take a ~ view** weit vorausblicken; **5.** ✝ langfristig, mit langer Laufzeit, auf lange Sicht; **6.** a) ✝ eingedeckt (**of** mit), b) **~ on** F reichlich versehen mit, fig. a. voller Ideen etc.; **II** adv. **7.** lang, lange: **~ dead** schon lange tot; **as** (**od. so**) **~ as** a) so lange (wie), b) sofern; vorausgesetzt, dass; **~ after** lange (da)nach; **~ ago** vor langer Zeit; **not ~ ago** vor kurzem; **as ~ ago as 1900** schon 1900; **all day ~** den ganzen Tag (lang); **be ~** a) lange dauern (Sache), b) lange brauchen ([**in**] **doing s.th.** et. zu tun); **don't be** (**too**) **~!** mach nicht so lang!, beeil dich!; **I shan't be ~!** (ich) bin gleich wieder da!; **not ~ before** kurz bevor; **it was not ~ before** es dauerte nicht lange, bis er kam etc.; **so ~!** tschüss!, bis später (dann)!; **no** (**od. not any**) **~er** nicht (mehr) länger, nicht mehr; **for how much ~er?** wie lange noch?; **~est** sup. am längsten; **III** s. **8.** (e-e) lange Zeit: **at the ~est** längstens, höchstens; **before ~** bald, binnen kurzem; **for ~** lange (Zeit); **it is ~ since** es ist lange her, dass; **9.** **take ~** lange brauchen; **the ~ and the short of it** a) die ganze Geschichte, b) mit 'einem Wort, kurz'um; **10.** Länge f: a) Phonetik: langer Laut, b) Metrik: lange Silbe; **11.** pl. a) lange Hose, b) 'Übergrößen pl.

long² [lɒŋ] v/i. sich sehnen (**for** nach): **~ for** a. j-n od. et. herbeisehnen; **I ~ed to see him** ich sehnte mich danach, ihn zu sehen; **the** (**much**) **~ed-for rest** die (heiß) ersehnte Ruhe.

'long·boat s. ⚓ Großboot n, großes Beiboot (e-s Segelschiffs); **'~·bow** [-bəʊ] s. hist. Langbogen m: **draw the ~** F übertreiben, dick auftragen; **'~·case clock** s. Standuhr f; **,~·dat·ed** adj. langfristig; **,~·'dis·tance I** adj. **1.** teleph. etc. Fern...(-gespräch, -empfang, -leitung etc.; a. -fahrt, -lastzug, -verkehr etc.); **2.** ✈, sport Langstrecken... (-bomber, -flug, -lauf etc.); **II** adv. **3.** **call ~** ein Ferngespräch führen; **III** s. **4.** teleph. Am. a) Fernamt n, b) Ferngespräch n; **,~·drawn-'out** adj. fig. langatmig, in die Länge gezogen.

longe [lʌndʒ] → **lunge²**.

lon·ge·ron ['lɒndʒərən] s. ✈ Rumpf(längs)holm m.

lon·gev·i·ty [lɒn'dʒevəti] s. Langlebigkeit f, langes Leben.

,long·'haired adj. **1.** langhaarig (a. contp.), zo. Langhaar...; **2.** (betont) intellektu'ell; **'~·hand** s. Langschrift f, (gewöhnliche) Schreibschrift; **,~·'head·ed** adj. **1.** langköpfig; **2.** gescheit, klug; **'~·horn** s. **1.** langhörniges Tier; **2.** langhörniges Rind, Am. Longhorn n.

long·ing ['lɒŋɪŋ] **I** adj. ☐ sehnsüchtig, verlangend; **II** s. Sehnsucht f, Verlangen n (**for** nach).

long·ish ['lɒŋɪʃ] adj. ziemlich lang.

lon·gi·tude ['lɒndʒɪtjuːd] s. geogr. Länge f; **lon·gi·tu·di·nal** [,lɒndʒɪ'tjuːdɪnl] adj. ☐ **1.** geogr. Längen...; **2.** Längs...; **lon·gi·tu·di·nal·ly** [,lɒndʒɪ'tjuːdɪnlɪ] adv. längs, der Länge nach.

long| johns s. pl. F lange 'Unterhose; **~ jump** s. sport Weitsprung m; **'~-legged** adj. langbeinig; **'~-life** adj. **1.** mit langer Lebensdauer (Batterie); **2.** haltbar gemacht (Milch etc.): **~ milk** H-Milch f; **,~-'lived** adj. langlebig; **'~-,play·ing rec·ord** s. Langspielplatte f; **~ prim·er** s. typ. Korpus f (Schriftgrad); **,~-'range** adj. **1.** ✕ weit tragend, Fernkampf..., Fern...; ✈ Langstrecken...: **~ bomber**, **2.** auf lange Sicht (geplant), langfristig; **'~-shore·man** [-mən] s. [irr.] Hafenarbeiter m; **~ shot** s. **1.** ⊞ Großaufnahme f, Film: To'tale f, **2.** sport etc. (krasser) Außenseiter; **3.** a) ris'kante Wette, b) (ziemlich) aussichtslose Sache, c) wilde Vermutung: **not by a ~** nicht entfernt, längst nicht (so gut etc.); **,~-'sight·ed** adj. **1.** ஃ weitsichtig; **2.** fig. weit blickend, 'umsichtig; **'~-,stand·ing** adj. seit langer Zeit bestehend, langjährig, alt; **,~-'suf·fer·ing I** s. Langmut f; **II** adj. langmütig; **'~-term** adj. langfristig, Langzeit...: **~ unemployed** Langzeitarbeitslose pl.; **'~-time** adj. → **long-standing**.

lon·gueur [lɒŋ'ɡɜː] (Fr.) s. Länge f (in e-m Roman etc.).

,long-'wind·ed [-'wɪndɪd] adj. fig. langatmig.

loo [luː] Brit. F **I** s. Klo n; **II** v/i. aufs Klo gehen.

loo·fa(h) ['luːfə] → **luffa**.

look [lʊk] **I** s. **1.** Blick m (**at** auf acc., nach): **have a ~ at s.th.** (sich) et. ansehen; **take a good ~** (**at it**)**!** sieh es dir genau an!; **have a ~ round** sich (mal) umsehen; **2.** Miene f, Ausdruck m; **3.** oft pl. Aussehen n: (**good**) **~s** gutes Aussehen; **I do not like the ~ of it** die Sache gefällt mir (gar) nicht; **II** v/i. **4.** schauen, blicken, (hin)sehen (**at, on** auf acc., nach): **don't ~!** nicht hersehen!; **don't ~ like that!** schau nicht so (drein)!; **~ here!** schau mal (her)!, hör mal (zu)!; → **leap** 1; **5.** (nach)schauen, nachsehen: **~ who is here!** schau, wer da kommt!, humor. ei, wer kommt denn da!; **~ and see!** überzeugen Sie sich (selbst)!; **6.** krank etc. aussehen (a. fig.): **things ~ bad for him** es sieht schlimm für ihn aus; **it ~s as if** es sieht (so) aus, als ob; **~ like** aussehen wie; **~s like snow** es sieht nach Schnee aus; **he ~s like winning** es sieht so aus, als ob er gewinnen sollte; **it ~s all right to me** es scheint (mir) in Ordnung zu sein; **it ~s well on you** es steht dir gut; **7.** aufpassen; → **Zssgn mit prp. look to**; **8.** nach e-r Richtung liegen, gehen (**toward, to** nach) (Zimmer etc.); **III** v/t. **9.** j-m in die Augen etc. sehen od. schauen: **~ s.o. in the eyes**; **10.** aussehen wie: **he ~s an idiot**; **he doesn't ~ his age** man sieht ihm sein Alter nicht an; **he ~s it!** so sieht er auch aus!; **11.** durch Blicke ausdrücken: **~ compassion** mitleidig dreinschauen; → **dagger** 1; **Zssgn mit prp.**:

look| a·bout v/i.: **~ one** sich 'umsehen, um sich blicken; **~ af·ter** v/i. **1.** j-m nachblicken; **2.** sehen nach, aufpassen auf (acc.), sich kümmern um, sorgen für: **~ o.s.** a) für sich selbst sorgen, b) auf sich aufpassen; **~ at** v/i. (a. sich j-n, et.) ansehen, -schauen, betrachten, blicken auf (acc.), fig. a. et. prüfen: **to ~ him** wenn man ihn (so) ansieht; **he wouldn't ~ it** er wollte nichts davon wissen; **he** (**it**) **isn't much to ~** er (es) sieht nicht ,berühmt' aus; **~ for** v/i. **1.** suchen (nach), sich 'umsehen nach; **2.**

erwarten; **~ in·to** v/i. **1.** blicken in (acc.); **2.** fig. et. unter'suchen, prüfen; **~ on** v/i. betrachten, ansehen (**as** als); **~ through** v/i. **1.** blicken durch; **2.** 'durchsehen, -lesen; **3.** fig. j-n od. et. durch'schauen; **~ to** v/i. **1.** achten od. Acht geben auf (acc.): **~ it that** achte darauf, dass; sieh zu, dass; **2.** zählen auf (acc.), von j-m erwarten, dass er ...: **I ~ you to help me** (od. **for help**) ich erwarte Hilfe von dir; **3.** sich wenden od. halten an (acc.); **~ up·on** → **look on**; **Zssgn mit adv.**:

look| a·bout v/i. sich 'umsehen (**for** nach); **~ a·head** v/i. **1.** nach vorn blicken od. schauen; **2.** fig. a) vor'ausschauen, b) Weitblick haben; **a·round** → **look about**; **~ back** v/i. **1.** sich 'umsehen; a. fig. zu'rückblicken (**upon** auf acc., **to** nach, zu); **2.** fig. schwankend werden; **~ down** v/i. **1.** her'ab-, her'untersehen (a. fig. [**up**]on s.o. auf j-n); **2.** bsd. ✝ sich verschlechtern; **~ for·ward** v/i.: **~ to** sich freuen auf (acc.): **I am looking forward to seeing him** ich freue mich darauf, ihn zu sehen; **~ in** v/i. als Besucher her'einod. hin'einschauen (**on** bei); **~ on** v/i. zusehen, -schauen (**at** bei); **~ out I** v/i. **1.** her'aus- od. hin'aussehen, -schauen (**of the window** zum od. aus dem Fenster); **2.** Ausschau halten (**for** nach); **3.** (**for**) gefasst sein (auf acc.), auf der Hut sein (vor dat.), aufpassen (auf acc.): **~!** pass auf!, Vorsicht!; **4.** Ausblick gewähren, (hin'aus)gehen (**on** auf acc.) (Fenster etc.); **II** v/t. **5.** (her'aus)suchen; **~ o·ver** v/t. **1.** 'durchsehen, (über)'prüfen; **2.** sich et. od. j-n ansehen, j-n mustern; **~ round** v/i. sich 'umsehen; **~ through** v/t. → **look over**; **~ up I** v/i. **1.** hin'aufblicken (**at** auf acc.); aufblicken (fig. **to s.o.** zu j-m); **2.** F a. ✝ sich bessern; steigen (Preise): **things are looking up** es geht bergauf; **II** v/t. **3.** Wort nachschlagen; **4.** j-n be- od. aufsuchen; **5.** **look s.o. up and down** j-n von oben bis unten mustern.

'look-a·like s. F Doppelgänger(in).

look·er ['lʊkə] s. F: **be a** (**good**) **~** gut od. ,toll' aussehen; **she is not much of a ~** sie sieht nicht besonders gut aus; **,~-'on** [-ər'ɒn] pl. **,look·ers-'on** s. Zuschauer(in) (**at** bei).

'look-in s. **1.** F kurzer Besuch; **2.** sl. Chance f.

'look·ing-glass ['lʊkɪŋ-] s. Spiegel m.

'look·out s. **1.** Ausschau f: **be on the ~ for** nach et. Ausschau halten; **keep a good ~** (**for**) auf der Hut sein (vor dat.); **2.** a. ⚓ Ausguck m; **4.** fig. Aussicht(en pl.) f; **5.** **that's his ~** F das ist s-e Sache od. sein Problem.

'look-see s.: **have a ~** sl. a) (kurz) mal nachgucken, b) sich mal umsehen.

loom¹ [luːm] s. Webstuhl m.

loom² [luːm] v/i. oft **~ up 1.** (drohend) auftragen; → **large** fig. a) sich auftürmen, b) von großer Bedeutung sein od. scheinen; **2.** undeutlich od. bedrohlich auftauchen; **3.** fig. a) sich abzeichnen, b) bedrohlich näher rücken, c) zs.-brauen.

loon¹ [luːn] s. orn. Seetaucher m.

loon² [luːn] s. F ,Blödmann' m.

loon·y ['luːnɪ] sl. **I** adj. ,bekloppt', verrückt; **II** s. Verrückte(r m) f, **~ bin** s. sl. ,Klapsmühle' f.

loop [luːp] **I** s. **1.** Schlinge f, Schleife f; **2.** ⚡, ⊞, Computer, Eislauf, Fingerabdruck, Fluss etc.: Schleife f; **3.** a) Schlaufe f, b) Öse f; **4.** ✈ etc. Looping *m, n;* **5.** ✍ Spi'rale *f* (*Verhütungsmittel*); **6.** → *loop aerial*; **II** *v/t.* **7.** in e-e Schleife *od.* in Schleifen legen, schlingen; **8.** ~ *the* ~ ✈ e-n Looping drehen; **9.** ↯ zur Schleife schalten; **III** *v/i.* **10.** e-e Schleife machen, sich schlingen *od.* winden; ~ **aer·i·al** *s.*, ~ **an·ten·na** *s.* ↯ 'Rahmen,tenne *f*, Peilrahmen *m*; '~**hole** *s.* **1.** (Guck)Loch *n*, ☒ a) Sehschlitz *m*, b) Schießscharte *f*; **3.** *fig.* Schlupfloch *n*, 'Hintertürchen *n*: *a ~ in the law* eine Lücke im Gesetz; ,~-**the-**-'**loop** *s. Am.* Achterbahn *f*.

loose [luːs] **I** *adj.* □ **1.** los(e): *come* (*od.* *get, work*) ~ a) abgehen (*Knöpfe*), b) sich ablösen (*Farbe etc.*), c) sich lockern, d) loskommen; *let* ~ a) loslassen, b) s-m *Ärger etc.* Luft machen; **2.** frei, befreit (*of, from* von): *break* ~ a) sich losreißen, b) sich lösen (*from* von), *fig. a.* sich frei machen (*from* von); **3.** lose (hängend) (*Haar etc.*): ~ *ends fig.* (noch zu erledigende) Kleinigkeiten; *be at a* ~ *end* a) nicht wissen, was man mit sich anfangen soll, b) ohne geregelte Tätigkeit sein; **4.** a) locker (*Boden, Glieder, Gürtel, Husten, Schraube, Zahn etc.*), b) offen, lose, unverpackt (*Ware*): *buy s.th.* ~ et. offen kaufen; ~ *bowels* offener Leib, *a.* Durchfall *m*; ~ *change* Kleingeld *n*; ~ *connection* ↯ Wackelkontakt *m*; *fig.* lose Beziehung; ~ *dress* weites *od.* lose sitzendes Kleid; ~ *leaves* lose Blätter; **5.** *fig.* einzeln, verstreut, zs.-hanglos; **6.** ungenau: ~ *translation* freie Übersetzung; **7.** *fig.* locker, lose (*unmoralisch*): ~ *girl* (*life, morals*); ~ *tongue* loses Mundwerk; **II** *adv.* **8.** lose, locker; **III** *v/t.* **9.** → *loos-en* 1; **10.** befreien, lösen (*from* von); **11.** lockern: ~ *one's hold* of et. loslassen; **12.** *mst* ~ *off* Waffe, Schuss abfeuern; **IV** *v/i.* **13.** *mst* ~ *off* schießen, feuern (*at* auf *acc.*): ~ *off at s.o. fig.* loswettern gegen j-n; **V** *s.* **14.** *be on the* ~ a) frei herumlaufen, b) die Gegend ,unsicher machen', c) ,einen draufmachen'; ,~-'**joint·ed** *adj.* **1.** (außerordentlich) gelenkig; **2.** schlaksig; '~-**leaf** *adj.* Loseblatt...: ~ *binder* (*od.* *book*) Loseblatt-, Ringbuch *n*, Schnellhefter *m*.

loos·en ['luːsn] **I** *v/t.* **1.** *Knoten etc., a.* ☒ Husten, *fig.* Zunge lösen; ✍ *Leib* öffnen; **2.** *Griff, Gürtel, Schraube etc., a.* Disziplin etc. lockern; ↗ *Boden* auflockern; **II** *v/i.* **3.** sich lockern (*a. fig.*), sich lösen; ~ *up v/t.* Muskeln lockern; *fig. j-n* auflockern; **II** *v/i. bsd. sport* sich (auf)lockern, *fig. a.* auftauen (*Person*).

loose·ness ['luːsnɪs] *s.* **1.** Lockerheit *f*; **2.** Schlaffheit *f*; **3.** Ungenauigkeit *f*, Unklarheit *f*; **4.** Freiheit *f* der Übersetzung; **5.** ✍ 'Durchfall *m*; **6.** lose Art, Liederlichkeit *f*.

loot [luːt] **I** *s.* **1.** (Kriegs-, Diebes)Beute *f*; **2.** *fig.* Beute *f*; **3.** F ,Kies' *m* (*Geld*); **II** *v/t.* **4.** erbeuten; **5.** plündern; **III** *v/i.* **6.** plündern; '**loot·er** [-tə] *s.* Plünderer *m*; '**loot·ing** [-tɪŋ] *s.* Plünderung *f*.

lop[1] [lɒp] *v/t.* **1.** *Baum etc.* beschneiden, stutzen; **2.** *oft* ~ *off* Äste, *a.* Kopf etc. abhauen, -hacken.

lop[2] [lɒp] *v/i. u. v/t.* schlaff (her'unter-) hängen (lassen).

lope [ləʊp] **I** *v/i.* (da'her)springen *od.* (-)trotten; **II** *s.*: *at a* ~ im Galopp, in großen Sprüngen.

'**lop**|**-eared** *adj.* mit Hängeohren; ,~-'**ears** *s. pl.* Hängeohren *pl.*; ,~-'**sid·ed** *adj.* **1.** schief (*a. fig.*), nach einer Seite hängend; **2.** einseitig (*a. fig.*).

lo·qua·cious [ləʊ'kweɪʃəs] *adj.* □ red-selig, geschwätzig; **lo'qua·cious·ness** [-nɪs], **lo'quac·i·ty** [-'kwæsətɪ] *s.* Redseligkeit *f*.

lord [lɔːd] **I** *s.* **1.** Herr *m*, Gebieter *m* (*of* über *acc.*): *her* ~ *and master bsd. humor.* ihr Herr u. Gebieter; *the* ~*s of creation a. humor.* die Herren der Schöpfung; **2.** *fig.* Ma'gnat *m*; **3.** Lehensherr *m*; → *manor*; **4.** *the* ♌ a) *a.* ♌ *God* (Gott) der Herr, b) *a. our* ♌ (Christus) der Herr; *the* ♌*'s day* der Tag des Herrn; *the* ♌*'s Prayer* das Vaterunser; *the* ♌*'s Supper* das (heilige) Abendmahl; *the* ♌*'s table* der Tisch des Herrn (*a. Abendmahl*), der Altar; *in the year of our* ♌ im Jahre des Herrn; (*good*) ♌*!* (du) lieber Gott *od.* Himmel!; **5.** ♌ Lord *m* (*Adliger od. Würdenträger, z. B. Bischof, hoher Richter*): *the* ♌*s Brit. parl.* das Oberhaus; *live like a* ~ leben wie ein Fürst; *my* ♌ [mɪ'lɔːd] *Brit. oft* mɪ'lʌd] My'lord, Euer Lordschaft, ⚖ Euer Ehren (*Anrede*); **II** *v/i.* **7.** *oft* ~ *it* den Herren spielen: ~ *it over* a) sich *j-m* gegenüber als Herr aufspielen, b) herrschen über (*acc.*).

Lord| **Cham·ber·lain (of the Household)** *s.* Hofmeister *m*; ~ **Chan·cel·lor** *s.* Lordkanzler *m* (*Präsident des Oberhauses, Präsident der Chancery Division des Supreme Court of Judicature sowie des Court of Appeal, Kabinettsmitglied, Bewahrer des Großsiegels*); ~ **Chief Jus·tice of Eng·land** *s.* ⚖ Lord'oberrichter *m* (*Vorsitzender der King's Bench Division des High Court of Justice*); ♌-**in-wait·ing** *s.* königlicher Kammerherr (*wenn e-e Königin regiert*); ~ **Jus·tice** *pl.* **Lords Jus·tic·es** *s. Brit.* Lordrichter *m* (*Richter des Court of Appeal*); ♌ **lieu·ten·ant** *pl.* **lords lieu·ten·ant** *s.* **1.** *hist.* Vertreter der Krone in den englischen Grafschaften; *jetzt oberster Exekutivbeamter*; **2. Lord Lieutenant** a) *hist.* Vizekönig *m* von Irland (*bis 1922*), b) *Vertreter der Krone in e-r Grafschaft*.

lord·li·ness ['lɔːdlɪnɪs] *s.* **1.** Großzügigkeit *f*; **2.** Würde *f*; **3.** Pracht *f*, Glanz *m*; **4.** Arro'ganz *f*.

lord·ling ['lɔːdlɪŋ] *s. contp.* Herrchen *n*, kleiner Lord.

lord·ly ['lɔːdlɪ] *adj. u. adv.* **1.** großzügig; **2.** vornehm, edel, Herren...; **3.** herrisch; **4.** stolz; **5.** arro'gant; **6.** prächtig.

Lord| **May·or** *pl.* **Lord May·ors** *s. Brit.* Oberbürgermeister *m*: ~*'s Day* Tag des Amtsantritts des Oberbürgermeisters von London (*9. November*); ~*'s Show* Festzug des Oberbürgermeisters von London am 9. November; ~ **Privy Seal** *s.* Lord'siegelbewahrer *m*; ~ **Prov·ost** *pl.* **Lord Prov·osts** *s.* Oberbürgermeister *m* (*der vier größten schottischen Städte*).

lord·ship ['lɔːdʃɪp] *s.* **1.** Lordschaft *f*: *your* (*his*) ~ Euer (Seine) Lordschaft; **2.** *hist.* Herrschaftsgebiet *n* e-s Lords; **3.** *fig.* Herrschaft *f*.

lord| **spir·it·u·al** *pl.* **lords spir·it·u·al** *s.* geistliches Mitglied des brit. Oberhauses; ~ **tem·po·ral** *pl.* **lords tem·po·ral** *s.* weltliches Mitglied des brit. Oberhauses.

lore [lɔː] *s.* **1.** (*Tier- etc.*)Kunde *f*, (über-'liefertes) Wissen *n*; **2.** Sagen- u. Märchengut *n*, Über'lieferungen *pl.*

lorn [lɔːn] *adj. obs. od. poet.* verlassen, einsam.

lor·ry ['lɒrɪ] *s. Brit.* Last(kraft)wagen *m*, Lastauto *n*: *it fell off the back of a ~* F es ist mir (uns, ihr etc.) ,zugeflo-

gen'; **2.** ⚒, ⚒ Lore *f*, Lori *f*.

lose [luːz] **I** *v/t.* [*irr.*] **1.** *allg.* Sache, *j-n*, Gesundheit, das Leben, Verstand, Weg, Zeit etc. verlieren: ~ *o.s.* a) sich verlieren (*a. fig.*), b) sich verirren; ~ *interest* a) das Interesse verlieren, b) uninteressant werden (*Sache*); *she lost the baby* sie verlor das Baby (*durch Fehlgeburt*); → *lost*; *s. a.* Verbindungen mit verschiedenen Substantiven; **2.** Vermögen, Stellung verlieren, einbüßen, kommen um; **3.** Vorrecht etc. verlieren, verlustig gehen (*gen.*); **4.** a) Schlacht, Spiel etc. verlieren, b) Preis etc. nicht erringen *od.* bekommen, c) Gesetzesantrag nicht 'durchbringen; **5.** Zug etc., *a.* Gelegenheit versäumen, verpassen; **6.** a) Worte etc. ,nicht mitbekommen', b) *he lost his listeners* F s-e Zuhörer kamen nicht mit; **7.** aus den Augen verlieren; → *sight* 3; **8.** vergessen, verlernen: *I have lost my French*; **9.** nachgehen, zu'rückbleiben (*Uhr*); **10.** Krankheit etc. loswerden, Verfolger *a.* abschütteln; **11.** *j-n s-e Stellung etc.* kosten, bringen um: *this will* ~ *you your position*; **12.** ~ *it mot. sl.* die Kontrolle über den Wagen verlieren; **II** *v/i.* [*irr.*] **13.** verlieren, Verluste erleiden (*on* bei, *by* durch); **14.** *fig.* verlieren: *the poem* ~*s in translation* das Gedicht verliert (sehr) in der Übersetzung; **15.** (*to*) verlieren (gegen), unter'liegen (*dat.*); **16.** ~ *out* F a) verlieren, b) ,in den Mond gucken' (*on* bei): ~ *on a. et.* nicht kriegen; '**los·er** [-zə] *s.* **1.** Verlierer(in): *a good* (*bad*) ~: *be a* ~ *by* Schaden *a.* e-n Verlust erleiden durch; *come off a* ~ den Kürzeren ziehen; **2.** F ,Verlierer' *m*, Versager *m*; '**los·ing** [-zɪŋ] *adj.* **1.** verlierend; **2.** Verlust bringend, Verlust...: ~ *bargain* ☨ Verlustgeschäft *n*; **3.** verloren, aussichtslos (*Schlacht, Spiel*).

loss [lɒs] *s.* **1.** Verlust *m*: a) Einbuße *f*, Ausfall *m* (*in* an *dat.*, von *od.* gen.): ~ *of blood* (*time*) Blut- (Zeit)verlust; ~ *of pay* Lohnausfall; *a dead* ~ totaler Verlust, *fig.* ,Pleite' *f*, totaler Reinfall (*Sache*), ,totaler Ausfall', ,Niete' *f* (*Person*), b) Nachteil *m*, Schaden *m*: *it's your* ~*!* das ist dein Problem!, c) *verlorene Sache od. Person*: *he is a great* ~ *to his firm*, d) Verschwinden *n*, Verlieren *n*, e) *verlorene Schlacht, Wette etc., a.* Niederlage *f*, f) Abnahme *f*, Schwund *m*: ~ *in weight* Gewichtsverlust, -abnahme; **2.** *mst pl.* ⚔ Verluste *pl.*, Ausfälle *pl.*; **3.** Versicherungswesen: Schadensfall *m*; **4.** *at a* ~ a) ☨ mit Verlust (*arbeiten, verkaufen etc.*), b) in Verlegenheit (*for* um): *be at a* ~ *a.* nicht mehr ein u. aus wissen; *be at a* ~ *for words* (*od. what to say*) keine Worte finden (können), nicht wissen, was man (dazu) sagen soll; *he is never at a* ~ *for an excuse* er ist nie um e-e Ausrede verlegen; ~ **lead·er** *s.* ☨ 'Lockar,tikel *m*; '~-,**mak·er** *s.* ☨ *Brit.* **1.** mit Verlust arbeitender Betrieb; **2.** Verlustgeschäft *n*.

lost [lɒst] **I** *pret. u. p.p. von* **lose**; **II** *adj.* **1.** verloren: ~ *articles* (*battle, friend, time etc.*); *a* ~ *chance* e-e verpasste Gelegenheit; ~ *property office* Fundbüro *n*; **2.** verloren (gegangen), vernichtet, (da)'hin: *be* ~ a) verloren gehen (*to* an *acc.*), b) zugrunde gehen, untergehen, c) umkommen, den Tod finden, d) verschwinden, e) verschwunden *od.* versunken sein, f) vergangen sein, g) versunken *od.* vertieft sein (*in* in *acc.*): ~ *in thought*; *I am* ~ *without my car!*

ohne mein Auto bin ich verloren *od.* ,aufgeschmissen'!; **3.** verirrt: *be* ~ sich verirrt *od.* verlaufen haben, sich nicht mehr zurechtfinden (*a. fig.*); *get* ~ sich verirren; *get* ~*!* F verschwinde!; *I'm* ~*!* F da komm ich nicht mehr mit!; **4.** *fig.* verschwendet, vergeudet (*on s.o.* an j-n): *that's* ~ *on him a.* a) das lässt ihn kalt, b) dafür hat er keinen Sinn, c) das versteht er nicht.

lot [lɒt] **I** *s.* **1.** Los *n*: *cast* (*od.* *draw*) ~*s* losen, Lose ziehen (*for* um); *throw in one's* ~ *with s.o.* das Los mit j-m teilen, sich (auf Gedeih u. Verderb) mit j-m zs.-tun; *by* ~ durch (das) Los; **2.** Anteil *m*; **3.** Los *n*, Schicksal *n*: *it falls to my* ~ es ist mein Los, es fällt mir zu (*et. zu tun*); **4.** *bsd. Am.* a) Stück *n* Land, Grundstück *n*, *bsd.* Par'zelle *f*, b) Bauplatz *m*, c) (Park- *etc.*)Platz *m*; **5.** *Am.* Filmgelände *n*, *bsd.* Studio *n*; **6.** ✝ a) Ar'tikel *m*, b) Par'tie *f*, Posten *m* (*von Waren*): *in* ~*s* partienweise; **7.** Gruppe *f*, Gesellschaft *f*, ,Verein' *m*: *the whole* ~ a) die ganze Gesellschaft, der ganze ,Laden', b) → **8**; **8.** *the* ~ alles, das Ganze: *take the* ~*!*; *that's the* ~ das ist alles; **9.** (Un)Menge *f*: *a* ~ *of*, ~*s of* viel, e-e Menge, ein Haufen *Geld etc.*; ~*s and* ~*s of people* e-e Unmasse Menschen; ~*s! in* Antworten: jede Menge!; **10.** F Kerl *m*: *a bad* ~ ein übler Bursche; **II** *adv.* **11.** *a* ~, F ~*s* a) (sehr) viel: *a* ~ *better*; *I read a* ~, b) (sehr) oft: *I see her a* ~.

loth [ləʊθ] → **loath**.

Lo·thar·i·o [ləʊˈθɑːrɪəʊ] *s.* Schwerenöter *m*.

lo·tion [ˈləʊʃn] *s.* (Augen-, Haut-, Rasier- *etc.*)Wasser *n*, Loti'on *f*.

lot·ter·y [ˈlɒtərɪ] *s.* **1.** Lotte'rie *f*: ~ *tick-et* a) Lotterielos *n*, b) *Lotto etc.*: Tippschein *m*; **2.** *fig.* Glückssache *f*, Lotte'riespiel *n*.

lo·tus [ˈləʊtəs] *s.* **1.** *Sage*: Lotos *m* (*Frucht*); **2.** ♀ a) Lotos(blume *f*) *m*, b) Honigklee *m*; '~·eat·er *s.* **1.** (*in der Odyssee*) Lotosesser *m*; **2.** Träumer *m*, Müßiggänger *m*, tatenloser Genussmensch.

loud [laʊd] *adj.* □ **1.** (*a. adv.*) laut (*a. fig.*): ~ *admiration*; **2.** schreiend, auffallend, grell: ~ *colo(u)rs*; '~·hail·er *s. Brit.* Mega'phon *n*; '~·mouth *s.* F **1.** Großmaul *n*; **2.** ,dummer Quatscher'; '~·mouthed *adj.* großmäulig.

loud·ness [ˈlaʊdnɪs] *s.* **1.** Lautheit *f*, *a. phys.* Lautstärke *f*; **2.** Lärm *m*; **3.** *das* Auffallende, Grellheit *f*.

'**loud·speak·er** *s.* ⚡ Lautsprecher *m*.

lounge [laʊndʒ] **I** *s.* **1.** a) Halle *f*, Diele *f*, Gesellschaftsraum *m* (*Hotel*), b) *thea.* Foy'er *n*, c) Abflug-, Wartehalle *f* (*Flughafen*), d) *a.* ~ *bar* ✈, ⚓, 🚗 Sa'lon *m*; **2.** Wohndiele *f*, -zimmer *n*; **3.** Sofa *n*, Liege *f*; **II** *v/i.* **4.** sich rekeln; **5.** faulenzen; **6.** ~ (*od.* *around*) he'rumliegen *od.* -sitzen *od.* -stehen *od.* -schlendern; **7.** schlendern; **III** *v/t.* **8.** ~ *away* Zeit verbummeln; ~ *bar* Sa'lon *m* (*e-s Restaurants*); ~ *chair s.* Klubsessel *m*; ~ *liz·ard s.* F Sa'lonlöwe *m*; ~ *suit s. Brit.* Straßenanzug *m*.

lour, lour·ing → **lower¹**, **lowering**.

louse [laʊs] **I** *pl.* **lice** [laɪs] *s.* **1.** *zo.* Laus *f*; **2.** *sl.* ,Fiesling' *m*, Scheißkerl *m*; **II** *v/t.* [laʊz] **3.** (ent)lausen; **4.** ~ *up sl.* versauen, -masseln; '**lous·y** [-zɪ] *adj.* **1.** verlaust; **2.** *sl.* a) ,fies', (hunds)gemein, b) mise'rabel, ,beschissen': *the film was* ~; *I feel* ~, c) ,lausig': *for* ~ *two dollars*; **3.** ~ *with sl.* wimmelnd von: ~ *with people*; ~ *with money* stinkreich.

lout [laʊt] *s.* Flegel *m*, Rüpel *m*; '**lout-ish** [-tɪʃ] *adj.* □ flegel-, rüpelhaft.

lou·ver, *Brit. a.* **lou·vre** [ˈluːvə] *s.* **1.** △ *hist.* Dachtürmchen *n*; **2.** Jalou'sie *f* (*a.* ⊕ *Luft-, Kühlschlitze*).

lov·a·ble [ˈlʌvəbl] *adj.* □ liebenswert, reizend, ,süß'.

lov·age [ˈlʌvɪdʒ] *s.* ♀ Liebstöckel *n*, *m*.

love [lʌv] **I** *s.* **1.** (*sinnliche od. geistige*) Liebe (*of, for, to*[*wards*] zu): ~ *of mu-sic* Liebe zur Musik, Freude *f* an der Musik; ~ *of adventure* Abenteuerlust *f*; *the* ~ *of God* a) die Liebe Gottes, b) die Liebe zu Gott; *for the* ~ *of God* um Gottes willen; *be in* ~ (*with s.o.*) verliebt sein (in j-n); *fall in* ~ (*with s.o.*) sich verlieben (in j-n); *make* ~ sich (*sexuell*) lieben; *make* ~ *to s.o.* a) j-n (*körperlich*) lieben, b) *obs.* j-m um'werben, j-m gegenüber zärtlich werden; *send one's* ~ *to s.o.* j-n grüßen lassen; *give her my* ~*!* grüße sie herzlich von mir!; ~ *als Briefschluss:* herzliche Grüße; *for* ~ a) umsonst, gratis, b) *a. for the* ~ *of it* (nur) zum Spaß; *play for* ~ um nichts spielen; *not for* ~ *or money* nicht für Geld u. gute Worte; *there is no* ~ *lost between them* sie haben nichts füreinander übrig; **2.** ♀ die Liebe, (Gott *m*) Amor *m*; **3.** *pl. Kunst*: Amo'retten *pl.*; **4.** Liebling *m*, Schatz *m*; **5.** F a) mein Lieber, b) m-e Liebe; **6.** Liebe *f*, Liebschaft *f*; **7.** F lieber *od.* goldiger Kerl: *he* (*she*) *is a* ~; **8.** F reizende *od.* goldige *od.* ,süße' Sache *od.* Per'son: *a* ~ *of a child* (*hat*); **9.** *bsd. Tennis*: null: ~ *all* null beide; ~ *fifteen* fünfzehn null; **II** *v/t.* **10.** *j-n* lieben; **11.** *et.* lieben, sehr mögen: ~ *to do* (*od. doing*) *s.th.* etwas (*schrecklich*) gern tun; *we* ~*d having you with us* wir haben uns sehr über deinen Besuch gefreut; ~ *af·fair s.* 'Liebesaf,färe *f*; '~·bird *s.* **1.** *orn.* Unzertrennliche(r) *m*; **2.** *pl.* F ,Turteltauben' *pl.*; ~ *child s.* [*irr.*] Kind *n* der Liebe; ~ *game s. Tennis*: Zu-'Null-Spiel *n*; ,~-'hate re·la·tion·ship *s.* Hassliebe *f*.

love·less [ˈlʌvlɪs] *adj.* □ **1.** ohne Liebe; **2.** lieblos.

love·| let·ter *s.* Liebesbrief *m*; ~ *life s.* Liebesleben *n*.

love·li·ness [ˈlʌvlɪnɪs] *s.* Lieblichkeit *f*, Schönheit *f*.

'**love·|lock** *s.* Schmachtlocke *f*; '~·lorn [-lɔːn] *adj.* liebeskrank, vor Liebeskummer *od.* Liebe vergehend.

love·ly [ˈlʌvlɪ] *adj.* □ **1.** a) lieblich, schön, hübsch, b) *allg., a.* F *u. iro.* schön, wunderbar, reizend, entzückend, c) lieb, nett (*of you* von dir); **2.** F ,süß', niedlich.

'**love·|,mak·ing** *s.* (*körperliche*) Liebe; Liebesspiele *pl.*, -kunst *f*; ~ *match s.* Liebesheirat *f*; ~ *nest s.* ,Liebesnest' *n*; ~ *po·tion s.* Liebestrank *m*.

love·| seat *s.* Plaudersofa *n*; ~ *set s. Tennis*: Zu-'null-Satz *m*; '~·sick *adj.* liebeskrank: *be* ~ *a.* Liebeskummer haben; ~ *song s.* Liebeslied *n*; ~ *sto·ry s.* Liebesgeschichte *f*; ~ *tri·an·gle s.* Dreiecksverhältnis *n*.

lov·ing [ˈlʌvɪŋ] *adj.* □ liebend, liebevoll, Liebes...: ~ *words*; *your* ~ *father* (*als Briefschluss*) dein dich liebender Vater; ~ *cup s.* Po'kal *m*; ~ *kind·ness s.*

1. (göttliche) Gnade *od.* Barm'herzigkeit; **2.** Herzensgüte *f*.

low¹ [ləʊ] **I** *adj. u. adv.* **1.** nieder, niedrig (*a. Preis, Temperatur, Zahl etc.*): *of* ~ *birth* von niedriger Abkunft; ~ *pres-sure* Tiefdruck *m*; ~ *speed* niedrige *od.* geringe Geschwindigkeit; ~ *water* ⚓ tiefster Gezeitenstand; *at the* ~*est* wenigstens, mindestens; *be at its* ~*est* auf dem Tiefpunkt angelangt sein; → *lower³*, *opinion* 2; **2.** tief (*a. fig.*): ~ *bow*; ~ *flying* Tiefflug *m*; *the sun is* ~ die Sonne steht tief; → *low-necked*; **3.** knapp (*Vorrat etc.*): *run* ~ knapp werden, zur Neige gehen; *I am* ~ *in funds* ich bin nicht gut bei Kasse; **4.** schwach: ~ *light*; ~ *pulse*; **5.** einfach, fru'gal (*Kost*); **6.** be-, gedrückt: ~ *spirits* gedrückte Stimmung; *feel* ~ a) in gedrückter Stimmung *od.* niedergeschlagen sein, b) sich elend fühlen; **7.** minderwertig, schlecht: ~ *quality*; **8.** a) niedrig (*denkend od. gesinnt*): ~ *think-ing* niedrige Denkungsart, b) ordi'när, vul'gär: *a* ~ *expression*; *a* ~ *fellow*, c) gemein, niederträchtig: *a* ~ *trick*; **9.** nieder, primi'tiv: ~ *forms of life* niedere Lebensformen; ~ *race* primitive Rasse; **10.** a) tief (*Ton etc.*), b) leise (*Ton, Stimme etc.*): *in a* ~ *voice* leise; **11.** *Phonetik*: offen (*Vokal*); **12.** ⊙, *mot.* erst, niedrigst (*Gang*): *in* ~ *gear*; **II** *adv.* **13.** niedrig (*zielen etc.*); **14.** tief: *bow* (*hit, etc.*) ~; *sunk thus* ~ *fig.* so tief gesunken; *bring s.o.* ~ *fig.* j-n zu Fall bringen *od.* ruinieren *od.* demütigen; *lay s.o.* ~ a) j-n niederstrecken, b) *fig.* j-n zur Strecke bringen; *be laid* ~ (*with*) daniederliegen (mit *e-r Krankheit*); **15.** a) leise, b) tief: *sing* ~; **16.** kärglich: *live* ~; **17.** billig: *buy* (*sell*) ~; **18.** niedrig, mit geringem Einsatz: *play* ~; **III** *s.* **19.** *meteor.* Tief(druckgebiet) *n*; **20.** *fig.* Tiefstand *m*: *reach a new* ~ e-n neuen Tiefstand erreichen; **21.** *mot.* erster Gang.

low² [ləʊ] **I** *v/i. u. v/t.* brüllen, muhen (*Rind*); **II** *s.* Brüllen *n*, Muhen *n*.

,**low·|-'born** *adj.* von niedriger Geburt; '~·boy *s. Am.* niedrige Kom'mode; '~·brow F **I** *s.* Ungebildete(r *m*) *f*, ,Unbedarfte(r' *m*) *f*; **II** *adj.* geistig anspruchslos, *Person: a.* ungebildet, ,unbedarft'; ⚱ Church *s. eccl.* Low Church *f* (*protestantisch-pietistische Sektion der anglikanischen Kirche*); ~ *com·e·dy s.* Schwank *m*, ,Klamotte' *f*; '~·cost *adj.* billig, preisgünstig; ⚱ Coun·tries *s. pl.* die Niederlande, Belgien u. Luxemburg; '~·down F **I** *adj.* fies, gemein; **II** *s.* (volle) Informati'onen *pl.*, *die* Wahrheit, genaue Tatsachen *pl.*, 'Hintergründe *pl.* (*on* über *acc.*); ,~-e'mis-sion *adj. mot.* abgas-, schadstoffarm.

low·er¹ [ˈlaʊə] *v/i.* **1.** finster *od.* drohend blicken: ~ *at* j-n drohend anblicken; **2.** *fig.* bedrohlich aussehen (*Himmel, Wolken etc.*); **3.** *fig.* drohen (*Ereignisse*).

low·er² [ˈləʊə] **I** *v/t.* **1.** niedriger machen; **2.** Augen, Gewehrlauf *etc.*, *a.* Stimme, Preis, Kosten, Niveau, Temperatur, Ton *etc.* senken; *fig. Moral* senken, *a.* Widerstand *etc.* schwächen; **3.** her'unter- *od.* hin'unterlassen, niederlassen; *Fahne, Segel* niederholen, *Rettungsboote* aussetzen; **4.** *fig.* erniedrigen: ~ *o.s.* sich herablassen (*et. zu tun*); **II** *v/i.* **5.** sinken, fallen, sich senken.

low·er³ [ˈləʊə] **I** *adj.* (*comp. von low¹* I) **1.** tiefer, niedriger; **2.** unter, Unter...: ⚱ *Chamber* (*od. House*) *parl.* Unter-,

Abgeordnetenhaus *n*; *the* ~ *class* so-
ciol. die untere Klasse *od.* Schicht; ~
deck Unterdeck *n*; ~ *jaw* Unterkiefer
m; ~ *region* Unterwelt *f* (*Hölle*); ~
school Unter- u. Mittelstufe *f*; **3.**
geogr. Unter..., Nieder...; ♔ *Austria*
Niederösterreich *n*; **II** *adv.* **4.** tiefer: ~
down the river (*list*) weiter unten am
Fluss (auf der Liste).

'**low·er**| *case s. coll. typ.* Kleinbuchsta-
ben *pl.*; '**~-case** *typ.* **I** *adj.* in Kleinbuchstaben (gedruckt *od.* geschrieben),
kleingeschrieben, Klein...; **II** *v/t.* in
Kleinbuchstaben drucken *od.* schreiben.

low·er·ing ['laʊərɪŋ] *adj.* □ finster, düster, drohend.

low·er·most ['laʊəməʊst] → *lowest*.

low·est ['laʊɪst] **I** *adj.* tiefst, niedrigst,
unterst (*etc.*, → *low*[1] I): ~ *bid* ✝ Mindestgebot *n*; **II** *adv.* am tiefsten (*etc.*).

'**low**|**-,fly·ing** *adj.* tief fliegend: ~ *plane*
Tiefflieger *m*; ~ **fre·quen·cy** *s.* ⚡ 'Nie-
derfre,quenz *f*; ~ **fu·el con·sump-**
tion en·gine *s.* Sparmotor *m*; ♔ **Ger-**
man *s. ling.* Niederdeutsch *n*, Plattdeutsch *n*; '**~-key(ed)** *adj.* gedämpft
(*Farbe, Ton, Stimmung etc.*), *fig. a.* a)
(sehr) zurückhaltend, b) bedrückt,
c) unaufdringlich; '**~-land** [-lənd] **I** *s.*
oft pl. Flach-, Tiefland *n*: *the* ♔*s* das
schottische Tiefland; **II** *adj.* Tief-
land(s)...; '**~-land·er** [-ləndə] *s.* **1.** Tief-
landbewohner(in); **2.** ♔ (schottischer)
Tiefländer; ♔ **Lat·in** *s. ling.* nichtklassi-
sches La'tein; '**~-lev·el** *adj.* niedrig (*a.
fig.*): ~ *officials*, ~ *talks pol.* Gespräche *pl.* auf unterer Ebene; ~ *attack* ✈
Tief(flieger)angriff *m*.

low·li·ness ['ləʊlɪnɪs] *s.* **1.** Niedrigkeit *f*;
2. Bescheidenheit *f*.

low·ly ['ləʊlɪ] *adj. u. adv.* **1.** niedrig,
gering, bescheiden; **2.** tief (stehend),
primi'tiv, niedrig; **3.** demütig, bescheiden.

Low| **Mass** *s. R.C.* Stille Messe; ,♔-
-'**mind·ed** *adj.* niedrig (gesinnt), gemein; ,♔-'**necked** *adj.* tief ausgeschnitten (*Kleid*).

low·ness ['ləʊnɪs] *s.* **1.** Niedrigkeit *f* (*a.
fig., contp.*); **2.** Tiefe *f* (*e-r Verbeugung,
e-s Tons etc.*); **3.** ~ *of spirits* Niedergeschlagenheit *f*; **4.** a) Gemeinheit *f*, b)
ordi'näre Art.

,**low**|-'**noise** *adj.* rauscharm (*Tonband*);
,**~-'pitched** *adj.* **1.** ♪ tief; **2.** mit geringer Steigung (*Dach*); ~ **pres·sure** *s.* **1.**
⚙ Nieder-, 'Unterdruck *m*; **2.** *meteor.*
Tiefdruck *m*; ,**~-'pres·sure** *adj.* a) Niederdruck..., b) *meteor.* Tiefdruck...; ,**~-**
-'**priced** *adj.* ✝ billig; ,**~-'pro·file** *adj.
attr.* **1.** *Politiker etc.*: a) wenig in den
Medien prä'sent, b) ziemlich unbekannt *od.* unbeachtet; **2.** *it was a* ~
campaign e-e Kampagne, die in
den Medien wenig Beachtung fand; ,**~-**
-'**spir·it·ed** *adj.* niedergeschlagen, gedrückt; ♔ **Sun·day** *s.* Weißer Sonntag
(*erster Sonntag nach Ostern*); ~ **ten-**
sion *s.* ⚡ Niederspannung *f*; ,**~-'ten-**
sion *adj.* ⚡ Niederspannungs...; ~ **tide**
s. ⚓ Niedrigwasser *n*; ,**~-'val·ue** *adj.* geringwertig; ,**~-'volt·age** *adj.* ⚡ **1.** Niederspannungs...; **2.** Schwachstrom...;
~ **wa·ter** *s.* ⚓ Ebbe *f*, Niedrigwasser
n: *be in* ~ *fig.* auf dem Trockenen sitzen; ,**~-'wa·ter mark** *s.* **1.** ⚓ Niedrig-
wassermarke *f*; **2.** *fig.* Tiefpunkt *m*,
-stand *m*.

loy·al ['lɔɪəl] *adj.* □ **1.** (*to*) loy'al (gegenüber), treu (ergeben) (*dat.*); **2.** (ge)treu
(*to dat.*); **3.** aufrecht, redlich; **loy·al·ist**
['lɔɪəlɪst] **I** *s.* Loya'list(in): a) *allg.* Treu-
gesinnte(r *m*) *f*, b) *hist.* Königstreue(r

m) *f*; **II** *adj.* loya'listisch; '**loy·al·ty** [-tɪ]
s. Loyali'tät *f*, Treue *f* (*to* zu, gegen).

loz·enge ['lɒzɪndʒ] *s.* **1.** *her.*, ♔ Raute *f*,
Rhombus *m*; **2.** *pharm.* (*bsd.* 'Husten-)
Pa,stille *f*.

L-plate ['elpleɪt] *s. Brit. Schild mit rotem
„L" an Privatautos, das auf e-n Fahr-
schüler (= learner) hinweist*.

lub·ber ['lʌbə] *s.* **1.** a) Flegel *m*, b) Trottel *m*; **2.** ⚓ Landratte *f*.

lu·bri·cant ['lu:brɪkənt] *s.* Gleit-, ⚙
Schmiermittel *n*; **lu·bri·cate** ['lu:brɪ-
keɪt] *v/t.* ⚙ *u. fig.* schmieren, ölen;
lu·bri·ca·tion [,lu:brɪ'keɪʃn] *s.* ⚙ *u. fig.*
Schmieren *n*, Schmierung *f*, Ölen *n*: ~
chart Schmierplan *m*; ~ *point* Schmierstelle *f*, -nippel *m*; '**lu·bri·ca·tor** [-keɪ-
tə] *s.* ⚙ Öler *m*, Schmiervorrichtung *f*;
lu·bric·i·ty ['lu:'brɪsətɪ] *s.* **1.** Gleitfähig-
keit *f*, Schlüpfrigkeit *f* (*a. fig.*); **2.** ⚙
Schmierfähigkeit *f*.

luce [lu:s] *s. ichth.* (ausgewachsener)
Hecht.

lu·cent ['lu:snt] *adj.* **1.** glänzend, strahlend; **2.** 'durchsichtig, klar.

lu·cern(e) [lu:'sɜ:n] *s.* ♣ Lu'zerne *f*.

lu·cid ['lu:sɪd] *adj.* □ **1.** *fig.* klar: ~ *interval psych.* lichter Augenblick; **2.** →
lucent; **lu·cid·i·ty** [lu:'sɪdətɪ], '**lu·cid-**
ness [-nɪs] *s. fig.* Klarheit *f*.

Lu·ci·fer ['lu:sɪfə] *s. bibl.* Luzifer *m* (*a.
ast.* Venus als Morgenstern).

luck [lʌk] *s.* **1.** Schicksal *n*, Geschick *n*,
Zufall *m*: *as* ~ *would have it* wie es der
Zufall wollte, (un)glücklicherweise;
bad (*od. hard, ill*) ~ a) Unglück *n*,
Pech *n*, b) *als Einschaltung*: Pech gehabt!; *good* ~ Glück *n*; *good* ~*!* viel
Glück!; *Hals- u.* Beinbruch!; *worse* ~
unglücklicherweise, leider; *be down
on one's* ~ e-e Pechsträhne haben; *just
my* ~*!* so geht es mir immer; **2.** Glück *n*:
for ~ als Glücksbringer; *be in* (*out of*)
~ (kein) Glück haben; *try one's* ~ sein
Glück versuchen; *with* ~ mit ein bisschen Glück; *here's* ~*!* F Prost!; **luck·i·ly**
['lʌkɪlɪ] *adv.* zum Glück, glücklicherweise; **luck·i·ness** ['lʌkɪnɪs] *s.* Glück *n*;
'**luck·less** [-lɪs] *adj.* □ glücklos.

luck·y ['lʌkɪ] *adj.* □ → *luckily*; **1.**
Glücks..., glücklich: *a* ~ *day* ein
Glückstag; ~ *hit* Glückstreffer *m*; *be*
~ Glück haben; *you* ~ *thing!* F du
Glückliche(r *m*) *f*!; *you are* ~ *to be
alive!* du kannst von Glück sagen, dass
du noch lebst!; *it was* ~ *that* ein Glück,
dass ..., zum Glück ...; **2.** Glück bringend, Glücks...: ~ *bag*, ~ *dip* Glücks-
beutel *m*, -topf *m*; ~ *star* Glücksstern
m.

lu·cra·tive ['lu:krətɪv] *adj.* □ einträglich, lukra'tiv.

lu·cre ['lu:kə] *s.* Gewinn(sucht *f*) *m*,
Geld(gier *f*) *n*: *filthy* ~ schnöder Mammon, gemeine Profitgier.

Lud·dite ['lʌdaɪt] *s.* Lud'dit *m*, Ma'schi-
nenstürmer *m*.

lu·di·crous ['lu:dɪkrəs] *adj.* □ **1.** lächerlich, ab'surd; **2.** spaßig, drollig.

lu·do ['lu:dəʊ] *s.* Mensch, ärgere dich
nicht *n* (*Würfelspiel*).

lu·es ['lu:i:z] *s.* ☤ Lues *f*, Syphilis *f*.

luff [lʌf] ⚓ **I** *s.* **1.** Luven *n*; **2.** Luv(seite)
f, Windseite *f*; **II** *v/t. u. v/i.* **3.** a. ~ *up*
anluven.

luf·fa ['lʌfə] *s.* ♣ *u.* ✝ Luffa *f*.

lug[1] [lʌɡ] *v/t.* zerren, schleppen: ~ *in fig.*
an den Haaren herbeiziehen, *Thema*
(mit Gewalt) hineinbringen.

lug[2] [lʌɡ] *s.* **1.** (Leder)Schlaufe *f*; **2.** ⚙
a) Henkel *m*, Öhr *n*, b) Knagge *f*, Zin-
ke *f*, c) Ansatz *m*; **3.** *Scot. od. Brit.* F
Ohr *n*; **4.** *sl.* Trottel *m*.

luge [lu:ʒ] **I** *s.* Renn-, Rodelschlitten *m*;
II *v/i.* rodeln.

lug·gage ['lʌɡɪdʒ] *s. Brit.* Gepäck *n*; ~
boot s. mot. Kofferraum *m*; ~ *car·ri·er
s.* Gepäckträger *m* (*am Fahrrad*); ~ *in-
sur·ance s.* (Reise)Gepäckversiche-
rung *f*; ~ *lock·er s.* (Gepäck)Schließ-
fach *n*; ~ *rack s.* **1.** Gepäcknetz *n*; **2.**
mot. Gepäckträger *m*; ~ *trol·ley s.* 🚂
Kofferkuli *m*; ~ *van s. Brit.* 🚂 Gepäck-,
Packwagen *m*.

lug·ger ['lʌɡə] *s.* ⚓ Logger *m* (*Schiff*).

lu·gu·bri·ous [lu:'ɡu:brɪəs] *adj.* □
schwermütig, kummervoll.

Luke [lu:k] *npr. u. s. bibl.* 'Lukas(evan-
,gelium *n*) *m*.

luke·warm ['lu:kwɔ:m] *adj.* □ lau
(-warm); *fig.* lau; '**luke·warm·ness**
[-nɪs] *s.* Lauheit *f* (*a. fig.*).

lull [lʌl] **I** *v/t.* **1.** *mst* ~ *to sleep* einlullen
(*a. fig.*); **2.** *fig.* beruhigen, *a. j-s* Befürchtungen etc. beschwichtigen: ~ *into*
(*a false sense of*) *security* in Sicher-
heit wiegen; **II** *s.* **3.** Pause *f*; **4.** (Wind-)
Stille *f*, Flaute *f* (*a.* ✝), *fig. a.* Stille *f*
(*vor dem Sturm*): *a* ~ *in conversation*
e-e Gesprächspause.

lull·a·by ['lʌləbaɪ] *s.* Wiegenlied *n*.

lu·lu ['lu:lu:] *s. Am. sl.* ,dolles Ding',
schicke Sache.

lum·ba·go [lʌm'beɪɡəʊ] *s.* ☤ Hexen-
schuss *m*, Lum'bago *f*.

lum·bar ['lʌmbə] *adj. anat.* Lenden...,
lum'bal.

lum·ber[1] ['lʌmbə] **I** *s.* **1.** *bsd. Am.* Bau-,
Nutzholz *n*; **2.** Gerümpel *n*, Plunder *m*;
II *v/t.* **3.** *bsd. Am. Holz* aufbereiten; **4.**
a. ~ *up* voll stopfen, voll pfropfen.

lum·ber[2] ['lʌmbə] *v/i.* **1.** trampeln, trap-
pen; **2.** (da'hin)rumpeln (*Fahrzeug*).

lum·ber·ing ['lʌmbərɪŋ] *adj.* □ schwerfällig.

'**lum·ber**|**·jack** *s. bsd. Am.* Holzfäller *m*;
'**~·jack·et** *s.* Lumberjack *m*; ~ *mill s.*
Sägewerk *n*; ~ *room s.* Rumpelkammer
f; ~ *trade s.* (Bau)Holzhandel *m*; ~
yard s. Holzplatz *m*.

lu·men ['lu:mən] *s. phys.* Lumen *n*.

lu·mi·nar·y ['lu:mɪnərɪ] *s.* Leuchtkörper
m, *bsd. ast.* Himmelskörper *m*; *fig.*
Leuchte *f* (*Person*); **lu·mi·nes·cence**
[,lu:mɪ'nesns] *s.* Lumines'zenz *f*; **lu·mi-**
nes·cent [,lu:mɪ'nesnt] *adj.* lumines-
zierend, leuchtend; **lu·mi·nos·i·ty** [,lu:-
mɪ'nɒsətɪ] *s.* **1.** Leuchten *n*, Glanz *m*; **2.**
ast., phys. Lichtstärke *f*, Helligkeit *f*;
'**lu·mi·nous** [-nəs] *adj.* □ **1.** leuchtend,
Leucht...(-farbe, -kraft, -uhr, -ziffer-
blatt etc.), *bsd. phys.* Licht...(-energie
etc.); **2.** *fig.* a) klar, b) lichtvoll, bril'lant.

lum·mox ['lʌməks] *s. Am.* F Trottel *m*.

lump [lʌmp] **I** *s.* **1.** Klumpen *m*: *have a*
~ *in one's throat fig.* e-n Kloß im Hals
haben; **2.** a) Schwellung *f*, Beule *f*, b)
Geschwulst *f*; **3.** Stück *n* Zucker etc.; **4.**
metall. Luppe *f*; **5.** *fig.* Masse *f*: *all of*
(*od. in*) *a* ~ alles auf einmal; *in the* ~ a)
pauschal, in Bausch u. Bogen, b) im
Großen; **6.** F ,Klotz' *m* (*langweiliger od.
stämmiger Kerl*); **7.** *the* ~ *Brit.* die Selbst-
ständigen *pl.* im Baugewerbe; **II** *adj.* **8.**
Stück...: ~ *coal*, ~ *sugar* Würfelzucker
m; **9.** Pauschal...(-fracht, -summe etc.);
III *v/t.* **10.** *oft* ~ *together* a) zs.-tun,
-legen, b) *fig. a. in* 'einen Topf werfen,
über 'einen Kamm scheren, c) *fig.* zs.-
fassen; **11.** *if you don't like it you can*
~ *it* a) wenn es dir nicht passt, kannst
dus ja bleiben lassen, b) du wirst dich
eben damit abfinden müssen; **IV** *v/i.*
12. Klumpen bilden; '**lump·ish** [-pɪʃ]
adj. □ **1.** schwerfällig, klobig, plump;
2. dumm; '**lump·y** [-pɪ] *adj.* □ **1.** klum-

pig; **2.** → *lumpish* 1; **3.** ♻ unruhig (*See*).

lu·na·cy ['luːnəsɪ] *s.* ✦ Wahn-, Irrsinn *m* (*a. fig.* F).

lu·nar ['luːnə] *adj.* Mond..., Lunar...: ~ *landing* Mondlandung *f*; ~ *landing vehicle* Mondlandefahrzeug *n*; ~ *module* Mondfähre *f*; ~ *rock* Mondgestein *n*; ~ *rover* Mondfahrzeug *n*; ~ *year* Mondjahr *n*.

lu·na·tic ['luːnətɪk] **I** *adj.* wahn-, irrsinnig, geisteskrank: ~ *fringe* F *pol.* extremistische Randgruppe; **II** *s.* Wahnsinnige(r *m*) *f*, Irre(r *m*) *f*: ~ *asylum* Irrenanstalt *f*.

lunch [lʌntʃ] **I** *s.* Mittagessen *n*, Lunch *m*: ~ *break* Mittagspause *f*; ~ *counter* Imbissbar *f*; ~ *hour*, ~ *time* Mittagszeit *f*, -pause *f*; *there is no such thing as a free* ~ für nichts gibts nichts; **II** *v/i.* das Mittagessen einnehmen; **III** *v/t.* j-n zum Mittagessen einladen, beköstigen.

lunch·eon ['lʌntʃən] → *lunch*: ~ *meat* Frühstücksfleisch *n*; ~ *voucher* Essen(s)marke *f*; **lunch·eon·ette** [ˌlʌntʃə'net] *s. Am.* Imbissstube *f*.

lu·nette [luː'net] *s.* **1.** Lü'nette *f*: a) ⚠ Halbkreis-, Bogenfeld *n*, b) ⚔ Brillschanze *f*, c) Scheuklappe *f* (*Pferd*); **2.** flaches Uhrglas.

lung [lʌŋ] *s. anat.* Lunge(nflügel *m*) *f*: *the* ~*s* die Lunge (*als Organ*); ~ *power* Stimmkraft *f*.

lunge¹ [lʌndʒ] **I** *s.* **1.** *fenc.* Ausfall *m*, Stoß *m*; **2.** Satz *m od.* Sprung *m* vorwärts; **II** *v/i.* **3.** *fenc.* ausfallen (*at* gegen); **4.** sich stürzen (*at* auf *acc.*); **III** *v/t.* **5.** *Waffe etc.* stoßen.

lunge² [lʌndʒ] **I** *s.* Longe *f*, Laufleine *f* (*für Pferde*); **II** *v/t.* longieren.

lu·pin(e)¹ ['luːpɪn] *s.* ♀ Lu'pine *f*.

lu·pine² ['luːpaɪn] *adj.* Wolfs..., wölfisch.

lurch¹ [lɜːtʃ] **I** *s.* **1.** Taumeln *n*, Torkeln *n*; **2.** ♻ Schlingern *n*, Rollen *n*; **3.** Ruck *m*; **II** *v/i.* **4.** ♻ schlingern; **5.** taumeln, torkeln.

lurch² [lɜːtʃ] *s.*: *leave in the* ~ *fig.* im Stich lassen.

lure [ljʊə] **I** *s.* **1.** Köder *m* (*a. fig.*); **2.** *fig.* Lockung *f*, Verlockungen *pl.*, Reiz *m*; **II** *v/t.* **3.** (an)locken, ködern: ~

away fortlocken; **4.** verlocken (*into* zu).

lu·rid ['ljʊərɪd] *adj.* □ **1.** grell; **2.** fahl, gespenstisch (*Beleuchtung etc.*); **3.** *fig.* a) düster, finster, unheimlich, b) grausig, grässlich.

lurk [lɜːk] **I** *v/i.* **1.** lauern (*a. fig.*); **2.** *fig.* a) verborgen liegen, b) (heimlich) drohen; **3.** *a.* ~ *about od.* ~ *around* her'umschleichen; **II** *s.* **4.** *on the* ~ auf der Lauer; **'lurk·ing** [-kɪŋ] *adj. fig.* versteckt, lauernd, heimlich.

lus·cious ['lʌʃəs] *adj.* □ **1.** köstlich, lecker, *a.* saftig; **2.** üppig; **3.** *Mädchen, Figur etc.*: prächtig, 'knackig'.

lush¹ [lʌʃ] *adj.* □ ♀ saftig, üppig (*a. fig.*).

lush² [lʌʃ] *s. Am. sl.* **1.** 'Stoff' *m* (*Whisky etc.*); **2.** Säufer(in).

lust [lʌst] **I** *s.* **1.** a) (sinnliche) Begierde, b) (Sinnes)Lust *f*, Wollust *f*; **2.** Gier *f*, Gelüste *n*, Sucht *f* (*of, for* nach): ~ *of power* Machtgier *f*; ~ *for life* Lebensgier *f*; **II** *v/i.* **3.** gieren (*for, after* nach): *they* ~ *for power* es gelüstet sie nach Macht.

lus·ter ['lʌstə] *Am.* → *lustre*.

lust·ful ['lʌstfʊl] *adj.* □ wollüstig, geil, lüstern.

lust·i·ly ['lʌstɪlɪ] *adv.* kräftig, mächtig, mit Macht *od.* Schwung, *a.* aus voller Kehle *singen*.

lus·tre ['lʌstə] *s.* **1.** Glanz *m* (*a. min. u. fig.*); **2.** Lüster *m*: a) Kronleuchter *m*, b) *Halbwollgewebe*, c) *Glanzüberzug auf Porzellan etc.*; **'lus·tre·less** [-lɪs] *adj.* glanzlos, stumpf; **lus·trous** ['lʌstrəs] *adj.* □ glänzend.

lust·y ['lʌstɪ] *adj.* (□ → *lustily*) **1.** kräftig, gesund u. munter; **2.** lebhaft, voller Leben, schwungvoll; **3.** kräftig, kraftvoll.

lu·ta·nist ['luːtənɪst] *s.* Lautenspieler (-in), Laute'nist(in).

lute¹ [luːt] *s.* ♪ Laute *f*.

lute² [luːt] **I** *s.* **1.** ⊕ Kitt *m*, Dichtungsmasse *f*; **2.** Gummiring *m*; **II** *v/t.* **3.** (ver)kitten.

lu·te·nist ['luːtənɪst] → *lutanist*.

Lu·ther·an ['luːθərən] **I** *s. eccl.* Luthe'raner(in); **II** *adj.* lutherisch; **'Lu·ther·an·ism** [-rənɪzəm] *s.* Luthertum *n*.

lu·tist ['luːtɪst] → *lutanist*.

lux [lʌks] *pl.* **lux**, **'lux·es** *s. phys.* Lux *n* (*Einheit der Beleuchtungsstärke*).

lux·ate ['lʌkseɪt] *v/t.* ✦ aus-, verrenken; **lux·a·tion** [lʌk'seɪʃn] *s.* Verrenkung *f*, Luxati'on *f*.

luxe [lʌks] *s.* Luxus *m*; → *de luxe*.

lux·u·ri·ance [lʌg'zjʊərɪəns], **lux·u·ri·an·cy** [-sɪ] *s.* **1.** Üppigkeit *f*; **2.** Fülle *f* (*of* an *dat.*), Pracht *f*; **lux·u·ri·ant** [-nt] *adj.* □ üppig (*Vegetation etc., a. fig.*); **lux·u·ri·ate** [lʌg'zjʊərɪeɪt] *v/i.* **1.** schwelgen (*a. fig.*) (*in* in *dat.*); **2.** üppig wachsen *od.* gedeihen; **lux·u·ri·ous** [-rəs] *adj.* □ **1.** Luxus..., luxuri'ös, üppig; **2.** schwelgerisch, verschwenderisch (*Person*); **3.** genüsslich, wohlig; **lux·ury** ['lʌkʃərɪ] **I** *s.* **1.** Luxus *m*: a) Wohlleben *n*: *live in* ~ im Überfluss leben, b) (Hoch)Genuss *m*: *permit o.s. the* ~ *of doing* sich den Luxus gestatten, *et.* zu tun, c) Aufwand *m*, Pracht *f*; **2.** a) 'Luxusar,tikel *m*, b) Genussmittel *n*; **II** *adj.* **3.** 'Luxus...: ~ *flat* (*Am. apartment*) Kom'fortwohnung *f*.

ly·chee [ˌlaɪ'tʃiː; 'lɪtʃɪ] *s. Obst:* 'Litschi *f*.

lych gate [lɪtʃ] → *lich gate*.

lye [laɪ] *s.* ♨ Lauge *f*.

ly·ing¹ ['laɪɪŋ] **I** *pres.p. von* **lie¹**; **II** *adj.* lügnerisch, verlogen; **III** *s.* Lügen *n od. pl.*

ly·ing² ['laɪɪŋ] **I** *pres.p. von* **lie²**; **II** *adj.* liegend; **,~-'in** *s.* a) Entbindung *f*, b) Wochenbett *n*: ~ *hospital* Entbindungsanstalt *f*, -heim *n*.

lymph [lɪmf] *s.* **1.** Lymphe *f*: a) *physiol.* Gewebeflüssigkeit *f*, b) ✦ Impfstoff *m*; **2.** *poet.* Quellwasser *n*; **lym·phat·ic** [lɪm'fætɪk] ✦ **I** *adj.* lym'phatisch, Lymph...: ~ *gland*; **II** *s.* Lymphgefäß *n*.

lynch [lɪntʃ] *v/t.* lynchen; ~ *law* *s.* 'Lynch·ju,stiz *f*.

lynx [lɪŋks] *s. zo.* Luchs *m*; '~**-eyed** *adj. fig.* luchsäugig.

lyre ['laɪə] *s.* ♪, *ast.* Leier *f*, Lyra *f*.

lyr·ic ['lɪrɪk] **I** *adj.* (□ ~*ally*) **1.** lyrisch (*a. fig.*); **2.** Musik...: ~ *drama*; **II** *s.* **3.** a) lyrisches Gedicht, b) *pl.* Lyrik *f*; **4.** *pl.* (Lied)Text *m*; **'lyr·i·cal** [-kl] *adj.* □ → *lyric* **I**; **'lyr·i·cism** [-ɪsɪzəm] *s.* **1.** Lyrik *f*, lyrischer Cha'rakter *od.* Stil; **2.** Schwärme'rei *f*; **'lyr·ist** [-ɪst] *s.* Lyriker(in).

L

M, m [em] *s.* M *n*, m *n* (*Buchstabe*).
ma [mɑː] *s.* F Ma'ma *f.*
ma'am [mæm] *s.* (*Anrede*) **1.** F für *madam*; **2.** [mɑːm; mæm] *Brit.* a) Maje'stät (*Königin*), b) Hoheit (*Prinzessin*).
Maas·tricht Trea·ty ['mɑːstrɪkt] *npr. pol.* Vertrag *m* von Maastricht.
mac¹ [mæk] *s. Brit.* F → *mackintosh.*
Mac² [mæk] *s. Am.* F ,Chef' *m.*
ma·ca·bre [mə'kɑːbrə], *Am. a.* **ma'ca·ber** [-bə] *adj.* ma'kaber: a) grausig, b) Toten...
ma·ca·co [mə'keɪkəʊ] *s. zo.* Maki *m.*
mac·ad·am [mə'kædəm] **I** *s.* **1.** Maka'dam-, Schotterdecke *f;* **2.** Schotterstraße *f;* **3.** a) Maka'dam *m*, b) Schotter *m;* **II** *adj.* **4.** beschottert, Schotter...: ~ *road;* **mac'ad·am·ize** [-maɪz] *v/t.* makadamisieren.
mac·a·ro·ni [,mækə'rəʊnɪ] *s. sg. u. pl.* Makka'roni *pl.*: ~ *cheese* mit Käse überbackene Makkaroni *pl.*
mac·a·roon [,mækə'ruːn] *s.* Ma'krone *f.*
ma·caw [mə'kɔː] *s. orn.* Ara *m.*
mac·ca·ro·ni → *macaroni.*
mace¹ [meɪs] *s.* Mus'katblüte *f.*
mace² [meɪs] *s.* **1.** ✕ *hist.* Streitkolben *m;* **2.** Amtsstab *m;* **3.** *a.* ~*-bearer* Träger *m* des Amtsstabes; **4.** (*Chemical*) ⚷ (*TM*) chemische Keule (*Reizgas*).
mac·er·ate ['mæsəreɪt] *v/t.* **1.** (*a. v/i.*) (aufquellen u.) aufweichen; **2.** *biol. Nahrungsmittel* aufschließen; **3.** ausmergeln; **4.** ka'steien.
Mach [mɑːk] *s.* ✕ *phys.* Mach *n*: *at* ~ *two* (mit) Mach 2 *fliegen.*
Mach·i·a·vel·li·an [,mækɪə'velɪən] *adj.* machiavel'listisch, skrupellos.
mach·i·nate ['mækɪneɪt] *v/i.* Ränke schmieden, intrigieren; **mach·i·na·tion** [,mækɪ'neɪʃn] *s.* Anschlag *m*, In'trige *f*, Machenschaft *f*, *pl. a.* Ränke; **'mach·i·na·tor** [-tə] *s.* Ränkeschmied *m*, Intri'gant(in).
ma·chine [mə'ʃiːn] **I** *s.* **1.** ⚙ Ma'schine *f* (F *a.* Auto, Motorrad, Flugzeug etc.); **2.** Appa'rat *m*, Vorrichtung *f*, (*thea.* 'Bühnen)Mecha,nismus *m*: *the god from the* ~ Deus *m* ex Machina (*e-e plötzliche Lösung*); **3.** *fig.* ,Ma'schine' *f*, ,Roboter' *m* (*Mensch*); **4.** *pol.* (Par'tei)Ma,schine *f*, (Re'gierungs)Appa,rat *m;* **II** *v/t.* **5.** ⚙ maschi'nell herstellen; maschi'nell drucken; (maschi'nell) bearbeiten; *engS. Metall* zerspanen; ~ *age s.* Ma'schinenzeitalter *m;* ~ **fit·ter** *s.* Ma'schinenschlosser *m;* ~ **gun** ✕ **I** *s.* Ma'schinengewehr *n;* **II** *v/t.* mit Ma'schinengewehrfeuer belegen; ~ **lan·guage** *s. Computer:* Ma'schinensprache *f;* ~**-made** *adj.* **1.** maschi'nell (hergestellt), Fabrik...: ~ *paper* Maschinenpapier *n;* **2.** *fig.* stereo'typ; ~ **pis·tol** *s.* Ma'schinenpis,tole *f;* ~**,read·a·ble** *adj.* ma'schinenlesbar.
ma·chin·er·y [mə'ʃiːnərɪ] *s.* **1.** Maschi'nerie *f*, Ma'schinen(park) *m*) *pl.*; **2.** Mecha'nismus *m*, (Trieb)Werk *n;* **3.** *fig.* Maschine'rie *f*, Räderwerk *n*, (*Regie-*

rungs)Ma'schine *f;* **4.** dra'matische Kunstmittel *pl.*
ma·chine| shop *s.* ⚙ Ma'schinenhalle *f*, -saal *m;* ~ **tool** *s.* ⚙ 'Werkzeugma,schine *f;* ~**,wash·a·ble** *adj.* 'waschma,schinenfest (*Stoff etc.*).
ma·chin·ist [mə'ʃiːnɪst] *s.* **1.** ⚙ a) Ma'schineningeni,eur *m*, b) Ma'schinenschlosser *m*, c) Maschi'nist *m* (*a. thea.*); **2.** Ma'schinennäherin *f.*
ma·chis·mo [mæ'tʃɪzməʊ] *s.* Ma'chismo *m*, Männlichkeitswahn *m.*
Mach num·ber [mɑːk] *s. phys.* Machzahl *f.*
ma·cho ['mætʃəʊ] **I** *s.* ,Macho' *m*, ,Kraft-od. Sexprotz' *m;* **II** *adj.* ,macho', (betont) männlich.
mac·in·tosh → *mackintosh.*
mack·er·el ['mækrəl] *pl.* **-el** *s. ichth.* Ma'krele *f;* ~ **sky** *s. meteor.* (Himmel *m* mit) Schäfchenwolken *pl.*
Mack·i·naw ['mækɪnɔː] *s. a.* ~ *coat Am.* Stutzer *m*, kurzer Plaidmantel.
mack·in·tosh ['mækɪntɒʃ] *s.* Regen-, Gummimantel *m.*
mack·le ['mækl] **I** *s.* **1.** dunkler Fleck; **2.** *typ.* Schmitz *m*, verwischter Druck; **II** *v/t. u. v/i.* **3.** *typ.* schmitzen.
ma·cle ['mækl] *s. min.* **1.** 'Zwillingskris,tall *m;* **2.** dunkler Fleck.
macro- [mækrəʊ] *in Zssgn* Makro..., (sehr) groß: ~*climate* Großklima *n.*
mac·ro ['mækrəʊ] *s. Computer:* Makro *n.*
mac·ro·bi·ot·ic [,mækrəʊbaɪ'ɒtɪk] *adj.* makrobi'otisch; **mac·ro·bi'ot·ics** [-ks] *s. pl. sg. konstr.* Makrobi'otik *f.*
mac·ro·cosm ['mækrəʊkɒzəm] *s.* Makro'kosmos *m.*
ma·cron ['mækrɒn] *s.* Längestrich *m* (*über Vokalen*).
mad [mæd] *adj.* □ → *madly;* **1.** wahnsinnig, verrückt, toll (*alle a. fig.*): ~ *cow disease* Rinderwahnsinn *m;* **go** ~ verrückt werden; *it's enough to drive one* ~ es ist zum Verrücktwerden; *like* ~ wie toll *od.* wie verrückt (*arbeiten etc.*); → *hatter, drive* 15; **2.** (*after, about, for, on*) versessen (auf *acc.*), verrückt (nach), vernarrt (in *acc.*): *she is* ~ *about music;* **3.** F außer sich, verrückt (*with* vor *Freude, Schmerzen, Wut etc.*); **4.** *bsd. Am.* F wütend, böse (*at, about* über *acc.*, auf *acc.*); **5.** toll, wild, 'übermütig: *they are having a* ~ *time* bei denen gehts toll zu, sie amüsieren sich toll; **6.** wild (geworden): *a* ~ *bull;* **7.** tollwütig (*Hund*).
Mad·a·gas·can [,mædə'gæskən] **I** *s.* Made'gasse *m*, Made'gassin *f;* **II** *adj.* made'gassisch.
mad·am ['mædəm] *s.* **1.** gnädige Frau *od.* gnädiges Fräulein (*Anrede*); **2.** Bor'dellwirtin *f*, Puffmutter *f.*
'mad·cap **I** *s.* ,verrückter Kerl'; **II** *adj.* ,verrückt', wild, verwegen.
mad·den ['mædn] **I** *v/t.* verrückt *od.* toll *od.* rasend machen (*a. fig.* wütend ma-

chen); **II** *v/i.* verrückt *etc.* werden; **'mad·den·ing** [-nɪŋ] *adj.* □ verrückt *etc.* machend: *it is* ~ es ist zum Verrücktwerden.
mad·der¹ ['mædə] *comp. von mad.*
mad·der² ['mædə] *s.* ♀, ⚙ Krapp *m.*
mad·dest ['mædɪst] *sup. von mad.*
mad·ding ['mædɪŋ] *adj. poet.* **1.** rasend, tobend: *the* ~ *crowd;* **2.** → *maddening.*
'mad-,doc·tor *s.* Irrenarzt *m.*
made [meɪd] **I** *pret. u. p.p. von make;* **II** *adj.* **1.** (künstlich) hergestellt: ~ *dish* aus mehreren Zutaten zs.-gestelltes Gericht; ~ *gravy* künstliche Bratensoße; ~ *road* befestigte Straße; *m ~ of wood* aus Holz, Holz...; *English-*~ ♀ Artikel englischer Fabrikation; **2.** gemacht, arriviert: *a* ~ *man; he had got it* ~ F er hatte es geschafft; **3.** *körperlich* gebaut: *a well-*~ *man.*
,made|-to-'meas·ure, **,~-to-'or·der** *adj.* ♀ nach Maß angefertigt, Maß..., *a. fig.* maßgeschneidert, nach Maß; ~**-'up** *adj.* **1.** (frei) erfunden: *a* ~ *story;* **2.** geschminkt; **3.** ♀ Fertig..., Fabrik...: ~ *clothes* Konfektionskleidung *f.*
'mad·house *s.* Irren-, *fig. a.* Tollhaus *n.*
mad·ly ['mædlɪ] *adv.* **1.** wie verrückt, wie wild: *they worked* ~ *all night;* **2.** F schrecklich, wahnsinnig: ~ *in love;* **3.** verrückt(erweise).
'mad·man [-mən] *s.* [*irr.*] Verrückte(r) *m*, Irre(r) *m.*
mad·ness ['mædnɪs] *s.* **1.** Wahnsinn *m*, Tollheit *f* (*a. fig.*); **2.** *bsd. Am.* Wut *f* (*at* über *acc.*).
mad·re·pore [,mædrɪ'pɔː] *s. zo.* Madre'pore *f*, 'Löcherko,ralle *f.*
mad·ri·gal ['mædrɪgl] *s.* ♪ Madri'gal *n.*
'mad,wom·an *s.* [*irr.*] Wahnsinnige *f*, Irre *f.*
mael·strom ['meɪlstrɒm] *s.* Mahlstrom *m*, Strudel *m* (*a. fig.*): ~ *of traffic* Verkehrsgewühl *n.*
Mae West [,meɪ'west] *s. sl.* **1.** ⚓ aufblasbare Schwimmweste; **2.** ✕ *Am.* Panzer *m* mit Zwillingsturm.
Maf·fi·a ['mæfɪə] → *Mafia.*
maf·fick ['mæfɪk] *v/i. Brit. obs.* ausgelassen feiern.
Ma·fi·a ['mæfɪə] *s.* Mafia *f;* **ma·fi·o·so** [,mæfɪ'əʊsəʊ] *pl.* **-sos** *od.* **-si** [-sɪ] *s.* Mafi'oso *m.*
mag¹ [mæg] F für *magazine* 4.
mag² [mæg] ⚙ *sl.* für *magneto:* ~ *generator* Magnetodynamo *m.*
mag·a·zine [,mægə'ziːn] *s.* **1.** ✕ a) ('Pulver)Maga,zin *n*, Muniti'onslager *n*, b) Versorgungslager *n*, c) Maga'zin *n* (*in Mehrladewaffen*): ~ *gun*, ~ *rifle* Mehrladegewehr *n;* **2.** ⚙ Maga'zin *n* (*a. Computer*), Vorratsbehälter *m;* **3.** ♀ Maga'zin *n*, Speicher *m*, Lagerhaus *n; fig.* Vorrats-, Kornkammer *f* (*fruchtbares Gebiet*); **4.** Maga'zin *n*, (*oft illustrierte*) Zeitschrift.
mag·da·len ['mægdəlɪn] *s. fig.* Magda'lena *f*, reuige Sünderin.

ma·gen·ta [mə'dʒentə] **I** *s.* 🜊 Ma'genta (-rot) *n*, Fuch'sin *n*; **II** *adj.* ma'gentarot, dunkelrot.

mag·got ['mægət] *s.* **1.** *zo.* Made *f*, Larve *f*; **2.** *fig.* Grille *f*; **'mag·got·y** [-tɪ] *adj.* **1.** madig; **2.** *fig.* schrullig.

Ma·gi ['meɪdʒaɪ] *s. pl.*: *the (three)* ~ die (drei) Weisen aus dem Morgenland, die Heiligen Drei Könige.

mag·ic ['mædʒɪk] **I** *s.* **1.** Ma'gie *f*, Zaube'rei *f*; **2.** Zauber(kraft *f*) *m (a. fig.)*: *it works like* ~ es ist die reinste Hexerei; **II** *adj.* (□ *~ally*) **3.** magisch, Wunder..., Zauber...: ~ *carpet* fliegender Teppich; ~ *eye* ⚡ magisches Auge; ~ *formula* Patentrezept *n*, -lösung *f*; ~ *lamp* Wunderlampe *f*; ~ *lantern* Laterna *f* magica; ~ *square* magisches Quadrat; **4.** zauberhaft: ~ *beauty*; **'mag·i·cal** [-kl] → *magic* II.

ma·gi·cian [mə'dʒɪʃn] *s.* **1.** Magier *m*, Zauberer *m*; **2.** Zauberkünstler *m*.

mag·is·te·ri·al [,mædʒɪ'stɪərɪəl] *adj.* □ **1.** obrigkeitlich, behördlich; **2.** maßgeblich; **3.** herrisch.

mag·is·tra·cy ['mædʒɪstrəsɪ] *s.* **1.** ⚖️, *pol.* Amt *e-s magistrate*; **2.** Richterschaft *f*; **3.** *pol.* Verwaltung *f*; **mag·is·tral** [mə'dʒɪstrəl] *adj. pharm.* magist·'ral *(nach ärztlicher Vorschrift)*; **'mag·is·trate** [-reɪt] *s.* **1.** a) ⚖️ Richter *m* (an e-m *magistrates' court*), b) *(police)* ~ *Am.* Poli'zeirichter *m*; **2.** (Ver'waltungs)Be,amte(r) *m*: *chief* ~ *Am.* a) Präsi'dent *m*, b) Gouver'neur *m*, c) Bürgermeister *m*; **mag·is·trates' court** *s.* ⚖️ erstinstanzliches Gericht für einfache Fälle.

mag·lev ['mæglev] *s.* 🚄 Ma'gnet(schwebe)bahn *f*.

Mag·na C(h)ar·ta [,mægnə'kɑːtə] *s.* **1.** *hist.* Magna Charta *f (der große Freibrief des englischen Adels [1215])*; **2.** Grundgesetz *n*.

mag·na·nim·i·ty [,mægnə'nɪmətɪ] *s.* Edelmut *m*, Großmut *f*; **mag·nan·i·mous** [mæg'nænɪməs] *adj.* □ großmütig, hochherzig.

mag·nate ['mægneɪt] *s.* **1.** Ma'gnat *m*: a) 'Großindustri,elle(r) *m*, b) Großgrundbesitzer *m*; **2.** Größe *f*, einflussreiche Per'sönlichkeit.

mag·ne·sia [mæg'niːʃə] *s.* 🜊 Ma'gnesia *f*, Ma'gnesiumo,xid *n*; **mag·ne·sian** [-ʃn] *adj.* **1.** Magnesia...; **2.** Magnesium...; **mag·ne·si·um** [-izjəm] *s.* 🜊 Ma'gnesium *n*.

mag·net ['mægnɪt] *s.* Ma'gnet *m (a. fig.)*; **mag·net·ic** [mæg'netɪk] *adj.* (□ *~ally*) **1.** ma'gnetisch, Magnet...(-feld, -kompass, -nadel, -pol etc.): ~ *attraction* magnetische Anziehung(skraft) *(a. fig.)*; ~ *declination* Missweisung *f*; ~ *resonance imaging* 🩻 Kernspintomo,gra,phie *f*; ~ *strip (od. stripe)* Magnetstreifen *m (auf Kreditkarte etc.)*; ~ *stripe* Magnetstreifen *m (bsd. Tonspur auf Film)*; ~ *tape* Magnet(ton)band *n*; ~ *tape recorder* Magnettongerät *n*; **2.** *fig.* faszinierend, fesselnd, ma'gnetisch; **mag·net·ics** [mæg'netɪks] *s. pl. (mst sg. konstr.)* Wissenschaft *f* vom Magne·'tismus; **'mag·net·ism** [-tɪzəm] *s.* **1.** *phys.* Magne'tismus *m*; **2.** *fig.* (ma'gnetische) Anziehungskraft; **mag·net·i·za·tion** [,mægnɪtaɪ'zeɪʃn] *s.* Magnetisierung *f*; **'mag·net·ize** [-taɪz] *v/t.* **1.** magnetisieren; **2.** *fig.* (wie ein Ma'gnet) anziehen, fesseln; **'mag·net·iz·er** [-taɪzə] *s.* ⚡ Magneti'seur *m*.

mag·ne·to [mæg'niːtəʊ] *pl.* **-tos** *s.* ⚡ Ma'gnetzünder *m*.

magneto- [mægniːtəʊ] *in Zssgn* Magne-

to...; **mag·ne·to·e·lec·tric** [mæg,niːtəʊɪ'lektrɪk] *adj.* ma'gnetoe,lektrisch.

mag·ni·fi·ca·tion [,mægnɪfɪ'keɪʃn] *s.* **1.** Vergrößern *n*; **2.** Vergrößerung *f*; **3.** *phys.* Vergrößerungsstärke *f*; **4.** ⚡ Verstärkung *f*.

mag·nif·i·cence [mæg'nɪfɪsns] *s.* Großartigkeit *f*, Herrlichkeit *f*; **mag'nif·i·cent** [-nt] *adj.* □ großartig, prächtig, herrlich *(alle a.* F *fig.)*.

mag·ni·fi·er ['mægnɪfaɪə] *s.* **1.** Vergrößerungsglas *n*, Lupe *f*; **2.** ⚡ Verstärker *m*; **3.** Verherrlicher *m*; **mag·ni·fy** ['mægnɪfaɪ] *v/t. opt. u. fig.* **1.** vergrößern: *~ing glass* → *magnifier* 1; **2.** *fig.* aufbauschen; **3.** ⚡ verstärken.

mag·nil·o·quence [mæg'nɪləʊkwəns] *s.* **1.** Großspreche'rei *f*; **2.** Schwulst *m*, Bom'bast *m*; **mag'nil·o·quent** [-nt] *adj.* □ **1.** großsprecherisch; **2.** hochtrabend, bom'bastisch.

mag·ni·tude ['mægnɪtjuːd] *s.* Größe *f*, Größenordnung *f (a. ast., ♄)*, *fig. a.* Ausmaß *n*, Schwere *f*: *a star of the first* ~ ein Stern erster Größe; *of the first* ~ von äußerster Wichtigkeit.

mag·no·li·a [mæg'nəʊljə] *s.* 🌿 Ma'gnolie *f*.

mag·num ['mægnəm] *s.* Zwei'quartflasche *f (etwa 2 l enthaltend)*; ~ **o·pus** [-'əʊpəs] *s.* Meister-, Hauptwerk *n*.

mag·pie ['mægpaɪ] *s.* **1.** *zo.* Elster *f*; **2.** *fig.* Schwätzer(in); **3.** *fig.* sammelwütiger Mensch; **4.** *Scheibenschießen:* zweiter Ring von außen.

ma·gus ['meɪgəs] *pl.* **-gi** [-dʒaɪ] *s.* **1.** ♈ *antiq. persischer* Priester; **2.** Zauberer *m*; **3.** *a.* ♈ *sg. von Magi*.

ma·ha·ra·ja(h) [,mɑːhə'rɑːdʒə] *s.* Maha'radscha *m*; **,ma·ha'ra·nee** [-ɑːniː] *s.* Maha'rani *f*.

mahl·stick ['mɔːlstɪk] → *maulstick*.

ma·hog·a·ny [mə'hɒgənɪ] **I** *s.* **1.** 🌿 Maha'gonibaum *m*; **2.** Maha'goni(holz) *n*; **3.** Maha'goni(farbe *f*) *n*; **4.** *have (od. put)* *one's feet under s.o.'s* ~ F j-s Gastfreundschaft genießen; **II** *adj.* **5.** Mahagoni...; **6.** maha'gonifarben.

ma·hout [mə'haʊt] *s. Brit. Ind.* Ele·'fantentreiber *m*.

maid [meɪd] *s.* **1.** (junges) Mädchen, *poet. u. iro.* Maid *f*: ~ *of hono(u)r* a) Ehren-, Hofdame *f*, b) *Am.* erste Brautjungfer; *old* ~ alte Jungfer; **2.** (Dienst-)Mädchen *n*, Magd *f*: ~*-of-all-work bsd. fig.* Mädchen für alles; **3.** *poet.* Jungfrau *f*: *the* ♈ *(of Orleans)*.

maid·en ['meɪdn] **I** *s.* **1.** mädchenhaft, Mädchen...: ~ *name* Mädchenname *m e-r Frau*; **2.** jungfräulich, unberührt *(a. fig.)*: ~ *soil*; **3.** unverheiratet: ~ *aunt*; **4.** Jungfern..., Antritts...: ~ *flight* ✈ Jungfernflug *m*; ~ *speech parl.* Jungfernrede *f*; ~ *voyage* ⚓ Jungfernfahrt *f*; **II** *s.* **5.** → *maid* 1; **6.** *Scot. hist.* Guillo·'tine *f*; **7.** *Rennsport:* a) Maiden *n (Pferd, das noch nie gesiegt hat)*, b) Rennen *n* für Maidens; **'~·hair (fern)** *s.* 🌿 Frauenhaar(farn *m*) *n*; **'~·head** *s.* **1.** → *maidenhood*; **2.** *anat.* Jungfernhäutchen *n*; **'~·hood** [-hʊd] *s.* **1.** Jungfräulichkeit *f*, Jungfernschaft *f*; **2.** Jung·'mädchenzeit *f*.

maid·en·like ['meɪdnlaɪk], **'maid·en·ly** [-lɪ] *adj.* **1.** → *maiden* 1; **2.** jungfräulich, züchtig.

'maid,serv·ant → *maid* 2.

mail¹ [meɪl] **I** *s.* **1.** Post(sendung) *f*, *bsd.* Brief- *od.* Pa'ketpost *f*: *by* ~ *Am.* mit der Post; *by return* ~ *Am.* postwendend, umgehend; *incoming* ~ Posteingang *m*; *outgoing* ~ Postausgang *m*; **2.** Briefbeutel *m*, Postsack *m*; **3.** Post®

(-dienst *m*) *f*: *the Federal* ⚲s *Am.* die Bundespost; **4.** Postversand *m*; **5.** Postauto *n*, -boot *n*, -bote *m*, -flugzeug *n*, -zug *m*; **II** *adj.* **6.** Post...: ~ *boat* Post-, Paketboot *n*; **III** *v/t.* **7.** *bsd. Am.* (ab-)schicken, aufgeben; zuschicken *(to dat.)*: *~ing list* 💌 Adressenliste *f*, -kartei *f*.

mail² [meɪl] **I** *s.* **1.** Kettenpanzer *m*: *coat of* ~ Panzerhemd *n*; **2.** (Ritter-) Rüstung *f*; **3.** *zo.* Panzer *m*; **II** *v/t.* **4.** panzern.

mail·a·ble ['meɪləbl] *adj. Am.* postversandfähig.

'mail·bag *s.* Postbeutel *m*; **'~·box** *s.* **1.** *Am.* Briefkasten *m*; **2.** *Computer etc.*: Mailbox *f (elektronischer Briefkasten)*; **'~·car** *s. Am.* Postwagen *m*; **'~,car·ri·er** *s.* → *mailman*; **'~·clad** *adj.* gepanzert; **'~·coach** *s. Brit.* **1.** Postwagen *m*; **2.** *hist.* Postkutsche *f*.

mailed [meɪld] *adj.* gepanzert *(a. zo.)*: *the* ~ *fist fig.* die eiserne Faust.

mail·ing ['meɪlɪŋ] *s.* Mailing *n*, (Werbe)Rundschreiben *n*; ~ **list** *s. Internet:* Mailing-Liste *f (mit E-Mail-Adressen)*.

'mail·man [-mən] *s. [irr.] Am.* Briefträger *m*; ~ **or·der** *s.* 💌 Bestellung *f (von Waren)* durch die Post; **'~-,or·der** *adj.* Postversand...: ~ *business* Versandhandel *m*; ~ *catalog(ue)* Versandhauskatalog *m*; ~ *house* (Post)Versandgeschäft *n*; **'~·shot** *s. Brit.* Mailing *n*, Werbebrief *m*.

maim [meɪm] *v/t.* verstümmeln *(a. fig. Text)*; zum Krüppel machen; lähmen *(a. fig.)*.

main [meɪn] **I** *adj.* □ → *mainly*; **1.** Haupt..., größt, wichtigst, vorwiegend, hauptsächlich: ~ *clause ling.* Hauptsatz *m*; ~ *deck* ⚓ Hauptdeck *n*; ~ *gird·er* 🔺 Längsträger *m*; ~ *office* Hauptbüro *n*; ~ *road* Hauptverkehrsstraße *f*; *the* ~ *sea* die offene *od.* hohe See; ~ *station* a) *teleph.* Hauptanschluss *m*, b) Hauptbahnhof *m*; *the* ~ *thing* die Hauptsache; *by* ~ *force* mit äußerster Kraft, mit (aller) Gewalt; **2.** ⚓ groß, Groß...: ~ *brace* Großbrasse *f*; **II** *s.* **3.** *mst pl.* a) Haupt(gas- etc.)leitung *f (gas)* ~s; *(water)* ~s, b) ⚡ Haupt-, Stromleitung *f*, c) (Strom)Netz *n*: *operating on the* ~s, ~s-*operated* mit Netzanschluss *od.* -betrieb; ~s *adapter* Netzteil *n*, b) Hauptkabel *n*; **5.** 🚄 *Am.* Hauptlinie *f*; **6.** Hauptsache *f*, Kern *m*: *in (Am. a. for) the* ~ hauptsächlich, in der Hauptsache; **7.** *poet.* die hohe See; **8.** → *might¹* 2; ~ *chance s.*: *have an eye to the* ~ s-n eigenen Vorteil im Auge haben; **'~·frame** *s. a.* ~ *computer* Großrechner *m*, Zent'ralrechner *m*; ~ *fuse* ⚡ Hauptsicherung *f*; **'~·land** [-lənd] *s.* Festland *n*, *bsd.* die ~ *land*; **1.** 🚄 etc., a. ⚔ Hauptlinie *f*: ~ *of resistance* Hauptkampflinie *f*; **2.** *Am.* Hauptverkehrsstraße *f*; **3.** *sl.* a) Hauptvene *f*, b) 'Schuss' *m (Heroin etc.)*; **'~·line** *v/i. sl.* ,fixen'; **'~,lin·er** *s.* ,Fixer(in)'.

main·ly ['meɪnlɪ] *adv.* hauptsächlich, vorwiegend.

'main·mast ['meɪnmɑːst; ⚓ -məst] *s.* ⚓ Großmast *m*; ~ **mem·o·ry** *s. Computer:* Hauptspeicher *m*; **'~·sail** ['meɪnseɪl; ⚓ -sl] *s.* ⚓ Großsegel *n*; **'~·spring** *s.* **1.** Hauptfeder *f (Uhr etc.)*; **2.** *fig.* (Haupt-)Triebfeder *f*, treibende Kraft; **'~·stay** *s.* **1.** ⚓ Großstag *n*; **2.** *fig.* Hauptstütze *f*; **'~·stream** *s. fig.* Hauptströmung *f*; ♈ **Street** *adj. Am.* provinzi'ell-materia'listisch.

main·tain [meɪn'teɪn] *v/t.* **1.** *Zustand, gute Beziehungen etc.* (aufrecht)erhalten, *e-e Haltung etc.* beibehalten, *Ruhe u. Ordnung etc.* (be)wahren: **~ a price** ♱ e-n Preis halten; **2.** in'stand halten, pflegen, ⚙ *a.* warten; **3.** *Briefwechsel etc.* unter'halten, (weiter)führen; **4.** (*in e-m bestimmten Zustand*) lassen, bewahren: **~ s.th. in (an) excellent condition**; **5.** *Familie etc.* unter'halten, versorgen; **6.** behaupten (*that* dass, *to* zu); **7.** *Meinung, Recht etc.* verfechten; auf *e-r Forderung* bestehen: **~ an action** ⚖ e-e Klage anhängig machen; **8.** *j-n* unter'stützen, *j-m* beipflichten; ⚖ *e-e Prozesspartei* 'widerrechtlich unter'stützen; **9.** nicht aufgeben, behaupten: **~ one's ground** *bsd. fig.* sich behaupten; **main·tain·a·ble** [-nəbl] *adj.* verfechtbar, haltbar; **main·tain·er** [-nə] *s.* Unter'stützer *m* (*Meinung etc.*), b) Versorger *m*; **main·tain·or** [-nə] *s.* ⚖ außenstehender Pro'zesstreiber; **main·te·nance** ['meɪntənəns] *s.* **1.** In'standhaltung *f*, Erhaltung *f*; **2.** ⚙ Wartung *f*: **~ man** Wartungsmonteur *m*; **~-free** wartungsfrei; **3.** 'Unterhalt(smittel *pl.*) *m*: **~ grant** Unterhaltszuschuss *m*; **~ order** ⚖ Anordnung *f* von Unterhaltszahlungen; **4.** Aufrechterhaltung *f*, Beibehalten *n*; **5.** Behauptung *f*, Verfechtung *f*; **6.** ⚖ 'ille‚gale Unter'stützung e-r pro'zessführenden Par'tei.

'main|·top *s.* ⚓ Großmars *m*; **~ yard** *s.* ⚓ Großrah(e) *f*.

mai·son·(n)ette [‚meɪzə'net] *s.* **1.** Maiso'nette *f*; **2.** Einliegerwohnung *f*.

maize [meɪz] *s. Brit.* 🌿 Mais *m*.

ma·jes·tic [mə'dʒestɪk] *adj.* (□ **~ally**) maje'stätisch; **maj·es·ty** ['mædʒəstɪ] *s.* **1.** Maje'stät *f*: *His* (*Her*) 👑 Seine (Ihre) Majestät; *Your* 👑 Eure Majestät; **2.** *fig.* Maje'stät *f*, Erhabenheit *f*, Hoheit *f*.

ma·jol·i·ca [mə'jɒlɪkə] *s.* Ma'jolika *f*.

ma·jor ['meɪdʒə] **I** *s.* **1.** Ma'jor *m*; **2.** ⚖ Volljährige(r *m*) *f*, Mündige(r *m*) *f*; **3.** *hinter Eigennamen:* der Ältere; **4.** ♪ a) Dur *n*, b) 'Durak‚kord *m*, c) Durtonart *f*; **5.** *phls.* a) *a.* **~ term** Oberbegriff *m*, b) *a.* **~ premise** Obersatz *m*; **6.** *univ. Am.* Hauptfach *n*; **II** *adj.* **7.** größer (*a. fig.*); *fig.* bedeutend: **~ attack** große Großangriff *m*; **~ event** *bsd. sport* Großveranstaltung *f*, *weitS.* ‚große Sache'; **~ repair** größere Reparatur; **~ shareholder** Großaktionär(in); → **operation** 2; **8.** ⚖ volljährig, mündig; **9.** ♪ a) groß (*Terz etc.*), b) Dur...: **~ key** Durtonart *f*; **C ~** C-Dur *n*; **III** *v/t.* **10.** (*v/i.* **~ in**) *Am.* als Hauptfach studieren (*in*); **‚~·'gen·er·al** *s.* ⚔ Gene'ralma‚jor *m*.

ma·jor·i·ty [mə'dʒɒrətɪ] *s.* **1.** Mehrheit *f*: **~ of votes** (Stimmen)Mehrheit, Majorität *f*; **~ decision** Mehrheitsbeschluss *m*; ♱ **~ holding** Mehrheitsbeteiligung *f*; **~ leader** *Am.* Fraktionsführer *m* der Mehrheitspartei; **~ rule** Mehrheitsregierung *f*; **in the ~ of cases** in der Mehrzahl der Fälle; **join the ~** a) sich der Mehrheit anschließen, b) zu den Vätern versammelt werden (*sterben*); **win by a large ~** mit großer Mehrheit gewinnen; **2.** ⚖ Voll-, Großjährigkeit *f*; **3.** ⚔ Ma'jorsrang *m*, -stelle *f*.

ma·jor| league *s. sport Am.* oberste Spielklasse; **~ mode** *s.* ♪ Dur(tonart *f*) *n*; **~ scale** *s.* Durtonleiter *f*.

ma·jus·cule ['mædʒəskjuːl] *s.* Ma'juskel *f*, großer Anfangsbuchstabe.

make [meɪk] **I** *s.* a) Mach-, Bauart *f*, Form *f*, b) Erzeugnis *n*, Fabri'kat *n*: **our own ~** (unser) eigenes Fabrikat; **of**

best English ~ beste englische Qualität; **2.** *Mode:* Schnitt *m*, Fas'son *f*; **3.** ♱ a) (Fa'brik)Marke *f*, b) ⚙ Typ *m*, Bau(-art *f*) *m*; **4.** (*Körper*)Bau *m*; **5.** Anfertigung *f*, Herstellung *f*; **6.** ⚡ Schließen *n* (*Stromkreis*): **be at ~** geschlossen sein; **7. be on the ~** *sl.* a) auf Geld (*od.* e-n Vorteil) aussein, ‚schwer dahinterher' sein, b) auf ein (sexuelles) Abenteuer aus sein; **II** *v/t.* [*irr.*] **8.** *allg. z. B. Einkäufe, Einwände, Feuer, Reise, Versuch* machen; *Frieden* schließen; *e-e Rede* halten; → **face** 2, **war** 1 *etc.*; **9.** machen: a) anfertigen, herstellen, erzeugen (*from, of, out of* von, aus), b) verarbeiten, bilden, formen (*to, into* in *acc.*, zu), c) *Tee etc.* (zu)bereiten, d) *Gedicht etc.* verfassen; **10.** errichten, bauen, *Garten, Weg etc.* anlegen; **11.** (er)schaffen: *God made man* Gott schuf den Menschen; *you are made for this job* du bist für diese Arbeit wie geschaffen; **12.** *fig.* machen zu: *he made her his wife*; *to ~ enemies of* sich zu Feinden machen; **13.** ergeben, bilden, entstehen lassen: *many brooks ~ a river*; *oxygen and hydrogen ~ water* Wasserstoff u. Sauerstoff bilden Wasser; **14.** verursachen: a) *ein Geräusch, Lärm, Mühe, Schwierigkeiten* machen, b) bewirken, (mit sich) bringen: *prosperity ~s contentment*; **15.** (er)geben, den Stoff abgeben zu, dienen als (*Sache*): *this ~s a good article* das gibt e-n guten Artikel; *this book ~s good reading* dieses Buch liest sich gut; **16.** sich erweisen als (*Person*): *he would ~ a good salesman* er würde e-n guten Verkäufer abgeben; *she made him a good wife* sie war ihm e-e gute Frau; **17.** bilden, (aus)machen: *this ~s the tenth time* ist das zehnte Mal; → **difference** 1, **one** 6, **party** 2; **18.** (*mit adj., p.p. etc.*) machen: **~ angry** zornig machen, erzürnen; **~ known** bekannt machen. od. geben; **~ make good**; **19.** (*mit folgendem s.*) machen zu, ernennen zu: *they made him a general*, *he was made a general* er wurde zum General ernannt; *he made himself a martyr* er wurde zum Märtyrer; **20.** *mit inf.* (*act. ohne to, pass. mit to*) *j-n* veranlassen, lassen, bringen, zwingen *od.* nötigen zu: **~ s.o. wait** j-n warten lassen; *we made him talk* wir brachten ihn zum Sprechen; *they made him repeat it* man ließ es ihn wiederholen; **~ s.th. do**, **~ do with s.th.** mit et. auskommen, sich mit et. behelfen; **21.** *fig.* machen: **~ much of** a) viel Wesens um et. *od. j-n* machen, b) sich viel aus et. machen, viel von et. halten; → **best** 7, **most** 3, **nothing** Redew.; **22.** sich e-e Vorstellung von et. machen, et. halten für: *what do you ~ of it?* was halten Sie davon?; **23.** F *j-n* halten für: *I ~ him a greenhorn*; **24.** schätzen auf (*acc.*): *I ~ the distance three miles*; **25.** feststellen: *I ~ it a quarter to five* nach m-r Uhr ist es Viertel vor fünf; **26.** erfolgreich 'durchführen; → **escape** 9; **27.** *j-m* zum Erfolg verhelfen, *j-s* Glück machen: *I can ~ and break you* ich kann aus Ihnen machen oder Sie auch fertig machen; **28.** sich *ein Vermögen etc.* erwerben, verdienen, *Geld, Profit etc.* machen, *Gewinn* erzielen; → **name** Redew.; **29.** ‚schaffen': a) *Strecke* zu'rücklegen: *can we ~ it in 3 hours?*, b) *Geschwindigkeit* erreichen: **~ 60 mph.**; **30.** F et. erreichen, ‚schaffen', *akademischen Grad* erlangen, *sport etc.* Punkte, *a. Schulno-*

te erzielen, *Zug* erwischen: **~ it** es schaffen; **~ the team** in die Mannschaft aufgenommen werden; **31.** *sl. Frau* ‚'umlegen' (*verführen*); **32.** ankommen in (*dat.*), erreichen: **~ port** ⚓ in den Hafen einlaufen; **33.** ⚓ sichten, ausmachen: **~ land**; **34.** *Brit. Mahlzeit* einnehmen; **35.** *Fest etc.* veranstalten; **36.** *Preis* festsetzen, machen; **37.** *Kartenspiel:* a) *Karten* mischen, b) *Stich* machen; **38.** ⚡ *Stromkreis* schließen; **39.** *ling. Plural etc.* bilden, werden zu; **40.** sich belaufen auf (*acc.*), ergeben, machen: *two and two ~ four* 2 u. 2 macht *od.* ist 4; **III** *v/i.* [*irr.*] **41.** sich anschicken, den Versuch machen (*to do* zu tun): *he made to go* er wollte eben gehen; **42.** (*to* nach) a) sich begeben *od.* wenden, b) führen, gehen (*Weg etc.*), sich erstrecken, c) fließen; **43.** einsetzen (*Ebbe, Flut*), (an)steigen (*Flut etc.*); **44. ~ as if** (*od.* **as though**) so tun als ob *od.* als wenn: **~ believe** (*that od.* **to do**) vorgeben (dass *od.* zu tun); **45. ~ like** *Am. sl.* sich verhalten wie: **~ like a father**;

Zssgn mit prp.:

make| af·ter *v/i. obs. j-m* nachsetzen, *j-n* verfolgen; **~ a·gainst** *v/i.* **1.** ungünstig sein für, schaden (*dat.*); **2.** sprechen gegen (*a. fig.*); **~ for** *v/i.* **1.** a) zugehen auf (*acc.*), sich aufmachen nach, zustreben (*dat.*), b) ⚓ lossteuern (*a. fig.*) *od.* Kurs halten auf (*acc.*), c) sich stürzen auf (*acc.*); **2.** beitragen zu, förderlich sein *od.* dienen (*dat.*): *it makes for his advantage* es wirkt sich für ihn günstig aus; *the aerial makes for better reception* die Antenne verbessert den Empfang; **~ to·ward(s)** *v/i.* zugehen auf (*acc.*), sich bewegen nach, sich nähern (*dat.*); **~ with** *v/i. Am. sl.* loslegen mit: **~ the feet!** nun lauf schon!

Zssgn mit adv.:

make| a·way *v/i.* sich da'vonmachen: **~ with** a) sich davonmachen mit (*Geld etc.*), b) *et. od. j-n* beseitigen, aus dem Weg(e) räumen, c) *Geld etc.* durchbringen, d) sich entledigen (*gen.*); **~ good I** *v/t.* **1.** a) (wieder) gutmachen, b) ersetzen, vergüten: **~ a deficit** ein Defizit decken; **2.** begründen, rechtfertigen, nachweisen; **3.** *Versprechen, sein Wort* halten; **4.** den *Erwartungen* entsprechen; **5.** *Flucht etc.* glücklich bewerkstelligen; **6.** (*berufliche etc.*) Stellung ausbauen; **II** *v/i.* **7.** sich 'durchsetzen, sein Ziel erreichen; **8.** sich bewähren, den *Erwartungen* entsprechen; **~ off** *v/i.* sich da'vonmachen, ausreißen (*with* mit *Geld etc.*); **~ out I** *v/t.* **1.** *Scheck etc.* ausstellen; *Urkunde* ausfertigen; *Liste etc.* aufstellen; **2.** ausmachen, erkennen; **3.** *Sachverhalt etc.* feststellen, herausbekommen; **4.** *a) j-n* ausfindig machen, b) aus *j-m od.* et. klug werden; **5.** entziffern; **6.** a) behaupten, b) beweisen, c) *j-n als Lügner etc.* hinstellen; **7.** *Am.* mühsam zustande bringen; **8.** *Summe* voll machen; **9.** halten für; **II** *v/i.* **10.** *bsd. Am.* F Erfolg haben: *how did you ~?* wie haben Sie abgeschnitten?; **11.** *bsd. Am.* (*mit j-m*) auskommen; **12.** vorgeben, (so) tun (als ob); **~ o·ver** *v/t.* **1.** *Eigentum* über'tragen, -'eignen, vermachen; **2.** 'umbauen; *Anzug etc.* 'umarbeiten; **~ up I** *v/t.* **1.** bilden, zs.-setzen: *be made up of* bestehen *od.* sich zs.-setzen aus; **2.** *Arznei, Bericht etc.* zs.-stellen; *Schriftstück* aufsetzen; *Liste etc.* aufstellen; *Paket* (ver)packen, verschnüren; **3.** *a. thea.* zu-

'rechtmachen, schminken, pudern; **4.** *Geschichte etc.* sich ausdenken, a. b.s. erfinden: *a made-up story*; **5.** a) *Versäumtes* nachholen; → *leeway* 2, b) 'wiedergewinnen: ~ *lost ground*; **6.** ersetzen, vergüten; **7.** *Rechnung, Konten* ausgleichen; *Bilanz* ziehen; → *account* 5; **8.** *Streit etc.* beilegen; **9.** ver'vollständigen, *Fehlendes* ergänzen, *Betrag, Gesellschaft etc.* voll machen; **10.** *make it up* a) es wieder gutmachen, b) → 17; **11.** *typ.* um'brechen; **II** *v/i.* **12.** sich zu'rechtmachen, *bsd.* sich pudern *od.* schminken; **13.** (*for*) Ersatz leisten, als Ersatz dienen (für), vergüten (*acc.*); **14.** aufholen, wieder gutmachen, wettmachen (*for acc.*): ~ *for lost time* die verlorene Zeit wieder wettzumachen suchen; **15.** *Am.* sich nähern (*to dat.*); **16.** (*to*) F (*j-m*) schöntun, sich anbiedern (bei *j-m*), sich her'anmachen (an *j-n*); **17.** sich versöhnen *od.* wieder vertragen (*with* mit).

make| and break s. ⚡ Unter'brecher *m*; **,~-and-'break** *adj.* ⚡ zeitweilig unter'brochen: ~ *contact* Unterbrecherkontakt *m*; **'~-be,lieve I** *s.* **1.** a) Verstellung *f*, b) Heuche'lei *f*; **2.** Vorwand *m*; **3.** Schein *m*, Spiegelfechte'rei *f*; **II** *adj.* **4.** vorgeblich, scheinbar, falsch: ~ *world* Scheinwelt *f*.

mak·er ['meɪkə] *s.* **1.** a) Macher *m*, Verfertiger *m*; Aussteller(in) *e-r Urkunde*, b) ✞ Hersteller *m*, Erzeuger *m*; **2.** *the* ⚴ *der* Schöpfer (*Gott*): *meet one's* ~ das Zeitliche segnen.

'make|-,read·y *s. typ.* Zurichtung *f*; **'~-shift I** *s.* Notbehelf *m*; **II** *adj.* behelfsmäßig, Behelfs..., Not...

'make-up *s.* **1.** Aufmachung *f*: a) *Film etc.*: Ausstattung *f*, Kostümierung *f*, Maske *f*: ~ *man* Maskenbildner *m*, b) Verpackung *f*, ✞ Ausstattung *f*: ~ *charge Schneiderei*: Macherlohn *m*; **2.** Schminke *f*, Puder *m*; **3.** Make-up *n*: a) Schminken *n*, b) Pudern *n*; **4.** *fig. humor.* Aufmachung *f*, (Ver)Kleidung *f*; **5.** Zs.-setzung *f*; *sport* (*Mannschafts*)Aufstellung *f*; **6.** Körperbau *m*; **7.** Veranlagung *f*, Na'tur *f*; **8.** *fig. humor.* Am. erfundene Geschichte; **9.** *typ.* 'Umbruch *m*.

'make-weight *s.* **1.** (Gewichts)Zugabe *f*, Zusatz *m*; **2.** Gegengewicht *n* (*a. fig.*); b) *fig.* a) Lückenbüßer *m* (*Person*), b) Notbehelf *m*.

mak·ing ['meɪkɪŋ] *s.* **1.** Machen *n*: *this is of my own* ~ das habe ich selbst gemacht; **2.** Erzeugung *f*, Herstellung *f*, Fabrikati'on *f*: *be in the* ~ a. *fig.* im Werden *od.* im Kommen *od.* in der Entwicklung sein; **3.** a) Zs.-setzung *f*, b) Verfassung *f*, c) Bau(art *f*) *m*, Aufbau *m*, d) Aufmachung *f*; **4.** Glück *n*, Chance *f*: *this will be the* ~ *of him* damit ist er ein gemachter Mann; **5.** *pl.* ('Roh)Materi,al *n* (*a. fig.*): *he has the* ~*s of* er hat das Zeug *od.* die Anlagen zu; **6.** *pl.* Pro'fit *m*, Verdienst *m*; **7.** *pl.* F *die* (nötigen) Zutaten *pl.*

mal- [mæl] *in Zssgn* a) schlecht, b) mangelhaft, c) übel, d) Miss..., un...

Mal·a·chi ['mæləkaɪ], *a.* **Mal·a·chi·as** [ˌmælə'kaɪəs] *npr. u. s. bibl.* (das Buch) Male'achi *m od.* Mala'chias *m*.

mal·a·chite ['mæləkaɪt] *s. min.* Mala-'chit *m*, Kupferspat *m*.

mal·ad·just·ed [ˌmælə'dʒʌstɪd] *adj. psych.* nicht angepasst, mi'lieugestört; **,mal·ad'just·ment** [-smənt] *s.* **1.** mangelnde Anpassung, Mi'lieustörung *f*; **2.** ⚙ Falscheinstellung *f*; **3.** 'Missverhältnis *n*.

'mal·ad,min·is'tra·tion *s.* **1.** schlechte

Verwaltung; **2.** *pol.* 'Misswirtschaft *f*.

,mal·a'droit *adj.* □ **1.** ungeschickt; **2.** taktlos.

mal·a·dy ['mælədɪ] *s.* Krankheit *f*, Gebrechen *n*, Übel *n* (*a. fig.*).

ma·la fi·de [ˌmeɪlə'faɪdɪ] (*Lat.*) *adj. u. adv.* arglistig, ✗ bösgläubig.

ma·laise [mæ'leɪz] *s.* **1.** Unpässlichkeit *f*; **2.** *fig.* Unbehagen *n*.

mal·a·prop·ism ['mæləprɒpɪzəm] *s.* (lächerliche) Wortverwechslung, 'Missgriff *m*; **mal·ap·ro·pos** [ˌmæl'æprəpəʊ] **I** *adj.* **1.** unangebracht; **2.** unschicklich; **II** *adv.* **3.** a) zur Unzeit, b) im falschen Augenblick; **III** *s.* **4.** *et.* Unangebrachtes.

ma·lar ['meɪlə] *anat.* **I** *adj.* Backen...; **II** *s.* Backenknochen *m*.

ma·lar·i·a [mə'leərɪə] *s.* 🌿 Ma'laria *f*; **ma'lar·i·al** [-əl], **ma'lar·i·an** [-ən], **ma'lar·i·ous** [-rəs] *adj.* Malaria..., ma-'lariaverseucht.

ma·lar·k(e)y [mə'lɑːkɪ] *s. Am. sl.* ,Quatsch' *m*, ,Käse' *m*.

Ma·lay [mə'leɪ] **I** *s.* **1.** Ma'laie *m*, Ma'laiin *f*; **2.** Ma'laiisch *n*; **II** *adj.* **3.** ma'laiisch; **Ma'lay·an** [-erən] *adj.* ma'laiisch.

'mal·con,tent I *adj.* unzufrieden (*a. pol.*); **II** *s.* Unzufriedene(r *m*) *f*.

male [meɪl] **I** *adj.* **1.** männlich (*a. biol. u. ⚙*): ~ *child* Knabe *m*; ~ *choir* Männerchor *m*; ~ *cousin* Vetter *m*; ~ *model* Dressman *m*; ~ *nurse* Krankenpfleger *m*; ~ *plug* ⚙ Stecker *m*; ~ *prostitute* Strichjunge *m*; ~ *rhyme* männlicher Reim; ~ *screw* Schraube(nspindel) *f*; **2.** *weitS.* männlich, mannhaft; **II** *s.* **3.** a) Mann *m*, b) Knabe *m*; **4.** *zo.* Männchen *n*; **5.** 🌿 männliche Pflanze.

mal·e·dic·tion [ˌmælɪ'dɪkʃn] *s.* Fluch *m*, Verwünschung *f*; **,mal·e'dic·to·ry** [-ktərɪ] *adj.* verwünschend, Verwünschungs..., Fluch...

mal·e·fac·tor ['mælɪfæktə] *s.* Misse-, Übeltäter *m*; **'mal·e·fac·tress** [-trɪs] *s.* Misse-, Übeltäterin *f*.

ma·lef·ic [mə'lefɪk] *adj.* (□ ~*ally*) ruchlos, bösartig; **ma'lef·i·cent** [-ɪsnt] *adj.* **1.** bösartig; **2.** schädlich (*to* für *od. dat.*); **3.** verbrecherisch.

ma·lev·o·lence [mə'levələns] *s.* 'Missgunst *f*, Feindseligkeit *f* (*to* gegen), Böswilligkeit *f*; **ma'lev·o·lent** [-nt] *adj.* □ **1.** 'missgünstig, widrig (*Umstände etc.*); **2.** feindselig, böswillig, übel wollend.

mal·fea·sance [mæl'fiːzəns] *s.* ✗ strafbare Handlung.

,mal·for'ma·tion *s. bsd.* 🌿 'Missbildung *f*.

,mal·func·tion I *s.* **1.** 🌿 Funkti'onsstörung *f*; **2.** ⚙ schlechtes Funktionieren, Versagen *n*, De'fekt *m*; **II** *v/i.* **3.** schlecht funktionieren, de'fekt sein, versagen.

mal·ice ['mælɪs] *s.* **1.** Böswilligkeit *f*, Bosheit *f*; Arglist *f*, Tücke *f*; **2.** Groll *m*: *bear s.o.* ~ j-m grollen, e-n Groll gegen j-n hegen; **3.** ✗ (böse) Absicht, Vorsatz *m*: *with* ~ *aforethought* (*od. prepense*) vorsätzlich; **4.** (schelmische) Bosheit: *with* ~ boshaft, maliziös; **ma·li·cious** [mə'lɪʃəs] *adj.* □ **1.** böswillig, boshaft; **2.** arglistig, (heim)tückisch; **3.** gehässig, **4.** hämisch; **5.** ✗ böswillig, vorsätzlich; **6.** malizi'ös, boshaft; **ma'li·cious·ness** [mə'lɪʃəsnɪs] → *malice* 1, 2.

ma·lign [mə'laɪn] **I** *adj.* □ **1.** verderblich, schädlich; **2.** unheilvoll; **3.** böswillig; **4.** 🌿 bösartig; **II** *v/t.* **5.** verleumden, beschimpfen.

ma·lig·nan·cy [mə'lɪgnənsɪ] *s.* Böswilligkeit *f*, Bösartigkeit *f* (*a.* 🌿); Bosheit *f*; Arglist *f*; Schadenfreude *f*; **ma'lig-**

---

nant [-nt] **I** *adj.* □ **1.** böswillig; bösartig (*a.* 🌿); **2.** arglistig, (heim)tückisch; **3.** schadenfroh; **4.** gehässig; **II** *s.* **5.** *hist. Brit.* Roya'list *m*; **6.** Übelgesinnte(r *m*) *f*; **ma'lig·ni·ty** [-nətɪ] → *malignancy*.

ma·lin·ger [mə'lɪŋɡə] *v/i.* sich krank stellen, simulieren, ,sich drücken'; **ma'lin·ger·er** [-ərə] *s.* Simu'lant *m*, Drückeberger *m*.

mall¹ [mɔːl] *s.* **1.** Prome'nade(nweg *m*) *f*; **2.** Mittelstreifen *m* e-r Autobahn; **3.** *Am.* Einkaufszentrum, Fußgängerzone *f*.

mall² [mɔːl] *s. orn.* Sturmmöwe *f*.

mal·lard ['mæləd] *pl.* **-lards**, *coll.* **-lard** *s. orn.* Stockente *f*.

mal·le·a·ble ['mælɪəbl] *adj.* **1.** ⚙ a) (kalt-) hämmerbar, b) dehn-, streckbar, c) verformbar, **2.** *fig.* gefügig, geschmeidig; ~ *cast i·ron* ⚙ **1.** Tempereisen *n*; **2.** Temperguss *m*; ~ *i·ron* *s.* ⚙ **1.** a) Schmiedeeisen *n*, b) schmiedbarer Guss; **2.** → *malleable cast iron*.

mal·le·o·lar [mæ'liːələ] *adj. anat.* Knöchel...

mal·let ['mælɪt] *s.* **1.** Holzhammer *m*, Schlägel *m*; **2.** ⚙, ✗ Fäustel *m*; ~ *toe* 🌿 Hammerzehe *f*; **3.** *sport* Schlagholz *n*, Schläger *m*.

mal·low ['mæləʊ] *s.* 🌿 Malve *f*.

malm [mɑːm] *s. geol.* Malm *m*.

,mal·nu'tri·tion *s.* 'Unterernährung *f*, schlechte Ernährung.

mal·o·dor·ous [mæl'əʊdərəs] *adj.* übel riechend.

,mal'prac·tice *s.* **1.** Übeltat *f*; **2.** ✗ a) Vernachlässigung *f* der beruflichen Sorgfalt, b) Kunstfehler *m*, Fahrlässigkeit *f* des Arztes, c) Untreue *f* im Amt *etc.*

malt [mɔːlt] **I** *s.* **1.** Malz *n*: ~ *kiln* Malzdarre *f*; ~ *liquor* gegorener Malztrank, *bsd.* Bier *n*; **II** *v/t.* **2.** mälzen, malzen: ~*ed milk* Malzmilch *f*; **3.** unter Zusatz von Malz herstellen; **III** *v/i.* **4.** zu Malz werden.

Mal·tese [ˌmɔːl'tiːz] **I** *s. sg. u. pl.* **1.** a) Mal'teser(in), b) Malteser *pl.*; **2.** *ling.* Mal'tesisch *n*; **II** *adj.* **3.** mal'tesisch, Maltese...; ~ *cross* **s.** **1.** Mal'teserkreuz *n*; **2.** 🌿 Brennende Liebe.

'malt·house *s.* Mälze'rei *f*.

malt·ose ['mɔːltəʊs] *s.* 🌿 Malzzucker *m*.

,mal'treat *v/t.* **1.** schlecht behandeln, malträtieren; **2.** miss'handeln; **,mal'treat·ment** *s.* **1.** schlechte Behandlung; **2.** Miss'handlung *f*.

mal·ver·sa·tion [ˌmælvəˈseɪʃn] *s.* ✗ **1.** Amtsvergehen *n*; **2.** Veruntreuung *f*, 'Unterschlief *m*.

ma·mil·la [mæ'mɪlə] *pl.* **-lae** [-liː] *s.* **1.** *anat.* Brustwarze *f*; **2.** *zo.* Zitze *f*; **mam·il·lar·y** ['mæmɪlərɪ] *adj.* **1.** *anat.* Brustwarzen...; **2.** brustwarzenförmig.

mam·ma¹ [mə'mɑː] *s.* Mutti *f*.

mam·ma² ['mæmə] *pl.* **-mae** [-miː] *s.* **1.** *anat.* (weibliche) Brust, Brustdrüse *f*; **2.** *zo.* Zitze *f*, Euter *n*.

mam·mal ['mæml] *s. zo.* Säugetier *n*; **mam·ma·li·an** [mæˈmeɪljən] *zo.* **I** *s.* Säugetier *n*; **II** *adj.* Säugetier...

mam·ma·ry ['mæmərɪ] *adj.* **1.** *anat.* Brust(warzen)..., Milch...: ~ *gland* Milchdrüse *f*; **2.** *zo.* Euter...

mam·mil·la *etc. Am.* → *mamilla etc.*

mam·mo·gram ['mæməʊɡræm] *s.* 🌿 Mammo'gramm *n*; **mam·mo·gra·phy** [mæ'mɒɡrəfɪ] *s.* Mammogra'phie *f*.

mam·mon ['mæmən] *s.* Mammon *m*; **'mam·mon·ism** [-nɪzəm] *s.* Mammonsdienst *m*, Geldgier *f*.

mam·moth ['mæməθ] **I** *s. zo.* Mammut

n; **II** *adj.* Mammut...(-*baum, -unternehmen etc.*), riesig, Riesen...

mam·my ['mæmı] *s.* **1.** F Mami *f*; **2.** *Am. obs.* (schwarzes) Kindermädchen.

man [mæn] **I** *pl.* **men** [men] *s.* **1.** Mensch *m*; **2.** *oft 2 coll.* (*mst ohne the*) der Mensch, die Menschen *pl.*, die Menschheit: *rights of* ~ Menschenrechte; → *measure* 5; **3.** Mann *m*: ~ *about town* Lebemann; *the* ~ *in the street* der Mann auf der Straße, der Durchschnittsmensch; ~ *of God* Diener *m* Gottes; ~ *of letters* a) Literat *m*, Schriftsteller *m*, b) Gelehrter *m*; ~ *of all work* a) Faktotum *n*, b) Allerweltskerl *m*; ~ *of straw* Strohmann; ~ *of the world* Weltmann; ~ *of few* (*many*) *words* Schweiger *m* (Schwätzer *m*); *Oxford* ~ Oxforder (Akademiker) *m*; *I have known him* ~ *and boy* ich kenne ihn von Jugend auf; *be one's own* ~ a) sein eigener Herr sein, b) im Vollbesitz s-r Kräfte sein; *the* ~ *Smith* (besagter) Smith; *my good* ~! herablassend: mein lieber Herr!; → *honour* 1; **4.** *weitS.* a) Mann *m*, Per'son *f*, b) jemand, c) man: *a* ~ jemand; *any* ~ irgendjemand, jedermann; *no* ~ niemand; *few men* wenige (Leute); *every* ~ *jack* F jeder Einzelne; ~ *by* ~ Mann für Mann, einer nach dem andern; *as one* ~ wie 'ein Mann, geschlossen; *to a* ~ bis auf den letzten Mann; *give a* ~ *a chance* einem e-e Chance geben; *what can a* ~ *do in such a case?* was kann man da schon machen?; **5.** F Mensch *m*, Menschenskind *n*: ~ *alive!* Menschenskind!; *hurry up,* ~! Mensch, beeil dich!; **6.** (Ehe)Mann *m*: ~ *and wife* Mann u. Frau; **7.** a) Diener *m*, b) Angestellte(r) *m*, c) Arbeiter *m*: *men working* Baustelle (*Hinweis auf Verkehrsschildern*), d) *hist.* Lehnsmann *m*; **8.** ✕, ⚓ Mann *m*: a) Sol'dat *m*, b) ⚓ Ma'trose *m*, c) *pl.* Mannschaft *f*: ~ *on leave* Urlauber *m*; *20 men* zwanzig Mann; **9.** *der* Richtige: *be the* ~ *for s.th.* der Richtige für et. (*e-e Aufgabe*) sein; *I am your* ~! ich bin Ihr Mann!; **10.** Brettspiel: Stein *m*, ('Schach)Fi,gur *f*; **II** *v/t.* **11.** ✕, ⚓ bemannen; *a.* e-n Arbeitsplatz besetzen; **12.** *fig.* j-n stärken: ~ *o.s.* sich ermannen; **III** *adj.* **13.** männlich: ~ *cook* Koch *m*.

man·a·cle ['mænəkl] **I** *s. mst pl.* (Hand-) Fessel *f*, -schelle *f* (*a. fig.*); **II** *v/t.* j-m Handfesseln *od.* -schellen anlegen, j-n fesseln (*a. fig.*).

man·age ['mænɪdʒ] **I** *v/t.* **1.** Geschäft *etc.* führen, verwalten; *Betrieb etc.* leiten; *Gut etc.* bewirtschaften; **2.** *Künstler etc.* managen; **3.** zu'stande bringen, bewerkstelligen, es fertig bringen (*to do* zu tun) (*a. iro.*): *he* ~*d to* (*inf.*) es gelang ihm zu (*inf.*); **4.** ,deichseln', ,managen': ~ *matters* die Sache managen'; **5.** F *Arbeit, Essen* bewältigen, ,schaffen'; **6.** 'umgehen (können) mit: a) *Werkzeug etc.* handhaben, bedienen, b) *j-n* zu behandeln *od.* zu ,nehmen' wissen, c) *j-n* bändigen, mit *j-m etc.* fertig werden: *I can* ~ *him* ich werde (schon) mit ihm fertig; **7.** lenken (*a. fig.*); **II** *v/i.* **8.** das Geschäft *od.* den *Betrieb etc.* führen; die Aufsicht haben; **9.** auskommen, sich behelfen (*with* mit); **10.** F a) ,es schaffen', 'durchkommen, zurande kommen, b) ermöglichen: *can you come?* *I'm afraid, I can't* ~ (*it*) es geht leider nicht *od.* es ist mir leider nicht möglich; '**man·age·a·ble** [-dʒəbl] *adj.* □ **1.** lenksam, fügsam; **2.** handlich, leicht zu handhaben(d); '**man-**

age·a·ble·ness [-dʒəblnıs] *s.* **1.** Lenk-, Fügsamkeit *f*; **2.** Handlichkeit *f*; '**man·age·ment** [-mənt] *s.* **1.** (Haus-*etc.*)Verwaltung *f*; **2.** ✝ Management *n*, Unter'nehmensführung *f*: ~ *consultancy* ✝ Unter'nehmensberatung *f*; ~ *consultant* Unternehmensberater *m*; → *industrial management*; **3.** ✝ Geschäftsleitung *f*, Direkti'on *f*: *under new* ~ unter neuer Leitung; *labo(u)r and* ~ Arbeitnehmer *pl.* u. Arbeitgeber *pl.*; **4.** ✎ Bewirtschaftung *f* (*Gut etc.*); **5.** Geschicklichkeit *f*, (kluge) Taktik; **6.** Kunstgriff *m*, Trick *m*; **7.** Handhabung *f*, Behandlung *f*; '**man·ag·er** [-dʒə] *s.* **1.** (Haus- *etc.*)Verwalter *m*; **2.** ✝ a) Manager *m*, b) Führungskraft *f*, c) Geschäftsführer *m*, Leiter *m*, Di'rektor *m*: *board of* ~s Direktorium *n*; **3.** *thea.* a) Inten'dant *m*, b) Regis'seur *m*, c) Manager *m* (*a. sport*), Impre'sario *m*; **4.** *be a good* ~ gut *od.* sparsam wirtschaften können; **man·ag·er·ess** [ˌmænɪdʒə'res] *s.* **1.** (Haus- *etc.*)Verwalterin *f*; **2.** ✝ a) Managerin *f*, b) Geschäftsführerin *f*, Leiterin *f*, Di'rektorin *f*, c) Haushälterin *f*; **man·a·ge·ri·al** [ˌmænə'dʒɪərɪəl] *adj.* geschäftsführend, Direktions..., leitend: ~ *functions*; *in* ~ *capacity* in leitender Stellung; ~ *qualities* Führungsqualitäten; ~ *staff* leitende Angestellte *pl.*

man·ag·ing ['mænɪdʒɪŋ] *adj.* geschäftsführend, leitend, Betriebs...; ~ *board* *s.* ✝ Direk'torium *n*; ~ *clerk* *s.* **1.** Geschäftsführer *m*; **2.** Bü'rovorsteher *m*; ~ *com·mit·tee* *s.* ✝ Vorstand *m*; ~ *di·rec·tor* *s.* ✝ Gene'raldi,rektor *m*, Hauptgeschäftsführer *m*.

Man·chu [ˌmæn't∫u:] **I** *s.* **1.** Mandschu *m* (*Eingeborener der Mandschurei*); **2.** *ling.* Mandschu *n*; **II** *adj.* **3.** mandschurisch; **Man·chu·ri·an** [mæn't∫ʊərɪən] → *Manchu* 1, 3.

man·da·mus [mæn'deıməs] *s.* ⚖ *hist.* (*heute: order of* ~) Befehl *m* e-s höheren Gerichts an ein untergeordnetes.

man·da·rin¹ ['mændərɪn] *s.* **1.** *hist.* Manda'rin *m* (*chinesischer Titel*); **2.** F ,hohes Tier' (*hoher Beamter*); **3.** 2 *ling.* Manda'rin *n*.

man·da·rin² ['mændərɪn] *s.* ♀ Manda'rine *f*.

man·da·tar·y ['mændətərı] *s.* ⚖ Manda'tar *m*: a) (Pro'zess)Be,vollmächtigte(r) *m*, Sachwalter *m*, b) Manda'tarstaat *m*.

man·date ['mændeıt] **I** *s.* **1.** ⚖ a) Man'dat *n* (*a. parl.*), (Pro'zess),Vollmacht *f*, b) Geschäftsbesorgungsauftrag *m*, c) Befehl *m* e-s übergeordneten Gerichts; **2.** *pol.* a) Man'dat *n* (*Schutzherrschaftsauftrag*), b) Man'dat(sgebiet) *n*; **3.** R.C. päpstlicher Entscheid; **II** *v/t.* **4.** *pol.* e-m Man'dat unter'stellen: ~*d territory* Mandatsgebiet *n*; **man·da·tor** ['mændeıtə] *s.* ⚖ Man'dant *m*, Vollmachtgeber *m*; '**man·da·to·ry** [-dətərı] **I** *adj.* **1.** ⚖ vorschreibend, Muss...: ~ *regulation* Mussvorschrift *f*; *to make s.th.* ~ *upon s.o.* j-m et. vorschreiben; **2.** obliga'torisch, verbindlich, zwangsweise; **II** *s.* **3.** → *mandatary*.

man·di·ble ['mændıbl] *s. anat.* **1.** Kinnbacken *m*, -lade *f*; **2.** 'Unterkieferknochen *m*.

man·do·lin(e) ['mændəlın] *s.* ♪ Mando'line *f*.

man·drake ['mændreık] *s.* ♀ Al'raun(e *f*) *m*; Al'raunwurzel *f*.

man·drel, a. man·dril ['mændrəl] *s.* ⊙ (Spann)Dorn *m*; (Drehbank)Spindel *f*; *für Holz:* Docke(nspindel) *f*.

mane [meın] *s.* Mähne *f* (*a. weitS.*).

'**man,eat·er** *s.* **1.** Menschenfresser *m*; **2.** Menschen fressendes Tier; **3.** F ,Männer mordendes Wesen' (*Frau*).

maned [meınd] *adj.* mit Mähne; Mähnen...: ~ *wolf*.

ma·nège, a. ma·nege [mæ'neıʒ] *s.* **1.** Ma'nege *f*: a) Reitschule *f*, b) Reitbahn *f*, c) Reitkunst *f*; **2.** Gang *m*, Schule *f*; **3.** Zureiten *n*.

ma·nes ['mɑ:neız] *s. pl.* Manen *pl.*

ma·neu·ver [mə'nu:və] *etc. Am.* → *manœuvre etc.*

man·ful ['mænfʊl] *adj.* □ mannhaft, beherzt; '**man·ful·ness** [-nıs] *s.* Mannhaftigkeit *f*; Beherztheit *f*.

man·ga·nate ['mæŋgəneıt] *s.* 🝆 man'gansaures Salz; **man·ga·nese** ['mæŋgəni:z] *s.* 🝆 Man'gan *n*; **man·gan·ic** [mæŋ'gænık] *adj.* man'ganhaltig, Mangan...

mange [meındʒ] *s. vet.* Räude *f*.

man·gel-wur·zel ['mæŋgl,wɜ:zl] *s.* ♀ Mangold *m*.

man·ger ['meındʒə] *s.* Krippe *f* (*a. ast.* 2); Futtertrog *m*; → *dog Redew.*

man·gle¹ ['mæŋgl] *v/t.* **1.** zerfleischen, -fetzen, -stückeln; **2.** *fig. Text* verstümmeln.

man·gle² ['mæŋgl] **I** *s.* (Wäsche)Mangel *f*; **II** *v/t.* mangeln.

man·gler ['mæŋglə] *s.* Fleischwolf *m*.

man·go ['mæŋgəʊ] *pl.* **-goes** [-z] *s.* Mango *f* (*Frucht*); Mangobaum *m*.

man·grove ['mæŋgrəʊv] *s.* ♀ Man'grove(nbaum *m*) *f*.

man·gy ['meındʒı] *adj.* □ **1.** *vet.* krätzig, räudig; **2.** *fig.* a) eklig, b) schäbig.

'**man,han·dle** *v/t.* **1.** F miss'handeln; **2.** mit Menschenkraft bewegen *od.* befördern *od.* meistern.

'**man,hole** *s.* ⊙ Mann-, Einsteigloch *n*; (Straßen)Schacht *m*.

man·hood ['mænhʊd] *s.* **1.** Menschentum *n*; **2.** Mannesalter *n*; **3.** Männlichkeit *f*; **4.** Mannhaftigkeit *f*; **5.** *coll.* die Männer *pl.*

'**man|-,hour** *s.* Arbeitsstunde *f*; '~·hunt *s.* Großfahndung *f*.

ma·ni·a ['meınıə] *s.* **1.** 🝨 Ma'nie *f*, Wahn(sinn) *m*, Besessensein *n*: *religious* ~ religiöses Irresein; **2.** *fig.* (*for*) Sucht *f* (nach), Leidenschaft *f* (für), Ma'nie *f*, ,Fimmel' *m*: *collector's* ~ Sammlerwut *f*; *sport* ~ ,Sportfimmel'; **ma·ni·ac** ['meınıæk] **I** *s.* Wahnsinnige(r *m*) *f*, Verrückte(r *m*) *f*; **II** *adj.* wahnsinnig, verrückt, irr(e); **ma·ni·a·cal** [mə'naıəkl] *adj.* □ → *maniac* II.

ma·nic ['mænık] *psych.* **I** *adj.* manisch: ~*-depressive* manisch-depressiv(e Person); **II** *s.* manische Per'son.

man·i·cure ['mænıˌkjʊə] **I** *s.* Mani'küre *f*: a) Hand-, Nagelpflege *f*, b) Hand-, Nagelpflegerin *f*; **II** *v/t. u. v/i.* mani'küren; '**man·i·cur·ist** [-ərıst] *s.* Mani'küre *f* (*Person*).

man·i·fest ['mænıfest] **I** *adj.* □ **1.** offenbar-, -kundig, augenscheinlich, mani'fest (*a.* 🝨); **II** *v/t.* **2.** offen'baren, bekunden, kundtun, manifestieren; **3.** be-, erweisen; **III** *v/i.* **4.** *pol.* Kundgebungen veranstalten; **5.** erscheinen (*Geister*); **IV** *s.* **6.** ⚓ Ladungsverzeichnis *n*; **7.** ✝ ('Schiffs)Mani,fest *n*, *bsd. Am.* ✈ Passa'gierliste *f*; **man·i·fes·ta·tion** [ˌmænıfes'teı∫n] *s.* **1.** Offen'barung *f*, Äußerung *f*, Manifestati'on *f*; **2.** (deutliches) Anzeichen, Sym'ptom *n*: ~ *of life* Lebensäußerung *f*; **3.** *pol.* Demonstrati'on *f*; **4.** Erscheinen *n* e-s Geistes; **man·i·fes·to** [ˌmænı'festəʊ] *s.* Mani'fest *n*: a) öffentliche Erklärung, b) *pol.* Grundsatzerklärung *f*, (Par'tei-, 'Wahl)Pro,gramm *n*.

man·i·fold ['mænɪfəʊld] **I** *adj.* □ **1.** mannigfaltig, vielfach, -fältig; **2.** ☉ Mehr(fach)..., Mehrzweck...; **II** *s.* **3.** ☉ a) Sammelleitung *f*, b) Rohrverzweigung *f*: *intake* ~ *mot.* Einlasskrümmer *m*; **4.** Ko'pie *f*, Abzug *m*; **III** *v/t.* **5.** *Text* vervielfältigen, hektographieren; ~ *pa·per* *s.* 'Manifold-Pa,pier *n* (*festes Durchschlagpapier*); ~ *plug* *s.* ⚡ Vielfachstecker *m*; ~ *writ·er* *s.* Ver'vielfältigungsappa,rat *m*.

man·i·kin ['mænɪkɪn] *s.* **1.** Männchen *n*, Knirps *m*; **2.** Glieder-, Schaufensterpuppe *f*, ('Anpro,bier)Mo,dell *n*; **3.** ✱ ana'tomisches Mo'dell, Phan'tom *n*; **4.** → *mannequin* 1.

Ma·nil·(l)a [mə'nɪlə] *s. abbr. für* a) ~ *cheroot*, b) ~ *hemp*, c) ~ *paper*; ~ *che·root* *s.* Ma'nilazi,garre *f*; ~ *hemp* *s.* Ma'nilahanf *m*; ~ *pa·per* *s.* Ma'nilapa,pier *n*.

ma·nip·u·late [mə'nɪpjʊleɪt] **I** *v/t.* **1.** manipulieren, (künstlich) beeinflussen: ~ *prices*; **2.** (geschickt) handhaben; ☉ bedienen; **3.** *j-n od. et.* manipulieren *od.* geschickt behandeln; **4.** *et.* ,deicheln', ,schaukeln'; **5.** *Konten etc.* ,frisieren'; **II** *v/i.* **6.** manipulieren; **ma·nip·u·la·tion** [mə,nɪpjʊ'leɪʃn] *s.* **1.** Manipulati'on *f*: ~ *of currency*; **2.** (Kunst)Griff *m*, Verfahren *n*; **3.** *b.s.* Machenschaft *f*, Manipulati'on *f*; **ma·nip·u·la·tive** [-lətɪv] → *manipulatory*; **ma·nip·u·la·tor** [-tə] *s.* **1.** (geschickter) Handhaber; **2.** Drahtzieher *m*, Manipulierer *m*; **ma·nip·u·la·to·ry** [-lətərɪ] *adj.* **1.** durch Manipulati'on her'beigeführt; **2.** manipulierend; **3.** Handhabungs...

man·kind [mæn'kaɪnd] *s.* **1.** die Menschheit; **2.** *coll.* die Menschen *pl.*, der Mensch; **3.** ['mænkaɪnd] *coll.* die Männer *pl.*

'man·like *adj.* **1.** menschenähnlich; **2.** wie ein Mann, männlich; **3.** → *mannish*.

man·li·ness ['mænlɪnɪs] *s.* **1.** Männlichkeit *f*; **2.** Mannhaftigkeit *f*; **man·ly** ['mænlɪ] *adj.* **1.** männlich; **2.** mannhaft; **3.** Mannes...: ~ *sports* Männersport *m*.

'man·made *adj.* Kunst..., künstlich: ~ *satellite*; ~ *fibre* (*Am. fiber*) ☉ Kunstfaser *f*.

man·na ['mænə] *s. bibl.* Manna *n*, *f* (*a.* ⚘ *u. fig.*).

man·ne·quin ['mænɪkɪn] *s.* **1.** Mannequin *n*: ~ *parade* Mode(n)schau *f*; **2.** → *manikin* 2.

man·ner ['mænə] *s.* **1.** Art *f* (*und Weise f*) (*et. zu tun*): *after* (*od. in*) *this* ~ auf diese Art *od.* Weise, so: *in such a* ~ (*that*) so *od.* derart (, dass); *in what* ~? wie?; *adverb of* ~ *ling.* Umstandswort der Art u. Weise, Modaladverb *n*; *in a* ~ auf e-e Art, gewissermaßen; *in a* ~ *of speaking* sozusagen; *all* ~ *of things* alles Mögliche; *no* ~ *of doubt* gar kein Zweifel; *by no* ~ *of means* in keiner Weise; **2.** Art *f*, Betragen *n*, Auftreten *n*, Verhalten *n* (*to* zu): *I don't like his* ~ ich mag ihn nicht; *to the* ~ *born* hineingeboren (*in bestimmte Verhältnisse*), von Kind auf damit vertraut; *as to the* ~ *born* wie selbstverständlich, als ob er *etc.* es immer so getan hätte; **3.** *pl.* Benehmen *n*, 'Umgangsformen *pl.*, Ma'nieren *pl.*: *bad* (*good*) ~*s*; *we shall teach them* ~*s* ,wir werden sie Mores lehren'; *it is bad* ~*s* es gehört sich nicht; **4.** *pl.* Sitten *pl.* (*u.* Gebräu-

che *pl.*); **5.** *paint. etc.* Stil(art *f*) *m*, Ma'nier *f*; **'man·nered** [-əd] *adj.* **1.** *mst in Zssgn* gesittet, geartet: *ill-~* von schlechtem Benehmen, ungezogen; **2.** gekünstelt, manie'riert; **'man·ner·ism** [-ərɪzəm] *s.* **1.** *Kunst etc.*: Manie'rismus *m*, Künste'lei *f*; **2.** Manie'riertheit *f*, Gehabe *n*; **3.** eigenartige Wendung (*in der Rede etc.*); **'man·ner·li·ness** [-əlɪnɪs] *s.* gutes Benehmen, Ma'nierlichkeit *f*; **'man·ner·ly** [-əlɪ] *adj.* ma'nierlich, gesittet.

man·ni·kin → *manikin*.

man·nish ['mænɪʃ] *adj.* masku'lin, unweiblich.

ma·nœu·vra·ble [mə'nuːvrəbl] *adj.* **1.** ✕ manövrierfähig; **2.** ☉ lenk-, steuerbar; *weitS.* (*a. fig.*) wendig, beweglich; **ma·nœu·vre** [mə'nuːvə] **I** *s.* **1.** ✕, ⚓ Ma'növer *n*: a) taktische Bewegung, b) Truppen-, ⚓ Flottenübung *f*, ✈ 'Luftma,növer *n*; **2.** *fig.* Ma'növer *n*, Schachzug *m*, List *f*; **II** *v/t. u. v/i.* **3.** manövrieren (*a. fig.*): ~ *s.o. into s.th.* j-n in et. hineinmanövrieren; **ma'nœu·vrer** [-vərə] *s. fig.* **1.** (schlauer) Taktiker; **2.** Intri'gant *m*.

man-of-war [,mænə'wɔː], *pl.* **,men-of-'war** [,men-] *s.* ⚓ Kriegsschiff *n*.

ma·nom·e·ter [mə'nɒmɪtə] *s.* ☉ Mano'meter *n*, Druckmesser *m*.

man·or ['mænə] *s.* **1.** Ritter-, Landgut *n*: *lord* (*lady*) *of the* ~ Gutsherr(in); **2.** *a.* ~ *house* Herrenhaus *n*; **ma·no·ri·al** [mə'nɔːrɪəl] *adj.* herrschaftlich, (Ritter-) Guts..., Herrschafts...

man·qué(e *f*) *m* ['mãːŋkeɪ] (*Fr.*) *adj.* verhindert, ,verkracht': *a poet manqué*.

'man,pow·er *s.* **1.** menschliche Arbeitskraft *od.* -leistung; **2.** 'Menschenpotenzi,al *n*: *bsd.* a) Kriegsstärke *f* (*e-s Volkes*), b) (verfügbare) Arbeitskräfte *pl.*

man·sard ['mænsɑːd] *s.* **1.** *a.* ~ *roof* Man'sardendach *n*; **2.** Man'sarde *f*.

'man,serv·ant *pl.* **'men,serv·ants** *s.* Diener *m*.

man·sion ['mænʃn] *s.* **1.** (herrschaftliches) Wohnhaus, Villa *f*; **2.** *bsd. pl. Brit.* (großes) Mietshaus; ~ *house* *s.* **1.** *Brit.* Herrenhaus *n*, -sitz *m*; **2.** *the* ☽ *Amtssitz des Lord Mayor von London*.

'man,slaugh·ter *s.* ⚖ Totschlag *m*, Körperverletzung *f* mit Todesfolge: *involuntary* ~ fahrlässige Tötung; *voluntary* ~ Totschlag im Affekt.

man·tel ['mæntl] *abbr. für* a) *mantelpiece*, b) *mantelshelf*; **'~piece** *s.* **1.** Ka'mineinfassung *f*, -mantel *m*; **2.** → **'~shelf** *s.* (*irr.*) Ka'minsims *m*, *n*.

man·tis ['mæntɪs] *pl.* **-tis·es** *s. zo.* Gottesanbeterin *f* (*Heuschrecke*).

man·tle ['mæntl] **I** *s.* **1.** Mantel *m* (*a. zo.*), (ärmelloser) 'Umhang *m*; **2.** *fig.* (Schutz-, Deck)Mantel *m*, Hülle *f*; **3.** ☉ Mantel *m*; (Glüh)Strumpf *m*; **4.** *Gusstechnik:* Formmantel *m*; **II** *v/i.* **5.** sich über'ziehen (*with* mit); sich röten (*Gesicht*); **III** *v/t.* **6.** über'ziehen; **7.** verhüllen (*a. fig.* bemänteln).

,man-to-'man *adj.* von Mann zu Mann: *a* ~ *talk*.

'man·trap *s.* **1.** Fußangel *f*; **2.** *fig.* Falle *f*.

man·u·al ['mænjʊəl] **I** *adj.* □ **1.** mit der Hand, Hand..., manu'ell: ~ *alphabet* Fingeralphabet *n*; ~ *exercises* ✕ Griffeüben *n*; ~ *labo(u)r* Handarbeit *f*; ~ *training* *ped.* Werkunterricht *m*; **~ly operated** ☉ mit Handbetrieb, handgesteuert; **2.** handschriftlich: ~ *bookkeeping*; **II** *s.* **3.** a) Handbuch *n*, Leitfaden *m*, *Computer:* Benutzerhand-

buch *n*: (*instruction*) ~ Bedienungsanleitung(en *pl.*) *f*, b) ✕ Dienstvorschrift *f*; **4.** ♪ Manu'al *n* (*Orgel etc.*).

man·u·fac·to·ry [,mænjʊ'fæktərɪ] *s. obs.* Fa'brik *f*.

man·u·fac·ture [,mænjʊ'fæktʃə] **I** *s.* **1.** Fertigung *f*, Erzeugung *f*, Herstellung *f*, Fabrikati'on *f*: *year of* ~ Herstellungs-, Baujahr *n*; **2.** Erzeugnis *n*, Fabri'kat *n*; **3.** Indu'strie(zweig *m*) *f*; **II** *v/t.* **4.** verfertigen, erzeugen, herstellen, fabrizieren (*a. fig. Beweismittel etc.*): ~*d goods* Fabrik-, Fertig-, Manufakturwaren; **5.** verarbeiten (*into* zu); **,man·u'fac·tur·er** [-tʃərə] *s.* Hersteller *m*, Erzeuger *m*; **2.** Fabri'kant *m*; **,man·u'fac·tur·ing** [-tʃərɪŋ] *adj.* **1.** Herstellungs..., Produktions...: ~ *cost* Herstellungskosten *pl.*; ~ *efficiency* Produktionsleistung *f*; ~ *industries* Fertigungsindustrien; ~ *plant* Fabrikationsbetrieb *m*; ~ *process* Herstellungsverfahren *n*; **2.** Industrie..., Fabrik..., Gewerbe...

man·u·mit [,mænjʊ'mɪt] *v/t. hist.* Sklaven freilassen, aus der Sklave'rei entlassen.

ma·nure [mə'njʊə] **I** *s.* **1.** Dünger *m*; **2.** Dung *m*: *liquid* ~ (Dung)Jauche *f*; **II** *v/t.* **3.** düngen.

man·u·script ['mænjʊskrɪpt] **I** *s.* Manu'skript *n*: a) Handschrift *f* (*alte Urkunde etc.*), b) Urschrift *f* (*e-s Autors*), c) *typ.* Satzvorlage *f*; **II** *adj.* Manuskript..., handschriftlich.

Manx [mæŋks] **I** *adj.* (von) der Insel Man; **II** *s. ling.* Manx *n* (*e-e keltische Sprache*).

man·y ['menɪ] **I** *adj.* **1.** viele, viel: ~ *times* oft; *as* ~ ebenso viel(e); *as* ~ *again* doppelt so viel(e); *as* ~ *as forty* (nicht weniger als) vierzig; *one too* ~ einer zu viel; *be one too* ~ *for* F j-m ,über' sein; *they behaved like so* ~ *children* sie benahmen sich wie (die) Kinder; **2.** ~ *a* manch, manch ein: ~ *a man* manch einer; ~ *a time* des Öfteren; **II** *s.* **3.** viele: *the* ~ *pl. konstr.* die (große) Masse; ~ *of us* viele von uns; *a good* ~ ziemlich viel(e); *a great* ~ sehr viele; **~-sid·ed** [,menɪ'saɪdɪd] *adj.* vielseitig (*a. fig.*); *fig.* vielschichtig (*Problem etc.*); **~-sid·ed·ness** [,menɪ'saɪdɪdnɪs] *s.* **1.** Vielseitigkeit *f* (*a. fig.*); **2.** *fig.* Vielschichtigkeit *f*.

Mao·ism ['maʊɪzəm] *s.* Mao'ismus *m*; **'Mao·ist** [-ɪst] **I** *s.* Mao'ist(in); **II** *adj.* mao'istisch.

map [mæp] **I** *s.* **1.** (Land- *etc.*, *a.* Himmels)Karte *f*: ~ *of the city* Stadtplan *m*; *by* ~ nach der Karte; *off the* ~ F a) abgelegen, ,hinter dem Mond' (gelegen), b) bedeutungslos; *on the* ~ F a) (noch) da *od.* vorhanden, b) beachtenswert; *put on the* ~ *fig.* Stadt etc. bekannt machen, Geltung verschaffen (*dat.*); **2.** *sl.* ,Vi'sage' *f*, ,Fresse' *f* (*Gesicht*); **II** *v/t.* **3.** e-e Karte machen von, karto'graphisch darstellen; **4.** *Gebiet* karto'graphisch erfassen; **5.** auf e-r Karte eintragen; **6.** ~ *out* *fig.* (vor'aus-) planen, ausarbeiten, *s-e Zeit* einteilen; ~ *case* *s.* Kartentasche *f*; ~ *ex·er·cise* *s.* ✕ Planspiel *n*.

ma·ple ['meɪpl] **I** *s.* **1.** ♀ Ahorn *m*; **2.** Ahornholz *n*; **II** *adj.* **3.** aus Ahorn (-holz), Ahorn...; ~ *sug·ar* *s.* Ahornzucker *m*.

map·per ['mæpə] *s.* Karto'graph *m*.

ma·quis ['mækiː] *pl.* **-quis** [-kiː] *s.* **1.** ♀ Macchia *f*; **2.** a) Ma'quis *m*, fran'zösische 'Widerstandsbewegung (*im 2.*

Weltkrieg), b) Maqui'sard *m*, (fran'zösischer) 'Widerstandskämpfer.

mar [mɑ:] *v/t.* **1.** (be)schädigen; **~-resistant** ⊜ kratzfest; **2.** ruinieren; **3.** *fig.* *Pläne etc.* stören, beeinträchtigen; *Schönheit, Spaß* verderben.

mar·a·bou ['mærəbu:] *s. orn.* Marabu *m*.

mar·a·schi·no [ˌmærə'ski:nəʊ] *s.* Maras-'chino(li,kör) *m*.

mar·a·thon ['mærəθn] **I** *s. sport* **1.** *a.* **~ race** Marathonlauf *m*; **2.** *fig.* Dauerwettkampf *m*; **II** *adj.* **3.** *sport* Marathon...; **~ runner**; **4.** *fig.* Marathon..., Dauer...; **~ session**.

ma·raud [mə'rɔ:d] ⚔ **I** *v/i.* plündern; **II** *v/t.* verheeren, (aus)plündern; **ma·'raud·er** [-də] *s.* Plünderer *m*.

mar·ble ['mɑ:bl] **I** *s.* **1.** *min.* Marmor *m*: **artificial ~** Gipsmarmor, Stuck *m*; **2.** Marmorstatue *f*, -bildwerk *n*; **3.** a) Murmel(kugel) *f*, b) *pl. sg. konstr.* Murmelspiel *n*: **play ~s** (mit) Murmeln spielen; **he's lost his ~s** *Brit. sl.* ,er hat nicht mehr alle'; **4.** marmorierter Buchschnitt; **II** *adj.* **5.** marmorn, aus Marmor; **6.** marmoriert, gesprenkelt; **7.** *fig.* steinern, gefühllos; **III** *v/t.* **8.** marmorieren, sprenkeln: **~d meat** durchwachsenes Fleisch.

mar·cel [mɑ:'sel] **I** *v/t.* Haar ondulieren; **II** *s. a.* **~ wave** Ondulati'on(swelle) *f*.

march¹ [mɑ:tʃ] **I** *v/i.* **1.** ⚔ *etc.* marschieren, ziehen: **~ off** abrücken; **~ past** (*s.o.*) (an j-m) vorbeiziehen *od.* -marschieren; **~ up** anrücken; **2.** *fig.* fortschreiten; Fortschritte machen; **II** *v/t.* **3.** *Strecke* marschieren, zu'rücklegen; **4.** marschieren lassen: **~ off prisoners** Gefangene abführen; **III** *s.* **5.** ⚔ Marsch *m* (*a.* ♪): **slow ~** langsamer Parademarsch; **~ order** *Am.* Marschbefehl *m*; **6.** Marsch(strecke *f*) *m*: **a day's ~** ein Tagesmarsch; **7.** ⚔ Vormarsch *m* (**on** auf *acc.*); **8.** *fig.* (Ab-)Lauf *m*, (Fort)Gang *m*: **the ~ of events**; **9.** *fig.* Fortschritt *m*: **the ~ of progress** die fortschrittliche Entwicklung; **10.** **steal a ~ (up)on s.o.** j-m ein Schnippchen schlagen, j-m zuvorkommen.

march² [mɑ:tʃ] **I** *s.* **1.** *hist.* Mark *f*; **2.** a) *mst pl.* Grenzgebiet *n*, -land *n*, b) Grenze *f*; **II** *v/i.* **3.** grenzen (**upon** *an acc.*); **4.** e-e gemeinsame Grenze haben (**with** mit).

March³ [mɑ:tʃ] *s.* März *m*: **in ~** im März; **as mad as a ~ hare** F total übergeschnappt.

march·ing ['mɑ:tʃɪŋ] *adj.* ⚔ Marsch..., marschierend: **~ order** a) Marschausrüstung *f*, b) Marschordnung *f*; **in heavy ~ order** feldmarschmäßig; **~ orders** *Brit.* Marschbefehl *m*; **he got his ~ orders** F er bekam den ,Laufpass'.

mar·chion·ess ['mɑ:ʃənɪs] *s.* Mar'quise *f*, Markgräfin *f*.

march·pane ['mɑ:tʃpeɪn] *s. obs.* Marzi-'pan *n*.

Mar·di Gras [ˌmɑ:dɪ'grɑ:] (*Fr.*) *s.* Fastnacht(sdienstag *m*) *f*.

mare [meə] *s.* Stute *f*: **the grey ~ is the better horse** *fig.* die Frau ist der Herr im Hause; **~'s nest** *fig.* a),Windei' *n, a.* (Zeitungs)Ente *f*, b) ,Saustall' *m*.

mar·ga·rine [ˌmɑ:dʒə'ri:n] *s.* Marga'rine *f*.

marge [mɑ:dʒ] *s. Brit.* F Marga'rine *f*.

mar·gin ['mɑ:dʒɪn] **I** *s.* **1.** Rand *m* (*a. fig.*); **2.** *a. pl.* (Seiten)Rand *m* (*bei Büchern etc.*): **as per ~** ✝ wie nebenstehend; **3.** Grenze *f* (*a. fig.*): **~ of income** Einkommensgrenze; **4.** Spielraum *m*:

leave a ~ Spielraum lassen; **5.** *fig.* 'Überschuss *m*, (*ein*) Mehr *n* (*an Zeit, Geld etc.*): **safety ~** Sicherheitsfaktor *m*; **by a narrow ~** mit knapper Not; **6.** *mst profit ~* ✝ (Gewinn-, Verdienst-) Spanne *f*, Marge *f*, Handelsspanne *f*: **interest ~** Zinsgefälle *n*; **7.** ✝, *Börse*: Hinter'legungssumme *f*, Deckung *f* (*von Kursschwankungen*), Marge *f*: **~ business** *Am.* Effektendifferenzgeschäft *n*; **8.** ✝ Rentabili'tätsgrenze *f*; **9.** *sport* (**by a ~ of four seconds** mit vier Sekunden) Abstand *m od.* Vorsprung *m*; **II** *v/t.* **10.** mit Rand(bemerkungen) versehen; **11.** an den Rand schreiben; **12.** ✝ durch Hinterlegung decken; **'mar·gin·al** [-nl] *adj.* □ **1.** am *od.* auf dem Rand, Rand...: **~ note** Randbemerkung *f*; **~ release** a) Randauslösung *f*, b) Randlöser *m* (*der Schreibmaschine*); **2.** am Rande, Grenz... (*a. fig.*); **3.** *fig.* Mindest...: **~ capacity**; **4.** ✝ a) vom Selbstkostenpreis, b) knapp über der Rentabili'tätsgrenze (liegend), Grenz...: **~ cost** Grenz-, Mindestkosten *pl.*; **~ sales** Verkäufe zum Selbstkostenpreis; **mar·gi·na·li·a** [ˌmɑ:dʒɪ-'neɪljə] *s. pl.* Margi'nalien *pl.*, Randmerkungen *pl.*; **'mar·gin·al·ize** *v/t.* **1.** *fig.* an den Rand drängen, zurückdrängen; **2.** (Rand)Bemerkungen schreiben an (*acc.*); **'mar·gin·al·ly** [-nəlɪ] *adv. fig.* **1.** geringfügig; **2.** (nur) am Rande.

mar·grave ['mɑ:greɪv] *s. hist.* Markgraf *m*; **mar·gra·vi·ate** [mɑ:'greɪvɪət] *s.* Markgrafschaft *f*; **'mar·gra·vine** [-grəvi:n] *s.* Markgräfin *f*.

mar·gue·rite [ˌmɑ:gə'ri:t] *s.* ♀ **1.** Marge'rite *f*; **2.** Gänseblümchen *n*.

mar·i·gold ['mærɪgəʊld] *s.* ♀ Ringelblume *f*; Stu'dentenblume *f*.

mar·i·jua·na, *a.* **mar·i·hua·na** [ˌmærɪ-'hwɑ:nə] *s.* **1.** Marihu'anahanf *m*; **2.** Marihu'ana *n* (*Droge*).

ma·ri·na [ˌmə'ri:nə] *s.* Jachthafen *m*.

mar·i·nade [ˌmærɪ'neɪd] *s.* **1.** Mari'nade *f*; **2.** marinierter Fisch; **mar·i·nate** ['mærɪneɪt] *v/t.* Fisch marinieren.

ma·rine [mə'ri:n] **I** *adj.* **1.** See...: **~ warfare**; **~ court** *Am.* ⚖ Seegericht *n*; **~ dumping** Verklappung *f* (*von Giftstoffen*); **~ insurance** See(transport)versicherung *f*; **2.** Meeres...: **~ plants**; **3.** Schiffs...; **4.** Marine...: **~ Corps** *Am.* ⚔ Marineinfanteriekorps *n*; **5.** Ma'rine *f*: **mercantile ~** Handelsmarine; **6.** ⚔ Ma'rineinfante‚rist *m*: **tell that to the ~s!** F das kannst du deiner Großmutter erzählen!; **7.** *paint.* Seestück *n*.

mar·i·ner ['mærɪnə] *s. poet. od.* ⚖ Seemann *m*, Ma'trose *m*: **master ~** Kapitän *m od.* e-s Handelsschiffs.

Mar·i·ol·a·try [ˌmeərɪ'ɒlətrɪ] *s.* Ma'rienkult *m*, -verehrung *f*.

mar·i·o·nette [ˌmærɪə'net] *s.* Mario'nette *f* (*a. fig.*).

mar·i·tal ['mærɪtl] *adj.* □ ehelich, Ehe..., Gatten...: **~ partners** Ehegatten; **~ relations** eheliche Beziehungen; **~ status** ⚖ Familienstand *m*; **disruption of ~ relations** Zerrüttung *f* der Ehe.

mar·i·time ['mærɪtaɪm] *adj.* **1.** See..., Schifffahrts...: **~ court** Seeamt *n*; **~ insurance** Seeversicherung *f*; **~ law** Seerecht *n*; **2.** a) seefahrend, Seemanns..., b) Seehandel (be)treibend; **3.** an der See liegend *od.* lebend, Küsten...; **4.** *zo.* an der Küste lebend, Strand... ⚓ **Com·mis·sion** *s. Am.* Oberste Handelsschifffahrtsbehörde der USA; **~ ter·ri·to·ry** *s.* ⚖ Seehoheitsge-

biet *n*.

mar·jo·ram ['mɑ:dʒərəm] *s.* ♀ Majoran *m*.

mark¹ [mɑ:k] **I** *s.* **1.** Markierung *f*, Marke *f*, Mal *n*; *engS.* Fleck *m*: **adjusting ~** ⊜ Einstellmarke; **2.** *fig.* Zeichen *n*: **~ of confidence** Vertrauensbeweis *m*; **~ of respect** Zeichen der Hochachtung; **3.** (Kenn)Zeichen *n*, (Merk)Mal *n*; *zo.* Kennung *f*: **distinctive ~** Kennzeichen; **4.** (Schrift-, Satz)Zeichen *n*: **question ~** Fragezeichen; **5.** (An)Zeichen *n*: **a ~ of great carelessness**; **6.** (Eigentums)Zeichen *n*, Brandmal *n*; **7.** Strieme *f*, Schwiele *f*; **8.** Narbe *f* (*a.* ⚕); **9.** Kerbe *f*, Einschnitt *m*; **10.** Kreuz *n* als *Unterschrift*; **11.** Ziel(scheibe *f*; *a. fig.*) *n*: **wide of (beside) the ~** *fig.* a) fehl am Platz, nicht zur Sache gehörig, b) ,fehlgeschossen'; **you are quite off (od. wide of) the ~** *fig.* Sie irren sich gewaltig; **hit the ~** ins (Schwarze) treffen; **miss the ~** a) fehl-, vorbeischießen, b) sein Ziel *od.* s-n Zweck verfehlen, ,danebenhauen'; **12.** *fig.* Norm *f*: **below the ~** unterdurchschnittlich, nicht auf der Höhe; **up to the ~** a) der Sache gewachsen, b) den Erwartungen entsprechend, c) *gesundheitlich etc.* auf der Höhe; **within the ~** innerhalb der erlaubten Grenzen, berechtigt (**in doing** zu tun); **overshoot the ~** über das Ziel hinausschießen, zu weit gehen; **13.** (aufgeprägter) Stempel, Gepräge *n*; **14.** Spur *f* (*a. fig.*): **leave one's ~ upon** a) s-n Stempel aufdrücken (*dat.*), b) bei *j-m* s-e Spuren hinterlassen; **make one's ~** sich e-n Namen machen (**in** *in dat.*, *upon* bei), Vorzügliches leisten; **15.** *fig.* Bedeutung *f*, Rang *m*: **a man of ~** e-e markante Persönlichkeit; **16.** ✝ a) (Waren)Zeichen *n*, Fa'brik-, Schutzmarke *f*, (Handels)Marke *f*, b) Preisangabe *f*; **17.** ⚔ *Brit.* Mo'dell *n*, Type *f* (*Panzerwagen etc.*); **18.** (Schul-) Note *f*, Zen'sur *f*: **obtain full ~s** in allen Punkten voll bestehen; **give s.o. full ~s (for)** *fig.* j-m höchstes Lob spenden (für); **bad ~** Note für schlechtes Benehmen; **bad ~s** (ein) schlechtes Zeugnis; **19.** *sport* a) Fußball *etc.*: (Strafstoß-) Marke *f*, b) *Laufsport*: Startlinie *f*, c) *Boxen: sl.* Magengrube *f*: **on your ~s!** auf die Plätze!; **get off the ~** starten; **20.** **not my ~** *sl.* nicht mein Geschmack, nicht das Richtige für mich; **21.** *sl.* ,Gimpel' *m*, leichtes Opfer: **be an easy ~** leicht ,reinzulegen' sein; **22.** *hist.* a) Mark *f* (*Grenzgebiet*), b) All-'mende *f*; **II** *v/t.* **23.** markieren (*a.* ⚔), (*a. fig.* j-n, et., ein Zeitalter*) kennzeichnen; bezeichnen; *Wäsche* zeichnen; ✝ *Waren* auszeichnen, *Preis* festsetzen; *Temperatur etc.* anzeigen; *fig.* ein Zeichen sein für: **to ~ the occasion** aus diesem Anlass, zur Feier des Tages; **the day was ~d by heavy fighting** der Tag stand im Zeichen schwerer Kämpfe; → **time** 18; **24.** brandmarken; **25.** Spuren hinter'lassen auf (*dat.*); **26.** zeigen, zum Ausdruck bringen; **27.** be-, vermerken, Acht geben auf (*acc.*), sich merken; **28.** *ped.* Arbeiten zensieren; **29.** bestimmen (**for** für); **30.** *sport* a) *Gegenspieler* decken, markieren; b) *Punkte etc.* notieren; **III** *v/i.* **31.** Acht geben, aufpassen: **~!** Achtung!; **~ you** wohlgemerkt; **~ down** *v/t.* **1.** ✝ (*im Preis*) her'absetzen; **2.** bestimmen, vormerken (**for** für, zu); **~ off** *v/t.* **1.** abgrenzen, -stecken; **2.** *auf e-r Liste* abhaken; **3.** *fig.* (ab)trennen; **4.** ⚓ *Strecke* ab-, auftragen; **~ out** *v/t.* **1.** bestimmen, ausersehen (*for* für, zu); **2.** abgrenzen, (*durch Striche etc.*) bezeichnen, markieren; **~ up** *v/t.* **✝ 1.** (*im Preis etc.*) hin'auf-, her'aufsetzen; **2.** *Diskontsatz etc.* erhöhen.

mark² [mɑːk] *s.* **✝ 1.** (deutsche) Mark: **blocked ~** Sperrmark; **2.** *hist.* Mark *f* (*Münze, Goldgewicht*).

Mark³ [mɑːk] *npr. u. s. bibl.* 'Markus (-evan‚gelium *n*) *m*.

'mark·down *s.* **✝** niedrigere Auszeichnung (*e-r Ware*), Preissenkung *f*.

marked [mɑːkt] *adj.* □ **1.** markiert, gekennzeichnet; mit e-r Aufschrift versehen; **2.** ✝ bestätigt (*Am.* gekennzeichnet) (*Scheck*); **3.** mar'kant, ausgeprägt; **4.** deutlich, merklich: **~ progress**; **5.** auffällig, ostenta'tiv: **~ indifference**; **6.** gezeichnet: **a face ~ with smallpox** ein pockennarbiges Gesicht; **a ~ man** *fig.* ein Gezeichneter; **'mark·ed·ly** [-kɪdlɪ] *adv.* deutlich, ausgesprochen.

mark·er ['mɑːkə] *s.* **1.** Anschreiber *m*; *Billard:* Mar'kör *m*; **2.** ✕ a) Anzeiger *m* (*beim Schießstand*), b) Flügelmann *m*; **3.** a) Kennzeichen *n*, b) (Weg- *etc.*) Markierung *f*; **4.** Lesezeichen *n*; **5.** *Am.* a) Straßenschild *n*, b) Gedenktafel *f*; **6.** ✈ a) Sichtzeichen *n*: **~ panel** Fliegertuch *n*, b) Leuchtbombe *f*.

mar·ket ['mɑːkɪt] **✝ I** *s.* **1.** Markt *m* (*Handel*): **be in the ~ for** Bedarf haben an (*a. fig.*); **come into the ~** (zum Verkauf) angeboten werden, auf den Markt kommen; *place* (*od.* *put*) **on the ~ → 11**; **sale in the open ~** freihändiger Verkauf; **2.** *Börse:* Markt *m*: **railway ~** Markt für Eisenbahnwerte; **3.** (*a.* Geld-) Markt *m*, Börse *f*, Handelsverkehr *m*: **active** (**dull**) **~** lebhafter (lustloser) Markt; **play the ~** an der Börse spekulieren; **4.** a) Marktpreis *m*, b) Marktpreise *pl.*: **the ~ is low** (**rising**); **at the ~** zum Marktpreis, *Börse:* zum „Bestens'-Preis; **5.** Markt(platz) *m*, Handelsplatz *m*: **in the ~** auf dem Markt; (**covered**) **~** Markthalle *f*; **6.** *Am.* (Lebensmittel)Geschäft *n*: **meat ~**; **7.** (Wochenod. Jahr)Markt *m*; **8.** Markt *m* (*Absatzgebiet*): **hold the ~** a) den Markt beherrschen, b) (durch Kauf *od.* Verkauf) die Preise halten; **9.** Absatz *m*, Verkauf *m*, Markt *m*: **find a ~** Absatz finden (*Ware*); **find a ~ for** et. an den Markt bringen; **meet with a ready ~** schnellen Absatz finden; **10.** (*for*) Nachfrage *f* (nach), Bedarf *m* (an *dat.*); **II** *v/t.* **11.** auf den Markt bringen; vertreiben; **III** *v/i.* **12.** einkaufen; auf dem Markt handeln; Märkte besuchen; **IV** *adj.* **13.** Markt...: **~ day**; **14.** Börsen...; **15.** Kurs...: **~ profit**; **'mar·ket·a·ble** [-təbl] *adj.* marktfähig, -gängig; börsenfähig.

mar·ket| a·nal·y·sis *s.* [*irr.*] ✝ 'Marktana‚lyse *f*; **~ con·di·tion** *s.* ✝ Marktlage *f*, Konjunk'tur *f*; **~ e·con·o·my** *s.* ✝ (**free ~, social ~**) freie, soziale) Marktwirtschaft *f*; **~ fluc·tu·a·tion** *s.* ✝ **1.** Konjunk'turbewegung *f*; **2.** *pl.* Konjunk'turschwankungen *pl.*; **~ gar·den** *s. Brit.* Handelsgärtne'rei *f*.

mar·ket·ing ['mɑːkɪtɪŋ] **I** *s.* **1.** ✝ Marketing *n*, Marktversorgung *f*, Absatzpoli‚tik *f*, -förderung *f*; **2.** Marktbesuch *m*; **II** *adj.* **3.** Markt...: **~ association** Marktverband *m*; **~ company** Vertriebsgesellschaft *f*; **~ organization** Absatzorganisation *f*; **~ research** Absatzforschung *f*.

mar·ket| in·ves·ti·ga·tion *s.* 'Marktun‚ter‚suchung *f*; **~ lead·ers** *s. pl.* führende Börsenwerte *pl.*; **~ let·ter** *s. Am.*

Markt-, Börsenbericht *m*; **~ niche** *s.* Marktnische *f*, -lücke *f*; **'~-‚o·ri·ent·ed** *adj.* ✝ marktorientiert; **'~·place** *s.* Marktplatz *m*; **~ price** *s.* **1.** Marktpreis *m*; **2.** *Börse:* Kurs(wert) *m*; **~ quo·ta·tion** *s.* Börsennotierung *f*, Marktkurs *m*: **list of ~s** Markt-, Börsenzettel *m*; **~ rate → market price**; **~ re·search** *s.* ✝ Marktforschung *f*; **~ re·search·er** *s.* ✝ Marktforscher *m*; **~ rig·ging** *s.* Kurstreibe'rei *f*, 'Börsenma‚növer *n*; **~ sat·u·ra·tion** *s.* Marktsättigung *f*; **~ share** *s.* Marktanteil *m*; **~ stud·y** *s.* ✝ 'Marktunter‚suchung *f*; **~ swing** *s. Am.* Konjunk'turperi‚ode *f*; **~ town** *s.* Markt (-flecken) *m*; **~ val·ue** *s.* Kurs-, Verkehrswert *m*.

mark·ing ['mɑːkɪŋ] **I** *s.* **1.** Kennzeichnung *f*, Markierung *f*; Bezeichnung *f* (*a.* ♪); *ped.* Zensieren *n*; ✈ Hoheitsabzeichen *n*; **2.** *zo.* (Haut-, Feder)Musterung *f*, Zeichnung *f*; **II** *adj.* **3.** ❂ markierend: **~ awl** Reißahle *f*; **~ ink** Zeichen-, Wäschetinte *f*.

marks·man ['mɑːksmən] *s.* [*irr.*] guter Schütze, Meisterschütze *m*, *bsd.* ✕ u. *Polizei:* Scharfschütze *m*; **'marks·man·ship** [-ʃɪp] *s.* **1.** Schießkunst *f*; **2.** Treffsicherheit *f*.

'mark·up *s.* **✝ 1.** a) höhere Auszeichnung (*e-r Ware*), b) Preiserhöhung *f*; **2.** Kalkulati'onsaufschlag *m*; **3.** *Am.* im Preis erhöhter Ar'tikel.

marl [mɑːl] **I** *s. geol.* Mergel *m*; **II** *v/t.* ✗ mergeln.

mar·ma·lade ['mɑːməleɪd] *s.* (*bsd.* O'rangen)Marme‚lade *f*.

Mar·mite ['mɑːmaɪt] *TM npr.* dunkle Paste aus Hefe- u. Gemüseextrakt.

mar·mite ['mɑːmaɪt] *s.* Kochtopf aus Ton.

mar·mo·set ['mɑːməʊzet] *s. zo.* Krallenaffe *m*.

mar·mot ['mɑːmət] *s. zo.* **1.** Murmeltier *n*; **2.** Prä'riehund *m*.

ma·roon¹ [məˈruːn] **I** *v/t.* **1.** (*auf e-r einsamen Insel etc.*) aussetzen; **2.** *fig.* a) im Stich lassen, b) von der Außenwelt abschneiden; **II** *v/i.* **3.** *Brit.* her'umlungern; **4.** *Am.* einsam zelten; **III** *s.* **5.** Busch-, Ma'ronneger *m* (*Westindien u. Guayana*); **6.** Ausgesetzte(r *m*) *f*.

ma·roon² [məˈruːn] **I** *s.* **1.** Ka'stanienbraun *n*; **2.** Ka'nonenschlag *m* (*Feuerwerk*); **II** *adj.* **3.** ka'stanienbraun.

mar·plot ['mɑːplɒt] *s.* **1.** Quertreiber *m*; **2.** Spielverderber *m*, Störenfried *m*.

marque [mɑːk] *s.* **✝** *hist.:* **letter(s) of ~** (**and reprisal**) Kaperbrief *m*.

mar·quee [mɑːˈkiː] *s.* **1.** großes Zelt; **2.** *Am.* Mar'kise *f*, Schirmdach *n* (*über e-m Hoteleingang etc.*); **3.** Vordach *n* (*über Haustür*).

mar·quess ['mɑːkwɪs] *s.* → **marquis**.

mar·que·try, *a.* **mar·que·te·rie** ['mɑːkɪtrɪ] *s.* In'tarsia *f*, Markete'rie *f*, Holzeinlegearbeit *f*.

mar·quis ['mɑːkwɪs] *s.* Mar'quis *m* (*englischer Adelstitel*).

mar·riage ['mærɪdʒ] *s.* **1.** Heirat *f*, Vermählung *f*, Hochzeit *f* (**to** mit); → *civil* 4; **2.** Ehe(stand *m*) *f*: **~ of convenience** Vernunftehe, Geldheirat *f*; **by ~** angeheiratet; **of his** (**her**) **first ~** aus erster Ehe; **related by ~** verschwägert; **contract a ~** die Ehe eingehen; **give s.o. in ~** j-n verheiraten; **take s.o. in ~** j-n heiraten; **3.** *fig.* Vermählung *f*, innige Verbindung; **'mar·riage·a·ble** [-dʒəbl] *adj.* heiratsfähig: **~ age** Ehemündigkeit *f*.

mar·riage| ar·ti·cles *s. pl.* ⚖ Ehever-

---

trag *m*; **~ bro·ker** *s.* Heiratsvermittler *m*; **~ bu·reau** *s.* 'Heiratsinsti‚tut *n*; **~ cer·e·mo·ny** *s.* Trauung *f*; **~ cer·tif·i·cate** *s.* Trauschein *m*; **~ con·tract** *s.* ⚖ Ehevertrag *m*; **~ flight** *s.* Bienenzucht: Hochzeitsflug *m*; **~ guid·ance** *s.* Eheberatung *f*: **~ counsel(l)or** Eheberater(in); **~ li·cence**, *Am.* **~ li·cense** *s.* ⚖ (kirchliche, *Am.* amtliche) Eheerlaubnis; **~ lines** *s. pl. Brit.* F Trauschein *m*; **~ por·tion** *s.* ✝ Mitgift *f*; **~ set·tle·ment** *s.* ⚖ Ehevertrag *m*.

mar·ried ['mærɪd] *adj.* **1.** verheiratet, Ehe..., ehelich: **~ life** Eheleben *n*; **~ man** Ehemann *m*; **~ state** Ehestand *m*; **2.** *fig.* eng *od.* innig (mitein'ander) verbunden.

mar·ron ['mærən] *s.* ❀ Ma'rone *f*.

mar·row¹ ['mærəʊ] *s.* **1.** *anat.* (Knochen-) Mark *n*; **2.** *fig.* Mark *n*, Kern *m*, das Innerste *od.* Wesentlichste; Lebenskraft *f*: **to the ~** (**of one's bones**) bis aufs Mark, bis ins Innerste; → *pith* 2.

mar·row² ['mærəʊ] *s. Am. mst* **~ squash**, *Brit. a.* **vegetable ~** ❀ Eier-, Markkürbis *m*.

'mar·row·bone *s.* **1.** Markknochen *m*; **2.** *pl. humor.* Knie *pl.*; **3.** *pl.* → **crossbones**.

mar·row·less ['mærəʊlɪs] *adj. fig.* mark-, kraftlos.

mar·row·y ['mærəʊɪ] *adj. a. fig.* markig, kernig, kräftig.

mar·ry¹ ['mærɪ] **I** *v/t.* **1.** heiraten, sich vermählen *od.* verheiraten mit: **be married to** verheiratet sein mit; **get married to** sich verheiraten mit; **2.** *a.* **~ off** Sohn, Tochter verheiraten (**to** an acc., mit); **3.** *ein* Paar trauen (*Geistlicher*); **4.** *fig.* eng verbinden *od.* verknüpfen (**to** mit); **II** *v/i.* **5.** (sich ver-) heiraten: **~ing man** F Heiratslustige(r) *m*, Ehekandidat *m*; **~ in haste and repent at leisure** schnell gefreit, lang bereut.

mar·ry² ['mærɪ] *int. obs.* für'wahr!

Mars [mɑːz] *npr. u. s.* Mars *m* (*Kriegsgott od.* Planet).

marsh [mɑːʃ] *s.* **1.** Sumpf(land *n*) *m*, Marsch *f*; **2.** Mo'rast *m*.

mar·shal ['mɑːʃl] **I** *s.* **1.** ✕ Marschall *m*; **2.** ⚖ *Brit.* Gerichtsbeamte(r) *m*; **3.** ⚖ *Am.* a) US ~ ('Bundes)Voll‚zugsbeamte(r) *m*, b) Be'zirkspoli‚zeichef *m*, c) *a.* **city ~** Poli'zeidi‚rektor *m*; d) *a.* **fire ~** 'Branddi‚rektor *m*; **4.** *hist.* 'Hofmar‚schall *m*; **5.** Zere'monienmeister *m*; Festordner *m*; *mot.* Rennwart *m*; **II** *v/t.* **6.** aufstellen (*a.* ✕), (an)ordnen, arrangieren: **~ wag(g)ons into trains** Züge zs.-stellen; **~ one's thoughts** *fig.* s-e Gedanken ordnen; **7.** (*bsd. feierlich*) (hin'ein)geleiten (*into* in acc.); **8.** ✈ einwinken; **'mar·shal·(l)ing yard** [-ʃlɪŋ] *s.* 🚂 Rangier-, Verschiebebahnhof *m*.

marsh| fe·ver *s.* 🦟 Sumpffieber *n*; **~ gas** *s.* Sumpfgas *n*; **'~·land** *s.* Sumpf-, Marschland *n*; **‚~·mal·low** *s.* **1.** ❀ Echter Eibisch, Al'thee *f*; **2.** Marsh'mallow *n* (*Süßigkeit*); **~ mar·i·gold** *s.* ❀ Sumpfdotterblume *f*.

marsh·y ['mɑːʃɪ] *adj.* sumpfig, mo'rastig, Sumpf...

mar·su·pi·al [mɑːˈsjuːpjəl] *zo.* **I** *adj.* **1.** Beuteltier...; **2.** Beutel...; **II** *s.* **3.** Beuteltier *n*.

mart [mɑːt] *s.* **1.** Markt *m*, Handelszentrum *m*; **2.** Aukti'onsraum *m*; **3.** *obs. od. poet.* Markt(platz) *m*, (Jahr)Markt *m*.

mar·ten ['mɑːtɪn] *s. zo.* Marder *m*.

mar·tial ['mɑːʃl] *adj.* □ **1.** kriegerisch,

streitbar; **2.** mili'tärisch, sol'datisch: ~ *music* Militärmusik *f*; **3.** Kriegs..., Militär...: ~ *law* Kriegs-, Standrecht *n*; **state of ~ law** Ausnahmezustand *m*; ~ *arts* asiatische Kampfsportarten.

Mar·ti·an ['mɑːʃjən] **I** *s.* **1.** Marsmensch *m*; **II** *adj.* **2.** Mars..., kriegerisch; **3.** *ast.* Mars...

mar·tin ['mɑːtɪn] *s. orn.* Mauerschwalbe *f*.

mar·ti·net [‚mɑːtɪ'net] *s.* Leuteschinder *m*, Zuchtmeister *m*.

mar·tyr ['mɑːtə] **I** *s.* **1.** Märtyrer(in), Blutzeuge *m*; **2.** *fig.* Märtyrer(in), Opfer *n*: *make a ~ of o.s.* sich für et. aufopfern, *iro.* den Märtyrer spielen: *die a ~ to* (*od. in the cause of*) *science* sein Leben im Dienst der Wissenschaft opfern; **3.** F Dulder *m*, armer Kerl: *be a ~ to gout* ständig von Gicht geplagt werden; **II** *v/t.* **4.** zum Märtyrer machen; **5.** zu Tode martern; **6.** martern, peinigen; **'mar·tyr·dom** [-dəm] *s.* **1.** Mar'tyrium *n* (*a. fig.*), Märtyrertod *m*; **2.** Marterqualen *pl.* (*a. fig.*); **'mar·tyr·ize** [-əraɪz] *v/t.* **1.** (*o.s.* sich) zum Märtyrer machen (*a. fig.*); **2.** → *martyr* 6.

mar·vel ['mɑːvl] **I** *s.* **1.** Wunder(ding) *n*: *engineering ~s* Wunder der Technik; *be a ~ at s.th.* et. fabelhaft können; **2.** Muster *n* (*of* an *dat.*): *he is a ~ of patience* er ist die Geduld selber; *he is a perfect ~* F er ist fantastisch *od.* ein Phänomen; **II** *v/i.* **3.** sich (ver)wundern, staunen (*at* über *acc.*); **4.** sich verwundert fragen, sich wundern (*that* dass, *how* wie, *why* warum).

mar·vel·(l)ous ['mɑːvələs] *adj.* □ **1.** erstaunlich, wunderbar; **2.** un'glaublich; **3.** F fabelhaft, fan'tastisch.

Marx·i·an ['mɑːksjən] → *Marxist*; **'Marx·ism** [-sɪzəm] *s.* Mar'xismus *m*; **'Marx·ist** [-sɪst] **I** *s.* Mar'xist(in); **II** *adj.* mar'xistisch.

mar·zi·pan [‚mɑːzɪ'pæn] *s.* Marzi'pan *n*.

mas·car·a [mæ'skɑːrə] *s.* Wimperntusche *f*.

mas·cot ['mæskət] *s.* Mas'kottchen *n*, Talisman *m*; Glücksbringer(in): *radiator ~* Kühlerfigur *f*.

mas·cu·line ['mæskjʊlɪn] **I** *adj.* **1.** männlich, masku'lin (*a. ling.*); Männer...; **2.** unweiblich, masku'lin; **II** *s.* **3.** *ling.* Masku'linum *n*; **mas·cu·lin·i·ty** [‚mæskjʊ'lɪnətɪ] *s.* **1.** Männlichkeit *f*; **2.** Mannhaftigkeit *f*.

mash¹ [mæʃ] **I** *s.* **1.** *Brauerei etc.*: Maische *f*; **2.** ✓ Mengfutter *n*; **3.** Brei *m*, Mansch *m*; **4.** *Brit.* Kar'toffelbrei *m*; **5.** *fig.* Mischmasch *m*; **II** *v/t.* **6.** (ein)maischen; **7.** zerdrücken, -quetschen: *~ed potatoes* Kartoffelbrei *m*.

mash² [mæʃ] *obs. sl.* **I** *v/t.* **1.** *j-m* den Kopf verdrehen; **2.** flirten mit; **II** *v/i.* **3.** flirten, schäkern.

mash·er¹ ['mæʃə] *s.* **1.** Stampfer *m* (*Küchengerät*); **2.** *Brauerei*: 'Maischappa‚rat *m*.

mash·er² ['mæʃə] *s. obs. sl.* Schwerenöter *m*, 'Schäker' *m*.

mask [mɑːsk] **I** *s.* **1.** Maske *f* (*a.* △), Larve *f*: *death ~* Totenmaske *f*; **2.** (Schutz-, Gesichts)Maske *f*: *fencing ~* Fechtmaske; *oxygen ~* ✿ Sauerstoffmaske; **3.** Gasmaske *f*; **4.** Maske *f*: a) Maskierte(r *m*) *f*, b) 'Maskenko‚stüm *n*, Maskierung *f*, c) *fig.* Verkappung *f*: *throw off the ~ fig.* die Maske fallen lassen; *under the ~ of* unter dem Deckmantel (*gen.*); **5.** maskenhaftes Gesicht; **6.** *Kosmetik*: (Gesichts)Maske *f*; **7.** → *masque*; **8.** ✕ Tarnung *f*, Blende

f; **9.** *phot.* Vorsatzscheibe *f*; **II** *v/t.* **10.** *j-n* maskieren, verkleiden, vermummen; *fig.* verschleiern, -hüllen; **11.** ✕ tarnen; **12.** *a.* ~ *out* ◉ korrigieren, retuschieren; *Licht* abblenden; **masked** [-kt] *adj.* **1.** maskiert (*a.* ♥); Masken...: ~ *ball* Maskenball *m*; **2.** ✕, ✝ getarnt; **'mask·er** [-kə] *s.* Maske *f*, Maskenspieler *m*.

mas·och·ism ['mæsəʊkɪzəm] *s.* ♂, *psych.* Maso'chismus *m*; **'mas·och·ist** [-ɪst] *s.* Maso'chist *m*.

ma·son ['meɪsn] **I** *s.* **1.** Steinmetz *m*; **2.** Maurer *m*; **3.** *oft* ♉ Freimaurer *m*; **II** *v/t.* **4.** mauern; **Ma·son·ic** [mə'sɒnɪk] *adj.* freimaurerisch, Freimaurer...; **'ma·son·ry** [-rɪ] *s.* **1.** Steinmetz-, Maurerarbeit *f od.* -handwerk *n*; **2.** Mauerwerk *n*; **3.** *mst.* ♉ Freimaure'rei *f*.

masque [mɑːsk] *s. thea. hist.* Maskenspiel *n*.

mas·quer·ade [‚mæskə'reɪd] **I** *s.* **1.** Maske'rade *f*: a) Maskenball *m*, b) Maskierung *f*, c) *fig.* The'ater *n*, Verstellung *f*, d) *fig.* Maske *f*, Verkleidung *f*; **II** *v/i.* **2.** an e-r Maske'rade teilnehmen; **3.** sich maskieren *od.* verkleiden (*a. fig.*); **4.** *fig.* sich ausgeben (*as* als).

mass¹ [mæs] **I** *s.* **1.** *allg.* Masse *f* (*a.* ◉ *u. phys.*): *a ~ of blood* ein Klumpen Blut; *a ~ of troops* e-e Truppenansammlung; *in the ~* im Großen u. Ganzen; **2.** Mehrzahl *f*: *the* (*great*) *~ of imports* der überwiegende Teil der Einfuhr; **3.** *the ~* die Masse, die Allgemeinheit: *the ~es* die ‚breite' Masse; **II** *v/t.* **4.** (*v/i.* sich) (an)sammeln *od.* (an)häufen, (*v/i.* sich) zs.-ballen; ✕ (*v/i.* sich) massieren *od.* konzentrieren; **III** *adj.* Massen...: ~ *acceleration phys.* Massenbeschleunigung *f*, ~ *communication* Massenkommunikation *f*, ~ *meeting* Massenversammlung *f*; ~ *murder* Massenmord *m*; ~ *society* Massengesellschaft *f*; ~ *unemployment* Massenarbeitslosigkeit *f*.

Mass² [mæs] *s. eccl.* (*a.* ♪) Messe *f*; → *High* (*Low*) *Mass*; ~ *was said* die Messe wurde gelesen; *to attend* (*the*) (*od. go to*) ~ zur Messe gehen; ~ *for the dead* Toten-, Seelenmesse.

mas·sa·cre ['mæsəkə] **I** *s.* Gemetzel *n*, Mas'saker *n*, Blutbad *n*; **II** *v/t.* niedermetzeln, massakrieren.

mas·sage ['mæsɑːʒ] **I** *s.* Mas'sage *f*: ~ *parlo(u)r* Massagesalon *m*; **II** *v/t.* massieren.

mas·seur [mæ'sɜː] (*Fr.*) *s.* Mas'seur *m*; **mas·seuse** [mæ'sɜːz] (*Fr.*) *s.* Mas'seurin *f*, Mas'seuse *f*.

mas·sif ['mæsiːf] *s. geol.* Ge'birgsmas‚siv *n*, -stock *m*.

mas·sive ['mæsɪv] *adj.* □ **1.** mas'siv (*a. geol., a. Gold etc.*), schwer, massig; **2.** *fig.* mas'siv, gewaltig, wuchtig, ‚klotzig'; **'mas·sive·ness** [-nɪs] *s.* **1.** Mas'sive(s) *n*, Schwere(s) *n*; **2.** Gediegenheit *f* (*Gold etc.*); **3.** *fig.* Wucht *f*.

mass | **me·di·a** *s. pl.* Massenmedien *pl.*; **'~·pro‚duce** *v/t.* serienmäßig herstellen: **~d articles** Massen-, Serienartikel; **~ pro·duc·tion** *s.* ✝ 'Massen-, 'Serienprodukti‚on *f*; *standardized ~* Fließarbeit *f*.

mass·y ['mæsɪ] → *massive*.

mast¹ [mɑːst] **I** *s.* **1.** ♉ (Schiffs)Mast *m*: *sail before the ~* (als Matrose) zur See fahren; **2.** (Gitter-, Leitungs-, An'tennen-, ✓ Anker)Mast *m*; **II** *v/t.* **3.** ♉ bemasten: *three-~ed* dreimastig.

mast² [mɑːst] *s.* ✓ Mast(futter *n*) *f*.

mas·tec·to·my [mæ'stektəmɪ] *s.* ♂

'Brustamputati‚on *f*.

mas·ter ['mɑːstə] **I** *s.* **1.** Meister *m* (*a. Kunst u. fig.*), Herr *m*, Gebieter *m*: *the ~* ♉ *eccl.* der Herr (*Christus*); *be ~ of s.th.* et. (*a. e-e Sprache*) beherrschen; *be ~ of o.s.* sich in der Gewalt haben; *be ~ of the situation* Herr der Lage sein; *be one's own ~* sein eigener Herr sein; *be ~ of one's time* über s-e Zeit (nach Belieben) verfügen können; **2.** Besitzer *m*, Eigentümer *m*, Herr *m*: *make o.s. ~ of s.th.* et. in s-n Besitz bringen; **3.** Hausherr *m*; **4.** Meister *m*, Sieger *m*; **5.** a) Lehrherr *m*, Meister *m*, b) *a.* ♉ Dienstherr *m*, Arbeitgeber *m*, c) (Handwerks)Meister *m*: ~ *tailor* Schneidermeister; *like ~ like man* wie der Herr, sos Gescherr; **6.** Vorsteher *m*, Leiter *m* e-r Innung etc.; **7.** ♉ ('Handels)Kapi‚tän *m*: ~'s certificate Kapitänspatent *n*; **8.** *bsd. Brit.* Lehrer *m*: ~ *in English* Englischlehrer; **9.** *Brit. univ.* Rektor *m* (*Titel der Leiter einiger Colleges*); **10.** *univ.* Ma'gister *m* (*Grad*): ♉ *of Arts* Magister Artium; ♉ *of Science* Magister der Naturwissenschaften; **11.** junger Herr (*a. als Anrede für Knaben bis zu 16 Jahren*); **12.** *Brit.* (*in Titeln*): Leiter *m*, Aufseher *m* (*am königlichen Hof etc.*): ♉ *of Ceremonies* a) Zeremonienmeister *m*, b) Conférencier *m*; ♉ *of the Horse* Oberstallmeister *m*; **13.** ♉ Proto'koll führender Gerichtsbeamter: ♉ *of the Rolls* Oberarchivar *m*; **14.** → *master copy* 1; **II** *v/t.* **15.** Herr sein *od.* werden über (*acc.*) (*a. fig.*), *a.* Sprache etc. beherrschen; *Aufgabe, Schwierigkeit* meistern; **16.** Tier zähmen; *a.* Leidenschaften etc. bändigen; **III** *adj.* **17.** Meister..., meisterhaft, -lich; **18.** Meister..., Herren...; **19.** Haupt..., hauptsächlich: ~ *file* Hauptkartei *f*, ~ *switch* ♭ Hauptschalter *m*; **20.** leitend, führend.

mas·ter|-at-'arms [-ərət'ɑː-] *pl.* ‚**mas·ters-at-'arms** [-əzət'ɑː-] *s.* ♉ 'Schiffspro‚fos *m* (*Polizeioffizier*); ~ **build·er** *s.* Baumeister *m*; ~ **car·pen·ter** *s.* Zimmermeister *m*; ~ **chord** *s.* ♪ Domi'nantdreiklang *m*; ~ **clock** *s.* Zen'traluhr *f* (*e-r Uhrenanlage*); ~ **cop·y** *s.* **1.** Origi'nalko‚pie *f* (*a. Film etc.*); **2.** 'Handexem‚plar *n* (*es literarischen etc. Werks*); ~ **file** *s.* Stammdatei *f*.

mas·ter·ful ['mɑːstəfʊl] *adj.* □ **1.** herrisch, gebieterisch; **2.** → *masterly*.

mas·ter| fuse *s.* ♭ Hauptsicherung *f*; ~ **ga(u)ge** *s.* ◉ Urlehre *f*; '~·**key** *s.* **1.** Hauptschlüssel *m*; **2.** *fig.* Schlüssel *m*.

mas·ter·less ['mɑːstəlɪs] *adj.* herrenlos; **'mas·ter·li·ness** [-lɪnɪs] *s.* meisterhafte Ausführung, Meisterschaft *f*; **'mas·ter·ly** [-lɪ] *adj. u. adv.* meisterhaft, -lich, Meister...

'mas·ter|·mind **I** *s.* **1.** über'ragender Geist, Ge'nie *n*; **2.** (führender) Kopf; **II** *v/t.* **3.** der Kopf (*gen.*) sein, leiten; '~·**piece** *s.* Meisterstück *n*, -werk *n*; ~ **plan** *s.* Gesamtplan *m*; ~ **ser·geant** *s.* ✕ *Am.* (Ober)Stabsfeldwebel *m*.

mas·ter·ship ['mɑːstəʃɪp] *s.* **1.** meisterhafte Beherrschung (*of gen.*), Meisterschaft *f*; **2.** Herrschaft *f*, Gewalt *f* (*over* über *acc.*); **3.** Vorsteheramt *n*; **4.** Lehramt *n*.

mas·ter| stroke *s.* Meisterstreich *m*, -stück *n*, Glanzstück *n*; ~ **tooth** *s.* [*irr.*] Eck-, Fangzahn *m*; ~ **touch** *s.* **1.** Meisterhaftigkeit *f*, -schaft *f*; **2.** Meisterzug *m*; **3.** ◉ *u. fig.* letzter Schliff; '~·**work** → *masterpiece*.

mas·ter·y ['mɑːstərɪ] *s.* **1.** Herrschaft *f*,

Gewalt *f* (*of*, *over* über *acc.*); **2.** Über'legenheit *f*, Oberhand *f*: *gain the ~ over s.o.* über j-n die Oberhand gewinnen; **3.** Beherrschung *f* (*e-r Sprache etc.*); **4.** → *master touch* 1.

'mast·head *s.* **1.** ♻ Masttopp *m*, Mars *m*: *~ light* Topplicht *n*; **2.** *typ.* Im'pressum *n* e-r Zeitung.

mas·tic ['mæstɪk] *s.* **1.** Mastix(harz *n*) *m*; **2.** ♀ Mastixstrauch *m*; **3.** Mastik *m*, 'Mastixze,ment *m*.

mas·ti·cate ['mæstɪkeɪt] *v/t.* (zer-) kauen; **mas·ti·ca·tion** [,mæstɪ'keɪʃn] *s.* Kauen *n*; **'mas·ti·ca·tor** [-tə] *s.* **1.** Kauende(r *m*) *f*; **2.** Fleischwolf *m*; **3.** ⚙ 'Mahlma,schine *f*; **'mas·ti·ca·to·ry** [-kətərɪ] *adj.* Kau..., Fress...

mas·tiff ['mæstɪf] *s.* Mastiff *m*, Bulldogge *f*, Englische Dogge.

mas·ti·tis [mæ'staɪtɪs] *s.* ♣ Brust(drüsen)entzündung *f*; **mas·toid** ['mæstɔɪd] *adj. anat.* masto'id, brust(warzen)förmig; **mas·tot·o·my** [mæ'stɒtəmɪ] *s.* ♣ 'Brustoperati,on *f*.

mas·tur·bate ['mæstəbeɪt] *v/i.* masturbieren; **mas·tur·ba·tion** [,mæstə'beɪʃn] *s.* Masturbati'on *f*.

mat¹ [mæt] **I** *s.* **1.** Matte *f* (*a. Ringen, Turnen*): *~ position* Ringen: Bank *f*; *be on the ~* a) am Boden sein, b) *sl. fig.* ,dran' sein, in der Tinte sitzen, *a.* e-e Zigarre verpasst kriegen; **2.** 'Untersetzer *m*, -satz *m*: *beer ~* Bierdeckel *m*; **3.** Vorleger *m*, Abtreter *m*; **4.** grober Sack; **5.** verfilzte Masse (*Haar etc.*), Gewirr *n*; **6.** (*glasloser*) Wechselrahmen; **II** *v/t.* **7.** mit Matten belegen; **8.** (*v/i.* sich) verflechten; **9.** (*v/i.* sich) verfilzen (*Haar*).

mat² [mæt] **I** *adj.* matt (*a. phot.*), glanzlos, mattiert; **II** *v/t.* mattieren.

match¹ [mætʃ] **I** *s.* **1.** *der od. die od. das gleiche od.* Ebenbürtige: *his ~* a) seinesgleichen, b) sein Ebenbild *n*, c) j-d, der es mit ihm aufnehmen kann; *meet one's ~* s-n Meister finden; *be a ~ for s.o.* j-m gewachsen sein; *be more than a ~ for s.o.* j-m überlegen sein; **2.** Gegenstück *n*, Passende(s) *n*; **3.** (zs.-passendes) Paar, Gespann *n* (*a. fig.*): *they are an excellent ~* sie passen ausgezeichnet zueinander; **4.** ✝ Ar'tikel *m* gleicher Quali'tät: *exact ~* genaue Bemusterung; **5.** (Wett)Kampf *m*, Wettspiel *n*, Par'tie *f*, Treffen *n*: *boxing ~* Boxkampf *m*; *singing ~* Wettsingen *n*; **6.** a) Heirat *f*, b) *gute etc.* Par'tie (*Person*): *make a ~ (of it)* e-e Ehe stiften od. zustande bringen; **II** *v/t.* **7.** j-n passend verheiraten (*to*, *with* mit); **8.** *j-n od. et.* vergleichen (*with* mit); **9.** *j-n* ausspielen (*against* gegen); **10.** passend machen, anpassen (*to*, *with* an *acc.*); *a. ehelich* verbinden, zs.-fügen; ⚡ angleichen: *~ing circuit* Anpassungskreis *m*; **11.** entsprechen (*dat.*), *a. farblich etc.* passen zu: *well-~ed* gut zs.-passend; **12.** *et.* Gleiches *od.* Passendes auswählen *od.* finden zu: *can you ~ this velvet for me?* haben Sie et. Passendes zu diesem Samtstoff?; **13.** *nur pass.: be ~ed j-m* ebenbürtig *od.* gewachsen sein, *e-r Sache* gleichkommen; *not to be ~ed* unerreichbar; **III** *v/i.* **14.** zs.-passen, über'einstimmen (*with* mit), entsprechen (*to dat.*): *a brown coat and gloves to ~* ein brauner Mantel u. dazu passende Handschuhe.

match² [mætʃ] *s.* **1.** Zünd-, Streichholz *n*; **2.** Zündschnur *f*; **3.** *hist.* Lunte *f*; **'~ box** *s.* Streichholzschachtel *f*.

match·less ['mætʃlɪs] *adj.* □ unvergleichlich, einzigartig.

'match,mak·er *s.* **1.** Ehestifter(in), *b.s.* Kuppler(in); **2.** Heiratsvermittler(in).

match| point *s. sport* (für den Sieg) entscheidender Punkt; *Tennis etc.*: Matchball *m*; **'~·wood** *s.* (Holz)Späne *pl.*, Splitter *pl.*: *make ~ of s.th.* aus et. Kleinholz machen, et. kurz u. klein schlagen.

mate¹ [meɪt] **I** *s.* **1.** a) ('Arbeits)Kame,rad *m*, Genosse *m*, Gefährte *m*, b) *als Anrede*: Kame'rad *m*, ,Kumpel' *m*, c) Gehilfe *m*, Handlanger *m*; **2.** a) (Lebens)Gefährte *m*, Gatte *m*, Gattin *f*, b) *bsd. orn.* Männchen *n od.* Weibchen *n*, c) Gegenstück *n* (*von Schuhen etc.*); **3.** *Handelsmarine*: 'Schiffsoffi,zier *m*; **4.** ♻ Maat *m*: *cook's ~* Kochsmaat; **II** *v/t.* **5.** (*paarweise*) verbinden, *bsd.* vermählen, -heiraten; *Tiere* paaren; **6.** *fig.* ein'ander anpassen: *~ words with deeds* auf Worte entsprechende Taten folgen lassen; **III** *v/i.* **7.** sich vermählen, (*a. weitS.*) sich verbinden; *zo.* sich paaren; **8.** ⚙ eingreifen (*Zahnräder*); aufein'ander arbeiten (*Flächen*): *mating surfaces* Arbeitsflächen.

mate² [meɪt] → *checkmate*.

ma·te·ri·al [mə'tɪərɪəl] **I** *adj.* □ **1.** materi'ell, physisch, körperlich; **2.** stofflich, Material...: *~ damage* Sachschaden *m*; *~ defect* Materialfehler *m*; *~ fatigue* ⚙ Materialermüdung *f*; *~ goods* Sachgüter; **3.** materia'listisch (*Anschauung etc.*); **4.** materi'ell, leiblich: *~ well-being*; **5.** a) sachlich wichtig, gewichtig, von Belang, b) wesentlich, ausschlaggebend (*to* für); ⚖ erheblich: *~ facts*; *a ~ witness* ein unentbehrlicher Zeuge; *Logik*: sachlich (*Folgerung etc.*); **7.** ♠ materi'ell (*Punkt etc.*); **II** *s.* **8.** Materi'al *n*, Stoff *m* (*beide a. fig.*: *for zu e-m Buch etc.*); ⚙ Werkstoff *m*; (Kleider-)Stoff *m*; **9.** *coll. od. pl.* Materi'al(ien *pl.*) *n*, Ausrüstung *f*: *building ~s* Baustoffe; *cleaning ~s* Putzzeug *n*; *war ~* Kriegsmaterial; *writing ~s* Schreibmaterial(ien); **10.** *oft pl. fig.* 'Unterlagen *pl.*, *urkundliches etc.* Materi'al; **ma'te·ri·al·ism** [-lɪzəm] *s.* Materia'lismus *m*; **ma'te·ri·al·ist** [-lɪst] **I** *s.* Materia'list(in); **II** *adj. a.* **ma·te·ri·al·is·tic** [mə,tɪərɪə'lɪstɪk] *adj.* (□ *~ally*) materia'listisch; **ma·te·ri·al·i·za·tion** [mə,tɪərɪəlaɪ'zeɪʃn] *s.* **1.** Verkörperung *f*; **2.** *Spiritismus*: Materialisati'on *f*; **ma'te·ri·al·ize** [-laɪz] **I** *v/t.* **1.** *e-r Sache* stoffliche Form geben, *et.* verkörperlichen; **2.** *et.* verwirklichen; **3.** *bsd. Am.* materia'listisch machen: *~ thought*; **4.** *Geister* erscheinen lassen; **II** *v/i.* **5.** (feste) Gestalt annehmen, sich verkörpern (*in in dat.*); **6.** sich verwirklichen, Tatsache werden, zu'stande kommen; **7.** sich materialisieren, erscheinen (*Geister*).

ma·té·ri·el [mə,tɪərɪ'el] *s.* Ausrüstung *f*, (✕ 'Kriegs)Materi,al *n*.

ma·ter·nal [mə'tɜːnl] *adj.* □ a) mütterlich, Mutter...: *~ instinct* (*love*), b) *Verwandte(r) etc.* mütterlicherseits, c) Mütter...: *~ mortality* Müttersterblichkeit *f*.

ma·ter·ni·ty [mə'tɜːnətɪ] **I** *s.* Mutterschaft *f*; **II** *adj.* Wöchnerinnen..., Schwangerschafts..., Umstands...(-*kleidung*): *~ allowance* (*od. benefit*) Mutterschaftsbeihilfe *f*; *~ dress* Umstandskleid *n*; *~ home*, *~ hospital* Entbindungsklinik *f*; *~ leave* Mutterschaftsurlaub *m*; *~ ward* Entbindungsstation *f*.

mat·ey ['meɪtɪ] **I** *adj.* kame'radschaftlich, vertraulich, famili'är; **II** *s. Brit.* F ,Kumpel' *m* (*Anrede*).

math [mæθ] *s. Am.* für **maths**.

math·e·mat·i·cal [,mæθə'mætɪkl] *adj.* □ **1.** mathe'matisch; **2.** *fig.* (mathe'matisch) ex'akt; **math·e·ma·ti·cian** [,mæθəmə'tɪʃn] *s.* Mathe'matiker(in); **,math·e'mat·ics** [-ks] *s. pl. mst sg. konstr.* Mathema'tik *f*: *higher* (*new*) *~* höhere (neue) Mathema'tik.

maths [mæθs] *s. Brit.* F ,Mathe' *f* (*Mathematik*).

mat·ins ['mætɪnz] *s. pl. oft 2* a) *R.C.* (Früh)Mette *f*, b) *Church of England*: 'Morgenlitur,gie *f*.

mat·i·nee, **mat·i·née** ['mætɪneɪ] *s. thea.* Mati'nee *f*, *bsd.* Nachmittagsvorstellung *f*.

mat·ing ['meɪtɪŋ] *s. bsd. orn.* Paarung *f*: *~ season* Paarungszeit *f*.

ma·tri·ar·chal [,meɪtrɪ'ɑːkl] *adj.* matriar'chalisch; **ma·tri·ar·chy** ['meɪtrɪɑːkɪ] *s.* Mutterherrschaft *f*, Matriar'chat *n*; **,ma·tri'cid·al** [-ɪ'saɪdl] *adj.* muttermörderisch; **ma·tri·cide** ['meɪtrɪsaɪd] *s.* **1.** Muttermord *m*; **2.** Muttermörder(in).

ma·tric·u·late [mə'trɪkjʊleɪt] **I** *v/t.* immatrikulieren (*an e-r Universität*); **II** *v/i.* sich immatrikulieren (lassen); **III** *s.* Immatrikulierte(r *m*) *f*; **ma·tric·u·la·tion** [mə,trɪkjʊ'leɪʃn] *s.* Immatrikulati'on *f*.

mat·ri·mo·ni·al [,mætrɪ'məʊnjəl] *adj.* □ ehelich, Ehe...: *~ agency* Heiratsinstitut *n*; *~ cases* ⚖ Ehesachen; *~ law* Eherecht *n*; **mat·ri·mo·ny** ['mætrɪmənɪ] *s.* Ehe(stand *m*) *f*.

ma·trix ['meɪtrɪks] *pl.* **-tri·ces** [-trɪsiːz] *s.* **1.** Mutter-, Nährboden *m* (*beide a. fig.*), 'Grundsub,stanz *f*; **2.** *physiol.* Matrix *f*: a) Mutterboden *m*, b) Gewebeschicht *f*, c) Gebärmutter *f*; **3.** *min.* a) Grundmasse *f*, b) Ganggestein *n*; **4.** ⚙, *typ.* Ma'trize *f* (*a. Schallplattenherstellung*); **5.** ⅍ Matrix *f*: *~ algebra* Matrizenrechnung *f*.

ma·tron ['meɪtrən] *s.* **1.** würdige Dame, Ma'trone *f*; **2.** Hausmutter *f* (*e-s Internats etc.*), Wirtschafterin *f* (*als Vorsteherin*), b) Oberschwester *f*, Oberin *f im Krankenhaus*, c) Aufseherin *f im Gefängnis etc.*; **'ma·tron·ly** [-lɪ] *adj.* ma'tronenhaft (*a. adv.*), gesetzt: *~ duties* hausmütterliche Pflichten.

mat·ted¹ ['mætɪd] *adj.* mattiert.

mat·ted² ['mætɪd] *adj.* **1.** mit Matten bedeckt: *a ~ floor*; **2.** verflochten: *~ hair* verfilztes Haar.

mat·ter ['mætə] **I** *s.* **1.** Ma'terie *f* (*a. phys., phls.*), Materi'al *n*, Stoff *m*; *biol.* Sub'stanz *f*: → *foreign* 2, *grey matter*; **2.** Sache *f* (*a. ⚖*), Angelegenheit *f*: *this is a serious ~*; *the ~ in hand* die vorliegende Angelegenheit; *a ~ of fact* e-e Tatsache; *as a ~ of fact* tatsächlich, eigentlich; *a ~ of course* e-e Selbstverständlichkeit; *as a ~ of course* selbstverständlich; *a ~ of form* e-e Formsache; *~ (in issue)* ⚖ Streitgegenstand *m*; *a ~ of taste* (e-e) Geschmackssache; *a ~ of time* e-e Frage der Zeit; *it is a ~ of life and death* es geht um Leben u. Tod; *it's no laughing ~* es ist nichts zum Lachen; *for that ~* was das (an)betrifft, schließlich; *in the ~ of* a) hinsichtlich (*gen.*), b) ⚖ in Sachen *A.* gegen *B.*; **3.** *pl.* (*ohne Artikel*) die 'Umstände *pl.*, die Dinge *pl.*: *to make ~s worse* was die Sache noch schlimmer macht; *as ~s stand* wie die Dinge liegen; **4.** *the ~* die Schwierigkeit: *what's the ~?* was ist los?, wo fehlts?; *what's the ~ with him (it)?* was ist los mit ihm (damit)?; *no ~!* es hat nichts zu sagen!; *it's no ~ whether* es spielt keine Rolle, ob; *no ~ what he says* was er auch sagt; *no ~ who* gleichgültig wer; **5.** *a ~ of* (*mit verblasster Bedeutung*) Sache *f*, etwas: *it's a ~ of £5* es kostet 5 Pfund; *a ~ of three weeks* ungefähr 3 Wochen; *it was a ~ of five minutes* es dauerte nur 5 Minuten; *it's a ~ of common knowledge* es ist allgemein bekannt; **6.** *fig.* Stoff *m* (*Dichtung*), Thema *n*, Gegenstand *m*, Inhalt *m* (*Buch*), innerer Gehalt; **7.** *mst postal ~* Postsache *f*: *printed ~* Drucksache *f*; **8.** *typ.* a) Manu'skript *n*, b) (Schrift)Satz *m*: *live ~, standing ~* Stehsatz *m*; **9.** ⚕ Eiter *m*; **II** *v/i.* **10.** von Bedeutung sein (*to* für), dar'auf ankommen (*to s.o.* j-m): *it doesn't ~* (es) macht nichts; *it ~s little* es ist ziemlich einerlei, es spielt kaum e-e Rolle; **11.** ⚕ eitern.

,**mat·ter|-of-'course** [-tərəv'k-] *adj.* selbstverständlich; ,**~-of-'fact** [-tərəv'f-] *adj.* sachlich, nüchtern; pro'saisch.

Mat·thew ['mæθjuː] *npr. u. s. bibl.* Mat'thäus(evan,gelium *n*) *m*.

mat·ting ['mætɪŋ] *s.* ⊕ **1.** Mattenstoff *m*; **2.** Matten(belag *m*) *pl.*

mat·tock ['mætək] *s.* (Breit)Hacke *f*, ✒ Karst *m*.

mat·tress ['mætrɪs] *s.* Ma'tratze *f*.

mat·u·ra·tion [,mætjuˈreɪʃn] *s.* **1.** ⚕ (Aus)Reifung *f*, Eiterung *f* (*Geschwür*); **2.** *biol., a. fig.* Reifen *n*.

ma·ture [məˈtjʊə] **I** *adj.* ☐ **1.** *allg.* reif (*a. Käse, Wein; a.* ⚕ *Geschwür*); **2.** reif (*Person*): a) voll entwickelt, b) *fig.* gereift, mündig; **3.** *fig.* reiflich erwogen, (wohl) durch'dacht: *upon ~ reflection* nach reiflicher Überlegung; *~ plans* ausgereifte Pläne; **4.** † fällig, zahlbar (*Wechsel*); **II** *v/t.* **5.** reifen (lassen), zur Reife bringen; *fig. Pläne* reifen lassen; **III** *v/i.* **6.** reif werden, (her'an-, aus)reifen; † fällig werden; **ma'tured** [-əd] *adj.* **1.** (aus)gereift; **2.** abgelagert; **3.** † fällig; **ma'tu·ri·ty** [-ərətɪ] *s.* **1.** Reife *f* (*a.* ⚕ *u. fig.*): *bring* (*come*) *to ~* zur Reife bringen (kommen); *~ of judg(e)ment* Reife des Urteils; **2.** † Fälligkeit *f*, Verfall(zeit *f*) *m*: *at* (*od. on*) *~* bei Fälligkeit; *~ date* Fälligkeitstag *m*; **3.** *fig. pol.* Mündigkeit *f* (*des Bürgers*).

ma·tu·ti·nal [,mætjuːˈtaɪnl] *adj.* morgendlich, Morgen..., früh.

mat·y ['meɪtɪ] *Brit.* → **matey**.

maud·lin ['mɔːdlɪn] **I** *s.* weinerliche Gefühlsduse'lei; **II** *adj.* weinerlich senti'men'tal, rührselig.

maul [mɔːl] **I** *s.* **1.** ⊕ Schlegel *m*, schwerer Holzhammer; **II** *v/t.* **2.** j-n, *et.* übel zurichten, j-n 'durchprügeln, miss'handeln: *~ about* roh umgehen mit; **3.** ,her'unterreißen' (*Kritiker*).

maul·stick ['mɔːlstɪk] *s. paint.* Malerstock *m*.

maun·der ['mɔːndə] *v/i.* **1.** schwafeln, faseln; **2.** ziellos um'herschlendern *od.* handeln.

Maun·dy Thurs·day ['mɔːndɪ] *s. eccl.* Grün'donnerstag *m*.

mau·so·le·um [,mɔːsəˈlɪəm] *s.* Mauso'leum *n*, Grabmal *n*.

mauve [məʊv] **I** *s.* Malvenfarbe *f*; **II** *adj.* malvenfarbig, mauve.

mav·er·ick ['mævərɪk] *s. Am.* **1.** herrenloses Vieh ohne Brandzeichen; **2.** mutterloses Kalb; **3.** F *pol.* Einzelgänger *m*, *allg.* Außenseiter *m*.

maw [mɔː] *s.* **1.** (Tier)Magen *m*, *bsd.* Labmagen *m* (*der Wiederkäuer*); **2.** *fig.* Rachen *m* des Todes etc.

mawk·ish ['mɔːkɪʃ] *adj.* ☐ **1.** süßlich, abgestanden (*Geschmack*); **2.** *fig.* rührselig, süßlich, kitschig.

'**maw·seed** *s.* Mohnsame(n) *m*.

'**maw·worm** *s. zo.* Spulwurm *m*.

max·i ['mæksɪ] **I** *s.* Maximode *f*: *wear ~* Maxi tragen; **II** *adj.* Maxi...: *~ dress*.

max·il·la [mækˈsɪlə] *pl.* **-lae** [-liː] *s.* **1.** *anat.* (Ober)Kiefer *m*; **2.** *zo.* Fußkiefer *m*, Zange *f*; **max'il·lar·y** [-ərɪ] **I** *adj. anat.* (Ober)Kiefer..., maxil'lar; **II** *s.* Oberkieferknochen *m*.

max·im ['mæksɪm] *s.* Ma'xime *f*.

max·i·mal ['mæksɪml] *adj.* maxi'mal, Maximal..., Höchst...; '**max·i·mize** [-maɪz] *v/t.* ✝, ⊕ maximieren; **max·i·mum** ['mæksɪməm] **I** *pl.* **-ma** [-mə], **-mums** *s.* **1.** Maximum *n*, Höchstgrenze *f*, -maß *n*, -stand *m*, -wert *m* (*a.* ℞): *smoke a ~ of 20 cigarettes a day* maximal 20 Zigaretten am Tag rauchen; **2.** † Höchstpreis *m*, -angebot *n*, -betrag *m*; **II** *adj.* **3.** höchst, größt, Höchst..., Maximal...: *~ credible accident* größter anzunehmender Unfall, GAU *m*; *~ load* ⊕, ⚡ Höchstbelastung *f*; *~ safety load* (*od. stress*) zulässige Beanspruchung; *~ performance* Höchst-, Spitzenleistung *f*; *~ permissible speed* zulässige Höchstgeschwindigkeit; *~ wages* Höchst-, Spitzenlohn *m*.

'**max·i,sin·gle** *s.* Maxisingle *f* (*Schallplatte*).

may¹ [meɪ] *v/aux.* [*irr.*] **1.** (*Möglichkeit, Gelegenheit*) *sg.* kann, mag, *pl.* können, mögen: *it ~ happen any time* es kann jederzeit geschehen; *it might happen* es könnte geschehen; *you ~ be right* du magst Recht haben; *he ~ not come* vielleicht kommt er nicht; *he might lose his way* er könnte sich verirren; **2.** (*Erlaubnis*) *sg.* darf, kann (*a.* 🕮), *pl.* dürfen können: *you ~ go; ~ I ask?* darf ich fragen?; *we might as well go* da können wir ebenso gut auch gehen; **3.** *ungewisse Frage*: *how old ~ she be?* wie alt mag sie wohl sein?; *I wondered what he might be doing* ich fragte mich, was er wohl tue; **4.** *Wunschgedanke, Segenswunsch*: *~ you be happy!* sei glücklich!; *~ it please your Majesty* Eure Majestät mögen geruhen; **5.** *familiäre od. vorwurfsvolle Aufforderung*: *you might help me* du könntest mir (eigentlich) helfen; *you might at least write me* du könntest mir wenigstens schreiben; **6.** *~ od. might* als Konjunktivumschreibung: *I shall write to him so that he ~ know our plans; whatever it ~ cost; difficult as it ~ be* so schwierig es auch sein mag; *we feared they might attack* wir fürchteten, sie könnten *od.* würden angreifen.

May² [meɪ] *s.* **1.** Mai *m*, *poet.* (*fig. a.* 🌑) Lenz *m*: *in ~* im Mai; **2.** 🌑 ♥ Weißdornblüte *f*.

may·be ['meɪbiː] *adv.* viel'leicht.

May| bug *s. zo.* Maikäfer *m*; **~ Day** *s.* der 1. Mai; '**🌑-day** *s. internationales Funknotsignal*; '**~,flow·er** *s.* **1.** ♥ a) Maiblume *f*, b) *Am.* Primelstrauch *m*; **2.** 🌑 *hist.* Name des Auswandererschiffs der *Pilgrim Fathers*; '**~fly** *s. zo.* Eintagsfliege *f*.

may·hap ['meɪhæp] *adv. obs. od. dial.* viel'leicht.

may·hem ['meɪhem] *s.* **1.** *bsd. Am.* 🕮 schwere Körperverletzung; **2.** *fig.* a) ,Gemetzel' *n*, b) Chaos *n*, Verwüstung *f*.

may·o ['meɪəʊ] *s. Am.* F Majo'näse *f*.

may·on·naise [,meɪəˈneɪz] *s.* Majo'näse (-gericht *n*) *f*: *~ of lobster* Hummermajonäse.

---

may·or [meə] *s.* Bürgermeister *m*; '**may·or·al** [-ərəl] *adj.* bürgermeisterlich; '**may·or·ess** [-ərɪs] *s.* **1.** Gattin *f* des Bürgermeisters; **2.** *Am.* Bürgermeisterin *f*.

'**May|·pole**, 🌑 *s.* Maibaum *m*; **~ queen** *s.* Mai(en)königin *f*; '**~·thorn** *s.* ♥ Weißdorn *m*.

maz·a·rine [,mæzəˈriːn] *adj.* maza'rin-, dunkelblau.

maze [meɪz] *s.* **1.** Irrgarten *m*, Laby'rinth *n*, *fig. a.* Gewirr *n*; **2.** *fig.* Verwirrung *f*: *in a ~* → **mazed** [-zd] *adj.* verdutzt, verblüfft.

Mc·Coy [məˈkɔɪ] *s. Am. sl.*: *the real ~* der wahre Jakob, der (die, das) Echte, das einzig Wahre.

'**M-day** *s.* Mo'bilmachungstag *m*.

me [miː; mɪ] **I** *pron.* **1.** (*dat.*) mir: *he gave ~ money*; *he gave it* (*to*) *~*; **2.** (*acc.*) mich: *he took ~ away* er führte mich weg; **3.** F ich: *it's ~* ich bins; **II** 🌑 *s.* **4.** *psych.* Ich *n*.

mead¹ [miːd] *s.* Met *m*.

mead² [miːd] *s. poet. für* **meadow**.

mead·ow ['medəʊ] *s.* Wiese *f*, **~ grass** *s.* ♥ Rispengras *n*; **~ saf·fron** *s.* ♥ (*bsd.* Herbst)Zeitlose *f*; '**~·sweet** *s.* ♥ **1.** Mädesüß *n*; **2.** *Am.* Spierstrauch *m*.

mead·ow·y ['medəʊɪ] *adj.* wiesenartig, -reich, Wiesen...

mea·ger *Am.*, **mea·gre** *Brit.* ['miːgə] *adj.* ☐ **1.** mager, dürr; **2.** *fig.* dürftig, kärglich; '**mea·ger·ness** *Am.*, '**mea·gre·ness** *Brit.* [-nɪs] *s.* **1.** Magerkeit *f*; **2.** Dürftigkeit *f*.

meal¹ [miːl] *s.* **1.** Schrotmehl *n*; **2.** Mehl *n*, Pulver *n* (*aus Nüssen, Mineralen etc.*).

meal² [miːl] *s.* Mahl(zeit *f*) *n*, Essen *n*: *have a ~* e-e Mahlzeit einnehmen; *make a ~ of sth.* et. verzehren; *~s on wheels* Essen *n* auf Rädern.

meal·ies ['miːlɪz] (*S.Afr.*) *s. pl.* Mais *m*.

meal| tick·et *s. Am.* **1.** Essensbon(s *pl.*) *m*; **2.** *sl.* a) *b.s.* ,Ernährer' *m*, b) Einnahmequelle *f*, ,Goldesel' *m*, c) Kapi'tal *n*: *his voice is his ~*; '**~·time** *s.* Essenszeit *f*.

meal·y ['miːlɪ] *adj.* **1.** mehlig: *~ potatoes*; **2.** mehlhaltig; **3.** (wie) mit Mehl bestäubt; **4.** blass (*Gesicht*); '**~-mouthed** *adj.* **1.** heuchlerisch, glattzüngig; **2.** leisetreterisch: *be ~ about it* um den (heißen) Brei herumreden.

mean¹ [miːn] **I** *v/t.* [*irr.*] **1.** *et.* beabsichtigen, vorhaben, im Sinn haben: *I ~ it* es ist mir Ernst damit; *~ to do s.th.* et. zu tun gedenken, et. tun wollen; *he ~s no harm* er meint es nicht böse; *I didn't ~ to disturb you* ich wollte dich nicht stören; *without ~ing it* ohne es zu wollen; → **business** 4; **2.** bestimmen (*for* zu): *he was meant to be a barrister* er war zum Anwalt bestimmt; *the cake is meant to be eaten* der Kuchen ist zum Essen da; *that remark was meant for you* das war auf dich abgezielt; **3.** meinen, sagen wollen: *by 'liberal' I ~* unter ,liberal' verstehe ich; *his father I ~ to say* ich will sagen; **4.** bedeuten: *that ~s a lot of work*; *he ~s all the world to me* er bedeutet mir alles; *that ~s war* das bedeutet Krieg; *what does 'fair' ~?* was bedeutet *od.* heißt (das Wort) ,fair'?; **II** *v/i.* [*irr.*] **5.** *~ well* (*ill*) *by* (*od. to*) *s.o.* j-m wohlgesinnt (übel gesinnt) sein.

mean² [miːn] *adj.* ☐ **1.** gering, niedrig: *~ birth* niedrige Herkunft; **2.** ärmlich, schäbig: *~ streets*; **3.** unbedeutend, gering: *no ~ artist* ein recht bedeutender

Künstler; *no* ~ *foe* ein nicht zu unterschätzender Gegner; **4.** schäbig, gemein; *feel* ~ sich schäbig vorkommen; **5.** geizig, schäbig, ‚filzig‘; **6.** *Am.* F a) bösartig, ‚ekelhaft‘, b) ‚bös‘, scheußlich (*Sache*), c) ‚toll‘, ‚wüst‘: *a* ~ *fighter*, d) *Am.* unpässlich: *feel* ~ sich elend fühlen.

mean³ [miːn] **I** *adj.* **1.** mittel, mittler, Mittel...; 'durchschnittlich, Durchschnitts...: ~ *life* a) mittlere Lebensdauer, b) *phys.* Halbwertzeit *f*; ~ *sea level* das Normalnull; ~ *value* Mittelwert *m*; **II** *s.* **2.** Mitte *f*, das Mittlere, Mittel *n*, 'Durchschnitt(szahl *f*) *m*; A Mittel(wert *m*) *n*: *hit the happy* ~ die goldene Mitte treffen; *arithmetical* ~ arithmetisches Mittel; → *golden mean*; **3.** *pl. sg. od. pl. konstr.* (Hilfs)Mittel *n od. pl.*, Werkzeug *n*, Weg *m*: *by all* ~*s* auf alle Fälle, unbedingt; *by any* ~*s* etwa, vielleicht, möglicherweise; *by no* ~*s* durchaus nicht, keineswegs, auf keinen Fall; *by some* ~*s or other* auf die eine oder andere Weise, irgendwie; *by* ~*s of* mittels, durch; *by this* (*od. these*) ~*s* hierdurch; ~ *of production* Produktionsmittel; ~*s of transport*(*ation*) Beförderungsmittel; *find the* ~*s* Mittel und Wege finden; → *end* 9, *way*¹ 1; **4.** *pl.* (Geld)Mittel *pl.*, Vermögen *n*, Einkommen *n*: *live within* (*beyond*) *one's* ~*s* s-n Verhältnissen entsprechend (über s-e Verhältnisse) leben; *a man of* ~*s* ein bemittelter Mann; ~*s test* *Brit.* (behördliche) Einkommens- *od.* Bedürftigkeitsermittlung.

me·an·der [mɪˈændə] **I** *s. bsd. pl.* Windung *f*, verschlungener Pfad, Schlängelweg *m*; △ Mä'ander(linien *pl.*) *m*, Schlangenlinie *f*; **II** *v/i.* sich winden, (sich) schlängeln.

mean·ing [ˈmiːnɪŋ] **I** *s.* **1.** Absicht *f*, Zweck *m*, Ziel *n*; **2.** Sinn *m*, Bedeutung *f*: *full of* ~ bedeutungsvoll, bedeutsam; *what's the* ~ *of this?* was soll das bedeuten?; *words with the same* ~ Wörter mit gleicher Bedeutung; *full of* ~ → 3; *if you take my* ~ wenn Sie verstehen, was ich meine; **II** *adj.* □ **3.** bedeutungsvoll, bedeutsam (*Blick etc.*); **4.** *in Zssgn* in ... Absicht: *well-*~ wohlmeinend, -wollend; **'mean·ing·ful** [-fʊl] *adj.* bedeutungsvoll; **'mean·ing·less** [-lɪs] *adj.* **1.** sinn-, bedeutungslos; **2.** ausdruckslos (*Gesicht*).

mean·ness [ˈmiːnnɪs] *s.* **1.** Niedrigkeit *f*, niedriger Stand; **2.** Wertlosigkeit *f*, Ärmlichkeit *f*; **3.** Schäbigkeit *f*: a) Gemeinheit *f*, Niederträchtigkeit *f*, b) Geiz *m*; **4.** *Am.* F Bösartigkeit *f*.

meant [ment] *pret. u. p.p. von* **mean¹**.

‚mean|'time I *adv.* in'zwischen, mittler'weile, unter'dessen; **II** *s.* Zwischenzeit *f*: *in the* ~ → I; ~ *time s. ast.* mittlere (Sonnen)Zeit; **‚~'while** → *meantime* I.

mea·sles [ˈmiːzlz] *s. pl. sg. konstr.* **1.** ✶ Masern *pl.*: *false* ~, *German* ~ Röteln *pl.*; **2.** *vet.* Finnen *pl.* (*der Schweine*); **'mea·sly** [-lɪ] *adj.* **1.** ✶ masernkrank; **2.** *vet.* finnig; **3.** *sl.* elend, schäbig, lumpig.

meas·ur·a·ble [ˈmeʒərəbl] *adj.* □ messbar: *within* ~ *distance of fig.* nahe (*dat.*); **'meas·ur·a·ble·ness** [-nɪs] *s.* Messbarkeit *f*.

meas·ure [ˈmeʒə] **I** *s.* **1.** Maß(einheit *f*) *n*: *long* ~ Längenmaß; ~ *of capacity* Hohlmaß; **2.** *fig.* richtiges Maß, Ausmaß *n*: *beyond* (*od. out of*) *all* ~ über alle Maßen, grenzenlos; *in a great* ~ in großem Maße, großenteils, überaus; *in*

some ~, *in a* (*certain*) ~ gewissermaßen, bis zu e-m gewissen Grade; *for good* ~ obendrein; **3.** Messen *n*, Maß *n*: *take the* ~ *of s.th.* et. abmessen; *take s.o.'s* ~ a) j-m (*zu e-m Anzug*) Maß nehmen, b) *fig.* j-n taxieren *od.* einschätzen; → *made-to-measure*; **4.** Maß *n*, Messgerät *n*; *weigh with two* ~*s fig.* mit zweierlei Maß messen; ~ *tape-measure*; **5.** Maßstab *m* (*of* für): *be a* ~ *of s.th.* e-r Sache als Maßstab dienen; *man is the* ~ *of all things* der Mensch ist das Maß aller Dinge; **6.** Anteil *m*, Porti'on *f*, gewisse Menge; **7.** a) A Maß(einheit *f*) *n*, Teiler *m*, Faktor *m*, b) ♪, *phys.* Maßeinheit *f*: ~ *of variation* Schwankungsmaß; *common* ~ gemeinsamer Teiler; **8.** (abgemessener) Teil, Grenze *f*: *set a* ~ *to s.th.* et. begrenzen; **9.** *Metrik:* a) Silbenmaß *n*, b) Versglied *n*, c) Versmaß *n*; **10.** ♪ Metrum *n*, Takt *m*, Rhythmus *m*: *tread a* ~ tanzen; **11.** *poet.* Weise *f*, Melo'die *f*; **12.** *pl. geol.* Lager *n*, Flöz *n*; **13.** *typ.* Zeilen-, Satz-, Ko'lumnenbreite *f*; **14.** *fig.* Maßnahme *f*, -regel *f*, Schritt *m*: *take* ~*s* Maßnahmen ergreifen; *take legal* ~*s* den Rechtsweg beschreiten; **15.** ᵗ₂ gesetzliche Maßnahme, Verfügung *f*: *coercive* ~ Zwangsmaßnahme; **II** *v/t.* **16.** (ver)messen, ab-, aus-, zumessen: ~ *one's length fig.* längelang hinfallen; ~ *swords* a) die Klingen messen, b) (*with*) die Klingen kreuzen (mit) (*a. fig.*); ~ *s.o. for a suit of clothes* j-m Maß nehmen zu e-m Anzug; **17.** ~ *out* ausmessen, die Ausmaße bestimmen; **18.** *fig.* ermessen; **19.** (ab)messen, abschätzen (*by* an *dat.*): ~*d by* gemessen an; **20.** beurteilen (*by* nach); **21.** vergleichen, messen (*with* mit): ~ *one's strength with s.o.* s-e Kräfte mit j-m messen; **III** *v/i.* **22.** Messungen vornehmen; **23.** messen, groß sein: *it* ~*s 7 inches* es misst 7 Zoll, es ist 7 Zoll lang; **24.** ~ *up* (*to*) die Ansprüche (*gen.*) erfüllen, her'anreichen (an *acc.*); **'meas·ured** [-əd] *adj.* **1.** (ab)gemessen: ~ *in the clear* (*od. day*) ⚙ *im* Lichten gemessen; ~ *value* Messwert *m*; **2.** richtig proportioniert; **3.** (ab)gemessen, gleich-, regelmäßig: ~ *tread* gemessener Schritt; **4.** wohl überlegt, abgewogen, gemessen: *to speak in* ~ *terms* sich maßvoll ausdrücken; **5.** im Versmaß, metrisch; **'meas·ure·less** [-lɪs] *adj.* unermesslich, unbeschränkt; **'meas·ure·ment** [-mənt] *s.* **1.** (Ver-)Messung *f*, (Ab)Messen *n*; **2.** Maß *n*; *pl.* Abmessungen *pl.*, Größe *f*, Ausmaße *pl.*; **3.** ⚓ Tonnengehalt *m*.

meas·ur·ing [ˈmeʒərɪŋ] *s.* **1.** Messen *n*, (Ver)Messung *f*; **2.** *in Zssgn:* Mess...; ~ *bridge* *s.* ⚡ Messbrücke *f*; ~ *di·al* *s.* Rundmaßskala *f*; ~ *glass* *s.* Messglas *n*; ~ *in·stru·ment* *s.* Messgerät *n*; ~ *range* *s.* Messbereich *m*; ~ *tape* *s.* Maß-, Messband *n*, Bandmaß *n*.

meat [miːt] *s.* **1.** Fleisch *n* (*als Nahrung; Am. a. von Früchten etc.*): ~*s* a) Fleischwaren, b) Fleichgerichte; *fresh* ~ Frischfleisch; *butcher's* ~ Schlachtfleisch; ~ *and drink to me* es ist mir e-e Wonne; *one man's* ~ *is another man's poison* des einen Freud ist des andern Leid; **2.** Fleischspeise *f*: *cold* ~ kalte Platte; ~ *tea* kaltes Abendbrot mit Tee, **3.** *fig.* Sub'stanz *f*, Gehalt *m*, Inhalt *m*: *full of* ~ gehaltvoll; ~ *ax*(*e*) *s.* Schlachtbeil *m*; ~*'ball* *s.* Bu'lette *f*, *südd.* Fleischpflanzerl *n*, *östr.* Fleischla(i)berl *n*; **2.** *Am. sl.* ‚Heini‘ *m*; ~ *broth*

s. Fleischbrühe *f*; '~·,chop·per *s.* **1.** Hackmesser *n*; **2.** → **grind·er** *s.* Fleischwolf *m*; ~ *ex·tract* *s.* 'Fleischex,trakt *m*; ~ *fly* *s. zo.* Schmeißfliege *f*; ~ *inspec·tion* *s.* Fleischbeschau *f*.

meat·less [ˈmiːtlɪs] *adj.* fleischlos.

meat| loaf *s.* Hackbraten *m*; '~·man [-mæn] *s.* [*irr.*] *Am.* Fleischer *m*; ~ *meal* *s.* Fleischmehl *n*; ~ *pie* *s.* 'Fleischpa,stete *f*; ~ *pud·ding* *s.* Fleischpudding *m*; ~ *safe* *s.* Fliegenschrank *m*.

meat·y [ˈmiːtɪ] *adj.* **1.** fleischig; **2.** fleischartig; **3.** *fig.* gehaltvoll, handfest, so'lid.

Mec·can·o [mɪˈkɑːnəʊ] (*TM*) *s.* Sta'bilbaukasten *m* (*Spielzeug*).

me·chan·ic [mɪˈkænɪk] **I** *adj.* **1.** → *mechanical*; **II** *s.* **2.** a) Me'chaniker *m*, Maschi'nist *m*, Mon'teur *m*, (Auto-) Schlosser *m*, b) Handwerker *m*; **3.** *pl. sg. konstr. phys.* a) Me'chanik *f*, Bewegungslehre *f*: ~*s of fluids* Strömungslehre *f*, b) a. *practical* ~*s* Ma'schinenlehre *f*; **4.** *pl. sg. konstr.* ⚙ Konstrukti'on *f* von Ma'schinen *etc.*: *precision* ~*s* Feinmechanik *f*; **5.** *pl. sg. konstr.* Mecha'nismus *m* (*a. fig.*); **6.** *pl. sg. konstr. fig.* Technik *f*: *the* ~*s of playwriting*; **me'chan·i·cal** [-kl] *adj.* □ **1.** ⚙ me'chanisch (*a. phys.*); maschi'nell, Maschinen...; auto'matisch: ~ *drawing* maschinelles Zeichnen; ~ *engineer* Maschinenbauingenieur *m*; ~ *engineering* Maschinenbau(kunde *f*) *m*; ~ *wood-pulp* Holzschliff *m*; **2.** *fig.* me'chanisch, auto'matisch: **me'chan·i·cal·ness** [-klnɪs] *s.* das Me'chanische; **mech·a·ni·cian** [ˌmekəˈnɪʃn] → *mechanic* 2.

mech·a·nism [ˈmekənɪzəm] *s.* **1.** Mecha'nismus *m*: ~ *of government fig.* Regierungs-, Verwaltungsapparat *m*; **2.** *biol., physiol., phls., psych.* Mecha'nismus *m*; **3.** *paint. etc.* Technik *f*; **mech·a·nis·tic** [ˌmekəˈnɪstɪk] *adj.* (□ ~*ally*) **1.** *phls.* mecha'nistisch; **2.** me'chanisch bestimmt; **3.** me'chanisch; **mech·a·ni·za·tion** [ˌmekənaɪˈzeɪʃn] *s.* Mechanisierung *f*; **'mech·a·nize** [-naɪz] *v/t.* mechanisieren, ✕ *a.* motorisieren: ~*d di·vision* ✕ Panzergrenadierdivision *f*.

me·co·ni·um [mɪˈkəʊnjəm] *s. physiol.* Kindspech *n*.

med·al [ˈmedl] *s.* Me'daille *f*: a) Denk-, Schaumünze *f*; → *reverse* 4, b) Orden *m*, Ehrenzeichen *n*, Auszeichnung *f*: ∠ *of Honor Am.* ✕ Tapferkeitsmedaille; ~ *ribbon* Ordensband *n*.

med·aled, med·al·ist *Am.* → *medalled, medallist*.

med·alled [ˈmedld] *adj.* ordengeschmückt.

me·dal·lion [mɪˈdæljən] *s.* **1.** große Denk- *od.* Schaumünze, Me'daille *f*; **2.** Medail'lon *n*; **med·al·list** [ˈmedlɪst] *s.* **1.** Me'daillenschneider *m*; **2.** *bsd. sport* (*Gold- etc.*)Medaillengewinner(in).

med·dle [ˈmedl] *v/i.* **1.** sich (ein-) mischen (*with, in* in *acc.*); **2.** sich (un-)aufgefordert) befassen, sich abgeben, sich einlassen (*with* mit); **3.** her'umhantieren, -spielen (*with* mit); **'med·dler** [-lə] *s.* j-d, der sich (ständig) in fremde Angelegenheiten mischt, aufdringlicher Mensch; **'med·dle·some** [-səm] *adj.* aufdringlich.

me·di·a¹ [ˈmedɪə] *pl.* -di·ae [-dɪiː] *s. ling.* Media *f*, stimmhafter Verschlusslaut.

me·di·a² [ˈmiːdjə] **1.** *pl. von* **medium**; **2.** Medien *pl.*: ~ *coverage* die Medienberichterstattung; ~ *research* Me-

M

dienforschung *f*; *mixed* ~ a) Multimedia *pl.*, b) *Kunst*: Mischtechnik *f*.
me·di·ae·val *etc.*→ *medieval etc.*
me·di·al ['miːdjəl] **I** *adj.* □ **1.** mittler, Mittel...: ~ *line* Mittellinie *f*; **2.** *ling.* medi'al, inlautend: ~ *sound* Inlaut *m*; **3.** Durchschnitts...; **II** *s.* **4.** → *media¹*.
me·di·an ['miːdjən] **I** *adj.* die Mitte bildend, mittler, Mittel...: ~ *salaries* ✝ mittlere Gehälter; ~ *strip Am. mot.* Mittelstreifen *m*; **II** *s.* Mittellinie *f*, -wert *m*; ~ *line s.* ⚥ a) Mittellinie *f* (*a. anat.*), b) Hal,bierungslinie *f*; ~ *point s.* ⚥ Mittelpunkt *m*, Schnittpunkt *m* der 'Winkelhal,bierenden.
me·di·ant ['miːdjənt] *s.* ♪ Medi'ante *f*.
me·di·ate ['miːdɪeɪt] **I** *v/i.* **1.** vermitteln (*a. v/t.*), den Vermittler spielen (*between* zwischen *dat.*); **2.** da'zwischenliegen, ein Bindeglied bilden; **II** *adj.* [-dɪət] □ **3.** mittelbar, 'indi,rekt; **4.** → *median* I; **me·di·a·tion** [,miːdɪ'eɪʃn] *s.* Vermittlung *f*, Fürsprache *f*; *eccl.* Fürbitte *f*: *through his* ~; **'me·di·a·tor** [-tə] *s.* Vermittler *m*; Fürsprecher *m*; *eccl.* Mittler *m*; **me·di·a·to·ri·al** [,miːdɪə'tɔːrɪəl] *adj.* □ vermittelnd, (Ver)Mittler...; **'me·di·a·tor·ship** [-tə-ʃɪp] *s.* (Ver)Mittleramt *n*, Vermittlung *f*; **'me·di·a·to·ry** [-dɪətərɪ] → *mediatorial*; **me·di·a·trix** [,miːdɪ'eɪtrɪks] *s.* Vermittlerin *f*.
med·ic ['medɪk] **I** *adj.* → *medical* 1; **II** *s.* F Medi'ziner *m* (*Arzt od. Student*), ✕ Sani'täter *m*.
Med·i·caid ['medɪkeɪd] *s. Am. Gesundheitsfürsorge(programm) für Bedürftige.*
med·i·cal ['medɪkl] **I** *adj.* □ **1.** medi'zinisch, ärztlich, Kranken..., *a.* inter'nistisch: ~ *attendance* ärztliche Behandlung; ~ *board* Gesundheitsbehörde *f*; ~ *certificate* ärztliches Attest; ⚥ *Corps* ✕ Sanitätstruppe *f*; ⚥ *Department* ✕ Sanitätswesen *n*; ~ *examiner* a) Amtsarzt *m*, -ärztin *f*, b) Vertrauensarzt *m*, -ärztin *f* (*Krankenkasse*), c) *Am.* Leichenbeschauer(in); ~ *history* Krankengeschichte *f*; ~ *jurisprudence* Gerichtsmedizin *f*; ~ *man* → 3 a; ~ *officer* Amtsarzt *m*, -ärztin *f*; ~ *practitioner* praktischer Arzt, praktische Ärztin; ~ *retirement* vorzeitige Pensionierung aus gesundheitlichen Gründen; ~ *science* medizinische Wissenschaft, Medizin *f*; ~ *specialist* Facharzt *m*, -ärztin *f*; ~ *student* Mediziner(in), Medizinstudent(in); ⚥ *Superintendent* Chefarzt *m*, -ärztin *f*; ~ *ward* innere Abteilung (*e-r Klinik*); *on* ~ *grounds* aus gesundheitlichen Gründen; **2.** Heil..., heilend; **II** *s.* **3.** F a) ,Doktor' *m* (*Arzt*), b) ärztliche Unter'suchung; **me·dic·a·ment** [me'dɪkəmənt] *s.* Medika'ment *n*, Heil-, Arz'neimittel *n*.
Med·i·care ['medɪkeə] *s. Am.* Gesundheitsfürsorge *f* (*bsd. für Senioren*).
med·i·cate ['medɪkeɪt] *v/t.* **1.** medi'zinisch behandeln; **2.** mit Arz'neistoff versetzen *od.* imprägnieren: ~*d cotton* medizinische Watte; ~*d bath* (*wine*) Medizinalbad *n* (-wein *m*); **med·i·ca·tion** [,medɪ'keɪʃn] *s.* **1.** Beimischung *f* von Arz'neistoffen; **2.** Verordnung *f*, medi'zinische *od.* medikamen'töse Behandlung; **'med·i·ca·tive** [-keɪtɪv] *adj.*, **me·dic·i·nal** [me'dɪsɪnl] *adj.* □ Medizinal..., medi'zinisch, heilkräftig, -sam, Heil...: ~ *herbs* Heilkräuter; ~ *spring* Heilquelle *f*.
med·i·cine ['medsɪn] *s.* **1.** Medi'zin *f*, Arz'nei *f* (*a. fig.*): *take one's* ~ a) s-e Medizin (ein)nehmen, b) *fig.* ,die Pille

schlucken'; **2.** a) Heilkunde *f*, ärztliche Wissenschaft, b) innere Medi'zin (*Ggs. Chirurgie*); **3.** Zauber *m*, Medi'zin *f* (*bei Indianern etc.*): *he is bad* ~ *Am. sl.* er ist ein gefährlicher Bursche; ~ *ball s. sport* Medi'zinball *m*; ~ *chest s.* Arz'neischrank *m*, 'Hausapo,theke *f*; ~ *man* [-mæn] *s.* [*irr.*] Medi'zinmann *m*.
med·i·co ['medɪkəʊ] *pl.* **-cos** → *medic* II.
medico- [medɪkəʊ] *in Zssgn* medi'zinisch, Mediko...: ~*legal* gerichtsmedizinisch.
me·di·e·val [,medɪ'iːvl] *adj.* □ mittelalterlich (*a.* F *fig.* altmodisch, vorsintflutlich); **,me·di·e·val·ism** [-vəlɪzəm] *s.* **1.** Eigentümlichkeit *f od.* Geist *m* des Mittelalters; **2.** Vorliebe *f* für das Mittelalter; **3.** Mittelalterlichkeit *f*, **,me·di·e·val·ist** [-vəlɪst] *s.* Mediä'vist(in), Erforscher(in) *od.* Kenner(in) des Mittelalters.
me·di·o·cre [,miːdɪ'əʊkə] *adj.* mittelmäßig, zweitklassig; **me·di·oc·ri·ty** [,miːdɪ'ɒkrɪtɪ] *s.* **1.** Mittelmäßigkeit *f*, mäßige Begabung; **2.** unbedeutender Mensch, kleiner Geist.
med·i·tate ['medɪteɪt] **I** *v/i.* nachsinnen, -denken, grübeln, meditieren (*on, upon* über *acc.*); **II** *v/t.* erwägen, planen, sinnen auf (*acc.*); **med·i·ta·tion** [,medɪ'teɪʃn] *s.* **1.** Meditati'on *f*, tiefes Nachdenken, Sinnen *n*; **2.** (*bsd.* fromme) Betrachtung, Andacht *f*: *book of* ~*s* Andachts-, Erbauungsbuch *n*; **'med·i·ta·tive** [-tətɪv] *adj.* □ **1.** nachdenklich; **2.** besinnlich (*a. Buch etc.*).
med·i·ter·ra·ne·an [,medɪtə'reɪnjən] **I** *adj.* **1.** von Land um'geben; binnenländisch; **2.** ⚥ mittelmeerisch, mediter'ran, Mittelmeer...: ⚥ *Sea* → 3; **II** *s.* **3.** ⚥ Mittelmeer *n*, Mittelländisches Meer *n*; **4.** ⚥ Angehörige(r *m*) *f* der mediter'ranen Rasse.
me·di·um ['miːdjəm] **I** *pl.* **-di·a** [-djə], **-di·ums** *s.* **1.** *fig.* Mitte *f*, Mittel *n*, Mittelweg *m*: *the happy* ~ die goldene Mitte, der goldene Mittelweg; **2.** *phys.* Mittel *n*, Medium *n*; **3.** ✝, *biol.* Medium *n*, Träger *m*, Mittel *n*: *circulating* ~, *currency* ~ ✝ Umlaufs-, Zahlungsmittel; *dispersion* ~ ⚛ Dispersionsmittel; **4.** 'Lebensele,ment *n*, -bedingungen *pl.*; **5.** *fig.* Um'gebung *f*, Mili'eu *n*; **6.** (*a. künstlerisches, a. Kommunikations-*) Medium *n*, (Hilfs-, Werbe- *etc.*)Mittel *n*; Werkzeug *n*, Vermittlung *f*: *by* (*od. through*) *the* ~ *of* durch, vermittels; ~ *media²*; **7.** *paint.* Bindemittel *n*; **8.** Spiritismus *etc.*: Medium *n*; **9.** *typ.* Medi'anpa,pier *n*; **II** *adj.* **10.** mittler, Mittel..., Durchschnitts..., *a.* mittelmäßig: ~ *quality* mittlere Qualität; ~ *price* Durchschnittspreis *m*; ~*-price car mot.* Wagen *m* der mittleren Preisklasse; ~ *brown s.* Mittelbraun *n*; '~*-,dat·ed adj.* ✝ mittelfristig; '~*-faced adj. typ.* halbfett.
me·di·um·is·tic [,miːdjə'mɪstɪk] *adj.* Spiritismus: medi'al (begabt).
me·di·um| *size s.* Mittelgröße *f*; '~*-size(d) adj.* mittelgroß: ~ *car* Mittelklassewagen *m*; '~*-term adj.* mittelfristig; ~ *wave s. Radio*: Mittelwelle *f*.
med·lar ['medlə] *s.* ♀ **1.** Mispelstrauch *m*; **2.** Mispel *f* (*Frucht*).
med·ley ['medlɪ] **I** *s.* **1.** Gemisch *n*; *contp.* Mischmasch *m*, Durchein'ander *n*; **2.** ♪ Potpourri *n*, Medley *n*; **II** *adj.* **3.** gemischt, wirr; bunt; **4.** *sport* Lagen...: ~ *swimming*; ~ *relay* a) Schwimmen: Lagenstaffel *f*, b) *Laufsport*: Schwellstaffel *f*.
me·dul·la [me'dʌlə] *s.* **1.** *anat.* (Kno-

chen)Mark *n*: ~ *spinalis* Rückenmark; **2.** ♀ Mark *n*; **me'dul·lar·y** [-ərɪ] *adj.* medul'lär, Mark...
meed [miːd] *s. poet.* Lohn *m*.
meek [miːk] *adj.* □ **1.** mild, sanft(mütig); **2.** demütig, unter'würfig; **3.** fromm (*Tier*): *as* ~ *as a lamb fig.* lammfromm; **'meek·ness** [-nɪs] *s.* **1.** Sanftmut *f*, Milde *f*; **2.** Demut *f*, Unter'würfigkeit *f*.
meer·schaum ['mɪəʃəm] *s.* Meerschaum(pfeife *f*) *m*.
meet [miːt] **I** *v/t.* [*irr.*] **1.** begegnen (*dat.*), treffen, zs.-treffen mit, treffen auf (*acc.*), antreffen: ~ *s.o. in the street*; *well met!* schön, dass wir uns treffen!; ~ *s.o. at the station* j-n von der Bahn abholen; *be met* abgeholt *od.* empfangen werden; *come* (*go*) *to* ~ *s.o.* j-m entgegengehen (-gehen); **2.** *fig.* j-n kennen lernen: *when I first met him* als ich s-e Bekanntschaft machte; *pleased to* ~ *you* F sehr erfreut, Sie kennen zu lernen; ~ *Mr. Brown! bsd. Am.* darf ich Sie mit Herrn B. bekannt machen?; **4.** *fig.* j-m entgegenkommen (*half-way* auf halbem Wege); **5.** (*feindlich*) zs.-treffen *od.* -stoßen mit, begegnen (*dat.*), stoßen auf (*acc.*); *sport* antreten gegen (*Konkurrenten*); **6.** *a. fig.* j-m gegen-'übertreten; → *fate* 1; **7.** *fig.* entgegentreten (*dat.*): a) *e-r Sache* abhelfen, *der Not* steuern, *Schwierigkeiten* über'winden, *e-m Übel* begegnen, *der Konkurrenz* Herr werden, b) *Einwände* wider'legen, entgegnen auf (*acc.*); **8.** *parl.* sich vorstellen (*dat.*): ~ (*the*) *parliament*; **9.** berühren, münden in (*acc.*) (*Straßen*), stoßen *od.* treffen auf (*acc.*), schneiden (*a.* ⚥): ~ *s.o.'s eye* a) j-m ins Auge fallen, b) j-s Blick erwidern; ~ *the eye* auffallen; *there is more in it than* ~*s the eye* da steckt mehr dahinter; **10.** *Anforderungen etc.* entsprechen, gerecht werden (*dat.*), über'einstimmen mit: *the supply* ~*s the demand* das Angebot entspricht der Nachfrage; *be well met* gut zs.-passen; *that won't* ~ *my case* das löst mein Problem nicht; **11.** *j-s Wünschen* entgegenkommen *od.* entsprechen, *Forderungen* erfüllen, *Verpflichtungen* nachkommen, *Unkosten* bestreiten (*out of* aus), *Nachfrage* befriedigen, *Rechnungen* begleichen, *j-s Auslagen* decken, *Wechsel* honorieren *od.* decken: ~ *the claims of one's creditors* s-e Gläubiger befriedigen; **II** *v/i.* [*irr.*] **12.** zs.-kommen, -treffen, -treten; **13.** sich begegnen, sich treffen, sich finden: ~ *again* sich wieder sehen; **14.** (*feindlich od. im Spiel*) zs.-stoßen, anein'ander geraten, sich messen; *sport* aufein'ander treffen (*Gegner*); **15.** sich kennen lernen, zs.-treffen; **16.** sich vereinigen (*Straßen etc.*), sich berühren; **17.** genau zs.-treffen *od.* -stimmen *od.* -passen, sich decken; zugehen (*Kleidungsstück*); → *end* 1; **18.** ~ *with* a) zs.-treffen mit, sich vereinigen mit, b) (an)treffen, finden, (zufällig) stoßen auf (*acc.*), c) erleben, erleiden, erfahren, betroffen werden von, erhalten, *Billigung* finden, *Erfolg* haben: ~ *with an accident* e-n Unfall erleiden, verunglücken; ~ *with a kind reception* freundlich aufgenommen werden; **III** *s.* **19.** *Am.* a) Treffen *n* (*von Zügen etc.*), b) → *meeting* 3 b; **20.** *Brit. hunt.* a) Jagdtreffen *n* (*zur Fuchsjagd*), b) Jagdgesellschaft *f*.
meet·ing ['miːtɪŋ] *s.* **1.** Begegnung *f*, Zs.-treffen *n*, -kunft *f*; **2.** (*at a* ~ auf

e-r) Versammlung *od.* Konfe'renz *od.* Sitzung *od.* Tagung: **~ of creditors** (**members**) Gläubiger- (Mitglieder-)versammlung; **3.** a) Zweikampf *m*, Du-'ell *n*, b) *sport* Treffen *n*, Wettkampf *m*, Veranstaltung *f*; **4.** Zs.-treffen *n* (*zweier Linien etc.*), Zs.-fluss *m* (*zweier Flüsse*); **~ place** *s.* Treffpunkt *m* (*a. weitS.*), Tagungs-, Versammlungsort *m*.

meg(a)- [meg(ə)] *in Zssgn* a) (riesen-)groß, b) Milli'on.

meg·a ['megə] **I** *adj.* ‚klasse‘, ‚mega‘, ‚geil‘; **II** *adv.* ‚wahnsinnig‘: **they are ~ rich** sie sind ‚stinkreich‘.

meg·a·buck ['megəbʌk] *s.* F Milli'on *f* Dollar; **'meg·a·byte** [-baɪt] *s.* Megabyte *n*; **meg·a·cy·cle** ['megə,saɪkl] *s.* ≠ Megahertz *n*; **'meg·a·death** [-deθ] *s.* Tod *m* von e-r Milli'on Menschen (*bsd. in e-m Atomkrieg*); **'meg·a·fog** [-fɒg] *s.* ♺ 'Nebel,signal,gnal(anlage *f*) *n*; **'meg·a·lith** [-lɪθ] *s.* Mega'lith *m*, großer Steinblock.

megalo- [megələʊ] *in Zssgn* groß.

meg·a·lo·car·di·a [,megələʊ'kɑːdɪə] *s.* ♣ Herzerweiterung *f*; **meg·a·lo·ma·ni·a** [,megələʊ'meɪnjə] *s. psych.* Größenwahn *m*; **meg·a·lop·o·lis** [,megə-'lɒpəlɪs] *s.* **1.** Riesenstadt *f*; **2.** Ballungsgebiet *n*.

meg·a·phone ['megəfəʊn] **I** *s.* Mega-'phon *n*; **II** *v/t. u. v/i.* durch ein Mega-'phon sprechen; **'meg·a·ton** [-tʌn] *s.* Megatonne *f* (*1 Million Tonnen*); **'meg·a·watt** [-wɒt] *s.* ≠ Megawatt *n*.

meg·ger ['megə] *s.* ≠ Megohm'meter *n*.

me·gilp [mə'gɪlp] **I** *s.* Leinöl-, Retuschierfirnis *m*; **II** *v/t.* firnissen.

meg·ohm ['megəʊm] *s.* ≠ Meg'ohm *n*.

me·grim ['miːgrɪm] *s.* **1.** ♣ *obs.* Mi'gräne *f*; **2.** *obs.* Grille *f*, Schrulle *f*; **3.** *pl. obs.* Schwermut *f*, Melancho'lie *f*; **4.** *pl. vet.* Koller *m* (*der Pferde*).

mel·an·cho·li·a [,melən'kəʊljə] *s.* ♣ Melancho'lie *f*, Schwermut *f*; **,mel·an·'cho·li·ac** [-lɪæk], **,mel·an·chol·ic** [-'kɒlɪk] **I** *adj.* melan'cholisch, schwermütig, traurig, schmerzlich; **II** *s.* Melan'choliker(in), Schwermütige(r *m*) *f*; **mel·an·chol·y** ['melənkəlɪ] **I** *s.* Melancho'lie *f*: a) ♣ Depressi'on *f*, b) Schwermut *f*, Trübsinn *m*; **II** *adj.* melan'cholisch: a) schwermütig, trübsinnig, b) *fig.* traurig, düster, trübe.

mé·lange [meɪ'lɑ̃ːʒ] (*Fr.*) *s.* Mischung *f*, Gemisch *n*.

mel·a·no·ma [,melə'nəʊmə] *s.* ♣ Mela-'nom *n*.

me·las·sic [mɪ'læsɪk] *adj.* ♺ Melassin...(-säure *etc.*).

Mel·ba toast ['melbə] *s.* dünne, hart geröstete Brotscheiben *pl*.

me·lee *Am.*, **mê·lée** ['meleɪ] (*Fr.*) *s.* Handgemenge *n*; *fig.* Tu'mult *m*; Gewühl *n*.

mel·io·rate ['miːljəreɪt] **I** *v/t.* **1.** (ver)-bessern; **2.** ✓ meliorieren; **II** *v/i.* sich (ver)bessern; **mel·io·ra·tion** [,miːljə-'reɪʃn] *s.* (Ver)Besserung *f*; ✓ Meliorati'on *f*.

me·lis·sa [mɪ'lɪsə] *s.* ♀, ♣ (Zi'tronen-)Me,lisse *f*.

mel·lif·er·ous [me'lɪfərəs] *adj.* **1.** ♀ honigerzeugend; **2.** *zo.* Honig tragend *od.* bereitend; **mel'lif·lu·ence** [-fluəns] *s.* **1.** Honigfluss *m*; **2.** *fig.* Süßigkeit *f*; **mel'lif·lu·ent** [-fluənt] *adj.* □ (wie Honig) süß *od.* glatt da'hinfließend; **mel'lif·lu·ous** [-fluəs] *adj.* □ *fig.* honigsüß.

mel·low ['meləʊ] **I** *adj.* □ **1.** reif, saftig, mürbe, weich (*Obst*); **2.** ✓ a) leicht zu bearbeiten(d), locker, b) reich (*Boden*); **3.** ausgereift, mild (*Wein*); **4.** sanft, mild, zart, weich (*Farbe, Licht,*

Ton etc.); **5.** *fig.* gereift u. gemildert, mild, freundlich, heiter (*Person*): **of ~ age** von gereiftem Alter; **6.** angeheitert, beschwipst; **II** *v/t.* **7.** weich *od.* mürbe machen, *Boden* auflockern; **8.** *fig.* sänftigen, mildern; **9.** (aus)reifen, reifen lassen (*a. fig.*); **III** *v/i.* **10.** weich *od.* mürbe *od.* mild *od.* reif werden (*Wein etc.*); **11.** *fig.* sich abklären *od.* mildern; **'mel·low·ness** [-nɪs] *s.* **1.** Weichheit *f* (*a. fig.*), Mürbheit *f*; **2.** ✓ Gare *f*; **3.** Gereiftheit *f*; **4.** Milde *f*, Sanftheit *f*.

me·lo·de·on [mɪ'ləʊdjən] *s.* ♪ **1.** Me'lodium(orgel *f*) *n* (*ein amer. Harmonium*); **2.** Art Ak'kordeon *n*; **3.** *obs. Am.* Varie'tee(the,ater) *n*.

me·lod·ic [mɪ'lɒdɪk] *adj.* me'lodisch; **me'lod·ics** [-ks] *s. pl. sg. konstr.* ♪ Melo'dielehre *f*, Me'lodik *f*; **me·lo·di·ous** [mɪ'ləʊdjəs] *adj.* □ melo'dienreich, wohlklingend; **mel·o·dist** ['melədɪst] *s.* **1.** 'Liedersänger(in), -kompo,nist(in); **2.** Me'lodiker *m*; **mel·o·dize** ['melədaɪz] **I** *v/t.* **1.** me'lodisch machen; **2.** *Lieder* vertonen; **II** *v/i.* **3.** Melo'dien singen *od.* komponieren; **mel·o·dra·ma** ['melə,drɑːmə] *s.* Melo'dram(a) *n* (*a. fig.*); **mel·o·dra·mat·ic** [,melədrə-'mætɪk] *adj.* (□ ~ally) melodra'matisch.

mel·o·dy ['melədɪ] *s.* **1.** ♪ (*a. ling. u. fig.*) Melo'die *f*, Weise *f*; **2.** Wohlklang *m*.

mel·on ['melən] *s.* **1.** ♀ Me'lone *f*: **water ~** Wassermelone; **2. cut a ~** ✝ *sl.* e-e Sonderdividende ausschütten.

melt [melt] **I** *v/i.* **1.** (zer)schmelzen, flüssig werden; sich auflösen, auf-, zergehen (**into** in *acc.*): **~ down** zerfließen; → **butter** 1; **2.** sich auflösen; **3.** aufgehen (**into** in *acc.*), sich verflüchtigen; **4.** zs.-schrumpfen; **5.** *fig.* zerschmelzen, zerfließen (**with** vor *dat.*): **~ into tears** in Tränen zerfließen; **6.** *fig.* auftauen, weich werden, schmelzen; **7.** verschmelzen, *ineinander* 'übergehen (*Ränder, Farben etc.*): **outlines ~ing into each other**; **8.** (ver)schmelzen, zur Neige gehen (*Geld etc.*): **~ away** dahinschwinden, -schmelzen; **9.** *humor.* vor Hitze vergehen, zerfließen; **II** *v/t.* **10.** schmelzen, lösen; **11.** (zer)schmelzen *od.* (zer)fließen lassen (**into** in *acc.*); *Butter* zerlassen; ♻ schmelzen: **~ down** einschmelzen; **12.** *fig.* rühren, erweichen: **~ s.o.'s heart**; **13.** *Farben etc.* verschmelzen lassen; **III** *s.* **14.** Schmelzen *n* (*Metall*); **15.** a) Schmelze *f*, geschmolzene Masse, b) → **melting charge**.

'melt·down *s.* **1.** Kernschmelze *f* (*im Reaktor*); **2.** a) Niedergang *m*, Abbau *m*, b) Absacken *n* (*der Börsenkurse*).

melt·ing ['meltɪŋ] *adj.* □ **1.** schmelzend, Schmelz...: **~ heat** schwüle Hitze; **2.** *fig.* a) weich, zart, b) schmelzend, schmachtend, rührend (*Worte etc.*); **~ charge** *s. metall.* Schmelzgut *n*; **~ furnace** *s.* ♻ Schmelzofen *m*; **~ point** *s. phys.* Schmelzpunkt *m*; **~ pot** *s.* Schmelztiegel *m* (*a. fig. Land etc.*): **put into the ~ pot** *fig.* von Grund auf ändern; **~ stock** *s. metall.* Charge *f*, Beschickungsgut *n* (*Hochofen*).

mem·ber ['membə] *s.* **1.** Mitglied *n*, Angehörige(r *m*) *f* (*e-s Klubs, e-r Familie, Partei etc.*): ♗ **of Parliament** *Brit.* Abgeordnete(r *m*) *f* des Unterhauses; ♗ **of the European Parliament** Europaabgeordnete(r *m*) *f*; ♗ **of Congress** *Am.* Kongressmitglied *n*; ♗ **state** Mitgliedstaat *m*; **2.** *anat.* a) Glied(maße *f*)

n, b) (männliches) Glied, Penis *m*; **3.** ♻ (Bau)Teil *n*; **4.** *ling.* Satzteil *m*; **5.** ♈ a) Glied *n* (*Reihe etc.*), b) Seite *f* (*Gleichung*); **'mem·bered** [-əd] *adj.* **1.** gegliedert; **2.** *in Zssgn* ...gliedrig: **four-~** viergliedrig; **'mem·ber·ship** [-ʃɪp] *s.* **1.** Mitgliedschaft *f*, Zugehörigkeit *f*: **~ card** Mitgliedsausweis *m*; **~ fee** Mitgliedsbeitrag *m*; **2.** Mitgliederzahl *f*; *coll.* die Mitglieder *pl*.

mem·brane ['membreɪn] *s.* **1.** *anat.* Mem'bran(e) *f*, Häutchen *n*: **drum ~** Trommelfell *n*; **~ of connective tissue** Bindegewebshaut *f*; **2.** *phys.*, ♻ Membran(e) *f*; **mem·bra·ne·ous** [mem-'breɪnjəs], **mem·bra·nous** [mem-'breɪnəs] *adj. anat.*, ♻ häutig, Membran...: **~ cartilage** Hautknorpel *m*.

me·men·to [mɪ'mentəʊ] *pl.* **-tos** [-z] *s.* Me'mento *n*, Mahnzeichen *n*; Erinnerung *f* (**of** an *acc.*).

mem·o ['meməʊ] *s.* F Memo *n*, No'tiz *f*.

mem·oir ['memwɑː] *s.* **1.** Denkschrift *f*, Abhandlung *f*, Bericht *m*; **2.** *pl.* Memo'iren *pl.*, Lebenserinnerungen *pl*.

mem·o·ra·bil·i·a [,memərə'bɪlɪə] (*Lat.*) *s. pl.* Denkwürdigkeiten *pl.*; **mem·o·ra·ble** ['memərəbl] *adj.* □ denkwürdig.

mem·o·ran·dum [,memə'rændəm] *pl.* **-da** [-də], **-dums** *s.* **1.** Vermerk *m* (*a.* 'Akten)No,tiz *f*: **make a ~ of** *et.* notieren; **urgent ~** Dringlichkeitsvermerk; **2.** ♇ Schriftsatz *m*; Vereinbarung *f*, Vertragsurkunde *f*: **~ of association** Gründungsurkunde (*e-r Gesellschaft*); **3.** ✝ a) Kommissi'onsnota *f*: **send on a ~** in Kommission senden, b) Rechnung *f*, Nota *f*; **4.** *pol.* diplo'matische Note, Denkschrift *f*, Memo'randum *n*; **5.** Merkblatt *n*; **~ book** *s.* No'tizbuch *n*, Kladde *f*.

me·mo·ri·al [mɪ'mɔːrɪəl] **I** *adj.* **1.** Gedächtnis...: **~ service** Gedenkgottesdienst *m*; **II** *s.* **2.** Denkmal *n*, Ehrenmal *n*; Gedenkfeier *f*; **3.** Andenken *n* (**for** an *acc.*); **4.** ♇ Auszug *m* (*aus e-r Urkunde etc.*); **5.** Denkschrift *f*, Eingabe *f*, Gesuch *n*; **6.** *pl.* → **memoir** 2; ♈ **Day** *s. Am.* Volkstrauertag *m* (*30. Mai*); **me'mo·ri·al·ize** [-laɪz] *v/t.* **1.** e-e Denk- *od.* Bittschrift einreichen bei: **~ Congress**; **2.** erinnern an (*acc.*), e-e Gedenkfeier abhalten für.

mem·o·rize ['meməraɪz] *v/t.* **1.** sich *et.* einprägen, auswendig lernen, memorieren; **2.** niederschreiben, festhalten, verewigen; **'mem·o·ry** [-rɪ] *s.* **1.** Gedächtnis *n*, Erinnerung(svermögen *n*) *f*: **from ~, by ~** aus dem Gedächtnis, auswendig; **call to ~** sich *et.* ins Gedächtnis zurückrufen; **escape s.o.'s ~** j-s Gedächtnis *od.* j-m entfallen; **if my ~ serves me** (**right**) wenn ich mich recht erinnere; → **commit** 1; **2.** Erinnerung(szeit) *f* (**of** an *acc.*): **within living ~** seit Menschengedenken; **before ~, beyond ~** in unvordenklichen Zeiten; **3.** Andenken *n*, Erinnerung *f*: **in ~ of** zum Andenken an (*acc.*); → **blessed** 1; **4.** Reminis'zenz *f*, Erinnerung *f* (*an Vergangenes*); **5.** *Computer:* Speicher *m*: **~ access** Speicherzugriff *m*; **~ bank** Speicherbank *f*; **~ capacity** Speicherkapazität *f*; **~ expansion** Speichererweiterung *f*; **~ function** Speicherfunktion *f*.

mem·sa·hib ['mem,sɑːhɪb] *s. Brit. Ind.* euro'päische Frau.

men [men] *pl. von* **man**.

men·ace ['menəs] **I** *v/t.* **1.** bedrohen, gefährden; **2.** *et.* androhen; **II** *v/i.* **3.** drohen, Drohungen ausstoßen; **III** *s.* **4.** (Be)Drohung *f* (**to** *gen.*), *fig. a.* dro-

M

hende Gefahr (**to** für); **5.** F ‚Scheusal‘ *n*, Nervensäge *f*; **'men·ac·ing** [-sɪŋ] *adj*. □ drohend.

mé·nage, me·nage [me'nɑːʒ] (*Fr.*) *s*. Haushalt(ung *f*) *m*.

me·nag·er·ie [mɪ'nædʒərɪ] *s*. Menage-'rie *f*, Tierschau *f*.

mend [mend] **I** *v/t*. **1.** ausbessern, flicken, reparieren: **~ stockings** Strümpfe stopfen; **~ a friendship** fig. e-e Freundschaft ‚kitten‘; **2.** fig. (ver)bessern: **~ one's efforts** s-e Anstrengungen verdoppeln; **~ one's pace** den Schritt beschleunigen; **~ one's ways** sich (*sittlich*) bessern; **least said soonest ~ed** je weniger geredet wird, desto rascher wird alles wieder gut; **II** *v/i*. **3.** sich bessern; **4.** genesen: **be ~ing** auf dem Wege der Besserung sein; **III** *s*. **5.** ✝ *u*. *allg*. Besserung *f*: **be on the ~** → 4; **6.** ausgebesserte Stelle, Stopfstelle *f*, Flicken *m*; **'mend·a·ble** [-dəbl] *adj*. (aus-)besserungsfähig.

men·da·cious [men'deɪʃəs] *adj*. □ lügnerisch, verlogen, lügenhaft; **men'dac·i·ty** [-'dæsətɪ] *s*. **1.** Lügenhaftigkeit *f*, Verlogenheit *f*; **2.** Lüge *f*, Unwahrheit *f*.

Men·de·li·an [men'diːljən] *adj*. *biol*. mendelsch, Mendel...; **'Men·de·lize** ['mendəlaɪz] *v/i*. mendeln.

men·di·can·cy ['mendɪkənsɪ] *s*. Bette'lei *f*, Betteln *n*; **'men·di·cant** [-nt] **I** *adj*. **1.** bettelnd, Bettel...: **~ friar** → 3; **II** *s*. **2.** Bettler(in); **3.** Bettelmönch *m*.

men·dic·i·ty [men'dɪsətɪ] *s*. **1.** Bette'lei *f*; **2.** Bettelstand *m*: **reduce to ~** fig. an den Bettelstab bringen.

mend·ing ['mendɪŋ] *s*. **1.** (Aus)Bessern *n*, Flicken *n*: **his boots need ~** seine Stiefel müssen repariert werden; **invisible ~** Kunststopfen *n*; **2.** ✝ Stopfgarn *n*.

'men·folk(s) *s*. *pl*. Mannsvolk *n*, -leute *pl*.

me·ni·al ['miːnjəl] **I** *adj*. □ **1.** *contp*. knechtisch, niedrig (*Arbeit*): **~ offices** niedrige Dienste; **2.** knechtisch, unter-'würfig; **II** *s*. **3.** Diener(in), Knecht *m*, La'kai *m* (*a. fig.*): **~s** Gesinde *n*.

me·nin·ge·al [mɪ'nɪndʒɪəl] *adj*. *anat*. Hirnhaut...; **men·in·gi·tis** [ˌmenɪn'dʒaɪtɪs] *s*. ✝ Menin'gitis *f*, (Ge)Hirnhautentzündung *f*.

me·nis·cus [mɪ'nɪskəs] *pl*. **-nis·ci** [-'nɪsaɪ] *s*. **1.** Me'niskus *m*: a) halbmondförmiger Körper, b) *anat*. Gelenkscheibe *f*; **2.** *opt*. Me'niskenglas *n*.

men·o·pause ['menəʊpɔːz] *s*. *physiol*. Wechseljahre *pl*., Klimak'terium *n*.

men·ses ['mensiːz] *s*. *pl*. *physiol*. Menses *pl*., Regel *f* (*der Frau*).

men·stru·al ['menstruəl] *adj*. **1.** *ast*. Monats...: **~ equation** Monatsgleichung *f*; **2.** *physiol*. Menstruations...: **~ flow** Regelblutung *f*; **'men·stru·ate** [-ʊeɪt] *v/i*. menstruieren, die Regel haben; **men·stru·a·tion** [ˌmenstrʊ'eɪʃn] *s*. Menstruati'on *f*, (monatliche) Regel, Peri'ode *f*.

men·su·ra·bil·i·ty [ˌmenʃʊrə'bɪlətɪ] *s*. Messbarkeit *f*; **men·su·ra·ble** ['menʃʊrəbl] *adj*. **1.** messbar; **2.** ♪ Mensural...: **~ music**.

men·tal ['mentl] **I** *adj*. □ **1.** geistig, innerlich, intellektu'ell, Geistes...(-*kraft*, -*zustand etc.*): **~ arithmetic** Kopfrechnen *n*; **~ reservation** geheimer Vorbehalt, Mentalreservation *f*; → **note** 2; **2.** (geistig-)seelisch; **3.** ✝ geisteskrank, -gestört, F verrückt: **~ disease** Geisteskrankheit *f*; **~ home**, **~ hospital** Nervenheilanstalt *f*; **~ patient**, **~ case** Geis-

teskranke(r *m*) *f*; **~ly handicapped** geistig behindert; **II** *s*. **4.** F Verrückte(r *m*) *f*; **~ age** *s*. *psych*. geistiges Alter; **~ cru·el·ty** *s*. ⚖ seelische Grausamkeit; **~ de·fi·cien·cy** *s*. ✝ Geistesbehinderung *f*; **~ de·range·ment** *s*. **1.** ✝ krankhafte Störung der Geistestätigkeit; **2.** ✝ Geistesstörung *f*, Irrsinn *m*; **~ hy·giene** *s*. ✝ 'Psychohygi,ene *f*.

men·tal·i·ty [men'tælətɪ] *s*. Mentali'tät *f*, Denkungsart *f*, Gesinnung *f*; Wesen *n*, Na'tur *f*.

men·thol ['menθɒl] *s*. 🜊 Men'thol *n*; **'men·tho·lat·ed** [-θəleɪtɪd] *adj*. Men'thol enthaltend, Menthol...

men·tion ['menʃn] **I** *s*. **1.** Erwähnung *f*: **to make** (**no**) **~ of s.th.** et. (nicht) erwähnen; **hono(u)rable ~** ehrenvolle Erwähnung; **2.** lobende Erwähnung; **II** *v/t*. **3.** erwähnen, anführen: (**please**) **don't ~ it!** bitte!, gern geschehen!, (es ist) nicht der Rede wert!; **not to ~** ganz zu schweigen von; **not worth ~ing** nicht der Rede wert; **'men·tion·a·ble** [-ʃnəbl] *adj*. erwähnenswert.

men·tor ['mentɔː] *s*. Mentor *m*, treuer Ratgeber.

men·u ['menjuː] (*Fr.*) *s*. **1.** Speise(n)-karte *f*, **2.** Speisenfolge *f*; **3.** *Computer*: Me'nü *n*.

me·ow [mɪ'aʊ] **I** *v/i*. mi'auen (*Katze*); **II** *s*. Mi'auen *n*.

me·phit·ic [me'fɪtɪk] *adj*. verpestet, giftig (*Luft, Geruch etc.*).

mer·can·tile ['mɜːkəntaɪl] *adj*. **1.** kaufmännisch, Handel treibend, Handels...: **~ agency** a) Handelsauskunftei *f*, b) Handelsvertretung *f*; **~ law** Handelsrecht *n*; **~ marine** Handelsmarine *f*; **~ paper** ✝ Warenpapier *n*; **2.** ✝ Merkantil...; **'mer·can·til·ism** [-tɪlɪzəm] *s*. **1.** Handels-, Krämergeist *m*; **2.** kaufmännischer Unter'nehmergeist; **3.** ✝ *hist*. Merkanti'lismus *m*.

mer·ce·nar·y ['mɜːsɪnərɪ] **I** *adj*. □ **1.** gedungen, Lohn...: **~ troops** Söldnertruppen; **2.** fig. feil, käuflich; **3.** fig. gewinnsüchtig: **~ marriage** Geldheirat *f*; **II** *s*. **4.** ⚔ Söldner *m*; *contp*. Mietling *m*.

mer·cer ['mɜːsə] *s*. *Brit*. Seiden- u. Tex-'tilienhändler *m*; **'mer·cer·ize** [-əraɪz] *v/t*. *Baumwollfasern* merzerisieren; **'mer·cer·y** [-ərɪ] *s*. ✝ *Brit*. **1.** Seiden-, Schnittwaren *pl*.; **2.** Seiden-, Schnittwarenhandlung *f*.

mer·chan·dise ['mɜːtʃəndaɪz] **I** *s*. **1.** *coll*. Ware(n *pl*.) *f*, Handelsgüter *pl*.: **an article of ~** eine Ware; **II** *v/i*. **2.** Handel treiben, Waren vertreiben; **III** *v/t*. **3.** Waren vertreiben; **4.** Werbung machen für *e-e Ware*, den Absatz *e-r Ware* steigern; **'mer·chan·dis·ing** [-zɪŋ] *s*. **1.** Merchandising *n*, Ver-'kaufspoli,tik *f* u. -förderung *f* (*durch Marktforschung, wirksame Gütergestaltung, Werbung etc.*); **2.** Handel(sgeschäfte *pl*.) *m*; **II** *adj*. **3.** Handels...

mer·chant ['mɜːtʃənt] ✝ **I** *s*. **1.** (Groß-)Kaufmann *m*, Handelsherr *m*, Großhändler *m*: **the ~s** die Kaufmannschaft, Handelskreise *pl*.; **2.** *bsd. Am.* Ladenbesitzer *m*, Krämer *m*; **3.** **~ of doom** *Brit. sl.* ‚Unke‘ *f*, Schwarzseher(in); **4.** ⚓ *obs*. Handelsschiff *n*; **II** *adj*. **5.** Handels..., Kaufmanns...; **'mer·chant·a·ble** [-təbl] *adj*. marktgängig.

mer·chant bank *s*. Handelsbank *f*; **~ fleet** *s*. ⚓ Handelsflotte *f*; **'~·man** [-mən] *s*. [*irr*.] ⚓ Kauffahr'tei-, Handelsschiff *n*; **~ na·vy** *s*. 'Handelsma,rine *f*; **~ prince** *s*. ✝ reicher Kaufherr, Han-

delsfürst *m*; **~ ship** *s*. Handelsschiff *n*.

mer·ci·ful ['mɜːsɪfʊl] *adj*. □ (**to**) barm-'herzig, mitleidvoll (gegen), gütig (gegen, zu); gnädig (*dat.*); **'mer·ci·ful·ly** [-fʊlɪ] *adv*. **1.** → **merciful**; **2.** glücklicherweise; **'mer·ci·ful·ness** [-nɪs] *s*. Barm'herzigkeit *f*, Erbarmen *n*, Gnade *f* (*Gottes*); **'mer·ci·less** [-ɪlɪs] *adj*. □ unbarmherzig, erbarmungslos, mitleidlos; **'mer·ci·less·ness** [-ɪlɪsnɪs] *s*. Erbarmungslosigkeit *f*.

mer·cu·ri·al [mɜː'kjʊərɪəl] *adj*. □ **1.** 🜍 Quecksilber...; **2.** fig. lebhaft, quecksilb(e)rig; **3.** *myth*. Merkur...; **♀ wand** Merkurstab *m*; **mer'cu·ri·al·ism** [-lɪzəm] *s*. ✝ Quecksilbervergiftung *f*; **mer'cu·ri·al·ize** [-laɪz] *v/t*. ✝, *phot*. mit Quecksilber behandeln; **mer'cu·ric** [-rɪk] *adj*. 🜍 Quecksilber...

mer·cu·ry ['mɜːkjʊrɪ] *s*. **1.** ♀ *myth*. *ast*. Mer'kur *m*; fig. Bote *m*; → 🜍, ♀; Quecksilber *n*: **~ column** → 3; **~ poisoning** Quecksilbervergiftung *f*; **3.** Quecksilber(säule *f*) *n*: **the ~ is rising** das Barometer steigt (*a. fig.*); **4.** ♀ Bingelkraut *n*; **~ pres·sure ga(u)ge** *s*. *phys*. 'Quecksilbermano,meter *n*.

mer·cy ['mɜːsɪ] *s*. **1.** Barm'herzigkeit *f*, Mitleid *n*, Erbarmen *n*; Gnade *f*: **be at the ~ of s.o.** in j-s Gewalt sein, j-m auf Gnade u. Ungnade ausgeliefert sein; **at the ~ of the waves** den Wellen preisgegeben; **throw o.s. on s.o.'s ~** sich j-m auf Gnade u. Ungnade ergeben; **be left to the tender mercies of** *iro*. der rauen Behandlung von ... ausgesetzt sein; **Sister of ♀** Barmherzige Schwester; **2.** Glück *n*, Segen *m*, (wahre) Wohltat: **it is a ~ that he left**; **~ kill·ing** *s*. Sterbehilfe *f*.

mere [mɪə] *adj*. □ bloß, nichts als, rein, völlig: **~(st) nonsense** purer Unsinn; **~ words** bloße Worte; **he is no ~ craftsman** er ist kein bloßer Handwerker; **the ~st accident** der reinste Zufall; **'mere·ly** [-lɪ] *adv*. bloß, rein, nur, lediglich.

mer·e·tri·cious [ˌmerɪ'trɪʃəs] *adj*. □ **1.** *obs*. dirnenhaft; **2.** fig. a) falsch, verlogen, b) protzig.

merge [mɜːdʒ] **I** *v/t*. **1.** (**in**) verschmelzen (mit), aufgehen lassen (in *dat.*), einverleiben (*dat.*): **be ~d in** et. aufgehen; **2.** ⚖ tilgen, aufheben; **3.** ✝ a) fusionieren, b) *Aktien* zs.-legen; **II** *v/i*. **4.** **~ in** sich verschmelzen mit, aufgehen in (*dat.*); **5.** a) *mot*. sich (in den Verkehr) einfädeln: **~ in turn** sich ‚im Reißverschlussverfahren‘ einfädeln, b) zs.-laufen (*Straßen*); **'mer·gence** [-dʒəns] *s*. Aufgehen *n* (**in** in *dat.*), Verschmelzung *f* (**into** mit); **'merg·er** [-dʒə] *s*. **1.** ✝ Fusi'on *f*, Fusionierung *f von Gesellschaften*; Zs.-legung *f von Aktien*; **2.** ⚖ a) Verschmelzung(svertrag *m*) *f*, Aufgehen *n* (*e-s Besitzes od. Vertrages in e-m anderen etc.*), b) Konsumpti'on *f* (*e-r Straftat durch e-e schwerere*).

me·rid·i·an [mə'rɪdɪən] *adj*. **1.** mittägig, Mittags...; **2.** *ast*. Kulminations-, Meridian...: **~ circle** Meridiankreis *m*; **3.** fig. höchst; **II** *s*. **4.** *geogr*. Meridi'an *m*, Längenkreis *m*: **prime ~** Nullmeridian; **5.** *poet*. Mittag(szeit *f*) *m*; **6.** *ast*. Kulminati'onspunkt *m*; **7.** fig. Höhepunkt *m*, Gipfel *m*; fig. Blüte(zeit) *f*; **me·rid·i·o·nal** [-dɪənl] *adj*. **1.** *ast*. meridio'nal, Meridian..., Mittags...; **2.** südlich, südländisch; **II** *s*. **3.** Südländer (-in), *bsd*. 'Südfran,zose *m*, -fran,zösin *f*.

me·ringue [mə'ræŋ] *s*. Me'ringe *f*, Schaumgebäck *n*, Bai'ser *n*.

me·ri·no [mə'riːnəʊ] *pl*. **-nos** [-z] *s*. **1.** *a*.

~ sheep zo. Me'rinoschaf n; **2.** ✝ a) Me'rinowolle f, b) Me'rino m (*Kammgarnstoff*).

mer·it ['merɪt] **I** s. **1.** Verdienst(lichkeit f) n: *according to one's* ~ nach Verdienst *belohnen etc.*; *a man of* ~ e-e verdiente Persönlichkeit; *Order of* ⚷ Verdienstorden m; ~ *pay* ✝ leistungsbezogene Bezahlung; ~ *rating* Leistungsbeurteilung f; **2.** Wert m, Vorzug m: *of architectural* ~ von architektonischem Wert, erhaltungswürdig; **3.** *the* ~*s* pl. fig. die Hauptpunkte, der sachliche Gehalt, die wesentlichen (⚖ a. materiell-rechtlichen) Gesichtspunkte: *on its* (*own*) ~*s* dem wesentlichen Inhalt nach, an (u. für) sich betrachtet; *on the* ~*s* ⚖ in der Sache selbst, nach materiellem Recht; *decision on the* ~*s* Sachentscheidung f; *inquire into the* ~*s of a case* e-r Sache auf den Grund gehen; **II** v/t. **4.** *Lohn, Strafe etc.* verdienen; 'mer·it·ed [-tɪd] adj. □ verdient; 'mer·it·ed·ly [-tɪdlɪ] adv. verdientermaßen.

me·ri·toc·ra·cy [ˌmerɪ'tɒkrəsɪ] s. sociol. **1.** (herrschende) E'lite; **2.** Leistungsgesellschaft f.

mer·i·to·ri·ous [ˌmerɪ'tɔːrɪəs] adj. □ verdienstvoll.

mer·lin ['mɜːlɪn] s. orn. Merlin-, Zwergfalke m.

mer·maid ['mɜːmeɪd] s. Meerweib n, Seejungfrau f, Nixe f; 'mer·man [-mæn] s. [*irr.*] Wassergeist m, Triton m, Nix m.

mer·ri·ly ['merɪlɪ] adv. von *merry*; 'mer·ri·ment [-ɪmənt] s. **1.** Fröhlichkeit f, Lustigkeit f; **2.** Belustigung f, Lustbarkeit f, Spaß m.

mer·ry ['merɪ] adj. □ **1.** lustig, fröhlich: *as* ~ *as a lark* (*od.* *cricket*) kreuzfidel; *make* ~ lustig sein, feiern, scherzen; **2.** scherzhaft, spaßhaft, lustig: *make* ~ *over* sich lustig machen über (*acc.*); **3.** beschwipst, angeheitert; ~ **an·drew** ['ændruː] s. Hans'wurst m, Spaßmacher m; '~-**go-,round** [-ɡəʊˌr-] s. Karus'sell n; fig. Wirbel m; '~,**mak·ing** s. Belustigung f, Lustbarkeit f, Fest n; '~-**thought** → *wishbone* 1.

me·sa ['meɪsə] s. geogr. Am. Tafelland n; ~ **oak** s. Am. Tischeiche f.

mes·en·ter·y ['mesəntərɪ] s. anat., zo. Gekröse n.

mesh [meʃ] **I** s. **1.** Masche f: ~ *stocking* Netzstrumpf m; **2.** ⊙ Maschenweite f; **3.** mst pl. fig. Netz n, Schlingen pl.: *be caught in the* ~*es of the law* sich in den Schlingen des Gesetzes verfangen (haben); **4.** ⊙ Inein'andergreifen n, Eingriff m (*von Zahnrädern*): *be in* ~ im Eingriff sein; **5.** → *mesh connection*; **II** v/t. **6.** in e-m Netz fangen, verwickeln; **7.** ⊙ in Eingriff bringen, einrücken; **8.** fig. (mitein'ander) verzahnen; **III** v/i. **9.** ⊙ ein-, inein'ander greifen (*Zahnräder*); ~ **con·nec·tion** s. ϟ Vieleck-, *bsd.* Deltaschaltung f.

meshed [meʃt] adj. netzartig; ...maschig: *close-*~ engmaschig.

'**mesh·work** s. Maschen pl., Netzwerk n; Gespinst n.

mes·mer·ic, mes·mer·i·cal [mez'merɪk(l)] adj. **1.** mesmerisch, 'heilma,gnetisch; **2.** fig. hyp'notisch, ma'gnetisch, faszinierend.

mes·mer·ism ['mezmərɪzəm] s. Mesmeˈrismus m, tierischer Magne'tismus; '**mes·mer·ist** [-ɪst] s. 'Heilmagneti,seur m; '**mes·mer·ize** [-raɪz] v/t. mesmerisieren; fig. faszinieren, bannen.

mesne [miːn] adj. ⚖ Zwischen..., Mit-

tel...: ~ *lord* Afterlehnsherr m; ~ **inter·est** s. ⚖ Zwischenzins m.

meso- [mesəʊ] in Zssgn Zwischen..., Mittel...; **mes·o·lith·ic** [-'lɪθɪk] adj. meso'lithisch, mittelsteinzeitlich.

mes·on ['miːzɒn] s. phys. Meson n.

Mes·o·zo·ic [ˌmesəʊˈzəʊɪk] geol. **I** adj. meso'zoisch; **II** s. Meso'zoikum n.

mess [mes] **I** s. **1.** obs. Gericht n, Speise f: ~ *of pottage* bibl. Linsengericht; **2.** Viehfutter n; **3.** ✕ Ka'sino n, Speiseraum m; ♣ Messe f, Back f: *officers'* ~ Offiziersmesse; **4.** fig. Mischmasch m, Mansche'rei f; **5.** fig. a) Durchein'ander n, Unordnung f, b) Schmutz m, ˌSchweine'rei f, c) ˌSchla'massel' m, ˌPatsche' f, Klemme f: *in a* ~ beschmutzt, in Unordnung, fig. in der Klemme; *get into a* ~ in die Klemme kommen; *make a* ~ Schmutz machen; *make a* ~ *of* → 6 c; *make a* ~ *of it* alles vermasseln *od.* versauen, Mist bauen; *you made a nice* ~ *of it* da hast du was Schönes angerichtet; *he was a* ~ er sah grässlich aus, fig. war völlig verwahrlost; → *pretty* 2; **II** v/t. **6.** a) ~ *up* a) beschmutzen, b) in Unordnung *od.* Verwirrung bringen, c) fig. verpfuschen, vermasseln, verhunzen; **III** v/i. **7.** (*an e-m gemeinsamen Tisch*) essen (*with* mit): ~ *together* ♣ zu 'einer Back gehören; **8.** manschen, pan(t)schen (*in* in *dat.*); **9.** ~ *with* sich einmischen; **10.** ~ *about*, ~ *around* her'ummurksen, (-)pfuschen, F fig. sich her'umtreiben.

mes·sage ['mesɪdʒ] s. **1.** Botschaft f (*a. bibl.*), Sendung f: *can I take a* ~*?* kann ich et. ausrichten?; **2.** Mitteilung f, Bescheid m, Nachricht, *Computer:* Meldung f: *get the* ~ F (es) kapieren; *radio* ~ Funkmeldung f, -spruch m; **3.** fig. Botschaft f, Anliegen n *e-s Dichters etc.*; '~-,**tak·ing ser·vice** s. teleph. (Fernsprech)Auftragsdienst m.

mes·sen·ger ['mesɪndʒə] s. **1.** (Post-*etc.*)Bote m: (*express od. special*) ~ Eilbote; *by* ~ durch Boten; **2.** Ku'rier m; ✕ a. Melder m; **3.** fig. (Vor)Bote m, Verkünder m; **4.** ♣ a) Anholtau n, b) Ankerkette f; ~ **air·plane** s. ✕ Ku'rierflugzeug n; ~ **boy** s. Laufbursche m, Botenjunge m; ~ **dog** s. Meldehund m; ~ **pi·geon** s. Brieftaube f.

mess hall s. ✕, ♣ Messe f, Ka'sino (-raum m) n, Speisesaal m.

Mes·si·ah [mɪ'saɪə] s. bibl. Mes'sias m, Erlöser m; **Mes·si·an·ic** [ˌmesɪ'ænɪk] adj. messi'anisch.

mess| jack·et s. ♣ kurze Uni'formjacke; ~ **kit** s. ✕ Kochgeschirr n, Essgerät n; '~-**mate** s. ✕, ♣ Messgenosse m, 'Tischkame,rad m; ~ **ser·geant** s. ✕ 'Küchen,unteroffi,zier m; '~-**tin** s. ✕, ♣ bsd. Brit. Essgeschirr n.

mes·suage ['meswɪdʒ] s. ⚖ Wohnhaus n (*mst mit Ländereien*), Anwesen n.

'**mess-up** s. F **1.** Durchein'ander n; **2.** Missverständnis n.

mess·y ['mesɪ] adj. □ **1.** unordentlich, schlampig; **2.** unsauber, schmutzig.

mes·ti·zo [me'stiːzəʊ] pl. -**zos** [-z] s. Me'stize m; Mischling m.

met [met] pret. u. p.p. von *meet*.

met·a·bol·ic [ˌmetə'bɒlɪk] adj. **1.** physiol. meta'bolisch, Stoffwechsel...; **2.** sich (ver)wandelnd; **me·tab·o·lism** [me'tæbəlɪzəm] s. **1.** biol. Metabo'lismus m, Formveränderung f; **2.** physiol., a. ☙ Stoffwechsel m: *general* ~, *total* ~ Gesamtstoffwechsel; → *basal* 2; **3.** ☙ Metabo'lismus m; **me·tab·o·lize** [me'tæbəlaɪz] v/t. 'umwandeln.

met·a·car·pal [ˌmetə'kɑːpl] anat. **I** adj. Mittelhand...; **II** s. Mittelhandknochen m; **met·a'car·pus** [-pəs] pl. -**pi** [-paɪ] s. **1.** Mittelhand f; **2.** Vordermittelfuß m.

met·age ['miːtɪdʒ] s. **1.** amtliches Messen (*des Inhalts od. Gewichts bsd. von Kohlen*); **2.** Messgeld n.

met·al ['metl] **I** s. **1.** 🜛, min. Me'tall n; **2.** ☉ a) 'Nichteisenme,tall n, b) Me'talllegierung f, bsd. 'Typen-, Ge'schützme,tall n, c) 'Gussme,tall n: *brittle* ~, *red* ~ Rotguss m; *fine* ~, *cupel* Weiß-, Feinmetall; *grey* ~ graues Gusseisen; **3.** min. a) Regulus m, Korn n, b) (Kupfer)Stein m; **4.** 🜨 Schieferton m; **5.** ☉ (flüssige) Glasmasse; **6.** pl. Brit. Eisenbahnschienen pl.: *run off the* ~*s* entgleisen; **7.** her. Me'tall n (*Gold- u. Silberfarbe*); **8.** *Straßenbau:* Beschotterung f, Schotter m; **9.** fig. Mut m; **II** v/t. **10.** mit Me'tall bedecken *od.* versehen; **11.** 🚂, *Straßenbau:* beschottern; **III** adj. **12.** Me'tall..., me'tallen; ~ **age** s. Bronze- u. Eisenzeitalter n; '~-**clad** adj. ☉ me'tallgekapselt; '~-**coat** v/t. mit Me'tall über-'ziehen; ~ **cut·ting** s. ☉ spanabhebende Bearbeitung; ~ **found·er** s. Me'tallgießer m; ~ **ga(u)ge** s. Blechlehre f.

met·al·ize Am. → *metallize*.

me·tal·lic [mɪ'tælɪk] adj. (□ ~**ally**) **1.** me'tallen, Metall...: ~ *cover* a) ☉ Me'tallüberzug m, b) ✝ Metalldeckung f; ~ *currency* Metallwährung f, Hartgeld n; **2.** me'tallisch (glänzend *od.* klingend): ~ *voice*; ~ *beetle* Prachtkäfer m; **met·al·lif·er·ous** [ˌmetə'lɪfərəs] adj. Me'tall führend, metallreich; **met·al·line** ['metəlaɪn] adj. **1.** me'tallisch; **2.** me'tallhaltig; **met·al·lize** ['metəlaɪz] v/t. metallisieren.

met·al·loid ['metəlɔɪd] **I** adj. metallo'idisch; **II** s. 🜛 Metallo'id n.

met·al·lur·gic, met·al·lur·gi·cal [ˌmetə'lɜːdʒɪk(l)] adj. metall'urgisch; **met·al·lur·gist** [me'tælədʒɪst] s. Metal'lurg(e) m; **met·al·lur·gy** [me'tælədʒɪ] s. Metallur'gie f, Hüttenkunde f, -wesen n.

met·al| plat·ing s. ☉ Plattierung f; '~-,**proc·ess·ing**, '~,**work·ing I** s. Me'tallbearbeitung f; **II** adj. Me'tall verarbeitend.

met·a·mor·phic [ˌmetə'mɔːfɪk] adj. **1.** geol. meta'morph; **2.** biol. gestaltverändernd; **met·a'mor·phose** [-fəʊz] **I** v/t. **1.** (*to, into*) 'umgestalten (zu), verwandeln (in *acc.*); **2.** verzaubern, -wandeln (*to, into* in *acc.*); **II** v/i. **3.** zo. sich verwandeln; **met·a'mor·pho·sis** [-fəsɪs] pl. -**ses** [-siːz] s. Metamor'phose f (*a. biol., physiol.*), Verwandlung f.

met·a·phor ['metəfə] s. Me'tapher f, bildlicher Ausdruck.

met·a·phor·i·cal [ˌmetə'fɒrɪkl] adj. □ meta'phorisch, bildlich.

met·a·phrase ['metəfreɪz] **I** s. Meta-'phrase f, wörtliche Über'setzung; **II** v/t. a) wörtlich über'tragen, b) um-'schreiben.

met·a·phys·i·cal [ˌmetə'fɪzɪkl] adj. □ **1.** phls. meta'physisch; **2.** 'übersinnlich; ab'strakt; **met·a·phy·si·cian** [ˌmetəfɪ'zɪʃn] s. phls. Meta'physiker m; **met·a·phys·ics** [-ks] s. pl. sg. konstr. phls. Metaphy'sik f.

met·a·plasm ['metəplæzəm] s. **1.** ling. Meta'plasmus m, Wortveränderung f; **2.** biol. Meta'plasma n.

me·tas·ta·sis [mɪ'tæstəsɪs] pl. -**ses** [-siːz] s. **1.** 🜏 Meta'stase f, Tochtergeschwulst f; **2.** biol. Stoffwechsel m.

met·a·tar·sal [ˌmetə'tɑːsl] anat. **I** adj.

Mittelfuß...; **II** s. Mittelfußknochen m; **,met·a·tar·sus** [-səs] pl. **-si** [-saɪ] s. anat., zo. Mittelfuß m.

mete [miːt] **I** v/t. **1.** poet. (ab-, aus)messen, durch'messen; **2.** mst **~ out** (a. Strafe) zumessen (**to** dat.); **3.** fig. ermessen; **II** s. mst pl. **4.** Grenze f: **know one's ~s and bounds** fig. Maß u. Ziel kennen.

me·tem·psy·cho·sis [,metempsɪ'kəʊsɪs] pl. **-ses** [-siːz] s. Seelenwanderung f, Metempsy'chose f.

me·te·or ['miːtjə] s. ast. a) Mete'or m (a. fig.), b) Sternschnuppe f; **me·te·or·ic** [,miːtɪ'ɒrɪk] adj. **1.** ast. mete'orisch, Meteor...: **~ shower** Sternschnuppenschwarm m; **2.** fig. mete'orhaft: a) glänzend: **~ fame**, b) ko'metenhaft, rasch: **his ~ rise to power**; **'me·te·or·ite** [-jə-raɪt] s. ast. Meteo'rit m, Mete'orstein m; **me·te·or·o·log·ic**, **me·te·or·o·log·i·cal** [,miːtjərə'lɒdʒɪk(l)] adj. □ phys. meteoro'logisch, Wetter..., Luft...: **~ conditions** Witterungsverhältnisse; **~ office** Wetteramt n; **~ satellite** Wettersatellit m; **me·te·or·ol·o·gist** [,miːtjə-'rɒlədʒɪst] s. phys. Meteoro'loge m, Meteoro'login f; **me·te·or·ol·o·gy** [,miːtjə'rɒlədʒɪ] s. phys. **1.** Meteorolo'gie f; **2.** meteoro'logische Verhältnisse pl. (e-r Gegend).

me·ter¹ ['miːtə] Am. → **metre**.

me·ter² ['miːtə] **I** s. ⊛ Messer m, Messgerät n, Zähler m: **electricity ~** elektrischer Strommesser od. Zähler; **II** v/t. (mit e-m Messinstrument) messen: **~ out** et. abgeben, dosieren; '**~-maid** s. F Poli'tesse f.

meth·a·done ['meθədəʊn] s. pharm. Metha'don n.

meth·ane ['miːθeɪn] s. ℞ Me'than n.

me·thinks [mɪ'θɪŋks] v/impers. obs. od. poet. mich dünkt, mir scheint.

meth·od ['meθəd] s. **1.** Me'thode f; bsd. ⊛ Verfahren n: **~ of doing s.th.** Art u. Weise f, et. zu tun; **by a ~** nach e-r Methode; **2.** 'Lehrme,thode f; **3.** Sys'tem n; **4.** phls. (logische) 'Denkme,thode; **5.** Ordnung f, Me'thode f, Planmäßigkeit f: **work with ~** methodisch arbeiten; **there is ~ in his madness** sein Wahnsinn hat Methode; **there is ~ in this** da ist System drin; **me·thod·ic**, **me·thod·i·cal** [mɪ'θɒdɪk(l)] adj. □ **1.** me'thodisch, syste'matisch; **2.** über'legt.

Meth·od·ism ['meθədɪzəm] s. eccl. Me-tho'dismus m; '**Meth·od·ist** [-ɪst] **I** s. **1.** eccl. Metho'dist(in); **2.** ⌂ fig. contp. Frömmler m, Mucker m; **II** adj. **3.** eccl. metho'distisch.

meth·od·ize ['meθədaɪz] v/t. me'thodisch ordnen; **'meth·od·less** [-dlɪs] adj. □ plan-, sy'stemlos.

meth·od·ol·o·gy [,meθə'dɒlədʒɪ] s. **1.** Methodolo'gie f; **2.** Me'thodik f.

Me·thu·se·lah [mɪ'θjuːzələ] npr. bibl. Me'thusalem m: **as old as ~** (so) alt wie Methusalem.

meth·yl ['meθɪl; ℞ 'miːθaɪl] s. ℞ Me'thyl n: **~ alcohol** Methylalkohol m; **meth·yl·ate** ['meθɪleɪt] ℞ **I** v/t. **1.** me'thylieren; **2.** denaturieren: **~d spirits** denaturierter Spiritus, Brennspiritus m; **II** s. **3.** Methy'lat n; **meth·yl·ene** ['meθɪliːn] s. ℞ Methy'len n; **me·thyl·ic** [mɪ'θɪlɪk] adj. ℞ Methyl...

me·tic·u·los·i·ty [mɪ,tɪkju'lɒsətɪ] s. peinliche Genauigkeit, Akri'bie f; **me·tic·u·lous** [mɪ'tɪkjʊləs] adj. □ peinlich genau, a'kribisch.

mé·tier ['meɪtɪeɪ] s. **1.** Gewerbe n; **2.** fig. (Spezi'al)Gebiet n, Meti'er n.

me·ton·y·my [mɪ'tɒnɪmɪ] s. Metony'mie f, Begriffsvertauschung f.

me·tre ['miːtə] s. Brit. **1.** Versmaß n, Metrum n; **2.** Meter m, n.

met·ric ['metrɪk] **I** adj. (□ **~ally**) **1.** metrisch: **~ system**; **~ method of analy·sis** ℞ Maßanalyse f; **2.** → **metrical** 2; **II** s. pl. sg. konstr. **3.** Metrik f, Verslehre f; ♪ Rhythmik f, Taktlehre f; **'met·ri·cal** [-kl] adj. □ **1.** → **metric** 1; **2.** a) metrisch, Vers..., b) rhythmisch; **'met·ri·cate** [-keɪt] v/t. u. v/i. Brit. (sich) auf das metrische Sy'stem 'umstellen.

met·ro·nome ['metrənəʊm] s. ♪ Metro-'nom n, Taktmesser m.

me·trop·o·lis [mɪ'trɒpəlɪs] s. **1.** Metro-'pole f, Haupt-, Großstadt f: **the ⌂** Brit. London; **2.** Hauptzentrum n; **3.** eccl. Sitz m e-s Metropo'liten od. Erzbischofs; **met·ro·pol·i·tan** [,metrə'pɒlɪtən] **I** adj. **1.** hauptstädtisch, Stadt...; **2.** eccl. erzbischöflich; **II** s. **3.** a) Metropo-'lit m (Ostkirche), Erzbischof m; **4.** Bewohner(in) der Hauptstadt; Großstädter(in).

met·tle ['metl] s. **1.** Veranlagung f; **2.** Eifer m, Mut m, Feuer n: **be on one's ~** vor Eifer brennen; **put s.o. on his ~** j-n zur Aufbietung aller s-r Kräfte ansporen; **try s.o.'s ~** j-n auf die Probe stellen; **horse of ~** feuriges Pferd; '**met·tled** [-ld], '**met·tle·some** [-səm] adj. feurig, mutig.

mew¹ [mjuː] s. orn. Seemöwe f.

mew² [mjuː] v/i. mi'auen (Katze).

mew³ [mjuː] s. **1.** Mauserkäfig m; **2.** pl. sg. konstr. a) Stall m: **the Royal ⌂s** der Königliche Marstall, b) Brit. zu Wohnungen umgebaute ehemalige Stallungen.

mewl [mjuːl] v/i. **1.** quäken, wimmern (Baby); **2.** mi'auen.

Mex·i·can ['meksɪkən] **I** adj. mexi'kanisch; **II** s. Mexi'kaner(in); **~ wave** s. sport La-'Ola-Welle f.

mez·za·nine ['metsəniːn] s. △ **1.** Mezza'nin n, Zwischengeschoss, östr. -geschoß n; **2.** thea. Raum m unter der Bühne.

mez·zo ['medzəʊ] (Ital.) **I** adj. **1.** ♪ mezzo, mittel, halb: **~ forte** halblaut; **II** s. **2.** → **mezzo-soprano**; **3.** → **mezzotint**; '**~-so'pra·no** s. ♪ 'Mezzoso,prano m; '**~-tint I** s. **1.** Kupferstecherei: Mezzo'tinto n, Schabkunst f; **2.** Schabkunstblatt n: **~ engraving** Stechkunst f in Mezzotintomanier; **II** v/t. **3.** in Mezzo-'tinto gravieren.

mi·aow [miː'aʊ] → **meow**.

mi·asm ['maɪæzəm], **mi·as·ma** [mɪ'æz-mə] pl. **-ma·ta** [-mətə] s. ℞ Mi'asma n, Krankheitsstoff m; **mi·as·mal** [mɪ-'æzml], **mi·as·mat·ic**, **mi·as·mat·i·cal** [,mɪəz'mætɪk(l)] adj. ansteckend.

mi·aul [mɪ'aʊl; mɪ'ɔːl] v/i. mi'auen.

mi·ca ['maɪkə] min. **I** s. Glimmer(erde f) m; **II** adj. Glimmer...: **~ capacitor** ƴ Glimmerkondensator m; **mi·ca·ceous** [maɪ'keɪʃəs] adj. Glimmer...

Mi·cah ['maɪkə] npr. u. s. bibl. (das Buch) Micha m od. Mi'chäas m.

mice [maɪs] pl. von **mouse**.

Mich·ael·mas ['mɪklməs] s. Micha'elis n, Michaelstag m (29. September); **~ Day** s. **1.** Michaelstag m (29. September); **2.** e-r der 4 brit. Quartalstage; **~ term** s. Brit. univ. 'Herbstse,mester n.

Mick [mɪk] → **Mike¹**.

Mick·ey ['mɪkɪ] s. **1.** Am. sl. ✈ Bordradar n; **2. take the ⌂ out of s.o.** j-n ,veräppeln; **3.** → **~ Finn** [fɪn] s. sl. a) präparierter Drink, b) Betäubungsmittel n.

micro- [maɪkrəʊ] in Zssgn: a) Mikro..., (sehr) klein, b) ein milli'onstel c) mikro'skopisch.

mi·crobe ['maɪkrəʊb] s. biol. Mi'krobe f; **mi·cro·bi·al** [maɪ'krəʊbjəl], **mi·cro·bic** [maɪ'krəʊbɪk] adj. mi'krobisch, Mikroben...; **mi·cro·bi·o·sis** [,maɪkrəʊ-baɪ'əʊsɪs] s. ℈ Mi'krobeninfekti,on f.

,mi·cro'chem·is·try s. Mikroche'mie f.

'mi·cro·chip s. Computer: Mikrochip m.

'mi·cro,cir·cuit s. Mikroschaltung f.

mi·cro·cosm ['maɪkrəʊkɒzəm] s. Mik-ro'kosmos m (a. phls. u. fig.); **mi·cro-cos·mic** [,maɪkrəʊ'kɒzmɪk] adj. mikro-'kosmisch.

'mi·cro,e·lec'tron·ics s. pl. sg. konstr. phys. Mikroelek'tronik f.

mi·cro·fiche ['maɪkrəʊfiːʃ] s. Mikrofiche m.

'mi·cro·film phot. **I** s. Mikrofilm m; **II** v/t. auf Mikrofilm aufnehmen.

'mi·cro·gram Am., **'mi·cro·gramme** Brit. s. phys. Mikro'gramm n (ein millionstel Gramm).

'mi·cro·groove s. **1.** Mikrorille f; **2.** Schallplatte f mit Mikrorillen.

'mi·cro·inch s. ein milli'onstel Zoll.

mi·crom·e·ter [maɪ'krɒmɪtə] s. **1.** phys. Mikro'meter n (ein millionstel Meter): **~ adjustment** ⊛ Feinstellung f; **~ (caliper)** Feinmessschraube f; **2.** opt. Oku'larmikro,meter n (an Fernrohren etc.).

mi·cron ['maɪkrɒn] pl. **-crons**, **-cra** [-krə] s. ℞, phys. Mikron n (ein tausendstel Millimeter).

,mi·cro'or·gan·ism s. Mikroorga'nismus m.

mi·cro·phone ['maɪkrəfəʊn] s. ƴ **1.** (**at the ~** am) Mikro'fon n; **2.** teleph. Sprechmuschel f; **3.** ℉ Radio n: **through the ~** durch den Rundfunk.

,mi·cro'pho·to·graph s. **1.** Mikrofoto (-gra'fie f) n; **2.** → **mi·cro·pho'tog·ra·phy** s. Mikrofotogra'fie f.

,mi·cro'pro·ces·sor s. Computer: Mikropro'zessor m.

mi·cro·scope ['maɪkrəskəʊp] **I** s. Mik-ro'skop n: **reflecting ~** Spiegelmikroskop; **~ stage** Objektivtisch m; **II** v/t. mikro'skopisch unter'suchen; **mi·cro·scop·ic**, **mi·cro·scop·i·cal** [,maɪkrə-'skɒpɪk(l)] adj. □ **1.** mikro'skopisch: **~ examination**; **~ slide** Objektträger m; **2.** (peinlich) genau; **3.** mikro'skopisch klein, verschwindend klein.

'mi·cro,sec·ond s. Mikrose'kunde f (eine millionstel Sekunde).

,mi·cro'sur·ger·y s. ℈ Mikrochirur'gie f.

'mi·cro·volt s. phys. Mikrovolt n.

'mi·cro·wave s. ƴ Mikrowelle f, Dezi-'meterwelle f: **~ engineering** Höchstfrequenztechnik f; **~ oven** Mikrowellenherd m.

mic·tu·ri·tion [,mɪktjʊə'rɪʃn] s. ℈ **1.** U'rindrang m; **2.** Harnen n.

mid¹ [mɪd] adj. attr. od. in Zssgn mittler, Mittel...: **in ~ air** mitten in der Luft, frei schwebend; **in the ~ 16th century** in der Mitte des 16. Jhs.; **in ~-April** Mitte April; **in ~ ocean** auf offener See.

mid² [mɪd] prp. poet. poet. mitten von (od. gen.).

Mi·das ['maɪdæs] **I** npr. antiq. Midas m (König von Phrygien): **he has the ~ touch** fig. er macht aus allem Geld; **II** s. ⌂ zo. Midasfliege f.

'mid·day I s. Mittag m; **II** adj. mittägig, Mittags...

mid·dle ['mɪdl] **I** adj. **1.** mittler, Mittel... (a. ling.): **~ finger** Mittelfinger m; **~**

quality ✝ Mittelqualität *f*; **II** *s.* **2.** Mitte *f*: *in the ~* in der Mitte; *in the ~ of speaking* mitten in der Rede; *in the ~ of July* Mitte Juli; **3.** Mittelweg *m*; **4.** Mittelstück *n* (*a. e-s Schlachttieres*); **5.** Mitte *f* (*des Leibes*), Taille *f*; **6.** Medium *n* (*griechische Verbalform*); **7.** *Logik:* Mittelglied *n* (*e-s Schlusses*); **8.** *Fußball:* Flankenball *m*; **9.** *a. ~ article Brit.* Feuille'ton *n*; **10.** *pl.* ✝ Mittelsorte *f*; **11.** Mittelsmann *m*; **III** *v/t.* **12.** in die Mitte platzieren; *Fußball:* zur Mitte flanken.

mid·dle| age *s.* mittleres Alter; ⚥-'**Age** *adj.* mittelalterlich; **;~-'aged** *adj.* mittleren Alters; ⚥ **Ag·es** *s. pl.* das Mittelalter; **~ A·mer·i·ca** *Am.* die (konserva'tive) ameri'kanische Mittelschicht; '**~·brow** F **I** *s.* geistiger ‚Nor'malverbraucher'; **II** *adj.* von 'durchschnittlichen geistigen Inter'essen; '**~·class** *adj.* zum Mittelstand gehörig, Mittelstands...; **~ class·es** *s. pl.* Mittelstand *m*; **~ course** *s. fig.* Mittelweg *m*; **~ dis·tance** *s.* **1.** *paint., phot.* Mittelgrund *m*; **2.** *sport* Mittelstrecke *f*; '**~-'dis·tance** *adj. sport* Mittelstrecken...: **~ runner** Mittelstreckler(in); **~ ear** *s. anat.* Mittelohr *m*; ⚥ **East** *s. geogr.* **1.** *der* Mittlere Osten; **2.** *Brit. der* Nahe Osten; ⚥ **Eng·lish** *s. ling.* Mittelenglisch *n*; ⚥ **High Ger·man** *s. ling.* Mittelhochdeutsch *n*; **;~-'in·come** *adj.* mit mittlerem Einkommen; **~ in·i·tial** *s. Am.* Anfangsbuchstabe *m* des zweiten Vornamens; **~ life** *s.* die mittleren Lebensjahre *pl.*; '**~-man** [-mæn] *s.* [*irr.*] **1.** Mittelsmann *m*; **2.** ✝ Zwischenhändler *m*; **~ man·age·ment** *s.* mittlere Unternehmensführung *f*; '**~·most** *adj.* ganz in der Mitte (liegend); **~ name** *s.* **1.** zweiter Vorname; **2.** *fig.* her'vorstechende Eigenschaft; **;~-of-the-'road** *adj.* **1.** *bsd. pol.* gemäßigt; neu'tral; **2.** gefällig (*Musik*), den 'Durchschnittsgeschmack treffend; **~ rhyme** *s.* Binnenreim *m*; '**~-sized** *adj.* von mittlerer Größe; **~ watch** *s.* ⚓ Mittelwache *f* (*zwischen Mitternacht u. 4 Uhr morgens*); '**~-weight** *s. sport* Mittelgewicht(ler *m*) *n*; ⚥ **West** *s. Am.* (*u. Kanada*) Mittelwesten *m, der* mittlere Westen.

mid·dling ['mɪdlɪŋ] **I** *adj.* □ → *a.* II; **1.** von mittlerer Güte *od.* Sorte, mittelmäßig, Mittel...: *fair to ~* ‚so lala', ‚mittelprächtig'; **~ quality** ✝ Mittelqualität *f*; **2.** F leidlich (*Gesundheit*); **3.** F ziemlich groß; **II** *adv.* F **4.** (*a. ~ly*) leidlich, ziemlich; **5.** ziemlich gut; **III** *s.* **6.** *mst pl.* ✝ Mittelsorte *f*; **7.** *pl.* Mittelmehl *n*; **8.** *pl. metall.* 'Zwischenpro,dukt *n*.

mid·dy ['mɪdɪ] *s.* F für **midshipman**; **2.** → **~ blouse** *s.* Ma'trosenbluse *f*.

'**mid·field** *s. sport* Mittelfeld *n* (*a. Spieler*): **~ man, ~ player** Mittelfeldspieler *m*.

midge [mɪdʒ] *s.* **1.** *zo.* kleine Mücke; **2.** → **midget** 1.

midg·et ['mɪdʒɪt] **I** *s.* **1.** Zwerg *m*, Knirps *m*; **2.** *et.* Winziges *n*; **II** *adj.* **3.** Zwerg..., Miniatur..., Kleinst...: **~ car** *mot.* Klein(st)wagen *m*; **~ railroad** Liliputbahn *f*.

MIDI ['mɪdɪ] *s. abbr. für musical instrument digital interface* ♪, *Computer:* Midi *n* (*digitale Schnittstelle für elektronische Musikinstrumente*).

mid·i ['mɪdɪ] **I** *s.* Midimode *f*: *wear ~* Midi tragen; **II** *adj.* Midi...: **~ skirt** → '**mid·i·skirt** *s.* Midirock *m*.

'**mid·land** *s.* **1.** *mst pl.* Mittelland *n*; **2.** *the* ⚥*s pl.* Mittelengland *n*; **II** *adj.* **3.** binnenländisch; **4.** ⚥ *geogr.* mit-

telenglisch.

'**mid·life cri·sis** *s.* [*irr.*] *psych.* Midlife-Crisis *f*, Krise *f* in der Lebensmitte.

'**mid·most** [-məʊst] **I** *adj.* ganz in der Mitte (liegend); innerst; **II** *adv.* (ganz) im Innern *od.* in der Mitte.

'**mid·night I** *s.* (*at ~* um) Mitternacht *f*; **II** *adj.* mitternächtlich, Mitternachts...: *burn the ~ oil* bis spät in die Nacht arbeiten *od.* aufbleiben; **~ blue** *s.* Mitternachtsblau *n* (*Farbe*); **~ sun** *s.* **1.** Mitternachtssonne *f*; **2.** ⚥ Nordersonne *f*.

'**mid**|'**noon** *s.* Mittag *m*; **;~-'off** (**;~-'on**) *s. Kricket:* **1.** links (rechts) vom Werfer po'stierter Spieler; **2.** links (rechts) vom Werfer liegende Seite des Spielfelds; '**~·riff** *s.* **1.** *anat.* Zwerchfell *n*; **2.** *Am.* a) Mittelteil *m e-s Damenkleids*, b) zweiteilige Kleidung, c) Obertaille *f*, d) Magengrube *f*; '**~·ship** ⚓ **I** *s.* Mitte *f* des Schiffs; **II** *adj.* Mittschiffs...: **~ section** Hauptspant *n*; '**~·ship·man** [-mən] *s.* [*irr.*] ⚓ **1.** *Brit.* Leutnant *m* zur See; **2.** *Am.* 'Seeoffi,ziersanwärter *m*; '**~·ships** *adv.* ⚓ mittschiffs.

midst [mɪdst] *s.*: *in the ~ of* inmitten (*gen.*), mitten unter (*dat.*); *in their* (*our*) *~* mitten unter ihnen (uns); *from our ~* aus unserer Mitte.

'**mid·stream** *s.* Strommitte *f*: *in ~ fig.* mittendrin.

'**mid·sum·mer I** *s.* **1.** Mitte *f* des Sommers, Hochsommer *m*; **2.** *ast.* Sommersonnenwende *f*; **II** *adj.* **3.** hochsommerlich, Hochsommer...; ⚥ **Day** *s.* **1.** Jo'hannistag *m* (*24. Juni*); **2.** *e-r der 4 brit. Quartalstage.*

'**mid**|'**way I** *s.* **1.** Hälfte *f* des Weges, halber Weg; **2.** *Am.* Haupt-, Mittelstraße *f* (*auf Ausstellungen etc.*); **II** *adj.* **3.** mittler; **III** *adv.* **4.** auf halbem Wege; **;~'week I** *s.* Mitte *f* der Woche; **II** *adj.* (in der) Mitte der Woche stattfindend.

mid·wife ['mɪdwaɪf] *s.* [*irr.*] Hebamme *f*, Geburtshelferin *f* (*a. fig.*); '**mid·wife·ry** [-wɪfərɪ] *s.* Geburtshilfe *f, fig. a.* Mithilfe *f*.

'**mid**|'**win·ter** *s.* **1.** Mitte *f* des Winters; **2.** *ast.* Wintersonnenwende *f*; **;~'year I** *adj.* **1.** in der Mitte des Jahres vorkommend, in der Jahresmitte; **II** *s.* **2.** Jahresmitte *f*; **3.** *Am.* F a) um die Jahresmitte stattfindende Prüfung, b) *pl.* Prüfungszeit *f* (*um die Jahresmitte*).

mien [miːn] *s.* Miene *f*, Gesichtsausdruck *m*; Gebaren *n*: *noble ~* vornehme Haltung.

miff [mɪf] *s.* F Verstimmung *f*.

miffed [mɪft] *adj.* beleidigt, eingeschnappt.

might¹ [maɪt] *s.* **1.** Macht *f*, Gewalt *f*: *~ is* (*above*) *right* Gewalt geht vor Recht; **2.** Stärke *f*, Kraft *f*: *with ~ and main, with all one's ~* aus Leibeskräften, mit aller Gewalt.

might² [maɪt] *pret. von* **may¹**.

'**might-have-,been** *s.* **1.** et., was hätte sein können; **2.** Per'son, die es zu et. hätte bringen können.

might·i·ly ['maɪtɪlɪ] *adv.* **1.** mit Macht, heftig, kräftig; **2.** F e'norm, mächtig, sehr; '**might·i·ness** [-ɪnɪs] *s.* Macht *f*, Gewalt *f*; **might·y** ['maɪtɪ] **I** *adj.* □ → *mightily u.* II; **1.** mächtig, gewaltig, heftig, groß, stark; → *high and mighty;* **2.** *fig.* gewaltig, riesig, mächtig; **II** *adv.* **3.** F mächtig, riesig, ungeheuer: **~ easy** kinderleicht; **~ fine** prima.

mi·graine ['miːgreɪn] (*Fr.*) *s.* ☞ Mi'gräne *f*; **'mi·grain·ous** [-nəs] *adj.* ☞ durch Mi'gräne verursacht, Migräne...

mi·grant ['maɪgrənt] **I** *adj.* **1.** Wan-

der..., Zug...; → *a. migratory;* **II** *s.* **2.** Wandernde(r *m*) *f*; 'Umsiedler(in); **3.** *zo.* Zugvogel *m;* Wandertier *n;* **mi·grate** [maɪ'greɪt] *v/i.* (aus-, ab)wandern, (*a. orn.* fort)ziehen; **mi·gra·tion** [maɪ'greɪʃn] *s.* Wanderung *f* (*a.* ☝, *zo.*, *geol.*); Zug *m* (*Menschen od. Wandertiere*); *orn.* (Vogel)Zug *m:* **~ of** (*the*) *peoples* Völkerwanderung; *intramolecular ~* ☝ intramolekulare Wanderung; → *ionic²;* **mi·gra·tion·al** [maɪ'greɪʃənl] *adj.* Wander..., Zug...; '**mi·gra·to·ry** [-rətərɪ] *adj.* **1.** (aus)wandernd; **2.** Zug..., Wander...: **~ bird** Zugvogel *m;* **~ instinct** Wandertrieb *m;* **3.** um'herziehend, no'madisch: **~ life** Wanderleben *n;* **~ worker** Wanderarbeiter(in).

Mike¹ [maɪk] *npr.* (*Kosename für*) Michael; **II** *s.* ⚥ *sl.* a) Ire *m,* b) Katho'lik *m.* **mike²** [maɪk] *v/i. sl.* her'umlungern. **mike³** [maɪk] *s.* F ‚Mikro' *n* (*Mikrofon*).

mil [mɪl] *s.* **1.** Tausend *n: per ~* per Mille; **2.** ⊙ ¹/₁₀₀₀ Zoll *m* (*Drahtmaß*); **3.** ✗ (Teil)Strich *m.*

mil·age ['maɪlɪdʒ] → *mileage.*

Mil·a·nese [,mɪlə'niːz] **I** *adj.* mailändisch; **II** *s. sg. u. pl.* Mailänder(in), Mailänder *pl.*

milch [mɪltʃ] *adj.* Milch gebend, Milch...; '**milch·er** [-tʃə] → *milker* 3.

mild [maɪld] *adj.* □ mild (*a. Strafe, Wein, Wetter etc.*); gelind, sanft; leicht (*Droge, Krankheit, Zigarre etc.*), schwach: **~ attempt** schüchterner Versuch; **~ steel** ⊙ Flussstahl *m; to put it ~(ly)* a) sich gelinde ausdrücken, b) gelinde gesagt; *draw it ~* machs mal halblang!

mil·dew ['mɪldjuː] **I** *s.* **1.** ✿ Mehltau (-pilz) *m,* Brand *m* (*am Getreide*); **2.** Schimmel *m,* Moder *m:* **spot of ~** Moder- *od.* Stockfleck *m* (*in Papier etc.*); **II** *v/t.* **3.** mit Mehltau *od.* Schimmel *od.* Moderflecken über'ziehen: *be ~ed* verschimmelt sein (*a. fig.*); **III** *v/i.* **4.** brandig *od.* schimm(e)lig *od.* mod(e)rig werden (*a. fig.*); '**mil·dewed** [-djuːd], '**mil·dew·y** [-djuːɪ] *adj.* **1.** brandig, mod(e)rig, schimm(e)lig; **2.** ✿ von Mehltau befallen; mehltauartig.

mild·ness ['maɪldnɪs] *s.* Milde *f*; Sanftheit *f*; Sanftmut *f*.

mile [maɪl] *s.* Meile *f* (*zu Land = 1,609 km*): *Admiralty ~ Brit.* englische Seemeile (= *1,8532 km*); *air ~* Luftmeile (= *1,852 km*); *nautical ~, sea ~* Seemeile (= *1,852 km*); *~ after ~ of fields, ~s and ~s of fields* meilenweite Felder; *~s apart* meilenweit auseinander, *fig.* himmelweit entfernt; *miss s.th. by a ~ fig.* et. (meilen)weit verfehlen.

mile·age ['maɪlɪdʒ] *s.* **1.** Meilenlänge *f,* -zahl *f;* **2.** zu'rückgelegte Meilenzahl *od.* Fahrstrecke, Meilenstand *m:* **~ indicator, ~ recorder** *mot.* Meilenzähler *m; unlimited ~ Autoverleih:* unbegrenzte Meilenzahl; **3.** *a.* **~ allowance** Meilengeld *n* (*Vergütung*); **4.** Fahrpreis *m* per Meile; **5.** *a.* **~ book** 🎟 *Am.* Fahrscheinheft *n;* **6.** F *get a lot of ~ out of it* jede Menge (dabei) rausholen; *there's no ~ in it* das bringt nichts (ein).

mile·om·e·ter [maɪ'lɒmɪtə] *s. mot.* Meilenzähler *m.*

'**mile·stone** *s.* Meilenstein *m* (*a. fig.*).

mil·foil ['mɪlfɔɪl] *s.* ✿ Schafgarbe *f.*

mil·i·ar·i·a [,mɪlɪ'eərɪə] *s.* ✚ Frieselfieber *n;* **mil·i·ar·y** ['mɪlɪərɪ] *adj.* ✚ mili'ar, hirsekornartig: **~ fever** → *miliaria;* **~ gland** Hirsedrüse *f.*

mil·i·tan·cy ['mɪlɪtənsɪ] *s.* **1.** Kriegszu-

stand *m*, Kampf *m*; **2.** Kampfgeist *m*;
mil·i·tant [-tənt] **I** *adj.* □ mili'tant: a)
streitend, kämpfend, b) streitbar, kriegerisch; **II** *s.* Kämpfer *m*, Streiter *m*;
mil·i·ta·rist [-tərɪst] *s.* **1.** *pol.* Milita-
'rist *m*; **2.** Wehr- od. Mili'tärexperte *m*;
mil·i·ta·ris·tic [ˌmɪlɪtə'rɪstɪk] *adj.* milita-
'ristisch; **mil·i·ta·rize** [-təraɪz] *v/t.*
militarisieren.
mil·i·tar·y ['mɪlɪtərɪ] **I** *adj.* □ **1.** militärisch, Militär...: *of ~ age* im wehrpflich-
tigen Alter; **2.** Heeres..., Kriegs...; **II**
s. pl. konstr. Mili'tär *n*, Sol'daten *pl.*,
Truppen *pl.*; ~ **a·cad·e·my** *s.* **1.** Mili-
'tärakade,mie *f*; **2.** *Am.* (*zivile*) Schule
mit mili'tärischer Ausbildung; ~ **college** *s. Am.* Mili'tärcollege *n*; ~ **gov-
ern·ment** *s.* Mili'tärre,gierung *f*; ~ **junta** *s.* Mili'tärjunta *f*; ~ **law** *s.* Wehr-
(straf)recht *n*; ~ **map** *s.* Gene'ralstabskarte *f*; ~ **po·lice** *s.* Mili'tärpoli,zei *f*; ~
serv·ice *s.* Mili'tär-, Wehrdienst *m*; ~
serv·ice book *s.* Wehrpass *m*; ~
stores *s. pl.* Mili'tärbedarf *m*, 'Kriegsmateri,al *n* (*Munition, Proviant etc.*); ~
tes·ta·ment *s.* 🏛 'Nottesta,ment *n*
(*von Militärpersonen im Krieg*); ~ **tri-
bu·nal** *s.* Mili'tärgericht *n*.
mil·i·tate ['mɪlɪteɪt] *v/i.* (*against*) sprechen (*gegen*), wider'streiten (*dat.*), e-r
Sache entgegenwirken; ~ *for* eintreten
od. kämpfen für.
mi·li·tia [mɪ'lɪʃə] *s.* ✕ Mi'liz *f*, Bürgerwehr *f*.
milk [mɪlk] **I** *s.* **1.** Milch *f*; ~ *and water*
fig. kraftloses Zeug, seichtes Gewäsch;
~ *of human kindness fig.* Milch der
frommen Denkungsart; ~ *of sulphur*
🌡 Schwefelmilch; *it is no use crying
over spilt* ~ geschehen ist geschehen,
hin ist hin; → *coconut* 1; **2.** 🌿 (*Pflan-
zen*)Milch *f*; **II** *v/t.* **3.** melken; **4.** *fig.* j-n
schröpfen, ,ausnehmen'; **5.** ⚡ *Leitung*
,anzapfen', abhören; **III** *v/i.* **6.** Milch
geben; ,~*and*'*wa·ter* *adj.* saft- u.
kraftlos, seicht; ~ **bar** *s.* Milchbar *f*; ~
crust *s.* 🩹 Milchschorf *m*; ~ **duct** *s.*
anat. Milchdrüsengang *m*.
milk·er ['mɪlkə] *s.* **1.** Melker(in); **2.** ⚙
'Melkma,schine *f*; **3.** Milchkuh *f od.*
-schaf *n od.* -ziege *f*.
milk **float** *s. Brit.* Milchwagen *m*;
,~·**man** [-mən] *s.* [*irr.*] Milchmann *m*; ~
run ✈ *sl.* **1.** Rou'tineeinsatz *m*; **2.**
,gemütliche Sache', gefahrloser Ein-
satz; '~·**shake** *s.* Milchshake *m*; '~·**sop**
s. fig. contp. Muttersöhnchen *n*; ~
sug·ar *s.* 🧪 Milchzucker *m*, Lak'tose *f*;
~ **tooth** *s.* [*irr.*] Milchzahn *m*; '~·**weed**
s. 🌿 **1.** Schwalbenwurzgewächs *n*; **2.**
Wolfsmilch *f*.
milk·y ['mɪlkɪ] *adj.* **1.** □ milchig,
Milch...; milchweiß; **2.** *min.* milchig,
wolkig (*bsd. Edelsteine*); **3.** *fig.* a)
sanft, b) weichlich, ängstlich; ⚗ *Way s.
ast.* Milchstraße *f*.
mill¹ [mɪl] **I** *s.* **1.** (Mehl-, Mahl)Mühle *f*;
→ *grist* 1; **2.** ⚙ (*Kaffee-, Öl-, Säge-
etc.*)Mühle *f*, Zerkleinerungsvorrich-
tung *f*: *go through the* ~ *fig.* e-e harte
Schule durchmachen; *put s.o. through
the* ~ j-n hart rannehmen; *have been
through the* ~ viel durchgemacht haben; **3.** *metall.* Hütten-, Hammer-,
Walzwerk *n*; **4.** *a.* spinning ~ 🧵 Spinne'rei *f*; **5.** ⚙ a) *Münzerei*: Prägwerk *n*,
b) *Glasherstellung*: Schleifkasten *m*; **6.**
Fa'brik *f*, Werk *n*; **7.** F Prüge'lei *f*; **II**
v/t. **8.** *Korn etc.* mahlen; **9.** ⚙ *allg.*
bearbeiten, *z. B. Holz, Metall* fräsen,
Papier, Metall walzen, *Tuch, Leder*
walken, *Münzen* rändeln, *Eier, Schokolade* quirlen, schlagen, *Seide* mouli-

nieren; **10.** F ,'durchwalken'; **III** *v/i.*
11. F sich prügeln; **12.** ~ *about od.*
around ('rund)her'umlaufen, her'umirren: ~*ing crowd* Gewühl *n*, wogende
Menge.
mill² [mɪl] *s. Am.* Tausendstel *n* (*bsd.*
¹/₁₀₀₀ *Dollar*).
mill **bar** *s.* ⚙ Pla'tine *f*; '~·**board** *s.* starke
Pappe, Pappdeckel *m*; '~·**course** *s.* **1.**
Mühlengerinne *n*; **2.** Mahlgang *m*.
mil·le·nar·i·an [ˌmɪlɪ'neərɪən] **I** *adj.* **1.**
tausendjährig; **2.** *eccl.* das Tausendjäh-
rige Reich (Christi) betreffend; **3.**
eccl. Chili'ast *m*; **mil·le·nar·i·an·ism**
[ˌmɪlɪ'neərɪənɪzəm] *s. eccl.* Mille,naria-
'nismus *m*; **mil·le·nar·y** [mɪ'lenərɪ] **I**
adj. **1.** aus tausend (Jahren) bestehend,
von tausend Jahren; **II** *s.* **2.** (Jahr')Tau-
send *n*; **3.** Jahr'tausendfeier *f*; **mil·len-
ni·al** [mɪ'lenɪəl] *adj.* **1.** Jahrtausend...,
Mil'lennium(s)...: ~ *doomsdayer* Jahr-
'tausendpro,phet(in); **2.** *eccl.* das Tau-
sendjährige Reich betreffend; **3.** e-e
Jahr'tausendfeier betreffend; **4.** tausendjährig; **mil·len·ni·um** [mɪ'lenɪəm]
pl. **-ni·ums** *od.* **-ni·a** [-nɪə] *s.* **1.** Jahr-
'tausend *n*: ~ *bug* Computer: Jahr-2000-
-Problem *n*, -fehler *m*; ~ *celebration*
Millennium(s)feier *f*, Jahrtausendfeier
f; ~ *compliance* Computer: Jahrtau-
sendfähigkeit *f*, -tauglichkeit *f*; ~*compliant* Computer: jahrtausendfähig,
-tauglich; ~ *date changeover* Datums-
wechsel *m* am Ende des Jahrtausends;
~*proof* jahrtausendsicher, -fähig; **2.**
Jahr'tausendfeier *f*; **3.** *eccl.* Tausend-
jähriges Reich (Christi); **4.** *fig.* Para-
'dies *n* auf Erden.
mil·le·pede ['mɪlɪpiːd] *s. zo.* Tausend-
füß(l)er *m*.
mill·er ['mɪlə] *s.* **1.** Müller *m*; **2.** ⚙ 'Fräsma,schine *f*.
mil·les·i·mal [mɪ'lesɪml] **I** *adj.* □ **1.** tausendst; **2.** aus Tausendsteln bestehend;
II *s.* Tausendstel *n*.
mil·let ['mɪlɪt] *s.* 🌿 (Rispen)Hirse *f*.
'**mill·hand** *s.* Mühlen-, Fa'brik-, Spinne-
'reiarbeiter *m*.
milli- [mɪlɪ] *in Zssgn* Tausendstel.
,**mil·li·am·me·ter** *s.* ⚡ 'Milliam,pere,me-
ter *n*.
mil·li·ard ['mɪljɑːd] *s. Brit.* Milli'arde *f*.
mil·li·bar ['mɪlɪbɑː] *s. meteor.* Milli'bar
n.
'**mil·li·gram(me)** *s.* Milli'gramm *n*; '**mil-
li·me·ter** *Am.*, '**mil·li·me·tre** *Brit.* *s.*
Milli'meter *m*, *n*.
mil·li·ner ['mɪlɪnə] *s.* Hut-, Putzmache-
rin *f*, Mo'distin *f*; '**mil·li·ner·y** [-nərɪ] *s.*
1. Putz-, Modewaren *pl.*; **2.** Hutma-
cherhandwerk *n*; **3.** 'Hutsa,lon *m*.
mill·ing ['mɪlɪŋ] *s.* **1.** Mahlen *n*; **2.** ⚙ a)
Walken *n*, b) Rändeln *n*, c) Fräsen *n*,
d) Walzen *n*; **3.** *sl.* Tracht *f* Prügel; ~
cut·ter *s.* ⚙ Fräser *m*; ~ **ma·chine** *s.*
1. 'Fräsma,schine *f*; **2.** Rändelwerk *n*; ~
prod·uct *s.* 'Mühlen- *od.* ⚙ 'Walzpro-
,dukt *n*.
mil·lion ['mɪljən] *s.* **1.** Milli'on *f*: *a ~
times* Millionen Mal; *two ~ men* 2 Millionen Mann; *by the* ~ nach Millionen;
~*s of people fig.* e-e Unmasse Menschen; **2.** *the* ~ die große Masse, das
Volk; **mil·lion·aire**, *bsd. Am.* **mil-
lion·naire** [ˌmɪljə'neə] *s.* Millio'när *m*;
mil·lion·air·ess [ˌmɪljə'neərɪs] *s.* Milli-
o'närin *f*; '**mil·lion·fold** *adj. u. adv.*
milli'onenfach; '**mil·lionth** [-nθ] **I** *adj.*
milli'onst; **II** *s.* Milli'onstel *n*.
mil·li·pede ['mɪlɪpiːd] *s.*, *a.* '**mil·li·ped**
[-ped] → *millepede*.
'**mil·li,sec·ond** *s.* 'Millise,kunde *f*.
'**mill·pond** *s.* Mühlteich *m*; '~·**race** *s.*

Mühlgerinne *n*.
Mills bomb [mɪlz], **Mills gre·nade** *s.*
✕ 'Eier,handgra,nate *f*.
'**mill·stone** *s.* Mühlstein *m* (*a. fig.
Last*): *be a ~ round s.o.'s neck fig.*
j-m ein Klotz am Bein sein; *see
through a ~ fig.* das Gras wachsen hören; '~·**wheel** *s.* Mühlrad *n*.
mi·lom·e·ter → *mileometer*.
milt¹ [mɪlt] *s. anat.* Milz *f*.
milt² [mɪlt] *ichth.* **I** *s.* Milch *f* (*der männlichen Fische*); **II** *v/t.* den Rogen mit
Milch befruchten; '**milt·er** [-tə] *s. ichth.*
Milchner *m*.
mime [maɪm] **I** *s.* **1.** *antiq.* Mimus *m*,
Possenspiel *n*; **2.** Mime *m*; **3.** Possenreißer *m*; **II** *v/t.* **4.** mimen, nachahmen.
mim·e·o·graph ['mɪmɪəɡrɑːf] **I** *s.* Mimeo'graph *m* (*Vervielfältigungsappa-
rat*); **II** *v/t.* vervielfältigen; **mim·e-
o·graph·ic** [ˌmɪmɪə'ɡræfɪk] *adj.* □ (~
ally) mimeo'graphisch, vervielfältigt.
mi·met·ic [mɪ'metɪk] *adj.* (□ ~*ally*) **1.**
nachahmend (*a. ling. lautmalend*); *b.s.*
nachäffend, Schein...; **2.** *biol.* fremde
Formen nachbildend.
mim·ic ['mɪmɪk] **I** *adj.* **1.** mimisch,
(durch Gebärden) nachahmend; **2.**
Schauspiel...: ~ *art* Schauspielkunst *f*;
3. nachgeahmt, Schein...; **II** *s.* **4.** Nachahmer *m*, Imi'tator *m*; **III** *v/t. pret. u.
p.p.* '**mim·icked** [-kt], *pres. p.* '**mim-
ick·ing** [-kɪŋ] **5.** nachahmen, -äffen; **6.**
♀, *zo.* sich *in der Farbe etc.* angleichen
(*dat.*); '**mim·ic·ry** [-krɪ] *s.* **1.** Nachahmen *n*, -äffung *f*; **2.** *zo.* Mimikry *f*, Angleichung *f*.
mi·mo·sa [mɪ'məʊzə] *s.* 🌿 Mi'mose *f*.
min·a·ret ['mɪnəret] *s.* 🕌 Mina'rett *n*.
min·a·to·ry ['mɪnətərɪ] *adj.* drohend, bedrohlich.
mince [mɪns] **I** *v/t.* **1.** zerhacken, in kleine Stücke zerschneiden; 'durchdrehen:
~ *meat* Hackfleisch machen; **2.** *fig.*
mildern, bemänteln: ~ *one's words* affektiert sprechen; *not to* ~ *matters*
(*od. one's words*) kein Blatt vor den
Mund nehmen; **3.** geziert tun: ~ *one's
steps* → 5 b; **II** *v/i.* **4.** Fleisch (*a. Fett,
Gemüse*) klein schneiden *od.* zerklei-
nern, Hackfleisch machen; **5.** a) sich
geziert benehmen, b) geziert gehen,
trippeln; **III** *s.* **6.** *bsd. Brit.* → *mincemeat* 2; '~·**meat** *s.* **1.** Pa'stetenfüllung *f*
(*aus Korinthen, Äpfeln, Rosinen, Rum
etc. mit od. ohne Fleisch*); **2.** Hackfleisch *n*, Gehacktes *n*: *make* ~ *of fig.*
a) ,aus j-m Hackfleisch machen', b) *Argument etc.* ,(in der Luft) zerreißen'; ~
pie *s.* mit *mincemeat gefüllte Pastete.
minc·er ['mɪnsə] *s.* → *mincing machine*.
minc·ing ['mɪnsɪŋ] *adj.* □ **1.** fig. geziert,
affektiert; ~ **ma·chine** *s.* 'Fleischhack-
ma,schine *f*, Fleischwolf *m*.
mind [maɪnd] **I** *s.* **1.** Sinn *m*, Gemüt *n*,
Herz *n*: *have s.th. on one's* ~ et. auf
dem Herzen haben; **2.** Seele *f*, Verstand *m*, Geist *m*: *presence of* ~ Geistesgegenwart *f*; (*the triumph of*) ~
over matter oft iro. der Sieg des Geistes über die Materie; *before one's* ~*'s
eye* vor s-m geistigen Auge; *be of
sound* ~, *be in one's right* ~ bei (vollem) Verstand sein; *of sound* ~ *and
memory* 🏛 im Vollbesitz s-r geistigen
Kräfte; *be out of one's* ~ nicht (recht)
bei Sinnen sein, verrückt sein; *lose
one's* ~ den Verstand verlieren; *close
one's* ~ *to s.th.* sich gegen et. verschließen; *have an open* ~ unvoreingenommen sein; *cast back one's* ~ sich
zurückversetzen (*to* nach, in *acc.*); *enter s.o.'s* ~ j-m in den Sinn kommen;

put (*od.* **give**) **one's ~ to s.th.** sich mit e-r Sache befassen; **put s.th. out of one's ~** sich et. aus dem Kopf schlagen; **read s.o.'s ~** j-s Gedanken lesen; **that blows your ~!** F da ist man (einfach) ‚fertig'!; **3.** Geist *m* (*a. phls.*): **the human ~; things of the ~** geistige Dinge; **history of the ~** Geistesgeschichte *f*; **his is a fine ~** er hat ein feinen Verstand, er ist ein kluger Kopf; **one of the greatest ~s of his time** *fig.* e-r der größten Geister *od.* Köpfe s-r Zeit; **4.** Meinung *f*, Ansicht *f*: **in** (*od.* **to**) **my ~** m-r Ansicht nach, m-s Erachtens; **be of s.o.'s ~** j-s Meinung sein; **change one's ~** sich anders besinnen; **speak one's ~** (**freely**) s-e Meinung frei äußern; **give s.o. a piece of one's ~** j-m gründlich die Meinung sagen; **know one's own ~** wissen, was man will; **be in two ~s about s.th.** mit sich selbst über et. nicht einig sein; **there can be no two ~s about it** darüber kann es keine geteilte Meinung geben; **5.** Neigung *f*, Lust *f*; Absicht *f*: **have** (**half**) **a ~ to do s.th.** (beinahe) Lust haben, et. zu tun; **have s.th. in ~** et. im Sinne haben; **I have you in ~** ich denke (dabei) an dich; **have it in ~ to do s.th.** beabsichtigen, et. zu tun; **make up one's ~** a) sich entschließen, e-n Entschluss fassen, b) zur Überzeugung kommen (**that** dass), sich klar werden (**about** über *acc.*); **I can't make up your ~** *iro.* ich kann mir nicht deinen Kopf zerbrechen; **6.** Erinnerung *f*, Gedächtnis *n*: **bear** (*od.* **keep**) **in ~** (immer) an et. denken, et. nicht vergessen, bedenken; **call to ~** sich et. ins Gedächtnis zurückrufen, sich an et. erinnern; **put s.o. in ~ of s.th.** j-n an et. erinnern; **nothing comes to ~** nichts fällt einem dabei ein; **time out of ~** seit (*od.* vor) undenklichen Zeiten; **II** *v/t.* **7.** merken, (be)achten, Acht geben, hören auf (*acc.*): **~ one's P's and Q's** F sich ganz gehörig in Acht nehmen; **~ you write** F denk daran (*od.* vergiss nicht) zu schreiben; **8.** sich in Acht nehmen, sich hüten vor (*dat.*): **~ the step!** Achtung, Stufe!; **9.** sorgen für, sehen nach: **~ the children** sich um die Kinder kümmern, die Kinder hüten; **~ your own business!** kümmere dich um deine eigenen Dinge!; **don't ~ me!** lass dich durch mich nicht stören!; **never ~ him!** kümmere dich nicht um ihn!; **10.** et. haben gegen, es nicht gern sehen *od.* mögen, sich stoßen an (*dat.*): **do you ~ my smoking?** haben Sie et. dagegen, wenn ich rauche?; **would you ~ coming?** würden Sie so freundlich sein zu kommen?; **I don't ~** (**it**) ich habe nichts dagegen, meinetwegen; **I wouldn't ~ a drink** ich hätte nichts gegen einen Drink; **III** *v/i.* **11.** Acht haben, aufpassen, bedenken: **~** (**you**)**!** wohlgemerkt; **never ~!** lass es gut sein!, es hat nichts zu sagen!, es macht nichts! (→ *a.* 12); **12.** et. da'gegen haben: **I don't ~** ich habe nichts dagegen, meinetwegen; **I don't ~ if I do** F ja, ganz gern *od.* ich möchte schon; **he ~s a great deal** er ist allerdings dagegen, es macht ihm sehr viel aus; **never ~!** mach dir nichts draus!
'**mind|-‚bend·ing**, '**~-‚blow·ing**, '**~-‚bog·gling** *adj. sl.* ‚irr(e)', ‚tonll'.
mind·ed ['maɪndɪd] *adj.* **1.** geneigt, gesonnen: **if you are so ~** wenn das deine Absicht ist; **2.** *in Zssgn* a) gesinnt: **evil-~** böse gesinnt; **small-~** kleinlich, b) *religiös, technisch etc.* veranlagt: **religious-~**, c) interes'siert an (*dat.*): **air-~**

flugbegeistert.
'**mind-ex‚pand·ing** *adj.* bewusstseinserweiternd, psyche'delisch.
mind·ful ['maɪndfʊl] *adj.* □ (**of**) aufmerksam, achtsam (auf *acc.*), eingedenk (*gen.*): **be ~ of** achten auf; '**mindless** ['maɪndlɪs] *adj.* □ **1.** (**of**) unbekümmert (um), ohne Rücksicht (auf *acc.*), uneingedenk (*gen.*); **2.** hirn-, gedankenlos, ‚blind'; **3.** geistlos, unbeseelt.
'**mind|-‚read·er** *s.* Gedankenleser(in); '**~-‚read·ing** *s.* Gedankenlesen *n*.
mine¹ [maɪn] **I** *poss. pron.* der (die, das) Mein(ig)e **what is ~** was mir gehört, das Meinige; **a friend of ~** ein Freund von mir; **me and ~** ich u. die Mein(ig)en *od.* meine Familie; **II** *poss. adj. poet. od. obs.* mein: **~ eyes** meine Augen; **~ host** (der) Herr Wirt.
mine² [maɪn] **I** *v/i.* **1.** minieren; **2.** schürfen, graben (**for** nach); **3.** sich eingraben (*Tiere*); **II** *v/t.* **4.** *Erz, Kohlen* abbauen, gewinnen; **5.** ♣, ✕ a) verminen, b) minieren; **6.** *fig.* unter'graben, -mi'nieren; **III** *s.* **7.** *oft pl.* ✕ Mine *f*, Bergwerk *n*, Zeche *f*, Grube *f*; **8.** ♣, ✕ (*Luft-, See*)Mine *f*: **spring a ~** e-e Mine springen lassen (*a. fig.*); **9.** *fig.* Fundgrube *f* (**of** an *dat.*): **a ~ of information**; **~ bar·ri·er** ✕ Minensperre *f*; **~ de·tec·tor** *s.* ✕ Minensuchgerät *n*; '**~-field** *s.* ✕ Minenfeld *n*; **~ fore·man** *s.* [*irr.*] ✕ Obersteiger *m*; **~ gas** *s.* Me'than *n*; **2.** ✕ Grubengas *n*, schlagende Wetter *pl.*; '**~-‚lay·er** [-‚leɪə] *s.* ♣, ✕ Minenleger *m*.
min·er ['maɪnə] *s.* **1.** ✕ Bergarbeiter *m*, -mann *m*, Grubenarbeiter *m*, Kumpel *m*: **~s' association** Knappschaft *f*; **~'s lamp** Grubenlampe *f*; **~'s lung** ♣ (Kohlen)Staublunge *f*; **2.** ♣, ✕ Minenleger *m*.
min·er·al ['mɪnərəl] **I** *s.* **1.** Mine'ral *n*; **2.** *bsd. pl.* Mine'ralwasser *n*; **II** *adj.* **3.** mine'ralisch, Mineral...; **4.** 🌱 'anor‚ganisch: **~ car·bon** *s.* Gra'phit *m*; **~ coal** *s.* Steinkohle *f*; **~ de·pos·it** *s.* Erzlagerstätte *f*.
min·er·al·ize ['mɪnərəlaɪz] *v/t. geol.* **1.** vererzen; **2.** mineralisieren, versteinern; **3.** mit 'anor‚ganischem Stoff durch'setzen; **min·er·al·og·i·cal** [‚mɪnərə'lɒdʒɪkl] *adj.* □ *min.* minera'logisch; **min·er·al·o·gy** [‚mɪnə'rælədʒɪ] *s.* Mineralo'gie *f*.
min·er·al| oil *s.* Erdöl *n*, Pe'troleum *n*, Mine'ralöl *n*; **~ spring** *s.* Mine'ralquelle *f*, Heilbrunnen *m*; **~ wa·ter** *s.* Mine'ralwasser *n*.
'**mine‚sweep·er** *s.* ♣, ✕ Minenräum-, Minensuchboot *n*.
min·e·ver ['mɪnɪvə] → **miniver**.
min·gle ['mɪŋgl] **I** *v/i.* **1.** verschmelzen, sich vermischen, sich verbinden (**with** mit): **with ~d feelings** *fig.* mit gemischten Gefühlen; **2.** *fig.* sich (ein)mischen (**in** in *acc.*), sich mischen (**among**, **with** unter *acc.*); **II** *v/t.* **3.** vermischen, -mengen.
min·i ['mɪnɪ] **I** *s.* **1.** Minimode *f*: **wear ~** Mini tragen; **2.** Minikleid *n*, -rock *m* *etc.*; **II** *adj.* **3.** Mini-.
min·i·a·ture ['mɪnətʃə] **I** *s.* **1.** Minia'tur(-gemälde *n*) *f*; **2.** *fig.* Minia'turausgabe *f*: **in ~** im Kleinen, en miniature, Miniatur...; **3.** ✕ kleine Ordensschnalle *f*; **II** *adj.* **4.** Miniatur..., Klein..., im kleinen: **~ cam·er·a** *s. phot.* Kleinbildkamera *f*; **~ cur·rent** *s.* ♪ Mini'mal-, 'Unterstrom *m*; **~ grand** *s.* ♪ Stutzflügel *m*; **~ ri·fle shoot·ing** *s.* 'Kleinka‚liberschießen *n*.

min·i·a·tur·ist ['mɪnə‚tjʊərɪst] *s.* Minia-'turmaler(in); **min·i·a·tur·ize** ['mɪnə-tʃəraɪz] *v/t. bsd. elektronische Elemente* miniaturisieren.
'**min·i|‚bar** *s.* Minibar *f*; '**~-bus** *s. mot.* Mini-, Kleinbus *m*; '**~-cab** *s. mot.* Minicar *m* (*Kleintaxi*); '**~-car** *s. mot.* Kleinwagen *m*; '**~-dress** *s.* Minikleid *n*.
min·i·kin ['mɪnɪkɪn] **I** *adj.* **1.** affektiert, geziert; **2.** winzig, zierlich; **II** *s.* **3.** kleine Stecknadel; **4.** *fig.* Knirps *m*.
min·im ['mɪnɪm] *s.* **1.** ♪ halbe Note; **2.** *et.* Winziges; Zwerg *m*; **3.** *pharm.* 1/60 Drachme *f* (*Apothekermaß*); **4.** Grundstrich *m* (*Kalligraphie*); '**min·i·mal** [-ml] *adj.* kleinst, mini'mal, Mindest...; '**min·i·mize** [-maɪz] *v/t.* **1.** auf das Mindestmaß zu'rückführen, möglichst gering halten; **2.** als geringfügig darstellen, bagatellisieren; '**min·i·mum** [-məm] **I** *pl.* **-ma** [-mə] *s.* Minimum *n* (*a.* A), Mindestmaß *n*, -betrag *m*, -stand *m*: **with a ~ of effort** mit e-m Minimum an *od.* von Anstrengung; **II** *adj.* mini'mal, Mindest..., kleinst: **~ output** Leistungsminimum *n*; **~ price** Mindestpreis *m*; **~ reserve holdings** *pl.* ✝ Mindestreserveguthaben *n od. pl*; **~ wage** Mindestlohn *m*.
min·ing ['maɪnɪŋ] **I** *s.* **1.** Bergbau *m*, Bergwerk(s)betrieb *m*; **II** *adj.* Bergwerks..., Berg(bau)..., Gruben..., Montan...: **~ academy** Bergakademie *f*; **~ law** Bergrecht *n*; **~ dis·as·ter** *s.* Grubenunglück *n*; **~ en·gi·neer** *s.* 'Berg(bau)inge‚nieur *m*; **~ in·dus·try** *s.* 'Bergbau-, Mon'tanindu‚strie *f*; **~ share** *s.* Kux *m*.
min·ion ['mɪnjən] *s.* **1.** Günstling *m*; **2.** *contp.* Speichellecker *m*: **~ of the law** *oft humor.* Gesetzeshüter *m*; **3.** *typ.* Kolo'nel *f* (*Schriftgrad*).
min·i·quake ['mɪnɪkweɪk] *s. geol.* kleines Erdbeben, Erdstoß *m*.
'**min·i·skirt** *s.* Minirock *m*.
'**min·i·state** *s. pol.* Zwergstaat *m*.
min·is·ter ['mɪnɪstə] **I** *s.* **1.** *eccl.* Geistliche(r) *m*, Pfarrer *m* (*bsd. e-r Dissenterkirche*); **2.** *pol. Brit.* Mi'nister(in), *a.* Premi'ermi‚nister(in): **2 of the Crown** (Kabinetts)Minister(in); **2 of Labour** Arbeitsminister(in); **3.** *pol.* Gesandte(r *m*) *f*: **~ plenipotentiary** bevollmächtigter Gesandter; **4.** *fig.* Diener *m*, Werkzeug *n*; **II** *v/t.* **5.** darreichen; *eccl.* die Sakramente spenden; **III** *v/i.* **6.** (**to**) behilflich *od.* dienlich sein (*dat.*) (*a. fig.* fördern): **~ to the wants of others** für die Bedürfnisse anderer sorgen; **7.** *eccl.* Gottesdienst halten; **min·is·te·ri·al** [‚mɪnɪ'stɪərɪəl] *adj.* □ **1.** amtlich, Verwaltungs..., 'untergeordnet: **~ officer** Verwaltungs-, Exekutivbeamte(r) *m*; **2.** *eccl.* geistlich; **3.** *pol.* a) Ministerial..., Minister..., b) Regierungs...: **~ bill** Regierungsvorlage *f*; **4.** Hilfs..., dienlich (**to** *dat.*); '**min·is·trant** [-trənt] **I** *adj.* **1.** (**to**) dienend (zu), dienstbar (*dat.*); **II** *s.* **2.** Diener(in); **3.** *eccl.* Minist-'rant *m*; **min·is·tra·tion** [‚mɪnɪ'streɪʃn] *s.* Dienst *m* (**to** an *dat.*); *bsd.* kirchliches Amt; '**min·is·try** [-trɪ] *s.* **1.** *eccl.* geistliches Amt; **2.** *pol. Brit.* a) Mini'sterium *n* (*a. Amtsdauer u. Gebäude*), b) Mi'nisterposten *m*, -amt *n*, c) Kabi'nett *n*, Regierung *f*; **3.** *pol. Brit.* Amt *n* e-s Gesandten; **4.** *eccl. coll.* Geistlichkeit *f*.
min·i·um ['mɪnɪəm] *s.* **1.** → **vermilion** 1; **2.** 🌱 Mennige *f*.
min·i·ver ['mɪnɪvə] *s.* Grauwerk *n*, Feh *n* (*Pelz*).
mink [mɪŋk] *s.* **1.** *zo.* Nerz *m*; **2.** Nerz (-fell *n*) *m*.
min·now ['mɪnəʊ] *s.* **1.** *ichth.* Elritze *f*;

2. *fig. contp.* (*eine*) ‚Null‘, (*ein*) Niemand *m*.

mi·nor [ˈmaɪnə] **I** *adj.* **1.** a) kleiner, geringer, b) klein, unbedeutend, geringfügig; 'untergeordnet (*a. phls.*): **~ casualty** ✕ Leichtverwundete(r) *m*; **~ offence** (*Am.* **-se**) ⚖ (leichtes) Vergehen; **the ⒉ Prophets** *bibl.* die kleinen Propheten; **of ~ importance** von zweitrangiger Bedeutung, c) Neben..., Hilfs..., Unter...: **a ~ group** eine Untergruppe; **~ premise** → 7; **~ subject** *Am. univ.* Nebenfach *n*; **2.** minderjährig; **3.** *Brit.* jünger (*in Schulen*): **Smith ~** Smith der Jüngere; **4.** ♪ a) klein (*Terz etc.*), b) Moll...: **C ~** c-Moll *n*; **~ key** Molltonart *f*; **in ~ key** *fig.* (etwas) gedämpft; **~ mode** Mollgeschlecht *n*; **II** *s.* **5.** Minderjährige(r *m*) *f*; **6.** ♪ a) Moll *n*, b) 'Mollak‚kord *m*, c) Molltonart *f*; **7.** *phls.* 'Untersatz *m*; **8.** *Am. univ.* Nebenfach *n*; **III** *v/i.* **9.** **~ in** *Am. univ.* als Nebenfach studieren; **mi·nor·i·ty** [maɪˈnɒrətɪ] *s.* **1.** Minderjährigkeit *f*, Unmündigkeit *f*; **2.** Minori'tät *f*, Minderheit *f*, -zahl *f*: **~ government** (*party*) Minderheitsregierung (-partei) *f*; **be in the ~** in der Minderheit *od.* -zahl sein.

min·ster [ˈmɪnstə] *s. eccl.* **1.** Münster *n*; **2.** Klosterkirche *f*.

min·strel [ˈmɪnstrəl] *s.* **1.** *hist.* Spielmann *m*; Minnesänger *m*; **2.** *poet.* Sänger *m*, Dichter *m*; **'min·strel·sy** [-sɪ] *s.* **1.** Musi'kantentum *n*; **2.** a) Minnesang *m*, -dichtung *f*, b) *poet.* Dichtkunst *f*, Dichtung *f*; **3.** *coll.* Spielleute *pl.*

mint¹ [mɪnt] *s.* **1.** ♀ Minze *f*: **~ sauce** (saure) Minzsoße *f*; **2.** 'Pfefferminz(li‚kör) *m*.

mint² [mɪnt] **I** *s.* **1.** Münze *f*: a) Münzstätte *f*, -anstalt *f*, b) Münzamt *n*: **a ~ of money** F ein Haufen Geld; **2.** *fig.* (reiche) Fundgrube, Quelle *f*; **II** *adj.* **3.** (wie) neu, tadellos erhalten, (*Buch etc.*): **in ~ condition**; **4.** postfrisch (*Briefmarke*); **III** *v/t.* **5.** Geld münzen, schlagen, prägen; **6.** *fig. Wort etc.* prägen; **'mint·age** [-tɪdʒ] *s.* **1.** Münzen *n*, Prägung *f* (*a. fig.*); **2.** das Geprägte, Geld *n*; **3.** Prägegebühr *f*.

min·u·end [ˈmɪnjʊend] *s.* ⅍ Minu'end *m*.

min·u·et [ˌmɪnjʊˈet] *s.* ♪ Menu'ett *n*.

mi·nus [ˈmaɪnəs] **I** *prp.* **1.** ⅍ minus, weniger; **2.** F ohne: **~ his hat**; **II** *adv.* **3.** minus, unter null (*Temperatur*); **III** *adj.* **4.** Minus..., negativ: **~ amount** Fehlbetrag *m*; **~ quantity** → 6; **~ sign** → 5; **IV** *s.* **5.** Minuszeichen *n*; **6.** Minus *n*, negative Größe; **7.** Mangel *m* (**of** an *dat.*).

mi·nus·cule [ˈmɪnəskjuːl] **I** *s.* Mi'nuskel *f*; **II** *adj.* winzig, sehr klein.

min·ute¹ [ˈmɪnɪt] **I** *s.* **1.** Mi'nute *f* (*a. ast.*, ⅍, △): **for a ~** e-e Minute (lang); **~ hand** Minutenzeiger *m* (*Uhr*): **~** auf die Minute genau; (**up**) **to the ~** hypermodern; **2.** Augenblick *m*: **in a ~** sofort; **just a ~!** Moment mal!; **the ~ that** sobald; **3.** ♪ a) Kon'zept *n*, kurzer Entwurf, b) No'tiz *f*, Memo'randum *n*: **~ book** Protokollbuch *n*; **4.** *pl.* ⅍, *pol.* ('Sitzungs)Proto‚koll *n*, Niederschrift *f*: (**the**) **~s of the proceedings** Verhandlungsprotokoll *n*; **keep the ~s** das Protokoll führen; **loose ~** Aktennotiz *f*; **II** *v/t.* **5.** a) entwerfen, aufsetzen, b) notieren, protokollieren.

mi·nute² [maɪˈnjuːt] *adj.* □ **1.** sehr klein, winzig: **in the ~st details** in den kleinsten Einzelheiten; **2.** *fig.* unbedeutend, geringfügig; **3.** peinlich genau, minuti'ös.

---

min·ute·ly¹ [ˈmɪnɪtlɪ] **I** *adj.* jede Mi'nute geschehend, Minuten...; **II** *adv.* jede Mi'nute, von Minute zu Minute.

min·ute·ly² [maɪˈnjuːtlɪ] *adv. von minute²*; **mi·nute·ness** [maɪˈnjuːtnɪs] *s.* **1.** Kleinheit *f*, Winzigkeit *f*; **2.** minuti'öse Genauigkeit.

mi·nu·ti·a [maɪˈnjuːʃɪə] *pl.* **-ti·ae** [-ʃiː] (*Lat.*) *s.* Einzelheit *f*, De'tail *n*.

minx [mɪŋks] *s.* Range *f*, ‚kleines Biest‘.

mir·a·belle [ˌmɪrəˈbel] *s. Obst*: Mira'belle *f*.

mir·a·cle [ˈmɪrəkl] *s.* Wunder *n* (*a. fig. of* an *dat.*); Wundertat *f*, -kraft *f*: **to a ~** fantastisch (gut); **work ~s** Wunder tun *od.* vollbringen; **~ drug** Wunderdroge *f*; **~ play** *hist. eccl.* Mirakelspiel *n*; **mi·rac·u·lous** [mɪˈrækjʊləs] *I adj.* □ 'überna‚türlich, wunderbar (*a. fig.*); Wunder...: **~ cure** Wunderkur *f*; **II** *s.* **das ~** das Wunderbare; **mi·rac·u·lous·ly** [mɪˈrækjʊləslɪ] *adv.* (wie) durch ein Wunder, wunderbar(erweise).

mi·rage [ˈmɪrɑːʒ] *s.* **1.** *phys.* Luftspiegelung *f*, Fata Mor'gana *f*; **2.** *fig.* Trugbild *n*.

mire [maɪə] **I** *s.* **1.** Schlamm *m*, Sumpf *m*, Kot *m* (*alle a. fig.*): **drag s.o. through the ~** *fig.* j-n in den Schmutz ziehen; **be deep in the ~** ‚tief in der Klemme sitzen‘; **II** *v/t.* **2.** in den Schlamm fahren *od.* setzen: **be ~d** im Sumpf *etc.* stecken (bleiben); **3.** beschmutzen, besudeln; **III** *v/i.* **4.** im Sumpf versinken.

mir·ror [ˈmɪrə] **I** *s.* **1.** Spiegel *m* (*a. zo.*): **hold up the ~ to s.o.** *fig.* j-m den Spiegel vorhalten; **2.** *fig.* Spiegel(bild *n*) *m*; **II** *v/t.* **3.** 'widerspiegeln: **be ~ed** sich (wider)spiegeln (**in** in *dat.*); **4.** mit Spiegel(n) versehen: **~ed room** Spiegelzimmer *n*; **~-fin·ish** *s.* ⊚ Hochglanz *m*; **'~-in‚vert·ed** *adj.* seitenverkehrt; **~ sym·me·try** *s.* ⅍, *phys.* 'Spiegelsymme‚trie *f*; **~ writ·ing** *s.* Spiegelschrift *f*.

mirth [mɜːθ] *s.* Fröhlichkeit *f*, Heiterkeit *f*, Freude *f*; **'mirth·ful** [-fʊl] *adj.* □ fröhlich, heiter, lustig; **'mirth·ful·ness** [-fʊlnɪs] *s.* → **mirth**; **'mirth·less** [-lɪs] *adj.* freudlos, trüb(e).

mir·y [ˈmaɪərɪ] *adj.* **1.** sumpfig, schlammig, kotig; **2.** *fig.* schmutzig, gemein.

mis- [mɪs] *in Zssgn* falsch, Falsch..., miss..., Miss...; schlecht; Fehl...

mis·ad·ven·ture *s.* Unfall *m*, Unglück *n*; 'Missgeschick *n*; **mis·a·lign·ment** *s.* ⊚ Flucht(ungs)fehler *m*; *Radio, TV*: schlechte Ausrichtung; **mis·al·li·ance** *s.* Mesal'liance *f*, 'Missheirat *f*.

mis·an·thrope [ˈmɪzənθrəʊp] *s.* Menschenfeind *m*, Misan'throp *m*; **mis·an·throp·ic, mis·an·throp·i·cal** [ˌmɪzənˈθrɒpɪk(l)] *adj.* □ menschenfeindlich, misan'thropisch; **mis·an·thro·pist** [mɪˈzænθrəpɪst] → **misanthrope**; **mis·an·thro·py** [mɪˈzænθrəpɪ] *s.* Menschenhass *m*, Misanthro'pie *f*.

mis·ap·pli·ca·tion *s.* falsche Verwendung; *b.s.* 'Missbrauch *m*; **mis·ap·ply** *v/t.* falsch anbringen *od.* anwenden; **2.** → **misappropriate** 1.

mis·ap·pre·hend *v/t.* 'missverstehen; **mis·ap·pre·hen·sion** *s.* 'Missverständnis *n*, falsche Auffassung: **be labo(u)r under a ~** sich in e-m Irrtum befinden.

mis·ap·pro·pri·ate *v/t.* **1.** sich *et.* 'widerrechtlich aneignen, unter'schlagen; **2.** falsch anwenden: **~d capital** ✝ fehlgeleitetes Kapital; **'mis·ap‚pro·pri·a·tion** *s.* ⚖ 'widerrechtliche Aneignung *od.* Verwendung, Unter'schlagung *f*, Veruntreuung *f*.

---

mis·be·come *v/t.* [*irr.* → **become**] j-m schlecht stehen, sich nicht schicken *od.* ziemen für; **mis·be·com·ing** *adj.* → **unbecoming**.

mis·be·got·ten *adj.* **1.** unehelich (gezeugt); **2.** → **misgotten**; **3.** mise'rabel, verkorkst.

mis·be·have *v/i. od. v/refl.* **1.** sich schlecht benehmen *od.* aufführen, sich da'nebenbenehmen; ungezogen sein (*Kind*); **2.** **~ with** sich einlassen *od.* in-'tim werden mit; **mis·be·hav·io(u)r** *s.* **1.** schlechtes Betragen, Ungezogenheit *f*; **2.** **~ before the enemy** ✕ *Am.* Feigheit *f* vor dem Feind.

mis·be·lief *s.* Irrglaube *m*; irrige Ansicht; **mis·be·lieve** *v/i.* irrgläubig sein.

mis·cal·cu·late I *v/t.* falsch berechnen *od.* (ab)schätzen; **II** *v/i.* sich verrechnen, sich verkalkulieren; **'mis·cal·cu·la·tion** *s.* Rechen-, Kalkulati'onsfehler *m*.

mis·call *v/t.* falsch *od.* zu Unrecht (be-)nennen.

mis·car·riage *s.* **1.** Fehlschlag(en *n*) *m*, Miss'lingen *n*: **~ of justice** ⚖ Fehlspruch *m*, -urteil *n*, Justizirrtum *m*; **2.** ✝ Versandfehler *m*; **3.** Fehlleitung *f* (*Brief*); **4.** ♞ Fehlgeburt *f*; **mis·car·ry** *v/i.* **1.** miss'lingen, -'glücken, fehlschlagen, scheitern; **2.** verloren gehen (*Brief*); **3.** ♞ e-e Fehlgeburt haben.

mis·cast *v/t.* [*irr.* → **cast**] *thea. etc.* Rolle fehlbesetzen: **be ~** a) e-e Fehlbesetzung sein (*Schauspieler*), b) *fig.* s-n Beruf verfehlt haben.

mis·ce·ge·na·tion [ˌmɪsɪdʒɪˈneɪʃn] *s.* Rassenmischung *f*.

mis·cel·la·ne·ous [ˌmɪsɪˈleɪnjəs] *adj.* □ **1.** ge-, vermischt, di'vers; **2.** mannigfaltig, verschiedenartig; **'mis·cel·la·ne·ous·ness** [-nɪs] *s.* **1.** Gemischtheit *f*; **2.** Vielseitigkeit *f*, Mannigfaltigkeit *f*; **mis·cel·la·ny** [mɪˈselənɪ] *s.* **1.** Gemisch *n*, Sammlung *f*, Sammelband *m*; **2.** *pl.* vermischte Schriften *pl.*, Mis'zellen *pl.*

mis·chance *s.* 'Missgeschick *n*: **by ~** durch e-n unglücklichen Zufall, unglücklicherweise.

mis·chief [ˈmɪstʃɪf] *s.* **1.** Unheil *n*, Unglück *n*, Schaden *m*: **do ~** Unheil anrichten; **mean ~** Böses im Schilde führen; **make ~** Zwietracht säen, böses Blut machen; **run into ~** in Gefahr kommen; **2.** Ursache *f* des Unheils, Übelstand *m*, Unrecht *n*, Störenfried *m*; **3.** Unfug *m*, Possen *m*: **get into ~** et. ‚anstellen‘; **keep out of ~** keine Dummheiten machen, brav sein; **that will keep you out of ~!** damit du auf keine dummen Gedanken kommst!; **4.** Racker *m* (*Kind*); **5.** 'Übermut *m*, Ausgelassenheit *f*: **be full of ~** immer Unfug im Kopf haben; **6.** *euphem.* der Teufel: **what** (*why*) **the ~ ...?** was (warum) zum Teufel ...?; **'~-‚mak·er** *s.* troublemaker.

mis·chie·vous [ˈmɪstʃɪvəs] *adj.* □ **1.** nachteilig, schädlich, verderblich; **2.** boshaft, mutwillig, schadenfroh, schelmisch; **'mis·chie·vous·ness** [-nɪs] *s.* **1.** Schädlichkeit *f*; **2.** Bosheit *f*; **3.** Schalkhaftigkeit *f*, Ausgelassenheit *f*.

mis·ci·ble [ˈmɪsɪbl] *adj.* mischbar.

mis·con·ceive *v/t.* falsch auffassen *od.* verstehen, sich e-n falschen Begriff machen von; **mis·con·cep·tion** *s.* 'Missverständnis *n*, falsche Auffassung.

mis·con·duct I *v/t.* [ˌmɪskənˈdʌkt] **1.** schlecht führen *od.* verwalten; **2.** **~ o.s.** sich schlecht betragen *od.* benehmen, e-n Fehltritt begehen; **II** *s.* [ˌmɪsˈkɒndʌkt] **3.** Ungebühr f, schlechtes Betragen od. Benehmen; **4.** Verfehlung f, bsd. Ehebruch m, Fehltritt m; ✕ schlechte Führung: ~ *in office* ⚖ Amtsvergehen n.

‚mis·con'struc·tion s. 'Missdeutung f, falsche Auslegung; **‚mis·con'strue** v/t. falsch auslegen, miss'deuten, 'missverstehen.

mis·cre·ant ['mɪskrɪənt] **I** adj. gemein, ab'scheulich; **II** s. Schurke m.

‚mis·date I v/t. falsch datieren; **II** s. falsches Datum.

‚mis'deal v/t. u. v/i. [irr. → *deal*] ~ (*the cards*) sich vergeben.

‚mis·deed s. Missetat f.

mis·de·mean [‚mɪsdɪ'miːn] v/i. u. v/refl. sich schlecht betragen, sich vergehen; **‚mis·de'mean·o(u)r** [-nə] ⚖ Vergehen n, minderes De'likt.

‚mis·di·rect v/t. **1.** j-n od. et. fehl-, irreleiten; ~*ed charity* falsch angebrachte Wohltätigkeit; **2.** ⚖ *die Geschworenen* falsch belehren; **3.** *Brief* falsch adressieren.

mise en scène [‚miːzɑ̃ːn'seɪn] (*Fr.*) s. thea. u. fig. Inszenierung f.

‚mis·em'ploy v/t. **1.** schlecht anwenden; **2.** miss'brauchen.

mi·ser ['maɪzə] s. Geizhals m.

mis·er·a·ble ['mɪzərəbl] adj. □ **1.** elend, jämmerlich, erbärmlich, armselig, kläglich (*alle a. contp.*); **2.** traurig, unglücklich: *make s.o.* ~; **3.** contp. allg. mise'rabel.

mi·ser·li·ness ['maɪzəlɪnɪs] s. Geiz m; **mi·ser·ly** ['maɪzəlɪ] adj. geizig.

mis·er·y ['mɪzərɪ] s. Elend n, Not f; Trübsal f, Jammer m; *put s.o. out of his* ~ mst iro. j-n von s-m Leiden erlösen.

mis·fea·sance [mɪs'fiːzəns] s. ⚖ **1.** pflichtwidrige Handlung; **2.** 'Missbrauch m (*der Amtsgewalt*).

‚mis'fire I v/i. **1.** versagen (*Waffe*); **2.** mot. fehlzünden, aussetzen; **3.** fig. ‚da'nebengehen'; **II** s. **4.** Versager m; **5.** mot. Fehlzündung f.

'mis·fit s. **1.** schlecht sitzendes Kleidungsstück; **2.** nicht passendes Stück; **3.** F fig. Außenseiter(in), Eigenbrötler(in).

mis'for·tune s. 'Missgeschick n.

mis'give v/t. [irr. → *give*] *Böses* ahnen lassen: *my heart* ~*s me* mir schwant (*that* dass, *about s.th.* et.); **mis'giv·ing** s. Befürchtung f, böse Ahnung, Zweifel m.

mis'got·ten adj. unrechtmäßig erworben.

‚mis'gov·ern v/t. schlecht regieren; **‚mis'gov·ern·ment** s. 'Missregierung f, schlechte Regierung.

‚mis'guide v/t. fehlleiten, verleiten, irreführen; **mis'guid·ed** adj. fehl-, irregeleitet; irrig, unangebracht.

‚mis'han·dle v/t. miss'handeln; weitS. falsch behandeln, schlecht handhaben; verpatzen.

mis'hap ['mɪshæp] s. Unglück n, Unfall m; mot. (*a. humor. fig.*) Panne f.

‚mis'hear v/t. u. v/i. [irr. → *hear*] falsch hören, sich verhören (bei).

mish·mash ['mɪʃmæʃ] s. Mischmasch m.

‚mis·in'form I v/t. j-m falsch berichten, j-n falsch unter'richten; **II** v/i. falsch aussagen (*against* gegen); **‚mis·in·for·'ma·tion** s. falscher Bericht, falsche Auskunft.

‚mis·in'ter·pret v/t. miss'deuten, falsch auffassen od. auslegen; **'mis·in‚ter·pre'ta·tion** s. 'Missdeutung f, falsche

Auslegung.

‚mis'join·der s. ⚖ unzulässige Klagehäufung; unzulässige Zuziehung (*e-s Streitgenossen*).

‚mis'judge v/i. u. v/t. **1.** falsch (be)urteilen, verkennen; **2.** falsch schätzen: *I* ~*d the distance*; **‚mis'judge·ment** s. irriges Urteil; falsche Beurteilung.

‚mis'lay v/t. [irr. → *lay*] et. verlegen.

‚mis'lead v/t. [irr. → *lead*] irreführen; fig. a. verführen, verleiten (*into doing* zu tun): *be misled* sich verleiten lassen; **‚mis'lead·ing** adj. irreführend.

‚mis'man·age I v/t. schlecht verwalten, unrichtig handhaben; **II** v/i. schlecht wirtschaften; **‚mis'man·age·ment** s. 'Miss‚management n, 'Misswirtschaft f.

‚mis'matched adj. nicht zs.-passend, ungleich (*Paar*).

‚mis'name v/t. falsch benennen.

mis·no·mer [‚mɪs'nəʊmə] s. **1.** ⚖ Namensirrtum m (*in e-r Urkunde*); **2.** falsche Benennung od. Bezeichnung.

mi·sog·a·mist [mɪ'sɒgəmɪst] s. Ehefeind m.

mi·sog·y·nist [mɪ'sɒdʒɪnɪst] s. Frauenfeind m; **mi'sog·y·ny** [-nɪ] s. Frauenhass m, Mysogy'nie f.

‚mis'place v/t. **1.** et. verlegen; **2.** an e-e falsche Stelle legen od. setzen; **3.** fig. falsch od. übel anbringen: ~*d* unangebracht, deplatziert.

mis·print I v/t. [‚mɪs'prɪnt] verdrucken, fehldrucken; **II** s. ['mɪsprɪnt] Druckfehler m.

‚mis·pro'nounce v/t. falsch aussprechen; **'mis·pro‚nun·ci·a·tion** s. falsche Aussprache.

‚mis·quo'ta·tion s. falsches Zi'tat; **‚mis'quote** v/t. u. v/i. falsch anführen od. zitieren.

‚mis'read v/t. [irr. → *read*] **1.** falsch lesen; **2.** miss'deuten.

'mis‚rep·re'sent v/t. **1.** falsch od. ungenau darstellen; **2.** entstellen, verdrehen; **'mis‚rep·re·sen'ta·tion** s. falsche Darstellung od. Angabe (a. ⚖), Verdrehung f.

‚mis'rule I v/t. **1.** schlecht regieren; **II** s. **2.** schlechte Re'gierung, 'Missregierung f; **3.** Unordnung f.

miss¹ [mɪs] s. **1.** 2 in der Anrede: Fräulein n: 2 *Smith*; 2 *America* Miss Amerika (*die Schönheitskönigin von Amerika*); **2.** humor. (junges) ‚Ding', Dämchen n; **3.** F (*ohne folgenden Namen*) Fräulein n.

miss² [mɪs] I v/t. **1.** *Chance, Zug etc.* verpassen, versäumen; *Beruf, Person, Schlag, Weg, Ziel* verfehlen: ~ *the point* (*of an argument*) das Wesentliche (e-s Arguments) nicht begreifen; *he didn't* ~ *much* a) er versäumte nicht viel, b) ihm entging fast nichts; ~*ed approach* ✈ Fehlanflug m; → *boat* 1, *bus* 1, *fire* 10, *etc.*; **2.** a. ~ *out* auslassen, über'gehen, -'springen; **3.** nicht haben, nicht bekommen; **4.** nicht hören können, über'hören; **5.** vermissen; **6.** (ver-) missen, entbehren: *we* ~ *her very much* sie fehlt uns sehr; **7.** vermeiden: *he just* ~*ed being hurt* er ist gerade (noch) e-r Verletzung entgangen; *I just* ~*ed running him over* ich hätte ihn beinahe überfahren; **II** v/i. **8.** fehlen, nicht treffen: a) da'nebenschießen, -werfen, -schlagen *etc.*, b) da'nebengehen (*Schuss etc.*); **9.** miss'glücken, -'lingen, fehlschlagen, ‚da'nebengehen'; **10.** ~ *out on* a) über'sehen, auslassen, b) sich entgehen lassen, c) et. nicht kriegen; **III** s. **11.** Fehlschuss m, -wurf m, -stoß m: *every shot a* ~ jeder Schuss

(ging) daneben; **12.** Verpassen n, Versäumen n, Verfehlen n, Entrinnen n: *a* ~ *is as good as a mile* a) knapp daneben ist auch daneben, b) mit knapper Not entrinnen ist immerhin entrinnen; *give s.th. a* ~ a) et. vermeiden, et. nicht nehmen, et. nicht tun *etc.*, die Finger lassen von et., b) → 10 a; **13.** Verlust m.

mis·sal ['mɪsl] s. eccl. Messbuch n.

mis·shap·en [‚mɪs'ʃeɪpən] adj. 'missgestaltet, ungestalt, unförmig.

mis·sile ['mɪsaɪl; *Am.* -səl] I s. **1.** (Wurf-) Geschoss, östr. Geschoß n, Projek'til n; **2.** a. *ballistic* ~, *guided* ~ ✕ Flugkörper m, Fernlenkwaffe f, Ra'kete(ngeschoss n) f; **II** adj. **3.** Wurf...; Raketen...: ~ *site* Raketenstellung f.

miss·ing ['mɪsɪŋ] adj. **1.** fehlend, weg, nicht ‚da, verschwunden: ~ *link* biol. fehlendes Glied, Zwischenstufe f (*zwischen Mensch u. Affe*); **2.** vermisst (✕ a. ~ *in action*), verschollen: *be* ~ vermisst sein od. werden; *the* ~ die Vermissten, die Verschollenen.

mis·sion ['mɪʃn] s. **1.** pol. Gesandtschaft f; Ge'sandtschaftsperso‚nal n; **2.** pol., ✕ Missi'on f im Ausland; **3.** (✕ Kampf)Auftrag m; ✈ Einsatz m, Feindflug m: *on* (a) *special* ~ mit besonderem Auftrag; ~ *accomplished!* Auftrag ausgeführt!; **4.** eccl. a) Missi'on f, Sendung f, b) Missio'narstätigkeit f: *foreign* (*home*) ~ äußere (innere) Mission, c) Missi'on(sgesellschaft) f, d) Missi'onsstati‚on f; **5.** Missi'on f, Sendung f, (innere) Berufung, Lebenszweck m: ~ *in life* Lebensaufgabe f; **mis·sion·a·ry** ['mɪʃnərɪ] I adj. missio'narisch, Missions...: ~ *work*; **II** s. Missio'nar(in); **mis·sion con·trol** s. Raumfahrt: Kon'troll‚zentrum n.

mis·sis ['mɪsɪz] s. **1.** sl. gnä' Frau (*Hausfrau*); **2.** F ‚Alte' f, ‚bessere Hälfte' (*Ehefrau*).

mis·sive ['mɪsɪv] s. Sendschreiben n.

‚mis'spell v/t. [a. irr. → *spell*] falsch buchstabieren od. schreiben; **‚mis'spell·ing** s. **1.** falsches Buchstabieren; **2.** Rechtschreibfehler m.

‚mis'spend v/t. [irr. → *spend*] falsch verwenden, a. s-e Jugend etc. vergeuden.

‚mis'state v/t. falsch angeben, unrichtig darstellen; **‚mis'state·ment** s. falsche Angabe od. Darstellung.

mis·sus ['mɪsəs] → *missis*.

miss·y ['mɪsɪ] s. F kleines Fräulein.

mist [mɪst] I s. **1.** (feiner) Nebel, feuchter Dunst, Am. a. Sprühregen m; **2.** fig. Nebel m, Schleier m: *be in a* ~ ganz irre od. verdutzt sein; Hauch m (*auf e-m Glas*); **II** v/i. **4.** a. ~ *over* nebeln, neblig sein (a. fig.); sich trüben (*Augen*); (sich) beschlagen (*Glas*); **III** v/t. **5.** um'nebeln.

mis·tak·a·ble [mɪ'steɪkəbl] adj. verkennbar, (leicht) zu verwechseln(d), 'missverstehen(d); **mis·take** [mɪ'steɪk] I v/t. [irr. → *take*] **1.** (*for*) verwechseln (mit), (fälschlich) halten (für), verfehlen, nicht erkennen, verkennen, sich irren in (dat.): ~ *s.o.'s character* sich in j-s Charakter irren; **2.** falsch verstehen, 'missverstehen; **II** v/i. [irr. → *take*] **3.** sich irren, sich versehen; **III** s. **4.** 'Missverständnis n; **5.** Irrtum m (a. ⚖), Fehler m, Versehen n, 'Missgriff m: *by* ~ irrtümlich, aus Versehen; *make a* ~ e-n Fehler machen, sich irren; *and no* ~ F bestimmt, worauf du dich verlassen kannst; **6.** (Schreib-, Sprach-, Rechen-) Fehler m; **mis'tak·en** [-kn] adj. □ **1.**

im Irrtum: *be* ~ sich irren; *unless I am very much* ~ wenn ich mich nicht sehr irre; *we were quite* ~ *in him* wir haben uns in ihm ziemlich getäuscht; **2.** irrtümlich, falsch, verfehlt (*Politik etc.*): (*case of*) ~ *identity* Personenverwechslung *f*; ~ *kindness* unangebrachte Freundlichkeit.

mis·ter ['mɪstə] *s.* **1.** ♃ Herr *m* (*abbr. Mr od. Mr.*): **Mr President** Herr Präsident; **2.** F *als bloße Anrede*: (mein) Herr!, ,Meister'!, ,Chef'!

,**mis'time** *v/t.* zur unpassenden Zeit sagen *od.* tun; e-n falschen Zeitpunkt wählen für, *bsd. sport* schlecht timen.

,**mis'timed** *adj.* unpassend, unangebracht, zur Unzeit, *bsd. sport* schlecht getimed.

mist·i·ness ['mɪstɪnɪs] *s.* **1.** Nebligkeit *f*, Dunstigkeit *f*; **2.** Unklarheit *f*, Verschwommenheit *f* (*a. fig.*).

mis·tle·toe ['mɪsltəʊ] *s.* ⚘ **1.** Mistel *f*; **2.** Mistelzweig *m*.

,**mis·trans'late** *v/t. u. v/i.* falsch übersetzen.

mis·tress ['mɪstrɪs] *s.* **1.** Herrin *f* (*a. fig.*), Gebieterin *f*, Besitzerin *f*: *she is* ~ *of herself* sie weiß sich zu beherrschen; **2.** Frau *f* des Hauses, Hausfrau *f*; **3.** *bsd. Brit.* Lehrerin *f*: *chemistry* ~ Chemielehrerin; **4.** Kennerin *f*, Meisterin *f in e-r Kunst etc.*; **5.** Mä'tresse *f*, Geliebte *f*; **6.** → *Mrs.*

,**mis'tri·al** *s.* ♃ fehlerhaft geführter (*Am. a.* ergebnisloser) Pro'zess.

,**mis'trust I** *s.* **1.** 'Misstrauen *n*, Argwohn *m* (*of* gegen); **II** *v/t.* **2.** j-m miss'trauen, nicht trauen; **3.** zweifeln an (*dat.*); **mis'trust·ful** *adj.* □ 'misstrauisch, argwöhnisch (*of* gegen).

mist·y ['mɪstɪ] *adj.* □ **1.** (leicht) neb(e)lig, dunstig; **2.** *fig.* nebelhaft, verschwommen, unklar.

,**mis·un·der'stand** *v/t. u. v/i.* (*irr.* → *understand*) 'missverstehen; ,**mis·un·der'stand·ing** *s.* **1.** 'Missverständnis *n*; **2.** 'Misshelligkeit *f*, Diffe'renz *f*; ,**mis·un·der'stood** *adj.* **1.** 'missverstanden; **2.** verkannt, nicht richtig gewürdigt.

,**mis'us·age** → *misuse* 1.

mis·use I *s.* [,mɪs'juːs] **1.** 'Missbrauch *m*, falscher Gebrauch, falsche Anwendung; **2.** Miss'handlung *f*; **II** *v/t.* [,mɪs'juːz] **3.** miss'brauchen, falsch *od.* zu unrechten Zwecken gebrauchen; falsch anwenden; **4.** miss'handeln.

mite¹ [maɪt] *s. zo.* Milbe *f*.

mite² [maɪt] *s.* **1.** Heller *m*; *weitS.* kleine Geldsumme: *contribute one's* ~ *to* sein Scherflein beitragen zu; *not a* ~ kein bisschen; **2.** F kleines Ding, Dingelchen *n*: *a* ~ *of a child* ein Würmchen.

mi·ter ['maɪtə] *Am.* → *mitre*.

mit·i·gate ['mɪtɪgeɪt] *v/t.* Schmerz etc. lindern; *Strafe etc.* mildern; *Zorn* besänftigen, mäßigen: *mitigating circumstances* ♃ (straf)mildernde Umstände; **mit·i·ga·tion** [,mɪtɪ'geɪʃn] *s.* **1.** Linderung *f*, Milderung *f*; **2.** Besänftigung *f*, Abschwächung *f*: *plead in* ~ ♃ a) für Strafmilderung plädieren, b) strafmildernde Umstände geltend machen; **3.** Besänftigung *f*, Mäßigung *f*.

mi·to·sis [maɪ'təʊsɪs] *pl.* **-ses** [-siːz] *s. biol.* Mi'tose *f*, 'indi,rekte *od.* chromoso'male (Zell)Kernteilung.

mi·tre ['maɪtə] *s.* **1.** a) Mitra *f*, Bischofsmütze *f*, b) *fig.* Bischofsamt *n*, -würde *f*; **2.** ⊙ a) → *mitre joint*, *mitre square*, b) Gehrungsfläche *f*; **II** *v/t.* **3.** mit der Mitra schmücken, zum Bischof machen; **4.** ⊙ a) auf Gehrung verbin-

den, b) gehren, auf Gehrung zurichten; **III** *v/i.* **5.** ⊙ sich in 'einem Winkel treffen; ~ **box** *s.* ⊙ Gehrlade *f*; ~ **gear** *s.* Kegelrad *n*, Winkelgetriebe *n*; ~ **joint** *s.* Gehrfuge *f*; ~ **square** *s.* Gehrdreieck *n*; ~ **valve** *s.* 'Kegelven,til *n*; ~ **wheel** *s.* Kegelrad *n*.

mitt [mɪt] *s.* **1.** Halbhandschuh *m*; **2.** *Baseball*: Fanghandschuh *m*; **3.** → *mitten* 1 *u.* 3; **4.** *Am. sl.* ,Flosse' *f* (*Hand*).

mit·ten ['mɪtn] *s.* **1.** Fausthandschuh *m*, Fäustling *m*: *get the* ~ F a) e-n Korb bekommen, abgewiesen werden, b) ,(hinaus)fliegen', entlassen werden; **2.** → *mitt* 1; **3.** *sl.* Boxhandschuh *m*.

mit·ti·mus ['mɪtɪməs] (*Lat.*) *s.* **1.** ♃ a) *richterlicher Befehl an die Gefängnisbehörde zur Aufnahme e-s Häftlings*, b) *Befehl zur Übersendung der Akten an ein anderes Gericht*; **2.** F ,blauer Brief', Entlassung *f*.

mix [mɪks] **I** *v/t.* **1.** (ver)mischen, vermengen (*with* mit); *Cocktail etc.* mixen, mischen; *Teig* anrühren, mischen: ~ *into* mischen in (*acc.*); ~ *up* zs.-, durcheinander mischen, *fig.* völlig durcheinander bringen, verwechseln (*with* mit); *be* ~*ed up fig.* a) verwickelt sein *od.* werden (*in, with* in *acc.*), b) (*geistig*) ganz durcheinander sein; **2.** *biol.* kreuzen; **3.** *Stoffe* melieren; **4.** *fig.* verbinden: ~ *business with pleasure* das Angenehme mit dem Nützlichen verbinden; **II** *v/i.* **5.** sich (ver)mischen; **6.** sich mischen lassen; **7.** *gut etc.* auskommen (*with* mit); **8.** verkehren (*with* mit, *in* in *dat.*): ~ *in the best society*; **III** *s.* **9.** (*Am. a.* koch- *od.* back-, gebrauchsfertige) Mischung: *cake* ~ Backmischung; **10.** F Durcheinander *n*, Mischmasch *m*; **11.** *sl.* Keile-'rei *f*.

mixed [mɪkst] *adj.* **1.** gemischt (*a. fig. Gefühl, Gesellschaft, Metapher*); **2.** vermischt, Misch...; **3.** F verwirrt, kon'fus; ~ **bag** *s.* F bunte Mischung; ~ **blood** *s.* **1.** gemischtes Blut; **2.** Mischling *m*; ~ **car·go** *s.* ♃ Stückgutladung *f*; ~ **con·struc·tion** *s.* Gemischtbauweise *f*; ~ **dou·bles** *s. pl. sg. konstr. sport* gemischtes Doppel: *play a* ~; ~ **e·con·o·my** *s.* ♃ gemischte Wirtschaftsform; ,~-e'**con·o·my** *adj.* ♃ gemischtwirtschaftlich; ~ **fi·nanc·ing** *s.* Mischfinanzierung *f*; ~ **for·est** *s.* Mischwald *m*; ~ **frac·tion** *s.* ♙ gemischter Bruch; ~ **mar·riage** *s.* Mischehe *f*; ~ **me·di·a** *s. pl.* **1.** Multimedia *pl.*; **2.** *Kunst*: Mischtechnik *f*; ~ **pick·les** *s. pl.* Mixed Pickles *pl.* (*Essiggemüse*).

mix·er ['mɪksə] *s.* **1.** Mischer *m*; **2.** Mixer *m* (*von Cocktails etc.*) (*a. Küchengerät*); **3.** ⊙ Mischer *m*, 'Mischma,schine *f*; **4.** ⚡ *Fernsehen etc.*: Mischpult *n*; **5.** *be a good* (*bad*) ~ F kontaktfreudig (kontaktarm) sein; **mix·ture** ['mɪkstʃə] *s.* **1.** Mischung *f* (*a. von Tee, Tabak etc.*), Gemisch *n* (*a.* ♗); **2.** *mot.* Gas-Luft-Gemisch *n*; **3.** *pharm.* Mix'tur *f*; **4.** *biol.* Kreuzung *f*; **5.** Beimengung *f*; '**mix-up** *s.* F **1.** Durchein'ander *n*; **2.** Verwechslung *f*; **3.** Handgemenge *n*.

miz·(z)en ['mɪzn] *s.* ⚓ **1.** Be'san(segel *n*) *m*; **2.** → '~-**mast**; '~-**mast** [-mɑːst, ⚓ -məst] *s.* Be'san-, Kreuzmast *m*; '~-**sail** → *miz(z)en* 1; ~ **top'gal·lant** *s.* Kreuzbramsegel *n*.

miz·zle ['mɪzl] *dial.* **I** *v/i.* nieseln; **II** *s.* Nieseln *n*, Sprühregen *m*.

mne·mon·ic [niː'mɒnɪk] **I** *adj.* **1.** mnemo'technisch; **2.** mne'monisch, Gedächtnis...; **II** *s.* **3.** Gedächtnishilfe *f*; → *mnemonics* 1; **mne'mon·ics** [-ks]

s. pl. **1.** *a. sg. konstr.* Mnemo'technik *f*, Gedächtniskunst *f*; **2.** mne'monische Zeichen *pl.*; **mne·mo·tech·nics** [,niːməʊ'tekniks] *s. pl. a. sg. konstr.* → *mnemonics* 1.

mo [məʊ] *s.* F Mo'ment *m*: *wait half a* ~! (eine) Sekunde!

moan [məʊn] **I** *s.* **1.** Stöhnen *n*, Ächzen *n* (*a. fig. des Windes etc.*); **II** *v/i.* **2.** stöhnen, ächzen; **3.** (weh)klagen, jammern; '**moan·ful** [-fʊl] *adj.* □ (weh-) klagend.

moat [məʊt] ✕ *hist.* **I** *s.* (Wall-, Burg-, Stadt)Graben *m*; **II** *v/t.* mit e-m Graben um'geben.

mob [mɒb] **I** *s.* **1.** Mob *m*, zs.-gerotteter Pöbel(haufen): ~ *law* Lynchjustiz *f*; ~ *psychology* Massenpsychologie *f*; **2.** Pöbel *m*, Gesindel *n*; **3.** *sl.* a) (Verbrecher)Bande *f*, b) *allg.* Bande *f*, Sippschaft *f*; **II** *v/t.* **4.** lärmend herfallen über (*acc.*); anpöbeln; angreifen, attackieren; *Geschäfte etc.* stürmen.

mo·bile ['məʊbaɪl] **I** *adj.* **1.** beweglich, wendig (*a. Geist etc.*); schnell (beweglich); **2.** unstet, veränderlich; lebhaft (*Gesichtszüge*); **3.** leichtflüssig; **4.** ⊙, ✕ fahrbar, beweglich, mo'bil, ✕ *a.* motorisiert: ~ *crane* Autokran *m*; ~ *home mot.* Wohnwagen *m*; ~ *phone* Mobiltelefon *n*, Handy *n*; ~ *warfare* Bewegungskrieg *m*; ~ *workshop* Werkstattwagen *m*; **5.** ♦ flüssig: ~ *funds*; **II** *s.* **6.** *Kunst*: Mobile *n*; *teleph.* F Handy *n*; **mo·bil·i·ty** [məʊ'bɪlətɪ] *s.* **1.** Beweglichkeit *f*, Wendigkeit *f*; **2.** Mobili'tät *f*, Freizügigkeit *f* (*der Arbeitnehmer etc.*).

mo·bi·li·za·tion [,məʊbɪlaɪ'zeɪʃn] *s.* Mobilisierung *f*: a) ✕ Mo'bilmachung *f*, b) *bsd. fig.* Aktivierung *f*, Aufgebot *n* (*der Kräfte etc.*), c) ♦ Flüssigmachung *f*; **mo·bi·lize** ['məʊbɪlaɪz] *v/t.* mobilisieren: a) ✕ mo'bil machen, *a.* dienstverpflichten, b) *fig. Kräfte etc.* aufbieten, einsetzen, c) ♦ *Kapital* flüssig machen.

mob·oc·ra·cy [mɒ'bɒkrəsɪ] *s.* **1.** Pöbelherrschaft *f*; **2.** (herrschender) Pöbel.

mobs·man ['mɒbzmən] *s.* [*irr.*] **1.** Gangster *m*; **2.** *Brit. sl.* (ele'ganter) Taschendieb.

mob·ster ['mɒbstə] *Am. sl. für mobsman* 1.

moc·ca·sin ['mɒkəsɪn] *s.* **1.** Mokas'sin *m* (*a. Damenschuh*); **2.** *zo.* Mokas'sinschlange *f*.

mo·cha¹ ['mɒkə] **I** *s.* **1.** a) ~ *coffee* 'Mokka(kaf,fee) *m*; **2.** Mochaleder *n*; **II** *adj.* **3.** Mokka...

mo·cha² ['məʊkə], ♃ *stone s. min.* Mochastein *m*.

mock [mɒk] **I** *v/t.* **1.** verspotten, -höhnen, lächerlich machen; **2.** (*zum Spott*) nachäffen; **3.** *poet.* nachahmen; **4.** täuschen, narren; **5.** spotten (*gen.*), trotzen (*dat.*), nicht achten (*acc.*); **II** *v/i.* **6.** sich lustig machen, spotten (*at* über *acc.*); **III** *s.* **7.** → *mockery* 1-3; **8.** Nachahmung *f*, Fälschung *f*; **IV** *adj.* **9.** nachgemacht, Schein..., Pseudo...: ~ *attack* ✕ Scheinangriff *m*; ~ *battle* ✕ Scheingefecht *n*; ~ *king* Schattenkönig *m*; **mock·er** ['mɒkə] *s.* **1.** Spötter(in); **2.** Nachäffer(in); **mock·er·y** ['mɒkərɪ] *s.* **1.** Spott *m*, Hohn *m*, Spötte'rei *f*; **2.** Gegenstand *m* des Spottes, Gespött *n*: *make a* ~ *of* zum Gespött (der Leute) machen; **3.** Nachäffung *f*; **4.** *fig.* Possenspiel *n*, Farce *f*.

,**mock-he'ro·ic** *adj.* (□ ~**ally**) 'komischhe'roisch (*Gedicht etc.*).

mock·ing ['mɒkɪŋ] **I** *s.* Spott *m*, Gespött *n*; **II** *adj.* □ spöttisch; '~-**bird** *s. orn.*

Spottdrossel *f.*
mock| moon *s. ast.* Nebenmond *m;* ~
tri·al *s.* 🜚 'Scheinpro,zess *m;* ~ **tur·tle**
s. Küche: Kalbskopf *m* en tor'tue; ~
tur·tle soup *s.* falsche Schildkrötensuppe; **'~-up** *s.* Mo'dell *n* (in na'türlicher Größe), At'trappe *f.*
mod·al ['mɔʊdl] *adj.* □ **1.** mo'dal *(a.
phls., ling.,* ♪): ~ *proposition Logik:*
Modalsatz *m;* ~ *verb* modales Hilfsverb; **2.** *Statistik:* typisch; **mo·dal·i·ty**
[mɔʊ'dælətɪ] *s.* Modali'tät *f (a.* 🕇, *pol.,
phls.),* Art *f* u. Weise *f,* Ausführungsart
f.
mod cons [ˌmɒd'kɒnz] *pl.* F *abbr.
für modern conveniences* moderner
Kom'fort.
mode[1] [mɔʊd] *s.* **1.** (Art *f* u.) Weise *f,*
Me'thode *f;* ~ *of action* 🚗 Wirkungs-
weise; ~ *of life* Lebensweise; ~ *of operation* Verfahrensweise; ~ *of payment*
🕇 Zahlungsweise; **2.** (Erscheinungs-)
Form *f,* Art *f: heat is a ~ of motion*
Wärme ist e-e Form der Bewegung; **3.**
Logik: a) Modali'tät *f,* b) Modus *m (e-r
Schlussfigur);* **4.** ♪ Modus *m,* Tonart *f,*
-geschlecht *n;* **5.** *ling.* Modus *m,* Aussageweise *f;* **6.** *Statistik:* Modus *m,* häu-
figster Wert. **7.** *Computer:* Modus *m,*
Funkti'onsweise *f.*
mode[2] [mɔʊd] *s.* Mode *f,* Brauch *m.*
mod·el ['mɒdl] **I** *s.* **1.** Muster *n,* Vorbild
n (for für): *after (od. on) the ~ of* nach
dem Muster von *(od. gen.); he is a ~ of
self-control* er ist ein Muster an Selbstbeherrschung; **2.** *(fig.* 'Denk)Mo,dell *n,*
Nachbildung *f: working ~* Arbeitsmo-
dell; **3.** Muster *n,* Vorlage *f;* **4.** *paint.
etc.* Mo'dell *n: act as a ~ to a painter*
e-m Maler Modell stehen *od.* sitzen; **5.**
Mode: a) Mannequin *n,* Vorführdame
f: male ~ Dressman *m,* b) Mo'dellkleid
n; **6.** 🚗 a) Bau(weise *f) m,* b) (Bau)Mus-
ter *n,* Mo'dell *n,* Typ(e *f) m;* **II** *adj.* **7.**
vorbildlich, musterhaft, Muster...: ~
farm landwirtschaftlicher Musterbetrieb; ~ *husband* Mustergatte *m;* ~
plant 🕇 Musterbetrieb *m;* ~ *school*
Musterschule *f;* **8.** Modell...: ~ *airplane;* ~ *builder* 🚗 Modellbauer *m;* ~
dress → 5 b; **III** *v/t.* **9.** nach Mo'dell
formen *od.* herstellen; **10.** modellieren, nachbilden; abformen; **11.** *fig.* formen, gestalten *(after, on, upon* nach
[dem Vorbild *gen.]):* ~ *o.s.* on sich *j*-n
zum Vorbild nehmen; **IV** *v/i.* **12.**
Kunst: modellieren; **13.** Mo'dell stehen
od. sitzen; **14.** Kleider vorführen, als
Mannequin *od.* Dressman arbeiten;
'mod·el·(l)er [-lə] *s.* **1.** Modellierer *m;*
2. Mo'dell-, Musterbauer *m;* **'mod·el-
(l)ing** [-lɪŋ] **I** *s.* **1.** Modellieren *n;* **2.**
Formgebung *f,* Formung *f;* **3.** Mo'dell-
stehen *od.* -sitzen *n;* **II** *adj.* **4.** Model-
lier...: ~ *clay.*
mo·dem ['mɔʊdem] *s. Computer, teleph.*
Modem *m, n (Datenübertragungsgerät).*
mod·er·ate ['mɒdərət] **I** *adj.* □ **1.** gemäßigt *(a. Sprache etc.; a. pol.),* mäßig;
2. mäßig *(im Trinken etc.;* fru'gal *(in
Lebensweise);* **3.** mild *(Winter, Strafe
etc.);* **4.** vernünftig, maßvoll *(Forderung etc.);* angemessen, niedrig *(Preis);*
5. mittelmäßig; **II** *s.* **6.** *(pol. mst* ⚹)
Gemäßigte(r *m) f;* **III** *v/t.* [-dəreɪt] **7.**
mäßigen, mildern; beruhigen; **8.** einschränken; **9.** 🚗, *phys.* dämpfen, abbremsen; **IV** *v/i.* [-dəreɪt] **10.** sich mäßigen; **11.** nachlassen *(Wind etc.);*
'mod·er·ate·ness [-nɪs] *s.* Mäßigkeit *f
etc.;* **mod·er·a·tion** [ˌmɒdə'reɪʃn] *s.* **1.**
Mäßigung *f,* Maß(halten) *n: in ~* mit
Maß; **2.** Mäßigkeit *f;* **3.** *pl. univ.* erste

öffentliche Prüfung *in Oxford;* **4.** Milderung *f;* **'mod·er·a·tor** [-dəreɪtə] *s.* **1.**
Mäßiger *m,* Beruhiger· *m;* Vermittler
m; **2.** Vorsitzende(r) *m;* Diskussi'onsleiter *m; univ.* Exami'nator *m (Oxford);* **3.** a) Mode'rator *m (Vorsitzender
e-s Kollegiums reformierter Kirchen),*
b) *TV:* Mode'rator *m,* Modera'torin *f,*
Pro'grammleiter(in); **4.** 🚗, *phys.* Mode'rator *m.*
mod·ern ['mɒdən] **I** *adj.* **1.** mo'dern,
neuzeitlich: ~ *times* die Neuzeit; *the ~
school (od. side) ped. Brit.* die Real-
abteilung; **2.** mo'dern, (neu)modisch;
3. *mst* ⚹ *ling.* a) mo'dern, Neu..., b)
neuer: ⚹ *Greek* Neugriechisch *n;* ~
languages neuere Sprachen; ⚹
Languages (als Fach) Neuphilologie *f;*
II *s.* **4.** mo'derner Mensch, Fortschritt-
liche(r *m) f;* **5.** Mensch *m* der Neuzeit;
6. *typ.* neuzeitliche An'tiqua;
'mod·ern·ism [-dənɪzəm] *s.* **1.** Moder-
'nismus *m:* a) mo'derne Einstellung, b)
mo'dernes Wort, mo'derne Redewen-
dung(en *pl.);* **2.** *eccl.* Moder'nismus *m;*
mo·der·ni·ty [mɒ'dɜːnətɪ] *s.* **1.** Moderni-
'tät *f, (das)* Mo'derne; **2.** *et.* Mo'dernes; **mod·ern·i·za·tion** [ˌmɒdənaɪ-
'zeɪʃn] *s.* Modernisierung *f;* **'mod·ern-
ize** [-dənaɪz] *v/t. u. v/i.* (sich) modernisieren.
mod·est ['mɒdɪst] *adj.* □ **1.** bescheiden,
anspruchslos *(Person od. Sache):* ~ *income* bescheidenes Einkommen; **2.**
anständig, sittsam; **3.** maßvoll, vernünftig; **'mod·es·ty** [-tɪ] *s.* **1.** Bescheidenheit *f (Person, Einkommen etc.): in
all ~* bei aller Bescheidenheit; **2.** Anspruchslosigkeit *f,* Einfachheit *f;* **3.**
Schamgefühl *n;* Sittsamkeit *f.*
mod·i·cum ['mɒdɪkəm] *s.* kleine Menge,
ein bisschen: a ~ of truth ein Körnchen
Wahrheit.
mod·i·fi·a·ble ['mɒdɪfaɪəbl] *adj.* modifizierbar, (ab)änderungsfähig; **mod·i·fi-
ca·tion** [ˌmɒdɪfɪ'keɪʃn] *s.* **1.** Modifikati'on *f:* a) Abänderung *f: make a ~ to
→ modify* 1 a, b) Abart *f,* modifizierte
Form, c) Einschränkung *f,* nähere Bestimmung, d) *biol.* nichterbliche Abänderung, e) *ling.* nähere Bestimmung, f)
ling. lautliche Veränderung, 'Umlau-
tung *f;* **2.** Mäßigung *f;* **mod·i·fy**
['mɒdɪfaɪ] *v/t.* **1.** modifizieren: a) abändern, teilweise 'umwandeln, b) einschränken, näher bestimmen; **2.** mildern, mäßigen; abschwächen; **3.** *ling.*
Vokal 'umlauten.
mod·ish ['mɔʊdɪʃ] *adj.* □ **1.** modisch,
mo'dern; **2.** Mode...
mods [mɒdz] *s. pl. Brit.* Halbstarke *pl.*
von betont dandyhaftem Äußeren *(in
den 60er Jahren) (Ggs. rockers).*
mod·u·lar ['mɒdjʊlə] *adj.* 🗝, 🚗 Modul...: ~ *design* Modulbauweise *f.*
mod·u·late ['mɒdjʊleɪt] **I** *v/t.* **1.** abstimmen, regulieren; **2.** anpassen *(to* an
acc.); **3.** dämpfen; **4.** *Stimme, Ton etc.,
a. Funk* modulieren: *~d reception* ⚡
Tonempfang *m;* **II** *v/i.* **5.** ♪ modulieren
(from von, *to* nach), die Tonart wechseln; **6.** all'mählich 'übergehen *(into* in
acc.); **mod·u·la·tion** [ˌmɒdjʊ'leɪʃn] *s.*
1. Abstimmung *f,* Regulierung *f;* **2.**
Anpassung *f;* **3.** Dämpfung *f;* **4.** ♪,
Funk, a. Stimme: Modulati'on *f;* **5.** Intonati'on *f,* Tonfall *m;* **'mod·u·la·tor**
[-tə] *s.* **1.** Regler *m;* ⚡ Modu'lator *m:* ~
of tonality Film: Tonblende *f;* **2.** ♪ die
Tonverwandtschaft *(nach der Tonic-
Solfa-Methode)* darstellende Skala;
'mod·ule [-dju:l] *s.* **1.** Modul *m,* Model
m, Maßeinheit *f,* Einheits-, Verhältnis-

zahl *f;* **2.** 🚗 Mo'dul *n (austauschbare
Funktionseinheit),* ⚹ *a.* Baustein *m;* **3.**
🚗 Baueinheit *f;* ~ *construction* Bau-
kastensystem *n;* **4.** *Raumfahrt: (Kom-
mando- etc.)*Kapsel *f;* **'mod·u·lus** [-ləs]
pl. **-li** [-laɪ] *s.* 🗝, *phys.* Modul *m:* ~ *of
elasticity* Elastizitätsmodul.
Mo·gul ['mɔʊgl] *s.* **1.** Mogul *m: the ~
(Great od. Grand) ~* der Großmogul;
2. ⚹ *Am. humor.* ,großes Tier', ,Bonze'
m, Ma'gnat *m.*
mo·gul ['mɔʊgl] *s. Skisport:* Buckel *m
(aus hartem Schnee).*
mo·hair ['mɔʊheə] *s.* **1.** Mo'här *m (An-
gorahaar);* **2.** Mo'hairstoff *m,* -klei-
dungsstück *n.*
Mo·ham·med·an [mɔʊ'hæmɪdən] **I** *adj.*
mohamme'danisch; **II** *s.* Mohamme-
'daner(in).
moi·e·ty ['mɔɪətɪ] *s.* **1.** Hälfte *f;* **2.** Teil
m.
moire [mwɑː] *s.* **1.** Moi'ré *m, n,* Wasser-
glanz *m auf Stoffen;* **2.** moirierter Stoff;
moi·ré ['mwɑːreɪ] **I** *adj.* moiriert, ge-
wässert, geflammt, mit Wellenmuster;
II *s.* → *moire* 1.
moist [mɔɪst] *adj.* □ feucht, nass; **'moisten** [-sn] **I** *v/t.* an-, befeuchten, benetzen; **II** *v/i.* feucht werden; nässen;
'moist·ness [-nɪs] *s.* Feuchte *f;*
'mois·ture [-tʃə] *s.* Feuchtigkeit *f; ~-
proof* feuchtigkeitsfest; **'mois·tur·ize**
[-tʃəraɪz] *v/t.* **1.** Haut mit e-r Feuchtigkeitscreme behandeln; **2.** *Luft* befeuchten; **'mois·tur·iz·er** [-tʃəraɪzə] *s.* **1.**
Feuchtigkeitscreme *f;* **2.** Luftbefeuch-
ter *m.*
moke [mɔʊk] *s. Brit. sl.* Esel *m (a. fig.).*
mo·lar[1] ['mɔʊlə] *anat.* **I** *s.* Backenzahn
m, Mo'lar *m;* **II** *adj.* Mahl..., Backen...: ~ *tooth* → I.
mo·lar[2] ['mɔʊlə] *adj.* **1.** *phys.* Massen...:
~ *motion* Massenbewegung *f;* **2.** 🜨
mo'lar, Mol...: ~ *weight* Mol-, Molar-
gewicht *n.*
mo·lar[3] ['mɔʊlə] *adj.* 🜨 Molen...
mo·las·ses [mɔʊ'læsɪz] *s. sg. u. pl.* **1.**
Me'lasse *f;* **2.** (Zucker)Sirup *m.*
mold [mɔʊld] *etc. Am.* → *mould etc.*
mole[1] [mɔʊl] *s. zo.* Maulwurf *m (a.* F
fig. eingeschleuster Agent).
mole[2] [mɔʊl] *s.* (kleines) Muttermal,
bsd. Leberfleck *m.*
mole[3] [mɔʊl] *s.* Mole *f,* Hafendamm *m.*
mole[4] [mɔʊl] *s.* 🜨 Mol *n,* 'Grammmole-
,kül *n.*
mole[5] [mɔʊl] *s.* 🜨 Mole *f,* Mondkalb *n.*
mole crick·et *s. zo.* Maulwurfsgrille *f.*
mo·lec·u·lar [mɔʊ'lekjʊlə] *adj.* 🜨,
phys. moleku'lar, Molekular...: ~ *biology;* ~ *weight;* **mo·lec·u·lar·i·ty**
[mɔʊˌlekjʊ'lærətɪ] *s.* 🜨, *phys.* Moleku-
'larzustand *m;* **mol·e·cule** ['mɒlɪkjuːl]
s. **1.** 🜨, *phys.* Mole'kül *n;* **2.** *fig.* winziges Teilchen.
'mole·hill *s.* Maulwurfshügel *m,* -hau-
fen *m;* → *mountain* I; **'~-skin** *s.* **1.**
Maulwurfsfell *n;* **2.** 🕇 Moleskin *m, n,*
Englischleder *n (Baumwollgewebe);* **3.**
pl. Hose *f* aus Moleskin.
mo·lest [mɔʊ'lest] *v/t.* belästigen; **mo-
les·ta·tion** [ˌmɔʊle'steɪʃn] *s.* Belästigung *f.*
Moll, *a.* ⚹ [mɒl] *s. sl.* **1.** ,Nutte' *f (Prostituierte);* **2.** Gangsterbraut *f.*
mol·li·fi·ca·tion [ˌmɒlɪfɪ'keɪʃn] *s.* **1.** Besänftigung *f,* **2.** Erweichung *f;* **mol·li·fy**
['mɒlɪfaɪ] *v/t.* **1.** besänftigen, beruhigen,
beschwichtigen; **2.** weich machen, erweichen.
mol·lusc ['mɒləsk] → *mollusk.*
mol·lus·can [mɒ'lʌskən] **I** *adj.* Weichtier...; **II** *s.* → **mol·lusk** ['mɒləsk] *s. zo.*

Mol'luske f, Weichtier n.

mol·ly·cod·dle ['mɒlɪˌkɒdl] **I** s. Weichling m, Muttersöhnchen n; **II** v/t. verhätscheln.

molt [məʊlt] Am. → **moult**.

mol·ten ['məʊltən] adj. **1.** geschmolzen, (schmelz)flüssig: ~ **metal** flüssiges Metall; **2.** gegossen, Guss...

mo·lyb·date [mɒ'lɪbdeɪt] s. 🜛 Molyb'dat n, molyb'dänsaures Salz; **mo'lyb·de·nite** [-dɪnaɪt] s. min. Molybdä'nit m.

mom [mɒm] s. F bsd. Am. **1.** Mami f; **2.** ‚Oma' f (alte Frau); **~-and-'pop store** s. Am. F Tante-Emma-Laden m.

mo·ment ['məʊmənt] s. **1.** Mo'ment m, Augenblick m: **one** (od. **just a**) ~! (nur) e-n Augenblick!; **in a** ~ in e-n Augenblick, sofort; **2.** Zeitpunkt m, Augenblick m: ~ **of truth** Stunde f der Wahrheit; **the very** ~ **I saw him** in dem Augenblick, in dem ich ihn sah; **at the** ~ im Augenblick, gerade (jetzt od. damals); **at the last** ~ im letzten Augenblick; **never a dull** ~ a) da od. hier ist was los, da od. hier ist es nie langweilig, b) man kommt (einfach) nicht zur Ruhe; **not for the** ~ im Augenblick nicht; **to the** ~ auf die Sekunde genau, pünktlich; **3.** Bedeutung f, Tragweite f, Belang m (**to** für); **4.** phys. Mo'ment n: ~ **of inertia** Trägheitsmoment; **mo·men·tal** [məʊ'mentl] adj. phys. Momenten...; **'mo·men·tar·y** [-tərɪ] adj. □ **1.** momen'tan, augenblicklich; **2.** vor'übergehend, flüchtig; **3.** jeden Augenblick geschehend od. möglich; **'mo·ment·ly** [-lɪ] adv. **1.** augenblicklich, in e-m Augenblick; **2.** von Se'kunde zu Se'kunde: **increasing** ~; **3.** e-n Augenblick lang; **mo·men·tous** [məʊ'mentəs] adj. □ bedeutsam, folgenschwer, von großer Tragweite; **mo·men·tous·ness** [məʊ'mentəsnɪs] s. Bedeutsam-, Wichtigkeit f, Tragweite f.

mo·men·tum [məʊ'mentəm] pl. **-ta** [-tə] s. **1.** phys. Im'puls m, Mo'ment n e-r Kraft: ~ **theorem** Momentensatz m; **2.** ⚙ Triebkraft f; **3.** allg. Wucht f, Schwung m, Fahrt f: **gather** (od. **gain**) ~ in Fahrt kommen, Stoßkraft gewinnen; **lose** ~ (an) Schwung verlieren.

mon·ad ['mɒnæd] s. **1.** phls. Mo'nade f; **2.** biol. Einzeller m; **3.** 🜛 einwertiges Ele'ment od. A'tom m; **mo·nad·ic** [mɒ'nædɪk] adj. **1.** mo'nadisch, Monaden...; **2.** ♐ eingliedrig, -stellig.

mon·arch ['mɒnək] s. Mon'arch(in), Herrscher(in); **mo·nar·chal** [mɒ'nɑːkl] adj. □ mon'archisch; **mo·nar·chic** adj., **mo·nar·chi·cal** [mɒ'nɑːkɪk(l)] adj. □ **1.** mon'archisch; **2.** mon'archistisch; **3.** königlich (a. fig.); **'mon·arch·ism** [-kɪzəm] s. Monar'chismus m; **'mon·arch·ist** [-kɪst] **I** s. Monar'chist(in); **II** adj. monar'chistisch; **'mon·arch·y** [-kɪ] s. Monar'chie f.

mon·as·ter·y ['mɒnəstərɪ] s. (Mönchs-) Kloster n; **mo·nas·tic** [mə'næstɪk] adj. (□ **~ally**) **1.** klösterlich, Kloster...; **2.** mönchisch (a. fig.), Mönchs...: ~ **vows** Mönchsgelübde n; **mo·nas·ti·cism** [mə'næstɪsɪzəm] s. **1.** Mönch(s)tum n; **2.** mönchisches Leben, As'kese f.

mon·a·tom·ic [ˌmɒnə'tɒmɪk] adj. 🜛 'eina,tomig.

Mon·day ['mʌndɪ] s. Montag m: **on** ~ am Montag; **on** ~s montags.

mon·e·tar·y ['mʌnɪtərɪ] adj. ♦ **1.** Geld..., geldlich, finanzi'ell: ~ **expansion** Ausweitung der Geldmenge; ~ **policy** Geldmengenpolitik f; ~ **restraint** restriktive Geldpolitik; ~ **tar-**

-geting Geldmengenpolitik f; **2.** Währungs...(-einheit, -reform etc.): ~ **area** Währungsgebiet n; ~ **policy** Währungs-, Geldpolitik f; ~ **stability** Geldwertstabilität; ~ **union** Währungsunion f; **3.** Münz...: ~ **standard** Münzfuß m; **'mon·e·tize** [-taɪz] v/t. **1.** zu Münzen prägen; **2.** zum gesetzlichen Zahlungsmittel machen; **3.** den Münzfuß (gen.) festsetzen.

mon·ey ['mʌnɪ] s. † **1.** Geld n; Geldbetrag m, -summe f: ~ **on** (od. **at**) **call** Tagesgeld m; **be out of** ~ kein Geld haben; **short of** ~ knapp an Geld, ‚schlecht bei Kasse'; ~ **due** ausstehendes Geld; ~ **on account** Guthaben n; ~ **on hand** verfügbares Geld; **get one's** ~'s **worth** et. (Vollwertiges) für sein Geld bekommen; **2.** Geld n, Vermögen n: **make** ~ Geld machen, gut verdienen (**by** bei); **marry** ~ sich reich verheiraten; **have** ~ **to burn** Geld wie Heu haben; **3.** Geldsorte f; **4.** Zahlungsmittel n; **5. monies** pl. 🜛 Gelder pl., (Geld-)Beträge pl.; **'~·bag** s. Geldbeutel m; ✗ Brustbeutel m; **2.** pl. F a) Geldsäcke pl., Reichtum m, b) sg. konstr. ‚Geldsack' m (reiche Person); ~ **bill** s. parl. Fi'nanzvorlage f; ~ **box** s. Sparbüchse f; ~ **bro·ker** s. Fi'nanzmakler m; **'~·chang·er** s. **1.** Geldwechsler m; **2.** 'Wechselauto,mat m.

mon·eyed ['mʌnɪd] adj. **1.** reich, vermögend; **2.** Geld...: ~ **corporation** ♣ Am. Geldinstitut n; ~ **interest** Finanzwelt f.

'mon·ey|**grub·ber** [-,grʌbə] s. Geldraffer m; **'~·grub·bing** [-,grʌbɪŋ] adj. Geld raffend, geldgierig; ~ **laun·der·ing** s. Geldwäsche f; ~ **laun·dry** s. Geldwaschanstalt f; **'~·lend·er** s. † Geldverleiher m; ~ **let·ter** s. Geld-, Wertbrief m; **'~·mak·er** s. **1.** guter Geschäftsmann; **2.** Bombengeschäft n, ‚Renner', ‚Goldgrube' f; **'~·mak·ing I** adj. Gewinn bringend, einträglich; **II** s. Geldverdienen n; ~ **mar·ket** s. † Geldmarkt m; ~ **mat·ters** s. pl. Geldangelegenheiten pl.; ~ **or·der** s. **1.** Postanweisung f; **2.** Zahlungsanweisung f; **'~·spin·ner** s. → **moneymaker** 2; ~ **sup·ply** s. Geldmenge f.

mon·ger ['mʌŋgə] s. (mst in Zssgn) Händler m, Krämer m: **fish~** Fischhändler; **2.** fig. contp. Verbreiter(in) von Gerüchten etc.; → **scaremonger, warmonger** etc.

Mon·gol ['mɒŋgɒl] **I** s. **1.** Mon'gole m, Mon'golin f; **2.** ling. Mon'golisch n; **II** adj. **3.** → **Mongolian** I; **Mon·go·li·an** [mɒŋ'gəʊljən] **I** adj. **1.** mon'golisch; **2.** mongo'lide, gelb (Rasse); **3.** → **Mongoloid** I; **II** s. **4.** → **Mongol** 1; **5.** → **Mongoloid** II; **'Mon·gol·oid** [-lɔɪd] bsd. ♂* **I** adj. mongolo'id; **II** s. Mongolo'ide(r m) f.

mon·goose ['mɒŋguːs] s. zo. Mungo m.

mon·grel ['mʌŋgrəl] **I** s. **1.** biol. Bastard m; **2.** Köter m, Prome'nadenmischung f; **3.** Mischling m (Mensch); **4.** Zwischending n; **II** adj. **5.** Bastard..., Misch...: ~ **race** Mischrasse f.

'mongst [mʌŋst] abbr. für **among(st)**.

mon·ick·er ['mɒnɪkə] s. sl. (Spitz)Name m.

mon·ies ['mʌnɪz] s. pl. → **money** 5.

mon·i·ker ['mɒnɪkə] s. sl. (Spitz)Name m.

mon·ism ['mɒnɪzəm] s. phls. Mo'nismus m.

mo·ni·tion [məʊ'nɪʃn] s. **1.** (Er)Mahnung f; **2.** Warnung f.

mon·i·tor ['mɒnɪtə] s. **1.** (Er)Mahner m; **2.** Warner m; **3.** ped. Klassenordner m; **4.** ♺ Art Panzerschiff n; **5.** ♫, tel. a)

Abhörer(in), b) Abhorchgerät n; **6.** ♫ etc. Monitor m, Kon'trollgerät n, -schirm m; **II** v/t. **7.** tel. ab-, mithören, über'wachen (a. fig.); **8.** ♫ Akustik etc. durch Abhören kontrollieren; **9.** auf Radioaktivi'tät über'prüfen; **'mon·i·tor·ing** [-tərɪŋ] **I** s. Über'wachen n, Über'wachung f; **II** adj. ♫, tel. Mithör..., Prüf..., Überwachungs...: ~ **desk** Misch-, Reglerpult n; **'mon·i·to·ry** [-tərɪ] adj. **1.** (er)mahnend, Mahn...; **2.** warnend, Warnungs...

monk [mʌŋk] s. **1.** eccl. Mönch m; **2.** zo. Mönchsaffe m; **3.** typ. Schmierstelle f.

mon·key ['mʌŋkɪ] **I** s. **1.** zo. a) Affe m (a. fig. humor.), b) engS. kleinerer (langschwänziger) Affe (Ggs. **ape**); **2.** ⚙ a) Ramme f, b) Fallhammer m; **3.** Brit. sl. Wut f: **get** (od. **put**) **s.o.'s** ~ **up** j-n auf die Palme bringen; **get one's** ~ **up** ‚hochgehen', in Wut geraten; **4.** sl. 500 Dollar od. brit. Pfund; **II** v/i. **5.** Possen treiben; **6.** F (**with**) spielen (mit), her'umfuschen (an dat.): ~ (**about**) (herum)albern; **III** v/t. **7.** nachäffen; **bread** s. ♀ Affenbrotbaumfrucht f; ~ **busi·ness** s. sl. **1.** ‚krumme Tour', ‚fauler Zauber'; **2.** ‚Blödsinn' m, Unfug m; ~ **en·gine** s. ⚙ (Pfahl)Ramme f; ~ **jack·et** s. ✗ Affenjäckchen n; **'~·shine** s. Am. sl. (dummer od. übermütiger) Streich, ‚Blödsinn' m; ~ **wrench** s. ⚙ ,Engländer' m, Univer'sal(schrauben)schlüssel m: **throw a** ~ **into s.th.** Am. F et. behindern od. beeinträchtigen.

monk·fish ['mʌŋkfɪʃ] s. Seeteufel m.

monk·ish ['mʌŋkɪʃ] adj. **1.** Mönchs...; **2.** mst contp. mönchisch, Pfaffen...

mon·o ['mɒnəʊ] F **I** s. Radio etc: Mono n; **II** adj. mono (abspielbar), Mono...

mono- [mɒnəʊ] in Zssgn ein..., einfach...; **mon·o·ac·id** [ˌmɒnəʊ'æsɪd] 🜛 **I** adj. einsäurig; **II** s. einbasige Säure; **mon·o·car·pous** [ˌmɒnəʊ'kɑːpəs] adj. ♀ **1.** einfrüchtig (Blüte); **2.** nur einmal fruchtend.

mon·o·chro·mat·ic [ˌmɒnəʊkrəʊ'mætɪk] adj. (□ **~ally**) monochro'matisch, einfarbig; **mon·o·chrome** ['mɒnəkrəʊm] **I** s. **1.** einfarbiges Gemälde; **2.** Schwarz'weißaufnahme f; **II** adj. **3.** mono'chrom.

mon·o·cle ['mɒnəkl] s. Mon'okel n.

mo·no·coque ['mɒnəkɒk] (Fr.) ✈ **1.** Schalenrumpf m; **2.** Flugzeug n mit Schalenrumpf: ~ **construction** ⚙ Schalenbau(weise f) m.

mo·noc·u·lar [mɒ'nɒkjʊlə] adj. mo'noku,lar, für 'ein Auge.

mon·o·cul·ture ['mɒnəʊˌkʌltʃə] s. ✔ 'Monokul,tur f; **mo·nog·a·mous** [mɒ'nɒgəməs] adj. mono'gam(isch); **mo·nog·a·my** [mɒ'nɒgəmɪ] s. Monoga'mie f, Einehe f; **mon·o·gram** ['mɒnəgræm] s. Mono'gramm n; **mon·o·graph** ['mɒnəgrɑːf] s. Monogra'phie f; **mon·o·hy·dric** [ˌmɒnəʊ'haɪdrɪk] adj. 🜛 einwertig: ~ **alcohol**; **mon·o·lith** ['mɒnəʊlɪθ] s. Mono'lith m; **mon·o·lith·ic** [ˌmɒnəʊ'lɪθɪk] adj. mono'lithisch; fig. gi'gantisch; **mo·nol·o·gize** [mɒ'nɒlədʒaɪz] v/i. monologisieren, ein Selbstgespräch führen; **mon·o·logue** ['mɒnəlɒg] s. Mono'log m, Selbstgespräch n; **mon·o·ma·ni·a** [ˌmɒnəʊ'meɪnjə] s. Monoma'nie f, fixe I'dee.

mo·no·mi·al [mɒ'nəʊmjəl] s. ♐ eingliedrige Zahlengröße.

mon·o·phase ['mɒnəʊfeɪz] adj. ♫ einphasig; **mon·o·pho·bi·a** [ˌmɒnəʊ'fəʊbjə] s. Monopho'bie f (Angst allein zu sein); **mon·o·phtong** ['mɒnəfθɒŋ] Mono'phthong m, einfacher Selbstlaut; **mon·o·plane** ['mɒnəʊpleɪn] s. ✈ Eindecker m.

mo·nop·o·list [mə'nɒpəlɪst] s. ✝ Monopo'list m; Mono'polbesitzer(in); **mo·'nop·o·lize** [-laɪz] v/t. monopolisieren: a) ✝ ein Mono'pol erringen od. haben für, b) fig. an sich reißen: ~ **the conversation** die Unterhaltung ganz allein bestreiten, c) fig. j-n od. et. mit Beschlag belegen; **mo·'nop·o·ly** [-lɪ] s. ✝ **1.** Mono'pol(stellung f) n; **2.** (**of**) Mono'pol n (auf acc.); Al'leinverkaufs-, Al'leinbetriebs-, Al'leinherstellungsrecht n (für): **market** ~ Marktbeherrschung f; **3.** fig. Mono'pol n, al'leiniger Besitz, al'leinige Beherrschung: ~ **of learning** Bildungsmonopol.

mon·o·rail ['mɒnəʊreɪl] s. ☶ Einschienenbahn f.

mon·o·syl·lab·ic [ˌmɒnəʊsɪ'læbɪk] adj. (□ **~ally**) ling. u. fig. einsilbig; **mon·o·syl·la·ble** ['mɒnəˌsɪləbl] s. einsilbiges Wort: **speak in ~s** einsilbige Antworten geben.

mon·o·the·ism ['mɒnəʊθiː‚ɪzəm] s. eccl. Monothe'ismus m; **'mon·o·the‚ist** [-‚ɪst] I s. Monothe'ist m; II adj. → **mon·o·the·is·tic, mon·o·the·is·ti·cal** [ˌmɒnəʊθiː'ɪstɪk(l)] adj. monothe'istisch.

mon·o·tone ['mɒnətəʊn] s. **1.** mono'tones Geräusch, gleichbleibender Ton; eintönige Wieder'holung; **2.** → **monotony**; **mo·not·o·nous** [mə'nɒtnəs] adj. □ mono'ton, eintönig (a. fig.); **mo·not·o·ny** [mə'nɒtnɪ] s. Monoto'nie f, Eintönigkeit f, fig. a. Einförmigkeit f, (ewiges) Einerlei n.

mon·o·type ['mɒnəʊtaɪp] (Fabrikmarke) s. typ. **1.** ⚙ Monotype f; **2.** mit der Monotype hergestellte Letter.

mon·o·va·lent ['mɒnəʊˌveɪlənt] adj. 🜛 einwertig; **mon·ox·ide** [mɒ'nɒksaɪd] s. 🜛 'Mono‚xid n.

mon·soon [mɒn'suːn] s. Mon'sun m.

mon·ster ['mɒnstə] I s. **1.** a. fig. Monster n, Ungeheuer n, Scheusal n; **2.** Monstrum n (a.) 'Missgeburt f, -bildung f, b) fig. Ungeheuer n, Ko'loss m; II adj. **3.** ungeheuer(lich), Riesen..., Monster...: ~ **film** Monsterfilm m; ~ **meeting** Massenversammlung f.

mon·strance ['mɒnstrəns] s. eccl. Monst'ranz f.

mon·stros·i·ty [mɒn'strɒsətɪ] s. **1.** Ungeheuerlichkeit f; **2.** → **monster** 2.

mon·strous ['mɒnstrəs] adj. □ **1.** monströs: a) ungeheuer, riesig, b) unge'heuerlich, grässlich, scheußlich, c) 'missgestaltet, unförmig, ungestalt; **2.** un-, 'widerna‚türlich; **3.** ab'surd, lächerlich; **'mon·strous·ness** [-nɪs] s. Unge'heuerlichkeit f; **2.** Riesenhaftigkeit f; **3.** 'Widerna‚türlichkeit f.

mon·tage [mɒn'tɑːʒ] s. **1.** ('Bild-, 'Foto-) Mon‚tage f; **2.** Film, Radio etc.: Mon'tage f.

month [mʌnθ] s. **1.** Monat m: **this day** ~ heute in od. vor e-m Monat; **by the** ~ (all)monatlich; **a** ~ **of Sundays** e-e ewig lange Zeit; **2.** F vier Wochen od. 30 Tage; **month·ly** ['mʌnθlɪ] I s. **1.** Monatsschrift f; **2.** pl. → **menses**; II adj. **3.** einen Monat dauernd; **4.** monatlich, Monats...: ~ **salary** Monatsgehalt n; III adv. **5.** monatlich, einmal im Monat, jeden Monat.

mon·ti·cule ['mɒntɪkjuːl] s. **1.** (kleiner) Hügel; **2.** Höckerchen n.

mon·u·ment ['mɒnjʊmənt] s. Monu'ment n, (a. Grab-, Na'tur- etc.)Denkmal n (**to** für, **of** gen.): **a** ~ **of literature**

fig. ein Literaturdenkmal; **mon·u·men·tal** [ˌmɒnjʊ'mentl] adj. □ **1.** monumen'tal, gewaltig, impo'sant; **2.** F kolos'sal, ungeheuer: ~ **stupidity**; **3.** Denkmal(s)..., Gedenk...; Grabmal(s)...

moo [muː] I v/i. muhen; II s. Muhen n.

mooch [muːtʃ] sl. I v/i. **1.** a. ~ **about** her'umlungern, -strolchen; ~ **along** dahinlatschen; II v/t. **2.** ‚klauen', stehlen; **3.** schnorren, erbetteln.

mood¹ [muːd] s. **1.** ling. Modus m, Aussageweise f; **2.** ♪ Tonart f.

mood² [muːd] s. **1.** Stimmung f (a. paint., ♪ etc.), Laune f: **be in the ~ to work** zur Arbeit aufgelegt sein; **be in no ~ for a walk** keine Lust haben spazieren zu gehen; **change of ~** Stimmungsumschwung m; ~ **music** stimmungsvolle Musik; **2.** paint., phot. Stimmungsbild n; **mood·i·ness** ['muːdɪnɪs] s. **1.** Launenhaftigkeit f; **2.** Übellaunigkeit f; **3.** Trübsinn(igkeit f) m; **mood·y** ['muːdɪ] adj. **1.** □ launisch, launenhaft; **2.** übellaunig, verstimmt; **3.** trübsinnig.

moon [muːn] I s. **1.** Mond m: **full** ~ Vollmond m; **new** ~ Neumond m; **once in a blue** ~ F alle Jubeljahre einmal, höchst selten; **be over the** ~ F ganz selig sein; **cry for the** ~ nach etwas Unmöglichem verlangen; **promise s.o. the** ~ j-m das Blaue vom Himmel (herunter) versprechen; **reach for the** ~ nach den Sternen greifen; **shoot the** ~ F bei Nacht u. Nebel ausziehen (Mieter); **2.** ast. Tra'bant m, Satel'lit m: **man-made** (od. 'baby) ~ (Erd)Satellit, 'Sputnik' m; **3.** poet. Mond m, Monat m; II v/i. **4.** mst ~ **about** her'umlungern, -geistern; III v/t. **5.** ~ **away** Zeit vertrödeln, verträumen; **'~beam** s. Mondstrahl m; **'~calf** s. [irr.] **1.** ‚Mondkalb' n, Trottel m; **2.** Träumer m; **'~faced** adj. vollmondsichtig; **'~light** I s. Mondlicht n, -schein m: ♬ **Sonata** ♪ Mondscheinsonate f; II adj. mondhell, Mondlicht...: ~ **flit(ting)** sl. heimliches Ausziehen bei Nacht (wegen Mietschulden); **'~light·er** s. Schwarzarbeiter m; **'~lit** adj. mondhell; **'~rak·er** s. ⚓ Mondsegel n; **'~rise** s. Mondaufgang m; **'~set** s. **1.** 'Mond‚untergang m; **2.** fig. a) Schwindel m, fauler Zauber, b) Unsinn m, Geschwafel m; **3.** sl. geschmuggelter od. schwarzgebrannter Alkohol; **~shin·er** s. Am. sl. Alkoholschmuggler m; Schwarzbrenner m; **'~stone** s. min. Mondstein m; **'~struck** adj. **1.** mondsüchtig; **2.** verrückt.

moon·y ['muːnɪ] adj. **1.** (halb)mondförmig; **2.** Mond...; **3.** mondhell, Mondlicht...; **4.** F a) verträumt, dösig, b) beschwipst, c) verrückt.

moor¹ [mʊə] s. **1.** Ödland n, bsd. Heideland n; **2.** Hochmoor n; Bergheide f.

moor² [mʊə] I v/t. **1.** ⚓ vertäuen, festmachen; fig. verankern, sichern; II v/i. ⚓ **2.** festmachen, ein Schiff vertäuen; **3.** sich festmachen; **4.** festgemacht od. vertäut liegen.

Moor³ [mʊə] s. Maure m; Mohr m.

moor·age ['mʊərɪdʒ] → **mooring**.

'moor|fowl, ~ game s. (Schottisches) Moorhuhn; **~hen** s. **1.** weibliches Moorhuhn; **2.** Gemeines Teichhuhn.

moor·ing ['mʊərɪŋ] s. ⚓ **1.** Festmachen n; **2.** mst pl. Vertäuung f (Schiff); **3.** pl. Liegeplatz m; **4.** Anlegegebühr f; ~ **buoy** ⚓ Festmacheboje f; ~ **rope** s. Halteleine f.

Moor·ish ['mʊərɪʃ] adj. maurisch.

'moor·land [-lənd] s. Heidemoor n.

moose [muːs] pl. **moose** s. zo. Elch m.

moot [muːt] I s. **1.** hist. (beratende) Volksversammlung; **2.** ⚖, univ. Diskussi'on f fik'tiver (Rechts)Fälle; II v/t. **3.** Frage aufwerfen, anschneiden; **4.** erörtern, diskutieren; III adj. **5.** a) strittig: ~ **point**, b) (rein) aka'demisch: ~ **question**.

mop¹ [mɒp] I s. **1.** Mopp m (Fransenbesen); Schrubber m; Wischlappen m; **2.** (Haar)Wust m; **3.** ⚙ Dweil m; ⚙ Schwabbelscheibe f; II v/t. **5.** auf-, abwischen: ~ **one's face** sich das Gesicht (ab)wischen; → **floor** 1; **6.** ~ **up** a) (mit dem Mopp) aufwischen, b) ⚔ sl. (vom Feinde) säubern, Wald durch'kämmen, c) sl. Profit etc. ‚schlucken', d) sl. aufräumen mit.

mop² [mɒp] I v/i. mst ~ **and mow** Gesichter schneiden; II s. Gri'masse f: ~**s and mows** Grimassen.

mope [məʊp] I v/i. **1.** den Kopf hängen lassen, Trübsal blasen; II v/t. **2.** (nur pass.) **be ~d** niedergeschlagen sein, ‚sich mopsen' (langweilen); III s. **3.** Trübsalbläser(in); **4.** pl. Trübsinn m.

mo·ped ['məʊped] s. mot. Brit. Moped n.

'mop·head s. F a) Wuschelkopf m, b) Struwwelpeter m.

mop·ing ['məʊpɪŋ] adj. □; **'mop·ish** [-ɪʃ] adj. □ trübselig, a'pathisch, kopfhängerisch; **'mop·ish·ness** [-ɪʃnɪs] s. Lustlosigkeit f, Griesgrämigkeit f, Trübsinn m.

mop·pet ['mɒpɪt] s. F Püppchen n (a. fig. Kind, Mädchen).

'mop·ping-up ['mɒpɪŋ-] s. ⚔ sl. **1.** Aufräumungsarbeit f; **2.** Säuberung f (vom Feinde): ~ **operation** Säuberungsaktion f.

mo·raine [mɒ'reɪn] s. geol. Mo'räne f.

mor·al ['mɒrəl] I adj. □ **1.** allg. mo'ralisch: a) sittlich: ~ **force**; ~ **sense** sittliches Empfinden, b) geistig: ~ **obligation** moralische Verpflichtung; ~ **support** moralische Unterstützung; ~ **victory** moralischer Sieg; c) vernunftgemäß: ~ **certainty** moralische Gewissheit, d) Moral..., Sitten...: ~ **law** Sittengesetz n; ~ **theology** Moraltheologie f, e) sittenstreng, tugendhaft: **a ~ life**; **2.** (sittlich) gut: **a ~ act**; **3.** cha'rakterlich: **~ly firm** innerlich gefestigt; II s. **4.** Mo'ral f, Nutzanwendung f (e-r Geschichte etc.): **draw the ~ from** die Lehre ziehen aus; **5.** mo'ralischer Grundsatz: **point the ~** den sittlichen Standpunkt betonen; **6.** pl. Mo'ral f, sittliches Verhalten, Sitten pl.: **code of ~s** Sittenkodex m; **7.** pl. sg. konstr. Sittenlehre f, Ethik f.

mo·rale [mɒ'rɑːl] s. Mo'ral f, Haltung f, Stimmung f, (Arbeits-, Kampf)Geist m: **the ~ of the army** die Kampfmoral od. Stimmung der Armee; **raise (lower) the ~** die Moral heben (senken).

mor·al| fac·ul·ty s. Sittlichkeitsgefühl n; ~ **haz·ard** s. Versicherungswesen: sub‚jek'tives Risiko, Risiko n falscher Angaben des Versicherten; ~ **in·san·i·ty** s. psych. mo'ralischer De'fekt.

mor·al·ist ['mɒrəlɪst] s. **1.** Mora'list m, Sittenlehrer m; **2.** Ethiker m.

mo·ral·i·ty [mə'rælətɪ] s. **1.** Mo'ral f, Sittlichkeit f, Tugend(haftigkeit) f; **2.** Morali'tät f, sittliche Gesinnung; **3.** Ethik f, Sittenlehre f; **4.** pl. mo'ralische Grundsätze pl., Ethik f (e-r Person); **5.** contp. Mo'ralpredigt f; **6.** → ~ **play** s. hist. thea. Morali'tät f.

M

mor·al·ize ['mɒrəlaɪz] **I** v/i. **1.** moralisieren (**on** über acc.); **II** v/t. **2.** mo'ralisch auslegen; **3.** versittlichen, die Mo'ral (gen.) heben; **'mor·al·iz·er** [-zə] s. Mo'ralprediger(in), -,apostel m.

mor·al| phi·los·o·phy, ~ sci·ence s. Mo'ralphiloso,phie f, Ethik f.

mo·rass [mə'ræs] s. **1.** Mo'rast m, Sumpf (-land n) m; **2.** fig. a) Wirrnis f, b) Klemme f, schwierige Lage.

mor·a·to·ri·um [,mɒrə'tɔːrɪəm] pl. **-ri·ums** s. ✝ Mora'torium n, Zahlungsaufschub m, Stillhalteabkommen n, Stundung f; **mor·a·to·ry** ['mɒrətərɪ] adj. Moratoriums..., Stundungs...

Mo·ra·vi·an [mə'reɪvjən] **I** s. **1.** Mähre m, Mährin f; **2.** ling. Mährisch n; **II** adj. **3.** mährisch: ~ **Brethren** eccl. die Herrnhuter Brüdergemein(d)e.

mor·bid ['mɔːbɪd] adj. □ mor'bid, krankhaft, patho'logisch: ~ **anatomy** ✱ pathologische Anatomie; **mor·bid·i·ty** [mɔː'bɪdɪtɪ] s. **1.** Krankhaftigkeit f; **2.** Erkrankungsziffer f.

mor·dan·cy ['mɔːdənsɪ] s. Bissigkeit f, beißende Schärfe; **'mor·dant** [-dənt] **I** adj. □ **1.** beißend: a) brennend (Schmerz), b) fig. scharf, sar'kastisch (Worte etc.); **2.** ⊙ a) beizend, ätzend, b) Farben fixierend; **II** s. **3.** ⊙ a) Ätzwasser n, b) (bsd. Färberei) Beize f.

more [mɔː] **I** adj. **1.** mehr: (no) ~ **than** (nicht) mehr als; **they are ~ than we** sie sind zahlreicher als wir; **2.** mehr, noch (mehr), weiter: **some ~ tea** noch etwas Tee; **one ~ day** noch ein(en) Tag; **so much the ~ courage** umso mehr Mut; **he is no ~** er ist nicht mehr (ist tot); **3.** größer (obs. außer in): **the ~ fool** der größere Tor; **the ~ part** der größere Teil; **II** adv. **4.** mehr: ~ **dead than alive** mehr od. eher tot als lebendig; ~ **and ~** immer mehr; ~ **and difficult** immer schwieriger; ~ **or less** mehr oder weniger, ungefähr; **the ~** umso mehr; **the ~ so because** umso mehr, da; **all the ~** so nur umso mehr; **no** (od. **not any**) ~ **than** ebenso wenig wie; **neither** (od. **no**) ~ **nor less than stupid** nicht mehr u. nicht weniger als dumm; **5.** (zur Bildung des comp.): ~ **important** wichtiger; ~ **often** öfter; **6.** noch: **once ~** noch einmal; **two hours ~** noch zwei Stunden; **7.** noch mehr, ja so'gar: **it is wrong and, ~, it is foolish**; **III** s. **8.** Mehr n (**of** an dat.); **9.** mehr: ~ **than one person has seen it** mehr als einer hat es gesehen; **we shall see ~ of him** wir werden ihn noch öfter sehen; **and what is ~** und was noch wichtiger ist; **no ~** nicht(s) mehr.

mo·rel [mɒ'rel] s. ♀ **1.** Morchel f; **2.** Nachtschatten m; **3.** → **mo·rel·lo** [mə'reləʊ] pl. **-los** s. ♀ Mo'relle f, Schwarze Sauerweichsel.

more·o·ver [mɔː'rəʊvə] adv. außerdem, über'dies, ferner, weiter.

mo·res ['mɔːriːz] s. pl. Sitten pl.

mor·ga·nat·ic [,mɔːgə'nætɪk] adj. (□ ~ally) morga'natisch.

morgue [mɔːg] s. **1.** Leichenschauhaus n; **2.** F Ar'chiv n (e-s Zeitungsverlages etc.).

mor·i·bund ['mɒrɪbʌnd] adj. **1.** sterbend, dem Tode geweiht; **2.** fig. zum Aussterben od. Scheitern verurteilt.

Mor·mon ['mɔːmən] eccl. **I** s. Mor'mone m, Mor'monin f; **II** adj. mor'monisch: ~ **Church** mormonische Kirche, Kirche Jesu Christi der Heiligen der letzten Tage; ~ **State** Beiname für Utah n (USA).

morn [mɔːn] s. poet. Morgen m.

morn·ing ['mɔːnɪŋ] **I** s. **1.** a) Morgen m, b) Vormittag m: **in the ~** morgens, am Morgen, vormittags; **early in the ~** frühmorgens, früh am Morgen; **on the ~ of May 5** am Morgen des 5. Mai; **one (fine) ~** eines (schönen) Morgens; **this ~** heute früh; **the ~ after** am Morgen darauf, am darauf folgenden Morgen; **good ~!** guten Morgen!; ~**!** F ('n) Morgen!; **2.** fig. Morgen m, Beginn m; **3.** poet. a) Morgendämmerung f, b) ♀ Au'rora f; **II** adj. **4.** a) Morgen..., Vormittags..., b) Früh...; ~**·af·ter pill** s. die Pille danach; ~ **call** s. Weckdienst m (im Hotel etc.); ~ **coat** s. Cut(away) m; ~ **dress** s. **1.** Hauskleid n; **2.** Besuchs-, Konfe'renzanzug m, ,Stresemann' m (schwarzer Rock mit gestreifter Hose); ~ **gift** s. ✝✝ hist. Morgengabe f; ~ **glo·ry** s. ♀ Winde f; ~ **gown** s. Morgenrock m; Hauskleid n (der Frau); ~ **per·form·ance** s. thea. Frühvorstellung f, Mati'nee f; ~ **prayer** s. eccl. **1.** Morgengebet n; **2.** Frühgottesdienst m; ~ **sick·ness** s. ✱ morgendliches Erbrechen (bei Schwangeren); ~ **star** s. **1.** ast., a. ✗ hist. Morgenstern m; **2.** ♀ Men'tzelie f.

Mo·roc·can [mə'rɒkən] **I** adj. marok'kanisch; **II** s. Marok'kaner(in).

mo·roc·co [mə'rɒkəʊ] pl. **-cos** [-z] s. a. ~ **leather** Saffian(leder n) m.

mo·ron ['mɔːrɒn] s. **1.** Schwachsinnige(r m) f; **2.** F Trottel m, Idi'ot m; **mo·ron·ic** [mə'rɒnɪk] adj. schwachsinnig.

mo·rose [mə'rəʊs] adj. □ mürrisch, grämlich, verdrießlich; **mo'rose·ness** [-nɪs] s. Verdrießlichkeit f.

mor·pheme ['mɔːfiːm] s. ling. Mor'phem n.

mor·phi·a ['mɔːfjə], **'mor·phine** [-fiːn] s. 🜍 Morphium n; **'mor·phin·ism** [-fɪnɪzəm] s. 🜍 Morphi'nismus m, Morphiumsucht f; 🜍 Morphiumvergiftung f; **'mor·phin·ist** [-fɪnɪst] s. Morphi'nist(in).

morpho- [mɔːfəʊ] in Zssgn Form..., Gestalt..., Morpho...

mor·pho·log·ic, mor·pho·log·i·cal [,mɔːfə'lɒdʒɪk(l)] adj. □ morpholo'gisch, Form...: ~ **element** Formelement n; **mor·phol·o·gy** [mɔː'fɒlədʒɪ] s. Morpholo'gie f.

mor·ris ['mɒrɪs] s. a. ~ **dance** Mo'riskentanz m; ~ **tube** s. Einstecklauf m (für Gewehre).

mor·row ['mɒrəʊ] s. mst poet. morgiger od. folgender Tag: **the ~ of** a) der Tag nach, b) fig. die Zeit unmittelbar nach.

Morse¹ [mɔːs] **I** adj. Morse...: ~ **code** Morsealphabet n; **II** v/t. u. v/i. ♩ morsen.

morse² [mɔːs] → **walrus**.

mor·sel ['mɔːsl] **I** s. **1.** Bissen m, Happen m; **2.** Stückchen n, das bisschen; **3.** Leckerbissen m; **II** v/t. **4.** in kleine Stückchen teilen, in kleinen Porti'onen austeilen.

mort¹ [mɔːt] s. hunt. ('Hirsch),Totsi,gnal n.

mort² [mɔːt] s. ichth. dreijähriger Lachs.

mor·tal ['mɔːtl] **I** adj. □ **1.** sterblich; **2.** tödlich (a.) verderblich, todbringend (**to** für): ~ **wound**, b) erbittert: ~ **battle**; ~ **hatred** tödlicher Hass; **3.** Tod(es)...: ~ **agony** Todeskampf m; ~ **enemies** Todfeinde pl.; ~ **fear** Todesangst f; ~ **hour** Todesstunde f; ~ **sin** Todsünde f; **4.** menschlich, irdisch, Menschen...: ~ **life** irdisches Leben, Vergänglichkeit f; **by no ~ means** F auf keine menschenmögliche Art; **of no ~ use** F absolut zwecklos; **every ~ thing** F alles Menschenmögliche; **5.** F Mords..., ,mordsmäßig': **I'm in a ~ hurry** ich habs furchtbar

eilig; **6.** ewig, sterbenslangweilig: **three ~ hours** drei endlose Stunden; **II** s. **7.** Sterbliche(r m) f; **mor·tal·i·ty** [mɔː'tælətɪ] s. **1.** Sterblichkeit f; **2.** die (sterbliche) Menschheit; **3.** a. ~ **rate** a) Sterblichkeit(sziffer) f, b) ⊙ Verschleiß(quote f) m.

mor·tar¹ ['mɔːtə] **I** s. **1.** 🍶 Mörser m; **2.** metall. Pochladen m; **3.** ✗ a) Mörser m (Geschütz), b) Gra'natwerfer m: ~ **shell** Werfergranate f; **4.** (Feuerwerks)Böller m; **II** v/t. **5.** ✗ mit Mörsern beschießen, mit Gra'natwerferfeuer belegen.

mor·tar² [mɔːtə] s. △ Mörtel m.

'mor·tar·board s. **1.** △ Mörtelbrett n; **2.** univ. qua'dratisches Ba'rett.

mort·gage ['mɔːgɪdʒ] ✝✝ **I** s. **1.** Verpfändung f; Pfandrecht n; ~ **give in** ~ verpfänden; **2.** Pfandbrief m; **3.** Hypo'thek f: **by** ~ hypothekarisch; **lend on** ~ auf Hypothek (ver)leihen; **raise a** ~ e-e Hypothek aufnehmen (**on** auf acc.); **4.** Hypo'thekenbrief m; **II** v/t. **5.** (a. fig.) verpfänden (**to** an acc.); **6.** hypothe'karisch belasten, e-e Hypo'thek aufnehmen auf (acc.); ~ **bond** s. Hypo'thekenpfandbrief m; ~ **deed** s. **1.** Pfandbrief m; **2.** Hypo'thekenbrief m.

mort·ga·gee [,mɔːgə'dʒiː] s. ✝✝ Hypothe'kar m, Pfand- od. Hypo'thekengläubiger m; **mort·ga·gor** [-'dʒɔː] s. Pfand- od. Hypo'thekenschuldner m.

mor·ti·cian [mɔː'tɪʃən] s. Am. Leichenbestatter m.

mor·ti·fi·ca·tion [,mɔːtɪfɪ'keɪʃn] s. **1.** Demütigung f, Kränkung f; **2.** Ärger m, Verdruss m; **3.** Ka'steiung f; Abtötung f (Leidenschaften); **4.** ✱ (kalter) Brand, Ne'krose f; **mor·ti·fy** ['mɔːtɪfaɪ] **I** v/t. **1.** demütigen, kränken; **2.** Gefühle verletzen; **3.** Körper, Fleisch ka'steien; Leidenschaften abtöten; **4.** ✱ brandig machen, absterben lassen; **II** v/i. **5.** ✱ brandig werden, absterben.

mor·tise ['mɔːtɪs] ⊙ **I** s. a) Zapfenloch n, b) Stemmloch n, c) (Keil)Nut f, d) Falz m, Fuge f; **II** v/t. a) verzapfen, b) einstemmen, c) einzapfen (**into** in acc.); ~ **chis·el** s. Lochbeitel m; ~ **ga(u)ge** s. Zapfenstreichmaß n; ~ **joint** s. Verzapfung f; ~ **lock** s. (Ein-) Steckschloss n.

mort·main ['mɔːtmeɪn] s. ✝✝ unveräußerlicher Besitz, Besitz m der Toten Hand: **in** ~ unveräußerlich.

mor·tu·ar·y ['mɔːtjʊərɪ] **I** s. Leichenhalle f; **II** adj. Leichen..., Begräbnis...

mo·sa·ic¹ [məʊ'zeɪɪk] **I** s. **1.** Mosa'ik n (a. fig.); **2.** ('Luftbild)Mosa,ik n, Reihenbild n; **II** adj. **3.** Mosaik...; mosa'ikartig.

Mo·sa·ic² adj., **Mo·sa·i·cal** [məʊ'zeɪɪk(l)] adj. mo'saisch.

Mo·selle [məʊ'zel] s. Mosel(wein) m.

mo·sey ['məʊzɪ] v/i. Am. sl. **1.** a. ~ **along** da'hinlatschen; **2.** ,abhauen'.

Mos·lem ['mɒzləm] → **Muslim**.

mosque [mɒsk] s. Mo'schee f.

mos·qui·to [mə'skiːtəʊ] s. **1.** pl. **-toes** zo. Stechmücke f, bsd. Mos'kito m; **2.** pl. **-toes** od. **-tos** ✈ Mos'kito m (brit. Bomber); ~ **boat** s., ~ **craft** s. Schnellboot n; ~ **net** s. Mos'kitonetz n; ~ **State** s. Am. (Beiname für) New Jersey n (USA).

moss [mɒs] s. **1.** ♀ Moos n; **2.** (Torf-) Moor n; **'~-grown** adj. **1.** moosbewachsen, bemoost; **2.** fig. altmodisch, über'holt.

moss·i·ness ['mɒsɪnɪs] s. **1.** 'Moos,überzug m; **2.** Moosartigkeit f, Weichheit f; **moss·y** ['mɒsɪ] adj. **1.** moosig, bemoost; **2.** moosartig; **3.** Moos...;

green Moosgrün n.

most [məʊst] **I** adj. □ → **mostly**; **1.** meist, größt; höchst, äußerst; **the ~ fear** die meiste od. größte Angst; **for the ~ part** größten-, meistenteils; **2.** (vor e-m Substantiv im pl.) die meisten: **~ people** die meisten Leute; **II** s. **3.** das meiste, das Höchste, das Äußerste: **at (the) ~** höchstens, bestenfalls; **make the ~ of** et. nach Kräften ausnützen, (noch) das Beste aus et. herausholen; **4.** das meiste, der größte Teil: **he spent ~ of his time there** er verbrachte die meiste Zeit dort; **5.** die meisten: **better than ~** besser als die meisten; **~ of my friends** die meisten m-r Freunde; **III** adv. **6.** am meisten: **~ of all** am allermeisten; **7.** zur Bildung des Superlativs: **the ~ important point** der wichtigste Punkt; **8.** vor adj. höchst, äußerst, 'überaus: **it's ~ kind of you.**

-most [məʊst] in Zssgn Bezeichnung des sup.: **in~**, **top~** etc.

'**most-ˌfa·vo(u)red-'na·tion clause** s. pol. Meistbegünstigungsklausel f.

most·ly ['məʊstlɪ] adv. **1.** größtenteils, im Wesentlichen, in der Hauptsache; **2.** hauptsächlich.

MOT [ˌeməʊ'tiː] s. Brit. **1.** abbr. für **Ministry of Transport** Ver'kehrsminis-,terium n; **2.** mot. als Test etwa: TÜV m; **go for one's ~** zum TÜV müssen; **pass (fail) one's ~** (nicht) durch den TÜV kommen.

mote [məʊt] s. (Sonnen)Stäubchen n: **the ~ in another's eye** bibl. der Splitter im Auge des anderen.

mo·tel [məʊ'tel] s. Mo'tel n.

mo·tet [məʊ'tet] s. ♪ Mo'tette f.

moth [mɒθ] s. **1.** pl. **moths** zo. Nachtfalter m; **2.** pl. **moths** od. coll. **moth** (Kleider)Motte f; '**~·ball I** s. Mottenkugel f: **put in ~s** od. **II** v/t. Kleidung, a. Maschinen etc. einmotten; fig. Plan etc. ,auf Eis legen'; '**~·ˌeat·en** adj. **1.** von Motten zerfressen; **2.** fig. veraltet, anti'quiert.

moth·er¹ ['mʌðə] **I** s. **1.** Mutter f (a. fig.); **II** adj. **2.** Mutter...: **~'s Day** Muttertag m; **III** v/t. **3.** (mst fig.) gebären, her'vorbringen; **4.** bemuttern; **5.** **~ a novel on s.o.** j-m e-n Roman zuschreiben.

moth·er² ['mʌðə] **I** s. Essigmutter f; **II** v/i. Essigmutter ansetzen.

Moth·er Car·ey's chick·en ['keərɪz] s. orn. Sturmschwalbe f.

moth·er| cell s. biol. Mutterzelle f; **~ church** s. Mutterkirche f; **2.** Hauptkirche f; **~ coun·try** s. **1.** Mutterland n; **2.** Vater-, Heimatland n; **~ earth** s. Mutter f Erde; **~ fix·a·tion** s. psych. Mutterfixierung f, -bindung f; '**~ˌfuck·er** s. fig. V ,Scheißkerl' m.

moth·er·hood ['mʌðəhʊd] s. **1.** Mutterschaft f; **2.** coll. die Mütter pl.

'**moth·er-in-law** [-ðərɪn-] pl. '**moth·ers-in-law** [-ðəzɪn-] s. Schwiegermutter f.

'**moth·er·land** → **mother country.**

moth·er·less ['mʌðəlɪs] adj. mutterlos.

'**moth·er·li·ness** ['mʌðəlɪnɪs] s. Mütterlichkeit f.

moth·er| liq·uor s. ♈ Mutterlauge f; **~ lode** s. ⚒ Hauptader f.

moth·er·ly ['mʌðəlɪ] adj. u. adv. mütterlich.

moth·er| of pearl s. Perlmutter f, Perlmutt n; '**~-of-'pearl** [-ðərəv'p-] adj. perlmuttern, Perlmutt...

moth·er| ship s. ⚓ Brit. Mutterschiff n; **~ su·pe·ri·or** s. eccl. Oberin f, Äb'tissin f; **~ tie** s. psych. Mutterbindung f; **~ tongue** s. Muttersprache f; **~ wit** s. Mutterwitz m.

moth·er·y ['mʌðərɪ] adj. hefig, trübe.

moth·y ['mɒθɪ] adj. **1.** voller Motten; **2.** mottenzerfressen.

mo·tif [məʊ'tiːf] s. **1.** ♪ ('Leit)Mo,tiv n; **2.** paint. etc., Literatur: Mo'tiv n, Vorwurf m; **3.** fig. Leitgedanke m.

mo·tile ['məʊtaɪl] adj. biol. frei beweglich; **mo·til·i·ty** [məʊ'tɪlətɪ] s. selbstständiges Bewegungsvermögen.

mo·tion ['məʊʃn] **I** s. **1.** Bewegung f (a. phys., ⚛, ♪): **go through the ~s of doing s.th.** fig. et. mechanisch od. pro forma tun; **2.** Gang m (a. ⚙): **set in ~** in Gang bringen, in Bewegung setzen; → **idle** 3; **3.** (Körper-, Hand)Bewegung f, Wink m: **~ of the head** Zeichen n mit dem Kopf; **4.** Antrieb m: **of one's own ~** aus eigenem Antrieb, a. freiwillig; **5.** pl. Schritte pl., Handlungen pl.: **watch s.o.'s ~s**; **6.** ♈, parl. etc. Antrag m: **carry a ~** e-n Antrag durchbringen; **~ of no confidence** Misstrauensantrag m; **7.** physiol. Stuhlgang m; **II** v/i. **8.** winken (with mit, to dat.); **III** v/t. **9.** j-m (zu)winken, j-n durch e-n Wink auffordern (**to do** zu tun), j-n wohin winken; '**mo·tion·less** [-lɪs] adj. bewegungslos, regungslos, unbeweglich.

mo·tion| pic·ture s. Film m; '**~-pic·ture** adj. Film...: **~ camera**; **~ projector** Filmprojektor m; **~ stud·y** s. Bewegungs-, Rationalisierungsstudie f; **~ ther·a·py** s. ♲ Be'wegungsthera,pie f.

mo·ti·vate ['məʊtɪveɪt] v/t. **1.** motivieren: a) et. begründen, b j-n anregen, anspornen; **2.** et. anregen, her'vorrufen; **mo·ti·va·tion** [ˌməʊtɪ'veɪʃn] s. **1.** Motivierung f: a) Begründung f, b) Motivati'on f, Ansporn m, Antrieb m: **~ research** Motivforschung f; **2.** Anregung f.

mo·tive ['məʊtɪv] **I** s. **1.** Mo'tiv n, Beweggrund m, Antrieb m (**for** zu); **2.** → **motif** 1 u. 2; **II** adj. **3.** bewegend, treibend (a. fig.): **~ power** Triebkraft f; **III** v/t. **4.** mst pass. der Beweggrund sein von, veranlassen: **an act ~d by hatred** e-e vom Hass diktierte Tat.

mo·tiv·i·ty [məʊ'tɪvətɪ] s. Bewegungsfähigkeit f, -kraft f.

mot·ley ['mɒtlɪ] **I** adj. **1.** bunt (a. fig. Menge etc.), scheckig; **II** s. **2.** hist. Narrenkleid n; **3.** Kunterbunt n.

mo·tor ['məʊtə] **I** s. **1.** ⚙ (bsd. E'lektro-, Verbrennungs)Motor m; **2.** fig. treibende Kraft; **3.** bsd. Brit. a) Kraftwagen m, Auto n, b) Motorfahrzeug n; **4.** anat. a) Muskel m, b) mo'torischer Nerv; **II** adj. **5.** bewegend, (an)treibend; **6.** Motor...; **7.** Auto...; **8.** anat. mo'torisch; **III** v/i. **9.** mot. fahren; **IV** v/t. **10.** in e-m Kraftfahrzeug befördern; **~ ac·ci·dent** s. Autounfall m; **~ am·bu·lance** s. Krankenwagen m, Ambu'lanz f; '**~-as,sist·ed** adj.: **~ bicycle** a) Fahrrad n mit Hilfsmotor, b) Mofa n; **~ bi·cy·cle** → **motorcycle**; '**~·bike** F für **motorcycle**; '**~·boat** s. Motorboot n; '**~·bus** s. Autobus m; '**~·cade** [-keɪd] s. 'Auto,ko,lonne f; '**~·car** s. **1.** Kraftwagen m, Auto(mo-'bil) n: **~ industry** Automobilindustrie f; **2.** ⚙ Triebwagen m; '**~·car·a·van** s. Brit. 'Wohnmo,bil n; **~ coach** s. Brit. 'Wohnmo,bil n; **~ coach** → **coach** 3; **~ court** → **motel**; '**~·cy·cle I** s. Motorrad n; **II** v/i. a) Motorrad fahren, b) mit dem Motorrad fahren; '**~·cy·clist** s. Motorradfahrer(in); '**~-·driv·en** adj. mit Motorantrieb, Motor...; '**~·drome** [-drəʊm] s. Moto'drom n.

mo·tored ['məʊtəd] adj. ⚙ s. motori-

siert, mit e-m Motor od. mit Mo'toren (versehen); **2.** ...motorig.

mo·tor| en·gine s. 'Kraftma,schine f; **~ fit·ter** s. Autoschlosser m; **~ home** 'Wohnmo,bil n. **~ in·dus·try** s. 'Auto-indus,trie f.

mo·tor·ing ['məʊtərɪŋ] s. Autofahren n; Motorsport m: **school of ~** Fahrschule f; '**mo·tor·ist** [-ɪst] s. Kraft-, Autofahrer(in).

mo·tor·i·za·tion [ˌməʊtəraɪ'zeɪʃn] s. Motorisierung f; **mo·tor·ize** ['məʊtəraɪz] v/t. ⚙ u. ✗ motorisieren: **~d unit** ✗ (voll) motorisierte Einheit.

mo·tor launch s. 'Motorbar,kasse f.

mo·tor·less ['məʊtəlɪs] adj. motorlos: **~ flight** Segelflug m.

mo·tor| lor·ry s. Brit. Lastkraftwagen m; '**~·man** [-mən] s. [irr.] Wagenführer m; **~ me·chan·ic** s. 'Autome,chaniker m; **~ nerve** s. anat. mo'torischer Nerv, Bewegungsnerv m; **~ oil** s. Motoröl n; **~ pool** s. Fahrbereitschaft f; **~ road** s. Autostraße f; **~ scoot·er** s. Motorroller m; **~ ship** s. Motorschiff n; **~ show** s. Automo'bilausstellung f; **~ start·er** s. (Motor)Anlasser m; **~ tor·pe·do boat** s. ⚓, ✗ Schnellboot n; **~ trac·tor** s. Traktor m, Schlepper m, 'Zugma-,schine f; **~ truck** s. **1.** bsd. Am. Lastkraftwagen m; **2.** ⚡ E'lektrokarren m; **~ van** s. Brit. Lieferwagen m; **~ ve·hi·cle** s. Kraftfahrzeug n; '**~·way** s. Brit. Autobahn f; '**~·way junc·tion** s. Brit. Autobahndreieck n.

mot·tle ['mɒtl] v/t. sprenkeln, marmorieren; '**mot·tled** [-ld] adj. gesprenkelt, gefleckt, bunt.

mot·to ['mɒtəʊ] pl. **-toes**, **-tos** s. Motto n, Wahl-, Sinnspruch m.

mou·jik ['muːʒɪk] → **muzhik**.

mould¹ [məʊld] s. **1.** ⚙ (Gieß-, Guss-) Form f: **cast in the same ~** fig. aus demselben Holz geschnitzt; **2.** (Körper-) Bau m, Gestalt f, (äußere) Form; **3.** Art f, Na'tur f, Cha'rakter m; **4.** ⚙ a) Hohlform f, b) Pressform f, c) Ko'kille f, Hartgussform f, d) Ma'trize f, e) ('Form)Mo,dell n, f) Gesenk n; **5.** ⚙ a) 'Gussmateri,al n, b) Guss(stück n) m; **6.** Schiffbau: Mall n; **7.** △ a) Sims m, n, b) Leiste f, c) Hohlkehle f; **8.** Küche: Form f (für Speisen): **jelly ~** Puddingform; **9.** geol. Abdruck m (Versteinerung); **II** v/t. **10.** ⚙ gießen; (ab)formen, modellieren; pressen; Holz profilieren; ⚓ abmallen; **11.** formen (a. fig. Charakter), bilden, gestalten (**on** nach dem Muster von); **III** v/i. **12.** Gestalt annehmen, sich formen.

mould² [məʊld] **I** s. **1.** Schimmel m, Moder m; **2.** ♣ Schimmelpilz m; **II** v/i. **3.** schimm(e)lig wcrden, (ver)schimmeln.

mould³ [məʊld] s. **1.** lockere Erde, Gartenerde f; **2.** Humus(boden) m.

mould·a·ble ['məʊldəbl] adj. (ver-) formbar, bildsam: **~ material** ⚙ Pressmasse f.

mould·er¹ ['məʊldə] s. **1.** ⚙ Former m, Gießer m; **2.** fig. Gestalter(in).

mould·er² ['məʊldə] v/i. a. **~ away** vermodern, (zu Staub) zerfallen.

mould·i·ness ['məʊldɪnɪs] s. Moder m, Schimm(e)ligkeit f; (a. fig.) Schalheit f; fig. sl. Fadheit f.

mould·ing ['məʊldɪŋ] s. **1.** Formen n, Formgebung f; **2.** Formgieße'rei f, -arbeit f; Modellieren n; **3.** Formstück n; Pressteil m; **4.** → **mould¹** 7; **~ board** s. **1.** Formbrett n; **2.** Küche: Kuchen-, Nudelbrett n; **~ clay** s. ⚙ Formerde f, -ton m; **~ ma·chine** s. **1.** Holzbearbeitung: 'Kehl(hobel)ma,schine f; **2.**

metall. 'Formma,schine *f*; **3.** 'Spritzma,schine *f* (*für Spritzguss etc.*); ~ **press** *s.* Formpresse *f*; ~ **sand** *s.* Formsand *m*.

mould·y ['məʊldɪ] *adj.* **1.** schimm(e)lig; **2.** Schimmel..., schimmelartig: ~ *fungi* Schimmelpilze; **3.** muffig, schal (*a. fig.*), *sl.* fad.

moult [məʊlt] *zo.* **I** *v/i.* (sich) mausern (*a. fig.*); sich häuten; **II** *v/t.* Federn, Haut abwerfen, verlieren; **III** *s.* Mauser(ung) *f*; Häutung *f*.

mound¹ [maʊnd] *s.* **1.** Erdwall *m*, -hügel *m*; **2.** Damm *m*; **3.** *Baseball*: Abwurfstelle *f*.

mound² [maʊnd] *s. hist.* Reichsapfel *m*.

mount¹ [maʊnt] **I** *v/t.* **1.** Berg, Pferd, Barrikaden etc., fig. den Thron besteigen; Treppen hin'aufgehen, ersteigen; Fluss hin'auffahren; **2.** beritten machen: ~ *troops*, ~*ed police* berittene Polizei; **3.** errichten; *a. Maschine* aufstellen, montieren (*a. phot.*, *TV*); anbringen, einbauen, befestigen; *Papier, Bild* aufkleben, -ziehen; *Edelstein* fassen; *Messer etc.* mit e-m Griff versehen, stielen; *⚓ Versuchsobjekt* präparieren; *Präparat im Mikroskop* fixieren; **4.** zs.-bauen, -stellen, arrangieren; *thea. Stück* inszenieren, *fig. a.* aufziehen; **5.** ✕ a) *Geschütz* in Stellung bringen, b) *Posten* aufstellen; → *guard* 9; **6.** ⚒ bewaffnet sein mit, *Geschütz* führen; **II** *v/i.* **7.** (auf-, em'por-, hoch)steigen; **8.** *fig.* (an)wachsen, steigen, sich auftürmen (*bsd. Schulden, Schwierigkeiten etc.*): ~*ing suspense* (*debts*) wachsende Spannung (Schulden); **9.** *oft* ~ *up* sich belaufen (*to* auf *acc.*); **III** *s.* **10.** Gestell *n*; ⚒ Ständer *m*, Halterung *f*, 'Untersatz *m*; Fassung *f*; (Wechsel)Rahmen *m*, Passepar'tout *m*; 'Aufziehkar,ton *m*; ✕ (Ge'schütz)La,fette *f*; Ob'jektträger *m* (*Mikroskop*); **11.** Pferd *n*, Reittier *n*.

mount² [maʊnt] *s.* **1.** *poet.* a) Berg *m*, b) Hügel *m*; **2.** ⚖ (*in Eigennamen*) Berg *m*: **☉** *Sinai*; **☉** *of Venus Handlesekunst f*: Venusberg *m*.

moun·tain ['maʊntɪn] **I** *s.* Berg *m* (*a. fig. von Arbeit etc.*); *pl.* Gebirge *n*: **make a** ~ *out of a molehill* aus e-r Mücke e-n Elefanten machen; **II** *adj.* Berg..., Gebirgs...: ~ *artillery* Gebirgsartillerie *f*; ~ **ash** *s. e-e* Eberesche *f*; ~ **bike** *s.* Mountainbike *n*, Geländefahrrad *n*; ~ **chain** *s.* Berg-, Gebirgskette *f*; ~ **crys·tal** *s.* 'Bergkri,stall *m*; ~ **cock** *s.* Auerhahn *m*.

moun·tained ['maʊntɪnd] *adj.* bergig, gebirgig.

moun·tain·eer [,maʊntɪ'nɪə] **I** *s.* **1.** Bergbewohner(in); **2.** Bergsteiger(in); **II** *v/i.* **3.** bergsteigen; ,**moun·tain'eer·ing** [-'nɪərɪŋ] **I** *s.* Bergsteigen *n*; **II** *adj.* bergsteigerisch; **moun·tain·ous** ['maʊntɪnəs] *adj.* **1.** bergig, gebirgig; **2.** Berg..., Gebirgs...; **3.** *fig.* riesig, gewaltig.

moun·tain| rail·way *s.* Bergbahn *f*; ~ **range** *s.* Gebirgszug *m*, -kette *f*; ~ **sick·ness** *s.* ⚕ Berg-, Höhenkrankheit *f*; '~**side** *s.* Berg(ab)hang *m*; ~ **slide** *s.* Bergrutsch *m*; **☉ State** *s. Am.* (*Beiname für*) a) Mon'tana *n*, b) West Vir'ginia *n* (*USA*); ~ **troops** *s. pl.* Gebirgstruppen *pl.*; ~ **wood** *s.* 'Holzas,best *m*.

moun·te·bank ['maʊntɪbæŋk] *s.* **1.** Quacksalber *m*; Marktschreier *m*; **2.** Scharlatan *m*.

mount·ing ['maʊntɪŋ] *s.* **1.** ⚒ a) Einbau

m, Aufstellung *f*, Mon'tage *f* (*a. phot.*, *TV etc.*), b) Gestell *n*, Rahmen *m*, c) Befestigung *f*, Aufhängung *f*, d) (Auf-)Lagerung *f*, e) Arma'tur *f*, f) (Ein)Fassung *f* (*Edelstein*), g) Ausstattung *f*, h) *pl.* Fenster-, Türbeschläge *pl.*, i) *pl.* Gewirre *n* (*an Türschlössern*), j) (*Weberei*) Geschirr *n*, Zeug *n*; **2.** ⚡ (Ver-)Schaltung *f*, Installati'on *f*; ~ **brack·et** *s.* Befestigungsschelle *f*.

mourn [mɔːn] **I** *v/i.* **1.** trauern, klagen (*at, over* über *acc.*; *for, over* um); **2.** Trauer(kleidung) tragen, trauern; **II** *v/t.* *j-n* betrauern, *a. et.* beklagen, trauern um *j-n*; '**mourn·er** [-nə] *s.* Trauernde(r *m*) *f*, Leidtragende(r *m*) *f*; '**mourn·ful** [-fʊl] *adj.* □ trauervoll, traurig, düster, Trauer...

mourn·ing ['mɔːnɪŋ] **I** *s.* **1.** Trauer(n *n*) *f*; *national* ~ Staatstrauer; **2.** Trauer(-kleidung) *f*: *in* ~ in Trauer; *go into* (*out of*) ~ Trauer anlegen (die Trauer ablegen); **II** *adj.* □ **3.** trauernd; **4.** Trauer...: ~ *band* Trauerband *n*, -flor *m*; ~ **bor·der**, ~ **edge** *s.* Trauerrand *m*; ~ **pa·per** *s.* Pa'pier *n* mit Trauerrand.

mouse [maʊs] **I** *pl.* **mice** [maɪs] *s.* **1.** *zo.* Maus *f*: ~*trap* Mausefalle *f* (*a. fig.*); **2.** *pl. a.* **mous·es** *Computer*: Maus *f*; **3.** ⚒ Zugleine *f* mit Gewicht; **4.** F Feigling *m*; **5.** *sl.* ,blaues Auge', ,Veilchen' *n*; **II** *v/i.* [maʊz] **6.** mausen, Mäuse fangen; ~ **but·ton** *s. Computer*: Maustaste *f*; '~**click** *s. Computer*: Mausklick *m*; '~**col·o(u)red** *adj.* mausfarbig, -grau; '~**mat** *s.*, '~**pad** *s. Computer*: 'Mousepad *n*; ~ **po·ta·to** *s. sl.* 'Mouse-Po,tato *f* (*j-d, der unentwegt am Computer sitzt*).

mousse [muːs] *s.* **1.** Mousse *f*, Schaumspeise *f*; **2.** *a. styling* ~ Schaumfestiger *m*.

mous·tache [mə'stɑːʃ] *s.* Schnurrbart *m* (*a. zo.*).

mous·y ['maʊsɪ] *adj.* **1.** von Mäusen heimgesucht; **2.** mausartig; mausgrau; **3.** *fig.* grau, trüb; **4.** *fig.* leise; furchtsam; farblos; unscheinbar.

mouth [maʊθ] **I** *pl.* **mouths** [maʊðz] *s.* **1.** Mund *m*: *give* ~ Laut geben, anschlagen (*Hund*); *by word* (*od. way*) *of* ~ mündlich; *keep one's* ~ *shut* F den Mund halten; *shut s.o.'s* ~ *j-m* den Mund stopfen; *stop s.o.'s* ~ *j-m* (durch Bestechung) den Mund stopfen; *down in the* ~ F niedergeschlagen, bedrückt; → *wrong* 2; **2.** Maul *n*, Schnauze *f*, Rachen *m* (*Tier*); **3.** Mündung *f* (*Fluss, Kanone etc.*); Öffnung *f* (*Flasche, Sack*); Ein-, Ausgang *m* (*Höhle, Röhre etc.*); Ein-, Ausfahrt *f* (*Hafen etc.*); ♪ → *mouthpiece* 1; **4.** ☉ *a)* Mundloch *n*, b) Schnauze *f*, c) Öffnung *f*, d) Gichtöffnung *f* (*Hochofen*), e) Abstichloch *n* (*Hoch-, Schmelzofen*); **II** *v/t.* [maʊð] **5.** (*bsd. affek'tiert od. gespreizt*) laut sprechen; **6.** *Worte* (*unhörbar*) mit den Lippen formen; **7.** in den Mund *od.* ins Maul nehmen; '**mouth·ful** [-fʊl] *pl.* **-fuls** *s.* **1.** *ein* Mund voll, Brocken *m* (*a. fig. ellenlanges Wort*); **2.** kleine Menge; **3.** *sl.* großes Wort.

mouth| or·gan *s.* ♪ **1.** 'Mundhar,monika *f*; **2.** Panflöte *f*; '~**piece** *s.* **1.** ♪ Mundstück *n*, Ansatz *m*; **2.** ☉ a) Schalltrichter *m*, Sprechmuschel *f*, b) Mundstück *n* (*a. e-r Tabakspfeife od. Gasmaske*), Tülle *f*; **3.** *fig.* Sprachrohr *n* (*a. Person*); ⚓ *sl.* (Straf)Verteidiger *m*; **4.** Gebiss *n* (*Pferdezaum*); **5.** *Boxen*: Zahnschutz *m*; ,~**to-**' **res·pi·ra·tion** *s.* ⚕ Mund-zu-Mund-Beatmung *f*; '~**wash** *s.* Mund-

wasser *n*; '~-,**wa·ter·ing** *adj.* lecker.

mov·a·bil·i·ty [,muːvə'bɪlətɪ] *s.* Beweglichkeit *f*, Bewegbarkeit *f*.

mov·a·ble ['muːvəbl] **I** *adj.* □ **1.** beweglich (*a.* ☉; *a.* ⚓ *Eigentum, Feiertag*); bewegbar; ~ *goods* → 5; **2.** a) verschiebbar, verstellbar, b) fahrbar; **3.** ☿ ortsveränderlich; **II** *s.* **4.** *pl.* Möbel *pl.*; **5.** *pl.* ⚓ Mo'bilien *pl.*, bewegliche Habe; ~ *kid·ney* *s.* ⚕ Wanderniere *f*.

move [muːv] *v/t.* **1.** fortbewegen, -rücken, von der Stelle bewegen, verschieben (*a. Textstelle, Datei auf dem Computer*); ✕ *Einheit* verlegen: ~ *up* a) *Truppen* heranbringen, b) *ped. Brit. Schüler* versetzen; F ~ *it* Tempo!; **2.** entfernen, fortbringen, -schaffen; **3.** bewegen (*a. fig.*), in Bewegung setzen *od.* halten, (an)treiben: ~ *on* vorwärts treiben; **4.** *fig.* bewegen, rühren, ergreifen: *be* ~*d to tears* zu Tränen gerührt sein; **5.** *j-n* veranlassen, bewegen, hinreißen (*to* zu): ~ *to anger* erzürnen; **6.** *Schach etc.*: e-n Zug machen mit, ziehen; **7.** *et.* beantragen, Antrag stellen auf (*acc.*), vorschlagen: ~ *an amendment* parl. e-n Abänderungsantrag stellen; **8.** *Antrag* stellen, einbringen; **II** *v/i.* **9.** sich bewegen, sich rühren, sich regen; ☉ laufen, in Gang sein (*Maschine etc.*); **10.** sich fortbewegen, gehen, fahren: ~ *on* weitergehen: ~ *with the times* *fig.* mit der Zeit gehen; **11.** sich entfernen, abziehen, abmarschieren; *wegen Wohnungswechsels* ('um)ziehen (*to* nach): ~ *in* einziehen; *if* ~*d* falls verzogen; **12.** fortschreiten, weitergehen (*Vorgang*); **13.** verkehren, sich bewegen: ~ *in good society* **14.** a) vorgehen, Schritte unter'nehmen (*in s.th.* in e-r Sache, *against* gegen), b) *a.* ~ *in* handeln, zupacken, losschlagen: *he* ~*d quickly*; **15.** ~ *for* beantragen, (e-n) Antrag stellen auf (*acc.*); ~ *that* beantragen, dass; **16.** *Schach etc.*: e-n Zug machen, ziehen; **17.** *a.* sich entleeren (*Darm*); **18.** ~ *up* ⚕ anziehen, steigen (*Preise*); **III** *s.* **19.** (Fort)Bewegung *f*, Aufbruch *m*; 'Übergang *m*: *on the* ~ in Bewegung, auf den Beinen; *get a* ~ *on! sl.* Tempo!, mach(t) schon!; *make a* ~ a) aufbrechen, sich (von der Stelle) rühren, b) → 14 b; **20.** 'Umzug *m*; **21.** *Schach etc.*: Zug *m*; *fig.* Schritt *m*, Maßnahme *f*: *a clever* ~ ein kluger Schachzug (*od.* Schritt); *make the first* ~ den ersten Schritt tun; '**move·ment** [-mənt] *s.* **1.** Bewegung *f* (*a. fig., pol., eccl., paint. etc.*); ✕, ⚒ (Truppen- *od.* Flotten)Bewegung *f*: ~ *by air* Lufttransport *m*; **2.** *mst pl.* Handeln *n*, Schritte *pl.*, Maßnahmen *pl.*; **3.** (rasche) Entwicklung, Fortschreiten *n* (*von Ereignissen, e-r Handlung*); **4.** Bestrebung *f*, Ten'denz *f*, (mo'derne) Richtung; **5.** ♪ a) Satz *m*: *a* ~ *of a sonata*, b) Tempo *n*; **6.** ☉ a) Bewegung *f*, b) Lauf *m* (*Maschine*), c) Gang-, Gehwerk *n* (*der Uhr*), 'Antriebsmecha,nismus *m*; **7.** *a.* ~ *of the bowels* ⚓ Stuhlgang *m*; **8.** ♀ (Kurs-, Preis)Bewegung *f*; 'Umsatz *m* (*Börse, Markt*): *downward* ~ Senkung *f*, Fallen *n*; *retrograde* ~ rückläufige Bewegung; *upward* ~ Steigen *n*, Aufwärtsbewegung *f* (*der Preise*); '**mov·er** [-və] *s.* **1.** *fig.* treibende Kraft, Triebkraft *f*, Antrieb *m* (*a. Person*); **2.** ☉ Triebwerk *n*, Motor *m*; → *prime mover*; **3.** Antragsteller(in); **4.** *Am.* a) Spedi'teur *m*, b) (Möbel)Packer *m*.

mov·ie ['muːvɪ] *Am.* F **I** *s.* **1.** Film(streifen) *m*; **2.** *pl.* a) Filmwesen *n*, b) Kino *n*, c) Kinovorstellung *f*: *go to the* ~*s* ins

Kino gehen; **II** *adj.* **3.** Film..., Kino..., Lichtspiel...: **~ camera** Filmkamera *f*; **~ projector** Filmprojektor *m*; **~ star** Filmstar *m*; '**~,go·er** *s. Am.* F Kinobesucher(in).

mov·ing ['muːvɪŋ] *adj.* □ **1.** beweglich, sich bewegend; **2.** bewegend, treibend: **~ power** treibende Kraft; **3.** a) rührend, bewegend, b) eindringlich, packend; **~ coil** ⚡ Drehspule *f*; **~ magnet** *s.* 'Drehma,gnet *m*; **~ pic·ture** F → **motion picture**; **~ stair·case** *s.* Rolltreppe *f*; **~ van** *s.* Möbelwagen *m*.

mow¹ [məʊ] **I** *v/t.* [*a. irr.*] (ab)mähen, schneiden; **~ down** niedermähen (*a. fig.*); **II** *v/i.* [*a. irr.*] mähen.

mow² [məʊ] *s.* **1.** Getreidegarbe *f*, Heuhaufen *m*; **2.** Heu-, Getreideboden *m*.

mow·er ['məʊə] *s.* **1.** Mäher(in), Schnitter(in); **2.** a) Rasenmäher *m*, b) → **mow·ing ma·chine** ['məʊɪŋ-] *s.* 'Mähma,schine *f*.

mown [məʊn] *p.p. von* **mow¹**.

Mr, Mr. → **mister** 1.

Mrs, Mrs. ['mɪsɪz] *s.* Frau *f* (*Anrede für verheiratete Frauen*): **Mrs Smith**.

Ms, Ms. [mɪz] *Anrede für Frauen ohne Berücksichtigung des Familienstandes.*

mu [mjuː] *s.* My *n* (*griechischer Buchstabe*).

much [mʌtʃ] **I** *s.* **1.** Menge *f*, große Sache, Besondere(s) *n*: **nothing ~** nichts Besonderes; **it did not come to ~** es kam nicht viel dabei heraus; **think ~ of s.o.** viel von j-m halten; **he is not ~ of a dancer** er ist kein großer Tänzer; → **make** 21; **II** *adj.* **2.** viel: **too ~** zu viel; **III** *adv.* **3.** sehr: **~ to my regret** sehr zu m-m Bedauern; **4.** (*in Zssgn*) viel...: **~-admired**; **5.** (*vor comp.*) viel, weit: **~ stronger**; **6.** (*vor sup.*) bei weitem, weitaus: **~ the oldest**; **7.** fast: **he did it in ~ the same way** er tat es auf ungefähr die gleiche Weise; **it is ~ the same thing** es ist ziemlich dasselbe; *Besondere Redewendungen:*

~ as I would like so gern ich (auch) möchte; **as ~ as** so viel wie; **he did not as ~ as write** er schrieb nicht einmal; **as ~ again** noch einmal so viel; **he said as ~** das war (ungefähr) der Sinn s-r Worte; **this is as ~ as to say** das heißt mit anderen Worten; **as ~ as to say** als wenn er (*etc.*) sagen wollte; **I thought as ~** das habe ich mir gedacht; **so ~** a) so sehr, b) so viel, c) lauter, nichts als; **so ~ the better** umso besser; **so ~ for our plans** so viel (wäre also) zu unseren Plänen (zu sagen); **not so ~ as** nicht einmal; **without so ~ as to move** ohne sich auch nur zu bewegen; **so ~ so** (und zwar) so sehr; **~ less** a) viel weniger, b) geschweige denn; **~ like a child** ganz wie ein Kind.

much·ly ['mʌtʃlɪ] *adv. obs. od. humor.* sehr, viel, besonders; '**much·ness** [-tʃnɪs] *s.* große Menge: **much of a ~** F ziemlich *od.* praktisch dasselbe.

mu·ci·lage ['mjuːsɪlɪdʒ] *s.* **1.** ♀ (Pflanzen)Schleim *m*; **2.** *bsd. Am.* Klebstoff *m*, Gummilösung *f*; **mu·ci·lag·i·nous** [,mjuːsɪ'lædʒɪnəs] *adj.* **1.** schleimig; **2.** klebrig.

muck [mʌk] **I** *s.* **1.** Mist *m*, Dung *m*; **2.** Kot *m*, Dreck *m*, Unrat *m*, Schmutz *m* (*a. fig.*); **3.** *Brit.* F Blödsinn *m*, 'Mist' *m*: **make a ~ of** → 6; **II** *v/t.* **4.** düngen; **a. ~ out** ausmisten; **5.** *oft* **~ up** F beschmutzen; **6.** *sl.* verpfuschen, verhunzen, 'vermasseln'; **III** *v/i.* **7.** *mst* **~ a-bout** *sl.* a) her'umlungern, b) her'umpfuschen (*with an dat.*), c) her'umal-

bern; **8.** **~ in** F mit anpacken; '**muck·er** [-kə] *s.* **1.** *sl.* a) ,Blödmann' *m*, b) ,Kumpel' *m*; **2.** ✗ Lader *m*: **~'s car** Minenhund *m*; **3.** *sl.* a) schwerer Sturz, b) *fig.* ,Reinfall' *m*: **come a ~** auf die ,Schnauze' fallen, *fig. a.* ,reinfallen'.

'**muck|·hill** *s.* Mist-, Dreckhaufen *m*; '**~·rake** *v/i. fig.* im Schmutz her'umwühlen; *Am. sl.* Skan'dale aufdecken; '**~,rak·er** *s. Am.* Skan'dalmacher *m*.

muck·y ['mʌkɪ] *adj.* schmutzig, dreckig (*a. fig.*).

mu·cous ['mjuːkəs] *adj.* schleimig, Schleim...: **~ membrane** Schleimhaut *f*; '**mu·cus** [-kəs] *s. biol.* Schleim *m*.

mud [mʌd] *s.* **1.** Schlamm *m*, Matsch *m*: **~ and snow tyres** (*Am.* **tires**) *mot.* Matsch-u.-Schnee-Reifen; **2.** Mo'rast *m*, Kot *m*, Schmutz *m* (*alle a. fig.*): **drag in the ~** *fig.* in den Schmutz ziehen; **stick in the ~** im Schlamm stecken bleiben, *fig.* aus dem Dreck nicht mehr herauskommen; **sling** (*od.* **throw**) **~ at s.o.** *fig.* j-n mit Schmutz bewerfen; **his name is ~ with me** er ist für mich erledigt; **~ in your eye!** F prost!; → **clear** 1; '**~·bath** *s.* ✿ Moor-, Schlammbad *n*.

mud·di·ness ['mʌdɪnɪs] *s.* **1.** Schlammigkeit *f*, Trübheit *f* (*a. des Lichts*); **2.** Schmutzigkeit *f*.

mud·dle ['mʌdl] **I** *s.* **1.** Durchein'ander *n*, Unordnung *f*, Wirrwarr *m*: **make a ~ of s.th.** et. durcheinander bringen *od.* ,vermasseln'; **get into a ~** in Schwierigkeiten geraten; **2.** Verworrenheit *f*, Unklarheit *f*: **be in a ~** in Verwirrung *od.* verwirrt sein; **II** *v/t.* **3.** *Gedanken etc.* verwirren: **~ up** verwechseln, durcheinander werfen; **4.** in Unordnung bringen, durchein'ander bringen; **5.** ,benebeln' (*bsd. durch Alkohol*): **~ one's brains** sich benebeln; **6.** verpfuschen, verderben; **III** *v/i.* **7.** pfuschen, stümpern, ,wursteln': **~ about** herumwursteln (*with an dat.*); **~ on** weiterwursteln; **~ through** sich durchwursteln; '**mud·dle·dom** [-dəm] *s. humor.* Durchein'ander *n*; '**mud·dle,head·ed** *adj.* wirr(köpfig), kon'fus; '**mud·dler** [-lə] *s.* **1.** j-d, der sich 'durchwurstelt; Wirrkopf *m*; Pfuscher *m*; **2.** *Am.* ('Um-) Rührlöffel *m*.

mud·dy ['mʌdɪ] **I** *adj.* □ **1.** schlammig, trüb(e) (*a. Licht*); Schlamm...: **~ soil 2.** schmutzig; **3.** *fig.* unklar, verworren, kon'fus; **4.** verschwommen (*Farbe*); **II** *v/t.* **5.** trüben; **6.** beschmutzen.

'**mud|·guard** *s.* **1.** a) *mot.* Kotflügel *m*, b) Schutzblech *n* (*Fahrrad*); **2.** ❂ Schmutzfänger *m*; '**~·hole** *s.* **1.** Schlammloch *n*; **2.** ❂ Schlammablass *m*; '**~·lark** *s.* Gassenjunge *m*, Dreckspatz *m*; '**~·pack** *s.* ✿ Fangopackung *f*; '**~,sling·er** [-,slɪŋə] *s.* F Verleumder(in); '**~,sling·ing** [-,slɪŋɪŋ] F **I** *s.* Beschmutzung *f*, Verleumdung *f*; **II** *adj.* verleumderisch.

mues·li ['mjuːzlɪ] *s.* Müsli *n*.

muff [mʌf] **I** *s.* **1.** Muff *m*; **2.** F *sport. u. fig.* ,Patzer' *m*; **3.** F ,Flasche' *f*, Stümper *m*; **4.** ❂ a) Stutzen *m*, b) Muffe *f*; **II** *v/t.* **5.** F *sport u. fig.* ,verpatzen'; **III** *v/i.* **6.** F ,patzen'.

muf·fin ['mʌfɪn] *s.* Muffin *n*: a) *Brit.* Hefeteigsemmel *f*, b) *Am.* kleine süße Semmel.

muf·fle ['mʌfl] **I** *v/t.* **1.** *oft* **~ up** einhüllen, einwickeln; *Ruder* um'wickeln; **2.** *Ton etc.* dämpfen (*a. fig.*); **II** *s.* **3.** *metall.* Muffel *f*: **~ furnace** Muffelofen *m*; '**muf·fler** [-lə] *s.* **1.** (dicker) Schal *m*, Halstuch *n*; **2.** ❂ Schalldämpfer *m*; *mot.* Auspufftopf *m*;

♪ Dämpfer *m*.

muf·ti ['mʌftɪ] *s.* **1.** Mufti *m*; **2.** ✗ Zi'vilkleidung *f*: **in ~** in Zivil.

mug [mʌg] *s.* **1.** Krug *m*; **2.** Becher *m*; **3.** *sl.* a) Vi'sage *f*, Gesicht *n*: **~ shot** Kopfbild *n* (*bsd. für das Verbrecheralbum*), *Film etc.*: Großaufnahme *f*, b) ,Fresse' *f*, Mund *m*, c) Gri'masse *f*; **4.** *Brit. sl.* a) Trottel *m*, b) Büffler *m*, Streber *m*; **5.** *Am. sl.* a) Boxer *m*, b) Ga'nove *m*; **II** *v/t.* **6.** *sl. bsd. Verbrecher* fotografieren; **7.** *sl.* über'fallen, niederschlagen u. ausrauben; **8.** *a.* **~ up** *Brit. sl.* ,büffeln', ,ochsen'; **III** *v/i.* **9.** *sl.* Gri'massen schneiden; **10.** *Am. sl.* schmunsen'; '**mug·ger** [-gə] *s. sl.* Straßenräuber *m*.

mug·gi·ness ['mʌgɪnɪs] *s.* **1.** Schwüle *f*; **2.** Muffigkeit *f*; '**mug·ging** [-gɪŋ] *s. sl.* 'Raub,überfall *m* (*auf der Straße*); **mug·gy** ['mʌgɪ] *adj.* **1.** schwül (*Wetter*); **2.** dumpfig, muffig.

'**mug·wort** *s.* ♀ Beifuß *m*.

mug·wump ['mʌgwʌmp] *s. Am.* **1.** F ,hohes Tier'; **2.** *pol. sl.* a) Unabhängige(r *m*) *f*, Einzelgänger(in), b) ,Rebell(in)', Abtrünnige(r *m*) *f*.

mu·lat·to [mjuː'lætəʊ] *I pl.* **-toes** *s.* Mu'latte *m*, Mu'lattin *f*; **II** *adj.* Mulatten...

mul·ber·ry ['mʌlbərɪ] *s.* **1.** Maulbeerbaum *m*; **2.** Maulbeere *f*.

mulch [mʌltʃ] ✿ **I** *s.* ✿ Mulch *m*; **II** *v/t.* mulchen.

mulct [mʌlkt] **I** *s.* **1.** Geldstrafe *f*; **II** *v/t.* **2.** mit e-r Geldstrafe belegen; **3.** a) j-n betrügen (*of* um), b) *Geld etc.* ,abknöpfen' (*from s.o.* j-m).

mule [mjuːl] *s.* **1.** *zo.* a) Maultier *n*, b) Maulesel *m*; **2.** *biol.* Bastard *m*, Hybride *f*; **3.** *fig.* sturer Kerl, Dickkopf *m*; **4.** ❂ a) (Motor)Schlepper *m*, Traktor *m*, b) 'Förderlokomo,tive *f*, c) 'Mule(spinn)ma,schine *f* (*Spinnerei*); **5.** Pan'toffel *m*; **mule jen·ny** → **mule** 4 c; **mule skin·ner**, *Am.* F **mu·le·teer** [,mjuːlɪ'tɪə] *s.* Maultiertreiber *m*; **mule track** *s.* Saumpfad *m*.

mul·ish ['mjuːlɪʃ] *adj.* □ störrisch, stur.

mull¹ [mʌl] **I** *v/t.* F verpatzen, verpfuschen; **II** *v/i.* **~ over** F *Am.* nachdenken, -grübeln über (*acc.*).

mull² [mʌl] *v/t. Getränk* heiß machen u. (süß) würzen: **~ed wine** Glühwein *m*.

mull³ [mʌl] *s.* (✿ Verband)Mull *m*.

mull⁴ [mʌl] *s. Scot.* Vorgebirge *n*.

mul·la(h) ['mʌlə] *s. eccl.* Mulla *m*.

mul·le(i)n ['mʌlɪn] *s.* ♀ Königskerze *f*, Wollkraut *n*.

mul·ler ['mʌlə] *s.* ❂ Reibstein *m*.

mul·let ['mʌlɪt] *s. ichth.* **1.** *a.* **grey ~** Meeräsche *f*; **2.** *a.* **red ~** Seebarbe *f*.

mul·li·gan ['mʌlɪgən] *s. Am.* F Eintopfgericht *n*.

mul·li·ga·taw·ny [,mʌlɪgə'tɔːnɪ] *s.* Currysuppe *f*.

mul·li·grubs ['mʌlɪgrʌbz] *s. pl.* F **1.** Bauchweh *n*; **2.** miese Laune.

mul·lion ['mʌlɪən] *s.* ◬ Mittelpfosten *m* (*Fenster etc.*).

mul·tan·gu·lar [mʌl'tæŋgjʊlə] *adj.* vielwink(e)lig, -eckig.

mul·te·i·ty [mʌl'tiːətɪ] *s.* Vielheit *f*.

multi- [mʌltɪ] *in Zssgn* viel..., mehr..., ...reich, Mehrfach..., Multi...

mul·ti ['mʌltɪ] *s.* ✞ F ,Multi' *m*.

'**mul·ti,ax·le drive** *s. mot.* Mehrachsenantrieb *m*; '**mul·ti,cast·ing** *s. Internet, Server-Technologie*: 'Multi,casting *n* (*Fähigkeit e-s Servers, einen einzigen Datenstrom gleichzeitig vielen Zugreifenden zur Verfügung zu stellen*); '**mul·ti,col·o(u)r**, '**mul·ti,col·o(u)red** *adj.* mehrfarbig, Mehrfarben...; ,**mul·ti'cul-**

tur·al *adj.* □ 'multikultu,rell; ,**mul·ti**-'**en·gine(d**) *adj.* 'mehrmo,torig.
mul·ti·far·i·ous [,mʌltɪ'feərɪəs] *adj.* □ mannigfaltig.
'**mul·ti·form** *adj.* vielförmig, -gestaltig; ,**mul·ti**'**func·tio·nal** *adj.* □ ,multifunktio'nal: ~ *keyboard Computer:* 'Multifunktionstasta'tur *f;* '**mul·ti·graph** *typ.* I *s.* Ver'vielfältigungsma,schine *f;* II *v/t. u. v/i.* vervielfältigen; '**mul·ti·grid tube** *s.* ⚡ Mehrgitterröhre *f;* '**mul·ti**'**lat·er·al** *adj.* **1.** vielseitig (*a. fig.*); **2.** *pol.* mehrseitig, multilate'ral; ,**mul·ti**'**lin·gual** *adj.* mehrsprachig; ,**mul·ti**'**me·di·a** I *s. pl.* Medienverbund *m,* Multi'media *pl.;* II *adj.* ,multimedi'al, Multimedia...: ~ *group* Medienkonzern *m;* ~ *presentation* Multimediapräsentation *f;* ,**mul·timil·lion**'**aire** *s.* 'Multimillio,när *m;* ,**mul·ti·na·tion·al** I *adj. bsd.* 🅣 multinatio'nal; II *s.* multinatio'naler Kon-'zern, ,Multi' *m;* **mul·tip·a·rous** [mʌl'tɪpərəs] *adj.* mehrgebärend; ,**mul·ti**'**par·tite** *adj.* **1.** vielteilig; **2.** → *multilateral* 2.

mul·ti·ple ['mʌltɪpl] I *adj.* □ **1.** viel-, mehrfach; **2.** mannigfaltig; **3.** *biol.,* 🌶, 🅰 mul'tipel; **4.** ⚙, ⚡ a) Mehr(fach)..., Vielfach...: ~ *switch,* b) Parallel...; **5.** *ling.* zs.-gesetzt (*Satz*); II *s.* **6.** Vielfache(s) *n* (*a.* 🅰); **7.** *a.* ~ *connection* ⚡ Paral'lelschaltung *f:* ~ *in* ~ parallel (geschaltet); ~ *birth s.* 🅑 Mehrlingsgeburt *f;* ,~'**choice ques·tion** *s.* Auswahlfrage *f;* ,~'**disk clutch** *s. mot.* La'mellenkupplung *f;* ~ *fac·tors s. pl. biol.* poly-'mere Gene *pl.;* ,~'**par·ty** *adj. pol.* Mehrparteien...: ~ *system;* ~ *plug s.* ⚡ Mehrfachstecker *m;* ~ **pro·duc·tion** *s.* 🅣 Serienherstellung *f;* ~ **re·tail·er** *s.* Einzelhandelskette *f,* Ladenkette *f;* ~ **root** *s.* 🅰 mehrwertige Wurzel; ~ **scle·ro·sis** *s.* 🅑 mul'tiple Skle'rose; ~ **shop** *s.,* ~ **store** *s.* 🅣 Ketten-, Fili'algeschäft *n;* ~ **thread** *s.* ⚙ mehrgängiges Gewinde.

mul·ti·plex ['mʌltɪpleks] I *adj.* **1.** mehr-, vielfach; **2.** ⚡, *tel.* Mehrfach...(-betrieb, -telegrafie *etc.*); II *v/t.* **3.** ⚡, *tel.* a) in Mehrfachschaltung betreiben, b) gleichzeitig senden; '**mul·ti·pli·a·ble** [-plaɪəbl] *adj.* multiplizierbar; **mul·ti·pli·cand** [,mʌltɪplɪ'kænd] *s.* 🅰 Multipli-'kand *m;* '**mul·ti·pli·cate** [-plɪkeɪt] *adj.* mehr-, vielfach; **mul·ti·pli·ca·tion** [,mʌltɪplɪ'keɪʃn] *s.* **1.** Vermehrung *f* (*a.* ♀); **2.** 🅰 a) Multiplikati'on *f:* ~ *sign* Mal-, Multiplikationszeichen *n;* ~ *table* das Einmaleins, b) Vervielfachung *f;* **3.** ⚙ (Ge'triebe)Über,setzung *f;* '**mul·ti·plic·i·ty** [,mʌltɪ'plɪsətɪ] *s.* **1.** Vielfalt *f;* **2.** Menge *f,* Vielzahl *f,* -heit *f;* **3.** 🅰 a) Mehr-, Vielwertigkeit *f,* b) Mehrfachheit *f;* '**mul·ti·pli·er** [-plaɪə] *s.* **1.** Vermehrer *m;* **2.** 🅰 a) Multipli'kator *m,* b) Multipli'zierma,schine *f;* **3.** *phys.* ⚡ Verstärker *m,* b) Vergrößerungslinse *f,* Lupe *f;* **4.** ⚡ 'Vor- od. 'Neben,widerstand *m;* **5.** ⚙ Über'setzung *f;* '**mul·ti·ply** [-plaɪ] I *v/t.* **1.** vermehren (*a. biol.*), vervielfältigen; ,~**ing glass** *opt.* Vergrö-ßerungsglas *n, pl.* Vergrö-ßerungsgläser; **2.** 🅰 multiplizieren (*by* mit); **3.** ⚡ vielfachschalten; II *v/i.* **4.** multiplizieren; **5.** sich vermehren *od.* vervielfachen.

,**mul·ti**'**po·lar** *adj.* ⚡ viel-, mehrpolig; ,~'**pur·pose** *adj.* Mehrzweck...: ~ *aircraft;* ,~'**ra·cial** *adj.* gemischtrassig, Vielvölker...: ~ *state;* '~,**seat·er** *s.* ✈ Mehrsitzer *m;* '~,**speed** *adj.* ⚙ Mehrgang...; '~**stage** *adj.* ⚙, ⚡ mehrstufig, Mehrstufen...: ~ *rocket;* ,~'**sto·r(e)y** *adj.* vielstöckig: ~ *building* Hochhaus

n; ~ *parking garage,* ~ *car park* Park-(hoch)haus *n;* '~,**task·ing** *s. Computer:* 'Multi,tasking *n* (*gleichzeitiger Betrieb mehrerer Programmabläufe*).
mul·ti·tude ['mʌltɪtjuːd] *s.* **1.** große Zahl, Menge *f;* **2.** Vielheit *f;* **3.** Menschenmenge *f: the* ~ der große Haufen, die Masse; **mul·ti·tu·di·nous** [,mʌltɪ'tjuːdɪnəs] *adj.* □ **1.** (sehr) zahlreich; **2.** mannigfaltig, vielfältig.
,**mul·ti**'**va·lent** *adj.* 🅰 mehr-, vielwertig; '~**way** *adj.* ⚡ mehrwegig: ~ *plug* Vielfachstecker *m.*

mum[1] [mʌm] F I *int.* pst!, still!; ~*'s the word!* (aber) Mund halten!; II *adj.* still, stumm.
mum[2] [mʌm] *v/i.* **1.** sich vermummen; **2.** Mummenschanz treiben.
mum[3] [mʌm] *s.* F Mami *f.*
mum·ble ['mʌmbl] I *v/t. u. v/i.* **1.** murmeln; **2.** mummeln, knabbern; II *s.* **3.** Gemurmel *n.*
Mum·bo Jum·bo [,mʌmbəʊ'dʒʌmbəʊ] *s.* **1.** Popanz *m;* **2.** ℘ a) Hokus'pokus *m,* fauler Zauber, b) Kauderwelsch *n.*
mum·mer ['mʌmə] *s.* **1.** Vermummte(r *m*) *f,* Maske *f* (*Person*); **2.** *contp.* Komödi'ant *m;* '**mum·mer·y** [-ərɪ] *s. contp.* Mummenschanz *m,* Maske'rade *f;* **2.** Hokus'pokus *m.*
mum·mi·fi·ca·tion [,mʌmɪfɪ'keɪʃn] *s.* **1.** Mumifizierung *f;* **2.** 🌶 trockener Brand; **mum·mi·fy** ['mʌmɪfaɪ] I *v/t.* mumifizieren; II *v/i. a. fig.* vertrocknen, -dorren.
mum·my[1] ['mʌmɪ] *s.* **1.** Mumie *f* (*a. fig.*); **2.** Brei *m,* breiige Masse.
mum·my[2] ['mʌmɪ] *s.* F Mutti *f.*
mump [mʌmp] *v/i.* **1.** schmollen, schlecht gelaunt sein; **2.** F schnorren, betteln; '**mump·ish** [-pɪʃ] *adj.* □ mürrisch.
mumps [mʌmps] *s. pl.* **1.** *sg. konstr.* 🌶 Mumps *m;* **2.** miese Laune.
munch [mʌntʃ] *v/t. u. v/i.* schmatzend kauen, ,mampfen'.
Mun·chau·sen·ism [mʌn'tʃɔːzɪzəm] *s.* Münchhausi'ade *f,* fan'tastische Geschichte.
mun·dane ['mʌndeɪn] *adj.* □ **1.** weltlich, Welt...; **2.** irdisch, weltlich: ~ *poetry* weltliche Dichtung; **3.** pro'saisch, nüchtern.
mu·nic·i·pal [mjuː'nɪsɪpl] *adj.* □ **1.** städtisch, Stadt...; kommu'nal, Gemeinde...: ~ *elections* Kommunalwahlen; **2.** Selbstverwaltungs...: ~ *town* → *municipality* 1; **3.** Land(es)...: ~ *law* Landesrecht *n;* ~ *bank s.* 🅣 Kommu'nalbank *f;* ~ *bonds s. pl.* 🅣 Kommu'nalobligati,onen *pl.,* Stadtanleihen *pl.;* ~ *cor·po·ra·tion s.* **1.** Gemeindebehörde *f;* **2.** Körperschaft *f* des öffentlichen Rechts.
mu·nic·i·pal loan *s.* Kommu'nalanleihe *f;* ~ **rates,** ~ **tax·es** *s. pl.* Gemeindesteuern *pl.,* -abgaben *pl.*
mu·nic·i·pal·i·ty [mjuː,nɪsɪ'pælətɪ] *s.* **1.** Stadt *f* mit Selbstverwaltung; Stadtbezirk *m;* **2.** Stadtbehörde *f,* -verwaltung *f;* **mu·nic·i·pal·ize** [mjuː'nɪsɪpəlaɪz] *v/t.* **1.** *Stadt* mit Obrigkeitsgewalt ausstatten; **2.** *Betrieb etc.* kommunalisieren.
mu·nif·i·cence [mjuː'nɪfɪsns] *s.* Freigebigkeit *f,* Großzügigkeit *f;* **mu·nif·i·cent** [-nt] *adj.* □ freigebig, großzügig.
mu·ni·ment ['mjuːnɪmənt] *s.* **1.** *pl.* 🖹 Rechtsurkunde *f;* **2.** Urkundensammlung *f,* Ar'chiv *n.*
mu·ni·tion [mjuː'nɪʃn] I *s. mst pl.* 'Kriegsmateri,al *n,* -vorräte *pl., bsd.* Muniti'on *f:* ~ *plant* Rüstungsfabrik *f;* ~ *worker* Munitionsarbeiter(in); II *v/t.*

mit Materi'al *od.* Muniti'on versehen, ausrüsten.
mu·ral ['mjʊərəl] I *adj.* Mauer..., Wand...; II *s. a.* ~ *painting* Wandgemälde *n.*
mur·der ['mɜːdə] I *s.* **1.** (*of*) Mord *m* (an *dat.*), Ermordung *f* (*gen.*): ~ *will out fig.* die Sonne bringt es an den Tag; *the* ~ *is out fig.* das Geheimnis ist gelüftet; *cry blue* ~ F zetermordio schreien; *get away with* ~ F sich alles erlauben können; *it was* ~! F es war fürchterlich!; II *v/t.* **2.** (er)morden; **3.** *fig.* (*a. Sprache*) verschandeln, verhunzen; **4.** *sport* F ,ausein'ander nehmen'; '**mur·der·er** [-ərə] *s.* Mörder *m;* '**mur·der·ess** [-ərɪs] *s.* Mörderin *f;* '**mur·der·ous** [-dərəs] *adj.* □ **1.** mörderisch (*a. fig. Hitze, Tempo etc.*); **2.** Mord...: ~ *intent;* **3.** tödlich, todbringend; **4.** blutdürstig; **mur·der squad** *s. Brit.* 'Mordkommissi,on *f.*
mure [mjʊə] *v/t.* **1.** einmauern; **2.** *mst* ~ *up* einsperren.
mu·ri·ate ['mjʊərɪət] *s.* 🌶 **1.** Muri'at *n,* Hydrochlo'rid *n;* **2.** 'Kaliumchlo,rid *n;* **mu·ri·at·ic** [,mjʊərɪ'ætɪk] *adj.* salzsauer: ~ *acid* Salzsäure *f.*
murk·y ['mɜːkɪ] *adj.* □ dunkel, düster, trüb (*alle a. fig.*).
mur·mur ['mɜːmə] I *s.* **1.** Murmeln *n,* (leises) Rauschen (*Wasser, Wind etc.*); **2.** Gemurmel *n;* **3.** Murren *n: without a* ~ ohne zu murren; **4.** 🌶 Geräusch *n;* II *v/i.* **5.** murmeln (*a. Wasser etc.*); **6.** murren (*at, against* gegen); III *v/t.* **7.** murmeln; '**mur·mur·ous** [-mərəs] *adj.* □ **1.** murmelnd; **2.** murrend.
Mur·phy's Law ['mɜːfɪz] *s.* Murphy's Gesetz *n* (*nach dem tatsächlich einmal schief geht, was schief gehen kann*).
mur·rain ['mʌrɪn] *s.* Viehseuche *f.*
mu·sac ['mjuːzæk] *s.* F *etwa:* leichte (*od.* sehr seichte) Musik, Hintergrundmusik *f.*
mus·ca·dine ['mʌskədɪn], '**mus·cat** [-kət], **mus·ca·tel** [,mʌskə'tel] *s.* Muska'teller(wein) *m,* -traube *f.*
mus·cle ['mʌsl] I *s.* **1.** *anat.* Muskel *m,* Muskelfleisch *n: not to move a* ~ *fig.* sich nicht rühren, nicht mit der Wimper zucken; **2.** *fig. a.* ~ *power* Muskelkraft *f;* **3.** *Am. sl.* Muskelprotz *m,* ,Schläger' *m;* **4.** *fig.* F Macht *f,* Einfluss *m,* ,Muskeln' *pl.;* II *v/i.* **5.** ~ *in bsd. Am.* F sich rücksichtslos eindrängen; '~**bound** *adj.: be* ~ eine überentwickelte Muskulatur haben; ~ **man** [mæn] *s. [irr.]* **1.** 'Muskelpa,ket *n,* -mann *m;* **2.** ,Schläger' *m.*
Mus·co·vite ['mʌskəʊvaɪt] I *s.* **1.** a) Mosko'witer(in), b) Russe *m,* Russin *f;* **2.** ℘ *min.* Musko'wit *m,* Kaliglimmer *m;* II *adj.* **3.** a) mosko'witisch, b) russisch.
mus·cu·lar ['mʌskjʊlə] *adj.* □ **1.** Muskel...: ~ *atrophy* Muskelschwund *m;* **2.** musku'lös; **mus·cu·lar·i·ty** [,mʌskjʊ'lærətɪ] *s.* Muskelkraft *f,* musku'löser Körperbau; '**mus·cu·la·ture** [-lətʃə] *s. anat.* Muskula'tur *f.*
Muse[1] [mjuːz] *s. myth.* Muse *f* (*fig. a.* ℘).
muse[2] [mjuːz] *v/i.* **1.** (nach)sinnen, (-)denken, (-)grübeln (*on, upon* über *acc.*); **2.** in Gedanken versunken sein, träumen; '**mus·er** [-zə] *s.* Träumer(in), Sinnende(r *m*) *f.*
mu·se·um [mjuː'zɪəm] *s.* Mu'seum *n:* ~ *piece* Museumsstück *n* (*a. fig.*).
mush[1] [mʌʃ] *s.* **1.** Brei *m,* Mus *n;* **2.** *Am.* (Mais)Brei *m;* **3.** F a) Gefühlsduse'lei *f,* b) sentimen'tales Zeug; **4.** *Radio:* Knistergeräusch *n:* ~ *area* Störgebiet *n.*

mush² [mʌʃ] *v/i. Am.* **1.** durch den Schnee stapfen; **2.** mit Hundeschlitten fahren.

mush·room ['mʌʃrʊm] **I** *s.* **1.** ♀ a) Ständerpilz *m*, b) *allg.* essbarer Pilz, *bsd.* Champignon *m*: *grow like* ~*s* → 6 a; **2.** *fig.* Em'porkömmling *m*; **II** *adj.* **3.** Pilz...; pilzförmig: ~ *bulb* ⚷ Pilzbirne *f*; ~ *cloud* Atompilz *m*; **4.** plötzlich entstanden; Eintags...: ~ *fame*; **III** *v/i.* **5.** Pilze sammeln; **6.** *fig.* a) wie Pilze aus dem Boden schießen, b) sich ausbreiten (*Flammen*); **IV** *v/t.* **7.** F Zigarette ausdrücken.

mush·y ['mʌʃɪ] *adj.* □ **1.** breiig, weich; **2.** *fig.* a) weichlich, b) F gefühlsduselig.

mu·sic ['mjuːzɪk] *s.* **1.** Mu'sik *f*, Tonkunst *f*; *konkr.* Kompositi'on(en *pl. coll.*) *f*: *face the* ~ F ,die Suppe auslöffeln'; *set to* ~ vertonen; **2.** Noten(blatt *n*) *pl.*: *play from* ~ vom Blatt spielen; **3.** *coll.* Musi'kalien *pl.*: ~ *shop* → *music house*; **4.** *fig.* Mu'sik *f*, Wohllaut *m*, Gesang *m*; **5.** (Mu'sik)Ka,pelle *f*.

mu·si·cal ['mjuːzɪkl] **I** *adj.* □ **1.** Musik...: ~ *history*; ~ *instrument*; **2.** me'lodisch; **3.** musi'kalisch (*Person, Komödie etc.*); **II** *s.* **4.** Musical *n*; **5.** F *für musical film*; ~ *art* *s.* (Kunst *f* der) Mu'sik *f*, Tonkunst *f*; ~ *box* *s. Brit.* Spieldose *f*; ~ *chairs* *s. pl.* ,Reise *f* nach Je'rusalem' (*Gesellschaftsspiel*); ~ *clock* *s.* Spieluhr *f*; ~ *film* *s.* Mu'sikfilm *m*; ~ *glass·es* *s. pl.* ♪ 'Glashar,monika *f*.

mu·si·cal·i·ty [,mjuːzɪ'kælətɪ], **mu·si·cal·ness** ['mjuːzɪklnɪs] *s.* **1.** Musikali'tät *f*; **2.** Wohlklang *m*.

'mu·sic|-ap,pre·ci'a·tion rec·ord *s.* Schallplatte *f* mit mu'sikkundlichem Kommen'tar; ~ *book* *s.* Notenheft *n*, -buch *n*; ~ *box* *s.* **1.** Spieldose *f*; **2.** → *jukebox*; ~ *hall* *s. Brit.* Varie'tee(the,ater) *n*; ~ *house* *s.* Musi'kalienhandlung *f*.

mu·si·cian [mjuː'zɪʃn] *s.* **1.** (*bsd.* Berufs)Musiker(in): *be a good* ~ a) gut spielen *od.* singen, b) sehr musikalisch sein; **2.** Musi'kant *m*.

mu·si·col·o·gy [,mjuːzɪ'kɒlədʒɪ] *s.* Mu'sikwissenschaft *f*.

mu·sic| pa·per *s.* 'Notenpa,pier *n*; ~ **rack**, ~ **stand** *s.* Notenständer *m*; ~ **stool** *s.* Kla'vierstuhl *m*.

mus·ing ['mjuːzɪŋ] **I** *s.* **1.** Sinnen *n*, Grübeln *n*, Nachdenken *n*; **2.** *pl.* Träume'reien *pl.*; **II** *adj.* □ **3.** nachdenklich, sinnend, in Gedanken (versunken).

musk [mʌsk] *s.* **1.** *zo.* Moschus *m* (*a. Duftstoff*), Bisam *m*; **2.** → *musk deer*; **3.** Moschuspflanze *f*; ~ **bag** *s. zo.* Moschusbeutel *m*; ~ **deer** *s. zo.* Moschustier *n*.

mus·ket ['mʌskɪt] *s.* ✕ *hist.* Mus'kete *f*, Flinte *f*; **mus·ket·eer** [,mʌskɪ'tɪə] *s. hist.* Muske'tier *m*; '**mus·ket·ry** [-trɪ] *s.* **1.** *hist. coll.* a) Mus'keten *pl.*, b) Muske'tiere *pl.*; **2.** *hist.* Mus'ketenschießen *n*; **3.** ✕ 'Schieß,unterricht *m*: ~ *manual* Schießvorschrift *f*.

musk| ox *s.* [*irr.*] *zo.* Moschusochse *m*; ~ **rat** *s. zo.* Bisamratte *f*; ~ **rose** *s.* ♀ Moschusrose *f*.

musk·y ['mʌskɪ] *adj.* □ **1.** nach Moschus riechend; **2.** Moschus...

Mus·lim ['mʊslɪm] **I** *s.* Mus'lim *m*; **II** *adj.* mus'limisch.

mus·lin ['mʌzlɪn] *s.* Musse'lin *m*.

mus·quash ['mʌskwɒʃ] → *muskrat*.

muss [mʌs] *bsd. Am.* F **I** *s.* Durchein'ander *n*, Unordnung *f*; **II** *v/t.* oft ~ *up* durchein'ander bringen, in Unordnung

bringen, *Haar* verwuscheln.

mus·sel ['mʌsl] *s.* Muschel *f*.

Mus·sul·man ['mʌslmən] **I** *pl.* -**mans**, *a.* -**men** [-mən] *s.* Muselman(n) *m*; **II** *adj.* muselmanisch.

muss·y ['mʌsɪ] *adj. Am.* F unordentlich; verknittert; schmutzig.

must¹ [mʌst] **I** *v/aux.* **1.** *pres.* muss, musst, müssen, müsst: *I* ~ *go now* ich muss jetzt gehen; *he* ~ *be over eighty* er muss über achtzig (Jahre alt) sein; **2.** *neg.* darf, darfst, dürfen, dürft: *you* ~ *not smoke here* du darfst hier nicht rauchen; **3.** *pret.* a) musste, musstest, mussten, musstet: *it was too late now, he* ~ *go on*; *just as I was busiest, he* ~ *come* gerade als ich am meisten zu tun hatte, musste er kommen, b) *neg.* durfte, durftest, durften, durftet; **II** *adj.* **4.** unerlässlich, abso'lut notwendig: *a* ~ *book* ein Buch, das man (unbedingt) gelesen haben muss; **III** *s.* **5.** Muss *n*: *it is a* ~ es ist unerlässlich *od.* unbedingt erforderlich (→ *a.* 4).

must² [mʌst] *s.* Most *m*.

must³ [mʌst] *s.* **1.** Moder *m*, Schimmel *m*; **2.** Modrigkeit *f*.

mus·tache [mə'stɑːʃ; *Am.* 'mʌstæʃ] *Am.* → *moustache*.

mus·tang ['mʌstæŋ] *s.* **1.** *zo.* Mustang *m* (*halbwildes Präriepferd*); **2.** ♀ ✈ Mustang *m* (*amer. Jagdflugzeug im 2. Weltkrieg*).

mus·tard ['mʌstəd] *s.* **1.** Senf *m*, Mostrich *m*; → *keen¹* 13; **2.** ♀ Senf *m*; **3.** *Am. sl.* a) ,Mordskerl' *m*, b) ,tolle' Sache, c) ,Pfeffer' *m*, Schwung *m*; ~ **gas** *s.* ✕ Senfgas *n*, Gelbkreuz *n*; ~ **plas·ter** *s.* ✚ Senfpflaster *n*; ~ **poul·tice** *s.* ✚ Senfpackung *f*; ~ **seed** *s.* **1.** ♀ Senfsame *m*: *grain of* ~ *bibl.* Senfkorn *n*; **2.** *hunt.* Vogeldunst *m*.

mus·ter ['mʌstə] **I** *v/t.* **1.** ✕ a) (zum Ap'pell) antreten lassen, mustern, b) aufbieten: ~ *in* (*out*) *Am.* einziehen (entlassen, ausmustern); **2.** zs.-bringen, auftreiben; **3.** *a.* ~ *up* *fig.* aufbieten, *s-e Kraft* zs.-nehmen, *Mut* fassen; **II** *v/i.* **4.** sich versammeln, ✕ *a.* antreten; **III** *s.* **5.** ✕ Ap'pell *m*, Pa'rade *f*; Musterung *f*: *pass* ~ *fig.* durchgehen, Billigung finden (*with* bei); **6.** ✕ → *muster roll* 2; **7.** Versammlung *f*; **8.** Aufgebot *n*; ~ **book** *s.* ✕ Stammrollenbuch *n*; ~ **roll** *s.* **1.** ⚓ Musterrolle *f*; **2.** ✕ Stammrolle *f*.

mus·ti·ness ['mʌstɪnɪs] *s.* **1.** Muffigkeit *f*, Modrigkeit *f*; **2.** *fig.* Verstaubtheit *f*; **mus·ty** ['mʌstɪ] *adj.* □ **1.** muffig; **2.** mod(e)rig; **3.** schal (*a. fig.*); **4.** *fig.* verstaubt.

mu·ta·bil·i·ty [,mjuːtə'bɪlətɪ] *s.* **1.** Veränderlichkeit *f*; **2.** *fig.* Unbeständigkeit *f*; **3.** *biol.* Mutati'onsfähigkeit *f*; **mu·ta·ble** ['mjuːtəbl] *adj.* □ **1.** veränderlich; **2.** *fig.* unbeständig; **3.** *biol.* mutati'onsfähig; **mu·tant** ['mjuːtənt] *biol.* **I** *adj.* **1.** mutierend; **2.** mutati'onsbedingt; **II** *s.* **3.** Vari'ante *f*, Mu'tant *m*; **mu·tate** [mjuː'teɪt] *v/t.* **1.** verändern; **2.** *ling.* 'umlauten: ~*d vowel* Umlaut *m*; **II** *v/i.* **3.** sich ändern; **4.** *ling.* 'umlauten; **5.** *biol.* mutieren; **mu·ta·tion** [mjuː'teɪʃn] *s.* **1.** (Ver)Änderung *f*; **2.** 'Umwandlung *f*: ~ *of energy* *phys.* Energieumformung *f*; **3.** *biol.* a) Mutati'on *f* (*a.* ♪), b) Mutati'onspro,dukt *n*; **4.** *ling.* 'Umlaut *m*.

mute [mjuːt] **I** *adj.* □ **1.** stumm (*a. ling.*), *weitS. a.* still, schweigend: ~ *sound* *ling.* Verschlusslaut *m*; **II** *s.* **2.** Stumme(r *m*) *f*; **3.** *thea.* Sta'tist(in); **4.** ♪ Dämpfer *m*; **5.** *ling.* a) stummer

Buchstabe, b) Verschlusslaut *m*; **III** *v/t.* **6.** ♪ Instrument dämpfen.

mu·ti·late ['mjuːtɪleɪt] *v/t.* verstümmeln (*a. fig.*); **mu·ti·la·tion** [,mjuːtɪ'leɪʃn] *s.* Verstümmelung *f*.

mu·ti·neer [,mjuːtɪ'nɪə] **I** *s.* Meuterer *m*; **II** *v/i.* meutern; **mu·ti·nous** ['mjuːtɪnəs] *adj.* □ **1.** meuterisch; **2.** aufrührerisch, re'bellisch (*a. fig.*); **mu·ti·ny** ['mjuːtɪnɪ] **I** *s.* **1.** Meute'rei *f*; **2.** Auflehnung *f*, Rebelli'on *f*; **II** *v/i.* **3.** meutern.

mut·ism ['mjuːtɪzəm] *s.* (Taub)Stummheit *f*.

mutt [mʌt] *s. Am. sl.* **1.** Trottel *m*, Schafskopf *m*; **2.** Köter *m*, Hund *m*.

mut·ter ['mʌtə] **I** *v/i.* **1.** (*a. v/t. et.*) murmeln: ~ *to o.s.* vor sich hinmurmeln; **2.** murren (*at* über *acc.*; *against* gegen); **II** *s.* **3.** Gemurmel *n*; **4.** Murren *n*.

mut·ton ['mʌtn] *s.* Hammelfleisch *n*: *leg of* ~ Hammelkeule *f*; → *dead* 1; ~ *chop* *s.* **1.** 'Hammelkote,lett *n*; **2.** *pl.* Kote'letten *pl.* (*Backenbart*); '~**head** *s.* F ,Schafskopf' *m*.

mu·tu·al ['mjuːtʃʊəl] *adj.* □ **1.** gegen-, wechselseitig: ~ *aid* gegenseitige Hilfe; ~ *building association* Baugenossenschaft *f*; *by* ~ *consent* in gegenseitigem Einvernehmen; ~ *contributory negligence* ⚖ beiderseitiges Verschulden; ~ *improvement society* Fortbildungsverein *m*; ~ *insurance* ✚ Versicherung *f* auf Gegenseitigkeit; ~ *investment trust*, ~ *fund* *Am.* Investmentfonds *m*; ~ *will* ⚖ gegenseitiges Testament; *it's* ~ *iro.* es beruht auf Gegenseitigkeit; **2.** gemeinsam: *our* ~ *friends*; **mu·tu·al·i·ty** [,mjuːtjʊ'ælətɪ] *s.* Gegenseitigkeit *f*.

Mu·zak ['mjuːzæk] *TM npr.* funktio'nelle Musik (*psychologisch gezielte Klangberieselung*).

mu·zhik, **mu·zjik** ['muːʒɪk] *s.* Muschik *m*, russischer Bauer.

muz·zle ['mʌzl] **I** *s.* **1.** Maul *n*, Schnauze *f* (*Tier*); **2.** Maulkorb *m*; **3.** Mündung *f* e-r Feuerwaffe; **4.** ⊗ Mündung *f*; Tülle *f*; **II** *v/t.* **5.** e-n Maulkorb anlegen (*dat.*); *fig. a.* Presse *etc.* knebeln, mundtot machen, den Mund stopfen (*dat.*); ~ **brake** *s.* ✕ Mündungsbremse *f*; ~ **burst** *s.* ✕ Mündungskrepierer *m*; '~-**,load·er** *s.* ✕ *hist.* Vorderlader *m*; ~ **ve·loc·i·ty** *s.* Ballistik: Mündungs-, Anfangsgeschwindigkeit *f*.

muz·zy ['mʌzɪ] *adj.* □ F **1.** zerstreut, verwirrt; **2.** dus(e)lig; **3.** stumpfsinnig.

my [maɪ] *poss. pron.* mein(e): *I must wash* ~ *face* ich muss mir das Gesicht waschen; (*oh*) ~*!* F (du) meine Güte!

my·al·gi·a [maɪ'ældʒɪə] *s.* ✚ 'Muskelrheuma(,tismus *m*) *n*.

my·col·o·gy [maɪ'kɒlədʒɪ] *s.* ♀ **1.** Pilzkunde *f*, Mykolo'gie *f*; **2.** Pilzflora *f*, Pilze *pl.* (*e-s Gebiets*).

my·cose ['maɪkəʊs] *s.* 🍄 My'kose *f*.

my·co·sis [maɪ'kəʊsɪs] *s.* ✚ Pilzkrankheit *f*, My'kose *f*.

my·e·li·tis [,maɪə'laɪtɪs] *s.* Mye'litis *f*: a) Rückenmarksentzündung *f*, b) Knochenmarksentzündung *f*; **my·e·lon** ['maɪəlɒn] *s.* Rückenmark *n*.

my·o·car·di·o·gram [,maɪəʊ'kɑːdɪəʊgræm] *s.* ✚ E,lektrokardio'gramm *n*; ,**my·o'car·di·o·graph** [-grɑːf] *s.* ✚ E,lektrokardio'graph *m*, EK'G-Appa,rat *m*; **my·o·car·di·tis** [,maɪəʊkɑː'daɪtɪs] *s.* Herzmuskelentzündung *f*.

my·ol·o·gy [maɪ'ɒlədʒɪ] *s.* Myolo'gie *f*, Muskelkunde *f*, -lehre *f*.

my·o·ma [maɪ'əʊmə] *s.* ✚ My'om *n*.

my·ope ['maɪəʊp] *s.* ✚ Kurzsichtige(r *m*) *f*; **my·o·pi·a** [maɪ'əʊpjə] *s.* ✚ Kurz-

M

sichtigkeit *f* (*a. fig.*); **my·op·ic** [maɪ-'ɒpɪk] *adj.* kurzsichtig; **my·o·py** ['maɪ-əpɪ] → *myopia*.

myr·i·ad ['mɪrɪəd] **I** *s.* Myri'ade *f*; *fig. a.* Unzahl *f*; **II** *adj.* unzählig.

myr·mi·don ['mɜːmɪdən] *s.* Scherge *m*, Häscher *m*; Helfershelfer *m*: ~ **of law** Hüter *m* des Gesetzes.

myrrh [mɜː] *s.* ♀ Myrr(h)e *f*.

myr·tle ['mɜːtl] *s.* ♀ **1.** Myrte *f*; **2.** *Am.* Immergrün *n*.

my·self [maɪ'self] *pron.* **1.** (*verstärkend*) (ich *od.* mir *od.* mich) selbst: *I did it* ~ ich selbst habe es getan; *I* ~ *wouldn't do it* ich (persönlich) würde es sein lassen; *it is for* ~ es ist für mich (selbst); **2.** *refl.* mir (*dat.*), mich (*acc.*): *I cut* ~ ich habe mich geschnitten.

mys·te·ri·ous [mɪ'stɪərɪəs] *adj.* □ mysteri'ös: a) geheimnisvoll, b) rätsel-, schleierhaft, unerklärlich; **mys·te·ri·ous·ness** [-nɪs] *s.* Rätselhaftigkeit *f*, Unerklärlichkeit *f*, *das* Geheimnisvolle

od. Mysteri'öse.

mys·ter·y ['mɪstərɪ] *s.* **1.** Geheimnis *n*, Rätsel *n* (**to** für *od. dat.*): *make a* ~ *of et.* geheim halten; *wrapped in* ~ in geheimnisvolles Dunkel gehüllt; *it's a complete* ~ *to me* es ist mir völlig schleierhaft; **2.** Rätselhaftigkeit *f*, Unerklärlichkeit *f*; **3.** *eccl.* My'sterium *n*; **4.** *pl.* Geheimlehre *f*, -kunst *f*; My'sterien *pl.*; **5.** → *mystery play* 1; **6.** *Am.* → ~ **nov·el** *s.* Krimi'nalro,man *m*; ~ **play** *s.* **1.** *hist.* My'sterienspiel *n*; **2.** *thea.* Krimi'nalstück *n*; ~ **ship** *s.* ⚓ U-Boot-Falle *f*; ~ **tour** *s.* Fahrt *f* ins Blaue.

mys·tic ['mɪstɪk] **I** *adj.* (□ ~*ally*) **1.** mystisch; **2.** *fig.* rätselhaft, mysteri'ös, geheimnisvoll; **3.** geheim, Zauber...; **II** *s.* **4.** Mystiker(in); Schwärmer(in); '**mys·ti·cal** [-kl] *adj.* □ **1.** sym'bolisch; **2.** → *mystic* 1, 2; '**mys·ti·cism** [-ɪsɪzəm] *s. phls., eccl.* a) Mysti'zismus *m*, Glaubensschwärme'rei *f*, b) Mystik *f*.

mys·ti·fi·ca·tion [ˌmɪstɪfɪ'keɪʃn] *s.* **1.** Täuschung *f*, Irreführung *f*; **2.** Foppe'rei *f*; **3.** Verwirrung *f*, Verblüffung *f*; **mys·ti·fy** ['mɪstɪfaɪ] *v/t.* **1.** täuschen, hinters Licht führen, foppen; **2.** verwirren, verblüffen; **3.** in Dunkel hüllen.

myth [mɪθ] *s.* **1.** (Götter-, Helden)Sage *f*, Mythos *m* (*a. pol.*), Mythus *m*, Mythe *f*; **2.** Märchen *n*, erfundene Geschichte; **3.** *fig.* Mythus *m* (*legendär gewordene Person od. Sache*).

myth·ic, myth·i·cal ['mɪθɪk(l)] *adj.* □ **1.** mythisch, sagenhaft; Sagen...; **2.** *fig.* erdichtet, fik'tiv.

myth·o·log·ic, myth·o·log·i·cal [ˌmɪθə-'lɒdʒɪk(l)] *adj.* □ mytho'logisch; **my·thol·o·gist** [mɪ'θɒlədʒɪst] *s.* Mytho'loge *m*; **my·thol·o·gize** [mɪ'θɒlədʒaɪz] *v/t.* mythologisieren; **my·thol·o·gy** [mɪ'θɒlədʒɪ] *s.* **1.** Mytholo'gie *f*, Götter- u. Heldensagen *pl.*; **2.** Sagenforschung *f*, -kunde *f*.

M

N, n [en] *s.* **1.** N *n*, n *n* (*Buchstabe*); **2.** ⚓ N *n* (*Stickstoff*); **3.** ℟ N *n*, n *n* (*unbestimmte Konstante*).

nab [næb] *v/t.* F **1.** schnappen, erwischen; **2.** sich *et.* schnappen.

na·bob ['neɪbɒb] *s.* Nabob *m* (*a. fig. Krösus*).

na·celle [næ'sel] *s.* ✈ **1.** (Flugzeug-)Rumpf *m*; **2.** (Motor-, Luftschiff)Gondel *f*; **3.** Bal'lonkorb *m*.

na·cre ['neɪkə] *s.* Perlmutt(er *f*) *n*; **'na·cre·ous** [-krɪəs], **'na·crous** [-krəs] *adj.* **1.** perlmutterartig; **2.** Perlmutt(er)...

na·dir ['neɪ,dɪə] *s.* **1.** *ast., geogr.* Na'dir *m*, Fußpunkt *m*; **2.** *fig.* Tief-, Nullpunkt *m*.

naff [næf] *Brit. sl.* **I** *adj.* **1.** geschmacklos (*Film etc.*); **2.** hirnrissig, blöd (*Idee etc.*); **3.** nutzlos, ,out'; **II** *v/i.* **4.** ~ **off!** verpiss dich!, Leine!; **'naff·ing** *adj. Brit. sl.* ,blöd', ,nervend'.

nag¹ [næg] *s.* **1.** kleines Reitpferd, Pony *n*; **2.** F *contp.* Gaul *m*.

nag² [næg] **I** *v/t.* **1.** her'umnörgeln an (*dat.*); *j-m* zusetzen; **II** *v/i.* **2.** nörgeln, keifen: ~ **at** → 1; **3.** *fig.* nagen, bohren; **III** *s.* **4.** → **'nag·ger** [-gə] *s.* Nörgler (-in); **'nag·ging** [-gɪŋ] **I** *s.* Nörge'lei *f*, Gekeife *n*; **II** *adj.* nörgelnd, keifend, *fig.* nagend.

nai·ad ['naɪæd] *s.* **1.** *myth.* Na'jade *f*, Wassernymphe *f*; **2.** *fig.* (Bade)Nixe *f*.

nail [neɪl] **I** *s.* **1.** (Finger-, Zehen)Nagel *m*; **2.** ⚙ Nagel *m*; Stift *m*; **3.** *zo.* a) Nagel *m*, b) Klaue *f*, Kralle *f*;
Besondere Redewendungen:
a ~ *in s.o.'s coffin* ein Nagel zu j-s Sarg; *on the* ~ auf der Stelle, sofort, bar *bezahlen*; *to the* ~ bis ins Letzte, vollendet; *hit the* (*right*) ~ *on the head fig.* den Nagel auf den Kopf treffen; *hard as* ~*s* eisern: a) fit, in guter Kondition, b) unbarmherzig; *right as* ~*s* ganz richtig.
II *v/t.* **4.** (an)nageln (*on* auf *acc.*, *to* an *acc.*): ~*ed to the spot* wie an- *od.* festgenagelt; ~ *to the barndoor fig.* Lüge *etc.* festnageln; → *colour* 10; **5.** benageln, mit Nägeln beschlagen; **6.** *a.* ~ *up* vernageln; **7.** *fig.* Augen *etc.* heften, *Aufmerksamkeit* richten (*to* auf *acc.*); **8.** → *nail down* 2; **9.** F a) schnappen, erwischen, b) sich *et.* schnappen, c) ,klauen', d) *et.* ,spitzkriegen' (*entdecken*); ~ *down* *v/t.* **1.** zunageln; **2.** *fig. j-n* festnageln (*to* auf *acc.*); **3.** *fig. et.* endgültig beweisen; ~ *up* *v/t.* **1.** zs.-nageln; **2.** zu-, vernageln; **3.** *fig.* zs.-basteln: *a nailed-up drama.*

nail| bed *s. anat.* Nagelbett *n*; **'~-,bit·ing** **I** *s.* Nägelkauen *n*; **II** *adj.* atemberaubend, atemlos (*Spannung*), aufregend, spannungsgeladen; ~ *brush* *s.* Nagelbürste *f*; ~ *en·am·el* *s.* Nagellack *m*; ~ *file* *s.* Nagelfeile *f*; ~ *head* *s.* ⚙ Nagelkopf *m*; ~ *pol·ish* *s.* Nagellack *m*; '~-,pull·er *s.* ⚙ Nagelzieher *m*; ~ *scis·sors* *s. pl.* Nagelschere *f*; ~ *var·nish* *s. Brit.* Nagellack *m*: ~ *re-*

mover Nagellackentferner *m*.

na·ïve [nɑː'iːv], *a.* **na·ive** [neɪv] *adj.* □ *allg.* na'iv (*a. Kunst*); **na·ïve·té** [nɑː'iːvteɪ], *a.* **na·ive·ty** ['neɪvtɪ] *s.* Naivi'tät *f*.

na·ked ['neɪkɪd] *adj.* □ **1.** nackt, bloß, unbedeckt: ⚲ *Lady* ⚘ Herbstzeitlose *f*; **2.** bloß, unbewaffnet (*Auge*); **3.** bloß, blank (*Schwert*; ⊙ *Draht*); **4.** nackt, kahl (*Feld, Raum, Wand etc.*); **5.** entblößt (*of* von): ~ *of all provisions* bar aller Vorräte; **6.** a) schutz-, wehrlos, b) preisgegeben (*to dat.*); **7.** nackt, unverhüllt: ~ *facts*; ~ *truth*; **8.** ⚖ bloß, unbestätigt: ~ *confession*; ~ *possession* tatsächlicher Besitz (*ohne Rechtsanspruch*); **'na·ked·ness** [-nɪs] *s.* **1.** Nacktheit *f*, Blöße *f*; **2.** Kahlheit *f*; **3.** Schutz-, Wehrlosigkeit *f*; **4.** Mangel *m* (*of* an *dat.*); **5.** *fig.* Unverhülltheit *f*.

nam·a·ble ['neɪməbl] *adj.* **1.** benennbar; **2.** nennenswert.

nam·by-pam·by [,næmbɪ'pæmbɪ] **I** *adj.* **1.** seicht, abgeschmackt; **2.** affektiert, ,etepe'tete'; **3.** sentimen'tal; **II** *s.* **4.** sentimentales Zeug; **5.** sentimentaler Mensch; **6.** Mutterkindchen *n*.

name [neɪm] **I** *v/t.* **1.** nennen; erwähnen, anführen; **2.** (be)nennen (*after, from* nach), e-n Namen geben (*dat.*): ~*d* genannt, namens; **3.** beim (richtigen) Namen nennen; **4.** a) ernennen (*zu*), b) nomi'nieren, vorschlagen (*for* für); **5.** *Datum etc.* bestimmen; **6.** *parl. Brit.* mit Namen zur Ordnung rufen; ~*!* a) zur Ordnung rufen!, b) *allg.* Namen nennen!; **II** *s.* **7.** Name *m*: *what is your* ~*?* wie heißen Sie?; *in* ~ *only* nur dem Namen nach; **8.** Name *m*, Bezeichnung *f*, Benennung *f*; **9.** Schimpfname *m*: *call s.o.* ~*s* j-n beschimpfen; **10.** Name *m*, Ruf *m*: *a bad* ~; → *Bes. Redew.*; **11.** (berühmter) Name, (guter) Ruf: *a man of* ~ ein Mann von Ruf; **12.** Name *m*, Berühmtheit *f* (*Person*): *the great* ~*s of our century*; **13.** Geschlecht *n*, Fa'milie *f*;
Besondere Redewendungen:
by ~ a) mit Namen, namentlich, b) namens, c) dem Namen nach; *a man by* (*od. of*) *the* ~ *of A.* ein Mann namens A.; *in the* ~ *of A.* a) um (*gen.*) willen, b) im Namen *des Gesetzes etc.*, c) auf j-s Namen *bestellen etc.*; *I haven't a penny to my* ~ ich besitze keinen Pfennig; *give one's* ~ s-n Namen nennen; *give it a* ~*!* F heraus damit!, sagen Sie, was Sie (haben) wollen!; *give s.o.* (*s.th.*) *a bad* ~ j-n (et.) in Verruf bringen; *give a dog a bad* ~ *and hang him* j-n wegen s-s schlechten Rufs *od.* auf Grund von Gerüchten verurteilen; *have a* ~ *for being* dafür bekannt sein, et. zu sein; *make one's* ~, *make* (*od. win*) *a* ~ *for o.s.* sich e-n Namen machen (*as* als, *by* durch); *put one's* ~ *down for* a) kandidieren für, b) sich anmelden für, c) sich vormerken lassen für:

send in one's ~ sich (an)melden (lassen); *what's in a* ~*?* was bedeutet schon ein Name?; *that's the* ~ *of the game!* darum dreht es sich!

'name|-,call·ing *s.* Beschimpfung(en *pl.*) *f*; ~ *child* *s.*: *my* ~ das nach mir benannte Kind.

named [neɪmd] *adj.* **1.** genannt, namens; **2.** genannt, erwähnt: ~ *above* oben genannt.

name| day *s.* **1.** Namenstag *m*; **2.** ✝ Abrechnungstag *m*; **'~-,drop·per** *s.* j-d, der ständig mit promi'nenten Bekannten angibt; **'~-,drop·ping** *s.* Wichtigtue'rei *f* durch Erwähnung von Promi-'nenten, die man angeblich kennt.

name·less ['neɪmlɪs] *adj.* □ **1.** namenlos, unbekannt, ob'skur; **2.** ungenannt, unerwähnt; ano'nym; **3.** unehelich (*Kind*); **4.** *fig.* namenlos, unbeschreiblich (*Furcht etc.*); **5.** unaussprechlich, ab'scheulich; **'name·ly** [-lɪ] *adv.* nämlich.

name| part *s. thea.* Titelrolle *f*; ~ *plate* *s.* **1.** Tür-, Firmen-, Namens-, Straßenschild *n*; **2.** ⊙ Typenschild *n*; '~-*sake* *s.* Namensvetter *m*, -schwester *f*.

nam·ing ['neɪmɪŋ] *s.* Namengebung *f*.

nan·cy ['nænsɪ] *s. sl.* **1.** Muttersöhnchen *n*; **2.** ,Homo' *m*.

nan·ny ['nænɪ] *s.* **1.** Kindermädchen *n*: ~ *state* *bsd. Brit.* Versorgerstaat *m*; **2.** Oma *f*; **3.** → ~ *goat* *s.* Ziege *f*.

nap¹ [næp] **I** *v/i.* **1.** ein Schläfchen *od.* ein Nickerchen machen; **2.** *fig.* ,schlafen': *catch s.o.* ~*ping* j-n überrumpeln; **II** *s.* **3.** Schläfchen *n*, ,Nickerchen' *n*: *take a* ~ → 1.

nap² [næp] **I** *s.* **1.** Haar(seite *f*) *n* e-s Gewebes; **2.** a) *Spinnerei:* Noppe *f*, b) *Weberei:* (Gewebe)Flor *m*; **II** *v/t. u. v/i.* **3.** noppen, rauen.

nap³ [næp] **I** *s.* **1.** Na'poleon *n* (*Kartenspiel*): *a* ~ *hand fig.* gute Chancen; *go* ~ a) die höchste Zahl von Stichen ansagen, b) *fig.* alles auf eine Karte setzen; **2.** Setzen *n* auf eine einzige Gewinnchance.

na·palm ['neɪpɑːm] *s.* ⚔ Napalm *n*.

nape [neɪp] *s. mst* ~ *of the neck* Genick *n*, Nacken *m*.

naph·tha ['næfθə] *s.* ⚗ **1.** Naphtha *n*, 'Leuchtpe,troleum *n*; **2.** ('Schwer)Ben-,zin *n*: *cleaner's* ~ Waschbenzin; *painter's* ~ Testbenzin; **'naph·tha·lene** [-liːn] *s.* Naphtha'lin *n*; **naph·tha·len·ic** [,næfθə'lenɪk] *adj.* naphtha'linsauer: ~ *acid* Naphthalinsäure *f*; **naph·thal·ic** [næf'θælɪk] *adj.* naph'thalsauer: ~ *acid* Naphthalsäure *f*; **'naph·tha·line** [-liːn] → *naphthalene.*

nap·kin ['næpkɪn] *s.* **1.** *a. table* ~ Servi'ette *f*; **2.** Wischtuch *n*; **3.** *bsd. Brit.* Windel *f*; **4.** *a. sanitary* ~ *Am.* Monatsbinde *f*.

napped [næpt] *adj.* genoppt, geraut (*Tuch*); **nap·ping** ['næpɪŋ] *s.* **1.** Ausnoppen *n* (*der Wolle*); **2.** Rauen *n*: ~ *comb* Aufstreichkamm *m*.

nap·py ['næpɪ] s. bsd. Brit. F Windel f.

nar·cis·sism [nɑːˈsɪsɪzəm] s. psych. Nar'zissmus m; **nar·cis·sist** [-ɪst] s. Nar'zisst (-in).

nar·cis·sus [nɑːˈsɪsəs] pl. **-sus·es** [-sɪz] s. ♀ Nar'zisse f.

'nar·co [nɑːkəʊ] s. sl. → narcotics agent.

nar·co·sis [nɑːˈkəʊsɪs] s. Nar'kose f.

nar·cot·ic [nɑːˈkɒtɪk] **I** adj. (□ **~ally**) **1.** nar'kotisch (a. fig. einschläfernd); **2.** Rauschgift...; **II** s. **3.** Nar'kotikum n, Betäubungsmittel n (a. fig.); **4.** Rauschgift n: **~s agent** Drogenfahnder m; **~s squad** Rauschgiftdezernat n; **nar·co·tism** [ˈnɑːkətɪzəm] s. **1.** Nar-ko'tismus m (Sucht); **2.** nar'kotischer Zustand od. Rausch; **nar·co·tize** [ˈnɑːkətaɪz] v/t. narkotisieren.

nard [nɑːd] s. **1.** ♀ Narde f; **2.** pharm. Nardensalbe f.

nark [nɑːk] sl. **I** s. **1.** Poli'zeispitzel m; **II** v/t. **2.** bespitzeln; **3.** ärgern; **nark·y** [ˈnɑːkɪ] adj. gereizt, grantig.

nar·rate [nəˈreɪt] v/t. u. v/i. erzählen; **nar·ra·tion** [-eɪʃn] s. Erzählung f; **nar·ra·tive** [ˈnærətɪv] **I** s. **1.** Erzählung f, Geschichte f; **2.** Bericht m, Schilderung f; **II** adj. □ **3.** erzählend: **~ poem**; **4.** Erzählungs...: **~ skill** Erzählergabe f; **nar·ra·tor** [-tə] s. Erzähler(in).

nar·row [ˈnærəʊ] **I** adj. □ **1.** eng, schmal: **the ~ seas** der Ärmelkanal u. die Irische See; **2.** eng (a. fig.), (räumlich) beschränkt, knapp: **within ~ bounds** in engen Grenzen; **in the ~est sense** im engsten Sinne; **3.** fig. eingeschränkt, beschränkt; **4.** → **narrow-minded**; **5.** knapp, beschränkt (Mittel, Verhältnisse); **6.** knapp (Entkommen, Mehrheit etc.); **7.** gründlich, eingehend; genau: **~ investigations**; **II** v/i. **8.** enger od. schmäler werden, sich verengen (**into** zu); **9.** knapper werden; **III** v/t. **10.** enger od. schmäler machen, verenge(r)n; **11.** einengen, beengen; **12.** a. **~ down** (**to** auf acc.) be-, einschränken, begrenzen, eingrenzen; **13.** Maschen abnehmen; **14.** engstirnig machen; **IV** s. **15.** Enge f, enge od. schmale Stelle; pl. a) (Meer)Enge f, b) bsd. Am. Engpass m.

nar·row| ga(u)ge s. ⬛ Schmalspur f; **'~-ga(u)ge** [-rəʊg-], a. **'~-'ga(u)ged** [-rəʊ'g-] adj. Schmalspur...; **'~-'minded** [-rəʊ'maɪndɪd] adj. engherzig, -stirnig, borniert, kleinlich; **'~-'mind·ed·ness** [-rəʊ'maɪndɪdnɪs] s. Engstirnigkeit f, Borniertheit f.

nar·row·ness [ˈnærəʊnɪs] s. **1.** Enge f, Schmalheit f; **2.** Knappheit f; **3.** → **narrow-mindedness**; **4.** Gründlichkeit f.

na·sal [ˈneɪzl] **I** adj. □ **~ nasally**: **1.** Nasen...: **~ bone; ~ cavity; ~ organ** humor. Riechorgan n; **~ septum** Nasenscheidewand f; **2.** ling. na'sal, Nasal...: **~ twang** Näseln n; **3.** ling. Na'sal(laut) m; **na·sal·i·ty** [neɪˈzælətɪ] s. Nasali'tät f; **na·sal·i·za·tion** [ˌneɪzəlaɪˈzeɪʃn] s. Nasalierung f, nasale Aussprache; **'na·sal·ize** [-zəlaɪz] **I** v/t. nasalieren; **II** v/i. näseln, durch die Nase sprechen; **'na·sal·ly** [-zəlɪ] adv. **1.** na'sal, durch die Nase; **2.** näselnd.

nas·cent [ˈnæsnt] adj. **1.** werdend, entstehend: **~ state** Entwicklungszustand m; **2.** 🜊 frei werdend.

nas·ti·ness [ˈnɑːstɪnɪs] s. **1.** Schmutzigkeit f; **2.** Ekligkeit f; **3.** Unflätigkeit f; **4.** Gefährlichkeit f; **5.** a) Bosheit f, b) Gemeinheit f, c) Übelgelauntheit f.

nas·tur·tium [nəˈstɜːʃəm] s. ♀ Kapu'ziner- od. Brunnenkresse f.

nas·ty [ˈnɑːstɪ] **I** adj. □ **1.** schmutzig; **2.** ekelhaft, eklig, widerlich (alle a. fig.): **~ taste; ~ fellow; 3.** fig. schmutzig, zotig; **4.** fig. böse, schlimm, gefährlich: **~ accident; 5.** fig. a) bös, gehässig, garstig (**to** zu, gegen), b) fies, niederträchtig, c) übel gelaunt, ‚eklig'; **II** s. **6.** mst pl. Video: ‚Schmutz- u. 'Horror-Kas-ˌsette' f.

na·tal [ˈneɪtl] adj. Geburts...: **~ day**; **na·tal·i·ty** [nəˈtælətɪ] s. bsd. Am. Geburtenziffer f.

na·ta·tion [nəˈteɪʃn] s. Schwimmen n; **na·ta·to·ri·al** [ˌneɪtəˈtɔːrɪəl] adj. Schwimm...: **~ bird; na·ta·to·ry** [ˈneɪtətərɪ] adj. Schwimm...

natch [nætʃ] adv. sl. abbr. für **naturally** selbstverständlich.

na·tion [ˈneɪʃn] s. **1.** Nati'on f: a) Volk n, b) Staat m; **2.** (Indi'aner)Stamm m.

na·tion·al [ˈnæʃənl] **I** adj. □ **1.** natio'nal, National..., Landes..., Volks...: **~ language** Landessprache f; **2.** staatlich, öffentlich, Staats...: **~ debt** Staatsschuld f, öffentliche Schuld; **3.** (ein)heimisch; **4.** landesweit (Streik etc.), 'überregio,nal (Zeitung etc.); **II** s. **5.** Staatsangehörige(r m) f; **~ an·them** s. Natio'nalhymne f; **~ as·sem·bly** s. pol. Na-tio'nalversammlung f; **~ bank** s. ♣ Landes-, Natio'nalbank f; **~ cham·pi·on** s. Landesmeister(in); **~ con·ven·tion** s. pol. Am. Par'teikonvent m (zur Nominierung des Präsidentschaftskandidaten etc.); **~ cur·ren·cy** s. ♣ Landeswährung f; **~ dish** s. Natio'nalgericht n; **~ e·con·o·my** s. ♣ Volkswirtschaft f; **♣ Gi·ro** s. 🐝 Brit. Postscheck-, Postgirodienst m; **♣ Guard** s. Am. Natio'nalgarde f (Art Miliz); **♣ Health Ser·vice** s. Brit. staatlicher Gesundheitsdienst; **~ in·come** s. ♣ Sozi'alpro,dukt n; **♣ In·sur·ance** s. Brit. Sozi'alversicherung f.

na·tion·al·ism [ˈnæʃnəlɪzəm] s. **1.** Natio'nalgefühl n, Nationa'lismus m; **2.** ♣ Am. Na'tionalisierungspoli,tik f; **'na·tion·al·ist** [-ɪst] **I** s. pol. Nationa'list (-in); **II** adj. nationa'listisch; **na·tion·al·i·ty** [ˌnæʃə'nælɪtɪ] s. **1.** Nationali'tät f, Staatsangehörigkeit f; **2.** Nati'on f; **na·tion·al·i·za·tion** [ˌnæʃnəlaɪˈzeɪʃn] s. **1.** bsd. Am. Einbürgerung f, Naturalisierung f; **2.** ♣ Verstaatlichung f; **3.** Verwandlung f in e-e (einheitliche, unabhängige etc.) Nation; **'na·tion·al·ize** [-laɪz] v/t. **1.** einbürgern, naturalisieren; **2.** ♣ verstaatlichen; **3.** zu e-r Nati'on machen; **4.** Problem etc. zur Sache der Nati'on machen.

na·tion·al| park s. Natio'nalpark m (Naturschutzgebiet); **~ prod·uct** s. ♣ Sozi'alpro,dukt n; **~ serv·ice** s. ✕ Wehrdienst m; **♣ So·cial·ism** s. pol. hist. Natio'nalsozia,lismus m.

'na·tion|·hood [-hʊd] s. (natio'nale) Souveräni'tät f; **'~-state** s. Natio'nalstaat m; **'~-'wide** adj. allgemein, das ganze Land um'fassend.

na·tive [ˈneɪtɪv] **I** adj. □ **1.** angeboren (**to s.o.** j-m), na'türlich (Recht etc.); **2.** gebürtig, eingeboren, Eingeborenen...: **~ quarter; ~ American** gebürtige(r) Amerikaner(in); **♣ American** Indianer (-in); **go ~** unter den od. wie die Eingeborenen leben, sich den Einheimischen anpassen; **3.** (ein)heimisch, inländisch, Landes...: **~ plant** ♀ einheimische Pflanze; **~ product**; **4.** heimatlich, Heimat...: **~ country** Heimat f, Vaterland n; **~ language** Muttersprache f; **~ speaker** ling. Muttersprachler(in); **~ town** Heimat-, Vaterstadt f; **5.** ursprünglich, ur-

wüchsig, na'turhaft: **~ beauty; 6.** ursprünglich, eigentlich: **the ~ sense of a word; 7.** gediegen (Metall etc.); **8.** min. a) roh, Jungfern..., b) na'türlich vorkommend; **II** s. **9.** Eingeborene(r m) f; **10.** Einheimische(r m) f, Landeskind n: **a ~ of Berlin** ein gebürtiger Berliner; **11.** ♀ einheimisches Gewächs; **12.** zo. einheimisches Tier; **13.** Na'tive f, (künstlich) gezüchtete Auster; **'~-born** adj. gebürtig: **a ~ American**.

na·tiv·i·ty [nəˈtɪvətɪ] s. **1.** Geburt f (a. fig.): **the ♣** eccl. a) die Geburt Christi (a. paint. etc.), b) Weihnachten f, Ma'riä Geburt (8. September); **♣ play** Krippenspiel n; **2.** ast. Nativi'tät f, (Ge-'burts)Horo,skop n.

na·tron [ˈneɪtrən] s. min. kohlensaures Natron.

nat·ter [ˈnætə] Brit. F **I** v/i. plauschen, plaudern; **II** s. Plausch m, Schwatz m.

nat·ty [ˈnætɪ] adj. □ F schick, piekfein (angezogen), ele'gant (a. fig.).

nat·u·ral [ˈnætʃrəl] **I** adj. □ → **naturally**; **1.** na'türlich, Natur...: **~ disaster** Naturkatastrophe f; **~ law** Naturgesetz n; **die a ~ death** e-s natürlichen Todes sterben; → **person** 1; **2.** na'turgemäß, -bedingt; **3.** angeboren, na'türlich, eigen (**to** dat.): **~ talent; 4.** → **natural-born; 5.** re'al, wirklich, physisch; **6.** selbstverständlich, na'türlich: **it comes quite ~ to him** es ist ihm ganz selbstverständlich; **7.** na'türlich, ungekünstelt (Benehmen etc.); **8.** na'turgetreu, na'türlich (wirkend) (Nachahmung, Bild etc.); **9.** unbearbeitet, Natur..., Roh...: **~ steel** Rohstahl m; **10.** na'turhaft, urwüchsig; **11.** na'türlich, unehelich (Kind, Vater etc.); **12.** 🜊 na'türlich: **~ number** natürliche Zahl; **13.** ♪ a) ohne Vorzeichen: **~ key** C-Dur-Tonart f, b) mit e-m Auflösungszeichen (versehen) (Note), c) Vokal...: **~ music; II** s. **14.** obs. Idi'ot(in); **15.** ♪ a) Auflösungszeichen n, b) mit e-m Auflösungszeichen versehene Note, c) Stammton m, d) weiße Taste (Klaviatur); **16.** F a) Na-'turta,lent n (Person), b) (sicherer) Erfolg (a. Person): **e-e ,klare Sache' (for s.o.** für j-n); **'~-born** adj. von Geburt, geboren: **~ genius; ~ fre·quen·cy** s. phys. 'Eigenfre,quenz f; **~ gas** s. geol. Erdgas n; **~ his·to·ry** s. Na'turgeschichte f

nat·u·ral·ism [ˈnætʃrəlɪzəm] s. phls., paint. etc. Natura'lismus m; **'nat·u·ral·ist** [-ɪst] **I** s. **1.** phls., paint. etc. Natura-'list m; **2.** Na'turwissenschaftler(in), -forscher(in), bsd. Zoo'loge m, Zoo'login f od. Bo'taniker(in); **3.** Brit. a) Tierhändler m, b) ('Tier)Präpa,rator m; **II** adj. **4.** natura'listisch; **nat·u·ral·is·tic** [ˌnætʃrə'lɪstɪk] adj. (□ **~ally**) **1.** phls., paint. etc. natura'listisch; **2.** na'turkundlich, -geschichtlich.

nat·u·ral·i·za·tion [ˌnætʃrəlaɪˈzeɪʃn] s. Naturalisierung f, Einbürgerung f; **nat·u·ral·ize** [ˈnætʃrəlaɪz] v/t. **1.** naturalisieren, einbürgern; **2.** einbürgern (a. ling. u. fig.), ♀, zo. heimisch machen; **3.** akklimatisieren (a. fig.).

nat·u·ral·ly [ˈnætʃrəlɪ] adv. **1.** von Na-'tur (aus); **2.** instink'tiv, spon'tan; **3.** auf na'türlichem Wege, na'türlich; **4.** a. int. na'türlich, selbstverständlich; **'nat·u·ral·ness** [-rəlnɪs] s. allg. Na'türlichkeit f.

nat·u·ral| phi·los·o·phy s. **1.** Na'turphilo,so,phie f, -kunde f; **2.** Phy'sik f; **~ re·li·gion** s. Na'turreli,gi,on f; **~ rights** s. pl. 🜊, pol. Na'turrechte pl. des Menschen; **~ scale** s. **1.** ♪ Stammtonleiter f; **2.** Ⓐ Achse f der na'türlichen Zahlen; **~ sci·ence** s. Na'turwissenschaft f; **~ se·lec·tion** s. biol. na'türliche Auslese; **~ sign** s. ♩ Auflösungszeichen n; **~ state** s. Na'turzustand m.

na·ture ['neɪtʃə] s. **1.** Na'tur f, Schöpfung f; **2.** (a. ⚋; ohne art.) Na'tur(kräfte pl.) f; **law of ~** Naturgesetz n; **from ~** nach der Natur malen etc.; **back to ~** zurück zur Natur; **in the state of ~** in natürlichem Zustand, nackt; → **debt, true** 4; **3.** Na'tur f, Veranlagung f, Cha'rakter m, (Eigen-, Gemüts)Art f, Natu'rell n: **animal ~** das Tierische im Menschen; **by ~** von Natur (aus); **human ~** die menschliche Natur; **of good ~** gutherzig, -mütig; **it is in her ~** es liegt in ihrem Wesen; → **second** 1; **4.** Art f, Sorte f: **of** (od. **in**) **the ~ of a trial** nach Art (od. in Form) e-s Verhörs; **~ of the business** Gegenstand m der Firma; **5.** (na'türliche) Beschaffenheit f; **6.** Na'tur f, na'türliche Landschaft: **~ conservation** Naturschutz m; **⚋ Conservancy** Brit. Naturschutzbehörde f; **~ reserve** Naturschutzgebiet n; **~ trail** Naturlehrpfad m; **7. ease** (od. **relieve**) **~** sich erleichtern (urinieren etc.).

-natured [neɪtʃəd] in Zssgn geartet, ...artig, ...mütig: **good-~** gutartig.

na·tur·ism ['neɪtʃərɪzəm] s. 'Freikörperkul,tur f; **'na·tur·ist** [-ɪst] s. FK'K-Anhänger(in).

na·tur·o·path ['neɪtʃərəʊpæθ] s. ⚗ **1.** Heilpraktiker(in); **2.** Na'turheilkundige(r m) f.

naught [nɔːt] **I** s. Null f: **bring** (**come**) **to ~** zunichte machen (werden); **set at ~ Mahnung** etc. in den Wind schlagen; **II** adj. obs. keineswegs.

naugh·ti·ness ['nɔːtɪnɪs] s. Ungezogenheit f, Unartigkeit f; **naugh·ty** ['nɔːtɪ] adj. □ **1.** ungezogen, unartig; **2.** ungehörig (Handlung); **3.** unanständig, schlimm (Wort etc.): **~, ~!** F aber, aber!

nau·se·a ['nɔːsjə] s. **1.** Übelkeit f, Brechreiz m; **2.** Seekrankheit f; **3.** fig. Ekel m; **'nau·se·ate** [-sɪeɪt] **I** v/i. **1.** (e-n) Brechreiz empfinden, sich ekeln (at vor dat.); **II** v/t. **2.** sich ekeln vor (dat.); **3.** anekeln, j-m Übelkeit erregen: **be ~d** (at) → 1; **'nau·se·at·ing** [-sɪeɪtɪŋ], **'nau·seous** [-sjəs] adj. □ Ekel erregend, widerlich.

nau·tic ['nɔːtɪk] → **nautical.**

nau·ti·cal ['nɔːtɪkl] adj. □ ⚓ nautisch, Schiffs...; See(fahrts)...; **~ al·ma·nac** s. nautisches Jahrbuch; **~ chart** s. Seekarte f; **~ mile** s. ⚓ Seemeile f (1,852 km).

na·val ['neɪvl] adj. ⚓ **1.** Flotten..., (Kriegs)Marine...; **2.** See..., Schiffs...; **~ a·cad·e·my** s. ⚓ **1.** Ma'rineakade,mie f; **2.** Navigati'onsschule f; **~ air·plane** s. Ma'rineflugzeug n; **~ ar·chi·tect** s. 'Schiffbauingeni,eur m; **~ base** s. Flottenstützpunkt m, -basis f; **~ bat·tle** s. Seeschlacht f; **~ ca·det** s. 'Seeka,dett m; **~ forc·es** s. pl. Seestreitkräfte pl.; **~ of·fi·cer** s. **1.** Ma'rineoffi,zier m; **2.** Am. (höherer) Hafenzollbeamter; **~ pow·er** s. pol. Seemacht f.

nave¹ [neɪv] s. ▲ Mittel-, Hauptschiff n: **~ of a cathedral.**

nave² [neɪv] s. ⊙ (Rad)Nabe f.

na·vel ['neɪvl] s. **1.** anat. Nabel m, fig. a. Mitte(lpunkt m) f; **2.** → **~ or·ange** s. 'Navelo,range f; **~ string** s. anat. Nabelschnur f.

nav·i·cert ['nævɪsɜːt] s. ✝, ⚓ Navi'cert n (Geleitschein).

na·vic·u·lar [nə'vɪkjʊlə] adj. nachen-, kahnförmig: **~** (**bone**) anat. Kahnbein n.

nav·i·ga·bil·i·ty [,nævɪgə'bɪlətɪ] s. **1.** ⚓ a) Schiffbarkeit f (e-s Gewässers), b) Fahrtüchtigkeit f; **2.** ✈ Lenkbarkeit f; **nav·i·ga·ble** ['nævɪgəbl] adj. **1.** ⚓ a) schiffbar, (be)fahrbar, b) fahrtüchtig; **2.** ✈ lenkbar (Luftschiff); **nav·i·gate** ['nævɪgeɪt] **I** v/i. **1.** schiffen, (zu Schiff) fahren; **2.** bsd. ⚓, ✈ steuern, orten (**to** nach); **II** v/t. **3.** Gewässer a) befahren, b) durch'fahren; **4.** ✈ durch'fliegen; **5.** steuern, lenken; **nav·i·ga·tion** [,nævɪ'geɪʃn] s. **1.** ⚓ Nautik f, Navigati'on f, Schiffsführung f, Schiffahrtskunde f; **2.** ✈ Navigati'onskunde f; **3.** ⚓ Schifffahrt f, Seefahrt f; **4.** ✈, ⚓ a) Navigati'on f, b) Ortung f; **nav·i·ga·tion·al** [,nævɪ'geɪʃnl] adj. Navigations...

nav·i·ga·tion| chan·nel s. Fahrwasser n; **~ chart** s. Navigati'onskarte f; **~ guide** s. Bake f; **~ light** s. Positi'onslicht n; **~ of·fi·cer** s. ⚓, ✈ Navigati'onsoffi,zier m.

nav·i·ga·tor ['nævɪgeɪtə] s. **1.** ⚓ a) Seefahrer m, b) Nautiker m, c) Steuermann m, d) Am. Navigati'onsoffi,zier m; **2.** ✈ a) (Aero)'Nautiker m, b) Beobachter m.

nav·vy ['nævɪ] s. **1.** Brit. Ka'nal-, Erd-, Streckenarbeiter m; **2.** ⊗ Exka'vator m, Löffelbagger m.

na·vy ['neɪvɪ] s. **1.** mst ⚋ 'Kriegsma,rine f; **2.** (Kriegs)Flotte f; **~ blue** s. Ma'rineblau n; **,~-'blue** adj. ma'rineblau; **⚋ Board** s. Brit. Admirali'tät f; **~ league** s. Flottenverein m; **⚋ List** s. Ma'rine,rangliste f; **~ yard** s. Ma'rinewerft f.

nay [neɪ] **I** adv. **1.** obs. nein; **2.** obs. ja so'gar; **II** s. **3.** parl. etc. Nein(stimme f) n: **the ~s have it!** der Antrag ist abgelehnt!

Naz·a·rene [,næzə'riːn] s. Naza'rener m (a. Christus).

naze [neɪz] s. Landspitze f.

Na·zi ['nɑːtsɪ] pol. contp. **I** s. Nazi m; **II** adj. Nazi...; **'Na·zism** [-ɪzəm] s. Na'zismus m.

neap [niːp] **I** adj. niedrig, abnehmend (Flut); **II** s. a. **~ tide** Nippflut f; **III** v/i. zu'rückgehen (Flut).

near [nɪə] **I** adj. **1.** nahe, (ganz) in der Nähe; **2.** nahe (bevorstehend) (Ereignis etc.): **~ upon five o'clock** ziemlich genau um 5 Uhr; **3.** F annähernd, nahezu, fast: **not ~ so bad** bei weitem nicht so schlecht;

Besondere Redewendungen:

~ at hand a) nahe, in der Nähe, dicht dabei, b) fig. nahe bevorstehend; **~ by** → **nearby** I; **come** (od. **go**) **~ to** a) sich ungefähr belaufen auf (acc.), b) e-r Sache sehr nahe kommen, fast er. sein; **come ~ to doing s.th.** et. beinahe tun; **draw ~** heranrücken (a. Zeitpunkt); **live ~** sparsam od. kärglich leben; **sail ~ to the wind** ⚓ hart am Wind segeln;

II adj. □ → **I** u. **nearly**; **4.** nahe (gelegen), in der Nähe: **the ~est place** der nächste Ort; **~ miss** a) ✕ Nahkrepierer m, b) ✈ Beinahezusammenstoß m, c) fig. fast ein Erfolg; **5.** kurz, nahe (Weg): **the ~est way** der kürzeste Weg; **6.** nahe (Zeit, Ereignis): **the ~ future**; **7.** nahe (verwandt): **the ~est relations** die nächsten Verwandten; **8.** eng (befreundet), in'tim: **a ~ friend**; **9.** a'kut, brennend (Frage, Problem etc.); **10.** knapp (Entkommen, Rennen etc.): **that was a ~ thing** F ,das hätte ins

Auge gehen können'; **11.** genau, (wort)getreu (Übersetzung etc.); **12.** sparsam, geizig; **13.** link (vom Fahrer aus; Pferd, Fahrbahnseite etc.): **~ horse** Handpferd n; **14.** Imitations...: **~ leather**, **~ beer** Dünnbier n; **~ silk** Halbseide f; **III** prp. **15.** nahe, in der Nähe von (od. gen.), nahe an (dat.) od. bei, unweit (gen.): **~ s.o.** j-m nahe; **~ doing s.th.** nahe daran, et. zu tun; **16.** (zeitlich) nahe, nicht weit von; **IV** v/t. u. v/i. **17.** sich nähern, näher kommen (dat.): **be ~ing completion** der Vollendung entgegengehen.

near·by [,nɪə'baɪ] adv. bsd. Am. in der Nähe, nahe; **II** ['nɪəbaɪ] adj. nahe (gelegen).

Near East s. geogr., pol. **1.** Brit. obs. die Balkanstaaten pl.; **2.** der Nahe Osten.

near·ly ['nɪəlɪ] adv. **1.** beinahe, fast; **2.** annähernd: **not ~** bei weitem nicht, nicht annähernd; **3.** genau, gründlich; **near·ness** ['nɪənɪs] s. **1.** Nähe f; **2.** Innigkeit f, Vertrautheit f; **3.** große Ähnlichkeit f; **4.** Knauserigkeit f.

near| point s. opt. Nahpunkt m; **'~-side** s. mot. Beifahrerseite f; **,~-'sight·ed** adj. kurzsichtig; **,~-'sight·ed·ness** s. Kurzsichtigkeit f.

neat¹ [niːt] adj. □ **1.** sauber: a) ordentlich, reinlich, b) hübsch, nett (a. fig.), a'drett, geschmackvoll, c) klar, 'übersichtlich, d) geschickt; **2.** treffend (Antwort etc.); **3.** a) rein: **~ silk**, b) pur: **~ whisky**; **4.** sl. prima.

neat² [niːt] **I** s. pl. **1.** coll. Rind-, Hornvieh n, Rinder pl.; **2.** Ochse m, Rind n; **II** adj. **3.** Rind(er)...

'neath, neath [niːθ] prp. poet. od. dial. unter (dat.), 'unterhalb (gen.).

neat·ness ['niːtnɪs] s. **1.** Ordentlichkeit f, Sauberkeit f; **2.** Gefälligkeit f, Nettigkeit f; Zierlichkeit f; **3.** schlichte Ele'ganz, Klarheit f (Stil etc.); **4.** Geschicklichkeit f; **5.** Unvermischtheit f (Getränke etc.).

'neat's-foot oil s. Klauenfett n; **'~-,leath·er** s. Rindsleder n.

neb·u·la ['nebjʊlə] pl. **-lae** [-liː] s. **1.** ast. Nebel(fleck) m; **2.** ✱ a) Trübheit f (des Urins), b) Hornhauttrübung f; **'neb·u·lar** [-lə] adj. ast. **1.** Nebel(fleck)..., Nebular...; **2.** nebelartig; **neb·u·los·i·ty** [,nebjʊ'lɒsɪtɪ] s. **1.** Nebel(igkeit f) f; **2.** Trübheit f; **3.** fig. Verschwommenheit f; **4.** → **nebula** 1; **'neb·u·lous** [-ləs] adj. □ **1.** neb(e)lig, wolkig (a. Flüssigkeit); ast. Nebel...; **2.** fig. verschwommen, nebelhaft.

nec·es·sar·i·ly ['nesəsərəlɪ] adv. **1.** notwendigerweise; **2.** unbedingt: **you need not ~ do it**; **nec·es·sar·y** ['nesəsərɪ] **I** adj. □ **1.** notwendig, nötig, erforderlich (**to** für): **it is ~ for me to do it** es ist nötig, dass ich es tue; **a ~ evil** ein notwendiges Übel; **if ~** nötigenfalls; **2.** unvermeidlich, zwangsläufig, notwendig: **a ~ consequence**; **3.** notgedrungen; **II** s. **4.** Erfordernis n, Bedürfnis n: **necessaries of life** Notbedarf m, Lebensbedürfnisse pl.; **strict necessaries** unentbehrliche Unterhaltsmittel; **5.** ✝ Be'darfsar,tikel m.

ne·ces·si·tar·i·an [nɪ,sesɪ'teərɪən] phls. **I** s. Determi'nist m; **II** adj. determi'nistisch.

ne·ces·si·tate [nɪ'sesɪteɪt] v/t. **1.** notwendig od. nötig machen, erfordern, verlangen; **2.** j-n zwingen, nötigen; **ne·ces·si·ta·tion** [nɪ,sesɪ'teɪʃn] s. Nötigung f, Zwang m; **ne·ces·si·tous** [-təs] adj. □ **1.** bedürftig, Not leidend; **2.** dürftig, ärmlich (Umstände); **3.** notgedrungen (*Handlung*); **ne'ces·si·ty** [-tɪ] s. **1.** Notwendigkeit f: a) Erforderlichkeit f, b) 'Unum‚gänglichkeit f, Unvermeidlichkeit f, c) Zwang m: **as a ~**, **of ~** notwendigerweise; **be under the ~ of doing** gezwungen sein zu tun; **2.** (dringendes) Bedürfnis: (**the bare**) **necessities of life** (die dringendsten) Lebensbedürfnisse; **3.** Not f, Zwangslage f, a. ⚖ Notstand m: **~ is the mother of invention** Not macht erfinderisch; **~ knows no law** Not kennt kein Gebot; **in case of ~** im Notfall; → **virtue** 3; **4.** Not(lage) f, Bedürftigkeit f.

neck [nek] **I** s. **1.** Hals m (a. Flasche, Gewehr, Saiteninstrument); **2.** Nacken m, Genick n: **break one's ~** sich das Genick brechen; **crane one's ~** sich den Hals ausrenken (**at** nach); **get it in the ~** sl. ‚eins aufs Dach bekommen'; **risk one's ~** Kopf u. Kragen riskieren; **stick one's ~ out** F viel riskieren, den Kopf hinhalten; **be up to one's ~ in s.th.** bis über die Ohren in et. stecken; **win by a ~** sport um e-e Kopflänge gewinnen (*Pferd*); **~ and ~** Kopf an Kopf (a. fig.); **~ and crop** mit Stumpf u. Stiel; **~ or nothing** a) (adv.) auf Biegen oder Brechen, b) (attr.) tollkühn, verzweifelt; **it is ~ or nothing** es geht um alles oder nichts; **3.** Hals-, Kammstück n (*Schlachtvieh*); **4.** Ausschnitt m (*Kleid*); **5.** anat. Hals m e-s Organs; **6.** △ Halsglied n (*Säule*); **7.** ☻ a) Hals m (*Welle*), b) Schenkel m (*Achse*), c) (abgesetzter) Zapfen, d) Ansatz m (*Schraube*), e) Einfüllstutzen m; **8.** a) Landenge f, b) Engpass m: **~ of the woods** ‚Ecke' f e-s Landes; **II** v/t. **9.** e-m Huhn etc. den Kopf abschlagen od. den Hals 'umdrehen; **10.** ☻ a. **~ out** aushalsen; **11.** sl. ‚knutschen' od. ‚schmusen' mit; **III** v/i. **12.** sl. ‚knutschen'; **'~·cloth** s. Halstuch n.

neck·er·chief ['nekətʃɪf] s. Halstuch n.

neck·ing ['nekɪŋ] s. **1.** △ Säulenhals m; **2.** ☻ a) Aushalsen n e-s Hohlkörpers, b) Querschnittverminderung f; **3.** sl. ‚Geknutsche' n.

neck·lace ['neklɪs], **'neck·let** [-lɪt] s. Halskette f.

neck| le·ver s. Ringen: Nackenhebel m; **'~·line** s. Ausschnitt m (am Kleid); **~ scis·sors** s. pl. sg. konstr. Ringen: Halsschere f; **'~·tie** s. Kra'watte f, Schlips m; **'~·wear** s. ✝ coll. Kra'watten pl., Kragen pl., Halstücher pl.

ne·crol·o·gy [ne'krɒlədʒɪ] s. **1.** Toten-, Sterbeliste f; **2.** Nachruf m; **nec·ro·man·cer** ['nekrəʊmænsə] s. **1.** Geister-, Totenbeschwörer m; **2.** allg. Schwarzkünstler m; **nec·ro·man·cy** ['nekrəʊmænsɪ] s. **1.** Geisterbeschwörung f, Nekroman'tie f; **2.** allg. schwarze Kunst; **nec·roph·i·lism** [ne'krɒfɪlɪzəm] s. psych. Nekrophi'lie f; **ne·cro·sis** [ne'krəʊsɪs] s. ✿ Ne'krose f, Brand m (a. ♥): **~ of the bone** Knochenfraß m; **ne·crot·ic** [ne'krɒtɪk] adj. ♥, ✿ brandig.

nec·tar ['nektə] s. myth. Nektar m (a. ♥ u. fig.), Göttertrank m; **'nec·ta·rine** [-rɪn] s. ♥ Obst: Nekta'rine f; **'nec·ta·ry** [-ərɪ] s. ♥, zo. Nek'tarium n, Honigdrüse f.

née, bsd. Am. **nee** [neɪ] adj. geborene (vor dem Mädchennamen e-r Frau).

need [niːd] **I** s. **1.** (**of**, **for**) (dringendes) Bedürfnis (nach), Bedarf m (an dat.): **one's own ~s** Eigenbedarf m; **be** (od. **stand**) **in ~ of s.th.** et. dringend brauchen, et. sehr nötig haben; **fill a ~** e-m

Bedürfnis entgegenkommen, e-m Mangel abhelfen; **in ~ of repair** reparaturbedürftig; **have no ~ to do** kein Bedürfnis od. keinen Grund haben zu tun; **2.** Mangel m (**of**, **for** an dat.): **feel the ~ of** (od. **for**) **s.th.** et. vermissen, Mangel an et. verspüren; **3.** dringende Notwendigkeit: **there is no ~ for you to come** du brauchst nicht zu kommen; **4.** Not(lage) f: **in case of ~**, **if ~ be**, **if ~ arise** nötigenfalls, im Notfall; **5.** Armut f, Not f; **6.** pl. Erfordernisse pl., Bedürfnisse pl.; **II** v/t. **7.** benötigen, nötig haben, brauchen; **8.** erfordern: **it ~s all your strength**; **it ~ed doing** es musste (einmal) getan werden; **III** v/aux. **9.** müssen, brauchen: **it ~s to be done** es muss getan werden; **it ~s but to become known** es braucht nur bekannt zu werden; **10.** (vor e-r Verneinung u. in Fragen, ohne to; 3. sg. pres. **need**) brauchen, müssen: **she ~ not do it**; **you ~ not have come** du hättest nicht zu kommen brauchen; **'need·ful** [-fʊl] **I** adj. □ nötig; **II** s. das Nötige: **the ~** F das nötige Kleingeld; **'need·i·ness** [-dɪnɪs] s. Bedürftigkeit f, Armut f.

nee·dle ['niːdl] **I** s. **1.** (Näh-, a. Grammophon-, Magnet- etc.)Nadel f (a. ✿, ♥): **knitting-~** Stricknadel; **as sharp as a ~** fig. äußerst intelligent, ‚auf Draht'; **~'s eye** Nadelöhr n; **get** (od. **take**) **the ~** F ‚hochgehen', e-e Wut kriegen; **give s.o. the ~** → 7; **2.** ☻ a) Ven'tilnadel f, b) mot. Schwimmernadel f (Vergaser), c) Zeiger m, d) Zunge f (Waage), e) Radiernadel f; **3.** Nadel f (Berg-, Felsspitze); **4.** Obe'lisk m; **5.** min. Kri'stallnadel f; **II** v/t. **6.** (mit e-r Nadel) nähen, durch'stechen; ✿ punktieren: **~ one's way through** fig. sich hindurchschlängeln; **7.** F durch Sticheleien aufheizen, reizen; **8.** anstacheln; **9.** F Getränk durch Alkoholzusatz schärfen; **~ bath** s. Strahldusche f; **'~·book** s. Nadelbuch n; **~ gun** s. ✗ Zündnadelgewehr n; **'~·like** adj. nadelartig; **~ point** s. **1.** Petit'pointsticke‚rei f; **2.** → **'~·point lace** s. Nadelspitze f (Ggs. Klöppelspitze).

need·less ['niːdlɪs] adj. □ unnötig, 'überflüssig: **~ to say** selbstredend, selbstverständlich; **~ly** adv. unnötig(erweise); **'need·less·ness** [-nɪs] s. Unnötigkeit f, 'Überflüssigkeit f.

nee·dle| valve s. ☻ 'Nadelven‚til n; **'~·wom·an** s. [irr.] Näherin f; **'~·work I** s. Handarbeit f, Nähe'rei f; **II** adj. Handarbeits...: **~ shop**.

needs [niːdz] adv. unbedingt, notwendigerweise: **if you must ~ do it** wenn du es durchaus tun willst.

need·y ['niːdɪ] adj. □ arm, bedürftig, notleidend.

ne'er [neə] poet. für **never**; **'~·do-well I** s. Tunichtgut m, Tunichtgut m; **II** adj. nichtsnutzig.

ne·far·i·ous [nɪ'feərɪəs] adj. □ ruchlos, schändlich; **ne'far·i·ous·ness** [-nɪs] s. Ruchlosigkeit f, Bosheit f.

ne·gate [nɪ'geɪt] v/t. **1.** verneinen, negieren, leugnen; **2.** annullieren, unwirksam machen, aufheben, verwerfen; **ne·ga·tion** [-eɪʃn] s. **1.** Verneinung f, Verneinen n, Negieren n; **2.** Verwerfung f, Annullierung f, Aufhebung f; **3.** phls. a) (Logik) Negati'on f, b) Nichts n.

neg·a·tive ['negətɪv] **I** adj. □ **1.** negativ, verneinend; **2.** abschlägig, ablehnend (Antwort etc.); **3.** erfolglos, ergebnislos; **4.** negativ (ohne positive Werte); **5.** 🜆, ⚡, ℟, ✇, phot., phys. negativ: **~**

conductor ⚡ Minusleitung f; **~ electrode** Kat(h)ode f; **~ lens** opt. Zerstreuungslinse f; **~ sign** ℟ Minuszeichen n, negatives Vorzeichen; **~!** Fehlanzeige!; **II** s. **6.** Verneinung f: **answer in the ~** verneinen; **7.** abschlägige Antwort; **8.** ling. Negati'on f; **9.** a) Einspruch m, Veto n, b) ablehnende Stimme; **10.** negative Eigenschaft, Negativum n; **11.** ⚡ negativer Pol; **12.** ℟ a) Minuszeichen n, b) negative Zahl; **13.** phot. Negativ n; **III** v/t. **14.** negieren, verneinen; **15.** verwerfen, ablehnen; **16.** wider'legen; **17.** unwirksam machen, neutralisieren, aufheben; **'neg·a·tiv·ism** [-vɪzəm] s. Negati'vismus m (a. phls., psych.); **ne·ga·tor** [nɪ'geɪtə] s. Verneiner m; **'neg·a·to·ry** [-tərɪ] adj. verneinend, negativ.

neg·lect [nɪ'glekt] **I** v/t. **1.** vernachlässigen; **2.** miss'achten; **3.** versäumen, unter'lassen (**to do** od. **doing** zu tun); **4.** über'sehen, -'gehen; außer Acht lassen; **II** s. **5.** Vernachlässigung f, Hint'ansetzung f; **6.** 'Missachtung f; **7.** Unter'lassung f, Versäumnis n, a. Fahrlässigkeit f: **~ of duty** Pflichtversäumnis f; **8.** Verwahrlosung f: **in a state of ~** verwahrlost; **9.** Über'gehen n, Auslassung f; **10.** Nachlässigkeit f; **neg'lect·ful** [-fʊl] adj. □ → **negligent** 1.

neg·li·gée ['neglɪʒeɪ] s. Negli'gee n: a) ungezwungene Hauskleidung, b) dünner Morgenmantel.

neg·li·gence ['neglɪdʒəns] s. **1.** Nachlässigkeit f, Unachtsamkeit f; **2.** ⚖ Fahrlässigkeit f: **contributory ~** mitwirkendes Verschulden; **'neg·li·gent** [-nt] adj. □ **1.** nachlässig, gleichgültig, unachtsam (**of** gegen): **be ~ of s.th.** et. vernachlässigen, et. außer Acht lassen; **2.** ℟ fahrlässig; **3.** lässig, sa'lopp.

neg·li·gi·ble ['neglɪdʒəbl] adj. □ **1.** nebensächlich, unwesentlich; **2.** geringfügig, unbedeutend; → **quantity** 2.

ne·go·ti·a·bil·i·ty [nɪ‚gəʊʃjə'bɪlətɪ] s. ✝ **1.** Verkäuflichkeit f, Begebbarkeit f; **2.** Begebbarkeit f; **3.** Bank-, Börsenfähigkeit f; **4.** Über'tragbarkeit f; **5.** Verwertbarkeit f; **ne·go·ti·a·ble** [nɪ'gəʊʃjəbl] adj. □ **1.** ✝ a) verkäuflich, veräußerlich, b) verkehrsfähig, c) bank-, börsenfähig, d) (durch Indossa'ment) über'tragbar, begebbar, e) verwertbar: **~ instrument** begebbares (Wert)Papier; **not ~** nur zur Verrechnung; **2.** über'windbar (Hindernis); befahrbar (Straße); **3.** auf dem Verhandlungsweg erreichbar: **salary ~** Gehalt nach Vereinbarung.

ne·go·ti·ate [nɪ'gəʊʃɪeɪt] **I** v/i. **1.** ver-, unter'handeln, in Unter'handlung stehen (**with** mit, **for**, **about** um, wegen): **negotiating table** Verhandlungstisch m; **II** v/t. **2.** Vertrag etc. zu'stande bringen, (ab)schließen; **3.** verhandeln über (acc.); **4.** ✝ Wechsel begeben: **~ back** zurückgeben; **5.** Hindernis etc. über'winden, a. Kurve nehmen; **ne·go·ti·a·tion** [nɪ‚gəʊʃɪ'eɪʃn] s. **1.** Ver-, Unter'handlung f: **enter into ~s** in Verhandlungen eintreten: **by way of ~** auf dem Verhandlungswege; **2.** Aushandeln n (Vertrag); **3.** ✝ Begebung f, Über'tragung f (Wechsel etc.): **further ~** Weiterbegebung; **4.** Über'windung f, Nehmen n von Hindernissen; **ne·go·ti·a·tor** [-tə] s. **1.** 'Unterhändler m; **2.** Vermittler m.

ne·gress ['niːgrɪs] s. obs. Negerin f.

ne·gro ['niːgrəʊ] **I** pl. **-groes** s. Neger (-in); **II** adj. Neger...: **~ question** Negerfrage f, -problem n; **~ spiritual** → **spiritual** 8; **'ne·groid** [-rɔɪd] adj. negro'id, negerartig.

Ne·gus¹ ['niːɡəs] *s. hist.* Negus *m (äthiopischer Königstitel).*

ne·gus² ['niːɡəs] *s.* Glühwein *m.*

neigh [neɪ] **I** *v/t. u. v/i.* wiehern; **II** *s.* Gewieher *n,* Wiehern *n.*

neigh·bo(u)r ['neɪbə] **I** *s.* **1.** Nachbar (-in); **2.** Nächste(r) *m,* Mitmensch *m;* **II** *adj.* **3.** → **neighbo(u)ring;** **III** *v/t.* **4.** (an)grenzen an (*acc.*); **IV** *v/i.* **5.** benachbart sein, in der Nachbarschaft wohnen; **6.** grenzen (*upon* an *acc.*); **'neigh·bo(u)r·hood** [-hʊd] *s.* **1.** Nachbarschaft *f* (*a. fig.*), Um'gebung *f,* Nähe *f: in the ~* of a) in der Umgebung von, b) *fig.* F ungefähr, etwa, um ... herum; **2.** *coll.* Nachbarn *pl.,* Nachbarschaft *f;* **3.** (Wohn)Gegend *f: a fashionable ~;* **'neigh·bo(u)ring** [-bərɪŋ] *adj.* benachbart, angrenzend, Nachbar...: *~ state a.* Anliegerstaat *m;* **'neighbo(u)r·li·ness** [-lɪnɪs] *s.* (gut)'nachbarliches Verhalten; Freundlichkeit *f;* **'neigh·bo(u)r·ly** [-lɪ] *adj.* **1.** (gut)'nachbarlich; **2.** freundlich, gesellig.

nei·ther ['naɪðə] **I** *adj. u. pron.* **1.** kein (von beiden): *~ of you* keiner von euch (beiden); **II** *cj.* **2.** weder: *~ you nor he knows* weder du weißt es noch er; **3.** noch (auch), auch nicht, ebenso wenig: *he does not know, ~ do I* er weiß es nicht, noch od. ebenso wenig weiß ich es.

nem·a·tode ['nemətəʊd] *zo. s.* Nema'tode *f,* Fadenwurm *m.*

nem con [ˌnem'kɒn] *adv.* einstimmig.

nem·e·sis, *a.* **Ɒ** ['nemɪsɪs] *s. myth. u. fig.* Nemesis *f,* (die Göttin der) Vergeltung *f.*

ne·mo ['niːməʊ] *pl.* **-mos** *s. Radio, TV:* 'Außenrepor,tage *f.*

neo- [niːəʊ] *in Zssgn* neu, jung, neo..., Neo...

ne·o·lith ['niːəʊlɪθ] *s.* jungsteinzeitliches Gerät; **ne·o·lith·ic** [ˌniːəʊ'lɪθɪk] *adj.* jungsteinzeitlich, neo'lithisch: **Ɒ** *period* Jungsteinzeit *f.*

ne·ol·o·gism [niːˈɒlədʒɪzəm] *s.* **1.** *ling.* Neolo'gismus *m,* Wortneubildung *f;* **2.** *eccl.* neue Dok'trin; **ne'ol·o·gy** [-dʒɪ] *s.* **1.** → **neologism** 1 *u.* 2; **2.** *ling.* Neolo'gie *f,* Bildung *f* neuer Wörter.

ne·on ['niːɒn] *s.* **Ⓡ** Neon *n: ~ lamp* Neonlampe *f,* Leucht(stoff)röhre *f; ~ signs* Leuchtreklame *f.*

ne·o·Na·zi [ˌniːəʊ'nɑːtsɪ] **I** *s.* Neonazi *m;* **II** *adj.* 'neona,zistisch.

ne·o·phyte ['niːəʊfaɪt] *s.* **1.** *eccl.* Neubekehrte(r *m) f,* Konver'tit(in); **2.** *R.C. a)* No'vize (*m, f,*) b) Jungpriester *m;* **3.** *fig.* Neuling *m,* Anfänger(in).

ne·o·plasm ['niːəʊplæzəm] *s.* **ℱ** Neo'plasma *n,* Gewächs *n.*

ne·o·ter·ic [ˌniːəʊ'terɪk] *adj.* (□ *~ally*) neuzeitlich, mo'dern.

Ne·o·zo·ic [ˌniːəʊ'zəʊɪk] *geol.* **I** *s.* Neo'zoikum *n,* Neuzeit *f;* **II** *adj.* neo'zoisch.

Nep·a·lese [ˌnepɔː'liːz] **I** *s.* Nepa'lese *m,* Nepalesin *f,* Bewohner(in) von Nepal; Nepa'lesen *pl.;* **II** *adj.* nepa'lesisch.

neph·ew ['nefjuː] *s.* Neffe *m.*

ne·phol·o·gy [nɪˈfɒlədʒɪ] *s.* Wolkenkunde *f.*

ne·phrit·ic [ne'frɪtɪk] *adj.* **ℱ** Nieren...; **ne·phri·tis** [ne'fraɪtɪs] *s.* **ℱ** Ne'phritis *f,* Nierenentzündung *f;* **neph·ro·lith** ['nefrəʊlɪθ] *s.* **ℱ** Nierenstein *m;* **ne·phrol·o·gist** [ne'frɒlədʒɪst] *s.* **ℱ** Nierenfacharzt *m,* Uro'loge *m.*

nep·o·tism ['nepətɪzəm] *s.* Nepo'tismus *m,* Vetternwirtschaft *f.*

Nep·tune ['neptjuːn] *s. myth. u. ast.* Neptun *m.*

nerd [nɜːd] *s.* **1.** Trottel *m,* Depp *m;* **2.**

(*Computer- etc.*)Freak *m.*

Ne·re·id ['nɪərɪɪd] *s. myth.* Nere'ide *f,* Wassernymphe *f.*

ner·va·tion [nɜː'veɪʃn], **nerv·a·ture** ['nɜːvə,tʃʊə] *s.* **1.** Anordnung *f* der Nerven; **2.** **♀** Aderung *f.*

nerve [nɜːv] **I** *s.* **1.** Nerv(enfaser *f) m: get on s.o.'s ~s* j-m auf die Nerven gehen; *be all ~s, be a bag of ~s* F ein Nervenbündel sein; *a fit of ~s* e-e Nervenkrise; *strain every ~* s-e ganze Kraft aufbieten; **2.** *fig. a)* Lebensnerv *m, b)* Stärke *f,* Ener'gie *f, c)* (innere) Ruhe, *d)* Mut *m, e) sl.* Frechheit *f: lose one's ~* die Nerven verlieren; *have the ~ to do s.th.* es wagen, et. zu tun; *he has got a ~! sl.* der hat vielleicht Nerven!; **3.** **♀** Nerv *m,* Ader *f (Blatt);* **4.** **⊿** (Gewölbe)Rippe *f;* **II** *v/t.* **5.** *fig.* (körperlich *od.* seelisch) stärken, ermutigen: *~ o.s.* sich aufraffen; *~ cen·ter Am., ~ cen·tre Brit. s.* Nervenzentrum *n (a. fig.); ~ cord s.* Nervenstrang *m.*

nerved [nɜːvd] *adj.* **1.** nervig (*mst in Zssgn*): *strong-~* nervenstark; **2.** **♀**, *zo.* geädert, gerippt.

nerve| gas *s.* Nervengas *n;* **'~·less** ['nɜːvlɪs] *adj.* □ **1.** *fig.* kraft-, ener'gielos; **2.** ohne Nerven; **3.** **♀** ohne Adern, nervenlos; *~ poi·son s.* Nervengift *n;* **'~·rack·ing** *adj.* nervenaufreibend.

nerv·ine ['nɜːviːn] *adj. u. s.* **ℱ** nervenstärkend(es Mittel).

nerv·ous ['nɜːvəs] *adj.* **1.** Nerven...(*-system, -zusammenbruch etc.*): *~ break·down* Nervenzs.-bruch *m; ~ excite·ment* nervöse Erregtheit; *~ wreck* ‚Nervenbündel' *n;* **2.** nervenreich; **3.** ner'vös: *a)* nervenschwach, erregbar, *b)* ängstlich, scheu, *c)* aufgeregt; **4.** aufregend; **5.** *obs.* kräftig, nervig; **'nervous·ness** [-nɪs] *s.* Nervosi'tät *f.*

nerv·y ['nɜːvɪ] *adj.* F **1.** frech; **2.** ner'vös; **3.** nervenaufreibend.

nes·ci·ence ['nesɪəns] *s.* (vollständige) Unwissenheit; **'nes·ci·ent** [-nt] *adj.* unwissend (*of* in *dat.*).

ness [nes] *s.* Vorgebirge *n.*

nest [nest] **I** *s.* **1.** *orn., zo., a. geol.* Nest *n;* **2.** *fig.* Nest *n,* Zufluchtsort *m,* behagliches Heim; **3.** *fig.* Schlupfwinkel *m,* Brutstätte *f: ~ of vice* Lasterhöhle *f;* **4.** Brut *f (junger Tiere): take a ~* ein Nest ausnehmen; **5.** **✕** (Widerstands-, M'G-)Nest *n;* **6.** Serie *f,* Satz *m (ineinander passender Dinge, z. B. Schüsseln);* **7.** **☉** Satz *m,* Gruppe *f: ~ of boiler tubes* Heizrohrbündel *n;* **II** *v/i.* **8.** *a)* ein Nest bauen, *b)* nisten; **9.** sich einnisten, sich 'niederlassen; **10.** Vogelnester ausnehmen; **III** *v/t.* **11.** Töpfe *etc.* inein'ander stellen *od.* setzen; *~ egg s.* **1.** Nestei *n;* **2.** *fig.* Spar-, Notgroschen *m.*

nes·tle ['nesl] **I** *v/i.* **1.** *a. ~ down* sich behaglich 'niederlassen; **2.** sich anschmiegen *od.* kuscheln (*to, against* an *acc.*); **3.** sich einnisten; **II** *v/t.* **4.** schmiegen, kuscheln (*on, to, against* an *acc.*); **nest·ling** ['nesl̩ɪŋ] *s.* **1.** *orn.* Nestling *m;* **2.** *fig.* Nesthäkchen *n.*

net¹ [net] **I** *s.* **1.** (*a. weitS.* Straßen- *etc.,* **☌** Koordi'naten)Netz *n: the* **Ɒ** (*od. ~*) das 'Internet; *a. network s;* **2.** *fig.* Falle *f,* Netz *n,* Garn *n;* **3.** netzartiges Gewebe, Netz *n;* **♀** Tüll *m,* Musse'lin *m: ~ curtain* Store *m;* **4.** *Tennis:* Netzball *m;* **II** *v/t.* **5.** mit e-m Netz fangen; **6.** *fig.* (ein)fangen; **7.** mit e-m Netz um'geben *od.* bedecken; **8.** *Gewässer* mit Netzen abfischen; **9.** in Fi'let arbeiten, knüpfen; **10.** *Tennis:* Ball ins Netz schlagen; **III** *v/i.* **11.** Netz- *od.* Fi'letarbeit ma-

---

chen.

net² [net] **I** *adj.* **✝ 1.** netto, Netto..., Rein..., Roh...: *~ income* Nettoeinkommen *n;* **II** *v/t.* **2.** netto einbringen, e-n Reingewinn von ... abwerfen; **3.** netto verdienen, e-n Reingewinn haben von; *~ a·mount s.* Nettobetrag *m,* Reinertrag *m; ~ as·sets s. pl.* Reinvermögen *n; ~ bor·row·ings s. pl.* 'Nettokre,ditaufnahme *f; ~ cash s.* **✝** netto Kasse: *~ in advance* Nettokasse im Voraus; *~ ef·fi·cien·cy s.* **☉** Nutzleistung *f.*

neth·er ['neðə] *adj.* **1.** unter, Unter...: *~ regions, ~ world* Unterwelt *f;* **2.** nieder, Nieder...

Neth·er·land·er ['neðələndə] *s.* Niederländer(in); **'Neth·er·land·ish** [-dɪʃ] *adj.* niederländisch.

'neth·er·most *adj.* unterst, tiefst.

net·i·quette ['netɪket] *s. Computer, Internet:* Neti'quette *f,* Neti'kette *f.*

net| load *s.* **✝,** **☉** Nutzlast *f; ~ price s.* **✝** Nettopreis *m; ~ pro·ceeds s. pl.* **✝** Nettoeinnahme(n *pl.) f,* Reinerlös *m; ~ prof·it s.* **✝** Reingewinn *m.*

net surf·er s., Net surf·er *s.* Internetsurfer(in).

net·ted ['netɪd] *adj.* **1.** netzförmig, maschig; **2.** von Netzen um'geben *od.* bedeckt; **'net·ting** [-tɪŋ] *s.* **1.** Netzstricken *n,* Fi'letarbeit *f;* **2.** Netz(werk) *n,* Geflecht *n (a. Draht);* **✕** Tarnnetze *pl.*

net·tle ['netl] **I** *s.* **♀** Nessel *f: grasp the ~ fig.* den Stier bei den Hörnern packen; **II** *v/t.* **2.** mit *od.* an Nesseln brennen; **3.** *fig.* ärgern, reizen: *be ~d at* aufgebracht sein über (*acc.*); *~ cloth s.* Nesseltuch *n; ~ rash s.* **ℱ** Nesselausschlag *m.*

net| weight *s.* **✝** Netto-, Rein-, Eigen-, Trockengewicht *n; ~ work s.* **1.** Netz-, Maschenwerk *n,* Geflecht *n;* Netz *n, Computer:* Netz(werk) *n: ~ ac·cess* Netzzugang *m; ~ driver* Netzwerktreiber *m; ~ server* Netzwerkserver *m;* **2.** Netz-, Fi'letarbeit *f;* **3.** *fig.* Netz *n: ~ of roads* Straßennetz *n; ~ of intrigues* Netz von Intrigen; **4.** **✏** *a)* Leitungs-, Verteilungsnetz *n, b) Rundfunk:* Sendernetz *n,* -gruppe *f;* **II** *v/t. Computer:* vernetzen; *~ yield s.* **✝** ef'fek'tive Ren'dite *od.* Verzinsung, Nettoertrag *m.*

neu·ral ['njʊərəl] *adj. physiol.* Nerven...: *~ axis* Nervenachse *f.*

neu·ral·gia [ˌnjʊə'rældʒə] *s.* **ℱ** Neural'gie *f,* Nervenschmerz *m;* **neu'ral·gic** [-dʒɪk] *adj.* (□ *~ally*) neur'algisch.

neu·ras·the·ni·a [ˌnjʊərəs'θiːnɪə] *s.* **ℱ** Neurasthe'nie *f,* Nervenschwäche *f;* **neu·ras·then·ic** [-'θenɪk] **ℱ I** *adj.* (□ *~ally*) neura'sthenisch; **II** *s.* Neura'stheniker(in).

neu·ri·tis [ˌnjʊə'raɪtɪs] *s.* Nervenentzündung *f.*

neu·rol·o·gist [njʊə'rɒlədʒɪst] *s.* Neuro'loge *m,* Nervenarzt *m;* **neu'rol·o·gy** [-dʒɪ] *s.* Neurolo'gie *f.*

neu·ro·path ['njʊərəʊpæθ] *s.* **ℱ** Nervenleidende(r *m) f;* **neu·ro·path·ic** [ˌnjʊərəʊ'pæθɪk] *adj.* (□ *~ally*) neuro'pathisch: *a)* ner'vös (*Leiden etc.*), *b)* nervenkrank; **neu·ro·pa·thist** [njʊə'rɒpəθɪst] → **neurologist; neu·rop·a·thy** [njʊə'rɒpəθɪ] *s.* Nervenleiden *n.*

neu·rop·ter·an [ˌnjʊə'rɒptərən] *zo.* **I** *adj.* Netzflügler...; **II** *s.* Netzflügler *m.*

neu·ro·sis [njʊə'rəʊsɪs] *pl.* **-ses** [-siːz] *s.* **ℱ** Neu'rose *f;* **neu·rot·ic** [-'rɒtɪk] **I** *adj.* (□ *~ally*) **1.** neu'rotisch; **2.** Nerven...(*-mittel, -leiden etc.*); **II** *s.* **3.** Neu'rotiker(in); **4.** Nervenmittel *n;* **neu-**

'**rot·o·my** [-'rɒtəmɪ] s. **1.** 'Nervenanato-,mie f; **2.** Nervenschnitt m.

neu·ter ['njuːtə] **I** adj. **1.** ling. a) sächlich, b) intransitiv (Verb); **2.** biol. geschlechtslos; **II** s. **3.** ling. a) Neutrum n, sächliches Hauptwort, b) intransitives Verb; **4.** ♀ Blüte f ohne Staubgefäße u. Stempel; **5.** zo. geschlechtsloses od. kastriertes Tier; **III** v/t. **6.** kastrieren.

neu·tral ['njuːtrəl] **I** adj. □ **1.** neu'tral (a. pol.), par'teilos, 'unpar,teiisch, unbeteiligt; **2.** neu'tral, unbestimmt, farblos; **3.** neu'tral (a. ♠, ♀), gleichgültig, 'indiffe,rent; **4.** ♀, zo. geschlechtslos; **5.** ⊕, mot. a) Ruhe..., Null... (Lage), b) Leerlauf... (Gang); **II** s. **6.** a) Neu'trale(r m) f, Par'teilose(r m) f, b) neu'traler Staat, c) Angehörige(r m) f e-s neu-'tralen Staates; **7.** mot., ⊕ Ruhelage f, Leerlaufstellung f: put the car in ~ den Gang herausnehmen; ~ ax·is s. [irr.] ⚡, phys., ⊕ neutrale Achse, Nulllinie f; ~ con·duc·tor s. ⚡ Nullleiter m; ~ gear s. ⊕ Leerlauf(gang) m.

neu·tral·ism ['njuːtrəlɪzəm] s. Neutra-'lismus m; '**neu·tral·ist** [-ɪst] **I** s. Neut-ra'list m; **II** adj. neutra'listisch.

neu·tral·i·ty [njuː'trælətɪ] s. Neutrali'tät f (a. ♠, pol.).

neu·tral·i·za·tion [,njuːtrəlaɪ'zeɪʃn] s. **1.** Neutralisierung f, Ausgleichung f, (gegenseitige) Aufhebung f; **2.** ♠ Neutrali-sati'on f; **3.** pol. Neutrali'tätserklärung f e-s Staates etc.; **4.** ⚡ Entkopplung f; **5.** ✕ Niederhaltung f, Lahmlegung f, a. sport: Ausschaltung f; **neu·tral·ize** ['njuːtrəlaɪz] v/t. **1.** neutralisieren (a. ♠), ausgleichen, aufheben: ~ each other sich gegenseitig aufheben; **2.** pol. für neu'tral erklären; **3.** ⚡ neutralisieren, entkoppeln; **4.** ✕ niederhalten, -kämpfen, a. sport: Gegner ausschalten; Kampfstoff entgiften.

neu·tral| line s. **1.** ⚡, phys. Neu'trale f, neu'trale Linie; **2.** phys. Nulllinie f; **3.** → neutral axis; ~ po·si·tion s. **1.** ⊕ Nullstellung f, -lage f; Ruhestellung f; **2.** ⚡ neu'trale Stellung (Anker etc.).

neu·tro·dyne ['njuːtrədaɪn] s. ⚡ Neut-ro'dyn n.

neu·tron ['njuːtron] phys. **I** s. Neu'tron n; **II** adj. Neutronen...(-bombe, -zahl etc.).

né·vé ['neveɪ] (Fr.) s. Firn(feld n) m.

nev·er ['nevə] adv. **1.** nie, niemals, nimmer(mehr); **2.** durch'aus nicht, (ganz und) gar nicht, nicht im Geringsten; **3.** (doch) wohl nicht;
Besondere Redewendungen:
~ ever noch nie; ~ fear nur keine Bange!; ~ mind das macht nichts!; well I ~! F nein, so was!, das ist ja unerhört!; ~ so auch noch so; he ~ so much as answered er hat noch nicht einmal geantwortet; ~ say die! nur nicht verzweifeln!

'**nev·er|-do-,well** s. Taugenichts m, Tunichtgut m; ',~-'end·ing [-ər'e-] adj. endlos, nicht enden wollend; ,~- '-fail·ing adj. **1.** unfehlbar, untrüglich; **2.** nie versiegend; ',~'more adv. nimmermehr, nie wieder; ,~-'nev·er s. F **1.** buy on the ~ 'abstottern', auf Pump kaufen; **2.** a. ~ land a) 'Arsch m der Welt', b) fig. Wolken'kuckucksheim n.

,**nev·er·the'less** adv. nichtsdesto'weniger, dennoch, trotzdem.

ne·vus ['niːvəs] s. ☀ Muttermal n, Leberfleck m: vascular ~ Feuermal.

new [njuː] **I** adj. □ → newly; **1.** allg. neu: nothing ~ nichts Neues; ~ broom² ; **2.** a. ling. neu, mo'dern; bsd. contp. neumodisch; **3.** neu (Obst etc.),

---

frisch (Brot, Milch etc.); **4.** neu (Ggs. alt), gut erhalten: as good as ~ so gut wie neu; **5.** neu(entdeckt od. -erschienen od. -erstanden od. -geschaffen): ~ facts; ~ star; ~ moon Neumond m; ~ publications Neuerscheinungen pl.; the ~ woman die Frau von heute; the ☾ World die Neue Welt (Amerika); that is not ~ to me das ist mir nichts Neues; **6.** unerforscht: ~ ground Neuland n (a. fig.); **7.** neu (gewählt, ernannt): the ~ president; **8.** (to) a) j-m unbekannt, b) nicht vertraut (mit e-r Sache), unerfahren (in dat.), c) j-m ungewohnt; **9.** neu, ander, besser: feel a ~ man sich wie neugeboren fühlen; **10.** erneut: a ~ start; **11.** (bsd. bei Ortsnamen) Neu...; **II** adv. **12.** neu(erlich), so'eben, frisch (bsd. in Zssgn): ~-built neu erbaut.

new·bie ['njuːbɪ] s. F bsd. Computer: Neuling m, Anfänger(in).

'**new|·born** adj. neugeboren (a. fig.); ~ build·ing s. Neubau m; '~-come adj. neu angekommen; '~,com·er s. **1.** Neuankömmling m, Fremde(r m) f; **2.** Neuling m (to in e-m Fach); ☾ Deal s. hist. New Deal m (Wirtschafts- u. Sozialpolitik des Präsidenten F. D. Roosevelt).

new·el ['njuːəl] s. ⊕ **1.** Spindel f (Wendeltreppe, Gussform etc.); **2.** Endpfosten m (Geländer).

'**new|,fan·gled** [-,fæŋgld] adj. contp. neu(modisch); '~-fledged adj. **1.** flügge geworden; **2.** fig. neu gebacken; ,~- '-found adj. **1.** neu gefunden; neu erfunden; **2.** neu entdeckt.

New·found·land (dog) [njuː'faʊnd-lənd], **New'found·land·er** [-də] s. Neu'fundländer m (Hund).

new·ish ['njuːɪʃ] adj. ziemlich neu; **new·ly** ['njuːlɪ] adv. **1.** neulich, kürzlich, jüngst: ~ married neu od. jung vermählt; **2.** von neuem; **new·ness** ['njuː-nɪs] s. Neuheit f, das Neue; fig. Unerfahrenheit f.

,**new-'rich I** adj. neureich; **II** s. Neureiche(r m) f, Parve'nü m.

news [njuːz] s. pl. sg. konstr. **1.** das Neue, Neuigkeit(en pl.) f, Neues n, Nachricht(en pl.) f: a piece of ~ e-e Nachricht od. Neuigkeit; at this ~ bei dieser Nachricht; commercial ~ ✝ Handelsteil m (Zeitung); break the (bad) ~ to s.o. j-m die (schlechte) Nachricht (schonend) beibringen; have ~ from s.o. von j-m Nachricht haben; it is ~ to me das ist mir (ganz) neu; what('s the) ~? was gibt es Neues?; ~ certainly travels fast! es macht sich alles herum!; he is bad ~s Am. sl. mit ihm werden wir Ärger kriegen; **2.** neueste (Zeitungs-, Radio)Nachrichten pl.: be in the ~ (in der Öffentlichkeit) von sich reden machen; ~ a·gen·cy s. 'Nachrichtenagen,tur f, -bü,ro n; '~,a·gent s. Zeitungshändler(in); ~ black·out s. Nachrichtensperre f; '~·boy s. Zeitungsjunge m; ~ butch·er s. 🚂 Am. Verkäufer m von Zeitungen, Süßigkeiten etc.; '~·cast s. Radio, TV: Nachrichtensendung f; '~,cast·er s. Nachrichtensprecher(in); ~ cin·e·ma s. Aktuali'tätenkino n; ~ con·fer·ence s. 'Pressekonfe,renz f; '~,deal·er Am. → newsagent; ~ flash s. (eingeblendete) Kurzmeldung; '~·group s. Internet: Newsgroup f (e-e Art öffentliches schwarzes Brett zum Nachrichtenaustausch); '~-hawk s. Am. F 'Zeitungsre,porter(in); ~ i·tem s. 'Presseno,tiz f; '~,let·ter s. (Nachrichten)Rundschrei-

---

ben n, Zirku'lar n; ~ mag·a·zine s. 'Nachrichtenmaga,zin n; '~·man [-mæn] s. [irr.] **1.** Zeitungshändler m, -austräger m; **2.** Journa'list m; '~,mon·ger s. Neuigkeitskrämer(in).

'**news,pa·per** s. Zeitung f; ~ ad·ver·tise·ment s. 'Zeitungsan,nonce f, -an-zeige f; ~ clip·ping Am., ~ cut·ting s. Zeitungsausschnitt m; '~·man [-mæn] s. [irr.] **1.** Zeitungsverkäufer m; **2.** Journa'list m; **3.** Zeitungsverleger m.

'**news|·print** s. 'Zeitungspa,pier n; '~,read·er s. Brit. für newscaster; '~·reel s. Wochenschau f; ~ re·lease s. Pressemitteilung f; '~·room [-rʊm] s. **1.** 'Nachrichtenraum m, -zen,trale f; **2.** Brit. Zeitschriftenlesesaal m; **3.** Am. 'Zeitungsladen m, -ki,osk m; ~ serv·ice s. Nachrichtendienst m; '~·sheet s. Informati'onsblatt n; '~·stall s. Brit. '~·stand s. Zeitungskiosk m, -stand m.

New Style s. neue Zeitrechnung (nach dem gregorianischen Kalender), neuer Stil.

news| ven·dor s. Zeitungsverkäufer(in); '~,wor·thy adj. von Inter'esse (für den Zeitungsleser), berichtenswert, schlagzeilenträchtig.

news·y ['njuːzɪ] adj. F voller Neuigkeiten.

newt [njuːt] s. zo. Wassermolch m.

new·ton ['njuːtn] s. phys. Newton n (Maßeinheit).

New·to·ni·an [njuː'təʊnjən] adj. new-ton(i)sch: ~ force newtonsche Kraft.

new| year s. Neujahr n, das neue Jahr; ☾ Year s. Neujahrstag m; ☾ Year's Day s. Neujahrstag m; ☾ Year's Eve s. Sil'vesterabend m; ☾ Zea·land·er ['ziːləndə] s. Neuseeländer(in).

next [nekst] **I** adj. adv. **1.** nächst, nächstfolgend, -stehend: the ~ house (train) das nächste Haus (der nächste Zug); (the) ~ day am nächsten od. folgenden Tag; ~ door (im Haus) nebenan; ~ door to fig. beinahe, fast unmöglich etc., so gut wie; ~ to a) (gleich) neben, b) (gleich) nach (Rang, Reihenfolge), c) fast unmöglich etc.; ~ to nothing fast gar nichts; ~ to last zweitletzt; the ~ but one der (die, das) Übernächste; ~ in size a) nächstgrößer, b) nächstkleiner; ~ friend ꝛꞇ Prozesspfleger m; the ~ of kin der (pl. die) nächste(n) Angehörige(n) od. Verwandte(n); be ~ best a) der (die, das) Zweitbeste sein, b) (to) fig. gleich kommen (nach), fast so gut sein (wie); week after ~ übernächste Woche; what ~? was (denn) noch?; **II** adv. **2.** (Ort, Zeit etc.) zu'nächst, gleich dar'auf, als Nächste(r) od. Nächstes: come ~ (als Nächstes) folgen; **3.** nächstens, demnächst, das nächste Mal; **4.** (bei Aufzählung) dann, dar'auf; **III** prp. **5.** (gleich) neben (dat.) od. bei (dat.) od. an (dat.); **6.** zu'nächst nach, (an Rang) gleich nach; **IV** s. **7.** der (die, das) Nächste; '**next-door** adj. neben'an, im Nachbar- od. Nebenhaus, benachbart.

nex·us ['neksəs] s. Verknüpfung f, Zs.-hang m.

nib [nɪb] s. **1.** Schnabel m (Vogel); **2.** (Gold-, Stahl)Spitze f (Schreibfeder); **3.** pl. Kaffee- od. Ka'kaobohnenstückchen pl.

nib·ble ['nɪbl] **I** v/t. **1.** nagen, knabbern an (dat.): ~ off abbeißen, -fressen; **2.** vorsichtig anbeißen (Fische am Köder); **II** v/i. **3.** nagen, knabbern (at an dat.): ~ at one's food im Essen herumstochern; **4.** Kekse etc. ,knabbern, naschen; **5.** (fast) anbeißen (Fisch) (a. fig.

Käufer); **6.** *fig.* kritteln, tadeln; **III** *s.* **7.** Nagen *n*, Knabbern *n*; **8.** (kleiner) Bissen, Happen *m*.

nib·lick ['nıblık] *s. Golf: obs.* Niblick *m* (*Schläger*).

nibs [nıbz] *s. pl. sg. konstr.* F ,großes Tier': *his* ~ ,seine Hoheit'.

nice [naıs] *adj.* □ **1.** fein (*Beobachtung, Sinn, Urteil, Unterschied etc.*); **2.** lecker, fein (*Speise etc.*); **3.** nett, freundlich (*to* zu *j-m*); **4.** nett, hübsch, schön (*alle a. iro.*): ~ *girl*; ~ *weather*; *a* ~ *mess iro.* e-e schöne Bescherung; ~ *and fat* schön fett; ~ *and warm* hübsch warm; **5.** niedlich, nett; **6.** heikel, wählerisch (*about* in *dat.*); **7.** (peinlich) genau, gewissenhaft; **8.** (*mst mit not*) anständig; **9.** *fig.* heikel, schwierig; '**nice-ly** [-lı] *adv.* **1.** nett, fein: *I was done* ~ *sl. iro.* ich wurde schön übers Ohr gehauen; **2.** gut, fein, befriedigend: *that will do* ~ das passt ausgezeichnet; *she is doing* ~ F es geht ihr gut (*od.* besser), sie macht gute Fortschritte; **3.** sorgfältig, genau; '**nice·ness** [-nıs] *s.* **1.** Feinheit *f*; **2.** Nettheit *f*, Niedlichkeit *f*; **3.** F Nettigkeit *f*; **4.** Schärfe *f des Urteils*; **5.** Genauigkeit *f*, Pünktlichkeit *f*; '**ni·ce·ty** [-sətı] **1.** Feinheit *f*, Schärfe *f des Urteils etc.*; **2.** peinliche Genauigkeit, Pünktlichkeit *f*: *to a* ~ aufs Genaueste, bis aufs Haar; **3.** Spitzfindigkeit *f*; **4.** *pl.* kleine 'Unterschiede *pl.*, Feinheiten *pl.*: *not to stand upon niceties* es nicht so genau nehmen; **5.** wählerisches Wesen; **6.** *the niceties of life* die Annehmlichkeiten des Lebens.

niche [nıtʃ] **I** *s.* **1.** △, *a.* ✹ Nische *f*; **2.** *fig.* Platz *m*, wo man hingehört: *he finally found his* ~ *in life* er hat endlich s-n Platz im Leben gefunden; **3.** *fig.* (ruhiges) Plätzchen; **II** *v/t.* **4.** mit e-r Nische versehen; **5.** in e-e Nische stellen.

ni·chrome ['naıkrəom] *s.* ⊗ Nickelchrom *n*.

Nick[1] [nık] *npr.* **1.** Niki *m* (*Koseform zu Nicholas*); **2.** *Old* ~ *sl.* der Teufel.

nick[2] [nık] **I** *s.* **1.** Kerbe *f*, Einkerbung *f*, Einschnitt *m*; **2.** Kerbholz *n*; **3.** *typ.* Signa'tur(rinne) *f*; **4.** *in the* (*very*) ~ (*of time*) a) im richtigen Augenblick, wie gerufen, b) im letzten Moment; *in good* ~ ,gut in Schuss'; **5.** *Würfelspiel etc.*: (hoher) Wurf, Treffer *m*; **II** *v/t.* **6.** (ein)kerben, einschneiden: ~ *out* auszacken, -furchen; ~ *o.s.* sich beim *Rasieren* schneiden; **7.** *et.* glücklich treffen: ~ *the time* gerade den richtigen Zeitpunkt treffen; **8.** erraten; **9.** *Zug etc.* erwischen, (noch) kriegen; **10.** *Brit. sl.* a) betrügen, reinlegen, b) ,klauen', c) *j-n* ,schnappen' *od.* ,einlochen'.

nick·el ['nıkl] **I** *s.* **1.** ♣, *min.* Nickel *n*; **2.** *Am.* F Nickel *m*, Fünf'centstück *n*; **II** *adj.* **3.** Nickel...; **II** *v/t.* **4.** vernickeln; ~ *bloom* ~ *min.* Nickelblüte *f*; '**~-clad sheet** *s.* ⊗ nickelplattiertes Blech.

nick·el·o·de·on [,nıkə'ləodıən] *s. Am.* **1.** *hist.* billiges ('Film-,Varie'tee)The,ater; **2.** Mu'sikauto,mat *m*.

'**nick·el|-plate** *v/t.* ⊗ vernickeln; '**~--plat·ing** *s.* Vernickelung *f*; ~ *sil·ver s.* Neusilber *n*; ~ *steel s.* Nickelstahl *m*.

nick·nack ['nıknæk] → *knickknack*.

nick·name ['nıkneım] **I** *s.* Spitzname *m*; ✗ Deckname *m*; **II** *v/t.* mit e-m Spitznamen bezeichnen, *j-m* e-n *od.* den Spitznamen geben.

nic·o·tine ['nıkətiːn] *s.* ♣ Niko'tin *n*; ~ *patch* Niko'tinpflaster *n*; '**nic·o·tin·ism** [-nızəm] *s.* Niko'tinvergiftung *f*.

nide [naıd] *s.* (Fa'sanen)Nest *n*.

---

nid·i·fy ['nıdıfaı] *v/i.* nisten.

nid-nod ['nıdnɒd] *v/i.* (mehrmals *od.* ständig) nicken.

ni·dus ['naıdəs] *pl. a.* **-di** [-daı] *s.* **1.** *zo.* Nest *n*, Brutstätte *f*; **2.** *fig.* Lagerstätte *f*, Sitz *m*; **3.** ✹ Herd *m e-r Krankheit*.

niece [niːs] *s.* Nichte *f*.

nif·ty ['nıftı] *adj. sl.* **1.** ,sauber': a) hübsch, fesch, b) prima, c) raffiniert; **2.** *Brit.* stinkend.

nig·gard ['nıgəd] **I** *s.* Knicker(in), Geizhals *m*, Filz *m*; **II** *adj.* □ geizig, knickerig, knickrig, kärglich; '**nig·gard·li·ness** [-lınıs] *s.* Knause'rei *f*, Geiz *m*; '**nig·gard·ly** [-lı] **I** *adv.* → *niggard* II; **II** *adj.* schäbig, kümmerlich: *a* ~ *gift*.

nig·ger ['nıgə] *s.* F *neg.!* Nigger *m*, Neger(in), Schwarze(r *m*) *f*: *work like a* ~ wie ein Pferd arbeiten, schuften; ~ *in the woodpile sl.* der Haken an der Sache.

nig·gle ['nıgl] *v/i.* **1.** her'umnörgeln (*at* an *dat.*); **2.** ~ *at fig.* nagen an (*dat.*), plagen, quälen: *the matter niggled at his brain* die Sache ging ihm nicht aus dem Kopf; **3.** stören, ärgerlich sein (*Dinge, Fakten*); **II** *v/t.* **4.** her'umnörgeln an (*dat.*); '**nig·gler** *s.* **1.** a) Tüftler(in), b) Pe'dant(in); **2.** Nörgler(in); '**nig·gling I** *adj.* □ **1.** a) tüftelig, b) pe'dantisch; **2.** nörglerisch; **3.** *fig.* nagend, quälend; **II** *s.* **4.** Nörgeln *n*, ,Meckern' *n*.

nigh [naı] *adv.* **1.** nahe (*to* an *dat.*): ~ (*un*)*to death* dem Tode nahe; ~ *but* beinahe; *draw* ~ *to* sich nähern (*dat.*); **2.** *mst well* ~ beinahe, nahezu; **II** *prp.* **3.** nahe bei, neben.

night [naıt] *s.* **1.** Nacht *f*: *at* ~, *by* ~, *in the* ~, F *o'nights* bei Nacht, nachts, des Nachts; ~*'s lodging* Nachtquartier *n*; *all* ~ (*long*) die ganze Nacht (hindurch); *over* ~ über Nacht; *bid* (*od.* *wish*) *s.o. good* ~ *j-m* gute (*od.* Gute) Nacht wünschen; *make a* ~ *of it* die ganze Nacht durchmachen, -feiern, sich die Nacht um die Ohren schlagen; *stay the* ~ *at* übernachten in *e-m Ort od.* bei *j-m*; **2.** Abend *m*: *last* ~ gestern Abend; *the* ~ *before last* vorgestern Abend; *first* ~ *thea.* Erstauffführung *f*, Premiere *f*; *a* ~ *of Wagner* Wagnerabend; *on the* ~ *of May 4th* am Abend des 4. Mai; ~ *out* freier Abend; *have a* ~ *out* e-n Abend ausspannen, ausgehen; **3.** *fig.* Nacht *f*, Dunkelheit *f*: ~ *at·tack s.* ✗ Nachtangriff *m*; ~ *bird s.* **1.** Nachtvogel *m*; **2.** *fig.* Nachtschwärmer *m*; '**~-blind** *adj.* ✹ nachtblind; '**~-cap** *s.* **1.** Nachtmütze *f*, -haube *f*; **2.** *fig.* Schlummertrunk *m*; '**~-club** *s.* Nachtklub *m*, 'Nachtlo,kal *n*; '**~-dress** *s.* Nachthemd *n* (*für Frauen u. Kinder*); ~ *ex·po·sure s. phot.* Nachtaufnahme *f*; '**~-fall** *s.* Einbruch *m* der Nacht; ~ *fight·er s.* ➤, ✗ Nachtjäger *m*; ~ *glass s.* Nachtfernrohr *n*, -glas *n*; '**~-gown** → *nightdress*.

night·in·gale ['naıtıŋgeıl] *s. orn.* Nachtigall *f*.

'**night|·jar** *s. orn.* Ziegenmelker *m*; ~ *leave s.* ✗ Urlaub *m* bis zum Wecken; '**~-life** *s.* Nachtleben *n*; '**~-long I** *adj.* e-e *od.* die ganze Nacht dauernd; **II** *adv.* die ganze Nacht (hin'durch).

night·ly ['naıtlı] **I** *adj.* **1.** nächtlich, Nacht...; **2.** jede Nacht *od.* jeden Abend stattfindend; **II** *adv.* **3.** a) (all-)nächtlich, jede Nacht, b) jeden Abend, (all)abendlich.

night·mare ['naıtmeə] *s.* **1.** Nachtmahr *m* (*böser Geist*); **2.** ✹ Alb(drücken *n*) *m*, böser Traum; **3.** *fig.* Schreckgespenst *n*, Albtraum *m*, Spuk *m*; '**night-**

---

mar·ish [-əərıʃ] *adj.* beklemmend, schauerlich.

night| nurse *s.* Nachtschwester *f*; ~ *owl s.* **1.** *orn.* Nachteule *f* (*a.* F *fig. Nachtmensch*); **2.** F Nachtschwärmer *m*; ~ *por·ter s.* 'Nachtporti,er *m*; ~ *rate s.* 'Nachtta,rif *m*.

nights [naıts] *adv.* F bei Nacht, nachts.

night| school *s.* Abend-, Fortbildungsschule *f*; '**~-shade** *s.* ♀ Nachtschatten *m*: *deadly* ~ Tollkirsche *f*; ~ *shift s.* Nachtschicht *f*: *be on* ~ Nachtschicht haben; '**~-shirt** *s.* Nachthemd *n* (*für Männer u. Knaben*); '**~-spot** *s.* F für *nightclub*; '**~-stand** *s. Am.* Nachttisch *m*; ~ *stick s. Am.* Schlagstock *m* der *Polizei*; '**~-stool** *s.* Nachtstuhl *m*; '**~-time** *s.* Nachtzeit *f*; ~ *vi·sion s.* **1.** nächtliche Erscheinung; **2.** Nachtsehvermögen *n*; ~ *watch s.* Nachtwache *f*; ,**~-'watch·man** [-mən] *s.* [*irr.*] Nachtwächter *m*; '**~-wear** *s.* Nachtzeug *n*.

night·y ['naıtı] *s.* F (Damen-, Kinder-) Nachthemd *n*.

ni·hil·ism ['naılızəm] *s. phls.*, *pol.* Nihi'lismus *m*; '**ni·hil·ist** [-ıst] *s.* Nihi'list (-in); **II** *adj.* → **ni·hil·is·tic** [,naıı'lıstık] *adj.* nihi'listisch.

nil [nıl] *s.* Nichts *n*, Null *f* (*bsd. in Spielresultaten*): *two goals to* ~ zwei zu null (2:0); ~ *report* Fehlanzeige *f*; *his influence is* ~ *fig.* sein Einfluss ist gleich null.

nim·ble ['nımbl] *adj.* □ flink, hurtig, gewandt, be'händ: ~ *mind fig.* beweglicher Geist, rasche Auffassungsgabe; ,**~--'fin·gered** *adj.* **1.** geschickt; **2.** langfingerig, diebisch; ,**~-'foot·ed** *adj.* leicht-, schnellfüßig.

nim·ble·ness ['nımblnıs] *s.* Flinkheit *f*, Gewandtheit *f*, *fig. a.* geistige Beweglichkeit.

nim·bus ['nımbəs] *pl.* **-bi** [-baı] *od.* **-bus-es** *s.* **1.** *a.* ~ *cloud* graue Regenwolke; **2.** Nimbus *m*: a) Heiligenschein *m*, b) *fig.* Ruhm *m*.

NIMBY, **nimby** ['nımbı] *abbr. für not in my back yard* **I** *s.* j-d, der nach dem Sankt-Florians-Prinzip handelt; **II** *adj.* F ablehnend: *a* ~ *attitude* e-e ,Ohnemich'-Haltung.

nim·i·ny-pim·i·ny [,nımını'pımını] *adj.* affektiert, ,etepe'tete'.

Nim·rod ['nımrɒd] *npr. Bibl. u. fig.* Nimrod *m* (*großer Jäger*).

nin·com·poop ['nıŋkəmpuːp] *s.* Einfaltspinsel *m*, Trottel *m*.

nine [naın] **I** *adj.* **1.** neun: ~ *days' wonder* Tagesgespräch *n*, sensationelles Ereignis; ~ *times out of ten* in neun von zehn Fällen; **II** *s.* **2.** Neun *f*, Neuner *m* (*Spielkarte etc.*): *the* ~ *of hearts* Herzneun; *to the* ~*s* in höchstem Maße; *dressed up to the* ~*s* piekfein gekleidet, aufgedonnert; **3.** *the* ♀ die neun Musen; **4.** *sport* Baseballmannschaft *f*; '**nine·fold I** *adj./adv.* neunfach; **II** *s.* das Neunfache; '**nine·pins** *s. pl.* **1.** Kegel *pl.*: ~ *alley* Kegelbahn *f*; **2.** *a. sg. konstr.* Kegelspiel *n*: *play* ~ Kegel spielen, kegeln.

nine·teen [,naın'tiːn] **I** *adj.* neunzehn; → *dozen* 2; **II** *s.* Neunzehn *f*; ,**nine-'teenth** [-θ] **I** *adj.* neunzehnt; **II** *s.* Neunzehntel *n*; **nine·ti·eth** [naıntııθ] **I** *adj.* neunzigst; **II** *s.* Neunzigstel *n*; **nine·ty** ['naıntı] **I** *s.* Neunzig *f*: *he is in his nineties* er ist in den Neunzigern; *in the nineties* in den Neunzigerjahren (*e-s Jahrhunderts*); **II** *adj.* neunzig.

nin·ny ['nını] F *s.* Trottel *m*.

ninth [naınθ] **I** *adj.* **1.** neunt: *in the* ~ *place* neuntens, an neunter Stelle; **II** *s.* **2.** *der* (*die, das*) Neunte; **3.** *a.* ~ *part*

Neuntel *n*; **4.** ♪ None *f*; **'ninth·ly** [-lɪ] *adv.* neuntens.

nip¹ [nɪp] **I** *v/t.* **1.** kneifen, zwicken, klemmen; **~ off** abzwicken, -kneifen, -beißen; **2.** (*durch Frost etc.*) beschädigen, vernichten, ka'puttmachen; **~ in the bud** *fig.* im Keim ersticken; **3.** *sl.* → **nick²** 10 b *u.* c; **II** *v/i.* **4.** schneiden (*Kälte, Wind*); ☉ klemmen (*Maschine*); **5.** F ,flitzen': **~ in** hineinschlüpfen; **~ on ahead** nach vorne flitzen; **III** *s.* **6.** Kneifen *n*, Kniff *m*, Biss *m*; **7.** Schneiden *n* (*Kälte etc.*); scharfer Frost; **8.** ♀ Frostbrand *m*; **9.** Knick *m* (*Draht etc.*); **10.** **~ and tuck**, *attr.* **~-and-tuck** *Am.* auf Biegen oder Brechen, scharf (*Kampf*), hart (*Rennen*).

nip² [nɪp] **I** *v/i. u. v/t.* nippen (an *dat.*); **II** *s.* Schlückchen *n*.

Nip [nɪp] *s. sl.* ,Japs' *m*.

nip·per ['nɪpə] *s.* **1.** *zo.* a) Vorder-, Schneidezahn *m* (*bsd. des Pferdes*), b) Schere *f* (*Krebs etc.*); **2.** *mst pl.* ☉ a) *a pair of* **~s** (Kneif)Zange *f*, b) Pin'zette *f*; **3.** *pl.* Kneifer *m*; **4.** *Brit.* F Bengel *m*, ,Stift' *m*; **5.** *pl.* F Handschellen *pl.*

nip·ping ['nɪpɪŋ] *adj.* □ **1.** kneifend; **2.** beißend, schneidend (*Kälte, Wind*); **3.** *fig.* bissig, scharf (*Worte*).

nip·ple ['nɪpl] *s.* **1.** *anat.* Brustwarze *f*; **2.** (Saug)Hütchen *n*, Sauger *m* (*e-r Saugflasche*); **3.** ☉ (Speichen-, Schmier)Nippel *m*; (Rohr)Stutzen *m*.

nip·py ['nɪpɪ] **I** *adj.* **1.** → *nipping* 2, 3; **2.** F schnell, ,fix'; spritzig (*Auto*); **II** *s.* **3.** *Brit.* F Kellnerin *f*.

ni·sei ['niːˌseɪ] *pl.* **-sei**, **-seis** *s.* Ja'paner (-in) geboren in den USA.

ni·si ['naɪsaɪ] (*Lat.*) *cj.* ♱♰ wenn nicht: *decree* **~** vorläufiges Scheidungsurteil.

Nis·sen hut ['nɪsn] *s.* ✕ Nissenhütte *f*, 'Wellblechba,racke *f*.

nit [nɪt] *s.* **1.** *Brit* F Schwachkopf *m*, Trottel *m*; **2.** *zo.* Nisse *f*, Niss *f*.

'nit,pick·ing I *adj.* F kleinlich, ,pingelig'; **II** *s.* ,Pingeligkeit' *f*.

ni·trate ['naɪtraɪd] **I** *s.* 🜁 Ni'trat *n*, sal-'petersaures Salz: **~ of silver** salpetersaures Silber, Höllenstein *m*; **~ of soda** (*od.* *sodium*) salpetersaures Natrium; **II** *v/t.* nitrieren; **III** *v/i.* sich in Sal'peter verwandeln.

ni·tre ['naɪtə] *s.* 🜁 Sal'peter *m*: **~ cake** Natriumkuchen *m*.

ni·tric ['naɪtrɪk] *adj.* 🜁 sal'petersauer, Salpeter..., Stickstoff...; **~ ac·id** *s.* Sal'petersäure *f*; **~ ox·ide** *s.* 'Stickstoffo,xid *n*.

ni·tride ['naɪtraɪd] **I** *s.* Ni'trid *n*; **II** *v/t.* nitrieren; **ni·trif·er·ous** [naɪ'trɪfərəs] *adj.* **1.** stickstoffhaltig; **2.** sal'peterhaltig; **'ni·tri·fy** [-trɪfaɪ] **I** *v/t.* nitrieren; **II** *v/i.* sich in Sal'peter verwandeln; **'ni·trite** [-aɪt] *s.* Ni'trit *n*, sal'pet(e)rigsaures Salz.

ni·tro·ben·zene [ˌnaɪtrəʊ'benziːn], **ni·tro·ben·zol(e)** [ˌnaɪtrəʊ'benzɒl] *s.* 🜁 Nitroben'zol *n*.

ni·tro·cel·lu·lose [ˌnaɪtrəʊ'seljʊləʊs] *s.* 🜁 Nitrozellu'lose *f*: **~ lacquer** Nitro-(zellulose)lack *m*.

ni·tro·gen ['naɪtrədʒən] *s.* 🜁 Stickstoff *m*: **~ carbide** Stickkohlenstoff *m*; **~ chloride** Chlorstickstoff *n*; **~ oxide** Stickoxid *n*; **~ oxide reduction** Entstickung *f*; **ni·trog·e·nize** [naɪ'trɒdʒɪnaɪz] *v/t.* mit Stickstoff verbinden *od.* anreichern *od.* sättigen: **~d foods** stickstoffhaltige Nahrungsmittel; **ni·trog·e·nous** [naɪ'trɒdʒɪnəs] *adj.* stickstoffhaltig.

ni·tro·glyc·er·in(e) [ˌnaɪtrəʊ'glɪsəriːn] *s.* 🜁 Nitroglyze'rin *n*.

ni·tro·hy·dro·chlo·ric ['naɪtrəʊˌhaɪdrəʊ-'klɒrɪk] *adj.* Salpetersalz...

ni·trous ['naɪtrəs] *adj.* 🜁 Salpeter..., sal'peterhaltig, sal'petrig; **~ ac·id** *s.* sal-'petrige Säure; **~ ox·ide** *s.* 'Stickstoffoxi,dul *n*, Lachgas *n*.

nit·ty-grit·ty [ˌnɪtɪ'grɪtɪ] *s.*: *get down to the* **~** F zur Sache kommen.

nit·wit ['nɪtwɪt] *s.* Schwachkopf *m*.

nix¹ [nɪks] *adv.* *Am. sl.* ,nix', nichts, *int.* a. nein.

nix² [nɪks] *pl.* **-es** *s.* Nix *m*, Wassergeist *m*; **'nix·ie** [-ksɪ] *s.* (Wasser)Nixe *f*.

no [nəʊ] **I** *adv.* **1.** nein: *answer* **~** Nein sagen; **2.** (*nach or am Ende e-s Satzes*) nicht (*jetzt mst* not): **~** *whether ... or ~* ob ... oder nicht; **3.** (*beim comp.*) um nichts, nicht: **~** *better a writer* kein besserer Schriftsteller; **~** *longer* (*ago*) *than yesterday* erst gestern; **~!** nicht möglich!, nein!; → *more* 2, 4, *soon* 1; **II** *adj.* **4.** kein(e): **~** *hope* keine Hoffnung; **~** *one* keiner; **~** *man* niemand; **~** *parking* Parkverbot; **~** *thoroughfare* Durchfahrt gesperrt; *in* **~** *time* im Nu; **~-claims bonus** Vergütung *f* für Schadenfreiheit; **~-fly zone** Flugverbotszone *f*; **5.** kein, alles andere als ein(e): *he is* **~** *artist*; **~** *such thing* nichts dergleichen; **6.** (*vor ger.*): *there is* **~** *denying* es lässt sich *od.* man kann nicht leugnen; **III** *pl.* **noes** *s.* **7.** Nein *n*, verneinende Antwort, Absage *f*, Weigerung *f*; **8.** *parl.* Gegenstimme *f*: *the ayes and* **~es** die Stimmen für u. wider; *the* **~es** *have it* die Mehrheit ist dagegen, der Antrag ist abgelehnt.

'no-ac,count *adj.* *Am. dial.* unbedeutend (*mst Person*).

nob¹ [nɒb] *s. sl.* ,Birne' *f* (*Kopf*).

nob² [nɒb] *s. sl.* ,feiner Pinkel' (*vornehmer Mann*), ,großes Tier'.

nob·ble ['nɒbl] *v/t. sl.* **1.** betrügen, ,reinlegen'; **2.** *j-n* auf s-e Seite ziehen, ,herumkriegen'; **3.** bestechen; **4.** ,klauen'.

nob·by ['nɒbɪ] *adj. sl.* schick.

No·bel Prize [nəʊ'bel] *s.* No'belpreis *m*: **~ winner** Nobelpreisträger(in); **Nobel Peace Prize** Friedensnobelpreis.

no·bil·i·a·ry [nəʊ'bɪlɪərɪ] *adj.* adlig, Adels...

no·bil·i·ty [nəʊ'bɪlətɪ] *s.* **1.** *fig.* Adel *m*, Würde *f*, Vornehmheit *f*: **~ of mind** vornehme Denkungsart; **~ of soul** Seelenadel; **2.** Adel(sstand) *m*, die Adligen *pl.*; (*bsd. in England*) *der* hohe Adel: *the* **~ and gentry** der hohe u. niedere Adel.

no·ble ['nəʊbl] **I** *adj.* □ **1.** adlig, von Adel; edel, erlaucht; **2.** *fig.* edel, nobel, erhaben, groß(mütig); vor'trefflich: *the* **~** *art* (*of self-defence*, *Am.* *self-defense*) die edle Kunst der Selbstverteidigung (*Boxen*); **3.** prächtig, stattlich: *a* **~** *edifice*; **4.** prächtig geschmückt (*with* mit); **5.** *phys.* Edel...(*-gas*, *-metall*); **II** *s.* **6.** Edelmann *m*, (hoher) Adliger; **7.** *hist.* Nobel *m* (*Goldmünze*); **'~-man** [-mən] *s.* [*irr.*] **1.** Edelmann *m*, (hoher) Adliger; **2.** *pl.* *Schach*: Offi'ziere *pl.*; **,~-'mind·ed** *adj.* edel denkend; **,~-'mind·ed·ness** *s.* vornehme Denkungsart, Edelmut *m*.

no·ble·ness ['nəʊblnɪs] *s.* **1.** Adel *m*, hohe Abstammung; **2.** *fig.* a) Adel *m*, Würde *f*, b) Edelsinn *m*, -mut *m*.

'no·ble,wom·an *s.* [*irr.*] Adlige *f*.

no·bod·y ['nəʊbədɪ] **I** *adj. pron.* niemand, keiner: **~** *else* sonst niemand, niemand anders; **II** *s.* unbedeutende Per'son, ,Niemand' *m*, ,Null' *f*: *be*

(a) **~** *a.* nichts sein, nichts zu sagen haben.

nock [nɒk] **I** *s.* *Bogenschießen*: Kerbe *f*; **II** *v/t.* a) *Pfeil* auf die Kerbe legen, b) *Bogen* einkerben.

no-claim(s) bo·nus [ˌnəʊkleɪm(z)'bəʊnəs] *s.* Versicherung: 'Schadenfreiheitsra,batt *m*.

noc·tam·bu·la·tion [nɒkˌtæmbjʊ'leɪʃn], *a.* **noc·tam·bu·lism** [nɒk'tæmbjʊlɪzəm] *s.* ♰ Somnambu'lismus *m*, Nachtwandeln *n*; **noc·tam·bu·list** [nɒk'tæmbjʊlɪst] *s.* Schlafwandler(in), Somnam'bule(r *m*) *f*.

noc·turn ['nɒktɜːn] *s.* *R.C.* Nachtmette *f*; **noc·tur·nal** [nɒk'tɜːnl] *adj.* □ nächtlich, Nacht...; **noc·turne** ['nɒktɜːn] *s.* **1.** *paint.* Nachtstück *n*; **2.** ♪ Not'turno *n*.

noc·u·ous ['nɒkjʊəs] *adj.* □ **1.** schädlich; **2.** giftig (*Schlangen*).

nod [nɒd] **I** *v/i.* **1.** nicken: **~** *to s.o.* j-m zunicken, j-n grüßen; **~ding acquaintance** oberflächliche(r) Bekannte(r), Grußbekanntschaft *f*; *we are on* **~ding terms** wir grüßen uns; **2.** sich neigen (*Blumen etc.*) (*a. fig.* *to* vor *dat.*); wippen (*Hutfeder*); **3.** nicken, (*sitzend*) schlafen: **~** *off* einnicken; **4.** *fig.* unaufmerksam sein, ,schlafen': *Homer sometimes* **~s** auch dem Aufmerksamsten entgeht manchmal etwas; **II** *v/t.* **5.** **~** *one's head* (mit dem Kopf) nicken; **6.** (*durch Nicken*) andeuten: **~** *one's assent* beifällig (zu)nicken; **~** *s.o. out* j-n hinauswinken; **III** *s.* **7.** (Kopf)Nicken *n*, Wink *m*: *give s.o. a* **~** j-m zunicken; *go to the land of* **~** einschlafen; *on the* **~** *Am. sl.* auf Pump.

nod·al ['nəʊdl] *adj.* Knoten...: **~** *point* a) ♪, *phys.* Schwingungsknoten *m*, b) ♣, *phys.* Knotenpunkt *m*.

nod·dle ['nɒdl] *s. sl.* Schädel *m*, ,Birne' *f*, *fig.* ,Grips' *m*.

node [nəʊd] *s.* **1.** *allg.* Knoten *m* (*a. ast.*, ♀, *a. fig. im Drama etc.*): **~** *of a curve* ♣ Knotenpunkt *m* e-r Kurve; **2.** ♰ Knoten *m*, Knötchen *n*: *gouty* **~** Gichtknoten; **3.** *phys.* Schwingungsknoten *m*.

no·dose [nəʊ'dəʊs] *adj.* knotig (*a.* ♰), voller Knoten; **no·dos·i·ty** [nəʊ'dɒsətɪ] *s.* **1.** knotige Beschaffenheit; **2.** → *node* 2.

nod·u·lar ['nɒdjʊlə] *adj.* knoten-, knötchenförmig: **~-ulcerous** ♰ tubero-ulzerös.

nod·ule ['nɒdjuːl] *s.* **1.** ♀, ♰ Knötchen *n*: *lymphatic* **~** Lymphknötchen *n*; **2.** *geol., min.* Nest *n*, Niere *f*.

no·dus ['nəʊdəs] *pl.* **-di** [-daɪ] *s.* Knoten *m*, Schwierigkeit *f*.

nog [nɒg] *s.* **1.** Holznagel *m*, -klotz *m*; **2.** △ a) Holm *m* (*querliegender Balken*), b) *Maurerei*: Riegel *m*.

nog·gin ['nɒgɪn] *s.* **1.** kleiner (Holz-) Krug; **2.** F ,Birne' *f* (*Kopf*).

nog·ging ['nɒgɪŋ] *s.* △ Riegelmauer *f*, (ausgemauertes) Fachwerk.

'no-good *Am.* F **I** *s.* Lump *m*, Nichtsnutz *m*; **II** *adj.* nichtsnutzig, elend, mise'rabel.

'no-how *adv.* F **1.** auf keinen Fall, durch-'aus nicht; **2.** nichts sagend, ungut: *feel* **~** nicht auf der Höhe sein; *look* **~** nach nichts aussehen.

noil [nɔɪl] *s. sg. u. pl.* ♉, ☉ Kämmling *m*, Kurzwolle *f*.

,no-'i·ron *adj.* bügelfrei (*Hemd etc.*).

noise [nɔɪz] **I** *s.* **1.** Geräusch *n*; Lärm *m*, Getöse *n*, Geschrei *n*: **~** *of battle* Gefechtslärm; **~** *abatement*, **~** *control* Lärmbekämpfung *f*; **~** *nuisance* Lärmbelästigung *f*; **hold your ~!** F halt den Mund!; **2.** Rauschen *n* (*a.* ♩ *Störung*), Summen *n*: **~ factor** ♩ Rauschfaktor *m*; **3.** *fig.* Streit *m*, Krach *m*: **make a ~** Krach machen (**about** wegen); → 4; **4.** *fig.* Aufsehen *n*, Geschrei *n*: **make a great ~ in the world** großes Aufsehen erregen; **make a ~** viel Tamtam machen (**about** um); **5. a big ~** *sl.* ein hohes (*od.* großes) Tier (*wichtige Persönlichkeit*); **II** *v/i.* **6. ~ it** lärmen; **III** *v/t.* **7. ~ abroad** verbreiten, aussprengen; **~ bar·ri·er** *s.* 'Lärmschutzwall *m*.

noise·less ['nɔɪzlɪs] *adj.* □ laut-, geräuschlos (*a.* ◎), still; **'noise·less·ness** [-nɪs] *s.* Geräuschlosigkeit *f*.

noise| lev·el *s.* Lärm-, ♩ Störpegel *m*; **~ sup·pres·sion** ♩ **1.** Störschutz *m*; **2.** Entstörung *f*; **~ pol·lu·tion** *s.* Lärmbelästigung *f*; **~ volt·age** *s.* ♩ **1.** Geräuschspannung *f*; **2.** Störspannung *f*.

nois·i·ness ['nɔɪzɪnɪs] *s.* Lärm *m*, Getöse *n*; lärmendes Wesen.

noi·some ['nɔɪsəm] *adj.* □ **1.** schädlich, ungesund; **2.** widerlich.

nois·y ['nɔɪzɪ] *adj.* □ **1.** geräuschvoll, laut; lärmend: **~ running** ◎ geräuschvoller Gang; **~ fellow** Krakeeler *m*, Schreier *m*; **2.** *fig.* grell, schreiend (*Farbe etc.*); laut, aufdringlich (*Stil*).

nol·le ['nɒlɪ], **nol·le·pros** [,nɒlɪ'prɒs] (*Lat.*) *ⁿ* *Am.* **I** *v/i.* a) die Zu'rücknahme e-r Klage einleiten, b) *im Strafprozess*: das Verfahren einstellen; **II** *s.* → **nolle prosequi.**

nol·le pros·e·qui [,nɒlɪ'prɒsɪkwaɪ] (*Lat.*) *s.* *ⁿ* a) Zu'rücknahme *f* der (*Zivil*)Klage, b) Einstellung *f* des (*Straf-*)Verfahrens.

,no·'load *s.* ♩ Leerlauf *m*: **~ speed** Leerlaufdrehzahl *f*.

nol-pros [nɒl'prɒs] → **nolle** I.

no·mad ['nəʊmæd] **I** *adj.* no'madisch, Nomaden...; **II** *s.* No'made *m*, No'madin *f*; **no·mad·ic** [nəʊ'mædɪk] *adj.* (□ **~ally**) **1.** → **nomad** I; **2.** *fig.* unstet; **'no·mad·ism** [-dɪzəm] *s.* No'madentum *n*, Wanderleben *n*.

'no-man's land *s.* ⚔ Niemandsland *n* (*a. fig.*).

nom·bril ['nɒmbrɪl] *s.* Nabel *m* (*des Wappenschilds*).

nom de plume [,nɔ̃mdə'pluːm] (*Fr.*) *s.* Pseudo'nym *n*, Schriftstellername *m*.

no·men·cla·ture [nəʊ'menklətʃə] *s.* **1.** Nomenkla'tur *f*: a) (*wissenschaftliche*) Namengebung, b) Namensverzeichnis *n*; **2.** (*fachliche*) Terminolo'gie; **3.** *coll.* die Namen *pl.*, Bezeichnungen *pl.* (*a.* ⚕).

nom·i·nal ['nɒmɪnl] *adj.* □ **1.** Namen...; **2.** nomi'nell, Nominal...: **~ consideration** *ⁿ* formale Gegenleistung; **~ fine** nominelle (*sehr geringe*) Geldstrafe; **~ rank** Titularrang *m*; **3.** *ling.* nomi'nal; **4.** ◎, ♩ Nominal..., Nenn..., Soll...; **~ ac·count** *s.* † Sachkonto *n*; **~ a·mount** *s.* † Nennbetrag *m*; **~ bal·ance** *s.* † Sollbestand *m*; **~ ca·pac·i·ty** *s.* ♩, ◎ Nennleistung *f*; **~ cap·i·tal** *s.* † 'Grund-, 'Stammkapi,tal *n*; **~ fre·quen·cy** *s.* ♩ 'Sollfre,quenz *f*; **~ in·ter·est** *s.* † Nomi'nalzinsfuß *m*.

nom·i·nal·ism ['nɒmɪnəlɪzəm] *s.* *phls.* Nomina'lismus *m*.

nom·i·nal| out·put *s.* ◎ Nennleistung *f*; **~ par** *s.* † Nenn-, Nomi'nalwert *m*; **~ par·i·ty** *s.* † 'Nennwertpari,tät *f*; **~ speed** *s.* ◎ Nenndrehzahl *f*; **~ stock** *s.* † 'Gründungs-, 'Stammkapi,tal *n*; **~ val·ue** *s.* †, ◎ Nennwert *m*.

nom·i·nate *v/t.* ['nɒmɪneɪt] **1.** (**to**) berufen, ernennen (zu e-r *Stelle*), einsetzen (in *ein Amt*); **2.** nominieren, als

('Wahl)Kandi,daten aufstellen; **nom·i·na·tion** [,nɒmɪ'neɪʃn] *s.* **1.** (**to**) Berufung *f*, Ernennung *f* (zu), Einsetzung *f* (in): **in ~** vorgeschlagen (**for** für); **2.** Vorschlagsrecht *n*; **3.** Nominierung *f*, Vorwahl *f* (*e-s Kandidaten*); **~ day** Wahlvorschlagstermin *m*; **nom·i·na·tive** ['nɒmɪnətɪv] **I** *adj. ling.* nominativ (-isch): **~ case** → **II**; **II** *s. ling.* Nominativ *m*, erster Fall; **'nom·i·na·tor** [-tə] *s.* Ernenn(end)er *m*; **nom·i·nee** [,nɒmɪ'niː] *s.* **1.** Vorgeschlagene(r *m*) *f*, Kandi'dat(in); **2.** *⚕* Begünstigte(r *m*) *f*, Empfänger(in) *e-r Rente etc.*

non- [nɒn] *in Zssgn*: nicht..., Nicht..., un..., miss...

,non(-)ac·cept·ance *s.* Annahmeverweigerung *f*, Nichtannahme *f e-s Wechsels etc.*

,non(-)a·chiev·er *s.* Versager *m*.

non·age ['nəʊnɪdʒ] *s.* Unmündigkeit *f*, Minderjährigkeit *f*.

non·a·ge·nar·i·an [,nəʊnədʒɪ'neərɪən] **I** *adj.* neunzigjährig; **II** *s.* Neunzigjährige(r *m*) *f*.

,non-ag'gres·sion *s.* Nichtangriff *m*: **~ treaty** *pol.* Nichtangriffspakt *m*.

non·a·gon ['nɒnəgən] *s.* ⚕ Nona'gon *n*, Neuneck *n*.

,non(-)al·co'hol·ic *adj.* alkoholfrei.

,non-a'ligned *adj. pol.* bündnis-, blockfrei.

,non(-)ap'pear·ance *s.* Nichterscheinen *n* vor Gericht etc.

,non(-)as'sess·a·ble *adj.* nicht steuerpflichtig, steuerfrei.

,non(-)at'tend·ance *s.* Nichterscheinen *n*.

,non(-)bel'lig·er·ent **I** *adj.* nicht Krieg führend; **II** *s.* nicht am Krieg teilnehmende Per'son *od.* Nati'on.

,non(-)'busi·ness *adj.* gemeinnützig.

nonce [nɒns] *s.* (*nur in*): **for the ~** a) für das 'eine Mal, nur für diesen Fall, b) einstweilen; **~ word** *s. ling.* Ad'hoc-Bildung *f*.

non·cha·lance ['nɒnʃələns] (*Fr.*) *s.* Noncha'lance *f*: a) (Nach)Lässigkeit *f*, Gleichgültigkeit *f*, b) Unbekümmertheit *f*; **'non·cha·lant** [-nt] *adj.* □ lässig: a) gleichgültig, b) unbekümmert.

,non(-)'chlo·rine bleached *adj.* chlorfrei (*Papier*).

,non(-)'col·le·gi·ate *adj.* **1.** *Brit. univ.* keinem College angehörend; **2.** nicht-aka'demisch; **3.** nicht aus Colleges bestehend (*Universität*).

non·com [,nɒn'kɒm] F *für* **non-commissioned** (*officer*).

,non(-)'com·bat·ant ⚔ **I** *s.* 'Nichtkämpfer *m*, -kombat,tant *m*; **II** *adj.* am Kampf nicht beteiligt.

,non(-)com'mis·sioned *adj.* **1.** unbestallt, nicht bevollmächtigt; **2.** 'Unteroffi,ziers,rang besitzend: **~ of·fi·cer** *s.* ⚔ 'Unteroffi,zier *m*.

,non-com'mit·tal **I** *adj.* **1.** unverbindlich, nichts sagend, neu'tral; **2.** zu'rückhaltend, sich nicht festlegen wollend (*Person*); **II** *s.* Unverbindlichkeit *f*.

,non(-)com'mit·ted → **non-aligned.**

,non(-)com'pli·ance *s.* **1.** Zu'widerhandeln *n* (**with** gegen), Weigerung *f*; **2.** Nichterfüllung *f*, Nichteinhaltung *f* (**with** von *od. gen.*).

non com·pos (men·tis) [,nɒn'kɒmpɒs-('mentɪs)] (*Lat.*) *adj.* *ⁿ* unzurechnungsfähig.

,non-con'duc·tor *s.* ♩ Nichtleiter *m*.

,non-con'form·ist **I** *s.* Nonkonfor'mist (-in): a) (sozi'aler *od.* po'litischer) Einzelgänger, b) *Brit. eccl.* Dissi'dent(in), Freikirchler(in); **II** *adj.* 'nonkonfor,mis-

tisch; **,non-con'form·i·ty** *s.* **1.** mangelnde Über'einstimmung (**with** mit) *od.* Anpassung (**to** an *acc.*); **2.** Nonkonfor'mismus *m*; **3.** *eccl.* Dissi'dententum *n*.

,non-con'tent *s.* *Brit. parl.* Neinstimme *f* (*im Oberhaus*).

,non(-)con'ten·tious *adj.* □ nicht strittig: **~ litigation** *ⁿ* freiwillige Gerichtsbarkeit.

,non-con'trib·u·to·ry *adj.* beitragsfrei (*Organisation*).

'non(-)co(-),op·er'a·tion *s.* Verweigerung *f* der Mit- *od.* Zu'sammenarbeit; *pol.* passiver 'Widerstand.

,non(-)'cor·rod·ing *adj.* ◎ **1.** korrosi'onsfrei; **2.** rostbeständig (*Eisen*).

,non(-)'creas·ing *adj.* ⚕ knitterfrei.

,non(-)'cut·ting *adj.* ◎ spanlos: **~ shaping** spanlose Formung.

,non(-)'daz·zling *adj.* ◎ blendfrei.

,non(-)'de·liv·er·y *s.* **1.** ⚕, *ⁿ* Nichtauslieferung *f*, Nichterfüllung *f*; **2.** ✍ Nichtbestellung *f*.

'non(-)de,nom·i'na·tion·al *adj.* nicht konfes'sionsgebunden: **~ school** Simultan-, Gemeinschaftsschule *f*.

non·de·script ['nɒndɪskrɪpt] **I** *adj.* schwer zu beschreiben(d), unbestimmbar, nicht klassifizierbar (*mst contp.*); **II** *s.* Per'son *od.* Sache, die schwer zu klassifizieren ist *od.* über die nichts Näheres bekannt ist, *etwas* 'Undefi,nierbares.

,non-di'rec·tion·al *adj. Funk, Radio*: ungerichtet: **~ aerial** (*bsd. Am.* **antenna**) Rundstrahlantenne *f*.

'non(-)dis,crim·i'na·tion prin·ci·ple *s.* Diskriminierungsverbot *n*.

,non(-)'du·ra·bles *s. pl.* kurzlebige Kon'sumgüter *pl.*

none [nʌn] **I** *pron. u. s. mst pl. konstr.* kein, niemand: **~ of them is here** keiner von ihnen ist hier; **I have ~** ich habe keine(n); **~ but fools** nur Narren; **it's ~ of your business** das geht dich nichts an; **~ of that** nichts dergleichen; **~ of your tricks!** lass deine Späße!; **he will have ~ of me** er will von mir nichts wissen; → **other** 8; **II** *adv.* in keiner Weise, nicht im Geringsten, keineswegs: **~ too high** keineswegs zu hoch; **~ the less** nichtsdestoweniger; **~ too soon** kein bisschen zu früh, im letzten Augenblick; → **wise** 3.

,non-ef'fec·tive ⚔ **I** *adj.* dienstuntauglich; **II** *s.* Dienstuntaugliche(r) *m*.

,non-'e·go *s. phls.* Nicht-Ich *n*.

non-en·ti·ty [nɒ'nentətɪ] *s.* **1.** Nicht(da)sein *n*; **2.** Unding *n*, Nichts *n*; *fig. contp.* Null *f* (*Person*).

nones [nəʊnz] *s. pl.* **1.** *antiq.* Nonen *pl.*; **2.** *R.C.* 'Mittagsof,fizium *n*.

,non(-)es'sen·tial *Brit.* **I** *adj.* unwesentlich; **II** *s.* unwesentliche Sache, Nebensächlichkeit *f*: **~s** *a.* nicht lebenswichtige Dinge.

'none·such I *adj.* **1.** unvergleichlich; **II** *s.* **2.** Per'son *od.* Sache, die nicht ihresgleichen hat, Muster *n*; **3.** ⚕ a) Brennende Liebe, b) Nonpa'reilleapfel *m*.

,none·the'less *adv.* nichtsdestoweniger, dennoch.

,non(-)'e·vent *s.* F ,Reinfall' *m*.

,non(-)ex'ist·ence *s.* Nicht(da)sein *n*; *weitS.* Fehlen *n*; **,non(-)ex'ist·ent** *adj.* nicht existierend.

,non(-)'fad·ing *adj.* ◎, ⚕ lichtecht.

non(-)fat [,nɒn'fæt] *adj.* fettarm, Mager...

non(-)'fea·sance [,nɒn'fiːzəns] *s.* *ⁿ* pflichtwidrige Unter'lassung.

,non(-)'fer·rous *adj.* **1.** nicht eisenhaltig; **2.** Nichteisen...: **~ metal**.

,non(-)'fic·tion s. Sachbücher pl.

,non(-)'flam·ma·ble adj. flammbeständig, nicht entflammbar.

,non(-)'freez·ing adj. ☺ kältebeständig: **~ mixture** Frostschutzmittel n.

,non(-)'ful·fil(l)·ment s. Nichterfüllung f.

,non(-)'glar·ing adj. blendfrei.

,non(-)'haz·ard·ous adj. ungefährlich.

,non(-)'hu·man adj. nicht zur menschlichen Rasse gehörig.

,non(-)in'duc·tive adj. ⚡ indukti'onsfrei.

,non(-)in'flam·ma·ble adj. nicht feuergefährlich.

,non-'in·ter·est-,bear·ing adj. ✝ zinslos.

'non(-),in·ter'ven·tion s. pol. Nichteinmischung f.

,non(-)'i·ron adj. bügelfrei.

,non(-)'ju·ry adj.: **~ trial** ⚖ summarisches Verfahren.

,non-'lad·der·ing adj. maschenfest.

,non(-)'lead·ed [-'ledɪd] adj. 🔥 bleifrei (Benzin).

,non(-)'met·al s. 🔥 'Nichtme,tall n; **,non(-)'me'tal·lic** adj. 'nichtme,tallisch: **~ element** Metalloid n.

,non(-)ne'go·ti·a·ble adj. ✝ 'unübertragbar, nicht begebbar: **~ bill** (cheque, Am. check) Rektawechsel m (-scheck m).

no-no ['nəʊnəʊ] s. F: **be a ~** verboten od. tabu sein, nicht infrage kommen.

no-'non·sense adj. sachlich, kühl.

,non(-)'nu·cle·ar adj. **1.** a) pol. ohne A'tomwaffen, b) ✕ konventio'nell; **2.** ☺ ohne A'tomkraft.

,non(-)'ob·jec·tion·a·ble adj. einwandfrei.

,non(-)ob'serv·ance s. Nichtbe(ob)achtung f; Nichterfüllung f.

non-pa·reil ['nɒnpərəl] (Fr.) **I** adj. **1.** unvergleichlich; **II** s. **2.** der (die, das) Unvergleichliche; **3.** typ. Nonpa'reille (-schrift) f; **4.** Liebesperlen(plätzchen n) pl.

,non(-)'par·ti·san adj. **1.** (par'tei)unabhängig; 'überpar,teilich; **2.** objek'tiv, 'unpar,teiisch.

,non(-)'par·ty → non(-)partisan.

,non(-)'pay·ment s. Nicht(be)zahlung f, Nichterfüllung f.

,non(-)per'form·ance s. ⚖ Nichterfüllung f.

,non(-)'per·ish·a·ble adj. haltbar: **~ foods**.

,non(-)'per·son s. 'Unper,son' f.

,non'plus I v/t. verblüffen, verwirren: **be ~(s)ed** a. verdutzt sein; **II** s. Verlegenheit f, Klemme f: **at a ~** ratlos, verdutzt.

,non(-)pol'lut·ing adj. 'umweltfreundlich, ungiftig.

,non(-)pro'duc·tive adj. ✝ 'unproduk,tiv (a. Person); unergiebig.

,non(-)'prof·it (mak·ing) adj. gemeinnützig: **a ~ institution**.

'non,pro·lif·er'a·tion s. pol. Nichtweitergabe f von A'tomwaffen: **~ treaty** Atomsperrvertrag m.

non-pros [,nɒn'prɒs] v/t. ⚖ e-n Kläger (wegen Nichterscheinens) abweisen; **non pro·se·qui·tur** [,nɒnprəʊ'sekwɪtə] (Lat.) s. Abweisung f e-s Klägers wegen Nichterscheinens.

,non(-)'quo·ta adj. ✝ nicht kontingentiert: **~ imports**.

,non(-)re'cov·er·a·ble adj.: **~ energy** nicht erneuerbare Energie.

,non-re'cur·ring adj. einmalig (Zahlung etc.).

'non(-),rep·re·sen'ta·tion·al adj. Kunst:

gegenstandslos, ab'strakt.

,non(-)'res·i·dent I adj. **1.** außerhalb des Amtsbezirks wohnend; abwesend (Amtsperson); **2.** nicht ansässig: **~ traffic** Durchgangsverkehr m; **3.** auswärtig (Klubmitglied); **II** s. **4.** Abwesende(r m) f; **5.** Nichtansässige(r m) f; nicht im Hause Wohnende(r m) f; **6.** ✝ De'visenausländer m.

,non(-)re'turn·a·ble adj. ✝ Einweg...: **~ bottle**.

,non(-)'rig·id adj. Brit. ✈ unstarr (Luftschiff; a. phys. Molekül).

,non(-)'sched·uled adj. **1.** außerplanmäßig; **2.** ✈ Charter...

non·sense ['nɒnsəns] **I** s. Unsinn m, dummes Zeug: **talk ~**; **stand no ~** sich nichts gefallen lassen; **make ~ of** a) ad absurdum führen, b) illusorisch machen; **there's no ~ about him** er ist ein ganz kühler Bursche; **II** int. Unsinn!, Blödsinn!; **III** adj. a) Nonsens...: **~ verses, ~ word**, b) → non·sen·si·cal [nɒn'sensɪkl] adj. □ unsinnig, ab'surd.

non se·qui·tur [,nɒn'sekwɪtə] (Lat.) s. Trugschluss m, irrige Folgerung.

,non(-)'skid adj. mot. rutschsicher, Gleitschutz...

,non(-)'slip adj. rutschfest.

,non(-)'smok·er s. **1.** Nichtraucher(in) (Person); **2.** 'Nichtraucher(ab,teil n) m (Zug, Restaurant); **,non(-)'smoking** adj. Nichtraucher...: **~ area** Nichtraucherbereich m, -zone f.

,non-'start·er s. fig. F **1.** ,Blindgänger' m (Person); **2.** ,Pleite' f, ,Reinfall' m (Plan etc.).

,non(-)'stick adj. mit Anti'haftbeschichtung, beschichtet.

,non(-)'stop adj. ohne Halt, pausenlos, Nonstop..., 'durchgehend (Zug), ohne Zwischenlandung (Flug), adv. a. non-'stop: **~ flight** Nonstopflug m; **~ operation** ☺ 24-Stunden-Betrieb m; **~ run** mot. Ohnehaltfahrt f.

'non·such → nonesuch.

,non(-)'suit ⚖ I s. **1.** (gezwungene) Zu-'rücknahme e-r Klage; **2.** Abweisung f e-r Klage; **II** v/t. **3.** den Kläger mit der Klage abweisen.

,non(-)sup'port s. ⚖ Nichterfüllung f einer 'Unterhaltsverpflichtung.

,non-'syn·chro·nous adj. ☺ Brit. asyn-'chron.

,non(-)'tox·ic adj. ungiftig.

,non-'U adj. Brit. F unfein.

,non(-)'u·ni·form adj. ungleichmäßig (a. phys., A), uneinheitlich.

,non(-)'un·ion Brit. adj. ✝ keiner Gewerkschaft angehörig, nicht organisiert: **~ shop** Am. gewerkschaftsfreier Betrieb; **,non(-)'un·ion·ist** s. **1.** nicht organisierter Arbeiter; **2.** Gewerkschaftsgegner m.

,non(-)'us·er s. ⚖ Nichtausübung f e-s Rechts.

,non(-)'va·lent adj. A, phys. nullwertig.

,non(-)'val·ue bill s. ✝ Gefälligkeitswechsel m.

,non(-)'vi·o·lent adj. gewaltlos.

,non(-)'war·ran·ty s. ⚖ Haftungsausschluss m.

noo·dle¹ ['nuːdl] s. **1.** F Trottel m; **2.** sl. ,Birne' f, Schädel m.

noo·dle² ['nuːdl] s. Nudel f: **~ soup** Nudelsuppe f.

nook [nʊk] s. (Schlupf)Winkel m, Ecke f, (stilles) Plätzchen.

nook·ie, nook·y ['nʊkɪ] s. F ,Nümmerchen' n (Sex).

noon [nuːn] **I** s. a. **'~-day**, **'~-tide**, **'~-time** Mittag(szeit f) m: **at ~** zu Mittag; **at high ~** am hellen Mittag; **II** adj. mit-

tägig, Mittags...

noose [nuːs] **I** s. Schlinge f (a. fig.): **running ~** Lauf-, Gleitschlinge; **slip one's head out of the hangman's ~** fig. mit knapper Not dem Galgen entgehen; **put one's head into the ~** fig. den Kopf in die Schlinge stecken; **II** v/t. a) et. schlingen (over über acc., round um), b) (mit e-r Schlinge) fangen.

,no-'par adj. ✝ nennwertlos (Aktie).

nope [nəʊp] adv. F ,ne(e)', nein.

nor [nɔː] cj. **1.** (mst nach neg.) noch: **neither ... ~** weder ... noch; **2.** (nach e-m verneinten Satzglied od. zu Beginn e-s angehängten verneinten Satzes) und nicht, auch nicht(s): **~ do** (od. am) **I** ich auch nicht.

Nor·dic ['nɔːdɪk] **I** adj. nordisch: **~ combined** Skisport: nordische Kombination; **II** s. nordischer Mensch.

norm [nɔːm] s. **1.** Norm f (a. A, ✝); **2.** biol. Typus m; **3.** bsd. ped. 'Durchschnittsleistung f; **'nor·mal** [-ml] **I** adj. □ → **normally**; **1.** nor'mal, Normal...; gewöhnlich, üblich: **~ school** pädagogische Hochschule; **~ speed** ☺ Betriebsdrehzahl f; **~ view** Computer: Normalansicht f; **2.** A nor'mal: a) richtig, b) lot-, senkrecht: **~ line** → 5; **II** s. **3.** → **normalcy**; **4.** Nor'maltyp m; **5.** A Nor'male f, Senkrechte f, (Einfalls)Lot n; **'nor·mal·cy** [-mlsɪ] s. Normali'tät f, Nor'malzustand m, das Nor'male: **return to ~** sich wieder normalisieren; **nor·mal·i·ty** [nɔː'mælətɪ] s. Normali-'tät f (a. A).

nor·mal·i·za·tion [,nɔːməlaɪ'zeɪʃn] s. **1.** Normalisierung f; **2.** Normung f, Vereinheitlichung f; **'nor·mal·ize** ['nɔːməlaɪz] v/t. **1.** normalisieren; **2.** normen, vereinheitlichen; **3.** metall. nor'malglühen; **'nor·mal·ly** ['nɔːməlɪ] adv. nor'malerweise, (für) gewöhnlich.

Nor·man ['nɔːmən] **I** s. **1.** hist. Nor'manne m, Nor'mannin f; **2.** Bewohner(in) der Norman'die; **3.** ling. Nor'mannisch n; **II** adj. **4.** nor'mannisch.

nor·ma·tive ['nɔːmətɪv] adj. norma'tiv.

Norse [nɔːs] **I** adj. **1.** skandi'navisch; **2.** altnordisch; **3.** (bsd. alt)norwegisch; **II** s. **4.** ling. a) Altnordisch n, b) (bsd. Alt)Norwegisch n; **5.** coll. a) die Skandinavier pl., b) die Norweger pl.; **'~·man** [-mən] s. [irr.] hist. Nordländer m, Norweger m.

north [nɔːθ] **I** s. **1.** mst the 🜨 Nord(en m) (Himmelsrichtung, Gegend etc.): **to the ~ of** nördlich von; **~ by east** ⚓ Nord zu Ost; **2. the 🜨** a) Brit. Nordengland n, b) Am. die Nordstaaten pl., c) die Arktis; **II** adj. **3.** nördlich, Nord...; **III** adv. **4.** nördlich, nach od. im Norden (of von); 🜨 **At·lan·tic Trea·ty** s. 'Nordat,lantik,pakt m; 🜨 **Brit·ain** s. Schottland n; 🜨 **Coun·try** s. Nordengland n; **~-east** [,nɔːθ'iːst; ⚓ nɔːr'iːst] **I** s. Nord'ost(en m); **~ by east** ⚓ Nordost zu Ost; **II** adj. nord'östlich, Nordost...; **III** adv. nord-'östlich, nach Nord'osten; **~-east·er** [,nɔːθ'iːstə; ⚓ nɔːr'iːstə] s. Nord'ostwind m; **~-east·er·ly** [,nɔːθ'iːstəlɪ; ⚓ nɔːr'iːstəlɪ] adj. u. adv. nord'östlich, Nordost...; **,~-'east·ern** adj. nord'östlich; **,~-'east·ward** I adj. u. adv. nord'östlich; **II** s. nord'östliche Richtung.

north·er·ly ['nɔːðəlɪ] adj. u. adv. nördlich; **'north·ern** [-ðn] adj. **1.** nördlich, Nord...: **~ Europe** Nordeuropa n; **~ lights** Nordlicht n; **2.** nordisch; **'north·ern·er** [-ðənə] s. Bewohner(in) des nördlichen Landesteils, bsd. der amer. Nordstaaten; **'north·ern·most** adj. nördlichst; **north·ing** ['nɔːθɪŋ] s. **1.** ast.

nördliche Deklinati'on (*Planet*); **2.** Weg *m od.* Di'stanz *f* nach Norden, nördliche Richtung.

'North·man [-mən] *s.* [*irr.*] Nordländer *m*; ⚥ **point** *s. phys.* Nordpunkt *m*; **~ Pole** *s.* Nordpol *m*; **~ Sea** *s.* Nordsee *f*; ⚥**-south di·vide** *s.* Nord-Süd-Gefälle *n*; **~ Star** *s. ast.* Po'larstern *m*.

north·ward ['nɔːθwəd] *adj. u. adv.* nördlich (**of**, **from** von), nordwärts, nach Norden; **'north·wards** [-dz] *adv.* → **northward**.

north-west [ˌnɔːθ'west; ⚓ nɔː'west] **I** *s.* Nord'west(en *m*); **II** *adj.* nord'westlich, Nordwest...: ⚥ **Passage** *geogr.* Nordwestpassage *f*; **III** *adv.* nord'westlich, nach *od.* von Nord'westen; **north-west·er** [ˌnɔːθ'westə; ⚓ nɔː'westə] *s.* **1.** Nord'westwind *m*; **2.** *Am.* Ölzeug *n*; **north-west·er·ly** [ˌnɔːθ'westəlɪ; ⚓ nɔː'westəlɪ] *adj. u. adv.* nord'westlich; **'north-'west·ern** *adj.* nord'westlich.

Nor·we·gian [nɔː'wiːdʒən] **I** *adj.* **1.** norwegisch; **II** *s.* **2.** Norweger(in); **3.** *ling.* Norwegisch *n*.

nose [nəʊz] **I** *s.* **1.** *anat.* Nase *f* (*a. fig.* **for** für); **2.** *Brit.* A'roma *n*, starker Geruch (*Tee, Heu etc.*); **3.** ⚙ *etc.* a) Nase *f*, Vorsprung *m*, (✕ Geschoss)Spitze *f*, Schnabel *m*, b) Schneidkopf *m* (*Drehstahl etc.*), Mündung *f*; **4.** a) ⚓ (Rumpf)Nase *f*, (*a.* ⚓ Schiffs)Bug *m*, b) *mot.* ‚Schnauze‘ *f* (*Vorderteil*); *Besondere Redewendungen:* **bite** (*od.* **snap**) **s.o.'s ~ off** j-n scharf anfahren; **cut off one's ~ to spite one's face** sich ins eigene Fleisch schneiden; **follow one's ~** a) immer der Nase nach gehen, b) s-m Instinkt folgen; **have a good ~ for s.th.** F e-e gute Nase *od.* e-n ‚Riecher‘ für et. haben; **hold one's ~** sich die Nase zuhalten; **lead s.o. by the ~** j-n völlig beherrschen; **keep one's ~ clean** F sich nichts zuschulden kommen lassen; **look down one's ~** ein verdrießliches Gesicht machen; **look down one's ~ at** j-n *od.* et. verachten; **pay through the ~** ‚bluten‘ *od.* übermäßig bezahlen müssen; **poke** (*od.* **put**, **thrust**) **one's ~ into** s-e Nase in et. stecken; **put s.o.'s ~ out of joint** a) j-n ausstechen, j-m die Freundin *etc.* ausspannen, b) j-m das Nachsehen geben; **not to see beyond one's ~** a) die Hand nicht vor den Augen sehen können, b) *fig.* e-n engen (*geistigen*) Horizont haben; **turn up one's ~** (**at**) die Nase rümpfen (über *acc.*); **as plain as the ~ in your face** sonnenklar; **under s.o.'s** (**very**) **~** direkt vor j-s Nase; **II** *v/t.* **5.** riechen, spüren, wittern; **6.** beschnüffeln; mit der Nase berühren *od.* stoßen; **7.** *fig.* a) sich *im Verkehr etc.* vorsichtig vortasten, b) *Auto etc.* vorsichtig (*aus der Garage etc.*) fahren; **8.** näseln(d aussprechen); **III** *v/i.* **9.** a. **~ around** (he-'rum)schnüffeln (**after**, **for** nach) (*a. fig.*); *Zssgn mit adv.:* **nose‖ down** ✈ **I** *v/t.* Flugzeug (an-)drücken; **II** *v/i.* im Steilflug niedergehen; **~ out** *v/t.* **1.** ausschnüffeln, -spionieren, her'ausbekommen; **2.** um e-e Handbreit schlagen; **~ o·ver** *v/i.* ✈ (sich) über'schlagen, e-n ‚Kopfstand‘ machen; **~ up** ✈ **I** *v/t.* Flugzeug hochziehen; **II** *v/i.* steil hochgehen.

nose‖ ape *s. zo.* Nasenaffe *m*; **'~·bag** *s.* Futterbeutel *m*; **'~·bleed** *s.* 🌸 Nasenbluten *n*; **~ cone** *s.* Ra'ketenspitze *f*.

nosed [nəʊzd] *adj. mst in Zssgn mit e-r* dicken *etc.* Nase, ...nasig.

'nose‖·dive I *s.* **1.** ✈ Sturzflug *m*; **2.** ✝ F (Kurs-, Preis)Sturz *m*; **II** *v/i.* **3.** e-n Sturzflug machen; **4.** ✝ ‚purzeln‘ (*Kurs, Preis*); **'~·gay** *s.* Sträußchen *n*; **'~-,heav·y** *adj.* ✈ vorderlastig; **'~-,o·ver** *s.* ✈ ‚Kopfstand‘ *m beim Landen*; **'~·piece** *s.* ⚙ a) Mundstück *n* (*Blasebalg, Schlauch etc.*), b) Re'volver *m* (*Objektivende e-s Mikroskops*), c) Steg *m* (*e-r Brille*); Nasensteg *m* (*Schutzbrille*); **'~·rag** *s. sl.* ‚Rotzfahne‘ *f* (*Taschentuch*); **~ tur·ret** *s.* ✈ vordere Kanzel; **'~,warm·er** *s. sl.* ‚Nasenwärmer‘ *m*, kurze Pfeife; **~ wheel** *s.* ✈ Bugrad *n*.

nos·ey → **nosy**.

'no-show *s.* ✈ *Am. sl.* **1.** *zur Abflugszeit nicht erschienener Flugpassagier*; **2.** ‚Phan'tom‘ *n* (*fiktiver Arbeitnehmer etc.*).

,no-'smok·ing *adj.* Nichtraucher...

nos·o·log·i·cal [ˌnɒsəʊ'lɒdʒɪkl] *adj.* □ 🌸 noso-, patho'logisch; **no·sol·o·gist** [nəʊ'sɒlədʒɪst] *s.* Patho'loge *m*.

nos·tal·gi·a [nɒ'stældʒɪə] *s.* 🌸 Nostal'gie *f* (*a.* 🌸): a) Heimweh *n*, b) Sehnsucht *f* nach etwas Vergangenem; **nos·tal·gic** [nɒ'stældʒɪk] *adj.* (□ **~ally**) **1.** Heimweh...; **2.** no'stalgisch, wehmütig.

nos·tril ['nɒstrɪl] *s.* Nasenloch *n, bsd. zo.* Nüster *f*: **it stinks in one's ~s** es ekelt einen an.

nos·trum ['nɒstrəm] *s.* **1.** 🌸 Geheimmittel *n*, ‚Quacksalbermedi,zin *f*; **2.** *fig.* (*soziales, politisches*) Heilmittel *n*, Pa'tentre,zept *n*.

nos·y ['nəʊzɪ] *adj.* **1.** F neugierig: **~ parker** *Brit.* neugierige Person; **2.** *Brit.* a) aro'matisch, duftend (*bsd. Tee*), b) muffig.

not [nɒt] *adv.* **1.** nicht; **~ that** nicht, dass, nicht als ob; **is it ~?**, F **isn't it?** nicht wahr?; → **at** 7; **2.** **~ a** kein(e): **~ a few** nicht wenige.

no·ta·bil·i·ty [ˌnəʊtə'bɪlətɪ] *s.* **1.** wichtige Per'sönlichkeit, 'Standesper,son *f*; **2.** her'vorragende Eigenschaft, Bedeutung *f*; **no·ta·ble** ['nəʊtəbl] **I** *adj.* □ **1.** beachtens-, bemerkenswert, denkwürdig, wichtig; **2.** beträchtlich: **a ~ difference**; **3.** angesehen, her'vorragend; **4.** 🌸 merklich; **II** *s.* **5.** → **notability** 1.

no·tar·i·al [nəʊ'teərɪəl] *adj.* □ ⚖ **1.** No'tariats..., notari'ell; **2.** notari'ell beglaubigt; **no·ta·rize** ['nəʊtəraɪz] *v/t.* notari'ell be'urkunden *od.* beglaubigen; **no·ta·ry** ['nəʊtərɪ] *s. mst* **~ public** (öffentlicher) No'tar.

no·ta·tion [nəʊ'teɪʃn] *s.* **1.** Aufzeichnung *f*, Notierung *f*; **2.** *bsd.* 🎵, ♈ Schreibweise *f*, Bezeichnung *f*: **chemical ~** chemisches Formelzeichen; **3.** ♪ (Aufzeichnen *n* in) Notenschrift *f*.

notch [nɒtʃ] **I** *s.* **1.** a. ⚙ Kerbe *f*, Einschnitt *m*, Aussparung *f*, Falz *m*, Nute *f*, Raste *f*: **be a ~ above** F e-e Klasse besser sein als; **2.** (Vi'sier)Kimme *f* (*Schusswaffe*): **~ and bead sights** Kimme und Korn; **3.** *Am.* Engpass *m*; **II** *v/t.* **4.** *bsd.* ⚙ (ein)kerben, (ein)schneiden, einfeilen; **5.** ⚙ a) ausklinken, b) nuten, falzen; **notched** [-tʃt] *adj.* **1.** ⚙ (ein)gekerbt, mit Nuten versehen; **2.** ♀ grob gezähnt (*Blatt*).

note [nəʊt] **I** *s.* **1.** (Kenn)Zeichen *n*, Merkmal *n*; *fig.* Ansehen *n*, Ruf *m*, Bedeutung *f*: **man of ~** bedeutender Mann; **nothing of ~** nichts von Bedeutung; **2.** *mst pl.* No'tiz *f*, Aufzeichnung *f*: **compare ~s** Meinungen *od.* Erfahrungen austauschen, sich beraten; **make a ~ of s.th.** sich et. vormerken *od.* notieren; **make a mental ~ of s.th.**

sich et. merken; **take ~s of s.th.** sich über et. Notizen machen; **take ~ of s.th.** *fig.* et. zur Kenntnis nehmen, et. berücksichtigen; **3.** *pol.* (diplo'matische) Note: **exchange of ~s** Notenwechsel *m*; **4.** Briefchen *n*, Zettelchen *n*; **5.** *typ.* a) Anmerkung *f*, b) (Satz-)Zeichen *n*; **6.** ✝ a) Nota *f*, Rechnung *f*: **as per ~** laut Nota, b) (Schuld)Schein *m*: **~ of hand** → **promissory**; **bought and sold ~** Schlussschein *m*; **~s payable** (**receivable**) *Am.* Wechselverbindlichkeiten (-forderungen), c) Banknote *f*, d) Vermerk *m*, Notiz *f*: **urgent ~** Dringlichkeitsvermerk *m*, e) Mitteilung *f*: **advice ~** Versandanzeige *f*; **~ of exchange** Kursblatt *n*; **7.** ♪ a) Note *f*, b) Ton *m*, c) Taste *f*; **8.** *weitS.* a) Klang *m*, Melo'die *f*; Gesang *m* (*Vogel*), b) *fig.* Ton(art *f*) *m*: **change one's ~** e-n anderen Ton anschlagen; **strike the right ~** den richtigen Ton treffen; **strike a false ~** a) sich im Ton vergreifen, b) sich danebenbenehmen; **on this** (*encouraging etc.*) **~** mit diesen (ermutigenden *etc.*) Worten; **9.** ✝ Brandmal *n*, Schandfleck *m*; **II** *v/t.* **10.** Kenntnis nehmen von, bemerken, be(ob)achten; **11.** besonders erwähnen; **12.** *a.* **~ down** niederschreiben, notieren, vermerken; **13.** ✝ *Wechsel* protestieren; *Preise* angeben.

note‖ bank *s.* ✝ Notenbank *f*; **'~·book** *s.* **1.** No'tizbuch *n*, ‚Kladde‘ *f*; **2.** *Computer:* Notebook *n* (*tragbarer Kleincomputer*); **~ bro·ker** *s.* ✝ *Am.* Wechselhändler *m*, Dis'kontmakler *m*.

not·ed ['nəʊtɪd] *adj.* □ **1.** bekannt, berühmt (**for** wegen); **2.** ✝ notiert: **~ before official hours** vorbörslich (*Kurs*); **'not·ed·ly** [-lɪ] *adv.* ausgesprochen, deutlich, besonders.

note·pad ['nəʊtpæd] *s.* **1.** No'tizblock *m*; **2.** *Computer:* Notepad *n* (*tragbarer Kleinstcomputer*).

note‖ pa·per *s.* 'Briefpa,pier *n*; **~ press** *s.* ✝ 'Banknotenpresse *f*, -drucke,rei *f*; **'~,wor·thy** *adj.* bemerkens-, beachtenswert.

noth·ing ['nʌθɪŋ] **I** *pron.* **1.** nichts (**of** von): **~ much** nichts Bedeutendes; **II** *s.* **2.** Nichts *n*: **to ~** zu *od.* in nichts; **for ~** vergebens, umsonst; **3.** *fig.* Nichts *n*, Unwichtigkeit *f*, Kleinigkeit *f*; *pl.* Nichtigkeiten *pl.*; Null *f* (*a. Person*): **whisper sweet ~s** Süßholz raspeln; **III** *adv.* **4.** durch'aus nicht, keineswegs: **~ like complete** alles andere als vollständig; **IV** *int.* **5.** F keine Spur!, Unsinn!; *Besondere Redewendungen:* **good for ~** zu nichts zu gebrauchen; **~ doing** F a) (das) kommt gar nicht in Frage, b) nichts zu machen; **~ but** nichts als, nur; **~ else** nichts anderes, sonst nichts; **~ if not courageous** über'aus mutig; **not for ~** nicht umsonst, nicht ohne Grund; **that is ~ to what we have seen** das ist nichts gegen das, was wir gesehen haben; **that's ~ to me** das bedeutet mir nichts; **that is ~ to you** das geht dich nichts an; **there is ~ like** es geht nichts über; **there is ~ to it** a) da ist nichts dabei, b) an der Sache ist nichts dran; **come to ~** *fig.* zunichte werden, sich zerschlagen; **feel like ~ on earth** sich hundeelend fühlen; **make ~ of s.th.** nicht viel Wesens von et. machen, sich nichts aus et. machen; **I can make ~ of it** ich kann daraus nicht klug werden; → **say** 2, **think** 3 e.

noth·ing·ness ['nʌθɪŋnɪs] *s.* **1.** Nichts *n*; **2.** Nichtigkeit *f*; **3.** Leere *f*.

no·tice ['nəʊtɪs] **I** *s.* **1.** Wahrnehmung *f*:

to avoid ~ (Redew.) um Aufsehen zu vermeiden; **come under s.o.'s** ~ j-m bekannt werden; **escape** ~ unbemerkt bleiben; **take** ~ **of** Notiz nehmen von et. od. j-m, beachten; ~! zur Beachtung!; **2.** No'tiz f, (a. Presse)Nachricht f, Anzeige f (a. ✝), (An)Meldung f, Ankündigung f, Mitteilung f; ⚖ Vorladung f; (Buch)Besprechung f; Kenntnis f: ~ **of acceptance** ✝ Annahmeerklärung f; ~ **of arrival** ✝ Eingangsbestätigung f; ~ **of assessment** Steuerbescheid m; ~ **of departure** (polizeiliche) Abmeldung f; ~ **previous** ~ Voranzeige f; **bring s.th. to s.o.'s** ~ j-m et. zur Kenntnis bringen; **give** ~ **that** bekannt geben, dass; **give s.o.** ~ **of s.th.** j-n von et. benachrichtigen; **give** ~ **of appeal** ⚖ Berufung einlegen; **give** ~ **of motion** parl. e-n Initiativantrag stellen; **give** ~ **of a patent** ein Patent anmelden; **have** ~ **of** Kenntnis haben von; **3.** Warnung f; Kündigung(sfrist) f: **give s.o.** ~ (**for Easter**) j-m (zu Ostern) kündigen; **I am under** ~ **to leave** mir ist gekündigt worden; **at a day's** ~ binnen eines Tages; **at a moment's** ~ sogleich, jederzeit; **at short** ~ kurzfristig, auf (kurzen) Abruf, sofort; **subject to a month's** ~ mit monatlicher Kündigung; **without** ~ fristlos; **until further** ~ bis auf weiteres; → **quit** 9; **II** v/t. **4.** bemerken, beobachten, wahrnehmen; **5.** beachten, achten auf (acc.); **6.** No'tiz nehmen von; **7.** Buch besprechen; **8.** anzeigen, melden, bekannt machen, ⚖ benachrichtigen; **no·tice·a·ble** ['nəʊtɪsəbl] adj. ☐ **1.** wahrnehmbar, merklich, spürbar; **2.** bemerkenswert, beachtlich; **3.** auffällig, ins Auge fallend.

no·tice| board s. **1.** Anschlagtafel f, schwarzes Brett; **2.** Warnschild n; ~ **pe·ri·od** s. Kündigungsfrist f.

no·ti·fi·a·ble ['nəʊtɪfaɪəbl] adj. meldepflichtig; **no·ti·fi·ca·tion** [ˌnəʊtɪfɪ'keɪʃn] s. Anzeige f, Meldung f, Mitteilung f, Bekanntmachung f, Benachrichtigung f; **no·ti·fy** ['nəʊtɪfaɪ] v/t. **1.** bekannt geben, anzeigen, avisieren, melden, (amtlich) mitteilen (**s.th. to s.o.** j-m et.); **2.** j-n benachrichtigen, in Kenntnis setzen (**of** von, **that** dass).

no·tion ['nəʊʃn] s. **1.** Begriff m (a. phls., ✗), Gedanke m, I'dee f, Vorstellung f (**of** von): **not to have the vaguest** ~ **of s.th.** nicht die leiseste Ahnung von et. haben; **I have a** ~ **that** ich denke mir, dass; **2.** Meinung f, Ansicht f: **fall into the** ~ **that** auf den Gedanken kommen, dass; **3.** Neigung f, Lust f, Absicht f (**of doing** zu tun); **4.** pl. Am. a) Kurzwaren pl., b) Kinkerlitzchen pl.; **'no·tion·al** [-ʃənl] adj. ☐ **1.** begrifflich, Begriffs...; **2.** phls. rein gedanklich, spekula'tiv; **3.** theo'retisch; **4.** fik'tiv, angenommen, imagi'när; **'no·tion·ate** [-nət] adj. ☐ Am. **1.** willensstark; stur; **2.** (leicht) verrückt.

no·to·ri·e·ty [ˌnəʊtə'raɪətɪ] s. **1.** bsd. contp. allgemeine Bekanntheit, (traurige) Berühmtheit, schlechter Ruf; **2.** Berüchtigtsein n, das No'torische; **3.** allbekannte Per'sönlichkeit od. Sache; **no·to·ri·ous** [nəʊ'tɔːrɪəs] adj. ☐ no'torisch: a) offenkundig, b) all-, stadt-, weltbekannt, c) berüchtigt (**for** wegen).

not·with·stand·ing [ˌnɒtwɪθ'stændɪŋ] **I** prp. ungeachtet, trotz (gen.): ~ **the objections** ungeachtet der Einwände; **his great reputation** ~ trotz s-s hohen Ansehens; **II** a. ~ **that** cj. ob'gleich; **III** adv. nichtsdesto'weniger, dennoch.

nou·gat ['nuːɡɑː] s. Art türkischer

Honig.

nought [nɔːt] s. u. pron. **1.** nichts: **bring to** ~ ruinieren, zunichte machen; **come to** ~ zunichte werden, misslingen, fehlschlagen; **2.** Null f (a. fig.): **set at** ~ et. in den Wind schlagen, verlachen, ignorieren.

noun [naʊn] ling. **I** s. Hauptwort n, Substantiv n: **proper** ~ Eigenname m; **II** adj. substantivisch.

nour·ish ['nʌrɪʃ] v/t. **1.** (er)nähren, erhalten (**on** von); **2.** fig. Gefühl nähren, hegen; **'nour·ish·ing** [-ʃɪŋ] adj. nahrhaft, Nähr...; **'nour·ish·ment** [-mənt] s. **1.** Ernährung f; **2.** Nahrung f (a. fig.), Nahrungsmittel n: **take** ~ Nahrung zu sich nehmen.

nous [naʊs] s. **1.** phls. Vernunft f, Verstand m; **2.** F Mutterwitz m, ‚Grütze' f, ‚Grips' m.

no·va ['nəʊvə] pl. **-vae** [-viː], a. **-vas** s. ast. Nova f, neuer Stern.

no·va·tion [nəʊ'veɪʃn] s. ⚖ Novati'on f (Forderungsablösung od. -übertragung).

nov·el ['nɒvl] **I** adj. neu(artig), ungewöhnlich, über'raschend; **II** s. Ro'man m: **short** ~ Kurzroman; ~ **writer** → **novelist**; **no·vel·la** [nəʊ'velə] s. No'velle f; **nov·el·ette** [ˌnɒvə'let] s. **1.** kurzer Ro'man; **2.** contp. seichter Unter'haltungsro,man; **nov·el·ist** ['nɒvəlɪst] s. Ro'manschriftsteller(in); **no·vel·is·tic** [ˌnɒvə'lɪstɪk] adj. ro'manhaft, Roman...; **'nov·el·ty** [-tɪ] s. **1.** Neuheit f: a) das Neue, b) et. Neues: **the** ~ **had soon worn off** der Reiz des Neuen war bald verflogen; **2.** Ungewöhnlichkeit f, et. Ungewöhnliches; **3.** pl. ✝ (billige) Neuheiten pl.: ~ **item** Neuheit f, Schlager m, (billiger) Modeartikel; **4.** Neuerung f.

No·vem·ber [nəʊ'vembə] s. No'vember m: **in** ~ im November.

nov·ice ['nɒvɪs] s. **1.** Anfänger(in), Neuling m (**at** auf **od** in em Gebiet); **2.** R.C. No'vize m, f, No'vizin f; **3.** bibl. Neubekehrte(r m) f.

now [naʊ] **I** adv. **1.** nun, gegenwärtig, jetzt: **from** ~ von jetzt an; **up to** ~ bis jetzt; **2.** so'fort, bald; **3.** eben, so'eben: **just** ~ gerade eben, vor ein paar Minuten; **4.** nun, dann, dar'auf, damals; **5.** (nicht zeitlich) nun (aber); **II** cj. **6.** a. ~ **that** nun aber, nun da, da nun, jetzt wo; **III** s. **7.** poet. Gegenwart f, Jetzt n; Besondere Redewendungen: **before** ~ schon einmal, schon früher; **by** ~ mittlerweile, jetzt; ~ **if** wenn nun aber; **how** ~? nun?, was gibts?, was soll das heißen?; **what is it** ~? was ist jetzt schon wieder los?; **now ... now** ... bald ... bald ...; ~ **and again**, (**every**) ~ **and then** von Zeit zu Zeit, hie(r) und da, dann und wann, gelegentlich; ~ **then** (nun) also; **come** ~! nur ruhig!, sachte, sachte!; **what** ~? was nun?; ~ **or never** jetzt oder nie.

now·a·days ['naʊədeɪz] **I** adv. heutzutage, jetzt; **II** s. das Heute od. Jetzt.

'no·way(s) [-weɪ(z)] F → **nowise**.

'no·where I adv. **1.** nirgends, nirgendwo: **be** ~ a) Sport: unter ‚ferner liefen' enden, b) nichts erreicht haben; **get** ~ nicht weiterkommen, nichts erreichen; ~ **near** auch nicht annähernd; **2.** nirgendwohin; **II** s. **3.** Nirgendwo n: **from** ~ aus dem Nichts; **in the middle of** ~ 🌍 auf freier Strecke halten.

'no·wise adv. in keiner Weise.

nox·ious ['nɒkʃəs] adj. ☐ schädlich (**to** für): ~ **substance** Schadstoff m; ~ **emission** Schadstoffausstoß m.

noz·zle ['nɒzl] s. **1.** Schnauze f, Rüssel m; **2.** sl. ‚Rüssel' m (Nase); **3.** ⊕ a) Schnauze f, Tülle f, Schnabel m, Mundstück n, Ausguss m, Röhre f, (an Gefäßen etc.), b) Stutzen m, Mündung f (an Röhren etc.), c) (Kraftstoff- etc.)Düse f, d) 'Zapfpis,tole f.

nth [enθ] adj. ✗ n-te(r), n-tes: **to the** ~ **degree** a) ✗ bis zum n-ten Grade, b) fig. im höchsten Maße; **for the** ~ **time** zum hundertsten Mal.

nu [njuː] s. Ny n (griech. Buchstabe).

nu·ance [nju'ɑ̃ːns] (Fr.) s. Nu'ance f: a) Schattierung f, b) Feinheit f, feiner 'Unterschied.

nub [nʌb] s. **1.** Knopf m, Auswuchs m, Knötchen n; **2.** (kleiner) Klumpen, Nuss f (Kohle etc.); **3. the** ~ F der springende Punkt (**of** bei); **'nub·bly** [-blɪ] adj. knotig.

nu·bile ['njuːbaɪl] adj. **1.** heiratsfähig, ehemündig (Frau); **2.** attrak'tiv; **nu·bil·i·ty** [njuː'bɪlətɪ] s. Heiratsfähigkeit f etc.

nu·cle·ar ['njuːklɪə] **I** adj. **1.** kernförmig; a. biol. etc. Kern...; **2.** phys. nukle'ar, Nuklear..., (Atom)Kern..., 'mar, Atom...: ~ **test**; ~ **weapon** Kernwaffe f; **3.** a. ~**-powered** mit A'tomantrieb, Atom...: ~ **submarine**; **II** s. **4.** Kernwaffe f, A'tomra,kete f; **5.** pol. A'tommacht f: ~ **bomb** s. A'tombombe f; ~ **charge** s. phys. Kernladung f; ~ **chem·is·try** s. 'Kernche,mie f; ~ **dis·in·te·gra·tion** s. phys. Kernzerfall m; ~ **en·er·gy** s. phys. **1.** 'Kernener,gie f; **2.** allg. A'tomener,gie f; ~ **fam·i·ly** s. 'Kernfa,milie f; ~ **fis·sion** s. phys. Kernspaltung f; ~**-free** adj. a'tomwaffenfrei; ~ **fu·el** s. Kernbrennstoff m: ~ **rod** Brennstab m; ~ **fu·sion** s. phys. 'Kernfus,ion f; ~ **par·ti·cle** s. phys. Kernteilchen n; ~ **phys·ics** s. pl. sg. konstr. 'Kernphy,sik f; ~ **pow·er** s. **1.** phys. Kernkraft f; ~ **plant** Kernkraftwerk n; **2.** pol. A'tommacht f; ~ **re·ac·tor** s. phys. 'Kernre,aktor m; ~ **re·search** s. (A'tom)Kernforschung f; ~ **ship** s. Re'aktorschiff n; ~ **smug·gling** s. A'tomschmuggel m; ~ **the·o·ry** s. phys. 'Kerntheo,rie f; ~ **war(·fare)** s. A'tomkrieg(führung f) m; ~ **war·head** s. ✗ A'tomsprengkopf m; ~ **waste** s. A'tommüll m.

nu·cle·i ['njuːklɪaɪ] pl. von **nucleus**.

nu·cle·o·lus [njuː'kliːələs] pl. **-li** [-laɪ] s. ⚕, biol. Kernkörperchen n.

nu·cle·on ['njuːklɪɒn] s. phys. Nukleon n, (A'tom)Kernbaustein m.

nu·cle·us ['njuːklɪəs] pl. **-e·i** [-ɪaɪ] s. **1.** allg. (a. A'tom-, Ko'meten-, Zell)Kern m (a. ✗); **2.** fig. Kern m: a) Mittelpunkt m, b) Grundstock m; **3.** opt. Kernschatten m.

nude [njuːd] **I** adj. **1.** nackt (a. fig. Tatsache etc.), bloß; **2.** nackt, kahl: ~ **hill**; **3.** ⚖ unverbindlich, nichtig: ~ **contract**; **II** s. **4.** paint. etc. Akt m: **study from the** ~ Aktstudie f; **5.** Nacktheit f: **in the** ~ nackt.

nudge [nʌdʒ] **I** v/t. j-n anstoßen, (an-)stupsen'; **II** s. Stups m.

nu·die ['njuːdɪ] s. sl. Nacktfilm m.

nud·ism ['njuːdɪzəm] s. 'Nackt-, 'Freikörperkul,tur f, Nu'dismus m; **'nud·ist** [-ɪst] s. Nu'dist(in), FK'K-Anhänger (-in): ~ **beach** Nacktbadestrand m; ~ **camp**, ~ **colony** FKK-Platz m; **'nu·di·ty** [-ətɪ] s. **1.** Nacktheit f, Blöße f; **2.** fig. Armut f; **3.** Kahlheit f; **4.** paint. etc. 'Akt(fi,gur f) m.

nu·ga·to·ry ['njuːɡətərɪ] adj. **1.** wertlos, albern; **2.** unwirksam (a. ⚖), eitel, leer.

nug·get ['nʌgɪt] s. **1.** Nugget n (Gold-klumpen); **2.** fig. Brocken m.

nui·sance ['njuːsns] s. **1.** Ärgernis n, Plage f, et. Lästiges od. Unangenehmes; Unfug m, 'Missstand m: *dust* ~ Staubplage; *what a* ~! wie ärgerlich!; **2.** ⚖ Poli'zeiwidrigkeit f: *public* ~ Störung f od. Gefährdung f der öffentlichen Sicherheit u. Ordnung, a. fig. iro. öffentliches Ärgernis; *private* ~ Besitzstörung f; *commit no* ~! das Verunreinigen (dieses Ortes) ist verboten!; **3.** (von Personen) ,Landplage' f, Quälgeist m, Nervensäge f: *be a* ~ *to s.o.* j-m lästig fallen; *make a* ~ *of o.s.* anderen auf die Nerven gehen; ~ *call* s. teleph. Schockanruf m, pl. a. Tele'fonterror m; ~ *raid* ✕, ✈ Störangriff m; ~ *tax* s. sl. ärgerliche kleine (Verbraucher)Steuer: ~ *val·ue* s. Wert m od. Wirkung f als störender Faktor.

nuke [nuːk] Am. sl. I s. **1.** Kernwaffe f; **2.** 'Kernre,aktor m; II v/t. **3.** mit Kernwaffen angreifen.

null [nʌl] I adj. **1.** ⚖ u. fig. nichtig, ungültig: *declare* ~ *and void* für null u. nichtig erklären; **2.** wertlos, leer, nichts sagend, unbedeutend; II s. **3.** A, ⌀ Null f: ~ *set* Nullmenge f.

nul·li·fi·ca·tion [ˌnʌlɪfɪˈkeɪʃn] s. **1.** Aufhebung f, Nichtigerklärung f; **2.** Zu-'nichtemachen n; **nul·li·fy** ['nʌlɪfaɪ] v/t. **1.** ungültig machen, für null u. nichtig erklären, aufheben; **2.** zu'nichte machen; **nul·li·ty** ['nʌlətɪ] s. **1.** Unwirksamkeit f; ⚖ Ungültigkeit f, Nichtigkeit f: *decree of* ~ Nichtigkeitsurteil n od. Annullierung f e-r Ehe; ~ *suit* Nichtigkeitsklage f; *be a* ~ (null u.) nichtig sein; **2.** Nichts n; fig. Null f (Person).

numb [nʌm] I adj. **1.** starr, erstarrt (*with* vor Kälte etc.); taub (empfindungslos); fig. a) (wie) betäubt, starr (*with fear* vor Angst), b) abgestumpft; II v/t. starr od. taub machen, erstarren lassen; fig. a. betäuben, b. abstumpfen.

num·ber ['nʌmbə] I s. **1.** Zahl(enwert m) f, Ziffer f; **2.** (Haus-, Tele'fon- etc.) Nummer f: *by* ~s nummernweise; ~ *engaged* teleph. besetzt; *have s.o.'s* ~ F j-n durchschaut haben; *his* ~ *is up* F s-e Stunde hat geschlagen, jetzt ist er dran; ~ *number one*; **3.** (An)Zahl f: *a* ~ *of* e-e Anzahl von (od. gen.), mehrere; *a great* ~ *of* sehr viele Leute etc.; *five in* ~ fünf an (der) Zahl; *in large* ~s in großen Mengen; *in round* ~ rund; *one of their* ~ einer aus ihrer Mitte; ~s *of times* zu wiederholten Malen; *times without* ~ unzählige Male; *five times the* ~ *of people* fünfmal so viele Leute; **4.** ✚ a) (An)Zahl f, Nummer f, b) Ar'tikel m, Ware f, **5.** Heft n, Nummer f, Ausgabe f (Zeitschrift etc.), Lieferung f e-s Werkes: *appear in* ~s in Lieferungen erscheinen; **6.** thea. etc. (Pro-'gramm)Nummer f; **7.** ♪ a) Nummer f (Satz), b) sl. Tanznummer f, Schlager m; **8.** poet. pl. Verse pl.; **9.** ling. Numerus m: *plural* (*singular*) ~ Mehrzahl (Einzahl) f; **10.** ⊕ Feinheitsnummer f (Garn); **11.** sl. ,Type' f, ,Nummer' f (Person); **12.** ~s bibl. Numeri pl., Viertes Buch Mose; II v/t. **13.** zs.-zählen, aufrechnen: ~ *off* abzählen; *his days are* ~*ed* s-e Tage sind gezählt; **14.** zählen, rechnen (a. fig. *among*, *in*, *with* zu od. unter acc.); **15.** nummerieren: ~ *consecutively* durchnummerieren; **16.** zählen, sich belaufen auf (acc.); **17.** Jahre zählen, alt sein; III v/i. **18.** (auf)zählen; **19.** zählen (*among* zu

j-s Freunden etc.); **num·ber block** s. Computer: Nummernblock m; '**num-ber-,crunch·ing** Computer: **1.** sehr schnelle Zahlenverarbeitung, sehr hohe Rechenleistung; II adj. 'rechenin,siv; **num·bered ac·count** s. Nummernkonto n; '**num·ber·ing** [-bərɪŋ] s. Nummerierung f; '**num·ber·less** [-lɪs] adj. unzählig, zahllos.

num·ber| one I adj. **1.** a) erstklassig, b) (aller)höchst: ~ *priority*; II s. **2.** Nummer f eins; der (die, das) Erste; erste Klasse; **3.** F das liebe Ich: *look after* ~ auf seinen Vorteil bedacht sein, nur an sich selbst denken; **4.** *do* ~ F sein ,kleines Geschäft' machen; '~·**plate** s. mot. Nummernschild n; ~ **pol·y·gon** s. A 'Zahlenvieleck n; -poly,gon n; ~ **two** s.: *do* ~ F sein ,großes Geschäft' machen.

numb·ness ['nʌmnɪs] s. Erstarrung f, Starr-, Taubheit f; fig. Betäubung f.

nu·mer·a·ble ['njuːmərəbl] adj. zählbar; '**nu·mer·al** [-rəl] I adj. **1.** Zahl..., Zahlen..., nu'merisch: ~ *language* Ziffernsprache f; II s. **2.** Ziffer f, Zahlzeichen n; **3.** ling. Zahlwort n; '**nu·mer·ar·y** [-ərɪ] adj. Zahl(en)...; '**nu·mer·ate** [-rət] adj. rechenkundig: *be* ~ rechnen können; **nu·mer·a·tion** [ˌnjuːməˈreɪʃn] s. **1.** Zählen n; Rechenkunst f; **2.** Nummerierung f; **3.** (Auf)Zählung f; '**nu-mer·a·tive** [-ətɪv] adj. zählend, Zahl(-en)...: ~ *system* Zahlensystem n; '**nu-mer·a·tor** [-məreɪtə] s. A Zähler m e-s Bruchs; **nu·mer·i·cal** [njuːˈmerɪkl] adj. □ nu'merisch: a) A Zahl(en)...: ~ *value*; ~ *equation* Zahlengleichung f, b) zahlenmäßig: ~ *superiority*.

nu·mer·ous ['njuːmərəs] adj. □ zahlreich: *a* ~ *assembly*; '**nu·mer·ous-ness** [-nɪs] s. große Zahl, Menge f, Stärke f.

nu·mis·mat·ic [ˌnjuːmɪzˈmætɪk] adj. (□ ~ally) numis'matisch, Münz(en)...; ˌ**nu·mis'mat·ics** [-ks] a. pl. sg. konstr. Numis'matik f, Münzkunde f; **nu·mis-ma·tist** [njuːˈmɪzmətɪst] s. Numis'matiker(in): a) Münzkenner(in), b) Münzsammler(in).

num·skull ['nʌmskʌl] s. Dummkopf m, Trottel m.

nun [nʌn] s. eccl. Nonne f.

nun·ci·a·ture ['nʌnʃɪətʃə] s. eccl. Nuntia'tur f; **nun·ci·o** ['nʌnʃɪəʊ] pl. -os s. Nuntius m.

nun·cu·pa·tive ['nʌnkjʊpeɪtɪv] adj. ⚖ mündlich: ~ *will* mündliches Testament, bsd. ✕ Not-, ⚓ Seetestament.

nun·ner·y ['nʌnərɪ] s. Nonnenkloster n.

nup·tial ['nʌptʃəl] I adj. hochzeitlich, Hochzeit(s)..., Ehe..., Braut...: ~ *bed* Brautbett n; ~ *flight* Hochzeitsflug m der Bienen; II s. mst pl. Hochzeit f.

nurse [nɜːs] I s. **1.** mst *wet* ~ (Säug-) Amme f; **2.** a. *dry* ~ Kinderfrau f, -mädchen n; **3.** Krankenschwester f, a. ~-*attendant* (Kranken)Pfleger(in): *head* ~ Oberschwester f; *sick children's* ~ Kinderkrankenschwester; → *male* 1; **4.** a) Stillen n, Stillzeit f, b) Pflege f: *at* ~ in Pflege; *put out to* ~ Kinder in Pflege geben; **5.** zo. a) Amme f, b) Arbeiterin f (Biene); **6.** fig. Nährmutter f; II v/t. **7.** Kind säugen, nähren, stillen, dem Kind die Brust geben; **8.** Kind auf-, großziehen; **9.** a) Kranke pflegen, b) Krankheit auskurieren, c) Glied, Stimme schonen, d) Knie etc. (schützend) um'fassen: ~ *one's leg* ein Bein über das andere schlagen, e) sparsam od. schonend 'umgehen mit: ~ *a glass of*

wine bedächtig ein Glas Wein trinken; **10.** fig. a) nähren, fördern, b) Gefühl etc. nähren, hegen; **11.** streicheln, hätscheln; weitS. a. pol. sich eifrig kümmern um ,warm halten': ~ *one's constituency*; III v/i. **12.** a) säugen, stillen, b) die Brust nehmen (Säugling); **13.** als (Kranken)Pfleger(in) arbeiten.

nurse·ling → *nursling*.

'**nurse·maid** s. Kindermädchen n.

nurs·er·y ['nɜːsrɪ] s. **1.** Kinderzimmer n: *day* ~ Spielzimmer n; *night* ~ Kinderschlafzimmer n; **2.** Kindertagesstätte f; **3.** Pflanz-, Baumschule f; Schonung f; fig. Pflanzstätte f, Schule f; **4.** Fischpflege f, Streckteich m; **5.** a. ~ *stakes* (Pferde-) Rennen n für Zweijährige; ~ **gov·er-ness** s. Kinderfräulein n; '~·**man** [-mən] s. [irr.] Pflanzenzüchter m; ~ **rhyme** s. Kinderlied n, -reim m; ~ **school** s. Kindergarten m; ~ **slope** s. Skisport: ,Idi'otenhügel' m, Anfängerhügel m; ~ **tale** s. Ammenmärchen n.

nurs·ing ['nɜːsɪŋ] I s. **1.** Säugen n, Stillen n; **2.** a. *sick*~, ~ *care* (Kranken-) Pflege f; II adj. **3.** Nähr..., Pflege..., Kranken...; ~ **ben·e·fit** s. Stillgeld n; ~ **bot·tle** s. Säuglingsflasche f; ~ **home** s. **1.** bsd. Brit. a) Pri'vatklinik f, b) pri'vate Entbindungsklinik; **2.** Pflegeheim n; ~ **moth·er** s. stillende Mutter; ~ **staff** s. 'Pflegeperso,nal n.

nurs·ling ['nɜːslɪŋ] s. **1.** Säugling m; **2.** Pflegling m; **3.** fig. a) Liebling m, Hätschelkind n, b) Schützling m.

nur·ture ['nɜːtʃə] I v/t. **1.** (er)nähren; **2.** auf-, erziehen; **3.** fig. Gefühle etc. hegen; II s. **4.** Nahrung f; fig. Pflege f, Erziehung f.

nut [nʌt] I s. **1.** ♀ Nuss f; **2.** ⊕ a) Nuss f, b) (Schrauben)Mutter f: ~*s and bolts* fig. praktische Grundlagen, wesentliche Details; **3.** ♪ a) Frosch m (am Bogen), b) Saitensattel m; **4.** pl. ☛ Nusskohle f; **5.** fig. schwierige Sache: *a hard* ~ *to crack* e-e harte Nuss; **6.** sl. a) ,Birne' f (Kopf): *be* (*go*) *off one's* ~ verrückt sein (werden), b) contp. ,Knülch' m, Kerl m, c) komischer Kauz, ,Spinner' m, d) Idi'ot m, e) Geck m; **7.** sl. *be* ~s verrückt sein (*on* nach); *he is* ~s *about her* er ist in sie total verschossen; *drive s.o.* ~s j-n verrückt machen; *go* ~s überschnappen; *do one's* ~ ,ausrasten', ,durchdrehen'; *that's* ~s *to him* das ist genau sein Fall; ~s! a) du spinnst wohl!, b) a. ~ *to you!* ,du kannst mich mal!'; **8.** pl. V ☛~s *pl.* (Hoden); **9.** *not for* ~s sl. überhaupt nicht; *he can't play for* ~s sl. er spielt miserabel; **10.** sl. a) ,Spinner' m, b) ... fan m, ... freak m; II v/i. **11.** Nüsse pflücken; III v/t. **12.** F j-n mit dem Kopf treffen, anstoßen.

nut| bolt ⊕ **1.** Mutterbolzen m; **2.** Bolzen m od. Schraube f mit Mutter; ~ **but·ter** s. Nussbutter f; '~·**case** s. sl. ,Spinner' m; '~·**crack·er** s. **1.** a. pl. Nussknacker m; **2.** orn. Tannenhäher m; '~·**gall** s. Gallapfel m: ~ *ink* Gallustinte f; '~·**hatch** s. orn. Kleiber m, Spechtmeise f; '~·**house** s. sl. ,Klapsmühle' f.

nut·meg ['nʌtmeg] s. Mus'kat(nuss f) m: ~ *butter* Muskatbutter f.

Nu·tra·Sweet TM, **nu·tra·sweet** ['njuː-trəswiːt] s. ein Süßstoff.

nu·tri·a ['njuːtrɪə] s. **1.** zo. Biberratte f, Nutria f; **2.** ☛ Nutriafell n.

nu·tri·ent ['njuːtrɪənt] I adj. **1.** nährend, nahrhaft; **2.** Ernährungs...: ~ *medium* biol. Nährsubstanz f; ~ *solution* Nährlösung f; II s. **3.** Nährstoff m; **4.** biol.

N

Baustoff *m*; **'nu·tri·ment** [-ɪmənt] *s.* Nahrung *f*, Nährstoff *m* (*a. fig.*); *biol.* Baustoff *m.*
nu·tri·tion [njuːˈtrɪʃn] *s.* **1.** Ernährung *f*; **2.** Nahrung *f*: **~ cycle** Nahrungskreislauf *m*; **nu·tri·tion·al** [-ʃənl] Ernährungs..., Nähr...: **~ value** Nährwert *m*; **nu·tri·tion·ist** [-ʃnɪst] *s.* Ernährungswissenschaftler(in), Diä'tetiker(in), Ernährungsberater(in); **nu·tri·tious** [-ʃəs] *adj.* □ nährend, nahrhaft; **nu·tri·tious·ness** [-ʃəsnɪs] *s.* Nahrhaftigkeit *f.*
nu·tri·tive [ˈnjuːtrətɪv] *adj.* □ **1.** nährend, nahrhaft: **~ value** Nährwert *m*; **2.** Ernährungs...: **~ tract** Ernährungsbahn

f.
nuts [nʌts] → *nut* 7.
nut| **screw** *s.* ⊛ **1.** Schraube *f* mit Mutter; **2.** Innengewinde *n*; '**~·shell** *s.* ⚕ Nussschale *f*: (*to put it*) *in a* **~** (*Redewendung*) mit 'einem Wort, kurz gesagt; **~·ter** [ˈnʌtə] *s. Brit.* F Spinner(in), Verrückte(r *m*) *f*; **~ tree** *s.* ⚕ **1.** Haselnussstrauch *m*; **2.** Nussbaum *m.*
nut·ty [ˈnʌtɪ] *adj.* **1.** voller Nüsse; **2.** nussartig, Nuss...; **3.** pi'kant; **4.** *sl.* verrückt (*on* nach).
nuz·zle [ˈnʌzl] **I** *v/t.* **1.** mit der Schnauze aufwühlen; **2.** mit der Schnauze *od.* Nase reiben an (*dat.*); *fig.* Kind liebkosen, hätscheln; **3.** *e-m Schwein etc.* e-n Ring

durch die Nase ziehen; **II** *v/i.* **4.** (mit der Schnauze) wühlen, schnüffeln (*in* in *dat.*, *for* nach); **5.** sich (an)schmiegen (*to* an *acc.*).
ny·lon [ˈnaɪlɒn] *s.* Nylon *n*: **~s** F Nylonstrümpfe, Nylons.
nymph [nɪmf] *s.* **1.** *myth.* Nymphe *f* (*a. poet. u. iro. Mädchen*); **2.** *zo.* a) Puppe *f*, b) Nymphe *f*; **'nymph·et** [nɪmˈfet] *s.* ‚Nymphchen' *n*; **nym·pho** [ˈnɪmfəʊ] *pl.* **-phos** *s.* F *für* **nymphomaniac** II.
nym·pho·ma·ni·a [ˌnɪmfəʊˈmeɪnjə] *s.* ✚ Nymphoma'nie *f*, Mannstollheit *f*; ‚**nym·pho·ma·ni·ac** [-nɪæk] **I** *adj.* nympho'man, mannstoll; **II** *s.* Nympho'manin *f.*

N

O, o¹ [əʊ] s. **1.** O n, o n (Buchstabe); **2.** bsd. teleph. Null f.

O, o² [əʊ] int. o(h)!, ah!, ach!

oaf [əʊf] s. **1.** Dummkopf m, ‚Esel‘ m; **2.** Lümmel m, Flegel m; **oaf·ish** ['əʊfɪʃ] adj. **1.** dumm, ‚blöd‘; **2.** lümmel-, flegelhaft.

oak [əʊk] I s. **1.** ♀ a. ~ tree Eiche f, Eichbaum m; **2.** poet. Eichenlaub n; **3.** Eichenholz n; **4.** Brit. univ. sl. Eichentür f: sport one's ~ die Tür verschlossen halten, nicht zu sprechen sein; **5.** the ℒs sport Stutenrennen in Epsom; II adj. **6.** eichen, Eichen...; ~ ap·ple s. ♀ Gallapfel m.

oak·en ['əʊkən] adj. **1.** bsd. poet. Eichen...; **2.** eichen, von Eichenholz; **oak·let** ['əʊklɪt], **oak·ling** ['əʊklɪŋ] s. ♀ junge od. kleine Eiche.

oa·kum ['əʊkəm] s. Werg n: pick ~ a) Werg zupfen, b) F ‚Tüten kleben‘, ‚Knast schieben‘.

'oak·wood s. **1.** Eichenholz n; **2.** Eichenwald(ung f) m.

oar [ɔː] I s. **1.** Ruder n (a. zo.), bsd. sport Riemen m: four-~ Vierer m (Boot); pull a good ~ gut rudern; put (od. shove) one's ~ in F sich einmischen, im Gespräch ‚s-n Senf dazugeben‘; rest on one's ~s fig. sich auf s-n Lorbeeren ausruhen; → ship 8; **2.** sport Ruderer m, Ruderin f: a good ~; **3.** fig. Flügel m, Arm m; **4.** Brauerei: Krücke f; II v/t. u. v/i. **5.** rudern; **oared** [ɔːd] adj. **1.** mit Rudern (versehen), Ruder...; **2.** in Zssgn ...rud(e)rig; **oar·lock** ['ɔːlɒk] s. Am. Riemendolle f, oars·man ['ɔːzmən] s. [irr.] Ruderer m; **oars·wom·an** ['ɔːz,wʊmən] s. [irr.] Ruderin f.

o·a·sis [əʊ'eɪsɪs] pl. -ses [-siːz] s. O'ase f (a. fig.).

oast [əʊst] s. Brauerei: Darre f.

oat [əʊt] s. mst pl. Hafer m: be off one's ~s F keinen Appetit haben; he feels his ~s F a) ihn sticht der Hafer, b) er ist ‚groß in Form‘; sow one's wild ~s sich austoben, sich die Hörner abstoßen; **oat·en** ['əʊtn] adj. **1.** Hafer...; **2.** Hafermehl...

oath [əʊθ; pl. əʊðz] s. **1.** Eid m, Schwur m: ~ of allegiance Fahnen-, Treueid; ~ of disclosure ⅁ Offenbarungseid; ~ of office Amts-, Diensteid; false ~ Falsch-, Meineid m; bind by ~ eidlich verpflichten; (up)on ~ unter Eid, eidlich; upon my ~! das kann ich beschwören!; administer (od. tender) an ~ to s.o., put s.o. to (od. on) his ~ j-m e-n Eid abnehmen, j-n schwören lassen; swear (od. take) an ~ e-n Eid leisten, schwören (on, to auf acc.); in lieu of an ~ an Eides statt; under ~ unter Eid, eidlich verpflichtet; be on one's ~ unter Eid stehen; **2.** Fluch m, Verwünschung f.

'oat·meal s. **1.** Hafermehl n, -grütze f; **2.** Haferschleim m.

ob·bli·ga·to [,ɒblɪ'gɑːtəʊ] ♪ I adj. obli-

'gat, hauptstimmig; II pl. **-tos** s. selbständige Begleitstimme.

ob·du·ra·cy ['ɒbdjʊərəsɪ] s. fig. Verstocktheit f, Halsstarrigkeit f; **'ob·du·rate** [-rət] adj. □ **1.** verstockt, halsstarrig; **2.** hartherzig.

o·be·di·ence [ə'biːdjəns] s. **1.** Gehorsam m (to gegen); **2.** fig. Abhängigkeit f (to von): in ~ to gemäß (dat.), im Verfolg (gen.); in ~ to s.o. auf j-s Verlangen; **o'be·di·ent** [-nt] adj. □ **1.** gehorsam (to dat.); **2.** ergeben, unter'würfig (to dat.): Your ~ servant Hochachtungsvoll (Amtsstil); **3.** fig. abhängig (to von).

o·bei·sance [əʊ'beɪsəns] s. **1.** Verbeugung f; **2.** Ehrerbietung f, Huldigung f: do (od. make od. pay) ~ to s.o. j-m huldigen; **o'bei·sant** [-nt] adj. huldigend, unter'würfig.

ob·e·lisk ['ɒbɪlɪsk] s. **1.** Obe'lisk m; **2.** typ. a) → obelus, b) Kreuz(zeichen) n (für Randbemerkungen).

ob·e·lus ['ɒbɪləs] pl. **-li** [-laɪ] s. typ. **1.** Obe'lisk m (Zeichen für fragwürdige Stellen); **2.** Verweisungszeichen n auf Randbemerkungen.

o·bese [əʊ'biːs] adj. fettleibig, korpu'lent, a. fig. fett, dick; **o'bese·ness** [-nɪs], **o'bes·i·ty** [-sətɪ] s. Fettleibigkeit f, Korpu'lenz f.

o·bey [ə'beɪ] v/t. **1.** j-m gehorchen, folgen (a. fig.); **2.** e-m Befehl etc. Folge leisten, befolgen (acc.); II v/i. **3.** gehorchen, folgen (to dat.).

ob·fus·cate ['ɒbfʌskeɪt] v/t. **1.** verfinstern, trüben (a. fig.); **2.** fig. Urteil etc. trüben, verwirren; die Sinne benebeln; **ob·fus·ca·tion** [,ɒbfʌs'keɪʃn] Verfinsterung f etc.

o·bit·u·ar·y [ə'bɪtjʊərɪ] I s. **1.** Todesanzeige f; **2.** Nachruf m; **3.** eccl. Totenliste f; II adj. **4.** Toten..., Todes...: ~ notice Todesanzeige f.

ob·ject¹ [əb'dʒekt] I v/t. **1.** fig. einwenden, vorbringen (to gegen); **2.** vorhalten, vorwerfen (to, against dat.); II v/i. **3.** Einwendungen machen, Einsprüche erheben, protestieren, reklamieren (to, against gegen); **4.** et. einwenden, et. dagegen haben: ~ to s.th. et. beanstanden; do you ~ to my smoking? haben Sie et. dagegen, wenn ich rauche?; if you don't ~ wenn Sie nichts dagegen haben.

ob·ject² ['ɒbdʒɪkt] s. **1.** Ob'jekt n (a. Kunst), Gegenstand m (a. fig. des Mitleids etc.): ~ of invention ⅁ Erfindungsgegenstand; money is no ~ Geld spielt keine Rolle; salary no ~ Gehalt Nebensache. **2.** Absicht f, Ziel m, Zweck m: make it one's ~ to do s.th. es sich zum Ziel setzen, et. zu tun; **3.** F komische od. scheußliche Per'son od. Sache: what an ~ you are! wie sehen Sie denn aus!; **4.** ling. a) Ob'jekt n: direct ~ Akkusativobjekt; ~ clause Objektsatz m, b) von e-r Präposi'tion abhängiges Wort; ~ draw·ing s. Zeich-

nen n nach Vorlagen od. Mo'dellen; '~-,find·er s. phot. (Objek'tiv)Sucher m; ~ glass s. opt. Objek'tiv(linse f) n.

ob·jec·ti·fy [ɒb'dʒektɪfaɪ] v/t. objektivieren.

ob·jec·tion [əb'dʒekʃn] s. **1.** a) Einwendung f (a. ⅁), Einspruch m, -wand m, -wurf m, Bedenken n (to gegen), b) weitS. Abneigung f, 'Widerwille m (against gegen): I have no ~ to him ich habe nichts gegen ihn od. an ihm nichts auszusetzen; make (od. raise) an ~ to s.th. gegen et. e-n Einwand erheben; take ~ to s.th. gegen et. protestieren; **2.** Beanstandung f, Reklamati'on f; **ob'jec·tion·a·ble** [-ʃnəbl] adj. □ **1.** nicht einwandfrei, zu beanstanden(d), unerwünscht, anrüchig; **2.** unangenehm (to dat. od. für); **3.** anstößig.

ob·jec·tive [əb'dʒektɪv] I adj. □ **1.** objek'tiv (a. phls.), sachlich, vorurteilslos; **2.** ling. Objekts...: ~ case → 5; ~ genitive objektiver Genitiv; **3.** Ziel...: ~ point → 6; II s. **4.** opt. Objek'tiv(linse f) n; **5.** ling. Ob'jektsfall m; **6.** (bsd. ✕ Kampf-, Angriffs)Ziel n; **ob'jec·tiveness** [-nɪs], **ob·jec·tiv·i·ty** [,ɒbdʒek'tɪvətɪ] s. Objektivi'tät f.

ob·ject lens s. opt. Objek'tiv(linse f) n.

ob·ject·less ['ɒbdʒɪktlɪs] adj. gegenstands-, zweck-, ziellos.

ob·ject les·son s. **1.** ped. u. fig. 'Anschauungs,unterricht m; **2.** fig. Schulbeispiel n; **3.** fig. Denkzettel m.

ob·jec·tor [əb'dʒektə] s. Gegner(in) (to gen.); → conscientious.

ob·ject| plate, ~ slide s. Ob'jektträger m (Mikroskop etc.); ~ teach·ing s. 'Anschauungs,unterricht m.

ob·jet d'art [,ɒbʒeɪ'dɑː] (Fr.) s. (bsd. kleiner) Kunstgegenstand.

ob·jur·gate ['ɒbdʒɜːgeɪt] v/t. tadeln, schelten. ·

ob·late¹ ['ɒbleɪt] adj. Å, phys. (an den Polen) abgeplattet.

ob·late² ['ɒbleɪt] R.C. Ob'lat(in) (Laienbruder od. -schwester).

ob·la·tion [əʊ'bleɪʃn] s. bsd. eccl. Opfer (-gabe f) n.

ob·li·gate v/t. ['ɒblɪgeɪt] a. ⅁ verpflichten; **ob·li·ga·tion** [,ɒblɪ'geɪʃn] s. **1.** Verpflichten n; **2.** Verpflichtung f, Verbindlichkeit f: of ~ obligatorisch; be under an ~ to s.o. j-m (zu Dank) verpflichtet sein; **3.** ⅁ a) Schuldverschreibung f, Obligati'on f, b) (Schuld-)Verpflichtung f, Verbindlichkeit f: financial ~ Zahlungsverpflichtung; ~ to buy Kaufzwang m; no ~, without ~ unverbindlich, freibleibend; **ob·li·ga·to·ry** [ə'blɪgətərɪ] adj. □ verpflichtend, bindend, (rechts)verbindlich, obliga'torisch (on, upon für), Zwangs...

o·blige [ə'blaɪdʒ] I v/t. **1.** nötigen, zwingen: I was ~d to go ich musste gehen; **2.** fig. j-n (zu Dank) verpflichten: much ~d! sehr verbunden!, danke bestens!; I am ~d to you for it ich habe es

Ihnen zu verdanken; *will you ~ me by* (*ger.*)*?* wären Sie so freundlich, zu (*inf.*)*?*, *iro.* würden Sie gefälligst *et. tun?*; **3.** *j-m* gefällig sein, e-n Gefallen tun, dienen: *to ~ you* Ihnen zu Gefallen; *~ the company with* die Gesellschaft mit *e-m Lied etc.* erfreuen; **4.** 🙼 *j-n* (*durch Eid etc.*) binden (**to** an *acc.*): **~ *o.s.*** sich verpflichten (**to do** *et.* zu tun); **II** *v/i.* **5. ~ with** F Lied etc. vortragen, zum Besten geben; **6.** erwünscht sein: *an early reply will* ~ um baldige Antwort wird gebeten; **ob·li·gee** [ˌɒblɪˈdʒiː] *s.* 🙼 Obligati'onsgläubiger (-in), Forderungsberechtigte(r *m*) *f*; **o'blig·ing** [-dʒɪŋ] *adj.* □ verbindlich, gefällig, zu'vor-, entgegenkommend; **o'blig·ing·ness** [-dʒɪŋnɪs] *s.* Gefälligkeit *f*, Zu'vorkommenheit *f*; **ob·li·gor** [ˌɒblɪˈɡɔː] *s.* 🙼 (Obligati'ons)Schuldner(in).

ob·lique [əˈbliːk] *adj.* □ **1.** *bsd.* 🗛 schief, schräg; **~(-angled)** schiefwink(e)lig; *at an ~ angle with* im spitzen Winkel zu; **2.** 'indi,rekt, versteckt, verblümt: *~ accusation*; *~ glance* Seitenblick *m*; **3.** unaufrichtig, unredlich; **4.** *ling.* abhängig, 'indi,rekt: *~ case* Beugefall *m*; *~ speech* indirekte Rede; **ob'lique·ness** [-nɪs], **ob·liq·ui·ty** [əˈblɪkwətɪ] *s.* **1.** Schiefe *f* (*a. ast.*), schiefe Lage *od.* Richtung, Schrägheit *f*; **2.** *fig.* Schiefheit *f*: *moral ~* Unredlichkeit *f*; *~ of judg(e)ment* Schiefe *f* des Urteils.

ob·lit·er·ate [əˈblɪtəreɪt] *v/t.* **1.** auslöschen, tilgen (*beide a. fig.*), *Schrift a.* ausstreichen, wegradieren; *Briefmarken* entwerten; 🐛 veröden; **ob·lit·er·a·tion** [əˌblɪtəˈreɪʃn] *s.* **1.** Verwischung *f*, Auslöschung *f*; **2.** *fig.* Vernichtung *f*, Vertilgung *f*.

ob·liv·i·on [əˈblɪvɪən] *s.* **1.** Vergessenheit *f*: *fall* (*od.* **sink**) *into* ~ in Vergessenheit geraten; **2.** Vergessen *n*, Vergesslichkeit *f*; **3.** 🙼, *pol.* Straferlass *m*: (*Act of*) 𝓔 Amne'stie *f*; **ob'liv·i·ous** [-ɪəs] *adj.* □ vergesslich: *be ~ of s.th.* et. vergessen (haben); *be ~ to s.th.* F *fig.* blind sein gegen et., et. nicht beachten.

ob·long [ˈɒblɒŋ] **I** *adj.* □ länglich: *~ hole* 🛈 Langloch *n*; **2.** 🗛 rechteckig; **II** *s.* **3.** 🗛 Rechteck *n*.

ob·lo·quy [ˈɒbləkwɪ] *s.* **1.** Verleumdung *f*, Schmähung *f*: *fall into* ~ in Verruf kommen; **2.** Schmach *f*.

ob·nox·ious [əbˈnɒkʃəs] *adj.* □ **1.** anstößig, anrüchig, verhasst, ab'scheulich; **2.** (*to*) unbeliebt (bei), unangenehm (*dat.*); **ob'nox·ious·ness** [-nɪs] *s.* **1.** Anstößigkeit *f*, Anrüchigkeit *f*; **2.** Verhasstheit *f*.

o·boe [ˈəʊbəʊ] *s.* ♪ O'boe *f*; **'o·bo·ist** [-əʊɪst] *s.* Obo'ist(in).

ob·scene [əbˈsiːn] *adj.* □ **1.** unzüchtig (*a.* 🙼), unanständig, zotig, ob'szön: *~ libel* 🙼 Veröffentlichung *f* unzüchtiger Schriften; *~ talker* Zotenreißer *m*; **2.** 'widerlich; **ob·scen·i·ty** [əbˈsenɪtɪ] *s.* **1.** Unanständigkeit *f*, Schmutz *m*, Zote *f*, *pl. a.* Obszöni'täten *pl.*; **2.** 'Widerlichkeit *f*.

ob·scur·ant [ˈɒbskjʊərənt] *s.* Obsku'rant *m*, Dunkelmann *m*, Bildungsfeind *m*; **ob·scur·ant·ism** [ˌɒbskjʊəˈræntɪzəm] *s.* Obskuran'tismus *m*, Bildungshass *m*; **ob·scur·ant·ist** [ˌɒbskjʊəˈræntɪst] **I** *s.* → obscurant; **II** *adj.* obskuran'tistisch.

ob·scu·ra·tion [ˌɒbskjʊˈreɪʃn] *s.* Verdunkelung *f* (*a. fig.*).

ob·scure [əbˈskjʊə] **I** *adj.* □ **1.** dunkel, düster; **2.** *fig.* dunkel, unklar; **3.** *fig.*

ob'skur, unbekannt, unbedeutend; **4.** *fig.* verborgen: *live an ~ life*; **II** *v/t.* **5.** verdunkeln, verfinstern (*a. fig.*); **6.** *fig.* verkleinern, in den Schatten stellen; **7.** *fig.* unverständlich *od.* undeutlich machen; **8.** verbergen; **ob'scu·ri·ty** [-ərɪtɪ] *s.* **1.** Dunkelheit *f* (*a. fig.*); **2.** *fig.* Unklarheit *f*, Undeutlichkeit *f*, Unverständlichkeit *f*; **3.** *fig.* Unbekanntheit *f*, Verborgenheit *f*, Niedrigkeit *f* der Herkunft: *be lost in ~* vergessen sein.

ob·se·quies [ˈɒbsɪkwɪz] *s. pl.* Trauerfeierlichkeit(en *pl.*) *f*.

ob·se·qui·ous [əbˈsiːkwɪəs] *adj.* □ unter'würfig (*to* gegen), ser'vil, kriecherisch; **ob'se·qui·ous·ness** [-nɪs] *s.* Unter'würfigkeit *f*.

ob·serv·a·ble [əbˈzɜːvəbl] *adj.* □ **1.** wahrnehmbar; **2.** bemerkenswert; **3.** zu be(ob)achten(d); **ob'serv·ance** [-vns] *s.* **1.** Befolgung *f*, Be(ob)achtung *f*, Ein-, Innehaltung *f von Gesetzen etc.*; **2.** *eccl.* Heilighaltung *f*, Feiern *n*; **3.** Brauch *m*, Sitte *f*; **4.** Regel *f*, Vorschrift *f*; **5.** *R.C.* Ordensregel *f*, Obser'vanz *f*; **ob'serv·ant** [-vnt] *adj.* □ **1.** beobachtend, befolgend (*of acc.*): *be very ~ of forms* sehr auf Formen halten; **2.** aufmerksam, acht-, wachsam (*of* auf *acc.*).

ob·ser·va·tion [ˌɒbzəˈveɪʃn] **I** *s.* **1.** Beobachtung *f* (*a.* 🐛, ⚓ *etc.*), Über'wachung *f*, Wahrnehmung *f*: *keep s.o. under ~* j-n beobachten (lassen); **2.** ✕ (Nah)Aufklärung *f*; **3.** Beobachtungsvermögen *n*; **4.** Bemerkung *f*; **5.** Befolgung *f*; **II** *adj.* **6.** Beobachtungs..., Aussichts...; **~ bal·loon** *s.* 'Fesselbal,lon *m*; **~ car** 🚃 Aussichtswagen *m*; **~ coach** *s.* Omnibus *m* mit Aussichtsplattform; **~ post** *s.* ✕ Beobachtungsstand *m*, -posten *m*; **~ tow·er** *s.* Beobachtungswarte *f*; Aussichtsturm *m*; **~ ward** *s.* 🐛 Be'obachtungsstati,on *f*; **~ win·dow** ⛭ *etc.* Beobachtungsfenster *n*.

ob·serv·a·to·ry [əbˈzɜːvətrɪ] *s.* Observa'torium *n*: a) Wetterwarte *f*, b) Sternwarte *f*.

ob·serve [əbˈzɜːv] **I** *v/t.* **1.** beobachten: a) über'wachen, b) (be)merken, wahrnehmen, c) *Gesetz etc.* befolgen, (ein)halten, beachten, *Fest etc.* feiern, begehen: *~ silence* Stillschweigen bewahren; **2.** bemerken, äußern, sagen; **II** *v/i.* **3.** Beobachtungen machen; **4.** Bemerkungen machen, sich äußern (*on, upon* über *acc.*); **ob'serv·er** [-və] *s.* **1.** Beobachter(in) (*a. pol.*), Zuschauer(in); **2.** Befolger(in); **3.** ✕, ✈ a) Beobachter *m*, b) *Flugmeldedienst:* Luftspäher *m*; **ob'serv·ing** [-vɪŋ] *adj.* □ aufmerksam, achtsam.

ob·sess [əbˈses] *v/t.* quälen, heimsuchen, verfolgen (*von Ideen etc.*): *~ed by* (*od.* **with**) besessen von; **ob·ses·sion** [əbˈseʃn] *s.* Besessenheit *f*, fixe I'dee; *psych.* Zwangsvorstellung *f*; **ob'ses·sive** [-sɪv] *adj. psych.* zwanghaft, Zwangs...: *~ neurosis*.

ob·so·les·cence [ˌɒbsəʊˈlesns] *s.* Veralten *n*: *planned ~* ⚗, ⛭ künstliche Veralterung; **ob·so·les·cent** [-nt] *adj.* veraltend.

ob·so·lete [ˈɒbsəliːt] *adj.* □ **1.** veraltet, über'holt, altmodisch; **2.** abgenutzt, verbraucht; **3.** *biol.* zu'rückgeblieben, rudimen'tär.

ob·sta·cle [ˈɒbstəkl] *s.* Hindernis *n* (*to* für) (*a. fig.*): *put ~s in s.o.'s way* *fig.* j-m Hindernisse in den Weg legen; **~ race** *sport* Hindernisrennen *n*.

ob·stet·ric, **ob·stet·ri·cal** [ɒbˈste-

trɪk(l)] *adj.* Geburts(hilfe)..., Entbindungs...; **ob·ste·tri·cian** [ˌɒbsteˈtrɪʃn] *s.* 🐛 Geburtshelfer(in); **ob'stet·rics** [-ks] *s. pl. mst sg. konstr.* Geburtshilfe *f*.

ob·sti·na·cy [ˈɒbstɪnəsɪ] *s.* Hartnäckigkeit *f* (*a. fig., 🐛 etc.*), Eigensinn *m*; **'ob·sti·nate** [-tənət] *adj.* □ hartnäckig (*a. fig.*), halsstarrig, eigensinnig.

ob·strep·er·ous [əbˈstrepərəs] *adj.* □ **1.** ungebärdig, tobend, 'widerspenstig; **2.** lärmend.

ob·struct [əbˈstrʌkt] **I** *v/t.* **1.** versperren, -stopfen, blockieren: *~ s.o.'s view* j-m die Sicht nehmen; **2.** *a. fig.* behindern, hemmen, lahm legen; **3.** *fig., a. pol.* blockieren, vereiteln; **4.** *sport:* sperren, (*a. Amtsperson*) behindern (*in* bei); **II** *v/i.* **5.** *pol.* Obstrukti'on treiben; **ob·struc·tion** [-kʃn] *s.* **1.** Versperrung *f*, Verstopfung *f*; **2.** Behinderung *f*, Hemmung *f*; **3.** Hindernis *n* (*to* für); **4.** *pol.* Obstrukti'on *f*; **ob'struc·tion·ism** [-kʃənɪzəm] *s. bsd. pol.* Obstrukti'onspoli,tik *f*; **ob'struc·tion·ist** [-kʃənɪst] **I** *s.* Obstrukti'onspo,litiker(in); **II** *adj.* Obstruktions...; **ob'struc·tive** [-tɪv] *adj.* □ **1.** versperrend (*etc.* → *obstruct* I); **2.** (*of, to*) hinderlich, hemmend (für): *be ~ to s.th.* et. behindern; **3.** Obstruktions...; **II** *s.* **4.** Hindernis *n*.

ob·tain [əbˈteɪn] **I** *v/t.* **1.** erlangen, erhalten, bekommen, erwerben, sich verschaffen, *Sieg* erringen: *~ by flattery* sich erschmeicheln; *~ legal force* Rechtskraft erlangen; *details can be ~ed from* Näheres ist zu erfahren bei; **2.** *Willen, Wünsche etc.* 'durchsetzen; **3.** erreichen; **4.** ✝ *Preis* erzielen; **II** *v/i.* **5.** (vor)herrschen, bestehen; Geltung haben, sich behaupten; **ob'tain·a·ble** [-nəbl] *adj.* erreichbar, erlangbar; erhältlich, zu erhalten(d) (*at* bei); **ob·tain·ment** [-mənt] *s.* Erlangung *f*.

ob·trude [əbˈtruːd] **I** *v/t.* aufdrängen, -nötigen, -zwingen (*upon, on dat.*): *~ o.s. upon* → **II** *v/i.* sich aufdrängen (*upon, on dat.*); **ob'tru·sion** [-uːʒn] *s.* **1.** Aufdrängen *n*, Aufnötigung *f*; **2.** Aufdringlichkeit *f*; **ob'tru·sive** [-uːsɪv] *adj.* □ aufdringlich (*a. Sache*).

ob·tu·rate [ˈɒbtjʊəreɪt] *v/t.* **1.** a. 🐛 verstopfen, verschließen; **2.** ⛭ (ab)dichten, lidern; **ob·tu·ra·tion** [ˌɒbtjʊəˈreɪʃn] *s.* **1.** Verstopfung *f*, Verschließung *f*; **2.** ⛭ (Ab)Dichtung *f*.

ob·tuse [əbˈtjuːs] *adj.* □ **1.** stumpf (*a.* 🗛): *~(-angled)* stumpfwink(e)lig; **2.** *fig.* begriffsstutzig, beschränkt; dumpf (*Ton, Schmerz etc.*); **ob'tuse·ness** [-nɪs] *s.* **1.** Stumpfheit *f* (*a. fig.*); **2.** Begriffsstutzigkeit *f*.

ob·verse [ˈɒbvɜːs] **I** *s.* **1.** Vorderseite *f*; Bildseite *f e-r Münze*; **2.** Gegenstück *n*, die andere Seite, Kehrseite *f*; **II** *adj.* □ **3.** Vorder..., dem Beobachter zugekehrt; **4.** entsprechend, 'umgekehrt; **ob·verse·ly** [ɒbˈvɜːslɪ] *adv.* 'umgekehrt.

ob·vi·ate [ˈɒbvɪeɪt] *v/t.* **1.** e-r Sache begegnen, zu'vorkommen, vorbeugen; et. verhindern, verhüten; **2.** aus dem Weg räumen, beseitigen; **3.** erübrigen; **ob·vi·a·tion** [ˌɒbvɪˈeɪʃn] *s.* **1.** Vorbeugen *n*, Verhütung *f*; **2.** Beseitigung *f*.

ob·vi·ous [ˈɒbvɪəs] *adj.* □ offensichtlich, augenfällig, klar, deutlich; nahe liegend, einleuchtend: *it is ~ that* es liegt auf der Hand, dass; *it was the ~ thing to do* es war das Nächstliegende; *he was the ~ choice* kein anderer kam dafür in Frage; **'ob·vi·ous·ness** [-nɪs] *s.* Offensichtlichkeit *f*.

oc·ca·sion [ə'keɪʒn] **I** s. **1.** (günstige) Gelegenheit; **2.** (of) Gelegenheit f (zu), Möglichkeit f (gen.); **3.** (besondere) Gelegenheit, Anlass m; (F festliches) Ereignis: **on this ~** bei dieser Gelegenheit; **on the ~ of** anlässlich (gen.); **on ~** a) bei Gelegenheit, b) gelegentlich, c) wenn nötig; **for the ~** für diese besondere Gelegenheit, eigens zu diesem Zweck; **a great ~** ein großes Ereignis; **improve the ~** die Gelegenheit (bsd. zu e-r Moralpredigt) benützen; **rise to the ~** sich der Lage gewachsen zeigen; **4.** Anlass m, Anstoß m: **give ~ to** → 6; **5.** (for) Grund m (zu), Ursache f (gen.), Veranlassung f (zu); **II** v/t. **6.** verursachen (s.o. s.th., s.th. to s.o. j-m et.), hervorrufen, bewirken, zeitigen; **7.** j-n veranlassen (to do zu tun); **oc'ca·sion·al** [-ʒənl] adj. □ **1.** gelegentlich, Gelegenheits...(-arbeit, -dichter, -gedicht etc.); vereinzelt; **2.** zufällig; **oc'ca·sion·al·ly** [-ʒnəlɪ] adv. gelegentlich, hin u. wieder.

Oc·ci·dent ['ɒksɪdənt] s. **1.** 'Okzident m, Westen m, Abendland n; **2.** ♃ Westen m; **Oc·ci·den·tal** [ˌɒksɪ'dentl] I adj. □ **1.** abendländisch, westlich; **2.** ♃ westlich; **II** s. **3.** Abendländer(in).

oc·cip·i·tal [ɒk'sɪpɪtl] anat. **I** adj. Hinterhaupt(s)...; **II** s. 'Hinterhauptsbein n; **oc·ci·put** ['ɒksɪpʌt] pl. **oc·cip·i·ta** [ɒk'sɪpɪtə] s. anat. 'Hinterkopf m.

oc·clude [ɒ'kluːd] v/t. **1.** a. 🜨 verstopfen, verschließen; **2.** a) einschließen, b) ausschließen (from von); **3.** 🜨 okkludieren, adsorbieren; **oc'clu·sion** [-uːʒn] s. **1.** a. 🜨 a) Verstopfung f, Verschließung f, b) Verschluss m; **2.** Okklusi'on f: a) 🜨 Adsorpti'on f, b) 🜨 Biss(stellung f) m; **ab·normal ~** Bissanomalie f.

oc·cult [ɒ'kʌlt] **I** adj. □ ok'kult: a) geheimnisvoll, verborgen (a. 🜨), b) magisch, 'übersinnlich, c) geheim, Geheim...: **~ sciences** Geheimwissenschaften; **II** v/t. verdecken; ast. verfinstern; **III** s.: **the ~** das Okkulte; **oc·cult·ism** ['ɒkəltɪzəm] s. Okkul'tismus m; **oc·cult·ist** ['ɒkəltɪst] **I** s. Okkul'tist (-in); **II** adj. okkul'tistisch.

oc·cu·pan·cy ['ɒkjʊpənsɪ] s. **1.** Besitzergreifung f (a. 🜨); Einzug m (of in e-e Wohnung); **2.** Innehaben n, Besitz m: **during his ~ of the post** solange er die Stelle innehatte; **3.** In'anspruchnahme f (von Raum etc.); **'oc·cu·pant** [-nt] s. **1.** bsd. 🜨 Besitzergreifer(in); **2.** Besitzer (-in), Inhaber(in); **3.** Bewohner(in), Insasse m, Insassin f (Haus etc.); **oc·cu·pa·tion** [ˌɒkjʊ'peɪʃn] s. **1.** Besitz m, Innehaben n; **2.** Besitznahme f, -ergreifung f; ✕, pol. Besetzung f, Besatzung f, Okkupati'on f: **~ troops** Besatzungstruppen; → **zone** 1; **4.** Beschäftigung f: **without ~** beschäftigungslos, **5.** Beruf m, Gewerbe n: **by ~** von Beruf; **employed in an ~** berufstätig; **in** (od. **as a**) **regular ~** hauptberuflich; **oc·cu·pa·tion·al** [ˌɒkjuː'peɪʃənl] adj. **1.** beruflich, Berufs...(-gruppe, -krankheit etc.), Arbeits...(-psychologie, -unfall etc.): **~ hazard** Berufsrisiko n; **2.** Beschäftigungs...: **~ therapy.**

oc·cu·pi·er ['ɒkjʊpaɪə] → occupant.

oc·cu·py ['ɒkjʊpaɪ] v/t. **1.** in Besitz nehmen, Besitz ergreifen von; Wohnung beziehen; ✕ besetzen; **2.** besitzen, innehaben; fig. Amt etc. bekleiden, innehaben: **~ the chair** den Vorsitz führen; **3.** bewohnen; **4.** Raum einnehmen, (a. Zeit) in Anspruch nehmen; **5.** j-n, j-s Geist beschäftigen: **~ o.s.** sich beschäf-

tigen (od. befassen (with mit); **be occupied with** (od. **in**) **doing** damit beschäftigt sein, et. zu tun.

oc·cur [ə'kɜː] v/i. **1.** sich ereignen, vorfallen, -kommen, passieren, eintreten; **2.** vorkommen (in Poe bei Poe); **3.** zustoßen, vorkommen, begegnen (to s.o. j-m); **4.** einfallen (to dat.): **it ~red to me that** es fiel mir ein od. es kam mir der Gedanke, dass; **oc·cur·rence** [ə'kʌrəns] s. **1.** Vorkommen n, Auftreten n; **2.** Ereignis n, Vorfall m, Vorkommnis n.

o·cean ['əʊʃn] s. **1.** Ozean m, Meer n: **~ lane** Schifffahrtsroute f; **~ liner** Ozeandampfer m; **2.** fig. Meer n: **~s of F** e-e Unmenge von; **~ bill of lad·ing** s. ♱ Konnosse'ment n, Seefrachtbrief m; **'~-,go·ing** adj. ♣ Hochsee..., hochseetüchtig.

o·ce·an·ic [ˌəʊʃɪ'ænɪk] adj. oze'anisch, Ozean..., Meer(es)...

o·ce·a·no·graph·ic, o·ce·a·no·graph·i·cal [ˌəʊʃɪənəʊ'græfɪk(l)] adj. ozeano'graphisch; **o·ce·a·nog·ra·phy** [ˌəʊʃə-'nɒgrəfɪ] s. Meereskunde f; **o·ce·a·nol·o·gy** [ˌəʊʃjə'nɒlədʒɪ] s. Ozeanolo'gie f, Meereskunde f.

oc·el·lat·ed ['ɒsəleɪtɪd] adj. zo. **1.** augenfleckig; **2.** augenähnlich; **o·cel·lus** [əʊ'seləs] pl. **-li** [-laɪ] s. zo. **1.** Punktauge n; **2.** Augenfleck m.

o·cher Am. → ochre.

och·loc·ra·cy [ɒk'lɒkrəsɪ] s. Ochlokra-'tie f, Pöbelherrschaft f.

o·chre ['əʊkə] **I** s. **1.** min. Ocker m: **blue** (od. **iron**) **~** Eisenocker m; **brown** (od. **spruce**) **~** brauner Eisenocker; **2.** Ockerfarbe f, -gelb n; **II** adj. **3.** ockergelb; **o·chre·ous** ['əʊkrɪəs] adj. **1.** Ocker...; **2.** ockerhaltig od. -artig od. -farbig.

o'clock [ə'klɒk] Uhr (bei Zeitangaben): **four ~** vier Uhr.

oc·ta·gon ['ɒktəgən] s. ♉ Achteck n; **oc·tag·o·nal** [ɒk'tægənl] adj. □ **1.** achteckig, -seitig; **2.** Achtkant...

oc·ta·he·dral [ˌɒktə'hedrəl] adj. ♉, min. okta'edrisch, achtflächig, **oc·ta·he·dron** [-drən] pl. **-drons** od. **-dra** [-drə] s. Okta'eder n.

oc·tal ['ɒktl] adj. ♫ Oktal...

oc·tane ['ɒkteɪn] s. 🜨 Ok'tan n: **~ number, ~ rating** Oktanzahl f.

oc·tant ['ɒktənt] s. ♉, ♣ Ok'tant m.

oc·tave ['ɒktɪv] s. ♪; eccl. 'ɒkteɪv] s. ♩, eccl., phys. Ok'tave f.

oc·ta·vo [ɒk'teɪvəʊ] pl. **-vos** s. **1.** Ok'tav(for,mat) n; **2.** Ok'tavband m.

oc·til·lion [ɒk'tɪljən] s. ♉ Brit. Oktilli'on f, Am. Quadrilli'arde f.

Oc·to·ber [ɒk'təʊbə] s. Ok'tober m: **in ~** im Oktober.

oc·to·dec·i·mo [ˌɒktəʊ'desɪməʊ] pl. **-mos** s. **1.** Okto'dezfor,mat n; **2.** Okto'dezband m.

oc·to·ge·nar·i·an [ˌɒktəʊdʒɪ'neərɪən] **I** adj. achtzigjährig; **II** s. Achtzigjährige(r m) f, Achtziger(in).

oc·to·pod ['ɒktəpɒd] s. zo. Okto'pode m, Krake m.

oc·to·pus ['ɒktəpəs] pl. **-pus·es** od. **'oc·to·pi** [-paɪ] s. **1.** zo. Krake m: a) 'Seepo,lyp m, b) Okto'pode m; **2.** fig. Po'lyp m.

oc·to·syl·lab·ic [ˌɒktəʊsɪ'læbɪk] **I** adj. achtsilbig; **II** s. Achtsilb(l)er m (Vers); **oc·to·syl·la·ble** ['ɒktəʊˌsɪləbl] s. **1.** achtsilbiges Wort; **2.** → **octosyllabic** II.

oc·u·lar ['ɒkjʊlə] **I** adj. □ **1.** Augen... (-bewegung, -zeuge etc.); **2.** sichtbar (Beweis), augenfällig; **II** s. **3.** opt. Oku'lar n; **'oc·u·lar·ly** [-lɪ] adv. **1.** augen-

scheinlich; **2.** durch Augenschein, mit eigenen Augen; **'oc·u·list** [-lɪst] s. Augenarzt m.

OD [ˌəʊ'diː] sl. abbr. für **overdose I** s. 'Überdosis f; **II** v/i. e-e 'Überdosis nehmen: **~ on ...** e-e 'Überdosis ... nehmen.

odd [ɒd] **I** adj. □ → **oddly**; **1.** sonderbar, seltsam, merkwürdig, kuri'os: **an ~ fellow** (od. F **fish**) ein sonderbarer Kauz; **2.** (nach Zahlen etc.) und etliche, und einige od. etwas dar'über: **50 ~** über 50, einige 50; **fifty ~ thousand** zwischen 50 000 u. 60 000; **it cost five pounds ~** es kostete etwas über 5 Pfund; **3.** (noch) übrig, 'überzählig, restlich; **4.** ungerade: **~ and even** gerade u. ungerade; **an ~ number** eine ungerade Zahl; **~ man out** Überzählige(r) m; **the ~ man** der Mann mit der entscheidenden Stimme (bei Stimmengleichheit) (→ 6); **5.** a) einzeln (Schuh etc.): **~ pair** Einzelpaar n, b) vereinzelt: **some ~ volumes** einige Einzelbände, c) ausgefallen, wenig gefragt (Kleidergröße); **6.** gelegentlich, Gelegenheits...: **~ jobs** Gelegenheitsarbeiten; **at ~ moments**, **at ~ times** dann und wann, zwischendurch; **~ man** Gelegenheitsarbeiter m; **II** s. **7.** → **odds**; **'odd·ball** s. Am. F → **oddity** 2.

odd·i·ty ['ɒdɪtɪ] s. **1.** Seltsamkeit f, Wunderlichkeit f, Eigenartigkeit f; **2.** komischer Kauz, Unikum n; **3.** seltsame od. kuri'ose Sache; **odd·ly** ['ɒdlɪ] adv. **1.** → **odd** 1; **2.** a. **~ enough** seltsamerweise; **odd·ments** ['ɒdmənts] s. pl. Reste pl., 'Überbleibsel pl.; Krimskrams m; ♱ Einzelstücke pl.; **odd·ness** ['ɒdnɪs] s. Seltsamkeit f, Sonderbarkeit f.

'odd,num·bered adj. ungeradzahlig.

odds [ɒdz] s. pl. oft sg. konstr. **1.** Verschiedenheit f, 'Unterschied m: **what's the ~?** F was macht es (schon) aus?; **it makes no ~** es macht nichts (aus); **2.** Vorgabe f (im Spiel): **give s.o. ~** j-m et. vorgeben; **take ~** sich vorgeben lassen; **take the ~** e-e ungleiche Wette eingehen; **3.** (Gewinn)Chancen pl.: **the ~ are 10 to 1** die Chancen stehen 10 zu 1; **the ~ are in our favo(u)r** (od. **on us**) a. fig. wir haben die besseren Chancen; **the ~ are against us** unsere Chancen stehen schlecht, wir sind im Nachteil; **against long ~** mit wenig Aussicht auf Erfolg; **by long ~** bei weitem; **the ~ are that he will come** es ist sehr wahrscheinlich, dass er kommt; **4.** Uneinigkeit f: **at ~ with** im Streit mit, uneins mit; **set at ~** uneinig machen, gegeneinander aufhetzen; **5.** **~ and ends** a) allerlei Kleinigkeiten, Krimskrams m, dies u. das, b) Reste, Abfälle; **,~-'on I** adj. aussichtsreich (z. B. Rennpferd): **~ certainty** sichere Sache; **it's ~ that** es ist so gut wie sicher, dass; **II** s. gute Chance.

ode [əʊd] s. Ode f.

o·di·ous ['əʊdjəs] adj. □ **1.** verhasst, hassenswert, ab'scheulich; **2.** widerlich, ekelhaft; **'o·di·ous·ness** [-nɪs] s. **1.** Verhasstheit f, Ab'scheulichkeit f; **2.** Widerlichkeit f; **'o·di·um** [-jəm] s. **1.** Verhasstheit f; **2.** Odium n, Vorwurf m, Makel m; **3.** Hass m, Gehässigkeit f.

o·dom·e·ter [əʊ'dɒmɪtə] s. **1.** Weg(strecken)messer m; **2.** Kilo'meterzähler m.

o·don·tic [ɒ'dɒntɪk] adj. Zahn...: **~ nerve**; **o·don·tol·o·gy** [ˌɒdɒn'tɒlədʒɪ] s. Zahn(heil)kunde f, Odontolo'gie f.

o·dor(·less) Am. → **odour(·less)**.

o·dor·ant ['əʊdərənt] adj., **o·dor·if·er-**

ous [ˌəʊdəˈrɪfərəs] *adj.* □ **1.** wohlriechend, duftend; **2.** *allg.* riechend.

o·dour [ˈəʊdə] *s.* **1.** Geruch *m*; **2.** Duft *m*, Wohlgeruch *m*; **3.** *fig.* Geruch *m*, Ruf *m*: the ~ of sanctity der Geruch der Heiligkeit; be in bad ~ with s.o. bei j-m in schlechtem Ruf stehen; 'o·dour·less [-lɪs] *adj.* geruchlos.

Od·ys·sey [ˈɒdɪsɪ] *s. lit.* (*fig. oft* 2) Odys-'see *f*.

oe·col·o·gy [iːˈkɒlədʒɪ] → *ecology.*

oec·u·men·i·cal [ˌiːkjʊˈmenɪkəl] *etc.* → *ecumenical etc.*

oe·de·ma [iːˈdiːmə] *pl.* -ma·ta [-mətə] *s.* ✠ Ö'dem *n*.

oe·di·pal [ˈiːdɪpl] *adj. psych.* ödi'pal, Ödipus...

Oed·i·pus com·plex [ˈiːdɪpəs] *s. psych.* 'Ödipuskom,plex *m*.

oen·o·lo·gy [iːˈnɒlədʒɪ] Wein(bau)kunde *f*, Önolo'gie *f*.

o'er [ˈɔːə] *poet. od. dial. für over.*

oe·so·phag·e·al [iːˌsɒfəˈdʒiːəl] *adj. anat.* Speiseröhren..., Schlund...: ~ orifice Magenmund *m*; **oe·soph·a·gus** [iːˈsɒfəgəs] *pl.* -gi [-gaɪ] *od.* -gus·es *s. anat.* Speiseröhre *f*.

of [ɒv, əv] *prp.* **1.** *allg.* von; **2.** *zur Bezeichnung des Genitivs:* the tail ~ the dog der Schwanz des Hundes; the tail ~ a dog der Hundeschwanz; **3.** *Ort:* bei: the battle ~ Hastings; **4.** *Entfernung, Trennung, Befreiung:* a) von: south ~ (within ten miles ~) London; cure (rid) ~ s.th.; free ~, b) *gen.:* robbed ~ his purse s-r Börse beraubt, c) um: cheat s.o. ~ s.th.; **5.** *Herkunft:* von, aus: ~ good family; Mr. X ~ London; **6.** *Teil:* von *od. gen.:* the best ~ my friends; a friend ~ mine ein Freund von mir, e-r m-r Freunde; that red nose ~ his diese rote Nase, die er hat; **7.** *Eigenschaft:* von, mit: a man ~ courage; a man ~ no importance ein unbedeutender Mensch; **8.** *Stoff:* aus, von: a dress ~ silk ein Kleid aus *od.* von Seide, ein Seidenkleid; (made) ~ steel aus Stahl (hergestellt), stählern, Stahl...; **9.** *Urheberschaft, Art u. Weise:* von: the works ~ Byron; it was clever ~ him; ~ o.s. von selbst, von sich aus; **10.** *Ursache, Grund:* a) von, an (*dat.*): die ~ cancer an Krebs sterben, b) aus: ~ charity, c) vor (*dat.*): afraid ~, d) auf (*acc.*): proud ~, e) über (*acc.*): a-shamed ~, f) nach: smell ~; **11.** *Beziehung:* hinsichtlich (*gen.*): quick ~ eye flinkäugig; nimble ~ foot leichtfüßig; **12.** *Thema:* a) von, über (*acc.*): speak ~ s.th., b) an (*acc.*): think ~ s.th.; **13.** *Apposition, im Deutschen nicht ausgedrückt:* a) the city ~ London; the University ~ Oxford; the month ~ April; the name ~ Smith, b) *Maß:* two feet ~ snow; a glass ~ wine; a piece ~ meat; **14.** *Genitivus objectivus:* zu: the love ~ God, b) vor (*dat.*): the fear ~ God die Furcht vor Gott, die Gottesfurcht, c) bei: an audience ~ the king; **15.** *Zeit:* a) an (*dat.*), in (*dat.*), mst *gen.:* ~ an evening e-s Abends; ~ late years in den letzten Jahren, b) von: your letter ~ March 3rd Ihr Schreiben vom 3. März, c) *Am.* F vor (*bei Zeitangaben*): ten minutes ~ three.

off [ɒf] **I** *adv.* **1.** mst *in Zssgn mit vb.* fort, weg, da'von: be ~ a) weg *od.* fort sein, b) (weg)gehen, sich davonmachen, (ab)fahren, c) wegmüssen: be ~!, ~ you go!, ~ with you! fort mit dir!, pack dich!; where are you ~ to? wo gehst du hin?; **2.** ab(-brechen, -kühlen, -rutschen, -schneiden etc.), her'un-

ter(...), los(...): the apple is ~ der Apfel ist ab; dash ~ losrennen; have one's shoes etc. ~ s-e *od.* die Schuhe etc. ausgezogen haben; ~ with your hat! herunter mit dem Hut!; **3.** entfernt, weg: 3 miles ~; **4.** *Zeitpunkt:* von jetzt an, hin: Christmas is a week ~ bis Weihnachten ist es eine Woche; ~ and on a) ab u. zu, hin u. wieder, b) ab u. an, mit (kurzen) Unterbrechungen; **5.** abgezogen, ab(züglich); **6.** a) aus(geschaltet), abgeschaltet, -gestellt (*Maschine, Radio etc.*), (ab)gesperrt (*Gas etc.*), zu (*Hahn etc.*), b) *fig.* aus, vor-'bei, abgebrochen; gelöst (*Verlobung*): the bet is ~ die Wette gilt nicht mehr; the whole thing is ~ die ganze Sache ist abgeblasen *od.* ins Wasser gefallen; **7.** aus(gegangen), verkauft, nicht mehr vorrätig; **8.** frei (*von Arbeit*): take a day ~ sich e-n Tag freinehmen; **9.** ganz, zu Ende: drink ~ (ganz) austrinken; kill ~ ausrotten; sell ~ ausverkaufen; **10.** ✠ flau: the market is ~; **11.** nicht frisch, (leicht) verdorben (*Nahrungsmittel*); **12.** *sport* außer Form; **13.** ♣ vom Land etc. ab; **14.** well (badly) ~ gut (schlecht) d(a)ran *od.* gestellt *od.* situiert; how are you ~ for ...? wie bist du dran mit ...?; **II** *prp.* **15.** von ... (weg, ab, her'unter): climb ~ the horse vom Pferd (herunter)steigen; eat ~ a plate von e-m Teller essen; take 3 percent ~ the price 3 Prozent vom Preis abziehen; be ~ a drug *sl.* von e-r Droge ,herunter sein'; **16.** abseits von *od. gen.*, von ... ab: ~ the street; a street ~ Piccadilly e-e Seitenstraße von Piccadilly; ~ one's balance aus dem Gleichgewicht; ~ form außer Form; **17.** frei von: ~ duty dienstfrei; **18.** ♣ auf der Höhe von Trafalgar etc., vor der Küste; **III** *adj.* **19.** (weiter) entfernt; **20.** Seiten..., Neben...: ~ street; **21.** recht (*von Tieren, Fuhrwerken etc.*): the ~ horse das rechte Pferd, das Handpferd; **22.** *Kricket:* abseitig (*rechts vom Schlagmann*); **23.** ab(-), los(gegangen); **24.** (arbeits-, dienst)frei: an ~ day; → **25.** (*verhältnismäßig*) schlecht: an ~ day ein schlechter Tag (*an dem alles misslingt etc.*); an ~ year for fruit ein schlechtes Obstjahr; **26.** ✠ a) flau, still, tot (*Saison*), b) von schlechter Quali'tät: ~ shade Fehlfarbe *f*; **27.** ,ab', unwohl, nicht auf dem Damm: I am feeling rather ~ today; **28.** on the ~ chance auf gut Glück: I went there on the ~ chance of seeing him ich ging in der vagen Hoffnung hin, ihn zu sehen; **IV** *int.* **29.** weg!, fort!, raus!: hands ~! Hände weg!; **30.** her'unter!, ab!

of·fal [ˈɒfl] *s.* **1.** Abfall *m*; **2.** *sg. od. pl. konstr.* Fleischabfall *m*, Inne'reien *pl.*; **3.** billige *od.* minderwertige Fische *pl.*; **4.** *fig.* Schund *m*, Ausschuss *m*.

off|'**beat** *adj.* F ausgefallen, extravagant (*Geschmack, Kleidung etc.*); '**~·cast** **I** *adj.* verworfen, abgetan; **II** *s.* abgetane Per'son *od.* Sache; **~·cen·ter** *Am.*, **~·cen·tre** *Brit. adj.* verrutscht; ❍ außermittig, ex'zentrisch (*a. fig.*); **~·col·o(u)r** *adj.* **1.** a) farblich abweichend, b) nicht lupenrein: ~ jewel; **2.** *fig.* nicht (ganz) in Ordnung; unpässlich; **3.** zweideutig, schlüpfrig: ~ jokes; **~·du·ty** *adj.* dienstfrei.

of·fence [əˈfens] *s.* **1.** *allg.* Vergehen *n*, Verstoß *m* (against gegen); **2.** ✠ a) *criminal* ~ Straftat *f*, strafbare Handlung, De'likt *n*, b) a. *lesser od. minor* ~ Über'tretung *f*; **3.** Anstoß *m*, Ärgernis *n*, Beleidigung *f*, Kränkung *f*: give ~

ter(...), los(...): the apple is ~ der Apfel ist ab; dash ~ losrennen; have one's shoes etc. ~ s-e *od.* die Schuhe etc. ausgezogen haben; ~ with your hat! herunter mit dem Hut!; **3.** entfernt, weg: 3 miles ~; **4.** *Zeitpunkt:* von jetzt an, hin: Christmas is a week ~ bis Weihnachten ist es eine Woche; ~ and on a) ab u. zu, hin u. wieder, b) ab u. an, mit (kurzen) Unterbrechungen; **5.** abgezogen, ab(züglich); **6.** a) aus(geschaltet), abgeschaltet, -gestellt (*Maschine, Radio etc.*), (ab)gesperrt (*Gas etc.*), zu (*Hahn etc.*), b) *fig.* aus, vor-'bei, abgebrochen; gelöst (*Verlobung*): the bet is ~ die Wette gilt nicht mehr; the whole thing is ~ die ganze Sache ist abgeblasen *od.* ins Wasser gefallen; **7.** aus(gegangen), verkauft, nicht mehr vorrätig; **8.** frei (*von Arbeit*): take a day ~ sich e-n Tag freinehmen; **9.** ganz, zu Ende: drink ~ (ganz) austrinken; kill ~ ausrotten; sell ~ ausverkaufen; **10.** ✠ flau: the market is ~; **11.** nicht frisch, (leicht) verdorben (*Nahrungsmittel*); **12.** *sport* außer Form; **13.** ♣ vom Land etc. ab; **14.** well (badly) ~ gut (schlecht) d(a)ran *od.* gestellt *od.* situiert; how are you ~ for ...? wie bist du dran mit ...?; **II** *prp.* **15.** von ... (weg, ab, her'unter): climb ~ the horse vom Pferd (herunter)steigen; eat ~ a plate von e-m Teller essen; take 3 percent ~ the price 3 Prozent vom Preis abziehen; be ~ a drug *sl.* von e-r Droge ,herunter sein'; **16.** abseits von *od. gen.*, von ... ab: ~ the street; a street ~ Piccadilly e-e Seitenstraße von Piccadilly; ~ one's balance aus dem Gleichgewicht; ~ form außer Form; **17.** frei von: ~ duty dienstfrei; **18.** ♣ auf der Höhe von Trafalgar etc., vor der Küste; **III** *adj.* **19.** (weiter) entfernt; **20.** Seiten..., Neben...: ~ street; **21.** recht (*von Tieren, Fuhrwerken etc.*): the ~ horse das rechte Pferd, das Handpferd; **22.** *Kricket:* abseitig (*rechts vom Schlagmann*); **23.** ab(-), los(gegangen); **24.** (arbeits-, dienst)frei: an ~ day; → **25.** (*verhältnismäßig*) schlecht: an ~ day ein schlechter Tag (*an dem alles misslingt etc.*); an ~ year for fruit ein schlechtes Obstjahr; **26.** ✠ a) flau, still, tot (*Saison*), b) von schlechter Quali'tät: ~ shade Fehlfarbe *f*; **27.** ,ab', unwohl, nicht auf dem Damm: I am feeling rather ~ today; **28.** on the ~ chance auf gut Glück: I went there on the ~ chance of seeing him ich ging in der vagen Hoffnung hin, ihn zu sehen; **IV** *int.* **29.** weg!, fort!, raus!: hands ~! Hände weg!; **30.** her'unter!, ab!

Anstoß *od.* Ärgernis erregen (to bei); take ~ (at) Anstoß nehmen (an *dat.*), beleidigt *od.* gekränkt sein (durch, über *acc.*), (et.) übel nehmen; no ~ (meant)! nichts für ungut!; **4.** Angriff *m*: arms of ~ Angriffswaffen *pl.*; **of'fence·less** [-lɪs] *adj.* harmlos.

of·fend [əˈfend] **I** *v/t.* **1.** j-n, j-s Gefühle etc. verletzen, beleidigen, kränken: it ~s the eye es beleidigt das Auge; be ~ed at (*od.* by) s.th. sich durch et. beleidigt fühlen; be ~ed with (*od.* by) s.o. sich durch j-n beleidigt fühlen; **II** *v/i.* **2.** Anstoß erregen; **3.** (against) verstoßen (gegen), sündigen, sich vergehen (an *dat.*); **of'fend·ed·ly** [-dɪdlɪ] *adv.* beleidigt; **of'fend·er** [-də] *s.* Übel-, Missetäter(in); ✠ Straffällige(r *m*) *f*: first ~ ✠ nicht Vorbestrafte(r *m*) *f*, Ersttäter(in); second ~ Rückfällige(r *m*) *f*; **of'fend·ing** [-dɪŋ] *adj.* **1.** verletzend, beleidigend; **2.** anstößig.

of·fense(·less) *Am.* → *offence(·less).*

of·fen·sive [əˈfensɪv] **I** *adj.* □ **1.** beleidigend, anstößig, anstöß- *od.* Ärgernis erregend; **2.** 'widerwärtig, ekelhaft, übel: ~ smell; **3.** angreifend, offen'siv: ~ war Angriffs-, Offensivkrieg *m*; ~ weapon Angriffswaffe *f*; **II** *s.* **4.** Offen'sive *f*, Angriff *m*: take the ~ die Offensive ergreifen, zum Angriff übergehen; **of'fen·sive·ness** [-nɪs] *s.* **1.** das Beleidigende, Anstößigkeit *f*; **2.** 'Widerlichkeit *f*.

of·fer [ˈɒfə] **I** *v/t.* **1.** Geschenk, Ware etc., a. Schlacht anbieten; ✝ a. offerieren; Preis, Summe bieten: ~ s.o. a cigarette; ~ one's hand (to) j-m die Hand bieten *od.* reichen; ~ for sale zum Verkauf anbieten; **2.** Ansicht, Entschuldigung etc. vorbringen, äußern; **3.** Anblick, Schwierigkeit etc. bieten: no opportunity ~ed itself es bot sich keine Gelegenheit; **4.** sich bereit erklären zu, sich (an)erbieten zu; **5.** Anstalten machen zu, sich anschicken zu; **6.** *fig.* Beleidigung zufügen; Widerstand leisten; Gewalt antun (to *dat.*); **7.** a. ~ up opfern, Opfer, Gebet, Geschenk darbringen (to *dat.*); **II** *v/i.* **8.** sich bieten, auftauchen: no opportunity ~ed es bot sich keine Gelegenheit; **III** *s.* **9.** *allg.* Angebot *n*, Anerbieten *n*; **10.** ✝ (An-)Gebot *n*, Of'ferte *f*, Antrag *m*: on ~ zu verkaufen, verkäuflich; **11.** Vorbringen *n* (*e-s Vorschlags, e-r Meinung etc.*); **of·fer·ing** [ˈɒfərɪŋ] *s.* **1.** *eccl.* Opfer *n*; **2.** *eccl.* Spende *f*; **3.** Angebot *n* (*Am. a.* ✝ *Börse*).

of·fer·to·ry [ˈɒfətərɪ] *s. eccl.* **1.** mst 2 Offer'torium *n*; **2.** Kol'lekte *f*, Geldsammlung *f*; **3.** Opfer(geld) *n*.

off|'**face** *adj.* stirnfrei (*Damenhut*); '**~·fla·vo(u)r** *s.* (unerwünschter) Beigeschmack; **~·grade** *adj.* ✝ von geringerer Quali'tät: ~ iron Ausfalleisen *n*.

off|**hand** [ˌɒfˈhænd] **I** *adv.* **1.** aus dem Stegreif *m*, Kopf, (so) ohne weiteres sagen können etc.; **II** *adj.* **2.** unvorbereitet, improvisiert, Stegreif...: an ~ speech; **3.** lässig (*Art etc.*), 'hingeworfen (*Bemerkung*); **4.** kurz (angebunden); **~·hand·ed** [-dɪd] → *offhand* II; **~·hand·ed·ness** [-dɪdnɪs] *s.* Lässigkeit *f*.

of·fice [ˈɒfɪs] *s.* **1.** Bü'ro *n*, Kanz'lei *f*, Kon'tor *n*; Geschäftsstelle *f* (*a.* ✠ *des Gerichts*), Amt *n*; Geschäfts-, Amtszimmer *n od.* -gebäude *n*; **2.** Behörde *f*, Amt *n*, (Dienst)Stelle *f*; mst 2 *bsd. Brit.* Mini'sterium *n*, (Ministeri'al)Amt *n*: Foreign 2; **3.** Zweigstelle *f*, Fili'ale *f*; **4.** (*bsd.* öffentliches, staatliches) Amt,

Posten *m*, Stellung *f*: *take* ~, *enter upon an* ~ ein Amt antreten; *be in* ~ im Amt *od.* an der Macht sein; *hold an* ~ ein Amt bekleiden *od.* innehaben; *resign one's* ~ zurücktreten, sein Amt niederlegen; **5.** Funkti'on *f*, Aufgabe *f*, Pflicht *f*: *it is my* ~ *to advise him*; **6.** Dienst(leistung *f*) *m*, Gefälligkeit *f*: *good* ~*s* *pol.* gute Dienste; *do s.o. a good* ~ j-m e-n guten Dienst erweisen; *through the good* ~*s of* durch die freundliche Vermittlung von; **7.** *eccl.* Gottesdienst *m*; *♀ for the Dead* Totenamt *n*; *perform the last* ~*s to* e-n Toten aussegnen; *divine* ~ das Brevier; **8.** *pl. bsd. Brit.* Wirtschaftsteil *m*, -raum *m od.* -räume *pl. od.* -gebäude *n od. pl.*; **9.** *sl.* Wink *m*, Tipp *m*.

of·fice| ac·tion *s.* (Prüfungs)Bescheid *m des Patentamts*; '~-,bear·er *s.* Amtsinhaber(in); ~ **block** *s.* Bü'rogebäude *n*; ~ **boy** *s.* Laufbursche *m*, Bü'rogehilfe *m*; ~ **clerk** *s.* Konto'rist(in), Bü'roangestellte(r *m*) *f*; ~ **girl** *s.* Bü'rogehilfin *f*; '~-,hold·er *s.* Amtsinhaber(in), (Staats)Beamte(r *m*), (Staats)Beamtin *f*; ~ **hours** *s. pl.* Dienststunden *pl.*, Geschäftszeit *f*; '~-,hunt·er *s.* Postenjäger(in).

of·fi·cer ['ɒfɪsə] **I** *s.* **1.** ✕, ♣ Offi'zier *m*: ~ *of the day* Offizier vom Tagesdienst; *commanding* ~ Kommandeur *m*, Einheitsführer *m*; ~ *cadet* Fähnrich *m*; ~ *candidate* Offiziersanwärter *m*; ~'*s' Training Corps Brit.* Offiziersausbildungskorps *n*; **2.** a) Poli'zist *m*, Poli'zeibeamte(r) *m*, b) Herr Wachtmeister (*Anrede*); **3.** Beamte(r) *m* (*a.* ✝ *etc.*), Beamtin *f*, Amtsträger(in): *medical* ~ Amtsarzt *m*; *public* ~ Beamte(r) im öffentlichen Dienst; **4.** Vorstandsmitglied *n*; **II** *v/t.* **5.** ✕ a) mit Offizieren versehen, b) *e-e Einheit* als Offizier befehligen (*mst pass.*): *be* ~*ed by* befehligt werden von; **6.** *fig.* leiten, führen.

of·fice| seek·er *s. bsd. Am.* **1.** Stellungssuchende(r *m*) *f*; **2.** *b.s.* Postenjäger(in); ~ **staff** *s.* Bü'roperso,nal *n*; ~ **sup·plies** *s. pl.* Bü'romateri,al *n*, -bedarf *m*.

of·fi·cial [əˈfɪʃl] **I** *adj.* □ **1.** offizi'ell, amtlich, dienstlich, behördlich: ~ *act* Amtshandlung *f*; ~ *business* ⚓ Dienstsache *f*; ~ *call teleph.* Dienstgespräch *n*; ~ *duties* Amtspflichten; ~ *language* Amtssprache *f*; ~ *oath* Amtseid *m*; ~ *residence* Amtssitz *m*; ~ *secret* Amts-, Dienstgeheimnis *n*; *through* ~ *channels* auf dem Dienst *od.* Instanzenweg; ~ *trip* Dienstreise *f*; **2.** offiziell, amtlich (*bestätigt od.* autorisiert): *an* ~ *report*; **3.** offizi'ell, for-'mell: *an* ~ *dinner*; **4.** ✿ offizi'nell; **II** *s.* **5.** Beamte(ɪ) *m*, Beamtin *f*; Funktio-'när(in); **of·fi·cial·dom** [-dəm] *s.* ~ *officialism* 2 *u.* 3; **of·fi·cial·ese** [ə,fɪʃə-'liːz] *s.* Behördensprache *f*, Amtsstil *m*; **of·fi·cial·ism** [-ˌʃəlɪzəm] *s.* **1.** 'Amtsme-,thoden *pl.*; **2.** Bürokra'tie *f*, Amtsschimmel *m*; **3.** *coll.* das Beamtentum, *die* Beamten *pl.*

of·fi·ci·ate [əˈfɪʃɪeɪt] *v/i.* **1.** amtieren, fungieren (*as* als); **2.** den Gottesdienst leiten: ~ *at the wedding* die Trauung vornehmen.

of·fic·i·nal [əˈfɪsɪnl] **I** *adj.* ✿ a) offizi'nell, als Arz'nei anerkannt, b) Arz-nei...: ~ *plants* Heilkräuter *n*; **II** *s.* offizinelle Arz'nei.

of·fi·cious [əˈfɪʃəs] *adj.* □ **1.** aufdringlich, über'trieben diensteifrig, 'übereifrig; **2.** offizi'ös, halbamtlich; **of'fi·cious·ness** [-nɪs] *s.* Zudringlichkeit *f*,

(aufdringlicher) Diensteifer.

of·fing ['ɒfɪŋ] *s.* ♣ offene See, Seeraum *m*: *in the* ~ a) auf offener See, b) *fig.* in (Aus)Sicht: *be in the* ~ *a.* sich abzeichnen.

off·ish ['ɒfɪʃ] *adj.* F reserviert, unnahbar, kühl, steif.

'**off|-key** *adj. u. adv.* ♪ falsch; '~-,li·cence *s. Brit.* 'Schankkonzessi,on *f* über die Straße; '**off(-)line** **I** *adj. Computer:* Offline...: ~ *mode* Offlinebetrieb *m*; **II** *adv. Computer:* offline; ,~'load *v/t. fig.* abladen (*on s.o.* auf j-n); ,~-'peak **I** *adj.* abfallend, unter der Spitze liegend: ~ *charges pl.* verbilligter Tarif; ~ *hours* verkehrsschwache Stunden; ~ *tariff* Nacht(strom)tarif *m*; **II** *s.* ⚡ Belastungstal *n*; '~-piste [-piːst] *adj.* abseits der Piste (*Skifahren*); ~ **po·si·tion** *s.* ⊙ Ausschalt-, Nullstellung *f*; '~-print **I** *s.* Sonder(ab)druck *m* (*from* aus); **II** *v/t.* als Sonder(ab)druck herstellen; '~-,put·ting *adj.* F störend, unangenehm; '~-road *adj. mot.* **1.** geländegängig, Gelände... **2.** im freien Gelände; ,~-'road·er *s. mot.* **1.** Geländefahrzeug *n*; **2.** Fahrer *m* e-s Geländefahrzeugs; '~-sales *s. pl. Brit.* Verkauf *m od.* Verkäufe *pl.* von alkoholischen Getränken ,über die Straße'; '~,scour·ings *s. pl.* **1.** Kehricht *m*, Schmutz *m*; **2.** Abschaum *m* (*bsd. fig.*): *the* ~*s of humanity*; '~-scum *s. fig.* Abschaum *m*, Auswurf *m*; ,~-'sea·son *s.* 'Nebensai,son *f*, stille Sai'son.

off·set ['ɒfset] **I** *s.* **1.** Ausgleich *m*, Kompensati'on *f*; ✝ Verrechnung *f*: ~ *account* Verrechnungskonto *n*; **2.** ♀ a) Ableger *m*, b) kurzer Ausläufer; **3.** Neben-, Seitenlinie *f* (*e-s Stammbaums etc.*); **4.** Abzweigung *f*, Ausläufer *m* (*bsd. e-s Gebirges*); **5.** *typ.* a) Offsetdruck *m*, b) Abziehen *n*, Abliegen *n* (*bsd. noch feuchten Druckes*), c) Abzug *m*, Pa'trize *f* (*Lithographie*); **6.** ⊙ a) Kröpfung *f*; Biegung *f e-s Rohrs*, b) ✖ kurze Sohle, c) ⚡ (Ab)Zweigleitung *f*; **7.** *surv.* Ordi'nate *f*; **8.** △ Absatz *m* e-r *Mauer etc.*; **II** *v/t.* [*irr.* → **set**] **9.** ausgleichen, aufwiegen, wettmachen: *the gains* ~ *the losses*; **10.** ✝ *Am.* aufrechnen, ausgleichen; **11.** ⊙ kröpfen; **12.** △ *Mauer etc.* absetzen; **13.** *typ.* im Offsetverfahren drucken; ~ *bulb s.* ♀ Brutzwiebel *f*; ~ **sheet** *s. typ.* 'Durchschussbogen *m*.

'**off|-shoot** *s.* **1.** ♀ Sprössling *m*, Ausläufer *m*, Ableger *m*; **2.** Abzweigung *f*, *fig.* Seitenlinie *f* (*e-s Stammbaums etc.*); '~-shore **I** *adv.* **1.** von der Küste ab *od.* her; **2.** in einiger Entfernung von der Küste; **II** *adj.* küstennah: ~ *drilling* Offshorebohrung *f*; **4.** ablandig (*Wind, Strömung*); **5.** Auslands...: ~ *order Am.* Offshoreauftrag *m*; ,~'side *adj. u. adv. sport* abseits: ~ *side* **I** *s.* **1.** *sport* Abseits(stellung *f*) *n*; **2.** *mot.* Fahrerseite *f*; **II** *adj. u. adv.* abseits: *be* ~ im Abseits stehen; ~ *trap* Abseitsfalle *f*; '~-size *s.* ⊙ Maßabweichung *f*; '~-spring *s.* **1.** Nachkommen(schaft *f*) *pl.*; **2.** (*pl. offspring*) Nachkomme *m*, Abkömmling *m*; ~ *stage adj.* hinter der Bühne, hinter den Ku'lissen (*a. fig.*); '~-take *s.* ✝ Abzug *m*; Einkauf *m*; **2.** ⊙ Abzug(srohr *n*) *m*; ,~-the-'cuff *adj. fig.* aus dem Handgelenk *od.* Stegreif; ,~-the-'peg *adj.* von der Stange, Konfektions...; ,~-the-'rec·ord *adj.* nicht für die Öffentlichkeit bestimmt, 'inoffizi,ell; ,~-the-'shelf *adj.* ✝ ⊙ Standard...: ~ *accessories*; ,~-'white *adj.* gebrochen

weiß.

oft [ɒft] *adv. obs., poet. u. in Zssgn* oft: ~-*told* oft erzählt.

of·ten ['ɒfn] *adv.* oft(mals), häufig: *as* ~ *as not, ever so* ~ sehr oft; *more* ~ *than not* meistens.

o·gee ['əʊdʒiː] *s.* **1.** S-Kurve *f*, S-förmige Linie; **2.** △ a) Kar'nies *n*, Rinnleiste *f*, b) *a.* ~ *arch* Eselsrücken *m* (*Bogenform*).

o·give ['əʊdʒaɪv] *s.* **1.** △ a) Gratrippe *f* *e-s Gewölbes*, b) Spitzbogen *m*; **2.** ✕ Geschossspitze *f*; **3.** *Statistik:* Häufigkeitsverteilungskurve *f*.

o·gle ['əʊgl] **I** *v/t.* liebäugeln mit; **II** *v/i.* (*with*) liebäugeln (mit, *a. fig.*), ,Augen machen' (*dat.*); **III** *s.* verliebter *od.* liebäugelnder Blick; '**o·gler** [-lə] *s.* Liebäugelnde(r *m*) *f*.

o·gre ['əʊgə] *s.* **1.** (Menschen fressendes) Ungeheuer, *bsd.* Riese *m* (*im Märchen*); **2.** *fig.* Scheusal *n*, Ungeheuer *n* (*Mensch*); **o·gress** ['əʊgrɪs] *s.* Menschenfresserin *f*, Riesin *f* (*im Märchen*).

oh [əʊ] *int.* oh!; ach!

ohm [əʊm], **ohm·ad** ['əʊmæd] *s.* ⚡ Ohm *n*: ♀'s *Law* ohmsches Gesetz; **ohm·age** ['əʊmɪdʒ] *s.* Ohmzahl *f*; **ohm·ic** ['əʊmɪk] *adj.* ohmsch: ~ *resistance*; **ohm·me·ter** ['əʊm,miːtə] *s.* ⚡ Ohmmeter *n*.

oi [ɔɪ] *int.* F he!, he du!

oi(c)k *s. Brit. sl.* Prolo *m*.

oil [ɔɪl] **I** *s.* **1.** Öl *n*: *pour* ~ *on the flames fig.* Öl ins Feuer gießen; *pour* ~ *on troubled waters fig.* die Gemüter beruhigen; *smell of* ~ *fig.* mehr Fleiß als Geist *od.* Talent verraten; **2.** (Erd-) Öl *n*, Pe'troleum *n*: *strike* ~ a) Erdöl finden, auf Öl stoßen, fündig werden (*a. fig.*), b) *fig.* Glück *od.* Erfolg haben; **3.** *mst pl.* Ölfarbe *f*: *paint in* ~*s* in Öl malen; **4.** *mst pl.* F Ölgemälde *n*; **5.** *pl.* Ölzeug *n*, -haut *f*; **II** *v/t.* **6.** ⊙ (ein-) ölen, einfetten, schmieren; → *palm[1]* 1; '~-,bear·ing *adj. geol.* ölhaltig, Öl führend; '~-berg [-bɜːg] *s.* ♣ Riesentanker *m*; ~ **box** *s.* ⊙ Schmierbüchse *f*; ~ **brake** *s. mot.* Öldruckbremse *f*; ~ **burn·er** *s.* ⊙ Ölbrenner *m*; '~-cake *s.* Ölkuchen *m*; '~-can *s.* 'Ölka,nister *m*, -kännchen *n*; ~ **change** *s. mot.* Ölwechsel *m*; '~-cloth *s.* **1.** Wachstuch *n*; **2.** → *oilskin*; ~ **col·o(u)r** *s. mst pl.* Ölfarbe *f*; ~ **cri·sis** *s.* [*irr.*] ✝ Ölkrise *f*; '~-cup *s.* ⊙ Öler *m*, Schmierbüchse *f*.

oiled [ɔɪld] *adj.* **1.** (ein)geölt; **2.** *bsd. well* ~ *sl.* ,blau', besoffen.

oil·er ['ɔɪlə] *s.* **1.** ♣, ⊙ Öler *m*, Schmierer *m* (*Person u. Gerät*); **2.** ⊙ Öl-, Schmierkanne *f*; **3.** *Am.* F → *oilskin* 2; **4.** *Am.* Ölquelle *f*; **5.** ♣ Öltanker *m*.

'**oil|-field** *s.* Ölfeld *n*; '~-,fired *adj.* mit Ölfeuerung, ölbeheizt: ~ *central heating* Ölzentralheizung *f*; ~ **fu·el** *s.* **1.** Heizöl *n*; **2.** Öltreibstoff *m*; ~ **gas** *s.* Ölgas *n*; ~ **ga(u)ge** *s.* ⊙ Ölstandsanzeiger *m*; ~ **glut** *s.* Ölschwemme *f*.

oil·i·ness ['ɔɪlɪnɪs] *s.* **1.** ölige Beschaffenheit, Fettigkeit *f*, Schmierfähigkeit *f*; **2.** *fig.* Glattheit *f*, aalglattes Wesen; **3.** *fig.* Öligkeit *f*, salbungsvolles Wesen.

oil| lev·el *s. mot.* Ölstand *m*; ~ **paint** *s.* Ölfarbe *f*; ~ **paint·ing** *s.* **1.** 'Ölmale,rei *f*; **2.** Ölgemälde *n*; **3.** ⊙ Ölanstrich *m*; ~ **pan** *s. mot.* Ölwanne *f*; '~-,pro·duc·ing coun·try *s.* Ölförderland *n*; ~ **rig** *s.* Bohrinsel *f*; ~ **seal** *s.* ⊙ **1.** Öldichtung *f*; **2.** *a.* ~ *ring* Simmerring *m*; '~-skin *s.* **1.** Ölleinwand *f*; **2.** *pl.* Ölzeug *n*, -kleidung *f*; ~ **slick** *s.* ⊙ Ölteppich *m*; **2.** Ölteppich *m* (*auf dem Meer etc.*); ~ **stove** *s.* Ölofen *m*; ~ **sump** *s.* ⊙ Ölwanne f; **~ switch** s. ⊖ Ölschalter m; **~ var·nish** s. Öllack m; **~ well** s. Ölquelle f.

oil·y [ˈɔɪlɪ] adj. □ **1.** ölig, ölhaltig, Öl...; **2.** fettig, schmierig; **3.** fig. glatt(züngig), aalglatt, schmeichlerisch; **4.** fig. ölig, salbungsvoll.

oint·ment [ˈɔɪntmənt] s. ⚕ Salbe f; → **fly²** 1.

O.K., OK, o·kay [ˌəʊˈkeɪ] F **I** adj. u. int. richtig, gut, in Ordnung, genehmigt; **II** v/t. genehmigen, gutheißen, e-r Sache zustimmen; **III** s. Zustimmung f, Genehmigung f.

old [əʊld] **I** adj. **1.** alt, betagt: **grow ~** alt werden, altern; **2.** zehn Jahre etc. alt: **ten years ~**; **3.** alt(ˈhergebracht): **~ tradition**; **as ~ as the hills** uralt; **4.** alt, vergangen, früher: **the ~ masters** paint. etc. die alten Meister; → **old boy**; **5.** alt(bekannt, -bewährt): **an ~ friend**; **6.** alt, abgenutzt; (ab)getragen (Kleider): **that is ~ hat** das ist ein alter Hut; **7.** alt(modisch), verkalkt; **8.** alt, erfahren, gewitz(ig)t: **~ offender** alter Sünder; → **hand** 6; **9.** F (guter) alter, lieber: **~ chap** od. **man** ˈaltes Haus`; **nice ~ boy** netter alter ˈKnabe`; **the ~ man** der ˈAlte` (Chef); **my ~ man** mein ˈAlter` (Vater); **my ~ woman** meine ˈAlte` (Ehefrau); **10.** sl. toll: **have a fine ~ time** sich toll amüsieren; **any ~ thing** irgend(et)was, egal was; **any ~ time** egal wann; **II** s. **11. the ~** die Alten pl; **12. of ~, in times of ~** ehedem, vor alters; **from of ~** seit alters; **times of ~** alte Zeiten; **a friend of ~** ein alter Freund.

old| age s. (hohes) Alter, Greisenalter n:~ **annuity, ~ pension** (Alters)Rente f, Ruhegeld n; **~ insurance** Altersversicherung f; **~ pensioner** (Alters)Rentner(in), Ruhegeldempfänger(in); **~ boy** s. Brit. ehemaliger Schüler, Ehemalige(r) m; **~-clothes·man** [ˌəʊldˈkləʊðzmæn] s. [irr.] Trödler m.

old·en [ˈəʊldən] adj. Brit. obs. od. poet. alt: **in ~ times**.

Old| Eng·lish s. ling. Altenglisch n; **,~-esˈtab·lished** adj. alteingesessen (Firma etc.), alt (Brauch etc.); **,~-ˈfash·ioned** adj. **1.** altmodisch: **an ~ butler** ein Butler der alten Schule; **2.** altklug (Kind); **,~-ˈfo·g(e)y·ish** adj. altmodisch, verknöchert, verkalkt; **~ girl** s. **1.** Brit. ehemalige Schülerin; **2.** F ˈaltes Mädchen`; **~ Glo·ry** s. Sternenbanner n (Flagge der USA); **~ Guard** s. pol. ˈalte Garde`: a) Am. der ultrakonservative Flügel der Republikaner, b) allg. jede streng konservative Gruppe.

old·ie [ˈəʊldɪ] s. F **1.** Oldie m (alter Schlager); **2.** alter Witz.

old·ish [ˈəʊldɪʃ] adj. ältlich.

,old-ˈline adj. **1.** konservaˈtiv; **2.** tradiˈtioˈnell; **3.** e-r alten Linie entstammend; **,~-ˈmaid·ish** adj. altˈjüngferlich; **,~-ˈworld** adj. **1.** altertümlich, anheimelnd; **2.** alt, anˈtik: **~ furniture**; **3.** altmodisch.

o·le·ag·i·nous [ˌəʊlɪˈædʒɪnəs] adj. ölig (a. fig.), ölhaltig, Öl...

o·le·ate [ˈəʊlɪeɪt] s. 🜊 ölsaures Salz: **~ of potash** ölsaures Kali.

o·le·fi·ant [ˈəʊlɪfaɪənt] adj. 🜊 Öl bildend: **~ gas**.

o·le·if·er·ous [ˌəʊlɪˈɪfərəs] adj. ♀ ölhaltig.

o·le·in [ˈəʊlɪɪn] s. 🜊 **1.** Oleˈin n; **2.** (handelsübliche) Ölsäure.

o·le·o·graph [ˈəʊlɪəʊgrɑːf] s. Öldruck m (Bild); **o·le·og·ra·phy** [ˌəʊlɪˈɒgrəfɪ] s. Öldruck(verfahren n) m.

o·le·o·mar·ga·rine [ˈəʊlɪəʊˌmɑːdʒəˈriːn] s. Margaˈrine f.

O lev·el s. Brit. ped. (etwa) mittlere Reife.

ol·fac·tion [ɒlˈfækʃn] s. Geruchssinn m; **ol·fac·to·ry** [ɒlˈfæktərɪ] adj. Geruchs...: **~ nerves**.

ol·i·garch [ˈɒlɪɡɑːk] s. Oligˈarch m; **'ol·i·garch·y** [-kɪ] s. Oligarˈchie f.

o·li·o [ˈəʊlɪəʊ] pl. **-os** s. **1.** Raˈgout n (a. fig.); **2.** ♪ Potpourri n.

ol·ive [ˈɒlɪv] **I** s. **1.** a. **~-tree** Olive f, Ölbaum m: **Mount of ~s** bibl. Ölberg m; **2.** Oˈlive f (Frucht); **3.** Ölzweig m; **4.** a. **~-green** Oˈlivgrün n; **II** adj. **5.** oˈlivenartig, Oliven...; **6.** oˈlivgrau, -grün; **~ branch** s. Ölzweig m (a. fig.): **hold out the ~** s-n Friedenswillen zeigen; **~ drab** s. **1.** Oˈlivgrün n; **2.** Am. oˈlivgrünes Uniˈformtuch; **,~-ˈdrab** adj. oˈlivgrün; **~ oil** s. Oˈlivenöl n.

ol·la po·dri·da [ˌɒlɑpɒˈdriːdə] → **olio**.

ol·o·gy [ˈɒlədʒɪ] s. humor. Wissenschaft(szweig m) f.

O·lym·pi·ad [əʊˈlɪmpiæd] s. allg. Olympiˈade f; **O·lym·pi·an** [-ɪən] adj. oˈlympisch; **O·lym·pic** [-ɪk] **I** adj. oˈlympisch: **~ Games** → **II** s. pl. Oˈlympische Spiele pl.

om·buds·man [ˈɒmbʊdzmən] s. [irr.] **1.** pol. Ombudsmann m (Beauftragter für Beschwerden von Staatsbürgern); **2.** Beschwerdestelle f, Schiedsrichter m.

om·e·let(te) [ˈɒmlɪt] s. Omeˈlett n: **you cannot make an ~ without breaking eggs** fig. wo gehobelt wird, (da) fallen Späne.

o·men [ˈəʊmen] **I** s. Omen n, (bsd. schlechtes) Vorzeichen (for für): **a good** (**bad, ill**) **~**; **II** v/i. u. v/t. deuten (auf acc.), ahnen (lassen), propheˈzeien, (ver)künden.

o·men·tum [əʊˈmentəm] pl. **-ta** [-tə] s. anat. (Darm)Netz n.

om·i·nous [ˈɒmɪnəs] adj. □ unheil-, verhängnisvoll, omiˈnös, drohend.

o·mis·si·ble [əʊˈmɪsɪbl] adj. auslassbar; **o·mis·sion** [əˈmɪʃn] s. **1.** Aus-, Weglassung f (from aus); **2.** Unterˈlassung f, Versäumnis n, Überˈgehung f: **sin of ~** Unterlassungssünde f; **o·mit** [əˈmɪt] v/t. **1.** aus-, weglassen (from aus od. von); überˈgehen; **2.** unterˈlassen, (es) versäumen (doing, to do et. zu tun).

om·ni·bus [ˈɒmnɪbəs] **I** s. **1.** Omnibus m, (Auto)Bus m; **2.** Sammelband m, Antholoˈgie f; **3.** Sammel... (-konto, -klausel etc.); **~ bar** s. ⚡ Sammelschiene f; **~ bill** s. parl. (Vorlage f zu e-m) Mantelgesetz n.

om·ni·di·rec·tion·al [ˌɒmnɪdɪˈrekʃənl] s. ⚡ Rundstrahl...(-antenne), Allrichtungs...(-mikrofon).

om·ni·far·i·ous [ˌɒmnɪˈfeərɪəs] adj. von aller(lei) Art, vielseitig.

om·nip·o·tence [ɒmˈnɪpətəns] s. Allmacht f; **om·ˈnip·o·tent** [-nt] adj. □ allˈmächtig.

om·ni·pres·ence [ˌɒmnɪˈprezns] s. Allˈgegenwart f; **om·ni·ˈpres·ent** [-nt] adj. allˈgegenwärtig, überˈall.

om·nis·cience [ɒmˈnɪsɪəns] s. Allˈwissenheit f; **om·ˈnis·cient** [-nt] adj. □ allˈwissend.

om·ni·um [ˈɒmnɪəm] s. ✝ Brit. Omnium n, Gesamtwert m e-r fundierten öffentlichen Anleihe; **,~-ˈgath·er·um** [-ˈɡæðərəm] s. **1.** Sammelˈsurium n; **2.** bunte Gesellschaft.

om·niv·o·rous [ɒmˈnɪvərəs] adj. alles fressend.

o·mo·plate [ˈəʊməʊpleɪt] s. anat. Schulterblatt n.

om·phal·ic [ɒmˈfælɪk] adj. anat. Nabel...; **om·pha·lo·cele** [ˈɒmfələʊsiːl] s. ⚕ Nabelbruch m.

om·pha·los [ˈɒmfələs] pl. **-li** [-laɪ] s. **1.** anat. Nabel m (a. fig. Mittelpunkt); **2.** antiq. Schildbuckel m.

on [ɒn; ən] **I** prp. **1.** mst auf (dat. od. acc.): siehe die mit **on** verbundenen Wörter; **2.** Lage: a) (getragen von): auf (dat.), an (dat.), in (dat.): **~ board** an Bord; **~ earth** auf Erden; **the scar ~ the face** die Narbe im Gesicht; **~ foot** zu Fuß; **~ all fours** auf allen vieren; **~ the radio** im Radio; **have you a match ~ you?** haben Sie ein Streichholz bei sich?, b) (festgemacht od. unmittelbar) an (dat.): **~ the chain**; **~ the Thames**; **~ the wall**; **3.** Richtung, Ziel: auf (acc.) ... (hin) (od. los), nach ... (hin), an (acc.), zu: **a blow ~ the chin** ein Schlag ans Kinn; **throw s.o. ~ the floor** j-n od. et. zu Boden werfen; **4.** fig. a) Grund: auf ... (hin): **~ his authority**; **~ suspicion**; **levy a duty ~ silk** einen Zoll auf Seide erheben; **~ his own theory** nach s-r eigenen Theorie; **~ these conditions** unter diesen Bedingungen, b) Aufeinanderfolge: auf (acc.), über (acc.), nach: **loss ~ loss** Verlust auf od. über Verlust, ein Verlust nach dem andern, c) gehörig zu, beschäftigt bei, an (dat.): **~ a committee** in e-m Ausschuss gehörend; **be ~ the Stock Exchange** an der Börse (beschäftigt) sein, d) Zustand: in, auf (dat.), zu: **~ duty** im Dienst; **~ fire** in Brand; **~ leave** auf Urlaub; **~ sale** verˈkäuflich, e) gerichtet auf (acc.): **an attack ~**; **~ business** geschäftlich; **a joke ~ me** ein Spaß auf m-e Kosten; **shut (open) the door ~ s.o.** j-m die Tür verschließen (öffnen); **have s.th. ~ s.o.** sl. et. Belastendes über j-n wissen; **have nothing ~ s.o.** sl. j-m nichts anhaben können, a. j-m nichts vorauszuhaben; **this is ~ me** F das geht auf m-e Rechnung; **be ~ a pill** e-e Pille (ständig) nehmen, f) Thema: über (acc.): **agreement** (**lecture, opinion**) **~**; **talk ~ a subject**; **5.** Zeitpunkt: an (dat.): **~ Sunday**; **~ the 1st of April**; **~ or before April 1st** bis zum 1. April; **~ his arrival** bei od. (gleich) nach seiner Ankunft; **~ being asked** als ich etc. (danach) gefragt wurde; **~ entering** beim Eintritt; **II** adv. **6.** (a. Zssgn mit vb.) daˈrauf (legen, schrauben etc.); **7.** bsd. Kleidung: a) an(-haben, -ziehen): **have (put) a coat ~**, b) auf: **keep one's hat ~**; **8.** (a. in Zssgn mit vb.) weiter(-gehen, -sprechen etc.): **and so ~** und so weiter; **~ and ~** immer weiter; **~ and off** a) ab u. zu, b) ab u. an, mit Unterbrechungen; **from that day ~** von dem Tage an; **~ with the show!** weiter im Programm!; **~ to ...** auf (acc.) ... (hinauf od. hinaus); **III** adj. pred. **9. be ~** a) im Gange sein (Spiel etc.), vor sich gehen: **what's ~?** was ist los?; **have you anything ~ tomorrow?** haben Sie morgen et. vor?; **that's not ~!** das ist nicht ˈdrin`!, b) an sein (Licht, Radio, Wasser etc.), an-, geschaltet sein, laufen; auf sein (Hahn): **~-off** ⊖ An – Aus, c) thea. gegeben werden, laufen (*Film*), *Radio*, *TV*: gesendet werden, d) d(a)ran (*an der Reihe*) sein, e) (mit) dabei sein, mitmachen; **10.** *be* **~** *to* *sl. et.* ‚spitzgekriegt' haben, über j-n *od. et.* im Bilde sein; *he is always* **~** *at me* er ‚bearbeitet' mich ständig (*about* wegen); **11.** *sl.* beschwipst: *be a bit* **~** e-n Schwips haben.

o·nan·ism ['əʊnənɪzəm] *s.* ⚕ **1.** Coitus *m* inter'ruptus; **2.** Ona'nie *f.*

'on·board *adj.* ✈ bordeigen, Bord...: **~** *computer*.

once [wʌns] **I** *adv.* **1.** einmal: **~** *again* (*od. more*) noch einmal; **~** *and again* (*od.* **~** *or twice*) einige Male, ab u. zu; **~** *in a while* (*od. way*) zuweilen, hin u. wieder; **~** (*and*) *for all* ein für alle Mal; *if* **~** *he should suspect* wenn er erst einmal misstrauisch würde; *not* **~** kein einziges Mal; **2.** einmal, einst: **~** (*upon a time*) *there was* es war einmal (*Märchenanfang*); **II** *s.* **3.** *every* **~** *in a while* von Zeit zu Zeit; *for* **~**, *this* **~** dieses 'eine Mal, (für) diesmal (*ausnahmsweise*); **4.** *at* **~** a) auf einmal, zugleich, gleichzeitig: *don't all speak at* **~**; *at* **~** *a soldier and a poet* Soldat u. Dichter zugleich, b) sogleich, sofort: *all at* **~** plötzlich, mit 'einem Male; **III** *cj.* **5.** *a.* **~** *that* so'bald *od.* wenn ... (einmal), wenn erst; **'-o·ver** *s.* F *give s.o. od. s.th. the* **~** a) j-n kurz mustern *od.* ab-schätzen, (sich) j-n *od. et.* (rasch) mal ansehen, b) j-n ‚in die Mache' nehmen.

'on·com·ing *adj.* **1.** (her'an)nahend, entgegenkommend: **~** *traffic* Gegen-verkehr *m*; **2.** *fig.* kommend: *the* **~** *generation*.

one [wʌn] **I** *adj.* **1.** ein (eine, ein): **~** *hundred* (ein)hundert; **~** *man in ten* jeder Zehnte; **~** *or two* ein paar, einige; **2.** (*betont*) ein (eine, ein), ein einziger ... (eine einzige ..., ein einziges ...): *all were of* **~** *mind* sie waren alle 'eines Sinnes; *for* **~** *thing* (zunächst) einmal; *his* **~** *thought* sein einziger Gedanke; *the* **~** *way to do it* die einzige Möglich-keit (es zu tun); **3.** ein gewisser (e-e ge-wisse, ein gewisses), ein (eine, ein): **~** *day* e-s Tages (*in Zukunft od. Vergan-genheit*); **~** *of these days* irgendwann (ein)mal; **~** *John Smith* ein gewisser J. S.; **II** *s.* **4.** Eins *f*, eins: *Roman* **~** römi-sche Eins; **~** *and a half* ein(und)ein-halb, anderthalb; *at* **~** *o'clock* um ein Uhr; **5.** *der* (*die*) *einzelne..., das einzel-ne* (*Stück*): **~** *by* **~**, **~** *after another* e-r nach dem andern, einzeln; *I for* **~** ich zum Beispiel; **6.** Einheit *f*: *be at* **~** *with s.o.* mit j-m 'einer Meinung *od.* einig sein; **~** *and all* alle miteinander; *all in* **~** alles in 'einem; *it is all* **~** (*to me*) es ist (mir) ganz einerlei; *be made* **~** ein (*Ehe*)Paar werden; *make* **~** mit von der Partie sein; **7.** *bsd.* Ein'dollar- *od.* Ein'pfundnote *f*; **III** *pron.* **8.** ein, einer, jemand: *like* **~** *dead* wie ein Toter; **~** *of the poets* einer der Dichter; **~** *another* einander; **~** *who* einer, der; *the* **~** *who* der(jenige), der; **~** *of these days* die-ser Tage; **~** *in the eye* F *fig.* ein Denk-zettel; **9.** (*Stützwort, mst unübersetzt*): *a sly* **~** ein (ganz) Schlauer; *the little* **~***s* die Kleinen; *a red pencil and a blue* **~** ein roter Bleistift u. ein blauer; *that* **~** der (die, das) da *od.* dort; *the* **~***s you mention* die (von Ihnen) Erwähnten; → *each etc.*; **10.** man: **~** *knows*; **11.** **~'***s* sein: *break* **~'***s leg* sich das Bein brechen; *take* **~'***s walk* s-n Spazier-gang machen; **'~-act play** *s.* *thea.* Einakter *m*; **,~-'armed** *adj.* einarmig: **~** *bandit* F Spielautomat *m*; **'~-crop**

sys·tem *s.* ✏ 'Monokul,tur *f*; **,~-'dig·it** *adj.* ✦ einstellig (*Zahl*); **,~-'eyed** *adj.* einäugig; **,~-'hand·ed** *adj.* **1.** einhän-dig; **2.** mit nur 'einer Hand zu bedie-nen(d); **,~-'horse** *adj.* **1.** einspännig; **2.** **~** *town* F (elendes) ‚Kaff' *n od.* ‚Nest' *n*; **,~-'legged** [-'legd] *adj.* **1.** einbeinig; **2.** *fig.* einseitig; **'~-line busi·ness** *s.* ✝ Fachgeschäft *n*; **,~-'man** *adj.* Ein-mann...: **~** *business* ✝ Einzelunter-nehmen *n*; **~** *bus* Einmannbus *m*; **~** *show* a) One-Man-Show *f* (*a. fig.*), b) Ausstellung *f* der Werke 'eines Künst-lers.

one·ness ['wʌnɪs] *s.* **1.** Einheit *f*; **2.** Gleichheit *f*, Identi'tät *f*; **3.** Einigkeit *f*, (völliger) Einklang.

'one|-night stand *s.* **1.** *thea.* einmaliges Gastspiel; **2.** Sex *m* für 'eine Nacht; **,~-'off** F *bsd. Brit.* **I** *adj.* einmalig: **~** *production* Einzelfertigung *f*; **II** *s.*: **~** *a.* et. Einmaliges, e-e Ausnahme (-erscheinung); *she's a* **~** *a.* sie ist einzigartig; **,~-'par·ent** *adj.*: **~** *family* Einelternfamilie *f*; **,~-'per·son** *adj.* Einpersonen...: **~** *household* Single-haushalt *m*; **,~-'piece** *adj.* **1.** einteilig: **~** *bathing-suit*; **2.** ⚙ aus 'einem Stück, Voll...; **,~-'price shop** *s.* Einheitspreis-laden *m*.

on·er ['wʌnə] *s.* **1.** *sl.* ‚Ka'none' *f* (*Kön-ner*) (*at* in *dat.*); **2.** *sl.* ‚Mordsding' *n* (*bsd. wuchtiger Schlag*).

on·er·ous ['ɒnərəs] *adj.* □ lästig, drü-ckend, beschwerlich (*to* für); **'on·er·ous·ness** [-nɪs] *s.* Beschwerlichkeit *f*, Last *f*.

one'self *pron.* **1.** *refl.* sich (selber): *by* **~** aus eigener Kraft, von selbst; **2.** selbst, selber; **3.** *mst one's self* man (selbst *od.* selber).

,one|-'shot F *Am.* **I** *adj.* **1.** einmalig (*nur einmal möglich*); **2.** auf Anhieb gefun-den (*Lösung etc.*); **II** *s.* **3.** et. Einmaliges *n*: a) einmalige Angelegenheit, b) ein-malige Veröffentlichung (*od.* Ausgabe), c) einmaliger Auftritt (*e-s Schauspielers etc.*); **4.** *Film:* Nahaufnahme *f* e-s Dar-stellers; **,~-'sid·ed** [-'saɪdɪd] *adj.* □ ein-seitig (*a. fig.*); **'~-time** *I adj.* einst-, ehe-malig; **II** *adv.* einst-, ehemals; **'~-track** *adj.* **1.** 🚃 eingleisig; **2.** *fig.* einseitig: *you have a* **~** *mind* du hast immer nur das-selbe im Kopf; **,~-'two** *s.* **1.** *Fußball:* Doppelpass *m*; **2.** *Boxen:* Rechts-'links--Kombinati,on *f*; **'~-up·man·ship** [wʌn-'ʌpmənʃɪp] *s.* die Kunst, dem andern immer (um eine Nasenlänge) vor'aus zu sein; **,~-'way** *adj.* **1.** Einweg...(-*flasche etc.*), Einbahn...(-*straße*, -*verkehr*): **~** *ticket* *Am.* einfache Fahrkarte; **2.** *fig.* einseitig.

on·ion ['ʌnjən] *s.* **1.** ♀ Zwiebel *f*; **2.** *sl.* ‚Rübe' *f* (*Kopf*): *off one's* **~** *sl.* (total) verrückt; **3.** *know one's* **~***s* F sein Ge-schäft verstehen; **'~-skin** *s.* **1.** Zwiebel-schale *f*; **2.** 'Durchschlag- *od.* 'Luftpost-pa,pier *n*.

'on(-)line **I** *adj.* *Computer*: Online...: **~** *mode* Onlinebetrieb *m*; **II** *adv.* on-line: *go* **~** a) *Computer*: online *od.* auf Onlinebetrieb gehen, b) in Betrieb ge-hen, den Betrieb aufnehmen (*Fabrik etc.*); *order* **~** online bestellen; **~** *ser·vice pro·vid·er* *s.* *Internet*: Online-dienst *m*.

'on,look·er *s.* Zuschauer(in) (*at* bei); **'on,look·ing** *adj.* zuschauend.

on·ly ['əʊnlɪ] **I** *adj.* **1.** einzig, al'leinig: *the* **~** *son* der einzige Sohn; *my one and* **~** *hope* meine einzige Hoffnung; *the* **~** *begotten Son of God* Gottes eingeborener Sohn; **2.** einzigartig: *the*

~ *and only Mr. X* *a. iro.* der unver-gleichliche, einzigartige Mr. X; **II** *adv.* **3.** nur, bloß: *not* **~** *...*, *but* (*also*) nicht nur ..., sondern auch; *if* **~** wenn nur; **4.** erst: **~** *yesterday* erst gestern, gestern noch; **~** *just* eben erst, gerade, kaum; *she's* **~** *young* sie ist noch jung; **III** *cj.* **5.** je'doch, nur (dass), aber; **6.** **~** *that* nur, dass; außer, wenn.

,on-'off switch *s.* ⚡ Ein-Aus-Schalter *m*.

on·o·mat·o·poe·ia [,ɒnəʊmætəʊ'piːə] *s.* Lautmale'rei *f*; **,on·o·mat·o·'poe·ic** [-'piːɪk], **on·o·mat·o·po·et·ic** [,ɒnəʊ-mætəʊpəʊ'etɪk] *adj.* (□ *ally*) laut-nachahmend, onomatopo'etisch.

'on|-,po·si·tion *s.* ⚙ Einschaltstellung *f*, -zustand *m*; **'~-rush** *s.* Ansturm *m* (*a. fig.*); **'~-set** *s.* **1.** Angriff *m*, At'tacke *f*; **2.** Anfang *m*, Beginn *m*, Einsetzen *n*: *at the first* **~** gleich beim ersten An-lauf; **3.** ⚕ Ausbruch *m* (*e-r Krankheit*), Anfall *m*; **'~shore** *adj. u. adv.* **1.** land-wärts; **2.** a) in Küstennähe, b) an Land; **3.** ✝ Inlands...: **~** *purchases*; **'on-(-)site** *adj.* Vor-Ort- ...; **~-slaught** ['ɒnslɔːt] *s.* (heftiger) Angriff *od.* An-sturm (*a. fig.*); **,~-the-'job** *adj.* prak-tisch: **~** *training*.

on·to ['ɒntʊ; -tə] *prp.* **1.** auf (*acc.*); **2.** *be* **~** *s.th.* *sl.* hinter et. gekommen sein; *he's* **~** *you* *sl.* er hat dich durchschaut.

on·to·gen·e·sis [,ɒntəʊ'dʒenɪsɪs] *s.* *biol.* Ontoge'nese *f*.

on·tol·o·gy [ɒn'tɒlədʒɪ] *s.* *phls.* Ontolo-'gie *f*.

o·nus ['əʊnəs] (*Lat.*) *s.* *nur sg.* **1.** *fig.* Last *f*, Verpflichtung *f*, Onus *m*; **2.** *a.* **~** *of proof*, **~** *probandi* 🏛 Beweislast *f*: *the* **~** *rests with him* die Beweislast trifft ihn.

on·ward ['ɒnwəd] **I** *adv.* vorwärts, wei-ter: *from the tenth century* **~** vom 10. Jahrhundert an; **II** *adj.* vorwärts schrei-tend, fortschreitend; **'on·wards** [-dz] → *onward* I.

on·yx ['ɒnɪks] *s.* **1.** *min.* Onyx *m*; **2.** ⚕ Nagelgeschwür *n* der Hornhaut, Onyx *m*.

o·o·blast ['əʊəblɑːst] *s.* *biol.* Eikeim *m*; **o·o·cyst** ['əʊəsɪst] *s.* Oo'zyste *f*.

oo·dles ['uːdlz] *s.* *pl.* F Unmengen *pl.*, ‚Haufen' *m*: *he has* **~** *of money* er hat Geld wie Heu.

oof [uːf] *s.* *Brit. sl.* ‚Kies' *m* (*Geld*).

oomph [ʊmf] *s.* *sl.* 'Sex-Ap'peal *m*.

o·o·sperm ['əʊəspɜːm] *s.* *biol.* befruch-tetes Ei *od.* befruchtete Eizelle, Zy'go-te *f*.

ooze [uːz] **I** *v/i.* **1.** ('durch-, aus-, ein)si-ckern (*through*, *out of*, *into*); ein-, hin-'durchdringen (*a. Licht etc.*): **~** *away* a) versickern, b) *fig.* (dahin)schwinden; **~** *out* a) entweichen (*Luft*, *Gas*), b) *fig.* durchsickern (*Geheimnis*); **~** *with sweat* von Schweiß triefen; **II** *v/t.* **2.** ausströmen, -schwitzen; **3.** *fig.* aus-strahlen, *iro.* triefen von; **III** *s.* **4.** ⚙ Lohbrühe *f*: **~** *leather* lohgares Leder; **5.** Schlick *m*, Schlamm(grund) *m*; **oo·zy** ['uːzɪ] *adj.* **1.** schlammig, schlick(er)ig; **2.** schleimig; **3.** feucht.

o·pac·i·ty [əʊ'pæsɪtɪ] *s.* **1.** 'Undurch-,sichtigkeit *f* (*a. fig.*); **2.** Dunkelheit *f* (*a. fig.*); **3.** *fig.* Borniertheit *f*; **4.** *phys.* ('Licht,)Undurch,lässigkeit *f*; **5.** Deck-fähigkeit *f* (*Farbe*).

o·pal ['əʊpl] *s.* *min.* O'pal *m*: **~** *blue* Opalblau *n*; **~** *glass* Opal-, Milchglas *n*; **~** *lamp* Opallampe *f*; **o·pal·esce** [,əʊpə'les] *v/i.* opalisieren, bunt schil-lern; **o·pal·es·cence** [,əʊpə'lesns] *s.* Opalisieren *n*, Schillern *n*; **o·pal·es-**

O

cent [ˌəʊpə'lesnt] *adj.* opalisierend, schillernd.

o·paque [əʊ'peɪk] *adj.* □ **1.** 'un,durchsichtig, o'pak: ~ *colo(u)r* Deckfarbe *f;* **2.** 'un,durchlässig (*to* für *Strahlen*): ~ *meal* ☢ Kontrastmahlzeit *f;* **3.** glanzlos, trüb; **4.** *fig.* a) unklar, dunkel, b) borniert, dumm; **o'paque·ness** [-nɪs] *s.* ('Licht)'Un,durchlässigkeit *f;* Deckkraft *f* (*Farben*).

op art [ɒp] *s. Kunst:* Op-Art *f.*

o·pen ['əʊpən] **I** *adj.* □ **1.** *allg.* offen (*z. B. Buch, Flasche,* ♞ *Kette,* ⚡ *Stromkreis,* ✕ *Stadt, Tür,* ⚕ *Wunde*); offen stehend, auf: ~ *prison* offenes Gefängnis; ~ *warfare* ✕ Bewegungskrieg *m;* **keep one's eyes** ~ *fig.* die Augen offen halten; → *arm¹* 1, *bowels* 1, *order* 5; **2.** zugänglich, frei, offen (*Gelände, Straße, Meer etc.*): ~ *field* freies Feld; ~ *spaces* öffentliche Plätze (*Parkanlagen etc.*); **3.** frei, bloß, offen (*Wagen etc.;* ⚡ *Motor*); → *lay open;* **4.** offen, eisfrei (*Wetter,* ⚓ *Hafen, Gewässer*); ⚓ klar (*Sicht*): ~ *winter* frostfreier Winter; **5.** ge-, eröffnet (*Laden, Theater etc.*), offen (*a. fig. to dat.*), öffentlich (*Sitzung, Versteigerung etc.*); (jedem) zugänglich: *a career ~ to talent;* ~ *competition* freier Wettbewerb; ~ *market* ✝ offener *od.* freier Markt; ~ *position* freie *od.* offene (*Arbeits*)Stelle; ~ *policy* a) ✝ Offenmarktpolitik *f,* b) *Versicherung:* Pauschalpolice *f;* ~ *scholarship Brit.* offenes Stipendium; ~ *for subscription* ✝ zur Zeichnung aufgelegt; *in ~ court* in öffentlicher Verhandlung, vor Gericht; **6.** (*to*) *fig.* der Kritik, dem Zweifel etc. ausgesetzt, unter'worfen: ~ *to question* anfechtbar; ~ *to temptation* anfällig gegen die Versuchung; *leave o.s. wide ~* (*to s.o.*) sich (j-m gegenüber) e-e (große) Blöße geben; **7.** zugänglich, aufgeschlossen (*to* für *od. dat.*): *an ~ mind; be ~ to conviction (an offer)* mit sich reden (handeln) lassen; *that is ~ to argument* darüber lässt sich streiten; **8.** offen(kundig), unverhüllt: ~ *contempt; an ~ secret* ein offenes Geheimnis; **9.** offen, freimütig: *an ~ character;* ~ *letter* offener Brief; *I will be ~ with you* ich will ganz offen mit dir reden; **10.** freigebig: *with an ~ hand; keep an ~house* ein offenes Haus führen, gastfrei sein; **11.** *fig.* unentschieden, offen (*Frage, Forderung, Kampf, Urteil etc.*); **12.** *fig.* frei (*ohne Verbote*): ~ *pattern* ⚖ ungeschütztes Muster; ~ *season* Jagd-, Fischzeit *f;* **13.** ✝ laufend (*Konto, Kredit, Rechnung*): ~ *cheque* Barscheck *m;* **14.** ⚙ durch-'brochen (*Gewebe, Handarbeit*); **15.** *ling.* offen (*Silbe, Vokal*): ~ *consonant* Reibelaut *m;* **16.** ♪ a) weit (*Lage, Satz*), b) leer (*Saite etc.*): ~ *note* Grundton *m;* **17.** *typ.* licht (*Satz*): ~ *type* Konturschrift *f;* **II** *s.* **18.** *the ~* a) offenes Land, b) offene See: *in the ~* im Freien, unter freiem Himmel; ✕ über Tag; *bring into the ~ fig.* an die Öffentlichkeit bringen; *come into the ~ fig.* sich erklären, offen reden, Farbe bekennen, (*with s.th.* mit et.) an die Öffentlichkeit treten; **19.** *the* ⚘ *bsd. Golf:* offenes Turnier *für Amateure u. Berufsspieler;* **III** *v/t.* **20.** *allg.* öffnen, aufmachen; *Buch a.* aufschlagen; ⚡ *Stromkreis* ausschalten, unter'brechen: ~ *the bowels* ☢ den Leib öffnen; ~ *s.o.'s eyes fig.* j-m die Augen öffnen; → *throttle* 2; **21.** *fig.* Aussicht, ✝ Akkreditiv, *Debatte,* ✕ *das Feuer,* ✝ *Konto,*

Geschäft, ⚖ *die Verhandlung etc.* eröffnen; *Verhandlungen* anknüpfen, in *Verhandlungen* eintreten; ✝ *neue Märkte* erschließen: ~ *s.th. to traffic* e-e Straße *etc.* dem Verkehr übergeben; **22.** *fig. Gefühle, Gedanken* enthüllen, *s-e Absichten* entdecken: ~ *o.s. to s.o.* sich j-m mitteilen; → *heart Redew.;* **IV** *v/i.* **23.** sich öffnen *od.* auftun, aufgehen; *fig.* sich *dem Auge, Geist etc.* erschließen, zeigen, auftun; **24.** führen, gehen (*Tür, Fenster*) (*on to* auf *acc., into* nach *dat.*); **25.** *fig.* a) anfangen, beginnen (*Schule, Börse etc.*), öffnen, aufmachen (*Laden etc.*), b) (e-n Brief, s-e Rede) beginnen (*with* mit e-m Kompliment *etc.*); **26.** *allg.* öffnen; (ein Buch) aufschlagen; ~ *out* **I** *v/t.* **1.** *et.* ausbreiten, -dehnen, sich erweitern; **3.** *mot.* Vollgas geben; ~ *up* **I** *v/t.* **1.** *Land,* ✝ *Markt etc.* erschließen; **II** *v/i.* **2.** ✕ das Feuer eröffnen; **3.** *fig.* a) ,loslegen' (*mit Worten, Schlägen etc.*), b) ,auftauen', mitteilsam werden: ~ *to s.o.* sich j-m gegenüber öffnen; **4.** sich auftun *od.* zeigen.

o·pen·|·ac·cess li·brar·y *s.* 'Freihandbiblio,thek *f;* ,~-'air *adj.* Freilicht..., Freiluft..., unter freiem Himmel: ~ *swimming pool* Freibad *n;* ,~-and--'shut *adj.* ganz einfach, sonnenklar; ,~-'armed *adj.* warm, herzlich (*Empfang*); '~-cast min·ing *s.* Tagebau *m;* ,~-'door *adj.* ✝ *politics* (*Handels*)Politik *f* der offenen Tür; ,~--'end·ed *adj.* **1.** zeitlich unbegrenzt: ~ *discussion* Open-'End-Diskussion *f;* **2.** ausbaufähig: ~ *program*(*me*).

o·pen·er ['əʊpnə] *s.* **1.** (*fig.* Er)Öffner (-in); **2.** (*Büchsen- etc.*)Öffner *m; sport etc.* Eröffnung(sspiel *n, thea.* -nummer *f*) *f.*

o·pen·|·eyed *adj.* **1.** mit großen Augen, staunend; **2.** wachsam; ,~-'hand·ed *adj.* □ freigebig; ,~-'heart *adj.:* ~ *surgery* ☢ Offenherzchirurgie *f;* ,~-'heart·ed *adj.* □ offen(herzig), aufrichtig; ,~--'hearth *adj.* ⚙ Siemens-Martin-(-*Ofen,* -*Stahl*).

o·pen·ing ['əʊpnɪŋ] **I** *s.* **1.** *das* Öffnen; Eröffnung *f* (*a. fig. Akkreditiv, Konto, Testament, Unternehmen*); *fig.* Inbetriebnahme *f* (*e-r Anlage etc.*); *fig.* Erschließung *f* (*Land,* ✝ *Markt*); **2.** Öffnung *f,* Loch *n,* Lücke *f,* Bresche *f,* Spalt *m,* 'Durchlass *m;* **3.** *Am.* (Wald-) Lichtung *f;* **4.** ⚙ (Spann)Weite *f;* **5.** *fig.* Eröffnung *f* (*a. Schach, Kampf etc.*), Beginn *m,* einleitender Teil (*a.* ⚖); (*of the*) *stock market* Börsenbeginn *m;* **6.** Gelegenheit *f,* (✝ Absatz)Möglichkeit *f;* **7.** ✝ offene *od.* freie Stelle; **II** *adj.* **8.** Öffnungs...; **9.** Eröffnungs...: ~ *speech;* ~ *price* ✝ Eröffnungskurs *m;* ~ *night thea.* Eröffnungsvorstellung *f.*

o·pen·|·mar·ket *adj.* Freimarkt...: ~ *paper* marktgängiges Wertpapier; ~ *policy* Offenmarktpolitik *f;* ,~-'mind·ed *adj.* □ aufgeschlossen, vorurteilslos; ,~-'mouthed *adj.* mit offenem Mund, *fig. a.* gaffend; '~-plan of·fice *s.* 'Großraumbü,ro *n;* ,~-'ses·a·me *s.* Sesam-'öffne-dich *n;* ~ *shop s. Am.* Betrieb, der auch Nichtgewerkschaftsmitglieder beschäftigt; ⚘ **U·ni·ver·si·ty** *s.* 'Fernsehuniversi,tät *f,* 'Telekol,leg *n;* '~-work *s.* 'Durchbrucharbeit *f* (*Handarbeit*); ~ **work·ing** *s.* ✕ Tagebau *m.*

op·er·a¹ ['ɒpərə] *s.* Oper *f* (*a. Gebäude*): *comic ~* komische Oper; *grand ~* große Oper.

op·er·a² ['ɒpərə] *pl. von* **opus.**

op·er·a·ble ['ɒpərəbl] *adj.* **1.** 'durchführbar; **2.** ⚙ betriebsfähig; **3.** ☢ ope-'rabel.

op·er·a|cloak *s.* Abendmantel *m;* ~ **glass**(·**es** *pl.*) *s.* Opern-, The'aterglas *n;* ~ **hat** *s.* 'Klappzy,linder *m,* Chapeau 'claque *m;* ~ **house** *s.* Opernhaus *n,* Oper *f;* ~ **pump** *s. Am.* glatter Pumps.

op·er·ate ['ɒpəreɪt] **I** *v/i.* **1.** arbeiten, in Betrieb sein, funktionieren, laufen (*Maschine etc.*): *be operating* in Betrieb sein; ~ *on batteries* von Batterien betrieben werden; ~ *at a deficit* ✝ mit Verlust arbeiten; **2.** wirksam werden *od.* sein, (ein)wirken (*on, upon* auf *acc., as* als), hinwirken (*for* auf *acc.*); **3.** ☢ (*on, upon*) j-n operieren: *be ~d on* operiert werden; **4.** ✝ F spekulieren, operieren: ~ *for a fall* auf e-e Baisse spekulieren; **5.** ✕ operieren; **II** *v/t.* **6.** bewirken, verursachen, (mit sich) bringen; **7.** ⚙ *Maschine* laufen lassen, bedienen, *Gerät* handhaben, *Schalter, Bremse etc.* betätigen, *Auto* fahren: *safe to ~* betriebssicher; **8.** *Unternehmen, Geschäft* betreiben, führen, *Vorhaben* ausführen.

op·er·at·ic [ˌɒpə'rætɪk] *adj.* (□ ~**ally**) opernhaft (*a. fig. contp.*), Opern...: ~ *performance* Opernaufführung *f;* ~ *singer* Opernsänger(in).

op·er·at·ing ['ɒpəreɪtɪŋ] *adj.* **1.** *bsd.* ⚙ in Betrieb befindlich, Betriebs..., Arbeits...: ~ *conditions* Betriebsbedingungen; ~ *instructions* Bedienungsvorschrift *f,* Betriebsanweisung *f;* ~ *lever* Betätigungshebel *m;* ~ *system* Computer: Betriebssystem *n;* **2.** ✝ Betriebs..., betrieblich: ~ *assets* Vermögenswerte; ~ *costs* (*od. expenses*) Betriebs-, Geschäfts(un)kosten; ~ *profit* Betriebsgewinn *m;* ~ *statement* Betriebsbilanz *f;* **3.** ☢ operierend, Operations...: ~ *room od.* ~ *theatre* (*Am. theater*) Operationssaal *m;* ~ *surgeon* → *operator* 4; ~ *table* Operationstisch *m.*

op·er·a·tion [ˌɒpə'reɪʃn] *s.* **1.** Wirken *n,* Wirkung *f* (*on* auf *acc.*); **2.** *bsd.* ⚖ Wirksamkeit *f,* Geltung *f:* **by ~ of law** kraft Gesetzes; *come into ~* in Kraft treten; **3.** ⚙ Betrieb *m,* Tätigkeit *f,* Lauf *m* (*Maschine etc.*): *in ~* in Betrieb; *put* (*od. set*) *in* (*out of*) ~ in (außer) Betrieb setzen; **4.** *bsd.* ⚙ Wirkungs-, Arbeitsweise *f;* Arbeits(vor)gang *m,* (*Arbeits-, Denk- etc. a. chemischer*) Pro'zess *m;* **5.** ⚙ Inbetriebsetzung *f,* Bedienung *f* (*Maschine, Gerät*), Betätigung *f* (*Bremse, Schalter*); **6.** Arbeit *f:* **building** ~**s** Bauarbeiten; **7.** ✝ a) Betrieb *m:* *continuous* ~ durchgehender Betrieb; *in* ~ a) in Betrieb, b) Unter'nehmen *n,* -'nehmung *f,* c) Geschäft *n:* **trading** ~ Tauschgeschäft; **8.** *Börse:* Transakti'on *f;* **9.** ☢ Operati'on *f,* (chirurgischer) Eingriff: ~ *for appendicitis* Blinddarmoperation; ~ *to* (*od. on*) *the neck* Halsoperation; *major* ~ a) größere Operation, b) *fig.* F große Sache, ,schwere Geburt'; **10.** ✕ Operati'on *f,* Einsatz *m,* Unter'nehmung *f;* **op·er·a·tion·al** [-ʃənl] *adj.* **1.** ⚙ a) Betriebs..., Arbeits..., b) betriebsbereit, -fähig; **2.** ✝ betrieblich, Betriebs...; **3.** ✕ Einsatz..., Operations..., einsatzfähig: ~ *objective* Operationsziel *n;* **4.** ⚓ klar, fahrbereit; **op·er·a·tive** ['ɒpərətɪv] **I** *adj.* □ **1.** wirkend, treibend: *an ~ motive;* **2.** wirksam: *an ~ dose; become ~* ⚖ (rechts)wirksam werden, in Kraft treten; *the ~ word* das Wort, auf das es ankommt, ⚖ *a.* das rechtsbegründende Wort; **3.** praktisch; **4.** ✞, ⊚ Arbeits..., Betriebs..., betriebsfähig; **5.** ⚕ opera'tiv, chir'urgisch: ～ **dentistry** Zahn- u. Kieferchirurgie f; **6.** arbeitend, tätig, beschäftigt; **II** s. **7.** (Fach)Arbeiter m, Me'chaniker m; → **operator** 2; **8.** Am. Pri'vatdetek-,tiv(in); **op·er·a·tor** ['ɒpəreɪtə] s. **1.** der (die, das) Wirkende; **2.** a) ⊚ Bedienungsperson f, Arbeiter(in), (Kran etc.)Führer m: **engine** ～ Maschinist m; ～**'s license** Am. Führerschein m, b) Telegra'fist(in), c) Telefo'nist(in), d) (Film)Vorführer m, a. Kameramann m; **3.** ✞ a) Unter'nehmer m, b) Börse: (berufsmäßiger) Speku'lant, b.s. Schieber m; **4.** ⚕ operierender Arzt, Opera'teur m; **5.** Computer: Ope'rator m.

o·per·cu·lum [əʊ'pɜːkjʊləm] pl. **-la** [-lə] s. **1.** ⚘ Deckel m; **2.** zo. a) Deckel m (Schnecken), b) Kiemendeckel m (Fische).

op·er·et·ta [,ɒpə'retə] s. Ope'rette f.

oph·thal·mi·a [ɒf'θælmɪə] s. ⚕ Bindehautentzündung f; **oph'thal·mic** [-ɪk] adj. Augen...; augenkrank: ～ **hospital** Augenklinik f; **oph·thal·mol·o·gist** [,ɒfθæl'mɒlədʒɪst] s. Augenarzt m, Augenärztin f; **oph·thal·mol·o·gy** [,ɒfθæl-'mɒlədʒɪ] s. Augenheilkunde f, Ophthalmolo'gie f; **oph·thal·mo·scope** [ɒf'θælməskəʊp] s. ⚕ Augenspiegel m, Ophthalmo'skop n.

o·pi·ate ['əʊpɪət] **I** s. **1.** ⚕ Opi'at n, 'Opiumpräpa,rat n; **2.** Schlaf- od. Beruhigungs- od. Betäubungsmittel n (a. fig.): ～ **for the people** Opium n fürs Volk; **II** adj. **3.** einschläfernd; betäubend (a. fig.).

o·pine [əʊ'paɪn] **I** v/i. da'fürhalten; **II** v/t. et. meinen.

o·pin·ion [ə'pɪnjən] s. **1.** Meinung f, Ansicht f, Stellungnahme f: **in my** ～ m-s Erachtens, nach m-r Meinung od. Ansicht; **be of (the)** ～ **that** der Meinung sein, dass; **that is a matter of** ～ das ist Ansichtssache f; **public** ～ die öffentliche Meinung; **2.** Achtung f, (gute) Meinung: **have a high (low** od. **poor)** ～ **of** e-e (keine) hohe Meinung haben von, (nicht) viel halten von; **she has no** ～ **of Frenchmen** sie hält nicht viel von (den) Franzosen; **3.** (schriftliches) Gutachten (**on** über acc.): **counsel's** ～ Rechtsgutachten f; **4.** mst pl. Über'zeugung f: **have the courage of one's** ～**s** zu s-r Überzeugung stehen; **5.** ⚖ (Urteils)Begründung f; **o·pin·ion·at·ed** [-neɪtɪd] adj. **1.** starr-, eigensinnig; dog'matisch; **2.** schulmeisterlich, über'heblich.

o·pin·ion|-,form·ing adj. meinungsbildend; ～ **form·er,** ～ **lead·er,** ～**-,mak·er** s. Meinungsbildner m; ～ **poll** s. 'Meinungsumfrage f; ～ **poll·ster** s. Meinungsforscher(in); ～ **re·search** s. Meinungsforschung f.

o·pi·um ['əʊpjəm] s. Opium n: ～ **eater** Opiumesser m; ～ **poppy** ⚘ Schlafmohn m; **'o·pi·um·ism** [-mɪzəm] s. ⚕ **1.** Opiumsucht f; **2.** Opiumvergiftung f.

o·pos·sum [ə'pɒsəm] s. zo. O'possum n, Beutelratte f.

op·po·nent [ə'pəʊnənt] **I** adj. entgegenstehend, -gesetzt, gegnerisch (**to** dat.); **II** s. Gegner(in) (a. ⚖, sport), Gegenspieler(in), 'Widersacher(in), Oppo'nent(in).

op·por·tune [,ɒpə'tjuːn] adj. □ **1.** günstig, passend, gut angebracht, opportun'; **2.** rechtzeitig: **'op·por·tune·ness** [-nɪs] s. Opportuni'tät f, Rechtzeitigkeit

f; günstiger Zeitpunkt.

op·por·tun·ism [,ɒpə'tjuːnɪzm] s. Opportu'nismus m; **op·por'tun·ist** [-ɪst] s. Opportu'nist(in).

op·por·tu·ni·ty [,ɒpə'tjuːnətɪ] s. (günstige) Gelegenheit, Möglichkeit f (**of** doing, **to do** zu tun; **for s.th.** zu et.): **miss the** ～ die Gelegenheit verpassen; **seize** (od. **take) an** ～ e-e Gelegenheit ergreifen; **at the first** ～ bei der ersten Gelegenheit; ～ **for advancement** Aufstiegsmöglichkeit; ～ **makes the thief** Gelegenheit macht Diebe.

op·pose [ə'pəʊz] v/t. **1.** (vergleichend) gegen'überstellen; **2.** entgegensetzen, -stellen (**to** dat.); **3.** entgegentreten (dat.), sich wider'setzen (dat.); angehen gegen, bekämpfen; **4.** ⚖ Am. gegen e-e Patentanmeldung Einspruch erheben; **op'posed** [-zd] adj. **1.** gegensätzlich, entgegengesetzt (a. ⚘); **2.** (to) abgeneigt (dat.), feind (dat.), feindlich (gegen): **be** ～ **to** j-m od. e-r Sache feindlich od. ablehnend gegenüberstehen, gegen j-n od. et. sein; **3.** ⊚ Gegen...: ～ **piston engine** Gegenkolben-, Boxermotor m; **op'pos·ing** [-zɪŋ] adj. **1.** gegen'überliegend; **2.** opponierend, gegnerisch; **3.** fig. entgegengesetzt, unvereinbar.

op·po·site ['ɒpəzɪt] **I** adj. □ **1.** gegen-'überliegend, -stehend (**to** dat.): ～ **angle** ⚘ Gegen-, Scheitelwinkel m; **2.** entgegengesetzt (gerichtet), 'umgekehrt: ～ **directions;** ～ **signs** ⚘ entgegengesetzte Vorzeichen; **of** ～ **sign** ⚘ ungleichnamig; ～ **pistons** ⊚ gegenläufige Kolben; **3.** gegensätzlich, entgegengesetzt, gegenteilig, (grund)verschieden, ander: **words of** ～ **meaning;** **4.** gegnerisch, Gegen...: ～ **side** sport Gegenpartei f, gegnerische Mannschaft; ～ **number** sport, pol. etc. Gegenspieler(in), ,Gegenüber' n, weitS. ,Kollege' m, ,Kollegin' f (von der anderen Seite); **5.** ⚘ Gegen... (Blätter); **II** s. **6.** Gegenteil n (a. ⚘), -satz m: **just the** ～ das genaue Gegenteil; **III** adv. **7.** gegen'über; **IV** prp. **8.** gegen'über (dat.): **the** ～ **house; play** ～ **X.** sport, Film etc. (der, die) Gegenspieler(in) von X sein.

op·po·si·tion [,ɒpə'zɪʃn] s. **1.** Gegen-'überstellung f; das Gegen'überstehen od. -liegen; ⊚ Gegenläufigkeit f; **2.** 'Widerstand m (**to** gegen): **offer** ～ (**to**) Widerstand leisten (gegen); **meet with** (od. **face) stiff** ～ auf heftigen Widerstand stoßen; **3.** Gegensatz m, 'Widerspruch m: **act in** ～ **to** zuwiderhandeln (dat.); **4.** pol. (a. ast. u. fig.) Opposition f; **5.** ✞ Konkur'renz f; **6.** ⚖ a) 'Widerspruch m, b) Am. Einspruch m (**to** gegen e-e Patentanmeldung); **7.** Logik: Gegensatz m; **,op·po'si·tion·al** [-ʃənl] adj. **1.** pol. oppositio'nell, Oppositions..., regierungsfeindlich; **2.** gegensätzlich, Widerstands...

op·press [ə'pres] v/t. **1.** seelisch bedrücken; **2.** unter'drücken, tyrannisieren, schikanieren; **op'pres·sion** [-eʃn] s. **1.** Unter'drückung f, Tyrannisierung f; ⚖ a) Schi'kane(n pl.) f, b) 'Missbrauch m der Amtsgewalt; **2.** Druck m, Bedrängnis f, Not f; **3.** Bedrücktheit f; **4.** ⚕ Beklemmung f; **op'pres·sive** [-sɪv] adj. □ **1.** seelisch (be)drückend; **2.** ty'rannisch, grausam, hart; ⚖ schika'nös; **3.** drückend (schwül); **op'pres·sive·ness** [-sɪvnɪs] s. **1.** Druck m; **2.** Schwere f, Schwüle f; **op'pres·sor** [-sə] s. Unter'drücker m, Ty'rann m.

op·pro·bri·ous [ə'prəʊbrɪəs] adj. □ **1.** schmähend, Schmäh...; **2.** schändlich,

in'fam; **op'pro·bri·um** [-ɪəm] s. Schmach f, Schande f.

op·pugn [ɒ'pjuːn] v/t. anfechten.

opt [ɒpt] v/i. wählen (**between** zwischen dat.), sich entscheiden (**for** für, **against** gegen), bsd. pol. optieren (**for** für); ～ **in** a) sich dafür entscheiden, b) mitmachen, c) beitreten; ～ **out** a) sich dagegen entscheiden, b) ,aussteigen' (**of** aus der Gesellschaft, e-r Unternehmung etc.), austreten (**of** aus), c) Versicherung etc. kündigen (**of** acc.); **op·ta·tive** ['ɒptətɪv] **I** adj. Wunsch..., ling. optativ(isch): ～ **mood** → **II** s. ling. Optativ m, Wunschform f.

op·tic ['ɒptɪk] **I** adj. **1.** Augen..., Seh..., Gesichts...: ～ **angle** Seh-, Gesichtswinkel m; ～ **axis** a) optische Achse, b) Sehachse f; ～ **nerve** Sehnerv m; **2.** → **optical; II** s. **3.** mst pl. humor. Auge n; **4.** pl. sg. konstr. phys. Optik f, Lichtlehre f; **'op·ti·cal** [-kl] adj. □ optisch: ～ **illusion** optische Täuschung; ～ **microscope** Lichtmikroskop n; ～ **viewfinder** TV optischer Sucher; **op·ti·cian** [ɒp'tɪʃn] s. Optiker(in).

op·ti·mal ['ɒptɪml] → **optimum** II.

op·ti·mism ['ɒptɪmɪzəm] s. Opti'mismus m; **'op·ti·mist** [-ɪst] s. Opti'mist(in); **op·ti·mis·tic** [,ɒptɪ'mɪstɪk] adj. (□ ～**al·ly**) opti'mistisch.

op·ti·mize ['ɒptɪmaɪz] v/t. ✞, ⊚ optimieren.

op·ti·mum ['ɒptɪməm] **I** pl. **-ma** [-mə] s. **1.** Optimum n, günstigster Fall, Bestfall m; **2.** ✞, ⊚ Bestwert m; **II** adj. **3.** opti'mal, günstigst, best.

op·tion ['ɒpʃn] s. **1.** Wahlfreiheit f, freie Wahl od. Entscheidung: ～ **of a fine** Recht n, e-e Geldstrafe (an Stelle der Haft) zu wählen; **2.** Wahl f: **at one's** ～ nach Wahl; **make one's** ～ s-e Wahl treffen; **3.** Alterna'tive f: **I had no** ～ **but to** ich hatte keine andere Wahl als; **4.** ✞ Opti'on f (a. Versicherung), Vorkaufsrecht n, Börse: Bezugsrecht n: **buyer's** ～ Kaufoption, Vorprämie f; ～ **for the call** (**the put**) Vor-(Rück-)prämiengeschäft n; ～ **rate** Prämiensatz m; ～ **of repurchase** Rückkaufsrecht n; **5.** ～**s** pl. Computer: Opti'onen pl; **op·tion·al** ['ɒpʃənl] adj. □ **1.** freigestellt, wahlfrei, freiwillig, fakulta'tiv: ～ **bonds** Am. kündbare Obligationen; ～ **extra(s)** Sonderausstattung f, ～ **subject** ped. Wahlfach n; **2.** ✞ Options...: ～ **bargain** Prämiengeschäft n.

'opt-out s. 'Opt-out n, Nichtbeteiligung f, Ausnahmeregelung f: ～ **clause** Rücktrittsklausel f.

op·u·lence ['ɒpjʊləns] s. Reichtum m, ('Über)Fülle f, 'Überfluss m: **live in** ～ im Überfluss leben; **'op·u·lent** [-nt] adj. □ **1.** (sehr) reich (a. fig.); **2.** üppig, opu'lent: ～ **meal.**

o·pus ['əʊpəs] pl. **op·er·a** ['ɒpərə] (Lat.) s. (einzelnes) Werk, Opus n; → **magnum opus; o·pus·cule** [ɒ'pʌskjuːl] s. ♪, lit. kleines Werk.

or¹ [ɔː] cj. **1.** oder: ～ **else** sonst, andernfalls; **one** ～ **two** ein bis zwei, einige; **2.** (nach neg.) noch, und kein, und auch nicht.

or² [ɔː] s. her. Gold n, Gelb n.

or·a·cle ['ɒrəkl] **I** s. **1.** O'rakel(spruch m) n; fig. a. Weissagung f: **work the** ～ F e-e Sache ,drehen'; **2.** fig. o'rakelhafter Ausspruch; **3.** fig. Pro'phet(in), unfehlbare Autori'tät; **II** v/t. u. v/i. **4.** o'rakeln; **o·rac·u·lar** [ɒ'rækjʊlə] adj. □ **1.** o'rakelhaft (a. fig.), Orakel...; **2.** fig. weise.

o·ra·cy ['ɔːrəsɪ] s. ped. Sprachgewandtheit *f.*

o·ral [ˈɔːrəl] **I** *adj.* □ **1.** mündlich: ~ **contract**; ~ **examination**; **2.** ⚕ o'ral (*a.* *ling.*), Mund...: **for ~ use** zum innerlichen Gebrauch; ~ **intercourse** Oralverkehr *m*; ~ **stage** *psych.* orale Phase; **II** *s.* **3.** F mündliche Prüfung.

or·ange [ˈɒrɪndʒ] **I** *s.* ♀ O'range *f*, Apfel'sine *f*: **bitter** ~ Pomeranze *f*; **squeeze the ~ dry** F j-n ausquetschen wie e-e Zitrone; **II** *adj.* Orangen...; o'range (-farben); ~ **lead** [led] *s.* ⚙ O'rangemennige *f*, Bleisafran *m*; ~ **peel** *s.* **1.** O'rangenschale *f*; **2.** *a.* ~ **effect** ⚙ O'rangenschalenstruk,tur *f* (*Lackierung*).

or·ange·ry [ˈɒrɪndʒərɪ] *s.* Orange'rie *f.*

o·rang-ou·tang [ɔːˌræŋuːˈtæŋ], **o,rang-u'tan** [-uːˈtæn] *s.* *zo.* 'Orang-'Utan *m.*

o·rate [ɔːˈreɪt] *v/i.* **1.** e-e Rede halten; **2.** *humor. od.* ,schwingen'. (lange) Reden halten *od.* ,schwingen', reden; **o·ra·tion** [-ˈeɪʃn] *s.* **1.** *förmliche od. feierliche* Rede; **2.** *ling.* (*direkte etc.*) Rede *f*; **or·a·tor** [ˈɒrətə] *s.* **1.** Redner(in); **2.** ⚖ *Am.* Kläger(in) (*in equity-Prozessen*); **or·a·tor·i·cal** [ˌɒrəˈtɒrɪkl] *adj.* □ rednerisch, Redner..., ora'torisch, rhe'torisch, Rede...; **or·a·to·ri·o** [ˌɒrəˈtɔːrɪəʊ] *pl.* **-ri·os** *s.* ♪ Ora'torium *n*; **or·a·tor·ize** [ˈɒrətəraɪz] → **orate** 2; **or·a·to·ry** [ˈɒrətərɪ] *s.* **1.** Redekunst *f*, Beredsamkeit *f*, Rhe'torik *f*; **2.** *eccl.* Ka'pelle *f*, Andachtsraum *m.*

orb [ɔːb] **I** *s.* **1.** Kugel *f*, Ball *m*; **2.** *poet.* Gestirn *n*, Himmelskörper *m*; **3.** *poet.* a) Augapfel *m*, b) Auge *n*; **4.** *hist.* Reichsapfel *m*; **or·bic·u·lar** [ɔːˈbɪkjʊlə] *adj.* □ **1.** kugelförmig; **2.** rund, kreisförmig; **3.** ringförmig; **or·bit** [ˈɔːbɪt] **I** *s.* **1.** (*ast. etc.* Kreis-, *phys.* Elek'tronen-) Bahn *f*: **get into** ~ in e-e Umlaufbahn gelangen (*Erdsatellit*); **put into** ~ → 5; **2.** *fig.* Bereich *m*, Wirkungskreis *m*; *pol.* Einflusssphäre *f*; **3.** *anat.* a) Augenhöhle *f*, b) Auge *n*; **II** *v/t.* **4.** *die Erde etc.* um'kreisen; **5.** in e-e 'Umlaufbahn bringen; **III** *v/i.* **6.** die Erde *etc.* um'kreisen; **7.** ✈ (über dem Flugplatz) kreisen; **'or·bit·al** [-bɪtl] **I** *adj.* **1.** *anat.* Augenhöhlen...: ~ **cavity** Augenhöhle *f*; **2.** *ast.*, *phys.* Bahn...: ~ **electron**; **II** *s.* **3.** *Brit.* Ringstraße *f.*

or·chard [ˈɔːtʃəd] *s.* Obstgarten *m*; 'Obstplan,tage *f*: **in** ~ mit Obstbäumen bepflanzt; **'or·chard·ing** [-dɪŋ] *s.* **1.** Obstbau *m*; **2.** *coll. Am.* 'Obstkul,turen *pl.*

or·ches·tic [ɔːˈkestɪk] **I** *adj.* Tanz...; **II** *s.* *pl.* Or'chestik *f.*

or·ches·tra [ˈɔːkɪstrə] *s.* **1.** ♪ Or'chester *n*; **2.** *thea.* a) Or'chester(raum *m*, -graben *m*) *n*, b) Par'terre *n*, c) *a.* ~ **stalls** Par'kett *n*; **or·ches·tral** [ɔːˈkestrəl] *adj.* ♪ **1.** Orchester...; **2.** orche'stral; **or·ches·trate** [-reɪt] *v/t.* **1.** *a. v/i.* ♪ orchestrieren, instrumentieren; **2.** *fig. Am.* ordnen, aufbauen; **or·ches·tra·tion** [ˌɔːkeˈstreɪʃn] *s.* Instrumentati'on *f.*

or·chid [ˈɔːkɪd] *s.* ♀ Orchi'dee *f.*

or·chis [ˈɔːkɪs] *pl.* **'or·chis·es** *s.* ♀ **1.** Orchi'dee *f*; **2.** Knabenkraut *n.*

or·dain [ɔːˈdeɪn] *v/t.* **1.** *eccl.* ordinieren, (*zum Priester*) weihen; **2.** bestimmen, fügen (*Gott, Schicksal*); **3.** anordnen, verfügen.

or·deal [ɔːˈdiːl] *s.* **1.** *hist.* Gottesurteil *n*: ~ **by fire** Feuerprobe *f*; **2.** *fig.* Zerreiß-, Feuerprobe *f*, schwere Prüfung; **3.** *fig.* Qual *f*, Nervenprobe *f*, Tor'tur *f*, Mar'tyrium *m.*

or·der [ˈɔːdə] **I** *s.* **1.** Ordnung *f*, geordneter Zustand: **love of** ~ Ordnungsliebe *f*;

in ~ in Ordnung (*a. fig.*); **out of** ~ in Unordnung; → 8; **2.** (öffentliche) Ordnung: **law and** ~ Ruhe *f* u. Ordnung; **3.** Ordnung *f* (*a.* ♀ *Kategorie*), Sy'stem *n*: **social** ~ soziale Ordnung; **4.** (An)Ordnung *f*, Reihenfolge *f*; *ling.* (Satz)Stellung *f*, Wortfolge *f*: **in alphabetical** ~ in alphabetischer Ordnung; ~ **of priority** Dringlichkeitsfolge *f*; ~ **of merit** (*od.* **precedence**) Rangordnung; **5.** Ordnung *f*, Aufstellung *f*; △ Stil *m*: **in close** (**open**) ~ ✕ in geschlossener (geöffneter) Ordnung; ~ **of battle** a) ✕ Schlachtordnung, Gefechtsaufstellung, b) ⚓ Gefechtsformation *f*; **Doric** ~ △ dorische Säulenordnung; **6.** ✕ vorschriftsmäßige Uni'form u. Ausrüstung; → **marching**; **7.** (Geschäfts-) Ordnung *f*: **standing** ~**s** *parl.* feststehende Geschäftsordnung; **a call to** ~ ein Ordnungsruf *m*; **call to** ~ zur Ordnung rufen; **rise to** (**a point of**) ~ zur Geschäftsordnung sprechen; **~!**, **~!** zur Ordnung!; **in** (**out of**) ~ (un)zulässig; ~ **of the day** Tagesordnung; → 9; **be the ~ of the day** *fig.* an der Tagesordnung sein; **pass to the ~ of the day** zur Tagesordnung übergehen; → **rule** 15; **8.** Zustand *m*: **in bad** ~ nicht in Ordnung, in schlechtem Zustand; **out of** ~ nicht in Ordnung, defekt; **in running** ~ betriebsfähig; **9.** Befehl *m*, Instrukti'on *f*, Anordnung *f*: ⚷ **in Council** *pol.* Kabinettsbefehl; ~ **of the day** ✕ Tagesbefehl; ~ **for remittance** Überweisungsauftrag *m*; **doctor's** ~**s** ärztliche Anordnung; **by** ~ a) befehls-, auftragsgemäß, b) im Auftrag (*vor der Unterschrift*); **by** (*od.* **on the**) ~ **of** auf Befehl von, im Auftrag von; **be under** ~**s to do s.th.** Befehl haben, et. zu tun; **till further** ~**s** bis auf weiteres; **in short** ~ *Am.* F sofort; **10.** ⚖ (Gerichts)Beschluss *m*, Befehl *m*, Verfügung *f*; **11.** ♣ Bestellung *f* (*a. Ware*), Auftrag *m* (**for** für): **a large** (**tall**) ~ F e-e (arge) Zumutung, (zu) viel verlangt; ~**s on hand** Auftragsbestand *m*; **give** (*od.* **place**) **an** ~ e-n Auftrag erteilen, e-e Bestellung aufgeben; **make to** ~ a) auf Bestellung anfertigen, b) nach Maß anfertigen; **shoes made to** ~ Maßschuhe; **last ~s, please** Polizeistunde!; **12.** ♣ Order *f* (*Zahlungsauftrag*): **pay to s.o.'s** ~ an j-s Order zahlen; **pay to the ~ of** für mich an ... (*Wechselindossament*); **payable to** ~ zahlbar an Order; **own** ~ eigene Order; **13.** → **post-office order, postal I**; **14.** ♣ Ordnung *f*, Grad *m*: **equation of the first** ~ Gleichung *f* ersten Grades; **15.** Größenordnung *f*: **of** (*od.* **in**) **the** ~ **of** in der Größenordnung von; **16.** Art *f*, Rang *m*: **of a high** ~ von hohem Rang; **of quite another** ~ von ganz anderer Art; **on the** ~ **of** nach Art von; **17.** (Gesellschafts)Schicht *f*, Klasse *f*, Stand *m*: **the higher** ~**s** die höheren Klassen; **the military** ~ *Am.* der Soldatenstand; **18.** Orden *m* (*Gemeinschaft*): **the Franciscan** ~ *eccl.* der Franziskanerorden; **the Teutonic** ~ *hist.* der Deutsche (*Ritter-*) Orden; **19.** Orden(szeichen *n*) *m*; → **Garter** 2; **20.** *pl. mst holy* ~**s** *eccl.* (heilige) Weihen, Priesterweihe *f*: **take** (**holy**) ~**s** die (heiligen) Weihen empfangen; **major** ~**s** höhere Weihen; **21.** Einlassschein *m*, *thea.* Freikarte *f*. **22.** **in** ~ **to** *inf.* um zu *inf.*; **in** ~ **that** damit; **II** *v/t.* **23.** j-m *od.* e-e *Sache* befehlen, *et.* anordnen: **he** ~**ed him to come** er befahl ihm zu kommen; **24.** j-n schicken, beordern (**to** nach); **25.** ⚕ j-m et.

verordnen; **26.** bestellen (*a.* ⚕; *a. im Restaurant*); **27.** regeln, leiten, (führen) **28.** ~ **arms!** ✕ Gewehr ab!; **29.** ordnen, einrichten: ~ **one's affairs** s-e Angelegenheiten in Ordnung bringen; ~ **a·bout** v/t. her'umkommandieren; ~ **a·way** v/t. **1.** weg-, fortschicken; **2.** abführen lassen; ~ **back** v/t. zu'rückbeordern; ~ **in** v/t. her'einkommen lassen; ~ **off** v/t. *sport* vom Platz stellen; ~ **out** v/t. **1.** hin'ausbeordern; **2.** hin'ausweisen.

or·der| bill *s.* ♣ 'Orderpa,pier *n*; ~ **bill of lad·ing** *s.* ♣, ⚙ 'Orderkonnosse-,ment *n*; ~ **book** *s.* ♣ **1.** ♣ Auftragsbuch *n*; **2.** *Brit. parl.* Liste *f* der angemeldeten Anträge; ~ **check** *Am.*, ~ **cheque** *Brit.* ♣ Orderscheck *m*; ~ **form** *s.* ♣ Bestellschein *m*, ~ **in·stru·ment** *s.* ♣ 'Orderpa,pier *n.*

or·der·less [ˈɔːdəlɪs] *adj.* unordentlich, regellos; **'or·der·li·ness** [-lɪnɪs] *s.* **1.** Ordnung *f*, Regelmäßigkeit *f*; **2.** Ordentlichkeit *f.*

or·der·ly [ˈɔːdəlɪ] **I** *adj.* **1.** ordentlich, (wohl) geordnet; **2.** plan-, regelmäßig, me'thodisch; **3.** *fig.* ruhig, friedlich: **an** ~ **citizen**; **4.** ✕ a) im *od.* vom Dienst, Dienst tuend, b) Ordonnanz...: **on** ~ **du·ty** auf Ordonnanz; **II** *adv.* **5.** ordnungsgemäß, planmäßig; **III** *s.* **6.** ✕ a) Or-don'nanz *f*, b) Sani'täter *m*, Krankenträger *m*, c) (Offi'ziers)Bursche *m*; **7.** *allg.* (Kranken)Pfleger *m*; ~ **of·fi·cer** *s.* ✕ **1.** Ordon'nanzoffi,zier *m*; **2.** Offi-'zier *m* vom Dienst; ~ **room** *s.* ✕ Schreibstube *f.*

or·der| num·ber *s.* ♣ Bestellnummer *f*; ~ **pad** *s.* ♣ Bestell(schein)block *m*; ~ **pa·per** *s.* **1.** 'Sitzungspro,gramm *n*, (*schriftliche*) Tagesordnung *f*; **2.** ♣ *Am.* 'Orderpa,pier *n*; ~ **proc·ess·ing** *s.* Auftragsabwicklung *f*; ~ **slip** *s.* ♣ Bestellzettel *m.*

or·di·nal [ˈɔːdɪnl] **I** *adj.* **1.** ♀ Ordnungs..., Ordinal...: ~ **number**; **2.** ♀, *zo.* Ordnungs...; **II** *s.* **3.** ♀ Ordnungszahl *f*; **4.** *eccl.* a) Ordi'nale *n* (*Regelbuch für die Ordinierung anglikanischer Geistlicher*), b) *oft* ⚷ Ordi'narium *n* (*Ritualbuch od. Gottesdienstordnung*).

or·di·nance [ˈɔːdɪnəns] *s.* **1.** *amtliche* Verordnung; **2.** *eccl.* (festgesetzter) Brauch, Ritus *m.*

or·di·nand [ˌɔːdɪˈnænd] *s. eccl.* Ordi-'nandus *m.*

or·di·nar·i·ly [ˈɔːdnrɪlɪ] *adv.* **1.** nor'malerweise, gewöhnlich; **2.** wie gewöhnlich *od.* üblich.

or·di·nar·y [ˈɔːdnrɪ] **I** *adj.* □ → **ordinarily**; **1.** gewöhnlich, nor'mal, üblich; **2.** gewöhnlich, mittelmäßig, Durchschnitts...: ~ **face** Alltagsgesicht *n*; **3.** ständig; ordentlich (*Gericht, Mitglied*); **II** *s.* **4.** *das* Übliche, *das* Nor'male: **nothing out of the** ~ nichts Ungewöhnliches; **above the** ~ außergewöhnlich; **5.** **in** ~ ordentlich, von Amts wegen; **judge in** ~ ordentlicher Richter; **physician in** ~ (*to a king*) Leibarzt *m* (e-s Königs); **6.** *eccl.* Ordi'narium *n*, Gottesdienst-, Messordnung *f*; **7.** *a.* ⚷ *eccl.* Ordi'narius *m* (*Bischof*); **8.** ⚖ a) ordentlicher Richter, b) *Am.* Nachlassrichter *m*; **9.** *Brit. obs.* a) Hausmannskost *f*, b) Tagesgericht *n*; **10.** *Brit. obs.* Gaststätte *f*; ~ **life in·sur·ance** *s.* Lebensversicherung *f* auf den Todesfall; ~ **sea·man** *s.* [*irr.*] 'Leichtma,trose *m*; ~ **share** *s.* ♣ Stammaktie *f.*

or·di·nate [ˈɔːdnət] *s.* ♀ Ordi'nate *f.*

or·di·na·tion [ˌɔːdɪˈneɪʃn] *s.* **1.** *eccl.* Priesterweihe *f*, Ordinati'on *f*; **2.** Ratschluss *m* (*Gottes etc.*).

ord·nance ['ɔːdnəns] s. ✕ **1.** Artille'rie f, Geschütze pl.: **a piece of ~** ein (schweres) Geschütz; **~ technician** Feuerwerker m; **2.** 'Feldzeugmateri,al n; **3.** Feldzeugwesen n: **Royal Army ⚹ Corps** Feldzeugkorps n des brit. Heeres; **⚹ De·part·ment** ✕ Zeug-, Waffenamt n; **~ de·pot** s. ✕ 'Feldzeug-, bsd. Artille'riede,pot n; **~ map** s. **1.** Am. Gene'ralstabskarte f; **2.** Brit. Messtischblatt n; **~ of·fi·cer** s. **1.** ⚓ Am. Artille'rieoffi,zier m; **2.** Offi'zier m der Feldzeugtruppe; **3.** 'Waffenoffi,zier m; **~ park** s. ✕ a) Geschützpark m, b) Feldzeugpark m; **~ ser·geant** s. ✕ 'Waffen-, Ge'räte,unteroffi,zier m; **⚹ Sur·vey** s. amtliche Landesvermessung: **⚹ map** Brit. a) Messtischblatt n, b) (1:100 000) Generalstabskarte f.

or·dure ['ɔː,djʊə] s. Kot m, Schmutz m, Unflat m (a. fig.).

ore [ɔː] s. **1.** Erz n; **2.** poet. (kostbares) Me'tall; **'~-,bear·ing** adj. geol. Erz führend, erzhaltig; **~ bed** s. Erzlager n.

or·gan ['ɔːgən] s. **1.** Or'gan n: a) anat. Körperwerkzeug n: **~ donor** Organspender m; **~ transplant** Organverpflanzung f; **~ of sight** Sehorgan, b) fig. Werkzeug n, Hilfsmittel n, c) Sprachrohr n (Zeitschrift): **party ~** Parteiorgan, d) laute etc. Stimme; **2.** ♪ a) Orgel f: **~ stop** Orgelregister n, b) Kla'vier n (e-r Orgel), c) a. **American ~** Art Har'monium n, d) → **barrel organ**; **'~- -grinder** Leier(kasten)mann m.

or·gan·die, or·gan·dy ['ɔːgəndɪ] s. Or'gandy m (Baumwollgewebe).

or·gan·ic [ɔːˈɡænɪk] adj. (☐ **~ally**) allg. **1.** or'ganisch; **2.** bio'logisch-or'ganisch, F Bio...: **~ vegetables**; **chem·is·try** s. or'ganische Che'mie; **~ dis·ease** s. ✚ or'ganische Krankheit; **~ e·lec·tric·i·ty** s. zo. tierische Elektrizi'tät; **~ farm·er** s. Ökobauer m; **~ food** s. Biokost f; **~ law** s. pol. Grundgesetz n; **~ waste** s. Biomüll m.

or·gan·ism ['ɔːgənɪzəm] s. biol. u. fig. Orga'nismus m.

or·gan·ist ['ɔːgənɪst] s. ♪ Orga'nist(in).

or·gan·i·za·tion [,ɔːgənaɪˈzeɪʃn] s. **1.** Organisati'on f: a) Organisierung f, Bildung f, Gründung f, b) (syste'matischer) Aufbau, Gliederung f, (Aus)Gestaltung f, c) Zs.-schluss m, Verband m, Gesellschaft f: **administrative ~** Verwaltungsapparat m; **2.** Orga'nismus m, Sy'stem n; **,or·gan·i·za·tion·al** [-ʃənl] adj. organisa'torisch; **or·gan·ize** ['ɔːgənaɪz] I v/t. **1.** organisieren: a) aufbauen, einrichten: **~d crime** (die) organisierte Kriminali'tät, das organisierte Verbrechen, b) gründen, ins Leben rufen, veranstalten, sport a. ausrichten: **~d tour** Gesellschaftsreise f, d) gestalten; **2.** in ein Sy'stem bringen; **3.** (gewerkschaftlich) organisieren: **~d la·bo(u)r**; II v/i. **4.** sich organisieren; **or·gan·iz·er** ['ɔːgənaɪzə] s. **1.** Organi'sator m, Veranstalter m, sport a. Ausrichter m; **2.** ⚖ Gründer m; **3.** a. **personal ~ Computer:** Organizer m: a) elek'tronisches Notizbuch, b) Programm für Termin- u. Adressverwaltung.

or·gan loft s. △ Orgelchor m.

or·gan·zine ['ɔːgənziːn] s. Organ'sin (-seide f) m, n.

or·gasm ['ɔːgæzəm] s. physiol. **1.** Or'gasmus m, (sexu'eller) Höhepunkt; **2.** heftige Erregung; **or·gi·as·tic** [,ɔːdʒɪˈæstɪk] adj. orgi'astisch; **or·gy** ['ɔːdʒɪ] s. Orgie f.

o·ri·el ['ɔːrɪəl] s. △ Erker m.

o·ri·ent ['ɔːrɪənt] I s. **1.** Osten m; **2. the ⚹**

---

der (Ferne) Osten, der Orient; II adj. **3.** aufgehend (Sonne); **4.** östlich; **5.** glänzend; III v/t. [-ɪent] **6.** orientieren, die Lage od. die Richtung bestimmen von, orten; Landkarte einnorden; Instrument einstellen; Kirche osten; **7.** fig. geistig (aus)richten, orientieren (**by** an dat.): **profit-~ed** gewinnorientiert; **8. ~ o.s.** sich orientieren (**by** an dat.), sich zu'rechtfinden, sich informieren; **o·ri·en·tal** [,ɔːrɪˈentl] I adj. **1.** östlich; **2.** mst ⚹ orien'talisch, bsd. Am. a. 'ostasi,atisch, östlich; II s. **3.** Orien'tale m, Orien'talin f, bsd. Am. a. 'Ostasi,at(in); **o·ri·en·tal·ist** [,ɔːrɪˈentəlɪst] s. Orienta'list(in); **o·ri·en·tate** ['ɔːrɪenteɪt] → **orient** 6, 7, 8; **o·ri·en·ta·tion** [,ɔːrɪenˈteɪʃn] s. **1.** △ Ostung f (Kirche); **2.** Anlage f, Richtung f; **3.** Orientierung f (a. 🧭 u. fig.), Ortung f; Ausrichtung f (a. fig.); **4.** a. fig. Orientierung f, (Sich)Zu'rechtfinden n: **~ course** Einführungskurs m; **5.** Orientierungssinn m; **or·i·en·teer·ing** [,ɔːrɪenˈtiːrɪŋ] s. Orientierungslauf m.

or·i·fice ['ɒrɪfɪs] s. Öffnung f (a. anat., ⚙), Mündung f.

or·i·flamme ['ɒrɪflæm] s. Banner n, Fahne f; fig. Fa'nal n.

or·i·gin ['ɒrɪdʒɪn] s. **1.** Ursprung f: a) Quelle f, b) fig. Herkunft f, Abstammung f: **certificate of ~** ✝ Ursprungszeugnis n; **country of ~** ✝ Ursprungsland n, c) Anfang m, Entstehung f: **the ~ of species** der Ursprung der Arten; **2.** ⅋ Koordi'natenursprung m, -nullpunkt m.

o·rig·i·nal [əˈrɪdʒənl] I adj. ☐ → **originally**; **1.** origi'nal, Original..., Ur..., ursprünglich, echt: **the ~ text** der Urod. Originaltext; **2.** erst, ursprünglich, Ur...: **~ bill** ✝ Am. **~ capital** ✝ Gründungskapital n; **~ copy** Erstausfertigung f; **~ cost** ✝ Selbstkosten pl.; **~ inhabitants** Ureinwohner; **~ jurisdiction** ⚖ erstinstanzliche Zuständigkeit; **~ share** ✝ Stammaktie f; **~ sin** 1; **3.** origi'nell, neu(artig); **an ~ idea**; **4.** schöpferisch, ursprünglich: **~ genius** Originalgenie n, Schöpfergeist m; **~ thinker** selbstständiger Geist; **~ nature** Urnatur f; II s. **6.** Origi'nal n: a) Urbild n, -stück n, b) Urfassung f, -text m: **in the ~** im Original, im Urtext, ⚖ urschriftlich; **7.** Origi'nal n (Mensch); **8.** ♀, zo. Stammform f; **o·rig·i·nal·i·ty** [əˈrɪdʒəˈnælətɪ] s. **1.** Originali'tät f: a) Ursprünglichkeit f, Echtheit f, b) Eigenart f, origi'neller Cha'rakter, c) Neuheit f; **2.** das Schöpferische; **o·rig·i·nal·ly** [-dʒənəlɪ] adv. **1.** ursprünglich, zu'erst; **2.** hauptsächlich, eigentlich; **3.** von Anfang an, schon immer; **4.** origi'nell.

o·rig·i·nate [əˈrɪdʒəneɪt] I v/i. **1.** (**from**) entstehen (aus), s-n Ursprung haben (in dat.), herrühren (von od. aus); **2.** (**with, from**) ausgehen (von j-m); II v/t. **3.** her'vorbringen, verursachen, erzeugen, schaffen, den Anfang machen mit, den Grund legen zu; **o·rig·i·na·tion** [ə,rɪdʒəˈneɪʃn] s. **1.** Her'vorbringung f, Schaffung f, Veranlassung f; **2.** → **origin** 1 b u. c; **o·rig·i·na·tive** [-tɪv] adj. schöpferisch; **o·rig·i·na·tor** [-tə] s. Urheber(in), Begründer(in), Schöpfer(in).

o·ri·ole ['ɔːrɪəʊl] s. orn. Pi'rol m.

or·mo·lu ['ɔːməʊluː] s. a) Malergold n, b) Goldbronze f.

or·na·ment I s. ['ɔːnəmənt] Orna'ment n, Verzierung f, Schmuck m; fig. Zier (-de) f (**to** für od. gen.): **rich in ~** reich verziert; II v/t. [-ment] verzieren, schmü-

---

cken; **or·na·men·tal** [,ɔːnəˈmentl] adj. ☐ ornamen'tal, schmückend, dekora'tiv, Zier...: **~ castings** ⚙ Kunstguss m; **~ plants** Zierpflanzen; **~ type** Zierschrift f; **or·na·men·ta·tion** [,ɔːnəmenˈteɪʃn] s. Ornamentierung f, Verzierung f.

or·nate [ɔːˈneɪt] adj. ☐ **1.** reich verziert; **2.** über'laden (Stil etc.); blumig (Sprache).

or·ni·tho·log·i·cal [,ɔːnɪθəˈlɒdʒɪkl] adj. ☐ ornitho'logisch; **or·ni·thol·o·gist** [,ɔːnɪˈθɒlədʒɪst] s. Ornitho'loge m; **or·ni·thol·o·gy** [,ɔːnɪˈθɒlədʒɪ] s. Ornitho'lo'gie f, Vogelkunde f; **or·ni·thop·ter** [,ɔːnɪˈθɒptə] s. ✈ Schwingenflügler m; **,or·ni·tho'rhyn·chus** [-əˈrɪŋkəs] s. zo. Schnabeltier m.

o·rol·o·gy [ɒˈrɒlədʒɪ] s. Gebirgskunde f.

o·ro·pha·ryn·ge·al [ˈɔːrəʊˌfærɪnˈdʒiːəl] adj. ✚ Mund-Rachen-...

o·ro·tund ['ɔːrəʊtʌnd] adj. **1.** volltönend; **2.** bom'bastisch (Stil).

or·phan ['ɔːfn] I s. **1.** (Voll)Waise f, Waisenkind n: **~s' home** → **orphanage** 1; II adj. **2.** Waisen...: **an ~ child**; III v/t. **3.** zur Waise machen: **be ~ed** (zur) Waise werden, verwaisen; **or·phan·age** ['ɔːfənɪdʒ] s. **1.** Waisenheim n, -haus n; **2.** Verwaistheit f; **or·phan·ize** ['ɔːfnaɪz] v/t. → **orphan** 3.

or·rer·y ['ɒrərɪ] s. Plane'tarium n.

or·tho·chro·mat·ic [,ɔːθəʊkrəʊˈmætɪk] adj. phot. orthochro'matisch, farb(wert)richtig.

or·tho·don·ti·a [,ɔːθəʊˈdɒnʃɪə] s. ✚ 'Kieferorthopä,die f.

or·tho·dox ['ɔːθədɒks] adj. ☐ **1.** eccl. ortho'dox: a) streng-, recht-, altgläubig, b) ⚹ 'griechisch-ortho'dox: ⚹ **Church**; **2.** fig. ortho'dox: a) streng: **an ~ opinion**, b) anerkannt, üblich, konventio'nell; **'or·tho·dox·y** [-ksɪ] s. eccl. Orthodo'xie f (a. fig. orthodoxes Denken).

or·thog·o·nal [ɔːˈθɒɡənl] adj. ⅋ ortho-go'nal, rechtwink(e)lig.

or·tho·graph·ic, or·tho·graph·i·cal [,ɔːθəʊˈɡræfɪk(l)] adj. ☐ **1.** ortho'graphisch; **2.** ⅋ senkrecht, rechtwink(e)lig; **or·thog·ra·phy** [ɔːˈθɒɡrəfɪ] s. Orthogra'phie f, Rechtschreibung f.

or·tho·p(a)e·dic [,ɔːθəʊˈpiːdɪk] adj. ✚ ortho'pädisch; **,or·tho'p(a)e·dics** [-ks] s. pl. oft sg. konstr. Orthopä'die f; **or·tho'p(a)e·dist** [-ɪst] s. Ortho'päde m; **or·tho·p(a)e·dy** ['ɔːθəʊpiːdɪ] → **orthop(a)edics**.

or·thop·ter [ɔːˈθɒptə] s. **1.** ✈ → **ornithopter**; **2.** → **or'thop·ter·on** [-ərɒn] s. zo. Geradflügler m.

or·tho·scope ['ɔːθəʊskəʊp] s. ✚ Ortho'skop n.

Os·car ['ɒskə] s. Oskar m (Filmpreis).

os·cil·late ['ɒsɪleɪt] I v/i. **1.** oszillieren, schwingen, pendeln, vibrieren: **oscillating axle** mot. Schwingachse f; **oscillating circuit** ⚡ Schwingkreis m; **2.** fig. (hin- u. her) schwanken; II v/t. **3.** in Schwingungen versetzen; **os·cil·la·tion** [,ɒsɪˈleɪʃn] s. **1.** Oszillati'on f, Schwingung f, Pendelbewegung f, Schwankung f; **2.** fig. Schwanken n; **3.** ⚡ a) Ladungswechsel m, b) Stoßspannung f, c) Peri'ode f; **'os·cil·la·tor** [-tə] s. ⚡ Oszil'lator m; **'os·cil·la·to·ry** [-lətərɪ] adj. oszilla'torisch, schwingend, schwingungsfähig: **~ circuit** ⚡ Schwingkreis m; **os·cil·lo·graph** [əˈsɪləʊɡrɑːf] s. Oszillo'graph m; **os·cil·lo·scope** [əˈsɪləʊskəʊp] s. phys., ⚡ Oszillo'skop n.

os·cu·late ['ɒskjʊleɪt] v/t. u. v/i. **1.** humor. (sich) küssen; **2.** ⅋ oskulieren.

o·sier ['əʊʒə] s. ♀ Korbweide f: **~ bas-**

ket Weidenkorb *m*; ~ *furniture* Korb-möbel *pl*.

os·mic ['ɒzmɪk] *adj.* 🜊 Osmium...

os·mo·sis [ɒz'məʊsɪs] *s. phys.* Os'mose *f*; **os·mot·ic** [ɒz'mɒtɪk] *adj.* (□ ~*ally*) os'motisch.

os·prey ['ɒsprɪ] *s.* **1.** *orn.* Fischadler *m*; **2.** † Reiherfederbusch *m*.

os·se·in ['ɒsiɪn] *s. biol.*, 🜊 Knochenleim *m*.

os·se·ous ['ɒsiəs] *adj.* knöchern, Knochen...; **os·si·cle** ['ɒsɪkl] *s. anat.* Knöchelchen *n*; **os·si·fi·ca·tion** [,ɒsɪfɪ-'keɪʃn] Verknöcherung *f*; **os·si·fied** ['ɒsɪfaɪd] *adj.* verknöchert (*a. fig.*); **os·si·fy** ['ɒsɪfaɪ] I *v/t.* **1.** verknöchern (lassen); **2.** *fig.* verknöchern; (*in Konventionen*) erstarren lassen; II *v/i.* **3.** verknöchern; **4.** *fig.* verknöchern, (*in Konventi'onen*) erstarren; **os·su·ar·y** ['ɒsjʊərɪ] *s.* Beinhaus *n*.

os·te·i·tis [,ɒstɪ'aɪtɪs] *s.* 🩺 Knochenentzündung *f*.

os·ten·si·ble [ɒ'stensəbl] *adj.* □ **1.** scheinbar; **2.** an-, vorgeblich: ~ *partner* † Strohmann *m*.

os·ten·ta·tion [,ɒsten'teɪʃn] *s.* **1.** (prot-zige) Schaustellung; **2.** Protze'rei *f*, Prahle'rei *f*; **os·ten·ta·tious** [-ʃəs] *adj.* □ **1.** großtuerisch, prahlerisch, prunkend; **2.** (*absichtlich*) auffällig, ostenta'tiv, betont; **os·ten·ta·tious·ness** [-ʃəsnɪs] → *ostentation*.

os·te·o·ar·thri·tis [,ɒstɪəʊɑː'θraɪtɪs] *s.* 🩺 Arth'rose *f*; **os·te·o·blast** ['ɒstɪəʊblɑːst] *s. biol.* Knochenbildner *m*; **os·te·oc·la·sis** [,ɒstɪ'ɒkləsɪs] *s.* 🩺 (opera-'tive) 'Knochenfrak,tur; **os·te·ol·o·gy** [,ɒstɪ'ɒlədʒɪ] *s.* Knochenlehre *f*; **os·te·o·ma** [,ɒstɪ'əʊmə] *s.* 🩺 Oste'om *n*, gutartige Knochengeschwulst; **os·te·o·ma·la·ci·a** [,ɒstɪəʊmə'leɪʃɪə] *s.* 🩺 Knochenerweichung *f*; **'os·te·o·path** [-ɪəʊpæθ] *s.* 🩺 Osteo'path *m*.

ost·ler ['ɒslə] *s.* Stallknecht *m*.

os·tra·cism ['ɒstrəsɪzəm] *s.* **1.** *antiq.* Scherbengericht *n*; **2.** *fig.* a) Verbannung *f*, b) Ächtung *f*; **'os·tra·cize** [-saɪz] *v/t.* **1.** verbannen (*a. fig.*); **2.** *fig.* ächten, (*aus der Gesellschaft*) ausstoßen, verfemen.

os·trich ['ɒstrɪtʃ] *s. orn.* Strauß *m*; ~ **pol·i·cy** *s.* Vogel-'Strauß-Poli,tik *f*.

oth·er ['ʌðə] I *adj.* **1.** ander; **2.** (*vor s. im pl.*) andere, übrige: *the* ~ *guests*; **3.** ander, weiter, sonstig: *one* ~ *person* e-e weitere Person, (noch) j-d anders; **4.** anders (*than* als): *no person* ~ *than yourself* niemand außer dir; **5.** (*from, than*) anders (als), verschieden (von); **6.** zweit (*nur in*): *every* ~ jeder (jede, jedes) zweite ...; *every* ~ *day* jeden zweiten Tag; **7.** (*nur in*): *the* ~ *day* neulich, kürzlich; *the* ~ *night* neulich abends; II *pron.* **8.** ander: *the* ~ der (die, das) andere; *each* ~ einander; *the two* ~s die beiden anderen; *of all* ~s vor allen anderen; *no* (*od. none*) ~ *than* kein anderer als; *some day* (*od. time*) *or* ~ eines Tages, irgendeinmal; *some way or* ~ irgendwie, auf irgendeine Weise; *someone* I; III *adv.* **9.** anders (*than* als); '~**wise** [-waɪz] *adv.* **1.** (*a. cj.*) sonst, andernfalls; **2.** sonst, im Übrigen: *stupid but* ~ *harmless*; **3.** anderweitig: *occupied*; *unless you are* ~ *engaged* wenn du nichts anderes vorhast; **4.** anders (*than* als): *we think* ~ wir denken anders; *berries edible and* ~ essbare u. nicht essbare Beeren; ,~**'world** *adj.* jenseitig; ,~**'world·ly** *adj.* **1.** jenseitig, Jenseits...; **2.** auf das Jen-

seits gerichtet; **3.** weltfremd.

o·ti·ose ['əʊʃɪəʊs] *adj.* □ müßig: a) un-tätig, b) zwecklos.

o·to·lar·yn·gol·o·gist ['əʊtəʊˌlærɪŋ'gɒlə-dʒɪst] *s.* 🩺 Hals-Nasen-Ohren-Arzt *m*; **o·tol·o·gy** [əʊ'tɒlədʒɪ] *s.* Ohrenheil-kunde *f*, **o·to·rhi·no·lar·yn·gol·o·gist** ['əʊtəʊ,raɪnəʊ,lærɪŋ'gɒlədʒɪst] → *oto-laryngologist*; **o·to·scope** ['əʊtə-skəʊp] *s.* 🩺 Ohr(en)spiegel *m*.

ot·ter ['ɒtə] *s.* **1.** *zo.* Otter *m*; **2.** Otter-fell *n*, -pelz *m*; '~**hound** *s. hunt.* Otter-hund *m*.

Ot·to·man ['ɒtəʊmən] I *adj.* **1.** os'ma-nisch, türkisch; II *s. pl.* **-mans 2.** Os-'mane *m*, Türke *m*; **3.** 2 Otto'mane *f* (*Sofa*).

ouch [aʊtʃ] *int.* autsch!, au!

ought¹ [ɔːt] I *v/aux.* ich, er, sie, es sollte, du solltest, ihr solltet, wir, sie, Sie soll-ten: *he* ~ *to do it* er sollte es (eigent-lich) tun; *he* ~ (*not*) *to have seen it* er hätte es (nicht) sehen sollen; *you* ~ *to have known better* du hättest es bes-ser wissen sollen *od.* müssen; II *s.* (mo-'ralische) Pflicht.

ought² [ɔːt] *s.* Null *f*.

ought³ [ɔːt] → *aught*.

ounce¹ [aʊns] *s.* **1.** Unze *f* (*28,35 g*): *by the* ~ nach (dem) Gewicht; **2.** *fig. ein* bisschen, Körnchen *n* (*Wahrheit etc.*): *an* ~ *of practice is worth a pound of theory* Probieren geht über Studieren.

ounce² [aʊns] *s.* **1.** *zo.* Irbis *m* (*Schnee-leopard*); **2.** *poet.* Luchs *m*.

our ['aʊə] *poss. adj.* unser: 2 *Father* das Vaterunser; **ours** ['aʊəz] *poss. pron.* **1.** der (die, das) Uns(e)re: *I like* ~ *better* mir gefällt das Unsere besser; *a friend of* ~ ein Freund von uns; *this world of* ~ diese unsere Welt; ~ *is a small group* unsere Gruppe ist klein; **2.** unser, der (die, das) Uns(e)re: *it is* ~ es gehört uns, es ist unser; ,**our'self** *pron.*: *We* 2 Wir höchstselbst; **our'selves** *pron.* **1.** *refl.* uns (selbst): *we blame* ~ wir geben uns (selbst) die Schuld; **2.** (wir) selbst: *let us do it* ~; **3.** uns (selbst): *good for the others, not for* ~ gut für die andern, nicht für uns (selbst).

oust [aʊst] *v/t.* **1.** vertreiben, entfernen, verdrängen, hin'auswerfen (*from* aus): ~ *s.o. from office*, ~ *from the market* † vom Markt verdrängen; **2.** 🏛 enteig-nen, um den Besitz bringen; **3.** berau-ben (*of gen.*); **'oust·er** [-tə] *s.* 🏛 a) Enteignung *f*, b) Besitzvorenthaltung *f*.

out [aʊt] I *adv.* **1.** (*a. in Zssgn mit vb.*) hin'aus (*-gehen, -werfen etc.*), her'aus (*-kommen, -schauen etc.*), aus (*-bre-chen, -pumpen, -sterben etc.*): *voyage* ~ Ausreise *f*; *way* ~ Ausgang *m*; *on the way* ~ beim Hinausgehen; ~ *with him!* hinaus mit ihm!; ~ *with it!* hinaus *od.* heraus damit!; *have a tooth* ~ sich e-n Zahn ziehen lassen; *insure* ~ *and home* † hin u. zurück versichern; *have it* ~ *with s.o. fig.* die Sache mit j-m ausfechten; *that's* ~! das kommt nicht in Frage!; **2.** außen, draußen, fort: *some way* ~ ein Stück draußen; *he is* ~ er ist draußen; **3.** nicht zu Hau-se, ausgegangen: *be* ~ *on business* ge-schäftlich verreist sein; *a day* ~ ein freier Tag; *an evening* ~ ein Ausgeh-abend *m*; *be* ~ *on account of illness* wegen Krankheit der Arbeit fernblei-ben; **4.** ausständig (*Arbeiter*): *be* ~ streiken; **5.** a) ins Freie, b) draußen, im Freien, c) ⚓ draußen, auf See, d) ✕ im Felde; **6.** a) ausgeliehen (*Buch*), b) ver-liehen (*Geld*), c) verpachtet, vermietet, d) (*aus dem Gefängnis etc.*) entlassen;

7. her'aus *sein*: a) (*just*) ~ (soeben) er-schienen (*Buch*), b) in Blüte (*Blumen*), entfaltet (*Blüte*), c) ausgeschlüpft (*Kü-ken*), d) verrenkt (*Glied*), e) *fig.* ent-hüllt (*Geheimnis*): *the girl is not yet* ~ das Mädchen ist noch nicht in die Ge-sellschaft eingeführt (worden); → *blood* 3, *murder* 1; **8.** *sport* aus, drau-ßen: a) nicht (mehr) im Spiel, b) im Aus; **9.** *Boxen*: ausgezählt, kampfunfä-hig; **10.** *pol.* draußen, raus, nicht (mehr) im Amt, nicht (mehr) am Ru-der; **11.** *aus*, außer der Mode; **12.** aus, vor'bei (*zu Ende*): *before the week is* ~ vor Ende der Woche; **13.** aus, erlo-schen (*Feuer, Licht*); **14.** aus(gegan-gen), verbraucht: *the potatoes are* ~; **15.** aus der Übung: *my hand is* ~; **16.** zu Ende, bis zum Ende, ganz: *hear s.o.* ~ j-n bis zum Ende *od.* ganz anhören; **17.** ausgetreten, über die Ufer getreten (*Fluss*); **18.** löch(e)rig, 'durchgescheu-ert; → *elbow* 1; **19.** ärmer um *1 Dollar etc.*; **20.** unrichtig, im Irrtum (befan-gen): *his calculations are* ~ s-e Be-rechnungen stimmen nicht; *be* (*far*) ~ sich (gewaltig) irren, (ganz) auf dem Holzweg sein; **21.** entzweit, verkracht: *be* ~ *with s.o.*; **22.** laut: *laugh* ~ *laut lachen etc.*; **23.** ~ *for* auf e-e Sache aus, auf der Jagd *od.* Suche nach: ~ *for prey* auf Raub aus; **24.** ~ *to do s.th.* darauf aus, et. zu tun; **25.** (*bsd. nach sup.*) das Beste etc. weit u. breit; **26.** ~ *and about* (wieder) auf den Beinen; ~ *and away* bei weitem; ~ *and* ~ durch u. durch; ~ *of* → 31; II *adj.* **27.** Außen...; ~ *edge*; ~ *party* Opposi-tionspartei *f*; **28.** *sport* auswärtig, Aus-wärts... (*-spiel*); **29.** *Kricket*: nicht schlagend: ~ *side* → 34; **30.** 'übernor-,mal, Über...; ~ *outsize*; III *prp.* **31.** ~ *of* a) aus (... her'aus), zu ... hin'aus, b) *fig.* aus *Furcht, Mitleid etc.*, c) aus, von: *two* ~ *of three* zwei von drei *Per-sonen etc.*, d) außerhalb, außer *Reich-weite, Sicht etc.*, e) außer *Atem, Übung etc.*, ohne: *be* ~ *of s.th.* et. nicht (mehr) haben, ohne et. sein; → *money* 1, *work* 1, f) aus der Mode, Richtung etc., nicht gemäß: ~ *of drawing* ver-zeichnet; → *focus* 1, *hand* Redew., *question* 4, g) außerhalb (*gen. od. von*): *6 miles* ~ *of Oxford*; ~ *of doors* im Freien, ins Freie; *be* ~ *of it* nicht dabei sein (dürfen); *feel* ~ *of it* sich aus-geschlossen *od.* nicht zugehörig fühlen, h) um et. betrügen: *cheat s.o.* ~ *of s.th.*, i) aus, von: *get s.th.* ~ *of s.o.* et. von j-m bekommen; *he got more* (*pleasure*) ~ *of it* er hatte mehr davon, j) hergestellt aus: *made* ~ *of paper*; IV *s.* **32.** *typ.* Auslassung *f*, ‚Leiche‘ *f*; **33.** *Tennis etc.*: Ausball *m*; **34.** *the* ~s *Kricket etc.*: die 'Feldpar,tei; **35.** *the* ~s *parl.* die Opposi'tion; **36.** *Am.* F Aus-weg *m*, Schlupfloch *n*; **37.** → *outage* 2; V *v/t.* **38.** hin'auswerfen, verjagen, F rausschmeißen; **39.** *sport*: a) den Gegner ausschalten, b) *Boxen*: k. 'o. schlagen, c) *Tennis*: Ball ins Aus schla-gen; **40.** F ‚outen‘, als schwul bloßstel-len: ~ *o.s.* a) sich zu erkennen geben (*as* als), b) sich ‚outen‘, öffentlich zu-geben, dass man homosexuell ist; VI *v/i.* her'auskommen, bekannt werden (*Wahrheit etc.*); VII *int.* **41.** hin'aus!, raus!

,**out'act** *v/t. thea. etc.* j-n ‚an die Wand spielen‘.

out·age ['aʊtɪdʒ] *s.* **1.** fehlende Menge; **2.** 🔌 (*Strom- etc.*)Ausfall *m*.

,**out'-and-out** *adj.* abso'lut, völlig: *an* ~ *villain* ein Erzschurke; ,~**-and-'out·er** *s. sl.* **1.** 'Hundertpro,zentige(r *m*) *f*, ,Waschechte(r' *m*) *f*; **2.** *et.* 'Hundertpro,zentiges *od.* ganz Typisches *s-r Art*; '**~·back** *s.* (*bsd. der* au'stralische) Busch, *das* Hinterland; ,**~'bal·ance** *v/t.* über'wiegen; ,**~'bid** *v/t.* [*irr.* → *bid*] über'bieten (*a. fig.*); '**~·board** ♪ **I** *adj.* Außenbord...: **~** *motor*; **II** *adv.* außenbords; '**~·bound** *adj.* **1.** ♪ nach auswärts bestimmt *od.* fahrend, auslaufend, ausgehend; **2.** ✈ im Abflug; **3.** ✈ nach dem Ausland bestimmt; ,**~'box** *v/t.* j-n ausboxen, im Boxen schlagen; ,**~'brave** *v/t.* **1.** trotzen (*dat.*); **2.** an Kühnheit *od.* Glanz über'treffen; '**~·break** *s. allg.* Ausbruch *m*; '**~,building** *s.* Außen-, Nebengebäude *n*; '**~·burst** *s.* Ausbruch *m* (*a. fig.*); '**~·cast I** *adj.* **1.** ausgestoßen, verstoßen; **II** *s.* **2.** Ausgestoßene(r *m*) *f*; **3.** Abfall *m*, Ausschuss *m*; ,**~'class** *v/t.* j-m weit über'legen sein, j-n weit über'treffen, *sport* j-n deklassieren; '**~,clear·ing** *s.* ✈ Gesamtbetrag *m* der Wechsel- u. Scheckforderungen e-r Bank an das *Clearing-House*; '**~·come** *s.* Ergebnis *n*, Resul'tat *n*, Folge *f*; '**~·crop I** *s.* **1.** *geol.* a) Zu'tageliegen *n*, Anstehen *n*, b) Anstehendes *n*, Ausbiss *m*; **2.** *fig.* Zu'tagetreten *n*; **II** *v/i.* ,**out'crop 3.** *geol.* zu'tage liegen *od.* treten (*a. fig.*); '**~·cry** *s.* Aufschrei *m*, Schrei *m* der Entrüstung; ,**~'dat·ed** *adj.* über'holt, veraltet; ,**~'dis·tance** *v/t.* (weit) über'holen *od.* hinter sich lassen (*a. fig.*); ,**~'do** *v/t.* [*irr.* → *do¹*] über'treffen (*o.s.* sich selbst); '**~·door** *adj.* Außen..., draußen, außerhalb des Hauses, im Freien: **~** *aerial* Außen-, Hochantenne *f*; **~** *dress* Ausgehanzug *m*; **~** *exercise* Bewegung *f* im Freien; **~** *performance thea.* Freiluftaufführung *f*; **~** *season bsd. sport* Freiluftsaison *f*; **~** *shot phot.* Außen-, Freilichtaufnahme *f*; ,**~'doors I** *adv.* **1.** draußen, im Freien; **2.** hin'aus, ins Freie; **II** *adj.* **3.** → *outdoor*; **III** *s.* **4.** das Freie; die freie Na'tur.

out·er ['autə] *adj.* Außen...: **~** *garments*, **~** *wear* Oberbekleidung *f*; **~** *cover* ✈ Außenhaut *f*; **~** *diameter* äußerer Durchmesser; **~** *harbo(u)r* ♪ Außenhafen *m*; *the* **~** *man* der äußere Mensch; **~** *skin* Oberhaut *f*, Epidermis *f*; **~** *space* Weltraum *m*; **~** *surface* Außenfläche *f*, -seite *f*; **~** *world* Außenwelt *f*; '**~·most** *adj.* äußerst.

,**out'face** *v/t.* **1.** Trotz bieten (*dat.*), mutig *od.* gefasst begegnen (*dat.*): **~** *a situation* e-r Lage Herr werden; **2.** j-n mit Blicken aus der Fassung bringen; '**~·fall** *s.* Mündung *f*; '**~·field** *s.* **1.** *Baseball u. Kricket*: a) Außenfeld *n*, b) Außenfeldspieler *pl.*; **2.** *fig.* fernes Gebiet; **3.** weitab liegende Felder *pl.* (*e-r Farm*); '**~,field·er** *s.* Außenfeldspieler(in); ,**~'fight** *v/t.* [*irr.* → *fight*] niederkämpfen, schlagen; '**~,fight·er** *s.* Di'stanzboxer *m*; '**~·fit I** *s.* **1.** Ausrüstung *f*, -stattung *f*: *travel(l)ing* **~** *of tools* Werkzeug *n*; *cooking* **~** Kochutensilien *pl.*; *puncture* **~** Reifenflickzeug *n*; *the whole* **~** F der ganze Kram; **2.** F a) ✗ Einheit *f*, Trupp(e *m*, b) Gruppe *f*, c) F ,Verein' *m*, ,Laden' *m*, Gesellschaft *f*; **II** *v/t.* **3.** ausrüsten, -statten; '**~·fit·ter** *s.* ✈ **1.** 'Ausrüstungsliefer,ant *m*; **2.** Herrenausstatter *m*; **3.** (Fach)Händler *m*: *electrical* **~** Elektrohändler; ,**~'flank** *v/t.* **1.** ✗ die Flanke um'fassen von: **~·ing attack** Umfassungsangriff *m*; **2.** *fig.* über'listen; '**~·flow** *s.* Ausfluss *m* (*a. ♣*): **~** *of gold* ✈ Goldabfluss *m*; ,**~'gen·er·al** → *outmanoeuvre*; ,**~'go**

I *v/t.* [*irr.* → *go*] *fig.* über'treffen; über'listen; **II** *s.* '**outgo** *pl.* '**~·goes** ✈ Ausgaben *pl.*; ,**~'going I** *adj.* weggehend; ♠, ♣, *teleph. etc.* abgehend (*a. Verkehr, ♪, Strom*); ausziehend (*Mieter*); zu'rückgehend (*Flut*); abtretend (*Regierung*): **~** *mail* Postausgang *m*; **II** *s.* Ausgehen *n*; *pl.* ✈ Ausgaben *pl.*; '**~·group** *s.* Fremdgruppe *f*; ,**~'grow** *v/t.* [*irr.* → *grow*] **1.** schneller wachsen als, hin'auswachsen über (*acc.*); **2.** j-m über den Kopf wachsen; **3.** her'auswachsen aus *Kleidern*; **4.** *fig.* Gewohnheit *etc.* (mit der Zeit) ablegen, her'auswachsen aus; '**~·growth** *s.* **1.** na'türliche Folge, Ergebnis *n*; **2.** Nebenerscheinung *f*; **3.** ✗ Auswuchs *m*; ,**~'guard** *s.* ✗ Vorposten *m*, Feldwache *f*; ,**~-'Her·od** [-'herəd] *v/t.*: **~** *Herod* der schlimmste Tyrann sein; '**~·house** *s.* **1.** Nebengebäude *n*, Schuppen *m*; **2.** *Am.* 'Außen,bort.*m*.

out·ing ['autɪŋ] *s.* Ausflug *m*: *go for an* **~** e-n Ausflug machen; *works* **~**, *company* **~** Betriebsausflug.

,**out'jump** *v/t.* höher *od.* weiter springen als; ,**~'land·ish** [-'lændɪʃ] *adj.* **1.** fremdartig, seltsam, e'xotisch; **2.** a) unkultiviert, b) rückständig; **3.** abgelegen; **4.** ausländisch; ,**~'last** *v/t.* über'dauern, -'leben.

out·law ['autlɔ:] **I** *s. hist.* Geächtete(r *m*) *f*, Vogelfreie(r *m*) *f*; **2.** Ban'dit *m*, Verbrecher *m*; **3.** *Am.* bösartiges Pferd; **II** *v/t.* **4.** *hist.* ächten, für vogelfrei erklären; **5.** ☆ *Am.* für verjährt erklären: **~·ed** *claim* verjährter Anspruch; **6.** für ungesetzlich erklären, verbieten; *Krieg etc.* ächten; '**out·law·ry** [-rɪ] *s. hist.* a) Acht *f* (u. Bann *m*), b) Ächtung *f*; **2.** Verbannung *f*, Verbot *n*, Ächtung *f*; **3.** Ge'setzesmiss,achtung *f*; **4.** Verbrechertum *n*.

'**out·lay** *s.* (Geld)Auslage(n *pl.*) *f*: *initial* **~** Anschaffungskosten *pl.*; '**~·let** *s.* **1.** Auslass *m*, Abzug *m*, Abzugsöffnung *f*, 'Durchlass *m*; *mot.* Abluftstutzen *m*; **2.** ⚡ Steckdose *f*; *weitS.* (*electric* **~**) Stromverbraucher *m*; **3.** *fig.* Ven'til *n*, Betätigungsfeld *n*: *find an* **~** *for one's emotions* s-n Gefühlen Luft machen können; **4.** ✈ a) Absatzmarkt *m*, -möglichkeit *f*, b) Abnehmer *m*, c) Verkaufsstelle *f*; '**~·line I** *s.* **1.** a) 'Umriss(li-nie *f*) *m*, b) *mst pl.* 'Umrisse *pl.*, Kon'turen *pl.*, Silhou'ette *f*; **2.** Zeichnen: a) Kon'turzeichnung *f*, b) 'Umriss-, Kon'turlinie *f*; **3.** Entwurf *m*, Skizze *f*; **4.** (*of*) *fig.* 'Umriss *m* (von), 'Überblick *m* (über *acc.*); **5.** Abriss *m*, Auszug *m*: *an* **~** *of history* Abriss der Ge'schichte; **6.** entwerfen, skizzieren; *fig. a.* um'reißen, e-n 'Überblick geben über (*acc.*), in groben Zügen darstellen; **7.** die 'Umrisse zeigen von: **~·d** *against* scharf abgehoben von; ,**~'live** *v/t.* j-n *od. et.* über'leben; *et.* über'dauern; '**~·look** *s.* **1.** Aussicht *f*, (Aus-)Blick *m*; *fig.* Aussichten *pl.*; **2.** *fig.* Auffassung *f*, Einstellung *f*; Anschauung *f*; *pol.* Zielsetzung *f*; **3.** Ausguck *m*, Warte *f*; **4.** Wacht *f*, Wache *f*; '**~·ly·ing** *adj.* **1.** außerhalb *od.* abseits gelegen, entlegen, Außen...: **~** *district* Außenbezirk *m*; **2.** *fig.* am Rande liegend, nebensächlich; ,**~·ma'neu·ver** *Am.*, '**~-ma'noeu·vre** *Brit. v/t.* ausmanövrieren (*a. fig.* über'listen); ,**~'match** *v/t.* über'treffen, (aus dem Felde) schlagen; ,**~'mod·ed** *adj.* 'unmo,dern, veraltet (*auch fig.*); '**~·most** [-məʊst] *adj.* äußerst (*auch fig.*); ,**~'num·ber** *v/t.* an Zahl über'treffen, zahlenmäßig über'legen sein (*dat.*): *be* **~·ed** *in*

der Minderheit sein.

,**out-of-'bal·ance** [,autə-] *adj.* ⚙ unausgeglichen: **~** *force* Unwuchtkraft *f*; ,**~-'date** *adj.* veraltet, 'unmo,dern; ,**~-'door(s)** → *outdoor(s)*; ,**~-'pock·et ex·pens·es** *s. pl.* Barauslagen *pl.*; ,**~-the-'way** [,autəðə-] *adj.* **1.** abgelegen, versteckt; **2.** ausgefallen, ungewöhnlich; **3.** ungehörig; ,**~'town** *adj.* auswärtig: **~** *bank* ✈ auswärtige Bank; **~** *bill* Distanzwechsel *m*; ,**~'turn** *adj.* unangebracht, taktlos, vorlaut; ,**~'work** *pay s.* Er'werbslosenunter,stützung *f*.

,**out'pace** *v/t.* j-n hinter sich lassen; '**~,pa·tient** *s.* ☆ ambu'lanter Pati'ent: **~** *treatment* ambulante Behandlung; ,**~'play** *v/t.* besser spielen als, schlagen; ,**~'point** *v/t. sport* nach Punkten schlagen; '**~·port** *s.* ♪ **1.** Vorhafen *m*; **2.** abgelegener Hafen; '**~·pour**, '**~,pour·ing** *s.* Erguss *m* (*a. fig.*); '**~·put** *s.* Output *m*: a) ✈, ⚙ (Arbeits)Leistung *f*, b) ✈ Ausstoß *m*, Produkti'on *f*, Ertrag *m*, c) ✗ Förderung *f*, Fördermenge *f*, d) ✍ Ausgang(sleistung *f*) *m*, e) Computer: (Daten)Ausgabe *f*: **~** *capacity* ⚙ Leistungsfähigkeit *f*, *e-r Maschine*: *a.* Stückleistung *f*; **~** *voltage* ✍ Ausgangsspannung *f*.

out·rage ['autreɪdʒ] **I** *s.* **1.** Frevel(tat *f*) *m*, Gräuel(tat *f*) *m*, Ausschreitung *f*, Verbrechen *n*, *a. fig.* Ungeheuerlichkeit *f*; **2.** (*on, upon*) Frevel(tat *f*) *m* (an *dat.*), Atten'tat *n* (auf *acc.*) (*bsd. fig.*): *an* **~** *upon decency* e-e grobe Verletzung des Anstandes; *an* **~** *upon justice* e-e Vergewaltigung der Gerechtigkeit; **3.** Schande *f*, Schmach *f*; **II** *v/t.* **4.** sich vergehen an (*dat.*), j-m Gewalt antun (*a. fig.*); **5.** *Gefühle etc.* mit Füßen treten, gröblich beleidigen *od.* verletzen; **6.** j-n em'pören, schockieren; **out·ra·geous** [aut'reɪdʒəs] *adj.* □ **1.** frevelhaft, abscheulich, verbrecherisch; **2.** schändlich, em'pörend, ungeheuerlich: **~** *behavio(u)r* *f*; **3.** heftig, unerhört: **~** *heat*.

,**out'range** *v/t.* **1.** ✗ e-e größere Reichweite haben als; **2.** hin'ausreichen über (*acc.*); **3.** *fig.* über'treffen; ,**~'rank** *v/t.* **1.** im Rang höher stehen als; **2.** *fig.* wichtiger sein als; ,**~'reach** → *outrange* 2, 3; ,**~'ride** *v/t.* [*irr.* → *ride*] **1.** besser *od.* schneller reiten *od.* fahren als; **2.** ♣ *e-n Sturm* ausreiten; '**~,rid·er** *s.* Vorreiter *m*; '**~,rig·ger** *s.* **1.** ♣, ⚙ *u. Rudern*: Ausleger *m*; **2.** Auslegerboot *n*; '**~·right I** *adj.* **1.** völlig, gänzlich, to'tal: *an* **~** *loss*; *an* **~** *lie* e-e glatte Lüge; **2.** vorbehaltlos, offen: *an* **~** *refusal* e-e glatte Weigerung; **3.** gerade (her)'aus, di'rekt; **II** *adv.* *out'right* **4.** → 1; **5.** ohne Vorbehalt, ganz: *refuse* **~** rundweg ablehnen; *sell* **~** fest verkaufen; **6.** auf der Stelle, so'fort: *kill* **~**; *buy* **~** *Am.* gegen sofortige Lieferung kaufen; *laugh* **~** laut lachen; ,**~'ri·val** *v/t.* über'treffen, über'bieten (*in* an *od.* in *dat.*), ausstechen; ,**~'run** *v/t.* [*irr.* → *run*] **1.** schneller laufen als, (im Laufen) besiegen; **2.** *fig.* über'schreiten; **II** *s.* '**outrun 3.** *Skisport:* Auslauf *m*; '**~,run·ner** *s.* **1.** (Vor)Läufer *m* (*Bedienter*); **2.** Leithund *m*; ,**~'sell** *v/t.* [*irr.* → *sell*] **1.** mehr verkaufen als; **2.** sich besser verkaufen als; mehr einbringen als; '**~·set** *s.* **1.** Anfang *m*, Beginn *m*: *at the* **~** am Anfang; *from the* **~** gleich von Anfang an; **2.** Aufbruch *m* zu e-r Reise; ,**~'shine** *v/t.* [*irr.* → *shine*] über'strahlen; *fig. a.* in den Schatten stellen.

,**out·side I** *s.* **1.** *das* Äußere (*a. fig.*), Außenseite *f*: *on the* **~** *of* außerhalb, jenseits (*gen.*); **2.** *fig. das* Äußerste: *at the ~* äußerstenfalls, höchstens; **3.** *sport* Außenstürmer *m*: *~ right* Rechtsaußen *m*; **II** *adj.* **4.** äußer, Außen... (*-antenne, -durchmesser etc.*), von außen: *~ broker* ✝ freier Makler; *~ capital* Fremdkapital *n*; *an ~ opinion* die Meinung e-s Außenstehenden; **5.** außerhalb, (dr)außen; **6.** *fig.* äußerst (*Schätzung, Preis*); **7.** *~ chance* winzige Chance, *sport* Außenseiterchance *f*; **III** *adv.* **8.** draußen, außerhalb; *~ of* a) außerhalb, b) *Am.* F außer, ausgenommen; **9.** her'aus, hin'aus; **10.** außen, an der Außenseite; **IV** *prp.* **11.** außerhalb, jenseits (*gen.*) (*a. fig.*); **'out'sid·er** *s.* **1.** *allg.* Außenseiter(in); **2.** ✝ freier Makler.

,out'sit *v/t.* [*irr. →* **sit**] länger sitzen (bleiben) als; **'~-size I** *s.* 'Übergröße *f* (*a. Kleidungsstück*); **II** *adj. a.* '~-**sized** 'übergroß, -dimensio,nal; **'~-skirts** *pl.* nahe Um'gebung, Stadtrand *m, a. fig.* Rand(gebiet *n*) *m*, Periphe'rie *f*; **,~'smart** → *outwit*; **,~'source** [-sɔːs] *v/t. Arbeit* ,outsourcen', an e-n externen Dienstleister vergeben'; **'~-sourc·ing** *s.* ✝ ,Outsourcing' *n*; **,~'speed** *v/t.* [*irr. →* **speed**] schneller sein als.

,out'spo·ken *adj.* □ offen, freimütig; unverblümt: *she was very ~ about it* sie äußerte sich sehr offen darüber; **,~'spo·ken·ness** [-'spəʊkənɪs] *s.* Offenheit *f*, Freimütigkeit *f*; Unverblümtheit *f*.

,out'stand·ing *adj.* **1.** her'vorragend (*bsd. fig. Leistung, Spieler etc.*); *fig.* her'vorstechend (*Eigenschaft etc.*), promi'nent (*Persönlichkeit etc.*); **2.** *bsd.* ✝ unerledigt, aus-, offen stehend (*Forderung etc.*), unbezahlt (*Zinsen etc.*): *~ capital stock* ausgegebenes Aktienkapital; *~ debts* → **'out,stand·ings** *s. pl.* ✝ Außenstände *pl.*, Forderungen *pl.*

,out'stare *v/t.* mit e-m Blick aus der Fassung bringen; **'~-sta·tion** *s.* **1.** 'Außenstati,on *f*; **2.** *Funk:* 'Gegenstati,on *f*; **,~'stay** *v/t.* länger bleiben als; → **welcome 1**; **,~'stretch** *v/t.* ausstrecken; **,~'strip** *v/t.* über'holen, hinter sich lassen, *fig. a.* über'flügeln, (aus dem Feld) schlagen; **,~'swim** *v/t.* [*irr. →* **swim**] schneller schwimmen als, schlagen; **,~'talk** *v/t.* in Grund u. Boden reden; **,über'fahren'**; *~* **tray** *s.* Ablagekorb *m* für ausgehende Post; **'~-turn** *s.* **1.** Ertrag *m*; **2.** ✝ Ausfall *m*: *~ sample* Ausfallmuster *n*; **,~'vote** *v/t.* über'stimmen.

out·ward ['aʊtwəd] **I** *adj.* □ → **outwardly**; **1.** äußer, sichtbar; Außen...; **2.** äußerlich (*a. ♣ u. fig. contr.*); **3.** nach (dr)außen gerichtet *od.* führend, Aus(wärts)..., Hin...: *~ cargo, ~ freight* ♣ ausgehende Ladung, Hinfracht *f*; *~ journey* Aus-, Hinreise *f*; *~ trade* Ausfuhrhandel *m*; **II** *adv.* **4.** (nach) auswärts, nach außen: *clear ~ Schiff* ausklarieren; → **bound²**; **'out·ward·ly** [-lɪ] *adv.* äußerlich; außen, nach außen (hin); **'out·ward·ness** [-nɪs] *s.* Äußerlichkeit *f*; äußere Form; **'out·wards** [-dz] → **outward II.**

,out'wear *v/t.* [*irr. →* **wear**] **1.** abnutzen; **2.** *fig.* erschöpfen; **3.** *fig.* über'dauern, haltbarer sein als; **,~'weigh** *v/t.* **1.** mehr wiegen als; **2.** *fig.* über'wiegen, gewichtiger sein als, *e-e Sache* aufwiegen; **,~'wit** *v/t.* über'listen, ,austricksen'; **'~-work** *s.* **1.** ✕ Außenwerk *n*; *fig.* Bollwerk *n*; **2.** ✝ Heimarbeit *f*; **'~-work·er** *s.* **1.** Außenarbeiter(in); **2.** Heimarbeiter(in); **'~-worn** *adj., pred.* **'out'worn 1.** abgetragen, abgenutzt; **2.**

---

veraltet, über'holt; **3.** erschöpft.

ou·zel ['uːzl] *s. orn.* Amsel *f.*

o·va ['əʊvə] *pl. von* **ovum.**

o·val ['əʊvl] **I** *adj.* o'val; **II** *s.* O'val *n.*

o·var·i·an [,əʊ'veərɪən] *adj.* **1.** *anat.* Eierstock(s)...; **2.** ♀ Fruchtknoten...; **o·va·ri·tis** [,əʊvə'raɪtɪs] *s.* Eierstockentzündung *f*; **o·va·ry** ['əʊvərɪ] *s.* **1.** *anat.* Eierstock *m*; **2.** ♀ Fruchtknoten *m.*

o·va·tion [əʊ'veɪʃn] *s.* Ovati'on *f*, begeisterte Huldigung.

ov·en ['ʌvn] *s.* **1.** Backofen *m*, -rohr *n*; **2.** ⊙ Ofen *m*; **'~-dry** *adj.* ofentrocken; **'~-read·y** *adj.* bratfertig; **'~-ware** *s.* feuerfestes Geschirr.

o·ver ['əʊvə] **I** *prp.* **1.** *Lage:* über (*dat.*): *the lamp ~ his head*; *be ~ the signature of Mr. N.* von Herrn N. unterzeichnet sein; **2.** *Richtung, Bewegung:* über (*acc.*), über (*acc.*) ... hin *od.* (hin-) 'weg: *jump ~, the fence*; *the bridge ~ the Danube* die Brücke über die Donau; *~ the radio* im Radio; *all ~ the town* durch die ganze *od.* in der ganzen Stadt; *from all ~ Germany* aus ganz Deutschland; *be all ~ s.o. sl.* ganz hingerissen sein von j-m; **3.** über (*dat.*), auf der anderen Seite von (*od. gen.*): *~ the sea* in Übersee, jenseits des Meeres; *~ the street* über die Straße, auf der anderen Seite; *~ the way* gegenüber; **4.** a) über *der Arbeit einschlafen etc.*, bei *e-m Glas Wein etc.*, b) über (*acc.*), wegen: *laugh ~* über *et.* lachen; **5.** *Herrschaft, Rang:* über (*dat. od. acc.*): *be ~ s.o.* über j-m stehen; **6.** über (*acc.*), mehr als: *~ a mile*; *~ and above* zusätzlich zu, außer; → **21**; **7.** über (*acc.*), während (*gen.*): *~ the weekend*; *~ night* die Nacht über; **8.** durch: *he went ~ his notes* er ging seine Notizen durch; **II** *adv.* **9.** hinüber, dar'über: *he jumped ~*; **10.** hinüber (*to* zu), auf die andere Seite; **11.** her'über: *come ~* herüberkommen (*a. weitS. zu Besuch*); **12.** drüben: *~ there* da drüben; *~ against* gegenüber (*dat.; a. fig.* im Gegensatz zu); **13.** (*genau*) dar'über: *the bird is directly ~*; **14.** über (*acc.*) ...; dar'über ... (*decken, legen etc.*); über'...: *to paint ~ et.* übermalen; **15.** (*mst in Verbindung mit vb.*) a) über'... (*-geben etc.*): *hand s.th. ~*, b) 'über... (*-kochen etc.*): *boil ~*; **16.** (*oft in Verbindung mit vb.*) a) 'um... (*-fallen, -werfen etc.*), b) (her)'um... (*-drehen etc.*): *see ~!* siehe umstehend; **17.** 'durch(weg), vom Anfang bis zum Ende: *the world ~* a) in der ganzen Welt, b) durch die ganze Welt; *read s.th. ~ et.* (ganz) durchlesen; **18.** (*gründlich*) über'... (*-denken, -legen*): *think s.th. ~; talk s.th. ~ et.* durchsprechen; **19.** nochmals, wieder: *do s.th. ~*; (*all*) *~ again* nochmals, (ganz) von vorn; *~ and ~* (*again*) immer wieder; *ten times ~* zehnmal hintereinander; **20.** 'übermäßig, allzu *sparsam etc.*, 'über... (*-vorsichtig etc.*); **21.** dar'über, mehr: *10 years and ~* 10 Jahre und darüber; *~ and above* außerdem, überdies; → **6**; **22.** übrig, über: *left ~* übrig (gelassen *od.* geblieben); *have s.th. ~ et.* übrig haben; **23.** zu Ende, vor'über, vor'bei: *the lesson is ~; ~ with* F erledigt, vorüber; *it's all ~* es ist aus und vorbei; *get s.th. ~* (*and done*) *with* F *et.* hinter sich bringen; *Funk: ~!* over!, Ende!; *~ and out!* over and out!, Ende (*der Gesamtdurchsage*)!

,o·ver·a'bun·dant [-vərə-] *adj.* □ 'überreich(lich), 'übermäßig; **,~'act** [-vər'æ-] **I** *v/t. e-e Rolle* über'treiben,

---

über'spielen; **II** *v/i.* (s-e Rolle) über'treiben; **'~-all** [-ɔːl] **I** *adj.* **1.** gesamt, Gesamt...: *~ length*; *~ efficiency* ⊙ Totalnutzeffekt *m*; **II** *s.* **2.** *a. pl.* Arbeits-, Mon'teur-, Kombinati'onsanzug *m*; (*Arzt- etc.*)Kittel *m*; **3.** *Brit.* Kittelschürze *f*; **4.** *pl. obs.* 'Überzieh-, Arbeitshose *f*; **,~-a'chiev·er** *s.* 'Überflieger *m*; **,~-am'bi·tious** [-əræ-] *adj.* □ allzu ehrgeizig; **,~-'anx·ious** [-ər'æ-] *adj.* □ **1.** 'überängstlich; **2.** allzu begierig; **'~-arm stroke** [-ərɑːm] *s.* Schwimmen: Hand-über-'Hand-Stoß *m*; **,~-'awe** [-ər'ɔː] *v/t.* **1.** einschüchtern; **2.** tief beeindrucken; **,~-'bal·ance I** *v/t.* **1.** über'wiegen (*a. fig.*); **2.** umstoßen, -kippen; **II** *v/i.* **3.** 'umkippen, das 'Übergewicht bekommen; **III** *s.* **'overbalance 4.** 'Übergewicht *n*; **5.** ✝ 'Überschuss *m*: *~ of exports*; **,~-'bear** *v/t.* [*irr. →* **bear¹**] **1.** niederdrücken; **2.** über'winden; **3.** tyrannisieren; **4.** *fig.* schwerer wiegen als; **,~-'bear·ance** *s.* Anmaßung *f*, Arro'ganz *f*; **,~-'bear·ing** *adj.* □ **1.** anmaßend, arro'gant, hochfahrend; **2.** von über'ragender Bedeutung; **,~-'bid** *v/t.* [*irr. →* **bid**] **1.** ✝ über'bieten; **2.** *Bridge:* über'reizen; **'~-blouse** *s.* Kasackbluse *f*; **,~-'blown** *adj.* **1.** am Verblühen (*a. fig.*); **2.** ♪ über'blasen (*Ton*); **3.** *metall.* 'übergar (*Stahl*); **4.** *fig.* schwülstig; **'~-board** *adv.* ♣ über Bord: *throw ~* über Bord werfen (*a. fig.*); *be ~* (*about od. for*) F hingerissen sein (von); **,~-'brim** *v/i. u. v/t.* überfließen (lassen); **,~-'build** *v/t.* [*irr. →* **build**] **1.** über'bauen; **2.** zu dicht bebauen; **3.** *~ o.s.* sich ,verbauen'; **,~-'bur·den** *v/t.* über'bürden, -'laden, -'lasten; **,~-'bus·y** *adj.* **1.** zu sehr beschäftigt; **2.** 'übergeschäftig; **,~-'buy** *v/t.* [*irr. →* **buy**] **I** *v/t.* zu viel kaufen von; **II** *v/i.* zu teuer *od.* über Bedarf (ein)kaufen; **,~-ca'pac·i·ty** *s.* 'Überkapazi,tät *f*; **,~-'cap·i·tal·ize** *v/t.* ✝ **1.** e-n zu hohen Nennwert für das 'Stammkapi,tal *e-s Unternehmens* angeben: *~ a firm*; **2.** 'überkapitalisieren; **,~-'cast I** *v/t.* [*irr. →* **cast**] **1.** mit Wolken über'ziehen, bedecken, verdunkeln, trüben (*a. fig.*); **2.** *Naht* um'stechen; **II** *v/i.* [*irr. →* **cast**] **3.** sich bewölken, sich beziehen (*Himmel*); **III** *adj.* **'overcast 4.** bewölkt, bedeckt (*Himmel*); **5.** trüb(e), düster (*a. fig.*); **6.** über'wendlich (*genäht*); **,~-'charge I** *v/t.* **1.** a) j-m zu viel berechnen, b) *e-n Betrag* zu viel verlangen, c) zu viel anrechnen *od.* verlangen für *et.*; **2.** ⊙, ⚡ über'laden (*a. fig.*); **II** *s.* **3.** ✝ a) Mehrbetrag *m*, Aufschlag *m*: *~ for arrears* Säumniszuschlag *m*, b) Über'forderung *f*, Über'teuerung *f*; **4.** Über'ladung *f*, 'Überbelastung *f*; **,~-'cloud** → **overcast** 1, 3; **'~-coat** *s.* Mantel *m*; **,~-'come** [*irr. →* **come**] **I** *v/t.* über'winden, -'wältigen, -'mannen, bezwingen; *e-r Sache* Herr werden: *he was ~ with* (*od. by*) *emotion* er wurde von s-n Gefühlen übermannt; **II** *v/i.* siegen, triumphieren: *we shall ~!*; **'~-com·pen·sate** *v/t. psych.* 'überkompensieren; **,~-'con·fi·dence** *s.* **1.** über'steigertes Selbstvertrauen *od.* -bewusstsein; **2.** zu großes Vertrauen; **3.** zu großer Opti'mismus; **,~-'con·fi·dent** *adj.* □ **1.** allzu sehr vertrauend (*of* auf *acc.*); **2.** über'trieben selbstbewusst; **3.** (all)zu opti'mistisch; **,~-'crop** *v/t.* ✓ Raubbau treiben mit; **,~-'crowd** *v/t.* über'füllen; *~ed profession* überlaufener Beruf; **,~-de'vel·op** *v/t. bsd. phot.* über'entwickeln; **,~-'do** *v/t.* [*irr. →* **do¹**] **1.** über'treiben, zu weit treiben; **2.** *fig.* zu weit gehen mit *od.* in (*dat.*), *et.*

zu arg treiben: ~ *it* (*od.* ***things***) a) zu weit gehen, b) des Guten zu viel tun; **3.** 'überbeanspruchen; **4.** zu stark *od.* zu lange kochen *od.* braten; ‚~'**done** *adj.* 'übergar; ~**dose I** *s.* ['əʊvədəʊs] 'Überdosis *f;* **II** *v/t.* [‚əʊvə'dəʊs] a) *j-m* e-e zu starke Dosis geben, b) *et.* 'überdosieren; **III** *v/i.* [‚əʊvə'dəʊs]: ~ *on* ... e-e 'Überdosis ... (*acc.*) nehmen; ‚~'**draft** *s.* ✝ a) ('Konto)Über‚ziehung *f,* b) Über'ziehung *f,* über'zogener Betrag; ‚~'**draw** *v/t.* [*irr.* → ***draw***] **1.** *Konto* über'ziehen; **2.** *Bogen* über'spannen; **3.** *fig.* über'treiben; ‚~'**dress** *v/t. u. v/i.* (sich) über'trieben anziehen; ‚~'**drive I** *v/t.* [*irr.* → ***drive***] **1.** abschinden, -hetzen; **2.** *et.* zu weit treiben; **II** *s.* '***over-drive 3.*** *mot.* Overdrive *m,* Schnell-, Schongang *m;* ‚~'**due** *adj.* 'überfällig (*a.* 🐚, ✝): **the train is ~** der Zug hat Verspätung; **she is ~** sie müsste längst hier sein; ‚~'**eat** *v/i.* [*irr.* → ***eat***] (*a.* ~ *o.s.*) sich über'essen; ‚~'**em·pha·size** [-ər'e-] *v/t.* 'überbetonen; ‚~**em'ploy·ment** *s.* 'Überbeschäftigung *f;* ‚~**es·ti·mate** [-ər'estɪmeɪt] **I** *v/t.* über'schätzen, 'überbewerten; **II** *s.* [-mət] Über'schätzung *f;* ‚~**ex'cite** [-vərɪ-] *v/t.* **1.** über'reizen; **2.** ⚡ 'übererregen; ‚~**ex'ert** [-vərɪ-] *v/t.* über'anstrengen; ‚~**ex'pose** [-vərɪ-] *v/t. phot.* 'überbelichten; ‚~**ex'po·sure** [-vərɪ-] *s. phot.* 'Überbelichtung *f;* ‚~**fa'tigue I** *v/t.* über'müden, über'anstrengen; **II** *s.* Über'müdung *f;* ‚~'**feed** *v/t.* [*irr.* → ***feed***] über'füttern, über'ernähren; ‚~**fer·ti·li'za·tion** *s.* Über'düngung *f;* ‚~'**fish·ing** *s.* Über'fischen *n;* ‚~'**flow I** *v/i.* **1.** 'überlaufen, 'überfließen, 'überströmen, sich ergießen (***into*** in *acc.*); **2.** *fig.* 'überquellen (***with*** von); **II** *v/t.* **4.** nicht mehr Platz finden in (*e-m Saal etc.*); **III** *s.* '***overflow 5.*** Über'schwemmung *f,* 'Überfließen *n;* **6.** ⊚ a) *a.* ⚡ 'Überlauf *m,* b) *a.* ~ *pipe* 'Überlaufrohr *n,* c) *a.* ~ *basin* 'Überlaufbas‚sin *n;* ~ *valve* Überström‚ventil *n;* **7.** 'Überschuss *m;* ~ *meeting* Parallelversammlung *f;* ‚~'**flow·ing I** *adj.* **1.** 'überfließend, -quellend, -strömend (*a. fig. Güte, Herz etc.*); **2.** 'überreich (*Ernte etc.*); **II** *s.* **3.** 'Überfließen *n:* *full to* ~ voll (bis) zum Überlaufen, *weitS.* zum Platzen voll; ‚~'**fly** *v/t.* [*irr.* → ***fly*¹**] über'fliegen; ‚~'**fond** *adj.:* *be* ~ *of doing s.th.* *et.* leidenschaftlich gern tun; ‚~'**freight** *s.* ✝ 'Überfracht *f;* '~**ground** *adj.* über der Erde (befindlich); ‚~'**grow** *v/t.* [*irr.* → ***grow***] **1.** über'wachsen, -'wuchern; **2.** hin'auswachsen über (*acc.*), zu groß werden für; ‚~'**grown** *adj.* **1.** über'wachsen; **2.** 'übermäßig gewachsen, 'übergroß; '~**growth** *s.* **1.** 'Überwucherung *f;* **2.** 'übermäßiges Wachstum; '~**hand** *adj. u. adv.* **1.** *Schlag etc.* von oben; **2.** *sport* 'überhand: ~ *stroke* a) *Tennis:* Überhandschlag *m,* b) *Schwimmen:* Hand-über-Hand-Stoß *m;* ~ *service* Hochaufschlag *m;* **3.** *Näherei:* über'wendlich; ‚~'**hang I** *v/t.* [*irr.* → ***hang***] **1.** her'vorstehen *od.* -ragen, 'überhangen über (*acc.*); **2.** *fig.* (drohend) schweben über (*dat.*), drohen (*dat.*); **II** *v/i.* [*irr.* → ***hang***] **3.** 'überhängen, -kragen (*a.* 🔺), her'vorstehen, -ragen; **III** *s.* '***overhang 4.*** 'Überhang *m* (*a.* 🔺, ⚓, ✈); ⊚ Ausladung *f;* ‚~'**hap·py** *adj.* 'überglücklich; ‚~'**hast·y** *adj.* über'eilt; ‚~'**haul I** *v/t.* **1.** *Maschine etc.* (gene'ral)über‚holen, (*a. fig.*) gründlich über'prüfen

(*a. fig.*) u. in'stand setzen; **2.** ⚓ *Tau,*

Taljen etc. 'überholen; **3.** a) einholen, b) über'holen; **II** *s.* '***overhaul 4.*** ⊚ Über'holung *f,* gründliche Über'prüfung (*a. fig.*); '~**head I** *adj.* **1.** oberirdisch, Frei..., Hoch...(*-antenne, -behälter etc.*): ~ *line* Frei-, Oberleitung *f;* ~ *railway* Hochbahn *f;* **2.** *mot.* a) oben gesteuert (*Motor, Ventil*), b) oben liegend (*Nockenwelle*); **3.** allgemein, Gesamt...: ~ *costs,* ~ *expenses* → 6; **4.** *sport* a) ~ *stroke* → 7, b) ~ *kick* (Fall-)Rückzieher *m;* **5.** Overhead...: ~ *projector* Overhead- *od.* Tageslichtprojektor *m;* ~ *transparency* Demo-, *Lehrmaterial:* Folie *f;* **II** *s.* **6.** *a. pl.* allgemeine Unkosten *pl.,* Gemeinkosten *pl.,* laufende Geschäftskosten *pl.;* **7.** *Tennis:* Über'kopfball *m;* **III** *adv.* ‚*over*-'head 8. (dr)oben: *works* ~ Vorsicht, Dacharbeiten!; ‚~'**hear** *v/t.* [*irr.* → ***hear***] belauschen, (zufällig) mit anhören; ‚~'**heat I** *v/t. Motor etc., a. fig.* über'hitzen, *Raum* über'heizen; ~ *itself* → II; **II** *v/i.* ⊚ heißlaufen; '~**house** *adj.* Dach...(*-antenne etc.*); ‚~'**hung** *adj.* fliegend (angeordnet), freitragend; 'überhängend; ‚~**in'dulge** [-vərɪ-] **I** *v/t.* **1.** zu nachsichtig behandeln; **2.** *e-r Leidenschaft etc.* übermäßig frönen; **3.** ~ *in* sich allzu sehr ergehen in (*dat.*); ‚~**in'dul·gence** [-vərɪ-] *s.* **1.** zu große Nachsicht; **2.** 'übermäßiger Genuss; ‚~**in'dul·gent** *adj.* allzu nachsichtig; ‚~**in'sure** [-vərɪ-] *v/t. u. v/i.* (sich) 'überversichern; ‚~**is·sue** [-ər'ɪ-] **I** *s.* 'Überemissi‚on *f;* **II** *v/t.* zu viel *Banknoten etc.* ausgeben; ‚~'**joyed** [-'dʒɔɪd] *adj.* außer sich vor Freude, 'überglücklich; '~**kill** *s.* **1.** ✕ Overkill *m;* **2.** *fig.* 'Übermaß *n,* Zu'viel *n* (*of* an *dat.*); '~**lad·en** *adj.* über'laden (*a. fig.*); ‚~'**land I** *adj.* über Land, auf dem Landweg; **II** *adj.* '***overland*** Überland...: ~ *route* Landweg *m;* ~ *transport* Überland-, Fernverkehr *m;* ‚~'**lap I** *v/t.* **1.** 'übergreifen auf (*acc.*) *od.* in (*acc.*), sich über'schneiden mit, teilweise zs.-fallen mit; ⊚ über'lappen; **2.** hin'ausgehen über (*acc.*); **II** *v/i.* ⊚ sich ein'ander über'schneiden, sich teilweise decken, auf *od.* inein'ander 'übergreifen; ⊚ über'lappen, 'übergreifen; **III** *s.* '***overlap 4.*** 'Übergreifen *n,* Über'schneiden *n;* ⊚ Über'lappung *f;* ‚~'**lay I** *v/t.* [*irr.* → ***lay*¹**] **1.** belegen; ⊚ über'lagern; **2.** über'ziehen (***with*** mit *Gold etc.*); **3.** *typ.* zurichten; **II** *s.* '***overlay 4.*** Bedeckung *f:* ~ *mattress* Auflegematratze *f;* **5.** Auflage *f,* 'Überzug *m;* **6.** *typ.* Zurichtung *f;* **7.** Planpause *f;* ‚~'**leaf** *adv.* 'umstehend, 'umseitig; ‚~'**lie** *v/t.* [*irr.* → ***lie*²**] **1.** liegen auf *od.* über (*dat.*); **2.** *geol.* über'lagern; ‚~'**load I** *v/t.* über'laden, 'überbelasten, *a.* ⚡ über'lasten; **II** *s.* '***overload*** Überladung *f,* -beanspruchung *f, a.* ⚡ Über'lastung *f;* ‚~'**long** *adj. u. adv.* 'überlang, (all)zu lang; ‚~'**look** *v/t.* **1.** *Fehler etc.* (geflissentlich) über'sehen, nicht beachten, *fig. a.* ignorieren, (nachsichtig) hin'wegsehen über (*acc.*); **2.** über'blicken; *weitS. a.* Aussicht gewähren auf (*acc.*); **3.** über'wachen; (prüfend) 'durchsehen; '~**lord** *s.* Oberherr *m;* '~**lord·ship** *s.* Oberherrschaft *f.*

o·ver·ly ['əʊvəlɪ] *adv.* allzu (sehr).

‚**o·ver**'**ly·ing** *adj.* da'rüber liegend; '~**man** [-mæn] *s.* [*irr.*] Aufseher *m,* Vorarbeiter *m;* ✕ Steiger *m;* ‚~'**manned** *adj.* 'überbelegt, zu stark bemannt; ‚~'**much I** *adj.* allzu viel; **II** *adv.* allzu (sehr, viel), 'übermäßig; ‚~'**nice** *adj.* 'überfein; ‚~'**night I** *adv.* über

Nacht; **II** *adj.* Nacht...; Übernachtungs...: ~ *lodgings*; ~ *bag* Reisetasche *f;* ~ *case* Handkoffer *m;* ~ *guests* Übernachtungsgäste; ~ *stay* Übernachtung *f;* ~ *stop* Aufenthalt *m* für e-e Nacht; '~**pass** *s.* ('Straßen-, 'Eisenbahn)Über‚führung *f;* ‚~'**pay** *v/t.* [*irr.* → ***pay***] **1.** zu teuer bezahlen; **2.** 'überreichlich belohnen; **3.** 'überbezahlen; ‚~'**peo·pled** *adj.* über'völkert; ‚~**per'suade** *v/t. j-n* (gegen s-n Willen) über'reden; ‚~'**play** *v/t.* **1.** über'treiben; **2.** ~ *one's hand fig.* sich über'nehmen, es übertreiben; '~**plus** *s.* 'Überschuss *m;* '~‚**pop·u'la·tion** *s.* 'Über(be)völkerung *f;* ‚~'**pow·er** *v/t.* über'wältigen (*a. fig.*); ‚~'**print I** *v/t.* **1.** *typ.* a) über'drucken, b) e-e zu große Auflage drucken von; **2.** *phot.* 'überkopieren; **II** *s.* '***overprint 3.*** *typ.* 'Überdruck *m;* **4.** a) Aufdruck *m* (*auf Briefmarken*), b) Briefmarke *f* mit Aufdruck; ‚~**pro'duce** *v/t.* ✝ 'überproduzieren; ‚~**pro'duc·tion** *s.* 'Überpro‚dukti‚on *f;* ‚~'**proof** *adj.* 'überpro‚zentig (*alkoholisches Getränk*); ‚~'**rate** *v/t.* **1.** über'schätzen, 'überbewerten (*a. sport*); **2.** ✝ zu hoch veranschlagen; ‚~'**reach** *v/t.* **1.** zu weit gehen für: ~ *one's purpose* über sein Ziel hinausschießen; ~ *o.s.* es zu weit treiben, sich übernehmen; **2.** *j-n* über'vorteilen, -'listen; ‚~**re'act** *v/i.* 'überreagieren; ‚~'**ride** *v/t.* [*irr.* → ***ride***] **1.** zu weit reiten; **2.** *fig.* sich (rücksichtslos) hin'wegsetzen über (*acc.*); **3.** *fig.* 'umstoßen, aufheben, nichtig machen; **4.** den Vorrang haben vor (*dat.*); ‚~'**rid·ing** *adj.* über'wiegend, hauptsächlich; vorrangig; ‚~'**ripe** *adj.* 'überreif; ‚~'**rule** *v/t.* **1.** *Vorschlag etc.* verwerfen, zu'rückweisen; 🏛 *Urteil* 'umstoßen; **2.** *fig.* die Oberhand gewinnen über (*acc.*); ‚~'**rul·ing** *adj.* beherrschend, 'übermächtig; ‚~'**run** *v/t.* [*irr.* → ***run***] **1.** *fig. Land etc.* über'fluten, -'schwemmen (*a. fig.*), einfallen in (*acc.*), über'rollen (*a. fig.*): *be* ~ *with* wimmeln von, überlaufen sein von; **2.** *fig.* rasch um sich greifen in (*dat.*); **3.** *typ.* 'umbrechen; ‚~'**run·ning** *adj.* Freilauf..., Überlauf...: ~ *clutch;* ‚~'**sea I** *adv. a.* ‚~'**seas** nach *od.* in 'Übersee; **II** *adj.* 'überseeisch, Übersee...; ‚~'**see** *v/t.* [*irr.* → ***see*¹**] beaufsichtigen, über'wachen; '~**‚se·er** [-‚sɪə] *s.* **1.** Aufseher(in), In'spektor *m,* Inspek'torin *f;* **2.** Vorarbeiter(in); ✕ Steiger *m;* ‚~'**sen·si·tive** *adj.* □ über'empfindlich; ‚~'**set** *v/t.* [*irr.* → ***set***] *upset*¹ I; ‚~'**sew** *v/t.* [*irr.* → ***sew***] über'wendlich nähen; ‚~'**sexed** *adj.* sexbesessen; ‚~'**shad·ow** *v/t.* **1.** *fig.* in den Schatten stellen; **2.** *bsd. fig.* über'schatten, e-n Schatten werfen auf (*acc.*), verdüstern; '~**shoe** *s.* 'Überschuh *m;* ‚~'**shoot** *v/t.* [*irr.* → ***shoot***] **1.** über ein Ziel hin'ausschießen (*a. fig.*): ~ *o.s.* (*od.* **the mark**) zu weit gehen, übers Ziel hinausschießen; ‚~'**shot** *adj.* oberschlächtig (*Wasserrad, Mühle*); '~**sight** *s.* **1.** Versehen *n:* *by an* ~ aus Versehen; **2.** Aufsicht *f;* ‚~'**sim·pli·fy** *v/t.* (zu) grob vereinfachen; ‚~'**size** *s.* 'Übergröße *f;* ‚~'**size(d)** *adj.* übergroß; ‚~'**slaugh** ['əʊvəslɔː] *v/t.* **1.** ✕ abkommandieren; **2.** *Am. bei der Beförderung* über'gehen; ‚~'**sleep I** *v/t.* [*irr.* → ***sleep***] *e-n Zeitpunkt* verschlafen: ~ *o.s.* → II; **II** *v/i.* [*irr.* → ***sleep***] (sich) verschlafen; '~**sleeve** *s.* Ärmelschoner *m;* ‚~'**speed** *v/t.* [*irr.* → ***speed***] *den Motor* über'drehen; ‚~'**spend** [*irr.* → ***spend***] **I** *v/i.* **1.** zu viel ausgeben; **II** *v/t.* **2.** *Ausgabensumme* über'schreiten; **3.** ~

o.s. über s-e Verhältnisse leben; '**~·spill** *s.* (*bsd.* Be'völkerungs),Über-schuss *m*; ,**~'spread** *v/t.* [*irr.* → *spread*] **1.** über'ziehen, sich ausbreiten über (*acc.*); **2.** (*with*) über'ziehen *od.* bede-cken (mit); ,**~'staffed** *adj.* (perso'nell) 'überbesetzt; ,**~'state** *v/t.* über'treiben: **~ one's case** in s-n Behauptungen zu weit gehen; ,**~'state·ment** *s.* Über'trei-bung *f*; ,**~'stay** *v/t. e-e Zeit* über'schrei-ten: **~ one's time** über s-e Zeit hinaus bleiben; → *welcome* 1; ,**~'steer** *v/i. mot.* über'steuern; ,**~'step** *v/t.* über-'schreiten (*a. fig.*); ,**~'stock I** *v/t.* **1.** 'überreichlich eindecken, ✝ *a.* 'überbe-liefern, *den Markt* über'schwemmen: **~ o.s.** → 3; **2.** ✝ in zu großen Mengen auf Lager halten; **II** *v/i.* **3.** sich zu hoch eindecken; ,**~'strain I** *v/t.* über'anstren-gen, 'überstrapazieren (*a. fig.*): **~ one's conscience** übertriebene Skrupel ha-ben; **II** *s.* '**overstrain** Über'anstrengung *f*; ,**~'strung** *adj.* **1.** über'reizt (*Nerven od. Person*); **2.** '**overstrung** ♪ kreuzsai-tig (*Klavier*); ,**~'sub'scribe** *v/t.* ✝ *An-leihe* über'zeichnen; ,**~'sub'scrip·tion** *s.* ✝ Über'zeichnung *f*; ,**~'sup'ply** *s.* (*of* an *dat.*) **1.** 'Überangebot *n*; **2.** zu großer Vorrat.

o·vert ['əʊvɜːt] *adj.* □ offen(kundig): **~ act** 🕮 Ausführungshandlung *f*; **~ hos-tility** offene Feindschaft; **~ market** ✝ offener Markt.

,**o·ver**|'**take** *v/t.* [*irr.* → *take*] **1.** einho-len (*a. fig.*); **2.** über'holen (*a. v/i.*); **3.** *fig.* über'raschen, -'fallen; **4.** *Versäum-tes* nachholen; ,**~'task** *v/t.* **1.** über'bür-den; **2.** über *j-s* Kräfte gehen; ,**~'tax** *v/t.* **1.** 'übersteuern; **2.** zu hoch einschät-zen; **3.** 'überbeanspruchen, zu hohe Anforderungen stellen an (*acc.*); *Ge-duld* strapazieren: **~ one's strength** sich (kräftemäßig) übernehmen; ,**~-the-'count·er** *adj.* **1.** ✝ freihändig (*Effektenverkauf*): **~ market** Freiver-kehrsmarkt *m*; **2.** *pharm.* re'zeptfrei; ,**~'throw I** *v/t.* [*irr.* → *throw*] **1.** ('um-)stürzen (*a. fig. Regierung etc.*); **2.** nie-derwerfen, besiegen; **3.** niederreißen, vernichten; **II** *s.* '**overthrow 4.** Sturz *m*, Niederlage *f* (*e-r Regierung etc.*); **5.** Vernichtung *f*, 'Untergang *m*; '**~-time I** *s.* ✝ a) 'Überstunden *pl.*, b) → **~ pay** Mehrarbeitszuschlag *m*, 'Überstunden-lohn *m*; **II** *adv.*: **work ~** Überstunden machen; ,**~'tire** *v/t.* über'müden; '**~-tone** *s.* **1.** ♪ Oberton *m*; **2.** *fig.* a) 'Un-terton *m*, b) *pl.* Neben-, Zwischentöne *pl.*: **it had ~s of** es schwang darin et. mit von; ,**~'top**, ,**~'tow·er** *v/t.* über'ra-gen (*a. fig.*); ,**~'train** *v/t. u. v/i.* über-trainieren; '**~-trump** *v/t. u. v/i.* über-'trumpfen.

o·ver·ture ['əʊvə,tjʊə] *s.* **1.** ♪ Ouver'tü-re *f*; **2.** *fig.* Einleitung *f*, Vorspiel *n*; **3.** (for'meller Heirats-, Friedens)Antrag *m*, Angebot *n*; **4.** *pl.* Annäherungsver-suche *pl.*

,**o·ver**|'**turn I** *v/t.* ('um)stürzen (*a. fig.*); 'umstoßen, -kippen; **II** *v/i.* 'umkippen, -schlagen, -stürzen, kentern; **III** *s.* '**overturn** ('Um)Sturz *m*; ,**~'type** *v/t. Computer: Text* über'schreiben; ,**~'val·ue** *v/t.* zu hoch einschätzen, 'überbe-werten; '**~-view** *s. fig.* 'Überblick *m*; ,**~'ween·ing** *adj.* **1.** anmaßend, über-'heblich; **2.** über'trieben; '**~-weight I** *s.* 'Übergewicht *n* (*a. fig.*); **II** *adj.* ,**over-'weight** 'übergewichtig, mit 'Überge-

wicht.

o·ver|**whelm** [,əʊvə'welm] *v/t.* **1.** über-'wältigen, -'mannen (*bsd. fig.*); **2.** *fig. mit Fragen, Geschenken etc.* über'schüt-ten, -'häufen: **~ed with work** überlas-tet; **3.** erdrücken; **o·ver'whelm·ing** [-mɪŋ] *adj.* über'wältigend.

o·ver|**wind** [,əʊvə'waɪnd] *v/t.* [*irr.* → *wind²*] *Uhr etc.* über'drehen; ,**~'work I** *v/t.* **1.** über'anstrengen, mit Arbeit über'lasten, 'überstrapazieren (*a. fig.*): **~ o.s.** → 2; **II** *v/i.* **2.** sich über'arbeiten; **III** *s.* **3.** 'Arbeitsüber,lastung *f*; **4.** Über-'arbeitung *f*; ,**~'wrought** *adj.* **1.** über-'arbeitet, erschöpft; **2.** über'reizt; ,**~'zeal·ous** *adj.* 'übereifrig.

o·vi·duct ['əʊvɪdʌkt] *s. anat.* Eileiter *m*; '**o·vi·form** [-ɪfɔːm] *adj.* eiförmig, o'val; **o·vip·a·rous** [əʊ'vɪpərəs] *adj.* ovi'par, Eier legend.

o·vo·gen·e·sis [,əʊvəʊ'dʒenɪsɪs] *s. biol.* Eibildung *f*; **o·void** ['əʊvɔɪd] *adj. u. s.* eiförmig(er Körper).

o·vu·lar ['ɒvjʊlə] *adj. biol.* Ei..., Ovu-lar...; **o·vu·la·tion** [,ɒvju'leɪʃn] *s.* Ovu-lati'on *f*, Eisprung *m*; **o·vule** ['əʊvjuːl] *s.* **1.** *biol.* Ovulum *n*, kleines Ei; **2.** ♀ Samenanlage *f*; **o·vum** ['əʊvəm] *pl.* **o·va** ['əʊvə] *s. biol.* Ovum *n*, Ei(zelle *f*) *n*.

owe [əʊ] **I** *v/t.* **1.** *Geld, Achtung, e-e Erklärung etc.* schulden, schuldig sein: **~ s.o. a grudge** gegen j-n e-n Groll hegen; **you ~ that to yourself** das bist du dir schuldig; **2.** bei *j-m* Schulden haben (**for** für); **3.** *et.* verdanken, zu verdanken haben, Dank schulden (*j-m*): **~ him much** ich habe ihm viel zu ver-danken; **II** *v/i.* **4.** Schulden haben; **5.** die Bezahlung schuldig sein (**for** für); **ow·ing** ['əʊɪŋ] *adj.* **1.** geschuldet: **be ~** zu zahlen sein, noch offen stehen; **have ~** ausstehen haben; **2. ~ to** infolge (*gen.*), wegen (*gen.*), dank (*dat.*): **be ~ to** zurückzuführen sein auf (*acc.*), zuzu-schreiben sein (*dat.*).

owl [aʊl] *s.* **1.** *orn.* Eule *f*; **2.** *fig.* ,alte Eule' (*Person*): **wise old ~** ,kluges Kind'; **owl·ish** ['aʊlɪʃ] *adj.* □ eulen-haft.

own [əʊn] **I** *v/t.* **1.** besitzen; **2.** *Erben, Kind, Schuld etc.* anerkennen; **3.** zuge-ben, (ein)gestehen, einräumen: **~ o.s. defeated** sich geschlagen geben; **II** *v/i.* **4.** sich bekennen (**to** zu): **~ to** → 3; **5. ~ up** es zugeben *od.* gestehen; **III** *adj.* **6.** eigen: **my ~ self** ich selbst; **~ brother to s.o.** j-s leiblicher Bruder; **~ re-sources** *pl.* ✝ Eigenmittel *pl.*; **7.** eigen (-artig), besonder: **it has a value all of its ~** es hat e-n ganz eigenen Wert; **8.** selbst: **I cook my ~ breakfast** ich ma-che mir das Frühstück selbst; **9.** (innig) geliebt, einzig: **my ~ child!; IV** *s.* **10.** **my ~** a) mein Eigentum *n*, b) meine Angehörigen *pl.*: **may I have it for my ~?** darf ich es haben?; **come into one's ~** a) s-n rechtmäßigen Besitz erlangen, b) zur Geltung kommen; **she has a car of her ~** sie hat ein eigenes Auto; **he has a way of his ~** er hat e-e eigene Art; **on one's ~** F a) selbstständig, un-abhängig, ohne fremde Hilfe, b) von sich aus, aus eigenem Antrieb, c) auf ei-gene Verantwortung; **be left on one's ~** F sich selbst überlassen sein; **get one's ~ back** F sich revanchieren, sich rächen (**on** an *dat.*); → *hold* 20.

-owned [əʊnd] *adj. in Zssgn* gehörig,

gehörend (*dat.*), in *j-s* Besitz: **state-~** staatseigen, Staats...

own·er ['əʊnə] *s.* Eigentümer(in), Inha-ber(in); **at ~'s risk** ✝ auf eigene Ge-fahr; **~-driver** j-d, der sein eigenes Au-to fährt; **~-occupation** Eigennutzung *f* (*e-s Hauses etc.*); '**own·er·less** [-lɪs] *adj.* herrenlos; '**own·er·ship** [-ʃɪp] *s.* **1.** Eigentum(srecht) *n*, Besitzerschaft *f*; **2.** Besitz *m*.

ox [ɒks] *pl.* **ox·en** ['ɒksn] *s.* **1.** Ochse *m*; **2.** (Haus)Rind *n*.

ox·a·late ['ɒksəleɪt] *s.* 🜪 Oxa'lat *n*; **ox·al·ic** [ɒks'ælɪk] *adj.* 🜪 o'xalsauer: **~ acid** Oxalsäure *f*.

Ox·bridge ['ɒksbrɪdʒ] *s. Brit.* F (die Uni-versi'täten) Oxford *u.* Cambridge *pl.*

Ox·ford | **man** *s.* [*irr.*] → *Oxonian* II; **~ move·ment** *s. eccl.* Oxfordbewegung *f*.

ox·i·dant ['ɒksɪdənt] *s.* 🜪 Oxidati'ons-mittel *n*; '**ox·i·date** [-deɪt] → *oxidize*; **ox·i·da·tion** [,ɒksɪ'deɪʃn] *s.* 🜪 Oxidati-'on *f*, Oxidierung *f*; **ox·ide** ['ɒksaɪd] *s.* 🜪 O'xid *m*; '**ox·i·dize** [-daɪz] *v/t. u. v/i.* 🜪 oxidieren; '**ox·i·diz·er** [-daɪzə] *s.* 🜪 Oxidati'onsmittel *n*.

'**ox·lip** *s.* ♀ Hohe Schlüsselblume.

Ox·o·ni·an [ɒk'səʊnjən] **I** *adj.* Oxforder, Oxford...; **II** *s.* Mitglied *n od.* Gradu-ierte(r *m*) *f* der Universi'tät Oxford; *weitS.* Oxforder(in).

'**ox·tail** *s.* Ochsenschwanz *m*: **~ soup**.

ox·y·a·cet·y·lene [,ɒksɪə'setɪliːn] *adj.* 🜪, ⚙ Sauerstoff-Azetylen...: **~ torch** *od.* **burner** Schweißbrenner *m*; **~ weld-ing** Autogenschweißen *n*.

ox·y·gen ['ɒksɪdʒən] *s.* 🜪 Sauerstoff *m*: **~ apparatus** Atemgerät *n*; **~ tent** 💉 Sauerstoffzelt *n*; **ox·yg·e·nant** [ɒk'sɪ-dʒənənt] *s.* Oxidati'onsmittel *n*; **ox·y·gen·ate** [ɒk'sɪdʒəneɪt], **ox·y·gen·ize** [ɒk'sɪdʒənaɪz] *v/t.* **1.** oxidieren, mit Sauerstoff verbinden *od.* behandeln; **2.** mit Sauerstoff anreichern.

ox·y·hy·dro·gen [,ɒksɪ'haɪdrədʒən] 🜪, ⊙ **I** *adj.* Hydrooxygen..., Knallgas...; **II** *s.* Knallgas *n*.

oy [ɔɪ] *int.* he!, he du!

o·yer ['ɔɪə] *s.* 🕮 **1.** *hist.* gerichtliche Un-ter'suchung. **2.** → **~ and ter·mi·ner** ['tɜːmɪnə] *s.* 🕮 **1.** *hist.* gerichtliche Un-tersuchung u. Entscheidung; **2.** *mst* **commission** (*od.* **writ**) **of ~** *Brit.* kö-nigliche Ermächtigung an die Richter der Assisengerichte, Gericht zu halten.

o·yez [əʊ'jes] *int.* hört (zu)!

oys·ter ['ɔɪstə] *s.* **1.** *zo.* Auster *f*: **~s on the shell** frische Austern; **he thinks the world is his ~** *fig.* er meint, er kann alles haben; **2.** F ,zugeknöpfter Mensch'; **~ bank**, **~ bed** *s.* Austern-bank *f*; **~ catch·er** *s. orn.* Austern-fischer *m*; **~ farm** *s.* Austernpark *m*.

o·zone ['əʊzəʊn] *s.* **1.** 🜪 O'zon *m*, *n*; **2.** F O'zon *n*, *n*, reine frische Luft; **~ a·lert** *s.* O'zona,larm *m*; ,**~-de'plet-ing** *adj.* o'zonschädlich; **~ de·ple·tion** *s.* O'zonabbau *m*; ,**~-'free** *adj.* o'zon-frei; ,**~-'friend·ly** *adj.* FCK'W-frei (*Spray etc.*); **~ hole** *s.* O'zonloch *n*; **~ lay·er** *s.* O'zonschicht *f*; **~ lev·els** *pl.* O'zonwerte *pl.*; **o·zon·ic** [əʊ'zɒnɪk] *adj.* **1.** o'zonisch, Ozon...; **2.** o'zonhaltig; **o·zo·nif·er·ous** [,əʊzəʊ'nɪfərəs] *adj.* **1.** o'zonhaltig; **2.** O'zon erzeugend; **o·zo·nize** ['əʊzəʊnaɪz] *v/t.* ozonisieren; **o·zo-niz·er** ['əʊzəʊnaɪzə] *s.* Ozoni'sator *m*.

P, p [pi:] *s.* P *n*, p *n* (*Buchstabe*): *mind one's P's and Q's* sich sehr in Acht nehmen.

pa [pɑː] *s.* F Pa'pa *m*, ,Paps' *m*.

pab·u·lum ['pæbjʊləm] *s.* Nahrung *f* (*a. fig.*).

pace¹ [peɪs] **I** *s.* **1.** Schritt *m* (*a. als Maß*); **2.** Gang(art *f*) *m*: *put a horse through its ~s* ein Pferd alle Gangarten machen lassen; *put s.o. through his ~s fig.* j-n auf Herz u. Nieren prüfen; **3.** Passgang *m* (*Pferd*); **4.** a) ✕ Marschschritt *m*, b) (Marsch)Geschwindigkeit *f*, Tempo *n* (*a. sport*; *a. fig. e-r Handlung etc.*), Fahrt *f*, Schwung *m*: *go the ~* a) ein scharfes Tempo anschlagen, b) *fig.* flott leben; *keep ~ with* Schritt halten mit (*a. fig.*); *set the ~ sport* das Tempo angeben (*a. fig.*) *od.* machen; *at a great ~* in schnellem Tempo; **II** *v/t.* **5.** a. *~ out* (*od. off*) abschreiten; **6.** Zimmer *etc.* durch'schreiten, -'messen; **7.** *fig.* das Tempo (*gen.*) bestimmen; **8.** *sport* Schrittmacher sein für; **9.** Pferd im Passgang gehen lassen; **III** *v/i.* **10.** (*auf u. ab etc.*) schreiten; **11.** im Passgang gehen (*Pferd*).

pa·ce² ['peɪsɪ] (*Lat.*) *prp.* ohne j-m zu nahe treten zu wollen.

'pace|,mak·er *s. sport* (*a. ♣* Herz-) Schrittmacher *m*: *~ race* Radsport: Steherrennen *n*; '*~,mak·ing s. sport* Schrittmacherdienste *pl.*

pac·er ['peɪsə] *s.* **1.** → *pacemaker*; **2.** Passgänger *m* (*Pferd*).

pach·y·derm ['pækɪdɜːm] *s. zo.* Dickhäuter *m* (*a. humor. fig.*); **pach·y·der·ma·tous** [,pækɪ'dɜːmətəs] *adj.* **1.** *zo.* dickhäutig; *fig. a.* dickfellig; **2.** ♀ dickwandig.

pa·cif·ic [pə'sɪfɪk] *adj.* (□ *~ally*) **1.** friedfertig, versöhnlich, Friedens...: *~ policy*; **2.** ruhig, friedlich; **3.** ♀ *geogr.* pa'zifisch, Pa'zifisch: *the ♀* (*Ocean*) der Pazifische *od.* Stille Ozean, der Pa'zifik; **pac·i·fi·ca·tion** [,pæsɪfɪ'keɪʃn] *s.* **1.** Befriedung *f*; **2.** Beschwichtigung *f*.

pac·i·fi·er ['pæsɪfaɪə] *s.* **1.** Friedensstifter(in); **2.** *Am.* a) Schnuller *m*, b) Beißring *m für Kleinkinder*; '**pac·i·fism** [-fɪzəm] *s.* Pazi'fismus *m*; '**pac·i·fist** [-fɪst] **I** *s.* Pazi'fist *m*; **II** *adj.* pazi'fistisch; '**pac·i·fy** [-faɪ] *v/t.* **1.** Land befrieden; **2.** besänftigen, beschwichtigen.

pack [pæk] **I** *s.* **1.** Pack(en) *m*, Ballen *m*, Bündel *n*; **2.** *bsd. Am.* Packung *f*, Schachtel *f Zigaretten etc.*, Päckchen *n*: *a ~ of films* ein Filmpack *m*; **3.** *♣*, *Kosmetik*: Packung *f*: *face ~*; **4.** (Karten)Spiel *n*; **5.** ✕ a) Tor'nister *m*, b) Rückentrage *f* (*Kabelrolle etc.*); **6.** Verpackungsweise *f*; **7.** (Schub *m*) Kon'serven *pl.*; **8.** Menge *f*: *a ~ of lies* ein Haufen Lügen; *a ~ of nonsense* lauter Unsinn; **9.** Packeis *n*; **10.** Pack *n*, Bande *f* (*Diebesgesindel*); **11.** Meute *f*, Koppel *f* (*Hunde*); Rudel *n* (*Wölfe*, ✕ U-Boote); **12.** *Rugby*: Sturm(reihe *f*) *m*; **II** *v/t.* **13.**

oft ~ up einpacken (*a. ♣*), zs.-, verpacken: *~ it in!* F *fig.* hör doch auf (damit)!; **14.** zs.-pressen, -pferchen; → *sardine*; **15.** voll stopfen: *a ~ed house thea. etc.* ein zum Bersten volles Haus; **16.** eindosen, konservieren; **17.** ☉ (ab)dichten; **18.** bepacken, -laden; **19.** *Geschworenenbank etc.* mit s-n Leuten besetzen; **20.** *Am.* F (bei sich) tragen: *~ a hard punch* Boxen: e-n harten Schlag haben; **21.** *a. ~ off* (fort)schicken, (-)jagen; **III** *v/i.* **22.** packen (*oft ~ up*); *~ up fig.* ,einpacken' (*es aufgeben*); **23.** sich *gut etc.* (ver)packen lassen; **24.** fest werden, sich fest zs.-ballen; **25.** *mst ~ off fig.* sich packen *od.* da'vonmachen: *send s.o. ~ing* j-n fortjagen; **26.** *~ up sl.* ,absterben', ,verrecken' (*Motor*) (*on s.o.* j-m).

pack·age ['pækɪdʒ] **I** *s.* **1.** Pack *m*, Ballen *m*; Frachtstück *n*; *bsd. Am.* Pa'ket *n*; **2.** Packung *f* (*Spaghetti etc.*): *~ insert* Beipackzettel *m*, Packungsbeilage *f*; **3.** Verpackung *f*; **4.** ☉ betriebsfertige Maschine *od.* Baueinheit; **5.** ♥, *pol.*, *fig.* Pa'ket *n* (*a. Computer*), *pol. a.* Junktim *n*: *~ deal* a) Kopplungsgeschäft *n*, b) Pau'schalarrange,ment *n*, -angebot *n*; *~ holiday* Pauschalurlaub *m*, *~ tour* Pauschalreise *f*, c) *pol.* Junktim *n*, d) (als Ganzes *od.* frei verkauftes) ('Fernseh- *etc.*)Pro,gramm *n*; **II** *v/t.* **6.** verpacken; **7.** *Lebensmittel etc.* abpacken; **8.** ♥ en bloc anbieten *od.* verkaufen; '**pack·ag·ing** [-dʒɪŋ] **I** *s.* (Einzel-) Verpackung *f*; **II** *adj.* Verpackungs...: *~ machine*; *~ waste* Verpackungsmüll *m*.

pack| an·i·mal *s.* Pack-, Lasttier *n*; '*~-cloth s.* Packleinwand *f*; *~ drill s.* ✕ Strafexerzieren *n* in voller Marschausrüstung.

pack·er ['pækə] *s.* **1.** (Ver)Packer(in); **2.** ♥ Verpacker *m*, Großhändler *m*; *Am.* Kon'serven,hersteller *m*; **3.** Ver'packungsma,schine *f*.

pack·et ['pækɪt] **I** *s.* **1.** kleines Pa'ket, Päckchen *n*, Schachtel *f* (*Zigaretten etc.*): *sell s.o. a ~* F j-n ,anschmieren'; **2.** ♣ *a. ~ boat* Postschiff *n*, Pa'ketboot *n*; **3.** *sl.* Haufen *m* Geld, e-e ,(hübsche) Stange Geld'; **4.** *sl.* ,Ding' *n* (*Schlag, Ärger etc.*); **II** *v/t.* **5.** verpacken, paketieren.

'**pack| horse** *s.* **1.** Packpferd *n*; **2.** *fig.* Lastesel *m*; *~ ice s.* Packeis *n*.

pack·ing ['pækɪŋ] *s.* **1.** (Ver)Packen *n*: *do one's ~* packen; **2.** Konservierung *f*; **3.** Verpackung *f* (*a. ♥*); **4.** ☉ a) (Ab-) Dichtung *f*, b) Dichtung *f*, c) 'Dichtungsmateri,al *n*, d) Füllung *f*, e) *Computer*: Verdichtung *f*; **5.** Zs.-ballen *n*; *~ box s.* **1.** Packkiste *f*; **2.** ☉ Stopfbüchse *f*; *~ case s.* Packkiste *f*; *~ de·part·ment s.* ♥ Packe'rei *f*, Versand *m*: **1.** *Am.* Abpackbetrieb *m*; **2.** Warenlager *n*; *~ pa·per s.* 'Packpa,pier *n*; *~ ring s.* ☉ Dichtring *m*, Man'schette *f*; *~ sleeve s.* ☉ Dichtungsmuffe *f*.

pack| rat *s. zo.* Packratte *f*; '*~-sack s. Am.* Rucksack *m*, Tor'nister *m*;

'*~,sad·dle s.* Pack-, Saumsattel *m*; '*~-thread s.* Packzwirn *m*, Bindfaden *m*; *~ train s.* 'Tragtierko,lonne *f*.

pact [pækt] *s.* Pakt *m*, Vertrag *m*.

pad¹ [pæd] **I** *s.* **1.** Polster *n*, (Stoß)Kissen *n*, Wulst *m*, Bausch *m*: *oil ~* ☉ Schmierkissen *n*; **2.** *sport* Knie- *od.* Beinschützer *m*; **3.** 'Unterlage *f*; ☉ Kon'sole *f für Hilfsgeräte*; → *mousepad*; **4.** ('Löschpa,pier-, Brief-, Schreib-) Block *m*; **5.** Stempelkissen *n*; **6.** *zo.* (Fuß)Ballen *m*; **7.** *hunt.* Pfote *f*; **8.** *sl.* ,Bude' *f* (*Zimmer od. Wohnung*); **9.** ✈ a) Startrampe *f*, b) (Ra'keten)Abschussrampe *f*; **10.** *Am. sl.* a) Schutzgelder *pl.*, b) Schmiergelder *pl.*; **II** *v/t.* **11.** (aus)polstern, wattieren: *~ded cell* Gummizelle *f* (*für Irre*): **12.** *fig.* Rede, Schrift ,garnieren', ,aufblähen'.

pad² [pæd] *v/t. u. v/i. a. ~ along sl.* (da'hin)trotten, (-)latschen.

pad·ding ['pædɪŋ] *s.* **1.** (Aus)Polstern *n*; **2.** Polsterung *f*, Wattierung *f*, Einlage *f*; **3.** (Polster)Füllung *f*; **4.** *fig.* leeres Füllwerk, (Zeilen)Füllsel *n*; **5.** *a. ~ capacitor ⚡* 'Paddingkonden,sator *m*.

pad·dle ['pædl] **I** *s.* **1.** Paddel *n*: **2.** ⚓ a) Schaufel(rad *n*) *f*, b) Raddampfer *m*; **3.** *obs.* Waschbleuel *m*; **4.** ☉ Kratze *f*, Rührstange *f*; **5.** ☉ a) Schaufel *f* (*Wasserrad*), b) Schütz *n*, Falltor *n* (*Schleuse*); **II** *v/i.* **6.** rudern, *bsd.* paddeln; → *canoe* **I**; **7.** *im Wasser* plan(t)schen; **8.** watscheln; **III** *v/t.* **9.** paddeln; **10.** *Am.* F verhauen; *~ steam·er s. ⚓* Raddampfer *m*; *~ wheel s.* Schaufelrad *n*.

pad·dling pool ['pædlɪŋ] *s.* Plan(t)schbecken *n*.

pad·dock¹ ['pædək] *s.* **1.** (Pferde)Koppel *f*; **2.** *sport* a) Sattelplatz *m*, b) *mot.* Fahrerlager *n*.

pad·dock² ['pædək] *s. zo.* **1.** *obs. od. dial.* Frosch *m*; **2.** *obs.* Kröte *f*.

Pad·dy¹ ['pædɪ] *s.* F ,Paddy' *m* (*Ire*).

pad·dy² ['pædɪ] *s.* ♥ roher Reis.

pad·dy³ ['pædɪ] *s.* F Wutanfall *m*; *~ wag·on s. Am.* F ,grüne Minna' (*Polizeigefangenenwagen*).

pad·lock ['pædlɒk] **I** *s.* Vorhänge-, Vorlegeschloss *n*; **II** *v/t.* mit e-m Vorhängeschloss verschließen.

pa·dre ['pɑːdrɪ] *s.* Pater *m* (*Priester*); ✕ Ka'plan *m*.

pae·an ['piːən] *s.* **1.** *antiq.* Pä'an *m*; **2.** *allg.* Freuden-, Lobgesang *m*.

paed·er·ast *etc.* → *pederast etc.*

pae·di·at·ric *etc.* → *pediatric etc.*

pa·gan ['peɪgən] **I** *s.* Heide *m*, Heidin *f*; **II** *adj.* heidnisch; '**pa·gan·ism** [-nɪzəm] *s.* Heidentum *n*.

page¹ [peɪdʒ] **I** *s.* **1.** Seite *f* (*Buch etc.*); *typ.* Schriftseite *f*, Ko'lumne *f*: *~ break Computer*: Seitenwechsel *m* (*in Textverarbeitung*); *~ printer tel.* Blattdrucker *m*; **2.** *fig.* Chronik *f*, Buch *n*; **3.** *fig.* Blatt *n aus der Geschichte etc.*; **II** *v/t.* **4.** paginieren.

page² [peɪdʒ] **I** *s.* **1.** *hist.* Page *m*; Edelknabe *m*; **2.** (Ho'tel)Page *m*; **II** *v/t.* **3.** *j-n* (durch e-n Pagen *od.* per Lautsprecher) ausrufen lassen; **4.** mit *j-m* über Funkrufempfänger Kon'takt aufnehmen, *j-n* ‚anpiepsen'.

pag·eant ['pædʒənt] *s.* **1.** a) (*bsd.* hi'storischer) Fest- *od.* 'Umzug, b) (historisches) Festspiel; **2.** (Schau)Gepränge *n*, Pomp *m*; **3.** *fig.* leerer Prunk; **'pageant·ry** [-rɪ] *s.* → **pageant** 2, 3.

page·boy ['peɪdʒbɔɪ] *s.* **1.** → *page²*; **2.** *Frisur:* Pagenkopf *m*.

pag·er ['peɪdʒə(r)] Funkrufempfänger *m*, ‚Piepser' *m*.

pag·i·nal ['pædʒɪnl] *adj.* Seiten...; **'pag·i·nate** [-neɪt] *v/t.* paginieren; **pag·i·na·tion** [ˌpædʒɪ'neɪʃn], *a.* **pag·ing** ['peɪdʒɪŋ] *s.* Paginierung *f*, 'Seitennumme‚rierung *f*.

pa·go·da [pə'gəʊdə] *s.* Pa'gode *f*; **~ tree** *s.* ♀ So'phora *f*: **shake the ~** *obs. fig.* in Indien schnell ein Vermögen machen.

pah [pɑː] *int. contp.* a) pfui!, b) pah!

paid [peɪd] **I** *pret. u. p.p. von* **pay**; **II** *adj.* bezahlt: **~ in** → **paid-in** → **paid-up**; **put ~ to s.th.** e-r Sache ein Ende setzen; **~-in** *adj.* **1.** ⴵ (voll) eingezahlt: **~ capital** Einlagekapital *n*; **2.** → **paid-up** 2; **~-'up** *adj.* **1.** → **paid-in** 1; **2. fully ~ member** Mitglied *n* ohne Beitragsrückstände, vollwertiges Mitglied.

pail [peɪl] *s.* Eimer *m*, Kübel *m*; **'pail·ful** [-fʊl] *s. ein* Eimer (voll): **by ~s** eimerweise.

pail·lasse ['pælɪæs] *s.* Strohsack *m* (*Matratze*).

pain [peɪn] **I** *s.* **1.** Schmerz(en *pl.*) *m*, Pein *f*; *pl.* ⚕ (Geburts)Wehen *pl.*: **be in ~** Schmerzen haben, leiden; **you are a ~ in the neck** F du gehst mir auf die Nerven; **2.** Schmerz(en *pl.*) *m*, Leid *n*, Kummer *m*: **give** (*od.* **cause**) **s.o. ~** j-m Kummer machen; **3.** *pl.* Mühe *f*, Bemühungen *pl.*: **be at ~s, take ~s** sich Mühe geben, sich anstrengen; **spare no ~s** keine Mühe scheuen; **all he got for his ~s** der (ganze) Dank (für s-e Mühe); **4.** Strafe *f*: (**up**)**on** (*od.* **under**) **~ of** bei Strafe von; **on** (*od.* **under**) **~ of death** bei Todesstrafe; **II** *v/t.* **5.** *j-m* wehtun, *j-n* schmerzen; *fig. a. j-n* schmerzlich berühren, peinigen; **pained** [-nd] *adj.* gequält, schmerzlich; **'pain·ful** [-fʊl] *adj.* □ **1.** schmerzhaft; **2.** a) schmerzlich, quälend, b) peinlich: **produce a ~ impression** peinlich wirken; **3.** mühsam; **'pain·ful·ness** [-fʊlnɪs] *s.* Schmerzhaftigkeit *f etc.*; **'pain,kill·er** *s.* F 'Schmerzmittel *n*, -ta‚blette *f*, schmerzstillendes Mittel; **'pain·less** [-lɪs] *adj.* □ schmerzlos (*a. fig.*).

pains·tak·ing ['peɪnzˌteɪkɪŋ] **I** *adj.* □ sorgfältig, gewissenhaft; eifrig; **II** *s.* Sorgfalt *f*, Mühe *f*.

paint [peɪnt] **I** *v/t.* **1.** *Bild* malen; *fig.* ausmalen, schildern: **~ s.o.'s portrait** j-n malen; **2.** an-, bemalen, (an)streichen; *Auto* lackieren: **~ out** übermalen; **~ the town red** *sl.* ‚auf die Pauke hauen', ‚(schwer) einen draufmachen'; → **lily**; **3.** *Mittel* auftragen, *Hals, Wunde* (aus)pinseln; **4.** schminken: **~ one's face** sich schminken, sich ‚anmalen'; **II** *v/i.* **5.** malen; **6.** streichen; **7.** sich schminken; **III** *s.* **8.** (Anstrich-, Öl)Farbe *f*; (Auto)Lack *m*; Tünche *f*; **9.** *a.* **coat of ~** Anstrich *m*: **as fresh as ~** F frisch u. munter; **10.** Schminke *f*; **11.** ⚕ Tink'tur *f*; **'~·box** *s.* Tusch-, Malkasten *m*; **2.** Schminkdose *f*; **'~·brush** *s.* Pinsel *m*.

paint·ed ['peɪntɪd] *p.p. u. adj.* **1.** ge-, bemalt, gestrichen; lackiert; **2.** *bsd.* ⚕ *zo.* bunt, scheckig; **3.** *fig.* gefärbt; ⚕ **La·dy** *s.* **1.** *zo.* Distelfalter *m*; **2.** ♀ Rote Wucherblume; **~ wom·an** *s.* [*irr.*] Hure *f*, ‚Flittchen' *n*.

paint·er¹ ['peɪntə] *s.* ⚓ Fangleine *f*: **cut the ~** *fig.* alle Brücken hinter sich abbrechen.

paint·er² ['peɪntə] *s.* **1.** (Kunst)Maler (-in); **2.** Maler *m*, Anstreicher *m*: **~'s colic** ⚕ Bleikolik *f*; **~'s shop** a) Malerwerkstatt *f*, b) (Auto)Lackiererei *f*; **'paint·ing** [-tɪŋ] *s.* **1.** Malen *n*, Male'rei *f*: **~ in oil** Ölmalerei; **2.** Gemälde *n*, Bild *n*; **3.** ⊚ a) Farbanstrich *m*, b) Spritzlackieren *n*.

paint| re·fresh·er *s.* 'Neuglanzpoli‚tur *f*; **~ re·mov·er** *s.* (Farben)Abbeizmittel *n*.

paint·ress ['peɪntrɪs] *s.* Malerin *f*.

'paint-,spray·ing pis·tol *s.* ⊚ ('Anstreich‚)Spritzpi‚stole *f*; **'~·work** *s. mot.* Lackierung *f*, Lack *m*.

pair [peə] **I** *s.* **1.** Paar *n*: **a ~ of boots**, **legs** *etc.*; **2.** (*Zweiteiliges, mst unübersetzt*): **a ~ of scales** (**scissors**, **spectacles**) eine Waage (Schere, Brille); **a ~ of trousers** ein Paar Hosen, eine Hose; **3.** Paar *n*, Pärchen *n* (*Mann u. Frau*; *zo.* Männchen u. Weibchen): **~ skating** *sport* Paarlauf(en *n*) *m*; **in ~s** paarweise; **4.** Partner *m*; Gegenstück *n* (*von e-m Paar*); *der (die, das)* Zweite: **where is the ~ to this shoe?**; **5.** *pol.* a) zwei Mitglieder verschiedener Parteien, die sich abgesprochen haben, sich der Stimme zu enthalten etc., b) dieses Abkommen, c) e-r dieser Partner; **6.** (Zweier)Gespann *n*: **carriage and ~** Zweispänner *m*; **7.** *sport* Zweier *m* (*Ruderboot*): **~ with cox** Zweier mit Steuermann; **8.** *a.* **kinematic ~** ⊚ Ele'mentenpaar *n*; **9.** *Brit.* **~ of stairs** (*od.* **steps**) Treppe *f*: **two ~ front** (**back**) (*Raum m od.* Mieter *m*) im zweiten Stock nach vorn (hinten); **II** *v/t.* **10.** *a.* **~ off** a) paarweise anordnen, b) F *fig.* verheiraten; **11.** *Tiere* paaren (**with** mit); **III** *v/i.* **12.** sich paaren (*Tiere*) (*a. fig.*); **13.** zs.-passen; **14.** **~ off** a) paarweise weggehen, b) F *fig.* sich verheiraten (**with** mit), c) *pol.* (**with** mit e-m Mitglied e-r anderen Partei) ein Abkommen treffen (→ 5a); **pair·ing** ['peərɪŋ] *s. biol.* Paarung *f* (*a. sport*): **~ season**, **~ time** Paarungszeit *f*.

pair-oar ['peərɔː] *s.* Zweier *m* (*Boot*); **II** *adj.* zweiruderig.

pa·ja·mas [pə'dʒɑːməs] *bsd. Am.* → **pyjamas**.

Pak·i ['pækɪ] *s. Brit. sl.* Paki'stani *m*.

Pak·i·stan·i [ˌpɑːkɪ'stɑːnɪ] **I** *adj.* pakis'tanisch; **II** *s.* Paki'staner(in), Paki'stani *m*.

pal [pæl] **I** *s.* F ‚Kumpel' *m*, ‚Spezi' *m*, Freund *m*; **II** *v/i. mst* **~ up** F sich anfreunden (**with s.o.** mit j-m).

pal·ace ['pælɪs] *s.* Schloss *n*, Pa'last *m*, Pa'lais *n*: **~ of justice** Justizpalast; **~ car** ⛟ Sa'lonwagen *m*; **~ guard** *s.* **1.** Pa'lastwache *f*; **2.** *fig. contp.* Clique *f* um e-n Regierungschef, Kama'rilla *f*; **~ rev·o·lu·tion** *s. pol. fig.* Pa'lastrevolu‚ti‚on *f*.

pal·a·din ['pælədɪn] *s. hist.* Pala'din *m* (*a. fig.*).

pa·lae·og·ra·pher *etc.* → **paleographer** *etc.*

pal·at·a·ble ['pælətəbl] *adj.* □ wohlschmeckend, schmackhaft (*a. fig.*); **'pal·a·tal** [-tl] **I** *adj.* **1.** Gaumen...; *ling.* **2.** Gaumenknochen *m*; **3.** *ling.* Pala'tal (-laut) *m*; **'pal·a·tal·ize** [-təlaɪz] *v/t.*

ling. Laut palatalisieren; **pal·ate** ['pælət] *s.* **1.** *anat.* Gaumen *m*: **bony** (*od.* **hard**) **~** harter Gaumen, Vordergaumen; **cleft ~** Wolfsrachen *m*; **soft ~** weicher Gaumen, Gaumensegel *n*; **2.** *fig.* (**for**) Gaumen *m*, Sinn *m* (für), Geschmack *m* (an *dat.*).

pa·la·tial [pə'leɪʃl] *adj.* pa'lastartig, Palast..., Schloss..., Luxus...

pa·lat·i·nate [pə'lætɪnət] **I** *s.* **1.** *hist.* Pfalzgrafschaft *f*; **2. the ~** die (Rhein-)Pfalz; **II** *adj.* **3.** ⚑ Pfälzer, pfälzisch.

pal·a·tine¹ ['pælətaɪn] **I** *adj.* **1.** *hist.* Pfalz..., pfalzgräflich: **Count ⚑** Pfalzgraf; **County ⚑** Pfalzgrafschaft *f*; **2.** ⚑ pfälzisch, Pfälzer(...); **II** *s.* **3.** Pfalzgraf *m*; **4.** ⚑ (Rhein)Pfälzer(in).

pal·a·tine² ['pælətaɪn] *adj. anat.* **I** *adj.* Gaumen...: **~ tonsil** Gaumen-, Halsmandel *f*; **II** *s.* Gaumenbein *n*.

pa·la·ver [pə'lɑːvə] **I** *s.* **1.** Unter'handlung *f*, -'redung *f*, Konfe'renz *f*; **2.** F ‚Pa'laver' *n*, Geschwätz *n*; **3.** F ‚Wirbel' *m*; **II** *v/i.* **4.** unter'handeln; **5.** pa'lavern, ‚quasseln'; **III** *v/t.* **6.** F *j-n* beschwatzen; *j-m* schmeicheln.

pale¹ [peɪl] **I** *s.* **1.** Pfahl *m* (*a. her.*); **2.** *bsd. fig.* um'grenzter Raum, Bereich *m*, (enge) Grenzen *pl.*: **beyond the ~** *fig.* jenseits der Grenzen des Erlaubten; **within the ~ of the Church** im Schoße der Kirche; **II** *v/t.* **3.** *a.* **~ in** einpfählen, -zäunen; *fig.* um'schließen; **4.** *hist.* pfählen.

pale² [peɪl] **I** *adj.* □ **1.** blass, bleich, fahl: **turn ~** → 3; **~ with fright** schreckensbleich; **as ~ as ashes** (**clay, death**) aschfahl (kreidebleich, totenblass); **2.** hell, blass, matt (*Farben*): **~ ale** helles Bier; **~ green** Blass-, Zartgrün *n*; **~ pink** (Blass)Rosa *n*; **II** *v/i.* **3.** blass werden, erbleichen, erblassen; **4.** *fig.* verblassen (**before** *od.* **beside** vor *dat.*); **III** *v/t.* **5.** bleich machen, erbleichen lassen.

'pale·face *s.* Bleichgesicht *n* (*Ggs. Indianer*).

pale·ness ['peɪlnɪs] *s.* Blässe *f*, Farblosigkeit *f* (*a. fig.*).

pa·le·og·ra·pher [ˌpælɪ'ɒgrəfə] *s.* Paläo'graph *m*, **pa·le'og·ra·phy** [-fɪ] *s.* **1.** alte Schriftarten *pl.*, alte Schriftdenkmäler *pl.*; **2.** Paläogra'phie *f*, Handschriftenkunde *f*.

pa·le·o·lith·ic [ˌpælɪəʊ'lɪθɪk] **I** *adj.* paläo'lithisch, altsteinzeitlich; **II** *s.* Altsteinzeit *f*.

pa·le·on·tol·o·gist [ˌpælɪɒn'tɒlədʒɪst] *s.* Paläonto'loge *m*; **pa·le·on'tol·o·gy** [-dʒɪ] *s.* Paläontolo'gie *f*.

pa·le·o·zo·ic [ˌpælɪəʊ'zəʊɪk] *geol.* **I** *adj.* paläo'zoisch: **~ era** → **II**; **II** *s.* Paläo'zoikum *n*.

Pal·es·tin·i·an [ˌpælɛ'stɪnɪən] **I** *adj.* paläs'ti'nensisch; **II** *s.* Paläs'ti'nenser(in).

pal·e·tot ['pæltəʊ] *s.* **1.** Paletot *m*, 'Überzieher *m* (für Herren); **2.** loser (Damen)Mantel.

pal·ette ['pælət] *s. paint.* Pa'lette *f*, *fig. a.* Farbenskala *f*; **~ knife** *s.* [*irr.*] Streichmesser *n*, Spachtel *m, f*.

pal·frey ['pɔːlfrɪ] *s.* Zelter *m*.

pal·ing ['peɪlɪŋ] *s.* Um'pfählung *f*, Pfahl-, Lattenzaun *m*, Sta'ket *n*.

pal·in·gen·e·sis [ˌpælɪn'dʒenɪsɪs] *s. bsd. eccl.* 'Wiedergeburt *f*, *a. biol.* Palinge-'nese *f*.

pal·i·sade [ˌpælɪ'seɪd] **I** *s.* **1.** Pali'sade *f*; Pfahlzaun *m*, Sta'ket *n*; **2.** Schanzpfahl *m*; **II** *v/t.* **3.** mit Pfählen *od.* mit e-r Pali'sade um'geben.

pall¹ [pɔːl] *s.* **1.** Bahr-, Leichentuch *n*; **2.** *fig.* Mantel *m*, Hülle *f*, Decke *f*; **3.** a) (Rauch)Wolke *f*, b) Dunstglocke *f*; **4.**

ecll. → **pallium** 2; **5.** *her.* Gabel(kreuz *n*) *f.*

pall² [pɔːl] **I** *v/i.* **1.** (**on**, **upon**) jeden Reiz verlieren (für), *j-n* kalt lassen *od.* langweilen; **2.** schal *od.* fade werden, s-n Reiz verlieren; **II** *v/t.* **3.** *a. fig.* über-'sättigen.

pal·la·di·um [pə'leɪdjəm] [-djə] *s.* Pal'ladium *n*: a) *pl.* **-di·a** *fig.* Hort *m*, Schutz *m*, b) 乃 *ein Element.*

'**pall,bear·er** *s.* Sargträger *m.*

pal·let¹ ['pælɪt] *s.* (Stroh)Lager *n*, Strohsack *m*, Pritsche *f.*

pal·let² ['pælɪt] *s.* **1.** ⊙ Dreh-, Töpferscheibe *f*; **2.** *paint.* Pa'lette *f*; **3.** Trockenbrett *n* (*für Keramik, Ziegel etc.*); **4.** ⊙ Pa'lette: **~ truck** Gabelstapler *m*; '**pal·let·ize** [-lətaɪz] *v/t.* ⊙ palettieren.

pal·liasse ['pæliæs] → **paillasse**.

pal·li·ate ['pælɪeɪt] *v/t.* **1.** ⚚ lindern; **2.** *fig.* bemänteln, beschönigen; **pal·li·a·tion** [,pælɪ'eɪʃn] *s.* **1.** Linderung *f*; **2.** Bemäntelung *f*, Beschönigung *f*; '**pal·li·a·tive** [-ɪətɪv] **I** *adj.* **1.** ⚚ lindernd, pallia'tiv; **2.** *fig.* bemäntelnd, beschönigend; **II** *s.* **3.** ⚚ Linderungsmittel *n*; **4.** *fig.* Bemäntelung *f.*

pal·lid ['pælɪd] *adj.* ☐ *a. fig.* blass, farblos; '**pal·lid·ness** [-nɪs] *s.* Blässe *f.*

pal·li·um ['pælɪəm] *pl.* **-li·a** [-lɪə], **-li·ums** *s.* **1.** *antiq.* Pallium *n*, Philo'sophenmantel *m*; **2.** *eccl.* a) Pallium *n* (*Schulterband des Erzbischofs*), b) Al'tartuch *n*; **3.** *anat.* (Ge)Hirnmantel *m*; **4.** *zo.* Mantel *m.*

pal·lor ['pælə] *s.* Blässe *f.*

pal·ly ['pælɪ] *adj.* **F 1.** (eng) befreundet; **2.** kumpelhaft.

palm¹ [pɑːm] **I** *s.* **1.** Handfläche *f*, -teller *m*, hohle Hand: **grease** (*od.* **oil**) *s.o.'s* **~** *j-n* ,schmieren', bestechen; **2.** Hand (-breite) *f* (*als Maß*); **3.** Schaufel *f* (*Anker, Hirschgeweih*); **II** *v/t.* **4.** betasten, streicheln; **5.** a) palmieren (*wegzaubern*), b) *Am. sl.* ,klauen', stehlen; **6.** **~ s.th. off on s.o.**, **~ s.o. off with s.th.** *j-m et.* ,aufhängen' *od.* ,andrehen'; **~ o.s. off** (**as**) sich ausgeben (als).

palm² [pɑːm] *s.* **1.** ⚘ Palme *f*; **2.** *fig.* Siegespalme *f*, Krone *f*, Sieg *m*: **bear** (*od.* **win**) **the ~** den Sieg davontragen; → **yield** 4.

pal·mate ['pælmɪt] *adj.* **1.** ⚘ handförmig (*gefingert od.* geteilt); **2.** *zo.* schwimmfüßig.

palm grease *s.* **F** Schmiergeld *n.*

pal·mi·ped ['pælmɪped], '**pal·mi·pede** [-ɪpiːd] *zo.* **I** *adj.* schwimmfüßig; **II** *s.* Schwimmfüßer *m.*

palm·ist ['pɑːmɪst] *s.* Handleser(in); '**palm·is·try** [-trɪ] *s.* Handlesekunst *f*, Chiroman'tie *f.*

palm| oil *s.* **1.** Palmöl *n*; **2.** → **palm grease**; ⚚ **Sun·day** *s.* Palm'sonntag *m*; '**~·top** *s.* *Computer:* Palmtop *m* (*tragbarer Kleinstcomputer*); **~ tree** *s.* Palme *f.*

palm·y ['pɑːmɪ] *adj.* **1.** palmenreich; **2.** *fig.* glorreich, Glanz..., Blüte...

pa·loo·ka [pə'luːkə] *s.* *Am. sl.* **1.** *bsd. sport* ,Niete', ,Flasche'; **2.** ,Ochse' *m*; **3.** Lümmel *m.*

palp [pælp] *s.* *zo.* Taster *m*, Fühler *m*; **pal·pa·bil·i·ty** [,pælpə'bɪlətɪ] *s.* **1.** Fühl-, Greif-, Tastbarkeit *f*; **2.** *fig.* Handgreiflichkeit *f*, Augenfälligkeit *f*; '**pal·pa·ble** [-pəbl] *adj.* ☐ **1.** fühl-, greif-, tastbar; **2.** *fig.* handgreiflich, augenfällig; '**pal·pa·ble·ness** [-pəblnɪs] → **palpability**; '**pal·pate** [-peɪt] *v/t.* befühlen, abtasten (*a.* ⚚); **pal·pa·tion** [pæl'peɪʃn] *s.* Abtasten *n* (*a.* ⚚).

pal·pe·bra ['pælpɪbrə] *s.* *anat.* Augenlid

---

n: **lower ~** Unterlid *n.*

pal·pi·tant ['pælpɪtənt] *adj.* klopfend, pochend; **pal·pi·tate** ['pælpɪteɪt] *v/i.* **1.** klopfen, pochen (*Herz*); **2.** (er)zittern; **pal·pi·ta·tion** [,pælpɪ'teɪʃn] *s.* Klopfen *n*, (heftiges) Schlagen: **~** (**of the heart**) ⚚ Herzklopfen *n.*

pal·sied ['pɔːlzɪd] *adj.* **1.** gelähmt; **2.** zittrig, wacklig; **pal·sy** ['pɔːlzɪ] **I** *s.* **1.** ⚚ Lähmung *f*: **shaking ~** Schüttellähmung; **wasting ~** progressive Muskelatrophie; → **writer** 1; **2.** *fig.* Ohnmacht *f*, Lähmung *f*; **II** *v/t.* **3.** lähmen.

pal·ter ['pɔːltə] *v/i.* **1.** (**with**) gemein handeln (an *dat.*), sein Spiel treiben (mit); **2.** feilschen.

pal·tri·ness ['pɔːltrɪnɪs] *s.* Armseligkeit *f*, Schäbigkeit *f*; **pal·try** ['pɔːltrɪ] *adj.* ☐ **1.** armselig, karg: *a* **~** *sum*; **2.** dürftig, fadenscheinig: *a* **~** *excuse*; **3.** schäbig, schofel, gemein: *a* **~** *fellow*; *a* **~** *lie*; *a* **~** *ten dollars* lumpige zehn Dollar.

pam·pas ['pæmpəs] *s. pl.* Pampas *pl.* (*südamer. Grasebene[n]*).

pam·per ['pæmpə] *v/t.* verwöhnen, -hätscheln; *fig.* Stolz etc. nähren, -hätscheln'; *e-m Gelüst* frönen.

pam·phlet ['pæmflɪt] *s.* **1.** Bro'schüre *f*, Druckschrift *f*, Heft *n*; **2.** Flugblatt *n*, -schrift *f*; **pam·phlet·eer** [,pæmflə'tɪə] *s.* Verfasser(in) von Flugschriften.

pan¹ [pæn] **I** *s.* **1.** Pfanne *f*: **frying ~** Bratpfanne; **2.** ⊙ Pfanne *f*, Tiegel *m*, Becken *n*, Mulde *f*, Trog *m*; **3.** Schale *f* (*e-r Waage*); **4.** ✗ *hist.* (Zünd)Pfanne *f*; → **flash** 2; **5.** *sl.* Vi'sage *f*, Gesicht *n*; **6.** **F** ,Verriss' *m*, vernichtende Kri'tik; **II** *v/t.* **7.** *oft* **~ out**, **~ off** Gold(sand) auswaschen; **8.** **F** ,verreißen', scharf kritisieren; **III** *v/i.* **9.** **~ out** *Am. sl.* sich bezahlt machen, ,klappen': **~ out well** a) *an Gold* ergiebig sein, b) *fig.* ,hinhauen', ,einschlagen'.

pan² [pæn] **I** *v/t.* Filmkamera schwenken, fahren; **II** *v/i.* a) panoramieren, die Filmkamera fahren *od.* schwenken, b) (her'um)schwenken (*Kamera*); **III** *s.* Film: Schwenk *m.*

pan- [pæn] *in Zssgn* all..., gesamt...; All..., Gesamt..., Pan...

pan·a·ce·a [,pænə'sɪə] *s.* All'heil-, Wundermittel *n*; *fig. a.* Pa'tentre,zept *n.*

pa·nache [pə'næʃ] *s.* **1.** Helm-, Federbusch *m*; **2.** *fig.* Großtue'rei *f.*

Pan-A·mer·i·can [,pænə'merɪkən] *adj.* panameri'kanisch.

'**pan·cake** *s.* **1.** Pfann-, Eierkuchen *m*: **~ roll** Frühlingsrolle *f*; **2.** Leder *n* geringerer Quali'tät (*aus Resten hergestellt*); **3.** *a.* **~ landing** ✈ Bumslandung *f*; **II** *v/i.* **4.** ✈ *bei Landung* 'durchsacken; **III** *v/t.* **5.** ✈ *Maschine* 'durchsacken lassen; **IV** *adj.* **6.** Pfannkuchen...: **~ Day** **F** Fastnachtsdienstag *m*; **7.** flach: **~ coil** ⚡ Flachspule.

pan·chro·mat·ic [,pænkrəʊ'mætɪk] *adj.* ♪, *phot.* panchro'matisch.

pan·cre·as ['pæŋkrɪəs] *s. anat.* Bauchspeicheldrüse *f*, Pankreas *n*; **pan·cre·at·ic** [,pæŋkrɪ'ætɪk] *adj.* Bauchspeicheldrüsen...: **~ juice** Bauchspeichel *m.*

pan·da ['pændə] *s. zo.* Panda *m*, Katzenbär *m*; **~ car** *s.* *Brit.* (Funk-, Poli-zei)Streifenwagen *m*; **~ cross·ing** *s.* *Brit.* 'Fußgänger,überweg *m* mit Druckampel.

pan·dem·ic [pæn'demɪk] *adj.* ⚚ pan'demisch, ganz allge'mein verbreitet.

pan·de·mo·ni·um [,pændɪ'məʊnjəm] *s. fig.* **1.** In'ferno *n*, Hölle *f*; **2.** Höllenlärm *m.*

pan·der ['pændə] **I** *s.* **1.** a) Kuppler(in), b) Zuhälter *m*; **2.** *fig.* j-d, der aus den

---

Schwächen u. Lastern anderer Kapi'tal schlägt; j-d, der *e-m* Laster Vorschub leistet; **II** *v/t.* **3.** verkuppeln; **III** *v/i.* **4.** kuppeln; **5.** **~ to** a) appellieren an (*acc.*), sich wenden an (*acc.*), b) *e-m Laster etc.* Vorschub leisten: **~ to s.o.'s ambition** j-s Ehrgeiz anstacheln.

Pan·do·ra's box [pæn'dɔːrəz] *s. myth. u. fig.* die Büchse der Pan'dora.

pane [peɪn] *s.* **1.** (Fenster)Scheibe *f*; **2.** ⊙ Feld *n*, Fach *n*, Platte *f*, Tafel *f*, Füllung *f* (*Tür*), △ Kas'sette *f* (*Decke*): **~ of glass** *e-e* Tafel Glas; **3.** ebene Seitenfläche; Finne *f* (*Hammer*); Fa-'cette *f* (*Edelstein*).

pan·e·gyr·ic [,pænɪ'dʒɪrɪk] **I** *s.* Lobrede *f*, -preisung *f*, -schrift *f*, Lobeshymne *f* (**on** über *acc.*); **II** *adj.* → **pan·e·gyr·i·cal** [-kl] *adj.* ☐ lobpreisend, Lob(es)-...; ,**pan·e·gyr·ist** [-ɪst] *s.* Lobredner *m*; **pan·e·gy·rize** ['pænɪdʒɪraɪz] **I** *v/t.* (lob)preisen, ,in den Himmel heben'; **II** *v/i.* sich in Lobeshymnen ergehen.

pan·el ['pænl] **I** *s.* **1.** △ (vertieftes) Feld, Fach *n*, Füllung *f* (*Tür*), Täfelung *f* (*Wand*); **2.** Tafel *f* (*Holz*), Platte *f* (*Blech etc.*); **3.** *paint.* Holztafel *f*, Gemälde *n* auf Holz; **4.** *phot.* (Bild *n* im) 'Hochfor,mat *n*; **5.** Einsatz(streifen) *m* *am Kleid*; **6.** ✈ a) ✗ 'Flieger-, Si'gnaltuch *n*, b) Stoffbahn *f* (*Fallschirm*), c) Streifen *m* der Bespannung (*am Flugzeugflügel*), Verkleidung(sblech *n*) *f* (*Flügelbauteil*); **7.** ⚡, ⊙ a) → *instrument* 6, b) Schalttafel(feld *n*) *f*, c) Radio etc.: Feld *n*, Einschub *m*, d) → *panel board* 2; **8.** (Bau)Abteilung *f*, Abschnitt *m*; **9.** ✗ (Abbau)Feld *n*; **10.** 🜨 a) Liste *f* der Geschworenen, b) Geschworene *pl.*; **11.** ('Unter)Ausschuss *m*, Kommissi'on *f*, Gremium *n*, Kammer *f*; **12.** a) → *panel discussion*, b) Diskussi'onsteilnehmer *pl.*; **13.** Meinungsforschung: Befragtengruppe *f*; **II** *v/t.* **14.** täfeln, paneelieren, in Felder einteilen; **15.** *Kleid* mit Einsatzstreifen verzieren.

pan·el| board *s.* **1.** ⊙ Füllbrett *n*, (Wand-, Par'kett)Tafel *f*; **2.** ⚡ Schaltbrett *n*, -tafel *f*; **~ dis·cus·sion** *s.* Podiumsgespräch *n*, öffentliche Diskussi'on; **~ game** *s.* *TV etc.* Ratespiel *n*, 'Quiz(pro,gramm) *n*; **~ heat·ing** *s.* Flächenheizung *f.*

pan·el·ist ['pænlɪst] *s.* **1.** Diskussi'onsteilnehmer(in); **2.** *TV etc.* Teilnehmer (-in) an *e-m* 'Quizpro,gramm.

pan·el·(l)ing ['pænlɪŋ] *s.* Täfelung *f*, Verkleidung *f.*

pan·el| sys·tem *s.* 'Listensy,stem *n* (*für die Auswahl von Abgeordneten etc.*); **~ saw** *s.* Laubsäge *f*; **~ truck** *s.* *Am.* (kleiner) Lieferwagen *m*; '**~·work** *s.* Tafel-, Fachwerk *n.*

pang [pæŋ] *s.* **1.** plötzlicher Schmerz, Stechen *n*, Stich *m*: **death ~s** Todesqualen; **~s of hunger** nagender Hunger; **~s of love** Liebesschmerz *m*; **2.** *fig.* aufschießende Angst, plötzlicher Schmerz, Qual *f*, Weh *n*, Pein *f*: **~s of remorse** heftige Gewissensbisse.

,**Pan-'Ger·man** **I** *adj.* 'panger,manisch, all-, großdeutsch; **II** *s.* 'Pangerma,nist *m*, Alldeutsche(r) *m.*

pan·han·dle ['pæn,hændl] **I** *s.* **1.** Pfannenstiel *m*; **2.** *Am.* schmaler Fortsatz (*bes. e-s Staatsgebiets*); **II** *v/i.* *Am. sl.* **3.** *Am. sl.* j-n (an)betteln, *et.* ,schnorren', erbetteln (*a. fig.*); '**pan,han·dler** [-lə] *s.* *Am. sl.* Bettler *m*, ,Schnorrer' *m.*

pan·ic¹ ['pænɪk] *s.* ⚘ (Kolben)Hirse *f.*

pan·ic² ['pænɪk] **I** *adj.* panisch: **~ fear**, **~ haste** blinde Hast; **~ braking**

mot. scharfes Bremsen; **~ buying** Angstkäufe; **push the ~ button** *fig.* F panisch reagieren; **be at ~ stations** F fast ,'durchdrehen'; **II** *s.* **2.** Panik *f*, panischer Schrecken; **3.** ✝ Börsenpanik *f*, Kurssturz *m*: **~-proof** krisenfest; **4.** *Am. sl.* etwas zum Totlachen; **III** *v/t. pret. u. p.p.* '**pan·icked** [-kt] **5.** in Panik versetzen; **6.** in Panik geraten, *Am. sl. Publikum* hinreißen; **IV** *v/i.* **7.** von panischem Schrecken erfasst werden: **don't ~!** nur die Ruhe!; **8.** sich zu e-r Kurzschlusshandlung hinreißen lassen, ,'durchdrehen'; '**pan·ick·y** [-kɪ] *adj.* F **1.** 'überängstlich, -ner‚vös; **2.** in Panik.

pan·i·cle ['pænɪkl] *s.* ♀ Rispe *f*.

'**pan·ic‚mon·ger** *s.* Bange-, Panikmacher(in); **~ re·ac·tion** *s.* Kurzschlusshandlung *f*; '**~-‚strick·en**, '**~-struck** *adj.* von panischem Schrecken gepackt.

pan·jan·drum [pən'dʒændrəm] *s. humor.* Wichtigtuer *m*.

pan·nier ['pænɪə] *s.* **1.** (Trag)Korb *m*: **a pair of ~s** e-e Doppelpacktasche (*Fahr-, Motorrad*); **2.** a) Reifrock *m*, b) Reifrockgestell *n*.

pan·ni·kin ['pænɪkɪn] *s.* **1.** Pfännchen *n*; **2.** kleines Trinkgefäß.

pan·ning ['pænɪŋ] *s. Film:* Panoramierung *f*, (Kamera)Schwenkung *f*: **~ shot** Schwenk *m*.

pan·o·plied ['pænəplɪd] *adj.* **1.** vollständig gerüstet (*a. fig.*); **2.** prächtig geschmückt; **pan·o·ply** ['pænəplɪ] *s.* **1.** vollständige Rüstung; **2.** *fig.* prächtige Um'rahmung *od.* Aufmachung, Schmuck *m*.

pan·o·ra·ma [‚pænə'rɑːmə] *s.* **1.** Pano'rama *n* (*a. paint.*), Rundblick *m*; **2.** a) *Film:* Schwenk *m*, b) *phot.* Rundbildaufnahme *f*: **~ lens** Weitwinkelobjektiv *n*; **3.** *fig.* vollständiger 'Überblick (**of** über *acc.*); **‚pan·o·ram·ic** [-'ræmɪk] *adj.* (□ **~ally**) pano'ramisch, Rundblick...: **~ camera** Panoramenkamera *f*; **~ sketch** Ansichtsskizze *f*; **~ windshield** *mot. Am.* Rundsichtverglasung *f*.

pan shot *s.* (Kamera)Schwenk *m*.

pan·sy ['pænzɪ] *s.* **1.** ♀ Stiefmütterchen *n*; **2.** *a.* **~ boy** F a) ,Bubi' *m*, b) ,Homo' *m*, ,Schwule(r)' *m*.

pant [pænt] **I** *v/i.* **1.** keuchen, japsen, schnaufen: **~ for breath** nach Luft schnappen; **2.** *fig.* lechzen, dürsten, gieren (**for** *od.* **after** nach); **II** *v/t.* **3.** **~ out** Worte (her'vor)keuchen.

pan·ta·loon [‚pæntə'luːn] *s.* **1.** *thea.* Hans'wurst *m*; **2.** *pl. hist.* Panta'lons *pl.* (*Herrenhose*).

pan·tech·ni·con [pæn'teknɪkən] *s. Brit.* **1.** Möbellager *n*; **2.** *a.* **~ van** Möbelwagen *m*.

pan·the·ism ['pænθiːˌɪzəm] *s. phls.* Panthe'ismus *m*; '**pan·the·ist** [-ɪst] *s.* Panthe'ist(in); **pan·the·is·tic** [‚pænθiː'ɪstɪk] *adj.* panthe'istisch.

pan·the·on ['pænθɪən] *s.* Pantheon *n*, Ehrentempel *m*, Ruhmeshalle *f*.

pan·ther ['pænθə] *s. zo.* Pant(h)er *m*.

pan·ties ['pæntɪz] *s. pl.* F **1.** Kinderhöschen *n od. pl.*; **2.** (Damen)Slip *m*.

pan·ti·hose ['pæntɪhəʊz] *s.* Strumpfhose *f*.

pan·tile ['pæntaɪl] *s.* Dachziegel *m*, -pfanne *f*, Hohlziegel *m*.

pan·to·graph ['pæntəʊgrɑːf] *s.* **1.** ⚡ Scherenstromabnehmer *m*; **2.** ◎ Storchschnabel *m*.

pan·to·mime ['pæntəmaɪm] **I** *s.* **1.** *thea.* Panto'mime *f*; **2.** *Brit.* (Laien)Spiel *n*, englisches Weihnachtsspiel; **3.** Mie-

nen-, Gebärdenspiel *n*; **II** *v/t.* **4.** panto-'mimisch darstellen, mimen; **pan·to·mim·ic** [‚pæntə'mɪmɪk] *adj.* (□ **~ally**) panto'mimisch.

pan·try ['pæntrɪ] *s.* Vorratskammer *f*, Speiseschrank *m*: **butler's ~** Anrichteraum *m*.

pants [pænts] *s. pl.* **1.** lange (Herren-) Hose; → **wear**[1] 1; **2.** *Brit.* Herrenunterhose *f*.

'**pant| skirt** [pænt] *s.* Hosenrock *m*; **~(s) suit** *s. Am.* Hosenanzug *m*.

pant·y ['pæntɪ] → **panties**; **~ gir·dle** *s.* Miederhös-chen *n*; **~ hose** *s.* Strumpfhose *f*; **~ lin·er** *s.* Slipeinlage *f*; '**~-waist** *Am. s.* **1.** Hemdhös-chen *n*; **2.** *sl.* Schwächling *m*.

pap [pæp] *s.* **1.** (Kinder)Brei *m*, Papp *m*; **2.** *fig. Am.* F Protekti'on *f*.

pa·pa [pə'pɑː] *s.* Pa'pa *m*.

pa·pa·cy ['peɪpəsɪ] *s.* **1.** päpstliches Amt; **2.** ⚴ Papsttum *n*; **3.** Pontifi'kat *n*; '**pa·pal** [-pl] *adj.* □ **1.** päpstlich; **2.** 'römisch-ka'tholisch; '**pa·pal·ism** [-əlɪzəm] *s.* Papsttum *n*; '**pa·pal·ist** [-əlɪst] *s.* Pa'pist(in).

pa·pa·ya [pə'paɪə] *s.* **1.** Pa'paya *f* (*Frucht*); **2.** Pa'paya *f*, Me'lonenbaum *m*.

pa·per ['peɪpə] **I** *s.* ◎ a) Pa'pier *n*, b) Pappe *f*, c) Ta'pete *f*; **2.** Blatt *n* Papier; **3.** Papier *n als Schreibmaterial*: **~ does not blush** das Papier ist geduldig; **on ~** *fig.* auf dem Papier, theoretisch; → **commit** 1; **4.** Doku'ment *n*, Schriftstück *n*; **5.** ✝ a) ('Wert)Pa‚pier *n*, b) Wechsel *m*, c) Pa'piergeld *n*: **best** erstklassiger Wechsel; **convertible ~** (*in Gold*) einlösbares Papiergeld; **~ currency** Papierwährung *f*; **6.** *pl.* a) 'Ausweis- *od.* Be'glaubigungspa‚piere *pl.*, Doku'mente *pl.*: **send in one's ~s** den Abschied nehmen, b) Akten *pl.*, Schriftstücke *pl.*: **~s on appeal** 🕮 Berufungsakten; **move for ~s** *bsd. parl.* die Vorlage der Unterlagen e-s *Falles* beantragen; **7.** Prüfungsarbeit *f*; **8.** Aufsatz *m*, Abhandlung *f*, Vortrag *m*, -lesung *f*, Refe-'rat *n*: **read a ~** e-n Vortrag halten, referieren (**on** über *acc.*); **9.** Zeitung *f*, Blatt *n*; **10.** Brief *m*, Heft *n* mit Nadeln *etc.*; **11.** *thea. sl.* a) Freikarte *f*, b) Besucher *m* mit Freikarte; **II** *adj.* **12.** pa-'pieren, Papier..., Papp...; **13.** *fig.* (hauch)dünn, schwach; **14.** nur auf dem Pa'pier vorhanden: **~ team**; **III** *v/t.* **15.** in Papier einwickeln; mit Papier ausschlagen: **~ over** überkleben, *fig.* (notdürftig) übertünchen; **16.** tapezieren; **17.** mit 'Sandpa‚pier polieren; **18.** *thea. sl.* Haus mit Freikarten füllen; '**~-back** *s.* Paperback *n*, Taschenbuch *n*; **~ bag** *s.* Tüte *f*; '**~-board** *s.* Pappdeckel *m*, Pappe *f*; **~ chase** *s.* Schnitzeljagd *f*; **~ clip** *s.* Bü'ro-, Heftklammer *f*; **~ cup** *s.* Pappbecher *m*; **~ cut·ter** *s.* Pa'pier‚schneidema‚schine *f*; **2.** → **paper knife**; **~ ex·er·cise** *s.* ✕ Planspiel *n*; **~ fas·ten·er** *s.* Heftklammer *f*; **~ feed** *s.* Pa'piereinzug *m*; '**~-‚hang·er** *s.* Tapezierer *m*; **~ jam** *s.* Pa'pierstau *m*; **~ knife** *s.* [*irr.*] Pa'piermesser *n*, Brieföffner *m*; **~ mill** *s.* Pa'pierfab‚rik *f*, -mühle *f*; **~ mon·ey** *s.* Pa'piergeld *n*; **~ plate** *s.* Pappteller *m*; **~ prof·it** *s.* ✝ rechnerischer Gewinn; **~ source** [sɔːs] *s. Drucker etc.*: Pa'pierzufuhr *f*; **~ stain·er** *s.* Ta'petenmaler *m*, -macher *m*; **~ tape** *s. Computer:* Lochstreifen *m*; '**~-thin** *adj.* hauchdünn (*a. fig.*); **~ ti·ger** *s. fig.* Pa'piertiger *m*; **~ tis·sue** *s.* Pa'piertuch *n*; **~ war(·fare)** *s.* Pressekrieg *m*, -fehde *f*, Feder-

krieg *m*; **2.** Pa'pierkrieg *m*; '**~-weight** *s.* **1.** Briefbeschwerer *m*; **2.** *sport* Pa'piergewicht(ler *m*) *n*; '**~-work** *s.* Schreib-, Bü'roarbeit *f*.

pa·per·y ['peɪpərɪ] *adj.* pa'pierähnlich; (pa'pier)dünn.

pa·pier-mâ·ché [‚pæpjeɪ'mæʃeɪ] *s.* Pa-'pierma‚ché, -ma‚schee *n*, 'Pappma‚ché, -ma‚schee *n*.

pa·pil·i·o·na·ceous [pə‚pɪlɪəʊ'neɪʃəs] *adj.* ♀ schmetterlingsblütig.

pa·pil·la [pə'pɪlə] *pl.* **-pil·lae** [-liː] *s. anat.* Pa'pille *f* (*a.* ♀), Warze *f*; **pap'il·lar·y** [-ərɪ] *adj.* **1.** warzenartig, papil-'lär; **2.** mit Pa'pillen versehen.

pa·pist ['peɪpɪst] *s. contp.* Pa'pist *m*; **pa·pis·tic** *adj.*; **pa·pis·ti·cal** [pə'pɪstɪk(l)] *adj.* □ **1.** päpstlich; **2.** *contp.* pa'pistisch; '**pa·pist·ry** [-rɪ] *s.* Pa'pismus *m*, Papiste'rei *f*.

pa·poose [pə'puːs] *s.* **1.** Indi'anerbaby *n*; **2.** *Am. humor.* ,Balg' *m*.

pap·pus ['pæpəs] *pl.* **-pi** [-aɪ] *s.* **1.** ♀ a) Haarkrone *f*, b) Federkelch *m*; **2.** Flaum *m*.

pap·py ['pæpɪ] *adj.* breiig, pappig.

Pap| test, **~ smear** [pæp] *s.* 🔬 Abstrich *m*.

pa·py·rus [pə'paɪərəs] *pl.* **-ri** [-raɪ] *s.* **1.** ♀ Pa'pyrus(staude *f*) *m*; **2.** *antiq.* Pa'pyrus(rolle *f*, -text) *m*.

par [pɑː] **I** *s.* **1.** ✝ Nennwert *m*, Pari *n*: **issue ~** Emissionskurs *m*; **nominal** (*od.* **face**) **~** Nennbetrag *m* (*Aktie*), Nominalwert *m*; **~ of exchange** Wechselpari(tät *f*) *n*, Parikurs *m*; **at ~** zum Nennwert, al pari; **above** (**below**) **~** über (unter) Pari; **2.** *fig.* **above ~** in bester Form; **up to** (**below**) **~** F (nicht) auf der Höhe; **be on a ~** (**with**) ebenbürtig *od.* gewachsen sein (*dat.*), entsprechen (*dat.*); **put on a ~ with** gleichstellen (*dat.*); **on a ~** *Brit.* im Durchschnitt; **3.** *Golf:* Par *n*, festgesetzte Schlagzahl; **II** *adj.* **4.** ✝ pari: **~ clearance** *Am.* Clearing *n* zum Pariwert; **~ value** Pari-, Nennwert *m*.

para- [pærə] *in Zssgn* **1.** neben, über ... hin'aus; **2.** ähnlich; **3.** falsch; **4.** 🐾 neben, ähnlich; Verwandtschaft bezeichnend; **5.** ⚕ a) fehlerhaft, ab'norm, b) ergänzend, c) um'gebend; **6.** Schutz...; **7.** Fallschirm...

pa·ra ['pærə] *s.* F **1.** ✕ Fallschirmjäger *m*; **2.** *typ.* Absatz *m*.

par·a·ble ['pærəbl] *s.* Pa'rabel *f*, Gleichnis *n* (*a. bibl.*).

pa·rab·o·la [pə'ræbələ] *s.* Å Pa'rabel *f*: **~ compasses** Parabelzirkel *m*.

par·a·bol·ic [‚pærə'bɒlɪk] *adj.* **1.** → **parabolical**; **2.** Å para'bolisch, Parabel...: **~ mirror** Parabolspiegel *m*; '**par·a·bol·i·cal** [-kl] *adj.* **1.** Å para'bolisch, gleichnishaft; **pa·rab·o·loid** [pə'ræbələɪd] *s.* Å Parabolo'id *n*.

'**par·a·brake** *v/t.* ✈ durch Bremsfallschirm abbremsen.

par·a·chute ['pærəʃuːt] **I** *s.* **1.** ✈ Fallschirm *m*: **~ jumper** Fallschirmspringer *m*; **2.** ♀ Schirmflieger *m*; **3.** ◎ Sicherheits-, Fangvorrichtung *f*; **II** *v/t.* **4.** (mit dem Fallschirm) absetzen, -werfen; **III** *v/i.* **5.** mit dem Fallschirm abspringen; **6.** (wie) mit e-m Fallschirm schweben; **~ flare** *s.* Leuchtfallschirm *m*; **~ troops** *s. pl.* ✕ Fallschirmtruppen *pl.*

par·a·chut·ist ['pærəʃuːtɪst] *s.* ✈ **1.** Fallschirmspringer(in); **2.** ✕ Fallschirmjäger *m*.

pa·rade [pə'reɪd] **I** *s.* **1.** Pa'rade *f*, Vorführung *f*, Zur'schaustellen *n*: **make a ~ of** → 7; **2.** ✕ a) Pa'rade *f* (*Truppenschau u. Vorbeimarsch*): **be on ~** e-e

Parade abhalten, b) Ap'pell *m*: ~ *rest!* Rührt Euch!, c) *a.* ~ *ground* Pa'rade-, Exerzierplatz *m*; **3.** ('Um)Zug *m*, (Auf-, Vor'bei)Marsch *m*; **4.** *bsd. Brit.* Prome'nade *f*; **5.** *fenc.* Pa'rade *f*; **II** *v/t.* **6.** zur Schau stellen, vorführen; **7.** zur Schau tragen, protzen mit; **8.** ✕ auf-, vor'beimarschieren lassen; **9.** *Straße* entlangstolzieren; **III** *v/i.* **10.** ✕ paradieren, (vor'bei)marschieren; **11.** e-n Umzug veranstalten, durch die Straßen ziehen; **12.** sich zur Schau stellen, stolzieren.

par·a·digm ['pærədaɪm] *s. ling.* Para'digma *n*, (Muster)Beispiel *n*; **par·a·dig·mat·ic** [ˌpærədɪg'mætɪk] *adj.* (□ ~*ally*) paradig'matisch.

par·a·dise ['pærədaɪs] *s. (bibl. ♫)* Para'dies *n* (*a. fig.*): **bird of** ~ Paradiesvogel *m*; → *fool's paradise*; **par·a·dis·i·ac** [ˌpærə'dɪsɪæk], **par·a·di·si·a·cal** [ˌpærədɪ'saɪəkl] *adj.* para'diesisch.

par·a·dox ['pærədɒks] *s.* Pa'radoxon *n*, Para'dox *n*; **par·a·dox·i·cal** [ˌpærə'dɒksɪkl] *adj.* □ para'dox.

'par·a·drop *v/t.* ⤴ mit dem Fallschirm abwerfen *od.* absetzen.

par·af·fin ['pærəfɪn], **par·af·fine** ['pærəfiːn] **I** *s.* Paraf'fin *n*: *liquid* ~, *Brit.* ~ (*oil*) Paraffinöl *n*; *solid* ~ Erdwachs *n*; ~ *wax* Paraffin (*für Kerzen*); **II** *v/t.* ⚙ paraffinieren.

par·a·glid·er ['pærəˌglaɪdə] *s. sport* **1.** Gleitschirm *m*; **2.** 'Para,glider(in), Gleitschirmflieger(in); **'par·a,glid·ing** *s.* 'Para,gliding *n*, Gleitschirmfliegen *n*.

par·a·gon ['pærəgən] *s.* **1.** Muster *n*, Vorbild *n*: ~ *of virtue* Muster *od. iro.* Ausbund *m* an Tugend; **2.** *typ.* Text *f* (*Schriftgrad*).

par·a·graph ['pærəgraːf] *s.* **1.** *typ.* a) Absatz *m*, Abschnitt *m*, Para'graph *m*: ~ *mark* Computer: Absatzzeichen *n*, b) Para'graphzeichen *n*; **2.** kurzer ('Zeitungs)Ar,tikel; **'par·a·graph·er** [-fə] *s.* **1.** Verfasser *m* kleiner Zeitungsartikel; **2.** 'Leitar,tikler *m* (*e-r Zeitung*).

Par·a·guay·an [ˌpærə'gwaɪən] **I** *adj.* para'guayisch; **II** *s.* Para'guayer(in).

par·a·keet ['pærəkiːt] *s. orn.* Sittich *m*: *Australian grass* ~ Wellensittich.

par·al·de·hyde [pə'rældɪhaɪd] *s.* 🝆 Paralde'hyd *n*.

par·al·lac·tic [ˌpærə'læktɪk] *adj. ast., phys.* paral'laktisch: ~ *motion* parallaktische Verschiebung; **par·al·lax** ['pærəlæks] *s.* Paral'laxe *f*.

par·al·lel ['pærəlel] **I** *adj.* **1.** (*with, to*) paral'lel (zu, mit), gleichlaufend (mit): ~ *bars* Turnen: Barren *m*; ~ *connection* ⚡ Parallelschaltung *f*; *run* ~ *to* parallel verlaufen zu; **2.** *fig.* paral'lel, gleich(gerichtet, -laufend), entsprechend: ~ *case* Parallelfall *m*; ~ *passage* Parallele *f* in e-m Text; **II** *s.* **3.** ↗ *u. fig.* Paral'lele *f* (*to* zu): *in* ~ *with* parallel zu; *draw a* ~ *between fig.* e-e Parallele ziehen zwischen (*dat.*), (mit'einander) vergleichen; **4.** ↗ Paralleli'tät *f* (*a. fig. Gleichheit*); **5.** *geogr.* Breitenkreis *m*; **6.** ⚡ Paral'lelschaltung *f*; **connect** (*od. join*) *in* ~ parallel schalten; **7.** Gegenstück *n*, Entsprechung *f*: *have no* ~ nicht seinesgleichen haben; *without* ~ ohnegleichen; **III** *v/t.* **8.** (*with, to*) anpassen, -gleichen (*dat.*); **9.** gleichkommen (*dat.*); **10.** et. Gleiches *od.* Entsprechendes finden zu; **11.** *bsd. Am.* ⊢ parallel laufen zu; **'par·al·lel·ism** [-lɪzəm] *s.* ↗ Paralle'lismus *m* (*a. ling., phls., fig.*), Paralleli'tät *f*; **par·al·lel·o·gram** [ˌpærə'leləʊɡræm] *s.* ↗ Parallelo'gramm *n*: ~ *of forces phys.*

Kräfteparallelogramm *n*.

pa·ral·o·gism [pə'rælədʒɪzəm] *s. phls.* Paralo'gismus *m*, Trugschluss *m*.

Par·a·lym·pics [ˌpærə'lɪmpɪks] *s. pl. sport* Para'lympics *pl.*, Be'hindertenolympi,ade *f*.

par·a·ly·sa·tion [ˌpærəlaɪ'zeɪʃn] *s.* **1.** Lähmung *f* (*a. fig.*); **2.** *fig.* Lahmlegung *f*; **par·a·lyse** ['pærəlaɪz] *v/t.* **1.** 🝆 paralysieren, lähmen (*a. fig.*); **2.** *fig.* lahm legen, lähmen, zum Erliegen bringen; **pa·ral·y·sis** [pə'rælɪsɪs] *pl.* **-ses** [-siːz] *s.* 🝆 Para'lyse *f*, Lähmung *f*; **2.** *fig.* a) Lähmung *f*, Lahmlegung *f*, b) Da'niederliegen *n*, c) Ohnmacht *f*; **par·a·lyt·ic** [ˌpærə'lɪtɪk] **I** *adj.* (□ ~*ally*) 🝆 para'lytisch: a) Lähmungs..., b) gelähmt (*a. fig.*), c) F volltrunken; **II** *s.* 🝆 Para'lytiker(in).

par·a·lyze *bsd. Am.* → *paralyse*.

par·a·med·ic [ˌpærə'medɪk] *s. Am.* **1.** ärztlicher Assi'stent, *a.* Sani'täter *m*; **2.** Arzt, der sich in abgelegenen Gegenden mit dem Fallschirm absetzen lässt.

pa·ram·e·ter [pə'ræmɪtə] *s.* ↗ **1.** Pa'rameter *m*; **2.** Nebenveränderliche *f*.

par·a·mil·i·tar·y *adj.* paramili,tärisch.

par·a·mount ['pærəmaʊnt] **I** *adj.* □ **1.** höher stehend (*to* als), oberst, höchst; **2.** *fig.* an der Spitze stehend, größt, über'ragend, ausschlaggebend: *of* ~ *importance* von (aller)größter Bedeutung; **'par·a·mount·cy** *s.* **1.** allergrößte Wichtigkeit *od.* Bedeutung; **2.** wichtigste Positi'on, Vorrangstellung *f*, oberste 'Führungspositi,on.

par·a·mour ['pærəˌmʊə] *s.* Geliebte(r *m*) *f*, Buhle *m*, *f*.

par·a·noi·a [ˌpærə'nɔɪə] *s.* 🝆 Para'noia *f*; **par·a·noi·ac** [-ɪæk] **I** *adj.* para'noisch; **II** *s.* Para'noiker(in); **par·a·noid** ['pærənɔɪd] *adj.* para'noid.

par·a·pet ['pærəpɪt] *s.* **1.** ✕ Wall *m*, Brustwehr *f*; **2.** △ (Brücken)Geländer *n*, (Bal'kon-, Fenster)Brüstung *f*.

par·aph ['pærəf] *s.* Pa'raphe *f*, ('Unterschrifts)Schnörkel *m*.

par·a·pher·na·li·a [ˌpærəfə'neɪljə] *s. pl.* **1.** Zubehör *n*, *m*, Uten'silien *pl.*, 'Drum u. 'Dran' *n*; **2.** 🝅 Parapher'nalgut *n* der Ehefrau.

par·a·phrase ['pærəfreɪz] **I** *s.* Para'phrase *f* (*a. ♪*), Um'schreibung *f*; freie 'Wiedergabe, Interpretati'on *f*; **II** *v/t. u. v/i.* paraphrasieren (*a. ♪*), interpretieren, e-n Text frei 'wiedergeben; um'schreiben.

par·a·ple·gi·a [ˌpærə'pliːdʒə] *s.* Paraple'gie *f*, doppelseitige Lähmung; **para·ple·gic** [-dʒɪk] *adj.* para'plegisch.

par·a·psy·chol·o·gy [ˌpærəsaɪ'kɒlədʒɪ] *s.* 'Parapsycholo,gie *f*.

par·a·scend·ing [ˌpærə'sendɪŋ] *s.* Fallschirmsport *m*, -springen *n*.

par·a·sit·al [ˌpærə'saɪtl] *adj.* para'sitisch (*a. fig.*); **par·a·site** ['pærəsaɪt] **I** *s.* **1.** *biol. u. fig.* Schma'rotzer *m*, Para'sit *m*; **2.** *ling.* para'sitischer Laut; **II** *adj.* **3.** → *parasitic* 4; **par·a·sit·ic**, **par·a·sit·i·cal** [-'sɪtɪk(l)] *adj.* □ **1.** *biol.* para'sitisch (*a. ling.*), schma'rotzend; **2.** 🝆 para'sitisch, parasi'tär; **3.** *fig.* schma'rotzerhaft, para'sitisch; **4.** ⊙, ⚡ (*nur parasitic*) störend, parasi'tär: ~ *current* Fremdstrom *m*; **par·a·sit·ism** ['pærəsaɪtɪzəm] *s.* Parasi'tismus *m* (*a.* 🝆), Schma'rotzertum *n*.

par·a·sol ['pærəsɒl] *s.* (Damen)Sonnenschirm *m*, *obs.* Para'sol *m*, *n*.

par·a·suit ['pærəsuːt] *s.* ⤴ 'Fallschirmkombinat,ion *f*.

par·a·thy·roid (**gland**) [ˌpærə'θaɪrɔɪd] *s. anat.* Nebenschilddrüse *f*.

'par·a,troop·er *s.* ✕ Fallschirmjäger *m*; **'par·a,troops** *s. pl.* ✕ Fallschirmtruppen *pl.*

par·a·ty·phoid (**fe·ver**) [ˌpærə'taɪfɔɪd] *s.* 🝆 Paratyphus *m*.

par·a·vane ['pærəveɪn] *s.* ⚓ Minenabweiser *m*, Ottergerät *n*.

par·boil ['paːbɔɪl] *v/t.* **1.** halb gar kochen, ankochen; **2.** *fig.* über'hitzen.

par·cel ['paːsl] *s.* **1.** Pa'ket *n*, Päckchen *n*; Bündel *n*; *pl.* Stückgüter *pl.*: ~ *of shares* Aktienpaket; *do up in* ~*s* einpacken; **2.** ✝ Posten *m*, Par'tie *f*, Los *n* (*Ware*): *in* ~*s* in kleinen Posten, stück-, packweise; **3.** *contp.* Haufe(n) *m*; **4.** *a.* ~ *of land* Par'zelle *f*; **II** *v/t.* **5.** *mst* ~ *out* auf-, aus-, abteilen, *Land* parzellieren; ~ **6.** *a.* ~ *up* einpacken, (ver)packen; ~ **bomb** *s.* Pa'ketbombe *f*; ~ **of·fice** *s.* Gepäckabfertigung(sstelle) *f*; ~ **post** *s.* Pa'ketpost *f*; ~**s count·er** *s.* 🝅 Pa'ketschalter *m*, -annahme *f*, -ausgabe *f*.

par·ce·nar·y ['paːsnərɪ] *s.* 🝅 Mitbesitz *m* (*durch Erbschaft*); **'par·ce·ner** [-nə] *s.* Miterbe *m*.

parch [paːtʃ] **I** *v/t.* **1.** rösten, dörren; **2.** ausdörren, -trocknen, (ver)sengen: *be* ~*ed* (*with thirst*), ,am Verdursten' sein; **II** *v/i.* **3.** ausdörren, -trocknen, dörren, schmoren; **'parch·ing** [-tʃɪŋ] *adj.* **1.** brennend (*Durst*); **2.** sengend (*Hitze*); **'parch·ment** [-mənt] *s.* **1.** Perga'ment *n*; **2.** *a.* **vegetable** ~ Perga'mentpa,pier *n*; **3.** Per'gament(urkunde *f*) *n*, Urkunde *f*.

pard [paːd], **'pard·ner** [-dnə] *s. bsd. Am.* F Partner *m*, ‚Kumpel' *m*.

par·don ['paːdn] **I** *v/t.* **1.** j-m *od.* e-e Sache verzeihen, j-n *od.* et. entschuldigen: ~ *me!* Verzeihung!, entschuldigen Sie!, verzeihen Sie!; ~ *me for interrupting you!* entschuldigen Sie, wenn ich Sie unterbreche!; **2.** *Schuld* vergeben; **3.** j-m das Leben schenken, j-m die Strafe erlassen, j-n begnadigen; **II** *s.* **4.** Verzeihung *f*: *a thousand* ~*s* ich bitte Sie tausendmal um Entschuldigung; *beg* (*od. ask*) *s.o.'s* ~ j-n um Verzeihung bitten; (*I*) *beg your* ~ a) entschuldigen Sie bitte!, Verzeihung!, b) F *a.* ~*?* wie sagten Sie (doch eben)?, wie bitte?, c) *empört:* erlauben Sie mal!; **5.** Vergebung *f*; *R.C.* Ablass *m*; 🝅 Begnadigung *f*, Straferlass *m*: *general* ~ (allgemeine) Amnestie; **6.** Par'don *m*, Gnade *f*; **'par·don·a·ble** [-nəbl] *adj.* □ verzeihlich (*Fehler*), lässlich (*Sünde*); **'par·don·er** [-nə] *s. eccl. hist.* Ablasskrämer *m*.

pare [peə] *v/t. Äpfel etc.* schälen; *Fingernägel etc.* (be)schneiden: ~ *down fig.* beschneiden, einschränken; ~ *off* (ab-) schälen (*a.* ⊙); → *claw* 1 b.

par·e·gor·ic [ˌpærə'gɒrɪk] *adj. u. s.* 🝆 schmerzstillend(es Mittel).

par·en·ceph·a·lon [ˌpæren'sefələn] *s. anat.* Kleinhirn *n*.

pa·ren·chy·ma [pə'reŋkɪmə] *s.* **1.** Paren'chym *n* (*biol.*, ♫ *Grund-*, *anat.* Organgewebe*); **2.** 🝆 Tumorgewebe *n*.

par·ent ['peərənt] **I** *s.* **1.** *pl.* Eltern *pl.*: ~*-teacher association* *ped.* (*amer.*, *a. brit.*) Eltern-Lehrer-Ausschuss *m*; ~*-teacher meeting* Elternabend *m*; **2.** *a.* 🝅 Elternteil *m*; **3.** Vorfahr *m*; **4.** *biol.* Elter *m*; **5.** *fig.* Ursache *f*: *the* ~ *of vice* aller Laster Anfang; **6.** ✝ F ‚Mutter' *f* (*Muttergesellschaft*); **II** *adj.* **7.** Stamm..., Mutter...: ~ *cell* Mutterzelle *f*; **8.** ursprünglich, Ur...: ~ *form* Urform *f*; **9.** *fig.* Mutter..., Stamm...: ~ *company* ✝ Stammhaus *n*, Muttergesellschaft *f*; ~ *material* Urstoff *m*, *geol.* Ausgangsgestein *n*; ~ *organization*

Dachorganisation *f*; ~ *patent* ✝ Stammpatent *n*; ~ *rock* geol. Urgestein *n*; ~ *ship* ♦ Mutterschiff *n*; ~ *unit* ✕ Stammtruppenteil *m*; **'par·ent·age** [-tɪdʒ] *s.* **1.** Abkunft *f*, Abstammung *f*, Fa'milie *f*; **2.** Elternschaft *f*; **3.** *fig.* Urheberschaft *f*; **pa·ren·tal** [pəˈrentl] *adj.* □ elterlich, Eltern...: ~ *authority* ⚖ elterliche Gewalt.

pa·ren·the·sis [pəˈrenθɪsɪs] *pl.* **-the·ses** [-siːz] *s.* **1.** *ling.* Paren'these *f*, Einschaltung *f*; *by way of* ~ *fig.* beiläufig; **2.** *mst pl. typ.* (runde) Klammer(n *pl.*): *put in parentheses* einklammern; **pa'ren·the·size** [-saɪz] *v/t.* **1.** einschalten, einflechten; **2.** *typ.* einklammern; **par·en·thet·ic**, **par·en·thet·i·cal** [ˌpærənˈθetɪk(l)] *adj.* □ **1.** paren'thetisch, eingeschaltet; *fig.* beiläufig; **2.** eingeklammert.

par·ent·less ['peərəntlɪs] *adj.* elternlos.

pa·re·sis ['pærɪsɪs] ✺ **1.** Pa'rese *f*, unvollständige Lähmung; **2.** *a.* **general** ~ progres'sive Para'lyse.

par·get ['pɑːdʒɪt] *s.* **1.** Gips(stein) *m*; **2.** Verputz *m*; **3.** Stuck *m*; **II** *v/t.* **4.** verputzen; **5.** mit Stuck verzieren.

par·he·li·on [pɑːˈhiːljən] *pl.* **-li·a** [-ljə] *s.* Nebensonne *f*, Par'helion *n*.

pa·ri·ah ['pærɪə] *s.* Paria *m* (*a. fig.*).

pa·ri·e·tal [pəˈraɪɪtl] **I** *adj.* **1.** *anat.* parie'tal: a) (*a.* ♀, *biol.*) wandständig, Wand..., b) seitlich, c) Scheitel (-bein)...; **2.** *ped. Am.* in'tern, Haus...; **II** *s.* **3.** *a.* ~ *bone* Scheitelbein *n*.

par·ing ['peərɪŋ] *s.* **1.** Schälen *n*; (Be-) Schneiden *n*, Stutzen *n* (*a. fig.*); **2.** *pl.* Schalen *pl.*: *potato* ~*s*; **3.** *pl.* ☺ Späne *pl.*, Schabsel *pl.*, Schnitzel *pl.*; ~ *knife* *s.* [*irr.*] **1.** Schälmesser *n* (*für Obst etc.*); **2.** Beschneidmesser.

pa·ri pas·su [ˌpærɪˈpæsuː] (*Lat.*) *adv.* gleichrangig, -berechtigt.

Par·is ['pærɪs] *adj.* Pa'riser; ~ *blue* *s.* Ber'liner Blau *n*; ~ *green* *s.* Pa'riser *od.* Schweinfurter Grün *n*.

par·ish ['pærɪʃ] **I** *s.* **1.** *eccl.* a) Kirchspiel *n*, Pfarrbezirk *m*, b) Gemeinde *f* (*a. coll.*); **2.** *a.* **civil** ~ (*od.* **poor-law**) ~ *Brit.* (po'litische) Gemeinde: **go** (*od.* **be**) **on the** ~ der Gemeinde zur Last fallen; **II** *adj.* **3.** Kirchen..., Pfarr...: ~ *church* Pfarrkirche *f*; ~ *clerk* Küster *m*; ~ *register* Kirchenbuch *n*; **4.** *pol.* Gemeinde...: ~ *council* Gemeinderat *m*; ~*-pump politics* Kirchturmpolitik *f*; **pa·rish·ion·er** [pəˈrɪʃənə] *s.* Gemeindeglied *n*.

Pa·ri·sian [pəˈrɪzjən] **I** *s.* Pa'riser(in); **II** *adj.* Pa'riser.

par·i·syl·lab·ic [ˌpærɪsɪˈlæbɪk] *ling.* **I** *adj.* parisyl'labisch, gleichsilbig; **II** *s.* Pari'syllabum *n*.

par·i·ty ['pærətɪ] *s.* **1.** Gleichheit *f*, *a.* gleichberechtigte Stellung; **2.** ✝ a) Pa'ri'tät *f*, b) 'Umrechnungskurs *m*: **at the** ~ *of* zum Umrechnungskurs von; ~ *clause* Paritätsklausel *f*; ~ *price* Parikurs *m*; **3.** *Computer:* Pari'tät *f*.

park [pɑːk] **I** *s.* **1.** Park *m*, (Park)Anlagen *pl.*; **2.** Na'turschutzgebiet *n*, Park *m*: *national* ~; **3.** *bsd.* ✕ (Geschütz-, Fahrzeug- *etc.*)Park *m*; **4.** *Am.* Parkplatz *m*; **5.** a) *Am.* (Sport)Platz *m*, b) *the* ~ *Brit.* F der Fußballplatz; **II** *v/t.* **6.** *mot. etc.* parken, ab-, aufstellen; F *et.* abstellen, *wo* lassen: ~ *o.s.* sich ,hinhocken'; **III** *v/i.* **7.** parken.

par·ka ['pɑːkə] *s.* Parka *m*, *f*.

,park-and-'ride sys·tem *s.* 'Park-and--'ride-Sy,stem *n*.

park·ing ['pɑːkɪŋ] *s. mot.* **1.** Parken *n*: *no* ~! Parken verboten!; **2.** Parkplatz

m, -plätze *pl.*, -fläche *f*; ~ *brake* *s.* Feststellbremse *f*; ~ *disc* *s.* Parkscheibe *f*; ~ *fee* *s.* Parkgebühr *f*; ~ *ga·rage* *s.* Parkhaus *n*; ~ *light* *s.* Park-, Standlicht *n*; ~ *lot* *s. Am.* Parkplatz *m*, -fläche *f*; ~ *me·ter* *s.* Park(zeit)uhr *f*; ~ *of·fend·er* *s.* Falschparker *m*, Parksünder *m*; ~ *place* *s.* **1.** Parkplatz *m*, -fläche *f*; **2.** Parklücke *f*; ~ *space* *s.* **1.** → *parking place*; **2.** Abstellfläche *f*, -lücke *f*; ~ *tick·et* *s.* Strafzettel *m* (für unerlaubtes Parken).

par·lance ['pɑːləns] *s.* Ausdrucksweise *f*, Sprache *f*: *in common* ~ auf gut Deutsch; *in legal* ~ in der Rechtssprache; *in modern* ~ im modernen Sprachgebrauch.

par·lay ['pɑːlɪ] *Am.* **I** *v/t.* **1.** *Wett-, Spielgewinn* wieder einsetzen; **2.** *fig.* aus *j-m od. et.* Kapi'tal schlagen; **3.** erweitern, ausbauen (*into* zu); **II** *v/i.* **4.** *e-n* Spielgewinn wieder einsetzen; **III** *s.* **5.** erneuter Einsatz e-s Gewinns; **6.** Auswertung *f*; **7.** Ausweitung *f*, Ausbau *m*.

par·ley ['pɑːlɪ] **I** *s.* **1.** Unter'redung *f*, Verhandlung *f*; **2.** ✕ (Waffenstillstands)Verhandlung(en *pl.*) *f*, Unter'handlung(en *pl.*) *f*; **II** *v/i.* **3.** sich besprechen (*with* mit); **4.** ✕ unter'handeln; **III** *v/t.* **5.** *humor.* parlieren: ~ *French*.

par·lia·ment ['pɑːləmənt] *s.* Parla'ment *n*: *enter* (*od.* *get into od. go into*) ♘ ins Parlament gewählt werden; *Member of* ♘ *Brit.* Mitglied des Unterhauses, Abgeordnete(r *m*) *f*; **par·lia·men·tar·i·an** [ˌpɑːləmenˈteərɪən] *pol.* **I** *s.* (erfahrener) Parlamen'tarier; **II** *adj.* → *parliamentary*; **par·lia·men·ta·rism** [ˌpɑːləˈmentərɪzəm] *s.* parlamen'tarisches Sy'stem, Parlamenta'rismus *m*; **par·lia·men·ta·ry** [ˌpɑːləˈmentərɪ] *adj.* **1.** parlamen'tarisch, Parlaments...: ♘ *Commissioner Brit.* → *ombudsman* 1; ~ *group* (*od.* *party*) Fraktion *f*; ~ *party leader Brit.* Fraktionsvorsitzende(r) *m*; **2.** *fig.* höflich (*Sprache*).

par·lo(u)r ['pɑːlə] **I** *s.* **1.** Wohnzimmer *n*; **2.** *obs.* Besuchszimmer *n*, Sa'lon *m*; **3.** Empfangs-, Sprechzimmer *n*; **4.** Klub-, Gesellschaftszimmer *n* (*Hotel*); **5.** *bsd. Am.* Geschäftsraum *m*, Sa'lon *m*: ~ *beauty parlo(u)r*; **II** *adj.* **6.** Wohnzimmer...: ~ *furniture*; **7.** *fig.* Salon...: ~ *radical*, *Am.* ~ *red pol.* Salonbolschewist(in); ~ *car* *s.* ⓇⒼ *Am.* Sa'lonwagen *m*; ~ *game* *s.* Gesellschaftsspiel *n*; '~*maid* *s.* Stubenmädchen *n*.

par·lous ['pɑːləs] *obs.* **I** *adj.* **1.** pre'kär; **2.** schlau; **II** *adv.* **3.** ,furchtbar'.

pa·ro·chi·al [pəˈrəʊkjəl] *adj.* □ **1.** parochi'al, Pfarr..., Gemeinde...: ~ *church council* Kirchenvorstand *m*; ~ *school Am.* Konfessionsschule *f*; **2.** *fig.* beschränkt, eng(stirnig): ~ *politics* Kirchturmpolitik *f*; **pa·ro·chi·al·ism** [-lɪzəm] *s.* **1.** Parochi'alsy,stem *n*; **2.** *fig.* Beschränktheit *f*, Spießigkeit *f*.

par·o·dist ['pærədɪst] *s.* Paro'dist(in); **par·o·dy** ['pærədɪ] **I** *s. a. fig.* Paro'die *f* (*of* auf *acc.*); **II** *v/t.* parodieren.

pa·role [pəˈrəʊl] **I** *s.* **1.** ⚖ a) bedingte Haftentlassung *od.* Strafaussetzung, b) Hafturlaub *m*: *put s.o. on* ~ → 4; ~ *officer Am.* Bewährungshelfer *m*; **2.** *a.* ~ *of hono(u)r* ✕ Ehrenwort *n*: *on* ~ auf Ehrenwort; **3.** ✕ Pa'role *f*, Kennwort *n*; **II** *v/t.* **4.** ⚖ a) *j-n* bedingt (aus

der Haft) entlassen, j-s Strafe bedingt aussetzen, b) *j-m* Hafturlaub gewähren; **pa·rol·ee** [pərəʊˈliː] *s.* ⚖ bedingt Haftentlassene(r *m*) *f*.

par·o·nym ['pærənɪm] *s. ling.* **1.** Paro'nym *n*, Wortableitung *f*; **2.** 'Lehnüber,setzung *f*; **pa·ron·y·mous** [pəˈrɒnɪməs] *adj.* □ a) (stamm)verwandt, b) 'lehnüber,setzt (*Wort*).

par·o·quet ['pærəket] → *parakeet*.

pa·rot·id [pəˈrɒtɪd] *s. a.* ~ *gland anat.* Ohrspeicheldrüse *f*; **par·o·ti·tis** [ˌpærəʊˈtaɪtɪs] *s.* Mumps *m*.

par·ox·ysm ['pærəksɪzəm] *s.* ✺ Paro'xysmus *m*, Krampf *m*, Anfall *m* (*a. fig.*): ~*s of laughter* Lachkrampf *m*; ~*s of rage* Wutanfall *m*; **par·ox·ys·mal** [ˌpærəkˈsɪzməl] *adj.* krampfartig.

par·quet ['pɑːkeɪ] **I** *s.* **1.** Par'kett(fußboden *m*) *n*; **2.** *thea. bsd. Am.* Par'kett *n*; **II** *v/t.* **3.** parkettieren; **'par·quet·ry** [-kɪtrɪ] *s.* Par'kett(arbeit *f*) *n*.

par·ri·cid·al [ˌpærɪˈsaɪdl] *adj.* vater-, muttermörderisch; **par·ri·cide** ['pærɪsaɪd] *s.* **1.** Vater-, Muttermörder(in); **2.** Vater-, Mutter-, Verwandtenmord *m*.

par·rot ['pærət] **I** *s. orn.* Papa'gei *m*, *fig. a.* Nachschwätzer(in); **II** *v/t.* nachplappern; ~ *dis·ease*, ~ *fe·ver* *s.* ✺ Papa'geienkrankheit *f*.

par·ry ['pærɪ] **I** *v/t. Stöße, Schläge, Fragen etc.* parieren, abwehren (*beide a. v/i.*); **II** *s. fenc. etc.* Pa'rade *f*, Abwehr *f*.

parse [pɑːz] *v/t. ling. Satz* gram'matisch zergliedern, *Satzteil* bestimmen, *Wort* gram'matisch definieren.

par·sec ['pɑːsek] *s. ast.* Parsek *n*, Sternweite *f* (*3,26 Lichtjahre*).

pars·er ['pɑːsə] *s. Computer:* Parser *m*.

par·si·mo·ni·ous [ˌpɑːsɪˈməʊnjəs] *adj.* □ **1.** sparsam, geizig, knauserig (*of* mit); **2.** armselig, kärglich; **,par·si'mo·ni·ous·ness** [-nɪs], **par·si·mo·ny** ['pɑːsɪmənɪ] *s.* Sparsamkeit *f*, Geiz *m*, Knauserigkeit *f*.

pars·ing ['pɑːsɪŋ] *s. Computer:* Parsing *n*, 'Syntaxana,lyse *f*.

pars·ley ['pɑːslɪ] *s.* ♀ Peter'silie *f*.

pars·nip ['pɑːsnɪp] *s.* ♀ Pastinak *m*.

par·son ['pɑːsn] *s.* Pastor *m*, Pfarrer *m*; F *contp.* Pfaffe *m*: ~*'s nose* Bürzel *m* (*e-r Gans etc.*); **'par·son·age** [-nɪdʒ] *s.* Pfar'rei *f*, Pfarrhaus *n*.

part [pɑːt] **I** *s.* **1.** Teil *m*, *n*, Stück *n*: ~ *by volume* (*weight*) *phys.* Raum(Gewichts)teil *m*; ~ *of speech ling.* Redeteil, Wortklasse *f*; *in* ~ teilweise; *payment in* ~ Abschlagszahlung *f*: *be* ~ *and parcel of* e-n wesentlichen Bestandteil bilden von (*od. gen.*); *for the best* ~ *of the year* fast das ganze Jahr (über); **2.** ♘ Bruchteil *m*: *three* ~*s* drei Viertel; **3.** ☺ (Bau-, Einzel)Teil *n*: ~*s list* Ersatzteil-, Stückliste *f*; **4.** ✝ Lieferung *f* e-s *Buches*; **5.** (Körper)Teil *m*, Glied *n*: *soft* ~ Weichteil *n*; *the* (*privy*) ~*s* die Geschlechtsteile; **6.** Anteil *m* (*of, in* an *dat.*): *have a* ~ *in* teilhaben an (*dat.*); *have neither* ~ *nor lot in* nicht das Geringste mit *et.* zu tun haben; *take* ~ (*in*) teilnehmen (an *dat.*), mitmachen (bei); *he wanted no* ~ *of it* er wollte davon nichts wissen *od.* damit zu tun haben; **7.** *fig.* Teil *m*, Seite *f*: *the most* ~ die Mehrheit, das meiste *von et.*; *for my* ~ ich für mein(en) Teil; *for the most* ~ meistens, größtenteils; *on the* ~ *of* vonseiten, seitens (*gen.*); *take in good* (*bad*) ~ *et.* gut (übel) aufnehmen; **8.** Seite *f*, Par'tei *f*: *he took my* ~ er ergriff m-e Partei; **9.** Pflicht *f*: *do one's* ~ das Seinige *od.* s-e Schuldigkeit tun; **10.** *thea.* Rolle *f* (*a. fig.*): *act* (*od.*

*a. fig. **play**) a ~ e-e Rolle spielen; **11.** ♪ Sing- *od.* Instrumen'talstimme *f*, Par'tie *f:* **for** (*od. in od. of*) **several ~s** mehrstimmig; **12.** *pl.* (geistige) Fähigkeiten *pl.*, Ta'lent *n:* **a man of ~s** ein fähiger Kopf; **13.** *oft pl.* Gegend *f*, Teil *m e-s* Landes, der Erde: **in these ~s** hierzulande; **in foreign ~s** im Ausland; **14.** *Am.* (Haar)Scheitel *m*; **II** *v/t.* **15.** teilen, ab-, ein-, zerteilen; trennen (**from** von); **16.** *Streitende* trennen, *Metalle* scheiden, *Haar* scheiteln; **III** *v/i.* **17.** ausein'ander gehen, sich lösen, zerreißen, brechen (*a.* ♨), aufgehen (*Vorhang*); **18.** ausein'ander gehen, sich trennen (*Menschen, Wege etc.*): ~ **friends** als Freunde auseinander gehen; ~ **with** sich von *j-m od. et.* trennen; ~ **with one's money** mit dem Geld herausrücken; **IV.** *adj.* **19.** Teil...: ~ **damage** Teilschaden *m*; ~ **delivery** Teillieferung *f*; **V** *adv.* **20.** teils, zum Teil: **made ~ of iron, ~ of wood** teils aus Eisen, teils aus Holz.
part- [pɑːt] *in Zssgn* teilweise, zum Teil: **~-done** zum Teil erledigt; **accept s.th. in ~-exchange** et. in Zahlung nehmen; **~-finished** halb fertig; **~-opened** ein Stück geöffnet.
par·take [pɑː'teɪk] **I** *v/i.* [*irr.* → **take**] **1.** teilnehmen, -haben (**in, of** an *dat.*); **2.** (**of**) *et.* an sich haben (von), *et.* teilen (mit): **his manner ~s of insolence** es ist et. Unverschämtes in s-m Benehmen; **3.** (**of**) mitessen, genießen, *j-s Mahlzeit* teilen; *Mahlzeit* einnehmen; **II** *v/t.* [*irr.* → **take**] **4.** *obs.* teilen, teilhaben (an *dat.*).
par·terre [pɑː'teə] *s.* **1.** französischer Garten; **2.** *thea. bsd. Am.* Par'terre *n*.
par·the·no·gen·e·sis [ˌpɑːθɪnəʊ'dʒenɪsɪs] *s.* Parthenoge'nese *f: a)* ♀ Jungfernfrüchtigkeit *f*, *b) zo.* Jungfernzeugung *f*, *c) eccl.* Jungfrauengeburt *f*.
Par·thi·an ['pɑːθjən] *adj.* parthisch: ~ **shot** → **parting shot**.
par·tial ['pɑːʃl] *adj.* □ → **partially**; **1.** teilweise, parti'ell, Teil...: ~ **eclipse** *ast.* partielle Finsternis; ~ **payment** Teilzahlung *f*; ~ **view** Teilansicht *f*; **2.** par'teiisch, eingenommen (**to** für), einseitig: **be ~ to s.th.** e-e besondere Vorliebe haben für et.; **par·ti·al·i·ty** [ˌpɑːʃɪ'ælətɪ] *s.* **1.** Par'teilichkeit *f*, Voreingenommenheit *f*; **2.** Vorliebe *f* (**to, for** für); '**par·tial·ly** [-ʃəlɪ] *adv.* teilweise, zum Teil: ~ **sighted** sehbehindert.
par·tic·i·pant [pɑː'tɪsɪpənt] **I** *s.* Teilnehmer(in) (**in** an *dat.*); **II** *adj.* teilnehmend, Teilnehmer..., (mit)beteiligt;
par·tic·i·pate [pɑː'tɪsɪpeɪt] *v/i.* **1.** teilhaben, -nehmen, sich beteiligen (**in** an *dat.*), mitmachen (bei): beteiligt sein (an *dat.*); ♣ am Gewinn beteiligt sein; **2.** ~ **of** *et.* an sich haben von; **par'tic·i·pat·ing** [-peɪtɪŋ] *adj.* **1.** ♣ gewinnberechtigt, mit Gewinnbeteiligung (*Versicherungspolice etc.*): ~ **share** dividendenberechtigte Aktie; ~ **rights** Gewinnbeteiligungsrechte; **2.** teilnehmend, Teilnehmer...: ~ **country** *EU etc.:* Teilnehmerland *n*; **par·tic·i·pa·tion** [pɑːˌtɪsɪ'peɪʃn] *s.* **1.** Teilnahme *f*, Beteiligung *f*, Mitwirkung *f*; **2.** ♣ Teilhaberschaft *f*, (Gewinn)Beteiligung *f*; **par'tic·i·pator** [-peɪtə] *s.* Teilnehmer(in) (**in** an *dat.*).
par·ti·cip·i·al [ˌpɑːtɪ'sɪpɪəl] *adj.* □ *ling.* partizipi'al; **par·ti·ci·ple** ['pɑːtɪsɪpl] *s. ling.* Parti'zip *n*, Mittelwort *n*.
par·ti·cle ['pɑːtɪkl] *s.* **1.** Teilchen *n*, Stückchen *n*; **2.** *phys.* Par'tikel *n* (*a. f*), (Stoff-, Masse-, Elemen'tar)Teilchen *n*;

3. *fig.* Fünkchen *n*, Spur *f: **not a ~ of truth in it*** nicht ein wahres Wort daran; **4.** *ling.* Par'tikel *f*.
par·ti·col·o(u)red ['pɑːtɪˌkʌləd] *adj.* bunt, vielfarbig.
par·tic·u·lar [pə'tɪkjʊlə] **I** *adj.* □ → **particularly**; **1.** besonder, einzeln, spezi'ell, Sonder...: ~ **average** ♣ kleine (besondere) Havarie; **for no ~ reason** aus keinem besonderen Grund; **this ~ case** dieser spezielle Fall; **2.** individu-'ell, ausgeprägt; **3.** ausführlich; 'umständlich; **4.** peinlich genau, eigen: **be ~ about** sehr genau nehmen mit, Wert legen auf (*acc.*); **5.** wählerisch (**in, about, as to** in *dat.*): **none too ~ about** *iro.* nicht gerade wählerisch (**in** s-n *Methoden etc.*); **6.** eigentümlich, sonderbar; **II** *s.* **7.** Einzelheit *f*, besonderer 'Umstand; *pl.* nähere Umstände *od.* Angaben *pl.*, *das* Nähere: **in ~** insbesondere; **enter into ~s** sich auf Einzelheiten einlassen; **further ~s from** Näheres (erfährt man) bei; **8.** Perso'nalien *pl.*, Angaben *pl.* zur Person; **9.** F Spezi'ali'tät *f*, *et.* Typisches; **par'tic·u·lar·ism** [-ərɪzəm] *s. pol.* Partikula'rismus *m: a)* Sonderbestrebungen *pl.*, *b)* ˌKleinstaate'rei *f*; **par·tic·u·lar·i·ty** [pəˌtɪkjʊ'lærətɪ] *s.* **1.** Besonderheit *f*, Eigentümlichkeit *f*; **2.** besonderer 'Umstand, Einzelheit *f*; **3.** Ausführlichkeit *f*; **4.** (peinliche) Genauigkeit; **5.** Eigenheit *f*; **par·tic·u·lar·i·za·tion** [pəˌtɪkjʊˌləraɪ'zeɪʃn] *s.* **1.** Detaillierung *f*, Spezifizierung *f*; **par'tic·u·lar·ize** [-əraɪz] **I** *v/t.* spezifizieren, einzeln (*a.* 'umständlich) anführen, ausführlich angeben; **II** *v/i.* ins Einzelne gehen; **par'tic·u·lar·ly** [-lɪ] *adv.* **1.** besonders, im Besonderen, insbesondere: **not ~** nicht sonderlich; (**more**) ~ **as** umso mehr als, zumal; **2.** ungewöhnlich; **3.** ausdrücklich.
part·ing ['pɑːtɪŋ] **I** *adj.* **1.** Scheide..., Abschieds...: ~ **kiss**; ~ **breath** letzter Atemzug; **2.** trennend, abteilend: ~ **wall** Trennwand *f*; **II** *s.* **3.** Abschied *m*, Scheiden *n*, Trennung *f* (**with** von); *fig.* Tod *m*; **4.** Trennlinie *f*, (Haar)Scheitel *m*: ~ **of the ways** Weggabelung, *fig.* Scheideweg; **5.** ⚒, *phys.* Scheidung *f*: ~ **silver** Scheidesilber; **6.** ⚒ *Gießerei:* a) *a.* ~ **sand** Streusand *m*, trockener Formsand, *b) a.* ~ **line** Teilfuge *f* (*Gussform*); **7.** ♣ Bruch *m*, Reißen *n*; ~ **shot** *s. fig.* letzte boshafte Bemerkung (*beim Abschied*).
par·ti·san¹ ['pɑːtɪzn] *s.* ⚔ *hist.* Parti'sane *f* (*Stoßwaffe*).
par·ti·san² [ˌpɑːtɪ'zæn] **I** *s.* **1.** Par'teigänger(in), -genosse *m*, -genossin *f*; **2.** ⚔ Parti'san *m*, Freischärler *m*; **II** *adj.* **3.** Partei...; **4.** par'teiisch: ~ **spirit** leidenschaftliche Parteilichkeit; **5.** ⚔ Partisanen..., ˌpar·ti·san·ship [-ʃɪp] *s.* **1.** *pl.* Par'teigängertum *n*; **2.** *fig.* Par'tei-, Vetternwirtschaft *f*.
par·tite ['pɑːtaɪt] *adj.* **1.** geteilt (*a.* ♀); **2.** *in Zssgn* ...teilig.
par·ti·tion [pɑː'tɪʃn] **I** *s.* **1.** (Auf-, Ver-) Teilung *f*; **2.** ✝ ('Erb)Auseinandersetzung *f*; **3.** Trennung *f*, Absonderung *f*; **4.** Scheide-, Querwand *f*, Fach *n* (*Schrank etc.*); (Bretter)Verschlag *m*: ~ **wall** Zwischenwand *f*; **II** *v/t.* **5.** (auf-, ver)teilen; **6.** *Erbschaft* ausein'ander setzen; **7.** *mst* ~ **off** abteilen, -fachen; **par·ti·tive** ['pɑːtɪtɪv] **I** *adj.* teilend, Teil...; *ling.* parti'tiv: ~ **genitive**; **II** *s. ling.* Parti'tivum *n*.
part·ly ['pɑːtlɪ] *adv.* zum Teil, teilweise, teils: ~ ..., teils ..., teils ...
part·ner ['pɑːtnə] **I** *s.* **1.** *allg.* (*a. sport, a.* Tanz)Partner(in); **2.** ♣ Gesellschaf-

ter *m*, (Geschäfts)Teilhaber(in), Kompagnon *m*: **general ~** (unbeschränkt) haftender Gesellschafter, Komplementär *m*; **special ~** *Am.* Kommanditist (-in); → **dormant** 3; **limited** I; **silent** 2; **sleeping partner**; **3.** 'Lebenskame,rad (-in), Gatte *m*, Gattin *f*; **II** *v/t.* **4.** zs.-bringen, -tun; **5.** sich zs.-tun, sich assoziieren (**with** mit *j-m*): **be ~ed with** *j-n* zum Partner haben; '**part·ner·ship** [-ʃɪp] *s.* **1.** Teilhaberschaft *f*, Partnerschaft *f*, Mitbeteiligung *f* (**in** an *dat.*); **2.** ✝ a) Handelsgesellschaft *f*, b) Perso-'nalgesellschaft *f*: **general ~** *od.* **ordinary ~** offene Handelsgesellschaft; → **limited** I; **special ~** *Am.* Kommanditgesellschaft *f*; **deed of ~** Gesellschaftsvertrag *m*; **enter into a ~ with** e-e Partner 5.
part·| own·er *s.* **1.** Miteigentümer(in); **2.** ♣ Mitreeder *m*; ~ **pay·ment** *s.* Teil-, Abschlagszahlung *f*.
par·tridge ['pɑːtrɪdʒ] *pl.* **par·tridge** *u.* **par·tridg·es** *s. orn.* Rebhuhn *n*.
part·| sing·ing *s.* ♪ mehrstimmiger Gesang; '**~-time** **I** *adj.* Teilzeit...: ~ **job** Teilzeitarbeit(sstelle) *f*; ~ **employee** Teilzeitbeschäftigte(r *m*) *f*; ~ **farmer** Nebenerwerbslandwirt *m*; **II** *adv.* Teilzeit ..., halbtags: **work ~** Teilzeit arbeiten; '**~,tim·er** *s.* Teilzeitbeschäftigte(r *m*) *f*, Halbtagskraft *f*.
par·tu·ri·ent [pɑː'tjʊərɪənt] *adj.* **1.** gebärend, kreißend; **2.** *fig.* (*mit e-r Idee*) schwanger; **par·tu·ri·tion** [ˌpɑːtjʊə-'rɪʃn] *s.* Gebären *n*.
par·ty ['pɑːtɪ] *s.* **1.** *pol.* Par'tei *f:* ~ **boss** Parteibonze *m*; ~ **spirit** Parteigeist *m*; → **whip** 4a; **2.** Par'tie *f*, Gesellschaft *f:* **hunting ~**; **make one of the ~** sich anschließen, mitmachen; **3.** Trupp *m:* a) ⚔ Kom'mando *n*, b) (Arbeits)Gruppe *f*, c) (Rettungs- *etc.*)Mannschaft *f*; **4.** Einladung *f*, Party *f*, Gesellschaft *f:* **give a ~**; ~ **pooper** *sl.* Partykiller *m*; **5.** ⚖ (Pro'zess- *etc.*)Par,tei *f: **contracting ~**, ~ **to a contract** Vertragspartei*, Kontrahent *m*; **a third ~** ein Dritter; **6.** Teilhaber(in), -nehmer(-in), Beteiligte(r *m*) *f:* **be a ~ to** beteiligt sein an, *et.* mitmachen; **the parties concerned** die Beteiligten; **7.** F ˌTyp' *m*, Per'son *f*; ~ **card** *s.* Par'teibuch *n*; ~ **in·fight·ing** *s.* par'tei,interne Que'relen; ~ **line** *s.* **1.** *teleph.* Gemeinschaftsanschluss *m*; **2.** *pol.* Par'teilinie *f*, -direk,tive *f: **follow the ~*** *parl.* linientreu sein; **voting was on ~s** bei der Abstimmung herrschte Fraktionszwang; ~ **lin·er** *s. Am.* Linientreue(r *m*) *f*; ~ **poop·er** *s.* F Spaßverderber *m*; ~ **tick·et** *s.* **1.** Gruppenfahrkarte *f*; **2.** *pol. Am.* (Kandi'daten)Liste *f e-r Partei*.
par·ve·nu ['pɑːvənjuː] (*Fr.*) *s.* Em'porkömmling *m*, Parve'nü *m*.
Pas·cal ['pæskl] Pas'cal *n: a) phys.* Einheit des Drucks, b) e-e Computersprache.
pa·sha ['pɑːʃə] *s.* Pascha *m*.
pasque·flow·er ['pæskˌflaʊə] *s.* ♀ Küchenschelle *f*.
pass¹ [pɑːs] *s.* **1.** (Eng)Pass *m*, Zugang *m*, 'Durchgang *m*, -fahrt *f*, Weg *m:* **hold the ~** die Stellung halten (*a. fig.*); **sell the ~** *fig.* alles verraten; **2.** Joch *n*, Sattel *m* (*Berg*); **3.** schiffbarer Ka'nal; **4.** Fischgang *m* (*Schleuse etc.*).
pass² [pɑːs] **I** *s.* **1.** (Reise)Pass *m*; (Perso'nal)Ausweis *m*; Passierschein *m*; 🎫, *thea. a.* **free ~** Frei-, Dauerkarte *f*; **2.** ⚔ a) Urlaubsschein *m*, b) Kurzurlaub *m*: **be on ~** auf (Kurz)Urlaub sein; **3.** a) Bestehen *n*, 'Durchkommen *n im* Examen *etc.*, b) bestandenes Ex'amen,

c) Note f, Zeugnis n, d) univ. Brit. einfacher Grad; **4. ♥**, ⚙ Abnahme f, Genehmigung f; **5.** Bestreichung f, Strich m beim Hypnotisieren etc.; **6.** Maltechnik: Strich m; **7.** (Hand)Bewegung f, (Zauber)Trick m; **8.** Fußball etc.: Pass m, (Ball)Abgabe f, Vorlage f: **~ back** Rückgabe f; **low ~** Flachpass; **9.** fenc. Ausfall m, Stoß m; **10.** sl. Annäherungsversuch m, oft **hard ~** Zudringlichkeit f: **make a ~ at** e-r Frau gegenüber zudringlich werden; **11.** fig. a) Zustand m, b) kritische Lage: **a pretty ~** F e-e ,schöne Geschichte'; **be at a desperate ~** hoffnungslos sein; **things have come to such a ~** die Dinge haben sich derart zugespitzt; **12.** ⚙ Arbeitsgang m (Werkzeugmaschine); **13.** ⚙ (Schweiß)Lage f; **14.** Walzwesen: a) Gang m, b) Zug m; **15.** ∮ Pass m (frequenzabhängiger Vierpol); **II** v/t. **16.** et. passieren, vor'bei-, vor'übergehen, -fahren, -fließen, -kommen, -reiten, -ziehen an (dat.); **17.** über'holen (a. mot.), vor'beilaufen, -fahren an (dat.); **18.** durch-, über'schreiten, passieren, durch'gehen, -'reisen etc.: **~ s.o.'s lips** über j-s Lippen kommen; **19.** über'steigen, -'treffen, hin'ausgehen über (acc.) (a. fig.): **it ~es my comprehension** es geht über m-n Verstand; **20.** fig. über'gehen, -'springen, keine No'tiz nehmen von; ♥ e-e Dividende ausfallen lassen; **21.** durch et. hin'durchleiten, -führen (a. ⚙), gleiten lassen: **~ (through a sieve)** durch ein Sieb passieren, durchseihen; ; **~ one's hand over** mit der Hand über et. reichen; **22.** Gegenstand reichen, (a. ⚖ Falschgeld) weitergeben; Geld in 'Umlauf setzen; (über-) 'senden, (a. Funkspruch) befördern; sport Ball abspielen, abgeben (zu an acc. passen), (zu): **~ the chair (to)** den Vorsitz abgeben (an j-n); **~ the hat (round** Brit.) e-e Sammlung veranstalten (for für j-n); **~ the time of day** guten (od. Guten) Tag etc. sagen, grüßen; **~ to s.o.'s account** j-m e-n Betrag in Rechnung stellen; **~ to s.o.'s credit** j-m gutschreiben; → **word** 5; **23.** Türschloss öffnen; **24.** vor'bei-, 'durchlassen, passieren lassen; **25.** fig. anerkennen, gelten lassen, genehmigen; **26.** ♣ a) Eiter, Nierenstein etc. ausscheiden, b) Eingeweide entleeren, Wasser lassen; **27.** Zeit verbringen, -leben, -treiben; **28.** parl. etc. a) Vorschlag 'durchbringen, -setzen, b) Gesetz verabschieden, ergehen lassen, c) Resolution annehmen; **29.** rechtskräftig machen; **30.** ⚖ Eigentum, Rechtstitel über'tragen, letztwillig zukommen lassen; **31.** a) Examen bestehen, b) Prüfling bestehen lassen, 'durchkommen lassen; **32.** Urteil äußern, s-e Meinung aussprechen (upon über acc.), Bemerkung fallen lassen, Kompliment machen: **~ criticism on** Kritik üben an (dat.); → **sentence** 2 a; **III** v/i. **33.** sich fortbewegen, von e-m Ort zum andern gehen od. fahren od. ziehen etc.; **34.** vor'bei-, vor'übergehen etc. (by an dat.); **35.** 'durchgehen, passieren (a. Linie): **it just ~ed through my mind** fig. es ging mir eben durch den Kopf; **36.** ♣ abgehen, abgeführt werden; **37.** 'durchkommen: a) ein Hindernis etc. bewältigen, b) (e-e Prüfung) bestehen; **38.** her'umgereicht werden, von Hand zu Hand gehen, herumgehen; im 'Umlauf sein: **harsh words ~ed between them** es fielen harte Worte bei ihrer Auseinandersetzung; **39.** a) sport passen, (den Ball)

zuspielen od. abgeben, b) (Kartenspiel u. fig.) passen: **I ~ on that!** da muss ich passen!; **40.** fenc. ausfallen; **41.** 'übergehen (**from ... [in]to** von ... zu), werden (**into** zu); **42.** in andere Hände 'übergehen, über'tragen werden (Eigentum); fallen (to an Erben etc.); unter j-s Aufsicht kommen, geraten; **43.** an-, hin-, 'durchgehen, leidlich sein, unbeanstandet bleiben, geduldet werden: **let that ~** reden wir nicht mehr davon; **44.** parl. etc. 'durchgehen, bewilligt od. zum Gesetz erhoben werden, Rechtskraft erlangen; **45.** gangbar sein, Geltung finden (Ideen, Grundsätze); **46.** angesehen werden, gelten (for als); **47.** urteilen, entscheiden (upon über acc.); **48.** ⚖ a. gefällt werden (Urteil); **48.** vergehen (a. Schmerz etc.), verstreichen (Zeit); endigen; sterben: **fashions ~** Moden kommen u. gehen; **49.** sich zutragen od. abspielen, passieren: **what ~ed between you and him?**; **bring to ~** bewirken; **it came to ~ that** bibl. es begab sich, dass;

Zssgn mit prp.:

pass| be·yond v/i. hin'ausgehen über (acc.) (a. fig.); **~ by** v/i. **1.** vor'bei-, vor'übergehen an (dat.); **2.** et. od. j-n über'gehen (**in silence** stillschweigend); **3.** unter dem Namen ... bekannt sein; **~ for** → **pass** 46; **~ in·to** I v/t. **1.** et. einführen in (acc.); **II** v/i. **2.** (hinein)gehen in (acc.); **3.** führen od. leiten in (acc.); **4.** 'übergehen in (acc.): **~ law** (zum) Gesetz werden; **~ through** I v/t. **1.** durch ... führen od. leiten od. stecken; 'durchschleusen; **II** v/i. **2.** durch'fahren, -'queren, -'schreiten etc.; durch ... gehen etc.; durch'fließen; **3.** durch ... führen (Draht, Tunnel etc.); **4.** durch'bohren; **5.** 'durchmachen, erleben;

Zssgn mit adv.:

pass| a·way I v/t. **1.** Zeit ver-, zubringen (doing s.th. mit et.); II v/i. **2.** vergehen (Zeit etc.); **3.** verscheiden, sterben; **~ by** v/i. vor'bei-, vor'übergehen (a. Zeit); **2.** → **pass over** 4; **~ down** v/t. Bräuche etc. über'liefern, weitergeben (**to** an dat.); **~ in** v/t. **1.** einlassen; **2.** einreichen, -händigen: **~ one's check** Am. sl. ,den Löffel abgeben' (sterben); **~ off** I v/t. **1.** j-n od. et. ausgeben (**for, as** für, als); II v/i. **2.** vergehen (Schmerz etc.); **3.** gut etc. vorübergehen, von'statten gehen; **4.** 'durchgehen (**as** als); **~ on** I v/t. **1.** weitergeben, -reichen (**to** dat. od. an acc.); befördern; **2.** ♥ abwälzen (**to** auf acc.); **II** v/i. **3.** weitergehen; **4.** 'übergehen (**to** zu); **5.** → **pass away** 3; **~ out** I v/i. **1.** hin'ausgehen, -fließen, -strömen; **2.** sl. ,umkippen', ohnmächtig werden; II v/t. **3.** ver-, austeilen; **~ o·ver** I v/i. **1.** hinüber'gehen; **2.** über'leiten, -führen; II v/t. **3.** über'reichen, -'tragen; **4.** über'gehen (**in silence** stillschweigend), ignorieren; **5.** → **pass up** 1; **~ through** v/i. 'hin'durchfahren; **3.** hin'durchgehen, -'reisen etc.: **be passing through** auf der Durchreise sein; **~ up** v/t. sl. **1.** a) sich e-e Chance entgehen lassen, b) et. ,sausen' lassen; verzichten auf (acc.); **2.** j-n über'gehen.

pass·a·ble ['pɑːsəbl] adj. □ **1.** passierbar; gang-, befahrbar; **2.** ♥ gangbar, gültig (Geld etc.); **3.** fig. leidlich, passabel.

pas·sage ['pæsidʒ] s. **1.** Her'ein-, He'raus-, Vor'über-, 'Durchgehen n, 'Durchgang m, -reise f, -fahrt f, 'Durchfließen n: **no ~!** kein Durchgang!, keine

Durchfahrt!; → **bird** 1; **2.** ♣ ('Waren-)Tran, sit m, 'Durchgang m; **3.** Pas'sage f, ('Durch-, Verbindungs)Gang m; bsd. Brit. Korridor m; **4.** Ka'nal m, Furt f; **5.** ⚙ 'Durchlass m, -tritt m; **6.** (See-, Flug)Reise f, ('Über)Fahrt f: **book one's ~** s-e Schiffskarte lösen (**to** nach); **work one's ~** s-e Überfahrt durch Arbeit abverdienen; **7.** Vergehen n, Ablauf m: **the ~ of time**; **8.** parl. 'Durchkommen n, Annahme f, In-'Kraft-Treten n e-s Gesetzes; **9.** Wortwechsel m; **10.** pl. Beziehungen pl., geistiger Austausch; **11.** (Text)Stelle f, Passus m; **12.** ♪ Pas'sage f (a. Reiten); **13.** fig. 'Übergang m, -tritt m (**from ... to, into** von ... in acc., zu); **14.** a) (Darm)Entleerung f, Stuhlgang m, b) anat. (Gehör- etc.)Gang m, (Harn- etc.) Weg(e pl.) m: **auditory (urinary) ~**; **~ at arms** s. **1.** Waffengang m; **2.** Wortgefecht n, ,Schlagabtausch' m; **~ boat** s. Fährboot n; **~·way** s. 'Durchgang m, Korridor m, Pas'sage f.

'pass|·book s. **1.** bsd. Brit. a) Bank-, Kontobuch n, b) Sparbuch n; **2.** Buch n über kreditierte Waren; **~ check** s. Am. Pas'sierschein m; **~ de·gree** → **pass²** 3c.

pas·sé, pas·sée ['pɑːsei] (Fr.) adj. pas'sé: a) vergangen, b) veraltet, c) verblüht: **a passée belle** e-e verblühte Schönheit.

pas·sel ['pæsl] s. bsd. Am. Gruppe f, Schar f; Reihe f.

passe·men·terie ['pɑːsməntri] (Fr.) s. Posamentierwaren pl.

pas·sen·ger ['pæsindʒə] s. **1.** Passa'gier m, Fahr-, Fluggast m, Reisende(r m) f, Insasse m: **~ cabin** ✈ Fluggastraum m; **2.** F a) Schma'rotzer m, b) Drückeberger m; **~ car** s. **1.** Per'sonen(kraft)wagen m, abbr. Pkw; **2.** ⚙ Am. Per'sonenwagen m, **~ lift** s. Brit. Per'sonenaufzug m; **~ pi·geon** s. orn. Wandertaube f; **~ plane** s. ✈ Per'sonenflugzeug n; **~ serv·ice** s. Per'sonenbeförderung f; **~ traf·fic** s. Per'sonenverkehr m; **~ train** s. ⚙ Per'sonenzug m.

passe-par·tout ['pæspɑːtuː] (Fr.) s. **1.** Hauptschlüssel m; **2.** Passepar'tout n (Bildumrahmung).

‚pass·er·'by pl. **‚pass·ers·'by** s. Pas'sant(in).

pass ex·am·i·na·tion s. univ. Brit. unterstes 'Abschlusse‚xamen.

pas·sim ['pæsim] (Lat.) adv. passim, hier u. da, an verschiedenen Orten.

pass·ing ['pɑːsiŋ] I adj. **1.** vor'über-, 'durchgehend: **~ axle** ⚙ durchgehende Achse; **2.** vergehend, vor'übergehend, flüchtig; **3.** beiläufig; II s. **4.** Vor'bei-, 'Durch-, Hin'übergehen n: **in ~** im Vorbeigehen, fig. beiläufig, nebenbei; **no ~!** mot. Überholverbot!; **5.** 'Übergang m: **~ of title** Eigentumsübertragung f; **6.** Da'hinschwinden n; **7.** Hinscheiden n, Ableben n; **8.** pol. 'Durchgehen n e-s Gesetzes; **~ beam** s. mot. Abblendlicht n; **~ lane** s. mot. 'Überholspur f; **~ note** s. ♪ 'Durchgangston m; **~ shot** s. Tennis: Pas'sierschlag m; **~ zone** s. Staffellauf: Wechselzone f.

pas·sion ['pæʃn] s. **1.** Leidenschaft f, heftige Gemütserregung, (Gefühls-) Ausbruch m; **2.** Zorn m: **fly into a ~** e-n Wutanfall bekommen; → **heat** 6; **3.** Leidenschaft f: a) heiße Liebe, heftige Neigung, b) heißer Wunsch, c) Passi'on f, Vorliebe f (**for** für), d) Liebhabe'rei f; Passi'on f: **it has become a ~ with him** es ist bei ihm zur Leidenschaft geworden, er tut es leidenschaftlich gern(e); **4.** ♀ *eccl.* Leiden *n* (Christi), Passion *f* (*a.* ♪, *paint. u. fig.*); **pas·sion·ate** ['pæʃənət] *adj.* □ **1.** leidenschaftlich (*a. fig.*); **2.** hitzig, jähzornig; **pas·sion·less** ['pæʃnlɪs] *adj.* □ leidenschaftslos.

pas·sion| play *s. eccl.* Passi'onsspiel *n*; ♀ **Sun·day** *s. eccl.* Passi'onssonntag *m*; **~ week** *s.* **1.** Karwoche *f*; **2.** Woche zwischen Passi'onssonntag u. Palm'sonntag.

pas·si·vate ['pæsiveit] *v/t.* ⊘, 🜚 passi-vieren.

pas·sive ['pæsiv] **I** *adj.* □ **1.** passiv (*a. ling.*, ⚡, 🜚, *sport*), leidend, teilnahmslos, 'widerstandslos: **~ air defence** Luftschutz *m*; **~ smoker** Passivraucher *m*; **~ smoking** Passivrauchen *n*; **~ verb** *ling.* passivisch konstruiertes Verb; **~ voice** → 3; **~ vocabulary** passiver Wortschatz; **2.** ✝ untätig, nicht zinstragend, passiv: **~ debt** unverzinsliche Schuld; **~ trade** Passivhandel *m*; **II** *s.* **3.** *ling.* Passiv *n*, Leideform *f*; **'pas·sive·ness** [-nis], **pas·siv·i·ty** [pæ'sivəti] *s.* Passivi'tät *f*, Teilnahmslosigkeit *f*.

'pass·key *s.* **1.** Hauptschlüssel *m*; **2.** Drücker *m*; **3.** Nachschlüssel *m*.

pas·som·e·ter [pæ'sɒmitə] *s.* ⊘ Schrittmesser *m*.

Pass·o·ver ['pɑːsˌəʊvə] *s. eccl.* **1.** Passah(fest) *n*; **2.** ♀ Osterlamm *n*.

pass·port ['pɑːspɔːt] *s.* **1.** (Reise)Pass *m*: **~ control** (*od. inspection*) Passkontrolle *f*; **2.** ✝ Passierschein *s*; **3.** *fig.* Zugang *m*, Weg *m*, Schlüssel *m* (**to** zu).

'pass·word *s.* Pa'role *f*, Losung *f*, Kennwort *n*; *Computer:* Passwort *n*.

past [pɑːst] **I** *adj.* **1.** vergangen, verflossen: **for some time ~** seit einiger Zeit; **2.** *ling.* Vergangenheits...: **~ participle** Mittelwort *n* der Vergangenheit, Partizip *n* Perfekt; **~ tense** Vergangenheit *f*, Präteritum *n*; **3.** vorig, früher, ehemalig, letzt: **~ president**; **~ master** *fig.* Altmeister *m*, großer Könner; **II** *s.* **4.** Vergangenheit *f* (*a. ling.*), *weitS. a.* Vorleben *n*: **a woman with a ~** eine Frau mit Vergangenheit; **III** *adv.* **5.** vorbei, vorüber: **to run ~**; **IV** *prp.* **6.** (*Zeit*) nach, über (*acc.*): **half ~ seven** halb acht; **she is ~ forty** sie ist über vierzig; **7.** an ... (*dat.*) vorbei: **he ran ~ the house**, **8.** über ... (*acc.*) hinaus: **~ comprehension** unfassbar, unfasslich; **~ cure** unheilbar; **~ hope** hoffnungslos; **he is ~ it** F er ist ,darüber hinaus'; **she is ~ caring** das kümmert sie nicht mehr; **I would not put it ~ him** *sl.* ich traue es ihm glatt zu.

pas·ta ['pæstə] *s.* Teigwaren *pl.*, Nudeln *pl.* (*als sg. konstr.*).

,past-'due *adj.* ✝ 'überfällig (*Wechsel etc.*); Verzugs...(-*zinsen*).

paste [peist] **I** *s.* **1.** Teig *m*, (*Fisch-, Zahn- etc.*)Paste *f*, Brei *m*; ⊘ Tonmasse *f*; Glasmasse *f*; **2.** Kleister *m*, Klebstoff *m*, Papp *m*; **3.** a) Paste *f* (*Diamantenherstellung*), b) künstlicher Edelstein, Simili *n*, *m*; **II** *v/t.* **4.** kleben, kleistern, pappen, bekleben (**with** mit); **5.** **~ up** a) auf-, ankleben (**on, in** auf, in *acc.*), b) verkleistern (*Loch*); **6.** *sl.* ('durch)hauen: **~ s.o. one** j-m ,eine kleben'; **7.** *Computer:* einfügen (**into** in *acc.*); **'~·board I** *s.* **1.** Pappe *f*, Pappendeckel *m*, Kar'ton *m*; **2.** *sl.* (Eintritts-, Spiel-, Vi'siten)Karte *f*; **II** *adj.* **3.** aus Pappe, Papp...: **~ box** Karton *m*; **4.** *fig.* unecht, wertlos, kitschig, nachgemacht.

pas·tel I *s.* [pæ'stel] **1.** ♀ Färberwaid *m*; **2.** ⊘ Waidblau *n*; **3.** Pa'stellstift *m*,

-farbe *f*; **4.** Pa'stellzeichnung *f*, -bild *n*; **II** *adj.* ['pæstl] **5.** zart, duftig, Pastell... (*Farbe*); **pas·tel·ist** ['pæstəlɪst], **pas·tel·list** [pæ'stelɪst] *s.* Pa'stellmaler(in).

pas·tern ['pæstɜːn] *s. zo.* Fessel *f* (*vom Pferd*).

'paste-up *s. typ.* 'Klebe,umbruch *m*.

pas·teur·i·za·tion [,pæstəraɪ'zeɪʃn] *s.* Pasteurisierung *f*; **pas·teur·ize** ['pæstəraɪz] *v/t.* pasteurisieren.

pas·tiche [pæ'stiːʃ] **1.** Pas'tiche *m*, Pas'ticcio *n*: a) *paint.* im Stil e-s anderen Malers angefertigtes Bild, b) ♪ aus Stücken verschiedener Komponisten zs.-gesetzte Oper; **2.** *fig.* Mischmasch *m*.

pas·tille ['pæstəl] *s.* **1.** Räucherkerzchen *n*; **2.** *pharm* Pa'stille *f*.

pas·time ['pɑːstaɪm] *s.* (**as a ~** zum) Zeitvertreib *m*.

past·i·ness ['peɪstɪnɪs] *s.* **1.** breiiger Zustand; breiiges Aussehen; **2.** *fig.* käsiges Aussehen.

past·ing ['peɪstɪŋ] *s.* **1.** Kleistern *n*, Kleben *n*; **2.** ⊘ Klebstoff *m*; **3.** *sl.* ,Dresche' *f*, (*Tracht f*) Prügel *pl.*

pas·tor ['pɑːstə] *s.* Pfarrer *m*, Pastor *m*, Seelsorger *m*; **'pas·to·ral** [-tərəl] **I** *adj.* □ **1.** Schäfer..., Hirten..., i'dyllisch, ländlich; **2.** *eccl.* pasto'ral, seelsorgerlich: **~ staff** Krummstab *m*; **II** *s.* **3.** Hirtengedicht *n*, I'dylle *f*; **4.** *paint.* ländliche Szene; **5.** ♪ a) Schäferspiel *n*, b) Pasto'rale *n*; **6.** *eccl.* a) Hirtenbrief *m*, b) *pl. a.* ♀ *Epistles* Pasto'ralbriefe *pl.* (*von Paulus*); **'pas·tor·ate** [-ərət] *s.* **1.** Pasto'rat *n*, Pfarramt *f*; **2.** *coll.* die Geistlichen *pl.*; **3.** *Am.* Pfarrhaus *n*.

past per·fect *ling. s.* Vorvergangenheit *f*, Plusquamperfekt *n*.

pas·try ['peɪstrɪ] *s.* **1.** a) *coll.* Kon'ditorwaren *pl.*, Feingebäck *n*, b) Kuchen *m*, Torte *f*; **2.** (Kuchen-, Torten)Teig *m*; **~ cook** *s.* Kon'ditor *m*.

pas·tur·age ['pɑːstjʊrɪdʒ] *s.* **1.** Weiden *n* (*Vieh*); **2.** Weidegras *n*; **3.** Weide (-land *n*) *f*; **4.** Bienenzucht *f* u. -fütterung *f*.

pas·ture ['pɑːstʃə] **I** *s.* **1.** Weidegras *n*, Viehfutter *n*; **2.** Weide(land *n*) *f*: **seek greener ~** *fig.* sich nach besseren Möglichkeiten umsehen; **retire to ~** (in den Ruhestand) abtreten; **II** *v/i.* **3.** grasen, weiden; **III** *v/t.* **4.** Vieh auf die Weide treiben, weiden; **5.** Wiese abweiden.

past·y¹ ['peɪstɪ] *adj.* **1.** teigig, kleisterig; **2.** *fig.* ,käsig', blass.

past·y² ['pæstɪ] *s.* ('Fleisch)Pa,stete *f*.

pat [pæt] **I** *s.* **1.** *Brit.* (*leichter*) Schlag, Klaps *m*: **~ on the back** *fig.* Schulterklopfen *n*, Lob *n*, Glückwunsch *m*; **2.** (Butter)Klümpchen *n*; **3.** Klopfen *n*, Getrappel *n*, Tapsen *n*; **II** *adj.* **4.** a) pa'rat, bereit, b) passend, treffend: **~ answer** schlagfertige Antwort; **~ solution** Patentlösung; **a ~ style** ein gekonnter Stil; **know s.th. off** (*od.* **have it down**) → F et. (wie) am Schnürchen können; **5.** fest: **stand ~** festbleiben, sich nicht beirren lassen; **6.** (*a. adv.*) im rechten Augenblick, rechtzeitig, wie gerufen; **III** *v/t.* **7.** *Brit.* klopfen, tätscheln: **~ s.o. on the back** j-m (anerkennend) auf die Schulter klopfen, *fig. a.* j-n beglückwünschen.

pat² [pæt] *s.* Ire *m* (*Spitzname*).

'pat-a-cake backe, backe Kuchen (*Kinderspiel*).

patch [pætʃ] **I** *s.* **1.** Fleck *m*, Flicken *m*, Lappen *m*; ⚔ *etc.* Tuchabzeichen *n*: **not a ~ on** F gar nicht zu vergleichen mit; **2.** a) Pflaster *n*, b) Augenbinde *f*; **3.** Schönheitspflästerchen *n*; **4.** Stück

n Land, Fleck *m*; Stück *n* Rasen; Stelle *f* (*a. im Buch*): **~** e-e Pechsträhne *od.* e-n schwarzen Tag haben; **5.** (Farb)Fleck *m* (*bei Tieren etc.*); **6.** *pl.* Bruchstücke *pl.*, *et.* Zs.-gestoppeltes; **II** *v/t.* **7.** flicken, ausbessern; mit Flicken versehen; **8.** **~ up** bsd. *fig.* a) zs.-stoppeln: **~ up a textbook**, b) ,zs.-flicken', c) *Ehe etc.* ,kitten', d) *Streit* beilegen, e) über'tünchen, beschönigen; **'~·board** *s. Computer:* Schaltbrett *n*; **~ kit** *s.* Flickzeug *n*.

patch·ou·li ['pætʃʊlɪ] *s.* Patschuli *n* (*Pflanze u. Parfüm*).

patch| pock·et *s.* aufgesetzte Tasche; **~ test** *s.* 🜚 Tuberku'linprobe *f*; **'~·word** *s. ling.* Flickwort *n*; **'~·work** *s. a. fig.* Flickwerk *n*.

patch·y ['pætʃɪ] *adj.* □ **1.** voller Flicken; **2.** *fig.* zs.-gestoppelt; **3.** fleckig; **4.** *fig.* ungleichmäßig.

pate [peɪt] *s.* F Schädel *m*, ,Birne' *f*.

pâté ['pæteɪ] (*Fr.*) *s.* Pa'stete *f*.

pat·en ['pæten] *s. eccl.* Pa'tene *f*, Hostienteller *m*.

pa·ten·cy ['peɪtənsɪ] *s.* **1.** Offenkundigkeit *f*; **2.** ⚡ 'Durchgängigkeit *f* (*e-s Kanals etc.*).

pat·ent ['peɪtənt] *bsd.* ⚖ *u. Am.* 'pæ-] **I** *adj.* □ **1.** offen(kundig): **to be ~** auf der Hand liegen; **2.** **letters ~** → 6 *u.* 7; **3.** patentiert, gesetzlich geschützt: **~ article** Markenartikel *m*; **~ fuel** Presskohlen *pl.*; **~ leather** Lack-, Glanzleder *n*; **~-leather shoe** Lackschuh *m*; **~ medicine** Marken-, Patentmedizin *f*; **4.** ⚖ Patent...: **~ agent** (*Am.* **attorney**) Patentanwalt *m*; **~ law** objektives Patentrecht; ♀ **Office** Patentamt *n*; **~ right** subjektives Patentrecht; **~ roll** *Brit.* Patentregister *n*; **~ specification** Patentschrift *f*, -beschreibung *f*; **5.** *Brit.* F ,pa'tent': **~ methods**; **II** *s.* **6.** Pa'tent *n*, Privi'leg(ium) *n*, Freibrief *m*, Bestallung *f*; **7.** ⚖ Pa'tent(urkunde *f*) *n*: **~ of addition** Zusatzpatent; **~ applied for**, **~ pending** Patent angemeldet; **take out a ~ for** → 10; **8.** *Brit.* F ,Re'zept' *n*; **III** *v/t.* **9.** patentieren, gesetzlich schützen; **10.** patentieren lassen; **'pat·enta·ble** [-təbl] *adj.* pa'tentfähig; **pat·ent·ee** [,peɪtən'tiː] *s.* Pa'tentinhaber(in).

pa·ter ['peɪtə] *s. ped. sl.* ,Alter Herr' (*Vater*).

pa·ter·nal [pə'tɜːnl] *adj.* □ väterlich, Vater...: **~ grandfather** Großvater *m* väterlicherseits; **pa·ter·ni·ty** [-nəti] *s.* Vaterschaft *f* (*a. fig.*): **~ suit** Vaterschaftsklage *f*; **declare ~** die Vaterschaft feststellen.

pa·ter·nos·ter [,pætə'nɒstə] **I** *s.* **1.** *R.C.* a) Vater'unser *n*, b) Rosenkranz *m*; **2.** ⊘ Pater'noster *m* (*Aufzug*); **II** *adj.* **3.** ⊘ Paternoster...

path [pɑːθ] *pl.* **paths** [pɑːðz] *s.* **1.** Pfad *m*, Weg *m* (*a. fig.*): **cross s.o.'s ~** j-m über den Weg laufen; **2.** ⊘, *phys.*, *sport* Bahn *f*: **~ of electrons** Elektronenbahn; **3.** *Computer:* Pfad *m*.

pa·thet·ic [pə'θetɪk] *adj.* (□ **~ally**) **1.** *obs.* pa'thetisch, allzu gefühlvoll: **~ fallacy** Vermenschlichung *f* der Natur (*in der Literatur*); **2.** Mitleid erregend; **3.** *Brit.* F kläglich, jämmerlich, ,zum Weinen'.

'path,find·er *s.* **1.** ✓, ⚔ Pfadfinder *m*; **2.** Forschungsreisende(r) *m*; **3.** *fig.* Bahnbrecher *m*.

path·less ['pɑːθlɪs] *adj.* weglos.

'path·name *s. Computer:* Pfadname *m*.

path·o·gen·ic [,pæθə'dʒenɪk] *adj.* ⚡ patho'gen, krankheitserregend.

path·o·log·i·cal [ˌpæθəˈlɒdʒɪkl] *adj.* □ ✸ pathoˈlogisch: a) krankhaft, b) *die Krankheitslehre betreffend;* **pa·thol·o·gist** [pəˈθɒlədʒɪst] *s.* ✸ Patho'loge *m;* **pa·thol·o·gy** [pəˈθɒlədʒɪ] *s.* ✸ **1.** Patholo'gie *f,* Krankheitslehre *f;* **2.** patho'logischer Befund.

pa·thos [ˈpeɪθɒs] *s.* **1.** *obs.* Pathos *n;* **2.** a) Mitleid *n,* b) *das* Mitleid Erregende.

'path·way *s.* Pfad *m,* Weg *m,* Bahn *f.*

pa·tience [ˈpeɪʃns] *s.* **1.** Geduld *f;* Ausdauer *f;* *lose one's* ~ die Geduld verlieren; *be out of* ~ *with s.o.* aufgebracht sein gegen j-n; *have no* ~ *with s.o.* j-n nicht leiden können, nichts übrig haben für j-n; *try s.o.'s* ~ j-s Geduld auf die Probe stellen; → *Job²; possess* 2 b; **2.** *bsd. Brit.* Pati'ence *f (Kartenspiel);* **'pa·tient** [-nt] *I adj.* □ **1.** geduldig; nachsichtig; beharrlich: *be* ~ *of* ertragen; ~ *of two interpretations* fig. zwei Deutungen zulassend; **II** *s.* **2.** Pati'ent(in), Kranke(r *m*) *f;* **3.** ✠ *Brit.* Geistesgestörte(r *m*) *f (in e-r Heil- und Pflegeanstalt).*

pat·i·o [ˈpætɪəʊ] *s.* **1.** Innenhof *m,* Patio *m;* **2.** Ter'rasse *f,* Ve'randa *f.*

pa·tri·arch [ˈpeɪtrɪɑːk] *s.* Patri'arch *m;* **pa·tri·ar·chal** [ˌpeɪtrɪˈɑːkl] *adj.* patriar'chalisch *(a. fig. ehrwürdig);* **'pa·tri·arch·ate** [-kɪt] *s.* Patriar'chat *n.*

pa·tri·cian [pəˈtrɪʃn] **I** *adj.* pa'trizisch; *fig.* aristo'kratisch; **II** *s.* Pa'trizier(in).

pat·ri·cide [ˈpætrɪsaɪd] → *parricide.*

pat·ri·mo·ni·al [ˌpætrɪˈməʊnjəl] *adj.* ererbt, Erb...; **pat·ri·mo·ny** [ˈpætrɪmənɪ] *s.* **1.** väterliches Erbteil *(a. fig.);* **2.** Vermögen *n;* **3.** Kirchengut *n.*

pa·tri·ot [ˈpætrɪət] *s.* Patri'ot(in); **pa·tri·ot·eer** [ˌpætrɪəˈtɪə] *s.* Hur'rapatri,ot *m;* **pa·tri·ot·ic** [ˌpætrɪˈɒtɪk] *adj.* (□ ~*ally*) patri'otisch; **'pa·tri·ot·ism** [-tɪzəm] *s.* Patri'otismus *m,* Vaterlandsliebe *f.*

pa·trol [pəˈtrəʊl] **I** *v/i.* **1.** ✕ patrouillieren, ✈ Pa'trouille fliegen; auf Streife sein *(Polizisten),* s-e Runde machen *(Wachmann);* **II** *v/t.* **2.** ✕ abpatrouillieren, ✈ *Strecke* abfliegen; auf Streife sein in *(dat.);* **III** *s.* **3.** *(on* ~ auf) Pa'trouille *f;* Streife *f;* Runde *f;* **4.** ✕ Pa'trouille, Späh-, Stoßtrupp *m;* (Poli'zei)Streife *f:* ~ *activity* ✕ Spähtrupptätigkeit *f;* ~ *car* a) ✕ (Panzer-) Spähwagen *m,* b) (Funk-, Poli'zei-) Streifenwagen *m;* ~ *wagon* Am. Polizeigefangenenwagen *m;* ~**man** [-mæn] *s. [irr.]* Streifenbeamte(r) *m.*

pa·tron [ˈpeɪtrən] *s.* **1.** Pa'tron *m,* Schutz-, Schirmherr *m;* **2.** Gönner *m,* Förderer *m;* **3.** *R.C.* a) 'Kirchenpa,tron *m,* b) → *patron saint;* **4.** a) ✝ (Stamm-) Kunde *m,* b) Stammgast *m, a. thea. etc.* regelmäßiger Besucher; **5.** *Brit. mot.* Pannenhelfer *m;* **pa·tron·age** [ˈpætrənɪdʒ] *s.* **1.** Schirmherrschaft *f;* **2.** Gönnerschaft *f,* Förderung *f;* **3.** ✝ Patro'natsrecht *n;* **4.** Kundschaft *f;* **5.** gönnerhaftes Benehmen; **6.** *Am.* Recht *n* der Ämterbesetzung; **pa·tron·ess** [ˈpeɪtrənɪs] *s.* Pa'tronin *f etc.* (→ *patron).*

pa·tron·ize [ˈpætrənaɪz] *v/t.* **1.** beschirmen, beschützen; **2.** fördern, unter'stützen; **3.** (Stamm)Kunde *od.* Stammgast sein bei, *Theater etc.* regelmäßig besuchen; **4.** gönnerhaft behandeln; **'pa·tron·iz·er** [-zə] *s.* → *patron* 2, 4; **'pa·tron·iz·ing** [-zɪŋ] *adj.* □ gönnerhaft, her'ablassend: ~ *air* Gönnermiene *f.*

pa·tron saint *R.C.* Schutzheilige(r) *m.*

pat·sy [ˈpætsɪ] *s. sl.* **1.** Sündenbock *m;* **2.**

Gimpel *m;* **3.** 'Witzfi,gur *f.*

pat·ten [ˈpætn] *s.* **1.** Holzschuh *m;* **2.** Stelzschuh *m;* **3.** △ Säulenfuß *m.*

pat·ter¹ [ˈpætə] **I** *v/i. u. v/t.* **1.** schwatzen, (da'her)plappern; ,he'runterlei-ern'; **II** *s.* **2.** Geplapper *n;* **3.** ('Fach-)Jar,gon *m;* **4.** Gaunersprache *f.*

pat·ter² [ˈpætə] **I** *v/i.* **1.** prasseln *(Regen etc.);* **2.** trappeln *(Füße);* **II** *s.* **3.** Prasseln *n (Regen);* **4.** (Fuß)Getrappel *n;* **5.** Klappern *n.*

pat·tern [ˈpætən] **I** *s.* **1.** *(a.* Schnitt-, Stick)Muster *n,* Vorlage *f,* Mo'dell *n:* *on the* ~ *of* nach dem Muster von *od. gen.;* **2.** ✠ Muster *n:* a) (Waren)Probe *f,* b) Des'sin *n,* Mo'tiv *n (Stoff): by* ~ *post* als Muster ohne Wert; **3.** *fig.* Muster *n,* Vorbild *n;* **4.** *fig.* Plan *m,* Anlage *f:* ~ *of one's life;* **5.** ✆ a) Scha'blone *f,* b) 'Gussmo,dell *n,* c) Lehre *f;* **6.** *Weberei:* Pa'trone *f,* **7.** *(behavio[u]r* ~) *psych.* (Verhaltens)Muster *n;* **II** *adj.* **8.** musterhaft, Muster...: *a* ~ *wife;* **III** *v/t.* **9.** (nach)bilden, gestalten *(after, on* nach): ~ *one's conduct on s.o.* sich (in s-m Benehmen) ein Beispiel an j-m nehmen; **10.** mit Muster(n) verzieren, mustern; ~ *bomb·ing* ✕ Flächenwurf *m;* ~ *book s.* ✝ Musterbuch *n;* ~ *mak·er s.* ✆ Mo'dellmacher *m;* ~ *paint·ing s.* ✕ Tarnanstrich *m.*

pat·ty [ˈpætɪ] *s.* Pa'stetchen *n.*

pau·ci·ty [ˈpɔːsɪtɪ] *s.* geringe Zahl *od.* Menge, Knappheit *f.*

Paul·ine [ˈpɔːlaɪn] *adj. eccl.* pau'linisch.

paunch [pɔːntʃ] *s.* **1.** (Dick)Bauch *m,* Wanst *m;* **2.** *zo.* Pansen *m;* **'paunch·y** [-tʃɪ] *adj.* dickbäuchig.

pau·per [ˈpɔːpə] **I** *s.* **1.** Arme(r *m*) *f;* **2.** *Am.* a) Unter'stützungsempfänger(in), b) ✠ unter Armenrecht Klagende(r *m*) *f;* **II** *adj.* **3.** Armen...; **'pau·per·ism** [-ərɪzəm] *s.* Verarmung *f,* Massenarmut *f;* **pau·per·i·za·tion** [ˌpɔːpəraɪˈzeɪʃn] *s.* Verarmung *f,* Verelendung *f;* **'pau·per·ize** [-əraɪz] *v/t.* bettelarm machen.

pause [pɔːz] **I** *s.* **1.** Pause *f,* Unter'brechung *f: make a* ~ innehalten, pausieren; *it gives one* ~ *to think* es gibt e-m zu denken; **2.** *typ.* Gedankenstrich *m;* **3.** ♪ Fer'mate *f;* **II** *v/i.* **4.** pausieren, innehalten, stehen bleiben; zögern; **5.** verweilen *(on, upon* bei): ~ *upon a note (od. tone)* ♪ e-n Ton aushalten.

pave [peɪv] *v/t. Straße* pflastern, *Fußboden* legen: ~ *the way for fig.* den Weg ebnen für; → *paving;* **'pave·ment** [-mənt] *s.* **1.** (Straßen)Pflaster *n;* **2.** *Brit.* Bürgersteig *m,* Trot'toir *n:* ~ *artist* Pflastermaler *m;* ~ *café* Straßencafé *n;* **3.** *Am.* Fahrbahn *f;* **4.** Fußboden(belag) *m;* **'pav·er** [-və] *s.* **1.** Pflasterer *m;* **2.** Fliesen-, Plattenleger *m;* **3.** Pflasterstein *m,* Fußbodenplatte *f;* **4.** *Am.* 'Straßenbe,tonmischer *m.*

pa·vil·ion [pəˈvɪljən] *s.* **1.** (großes) Zelt; **2.** Pavillon *m,* Gartenhäuschen *n;* **3.** ✝ (Messe)Pavillon *m.*

pav·ing [ˈpeɪvɪŋ] *s.* Pflastern *n;* (Be)Pflasterung *f,* Straßendecke *f;* Fußbodenbelag *m;* ~ *stone s.* Pflasterstein *m;* ~ *tile s.* Fliese *f.*

pav·io(u)r [ˈpeɪvjə] *s.* Pflasterer *m.*

paw [pɔː] **I** *s.* **1.** Pfote *f,* Tatze *f;* **2.** F ,Pfote' *f (Hand);* **3.** F *humor.* ,Klaue' *f (Handschrift);* **II** *v/t.* **4.** mit dem Vorderfuß *od.* der Pfote scharren; **5.** F ,betatschen': a) derb *od.* ungeschickt anfassen, b) j-n ,begrapschen': ~ *the air* (in der Luft) herumfuchteln; **III** *v/i.* **6.** stampfen, scharren; **7.** ,(he'rum)fummeln'.

---

pawl [pɔːl] *s.* **1.** ✆ Sperrhaken *m,* -klinke *f,* Klaue *f;* **2.** ⚓ Pall *n.*

pawn¹ [pɔːn] *s.* **1.** *Schach:* Bauer *m;* **2.** *fig.* 'Schachfi,gur *f:* ~ *sacrifice a* ~ ein Bauernopfer bringen.

pawn² [pɔːn] **I** *s.* **1.** Pfand(sache *f*) *n;* ✠ *u. fig. a.* Faustpfand *n (od.* at); ~ verpfändet, versetzt; **II** *v/t.* **2.** verpfänden *(a. fig.),* versetzen; **3.** ✝ lombardieren; ~**bro·ker** *s.* Pfandleiher *m.*

pawn·ee [ˌpɔːˈniː] *s.* ✠ Pfandinhaber *m,* -nehmer *m;* **pawn·er, pawn·or** [ˈpɔːnə] *s.* Pfandschuldner *m.*

'pawn·shop *s.* Pfandhaus *n,* Pfandleihe *f;* ~**tick·et** *s.* Pfandschein *m.*

pay [peɪ] **I** *s.* **1.** Bezahlung *f;* (Arbeits-) Lohn *m,* Löhnung *f;* Gehalt *n;* Sold *m (a. fig.);* ✕ (Wehr)Sold *m: in the* ~ *of s.o.* bei j-m beschäftigt, in j-s Sold; **2.** *fig.* Belohnung *f,* Lohn *m;* **II** *v/t.* [*irr.*] **3.** zahlen, entrichten; *Rechnung* bezahlen *od.* begleichen, *Wechsel* einlösen, *Hypothek* ablösen; j-n bezahlen, *Gläubiger* befriedigen: ~ *into* einzahlen auf *ein Konto;* ~ *one's way* ohne Verlust arbeiten, s-n Verbindlichkeiten nachkommen, auskommen mit dem, was man hat; **4.** *fig.* (be)lohnen, vergelten *(for et.):* ~ *home* heimzahlen; **5.** *fig. Achtung* zollen; *Aufmerksamkeit* schenken; *Besuch* abstatten; *Ehre* erweisen; *Kompliment* machen; → *court* 10; *homage* 2; **6.** *fig.* sich lohnen für j-n; **III** *v/i.* [*irr.*] **7.** zahlen, Zahlung leisten: ~ *for* (für) et. bezahlen *(a. fig. et.* büßen), die Kosten tragen für; *he had to* ~ *dearly for it fig.* er mußte es bitter büßen, es kam ihn teuer zu stehen; **8.** *fig.* sich lohnen, sich rentieren, sich bezahlt machen;

Zssgn mit adv.:

pay| back *v/t.* **1.** zu'rückzahlen, -erstatten; **2.** *fig.* a) *Besuch etc.* erwidern, b) j-m heimzahlen *(for s.th.* et.); → *coin* 1; ~ *down v/t.* **1.** bar bezahlen; **2.** e-e Anzahlung machen von; ~ *in v/t. v/i.* (auf ein Konto) einzahlen; → *paid-in;* ~ *off* **I** *v/t.* **1.** j-n auszahlen, entlohnen; ⚓ abmustern; **2.** *et.* abbezahlen, tilgen; **3.** *Am.* für *pay back* 2b; **II** *v/i.* **4.** F → *pay* 8; ~ *out v/t.* **1.** auszahlen; **2.** F *fig.* → *pay back* 2b; **3.** *(pret. u. p.p.* **payed**) *Kabel, Kette etc.* ausstecken, -legen, abrollen; ~ *up v/t.* j-n *od.* et. voll *od.* so'fort bezahlen; *Schuld* tilgen; ✝ *Anteile, Versicherung etc.* voll einzahlen; → *paid-up.*

pay·a·ble [ˈpeɪəbl] *adj.* **1.** zahlbar, fällig: ~ *to bearer* auf den Überbringer lautend; *make a cheque (Am. check)* ~ *to s.o.* e-n Scheck auf j-n ausstellen; **2.** ✝ ren'tabel.

,pay-as-you-'earn *s. Brit.* Lohnsteuerabzug *m;* **,~-as-you-'see tel·e·vi·sion** *s.* Münzfernsehen *n;* ~ *bed s.* ✸ Pri'vatbett *n;* ~ *check s. Am.* Lohn-, Gehaltsscheck *m;* ~ *claim s.* Lohn-, Gehaltsforderung *f;* ~ *clerk s.* ✝ Lohnauszahler *m;* **2.** ✕ Rechnungsführer *m;* **'~-day** *s.* Zahl-, Löhnungstag *m;* ~ *desk s.* ✝ Kasse *f (im Kaufhaus);* ~ *dirt s. geol.* Gold führendes Erdreich; **2.** *fig. Am.* Geld *n,* Gewinn *m:* *strike* ~ *dirt* Glück haben.

pay·ee [peɪˈiː] *s.* **1.** Zahlungsempfänger (-in); **2.** Wechselnehmer(in).

pay en·ve·lope *s.* Lohntüte *f.*

pay·er [ˈpeɪə] *s.* **1.** (Be)Zahler *m;* **2.** *(Wechsel)Bezogene(r) m,* Tras'sat *m.*

pay freeze *s.* Lohnstopp *m.*

pay·ing [ˈpeɪɪŋ] *adj.* **1.** lohnend, einträglich, ren'tabel: *not* ~ unrentabel; ~ *concern* lohnendes Geschäft; **2.** Kas-

sen..., Zahl(ungs)...: ~ *guest* zahlender Gast; **,~-'in slip** *s.* Einzahlungsschein *m*.
'**pay|·load** *s.* **1.** ◎, ⚓, ✈ Nutzlast *f*: ~ *capacity* Ladefähigkeit *f*; **2.** ✕ Sprengladung *f*; **3.** ✞ *Am.* Lohnanteil *m*; '**~·mas·ter** *s.* ✕ Zahlmeister *m*.
pay·ment ['peɪmənt] *s.* **1.** (Ein-, Aus-, Be)Zahlung *f*, Entrichtung *f*, Abtragung *f von Schulden*, Einlösung *f e-s Wechsels*: ~ *in kind* Sachleistung *f*; *in* ~ *of* zum Ausgleich (*gen.*); *on* ~ (*of*) nach Eingang (*gen.*), gegen Zahlung (von *od. gen.*); *accept in* ~ in Zahlung nehmen; **2.** gezahlte Summe, Bezahlung *f*; **3.** Lohn *m*, Löhnung *f*, Besoldung *f*; **4.** *fig.* Lohn *m* (*a. Strafe*).
'**pay|·off** *s. sl.* **1.** Aus- *od.* Abzahlung *f*; **2.** *fig.* Abrechnung *f* (*Rache*); **3.** Resul·'tat *n*; Entscheidung *f*; **4.** *Am.* Clou *m* (*Höhepunkt*); ~ *of·fice s.* **1.** 'Lohnbü·,ro *n*; **2.** Zahlstelle *f*.
pay·o·la [peɪ'əʊlə] *s. Am. sl.* Bestechungs-, Schmiergeld(er *pl.*) *n*.
pay| pack·et Lohntüte *f*; ~ *pause s.* Lohnpause *f*; '**~·roll** *s.* Lohnliste *f*: *have* (*od. keep*) *s.o. on one's* ~ j-n (bei sich) beschäftigen; *he is no longer on our* ~ er arbeitet nicht mehr für *od.* bei uns; ~ *round s.* Ta'rifrunde *f*; ~ *scale s.* 'Lohn- u. Ge'haltsta,rif *m*; ~ *slip* Lohn-, Gehaltsstreifen *m*; ~ *tel·e·phone s.* Münzfernsprecher *m*; ~ *TV s.* 'Pay-T,V *n*.
pea [piː] **I** *s.* ♀ Erbse *f*: *as like as two* ~*s* sich gleichend wie ein Ei dem andern; → *sweet pea*; **II** *adj.* erbsengroß, -förmig.
peace [piːs] **I** *s.* **1.** Friede(n) *m*: *at* ~ a) in Frieden, im Friedenszustand, b) in Frieden ruhend (*tot*); **2.** *a.* *the King's* (*od. Queen's*) ~, *public* ~ Landfrieden *m*, öffentliche Ruhe und Ordnung, öffentliche Sicherheit: *breach of the* ~ ♯ (öffentliche) Ruhestörung; *disturb the* ~ die öffentliche Ruhe stören; *keep the* ~ die öffentliche Sicherheit wahren; **3.** *fig.* Ruhe *f*, Friede(n) *m*: ~ *of mind* Seelenruhe *f*; *hold one's* ~ sich ruhig verhalten; *leave in* ~ in Ruhe *od.* Frieden lassen; **4.** Versöhnung *f*, Eintracht *f*: *make one's* ~ *with s.o.* sich mit j-m versöhnen; **II** *int.* **5.** sst!, still!, ruhig!; **III** *adj.* **6.** Friedens...: ~ *conference*; ~ *feelers*; ~ *movement*; ~ *offensive*; ~ *corps* Friedenstruppe *f*; '**peace·a·ble** [-səbl] *adj.* □ friedlich: a) friedfertig, -liebend, b) ruhig, ungestört; '**peace·ful** [-ful] *adj.* □ friedlich; '**~·,keep·ing** *adj.*: ~ *force pol.* ✕ Friedenstruppe *f*; '**peace·less** [-lɪs] *adj.* friedlos.
peace·nik ['piːsnɪk] *s. Am. sl.* Kriegsgegner(in).
peace| of·fer·ing *s.* **1.** *eccl.* Sühneopfer *n*; **2.** Versöhnungsgeschenk *n*, versöhnliche Geste, Friedenszeichen *n*; ~ *of·fi·cer s.* Sicherheitsbeamte(r) *m*, Schutzmann *m*; ~ *pro·cess s.* 'Friedenspro,zess *m*; ~ *re·search s.* Friedensforschung *f*; ~ *set·tle·ment s.* Friedensregelung *f*; ~ *stud·ies s. pl.* Friedensforschung *f*; '**~·time I** *s.* Friedenszeit *f*; **II** *adj.* in Friedenszeiten, Friedens...; ~ *trea·ty s. pol.* Friedensvertrag *m*.
peach¹ [piːtʃ] *s.* ♀ Pfirsich(baum) *m*; **2.** *sl.* ,klasse' Per'son *od.* Sache: *a* ~ *of a car* ein ,todschicker' Wagen; *a* ~ *of a girl* ein bildhübsches Mädchen.
peach² [piːtʃ] *v/i.* ~ *against* (*od. on*) Komplicen ,verpfeifen', Schulkameraden verpetzen.
peach·y ['piːtʃɪ] *adj.* **1.** pfirsichartig; **2.** *sl.* ,prima', ,schick', ,klasse'.
pea·cock ['piːkɒk] *s. orn.* Pfau(hahn)

m; **2.** *fig.* (eitler) Fatzke *m*; ~ *blue s.* Pfauenblau *n* (*Farbe*).
'**pea|·fowl** *s. orn.* Pfau *m*; '~·**hen** *s. orn.* Pfauhenne *f*; ~ *jack·et s.* ⚓ Ko'lani *m* (*Uniformjacke*).
peak¹ [piːk] **I** *s.* **1.** Spitze *f*; **2.** Bergspitze *f*; Horn *n*, spitzer Berg; **3.** (Mützen-) Schirm *m*; **4.** ⚓ Piek *f*; **5.** ♫, *phys.* Höchst-, Scheitelwert *m*; **6.** *fig.* (Leistungs- *etc.*)Spitze *f*, Höchststand *m*; Gipfel *m des Glücks etc.*: ~ *of traffic* Verkehrsspitze; *reach the* ~ den Höchststand erreichen; **II** *adj.* **7.** Spitzen..., Höchst..., Haupt...: ~ *factor phys.*, ♫ Scheitelfaktor *m*; ~ *load* Spitzenbelastung *f* (*a.* ♫); ~ *season* Hochsaison *f*, -konjunktur; ~ *time* a) Hochkonjunktur *f*, b) Stoßzeit *f*, c) = ~ (*traffic*) *hours* Hauptverkehrszeit *f*; d) *Stromverbrauch:* Hauptbelastungszeit *f*, Spitzenzeit *f*, e) → ~ *viewing time TV* Hauptsendezeit *f*.
peak² [piːk] *v/i.* **1.** kränkeln, abmagern; **2.** spitz aussehen.
peaked [piːkt] *adj.* **1.** spitz(ig): ~ *cap* Schirmmütze *f*; **2.** F ,spitz', kränklich.
peak·y ['piːkɪ] *adj.* **1.** gipfelig; **2.** spitz (-ig); **3.** → *peaked* 2.
peal [piːl] **I** *s.* **1.** (Glocken)Läuten *n*; **2.** Glockenspiel *n*; **3.** (*Donner*)Schlag *m*, Dröhnen *n*: ~ *of laughter* schallendes Gelächter; **II** *v/i.* **4.** läuten; erschallen, dröhnen, schmettern; **III** *v/t.* **5.** erschallen lassen.
'**pea·nut I** *s.* **1.** ♀ Erdnuss *f*; **2.** *Am. sl.* a) *pl.* ,Peanuts' *pl.*, ,kleine Fische' *pl.* (*geringer Betrag*), b) ,kleines Würstchen' (*Person*); **II** *adj.* **3.** *Am. sl.* klein, unbedeutend, lächerlich: *a* ~ *politician*; ~ *but·ter s.* Erdnussbutter *f*.
pear [peə] *s.* ♀ **1.** Birne *f* (*a. weitS. Objekt*); **2.** *a.* ~ *tree* Birnbaum *m*.
pearl [pɜːl] **I** *s.* **1.** Perle *f* (*a. fig. u. pharm.*): *cast* ~*s before swine* Perlen vor die Säue werfen; **2.** Perl'mutt *n*; **3.** *typ.* Perl(schrift) *f*; **II** *adj.* **4.** Perlen...; Perlmutt(er)...; **III** *v/i.* **5.** Perlen bilden, perlen, tropfen; ~ *bar·ley s.* Perlgraupen *pl.*; ~ *div·er s.* Perlentaucher *m*; ~ *oys·ter s. zo.* Perlmuschel *f*.
pearl·y ['pɜːlɪ] *adj.* **1.** Perlen..., perlenartig, perlmutterartig; **2.** perlenreich.
'**pearl|·quince** *s.* ♀ Echte Quitte, Birnenquitte *f*; '~·**shaped** *adj.* birnenförmig.
peas·ant ['peznt] **I** *s.* **1.** (Klein)Bauer *m*; **2.** *fig.* ,Bauer' *m*; **II** *adj.* **3.** (klein-) bäuerlich, Bauern...: ~ *woman* Bäuerin *f*; '**peas·ant·ry** [-rɪ] *s. die* (Klein-) Bauern *pl.*, Landvolk *n*.
pease [piːz] *s. pl. Br. dial.* Erbsen *pl.*: ~ *pudding* Erbs(en)brei *m*.
'**pea|·shoot·er** *s.* **1.** Blas-, Pusterohr *n*; **2.** *Am.* Kata'pult *m*, *n*; **3.** *Am. sl.* ,Ka-'none' *f* (*Pistole*); ~ *soup s.* **1.** Erbsensuppe *f*; **2.** *a.* ,~·'soup·er [-'suːpə] *s.* F ,Waschküche' *f* (*dichter Nebel*); **2.** 'Frankoka,nadier; *m*; ,~·'soup·y [-'suːpɪ] *adj.* F dicht u. gelb (*Nebel*).
peat [piːt] *s.* **1.** Torf *m*: ~ *cut* (*od. dig*) ~ Torf stechen: ~ *bath* ♯ Moorbad *n*; ~ *coal* Torfkohle *f*; ~ *moss* Torfmoos *n*; **2.** Torfstück *n*, -sode *f*.
peb·ble ['pebl] **I** *s.* **1.** Kiesel(stein) *m*: *you are not the only* ~ *on the beach* F man (*od.* ich) kann auch ohne dich auskommen; **2.** A'chat *m*; **3.** 'Bergkri,stall *m*; **4.** *opt.* Linse *f* aus 'Bergkri,stall; **II** *v/t.* **5.** *Weg* mit Kies bestreuen; **6.** ⊚ *Leder* krispeln; '**peb·bly** [-lɪ] *adj.* kieselig.
pec·ca·dil·lo [,pekə'dɪləʊ] *pl.* -**loes** *s.*

,kleine Sünde', Kava'liersde,likt *n*.
peck¹ [pek] *s.* **1.** Viertelscheffel *m* (*Brit. 9,1, Am. 8,8 Liter*); **2.** *fig.* Menge *f*, Haufen *m*: *a* ~ *of trouble*.
peck² [pek] **I** *v/t.* **1.** mit dem Schnabel *etc.* (auf)picken, (-)hacken; **2.** j-m ein Küsschen geben; **II** *v/i.* **3.** (*at*) picken, hacken (nach), einhacken (auf *acc.*): ~*ing order zo. u. fig.* Hackordnung *f*; ~ *at s.o. fig.* auf j-m ,herumhacken'; ~ *at one's food* lustlos im Essen herumstochern; **III** *s.* **4.** Schlag *m*, (Schnabel-) Hieb *m*; **5.** Loch *n*; **6.** leichter *od.* flüchtiger Kuss; **7.** *Brit. sl.* ,Futter' *n* (*Essen*); '**peck·er** [-kə] *s.* **1.** Picke *f*, Haue *f*; **2.** ⊚ Abfühlnadel *f*; **3.** *sl.* ,Zinken' *m* (*Nase*): *keep your* ~ *up!* halt die Ohren steif!; **4.** *Am. sl.* ,Schwanz' *m* (*Penis*); **peck·ish** ['pekɪʃ] *adj.* F **1.** hungrig; **2.** *Am.* reizbar.
pecs [peks] *s. pl.* F Muckis *pl.* (*Muskeln*).
pec·to·ral ['pektərəl] **I** *adj.* **1.** *anat.*, ♯ Brust...; **II** *s.* **2.** *hist.* Brustplatte *f*; **3.** *anat.* Brustmuskel *m*; **4.** *pharm.* Brustmittel *n*; **5.** *zo. a.* ~ *fin* Brustflosse *f*; **6.** *R.C.* Brustkreuz *n*.
pec·u·late ['pekjʊleɪt] *v/t.* (*v/i.* öffentliche Gelder) unter'schlagen, veruntreuen; **pec·u·la·tion** [,pekjʊ'leɪʃn] *s.* Unter'schlagung *f*, Veruntreuung *f*, 'Unterschleif *m*; '**pec·u·la·tor** [-tə] *s.* Veruntreuer *m*.
pe·cul·iar [pɪ'kjuːljə] **I** *adj.* □ **1.** eigen (-tümlich) (*to dat.*); **2.** eigen, seltsam, absonderlich; **3.** besonder; **II** *s.* **4.** ausschließliches Eigentum; **pe·cu·li·ar·i·ty** [pɪ,kjuːlɪ'ærətɪ] *s.* **1.** Eigenheit *f*, Eigentümlichkeit *f*, Besonderheit *f*; **2.** Eigenartigkeit *f*, Seltsamkeit *f*.
pe·cu·ni·ar·y [pɪ'kjuːnjərɪ] *adj.* □ Geld..., pekuni'är, finanzi'ell: ~ *advantage* Vermögensvorteil *m*.
ped·a·gog·ic, ped·a·gog·i·cal [,pedə-'gɒdʒɪk(l)] *adj.* □ päda'gogisch, erzieherisch, Erziehungs...; **,ped·a·'gog·ics** [-ks] *s. pl. sg. konstr.* Päda'gogik *f*; **ped·a·gogue** ['pedəgɒg] *s.* **1.** Päda'goge *m*, Erzieher *m*; **2.** *contp. fig.* Pe'dant *m*, Schulmeister *m*; **ped·a·go·gy** ['pedəgɒdʒɪ] *s.* Päda'gogik *f*.
ped·al ['pedl] **I** *s.* **1.** Pe'dal *n* (*a.* ♪), Fußhebel *m*, Tretkurbel *f*; → *soft pedal*; **2.** *a.* ~ *note* ♪ Pe'dal- *od.* Orgelton *m*; **II** *v/i.* **3.** ⊚, ♪ Pe'dal treten; **4.** Rad fahren, strampeln'; **III** *v/t.* **5.** treten, fahren; **IV** *adj.* **6.** Pedal..., Fuß...: ~ *bin* Treteimer *m*; ~ *car* Tretauto *n*; ~ *brake mot.* Fußbremse *f*; ~ *control* ✈ Pedalsteuerung *f*; ~ *switch* ⊚ Fußschalter *m*.
ped·a·lo ['pedələʊ] *pl.* -**lo(e)s** *s.* Tretboot *n*.
ped·ant ['pedənt] *s.* Pe'dant(in), Kleinigkeitskrämer(in); **pe·dan·tic** [pɪ'dæntɪk] *adj.* (□ ~*ally*) pe'dantisch, kleinlich; '**ped·ant·ry** [-trɪ] *s.* Pedante'rie *f*.
ped·dle ['pedl] **I** *v/i.* **1.** hausieren gehen; **2.** sich mit Kleinigkeiten abgeben, tändeln; **II** *v/t.* **3.** hausieren gehen mit (*a. fig.*), handeln mit: ~ *drugs*; ~ *new ideas*; '**ped·dler** [-lə] *Am.* → *pedlar*; '**ped·dling** [-lɪŋ] *adj. fig.* kleinlich; geringfügig, unbedeutend, wertlos.
ped·er·ast ['pedəræst] *s.* Päde'rast *m*; '**ped·er·as·ty** [-tɪ] *s.* Päde'rastie *f*, Knabenliebe *f*.
ped·es·tal ['pedɪstl] *s.* **1.** △ Sockel *m*, Postament *n*, Säulenfuß *m*: *set s.o. on a* ~ *fig.* j-n aufs Podest erheben; **2.** *fig.* Basis *f*, Grundlage *f*; **3.** ⊚ 'Untergestell *n*, Sockel *m*, (Lager)Bock *m*.
pe·des·tri·an [pɪ'destrɪən] **I** *adj.* **1.** zu Fuß, Fuß...; Spazier...; Fußgänger...: ~

precinct (*od. area*) Fußgängerzone *f*; **2.** *fig.* pro'saisch, nüchtern; langweilig; **II** *s.* **3.** Fußgänger(in); **pe'des·tri·an·ize** [-naɪz] *v/t.* in e-e Fußgängerzone verwandeln.

pe·di·at·ric [ˌpiːdɪˈætrɪk] *adj.* ⚕ pädi'atrisch, Kinder(heilkunde)...; **~ nurse** Kinderkrankenschwester *f*; **pe·di·a·tri·cian** [ˌpiːdɪəˈtrɪʃn] *s.* Kinderarzt *m*, -ärztin *f*; **pe·di·at·rics** [-ks] *s. pl. sg. konstr.* Kinderheilkunde *f*, Pädia'trie *f*; **pe·di·at·rist** [-ɪst] → **pediatrician**; **ped·i·at·ry** [ˈpiːdɪætrɪ] → **pediatrics**.

ped·i·cel [ˈpedɪsəl] *s.* **1.** ♀ Blütenstängel *m*; **2.** *anat., zo.* Stiel(chen *n*) *m*; **ped·i·cle** [-kl] *s.* **1.** ♀ Blütenstängel *m*; **2.** ⚕ Stiel *m* (*Tumor*).

ped·i·cure [ˈpedɪkjʊə] **I** *s.* Pedi'küre *f*: a) Fußpflege *f*, b) Fußpfleger(in); **II** *v/t.* j-s Füße behandeln *od.* pflegen; **ped·i·cur·ist** [-ərɪst] → **pedicure** I b.

ped·i·gree [ˈpedɪɡriː] *s.* **1.** Stammbaum *m* (*a. zo. u. fig.*), Ahnentafel *f*; **2.** Entwicklungstafel *f*; **3.** Ab-, Herkunft *f*; **4.** lange Ahnenreihe; **II** *adj. a.* **'ped·i·greed** [-iːd] **5.** mit Stammbaum, reinrassig, Zucht...

ped·i·ment [ˈpedɪmənt] *s.* △ **1.** Giebel (-feld *n*) *m*; **2.** Ziergiebel *m*.

ped·lar [ˈpedlə] *s.* Hausierer *m*.

pe·dom·e·ter [pɪˈdɒmɪtə] *s. phys.* Schrittmesser *m*, -zähler *m*.

pe·dun·cle [pɪˈdʌŋkl] *s.* **1.** ♀ Blütenstandstiel *m*, Blütenzweig *m*; **2.** *zo.* Stiel *m*, Schaft *m*; **3.** *anat.* Zirbel-, Hirnstiel *m*.

pee [piː] *v/i.* F ,Pi'pi machen', ,pinkeln'.

peek¹ [piːk] **I** *v/i.* **1.** gucken, spähen (*into* to in *acc.*); **2. ~ out** her'ausgucken (*a. fig.*); **II** *s.* **3.** flüchtiger *od.* heimlicher Blick.

peek² [piːk] *s.* Piepsen *n* (*Vogel*).

peek·a·boo [ˌpiːkəˈbuː] *s.* ,Guck-Guck-Spiel' *n* (*kleiner Kinder*).

peel¹ [piːl] **I** *v/t.* **1.** *Frucht, Kartoffeln, Bäume* schälen: **~ off** abschälen, -lösen; **~ed barley** Graupen *pl.*; **keep your eyes ~ed** *sl.* halt die Augen offen; **2.** *sl. Kleider* abstreifen; **II** *v/i.* **3.** *a.* **~ off** sich abschälen, sich abblättern, abbröckeln, abschilfern; **4.** *sl.* ,sich entblättern', ,strippen'; **5. ~ off** ✈ aus e-m Verband ausscheren; **III** *s.* **6.** (*Zitronen- etc.*)Schale *f*; Rinde *f*; Haut *f*.

peel² [piːl] *s.* **1.** Backschaufel *f*, Brotschieber *m*; **2.** *typ.* Aufhängekreuz *n*.

peel·er¹ [ˈpiːlə] *s.* **1.** (*Kartoffel- etc.*) Schäler *m*; **2.** *sl.* Stripperin *f*.

peel·er² [ˈpiːlə] *s. sl. obs.* ,Bulle' *m* (*Polizist*).

peel·ing [ˈpiːlɪŋ] *s.* (*lose*) Schale, Rinde *f*, Haut *f*.

peen [piːn] *s.* ☉ Finne *f*, Hammerbahn *f*.

peep¹ [piːp] **I** *v/i.* **1.** piep(s)en (*Vogel etc.*): **he never dared ~ again** er hat es nicht mehr gewagt, den Mund aufzumachen; **II** *s.* **2.** Piep(s)en *n*; **3.** *sl.* ,Pieps' *m* (*Wort*).

peep² [piːp] **I** *v/i.* **1.** gucken, neugierig *od.* verstohlen blicken (*into* in *acc.*): **~ at** e-n Blick werfen auf (*acc.*); **2.** *oft.* **~ out** her'vorgucken, -schauen, -lugen (*a. fig. sich zeigen, zum Vorschein kommen*); **II** *s.* **3.** neugieriger *od.* verstohlener Blick: **have** (*od.* **take**) **a ~** → 1; **4.** Blick *m* (*of* in *acc.*), ('Durch)Sicht *f*; **5. at ~ of day** bei Tagesanbruch; **'peep·er** [-pə] *s.* **1.** Spitzel *m*; **2.** *sl.* ,Gucker' *m* (*Auge*); **3.** *sl.* Spiegel *m*; Fenster *n*; Brille *f*.

'peep·hole *s.* Guckloch *n*.

Peep·ing Tom [ˈpiːpɪŋ] *s.* ,Spanner' *m* (*Voyeur*).

'peep|·scope *s.* ,Spi'on' *m* (*an der Tür*); **~ show** *s.* **1.** Guckkasten *m*; **2.** Peep-Show *f*.

peer¹ [pɪə] *v/i.* **1.** spähen, gucken (*into* in *acc.*): **~ at** sich *et.* genau an- *od.* begucken; **2.** *poet.* sich zeigen; **3.** → **peep²** 2.

peer² [pɪə] *s.* **1.** Gleiche(r *m*) *f*, Ebenbürtige(r *m*) *f*: **without a ~** ohnegleichen, unvergleichlich; **he associates with his ~s** er gesellt sich zu seinesgleichen; **~ group** *sociol.* Peer-Group *f*; **~ pressure** *sociol.* Peer-Pressure *m*, (Erwartungs)Druck *m* von Gleichaltrigen *od.* sozial Gleichgestellten; **2.** Angehörige(r) *m* des (brit.) Hochadels: **~ of the realm** *Brit.* Peer *m* (*Mitglied des Oberhauses*); **peer·age** [ˈpɪərɪdʒ] *s.* **1.** Peerage *f*: a) Peerswürde *f*, b) Hochadel *m*, (*die*) Peers *pl.*; **2.** 'Adels,lender *m*; **peer·ess** [ˈpɪərɪs] *s.* **1.** Gemahlin *f* e-s Peers; **2.** hohe Adlige: **~ in her own right** Peeress *f* im eigenen Recht; **peer·less** [ˈpɪəlɪs] *adj.* ☐ unvergleichlich, einzig(artig).

peeve [piːv] *v/t.* F (ver)ärgern; **peeved** [-vd] *adj.* F ,eingeschnappt', verärgert; **'pee·vish** [-vɪʃ] *adj.* ☐ grämlich, übellaunig, verdrießlich.

peg [peɡ] **I** *s.* **1.** (Holz-, *surv.* Absteck-) Pflock *m*; (Holz)Nagel *m*; (Schuh)Stift *m*; ☉ Dübel *m*; Sprosse *f* (*a. fig.*): **take s.o. down a ~** (*or two*) j-m ,einen Dämpfer aufsetzen'; **come down a ~** gelindere Saiten aufziehen, ,zurückstecken'; **a round ~ in a square hole**, **a square ~ in a round hole** ein Mensch am falschen Platze; **2.** (Kleider)Haken *m*: **off the ~** von der Stange (*Anzug*); **3.** (Wäsche)Klammer *f*; **4.** (Zelt)Hering *m*; **5.** ♪ Wirbel *m* (*Saiteninstrument*); **6.** *fig.* ,Aufhänger' *m*: **a good ~ on which to hang a story**; **7.** *Brit.* ,Gläs·chen' *n*, *bsd.* Whisky *m* mit Soda; **II** *v/t.* **8.** anpflöcken, -nageln; **9.** ☉ (ver)dübeln; **10.** *a.* **~ out** *surv.* Grenze, *Land* abstecken: **~ out one's claim** *fig.* s-e Ansprüche geltend machen; **11.** ✝ *Löhne, Preise* stützen, halten: **~ged price** Stützkurs; **12.** F schmeißen (*at* nach); **III** *v/i.* **13. ~ away** (*od.* **along**) F drauf'losarbeiten; **14. ~ out** F a) ,zs.-klappen', b) ,abkratzen' (*sterben*); **'~-top** *s.* Kreisel *m*.

peign·oir [ˈpeɪnwɑː] (*Fr.*) *s.* Morgenrock *m*.

pe·jo·ra·tive [ˈpiːdʒərətɪv] **I** *adj.* ☐ abschätzig, her'absetzend, pejora'tiv; **II** *s. ling.* abschätziges Wort, Pejora'tivum *n*.

peke [piːk] F *für* **Pekingese** 2.

Pe·king·ese [ˌpiːkɪŋˈiːz] *s. sg. u. pl.* **1.** Bewohner(in) von Peking; **2.** ⚥ Peki'nese *m* (*Hund*).

pel·age [ˈpelɪdʒ] *s. zo.* Körperbedeckung *f* wilder Tiere (*Fell etc.*).

pel·ar·gon·ic [ˌpelɑːˈɡɒnɪk] *adj.* 🜚 Pelargon...: **~ acid**, **pel·ar·go·ni·um** [-ˈɡəʊnjəm] *s.* ♀ Pelar'gonie *f*.

pelf [pelf] *s. contp.* Mammon *m*.

pel·i·can [ˈpelɪkən] *s. orn.* Pelikan *m*; **~ cross·ing** *s.* mit Ampeln gesicherter 'Fußgänger,überweg *m*.

pe·lisse [peˈliːs] *s.* (*langer*) Damen- *od.* Kindermantel.

pel·let [ˈpelɪt] *s.* **1.** Kügelchen *n*, Pille *f*; **2.** Schrotkorn *n* (*Munition*).

pel·li·cle [ˈpelɪkl] *s.* Häutchen *n*; Memb'ran *f*; **pel·lic·u·lar** [peˈlɪkjʊlə] *adj.* häutchenförmig, Häutchen...

pell-mell [ˌpelˈmel] **I** *adv.* **1.** durcheinander, ,wie Kraut u. Rüben'; **2.** 'unterschiedslos; **3.** Hals über Kopf; **II** *adj.* **4.** verworren, kunterbunt; **5.** hastig, über'eilt; **III** *s.* **6.** Durchein'ander *n*.

pel·lu·cid [peˈljuːsɪd] *adj.* ☐ 'durchsichtig, klar (*a. fig.*).

pelt¹ [pelt] *s.* Fell *n*, (Tier)Pelz *m*; ✝ rohe Haut.

pelt² [pelt] **I** *v/t.* **1.** j-n mit Steinen *etc.* bewerfen, (*fig. mit Fragen*) bombardieren; **2.** verhauen, prügeln; **II** *v/i.* **3.** *mit Steinen etc.* werfen (*at* nach); **4.** niederprasseln: **~ing rain** Platzregen *m*; **III** *s.* **5.** Schlag *m*, Wurf *m*; **6.** Prasseln *n* (*Regen*); **7.** Eile *f*: (*at*) **full ~** in voller Geschwindigkeit.

pelt·ry [ˈpeltrɪ] *s.* **1.** Rauch-, Pelzwaren *pl.*; **2.** Fell *n*, Haut *f*.

pel·vic [ˈpelvɪk] *adj. anat.* Becken...: **~ cavity** Beckenhöhle *f*; **pel·vis** [ˈpelvɪs] *pl.* **-ves** [-viːz] *s. anat.* Becken *n*.

pem·(m)i·can [ˈpemɪkən] *s.* Pemmikan *n* (*Dörrfleisch*).

pen¹ [pen] *s.* **1.** Pferch *m*, Hürde *f* (*Schafe*), Verschlag *m* (*Geflügel*), Hühnerstall *m*; **2.** kleiner Behälter *od.* Raum; **3.** ⚓ (U-Boot-)Bunker *m*; **4.** *Am. sl.* ,Kittchen' *n*, ,Knast' *m*; **II** *v/t.* **5.** *a.* **~ in**, **~ up** einpferchen, -schließen, -sperren.

pen² [pen] **I** *s.* **1.** (Schreib)Feder *f*, *a.* Federhalter *m*; Füller *m*; Kugelschreiber *m*: **set ~ to paper** die Feder ansetzen; **~ and ink** Schreibzeug *n*; **2.** *fig.* Feder *f*, Stil *m*: **he has a sharp ~** er führt e-e spitze Feder; **II** *v/t.* **3.** (nieder)schreiben; ab-, verfassen.

pe·nal [ˈpiːnl] *adj.* ☐ **1.** strafrechtlich, Straf...: **~ code** Strafgesetzbuch *n*; **~ colony** Sträflingskolonie *f*; **~ duty** Strafzoll *m*; **~ institution** Strafanstalt *f*; **~ law** Strafrecht *n*; **~ reform** Strafrechtsreform *f*; **~ sum** Vertrags-, Konventionalstrafe *f*; **~ servitude** 2; **2.** sträflich, strafbar: **~ act**; **'pe·nal·ize** [-nəlaɪz] *v/t.* **1.** mit e-r Strafe belegen, bestrafen; **2.** benachteiligen, ,bestrafen'; **pen·al·ty** [ˈpenltɪ] *s.* **1.** gesetzliche Strafe *n* (*od. under*) **~ of** bei Strafe von; → **extreme** 2; **pay** (*od.* **bear**) **the ~ of** *et.* büßen; **2.** (Geld)Buße *f*, Vertragsstrafe *f*; **3.** *fig.* Nachteil *m*, Fluch *m des Ruhms etc.*; **4.** *sport* a) Strafe *f*, Strafpunkt *m*, b) *Fußball*: Elf'meter *m*, c) *Hockey*: Sieben'meter *m*, *Eishockey*: Penalty *m*: **~ area** Fußball: Strafraum *m*; **~ box** a) *Eishockey*: Strafbank, b) *Fußball*: Strafraum *m*; **~ kick** Fußball: Strafstoß *m*; **~ shot** Eishockey: Penalty *m*; **~ shootout** Fußball: Elfmeterschießen *n*; **~ spot** a) Fußball: Elfmeterpunkt *m*, b) Hockey: Siebenmeterpunkt *m*.

pen·ance [ˈpenəns] *s.* Buße *f*: **do ~** Buße tun.

pen-and-ink *adj.* Feder..., Schreiber...: **~ (drawing)** Federzeichnung *f*.

pence [pens] *pl. von* **penny**.

pen·chant [ˈpɑ̃ːʃɑ̃ːŋ] (*Fr.*) *s.* (*for*) Neigung *f*, Hang *m* (für, zu), Vorliebe *f* (für).

pen·cil [ˈpensl] **I** *s.* **1.** Blei-, Zeichenstift *m*: **red ~** Rotstift; **in ~** mit Bleistift; **2.** *paint. obs.* Pinsel *m*; *fig.* Stil *m* e-s Malers; **3.** *rhet.* Griffel *m*, Stift *m*; **4.** ☉, ✗, *Kosmetik*: Stift *m*; **5.** ✗, *phys.* (Strahlen)Büschel *m*, *n*: **~ of light** *phot.* Lichtbündel *n*; **II** **6.** *v/t.* zeichnen; **7.** mit e-m Bleistift aufschreiben, anzeichnen *od.* anstreichen; **8.** mit e-m Stift behandeln, *z.B. die Augenbrauen* nachziehen; **'pen·cil(l)ed** [-ld] *adj.* **1.** fein gezeichnet *od.* gestrichelt; **2.** mit e-m Bleistift gezeichnet *od.* angestrichen; **3.** ✗, *phys.* gebündelt

(*Strahlen etc.*).

pen·cil| push·er *s. humor.* ,Bürohengst' *m*; ~ **sharp·en·er** *s.* Bleistiftspitzer *m*.

'pen·craft *s.* **1.** → *penmanship*; **2.** Schriftstelle'rei *f*.

pend·ant ['pendənt] **I** *s.* **1.** Anhänger *m*, (*Schmuckstück*), Ohrgehänge *n*; **2.** a) Behang *m*, b) Hängeleuchter *m*; **3.** Bügel *m* (*Uhr*); **4.** △ Hängezierrat *m*; **5.** *fig.* Anhang *m*, Anhängsel *n*; **6.** *fig.* Pen'dant *n*, Seiten-, Gegenstück *n* (*to* zu); **7.** ♍ → *pennant* 1; **II** *adj.* → *pendent*; **'pend·en·cy** [-dənsɪ] *s. fig. bsd.* ⚖ Schweben *n*, Anhängigkeit *f* (*e-s Prozesses*); **'pend·ent** [-nt] **I** *adj.* **1.** (her'ab)hängend; 'überhängend; Hänge...; **2.** *fig.* unentschieden; (noch) unentschieden (*Klage*); → *patent* 7; **II** *prp.* **4.** a) während, b) bis zu.

pen·du·late ['pendjuleɪt] *v/i.* **1.** pendeln; **2.** *fig.* fluktuieren, schwanken; **'pen·du·lous** [-ləs] *adj.* hängend, pendelnd; Hänge...(*bauch etc.*), Pendel...(*-bewegung etc.*); **'pen·du·lum** [-ləm] *s.* **1.** *phys.* Pendel *n*; **2.** ☉ a) Pendel *n*, Perpen'dikel *m*, *n* (*Uhr*), b) Schwunggewicht *n*; **3.** *fig.* Pendelbewegung *f*, wechselnde Stimmung *od.* Haltung; → *swing* 20; **II** *adj.* **4.** Pendel... (*-säge, -uhr, -waage etc.*): ~ *wheel* Unruh *f der Uhr*.

pen·e·tra·bil·i·ty [,penɪtrə'bɪlətɪ] *s.* Durch'dringbarkeit *f*, Durch'dringlichkeit *f*; **pen·e·tra·ble** ['penɪtrəbl] *adj.* ☐ durch'dringlich, erfassbar, erreichbar; **pen·e·tra·li·a** [,penɪ'treɪljə] (*Lat.*) *s. pl.* **1.** das Innerste, das Aller'heiligste; **2.** *fig.* Geheimnisse *pl.*; in'time Dinge *pl.*

pen·e·trate ['penɪtreɪt] **I** *v/t.* **1.** durch'dringen, eindringen in (*acc.*), durch'bohren, *a.* ✕ durch'stoßen; **2.** *fig.* seelisch durch'dringen, erfüllen; **3.** *fig.* geistig eindringen in (*acc.*), ergründen, durch'schauen; **II** *v/i.* **4.** eindringen, 'durchdringen (*into, to* in *acc.*, zu); ✈, ✕ einfliegen; **5.** 'durch-, vordringen (*to* zu); **6.** *fig.* ergründen: ~ *into a secret*; **'pen·e·trat·ing** [-tɪŋ] *adj.* ☐ **1.** 'durchdringend, durch'bohrend (*a. Blick*): ~ *power* ✕ Durchschlagskraft *f*; **2.** *fig.* durch'dringend, scharf(sinnig); **pen·e·tra·tion** [,penɪ'treɪʃn] *s.* **1.** Ein-, 'Durchdringen, Durch'bohren *n*; **2.** Eindringungsvermögen *n*, 'Durchschlagskraft *f* (*e-s Geschosses*); Tiefenwirkung *f*; **3.** ✕ 'Durch-, Einbruch *m*; ✈ Einflug *m*; **4.** *phys.* Schärfe *f*, Auflösungsvermögen *n* (*Auge, Objektiv etc.*); **5.** *fig.* Ergründung *f*; **6.** *fig.* Einflussnahme *f*, Durch'dringung *f*: *peaceful* ~ friedliche Durchdringung *e-s Landes*; **7.** *fig.* Scharfsinn *m*, durch'dringender Verstand; **'pen·e·tra·tive** [-trətɪv] *adj.* ☐ → *penetrating*.

pen friend *s.* Brieffreund(in).

pen·guin ['peŋgwɪn] *s.* **1.** Pinguin *m*; **2.** ✈ Übungsflugzeug *n*; ~ *suit* *s.* Raumanzug *m*.

'pen,hold·er *s.* Federhalter *m*.

pen·i·cil·lin [,penɪ'sɪlɪn] *s.* ☤ Penizil'lin *n*.

pen·in·su·la [pɪ'nɪnsjulə] *s.* Halbinsel *f*; **pen·in·su·lar** [-lə] *adj.* **1.** Halbinsel...; **2.** halbinselförmig.

pe·nis ['pi:nɪs] *s. anat.* Penis *m*.

pen·i·tence ['penɪtəns] *s.* Bußfertigkeit *f*, Buße *f*, Reue *f*; **'pen·i·tent** [-nt] **I** *adj.* ☐ **1.** bußfertig, reuig, zerknirscht;

II *s.* **2.** Bußfertige(r *m*) *f*, Büßer(in); **3.** Beichtkind *n*; **pen·i·ten·tial** [,penɪ'tenʃl] *eccl.* **I** *adj.* ☐ bußfertig, Buß...; **II** *s. a.* ~ *book* R.C. Buß-, Pöni'tenzbuch *n*; **pen·i·ten·tia·ry** [,penɪ'tenʃərɪ] **I** *s.* **1.** *eccl.* Bußpriester *m*; **2.** *Am.* 'Straf(voll,zugs)anstalt *f*; **3.** *hist.* Besserungsanstalt *f*; **II** *adj.* **4.** *eccl.* Buß...

'pen|·knife *s.* [*irr.*] Feder-, Taschenmesser *n*; '~·man [-mən] *s.* [*irr.*] **1.** Kalli'graph *m*; **2.** Schriftsteller *m*; '~·man·ship [-mənʃɪp] *s.* **1.** Schreibkunst *f*; **2.** Stil *m*; schriftstellerisches Können; ~ *name* *s.* Schriftstellername *m*, Pseudo'nym *n*.

pen·nant ['penənt] *s.* **1.** ♍, ✕ Wimpel *m*, Stander *m*, kleine Flagge; **2.** (Lanzen)Fähnchen *n*; **3.** *sport Am.* Siegeswimpel *m*; *fig.* Meisterschaft *f*; **4.** ♪ *Am.* Fähnchen *n*.

pen·ni·less ['penɪlɪs] *adj.* ☐ ohne (e-n Pfennig) Geld, mittellos.

pen·non ['penən] *s.* **1.** *bsd.* ✕ Fähnlein *n*, Wimpel *m*, Lanzenfähnchen *n*; **2.** Fittich *m*, Schwinge *f*.

Penn·syl·va·nia Dutch [,pensɪl'veɪnjə] *s.* **1.** *coll.* in Pennsyl'vania lebende 'Deutschameri,kaner *pl.*; **2.** *ling.* Pennsyl'vanisch-Deutsch *n*.

pen·ny ['penɪ] *pl.* **-nies** *od. coll.* **pence** [pens] *s.* **1.** a) *Brit.* Penny *m* (= £ 0.01 = 1 p), b) *Am.* Centstück *n*: *in for a* ~, *in for a pound* wer A sagt, muss auch B sagen; *the* ~ *dropped! humor.* ,der Groschen ist gefallen'!; *spend a* ~ F ,mal verschwinden' (*auf die Toilette*); **2.** *fig.* Pfennig *m*, Heller *m*, Kleinigkeit *f*: *not worth a* ~ keinen Heller wert; *he hasn't a* ~ *to bless himself with* er hat keinen roten Heller; *a* ~ *for your thoughts!* (an) was denkst du denn (eben)?; **3.** *fig.* Geld *n*: *turn an honest* ~ sich et. (durch ehrliche Arbeit) (dazu)verdienen; *a pretty* ~ ein hübsches Sümmchen.

,pen·ny|-a-'lin·er *s. bsd. Brit.* Schreiberling *m*, Zeilenschinder *m*; ~ *ar·cade* *s.* 'Spielsa,lon *m*; ~ *dread·ful s.* 'Groschenro,man *m*; Groschenblatt *n*; ,~*-in-the-'slot ma·chine* *s.* (Ver'kaufs)Auto,mat *m*; '~-,pinch·er *s.* F Pfennigfuchser *m*; '~·weight *s. Brit.* Pennygewicht *n* (*1¹/₂ Gramm*); ,~-'wise *adj.* am falschen Ende sparsam: ~ *and pound-foolish* im Kleinen sparsam, im Großen verschwenderisch; '~·worth ['penəθ] *s.* **1.** was man für e-n Penny kaufen kann: *a* ~ *of tobacco* für e-n Penny Tabak; **2.** (*bsd.* guter) Kauf: *a good* ~.

pe·no·log·ic, pe·no·log·i·cal [,pi:nə'lɒdʒɪk(l)] *adj.* ☐ krimi'nalkundlich, Strafvollzugs...; **pe·nol·o·gy** [pi:'nɒlədʒɪ] *s.* Krimi'nalstrafkunde *f, bsd.* 'Strafvoll,zugslehre *f*.

pen pal *Am.* für *pen friend*.

pen·sion[1] ['pɑ̃:ŋsiɔ̃:ŋ] (*Fr.*) *s.* Pensi'on *f*: a) Fremdenheim *n*, b) 'Unterkunft u. Verpflegung *f*: *full* ~.

pen·sion[2] ['penʃn] **I** *s.* Pensi'on *f*, Ruhegeld *n*, Rente *f*: ~ *fund* Pensionskasse *f*; ~ *plan*, ~ *scheme* (Alters)Versorgungsplan *m*; *entitled to a* ~ pensionsberechtigt; *be on a* ~ in Rente *od.* Pension sein; **II** *v/t. oft* ~ *off* *j-n* pensionieren; **'pen·sion·a·ble** [-ʃnəbl] *adj.* pensi'onsberechtigt, -fähig: *of* ~ *age* im Renten- *od.* Pensionsalter; **'pen·sion·er** [-ʃənə] *s.* **1.** Pensio'när *m*, Ruhegeldempfänger(in), Rentner(in); **2.** *Brit.* Stu'dent *m* (*in Cambridge*), der für Kost u. Wohnung im College zahlt.

pen·sive ['pensɪv] *adj.* ☐ **1.** nachdenk-

---

lich, sinnend, gedankenvoll; **2.** ernst, tiefsinnig; **'pen·sive·ness** [-nɪs] *s.* Nachdenklichkeit *f*; Tiefsinn *m*, Ernst *m*.

'pen·stock *s.* **1.** Wehr *n*, Stauanlage *f*; **2.** *Am.* Druckrohr *n*.

pen·ta·cle ['pentəkl] → *pentagram*.

pen·ta·gon ['pentəgən] *s.* ⅍ Fünfeck *n*: *the* ⅊ *Am.* das Pentagon (*das amer. Verteidigungsministerium*); **pen·tag·o·nal** [pen'tægənl] *adj.* fünfeckig; **'pen·ta·gram** [-græm] *s.* Penta'gramm *n*, Drudenfuß *m*; **pen·ta·he·dral** [,pentə'hi:drəl] *adj.* ⅍ fünfflächig; **pen·ta·he·dron** [,pentə'hi:drɒn] *pl.* **-drons** *od.* **-dra** [-drə] *s.* ⅍ ,Penta'eder *n*; **pen·tam·e·ter** [pen'tæmɪtə] *s.* Pen'tameter *m*.

Pen·ta·teuch ['pentətju:k] *s. bibl.* Penta'teuch *m*, die fünf Bücher Mose.

pen·tath·lete [pen'tæθli:t] *s. sport* Fünfkämpfer(in); **pen'tath·lon** [-lɒn] *s. sport* Fünfkampf *m*.

pen·ta·va·lent [,pentə'veɪlənt] *adj.* ⅍ fünfwertig.

Pen·te·cost ['pentɪkɒst] *s.* Pfingsten *n od. pl.*, Pfingstfest *n*; **Pen·te·cos·tal** [,pentɪ'kɒstl] *adj.* pfingstlich; Pfingst...

pent·house ['penthaʊs] *s.* △ **1.** Penthouse *n*, 'Dachter,rassenwohnung *f*; **2.** Wetter-, Vor-, Schirmdach *n*; **3.** Anbau *m*, Nebengebäude *n*, angebauter Schuppen.

pen·tode ['pentəʊd] *s.* ⚡ Pen'tode *f*, Fünfpolröhre *f*.

,pent-'up *adj.* **1.** eingepfercht; **2.** *fig.* angestaut (*Gefühle*): ~ *demand* ♥ *Am.* Nachholbedarf *m*.

pe·nult [pe'nʌlt] *s. ling.* vorletzte Silbe; **pe'nul·ti·mate** [-tɪmət] **I** *adj.* vorletzt; **II** *s.* → *penult*.

pe·num·bra [pɪ'nʌmbrə] *pl.* **-bras** *s.* Halbschatten *m*.

pe·nu·ri·ous [pɪ'njʊərɪəs] *adj.* ☐ **1.** geizig, knauserig; **2.** karg; **pen·u·ry** ['penjʊrɪ] *s.* Knappheit *f*, Armut *f*, Not *f*, Mangel *m*.

pe·on ['pi:ən] *s.* **1.** Sol'dat *m*, Poli'zist *m*, Bote *m* (*in Indien u. Ceylon*); **2.** Tagelöhner *m* (*in Südamerika*); **3.** (*wegen Geldschulden*) zu Dienst verpflichteter Arbeiter (*Mexiko*); **4.** *Am.* zu Arbeit her'angezogener Sträfling; **'pe·on·age** [-nɪdʒ] **'pe·on·ism** [-nɪzəm] *s.* Dienstbarkeit *f*, Leibeigenschaft *f*.

pe·o·ny ['pi:ənɪ] *s.* ♀ Pfingstrose *f*.

peo·ple ['pi:pl] **I** *s.* **1.** *pl. konstr.* die Leute *pl.*, die Menschen *pl.*: *English* ~ (die) Engländer; *London* ~ die Londoner (Bevölkerung); *country* ~ Landleute, -bevölkerung *f*; *literary* ~ (die) Literaten; *a great many* ~ sehr viele Leute; *some* ~ manche; *he of all* ~ ausgerechnet er; **2.** *the* ~ a) *a. sg. konstr.* das gemeine Volk, b) die Bürger *pl.*, die Wähler *pl.*; **3.** *pl.* ~*s* Volk *n*, Nati'on *f*: *the* ~*s of Europe*; *the chosen* ~ das auserwählte Volk; **4.** *pl. konstr.* F *j-s* Angehörige *pl.*, Fa'milie *f*: *my* ~ m-e Leute; *S* F man: ~ *say* man sagt; **II** *v/t.* **6.** bevölkern (*with* mit).

peo·ple's re·pub·lic *s. pol.* 'Volksrepu-,blik *f*: *the* ⅊ *of China*.

pep [pep] *sl.* **I** *s.* E'lan *m*, Schwung *m*, ,Schmiss' *m*: ~ *pill* Aufputschtablette *f*; ~ *talk* Anfeuerung *f*, ermunternde Worte; **II** *v/t.* ~ *up* a) *j-n* ,aufmöbeln', in Schwung bringen, b) *j-n* anfeuern, c) *Geschichte* ,pfeffern', d) *et.* in Schwung bringen.

pep·per ['pepə] *s.* **1.** Pfeffer *m* (*a. fig. et. Scharfes*); **2.** ♀ Pfefferstrauch *m*, *bsd.* a) Spanischer Pfeffer, b) Roter

Pfeffer, c) Paprika *m*; **3.** pfefferähnliches Gewürz: **~ cake** Ingwerkuchen *m*; **II** *v/t.* **4.** pfeffern; **5.** *fig. Stil etc.* würzen; **6.** *fig.* sprenkeln, bestreuen; **7.** *fig.* ‚bepfeffern‘, bombardieren (*a. mit Fragen etc.*); **8.** *fig.* 'durchprügeln'; **‚~-and- -'salt I** *adj.* pfeffer-und-salz-farbig (*Stoff*); **II** *s.* a) Pfeffer u. Salz *n* (*Stoff*), b) Anzug *m* in Pfeffer u. Salz; **'~-box** *s. bsd. Brit.*, **~ cas·tor** *s.* Pfefferbüchse *f*, -streuer *m*; **'~-corn** *s.* Pfefferkorn *n*; **'~-mint** *s.* **1.** ♀ Pfefferminze *f*; **2.** Pfefferminzöl *n*; **3.** *a.* **~ drop**, **~ lozenge** Pfefferminzplätzchen *n*.

pep·per·y ['pepərɪ] *adj.* **1.** pfefferig, scharf; **2.** *fig.* hitzig, jähzornig; **3.** gepfeffert, scharf (*Stil*).

pep·py ['pepɪ] *adj. sl.* schwungvoll, ‚schmissig', forsch.

pep·sin ['pepsɪn] *s.* ♀ Pep'sin *n*; **pep·tic** ['peptɪk] *anat. adj.* **1.** Verdauungs...: **~ gland** Magendrüse *f*, **~ ulcer** Magengeschwür *n*; **2.** verdauungsfördernd, peptisch; **pep·tone** ['peptəʊn] *s. physiol.* Pep'ton *n*.

per [pɜː; pə] *prp.* **1.** per, durch: **~ bearer** durch Überbringer; **~ post** durch die Post®; **~ rail** per Bahn; **2.** pro, je, für: **~ annum** [pər'ænəm] pro Jahr, jährlich; **~ capita** ['kæpɪtə] pro Kopf, pro Person; **~ capita income** Pro-Kopf-Einkommen *n*; **~ capita quota** Kopfbetrag *m*; **~ cent** pro *od.* vom Hundert; **~ second** in der *od.* pro Sekunde; **3.** laut, gemäß (♥ *a. as ~*).

per·ad·ven·ture [ˌpərəd'ventʃə] *adv. obs.* viel'leicht, ungefähr.

per·am·bu·late [pə'ræmbjʊleɪt] **I** *v/t.* **1.** durch'wandern, -'reisen, -'ziehen; **2.** bereisen, besichtigen; **3.** die Grenzen *e-s Gebiets* abschreiten; **II** *v/i.* **4.** um'herwandern; **per·am·bu·la·tion** [pəˌræmbjʊ'leɪʃn] *s.* **1.** Durch'wanderung *f*; **2.** Bereisen *n*, Besichtigung(sreise) *f*; **3.** Grenzbegehung *f*; **per·am·bu·la·tor** [pə'ræmbjʊleɪtə] *s. bsd. Brit.* Kinderwagen *m*.

per·ceiv·a·ble [pə'siːvəbl] *adj.* □ **1.** wahrnehmbar, spürbar, merklich; **2.** verständlich; **per·ceive** [pə'siːv] *v/t. u. v/i.* **1.** wahrnehmen, empfinden, (be-) merken, spüren; **2.** verstehen, erkennen, begreifen.

per·cent, *Brit.* **per cent** [pə'sent] **I** *adj.* **1.** ...prozentig; **II** *s.* **2.** Pro'zent *n* (%); **3.** *pl.* 'Wertpa,piere *pl.* mit feststehendem Zinssatz: *three per cents* dreiprozentige Wertpapiere; **per'cent·age** [-tɪdʒ] *s.* **1.** Pro'zent-, Hundertsatz *m*; Prozentgehalt *m*: **~ by weight** Gewichtsprozent *n*; **2.** ♥ Pro'zente *pl.*; **3.** *weitS.* Teil *m*, Anteil *m* (*of* an *dat.*); **4.** ♥ Gewinnanteil *m*, Provisi'on *f*, Tanti'eme *f*; **per'cen·tal** [-tl], **per'cen·tile** [-taɪl] *adj.* prozentu'al, Prozent...

per·cep·ti·bil·i·ty [pəˌseptə'bɪlətɪ] *s.* Wahrnehmbarkeit *f*; **per·cep·ti·ble** [pə'septəbl] *adj.* □ wahrnehmbar, merklich; **per·cep·tion** [pə'sepʃn] *s.* **1.** (sinnliche *od.* geistige) Wahrnehmung, Empfindung *f*; **2.** Wahrnehmungsvermögen *n*; **3.** Auffassung(skraft) *f*; **4.** Begriff *m*, Vorstellung *f*; **5.** Erkenntnis *f*; **per·cep·tion·al** [pə'sepʃənl] *adj.* Wahrnehmungs..., Empfindungs...; **per·cep·tive** [pə'septɪv] *adj.* □ **1.** wahrnehmend, Wahrnehmungs...; **2.** auffassungsfähig, scharfsichtig; **per·cep·tiv·i·ty** [ˌpɜːsep'tɪvətɪ] *s.* → **perception** 2.

perch¹ [pɜːtʃ] *pl.* 'perch·es [-ɪz] *od.* **perch** *s. ichth.* Flussbarsch *m*.

perch² [pɜːtʃ] **I** *s.* **1.** (Auf)Sitzstange *f*

für Vögel, Hühnerstange *f*; **2.** F *fig.* hoher (sicherer) Sitz, ‚Thron': *knock s.o. off his ~ fig.* j-n von s-m Sockel herunterstoßen; *come off your ~!* F nicht so überlegen!; **3.** *surv.* Messstange *f*; **4.** Rute *f* (*Längenmaß = 5,029 m*); **5.** ⚓ Pricke *f*; **6.** Lang-, Lenkbaum *m e-s Wagens*; **II** *v/i.* **7.** sich setzen *od.* niederlassen (*on* auf *acc.*), sitzen (*Vögel*), *fig.* hoch sitzen *od.* ‚thronen'; **III** *v/t.* **8.** (*auf et. Hohes*) setzen: *~ o.s.* sich setzen; *be ~ed* sitzen, ‚thronen'.

per·chance [pə'tʃɑːns] *adv. poet.* viel'leicht, zufällig.

perch·er ['pɜːtʃə] *s. orn.* Sitzvogel *m*.

per·chlo·rate [pə'klɔːreɪt] *s.* ♀ Perchlo'rat *n*; **per'chlo·ric** [-ɪk] *adj.* 'überchlorig: **~ acid** Über- *od.* Perchlorsäure *f*; **per'chlo·ride** [-raɪd] *s.* Perchlo'rid *n*.

per·cip·i·ence [pə'sɪpɪəns] *s.* **1.** Wahrnehmen *n*; **2.** Wahrnehmung(svermögen *n*) *f*; **per'cip·i·ent** [-nt] → **perceptive** 1.

per·co·late ['pɜːkəleɪt] **I** *v/t.* **1.** *Kaffee etc.* filtern, 'durchseihen, 'durchsickern lassen; **II** *v/i.* **2.** 'durchsickern (*a. fig.*): *percolating tank* Sickertank *m*; **3.** gefiltert werden; **per·co·la·tion** [ˌpɜːkə'leɪʃn] *s.* 'Durchseihung *f*, Filtrati'on *f*; **'per·co·la·tor** [-tə] *s.* Fil'triertrichter *m*, Filterkaffee *m*, 'Kaffeema,schine *f*.

per·cuss [pə'kʌs] *v/t. u. v/i.* ♫ perkutieren, abklopfen; **per'cus·sion** [-ʌʃən] **I** *s.* **1.** Schlag *m*, Stoß *m*, Erschütterung *f*, Aufschlag *m*; **2.** ♫ a) Perkussi'on *f*, Abklopfen *n*, b) 'Klopfmas,sage *f*; **3.** ♪ *coll.* 'Schlaginstru,mente *pl.*, -zeug *n*; **II** *adj.* **4.** Schlag..., Stoß..., Zünd...: **~ cap** Zündhütchen *n*; **~ drill** ⊙ Schlagbohrer *m*; **~ fuse** ✗ Aufschlagzünder *m*; **~ instrument** ♪ Schlaginstrument *n*; **~ welding** ⊙ Schlag-, Stoßschweißen *n*; **III** *v/t.* **5.** ♫ a) perkutieren, abklopfen, b) durch Beklopfen massieren; **per'cus·sion·ist** [-ʌʃnɪst] *s.* ♪ Schlagzeuger *m*; **per'cus·sive** [-sɪv] → **percussion** 4.

per·cu·ta·ne·ous [ˌpɜːkjuː'teɪnjəs] *adj.* □ ♫ perku'tan, durch die Haut.

per di·em [ˌpɜː'daɪem] **I** *adj. u. adv.* täglich, pro Tag: **~ rate** Tagessatz *m*; **II** *s.* Tagegeld *n*.

per·di·tion [pə'dɪʃn] *s.* **1.** Verderben *n*; **2.** a) ewige Verdammnis, b) Hölle *f*.

per·e·gri·nate ['perɪgrɪneɪt] **I** *v/i.* wandern, um'herreisen; **II** *v/t.* durch'wandern, bereisen; **per·e·gri·na·tion** [ˌperɪgrɪ'neɪʃn] *s.* **1.** Wanderschaft *f*; **2.** Wanderung *f*; **3.** *fig.* Weitschweifigkeit *f*.

per·emp·to·ri·ness [pə'remptərɪnɪs] *s.* **1.** Entschiedenheit *f*, Bestimmtheit *f*; herrisches Wesen; **2.** Endgültigkeit *f*; **per·emp·to·ry** [pə'remptərɪ] *adj.* □ **1.** entschieden, bestimmt, ‚gebieterisch, herrisch; **2.** entscheidend, endgültig; zwingend, defini'tiv: **~ command** Machtgebot *n*.

per·en·ni·al [pə'renjəl] *adj.* □ **1.** das ganze Jahr *od.* Jahre hin'durch dauernd, beständig; **2.** immer während, anhaltend; **3.** ♀ perennierend, winterhart; **II** *s.* **4.** ♀ perennierende Pflanze.

per·fect ['pɜːfɪkt] **I** *adj.* □ → **perfectly**; **1.** per'fekt, voll'endet: a) fehler-, ‚ideal, b) fertig, abgeschlossen: *make ~* vervollkommnen, **~ pitch** ♪ absolutes Gehör; **~ participle** *ling.* Mittelwort *n* der Vergangenheit, Partizip *n* Perfekt; **~ tense** Perfekt *n*; **2.** gründlich (ausgebildet), per'fekt (*in* in *dat.*); **3.** gänzlich, 'vollständig: *a ~ circle*; **~ strangers** wildfremde Leute; **4.** F rein, ‚kom'plett': **~ nonsense**; *a ~ fool* ein

ausgemachter Narr; **II** *s.* **5.** *ling.* Perfekt *n*: *past ~* Plusquamperfekt; **III** *v/t.* [pə'fekt] **6.** voll'enden; ver'vollkommnen (*o.s.* sich); **per·fect·i·ble** [pə'fektəbl] *adj.* ver'vollkommnungsfähig; **per·fec·tion** [pə'fekʃn] *s.* **1.** Ver'vollkommnung *f*, *fig.* Voll'kommenheit *f*, Voll'endung *f*, Perfekti'on *f*: **bring to ~** vervollkommnen; **to ~** vollkommen, meisterlich; **2.** Vor'trefflichkeit *f*; **4.** Fehler-, Makellosigkeit *f*; **5.** *fig.* Gipfel *m*; **6.** *pl.* Fertigkeiten *pl.*; **per·fec·tion·ist** [pə'fekʃnɪst] **I** *s.* Perfektio'nist *m*; **II** *adj.* perfektio'nistisch; **'per·fect·ly** [-klɪ] *adv.* **1.** voll'kommen, fehlerlos; gänzlich, völlig; **2.** F ganz, abso'lut, einfach *wunderbar etc.*

per·fid·i·ous [pə'fɪdɪəs] *adj.* □ verräterisch, falsch, heimtückisch, per'fid; **per'fid·i·ous·ness** [-nɪs], **per·fi·dy** ['pɜːfɪdɪ] *s.* Falschheit *f*, Perfi'die *f*, Tücke *f*, Verrat *m*.

per·fo·rate I *v/t.* ['pɜːfəreɪt] durch'bohren, -'löchern, lochen, perforieren: **~d disk** ⊙ (Kreis)Lochscheibe *f*; **~d tape** Lochstreifen *m*; **II** *adj.* [-rɪt] durch'löchert, gelocht; **per·fo·ra·tion** [ˌpɜːfə'reɪʃn] *s.* **1.** Durch'bohrung *f*, -'lochung *f*, -'löcherung *f*, Perforati'on *f*: **~ of the stomach** ♫ Magendurchbruch *m*; **2.** Lochung *f*, gelochte Linie; **3.** Loch *n*, Öffnung *f*; **'per·fo·ra·tor** [-tə] *s.* Locher *m*.

per·force [pə'fɔːs] *adv.* notgedrungen, gezwungenermaßen.

per·form [pə'fɔːm] **I** *v/t.* **1.** *Arbeit, Dienst etc.* verrichten, leisten, machen, tun, ausführen; ♫ *e-e Operation* 'durchführen (*on* bei); **2.** voll'bringen, -'ziehen, 'durchführen; *e-r Verpflichtung* nachkommen, *e-e Pflicht, a. e-n Vertrag* erfüllen; **3.** *Theaterstück, Konzert etc.* aufführen, geben, spielen; *e-e Rolle* spielen, darstellen; **II** *v/i.* **4.** et. ausführen *od.* leisten; ⊙ funktionieren, arbeiten: **~ well** e-e gute Leistung bringen; **5.** *thea. etc.* e-e Vorstellung geben, auftreten, spielen: **~ on the piano** Klavier spielen, auf dem Klavier et. vortragen; **per'form·ance** [-məns] *s.* **1.** Aus-, 'Durchführung *f*: **in the ~ of his duty** in Ausübung s-r Pflicht; **2.** Leistung *f* (*a.* ⚖, ⊙), Erfüllung *f* (*Pflicht, Versprechen, Vertrag*), Voll'ziehung *f* (*in kind* Sachleistung; **~ data** ⊙ Leistungswerte *pl.*; **~ principle** *sociol.* Leistungsprinzip *n*; **~ test** *ped.* Leistungsprüfung *f*; **~ of a machine** ⊙ Arbeitsweise *f* e-r Maschine; **3.** ♪, *thea.* Aufführung *f*; Vorstellung *f*; Vortrag *m*; **4.** *thea.* Darstellung(skunst *f*), Spiel *n*; **5.** *ling.* Perfor'manz *f*; **per'form·er** [-mə] *s.* **1.** Ausführende(r *m*) *f*; **2.** Leistungsträger(in): *top ~*; **3.** Schauspieler(in); Darsteller(in); Musiker(in); Künstler(in); **per'form·ing** [-mɪŋ] *adj.* **1.** *thea.* Aufführungs...: **~ rights**; **2.** darstellend: **~ arts**; **3.** dressiert (*Tier*).

per·fume I *v/t.* [pə'fjuːm] **1.** mit Duft erfüllen, parfümieren (*a. fig.*); **II** *s.* ['pɜːfjuːm] **2.** Duft *m*, Wohlgeruch *m*; **3.** Par'füm *n*, Duftstoff *m*; **per'fum·er** [-mə] *s.* Parfüme'riehändler *m*, Parfü'meur *m*; **per'fum·er·y** [-mərɪ] *s.* Parfüme'rien *pl.*; Parfüme'rie(geschäft *n*) *f*.

per·func·to·ry [pə'fʌŋktərɪ] *adj.* □ **1.** oberflächlich, obenhin, flüchtig; **2.** me'chanisch, inter'esselos.

per·go·la ['pɜːgələ] *s.* Laube *f*, offener Laubengang, Pergola *f*.

per·haps [pə'hæps; præps] *adv.* viel'leicht.

per·i·car·di·tis [ˌperɪkɑːˈdaɪtɪs] s. ✒ Herzbeutelentzündung f, Perikar'ditis f; **per·i·car·di·um** [ˌperɪˈkɑːdjəm] pl. **-di·a** [-djə] s. anat. **1.** Herzbeutel m; **2.** Herzfell n.

per·i·carp [ˈperɪkɑːp] s. ♀ Fruchthülle f, Peri'karp n.

per·i·gee [ˈperɪdʒiː] s. ast. Erdnähe f.

per·i·he·li·on [ˌperɪˈhiːljən] s. ast. Sonnennähe f e-s Planeten.

per·il [ˈperəl] **I** s. Gefahr f, Risiko n (a. ✝): **in ~ of one's life** in Lebensgefahr; **at (one's) ~** auf eigene Gefahr; **at the ~ of** auf die Gefahr hin, dass; **II** v/t. gefährden; **per·il·ous** [-rələs] adj. □ gefährlich.

per·im·e·ter [pəˈrɪmɪtə] s. **1.** Peri'pherie f: a) ♈ 'Umkreis m, b) allg. Rand m: ~ **position** ✕ Randstellung f, **2.** ✒, opt. Peri'meter n (Instrument).

per·i·ne·um [ˌperɪˈniːəm] pl. **-ne·a** [-ə] s. anat. Damm m, Peri'neum n.

pe·ri·od [ˈpɪərɪəd] **I** s. **1.** Peri'ode f (a. ♈, ♫, ♪), Zeit(dauer f, -raum m, -spanne f) f, Frist f: **~ of appeal** ✝ Berufungsfrist; **~ of exposure** phot. Belichtungszeit; **~ of office** Amtsdauer f; **for a ~** für einige Zeit; **for a ~ of** auf die Dauer von; **2.** ast. 'Umlaufzeit f; **3.** (vergangenes od. gegenwärtiges) Zeitalter: **glacial ~** Eiszeit f; **dresses of the ~** zeitgenössische Kleider; **a girl of the ~** ein modernes Mädchen; **4.** ped. ('Unterrichts)Stunde f; **5.** Sport: Spielabschnitt m, z. B. Eishockey: Drittel n; **6.** a. **monthly ~** (od. **~s** pl.) ✒ Peri'ode f der Frau; **7.** (Sprech)Pause f, Absatz m; **8.** ling. a) Punkt m: **put a ~ to** fig. e-r Sache ein Ende setzen, b) Satzgefüge n, c) allg. wohlgefügter Satz; **II** adj. **9.** a) zeitgeschichtlich, Zeit...: **~ play** Zeitstück n; b) Stil...: **~ furniture; ~ house** Haus n im Zeitstil; **~ dress** historisches Kostüm.

pe·ri·od·ic¹ [ˌpɪərɪˈɒdɪk] adj. (□ **~ ally**) **1.** peri'odisch, Kreis..., regelmäßig 'wiederkehrend; **2.** ling. rhe'torisch, wohlgefügt (Satz).

per·i·od·ic² [ˌpɜːraɪˈɒdɪk] adj. ♈ per'jod-, 'überjodsauer: **~ acid** Überjodsäure f.

pe·ri·od·i·cal [ˌpɪərɪˈɒdɪkl] **I** adj. □ **1.** → **periodic¹**; **2.** regelmäßig erscheinend; **3.** Zeitschriften...; **II** s. **4.** Zeitschrift f; **pe·ri·o·dic·i·ty** [ˌpɪərɪəˈdɪsətɪ] s. **1.** Periodizi'tät f (a. ✒); **2.** ♈ Stellung f e-s Ele'ments in der A'tomgewichtstafel; **3.** ⚡ Fre'quenz f.

per·i·os·te·um [ˌperɪˈɒstɪəm] pl. **-te·a** [-ə] s. anat. Knochenhaut f; **per·i·os·ti·tis** [ˌperɪəˈstaɪtɪs] s. ✒ Knochenhautentzündung f.

per·i·pa·tet·ic [ˌperɪpəˈtetɪk] adj. (□ **~ally**) **1.** um'herwandelnd; **2.** ♀ phls. peripa'tetisch; **3.** fig. weitschweifig.

pe·riph·er·al [pəˈrɪfərəl] adj. □ **1.** peri'pherisch, Rand...: **~ (equipment)** Com'puter: Peripheriegerät n; **~s** Peripheriegeräte pl.; **2.** anat. peri'pher; **pe·riph·er·y** [pəˈrɪfərɪ] s. Periphe'rie f; fig. a. Rand m, Grenze f.

pe·riph·ra·sis [pəˈrɪfrəsɪs] pl. **-ses** [-siːz] s. Um'schreibung f, Peri'phrase f; **per·i·phras·tic** [ˌperɪˈfræstɪk] adj. (□ **~ally**) um'schreibend, peri'phrastisch.

per·i·scope [ˈperɪskəʊp] s. ✕ **1.** Sehrohr n (U-Boot, Panzer); **2.** Beobachtungsspiegel m.

per·ish [ˈperɪʃ] **I** v/i. **1.** 'umkommen, 'untergehen, zu'grunde gehen, sterben, (tödlich) verunglücken (**by, of, with** durch, von, an dat.): **to ~ by drowning** ertrinken; **~ the thought!** Gott behü-

te!; **2.** hinschwinden, absterben, eingehen; **II** v/t. **3.** vernichten (mst pass.): **be ~ed with** F (fast) umkommen vor Kälte etc.; **'per·ish·a·ble** [-ʃəbl] **I** adj. □ vergänglich; leicht verderblich (Lebensmittel etc.); **II** s. pl. leicht verderbliche Waren pl.; **'per·ish·er** [-ʃə] s. Brit. **little ~** kleiner Räuber (Kind); **'per·ish·ing** [-ʃɪŋ] **I** adj. □ vernichtend, tödlich (a. fig.); **II** adv. F scheußlich, verflixt: **~ cold.**

per·i·style [ˈperɪstaɪl] s. ⌂ Säulengang m, Peri'styl n.

per·i·to·n(a)e·um [ˌperɪtəʊˈniːəm] pl. **-ne·a** [-ə] s. anat. Bauchfell n; **per·i·to'ni·tis** [-təˈnaɪtɪs] s. ✒ Bauchfellentzündung f.

per·i·wig [ˈperɪwɪg] s. Pe'rücke f.

per·i·win·kle [ˈperɪˌwɪŋkl] s. **1.** ♀ Immergrün n.; **2.** zo. (essbare) Uferschnecke.

per·jure [ˈpɜːdʒə] v/t.: **~ o.s.** e-n Meineid leisten, meineidig werden; **~d** meineidig; **'per·jur·er** [-dʒərə] s. Meineidige(r m) f; **'per·ju·ry** [-dʒərɪ] s. Meineid m.

perk¹ [pɜːk] s. mst pl. bsd. Brit F für **perquisite** 1.

perk² [pɜːk] **I** v/i. mst **~ up 1.** (lebhaft) den Kopf recken, munter werden; **2.** fig. die Nase hoch tragen, selbstbewusst od. forsch auftreten; **3.** fig. sich erholen, munter werden; **II** v/t. mst **~ up 4.** den Kopf recken; die Ohren spitzen; **5.** **~ up** j-n 'aufmöbeln'; **6.** **~ o.s.** (**up**) sich schönmachen; **'perk·i·ness** [-kɪnɪs] s. Keckheit f, Selbstbewusstsein n; **'perk·y** [-kɪ] adj. □ **1.** flott, forsch; **2.** keck, dreist, frech.

perm [pɜːm] s. F Dauerwelle f.

per·ma·frost [ˈpɜːməfrɒst] s. Dauerfrostboden m.

per·ma·nence [ˈpɜːmənəns] s. **1.** Perma'nenz f (a. phys.), Ständigkeit f, (Fort)Dauer f; **2.** Beständigkeit f; **'per·ma·nen·cy** [-sɪ] s. **1.** → **permanence**; **2.** et. Dauerhaftes od. Bleibendes; feste Anstellung, Dauerstellung f; **'per·ma·nent** [-nt] adj. □ **1.** (fort)dauernd, bleibend, perma'nent; ständig (Ausschuss, Bauten, Personal, Wohnsitz etc.); dauerhaft, Dauer... (-magnet, -stellung, -ton, -wirkung etc.), mas'siv (Bau): **~ assets** ✝ Anlagevermögen n; **~ call** teleph. Dauerbelegung f; **~ disposal** Endlagerung f; **⚿ Secretary** Brit. ständiger (fachlicher) Staatssekretär; **~ situation** ✝ Dauer-, Lebensstellung f; **~ wave** Dauerwelle f; **~ way** 🚂 Bahnkörper m; Oberbau m.

per·man·ga·nate [pɜːˈmæŋgəneɪt] s. ♈ Permanga'nat n: **~ of potash** Kaliumpermanganat; **per·man·gan·ic** [ˌpɜːmæŋˈgænɪk] adj. Übermangan...: **~ acid.**

per·me·a·bil·i·ty [ˌpɜːmjəˈbɪlətɪ] s. **1.** Durch'dringbarkeit f, bsd. phys. Permeabili'tät f: **~ to gas(es)** phys. Gasdurchlässigkeit f.

per·me·a·ble [ˈpɜːmjəbl] adj. □ 'durchlässig (**to** für); **per·me·ance** [ˈpɜːmɪəns] s. **1.** Durch'dringung f; **2.** phys. ma'gnetischer Leitwert; **per·me·ate** [ˈpɜːmɪeɪt] **I** v/t. durch'dringen; **II** v/i. dringen (**into** in acc.), sich verbreiten (**among** unter dat.), 'durchsickern; **per·me·a·tion** [ˌpɜːmɪˈeɪʃn] s. Eindringen n, Durch'dringung f.

per·mis·si·ble [pəˈmɪsəbl] adj. □ zulässig; **per·mis·sion** [-ˈmɪʃn] s. Erlaubnis f, Genehmigung f, Zulassung f: **by special ~** mit besonderer Erlaubnis; **ask s.o. for ~, ask s.o.'s ~** j-n um Erlaub-

nis bitten; **per·mis·sive** [-sɪv] adj. □ **1.** gestattend, zulassend; ✝ fakulta'tiv; **2.** tole'rant, libe'ral; (sexu'ell) freizügig: **~ society** tabufreie Gesellschaft; **per·mis·sive·ness** [-sɪvnɪs] s. **1.** Zulässigkeit f; **2.** Tole'ranz f; **3.** (sexu'elle) Freizügigkeit f.

per·mit [pəˈmɪt] **I** v/t. **1.** et. erlauben, gestatten, zulassen, dulden: **am I ~ted to** darf ich?; **~ o.s. s.th.** sich et. erlauben; **II** v/i. **2.** erlauben: **weather (time) ~ting** wenn es das Wetter (die Zeit) erlaubt; **3.** **~ of** fig. zulassen: **the rule ~s of no exception**; **III** s. [ˈpɜːmɪt] **4.** Genehmigung(sschein m) f, Li'zenz f, Zulassung f (**to** für); ✝ Aus-, Einfuhrerlaubnis f; **5.** Aus-, Einreiseerlaubnis f; **6.** Passierschein m; **per·mit·tiv·i·ty** [ˌpɜːmɪˈtɪvətɪ] s. phys. Permittivi'tät f, Dielektrizi'tätskon,stante f.

per·mu·ta·tion [ˌpɜːmjuˈteɪʃn] s. **1.** Vertauschung f, Versetzung f: **~ lock** Vexierschloss n; **2.** ♈ Permutati'on f.

per·ni·cious [pəˈnɪʃəs] adj. □ **1.** verderblich, schädlich; **2.** ✒ bösartig, perni'ziös; **per·ni·cious·ness** [-nɪs] s. Schädlichkeit f; Bösartigkeit f.

per·nick·et·y [pəˈnɪkətɪ] adj. **1.** F ‚pingelig', kleinlich, wählerisch, pe'dantisch (**about** mit); **2.** heikel (a. Sache).

per·o·rate [ˈperəreɪt] v/i. **1.** große Reden schwingen; **2.** e-e Rede abschließen; **per·o·ra·tion** [ˌperəˈreɪʃn] s. (zs.-fassender) Redeschluss.

per·ox·ide [pəˈrɒksaɪd] ♈ 'Supero,xid n; engS. 'Wasserstoff,supero,xid n: **~ blonde** ♈ ‚Wasserstoffblondine' f; **per·ox·i·dize** [-sɪdaɪz] v/t. u. v/i. peroxidieren.

per·pen·dic·u·lar [ˌpɜːpənˈdɪkjʊlə] **I** adj. □ **1.** senk-, lotrecht (**to** zu): **~ style** ⌂ englische Spätgotik; **2.** rechtwinklig (**to** auf dat.); **3.** ♈ seiger; **4.** steil; **5.** aufrecht (a. fig.); **II** s. **6.** (Einfalls)Lot n, Senkrechte f, Perpen'dikel n, m: **out of (the) ~** schief, nicht senkrecht; **raise (let fall) a ~** ein Lot errichten (fällen); **7.** ⊙ (Senk)Lot n, Senkwaage f.

per·pe·trate [ˈpɜːpɪtreɪt] v/t. Verbrechen etc. begehen, verüben; F fig. Buch etc. ‚verbrechen'; **per·pe·tra·tion** [ˌpɜːpɪˈtreɪʃn] s. Begehung f, Verübung f; **'per·pe·tra·tor** [-tə] s. Ver'ursacher m, Täter m.

per·pet·u·al [pəˈpetjʊəl] adj. □ **1.** fortwährend, immer während, unaufhörlich, beständig, ewig, andauernd: **~ check** Dauerschach n; **~ motion machine** Perpetuum mobile n; **~ snow** ewiger Schnee, Firn m; **2.** lebenslänglich, unabsetzbar: **~ officer**; ✝ unablösbar, unkündbar: **~ lease; ~ bonds** Rentenanleihen; **4.** ♀ perennierend; **per·pet·u·ate** [-tʃueɪt] verewigen, fortbestehen lassen, (immer während) fortsetzen; **per·pet·u·a·tion** [pəˌpetʃuˈeɪʃn] s. Fortdauer f, endlose Fortsetzung, Verewigung f, Fortbestehenlassen n; **per·pe·tu·i·ty** [ˌpɜːpɪˈtjuːətɪ] s. **1.** Fortdauer f, unaufhörliches Bestehen, Unaufhörlichkeit f, Ewigkeit f: **in** (od. **to od. for**) **~** auf ewig; **2.** ✝ Unveräußerlichkeit(sverfügung) f; **3.** lebenslängliche (Jahres)Rente.

per·plex [pəˈpleks] v/t. verwirren, verblüffen, bestürzt machen; **per·plexed** [-kst] adj. □ **1.** verwirrt, verblüfft, verdutzt, bestürzt (Person); **2.** verworren, verwickelt (Sache); **per·plex·i·ty** [-ksətɪ] s. **1.** Verwirrung f, Bestürzung f, Verlegenheit f; **2.** Verworrenheit f.

per·qui·site [ˈpɜːkwɪzɪt] s. **1.** mst pl.

bsd. Brit. a) Nebeneinkünfte *pl.*, -verdienst *m*, b) Vergünstigung *f*; **2.** Vergütung *f*, Gehalt *n*; **3.** per'sönliches Vorrecht.

per·se·cute ['pɜːsɪkjuːt] *v/t.* **1.** *bsd. pol., eccl.* verfolgen; **2.** a) plagen, belästigen, b) drangsalieren, schikanieren; **per·se·cu·tion** [ˌpɜːsɪ'kjuːʃn] *s.* **1.** Verfolgung *f*: ~ *mania*, ~ *complex* Verfolgungswahn *m*; **2.** Drangsalierung *f*, Schi'kane(n *pl.*) *f*; '**per·se·cu·tor** [-tə] *s.* **1.** Verfolger *m*; **2.** Peiniger(in).

per·se·ver·ance [ˌpɜːsɪ'vɪərəns] *s.* Beharrlichkeit *f*, Ausdauer *f*; **per·sev·er·ate** [pə'sevəreɪt] *v/i. psych.* ständig *od.* immer 'wiederkehren (*Melodie, Motiv, Gedanken etc.*); **per·se·vere** [ˌpɜːsɪ'vɪə] *v/i.* (*in*) beharren, ausdauern, aushalten (bei), fortfahren (mit), festhalten (an *dat.*); **per·se'ver·ing** [-'vɪərɪŋ] *adj.* ☐ beharrlich, standhaft.

Per·sian ['pɜːʃn] **I** *adj.* **1.** persisch; **II** *s.* **2.** Perser(in); **3.** *ling.* Persisch *n*; ~ **blinds** *s. pl.* Jalou'sien *pl.*; ~ **car·pet** *s.* Perserteppich *m*; ~ **cat** *s.* An'gorakatze *f*.

per·si·flage [ˌpɜːsɪ'flɑːʒ] *s.* Persi'flage *f*, (*feine*) Verspottung *f*.

per·sim·mon [pɜː'sɪmən] *s.* ♥ Persi'mone *f*, Kaki-, Dattelpflaume *f*.

per·sist [pə'sɪst] *v/i.* **1.** (*in*) aus-, verharren (bei), hartnäckig bestehen (auf *dat.*), beharren (auf *dat.*, bei), unbeirrt fortfahren (mit); **2.** weiterarbeiten (*with* an *dat.*); **3.** fortdauern, anhalten; fortbestehen, weiter bestehen; **per'sist·ence** [-təns], **per'sist·en·cy** [-tənsɪ] *s.* **1.** Beharren *n* (*in* bei); Beharrlichkeit *f*; Fortdauer *f*; **2.** beharrliches *od.* hartnäckiges Fortfahren (*in* in *dat.*); **3.** Hartnäckigkeit *f*, Ausdauer *f*; **4.** *phys.* Beharrung(szustand *m*) *f*, Nachwirkung *f*; Wirkungsdauer *f*; *TV etc.* Nachleuchten *n*; *opt.* (Augen)Trägheit *f*; **per'sist·ent** [-tənt] *adj.* ☐ **1.** beharrlich, ausdauernd, hartnäckig; **2.** ständig, nachhaltig, anhaltend (*a.* ♥ Nachfrage; *a.* Regen); ✗ sesshaft (*Kampfstoff*), schwerflüchtig (*Gas*).

per·snick·et·y [pə'snɪkətɪ] *adj. Am.* → **pernickety**.

per·son ['pɜːsn] *s.* **1.** Per'son *f* (*a. contr.*), (Einzel)Wesen *n*, Indi'viduum *n*; *weitS.* Per'sönlichkeit *f*: *any* ~ irgendjemand: *in* ~ in eigener Person, persönlich; *no* ~ niemand; *natural* ~ ꞔꞔ natürliche Person; *v/t.-to-* ~ *call teleph.* Voranmeldung(sgespräch *n*) *f*; **2.** das Äußere, Körper *m*: *carry s.th. on one's* ~ et. bei sich tragen; **3.** *thea.* Rolle *f*.

per·so·na [pɜː'səʊnə] *pl.* **-nae** [-niː] *s.* (*Lat.*) **1.** a) *thea.* Cha'rakter *m*, Rolle *f*, b) Gestalt *f* (*in der Literatur*); **2.** ~ (*non*) *grata* Persona (non) grata *f*, (nicht) genehme Person.

per·son·a·ble ['pɜːsnəbl] *adj.* **1.** von angenehmem Äußeren; **2.** sym'pathisch; '**per·son·age** [-nɪdʒ] *s.* **1.** (hohe) Per'sönlichkeit; **2.** → *persona* 1; '**per·son·al** [-nl] **I** *adj.* ☐ **1.** per'sönlich (*a. ling.*); Personal...(*-konto, -kredit, -steuer etc.*); Privat...(*-einkommen, -leben etc.*); eigen (*a. Meinung*): ~ *column* → 5; ~ *damage* Personenschaden *m*; ~ *data* Personalien *pl.*; ~ *digital assistant* Computer: PDA *m* (*Palmtop-Computer*); ~ *file* Personalakte *f*; ~ *injury* Körperverletzung *f*; ~ *property* (*od. estate*) → *personalty*; ~ *union* *pol.* Personalunion *f*; **2.** per'sönlich, pri'vat, vertraulich (*Brief etc.*); mündlich (*Auskunft etc.*): ~ *matter* Privat-

sache *f*; ~ *stereo* a) 'Walkman *TM m*, b) tragbarer CD-Player; **3.** äußer, körperlich: ~ *charms*; ~ *hygiene* Körperpflege *f*; **4.** persönlich, anzüglich (*Bemerkung etc.*): *become* ~ anzüglich werden; **II** *s.* **5.** Per'sönliches *n* (*Zeitung*); **per·son·al·i·ty** [ˌpɜːsə'nælətɪ] *s.* **1.** Per'sönlichkeit *f* (*a. jur.*), Per'son *f*: ~ *clash psych.* Persönlichkeitskonflikt *m*; ~ *cult pol.* Personenkult *m*; ~ *test psych.* Persönlichkeitstest *m*; **2.** Individuali'tät *f*; **3.** *pl.* Anzüglichkeiten *pl.*, anzügliche Bemerkungen *pl.*; **per·son·al·ize** ['pɜːsnəlaɪz] → *personify*; '**per·son·al·ty** [-nltɪ] ꞔꞔ bewegliches Vermögen; '**per·son·ate** [-səneɪt] *v/t.* **1.** → *personify*; **2.** vor-, darstellen; **3.** nachahmen; **4.** sich (fälschlich) ausgeben als; **per·son·a·tion** [ˌpɜːsə'neɪʃn] *s.* **1.** Vor-, Darstellung *f*; **2.** Personifikati'on *f*, Verkörperung *f*; **3.** Nachahmung *f*; **4.** ꞔꞔ fälschliches Sich'ausgeben.

per·son·i·fi·ca·tion [pɜːˌsɒnɪfɪ'keɪʃn] *s.* Verkörperung *f*; **per·son·i·fy** [pɜː'sɒnɪfaɪ] *v/t.* personifizieren, verkörpern, versinnbildlichen.

per·son·nel [ˌpɜːsə'nel] *s.* Perso'nal *n*, Belegschaft *f*; ✗, ⚓ Mannschaft(en *pl.*) *f*, Besatzung *f*: ~ *manager* ✝ Personalchef *m*.

per·spec·tiv·al [ˌpɜːspek'taɪvl] *adj.* perspek'tivisch; **per·spec·tive** [pə'spektɪv] **I** *s.* **1.** ꞔꞔ, *paint. etc.* Perspek'tive *f*: *in* (*true*) ~ in richtiger Perspektive; **2.** *a.* ~ *drawing* perspektivische Zeichnung; **3.** Perspek'tive *f*: a) Aussicht *f*, -blick *m* (*beide a. fig.*), b) *fig.* klarer Blick: *he has no* ~ er sieht die Dinge nicht im richtigen Verhältnis (zueinander); **II** *adj.* ☐ **4.** → *perspectival*.

per·spex ['pɜːspeks] (*TM*) *s. Brit.* Sicherheits-, Plexiglas *n*.

per·spi·ca·cious [ˌpɜːspɪ'keɪʃəs] *adj.* ☐ scharfsinnig, 'durchdringend; **per·spi·'cac·i·ty** [-'kæsətɪ] *s.* Scharfblick *m*, -sinn *m*; **per·spi'cu·i·ty** [-'kjuːətɪ] *s.* Klarheit *f*, Verständlichkeit *f*; **per·spic·u·ous** [pə'spɪkjʊəs] *adj.* ☐ deutlich, klar, (leicht) verständlich.

per·spi·ra·tion [ˌpɜːspə'reɪʃn] *s.* **1.** Ausdünsten *n*, Schwitzen *n*; **2.** Schweiß *m*; **per·spi·ra·to·ry** [pə'spaɪərətərɪ] *adj.* Schweiß...: ~ *gland* Schweißdrüse *f*; **per·spire** [pə'spaɪə] **I** *v/i.* schwitzen, transpirieren; **II** *v/t.* ausschwitzen, -dünsten.

per·suade [pə'sweɪd] *v/t.* **1.** über'reden, bereden (*to inf., into ger.* zu *inf.*); **2.** über'zeugen (*of* von, *that* dass): ~ *o.s.* a) sich überzeugen, b) sich einbilden *od.* einreden; *be* ~*d that* überzeugt sein, dass; **per'suad·er** [-də] *s.* **1.** Über-'redungskünstler(in), ,Verführer' *m*; **2.** *sl.* Über'redungsmittel *n* (*a. Pistole etc.*).

per·sua·sion [pə'sweɪʒn] *s.* **1.** Über'redung *f*; **2.** *a.* **powers of** ~ Über'redungsgabe *f*, -künste *pl.*; **3.** Über'zeugung *f*, fester Glaube; **4.** *eccl.* Glaube(nsrichtung *f*) *m*; **5.** F *humor.* a) Art *f*, Sorte *f*, b) Geschlecht *n*: *female* ~, *male* ~; **per'sua·sive** [-eɪsɪv] *adj.* ☐ **1.** über're-dend; **2.** über'zeugend; **per'sua·sive·ness** [-eɪsɪvnɪs] *s.* **1.** → *persuasion* 2; **2.** über'zeugende Art.

pert [pɜːt] *adj.* ☐ keck (*a. fig. Hut etc.*), schnippisch, vorlaut.

per·tain [pɜː'teɪn] *v/i.* (*to*) a) gehören (*dat. od.* zu), b) betreffen (*acc.*), sich beziehen (auf *acc.*): ~*ing to* betreffend.

per·ti·na·cious [ˌpɜːtɪ'neɪʃəs] *adj.* ☐ **1.** hartnäckig, zäh; **2.** beharrlich, standhaft; **per·ti'nac·i·ty** [-'næsətɪ] *s.* Hartnäckigkeit *f*; Zähigkeit *f*; Beharrlich-

keit *f*.

per·ti·nence ['pɜːtɪnəns], '**per·ti·nen·cy** [-sɪ] *s.* **1.** Angemessenheit *f*, Gemäßheit *f*; **2.** Sachdienlichkeit *f*, Rele-'vanz *f*; '**per·ti·nent** [-nt] *adj.* ☐ **1.** angemessen, passend, gemäß; **2.** zur Sache gehörig, einschlägig, sachdienlich, gehörig (*to* zu): *be* ~ *to* Bezug haben auf (*acc.*).

pert·ness ['pɜːtnɪs] *s.* Keckheit *f*, schnippisches Wesen, vorlaute Art.

per·turb [pə'tɜːb] *v/t.* beunruhigen, stören, verwirren, ängstigen; **per·tur·ba·tion** [ˌpɜːtə'beɪʃn] *s.* **1.** Unruhe *f*, Bestürzung *f*; **2.** Beunruhigung *f*, Störung *f*; **3.** *ast.* Perturbati'on *f*.

pe·ruke [pə'ruːk] *s. hist.* Pe'rücke *f*.

pe·rus·al [pə'ruːzl] *s.* sorgfältiges 'Durchlesen, 'Durchsicht *f*, Prüfung *f*: *for* ~ zur Einsicht; **pe·ruse** [pə'ruːz] *v/t.* (*durch*)lesen; *weitS.* 'durchgehen, prüfen.

Pe·ru·vi·an [pə'ruːvjən] **I** *adj.* peru'a-nisch: ~ *bark* ♥ Chinarinde *f*; **II** *s.* Peru'aner(in).

per·vade [pə'veɪd] *v/t.* durch'dringen, -'ziehen, erfüllen (*a. fig.*); **per'va·sion** [-eɪʒn] *s.* Durch'dringung *f* (*a. fig.*); **per'va·sive** [-eɪsɪv] *adj.* ☐ 'durchdringend; *fig.* 'überall vor'handen, beherrschend.

per·verse [pə'vɜːs] *adj.* ☐ **1.** verkehrt, Fehl...; **2.** verderbt, böse; **3.** verdreht, wunderlich; **4.** verstockt; **5.** launisch; **6.** *psych.* per'vers (*a. fig.*), 'widernatürlich; **per'ver·sion** [-ɜːʒn] *s.* **1.** Verdrehung *f*, 'Umkehrung *f*; Entstellung *f*: ~ *of justice* Rechtsbeugung *f*; ~ *of history* Geschichtsklitterung *f*; **2.** *bsd. eccl.* Verirrung *f*, Abkehr *f* vom Guten etc.; **3.** *psych.* Perversi'on *f*; **4.** ꞔꞔ 'Umkehrung *f* (*e-r Figur*); **per'ver·si·ty** [-sətɪ] *s.* **1.** Verdrehtheit *f*; Halsstarrigkeit *f*; **3.** Verderbtheit *f*; **4.** 'Widerna,türlichkeit *f*, Perversi'tät *f* (*a. fig.*); **per'ver·sive** [-sɪv] *adj.* verderblich (*of* für).

per·vert **I** *v/t.* [pə'vɜːt] **1.** verdrehen, verkehren, entstellen, fälschen, pervertieren (*a. psych.*); miss'brauchen; **2.** *j-n* verderben, verführen; **II** *s.* ['pɜːvɜːt] **3.** Abtrünnige(r *m*) *f*; **4.** *a. sexual* ~ *psych.* per'verser Mensch; **per'vert·er** [-tə] *s.* Verdreher(in); Verführer(in).

per·vi·ous ['pɜːvjəs] *adj.* ☐ **1.** 'durchlässig (*a. phys.*), durch'dringbar, gangbar (*to* für); **2.** *fig.* zugänglich (*to* für), offen (*to dat.*); **3.** ⊙ undicht.

pes·ky ['peskɪ] *adj. u. adv. Am.* F ,ver-flixt'.

pes·sa·ry ['pesərɪ] *s.* ✿ Pes'sar *n*.

pes·si·mism ['pesɪmɪzəm] *s.* Pessi'mismus *m*, Schwarzsehe'rei *f*; '**pes·si·mist** [-ɪst] **I** *s.* Pessi'mist(in), Schwarzseher (-in); **II** *adj.* **pes·si·mis·tic** [ˌpesɪ'mɪs-tɪk] *adj.* (☐ ~*ally*) pessi'mistisch.

pest [pest] *s.* **1.** Pest *f*, Plage *f* (*a. fig.*); **2.** *fig.* Pestbeule *f*; **3.** *fig.* a) ,Ekel' *n*, ,Nervensäge' *f*, b) Plage *f*, lästige Sache; **4.** *bsd. insect* → *biol.* Schädling *m*: ~ *control* Schädlingsbekämpfung *f*.

pes·ter ['pestə] *v/t.* plagen, quälen, belästigen, *j-m* auf die Nerven gehen.

pes·ti·cide ['pestɪsaɪd] *s.* Schädlingsbe-kämpfungsmittel *n*, Pesti'zid *n*.

pes·ti·lence ['pestɪləns] *s.* Seuche *f*, Pest *f*, Pesti'lenz *f* (*a. fig.*); '**pes·ti·lent** [-nt] *adj.* → **pes·ti·len·tial** [ˌpestɪ'lenʃl] *adj.* ☐ **1.** verpestend, ansteckend; **2.** *fig.* verderblich, schädlich; **3.** *oft humor.* ekelhaft.

pes·tle ['pesl] **I** *s.* **1.** Mörserkeule *f*, Stö-ßel *m*; **2.** ꞔꞔ Pi'still *n*; **II** *v/t.* **3.** zerstoßen.

pet¹ [pet] **I** *s.* **1.** (zahmes) Haustier; Stubentier *n*; **2.** gehätscheltes Tier *od.* Kind, Liebling *m*, ‚Schatz‘ *m*, ‚Schätzchen‘ *n*; **II** *adj.* **3.** Lieblings...: ~ *dog* Schoßhund *m*; ~ *hate* bevorzugtes Hassobjekt; ~ *mistake* Lieblingsfehler *m*; ~ *name* Kosename *m*; ~ *shop* Tierhandlung *f*; → *aversion* 3; **III** *v/t.* **4.** (ver)hätscheln, liebkosen; **5.** F ‚abfummeln‘, Petting machen mit; **IV** *v/i.* **6.** F ‚fummeln‘, knutschen, Petting machen.
pet² [pet] *s.* schlechte Laune: *in a* ~ verärgert, schlecht gelaunt.
pet·al [ˈpetl] *s.* ♀ Blumenblatt *n*.
pe·tard [peˈtɑːd] *s.* **1.** ✕ *hist.* Peˈtarde *f*, Sprengbüchse *f*; → *hoist¹*; **2.** Schwärmer *m* (*Feuerwerk*).
pe·ter¹ [ˈpiːtə] *v/i.*: ~ *out* a) (allmählich) zu Ende gehen, abebben (*Erregung, Sturm etc.*), b) sich verlieren, c) sich totlaufen, versanden.
pe·ter² [ˈpiːtə] *s. sl.* ‚Zipfel‘ *m* (*Penis*).
pe·ter³ [ˈpiːtə] *s. sl.* **1.** Geldschrank *m*; **2.** (Laden)Kasse *f*.
Pe·ter [ˈpiːtə] *npr. u. s. bibl.* Petrus *m*: (*the Epistles of*) ~ die Petrusbriefe.
pet·it [ˈpeti] → *petty*.
pe·ti·tion [piˈtiʃn] **I** *s.* Bitte *f*, bsd. Bittschrift *f*, Gesuch *n*; Eingabe *f* (*a. Patentrecht*); ♊ (schriftlicher) Antrag: ~ *for divorce* Scheidungsklage *f*; ~ *in bankruptcy* Konkursantrag *m*; *file one's* ~ *in bankruptcy* Konkurs anmelden; ~ *for clemency* Gnadengesuch; **II** *v/i.* (*u. v/t. j-n*) bitten, an-, ersuchen (*for* um), schriftlich einkommen (*s.o.* bei j-m), e-e Bittschrift einreichen (*s.o.* an j-n): ~ *for divorce* die Scheidungsklage einreichen; **pe·ti·tion·er** [-ʃnə] *s.* Antragsteller(in): a) Bitt-, Gesuchsteller(in), Peˈtent *m*, b) ♊ (Scheidungs)Kläger(in).
pet·rel [ˈpetrəl] *s.* **1.** *orn.* Sturmvogel *m*; → *stormy petrel*; **2.** Unruhestifter *m*.
pet·ri·fac·tion [ˌpetriˈfækʃn] *s.* Versteinerung *f* (*Vorgang u. Ergebnis; a. fig.*); **pet·ri·fy** [ˈpetrifai] **I** *v/t.* **1.** versteinern (*a. fig.*); **2.** *fig. durch Schrecken etc.* versteinern, erstarren lassen: *petrified with horror* starr vor Schrecken; **II** *v/i.* **3.** sich versteinern (*a. fig.*).
pe·tro·chem·is·try [ˌpetrəʊˈkemistri] *s.* Petroˈcheˈmie *f*; **pe·trog·ra·phy** [piˈtrɒɡrəfi] *s.* Gesteinsbeschreibung *f*, -kunde *f*.
pet·rol [ˈpetrəl] *s. mot. Brit.* Benˈzin *n*, Kraftstoff *m*: ~ *bomb* Molotowcocktail *m*; ~ *coupon* Benzingutschein *m*; ~ *engine* Benzin-, Vergasermotor *m*; ~ *ga(u)ge* Kraftstoffanzeige *f*; ~ *station* Tankstelle *f*; **pet·ro·la·tum** [ˌpetrəˈleitəm] *s.* **1.** ♐ Petroˈlatum *n*, Vaseˈlin *n*; **2.** ☀ Parafˈfinöl *n*; **pe·tro·le·um** [piˈtrəʊljəm] *s.* Petroleum *n*, Erd-, Mineˈralöl *n*: ~ *jelly* → *petrolatum*; **pe·trol·o·gy** [piˈtrɒlədʒi] *s.* Gesteinskunde *f*.
pet·ti·coat [ˈpetikəʊt] **I** *s.* **1.** ‚Unterrock‘ *m*, Petticoat *m*; **2.** *fig.* Frauenzimmer *n*, Weibsbild *n*, ‚Unterrock‘ *m*; **3.** Kinderröckchen *n*; **4.** ⊕ Glocke *f*; **5.** ⚡ a) ~ *insulator* ‚Glockeniso‚lator *m*, b) Isolierglocke *f*; **6.** *mot.* (Venˈtil)Schutzhaube *f*; **II** *adj.* **7.** Weiber...: ~ *government* Weiberregiment *n*.
pet·ti·fog·ger [ˈpetifɒɡə] *s.* ‚Winkeladvo‚kat *m*; Haarspalter *m*, Rabuˈlist *m*; **'pet·ti·fog·ging** [-ɡɪŋ] **I** *adj.* **1.** rechtsverdrehend; **2.** schikaˈnös, rabuˈlistisch; **3.** gemein, lumpig; **II** *s.* **4.** Rabuˈlistik *f*, Haarspalteˈrei *f*, Rechtskniffe *pl.*
pet·ti·ness [ˈpetinis] *s.* **1.** Geringfügigkeit *f*; **2.** Kleinlichkeit *f*.

pet·ting [ˈpetiŋ] *s.* F ‚Fummeˈlei‘ *f*, Petting *n*.
pet·tish [ˈpetiʃ] *adj.* ☐ reizbar, mürrisch; **'pet·tish·ness** [-nis] *s.* Gereiztheit *f*.
pet·ti·toes [ˈpetitəʊz] *s. pl. Küche:* Schweinsfüße *pl.*
pet·ty [ˈpeti] *adj.* ☐ **1.** unbedeutend, geringfügig, klein, Klein...: ~ *cash* ♥ a) geringfügige Beträge, b) kleine Kasse, Portokasse; ~ *offence* ♊ Bagatelldelikt *n*; ~ *wares* Kurzwaren; **2.** kleinlich; ~ *bour·gois* [ˈbʊəʒwɑː] **I** *s.* (*Fr.*) Kleinbürger(in); **II** *adj.* kleinbürgerlich; ~ *bour·geoi·sie* [ˌbʊəʒwɑːˈziː] *s.* (*Fr.*) Kleinbürgertum *n*; ~ *ju·ry* *s.* ♊ kleine Jury; ~ *lar·ce·ny* *s.* ♊ leichter Diebstahl; ~ *of·fi·cer* *s.* ✕, ♣ Maat *m* (*Unteroffizier*); ~ *ses·sions* *s. pl.* → *magistrate*.
pet·u·lance [ˈpetjʊləns] *s.* Gereiztheit *f*; **'pet·u·lant** [-nt] *adj.* ☐ gereizt.
pe·tu·ni·a [piˈtjuːnjə] *s.* ♀ Peˈtunie *f*.
pew [pjuː] *s.* **1.** Kirchenstuhl *m*, -sitz *m*, Bank(reihe) *f*; **2.** *Brit.* F Platz *m*: *take a* ~ sich ‚platzen‘.
pe·wit [ˈpiːwit] *s. orn.* **1.** Kiebitz *m*; **2.** *a.* ~ *gull* Lachmöwe *f*.
pew·ter [ˈpjuːtə] **I** *s.* **1.** brit. Schüsselzinn *n*, Hartzinn *n*; **2.** *coll.* Zinngerät *n*; **3.** Zinnkrug *m*, -gefäß *n*; **4.** *Brit. sl. bsd. Sport:* Poˈkal *m*; **II** *adj.* **5.** (Hart-)Zinn..., zinnern; **'pew·ter·er** [-ərə] *s.* Zinngießer *m*.
pH [ˌpiːˈeitʃ] *s.* ♐ pˈH-Wert *m*.
pha·e·ton [ˈfeitn] *s.* Phaeton *m* (*Kutsche; mot. obs. Tourenwagen*).
phag·o·cyte [ˈfæɡəʊsait] *s. biol.* Phagoˈzyt *m*, Fresszelle *f*.
phal·ange [ˈfælændʒ] *s.* **1.** *anat.* Finger-, Zehenknochen *m*; **2.** ♀ Staubfädenbündel *n*; **3.** *zo.* Tarsenglied *n*.
pha·lanx [ˈfælæŋks] *pl.* **-lanx·es** *od.* **-lan·ges** [fæˈlændʒiːz] *s.* **1.** ✕ *hist.* Phalanx *f*, *fig. a.* geschlossene Front; **2.** → *phalange* 1 *u.* 2.
phal·lic [ˈfælik] *adj.* phallisch, Phallus...: ~ *symbol*; **phal·lus** [ˈfæləs] *pl.* **-li** [-lai] *s.* Phallus *m*.
phan·tasm [ˈfæntæzəm] → *phantom* 1 a *u.* b; **phan·tas·ma·go·ri·a** [ˌfæntæzməˈɡɔːriə] *s.* Phantasmagoˈrie *f*, Gaukelbild *n*, Blendwerk *n*; **phan·tas·ma·gor·ic** [ˌfæntæzməˈɡɔrik] *adj.* (☐ ~ally) phantasmaˈgorisch, gespensterhaft, trügerisch; **phan·tas·mal** [fænˈtæzml] *adj.* ☐ **1.** halluziˈnatorisch, eingebildet; **2.** geisterhaft; **3.** illuˈsorisch, unwirklich, trügerisch.
phan·tom [ˈfæntəm] **I** *s.* **1.** Phanˈtom *n*: a) Erscheinung *f*, Gespenst *n*, *a. fig.* Geist *m*, b) Wahngebilde *n*, Hirngespinst *n*; Trugbild *n*, c) *fig.* Alptraum *m*, Schreckgespenst *n*; **2.** *fig.* Schatten *m*, Schein *m*; **3.** ☀ Phanˈtom *n* (*Körpermodell*); **II** *adj.* **4.** Phantom..., Gespenster..., Geister...; **5.** scheinbar, Schein...; ~ *cir·cuit* *s.* ⚡ Phanˈtomkreis *m*, Duplexleitung *f*; ~ (*limb*) *pain* *s.* Phanˈtomschmerz *m*; ~ *ship* *s.* Geisterschiff *n*; ~ *view* *s.* ⊕ (Konstrukti'ons)Durchsicht *f*.
phar·i·sa·ic, **phar·i·sa·i·cal** [ˌfæriˈseiik(l)] *adj.* ☐ phariˈsäisch, selbstgerecht, scheinheilig; **phar·i·sa·ism** [ˈfæriseiizəm] *s.* Phariˈsäertum *n*, Scheinheiligkeit *f*; **Phar·i·see** [ˈfærisiː] *s.* **1.** *eccl.* Phariˈsäer *m*; **2.** ♊ *fig.* Phariˈsäer(in), Selbstgerechte(r *m*) *f*, Heuchler(in).
phar·ma·ceu·ti·cal [ˌfɑːməˈsjuːtikl] *adj.* ☐ pharmaˈzeutisch; Apotheker...: ~ *industry* Pharmaindustrie *f*; **phar·ma-**

'ceu·ti·cals *s. pl.* Arzˈneimittel *pl.*; **phar·ma'ceu·tics** [-ks] *s. pl. sg. konstr.* Pharmaˈzeutik *f*, Arzˈneimittelkunde *f*; **phar·ma·cist** [ˈfɑːməsist] *s.* **1.** Pharmaˈzeut *m*, Apoˈtheker *m*; **2.** pharmaˈzeutischer Chemiker; **phar·ma·col·o·gy** *s.* [ˌfɑːməˈkɒlədʒi] ‚Pharmakolo'gie *f*, Arzˈneimittellehre *f*; **phar·ma·co·poe·ia** [ˌfɑːməkəˈpiːə] *s.* **1.** ‚Pharmako'pöe *f*, amtliches Arzˈneibuch; **2.** Arzˈneimittelvorrat *m*; **phar·ma·cy** [ˈfɑːməsi] *s.* **1.** → *pharmaceutics*; **2.** Apoˈtheke *f*.
pha·ryn·gal [fəˈriŋɡl]; **pha·ryn·ge·al** [ˌfærinˈdʒiːl] **I** *adj. anat.* Rachen... (*-mandeln etc.; a. ling. -laut*); **II** *s. anat.* Schlundknochen *m*; **phar·yn·gi·tis** [ˌfærinˈdʒaitis] *s.* 'Rachenka‚tarr(h) *m*; **pha·ryn·go·na·sal** [-ɡəʊˈneizl] *adj.* Rachen u. Nase betreffend; **phar·ynx** [ˈfæriŋks] *s.* Schlund *m*, Rachen(höhle *f*) *m*.
phase [feiz] **I** *s.* **1.** ♐, ♄, ♈, *ast., biol., phys.* Phase *f*: *the ~s of the moon ast.* die Mondphasen; ~ *advancer* [a. ♊] *converter*] ⚡ Phasenverschieber *m*; *in* ~ (*out of* ~) ⚡ phasengleich (phasenverschoben); **2.** (Entwicklungs)Stufe *f*, Stadium *m*, Phase *f* (*a. psych.*); **3.** ✕ (Front)Abschnitt *m*; **II** *v/t.* **4.** ⚡ in Phase bringen; **5.** aufeinˈander abstimmen, ⊚ synchronisieren; **6.** stufenweise durchführen, staffeln: ~ *down* einstellen; ~ *in* stufenweise einführen; ~ *out* etc. stufenweise einstellen *od.* abwickeln *od.* auflösen, *Produkt etc.* auslaufen lassen; **III** *v/i.* **7.** ~ *out* sich stufenweise zurückziehen (*of* aus).
pH-bal·anced [ˌpiːˈeitʃˌbælənst] *adj.* ♐ pˈH-neut‚ral.
pheas·ant [ˈfeznt] *s. orn.* Faˈsan *m*; **'pheas·ant·ry** [-ri] *s.* Fasaneˈrie *f*.
phe·nic [ˈfiːnik] *adj.* ♐ karˈbolsauer, Karbol...: ~ *acid* → **phe·nol** [ˈfiːnɒl] *s.* ♐ Pheˈnol *n*, Karˈbolsäure *f*; **phe·nol·ic** [fiˈnɒlik] **I** *adj.* Phenol...: ~ *resin* ♐; **II** *s.* Pheˈnolharz *n*.
phe·nom·e·nal [fiˈnɒminl] *adj.* ☐ phänomeˈnal: a) *phls.* Erscheinungs... (*-welt etc.*), b) unglaublich, ‚toll‘; **phe·nom·e·nal·ism** [-nəlizəm] *s. phls.* Phänomeˈnalismus *m*; **phe·nom·e·non** [fiˈnɒminən] *pl.* **-na** [-nə] *s.* **1.** Phänoˈmen *n*, Erscheinung *f* (*a. phys. u. phls.*); **2.** *pl.* **-nons** *fig.* wahres Wunder; *a. infant* ~ Wunderkind *n*.
phe·no·type [ˈfiːnəʊtaip] *s. biol.* 'Phäno‚typus *m*, Erscheinungsbild *n*.
phen·yl [ˈfiːnil] *s.* Pheˈnyl *n*; **phe·nyl·ic** [fiˈnilik] *adj.* Phenyl..., pheˈnolisch: ~ *acid* → *phenol*.
phew [fjuː] *int.* puh!
pH fac·tor [ˌpiːˈeitʃ] *s.* ♐ pˈH-Wert *m*.
phi·al [ˈfaiəl] *s.* Phiˈole *f*, (*bsd.* Arzˈnei-) Fläschchen *n*, Amˈpulle *f*.
Phi Be·ta Kap·pa [ˌfaiˌbiːtəˈkæpə] *s. Am.* a) *studentische Vereinigung hervorragender Akademiker*, b) *ein Mitglied dieser Vereinigung*.
phi·lan·der [fiˈlændə] *v/i.* ‚poussieren‘, schäkern; **phi·lan·der·er** [-ərə] *s.* Schäker *m*, Schürzenjäger *m*.
phil·an·throp·ic, **phil·an·throp·i·cal** [ˌfilənˈθrɒpik(l)] *adj.* ☐ philanˈthropisch, menschenfreundlich; **phi·lan·thro·pist** [fiˈlænθrəpist] *s.* Philanthˈrop *m*, Menschenfreund *m*; **II** *adj.* → *philanthropic*; **phi·lan·thro·py** [fiˈlænθrəpi] *s.* Philanthroˈpie *f*, Menschenliebe *f*.
phi·la·tel·ic [ˌfiləˈtelik] *adj.* philateˈlistisch; **phi·lat·e·list** [fiˈlætəlist] **I** *s.* Phi-

late'list *m*; **II** *adj.* philate'listisch; **phi-lat·e·ly** [fɪ'lætəlɪ] *s.* Philate'lie *f.*

phil·har·mon·ic [ˌfɪlɑː'mɒnɪk] *adj.* phil-har'monisch (*Konzert, Orchester*): ~ **society** Philharmonie *f.*

Phi·lip·pi·ans [fɪ'lɪpɪənz] *s. pl. sg. konstr. bibl.* (Brief *m* des Paulus an die) Phi'lipper *pl.*

phi·lip·pic [fɪ'lɪpɪk] *s.* Phi'lippika *f,* Strafpredigt *f.*

Phil·ip·pine ['fɪlɪpiːn] *adj.* **1.** philip'pi-nisch, Philippinen...; **2.** Filipino...

Phi·lis·tine ['fɪlɪstaɪn] **I** *s. fig.* Phi'lister *m,* Spießbürger *m,* Spießer *m;* **II** *adj.* phi'listerhaft, spießbürgerlich; **'phi·lis-tin·ism** [-tɪnɪzəm] *s.* Phi'listertum *n,* Philiste'rei *f,* Spießbürgertum *n,* Ba-'nausentum *n.*

Phil·lips *TM* **screw·driv·er** ['fɪlɪps] *s.* Kreuzschlitzschraubendreher *m,* F -zieher *m.*

phil·o·log·i·cal [ˌfɪlə'lɒdʒɪkl] *adj.* □ philo'logisch, sprachwissenschaftlich; **phi-lol·o·gist** [fɪ'lɒlədʒɪst] *s.* Philo'loge *m,* Philo'login *f,* Sprachwissenschaftler (-in); **phi·lol·o·gy** [fɪ'lɒlədʒɪ] *s.* Philolo-'gie *f,* (Litera'tur- u.) Sprachwissen-schaft *f.*

phi·los·o·pher [fɪ'lɒsəfə] *s.* Philosoph *m* (*a. fig.* Lebenskünstler): **natural ~** Na-turforscher *m;* **~s' stone** Stein *m* der Weisen; **phil·o·soph·ic, phil·o·soph-i·cal** [ˌfɪlə'sɒfɪk(l)] *adj.* □ philo'so-phisch (*a. fig. weise, gleichmütig*); **phi-'los·o·phize** [-faɪz] *v/i.* philosophieren; **phi'los·o·phy** [-fɪ] *s.* **1.** Philoso'phie *f:* **natural ~** Naturwissenschaft *f;* **~ of his-tory** Geschichtsphilosophie; **2.** a) *a.* **of life** ('Lebens)Philoso,phie *f,* Weltan-schauung *f,* b) *fig.* (philo'sophische) Gelassenheit, c) 'Philoso'phie *f,* 'Denk-bild *n,* -mo,dell *n.*

phil·ter *Am.,* **phil·tre** *Brit.* ['fɪltə] *s.* **1.** Liebestrank *m;* **2.** Zaubertrank *m.*

phiz [fɪz] *s. sl.* Vi'sage *f,* Gesicht *n.*

phle·bi·tis [flɪ'baɪtɪs] *s.* 🗡 Venenentzün-dung *f,* Phle'bitis *f.*

phlegm [flem] *s.* **1.** *physiol.* Phlegma *n,* Schleim *m;* **2.** *fig.* Phlegma *n:* a) stump-fer Gleichmut, b) (geistige) Trägheit; **phleg·mat·ic** [fleg'mætɪk] **I** *adj.* (□ **~ally**) *physiol. u. fig.* phleg'matisch; **II** *s.* Phleg'matiker(in).

pH lev·el [ˌpiː'eɪtʃ] *s.* 🗡 p'H-Wert *m.*

pho·bi·a ['fəʊbɪə] *s. psych.* (**about**) Pho-'bie *f,* krankhafte Furcht (vor *dat.*) *od.* Abneigung (*gegen*).

Phoe·ni·cian [fɪ'nɪʃɪən] **I** *s.* **1.** Phö'nizier (-in); **2.** *ling.* Phö'nikisch *n;* **II** *adj.* **3.** phö'nizisch.

phoe·nix ['fiːnɪks] *s. myth.* Phönix *m* (*le-gendärer Vogel*), *fig. a.* Wunder *n.*

phon [fɒn] *s. phys.* Phon *n.*

phone[1] [fəʊn] *s. ling.* (Einzel)Laut *m.*

phone[2] [fəʊn] *s., v/t. u. v/i.* F → **tele-phone**

phone| book *s.* Tele'fonbuch *n;* **~ booth** *s.* Tele'fonzelle *f;* **'~card** *s.* Tele'fon-karte *f;* **'~-in** *s.* Radio, TV: *Sendung mit Hörer- bzw. Zuschauerbeteiligung per Telefon.*

pho·neme ['fəʊniːm] *s. ling.* **1.** Pho'nem *n;* **2.** → **phone**[1].

pho·net·ic [fəʊ'netɪk] *adj.* (□ **~ally**) pho'netisch, lautlich: ~ **spelling,** ~ **transcription** Lautschrift *f;* **pho·ne·ti-cian** [ˌfəʊnɪ'tɪʃn] *s.* Pho'netiker *m;* **pho'net·ics** [-ks] *s. pl. mst sg. konstr.* Pho'netik *f,* Laut(bildungs)lehre *f.*

pho·ney ['fəʊnɪ] → **phony.**

phon·ic ['fəʊnɪk] *adj.* **1.** lautlich, a'kus-tisch; **2.** pho'netisch; **3.** ☺ phonisch.

pho·no·gram ['fəʊnəgræm] *s.* Lautzei-

chen *n;* **'pho·no·graph** [-grɑːf] *s.* ☺ **1.** Phono'graph *m,* 'Sprechma,schine *f;* **2.** *Am.* Plattenspieler *m,* Grammo'phon *n;* **pho·no·graph·ic** [ˌfəʊnə'græfɪk] *adj.* (□ **~ally**) phono'graphisch.

pho·nol·o·gy [fəʊ'nɒlədʒɪ] *s. ling.* Pho-nolo'gie *f,* Lautlehre *f.*

pho·nom·e·ter [fəʊ'nɒmɪtə] *s. phys.* Phono'meter *n,* Schall(stärke)messer *m.*

pho·ny ['fəʊnɪ] F **I** *adj.* **1.** falsch, ge-fälscht, unecht; Falsch..., Schwindel..., Schein...: ~ **war** *hist.* 'Sitzkrieg *m;* **II** *s.* **2.** Schwindler(in), 'Schauspieler(in)', Scharlatan *m:* **he is** ~ *a.* der ist nicht ,echt'; **3.** Fälschung *f,* Schwindel *m.*

phos·gene ['fɒzdʒiːn] *s.* 🜍 Phos'gen *n,* Chlor'kohleno,xid *n;* **phos·phate** ['fɒsfeɪt] *s.* 🜍 **1.** Phos'phat *n:* ~ **of lime** phosphorsaurer Kalk; **2.** ✓ Phos'phat (-düngemittel) *n;* **,phos·phate-'free** *adj.* phos'phatfrei (*Waschmittel etc.*).

phos·phat·ic [fɒs'fætɪk] *adj.* 🜍 phos-'phathaltig; **phos·phide** ['fɒsfaɪd] *s.* 🜍 Phos'phid *n;* **phos·phite** ['fɒsfaɪt] *s.* **1.** 🜍 Phos'phit *n;* **2.** *min.* 'Phosphorme,tall *n;* **phos·phor** ['fɒsfə] **I** *s.* **1.** *poet.* Phosphor *m;* **2.** ☺ Leuchtmasse *f;* **II** *adj.* **3.** Phosphor...; **phos·pho·rate** ['fɒsfə-reɪt] *v/t.* 🜍 **1.** phosphorisieren; **2.** phos-phoreszierend machen; **phos·pho-resce** [ˌfɒsfə'res] *v/i.* phosphoreszieren, (nach)leuchten; **phos·pho·res·cence** [ˌfɒsfə'resns] *s.* **1.** 🜍 *phys.* Chemolu-mines'zenz *f;* **2.** *phys.* Phosphores'zenz *f,* Nachleuchten *n;* **phos·pho·res·cent** [ˌfɒsfə'resnt] *adj.* phosphoreszierend; **phos·phor·ic** [fɒs'fɒrɪk] *adj.* phos-phorsauer, -haltig, Phosphor...; **phos-pho·rous** ['fɒsfərəs] *adj.* 🜍 phos'pho-rig(sauer); **phos·pho·rus** ['fɒsfərəs] *pl.* **-ri** [-raɪ] *s.* **1.** 🜍 Phosphor *m;* **2.** *phys.* 'Leuchtphos,phore *f,* -masse *f.*

phot [fɒt] *s. phys.* Phot *n.*

pho·to ['fəʊtəʊ] F → **photograph.**

photo- [fəʊtəʊ] *in Zssgn* Photo..., Foto...: a) Licht..., b) foto'grafisch; **'~-cell** *s.* ⚡ Fotozelle *f;* **,~'chem·i·cal** *adj.* □ photo-'chemisch; **,~·com'pose** *v/t.* im Fotosatz herstellen; **'~,cop·i·er** *s.* Fotoko-'piergerät *n;* **'~,cop·y** → **photostat** 1 *u.* 3; **,~·e'lec·tric** [-təʊ-] *adj.;* **,~·e'lec·tri-cal** [-təʊ-] *adj.* □ *phys.* photoe'lek-trisch: ~ **barrier** Lichtschranke *f;* ~ **cell** Fotozelle *f;* **,~-en'grav·ing** [-təʊ-] *s.* Lichtdruck(verfahren *n*) *m;* ~ **fin·ish** *s. sport* a) Fotofinish *n,* b) äußerst knappe Entscheidung; **'☺-fit** *TM,* **~fit** (*pic-ture*) *s. Brit. Polizei:* Phan'tombild *n;* **'~-flash** (**lamp**) *s.* Blitzlicht(birne *f*) *n.*

pho·to·gen·ic [ˌfəʊtəʊ'dʒenɪk] *adj.* **1.** foto'gen, bildwirksam; **2.** *biol.* licht-erzeugend, Leucht...; **~-gram·me·try** [ˌfəʊtə'græmɪtrɪ] *s.* Photogramme'trie *f,* Messbildverfahren *n.*

pho·to·graph ['fəʊtəgrɑːf] **I** *s.* Fotogra-'fie *f,* (Licht)Bild *n,* Aufnahme *f:* **take a ~** e-e Aufnahme machen (**of** von); **II** *v/t.* fotografieren, aufnehmen, ,knip-sen'; **III** *v/i.* fotografieren; fotografiert werden: **he does not ~ well** er wird nicht gut auf den Bildern, er lässt sich schlecht fotografieren; **pho·tog·ra-pher** [fə'tɒgrəfə] *s.* Foto'graf(in); **pho-to·graph·ic** [ˌfəʊtə'græfɪk] *adj.* (□ **~ally**) **1.** foto'grafisch; **2.** *fig.* foto'gra-fisch genau; **pho·tog·ra·phy** [fə'tɒgrə-fɪ] *s.* Fotogra'fie *f,* Lichtbildkunst *f.*

pho·to·gra·vure [ˌfəʊtəgrə'vjʊə] *s.* 'Photogra,vüre *f,* Kupferlichtdruck *m;* **,pho·to'jour·nal·ism** *s.* 'Bildjourna,lis-mus *m;* **,pho·to'lith·o·graph** *typ.* **I** *s.* ,Photolithogra'phie *f* (*Erzeugnis*); **II** *v/t.*

photolithographieren; **,pho·to·li'thog-ra·phy** *s.* ,Photolithogra'phie *f* (*Ver-fahren*).

pho·tom·e·ter [fəʊ'tɒmɪtə] *s. phys.* Pho-to'meter *n,* Lichtstärkemesser *m;* **pho-'tom·e·try** [-trɪ] *s.* Lichtstärkemessung *f.*

,pho·to'mi·cro·graph *s. phot.* 'Mikrofo-togra,fie *f* (*Bild*).

,pho·to'mon·tage *s.* 'Fotomon,tage *f;* **,~'mu·ral** *s.* Riesenvergrößerung *f* (*Wandschmuck*), *a.* 'Fotota,pete *f;* **,~'off·set** *s. typ.* foto'grafischer Offset-druck *m.*

pho·ton ['fəʊtɒn] *s.* **1.** *phys.* Photon *n,* Lichtquant *n;* **2.** *opt.* Troland *n.*

'pho·to·play *s.* Filmdrama *n.*

pho·to·stat ['fəʊtəʊstæt] *phot.* **I** *s.* **1.** Fotoko'pie *f,* Ablichtung *f;* **2.** ♀ Foto-ko'piergerät *n* (*Handelsname*); **II** *v/t.* **3.** fotokopieren, ablichten; **pho·to·stat-ic** [ˌfəʊtəʊ'stætɪk] *adj.* Kopier..., Ab-lichtungs...: ~ **copy** → **photostat** 1.

,pho·to·te'leg·ra·phy *s.* 'Bildtelegra-,fie *f;* **'pho·to·type** *s. typ.* **1.** Licht-druck(bild *n,* -platte *f*) *m;* **II** *v/t.* im Lichtdruckverfahren vervielfältigen; **,pho·to'type·set** → **photocompose.**

phrase [freɪz] **I** *s.* **1.** (Rede)Wendung *f,* Redensart *f,* Ausdruck *m:* ~ **of civility** Höflichkeitsfloskel *f;* ~ **book** a) Samm-lung *f* von Redewendungen, b) Sprach-führer *m;* **2.** Phrase *f,* Schlagwort *n:* ~ **monger** Phrasendrescher *m;* **as the ~ goes** wie man so schön sagt; **3.** *ling.* a) Wortverbindung *f,* b) kurzer Satz, c) Sprechtakt *m;* **4.** ♪ Satz *m;* Phrase *f;* **II** *v/t.* **5.** ausdrücken, formulieren; **6.** ♪ phrasieren; **phra·se·ol·o·gy** [ˌfreɪzɪ-'ɒlədʒɪ] *s.* Phraseolo'gie *f* (*a. Buch*), Ausdrucksweise *f.*

phren·ic ['frenɪk] *anat.* **I** *adj.* Zwerch-fell...; **II** *s.* Zwerchfell *n.*

phre·nol·o·gist [frɪ'nɒlədʒɪst] *s.* Phre-no'loge *m;* **phre'nol·o·gy** [-dʒɪ] *s.* Phrenolo'gie *f,* Schädellehre *f.*

phthi·sis ['θaɪsɪs] *s.* Tuberku'lose *f,* Schwindsucht *f.*

phut [fʌt] **I** *int.* fft'; **II** *adj. sl.:* **go ~** a) futschgehen, b) ,platzen'.

pH val·ue [ˌpiː'eɪtʃ] *s.* 🗡 p'H-Wert *m.*

phy·col·o·gy [faɪ'kɒlədʒɪ] *s.* Algenkun-de *f.*

phyl·lox·e·ra [ˌfɪlɒk'sɪərə] *pl.* **-rae** [-riː] *s. zo.* Reblaus *f.*

phy·lum ['faɪləm] *pl.* **-la** [-lə] *s.* **1.** *bot. zo.* 'Unterab,teilung *f,* Ordnung; **2.** *biol.* Stamm *m;* **3.** *ling.* Sprachstamm *m.*

phys·ic ['fɪzɪk] **I** *s.* **1.** Arz'nei(mittel *n*) *f,* *bsd.* Abführmittel *n;* **2.** *obs.* Heilkunde *f;* **3.** *pl. sg. konstr.* Phy'sik *f;* **II** *v/t. pret. u. p.p.* **'phys·icked** [-kt] **4.** *obs.* j-n (ärztlich) behandeln; **'phys·i·cal** [-kl] **I** *adj.* □ **1.** physisch, körperlich (*a. Liebe etc.*): ~ **condition** Gesundheitszustand *m;* ~ **culture** Körperkultur *f;* ~ **educa-tion,** ~ **training** *ped.* Leibeserziehung *f;* ~ **examination** → 3; ~ **force** physische Gewalt; ~ **impossibility** absolute Un-möglichkeit; ~ **inventory** ♥ Bestands-aufnahme *f;* ~ **stock** ♥ Lagerbestand *m;* **2.** physi'kalisch; na'turwissenschaft-lich: ~ **geography** physikalische Geo-graphie; ~ **science** a) Physik *f,* b) Na-turwissenschaft(en *pl.*) *f;* **II** *s.* **3.** ärztli-che Unter'suchung, ✗ Musterung *f;* **phy·si·cian** [fɪ'zɪʃn] *s.* Arzt *m;* **'phys·i·cist** [-ɪsɪst] *s.* Physiker *m.*

,phys·i·co-'chem·i·cal [ˌfɪzɪkəʊ-] *adj.* □ physiko'chemisch.

phys·i·og·no·my [ˌfɪzɪ'ɒnəmɪ] *s.* **1.** Phy-siogno'mie *f* (*a. fig.*), Gesichtsausdruck *m*, -züge *pl.*; **2.** Physio'gnomik *f*; **phys·i'og·ra·phy** [-'ɒgrəfɪ] *s.* **1.** Physio(geo)gra'phie *f*; **2.** Na'turbeschreibung *f*; **phys·i·o·log·i·cal** [ˌfɪzɪə'lɒdʒɪkl] *adj.* □ physio'logisch; **phys·i·ol·o·gist** [-'ɒlədʒɪst] *s.* Physi'ologe *m*; **phys·i·ol·o·gy** [-'ɒlədʒɪ] *s.* Physiolo'gie *f*; **phys·i·o·ther·a·pist** [ˌfɪzɪəʊ'θerəpɪst] *s.* ✚ Physiothera'peut(in), *weitS.* Heilgymnastiker(in); **phys·i·o·ther·a·py** [ˌfɪzɪəʊ'θerəpɪ] *s.* Physiothera'pie *f*, 'Heilgym,nastik *f*.

phy·sique [fɪ'ziːk] *s.* Körperbau *m*, -beschaffenheit *f*, Konstituti'on *f*.

phy·to·gen·e·sis [ˌfaɪtəʊ'dʒenɪsɪs] *s.* ♀ Lehre *f* von der Entstehung der Pflanzen; **phy·tol·o·gy** [faɪ'tɒlədʒɪ] *s.* Pflanzenkunde *f*; **phy·to·to·my** [faɪ'tɒtəmɪ] *s.* ♀ 'Pflanzenanato,mie *f*.

pi·an·ist ['pɪənɪst] *s.* ♪ Pia'nist(in), Kla'vierspieler(in).

pi·an·o¹ [pɪ'ænəʊ] *pl.* **-os** *s.* ♪ Kla'vier *n*, Pi,ano('forte) *n*: **at** (**on**) **the ~** am (auf dem) Klavier.

pi·a·no² ['pjɑːnəʊ] ♪ **I** *pl.* **-nos** *s.* Pi'ano *n* (*leises Spiel*): **~ pedal** Pianopedal *n*; **II** *adv.* pi'ano, leise.

pi·an·o·for·te [ˌpjænəʊ'fɔːtɪ] → **piano¹**.

pi·an·o play·er 1. → **pianist; 2.** Pia'no·la *n*.

pi·az·za [pɪ'ætsə] *pl.* **-zas** (*Ital.*) *s.* **1.** öffentlicher Platz; **2.** *Am.* (große) Ve'randa.

pi·broch ['piːbrɒk; -ɒx] *s.* 'Kriegsmu,sik *f* der Bergschotten; 'Dudelsackvaria·ti,onen *pl.*

pi·ca ['paɪkə] *s. typ.* Cicero *f*, Pica *f*.

pic·a·resque [ˌpɪkə'resk] *adj.* pika'resk: **~ novel** Schelmenroman *m*.

pic·a·roon [ˌpɪkə'ruːn] *s.* **1.** Gauner *m*, Abenteurer *m*; **2.** Pi'rat *m*.

pic·a·yune [ˌpɪkɪ'juːn] *Am.* **I** *s.* **1.** *mst fig.* Pfennig *m*, Groschen *m*; **2.** *fig.* Lap'palie *f*; Tinnef *m*, *n*; **3.** *fig.* ,Null' *f* (*unbedeutender Mensch*); **II** *adj.*, *a.* ,pic·a'yun·ish [-nɪʃ] **4.** unbedeutend, schäbig; klein(lich).

pic·ca·lil·li ['pɪkəlɪlɪ] *s. pl.* Picca'lilli *pl.* (*eingemachtes, scharf gewürztes Mischgemüse*).

pic·ca·nin·ny ['pɪkənɪnɪ] **I** *s. humor.* (*bsd.* Neger)Kind *n*, Gör *n*; **II** *adj.* kindlich; winzig.

pic·co·lo ['pɪkələʊ] *pl.* **-los** *s.* ♪ Pikkoloflöte *f*; **~ pi·an·o** *s.* ♪ 'Kleinkla,vier *n*.

pick [pɪk] **I** *s.* **1.** ⊛ *a)* Spitz-, Kreuzhacke *f*, Picke *f*, Pickel *m*, *b)* ✂ (Keil)Haue *f*; **2.** Schlag *m*; **3.** Auswahl *f*, -lese *f*: **the ~ of the bunch** der (die, das) Beste von allen; **take your ~!** suchen Sie sich etwas aus!; Sie haben die Wahl!; **4.** *typ.* unreiner Buchstabe; **5.** ♪ Ernte *f*; **II** *v/t.* **6.** aufhacken, -picken: → **brain** 2, **hole** 1; **7.** Körner aufpicken; auflesen; sammeln; *Blumen, Obst* pflücken; *Beeren* abzupfen; *Hühner* rupfen; *Metall* scheiden; *Wolle* zupfen; in *der Nase* bohren; in *den Zähnen* stochern; *e-n Knochen* (ab)nagen; → **bone** 1; **10.** *Schloss* mit e-m Dietrich öffnen, ,knacken'; *j-m die Tasche* ausräumen (*Dieb*); **11.** ♪ *Am.* Banjo etc. spielen; **12.** ausfasern, zerpflücken: → **to pieces** *fig.* *Theorie etc.* zerpflücken, herunterreißen; **III** *v/i.* **13.** hacken, picke(l)n; **14.** (*lustlos*) im Essen her'umstochern; **15.** sorgfältig wählen: **~ and choose** *a.* wählerisch sein; **16.** ,sti'bitzen', stehlen; *Zssgn mit prp. u. adv.:*

pick at *v/i.* **1.** *im Essen* her'umstochern; **2.** F her'ummäkeln *od.* -nörgeln an (*dat.*); auf *j-m* her'umhacken; **~ off** *v/t.* **1.** (ab)pflücken, -rupfen; **2.** wegnehmen; **3.** (einzeln) abschießen, ,wegputzen'; **~ on** *v/i.* **1.** aussuchen, sich entscheiden für; **2.** → **pick at** 2; **~ out** *v/t.* **1.** (sich) *et. od. j-n* auswählen; **2.** ausmachen, erkennen; *fig.* her'ausfinden, -bekommen; **3.** ♪ sich *e-e Melodie auf dem Klavier etc.* zs.-suchen; **4.** *mit e-r anderen Farbe* absetzen; **~ o·ver** *v/t.* **1.** (gründlich) 'durchsehen, -gehen; **2.** (*das Beste*) auslesen; **~ up I** *v/t.* **1.** *Boden* aufhacken; **2.** aufheben, -nehmen, -lesen; in die Hand nehmen: **pick o.s. up** sich ,hochrappeln' (*a. fig.*); → **gauntlet¹** 2; **3.** *j-n im Fahrzeug* mitnehmen, abholen; **4.** F *a) j-n* ,auflesen, -gabeln, -reißen', *b)* ,hochnehmen' (*verhaften*), *c)* ,klauen' (*stehlen*); **5.** *Strickmaschen* aufnehmen; **6.** *a) Rundfunksender* ,(rein)kriegen', *b) Sendung* empfangen, aufnehmen, abhören, *c) Funkspruch etc.* auffangen; **7.** in Sicht bekommen; **8.** *fig. et.* ,mitkriegen', *Wort, Sprache etc.* ,aufschnappen'; **9.** erstehen, gewinnen: **~ a livelihood** sich mit Gelegenheitsarbeiten *etc.* durchschlagen; **~ courage** Mut fassen; **~ speed** auf Touren (*od.* in Fahrt) kommen; **II** *v/i.* **10.** sich (wieder) erholen (*a.* ✚); **11.** sich anfreunden (**with** mit); **12.** auf Touren kommen, Geschwindigkeit aufnehmen; *fig.* stärker werden.

pick-a-back ['pɪkəbæk] *adj. u. adv.* huckepack *tragen etc.*: **~ plane** ✈ Huckepackflugzeug *n*.

pick·a·nin·ny → **piccaninny**.

'pick·ax(e) *s.* (Spitz)Hacke *f*, (Beil)Pike *f*, Pickel *m*.

picked [pɪkt] *adj. fig.* ausgewählt, -gesucht, (aus)erlesen: **~ troops** ✕ Kerntruppen *pl.*

pick·er·el ['pɪkərəl] *s. ichth.* (*Brit.* junger) Hecht.

pick·et ['pɪkɪt] **I** *s.* **1.** (Holz-, Absteck-) Pfahl *m*; Pflock *m*; **2.** ✕ Vorposten *m*; **3.** Streikposten *m*; **II** *v/t.* **4.** einpfählen; **5.** an e-n Pfahl binden, aufpflocken; **6.** Streikposten aufstellen vor (*dat.*), mit Streikposten besetzen; (als Streikposten) anhalten *od.* belästigen; **7.** ✕ als Vorposten ausstellen; **III** *v/i.* **8.** Streikposten stehen.

pick·ings ['pɪkɪŋz] *s. pl.* **1.** Nachlese *f*, 'Überbleibsel *pl.*, Reste *pl.*; **2.** *a.* **~ and stealings** *a)* unehrliche Nebeneinkünfte *pl.*, *b)* Diebesbeute *f*, Fang *m*; **3.** Pro'fit *m*.

pick·le ['pɪkl] **I** *s.* **1.** Pökel *m*, Salzlake *f*, Essigsoße *f* (*zum Einlegen*); **2.** (saure) Gewürzgurke *f*; **3.** *pl.* Eingepökelte(s) *n*, Pickles *pl.*; → **mixed pickles**; **4.** ⊛ Beize *f*; **5.** F *a.* **nice** (*od.* **sad** *od.* **sorry**) **~** missliche Lage, ,böse Sache': **be in a ~** (schön) in der Patsche sitzen; **6.** F Balg *m*, *n*, Gör *n*; **II** *v/t.* **7.** einpökeln, -salzen, -legen; **8.** ⊛ *Metall* (ab)beizen; *Bleche* dekapieren: **pickling agent** Abbeizmittel *n*; **9.** ♪ *Saatgut* beizen; **'pick·led** [-ld] *adj.* **1.** gepökelt, eingesalzen; Essig..., Salz...: **~ herring** Salzhering *m*; **2.** *sl.* ,blau' (*betrunken*).

'pick·lock *s.* **1.** Einbrecher *m*; **2.** Dietrich *m*; '**~-me-up** *s.* F Schnäps-chen *n*, *a. fig.* Stärkung *f*; '**~-off** *adj.* ⊛ *Am.* 'abmon,tierbar, Wechsel...; '**~,pock·et** *s.* Taschendieb *m*; '**~-up** *s.* **1.** Ansteigen *n*; ✚ Erholung *f*: **~ (in prices)** Anziehen *n* der Preise, Hausse *f*; **2.** *mot.* Start-, Beschleunigungsvermögen *n*; **3.** *a.* **~ truck** (kleiner) Lieferwagen; **4.** *Am.* → **pick-me-up; 5.** ⊛ Tonabnehmer *m*, Pick-up *m* (*am Plattenspieler*); Empfänger *m* (*Mikrophon*); Geber *m* (*Messgerät*); **6.** *TV: a)* Abtasten *n*, *b)* Abtastgerät *n*, *c) a. Radio:* 'Aufnahme·u. Über'tragungsappara,tur *f*; **7.** ✚ *a)* Schalldose *f*, *b)* Ansprechen *n* (*Relais*); **8.** F *a)* Zufallsbekanntschaft *f*, *b)* ,Flittchen' *n*, *c)* ,Anhalter' *m*; **9.** *mst* → **dinner** *sl.* improvisierte Mahlzeit, Essen *n* aus (Fleisch)Resten; **10.** *sl. a)* Verhaftung *f*, *b)* Verhaftete(r *m*) *f*; **11.** *sl.* Fund *m*.

pick·y ['pɪkɪ] *adj.* F wählerisch.

pic·nic ['pɪknɪk] **I** *s.* **1.** *a)* Picknick *n*, *b)* Ausflug *m*; **2.** F *a)* (reines) Vergnügen, *b)* Kinderspiel *n*: **~ no ~** keine leichte Sache, kein Honiglecken; **II** *v/i.* **3.** ein Picknick *etc.* machen; picknicken.

pic·to·gram ['pɪktəʊgræm] Pikto'gramm *n*.

pic·to·ri·al [pɪk'tɔːrɪəl] **I** *adj.* □ **1.** malerisch, Maler...: **~ art** Malerei *f*; **2.** Bild(er)..., illustriert: **~ advertising** Bildwerbung *f*; **3.** *fig.* bildmäßig (*a. phot.*), -haft; **II** *s.* **4.** Illustrierte *f* (*Zeitung*).

pic·ture ['pɪktʃə] **I** *s.* **1.** *allg.*, *a. TV* Bild *n*: *(clinical)* **~** ✚ Krankheitsbild, Befund *m*; **2.** Abbildung *f*, Illustrati'on *f*, Bild *n*; **3.** Gemälde *n*, Bild *n*: **sit for one's ~** sich malen lassen; **4.** (geistiges) Bild, Vorstellung *f*: **form a ~ of s.th.** sich von *et.* ein Bild machen; **get the ~** F *et.* verstehen *od.* kapieren; **5.** *fig.* F Bild *n*, Verkörperung *f*: **he looks the very ~ of health** er sieht aus wie das blühende Leben; **be the ~ of misery** ein Bild des Jammers sein; **6.** Ebenbild *n*: **the child is the ~ of his father; 7.** *fig.* anschauliche Darstellung *od.* Schilderung (*in Worten*), Bild *n*; **8.** F bildschöne Sache *od.* Per'son: **she is a perfect ~** sie ist bildschön; **the hat is a ~** der Hut ist ein Gedicht; **9.** *fig.* F Blickfeld *n*: **be in the ~** *a)* sichtbar sein, e-e Rolle spielen, *b)* im Bilde (*informiert*) sein; **come into the ~** in Erscheinung treten; **put s.o. in the ~** j-n ins Bild setzen; **quite out of the ~** gar nicht von Interesse, ohne Belang; **10.** *phot.* Aufnahme *f*, Bild *n*; **11.** *a)* Film *m*, Streifen *m*, *b) pl.* F Kino *n*, Film *m* (*Filmvorführung od. Filmwelt*): **go to the ~s** *Brit.* ins Kino gehen; **II** *v/t.* **12.** abbilden, darstellen, malen; **13.** *fig.* anschaulich schildern, beschreiben, ausmalen; **14.** *a.* **~ to o.s.** *fig.* sich ein Bild machen von, sich *et.* ausmalen *od.* vorstellen; **15.** *s-e Empfindung etc.* spiegeln, zeigen; **III** *adj.* **16.** Bild..., Bilder...; **17.** Film...: **~ play** Filmdrama *n*; **~ book** Bilderbuch *n*; **~ card** *s.* Kartenspiel: Fi'gurenkarte *f*, Bild *n*; **~ ed·i·tor** *s.* 'Bildredak,teur *m*; **~ ,go·er** *s. Brit.* Kinobesucher(in); **~ post·card** *s.* Ansichtskarte *f*; **~ puz·zle** *s.* **1.** Vexierbild *n*; **2.** Bilderrätsel *n*.

pic·tur·esque [ˌpɪktʃə'resk] *adj.* □ malerisch (*a. fig.*).

pic·ture te·leg·ra·phy *s.* 'Bildtelegra-,fie *f*; **~ the·a·ter** *Am.*, **~ the·a·tre** *Brit.* 'Filmthe,ater *n*, Lichtspielhaus *n*, Kino *n*; **~ trans·mis·sion** *s.* 'Bildüber,tragung *f*, Bildfunk *m*; **~ tube** *s. TV* Bildröhre *f*; **~ writ·ing** *s.* Bilderschrift *f*.

pic·tur·ize ['pɪktʃəraɪz] *v/t.* **1.** *Am.* verfilmen; **2.** bebildern.

pid·dle ['pɪdl] *v/i.* **1.** (*v/t.* ver)trödeln; **2.** F ,Pi'pi machen', ,pinkeln'; **'pid·dling** [-lɪŋ] *adj.* ,lumpig'.

pidg·in ['pɪdʒɪn] *s.* **1.** *sl.* Angelegenheit *f: that is your* ~ das ist deine Sache; **2.** ~ *English* Pidginenglisch *n* (*Verkehrssprache zwischen Europäern u. Ostasiaten*); *weitS.* Kauderwelsch *n.*

pie¹ [paɪ] *s.* **1.** *orn.* Elster *f;* **2.** *zo.* Scheck(e) *m* (*Pferd*).

pie² [paɪ] *s.* **1.** ('Fleisch-, 'Obst- *etc.*)Pas,tete *f,* Pie *f:* ~ *in the sky* F a) ein ,schöner Traum', b) leere Versprechung(en); *a share in the* ~ ☂ F ein ,Stück vom Kuchen'; **~-flinging** ,Tortenschlacht' *f; it's* (*as easy as*) ~ *sl.* es ist kinderleicht; → *finger* 1; *humble* I; **2.** (Obst)Torte *f;* **3.** *pol. Am. sl.* Protekti'on *f,* Bestechung *f:* ~ *counter* ,Futterkrippe' *f;* **A** F e-e feine Sache, *ein ,gefundenes Fressen'.*

pie³ [paɪ] I *s.* **1.** *typ.* Zwiebelfisch(e *pl.*) *m;* **2.** *fig.* Durchein'ander *n;* II *v/t.* **3.** *typ.* Satz zs.-werfen; **4.** *fig.* durcheinander bringen.

pie·bald ['paɪbɔːld] I *adj.* scheckig, bunt; II *s.* scheckiges Tier; Schecke *m, f* (*Pferd*).

piece [piːs] I *s.* **1.** Stück *n: a* ~ *of land* ein Stück Land; *a* ~ *of furniture* ein Möbel(stück) *n; a* ~ *of luggage* ein Gepäckstück; *a* ~ *of wallpaper* e-e Rolle Tapete; *a* ~ je, das Stück (*im Preis*); *by the* ~ a) stückweise *verkaufen,* b) im Akkord *od.* Stücklohn *arbeiten od. bezahlen; in* ~*s* entzwei, ,kaputt'; *of a* ~ gleichmäßig; *all of a* ~ aus 'einem Guss; *be all of a* ~ *with* ganz passen zu; *break* (*od. fall*) *to* ~*s* entzweigehen, zerbrechen; *go to* ~*s* a) in Stücke gehen (*a. fig.*), b) *fig.* zs.-brechen (*Person*); *take to* ~*s* auseinander nehmen, zerlegen; *it's a* ~ *of a cake* F *fig.* es ist kinderleicht (*od.* ein Kinderspiel); → *pick* 12, *pull* 16; **2.** *fig.* Beispiel *n,* Fall *m, mst* ein(e): *a* ~ *of advice* ein Rat(schlag) *m; a* ~ *of folly* e-e Dummheit; *a* ~ *of news* e-e Neuigkeit; → *mind* 4; **3.** Teil *m* (*e-s Service etc.*): *two-*~ *set* zweiteiliger Satz; **4.** (Geld-)Stück *n,* Münze *f;* **5.** ✕ Geschütz *n;* Gewehr *n;* **6.** ✕ *a* ~ *of work* Arbeit *f,* Stück *n: a nasty* ~ *of work fig.* F ein ,fieser' Kerl, b) *paint.* Stück *n,* Gemälde *n,* c) *thea.* (Bühnen)Stück *n,* d) ♪ (Mu'sik)Stück *n,* e) (kleines) *literarisches* Werk; **7.** ('Spiel)Fi,gur *f,* Stein *m;* Schach: Offi'zier *m,* Figur *f: minor* ~*s* leichtere Figuren (*Läufer u. Springer*); **8.** F a) Stück *n* Wegs, kurze Entfernung, b) Weilchen *n;* **9.** ∨ *a.* ~ *of ass* a) ,heiße Biene', b) ,Nummer' *f* (*Koitus*); II *v/t.* **10.** *a.* ~ *up* flicken, ausbessern, zs.-stücken; **11.** verlängern, anstücken, -setzen (*on to* an *acc.*); **12.** *oft* ~ *together* zs.-setzen, -stücke(l)n (*a. fig.*); **13.** ver'vollständigen, ergänzen; ~ *goods pl.* ☂ Meter-, Schnittware *f;* **'~-meal** *adv. u. adj.* stückchenweise, all'mählich; ~ *rate s.* Ak'kordsatz *m;* ~ **wag·es** *s. pl.* Ak'kord-, Stücklohn *m;* **'~-work** *s.* Ak'kordarbeit *f;* **'~,work·er** *s.* Ak'kordarbeiter(in).

pièce de ré·sis·tance [pɪˌesdərezɪ-'stãːs] (*Fr.*) *s.* **1.** Hauptgericht *n;* **2.** *fig.* Glanzstück *n,* Krönung *f.*

pie| chart *s. Statistik:* 'Kreisdia,gramm *n;* **'~-crust** *s.* Pa'stetenkruste *f,* ungefüllte Pa'stete.

pied¹ [paɪd] *adj.* gescheckt, buntscheckig: ♫ *Piper* (*of Hamelin*) *der* Rattenfänger von Hameln.

pied² [paɪd] *pret. u. p.p. von pie³* II.

'pie|-eyed *adj. Am. sl.* ,blau', ,besoffen'; **'~-plant** *s. Am.* Rha'barber *m.*

pier [pɪə] *s.* **1.** Pier *m, f* (*feste Landungsbrücke*); **2.** Kai *m;* **3.** Mole *f,* Hafendamm *m;* (Brücken- *od.* Tor- *od.* Stütz-)Pfeiler *m;* **pier·age** ['pɪərɪdʒ] *s.* Kaigeld *n.*

pierce [pɪəs] I *v/t.* **1.** durch'bohren, -'dringen, -'stechen, -'stoßen; ⊕ lochen; ✕ durch'brechen, -'stoßen, eindringen in (*acc.*); **2.** *fig.* durch'dringen (*Kälte, Schrei, Schmerz etc.*): ~ *s.o.'s heart* j-m ins Herz schneiden; **3.** *fig.* durch'schauen, ergründen, eindringen in *Geheimnisse etc.;* II *v/i.* **4.** (ein)dringen (*into* in *acc.*) (*a. fig.*); dringen (*through* durch); **'pierc·ing** [-sɪŋ] *adj.* □ 'durchdringend, scharf, schneidend, stechend (*a. Kälte, Blick, Schmerz*); gellend (*Schrei*).

pier| glass *s.* Pfeilerspiegel *m;* **'~-head** *s.* Molenkopf *m.*

pi·er·rot ['pɪərəʊ] *s.* Pier'rot *m,* Hans'wurst *m.*

pi·e·tism ['paɪətɪzəm] *s.* **1.** Pie'tismus *m;* **2.** → *piety* 1; **3.** *contp.* Frömme'lei *f;* **'pi·e·tist** [-ɪst] *s.* **1.** Pie'tist(in); **2.** *contp.* Frömmler(in).

pi·e·ty ['paɪətɪ] *s.* **1.** Frömmigkeit *f;* **2.** Pie'tät *f,* Ehrfurcht *f* (*to* vor *dat.*).

pi·e·zo·e·lec·tric [paɪˌiːzəʊ'lektrɪk] *adj.* *phys.* pie'zoe,lektrisch.

pif·fle ['pɪfl] F I *v/i.* Quatsch reden *od.* machen; II *s.* Quatsch *m.*

pig [pɪg] I *pl.* **pigs** *od.* **coll. pig** *s.* **1.** Ferkel *n;* Schwein *n: sow in* ~ trächtiges Mutterschwein; *sucking* ~ Spanferkel; *buy a* ~ *in a poke fig.* die Katze im Sack kaufen; ~*s might fly iron.* ,man hat schon Pferde kotzen sehen'; *in a* (*od. the*) ~*'s eye! Am. sl.* Quatsch!, ,von wegen'!; **2.** *fig. contp.* a) ,Fresssack' *m,* b) ,Ekel' *n,* c) sturer Kerl, d) gieriger Kerl; **3.** *sl.* ,Bulle' *m* (*Polizist*); **4.** ⊕ a) Massel *f* (Roheisen)Barren *m,* b) Roheisen *n,* c) Block *m,* Mulde *f* (*bsd. Blei*); II *v/i.* **5.** ferkeln, frischen; **6.** *mst* ~ *it* F ,aufeinander hocken', eng zs.-hausen.

pi·geon ['pɪdʒɪn] *s.* **1.** *pl.* **-geons** *od.* **coll. -geon** Taube *f: that's not my* ~ F a) das ist nicht mein Fall, b) das ist nicht mein ,Bier'; **2.** *sl.* ,Gimpel' *m;* **3.** → *clay pigeon;* ~ *breast s.* ✿ Hühnerbrust *f;* **'~-hole** I *s.* **1.** (Ablege-, Schub-)Fach *n;* **2.** Taubenloch *n;* II *v/t.* **3.** in ein Schubfach legen, einordnen, *Akten* ablegen; **4.** *fig.* zu'rückstellen, zu den Akten legen, auf die lange Bank schieben, die Erledigung *e-r Sache* verschleppen; **5.** *fig. Tatsachen, Wissen* (ein)ordnen, klassifizieren; **6.** mit Fächern versehen; ~ *house,* ~ *loft s.* Taubenschlag *m;* **'~-,liv·ered** *adj.* feige.

pi·geon·ry ['pɪdʒɪnrɪ] *s.* Taubenschlag *m.*

pig·ger·y ['pɪgərɪ] *s.* **1.** Schweinezucht *f;* **2.** Schweinestall *m;* **3.** *fig. contp.* Saustall *m;* **pig·gish** ['pɪgɪʃ] *adj.* **1.** schweinisch, unflätig; **2.** gierig; **3.** dickköpfig; **pig·gy** ['pɪgɪ] I *s.* F **1.** Schweinchen *n:* ~ *bank* Sparschwein(chen); **2.** *Am.* Zehe *f;* II *adj.* **3.** → *piggish;* **'pig·gy·back** → *pick-a-back.*

,pig|'head·ed *adj.* □ dickköpfig, stur; ~ **i·ron** *s.* Massel-, Roheisen *n;* ⊿ **Lat·in** *s.* e-e Kindergeheimsprache.

pig·let ['pɪglɪt] *s.* Ferkel *n.*

pig·ment ['pɪgmənt] I *s.* **1.** *a. biol.* Pig'ment *n;* **2.** Farbe *f,* Farbstoff *m,* -körper *m;* II *v/t. u. v/i.* **3.** (sich) pigmentieren, (sich) färben; **'pig·men·tar·y** [-tə-

ri], *a.* **pig·men·tal** [pɪg'mentl] *adj.* Pigment...; **pig·men·ta·tion** [,pɪgmən-'teɪʃn] *s.* **1.** *biol.* Pigmentati'on *f,* Färbung *f;* **2.** ✿ Pigmentierung *f.*

pig·my ['pɪgmɪ] → *pygmy.*

'pig|·nut *s.* ♀ 'Erdka,stanie *f,* -nuss *f;* **'~-skin** *s.* **1.** Schweinehaut *f;* **2.** Schweinsleder *n;* **'~,stick·ing** *s.* **1.** Wildschweinjagd *f,* Sauhatz *f;* **2.** Schweineschlachten *n;* **'~-sty** [-staɪ] *s.* Schweinestall *m* (*a. fig.*); **'~-tail** *s.* **1.** Zopf *m;* **2.** Rolle *f* (Kau)Tabak.

pi-jaw ['paɪdʒɔː] *s. Brit. sl.* Mo'ralpredigt *f,* Standpauke *f.*

pike¹ [paɪk] *pl.* **pikes** *od. bsd. coll.* **pike** *s.* **1.** *ichth.* Hecht *m;* **2.** *Sport:* Hechtsprung *m.*

pike² [paɪk] *s.* **1.** ✕ *hist.* Pike *f,* (Lang-)Spieß *m;* **2.** (Speer- *etc.*)Spitze *f,* Stachel *m;* **3.** a) Schlagbaum *m* (*Mautstraße*), b) Maut *f,* Straßenbenutzungsgebühr *f,* c) Mautstraße *f,* gebührenpflichtige Straße; **4.** *Brit. dial.* Bergspitze *f.*

'pike·man [-mən] *s.* [*irr.*] **1.** ✕ Hauer *m;* **2.** Mauteinnehmer *m;* **3.** ✕ *hist.* Pike'nier *m.*

pik·er ['paɪkə] *s. Am. sl.* **1.** Geizhals *m;* **2.** vorsichtiger Spieler.

'pike·staff *s.: as plain as a* ~ sonnenklar.

pi·las·ter [pɪ'læstə] *s.* ⌂ Pi'laster *m,* (viereckiger) Stützpfeiler.

pil·chard ['pɪltʃəd] *s.* Sar'dine *f.*

pile¹ [paɪl] I *s.* **1.** Haufen *m,* Stoß *m,* Stapel *m* (*Akten, Holz etc.*): *a* ~ *of arms* e-e Gewehrpyramide; **2.** Scheiterhaufen *m;* **3.** großes Gebäude, Ge'bäudekom,plex *m;* **4.** F ,Haufen' *m,* ,Masse' *f* (*bsd. Geld*): *make a* (*od. one's*) ~ e-e Menge Geld machen, ein Vermögen verdienen; *make a* ~ *of money* e-e Stange Geld verdienen; **5.** ⚡ a) (gal'vanische *etc.*) Säule: *thermoelectrical* ~ Thermosäule, b) Batte-'rie *f;* **6.** *a. atomic* ~ (A'tom)Meiler *m,* Re'aktor *m;* **7.** *metall.* 'Schweiß(eisen)-pa,ket *n;* **8.** *Am. sl.* ,Schlitten' *m* (*Auto*); **9.** → *piles;* II *v/t.* **10.** *a.* ~ *up* (*od. on*) (an-, auf)häufen, (auf)stapeln, aufschichten: ~ *arms* ✕ Gewehre zs.-setzen; **11.** aufspeichern (*a. fig.*); **12.** über'häufen, -'laden (*a. fig.*): ~ *a table with food;* ~ *up* (*od. on*) *the agony* F Schrecken auf Schrecken häufen; ~ *it on* F dick auftragen; **13.** ~ *up* F a) ⚓ Schiff auflaufen lassen, b) ✈ mit *dem Flugzeug* ,Bruch machen', c) *mot. sein Auto* ka'puttfahren; III *v/i.* **14.** *mst* ~ *up* sich (auf- *od.* an)häufen, sich ansammeln *od.* stapeln (*a. fig.*); **15.** F sich (scharenweise) drängen (*into* in *acc.*); **16.** ~ *up* a) ⚓ auffahren, b) ✈ ,Bruch machen', c) *mot.* aufein'ander prallen.

pile² [paɪl] I *s.* **1.** ⊕ (Stütz)Pfahl *m,* Pfeiler *m;* Bock *m,* Joch *n e-r Brücke;* **2.** *her.* Spitzpfahl *m;* II *v/t.* **3.** auspfählen, unter'pfählen, durch Pfähle verstärken; **4.** (hin'ein)treiben *od.* (ein)rammen (*into* in *acc.*).

pile³ [paɪl] I *s.* **1.** Flaum *m;* **2.** (Woll-)Haar *n,* Pelz *m* (*des Fells*); **3.** *Weberei:* a) Samt *m,* Ve'lours *n,* b) Flor *m,* Pol *m* (*e-s Gewebes*); II *adj.* **4.** ...lach gewebt (*Teppich etc.*): *a three-*~ *carpet.*

pile| bridge *s.* (Pfahl)Jochbrücke *f;* ~ **driv·er** *s.* ⊕ **1.** (Pfahl)Ramme *f;* **2.** Rammklotz *m;* ~ **dwell·ing** *s.* Pfahlbau *m;* ~ **fab·ric** *s.* Samtstoff *m; pl.* Polgewebe *pl.*

piles [paɪlz] *s. pl.* ✿ Hämorr(ho)'iden *pl.*

'pile-up *s. mot.* 'Massenkarambo,lage *f.*

pil·fer ['pɪlfə] *v/t. u. v/i.* stehlen, sti'bitzen; **'pil·fer·age** [-ərɪdʒ] s. Diebe'rei f; **'pil·fer·er** [-ərə] s. Dieb(in).

pil·grim ['pɪlgrɪm] s. **1.** Pilger(in), Wallfahrer(in); **2.** fig. Pilger m, Wanderer m; **3.** ♀ (pl. a. ♀ **Fathers**) hist. Pilgervater m; **'pil·grim·age** [-mɪdʒ] **I** s. **1.** Pilger-, Wallfahrt f (a. fig.); **2.** fig. lange Reise; **II** v/i. **3.** pilgern, wallfahren.

pill [pɪl] **I** s. **1.** Pille f (a. fig.), Ta'blette f: **swallow the** ~ die bittere Pille schlucken, in den sauren Apfel beißen; ~ **popper** F Pillenschlucker m; → **gild²** 2; **2.** sl. ,Brechmittel' n, ,Ekel' n (Person); **3.** sport sl. Ball m; Brit. a. Billard n; **4.** ✕ sl. od. humor. ,blaue Bohne' (Gewehrkugel), ,Ei' n, ,Koffer' m (Granate, Bombe); **5.** sl. ,Stäbchen' n (Zigarette); **6. the** ~ die (Anti'baby-) Pille: **be on the** ~ die Pille nehmen; **II** v/t. **7.** sl. bei e-r Wahl durchfallen lassen.

pil·lage ['pɪlɪdʒ] **I** v/t. **1.** (aus)plündern; **2.** rauben, erbeuten; **II** v/i. **3.** plündern; **III** s. **4.** Plünderung f, Plündern n; **5.** Beute f.

pil·lar ['pɪlə] **I** s. **1.** Pfeiler m, Ständer m (a. Reitsport): ~ **of coal** ⚒ Kohlenpfeiler; **run from** ~ **to post** fig. von Pontius zu Pilatus laufen; **2.** △ (a. weitS. Luft-, Rauch- etc.)Säule f; **3.** fig. Säule f, (Haupt)Stütze f: **the** ~**s of society** (**wisdom**) die Säulen der Gesellschaft (der Weisheit); **he was a** ~ **of strength** er stand da wie ein Fels in der Brandung; **4.** ◎ Stütze f, Sup'port m, Sockel m; **II** v/t. **5.** mit Pfeilern od. Säulen stützen od. schmücken; **'~·box** s. Brit. Briefkasten m (in Säulenform).

pil·lared ['pɪləd] adj. **1.** mit Säulen od. Pfeilern (versehen); **2.** säulenförmig.

'pill·box s. **1.** Pillenschachtel f; **2.** ✕ sl. Bunker m, 'Unterstand m.

pil·lion ['pɪljən] s. **1.** leichter (Damen-) Sattel; **2.** Sattelkissen n; **3.** a. ~ **seat** mot. Soziussitz m: **ride** ~ auf dem Soziussitz (mit)fahren; '~·**rid·er** s. Soziusfahrer(in).

pil·lo·ry ['pɪlərɪ] **I** s. (**in the** ~ am) Pranger m (a. fig.); **II** v/t. an den Pranger stellen; fig. anprangern.

pil·low ['pɪləʊ] **I** s. **1.** (Kopf)Kissen n, Polster n: **take counsel of one's** ~ fig. die Sache beschlafen; **2.** ◎ (Zapfen)Lager n, Pfanne f; **II** v/t. **3.** (auf ein Kissen) betten, stützen (**on** auf acc.): ~ **up** hoch betten; '~·**case** s. (Kopf)Kissenbezug m; ~ **fight** s. Kissenschlacht f; ~ **lace** s. Klöppel-, Kissenspitzen pl.; ~ **slip** → **pillowcase**.

pi·lose ['paɪləʊs] adj. ♀, zo. behaart.

pi·lot ['paɪlət] **I** s. **1.** ⚓ Lotse m: **drop the** ~ fig. den Lotsen von Bord schicken; **2.** ✈ Flugzeug-, Bal'lonführer m, Pi'lot m: ~**'s licence** Flug-, Pilotenschein m; **second** ~ Kopilot m; **3.** fig. a) Führer m, Wegweiser m, b) Berater m; **4.** ◎ a) Be'tätigungsele‚ment n, b) Führungszapfen m; **5.** → a) **pilot program(me)**, b) **pilot film**; **II** v/t. **6.** ⚓ lotsen (a. mot. u. fig.), steuern: ~ **through** durchlotsen (a. fig.); **7.** ✈ steuern, fliegen; **8.** bsd. fig. führen, lenken, leiten; **III** adj. **9.** Versuchs..., Pilot...; **10.** Hilfs-...: ~ **parachute**; **11.** Steuer..., Kontroll..., Leit...: ~ **relay** Steuer-, Kontrollrelais n; '**pi·lot·age** [-tɪdʒ] s. **1.** ⚓ Lotsen(kunst f) n: **cer·tificate of** ~ Lotsenpatent n; **2.** Lotsengeld n; **3.** ✈ a) Flugkunst f, b) 'Bodennavigati‚on f; **4.** fig. Leitung f, Führung f.

pi·lot| bal·loon s. ✈ Pi'lotbal‚lon m; ~ **boat** s. Lotsenboot n; ~ **burn·er** s. ◎

Zündbrenner m; ~ **cloth** s. dunkelblauer Fries; ~ **en·gine** s. 🚂 'Leerfahrtlokomo‚tive f; ~ **film** s. Pi'lotfilm m; ~ **in·jec·tion** s. mot. Voreinspritzung f; ~ **in·struc·tor** s. ✈ Fluglehrer(in); ~ **jet** s. ◎ Leerlaufdüse f; ~ **lamp** s. ◎ Kon'trollampe f.

pi·lot·less ['paɪlətlɪs] adj. führerlos, unbemannt: ~ **airplane**.

pi·lot| light s. **1.** → **pilot burner**; **2.** → **pilot lamp**; ~ **of·fi·cer** s. ✕ Fliegerleutnant m; ~ **plant** s. **1.** Versuchsanlage f; **2.** Musterbetrieb m; ~ **pro·gram(me** Brit.) s. Radio, TV: Pi'lotsendung f; ~ **pro·ject** s., ~ **scheme** s. Pi'lot-, Ver'suchspro‚jekt n; ~ **stud·y** s. Pi'lotstudie f; ~ **train·ee** s. Flugschüler (-in); ~ **valve** s. ◎ 'Steuerven‚til n.

pi·lous ['paɪləs] → **pilose**.

pil·ule ['pɪljuːl] s. kleine Pille.

pi·men·to [pɪ'mentəʊ] pl. **-tos** s. ♀ bsd. Brit. **1.** kleine rote Paprikaschote, Spanischer Pfeffer; **2.** Pi'ment m, n, Nelkenpfeffer m; **3.** Pi'mentbaum m; **4.** leuchtendes Rot; **pi·mi·en·to** [‚pɪmi-'entəʊ] pl. **-tos** → **pimento** 1–3.

pimp [pɪmp] **I** s. a) Kuppler m, b) Zuhälter m; **II** v/i. Kuppler od. Zuhälter sein.

pim·per·nel ['pɪmpənel] s. ♀ Pimper'nell m.

pim·ple ['pɪmpl] **I** s. Pustel f, (Haut)Pickel m; **II** v/i. pickelig werden; '**pim·pled** [-ld], '**pim·ply** [-lɪ] adj. pickelig.

pin [pɪn] **I** s. **1.** (Steck)Nadel f: ~**s and needles** ,Kribbeln' n (in eingeschlafenen Gliedern); **I've got** ~**s and needles in my left leg** mir ist das linke Bein ,eingeschlafen'; **sit on** ~**s and needles** fig. wie auf Kohlen sitzen; **I don't care a** ~ das ist mir völlig schnuppe; **2.** (Schmuck-, Haar-, Hut)Nadel f: **scarf** ~ Vorstecknadel; **3.** (Ansteck)Nadel f, Abzeichen n; **4.** ◎ Pflock m, Dübel m, Bolzen m, Zapfen m, Stift m: **split** ~ Splint m; ~ **with thread** Gewindezapfen; ~ **bearing** Nadel-, Stiftlager n; **5.** ◎ Dorn m; **6.** a. **drawing** ~ Brit. Reißnagel m, -zwecke f; **7.** a. **clothes-** ~ Wäscheklammer f; **8.** a. **rolling** ~ Nudel-, Wellholz n; **9.** F ,Stelzen' pl. (Beine): **that knocked him off his** ~**s** das hat ihn ‚umgehauen'; **10.** ♪ Wirbel m (Streichinstrument); **11.** a) Kegelsport: Kegel m, b) Bowling: Pin m; **II** v/t. **12.** (an)heften, -stecken, befestigen (**to, on** an acc.): ~ **up** auf-, hochstecken; **one's faith on** sein Vertrauen auf j-n setzen; ~ **one's hopes on** s-e (ganze) Hoffnung setzen auf (acc.); ~ **a murder on** s.o. F j-m e-n Mord ‚anhängen'; **13.** pressen, drücken, heften (**against, to** gegen, an acc.), festhalten; **14.** a. ~ **down** a) zu Boden pressen, b) fig. j-n festnageln (**to** auf et.), e-e Aussage etc.), c) ✕ Feindkräfte fesseln (a. Schach), d) et. genau bestimmen od. definieren; **15.** ◎ verbolzen, -dübeln, -stiften.

pin·a·fore ['pɪnəfɔː] s. (Kinder)Lätzchen n, (-)Schürze f.

'pin| ball ma·chine s. Flipper m (Spielautomat); ~ **bit** s. ◎ Bohrspitze f; ~ **bolt** s. Federbolzen m.

pince-nez ['pæːnsneɪ] (Fr.) s. Kneifer m, Klemmer m.

pin·cer ['pɪnsə] adj. Zangen...: ~ **movement** ✕ Zangenbewegung f; '**pin·cers** [-əz] s. pl. **1.** (Kneif-, Beiß)Zange f: **a pair of** ~ eine Kneifzange; **2.** ♒, typ. Pin'zette f; **3.** zo. Krebsschere f.

pinch [pɪntʃ] **I** v/t. **1.** zwicken, kneifen, (ein)klemmen, quetschen: ~ **off** ab-

kneifen; **2.** beengen, einengen, -zwängen; fig. (be)drücken, beengen, beschränken: **be** ~**ed for time** wenig Zeit haben; **be** ~**ed** in Bedrängnis sein, Not leiden, knapp sein (**for, in, of** an dat.); **be** ~**ed for money** knapp bei Kasse sein; ~**ed circumstances** beschränkte Verhältnisse; **3.** fig. quälen: **be** ~**ed with hunger** ausgehungert sein; **a** ~**ed face** ein spitzes od. abgehärmtes Gesicht; **4.** sl. et. ‚klauen' (stehlen); **5.** sl. j-n ‚schnappen' (verhaften); **II** v/i. **6.** drücken, kneifen, zwicken: ~**ing want** drückende Not; → **shoe** 1; **7.** fig. a. ~ **and scrape** knausern, darben, sich nichts gönnen; **III** s. **8.** Kneifen n, Zwicken n; **9.** fig. Druck m, Qual f, Not(lage) f: **at a** ~ im Notfall; **if it comes to a** ~ wenn es zum Äußersten kommt; **10.** Prise f (Tabak etc.); **11.** Quäntchen n, (kleines) bisschen: **a** ~ **of butter**; **with a** ~ **of salt** fig. mit Vorbehalt; **12.** sl. Festnahme f, Verhaftung f.

pinch·beck ['pɪntʃbek] **I** s. **1.** Tombak m, Talmi n (a. fig.); **II** adj. **2.** Talmi... (a. fig.); **3.** unecht.

'pinch| hit v/i. [irr. → **hit**] Am. Baseball u. fig. einspringen (**for** für); '~·**hit·ter** s. Am. Ersatz(mann) m.

'pinch·pen·ny I adj. knick(e)rig; **II** s. knick(e)riger Mensch, Knicker m.

'pin·cush·ion s. Nadelkissen n.

pine¹ [paɪn] s. **1.** ♀ Kiefer f, Föhre f, Pinie f; **2.** Kiefernholz n; **3.** F Ananas f.

pine² [paɪn] v/i. **1.** sich sehnen, schmachten (**after, for** nach); **2.** mst ~ **away** verschmachten, vor Gram vergehen; **3.** sich grämen od. abhärmen (**at** über acc.).

pin·e·al gland ['paɪnɪəl] s. anat. Zirbeldrüse f.

'pine| ap·ple s. **1.** ♀ Ananas f; **2.** ✕ sl. a) 'Handgra‚nate f, b) (kleine) Bombe; ~ **cone** s. ♀ Kiefernzapfen m; ~ **marten** s. zo. Baummarder m; ~ **nee·dle** s. ♀ Fichtennadel f; ~ **oil** s. Kiefernöl n.

pine| tar s. Kienteer m; ~ **tree** → **pine¹** 1.

ping [pɪŋ] **I** v/i. **1.** pfeifen (Kugel), schwirren (Mücke etc.); mot. klingeln; **II** s. **2.** Peng n; **3.** Pfeifen n, Schwirren n; mot. Klingeln n; '~·**pong** [-pɒŋ] s. Tischtennis n.

'pin·head s. **1.** (Steck)Nadelkopf m; **2.** fig. Kleinigkeit f; **3.** F Dummkopf m; '~·**hole** s. **1.** Nadelloch n; **2.** kleines Loch (a. opt.): ~ **camera** Lochkamera f.

pin·ion¹ ['pɪnjən] s. ◎ **1.** Ritzel n, Antriebs(kegel)rad n: **gear** ~ Getriebezahnrad n; ~ **drive** Ritzelantrieb m; **2.** Kammwalze f.

pin·ion² ['pɪnjən] **I** s. **1.** orn. Flügelspitze f; **2.** orn. (Schwung)Feder f; **3.** poet. Schwinge f, Fittich m; **II** v/t. **4.** die Flügel stutzen (dat.) (a. fig.); **5.** fesseln (**to** an acc.).

pink¹ [pɪŋk] **I** s. **1.** ♀ Nelke f: **plumed** (od. **feathered**) ~ Federnelke; **2.** Blassrot n, Rosa n; **3.** bsd. Brit. (scharlach-) roter Jagdrock; **4.** pol. Am. sl. ,Rotangehauchte(r)' m, Sa'lonbolsche‚wist m; **5.** fig. Gipfel m, Krone f, höchster Grad: **in the** ~ **of health** bei bester Gesundheit; **the** ~ **of perfection** die höchste Vollendung; **be in the** ~ (**of condition**) in ,Hochform' sein; **II** adj. **6.** rosa(farben), blassrot; ~ **slip** ,blauer Brief', Kündigungsschreiben n; **7.** pol. sl. ,rötlich', kommu'nistisch angehaucht.

pink² [pɪŋk] v/t. **1.** a. ~ **out** auszacken: ~**ing shears** pl. Zickzackschere f; **2.** durch'bohren, -'stechen.

pink³ [pɪŋk] *s.* ⚓ Pinke *f* (*Boot*).

pink⁴ [pɪŋk] *v/i.* klopfen (*Motor*).

pink·ish ['pɪŋkɪʃ] *adj.* rötlich (*a. pol. sl.*), blassrosa.

pin mon·ey *s.* (*a.* selbst verdientes) Taschengeld (*der Frau*).

pin·na ['pɪnə] *pl.* **-nae** [-niː] *s.* **1.** *anat.* Ohrmuschel *f*; **2.** *zo.* a) Feder *f*, Flügel *m*, b) Flosse *f*; **3.** ♀ Fieder(blatt *n*) *f*.

pin·nace ['pɪnɪs] *s.* ⚓ Pi'nasse *f*.

pin·na·cle ['pɪnəkl] *s.* **1.** △ a) Spitzturm *m*, b) Zinne *f*; **2.** (Fels-, Berg)Spitze *f*, Gipfel *m*; **3.** *fig.* Gipfel *m*, Spitze *f*, Höhepunkt *m*.

pin·nate ['pɪnɪt] *adj.* gefiedert.

pin·ni·grade ['pɪnɪgreɪd], '**pin·ni·ped** [-ped] *zo.* **I** *adj.* flossen-, schwimmfüßig; **II** *s.* Flossen-, Schwimmfüßer *m*.

pin·nule ['pɪnjuːl] *s.* **1.** Federchen *n*; **2.** *zo.* Flössel *n*; **3.** ♀ Fiederblättchen *n*.

pin·ny ['pɪnɪ] F → *pinafore*.

pi·noch·le, **pi·noc·le** ['piːnʌkl] *s. Am.* Bi'nokel *n* (*Kartenspiel*).

'**pin·point** **I** *v/t.* Ziel genau festlegen *od.* lokalisieren *od.* bombardieren, *fig. et.* genau bestimmen; **II** *adj.* genau, Punkt...: ~ **bombing** Bombenpunktwurf *m*; ~ **strike** ✠ Schwerpunktstreik *m*; ~ **target** Punktziel *n*; '~**prick** *s.* **1.** Nadelstich *m* (*a. fig.*): *policy of* ~*s* Politik *f* der Nadelstiche; **2.** *fig.* Stiche'lei *f*, spitze Bemerkung; '~**striped** *adj.* mit Nadelstreifen (*Anzug*).

pint [paɪnt] *s.* **1.** Pint *n* (*Brit.* 0,57, *Am.* 0,47 *Liter*); **2.** F Halbe *f* (*Bier*); '**pint**- **-size(d)** *adj.* F winzig.

pin·tle ['pɪntl] *s.* **1.** ⚙ (Dreh)Bolzen *m*; **2.** *mot.* Düsennadel *f* -zapfen *m*; **3.** ⚓ Fingerling *m*, Ruderhaken *m*.

pin·to ['pɪntəʊ] *pl.* **-tos** *s. Am.* Scheck(e) *m*, Schecke *f* (*Pferd*).

'**pin-up** (**girl**) *s.* Pin-'up-Girl *n*.

pi·o·neer [ˌpaɪə'nɪə] **I** *s.* **1.** ✠ Pio'nier *m*; **2.** *fig.* Pio'nier *m*, Bahnbrecher *m*, Vorkämpfer *m*, Wegbereiter *m*; **II** *v/i.* **3.** *fig.* den Weg bahnen, bahnbrechende Arbeit leisten; **III** *v/t.* **4.** den Weg bahnen für (*a. fig.*); **IV.** *adj.* **5.** Pionier...: ~ *work*; **6.** *fig.* bahnbrechend, wegbereitend, Versuchs..., erst.

pi·ous ['paɪəs] *adj.* □ **1.** fromm (*a. iro.*), gottesfürchtig: ~ *fraud* (*wish*) *fig.* frommer Betrug (Wunsch); ~ *effort* F gut gemeinter Versuch; **2.** lieb (*Kind*).

pip¹ [pɪp] *s.* **1.** *vet.* Pips *m* (*Geflügelkrankheit*); **2.** *Brit.* F miese Laune: *he gives me the* ~ er geht mir auf den ,Wecker'.

pip² [pɪp] *s.* **1.** Auge *n* (*auf Spielkarten*), Punkt *m* (*auf Würfeln etc.*); **2.** (Obst-) Kern *m*; **3.** ✠ *bsd. Brit. sl.* Stern *m* (*Rangabzeichen*); **4.** *Radar*: Blip *m* (*Bildspur*); **5.** *Brit. Radio*: Ton *m* (*Zeitzeichen*).

pip³ [pɪp] *Brit.* F **I** *v/t.* **1.** 'durchfallen lassen (*bei e-r Wahl etc.*); **2.** *fig.* knapp besiegen, im Ziel abfangen; **3.** ,abknallen' (*erschießen*); **II** *v/i.* **4.** a. ~ *out* ,abkratzen' (*sterben*).

pipe [paɪp] **I** *s.* **1.** ⚙ a) Rohr *n*, Röhre *f*, b) (Rohr)Leitung *f*; **2.** (Tabaks)Pfeife *f*: *put that in your* ~ *and smoke it* F lass dir das gesagt sein; **3.** ♪ Pfeife *f* (*Flöte*); Orgelpfeife *f*, ('Holz)Blasin,strument *n*; *mst pl.* Dudelsack *m*; **4.** a) Pfeifen *n* (*e-s Vogels*), Piep(s)en *n*, b) Pfeifenton *m*, c) Stimme *f*; **5.** F Luftröhre *f*: *clear one's* ~ sich räuspern; **6.** *metall.* Lunker *m*; **7.** ✠ (Wetter)Lutte *f*; **8.** ♀ Pipe *f* (*Weinfass = Brit.* 477,3, *Am.* 397,4 *Liter*); **II** *v/t.* **9.** (durch Röhren, *weitS.* durch Kabel) leiten, *weitS. a.* schleusen, *a.* e-e Radiosendung über-

'tragen: ~*d* *music* Musik *f* aus dem Lautsprecher, Musikberieselung *f*; **10.** Röhren *od.* e-e Rohrleitung legen in (*acc.*); **11.** pfeifen, flöten; *Lied* anstimmen, singen; **12.** quieken, piepsen; **13.** ⚓ *Mannschaft* zs.-pfeifen; **14.** *Schneiderei*: paspelieren, mit Biesen besetzen; **15.** *Torte etc.* mit feinem Guss verzieren, spritzen; **16.** ~ *one's eye* F ,flennen', weinen; **III** *v/i.* **17.** pfeifen (*a. Wind etc.*), flöten; piep(s)en: ~ *down* *sl.* ,die Luft anhalten', ,die Klappe halten'; ~ *up* loslegen, anfangen; ~ *bowl* *s.* Pfeifenkopf *m*; ~ *burst* *s.* Rohrbruch *m*; ~ *clamp* *s.* ⚙ Rohrschelle *f*; '~*clay* **I** *s.* **1.** *min.* Pfeifenton *m*; **2.** ✠ *fig.* ,Kom'miss' *m*; **II** *v/t.* **3.** mit Pfeifenton weißen; ~ *clip* *s.* ⚙ Rohrschelle *f*; ~ *dream* *s.* F Luftschloss *n*, Hirngespinst *n*; ~ *fit·ter* *s.* ⚙ Rohrleger *m*; '~*line* *s.* **1.** Rohrleitung *f*; *für Erdöl, Erdgas*: Pipeline *f*: *in the* ~ *fig.* in Vorbereitung (*Pläne etc.*), im Kommen (*Entwicklung etc.*); **2.** *fig.* ,Draht' *m*, (geheime) Verbindung *f* (*Informati'ons*)Quelle; **3.** (*bsd.* Ver'sorgungs)Sy,stem *n*.

pip·er ['paɪpə] *s.* Pfeifer *m*: *pay the* ~ *fig.* die Zeche bezahlen, *weitS.* der Dumme sein.

pipe rack *s.* Pfeifenständer *m*; ~ *tongs* *s. pl.* ⚙ Rohrzange *f*.

pi·pette [pɪ'pet] *s.* 🜊 Pi'pette *f*.

pipe wrench *s.* ⚙ Rohrzange *f*.

pip·ing ['paɪpɪŋ] **I** *s.* **1.** ⚙ a) Rohrleitung *f*, -netz *n*, Röhrenwerk *n*, b) Rohrverlegung *f*; **2.** *metall.* a) Lunker *m*, b) Lunkerbildung *f*; **3.** Pfeifen, Piep(s)en *n*; Pfiff *m*; **4.** *Schneiderei*: Paspel *f*, (*an Uniformen*) Biese *f*; **5.** (feiner) Zuckerguss, Verzierung *f* (*Kuchen*); **II** *adj.* **6.** pfeifend, schrill; **7.** friedlich, i'dyllisch (*Zeit*); **III** *adv.* **8.** ~ *hot* siedend heiß, *fig.* ,brühwarm'.

pip·pin ['pɪpɪn] *s.* **1.** Pippinapfel *m*; **2.** *sl.* a) ,tolle Sache', b) ,toller Kerl'.

'**pip·squeak** *s.* F ,Grashüpfer' *m*, ,Würstchen' *n* (*Person*).

pi·quan·cy ['piːkənsɪ] *s.* Pi'kantheit *f*, *das* Pi'kante; '**pi·quant** [-nt] *adj.* □ pi'kant (*a. fig.*).

pique [piːk] **I** *v/t.* **1.** (auf)reizen, sticheln, ärgern, *j-s Stolz etc.* verletzen: *be* ~*d at* über *et.* pikiert *od.* verärgert sein; **2.** *Neugier etc.* reizen, wecken; **3.** ~ *o.s.* (*on*) sich *et.* einbilden (auf *acc.*), sich brüsten (mit); **II** *s.* **4.** Groll *m*; Gereiztheit *f*, Gekränktsein *n*, Ärger *m*.

pi·qué ['piːkeɪ] *s.* Pi'kee *m* (*Gewebe*).

pi·quet [pɪ'ket] *s.* Pi'kett *n* (*Kartenspiel*).

pi·ra·cy ['paɪərəsɪ] *s.* **1.** Pirate'rie *f*, Seeräube'rei *f*; **2.** Plagi'at *n*, *bsd.* a) Raubdruck *m*, b) Raubpressung *f* (*e-r Schallplatte*); **3.** Pa'tentverletzung *f*; **pi·rate** ['paɪərət] **I** *s.* **1.** a) Pi'rat *m*, Seeräuber *m*, b) Seeräuberschiff *n*; **2.** Plagi'ator *m*, *bsd.* a) Raubdrucker *m*, b) Raubpresser *m* (*von Schallplatten*); **II** *adj.* **3.** Piraten...: ~ *ship*; **4.** 🜊 Raub...: ~ *copy* Raubkopie *f*; ~ *edition* Raubdruck *m*; **5.** Schwarz...: ~ *listener*; ~ (*radio*) *station* Piraten-, Schwarzsender *m*; **III** *v/t.* **6.** kapern, (aus)plündern (*a. weitS.*); **7.** a) plagiieren, *bsd.* unerlaubt nachdrucken, b) e-e 'Raubko,pie machen von; **pi·rat·i·cal** [paɪ'rætɪkl] *adj.* □ **1.** (see-)räuberisch, Piraten...; **2.** ~ *edition* Raubdruck *m*.

pi·rogue [pɪ'rəʊg] *s.* Boot: Einbaum *m*, Kanu *n*.

pir·ou·ette [ˌpɪru'et] **I** *s.* Tanz etc.: Pi'rou'ette *f*; **II** *v/i.* pirouettieren.

Pis·ces ['pɪsiːz] *s. pl. ast.* **1.** Fische *pl.*;

2. *Person*: ein Fisch *m*.

pis·ci·cul·ture ['pɪsɪkʌltʃə] *s.* Fischzucht *f*; **pis·ci·cul·tur·ist** [ˌpɪsɪ'kʌltʃərɪst] *s.* Fischzüchter *m*.

pish [pɪʃ] *int.* **1.** pfui!; **2.** pah!

pi·si·form ['paɪsɪfɔːm] *adj.* erbsenförmig, Erbsen...

piss [pɪs] *sl.* **I** *v/i.* ,pissen', ,pinkeln': ~ *on s.th. fig.* ,auf *et.* scheißen'; ~ *off!* verpiss dich!; **II** *v/t.* ,be-, anpissen': ~ *the bed* ins Bett pinkeln; **III** *s.* ,Pisse' *f*; **piss art·ist** *s. Brit.* V **1.** Säufer(in); **2.** ,Niete' *f*; **3.** Großmaul *n*; **4.** ,Arsch(loch *n*) *m*; **pissed** [-st] *adj. sl.* **1.** ,blau', besoffen; **2.** ~ *off* ,(stock)sauer'.

pis·tach·i·o [pɪ'stɑːʃɪəʊ] *pl.* **-i·os** *s.* ♀ Pi'stazie *f*.

piste [piːst] *s.* (Ski)Piste *f*.

pis·til ['pɪstɪl] *s.* ♀ Pi'still *n*, Stempel *m*, Griffel *m*; '**pis·til·late** [-lət] *adj.* mit Stempel(n), weiblich (*Blüte*).

pis·tol ['pɪstl] *s.* Pi'stole *f* (*a. phys.*): *hold a* ~ *to s.o.'s head fig.* j-m die Pistole auf die Brust setzen; ~ *point s.*: *at* ~ mit vorgehaltener Pistole; ~ *shot* *s.* **1.** Pi'stolenschuss *m*; **2.** *Am.* Pi'stolenschütze *m*.

pis·ton ['pɪstən] *s.* **1.** ⊙ Kolben *m*: ~ *engine* Kolbenmotor *m*; **2.** ⊙ (Druck-) Stempel *m*; ~ *dis·place·ment* *s.* Kolbenverdrängung *f*, Hubraum *m*; ~ *rod* *s.* Kolben-, Pleuelstange *f*; ~ *stroke* *s.* Kolbenhub *m*.

pit¹ [pɪt] **I** *s.* **1.** Grube *f* (*a. anat.*): *ref-use* ~ Müllgrube; ~ *of the stomach* Magengrube; *sl. the* ~*s* das Letzte, Mist *m*; **2.** Abgrund *m* (*a. fig.*): (*bottomless*) ~, ~ (*of hell*) (Abgrund der) Hölle *f*, Höllenschlund *m*; **3.** ✠ a) (*bsd.* Kohlen)Grube *f*, Zeche *f*, b) (*bsd.* Kohlen)Schacht *m*; **4.** ♪ (*Rüben- etc.*)Miete *f*; **5.** ⊙ a) Gießerei: Dammgrube *f*, b) Abstichherd *m*, Schlackengrube *f*; **6.** *thea.* a) *bsd. Brit.* Par'kett *n*, b) Or'chestergraben *m*; **7.** *mot. Sport*: Box *f*: ~ *stop* Boxenstopp *m*; **8.** ✠ *Am.* Börse *f*, Maklerstand *m*: *grain* ~ Getreidebörse; **9.** ♪ (Blattern-, Pocken)Narbe *f*; **10.** ⊙ Rostgrübchen *n*; **II** *v/t.* **11.** Löcher *od.* Vertiefungen bilden in (*dat.*) *od.* graben in (*acc.*); ⊙ an-, zerfressen (*Korrosion*); ♪ mit Narben bedecken; ~*ted with smallpox* pockennarbig; **12.** ♪ *Rüben etc.* einmieten; **13.** (*against*) a) feindlich gegen-'überstellen (*dat.*), b) j-n ausspielen (gegen), c) s-e Kraft etc. messen (mit), *Argument* ins Feld führen (gegen); **III** *v/i.* **14.** Löcher *od.* Vertiefungen bilden; ♪ narbig werden; ⊙ sich festfressen (*Kolben*).

pit² [pɪt] *Am.* **I** *s.* (Obst)Stein *m*; **II** *v/t.* entsteinen.

pit·a *bsd. Am.* → *pitta*.

pit-a-pat [ˌpɪtə'pæt] **I** *adv.* ticktack (*Herz*); klippklapp (*Schritte*); **II** *s.* Getrappel *n*, Getrippel *n*.

pitch¹ [pɪtʃ] **I** *s.* Pech *n*; **II** *v/t.* (ver)pichen, teeren (*a.* ⚓).

pitch² [pɪtʃ] **I** *s.* **1.** Wurf *m* (*a. sport*): *queer s.o.'s* ~ F j-m ,die Tour vermasseln', j-m e-n Strich durch die Rechnung machen; *what's the* ~*?* *Am. sl.* was ist los?; **2.** F (Waren)Angebot *n*; **3.** ⚓ Stampfen *n*; **4.** Neigung *f*, Gefälle *n* (*Dach etc.*); **5.** ⊙ a) Teilung *f* (*Gewinde, Zahnrad*), b) Schränkung *f* (*Säge*), c) Steigung *f* (*Luftschraube* ✔); **6.** ♪ a) Tonhöhe *f*, b) (*absolute*) Stimmung *e-s Instruments*, c) Nor'malstimmung *f*, Kammerton *m*: *above* ~ zu hoch; *have absolute* ~ das absolute Gehör haben; *sing true to* ~ tonrein singen; **7.** Grad *m*, Stufe *f*, Höhe *f* (*a. fig.*); *fig.* höchster Grad, Gipfel *m*: **to the highest ~** aufs Äußerste; **8.** ✝ a) Stand *m e-s Händlers*, b) *sl.* Anpreisung *f*, Verkaufsgespräch *n*, c) *sl.* ‚Platte‘ *f*, ‚Masche‘ *f*; **9.** *sport Brit.* Spielfeld *n*; *Kricket:* (Mittel)Feld *n*; **II** *v/t.* **10.** (*gezielt*) werfen (*a. sport*), schleudern; *Golf: den Ball* heben (*hoch schlagen*); **11.** *Heu etc.* aufladen, -gabeln; **12.** *Pfosten etc.* einrammen, befestigen; *Zelt, Verkaufsstand etc.* aufschlagen; *Leiter, Stadt etc.* anlegen; **13.** ♪ a) *Instrument* stimmen, b) *Grundton* angeben, c) *Lied etc. in e-r Tonart* anstimmen *od.* singen *od.* spielen: **high-~ed voice** hohe Stimme; **~ one's hopes too high** *fig.* s-e Hoffnungen zu hoch stecken; **~ a yarn** *fig.* ein Garn spinnen; **14.** *fig. Rede etc.* abstimmen (**on** auf *acc.*), *et.* ausdrücken; **15.** *Straße* beschottern, *Böschung* verpacken; *Brit. Ware* ausstellen, feilhalten; **17.** ✕ **~ed battle** regelrechte *od.* offene (Feld)Schlacht; **III** *v/i.* **18.** (kopf'über) hinstürzen, -schlagen; **19.** ✕ (sich) lagern; **20.** ✝ e-n (Verkaufs-)Stand aufschlagen; **21.** ⚓ stampfen (*Schiff*); *fig.* taumeln; **22.** sich neigen (*Dach etc.*); **23. ~ in** F a) sich (tüchtig) ins Zeug legen, loslegen, b) tüchtig ‚zulangen‘ (*essen*); **24. ~ into** F a) herfallen über *j-n* (*a. fig.*), b) herfallen über *das Essen*, c) sich (mit Schwung) an *die Arbeit* machen; **25. ~ on, ~ upon** sich entscheiden für, verfallen auf (*acc.*); **,~--and-'toss** *s.* ‚Kopf oder Schrift‘ (*Spiel*); **~ an·gle** *s.* ⊙ Steigungswinkel *m*; **,~-'black** *adj.* pechschwarz; **'~-blende** [-blend] *s. min.* (U'ran)Pechblende *f*; **~ cir·cle** *s.* ⊙ Teilkreis *m* (*Zahnrad*); **,~-'dark** *adj.* pechschwarz, stockdunkel (*Nacht*).

pitch·er¹ ['pɪtʃə] *s. sport* Werfer *m*.

pitch·er² ['pɪtʃə] *s.* (irdener) Krug (*mit Henkel*).

'pitch·fork I *s.* **1.** ⚷ Heu-, Mistgabel *f*; **2.** ♪ Stimmgabel *f*; **II** *v/t.* **3.** mit der Heugabel werfen; **4.** *fig.* rücksichtslos werfen: **~ troops into a battle**; **5.** ‚schubsen‘ (*into* in *ein Amt etc.*); **pine** *s.* ♀ Pechkiefer *f*; **~ pipe** *s.* ♪ Stimmpfeife *f*.

pitch·y ['pɪtʃɪ] *adj.* **1.** pechartig; **2.** voll Pech; **3.** pechschwarz (*a. fig*.)

pit coal *s.* Schwarz-, Steinkohle *f*.

pit·e·ous ['pɪtɪəs] → *pitiable* 1.

'pit·fall *s.* Fallgrube *f*, Falle *f*, *fig. a.* Fallstrick *m*.

pith [pɪθ] *s.* **1.** ♀, *anat.* Mark *n*; **2.** *a.* **~ and marrow** *fig.* Mark *n*, Kern *m*, 'Quintes,senz *f*; **3.** *fig.* Kraft *f*, Präg'nanz *f* (*e-r Rede etc.*); **4.** *fig.* Gewicht *n*, Bedeutung *f*.

'pit·head *s.* ✕ **1.** Füllort *m*, Schachtöffnung *f*; **2.** Fördergerüst *n*.

pith·e·can·thro·pus [,pɪθɪkæn'θrəʊpəs] *s.* Javamensch *m*.

pith| hat, ~ hel·met *s.* Tropenhelm *m*.

pith·i·ness ['pɪθɪnɪs] *s.* **1.** *das* Markige, Markigkeit *f*; **2.** *fig.* Kernigkeit *f*, Präg'nanz *f*, Kraft *f*; **pith·less** ['pɪθlɪs] *adj.* marklos; *fig.* kraftlos, schwach; **pith·y** ['pɪθɪ] *adj.* ☐ **1.** mark(art)ig; **2.** *fig.* markig, kernig, präg'nant.

pit·i·a·ble ['pɪtɪəbl] *adj.* ☐ **1.** Mitleid erregend, bedauernswert; *a. contp.* erbärmlich, jämmerlich, elend, kläglich; **2.** *contp.* armselig, dürftig; **'pit·i·ful** [-fʊl] *adj.* ☐ **1.** mitleidig, mitleidsvoll; **2.** → *pitiable*; **'pit·i·less** [-lɪs] *adj.* ☐ **1.** unbarmherzig; **2.** erbarmungslos, mitleidlos.

'pit|·man [-mən] *s.* [*irr.*] Bergmann *m*,

Knappe *m*, Grubenarbeiter *m*; **~ prop** *s.* ✕ (Gruben)Stempel *m*; *pl.* Grubenholz *n*; **~ saw** *s.* ⊙ Schrot-, Längensäge *f*.

pit·ta ['pɪtə] *s. a.* **~ bread** Fladenbrot *n*.

pit·tance ['pɪtəns] *s.* **1.** Hungerlohn *m*, ‚paar Pfennige‘ *pl.*; **2.** (kleines) bisschen: **the small ~ of learning** das kümmerliche Wissen.

pit·ting ['pɪtɪŋ] *s. metall.* Körnung *f*, Lochfraß *m*, 'Grübchenkorrosi,on *f*.

pi·tu·i·tar·y [pɪ'tjuːɪtərɪ] *physiol.* **I** *adj.* pi-tui'tär, Schleim absondernd, Schleim...; **II** *s. a.* **~ gland** Hirnanhang(drüse *f*) *m*, Hypo'physe *f*.

pit·y ['pɪtɪ] **I** *s.* **1.** Mitleid *n*, Erbarmen *n*: **feel ~ for, have** (*od.* **take**) **~ on** Mitleid haben mit; **for ~'s sake!** um Himmels willen!; **2.** Jammer *m*: **it is a** (**great**) **~** es ist (sehr) schade; **what a ~!** wie schade!; **it is a thousand pities** es ist jammerschade; **the ~ of it is that** es ist ein Jammer, dass; **II** *v/t.* **3.** bemitleiden, bedauern, Mitleid haben mit; **I ~ him** er tut mir Leid; **pit·y·ing** ['pɪtɪɪŋ] *adj.* ☐ mitleidig.

piv·ot ['pɪvət] **I** *s.* **1.** a) (Dreh)Punkt *m*, b) (Dreh)Zapfen *m*: **~ bearing** Zapfenlager, c) Stift *m*, d) Spindel *f*; **2.** (Tür-)Angel *f*; **3.** ✕ stehender Flügel(mann), Schwenkungspunkt *m*; **4.** *fig. a.* Dreh-, Angelpunkt *m*, b) → *pivot man*, c) *Fußball:* 'Schaltstati,on *f* (*Spieler*); **II** *v/t.* **5.** ⊙ a) mit Zapfen *etc.* versehen, b) drehbar lagern, c) (ein)schwenken; **III** *v/i.* **6.** sich drehen (**upon, on** um) (*a. fig.*); ✕ schwenken; **'piv·ot·al** [-tl] *adj.* **1.** Zapfen..., Angel...; **~ point** Angelpunkt *m*; **2.** *fig.* zen'tral, Kardinal...: **a ~ question**.

piv·ot| bolt *s.* Drehbolzen *m*; **~ bridge** *s.* Drehbrücke *f*; **~ man** [-mən] *s.* [*irr.*] *fig.* 'Schlüsselfi,gur *f*; **'~-,mount·ed** *adj.* schwenkbar; **~ tooth** *s.* [*irr.*] ⚶ Stiftzahn *m*.

pix·el ['pɪksl] *s. TV, Computer:* Pixel *n*, Bildpunkt *m*.

pix·ie → *pixy*.

pix·i·lat·ed ['pɪksɪleɪtɪd] *adj. Am.* F **1.** ‚verdreht‘, leicht verrückt; **2.** ‚blau‘ (*betrunken*).

pix·y ['pɪksɪ] *s.* Fee *f*, Elf *m*, Kobold *m*.

pi·zazz, piz·zazz [pɪ'zæz] *s.* **1.** Mode *etc.*: ‚Pfiff‘ *m*, Elc'ganz *f*, Flair *n*; **2.** E'lan *m*, Ener'gie *f*.

piz·zle ['pɪzl] *s.* **1.** *zo.* Fiesel *m*; **2.** Ochsenziemer *m*.

pla·ca·ble ['plækəbl] *adj.* ☐ versöhnlich, nachgiebig.

plac·ard ['plækɑːd] **I** *s.* **1.** a) Pla'kat *n*, b) Transpa'rent *n*; **II** *v/t.* **2.** mit Pla'katen bekleben; **3.** durch Pla'kate bekannt geben, anschlagen.

pla·cate [plə'keɪt] *v/t.* beschwichtigen, besänftigen, versöhnlich stimmen.

place [pleɪs] *s.* **1.** Ort *m*, Stelle *f*, Platz *m*: **from ~ to ~** von Ort zu Ort; **in ~** am Platze (*a. fig. angebracht*); **in ~s** stellenweise; **in ~ of** anstelle (*gen.*), anstatt (*gen.*); **out of ~** *fig.* fehl am Platz, unangebracht; **take ~** stattfinden; **take s.o.'s ~** j-s Stelle einnehmen; **take the ~ of** ersetzen, an die Stelle treten von; **if I were in your ~** an Ihrer Stelle (*würde ich ...*); **put yourself in my ~** versetzen Sie sich in meine Lage; **2.** Ort *m*, Stätte *f*: **~ of amusement** Vergnügungsstätte; **~ of birth** Geburtsort; **~ of business** ✝ Geschäftssitz *m*; **~ of delivery** ✝ Erfüllungsort *m*; **~ of jurisdiction** Gerichtsstand *m*; **~ of worship** Gotteshaus *n*, Kultstätte *f*; **from this ~** ✝ ab hier; **in** (*od.* **of**) **your ~** ✝ dort; **go**

~s *Am.* a) ‚groß ausgehen‘, b) die Sehenswürdigkeiten *e-s Ortes* ansehen, c) *fig.* es weit bringen (*im Leben*); **3.** Wohnsitz *m*; F Wohnung *f*, Haus *n*: **at his ~** bei ihm (zu Hause); **4.** Wohnort *m*; Ort(schaft *f*) *m*, Stadt *f*, Dorf *n*: **in this ~** hier; **5.** ⚓ Platz *m*, Hafen *m*: **~ for tran(s)shipment** Umschlagplatz; **6.** ✕ Festung *f*; **7.** F Gaststätte *f*, Lo'kal *n*; **8.** (Sitz)Platz *m*; **9.** *fig.* Platz *m* (*in e-r Reihenfolge; a. sport*), Stelle *f* (*a. in e-m Buch*): **in the first ~** a) an erster Stelle, erstens, b) zuerst, von vornherein, c) in erster Linie, d) überhaupt (erst); **in third ~** *sport* auf dem dritten Platz; **10.** A (Dezi'mal)Stelle *f*; **11.** Raum *m* (*a. fig., a. für Zweifel etc.*); **12.** *thea.* Ort *m* (*der Handlung*); **13.** (An)Stellung *f*, (Arbeits)Stelle *f*: **out of ~** stellenlos; **14.** Dienst *m*, Amt *n*: **it is not my ~** *fig.* es ist nicht meines Amtes; **15.** (sozi'ale) Stellung, Rang *m*, Stand *m*: **keep s.o. in his ~** j-n in s-n Schranken *od.* Grenzen halten; **know one's ~** wissen, wohin man gehört; **put s.o. in his ~** j-n in s-e Schranken weisen; **16.** *univ.* (Studien)Platz *m*; **II** *v/t.* **17.** stellen, setzen, legen (*a. fig.*); *teleph. Gespräch* anmelden; → *disposal* 3; **18.** ✕ *Posten* aufstellen, (*o.s.* sich) postieren; **19.** *j-n* an-, einstellen; ernennen, in ein Amt einsetzen; **20.** *j-n* 'unterbringen (*a. Kind*), *j-m* Arbeit *od.* e-e Anstellung verschaffen; **21.** ✝ *Anleihe, Kapital* 'unterbringen; *Auftrag* erteilen *od.* vergeben; *Bestellung* aufgeben; *Vertrag* abschließen; → *account* 5, *credit* 1; **22.** ✝ *Ware* absetzen; **23.** (*der Lage nach*) näher bestimmen; *fig. j-n* ,'unterbringen‘ (*identifizieren*): **I can't ~ him** ich weiß nicht, wo ich ihn ,unterbringen‘ *od.* ,hintun‘ soll; **24.** *sport* platzieren: **be ~d** unter den ersten drei sein, sich platzieren; **~ bet** *s. Rennsport:* Platzwette *f*.

pla·ce·bo [plə'siːbəʊ] *pl.* **-bos** *s.* ⚶ Pla'cebo *n*, 'Blindpräpa,rat *n*; **2.** *fig.* Beruhigungspille *f*.

place| card *s.* Platz-, Tischkarte *f*; **~ hunt·er** *s.* Pöstchenjäger *m*; **~ hunt·ing** *s.* Pöstchenjäge'rei *f*; **~ kick** *s. sport* a) *Fußball:* Stoß *m* auf den ruhenden Ball (*Freistoß etc.*), b) *Rugby:* Platztritt *m*; **'~-man** [-mən] *s.* [*irr.*] *pol. contp.* ‚Pöstcheninhaber‘ *m*, 'Futterkrippenpo,litiker‘ *m*; **~ mat** *s.* Set *n*, Platzdeckchen *n*.

place·ment ['pleɪsmənt] *s.* **1.** (Hin-, Auf)Stellen *n*, Platzieren *n*; **2.** a) Einstellung *f e-s Arbeitnehmers*, b) Vermittlung *f e-s Arbeitsplatzes*, c) 'Unterbringung *f von Arbeitskräften, Waisen*; **3.** Stellung *f*, Lage *f*; Anordnung *f*; **4.** ✝ a) Anlage *f*, 'Unterbringung *f von Kapital*, b) Vergabe *f von Aufträgen*; **5.** *ped. Am.* Einstufung *f*.

place name *s.* Ortsname *m*.

pla·cen·ta [plə'sentə] *pl.* **-tae** [-tiː] *s.* **1.** *anat.* Pla'zenta *f*, Mutterkuchen *m*; **2.** ♀ Samenleiste *f*.

plac·er ['plæsə] *s. min.* **1.** *bsd. Am.* (*Gold- etc.*)Seife *f*; **2.** seifengold- *od.* erzseifenhaltige Stelle; **~ gold** *s.* Seifen-, Waschgold *n*; **~ min·ing** *s.* Goldwaschen *n*.

pla·cet ['pleɪset] (*Lat.*) *s.* Plazet *n*, Zustimmung *f*, Ja *n*.

plac·id ['plæsɪd] *adj.* ☐ **1.** (seelen)ruhig, ‚gemütlich‘; **2.** mild, sanft; **3.** selbstgefällig; **pla·cid·i·ty** [plæ'sɪdətɪ] *s.* Milde *f*, Gelassenheit *f*, (Seelen)Ruhe *f*.

plack·et ['plækɪt] *s. Mode:* a) Schlitz *m* an Frauenkleid, b) Tasche *f*.

pla·gi·a·rism ['pleɪdʒjərɪzəm] *s.* Plagi'at

n; **'pla·gi·a·rist** [-ɪst] s. Plagi'ator m;
'pla·gi·a·rize [-raɪz] I v/t. plagiieren,
abschreiben; II v/i. ein Plagi'at begehen.

plague [pleɪg] I s. **1.** ☞ Seuche f, Pest f:
avoid like the ~ fig. wie die Pest meiden; **2.** *bsd. fig.* Plage f, Heimsuchung
f, Geißel f: *the ten ~s bibl.* die Zehn
Plagen; *a ~ on it!* zum Henker damit!;
3. *fig.* F a) Plage f, b) Quälgeist m
(*Mensch*); II v/t. **4.** plagen, quälen; **5.** F
belästigen, peinigen; **6.** *fig.* heimsuchen; *~ spot s. mst fig.* Pestbeule f.

plaice [pleɪs] *pl. coll.* **plaice** s. *ichth.*
Scholle f.

plaid [plæd] I s. schottisches Plaid(tuch);
II *adj.* bunt kariert.

plain [pleɪn] I *adj.* □ **1.** einfach,
schlicht: *~ clothes* Zivil(kleidung f) n;
~-clothes man Kriminalbeamte(r) m
od. Polizist m in Zivil; *~ cooking* bürgerliche Küche; *~ fare* Hausmannskost
f; *~ paper* unliniertes Papier; *~ postcard* gewöhnliche Postkarte; **2.** schlicht,
schmucklos, kahl (*Zimmer etc.*); unge-
mustert, einfarbig (*Stoff*): *~ knitting*
Rechts-, Glattstrickerei f; *~ sewing*
Weißnäherei f; **3.** unscheinbar, reizlos,
hausbacken (*Gesicht, Mädchen etc.*); **4.**
klar, leicht verständlich: *in ~ language*
tel. im Klartext (*a. fig.*), offen; **5.** klar,
offenbar, -kundig (*Irrtum etc.*); **6.** klar
(und deutlich), unmissverständlich,
'unum,wunden: *~ talk; the ~ truth* die
nackte Wahrheit; **7.** offen, ehrlich: *~
dealing* ehrliche Handlungsweise; **8.**
pur, unverdünnt (*Getränk*); *fig.* bar,
rein (*Unsinn etc.*): *~ folly* heller Wahnsinn; **9.** *bsd. Am.* flach; ◎ glatt: *~
country Am.* Flachland n; *~ roll* ◎
Glattwalze f; *~ bearing* Gleitlager n; *~
fit* ◎ Schlichtsitz m; *fig.* → *sailing* 1;
10. ohne Filter (*Zigarette*); II *adv.* **11.**
klar, deutlich; III s. **12.** Ebene f, Fläche f; Flachland n; *pl. bsd. Am.* Prä'rie
f; **'plain·ness** [-nɪs] s. **1.** Einfachheit f,
Schlichtheit f; **2.** Deutlichkeit f, Klarheit f; **3.** Offenheit f, Ehrlichkeit f; **4.**
Reizlosigkeit f (*e-r Frau etc.*); **,plain-
'spo·ken** *adj.* offen, freimütig: *he is a
~ man* er nimmt (sich) kein Blatt vor
den Mund.

plaint [pleɪnt] s. **1.** Beschwerde f, Klage
f; **2.** ⅓ (An)Klage(schrift) f; **'plain·tiff**
[-tɪf] s. ⅓ (Zi'vil)Kläger(in): *party ~*
klagende Partei; **'plain·tive** [-tɪv] *adj.*
□ traurig, kläglich; wehleidig (*Stimme*); Klage...: *~ song.*

plait [plæt] I s. **1.** Zopf m, Flechte f;
(Haar-, Stroh)Geflecht n; **2.** Falte f; II
v/t. **3.** Haar, Matte etc. flechten; **4.** verflechten.

plan [plæn] I s. **1.** (Spiel-, Wirtschafts-,
Arbeits)Plan m, Entwurf m, Pro'jekt n,
Vorhaben n: *~ of action* Schlachtplan
(*a. fig.*); *according to ~* planmäßig;
make ~s (for the future) (Zukunfts-)
Pläne schmieden; **2.** (Lage-, Stadt-)
Plan m: *general ~* Übersichtsplan; **3.**
◎ (Grund)Riss m: *~ view* Draufsicht f;
II v/t. **4.** planen, entwerfen, e-n Plan
entwerfen für *od.* zu: *~ ahead* (*a. v/i.*)
vorausplanen; *~ning board* Planungs-
amt n; **5.** *fig.* planen, beabsichtigen.

plane¹ [pleɪn] s. ♀ Pla'tane f.

plane² [pleɪn] I *adj.* **1.** flach, eben; ◎
plan; **2.** Å eben: *~ figure; ~ curve*
einfach gekrümmte Kurve; II s. **3.** Ebene f, (ebene) Fläche f: *~ of refraction*
phys. Brechungsebene f; *on the upward
~ fig.* im Anstieg; **4.** *fig.* Ebene f, Stufe
f, Ni'veau n, Bereich m: *on the same ~
as* auf dem gleichen Niveau wie; **5.** ◎

Hobel m; **6.** ⚒ Förderstrecke f; **7.** ✈ a)
Tragfläche f: *elevating (depressing)
~s* Höhen-(Flächen)steuer n, b) Flugzeug n; III v/t. **8.** (ein)ebnen, planieren, ◎ *a.* schlichten, *Bleche* abrichten;
9. (ab)hobeln; **10.** *typ.* bestoßen; IV.
v/i. **11.** ✈ gleiten; fliegen; **'plan·er**
[-nə] s. **1.** ◎ 'Hobel(ma,schine f) m; **2.**
typ. Klopfholz n.

plane sail·ing s. ⚓ Plansegeln n.
plan·et ['plænɪt] s. *ast.* Pla'net m.
plane ta·ble s. *surv.* Messtisch m: *~ map*
Messtischblatt n.
plan·e·tar·i·um [,plænɪ'teərɪəm] s. Plane'tarium n; **plan·e·tar·y** ['plænɪtərɪ]
adj. **1.** *ast.* plane'tarisch, Planeten...; **2.**
fig. um'herirrend; **3.** ◎ Planeten...: *~
gear* Planetengetriebe n; *~ wheel* Um-
laufrad n; **plan·et·oid** ['plænɪtɔɪd] s.
ast. Planeto'id m.

plane tree → **plane¹**.

pla·nim·e·ter [plæ'nɪmɪtə] s. ◎ Plani-
'meter n, Flächenmesser m; **pla'nim·e-
try** [-trɪ] s. Planime'trie f.

plan·ish ['plænɪʃ] ◎ v/t. **1.** glätten, (ab-)
schlichten, planieren; **2.** *Holz* glatt hobeln; **3.** *Metall* glatt hämmern; polieren.

plank [plæŋk] I s. **1.** (a. Schiffs)Planke f,
Bohle f, (Fußboden)Diele f, Brett n: *~
flooring* Bohlenbelag m; *walk the ~* a)
⚓ *hist.* ertränkt werden, b) *fig. pol. etc.*
,abgeschossen' werden; **2.** *pol. bsd.
Am.* (Pro'gramm)Punkt m e-r Partei; **3.**
⚒ Schwarte f; II v/t. **4.** mit Planken *etc.*
belegen, beplanken, dielen; **5.** verschalen, ⚒ verzimmern; **6.** *Speise* auf e-m
Brett servieren; **7.** *~ down* (*od. out*) F
Geld auf den Tisch legen, hinlegen,
,blechen'; *~ bed* s. (Holz)Pritsche f (*im
Gefängnis etc.*).

plank·ing ['plæŋkɪŋ] s. Beplankung f,
(Holz)Verschalung f, Bohlenbelag m;
coll. Planken *pl.*

plank·ton ['plæŋktən] s. *zo.* Plankton n.
plan·less ['plænlɪs] *adj.* planlos; **'planning** [-nɪŋ] s. **1.** Planen n, Planung f; **2.**
♀ Bewirtschaftung f, Planwirtschaft f.

pla·no-con·cave [,pleɪnəʊ'kɒnkeɪv]
adj. phys. 'plankon,kav (*Linse*).

plant [plɑːnt] I s. **1.** a) Pflanze f, Gewächs n, b) Setz-, Steckling m: *in ~* in
Wachstum befindlich; **2.** ◎ (Betriebs-,
Fa'brik)Anlage f, Werk n, Fa'brik f,
(Fabrikati'ons)Betrieb m: *~ engineer*
Betriebsingenieur m; **3.** ◎ (Ma'schinen)Anlage f, Aggre'gat n; Appara'tur
f; **4.** (Be'triebs)Materi,al n, Betriebs-
einrichtung f, Inven'tar n: *~ equipment*
Werksausrüstung f; **5.** *sl.* a) *et.* Einge-
schmuggeltes, Schwindel m, (*a. Poli-
'zei*)Falle f, b) (Poli'zei)Spitzel m; II v/t.
6. (ein-, an)pflanzen: *~ out* aus-, um-,
verpflanzen; **7.** *Land* a) bepflanzen, b)
besiedeln, kolonisieren; **8.** *Kolonisten*
ansiedeln; **9.** *Garten etc.* anlegen; *et.*
errichten; *Kolonie etc.* gründen; **10.**
fig. (*o.s.* sich) wo aufpflanzen, (auf-)
stellen, postieren; **11.** *Faust, Fuß wohin* setzen, ,pflanzen'; **12.** *fig. Ideen
etc.* (ein)pflanzen, einimpfen; **13.** *sl.
Schlag* ,landen', ,verpassen'; *Schuss* setzen, knallen; **14.** *Spitzel* einschleusen;
15. *sl. Belastendes etc.* (ein)schmug-
geln, ,deponieren', *~ s.th. on j-m* et.
,unterschieben'; **16.** *j-n* im Stich lassen.

plan·tain¹ ['plæntɪn] s. ♀ Wegerich m.
plan·tain² ['plæntɪn] s. ♀ **1.** Pi'sang m;
2. Ba'nane f (*Frucht*).
plan·ta·tion [plæn'teɪʃn] s. **1.** Pflanzung
f (*a. fig.*), Plan'tage f; **2.** (Wald-)Scho-
nung f; **3.** *hist.* Ansiedlung f, Kolo'nie f.

plant·er ['plɑːntə] s. **1.** Pflanzer m,
Plan'tagenbesitzer m; **2.** *hist.* Siedler m;

3. 'Pflanzma,schine f.
plan·ti·grade ['plæntɪgreɪd] *zo.* I *adj.*
auf den Fußsohlen gehend; II s. Soh-
lengänger m (*Bär etc.*).

plant louse s. [*irr.*] *zo.* Blattlaus f.

plaque [plɑːk] s. **1.** (Schmuck)Platte f;
2. A'graffe f, (Ordens)Schnalle f, Spange f; **3.** Gedenktafel f; **4.** (Namens-)
Schild n; **5.** ☞ Fleck m: *dental ~* Zahnbelag m.

plash¹ [plæʃ] v/t. u. v/i. (Zweige) zu e-r
Hecke verflechten.

plash² [plæʃ] I v/i. **1.** platschen, plätschern (*Wasser*); *im Wasser* plan(t)schen;
II v/t. **2.** platschen *od.* klatschen auf
(*acc.*): *~!* platsch!; III s. **3.** Platschen n,
Plätschern n, Spritzen n; **4.** Pfütze f,
Lache f; **'plash·y** [-ʃɪ] *adj.* **1.** plät-
schernd, klatschend, spritzend; **2.** voller Pfützen, matschig, feucht.

plasm ['plæzəm], **'plas·ma** [-zmə] s. **1.**
biol. ('Milch-, 'Blut-, 'Muskel),Plasma
n; **2.** *biol.* Proto'plasma n; **3.** *min.-
phys.* 'Plasma n; **plas·mat·ic** [plæz-
'mætɪk], **'plas·mic** [-zmɪk] *adj. biol.*
plas'matisch, Plasma...

plas·ter ['plɑːstə] I s. **1.** *pharm.* (Heft-,
Senf)Pflaster n; **2.** a) Gips m (*a.* ☞), b)
◎ Mörtel m, Verputz m, Bewurf m,
Tünche f: *~ cast* a) Gipsabdruck m, b)
☞ Gipsverband m; **3.** *mst ~ of Paris* a)
(gebrannter) Gips (*a.* ☞), b) Stuck m,
Gips(mörtel) m; II v/t. **4.** ◎ (ver)gip-
sen, über'tünchen, verputzen; **5.** bepflastern (*a. fig. mit Plakaten, Stein-
würfen etc.*); **6.** *fig.* über'schütten (*with
mit Lob etc.*); **7.** *be ~ed sl.* ,besoffen'
sein; **'plas·ter·er** [-ərə] s. Stucka'teur
m; **'plas·ter·ing** [-ərɪŋ] s. **1.** Verputz
m, Bewurf m; **2.** Stuck m; **3.** Gipsen n;
4. Stucka'tur f.

plas·tic ['plæstɪk] I *adj.* (□ *~ally*) **1.**
plastisch: *~ art* bildende Kunst, Plastik
f; **2.** formgebend, gestaltend; **3.** ◎
(ver)formbar, knetbar, plastisch: *~
clay* bildfähiger Ton; **4.** Kunststoff...:
~ bag Plastikbeutel m, -tüte f; (*synthetic*) *~ material* → 9; **5.** ☞ plastisch:
~ surgery; *~ surgeon* Facharzt m für
plastische Chirurgie; **6.** *fig.* plastisch,
anschaulich; **7.** *fig.* formbar (*Geist*); **8.**
~ bomb Plastikbombe f; II s. **9.** ◎
(Kunstharz)Pressstoff m, Plastik-,
Kunststoff m; **'plas·ti·cine** [-ɪsiːn] s.
Plasti'lin n, Knetmasse f; **plas·tic·i·ty**
[plæ'stɪsətɪ] s. Plastizi'tät f (*a. fig. Bildhaftigkeit*), (Ver)Formbarkeit f; **'plas-
ti·ciz·er** [-ɪsaɪzə] s. ◎ Weichmacher m.

plat [plæt] → **plait**, **plot** 1.

plate [pleɪt] I s. **1.** *allg.* Platte f (*a.
phot.*); (Me'tall)Schild n, Tafel f; (Na-
men-, Firmen-, Tür)Schild n; **2.** *paint.*
(Kupfer- *etc.*)Stich m; *weitS.* Holzschnitt m: *etched ~* Radierung f; **3.**
(Bild)Tafel f (*Buch*); **4.** (Ess-, *eccl.* Kol-
'lekten)Teller m; Platte f (*a. Gang e-r
Mahlzeit*); *coll.* (Gold-, Silber-, Tafel-)
Geschirr n *od.* (-)Besteck n: *German ~*
Neusilber n; *have a lot on one's ~* F
viel am Hals haben; *hand s.o. s.th. on
a ~* j-m et. ,auf dem Tablett servieren';
5. ◎ (Glas-, Me'tall)Platte f; Scheibe f,
La'melle f (*Kupplung etc.*); Deckel m;
6. ◎ Grobblech n; Blechtafel f; **7.** ⚡
Radio: A'node f e-r Röhre; Platte f,
Elek'trode f e-s Kondensators; **8.** *typ.*
(Druck-, Stereo'typ)Platte f; **9.** Po'kal
m, Preis m beim Rennen; **10.** *Am.
Baseball:* (Schlag)Mal n; **11.** *a. dental
~* a) (Gaumen)Platte f, b) *weitS.*
(künstliches) Gebiss; **12.** *Am. sl.* a)
('hyper)ele,gante Per'son, ,tolle
Frau'; **13.** *pl. sl.* ,Plattfüße' *pl.* (*Füße*);

II *v/t.* **14.** mit Platten belegen; ✕, ⚓ panzern, blenden; **15.** plattieren, (mit Me'tall) über'ziehen; **16.** *typ.* a) stereotypieren, b) *Typendruck*: in Platten formen; ~ **ar·mo(u)r** *s.* ⚓, ⊙ Plattenpanzer(ung *f*) *m*.

pla·teau ['plætəʊ] *pl.* **-teaux, teaus** [-z] (*Fr.*) *s.* Pla'teau *n* (*a. fig. psych. etc.*), Hochebene *f*.

plate cir·cuit *s.* ♮ An'odenkreis *m*.

plat·ed ['pleɪtɪd] *adj.* ⊙ plattiert, me'tallüber,zogen, versilbert, -goldet, dubliert; '**plate·ful** [-fʊl] *pl.* **-fuls** *s.* ein Teller *m* (voll).

plate| **glass** *s.* Scheiben-, Spiegelglas *n*; '~**hold·er** *s. phot.* ('Platten)Kas,sette *f*; '~**lay·er** *s.* ⚓ Streckenarbeiter *m*; '~**mark** → **hallmark**.

plat·en ['plætən] *s.* **1.** *typ.* Drucktiegel *m*, Platte *f*: ~ **press** Tiegeldruckpresse *f*; **2.** ('Schreibma,schinen)Walze *f*; **3.** 'Druckzy,linder *m* (*Rotationsmaschine*).

plat·er ['pleɪtə] *s.* **1.** ⊙ Plattierer *m*; **2.** (minderwertiges) Rennpferd.

plate| **shears** *s. pl.* Blechschere *f*; ~ **spring** *s.* ⊙ Blattfeder *f*.

plat·form ['plætfɔ:m] *s.* **1.** Plattform *f* (*a. Computerhardware od. -software*), ('Redner)Tri,büne *f*, Podium *n*; **2.** ⊙ Rampe *f*; (Lauf-, Steuer)Bühne *f*: **lifting ~** Hebebühne *f*; **3.** Treppenabsatz *m*; **4.** *geogr.* a) Hochebene *f*, b) Ter'rasse *f* (*a. engS.*); **5.** ⚓ a) Bahnsteig *m*, b) Plattform *f am Wagenende*; **6.** ✕ Bettung *f e-s Geschützes*; **7.** a) *a.* ~ **sole** Pla'teausohle *f*, b) *pl., a.* ~ **shoes** Schuhe *pl.* mit Plateausohle; **8.** *fig.* öffentliches Forum, Podiumsgespräch *n*; **9.** *pol.* Par'teipro,gramm *n*, Plattform *f*; *bsd. Am.* program'matische Wahlerklärung; ~ **car** *bsd. Am.* → **flatcar**; ~ **scale** *s.* ⊙ Brückenwaage *f*; ~ **tick·et** *s.* Bahnsteigkarte *f*.

plat·ing ['pleɪtɪŋ] *s.* **1.** Panzerung *f*; **2.** ⊙ Beplattung *f*, Me'tall,auflage *f*, Verkleidung *f* (*mit Metallplatten*); **3.** Plattieren *n*, Versilberung *f*.

pla·tin·ic [plə'tɪnɪk] *adj.* Platin...: ~ **acid** 🜨 Platinchlorid *n*; **plat·i·nize** ['plætɪnaɪz] *v/t.* **1.** ⊙ platinieren, mit Platin über'ziehen; **2.** 🜨 mit Platin verbinden; **plat·i·num** ['plætɪnəm] *s.* Platin *n*: ~ **blonde** F Platinblondine *f*.

plat·i·tude ['plætɪtju:d] *s. fig.* Plattheit *f*, Gemeinplatz *m*, Platti'tüde *f*; **plat·i·tu·di·nar·i·an** ['plætɪ,tju:dɪ'neərɪən] *s.* Phrasendrescher *m*, Schwätzer *m*; **plat·i·tu·di·nize** [,plætɪ'tju:dɪnaɪz] *v/i.* sich in Gemeinplätzen ergehen, quatschen; **plat·i·tu·di·nous** [,plætɪ'tju:dɪnəs] *adj.* □ platt, seicht, phrasenhaft.

Pla·ton·ic [plə'tɒnɪk] *adj.* (□ ~**ally**) pla'tonisch.

pla·toon [plə'tu:n] *s.* **1.** ✕ Zug *m* (*Kompanieabteilung*): **in** (*od. by*) ~**s** zugweise; **2.** Poli'zeiaufgebot *n*.

plat·ter ['plætə] *s.* **1.** (Servier)Platte *f*: **hand s.o. s.th. on a ~** *fig.* F j-m et. ,auf e-m Tablett servieren'; **2.** *Am. sl.* Schallplatte *f*.

plat·y·pus ['plætɪpəs] *pl.* **-pus·es** *s. zo.* Schnabeltier *n*.

plat·y(r)·rhine ['plætɪraɪn] *zo.* **I** *adj.* breitnasig; **II** *s.* Breitnase *f* (*Affe*).

plau·dit ['plɔ:dɪt] *s. mst pl.* lauter Beifall, Ap'plaus *m*.

plau·si·bil·i·ty [,plɔ:zə'bɪlətɪ] *s.* **1.** Glaubwürdigkeit *f*, Wahr'scheinlichkeit *f*; **2.** gefälliges Äußeres, einnehmendes Wesen; **3.** *Computer*: ,Plausibili'tät *f*; **plau·si·ble** ['plɔ:zəbl] *adj.* □ **1.** glaubhaft, einleuchtend, annehmbar, plau'si-

bel; **2.** einnehmend, gewinnend (*Äußeres*); **3.** glaubwürdig.

play [pleɪ] **I** *s.* **1.** (Glücks-, Wett-, Unter'haltungs)Spiel *n* (*a. sport*): **be at ~** a) spielen, b) *Kartenspiel*: am Ausspielen sein, c) *Schach*: am Zuge sein; **it is your ~** Sie sind am Spiel; **in** (**out of**) ~ *sport*: (noch) im Spiel (im Aus) (*Ball*); **lose money at ~** Geld verwetten; **2.** Spiel(weise *f*) *n*: **that was pretty ~** das war gut (gespielt); → **fair¹** 9, **foul play**; **3.** Spiele'rei *f*, Kurzweil *f*, *a.* Liebesspiel(e *pl.*) *n*: **a ~ of words** ein Spiel mit Worten; **a ~** (**up**)**on words** ein Wortspiel; **in ~** im Scherz; **4.** *thea.* (Schau)Spiel *n*, (The'ater)Stück *n*: **at the ~** im Theater; **go to the ~** ins Theater gehen; **as good as a ~** äußerst amüsant *od.* interessant; **5.** Spiel *n*, Vortrag *m*; **6.** *fig.* Spiel *n des Lichtes auf Wasser etc.*, spielerische Bewegung, (*Muskel etc.*)Spiel *n*: ~ **of colo(u)rs** Farbenspiel; **7.** Bewegung *f*, Gang *m*: **bring into ~** a) in Gang bringen, b) ins Spiel *od.* zur Anwendung bringen; **come into ~** ins Spiel kommen; **make ~** a) Wirkung haben, b) s-n Zweck erfüllen; **make ~ with** zur Geltung bringen, sich brüsten mit; **make a ~ for** *Am. sl.* e-m *Mädchen* den Kopf verdrehen wollen; **8.** Spielraum *m* (*a. fig.*), ⊙ *mst* Spiel *n*: **allow** (*od.* **give**) **full** (*od.* **free**) ~ **to** e-r *Sache*, s-r *Fantasie etc.* freien Lauf lassen; **II** *v/i.* **9.** a) spielen (*a. sport, thea. u. fig.*) (**for** um *Geld etc.*), b) mitspielen (*a. fig. mitmachen*): ~ **at** a) *Ball, Karten etc.* spielen, b) *fig.* sich nur so nebenbei mit et. beschäftigen; ~ **at business** ein bisschen in Geschäften machen; ~ **for time** a) Zeit zu gewinnen suchen, b) *sport*: auf Zeit spielen; ~ **into s.o.'s hands** j-m in die Hände spielen; ~ (**up**)**on** a) ♪ auf *einem Instrument* spielen, b) mit *Worten* spielen, c) *fig.* j-s *Schwächen* ausnutzen; ~ **with** spielen mit (*a. fig. e-m Gedanken*; *a.* leichtfertig *umgehen mit*; *a. engS.* herumfingern *an*); ~ **safe** ,auf Nummer sicher' gehen; ~**!** *Tennis etc.*: bitte! (= fertig); → **fair¹** 15, **false** II, **fast²** 3, **gallery** 2; **10.** a) *Kartenspiel*: ausspielen, b) *Schach*: am Zug sein, ziehen; **11.** a) ,her'umspielen', sich amüsieren, b) Unsinn treiben, c) scherzen; **12.** a) sich tummeln, b) flattern, gaukeln, c) spielen (*Lächeln, Licht etc.*) (**on** auf *dat.*), d) schillern (*Farbe*), e) in Tätigkeit sein (*Springbrunnen*); **13.** a) schießen, spritzen, c) strahlen, streichen: ~ **on** gerichtet sein auf (*acc.*), bestreichen, bespritzen (*Schlauch, Wasserstrahl*), anstrahlen, absuchen (*Scheinwerfer*); **14.** ⊙ a) Spiel(raum) haben, b) sich bewegen (*Kolben etc.*); **15.** sich *gut etc.* zum Spielen eignen (*Boden etc.*); **III** *v/t.* **16.** *Karten, Tennis etc.*, *a.* ♪, *a. thea.* Rolle *od.* Stück, *a. fig.* spielen: ~ (**s.th. on**) **the piano** (et. auf dem) Klavier spielen; ~ **both ends against the middle** *fig.* vorsichtig lavieren; ~ **it safe** a) kein Risiko eingehen, b) (*Wendung*) um (ganz) sicherzugehen; ~ **it low down** *sl.* ein gemeines Spiel treiben (**on** mit *j-m*); → **the races** bei (Pferde)Rennen wetten; → **deuce** 3, **fool¹** 2, **game¹** 4, **havoc, hooky²**, **trick** 2, **truant** 1; **17.** a) *Karte* ausspielen (*a. fig.*): ~ **one's cards well** s-e Chancen gut (aus)nutzen, b) *Schachfigur* ziehen; **18.** spielen, Vorstellungen geben in (*dat.*): → **the larger cities**; **19.** *Geschütz, Scheinwerfer, Licht etc.*, *Wasserstrahl etc.* richten (**on** auf *acc.*): ~ **a**

hose on et. bespritzen; ~ **colo(u)red lights on** et. bunt anstrahlen; **20.** *Fisch* auszappeln lassen;

Zssgn mit prp.:

play| **at** → *play* 9; ~ (**up·**)**on** → *play* 9, 12, 13, 19; ~ **up to** → *play* 9; ~ **with** → *play* 9;

Zssgn mit adv.:

play| **a·round** *v/i.* → *play* 11a; ~ **a·way** **I** *v/t.* Geld verspielen; **II** *v/i.* drauf'losspielen; ~ **back** *v/t. Platte, Band* abspielen; ~ **down** *v/t. fig.* ,herunterspielen'; ~ **off** *v/t.* **1.** *sport Spiel* a) beenden, b) *durch Stichkampf* entscheiden; **2.** *fig.* j-n ausspielen (**against** gegen *e-n andern*); **3.** *Musik* her'unterspielen; ~ **out** *v/t.* erschöpfen: **played out** erschöpft, ,fertig'; ~ **up** **I** *v/i.* **1.** ♪ lauter spielen; **2.** *sport* F ,aufdrehen'; **3.** *Brit.* F ,verrückt spielen' (*Auto etc.*); **4.** ~ **to** a) j-m schöntun, b) j-n unter'stützen; **II** *v/t.* **5.** *e-e Sache* ,hochspielen'; **6.** F j-n ,auf die Palme bringen' (*reizen*).

play·a·ble ['pleɪəbl] *adj.* **1.** spielbar; **2.** *thea.* bühnenreif, -gerecht.

'**play·act** *v/i. contp.* ,schauspielern'; ~ **ac·tor** *s. mst contp.* Schauspieler *m* (*a. fig.*); '~**back** *s.* ♮ **1.** Play-back *n*, spielen *n*: ~ **head** Tonabnehmerkopf *m*; **2.** Wiedergabegerät *n*; '~**bill** *s.* The'aterpla,kat *n*; '~**book** *s. thea.* Textbuch *n*; '~**boy** *s.* Playboy *m*; '~**day** *s.* (schul)freier Tag.

play·er ['pleɪə] *s.* **1.** *sport, a.* ♪ Spieler (-in); **2.** *Brit. sport* Berufsspieler *m*; **3.** (Glücks)Spieler *m*; **4.** Schauspieler(in); ~ **pi·an·o** *s.* me'chanisches Kla'vier.

'**play·fel·low** → **playmate**.

play·ful ['pleɪfʊl] *adj.* □ **1.** spielerisch; **2.** verspielt; **3.** ausgelassen, neckisch; '**play·ful·ness** [-nɪs] *s.* **1.** Munterkeit *f*; Ausgelassenheit *f*; **2.** Verspieltheit *f*.

'**play**| **girl** *s.* Playgirl *n*; '~**go·er** *s.* The'aterbesucher(in); '~**ground** *s.* **1.** Spielplatz *m* (*a. fig.*); **2.** Schulhof *m*; '~**house** *s.* **1.** *thea.* Schauspielhaus *n*; **2.** Spielhaus *n*, -hütte *f*.

play·ing card *s.* Spielkarte *f*; ~ **field** *s. Brit.* Sport-, Spielplatz *m*.

play·let ['pleɪlɪt] *s.* kurzes Schauspiel.

'**play·mate** *s.* 'Spielkame,rad(in), Gespiele *m*, Gespielin *f*; '~**off** *s. sport* Entscheidungsspiel *n*; '~**pen** Laufgitter *n*; '~**suit** *s.* Spielhöschen *n*; '~**thing** *s.* Spielzeug *n* (*fig. a. Person*); '~**time** *s.* **1.** Freizeit *f*; **2.** *ped.* große Pause; '~**wright** *s.* Bühnenschriftsteller *m*, Dra'matiker *m*.

plea [pli:] *s.* **1.** Vorwand *m*, Ausrede *f*: **on the ~ of** (*od. that*) unter dem Vorwand (*gen.*) *od.* dass; **2.** 🜨 a) Verteidigung *f*, b) Antwort *f* des Angeklagten: ~ **of guilty** Schuldgeständnis *n*; **3.** 🜨 Einrede *f*: **make a ~** Einspruch erheben; ~ **of the crown** *Brit.* Strafklage *f*. **4.** *fig.* (dringende) Bitte (**for** um), Gesuch *n*; **5.** *fig.* Befürwortung *f*; ~ **bar·gain·ing** *s. Brit.* 🜨 Verfahrensabsprache *f* (*inoffizielle Absprache, nach der ein Angeklagter durch Schuldbekenntnis e-e milde Strafe zugesichert bekommt*).

plead [pli:d] **I** *v/i.* **1.** 🜨 *u. fig.* plädieren (**for** für); **2.** 🜨 (*vor Gericht*) e-n Fall erörtern, Beweisgründe vorbringen; **3.** 🜨 sich zu s-r Verteidigung äußern: ~ **guilty** sich schuldig bekennen (**to** *gen.*); **4.** dringend bitten (**for** um, **with s.o.** j-n); **5.** sich einsetzen *od.* verwenden (**for** für, **with s.o.** bei *j-m*); **6.** einwenden *od.* geltend machen (**that** dass); **II** *v/t.* **7.** 🜨 *u. fig.* als Verteidigung *od.*

Entschuldigung anführen, *et.* vorschützen: ~ *ignorance*; **8.** ⚖ erörtern; **9.** ⚖ a) *Sache* vertreten, verteidigen: ~ *s.o.'s cause*, b) (als Beweisgrund) vorbringen, anführen; **'plead·er** [-də] *s.* ⚖ *u. fig.* Anwalt *m*, Sachwalter *m*; **'pleading** [-dɪŋ] **I** *s.* **1.** ⚖ a) Plädo'yer *n*, b) Plädieren *n*, Führen *n* e-r Rechtssache, c) Parteivorbringen *n*, d) *pl.*, gerichtliche Verhandlungen *pl.*, e) *bsd. Brit.* vorbereitete Schriftsätze *pl.*, Vorverhandlung *f*; **2.** Fürsprache *f*; **3.** Bitten *n* (*for* um); **II** *adj.* □ **4.** flehend, bittend, inständig.

pleas·ant ['pleznt] *adj.* □ **1.** angenehm (*a. Geruch, Traum etc.*), wohltuend, erfreulich (*Nachrichten etc.*), vergnüglich; **2.** freundlich (*a. Wetter, Zimmer*): *please look ~!* bitte recht freundlich!; **'pleas·ant·ness** [-nɪs] *s.* **1.** *das* Angenehme; angenehmes Wesen; **2.** Freundlichkeit *f*; **3.** Heiterkeit *f* (*a. fig.*); **'pleas·ant·ry** [-trɪ] *s.* **1.** Heiter-, Lustigkeit *f*; **2.** Scherz *m*: a) Witz *m*, b) Hänse'lei *f*.

please [pliːz] **I** *v/i.* **1.** gefallen, angenehm sein, befriedigen, Anklang finden: *~!* bitte (sehr)!; *as you ~* wie Sie wünschen; *if you ~* a) wenn ich bitten darf, wenn es Ihnen recht ist, b) *iro.* gefälligst, c) man stelle sich vor, denken Sie nur; *~ come in!* bitte, treten Sie ein!; **2.** befriedigen, zufrieden stellen: *anxious to ~* dienstbeflissen, sehr eifrig; **II** *v/t.* **3.** *j-m* gefallen *od.* angenehm sein *od.* zusagen, *j-n* erfreuen: *be ~d to do* sich freuen *et.* zu tun; *I am only too ~d to do it* ich tue es mit dem größten Vergnügen; *be ~d with* a) befriedigt sein von, b) Vergnügen haben an (*dat.*), c) Gefallen finden an (*dat.*): *I am ~d with it* es gefällt mir; **4.** befriedigen, zufrieden stellen: *~ o.s.* tun, was man will; *~ yourself* a) wie Sie wünschen, b) bitte, bedienen Sie sich; *only to ~ you* nur Ihnen zuliebe; → *hard* 3; **5.** (*a. iro.*) geruhen, belieben (*to do et.* zu tun): *~ God* so Gott will; **pleased** [-zd] *adj.* zufrieden (*with* mit), erfreut (*at* über *acc.*); → *Punch*[4]; **'pleas·ing** [-zɪŋ] *adj.* □ angenehm, wohltuend, gefällig.

pleas·ur·a·ble ['pleʒərəbl] *adj.* □ angenehm, vergnüglich, ergötzlich.

pleas·ure ['pleʒə] **I** *s.* **1.** Vergnügen *n*, Freude *f*, (*a. sexueller*) Genuss, Lust *f*: *with ~!* mit Vergnügen!; *give s.o. ~* j-m Vergnügen (*od.* Freude) machen; *have the ~ of doing* das Vergnügen haben, *et.* zu tun; *take ~ in* (*od. at*) Vergnügen *od.* Freude finden an (*dat.*): *he takes (a) ~ in contradicting* es macht ihm Spaß zu widersprechen; *take one's ~* sich vergnügen; *a man of ~* ein Genussmensch; **2.** Gefallen *m*, Gefälligkeit *f*: *do so. a ~* j-m e-n Gefallen tun; **3.** Belieben *n*, Gutdünken *n*: *at ~* nach Belieben; *at the Court's ~* nach dem Ermessen des Gerichts; ⚖ *during Her Majesty's ~ Brit.* auf unbestimmte Zeit (*Freiheitsstrafe*); **II** *v/i.* **4.** sich erfreuen *od.* vergnügen; *~ boat s.* Vergnügungsdampfer *m*; *~ ground s.* Vergnügungs-, Rasenplatz *m*; *~ princip* *psych.* 'Lustprin,zip *n*; *'~-,seeking adj.* vergnügungssüchtig; *~ tour s.*, *~ trip s.* Vergnügungsreise *f*.

pleat [pliːt] **I** *s.* (*Rock- etc.*)Falte *f*; **II** *v/t.* falten, fälteln, plissieren.

ple·be·ian [plɪ'biːən] **I** *adj.* ple'bejisch; **II** *s.* Ple'bejer(in); **ple'be·ian·ism** [-nɪzəm] *s.* Ple'bejertum *n*.

pleb·i·scite ['plebɪsɪt] *s.* Plebis'zit *n*, Volksabstimmung *f*, -entscheid *m*.

plec·trum ['plektrəm] *pl.* **-tra** [-ə] *s.* ♪ Plektron *n*.

pledge [pledʒ] **I** *s.* **1.** (Faust-, 'Unter-) Pfand *n*, Pfandgegenstand *m*; Verpfändung *f*; Bürgschaft *f*, Sicherheit *f*; *hist.* Bürge *m*, Geisel *f*: *in ~* a) als Pfand für, b) *fig.* als Beweis für, zum Zeichen, dass; *hold in ~* als Pfand halten; *put in ~* verpfänden; *take out of ~* Pfand auslösen; **2.** Versprechen *n*, feste Zusage, Gelübde *n*, Gelöbnis *n*: *take the ~* dem Alkohol abschwören; **3.** *fig.* 'Unterpfand *n*, Beweis *m* (*der Freundschaft etc.*): *under the ~ of secrecy* unter dem Siegel der Verschwiegenheit; **4.** *a.* ~ *of love fig.* Pfand *n* der Liebe (*Kind*); **5.** Zutrinken *n*, Toast *m*; **6.** *bsd. univ. Am.* a) Versprechen *n*, e-r Verbindung *od.* e-m (Geheim)Bund beizutreten, b) Anwärter(in) auf solche Mitgliedschaft; **II** *v/t.* **7.** verpfänden (*s.th. to s.o.* j-m *et.*); Pfand bestellen für, e-e Sicherheit leisten für; als Sicherheit *od.* zum Pfand geben: ~ *one's word fig.* sein Wort verpfänden; *~d article* Pfandobjekt *n*; *~d merchandise* ✝ sicherungsübereignete Ware(n); *~d securities* ✝ lombardierte Effekten; **8.** *j-n* verpflichten (*to* zu, auf *acc.*): ~ *o.s.* geloben, sich verpflichten; **9.** *j-m* zutrinken, auf das Wohl (*gen.*) trinken; **'pledge·a·ble** [-dʒəbl] *adj.* verpfändbar; **pledg·ee** [ple'dʒiː] *s.* Pfandnehmer(in), -inhaber (-in), -gläubiger(in); **pledge·or** [ple-'dʒɔː], **'pledg·er** [-dʒə], **pledg·or** [ple-'dʒɔː] *s.* ⚖ Pfandgeber(in), -schuldner(in).

Ple·iad ['plaɪəd] *pl.* **'Ple·ia·des** [-diːz] *s. ast.*, *fig.* Siebengestirn *n*.

Pleis·to·cene ['plaɪstəʊsiːn] *s. geol.* Pleisto'zän *n*, Di'luvium *n*.

ple·na·ry ['pliːnərɪ] *adj.* **1.** □ voll(ständig), Voll..., Plenar...: ~ *session* Plenarsitzung *f*; **2.** voll('kommen), uneingeschränkt: ~ *indulgence R.C.* vollkommener Ablass; ~ *power* Generalvollmacht *f*.

plen·i·po·ten·ti·ar·y [,plenɪpəʊ'tenʃərɪ] **I** *s.* **1.** (Gene'ral)Be,vollmächtigte(r *m*) *f*, bevollmächtigter Gesandter *od.* Mi'nister; **II** *adj.* **2.** bevollmächtigt; **3.** abso'lut, unbeschränkt.

plen·i·tude ['plenɪtjuːd] *s.* **1.** → *plenty* 1; **2.** Vollkommenheit *f*.

plen·te·ous ['plentjəs] *adj.* □ *poet.* reich(lich); **'plen·te·ous·ness** [-nɪs] *s. poet.* Fülle *f*.

plen·ti·ful ['plentɪfʊl] *adj.* □ reich(lich), im 'Überfluss (vor'handen); **'plen·ti·ful·ness** [-nɪs] → *plenty* 1.

plen·ty ['plentɪ] **I** *s.* Fülle *f*, 'Überfluss *m*, Reichtum *m* (*of* an *dat.*): *have ~ of s.th.* mit et. reichlich versehen sein, et. in Hülle u. Fülle haben; *in ~* im Überfluss; ~ *of money* (*time*) jede Menge *od.* viel Geld (Zeit); ~ *of times* sehr oft; → *horn* 4; **II** *adj. bsd. Am.* reichlich, jede Menge; **III** *adv.* F a) bei weitem, 'lange', b) *Am.* 'mächtig'.

ple·num ['pliːnəm] *s.* **1.** Plenum *n*, Vollversammlung *f*; **2.** *phys.* (vollkommen) ausgefüllter Raum.

ple·o·nasm ['plɪəʊnæzəm] *s.* Pleo'nasmus *m*; **ple·o·nas·tic** [,plɪəʊ'næstɪk] *adj.* (□ *~ally*) pleo'nastisch.

pleth·o·ra ['pleθərə] *s.* **1.** ✿ Blutandrang *m*; **2.** *fig.* 'Überfülle *f*, Zu'viel *n* (*of* an *dat.*); **ple·thor·ic** [ple'θɒrɪk] *adj.* (□ *~ally*) **1.** ✿ ple'thorisch; **2.** *fig.* 'übervoll, über'laden.

pleu·ra ['plʊərə] *pl.* **-rae** [-riː] *s. anat.* Brust-, Rippenfell *n*; **'pleu·ral** [-rəl] *adj.* Brust-, Rippenfell...; **'pleu·ri·sy**

[-rəsɪ] *s.* ✿ Pleu'ritis *f*, Brustfell-, Rippenfellentzündung *f*.

pleu·ro·car·pous [,plʊərəʊ'kɑːpəs] *adj.* ❀ seitenfrüchtig; **pleu·ro·pneu'mo·ni·a** [-nju'məʊnjə] *s.* **1.** ✿ Lungen- u. Rippenfellentzündung *f*; **2.** *vet.* Lungen- u. Brustseuche *f*.

plex·or ['pleksə] *s.* ✿ Perkussi'onshammer *m*.

plex·us ['pleksəs] *pl.* **-es** [-ɪz] *s.* **1.** *anat.* Plexus *m*, (Nerven)Geflecht *n*; **2.** *fig.* Flechtwerk *n*, Netz(werk) *n*, Kom'plex *m*.

pli·a·bil·i·ty [,plaɪə'bɪlətɪ] *s.* Biegsamkeit *f*, Geschmeidigkeit *f* (*a. fig.*); **pli·a·ble** ['plaɪəbl] *adj.* □ **1.** biegsam, geschmeidig (*a. fig.*); **2.** *fig.* nachgiebig, fügsam, leicht zu beeinflussen(d).

pli·an·cy ['plaɪənsɪ] *s.* Biegsamkeit *f*, Geschmeidigkeit *f* (*a. fig.*); **'pli·ant** [-nt] *adj.* □ → *pliable*.

pli·ers ['plaɪəz] *s. pl.* (*a. als sg. konstr.*) ⊕ (*a pair of* ~ e-e) (Draht-, Kneif)Zange: *round(-nosed)* ~ Rundzange *f*.

plight[1] [plaɪt] *s.* (missliche) Lage, Not-, Zwangslage *f*.

plight[2] [plaɪt] *bsd. poet.* **I** *v/t.* **1.** *Wort, Ehre* verpfänden, *Treue* geloben: *~ed troth* gelobte Treue; **2.** verloben (*to dat.*); **II** *s.* **3.** *obs.* Gelöbnis *n*, feierliches Versprechen; **4.** *a.* ~ *of faith* Verlobung *f*.

plim·soll ['plɪmsəl] *s.* Turnschuh *m*.

plinth [plɪnθ] *s.* △ **1.** Plinthe *f*, Säulenplatte *f*; **2.** Fußleiste *f*.

Pli·o·cene ['plaɪəʊsiːn] *s. geol.* Plio'zän *n*.

plod [plɒd] **I** *v/i.* **1.** *a.* ~ *along*, ~ *on* mühsam *od.* schwerfällig gehen, sich da'hinschleppen, trotten, (ein'her)stapfen; **2.** ~ *away fig.* sich abmühen *od.* -plagen (*at* mit), 'schuften'; **II** *v/t.* **3.** ~ *one's way* → 1; **'plod·der** [-də] *s. fig.* Arbeitstier *n*; **'plod·ding** [-dɪŋ] **I** *adj.* □ **1.** stapfend; **2.** arbeitsam, angestrengt *od.* unverdrossen (*arbeitend*); **II** *s.* **3.** Placke'rei *f*, Schufte'rei *f*.

plonk[1] [plɒŋk] *s.* F billiger u. schlechter Wein, *humor.* Fusel *m*.

plonk[2] [plɒŋk] F **I** *v/t.* **1.** *a.* ~ *down et.* ,hinschmeißen'; **2.** ♪ zupfen auf (*acc.*): **3.** ~ *down Am. sl.* ,blechen', bezahlen; **II** *v/i.* **4.** ,knallen'; **III** *adv.* **5.** knallend; **6.** ,zack', genau: ~ *in the eye*; *~!* wamm!

plop [plɒp] **I** *v/i.* plumpsen; **II** *v/t.* plumpsen lassen; **III** *s.* Plumps *m*, Plumpsen *n*; **IV** *adv.* mit e-m Plumps; **V** *int.* plumps!

plo·sion ['pləʊʒn] *s. ling.* Verschluss(-sprengung *f*) *m*; **plo·sive** ['pləʊsɪv] **I** *adj.* Verschluss...; **II** *s.* Verschlusslaut *m*.

plot [plɒt] **I** *s.* **1.** Stück(chen) *n* Land, Par'zelle *f*, Grundstück *n*: *a garden-~* ein Stück Garten; **2.** *bsd. Am.* (Lage-, Bau)Plan *m*, (Grund)Riss *m*, Dia'gramm *n*, grafische Darstellung; **3.** ✗ *a) Artillerie:* Zielort *m*, b) *Radar:* Standort *m*; **4.** (geheimer) Plan, Kom'plott *n*, Anschlag *m*, Verschwörung *f*, In'trige *f*: *lay a ~* ein Komplott schmieden; **5.** Handlung *f*, Fabel *f* (*Roman, Drama etc.*), *a.* In'trige *f* (*Komödie*); **II** *v/t.* **6.** e-n Plan von *et.* anfertigen, *et.* planen, entwerfen; aufzeichnen (*a.* ~ *down*) (*on* in *dat.*); ⚓, ✈ Kurs abstecken, -setzen, ermitteln; Å *Kurve* (grafisch) darstellen *od.* auswerten; *Luftbilder* auswerten: *~ted fire* ✗ Planfeuer *n*; **7.** *a.* ~ *out Land* parzellieren; **8.** *Verschwörung* planen, ausdenken, *Meuterei etc.* anzetteln; **9.** *Romanhand-*

lung etc. entwickeln, ersinnen; **III** *v/i.* **10.** (*against*) Ränke *od.* ein Komplott schmieden, intrigieren, sich verschwören (gegen), e-n Anschlag verüben (auf *acc.*); **'plot·ter** [-tə] *s.* **1.** Planzeichner (-in); **2.** Anstifter(in); **3.** Ränkeschmied *m*, Intri'gant(in), Verschwörer(in).

plough [plaʊ] **I** *s.* **1.** Pflug *m*: *put one's hand to the* ~ s-e Hand an den Pflug legen; **2.** *the* ♌ *ast.* der Große Bär *od.* Wagen; **3.** *Tischlerei:* Falzhobel *m*; **4.** *Buchbinderei:* Beschneidhobel *m*; **5.** *univ. Brit. sl.* ,('Durch)Rasseln' *n*, 'Durchfall' *m*; **II** *v/t.* **6.** *Boden* ('um-)pflügen: ~ *back* unterpflügen, *fig. Gewinn* wieder in das Geschäft stecken; ~ *sand* 2; **7.** *fig.* a) *Wasser, Gesicht* (durch)'furchen, *Wellen* pflügen, b) sich (*e-n Weg*) bahnen: ~ *one's way*; **8.** *univ. Brit. sl.* 'durchfallen lassen: *be od. get* ~*ed* durchrasseln; **III** *v/i.* **9.** *fig.* sich e-n Weg bahnen: ~ *through a book* F ein Buch durchackern; '~·land *s.* Ackerland *n*; '~·man [-mən] *s.* [*irr.*] Pflüger *m*: ~*'s lunch* Imbiss *m* aus Brot, Käse *etc.*; ~ *plane s.* ☉ Nuthobel *m*; '~·share *s.* ⚒ Pflugschar *f.*

plov·er ['plʌvə] *s. orn.* **1.** Regenpfeifer *m*; **2.** Gelbschenkelwasserläufer *m*; **3.** Kiebitz *m.*

plow [plaʊ] *etc. Am.* → *plough etc.*

ploy [plɔɪ] *s.* F Trick *m*, ,Masche' *f.*

pluck [plʌk] **I** *s.* **1.** Rupfen *n*, Zupfen *n*, Zerren *n*; **2.** Ruck *m*, Zug *m*; **3.** Geschlinge *n von Schlachttieren*; **4.** *fig.* Schneid *m*, Mut *m*; **5.** → *plough* 5; **II** *v/t.* **6.** *Obst, Blumen etc.* pflücken, abreißen; **7.** *Federn, Haar, Unkraut etc.* ausreißen, -zupfen, *Geflügel* rupfen; ☉ *Wolle* plüsen; → *crow*¹ 1; **8.** zupfen, ziehen, zerren, reißen: ~ *s.o. by the sleeve* j-n am Ärmel zupfen; ~ *up courage fig.* Mut fassen; **9.** *sl.* j-n ,rupfen', ausplündern; **10.** → *plough* 8; **III** *v/i.* **11.** (*at*) zupfen, ziehen, zerren (an *dat.*), schnappen, greifen (nach); **'pluck·i·ness** [-kɪnɪs] *s.* Schneid *m*, Mut *m*; **'pluck·y** [-kɪ] *adj.* □ F mutig, schneidig.

plug [plʌg] **I** *s.* **1.** Pflock *m*, Stöpsel *m*, Dübel *m*, Zapfen *m*; (Fass)Spund *m*; Pfropf(en) *m* (*a.* ❀); Verschlussschraube *f*, (Hahn-, Ven'til)Küken *n*: *drain* ~ Ablassschraube; **2.** ⚡ Stecker *m*, Stöpsel *m*: ~*-ended cord* Stöpselschnur *f*; ~ *socket* Steckdose *f*; **3.** *mot.* Zündkerze *f*; **4.** ('Feuer)Hy,drant *m*; **5.** (Klo'sett)Spülvorrichtung *f*; **6.** (Zahn)Plombe *f*; **7.** Priem *m* (*Kautabak*); **8.** → *plug hat*; **9.** ♰ *sl.* Ladenhüter *m*; **10.** *sl.* alter Gaul; **11.** *sl.* a) (Faust)Schlag *m*, b) Schuss *m*, c) Kugel *f*: *take a* ~ *at* → 18; **12.** *Am. Radio:* Re'klame(hinweis *m*) *f*; **13.** F falsches Geldstück; **II** *v/t.* **14.** *a.* ~ *up* zu-, verstopfen, zustöpseln; **15.** *Zahn* plombieren; **16.** ~ *in* ⚡ *Gerät* einstecken, -stöpseln, *durch Steckkontakt* anschließen; **17.** F *im Radio etc.* (ständig) Re'klame machen für; *Lied etc.* ständig spielen (lassen); **18.** *sl.* j-m ,eine (*e-n Schlag, e-e Kugel*) verpassen'; **III** *v/i.* **19.** F *a.* ~ *away* ,schuften' (*at* an *dat.*); ~ *box s.* 'Steckdose *f*, -kon,takt *m*; ~ *fuse s.* Stöpselsicherung *f*; ~ *hat s. Am. sl.* ,Angströhre' *f* (*Zylinder*); '~·in *adj.* ☉ Steck..., Einschub...: ~ *board Computer:* Steckkarte *f*; ~ *telephone* umsteckbares Telefon; '~·ug·ly **I** *s. Am. sl.* Schläger *m*, Ra'bauke *m*; **II** *adj.* F abgrundhässlich; ~ *wrench s. mot.* Zündkerzenschlüssel *m.*

---

plum [plʌm] *s.* **1.** Pflaume *f*, Zwetsch(g)e *f*; **2.** Ro'sine (*im Pudding etc.*): ~ *cake* Rosinenkuchen *m*; **3.** *fig.* a) ,Ro'sine' *f* (*das Beste*), b) *a.* ~ *job* ,Bombenjob' *m*, c) *Am. sl.* Belohnung *f* für Unterstützung *bei der Wahl* (*Posten, Titel etc.*); **4.** *Am. sl.* unverhoffter Gewinn, ♰ 'Sonderdivi,dende *f.*

plum·age ['pluːmɪdʒ] *s.* Gefieder *n.*

plumb [plʌm] **I** *s.* **1.** (Blei)Lot *n*, Senkblei *n*: *out of* ~ aus dem Lot, nicht (mehr) senkrecht; **2.** ⚓ (Echo)Lot *n*; **II** *adj.* **3.** lot-, senkrecht; **4.** F völlig, rein (*Unsinn etc.*); **III** *adv.* **5.** *fig.* genau, ,peng', platsch (*ins Wasser etc.*); **6.** *Am.* F ,to'tal' (*verrückt etc.*); **IV** *v/t.* **7.** lotrecht machen; **8.** ⚓ *Meerestiefe* (ab-, aus)loten, sondieren; **9.** *fig.* sondieren, ergründen; **10.** ☉ (mit Blei) verlöten, verbleien; **11.** F *Wasser- od.* Gasleitungen legen in (*e-m Haus*); **V** *v/i.* **12.** klempnern; **plum·ba·go** [plʌm'beɪɡəʊ] *s.* **1.** *min.* a) Gra'phit *m*, b) Bleiglanz *m*; **2.** ♀ Bleiwurz *f.*

plumb bob → *plumb* 1.

plum·be·ous ['plʌmbɪəs] *adj.* **1.** bleiartig; **2.** bleifarben; **3.** *Keramik:* mit Blei glasiert; **plumb·er** ['plʌmə(r)] *s.* **1.** Klempner *m*, Installa'teur *m*; **2.** Bleiarbeiter *m*; **'plum·bic** [-bɪk] *adj.* Blei...: ~ *chloride* ❀ Bleitetrachlorid *n*; **plum·bif·er·ous** [plʌm'bɪfərəs] *adj.* bleihaltig; **'plumb·ing** [-mɪŋ] *s.* **1.** Klempner-, Installa'teurarbeit *f*; Rohr-, Wasser-, Gasleitung *f*; sani'täre Einrichtung; **3.** Blei(gießer)arbeit *f*; **4.** ⚓, ⚓ Ausloten *n*; **'plum·bism** [-bɪzəm] *s.* ⚕ Bleivergiftung *f.*

plumb line I *s.* **1.** Senkschnur *f*, -blei *n*; **II** *v/t.* **2.** ⚓, ⚓ ausloten; **3.** *fig.* sondieren, prüfen.

plum·bo- [plʌmbəʊ] ❀ *in Zssgn* Blei..., *z.B.* **plumbosolvent** Blei zersetzend.

plumb rule *s.* ☉ Lot-, Senkwaage *f.*

plume [pluːm] **I** *s.* **1.** *orn.* (Straußen- *etc.*) Feder *f*: *adorn o.s. with borrowed* ~*s fig.* sich mit fremden Federn schmücken; **2.** (Hut-, Schmuck)Feder *f*; **3.** Feder-, Helmbusch *m*; **4.** *fig.* ~ (*of cloud*) Wolkenstreifen *m*; ~ (*of smoke*) Rauchfahne *f*; **II** *v/t.* **5.** mit Federn schmücken: ~ *o.s.* (*up*)*on fig.* sich brüsten mit; ~*d* a) gefiedert, b) mit Federn geschmückt; **6.** *Gefieder* putzen; **'plume·less** [-lɪs] *adj.* ungefiedert.

plum·met ['plʌmɪt] **I** *s.* **1.** (Blei)Lot *n*, Senkblei *n*; **2.** ☉ Senkwaage *f*; **3.** *Fischen:* (Blei)Senker *m*; **4.** *fig.* Bleigewicht *n*; **II** *v/i.* **5.** absinken, (ab)stürzen (*a. fig.*).

plum·my ['plʌmɪ] *adj.* **1.** pflaumenartig, Pflaumen...; **2.** reich an Pflaumen *od.* Ro'sinen; **3.** F ,prima', schick'; **4.** so'nor: ~ *voice.*

plu·mose ['pluːməʊs] *adj.* **1.** *orn.* gefiedert; **2.** ♀, *zo.* federartig.

plump¹ [plʌmp] **I** *adj.* drall, mollig, ,pummelig': ~ *cheeks* Pausbacken; **II** *v/t. u. v/i. oft* ~ *out* prall *od.* fett machen (werden).

plump² [plʌmp] **I** *v/i.* **1.** (hin)plumpsen, schwer fallen, sich (*in e-n Sessel etc.*) fallen lassen; **2.** *pol.* kumulieren: ~ *for* a) *e-m Wahlkandidaten* s-e Stimme ungeteilt geben, j-n rückhaltlos unterstützen, c) sich sofort für *et.* entscheiden; **II** *v/t.* **3.** plumpsen lassen; **4.** mit *s-r Meinung etc.* her'ausplatzen, unverblümt her'aussagen; **III** *s.* **5.** F Plumps *m*; **IV** *adv.* **6.** plumpsend, mit e-m

---

Plumps; **7.** F unverblümt, geradeheraus; **V** *adj.* □ **8.** F plump (*Lüge etc.*), deutlich, glatt (*Ablehnung etc.*); **'plump·er** [-pə] *s.* **1.** Plumps *m*; **2.** Bausch *m*; **3.** *pol.* ungeteilte Wahlstimme; **4.** *sl.* plumpe Lüge.

plum pud·ding *s.* Plumpudding *m.*

plum to·ma·to *s.* 'Eierto,mate *f.*

plum·y ['pluːmɪ] *adj.* **1.** gefiedert; **2.** federartig.

plun·der ['plʌndə] **I** *v/t.* **1.** *Land, Stadt etc.* plündern; **2.** rauben, stehlen; **3.** *j-n* ausplündern; **II** *v/i.* **4.** plündern, räubern; **III** *s.* **5.** Plünderung *f*; **6.** Beute *f*, Raub *m*; **7.** *Am.* F Plunder *m*; **'plun·der·er** [-ərə] *s.* Plünderer *m*, Räuber *m.*

plunge [plʌndʒ] **I** *v/t.* **1.** (ein-, 'unter-)tauchen, stürzen (*in, into* in *acc.*); *fig. j-n in Schulden etc.* stürzen; *e-e Nation in e-n Krieg* stürzen *od.* treiben; *Zimmer in Dunkel* tauchen *od.* hüllen; **2.** *Waffe* stoßen; **II** *v/i.* **3.** (ein-, 'unter-)tauchen (*into* in *acc.*); **4.** (ab)stürzen (*a. fig. Klippe etc.*, ♰ *Preise*); **5.** *fig.* sich *in Zimmer etc.* stürzen, stürmen; *fig.* sich *in e-e Tätigkeit, in Schulden etc.* stürzen; **6.** ⚓ stampfen (*Schiff*); **7.** sich nach vorne werfen, ausschlagen (*Pferd*); **8.** *sl. et.* riskieren, alles auf 'eine Karte setzen; **III** *s.* **9.** (Ein-, 'Unter)Tauchen *n*; *sport* (Kopf)Sprung *m*: *take the* ~ *fig.* den entscheidenden Schritt *od.* den Sprung wagen; **10.** Sturz *m*, Stürzen *n*; **11.** Ausschlagen *n e-s Pferdes*; **12.** Sprung-, Schwimmbecken *n*; **13.** Schwimmen *n*, Bad *n*; **'plung·er** [-dʒə] *s.* **1.** Taucher *m*; **2.** ☉ Tauchkolben *m*; **3.** ⚡ a) Tauchkern *m*, b) Tauchspule *f*; **4.** *mot.* Ven'tilkolben *m*; **5.** ✕ Schlagbolzen *m*; **6.** *sl.* a) Ha'sar'deur *m*, Spieler *m*, b) wilder Speku'lant.

plunk [plʌŋk] → *plonk*².

plu·per·fect [,pluː'pɜːfɪkt] *s. a.* ~ *tense ling.* Plusquamperfekt *n*, Vorvergangenheit *f.*

plu·ral ['plʊərəl] **I** *adj.* □ **1.** mehrfach: ~ *marriage* Mehrehe *f*; ~ *society* pluralistische Gesellschaft; ~ *vote* Mehrstimmenwahlrecht *n*; **2.** *ling.* Plural..., im Plural, plu'ralisch: ~ *number* → 3; **II** *s.* **3.** *ling.* Plural *m*, Mehrzahl *f*; **'plu·ral·ism** [-rəlɪzəm] *s.* **1.** Vielheit *f*; **2.** *eccl.* Besitz *m* mehrerer Pfründen *od.* Ämter; **3.** *phls., pol.* Plura'lismus *m*; **'plu·ral·ist** [-rəlɪst] *adj. phls., pol.* plura'listisch; **plu·ral·i·ty** [,plʊə'rælətɪ] *s.* **1.** Mehrheit *f*, 'Über-, Mehrzahl *f*; **2.** Vielheit *f*, -zahl *f*; **3.** *pol.* (*Am. bsd.* rela'tive) Stimmenmehrheit; **4.** → *plu·ralism* 2; **'plu·ral·ize** [-rəlaɪz] *v/t. ling.* **1.** in den Plural setzen; **2.** als *od.* im Plural gebrauchen.

plus [plʌs] **I** *prp.* **1.** plus, und; **2.** *bsd.* ♰ zuzüglich (*gen.*); **II** *adj.* **3.** Plus..., *a.* extra, Extra...; **4.** A, ⚡ positiv, Plus...: ~ *quantity* positive Größe; **5.** F plus, mit; **II** *s.* **6.** Plus(zeichen) *n*; **7.** Plus *n*, Mehr *n*, 'Überschuss *m*; **8.** *fig.* Plus (-punkt *m*) *n*; ~*-'fours s. pl.* weite Knickerbocker- *od.* Golfhose.

plush [plʌʃ] **I** *s.* **1.** Plüsch *m*; **II** *adj.* **2.** Plüsch...; **3.** *sl.* (stink)vornehm, ,feu'dal'; **'plush·y** [-ʃɪ] *adj.* **1.** plüschartig; **2.** → *plush* 3.

plus·(s)age ['plʌsɪdʒ] *s. Am.* 'Überschuss *m.*

Plu·to ['pluːtəʊ] *s. myth. u. ast.* Pluto *m* (*Gott u. Planet*).

plu·toc·ra·cy [pluː'tɒkrəsɪ] *s.* **1.** Plutokra'tie *f*, Geldherrschaft *f*; **2.** 'Geldaristokra,tie *f*, *coll.* Pluto'kraten *pl.*; **plu-**

to·crat ['plu:təʊkræt] s. Pluto'krat m, Kapita'list m; **plu·to·crat·ic** [ˌplu:təʊ'krætɪk] adj. pluto'kratisch.

plu·ton·ic [plu:'tɒnɪk] adj. geol. plu'tonisch; **plu·to·ni·um** [-'təʊnjəm] s. 🜨 Plu'tonium n.

plu·vi·al ['plu:vjəl] adj. regnerisch; Regen...; **plu·vi·o·graph** [-əʊgrɑ:f] s. phys. Regenschreiber m; **plu·vi·om·eter** [ˌplu:vɪ'ɒmɪtə] s. phys. Pluvio'meter n, Regenmesser m; **plu·vi·ous** [-jəs] → **pluvial**.

ply¹ [plaɪ] I v/t. **1.** Arbeitsgerät handhaben, hantieren mit; **2.** Gewerbe betreiben, ausüben; **3.** (with) bearbeiten (mit) (a. fig.); fig. j-m (mit Fragen etc.) zusetzen, j-n (mit et.) über'häufen: ~ s.o. with drink j-n zum Trinken nötigen; **4.** Strecke (regelmäßig) befahren; II v/i. **5.** verkehren, fahren, pendeln (between zwischen dat.); **6.** ⚓ aufkreuzen.

ply² [plaɪ] I s. **1.** Falte f; (Garn)Strähne f; (Stoff-, Sperrholz- etc.)Lage f, Schicht f: three-~ dreifach (z. B. Garn, Teppich); **2.** fig. Hang m, Neigung f; II v/t. **3.** falten; Garn fachen; **'ply·wood** s. Sperrholz n.

pneu·mat·ic [nju:'mætɪk] I adj. (□ ~al·ly) **1.** ⚙, phys. pneu'matisch, Luft...; ⚙ Druck-, Pressluft...: ~ brake Druckluftbremse f; ~ tool Pressluftwerkzeug n; **2.** zo. lufthaltig; II s. **3.** Luftreifen m; **4.** Fahrzeug n mit Luftbereifung; ~ dis·patch s. Rohrpost f; ~ drill s. Pressluftbohrer m; ~ float s. Floßsack m; ~ ham·mer s. Presslufthammer m.

pneu·mat·ics [nju:'mætɪks] s. pl. sg. konstr. phys. Pneu'matik f.

pneu·mat·ic| tire (od. tyre) s. Luftreifen m; pl. a. Luftbereifung f; ~ tube s. pneu'matische Röhre; weitS., a. pl. Rohrpost f.

pneu·mo·ni·a [nju:'məʊnjə] s. 🜊 Lungenentzündung f, Pneumo'nie f; **pneu·'mon·ic** [-'mɒnɪk] adj. pneu'monisch, die Lunge od. Lungenentzündung betreffend.

poach¹ [pəʊtʃ] I v/t. **1.** a. ~ up Erde aufwühlen, Rasen zertrampeln; **2.** (zu e-m Brei) anrühren; **3.** wildern, unerlaubt jagen od. fangen; **4.** räubern (a. fig.); **5.** sl. wegschnappen; **6.** ⚙ Papier bleichen; II v/i. **7.** weich od. matschig werden (Boden); **8.** unbefugt eindringen (on in acc.); → preserve 8b; **9.** hunt. wildern.

poach² [pəʊtʃ] v/t. Eier pochieren: ~ed egg pochiertes od. verlorenes Ei.

poach·er¹ ['pəʊtʃə] s. Wilderer m, Wilddieb m.

poach·er² ['pəʊtʃə] s. Po'chierpfanne f.

poach·ing ['pəʊtʃɪŋ] s. Wildern n, Wilde'rei f.

PO Box [ˌpi: əʊ 'bɒks] s. Postfach n.

po·chette [pɒ'ʃet] (Fr.) s. Handtäschchen n.

pock [pɒk] s. 🜊 **1.** Pocke f, Blatter f; **2.** → pockmark.

pock·et ['pɒkɪt] I s. **1.** (Hosen- etc., a. zo. Backen- etc.)Tasche f: have s.o. in one's ~ fig. j-n in der Tasche od. Gewalt haben; put s.o. in one's ~ fig. j-n in die Tasche stecken; put one's pride in one's ~ s-n Stolz überwinden, klein beigeben; **2.** fig. Geldbeutel m, Fi'nanzen pl.: be in ~ gut bei Kasse sein; be 3 dollars in (out of) ~ drei Dollar profitiert (verloren) haben; put one's hand in one's ~ (tief) in die Tasche greifen; → line² 2; **3.** Brit. Sack m Hopfen, Wolle (= 76 kg); **4.** geol. Einschluss m; **5.** min. (Erz-, Gold)Nest n; **6.** Billard:

Tasche f, Loch n; **7.** ✈ (Luft)Loch n, Fallbö f; **8.** ✕ Kessel m: ~ of resistance Widerstandsnest n; II adj. **9.** Taschen..., im (fig. Westen)Taschenformat; III v/t. **10.** in die Tasche stecken, einstecken (a. fig. einheimsen); **11.** a) fig. Kränkung einstecken, hinnehmen, b) Gefühle unter'drücken, s-n Stolz über'winden; **12.** Billardkugel einlochen; **13.** pol. Am. Gesetzesvorlage nicht unter'schreiben, sein Veto einlegen gegen (Präsident etc.); **14.** ✕ Feind einkesseln; ~ bat·tle·ship s. ⚓ Westentaschenkreuzer m; ~ bil·liards s. pl. sing. konstr. Poolbillard n; ~ book s. **1.** Taschen-, No'tizbuch n; **2.** a) Brieftasche f, b) Geldbeutel m (beide a. fig.); **3.** Am. Handtasche f; **4.** Taschenbuch n; ~ cal·cu·la·tor s. Taschenrechner m; ~ e·di·tion s. Taschenausgabe f.

pock·et·ful ['pɒkɪtfʊl] pl. -fuls s. e-e Tasche (voll): a ~ of money.

'pock·et·knife s. [irr.] Taschenmesser n; ~ lamp s. Taschenlampe f; ~ light·er s. Taschenfeuerzeug n; ~ mon·ey s. Taschengeld n; '~-size(d) adj. im (fig. Westen)Taschenformat; ~ ve·to s. pol. Am. Zu'rückhalten n od. Verzögerung f e-s Gesetzentwurfs (bsd. durch den Präsidenten etc.).

'pock|·mark s. Pockennarbe f; '~-marked adj. pockennarbig.

pod¹ [pɒd] s. zo. **1.** Herde f (Wale, Robben); **2.** Schwarm m (Vögel).

pod² [pɒd] I s. **1.** ♀ Hülse f, Schale f, Schote f: ~ pepper Paprika f; **2.** zo. (Schutz)Hülle f, a. Ko'kon m (der Seidenraupe), Beutel m (des Moschustiers); **3.** sl. ,Wampe' f, Bauch m: in ~ ,dick' (schwanger); II v/i. **4.** Hülsen ansetzen; **5.** Erbsen etc. aushülsen, -schoten.

po·dag·ra [pəʊ'dægrə] s. 🜊 Podagra n, (Fuß)Gicht f.

podg·y ['pɒdʒɪ] adj. F unter'setzt, dicklich.

po·di·a·trist [pəʊ'daɪətrɪst] s. Am. Fußpfleger(in); **po'di·a·try** [-trɪ] s. Fußpflege f, Pedi'küre f.

Po·dunk ['pəʊdʌŋk] s. Am. contp. ,Krähwinkel' n.

po·em ['pəʊɪm] s. Gedicht n (a. fig.), Dichtung f; **po·et** ['pəʊɪt] s. Dichter m, Po'et m: ~ laureate a) Dichterfürst m, b) Brit. Hofdichter m; **po·et·as·ter** [pəʊɪ'tæstə] s. Dichterling m; **po·et·ess** ['pəʊɪtɪs] s. Dichterin f.

po·et·ic, po·et·i·cal [pəʊ'etɪk(l)] adj. □ **1.** po'etisch, dichterisch: ~ justice fig. ausgleichende Gerechtigkeit; ~ li·cence 4; **2.** fig. po'etisch, ro'mantisch, stimmungsvoll; **po'et·ics** [-ks] s. pl. sg. konstr. Po'etik f; **po·et·ize** ['pəʊɪtaɪz] I v/i. **1.** dichten; II v/t. **2.** in Verse bringen; **3.** (im Gedicht) besingen; **po·et·ry** ['pəʊɪtrɪ] s. **1.** Poe'sie f (a. Ggs. Prosa) (a. fig.), Dichtkunst f; **2.** Dichtung f, coll. Dichtungen pl., Gedichte pl.: dra·matic ~ dramatische Dichtung.

po-faced [ˌpəʊ'feɪst] Brit. F grimmig (dreinschauend).

po·grom ['pɒgrəm] s. Po'grom m, n, (bsd. Juden)Verfolgung f.

poign·an·cy ['pɔɪnənsɪ] s. **1.** Schärfe f von Gerüchen etc.; **2.** fig. Bitterkeit f, Heftigkeit f, Schärfe f; **3.** Schmerzlichkeit f; **'poign·ant** [-nt] adj. □ **1.** scharf, beißend (Geruch, Geschmack); **2.** pi·'kant (a. fig.); **3.** fig. a) bitter, quälend (Reue, Hunger etc.), b) ergreifend: a ~ scene c) beißend, scharf: ~ wit, d) treffend, präg'nant: ~ remark; **4.**

'durchdringend: a ~ look.

point [pɔɪnt] I s. **1.** (Nadel-, Messer-, Bleistift- etc.)Spitze f: (not) to put too fine a ~ upon s.th. fig. et. (nicht gerade) gewählt ausdrücken; at the ~ of the pistol → pistol point; at the ~ of the sword fig. unter Zwang, mit Gewalt; **2.** ⊙ a) Stecheisen n, b) Grabstichel m, Griffel m, c) Radiernadel f, d) Ahle f; **3.** geogr. a) Landspitze f, b) Himmelsrichtung f; → cardinal 1; **4.** hunt. a) (Geweih)Ende n, b) Stehen n des Jagdhundes; **5.** ling. a) ⏷ Punkt m am Satzende, b) ~ of exclamation Ausrufezeichen n; → interrogation 1; **6.** typ. a) Punk'tur f, b) typo'graphischer Punkt (= 0,376 mm im Didot-System); **7.** ✶ a) Punkt m: ~ of intersection Schnittpunkt, b) (Dezi'mal)Punkt m, Komma n; **8.** (Kompass)Strich m; **9.** Auge n, Punkt m auf Karten, Würfeln; **10.** → point lace; **11.** phys. Grad m e-r Skala (a. ast.), Stufe f (a. ⊙ e-s Schalters), Punkt m: ~ of action Angriffspunkt (der Kraft); ~ of contact Berührungspunkt; ~ of culmination Kulminations-, Gipfelpunkt; boiling ~ Siedepunkt; freezing ~ Gefrierpunkt; 3 ~s below zero 3 Grad unter null; to bursting ~ zum Bersten (voll); frankness to the ~ of insult fig. an Beleidigung grenzende Offenheit; up to a ~ bis zu e-m gewissen Grad; when it came to the ~ fig. als es so weit war, als es darauf ankam; → stretch 10; **12.** Punkt m, Stelle f, Ort m: ~ of departure Ausgangsort; ~ of destination Bestimmungsort; ~ of entry ✚ Eingangshafen m; ~ of lubrication ⊙ Schmierstelle; ~ of view fig. Gesichts-, Standpunkt; **13.** ⚡ a) Kon'takt(punkt) m, b) Brit. 'Steckkon,takt m; **14.** Brit. (Kon'troll)Posten m e-s Verkehrspolizisten; **15.** pl. 🚉 Brit. Weichen pl.; **16.** Punkt m e-s Bewertungs- od. Bewirtschaftungssystems (a. Börse u. sport): bad ~ sport Strafpunkt; beat (win) on ~s nach Punkten schlagen (gewinnen); winner on ~s Punktsieger m; level on ~s punktgleich; give ~s to s.o. a) sport j-m vorgeben, b) fig. j-m überlegen sein; **17.** Boxen: ,Punkt' m (Kinnspitze); **18.** a. ~ of time Zeitpunkt m, Augenblick m: at the ~ of death; at this ~ a) in diesem Augenblick, b) an dieser Stelle, hier (a. in e-r Rede etc.); be on the ~ of doing s.th. im Begriff sein, et. zu tun; **19.** Punkt m e-r Tagesordnung etc., (Einzel-, Teil)Frage f: a case in ~ ein einschlägiger Fall, ein Beispiel; the case in ~ der vorliegende Fall; at all ~s in allen Punkten, in jeder Hinsicht; ~ of interest interessante Einzelheit; ~ of law Rechtsfrage; ~ of order a) (Punkt der) Tagesordnung f, b) Verfahrensfrage f; differ on many ~s in vielen Punkten nicht übereinstimmen; **20.** Kernpunkt m, -frage f, springender Punkt, Sache f: beside (od. off) the ~ nicht zur Sache gehörig, abwegig, unerheblich; come to the ~ zur Sache kommen; the ~ zur Sache gehörig, (zu)treffend, exakt; keep (od. stick) to the ~ bei der Sache bleiben; make (od. score) a ~ ein Argument anbringen, s-e Ansicht durchsetzen; make a ~ of s.th. Wert od. Gewicht auf et. legen, auf et. bestehen; make the ~ that die Feststellung machen, dass; that's the ~ I wanted to make darauf wollte ich hinaus; in ~ of hinsichtlich (gen.); in ~ of fact tatsächlich; that is the ~! das ist die Frage!; the ~ is that die Sache ist

die, dass; *it's a* ~ *of hono(u)r to him* das ist Ehrensache für ihn; *you have a* ~ *there!* da haben Sie nicht Unrecht!; *I take your* ~*!* ich verstehe, was Sie meinen!; → *miss²*, *press* 8; **21.** Pointe *f e-s Witzes etc.*; **22.** Zweck *m*, Ziel *n*, Absicht *f*: *what's your* ~ *in coming?*; *carry* (*od. gain od. make*) *one's* ~ sich (*od.* s-e Ansicht) durchsetzen, sein Ziel erreichen; *there is no* ~ *in doing* es hat keinen Zweck *od.* es ist sinnlos, zu tun; **23.** Nachdruck *m*: *give* ~ *to one's words* s-n Worten Nachdruck *od.* Gewicht verleihen; **24.** (her)vorstechende) Eigenschaft, (Vor)Zug *m*: *a noble* ~ *in her* ein edler Zug an ihr; *it has its* ~*s* es hat so s-e Vorzüge; *strong* ~ starke Seite, Stärke; *weak* ~ schwache Seite, wunder Punkt; **II** *v/t.* **25.** (an-, zu)spitzen; **26.** *fig.* pointieren; **27.** *Waffe etc.* richten (*at auf acc.*): ~ *one's finger at* (mit dem Finger) auf *j-n* deuten *od.* zeigen; ~ (*up*)*on Augen, Gedanken etc.* richten auf (*acc.*); ~ *to Kurs, Aufmerksamkeit* lenken auf (*acc.*), *j-n* bringen auf (*acc.*); **28.** ~ *out* a) zeigen, b) *fig.* hinweisen *od.* aufmerksam machen auf (*acc.*), betonen, c) *fig.* aufzeigen (*a. Fehler*), klarmachen, d) ausführen, darlegen; **29.** ~ *off places* A (Dezimal-) Stellen abstreichen; **30.** ~ *up* a) △ verfugen, b) ☉ *Fugen* glatt streichen, c) *Am. fig.* unter'streichen; **III** *v/i.* **31.** (mit dem Finger) zeigen, deuten, weisen (*at auf acc.*); **32.** ~ *to* nach e-r *Richtung* weisen *od.* liegen (*Haus etc.*); *fig.* a) hinweisen, -deuten auf (*acc.*), b) ab-, hinzielen auf (*acc.*); **33.** *hunt.* (vor)stehen (*Jagdhund*); **34.** ✻ reifen (*Abszess etc.*); '~-**blank I** *adj.* **1.** schnurgerade; **2.** ✕ *Kernschuss...*(*-Weite etc.*): *at* ~ *range* aus kürzester Entfernung; ~ *shot* Fleckschuss *m*; **3.** unverblümt, offen; glatt (*Ablehnung*); **II** *adv.* **4.** geradewegs; **5.** *fig.* 'rundheraus, klipp u. klar; ~ **du·ty** *s. Brit.* (Verkehrs)Postendienst *m* (*Polizei*).
point·ed ['pɔɪntɪd] *adj.* □ **1.** spitz, zugespitzt, Spitz...(*-bogen, -geschoss etc.*); **2.** scharf, pointiert (*Stil, Bemerkung*), anzüglich; **3.** treffend; '**point·ed·ness** [-nɪs] *s.* **1.** Spitzigkeit *f*; **2.** *fig.* Schärfe *f*, Deutlichkeit *f*; **3.** Anzüglichkeit *f*, Spitze *f*; '**point·er** [-tə] *s.* **1.** ✕ 'Richtschütze *m*, -kano,nier *m*; **2.** Zeiger *m*, Weiser *m* (*Uhr, Messgerät*); **3.** Zeigestock *m*; **4.** Radiernadel *f*; **5.** *hunt.* Vorsteh-, Hühnerhund *m*; **6.** F Fingerzeig *m*, Tipp *m*.
point lace *s.* genähte Spitze(n *pl.*).
point·less ['pɔɪntlɪs] *adj.* □ **1.** ohne Spitze, stumpf; **2.** *sport etc.* punktlos; **3.** *fig.* witzlos, ohne Pointe; **4.** *fig.* sinn-, zwecklos.
point po·lice·man [-mən] *s.* [*irr.*] → **pointsman**; **2.** **points·man** ['pɔɪntsmən] *s.* [*irr.*] *Brit.* **1.** ⚐ Weichensteller *m*; **2.** Ver'kehrspoli,zist *m*; **point system** *s. sport, ped. etc.* 'Punktsys,tem *n* (*a. typ.*); **2.** Punktschrift *f für Blinde*; ,**point-to-'point** (**race**) *s.* Geländejagdrennen *n*.
poise [pɔɪz] **I** *s.* **1.** Gleichgewicht *n*; **2.** Schwebe *f* (*a. fig. Unentschiedenheit*); **3.** (*Körper-, Kopf*)Haltung *f*; **4.** *fig.* sicheres Auftreten; Gelassenheit *f*; Haltung *f*; **II** *v/t.* **5.** im Gleichgewicht halten; *et.* balancieren: *be* ~*d* a) im Gleichgewicht sein, b) gelassen *od.* ausgeglichen sein, c) *fig.* schweben: ~*d for* bereit zu; **6.** *Kopf, Waffe etc.* halten; **III** *v/i.* **7.** schweben.
poi·son ['pɔɪzn] **I** *s.* **1.** Gift *n* (*a. fig.*):

what is your ~*?* F was wollen Sie trinken?; **II** *v/t.* **2.** (*o.s.* sich) vergiften (*a. fig.*); **3.** ✻ infizieren; '**poi·son·er** [-nə] *s.* **1.** Giftmörder(in), Giftmischer(in); **2.** *fig.* Vergifter(in), 'Giftspritze' *f*.
poi·son fang *s. zo.* Giftzahn *m*; ~ **gas** *s.* ✕ Kampfstoff *m, bsd.* Giftgas *n*.
poi·son·ing ['pɔɪznɪŋ] *s.* **1.** Vergiftung *f*; **2.** Giftmord *m*; '**poi·son·ous** [-nəs] *adj.* □ **1.** giftig (*a. fig.*) Gift...; **2.** F ekelhaft.
,**poi·son-'pen let·ter** *s.* verleumderischer *od.* ob'szöner (*anonymer*) Brief.
poke¹ [pəʊk] **I** *v/t.* **1.** *j-n* stoßen, puffen, knuffen: ~ *s.o. in the ribs* j-m e-n Rippenstoß geben; **2.** *Loch* stoßen (*in in acc.*); **3.** a. ~ *up Feuer* schüren; **4.** *Kopf* vorstrecken, *Nase etc. wohin* stecken: *she* ~*s her nose into everything* sie steckt überall ihre Nase hinein; **5.** ~ *fun at s.o.* sich über *j-n* lustig machen; **II** *v/i.* **6.** stoßen (*at* nach); stöbern (*into* in *dat.*): ~ *about* (herum)tasten, -tappen (*for* nach); **7.** *fig.* a) ~ *and pry* (herum)schnüffeln, b) sich einmischen (*into* in *acc.*); **8.** a. ~ *about* F (her'um)trödeln, bummeln; **III** *s.* **9.** (Rippen)Stoß *m*, Puff *m*, Knuff *m*; **10.** *Am.* → **slowpoke**.
poke² [pəʊk] *s. obs.* Spitztüte *f*; → **pig** 1.
poke bon·net *s.* Kiepe(nhut *m*) *f*.
pok·er¹ ['pəʊkə] *s.* Schürhaken *m*: *be as stiff as a* ~ steif wie ein Stock sein.
pok·er² ['pəʊkə] *s.* Poker(spiel) *n*.
pok·er face *s.* Pokergesicht *n* (*unbewegtes, undurchdringliches Gesicht, a. Person*); ~ **work** *s.* Brandmale'rei *f*.
pok·y ['pəʊkɪ] *adj.* **1.** eng, winzig; **2.** 'unele,gant: ~ *dress*; **3.** langweilig, ,lahm' (*a. Mensch*).
po·lar ['pəʊlə] **I** *adj.* □ **1.** po'lar (*a. phys.*, A), Polar...: ~ *air* Polarluft *f*, polare Kaltluft; ~ *fox* Polarfuchs *m*; ~ *lights* Polarlicht *n*; ⊉ *Sea* Polar-, Eismeer *n*; **2.** *fig.* po'lar, genau entgegengesetzt (*wirkend*); **II** *s.* A Po'lare *f*; ~ **ax·is** *s.* [*irr.*] A, *ast.* Po'larachse *f*; ~ **bear** *s. zo.* Eisbär *m*; ~ **cir·cle** *s. geogr.* Po'larkreis *m*.
po·lar·i·ty [pəʊˈlærətɪ] *s. phys.* Polari'tät *f* (*a. fig.*): ~ *indicator* ⚡ Polsucher *m*; **po·lar·i·za·tion** [,pəʊləraɪˈzeɪʃn] *s.* ⚡, *phys.* Polarisation *f*; *fig.* Polarisierung *f*; **po·lar·ize** ['pəʊləraɪz] *v/t.* ⚡, *phys.* polarisieren (*a. fig.*); **po·lar·iz·er** ['pəʊləraɪzə] *s. phys.* Polari'sator *m*.
pole¹ [pəʊl] **I** *s.* **1.** Pfosten *m*, Pfahl *m*; **2.** (*Bohnen-, Telegrafen-, Zelt- etc.*) Stange *f*; (*sport* Sprung)Stab *m*; (*Wagen*)Deichsel *f*; ⚡ (Leitungs)Mast *m*; (Ski)Stock *m*: ~ *jumper sport* Stabhochspringer *m*; *be up the* ~ *sl.* a) in der Tinte sitzen, b) verrückt sein; **3.** ♆ a) Flaggenmast *m*, b) Schifferstange *f*: *under bare* ~*s* ♆ vor Topp und Takel; **4.** (Mess)Rute *f* (*5,029 Meter*); **II** *v/t.* **5.** *Boot* staken; **6.** *Bohnen etc.* stängen.
pole² [pəʊl] *s.* **1.** *ast., biol., geogr., phys.* Pol *m*: *celestial* ~ Himmelspol; *the North* (*South*) ⊉ der Nordpol (Südpol); *negative* ~ *phys.* negativer Pol, ⚡ a. Kat(h)ode *f*; *positive* 8; **2.** *fig.* Gegenpol *m*, entgegengesetztes Ex'trem: *they are* ~*s apart* Welten trennen sie.
Pole³ [pəʊl] *s.* Pole *m*, Polin *f*.
pole aer·i·al *s.* 'Staban,tenne *f*; '~-**ax**(**e**) *s.* **1.** Streitaxt *f*; **2.** ♆ a) *hist.* Enterbeil *n*, b) Kappbeil *n*; **3.** Schlächterbeil *n*; '~-**cat** *s. zo.* **1.** Iltis *m*; **2.** *Am.* Skunk *m*; ~ **chang·er** *s.* ⚡ Polwechsler *m*; ~ **charge** *s.* ✕ gestreckte Ladung; ~

jump etc. → *pole vault etc.*
po·lem·ic [pɒˈlemɪk] **I** *adj.* (□ ~*ally*) **1.** po'lemisch, Streit...; **II** *s.* **2.** Po'lemiker (-in); **3.** Po'lemik *f*; **po·lem·i·cist** [-ɪsɪst] *s.* Po'lemiker(in); **po·lem·ics** [-ks] *s. pl. sg. konstr.* Po'lemik *f*.
pole star *s. ast.* Po'larstern *m*; *fig.* Leitstern *m*; ~ **vault** *s. sport* Stabhochsprung *m*; '~-**vault** *v/i.* Stabhochspringen; ~ **vault·er** *s. sport* Stabhochspringer *m*.
po·lice [pəˈliːs] **I** *s.* **1.** Poli'zei(behörde, -truppe) *f*; **2.** *coll. pl.* Poli'zisten *pl.*, einzelne Poli'zisten *pl.*: *five* ~; **3.** ✕ *Am.* Ordnungsdienst *m*: *kitchen* ~ Küchendienst; **II** *v/t.* **4.** (poli'zeilich) über'wachen; **5.** *fig.* kontrollieren, über'wachen; **6.** ✕ *Am. Kaserne etc.* säubern, in Ordnung halten; **III** *adj.* **7.** poli'zeilich, Polizei...(*-gericht, -gewalt, -staat etc.*): ~ *blot·ter s. Am.* Dienstbuch *n*; ~ **car** *s.* Poli'zeiauto *n*; ~ **con·sta·ble** → *policeman* 1; ~ **dog** *s.* **1.** Poli'zeihund *m*; **2.** (*Deutscher*) Schäferhund *m*; ~ **force** *s.* Poli'zei(truppe) *f*; ~*man* [-mən] *s.* [*irr.*] **1.** Poli'zist *m*, Schutzmann *m*; **2.** *zo.* Sol'dat *m* (*Ameise*); ~ **mes·sage** *s. Radio:* a) 'Durchsage *f* der Poli'zei, b) Reiseruf *m*; ~ **of·fi·cer** *s.* Poli'zeibeamte(r) *m*, Poli'zist *m*; ~ **rec·ord** *s.* 'Vorstrafenre,gister *n*; ~ **sta·tion** *s.* Poli'zeiwache *f*, -re,vier *n*; ~ **trap** *s.* Autofalle *f*; ~,**woman** *s.* [*irr.*] Poli'zistin *f*.
pol·i·clin·ic [,pɒlɪˈklɪnɪk] *s.* ✻ Poliklinik *f*, Ambu'lanz *f*.
pol·i·cy¹ ['pɒlɪsɪ] *s.* **1.** Verfahren(sweise *f*) *n*, Taktik *f*, Poli'tik *f*: *marketing* ~ ✝ Absatzpolitik *e-r Firma*; *honesty is the best* ~ ehrlich währt am längsten; *the best* ~ *would be to* (*inf.*) das Beste *od.* Klügste wäre, zu (*inf.*); **2.** Poli'tik *f* (*Wege u. Ziele der Staatsführung*), po'litische Linie: *foreign* ~ Außenpolitik; ~ *adviser* (politischer) Berater; **3.** *public* ~ ✁ Rechtsordnung *f*: *against public* ~ sittenwidrig; **4.** Klugheit *f*: a) Zweckmäßigkeit *f*, b) Schlauheit *f*.
pol·i·cy² ['pɒlɪsɪ] *s.* **1.** (Ver'sicherungs-) Po,lice *f*, Versicherungsschein *m*; **2.** a. ~ *racket Am.* Zahlenlotto *n*; '~,**hold·er** *s.* Versicherungsnehmer(in), Poli'ceninhaber(in); '~-,**mak·ing** *adj.* die Richtlinien der Poli'tik bestimmend.
pol·i·o ['pəʊlɪəʊ] *s.* **1.** ✻ F Polio *f*; **2.** Poliofall *m*.
pol·i·o·my·e·li·tis [,pəʊlɪəʊmaɪəˈlaɪtɪs] *s.* ✻ spi'nale Kinderlähmung, Poliomye'litis *f*.
Pol·ish¹ ['pəʊlɪʃ] **I** *adj.* polnisch; **II** *s. ling.* Polnisch *n*.
pol·ish² ['pɒlɪʃ] **I** *v/t.* **1.** polieren, glätten; *Schuhe etc.* wichsen, ☉ abschleifen, -schmirgeln, glanzschleifen; **2.** *fig.* abschleifen, verfeinern: ~ *off* F a) *Gegner* 'erledigen', b) *Arbeit* 'hinhauen' (*schnell erledigen*), c) *Essen* ,wegputzen', ,verdrücken' (*verschlingen*); ~ *up* aufpolieren (*a. fig. Wissen auffrischen*); **II** *v/i.* **3.** glänzend werden; sich polieren lassen; **III** *s.* **4.** Poli'tur *f*, (Hoch)Glanz *m*, Glätte *f*: *give s.th. a* ~ *et.* polieren; **5.** Poliermittel *n*, Poli'tur *f*; Schuhcreme *f*; Bohnerwachs *n*; **6.** *fig.* Schliff *m* (*feine Sitten*); **7.** *fig.* Glanz *m*; '**pol·ished** [-ʃt] *adj.* **1.** poliert, glatt, glänzend; **2.** *fig.* geschliffen, a) höflich, b) gebildet, fein, c) bril'lant; '**pol·ish·er** [-ʃə] *s.* **1.** Polierer *m*, Schleifer *m*; **2.** ☉ a) Polierfeile *f*, -stahl *m*, -scheibe *f*, -bürste *f*, b) Po'liermaschine *f*; **3.** Poliermittel *n*, Poli'tur *f*; '**pol·ish·ing** [-ʃɪŋ] *s.* **1.** Polieren *n*, Glätten *n*, Schleifen *n*; **II** *adj.* Polier..., Putz...: ~ *file* Polierfeile *f*; ~

powder Polier-, Schleifpulver *n*; ~ ***wax*** Bohnerwachs *n*.

po·lite [pəˈlaɪt] *adj.* □ **1.** höflich, artig (**to** gegen); **2.** verfeinert, fein: ~ ***arts*** schöne Künste; ~ ***letters*** schöne Literatur, Belletristik *f*; **poˈlite·ness** [-nɪs] *s.* Höflichkeit *f*.

pol·i·tic [ˈpɒlɪtɪk] *adj.* □ **1.** diploˈmatisch; **2.** *fig.* diploˈmatisch, (welt)klug, berechnend, poˈlitisch; **3.** poˈlitisch: *body* ~ Staatskörper *m*; **po·lit·i·cal** [pəˈlɪtɪkl] *adj.* □ **1.** poˈlitisch: ~ *cor-rectness* Poˈlitical Correctness *f*, politische Korrektheit *f*, *~ly correct* politisch korrekt (*Wortwahl*); ~ *econo-my* Volkswirtschaft *f*; ~ *science* Politologie *f*; ~ *scientist* Politologe *m*, Politikwissenschaftler *m*; *a ~ issue* ein Politikum; **2.** staatlich, Staats...: ~ *sys-tem* Regierungssystem *n*; **pol·i·ti·cian** [ˌpɒlɪˈtɪʃn] *s.* **1.** Poˈlitiker *m*; **2.** a) (Parˈtei)Poˌlitiker *m* (*a. contp.*), b) *Am.* poˈlitischer Opportuˈnist; **po·lit·i·cize** [pəˈlɪtɪsaɪz] *v/i. u. v/t. allg.* politisieren; **po·lit·i·co** [pəˈlɪtɪkəʊ] *pl.* **-cos** *Am.* F *für politician* 2.

po·lit·i·co- [pɒˈlɪtɪkəʊ] *in Zssgn* politisch-...: *~-economical* wirtschaftspolitisch.

pol·i·tics [ˈpɒlɪtɪks] *s. pl. oft sg. konstr.* **1.** Poliˈtik *f*, Staatskunst *f*; **2.** (Parˈtei-, ˈStaats)Poliˌtik: *enter ~* ins politische Leben (ein)treten; **3.** poˈlitische Überˈzeugung *od.* Richtung: *what are his ~?* wie ist er politisch eingestellt?; **4.** *fig.* (Interˈessen)Poliˌtik *f*; **5.** *Am.* (poˈlitische) Machenschaften *pl.*: *play ~* Winkelzüge machen, manipulieren; **'pol·i·ty** [-ɪtɪ] *s.* **1.** Regierungsform *f*, Verfassung *f*, politische Ordnung; **2.** Staats-, Gemeinwesen *n*, Staat *m*.

pol·ka [ˈpɒlkə] **I** *s.* ♪ Polka *f*; **II** *v/i.* Polka tanzen; ~ *dot s.* Punktmuster *n* (*auf Textilien*).

poll¹ [pəʊl] **I** *s.* **1.** *bsd. dial. od. humor.* (Hinter)Kopf *m*; **2.** (ˈEinzel)Perˌson *f*; **3.** Abstimmung *f*, Stimmabgabe *f*, Wahl *f*: *poor ~* geringe Wahlbeteiligung; **4.** Wählerliste *f*; **5.** a) Stimmenzählung *f*, b) Stimmenzahl *f*; **6.** *mst pl.* ˈWahllo‚kal *n*: *go to the ~s* zur Wahl (-urne) gehen; **7.** (Ergebnis *n* e-r) (ˈMeinungs)Umfrage *f*; **II** *v/t.* **8.** *Haar etc.* stutzen, (*a. Tier*) scheren; *Baum* kappen; *Pflanze* köpfen; *e-m Rind die* Hörner stutzen; **9.** in die Wahlliste eintragen; **10.** *Wahlstimmen* erhalten, auf sich vereinigen; **11.** *Bevölkerung* befragen; **III** *v/i.* **12.** s-e Stimme abgeben, wählen: ~ *for* stimmen für.

poll² [pɒl] *s. univ. Brit. sl.* **1.** *coll.* **the *℔** Studenten, die sich nur auf den *poll degree* (→ 2) vorbereiten; **2.** *a.* ~ *ex-amination* (leichteres) Bakkalaureˈatsex‚amen: *~ degree* nach Bestehen dieses Examens erlangter Grad.

poll³ [pəʊl] **I** *adj.* hornlos: ~ *cattle*; **II** *s.* hornloses Rind.

pol·lack [ˈpɒlək] *pl.* **-lacks**, *bsd. coll.* **-lack** *s.* Pollack *m*, Steinköhler *m* (*Dorsch*).

pol·lard [ˈpɒləd] **I** *s.* **1.** gekappter Baum; **2.** *zo.* a) hornloses Tier, b) Hirsch, der sein Geweih abgeworfen hat; **3.** (Weizen)Kleie *f*; **II** *v/t.* **4.** *Baum etc.* kappen, stutzen.

ˈpoll·book *s.* Wählerliste *f*.

pol·len [ˈpɒlən] *s.* ♥ Pollen *m*, Blütenstaub *m*: ~ *catarrh* Heuschnupfen *m*; ~ *sac* Pollensack *m*; ~ *count* Pollenwerte *pl.*; *a high ~ count* starker Pollenflug; ~ *tube* Pollenschlauch *m*; **'pol·li·nate** [-neɪt] *v/t. bot.* bestäuben, befruchten.

poll·ing [ˈpəʊlɪŋ] **I** *s.* **1.** Wählen *n*, Wahl *f*; **2.** Wahlbeteiligung *f*: *heavy (poor) ~* starke (geringe) Wahlbeteiligung; **II** *adj.* **3.** Wahl...: ~ *booth* Wahlzelle *f*; ~ *district* Wahlkreis *m*; ~ *place Am.*, ~ *station bsd. Brit.* Wahllokal *n*.

pol·lock [ˈpɒlək] → *pollack*.

poll·ster [ˈpəʊlstə] *s.* Meinungsforscher(in).

poll tax *s.* Kopfsteuer *f*, -geld *n*.

pol·lu·tant [pəˈluːtənt] *s.* Schadstoff *m*; **pol·lute** [pəˈluːt] *v/t.* **1.** beflecken (*a. fig. Ehre etc.*), beschmutzen; **2.** *Wasser etc.* verunreinigen, *Umwelt etc.* verschmutzen; **3.** *fig.* besudeln; *eccl.* entweihen; *moralisch* verderben; **pol·lut·er** [-tə] *s.* ˈUmweltverschmutzer *m*, -sünder *m*: ~ *pays principle* Verursacherprinzip *n* (*bei Bereinigung von Umweltschäden*); **pol·lu·tion** [-uːʃn] *s.* **1.** Befleckung *f*, Verunreinigung *f* (*a. fig.*); **2.** *fig.* Entweihung *f*, Schändung *f*; **3.** *physiol.* Polluti'on *f*; **4.** (ˈUmwelt-, Luft-, Wasser)Verschmutzung *f*: ~ *control* Umweltschutz *m*; ~ *level* Schadstoffbelastung *f*; **pol·lu·tive** [-tɪv] *adj.* ˈumweltverschmutzend, -feindlich.

po·lo [ˈpəʊləʊ] *s. sport* Polo *n*: ~ (*neck*) Rollkragen(pullover) *m*; ~ *shirt* Polohemd *n*.

po·lo·ny [pəˈləʊnɪ] *s.* grobe Zerveˈlatwurst.

pol·troon [pɒlˈtruːn] *s.* Feigling *m*.

poly- [pɒlɪ] *in Zssgn* Viel..., Mehr..., Poly...; **pol·y·an·drous** [ˌpɒlɪˈændrəs] *adj.* ♥, *zo., sociol.* poly'andrisch; **pol·y·a·tom·ic** *adj.* ⚛ 'viel-, ˈmehra‚tomig; **pol·y·bas·ic** *adj.* ⚛ mehrbasig; **pol·y·chro·mat·ic** *adj.* (□ *~ally*) viel-, mehrfarbig; **pol·y·chrome** **I** *adj.* **1.** viel-, mehrfarbig, bunt: ~ *printing* Bunt-, Mehrfarbendruck; **II** *s.* **2.** Vielfarbigkeit *f*; **3.** bunt bemalte Plastik; **pol·y·clin·ic** *s.* Klinik *f* (für alle Krankheiten); **po·lyg·a·mist** [pəˈlɪgəmɪst] *s.* Polygaˈmist(in); **po·lyg·a·mous** [-məs] *adj.* poly'gam(isch ♥, *zo.*); **po·lyg·a·my** [-mɪ] *s.* Polygaˈmie *f* (*a. zo.*), Mehrehe *f*, Vielweibeˈrei *f*.

pol·y·glot [ˈpɒlɪglɒt] **I** *adj.* **1.** vielsprachig; **II** *s.* **2.** Polyˈglotte *f* (*Buch in mehreren Sprachen*); **3.** Polyˈglotte(r *m*) *f* (*Person*).

pol·y·gon [ˈpɒlɪgən] *s.* ♈ a) Polyˈgon *n*, Vieleck *n*, b) Polygoˈnalzahl *f*: ~ *of forces phys.* Kräftepolygon; **po·lyg·o·nal** [pɒˈlɪgənl] *adj.* polygoˈnal, vieleckig.

po·lyg·y·ny [pəˈlɪdʒɪnɪ] *s. allg.* Polygyˈnie *f*.

pol·y·he·dral [ˌpɒlɪˈhedrl] *adj.* ♈ poly'edrisch, vielflächig, Polyeder...; **pol·y·he·dron** [-rən] *s.* ♈ Poly'eder *n*.

pol·y·mer·ic [ˌpɒlɪˈmerɪk] *adj.* ⚛ ‚poly'mer; **po·lym·er·ism** [pəˈlɪmərɪzəm] *s.* Polymeˈrie *f*; **pol·y·mer·ize** [pəˈlɪməraɪz] ⚛ **I** *v/t.* polymerisieren; **II** *v/i.* poly'mere Körper bilden.

pol·y·mor·phic [ˌpɒlɪˈmɔːfɪk] *adj.* poly'morph, vielgestaltig.

Pol·y·ne·sian [ˌpɒlɪˈniːzjən] **I** *adj.* **1.** polyˈnesisch; **II** *s.* **2.** Polyˈnesier(in); **3.** *ling.* Polyˈnesisch *n*.

pol·y·nom·i·al [ˌpɒlɪˈnəʊmjəl] **I** *adj.* ♈ poly'nomisch, vielglied(e)rig; **II** *s.* ♈ Poly'nom *n*.

pol·yp(e) [ˈpɒlɪp] *s. ⚕, zo.* Po'lyp *m*.

'pol·y·phase *adj.* ⚡ mehrphasig: ~ *cur-rent* Mehrphasen-, Drehstrom *m*; **'pol·y·phon·ic** [-ˈfɒnɪk] *adj.* **1.** vielstimmig, mehrtönig; **2.** ♪ poly'phon, kontraˈpunktisch; **3.** *ling.* pho'netisch mehr-

deutig; **'pol·y·pod** [-pɒd] *s. zo.* Vielfüßer *m*.

pol·y·pus [ˈpɒlɪpəs] *pl.* **-pi** [-paɪ] *s.* **1.** *zo.* Po'lyp *m*, Tintenfisch *m*; **2.** ⚕ Po'lyp *m*.

pol·y·sty·rene [ˌpɒlɪˈstaɪriːn] *s.* 🜀 ‚Polysty'rol *n*, *bsd.* ‚Styro'por *TM n*.

pol·y·syl·lab·ic *adj.* mehr-, vielsilbig; **'pol·y·syl·la·ble** *s.* vielsilbiges Wort; **'pol·y·tech·nic** **I** *adj.* poly'technisch; **II** *s.* poly'technische Schule, Poly'technikum *n*; **'pol·y·the·ism** *s.* Polythe'ismus *m*, Vielgötteˈrei *f*; **pol·y·thene** [ˈpɒlɪθiːn] *s.* 🜀 Polyäthy'len *n*: ~ *bag* Plastiktüte *f*; **pol·y·trop·ic** *adj.* ⚗, *biol.* poly'trop(isch); **pol·y·va·lent** *adj.* 🜀 polyva'lent, mehrwertig.

pol·y·zo·on [ˌpɒlɪˈzəʊɒn] *pl.* **-'zo·a** [-ə] *s.* Moostierchen *n*.

pom [pɒm] → *pommy*.

po·made [pəˈmɑːd] **I** *s.* Po'made *f*; **II** *v/t.* pomadisieren, mit Po'made einreiben.

po·man·der [pəʊˈmændə] *s.* Duftkugel *f*.

po·ma·tum [pəʊˈmeɪtəm] → *pomade*.

pome [pəʊm] *s.* **1.** ♥ Apfel-, Kernfrucht *f*; **2.** *hist.* Reichsapfel *m*.

pome·gran·ate [ˈpɒmɪˌgrænɪt] *s.* **1.** *a.* ~ *tree* Graˈnatapfelbaum *m*; **2.** *a.* ~ *ap-ple* Graˈnatapfel *m*.

Pom·er·a·nian [ˌpɒməˈreɪnjən] **I** *adj.* **1.** pommer(i)sch; **II** *s.* **2.** Pommer(in); **3.** *a.* ~ *dog* Spitz *m*.

po·mi·cul·ture [ˈpəʊmɪˌkʌltʃə] *s.* Obstbaumzucht *f*.

pom·mel [ˈpʌml] **I** *s.* (Degen-, Sattel-, Turm)Knopf *m*, Knauf *m*; **II** *v/t.* mit den Fäusten bearbeiten, schlagen.

pom·my [ˈpɒmɪ] *s. sl. brit.* Einwanderer *m* (in Auˈstralien *od.* Neu'seeland).

pomp [pɒmp] *s.* Pomp *m*, Prunk *m*.

pom·pon [ˈpɔ̃ːmpɔ̃ːŋ] (*Fr.*) *s.* Troddel *f*, Quaste *f*.

pom·pos·i·ty [pɒmˈpɒsətɪ] *s.* **1.** Prunk *m*; Pomphaftigkeit *f*, Prahleˈrei *f*; wichtigtuerisches Wesen; **2.** Bom'bast *m*, Schwülstigkeit *f* (*im Ausdruck*); **pomp·ous** [ˈpɒmpəs] *adj.* □ **1.** pom'pös, prunkvoll; **2.** wichtigtuerisch, aufgeblasen; **3.** bom'bastisch, schwülstig (*Sprache*).

ponce [pɒns] *Brit. sl.* **I** *s.* **1.** Zuhälter *m*; **2.** ‚Homo' *m*; **II** *v/i.* **3.** Zuhälter sein; **'ponc·ing** [-sɪŋ] *s. Brit. sl.* Zuhälteˈrei *f*.

pon·cho [ˈpɒntʃəʊ] *pl.* **-chos** [-z] *s.* Poncho *m*, ˈUmhang *m*.

pond [pɒnd] *s.* Teich *m*, Weiher *m*: *horse ~* Pferdeschwemme *f*; *big ~* ‚Großer Teich' (*Atlantik*).

pon·der [ˈpɒndə] **I** *v/i.* nachdenken, -sinnen, (nach)grübeln (*on, upon, over* über *acc.*): ~ *over s.th.* et. überlegen; **II** *v/t.* über'legen, nachdenken über (*acc.*): ~ *one's words* s-e Worte abwägen; *~ing silence* nachdenkliches Schweigen; **pon·der·a·bil·i·ty** [ˌpɒndərəˈbɪlətɪ] *s. phys.* Wägbarkeit *f*; **'pon·der·a·ble** [-dərəbl] *adj.* wägbar (*a. fig.*); **pon·der·os·i·ty** [ˌpɒndəˈrɒsətɪ] *s.* **1.** Gewicht *n*, Schwere *f*, Gewichtigkeit *f*; **2.** *fig.* Schwerfälligkeit *f*; **'pon·der·ous** [-dərəs] *adj.* □ **1.** schwer, massig, gewichtig; **2.** *fig.* schwerfällig (*Stil*); **'pon·der·ous·ness** [-dərəsnɪs] → *pon-derosity*.

pone¹ [pəʊn] *s. Am.* Maisbrot *n*.

po·ne² [ˈpəʊnɪ] *s. Kartenspiel:* **1.** Vorhand *f*; **2.** Spieler, der abhebt.

pong [pɒŋ] **I** *s.* **1.** dumpfes Dröhnen; **2.** *Br. sl.* Gestank *m*, ‚Mief' *m*; **II** *v/i.* **3.** dröhnen; **4.** *Br. sl.* stinken; **5.** *sl. thea.* improvisieren.

pon·tiff [ˈpɒntɪf] *s.* **1.** Hohe'priester *m*; **2.** Papst *m*; **pon·tif·i·cal** [pɒnˈtɪfɪkl] *adj.* □ **1.** *antiq.* (ober)priesterlich; **2.** *R.C.* pontifi'kal: a) bischöflich, b) *bsd.* päpstlich: ☿ **Mass** Pontifikalamt *n*; **3.** *fig.* a) feierlich, würdig, b) päpstlich, über'heblich; **pon·tif·i·cate I** *s.* [pɒn'tɪfɪkət] Pontifi'kat *n*; **II** *v/i.* [-keɪt] a) sich päpstlich gebärden, b) ~ (**on**) sich dogmatisch auslassen (über *acc.*); **'pon·ti·fy** [-ɪfaɪ] → **pontificate** II.

pon·toon¹ [pɒn'tu:n] *s.* **1.** Pon'ton *m*, Brückenkahn *m*: ~ **bridge** Ponton-, Schiffsbrücke *f*; ~ **train** ✕ Brückenkolonne *f*; **2.** ⚓ Kielleichter *m*, Prahm *m*; **3.** ✈ Schwimmer *m*.

pon·toon² [pɒn'tu:n] *s. Brit.* 'Siebzehnund'vier *n* (*Kartenspiel*).

po·ny ['pəʊnɪ] **I** *s.* **1.** *zo.* Pony *n*: a) kleines Pferd, b) *Am. a.* Mustang *m*, c) *pl. sl.* Rennpferde *pl.*; **2.** *Brit. sl.* £ 25; **3.** *Am.* F ‚Klatsche' *f*, Eselsbrücke *f* (*Übersetzungshilfe*); **4.** *Am.* F a) kleines (Schnaps- *etc.*)Glas, b) Gläs·chen *n* Schnaps *etc.*; **5.** *Am. et.* ‚im 'Westentaschenfor,mat', Miniatur... (*z. B. Auto, Zeitschrift*); **II** *v/t.* **6.** ~ **up** *Am. sl.* berappen, bezahlen; ~ **en·gine** 🚂 Ran-'gierlokomo,tive *f*; ~ **tail** *s.* Pferdeschwanz *m* (*Frisur*).

pooch [pu:tʃ] *s. Am. sl.* Köter *m*.

poo·dle ['pu:dl] *s. zo.* Pudel *m*.

poof [pu:f] *Brit. sl.* ‚Schwule(r)' *m*, ‚Homo' *m*.

pooh [pu:] *int. contp.* pah!; **,~·'pooh** *v/t.* geringschätzig behandeln, *et.* als unwichtig abtun, die Nase rümpfen über (*acc.*), *et.* verlachen.

pool¹ [pu:l] *s.* **1.** Teich *m*, Tümpel *m*; **2.** Pfütze *f*, Lache *f*: ~ **of blood** Blutlache; **3.** (Schwimm)Becken *n*; **4.** *geol.* pe'troleumhaltige Ge'steinspar,tie; **5.** ◎ Schmelzbad *n*.

pool² [pu:l] **I** *s.* **1.** *Kartenspiel:* a) (Gesamt)Einsatz *m*, b) (Spiel)Kasse *f*; **2.** *mst pl.* (Fußball- *etc.*)Toto *m*, *n*: ~**s coupon** *Brit.* Tippschein *m* (*im Toto*); **3.** *Billard:* a) *Brit.* Poulespiel *n* (*mit Einsatz*), b) *Am.* Poolbillard *n*; **4.** *fenc.* Ausscheidungsrunde *f*; **5.** ✝ a) Pool *m*, Kar'tell *n*, Ring *m*, Inter'essengemeinschaft *f*, b) a. **working** a) Arbeitsgemeinschaft *f*, c) (Preis- *etc.*)Abkommen *n*; **6.** ✝ gemeinsamer Fonds; **7.** ~ (**of players**) *sport* a) Kader *m*, b) Aufgebot *n*, Auswahl *f*; **II** *v/t.* **8.** ✝ *Geld, Kapital* zs.-legen; ~ **funds** zs.-schießen; *Gewinn* unterein'ander (ver)teilen; *Geschäftsrisiko* verteilen; **9.** ✝ zu e-m Ring vereinigen; **10.** *fig. Kräfte, Wissen etc.* vereinigen, zs.-tun; **III** *v/i.* **11.** ein Kar'tell bilden; **'~·room** *s. Am.* **1.** Billardzimmer *n*; **2.** 'Spielsa,lon *m*; **3.** Wettannahmestelle *f*.

poop¹ [pu:p] ⚓ **I** *s.* **1.** Heck *n*; **2.** *a.* ~ **deck** Achterdeck *n*; **3.** *obs.* Achterhütte *f*; **II** *v/t.* **4.** *Schiff* von hinten treffen (*Sturzwelle*): **be ~ed** e-e Sturzsee von hinten bekommen.

poop² [pu:p] **I** *v/i.* **1.** tuten; **2.** ‚pupen', furzen; **II** *v/t.* **3.** *sl. j-n* ‚auspumpen': **~ed** (**out**) ‚fix u. fertig'.

poor [pʊə] **I** *adj.* □ → **poorly** II; **1.** arm, mittellos, (unter'stützungs)bedürftig: ~ **person** ⚖ Arme(r *m*) *f*; **2.** *fig.* arm(selig), ärmlich, dürftig (*Kleidung, Mahlzeit etc.*); **3.** dürr, mager (*Boden, Erz, Vieh etc.*), schlecht, unergiebig (*Ernte etc.*): ~ **coal** Magerkohle *f*; **4.** *fig.* arm (**in** an *dat.*); schlecht, mangelhaft, schwach (*Gesundheit, Leistung, Spieler, Sicht, Verständigung etc.*): ~ **consolation** schwacher Trost; **a** ~ **lookout** schlechte Aussichten; **a** ~ **night** e-e schlechte Nacht; **5.** *fig.*

contp. jämmerlich, traurig: **in my** ~ **opinion** *iro.* m-r unmaßgeblichen Meinung nach; **6.** F arm, bedauernswert: ~ **me!** *humor.* ich Ärmste(r)!; **II** *s.* **7. the** ~ die Armen *pl.*; '**~·house** *s. hist.* Armenhaus *n*; ~ **law** *s. hist.* **1.** ⚖ Armenrecht *n*; **2.** *pl.* öffentliches Fürsorgerecht.

poor·ly ['pʊəlɪ] **I** *adj.* **1.** unpässlich, kränklich: **he looks** ~ er sieht schlecht aus; **II** *adv.* **2.** armselig, dürftig: **he is** ~ **off** es geht ihm schlecht; **3.** *fig.* schlecht, dürftig, schwach: ~ **gifted** schwach begabt; **think** ~ **of** nicht viel halten von; '**poor·ness** [-nɪs] *s.* **1.** Armut *f*, Mangel *m*; *fig.* Armseligkeit *f*, Ärmlichkeit *f*, Dürftigkeit *f*; **2.** ✒ Magerkeit *f*, Unfruchtbarkeit *f* (*des Bodens*); *min.* Unergiebigkeit *f*.

poove [pu:v] *s.* → **poof**; '**poov·y** *adj.* ‚schwul'.

pop¹ [pɒp] **I** *v/i.* **1.** knallen, puffen, losgehen (*Flaschenkork, Feuerwerk etc.*); **2.** aufplatzen (*Kastanien, Mais*); **3.** F knallen, ‚ballern' (**at** auf *acc.*); **4.** *mit adv.* flitzen, huschen: ~ **in** hereinplatzen, auf e-n Sprung vorbeikommen (*Besuch*); ~ **off** F a) ‚abhauen', sich aus dem Staub machen, plötzlich verschwinden, b) einnicken, c) ‚abkratzen' (*sterben*), d) *Am. sl.* ‚das Maul aufreißen'; ~ **up** (plötzlich) auftauchen; **5.** *a.* ~ **out** aus den Höhlen treten (*Augen*); **II** *v/t.* **6.** knallen od. platzen lassen; *Am. Mais* rösten; **7.** F *Gewehr etc.* abfeuern; **8.** abknallen, -schießen; **9.** schnell *wohin* tun od. stecken: ~ **one's head into the door**; ~ **on** Hut aufstülpen; **10.** her'ausplatzen mit (*e-r Frage etc.*): ~ **the question** F (**to** e-r *Dame*) e-n Heiratsantrag machen; **11.** *Brit. sl.* versetzen, verpfänden; **III** *s.* **12.** Knall *m*, Puff *m*, Paff *m*; **13.** F Schuss *m*: **take a** ~ **at** schießen nach; **14.** *Am. sl.* Pi'stole *f*; **15.** *bsd. Am.* kohlensäurehaltiges Getränk: a) F Cola *f*, b) F ‚Limo' *f* (*Limonade*); **16. in** ~ *Brit. sl.* versetzt, verpfändet; **IV** *int.* **17.** puff!, paff!, husch!, zack!; **V** *adv.* **18.** a) mit e-m Knall, b) plötzlich: **go** ~ knallen, platzen.

pop² [pɒp] *s. Am.* F **1.** Pa'pa *m*, Papi *m*; **2.** ‚Opa' *m*, Alter *m*.

pop³ [pɒp] F **I** *s.* **1.** *a.* ~ **music** 'Schlager', 'Popmu,sik *f*; **2.** *a.* ~ **song** Schlager *m*; **II** *adj.* **3.** Schlager...: ~ **group** Popgruppe *f*; ~ **singer** Schlager-, Popsänger(in).

pop⁴ [pɒp] → **popsicle**.

pop art *s. Kunst:* Pop-Art *f*.

'**pop·corn** *s.* Puffmais *m*, Popcorn *n*.

pope [pəʊp] *s. R.C.* Papst *m* (*a. fig.*): **is the ☿** (**a**) **Catholic?** worauf du dich verlassen kannst!, da fragst du noch?; '**pope·dom** [-dəm] *s.* Papsttum *n*; '**pop·er·y** [-pərɪ] *s. contp.* Papiste'rei *f*, Pfaffentum *n*.

'**pop|·eyed** *adj.* F glotzäugig: **be** ~ Stielaugen machen (**with** vor *dat.*); '**~·gun** *s.* Kindergewehr *n*; ‚Knallbüchse' *f* (*a. fig. schlechtes Gewehr*).

pop·in·jay ['pɒpɪndʒeɪ] *s. obs.* Geck *m*, Laffe *m*, Fatzke *m*.

pop·ish ['pəʊpɪʃ] *adj.* □ *contp.* pa'pistisch.

pop·lar ['pɒplə] *s.* ✿ Pappel *f*.

pop·lin ['pɒplɪn] *s.* Pope'lin *m*, Pope'line *f* (*Stoff*).

pop·per ['pɒpə] *s.* F Druckknopf *m*.

pop·pet ['pɒpɪt] *s.* **1.** *obs. od. dial.* Püppchen *n* (*a. Kosewort*); **2.** ◎ a) *a.* ~ **head** Docke *f* e-r *Drehbank*, b) *a.* ~ **valve** 'Schnüffelven,til *n*.

pop·py ['pɒpɪ] *s.* **1.** ✿ Mohn(blume *f*) *m*;

2. a) Mohnsaft *m*, b) Mohnrot *n*; '**~·cock** *s. Am.* F Quatsch *m*; ☿ **Day** *s. Brit.* F Volkstrauertag *m* (*Sonntag vor od. nach dem 11. November*); ~ **seed** *s.* Mohn(samen) *m*.

pops [pɒps] → **pop²** 2.

pop·si·cle ['pɒpsɪkl] *s. Am.* Eis *n* am Stiel.

pop·sy ['pɒpsɪ], *a.* **,~·'wop·sy** [-'wɒpsɪ] *s.* ‚süße Puppe', ‚Mädchen' *n*, ‚Schatz' *m*.

pop·u·lace ['pɒpjʊləs] *s.* **1.** Pöbel *m*; **2.** (gemeines) Volk, *der* große Haufen.

pop·u·lar ['pɒpjʊlə] *adj.* □ → **popularly**; **1.** Volks...: ~ **election** allgemeine Wahl; ~ **front** *pol.* Volksfront *f*; ~ **government** Volksherrschaft *f*; **2.** allgemein, weit verbreitet (*Irrtum, Unzufriedenheit etc.*); **3.** popu'lär, (allgemein) beliebt (**with** bei): **the** ~ **hero** der Held des Tages; **make o.s.** ~ **with** sich bei *j-m* beliebt machen; **4.** a) popu'lär, volkstümlich, b) gemeinverständlich, Popular...: ~ **magazine** populäre Zeitschrift; ~ **music** volkstümliche Musik; ~ **newspaper** Boulevardblatt *n*; ~ **science** Popularwissenschaft *f*; ~ **song** Schlager *m*; ~ **writer** Volksschriftsteller(in); **5.** (für jeden) erschwinglich, Volks...: ~ **edition** Volksausgabe *f*; ~ **prices** volkstümliche Preise; **pop·u·lar·i·ty** [,pɒpjʊ'lærətɪ] *s.* Populari'tät *f*, Volkstümlichkeit *f*, Beliebtheit *f* (**with** bei, **among** unter *dat.*); '**pop·u·lar·ize** [-əraɪz] *v/t.* **1.** popu'lär machen, (*beim Volk*) einführen; **2.** popularisieren, volkstümlich *od.* gemeinverständlich darstellen; '**pop·u·lar·ly** [-lɪ] *adv.* **1.** allgemein; im Volksmund; **2.** populär *od.* volkstümlich, gemeinverständlich.

pop·u·late ['pɒpjʊleɪt] *v/t.* bevölkern, besiedeln; **pop·u·la·tion** [,pɒpjʊ'leɪʃn] *s.* **1.** Bevölkerung *f*, Einwohnerschaft *f*: ~ **density** Bevölkerungsdichte *f*; ~ **explosion** Bevölkerungsexplosion *f*; **2.** Bevölkerungszahl *f*; **3.** Gesamtzahl *f*, Bestand *m*: ~ **swine** Schweinebestand (*e-s Landes*); '**pop·u·lous** [-ləs] *adj.* □ dicht besiedelt, volkreich; '**pop·u·lousness** [-ləsnɪs] *s.* dichte Besied(e)lung, Bevölkerungsdichte *f*.

por·ce·lain ['pɔ:səlɪn] **I** *s.* Porzel'lan *n*; **II** *adj.* Porzellan...: ~ **clay** *min.* Porzellanerde *f*, Kaolin *n*.

porch [pɔ:tʃ] *s.* **1.** (über'dachte) Vorhalle, Por'tal *n*; **2.** *Am.* Ve'randa *f*: ~ **climber** *sl.* ‚Klettermaxe' *m*, Einsteigdieb *m*.

por·cine ['pɔ:saɪn] *adj.* **1.** *zo.* zur Fa'milie der Schweine gehörig; **2.** schweineartig; **3.** *fig.* schweinisch.

por·cu·pine ['pɔ:kjʊpaɪn] *s. zo.* Stachelschwein *n*.

pore¹ [pɔ:] *v/i.* **1.** (**over**) brüten (über *dat.*): ~ **over one's books** über s-n Büchern hocken; **2.** (nach)grübeln (**on**, **upon** über *acc.*).

pore² [pɔ:] *s. biol. etc.* Pore *f*.

pork [pɔ:k] *s.* **1.** Schweinefleisch *n*; **2.** *Am.* F *von der Regierung aus politischen Gründen gewährte (finanzielle) Begünstigung od. Stellung;* ~ **bar·rel** *s. Am.* F *politisch berechnete Geldzuwendung der Regierung;* ~ **butch·er** *s.* Schweineschlächter *m*; ~ **chop** *s.* 'Schweinekote,lett *n*.

pork·er ['pɔ:kə] *s.* Mastschwein *n*; '**pork·ling** [-klɪŋ] *s.* Ferkel *n*.

pork pie *s.* 'Schweinefleischpa,stete *f*.

'**pork-pie hat** *s.* runder Filzhut.

pork·y¹ ['pɔ:kɪ] *adj.* fett(ig), dick.

por·ky² ['pɔ:kɪ] *s. Am.* F Stachelschwein *n*.

porn [pɔ:n], **por·no** ['pɔ:nəʊ] *sl.* **I** *s.* **1.**

Porno(gra'phie f) m; **2.** Porno(film) m; **II** adj. **3.** → **pornographic**.

por·no·graph·ic [ˌpɔːnəʊˈgræfɪk] adj. porno'graphisch, Porno...: ~ **film** Porno(film) m; **por·nog·ra·phy** [pɔːˈnɒgrəfɪ] s. Pornogra'phie f.

por·ny [ˈpɔːnɪ] adj. sl. → **pornographic**.

po·ros·i·ty [pɔːˈrɒsətɪ] s. **1.** Porosi'tät f, ('Luft-, 'Wasser),Durchlässigkeit f; **2.** Pore f, po'röse Stelle; **po·rous** [ˈpɔːrəs] adj. po'rös: a) löch(e)rig, porig, b) ('luft-, 'wasser),durchlässig.

por·poise [ˈpɔːpəs] pl. **-pois·es**, coll. **-poise** s. zo. **1.** Tümmler m; **2.** Del-'phin m.

por·ridge [ˈpɒrɪdʒ] s. Porridge n, m, Hafer(flocken)brei m, -grütze f: **pease ~** Erbsenbrei.

por·ri·go [pəˈraɪgəʊ] s. ✻ Grind m.

port¹ [pɔːt] s. **1.** ♘, ✓ (See-, Flug)Hafen m: **free ~** Freihafen; **inner ~** Binnenhafen; **~ of call** a) ♘ Anlaufhafen, b) ✓ Anflughafen; **~ of delivery** (od. **discharge**) Löschhafen, -platz m; **~ of departure** a) ♘ Abgangshafen, b) ✓ Abflughafen; **~ of destination** a) ♘ Bestimmungshafen, b) ✓ Zielflughafen; **~ of entry** Einlaufhafen; **~ of registry** Heimathafen; **~ of tran(s)shipment** Umschlaghafen; **any ~ in a storm** fig. in der Not frisst der Teufel Fliegen; **2.** Hafenplatz m, -stadt f; **3.** fig. (sicherer) Hafen, Ziel n: **come safe to ~.**

port² [pɔːt] ♘ **I** s. Backbord(seite f) n: **on the ~ beam** an Backbord dwars; **on the ~ bow** an Backbord voraus; **on the ~ quarter** Backbord achtern; **cast to ~** nach Backbord abfallen; **II** v/t. Ruder nach der Backbordseite 'umlegen; **III** v/i. nach Backbord drehen (Schiff); **IV** adj. a) ♘ Backbord..., b) ✓ link.

port³ [pɔːt] s. **1.** Tor n, Pforte f; **city ~** Stadttor; **2.** ♘ a) (Pfort-, Lade)Luke f, b) (Schieß)Scharte f (a. ✗ Panzer); **3.** ⊚ (Auslass-, Einlass)Öffnung f, Abzug m; **4.** ⚡ Anschlussbuchse f.

port⁴ [pɔːt] s. Portwein m.

port⁵ [pɔːt] v/t. **1.** obs. tragen; **2.** ✗ Am. **~ arms!** Gewehr in Schräghalte nach links!

port·a·ble [ˈpɔːtəbl] **I** adj. **1.** tragbar: **~ radio** (**set**) a) → 3a, b) ✗ Tornisterfunkgerät; **~ typewriter** → 4; **2.** transpor'tabel, beweglich: **~ derrick** fahrbarer Kran; **~ firearm** Handfeuerwaffe f; **~ railway** Feldbahn f; **~ searchlight** Handscheinwerfer m; **II** s. **3.** a) Kofferradio n, b) Portable m, n, tragbares Fernsehgerät, c) Phonokoffer m, d) Koffertonbandgerät n; **4.** 'Reiseschreibma,schine f.

por·tage [ˈpɔːtɪdʒ] s. **1.** (bsd. 'Trage-) Trans,port m; **2.** ✝ Fracht f, Rollgeld n; **3.** ♘ a) Por'tage f, Trageplatz m, b) Tragen n (von Kähnen etc.) über e-e Portage.

por·tal¹ [ˈpɔːtl] s. **1.** Δ Por'tal n, (Haupt)Eingang m, Tor n: **~ crane** ⊚ Portalkran m; **2.** poet. Pforte f, Tor n; **of heaven**; **3.** Computer: Portal n, Startseite f (mit Themenauswahl).

por·tal² [ˈpɔːtl] anat. **I** adj. Pfort (-ader)...; **II** s. Pfortader f.

ˌpor·tal-to-ˈpor·tal pay s. ✝ Arbeitslohn, berechnet für die Zeit vom Betreten der Fabrik etc. bis zum Verlassen.

port·cul·lis [ˌpɔːtˈkʌlɪs] s. ✗ hist. Fallgatter n.

por·tend [pɔːˈtend] v/t. vorbedeuten, anzeigen, deuten auf (acc.); **por·tent** [ˈpɔːtent] s. **1.** Vorbedeutung f; **2.** (bsd. schlimmes) (Vor-, An)Zeichen, Omen

n; **3.** Wunder n (Sache od. Person); **por'ten·tous** [-ntəs] adj. □ **1.** omi'nös, unheil-, verhängnisvoll; **2.** ungeheuer, wunderbar, a. humor. unheimlich.

por·ter¹ [ˈpɔːtə] s. a) Pförtner m, b) Por-'tier m.

por·ter² [ˈpɔːtə] s. **1.** ☙ (Gepäck)Träger m, Dienstmann m; **2.** ☙ Am. (Schlafwagen)Schaffner m.

por·ter³ [ˈpɔːtə] s. Porter(bier n) m.

'por·ter·house s. **1.** obs. Bier-, Speisehaus n; **2.** a. **~ steak** Porterhousesteak n.

'port|,fire s. ✗ Zeitzündschnur f, Lunte f; **,~'fo·li·o** s. **1.** a) Aktentasche f, (a. Künstler- etc.)Mappe f, b) Porte'feuille n (für Staatsdokumente); **2.** fig. (Mi'nister)Porte,feuille n: **without ~** ohne Geschäftsbereich; **3.** ✝ ('Wechsel-) Porte,feuille n; **'~·hole** s. **1.** ♘ a) (Pfort)Luke f, b) Bullauge n; **2.** ⊚ → **port³** 3.

por·ti·co [ˈpɔːtɪkəʊ] pl. **-cos** s. Δ Säulengang m.

por·tion [ˈpɔːʃn] **I** s. **1.** (An)Teil m (of an dat.); **2.** Porti'on f (Essen); **3.** Teil m, Stück n (Buch, Gebiet, Strecke etc.); **4.** Menge f, Quantum n; **5.** ⚕ a) Mitgift f, Aussteuer f, b) Erbteil n: **legal ~** Pflichtteil n; **6.** fig. Los n, Schicksal n; **II** v/t. **7.** aufteilen: **~ out** aus-, verteilen; **8.** zuteilen; **9.** Tochter aussteuern.

port·li·ness [ˈpɔːtlɪnɪs] s. **1.** Stattlichkeit f; **2.** Wohlbeleibtheit f; **port·ly** [ˈpɔːtlɪ] adj. **1.** stattlich, würdevoll; **2.** wohlbeleibt.

port·man·teau [ˌpɔːtˈmæntəʊ] pl. **-s** u. **-x** [-z] s. **1.** Handkoffer m; **2.** obs. Mantelsack m; **3.** mst **~ word** ling. Schachtelwort n.

por·trait [ˈpɔːtrɪt] s. **1.** a) Por'trät n, Bild(nis) n, b) phot. Por'trät(aufnahme f) n; **take s.o.'s ~** j-n porträtieren od. malen; → **sit for** 3; **2.** fig. Bild n, (lebenswahre) Schilderung f; **'por·trait·ist** [-tɪst] s. Por'trätmaler(in); **'portrai·ture** [-tʃə] s. **1.** → **portrait**; **2.** a) Por'trätmale,rei f, b) phot. Por'trätfotogra,fie f; **por·tray** [pɔːˈtreɪ] v/t. **1.** porträ'tieren, (ab)malen; **2.** fig. schildern, darstellen; **por·tray·al** [pɔːˈtreɪəl] s. **1.** Porträtieren n; **2.** Por'trät n; **3.** fig. Schilderung f.

Por·tu·guese [ˌpɔːtjʊˈgiːz] **I** pl. **-guese** s. **1.** Portu'giese m, Portu'giesin f; **2.** ling. Portu'giesisch n; **II** adj. **3.** portu-'giesisch.

pose¹ [pəʊz] **I** s. **1.** Pose f (a. fig.), Posi-'tur f, Haltung f; **II** v/t. **2.** aufstellen, in Posi'tur setzen; **3.** Frage stellen, aufwerfen; **4.** Behauptung aufstellen, Anspruch erheben; **5.** (as) hinstellen (als), ausgeben (für); **III** v/i. **6.** sich in Posi-'tur setzen; **7.** a) paint etc. Mo'dell stehen od. sitzen, b) sich fotografieren lassen; **8.** posieren, sich in Pose werfen; **9.** auftreten od. sich ausgeben (as als).

pose² [pəʊz] v/t. durch Fragen verwirren, verblüffen.

pos·er [ˈpəʊzə] s. **1.** → **poseur**; **2.** ,harte Nuss', knifflige Frage.

po·seur [pəʊˈzɜː] (Fr.) s. Po'seur m, ,Schauspieler' m.

posh [pɒʃ] adj. F ,piekfein', ,todschick', ,feu'dal'.

pos·it [ˈpɒzɪt] phls. **I** v/t. postulieren; **II** n Postu'lat n.

po·si·tion [pəˈzɪʃn] **I** s. **1.** Positi'on f, Lage f, Standort m; ⊚ (Schalt- etc.) Stellung f: **~ of the sun** ast. Sonnenstand m; **in** (**out of**) **~** (nicht) in der richtigen Lage; **2.** körperliche Lage,

Stellung f: **horizontal ~**; **3.** ♘, ✓ Positi'on f (a. sport), ♘ a. Besteck n: **~ lights** a) ♘, ✓ Positionslichter, b) mot. Begrenzungslichter; **4.** ✗ Stellung f: **~ warfare** Stellungskrieg m; **5.** (Arbeits-) Platz m, Stellung f, Posten m, Amt n: **hold a responsible ~** e-e verantwortliche Stellung innehaben; **6.** fig. (sozi'ale) Stellung, (gesellschaftlicher) Rang: **people of ~** Leute von Rang; **7.** fig. Lage f, Situati'on f: **an awkward ~**; **be in a ~ to do s.th.** in der Lage sein, et. zu tun; **8.** fig. (Sach)Lage f, Stand m der Dinge: **financial ~** Finanzlage, Vermögensverhältnisse pl.; **legal ~** Rechtslage; **9.** Standpunkt m, Haltung f: **take up a ~ on a question** zu e-r Frage Stellung nehmen; **10.** ⚔, phls. (Grund-, Lehr)Satz m; **II** v/t. **11.** bsd. ⊚ in die richtige Lage bringen, (ein-) stellen; anbringen; Cursor etc. positio-'nieren; **12.** lokalisieren; **13.** Polizisten etc. postieren; **po·si·tion·al** [-ʃənl] adj. Stellungs..., Lage...: **~ play** sport Stellungsspiel n; **po·si·tion find·er** s. Ortungsgerät n; **po·si·tion pa·per** s. pol. 'Grundsatzpa,pier n.

pos·i·tive [ˈpɒzɪtɪv] **I** adj. □ **1.** bestimmt, defini'tiv, ausdrücklich (Befehl etc.), fest (Versprechen etc.), unbedingt: **~ law** ⚕ positives Recht; **2.** sicher, 'unum,stößlich, eindeutig (Beweis, Tatsache); **3.** positiv, tatsächlich; **4.** positiv, zustimmend: **~ reaction**; **5.** über'zeugt, (abso'lut) sicher: **be ~ about s.th.** e-r Sache ganz sicher sein; **6.** rechthaberisch; **7.** F ausgesprochen, abso'lut: **a ~ fool** ein ausgemachter Narr; **8.** ⚡, ⚔, ✻, biol., phys., phot., phls. positiv: **~ electrode** ⚡ Anode f; **~ pole** ⚡ Pluspol m; **9.** ⊚ zwangsläufig, Zwangs... (Getriebe, Steuerung etc.); **10.** ling. im Positiv stehend: **~ degree** Positiv m; **II** s. **11.** et. Positives, Positivum n; **12.** phot. Positiv n; **13.** ling. Positiv m; **'pos·i·tive·ness** [-nɪs] s. **1.** Bestimmtheit f; Wirklichkeit f; **2.** fig. Hartnäckigkeit f; **'pos·i·tiv·ism** [-vɪzəm] s. phls. Positi'vismus m.

pos·se [ˈpɒsɪ] s. (Poli'zei- etc.)Aufgebot n; allg. Haufen m, Schar f.

pos·sess [pəˈzes] v/t. **1.** allg. (a. Eigenschaften, Kenntnisse etc.) besitzen, haben; im Besitz (inne)haben: **~ed of** im Besitz e-r Sache; **~ o.s. of** et. in Besitz nehmen, sich e-r Sache bemächtigen; **~ed noun** ling. Besitzsubjekt n; **2.** a) (a. die e-e Sprache etc.) beherrschen, Gewalt haben über (acc.), b) erfüllen (**with** mit e-r Idee, mit Unwillen etc.): **like a man ~ed** wie ein Besessener, wie toll; **~ one's soul in patience** sich in Geduld fassen; **pos'ses·sion** [-eʃn] s. **1.** abstrakt: Besitz m (a. ⚕): **actual ~** tatsächlicher od. unmittelbarer Besitz; **adverse ~** Ersitzung(sbesitz m) f; **in the ~ of** in j-s Besitz; **in ~ of s.th.** im Besitz e-r Sache; **have ~ of** im Besitze von et. sein; **take ~ of** Besitz ergreifen von, in Besitz nehmen; **2.** Besitz(tum n) m, Habe f; **3.** pl. Besitzungen pl., Liegenschaften pl.: **foreign ~s** auswärtige Besitzungen; **4.** fig. Besessenheit f; **5.** fig. Beherrscht-, Erfülltsein n (**by** von e-r Idee etc.); **6.** mst **self-~** fig. Fassung f, Beherrschung f; **pos'ses·sive** [-sɪv] **I** adj. □ **1.** Besitz...; **2.** besitzgierig, -betonend: **~ instinct** Sinn m für Besitz; **3.** fig. besitzergreifend (Mutter etc.); **4.** ling. posses-'siv, besitzanzeigend: **~ case** → 5 b; **II** s. **5.** ling. a) Posses'siv(um) n, besitzanzeigendes Fürwort, b) Genitiv m, zweiter Fall; **pos'ses·sor** [-sə] *s.* Besitzer (-in), Inhaber(in); **pos'ses·so·ry** [-sərɪ] *adj.* Besitz...: **~ action** ⚖ Besitzstörungsklage *f*; **~ right** Besitzrecht *n.*

pos·si·bil·i·ty [ˌpɒsəˈbɪlətɪ] *s.* **1.** Möglichkeit *f* (**of** zu, für, **of doing** *et.* zu tun): **there is no ~ of his coming** es besteht keine Möglichkeit, dass er kommt; **2.** *pl.* (Entwicklungs)Möglichkeiten *pl.*, (-)Fähigkeiten *pl.*; **pos·si·ble** [ˈpɒsəbl] **I** *adj.* ☐ **1.** möglich (**with** bei, **to** *dat.*, **for** für): **this is ~ with him** das ist bei ihm möglich; **highest ~** größtmöglich; **2.** eventu'ell, etwaig, denkbar; **3.** F annehmbar, pas'sabel, leidlich; **II** *s.* **4. the ~** das (Menschen-)Mögliche, das Beste; *sport* die höchste Punktzahl; **5.** infrage kommende Per'son (*bei Wettbewerb etc.*); **pos·si·bly** [ˈpɒsəblɪ] *adv.* **1.** möglicherweise, viel'leicht; **2.** (irgend) möglich: **when I ~ can** wenn ich irgend kann; **I cannot ~ do this** ich kann das unmöglich tun; **how can I ~ do it?** wie kann ich es nur *od.* bloß machen?

pos·sum [ˈpɒsəm] *s.* F *abbr. für* **opossum**: **play ~** sich nicht rühren, sich tot *od.* krank *od.* dumm stellen.

post[1] [pəʊst] **I** *s.* **1.** Pfahl *m*, Pfosten *m*, Ständer *m*, Stange *f*, Stab *m*: **as deaf as a ~** *fig.* stocktaub; **2.** Anschlagsäule *f*; **3.** *sport* (Start- *od.* Ziel)Pfosten *m*, Start- (*od.* Ziel)linie *f*: **be beaten at the ~** kurz vor dem Ziel geschlagen werden; **II** *v/t.* **4.** *mst* **~ up** *Plakate etc.* anschlagen, -kleben; **5.** *mst* **~ over** *Mauer mit Zetteln* bekleben; **6.** a) *et.* (durch Aushang *etc.*) bekannt geben: **~ as missing** ⚓, ✈ als vermisst melden, b) *fig.* (öffentlich) anprangern.

post[2] [pəʊst] **I** *s.* **1.** ⚔ Posten *m* (*Stelle od. Soldat*): **advanced ~** vorgeschobener Posten; **last ~** *Brit.* Zapfenstreich *m*; **at one's ~** auf (s-m) Posten; **2.** ⚔ Standort *m*, Garni'son *f*: **2 Exchange** (*abbr.* **PX**) *Am.* Einkaufsstelle *f*; **~ headquarters** Standortkommandantur *f*; **3.** Posten *m*, Platz *m*, Stand *m*; ✝ Börsenstand *m*; **4.** Handelsniederlassung *f*, -platz *m*; **5.** ✝ (Rechnungs)Posten *m*; **6.** Posten *m*, (An)Stellung *f*, Stelle *f*, Amt *n*: **~ of a secretary** Sekretärsposten; **II** *v/t.* **7.** *Soldaten etc.* aufstellen, postieren; **8.** ⚔ a) ernennen, b) versetzen, (ab)kommandieren; **9.** ✝ eintragen, verbuchen; *Konto* (ins Hauptbuch) über'tragen: **~ up** *Bücher* nachtragen, in Ordnung bringen.

post[3] [pəʊst] **I** *s.* **1.** ☎ *bsd. Brit.* Post® *f*: a) *als Einrichtung*, b) *Brit.* Postamt *n*, c) *Brit.* Post-, Briefkasten *m*, d) Postzustellung *f*, e) Postsendung(en *pl.*) *f*, -sachen *pl.*, *f*) Nachricht *f*: **by ~** per (*od.* mit der) Post; **2.** *hist.* a) Post(kutsche) *f*, b) Ku'rier *m*; **3.** *bsd. Brit.* 'Brief,papier *n* (*Format*); **II** *v/t.* **4.** *Brit.* zur Post® geben, mit der Post® (zu)senden, aufgeben, in den Briefkasten werfen; **5.** F *mst* **~ up** *j-n* informieren: **keep s.o. ~ed** j-n auf dem Laufenden halten; **well ~ed** gut unterrichtet.

post- [pəʊst] *in Zssgn* nach, später, hinter, post...

post·age [ˈpəʊstɪdʒ] *s.* Porto *n*, Postgebühr *f*, -spesen *pl.*: **additional** (*od.* **extra**) **~** Nachporto, Portozuschlag *m*; **~ free, ~ paid** portofrei, franko; **~ due** *s.* Nach-, Strafporto *n*; **~ stamp** *s.* Briefmarke *f*, Postwertzeichen *n.*

post·al [ˈpəʊstəl] **I** *adj.* po'stalisch, Post...: **~ card** → II; **~ cash order** Postnachnahme *f*; **~ code** → **postcode**; **~ district** Postzustellbezirk *m*; **~ order** *Brit.* Postanweisung *f*; **~ parcel** Postpaket *n*; **~ service** *bsd. Am.* Postzustelldienst *m*: **~ tuition** Fernunterricht *m*; **~ vote** *Brit.* Briefwahl *f*; **~ voter** Briefwähler(in); **2 Union** Weltpostverein *m*; **II** *s. Am.* Postkarte *f* (*mit aufgedruckter Marke*).

'**post|·box** *s. Brit.* **1.** Briefkasten *m*; **2.** Mailbox *f* (*elektronischer Briefkasten*); '**~·card** [-sk] *s.* Postkarte *f*; '**~·code** *s. Brit.* Postleitzahl *f.*

ˌ**post|-'date** *v/t.* **1.** *Brief etc.* vo'rausdaˌtieren; **2.** nachträglich *od.* später datieren; 'ˌ**~en·try** *s.* **1.** ✝ nachträgliche (Ver)Buchung; **2.** ✝ Nachverzollung *f*; **3.** *sport* Nachnennung *f.*

post·er [ˈpəʊstə] *s.* **1.** Pla'katankleber *m*; **2.** Pla'kat *n*: **~ paint** Plakatfarbe *f*; **3.** Poster *m*, *n.*

poste res·tante [ˌpəʊstˈrestɑ̃ːnt] (*Fr.*) **I** *adj.* postlagernd; **II** *s. bsd. Brit.* Aufbewahrungsstelle *f* für postlagernde Sendungen.

pos·te·ri·or [pɒˈstɪərɪə] **I** *adj.* ☐ a) später (**to** als), b) hinter, Hinter...: **be ~ to** *zeitlich od. örtlich* kommen nach, folgen auf (*acc.*); **II** *s.* Hinterteil *n*, Hintern *m*; **pos·ter·i·ty** [pɒˈsterətɪ] *s.* **1.** Nachkommen(schaft *f*) *pl.*; **2.** Nachwelt *f.*

pos·tern [ˈpəʊstɜːn] *s. a.* **~ door, ~ gate** Hinter-, Neben-, Seitentür *f.*

ˌ**post-'free** *adj.* portofrei.

ˌ**post'grad·u·ate** [-st'g-] **I** *adj.* nach dem ersten aka'demischen Grad: **~ studies**; **II** *s.* j-d, der nach dem ersten aka'demischen Grad weiterstudiert.

ˌ**post'haste** *adv.* eiligst.

post·hu·mous [ˈpɒstjʊməs] *adj.* ☐ po'stum, post'hum: a) *nach des Vaters Tod geboren*, b) nachgelassen, hinter'lassen (*Schriftwerk*), c) nachträglich (*Ordensverleihung etc.*): **~ fame** Nachruhm *m.*

pos·til·(l)ion [pəˈstɪljən] *s. hist.* Postillion *m.*

post·ing [ˈpəʊstɪŋ] *s.* Versetzung *f*, ⚔ 'Abkomman,dierung *f.*

post|·man [ˈpəʊstmən] *s.* [*irr.*] Briefträger *m*, Postbote *m*; '**~·mark** [-stm-] **I** *s.* Poststempel *m*; **II** *v/t.* (ab)stempeln; '**~,mas·ter** [-st,m-] *s.* Postamtsvorsteher *m*, Postmeister *m*: **2 General** Postminister *m.*

post·me·rid·i·an [ˌpəʊstməˈrɪdɪən] *adj.* Nachmittags..., nachmittägig; **post me·rid·i·em** [-məˈrɪdɪəm] (*Lat.*) *adv.* (*abbr.* **p.m.**) nachmittags.

'**post,mis·tress** [-st,m-] *s.* Postmeisterin *f.*

post|·mod·ern [ˌpəʊstˈmɒdn] *adj. bsd.* ⚠ 'postmo,dern; ˌ**~'mod·ern·ism** *s. bsd.* ⚠ **1.** die 'Postmo,derne, (der) ,Postmoder'nismus; ˌ**~'mod·ern·ist I** *adj.* postmoder'nistisch, 'postmo,dern; **II** *s.* 'Postmoderne(r *m*) *f*, Vertreter(in) der 'Postmo,derne; **~-mor·tem** [ˌpəʊstˈmɔːtəm] ⚖, ✱ **I** *adj.* Leichen..., nach dem Tode (stattfindend); **II** *s.* (*abbr. für* **~ examination**) Leichenöffnung *f*, Auto'psie *f*; *fig.* Ma'növerkri,tik *f*, nachträgliche Ana'lyse; ˌ**~'na·tal** *adj.* nach der Geburt (stattfindend); ˌ**~'nup·tial** *adj.* nach der Hochzeit (stattfindend).

post of·fice *s.* **1.** Post(amt *n*) *f*: **General 2** Hauptpost(amt); **2 Department** *Am.* Postministerium *n*; **2.** *Am. ein Gesellschaftsspiel*; **~ box** *s.* Post(schließ)fach *n*; **~ or·der** *s.* Postanweisung *f*; **~ savings bank** *s.* Postsparkasse *f.*

ˌ**post'op·er·a·tive** *adj.* ✱ postopera'tiv, nachträglich.

ˌ**post-'paid** *adj. u. adv.* freigemacht, frankiert.

post·pone [ˌpəʊsˈpəʊn] *v/t.* **1.** verschieben, auf-, hin'ausschieben; **2.** 'unterordnen (**to** *dat.*), hint'ansetzen; ˌ**post'pone·ment** [-mənt] *s.* **1.** Verschiebung *f*, Aufschub *m*; **2.** ⚙, *a. ling.* Nachstellung *f.*

ˌ**post·po'si·tion** *s.* **1.** Nachstellung *f* (*a. ling.*); **2.** *ling.* nachgestelltes (Verhältnis)Wort; ˌ**post'pos·i·tive** *ling.* **I** *adj.* nachgestellt; **II** *s.* → **postposition** 2.

ˌ**post'pran·di·al** *adj.* nach dem Essen, nach Tisch (*Rede, Schläfchen etc.*).

post·script [ˈpəʊsskrɪpt] *s.* **1.** Post'skriptum *n* (*zu e-m Brief*), Nachschrift *f*; **2.** Nachtrag *m* (*zu e-m Buch*); **3.** Nachbemerkung *f.*

pos·tu·lant [ˈpɒstjʊlənt] *s.* **1.** Antragsteller(in); **2.** *R.C.* Postu'lant(in); **pos·tu·late I** *v/t.* [ˈpɒstjʊleɪt] **1.** fordern, verlangen, begehren; **2.** postulieren, (als gegeben) vor'aussetzen; **II** *s.* [-lət] **3.** Postu'lat *n*, ('Grund)Vor,aussetzung *f.*

pos·ture [ˈpɒstʃə] **I** *s.* **1.** (Körper)Haltung *f*, Stellung *f*; (*a. thea., paint.*) Posi'tur *f*, Pose *f*; **2.** Lage *f* (*a. fig. Situation*), Anordnung *f*; **3.** *fig. geistige* Haltung; **II** *v/t.* **4.** zu'rechtstellen, arrangieren; **III** *v/i.* **5.** sich in Posi'tur stellen *od.* in Pose werfen; posieren (*a. fig.* **as** als); '**pos·tur·er** [-ərə] *s.* **1.** Schlangenmensch *m* (*Artist*); **2.** → **poseur**.

ˌ**post'war** *adj.* Nachkriegs...: **~ Germany** Deutschland *n* nach dem (Zweiten Welt)Krieg, 'Nachkriegs,deutschland *n.*

po·sy [ˈpəʊzɪ] *s.* **1.** Sträußchen *n*; **2.** *obs.* Motto *n*, Denkspruch *m.*

pot [pɒt] **I** *s.* **1.** (*Blumen-, Koch-, Nacht- etc.*)Topf *m*: **go to ~** *sl.* a) kaputtgehen, b) ‚vor die Hunde gehen' (*Person*); **keep the ~ boiling** a) die Sache in Gang halten, b) sich über Wasser halten; **the ~ calls the kettle black** ein Esel schilt den andern Langohr; **big ~** *sl.* ‚großes Tier'; **a ~ of money** F ‚ein Heidengeld'; **he has ~s of money** F er hat Geld wie Heu; **2.** Kanne *f*; **3.** ⚙ Tiegel *m*, Gefäß *n*: **~ annealing** Kastenglühen *n*; **~ galvanization** Feuerverzinken *n*; **4.** *sport sl.* Po'kal *m*; **5.** (Spiel)Einsatz *m*; **6.** → **pot shot**; **7.** *sl.* Pot *n*, Marihu'ana *n*; **II** *v/t.* **8.** in e-n Topf tun; *Pflanze* eintopfen; **9.** *Fleisch* einlegen, einmachen: **~ted meat** Fleischkonserven *pl.*; **10.** *Billardball* einlochen; **11.** *hunt.* (ab)schießen; **12.** F einheimsen, erbeuten; **13.** *Baby* aufs Töpfchen setzen; **14.** *fig.* F a) *Musik* ‚konservieren', b) *Stoff* mundgerecht machen; **III** *v/i.* **15.** (los)ballern, schießen (**at** auf *acc.*).

po·ta·ble [ˈpəʊtəbl] **I** *adj.* trinkbar; **II** *s.* Getränk *n.*

po·tage [pɒˈtɑːʒ] (*Fr.*) *s.* (dicke) Suppe.

pot·ash [ˈpɒtæʃ] *s.* ⚗ **1.** Pottasche *f*, 'Kaliumkarbo,nat *n*: **bicarbonate of ~** doppeltkohlensaures Kali; **~ fertilizer** Kalidünger *m*; **~ mine** Kalibergwerk *n*; **2.** → **caustic** 1.

po·tas·si·um [pəˈtæsjəm] *s.* ⚗ Kalium *n*; **~ bro·mide** *s.* 'Kaliumbro,mid *n*; **~ car·bon·ate** *s.* 'Kaliumkarbo,nat *n*, Pottasche *f*; **~ cy·a·nide** *s.* 'Kaliumcya,nid *n*, Zyan'kali *n*; **~ hy·drox·ide** *s.* 'Kaliumhydro,xid *n*, Ätzkali *n*; **~ ni·trate** *s.* 'Kaliumni,trat *n.*

po·ta·tion [pəʊˈteɪʃn] *s.* **1.** Trinken *n*; Zeche'rei *f*; **2.** Getränk *n.*

po·ta·to [pəˈteɪtəʊ] *pl.* **-toes** *s.* **1.** Kar'toffel *f*: **fried ~es** Bratkartoffeln; **small ~es** *Am.* F ‚kleine Fische'; **hot ~**

F ‚heißes Eisen'; *drop s.th. like a hot ~*
et. wie eine heiße Kartoffel fallen lassen; *think o.s. no small ~es sl.* sehr
von sich eingenommen sein; *one ~, two
~es, three ~es etc.* beim Sekunden-
zählen: einundzwanzig, zweiundzwan-
zig, dreiundzwanzig *etc.*; **2.** *Am. sl.* a)
‚Rübe' *f* (*Kopf*), b) Dollar *m*; **~ bee·tle**
s. zo. Kar'toffelkäfer *m*; **~ blight → potato disease**; **~ bug → potato beetle**;
~ chips *s. pl.* a) *Brit.* Pommes frites *pl.*,
b) *Am.* → **~ crisps** *s. pl.* Kar'toffelchips
pl.; **~ dis·ease** *s.* Kar'toffelkrankheit *f*;
~ soup *s.* Kar'toffelsuppe *f*; **~ trap** *s. sl.*
‚Klappe' *f*, ‚Maul' *n*.
pot| bar·ley *s.* Graupen *pl.*; **'~‚bel·lied**
adj. dickbäuchig; **'~‚bel·ly** *s.* Schmerbauch *m*; **'~‚boil·er** *s.* F *Kunst etc.*: reine Brotarbeit; **'~·boy** *s. Brit.* Schank-
kellner *m*.
po·teen [pɒ'tiːn] *s.* heimlich gebrannter
Whisky (*in Irland*).
po·ten·cy ['pəʊtənsɪ] *s.* **1.** Stärke *f*,
Macht *f*; *fig. a.* Einfluss *m*; **2.** Wirksamkeit *f*, Kraft *f*; **3.** *physiol.* Po'tenz *f*;
'po·tent [-nt] *adj.* □ **1.** mächtig, stark;
2. einflussreich; **3.** po'tent, fi'nanzstark:
a ~ bidder; **4.** zwingend, über'zeugend
(*Argumente etc.*); **5.** stark (*Drogen, Getränk*); **6.** *physiol.* po'tent; **'po·ten·tate**
[-teɪt] *s.* Poten'tat *m*, Machthaber *m*,
Herrscher *m*; **po·ten·tial** [pəʊ'tenʃl] I
adj. □ **1.** potenzi'ell: a) möglich, eventu'ell, b) in der Anlage vorhanden, la-
'tent: **~ market** (*murderer*) potenzieller Markt (*Mörder*); **2.** *ling.* Möglich-
keits...: **~ mood** → 4; **3.** *phys.* potenzi-
'ell, gebunden: **~ energy** potenzielle
Energie, Energie der Lage; II *s.* **4.** *ling.*
Potenti'alis *m*, Möglichkeitsform *f*; **5.**
phys. Potenzi'al *n* (*a. ⚡*); **~** Spannung *f*:
~ equation ⓐ Potenzialgleichung *f*; **6.**
(*Kriegs-, Menschen- etc.*)Potenzi'al *n*,
Re'serven *pl.*; **7.** Leistungsfähigkeit *f*,
Kraftvorrat *m*; **po·ten·ti·al·i·ty** [pəʊ-
tenʃɪ'ælətɪ] *s.* **1.** Potenziali'tät *f*, (Entwicklungs)Möglichkeit *f*; **2.** Wirkungs-
vermögen *n*, innere Kraft; **po·ten·ti-
om·e·ter** [pəʊˌtenʃɪ'ɒmɪtə] *s.* ⚡ Poten-
tio'meter *n* (*veränderbarer Widerstand*).
'pot·head *s. sl.* ‚Hascher' *m*.
po·theen [pɒ'θiːn] → **poteen**.
poth·er ['pɒðə] I *s.* **1.** Aufruhr *m*, Lärm
m, Aufregung *f*, ‚The'ater' *n*: *be in a ~
about s.th.* e-n großen Wirbel wegen
et. machen; **2.** Rauch-, Staubwolke *f*,
Dunst *m*; II *v/t.* **3.** verwirren, aufregen;
III *v/i.* **4.** sich aufregen.
'pot|·herb *s.* Küchenkraut *n*; **'~·hole** *s.*
1. *mot.* Schlagloch *n*; **2.** *geol.* Gle-
schertopf *m*, Strudelkessel *m*; **'~‚hol·er**
s. Höhlenforscher *m*; **'~·hook** *s.* **1.**
Kesselhaken *m*; **2.** Schnörkel *m* (*Kin-
derschrift*); *pl.* Gekritzel *n*; **'~·house** *s.*
Wirtschaft *f*, Kneipe *f*; **'~‚hunt·er** *s. sl.*
1. Aasjäger *m*; **2.** *sport* F Preisjäger *m*.
po·tion ['pəʊʃn] *s.* (Arz'nei-, Gift-, Zauber)Trank *m*.
pot luck *s.*: *take ~* a) (*with s.o.*) (bei
j-m) mit dem vorlieb nehmen, was es
gerade (zu essen) gibt, b) es aufs Geratewohl probieren.
pot·pour·ri [ˌpəʊ'pʊrɪ] *s.* Potpourri *n*: a)
Dufttopf *m*, b) musi'kalisches Aller'lei,
c) *fig.* Kunterbunt *n*, Aller'lei *n*.
pot| roast *s.* Schmorfleisch *n*; **'~·sherd**
[-ʃɜːd] *s.* (Topf)Scherbe *f*; **~ shot** *s.* **1.**
unweidmännischer Schuss; **2.** Nahschuss
m, ‚hinterhältiger Schuss; **3.** (wahllos
abgegebener) Schuss; **4.** *fig.* Seitenhieb
m.
pot·tage ['pɒtɪdʒ] *s.* dicke Gemüsesup-

pe (mit Fleisch).
pot·ter¹ ['pɒtə] I *v/i.* **1.** *oft ~ about* her-
'umwerkeln, -hantieren; **2.** (her'um-)
trödeln: **~ at** herumspielen, -pfuschen
an od. in (*dat.*); II *v/t.* **3. ~ away** Zeit
vertrödeln.
pot·ter² ['pɒtə] *s.* Töpfer(in): **~'s clay**
Töpferton *m*; **~'s lathe** Töpferschei-
bentisch *m*; **~'s wheel** Töpferscheibe *f*;
'pot·ter·y [-ərɪ] *s.* **1.** Töpfer-, Tonwa-
re(n *pl.*) *f*, Steingut *n*, Ke'ramik *f*; **2.**
Töpfe'rei(werkstatt) *f*; **3.** Töpfe'rei *f*
(*Kunst*), Ke'ramik *f*.
pot·ty ['pɒtɪ] *adj.* F **1.** verrückt; **2.** klein,
unbedeutend.
'pot-‚val·o(u)r *s.* angetrunkener Mut.
pouch [paʊtʃ] I *s.* **1.** Beutel (*a. zo.*, ♀),
(Leder-, Trage-, *a.* Post)Tasche *f*, (kleiner) Sack; **2.** Tabaksbeutel *m*; **3.** Geldbeutel *m*; **4.** ✕ Pa'tronentasche *f*; **5.**
anat. (Tränen)Sack *m*; II *v/t.* **6.** in e-n
Beutel tun; **7.** *fig.* einstecken; **8.** (*v/i.*
sich) beuteln *od.* bauschen; **pouched**
[-tʃt] *adj. zo.* Beutel...
pouf(fe) [puːf] *s.* **1.** a) Haarknoten *m*,
-rolle *f*, b) Einlage *f*; **2.** Puff *m* (*Sitzpols-
ter*); **3.** Tur'nüre *f*; **4.** → *poof*.
poul·ter·er ['pəʊltərə] *s.* Geflügelhänd-
ler *m*.
poul·tice ['pəʊltɪs] ✚ I *s.* ‚Brei‚umschlag
m, Packung *f*; II *v/t.* e-n ‚Brei‚umschlag
auflegen auf (*acc.*), e-e Packung machen un.
poul·try ['pəʊltrɪ] *s.* (Haus)Geflügel *n*,
Federvieh *n*: **~ farm** Geflügelfarm *f*;
'~·man [-mən] *s. irr.* Geflügelzüchter *m*
od. -händler *m*.
pounce¹ [paʊns] I *s.* **1.** a) Her'abstoßen
n e-s Raubvogels, b) Sprung *m*, Satz *m*:
on the ~ sprungbereit; II *v/i.* **2.** (he-
'rab)stoßen, sich stürzen (*on, upon auf
acc.*) (*Raubvogel*); **3.** *fig.* a) (*on, upon*)
sich stürzen (auf *j-n*, e-n Fehler, e-e Gelegenheit etc.), losgehen (auf *j-n*), b)
‚zuschlagen'; **4.** (plötzlich) stürzen: **~
into the room.**
pounce² [paʊns] I *s.* **1.** Glättpulver *n*,
bsd. Bimssteinpulver *n*; **2.** Pauspulver
n; **3.** ‚durchgepaustes (*bsd.* Stick)Mus-
ter; II *v/t.* **4.** glatt abreiben, bimsen; **5.**
'durchpausen.
pound¹ [paʊnd] *s.* **1.** Pfund *n* (*abbr. lb.*
= 453,59 *g*): **~ cake** *Am.* (reichhalti-
ger) Früchtekuchen; **2.** *a.* **~ sterling**
Pfund *n* (Sterling) (*abbr. £*): *pay twenty shillings in the ~ fig. obs.* voll bezahlen.
pound² [paʊnd] I *s.* **1.** schwerer Stoß
od. Schlag, Stampfen *n*; II *v/t.* **2.** (zer-)
stoßen, (zer)stampfen; **3.** feststampfen,
rammen; **4.** hämmern (auf), trommeln
auf, schlagen: **~ sense into s.o.** *fig.*
j-m Vernunft einhämmern; **~ out** a)
glatt hämmern, b) *Melodie* herunter-
hämmern (*auf dem Klavier*); **5.** ✕
beschießen; III *v/i.* **6.** hämmern (*a.
Herz*), pochen, schlagen; **7.** *mst ~
along* (ein'her)stampfen, wuchtig gehen; **8.** stampfen (*Maschine etc.*); **9.** ~
(*away*) *at* ✕ unter schweren Beschuss
nehmen.
pound³ [paʊnd] I *s.* **1.** 'Tiera‚syl *n*; **2.**
Hürde *f*, Pferch *m*; **3.** Abstellplatz *m*
für abgeschleppte Autos; II *v/t.* **4.** *oft ~
up* einpferchen.
pound·age ['paʊndɪdʒ] *s.* **1.** Anteil *m*
od. Gebühr *f* pro Pfund (*Sterling*); **2.**
Bezahlung *f* pro Pfund (*Gewicht*); **3.**
Gewicht *n* in Pfund.
pound·er ['paʊndə] *s. in Zssgn*
...pfünder.
‚pound-'fool·ish *adj.* unfähig, mit großen Summen *od.* Pro'blemen 'umzuge-

hen; → **penny-wise.**
pour [pɔː] I *s.* **1.** Strömen *n*; **2.** (Regen-)
Guss *m*; **3.** *metall.* Einguss *m*: **~ test**
Stockpunktbestimmung *f*; II *v/t.* **4.** gießen, schütten (*from, out of* aus, *into,
in* in *acc.*, *on, upon* auf *acc.*): **~ forth**
(*od. out*) a) ausgießen, (aus)strömen
lassen, b) *fig. Herz* ausschütten, *Kummer* ausbreiten, c) *Flüche etc.* ausstoßen; **~ out drinks** Getränke eingießen,
-schenken; **~ off** abgießen; **~ it on** *Am.
sl.* a) ‚rangehen', b) *a.* **~ on the speed**
‚volle Pulle' fahren; **5.** **~ itself** sich ergießen (*Fluss*); III *v/i.* **6.** strömen, gießen: **~ down** niederströmen; **~ forth**
(*od. out*) (*a. fig.*) sich ergießen, strömen (*from* aus); *it ~s with rain* es gießt
in Strömen; *it never rains but it ~s fig.*
ein Unglück kommt selten allein; **7.** *fig.*
strömen (*Menschenmenge etc.*): **~ in**
hereinströmen (*a. Aufträge, Briefe
etc.*); **8.** *metall.* in die Form gießen;
pour·a·ble ['pɔːrəbl] *adj.* ⊘ vergießbar:
~ compound Gussmasse *f*; **pour·ing**
['pɔːrɪŋ] I *adj.* **1.** strömend (*a. Regen*);
2. ⊘ Gieß..., Guss...: **~ gate** Gießtrich-
ter *m*; II *s.* **3.** ⊘ (Ver)Gießen *n*, Guss *m*.
pout¹ [paʊt] I *v/i.* **1.** die Lippen spitzen
od. aufwerfen; **2.** a) e-e Schnute *od.* e-n
Flunsch ziehen, b) *fig.* schmollen; **3.**
vorstehen (*Lippen*); II *v/t.* **4.** *Lippen,
Mund* (schmollend) aufwerfen, (*a. zum
Kuss*) spitzen; **5.** schmollen(d sagen);
III *s.* **6.** Flunsch *m*, Schnute *f*, Schmollmund *m*; **7.** Schmollen *n*: *have the ~s*
schmollen, im Schmollwinkel sitzen.
pout² [paʊt] *s. ein* Schellfisch *m*.
pout·er ['paʊtə] *s.* **1.** *a.* **~ pigeon** *orn.*
Kropftaube *f*; **2.** → *pout²*.
pov·er·ty ['pɒvətɪ] *s.* **1.** (*of* an *dat.*) Armut *f*, Mangel *m* (*beide a. fig.*): (*of*
ideas Ideenarmut); **2.** *fig.* Armseligkeit
f, Dürftigkeit *f*; **3.** Armut *f*, geringe
Ergiebigkeit (*des Bodens etc.*); **'~-
‚strick·en** *adj.* **1.** in Armut lebend,
verarmt; **2.** *fig.* armselig.
pow·der ['paʊdə] I *s.* **1.** (Back-, Schieß-
etc.)Pulver *n*: *not worth ~ and shot*
keinen Schuss Pulver wert; *keep your ~
dry!* sei auf der Hut!; *take a ~ Am. sl.*
‚türmen'; **2.** Puder *m*: *face ~*; II *v/t.* **3.**
pulvern, pulverisieren: **~ed milk** Trockenmilch *f*; **~ed sugar** Staubzucker *m*;
4. (be)pudern: **~ one's nose** a) sich die
Nase pudern, b) F ‚mal kurz verschwinden'; **5.** bestäuben, bestreuen (*with*
mit); III *v/i.* **6.** zu Pulver werden; **~ box**
s. Puderdose *f*; **~ keg** *s. fig.* Pulverfass
n; **~ met·al·lur·gy** *s.* 'Sintermetallur-
‚gie *f*, Me'tallke‚ramik *f*; **~ mill** *s.* 'Pul-
vermühle *f*, -fa‚brik *f*; **~ puff** *s.* Puderquaste *f*; **~ room** *s.* 'Damentoi‚lette *f*.
pow·der·y ['paʊdərɪ] *adj.* **1.** pulverig,
Pulver...: **~ snow** Pulverschnee *m*; **2.**
bestäubt.
pow·er ['paʊə] I *s.* **1.** Kraft *f*, Stärke *f*,
Macht *f*, Vermögen *n*: *do all in one's ~*
alles tun, was in s-r Macht steht; *it was
out of* (*od. not in*) *his ~* es stand nicht
in s-r Macht (*to do* zu tun); *more ~ to
you(r elbow)!* nur zu!, viel Erfolg!; **2.**
Kraft *f*, Ener'gie *f*; *weitS.* Wucht *f*, Gewalt *f*; **3.** *mst pl.* Fähigkeiten *pl.*, Kräfte
pl., (geistige) Fähigkeiten *pl.*, Ta'lent
n: *reasoning ~* Denkvermögen *f*; **4.**
Macht *f*, Gewalt *f*, Herrschaft *f*, Einfluss *m* (*over* über *acc.*): *be in ~ pol.* an
der Macht sein; *am Ruder sein; be in
s.o.'s ~* in j-s Gewalt sein; *come into ~
pol.* an die Macht kommen; **~ politics**
Machtpolitik *f*; **5.** *pol.* Gewalt *f* als
Staatsfunktion: *legislative ~*; *separation of ~s* Gewaltenteilung *f*; **6.** *pol.*

(Macht)Befugnis f, (Amts)Gewalt f; **7. ⚖** (Handlungs-, Vertretungs)Vollmacht f, Befugnis f, Recht n: **~ of testation** Testierfähigkeit f; → **attorney**; **8.** pol. Macht f, Staat m; **9.** Macht(faktor m) f, einflussreiche Stelle od. Per-'son: **the ~s that be** die maßgeblichen (Regierungs)Stellen; **~ behind the throne** graue Eminenz; **10.** mst pl. höhere Macht: **heavenly ~s**; **11.** F Masse f: **a ~ of people**; **12.** A Po'tenz f: **raise to the third ~** in die dritte Potenz erheben; **13. ⚡, phys.** Kraft f, Ener'gie f, Leistung f; a. **~ current ⚡** (Stark)Strom m; Funk, Radio, TV: Sendestärke f; opt. Stärke f e-r Linse: **~ cable** Starkstromkabel n; **~ economy** Energiewirtschaft f; **14. ⚙** me'chanische Kraft, Antriebskraft f: **~-propelled** kraftbetrieben, Kraft...; **~ on** (mit) Vollgas; **~ off** a) mit abgestelltem Motor, b) im Leerlauf; **II** v/t. **15.** mit (elektrischer etc.) Kraft versehen od. betreiben, antreiben: **rocket-~ed** raketengetrieben; **~ am·pli·fi·er** s. Radio: Kraft-, Endverstärker m; **~-as,sis·ted** adj. mot. Servo... (-lenkung etc.); **~ brake** s. mot. Servobremse f; **~ con·sump·tion** s. ⚡ Strom-, Ener'gieverbrauch m; **~ cut** s. ⚡ **1.** Stromsperre f; **2.** → **power failure**; **~ dress·ing** s Karri'erelook m, 'durchgestyltes Outfit; **~ drive** s. ⚙ Kraftantrieb m; **~-,driv·en** adj. ⚙ kraftbetrieben, Kraft...; **~ en·gi·neer·ing** s. ⚡ Starkstromtechnik f; **~ fac·tor** s. ⚡, phys. Leistungsfaktor m; **~-'fail pro·tec·tion** s. Netzausfallschutz m; **~ fail·ure** s. ⚡ Strom-, Netzausfall m.

pow·er·ful ['paʊəfʊl] adj. □ **1.** mächtig (a. Körper, Schlag, Mensch), stark (a. opt. u. Motor), gewaltig, kräftig; **2.** fig. kräftig, wirksam (a. Argument); wuchtig (Stil); packend (Roman etc.); **3.** F ,massig', gewaltig.

pow·er| glid·er s. ✈ Motorsegler m; **'~·house** s. ⚡ → **power station**; **2.** ⚙ Ma'schinenhaus n; **3.** Am. sl. a) sport ,Bombenmannschaft' f, b) sport ,Ka-'none' f (Spitzenspieler), c) Riesenkerl m, d) ,Wucht' f, ,tolle' Person od. Sache; **~ lathe** s ⚙ Hochleistungsdrehbank f.

pow·er·less ['paʊəlɪs] adj. □ kraft-, machtlos, ohnmächtig.

pow·er| line s. ⚡ **1.** Starkstromleitung f; **2.** 'Überlandleitung f; **~-'op·er·at·ed** adj. ⚙ kraftbetätigt, -betrieben; **~ out·put** s. ⚡ Ausgangs-, Nennleistung f; **~ pack** s. ⚡ Netzteil n (Radio etc.); **~ plant** s. **1.** → **power station**; **2.** Ma-'schinensatz m, Aggre'gat n, Triebwerk(anlage f) n; **~ play** s. sport Powerplay n; **~ point** s. ⚡ Steckdose f; **~ pol·i·tics** s. pl. sg. konstr. 'Machtpoli-,tik f; **~ saw** s. ⚙ Motorsäge f; **~ shar·ing** s. Teilhabe f an der Macht; **~ shov·el** s. ⚙ Löffelbagger m; **~ sta·tion** s. ⚡ Elektrizi'täts-, Kraftwerk n: **long-distance ~** Überlandzentrale f; **~ steer·ing** s. mot. Servolenkung f; **~ stroke** s. ⚙, ⚡, mot. Arbeitshub m, -takt m; **~ strug·gle** s. Machtkampf m; **~ sup·ply** s. ⚡ **1.** Ener'gieversorgung f, Netz(anschluss m) n; **2.** → **power pack**; **~ trans·mis·sion** s. ⚙ 'Leistungs-, Ener'gieüber,tragung f; **~ un·it** s. **1.** → **power station**; **2.** → **power plant** 2.

pow·wow ['paʊwaʊ] **I** s. **1.** a) indi'anisches Fest, b) Ratsversammlung f, c) indi'anischer Medi'zinmann; **2.** Am. F a) (lärmende, a. po'litische) Versammlung, b) Konfe'renz f, Besprechung f; **II**

v/i. **3.** bsd. Am. F e-e Versammlung etc. abhalten; debattieren.

pox [pɒks] s. ✱ **1.** Pocken pl., Blattern pl.; Pusteln pl.; **2.** V Syphilis f.

prac·ti·ca·bil·i·ty [ˌpræktɪkəˈbɪlətɪ] s. 'Durchführbarkeit f etc.; **prac·ti·ca·ble** ['præktɪkəbl] adj. □ **1.** 'durch-, ausführbar, möglich; **2.** anwendbar, brauchbar; **3.** gang-, (be)fahrbar (Straße, Furt etc.).

prac·ti·cal ['præktɪkl] adj. □ → **practically**; **1.** (Ggs. theoretisch) praktisch (Kenntnisse, Landwirtschaft etc.); angewandt: **~ chemistry**; **~ fact** Erfahrungstatsache f; **2.** praktisch (Anwendung, Versuch etc.); **3.** praktisch, geschickt (Person); **4.** praktisch, in der Praxis tätig, ausübend: **~ politician**; **~ man** Mann der Praxis, Praktiker; **5.** praktisch (Denken); **6.** praktisch, faktisch, tatsächlich; **7.** sachlich; **8.** praktisch anwendbar, 'durchführbar; **9.** handgreiflich, grob: **~ joke**; **prac·ti·cal·i·ty** [ˌpræktɪˈkælətɪ] s. das Praktische, praktisches Wesen, Sachlichkeit f; praktische Anwendbarkeit; **'prac·ti·cal·ly** adv. **1.** [-kəlɪ] → **practical**; **2.** [-klɪ] praktisch, so gut wie nichts etc.

prac·tice ['præktɪs] **I** s. **1.** Praxis f (Ggs. Theorie): **in ~** in der Praxis; **put into ~** in die Praxis umsetzen, ausführen, verwirklichen; **2.** Übung f (a. ♪, ✗), mot. sport Training n: **in (out of) ~** in (aus) der Übung; **~ makes perfect** Übung macht den Meister; **3.** Praxis f (Arzt, Anwalt): **be in ~** praktizieren, s-e Praxis ausüben (Arzt); **4.** Brauch m, Gewohnheit f, übliches Verfahren, Usus m; **5.** Handlungsweise f, Praktik f; oft pl. contp. (unsaubere) Praktiken pl., Machenschaften pl., Schliche pl.; **6.** Verfahren n; ⚙ a. Technik f: **welding ~** Schweißtechnik; **7.** ⚖ Verfahren(sregeln pl.) n, for'melles Recht; **8.** Übungs..., Probe...: **~ alarm**, **~ alert** Probealarm m; **~ ammunition** ✗ Übungsmunition f; **~ cartridge** ✗ Exerzierpatrone f; **~ flight** ✈ Übungsflug m; **~ run** mot. Trainingsfahrt f; **II** v/t. u. v/i. **9.** Am. → **practise**.

prac·tise ['præktɪs] **I** v/t. **1.** Beruf ausüben; Geschäft etc. betreiben; tätig sein als od. in (dat.), als Arzt, Anwalt praktizieren: **~ medicine** (law); **2.** ♪ etc. (ein)üben, sich üben in (dat.); et. auf e-m Instrument üben; j-n schulen: **~ Bach** Bach üben; **3.** fig. Höflichkeit etc. üben: **~ politeness**; **4.** verüben: **~ a fraud on** j-n arglistig täuschen; **II** v/i. **5.** praktizieren (als Arzt, Jurist, a. Katholik); **6.** (sich) üben (**on the piano** auf dem Klavier, **at shooting** im Schießen); **7.** **~ on** (od. **upon**) a) j-n ,bearbeiten', b) j-s Schwäche etc. ausnutzen, miss'brauchen; **'prac·tised** [-st] adj. geübt (Person, a. Auge, Hand).

prac·ti·tion·er [prækˈtɪʃnə] s. **1.** Praktiker m; **2.** **general** (od. **medical**) **~** praktischer Arzt; **3.** **legal** (od. **general**) **~** ⚖ (Rechts)Anwalt m.

prag·mat·ic [præɡˈmætɪk] adj. (□ **~al·ly**) **1.** phls. prag'matisch; **2.** → **prag·mat·i·cal** [-kl] adj. □ **1.** phls. prag'matisch, fig. a. praktisch (denkend), sachlich; **2.** belehrend; **3.** geschäftig; **4.** 'übereifrig, aufdringlich; **5.** rechthaberisch; **prag·ma·tism** ['præɡmətɪzəm] s. **1.** phls. Pragma'tismus m, fig. a. Sachlichkeit f, praktisches Denken; **2.** 'Übereifer m; **3.** rechthaberisches Wesen; **prag·ma·tize** ['præɡmətaɪz] v/t. **1.** als re'al darstellen; **2.** vernunftmäßig erklären, rationalisieren.

prai·rie ['preərɪ] s. **1.** Grasebene f, Steppe f; **2.** Prä'rie f (in Nordamerika); **3.** Am. (grasbewachsene) Lichtung; **~ dog** s. zo. Prä'riehund m; **~ schoon·er** s. Am. Planwagen m der frühen Siedler.

praise [preɪz] **I** v/t. **1.** loben, rühmen, preisen; → **sky** 2; **2.** (bsd. Gott) (lob-)preisen, loben; **II** s. **3.** Lob n: **sing s.o.'s** j-s Lob singen; **in ~ of s.o.** in s.o.'s zu j-s Lob; **'~,wor·thi·ness** s. Löblichkeit f, lobenswerte Eigenschaft; **'~,wor·thy** adj. □ lobenswert, löblich.

pram[1] [præm] s. ⚓ Prahm m.

pram[2] [præm] s. F → **perambulator**.

prance [prɑːns] v/i. **1.** a) sich bäumen, b) tänzeln (Pferd); **2.** (ein'her)stolzieren, paradieren; sich brüsten; **3.** F herumtollen.

pran·di·al ['prændɪəl] adj. Essens..., Tisch...

prang [præŋ] Brit. F I s. **1.** ✈ Bruchlandung f; **2.** mot. schwerer Unfall; **3.** Luftangriff m; **4.** fig. ,tolles Ding'; **II** v/i. **5.** ,knallen', ,krachen'.

prank[1] [præŋk] s. **1.** Streich m, Ulk m, Jux m; **2.** weitS. Kapri'ole f, Faxe.

prank[2] [præŋk] **I** v/t. mst **~ out** (od. **up**) (her'aus)putzen, schmücken; **II** v/i. prunken, prangen.

prat [præt] s. **1.** Brit. F Trottel m; **2.** sl. ,Hintern' m.

prate [preɪt] **I** v/i. schwatzen, schwafeln (of von); **II** v/t. (da'her)schwafeln; **III** s. Geschwätz n, Geschwafel n; **'prat·er** [-tə] s. Schwätzer(in).

prat·fall ['prætfɔːl] s. F a) Sturz m auf den ,Hintern', b) fig. ,Bauchlandung' f, Bla'mage f: **have** (od. **take**) **a ~** sich ,auf den Hintern setzen', e-e Bauchlandung machen, sich blamieren; **until the next ~** bis er (od. sie) wieder mal ,auf den Hintern fällt'.

'prat·ing [-tɪŋ] adj. □ schwatzhaft, geschwätzig; **prat·tle** ['prætl] → **prate**.

prawn [prɔːn] s. zo. Gar'nele f.

pray [preɪ] **I** v/i. **1.** beten (**to** zu, **for** um, für); **2.** bitten, ersuchen (**for** um); ⚖ beantragen (**that** dass); **II** v/t. **3.** j-n inständig bitten, ersuchen, anflehen (**for** um): **~, consider!** bitte, bedenken Sie doch!; **4.** et. erbitten, erflehen.

prayer [preə] s. **1.** Ge'bet n: **put up a ~** ein Gebet emporsenden; **say one's ~s** beten, s-e Gebete verrichten; **he hasn't got a ~** Am. sl. er hat nicht die geringste Chance; **2.** oft pl. Andacht f: **evening ~** Abendandacht; **3.** inständige Bitte, Flehen n; **4.** Gesuch n; ⚖ a. Antrag m, Klagebegehren n; **5.** ['preɪə] Beter(in); **~ book** s. Ge'betbuch n; **~ meet·ing** s. Ge'betsversammlung f; **~ wheel** s. Ge'betsmühle f.

pre- [priː; prɪ] in Zssgn a) (zeitlich) vor (-her); vor...; früher als, b) (räumlich) vor, da'vor.

preach [priːtʃ] **I** v/i. **1.** (**to**) predigen (zu od. vor dat.), e-e Predigt halten (dat. od. vor dat.); **2.** fig. ,predigen': **~ at s.o.** j-m e-e (Moral)Predigt halten; **II** v/t. **3.** et. predigen: **~ the gospel** das Evangelium verkünden; **~ a sermon** e-e Predigt halten; **4.** ermahnen zu: **~ charity** Nächstenliebe predigen; **'preach·er** [-tʃə] s. Prediger(in); **'preach·i·fy** [-tʃɪfaɪ] v/i. sal'badern, Mo'ral predigen; **'preach·ing** [-tʃɪŋ] s. **1.** Predigen n; **2.** bibl. Lehre f; **'preach·y** [-tʃɪ] adj. □ F sal'badernd, moralisierend.

pre·am·ble [priːˈæmbl] s. **1.** Prä'ambel f (a. ⚖), Einleitung f; Oberbegriff m e-r Patentschrift; Kopf m e-s Funkspruchs *etc.*; **2.** *fig.* Vorspiel *n*, Auftakt *m*.

pre·ar·range [ˌpriːəˈreɪndʒ] *v/t.* **1.** vorher abmachen *od.* anordnen *od.* bestimmen; **2.** vorbereiten.

preb·end [ˈprebənd] *s. eccl.* Prä'bende *f*, Pfründe *f*; **ˈpreb·en·dar·y** [-bəndərɪ] *s.* Pfründner *m*.

pre·cal·cu·late [ˌpriːˈkælkjuleɪt] *v/t.* vor'ausberechnen.

pre·car·i·ous [prɪˈkeərɪəs] *adj.* □ **1.** pre'kär, unsicher (*a. Lebensunterhalt*), bedenklich (*a. Gesundheitszustand*); **2.** gefährlich; **3.** anfechtbar; **4.** ˌ'widerruflich; **pre·car·i·ous·ness** [-nɪs] *s.* **1.** Unsicherheit *f*; **2.** Gefährlichkeit *f*; **3.** Zweifelhaftigkeit *f*.

pre·cau·tion [prɪˈkɔːʃn] *s.* **1.** Vorkehrung *f*, Vorsichtsmaßregel *f*: **take** ∼**s** Vorsichtsmaßregeln *od.* Vorsorge treffen; **as a** ∼ vorsichtshalber, vorsorglich; **2.** Vorsicht *f*; **pre·cau·tion·ar·y** [-ʃnərɪ] *adj.* **1.** vorbeugend, Vorsichts...: ∼ **measures** Vorkehrungen; **2.** Warn...: ∼ **signal** Warnsignal *n*.

pre·cede [ˌpriːˈsiːd] **I** *v/t.* **1.** vor'aus-, vor'angehen (*dat.*) (*a. fig. Buchkapitel, Zeitraum etc.*); **2.** den Vorrang *od.* Vortritt *od.* Vorzug haben vor (*dat.*), vorgehen (*dat.*); **3.** *fig.* (**by, with s.th.**) (durch et.) einleiten, (e-r Sache et.) vor'ausschicken; **II** *v/i.* **4.** vor'an-, vo'rausgehen; **5.** den Vorrang *od.* Vortritt haben; **pre·ced·ence** [ˈpresɪdəns] *s.* **1.** Vor'hergehen *n*, Priori'tät *f*: **have the** ∼ **of e-r Sache** *zeitlich* vorangehen; **2.** Vorrang *m*, Vorzug *m*, Vortritt *m*, Vorrecht *n*: **take** ∼ **of** (*od.* **over**) → **precede** 2; (**order of**) ∼ Rangordnung *f*; **prec·e·dent** [ˈpresɪdənt] **I** *s.* ˌ'Präze·'denzfall *m*, Präju'diz *n*: **without** ∼ ohne Beispiel, nie dagewesen; **set a** ∼ e·n Präzedenzfall schaffen; **II** [prɪˈsiːdənt] *adj.* □ vor'hergehend; **pre·ced·ing** [-dɪŋ] **I** *adj.* vor'hergehend: ∼ **indorser** ✝ Vor(der)mann *m* (*Wechsel*); **II** *prp.* vor (*dat.*).

pre·cen·sor [ˌpriːˈsensə] *v/t.* e·r 'Vorzen·ˌsur unter'werfen.

pre·cen·tor [ˌpriːˈsentə] *s.* ♪, *eccl.* Kantor *m*, Vorsänger *m*.

pre·cept [ˈpriːsept] *s.* **1.** (*a.* göttliches) Gebot; **2.** Regel *f*, Richtschnur *f*; **3.** Lehre *f*, Unter'weisung *f*; **4.** ✝ Gerichtsbefehl *m*; **pre·cep·tor** [prɪˈseptə] *s.* Lehrer *m*.

pre·cinct [ˈpriːsɪŋkt] *s.* **1.** Bezirk *m*: **ca·thedral** ∼**s** Domfreiheit *f*; **2.** *bsd. Am.* Poli'zei-, Wahlbezirk *m*; **3.** *pl.* Bereich *m*, *pl. fig. a.* Grenzen *pl.*

pre·ci·os·i·ty [ˌpreʃɪˈɒsətɪ] *s.* Geziertheit *f*, Affektiertheit *f*.

pre·cious [ˈpreʃəs] **I** *adj.* □ **1.** kostbar, wertvoll (*a. fig.*): ∼ **memories**; **2.** edel (*Steine etc.*): ∼ **metals** Edelmetalle; **3.** F ˌschön': a) *iro.* ˌnett': *a* ∼ **mess**, b) beträchtlich: *a* ∼ **lot better than** bei weitem besser als; **4.** *fig.* prezi'ös, affektiert, geziert: ∼ **style**; **II** *adv.* **5.** F reichlich, äußerst: ∼ **little**; **III** *s.* **6.** Schatz *m*, Liebling *m*: **my** ∼**!**; '**pre·cious·ness** [-nɪs] *s.* **1.** Köstlichkeit *f*, Kostbarkeit *f*; **2.** → **preciosity**.

prec·i·pice [ˈpresɪpɪs] *s.* Abgrund *m*, *fig. a.* Klippe *f*.

pre·cip·i·ta·ble [prɪˈsɪpɪtəbl] *adj.* ♠ abscheidbar, fällbar, niederschlagbar; **pre·cip·i·tance** [-təns], **pre·cip·i·tan·cy** [-tənsɪ] *s.* **1.** Eile *f*; **2.** Hast *f*, Über'stürzung *f*; **pre·cip·i·tant** [-tənt] **I** *adj.* □ **1.** (steil) abstürzend, jäh; **2.** *fig.* hastig, eilig; **3.** *fig.* über'eilt; **II** *s.* **4.** ♠ Fällungsmittel *n*; **pre·cip·i·tate** [-teɪt] **I** *v/t.* **1.** hin'abstürzen (*a. fig.*); **2.** *fig.*

Ereignisse her'aufbeschwören, (plötzlich) her'beiführen, beschleunigen; **3.** *j-n* (hin'ein)stürzen (**into** in *acc.*): ∼ *a* **country into war**; **4.** ♠ (aus)fällen; **5.** *meteor.* niederschlagen, verflüssigen; **II** *v/i.* **6.** ♠ *u. meteor.* sich niederschlagen; **III** *adj.* [-tət] **7.** jäh(lings) hin'abstürzend, steil abfallend; **8.** *fig.* über'stürzt, -'eilt, 'voreilig; eilig, hastig; **9.** plötzlich; **IV** *s.* [-teɪt] **10.** ♠ Niederschlag *m*, 'Fällpro·ˌdukt *n*; **pre·cip·i·tate·ness** [-tətnɪs] *s.* Über'eilung *f*, 'Voreiligkeit *f*; **pre·cip·i·ta·tion** [prɪˌsɪpɪˈteɪʃn] *s.* **1.** jäher Sturz, (Her'ab)Stürzen *n*; **2.** *fig.* Über'stürzung *f*; Hast *f*; **3.** ♠ Fällung *f*; **4.** *meteor.* Niederschlag *m*; **5.** *Spiritismus*: Materialisati'on *f*; **pre·cip·i·tous** [-təs] *adj.* □ **1.** jäh, steil (abfallend), abschüssig; **2.** *fig.* über'stürzt.

pré·cis [ˈpreɪsiː] (*Fr.*) **I** *pl.* **-cis** [-siːz] *s.* (kurze) 'Übersicht, Zs.-fassung *f*; **II** *v/t.* kurz zs.-fassen.

pre·cise [prɪˈsaɪs] *adj.* □ **1.** prä'zis(e), klar, genau; **2.** ex'akt, (peinlich) genau, kor'rekt; *contp.* pe'dantisch; **3.** genau, richtig (*Betrag, Moment etc.*); **pre·'cise·ly** [-lɪ] *adv.* **1.** → **precise**; **2.** gerade, genau, ausgerechnet; **3.** ∼**!** genau!; **pre·'cise·ness** [-nɪs] *s.* **1.** (über-'triebene) Genauigkeit; **2.** (ängstliche) Gewissenhaftigkeit, Pedante'rie *f*; **pre·ci·sion** [prɪˈsɪʒn] *s.* **1.** Genauigkeit *f*, Ex'aktheit *f* (*a.* ♠, ✕ Präzisi'on *f*; **II** *adj.* ♠, ✕ Präzisions..., Fein...: ∼ **adjustment** a) ♠ Feineinstellung, b) ✕ genaues Einschießen; ∼ **bombing** gezielter Bombenwurf; ∼ **instrument** Präzisionsinstrument *n*; ∼ **mechanics** Feinmechanik *f*; ∼**-made** Präzisions...

pre·clude [prɪˈkluːd] *v/t.* **1.** ausschließen (**from** von); **2.** e-r Sache vorbeugen *od.* zu'vorkommen; *Einwände* vor'wegnehmen; **3.** *j-n* hindern (**from** an *dat.*, **from** **doing** zu tun); **pre·clu·sion** [-uːʒn] *s.* **1.** Ausschließung *f*, Ausschluss *m* (**from** von); **2.** Verhinderung *f*; **pre·clu·sive** [-uːsɪv] *adj.* □ **1.** ausschließend (**of** von); **2.** (ver)hindernd.

pre·co·cious [prɪˈkəʊʃəs] *adj.* □ **1.** frühreif, frühzeitig (entwickelt); **2.** *fig.* frühreif, altklug; **pre·co·cious·ness** [-nɪs], **pre·coc·i·ty** [-ˈkɒsətɪ] *s.* **1.** Frühreife *f*, -zeitigkeit *f*; **2.** *fig.* Frühreife *f*, Altklugheit *f*.

pre·cog·ni·tion [ˌpriːkɒgˈnɪʃn] *s.* Präkogniti'on *f*, Vorauswissen *n*.

pre·con·ceive [ˌpriːkənˈsiːv] *v/t.* (sich) vorher ausdenken, sich vorher vorstellen: ∼**d opinion** → **pre·con·cep·tion** [ˌpriːkənˈsepʃn] *s.* vorgefasste Meinung, *a.* Vorurteil *n*.

pre·con·cert [ˌpriːkənˈsɜːt] *v/t.* vorher vereinbaren, ∼**ed** verabredet, *b.s.* abgekartet.

pre·con·di·tion [ˌpriːkənˈdɪʃn] **I** *s.* **1.** Vorbedingung *f*, Vor'aussetzung *f*: ∼**s for accession** Beitrittsvorraussetzungen *pl.* (*zur EU etc.*); **II** *v/t.* **2.** ♠ vorbehandeln; **3.** *fig. j-n* einstimmen.

pre·co·nize [ˈpriːkənaɪz] *v/t.* **1.** öffentlich verkündigen; **2.** *R. C. Bischof* präkonisieren.

pre·cook [ˌpriːˈkʊk] *v/t.* vorkochen.

pre·cool [ˌpriːˈkuːl] *v/t.* vorkühlen.

pre·cur·sor [ˌpriːˈkɜːsə] *s.* **1.** Vorläufer (-in), Vorbote *m*, -botin *f*; **2.** (Amts-)Vorgänger(in); **pre·cur·so·ry** [-ərɪ] *adj.* **1.** vor'ausgehend; **2.** einleitend, vorbereitend.

pre·da·ceous *Am.*, **pre·da·cious** *Brit.* [prɪˈdeɪʃəs] *adj.* räuberisch: ∼ **animal** Raubtier *n*; ∼ **instinct** Raub(tier)ins-

tinkt *m*.

pre·date [ˌpriːˈdeɪt] *v/t.* **1.** zu'rück-, vordatieren; **2.** *zeitlich* vor'angehen.

pred·a·to·ry [ˈpredətərɪ] *adj.* □ räuberisch, Raub...(*-krieg, -vogel etc.*).

pre·de·cease [ˌpriːdɪˈsiːs] *v/t.* früher sterben als *j-d*, vor *j-m* sterben: ∼**d parent** ✝ vorverstorbener Elternteil.

pred·e·ces·sor [ˈpriːdɪsesə] *s.* **1.** Vorgänger(in) (*a. fig. Buch etc.*): ∼ **in interest** ✝ Rechtsvorgänger; ∼ **in office** Amtsvorgänger; **2.** Vorfahr *m*.

pre·des·ti·nate [ˌpriːˈdestɪneɪt] **I** *v/t. eccl. u. weitS.* prädestinieren, aus(er)wählen, (vor'her)bestimmen, ausersehen (**to** für, zu); **II** *adj.* [-neɪt] prädestiniert, auserwählt; **pre·des·ti·na·tion** [priːˌdestɪˈneɪʃn] *s.* **1.** Vor'herbestimmung *f*; **2.** *eccl.* Prädestinati'on *f*, Gnadenwahl *f*; **pre·des·tine** [-tɪn] → **predestinate** I.

pre·de·ter·mi·na·tion [ˈpriːdɪˌtɜːmɪˈneɪʃn] *s.* Vor'herbestimmung *f*; **pre·de·ter·mine** [ˌpriːdɪˈtɜːmɪn] *v/t.* **1.** *eccl.*, *a.* ♠ vor'herbestimmen; **2.** *Kosten etc.* vorher festsetzen *od.* bestimmen: ∼ **s.o. to s.th.** *j-n* für et. vorbestimmen.

pred·i·ca·ble [ˈpredɪkəbl] **I** *adj.* aussagbar, *j-m* zuzuschreiben(d); **II** *s. pl. phls.* Prädika'bilien *pl.*, Allgemeinbegriffe *pl.*; **pre·dic·a·ment** [prɪˈdɪkəmənt] *s.* **1.** *phls.* Katego'rie *f*; **2.** (missliche) Lage; **pred·i·cate** [ˈpredɪkeɪt] **I** *v/t.* **1.** behaupten, aussagen; **2.** *phls.* prädizieren, aussagen; **3.** gründen, basieren (**on** auf *dat.*): **be** ∼**d on** basieren auf (*dat.*); **II** *s.* [-kət] **4.** *phls.* Aussage *f*; **5.** *ling.* Prädi'kat *n*, Satzaussage *f*: ∼ **adjective** prädikatives Adjektiv; ∼ **noun** Prädikatsnomen *n*; **pred·i·ca·tion** [ˌpredɪˈkeɪʃn] *s.* Aussage *f* (*a. ling. im Prädikat*), Behauptung *f*; **pred·i·ca·tive** [prɪˈdɪkətɪv] *adj.* □ **1.** aussagend, Aussage...; **2.** *ling.* prädika'tiv; **pred·i·ca·to·ry** [prɪˈdɪkətərɪ] *adj.* **1.** predigend, Prediger...; **2.** gepredigt.

pre·dict [prɪˈdɪkt] *v/t.* vor'her-, vor'aussagen, prophe'zeien; **pre·dict·a·ble** [-təbl] *adj.* vor'aussagbar, berechenbar (*a. Person, Politik etc.*): **he's so** ∼ bei ihm weiß man immer genau, was er tun wird; **pre·dict·a·bly** [-təblɪ] *adv.* a) wie vorherzusehen war, b) man kann jetzt schon sagen, dass; **pre·dic·tion** [-kʃn] *s.* Vor'her-, Vor'aussage *f*, Weissagung *f*, Prophe'zeiung *f*; **pre·dic·tor** [-tə] *s.* **1.** Pro'phet(in); **2.** ✕ Kom'mandogerät *n*.

pre·di·lec·tion [ˌpriːdɪˈlekʃn] *s.* Vorliebe *f*, Voreingenommenheit *f*.

pre·dis·pose [ˌpriːdɪˈspəʊz] *v/t.* **1.** (**for**) *j-n* (im Vor'aus) geneigt *od.* empfänglich machen *od.* einnehmen (für); **2.** (**to**) *bsd.* ♠ prädisponieren, empfänglich *od.* anfällig machen (für); **pre·dis·po·si·tion** [ˌpriːdɪspəˈzɪʃn] *s.* (**to**) Neigung *f* (zu); Empfänglichkeit *f* (für); Anfälligkeit *f* (für) (*alle a.* ♠).

pre·dom·i·nance [prɪˈdɒmɪnəns] *s.* **1.** Vorherrschaft *f*; Vormacht(stellung) *f*; **2.** *fig.* Vorherrschen *n*, Über'wiegen *n*, 'Übergewicht *n* (**in** in *dat.*, **over** über *acc.*); **3.** Über'legenheit *f*; **pre·dom·i·nant** [-nt] *adj.* □ **1.** vorherrschend, über'wiegend, vorwiegend; **2.** über'legen; **pre·dom·i·nate** [-neɪt] *v/i.* **1.** vorherrschen, über'wiegen, vorwiegen; **2.** zahlenmäßig, geistig, körperlich etc. über'legen sein; **3.** die Oberhand *od.* das 'Übergewicht haben (**over** über *acc.*); **4.** herrschen, die Herrschaft haben (**over** über *acc.*).

pre·em·i·nence [ˌpriːˈemɪnəns] *s.* **1.**

Her'vorragen n, Über'legenheit f (*above*, *over* über acc.); **2.** Vorrang m, -zug m (*over* vor dat.); **3.** her'vorragende Stellung; ˌ**pre-'em·i·nent** [-nt] adj. □ her'vorragend, über'ragend: *be ~* hervorstechen, sich hervortun.

pre-empt [ˌpriːˈempt] v/t. **1.** (v/i. Land) durch Vorkaufsrecht erwerben; **2.** (im Vor'aus) mit Beschlag belegen; ˌ**pre-'emp·tion** [-pʃn] s. Vorkauf(srecht n) m: ~ *price* Vorkaufspreis m; ˌ**pre-'emp·tive** [-tɪv] adj. **1.** Vorkaufs...: ~ *right*; **2.** ✕ Präventiv...: ~ *strike* Präventivschlag m; ˌ**pre'emp·tor** [-tə] s. Vorkaufsberechtigte(r m) f.

preen [priːn] v/t. Gefieder etc. putzen; *sein Haar* (her)richten: ~ *o.s.* sich putzen (a. Person); ~ *o.s. on* sich et. einbilden auf (acc.).

pre-en·gage [ˌpriːɪnˈgeɪdʒ] v/t. **1.** im Vor'aus *vertraglich* verpflichten; **2.** im Vor'aus in Anspruch nehmen; **3.** ⚓ vorbestellen; ˌ**pre-en'gage·ment** [-mənt] s. vorher eingegangene Verpflichtung, frühere Verbindlichkeit.

pre-ex·am·i·na·tion [ˈpriːɪgˌzæmɪˈneɪʃn] s. vor'herige Vernehmung, 'Vorunter-ˌsuchung f, -prüfung f.

pre-ex·ist [ˌpriːɪgˈzɪst] v/i. vorher vor'handen sein od. existieren; ˌ**pre-ex'ist·ence** [-təns] s. bsd. eccl. früheres Dasein, Präexi'stenz f.

pre·fab [ˈpriːfæb] I adj. → *prefabricated*; II s. Fertighaus n.

pre·fab·ri·cate [ˌpriːˈfæbrɪkeɪt] v/t. vorfabrizieren, *genormte* Fertigteile für *Häuser etc.* herstellen; ˌ**pre'fab·ri·cat·ed** [-tɪd] adj. vorgefertigt, zs.-setzbar, Fertig...: ~ *house* Fertighaus n; ~ *piece* Bauteil n.

pref·ace [ˈprefɪs] I s. Vorwort n, -rede f; Einleitung f (a. fig.); II v/t. Rede etc. einleiten (a. fig.), ein Vorwort schreiben zu e-m Buch.

pref·a·to·ry [ˈprefətərɪ] adj. □ einleitend, Einleitungs...

pre·fect [ˈpriːfekt] s. **1.** pol. Prä'fekt m; **2.** Brit. Vertrauensschüler m.

pre·fer [prɪˈfɜː] v/t. **1.** (es) vorziehen (*to dat.*, *rather than* statt) bevorzugen: *I ~ to go today* ich gehe lieber heute; ~*red* ⚓ bevorzugt, Vorzugs...(-aktie etc.); **2.** befördern (*to* [*the rank of*] zum); **3.** ⚖ *Gläubiger etc.* begünstigen, bevorzugt befriedigen; **4.** ⚖ *Gesuch*, *Klage* einreichen (*to* bei, *against* gegen); *Ansprüche* erheben; **pref·er·a·ble** [ˈprefərəbl] adj. □ (*to*) vorzuziehen(d) (*dat.*); vorzüglicher (als); **pref·er·a·bly** [ˈprefərəblɪ] adv. vorzugsweise, lieber, am besten; **pref·er·ence** [ˈprefərəns] s. **1.** Bevorzugung f, Vorzug m (*above*, *before*, *over*, *to* vor dat.); **2.** Vorliebe f (*for* für): *by* ~ mit (besonderer) Vorliebe; **3.** ⚓, ⚖ a) Vor(zugs)recht n, Priori'tät f: ~ *bond* Prioritätsobligation f; ~ *dividend* Brit. Vorzugsdividende f; ~ *share* (od. *stock*) → e), b) Vorzug m, Bevorrechtigung f: ~ *as to dividends* Dividendenbevorrechtigung f, c) bevorzugte Befriedigung (a. Konkurs): *fraudulent* ~ Gläubigerbegünstigung f, d) Zoll: 'Meistbegünstigung(sta,rif m) f, e) Brit. 'Vorzugsˌaktie f; **pref·er·en·tial** [ˌprefəˈrenʃl] adj. □ bevorzugt; a. ⚓, ⚖ bevorrechtigt (*Forderung*, *Gläubiger etc.*), Vorzugs...(-aktie, -dividende, -recht, -zoll): ~ *treatment* Vorzugsbehandlung f; **pref·er·en·tial·ly** [ˌprefəˈrenʃəlɪ] adv. vorzugsweise; **pre·fer·ment** [-mənt] s. **1.** Beförderung f (*to* zu); **2.** höheres Amt, Ehrenamt n (bsd. eccl.); **3.** ⚖ Einreichung f (*Klage*).

pre·fig·u·ra·tion [ˈpriːˌfɪgjʊˈreɪʃn] s. **1.** vorbildhafte Darstellung, Vor-, Urbild n; **2.** vor'herige Darstellung.

pre·fix I v/t. [ˌpriːˈfɪks] **1.** (a. ling. Wort, Silbe) vorsetzen, vor'ausgehen lassen (*to dat.*); II s. [ˈpriːfɪks] **2.** ling. Prä'fix n, Vorsilbe f; **3.** bsd. Am. teleph. Vorwahl f; **4.** Namenszu- od. -vorsatz m.

ˌ**pre-'for·mat** v/t. Computer: vorformatieren.

preg·gers [ˈpregəz] adj. F schwanger.

preg·nan·cy [ˈpregnənsɪ] s. **1.** Schwangerschaft f, zo. Trächtigkeit f; **2.** fig. Fruchtbarkeit f, Schöpferkraft f, Gedankenfülle f; **3.** fig. Prä'gnanz f, Bedeutungsgehalt m, -schwere f; **'preg·nant** [-nt] adj. □ **1.** a) schwanger (*Frau*), b) trächtig (*Tier*); **2.** fig. fruchtbar, reich (*in* an dat.); **3.** einfalls-, geistreich; **4.** fig. bedeutungsvoll, gewichtig; voll (*with* von).

pre·heat [ˌpriːˈhiːt] v/t. vorwärmen (a. ⚙).

pre·hen·sile [prɪˈhensaɪl] adj. zo. Greif...: ~ *organ*.

pre·his·tor·ic, **pre·his·tor·i·cal** [ˌpriːhɪˈstɒrɪk(l)] adj. □ prähi'storisch, vorgeschichtlich; **pre·his·to·ry** [ˌpriːˈhɪstərɪ] s. Vor-, Urgeschichte f.

pre·ig·ni·tion [ˌpriːɪgˈnɪʃn] s. mot. Frühzündung f.

pre·judge [ˌpriːˈdʒʌdʒ] v/t. im Vor'aus od. vorschnell be- od. verurteilen.

prej·u·dice [ˈpredʒʊdɪs] I s. **1.** Vorurteil n, Voreingenommenheit f, a. ⚖ Befangenheit f; **2.** (a. ⚖) Nachteil m, Schaden m: *to the* ~ *of* zum Nachteil (gen.); *without* ~ ohne Verbindlichkeit; *without* ~ *to* ohne Schaden für, unbeschadet (gen.); II v/t. **3.** mit e-m Vorurteil erfüllen, einnehmen (*in favo[u]r of* für, *against* gegen): ~*d* a) (vor)eingenommen, b) ⚖ befangen, c) vorgefasst (*Meinung*); **4.** a. ⚖ beeinträchtigen, benachteiligen, schaden (dat.), e-r Sache abträglich sein; **prej·u·di·cial** [ˌpredʒʊˈdɪʃl] adj. □ nachteilig, schädlich (*to* für): *be* ~ *to* → *prejudice* 4.

prel·a·cy [ˈpreləsɪ] s. eccl. **1.** Präla'tur f (*Würde od. Amtsbereich*); **2.** coll. Prä'laten(stand m, -tum n) pl.; **prel·ate** [ˈprelɪt] s. Prä'lat m.

pre·lect [prɪˈlekt] v/i. lesen, e-e Vorlesung od. Vorlesungen halten (*on*, *upon* über acc., *to* vor dat.); **pre'lec·tion** [-kʃn] s. Vorlesung f, Vortrag m; **pre·'lec·tor** [-tə] s. Vorleser m, (Universi'täts)Lektor m.

pre·lim [ˈpriːlɪm] **1.** F → *preliminary examination*; **2.** pl. typ. Tite'lei f.

pre·lim·i·nar·y [prɪˈlɪmɪnərɪ] I adj. □ **1.** einleitend, vorbereitend, Vor...: ~ *discussion* Vorbesprechung f; ~ *inquiry* ⚖ Voruntersuchung f; ~ *measures* vorbereitende Maßnahmen; ~ *round* sport Vorrunde f; ~ *work* Vorarbeit f; **2.** vorläufig; ~ *dressing* ⚕ Notverband m; II s. **3.** mst pl. Einleitung f, Vorbereitung(en pl.) f, vorbereitende Maßnahmen pl.; pl. Präli'mi'narien pl. (a. e-s Vertrags); **4.** ⚖ Vorverhandlungen pl.; **5.** → ex·am·i·na·tion s. univ. **1.** Aufnahmeprüfung f; **2.** a) Vorprüfung f, b) ⚗ Physikum n.

prel·ude [ˈpreljuːd] I s. **1.** ♪ Vorspiel n, Einleitung f (*beide a. fig.*), Prä'ludium n; fig. Auftakt m; II v/t. **2.** ♪ a) einleiten, b) als Prä'ludium spielen; **3.** bsd. fig. einleiten, das Vorspiel od. der Auftakt sein zu; III v/i. **4.** ♪ a) ein Prä'ludium spielen, b) als Vorspiel dienen (*to* für, zu); **5.** fig. das Vorspiel od. die Einleitung bilden (*to* zu).

pre·mar·i·tal [ˌpriːˈmærɪtl] adj. vorehelich.

pre·ma·ture [ˌpreməˈtjʊə] adj. □ **1.** früh-, vorzeitig, verfrüht: ~ *birth* Frühgeburt f; ~ *ignition* mot. Frühzündung f; **2.** fig. voreilig, -schnell; über'eilt; **3.** frühreif; ˌ**pre·ma'ture·ness** [-nɪs], ˌ**pre·ma'tu·ri·ty** [-ərətɪ] s. **1.** Frühreife f; **2.** Früh-, Vorzeitigkeit f; **3.** Über'eiltheit f.

pre·med·i·cal [ˌpriːˈmedɪkl] adj. univ. Am. 'vormedi,zinisch, in die Medi'zin einführend: ~ *course* Einführungskurs m in die Medizin; ~ *student* Medizinstudent(in), der (die) e-n Einführungskurs besucht.

pre·me·di·e·val [ˈpriːˌmedɪˈiːvl] adj. frühmittelalterlich.

pre·med·i·tate [ˌpriːˈmedɪteɪt] v/t. u. v/i. vorher über'legen: ~*d murder* vorsätzlicher Mord; ˌ**pre'med·i·tat·ed·ly** [-tɪdlɪ] adv. mit Vorbedacht, vorsätzlich; **pre·med·i·ta·tion** [priːˌmedɪˈteɪʃn] s. Vorbedacht m; Vorsatz m.

pre·men·stru·al [ˌpriːˈmenstrʊəl] adj. prämenstru'ell, vor der Menstruati'on: ~ *syndrome* ⚗ prämenstruelles Syndrom, prämenstruelle Phase.

pre·mi·er [ˈpremjə] I adj. erst; oberst, Haupt...; II s. Premi'er(mi,nister) m, Mi'nisterpräsi,dent(in).

pre·mière [prəˈmjeə] (Fr.) thea. I s. **1.** Premi'ere f, Ur-, Erstaufführung f; **2.** a) Darstellerin f, b) Primaballe'rina f; II v/t. **3.** ur-, erstaufführen.

pre·mi·er·ship [ˈpremjəʃɪp] s. Amt n od. Würde f des Premi'ermi,nisters.

pre·mil·len·ni·al [ˌpriːmɪˈlenjəl] adj. ... vor dem neuen Jahr'tausend, ... vor der Jahr'tausendwende: ~ *angst* Millenniumsangst f; ~ *tension* Stress m vor der Jahrtausendwende, Millenniumsangst f.

prem·ise[1] [ˈpremɪs] s. **1.** phls. Prä'misse f, Vor'aussetzung f, Vordersatz m e-s Schlusses; **2.** ⚖ a) pl. das Obenerwähnte: *in the* ~*s* im Vorstehenden; *in these* ~*s* in Hinsicht auf das eben Erwähnte, b) oben erwähntes Grundstück; **3.** pl. a) Grundstück n, b) Haus n nebst Zubehör (*Nebengebäude*, *Grund u. Boden*), c) Lo'kal n, Räumlichkeiten pl.: *business* ~*s* Geschäftsräume pl., Werksgelände n; *licensed* ~ Schanklokal n; *on the* ~*s* an Ort u. Stelle, auf dem Grundstück, im Hause od. Lokal.

pre·mise[2] [prɪˈmaɪz] v/t. **1.** vor'ausschicken; **2.** phls. postulieren.

pre·mi·um [ˈpriːmjəm] s. **1.** (Leistungs- etc.)Prämie f, Bonus m; Belohnung f, Preis m; Zugabe f: ~ *offers* ⚓ Verkauf m mit Zugaben; ~ *system* Prämienlohnsystem n; **2.** (Versicherungs)Prämie f: *free of* ~ prämienfrei; **3.** ⚓ Aufgeld n, Agio n: *at a* ~ a) ⚓ über Pari, b) fig. hoch im Kurs (stehend), sehr gesucht: *sell at a* ~ a) (v/i.) über Pari stehen, b) (v/t.) mit Gewinn verkaufen; **4.** a. ~ *petrol* Brit., ~ *gas* Am. 'Super(ben,zin) n; **5.** Lehrgeld n e-s Lehrlings, 'Ausbildungshono,rar n.

pre·mo·ni·tion [ˌpriːməˈnɪʃn] s. **1.** Warnung f; **2.** (Vor)Ahnung f, (Vor)Gefühl n; **pre·mon·i·to·ry** [prɪˈmɒnɪtərɪ] adj. warnend: ~ *symptom* ⚗ Frühsymptom n.

pre·na·tal [ˌpriːˈneɪtl] adj. ⚗ vor der Geburt, vorgeburtlich, präna'tal: ~ *care* Schwangerenvorsorge f.

pre·oc·cu·pan·cy [ˌpriːˈɒkjʊpənsɪ] s. **1.** (Recht n der) frühere(n) Besitznahme; **2.** (*in*) Beschäftigtsein n (mit), Vertieftsein n (in acc.); **pre·oc·cu·pa·tion**

[pri:ˌɒkjuˈpeɪʃn] *s.* **1.** vor'herige Besitz-nahme; **2.** (*with*) Beschäftigtsein *n* (mit), Vertieftsein *n* (in *acc.*), In'an-spruchnahme *f* (durch); **3.** Hauptbe-schäftigung *f*; **4.** Vorurteil *n*, Voreinge-nommenheit *f*; **pre'oc·cu·pied** [-paɪd] *adj.* vertieft (*with* in *acc.*), gedanken-verloren; **preoc·cu·py** [ˌpriːˈɒkjupaɪ] *v/t.* **1.** vorher *od.* vor anderen in Besitz nehmen; **2.** *j-n* (völlig) in Anspruch nehmen, *j-s Gedanken* ausschließlich beschäftigen, erfüllen.

pre·or·dain [ˌpriːɔːˈdeɪn] *v/t.* vorher an-ordnen, vor'herbestimmen.

prep [prep] *s.* F **1.** a) *a.* **~ school** → **preparatory school**, b) *Am.* Schüler (-in) e-r *preparatory school*; **2.** *Brit.* → *preparation* 5.

pre·pack [ˌpriːˈpæk], **pre·pack·age** [ˌpriːˈpækɪdʒ] *v/t.* ✝ abpacken.

pre·paid [ˌpriːˈpeɪd] *adj.* vor'ausbezahlt; ✆ frankiert, (porto)frei.

prep·a·ra·tion [ˌprepəˈreɪʃn] *s.* **1.** Vor-bereitung *f*: *in* ~ *for* als Vorbereitung auf (*acc.*); *make* ~*s* Vorbereitungen *od.* Anstalten treffen (*for* für); **2.** (Zu-) Bereitung *f* (*von Tee, Speisen etc.*); Herstellung *f*, ⚒, ⚙ Aufbereitung *f* (*von Erz, Kraftstoff etc.*); Vorbehand-lung *f*, Imprägnieren *n* (*von Holz etc.*); **3.** ⚒, ⚕ Präpa'rat *n*, *pharm. a.* Arz'nei (-mittel *n*) *f*; **4.** Abfassung *f* e-r *Urkun-de etc.*; Ausfüllen *n* e-s *Formulars*; **5.** *ped. Brit.* (Anfertigung *f* der) Hausauf-gaben *pl.*, Vorbereitung(sstunde) *f*; **6.** ♪ a) (Disso'nanz)Vorbereitung *f*, b) Einleitung *f*; **pre·par·a·tive** [prɪˈpærə-tɪv] **I** *adj.* □ → **preparatory** **I**; **II** *s.* Vorbereitung *f*, vorbereitende Maß-nahme (*for* auf *acc.*, *to* zu).

pre·par·a·to·ry [prɪˈpærətərɪ] **I** *adj.* □ **1.** vorbereitend, als Vorbereitung dienend (*to* für); **2.** Vor(bereitungs)...; **3.** ~ *to* *adv.* im Hinblick auf (*acc.*), vor (*dat.*): ~ *to doing s.th.* bevor *od.* ehe man etwas tut; *Brit.* → ~ *school* **s. 1.** *Brit.* (*mit Ausnahme Schottlands*) Vor-bereitungsschule auf e-e *public school*; **2.** *Am.* Vorbereitungsschule auf e-e *Hochschule*.

pre·pare [prɪˈpeə] **I** *v/t.* **1.** (*a. Rede, Schularbeiten, Schüler etc.*) vorberei-ten; zu'rechtmachen, fertig machen, (her)richten; *Speise etc.* (zu)bereiten; **2.** (aus)rüsten, bereitstellen; **3.** *j-n seelisch* vorbereiten (*to do* zu tun, *for* auf *acc.*): a) geneigt *od.* bereit machen, b) gefasst machen: ~ *o.s. to do s.th.* sich anschik-ken, et. zu tun; **4.** anfertigen, ausarbei-ten, *Plan* entwerfen, *Schriftstück* abfas-sen; **5.** ⚒, ⚙ a) herstellen, anfertigen, b) präparieren, zurichten; **6.** *Kohle* auf-bereiten; **II** *v/i.* **7.** (*for*) sich (*a. seelisch*) vorbereiten (auf *acc.*), sich anschicken *od.* rüsten, Vorbereitungen *od.* Anstal-ten treffen (für): ~ *for war* sich zum Krieg rüsten; ~ *to* ...! ✗ fertig zum ...!; **pre'pared** [-eəd] *adj.* **1.** vor-, zuberei-tet, bereit; **2.** *fig.* bereit, gewillt; **3.** ge-fasst (*for* auf *acc.*); **pre'par·ed·ness** [-eədnɪs] *s.* **1.** Bereitschaft *f*, -sein *n*; **2.** Gefasstsein *n* (*for* auf *acc.*).

pre·pay [ˌpriːˈpeɪ] *v/t.* [*irr.* → *pay*] vo-'rausbezahlen, *Brief etc.* frankieren; **pre'pay·ment** [-mənt] *s.* Vor'aus(be)-zahlung *f*; ✆ Frankierung *f*.

pre·pense [prɪˈpens] *adj.* □ ♯♯ vorsätz-lich, vorbedacht: *with* (*od.* *of*) *malice* ~ in böswilliger Absicht.

pre·pon·der·ance [prɪˈpɒndərəns] *s.* **1.** 'Übergewicht *n* (*a. fig. over* über *acc.*); **2.** *fig.* Über'wiegen *n* (*an Zahl etc.*), über'wiegende Zahl (*over* über *acc.*);

pre'pon·der·ant [-nt] *adj.* □ über'wie-gend, entscheidend; **pre'pon·der·ate** [prɪˈpɒndəreɪt] *v/i. fig.* über'wiegen, vorherrschen: ~ *over* (an Zahl) über-steigen, überlegen sein (*dat.*).

prep·o·si·tion [ˌprepəˈzɪʃn] *s. ling.* Prä-positi'on *f*, Verhältniswort *n*; **prep·o-'si·tion·al** [-ʃənl] *adj.* □ präpositio'nal.

pre·pos·sess [ˌpriːpəˈzes] *v/t.* **1.** *mst pass. j-n*, *j-s Geist* einnehmen (*in fa-vo[u]r of* für): ~*ed* voreingenommen; ~*ing* einnehmend, anziehend; **2.** erfül-len (*with* mit *Ideen etc.*); **prep·os-'ses·sion** [-eʃn] *s.* Voreingenommen-heit *f* (*in favo[u]r of* für), Vorurteil *n* (*against* gegen); vorgefasste (günstige) Meinung (*for* von).

pre·pos·ter·ous [prɪˈpɒstərəs] *adj.* □ **1.** ab'surd, un-, 'widersinnig; **2.** lächerlich, gro'tesk.

pre·po·tence [prɪˈpəʊtəns], **pre'po·ten-cy** [-sɪ] *s.* **1.** Vorherrschaft *f*, Über'legen-heit *f*; **2.** *biol.* stärkere Vererbungskraft; **pre'po·tent** [-nt] *adj.* **1.** vorherrschend, (an Kraft) über'legen; **2.** *biol.* sich stärker fortpflanzend *od.* vererbend.

pre·pie, **prep·py** [ˈprepɪ] *adj. bsd. Am. mst b. s.* ad'rett, geschniegelt.

pre·print **I** *s.* [ˈpriːprɪnt] **1.** Vorabdruck *m* (*e-s Buches etc.*); **2.** Teilausgabe *f*; **II** *v/t.* [ˌpriːˈprɪnt] **3.** vorabdrucken.

prep school [prep] → **preparatory school**.

pre·puce [ˈpriːpjuːs] *s. anat.* Vorhaut *f*.

Pre-Raph·a·el·ite [ˌpriːˈræfəlaɪt] *paint.* **I** *adj.* präraffae'litisch; **II** *s.* Präraffae-'lit(in).

pre·re·cord·ed [ˌpriːrɪˈkɔːdɪd] *adj.* be-spielt (*Musikkassette etc.*).

pre·req·ui·site [ˌpriːˈrekwɪzɪt] **I** *adj.* vor'auszusetzen(d), erforderlich (*for*, *to* für); **II** *s.* Vorbedingung *f*, ('Grund-) Vor,aussetzung *f* (*for*, *to* für).

pre·rog·a·tive [prɪˈrɒgətɪv] **I** *s.* Privi'leg *n*, Vorrecht *n*: *royal* ~ Hoheitsrecht *n*; **II** *adj.* bevorrechtigt: ~ *right* Vorrecht *n*.

pre·sage [ˈpresɪdʒ] **I** *v/t.* **1.** *mst Böses* ahnen; **2.** (vorher) anzeigen *od.* ankün-digen; **3.** weissagen, prophe'zeien; **II** *s.* **4.** Omen *n*, Warnungs-, Anzeichen *n*; **5.** (Vor)Ahnung *f*, Vorgefühl *n*; **6.** Vorbedeutung *f*: *of evil* ~.

pres·by·op·ic [ˌprezbɪˈɒpɪk] *adj.* alters-(weit)sichtig.

pres·by·ter [ˈprezbɪtə] *s. eccl.* **1.** (Kir-chen)Älteste(r) *m*; **2.** (Hilfs)Geistli-che(r) *m* (*in Episkopalkirchen*); **Pres-by·te·ri·an** [ˌprezbɪˈtɪərɪən] **I** *adj.* pres-byteri'anisch; **II** *s.* Presbyteri'aner(in); **'pres·by·ter·y** [-tərɪ] *s.* **1.** Presby'te-rium *n* (*a.* ⌂ *Chor*); **2.** Pfarrhaus *n*.

pre·school *ped.* **I** [ˌpriːˈskuːl] vor-schulisch, Vorschul...: ~ *child* noch nicht schulpflichtiges Kind; **II** *s.* [ˈpriː-skuːl] Vorschule *f*.

pre·sci·ence [ˈpresɪəns] *s.* Vor'herwis-sen *n*, Vor'aussicht *f*; **'pre·sci·ent** [-nt] *adj.* □ vor'herwissend, -sehend (*of acc.*).

pre·scribe [prɪˈskraɪb] **I** *v/t.* **1.** vorschrei-ben (*to s.o.* j-m), *et.* anordnen: (*as*) ~*d* (wie) vorgeschrieben, vorschriftsmä-ßig; **2.** ⚕ verordnen, -schreiben (*for od. to s.o.* j-m, *for s.th.* gegen et.); **II** *v/i.* **3.** ⚕ *et.* verschreiben, ein Re'zept ausstellen (*for s.o.* j-m); **4.** ♯♯ a) ver-jähren, b) Verjährung *od.* Ersitzung geltend machen (*for*, *to* für, auf *acc.*).

pre·scrip·tion [prɪˈskrɪpʃn] **I** *s.* **1.** Vor-schrift *f*, Verordnung *f*; **2.** ⚕ a) Re'zept *n*, b) verordnete Medi'zin; **3.** ♯♯ a) (*positive*) ~ Ersitzung *f*, b) (*negative*)

~ Verjährung *f*; **II** *adj.* **4.** ärztlich ver-ordnet: ~ *glasses*; ~ *pad* Rezeptblock *m*; **pre'scrip·tive** [-ptɪv] *adj.* □ **1.** ver-ordnend, vorschreibend; **2.** ♯♯ a) erses-sen: ~ *right*, b) Verjährungs...: ~ *pe-riod*; ~ *debt* verjährte Schuld.

pre·se·lec·tion [ˌpriːsɪˈlekʃn] *s.* **1.** ⚙ Vorwahl *f*; **2.** *Radio*: 'Vorselekti,on *f*; **pre·se'lec·tive** [-ktɪv] *adj.* ⚙, *mot.* Vorwähler...: ~ *gears*; **pre·se'lec·tor** [-ktə] *s.* ⚙ Vorwähler *m*.

pres·ence [ˈprezns] *s.* **1.** Gegenwart *f*, Anwesenheit *f*, ✗ *pol.* Prä'senz *f*: *in the* ~ *of* in Gegenwart *od.* in Anwesen-heit von *od. gen.*, vor Zeugen; *saving your* ~ sosehr ich es bedaure, dies in Ihrer Gegenwart sagen zu müssen; → *mind* 2; **2.** (unmittelbare) Nähe, Vor-'handensein *n*: *be admitted into the* ~ (zur Audienz) vorgelassen werden; *in the* ~ *of danger* angesichts der Gefahr; **3.** hohe Per'sönlichkeit(en *pl.*); **4.** Äu-ßere(s) *n*, Aussehen *n*, (stattliche) Er-scheinung; *weitS.* Auftreten *n*, Haltung *f*; **5.** Anwesenheit *f* e-s unsichtbaren Geistes; ~ *cham·ber* *s.* Audi'enzsaal *m*.

pres·ent¹ [ˈpreznt] **I** *adj.* □ → *present-ly*; **1.** (*räumlich*) gegenwärtig, anwe-send; vor'handen (*a.* ⚛ *etc.*): ~ *com-pany, those* ~ die Anwesenden; *be* ~ *at* teilnehmen an (*dat.*), beiwohnen (*dat.*), zugegen sein bei; ~! (*bei Na-mensaufruf*) hier!; *it is* ~ *to my mind fig.* es ist mir gegenwärtig; **2.** (*zeitlich*) gegenwärtig, jetzig, augenblicklich, momen'tan: *the* ~ *day* (*od. time*) die Gegenwart; ~ *value* Gegenwartswert *m*; **3.** heutig (*bsd. Tag*), laufend (*bsd. Jahr, Monat*); **4.** vorliegend (*Fall, Ur-kunde etc.*): *the* ~ *writer* der Schreiber *od.* Verfasser (dieser Zeilen); **5.** *ling.* ~ *participle* Mittelwort *n* der Gegenwart, Partizip *n* Präsens; ~ *perfect* Perfekt *n*, zweite Vergangenheit; ~ *tense* → 7; **II** *s.* **6.** Gegenwart *f*: *at* ~ gegenwärtig, im Augenblick, jetzt, momentan; *for the* ~ für den Augenblick, vorläufig, einst-weilen; *up to the* ~ bislang, bis dato; **7.** *ling.* Präsens *n*, Gegenwart *f*; **8.** *pl.* ♯♯ (vorliegendes) Schriftstück *od.* Doku-'ment: *by these* ~*s* hiermit, hierdurch; *know all men by these* ~*s* hiermit je-dermann kund und zu wissen(, *dass*).

pres·ent² [prɪˈzent] **I** *v/t.* **1.** (dar)bieten, (über)'reichen; *Nachricht etc.* über-'bringen: ~ *one's compliments to* sich *j-m* empfehlen; ~ *s.o. with* j-n mit *et.* beschenken; ~ *s.th. to* j-m et. schen-ken; **2.** *Gesuch etc.* einreichen, vorle-gen, unter'breiten; ✝ *Scheck, Wechsel* (zur Zahlung) vorlegen, präsentieren; ♯♯ *Klage* erheben: ~ *a case* e-n Fall vor Gericht vertreten; **3.** j-n für ein Amt vorschlagen; **4.** *Bitte, Klage* vorbrin-gen; *Gedanken, Wunsch etc.* äußern, unterbreiten; **5.** *j-n* vorstellen (*to dat.*), einführen (*at* bei *Hofe*): ~ *o.s.* a) sich vorstellen, b) sich einfinden, erschei-nen, sich melden (*for* zu), c) *fig.* sich bieten (*Möglichkeit etc.*); **6.** *Schwierig-keiten* bieten, *Problem* darstellen; **7.** *thea. etc.* darbieten, *Film* vorführen, zeigen, *Sendung* bringen *od.* moderie-ren, *Rolle* spielen *od.* verkörpern; *fig.* vergegenwärtigen, darstellen, schil-dern; **8.** ✗ a) *Gewehr* präsentieren, b) *Waffe* anlegen, richten (*at* auf *acc.*).

pres·ent³ [ˈpreznt] *s.* Geschenk *n*: *make s.o. a* ~ *of s.th.* j-m et. zum Geschenk machen.

pre·sent·a·ble [prɪˈzentəbl] *adj.* □ **1.** darstellbar; **2.** präsen'tabel (*Geschenk*); **3.** präsen'tabel (*Erscheinung*), anständig angezogen.

pres·en·ta·tion [ˌprezənˈteɪʃn] *s.* **1.** Schenkung *f*, (feierliche) Überreichung *od.* 'Übergabe: **~** *copy* Widmungsexemplar *n*; **2.** Gabe *f*, Geschenk *n*; **3.** Vorstellung *f*, Einführung *f e-r Person*; **4.** Vorstellung *f*, Erscheinen *n*; **5.** *fig.* Darstellung *f*, Schilderung *f*, Behandlung *f e-s Falles*, *Problems etc.*; **6.** *thea.*, *Film*: Darbietung *f*, Vorführung *f*; *Radio*, *TV*: Moderati'on *f*; ♣ Demonstrati'on *f* (*im Kolleg*); **7.** Einreichung *f e-s Gesuchs etc.*; ✝ Vorlage *f e-s Wechsels*: (**up**)**on ~** gegen Vorlage; *payable on* **~** zahlbar bei Sicht; **8.** Vorschlag(srecht *n*) *m*; Ernennung *f* (*Brit. a. eccl.*); **9.** ♣ (Kinds)Lage *f im Uterus*; **10.** *psych.* a) Wahrnehmung *f*, b) Vorstellung *f*.

pres·ent-'day [ˌpreznt-] *adj.* heutig, gegenwärtig, mo'dern.

pre·sent·er [prɪˈzentə] *s. Brit.* ('Fernseh)Mode,rator *m*.

pre·sen·tient [prɪˈsenʃɪənt] *adj.* im Vo'raus fühlend, ahnend (*of acc.*); **pre·sen·ti·ment** [prɪˈsentɪmənt] *s.* (Vor-)Gefühl *n*, (*mst* böse Vor)Ahnung.

pres·ent·ly [ˈprezntlɪ] *adv.* **1.** (so-) 'gleich, bald (dar'auf), als'bald; **2.** jetzt, gegenwärtig; **3.** so'fort.

pre·sent·ment [prɪˈzentmənt] *s.* **1.** Darstellung *f*, 'Wiedergabe *f*, Bild *n*; **2.** *thea. etc.* Darbietung *f*, Aufführung *f*; **3.** ✝ (*Wechsel- etc.*)Vorlage *f*; **4.** ⚖ Anklage(schrift) *f*; Unter'suchung *f* von Amts wegen.

pre·serv·a·ble [prɪˈzɜːvəbl] *adj.* erhaltbar, zu erhalten(d), konservierbar; **pres·er·va·tion** [ˌprezəˈveɪʃn] *s.* **1.** Bewahrung *f*, (Er)Rettung *f*, Schutz *m* (*from* vor *dat.*): **~** *of natural beauty* Naturschutz; **2.** Erhaltung *f*, Konservierung *f*: *in good* **~** gut erhalten: **~** *of evidence* ⚖ Beweissicherung *f*; **3.** Einmachen *n*, -kochen *n*, Konservierung *f* (*von Früchten etc.*); **pre·serv·a·tive** [-vətɪv] **I** *adj.* **1.** bewahrend, Schutz...: **~** *coat* ⚙ Schutzanstrich *m*; **2.** erhaltend, konservierend; **II** *s.* **3.** Konservierungsmittel *n* (*a.* ⚙); **pre·serve** [prɪˈzɜːv] **I** *v/t.* **1.** bewahren, behüten, (er)retten, (be)schützen (*from* vor *dat.*); **2.** erhalten, vor dem Verderb schützen, *well-~d* gut erhalten; **3.** aufbewahren, -heben; ⚖ *Beweise* sichern; **4.** konservieren (*a.* ⚙), *Obst etc.* einkochen, -machen, -legen: **~d** *meat* Büchsenfleisch *n*, *coll.* Fleischkonserven *pl.*; **5.** *hunt. bsd. Brit. Wild*, *Fische* hegen; **6.** *fig. Haltung*, *Ruhe*, *Andenken etc.* (be)wahren: **~** *silence*; **II** *s.* **7.** *mst pl.* Eingemachte(s) *n*, Kon'serve(n *pl.*) *f*; **8.** *oft pl.* a) *hunt. bsd. Brit.* ('Wild)Reser,vat *n*, (Jagd-, Fisch)Gehege *n*, b) *fig.* Gehege *n*: *poach on s.o.'s* **~s** j-m ins Gehege kommen (*a. fig.*); **pre·'serv·er** [-və] *s.* **1.** Bewahrer(in), Erhalter(in), (Er)Retter(in); **2.** Konservierungsmittel *n*; **3.** 'Einkochappa,rat *m*; **4.** *hunt. Brit.* Heger *m*, Wildhüter *m*.

pre·set [ˌpriːˈset] *v/t.* [*irr.* → *set*] ⚙ voreinstellen.

pre·shrink [ˌpriːˈʃrɪŋk] *v/t.* [*irr.* → *shrink*] ⚙ *Stoffe* krumpfen; vorwaschen.

pre·side [prɪˈzaɪd] *v/i.* **1.** den Vorsitz haben *od.* führen (*at* bei, *over* über *acc.*), präsidieren: **~** *over (od. at) a meeting* e-e Versammlung leiten; *presiding judge* ⚖ Vorsitzende(r *m*) *f*; **2.** ♪ *u. fig.* führen.

pres·i·den·cy [ˈprezɪdənsɪ] *s.* **1.** Prä'si-

---

dium *n*, Vorsitz *m*, (Ober)Aufsicht *f*; **2.** *pol.* a) Präsi'dentschaft *f*, b) Amtszeit *f e-s Präsidenten*; **3.** *eccl.* (*First* ♪ oberste) Mor'monenbehörde *f*; **'pres·i·dent** [-nt] *s.* **1.** Präsi'dent *m* (*a. pol. u.* ⚖), Vorsitzende(r *m*) *f*, Vorstand *m e-r Körperschaft*; *Am.* ✝ (Gene'ral)Di,rektor *m*: ♪ *of the Board of Trade Brit.* Handelsminister *m*; **2.** *univ. bsd. Am.* Rektor *m*; **pres·i·dent e·lect** *s.* der gewählte Präsi'dent (*vor Amtsantritt*); **pres·i·den·tial** [ˌprezɪˈdenʃl] *adj.* □ Präsidenten..., Präsidentschafts...: **~** *message Am.* Botschaft *f* des Präsidenten an den Kongress; **~** *primary Am.* Vorwahl *f* zur Nominierung des Präsidentschaftskandidaten *e-r Partei*; **~** *system* Präsidialsystem *n*; **~** *term Am.* Amtsperiode *f* des Präsidenten; **~** *year Am.* F Jahr *n* der Präsidentenwahl.

press [pres] **I** *v/t.* **1.** *allg.*, *a.* j-m die *Hand* drücken, pressen (*a.* ⚙); **2.** drücken auf (*acc.*): **~** *the button* auf den Knopf drücken (*a. fig.*); **3.** *Saft*, *Frucht etc.* (aus)pressen, keltern; **4.** (*vorwärts*) drängen *od.* treiben, (*weiter- etc.*)drängen, (-)treiben: **~** *on*; **5.** j-n (be)drängen: a) in die Enge treiben, zwingen (*to do* zu tun), b) j-m zusetzen, j-n bestürmen: **~** *s.o. for* j-n dringend um *et.* bitten, von j-m *Geld* erpressen; *be* **~ed** *for money* (*time*) in Geldverlegenheit sein (unter Zeitdruck stehen, es eilig haben); *hard* **~ed** in Bedrängnis; **6.** ([*up*]*on* j-m) *et.* aufdrängen, -nötigen; **7.** *Kleidungsstück* plätten; **8.** Nachdruck legen auf (*acc.*): **~** *a charge* Anklage erheben; **~** *one's point* auf s-r Forderung *od.* Meinung nachdrücklich bestehen; **~** *the point that* nachdrücklich betonen, dass; **~** *home* a) *Forderung etc.* 'durchsetzen, b) *Angriff* energisch 'durchführen, c) *Vorteil* ausnutzen (wollen); **9.** ⚔, ⚓ *in den Dienst* pressen; **II** *v/i.* **10.** drücken, (e-n) Druck ausüben (*a. fig.*); **11.** drängen, pressieren: *time* **~es** die Zeit drängt; **12.** **~** *for* dringen *od.* drängen auf (*acc.*), fordern; **13.** (sich) *wohin* drängen: **~** *forward* (sich) vordrängen, vorwärts drängen; **~** *on* vorwärts drängen, weitereilen; **~** *in upon s.o.* auf j-n eindringen (*a. fig.*); **III** *s.* **14.** (*Frucht-*, *Wein- etc.*)Presse *f*; **15.** *typ.* a) (Drucker)Presse *f*, b) Drucke'rei(anstalt *f*, -raum *m*, -wesen *n*) *f*, c) Druck(en *n*) *m*: *correct the* **~** Korrektur lesen; *go to* (*the*) **~** in Druck gehen; *send to* (*the*) **~** in Druck geben; *in the* **~** im Druck; *ready for the* **~** druckfertig; **16.** *the* **~** die Presse (*Zeitungswesen*, *a. coll.* die Zeitungen *od.* die Presseleute): **~** *campaign* Pressefeldzug *m*; **~** *conference* Pressekonferenz *f*; **~** *photographer* Pressefotograf *m*; *have a good* (*bad*) **~** e-e gute (schlechte) Presse haben; **17.** Spanner *m für Skier od. Tennisschläger*; **18.** (*Bücher- etc.*, *bsd. Wäsche*)Schrank *m*; **19.** *fig.* a) Druck *m*, Hast *f*, b) Dringlichkeit *f*, Drang *m der Geschäfte*: *the* **~** *of business*; **20.** ⚔, ⚓ *hist.* Zwangsaushebung *f*; **~** *a·gen·cy s.* 'Presseagen,tur *f*; **~** *a·gent s. thea. etc.* 'Pressea,gent *m*; **~** *bar·on s.* Pressezar *m*; **~** *box s.* 'Pressetri,büne *f*; **~** *but·ton s.* ⚡ (Druck)Knopf *m*; **~** *clip·ping Am.* → *press cutting*; **~** *cop·y s.* **1.** 'Durchschlag *m*; **2.** Rezensi'onsexem,plar *n*; **~** *cor·rec·tor s. typ.* Kor'rektor *m*; ♪ *Coun·cil s. Brit.* Presserat *m*; **~** *cut·ting s. Brit.* Zeitungsausschnitt *m*.

pressed [prest] *adj.* gepresst, Press... (*-glas*, *-käse*, *-öl*, *-ziegel etc.*); **'press·er**

[-sə] *s.* **1.** ⚙ Presser(in); **2.** *typ.* Drucker *m*; **3.** Bügler(in); **4.** ⚙ Pressvorrichtung *f*; **5.** *typ. etc.* Druckwalze *f*.

press| gal·ler·y *s. parl. bsd. Brit.* 'Pressetri,büne *f*; **'~·gang I** *s.* ⚓ *hist.* 'Presspa,trouille *f*; **II** *v/t.*: **~** *s.o. into doing s.th.* F j-n zu *et.* zwingen.

press·ing [ˈpresɪŋ] **I** *adj.* □ **1.** pressend, drückend; **2.** *fig.* a) (be)drückend, b) dringend, dringlich; **II** *s.* **3.** (Aus)Pressen *n*; **4.** ⚙ a) Stanzen *n*, b) *Papierfabrikation*: Satinieren *n*; **5.** ⚙ Pressling *m*; **6.** *Schallplattenfabrikation*: a) Pressplatte *f*, b) Pressung *f*, c) Auflage *f*.

press| law *s. mst pl.* Pressegesetz(e *pl.*) *n*; **~** *lord s.* Pressezar *m*; **'~·man** [-mən] *s.* [*irr.*] **1.** (Buch)Drucker *m*; **2.** Zeitungsmann *m*, Pressevertreter *m*; **'~·mark** *s.* Signa'tur *f*, Bibliotheksnummer *f e-s Buches*; **~** *proof s. typ.* letzte Korrek'tur, Ma'schinenrevisi,on *f*; **~** *re·lease s.* Presseverlautbarung *f*; **~** *room s.* Drucke'rei(raum *m*) *f*, Ma'schinensaal *m*; **'~·stud** *s.* Druckknopf *m*; **'~-to-'talk but·ton** *s.* Sprechtaste *f*; **'~-up** *s. sport* Liegestütz *m*.

pres·sure [ˈpreʃə] **I** *s.* **1.** Druck *m* (*a.* ⚙, *phys.*): **~** *hose* (*pump*, *valve*) ⚙ Druckschlauch *m* (-pumpe *f*, -ventil *n*); *work at high* **~** mit Hochdruck arbeiten (*a. fig.*); **2.** *meteor.* (Luft)Druck *m*: *high* (*low*) **~** Hoch-(Tief)druck; **3.** *fig.* Druck *m* (*Last od. Zwang*): *act under* **~** unter Druck handeln; *bring* **~** *to bear upon* auf j-n Druck ausüben; *the* **~** *of business* der Drang *od.* Druck der Geschäfte; **~** *of taxation* Steuerdruck *m*, -last *f*; **4.** *fig.* Drangsal *f*, Not *f*: *monetary* **~** Geldknappheit *f*, **~** *of conscience* Gewissensnot *f*; **II** *v/t.* **5.** → *pressurize* 1; **6.** *fig.* j-n (dazu) treiben *od.* zwingen (*to* et. zu tun); **~** *cab·in s.* ✈ 'Druckausgleichska,bine *f*; **~** *cook·er s.* Schnellkochtopf *m*; **~** *drop s.* **1.** ⚙ Druckgefälle *n*; **2.** ⚡ Spannungsabfall *m*; **~** *e·qual·i·za·tion s.* Druckausgleich *m*; **~** *ga(u)ge s.* ⚙ Druckmesser *m*, Mano'meter *n*; **~** *group s. pol.* Inter'essengruppe *f*; **~** *lu·bri·ca·tion s.* ⚙ 'Druck(umlauf)-,schmierung *f*; **'~-,sen·si·tive** *adj.* ♣ druckempfindlich; **~** *suit s.* ✈ ('Über-)Druckanzug *m*; **~** *tank s.* ⚙ Druckbehälter *m*.

pres·sur·ize [ˈpreʃəraɪz] *v/t.* **1.** ✈, unter Druck setzen (*a. fig.*), unter 'Überdruck halten, *bsd.* ✈ druckfest machen: **~d** *cabin* → *pressure cabin*; **2.** ✈ belüften.

'press·work *s. typ.* Druckarbeit *f*.

pres·ti·dig·i·ta·tion [ˈprestɪˌdɪdʒɪˈteɪʃn] *s.* **1.** Fingerfertigkeit *f*; **2.** Taschenspielerkunst *f*; **pres·ti·dig·i·ta·tor** [ˌprestɪˈdɪdʒɪteɪtə] *s.* Taschenspieler *m* (*a. fig.*).

pres·tige [preˈstiːʒ] (*Fr.*) *s.* Pre'stige *n*, Geltung *f*, Ansehen *n*.

pres·tig·ious [preˈstɪdʒəs] *adj.* berühmt, renom'miert.

pres·to [ˈprestəʊ] (*Ital.*) **I** *adv.* ♪ presto, (sehr) schnell (*a. fig.*): *hey* **~**, *pass!* Hokuspokus (Fidibus)! (*Zauberformel*); **II** *adj.* blitzschnell.

pre·stressed [ˌpriːˈstrest] *adj.* ⚙ vorgespannt: **~** *concrete* Spannbeton *m*.

pre·sum·a·ble [prɪˈzjuːməbl] *adj.* □ vermutlich, mutmaßlich, wahr'scheinlich; **pre·sume** [prɪˈzjuːm] **I** *v/t.* **1.** *als wahr* annehmen, vermuten; vor'aussetzen; schließen (*from* aus): **~d** *dead* verschollen; **2.** sich *et.* erlauben; **II** *v/i.* **3.** vermuten, mutmaßen: *I* **~** (wie) ich vermute, vermutlich; **4.** sich her'ausnehmen, sich erdreisten, (es) wagen (*to inf.* zu *inf.*); anmaßend sein; **5.** (*up*)*on* ausnutzen *od.* miss'brauchen (*acc.*); **pre'sum·ed·ly** [-mɪdlɪ] *adv.* vermutlich; **pre'sum·ing** [-mɪŋ] *adj.* □ → *presumptuous* 1.

pre·sump·tion [prɪ'zʌmpʃn] *s.* **1.** Vermutung *f*, Annahme *f*, Mutmaßung *f*; **2.** ⚖ Vermutung *f*, Präsumti'on *f*: *~ of death* Todesvermutung, Verschollenheit *f*; *~ of innocence* Unschuldsvermutung *f*; *~ of law* Rechtsvermutung *f* (*der Wahrheit bis zum Beweis des Gegenteils*); **3.** Wahrscheinlichkeit *f*: *there is a strong ~ of his death* es ist (mit Sicherheit) anzunehmen, dass er tot ist; **4.** Vermessenheit *f*, Anmaßung *f*, Dünkel *m*; **pre'sump·tive** [-ptɪv] *adj.* □ vermutlich, mutmaßlich, präsum'tiv: *~ evidence* ⚖ Indizienbeweis *m*; *~ title* ⚖ präsumtives Eigentum; **pre·'sump·tu·ous** [-ptjʊəs] *adj.* □ **1.** anmaßend, vermessen, dreist; **2.** über'heblich, dünkelhaft.

pre·sup·pose [ˌpriːsə'pəʊz] *v/t.* vor'aussetzen: a) im Vor'aus annehmen, b) zur Vor'aussetzung haben; **pre·sup·po·si·tion** [ˌpriːsʌpə'zɪʃn] *s.* Vor'aussetzung *f*.

pre·tax [ˌpriː'tæks] *adj.* ✝ vor Abzug der Steuern, *a.* Brutto...

pre·teen [ˌpriː'tiːn] *adj. u. s.* (Kind *n*) im Alter zwischen 10 u. 12.

pre·tence [prɪ'tens] *s.* **1.** Anspruch *m*: *make no ~ to* keinen Anspruch erheben auf (*acc.*); **2.** Vorwand *m*, Scheingrund *m*, Vortäuschung *f*: *false ~s* ⚖ Arglist *f*; *under false ~s* arglistig, unter Vorspiegelung falscher Tatsachen; **3.** *fig.* Schein *m*, Verstellung *f*: *make ~ of doing s.th.* sich den Anschein geben, als tue man etwas.

pre·tend [prɪ'tend] **I** *v/t.* **1.** vorgeben, -täuschen, -schützen, -heucheln; so tun als ob: *~ to be sick* sich krank stellen, krank spielen; **2.** → *presume* 2–4; **II** *v/i.* **3.** sich verstellen, heucheln: *he is only ~ing* er tut nur so; **4.** Anspruch erheben (*to* auf *den Thron etc.*); **pre·'tend·ed** [-dɪd] *adj.* □ vorgetäuscht, an-, vorgeblich; **pre'tend·er** [-də] *s.* **1.** Beanspruchende(r *m*) *f*; **2.** ('Thron-)Präten,dent *m*, Thronbewerber *m*.

pre·tense *Am.* → *pretence*.

pre·ten·sion [prɪ'tenʃn] *s.* **1.** Anspruch *m* (*to* auf *acc.*): *of great ~s* anspruchsvoll; **2.** Anmaßung *f*, Dünkel *m*; **pre·'ten·tious** [-ʃəs] *adj.* □ **1.** anmaßend; **2.** prätenti'ös, anspruchsvoll; **3.** protzig; **pre'ten·tious·ness** [-ʃəsnɪs] *s.* Anmaßung *f*.

preter- [priːtə] *in Zssgn* (hin'ausgehend) über (*acc.*), mehr als.

pret·er·it(e) ['pretərɪt] *ling.* **I** *adj.* Vergangenheits...; **II** *s.* Prä'teritum *n*, (erste) Vergangenheit; *~·'pres·ent* [-'preznt] *s.* Prä'terito,präsens *n*.

pre·ter·nat·u·ral [ˌpriːtə'nætʃrəl] *adj.* □ **1.** ab'norm, außergewöhnlich; **2.** 'übernat,türlich.

pre·text ['priːtekst] *s.* Vorwand *m*, Ausrede *f*: *under* (*od.* *on*) *the ~ of* unter dem Vorwand (*gen.*).

pre·tri·al [ˌpriː'traɪəl] ⚖ **I** *s.* Vorverhandlung *f*; **II** *adj.* vor der (Haupt)Verhandlung, Untersuchungs...

pret·ti·fy ['prɪtɪfaɪ] *v/t.* F verschönern, hübsch machen; **'pret·ti·ly** [-ɪlɪ] *adv.* → *pretty* 1; **'pret·ti·ness** [-ɪnɪs] *s.* **1.** Hübschheit *f*, Niedlichkeit *f*; Anmut *f*; **2.** Geziertheit *f*; **pret·ty** ['prɪtɪ] **I** *adj.* □ **1.** hübsch, nett, niedlich; **2.** (*a. iro.*) schön, fein, tüchtig: *a ~ mess!* e-e schöne Geschichte!; **3.** F ,(ganz)

schön', ,hübsch', beträchtlich: *it costs a ~ penny* es kostet e-e schöne Stange Geld; **II** *adv.* **4.** a) ziemlich, ganz, b) einigermaßen, leidlich: *~ cold* ganz schön kalt; *~ good* recht gut, nicht schlecht; *~ much the same thing* so ziemlich dasselbe; *~ near* nahe daran, ziemlich nahe; **5.** *sitting ~ sl.* wie der Hase im Kohl, ,warm' (sitzend); **III** *v/t.* **6.** *~ up et.* hübsch machen, ,aufpolieren'.

pret·zel ['pretsəl] *s.* (Salz)Brezel *f*.

pre·vail [prɪ'veɪl] *v/i.* **1.** (*over, against*) die Oberhand *od.* das 'Übergewicht gewinnen (über *acc.*), (*a.* ⚖ ob)'siegen; *fig. a.* sich 'durchsetzen *od.* behaupten (gegen); **2.** *fig.* ausschlag-, maßgebend sein; **3.** *fig.* (vor)herrschen; (weit) verbreitet sein; **4.** *~ (up)on s.o. to do* j-n dazu bewegen *od.* bringen, et. zu tun; **pre'vail·ing** [-lɪŋ] *adj.* □ **1.** über'legen: *~ party* ⚖ obsiegende Partei; **2.** (vor)herrschend, maßgebend: *the ~ opinion* die herrschende Meinung; *under the ~ circumstances* unter den obwaltenden Umständen; *tone* ✝ Grundstimmung *f*; **prev·a·lence** ['prevələns] *s.* **1.** (Vor)Herrschen *n*; Über'handnehmen *n*; **2.** (allgemeine) Gültigkeit; **prev·a·lent** ['prevələnt] *adj.* □ **1.** (vor)herrschend, über'wiegend; häufig, weit verbreitet.

pre·var·i·cate [prɪ'værɪkeɪt] *v/i.* Ausflüchte machen; die Wahrheit verdrehen; **pre·var·i·ca·tion** [prɪˌværɪ'keɪʃn] *s.* **1.** Ausflucht *f*, Tatsachenverdrehung *f*, Winkelzug *m*; **2.** ⚖ Anwaltstreubruch *m*; **pre'var·i·ca·tor** [-tə] *s.* Ausflüchtemacher(in), Wortverdreher(in).

pre·vent [prɪ'vent] *v/t.* **1.** verhindern, -hüten; *e-r Sache* vorbeugen *od.* zu'vorkommen; **2.** (*from*) j-n hindern (an *dat.*), abhalten (von): *~ s.o. from coming* j-n am Kommen hindern, j-n vom Kommen abhalten; **pre'vent·a·ble** [-təbl] *adj.* verhütbar, abwendbar; **pre·'ven·tion** [-nʃn] *s.* **1.** Verhinderung *f*, Verhütung *f*: *~ of accidents* Unfallverhütung; **2.** *bsd.* ⚕ Vorbeugung *f*; **pre·'ven·tive** [-tɪv] **I** *adj.* □ **1.** *a.* ⚕ vorbeugend, prophy'laktisch, Vorbeugungs...: *~ medicine* Vorbeugungsmedizin *f*; **2.** *bsd.* ⚖ präven'tiv: *~ arrest* Schutzhaft *f*; *~ detention* a) Sicherungsverwahrung *f*, b) *Am.* Vorbeugehaft *f*; *~ war* pol. Präventivkrieg *m*; **II** *s.* **3.** *a.* ⚕ Vorbeugungs-, Schutzmittel *n*; **4.** Schutz-, Vorsichtsmaßnahme *f*.

pre·view ['priːvjuː] *s.* **1.** Vorbesichtigung *f*; *Film:* a) Probeaufführung *f*, b) (Pro'gramm)Vorschau *f*; *Radio, TV:* Probe *f*; **2.** Vorbesprechung *f e-s Buches*; **3.** (Vor)'Ausblick *m*; **4.** F → *print preview*.

pre·vi·ous ['priːvjəs] **I** *adj.* □ → *previously*; **1.** vor'her-, vor'ausgehend, früher, vor'herig, Vor...: *~ conviction* ⚖ Vorstrafe *f*; *~ holder* ✝ Vor(der)mann *m*; *~ question* parl. Vorfrage, ob ohne weitere Debatte abgestimmt werden soll: *move the ~ question* Übergang zur Tagesordnung beantragen; *without ~ notice* ohne vorherige Ankündigung; **2.** *mst too ~* F verfrüht, voreilig; **II** *adv.* **3.** *~ to* bevor, vor (*dat.*); *~ to that* zuvor; **'pre·vi·ous·ly** [-lɪ] *adv.* vorher, früher.

pre·vo·ca·tion·al [ˌpriːvəʊ'keɪʃənl] *adj.* vorberuflich.

pre·vue ['priːvjuː] *s. Am.* (Film)Vorschau *f*.

pre·war [ˌpriː'wɔː] *adj.* Vorkriegs...

prey [preɪ] **I** *s.* **1.** *zo. u. fig.* Raub *m*,

Beute *f*, Opfer *n*: → *beast* 1, *bird* 1; **become** (*od.* *fall*) *a ~ to* j-m *od.* e-r Sache zum Opfer fallen; **II** *v/i.* **2.** auf Raub *od.* Beute ausgehen; **3.** *~ (up)on* a) *zo.* Jagd machen auf (*acc.*), erbeuten, fressen, b) *fig.* berauben, aussaugen, c) *fig.* nagen *od.* zehren an (*dat.*): *it ~ed upon his mind* es ließ ihm keine Ruhe, der Gedanke quälte ihn.

price [praɪs] **I** *s.* ✝ a) (Kauf)Preis *m*, Kosten *pl.*, b) *Börse:* Kurs(wert) *m*: *~ of issue* Emissionspreis; *bid ~* gebotener Preis, *Börse:* Geldkurs; *share* (*od.* *stock*) *~* Aktienkurs; *secure a good ~* e-n guten Preis erzielen; *every man has his ~ fig.* keiner ist unbestechlich; (*not*) *at any ~* um jeden (keinen) Preis; **2.** (Kopf)Preis *m*: *set a ~ on s.o.'s head* e-n Preis auf j-s Kopf aussetzen; **3.** *fig.* Lohn *m*, Preis *m*; **4.** (Wett-)Chance(n *pl.*) *f*: *what ~ ...? sl.* wie steht es mit ...?, welche Chance hat ...?; **II** *v/t.* **5.** ✝ a) den Preis festsetzen für, b) *Waren* auszeichnen: *~d* mit Preisangaben (*Katalog*); *high-~d* hoch im Preis, teuer; **6.** bewerten: *~ s.th. high* (*low*) e-r Sache großen (geringen) Wert beimessen; **7.** F nach dem Preis e-r Ware fragen; *~ a·gree·ment* *s.* Preisabsprache *f*; *~ ceil·ing* *s.* oberste Preisgrenze; *'~-,con·scious* *adj.* preisbewusst; *~ con·trol* *s.* 'Preiskon,trolle *f*, -über,wachung *f*; *~ cut* *s.* Preissenkung *f*; *~ cut·ting* *s.* Preisdrücke'rei *f*, 'Preissenkung *f*, -unter,bietung *f*; *~ dif·fer·en·tial* *s.* 'Preis,unterschied *m*, -gefälle *n*; *~ floor* *s.* unterste Preisgrenze; *~ freeze* *s.* Preisstopp *m*.

price·less ['praɪslɪs] *adj.* unschätzbar, unbezahlbar (*a.* F köstlich).

price| **lev·el** *s.* 'Preisni,veau *n*; *~ lim·it* *s.* (Preis)Limit *n*, Preisgrenze *f*; *~ list* *s.* **1.** Preisliste *f*; **2.** *Börse:* Kurszettel *m*; *'~-main,tained* *adj.* ✝ preisgebunden (*Ware*); *~ main·te·nance* *s.* ✝ Preisbindung *f*; *~ peg·ging* *s.* Preisstützung *f*; *~ range* *s.* Preisklasse *f*; *~ tag*, *~ tick·et* *s.* Preisschild *n*, -zettel *m*.

pric·ey ['praɪsɪ] *adj.* F (ganz schön) teuer.

prick [prɪk] **I** *s.* **1.** (Insekten-, Nadel- etc.)Stich *m*; **2.** stechender Schmerz, Stich *m*: *~s of conscience* *fig.* Gewissensbisse; **3.** spitzer Gegenstand; Stachel *m* (*a. fig.*): *kick against the ~s* wider den Stachel löcken; **4.** V a) ,Schwanz' *m*, b) ,blöder Hund'; **II** *v/t.* **5.** (ein-, 'durch)stechen, ,piken': *~ one's finger* sich in den Finger stechen; *his conscience ~ed him* *fig.* er bekam Gewissensbisse; **6.** *a.* *~ out* (aus)stechen, lochen; *Muster etc.* punktieren; **7.** ✗ pikieren; *~ in* (*out*) ein(aus)pflanzen; **8.** prickeln auf *od.* in (*dat.*); **9.** *~ up one's ears* die Ohren spitzen (*a. fig.*); **III** *v/i.* **10.** stechen (*a. Schmerzen*); **11.** prickeln; **12.** *~ up* sich aufrichten (*Ohren etc.*); **'prick·er** [-kə] *s.* **1.** ⊕ Pfriem *m*, Ahle *f*; **2.** me·tall. Schießnadel *f*; **'prick·et** [-kɪt] *s.* zo. Spießbock *m*.

prick·le ['prɪkl] **I** *s.* **1.** Stachel *m*, Dorn *m*; **2.** Prickeln *n*, Kribbeln *n* (*der Haut*); **II** *v/i.* **3.** stechen; **4.** prickeln, kribbeln; **'prick·ly** [-lɪ] *adj.* **1.** stachelig, dornig; **2.** stechend, pickelnd: *~ heat* ⚕ Frieselausschlag *m*, Hitzebläschen *pl.*; **3.** *fig.* reizbar.

pric·y ['praɪsɪ] → *pricey*.

pride [praɪd] **I** *s.* **1.** Stolz *m* (*a. Gegenstand des Stolzes*): *civic ~* Bürgerstolz; *~ of place* Ehrenplatz *m*, *fig.* Vorrang *m*, *b.s.* Standesdünkel *m*; *take ~ of*

place die erste Stelle einnehmen; **take** *(a)* ~ *in* stolz sein auf *(acc.)*; *he is the* ~ *of his family* er ist der Stolz s-r Familie; **2.** *b.s.* Stolz *m*, Hochmut *m*: ~ *goes before a fall* Hochmut kommt vor dem Fall; **3.** *rhet.* Pracht *f*; **4.** Höhe *f*, Blüte *f*: ~ *of the season* beste Jahreszeit; *in the* ~ *of his years* in s-n besten Jahren; **5.** *zo.* (Löwen)Rudel *n*; **6.** *in his* ~ *her.* Rad schlagend (*Pfau*); **II** *v/t.* **7.** ~ *o.s.* *(on, upon)* stolz sein (auf *acc.*), sich et. einbilden (auf *acc.*), sich brüsten (mit).

priest [priːst] *s.* Priester *m*, Geistliche(r) *m*; '**priest·craft** *s. contp.* Pfaffenlist *f*; '**priest·ess** [-tɪs] *s.* Priesterin *f*; '**priest·hood** [-hʊd] *s.* **1.** Priesteramt *n*, -würde *f*; **2.** Priesterschaft *f*, Priester *pl.*; '**priest·ly** [-lɪ] *adj.* priesterlich, Priester...

prig [prɪg] *s.* (selbstgefälliger) Pe'dant; eingebildeter Mensch; Tugendbold *m*; '**prig·gish** [-gɪʃ] *adj.* □ **1.** selbstgefällig, eingebildet; **2.** pe'dantisch; **3.** tugendhaft.

prim [prɪm] **I** *adj.* □ **1.** steif, for'mell, *a.* affektiert, gekünstelt; **2.** spröde, ,etepe'tete'; **3.** → *priggish*; **II** *v/t.* **4.** *Mund, Gesicht* affektiert verziehen.

pri·ma·cy ['praɪməsɪ] *s.* **1.** Pri'mat *m, n*, Vorrang *m*, Vortritt *f*; **2.** *eccl.* Pri'mat *m, n (Würde, Sprengel e-s Primas)*; **3.** *R.C.* Pri'mat *m, n (Gerichtsbarkeit des Papstes)*.

pri·ma don·na [ˌpriːməˈdɒnə] *s.* ♪ Pri'ma'donna *f (a. fig.)*.

pri·ma fa·ci·e [ˌpraɪməˈfeɪʃɪ] *(Lat.) adj. u. adv.* dem (ersten) Anschein nach: ~ *case* 🏛 Fall, bei dem der Tatbestand einfach liegt; ~ *evidence* 🏛 a) glaubhafter Beweis, b) Beweis *m* des ersten Anscheins.

pri·mal ['praɪml] *adj.* □ **1.** erst, frühest, ursprünglich; **2.** wichtigst, Haupt...; '**pri·ma·ri·ly** [-mərəlɪ] *adv.* in erster Linie; **pri·ma·ry** ['praɪmərɪ] **I** *adj.* □ **1.** erst, ursprünglich, Anfangs..., Ur...: ~ *instinct* Urinstinkt *m*; ~ *matter* Urstoff *m*; ~ *rocks* Urgestein *n*, -gebirge *n*; ~ *scream* *psych.* Urschrei *m*; **2.** pri'mär, hauptsächlich, wichtigst, Haupt...: ~ *accent* *ling.* Hauptakzent *m*; ~ *concern* Hauptsorge *f*; ~ *industry* Grundstoffindustrie *f*; ~ *liability* unmittelbare Haftung; ~ *road* Straße *f* erster Ordnung; ~ *share* ♥ Stammaktie *f*; *of* ~ *importance* von höchster Wichtigkeit; **3.** grundlegend, elemen'tar, Grund...: ~ *education* Volksschul-, *Am.* Grundschul(aus)bildung *f*; ~ *school* Volks-, *Am.* Grundschule *f*; **4.** ⚡ Primär...(-*batterie*, -*spule*, -*strom etc.*); **5.** 🖋 Primär...: ~ *tumo(u)r* Primärtumor *m*; **II** *s.* **6.** *a.* ~ *colo(u)r* Pri'mär-, Grundfarbe *f*; **7.** *a.* ~ *feather* *orn.* Schwungfeder *f*; **8.** *pol. Am.* a) *a.* ~ *election* Vorwahl *f (zur Aufstellung von Wahlkandidaten)*, b) *a.* ~ *meeting* (innerparteiliche) Versammlung zur Nominierung der Wahlkandidaten; **9.** *a.* ~ *planet* *ast.* 'Hauptpla,net *m.*

pri·mate ['praɪmət] *s. eccl. Brit.* Primas *m*: ⁂ *of England (Titel des Erzbischofs von York)*; ⁂ *of All England (Titel des Erzbischofs von Canterbury)*; **pri·ma·tes** [praɪˈmeɪtiːz] *s. pl. zo.* Pri'maten *pl.*

prime [praɪm] **I** *adj.* □ **1.** erst, wichtigst, wesentlichst, Haupt...(-*grund etc.*): *of* ~ *importance* von größter Wichtigkeit; **2.** erstklassig *(Kapitalanlage, Qualität etc.)*, prima: ~ *bill* ♥ vorzüglicher Wechsel; ~ *rate* Vorzugszins *m* für ers-

te Adressen; ~ *time* *TV* Hauptsendezeit *f*; **3.** pri'mär, grundlegend; **4.** erst, Erst..., Ur...; **5.** ♈ a) unteilbar, b) teilerfremd *(to* zu): ~ *factor (number)* Primfaktor *m* (Primzahl *f*); **II** *s.* **6.** Anfang *m*: ~ *of the day (year)* Tagesanbruch *m* (Frühling *m*); **7.** *fig.* Blüte(zeit) *f*: *in his* ~ in der Blüte s-r Jahre, im besten (Mannes)Alter; **8.** *das* Beste, höchste Voll'kommenheit; ✝ Primasorte *f*, auserlesene Quali'tät; **9.** *eccl.* Prim *f*, erste Gebetsstunde; Frühgottesdienst *m*; **10.** ♈ a) Primzahl *f*, b) Strich *m (erste Ableitung e-r Funktion)*: **x** = (**x'**) x Strich (x'); **11.** Strichindex *m*; **12.** ♪ *u. fenc.* Prim *f*; **III** *v/t.* **13.** ✕ *Bomben, Munition* scharfmachen: ~*d* zündfertig; **14.** a) ⚙ *Pumpe* anlassen, b) *sl.* ,voll laufen lassen': ~*d* ,besoffen'; **15.** *mot.* a) *Kraftstoff* vorpumpen, b) Anlasskraftstoff einspritzen in *(acc.)*; **16.** ⚙, *paint.* grundieren; **17.** mit Strichindex versehen; **18.** *fig.* instruieren, vorbereiten; ~ *cost* *s.* ✝ **1.** Selbstkosten(preis *m) pl.*, Gestehungskosten *pl.*; **2.** Einkaufspreis *m*, Anschaffungskosten *pl.*; ~ *min·is·ter* *s.* Premi'ermi,nister *m*, Mi'nisterpräsi,dent *m*; ~ *mov·er* *s.* **1.** *phys.* Antriebskraft *f*, *fig.* Triebfeder *f*, treibende Kraft; **2.** ⚙ 'Antriebsma,schine *f*; 'Zugma,schine *f (Sattelschlepper)*; ✕ *Am.* Geschützschlepper *m*; Triebwagen *m (Straßenbahn)*.

prim·er[1] ['praɪmə] *s.* **1.** ✕ Zündvorrichtung *f*, -hütchen *n*, -pille *f*; Sprengkapsel *f*; **2.** ✕ Zündbolzen *m (am Gewehr)*; **3.** ✕ Zünddraht *m*; **4.** ⚙ Einspritzvorrichtung *f (bsd. mot.)*: ~ *pump* Anlasseinspritzpumpe *f*; ~ *valve* Anlassventil *n*; **5.** ⚙ Grundier-, Spachtelmasse *f*: ~ *coat* Voranstrich *m*; **6.** Grundierer *m.*

prim·er[2] ['praɪmə] *s.* **1.** a) Fibel *f*, b) Elemen'tarbuch *n*, c) *fig.* Leitfaden *m*; **2.** ['praɪmə] *typ.* a) *great* ~ Tertia (-schrift) *f*, b) *long* ~ Korpus(schrift) *f*, (-), Garmond(schrift) *f.*

pri·me·val [praɪˈmiːvl] *adj.* □ urzeitlich, Ur...(-*wald etc.*).

prim·ing ['praɪmɪŋ] *s.* **1.** ✕ Zündmasse *f*, Zündung *f*: ~ *charge* Zünd-, Initialladung *f*; **2.** ⚙ Grundierung *f*: ~ *col·o(u)r* Grundierfarbe *f*; **3.** *a.* ~ *material* Spachtelmasse *f*; **4.** *mot.* Einspritzen *n* von Anlasskraftstoff: ~ *fuel injector* Anlasseinspritzanlage *f*; **5.** ⚙ Angießen *n* e-r Pumpe; **6.** *a.* ~ *of the tide* verfrühtes Eintreten der Flut; **7.** *fig.* Instrukti'on *f*, Vorbereitung *f.*

prim·i·tive ['primitɪv] **I** *adj.* □ **1.** erst, ursprünglich, urzeitlich, Ur...: ⁂ *Church* Urkirche *f*; ~ *races* Urvölker; ~ *rocks* *geol.* Urgestein *n*; **2.** *allg.* (*a. contp.*) primi'tiv *(Kultur, Mensch, a. fig. Denkweise, Konstruktion etc.)*; **3.** *ling.* Stamm...: ~ *verb* Stammverb *n*, ~ *colo(u)r* Grundfarbe *f*; **II** *s.* **5.** *der (die, das)* Primi'tive: *the* ~*s* die Primitiven *(Naturvölker)*; **6.** *Kunst:* a) primi'tiver Künstler, b) Frühmeister *m*, c) Früher Meister *(der Frührenaissance, a. Bild)*; **7.** *ling.* Stammwort *n*; '**prim·i·tive·ness** [-nɪs] *s.* **1.** Ursprünglichkeit *f*; **2.** Primitivi'tät *f*; '**prim·i·tiv·ism** [-vɪzəm] *s.* **1.** Primitivi'tät *f*; **2.** *Kunst:* Primiti'vismus *m.*

prim·ness ['prɪmnɪs] *s.* **1.** Steifheit *f*, Förmlichkeit *f*; **2.** Sprödigkeit *f*, Zimperlichkeit *f.*

pri·mo·gen·i·tor [ˌpraɪməʊˈdʒenɪtə] *s.* (Ur)Ahn *m*, Stammvater *m*; ˌ**pri·mo-'gen·i·ture** [-ɪtʃə] *s.* Erstgeburt(srecht *n* 🏛) *f.*

pri·mor·di·al [praɪˈmɔːdjəl] □ primor-

di'al *(a. biol.)*, Ur...

prim·rose ['prɪmrəʊz] *s.* **1.** ♀ Primel *f*, Gelbe Schlüsselblume: ~ *path* *fig.* Rosenpfad *m*; **2.** *evening* ~ ♀ Nachtkerze *f*; **3.** *a.* ~ *yellow* Blassgelb *n.*

prim·u·la ['prɪmjʊlə] *s.* ♀ Primel *f.*

prince [prɪns] *s.* **1.** Fürst *m (Landesherr u. Adelstitel)*: ⁂ *of the Church* Kirchenfürst; ⁂ *of Darkness* Fürst der Finsternis *(Satan)*; ⁂ *of Peace* Friedensfürst *(Christus)*; ~ *of poets* Dichterfürst; *merchant* ~ Kaufherr *m*; ~ *consort* Prinzgemahl *m*; **2.** Prinz *m*: ~ *of the blood* Prinz von (königlichem) Geblüt; ⁂ *Albert* *Am.* Gehrock *m*; '**prince·dom** ['prɪnsdəm] *s.* **1.** Fürstenwürde *f*; **2.** Fürstentum *n*; '**prince·ling** [-lɪŋ] *s.* **1.** Prinzchen *n*; **2.** kleiner Herrscher, Duo'dezfürst *m*; '**prince·ly** [-lɪ] *adj.* fürstlich *(a. fig.)*; prinzlich, königlich; **prin·cess** [prɪn'ses] **I** *s.* **1.** Prin-'zessin *f*: ~ *royal* älteste Tochter e-s Herrschers; **2.** Fürstin *f*; **II** *adj.* **3.** *Damenmode:* Prinzess...(-*kleid etc.*).

prin·ci·pal ['prɪnsəpl] **I** *adj.* □ → *principally*; **1.** erst, hauptsächlich, Haupt...: ~ *actor* Haupt(rollen)darsteller *m*; ~ *office*, ~ *place of business* Hauptgeschäftsstelle *f*, -niederlassung *f*; **2.** ♪, *ling.* Haupt..., Stamm...: ~ *chord* Stammakkord *m*; ~ *clause* Hauptsatz *m*; ~ *parts* Stammformen *des Verbs*; **3.** ✝ Kapital...: ~ *amount* Kapitalbetrag *m*; **II** *s.* **4.** 'Haupt(per,son *f) m*; Vorsteher (-in), *bsd. Am.* ('Schul)Di,rektor *m*, Rektor *m*; **5.** ✝ Chef(in), Prinzi'pal (-in); **6.** ✝, 🏛 Auftrag-, Vollmachtgeber (-in), Geschäftsherr *m*; **7.** 🏛 *a.* ~ *in the first degree* Haupttäter(in), -schuldige(r *m) f*; ~ *in the second degree* Mittäter(in); **8.** *a.* ~ *debtor* Hauptschuldner(in); **9.** Duel'lant *m (bsd. Sekundant)*; **10.** ✝ ('Grund)Kapi,tal *n*, Hauptsumme *f*; *(Nachlass- etc.)*Masse *f*: ~ *and interest* Kapital u. Zins(en); **11.** *a.* ~ *beam* ♈ Hauptbalken *m*; **prin·ci·pal·i·ty** [ˌprɪnsɪˈpælɪtɪ] *s.* Fürstentum *n*; '**prin·ci·pal·ly** [-plɪ] *adv.* hauptsächlich, in der Hauptsache.

prin·ci·ple ['prɪnsəpl] *s.* **1.** Prin'zip *n*, Grundsatz *m*, -regel *f*: *a man of* ~*s* ein Mann mit Grundsätzen; ~ *of law* Rechtsgrundsatz *m*; *in* ~ im Prinzip, an sich; *on* ~ aus Prinzip, grundsätzlich; *on the* ~ *that* nach dem Grundsatz, dass; **2.** *phys. etc.* Prinzip *n*, (Na'tur-) Gesetz *n*, Satz *m*: ~ *of causality* Kausalitätsprinzip; ~ *of averages* Mittelwertsatz: ~ *of relativity* Relativitätstheorie *f*; **3.** Grund(lage *f) m*; **4.** 🜍 Grundbestandteil *m*; '**prin·ci·pled** [-ld] *adj.* mit hohen etc. Grundsätzen.

prink [prɪŋk] **I** *v/i.* *a.* ~ *up* sich (auf)putzen, sich schniegeln; **II** *v/t.* (auf)putzen: ~ *o.s.* (*up*).

print [prɪnt] **I** *v/t.* **1.** *typ.* drucken (lassen), in Druck geben: ~ *in italics* kursiv drucken; **2.** (ab)drucken: ~*ed form* Vordruck *m*; ~*ed matter* ✉ Drucksache(n *pl.) f*: ~*ed circuit* ⚡ gedruckte Schaltung; **3.** bedrucken: ~*ed goods* bedruckte Stoffe; **4.** in Druckschrift schreiben: ~*ed characters* Druckbuchstaben; **5.** *Stempel etc.* (auf)drücken *(on dat.)*, Eindruck, Spur hinter-'lassen *(on* auf *acc.)*, *Muster etc.* ab-, aufdrucken, drücken *(in* in *acc.)*; **6.** *fig.* einprägen *(on s.o.'s mind* j-m); **7.** ~ *out* a) *Computer:* ausdrucken, b) *a.* ~ *off* *phot.* abziehen, kopieren; **II** *v/i.* **8.** *typ.* drucken; **9.** gedruckt werden, sich im Druck befinden: *the book is* ~*ing*; **10.** sich drucken *(phot.* abziehen) lassen; **III** s. **11.** (*Finger- etc.*)Abdruck m, Eindruck m, Spur f, Mal n; **12.** *typ.* Druck m: *colo(u)red* ~ Farbdruck; *in* ~ a) im Druck (erschienen), b) vorrätig; *out of* ~ vergriffen; *in cold* ~ *fig.* schwarz auf weiß; **13.** Druckschrift f, *bsd. Am.* Zeitung f, Blatt n: *rush into* ~ sich in die Öffentlichkeit flüchten; *appear in* ~ im Druck erscheinen; **14.** Druckschrift f, -buchstaben *pl.*; **15.** 'Zeitungspa,pier n; **16.** (*Stahl- etc.*) Stich m; Holzschnitt m; Lithogra'phie f; **17.** bedruckter Kat'tun, Druckstoff m: ~ *dress* Kattunkleid n; **18.** *phot.* Abzug m, Ko'pie f; **19.** ⊕ Stempel m, Form f: ~ *cutter* Formenschneider m; **20.** *metall.* Gesenk n; *Eisengießerei*: Kernauge n; **21.** *fig.* Stempel m; '**print-a·ble** [-təbl] *adj.* **1.** druckfähig; **2.** druckfertig, -reif (*Manuskript*); '**print-er** [-tə] s. **1.** (*Buch- etc.*)Drucker m: ~*'s devil* Setzerjunge m; ~*'s error* Druckfehler m; ~*'s flower* Vignette f; ~*'s ink* Druckerschwärze f; **2.** Drucke'reibesitzer m; **3.** *Computer*: Drucker m (*Gerät*); '**print·er·y** [-təri] s. *bsd. Am.* Drucke-'rei f.

print·ing ['prɪntɪŋ] s. **1.** Drucken n; (Buch)Druck m, Buchdruckerkunst f; **2.** Tuchdruck m; **3.** *phot.* Abziehen n, Kopieren n; ~ *block* s. Kli'schee n; ~ *frame* s. *phot.* Ko'pierrahmen m; ~ *ink* s. Druckerschwärze f, -farbe f; ~ *ma·chine* s. *typ.* Schnellpresse f, ('Buch-)Druckma,schine f; ~ *of·fice* s. (Buch-) Drucke'rei f: *lithographic* ~ lithographische Anstalt; ~ *me·di·a* s. *pl.* Druckmedien *pl.*; '~*-out adj. phot.* Kopier...; ~ *pa·per* s. **1.** 'Druckpa,pier n; **2.** 'Lichtpauspa,pier n; **3.** Ko'pierpa-,pier n; ~ *press* s. Druckerpresse f: ~ *type* Letter f, Type f; ~ *space* s. Satzspiegel m; ~ *tel·e·graph* s. 'Drucktele-,graf m; ~ *types* s. *pl.* Lettern *pl.*; ~ *works* s. *pl. oft sg. konstr.* Drucke'rei f.

'**print**,**mak·er** s. Grafiker(in); '~*-out* s. *Computer*: Ausdruck m, Print-out m; ~ *pre·view* s. *Computer*: Seitenansicht f (*in Textverarbeitung*).

pri·or ['praɪə] I *adj.* **1.** (*to*) früher, älter (als): ~ *art Patentrecht*: Stand m der Technik, Vorwegnahme f; ~ *patent* älteres Patent; ~ *subject to* ~ *sale* ↑ Zwischenverkauf vorbehalten; **2.** vordringlich, Vorzugs...: ~ *right* (*od. claim*) Vorzugsrecht n; ~ *condition* erste Voraussetzung; **II** *adv.* **3.** ~ *to* vor (*dat.*) (*zeitlich*); **III** s. *eccl.* **4.** Prior m; '**pri·or·ess** [-əris] s. Pri'orin f; **pri·or·i·ty** [praɪ'ɒrɪtɪ] s. **1.** Priori'tät f (*a.* ↕), Vorrang m (*a. e-s Anspruchs etc.*), Vorzug m (*over, to* vor *dat.*): *take* ~ *of* den Vorrang haben *od.* genießen vor (*dat.*); *set priorities* Prioritäten setzen, Schwerpunkte bilden; ~ *share* ↑ Vorzugsaktie f; **2.** Dringlichkeit(sstufe) f: ~ *call* *teleph.* Vorrangsgespräch n; ~ *list* Dringlichkeitsliste f (*od. top*) ~ von größter Dringlichkeit; *give* ~ *to* et. vordringlich behandeln; **3.** Vorfahrt(srecht n) f; '**pri·o·ry** [-əri] s. *eccl.* Prio-'rei f.

prise [praɪz] *bsd. Brit.* → **prize³**.

prism ['prɪzəm] s. Prisma n (*a. fig.*): ~ *binoculars* Prismen(fern)glas n; **pris-mat·ic** [prɪz'mætɪk] *adj.* (□ ~*ally*) pris-'matisch, Prismen...: ~ *colo(u)rs* Regenbogenfarben.

pris·on ['prɪzn] s. Gefängnis n (*a. fig.*), Strafanstalt f; '~*-,break·ing* s. Ausbruch m aus dem Gefängnis; ~ *camp* s.

---

1. (Kriegs)Gefangenenlager n; **2.** ,offenes' Gefängnis; ~ *ed·i·tor* s. (*presse-rechtlich verantwortlicher*) ,'Sitzredak-,teur' m.

pris·on·er ['prɪznə] s. Gefangene(r m) f (*a. fig.*), Häftling m: ~ (*at the bar*) Angeklagte(r m) f; ~ (*on remand*) Untersuchungsgefangene(r); ~ *of state* Staatsgefangene(r), politischer Häftling; ~ (*of war*) Kriegsgefangene(r); *hold* (*take*) *s.o.* ~ j-n gefangen halten (nehmen); *he is a* ~ *to fig.* er ist gefesselt an (*acc.*); ~*'s bar(s)*, ~*'s base* s. Barlauf(spiel n) m.

pris·on| *of·fi·cer* s. Strafvollzugsbeamte(r) m; ~ *psy·cho·sis* s. [*irr.*] 'Haftpsy,chose f.

pris·sy ['prɪsɪ] *adj. Am.* F zimperlich, etepe'tete.

pris·tine ['prɪstiːn] *adj.* **1.** ursprünglich, -tümlich, unverdorben; **2.** vormalig, alt.

pri·va·cy ['prɪvəsɪ] s. **1.** Zu'rückgezogenheit f, Alleinsein n; Ruhe f: *disturb s.o.'s* ~ j-n stören; **2.** Pri'vatleben n, *a.* ↕ Pri'vat-, In'timsphäre f: *right of* ~ Persönlichkeitsrecht n; **3.** Heimlichkeit f, Geheimhaltung f: ~ *of letters* ↕ Briefgeheimnis n; *talk to s.o. in* ~ mit j-m unter vier Augen sprechen; *in strict* ~ streng vertraulich.

pri·vate ['praɪvɪt] I *adj.* □ **1.** pri'vat, Privat...(-*konto, -leben, -person, -recht etc.*), per'sönlich: ~ *affair* Privatangelegenheit f; ~ *member's bill parl.* Antrag m e-s Abgeordneten; ~ *eye Am. sl.* Privatdetektiv m; ~ *firm* ↑ Einzelfirma f; ~ *gentleman* Privatier m; ~ *health insurance* private Krankenversicherung; ~ *means* Privatvermögen n; → *nuisance* 2; ~ *property* Privateigentum n; -besitz m; **2.** pri'vat, Privat... (-*pension, -schule etc.*), nichtöffentlich: ~ (*limited*) *company* ↑ *Brit.* Gesellschaft f mit beschränkter Haftung; ~ *corporation* a) ↕ privatrechtliche Körperschaft, b) ↑ *Am.* Gesellschaft f mit beschränkter Haftung; *sell by* ~ *contract* unter der Hand verkaufen; ~ *hotel* Fremdenheim n; ~ *industry* Privatwirtschaft f; ~ *road* Privatweg m; ~ *theatre* Liebhabertheater n; ~ *view* Besichtigung f durch geladene Gäste; **3.** al'lein, zu'rückgezogen, einsam; **4.** geheim (*Gedanken, Verhandlungen etc.*), heimlich; vertraulich (*Mitteilung etc.*): ~ *parts* → 10; ~ *prayer* stilles Gebet; ~ *reasons* Hintergründe; *keep s.th.* ~ et. geheim halten *od.* vertraulich behandeln; *this is for your* ~ *ear* dies sage ich Ihnen ganz im Vertrauen; **5.** außeramtlich (*Angelegenheit*); **6.** nicht beamtet; **7.** ↕ außergerichtlich: ~ *arrangement* gütlicher Vergleich; **8.** ~ *soldier* → 9; **II** s. **9.** ✕ (gewöhnlicher) Sol'dat; *pl.* Mannschaften *pl.*: ~ *1st Class Am.* Obergefreite(r) m; **10.** *pl.* Geschlechtsteile *pl.*; **11.** *in* ~ a) pri'vat(im), b) insge'heim, unter vier Augen.

pri·va·teer [,praɪvə'tɪə] I s. **1.** ♣ Freibeuter m, Kaperschiff n; **2.** Kapi'tän m e-s Kaperschiffes, Kaperer m; **3.** *pl.* Mannschaft f e-s Kaperschiffes; **II** *v/i.* **4.** Kape'rei treiben.

pri·va·tion [praɪ'veɪʃn] s. **1.** *a. fig.* Wegnahme f, Entziehung f, Entzug m; **2.** Not f, Entbehrung f.

priv·a·tive ['prɪvətɪv] I *adj.* □ **1.** entziehend, beraubend; **2.** *a. ling. od. phls.* verneinend, negativ; **II** s. **3.** *ling.* a) Ver'neinungspar,tikel f, b) priva'tiver Ausdruck.

priv·et ['prɪvɪt] s. ♣ Li'guster m.

priv·i·lege ['prɪvɪlɪdʒ] I s. **1.** Privi'leg n,

Sonder-, Vorrecht n, Vergünstigung f, *Am. pol.* Grundrecht n; *breach of a* ~ a) Übertretung f der Machtbefugnis, b) *parl.* Vergehen n gegen die Vorrechte des Parlaments; *Committee of* ~s Ausschuss m zur Untersuchung von Rechtsübergriffen; ~ *of Parliament pol.* Immunität f e-s Abgeordneten; ~ *of self-defence* (Recht n der) Notwehr f; *with kitchen* ~s mit Küchenbenutzung; **2.** *fig.* (besonderer) Vorzug: *have the* ~ *of being admitted* den Vorzug haben, zugelassen zu sein; *it is a* ~ *to do* es ist e-e besondere Ehre, et. zu tun; **3.** *pl.* † Prämien- *od.* Stellgeschäft n; **II** *v/t.* **4.** privilegieren, bevorrecht(ig)en: *the* ~*d classes* die privilegierten Stände; ~*d debt* bevorrechtigte Forderung; ~*d communication* ↕ a) vertrauliche Mitteilung (*für die Schweigepflicht besteht*), b) Berufsgeheimnis n.

priv·i·ty ['prɪvɪtɪ] s. **1.** ↕ (Inter'essen-) Gemeinschaft f; **2.** ↕ Rechtsbeziehung f; **3.** ↕ Rechtsnachfolge f; **4.** Mitwisserschaft f.

priv·y ['prɪvɪ] I *adj.* □ **1.** eingeweiht (*to* in *acc.*); **2.** ↕ (mit)beteiligt (*to* an *dat.*); **3.** *mst poet.* heimlich, geheim: ~ *parts* Scham-, Geschlechtsteile; ~ *stairs* Hintertreppe f; **II** s. **4.** 'Mitinteres,sent(in) (*to* an *dat.*); **5.** A'bort m, Abtritt m; ♃ *Coun·cil* s. *Brit.* (Geheimer) Staats- *od.* Kronrat m; *Judicial Committee of the* ~ ↕ Justizausschuss m des Staatsrats (*höchste Berufungsinstanz für die Dominions*); ♃ *Coun·cil·lor* s. *Brit.* Geheimer (Staats)Rat (*Person*); ♃ *Purse* s. königliche Pri'vatscha-,tulle; ♃ *Seal* s. *Brit.* Geheimsiegel n: *Lord* ~ königlicher Geheimsiegelbewahrer.

prize¹ [praɪz] I s. **1.** (Sieger)Preis m (*a. fig.*), Prämie f: *the* ~*s of a profession* die höchsten Stellungen in e-m Beruf; **2.** (*a.* Lotte'rie)Gewinn m: *the first* ~ das große Los; **3.** Lohn m, Belohnung f; **II** *adj.* **4.** preisgekrönt, prämiiert; **5.** Preis...: ~ *medal*; **6.** a) erstklassig (*a. iro.*), b) F *contp.* Riesen...: ~ *idiot*; **III** *v/t.* **7.** (hoch) schätzen, würdigen.

prize² [praɪz] I s. ♣ Prise f, Beute f (*a. fig.*): *make* ~ *of* → **II** *v/t.* (als Prise) aufbringen, kapern.

prize³ [praɪz] *bsd. Brit.* I *v/t.* **1.** (auf-) stemmen: ~ *open* (mit e-m Hebel) aufbrechen; ~ *up* hochwuchten *od.* -stemmen; **II** s. **2.** Hebelwirkung f, -kraft f; **3.** Hebel m.

prize| *com·pe·ti·tion* s. Preisausschreiben n; ~ *court* s. ♣ Prisengericht n; ~ *fight* s. Preisboxkampf m; ~ *fight·er* s. Preis-, Berufsboxer m; ~ *list* s. Gewinnliste f; '~*-man* [-mən] s. [*irr.*] Preisträger m; ~ *mon·ey* s. **1.** ♣ Prisengeld(er pl.) n; **2.** Geldpreis m; ~ *ques·tion* s. Preisfrage f; ~ *ring* s. (Box)Ring m, das Berufsboxen; ~ *win·ner* s. Preisträger(in); '~*-,win·ning adj.* preisgekrönt, präm(i)iert.

pro¹ [prəʊ] *pl.* **pros** s. **1.** Jastimme f, Stimme f da'für: *the* ~*s and cons* das Für und Wider; **II** *adv.* da'für.

pro² [prəʊ] (*Lat.*) *prp.* für; pro, per; → *pro forma, pro rata*.

pro³ [prəʊ] s. F **1.** *sport* Profi m (*a. fig.*); **2.** ,Nutte' f.

pro- [prəʊ] *in Zssgn* **1.** pro..., ...freundlich, *z. B.* ~*German*; **2.** stellvertretend, Vize..., Pro...; **3.** vor (*räumlich u. zeitlich*).

prob·a·bil·i·ty [,prɒbə'bɪlətɪ] s. Wahrscheinlichkeit f (*a.* ♄): *in all* ~ aller

Wahrscheinlichkeit nach, höchstwahrscheinlich; *theory of* ~, ~ *calculus* ℟ Wahrscheinlichkeitsrechnung *f*; *the* ~ *is that* es besteht die Wahrscheinlichkeit, dass; **prob·a·ble** ['prɒbəbl] *adj.* □ **1.** wahrscheinlich, vermutlich, mutmaßlich: ~ *cause* ☆ hinreichender Verdacht; **2.** wahrscheinlich, glaubhaft, einleuchtend.

pro·bate ['prəʊbeɪt] ⚖ **I** *s.* **1.** gerichtliche (*bsd.* Testa'ments)Bestätigung; **2.** Testa'mentser,öffnung *f*; **3.** Abschrift *f* e-s gerichtlich bestätigten Testaments; **II** *v/t.* **4.** *bsd. Am. Testament* a) gerichtlich bestätigen, b) eröffnen u. als rechtswirksam bestätigen lassen; ~ *court s.* Nachlassgericht *n*, (*in U.S.A. a. zuständig in Sachen der freiwilligen Gerichtsbarkeit, bsd. als*) Vormundschaftsgericht *n*; ~ *du·ty s.* ⚖ Erbschaftssteuer *f*.

pro·ba·tion [prə'beɪʃn] *s.* **1.** (Eignungs-)Prüfung *f*, Probe(zeit) *f*: *on* ~ auf Probe(zeit); **2.** ⚖ Bewährungsfrist *f*, bedingte Freilassung *f*: *place s.o. on* ~ j-m Bewährungsfrist zubilligen, j-n unter Zubilligung von Bewährungsfrist freilassen: ~ *officer* Bewährungshelfer (-in); **3.** *eccl.* Novizi'at *n*; **pro'ba·tion·ar·y** [-ʃnərɪ], **pro'ba·tion·al** [-ʃənl] *adj.* Probe...: ~ *period* ⚖ Bewährungsfrist *f*; **pro'ba·tion·er** [-ʃnə] *s.* **1.** 'Probekandi,dat(in), Angestellte(r *m*) *f* auf Probe, *z.B.* Lernschwester *f*; **2.** *fig.* Neuling *m*; **3.** *eccl.* No'vize *m*, *f*; **4.** ⚖ a) j-d, dessen Strafe zur Bewährung ausgesetzt ist, b) auf Bewährung bedingt Strafentlassene(r).

pro·ba·tive ['prəʊbətɪv] als Beweis dienend (*of* für): ~ *facts* ⚖ beweiserhebliche Tatsachen; ~ *force* Beweiskraft *f*.

probe [prəʊb] **I** *v/t.* **1.** 🩺 sondieren (*a. fig.*); **2.** *fig.* eindringen in (*acc.*), erforschen, (gründlich) unter'suchen; **II** *v/i.* **3.** *fig.* (forschend) eindringen (*into* in *acc.*); **III** *s.* **4.** 🩺, *a.* Raumforschung *etc.*: Sonde *f*; **5.** *fig.* Sondierung *f*; *bsd. Am.* Unter'suchung *f*.

prob·i·ty ['prəʊbətɪ] *s.* Rechtschaffenheit *f*, Redlichkeit *f*.

prob·lem ['prɒbləm] **I** *s.* **1.** Pro'blem *n* (*a. phls.*, *Schach etc.*), proble'matische Sache, Schwierigkeit *f*: *set a* ~ ein Problem stellen; **2.** ℟ Aufgabe *f*, Pro'blem *n*; **3.** *fig.* Rätsel *n* (*to* für *j-n*); **II** *adj.* **4.** proble'matisch: ~ *play* Problemstück *n*; ~ *child* schwer erziehbares Kind, Sorgenkind *n*; ~ *drinker* Alkoholiker(in); **prob·lem·at·ic**, **prob·lem·at·i·cal** [,prɒblə'mætɪk(l)] *adj.* □ proble'matisch, zweifelhaft.

pro·bos·cis [prəʊ'bɒsɪs] *pl.* **-cis·es** [-sɪ:sɪ:z] *s. zo.* Rüssel *m* (*a. humor.*).

pro·ce·dur·al [prə'si:dʒərəl] *adj.* ⚖ verfahrensrechtlich; Verfahrens...: ~ *law*; **pro·ce·dure** [prə'si:dʒə] *s.* **1.** *allg.* Verfahren *n* (*a.* ⚙), Vorgehen *n*; **2.** ⚖ (*bsd. prozessrechtliches*) Verfahren: *rules of* ~ Prozessvorschriften, Verfahrensbestimmungen; **3.** Handlungsweise *f*, Verhalten *n*.

pro·ceed [prə'si:d] *v/i.* **1.** weitergehen, -fahren *etc.*; sich begeben (*to* nach); **2.** *fig.* weitergehen (*Handlung etc.*), fortschreiten; **3.** vor sich gehen, von'statten gehen; **4.** *fig.* fortfahren (*with, in* mit, in *s-r Rede etc.*), s-e Arbeit *etc.* fortsetzen: ~ *on one's journey* s-e Reise fortsetzen, weiterreisen; **5.** *fig.* vorgehen, verfahren: ~ *with et.* durchführen *od.* in Angriff nehmen; ~ *on the assumption that* davon ausgehen, dass; **6.** schreiten *od.* 'übergehen (*to* zu), sich anschicken (*to do* zu tun): ~ *to business* an die

Arbeit gehen, anfangen; **7.** (*from*) ausgehen *od.* herrühren *od.* kommen (von) (*Geräusch, Hoffnung, Krankheit etc.*), (*e-r Hoffnung etc.*) entspringen; **8.** ⚖ (gerichtlich) vorgehen, e-n Pro'zess anstrengen (*against* gegen); **9.** *univ. Brit.* promovieren (*to* [*the degree of*] zum); **pro'ceed·ing** [-dɪŋ] *s.* **1.** Vorgehen *n*, Verfahren *n*; **2.** *pl.* ⚖ Verfahren *n*, (Gerichts)Verhandlung(en *pl.*) *f*: *take* (*od. institute*) ~*s against* ein Verfahren einleiten *od.* gerichtlich vorgehen gegen; **3.** *pl.* (Sitzungs-, Tätigkeits)Bericht(e *pl.*) *m*, (⚖ Pro'zess)Akten *pl.*; **pro·ceeds** ['prəʊsi:dz] *s. pl.* **1.** Erlös *m* (*from a sale* aus e-m Verkauf), Ertrag *m*, Gewinn *m*; **2.** Einnahmen *pl.*

pro·cess ['prəʊses] **I** *s.* **1.** Verfahren *n*, Pro'zess *m* (*a.* ⚙, 🎞): ~ *engineering* Verfahrenstechnik *f*; ~ *chart* Arbeitsablaufdiagramm *n*; ~ *control* Computer: Prozesssteuerung *f*; ~ *of manufacture* Herstellungsvorgang *m*, Werdegang *m*; *in* ~ *of construction* im Bau (befindlich); **2.** Vorgang *m*, Verlauf *m*, Pro'zess *m* (*a. phys.*): ~ *of combustion* Verbrennungsvorgang; *mental* ~ Denkprozess; **3.** Arbeitsgang *m*; **4.** Fortgang *m*, -schreiten *n*, (Ver)Lauf *m*: *in* ~ *of time* im Laufe der Zeit; *be in* ~ im Gange sein; **5.** *typ.* 'photome,chanisches Reprodukti'onsverfahren: ~ *printing* Mehrfarbendruck *m*; **6.** *anat.* Fortsatz *m*; **7.** 🌿 Auswuchs *m*; **8.** ⚖ a) Zustellung(en *pl.*) *f*, *bsd.* Vorladung *f*, b) (ordentliches) Verfahren: *due* ~ *of law* rechtliches Gehör; **II** *v/t.* **9.** ⚙ *etc.* bearbeiten, (chemisch *etc.*) behandeln, e-m Verfahren unter'werfen; *Material*, *a. Daten* verarbeiten; *Lebensmittel* haltbar machen, *Milch etc.* sterilisieren: ~ *into* verarbeiten zu; **10.** ⚖ j-n gerichtlich belangen; **11.** *Am. fig.* j-n 'durchschleusen, abfertigen, *j-s Fall etc.* bearbeiten; **III** *v/i.* ['prɒ'ses] **12.** F in e-r Prozessi'on (mit)gehen; **pro·cess·ing** [-sɪŋ] *s.* **1.** ⚙ Vered(e)lung *f*: ~ *industry* weiterverarbeitende Industrie, Veredelungsindustrie *f*; **2.** ⚙, *a. Computer*: Verarbeitung *f*; *von Abfall*: Aufbereitung *f*; **3.** *bsd. Am. fig.* Bearbeitung *f*.

pro·ces·sion [prə'seʃn] *s.* **1.** Prozessi'on *f*, (*feierlicher*) (Auf-, 'Um)Zug *m*: *go in* ~ e-e Prozession abhalten *od.* machen; **2.** Reihe(nfolge) *f*; **3.** *a.* ~ *of the Holy Spirit eccl.* Ausströmen *n* des Heiligen Geistes; **pro'ces·sion·al** [-ʃənl] **I** *adj.* Prozessions...; **II** *s. eccl.* a) Prozessi'onsbuch *n*, b) Prozessi'onshymne *f*.

pro·ces·sor ['prəʊsesə] *s.* **1.** ⚙ Verarbeiter *m*; Hersteller(in); **2.** *Am.* (Sach-)Bearbeiter(in); **3.** *Computer*: Pro'zessor *m*.

pro·claim [prə'kleɪm] *v/t.* **1.** proklamieren, (öffentlich) verkünd(ig)en, kundgeben: ~ *war* den Krieg erklären; ~ *s.o. a traitor* j-n zum Verräter erklären; ~ *s.o. king* j-n zum König ausrufen; **2.** den Ausnahmezustand verhängen über *ein Gebiet etc.*; **3.** in die Acht erklären; **4.** *Versammlung etc.* verbieten.

proc·la·ma·tion [,prɒklə'meɪʃn] *s.* **1.** Proklamati'on *f* (*to* an *acc.*), (öffentliche *od.* feierliche) Verkündigung *od.* Bekanntmachung, Aufruf *m*: ~ *of martial law* Verhängung *f* des Standrechts; **2.** Erklärung *f*, Ausrufung *f* zum König *etc.*; **3.** Verhängung *f* des Ausnahmezustandes.

pro·cliv·i·ty [prə'klɪvətɪ] *s.* Neigung *f*, Hang *m* (*to, toward* zu).

pro·cras·ti·nate [prəʊ'kræstɪneɪt] **I** *v/i.* zaudern, zögern; **II** *v/t.* hi'nausziehen, verschleppen.

pro·cre·ant ['prəʊkrɪənt] *adj.* (er)zeugend; **pro·cre·ate** ['prəʊkrɪeɪt] *v/t.* (er-)zeugen, her'vorbringen (*a. fig.*); **pro·cre·a·tion** [,prəʊkrɪ'eɪʃn] *s.* 'pro·cre·a·tive [-ɪeɪtɪv] *adj.* **1.** zeugungsfähig, Zeugungs...: ~ *capacity* Zeugungsfähigkeit *f*, **2.** fruchtbar; **'pro·cre·a·tor** [-ɪeɪtə] *s.* Erzeuger *m*.

Pro·crus·te·an [prəʊ'krʌstɪən] *adj.* Prokrustes... (*a. fig.*): ~ *bed*.

proc·tor ['prɒktə] **I** *s.* **1.** *univ. Brit.* a) Diszipli'narbe,amte(r) *m*, b) Aufsicht Führende(r) *m*, (*bsd. bei Prüfungen*): ~*'s man*, ~*'s* (*bull*)*dog sl.* Pedell *m*; **2.** ⚖ a) Anwalt *m* (*an Spezialgerichten*), b) *a. King's* (*od. Queen's*) ~ Proku'rator *m* der Krone; **II** *v/t.* **3.** beaufsichtigen.

pro·cur·a·ble [prə'kjʊərəbl] *adj.* zu beschaffen(d), erhältlich; **proc·u·ra·tion** [,prɒkjʊə'reɪʃn] *s.* **1.** → *procurement* 1 *u.* 3; **2.** (Stell)Vertretung *f*; **3.** ✝ Pro'kura *f*, Vollmacht *f*: *by* ~ per Prokura; *joint* ~ Gesamthandlungsvollmacht; *single* (*od. sole*) ~ Einzelprokura; **4.** → *procuring* 2; **proc·u·ra·tor** ['prɒkjʊəreɪtə] *s.* **1.** ⚖ Anwalt *m*: ⚖ *General Brit.* Königlicher Anwalt des Schatzamtes; **2.** ⚖ Bevollmächtigte(r) *m*, Sachwalter *m*; **3.** ~ *fiscal* ⚖ *Scot.* Staatsanwalt *m*.

pro·cure [prə'kjʊə] **I** *v/t.* **1.** (sich) be-, verschaffen, besorgen (*s.th. for s.o.*, *s.o. s.th.* j-m et.); *a. Beweise etc.* liefern, beibringen; **2.** erwerben, erlangen; **3.** verkuppeln; **4.** *fig.* bewirken, her'beiführen; **5.** veranlassen: ~ *s.o. to commit a crime* j-n zu e-m Verbrechen anstiften; **II** *v/i.* **6.** kuppeln; Zuhälte'rei treiben; **pro'cure·ment** [-mənt] *s.* **1.** Besorgung *f*, Beschaffung *f*; **2.** Erwerbung *f*; **3.** Vermittlung *f*; **4.** Veranlassung *f*; **pro'cur·er** [-ərə] *s.* **1.** Beschaffer(in), Vermittler(in); **2.** a) Kuppler *m*, b) Zuhälter *m*; **pro'cur·ess** [-ərɪs] *s.* Kupplerin *f*; **pro'cur·ing** [-ərɪŋ] *s.* **1.** Beschaffen *n etc.*; **2.** a) Kuppe'lei *f*, b) Zuhälte'rei *f*.

prod [prɒd] **I** *v/t.* **1.** stechen, stoßen; **2.** *fig.* anstacheln, -spornen (*into* zu et.); **II** *s.* **3.** Stich *m*, Stechen *n*, Stoß *m* (*a. fig.*); **4.** *fig.* Ansporn *m*; **5.** Stachelstock *m*; **6.** Ahle *f*.

prod·i·gal ['prɒdɪgl] **I** *adj.* □ **1.** verschwenderisch (*of* mit): *be* ~ *of* → *prodigalize*; *the* ~ *son bibl.* der verlorene Sohn; **II** *s.* **2.** Verschwender(in); **3.** reuiger Sünder; **prod·i·gal·i·ty** [,prɒdɪ'gælɪtɪ] *s.* **1.** Verschwendung *f*, Üppigkeit *f*, Fülle *f* (*of* an *dat.*); **'prod·i·gal·ize** [-gəlaɪz] *v/t.* verschwenden, verschwenderisch umgehen mit.

pro·di·gious [prə'dɪdʒəs] *adj.* □ **1.** erstaunlich, wunderbar, großartig; **2.** gewaltig, ungeheuer; **prod·i·gy** ['prɒdɪdʒɪ] *s.* **1.** Wunder *n* (*of gen. od.* an *dat.*): *a* ~ *of learning* ein Wunder der *od.* an Gelehrsamkeit; **2.** *mst infant* ~ Wunderkind *n*.

pro·duce¹ [prə'dju:s] *v/t.* **1.** *allg.* erzeugen, machen, schaffen; ✝ *Waren etc.* produzieren, herstellen, erzeugen; *Kohle etc.* gewinnen, fördern; *Buch* a) verfassen, b) her'ausbringen; *thea. Stück* a) inszenieren, b) aufführen; *Film* produzieren; *Brit. thea., Radio*: Re'gie führen bei: ~ *o.s. fig.* sich produzieren; **2.** 🌿 *Früchte etc.* her'vorbringen; **3.** ✝ *Gewinn, Zinsen* (ein)bringen, abwerfen; **4.** *fig.* erzeugen, bewirken, her'vorrufen, zeitigen; *Wirkung* erzielen; **5.** her'vorziehen, -holen (**from** aus *der Tasche etc.*); *Ausweis etc.* (vor)zeigen, vorlegen; *Beweise, Zeugen etc.* beibringen; *Gründe* anführen; **6.** A *Linie* verlängern.

prod·uce² ['prɒdjuːs] *s.* (*nur sg.*) **1.** (*bsd.* 'Boden)Pro,dukt(e *pl.*) *n*, (Na'tur)Erzeugnis(se *pl.*) *n*: ~ **market** Produkten-, Warenmarkt *m*; **2.** Ertrag *m*, Gewinn *m*.

pro·duc·er [prə'djuːsə] *s.* **1.** *a.* ♀ Erzeuger(in), 'Hersteller(in): ~ **country** ♀ Erzeugerland *n*; **2.** ♀ Produ'zent *m*, Fabri'kant *m*: ~ **goods** Produktionsgüter; **3.** a) *Film:* Produ'zent *m*, Produkti'onsleiter *m*, b) *Brit. thea., Radio:* Re'gis'seur *m*, Spielleiter *m*; **4.** ⊚ Gene'rator *m*: ~ **gas** Generatorgas *n*; **pro'duc·i·ble** [-səbl] *adj.* **1.** erzeug-, herstellbar, produzierbar; **2.** vorzuzeigen(d), beizubringen(d); **pro'duc·ing** [-sɪŋ] *adj.* Produktions..., Herstellungs...

prod·uct ['prɒdʌkt] *s.* **1.** *a.* ♀, ⊚ Pro'dukt *n* (*a.* A, ⚗), Erzeugnis *n*: **intermediate** ~ Zwischenprodukt *n*; ~ **liability** Produkthaftung *f*; ~ **line** Erzeugnis(gruppe *f*) *n*; ~ **manager** Pro'dukt,manager *m*; ~ **patent** Stoffpatent *n*; ~ **range** Produktpalette *f*; **2.** *fig.* (a. 'Geistes)Pro,dukt *n*, Ergebnis *n*, Werk *n*; **3.** *fig.* Pro'dukt *n* (*Person*).

pro·duc·tion [prə'dʌkʃn] *s.* **1.** (*z.B. Kälte-, Strom*)Erzeugung *f*, (*z.B. Rauch*)Bildung *f*; **2.** ♀ Produkti'on *f*, Herstellung *f*, Erzeugung *f*, Fertigung *f*; ♠, ⚒, *min.* Gewinnung *f*; ⚒ Förderleistung *f*: ~ **of gold** Goldgewinnung; **be in** ~ serienmäßig hergestellt werden; **be in good** ~ genügend hergestellt werden; **go into** ~ a) in Produktion gehen, b) die Produktion aufnehmen (*Fabrik*); **3.** (*Arbeits*)Erzeugnis *n*, (*a.* Na'tur)Pro,dukt *n*, Fabri'kat *n*; **4.** *fig.* (*mst* lite'rarisches) Pro'dukt, Ergebnis *n*, Werk *n*, Schöpfung *f*, Frucht *f*; **5.** Her'vorbringen *n*, Entstehung *f*; **6.** Vorlegung *f*, -zeigung *f* *e-s Dokuments etc.*, Beibringung *f* *e-s Zeugen*, Erbringen *n* *e-s Beweises*; Vorführen *n*, Aufweisen *n*; **7.** Her'vorholen *n*, -ziehen *n*; **8.** *thea.* Vor-, Aufführung *f*, Inszenierung *f*; **9.** a) *Brit. thea., Radio, TV:* Re'gie *f*, Spielleitung *f*, b) *Film:* Produkti'on *f*; **pro'duc·tion·al** [-ʃənl] *adj.* Produktions...

pro·duc·tion| ca·pac·i·ty *s.* Produkti'onskapazi,tät *f*, Leistungsfähigkeit *f*; ~ **car** *s. mot.* Serienwagen *m*; ~ **costs** *s. pl.* Gestehungskosten *pl.*; ~ **di·rector** *s. Radio:* Sendeleiter *m*; ~ **en·gineer** *s.* Be'triebsingeni,eur *m*; ~ **goods** *s. pl.* Produkti'onsgüter *pl.*; ~ **line** *s.* ⊚ Fließband *n*, Fertigungsstraße *f*; ~ **lo·ca·tion** *s.* Produktionsstandort *m*; ~ **man·ag·er** *s.* Herstellungsleiter *m*.

pro·duc·tive [prə'dʌktɪv] *adj.* □ **1.** (*of acc.*) her'vorbringend, erzeugend, schaffend: **be** ~ **of** führen zu, erzeugen; **2.** produk'tiv, ergiebig, ertragreich, fruchtbar, ren'tabel; **3.** produzierend, leistungsfähig; ⚒ abbauwürdig; **4.** *fig.* produk'tiv, fruchtbar, schöpferisch; **pro'duc·tive·ness** [-nɪs], **pro·duc·tiv·i·ty** [,prɒdʌk'tɪvətɪ] *s.* Produktivi'tät *f*: a) ♀ Rentabili'tät *f*, Ergiebigkeit *f*, b) ♀ Leistungs-, Ertragsfähigkeit *f*, c) *fig.* Fruchtbarkeit *f*.

pro·em ['prəʊem] *s.* Einleitung *f* (*a. fig.*), Vorrede *f*.

prof [prɒf] *s.* F Prof *m* (*Professor*).

prof·a·na·tion [,prɒfə'neɪʃn] *s.* Entweihung *f*, Profanierung *f*; **pro·fane**

[prə'feɪn] **I** *adj.* □ **1.** weltlich, pro'fan, ungeweiht, Profan...(-*bau, -geschichte*); **2.** lästerlich, gottlos: ~ **language**; **3.** uneingeweiht (**to** in *acc.*); **II** *v/t.* **4.** entweihen, profanieren; **pro·fan·i·ty** [prə'fænətɪ] *s.* **1.** Gott-, Ruchlosigkeit *f*; **2.** Weltlichkeit *f*; **3.** Fluchen *n*; *pl.* Flüche *pl.*

pro·fess [prə'fes] *v/t.* **1.** (*a.* öffentlich) erklären, *Reue etc.* bekunden, sich bezeichnen (**to be** als), sich bekennen zu (*e-m Glauben etc.*) *od.* als (*Christ etc.*): ~ **o.s. a communist**; ~ **Christianity**; **2.** beteuern, versichern, *b.s.* heucheln, zur Schau tragen; **3.** eintreten für, *Grundsätze etc.* vertreten; **4.** (*als Beruf*) ausüben, betreiben; **5.** *Brit.* Pro'fessor sein in (*dat.*), lehren; **pro'fessed** [-st] *adj.* □ **1.** erklärt (*Feind etc.*), ausgesprochen; **2.** an-, vorgeblich; **3.** Berufs..., berufsmäßig; **4.** (in einen Orden) aufgenommen: ~ **monk** Profess *m*; **pro'fess·ed·ly** [-sɪdlɪ] *adv.* **1.** angeblich; **2.** erklärtermaßen; **3.** offenkundig; **pro'fes·sion** [-eʃn] *s.* **1.** (*bsd.* aka'demischer *od.* freier) Beruf, Stand *m*: **learned** ~ gelehrter Beruf; **the** ~**s** die akademischen Berufe; **the military** ~ der Soldatenberuf; **by** ~ von Beruf; **2.** **the** ~ *coll.* der Beruf *od.* Stand: **the medical** ~ die Ärzteschaft; **3.** (*bsd.* Glaubens)Bekenntnis *n*; **4.** Bekundung *f*, (*a.* falsche) Versicherung *od.* Behauptung, Beteuerung *f*: ~ **of friendship** Freundschaftsbeteuerung *f*; **5.** *eccl.* Pro'fess *f*, Gelübde(ablegung *f*) *n*; **pro'fes·sion·al** [-eʃənl] **I** *adj.* □ **1.** Berufs..., beruflich, Amts..., Standes...: ~ **discretion** Schweigepflicht *f* *des Arztes etc.*; ~ **ethics** Berufsethos *n*; **2.** Fach..., Berufs..., fachlich: ~ **association** Berufsgenossenschaft *f*; ~ **school** Fach-, Berufsschule *f*; ~ **studies** Fachstudium *n*; ~ **terminology** Fachsprache *f*; ~ **man** Mann vom Fach (→ 4); **3.** professio'nell, Berufs... (*a. sport*): ~ **player** 5. freiberuflich, aka'demisch; ~ **man** Akademiker, Geistesarbeiter; **the** ~ **classes** die höheren Berufsstände; **5.** gelernt, fachlich ausgebildet: ~ **gardener**; **6.** *fig. iro.* unentwegt, ,Berufs...': ~ **patriot**; **II** *s.* **7.** *sport* Berufssportler(in) *od.* -spieler (-in); **8.** Berufskünstler *m etc.*, Künstler *m vom* Fach; **9.** Fachmann *m*; **10.** Geistesarbeiter *m*; **pro'fes·sion·al·ism** [-eʃnəlɪzəm] *s.* Berufssportlertum *n*, -spielertum *n*, Profitum *n*.

pro·fes·sor [prə'fesə] *s.* **1.** Pro'fessor *m*, Profes'sorin *f*; → **associate** 8; **2.** *Am.* Hochschullehrer *m*; **3.** *a. humor.* Lehrmeister *m*; **4.** *bsd. Am. od. Scot.* (Glaubens)Bekenner *m*; **pro·fes·so·ri·al** [,prɒfɪ'sɔːrɪəl] *adj.* □ professo'ral; Professoren...: ~ **chair** Lehrstuhl *m*, Professur *f*; **pro·fes·so·ri·ate** [prɒfɪ'sɔːrɪət] *s.* **1.** Profes'soren(schaft *f*) *pl.*; **2.** → **pro'fes·sor·ship** [-ʃɪp] *s.* Profes'sur *f*, Lehrstuhl *m*.

prof·fer ['prɒfə] **I** *s.* Angebot *n*; **II** *v/t.* (an)bieten.

pro·fi·cien·cy [prə'fɪʃnsɪ] *s.* Können *n*, Tüchtigkeit *f*, (gute) Leistungen *pl.*; Fertigkeit *f*; **pro'fi·cient** [-nt] **I** *adj.* □ tüchtig, geübt, bewandert, erfahren (**in, at** in *dat.*); **II** *s.* Fachmann *m*, Meister *m*.

pro·file ['prəʊfaɪl] **I** *s.* **1.** Pro'fil *n*: a) Seitenansicht *f*, b) Kon'tur *f*: **keep a low** ~ *fig.* sich ,bedeckt' *od.* im Hintergrund halten; **2.** (*a.* △, ⊚) Pro'fil *n*, Längsschnitt *m*; **3.** Querschnitt *m* (*a. fig.*); **4.** 'Kurzbiogra,phie *f*; **II** *v/t.* **5.** im

Pro'fil darstellen, profilieren; ⊚ im Quer- *od.* Längsschnitt zeichnen; **6.** ⊚ profilieren, fassonieren; kopierfräsen: ~ **cutter** Fassonfräser *m*.

prof·it ['prɒfɪt] **I** *s.* **1.** (♀ *oft pl.*) Gewinn *m*, Pro'fit *m*: ~ **and loss account** Gewinn- u. Verlustkonto *n*, Erfolgsrechnung *f*; ~ **margin** Gewinnspanne *f*; ~ **maximization** Gewinnmaximierung *f*; ~-**sharing** Gewinnbeteiligung *f*; ~-**taking** *Börse:* Gewinnmitnahme *f*; **sell at a** ~ mit Gewinn verkaufen; **leave a** ~ e-n Gewinn abwerfen; **2.** *oft pl.* a) Ertrag *m*, Erlös *m*, b) Reinertrag *m*; **3.** ♱ Nutzung *f*, Früchte *pl.* (*aus Land*); **4.** Nutzen *m*, Vorteil *m*: **turn s.th. to** ~ aus et. Nutzen ziehen; **to his** ~ zu s-m Vorteil; **II** *v/i.* **5.** (**by, from**) (e-n) Nutzen *od.* Gewinn ziehen (aus), profitieren (von): ~ **by** a. sich et. zunutze machen, *e-e Gelegenheit* ausnützen; **III** *v/t.* **6.** nützen, nutzen (*dat.*), von Nutzen sein für: '**prof·it·a·ble** [-təbl] *adj.* □ **1.** Gewinn bringend, einträglich, lohnend, ren'tabel: **be** ~ a. sich rentieren; **2.** vorteilhaft, nützlich (**to** für); '**prof·it·a·ble·ness** [-təblnɪs] *s.* **1.** Einträglichkeit *f*, Rentabili'tät *f*; **2.** Nützlichkeit *f*; **prof·it·eer** [,prɒfɪ'tɪə] **I** *s.* Pro'fitmacher *m*, (Kriegs- *etc.*)Gewinnler *m*, ,Schieber' *m*, Wucherer *m*; **II** *v/i.* Schieber *od.* Wuchergeschäfte machen, ,schieben'; **prof·it·eer·ing** [,prɒfɪ'tɪərɪŋ] *s.* Schieber-, Wuchergeschäfte *pl.*, Preistreibe'rei *f*; '**prof·it·less** [-lɪs] *adj.* □ **1.** 'unren,tabel, ohne Gewinn; **2.** nutzlos.

prof·li·ga·cy ['prɒflɪgəsɪ] *s.* **1.** Lasterhaftigkeit *f*, Verworfenheit *f*; **2.** Verschwendung(ssucht) *f*; '**prof·li·gate** [-gət] **I** *adj.* □ **1.** verworfen, liederlich; **2.** verschwenderisch; **II** *s.* **3.** lasterhafter Mensch, Liederjan *m*; **4.** Verschwender(in).

pro for·ma [,prəʊ'fɔːmə] (*Lat.*) *adv. u. adj.* **1.** pro forma, zum Schein; **2.** ♀ Pro-forma-...(-*Rechnung*), Schein...(-*geschäft*): ~ **bill** Pro-forma-Wechsel *m*, Gefälligkeitswechsel *m*.

pro·found [prə'faʊnd] *adj.* □ **1.** tief (*mst fig. Friede, Seufzer, Schlaf etc.*); **2.** tief schürfend, inhaltsschwer, gründlich, pro'fund; **3.** *fig.* unergründlich, dunkel; **4.** *fig.* tief, groß (*Hochachtung etc.*), stark (*Interesse etc.*), vollkommen (*Gleichgültigkeit*); **pro'found·ness** [-nɪs], **pro'fun·di·ty** [-'fʌndətɪ] *s.* **1.** Tiefe *f*, Abgrund *m* (*a. fig.*); **2.** Tiefgründigkeit *f*, -sinnigkeit *f*; **3.** Gründlichkeit *f*; **4.** *pl.* tiefgründige Pro'bleme *od.* Theo'rien; **5.** *oft pl.* Weisheit *f*, pro'funder Ausspruch; **6.** Stärke *f*, hoher Grad (*der Erregung etc.*).

pro·fuse [prə'fjuːs] *adj.* □ **1.** (*a.* 'über-)reich (**of, in** an *dat.*), 'überfließend, üppig; **2.** (*oft allzu*) freigebig, verschwenderisch (**of, in** mit): **be** ~ **in one's thanks** überschwänglich danken; ~**ly illustrated** reich(haltig) illustriert; **pro'fuse·ness** [-nɪs], **pro'fu·sion** [-uːʒn] *s.* **1.** ('Über)Fülle *f*, 'Überfluss *m* (*of* an *dat.*): **in** ~ in Hülle u. Fülle; **2.** Verschwendung *f*, Luxus *m*, allzu große Freigebigkeit.

pro·gen·i·tive [prəʊ'dʒenɪtɪv] *adj.* **1.** Zeugungs...: ~ **act**; **2.** zeugungsfähig; **pro'gen·i·tor** [-tə] *s.* **1.** Vorfahr *m*, Ahn *m*; **2.** *fig.* Vorläufer *m*; **pro'gen·i·tress** [-trɪs] *s.* Ahne *f*; **pro'gen·i·ture** [-tʃə] *s.* **1.** Zeugung *f*; **2.** Nachkommenschaft *f*; **prog·e·ny** ['prɒdʒənɪ] *s.* **1.** Nachkommen(schaft *f a.* ♀) *pl.*; *zo.* die Jungen *pl.*, Brut *f*; **2.** *fig.* Frucht *f*, Pro'dukt *n*.

pro·gna·thy ['prɒgnəθɪ] s. ⚔ **1.** Progna'thie f; **2.** Proge'nie f.

prog·no·sis [prɒg'nəʊsɪs] pl. **-ses** [-siːz] s. ⚔ etc. Pro'gnose f, Vor'hersage f; **prog'nos·tic** [-'nɒstɪk] **I** adj. **1.** prog'nostisch (bsd. ⚔), vor'aussagend (of acc.); **2.** warnend, vorbedeutend; **II** s. **3.** Vor'hersage f; **4.** (An-, Vor)Zeichen n; **prog·nos·ti·cate** [prɒg'nɒstɪkeɪt] v/t. **1.** (a. v/i.) vor'her-, vor'aussagen, prognostizieren; **2.** anzeigen; **prog·nos·ti·ca·tion** [prəg,nɒstɪ'keɪʃn] s. **1.** Vor'her-, Vor'aussage f, Pro'gnose f (a. ⚔); **2.** Prophe'zeiung f; **3.** Vorzeichen n.

pro·gram(me) ['prəʊgræm] **I** s. **1.** ('Studien-, Par'tei- etc.)Pro,gramm n, Plan m (a. fig. F): **manufacturing ~** Herstellungsprogramm; **2.** Pro'gramm n: a) thea. Spielplan m, b) Pro'grammheft n, c) Darbietung f, d) Radio, TV: Sendefolge f, Sendung f; **~ director** Programmdirektor m; **~ music** Programmmusik f; **~ picture** Beifilm m; **~ rating** TV Einschaltquote f; **3.** Computer: Pro'gramm n: **~-controlled** programmgesteuert; **~ step** Programmschritt m; **II** v/t. **4.** ein Pro'gramm aufstellen für; **5.** auf das Pro'gramm setzen, planen, ansetzen; **6.** Computer programmieren; **'pro·grammed** [-md] adj. programmiert: **~ instruction**, **~ learning**; **'pro·gram·mer** [-mə] s. Computer: Program'mierer(in); **'pro·gram·ming** [-mɪŋ] s. **1.** Rundfunk, TV: Pro'grammgestaltung f; **2.** Computer: Programmierung f: **~ language** Programmiersprache f.

pro·gress I ['prəʊgres] s. (nur sg. außer 6) **1.** fig. Fortschritt(e pl.) m: **make ~** Fortschritte machen; **~ engineer** Entwicklungsingenieur m; **~ report** Zwischenbericht m; **2.** (Weiter)Entwicklung f: **in ~** im Werden (begriffen); **3.** Fortschreiten n, Vorrücken n; ⚔ Vordringen n; **4.** Fortgang m, (Ver)Lauf m: **be in ~** im Gange sein; **5.** Über'handnehmen n, 'Um-sich-Greifen n: **the disease made rapid ~** die Krankheit griff schnell um sich; **6.** obs. Reise f, Fahrt f; Brit. mst hist. Rundreise f e-s Herrschers etc.; **II** [prəʊ'gres] v/i. **7.** fortschreiten, weitergehen, s-n Fortgang nehmen; **8.** sich (fort-, weiter)entwickeln: **~ towards completion** s r Vollendung entgegengehen; **9.** fig. Fortschritte machen, vo'rankommen, vorwärts kommen.

pro·gres·sion [prəʊ'greʃn] s. **1.** Vorwärts-, Fortbewegung f; **2.** Weiterentwicklung f, Verlauf m; **3.** (Aufein'ander)Folge f; **4.** Progressi'on f: a) ♪ Rei he f, b) Staffelung f e-r Steuer etc.; **5.** ♪ a) Se'quenz f, b) Fortschreitung f (Stimmbewegung); **pro'gres·sion·ist** [-ʃnɪst], **pro'gress·ist** [-esɪst] s. pol. Fortschrittler m; **pro'gres·sive** [-esɪv] **I** adj. □ **1.** fortschrittlich (Person u. Sache): **~ party** pol. Fortschrittspartei f; **2.** fortschreitend, -laufend, progres'siv: **a ~ step** fig. ein Schritt nach vorn; **~ assembly** ⚙ Fließbandmontage f; **3.** gestaffelt, progres'siv (Besteuerung etc.); **4.** (fort)laufend: **~ numbers**; **5.** a. ⚔ zunehmend, progres'siv: **~ paralysis**; **6.** ling. progres'siv: **~ form** Verlaufsform f; **II** s. **7.** pol. Progres'sive(r) m) f, Fortschrittler m; **pro'gres·sive·ly** [-esɪvlɪ] adv. schritt-, stufenweise, nach u. nach, all'mählich.

pro·hib·it [prə'hɪbɪt] v/t. **1.** verbieten, unter'sagen (s.th. et., s.o. from doing j-m et. zu tun); **2.** verhindern (s.th. being done dass et. geschieht); **3.** hindern

(s.o. from doing j-n daran, et. zu tun); **pro·hi·bi·tion** [,prəʊɪ'bɪʃn] s. **1.** Verbot n; **2.** (hist. Am. mst ⚒) Prohibiti'on(s-zeit) f, Alkoholverbot n; **pro·hi·bi·tion·ist** [,prəʊɪ'bɪʃnɪst] s. hist. Am. Prohibitio'nist m, Verfechter m des Alkoholverbots; **pro'hib·i·tive** [-tɪv] adj. □ **1.** verbietend, unter'sagend; **2.** ♱ Prohibitiv..., Schutz..., Sperr...: **~ duty** Prohibitivzoll m; **~ tax** Prohibitivsteuer f; **3.** unerschwinglich (Preis), untragbar (Kosten); **pro'hib·i·to·ry** [-tərɪ] → prohibitive.

pro·ject I v/t. [prə'dʒekt] **1.** planen, entwerfen, projektieren; **2.** werfen, schleudern; **3.** Bild, Licht, Schatten etc. werfen, projizieren; **4.** fig. projizieren (a. ♈): **~ o.s.** (od. **one's thoughts**) **into** sich versetzen in (acc.); **~ one's feelings into** s-e Gefühle übertragen auf (acc.); **II** v/i. **5.** vorspringen, -stehen, -ragen (over über acc.); **III** s. ['prɒdʒekt] **6.** Pro'jekt n (a. Am. ped.), Plan m, (a. Bau)Vorhaben n, Entwurf m: **~ engineer** Projektingenieur m; **~ manager** Projektmanager m.

pro·jec·tile [prəʊ'dʒektaɪl] **I** s. **1.** ⚔ Geschoss, östr. Geschoß n, Projek'til n; **2.** (Wurf)Geschoss n; östr. (-)Geschoß n; **II** adj. **3.** (an)treibend, Stoß..., Trieb...: **~ force**; **4.** Wurf...

pro·jec·tion [prə'dʒekʃn] s. **1.** Vorsprung m, vorspringender Teil od. Gegenstand etc.; ⚙ Auskragung f, -ladung f, 'Überhang m; **2.** Fortsatz m; **3.** Werfen n, Schleudern n, (Vorwärts)Treiben n; **4.** Wurf m, Stoß m; **5.** ♈, ast. Projekti'on f: **upright ~** Aufriss m; **6.** phot. Projekti'on f: a) Projizieren n (Lichtbilder), b) Lichtbild n; **7.** Vorführen n (Film): **~ booth** Vorführkabine f; **~ screen** Projektions-, Leinwand f, Bildschirm m; **8.** psych. Projekti'on f; **9.** fig. 'Widerspiegelung f; **10.** a) Planen n, Entwerfen n, b) Plan m, Entwurf m; **11.** Statistik etc.: Hochrechnung f; **pro'jec·tion·ist** [-kʃnɪst] s. Filmvorführer m; **pro'jec·tor** [-ktə] s. **1.** Projekti'onsappa,rat m, Vorführgerät n, Bildwerfer m, Pro'jektor m; ⚔ ❂ Scheinwerfer m; **3.** ⚔ (Raketen-, Flammen- etc.)Werfer m; **4.** a) Planer m, b) contp. Pläneschmied m, Pro'jektemacher m.

pro·lapse ['prəʊlæps] ⚔ **I** s. Vorfall m, Pro'laps(us) m; **II** v/i. [prə'læps] prolabieren, vorfallen; **pro·lap·sus** [prəʊ-'læpsəs] → prolapse I.

prole [prəʊl] s. F Pro'let(in).

pro·le·tar·i·an [,prəʊlɪ'teərɪən] **I** adj. prole'tarisch, Proletarier...; **II** s. Prole-'tarier(in); **pro·le·tar·i·at(e)** [-ɪət] s. Proletari'at n.

pro·li·cide ['prəʊlɪsaɪd] s. ♃ Tötung f der Leibesfrucht, Abtreibung f.

pro·lif·er·ate [prəʊ'lɪfəreɪt] v/i. biol. **1.** wuchern; **2.** sich fortpflanzen (durch Zellteilung etc.); **3.** sich stark vermehren; **pro·lif·er·a·tion** [prəʊ,lɪfə'reɪʃn] s. **1.** Wuchern n; **2.** Fortpflanzung f; **3.** starke Vermehrung od. Ausbreitung; **pro'lif·ic** [-fɪk] adj. (□ ~ally) **1.** bsd. biol. (oft 'überaus) fruchtbar; **2.** fig. reich (of, in an dat.); **3.** fig. fruchtbar, produk'tiv (Schriftsteller etc.).

pro·lix ['prəʊlɪks] adj. □ weitschweifig; **pro·lix·i·ty** [,prəʊ'lɪksətɪ] s. Weitschweifigkeit f.

pro·log Am. → prologue.

pro·logue ['prəʊlɒg] s. **1.** bsd. thea. Pro'log m, Einleitung f (to zu); **2.** fig. Vorspiel n, Auftakt m; **'pro·logu·ize** [-gaɪz] v/i. e-n Pro'log verfassen od. sprechen.

pro·long [prə'lɒŋ] v/t. **1.** verlängern, (aus)dehnen; **2.** ♱ prolongieren; **pro'longed** [-ŋd] adj. anhaltend (Beifall, Regen etc.): **for a ~ period** längere Zeit; **pro·lon·ga·tion** [,prəʊ-lɒŋ'geɪʃn] s. **1.** Verlängerung f; **2.** Prolongierung f e-s Wechsels etc., Fristverlängerung f, Aufschub m: **~ business** ♱ Prolongationsgeschäft n.

prom [prɒm] s. **1.** Am. F High-School-, College-Ball m; **2.** bsd. Brit. F a) 'Strandprome,nade f, b) → promenade concert.

prom·e·nade [,prɒmə'nɑːd] **I** s. **1.** Prome'nade f: a) Spaziergang m, -fahrt f, -ritt m, b) Spazierweg m, Wandelhalle f; **2.** [a. -'neɪd] feierlicher Einzug der (Ball)Gäste, Polo'naise f; **3.** → prom 1; **4.** → promenade concert; **II** v/i. **5.** promenieren, spazieren (gehen etc.); **III** v/t. **6.** promenieren od. (her'um)spazieren in (dat.) od. auf (dat.); **7.** spazieren führen, (um'her)führen; **~ con·cert** s. Konzert in ungezwungener Atmosphäre; **~ deck** s. ♘ Prome'nadendeck n.

prom·i·nence ['prɒmɪnəns] s. **1.** (Her-) 'Vorragen n, -springen n; **2.** Vorsprung m, vorstehender Teil; ast. Protube'ranz f; **3.** fig. a) Berühmtheit f, b) Bedeutung f: **bring into ~** a) berühmt machen, b) klar herausstellen, hervorheben, **come into ~** in den Vordergrund rücken, hervortreten; **~ blaze** 7; **'prom·i·nent** [-nt] adj. □ **1.** vorstehend, -springend (a. Nase etc.); **2.** mar-'kant, auffallend, her'vorstehend (Eigenschaft); **3.** promi'nent: a) führend (Persönlichkeit), her'vorragend, b) berühmt.

prom·is·cu·i·ty [,prɒmɪ'skjuːɪtɪ] s. **1.** Vermischt-, Verworrenheit f, Durchein'ander n; **2.** Wahllosigkeit f; **3.** Promiskui'tät f, wahllose od. ungebundene Geschlechtsbeziehungen pl.; **pro·mis·cu·ous** [prə'mɪskjʊəs] adj. □ **1.** (kunter)bunt, verworren; **2.** wahl-, 'unterschiedslos; **3.** gemeinsam (beider Geschlechter): **~ bathing**.

prom·ise ['prɒmɪs] **I** s. **1.** Versprechen n, -heißung f, Zusage f (to j-m gegen-'über): **~ to pay** ♱ Zahlungsversprechen; **break (keep) one's ~** sein Versprechen brechen (halten); **make a ~** ein Versprechen geben; **breach of ~** Bruch m des Eheversprechens; **Land of ⚒** → Promised Land; **2.** fig. Hoffnung f od. Aussicht f (of auf acc., zu inf.): **of great ~** viel versprechend (Aussicht, junger Mann etc.); **show some ~** gewisse Ansätze zeigen; **II** v/t. **3.** versprechen, zusagen, in Aussicht stellen (s.o. s.th., s.th. to s.o. j-m et.): **I ~ you** a) das kann ich Ihnen versichern, b) ich warne Sie!; **4.** fig. versprechen, erwarten od. hoffen lassen, ankündigen: **be ~d** (in die Ehe) versprochen sein; **6. ~ o.s. s.th.** sich et. versprechen od. erhoffen; **III** v/i. **7.** versprechen, zusagen; **8.** fig. Hoffnungen erwecken: **he ~s well** er lässt sich gut an; **the weather ~s fine** das Wetter verspricht gut zu werden; **Prom·ised Land** ['prɒmɪst] s. bibl. u. fig. das Gelobte Land, Land n der Verheißung; **prom·is·ee** [,prɒmɪ-'siː] s. ♃ Versprechensempfänger(in), Berechtigte(r m) f; **prom·is·ing** [-sɪŋ] adj. □ fig. viel versprechend, hoffnungs-, verheißungsvoll, aussichtsreich; **'prom·i·sor** [-sɔː] s. ♃ Versprechensgeber(in); **'prom·is·so·ry** [-sərɪ] adj. versprechend: **~ note** ♱ Schuldschein m, Eigen-, Solawechsel m.

pro·mo ['prəʊməʊ] F I *adj.* Reklame...; II *pl.* **-mos** *s. Radio, TV:* (Werbe)Spot *m; Zeitung:* Anzeige *f.*

prom·on·to·ry ['prɒməntrɪ] *s.* Vorgebirge *n.*

pro·mote [prə'məʊt] *v/t.* **1.** fördern, unter'stützen; *b.s.* Vorschub leisten (*dat.*); **2.** *j-n* befördern: *be ~d* a) befördert werden, b) *sport* aufsteigen; **3.** *parl.* Antrag a) unter'stützen, b) einbringen; **4.** † *Gesellschaft* gründen; **5.** † a) *Verkauf (durch Werbung)* steigern, b) werben für; **6.** *Boxkampf etc.* veranstalten; **7.** *ped. Am. Schüler* versetzen; **8.** *Schach: Bauern* verwandeln; **9.** *Am. sl.* ,organisieren'; **pro'mot·er** [-tə] *s.* **1.** Förderer *m;* *b.s.* Anstifter *m;* **2.** † Gründer *m:* ~'s *shares* Gründeraktien; **3.** *sport* Veranstalter *m;* **pro'mo·tion** [-əʊʃn] *s.* **1.** Beförderung *f* (*a.* ✕): ~ *list* Beförderungsliste *f; get one's* ~ befördert werden; ~ *prospects pl.* Aufstiegschancen *pl.;* **2.** Förderung *f,* Befürwortung *f:* *export* ~ † Exportförderung; **3.** † Gründung *f;* ~ † Verkaufsförderung *f,* Werbung *f.* **5.** *ped. Am.* Versetzung *f;* **6.** *sport* Aufstieg *m:* *gain* ~ aufsteigen; **7.** *Schach:* Umwandlung *f;* **pro'mo·tion·al** [-əʊʃənl] *adj.* **1.** Beförderungs...; **2.** fördernd; **3.** † Reklame..., Werbe...; **pro'mo·tive** [-tɪv] *adj.* fördernd, begünstigend (*of acc.*).

prompt [prɒmpt] I *adj.* ☐ **1.** unverzüglich, prompt, so'fortig, 'umgehend: *a ~ reply* e-e prompte *od.* schlagfertige Antwort; **2.** schnell, rasch; **3.** bereit (-willig); **4.** † a) pünktlich, b) bar, c) sofort liefer- u. zahlbar: *for* ~ *cash* gegen sofortige Kasse; II *adv.* **5.** pünktlich; III *v/t.* **6.** *j-n* antreiben, bewegen, (*a. et.*) veranlassen (*to* zu); **7.** *Gedanken, Gefühl etc.* eingeben, wecken; **8.** *j-m* das Stichwort geben, ein-, vorsagen; *thea. j-m* soufflieren: ~ *book* Soufflierbuch *n;* ~ *box* Souffleurkasten; ~ *facility Computer:* Bedienerführung *f;* IV *s.* **9.** *Computer:* Prompt *m,* Eingabeaufforderung *f;* **10.** † *Ziel n,* Zahlungsfrist *f;* **'prompt·er** [-tə] *s.* **1.** *thea.* Souf'fleur *m,* Souf'fleuse *f;* **2.** Vorsager(in); **3.** Anreger(in), Urheber(in); *b.s.* Anstifter(in); **'prompt·ing** [-tɪŋ] *s.* (*oft pl.*) *fig.* Eingebung *f,* Stimme *f des Herzens;* **'promp·ti·tude** [-tɪtjuːd]; **'prompt·ness** [-nɪs] *s.* **1.** Schnelligkeit *f;* **2.** Bereitwilligkeit *f;* **3.** *bsd.* † Promptheit *f,* Pünktlichkeit *f.*

prompt note *s.* † Verkaufsnota *f* mit Angabe der Zahlungsfrist.

pro·mul·gate ['prɒmlgeɪt] *v/t.* **1.** *Gesetz etc.* (öffentlich) bekannt machen *od.* verkündigen; **2.** *Lehre etc.* verbreiten; **pro·mul·ga·tion** [,prɒml'geɪʃn] *s.* **1.** (öffentliche) Bekanntmachung, Verkündung *f,* -öffentlichung *f;* **2.** Verbreitung *f.*

prone [prəʊn] *adj.* ☐ **1.** auf dem Bauch *od.* mit dem Gesicht nach unten liegend, hingestreckt: ~ *position* a) Bauchlage *f,* b) ✕ *etc.* Anschlag liegend; **2.** (vorn'über)gebeugt; **3.** abschüssig; **4.** *fig.* (*to*) neigend (zu), veranlagt (zu), anfällig (für); **'prone·ness** [-nɪs] *s.* (*to*) Neigung *f,* Hang *m* (zu), Anfälligkeit *f* (für).

prong [prɒŋ] I *s.* **1.** Zinke *f* e-r (*Heu- etc.*)*Gabel;* Zacke *f,* Spitze *f,* Dorn *m;* **2.** (Geweih)Sprosse *f,* (-)Ende *n;* **3.** Horn *n;* **4.** (Heu-, Mist- *etc.*)Gabel *f;* II *v/t.* **5.** mit e-r Gabel stechen *od.* heben; **6.** aufspießen; **pronged** [-ŋd] *adj.* gezinkt, zackig: *two-~* zweizinkig.

---

pro·nom·i·nal [prə'nɒmɪnl] *adj.* ☐ *ling.* pronomi'nal.

pro·noun ['prəʊnaʊn] *s. ling.* Pro'nomen *n,* Fürwort *n.*

pro·nounce [prə'naʊns] I *v/t.* **1.** aussprechen (*a. ling.*); **2.** erklären für, bezeichnen als; **3.** *Urteil* aussprechen *od.* verkünden, *Segen* erteilen: ~ *sentence of death* das Todesurteil fällen, auf Todesstrafe erkennen; **4.** behaupten (*that* dass); II *v/i.* **5.** Stellung nehmen, s-e Meinung äußern (*on* zu): ~ *in favo(u)r of* (*against*) *s.th.* sich für (gegen) et. aussprechen; **pro'nounced** [-st] *adj.* ☐ **1.** ausgesprochen, ausgeprägt, deutlich (*Tendenz etc.*), sichtlich (*Besserung etc.*); **2.** bestimmt, entschieden (*Ansicht etc.*); **pro'nounc·ed·ly** [-sɪdlɪ] *adv.* ausgesprochen *gut, schlecht etc.;* **pro'nounce·ment** [-mənt] *s.* **1.** Äußerung *f;* **2.** Erklärung *f,* (₤ *Urteils*)Verkünd(ig)ung *f;* **3.** Entscheidung *f.*

pron·to ['prɒntəʊ] *adv. Am.* F fix, schnell, ,aber dalli'.

pro·nun·ci·a·tion [prə,nʌnsɪ'eɪʃn] *s.* Aussprache *f.*

proof [pruːf] I *adj.* **1.** fest (*against, to* gegen), 'undurch,lässig, (*wasser- etc.*) dicht, (*hitze*)beständig, (*kugel*)sicher; **2.** gefeit (*against* gegen) (*a. fig.*); *fig. a.* unzugänglich: ~ *against bribes* unbestechlich; **3.** ♫ *obs.* probehaltig, nor'malstark (*alkoholische Flüssigkeit*); II *s.* **4.** Beweis *m,* Nachweis *m:* *in* ~ *of* zum *od.* als Beweis (*gen.*); *give* ~ *of* et. beweisen; **5.** (*a.* ₤) Beweis(mittel *n,* -stück *n*) *m;* Beleg(e *pl.*) *m;* **6.** Probe *f* (*a.* ♣), (*a.* Materi'al)Prüfung *f:* *put to* (*the*) ~ auf die Probe stellen; *the* ~ *of the pudding is in the eating* Probieren geht über Studieren; **7.** *typ.* a) Korrek'turfahne *f,* -bogen *m,* b) Probeabzug *m* (*a. phot.*): *clean* ~ Revisionsbogen *m;* **8.** Nor'malstärke *f* alkoholischer Getränke; III *v/t.* **9.** ❂ (*wasser- etc.*)dicht *od.* (*hitze- etc.*)beständig *od.* (*kugel- etc.*)fest machen, imprägnieren; **'~read·er** *s. typ.* Kor'rektor *m;* **'~read·ing** *s. typ.* Korrek'turlesen *n;* ~ *sheet* → *proof* 7 a; ~ *spir·it* *s.* Nor'malweingeist *m.*

prop[1] [prɒp] I *s.* **1.** Stütze *f* (*a.* ♣), (Stütz)Pfahl *m;* **2.** *fig.* Stütze *f,* Halt *m;* **3.** △, ❂ Stempel *m;* **4.** Stützbalken *m,* Strebe *f;* **4.** ❂ Drehpunkt *m* e-s *Hebels;* **5.** *pl. sl.* ,Stelzen' *pl.* (*Beine*); II *v/t.* **6.** stützen (*a. fig.*); **7.** *a.* ~ *up* a) (ab)stützen, ❂ *a.* absteifen, verstreben, *mot.* aufbocken, b) *sich, et.* lehnen (*against* gegen).

prop[2] [prɒp] *s. thea.* Requi'sit *n* (*a. fig.*).

prop[3] [prɒp] *s. F* Pro'peller *m.*

prop·a·gan·da [,prɒpə'gændə] *s.* Propa'ganda *f;* † Werbung *f,* Re'klame *f:* *make* ~ *for;* ~ *week* Werbewoche *f;* **,prop·a'gan·dist** [-dɪst] *s.* Propagan'dist(in); II *adj.* propagan'distisch; **prop·a·gan·dis·tic** [,prɒpəgæn'dɪstɪk] *adj.* propagan'distisch; **,prop·a'gan·dize** [-daɪz] *v/t.* **1.** Propa'ganda machen für, propagieren; **2.** *j-n* durch Propa'ganda beeinflussen; II *v/i.* **3.** Propa'ganda machen.

prop·a·gate ['prɒpəgeɪt] I *v/t.* **1.** *biol., a. phys. Ton, Bewegung, Licht* fortpflanzen; **2.** *Nachricht etc.* aus-, verbreiten, propagieren; II *v/i.* **3.** sich fortpflanzen; **prop·a·ga·tion** [,prɒpə'geɪʃn] *s.* **1.** Fortpflanzung *f* (*a. phys.*), Vermehrung *f;* **2.** Aus-, Verbreitung *f;* **prop·a·ga·tor** ['prɒpəgeɪtə] *s.* **1.** Fortpflanzer *m;* **2.** Verbreiter *m,* Propagan'dist *m.*

---

pro·pane ['prəʊpeɪn] *s.* ♫ Pro'pan *n.*

pro·pel [prə'pel] *v/t.* antreiben, (vorwärts) treiben (*a. fig. od.* ❂); **pro'pel·lant** [-lənt] *s.* ❂ Treibstoff *m,* -mittel *n:* ~ (*charge*) Treibladung *f* e-r Rakete etc.; **pro'pel·lent** [-lənt] I *adj.* **1.** antreibend, (vorwärts) treibend: ~ *gas* Treibgas; ~ *power* Antriebs-, Triebkraft *f;* II *s.* **2.** *fig.* treibende Kraft; **3.** → *propellant;* **pro'pel·ler** [-lə] *s.* Pro'peller *m:* a) ✈ Luftschraube *f,* b) ♣ Schiffsschraube *f:* ~ *blade* ✈ Luftschraubenblatt *n;* **pro'pel·ling** [-lɪŋ] *adj.* Antriebs..., Trieb..., Treib...: ~ *charge* Treibladung *f,* -satz *m* e-r Rakete etc.; ~ *nozzle* ✈ Schubdüse *f;* ~ *pencil* Drehbleistift *m.*

pro·pen·si·ty [prə'pensətɪ] *s. fig.* Hang *m,* Neigung *f* (*to, for* zu).

prop·er ['prɒpə] *adj.* ☐ **1.** richtig, passend, geeignet, angemessen, ordnungsgemäß, zweckmäßig: *in* ~ *form* in gebührender *od.* angemessener Form; *in the* ~ *place* am rechten Platz; *do as you think* (*it*) ~ tun Sie, was Sie für richtig halten; ~ *fraction* Å echter Bruch; **2.** anständig, schicklich, kor'rekt, einwandfrei (*Benehmen etc.*): *it is* ~ es (ge)ziemt *od.* schickt sich; **3.** zulässig; **4.** eigen(tümlich) (*to dat.*), besonder; **5.** genau: *in the* ~ *meaning of the word* streng genommen; **6.** (*mst nachgestellt*) eigentlich: *philosophy* ~ die eigentliche Philosophie; *in the Middle East* ~ im Mittleren Osten selbst; **7.** maßgebend, zuständig (*Dienststelle etc.*); **8.** F ,richtig', ,ordentlich', ,anständig': *a* ~ *licking* e-e gehörige Tracht Prügel; **9.** *ling.* Eigen...: ~ *name* (*od. noun*) Eigenname *m;* **'proper·ly** [-lɪ] *adv.* **1.** richtig (*etc.* → *proper* 1, 2), passend, wie es sich gehört: *behave* ~ sich (anständig) benehmen; **2.** genau: ~ *speaking* eigentlich, streng genommen; **3.** F gründlich, ,anständig', ,tüchtig'.

prop·er·tied ['prɒpətɪd] *adj.* besitzend, begütert: *the* ~ *classes.*

prop·er·ty ['prɒpətɪ] *s.* **1.** Eigentum *n,* Besitz(tum *n*) *m,* Gut *n,* Vermögen *n:* *common* ~ Gemeingut; *damage to* ~ Sachschaden *m;* *law of* ~ ₤ Sachenrecht *n; left* ~ Hinterlassenschaft *f; lost* ~ Fundsache *f; man of* ~ begüterter Mann; *personal* ~ → *personalty;* **2.** *a. landed* ~ (Grund-, Land)Besitz *m,* Grundstück *n,* Liegenschaft *f,* Ländereien *pl.;* **3.** ₤ Eigentum(srecht) *n: industrial* ~ gewerbliches Schutzrecht; *intellectual* ~ geistiges Eigentum; *literary* ~ literarisches Eigentum, Urheberrecht; **4.** *mst pl. thea.* Requi'sit(en *pl.*) *n;* **5.** Eigenart *f,* -heit *f;* Merkmal *n;* **6.** *phys. etc.* Eigenschaft *f,* ❂ Fähigkeit *f:* ~ *of material* Werkstoffeigenschaft; *insulating* ~ Isolationsvermögen *n;* ~ *as·sets s. pl.* † Vermögenswerte *pl.;* ~ *in·sur·ance s.* Sachversicherung *f;* ~ *man* [mæn] *s.* [*irr.*] *thea.* Requi'steur *m;* ~ *mar·ket s.* Immo'bilienmarkt *m;* ~ *tax s.* **1.** Vermögenssteuer *f;* **2.** Grundsteuer *f.*

proph·e·cy ['prɒfɪsɪ] *s.* Prophe'zeiung *f,* Weissagung *f;* **'proph·e·sy** [-saɪ] *v/t.* prophe'zeien, weis-, vor'aussagen (*s.th. for s.o.* j-m et.).

proph·et ['prɒfɪt] *s.* Pro'phet *m* (*a. fig.*): *the Major* (*Minor*) ♫s *bibl.* die großen (kleinen) Propheten; **'proph·et·ess** [-tɪs] *s.* Pro'phetin *f;* **pro·phet·ic, pro·phet·i·cal** [prə'fetɪk(l)] *adj.* ☐ pro'phetisch.

pro·phy·lac·tic [,prɒfɪ'læktɪk] I *adj. bsd.* ♣ prophy'laktisch, vorbeugend, Vorbeugungs..., Schutz...; II *s.* ♣ Prophy-

'laktikum *n*, vorbeugendes Mittel; *fig.* vorbeugende Maßnahme; **ˌpro·phy·'lax·is** [-ksɪs] *s.* ⚕ Prophy'laxe *f*, Präven'tivbeˌhandlung *f*, Vorbeugung *f*.

pro·pin·qui·ty [prə'pɪŋkwətɪ] *s.* **1.** Nähe *f*; **2.** nahe Verwandtschaft.

pro·pi·ti·ate [prə'pɪʃɪeɪt] *v/t.* versöhnen, besänftigen, günstig stimmen; **pro·pi·ti·a·tion** [prəˌpɪʃɪ'eɪʃn] *s.* **1.** Versöhnung *f*; Besänftigung *f*; **2.** *obs.* (Sühn-)Opfer *n*, Sühne *f*; **pro'pi·ti·a·to·ry** [-ɪətərɪ] *adj.* □ versöhnend, sühnend, Sühn...

pro·pi·tious [prə'pɪʃəs] *adj.* □ **1.** günstig, vorteilhaft (*to* für); **2.** gnädig, geneigt.

'prop·jet *s.* ✈ **1.** *a.* ~ ***engine*** Pro'pellerturˌbine(ntriebwerk *n*) *f*; **2.** *a.* ~ ***plane*** Flugzeug *n* mit Pro'pellerturˌbine(n).

pro·po·nent [prə'pəʊnənt] *s.* **1.** Vorschlagende(r *m*) *f*; *fig.* Befürworter(in); **2.** ⚖ präsum'tiver Testa'mentserbe.

pro·por·tion [prə'pɔːʃn] **I** *s.* **1.** (richtiges) Verhältnis; Gleich-, Ebenmaß *n*; *pl.* (Aus)Maße *pl.*, Größenverhältnisse *pl.*, Dimensi'onen *pl.*, Proporti'onen *pl.*: ***in ~ as*** in dem Maße wie, je nachdem wie; ***in ~ to*** im Verhältnis zu; ***be out of (all) ~ to*** in keinem Verhältnis stehen zu; ***sense of ~*** *fig.* Augenmaß *n*; **2.** *fig.* a) Ausmaß *n*, Größe *f*, Umfang *m*, b) Symmet'rie *f*, Harmo'nie *f*; **3.** A, ⛫ Proporti'on *f*; **4.** A a) Dreisatz(rechnung *f*) *m*, *obs.* Regelde'tri *f*, b) *a.* ***geometric ~*** Verhältnisgleichheit *f*; **5.** Anteil *m*, Teil *m*: ***in ~*** anteilig; **II** *v/t.* **6.** (*to*) in das richtige Verhältnis bringen (mit, zu), anpassen (*dat.*); **7.** verhältnismäßig verteilen; **8.** proportionieren, bemessen; **9.** sym'metrisch gestalten: ***well-~d*** ebenmäßig, wohlgestaltet; **pro'por·tion·al** [-ʃənl] **I** *adj.* □ **1.** proportio'nal, verhältnismäßig; anteilmäßig: ~ ***numbers*** A Proportionalzahlen *pl.*; ~ ***representation*** *pol.* Verhältniswahl(system *n*) *f*; **2.** → ***proportionate***; **II** *s.* **3.** A Proportio'nale *f*; **pro'por·tion·ate** [-ʃnət] *adj.* □ (*to*) im richtigen Verhältnis (stehend) (zu), angemessen (*dat.*), entsprechend (*dat.*): ~ ***share*** ✝ Verhältnisanteil *m*, anteilmäßige Befriedigung.

pro·pos·al [prə'pəʊzl] *s.* **1.** Vorschlag *m*, (*a.* ✝, *a. Friedens*)Angebot *n*, (*u.* Heirats)Antrag *m*; **2.** Plan *m*; **pro·pose** [prə'pəʊz] **I** *v/t.* **1.** vorschlagen (***s.th. to s.o.*** j-m et., ***s.o. for*** j-n zu *od.* als); **2.** *Antrag* stellen; *Resolution* einbringen; *Misstrauensvotum* stellen *od.* beantragen; **3.** *Rätsel* aufgeben; *Frage* stellen; **4.** beabsichtigen, sich vornehmen; **5.** e-n Toast ausbringen auf (*acc.*), auf *et.* trinken; **II** *v/i.* **6.** beabsichtigen, vorhaben; planen: ***man ~s (but) God disposes*** der Mensch denkt, Gott lenkt; **7.** e-n Heiratsantrag machen (***to*** *dat.*), anhalten (***for*** um *j-n, j-s Hand*); **pro'pos·er** [-zə] *s. pol.* Antragsteller *m*; **prop·o·si·tion** [ˌprɒpə'zɪʃn] **I** *s.* **1.** Vorschlag *m*, Antrag *m*; **2.** (vorgeschlagener) Plan, Pro'jekt *n*; **3.** ✝ Angebot *n*; **4.** Behauptung *f*; **5.** F a) Sache *f*, b) Geschäft *n*: ***an easy ~*** ‚kleine Fische', Kleinigkeit *f*; **6.** *phls.* Satz *m*; **7.** A (Lehr)Satz *m*; **II** *v/t.* **8.** *j-m* e-n Vorschlag machen; **9.** *e-m Mädchen* e-n unsittlichen Antrag machen.

pro·pound [prə'paʊnd] *v/t.* **1.** *Frage etc.* vorlegen, -tragen (***to*** *dat.*); **2.** vorschlagen; **3.** ***~ a will*** ⚖ auf Anerkennung e-s Testaments klagen.

pro·pri·e·tar·y [prə'praɪətərɪ] **I** *adj.* **1.** Eigentums...(*-recht etc.*), Vermögens...; **2.** Eigentümer..., Besitzer...: ~ ***company*** ✝ a) *Am.* Holding-, Dachgesellschaft *f*, b) *Brit.* Familiengesellschaft *f*; ***the ~ classes*** die besitzenden Schichten; **3.** gesetzlich geschützt (*Arznei, Ware*): ~ ***article*** Markenartikel *m*; ~ ***name*** Markenbezeichnung *f*; **II** *s.* **4.** Eigentümer *m od. pl.*; **5.** ⚕ a) medi'zinischer 'Markenarˌtikel, b) nicht re'zeptpflichtiges Medika'ment; **pro·pri·e·tor** [prə'praɪətə] *s.* Eigentümer *m*, Besitzer *m*, (Geschäfts)Inhaber *m*, Anteilseigner *m*, Gesellschafter *m*: ***~s' capital*** Eigenkapital *n e-r Gesellschaft*; ***sole ~*** a) Alleininhaber(in), b) ✝ *Am.* Einzelkaufmann *m*; **pro'pri·e·tor·ship** [-təʃɪp] *s.* **1.** Eigentum(srecht) *n* (***in*** an *dat.*); **2.** Verlagsrecht *n*; **3.** *Bilanz*: 'Eigenkapiˌtal *n*; **4.** ***sole ~*** a) alleiniges Eigentumsrecht, b) ✝ *Am.* Einzelunternehmen *n*; **pro'pri·e·tress** [-trɪs] *s.* Eigentümerin *f etc.*; **pro'pri·e·ty** [-tɪ] *s.* **1.** Schicklichkeit *f*, Anstand *m*; **2.** *pl.* Anstandsformen *pl.*; **3.** Angemessenheit *f*, Richtigkeit *f*.

props [prɒps] *s. pl. thea. sl.* **1.** Requi'siten *pl.*; **2.** *sg. konstr.* Requisi'teur *m*.

pro·pul·sion [prə'pʌlʃn] *s.* **1.** ⚙ Antrieb *m* (*a. fig.*), Antriebskraft *f*: ~ ***nozzle*** Rückstoßdüse *f*; **2.** Fortbewegung *f*; **pro'pul·sive** [-lsɪv] *adj.* antreibend, (vorwärts) treibend (*a. fig.*): ~ ***force*** Triebkraft *f*; ~ ***jet*** Treibstrahl *m*.

pro ra·ta [ˌprəʊ'rɑːtə] (*Lat.*) *adj. u. adv.* verhältnis-, anteilmäßig, pro 'rata; **pro·rate** ['prəʊreɪt] *Am v/t.* anteilmäßig ver-, aufteilen.

pro·ro·ga·tion [ˌprəʊrə'geɪʃn] *s. pol.* Vertagung *f*; **pro·rogue** [prə'rəʊg] *v/t. u. v/i.* (sich) vertagen.

pro·sa·ic [prəʊ'zeɪɪk] *adj.* (□ ***~ally***) *fig.* pro'saisch: a) all'täglich, b) nüchtern, trocken, c) langweilig.

pro·sce·ni·um [prəʊ'siːnjəm] *pl.* **-ni·a** [-njə] *s. thea.* Pro'szenium *n*.

pro·scribe [prəʊ'skraɪb] *v/t.* **1.** ächten, für vogelfrei erklären; **2.** *mst fig.* verbannen; **3.** *fig.* a) verurteilen, b) verbieten; **pro'scrip·tion** [-'skrɪpʃn] *s.* **1.** Ächtung *f*, Acht *f*, Proskripti'on *f* (*mst hist.*); **2.** Verbannung *f*; **3.** *fig.* Verurteilung *f*, Verbot *n*; **pro'scrip·tive** [-'skrɪptɪv] *adj.* □ **1.** Ächtungs..., ächtend; **2.** verbietend, Verbots...

prose [prəʊz] **I** *s.* **1.** Prosa *f*; **2.** *fig.* Prosa *f*, Nüchternheit *f*, All'täglichkeit *f*; **3.** *ped.* Über'setzung *f in die Fremdsprache*; **II** *adj.* **4.** Prosa...: ~ ***writer*** Prosaschriftsteller(in); **5.** *fig.* pro'saisch; **III** *v/t. u. v/i.* **6.** in Prosa schreiben; **7.** langweilig erzählen.

pros·e·cute ['prɒsɪkjuːt] **I** *v/t.* **1.** *Plan etc.* verfolgen, weiterführen: ~ ***an action*** ⚖ e-n Prozess führen; **2.** *Gewerbe, Studien etc.* betreiben; **3.** *Untersuchung* 'durchführen; **4.** ⚖ a) strafrechtlich verfolgen, b) gerichtlich verfolgen, belangen, anklagen (***for*** wegen), c) *Forderung* einklagen; **II** *v/i.* **5.** gerichtlich vorgehen; **6.** ⚖ als Kläger auftreten, die Anklage vertreten: ***prosecuting counsel*** (*Am.* ***attorney***) → ***prosecutor***; **pros·e·cu·tion** [ˌprɒsɪ'kjuːʃn] *s.* **1.** Verfolgung *f*, Fortsetzung *f*, 'Durchführung *f e-s Plans etc.*; **2.** Betreiben *n e-s Gewerbes etc.*; **3.** ⚖ a) strafrechtliche Verfolgung, Strafverfolgung *f*, b) Einklagen *n e-r Forderung etc.*: ***liable to ~*** strafbar; ***Director of Public ≈s*** Leiter *m* der Anklagebehörde; **4.** ***the ~*** ⚖ die Staatsanwaltschaft, die Anklage(behörde); → ***witness*** 1; **'pros·e·cu·tor** [-tə] *s.* ⚖ (An)Kläger *m*, Anklagevertreter *m*: ***public ~*** Staatsanwalt *m*.

pros·e·lyte ['prɒsɪlaɪt] *s. eccl.* Prose'lyt(-in), Konver'tit(in), *a. fig.* Neubekehrte(r *m*) *f*; **'pros·e·lyt·ism** [-lɪtɪzəm] *s.* Prosely'tismus *m*: a) Bekehrungseifer *m*, b) Prose'lytentum *n*; **'pros·e·lyt·ize** [-lɪtaɪz] **I** *v/t.* (***to***) bekehren (zu), *fig. a.* gewinnen (für); **II** *v/i.* Anhänger gewinnen.

pros·i·ness ['prəʊzɪnɪs] *s.* **1.** Eintönigkeit *f*, Langweiligkeit *f*; **2.** Weitschweifigkeit *f*.

pros·o·dy ['prɒsədɪ] *s.* Proso'die *f* (*Silbenmessungslehre*).

pros·pect **I** *s.* ['prɒspekt] **1.** (Aus)Sicht *f*, (-)Blick *m* (***of*** auf *acc.*); **2.** *fig.* Aussicht *f*: ***hold out a ~ of*** et. in Aussicht stellen; ***have s.th. in ~*** auf et. Aussicht haben, et. in Aussicht haben; **3.** *fig.* Vor('aus)schau *f* (***of*** auf *acc.*); **4.** ✝ *etc.* Interes'sent *m*, Reflek'tant *m*; ✝ möglicher Kunde; **5.** ⚒ a) (*Erz- etc.*) Anzeichen *n*, b) Schürfprobe *f*, c) Schürfstelle *f*; **II** *v/t.* [prə'spekt] **6.** *Gebiet* durch'forschen, unter'suchen (***for*** nach *Gold etc.*); **III** *v/i.* [prə'spekt] **7.** (***for***) ⚒ suchen (nach, *a. fig.*), schürfen (nach); (nach *Öl*) bohren; **pro·spec·tive** [prə'spektɪv] *adj.* □ **1.** (zu)künftig, vor'aussichtlich, in Aussicht stehend, potenzi'ell: ~ ***buyer*** Kaufinteressent *m*, potenzieller Käufer; **2.** *fig.* vor'ausschauend; **pros·pec·tor** [prə'spektə] *s.* Pro'spektor *m*, Schürfer *m*, Goldsucher *m*; **pro·spec·tus** [prə'spektəs] *s.* Pros'pekt *m*: a) Werbeschrift *f*, b) ✝ Subskripti'onsanzeige *f*, c) *Brit.* 'Schulprosˌpekt *m*.

pros·per ['prɒspə] **I** *v/i.* Erfolg haben (***in*** bei); gedeihen, florieren, blühen (*Unternehmen etc.*); **II** *v/t.* begünstigen, *j-m* hold *od.* gewogen sein; segnen, *j-m* gnädig sein (*Gott*); **pros·per·i·ty** [prɒ'sperətɪ] *s.* **1.** Wohlstand *m* (*a.* ✝), Gedeihen *n*, Glück *n*; **2.** ✝ Prosperi'tät *f*, Blüte(zeit) *f*, (*a.* ***peak ~*** 'Hoch)Konjunkˌtur *f*; **'pros·per·ous** [-pərəs] *adj.* □ **1.** gedeihend, blühend, erfolgreich, glücklich; **2.** wohlhabend, Wohlstands...; **3.** günstig (*Wind etc.*).

pros·tate (gland) ['prɒsteɪt] *s. anat.* Prostata *f*, Vorsteherdrüse *f*.

pros·the·sis ['prɒsθɪsɪs] *pl.* **-ses** [-siːz] *s.* **1.** ⚕ Pro'these *f*, künstliches Glied; **2.** ⚕ Anfertigung *f* e-r Pro'these; **3.** *ling.* Pros'these *f* (*Vorsetzen e-s Buchstabens od. e-r Silbe vor ein Wort*).

pros·ti·tute ['prɒstɪtjuːt] **I** *s.* **1.** a) Prostituierte *f*, b) *a.* ***male ~*** Strichjunge *m*; **II** *v/t.* **2.** prostituieren: ***~ o.s.*** sich prostituieren *od.* verkaufen (*a. fig.*); **3.** *fig.* (für ehrlose Zwecke) her-, preisgeben, entwürdigen, *Talente etc.* wegwerfen; **pros·ti·tu·tion** [ˌprɒstɪ'tjuːʃn] *s.* **1.** Prostituti'on *f*; **2.** *fig.* Her'ab-, Entwürdigung *f*.

pros·trate **I** *v/t.* [prɒ'streɪt] **1.** zu Boden werfen *od.* strecken, niederwerfen; **2.** ***~ o.s.*** *fig.* sich in den Staub werfen, sich demütigen (***before*** vor *dat.*); **3.** entkräften, erschöpfen; *fig.* niederschmettern; **II** *adj.* ['prɒstreɪt] **4.** hingestreckt; **5.** *fig.* erschöpft (***with*** vor *dat.*), da'niederliegend, kraftlos; *weitS.* gebrochen (***with grief*** vom Gram); **6.** *fig.* a) demütig, b) fußfällig, im Staube liegend; **pros'tra·tion** [-eɪʃn] *s.* **1.** Fußfall *m* (*a. fig.*); **2.** *fig.* Niederwerfung *f*; Demütigung *f*; **3.** Erschöpfung, Entkräftung *f*; **4.** *fig.* Niedergeschlagenheit *f*.

pros·y ['prəʊzɪ] *adj.* □ **1.** langweilig, weitschweifig; **2.** nüchtern, pro'saisch.

pro·tag·o·nist [prəʊ'tægənɪst] *s.* **1.** *thea.*

P

'Hauptfi‚gur f, Held(in), Träger(in) der Handlung; **2.** fig. Vorkämpfer(in).

pro·te·an [prəʊ'tiːən] adj. **1.** fig. pro-'teisch, vielgestaltig; **2.** zo. a'möbenartig: **~ animalcule** Amöbe f.

pro·tect [prə'tekt] v/t. **1.** (be)schützen (**from** vor dat., **against** gegen): **~ interests** Interessen wahren; **2.** ✝ (durch Zölle) schützen; **3.** ✝ a) Sichtwechsel honorieren, einlösen, b) Wechsel mit Laufzeit schützen; **4.** ⊛ (ab)sichern, abschirmen; weitS. schonen: **~ed against corrosion** korrosionsgeschützt; **~ed motor** ⚡ geschützter Motor; **5.** ✕ (taktisch) sichern, abschirmen; **6.** Schach: Figur decken; **pro-'tec·tion** [-kʃn] s. **1.** Schutz m, Be-schützung f (**from** vor dat.); Sicherheit f: **~ factor** (Licht)Schutzfaktor m; **~ money** Schutzgeld n; **~ racket** (organisierte) Schutzgelderpressung; **~ of interests** Interessenwahrung f; (**legal**) **~ of registered designs** ✐ Gebrauchsmusterschutz; **~ of industrial property** gewerblicher Rechtsschutz; **2.** ✝ Wirtschaftsschutz m, 'Schutzzoll (-poli‚tik f, -sy‚stem n) m; **3.** ✝ Honorierung f e-s Wechsels: **find due ~** honoriert werden; **4.** Protekti'on f, Gönnerschaft f, Förderung f: **~** (**money**) Am. ‚Schutzgebühr' f; **5.** ⊛ Schutz m, Abschirmung f; **pro'tec·tion·ism** [-kʃnizəm] s. ✝ 'Schutzzollpoli‚tik f; **pro'tec·tion·ist** [-kʃənist] **I** s. **1.** Protektio'nist m, Verfechter m der 'Schutzzollpoli‚tik; **2.** Na'turschützer m; **II** adj. **3.** protektio'nistisch, Schutzzoll...; **pro'tec·tive** [-tɪv] adj. □ **1.** (be)schützend, Schutz gewährend, Schutz...: **~ conveyance** ✐ Sicherungsübereignung f; **~ custody** ✐ Schutzhaft f; **~ duty** ✝ Schutzzoll m; **~ goggles** Schutzbrille f; **2.** ✝ Schutzzoll...; **3.** beschützerisch; **pro'tec·tor** [-tə] s. **1.** Beschützer m, Schutz-, Schirmherr m, Gönner m; **2.** ⊛ etc. Schutz(vorrichtung f, -mittel n) m, Schützer m, Schoner m; **3.** hist. Pro-'tektor m, Reichsverweser m; **pro'tec·tor·ate** [-tərət] s. Protekto'rat n: a) Schutzherrschaft f, b) Schutzgebiet n; **pro'tec·tress** [-trɪs] s. Beschützerin f, Schutz-, Schirmherrin f.

pro·té·gé ['prəʊteʒeɪ] (Fr.) s. Schützling m, Prote'gé m.

pro·te·in ['prəʊtiːn] s. biol. Prote'in n, Eiweiß(körper m od. pl.) n.

pro·test I s. ['prəʊtest] **1.** Pro'test m, Ein-, 'Widerspruch m: **in ~, as a ~** aus (od. als) Protest; **enter** (od. **lodge**) **a ~** Protest erheben od. Verwahrung einlegen (**with** bei); **accept under ~** unter Vorbehalt od. Protest annehmen; **2.** ✝, ✐ ('Wechsel)Pro‚test m; **3.** ♣, ✐ 'Seepro‚test m, Verklarung f; **II** v/i. [prə'test] **4.** protestieren, Verwahrung einlegen, sich verwahren (**against** gegen); **III** v/t. [prə'test] **5.** protestieren gegen, reklamieren; **6.** beteuern (**s.th.** et., **that** dass): **~ one's loyalty**; **7.** ✝ Wechsel protestieren: **have a bill ~ed** e-n Wechsel zu Protest gehen lassen.

Prot·es·tant ['prɒtɪstənt] **I** s. Prote'stant (-in); **II** adj. prote'stantisch; **'Prot·es·tant·ism** [-tɪzəm] s. Protestan'tismus m.

prot·es·ta·tion [‚prəʊteˈsteɪʃn] s. **1.** Beteuerung f; **2.** Pro'test m.

pro·to·col ['prəʊtəkɒl] **I** s. **1.** (Ver'handlungs)Proto‚koll n; **2.** pol. Proto'koll n: a) diplomatische Etikette, b) kleinere Vertragswerk; **3.** pol. Einleitungs- u. Schlussformeln pl. e-r Urkunde etc.; **II** v/t. u. v/i. **4.** protokollieren.

pro·ton ['prəʊtɒn] s. phys. Proton n.

pro·to·plasm ['prəʊtəʊplæzəm] s. biol. **1.** Proto'plasma n (Zellsubstanz); **2.** Urschleim m; **'pro·to·plast** [-plæst] s. biol. Proto'plast m.

pro·to·type ['prəʊtəʊtaɪp] s. Proto'typ m (a. biol.): a) Urbild n, -typ m, -form f, b) (Ur)Muster n; ⊛ ('Richt)Mo‚dell n, Ausgangsbautyp m.

pro·to·zo·on [‚prəʊtəʊˈzəʊən] pl. -'zo·a [-ˈzəʊə] s. zo. Proto'zoon n, Urtierchen n, Einzeller m.

pro·tract [prə'trækt] v/t. **1.** in die Länge ziehen, hin'ausziehen, verschleppen: **~ed illness** langwierige Krankheit; **~ed defence** ✕ hinhaltende Verteidigung; **2.** ⊿ mit e-m Winkelmesser od. maßstabsgetreu zeichnen od. auftragen; **pro'trac·tion** [-kʃn] s. **1.** Hin'ausschieben n, -ziehen n, Verschleppen n (a. 🐾); **2.** ⊿ maßstabsgetreue Zeichnung; **pro-'trac·tor** [-tə] s. **1.** ⊿ Transpor'teur m, Gradbogen m, Winkelmesser m; **2.** anat. Streckmuskel m.

pro·trude [prə'truːd] **I** v/i. her'aus-, (her)'vortreten, -ragen, -treten; **II** v/t. her'ausstrecken, (her)'vortreten lassen; **pro'tru·sion** [-uːʒn] s. **1.** Her'vorstehen n, -treten n, Vorspringen n; **2.** Vorwölbung f, (her)'vorstehender Teil; **pro'tru·sive** [-uːsɪv] adj. □ vorstehend, her'vortretend.

pro·tu·ber·ance [prə'tjuːbərəns] s. **1.** Auswuchs m, Beule f, Höcker m; **2.** ast. Protube'ranz f; **3.** (Her)'Vortreten n, -stehen n; **pro'tu·ber·ant** [-nt] adj. □ (her)'vorstehend, -tretend, -quellend (a. Augen).

proud [praʊd] **I** adj. □ **1.** stolz (**of** auf acc., **to** inf. zu inf.): **a ~ day** fig. ein stolzer Tag für uns etc.; **2.** hochmütig, eingebildet; **3.** fig. stolz, prächtig; **4. ~ flesh** 🐾 wildes Fleisch; **II** adv. **5.** F stolz: **do s.o. ~** a) j-m große Ehre erweisen, b) j-n königlich bewirten; **do o.s. ~** a) stolz auf sich sein können, b) es sich gut gehen lassen.

prov·a·ble ['pruːvəbl] adj. □ be-, nachweisbar, erweislich; **prove** [pruːv] **I** v/t. **1.** er-, nach-, beweisen, **2.** ✐ Testament bestätigen (lassen); **3.** bekunden, unter Beweis stellen, zeigen; **4.** (a. ⊛) prüfen, erproben: **a ~d remedy** ein erprobtes od. bewährtes Mittel; **~ o.s.** a) sich bewähren, b) sich erweisen als; → **proving** 1; **5.** ⊿ die Probe machen auf (acc.); **II** v/i. **6.** sich her'ausstellen od. erweisen (als): **he will ~** (**to be**) **the heir** es wird sich herausstellen, dass er der Erbe ist; **~ true** (**false**) a) sich als richtig (falsch) herausstellen, b) sich (nicht) bestätigen (Voraussage etc.); **7.** ausfallen, sich ergeben; **'prov·en** [-vən] adj. be-, erwiesen, nachgewiesen, fig. bewährt.

prov·e·nance ['prɒvənəns] s. Herkunft f, Ursprung m, Proveni'enz f.

prov·en·der ['prɒvɪndə] s. **1.** ➹ (Trocken)Futter n; **2.** F humor. ‚Futter' n (Lebensmittel).

prov·erb ['prɒvɜːb] **1.** s. Sprichwort n: **he is a ~ for shrewdness** s-e Schläue ist sprichwörtlich (b.s. berüchtigt); **2.** (**The Book of**) **~s** pl. bibl. die Sprüche pl. (Salo'monis; **pro·ver·bi·al** [prə'vɜːbjəl] adj. □ sprichwörtlich (a. fig.).

pro·vide [prə'vaɪd] **I** v/t. **1.** versehen, -sorgen, ausstatten, beliefern (**with** mit); **2.** ver-, beschaffen, besorgen, liefern; zur Verfügung (od. bereit)stellen; Gelegenheit schaffen; **3.** ✐ vorsehen, -schreiben, bestimmen (a. Gesetze, Vertrag etc.); **II** v/i. **4.** Vorsorge od.

Vorkehrungen treffen, vorsorgen, sich sichern (**against** vor dat., gegen): **~ against** a) sich schützen vor (dat.), b) et. unmöglich machen, verhindern; **~ for** a) sorgen für (j-s Lebensunterhalt), b) Maßnahmen vorsehen, e-r Sache Rechnung tragen, Bedürfnisse befriedigen, Gelder etc. bereitstellen; **5.** ✐ den Vorbehalt machen (**that** dass): **unless otherwise ~d** sofern nichts Gegenteiliges bestimmt ist; **providing** (**that**) → **pro'vid·ed** [-dɪd] cj. a. **~ that 1.** vor-'ausgesetzt (dass), unter der Bedingung, dass; **2.** wenn, sofern.

prov·i·dence ['prɒvɪdəns] s. **1.** (göttliche) Vorsehung; **2.** **the ℘** die Vorsehung, Gott m; **3.** Vorsorge f, (weise) Vor'aussicht; **'prov·i·dent** [-nt] adj. □ **1.** vor'ausblickend, vor-, fürsorglich: **~ bank** Sparkasse f; **~ fund** Unterstützungskasse f; **~ society** Versicherungsverein m auf Gegenseitigkeit; **2.** haushälterisch, sparsam; **prov·i·den·tial** [‚prɒvɪˈdenʃl] adj. □ **1.** schicksalhaft; **2.** glücklich, gnädig (Geschick etc.).

pro·vid·er [prə'vaɪdə] s. **1.** Versorger (-in), Ernährer m: **good ~** F treu sorgende(r) Mutter (Vater); **2.** Liefe'rant m; **3.** Internet etc.: Pro'vider m.

prov·ince ['prɒvɪns] s. **1.** Pro'vinz f (a. Ggs. Stadt), Bezirk m; **2.** fig. a) (Wissens)Gebiet n, Fach n, b) (Aufgaben-) Bereich m, Amt n: **it is not within my ~** a) es schlägt nicht in mein Fach, b) es ist nicht m-s Amtes (**to** inf. zu inf.).

pro·vin·cial [prə'vɪnʃl] **I** adj. □ **1.** Provinz..., provinzi'ell (a. fig. engstirnig, spießbürgerlich): **~ town; 2.** provinzi'ell, ländlich, kleinstädtisch; **3.** fig. contp. pro'vinzlerisch (ungebildet, plump); **II** s. **4.** Pro'vinzbewohner(in); contp. Pro'vinzler(in); **pro'vin·cial·ism** [-ʃəlɪzəm] s. Provinzia'lismus m (a. mundartlicher Ausdruck, a. contp. Kleingeisterei, Lokalpatriotismus, Plumpheit); contp. Pro'vinzlertum n.

prov·ing ['pruːvɪŋ] s. **1.** Prüfen n, Erprobung f: **~ flight** Probe-, Erprobungsflug m; **~ ground** Versuchsgelände n; **2.** **~ of a will** ✐ Eröffnung f u. Bestätigung f e-s Testaments.

pro·vi·sion [prə'vɪʒn] **I** s. **1.** a) Vorkehrung f, -sorge f, Maßnahme f, b) Vor-, Einrichtung f: **make ~** sorgen od. Vorkehrungen treffen (**for** für), sich schützen (**against** vor dat. od. gegen); **2.** ✐ Bestimmung f, Vorschrift f: **come within the ~s of the law** unter die gesetzlichen Bestimmungen fallen; **3.** ✐ Bedingung f, Vorbehalt m; **4.** Beschaffung f, Besorgung f, Bereitstellung f; **5.** pl. (Lebensmittel)Vorräte pl., Vorrat m (**of** an dat.), Nahrungsmittel pl., Pro-vi'ant m: **~s dealer** (od. **merchant**) Lebensmittel-, Feinkosthändler m; **~s industry** Nahrungsmittelindustrie f; **6.** oft pl. Rückstellungen pl., -lagen pl., Re'serven pl.: **~ for taxes** Steuerrückstellungen pl.; **II** v/t. **7.** mit Lebensmitteln versehen, verproviantieren; **pro-'vi·sion·al** [-ʒənl] adj. □ provi'sorisch, einstweilig, behelfsmäßig: **~ agreement** Vorvertrag m; **~ arrangement** Provisorium n; **~ receipt** Interimsquittung f; **~ regulations** Übergangsbestimmungen pl.; **~ result** sport vorläufiges od. inoffizielles Endergebnis.

pro·vi·so [prə'vaɪzəʊ] pl. -**so(e)s** s. ✐ Vorbehalt m, (Bedingungs)Klausel f, Bedingung f: **~ clause** Vorbehaltsklausel f; **pro'vi·so·ry** [-zərɪ] adj. □ **1.** bedingend, bedingt, vorbehaltlich; **2.** provi'sorisch, vorläufig.

pro·vo ['prəʊvəʊ] *pl.* **-vos** *s. Mitglied der provisorischen irisch-republikanischen Armee.*

prov·o·ca·tion [ˌprɒvə'keɪʃn] *s.* **1.** He'rausforderung *f,* Provokati'on *f (a.* ⚖); **2.** Aufreizung *f,* Erregung *f;* **3.** Verärgerung *f,* Ärger *m: at the slightest ~* beim geringsten Anlass; **pro·voc·a·tive** [prə'vɒkətɪv] **I** *adj. (a.* zum 'Widerspruch) her'ausfordernd, aufreizend (*of* zu), provozierend; **II** *s.* Reiz(mittel *n) m,* Antrieb *m (of* zu).

pro·voke [prə'vəʊk] *v/t.* provozieren: a) erzürnen, aufbringen, b) *et.* her'vorrufen, *Gefühl a.* erregen, c) *j-n* (auf)reizen, her'ausfordern; *~ s.o. to do s.th.* j-n dazu bewegen, et. zu tun; **pro'vok·ing** [-kɪŋ] *adj.* □ **1.** → *provocative* I; **2.** unerträglich, unausstehlich.

prov·ost ['prɒvəst] *s.* **1.** Vorsteher *m (a. univ. Brit. e-s College);* **2.** *Scot.* Bürgermeister *m;* **3.** *eccl.* Propst *m;* **4.** [prə'vəʊ] ✗ Pro'fos *m,* Offi'zier *m* der Mili'tärpoli,zei; *~ mar·shal* [prə'vəʊ] *s.* ✗ Komman'deur *m* der Mili'tärpoli,zei.

prow [praʊ] *s.* ⚓, ✈ Bug *m.*

prow·ess ['praʊɪs] *s.* **1.** Tapferkeit *f,* Kühnheit *f;* **2.** über'ragendes Können, Tüchtigkeit *f.*

prowl [praʊl] **I** *v/i.* um'herschleichen, -streichen; **II** *v/t.* durch'streifen; **III** *s.* Um'herstreifen *n,* Streife *f: be on the ~* → I; *~ car Am.* (Polizei)Streifenwagen *m;* **'prowl·er** [-lə] *s.* Her'umtreiber *m.*

prox·i·mal ['prɒksɪml] *adj.* □ *anat.* proxi'mal, körpernah; **'prox·i·mate** [-mət] *adj.* □ **1.** nächst, folgend, (sich) unmittelbar (anschließend): *~ cause* unmittelbare Ursache; **2.** nahe liegend; **3.** annähernd; **prox·im·i·ty** [prɒk'sɪmətɪ] *s.* Nähe *f: ~ fuse* ✗ Annäherungszünder *m;* **'prox·i·mo** [-məʊ] *adv.* (des) nächsten Monats.

prox·y ['prɒksɪ] *s.* **1.** (Stell)Vertretung *f,* (Handlungs)Vollmacht *f: by ~* in Vertretung (→ 2); *marriage by ~* Ferntrauung *f;* **2.** (Stell)Vertreter(in), Bevollmächtigte(r *m) f: by ~* durch e-n Bevollmächtigten; *stand ~ for s.o.* als Stellvertreter fungieren für j-n; **3.** Vollmacht(surkunde) *f.*

prude [pruːd] *s.* prüder Mensch: *be a ~* prüde sein.

pru·dence ['pruːdəns] *s.* **1.** Klugheit *f,* Vernunft *f;* **2.** 'Um-, Vorsicht *f,* Über'legtheit *f: ordinary ~* ⚖ die im Verkehr erforderliche Sorgfalt; **'pru·dent** [-nt] *adj.* □ **1.** klug, vernünftig; **2.** 'um-, vorsichtig, besonnen; **pru·dential** [prʊ'denʃl] *adj.* □ a) → *prudent,* b) sachverständig: *for ~ reasons* aus Gründen praktischer Überlegung.

prud·er·y ['pruːdərɪ] *s.* Prüde'rie *f;* **'prud·ish** [-dɪʃ] *adj.* □ prüde.

prune¹ [pruːn] *s.* **1.** (*a.* Back)Pflaume *f;* **2.** *sl.* ˌBlödmann' *m.*

prune² [pruːn] *v/t.* **1.** *Bäume etc.* (aus-)putzen, beschneiden; **2.** *a. ~ off, ~ away* wegschneiden; **3.** *fig.* zu('recht-) stutzen, befreien (*of* von), säubern, *Text etc.* zs.-streichen, straffen, kürzen, *Überflüssiges* entfernen.

pru·nel·la¹ [prʊ'nelə] *s.* ✝ Pru'nell *m,* Lasting *m (Gewebe).*

pru·nel·la² [prʊ'nelə] *s.* ✍ *obs.* Halsbräune *f.*

pru·nelle [prʊ'nel] *s.* Prü'nelle *f (getrocknete entkernte Pflaume).*

pru·nel·lo [prʊ'neləʊ] → *prunelle.*

prun·ing knife ['pruːnɪŋ] *s. [irr.]* Gartenmesser *n; ~ shears s. pl.* Baumschere *f.*

---

pru·ri·ence ['prʊərɪəns], **'pru·ri·en·cy** [-sɪ] *s.* **1.** Geilheit *f,* Lüsternheit *f;* (Sinnen)Kitzel *m;* **2.** Gier *f (for* nach); **'pru·ri·ent** [-nt] *adj.* □ geil, lüstern, las'ziv.

Prus·sian ['prʌʃn] **I** *adj.* preußisch; **II** *s.* Preuße *m,* Preußin *f; ~ blue s.* Preußischblau *n.*

prus·si·ate ['prʌʃɪət] *s.* 🝆 Prussi'at *n; ~ of pot·ash s.* 🝆 'Kaliumferrozya,nid *n.*

prus·sic ac·id ['prʌsɪk] *s.* 🝆 Blausäure *f,* Zy'anwasserstoff(säure *f) m.*

pry¹ [praɪ] *v/i.* neugierig gucken *od.* sein, (*about* her'um)spähen, (-)schnüffeln: *~ into* a) *et.* zu erforschen suchen, b) *contp.* s-e Nase stecken in (*acc.*).

pry² [praɪ] **I** *v/t.* **1.** *a. ~ open* mit e-m *Hebel etc.* aufbrechen, -stemmen: *~ up* hochstemmen, -heben; **2.** *fig.* her'ausholen; **II** *s.* **3.** Hebel *m;* Brecheisen *n;* **4.** Hebelwirkung *f.*

pry·ing ['praɪɪŋ] *adj.* □ neugierig, naseweis.

psalm [sɑːm] *s.* Psalm *m: the (Book of) ₂s bibl.* die Psalmen; **'psalm·ist** [-mɪst] *s.* Psal'mist *m;* **psal·mo·dy** ['sælmədɪ] *s.* **1.** Psalmo'die *f,* Psalmengesang *m;* **2.** Psalmen *pl.*

Psal·ter ['sɔːltə] *s.* Psalter *m,* (Buch *n* der) Psalmen *pl.;* **psal·te·ri·um** [sɔːl'tɪərɪəm] *pl.* **-ri·a** [-rɪə] *s. zo.* Blättermagen *m.*

pse·phol·o·gy [pse'fɒlədʒɪ] *s.* (wissenschaftliche) Ana'lyse von Wahlergebnissen u. -trends.

pseu·do- ['sjuː|dəʊ] *in Zssgn* Pseudo..., pseudo..., falsch, unecht; **ˌpseu·do'carp** [-'kɑːp] *s.* ♀ Scheinfrucht *f;* **'pseu·do·nym** [-dənɪm] *s.* Pseudo'nym *n,* Deckname *m;* **ˌpseu·do'nym·i·ty** [-də'nɪmətɪ] *s.* **1.** Pseudonymi'tät *f;* **2.** Führen *n* e-s Pseudo'nyms; **pseu'don·y·mous** [-'dɒnɪməs] *adj.* □ pseudo'nym.

pshaw [pʃɔː] *int.* pah!

psit·ta·co·sis [ˌpsɪtə'kəʊsɪs] *s.* ✍ Papa'geienkrankheit *f.*

pso·ri·a·sis [psɒ'raɪəsɪs] *s.* ✍ Schuppenflechte *f,* Pso'riasis *f.*

Psy·che ['saɪkɪ] *s.* **1.** *myth.* Psyche *f;* **2.** ₂ Psyche *f,* Seele *f,* Geist *m.*

psy·che·del·ic [ˌsaɪkɪ'delɪk] *adj.* psyche'delisch, bewusstseinserweiternd.

psy·chi·at·ric, psy·chi·at·ri·cal [ˌsaɪkɪ'ætrɪk(l)] *adj.* psychi'atrisch; **psy·chi·a·trist** [saɪ'kaɪətrɪst] *s.* ✍ Psychi'ater *m;* **psy'chi·a·try** [saɪ'kaɪətrɪ] *s.* ✍ Psychiat'rie *f.*

psy·chic ['saɪkɪk] **I** *adj.* (□ *~ally*) **1.** psychisch, seelisch(-geistig), Seelen...; **2.** 'übersinnlich: *~ forces* übersinnliche Kräfte *pl.; ~ healer* Geistheiler(in); **3.** medi'al (veranlagt), F ˌhellseherisch'; **4.** parapsycho'logisch: *~ research* Para'Forschung *f;* **II** *s.* **5.** medi'al veranlagte Per'son, Medium *n;* **6.** das Psychische; **7.** *pl. sg. konstr.* a) Seelenkunde *f,* -forschung *f,* b) Parapsycholo'gie *f;* **'psy·chi·cal** [-kl] *adj.* □ → *psychic* I.

psy·cho·a·nal·y·sis [ˌsaɪkəʊ'næləsɪs] *s.* ˌPsychoana'lyse *f;* **psy·cho·an·a·lyst** [ˌsaɪkəʊ'ænəlɪst] *s.* ˌPsychoana'lytiker (-in).

psy·cho·graph ['saɪkəʊgrɑːf] *s.* Psycho'gramm *n.*

psy·cho·log·ic [ˌsaɪkə'lɒdʒɪk] → *psychological;* **ˌpsy·cho'log·i·cal** [-kl] *adj.* □ psycho'logisch: *~ moment* richtiger Augenblick; *~ warfare* a) psychologische Kriegführung, b) *fig.* Nervenkrieg *m;* **psy·chol·o·gist** [saɪ'kɒlədʒɪst] *s.* Psycho'loge *m,* Psycho'login *f;* **psy·chol·o·gy** [saɪ'kɒlədʒɪ] *s.* Psycholo'gie *f*

(*Wissenschaft od. Seelenleben*): *good ~ fig.* das psychologisch Richtige.

psy·cho·path ['saɪkəʊpæθ] *s.* Psycho'path(in); **psy·cho·path·ic** [ˌsaɪkəʊ'pæθɪk] I *adj.* psycho'pathisch; II *s.* Psycho'path(in); **psy·cho·pa·thy** [saɪ'kɒpəθɪ] *s.* Psychopa'thie *f,* Gemütskrankheit *f.*

psy·cho·sis [saɪ'kəʊsɪs] *pl.* **-ses** [-siːz] *s.* Psy'chose *f (a. fig.).*

psy·cho·ther·a·py [ˌsaɪkəʊ'θerəpɪ] *s.* ✍ ˌPsychothera'pie *f.*

psy·chot·ic [saɪ'kɒtɪk] I *adj.* □ psy'chotisch; II *s.* Psy'chotiker(in).

ptar·mi·gan ['tɑːmɪgən] *s. zo.* Schneehuhn *n.*

pto·maine ['təʊmeɪn] *s.* ✍ Ptoma'in *n,* Leichengift *n.*

pub [pʌb] *s. bsd. Brit.* F Pub *n od.* m, Kneipe *f; ~ crawl s. bsd. Brit.* F Kneipenbummel *m.*

pu·ber·ty ['pjuːbətɪ] *s.* **1.** Puber'tät *f,* Geschlechtsreife *f;* **2.** *a. age of ~* Puber'tät(salter *n) f: ~ vocal change* Stimmbruch *m.*

pu·bes¹ ['pjuːbiːz] *s. anat.* a) Schamgegend *f,* b) Schamhaare *pl.*

pu·bes² ['pjuːbiːz] *pl. von pubis.*

pu·bes·cence [pjuː'besns] *s.* **1.** Geschlechtsreife *f;* **2.** ♀, *zo.* Flaumhaar *n;* **pu'bes·cent** [-nt] *adj.* **1.** geschlechtsreif (werdend); **2.** Pubertäts...; **3.** ♀, *zo.* fein behaart.

pu·bic ['pjuːbɪk] *adj. anat.* Scham...

pu·bis ['pjuːbɪs] *pl.* **-bes** [-biːz] *s. anat.* Schambein *n.*

pub·lic ['pʌblɪk] **I** *adj.* □ **1.** öffentlich stattfindend (*z.B.* Verhandlung, Versammlung, Versteigerung): *~ notice* öffentliche Bekanntmachung, Aufgebot *n; in the ~ eye* im Lichte der Öffentlichkeit; **2.** öffentlich, allgemein bekannt: *~ figure* Persönlichkeit *f* des öffentlichen Lebens, prominente Gestalt; *go ~* a) sich an die Öffentlichkeit wenden, b) ✝ sich in e-e AG umwandeln; *make ~* (allgemein) bekannt machen; **3.** a) öffentlich (*z.B. Anstalt, Bad, Dienst, Feiertag, Kredit, Sicherheit, Straße, Verkehrsmittel*), b) Staats..., staatlich (*z.B. Anleihe, Behörde, Papiere, Schuld, Stellung*), c) Volks... (*-bücherei, -gesundheit etc.*), d) Gemeinde..., Stadt...: *~ accountant Am.* Wirtschaftsprüfer (in); *~-address system* öffentliche Lautsprecheranlage; *₂ Assistance Am.* Sozialhilfe *f; ~ borrowing* staatliche Kreditaufnahme; *~ charge* Sozialhilfeempfänger(in); *~ (limited) company* ✝ *Brit.* Aktiengesellschaft *f; ~ convenience* öffentliche Bedürfnisanstalt; *~ corporation* ⚖ öffentlich-rechtliche Körperschaft; *~ economy* Volkswirtschaft(slehre) *f; ~ enemy* Staatsfeind *m; ~ expenditure* öffentliche Ausgaben *pl.; ~ health policy* Gesundheitspolitik *f; ~ house bsd. Brit.* → *pub; ~ information* Unterrichtung *f* der Öffentlichkeit; *~ law* öffentliches Recht; *~ opinion* öffentliche Meinung; *~ opinion poll* öffentliche Umfrage, Meinungsbefragung *f; ~ relations* a) Public Relations *pl.,* Öffentlichkeitsarbeit *f,* b) *attr.* Presse..., Werbe..., Public-Relations...; *~ revenue* Staatseinkünfte *pl.; ~ school* a) *Brit.* Public School *f,* höhere Privatschule mit Internat, b) *Am.* staatliche Schule; *~ sector spending* öffentliche Ausgaben *pl.; ~ service* a) Staatsdienst *m,* b) öffentliche Versorgung (*Gas, Wasser, Elektrizität etc.*); *~ servant* a) (Staats)Beamte(r *m) m,* b) Angestellte(r) *m* im öffentlichen Dienst; *~ works* öffentliche (Bau)Arbeiten; → *nuisance* 2, *policy*[1] 3, *prosecutor*, *utility* 3; **4.** natio'nal: ~ *disaster*; **II** *s.* **5.** Öffentlichkeit *f*: *in* ~ in der Öffentlichkeit, öffentlich; **6.** *sg. u. pl. konstr.* Öffentlichkeit *f*, *die* Leute *pl.*; *das* Publikum; Kreise *pl.*, Welt *f*: *appear before the* ~ an die Öffentlichkeit treten; *exclude the* ~ ᵗⁱ die Öffentlichkeit ausschließen; **7.** *Brit.* F → *pub*; '**pub·li·can** [-kən] *s.* **1.** *Brit.* (Gast)Wirt *m*; **2.** *hist., bibl.* Zöllner *m*; **pub·li·ca·tion** [ˌpʌblɪ'keɪʃn] *s.* **1.** Bekanntmachung *f*, -gabe *f*; **2.** Her'ausgabe *f*, Veröffentlichung *f* (*von Druckwerken*); **3.** Publikati'on *f*, Veröffentlichung *f*, Verlagswerk *n*; (Druck)Schrift *f*: *monthly* ~ Monatsschrift *f*; *new* ~ Neuerscheinung *f*; '**pub·li·cist** [-ɪsɪst] *s.* **1.** Publi'zist *m*, Tagesschriftsteller *m*; **2.** Völkerrechtler *m*; **pub·lic·i·ty** [pʌb'lɪsətɪ] *s.* **1.** Publizi'tät *f*, Öffentlichkeit *f* (*a.* ᵗⁱ *des Verfahrens*): *give s.th.* ~ et. allgemein bekannt machen; *seek* ~ bekannt werden wollen; **2.** Re'klame *f*, Werbung *f*, Pu'blicity *f*: ~ *agent*, ~ *man* Werbefachmann *m*; ~ *campaign* Werbefeldzug *m*; ~ *manager* Werbeleiter *m*; '**pub·li·cize** [-ɪsaɪz] *v/t.* **1.** publizieren, (öffentlich) bekannt machen; **2.** Re'klame machen für, propagieren; ˌ**pub·lic|-'pri·vate** *adj.* ✝ gemischtwirtschaftlich; ˌ~-'**spir·it·ed** *adj.* gemeinsinnig, sozi'al gesinnt.

pub·lish ['pʌblɪʃ] *v/t.* **1.** (offizi'ell) bekannt machen *od.* geben; *Aufgebot etc.* verkünd(ig)en; **2.** publizieren, veröffentlichen; **3.** *Buch etc.* verlegen, he'rausbringen: *just* ~*ed* (so)eben erschienen; ~*ed by Methuen* im Verlag Methuen erschienen; ~*ed by the author* im Selbstverlag; **4.** ᵗⁱ *Beleidigendes* äußern, verbreiten; '**pub·lish·er** [-ʃə] *s.* **1.** Verleger *m*, Her'ausgeber *m*; *bsd. Am.* Zeitungsverleger *m*; **2.** *pl.* Verlag *m*, Verlagsanstalt *f*; '**pub·lish·ing** [-ʃɪŋ] **I** *s.* Her'ausgabe *f*, Verlag *m*; **II** *adj.* Verlags...: ~ *business* Verlagsgeschäft *n*, -buchhandel *m*; ~ *house* → *publisher* 2.

puce [pjuːs] *adj.* braunrot.

puck [pʌk] *s.* **1.** Kobold *m*; **2.** *Eishockey*: Puck *m*, Scheibe *f*.

puck·a ['pʌkə] *adj. Brit.* F **1.** echt, wirklich; **2.** erstklassig, tadellos.

puck·er ['pʌkə] **I** *v/t. oft* ~ *up* **1.** runzeln, fälteln, Runzeln *od.* Falten bilden in (*dat.*); **2.** *Mund, Lippen etc.* spitzen; *a. Stirn, Stoff* kräuseln; **II** *v/i.* **3.** sich kräuseln, sich zs.-ziehen, sich falten, Runzeln bilden; **III** *s.* **4.** Runzel *f*, Falte *f*; **5.** Bausch *m*; **6.** F Aufregung *f* (*about* über *acc.*, wegen).

pud·ding ['pʊdɪŋ] *s.* **1.** a) Pudding *m*, b) Nach-, Süßspeise *f*; → *proof* 6; **2.** *Art* 'Fleischpaˌstete *f*; **3.** *e-e Wurstsorte*: *black* ~ Blutwurst *f*; *white* ~ Presssack *m*; '~-**faced** *adj.* mit e-m Vollmondgesicht.

pud·dle ['pʌdl] **I** *s.* **1.** Pfütze *f*, Lache *f*; **2.** ⊙ Lehmschlag *m*; **II** *v/t.* **3.** mit Pfützen bedecken; in Matsch verwandeln; **4.** *Wasser* trüben (*a. fig.*); **5.** *Lehm* zu Lehmschlag verarbeiten; **6.** mit Lehmschlag abdichten *od.* auskleiden; **7.** *metall.* puddeln: ~(*d*) *steel* Puddelstahl *m*; **III** *v/i.* **8.** he'rumplan(t)schen *od.* -waten; **9.** *fig.* her'umpfuschen; '**pud·dler** [-lə] *s.* ⊙ Puddler *m* (*Arbeiter od. Gerät*).

pu·den·cy ['pjuːdənsɪ] *s.* Verschämtheit *f*.

pu·den·dum [pjuː'dendəm] *mst im pl.* **-da** [-də] *s.* (weibliche) Scham, Vulva *f*.

pu·dent ['pjuːdənt] *adj.* verschämt.

pudg·y ['pʌdʒɪ] *adj.* dicklich.

pu·er·ile ['pjʊəraɪl] *adj.* □ pue'ril, knabenhaft, kindlich, *contp.* kindisch; **pu·er·il·i·ty** [pjʊə'rɪlətɪ] *s.* **1.** Puerili'tät *f*, kindliche *od.* kindisches Wesen; **2.** Kinde'rei *f*.

pu·er·per·al [pjuː'ɜːpərəl] *adj.* Kindbett...: ~ *fever*.

puff [pʌf] **I** *s.* **1.** Hauch *m*; (leichter) Windstoß; **2.** Zug *m beim Rauchen*; Paffen *n der Pfeife etc.*; **3.** (Rauch-, Dampf)Wölkchen *n*; **4.** leichter Knall; **5.** *Bäckerei*: Windbeutel *m*; **6.** Puderquaste *f*; **7.** Puffe *f*, Bausch *m* an *Kleidern*; **8.** a) marktschreierische Anpreisung, aufdringliche Re'klame, b) lobhudelnde Kri'tik: ~ *is part of the trade* Klappern gehört zum Handwerk; **II** *v/t.* **9.** blasen, pusten (*away* weg, *out* aus); **10.** auspuffen, -paffen, -stoßen; **11.** *Zigarre etc.* paffen; **12.** *oft* ~ *out*, ~ *up* aufblasen, (-)blähen; *fig.* aufgeblasen machen: ~*ed up with pride* stolzgeschwellt; ~*ed eyes* geschwollene Augen; ~*ed sleeve* Puffärmel *m*; ~*ed* außer Atem bringen: ~*ed* außer Atem; **14.** marktschreierisch anpreisen: ~ *up Preise* hochtreiben; **III** *v/i.* **15.** paffen (*at* an *e-r Zigarre etc.*); Rauch- *od.* Dampfwölkchen ausstoßen; **16.** pusten, schnaufen, keuchen; **17.** *Lokomotive etc.* (da'hin)dampfen, keuchen; **18.** ~ *out* (*od.* ~ *up*) sich (auf)blähen; **ad·der** *s. zo.* Puffotter *f*; '~·**ball** *s.* ♀ Bofist *m*.

puff·er ['pʌfə] *s.* **1.** Paffer *m*; **2.** Marktschreier *m*; **3.** Preistreiber *m*, Scheinbieter *m bei Auktionen*; '**puff·er·y** [-ərɪ] *s.* Marktschreie'rei *f*.

puf·fin ['pʌfɪn] *s. orn.* Lund *m*, Papa'geientaucher *m*.

puff·i·ness ['pʌfɪnɪs] *s.* **1.** Aufgeblähtheit *f*, Aufgeblasenheit *f* (*a. fig.*); **2.** (Auf)Gedunsenheit *f*; **3.** Schwulst *m*; **puff·ing** ['pʌfɪŋ] *s.* **1.** Aufbauschung *f*, Aufblähung *f*; **2.** → *puff* 8 a; **3.** Scheinbieten *n bei Auktionen*, Preistreibe'rei *f*; **puff paste** *s.* Blätterteig *m*; **puff·y** ['pʌfɪ] *adj.* □ **1.** bög (*Wind*); **2.** kurzatmig, keuchend; **3.** aufgebläht, (an)geschwollen; **4.** bauschig (*Ärmel*); **5.** aufgedunsen, dick; **6.** *fig.* schwülstig.

pug[1] [pʌg] *s. a.* ~ *dog* Mops *m*.

pug[2] [pʌg] *v/t.* **1.** *Lehm etc.* mischen u. kneten; schlagen; **2.** mit Lehmschlag *etc.* ausfüllen *od.* abdichten.

pug[3] [pʌg] *s. sl.* Boxer *m*.

pu·gil·ism ['pjuːdʒɪlɪzəm] *s.* (Berufs-) Boxen *n*; '**pu·gil·ist** [-ɪst] *s.* (Berufs-) Boxer *m*.

pug·na·cious [pʌg'neɪʃəs] *adj.* □ **1.** kampflustig, kämpferisch; **2.** streitsüchtig; **pug·nac·i·ty** [-'næsətɪ] *s.* **1.** Kampflust *f*; **2.** Streitsucht *f*.

pug nose *s.* Stupsnase *f*; '~-**nosed** *adj.* stupsnasig.

puis·ne ['pjuːnɪ] **I** *adj.* ᵗⁱ rangjünger, 'untergeordnet: ~ *judge* → **II**; **II** *s.* 'Unterrichter *m*, dem Beisitzer *m*.

puke [pjuːk] F **I** *v/t. u. v/i.* (sich) erbrechen, ˌkotzen'; **II** *s.* ˌKotze' *f*.

puk·ka ['pʌkə] → *pucka*.

pul·chri·tude ['pʌlkrɪtjuːd] *s. bsd. Am.* (weibliche) Schönheit; **pul·chri·tu·di·nous** [ˌpʌlkrɪ'tjuːdɪnəs] *adj. Am.* schön.

pule [pjuːl] *v/i.* **1.** wimmern, winseln; **2.** piepsen.

pull [pʊl] **I** *s.* **1.** Ziehen *n*, Zerren *n*; **2.** Zug *m*, Ruck *m*: *give a strong* ~ (*at*) kräftig ziehen (an *dat.*); **3.** *mot. etc.* Zug(kraft *f*) *m*, Ziehkraft *f*; **4.** Anzie-

hungskraft *f* (*a. fig.*); **5.** *fig.* Zug-, Werbekraft *f*; **6.** Zug *m*, Schluck *m* (*at* aus); **7.** Zug(griff) *m*, -leine *f*: *bell* ~ Glockenzug; **8.** a) Bootsfahrt *f*, 'Ruderparˌtie *f*, b) Ruderschlag *m*; **9.** (*long* ~ große) Anstrengung, ˌSchlauch' *m*, *fig.* Durststrecke *f*; **10.** ermüdende Steigung; **11.** Vorteil *m* (*over, of* vor *dat.*, gegen'über); **12.** *sl.* (*with*) (heimlicher) Einfluss (auf *acc.*), Beziehungen *pl.* (zu); **13.** *typ.* Fahne *f*, (erster) Abzug; **II** *v/t.* **14.** ziehen, schleppen; **15.** zerren (an *dat.*), zupfen (an *dat.*): ~ *about* umherzerren; ~ *a muscle* sich e-e Muskelzerrung zuziehen; → *face* 2, *leg Bes. Redew.*, *string* 3, *trigger* 2; **16.** reißen: ~ *apart* auseinander reißen; ~ *to pieces* a) zerreißen, in Stücke reißen, b) *fig.* (in e-r *Kritik etc.*) ˌverreißen'; ~ *o.s. together fig.* sich zs.-reißen; **17.** *Pflanze* ausreißen; *Korken, Zahn* ziehen; *Blumen, Obst* pflücken; *Flachs* raufen; *Gans etc.* rupfen; *Leder* enthaaren; **18.** ~ *one's punches Boxen*: verhalten schlagen, *fig.* sich zurückhalten; *not to* ~ *one's punches fig.* vom Leder ziehen, kein Blatt vor den Mund nehmen; **19.** *Pferd* zügeln; *Rennpferd* pullen; **20.** *Boot* rudern: ~ *a good oar* gut rudern; → *weight* 1; **21.** *Am. Messer etc.* ziehen: ~ *a pistol on* j-n mit der Pistole bedrohen; **22.** *typ. Fahne* abziehen; **23.** *sl. et.* ˌdrehen', ˌschaukeln' (*ausführen*): ~ *the job* das Ding drehen; ~ *a fast one on s.o.* j-n ˌreinlegen'; **24.** *sl.* ˌschnappen' (*verhaften*); **25.** *sl.* e-e Razzia machen auf (*acc.*), *Spielhölle etc.* ausheben; **III** *v/i.* **26.** ziehen (*at* an *dat.*); **27.** zerren, reißen (*at* an *dat.*); **28.** *a.* ~ *against the bit* am Zügel reißen (*Pferd*); **29.** a) e-n Zug machen, trinken (*at* an *e-r Flasche*), b) ziehen (*at* an *e-r Pfeife etc.*); **30.** *gut etc.* ziehen (*Pfeife etc.*); **31.** sich vorwärts arbeiten, bewegen *od.* schieben: ~ *into the station* ᵗⁱ (in den Bahnhof) einfahren; **32.** rudern, pullen: ~ *together fig.* zs.-arbeiten; **33.** (her'an)fahren (*to the kerb* an den Bordstein); **34.** *sl.* ˌziehen', Zugkraft haben (*Reklame*).

Zssgn mit adv.:

pull a·way **I** *v/t.* **1.** wegziehen, -reißen; **II** *v/i.* **2.** anfahren (*Bus etc.*); **3.** sich losreißen; **4.** *a. sport* sich absetzen (*from* von); ~ **down** *v/t.* **1.** her'unterziehen, -reißen; *Gebäude* abreißen; **2.** *fig.* he'runterreißen, her'absetzen; **3.** j-n schwächen; *j-n* entmutigen; ~ **in I** *v/t.* **1.** (her)'einziehen; **2.** *Pferd* zügeln, parieren; **II** *v/i.* **3.** anhalten, stehen bleiben; **4.** hin'einrudern; ᵗⁱ einfahren; ~ **off I** *v/t.* **1.** wegziehen, -reißen; **2.** *Schuhe etc.* ausziehen; *Hut* abnehmen (*to* vor *dat.*); **3.** *Preis, Sieg* da'vontragen, erringen; **4.** F *et.* ˌschaukeln', ˌschaffen'; **II** *v/i.* **5.** sich in Bewegung setzen, abfahren; abstoßen (*Boot*); ~ **on** *v/t.* *Kleid etc.* anziehen; ~ **out I** *v/t.* **1.** her'ausziehen; ✕ *Truppen* abziehen; **2.** ✈ *Flugzeug* hochziehen, aus dem Sturzflug abfangen; **3.** *fig.* in die Länge ziehen; **II** *v/i.* **4.** hin'ausrudern; abfahren (*Zug etc.*); ausscheren (*Fahrzeug*); ✕ abziehen; *fig.* ˌaussteigen' (*of* aus); ~ **round I** *v/t.* *Kranken* wieder ˌhinkriegen', 'durchbringen; **II** *v/i.* wieder auf die Beine kommen, 'durchkommen, sich erholen; ~ **through I** *v/t.* **1.** (hin-) 'durchziehen; **2.** *fig.* a) j-m 'durchhelfen, b) → *pull round* I; **3.** *et.* erfolgreich 'durchführen; **II** *v/i.* **4.** → *pull round* II; **5.** sich 'durchschlagen; ~ **up** *v/t.* **1.** hochziehen (*a.* ✈); ⚓ *Flagge* hissen; **2.** *Pferd, Wagen* anhalten; **3.** *j-n* zu'rückhalten, *j-m* Einhalt gebieten; *j-n* zur Rede stellen; **II** *v/i.* **4.** (an)halten, vorfahren; **5.** *fig.* bremsen; **6.** *sport* sich nach vorn schieben: ~ *to* (*od.* *with*) *j-n* einholen.

'**pull**|·**back** *s.* **1.** Hemmnis *n*; **2.** ✕ Rückzug *m*; ~ **date** *s.* ✝ Haltbarkeitsdatum *n*.

pul·let ['pʊlɪt] *s.* Hühnchen *n*.

pul·ley ['pʊlɪ] ⊕ *s.* **1.** a) Rolle *f* (*bsd. Flaschenzug*): *rope* ~ Seilrolle *f*; *block and* ~, *set of* ~*s* Flaschenzug *m*, b) Flasche *f* (*Verbindung mehrerer Rollen*), c) Flaschenzug *m*; **2.** ⚓ Talje *f*; **3.** *a.* **belt** ~ Riemenscheibe *f*; ~ **block** *s.* ⊕ (Roll)Kloben *m*; ~ **chain** *s.* Flaschenzugkette *f*; ~ **drive** *s.* Riemenscheibenantrieb *m*.

Pull·man (**car**) ['pʊlmən] *pl.* **-mans** *s.* 🚃 Pullmanwagen *m*.

'**pull**|·**off** **I** *s.* ➹ Lösen *n* des Fallschirms (*beim Absprung*); **2.** *leichter etc.* Abzug (*Schusswaffe*); **II** *adj.* **3.** ⊕ Abzieh...(-*feder*); '~·**out** **I** *s.* **1.** Faltblatt *n*; **2.** (*Zeitschriften*)Beilage *f*; **3.** ✕ (Truppen)Abzug *m*; **II** *adj.* **4.** ausziehbar: ~ *map* Faltkarte *f*; ~ *seat* Schiebesitz *m*; '~·**o·ver** *s.* Pull'over *m*; ~ **switch** *s.* 🗲 Zugschalter *m*.

pul·lu·late ['pʌljʊleɪt] *v/i.* **1.** (her'vor-) sprossen, knospen; **2.** Knospen treiben; **3.** keimen (*Samen*); **4.** *biol.* sich (*durch Knospung*) vermehren; **5.** *fig.* wuchern, grassieren; **6.** *fig.* wimmeln.

'**pull**·**up** *s.* **1.** *Brit. mot.* Raststätte *f*; **2.** Klimmzug *m*.

pul·mo·nar·y ['pʌlmənərɪ] *adj. anat.* Lungen...; '**pul·mo·nate** [-neɪt] *zo. adj.* Lungen..., mit Lungen (ausgestattet): ~ (*mollusc*) Lungenschnecke *f*; **pul·mon·ic** [pʌl'mɒnɪk] **I** *adj.* Lungen...; **II** *s.* Lungenheilmittel *n*.

pulp [pʌlp] **I** *s.* **1.** Fruchtfleisch *n*, -mark *n*; **2.** ♀ Stängelmark *n*; **3.** *anat.* (Zahn-) Pulpa *f*; **4.** Brei *m*, breiige Masse: *beat to a* ~ *fig. j-n* zu Brei schlagen; **5.** ⊕ a) Pa'pierbrei *m*, Pulpe *f*, *bsd.* Ganzzeug *n*, b) Zellstoff *m*: ~ *board* Zellstoffpappe *f*; ~ *engine* → *pulper* 1; ~ *factory* Holzschleiferei *f*; **6.** Maische *f*, Schnitzel *pl.* (*Zucker*); **7.** *Am.* a) Schund *m*, b) *a.* ~ *magazine Am.* Schundblatt *n*; **II** *v/t.* **8.** in Brei verwandeln; **9.** *Papier* einstampfen; **10.** *Früchte* entfleischen; **III** *v/i.* **11.** breiig werden *od.* sein; '**pulp·er** [-pə] *s.* **1.** ⊕ (Ganzzeug)Holländer *m* (*Papier*); **2.** ✔ (Rüben)Breimühle *f*; '**pulp·i·fy** [-pɪfaɪ] *v/t.* in Brei verwandeln; '**pulp·i·ness** [-pɪnɪs] *s.* **1.** Weichheit *f*; **2.** Fleischigkeit *f*; **3.** Matschigkeit *f*.

pul·pit ['pʊlpɪt] *s.* **1.** Kanzel *f*: *in the* ~ auf der Kanzel; ~ *orator* Kanzelredner *m*; **2.** *the* ~ *coll.* die Geistlichkeit; **3.** *fig.* Kanzel *f*; **4.** ⊕ Bedienungsstand *m*.

pulp·y ['pʌlpɪ] *adj.* □ **1.** weich u. saftig; **2.** fleischig; **3.** schwammig; **4.** breiig, matschig.

pul·sate [pʌl'seɪt] *v/i.* **1.** pulsieren (*a.* 🗲), (rhythmisch) pochen *od.* schlagen; **2.** vibrieren; **3.** *fig.* pulsieren (*with* von *Leben, Erregung*); **pul·sa·tile** ['pʌlsətaɪl] *adj.* ♪ Schlag...: ~ *instrument*; **pul·sat·ing** [-tɪŋ] *adj.* **1.** 🗲 pulsierend (*a. fig.*), stoßweise; **2.** *fig.* beschwingt (*Rhythmus, Weise*); **pul·sa·tion** [-eɪʃn] *s.* **1.** Pulsieren *n* (*a. fig.*), Pochen *n*, Schlagen *n*; **2.** Pulsschlag *m* (*a. fig.*); **3.** Vibrieren *n*.

pulse¹ [pʌls] **I** *s.* **1.** Puls(schlag) *m* (*a. fig.*): *quick* ~ schneller Puls; ~ *rate* 🖉

Pulszahl *f*; *feel s.o.'s* ~ a) j-m den Puls fühlen, b) *fig.* j-m auf den Zahn fühlen, bei j-m vorfühlen; **2.** 🗲, *phys.* Im'puls *m*, (Strom)Stoß *m*; **II** *v/i.* **3.** → *pulsate*.

pulse² [pʌls] *s.* Hülsenfrüchte *pl.*

pul·ver·i·za·tion [,pʌlvəraɪ'zeɪʃn] *s.* **1.** Pulverisierung *f*, (Feinst)Mahlung *f*; **2.** Zerstäubung *f von Flüssigkeiten*; **3.** *fig.* Zermalmung *f*; **pul·ver·ize** ['pʌlvəraɪz] **I** *v/t.* **1.** pulverisieren, *zu Staub* zermahlen, -stoßen, -reiben: ~*d coal* fein gemahlene Kohlen *pl.*, Kohlenstaub *m*; **2.** *Flüssigkeit* zerstäuben; **3.** *fig.* zermalmen; **II** *v/i.* **4.** (in Staub) zerfallen; **pul·ver·iz·er** ['pʌlvəraɪzə] *s.* **1.** ⊕ Zerkleinerer *m*, Pulverisiermühle *f*, Mahlanlage *f*; **2.** Zerstäuber *m*; **pul·ver·u·lent** [pʌl'verjələnt] *adj.* **1.** (fein)pulverig; **2.** (leicht) zerbröckelnd; **3.** staubig.

pu·ma ['pjuːmə] *s. zo.* Puma *m*.

pum·ice ['pʌmɪs] **I** *s. a.* ~ *stone* Bimsstein *m*; **II** *v/t.* mit Bimsstein abreiben, (ab)bimsen.

pum·mel ['pʌml] → *pommel* II.

pump¹ [pʌmp] **I** *s.* **1.** Pumpe *f*: (*dispensing*) ~ *mot.* Zapfsäule *f*; ~ *priming* a) Anlassen *n* der Pumpe, b) ✝ Ankurbelung *f* der Wirtschaft; **2.** Pumpen(stoß *m*) *n*; **II** *v/t.* **3.** pumpen: ~ *dry* auspumpen, leer pumpen; ~ *out* auspumpen (*a. fig. erschöpfen*); ~ *up* a) hochpumpen, b) *Reifen* aufpumpen (*a. fig.*); ~ *bullets into fig. j-m* Kugeln in den Leib jagen; ~ *money into* ✝ Geld in *et.* hineinpumpen; **4.** *fig. j-n* ausholen, -fragen, -horchen; **III** *v/i.* **5.** pumpen (*a. fig. Herz etc.*).

pump² [pʌmp] *s.* **1.** Pumps *m* (*Halbschuh*); **2.** *Brit.* Turnschuh *m*.

'**pump-**,**han·dle I** *s.* Pumpenschwengel *m*; **II** *v/t.* F *j-s Hand* 'überschwänglich schütteln.

pump·kin ['pʌmpkɪn] *s.* ♀ (*bsd.* Garten-) Kürbis *m*.

pump room *s.* Trinkhalle *f in Kurbädern*.

pun [pʌn] **I** *s.* Wortspiel *n* (*on* über *acc.*, mit); **II** *v/i.* Wortspiele *od.* ein Wortspiel machen, witzeln.

punch¹ [pʌntʃ] **I** *s.* **1.** (Faust)Schlag *m*: *beat s.o. to the* ~ *Am. fig.* j-m zuvorkommen; → *pull* 18; **2.** Schlagkraft *f* (*a. fig.*); → *pack* 20; **3.** F Wucht *f*, Schmiss *m*, Schwung *m*; **II** *v/t.* **4.** (*mit der Faust*) schlagen, boxen, knuffen; **5.** (ein)hämmern auf (*acc.*): ~ *the typewriter*.

punch² [pʌntʃ] ⊕ **I** *s.* **1.** Stanzwerkzeug *n*, Lochstanze *f*, -eisen *n*, Stempel *m*, 'Durchschlag *m*, Dorn *m*; **2.** Pa'trize *f*; **3.** Prägestempel *m*; **4.** Lochzange *f* (*a.* 🚃 *etc.*); **5.** (Pa'pier)Locher *m*; **II** *v/t.* **6.** (aus-, loch)stanzen, durch'schlagen, lochen; **7.** *Zahlen etc.* punzen, stempeln; **8.** *Fahrkarten etc.* lochen, knipsen: ~*ed card* Lochkarte *f*; ~*ed tape* Lochstreifen *m*.

punch³ [pʌntʃ] *s.* Punsch *m*.

punch⁴ [pʌntʃ] *s. Brit.* **1.** kurzbeiniges schweres Zugpferd; **2.** F ,Stöpsel' *m* (*kleine dicke Person*).

Punch [pʌntʃ] *s.* Kasperle *n*, Hans'wurst *m*: ~ *and Judy show* Kasperletheater *n*; *he was as pleased as* ~ er hat sich königlich gefreut.

'**punch**|·**ball** *s.* Boxen: Punchingball *m*, (Mais)Birne *f*; ~ **card** *s.* Lochkarte *f*; ,~·'**drunk** *adj.* **1.** (von vielen Boxhieben) blöde (geworden); **2.** groggy.

pun·cheon¹ ['pʌntʃən] *s.* **1.** (Holz-, Stütz)Pfosten *m*; **2.** ⊕ → *punch²* 1.

pun·cheon² ['pʌntʃən] *s. hist.* Puncheon *n* (*Fass von 315–540 l*).

punch·er ['pʌntʃə] *s.* **1.** ⊕ Locheisen *n*,

Locher *m*; **2.** F Schläger *m* (*a. Boxer*); **3.** *Am.* F Cowboy *m*.

punch·ing| **bag** ['pʌntʃɪŋ] *s.* Boxen: Sandsack *m*; ~ **ball** *s.* Boxen: Punchingball *m*; ~ **die** *s.* ⊕ 'Stanzma,trize *f*.

punch| **line** *s. Am.* Po'inte *f*, 'Knallef,fekt *m*; ~ **press** *s.* ⊕ Lochpresse *f*; '~·**up** *s.* F Schläge'rei *f*.

punc·til·i·o [pʌŋk'tɪlɪəʊ] *pl.* **-i·os** *s.* **1.** Punkt *m* der Eti'kette; Feinheit *f des Benehmens etc.*; **2.** heikler *od.* kitzliger Punkt: ~ *of hono(u)r* Ehrenpunkt *m*; **3.** → *punctiliousness*; **punc·til·i·ous** [-ɪəs] *adj.* □ **1.** peinlich (genau), pe'dantisch, spitzfindig; **2.** (über'trieben) förmlich; **punc·til·i·ous·ness** [-ɪəsnɪs] *s.* pe'dantische Genauigkeit, Förmlichkeit *f*.

punc·tu·al ['pʌŋktjʊəl] *adj.* □ pünktlich; **punc·tu·al·i·ty** [,pʌŋktjʊ'ælətɪ] *s.* Pünktlichkeit *f*.

punc·tu·ate ['pʌŋktjʊeɪt] *v/t.* **1.** interpunktieren, Satzzeichen setzen in (*acc.*); **2.** *fig.* a) unter'brechen (*with* durch, mit), b) unter'streichen; **punc·tu·a·tion** [,pʌŋktjʊ'eɪʃn] *s.* **1.** Interpunkti'on *f*, Zeichensetzung *f*: *close* (*open*) ~ (weniger) strikte Zeichensetzung; ~ *mark* Satzzeichen *n*; **2.** *fig.* a) Unter'brechung *f*, b) Unter'streichung *f*.

punc·ture ['pʌŋktʃə] **I** *v/t.* **1.** durch'stechen, -'bohren; **2.** ⚕ punktieren; **II** *v/i.* **3.** ein Loch bekommen, platzen (*Reifen*); **4.** 🗲 'durchschlagen; **III** *s.* **5.** (Ein-) Stich *m*, Loch *n*; **6.** Reifenpanne *f*: ~ *outfit* Flickzeug *n*; **7.** ⚕ Punk'tur *f*; **8.** 🗲 'Durchschlag *m*; '~·**proof** *adj. mot.* pannen-, 🗲 'durchschlagsicher.

pun·dit ['pʌndɪt] *s.* **1.** Pandit *m* (*brahmanischer Gelehrter*); **2.** *humor.* a) ,gelehrtes Haus', b) ,Weise(r)' *m* (*Experte*).

pun·gen·cy ['pʌndʒənsɪ] *s.* Schärfe *f* (*a. fig.*); '**pun·gent** [-nt] *adj.* □ **1.** scharf (*im Geschmack*); **2.** stechend (*Geruch etc.*), *a. fig.* beißend, scharf; **3.** *fig.* prickelnd, pi'kant.

pu·ni·ness ['pjuːnɪnɪs] *s.* **1.** Schwächlichkeit *f*; **2.** Kleinheit *f*.

pun·ish ['pʌnɪʃ] *v/t.* **1.** *j-n* (be)strafen (*for* für, wegen); **2.** *Vergehen* bestrafen, ahnden; **3.** F *fig. Boxer etc.* übel zurichten, arg mitnehmen (*a. weitS.* strapazieren): *~ing* ,mörderisch', zermürbend; **4.** F ,reinhauen' (*ins Essen*); '**pun·ish·a·ble** [-ʃəbl] *adj.* □ strafbar; '**pun·ish·ment** [-mənt] *s.* **1.** Bestrafung *f* (*by* durch); **2.** Strafe *f* (*a.* 🏛): *for* (*od. as*) *a* ~ als *od.* zur Strafe; **3.** F a) grobe Behandlung, b) Boxen: ,Prügel' *pl.*: *take* ~ ,schwer einstecken' müssen; c) Stra'paze *f*, ,Schlauch' *m*, d) ⊕, ✝ harte Beanspruchung.

pu·ni·tive ['pjuːnətɪv] *adj.* Straf...

punk [pʌŋk] **I** *s.* **1.** Zunder(holz *n*) *m*; **2.** *sl. contp.* a) ,Flasche' *f*, b) ,Blödmann' *m*, c) ,Mist' *m*; **3.** ,Punk' *m* (*Bewegung u. Anhänger*), Punker(in); **II** *adj. sl.* **4.** mise'rabel; **5.** Punk... (*a.* ♪).

pun·ster ['pʌnstə] *s.* Wortspielmacher (-in), Witzbold *m*.

punt¹ [pʌnt] **I** *s.* Punt *n*, Stakkahn *m*; **II** *v/t. Boot* staken; **III** *v/i.* punten, im Punt fahren.

punt² [pʌnt] **I** *s. Rugby etc.*: Falltritt *m*; **II** *v/t. u. v/i.* (den Ball) aus der Hand (ab)schlagen.

punt³ [pʌnt] *v/i.* **1.** *Glücksspiel*: gegen die Bank setzen; **2.** (*auf ein Pferd*) setzen, *allg.* wetten.

punt⁴ [pʌnt] *s. Währung*: Punt *n*, irisches Pfund.

punt·er¹ ['pʌntə] *s. bsd. Brit.* **1.** Wetter

(-in); **2.** (Glücks)Spieler(in); **3.** F *a. b. s.* Kunde *m*, Kundin *f*: *the average ~* ‚Otto Normalverbraucher'; *the ~s pl.* die Leutchen *pl.*, das Publikum; **4.** F Freier *m* (*e-r* Prostituierten).

punt·er² ['pʌntə] *s.* Stechkahnfahrer(in).

pu·ny ['pjuːnɪ] *adj.* □ schwächlich; winzig, *a. fig.* kümmerlich.

pup [pʌp] **I** *s.* junger Hund: *in ~* trächtig (*Hündin*); *conceited ~ → puppy* 2; *sell s.o. a ~* F j-m et. andrehen, j-n ‚reinlegen'; **II** *v/t. u. v/i.* (Junge) werfen.

pu·pa ['pjuːpə] *pl.* **-pae** [-piː] *s. zo.* Puppe *f*; **'pu·pate** [-peɪt] *v/i. zo.* sich verpuppen; **pu·pa·tion** [pjuːˈpeɪʃən] *s. zo.* Verpuppung *f*.

pu·pil¹ ['pjuːpl] *s.* **1.** Schüler(in): *~ teacher* Junglehrer(in); **2.** ✝ Prakti'kant(in); **3.** ⚖ Mündel *m, n*.

pu·pil² ['pjuːpl] *s. anat.* Pu'pille *f*.

pu·pil·(l)age ['pjuːpɪlɪdʒ] *s.* **1.** Schüler-, Lehrjahre *pl.*; **2.** Minderjährigkeit *f*, Unmündigkeit *f*; **'pu·pil·(l)ar** [-lə] → **'pu·pil·(l)ar·y** [-lərɪ] *adj.* **1.** ⚖ Mündel...; **2.** *anat.* Pupillen...

pup·pet ['pʌpɪt] *s. a. fig.* Mario'nette *f*, Puppe *f*: *~ government* Marionettenregierung *f*; *~ show* (*od.* *play*) Puppenspiel *n*, Mario'nettenthe,ater *m*.

pup·py ['pʌpɪ] *s.* **1.** *zo.* junger Hund, Welpe *m, a. weitS.* Junge(s) *n*: *~ love → calf love*; **2.** *fig.* (junger) Schnösel, Fatzke *m*; **'pup·py·hood** [-hʊd] *s.* Jugend-, Flegeljahre *pl.*

pup tent *s.* kleines Schutzzelt.

pur [pɜː] → **purr.**

pur·blind ['pɜːblaɪnd] *adj.* **1.** *fig.* kurzsichtig, dumm; **2.** a) halb blind, b) *obs.* (ganz) blind.

pur·chas·a·ble ['pɜːtʃəsəbl] *adj.* käuflich (*a. fig.*); **pur·chase** ['pɜːtʃəs] **I** *v/t.* **1.** kaufen, erstehen, (käuflich) erwerben; **2.** *fig.* erkaufen, erringen (*with* mit, durch); **3.** *fig.* kaufen (*bestechen*); **4.** ⊙, ⚓ u.) hochwinden; b) (mit Hebelkraft) heben *od.* bewegen; **II** *s.* **5.** (An-, Ein)Kauf *m*: *by ~* durch Kauf, käuflich; *make ~s* Einkäufe machen; **6.** 'Kauf (-ob,jekt *m*) *n*, Anschaffung *f*; *~s Bilanz*: Wareneingänge *f*; **7.** ⚖ Erwerbung *f*; **8.** (Jahres)Ertrag *m*: *at ten years'* ~ zum Zehnfachen des Jahresertrages; *his life is not worth a day's ~* er lebt keinen Tag mehr, er macht es nicht mehr lange; **9.** ⊙ Hebevorrichtung *f, bsd.* a) Flaschenzug *m*, b) ⚓ Talje *f*; **10.** Hebelkraft *f*, -wirkung *f*; **11.** (guter) Angriffs- *od.* Ansatzpunkt *m*; **12.** *fig.* a) Machtstellung *f*, Einfluss *m*, b) Machtmittel *n*, Handhabe *f*.

pur·chase| ac·count *s.* ✝ Warengangskonto *n*; **~ dis·count** *s.* 'Einkaufsra,batt *m*; **~ mon·ey** *s.* Kaufsumme *f*; **~ pat·tern** *s.* Käuferverhalten *n*; **~ price** *s.* Kaufpreis *m*.

pur·chas·er ['pɜːtʃəsə] *s.* **1.** Käufer(in); Abnehmer(in); **2.** ⚖ Erwerber *m*: *first ~* Ersterwerber.

pur·chase tax *s. Brit.* Kaufsteuer *f*.

pur·chas·ing| a·gent ['pɜːtʃəsɪŋ] *s.* ✝ Einkäufer *m*; **~ as·so·ci·a·tion** *s.* Einkaufsgenossenschaft *f*; **~ de·part·ment** *s.* Einkauf(sabteilung *f*) *m*; **~ man·ag·er** *s.* Einkaufsleiter *m*; **~ pow·er** *s.* Kaufkraft *f*.

pure [pjʊə] *adj.* □ **1.** rein: a) sauber, makellos (*a. fig.* Freundschaft, Sprache, Ton etc.), b) unschuldig, unberührt: *a ~ girl*, c) unvermischt: *~ gold* pures *od.* reines Gold, d) theo'retisch: *~ mathematics* reine Mathematik, e) völlig, bloß, pur: *~ nonsense*; *~ly adv. fig.*

rein, bloß, ausschließlich; **2.** *biol.* reinrassig; **'~·bred I** *adj.* reinrassig, rasserein; **II** *s.* reinrassiges Tier.

pu·rée ['pjʊreɪ] (*Fr.*) *s.* **1.** Pü'ree *n*; **2.** (Pü'ree)Suppe *f*.

pur·ga·tion [pɜːˈgeɪʃn] *s.* **1.** *mst eccl. u. fig.* Reinigung *f*; **2.** ♣ Darmentleerung *f*; **pur·ga·tive** ['pɜːgətɪv] **I** *adj.* □ **1.** reinigend; **2.** ♣ abführend, Abführ...; **II** *s.* **3.** ♣ Abführmittel *n*; **pur·ga·to·ry** ['pɜːgətərɪ] *s. R.C.* Fegefeuer *n* (*a. fig.*).

purge [pɜːdʒ] **I** *v/t.* **1.** *mst fig.* j-n reinigen (*of, from von Schuld, Verdacht*); **2.** *Flüssigkeit* klären, läutern; **3.** ♣ a) *Darm* abführen, entschlacken, b) j-m Abführmittel geben; **4.** *Verbrechen* sühnen; **5.** *pol.* a) *Partei etc.* säubern, b) (aus der Par'tei) ausschließen, c) liquidieren (*töten*); **II** *v/i.* **6.** sich läutern; **7.** ♣ a) abführen (*Medikament*), b) Stuhlgang haben; **III** *s.* **8.** Reinigung *f*; **9.** ♣ a) Entleerung *f*, -schlackung *f*, b) Abführmittel *n*; **10.** *pol.* 'Säuberung(s-akti,on) *f*.

pu·ri·fi·ca·tion [,pjʊərɪfɪˈkeɪʃn] *s.* **1.** Reinigung *f* (*a. eccl.*); **2.** ⊙ Reinigung *f* (*a. metall.*), Klärung *f*, Abläuterung *f*; Regenerierung *f von Altöl*; **pu·ri·fi·er** ['pjʊərɪfaɪə] *s.* ⊙ Reiniger *m*, 'Reinigungsappa,rat *m*; **pu·ri·fy** ['pjʊərɪfaɪ] **I** *v/t.* **1.** reinigen (*of, from* von) (*a. fig.* läutern); **2.** ⊙ reinigen, läutern, klären; aufbereiten, Öl regenerieren; **II** *v/i.* **3.** sich läutern.

pur·ism ['pjʊərɪzəm] *s. a. ling. u. Kunst:* Pu'rismus *m*; **'pur·ist** [-ɪst] *s.* Pu'rist *m, bsd.* Sprachreiniger *m*.

Pu·ri·tan ['pjʊərɪtən] **I** *s.* **1.** *hist.* (*fig. mst 2*) Puri'taner(in); **II** *adj.* **2.** puri'tanisch; **3.** *fig.* (*mst 2*) → **puritanical**; **pu·ri·tan·i·cal** [,pjʊərɪˈtænɪkəl] *adj.* □ puritanisch, über'trieben sittenstreng; **'Pu·ri·tan·ism** [-tənɪzəm] *s.* Purita'nismus *m*.

pu·ri·ty ['pjʊərətɪ] *s.* Reinheit *f*: ⚖ *Campaign fig.* Sauberkeitskampagne *f*.

purl¹ [pɜːl] **I** *v/i.* murmeln, rieseln (*Bach*); **II** *s.* Murmeln *n*.

purl² [pɜːl] **I** *v/t.* **1.** (um)'säumen, einfassen; **2.** (*a. v/i.*) links stricken; **II** *s.* **3.** Gold-, Silberdrahtlitze *f*; **4.** Zäckchen (-borte *f*) *n*; **5.** Häkelkante *f*; **6.** Linksstricken *n*.

purl·er ['pɜːlə] *s.* F **1.** schwerer Sturz: *come* (*od.* *take*) *a ~* schwer stürzen; **2.** schwerer Schlag.

pur·lieus ['pɜːljuːz] *s. pl.* Um'gebung *f*, Randbezirk(e *pl.*) *m*.

pur·loin [pɜːˈlɔɪn] *v/t.* entwenden, stehlen (*a. fig.*); **pur'loin·er** [-nə] *s.* Dieb *m; fig.* Plagi'ator *m*.

pur·ple ['pɜːpl] **I** *adj.* **1.** vio'lett, lila: ⚕ *Heart* a) ✕ *Am.* Verwundetenabzeichen *n*, b) *Brit.* F Amphetamintablette *f*; **2.** *fig.* bril'lant (*Stil*): *~ passage* Glanzstelle *f*; **3.** *Am.* lästerlich; **II** *s.* **4.** Vio'lett *n*, Lila *n*; Purpur *m* (*a. fig. Herrscher-, Kardinalswürde*): *raise to the ~* zum Kardinal ernennen; **III** *v/i.* **5.** sich vio'lett *od.* lila färben.

pur·port ['pɜːpət] **I** *v/t.* **1.** behaupten, vorgeben: *~ to be* (*do*) angeblich sein (tun), sein (tun) wollen; **2.** besagen, beinhalten, zum Inhalt haben, ausdrücken (wollen); **II** *s.* **3.** Tenor *m*, Inhalt *m*, Sinn *m*.

pur·pose ['pɜːpəs] **I** *s.* **1.** Zweck *m*, Ziel *n*; Absicht *f*, Vorsatz *m*: *for what ~?* zu welchem Zweck?, wozu?; *for all practical ~s* praktisch; *for the ~ of* a) um zu, zwecks, b) im Sinne *e-s Gesetzes*; *of set ~* ⚖ vorsätzlich; *on ~* absichtlich;

to the ~ a) zur Sache (gehörig), b) zweckdienlich; *to no ~* vergeblich, umsonst; *answer* (*od.* *serve*) *the ~* dem Zweck entsprechen; *be to little ~* wenig Zweck haben; *turn to good ~* gut anwenden *od.* nützen; *novel with a ~, ~ novel* Tendenzroman *m*; **2.** *a. strength of ~* Entschlusskraft *f*; **3.** Zielbewusstheit *f*; **4.** Wirkung *f*; **II** *v/t.* **5.** vorhaben, beabsichtigen, bezwecken; **'~·built** *adj.* spezi'algefertigt, Spezial..., Zweck...

pur·pose·ful ['pɜːpəsfʊl] *adj.* □ **1.** zielbewusst, entschlossen; **2.** zweckmäßig, -voll; **3.** absichtlich; **'pur·pose·less** [-lɪs] *adj.* □ **1.** zwecklos; **2.** ziel-, planlos; **'pur·pose·ly** [-lɪ] *adv.* absichtlich, vorsätzlich; **'pur·pose-trained** *adj.* mit Spezi'alausbildung; **'pur·pos·ive** [-sɪv] *adj.* □ **1.** zweckmäßig, -voll, -dienlich; **2.** absichtlich, bewusst, *a.* gezielt; **3.** zielstrebig.

purr [pɜː] **I** *v/i.* **1.** schnurren (*Katze etc.*); **2.** *fig.* surren, summen (*Motor etc.*); **3.** *fig.* vor Behagen schnurren; **II** *v/t.* **4.** et. summen, säuseln (*sagen*); **III** *s.* **5.** Schnurren *n*; Surren *n*.

purse [pɜːs] **I** *s.* **1.** a) Geldbeutel *m*, Börse *f*, b) (Damen)Handtasche *f*: *a light* (*long*) *~ fig.* ein magerer (voller) Geldbeutel; *public ~* Staatssäckel *m*; **2.** Fonds *m*: *common ~* gemeinsame Kasse; **3.** Geldsammlung *f*, -geschenk *n*: *make up a ~ for* Geld sammeln für; **4.** *sport:* a) Siegprämie *f*, b) *Boxen:* Börse *f*; **II** *v/t.* **5.** *oft ~ up* in Falten legen; *Stirn* runzeln; *Lippen* schürzen, *Mund* spitzen; **'~·proud** *adj.* geldstolz, protzig.

purs·er ['pɜːsə] *s.* **1.** ⚓ Zahl-, Provi'antmeister *m*; **2.** ✈ Purser(in).

purse strings *s. pl.:* *hold the ~* den Geldbeutel verwalten; *tighten the ~* den Daumen auf dem Beutel halten.

purs·lane ['pɜːslɪn] *s.* ♣ Portulak(gewächs *n*) *m*.

pur·su·ance [pəˈsjʊəns] *s.* Verfolgung *f*, Ausführung *f*: *in ~ of* a) im Verfolg (*gen.*), b) → **pursuant**; **pur'su·ant** [-nt] *adj.* □: *~ to* gemäß *od.* laut *e-r Vorschrift etc.*

pur·sue [pəˈsjuː] **I** *v/t.* **1.** (*a.* ✕) verfolgen, j-m nachsetzen, j-n jagen; **2.** *fig. Zweck, Ziel, Plan* verfolgen; **3.** *nach Glück etc.* streben; *dem Vergnügen* nachgehen; **4.** *Kurs, Weg* einschlagen, folgen (*dat.*); **5.** *Beruf, Studien etc.* betreiben, nachgehen (*dat.*); **6.** et. weiterführen, fortsetzen, fortfahren in (*dat.*); **7.** *Thema etc.* weiterführen, (weiter-) diskutieren; **II** *v/i.* **8.** *~ after* → 1; **9.** *im Sprechen etc.* fortfahren; **pur'su·er** [-juːə] *s.* **1.** Verfolger(in); **2.** ⚖ *Scot.* (An)Kläger(in).

pur·suit [pəˈsjuːt] *s.* **1.** Verfolgung *f*, Jagd *f* (*of auf acc.*): *~ action* ✕ Verfolgungskampf *m*; *in hot ~* in wilder Verfolgung *od.* Jagd; **2.** *fig.* Streben *n*, Trachten *n*, Jagd *f* (*of* nach); **3.** Verfolgung *f*, Verfolg *m e-s Plans etc.*: *in ~ of* im Verfolg *e-r Sache*; **4.** Beschäftigung *f*, Betätigung *f*; Ausübung *f e-s Gewerbes*, Betreiben *n von Studien etc.*; **5.** *pl.* Arbeiten *pl.*, Geschäfte *pl.*; Studien *pl.*; *~ in·ter·cep·tor* ✈ Zerstörer *m*; *~ plane* ✈ Jagdflugzeug *n*.

pur·sy¹ ['pɜːsɪ] *adj.* **1.** kurzatmig; **2.** korpu'lent; **3.** protzig.

pur·sy² ['pɜːsɪ] *adj.* □ zs.-gekniffen.

pu·ru·lence ['pjʊərʊləns] *s.* ♣ **1.** Eitrigkeit *f*; **2.** Eiter *m*; **'pu·ru·lent** [-nt] *adj.* □ ♣ eiternd, eit(e)rig; Eiter...: *~ matter* Eiter *m*.

pur·vey [pə'veɪ] **I** v/t. (**to**) mst Lebensmittel liefern (an acc.), (j-n) versorgen mit; **II** v/i. (**for**) liefern (an acc.), sorgen (für): ~ **for** j-n beliefern; **pur-'vey·ance** [-erəns] s. **1.** Lieferung f, Beschaffung f; **2.** (Mund)Vorrat m, Lebensmittel pl.; **pur'vey·or** [-erə] s. **1.** Liefe'rant m: 2 **to Her Majesty** Hoflieferant; **2.** Lebensmittelhändler m.

pur·view ['pɜːvjuː] s. **1.** ⅍ verfügender Teil e-s Gesetzes; **2.** bsd. ⅍ (Anwendungs)Bereich m e-s Gesetzes, b) Zuständigkeit(sbereich m) f; **3.** Wirkungskreis m, Sphäre f, Gebiet n; **4.** Gesichtskreis m, Blickfeld n (a. fig.).

pus [pʌs] s. ☞ Eiter m.

push [pʊʃ] **I** s. **1.** Stoß m, Schub m: **give s.o. a** ~ a) j-m e-n Stoß versetzen, b) mot. j-n anschieben; **give s.o. the** ~ sl. j-n ‚rausschmeißen' (entlassen); **get the** ~ sl. ‚rausfliegen' (entlassen werden); **2.** △, ⊖, geol. (horizon'taler) Druck, Schub m; **3.** Anstoß m, -trieb m; **4.** Anstrengung f, Bemühung f; **5.** bsd. ✕ Vorstoß m (**for** auf acc.); Offen'sive f; **6.** fig. Druck m, Drang m der Verhältnisse; **7.** kritischer Augenblick: **at a** ~ im Notfall; **bring to the last** ~ aufs Äußerste treiben; **when it came to the** ~ als es darauf ankam; **8.** F Schwung m, Ener'gie f, Tatkraft f, Draufgängertum n; **9.** Protekti'on f: **get a job by** ~; **10.** F Menge f, Haufen m Menschen; **11.** sl. a) (exklu'sive) Clique, b) ‚Verein' m, ‚Bande' f; **II** v/t. **12.** stoßen, Karren etc. schieben: ~ **open** aufstoßen; **13.** stecken, schieben (**into** in acc.); **14.** drängen: ~ **one's way ahead** (**through**) sich vor- (durch)drängen; **15.** fig. (an)treiben, drängen (**to** zu, **to do** zu tun): ~ **s.o. for** j-n bedrängen od. j-m zusetzen wegen; ~ **s.o. for payment** bei j-m auf Zahlung drängen; ~ **s.th. on s.o.** j-m et. aufdrängen; **be** ~**ed for time** in Zeitnot od. im Gedränge sein; **be** ~**ed for money** in Geldverlegenheit sein; **16.** a. ~ **forward** od. **on**) Angelegenheit (e'nergisch) betreiben od. verfolgen, vor'antreiben; **17.** a. ~ **through** 'durchführen, -setzen; Anspruch 'durchdrücken; Vorteil ausnutzen: ~ **s.th. too far** et. zu weit treiben; **18.** Re'klame machen für, die Trommel rühren für; **19.** F verkaufen, mit Rauschgift etc. handeln: ~ **forty** sich e-m Alter nähern: **be** ~**ing 70**; **III** v/i. **21.** stoßen, schieben; **22.** (sich) drängen; **23.** sich vorwärts drängen, sich vor'ankämpfen; **24.** sich tüchtig ins Zeug legen; **25.** Billard: schieben; ~ **a·round** v/t. her'umschubsen (a. fig.); ~ **off I** v/t. **1.** Boot abstoßen; **2.** ✝ Waren abstoßen, losschlagen; **II** v/i. **3.** ✿ abstoßen (**from** von); **4.** ‚abhauen'; **5.** ~! F ‚schieß los'!; ~ **up** v/t. hoch-, hin'aufschieben, -stoßen; ✝ Preise hochtreiben; ~ **un·der** v/t. F j-n ‚unterbuttern'.

'push|·ball s. Pushball(spiel n) m; **'~-bike** s. Brit. F Fahrrad n; **'~-,but·ton I** s. ⊖ Druckknopf m, -taste f; **II** adj. druckknopfgesteuert, Druckknopf...: ~ **switch**; ~ **telephone** Tastentelefon n; ~ **warfare** automatische Kriegsführung; **'~-cart** s. **1.** (Hand)Karren m; **2.** Am. Einkaufswagen m; **'~-chair** s. (Kinder)Sportwagen m.

push·er ['pʊʃə] s. **1.** ⊖ Schieber m (a. Kinderlöffel); **2.** 🚂 'Hilfslokomo,tive f; **3.** a. ~ **airplane** Flugzeug n mit Druckschraube; **4.** F Streber m; Draufgänger m; **5.** sl. ‚Pusher' m, ‚Dealer' m (Rauschgifthändler).

push·ful ['pʊʃfʊl] adj. ☐ e'nergisch, unter'nehmend, draufgängerisch.

push·ing ['pʊʃɪŋ] adj. ☐ **1.** → pushful; **2.** streberisch; **3.** zudringlich.

'push|-off s. F Anfang m, Start m; **'~,o·ver** s. F **1.** leicht zu besiegender Gegner; **2.** Gimpel m: **he is a** ~ **for that** darauf fällt er prompt herein; **3.** leichte Sache, Kinderspiel n; **,~-'pull** adj. ✠ Gegentakt...; ~ **start** s. mot. Anschieben n; **,~-to-'talk but·ton** s. ✠ Sprechtaste f; **'~-up** s. Liegestütz m; **'~-up bra** [brɑː] s. 'Push-up-B,H m.

push·y ['pʊʃɪ] adj. F aufdringlich, penet'rant; aggres'siv.

pu·sil·la·nim·i·ty [,pjuːsɪlə'nɪmətɪ] s. Kleinmütigkeit f, Verzagtheit f; **pu·sil·lan·i·mous** [,pjuːsɪ'lænɪməs] adj. ☐ kleinmütig, verzagt.

puss¹ [pʊs] s. **1.** Mieze f, Kätzchen n (a. F fig. Mädchen): 2 **in Boots** der Gestiefelte Kater; ~ **in the corner** Kämmerchen vermieten (Kinderspiel); **2.** hunt. Hase m.

puss² [pʊs] s. sl. ‚Fresse' f, Vi'sage f.

puss·l(e)y ['pʊslɪ] s. ♀ Am. Kohlportulak m.

puss·y ['pʊsɪ] s. **1.** Mieze(kätzchen n) f, Kätzchen n; **2.** → tipcat; **3.** et. Weiches u. Wolliges, bsd. ♀ (Weiden)Kätzchen n; **4.** vulg. ‚Muschi' f (Vulva): **have some** ~ ‚bumsen'; **'~-cat 1.** → pussy 1; **2.** → pussy willow; **'~-foot I** v/i. **1.** (wie e-e Katze) schleichen; **2.** fig. F a) leisetreten, sich nicht festlegen (on auf acc.), her'umreden (um); **II** pl. **-foots** [-fʊts] s. **3.** Schleicher m; **4.** fig. F Leisetreter m; ~ **wil·low** s. ♀ Verschiedenfarbige Weide.

pus·tule ['pʌstjuːl] s. **1.** ☞ Pustel f, Eiterbläschen n; **2.** ♀, zo. Warze f.

put [pʊt] **I** s. **1.** bsd. sport Stoß m, Wurf m; **2.** ✝, Börse: Rückprämie f: ~ **and call** Stellagegeschäft n; ~ **of more** Nochgeschäft n ‚auf Geben'; **II** adj. **3.** F an Ort u. Stelle, unbeweglich: **stay** ~ a) sich nicht (vom Fleck) rühren, b) festbleiben (a. fig.); **III** v/t. [irr.] **4.** legen, stellen, setzen, wohin tun; befestigen (**to** an dat.): **I shall** ~ **the matter before him** ich werde ihm die Sache vorlegen; **I** ~ **him above his brother** ich stelle ihn über seinen Bruder; ~ **s.th. in hand** fig. et. in die Hand nehmen, anfangen; **5.** stecken (**in one's pocket** in die Tasche, **in prison** ins Gefängnis); **6.** j-n in e-e unangenehme Lage, ✝ et. auf den Markt, in Ordnung, thea. ein Stück auf die Bühne etc. bringen: ~ **s.o. across a river** j-n über e-n Fluss übersetzen; ~ **it across s.o.** F j-n ‚reinlegen'; ~ **one's brain to it** sich darauf konzentrieren, die Sache in Angriff nehmen; ~ **s.o. in mind of** j-n erinnern an (acc.); ~ **s.th. on paper** et. zu Papier bringen; ~ **s.o. right** j-n berichtigen; **7.** ein Ende, in Kraft, in Umlauf, in den Besitz, in ein gutes od. schlechtes Licht, ins Unrecht, über ein Land, sich et. in den Kopf, j-n an e-e Arbeit setzen: ~ **one's signature to** s-e Unterschrift darauf od. darunter setzen; ~ **yourself in my place** versetze dich in m-e Lage; **8.** ~ **o.s.** sich in j-s Hände etc. begeben: ~ **o.s. under s.o.'s care** sich in j-s Obhut begeben; ~ **yourself in(to) my hands** vertraue dich mir ganz an; **9.** ~ **out of** aus ... hin'ausstellen etc.; werfen od. verdrängen aus; außer Betrieb od. Gefecht etc. setzen; → action 2, 9, running 1; **10.** unter'werfen, -'ziehen (**to** e-r Probe etc.; **through** e-m Verhör etc.): ~ **s.o. through it** j-n auf Herz u.

Nieren prüfen; → confusion 3, death 1, expense 2, shame 2, sword, test 1; **11.** Land bepflanzen (**into**, **under** mit): **land was** ~ **under potatoes**; **12.** (**to**) setzen (an acc.), (an)treiben od. zwingen (zu): ~ **s.o. to work** j-n an die Arbeit setzen, j-n arbeiten lassen; ~ **to school** zur Schule schicken, einschulen; ~ **to trade** j-n ein Handwerk lernen lassen; ~ **s.o. to a joiner** j-n bei e-m Schreiner in die Lehre geben; ~ **s.o. to it** j-m zusetzen, j-n bedrängen; **be hard** ~ **to it** arg bedrängt werden; → flight¹, pace¹ 2; **13.** veranlassen, verlocken (**on**, **to** zu); **14.** in Furcht, Wut etc. versetzen; → countenance 2, ease 2, guard 11, mettle 2, temper 4; **15.** über'setzen (**into French etc.** ins Fran-zösische etc.); **16.** (un)klar etc. ausdrücken, sagen klug etc. formulieren, in Worte fassen: **the case was cleverly** ~; **to** ~ **it mildly** gelinde gesagt; **how shall I** ~ **it?** wie soll ich mich (od. es) ausdrücken; **17.** schätzen (**at** auf acc.); **18.** (**to**) verwenden (für), anwenden (zu): ~ **s.th. to a good use** et. gut verwenden; **19.** Frage, Antrag etc. vorlegen, stellen; **den Fall setzen: I** ~ **it to you** a) ich appelliere an Sie, b) ich stelle es Ihnen anheim; **I** ~ **it to you that** geben Sie zu, dass; **20.** Geld setzen, wetten (**on** auf acc.); **21.** (**into**) Geld stecken (in acc.), anlegen (in dat.), investieren (in dat.); **22.** Schuld zuschieben, geben (**on** dat.): **they** ~ **the blame on him**; **23.** Uhr stellen; **24.** bsd. sport werfen, schleudern; Kugel, Stein stoßen; **25.** Waffe stoßen, Kugel schießen (**in**[**to**] in acc.); **IV** v/i. [irr.] **26.** sich begeben (**to land** an Land), fahren: ~ **to sea** in See stechen; **27.** Am. münden, sich ergießen (Fluss) (**into** in e-n See etc.); **28.** ~ **upon** mst pass. a) j-m zusetzen, b) j-n ausnutzen, c) j-n ‚reinlegen';

Zssgn mit prp.:
→ Beispiele unter put 4 → 28;

Zssgn mit adv.:
put| a·bout I v/t. **1.** ✿ wenden; **2.** Gerücht verbreiten; **3.** a) beunruhigen, b) quälen, c) ärgern; **II** v/i. ✿ wenden; ~ **a·cross** v/t. **1.** ✿ 'übersetzen; **2.** sl. et. ‚schaukeln', erfolgreich 'durchführen, Idee etc. ‚verkaufen': **put it across** ,es schaffen', Erfolg haben; ~ **a·side** v/t. **1.** → put away 1 u. 3; **2.** fig. beiseite schieben; ~ **a·way I** v/t. **1.** weglegen, -stecken, -tun, beiseite legen; **2.** Geld zu'rücklegen, ,auf die hohe Kante legen'; **3.** Laster etc. ablegen; **4.** F Speisen ,verdrücken', Getränke ,runterstellen'; **5.** F j-n ,einsperren'; **6.** F j-n ,beseitigen' (umbringen); **7.** sl. et. versetzen; **II** v/i. **9.** ✿ auslaufen (**for** nach); ~ **back I** v/t. **1.** zu'rückschieben, -stellen, -tun; **2.** Uhr zu'rückstellen, Zeiger zu'rückdrehen; **3.** fig. aufhalten, hemmen; → clock¹ 1; **4.** Schüler zu'rückversetzen; **II** v/i. **5.** ✿ 'umkehren; ~ **by** v/t. **1.** → put away 1 u. 3; **2.** Frage etc. ausweichen; **3.** fig. bei'seite schieben, j-n über'gehen; ~ **down** v/t. **1.** hin-, niederlegen, -stellen, -setzen; → foot 1; **2.** j-n auf der Fahrt absetzen, aussteigen lassen; **3.** Weinkeller anlegen; **4.** Aufstand niederwerfen, a. Missstand unter'drücken; **5.** j-n demütigen, ducken, kurz abweisen; he'runtersetzen; **6.** zum Schweigen bringen; **7.** a) Preise her'untersetzen, b) Ausgaben einschränken; **8.** (auf-, nieder)schreiben; **9.** (**to**) ✝ a) j-m anschreiben, b) auf j-s Rechnung setzen:

put s.th. down to s.o.'s account; **10.** j-n eintragen od. vormerken (**for** für e-e Spende etc.): **put o.s. down** sich eintragen; **11.** zuschreiben (**to** dat.); **12.** schätzen (**at, for** auf acc.); **13.** ansehen (**as, for** als); **~ forth** v/t. **1.** her'vor-, hin'auslegen, -stellen, -schieben; **2.** Hand etc. ausstrecken; **3.** Kraft etc. aufbieten; **4.** ♀ Knospen etc. treiben; **5.** veröffentlichen, bsd. Buch her'ausbringen; **6.** behaupten; **~ for·ward** v/t. **1.** vorschieben; Uhr vorstellen, Zeiger vorrücken; **2.** in den Vordergrund schieben: **put o.s. forward** a) sich hervortun, b) sich vordrängen; **3.** fig. vo-'ranbringen, weiterhelfen (dat.); **4.** Meinung etc. vorbringen, et. vorlegen, unter'breiten; Theorie aufstellen; **~ in I** v/t. **1.** her'ein-, hin'einlegen etc.; **2.** einschieben, -schalten; **~ a word** a) e-e Bemerkung einwerfen od. anbringen, b) ein Wort mitsprechen, c) ein Wort einlegen (**for** für); **~ an extra hour's work** e-e Stunde mehr arbeiten; **3.** Schlag etc. anbringen; **4.** Gesuch etc. einreichen, Dokument vorlegen; Anspruch stellen od. erheben (**to, for** auf acc.); **5.** j-n anstellen, in ein Amt einsetzen; **6.** Annonce einrücken; **7.** F Zeit verbringen; **II** v/i. **8.** ♧ einlaufen; **9.** einkehren (**at** in e-m Gasthaus etc.); **10.** sich bewerben (**for** um): **~ for s.th.** et. fordern od. verlangen; **~ in·side** v/t. F j-n ‚einlochen'; **~ off I** v/t. **1.** weg-, bei'seite legen, -stellen; **2.** Kleider, bsd. fig. Zweifel etc. ablegen; **3.** auf-, verschieben; **4.** j-n vertrösten, abspeisen (**with** mit Worten etc.); j-m absagen; **6.** sich drücken vor (dat.); **7.** j-n abbringen, j-m abraten (**from** von); **8.** hindern (**from** an dat.); **9.** **put s.th. off** (**up**)**on s.o.** j-m et. ‚andrehen'; **10.** F a) j-n aus der Fassung od. aus dem Kon-'zept bringen, b) j-m die Lust nehmen, j-n abstoßen; **II** v/i. **11.** ♧ auslaufen; **~ on** v/t. **1.** Kleider anziehen; Hut, Brille aufsetzen; Rouge auflegen; **2.** Fett ansetzen; → **weight** 1; **3.** Charakter, Gestalt annehmen; **4.** vortäuschen, -spiegeln, (er)heucheln: → **air**¹ 14, **dog** Bes. Redew.; **put it on** F a) angeben, b) übertreiben, c) ‚schwer draufschlagen' (auf den Preis), d) heucheln; **put it on thick** F dick auftragen; **his modesty is all ~** s-e Bescheidenheit ist nur Mache; **5.** Summe aufschlagen (**on** auf den Preis); **6.** Uhr vorstellen, Zeiger vorrücken; **7.** an-, einschalten, Gas etc. aufdrehen, Dampf anlassen, Tempo beschleunigen; **8.** Kraft, a. Arbeitskräfte, Sonderzug etc. einsetzen; **9.** Schraube, Bremse anziehen; **10.** thea. etc. Stück, Sendung bringen; **11.** put s.o. on to j-m e-n Tipp geben für, j-n auf e-e Idee bringen; **12.** sport Tor etc. erzielen; **~ out I** v/t. **1.** hin'auslegen, -stellen etc.; **2.** Hand, Fühler ausstrecken; Zunge her'ausstrecken; Ankündigung etc. aushängen; **3.** sport zum Ausscheiden zwingen, ‚aus dem Rennen werfen'; **4.** Glied aus-, verrenken; **5.** Feuer, Licht (aus-)löschen; **6.** a) verwirren, außer Fassung bringen, b) verstimmen, ärgern: **be ~ about s.th.**, c) j-m Ungelegenheiten bereiten, j-n stören; **7.** Kraft etc. aufbieten; **8.** Geld ausleihen (**at interest** auf Zinsen), investieren; **9.** Boot aussetzen; **10.** Augen ausstechen; **11.** Arbeit, a. Kind, Tier außer Haus geben; ♀ in Auftrag geben; → **grass** 3, **nurse** 4; **12.** Knospen etc. treiben; **II** v/i. **13.** ♧ auslaufen; **~ (to sea)** in See stechen; **~ o·ver I** v/t. **1.** sl. → **put across** 2; **2.**

e-m Film etc. Erfolg sichern, popu'lär machen (acc.): **put o.s. over** sich durchsetzen, ‚ankommen'; **3.** put it over on j-n ‚reinlegen'; **II** v/i. **4.** ♧ hin'überfahren; **~ through** v/t. **1.** 'durch-, ausführen; **2.** teleph. j-n verbinden (**to** mit); **~ to** v/t. Pferd anspannen, Lokomotive vorspannen; **~ to·geth·er** v/t. **1.** zs.-setzen (a. Schriftwerk) zs.-stellen; **2.** zs.-zählen; → **two** 2; **3.** zs.-stecken; → **head** Bes. Redew.; **~ up I** v/t. **1.** hin'auflegen, -stellen; **2.** hochschieben, -ziehen; → **back**¹ 7, **shutter** 1; **3.** Hände etc. heben, b) zum Kampf hochnehmen; **4.** Bild etc. aufhängen; Plakat anschlagen; **5.** Haar aufstecken; **6.** Schirm aufspannen; **7.** Zelt etc. aufstellen, Gebäude errichten; **8.** F et. aushecken, et. ‚drehen', fingieren; **9.** Gebet em'porsenden; **10.** Gast (bei sich) aufnehmen, 'unterbringen; **11.** weglegen; **12.** aufbewahren; **13.** ein-, ver-, wegpacken; zs.-legen; **14.** Schwert einstecken; **15.** konservieren, einkochen, -machen; **16.** Spiel etc. zeigen; e-n Kampf liefern; Widerstand leisten; **17.** (als Kandi'daten) aufstellen; **18.** Auktion: an-, ausbieten; **~ for sale** meistbietend verkaufen; **19.** Preis etc. hi'naufsetzen, erhöhen; **20.** Wild aufjagen; **21.** Eheaufgebot verkünden; **22.** bezahlen; **23.** (ein)setzen (Wette etc.), Geld bereitstellen, od. hinter'legen; **24. ~ to** a) j-n anstiften zu, b) j-n informieren über (acc.), a. j-m e-n Tipp geben für; **II** v/i. **25.** absteigen, einkehren (**at** in dat.); **26.** (**for**) sich aufstellen lassen, kandidieren (für), sich bewerben (um); **27. ~ with** sich abfinden mit, sich gefallen lassen, hinnehmen.

put and call op·tion s. ♦ Stel'lagegeschäft n.

pu·ta·tive ['pju:tətɪv] adj. ☐ **1.** vermeintlich; **2.** mutmaßlich; **3.** ♣ pu'ta·tiv.

'put|·down s.: **that was a ~** damit wollte er mich etc. fertig machen; **'~·off** s. **1.** Ausflucht f; **2.** Verschiebung f; **'~-on I** adj. **1.** vorgetäuscht; **II** s. Am. sl. **2.** Bluff m; **3.** Getue n, ‚Mache' f, ‚Schau' f.

put-put ['pʌtpʌt] s. Tuckern n (e-s Motors etc.).

pu·tre·fa·cient [ˌpju:trɪ'feɪʃənt] → putrefactive; **ˌpu·tre'fac·tion** [-'fækʃn] s. **1.** Fäulnis f, Verwesung f; **2.** Faulen n; **ˌpu·tre'fac·tive** [-'fæktɪv] **I** adj. **1.** faulig, Fäulnis...; **2.** Fäulnis erregend; **II** s. **3.** Fäulniserreger m; **pu·tre·fy** ['pju:trɪfaɪ] **I** v/i. (ver)faulen, verwesen; **II** v/t. verfaulen lassen.

pu·tres·cence [pju:'tresns] s. (Ver-) Faulen n, Fäulnis f; **pu'tres·cent** [-nt] adj. **1.** (ver)faulend, verwesend; **2.** faulig, Fäulnis...

pu·trid ['pju:trɪd] adj. ☐ **1.** verfault, verwest; faulig (Geruch), stinkend; **2.** fig. verderbt, kor'rupt; **3.** fig. verderblich; **4.** fig. ekelhaft; **5.** sl. mise'rabel.

putsch [putʃ] (Ger.) s. pol. Putsch m, Staatsstreich m.

putt [pʌt] Golf: **I** v/t. u. v/i. putten; **II** s. Putt m.

put·tee ['pʌtɪ] s. 'Wickelga,masche f.

putt·er ['pʌtə] s. Golf: Putter m (Schläger od. Spieler).

putt·ing green ['pʌtɪŋ] s. Golf: Putting- -Green n (Platzteil).

put·ty ['pʌtɪ] **I** s. **1.** ⊙ Kitt m, Spachtel m: (glaziers') ~ Glaserkitt m, (plasterers') ~ Kalkkitt m, (jewellers') ~ Zinnasche f; **2.** fig. Wachs n: **he is ~ in her hand**; **II** v/t. **3.** a. ~ **up** (ver)kitten; ~

knife s. [irr.] Spachtelmesser n.

'put-up adj. F abgekartet: **a ~ job** e-e ‚Schiebung', ‚Schiebung'.

puz·zle ['pʌzl] **I** s. **1.** Rätsel n; **2.** Puzzle-, Geduldspiel n; **3.** schwierige Sache, Prob'lem n; **4.** Verwirrung f, Verlegenheit f; **II** v/t. **5.** verwirren, vor ein Rätsel stellen, verdutzen; **6.** et. kompli'zieren, durchein'ander bringen; **7.** j-m Kopfzerbrechen machen, zu schaffen machen: ~ **one's brains** (od. **head**) sich den Kopf zerbrechen (**over** über acc.); **8. ~ out** austüfteln, -knobeln, her'auskommen; **III** v/i. **9.** verwirrt sein (**over, about** über acc.); **10.** sich den Kopf zerbrechen (**over** über acc.); **'~-,head·ed** adj. wirrköpfig, kon'fus; ~ **lock** s. Vexier-, Buchstabenschloss n.

puz·zle·ment ['pʌzlmənt] s. Verwirrung f; **'puz·zler** [-lə] → **puzzle** 3; **'puz·zling** [-lɪŋ] adj. ☐ **1.** rätselhaft; **2.** verwirrend.

py·e·li·tis [paɪə'laɪtɪs] s. ♣ Nierenbeckenentzündung f.

pyg·m(a)e·an [pɪg'mi:ən] → **pygmy** II.

pyg·my ['pɪgmɪ] **I** s. **1.** ♀ Pyg'mäe m, Pyg'mäin f (Zwergmensch); **2.** fig. Zwerg m; **II** adj. **3.** Pygmäen...; **4.** winzig, Zwerg...; **5.** unbedeutend.

py·ja·mas [pə'dʒɑ:məz] s. pl. Schlafanzug m, Py'jama m.

py·lon ['paɪlən] s. **1.** ⚡ (freitragender) Mast (für Hochspannungsleitungen etc.); **2.** ✈ Orientierungsturm m, bsd. Wendeturm m.

py·lo·rus [paɪ'lɔ:rəs] pl. **-ri** [-raɪ] s. anat. Py'lorus m, Pförtner m.

pyr·a·mid ['pɪrəmɪd] s. Pyra'mide f (a. ♣ u. fig.): ~ **of ages** Alterspyramide f; **py·ram·i·dal** [pɪ'ræmɪdl] adj. ☐ **1.** Pyramiden...; **2.** pyrami'dal (a. fig. gewaltig), pyra'midenartig, -förmig.

pyre ['paɪə] s. Scheiterhaufen m.

py·ret·ic [paɪ'retɪk] adj. ♣ fieberhaft, Fieber...; **py·rex·i·a** [-eksɪə] s. ♣ Fieberzustand m.

py·rite ['paɪraɪt] s. min. Py'rit m, Schwefel-, Eisenkies m; **py·ri·tes** [paɪ'raɪtiːz] s. min. Py'rit m: **copper ~** Kupferkies m; **iron ~ → pyrite**.

pyro- [paɪərəʊ] in Zssgn Feuer..., Brand..., Wärme..., Glut...; **'py·ro·gen** [-rədʒən] s. ♣ Fieber erregender Stoff; **py·rog·e·nous** [paɪ'rɒdʒɪnəs] adj. **1.** a) wärmeerzeugend, b) durch Wärme erzeugt; **2.** ♣ a) Fieber erregend, b) durch Fieber verursacht; **3.** geol. pyro'gen; **py·rog·ra·phy** [paɪ'rɒgrəfɪ] s. Brandmale'rei f; **py·ro·ma·ni·a** [ˌpaɪrəʊ'meɪnɪə] s. Pyroma'nie f, Brandstiftungstrieb m; **py·ro·ma·ni·ac** [ˌpaɪrəʊ'meɪnɪæk] s. Pyro'mane m, Pyro'manin f.

py·ro·tech·nic, py·ro·tech·ni·cal [ˌpaɪrəʊ'teknɪk(l)] adj. ☐ **1.** pyro'technisch; **2.** Feuerwerks..., feuerwerkartig; **3.** fig. bril'lant; **ˌpy·ro'tech·nics** [-ks] s. pl. **1.** Pyro'technik f, Feuerwerke'rei f; **2.** fig. Feuerwerk n von Witz etc.; **ˌpy·ro'tech·nist** [-ɪst] s. Pyro'techniker m.

Pyr·rhic vic·to·ry ['pɪrɪk] s. Pyrrhussieg m.

Py·thag·o·re·an [paɪˌθægə'rɪən] **I** adj. pythago'reisch; **II** s. phls. Pythago'reer m.

py·thon ['paɪθn] s. zo. **1.** Python(schlange f) m; **2.** allg. Riesenschlange f.

pyx [pɪks] **I** s. **1.** R.C. Pyxis f, Monst-'ranz f; **2.** Brit. Büchse f mit Probemünzen; **II** v/t. **3.** Münze a) in die **Pyx** hinter'legen, b) auf Gewicht u. Feinheit prüfen.

pzazz [psæz] → **piz(z)azz**.

Q, q [kjuː] s. Q n, q n (*Buchstabe*).
'Q-boat s. ♣ U-Boot-Falle f.
quack¹ [kwæk] I v/i. **1.** quaken; **2.** fig. schnattern, schwatzen; II s. **3.** Quaken n; fig. Geplapper n.
quack² [kwæk] I s. **1.** a. ~ **doctor** Quacksalber m, Kurpfuscher m; **2.** Scharlatan m; Marktschreier m; II adj. **3.** quacksalberisch, Quacksalber...; **4.** marktschreierisch; **5.** Schwindel...; III v/i. u. v/t. **6.** quacksalbern, her'umpfuschen (an dat.); **7.** marktschreierisch auftreten (v/t. anpreisen); **'quack·er·y** [-kərı] s. **1.** Quacksalbe'rei f, Kurpfusche'rei f; **2.** Scharlatane'rie f; **3.** marktschreierisches Auftreten.
quad¹ [kwɒd] F → *quadrangle*, *quadrat*, *quadruped*, *quadruplet*.
quad² [kwɒd] I s. ⚡ Viererkabel n; II v/t. zum Vierer verseilen.
quad·ra·ble ['kwɒdrəbl] adj. ⅄ quadrierbar.
quad·ra·ge·nar·i·an [ˌkwɒdrədʒɪ'neərıən] I adj. a) vierzigjährig, b) in den Vierzigern; II s. Vierziger(in), Vierzigjährige(r m) f.
quad·ran·gle ['kwɒdræŋgl] s. **1.** ⅄ u. weitS. Viereck n; **2.** a) (bsd. Schul)Hof m, b) viereckiger Ge'bäudekom‚plex; **quad·ran·gu·lar** [kwɒ'dræŋgjulə] adj. □ ⅄ viereckig.
quad·rant ['kwɒdrənt] s. **1.** ⅄ Quad'rant m, Viertelkreis m, ('Kreis)Seg‚ment n; **2.** ♣, ast. Qua'drant m.
quad·ra·phon·ic [ˌkwɒdrə'fɒnık] adj. ♪, phys. quadro'phonisch; **‚quad·ra·'phon·ics** [-ks] s. pl. sg. konstr. Quadropho'nie f.
quad·rat ['kwɒdrət] s. typ. Qua'drat n, (großer) Ausschluss: **em** ~ Geviert n; **en** ~ Halbgeviert n.
quad·rate ['kwɒdrət] I adj. (annähernd) qua'dratisch, bsd. anat. Quadrat...; II v/t. [kwɒ'dreıt] in Über'einstimmung bringen (**with**, **to** mit); III v/i. [kwɒ'dreıt] über'einstimmen; **quad·rat·ic** [kwɒ'drætık] I adj. qua'dratisch (Form, Gleichung): ~ **curve** Kurve f zweiter Ordnung; II s. ⅄ qua'dratische Gleichung; **quad·ra·ture** ['kwɒdrətʃə] s. **1.** ⅄, ast. Quadra'tur f (**of the circle** des Kreises); **2.** ⚡ (Phasen)Verschiebung f um 90 Grad.
quad·ren·ni·al [kwɒ'drenıəl] I adj. □ **1.** vierjährig, vier Jahre dauernd; **2.** vierjährlich, alle vier Jahre stattfindend; II s. **3.** Zeitraum m von vier Jahren; **4.** vierter Jahrestag.
quad·ri·lat·er·al [ˌkwɒdrı'lætərəl] I adj. vierseitig; II s. Vierseit n, -eck n.
qua·drille [kwə'drıl] s. Qua'drille f (Tanz).
quad·ril·lion [kwɒ'drıljən] s. ⅄ **1.** Brit. Quadrilli'on f; **2.** Am. Billi'arde f.
quad·ri·par·tite [ˌkwɒdrı'pɑːtaıt] adj. **1.** vierteilig (a. ♀); **2.** Vierer..., zwischen vier Partnern abgeschlossen etc.: ~ **pact** Viererpakt m.
quad·ro ['kwɒdrəu] adj. u. adv. ♪, Ra-

---

dio: quadro.
quad·ro- ['kwɒdrəu] in Zssgn quadro...
‚quad·ro'phon·ic [-'fɒnık] etc. → *quadraphonic* etc.
quad·ru·ped ['kwɒdruped] I s. Vierfüßer m; II adj. a. **quad·ru·pe·dal** [ˌkwɒdrə'piːdl] vierfüßig; **'quad·ru·ple** [-pl] I adj. a. ~ **to** (od. **of**) vierfach, -fältig; viermal so groß wie; **2.** Vierer...: ~ **machinegun** ⚔ Vierlings-MG n; ~ **measure** ♪ Viervierteltakt m; ~ **thread** ⚙ viergängiges Gewinde; II adv. **3.** vierfach; III s. **4.** das Vierfache; IV v/t. **5.** vervierfachen; **6.** viermal so groß od. so viel sein wie; V v/i. **7.** sich vervierfachen; **'quad·ru·plet** [-plıt] s. **1.** Vierling m (Kind); **2.** Vierergruppe f; **'quad·ru·plex** [-pleks] I adj. **1.** vierfach; **2.** ⚡ Quadruplex..., Vierfach...: ~ **system** Vierfachbetrieb m, Doppelgegensprechen n; II s. **3.** 'Quadruplextele‚graf m; **quad·ru·pli·cate** I v/t. [kwɒ'druːplıkeıt] **1.** vervierfachen; **2.** Dokument vierfach ausfertigen; II adj. [kwɒ'druːplıkət] **3.** vierfach; III s. [-kət] **4.** vierfache Ausfertigung.
quaff [kwɑːf] I v/i. zechen; II v/t. schlürfen, in langen Zügen (aus)trinken: ~ **off** Getränk hinunterstürzen.
quag [kwæg] → *quagmire*; **'quag·gy** [-gı] adj. **1.** sumpfig; **2.** schwammig; **'quag·mire** [-maıə] s. Mo'rast m, Moor(boden m) n, Sumpf(land n) m: **be caught in a** ~ fig. in der Patsche sitzen.
quail¹ [kweıl] pl. **quails**, coll. **quail** s. orn. Wachtel f.
quail² [kweıl] v/i. **1.** verzagen; **2.** (vor Angst) zittern (**before** vor dat.; **at** bei).
quaint [kweınt] adj. □ **1.** wunderlich, drollig, kuri'os; **2.** malerisch, anheimelnd (altmodisch); **3.** seltsam, merkwürdig; **'quaint·ness** [-nıs] s. **1.** Wunderlichkeit f; Seltsamkeit f; **2.** anheimelndes (bsd. altmodisches) Aussehen.
quake [kweık] I v/i. zittern, beben (**with**, **for** vor dat.); II s. Zittern n, (a. Erd)Beben n, Erschütterung f.
Quak·er ['kweıkə] s. **1.** eccl. Quäker m: ~**(s') meeting** fig. schweigsame Versammlung; **2.** a. ~ **gun** ⚔ Am. Ge'schützat‚trappe f; **3.** ♀, a. ⚘ **bird** orn. schwarzer Albatros; **'Quak·er·ess** [-ərıs] s. Quäkerin f; **'Quak·er·ism** [-ərızəm] s. Quäkertum n.
quak·ing grass ['kweıkıŋ-] s. ♀ Zittergras n.
qual·i·fi·ca·tion [ˌkwɒlıfı'keıʃn] s. **1.** Qualifikati'on f, Befähigung f, Eignung f (**for** für, zu): ~ **test** Eignungsprüfung f; **have the necessary ~s** den Anforderungen entsprechen; **2.** Vorbedingung f, (notwendige) Vor'aussetzung (**of**, **for** für); **3.** Eignungszeugnis n; Einschränkung f, Modifikati'on f: **without any** ~ ohne jede Einschränkung; **5.** ling. nähere Bestimmung; **6.** ✝ 'Mindest‚aktienkapi‚tal n (e-s Aufsichtsratsmitglieds); **qual·i·fied** ['kwɒlıfaıd] adj.

---

1. qualifiziert, geeignet, befähigt (**for** für); **2.** berechtigt: ~ **for a post** anstellungsberechtigt; ~ **voter** Wahlberechtigte(r m) f; **3.** eingeschränkt, bedingt, modifiziert: ~ **acceptance** ✝ bedingte Annahme (e-s Wechsels); ~ **sale** ✝ Konditionskauf m; **in a** ~ **sense** mit Einschränkungen; **qual·i·fy** ['kwɒlıfaı] I v/t. **1.** qualifizieren, befähigen, geeignet machen (**for** für; **for being**, **to be** zu sein); **2.** berechtigen (**for** zu); **3.** bezeichnen, charakterisieren (**as** als); **4.** einschränken, modifizieren; **5.** abschwächen, mildern; **6.** Getränke verdünnen; **7.** ling. modifizieren, näher bestimmen; II v/i. **8.** sich qualifizieren od. eignen, die Eignung besitzen od. nachweisen, infrage kommen (**for** für; **as** als): ~**ing examination** Eignungsprüfung f; ~**ing period** Anwartschafts-, Probezeit f; **9.** sport sich qualifizieren (**for** für): ~**ing round** Ausscheidungsrunde f; **10.** die nötigen Fähigkeiten erwerben; **11.** die (ju'ristischen) Vorbedingungen erfüllen, bsd. Am. den Eid ablegen; **qual·i·ta·tive** ['kwɒlıtə‚tıv] adj. □ qualita'tiv (a. 🜍 Analyse, a. ⅄ Verteilung); **qual·i·ty** ['kwɒlətı] s. **1.** Eigenschaft f (Person u. Sache): (**good**) ~ gute Eigenschaft; **in the** ~ **of** (in der Eigenschaft) als; **2.** Art f, Na'tur f, Beschaffenheit f; **3.** Fähigkeit f, Ta'lent n; **4.** bsd. ✝, ⚙ Quali'tät f: **in** ~ qualitativ; **5.** ✝ (Güte)Sorte f, Klasse f; **6.** gute Quali'tät, Güte f: ~ **goods** Qualitätswaren; ~ **of life** Lebensqualität f; **7.** a) ♪ 'Tonquali‚tät f, -farbe f, b) ling. Klangfarbe f; **8.** phls. Quali'tät f; **9.** vornehmer Stand: **person of** ~ Standesperson f; **the people of** ~ die vornehme Welt.
qualm [kwɑːm] s. **1.** Übelkeitsgefühl n, Schwäche(anfall m) f; **2.** Bedenken pl., Zweifel pl.; Skrupel pl.; **'qualm·ish** [-mıʃ] adj. □ **1.** (sich) übel (fühlend), unwohl; **2.** Übelkeits...: ~ **feelings**.
quan·da·ry ['kwɒndərı] s. Verlegenheit f, verzwickte Lage: **be in a** ~ sich in e-m Dilemma befinden; nicht wissen, was man tun soll.
quan·go [kwæŋgəu] pl. **-gos** s. halbstaatliche Organisati'on.
quan·ta ['kwɒntə] pl. von *quantum*.
quan·ti·fi·a·ble ['kwɒntıfaıəbl] s. quantita'tiv bestimmbar, messbar; **quan·ti·fy** [-faı] vt. quantita'tiv bestimmen, messen.
quan·ti·ta·tive ['kwɒntıtətıv] adj. □ quantita'tiv (a. ling.), Mengen...: ~ **analysis** 🜍 quantitative Analyse; ~ **ratio** Mengenverhältnis n; **quan·ti·ty** ['kwɒntətı] s. **1.** Quanti'tät f, (bestimmte od. große) Menge, Quantum n; ~ **of heat** phys. Wärmemenge; **a** ~ **of cigars** e-e Anzahl Zigarren; **in** (**large**) **quantities** in großen Mengen; ~ **discount** ✝ Mengenrabatt m; ~ **count** Massenerzeugung f, Serienfertigung f; ~ **purchase** Großeinkauf m; ~

surveyor *Brit.* Bausachverständige(r) *m*; **2.** *A* Größe *f*: *negligible* ~ a) unwesentliche Größe, b) *fig.* völlig unbedeutende Person *etc.*; *numerical* ~ Zahlengröße; *(un)known* ~ (un)bekannte Größe (*a. fig.*); **3.** *ling.* Quanti'tät *f*, Lautdauer *f*; (Silben)Zeitmaß *n*.

quan·ti·za·tion [ˌkwɒntɪ'zeɪʃn] *s. phys.* Quantelung *f*; **quan·tize** ['kwɒntaɪz] *v/t.* **1.** *phys.* quanteln; **2.** *Computer:* quantisieren.

quan·tum ['kwɒntəm] *pl.* **-ta** [-tə] *s.* **1.** Quantum *n*, Menge *f*; **2.** (An)Teil *m*; **3.** *phys.* Quant *n*: ~ *of radiation* Lichtquant; ~ *jump* *s.*, ~ *leap* *s.* **1.** *phys.* Quantensprung *m* (*a. fig.*); **2.** *fig.* gewaltiger Fortschritt, Riesenschritt *m*; ~ *me·chan·ics* *s. pl. sg. konstr.* 'Quantenme,chanik *f*; ~ *or·bit*, ~ *path* *s.* Quantenbahn *f*.

quar·an·tine ['kwɒrənti:n] **I** *s.* *♮* **1.** Quaran'täne *f*: *absolute* ~ Isolierung *f*; ~ *flag* *♮* Quarantäneflagge *f*; *put in* ~ → 2; **II** *v/t.* **2.** unter Quaran'täne stellen; **3.** *fig. pol.*, *♱* *Land* völlig isolieren.

quar·rel ['kwɒrəl] **I** *s.* **1.** Streit *m*, Zank *m*, Hader *m* (*with* mit; *between* zwischen *dat.*): *have no* ~ *with* (*od. against*) keinen Grund zum Streit haben mit, nichts auszusetzen haben an (*dat.*); → *pick* 8; **II** *v/i.* **2.** (sich) streiten, (sich) zanken (*with* mit; *for* wegen; *about* über *acc.*); **3.** sich entzweien; **4.** hadern (*with one's lot* mit s-m Schicksal); **5.** *et.* auszusetzen haben (*with* an *dat.*); → *bread* 2; **'quar·rel·(l)er** [-rələ] *s.* Zänker(in), 'Streithammel' *m*; **'quar·rel·some** [-səm] *adj.* □ streitsüchtig; **'quar·rel·some·ness** [-səmnɪs] *s.* Streitsucht *f*.

quar·ri·er ['kwɒrɪə] *s.* Steinbrecher *m*.

quar·ry¹ ['kwɒrɪ] *s.* **1.** *hunt.* (verfolgtes) Wild, Jagdbeute *f*; **2.** *fig.* Wild *n*, Opfer *n*, Beute *f*.

quar·ry² ['kwɒrɪ] **I** *s.* **1.** Steinbruch *m*; **2.** Quaderstein *m*; **3.** unglasierte Kachel; **4.** *fig.* Fundgrube *f*, Quelle *f*; **II** *v/t.* **5.** *Steine* brechen, abbauen; **6.** *fig.* zs.-tragen, (mühsam) erarbeiten, ausgraben; stöbern (*for* nach); **'~·man** [-mən] *s.* [*irr.*] → *quarrier*; **'~·stone** *s.* Bruchstein *m*.

quart¹ [kwɔ:t] *s.* **1.** Quart *n* (*Maß =* *Brit.* 1,14 *l*, *Am.* 0,95 *l*); **2.** *a.* **~·pot** Quartkrug *m*.

quart² [ka:t] *s.* **1.** *fenc.* Quart *f*; **2.** *Kartenspiel:* Quart *f* (*Sequenz von 4 Karten gleicher Farbe*); **3.** *♪* Quart(e) *f*.

quar·tan ['kwɔ:tn] *♯* **I** *adj.* viertägig: ~ *fever* → **II** *s.* Quar'tan-, Vier'tagefieber *n*.

quar·ter ['kwɔ:tə] **I** *s.* **1.** Viertel *n*, vierter Teil: *~ of a century* Vierteljahrhundert *n*; *for a* ~ *the price* zum viertel Preis; *not a* ~ *as good* nicht annähernd so gut; **2.** *a.* ~ *of an hour* Viertel(stunde *f*) *n*: *a* ~ *to six* (ein) Viertel vor sechs, drei Viertel sechs; **3.** *a.* ~ *of a year* Vierteljahr *n*, Quar'tal *n*; **4.** Viertel(pfund *n*, -zentner *m*) *n*; **5.** *bsd.* Hinter)Viertel *n* e-s Schlachttieres; Kruppe *f* e-s Pferdes; **6.** *sport* a) (Spiel)Viertel *n*, b) Viertelmeile(nlauf *m*, ~ *mile race*) *f*, c) → *quarterback* I; **7.** *Am.* Vierteldollar *m*, 25 Cent; **8.** Quarter *n*: a) *Handelsgewicht* (*Brit.* 12,7 *kg*, *Am.* 11,34 *kg*), b) *Hohlmaß* (2,908 *hl*); **9.** Himmelsrichtung *f*; **10.** Gegend *f*, Teil *m* e-s *Landes etc.*: *at close* ~s nahe aufeinander; *come to close* ~s handgemein werden; *from all* ~s von überall (her); *in this* ~ hierzulande, in dieser Gegend; **11.** (Stadt)Viertel *n*: *poor* ~ Armenviertel; *residential* ~ Wohnbezirk *m*; **12.** *mst pl.* Quar'tier *n*, 'Unterkunft *f*, Wohnung *f*: *have free* ~s freie Wohnung haben; **13.** *mst pl.* *✕* Quar'tier *n*, ('Truppen)Unterkunft *f*: *be confined to* ~s Stubenarrest haben; **14.** Stelle *f*, Seite *f*, Quelle *f*: *higher* ~s höhere Stellen; *in the proper* ~ bei der zuständigen Stelle; *from official* ~s von amtlicher Seite; *from a good* ~ aus guter Quelle; → *informed* 1; **15.** *bsd.* *✕* Par'don *m*, Schonung *f*: *find no* ~ keine Schonung finden; *give no* ~ keinen Pardon geben; *give fair* ~ *fig.* Nachsicht üben; **16.** *♮* Achterschiff *n*; **17.** *♮* Posten *m*; **18.** *her.* Quar'tier *n*, (Wappen)Feld *n*; **19.** *Ⓐ*, *Δ* Stollenholz *n*; **II** *v/t.* **20.** *et.* vierteln, *weitS.* aufteilen, zerstückeln; **21.** *j-n* vierteilen; **22.** *Wappenschild* vieren; **23.** *j-n* beherbergen; *✕* einquartieren, *Truppen* 'unterbringen ([*up*]*on* bei): *~ed in barracks* kaserniert; *be* ~*ed at* (*od. in*) in Garnison liegen in (*dat.*); *be* ~*ed* (*up*)*on* bei *j-m* in Quartier liegen; ~ *o.s. upon s.o.* *fig.* sich bei j-m einquartieren; **24.** *Gegend* durch'stöbern (*Jagdhunde*).

'quar·ter|·back **I** *s. American Football:* ,'Angriffsdiri,gent' *m*; **II** *v/t. den Angriff dirigieren* (*a. fig.*); ~ *bind·ing* *s. Buchbinderei:* Halbfranz(band *m*) *n*; ~ *cir·cle* *s.* **1.** *A* Viertelkreis *m*; **2.** *Ⓐ* Abrundung *f*; ~ *day* *s.* Quar'talstag *m* für fällige Zahlungen (*in England:* 25. 3., 24. 6., 29. 9., 25. 12.; *in USA:* 1. 1., 1. 4., 1. 7., 1. 10.); **'~·deck** *s.* *♮* **1.** Achterdeck *n*; **2.** *coll.* Offi'ziere *pl.*; ,~·**fi·nal** *s. sport* **1.** *mst pl.* 'Viertelfi,nale *n*; **2.** 'Viertelfi,nalspiel *n*; ,~·**fi·nal·ist** *s. sport* Teilnehmer(in) am 'Viertelfi,nale.

quar·ter·ly ['kwɔ:təlɪ] **I** *adj.* **1.** Viertel...; **2.** vierteljährlich, Quartals...; **II** *adv.* **3.** in *od.* nach Vierteln; **4.** vierteljährlich, quar'talsweise; **III** *s.* **5.** Vierteljahresschrift *f*.

'quar·ter,mas·ter *s.* **1.** *✕* Quar'tiermeister *m*; **2.** *♮* a) Steuerer *m* (*Handelsmarine*), b) Steuermannsmaat *m* (*Kriegsmarine*); ,~·**'Gen·er·al** *s.* *✕* Gene'ralquar,tiermeister *m*.

quar·tern ['kwɔ:tən] *s. bsd. Brit.* **1.** Viertel *n* (*bsd. e-s Maßes od. Gewichtes*): a) Viertelpint *n*, b) Viertel *n* e-s engl. Pfunds; **2.** *a.* ~ *loaf* Vier'pfundbrot *n*.

quar·ter| ses·sions *s. pl.* *♮* **1.** *Brit. obs.* Krimi'nalgericht *n* (*mit vierteljährlichen Sitzungen, a. Berufungsinstanz für Zivilsachen; bis 1971*); **2.** *Am.* (*in einigen Staaten*) ähnliches Gericht für Strafsachen; ~ *tone* *s.* *♪* **1.** 'Vierteltoninter,vall *n*; **2.** Viertelton *m*.

quar·tet(te) [kwɔ:'tet] *s.* **1.** *♪* Quar'tett *n* (*a. humor. 4 Personen*); **2.** Vierergruppe *f*.

quar·tile ['kwɔ:taɪl] *s.* **1.** *ast.* Quadra'tur *f*, Geviertschein *m*; **2.** *Statistik:* Quar'til *n*, Viertelwert *m*.

quar·to ['kwɔ:təʊ] *pl.* **-tos** *typ.* **I** *s.* 'Quartfor,mat *n*; **II** *adj.* im 'Quartfor,mat.

quartz [kwɔ:ts] *s. min.* Quarz *m*: *crystallized* ~ Bergkristall *m*; ~ *clock* Quarzuhr *f*; ~ *lamp* a) *Ⓐ* Quarz(glas)lampe *f*, b) *♯* Quarzlampe *f* (*Höhensonne*).

qua·sar ['kweɪza:] *s. ast.* Qua'sar *m*.

quash¹ [kwɒʃ] *v/t.* *♮* **1.** *Verfügung etc.* aufheben, annullieren, verwerfen; **2.** *Klage* abweisen; **3.** *Verfahren* niederschlagen.

quash² [kwɒʃ] *v/t.* **1.** zermalmen, -stören; **2.** *fig.* unter'drücken.

qua·si ['kweɪzaɪ] *adv.* gleichsam, gewissermaßen, sozu'sagen; Quasi..., Schein..., ...ähnlich: ~ *contract* vertragsähnliches Verhältnis; *~·judicial* quasigerichtlich; *~·official* halbamtlich.

qua·ter·na·ry [kwə'tɜ:nərɪ] **I** *adj.* **1.** aus vier bestehend; **2.** *⅔ geol.* Quartär...; **3.** *♠* vierbindig, quater'när; **II** *s.* **4.** Gruppe *f* von 4 Dingen; **5.** Vier *f* (*Zahl*); **6.** *geol.* Quar'tär(peri,ode *f*) *n*.

quat·rain ['kwɒtreɪn] *s.* Vierzeiler *m*.

quat·re·foil ['kætrəfɔɪl] *s.* **1.** *Δ* Vierpass *m*; **2.** *♀* vierblättriges (Klee)Blatt.

qua·ver ['kweɪvə] **I** *v/i.* **1.** zittern; **2.** *♪* tremolieren (*weitS. a. beim Sprechen*); **II** *v/t. mst* ~ *out* **3.** mit über'triebenem Vi'brato singen; **4.** mit zitternder Stimme sagen, stammeln; **III** *s.* **5.** *♪* Trillern *n*, Tremolo *n*; **6.** *♪* *Brit.* Achtelnote *f*; **'qua·ver·y** [-vərɪ] *adj.* zitternd.

quay [ki:] *s.* *♮* (*on the* ~ am) Kai *m*; **quay·age** ['ki:ɪdʒ] *s.* **1.** Kaigeld *n*, -gebühr *f*; **2.** Kaianlagen *pl.*

quea·si·ness ['kwi:zɪnɪs] *s.* **1.** Übelkeit *f*; **2.** ('Über)Empfindlichkeit *f*; **quea·sy** ['kwi:zɪ] *adj.* □ **1.** ('über)empfindlich (*Magen etc.*); **2.** heikel, mäkelig (*beim Essen etc.*); **3.** Ekel erregend; **4.** unwohl: *I feel* ~ mir ist übel; **5.** bedenklich.

queen [kwi:n] **I** *s.* **1.** Königin *f* (*a. fig.*): *♀ of* (*the*) *May* Maikönigin; *the* ~ *of the watering places* *fig.* die Königin *od.* Perle der Badeorte; *~'s metal* Weißmetall *n*; *~'s ware* gelbes Steingut; *♀ Anne is dead!* *humor.* so'n Bart!; **2.** *zo.* Königin *f*: a) *a.* ~ *bee* Bienenkönigin, b) *a.* ~ *ant* Ameisenkönigin; **3.** *Kartenspiel, Schach:* Dame *f*: *~'s pawn* Damenbauer *m*; **4.** *sl.* a) ,Schwule(r)' *m*, ,Tunte' *f*, b) *Am.* ,Prachtweib' *n*; **II** *v/i.* **5.** *mst* ~ *it* die große Dame spielen: ~ *it over* *j-n* von oben herab behandeln; **6.** *Schach:* in e-e Dame verwandelt werden (*Bauer*); **III** *v/t.* **7.** zur Königin machen; **8.** *Bienenstock* beweiseln; **9.** *Schach:* Bauern (in e-e Dame) verwandeln; **'~·dow·ger** *s.* Königinwitwe *f*; **'~·like** → *queenly*.

queen·ly ['kwi:nlɪ] *adj. u. adv.* wie e-e Königin, maje'stätisch.

queen moth·er *s.* Königinmutter *f*.

Queen's| Bench → *King's Bench*; **~ Coun·sel** → *King's Counsel*; **~ Eng·lish** → *English* 3; **~ Speech** → *King's Speech*.

queer [kwɪə] **I** *adj.* □ **1.** seltsam, sonderbar, wunderlich, kuri'os, ,komisch': ~ (*in the head*) F leicht verrückt; ~ *fellow* komischer Kauz; **2.** F fragwürdig, ,faul' (*Sache*): *be in ♀ Street* a) ,auf dem Trockenen sitzen', b) ,in der Tinte sitzen'; **3.** unwohl, schwummerig: *feel* ~ sich ,komisch' fühlen; **4.** *sl.* gefälscht; **5.** *sl.* ,schwul' (*homosexuell*); **II** *v/t.* **6.** *sl.* verpfuschen, verderben; → *pitch²* 7; **7.** *sl.* *j-n* in ein falsches Licht setzen (*with* bei); **III** *s.* **8.** *sl.* ,Blüte' *f* (*Falschgeld*); **9.** *sl.* ,Schwule(r)' *m*, ,Homo' *m*.

quell [kwel] *v/t. rhet.* **1.** bezwingen; **2.** *Aufstand etc.*, *a. Gefühle* unter'drücken, ersticken.

quench [kwentʃ] *v/t.* **1.** *rhet. Flammen, Durst etc.* löschen; **2.** *fig.* a) → *quell* 2, b) *Hoffnung* zu'nichte machen, c) *Verlangen* stillen; **3.** *Ⓐ* Asche, Koks etc. (ab)löschen; **4.** *metall.* abschrecken, härten: *~·ing and tempering* (Stahl-)Vergütung *f*; **5.** *⚡ Funken* löschen: *~·ed spark gap* Löschfunkenstrecke *f*; **6.**

fig. j-m den Mund stopfen; '**quench·er** [-tʃə] *s.* F Schluck *m*; '**quench·less** [-lɪs] *adj.* □ un(aus)löschbar.

que·nelle [kə'nel] *s.* Fleisch- *od.* Fischknödel *m*.

que·rist ['kwɪərɪst] *s.* Fragesteller(in).

quer·u·lous ['kwerʊləs] *adj.* □ quengelig, nörgelnd, verdrossen.

que·ry ['kwɪərɪ] I *s.* **1.** (*bsd.* zweifelnde *od.* unangenehme) Frage; ⳨ Rückfrage *f*: ~ (*abbr.* **qu.**), *was the money ever paid?* Frage, wurde das Geld je bezahlt?; **2.** *typ.* (anzweifelndes) Fragezeichen; **3.** *fig.* Zweifel *m*; II *v/t.* **4.** fragen; **5.** j-n (aus-, be)fragen; **6.** *et.* in Zweifel ziehen, infrage stellen, beanstanden; **7.** *typ.* mit e-m Fragezeichen versehen.

quest [kwest] I *s.* **1.** Suche *f*, Streben *n*, Trachten *n* (*for, of* nach): *knightly* ~ Ritterzug *m*; *the ~ for the* (*Holy*) *Grail* die Suche nach dem (Heiligen) Gral; *in ~ of* auf der Suche nach; **2.** Nachforschung(en *pl.*) *f*; II *v/i.* **3.** suchen (*for, after* nach); **4.** Wild suchen (*Jagdhund*); III *v/t.* **5.** suchen *od.* trachten nach.

ques·tion ['kwestʃən] I *s.* **1.** Frage *f* (*a. ling.*): *beg the* ~ die Antwort auf eine Frage schuldig bleiben; *put a* ~ *to s.o.* j-m e-e Frage stellen; *the* ~ *does not arise* die Frage ist belanglos; → *pop¹* 10; **2.** Frage *f*, Pro'blem *n*, Thema *n*, (Streit)Punkt *m*: *the social* ~ die soziale Frage; *~s of the day* Tagesfragen; ~ *of fact* ⳨ Tatfrage; ~ *of law* ⳨ Rechtsfrage; *the point in* ~ die fragliche *od.* vorliegende *od.* zur Debatte stehende Sache; *come into* ~ infrage kommen, wichtig werden; *there is no* ~ *of s.th. od. ger.* es ist nicht die Rede von *et. od.* davon, dass; ~*! parl.* zur Sache!; **3.** Frage *f*, Sache *f*, Angelegenheit *f*: *only a* ~ *of time* nur e-e Frage der Zeit; **4.** Frage *f*, Zweifel *m*: *beyond* (*all*) ~ ohne Frage, fraglos; *call in* ~ → 8; *there is no* ~ *but* (*od.* *that*) es steht außer Frage, dass; *out of* ~ außer Frage; *that is out of the* ~ das kommt nicht infrage; **5.** *pol.* Anfrage *f*: *put to the* ~ zur Abstimmung über *e-e Sache* schreiten; **6.** ⳨ Vernehmung *f*; Unter'suchung *f*: *put to the* ~ *hist.* j-n foltern; II *v/t.* **7.** j-n (aus-, be)fragen; vernehmen, -hören; **8.** *et.* an-, bezweifeln, in Zweifel ziehen; '**ques·tion·a·ble** [-tʃənəbl] *adj.* □ **1.** fraglich, zweifelhaft, ungewiss; **2.** bedenklich, fragwürdig; '**ques·tion·ar·y** [-tʃənərɪ] → *questionnaire*; '**ques·tion·er** [-tʃənə] *s.* Fragesteller(in), Frager(in); '**ques·tion·ing** [-tʃənɪŋ] I *adj.* □ fragend (*a. Blick, Stimme*); II *s.* Befragung *f*; ⳨ Vernehmung *f*.

ques·tion| mark *s.* Fragezeichen *n*; ~ **mas·ter** *s.* Mode'rator *m* e-r Quizsendung.

ques·tion·naire [ˌkwestɪə'neə] (*Fr.*) *s.* Fragebogen *m*.

ques·tion time *s. parl.* Fragestunde *f*.

queue [kjuː] I *s.* **1.** (Haar)Zopf *m*; **2.** *bsd. Brit.* Schlange *f*, Reihe *f* vor Geschäften *etc.*: *stand* (*od.* *wait*) *in a* ~ Schlange stehen; → *jump* 25; II *v/i.* **3.** *mst* ~ *up Brit.* Schlange stehen, sich anstellen; '~*,*jump·er *s.* F j-d., der sich vordrängelt, *mot.* Ko'lonnenspringer *m*.

quib·ble ['kwɪbl] I *s.* **1.** Spitzfindigkeit *f*, Wortklaube'rei *f*, Ausflucht *f*; **2.** *obs.* Wortspiel *n*; II *v/i.* **3.** her'umreden, Ausflüchte machen; **4.** spitzfindig sein, Haarspalte'rei betreiben; **5.** witzeln; '**quib·bler** [-lə] *s.* **1.** Wortklauber(in);

-verdreher(in); **2.** Krittler(in); '**quib·bling** [-lɪŋ] *adj.* □ spitzfindig, haarspalterisch, wortklauberisch.

quick [kwɪk] I *adj.* □ **1.** schnell, so'fortig: ~ *answer* (*service*) prompte Antwort (Bedienung); ~ *returns* ⳨ schneller Umsatz; **2.** schnell, hurtig, geschwind, rasch: *be* ~*!* mach schnell!, beeile dich!; *be* ~ *about s.th.* sich mit *et.* beeilen; **3.** (geistig) gewandt, flink, aufgeweckt, schlagfertig, ‚fix'; beweglich, flink (*Geist*): ~ *wit* Schlagfertigkeit *f*; **4.** scharf (*Auge, Ohr, Verstand*): *a* ~ *ear* ein feines Gehör; **5.** scharf (*Geruch, Geschmack, Schmerz*); **6.** voreilig, hitzig: *a* ~ *temper*; **7.** *obs.* lebend (*a.* ⚕ *Hecke*), lebendig: ~ *with child* (hoch)schwanger; **8.** *fig.* lebhaft (*a. Gefühle*; *a. Handel etc.*); **9.** lose, treibend (*Sand etc.*); **10.** *min.* erzhaltig, ergiebig; **11.** ⳨ flüssig (*Anlagen, Aktiva*); II *s.* **12.** *the* ~ die Lebenden *pl.*; **13.** (lebendes) Fleisch; *fig.* Mark *n*: *to the* ~ a) (bis) ins Fleisch, b) *fig.* bis ins Mark *od.* Herz, c) durch u. durch; *cut s.o. to the* ~ j-n tief verletzen; *touched to the* ~ bis ins Mark getroffen; *a Socialist to the* ~ ein Sozialist bis auf die Knochen; *paint s.o. to the* ~ j-n malen wie er leibt u. lebt; **14.** *Am.* → *quicksilver*; III *adv.* **15.** schnell, geschwind; ‚~-'**ac·tion** *adj.* ⊕ Schnell...; '~-**break switch** *s.* ⚡ Mo'mentschalter *m*; '~-**change** *adj.* ~ *artist thea.* Verwandlungskünstler(in); ⊕ Schnellwechsel...(-*futter, -getriebe etc.*); '~-**dry·ing** *adj.* schnell trocknend (*Lack*); ä'therisch (*Öl*); '~-**eared** *adj.* mit e-m feinen Gehör.

quick·en ['kwɪkən] I *v/t.* **1.** beschleunigen; **2.** (wieder) lebendig machen; beseelen; **3.** *Interesse etc.* an-, erregen; **4.** beleben, j-m neuen Auftrieb geben; II *v/i.* **5.** sich beschleunigen (*Puls, Schritte etc.*); **6.** (wieder) lebendig werden; **7.** gekräftigt werden; **8.** hoch'schwanger werden; **9.** sich bewegen (*Fötus*).

quick-ie ['kwɪkɪ] *s.* F **1.** *et.* ‚'Hingehauenes', ‚auf die Schnelle' gemachte Sache, *z. B.* billiger, improvisierter Film; **2.** ‚kurze Sache', *z. B.* kurzer Werbefilm; **3.** *have a* ~ F rasch einen ‚kippen'.

'**quick|·lime** *s.* 🜨 gebrannter, ungelöschter Kalk, Ätzkalk *m*; ~ **march** *s.* ✕ Eilmarsch *m*; '~-**match** *s.* ✕, ⚒ Zündschnur *f*; ~ **mo·tion** *s.* ⊕ Schnellgang *m*; ‚~-'**mo·tion cam·er·a** *s. phot.* Zeitraffer(kamera *f*) *m*.

quick·ness ['kwɪknɪs] *s.* **1.** Schnelligkeit *f*; **2.** (geistige) Beweglichkeit *od.* Flinkheit *f*; **3.** Hitzigkeit *f*: ~ *of temper*; **4.** ~ *of sight* gutes Sehvermögen; **5.** Lebendigkeit *f*, Kraft *f*.

'**quick|·sand** *s. geol.* Treibsand *m*; '~-**set** *s.* **1.** heckenbildende Pflanze, *bsd.* Weißdorn *m*; **2.** Setzling *m*; **3.** *a.* ~ *hedge* lebende Hecke; ‚~-'**set·ting** *adj.* ⊕ schnell abbindend (*Zement etc.*); ‚~-'**sight·ed** *adj.* scharfsichtig; '~-**sil·ver** *s.* Quecksilber *n* (*a. fig.*); '~-**step** *s.* **1.** ✕ Schnellschritt *m*; **2.** ♪ Quickstep *m* (*schneller Foxtrott*); ‚~-'**tem·pered** *adj.* hitzig, jäh; ~ **time** *s.* ✕ **1.** schnelles Marschtempo; **2.** exerziermäßiges Marschtempo: ~ *march!* Im Gleichschritt, marsch!; ‚~-'**wit·ted** *adj.*

schlagfertig, aufgeweckt, ‚fix'.

quid¹ [kwɪd] *s.* **1.** Priem *m* (*Kautabak*); **2.** wiedergekäutes Futter.

quid² [kwɪd] *pl. mst* **quid** *s. Brit. sl.* Pfund *n* (*Sterling*).

quid·di·ty ['kwɪdətɪ] *s.* **1.** *phls.* Es'senz *f*, Wesen *n*; **2.** Feinheit *f*; **3.** Spitzfindigkeit *f*.

quid·nunc ['kwɪdnʌŋk] *s.* Neuigkeitskrämer *m*, Klatschtante *f*.

quid pro quo [ˌkwɪdprəʊ'kwəʊ] *pl.* **quid pro quos** (*Lat.*) *s.* Gegenleistung *f*, Vergütung *f*.

qui·es·cence [kwaɪ'esns] *s.* Ruhe *f*, Stille *f*; **qui'es·cent** [-nt] *adj.* □ **1.** ruhig, bewegungslos; *fig.* ruhig, still: ~ *state* Ruhezustand *m*; **2.** *ling.* stumm (*Buchstabe*).

qui·et ['kwaɪət] I *adj.* □ **1.** ruhig, still (*a. fig. Person, See, Straße etc.*); **2.** ruhig, leise, geräuschlos (*a.* ◎): ~ *running mot.* ruhiger Gang; *be* ~*! sei still!; ~, please!* ich bitte um Ruhe!; *keep* ~ a) sich ruhig verhalten, b) den Mund halten; **3.** bewegungslos, still; **4.** ruhig, friedlich (*a. Leben, Zeiten*); beschaulich: ~ *conscience* ruhiges Gewissen; ~ *enjoyment* ⳨ ruhiger Besitz, ungestörter Genuss; **5.** ruhig, unauffällig (*Farbe etc.*); **6.** versteckt, geheim, leise: *keep s.th.* ~ *et.* geheim halten, et. für sich behalten; **7.** ⳨ ruhig, still, ‚flau' (*Geschäft etc.*); II *s.* **8.** Ruhe *f*, Stille *f*; Frieden *m*: *on the* ~ (*od.* *on the q.t.*) F ‚klammheimlich', stillschweigend; III *v/t.* **9.** beruhigen, zur Ruhe bringen; **10.** besänftigen; **11.** zum Schweigen bringen; IV *v/i.* **12.** *mst* ~ *down* ruhig *od.* still werden, sich beruhigen; '**qui·et·en** [-tn] → *quiet* III *u.* IV.

qui·et·ism ['kwaɪɪtɪzəm] *s. eccl.* Quie'tismus *m*.

qui·et·ness ['kwaɪətnɪs] *s.* **1.** → *quietude*; **2.** Geräuschlosigkeit *f*; **qui·e·tude** ['kwaɪɪtjuːd] *s.* **1.** Stille *f*, Ruhe *f*; **2.** *fig.* Friede(n) *m*; **3.** (Gemüts)Ruhe *f*.

qui·e·tus [kwaɪ'iːtəs] *s.* **1.** Ende *n*, Tod *m*; **2.** Todesstoß *m*: *give s.o. his* ~ j-m den Garaus machen; **3.** (restlose) Tilgung *e-r Schuld*; **4.** ⳨ a) *Brit.* Endquittung *f*, b) *Am.* Entlastung *f* des Nachlassverwalters.

quill [kwɪl] *s.* **1.** *a.* ~ *feather orn.* (Schwung-, Schwanz)Feder *f*; **2.** *a.* ~ *pen* Federkiel *m*; *fig.* Feder *f*; **3.** *zo.* Stachel *m* (*Igel etc.*); **4.** ♪ a) *hist.* Pan-flöte *f*, b) Plektrum *n*; **5.** Zahnstocher *m*; **6.** Zimtstange *f*; **7.** ⊕ Weberspule *f*; **8.** ⊕ Hohlwelle *f*; II *v/t.* **9.** rund fälteln, kräuseln; **10.** *Faden* aufspulen; '~-**,driv·er** *s. contp.* Federfuchser *m*.

quilt [kwɪlt] I *s.* **1.** Steppdecke *f*; **2.** gesteppte (Bett)Decke; II *v/t.* **3.** steppen, 'durchnähen; **4.** wattieren, (aus)polstern; *~ed* *jacket* Steppjacke *f*; '**quilt·ing** [-tɪŋ] *s.* **1.** 'Durchnähen *n*, Steppen *n*: ~ *seam* Steppnaht *f*; **2.** gesteppte Arbeit; **3.** Füllung *f*, Wattierung *f*; **4.** Pi'kee *n* (*Gewebe*).

quim [kwɪm] *s.* V ‚Möse' *f*.

quince [kwɪns] *s.* ⚘ Quitte *f*.

qui·nine [*Brit.* kwɪ'niːn; *Am.* 'kwaɪnaɪn] *s.* 🜨, *pharm.* Chi'nin *n*.

quin·qua·ge·nar·i·an [ˌkwɪŋkwədʒɪ-'neərɪən] I *adj.* fünfzigjährig, in den Fünfzigern; II *s.* Fünfzigjährige(r *m*) *f*, Fünfziger(in); **quin·quen·ni·al** [kwɪŋ-'kwenɪəl] *adj.* □ fünfjährig; fünfjährlich (*wiederkehrend*).

quins [kwɪnz] *s. pl.* F Fünflinge *pl.*

quin·sy ['kwɪnzɪ] *s.* ⚕ (Hals)Bräune *f*, Mandelentzündung *f*.

          Q

quint *s.* **1.** [kɪnt] *Pikett*: Quinte *f*; **2.** [kwɪnt] ♪ Quint(e) *f*.

quin·tal ['kwɪntl] *s.* Doppelzentner *m*.

quinte [kɛ̃t; kænt] (*Fr.*) *s.* fenc. Quinte *f*.

quint·es·sence [kwɪn'tesns] *s.* **1.** 🜊 'Quintes,senz *f* (*a. phls. u. fig.*); **2.** *fig.* Kern *m*, Inbegriff *m*; **3.** a) Urtyp *m*, b) klassisches Beispiel, c) (höchste) Voll-'kommenheit *f*.

quin·tet(te) [kwɪn'tet] *s.* **1.** ♪ Quin'tett *n* (*a. humor.* 5 *Personen*); **2.** Fünfergruppe *f*.

quin·tu·ple ['kwɪntjʊpl] I *adj.* fünffach; II *s. das* Fünffache; III *v/t. u. v/i.* (sich) verfünffachen; '**quin·tu·plets** [-plɪts] *s. pl.* Fünflinge *pl.*

quip [kwɪp] I *s.* **1.** witziger Einfall, geistreiche Bemerkung, Bon'mot *n*; **2.** (Seiten)Hieb *m*, Stich(e'lei *f*) *m*; II *v/i.* **3.** witzeln, spötteln.

quire ['kwaɪə] *s.* **1.** *typ.* Buch *n* (*24 Bogen*); **2.** *Buchbinderei*: Lage *f*.

quirk [kwɜːk] *s.* **1.** → *quip* 1, 2; **2.** Kniff *m*, Trick *m*; **3.** Zucken *n des Mundes etc.*; **4.** Eigenart *f*, seltsame Angewohnheit: *by a ~ of fate* durch e-n verrückten Zufall, wie das Schicksal so spielt; **5.** Schnörkel *m*; **6.** 🜂 Hohlkehle *f*; '**quirk·y** [-kɪ] *adj.* F **1.** ,gerissen' (*Anwalt etc.*); **2.** eigenartig, schrullig, ,komisch'.

quis·ling ['kwɪzlɪŋ] *s. pol.* F Quisling *m*, Kollabora'teur *m*.

quit [kwɪt] I *v/t.* **1.** verzichten auf (*acc.*); **2.** *a.* Stellung aufgeben; *Dienst* quittieren; sich vom *Geschäft* zu'rückziehen; **3.** F aufhören (*s.th.* mit et.; *doing* zu tun); **4.** verlassen; **5.** *Schuld* bezahlen, tilgen; **6.** ~ *o.s.* sich befreien (*of* von); **7.** *poet.* vergelten (*love with hate* Liebe mit Hass); II *v/i.* **8.** aufhören; **9.** weggehen; **10.** ausziehen (*Mieter*): *notice to ~* Kündigung *f*; *give notice to ~* (*j-m die Wohnung*) kündigen; III *adj. pred.* **11.** quitt, frei: *go ~* frei ausgehen; *be ~ for* davonkommen mit; **12.** frei, los (*of* von): ~ *of charges* ✝ nach Abzug der Kosten, spesenfrei; '**~claim** *s.* ⚖ **1.** Verzicht(leistung *f*) *m auf Rechte*; **2.** ~ *deed* a) Grundstückskaufver-

trag *m*, b) *Am.* Zessi'onsurkunde *f* (*beide*: *ohne Haftung für Rechts- od. Sachmängel*).

quite [kwaɪt] *adv.* **1.** ganz, völlig: ~ *another* ein ganz anderer; ~ *wrong* völlig falsch; **2.** wirklich, tatsächlich, ziemlich: ~ *a disappointment* e-e ziemliche Enttäuschung; ~ *good* recht gut; ~ *a few* ziemlich viele; ~ *a gentleman* wirklich ein feiner Herr; **3.** F ganz, durch'aus: ~ *nice* ganz od. sehr nett; ~ *the thing* genau das Richtige; ~ (*so*)! ganz recht!

quit rent *s.* ⚖ Miet-, Pachtzins *m*.

quits [kwɪts] *adj.* quitt (*mit j-m*): *call it* ~ quitt sein; *get ~ with s.o.* mit j-m quitt werden; → *double* 10.

quit·tance ['kwɪtəns] *s.* **1.** Vergeltung *f*, Entgelt *n*; **2.** Erledigung *f* e-r *Schuld etc.*; **3.** ✝ Quittung *f*.

quit·ter ['kwɪtə] *s. Am. u.* F **1.** Drückeberger *m*; **2.** Feigling *m*.

quiv·er¹ ['kwɪvə] I *v/i.* beben, zittern (*with* vor *dat.*); II *s.* Beben *n*, Zittern *n*: *in a ~ of excitement fig.* zitternd vor Aufregung.

quiv·er² ['kwɪvə] *s.* Köcher *m*: *have an arrow left in one's ~ fig.* noch ein Eisen im Feuer haben; *a ~ full of children fig.* e-e ganze Schar Kinder.

qui vive [,kiː'viːv] (*Fr.*) *s.*: *be on the ~* auf dem Quivive *od.* auf der Hut sein.

quix·ot·ic [kwɪk'sɒtɪk] *adj.* (□ ~*ally*) donqui'chotisch (*weltfremd, überspannt*); **quix·ot·ism** ['kwɪksətɪzəm], **quix·ot·ry** ['kwɪksətrɪ] *s.* Donquichot-te'rie *f*, Narre'tei *f*.

quiz [kwɪz] I *v/t.* **1.** *Am.* j-n prüfen, abfragen; **2.** (aus)fragen; **3.** *bsd. Brit.* aufziehen, hänseln; **4.** (spöttisch) anstarren, fixieren; II *pl.* '**quiz·zes** [-zɪz] *s.* **5.** *ped. Am.* Prüfung *f*, Klassenarbeit *f*; **6.** Ausfragen *n*; **7.** *Radio, TV*: Quiz *n*: ~ *game* Ratespiel *n*, Quiz, ~*master* Quizmaster *m*; ~ *program(me)*, ~ *show* Quizsendung *f*; **8.** Denksportaufgabe *f*; **9.** *obs.* Foppe'rei *f*, Ulk *m*.

quiz·zi·cal ['kwɪzɪkl] *adj.* □ **1.** seltsam, komisch; **2.** spöttisch.

quod [kwɒd] *s. sl.* ,Kittchen' *n*: *be in* ~

a. ,sitzen'.

quoin [kɔɪn] I *s.* **1.** 🜂 a) (vorspringende) Ecke, b) Eckstein *m*; **2.** *typ.* Schließkeil *m*; II *v/t.* **3.** *typ. Druckform* schließen; **4.** ⊕ verkeilen; **5.** 🜂 *Ecke* mit Keilsteinen versehen.

quoit [kɔɪt] *s.* **1.** Wurfring *m*; **2.** *pl. sg. konstr.* Wurfringspiel *n*.

quon·dam ['kwɒndæm] *adj.* ehemalig, früher.

Quon·set hut ['kwɒnsɪt] *s. Am.* (*Warenzeichen*) e-e Nissenhütte.

quo·rum ['kwɔːrəm] *s.* **1.** beschlussfähige Anzahl *od.* Mitgliederzahl: *be* (*od. constitute*) *a* ~ beschlussfähig sein; **2.** ⚖ handlungsfähige Besetzung *e-s Gerichts.*

quo·ta ['kwəʊtə] *s.* **1.** *bsd.* ✝ Quote *f*, Anteil *m*; **2.** ✝ (*Einfuhr- etc.*)Kontin-'gent *n*: ~ *goods* kontingentierte Waren; ~ *system* Quotensystem *n*, -regelung *f*, Zuteilungssystem *n*; **3.** ⚖ Kon-'kursdivi,dende(nquote) *f*; **4.** *Am.* Einwanderungsquote *f*.

quot·a·ble ['kwəʊtəbl] *adj.* zi'tierbar.

quo·ta·tion [kwəʊ'teɪʃn] *s.* **1.** Zi'tat *n*, Anführung *f*, Her'anziehung *f* (*a.* ⚖): *familiar* ~*s* geflügelte Worte; **2.** Beleg (-stelle *f*) *m*; **3.** ✝ a) Preisangabe *f*, -ansatz *m*, b) (*Börsen-, Kurs*)Notierung *f*, Kurs *m*: *final* ~ Schlussnotierung; **4.** *typ.* Steg *m*; ~ *marks s. pl.* Anführungszeichen *pl.*, ,Gänsefüßchen' *pl.*

quote [kwəʊt] I *v/t.* **1.** zitieren (*from* aus), (*a. als Beweis*) anführen, *weitS. a.* Bezug nehmen auf (*acc.*), sich auf *ein Dokument etc.* berufen, e-e *Quelle*, e-n *Fall* her'anziehen; **2.** ✝ *Preis* aufgeben, ansetzen, berechnen; **3.** *Börse*: notieren: *be* ~*d at* (*od. with*) notiert *od.* im Kurs stehen mit; **4.** *Am.* in Anführungszeichen setzen; II *v/i.* **5.** zitieren (*from* aus): ~: ... ich zitiere: ...; *Zitat*: ...; III *s.* F **6.** Zi'tat *n*; **7.** *pl.* → *quotation marks*.

quoth [kwəʊθ] *obs.* ich, er, sie, es sprach, sagte.

quo·tid·i·an [kwɒ'tɪdɪən] I *adj.* **1.** täglich: ~ *fever* → 3; **2.** all'täglich, gewöhnlich; II *s.* **3.** 🜊 Quotidi'anfieber *n*.

quo·tient ['kwəʊʃnt] *s.* Ⱥ Quoti'ent *m*.

R

R, r [ɑː] *s.* R *n*, r *n* (*Buchstabe*): *the three Rs* (*reading*, [*w*]*riting*, [*a*]*rithmetic*) (das) Lesen, Schreiben, Rechnen.

rab·bet ['ræbɪt] ⊕ **I** *s.* **1.** a) Fuge *f*, Falz *m*, Nut *f*, b) Falzverbindung *f*; **2.** Stoßstahl *m*; **II** *v/t.* **3.** einfügen, (zs.-)fugen, falzen; **~ joint** *s.* Fuge *f*, Falzverbindung *f*; **~ plane** *s.* Falzhobel *m*.

rab·bi ['ræbaɪ] *s.* **1.** Rab'biner *m*; **2.** Rabbi *m* (*Schriftgelehrter*); **rab·bin·ate** ['ræbɪnət] *s.* **1.** Rabbi'nat *n*; **2.** *coll.* Rab'biner *pl.*; **rab·bin·i·cal** [ræ'bɪnɪkl] *adj.* □ rab'binisch.

rab·bit ['ræbɪt] *s.* **1.** *zo.* Ka'ninchen *n*; **2.** *zo. allg.* Hase *m*; **3.** → **Welsh rabbit**; **4.** *sport* F a) Anfänger(in), b) ‚Flasche' *f*, c) *Laufsport:* Tempomacher *m*; **~ fe·ver** *s.* Hasenpest *f*; **~ hutch** *s.* Ka'ninchenstall *m*; **~ punch** *s. Boxen:* Genickschlag *m*.

rab·ble¹ ['ræbl] *s.* **1.** Mob *m*, Pöbelhaufen *m*; **2.** **the ~** der Pöbel; **~-rousing** aufwieglerisch, demagogisch.

rab·ble² ['ræbl] ⊕ **I** *s.* Rührstange *f*, Kratze *f*; **II** *v/t.* ‚umrühren.

Rab·e·lai·si·an [,ræbə'leɪzɪən] *adj.* **1.** des Rabe'lais; **2.** im Stil von Rabe'lais (*grob-satirisch, geistvoll-frech*).

rab·id ['ræbɪd] *adj.* □ **1.** wütend (*a. Hass etc.*), rasend (*a. fig. Hunger etc.*); **2.** rabi'at; *fanatisch*: *a ~ anti-Semite*; **3.** toll(wütig): *a ~ dog*; **'rab·id·ness** [-nɪs] *s.* **1.** Rasen *n*, Wut *f*; **2.** (wilder) Fana'tismus.

ra·bies ['reɪbiːz] *s. vet.* Tollwut *f*.

rac·coon [rə'kuːn] *s.* Waschbär *m*.

race¹ [reɪs] *s.* **1.** Rasse *f*: *the white ~*; **2.** Rasse *f*: a) Rassenzugehörigkeit *f*, b) rassische Eigenart: *differences of ~* Rassenunterschiede; **3.** a) Geschlecht *n*, Fa'milie *f*, b) Volk *n*; **4.** *biol.* Rasse *f*, Gattung *f*, 'Unterart *f*; **5.** (*Menschen- etc.*)Geschlecht *n*: *the human ~*, *a. fig.* Kaste *f*, Schlag *m*: *the ~ of politicians*; **7.** Rasse *f des Weins etc.*

race² [reɪs] **I** *s.* **1.** *sport* (Wett)Rennen *n*, (Wett)Lauf *m*: **motor ~** Autorennen; **2.** *pl. sport* Pferderennen *n*; → **play** 16; **3.** *fig.* (*for*) Wettlauf *m*, Kampf *m* (um), Jagd *f* (nach): *~ against time* Wettlauf mit der Zeit; **4.** *ast.* Lauf *m* (*a. fig. des Lebens etc.*): *his ~ is run* er hat die längste Zeit gelebt; **5.** a) starke Strömung, b) Stromschnelle *f*, c) Flussbett *n*, d) Ka'nal *m*, Gerinne *n*, e) Ka'nalgewässer *n*; **6.** ⊕ a) Laufring *m* (*Kugellager*), (Gleit)Bahn *f*, b) *Weberei:* Schützenbahn *f*; **7.** → **slipstream**; **II** *v/i.* **8.** an e-m Rennen teilnehmen, *bsd.* um die Wette laufen *od.* fahren (**with** mit); laufen *etc.* (**for** um); **9.** (da'hin)rasen, (-)schießen, rennen; **10.** ⊕ 'durchdrehen (*Rad*); **III** *v/t.* **11.** um die Wette laufen *od.* fahren *etc.* mit; **12.** *Pferde* rennen *od.* laufen lassen; **13.** *Fahrzeug* rasen lassen, rasen mit; **14.** *fig.* (durch)hetzen, (-)jagen; *Gesetz* 'durchpeitschen; **15.** ⊕ a) Mo-

tor 'durchdrehen lassen, b) *Motor* hochjagen: **~ up** *Flugzeugmotor* abbremsen; **~ boat** *s.* Rennboot *n*; **'~·course** *s.* (Pferde)Rennbahn *f*; **~ di·rec·tor** *s. mot.* Rennleiter *m*; **'~·go·er** *s.* Rennplatzbesucher(in); **'~·horse** *s.* Rennpferd *n*.

ra·ceme [rə'siːm] *s.* ♀ Traube *f* (*Blütenstand*).

race meet·ing *s.* (Pferde)Rennen *n*.

rac·er ['reɪsə] *s.* **1.** a) (Renn)Läufer(in), b) Rennfahrer(in); **2.** Rennpferd *n*; **3.** Rennrad *n*, -boot *n*, -wagen *m*.

Race Re·la·tions Board *s. Brit.* Ausschuss *m* zur Verhinderung von 'Rassendiskrimi,nierung.

race| ri·ot *s.* 'Rassenkra,wall *m*; **'~·track** *s.* **1.** *mot.* Rennstrecke *f*; **2.** → **racecourse**; **'~·way** *s.* **1.** (Mühl)Gerinne *n*; **2.** ⊕ Laufring *m*.

ra·chis ['reɪkɪs] *pl.* **rach·i·des** ['reɪkɪdiːz] *s.* **1.** ♀, *zo.* Rhachis *f*, Spindel *f*; **2.** *anat., zo.* Rückgrat *n*; **ra·chi·tis** [ræ'kaɪtɪs] *s.* ✠ Ra'chitis *f*.

ra·cial ['reɪʃl] *adj.* □ rassisch, Rassen...: **~ equality** Rassengleichheit *f*; **~ discrimination** Rassendiskriminierung *f*; **~ segregation** Rassentrennung *f*; **'ra·cial·ism** [-ʃəlɪzəm] *s.* **1.** Ras'sismus *m*; **2.** Rassenkult *m*; **3.** 'Rassenpoli,tik *f*; **'ra·cial·ist** [-ʃəlɪst] **I** *s.* Ras'sist(in); **II** *adj.* ras'sistisch.

rac·i·ness ['reɪsɪnɪs] *s.* **1.** Rassigkeit *f*, Rasse *f*; **2.** Urwüchsigkeit *f*; **3.** *das* Pi'kante, Würze *f*; **4.** Schwung *m*, 'Schmiss' *m*.

rac·ing ['reɪsɪŋ] **I** *s.* **1.** Rennen *n*; **2.** (Pferde)Rennsport *m*; **II** *adj.* **3.** Renn...(*-boot, -wagen etc.*): **~ circuit** *mot.* Rennstrecke *f*; **~ cyclist** Radrennfahrer *m*; **~ driver** Rennfahrer(in); **~ man** Pferdesportliebhaber *m*; **~ world** die Rennwelt.

rac·ism ['reɪsɪzəm] → **racialism**; **'rac·ist** → **racialist**.

rack¹ [ræk] **I** *s.* **1.** Gestell *n*, Gerüst *n*; (*Gewehr-, Kleider- etc.*)Ständer *m*; (*Streck-, Stütz*)Rahmen *m*; ✗ Raufe *f*, Futtergestell *n*; 🖾 Gepäcknetz *n*; (Handtuch)Halter *m*; **2.** 'Fächerre,gal *n*; **3.** *typ.* 'Setze,gal *n*; **4.** ⊕ Zahnstange *f*: **~-and-pinion gear** Zahnstangengetriebe *n*; **5.** *hist.* Folterbank *f*, (Streck)Folter *f*; *fig.* (Folter)Qualen *pl.*: *put on the ~ bsd. fig.* j-n auf die Folter spannen; **II** *v/t.* **6.** (aus)recken, strecken; **7.** auf *od.* in ein Gestell *od.* Re'gal legen; **8.** *bsd. fig.* foltern, martern: *~ one's brains* sich den Kopf zermartern; *~ed with pain* schmerzgequält; *~ing pains* rasende Schmerzen; **9.** a) *Miete* (wucherisch) hoch schrauben, b) → **rack-rent** 3; **10.** **~ up** ✗ mit Futter versehen.

rack² [ræk] *s.:* *go to ~ and ruin* *a.* *fig.* kaputtgehen.

rack³ [ræk] *s.* Passgang *m* (*Pferd*).

rack⁴ [ræk] **I** *s.* fliegendes Gewölk; **II** *v/i.* (da'hin)ziehen (*Wolken*).

rack⁵ [ræk] *v/t. oft* **~ off** *Wein etc.* abziehen, -füllen.

rack·et¹ ['rækɪt] *s.* **1.** *sport* Ra'kett *n*, (*Tennis- etc.*)Schläger *m*: **~ press** Spanner *m*; **2.** *pl. oft sg. konstr.* Ra'kettspiel *n*, Wandballspiel *n*; **3.** Schneeteller *m*.

rack·et² ['rækɪt] **I** *s.* **1.** Krach *m*, Lärm *m*, Ra'dau *m*, Spek'takel *m*; **2.** ‚Wirbel' *m*, Aufregung *f*; **3.** a) ausgelassene Gesellschaft, rauschendes Fest, b) Vergnügungstaumel *m*, c) Trubel *m des Gesellschaftslebens*: *go on the ~* ‚auf die Pauke hauen'; **4.** harte (Nerven-)Probe, ‚Schlauch' *m*: *stand the ~* F a) die Sache durchstehen, b) die Folgen zu tragen haben, c) (alles) berappen; **5.** *sl.* a) Schwindel *m*, ‚Schiebung' *f*, b) Erpresserbande *f*, Racket *n*, c) organisierte Erpressung, d) ‚Masche' *f*, (einträgliches) Geschäft, e) *Am.* Beruf *m*, Branche *f*; **II** *v/i.* **6.** Krach machen, lärmen; **7.** *mst* **~ about** ‚(he'rum)sumpfen'; **rack·et·eer** [,rækə'tɪə] **I** *s.* **1.** Gangster *m*, Erpresser *m*; **2.** Schieber *m*, Geschäftemacher *m*; **II** *v/i.* **3.** dunkle Geschäfte machen; **4.** organisierte Erpressung betreiben; **rack·et·eer·ing** [,rækə'tɪərɪŋ] *s.* **1.** Gangstertum *n*, organisierte Erpressung; **2.** Geschäftemache'rei *f*; **'rack·et·y** [-tɪ] *adj.* **1.** lärmend; **2.** turbu'lent; **3.** ausgelassen, ausschweifend.

rack| rail·way *s.* Zahnradbahn *f*; **'~·rent I** *s.* **1.** Wuchermiete *f*; **2.** *Brit.* höchstmögliche Jahresmiete; **II** *v/t.* **3.** e-e Wuchermiete *od.* von *j-m* verlangen; **~ wheel** *s.* Zahnrad *n*.

ra·coon → **raccoon**.

rac·y ['reɪsɪ] *adj.* **1.** rassig (*a. fig. Auto, Stil etc.*), feurig (*Pferd, a. Musik etc.*); **2.** urtümlich, kernig: **~ of the soil** urwüchsig, bodenständig; **3.** *fig.* a) le'bendig, geistreich, ‚spritzig', b) schwungvoll, schmissig: **~ melody**; **4.** pi'kant, würzig (*Geruch etc.*) (*a. fig.*); **5.** F *u. Am.* schlüpfrig, gewagt.

rad [ræd] *s. pol.* Radi'kale(r) *f*.

ra·dar ['reɪdɑː] **I** *s.* **1.** Ra'dar *m*, *n*, Funkmesstechnik *f*, -ortung *f*; **2.** *a.* **~ set** Ra'dargerät *n*; **II** *adj.* **3.** Radar...: **~ display** Radarschirmbild *n*; **~ gun** Radarpistole *f*; **~ scanner** Radarsuchgerät *n*; **~ screen** Radarschirm *m*; **~ scope** Radarsichtgerät *n*; **~ trap** Radarfalle *f* (*der Polizei*).

rad·dle ['rædl] **I** *s.* **1.** *min.* Rötel *m*; **II** *v/t.* **2.** mit Rötel bemalen; **3.** rot anmalen.

ra·di·al ['reɪdjəl] **I** *adj.* □ **1.** radi'al, Radi-al..., Strahl(en)...; sternförmig; **2.** *anat.* Speichen...; **3.** ♀, *zo.* radi'alsym,metrisch; **II** *s.* **4.** *anat.* → a) *radial artery*, b) *radial nerve*; **~ ar·ter·y** *s.* Speichenschlagader *f*; **~ drill** *s.* ⊕ Radi'albohr,maschine *f*; **~ en·gine** *s.* Sternmotor *m*; **'~-flow tur·bine** *s.* Radi'altur,bine *f*; **~ nerve** *s.* Speichennerv *m*; **'~-(-ply) tire** (*Brit.* **tyre**) *s.* ⊕ Gür-

telreifen *m*; ~ **route** *s*. Ausfallstraße *f*.
ra·di·ance ['reɪdjəns], **'ra·di·an·cy** [-sɪ] *s*. **1.** *a. fig.* Strahlen *n*, strahlender Glanz; **2.** → *radiation*; **'ra·di·ant** [-nt] **I** *adj.* □ **1.** strahlend (*a. fig.* **with** vor *dat.*, von): ~ *beauty*; ~ *with joy* freudestrahlend; *be* ~ *with health* vor Gesundheit strotzen; **2.** *phys.* Strahlungs...(-*energie etc.*): ~ *heating* ⊚ Flächenheizung *f*; **3.** strahlenförmig (angeordnet); **II** *adj.* **4.** Strahl(ungs)punkt *m*; **'ra·di·ate** [-dɪeɪt] **I** *v/i.* **1.** ausstrahlen (*from* von) (*a. fig.*); **2.** *a. fig.* strahlen, leuchten; **II** *v/t.* **3.** *Licht, Wärme etc.* ausstrahlen; **4.** *fig. Liebe etc.* ausstrahlen, -strömen: ~ *health* vor Gesundheit strotzen; **5.** *Radio, TV:* ausstrahlen, senden; **III** *adj.* strahlenförmig, Strahl(en)...; **ra·di·a·tion** [ˌreɪdɪ'eɪʃn] *s*. **1.** *phys.* (Aus)Strahlung *f* (*a. fig.*): ~ *detection team* ✕ Strahlenspürtrupp *m*; ~ *level* Strahlenbelastung *f*; **2.** *a.* ~ *therapy* ✚ Strahlenbehandlung *f*, Bestrahlung *f*; **'ra·di·a·tor** [-dɪeɪtə] *s*. **1.** ⊚ Heizkörper *m*; Strahlkörper *m*, -ofen *m*; **2.** ⚡ 'Raumstrahlan,tenne *f*; **3.** *mot.* Kühler *m*: ~ *core* Kühlerblock *m*; ~ *grid*, ~ *grill* Kühlergrill *m*; ~ *mascot* Kühlerfigur *f*.
rad·i·cal ['rædɪkl] **I** *adj.* □ → *radically*; **1.** radi'kal (*pol. oft ⚐*); *weitS. a.* drastisch, gründlich: ~ *cure* Radikal-, Rosskur *f*; *undergo a* ~ *change* sich von Grund auf ändern; **2.** ursprünglich, eingewurzelt; fundamen'tal (*Fehler etc.*); grundlegend, Grund...: ~ *difference*; ~ *idea*; **3.** *bsd.* ♀, ⚓ Wurzel...: ~ *sign* → 8b; ~ *plane* ⚓ Potenzebene *f*; **4.** *ling.* Wurzel..., Stamm...: ~ *word* Stamm(wort *n*) *m*; **5.** ♪ Grund(ton)...; **6.** *a.* 🜋 Radikal...; **II** *s*. **7.** *pol.* (*a. ⚐*) Radi'kale(r *m*) *f*; **8.** ⚓ *a.* Wurzel(zeichen *n*); **9.** *ling.* Wurzel(buchstabe *m*) *f*; **10.** ♪ Grundton *m* (*Akkord*); **11.** 🜋 Radi'kal *n*; **'rad·i·cal·ism** [-kəlɪzəm] *s*. Radika'lismus *m*; **'rad·i·cal·ize** [-kəlaɪz] *v/t.* (*v/i.* sich) radikalisieren; **'rad·i·cal·ly** [-kəlɪ] *adv.* **1.** radi'kal, von Grund auf; **2.** ursprünglich.
ra·dic·chi·o [ræ'dɪkɪəʊ] *pl.* **-chi·os** *s*. ♀ Ra'dicchio *m*.
rad·i·ces ['reɪdɪsiːz] *pl. von* **radix**.
rad·i·cle ['rædɪkl] *s*. **1.** ♀ a) Keimwurzel *f*, b) Würzelchen *n*; **2.** *anat.* (Gefäß-, Nerven)Wurzel *f*.
ra·di·i ['reɪdɪaɪ] *pl. von* **radius**.
ra·di·o ['reɪdɪəʊ] **I** *pl.* **-di·os** *s*. **1.** Funk (-betrieb) *m*; **2.** Radio *n*, Rundfunk *m*: *on the* ~ im Rundfunk; **3.** a) Radio(gerät) *n*, Rundfunkempfänger *m*, b) Funkgerät *n*; **4.** (Radio)Sender *m*; **5.** Rundfunkgesellschaft *f*; **6.** F Funkspruch *m*; **II** *v/t.* **7.** senden, funken, *e-e Funkmeldung* 'durchgeben; **8.** ✚ a) *e-e* Röntgenaufnahme machen von, b) durch'leuchten; **9.** ✚ mit Radium bestrahlen.
ˌra·di·o·'ac·tive *adj.* □ radioak'tiv: ~ *waste* radioaktiver Müll, Atommüll *m*; **~ly contaminated** (radioaktiv) verstrahlt; **ˌ~·ac'tiv·i·ty** *s*. Radioaktivi'tät *f*; ~ *am·a·teur* *s*. 'Funkama,teur *m*; ~ *bea·con* *s*. Funkbake *f*; ~ *beam* *s*. Funk-, Richtstrahl *m*; ~ *bear·ing* *s*. **1.** Funkpeilung *f*; **2.** Peilwinkel *m*; ~ *cab* *s*. Funktaxi *n*; ~ *car* *s*. Funk(streifen)wagen *m*; **ˌ~·car·bon dat·ing** *s*. Radiokar'bon,thode, C-'14-Me,thode *f*; **ˌ~·chem·is·try** *s*. 'Radio-, 'Strahlenche,mie *f*; **ˌ~·con'trol** **I** *s*. Funksteuerung *f*; **II** *v/t.* fernsteuern; **ˌ~·el·e·ment** *s*. radioak'tives Ele'ment; **ˌ~·en·gi·neer·ing** *s*. Funktechnik *f*; ~ *fre·quen·cy* *s*.

⚡ 'Hochfre,quenz *f*.
ra·di·o·gram ['reɪdɪəʊɡræm] *s*. **1.** 'Funkmeldung *f*, -tele,gramm *n*; **2.** *Brit.* a) → *radiograph* **I**, b) Mu'siktruhe *f*.
ra·di·o·graph ['reɪdɪəʊɡrɑːf] ✚ **I** *s*. Radio'gramm *n*, *bsd.* Röntgenaufnahme *f*; **II** *v/t.* ein Radio'gramm *etc.* machen von; **ra·di·o·gra·phy** [ˌreɪdɪ'ɒɡrəfɪ] *s*. Röntgenogra'phie *f*.
ra·di·o·log·i·cal [ˌreɪdɪəʊ'lɒdʒɪkl] *adj.* ✚ radio'logisch, Röntgen...; **ra·di·o·lo·gist** [ˌreɪdɪ'ɒlədʒɪst] *s*. Röntgeno'loge *m*; **ra·di·ol·o·gy** [ˌreɪdɪ'ɒlədʒɪ] *s*. Strahlen-, Röntgenkunde *f*.
ra·di·o| mark·er *s*. ✈ (Anflug)Funkbake *f*; ~ *mes·sage* *s*. Funkmeldung *f*; ~ *op·er·a·tor* *s*. (✈ Bord)Funker *m*.
ra·di·o·phone ['reɪdɪəʊfəʊn] *s*. **1.** *phys.* Radio'phon *n*; **2.** → *radiotelephone*.
ˌra·di·o·'pho·no·graph *s*. *Am.* Mu'siktruhe *f*; **ˌ~·'pho·to·graph** *s*. Funkbild *n*; **ˌ~·'pho·tog·ra·phy** *s*. Bildfunk *m*.
ra·di·os·co·py [ˌreɪdɪ'ɒskəpɪ] *s*. ✚ Röntgenosko'pie *f*, 'Röntgenunter,suchung *f*.
ra·di·o| set *s*. → *radio* 3; ~ *sonde* [sɒnd] *s*. *meteor.* Radiosonde *f*; ~ *tax·i* *s*. Funktaxi *n*; **ˌ~·'tel·e·gram** *s*. 'Funkte,gramm *n*; **ˌ~·te'leg·ra·phy** *s*. drahtlose Telegra'fie; **ˌ~·'tel·e·phone** *s*. Funksprechgerät *n*; **ˌ~·te'leph·o·ny** *s*. drahtlose Telefo'nie; **ˌ~·'ther·a·py** *s*. 'Strahlen-, 'Röntgenthera,pie *f*.
rad·ish ['rædɪʃ] *s*. **1.** *a. large* ~ Rettich *m*; **2.** *a. red* ~ Ra'dieschen *n*.
ra·di·um ['reɪdjəm] *s*. 🜚 Radium *n*.
ra·di·us ['reɪdjəs] *pl.* **-di·i** [-dɪaɪ] *od.* **-di·us·es** *s*. **1.** ⚓ Radius *m*, Halbmesser *m*: ~ *of turn mot.* Wendehalbmesser; **2.** ⊚, *anat.* Speiche *f*; **3.** ♀ Strahl (-blüte *f*) *m*; **4.** 'Umkreis *m*: *within a* ~ *of*; **5.** *fig.* (Wirkungs-, Einfluss)Bereich *m*: ~ *(of action)* Aktionsradius *m*, *mot.* Fahrbereich *m*.
ra·dix ['reɪdɪks] *pl.* **rad·i·ces** ['reɪdɪsiːz] *s*. **1.** ⚓ Basis *f*, Grundzahl *f*; **2.** ♀, *a. ling.* Wurzel *f*.
raf·fi·a ['ræfɪə] *s*. Raffiabast *m*.
raff·ish ['ræfɪʃ] *adj.* □ **1.** liederlich; **2.** pöbelhaft, ordi'när.
raf·fle ['ræfl] **I** *s*. Tombola *f*, Verlosung *f*; **II** *v/t. oft* ~ *off et.* (in *e-r* Tombola) verlosen; **III** *v/i.* losen (*for* um).
raft [rɑːft] **I** *s*. **1.** Floß *n*; **2.** zs.-gebundenes Holz; **3.** *Am.* Treibholz(ansammlung *f*) *n*; **4.** F Unmenge *f*, 'Haufen' *m*, 'Latte' *f*; **II** *v/t.* **5.** flößen, als *od.* mit dem Floß beförder; **6.** zu e-m Floß zs.-binden; **7.** mit e-m Floß befahren; **'raft·er** [-tə] *s*. **1.** Flößer *m*; **2.** ⊚ (Dach)Sparren *m*; **rafts·man** ['rɑːftsmən] *s*. [*irr.*] Flößer *m*.
rag¹ [ræɡ] *s*. **1.** Fetzen *m*, Lumpen *m*, Lappen *m*: *in ~s* a) in Fetzen (*Stoff etc.*), b) zerlumpt (*Person*); *not a* ~ *of evidence* nicht der geringste Beweis; *chew the* ~ a) 'quatschen', plaudern, b) 'meckern'; *cook to ~s* zerkochen; *it's a red* ~ *to him fig.* es ist für ihn ein rotes Tuch; → *ragtag* 2; **2.** *pl. Papierherstellung:* Hadern *pl.*, Lumpen *pl.*; **3.** *humor.* 'Fetzen' *m* (*Kleid, Anzug*): *not a* ~ *to put on* keinen Fetzen zum Anziehen haben; → *glad* 2; **4.** *humor.* 'Lappen' *m* (*Geldschein, Taschentuch etc.*); **5.** (*contp.* Käse-, Wurst)Blatt *n* (*Zeitung*); **6.** ♪ F → *ragtime*.
rag² [ræɡ] *sl.* **I** *v/t.* **1.** *j-n* 'anschnauzen'; **2.** *j-n* 'aufziehen'; **3.** *j-m e-n* Streich spielen; **4.** *j-n* 'piesacken', übel mitspielen (*dat.*); **II** *v/i.* **5.** Ra'dau machen; **III** *s*. **6.** Ra'dau *m*; **7.** Ulk *m*, Jux *m*.
rag·a·muf·fin ['ræɡəˌmʌfɪn] *s*. **1.** zer-

lumpter Kerl; **2.** Gassenkind *n*.
ˌrag|-and-'bone man [-ɡən'b-] *s*. Lumpensammler *m*; ~ *bag* *s*. Lumpensack *m*; *fig.* Sammel'surium *n*: *out of the* ~ aus der 'Klamottenkiste'; ~ *doll* *s*. Stoffpuppe *f*.
rage [reɪdʒ] **I** *s*. **1.** Wut(anfall *m*) *f*, Zorn *m*, Rage *f*: *be in a* ~ vor Wut schäumen, toben; *fly into a* ~ in Wut geraten; **2.** Wüten *n*, Toben *n*, Rasen *n* (*der Elemente, der Leidenschaft etc.*); **3.** Sucht *f*, Ma'nie *f*, Gier *f* (*for* nach): ~ *for collecting things* Sammelwut *f*; **4.** Begeisterung *f*, Taumel *m*, Rausch *m*, Ek'stase *f*: *it is all the* ~ es ist jetzt die große Mode, alles ist wild darauf; **II** *v/i.* **5.** (*a. fig.*) toben, rasen, wüten (*at, against* gegen).
rag fair *s*. Trödelmarkt *m*.
rag·ged ['ræɡɪd] *adj.* □ **1.** zerlumpt, abgerissen (*Person, Kleidung*); **2.** zottig, struppig; **3.** zerfetzt, ausgefranst (*Wunde*); **4.** zackig, gezackt (*Glas, Stein*); **5.** holp(e)rig: ~ *rhymes*; **6.** verwildert: *a* ~ *garden*; **7.** roh, unfertig, fehler-, mangelhaft; *zs.*-hanglos; **8.** rau (*Stimme, Ton*).
'rag·man [-mən] *s*. [*irr.*] Lumpensammler *m*.
ra·gout ['ræɡuː] *s*. Ra'gout *n*.
rag| pa·per *s*. ⊚ 'Hadernpa,pier *n*; **'~·pick·er** *s*. Lumpensammler(in); **'~·tag** *s*. Pöbel *m*, Gesindel *n*: ~ *and bobtail* Krethi u. Plethi *pl.*; **'~·time** *s*. ♪ Ragtime *m* (*Jazzstil*).
raid [reɪd] **I** *s*. **1.** Ein-, 'Überfall *m*; Raub-, Streifzug *m*; ✕ 'Stoßtruppunter,nehmen *n*; ⚓ Kaperfahrt *f*; ✈ (Luft-) Angriff *m*; **2.** (Poli'zei)Razzia *f*; **3.** *fig.* a) (An)Sturm *m* (*on, upon* auf *acc.*), b) *sport* Vorstoß *m*; **II** *v/t.* **4.** *e-n* 'Überfall machen auf (*acc.*), über'fallen, angreifen (*a.* ✈): *~ing party* ✕ Stoßtrupp *m*; **5.** stürmen, plündern; **6.** *e-e* Razzia machen in (*dat.*); **7.** ~ *the market* ✝ den Markt drücken.
rail¹ [reɪl] **I** *s*. **1.** ⊚ Schiene *f*, Riegel *m*, Querstange *f*; **2.** Geländer *n*; (*main*) ~ ⚓ Reling *f*; **3.** 🚢 a) Schiene *f*, b) *pl.* Gleis *n*: *by* ~ mit der Bahn; *run off the ~s* entgleisen; *off the* ~s *fig.* aus dem Geleise, durcheinander; **4.** *pl.* ✝ Eisenbahnaktien *pl.*; **II** *v/t.* **5.** *a.* ~ *in* mit *e-m* Geländer um'geben: ~ *off* durch ein Geländer (ab)trennen.
rail² [reɪl] *s. orn.* Ralle *f*.
rail³ [reɪl] *v/i.* schimpfen, lästern, fluchen (*at, against* über *acc.*): ~ *at* (*od. against*) über *et.* herziehen, gegen *et.* wettern.
rail| bus *s*. Schienenbus *m*; **'~·car** *s*. Triebwagen *m*; **'~·head** *s*. **1.** Kopfbahnhof *m*; ✕ Ausladebahnhof *m*; **2.** 🚢 a) Schienenkopf *m*, b) im Bau befindliches Ende (*e-r neuen Strecke*).
rail·ing ['reɪlɪŋ] *s*. **1.** *a. pl.* Geländer *n*, Gitter *n*; **2.** 🚢 Reling *f*.
rail·ler·y ['reɪlərɪ] *s*. Necke'rei *f*, Stiche'lei *f*, (gutmütiger) Spott.
rail·road ['reɪlrəʊd] *bsd. Am.* **I** *s*. **1.** *allg.* Eisenbahn *f*; **2.** *pl.* ✝ Eisenbahnaktien *pl.*; **II** *adj.* **3.** Eisenbahn...: ~ *accident*; **III** *v/t.* **4.** mit der Eisenbahn befördern; **5.** F *Gesetzesvorlage etc.* 'durchpeitschen'; **6.** F a) *j-n* 'über'fahren', zwingen (*into doing et.* zu tun), b) *j-n* ,abservieren'; **'rail,road·er** [-də] *s. Am.* Eisenbahner *m*.
rail·way ['reɪlweɪ] **I** *s*. **1.** *bsd. Brit. allg.* Eisenbahn *f*; **2.** Lo'kalbahn *f*; **II** *adj.* **3.** Eisenbahn...: ~ *accident*; ~ *car·riage* *s*. Per'sonenwagen *m*; ~ *guard* *s*. Zugbegleiter *m*; ~ *guide* *s*. Kursbuch *n*; **'~·man** [-weɪmən] *s*. [*irr.*] Eisenbahner

m.

rai·ment ['reɪmənt] *s. poet.* Kleidung *f*, Gewand *n*.

rain [reɪn] **I** *s.* **1.** Regen *m*; *pl.* Regenfälle *pl.*, -güsse *pl.*: **the** ~**s** die Regenzeit (*in den Tropen*); ~ **or shine** bei jedem Wetter; **as right as** ~ F ganz richtig, in Ordnung; **II** *v/i.* **2.** *impers.* regnen; → **pour** 6; **3.** *fig.* regnen; niederprasseln (*Schläge*); strömen (*Tränen*); **III** *v/t.* **4.** *Tropfen etc.* (her)'niedersenden, regnen: **it's** ~**ing cats and dogs** es gießt in Strömen; **5.** *fig.* (nieder)regnen *od.* (-)hageln lassen; '~**bow** [-bəʊ] *s.* Regenbogen *m*; ~ **check** *s. Am.* Einlasskarte *f* für die Neuansetzung e-r wegen Regens abgebrochenen (Sport)Veranstaltung: **may I take a** ~ **on it?** *fig.* darf ich darauf (*auf Ihr Angebot etc.*) später einmal zurückkommen?; '~**coat** *s.* Regenmantel *m*; '~**drop** *s.* Regentropfen *m*; '~**fall** *s.* **1.** Regen(schauer) *m*; **2.** *meteor.* Niederschlagsmenge *f*; ~ **forest** *s.* Regenwald *m*.

rain·i·ness ['reɪnɪnɪs] *s.* **1.** Regenneigung *f*; **2.** Regenwetter *n*.

'**rain|·proof I** *adj.* wasserdicht; **II** *s.* Regenmantel *m*; '~**storm** *s.* heftiger Regenguss.

rain·y ['reɪnɪ] *adj.* □ regnerisch, verregnet; Regen...(-*wetter, -wind etc.*): **save up for a** ~ **day** *fig.* e-n Notgroschen zurücklegen.

raise [reɪz] **I** *v/t.* **1.** *oft* ~ **up** (in die Höhe) heben, auf-, em'por-, hochheben, erheben, erhöhen; *mit Kran etc.* hochwinden, -ziehen; *Augen* erheben, aufschlagen; ♪ *Blasen* ~ *Kohle* fördern; *Staub* aufwirbeln; *Vorhang* hochziehen; *Teig, Brot* treiben: ~ **one's glass to** auf *j-n* das Glas erheben, *j-m* zutrinken; ~ **a toast to s.o.** e-n Toast auf j-n ausbringen; ~ **one's hat** (**to s.o.**) den Hut ziehen (vor j-m, *a. fig.*); → **power** 12; **2.** aufrichten, -stellen, aufrecht stellen; **3.** errichten, erstellen, (er)bauen; **4.** *Familie* gründen; *Kinder* auf-, großziehen; **5.** a) *Pflanzen* ziehen, b) *Tiere* züchten; **6.** aufwecken: ~ **from the dead** von den Toten erwecken; **7.** *Geister* zitieren, beschwören; **8.** *Gelächter, Sturm etc.* her'vorrufen, verursachen; *Erwartungen, Verdacht, Zorn* erwecken, erregen; *Gerücht* aufkommen lassen; *Schwierigkeiten* machen; **9.** *Geist, Mut* beleben, anfeuern; **10.** aufwiegeln (**against** gegen); *Aufruhr* anstiften, -zetteln; **11.** *Geld etc.* beschaffen; *Anleihe, Hypothek, Kredit* aufnehmen; *Steuern* erheben; *Heer* aufstellen; **12.** *Stimme, Geschrei* erheben; **13.** *An-, Einspruch* erheben, *Einwand a.* vorbringen, geltend machen, *Forderung a.* stellen; *Frage* aufwerfen; *Sache* zur Sprache bringen; **14.** (ver)stärken, vergrößern, vermehren; **15.** *Lohn, Preis, Wert etc.* erhöhen, hin'aufsetzen; *Temperatur, Wette etc.* steigern; **16.** (im Rang) erhöhen: ~ **to the throne** auf den Thron erheben; **17.** *Belagerung, Blockade etc., a. Verbot* aufheben; **18.** ♪ sichten; **II** *s.* **19.** Erhöhung *f*; *Am.* Steigung *f* (*Straße*); **20.** *bsd. Am.* (Gehalts-, Lohn)Erhöhung *f*, Aufbesserung *f*; **raised** [-zd] *adj.* **1.** erhöht; **2.** gesteigert; **3.** ❷ erhaben; **4.** Hefe...: ~ **cake**.

rai·sin ['reɪzn] *s.* Ro'sine *f*.

rai·son| d'é·tat [ˌreɪzɔ̃ːndeɪˈtɑː] (*Fr.*) *s.* 'Staatsräˌson *f*; ~ **d'ê·tre** [-ˈdeɪtrə] (*Fr.*) *s.* Daseinsberechtigung *f*, -zweck *m*.

raj [rɑːdʒ] *s. Brit. Ind.* Herrschaft *f*.

ra·ja(h) ['rɑːdʒə] *s.* Radscha *m* (*indi-*

---

scher Fürst).

rake¹ [reɪk] **I** *s.* **1.** Rechen *m* (*a. des Croupiers etc.*), Harke *f*; **2.** ❷ a) Rührstange *f*, b) Kratze *f*, c) Schürhaken *m*; **II** *v/t.* **3.** (glatt-, zs.-)rechen, (-)harken; **4.** *mst* ~ **together** zs.-scharren (*a. fig. zs.-raffen*); **5.** durch'stöbern (*a.* ~ **up**, ~ **over**): ~ **up** *fig.* alte Geschichten aufrühren; **6.** ✕ (mit Feuer) bestreichen, ‚beharken'; **7.** über'blicken, absuchen; **III** *v/i.* **8.** rechen, harken; **9.** *fig.* he'rumstöbern, -suchen (**for** nach).

rake² [reɪk] *s.* Lebemann *m*.

rake³ [reɪk] **I** *v/i.* **1.** Neigung haben; **2.** ♪ a) 'überhängen (*Steven*), b) Fall haben (*Mast, Schornstein*); **II** *v/t.* **3.** (nach rückwärts) neigen; **III** *s.* **4.** Neigung(swinkel *m*) *f.*

'**rake-off** *s.* F (Gewinn)Anteil *m*.

rak·ish¹ ['reɪkɪʃ] *adj.* □ ausschweifend, liederlich, wüst.

rak·ish² ['reɪkɪʃ] *adj.* **1.** ♪, *mot.* schnittig (gebaut); **2.** *fig.* flott, verwegen, keck.

ral·ly¹ ['rælɪ] **I** *v/t.* **1.** *Truppen etc.* (wieder) sammeln *od.* ordnen; **2.** vereinigen, scharen (**round, to** um), zs.-trommeln; **3.** aufrütteln, -muntern, in Schwung bringen; **4.** *Kräfte etc.* sammeln, zs.-raffen; **II** *v/i.* **5.** sich (wieder) sammeln; **6.** *a.* sich scharen (**round, to** um); sich zs.-tun; sich anschließen (**to** *dat. od.* an *acc.*); **7.** *a.* ~ **round** sich erholen (*a. fig. u.* ♥), neue Kräfte sammeln; *sport etc.* sich (wieder) ‚fangen'; **8.** *Tennis etc.*: a) e-n Ballwechsel ausführen, b) sich einschlagen; **III** *s.* **9.** ✕ Sammeln *n*; **10.** Zs.-kunft *f*, Treffen *n*, Tagung *f*, Kundgebung *f*, (Massen)Versammlung *f*; **11.** Erholung *f* (*a.* ✝ *der Preise, des Marktes*); **12.** *Tennis:* Ballwechsel *m*; **13.** *mot.* Rallye *f*, Sternfahrt *f*.

ral·ly² ['rælɪ] *v/t.* hänseln.

ral·ly·ing ['rælɪɪŋ] *adj.* Sammel...: ~ **cry** Parole *f*, Schlagwort *n*; ~ **point** Sammelpunkt *m*, -platz *m*.

ram [ræm] **I** *s.* **1.** *zo.* (*ast.* ♈) Widder *m*; **2.** ✕ *hist.* Sturmbock *m*; **3.** ❷ a) Ramme *f*, b) Rammbock *m*, -bär *m*, c) Presskolben *m*; **4.** ♪ Rammsporn *m*; **II** *v/t.* **5.** (fest-, ein)rammen (*a.* ~ **down** *od.* **in**); *weitS.* (gewaltsam) stoßen, drücken; **6.** (hin'ein)stopfen: ~ **up** a) voll stopfen, b) verrammeln, verstopfen; **7.** *fig.* eintrichtern, -pauken: ~ **s.th. into s.o.** j-m et. einbläuen; → **throat** 1; **8.** ♪, ✈ *etc.* rammen; *weitS.* stoßen, schmettern, ‚knallen'.

ram·ble ['ræmbl] **I** *v/i.* **1.** um'herwandern, -streifen, bummeln; **2.** sich winden (*Fluss etc.*); **3.** ♥ wuchern, (üppig) ranken; **4.** *fig.* (vom Thema) abschweifen; drauf'losreden; **II** *s.* **5.** (Fuß)Wanderung *f*, Streifzug *m*; Bummel *m*; '**ram·bler** [-lə] *s.* **1.** Wand(e)rer *m*, Wand(r)erin *f*; **2.** *a.* **crimson** ~ ♥ Kletterrose *f*; '**ram·bling** [-lɪŋ] **I** *adj.* □ **1.** um'herwandernd, -streifend: ~ **club** Wanderverein *m*; **2.** ♥ (üppig) rankend, wuchernd; **3.** weitläufig, verschachtelt (*Gebäude*); **4.** *fig.* abschweifend, weitschweifig, planlos; **II** *s.* **5.** Wandern *n*, Um'herstreifen *n*.

ram·bo ['ræmbəʊ] *pl.* -**bos** *s.* F Rambo *m*; '~**-style** *adj.* nach Ramboart, angriffslustig, draufgängerisch.

ram·bunc·tious [ræmˈbʌŋkʃəs] *adj.* laut, lärmend, wild.

ram·ie ['ræmiː] *s.* Ra'mie(faser) *f.*

ram·i·fi·ca·tion [ˌræmɪfɪˈkeɪʃn] *s.* Verzweigung *f*, -ästelung *f* (*a. fig.*); **ram·i·fy** ['ræmɪfaɪ] *v/t. u. v/i.* (sich) verzweigen

---

(*a. fig.*).

ram·jet (**en·gine**) ['ræmdʒet] *s.* ❷ Staustrahltriebwerk *n*.

ramp¹ [ræmp] **I** *s.* **1.** Rampe *f* (*a.* △ *Abdachung*); **2.** (schräge) Auffahrt, (Lade)Rampe *f*; **3.** Krümmling *m* (*am Treppengeländer*); **4.** ✈ (fahrbare) Treppe *f*; **II** *v/i.* **5.** sich (drohend) aufrichten, zum Sprung ansetzen (*Tier*); **6.** toben, wüten; **7.** ♥ wuchern; **III** *v/t.* **8.** mit e-r Rampe versehen.

ramp² [ræmp] *s. Brit. sl.* Betrug *m.*

ram·page [ræmˈpeɪdʒ] **I** *v/i.* toben, wüten; **II** *s.*: **be on the** ~ a) (sich aus)toben, b) *fig.* grassieren, um sich greifen, wüten; **ram'pa·geous** [-dʒəs] *adj.* □ wild, wütend.

ramp·an·cy ['ræmpənsɪ] *s.* **1.** Über'handnehmen *n*, 'Umsichgreifen *n*, Grassieren *n*; **2.** *fig.* wilde Ausgelassenheit, Wildheit *f*; '**ramp·ant** [-nt] *adj.* □ **1.** wild, zügellos, ausgelassen; **2.** über'hand nehmend: **be** ~ → **rampage** II b; **3.** üppig, wuchernd (*Pflanzen*); **4.** (drohend) aufgerichtet, sprungbereit (*Tier*); **5.** *her.* steigend.

ram·part ['ræmpɑːt] *s.* ✕ a) Brustwehr *f*, b) (Schutz)Wall *m* (*a. fig.*).

ram raid *s.* F Blitzeinbruch *m* (*in ein Geschäft, bei dem das Schaufenster od. die Tür mit e-m Auto eingefahren wird*); '**ram-raid** *v/t.* F e-n Blitzeinbruch machen in (*acc.*); **ram raid·er** *s.* F Blitzeinbrecher(in); **ram raid·ing** *s.* F Blitzeinbruch *m*, -einbrüche *pl.*

ram·rod ['ræmrɒd] *s.* ✕ *hist.* Ladestock *m*: **as stiff as a** ~ als hätte *er etc.* e-n Ladestock verschluckt.

ram·shack·le ['ræmˌʃækl] *adj.* baufällig, wack(e)lig; klapp(e)rig.

ran¹ [ræn] *pret. von* **run**.

ran² [ræn] *s.* **1.** Docke *f* Bindfaden; **2.** ♪ aufgehaspeltes Kabelgarn.

ranch [rɑːntʃ; *bsd. Am.* ræntʃ] **I** *s.* Ranch *f*, (*bsd.* Vieh)Farm *f*; **II** *v/i.* Viehzucht treiben; '**ranch·er** [-tʃə] *s. Am.* **1.** Rancher *m*, Viehzüchter *m*; **2.** Farmer *m*; **3.** Rancharbeiter *m.*

ran·cid ['rænsɪd] *adj.* **1.** ranzig (*Butter etc.*); **2.** *fig.* widerlich; **ran·cid·i·ty** [rænˈsɪdətɪ], '**ran·cid·ness** [-nɪs] *s.* Ranzigkeit *f.*

ran·cor *Am.* → **rancour**.

ran·cor·ous ['ræŋkərəs] *adj.* □ erbittert, voller Groll, giftig; **ran·cour** ['ræŋkə] *s.* Groll *m*, Hass *m.*

ran·dom ['rændəm] **I** *adj.* □ ziel-, wahllos, zufällig, aufs Gerate'wohl, Zufalls...: ~ **mating** *biol.* Zufallspaarung *f*, ~ **sample** (*od.* **test**) Stichprobe *f*; ~ **shot** Schuss ins Blaue; ~ **access** *Computer*: wahlfreier *od.* direkter Zugriff; ~ **access memory** *Computer*: Arbeitsspeicher *m*; **II** *s.*: **at** ~ aufs Geratewohl, auf gut Glück, blindlings, zufällig: **talk at** ~ (wild) drauflosreden.

rand·y ['rændɪ] *adj.* F geil.

ra·nee [ˌrɑːˈniː] *s.* Rani *f* (*indische Fürstin*).

rang [ræŋ] *pret. von* **ring²**.

range [reɪndʒ] **I** *s.* **1.** Reihe *f*; (*a.* Berg-) Kette *f*; **2.** (Koch-, Küchen)Herd *m*; **3.** Schießstand *m*, -platz *m*; **4.** Entfernung *f zum Ziel*, Abstand *m*: **at a** ~ **of** aus (*od.* in) e-r Entfernung von; **at close** ~ aus der Nähe; **find the** ~ ✕ sich einschießen; **take the** ~ die Entfernung schätzen; **5.** *bsd.* ✕ Reich-, Trag-, Schussweite *f*; ♪ Laufstrecke *f* (*Torpedo*); ✈ Flugbereich *m*: **at close** ~ aus nächster Nähe; **out of** ~ außer Schussweite; **within** *od.* **out of vision** in Sichtweite; → **long-range**; **6.** Ausdehnung *f*, (ausgedehnte) Fläche; **7.** *fig.* Bereich *m*, Spielraum *m*, Grenzen *pl.*; (♥, *zo.* Verbreitungs)Gebiet *n*: **~** (*of action*) Aktionsbereich; **~** (*of activities*) (Betätigungs)Feld *n*; **~ of application** Anwendungsbereich; **~ of prices** ♥ Preislage *f*, -klasse *f*; **~ of reception** *Funk.* Empfangsbereich; **boiling ~** *phys.* Siedebereich; **8.** ♥ Kollekti'on *f*, Sorti'ment *n*: **a wide ~** (*of goods*) e-e große Auswahl, ein großes Angebot; **9.** Bereich *m*, Gebiet *n*, Raum *m*: **~ of knowledge** Wissensbereich; **~ of thought** Ideenkreis *m*; **10.** ♪ a) 'Ton-, 'Stimm,umfang *m*, b) Ton-, Stimmlage *f*; **II** *v/t.* **11.** (in Reihen) aufstellen *od.* anordnen; **12.** einreihen, -ordnen: **~ o.s. with** (*od.* **on the side of**) zu *j-m* halten; **13.** *Gebiet etc.* durch'streifen, -'wandern; **14.** längs *der Küste* fahren, entlangfahren; **15.** *Teleskop etc.* einstellen; **16.** ✕ a) *Geschütz* richten (**on** auf *acc.*), b) e-e Reichweite haben von, tragen; **III** *v/i.* **17.** (**with**) e-e Reihe *od.* Linie bilden (mit), in e-r Reihe *od.* Linie stehen (mit); **18.** sich erstrecken, verlaufen, reichen; **19.** *fig.* rangieren (**among** unter *dat.*), im gleichen Rang stehen (**with** mit); zählen, gehören (**with** zu); **20.** (um'her)streifen, (-)schweifen, wandern (*a. Auge, Blick*); **21.** ♥, *zo.* vorkommen, verbreitet *od.* zu finden sein; **22.** schwanken, sich bewegen (**from ... to ...** *od.* **between ... and ...** zwischen *... dat.* und ...) (*Zahlenwert, Preis etc.*); **23.** ✕ sich einschießen (*Geschütz*). **'range,find·er** *s.* ✕, *phot.* Entfernungsmesser *m* (✕ *a. Mann*).

rang·er ['reɪndʒə] *s.* **1.** *Am.* Ranger *m*: a) *Wächter e-s Nationalparks*, b) *mst* **⚷** *Angehöriger e-r Schutztruppe e-s Bundesstaates*, c) ✕ *Angehöriger e-r Kommandotruppe*; **2.** *Brit.* Aufseher *m* e-s königlichen Forsts *od.* Parks (*Titel*); **3.** *a.* **~ guide** *Brit.* Ranger *f* (*Pfadfinderin über 16 Jahre*).

rank¹ [ræŋk] **I** *s.* **1.** Reihe *f*, Linie *f*; **2.** ✕ a) Glied *n*, b) Rang *m*, Dienstgrad *m*: **the ~s** (Unteroffiziere und) Mannschaften; **~ and file** ✕ *der Mannschaftsstand, pol.* die Basis (*e-r Partei*); **in ~ and file** in Reih und Glied; **close the ~s** die Reihen schließen; **join the ~s** ins Heer eintreten; **rise from the ~s** von der Pike auf dienen (*a. fig.*); **3.** (sozi'ale) Klasse, Stand *m*, Schicht *f*, Rang *m*: **man of ~** Mann von Stand; **~ and fashion** die vornehme Welt; **of second ~** zweitrangig; **take ~ of** den Vorrang haben vor (*dat.*); **take ~ with** mit *j-m* gleichrangig sein; **II** *v/t.* **4.** (ein)reihen, (-)ordnen, klassifizieren; **5.** *Truppe etc.* aufstellen, formieren; **6.** *fig.* rechnen, zählen (**with, among** zu): **I ~ him above Shaw** ich stelle ihn über Shaw; **III** *v/i.* **7.** sich reihen *od.* ordnen; ✕ (in geschlossener Formati'on) marschieren; **8.** e-n Rang *od.* e-e Stelle einnehmen, rangieren (**above** über *dat.*, **below** unter *dat.*, **next to** hinter *dat.*): **~ as** gelten als; **~ first** an erster Stelle stehen; **~ high** e-n hohen Rang einnehmen, *a.* e-n hohen Stellenwert haben; **~ing officer** *Am.* rangältester Offizier; **9.** **~ among** ... mit gehören *od.* zählen zu.

rank² [ræŋk] *adj.* □ **1.** a) üppig, geil wachsend (*Pflanzen*), b) verwildert (*Garten*); **2.** fruchtbar, fett (*Boden*); **3.** stinkend, ranzig; **4.** widerlich, scharf (*Geruch od. Geschmack*); **5.** krass: **~ outsider**; **~ beginner** blutiger Anfänger; **~ nonsense** blühender Unsinn; **6.** ekelhaft, unanständig.

rank·er ['ræŋkə] *s.* ✕ a) einfacher Sol'dat, b) aus dem Mannschaftsstand her'vorgegangener Offi'zier.

ran·kle ['ræŋkl] *v/i.* **1.** eitern, schwären (*Wunde*); **2.** *fig.* nagen, fressen, weh tun: **~ with** *j-n* wurmen, *j-m* wehtun.

ran·sack ['rænsæk] *v/t.* **1.** durch'wühlen; **2.** plündern, ausrauben.

ran·som ['rænsəm] **I** *s.* **1.** Loskauf *m*, Auslösung *f*; **2.** Lösegeld *n*: **a king's ~** e-e Riesensumme; **hold to ~** a) *j-n* gegen Lösegeld gefangen halten, b) *fig. j-n* erpressen; **3.** *eccl.* Erlösung *f*; **II** *v/t.* **4.** los-, freikaufen; **5.** *eccl.* erlösen.

rant [rænt] *v/i.* **1.** toben, lärmen; **2.** schwadronieren, Phrasen dreschen; **3.** *obs.* geifern (**at, against** über *acc.*); **II** *v/t.* **4.** pa'thetisch vortragen; **II** *s.* **5.** Wortschwall *m*; Schwulst *m*, leeres Gerede, ‚Phrasendresche'rei‘; **'rant·er** [-tə] *s.* **1.** pa'thetischer Redner, Kanzelpauker *m*; **2.** Schwadro'neur *m*, Großsprecher *m*.

ra·nun·cu·lus [rə'nʌŋkjuləs] *pl.* **-lus·es, -li** [-laɪ] *s.* ♥ Ra'nunkel *f*.

rap¹ [ræp] **I** *v/t.* **1.** klopfen *od.* pochen an *od.* auf (*acc.*): **~ s.o.'s fingers, ~ s.o. over the knuckles** *bsd. fig.* j-m auf die Finger klopfen; **2.** *Am. sl.* a) *j-m* e-e ‚Zi'garre‘ verpassen, b) *j-n, et.* scharf kritisieren, c) *j-n* ‚verdonnern‘; d) *j-n* ‚schnappen‘; **3.** **~ out** a) durch Klopfen mitteilen (*Geist*), b) *Worte* her'auspoltern, ‚bellen‘; **II** *v/i.* **4.** klopfen, pochen, schlagen (**at** an *acc.*); **III** *s.* **5.** Klopfen *n*; **6.** Schlag *m*; **7.** *Am.* F a) scharfe Kri'tik, b) ‚Zi'garre‘ *f*, Rüge *f*; **8.** *Am. sl.* a) Anklage *f*, b) Strafe *f*, c) Schuld *f*: **~ sheet** Strafregister *n*; **beat the ~** sich rauswinden; **take the ~** (zu e-r Strafe ‚verdonnert‘ werden; **9.** *Am.* F ‚Plausch‘ *m*: **~ session** (Gruppen-) Diskussion *f*.

rap² [ræp] *s. fig.* Heller *m*, Deut *m*: **I don't care** (*od.* **give**) **a ~** (**for it**) das ist mir ganz egal; **it is not worth a ~** es ist keinen Pfifferling wert.

ra·pa·cious [rə'peɪʃəs] *adj.* □ raubgierig, Raub...(-*tier, -vogel*); *fig.* (hab)gierig; **ra'pa·cious·ness** [-nɪs], **ra'pac·i·ty** [-'pæsətɪ] *s.* **1.** Raubgier *f*; **2.** *fig.* Habgier *f*.

rape¹ [reɪp] **I** *s.* **1.** Vergewaltigung *f* (*a. fig.*), ⚖ Notzucht *f*: **~ and murder** Lustmord *m*; ~ *Am.* Unzucht *f* mit Minderjährigen; **2.** Entführung *f*, Raub *m*; **II** *v/t.* **3.** vergewaltigen; **4.** *obs.* rauben.

rape² [reɪp] *s.* ♥ Raps *m*.

rape³ [reɪp] *s.* Trester *pl.*

rape oil *s.* Rüb-, Rapsöl *n*; **'~·seed** *s.* Rübsamen *m*.

rap·id ['ræpɪd] **I** *adj.* □ **1.** schnell, rasch, ra'pid(e); reißend (*Fluss*; ♥ *Absatz*): **Schnell...**: **~ deployment force** schnelle Eingreiftruppe; **~ fire** ✕ Schnellfeuer *n*; **~ transit** *Am.* Nahschnellverkehr *m*; **2.** jäh, steil (*Hang*); **3.** *phot.* a) lichtstark (*Objektiv*), b) hoch empfindlich (*Film*); **II** *s.* **4.** *pl.* Stromschnelle(n *pl.*) *f*; **ra'pid·i·ty** [rə'pɪdətɪ] *s.* Schnelligkeit *f*, (rasende) Geschwindigkeit.

ra·pi·er ['reɪpjə] *s. fenc.* Ra'pier *n*: **~ thrust** *fig.* sarkastische Bemerkung.

rap·ist ['reɪpɪst] *s.* Vergewaltiger *m*: **~-killer** Lustmörder *m*.

rap·port [ræ'pɔː] *s.* (enge, per'sönliche) Beziehung: **be in** (*od.* **en**) **~ with** mit *j-m* in Verbindung stehen, *fig.* gut harmonieren mit.

rap·proche·ment [ræ'prɔʃmãː] (*Fr.*) *s. bsd. pol.* (Wieder)'Annäherung *f*.

rapt [ræpt] *adj.* **1.** versunken, verloren (**in** in *acc.*): **~ in thought**; **2.** hingerissen, entzückt (**with, by** von); **3.** verzückt (*Lächeln etc.*); gespannt (**upon** auf *acc.*) (*a. Aufmerksamkeit*).

rap·to·ri·al [ræp'tɔːrɪəl] *orn.* **I** *adj.* Raub...; **II** *s.* Raubvogel *m*.

rap·ture ['ræptʃə] *s.* **1.** Entzücken *n*, Verzückung *f*, Begeisterung *f*, Taumel *m*: **in ~s** hingerissen (**at** von); **go into ~s** in Verzückung geraten (**over** über *acc.*); **~ of the deep** ⚓ Tiefenrausch *m*; **2.** *pl.* Ausbruch *m* des Entzückens, Begeisterungstaumel *m*; **'rap·tur·ous** [-tʃərəs] *adj.* □ **1.** entzückt, hingerissen; **2.** stürmisch, begeistert (*Beifall etc.*); **3.** verzückt (*Gesicht*).

rare¹ [reə] *adj.* □ **1.** selten, rar (*a. fig.* ungewöhnlich, hervorragend, köstlich): **~ earth** 🜍 seltene Erde; **~ fun** F Mordsspaß *m*; **~ gas** Edelgas *n*; **2.** *phys.* dünn (*Luft*).

rare² [reə] *adj.* halbgar, nicht 'durchgebraten (*Fleisch*); englisch (*Steak*).

rare·bit ['reəbɪt] *s.*: **Welsh ~** überbackene Käseschnitte.

rar·ee show ['reərɪː] *s.* **1.** Guckkasten *m*; **2.** Straßenzirkus *m*; **3.** *fig.* Schauspiel *n*.

rar·e·fac·tion [,reərɪ'fækʃn] *s. phys.* Verdünnung *f*; **rar·e·fy** ['reərɪfaɪ] **I** *v/t.* **1.** verdünnen; **2.** *fig.* verfeinern; **II** *v/i.* **3.** sich verdünnen.

rare·ness ['reənɪs] → *rarity*.

rar·ing ['reərɪŋ] *adj.*: **~ to do s.th.** F ganz wild darauf, et. zu tun.

rar·i·ty ['reərətɪ] *s.* **1.** Seltenheit *f*: a) *seltenes Vorkommen*, b) Rari'tät *f*, Kostbarkeit *f*; **2.** Vor'trefflichkeit *f*; **3.** *phys.* Verdünnung *f*.

ras·cal ['rɑːskəl] *s.* **1.** Schuft *m*, Schurke *m*, Ha'lunke *m*; **2.** *humor.* a) Gauner *m*, b) Frechdachs *m* (*Kind*); **ras·cal·i·ty** [rɑː'skælətɪ] *s.* Schurke'rei *f*; **'ras·cal·ly** [-kəlɪ] *adj u. adv.* niederträchtig, gemein.

rash¹ [ræʃ] *adj.* □ **1.** hastig, über'eilt, -'stürzt, vorschnell: **a ~ decision**; **2.** unbesonnen.

rash² [ræʃ] *s.* ♥ (Haut)Ausschlag *m*.

rash·er ['ræʃə] *s.* (dünne) Scheibe Frühstücksspeck *od.* Schinken.

rash·ness ['ræʃnɪs] *s.* **1.** Hast *f*, Über'eiltheit *f*, -'stürztheit *f*; **2.** Unbesonnenheit *f*.

rasp [rɑːsp] **I** *v/t.* **1.** raspeln, feilen, schaben; **2.** *fig. Gefühle etc.* verletzen; *Ohren* beleidigen; *Nerven* reizen; **3.** krächzen(d sprechen); **II** *s.* **4.** Raspel *f*, Grobfeile *f*; Reibeisen *n*.

rasp·ber·ry ['rɑːzbərɪ] *s.* **1.** ♥ Himbeere *f*; **2.** *a.* **~ cane** ♥ Himbeerstrauch *m*; **3.** **give** (*od.* **blow**) **a ~** *fig. sl.* verächtlich schnauben.

rasp·ing ['rɑːspɪŋ] **I** *adj.* □ **1.** kratzend, krächzend (*Stimme etc.*); **II** *s.* **2.** Raspeln *n*; **3.** *pl.* Raspelspäne *pl.*

ras·ter ['ræstə] *s. opt.*, TV Raster *m*.

rat [ræt] **I** *s.* **1.** *zo.* Ratte *f*: **smell a ~** *fig.* Lunte *od.* den Braten riechen, Unrat wittern; **like a drowned ~** pudelnass; **~s!** *Quatsch!*; **2.** *pol.* F 'Überläufer *m*, Abtrünnige(r *m*) *f*; **3.** F a) allg. Verräter *m*, b) ‚Schwein‘ *n*, c) Spitzel *m*, d) Streikbrecher *m*; **II** *v/i.* **4.** *pol.* F 'überlaufen, allg. Verrat begehen: **~ on** a) *j-n* verraten *od.* im Stich lassen, b) *Kumpane* ‚verpfeifen‘, c) *et.* widerrufen, d) aus *et.* ‚aussteigen‘; **5.** Ratten fangen.

rat·a·bil·i·ty [,reɪtə'bɪlətɪ] *s.* **1.** (Ab-) Schätzbarkeit *f*; **2.** Verhältnismäßigkeit *f*; **3.** *bsd. Brit.* Steuerbarkeit *f*, 'Umlagepflicht *f*; **rat·a·ble** ['reɪtəbl] *adj.* □ **1.**

(ab)schätzbar, abzuschätzen(d), bewertbar; **2.** anteilmäßig, proportio'nal; **3.** *bsd. Brit.* (kommu'nal)steuerpflichtig; zollpflichtig: **~** *value* Bemessungsgrundlage *f* (*für Steuer*); *a.* Einheitswert *m.*

ratch [ræt∫] *s.* ⊘ **1.** (gezahnte) Sperrstange; **2.** Auslösung *f* (*Uhr*).
ratch·et ['ræt∫ɪt] *s.* ⊘ Sperrklinke *f*; **~ wheel** *s.* ⊘ Sperrad *n.*
rate¹ [reɪt] **I** *s.* **1.** (Verhältnis)Ziffer *f*, Quote *f*, Maß(stab *m*) *n*, (*Wachstums-*, *Inflations- etc.*)Rate *f*: *birth* **~** Geburtenziffer; *death* **~** Sterblichkeitsziffer; *at the* **~** *of* im Verhältnis von (→ 2 *u.* 6); *at a fearful* **~** in erschreckendem Ausmaß; **2.** (*Diskont-, Lohn-, Steueretc.*)Satz *m*, Kurs *m*, Ta'rif *m*: **~** *of exchange* (Umrechnungs-, Wechsel-)Kurs; **~** *of the day* Tageskurs; *at the* **~** *of* zum Satz(e) von; **3.** (festgesetzter) Preis, Betrag *m*, Taxe *f*: *at any* **~** *fig.* a) auf jeden Fall, b) wenigstens; *at that* **~** unter diesen Umständen; **4.** (Post- *etc.*) Gebühr *f*, Porto *n*; (Gas-, Strom-)Preis *m*: *inland* **~** Inlandporto; **5.** *Brit.* (Kommu'nal)Steuer *f*, (Gemeinde)Abgabe *f*, **6.** (rela'tive) Geschwindigkeit: **~** *of climb* ✈ Steiggeschwindigkeit; **~** *of energy phys.* Energiemenge *f* pro Zeiteinheit; **~** *of an engine* Motorleistung *f*; **~** *plate* ⊘ Leistungsschild *n*; *at the* **~** *of* mit e-r Geschwindigkeit von; **7.** Grad *m*, Rang *m*, Klasse *f*; **8.** ♣ a) Klasse *f* (*Schiff*), b) Dienstgrad *m* (*Matrose*); **II** *v/t.* **9.** *et.* abschätzen, taxieren (*at* auf *acc.*); **10.** *j-n* einschätzen, beurteilen; ♣ *Seemann* einstufen; **11.** *Preis etc.* bemessen, ansetzen; *Kosten* veranschlagen: **~** *up* höher versichern; **12.** *j-n* betrachten als, halten für; **13.** rechnen, zählen (*among* zu); **14.** *Brit.* a) (zur Steuer) veranlagen, b) besteuern; **15.** *Am. sl. et.* wert sein, Anspruch haben auf (*acc.*); **III** *v/i.* **16.** angesehen werden, gelten (*as* als): **~** *high* (*low*) hoch (niedrig) ,im Kurs stehen', e-n hohen Stellenwert haben; **~** *above* (*below*) rangieren, stehen über (unter) *j-m od. e-r Sache*; **~** *high with s.o.* bei *j-m* e-n Stein im Brett haben; *she* (*it*) **~***d high with him* sie (es) galt viel bei ihm; **17.** **~** *among* zählen zu.
rate² [reɪt] *v/t.* ausschelten (*for, about* wegen); **II** *v/i.* schimpfen (*at* auf *acc.*).
rate·a·bil·i·ty *etc.* → *ratability etc.*
rat·ed ['reɪtɪd] *adj.* **1.** (gemeinde)steuerpflichtig; **2.** ⊘ Nenn...: **~** *power* Nennleistung *f.*
'rate,pay·er *s. Brit.* (Gemeinde)Steuerzahler(in).
rath·er ['rɑːðə] *adv.* **1.** ziemlich, fast, etwas: **~** *cold* ziemlich kalt; *I would* **~** *think* ich möchte fast glauben; *I* **~** *expected it* ich habe es fast erwartet; **2.** lieber, eher (*than* als): *I would* (*od. had*) *much* **~** *go* ich möchte viel lieber gehen; **3.** (*or* oder) vielmehr, eigentlich, besser gesagt; **4.** *bsd. Brit.* F (ja) freilich!, aller'dings!
rat·i·fi·ca·tion [,rætɪfɪ'keɪ∫n] *s.* **1.** Bestätigung *f*, Genehmigung *f*; **2.** *pol.* Ratifizierung *f*; **rat·i·fy** ['rætɪfaɪ] *v/t.* **1.** bestätigen, genehmigen, gutheißen; **2.** *pol.* ratifizieren.
rat·ing¹ ['reɪtɪŋ] *s.* **1.** (Ab)Schätzung *f*, Bewertung *f*, (*a.* Leistungs)Beurteilung *f*; *ped.* (Zeugnis)Note *f*; *Radio, TV:* Einschaltquote *f*; **2.** (Leistungs-)Stand *m*, Ni'veau *n*; **3.** *fig.* Stellenwert *m*; **4.** ♣ a) Dienstgrad *m*, b) *Brit.* Mat'rose *m*, c) *pl. Brit.* Leute *pl.* bestimmten Dienstgrades; **5.** ♣ (Segel-)

Klasse *f*; **6.** ✝ Kre'ditwürdigkeit *f*; **7.** Ta'rif *m*; **8.** *Brit.* a) (Gemeindesteuer-) Veranlagung *f*, b) Steuersatz *m*; **9.** ⊘ (Nenn)Leistung *f*, Betriebsdaten *pl.*
rat·ing² ['reɪtɪŋ] *s.* heftige Schelte.
ra·tio ['reɪ∫ɪəʊ] *pl.* **-tios** *s.* **1.** ᚕ *etc.* Verhältnis *n*: **~** *of distribution* Verteilungsschlüssel *m*; *be in the inverse* **~** a) im umgekehrten Verhältnis stehen, b) ᚕ umgekehrt proportional sein (*to* zu); **2.** ᚕ Quoti'ent *m*; **3.** ✝ Wertverhältnis *n* zwischen Gold u. Silber; **4.** ⊘ Über'setzungsverhältnis *n* (*e-s Getriebes*).
ra·ti·oc·i·na·tion [,rætɪɒsɪ'neɪ∫n] *s.* **1.** logisches Denken; **2.** logischer Gedankengang *od.* Schluss.
ra·tion ['ræ∫n] **I** *s.* **1.** Rati'on *f*, Zuteilung *f*: **~** *card* Lebensmittelkarte *f*; *off the* **~** markenfrei; **2.** ✕ (Tages-) Verpflegungssatz *m*; **3.** *pl.* Lebensmittel *pl.*, Verpflegung *f*; **II** *v/t.* **4.** rationieren, (zwangs)bewirtschaften; **5.** *a.* **~** *out* (in Rationen) zuteilen; **6.** ✕ verpflegen.
ra·tion·al ['ræ∫ənl] *adj.* ☐ **1.** vernünftig: a) vernunftmäßig, ratio'nal, b) vernunftbegabt, c) verständig; **2.** zweckmäßig, ratio'nal (*a.* ᚕ); **ra·tion·ale** [,ræ∫ə'nɑːl] *s.* **1.** 'Grundprin,zip *n*; **2.** vernunftmäßige Erklärung.
ra·tion·al·ism ['ræ∫nəlɪzəm] *s.* Rationa'lismus *m*; **'ra·tion·al·ist** [-ɪst] **I** *s.* Rationa'list *m*; **II** *adj.* → **ra·tion·al·is·tic** [,ræ∫nə'lɪstɪk] *adj.* (**~ally**) rationa'listisch; **ra·tion·al·i·ty** [,ræ∫ə'nælətɪ] *s.* **1.** Vernünftigkeit *f*; **2.** Vernunft *f*, Denkvermögen *n*; **ra·tion·al·i·za·tion** [,ræ∫nələ'zeɪ∫n] *s.* **1.** Rationalisieren *n*; **2.** ✝ Rationalisierung *f*; **'ra·tion·al·ize** [-laɪz] **I** *v/t.* **1.** ratio'nal erklären, vernunftgemäß deuten; **2.** ✝ rationalisieren; **II** *v/i.* **3.** ratio'nell verfahren; **4.** rationa'listisch denken.
ra·tion·ing ['ræ∫nɪŋ] *s.* Rationierung *f.*
rat| race *s.* **1.** ,Hetzjagd' *f* (*des Lebens*); **2.** harter (Konkur'renz)Kampf; **3.** Teufelskreis *m*; **~** *run s. Brit.* F *mot.* Ausweichroute *f*, Schleichweg *m.*
rats·bane ['rætsbeɪn] *s.* Rattengift *n.*
rat-tat [,ræt'tæt], *a.* **rat-tat-tat** [,rætə-'tæt] **I** *s.* Rattern *n*, Geknatter *n*; **II** *v/i.* knattern.
rat·ten [rætn] *v/i. bsd. Brit.* (die Arbeit) sabotieren, Sabo'tage treiben.
rat·ter ['rætə] *s.* Rattenfänger *m* (*Hund od. Katze*).
rat·tle ['rætl] **I** *v/i.* **1.** rattern, klappern, rasseln, klirren: **~** *at the door* an der Tür rütteln; **~** *off* losrattern, davonjagen; **2.** röcheln; rasseln (*Atem*); **3.** *a.* **~** *away od. on* plappern; **II** *v/t.* **4.** rasseln mit *od. an* (*dat.*); an der Tür *etc.* rütteln; mit *Geschirr etc.* klappern; → *sabre* 1; **5.** *a.* **~** *off Rede etc.* ,her'unterrasseln'; **6.** F *j-n* aus der Fassung bringen, verunsichern; **III** *s.* **7.** Rattern *n*, Gerassel *n*, Klappern *n*; **8.** Rassel *f*, (Kinder)Klapper *f*; **9.** Röcheln *n*; **10.** Lärm *m*, Trubel *m*; **11.** ♀ a) *red* **~** Sumpfläusekraut *n*, b) *yellow* **~** Klappertopf *m*; **'~·brain** *s.* Hohl-, Wirrkopf *m*; **'~·brained** [-breɪnd] **'~·pat·ed** [-,peɪtɪd] *adj.* hohl-, wirrköpfig; **'~·snake** *s. zo.* Klapperschlange *f*; **'~·trap** F **I** *s.* **1.** Klapperkasten *m* (*Fahrzeug etc.*); **2.** *mst pl.* (Trödel)Kram *m*; **II** *adj.* **3.** klapperig.
rat·tling ['rætlɪŋ] **I** *adj.* **1.** ratternd, klappernd; **2.** lebhaft; **3.** F schnell: *at a* **~** *pace* in rasendem Tempo; **4.** F ,toll'; **II** *adv.* **~** äußerst.
rat·ty ['rætɪ] *adj.* **1.** rattenverseucht; **2.** Ratten...; **3.** *sl.* gereizt, bissig.

rau·cous ['rɔːkəs] *adj.* ☐ rau, heiser.
raunch·y ['rɔːnt∫ɪ] *adj.* F **1.** a) ordi'när, *Witz etc.* a. ,dreckig', b) geil, ,scharf'; **2.** derb, di'rekt u. sehr freizügig (*Roman etc.*); **3.** *bsd. Am.* a) ,vergammelt', b) dreckig.
rav·age ['rævɪdʒ] **I** *s.* **1.** Verwüstung *f*, Verheerung *f*; **2.** *pl.* verheerende (Aus-)Wirkungen *pl.*: *the* **~***s of time* der Zahn der Zeit; **II** *v/t.* **3.** verwüsten, verheeren; plündern: *a face* **~***d by grief fig.* ein gramzerfurchtes Gesicht; **III** *v/i.* **4.** Verheerungen anrichten.
rave [reɪv] **I** *v/i.* **1.** a) fantasieren, irrereden, b) toben, wüten (*a. fig. Sturm etc.*), c) *fig.* wettern; **2.** schwärmen (*about, of* von); **II** *s.* **3.** Pracht *f*; **4.** F Schwärme'rei *f*: **~** *review* ,Bombenkritik' *f*; **5.** ♪ a) Rave *m*, b) Raveparty *f*; **6.** *Brit. sl.* a) Mode *f*, b) → *rave-up*.
rav·el ['rævl] *v/t.* **1.** *a.* **~** *out* ausfasern, auftrennen; entwirren (*a. fig.*); **2.** verwirren, -wickeln (*a. fig.*); **II** *v/i.* **3.** *a.* **~** *out* sich auftrennen, sich ausfasern; sich entwirren (*a. fig.*); **III** *s.* **4.** Verwirrung *f*, -wicklung *f*; **5.** loser Faden.
ra·ven¹ ['reɪvn] **I** *s. orn.* Rabe *m*; **II** *adj.* (kohl)rabenschwarz.
rav·en² ['rævn] **I** *v/i.* **1.** rauben, plündern; **2.** gierig (fr)essen; **3.** Heißhunger haben; **4.** lechzen (*for* nach); **II** *v/t.* **5.** (gierig) verschlingen.
rav·en·ous ['rævənəs] *adj.* ☐ **1.** ausgehungert, heißhungrig (*beide a. fig.*); **2.** gierig (*for* auf *acc.*): **~** *hunger* Bärenhunger *m*; **3.** gefräßig; **4.** raubgierig (*Tier*).
'rave-up *s. Brit. sl.* ,tolle Party'.
ra·vine [rə'viːn] *s.* (Berg)Schlucht *f*, Klamm *f*; Hohlweg *m.*
rav·ing ['reɪvɪŋ] *adj.* ☐ **1.** tobend, rasend; **2.** fantasierend, delirierend; **3.** F ,toll', fan'tastisch: *a* **~** *beauty*; **II** *s.* **4.** *mst pl.* a) Rase'rei *f*, b) De'lirien *pl.*, Fieberwahn *m.*
rav·ish ['rævɪ∫] *v/t.* **1.** entzücken, hinreißen; **2.** *obs. Frau* a) vergewaltigen, schänden, b) entführen; **3.** *rhet.* rauben, entreißen; **'rav·ish·er** [-∫ə] *s. obs.* **1.** Schänder *m*; **2.** Entführer *m*; **'rav·ish·ing** [-∫ɪŋ] *adj.* ☐ hinreißend, entzückend.
raw [rɔː] **I** *adj.* ☐ **1.** roh (*a. fig. grob*); **2.** roh, ungekocht; **3.** ⊘, ✝ roh, Roh..., unbearbeitet, *a.* ungegerbt (*Leder*), ungewalkt (*Tuch*), ungesponnen (*Wolle etc.*), unvermischt, unverdünnt (*Spirituosen*): **~** *material* Rohmaterial *n*, -stoff *m* (*a. fig.*); **~** *silk* Rohseide *f*; **4.** *phot.* unbelichtet; **5.** roh, noch nicht ausgewertet: **~** *data; 6. Am.* nagelneu; **7.** wund (gerieben); offen (*Wunde*); **8.** unwirtlich, rau, nasskalt (*Wetter, Klima etc.*); **9.** unerfahren, ,grün'; **10.** *sl.* gemein: *a* **~** *deal* e-e Gemeinheit; **II** *s.* **11.** wunde *od.* wund geriebene Stelle; **12.** *fig.* wunder Punkt: *touch s.o. on the* **~** *j-n* an s-r empfindlichen Stelle treffen; **13.** ✝ Rohstoff *m*; **14.** *in the* **~** a) im Naturzustand, b) nackt: *life in the* **~** *fig.* die grausame Härte des Lebens; **'~·boned** *adj.* hager, (grob)knochig; **'~·hide** *s.* **1.** Rohhaut *f*, -leder *n*; **2.** Peitsche *f.*
raw·ness ['rɔːnɪs] *s.* **1.** Rohzustand *m*; **2.** Unerfahrenheit *f*; **3.** Wundsein *n*; **4.** Rauheit *f des Wetters.*
ray¹ [reɪ] **I** *s.* **1.** (Licht)Strahl *m*; **2.** *fig.* (*Hoffnungs- etc.*)Strahl *m*, Schimmer *m*; **3.** *phys.*, ᚕ, ♀ Strahl *m*: **~** *treatment* ☢ Strahlenbehandlung *f*, Bestrahlung *f*; **II** *v/i.* **4.** Strahlen aussen-

den; **5.** sich strahlenförmig ausbreiten; **III** *v/t.* **6.** *a.* ~ *out* ausstrahlen; **7.** bestrahlen (*a. phys.*, ⚡), ⚡ F röntgen.

ray² [reɪ] *s. ichth.* Rochen *m.*

ray·on ['reɪɒn] *s.* ✝ 'Kunstseide(npro-,dukt *n*) *f.*: ~ **staple** Zellwolle *f.*

raze [reɪz] *v/t.* **1.** *Gebäude* niederreißen; *Festung* schleifen; ~ **s.th. to the ground** et. dem Erdboden gleichmachen; **2.** *fig.* ausmerzen; **3.** ritzen, kratzen, streifen.

ra·zor ['reɪzə] *s.* Rasiermesser *n*: (*safe-ty*) ~ Rasierapparat *m*; ~ *blade* Rasierklinge *f*; *as sharp as a* ~ messerscharf; *be on a* ~*'s edge* auf des Messers Schneide stehen; ~ *cut s.* Messerschnitt *m* (*a. Frisur*); ~ *strop s.* Streichriemen *m.*

razz [ræz] *v/t. Am. sl.* hänseln, ,aufziehen'.

raz·zi·a ['ræzɪə] *s. hist.* Raubzug *m.*

raz·zle-daz·zle ['ræzl,dæzl] *s. sl.* **1.** Saufe'rei *f*: *go on the* ~ ,auf die Pauke hauen'; **2.** ,Rummel' *m*; **3.** *Am. sl.* a) ,Kuddelmuddel' *m, n*, b) ,Wirbel' *m*, Tam'tam *n.*

re [riː] (*Lat.*) *prp.* **1.** ⚖ in Sachen; **2.** *bsd.* ✝ betrifft, betreffs, bezüglich.

re- *in Zssgn* **1.** [riː] wieder, noch einmal, neu: *reprint*, *rebirth*; **2.** [rɪ] zu'rück, wider: *revert*, *retract*.

're [ə] F *für are.*

re·ab·sorb [,riːəb'sɔːb] *v/t.* resorbieren.

reach [riːtʃ] **I** *v/t.* **1.** (hin-, her)reichen, über'reichen, geben (*s.o. s.th.* j-m et.): *j-m e-n Schlag versetzen*; **2.** (her)langen, nehmen: ~ *s.th. down* et. herunterlangen; **3.** *oft* ~ *out* (*od. forth*) *Hand etc.* reichen, ausstrecken; **4.** reichen *od.* sich erstrecken bis an (*acc.*) *od.* zu: *the water* ~*ed his knees* das Wasser ging ihm bis an die Knie; **5.** *Zahl*, *Alter* erreichen; sich belaufen auf (*acc.*); *Auflagenzahl* erleben; **6.** erreichen, erzielen, gelangen zu: ~ *an understanding*; ~ *no conclusion* zu keinem Schluss gelangen; **7.** *Ziel* erreichen, treffen; **8.** *Ort* erreichen, eintreffen in *od.* an (*dat.*): ~ *home* nach Hause gelangen; ~ *s.o.'s ear* j-m zu Ohren kommen; **9.** *j-n* erreichen (*Brief etc.*); **10.** *fig.* (ein)wirken auf (*acc.*), durch Werbung etc. ansprechen *od.* gewinnen *od.* erreichen, bei *j-m* (*geistig*) 'durchdringen; **II** *v/i.* **11.** (mit der Hand) reichen *od.* greifen *od.* langen; **12.** *a.* ~ *out* langen, greifen (*after, for, at* nach); **13.** reichen, sich erstrecken *od.* ausdehnen (*to* bis [zu]): *as far as the eye can* ~ so weit das Auge reicht; **14.** sich belaufen (*to* auf *acc.*); **III** *s.* **15.** Griff *m*: *make a* ~ *for s.th.* nach et. greifen *od.* langen; **16.** Reich-, Tragweite *f* (*Geschoss*, *Waffe*, *Stimme etc.*) (*a. fig.*): *within* ~ erreichbar; *within s.o.'s* ~ in j-s Reichweite, für j-n erreichbar *od.* erschwinglich, j-m zugänglich; *above* (*od. beyond od. out of*) ~ unerreichbar *od.* unerschwinglich (*of* für); *within easy* ~ *of the station* vom Bahnhof aus leicht zu erreichen; **17.** Bereich *m*, 'Umfang *m*, Ausdehnung *f*; **18.** (geistige) Fassungskraft, Hori'zont *m*; **19.** a) Ka'nalabschnitt *m* (*zwischen zwei Schleusen*), b) Flussstrecke *f*; **'reach·a·ble** [-tʃəbl] *adj.* erreichbar.

'reach-me-,down F **I** *adj.* **1.** Konfektions..., von der Stange; **2.** abgelegt (*Kleider*); **II** *s.* **3.** *mst pl.* Konfekti'onsanzug *m*, Kleid *n* von der Stange, *pl.* Konfekti'onskleidung *f*; **4.** abgelegtes Kleidungsstück *n* (*das vom jüngeren Geschwistern etc. weiter getragen wird*).

re·act [rɪ'ækt] **I** *v/i.* **1.** 🜪, ⚡ reagieren (*to* auf *acc.*): *slow to* ~ reaktionsträge; **2.** *fig.* (*to*) reagieren, antworten, eingehen (auf *acc.*), (*et.*) aufnehmen; sich verhalten (auf *acc.*, bei): ~ *against e-r Sache* entgegenwirken *od.* widerstreben; **3.** ein-, zu'rückwirken, Rückwirkungen haben ([*up*]*on* auf *acc.*): ~ *on each other* sich gegenseitig beeinflussen; **4.** ✕ e-n Gegenschlag führen; **II** *v/t.* **5.** 🜪 zur Reakti'on bringen.

re·act [,riː'ækt] *v/t. thea. etc.* wieder aufführen.

re·act·ance [rɪ'æktəns] *s.* ⚡ Reak'tanz *f*, Blindwiderstand *m.*

re·ac·tion [rɪ'ækʃn] *s.* **1.** 🜪, ⚡, *phys.* Reakti'on *f*; **2.** Rückwirkung *f*, -schlag *m*, Gegen-, Einwirkung *f* (*from*, *against* gegen, [*up*]*on* auf *acc.*); **3.** *fig.* (*to*) Reakti'on *f* (auf *acc.*), Verhalten *n* (bei), Stellungnahme *f* (zu); **4.** *pol.* Reakti'on *f* (*a. Bewegung*), Rückschritt (-lertum *n*) *m*; **5.** ✝ rückläufige Bewegung, (*Kurs-*, *Preis- etc.*)Rückgang *m*; **6.** ✕ Gegenstoß *m*, -schlag *m*; **7.** ⊖ Gegendruck *m*; **8.** ⚡ Rückkopplung *f*, -wirkung *f*; **re'ac·tion·ar·y** [-ʃnərɪ] **I** *adj. bsd. pol.* reaktio'när; **II** *s. pol.* Reaktio'när(in).

re·ac·tion| drive *s.* ⊖ Rückstoßantrieb *m*; ~ **time** *s. psych.* Reakti'onszeit *f.*

re'ac·ti·vate [rɪ'æktɪveɪt] *v/t.* reaktivieren; **re·ac·tive** [rɪ'æktɪv] *adj.* □ **1.** re-ak'tiv, rück-, gegenwirkend; **2.** empfänglich (*to* für), Reaktions...; **3.** ⚡ Blind...(-*strom*, -*leistung etc.*); **re·ac·tor** [rɪ'æktə] *s.* **1.** *phys.* ('Kern)Re,aktor *m*: ~ *block* Reaktorblock *m*; ~ *core* Reaktorkern *m*; **2.** ⚡ Drossel(spule) *f.*

read¹ [riːd] **I** *v/t.* [*irr.*] **1.** lesen (*a. fig.*): ~ *s.th. into* et. in e-n Text hineinlesen; ~ *off* et. ablesen; ~ *out* a) et. (laut) vorlesen, b) *Buch etc.* auslesen; ~ *over* a) durchlesen, b) *formell* vor-, verlesen (*Notar etc.*); ~ *up* a) sich in et. einlesen, b) et. nachlesen; ~ *s.o.'s face* in j-s Gesicht lesen; **2.** vor-, verlesen; *Rede etc.* ablesen; **3.** *parl. Vorlage* lesen: *was read for the third time die Vorlage* wurde in dritter Lesung behandelt; **4.** *Kurzschrift etc.* lesen können; *die Uhr kennen*; ~ *music* a) Noten lesen, b) nach Noten spielen etc.; **5.** *Traum etc.* deuten; → *fortune* 3; **6.** et. auslegen, auffassen, verstehen: *do you* ~ *me?* a) *Funk:* können Sie mich verstehen?, b) *fig.* haben Sie mich verstanden?; *we can take it as* ~ *that* wir können (also) davon ausgehen, dass; **7.** *Charakter etc.* durch'schauen: *I* ~ *you like a book* ich lese in dir wie in e-m Buch; **8.** ⊖ *a*) anzeigen (*Messgerät*) *Barometerstand etc.* ablesen; **9.** *Rätsel* lösen; **II** *v/i.* [*irr.*] **10.** lesen: ~ *to s.o.* j-m vorlesen; **11.** e-e Vorlesung *od.* e-n Vortrag halten; **12.** *bsd. Brit.* (*for*) sich vorbereiten (auf *e-e Prüfung etc.*), et. studieren: ~ *for the bar* sich auf den Anwaltsberuf vorbereiten; ~ *up on* sich in et. einlesen *od.* einarbeiten; **13.** sich *gut etc.* lesen lassen; **14.** *so u. so* lauten, heißen: *the passage* ~*s as follows.*

read² [red] **I** *pret. u. p.p. von read¹*; **II** *adj.* **1.** gelesen: *the most-*~ *book* das meistgelesene Buch; **2.** belesen (*in* in *dat.*); → *well-read.*

read·a·ble ['riːdəbl] *adj.* □ lesbar: a) lesenswert, b) leserlich.

re·ad·dress [,riːə'dres] *v/t.* **1.** *Brief* neu adressieren; **2.** ~ *o.s.* sich nochmals wenden (*to* an *j-n*).

read·er ['riːdə] *s.* **1.** Leser(in); **2.** Vorle-ser(in); **3.** (Verlags)Lektor *m*, (Ver-'lags)Lek,torin *f*; **4.** *typ.* Kor'rektor *m*; **5.** *univ. Brit.* außerordentlicher Pro'fessor, Do'zent(in); **6.** a) *ped.* Lesebuch *n*, b) Antholo'gie *f*; **7.** *Computer:* Lesegerät *n*; **'read·er·ship** [-ʃɪp] *s.* **1.** Vorleseramt *n*; **2.** *univ. Brit.* Do'zentenstelle *f.*

read·i·ly ['redɪlɪ] *adv.* **1.** so'gleich, prompt; **2.** bereitwillig, gern; **3.** leicht, ohne weiteres; **'read·i·ness** [-ɪnɪs] *s.* **1.** Bereitschaft *f*: ~ *for war* Kriegsbereitschaft; *in* ~ bereit, in Bereitschaft; *place in* ~ bereitstellen; **2.** Schnelligkeit *f*, Raschheit *f*, Promptheit *f*: ~ *of mind od. wit* Geistesgegenwart *f*; **3.** Gewandtheit *f*; **4.** Bereitwilligkeit *f*: ~ *to help others* Hilfsbereitschaft *f.*

read·ing ['riːdɪŋ] **I** *s.* **1.** Lesen *n*; *weitS.* Bücherstudium *n*; **2.** (Vor)Lesung *f*, Vortrag *m*; **3.** *parl.* Lesung *f*; **4.** Belesenheit *f*: *a man of vast* ~ ein sehr belesener Mann; **5.** Lek'türe *f*, Lesestoff *m*: *this book makes good* ~ dieses Buch liest sich gut; **6.** Lesart *f*, Versi'on *f*; **7.** Deutung *f*, Auslegung *f*, Auffassung *f*; **8.** ⊖ Anzeige *f*, Ablesung *f* (*Messgerät*), (*Barometer- etc.*)Stand *m*; **II** *adj.* **9.** Lese...: ~ *lamp*; ~ *desk s.* Lesepult *m*; ~ *glass s.* Vergrößerungsglas *n*, Lupe *f*; ~ *glass·es s. pl.* Lesebrille *f*; ~ *head s. Computer:* Lesekopf *m*; ~ *mat·ter s.* **1.** Lesestoff *m*; **2.** redaktio'neller Teil (*e-r Zeitung*); ~ *pub·lic s.* Leserschaft *f*, Leserpublikum *n*; ~ *room s.* Lesezimmer *n*, -saal *m.*

re·ad·just [,riːə'dʒʌst] *v/t.* **1.** wieder anpassen; ⊖ nachstellen, -richten; **2.** wieder in Ordnung bringen; ✝ sanieren; *pol. etc.* neu orientieren; **re·ad'just-ment** [-stmənt] *s.* **1.** Wieder'anpassung *f*; **2.** Neuordnung *f*; ✝ wirtschaftliche Sanierung; **3.** ⊖ Korrek'tur *f.*

re·ad·mis·sion [,riːəd'mɪʃn] *s.* Wieder-'zulassung *f* (*to* zu); **,re·ad'mit** [-'mɪt] *v/t.* wieder zulassen.

'read|-,on·ly mem·o·ry *s. Computer:* (Nur)Lesespeicher *m*, Festwertspeicher *m*; '~**out** *s. Computer:* Ausgabe *f* (*von lesbaren Worten*); ~ *pulse* Leseimpuls *m*; '~**through** *s. thea.* Leseprobe *f.*

read·y ['redɪ] **I** *adj.* □ → *readily*; **1.** bereit, fertig (*for* zu et.): ~ *for action* ✕ einsatzbereit; ~ *for sea* ⚓ seeklar; ~ *for service* ⊖ betriebsfertig; ~ *for take-off* ✈ startbereit; ~ *to operate* ⊖ betriebsbereit; *be* ~ *with s.th.* et. bereithaben *od.* -halten; *get od. make* ~ (sich) bereitmachen *od.* fertig machen; *are you* ~*? go! sport* Achtung, fertig, los!; **2.** bereit(willig), willens, geneigt (*to* zu); **3.** schnell, rasch, prompt: *find a* ~ *market* (*od. sale*) ✝ raschen Absatz finden, gut gehen; **4.** schlagfertig, prompt (*Antwort*), geschickt (*Arbeiter etc.*), gewandt: *a* ~ *pen* e-e gewandte Feder; ~ *wit* Schlagfertigkeit *f*; **5.** im Begriff, nahe dar'an (*to do* zu tun); **6.** ✝ verfügbar, greifbar (*Vermögenswerte*), bar (*Geld*): ~ *cash od. money* Bargeld *n*, -zahlung *f*; ~ *money business* Bar-, Kassageschäft *n*; **7.** bequem, leicht: ~ *at* (*od. to*) *hand* gleich zur Hand; **II** *adv.* **8.** bereitmachen, fertig machen; **III** *s.* **9.** *mst the* ~ *sl.* Bargeld *n*; **10.** ✕ *at the* ~ schussbereit (*a. Kamera*); **IV** *adv.* **11.** fertig: '~*built house* Fertighaus *n*; **12.** *readier* schneller; *readiest* am schnellsten; ,~**'made** *adj.* **1.** Konfektions..., von der Stange: ~ *clothes* Konfektion(sbekleidung *f*) *f*; ~ *shop* Konfektionsgeschäft *n*; **2.** gebrauchsfertig, Fertig...; **3.** *fig.* schablonisiert,

‚fertig', ‚vorgekaut'; **4.** *fig.* Patent...: **~ solution**; **~ reck·on·er** *s.* 'Rechenta- ‚belle *f*; **‚~-to-'serve** *adj.* tischfertig (*Speise*); **‚~-to-'wear** → *ready-made* 1; **‚~-'wit·ted** *adj.* schlagfertig.

re·af·firm [ˌriːəˈfɜːm] *v/t.* nochmals versichern *od.* beteuern.

re·af·for·est [ˌriːæˈfɒrɪst] *v/t.* wieder aufforsten.

re·a·gent [riːˈeɪdʒənt] *s.* **1.** 🔥 Re'agens *n*; **2.** *fig.* Gegenkraft *f*, -wirkung *f*; **3.** *psych.* 'Testper‚son *f*.

re·al [rɪəl] **I** *adj.* □ → *really*; **1.** re'al (*a. phls.*), tatsächlich, wirklich, wahr, eigentlich: **~ life** das wirkliche Leben; *the* **~ thing** *sl.* das einzig Wahre; **2.** echt (*Seide etc., a. fig. Gefühle, Mann etc.*); **3.** 🏛 a) dinglich, b) unbeweglich: **~ account** ♦ Sach(wert)konto *n*; **~ action** dingliche Klage; **~ assets** unbewegliches Vermögen; **~ estate** *od.* **property** Grundeigentum *n*, Liegenschaften *pl.*, Immobilien *pl.*; **~ stock** ♦ Istbestand *m*; **~ time** *Computer*: Echtzeit *f*; **~ wage** Reallohn *m*; **4.** *phys.*, 🅰 re'ell (*Bild, Zahl etc.*); **5.** ⚡ ohmsch, Wirk...: **~ power** Wirkleistung *f*; **II** *adv.* **6.** *bsd. Am.* F sehr, äußerst, ‚richtig': **for ~** echt, im Ernst; **III** *s.* **7. the ~** *phls.* das Reale, die Wirklichkeit; **re·al ale** *s. bsd. Brit.* Real Ale *n* (*nach traditionellen Methoden hergestelltes, fassvergorenes, ungefiltertes u. nicht pasteurisiertes Bier*); **'re·al·ism** [-lɪzəm] *s.* Rea'lismus *m* (*a. phls., lit., paint.*); **'re·al·ist** [-lɪst] **I** *s.* Rea'list(in); **II** *adj.* → **re·al·is·tic** [ˌrɪəˈlɪstɪk] *adj.* (□ **~ally**) rea'listisch (*a. phls., lit., paint.*), wirklichkeitsnah, -getreu, sachlich; **re·al·i·ty** [rɪˈælətɪ] *s.* **1.** Reali'tät *f*, Wirklichkeit *f*: **in ~** in Wirklichkeit, tatsächlich; **2.** Wirklichkeits-, Na'turtreue *f*; **3.** Tatsache *f*, Faktum *n*, Gegebenheit *f*; **re·al·iz·a·ble** [ˈrɪəlaɪzəbl] *adj.* □ **1.** realisierbar, aus-, 'durchführbar; **2.** ♦ realisierbar, verwertbar, kapitalisierbar, verkäuflich; **re·al·i·za·tion** [ˌrɪəlaɪˈzeɪʃn] *s.* **1.** Realisierung *f*, Verwirklichung *f*, Aus-, 'Durchführung *f*; **2.** Vergegen-'wärtigung *f*, Erkenntnis *f*; **3.** ♦ a) Realisierung *f*, Verwertung *f*, b) Liquidati'on *f*, Glattstellung *f*, c) Erzielung *f* e-s Gewinns: **~ account** Liquidationskonto *n*; **re·al·ize** [ˈrɪəlaɪz] *v/t.* **1.** (klar) erkennen, sich klarmachen, begreifen, erfassen: *he* **~d that** er sah ein, dass; ihm wurde klar *od.* es kam ihm zum Bewusstsein, dass; **2.** verwirklichen, realisieren, aus-, 'durchführen; **3.** sich *et.* vergegen'wärtigen, sich *et.* (lebhaft) vorstellen; **4.** ♦ a) realisieren, verwerten, zu Geld *et.* flüssig machen, b) *Gewinn, Preis* erzielen; **re·al·ly** [ˈrɪəlɪ] *adv.* **1.** wirklich, tatsächlich, eigentlich: *not* **~** eigentlich nicht; *not* **~!** nicht möglich!; **2.** (*rügend*) *you* **~ must come!** unbedingt: *you* **~ must come!**

realm [relm] *s.* **1.** Königreich *n*: *Peer of the* ♌ Mitglied *n* des Oberhauses; **2.** *fig.* Reich *n*, Sphäre *f*; **3.** Bereich *m*, (Fach-) Gebiet *n*.

're·al-time clock *s. Computer*: Echtzeituhr *f*.

re·al·tor [ˈrɪəltə] *s. Am.* Immo'bilienmakler *m*; **'re·al·ty** [-tɪ] *s.* Grundeigentum *n*, -besitz *m*, Liegenschaften *pl.*

ream¹ [riːm] *s.* Ries *n* (*480 Bogen Papier*): *printer's* **~** 516 Bogen Druckpapier; **~s and ~s of** *fig.* zahllose, große Mengen von.

ream² [riːm] *v/t.* ⊕ **1.** Bohrloch *etc.* erweitern; **2.** *oft* **~ out** a) *Bohrung* (auf-, aus)räumen, b) *Kaliber* ausbohren, c)

nachbohren; **'ream·er** [-mə] *s.* **1.** ⊕ Reib-, Räumahle *f*; **2.** *Am.* Fruchtpresse *f*.

re·an·i·mate [ˌriːˈænɪmeɪt] *v/t.* **1.** wieder beleben; **2.** *fig.* neu beleben.

reap [riːp] **I** *v/t.* **1.** *Getreide etc.* schneiden, ernten; **2.** *Feld* mähen, abernten; **3.** *fig.* ernten; **II** *v/i.* **4.** mähen, ernten: *he* **~s where he has not sown** *fig.* er erntet, wo er nicht gesät hat; **'reap·er** [-pə] *s.* **1.** Schnitter(in), Mäher(in): *the Grim* ♌ *fig.* der Sensenmann; **2.** 'Mähma‚schine *f*: **~-binder** Mähbinder *m*.

re·ap·pear [ˌriːəˈpɪə] *v/i.* wieder erscheinen; **‚re·ap'pear·ance** [-ərəns] *s.* 'Wiedererscheinen *n*.

re·ap·pli·ca·tion [ˈriːˌæplɪˈkeɪʃn] *s.* **1.** wieder'holte Anwendung; **2.** erneutes Gesuch; **re·ap·ply** [ˌriːəˈplaɪ] **I** *v/t.* wieder *od.* wieder'holt anwenden; **II** *v/i.* (*for*) (*et.*) wieder'holt beantragen, erneut e-n Antrag stellen (auf *acc.*); sich erneut bewerben (um).

re·ap·point [ˌriːəˈpɔɪnt] *v/t.* wieder ernennen *od.* einsetzen *od.* anstellen.

re·ap·prais·al [ˌriːəˈpreɪzl] *s.* Neubewertung *f*, -beurteilung *f*.

rear¹ [rɪə] **I** *v/t.* **1.** *Kind* auf-, großziehen, erziehen; *Tiere* züchten; *Pflanzen* ziehen; **2.** *Leiter etc.* aufrichten, -stellen; **3.** *rhet.* Gebäude errichten; **4.** *Haupt, Stimme etc.* (er)heben; **II** *v/i.* **5.** *a.* **~ up** sich (auf)bäumen (*Pferd etc.*); **6.** *oft* **~ up** (auf-, hoch)ragen.

rear² [rɪə] *s.* **1.** 'Hinter-, Rückseite *f*; *mot.*, ♦ Heck *n*: *at* (*Am. in*) *the* **~ of** hinter (*dat.*); **2.** 'Hintergrund *m*: *in the* **~ of** im Hintergrund (*gen.*); **3.** ✕ Nachhut *f*: *bring up the* **~** *allg.* die Nachhut bilden, den Zug beschließen; *take in the* **~** den *Feind* im Rücken fassen; **4.** F a) ‚Hintern' *m*, b) *Brit.* ‚Lokus' *m* (*Abort*); **II** *adj.* **5.** hinter, Hinter..., Rück... **~ axle**: *mot.* Hinterachse *f*; **~ echelon** ✕ rückwärtiger Stab; **~ engine** *mot.* Heckmotor *m*; **~ ad·mi·ral** ♦ 'Konteradmi‚ral *m*; **~ drive** *s. mot.* Heckantrieb *m*; **~ end** *s.* **1.** hinter(st)er Teil, Ende *n*; **2.** F ‚Hintern' *m*; **'~-guard** *s.* ✕ Nachhut *f*: **~ action** Rückzugsgefecht *n* (*a. fig.*); **~ gun·ner** *s.* ✈ Heckschütze *m*; **~ lamp**, **~ light** *s. mot.* Schlusslicht *n*.

re·arm [ˌriːˈɑːm] **I** *v/t.* wieder bewaffnen; **II** *v/i.* wieder aufrüsten; **‚re'ar·ma·ment** [-məmənt] *s.* Wieder'aufrüstung *f*, 'Wiederbewaffnung *f*.

re·ar·range [ˌriːəˈreɪndʒ] *v/t.* neu-, 'umordnen, ändern; **‚re·ar'range·ment** [-mənt] *s.* **1.** 'Um-, Neuordnung *f*, Neugestaltung *f*; Änderung *f*; **2.** 🔥 'Umlagerung *f*; **3.** 🅰 'Umschreibung *f*.

rear| sight *s.* ✕ Kimme *f*; **'~-view mirror**, **'~-vi·sion mir·ror** *s. mot.* Rückspiegel *m*.

rear·ward [ˈrɪəwəd] **I** *adj.* **1.** hinter, rückwärtig; **2.** Rückwärts...; **II** *adv. a.* 'rear·wards [-dz] nach hinten, rückwärts, zu'rück.

rea·son [ˈriːzn] **I** *s.* ohne *art.* Vernunft *f* (*a. phls.*): Vernunft, Einsicht *f*: *Age of* ♌ *hist.* die Aufklärung; *bring s.o. to* **~** j-n zur Vernunft bringen; *listen to* **~** Vernunft annehmen; *lose one's* **~** den Verstand verlieren; *it stands to* **~** es ist klar, es leuchtet ein (*that* dass); *there is* **~ in what you say** was du sagst, hat Hand u. Fuß; *in* (*all*) **~** in Grenzen, mit Maß u. Ziel, b) mit Recht; *do everything in* **~** sein Möglichstes tun (in gewissen Grenzen); **2.** Grund *m* (*of, for gen. od.* für), Ursache *f* (*for gen.*), Anlass *m*: *the* **~ why** (der Grund) wes-

halb; *by* **~ of** wegen (*gen.*), infolge (*gen.*); *for this* **~** aus diesem Grund, deshalb; *with* **~** aus gutem Grund, mit Recht; *have* **~ to do** Grund *od.* Anlass haben, zu tun; *there is no* **~ to suppose** es besteht kein Grund zu der Annahme; *there is every* **~ to believe** alles spricht dafür (*that* dass); *for* **~s best known to oneself** *iro.* aus unerfindlichen Gründen; **3.** Begründung *f*, Rechtfertigung *f*: **~ of state** Staatsräson *f*; **II** *v/i.* **4.** logisch denken; vernünftig urteilen; **5.** schließen, folgern (*from* aus); **6.** (*with*) vernünftig reden (mit *j-m*), (*j-m*) gut zureden, (*j-n*) zu über-'zeugen suchen: *he is not to be* **~ed with** er lässt nicht mit sich reden; **III** *v/t.* **7.** *a.* **~ out** durch'denken: **~ed** wohl durchdacht; **8.** ergründen (*why* warum, *what* was); **9.** erörtern: **~ away** *et.* wegdisputieren; **~ s.o. into** (*out of*) *s.th.* j-m et. ein-(aus)reden; **10.** schließen, geltend machen (*that* dass); **'rea·son·a·ble** [-nəbl] *adj.* □ → *reasonably*; vernünftig: a) vernunftgemäß, b) verständig, einsichtig (*Person*), c) angemessen, annehmbar, tragbar, billig (*Forderung*), zumutbar (*Bedingung, Frist, Preis etc.*): **~ doubt** berechtigter Zweifel; **~ care and diligence** 🏛 die im Verkehr erforderliche Sorgfalt; **'rea·son·a·ble·ness** [-nəblnɪs] *s.* **1.** Vernünftigkeit *f*, Verständigkeit *f*; **2.** Annehmbarkeit *f*, Zumutbarkeit *f*, Billigkeit *f*; **'rea·son·a·bly** [-nəblɪ] *adv.* **1.** vernünftig; **2.** vernünftiger-, billigerweise; **3.** ziemlich, leidlich: **~ good**; **'rea·son·er** [-nə] *s.* logischer Geist (*Person*); **'rea·son·ing** [-nɪŋ] **I** *s.* **1.** Denken *n*, Folgern *n*, Urteilen *n*; **2.** *a.* **line of** **~** Gedankengang *m*; **3.** Argumentati'on *f*, Beweisführung *f*; **4.** Schluss(folgerung *f*) *m*, Schlüsse *pl.*; Argu'ment *n*, Beweis *m*; **II** *adj.* **6.** Denk..., Urteils...

re·as·sem·ble [ˌriːəˈsembl] *v/t.* **1.** (*v/i.* sich) wieder versammeln; **2.** ⊕ wieder zs.-bauen.

re·as·sert [ˌriːəˈsɜːt] *v/t.* **1.** erneut feststellen; **2.** wieder behaupten; **3.** wieder geltend machen.

re·as·sess·ment [ˌriːəˈsesmənt] *s.* **1.** neuerliche (Ab)Schätzung; **2.** ♦ Neuveranlagung *f*; **3.** *fig.* Neubeurteilung *f*.

re·as·sur·ance [ˌriːəˈʃʊərəns] *s.* **1.** Beruhigung *f*; **2.** nochmalige Versicherung, Bestätigung *f*; **3.** ♦ Rückversicherung *f*; **re·as·sure** [ˌriːəˈʃʊə] *v/t.* **1.** j-n beruhigen; **2.** *et.* nochmals versichern *od.* beteuern; **3.** ♦ wieder versichern; **‚re·as'sur·ing** [-ərɪŋ] *adj.* □ beruhigend.

re·bap·tism [ˌriːˈbæptɪzəm] *s.* 'Wiedertaufe *f*; **re·bap·tize** [ˌriːbæpˈtaɪz] *v/t.* **1.** 'wiedertaufen; **2.** 'umtaufen.

re·bate¹ [ˈriːbeɪt] *s.* **1.** Ra'batt *m*, (Preis-) Nachlass *m*, Abzug *m*; **2.** Zu'rückzahlung *f*, (Rück)Vergütung *f*.

re·bate² [ˈræbɪt] → *rabbet*.

reb·el [ˈrebl] **I** *s.* Re'bell(in), Empörer (-in) (*beide a. fig.*), Aufrührer(in); **II** *adj.* re'bellisch, aufrührerisch; Rebellen...; **III** *v/i.* [rɪˈbel] rebellieren, sich empören *od.* auflehnen (*against* gegen); **re·bel·lion** [rɪˈbeljən] *s.* **1.** Rebelli'on *f*, Aufruhr *m*, Aufstand *m*, Empörung *f* (*against, to* gegen); **2.** Auflehnung *f*, offener Widerstand; **re'bel·lious** [rɪˈbeljəs] *adj.* □ **1.** re'bellisch: a) aufrührerisch, -ständisch, b) *fig.* aufsässig, widerspenstig (*a. Sache*); **2.** 🎗 hartnäckig (*Krankheit*).

re·birth [ˌriːˈbɜːθ] *s.* 'Wiedergeburt *f* (*a.*

fig.).

re·boot [ˌriːˈbuːt] *v/t. Computer:* neu starten.

re·bore [ˌriːˈbɔː] *v/t.* ⊚ **1.** *Loch* nachbohren; **2.** *Motorzylinder* ausschleifen.

re·born [ˌriːˈbɔːn] *adj.* wieder geboren, neugeboren (*a. fig.*).

re·bound¹ **I** *v/i.* [rɪˈbaʊnd] **1.** zu'rückprallen, -schnellen; **2.** *fig.* zu'rückfallen (*upon* auf *acc.*); **II** *s.* [ˈriːbaʊnd] **3.** Zu'rückprallen *n*; **4.** Rückprall *m*; **5.** Widerhall *m*; **6.** *fig.* Reakti'on *f* (*from* auf e-n Rückschlag *etc.*): **on the ~** a) als Reaktion darauf, b) in e-r Krise (befindlich); **take s.o. on** (*od.* **at**) **the ~** j-s Enttäuschung ausnutzen; **7.** *sport* Abpraller *m*.

re·bound² [ˌriːˈbaʊnd] *adj.* neu gebunden (*Buch*).

re·broad·cast [ˌriːˈbrɔːdkɑːst] **I** *v/t.* [*irr.* → *cast*] **1.** *Radio, TV:* e-e Sendung wieder'holen; **2.** durch Re'lais(stati,onen) über'tragen; **II** *v/i.* [*irr.* → *cast*] **3.** über Re'lais(stati,onen) senden: **~ing station** Ballsender *m*; **III** *s.* **4.** Wieder'holungssendung *f*; **5.** Re'laisüber,tragung *f*, Ballsendung *f*.

re·buff [rɪˈbʌf] **I** *s.* **1.** (schroffe) Abweisung, Abfuhr *f*: **meet with a ~** abblitzen; **II** *v/t.* **2.** zu'rück-, abweisen, abblitzen lassen; **3.** *Angriff* abweisen, zu'rückschlagen.

re·build [ˌriːˈbɪld] *v/t.* [*irr.* → *build*] **1.** wieder aufbauen (*a. fig.*); **2.** 'umbauen; **3.** *fig.* wieder'herstellen.

re·buke [rɪˈbjuːk] **I** *v/t.* **1.** j-n rügen, rüffeln, zu'rechtweisen, j-m e-n scharfen Verweis erteilen; **2.** *et.* scharf tadeln, rügen; **II** *s.* **3.** Rüge *f*, (scharfer) Tadel, Rüffel *m*.

re·bus [ˈriːbəs] *pl.* **-bus·es** [-sɪz] *s.* Rebus *m, n*, Bilderrätsel *n*.

re·but [rɪˈbʌt] *bsd.* ⟨⟩ **I** *v/t.* wider'legen, entkräften; **II** *v/i.* den Gegenbeweis antreten; **re·but·tal** [-tl] *s. bsd.* ⟨⟩ Wider'legung *f*, Entkräftung *f*; **re·but·ter** [-tə] *s. bsd.* ⟨⟩ Gegenbeweis *m*.

re·cal·ci·trance [rɪˈkælsɪtrəns] *s.* Widerspenstigkeit *f*; **re·cal·ci·trant** [-nt] *adj.* widerspenstig.

re·call [rɪˈkɔːl] **I** *v/t.* **1.** zu'rückrufen, *Gesandten etc.* abberufen; ⟨⟩ *defekte Autos etc.* (in die Werkstatt) zu'rückrufen; **2.** sich erinnern an (*acc.*), sich *et.* ins Gedächtnis zurückrufen; **3.** j-n erinnern (**to** an *acc.*): **~ s.th. to s.o.** (*od.* **to s.o.'s mind**) j-m *et.* ins Gedächtnis zurückrufen; **4.** *poet. Gefühl* wieder wachrufen; **5.** *Versprechen etc.* zu'rücknehmen, wider'rufen: **until ~ed** bis auf Widerruf; **6.** ⟨⟩ *Kapital, Kredit etc.* (auf)kündigen; **II** *s.* **7.** Zu'rückrufung *f*, Abberufung *f* e-s *Gesandten etc.*; ⟨⟩, ⟨⟩ Rückruf *m* (*in die Werkstatt*); **8.** Widerruf *m*, Zu'rücknahme *f*: **beyond** (*od.* **past**) **~** unwiderruflich, unabänderlich; **9.** ⟨⟩ (Auf)Kündigung *f*, Aufruf *m*; **10.** ✕ Si'gnal *n* zum Sammeln; **11.** (**total** abso'lutes) Gedächtnis; **~ test** *s. ped.* Nacherzählung *f*.

re·cant [rɪˈkænt] **I** *v/t. Behauptung* (for'mell) zu'rücknehmen, wider'rufen; **II** *v/i.* (öffentlich) wider'rufen, Abbitte tun; **re·can·ta·tion** [ˌriːkænˈteɪʃn] *s.* Wider'rufung *f*.

re·cap¹ [ˌriːˈkæp] *v/t.* ⟨⟩ *Am. Autoreifen* runderneuern.

re·cap² [ˈriːkæp] F *für* **recapitulate, recapitulation**.

re·cap·i·tal·i·za·tion [ˈriːkæpɪtəlaɪ-ˈzeɪʃn] *s.* ⟨⟩ Neukapitalisierung *f*.

re·ca·pit·u·late [ˌriːkəˈpɪtjʊleɪt] *v/t. u.*

---

v/i. rekapitulieren (*a. biol.*), (kurz) zs.-fassen *od.* wieder'holen; **re·ca·pit·u·la·tion** [ˈriːkəˌpɪtjʊˈleɪʃn] *s.* ˌRekapitulati'on *f* (*a. biol.*), kurze Wieder'holung *od.* Zs.-fassung.

re·cap·ture [ˌriːˈkæptʃə] **I** *v/t.* **1.** *et.* wieder (in Besitz) nehmen, 'wiedererlangen; *j-n* wieder ergreifen; **2.** ✕ zu'rückerobern; **II** *s.* **3.** 'Wiedererlangung *f*, -ergreifung *f*; ✕ Zu'rückeroberung *f*.

re·cast [ˌriːˈkɑːst] **I** *v/t.* [*irr.* → *cast*] **1.** ⟨⟩ 'umgießen; **2.** 'umformen, neu-, 'umgestalten; **3.** *thea. Stück, Rolle* 'umbesetzen; *Rollen* neu verteilen; **4.** 'durchrechnen; **II** *s.* **5.** ⟨⟩ 'Umguss *m*; **6.** 'Umarbeitung *f*, 'Umgestaltung *f*; **7.** *thea.* Neu-, 'Umbesetzung *f*.

re·cede [rɪˈsiːd] *v/i.* **1.** zu'rücktreten, -weichen: **receding** fliehend (*Kinn, Stirn*); **2.** ent-, verschwinden; *fig.* in den Hintergrund treten; **3.** *fig.* (**from**) zu'rücktreten (von *e-m Amt, Vertrag*), (von *e-r Sache*) Abstand nehmen, (*e-e Ansicht*) aufgeben; *bsd.* ⟨⟩ zu'rückgehen, im Wert fallen.

re·ceipt [rɪˈsiːt] **I** *s.* **1.** Empfang *m* e-s *Briefes etc.*, Erhalt *m*; Annahme *f* e-r *Sendung*; Eingang *m* von *Waren*: **on ~ of** bei *od.* nach Empfang (*gen.*); **be in ~ of** im Besitz *od.* e-r *Sendung etc.* sein; **2.** Empfangsbestätigung *f*, Quittung *f*, Beleg *m*: **~ stamp** Quittungsstempel *m*; **3.** *pl.* ⟨⟩ Einnahmen *pl.*, Eingänge *pl.*, eingehende Gelder *pl. od.* Waren *pl.*; **4.** *obs.* (ˈKoch)Re,zept *n*; **II** *v/t. u. v/i.* **5.** quittieren.

re·ceiv·a·ble [rɪˈsiːvəbl] *adj.* **1.** annehmbar, zulässig (*Beweis etc.*): **be ~** als gesetzliches Zahlungsmittel gelten; **2.** ⟨⟩ ausstehend (*Forderung, Gelder, Guthaben*), debi'torisch (*Posten*): **accounts ~, ~s** *s. pl.* Außenstände, Forderungen; **bills ~** Rimessen; **re·ceive** [rɪˈsiːv] **I** *v/t.* **1.** *Brief etc., a weitS.* Befehl, Eindruck, Radiosendung, Sakramente, Wunde empfangen, *a. Namen, Schock, Treffer* erhalten, bekommen; *Aufmerksamkeit* finden, auf sich ziehen; *Neuigkeit* erfahren; **2.** in Empfang nehmen, annehmen, *a. Beichte, Eid* entgegennehmen; *Geld etc.* einnehmen: **~ stolen goods** ⟨⟩ Hehlerei treiben; **3.** *j-n* bei sich aufnehmen, beherbergen; **4.** *Besucher, a. weitS. Schauspieler etc.* empfangen (**with applause** mit Beifall); **5.** *j-n* aufnehmen (**into** in e-e *Gemeinschaft*); *j-n* zulassen; **6.** *Nachricht etc.* aufnehmen, reagieren auf (*acc.*): **how did he ~ this offer?**; **7.** *et.* erleben, erleiden, erfahren; *Beleidigung* einstecken; *Armbruch etc.* da'vontragen; **8.** ⟨⟩ *Flüssigkeit, Schraube etc.* aufnehmen; **9.** *et.* (als gültig) anerkennen; **II** *v/i.* **10.** (Besuch) empfangen; **11.** *eccl.* das Abendmahl empfangen, *R.C.* kommunizieren; **re·ceived** [-vd] *adj.* **1.** erhalten: **~ with thanks** dankend erhalten; **2.** allgemein anerkannt: **~ text** echter *od.* authentischer Text; **3.** gültig, korrekt, vorschriftsmäßig; **re·ceiv·er** [-və] *s.* **1.** Empfänger(in); **2.** (Steuer-, Zoll)Einnehmer *m*; **3.** *a.* offi**cial ~** ⟨⟩ a) (gerichtlich bestellter) Zwangs- *od.* Kon'kurs- *od.* Masseverwalter, b) Liqui'dator *m*, c) Treuhänder *m*; **4.** *a.* **~ of stolen goods** ⟨⟩ Hehler (-in); **5.** (Radio-, Funk)Empfänger, (-)Empfangsgerät *n*; **6.** *teleph.* Hörer *m*; **7.** ⟨⟩ (Sammel)Becken *n*, (-)Behälter *m*; **8.** ⟨⟩, *phys.* Rezipi'ent *m*; **re·ceiv·er·ship** [-vəʃɪp] *s.* ⟨⟩ Zwangs-, Kon'kursverwaltung *f*, Geschäftsaufsicht *f*; **re·ceiv·ing** [-vɪŋ] *s.* **1.** Annahme *f*; **~**

---

hopper ⟨⟩ Schüttrumpf *m*; **~ office** Annahmestelle *f*; **~ order** ⟨⟩ Konkurseröffnungsbeschluss *m*; **2.** *Funk:* Empfang *m*: **~ set** → **receiver** 5; **~ station** Empfangsstation *f*; **3.** ⟨⟩ Hehle'rei *f*.

re·cen·cy [ˈriːsnsɪ] *s.* Neuheit *f*.

re·cen·sion [rɪˈsenʃn] *s.* **1.** Prüfung *f*, Revisi'on *f*, 'Durchsicht *f* e-s *Textes etc.*; **2.** revidierter Text.

re·cent [ˈriːsnt] *adj.* □ **1.** vor kurzem *od.* unlängst (geschehen *od.* entstanden *etc.*): **the ~ events** die jüngsten Ereignisse; **2.** neu, jung, frisch: **of ~ date** neueren *od.* jüngeren Datums; **3.** neu, mo'dern; **re·cent·ly** [-lɪ] *adv.* kürzlich, vor kurzem, unlängst, neulich.

re·cep·ta·cle [rɪˈseptəkl] *s.* **1.** Behälter *m*, Gefäß *n*; **2.** *a.* **floral ~** ⟨⟩ Fruchtboden *m*; **3.** ⟨⟩ a) Steckdose *f*, b) Gerätbuchse *f*.

re·cep·tion [rɪˈsepʃn] *s.* **1.** Empfang *m* (*a. Funk, TV*), Annahme *f*; **2.** Zulassung *f*; **3.** Aufnahme *f* (*a. fig.*): **meet with a favo(u)rable ~** e-e günstige Aufnahme finden (*Buch etc.*); **4.** (offizi'eller) Empfang, *a.* Empfangsabend *m*: **a warm** (**cool**) **~** ein herzlicher (kühler) Empfang; **~ room** Empfangszimmer *n*; **re·cep·tion·ist** [-ʃənɪst] *s.* **1.** Empfangsdame *f*; **2.** 🖊 Sprechstundenhilfe *f*.

re·cep·tive [rɪˈseptɪv] *adj.* □ aufnahmefähig, empfänglich (**of** für); **re·cep·tiv·i·ty** [ˌresepˈtɪvətɪ] *s.* Aufnahmefähigkeit *f*, Empfänglichkeit *f*.

re·cess [rɪˈses] **I** *s.* **1.** (zeitweilige) Unter'brechung (*a. der Verhandlung*), (*Am. a.* Schul)Pause *f*, *bsd. parl.* Ferien *pl.*; **2.** Schlupfwinkel *m*, stiller Winkel; **3.** △ (Wand)Aussparung *f*, Nische *f*, Al'koven *m*; ⟨⟩ Aussparung *f*, Vertiefung *f*, Einschnitt *m*; **5.** *pl. fig.* das Innere, Tiefe(n *pl.*) *f*, geheime Winkel *pl.* des *Herzens etc.*; **II** *v/t.* **6.** in e-e Nische einbauen, zu'rücksetzen; **7.** aussparen; ausbuchten, einsenken, vertiefen; **III** *v/i.* **8.** *Am.* e-e Pause *od.* Ferien machen, unter'brechen, sich vertagen.

re·ces·sion [rɪˈseʃn] *s.* **1.** Zu'rücktreten *n*; **2.** *eccl.* Auszug *m*; **3.** △ *etc.* Vertiefung *f*; **4.** ⟨⟩ Rezessi'on *f*, (leichter) Konjunk'turrückgang: **period of ~** Rezessionsphase *f*; **re·ces·sion·al** [-ʃənl] **I** *adj.* **1.** *eccl.* Schluss...; **2.** *parl.* Ferien...; **3.** ⟨⟩ Rezessions...; **II** *s.* **4.** *a.* **~ hymn** 'Schlusscho,ral *m*.

re·charge [ˌriːˈtʃɑːdʒ] *v/t.* **1.** wieder (be-)laden; **2.** ✕ a) von neuem angreifen, b) nachladen; **3.** ⟨⟩ *Batterie* wieder aufladen.

re·cher·ché [rəˈʃeəʃeɪ] (*Fr.*) *adj. fig.* **1.** ausgesucht, exqui'sit; **2.** *iro.* gesucht, prezi'ös.

re·chris·ten [ˌriːˈkrɪsn] → **rebaptize**.

re·cid·i·vism [rɪˈsɪdɪvɪzəm] *s.* ⟨⟩ Rückfall *m*, -fälligkeit *f*; **re·cid·i·vist** [-ɪst] *s.* Rückfällige(r *m*) *f*; **re·cid·i·vous** [-vəs] *adj.* rückfällig.

rec·i·pe [ˈresɪpɪ] *s.* (ˈKoch)Re,zept *n*.

re·cip·i·ent [rɪˈsɪpɪənt] **I** *s.* **1.** Empfänger (-in); **II** *adj.* **2.** aufnehmend; **3.** empfänglich (**of, to** für).

re·cip·ro·cal [rɪˈsɪprəkl] **I** *adj.* □ **1.** wechsel-, gegenseitig, *Vertrag, Versicherung* auf Gegenseitigkeit: **~ service** Gegendienst *m*; **~ relationship** Wechselbeziehung *f*; **2.** 'umgekehrt; **3.** ⟨⟩, *ling., phls.* rezi'prok; **II** *s.* **4.** Gegenstück *n*; ⟨⟩ a. **~ value** ⟨⟩ rezi'proker Wert, Kehrwert *m*; **re·cip·ro·cate** [-keɪt] **I** *v/t.* **1.** *Gefühle etc.* erwidern, vergelten; *Glückwünsche etc.* austauschen; **II** *v/i.* **2.** sich erkenntlich zeigen, sich revanchieren (**for** für, **with** mit): **glad to** ~ zu Gegendiensten gern bereit; **3.** in Wechselbeziehung stehen; **4.** ☼ sich hin- u. herbewegen: *reciprocating engine* Kolbenmaschine *f*, -motor *m*; **re·cip·ro·ca·tion** [rɪ,sɪprə'keɪʃn] *s.* **1.** Erwiderung *f*; **2.** Erkenntlichkeit *f*; **3.** Austausch *m*; **4.** Wechselwirkung *f*; **5.** ☼ ,Hinund'herbewegung *f*; **rec·i·proc·i·ty** [,resɪ'prɒsətɪ] *s.* Rezipro'zität *f*; Gegenseitigkeit *f* (*a.* ✝ *in Verträgen etc.*): ~ *clause* Gegenseitigkeitsklausel *f*.

re·cit·al [rɪ'saɪtl] *s.* **1.** Vortrag *m*, -lesung *f*; **2.** ♪ (Solo)Vortrag *m*, (*Orgel- etc.*) Kon'zert *n*: *lieder* ~ Liederabend *m*; **3.** Bericht *m*, Schilderung *f*; **4.** Aufzählung *f*; **5.** ⚖ a) *a.* ~ *of fact* Darstellung *f* des Sachverhalts, b) Prä'ambel *f e-s Vertrags etc.*; **rec·i·ta·tion** [,resɪ'teɪʃn] *s.* **1.** Auf-, Hersagen *n*, Rezitieren *n*; **2.** Vortrag *m*, Rezitati'on *f*; **3.** *ped. Am.* Abfrage-, Übungsstunde *f*; **4.** Vortragsstück *n*, rezitierter Text; **rec·i·ta·tive** [,resɪtə'tiːv] ♪ **I** *adj.* rezita'tivartig; **II** *s.* Rezita'tiv *n*, Sprechgesang *m*; **re·cite** [rɪ'saɪt] *v/t.* **1.** (auswendig) her- *od.* aufsagen; **2.** rezitieren, vortragen, deklamieren; **3.** ⚖ a) *Sachverhalt* darstellen, b) anführen, zitieren; **re·cit·er** [-tə] *s.* **1.** Rezi'tator *m*, Rezita'torin *f*, Vortragskünstler(in); **2.** Vortragsbuch *n*.

reck·less ['reklɪs] *adj.* ☐ **1.** unbesorgt, unbekümmert (**of** um); *be* ~ *of* sich nicht kümmern um; **2.** sorglos; leichtsinnig; verwegen; **3.** rücksichtslos; ⚖ (bewusst *od.* grob) fahrlässig; '**reck·less·ness** [-nɪs] *s.* **1.** Unbesorgtheit *f*, Unbekümmertheit *f* (**of** um); **2.** Sorglosigkeit *f*, Leichtsinn *m*, Verwegenheit *f*; **3.** Rücksichtslosigkeit *f*.

reck·on ['rekən] **I** *v/t.* **1.** (be-, er)rechnen: ~ *in* einrechnen; ~ *over* nachrechnen; ~ *up* a) auf-, zs.-zählen, b) *j-n* einschätzen; **2.** halten für: ~ *as od.* *for* betrachten als; ~ *among od.* *with* rechnen *od.* zählen zu (*od.* unter *acc.*); **3.** der Meinung sein (**that** dass) **II** *v/i.* **4.** zählen, rechnen: ~ *with* a) rechnen mit (*a. fig.*), b) abrechnen mit (*a. fig.*); *he is to be* ~*ed with* mit ihm muss man rechnen; ~ *without* nicht rechnen mit; ~ (**up**)**on** *fig.* rechnen *od.* zählen auf *j-n, j-s Hilfe etc.*; *I* ~ schätze ich, glaube ich; → *host*² **2**; **reck·on·er** ['rekənə] *s.* **1.** Rechner(in); **2.** → *ready reckoner*; '**reck·on·ing** ['rekənɪŋ] *s.* **1.** Rechnen *n*; **2.** Berechnung *f*, Kalkulati'on *f*; ♣ Gissung *f*: *dead* ~ gegisstes Besteck; *be out of* (*od.* *out in*) *one's* ~ sich verrechnet haben (*a. fig.*); **3.** Abrechnung *f*: *day of* ~ a) *bsd. fig.* Tag *m* der Abrechnung, b) *eccl. der* Jüngste Tag; **4.** *obs.* Rechnung *f*, Zeche *f*.

re·claim [rɪ'kleɪm] *v/t.* **1.** *Eigentum, Rechte etc.* zu'rückfordern, her'ausverlangen, reklamieren; **2.** *Land* urbar machen, kultivieren, trockenlegen; **3.** *Tiere* zähmen; **4.** *Volk* zivilisieren; **5.** ☼ aus Altmaterial gewinnen, *Altöl, Gummi etc.* regenerieren; **6.** *fig.* a) *j-n* bekehren, bessern, b) *j-n* zu'rückbringen, -führen (**from** von, **to** zu); **re'claim·a·ble** [-məbl] *adj.* ☐ **1.** (ver)besserungsfähig; **2.** kul'turfähig (*Land*); **3.** ☼ regenerierfähig.

rec·la·ma·tion [,reklə'meɪʃn] *s.* **1.** Reklamati'on *f*: a) Rückforderung *f*, b) Beschwerde *f*; **2.** *fig.* Bekehrung *f*, Besserung *f*, Heilung *f* (**from** von); **3.** Urbarmachung *f*, Neugewinnung *f* (*von*

Land); **4.** ☼ Rückgewinnung *f*.

re·cline [rɪ'klaɪn] **I** *v/i.* **1.** sich (an-, zu'rück)lehnen: *reclining chair* (verstellbarer) Lehnstuhl; **2.** ruhen, liegen (**on**, **upon** an, auf *dat.*); **3.** *fig.* ~ *upon* sich stützen auf (*acc.*); **II** *v/t.* **4.** (an-, zu'rück)lehnen, legen (**on**, **upon** auf *acc.*).

re·cluse [rɪ'kluːs] **I** *s.* **1.** Einsiedler(in); **II** *adj.* **2.** einsam, abgeschieden (**from** von); **3.** einsiedlerisch.

rec·og·ni·tion [,rekəg'nɪʃn] *s.* **1.** ('Wieder)Erkennen *n*: ~ *vocabulary* ling. passiver Wortschatz; *beyond* ~, *out of* ~, *past* (**all**) ~ (bis) zur Unkenntlichkeit *verändert, verstümmelt etc.*; *the capital has changed beyond* (**all**) ~ die Hauptstadt ist (überhaupt) nicht wieder zu erkennen; **2.** Erkenntnis *f*; **3.** Anerkennung *f* (*a. pol.*): *in* ~ *of* als Anerkennung für; *win* ~ sich durchsetzen, Anerkennung finden; **rec·og·niz·a·ble** ['rekəgnaɪzəbl] *adj.* ☐ (wieder) erkennbar, kenntlich; **re·cog·ni·zance** [rɪ'kɒgnɪzəns] *s.* **1.** ⚖ schriftliche Verpflichtung; (Schuld)Anerkenntnis *n, f*: *enter into* ~*s* sich gerichtlich binden; **2.** ⚖ Sicherheitsleistung *f*, Kauti'on *f*; **re·cog·ni·zant** [rɪ'kɒgnɪzənt] *adj.*: *be* ~ *of* anerkennen; **rec·og·nize** ['rekəgnaɪz] *v/t.* **1.** (wieder) erkennen; **2.** *j-n, e-e Regierung, Schuld etc., a. lobend* anerkennen; ~ *that* zugeben, dass; **3.** No'tiz nehmen von; **4.** *auf der Straße* grüßen; **5.** *j-m* das Wort erteilen.

re·coil **I** *v/i.* [rɪ'kɔɪl] **1.** zu'rückprallen; zu'rückstoßen (*Gewehr etc.*); **2.** *fig.* zu'rückprallen, -schrecken, -schaudern (**at**, **from** vor *dat.*); **3.** ~ *on fig.* zu'rückfallen auf (*acc.*) **II** *s.* ['riːkɔɪl] **4.** Rückprall *m*; **5.** ✕ a) Rückstoß *m* (*Gewehr*), b) (Rohr)Rücklauf *m* (*Geschütz*); **re·'coil·less** [-lɪs] *adj.* ✕ rückstoßfrei.

rec·ol·lect [,rekə'lekt] *v/t.* sich erinnern (*gen.*) *od.* an (*acc.*), sich *et.* ins Gedächtnis zu'rückrufen.

re·col·lect [,riːkə'lekt] *v/t.* wieder sammeln (*a. fig.*): ~ *o.s.* sich fassen.

rec·ol·lec·tion [,rekə'lekʃn] *s.* Erinnerung *f* (*Vermögen u. Vorgang*), Gedächtnis *n*: *it is within my* ~ es ist mir erinnerlich; *to the best of my* ~ soweit ich mich (daran) erinnern kann.

re·com·mence [,riːkə'mens] *v/t. u. v/i.* wieder beginnen.

rec·om·mend [,rekə'mend] *v/t.* **1.** empfehlen (*s.th. to s.o.* j-m et.): ~ *s.o. for a post* j-n für e-n Posten empfehlen; ~ *caution* Vorsicht empfehlen, zu Vorsicht raten; **2.** empfehlen, anziehend machen: *his manners* ~ *him*; **3.** (an-) empfehlen, anvertrauen: ~ *s.o. to s.o.*; ,**rec·om'mend·a·ble** [-dəbl] *adj.* ☐ empfehlenswert; **rec·om·men·da·tion** [,rekəmen'deɪʃn] *s.* **1.** Empfehlung *f* (*a. fig. Eigenschaft*); **2.** Empfehlung *f*, Vorschlag *m*: *on the* ~ *of* auf Empfehlung von; **2.** *a.* *letter of* ~ Empfehlungsschreiben *n*; ,**rec·om'mend·a·to·ry** [-dətərɪ] *adj.* empfehlend, Empfehlungs...

re·com·mis·sion [,riːkə'mɪʃn] *v/t.* **1.** wieder anstellen *od.* beauftragen; ✕ *Offizier* reaktivieren; **2.** ♣ *Schiff* wieder in Dienst stellen.

re·com·mit [,riːkə'mɪt] *v/t.* **1.** *parl. Gesetzesvorlage* an e-n Ausschuss zu'rückverweisen; **2.** ⚖ *j-n* erneut einweisen (**to** in *e-e Strafanstalt etc.*).

re·com·pense ['rekəmpens] **I** *v/t.* **1.** *j-n* belohnen, entschädigen (**for** für); **2.** *et.* vergelten, belohnen (**to s.o.** j-m); **3.** *et.* erstatten, ersetzen, wieder gutmachen; **II** *s.* **4.** Belohnung *f*; *a. b.s.* Vergeltung

f; **5.** Entschädigung *f*, Ersatz *m*.

re·com·pose [,riːkəm'pəuz] *v/t.* **1.** wieder zs.-setzen; **2.** neu (an)ordnen, 'umgestalten, -gruppieren; **3.** *fig.* wieder beruhigen; **4.** *typ.* neu setzen.

rec·on·cil·a·ble ['rekənsaɪləbl] *adj.* **1.** versöhnbar; **2.** vereinbar (**with** mit); **rec·on·cile** ['rekənsaɪl] *v/t.* **1.** *j-n* ver-, aussöhnen (**to, with** mit): ~ *o.s. to, become* ~*d to fig.* sich versöhnen *od.* abfinden *od.* befreunden mit *et.*, sich fügen *od.* finden in (*acc.*); **2.** *fig.* in Einklang bringen, abstimmen (**with, to** mit); **3.** *Streit* beilegen, schlichten; **rec·on·cil·i·a·tion** [,rekənsɪlɪ'eɪʃn] *s.* **1.** Ver-, Aussöhnung *f* (**to, with** mit); **2.** Beilegung *f*, Schlichtung *f*; **3.** Ausgleich(ung *f*) *m*, Einklang *m* (**between** zwischen *dat.*, unter *dat.*).

rec·on·dite [rɪ'kɒndaɪt] *adj.* ☐ *fig.* tief (-gründig), ab'strus, dunkel.

re·con·di·tion [,riːkən'dɪʃn] *v/t. bsd.* ☼ wieder in'standsetzen, über'holen, erneuern.

re·con·nais·sance [rɪ'kɒnɪsəns] *s.* ✕ a) Erkundung *f*, Aufklärung *f*, b) *a.* ~ *party od. patrol* Spähtrupp *m*: ~ *car* Spähwagen *m*; ~ *plane* Aufklärungsflugzeug *n*, Aufklärer *m*.

re·con·noi·ter *Am.*, **re·con·noi·tre** *Brit.* [,rekə'nɔɪtə] *v/t.* ✕ erkunden, aufklären, auskundschaften (*a. fig.*), rekognoszieren (*a. geol.*).

re·con·quer [,riː'kɒŋkə] *v/t.* 'wieder-, zu'rückerobern; ,**re·con·quest** [-kwest] *s.* 'Wiedereroberung *f*.

re·con·sid·er [,riːkən'sɪdə] *v/t.* **1.** von neuem erwägen, nochmals über'legen, nachprüfen; **2.** *pol.,* ⚖ *Antrag, Sache* nochmals behandeln; **re·con·sid·er·a·tion** ['riːkən,sɪdə'reɪʃn] *s.* nochmalige Über'legung *od.* Erwägung *od.* Prüfung.

re·con·stit·u·ent [,riːkən'stɪtjʊənt] **I** *s.* ❀ Roborans *n*; **II** *adj. bsd.* ❀ wieder aufbauend.

re·con·sti·tute [,riː'kɒnstɪtjuːt] *v/t.* **1.** wieder einsetzen; **2.** wieder herstellen; neu bilden; ✕ neu aufstellen; **3.** im Wasser auflösen.

re·con·struct [,riːkən'strʌkt] *v/t.* **1.** wieder aufbauen (*a. fig.*), wieder herstellen; **2.** 'umbauen (*a.* ☼ *neu konstruieren*), 'umformen, -bilden; **3.** ✝ wieder aufbauen, sanieren; ,**re·con·struc·tion** [,riːkən'strʌkʃn] *s.* **1.** Wieder'aufbau *m*, -'herstellung *f*; **2.** 'Umbau *m* (*a.* ☼ *Neukonstruktion*), 'Umformung *f*; **3.** Rekonstrukti'on *f* (*a. e-s Verbrechens etc.*); **4.** ✝ Sanierung *f*, Wieder'aufbau *m*.

re·con·ver·sion [,riːkən'vɜːʃn] *s.* ('Rück),Umwandlung *f*, 'Umstellung *f* (*bsd.* ✝ *e-s Betriebs, auf Friedensproduktion etc.*); ,**re·con'vert** [-'vɜːt] *v/t.* (wieder) 'umstellen.

rec·ord¹ ['rekɔːd] *s.* **1.** Aufzeichnung *f*, Niederschrift *f*: *on* ~ a) (geschichtlich *etc.*) verzeichnet, schriftlich belegt, b) → **4 b**, c) *fig.* das beste *etc.* aller Zeiten, bisher; *off the* ~ inoffiziell, nicht für die Öffentlichkeit bestimmt; *on the* ~ offiziell; *matter of* ~ verbürgte Tatsache; **2.** (schriftlicher) Bericht; **3.** *a.* ⚖ Urkunde *f*, Doku'ment *n*, 'Unterlage *f*; **4.** ⚖ a) Proto'koll *n*, Niederschrift *f*, b) (Gerichts)Akte *f*, Aktenstück *n*: *on* ~ aktenkundig; *on the* ~ *of the case* nach Aktenlage; *go on* ~ *fig.* a) sich erklären *od.* festlegen, b) sich erweisen (*as* als); *place on* ~ aktenkundig machen; *court of* ~ ordentliches Gericht; ~ *office* Archiv *n*; (*just*) *to put the* ~

straight! (nur) um das mal klarzustellen!; *just for the ~!* (nur) um das mal festzuhalten!; **5.** Re'gister *n*, Liste *f*, Verzeichnis *n*, Bi'lanz *f*: *criminal ~* a) Strafregister, b) *weitS.* Vorstrafen *pl.*; *have a (criminal) ~* vorbestraft sein; *his human rights record ...* die Art u. Weise, wie er mit den Menschenrechten umgeht *od.* umging, ...; **6.** *a.* ◎ Registrierung *f*; **7.** a) Ruf *m*, Leumund *m*, Vergangenheit *f*: *a bad ~*, b) gute *etc.* Leistung(en *pl.*) *in der Vergangenheit*; **8.** *fig.* Urkunde *f*, Zeugnis *n*: *be a ~ of et.* bezeugen; **9.** (Schall)Platte *f*: *~ changer* Plattenwechsler *m*; *~ library* a) Plattensammlung *f*, -archiv *n*, b) Plattenverleih *m*; *~ machine* Am. Musikautomat *m*; *~ player* Plattenspieler *m*; **10.** *sport, a. weitS.* Re'kord *m*, Best-, Höchstleistung *f*: *~ high (low)* ✝ Rekordhoch (-tief) *n*; *~ attendance* Zuschauerrekord *m*; *~ performance* *allg.* Spitzenleistung *f*; *~ prices* ✝ Rekordpreise; *in ~ time* in Rekordzeit.

re·cord² [rɪ'kɔːd] *v/t.* **1.** schriftlich niederlegen; (*a.* ◎) aufzeichnen, -schreiben; ♫ beurkunden, protokollieren; zu den Akten nehmen; ✝ *etc.* eintragen, registrieren, erfassen: *by ~ed delivery* ⓥ per Einschreiben; **2.** ◎ Messwerte registrieren, verzeichnen; **3.** (*auf Tonband etc.*) aufnehmen, -zeichnen, *Sendung* mitschneiden, *a. fotografisch* festhalten: *~ a CD (CD-ROM)* a. e-e CD (CD-ROM) brennen; **4.** *fig.* aufzeichnen, festhalten, der Nachwelt über'liefern; **5.** *Stimme* abgeben; **re'cord·a·ble** [-əbl] *adj.* **1.** dokumentierbar, protokollierbar; **2.** registrierbar; **3.** a) bespielbar (*CD*), b) beschreibbar (*CD-ROM*); **re'cord·er** [-də] *s.* **1.** Regi'strator *m*; *weitS.* Chro'nist *m*; **2.** Schrift-, Proto'kollführer(in); **3.** ♫ *Brit. obs.* Einzelrichter *m* der *Quarter Sessions*; **4.** ◎ Aufnahmegerät *n*: a) Regi'strierappa·,rat *m*, (Bild-, Selbst)Schreiber *m*, b) 'Wiedergabegerät *n*; → *tape recorder etc.*; **5.** ♪ Blockflöte *f*; **re'cord·ing** [-dɪŋ] I *s.* **1.** *a.* ◎ Aufzeichnung *f*, Registrierung *f*; **2.** Beurkundung *f*, Protokollierung *f*; **3.** *Radio etc.*: Aufnahme *f*, Aufzeichnung *f*, Mitschnitt *m*; II *adj.* **4.** Protokoll...; **5.** registrierend: *~ chart* Registrierpapier *n*; *~ head* a) ♫ Tonkopf *m* (*Tonbandgerät*), b) Schreibkopf *m* (*Computer*).

re·count¹ [riː'kaʊnt] *v/t.* **1.** (im Einzelnen) erzählen; **2.** aufzählen.

re·count² [,riː'kaʊnt] *v/t.* nachzählen.

re·coup [rɪ'kuːp] *v/t.* **1.** 'wiedergewinnen, *Verlust etc.* wieder'einbringen; **2.** *j-n* entschädigen (*for* für); **3.** ✝, ♫ einbehalten.

re·course [rɪ'kɔːs] *s.* **1.** Zuflucht *f* (*to* zu): *have ~ to s.th.* s-e Zuflucht zu et. nehmen; *have ~ to foul means* zu unredlichen Mitteln greifen; **2.** ✝, ♫ Re'gress *m*, Re'kurs *m*: *with (without) ~* mit (ohne) Rückgriff; *liable to ~* regresspflichtig.

re·cov·er [rɪ'kʌvə] I *v/t.* **1.** (*a. fig. Appetit, Bewusstsein, Fassung etc.*) 'wiedererlangen, wieder finden; zu'rückerlangen, -gewinnen; ✕ 'wieder-, zu'rückerobern; *Fahrzeug, Schiff* bergen: *~ data* Computer: Daten wiederherstellen; *~ one's breath* wieder zu Atem kommen; *~ one's legs* wieder auf die Beine kommen; *~ land from the sea* dem Meer Land abringen; **2.** *Verluste etc.* wieder gutmachen, wieder'einbringen, ersetzen; *Zeit* wieder'aufholen; **3.** *a) Schuld etc.* einziehen, beitreiben, b)

Urteil erwirken (*against* gegen): *~ damages for* Schadensersatz erhalten für; **4.** ◎ *aus Altmaterial* regenerieren, 'wiedergewinnen; **5.** *~ o.s.* → 8 *u.* 9.: *be ~ed from* wiederhergestellt sein von; **6.** (er)retten, befreien (*from* aus); **7.** *fenc. etc.* in die Ausgangsstellung bringen; II *v/i.* **8.** genesen, wieder gesund werden; sich erholen (*from, of* von *e-m Schock etc.*) (*a.* ✝); **10.** wieder zu sich kommen, das Bewusstsein 'wiederererlangen; **11.** ♫ a) Recht bekommen, b) entschädigt werden, sich schadlos halten: *~ in one's (law)suit* s-n Prozess gewinnen, obsiegen.

re·cov·er·a·ble [rɪ'kʌvərəbl] *adj.* **1.** 'wiedererlangbar; **2.** wieder gutzumachen(d); **3.** ♫ ein-, beitreibbar (*Schuld*); **4.** wieder'herstellbar; **5.** ◎ regenerierbar; **re·cov·er·y** [rɪ'kʌvərɪ] *s.* **1.** (Zu)'Rück-, 'Wiedererlangung *f*, -gewinnung *f*; **2.** ♫ a) Ein-, Beitreibung *f*, b) *mst ~ of damages* (Erlangung *f* von) Schadenersatz *m*; **3.** ◎ Rückgewinnung *f aus Abfallstoffen etc.*; **4.** ♦ *etc.* Bergung *f*, Rettung *f*: *~ vehicle* mot. Bergungsfahrzeug *n*; Abschleppwagen *m*; **5.** *fig.* Rettung *f*, Bekehrung *f*; **6.** Genesung *f*, Gesundung *f*, Erholung *f* (*a.* ✝), (gesundheitliche) 'Wieder'herstellung: *economic ~* Konjunkturaufschwung *m*, -belebung *f*; *be past (od. beyond) ~* unheilbar krank sein, *fig.* hoffnungslos darniederliegen; **7.** *sport* a) *fenc. etc.* Zu'rückgehen *n* in die Ausgangsstellung, b) *Golf:* Bunkerschlag *m*.

rec·re·an·cy ['rekrɪənsɪ] *s.* **1.** Feigheit *f*; **2.** Abtrünnigkeit *f*; **'rec·re·ant** [-nt] I *adj.* □ **1.** feig(e); **2.** abtrünnig, treulos; II *s.* **3.** Feigling *m*; **4.** Abtrünnige(r *m*) *f*.

rec·re·ate ['rekrɪeɪt] I *v/t.* **1.** erfrischen, *j-m* Erholung *od.* Entspannung gewähren; **2.** erheitern, unter'halten; **3.** *~ o.s.* a) ausspannen, sich erholen, b) sich ergötzen *od.* unterhalten; II *v/i.* **4.** → 3.

re·cre·ate [,riːkrɪ'eɪt] *v/t.* neu *od.* wieder (er)schaffen.

rec·re·a·tion [,rekrɪ'eɪʃn] *s.* Erholung *f*, Entspannung *f*, Erfrischung *f*, Belustigung *f*, Unter'haltung *f*: *~ area* Erholungsgebiet *n*; *~ centre, Am. ~ center* Freizeitzentrum *n*; *~ ground* Spiel-, Sportplatz *m*; **,rec·re·a·tion·al** [-ʃənl] *adj.* Erholungs..., Entspannungs..., *Ort etc.* der Erholung; Freizeit...: *~ value* Freizeitwert *m*; *~ vehicle* Am. Wohnmobil *n*; **rec·re·a·tive** ['rekrɪeɪtɪv] *adj.* **1.** erholsam, entspannend, erfrischend; **2.** unter'haltend.

re·crim·i·nate [rɪ'krɪmɪneɪt] *v/i. u. v/t.* Gegenbeschuldigungen vorbringen (gegen); **re·crim·i·na·tion** [rɪ,krɪmɪ'neɪʃn] *s.* Gegenbeschuldigung *f*.

re·cru·desce [,riːkruː'des] *v/i.* **1.** wieder aufbrechen (*Wunde*); **2.** sich wieder verschlimmern (*Zustand*); **3.** *fig.* wieder ausbrechen, wieder aufflackern (*Übel*); **,re·cru'des·cence** [-sns] *s.* **1.** Wieder'aufbrechen *n* (*e-r Wunde etc.*); **2.** *fig.* a) Wieder'ausbrechen *n*, b) Wieder'aufleben *n*.

re·cruit [rɪ'kruːt] I *s.* **1.** ✕ a) Re'krut *m*, b) *Am.* (einfacher) Sol'dat *m*; **2.** Neuling *m* (*a. contp.*); II *v/t.* **3.** ✕ rekrutieren: a) *Rekruten* ausheben, einziehen, b) anwerben, c) *Einheit* ergänzen, erneuern, d) *weitS. Leute* her'anziehen: *be ~ed from* sich rekrutieren aus, *fig. a.* sich zs.-setzen *od.* ergänzen aus; **4.** *j-n*, *j-s Gesundheit* wieder'herstellen, stärken, erfrischen; III *v/i.* **6.** Rekruten ausheben *od.* anwerben; **7.** sich erho-

len; **re'cruit·al** [-tl] *s.* Erholung *f*, Wieder'herstellung *f*; **re'cruit·ing** [-tɪŋ] ✕ I *s.* Rekrutierung *f*, (An)Werben *n*; II *adj.* Werbe...(-büro, -offizier etc.); Rekrutierungs...(-stelle); **re'cruit·ment** [-mənt] *s.* **1.** Verstärkung *f*, Auffrischung *f*; **2.** *bsd.* ✕ Rekrutierung *f*; **3.** Erholung *f*.

rec·tal ['rektəl] *adj.* □ *anat.* rek'tal: *~ syringe* Klistierspritze *f*.

rec·tan·gle ['rek,tæŋgl] *s.* ♠ Rechteck *n*; **rec·tan·gu·lar** [rek'tæŋgjʊlə] *adj.* □ ♠ **1.** rechteckig; **2.** rechtwink(e)lig.

rec·ti·fi·a·ble ['rektɪfaɪəbl] *adj.* **1.** zu berichtigen(d), korrigierbar; **2.** ♠, ◎, ♯ rektifizierbar; **rec·ti·fi·ca·tion** [,rektɪfɪ'keɪʃn] *s.* **1.** Berichtigung *f*, Verbesserung *f*, Richtigstellung *f*; **2.** ♠, ♯ Rektifikati'on *f*; **3.** ♯ Gleichrichtung *f*; **4.** *phot.* Entzerrung *f*; **'rec·ti·fi·er** [-aɪə] *s.* **1.** Berichtiger *m*; **2.** ♠ *etc.* Rektifizierer *m*; **3.** ♯ Gleichrichter *m*; **4.** *phot.* Entzerrungsgerät *n*; **rec·ti·fy** ['rektɪfaɪ] *v/t.* berichtigen, korrigieren, richtigstellen; *Missstand etc.* beseitigen; ♠, ♯, ◎ rektifizieren; ♯ gleichrichten.

rec·ti·lin·e·al [,rektɪ'lɪnɪəl] *adj.*, **,rec·ti·'lin·e·ar** [-ɪə] *adj.* □ geradlinig; **rec·ti·tude** ['rektɪtjuːd] *s.* Geradheit *f*, Rechtschaffenheit *f*.

rec·tor ['rektə] *s.* **1.** *eccl.* Pfarrer *m*; **2.** *univ.* Rektor *m*; **3.** *Scot.* ('Schul)Di,rektor *m*; **'rec·tor·ate** [-ərət], **'rec·tor·ship** [-ʃɪp] *s.* **1.** *ped.* Rekto'rat *n*; **2.** *eccl.* a) Pfarrstelle *f*, b) Amt *n od.* Amtszeit *f* e-s Pfarrers; **'rec·to·ry** [-tərɪ] *s.* Pfar'rei *f*, Pfarre *f*: a) Pfarrhaus *n*, b) *Brit.* Pfarrstelle *f*, c) Kirchspiel *n*.

rec·tum ['rektəm] *pl.* **-ta** [-tə] *s. anat.* Mastdarm *m*, Rektum *n*.

re·cum·ben·cy [rɪ'kʌmbənsɪ] *s.* **1.** liegende Stellung, Liegen *n*; **2.** *fig.* Ruhe *f*; **re'cum·bent** [-nt] *adj.* □ (sich zu'rück)lehnend, liegend, *a. fig.* ruhend.

re·cu·per·ate [rɪ'kjuːpəreɪt] I *v/i.* **1.** sich erholen (*a.* ✝); II *v/t.* **2.** 'wiedererlangen; **3.** *Verluste etc.* wettmachen; **re·cu·per·a·tion** [rɪ,kjuːpə'reɪʃn] *s.* Erholung *f* (*a. fig.*); **re'cu·per·a·tive** [-rətɪv] *adj.* **1.** stärkend, kräftigend; **2.** Erholungs...

re·cur [rɪ'kɜː] *v/i.* **1.** 'wiederkehren, wieder auftreten (*Ereignis, Erscheinung etc.*); **2.** *fig.* in Gedanken, im Gespräch zu'rückkommen (*to* auf *acc.*); **3.** *fig.* 'wiederkehren (*Gedanken*); **4.** zu'rückgreifen (*to* auf *acc.*); **5.** ♠ (peri'odisch) wiederkehren (*Kurve etc.*): *~ring decimal* periodische Dezimalzahl; **re·cur·rence** [rɪ'kʌrəns] *s.* **1.** 'Wiederkehr *f*, Wieder'auftreten *n*; **2.** Zu'rückgreifen *n* (*to* auf *acc.*); **3.** *fig.* Zu'rückkommen *n* (*im Gespräch etc.*) (*to* auf *acc.*); **re·cur·rent** [rɪ'kʌrənt] *adj.* □ **1.** 'wiederkehrend (*a. Zahlungen, Träume*), sich wieder'holend; **2.** peri'odisch auftretend: *~ fever* ✿ Rückfallfieber *n*; **3.** ♀, *anat.* rückläufig (*Nerv, Arterie etc.*).

re·cy·cla·ble [,riː'saɪkləbl] *adj.* recyclingfähig, wieder verwertbar; **re·cy·cle** [,riː'saɪkl] *v/t.* **1.** ◎ Abfälle 'wieder verwerten; *~d paper* Umweltpapier *n*; **2.** ✝ Kapital zu'rückschleusen; **re·cy·cle bin** *s.* Computer: 'Pa'pierkorb' *m*; **re·'cy·cling** [-lɪŋ] *s.* ◎, ✝ Re'cycling *n*: a) ◎ 'Wiederverwertung *f*: *~ of waste material*, b) ✝ Rückschleusung *f*: *~ of funds*.

red [red] I *adj.* **1.** rot: *~ ant* Rote Waldameise; *⚹ Book* a) Adelskalender *m*, b) *pol.* Rotbuch *m*; *~ cabbage* Rotkohl *m*; *⚹ Cross* Rotes Kreuz; *~ deer* Edel-, Rothirsch *m*; *⚹ Ensign* brit. Handels-

flagge *f*; **~ hat** Kardinalshut *m*; **~ heat** Rotglut *f*; **~ herring** a) Bückling *m*, b) *fig.* Ablenkungsmanöver *n*, falsche Spur; **draw a ~ herring across the path** a) ein Ablenkungsmanöver durchführen, b) e-e falsche Spur zurücklassen; **~ lead** [led] *min.* Mennige *f*; **~ lead ore** [led] Rotbleierz *n*; **~ light** Warn-, Stopplicht *n*; **see the ~ light** *fig.* die Gefahr erkennen; **the lights are at ~** *mot.* die Ampel steht auf Rot; **~ tape** Amtsschimmel *m*, Bürokratismus *m*, Papierkrieg *m*; **see ~** ‚rotsehen'; **→ paint** 2; **rag¹** 1; **2.** rot (glühend); **3.** rot(haarig); **4.** rot(häutig); **5.** *oft ♐ pol.* rot: a) kommu'nistisch, sozia'listisch, b) sow'jetisch: **the ♐ Army** die Rote Armee; **II** *s.* **6.** Rot *n*; **7.** *a.* **~skin** Rothaut *f* (*Indianer*); **8.** *oft ♐ pol.* Rote(r *m*) *f*; **9.** *bsd.* ✝ **be in the ~** in den roten Zahlen sein; **get out of the ~** aus den roten Zahlen herauskommen.
re·dact [rɪ'dækt] *v/t.* **1.** redigieren, he'rausgeben; **2.** *Erklärung etc.* abfassen; **re'dac·tion** [-kʃn] *s.* **1.** Redakti'on *f* (*Tätigkeit*), Her'ausgabe *f*; **2.** (Ab)Fassung *f*; **3.** Neubearbeitung *f*.
‚**red|-'blood·ed** *adj. fig.* lebensprühend, vi'tal, feurig; '**~·breast** *s. orn.* Rotkehlchen *n*; '**~·cap** *s.* ‚Rotkäppchen' *n*: a) *Brit. sl.* Mili'tärpoli‚zist *m*, b) *Am.* (Bahnhofs)Gepäckträger *m*; **~ car·pet** *s.* roter Teppich; **~ treatment** ‚großer Bahnhof'; '**red-cur·rant** *s.* ♥ Rote Jo'hannisbeere.
red·den ['redn] **I** *v/t.* röten, rot färben; **II** *v/i.* rot werden: a) sich röten, b) erröten (**at** über *acc.*, **with** vor *dat.*).
red·dish ['redɪʃ] *adj.* rötlich.
red·dle ['redl] *s.* Rötel *m*.
re·dec·o·rate [‚riː'dekəreɪt] *v/t.* Zimmer *etc.* renovieren, neu streichen *od.* tapezieren.
re·deem [rɪ'diːm] *v/t.* **1.** *Verpflichtung* abzahlen, -lösen, tilgen, amortisieren; **2.** zu'rückkaufen; **3.** ✝ *Staatspapier* auslosen; **4.** *Pfand* einlösen; **5.** *Gefangene etc.* los-, freikaufen; **6.** *Versprechen* erfüllen, einlösen; **7.** *Fehler etc.* wieder gutmachen, *Sünde* abbüßen; **8.** *schlechte Eigenschaft* aufwiegen, wettmachen, versöhnen mit: **~ing feature** a) versöhnender Zug, b) ausgleichendes Moment; **9.** *Ehre, Rechte* 'wiedererlangen, wieder'herstellen; **10.** (*from*) bewahren (vor *dat.*); (er)retten (von); befreien (von); **11.** *eccl.* erlösen (**from** von); **12.** *Zeitverlust* wettmachen; **re·'deem·a·ble** [-məbl] *adj.* ☐ **1.** abzahlbar, -lösbar, tilgbar; kündbar (*Anleihe*); rückzahlbar (*Wertpapier*): **~ loan** Tilgungsdarlehen *n*; **2.** zu'rückkaufbar; **3.** ✝ auslosbar (*Staatspapier*); **4.** einlösbar (*Pfand, Versprechen etc.*); **5.** wieder gutzumachen(d) (*Fehler*), abzubüßen(d) (*Sünde*); **6.** 'wiedererlangbar; **7.** *eccl.* erlösbar; **re'deem·er** [-mə] *s.* **1.** Einlöser(in) *etc.*; **2.** ♐ *eccl.* Erlöser *m*, Heiland *m*.
re·de·liv·er [‚riːdɪ'lɪvə] *v/t.* **1.** *j-n* wieder befreien; **2.** *et.* zu'rückgeben; rückliefern.
re·demp·tion [rɪ'dempʃn] *s.* **1.** Abzahlung *f*, Ablösung *f*, Tilgung *f*, Amorti‚sati'on *f* e-r *Schuld etc.*: **~ fund** *Am.* ✝ Tilgungsfonds *m*; **~ loan** ✝ Ablösungsanleihe *f*; **2.** Rückkauf *m*; **3.** Auslosung *f* von *Staatspapieren*; **4.** Einlösung *f* e-s *Pfandes* (*fig.* e-s *Versprechens*); **5.** Los-, Freikauf *m* e-r *Geisel etc.*; **6.** Wieder'gutmachung *f* e-s *Fehlers*; Abbüßung *f* e-r *Sünde*; **7.** Ausgleich *m* (**of** für),

Wettmachen *n* e-s *Nachteils*; **8.** 'Wiedererlangung *f*, Wieder'herstellung *f* e-s *Rechts etc.*; **9.** *bsd. eccl.* Erlösung *f* (**from** von): **past od. beyond ~** hoffnungs- *od.* rettungslos (verloren); **re·'demp·tive** [-ptɪv] *adj. eccl.* erlösend, Erlösungs...
re·de·ploy [‚riːdɪ'plɔɪ] *v/t.* **1.** *bsd.* ✖ 'umgrup‚pieren; **2.** ✖, *a.* ✝ verlegen; ‚**re·de'ploy·ment** [-mənt] *s.* **1.** 'Umgrup‚pierung *f*; (Truppen)Verschiebung *f*; **2.** Verlegung *f*.
re·de·vel·op [‚riːdɪ'veləp] *v/t.* **1.** neu entwickeln; **2.** *phot.* nachentwickeln; **3.** *Stadtteil etc.* sanieren; ‚**re·de'vel·op·ment** [-mənt] *s.* **1.** Neuentwicklung *f etc.*; **2.** (Stadt- *etc.*)Sanierung *f*: **~ area** Sanierungsgebiet *n*.
‚**red-'hand·ed** *adj.*: **catch s.o. ~** j-n auf frischer Tat ertappen.
red·hi·bi·tion [‚redhɪ'bɪʃn] *s.* ⚄ Wandlung *f beim Kauf*; **red·hib·i·to·ry** [red'hɪbɪtərɪ] *adj.* Wandlungs...(*-klage etc.*): **~ defect** Fehler *m* der Sache beim Kauf.
‚**red-'hot** *adj.* **1.** rot glühend; **2.** glühend heiß; **3.** *fig.* wild, toll; **4.** hitzig, jähzornig; **5.** allerneuest, 'brandaktu‚ell: **~ news.**
red·in·te·grate [re'dɪntɪgreɪt] *v/t.* **1.** wieder'herstellen; **2.** erneuern.
re·di·rect [‚riːdɪ'rekt] *v/t.* **1.** *Brief etc.* 'umadres‚sieren; **2.** *Verkehr* 'umleiten; **3.** *fig.* e-e neue Richtung geben (*dat.*), ändern.
re·dis·count [‚riː'dɪskaʊnt] ✝ **I** *v/t.* **1.** rediskontieren; **II** *s.* **2.** Rediskon'tierung *f*; **3.** Redis'kont *m*: **~ rate** *Am.* Rediskontsatz *m*; **4.** rediskon'tierter Wechsel.
re·dis·cov·er [‚riːdɪ'skʌvə] *v/t.* 'wieder entdecken.
re·dis·trib·ute [‚riːdɪ'strɪbjuːt] *v/t.* **1.** neu verteilen; **2.** wieder verteilen.
‚**red|-'let·ter day** *s. fig.* Freuden-, Glückstag *m*; ‚**~·'light dis·trict** *s.* Rotlichtbezirk *m*.
red·ness ['rednɪs] *s.* Röte *f*.
re·do [‚riː'duː] *v/t.* [*irr.* → **do¹**] **1.** nochmals tun *od.* machen; **2.** *Haar etc.* nochmals richten *etc.*; **3.** *Computer:* *Datei* wieder'herstellen.
red·o·lence ['redəʊləns] *s.* Duft *m*, Wohlgeruch *m*; '**red·o·lent** [-nt] *adj.* duftend (**of, with** nach): **be ~ of** *fig. et.* atmen, stark gemahnen an (*acc.*), um'wittert sein von.
re·dou·ble [‚riː'dʌbl] **I** *v/t.* **1.** verdoppeln; **2.** *Bridge:* *j-m* Re'kontra geben; **II** *v/i.* **3.** sich verdoppeln; **4.** *Bridge:* Re'kontra geben.
re·doubt [rɪ'daʊt] *s.* ✖ Re'doute *f*; Schanze *f*; **re'doubt·a·ble** [-təbl] *adj. rhet. od. iro.* **1.** furchtbar, schrecklich; **2.** gewaltig.
re·dound [rɪ'daʊnd] *v/i.* **1.** ausschlagen *od.* gereichen (**to** zu *j-s Ehre, Vorteil etc.*); **2.** zu'teil werden, erwachsen (**to** *dat.*, **from** aus); **3.** zu'rückfallen, -wirken (**upon** auf *acc.*).
re·draft [‚riː'drɑːft] **I** *s.* **1.** neuer Entwurf; **2.** ✝ Rück-, Ri'kambiowechsel *m*; **II** *v/t.* **3.** → **redraw** I.
re·draw [‚riː'drɔː] [*irr.* → **draw**] **I** *v/t.* neu entwerfen; **II** *v/i.* ✝ zu'rücktras‚sieren (**on** auf *acc.*).
re·dress [rɪ'dres] **I** *s.* **1.** Abhilfe *f* (*a.* ⚄): **legal ~** Rechtshilfe *f*: **obtain ~ from s.o.** gegen j-n Regress nehmen; **2.** Behebung *f*, Beseitigung *f* e-s *Übelstandes*; **3.** Wieder'gutmachung *f* e-s *Unrechts, Fehlers etc.*; **4.** Entschädigung *f* (**for** für); **II** *v/t.* **5.** *Missstand* beheben,

beseitigen, (*dat.*) abhelfen; *Unrecht* wieder gutmachen; *Gleichgewicht etc.* wieder 'herstellen; **6.** ✈ *Flugzeug* in die nor'male Fluglage zu'rückbringen.
‚**red|-'short** *adj. metall.* rotbrüchig; '**~·start** *s. orn.* Rotschwänzchen *n*; ‚**~·'tape** *adj.* büro'kratisch; ‚**~·'tap·ism** [-'teɪpɪzəm] *s.* Bürokra'tismus *m*; ‚**~·'tap·ist** [-'teɪpɪst] *s.* Büro'krat(in), Aktenmensch *m*.
re·duce [rɪ'djuːs] **I** *v/t.* **1.** her'absetzen, vermindern, -ringern, -kleinern, reduzieren, *fig. a.* abbauen: **~d scale** verjüngter Maßstab; **on a ~d scale** in verkleinertem Maßstab; **2.** *Preise* her'absetzen, ermäßigen: **at ~d prices** zu herabgesetzten Preisen; **at a ~d fare** zu ermäßigtem Fahrpreis; **3.** *im Rang, Wert etc.* her'absetzen, -mindern, -drücken, erniedrigen; *a.* **~ to the ranks** ✖ degradieren; **4.** schwächen, erschöpfen; (*finanziell*) erschüttern: **in ~d circumstances** in beschränkten Verhältnissen, verarmt; **5.** (**to**) verwandeln (in *acc.*, zu), machen (zu): **~ to pulp** zu Brei machen; **~d to a skeleton** zum Skelett abgemagert; **6.** bringen (**to** zu): **~ to a system** in ein System bringen; **~ to rules** in Regeln fassen; **~ to writing** schriftlich niederlegen, aufzeichnen; **~ theories into practice** Theorien in die Praxis umsetzen; **7.** zu'rückführen, reduzieren (**to** auf *acc.*): **~ to absurdity** ad absurdum führen; **8.** zerlegen (**to in** *acc.*); **9.** einteilen (**to in** *acc.*); **10.** anpassen (**to** *dat. od.* an *acc.*); **11.** A, ⚗, *biol.* reduzieren; *Gleichung* auflösen; **~ to a common denominator** auf e-n gemeinsamen Nenner bringen; **12.** *metall.* (aus)schmelzen (**from** aus); **13.** zwingen, *zur Verzweiflung etc.* bringen: **~ to obedience** zum Gehorsam zwingen; **he was ~d to sell** (*-ing*) **his house** er war gezwungen, sein Haus zu verkaufen; **~d to tears** zu Tränen gerührt; **14.** unter'werfen, erobern; *Festung* zur 'Übergabe zwingen; **15.** beschränken (**to** auf *acc.*); **16.** *Farben etc.* verdünnen; **17.** *phot.* abschwächen; **18.** ✈ einrenken, (wieder) einrichten; **II** *v/i.* **19.** (an Gewicht) abnehmen; e-e Abmagerungskur machen; **re‚duced-e'mis·sion** *adj. attr. mot. etc.* 'abgasredu‚ziert; **re'duc·er** [-sə] *s.* **1.** ✈ Redukti'onsmittel *n*; **2.** *phot.* a) Abschwächer *m*, b) Entwickler *m*; **3.** ⊙ a) Redu'zierstück *n od.* -ma‚schine *f*, b) → **reducing gear**; **re'duc·i·ble** [-səbl] *adj.* **1.** reduzierbar (*a.* ✈), zu'rückführbar (**to** auf *acc.*): **be ~ to** sich reduzieren *od.* zurückführen lassen auf (*acc.*); **2.** verwandelbar (**to, into** in *acc.*); **3.** her'absetzbar.
re·duc·ing| a·gent [rɪ'djuːsɪŋ] *s.* ✈ Redukti'onsmittel *n*; **~ di·et** *s.* Abmagerungskur *f*; **~ gear** *s.* ⊙ Unter'setzungsgetriebe *n*.
re·duc·tion [rɪ'dʌkʃn] *s.* **1.** Her'absetzung *f*, Verminderung *f*, -ringerung *f*, -kleinerung *f*, Reduzierung *f*, *fig. a.* Abbau *m*: **~ in** (*od.* **of**) **prices** Preisherabsetzung, -ermäßigung *f*; **~ in** (*od.* **of**) **wages** Lohnkürzung *f*; **~ of interest** Zinsherabsetzung; **~ of staff** Personalabbau; **2.** (Preis)Nachlass *m*, Abzug *m*, Ra'batt *m*; **3.** Verminderung *f*, Rückgang *m*: **import ~** ✝ Einfuhrrückgang; **4.** Verwandlung *f* (**into, to** in *acc.*): **~ into gas** Vergasung *f*; **5.** Zu'rückführung *f*, Reduzierung *f* (**to** auf *acc.*); **6.** Zerlegung *f* (**to in** *acc.*); **7.** A Redukti'on *f*; **8.** A Redukti'on *f*, Kürzung *f*, Vereinfachung *f*; Auflösung *f*

von Gleichungen; **9.** *metall.* (Aus-) Schmelzung *f*; **10.** Unter'werfung *f* (**to** unter *acc.*); Bezwingung *f*, ✕ Niederkämpfung *f*; **11.** *phot.* Abschwächung *f*; **12.** *biol.* Redukti'on *f*; **13.** ✻ Einrenkung *f*; **14.** Verkleinerung *f* (*e-s Bildes etc.*); ~ **com·pass·es** *s. pl.* Redukti'onszirkel *m*; ~ **di·vi·sion** *s. biol.* Redukti'onsteilung *f*; ~ **gear** *s.* ☉ Redukti'ons-, Unter'setzungsgetriebe *n*; ~ **ratio** *s.* ☉ Unter'setzungsverhältnis *n*.

re·dun·dance [rɪ'dʌndəns], **re'dun·dan·cy** [-sɪ] *s.* **1.** 'Überfluss *m*, -fülle *f*; **2.** 'Überflüssigkeit *f*, ✝ *a.* Arbeitslosigkeit *f*: *redundancies pl.* Freistellungen *pl.*, Entlassungen *pl.*; ~ **letter** *od.* **notice** Entlassungsschreiben *n*; ~ **pay** Abfindung *f*, Abstandszahlung *f*; **3.** Wortfülle *f*; **4.** *ling.*, *Informatik*: Redun'danz *f*; **re'dun·dant** [-nt] *adj.* ☐ **1.** 'überreichlich, -mäßig; **2.** 'überschüssig, -zählig: ~ **workers** freigesetzte (*entlassene*) Arbeitskräfte; **make s.o.** ~ j-n freisetzen, -stellen; **3.** 'überflüssig; **4.** üppig; **5.** 'überfließend (**of**, **with** von); **6.** über'laden (*Stil etc.*), *bsd.* weitschweifig; **7.** *ling.*, *Informatik*: redun-'dant.

re·du·pli·cate [rɪ'dju:plɪkeɪt] *v/t.* **1.** verdoppeln; **2.** wieder'holen; **3.** *ling.* reduplizieren.

re·dye [ˌri:'daɪ] *v/t.* **1.** nachfärben; **2.** 'umfärben.

re·ech·o [ri:'ekəʊ] **I** *v/i.* widerhallen (**with** von); **II** *v/t.* widerhallen lassen.

reed [ri:d] *s.* **1.** ♀ Schilf *n*; (Schilf)Rohr *n*; Ried(gras) *n*: **broken** ~ *fig.* schwankes Rohr; **2.** *pl. Brit.* (Dachdecker-) Stroh *n*; **3.** Pfeil *m*; **4.** Rohrflöte *f*; **5.** ♪ a) (Rohr)Blatt *n*: ~ **instruments**, **the** ~s Rohrblattinstrumente, b) *a.* ~ **stop** Zungenstimme *f* (*Orgel*); **6.** ☉ Weberkamm *m*, Blatt *n*.

re·ed·it [ri:'edɪt] *v/t.* neu her'ausgeben; **re-e·di·tion** [ˌri:ɪ'dɪʃn] *s.* Neuausgabe *f*.

re·ed·u·cate [ˌri:'edʊkeɪt] *v/t.* 'umschulen; **re-ed·u·ca·tion** ['ri:ˌedjʊ'keɪʃn] *s.* 'Umschulung *f*.

reed·y ['ri:dɪ] *adj.* **1.** schilfig, schilfreich; **2.** lang u. schlank; **3.** dünn, quäkend (*Stimme*).

reef[1] [ri:f] *s.* **1.** (Felsen)Riff *n*; **2.** *min.* Ader *f*, (Quarz)Gang *m*.

reef[2] [ri:f] ♣ **I** *s.* Reff *n*; **II** *v/t.* Segel reffen.

reef·er ['ri:fə] *s.* **1.** ♣ a) Reffer *m*, b) *sl.* 'Seeka,dett *m*, c) Bord-, Ma'trosenjacke *f*, d) *Am. sl.* Kühlschiff *n*; **2.** *Am. sl.* a) 🚗, *mot.* Kühlwagen *m*, b) Kühlschrank *m*; **3.** *sl.* Marihu'anaziga,rette *f*.

reek [ri:k] **I** *s.* **1.** Gestank *m*, (üble) Ausdünstung, Geruch *m*; **2.** Dampf *m*, Dunst *m*, Qualm *m*; **II** *v/i.* **3.** stinken, riechen (**of**, **with** nach), üble Dünste ausströmen; **4.** dampfen, rauchen (**with** von); **5.** *fig.* (**of**, **with**) stark riechen (nach), voll sein (von); **'reek·y** [-kɪ] *adj.* **1.** dampfend, dunstend; **2.** rauchig.

reel[1] [ri:l] **I** *s.* **1.** Haspel *f*, (*Garn- etc.*) Winde *f*; **2.** (*Garn-, Schlauch- etc.*) Rolle *f*, (*Bandmaß-, Farbband-, Film-etc.*)Spule *f*; ⚡ Kabeltrommel *f*; **3.** a) Film(streifen) *m*, b) (Film)Akt *m*; **II** *v/t.* **4.** a. ~ **up** aufspulen, -wickeln, -rollen: ~ **off** abhaspeln, -spulen, *fig.* ,herunterrasseln': ~ **off a poem**.

reel[2] [ri:l] *v/i.* **1.** sich (schnell) drehen, wirbeln: **my head** ~s mir schwindelt; **2.** wanken, taumeln: ~ **back** zurücktaumeln.

reel[3] [ri:l] *s.* Reel *m* (*schottischer Volks-*

tanz).

re·e·lect [ˌri:ɪ'lekt] *v/t.* wieder wählen; **re-e·lec·tion** [-kʃn] *s.* 'Wiederwahl *f*; **re-el·i·gi·ble** [ˌri:'elɪdʒəbl] *adj.* wieder wählbar.

re·em·bark [ˌri:ɪm'bɑ:k] *v/t.* (*v/i.* sich) wieder einschiffen.

re·e·merge [ˌri:ɪ'mɜːdʒ] *v/i.* wieder auftauchen, wieder auftreten.

re·en·act [ˌri:ɪ'nækt] *v/t.* **1.** wieder in Kraft setzen; **2.** *thea.* neu inszenieren; **3.** *fig.* wieder'holen; **re-en'act·ment** [-mənt] *s.* **1.** ,Wiederin'kraftsetzung *f*; **2.** *thea.* Neuinszenierung *f*.

re·en·gage [ˌri:ɪn'geɪdʒ] *v/t.* j-n wieder an- *od.* einstellen.

re·en·list [ˌri:ɪn'lɪst] ✕ *v/t. u. v/i.* (sich) weiterverpflichten, wieder verpflichten; (*nur v/i.*) kapitulieren: ~**ed man** Kapitulant *m*; **re-en'list·ment** [-mənt] *s.* Wieder'anwerbung *f*.

re·en·ter [ˌri:'entə] *v/t.* **1.** wieder betreten, wieder eintreten in (*acc.*); **2.** wieder eintragen (*in e-e Liste etc.*); **3.** ☉ *Farben* auftragen; **re-en·trant** [ri:'entrənt] **I** *adj.* ⚓ einspringend (*Winkel*); **II** *s.* einspringender Winkel; **re-en·try** [ri:'entrɪ] *s.* Wieder'eintritt *m* (*a. Raumfahrt: in die Erdatmosphäre*; *a.* 📱 *etc.*).

re·es·tab·lish [ˌri:ɪ'stæblɪʃ] *v/t.* **1.** wieder'herstellen; **2.** wieder einführen, neu gründen.

reeve[1] [ri:v] *s. Brit.* a) *hist.* Vogt *m*, b) Gemeindevorsteher *m*.

reeve[2] [ri:v] *v/t.* ⚓ *Tauende* einscheren; *das Tau* ziehen (**around** um).

re·ex·am·i·na·tion ['ri:ɪgˌzæmɪ'neɪʃn] *s.* **1.** Nachprüfung *f*, Wieder'holungsprüfung *f*; **2.** 📱 a) nochmaliges (Zeugen-) Verhör, b) nochmalige Unter'suchung.

re·ex·change [ˌri:ɪks'tʃeɪndʒ] *s.* **1.** Rücktausch *m*; **2.** ✝ Rück-, Gegenwechsel *m*; **3.** ✝ Rückwechselkosten *pl.*

re·ex·port ✝ **I** *v/t.* [ˌri:ek'spɔ:t] **1.** wieder'ausführen; **II** *s.* [ˌri:'ekspɔ:t] **2.** Wieder'ausfuhr *f*; **3.** wieder'ausgeführte Ware.

ref[1] [ref] *s. sport* F a) Schiri *m* (*Schiedsrichter*), b) *Boxen:* Ringrichter *m*.

ref[2] [ref] *abbr. für* **reference** *in Briefen, auf Rechnungen etc.:* betrifft, Betr.

re·fash·ion [ˌri:'fæʃn] *v/t.* 'umgestalten, -modeln.

re·fec·tion [rɪ'fekʃn] *s.* **1.** Erfrischung *f*; **2.** Imbiss *m*; **re'fec·to·ry** [-ktərɪ] *s.* **1.** R.C. Refek'torium *n* (*Speiseraum*); **2.** *univ.* Mensa *f*.

re·fer [rɪ'fɜː] **I** *v/t.* **1.** verweisen, hinweisen (**to** auf *acc.*); **2.** j-n um Auskunft, *Referenzen etc.* verweisen (**to** an j-n); **3.** *zur Entscheidung etc.* über'geben, -'weisen (**to** an *acc.*): ~ **back to** 📱 *Rechtssache* zurückverweisen an *die Unterinstanz*; ~ **to drawer** ✝ an Aussteller zurück; **4.** (**to**) zuschreiben (*dat.*), zu'rückführen (auf *acc.*); **5.** zuordnen, -weisen (**to** *e-r Klasse etc.*); **II** *v/i.* **6.** (**to**) verweisen, hinweisen, sich beziehen, Bezug haben (auf *acc.*), betreffen (*acc.*): ~ **to s.th. briefly** et. kurz berühren; ~**ring to my letter** Bezug nehmend auf mein Schreiben; **the point** ~**red to** der erwähnte *od.* betreffende Punkt; **7.** sich beziehen *od.* berufen, Bezug nehmen (**to** auf j-n); **8.** (**to**) sich wenden (an *acc.*), (*a. Uhr, Wörterbuch etc.*) befragen; (in *e-m Buch*) nachschlagen, -sehen; **ref·er·a·ble** [rɪ-'fɜːrəbl] *adj.* **1.** (**to**) zuzuschreiben(d) (*dat.*), zu'rückführen(d) (auf *acc.*); **2.** (**to**) zu beziehen(d) (auf *acc.*), bezüglich (*gen.*); **ref·er·ee** [ˌrefə'ri:] **I** *s.* **1.**

📱, *sport* Schiedsrichter *m*, 📱 *a.* beauftragter Richter; *Boxen:* Ringrichter *m*; **2.** *parl. etc.* Refe'rent *m*, Berichterstatter *m*; **3.** 📱 *etc.* Sachbearbeiter(in), -verständige(r *m*) *f*; **II** *v/i. u. v/t.* **4.** als Schiedsrichter *etc.* fungieren (bei); **ref·er·ence** ['refrəns] **I** *s.* **1.** Verweis(ung *f*) *m*, Hinweis *m* (**to** auf *acc.*): **cross** ~ Querverweis: (**list of**) ~s Quellenangabe *f*, Literaturverzeichnis *n*; **mark of** ~ → **2** *a u.* **4**; **2.** a) Verweiszeichen *n*, b) Verweisstelle *f*, c) Beleg *m*, 'Unterlage *f*; **3.** Bezugnahme *f* (**to** auf *acc.*); *Patentrecht:* Entgegenhaltung *f* (*od.* **with**) ~ **to** bezüglich (*gen.*); **for future** ~ zu späterer Verwendung; **terms of** ~ Richtlinien (*acc.*); **have** ~ **to** sich beziehen auf (*acc.*); **4.** *a.* ~ **number** Akten-, Geschäftszeichen *n*; **5.** (**to**) Anspielung *f* (auf *acc.*), Erwähnung *f* (*gen.*): **make** ~ **to** auf et. anspielen, et. erwähnen; **6.** (**to**) Zs.-hang *m* (mit), Beziehung *f* (zu): **have no** ~ **to** nichts zu tun haben mit; **with** ~ **to him** was ihn betrifft; **7.** Rücksicht *f* (**to** auf *acc.*): **without** ~ **to** ohne Berücksichtigung (*gen.*); **8.** (**to**) Nachschlagen *n*, -sehen *n* (in *dat.*), Befragen *n* (*gen.*): **book** (*od.* **work**) **of** ~ Nachschlagewerk *n*; ~ **library** Handbibliothek *f*; **9.** (**to**) Befragung *f* (*gen.*), Rückfrage *f* (bei); **10.** 📱 Über'weisung *f e-r Sache* (**to** an *ein Schiedsgericht etc.*); **11.** a) Refe'renz *f*, Empfehlung *f*, *allg.* Zeugnis *n*, b) Refe'renz *f* (*Auskunftgeber*); **II** *adj.* **12.** ☉, ⚓ Bezugs...: ~ **frequency**; ~ **value**; **III** *v/t.* **13.** Verweise anbringen in *e-m Buch*; **ref·er·en·dum** [ˌrefə'rendəm] *pl.* **-dums** *s. pol.* Volksentscheid *m*, -befragung *f*, Refe'rendum *n*.

re·fill [ˌri:'fɪl] **I** *v/t.* wieder füllen, nach-, auffüllen; **II** *v/i.* sich wieder füllen; **III** *s.* ['ri:fɪl] Nach-, Ersatzfüllung *f*; ⚡ Ersatzbatte,rie *f*; Ersatzmine *f* (*Bleistift etc.*); Einlage *f* (*Ringbuch*); ~ **pack** *s.* Nachfüllpack(ung *f*) *m*.

re·fine [rɪ'faɪn] *v/t.* **1.** ☉ veredeln, raffinieren, *bsd.* a) *Eisen* frischen, b) *Metall* feinen, c) *Stahl* gar machen, d) *Glas* läutern, e) *Petroleum, Zucker* raffinieren; **2.** *fig.* bilden, verfeinern, kultivieren; **3.** *fig.* läutern, vergeistigen; **II** *v/i.* **4.** sich läutern; **5.** sich verfeinern *od.* kultivieren; **6.** (her'um)tüfteln ([*up*]on an *dat.*); **7.** ~ (**up**)**on** verbessern, weiterentwickeln; **re'fined** [-nd] *adj.* ☐ **1.** geläutert, raffiniert: ~ **sugar** Feinzucker *m*, Raffinade *f*; ~ **steel** Raffinierstahl *m*; **2.** *fig.* fein, gebildet, kultiviert; **3.** *fig.* raffiniert, sub'til; **4.** ('über)fein, (-)genau; **re'fine·ment** [-mənt] *s.* **1.** ☉ Veredelung *f*, Vergütungs-, Raffinati'onsbehandlung *f*; **2.** Verfeinerung *f*; **3.** Feinheit *f* der Sprache, *e-r Konstruktion etc.*, Raffi'nesse *f* (*des Luxus etc.*); **4.** Vornehm-, Feinheit *f*, Kultiviertheit *f*, gebildetes Wesen; **5.** Klüge'lei *f*, Spitzfindigkeit *f*; **re'fin·er** [-nə] *s.* ☉ a) (Eisen)Frischer *m*, b) Raffi'neur *m*, (Zucker)Sieder *m*, c) *metall.* Vorfrischofen *m*; **2.** Verfeinerer *m*; **3.** Klügler (-in), Haarspalter(in); **re'fin·er·y** [-nərɪ] *s.* ☉ **1.** (*Öl-, Zucker- etc.*)Raffine'rie *f*; **2.** *metall.* (Eisen-, Frisch)Hütte *f*; **re-'fin·ing fur·nace** [-nɪŋ] *s. metall.* Frisch-, Feinofen *m*.

re·fit [ˌri:'fɪt] **I** *v/t.* **1.** wieder in'stand setzen, ausbessern; **2.** neu ausrüsten; **II** *v/i.* **3.** ausgebessert *od.* über'holt werden; **III** *s.* **4.** *a.* **re·fit·ment** [rɪ'fɪtmənt] Wiederin'standsetzung *f*, Ausbesserung *f*.

re·fla·tion [ri:'fleɪʃn] *s.* ✝ Reflati'on *f*.

re·flect [rɪ'flekt] **I** *v/t.* **1.** *Strahlen etc.* reflektieren, zu'rückwerfen, -strahlen: **~ing power** Reflexionsvermögen *n*; **2.** *Bild etc.* (wider)spiegeln: **~ing tele·scope** Spiegelteleskop *n*; **3.** *fig.* (wider)spiegeln, zeigen: **be ~ed in** sich (wider)spiegeln in (*dat.*); **~ credit on s.o.** j-m Ehre machen; **our prices ~ your commission** ✝ unsere Preise enthalten Ihre Provision; **4.** über'legen (**that** dass, **how** wie); **II** *v/i.* **5.** (**[up]on**) nachdenken, -sinnen (über *acc.*), (*et.*) über'legen; **6.** **~ (up)on a)** sich abfällig äußern über (*acc.*), *et.* her'absetzen, b) ein schlechtes Licht werfen auf (*acc.*), j-m nicht gerade zur Ehre gereichen, c) *et.* ungünstig beeinflussen; **re'flec·tion** [-kʃn] *s.* **1.** *phys.* Reflexi'on *f*, Zu'rückstrahlung *f*; **2.** (Wider)Spiegelung *f* (*a. fig.*); Re'flex *m*, Widerschein *m*: **a faint ~ of** ein schwacher Abglanz (*gen.*); **3.** Spiegelbild *n*; **4.** *fig.* Nachwirkung *f*, Einfluss *m*; **5. a)** Über'legung *f*, Erwägung *f*, b) Betrachtung *f*, Gedanke *m* (**on** über *acc.*): **~ on** nach einigem Nachdenken; **6.** abfällige Bemerkung (**on** über *acc.*), Anwurf *m*: **cast ~s upon** herabsetzen, in ein schlechtes Licht setzen; **7.** *anat.* a) Zu'rückbiegung *f*, b) zu'rückgebogener Teil *m*; **8.** *physiol.* Re'flex *m*; **re'flec·tive** [-tɪv] *adj.* □ **1.** reflektierend, zu'rückstrahlend; **2.** nachdenklich; **re'flec·tor** [-tə] *s.* **1.** Re'flektor *m*; **2.** Spiegel *m*; **3.** *mot. etc.* Rückstrahler *m*; Katzenauge *n* (*Fahrrad etc.*); **4.** Scheinwerfer *m*; **re·flex** ['riːfleks] **I** *s.* **1.** *physiol.* Re'flex *m*: **~ action** (*od.* **movement**) Reflexbewegung *f*; **2.** ('Licht)Re,flex *m*, Widerschein *m*; *fig.* Abglanz *m*: **~ camera** (Spiegel)Reflexkamera *f*; **3.** Spiegelbild *n* (*a. fig.*); **II** *adj.* **4.** zu'rückgebogen; **5.** Reflex..., Rück...; **re·flex·i·ble** [rɪ'fleksəbl] *adj.* reflektierbar; **re·flex·ion** [rɪ'flekʃn] *s.* → **reflection**; **re·flex·ive** [rɪ'fleksɪv] **I** *adj.* □ **1.** zu'rückwirkend; **2.** *ling.* refle'xiv, rückbezüglich, Reflexiv...; **II** *s.* **3.** *ling.* a) rückbezügliches Fürwort *od.* Zeitwort, b) reflexive Form.

re·flex·ol·o·gy [ˌriːflek'sɒlədʒɪ] *s.* ♣ **1.** Reflexolo'gie *f*; **2.** Re'flexzonenmas,sage *f*.

re·float [ˌriː'fləʊt] ⚓ **I** *v/t.* wieder flottmachen; **II** *v/i.* wieder flott werden.

re·flux ['riːflʌks] *s.* Zu'rückfließen *n*, Rückfluss *m* (*a.* ✝ *von Kapital*).

re·for·est [ˌriː'fɒrɪst] *v/t.* Land aufforsten.

re·form¹ [rɪ'fɔːm] **I** *s.* **1.** *pol. etc.* Re'form *f*, Verbesserung *f*; **2.** Besserung *f*: **~ school** Besserungsanstalt *f*; **II** *v/t.* **3.** reformieren, verbessern; **4.** *j-n* bessern; **5.** *Missstand etc.* beseitigen; **6.** ⚖ *Am.* Urkunde berichtigen; **III** *v/i.* **7.** sich bessern.

re·form², **re-form** [ˌriː'fɔːm] **I** *v/t.* 'umformen, -gestalten, -bilden, neu gestalten; **II** *v/i.* sich 'umformen, sich neu gestalten.

ref·or·ma·tion¹ [ˌrefə'meɪʃn] *s.* **1.** Reformierung *f*, Verbesserung *f*; **2.** Besserung *f des Lebenswandels etc.*; **3.** ⚖ *eccl.* Reformati'on *f*; **4.** ⚖ *Am.* Berichtigung *f e-r Urkunde*.

re·for·ma·tion², **re-for·ma·tion** [ˌriːfɔː'meɪʃn] *s.* 'Umbildung *f*, 'Um-, Neugestaltung *f*.

re·form·a·to·ry [rɪ'fɔːmətərɪ] **I** *adj.* **1.** Besserungs...: **~ measures** Besserungsmaßnahmen; **2.** Reform...; **II** *s.* **3.** Besserungsanstalt *f*; **re'formed** [-md] *adj.* **1.** verbessert, neu u. besser

gestaltet; **2.** gebessert: **~ drunkard** geheilter Trinker; **3.** ⚖ *eccl.* reformiert; **re'form·er** [-mə] *s.* **1.** *bsd. eccl.* Refor'mator *m*; **2.** *pol.* Re'former(in); **re'form·ist** [-mɪst] *s.* **1.** *eccl.* Reformierte(r *m*) *f*; **2.** → **reformer**.

re·fract [rɪ'frækt] *v/t. phys. Strahlen* brechen; **re'fract·ing** [-tɪŋ] *adj. phys.* lichtbrechend, Brechungs..., Refraktions...: **~ angle** Brechungswinkel *m*; **~ telescope** Refraktor *m*; **re'frac·tion** [-kʃn] *s. phys.* **1.** (*Licht-, Strahlen*)Brechung *f*, Refrakti'on *f*; **2.** *opt.* Brechungskraft *f*; **re'frac·tive** [-tɪv] *adj. phys.* Brechungs..., Refraktions...; **re'frac·tor** [-tə] *s. phys.* **1.** Lichtbrechungskörper *m*; **2.** Re'fraktor *m*; **re'frac·to·ri·ness** [-tərɪnɪs] *s.* **1.** Widerspenstigkeit *f*; **2.** Widerstandskraft *f*, *bsd.* a) 🔥 Strengflüssigkeit *f*, b) ⊕ Feuerfestigkeit *f*; 🌿 a) Widerstandsfähigkeit *f gegen Krankheiten*, b) Hartnäckigkeit *f e-r Krankheit*; **re'frac·to·ry** [-tərɪ] **I** *adj.* **1.** widerspenstig, aufsässig; **2.** 🔥 strengflüssig; **3.** ⊕ feuerfest: **~ clay** Schamotte(ton *m*) *f*; **4.** 🌿 a) widerstandsfähig (*Person*), b) hartnäckig (*Krankheit*); **II** *s.* **5.** ⊕ feuerfester Baustoff.

re·frain¹ [rɪ'freɪn] *v/i.* (**from**) Abstand nehmen *od.* absehen (von), sich (*gen.*) enthalten: **~ from doing s.th.** *et.* unterlassen, es unterlassen, et. zu tun.

re·frain² [rɪ'freɪn] *s.* Re'frain *m*.

re·fran·gi·ble [rɪ'frændʒɪbl] *adj. phys.* brechbar.

re·fresh [rɪ'freʃ] **I** *v/t.* **1.** erfrischen, erquicken (*a. fig.*); **2.** *fig. sein Gedächtnis* auffrischen; *Vorrat etc.* erneuern; **II** *v/i.* **3.** sich erfrischen; **4.** frische Vorräte fassen (*Schiff etc.*); **re'fresh·er** [-ʃə] *s.* **1.** Erfrischung *f*; ,Gläs·chen' *n* (*Trunk*); **2.** *fig.* Auffrischung *f*: **~ course** Auffrischungs-, Wiederholungskurs *m*; **paint ~** Neuglanzpolitur *f*; **3.** ⚖ 'Nachschuss (-hono,rar *n*) *m e-s Anwalts*; **re'fresh·ing** [-ʃɪŋ] *adj.* □ erfrischend (*a. fig. wohltuend*); **re'fresh·ment** [-mənt] *s.* Erfrischung *f* (*a. Getränk etc.*): **~ room** (Bahnhofs)Büfett *n*.

re·frig·er·ant [rɪ'frɪdʒərənt] **I** *adj.* **1.** kühlend, Kühl...; **II** *s.* **2.** 🌿 kühlendes Mittel, Kühlmittel *n*; **3.** ⊕ Kühlmittel *n*; **re·frig·er·ate** [rɪ'frɪdʒəreɪt] *v/t.* ⊕ kühlen; **re'frig·er·at·ing** [-reɪtɪŋ] *adj.* ⊕ Kühl...(-raum *etc.*), Kälte...(-maschine etc.); **re·frig·er·a·tion** [rɪˌfrɪdʒə'reɪʃn] *s.* Kühlung *f*; Kälteerzeugung *f*, -technik *f*; **re'frig·er·a·tor** [-reɪtə] *s.* ⊕ Kühlschrank *m*, -raum *m*, -anlage *f*; 'Kältema,schine *f*: **~ van** *Brit.*, **~ car** *Am.* 🚂 Kühlwagen *m*; **~ van** *od.* **lorry** *Brit.*, **~ truck** *Am. mot.* Kühlwagen *m*; **~ vessel** ⚓ Kühlschiff *n*.

re·fu·el [ˌriː'fjʊəl] *v/t. u. v/i. mot.,* ✈ (auf)tanken.

ref·uge ['refjuːdʒ] **I** *s.* **1.** Zuflucht *f* (*a. fig. Ausweg, a. Person, Gott*), Schutz *m* (**from** vor): **seek ~ in** *fig.* s-e Zuflucht suchen in (*dat.*) *od.* nehmen zu; **house of ~** Obdachlosenasyl *n*; **2.** Zuflucht *f*, Zufluchtsort *m*; **3.** *a.* **~ hut** mount. Schutzhütte *f*; **4.** Verkehrsinsel *f*; **II** *v/i.* **5.** Schutz suchen; **ref·u·gee** [ˌrefjʊ'dʒiː] *s.* Flüchtling *m*: **~ camp** Flüchtlingslager *n*.

re·ful·gent [rɪ'fʌldʒənt] *adj.* □ glänzend, strahlend.

re·fund¹ I *v/t.* [riː'fʌnd] **1.** *Geld* zu'rückzahlen, -erstatten, *Verlust, Auslagen* ersetzen, zu'rückzahlen; **2.** *j-m* Rückzahlung leisten, j-m seine Auslagen ersetzen; **II** *s.* ['riːfʌnd] **3.** Rückvergütung *f*.

re·fund² [ˌriː'fʌnd] *v/t.* ✝ *Anleihe etc.* neu fundieren.

re·fund·ment [rɪ'fʌndmənt] *s.* Rückvergütung *f*.

re·fur·bish [ˌriː'fɜːbɪʃ] *v/t.* aufpolieren (*a. fig.*).

re·fur·nish [ˌriː'fɜːnɪʃ] *v/t.* wieder *od.* neu möblieren *od.* ausstatten.

re·fu·sal [rɪ'fjuːzl] *s.* **1.** Ablehnung *f*, Zu'rückweisung *f e-s Angebots etc.*; **2.** Verweigerung *f e-r Bitte, des Gehorsams etc., a. Reitsport*; **3.** abschlägige Antwort: **he will take no ~** er lässt sich nicht abweisen; **4.** Weigerung *f* (**to do s.th.** et. zu tun); **5.** ✝ Vorkaufsrecht *n*, Vorhand *f*: **first ~ of** erstes Anrecht auf (*acc.*); **give s.o. the ~ of s.th.** j-m das Vorkaufsrecht auf e-e Sache einräumen.

re·fuse¹ [rɪ'fjuːz] **I** *v/t.* **1.** *Amt, Antrag, Kandidaten etc.* ablehnen; *Angebot* ausschlagen; *et. od. j-n* zu'rückweisen; *j-n* abweisen; *j-m e-e Bitte* abschlagen; **2.** *Befehl, Forderung, Gehorsam* verweigern; *Bitte* abschlagen; **3.** *Kartenspiel: Farbe* verweigern; **4.** *Hindernis* verweigern, scheuen vor (*dat.*) (*Pferd*); **II** *v/i.* **5.** sich weigern, es ablehnen (**to do** zu tun): **he ~d to believe it** er wollte es einfach nicht glauben; **he ~d to be bullied** er ließ sich nicht tyrannisieren; **it ~d to work** es wollte nicht funktionieren, es ,streikte'; **6.** absagen (*Gast*); **7.** scheuen (*Pferd*).

ref·use² ['refjuːs] **I** *s.* **1.** ⊕ Abfall *m*, Ausschuss *m*; **2.** (Küchen)Abfall *m*, Müll *m*; **II** *adj.* **3.** wertlos; **4.** Abfall..., Müll...: **~ skip** *s. Brit.* 'Müllcon,tainer *m*.

ref·u·ta·ble ['refjʊtəbl] *adj.* □ wider'legbar; **ref·u·ta·tion** [ˌrefjʊ'teɪʃn] *s.* Wider'legung *f*; **re·fute** [rɪ'fjuːt] *v/t.* wider'legen.

re·gain [rɪ'geɪn] *v/t.* 'wiedergewinnen; *a. Bewusstsein etc.* 'wiedererlangen: **~ one's feet** wieder auf die Beine kommen; **~ the shore** den Strand wiedergewinnen (*erreichen*).

re·gal ['riːgl] *adj.* □ königlich (*a. fig. prächtig*); Königs...

re·gale [rɪ'geɪl] **I** *v/t.* **1.** erfreuen, ergötzen; **2.** festlich bewirten: **~ o.s. on** sich laben an (*dat.*); **II** *v/i.* **3.** (**on**) schwelgen (in *dat.*), sich gütlich tun (an *dat.*).

re·ga·li·a [rɪ'geɪljə] *s. pl.* ('Krönungs-, 'Amts)In,signien *pl.*

re·gard [rɪ'gɑːd] **I** *v/t.* **1.** ansehen; betrachten (*a. fig.* mit **with** Abneigung *etc.*); **2.** *fig.* **~ as** betrachten als, halten für: **be ~ed as** gelten als *od.* für; **3.** *fig.* beachten, berücksichtigen; **4.** respektieren; **5.** achten, (hoch) schätzen; **6.** betreffen, angehen: **as ~s** was ... betrifft; **II** *s.* **7.** (*fester od. bedeutsamer*) Blick; **8.** Hinblick *m*, -sicht *f* (**to** auf *acc.*): **in this ~** in dieser Hinsicht; **in ~ to** (*od. of*), **with ~ to** hinsichtlich, be'züglich, was ... betrifft; **have ~ to** a) sich beziehen auf (*acc.*), b) in Betracht ziehen; **9.** (**to, for**) Rücksicht(nahme) *f* (auf *acc.*), Beachtung *f* (*gen.*): **pay no ~ to s.th.** sich um et. nicht kümmern; **without ~ to** (*od. for*) ohne Rücksicht auf (*acc.*); **have no ~ for s.o.'s feelings** auf j-s Gefühle keine Rücksicht nehmen; **10.** (Hoch)Achtung *f* (**for** vor *dat.*); **11.** *pl.* Grüße *pl.*, Empfehlungen *pl.*: **with kind ~s** mit herzlichen Grüßen an (*acc.*); **give him my (best) ~s** grüße ihn (herzlich) von mir; **re'gard·ful** [-fʊl] *adj.* □ **1.** achtsam, aufmerksam (**of** auf *acc.*); **2.** rücksichtsvoll (**of** gegen); **re'gard·ing** [-dɪŋ] *prp.* be'züglich, betreffs, hinsichtlich (*gen.*);

re'gard·less [-lɪs] **I** *adj.* ☐ **1.** ~ ***of*** ungeachtet (*gen.*), ohne Rücksicht auf (*acc.*); **2.** rücksichts-, achtlos; **II** *adv.* **3.** F trotzdem, dennoch; ganz gleich, was passiert *od.* passieren würde; ohne Rücksicht auf Kosten *etc.*

re·gat·ta [rɪ'gætə] *s.* Re'gatta *f.*

re·gen·cy ['riːdʒənsɪ] *s.* **1.** Re'gentschaft *f* (*Amt, Gebiet, Periode*); **2.** ℛ *hist.* Regentschaft(szeit) *f*, *bsd.* a) Ré'gence *f* (*in Frankreich, des Herzogs Philipp von Orléans* [*1715–23*]), b) *in England* (*1811–30*), *von Georg, Prinz von Wales* (*später Georg IV.*).

re·gen·er·ate [rɪ'dʒenəreɪt] **I** *v/t. u. v/i.* **1.** (sich) regenerieren (*a. biol., phys.*, ⚙) (sich) erneuern, (sich) neu *od.* wieder bilden; (sich) wieder erzeugen: ***be ~d*** *eccl.* wieder geboren werden; **2.** *fig.* (sich) bessern *od.* reformieren; **3.** *fig.* (sich) neu beleben; **4.** ⚡ rückkoppeln; **II** *adj.* [-rət] **5.** ge- *od.* verbessert, reformiert; wieder geboren; **re·gen·er·a·tion** [rɪˌdʒenə'reɪʃn] *s.* **1.** Regenerati'on *f* (*a. biol.*), Erneuerung *f*; **2.** *eccl.* 'Wiedergeburt *f*; **3.** Besserung *f*; **4.** ⚡ Rückkopplung *f*; **5.** ⚙ Regenerierung *f*, 'Wiedergewinnung *f*; **re'gen·er·a·tive** [-nərətɪv] *adj.* ☐ **1.** (ver)bessernd; **2.** neu schaffend; **3.** Erneuerungs..., Verjüngungs...; **4.** ⚡ Rückkopplungs...

re·gent ['riːdʒənt] *s.* **1.** Re'gent(in): ***Queen*** ℛ Regentin *f*; ***Prince*** ℛ Prinzregent *m*; **2.** *univ. Am.* Mitglied *n* des 'Aufsichtskomiˌtees; **'re·gent·ship** [-ʃɪp] *s.* Re'gentschaft *f.*

reg·gae ['regeɪ] *s.* ♪ Reggae *m*

reg·i·cide ['redʒɪsaɪd] *s.* **1.** Königsmörder *m*; **2.** Königsmord *m.*

re·gime, *a.* **ré·gime** [reɪ'ʒiːm] *s.* **1.** *pol.* Re'gime *n*, Regierungsform *f*; **2.** (vor-)herrschendes Sy'stem: ***matrimonial ~*** ⚖ eheliches Güterrecht; **3.** → ***regimen*** 1.

reg·i·men ['redʒɪmən] *s.* **1.** ⚕ gesunde Lebensweise, *bsd.* Di'ät *f*; **2.** Regierung *f*, Herrschaft *f*; **3.** *ling.* Rekti'on *f.*

reg·i·ment I *s.* ['redʒɪmənt] **1.** ⚔ Regi'ment *n*; **2.** *fig.* (große) Schar; **II** *v/t.* ['redʒɪment] **3.** *fig.* reglementieren, bevormunden; **4.** organisieren, syste'matisch einteilen.

reg·i·men·tal [ˌredʒɪ'mentl] *adj.* ☐ Regiments...: ***~ officer*** *Brit.* Truppenoffizier *m*; **reg·i·men·tals** [ˌredʒɪ'mentlz] *s. pl.* ⚔ (Regi'ments)Uniˌform *f*; **reg·i·men·ta·tion** [ˌredʒɪmen'teɪʃn] *s.* **1.** Organisierung *f*, Einteilung *f*; **2.** Reglementierung *f*, Diri'gismus *m*, Bevormundung *f.*

Re·gi·na [rɪ'dʒaɪnə] (*Lat.*) *s. Brit.* ⚖ *die* Königin; *weitS. die* Krone, *der* Staat: ***~ versus John Doe.***

re·gion ['riːdʒən] *s.* **1.** Gebiet *n* (*a. meteor.*), (*a.* ⚕ *Körper*)Gegend *f*, (*a. Höhen-, Tiefen*)Regi'on *f*, Landstrich *m*; (Verwaltungs)Bezirk *m*; **2.** *fig.* Gebiet *n*, Bereich *m*, Sphäre *f*; (*a. himmlische etc.*) Regi'on: ***in the ~ of*** von ungefähr ...; **'re·gion·al** [-dʒənl] *adj.* ☐ regio'nal; örtlich, lo'kal (*beide a.* ⚕); Orts...; Bezirks...: ***~ (station)*** *Radio*: Regionalsender *m*; **'re·gion·al·ism** [-dʒənəlɪzəm] *s.* **1.** Regiona'lismus *m*, Lo'kalpatrioˌtismus *m*; **2.** Heimatkunst *f*; **3.** *ling.* nur regio'nal gebrauchter Ausdruck.

reg·is·ter ['redʒɪstə] **I** *s.* **1.** Re'gister *n* (*a. Computer*), (Eintragungs)Buch *n*, (*a.* Inhalts)Verzeichnis *n*; (*Wähler- etc.*)Liste *f*: ***~ of births, marriages, and deaths*** Personenstandsregister; ***~ of companies*** Handelsregister; (***ship's***) ***~*** Schiffsregister; ***~ ton*** ⚓ Registertonne *f*; **2.** ⚙ a) Registriervorrichtung *f*, Zählwerk *n*: ***cash ~*** Registrier-, Kontrollkasse *f*, b) Schieber *m*, Klappe *f*, Ven'til *n*; **3.** ♪ a) ('Orgel)ReˌRegister *n*, b) Stimm-, Tonlage *f*, c) 'Stimmˌumfang *m*; **4.** *typ.* Re'gister *n*; **5.** *phot.* genaue Einstellung; **6.** → ***registrar***; **II** *v/t.* **7.** registrieren, (in ein Register *etc.*) eintragen *od.* -schreiben (lassen), anmelden (***for school*** zur Schule); *weitS.* amtlich erfassen; (*a. fig. Erfolg etc.*) verzeichnen, -buchen: ***~ a company*** e-e Firma handelsgerichtlich eintragen; **8.** ✝ *Warenzeichen* anmelden; *Artikel* gesetzlich schützen; **9.** *Postsachen* einschreiben (lassen); *Gepäck* aufgeben; **10.** ⚙ *Messwerte* registrieren, anzeigen; **11.** *fig. Empfindung* zeigen, ausdrücken, registrieren; **12.** *typ.* in das Re'gister bringen; **13.** ⚔ *Geschütz* einschießen; **III** *v/i.* **14.** sich (in das Ho'telreˌgister, in die Wählerliste *etc.*) eintragen (lassen); *univ. etc.* sich einschreiben (***for*** für); **15.** sich (an)melden (***at, with*** bei *der Polizei etc.*); **16.** *typ.* Re'gister halten; **17.** ⚙ a) sich decken, genau passen, b) einrasten; **18.** ♪ registrieren; **19.** ⚔ sich einschießen; **'reg·is·tered** [-əd] *adj.* **1.** eingetragen (✝ *Geschäftssitz, Gesellschaft, Warenzeichen*); **2.** ✝ gesetzlich geschützt: ***~ design*** (*od.* ***pattern***) Gebrauchsmuster *n*; **3.** ✝ registriert, Namens...: ***~ bonds*** Namensschuldverschreibungen; ***~ capital*** autorisiertes (Aktien)Kapital; ***~ share*** (*Am.* ***stock***) Namensaktie *f*; **4.** ✉ eingeschrieben, Einschreibe...(*-brief etc.*): ***~!*** Einschreiben!; **reg·is·trar** [ˌredʒɪ'strɑː] *s.* Regi'strator *m*, Archi'var(in), Urkundsbeamte(r) *m*; *Brit.* Standesbeamte(r) *m*; ⚕ *Brit.* Krankenhausarzt *m*, -ärztin *f*: ***~'s office*** a) Standesamt *n*, b) Registratur *f*; ℛ ***General*** *Brit.* oberster Standesbeamter; ***~ in bankruptcy*** ⚖ *Brit.* Konkursrichter *m*; **reg·is·tra·tion** [ˌredʒɪ'streɪʃn] *s.* **1.** (*bsd.* amtliche) Registrierung, Erfassung *f*; Eintragung *f* (*a.* ✝ *e-r Gesellschaft, e-s Warenzeichens*); *mot.* Zulassung *f e-s Fahrzeugs*; **2.** (*polizeiliche, a. Hotel-, Schul- etc.*) Anmeldung, Einschreibung *f*: ***compulsory ~*** (An)Meldepflicht *f*; ***~ fee*** Anmelde-, Einschreibgebühr *f*; ✝ Umschreibungsgebühr *f* (*Aktien*); ***~ form*** (An)Meldeformular *n*; ***~ office*** Meldestelle *f*, Einwohnermeldeamt *n*; **3.** Zahl *f* der Erfassten, registrierte Zahl; **4.** ✉ Einschreibung *f*; **5.** *a.* ***~ of luggage*** *bsd. Brit.* Gepäckaufgabe *f*: ***~ window*** Gepäckschalter *m*; **'reg·is·try** [-trɪ] *s.* **1.** Registrierung *f* (*a. e-s Schiffs*): ***~ fee*** *Am.* Anmelde-, Einschreibegebühr *f*; ***port of ~*** ⚓ Registerhafen *m*; **2.** Re'gister *n*; **3.** *a.* ***~ office*** a) Registra'tur *f*, b) Standesamt *n*, c) 'Stellenverˌmittlungsbüˌro *n.*

reg·let ['reglɪt] *s.* **1.** ⚠ Leistchen *n*; **2.** *typ.* a) Re'glette *f*, b) ('Zeilen)ˌDurchschuss *m.*

reg·nant ['regnənt] *adj.* regierend; *fig.* (vor)herrschend.

re·gress I *v/i.* [rɪ'gres] **1.** sich rückwärts bewegen; **2.** *fig.* a) sich rückläufig entwickeln, b) *biol., psych.* sich zu'rückbilden *od.* -entwickeln; **II** *s.* ['riːgres] **3.** Rückwärtsbewegung *f*; **4.** rückläufige Entwicklung; **re'gres·sion** [-eʃn] *s.* **1.** → ***regress*** II; **2.** Regressi'on *f*: a) *biol. psych.* Rückentwicklung *f*, b) ⚠ Beziehung *f*; **re'gres·sive** [-sɪv] *adj.* ☐ **1.** rückläufig; **2.** rückwirkend (*Steuer etc.*, *a. ling. Akzent*); **3.** *biol.* regres'siv.

re·gret [rɪ'gret] **I** *s.* **1.** Bedauern *n* (***at*** über *acc.*): ***to my ~*** zu m-m Bedauern, leider; **2.** Reue *f*; **3.** Schmerz *m*, Trauer *f* (***for*** um); **II** *v/t.* **4.** bedauern, bereuen: ***it is to be ~ted*** es ist bedauerlich; ***I ~ to say*** ich muss leider sagen; **5.** *Vergangenes etc., a. Tote* beklagen, trauern um, *j-m od. e-r Sache* nachtrauern; **re'gret·ful** [-fʊl] *adj.* ☐ bedauernd, reue-, kummervoll; **re'gret·ta·ble** [-təbl] *adj.* ☐ **1.** bedauerlich; **2.** bedauernswert, zu bedauern(d); **re'gret·ta·bly** [-təblɪ] *adv.* bedauerlicherweise.

re·grind [ˌriː'graɪnd] *v/t.* [*irr.* → ***grind***] ⚙ nachschleifen.

re·group [ˌriː'gruːp] *v/t.* 'umgruppieren, neu gruppieren, (*a.* ✝ *Kapital*) 'umschichten; **re'group·ment** [-mənt] *s.* 'Umgrupˌpierung *f.*

reg·u·lar ['regjʊlə] **I** *adj.* ☐ **1.** *zeitlich* regelmäßig; 🚂 *etc.* fahrplanmäßig: ***~ air service*** regelmäßige Flugverbindung; ***~ business*** ✝ laufende Geschäfte; ***~ customer*** → 14; ***at ~ intervals*** in regelmäßigen Abständen; **2.** regelmäßig (*in Form od. Anordnung*), ebenmäßig; sym'metrisch; **3.** regelmäßig, geregelt, geordnet (*Lebensweise etc.*); **4.** pünktlich, genau; **5.** regu'lär, nor'mal, gewohnt; **6.** richtig, geprüft, gelernt: ***a ~ cook***; ***~ doctor*** approbierter Arzt; **7.** richtig, vorschriftsmäßig, formgerecht; **8.** F ˌrichtig(gehend)': ***~ rascal***; ***a ~ guy*** *Am.* ein Pfundskerl; **9.** ⚔ a) regu'lär (*Kampftruppe*), b) Berufs..., ak'tiv (*Heer, Soldat*); **10.** *sport*: Stamm...: ***~ player***; ***make the ~ team*** sich e-n Stammplatz (*in der Mannschaft*) erobern; *eccl.* Ordens...; **II** *s.* **11.** Ordensgeistliche(r) *m*; **12.** ⚔ ak'tiver Sol'dat, Be'rufssolˌdat *m*; *pl.* regu'läre Truppen *pl.*; **13.** *pol. Am.* treuer Par'teianhänger; **14.** F Stammkunde *m*, -kundin *f*, -gast *m*; **reg·u·lar·i·ty** [ˌregjʊ'lærətɪ] *s.* **1.** Regelmäßigkeit *f*: a) Gleichmäßigkeit *f*, Stetigkeit *f*, b) regelmäßige Form; **2.** Ordnung *f*, Richtigkeit *f*; **'reg·u·lar·ize** [-əraɪz] *v/t.* regeln, festlegen.

reg·u·late ['regjʊleɪt] *v/t.* **1.** *Geschäft, Verdauung, Verkehr etc.* regeln; ordnen; (*a.* ✝ *Wirtschaft*) lenken; **2.** ⚖ (gesetzlich) regeln; **3.** ⚙ a) *Geschwindigkeit etc.* regulieren, regeln, b) *Gerät, Uhr* (ein)stellen; **4.** anpassen (***according to*** an *acc.*); **'reg·u·lat·ing** [-tɪŋ] *adj.* ⚙ Regulier..., (Ein)Stell...: ***~ screw*** Stellschraube *f*; ***~ switch*** Regelschalter *m*; **reg·u·la·tion** [ˌregjʊ'leɪʃn] **I** *s.* **1.** Regelung *f*, Regulierung *f* (*a.* ⚙); ⚙ Einstellung *f*; **2.** Verfügung *f*, (Ausführungs)Verordnung *f*; *pl.* a) 'Durchführungsbestimmungen *pl.*, b) Satzung(en *pl.*) *f*, Sta'tuten *pl.*, c) (Dienst-, Betriebs)Vorschrift *f*: ***~s of the works*** Betriebsordnung *f*; ***traffic ~s*** Verkehrsvorschriften; ***according to ~s*** nach Vorschrift, vorschriftsmäßig; ***contrary to ~s*** vorschriftswidrig; **II** *adj.* **3.** vorschriftsmäßig; ⚔ *a.* Dienst...(*-mütze etc.*); **'reg·u·la·tive** [-lətɪv] *adj.* regelnd, regulierend, *a. phls.* regula'tiv; **'reg·u·la·tor** [-tə] *s.* **1.** ⚡ Regler *m*; **2.** *Uhrmacherei*: Regu'lator *m* (*a. Uhr*); **3.** ⚙ Regulier-, Stellvorrichtung *f*: ***~ valve*** Reglerventil *n*; **4.** ⚗ Regu'lator *m*; **'reg·u·la·to·ry** [-leɪtərɪ] *adj.* Durch-, Ausführungs...

re·gur·gi·tate [rɪ'gɜːdʒɪteɪt] **I** *v/i.* zu'rückfließen; **II** *v/t.* wieder ausströmen *od.* -speien; *Essen* erbrechen.

re·ha·bil·i·tate [ˌriːə'bɪlɪteɪt] *v/t.* **1.** rehabilitieren: a) wieder einsetzen (*in* in *acc.*), b) *j-s* Ruf wiederherstellen, c) *e-n Versehrten* wieder ins Berufsleben eingliedern; **2.** *et. od. j-n* wieder'herstellen; **4.** ✝ *Strafentlassenen* resozialisieren; **4.** *Altbauten*, ✝ *e-n Betrieb etc.* sanieren; **re·ha·bil·i·ta·tion** ['riːə,bɪlɪ'teɪʃn] *s.* **1.** Rehabilitierung *f*: a) Wieder'einsetzung *f* (*in frühere Rechte*), b) Ehrenrettung *f*, c) *a.* **vocational ~** Wieder'eingliederung *f* ins Berufsleben: **~ centre** (*Am.* **center**) Rehabilitationszentrum *n*; **2.** Wieder'herstellung *f*; ✝ Sanierung *f*: **industrial ~** wirtschaftlicher Wiederaufbau; **3.** *a.* **social ~** ✝ Resozialisierung *f*.

re·hash ['riːhæʃ] **I** *s.* **1.** *fig. et.* Aufgewärmtes, Wieder'holung *f*, ,Aufguss' *m*; **2.** Wieder'aufwärmen *n*; **II** *v/t.* [,riː'hæʃ] **3.** *fig.* wieder aufwärmen, 'wiederkäuen.

re·hear·ing [,riː'hɪərɪŋ] *s.* ✝ erneute Verhandlung.

re·hears·al [rɪ'hɜːsl] *s.* **1.** *thea.*, ♪ *u. fig.* Probe *f*: **be in ~** einstudiert werden; **final ~** Generalprobe *f*. Einstudierung *f*; **3.** Wieder'holung *f*. **4.** Aufsagen *n*, Vortrag *m*; **5.** *fig.* Lita'nei *f*; **re·hearse** [rɪ'hɜːs] *v/t.* **1.** *thea.*, ♪ *et.* proben (*a. v/i. u. fig.*), *Rolle etc.* einstudieren; **2.** wieder'holen; **3.** aufzählen; **4.** aufsagen, rezitieren; **5.** *fig. Möglichkeiten etc.* 'durchspielen.

reign [reɪn] **I** *s.* **1.** Regierung *f*, Regierungszeit *f*: **in** (*od.* **under**) **the ~ of** unter der Regierung (*gen.*); **2.** Herrschaft *f* (*a. fig. der Mode etc.*): **~ of law** Rechtsstaatlichkeit *f*; **≈ of Terror** Schreckensherrschaft; **II** *v/i.* **3.** regieren, herrschen (**over** über *acc.*); **4.** *fig.* (vor)herrschen: **silence ~ed** es herrschte Stille.

re·im·burs·a·ble [,riːɪm'bɜːsəbl] *adj.* rückzahlbar; **re·im·burse** [,riːɪm'bɜːs] *v/t. j-n* entschädigen (**for** für): **~ o.s.** sich entschädigen *od.* schadlos halten; **2.** *et.* zu'rückzahlen, vergüten, *Auslagen* erstatten, *Kosten* decken; **re·im·burse·ment** [-mənt] *s.* **1.** Entschädigung *f*; **2.** ('Wieder)Erstattung *f*, (Rück)Vergütung *f*, (Kosten)Deckung *f*: **~ credit** ✝ Rembourskredit *m*.

re·im·port ✝ **I** *v/t.* [,riːɪm'pɔːt] **1.** wieder'einführen; **II** *s.* [,riː'ɪmpɔːt] **2.** 'Wiedereinfuhr *f*; **3.** *pl.* wieder'eingeführte Waren *pl.*

rein [reɪn] **I** *s.* **1.** *oft pl.* Zügel *m mst pl.* (*a. fig.*): **draw ~** (an)halten, zügeln (*a. fig.*); **give a horse the ~(s)** die Zügel locker lassen; **give free ~(s) to** *s-r* Fantasie freien Lauf lassen *od.* die Zügel schießen lassen; **keep a tight ~ on** *j-n* fest an der Kandare haben; **take** (*od.* **assume**) **the ~s of government** die Zügel (der Regierung) in die Hand nehmen; **II** *v/t.* **2.** *Pferd* aufzäumen; **3.** lenken: **~ back** (*od.* **in, up**) (*a. v/i.*) a) anhalten, b) verhalten; **4.** *a.* **~ in** *fig.* zügeln, im Zaum halten.

re·in·car·na·tion [,riːɪnkɑː'neɪʃn] *s.* Reinkarnati'on *f*: a) (Glaube *m* an die) Seelenwanderung *f*, b) 'Wiederverkörperung *f*, -geburt *f*.

rein·deer ['reɪn,dɪə] *pl.* **-deer** *od.* **-deers** *s. zo.* Ren(tier) *n*.

re·in·force [,riːɪn'fɔːs] **I** *v/t.* **1.** verstärken (*a.* ⊕, *Gewebe etc.*, *a.* ✕ *u. fig.*), ⊕ *Beton* armieren: **~d concrete** Eisen-, Stahlbeton *m*; **2.** *fig. Gesundheit* kräftigen, *Worte* bekräftigen, *Beweis* unter'mauern; **II** *s.* **3.** ⊕ Verstärkung *f*; **,re·in'force·ment** [-mənt] *s.* **1.** Verstärkung *f*; Armierung *f* (*Beton*); *pl.* ✕

Verstärkungstruppen *pl.*; **2.** *fig.* Unter'mauerung *f*, Bekräftigung *f*.

re·in·stall [,riːɪn'stɔːl] *v/t.* wieder einsetzen; **,re·in'stal(l)·ment** [-mənt] *s.* Wieder'einsetzung *f*.

re·in·state [,riːɪn'steɪt] *v/t.* **1.** *j-n* wieder einsetzen (**in** in *acc.*); **2.** *et.* (wieder) in'stand setzen; **3.** *j-n od. et.* wieder'herstellen; *Versicherung etc.* wieder aufleben lassen; **,re·in'state·ment** [-mənt] *s.* **1.** Wieder'einsetzung *f*; **2.** Wieder'herstellung *f*.

re·in·sur·ance [,riːɪn'ʃʊərəns] *s.* ✝ Rückversicherung *f*; **re·in·sure** [,riːɪn-'ʃʊə] *v/t.* **1.** rückversichern; **2.** nachversichern.

re·in·vest·ment [,riːɪn'vesmənt] *s.* ✝ Neu-, 'Wiederanlage *f*.

re·is·sue [,riː'ɪʃuː] **I** *v/t.* **1.** *Banknoten etc.* wieder ausgeben; **2.** *Buch* neu he'rausgeben; **II** *s.* **3.** 'Wieder-, Neuausgabe *f*: **~ patent** Abänderungspatent *n*.

re·it·er·ate [riː'ɪtəreɪt] *v/t.* (ständig) wieder'holen; **re·it·er·a·tion** [riː,ɪtə'reɪʃn] *s.* Wieder'holung *f*.

re·ject I *v/t.* [rɪ'dʒekt] **1.** *Antrag, Kandidaten, Lieferung, Verantwortung etc.* ablehnen; *Ersuchen, Freier etc.* ab-, zu'rückweisen; *Bitte* abschlagen; *et.* verwerfen; *Nahrung* verweigern: **be ~ed** *pol. u. thea.* durchfallen; **2.** (als wertlos) ausscheiden; **3.** *Essen* wieder von sich geben (*Magen*); **4.** 🇸 *körperfremdes Gewebe etc.* abstoßen; **II** *s.* ['riːdʒekt] **5.** ✕ Ausgemusterte(r) *m*, Untaugliche(r) *m*; **6.** ✝ 'Ausschussar,tikel *m*; **re·jec·ta·men·ta** [rɪ,dʒektə'mentə] *s. pl.* **1.** Abfälle *pl.*; **2.** Strandgut *n*; **3.** *physiol.* Exkre'mente *pl.*; **re'jec·tion** [-kʃn] *s.* **1.** Ablehnung *f*, Zu'rückweisung *f*, Verwerfung *f*; ✝, ⊕ Abnahmeverweigerung *f*; **2.** Ausscheidung *f* **3.** *pl.* Ausschussartikel *pl.*; **4.** 🇸 Abstoßung *f*; **5.** *pl. physiol.* Exkre'mente *pl.*; **re'jec·tor** [-tə] *s. a.* **~ circuit** ⚡ Sperrkreis *m*.

re·joice [rɪ'dʒɔɪs] **I** *v/i.* **1.** sich freuen, froh'locken (**in, at** über *acc.*); **2.** **~ in** sich *e-r Sache* erfreuen; **II** *v/t.* **3.** erfreuen: **~d at** (*od.* **by**) erfreut über (*acc.*); **re'joic·ing** [-sɪŋ] **I** *s.* **1.** Freude *f*, Froh-'locken *n*; **2.** *oft pl.* (Freuden)Fest *n*, Lustbarkeit (*pl.*) *f*; **II** *adj.* □ **3.** erfreut, froh (**in, at** über *acc.*).

re·join [,riː'dʒɔɪn] *v/t. u. v/i.* (sich) wieder vereinigen (**to, with** mit), (sich) wieder zs.-fügen.

re·join[1] [,riː'dʒɔɪn] *v/t.* sich wieder anschließen (*dat.*) *od.* an (*acc.*), wieder eintreten in *e-e Partei etc.*; wieder zu-'rückkehren zu, *j-n* wieder treffen.

re·join[2] [rɪ'dʒɔɪn] **I** *v/t.* erwidern; **II** *v/i.* ✝ *e-e Gegenerklärung* auf *e-e* Re'plik abgeben; **re'join·der** [-ndə] *s.* Erwiderung *f*; ✝ Gegenerklärung *f* (*des Beklagten auf e-e Replik*).

re·ju·ve·nate [rɪ'dʒuːvɪneɪt] *v/t.* (*v/i.* sich) verjüngen; **re·ju·ve·na·tion** [rɪ-,dʒuːvɪ'neɪʃn] *s.* Verjüngung *f*.

re·ju·ve·nesce [,riːdʒuːvɪ'nes] *v/t. u. v/i.* (sich) verjüngen (*a. biol.*); **,re·ju·ve-'nes·cence** [-sns] *s.* (*biol.* Zell)Verjüngung *f*.

re·kindle [,riː'kɪndl] **I** *v/t.* **1.** wieder anzünden; **2.** *fig.* wieder entfachen, neu beleben; **II** *v/i.* **3.** sich wieder entzünden; **4.** *fig.* wieder entbrennen, wieder aufleben.

re·lapse [rɪ'læps] **I** *v/i.* **1.** zu'rückfallen, wieder (ver)fallen (**into** in *acc.*); **2.** rückfällig werden; 🇸 e-n Rückfall bekommen; **II** *s.* **3.** 🇸 Rückfall *m*.

re·late [rɪ'leɪt] **I** *v/t.* **1.** berichten, erzäh-

len (**to s.o.** j-m); **2.** in Beziehung *od.* Zs.-hang bringen, verbinden (**to, with** mit); **II** *v/i.* **3.** sich beziehen, Bezug haben (**to** auf *acc.*): **relating to** in Bezug auf (*acc.*), bezüglich (*gen.*); **4.** **~ to s.o.** a) sich j-m gegenüber verhalten, b) zu j-m *e-e* (*gute, innere etc.*) Beziehung haben; **re'lat·ed** [-tɪd] *adj.* verwandt (**to, with** mit) (*a. fig.*): **~ by marriage** verschwägert.

re·la·tion [rɪ'leɪʃn] *s.* **1.** Bericht *m*, Erzählung *f*; **2.** Beziehung *f* (*a. pol.*, ✝, ♣), (*a. Vertrags-, Vertrauens- etc.*)Verhältnis *n*; (*kausaler etc.*) Zs.-hang; Bezug *m*: **business ~s** Geschäftsbeziehungen; **human ~s** a) zwischenmenschliche Beziehungen, b) (innerbetriebliche) Kontaktpflege; **in ~ to** in Bezug auf (*acc.*); **be out of all ~ to** in keinem Verhältnis stehen zu; **bear no ~ to** nichts zu tun haben mit; → **public** 3; **3.** a) Verwandte(r *m*) *f*, b) Verwandtschaft *f* (*a. fig.*): **what ~ is he to you?** wie ist er mit dir verwandt?; **re'la·tion·al** [-ʃənl] *adj.* **1.** verwandtschaftlich, Verwandtschafts...; **2.** Beziehungs..., Bezugs...; **3.** *EDV* relatio'nal: **~ database** relationale Datenbank; **re'la·tion·ship** [-ʃɪp] *s.* **1.** Beziehung *f*, (*a. Rechts*)Verhältnis *n* (**to** zu); **2.** Verwandtschaft *f* (**to** mit) (*a. coll. u. fig.*).

rel·a·tive ['relətɪv] **I** *adj.* □ **1.** bezüglich, sich beziehend (**to** auf *acc.*): **~ value** ♣ Bezugswert *m*; **~ to** bezüglich, hinsichtlich (*gen.*); **2.** rela'tiv, verhältnismäßig, Verhältnis...; **3.** (**to**) abhängig (von), bedingt (durch); **4.** gegenseitig, entsprechend, jeweilig; **5.** *ling.* bezüglich, Relativ...; **6.** ♪ paral'lel (*Tonart*); **II** *s.* **7.** Verwandte(r *m*) *f*; **8.** *ling.* a) Rela-'tivpro,nomen *n*, b) Rela'tivsatz *m*; **'rel·a·tive·ness** [-nɪs] *s.* Relativi'tät *f*; **'rel·a·tiv·ism** [-vɪzəm] *s. phls.* Relati'vismus *m*; **rel·a·tiv·i·ty** [,relə'tɪvətɪ] *s.* **1.** Relativi'tät *f*: **theory of ~** *phys.* Relativitätstheorie *f*; **2.** Abhängigkeit *f* (**to** von).

re·lax [rɪ'læks] **I** *v/t.* **1.** *Muskeln etc.*, ⊕ *Feder* entspannen; (*a. fig. Disziplin, Vorschrift etc.*) lockern: **~ing climate** Schonklima *n*; **2.** in *s-n Anstrengungen etc.* nachlassen; **3.** 🇸 abführend wirken; **II** *v/i.* **4.** sich entspannen (*Muskeln etc.*, *a. Geist, Person*); ausspannen, sich erholen (*Person*); es sich bequem machen: **~ing** entspannend, erholsam, Erholungs...; **5.** sich lockern (*Griff, Seil etc.*) (*a. fig.*); **6.** nachlassen (in in *e-r Bemühung etc.*) (*a. Sturm etc.*); **7.** milder *od.* freundlicher werden; **re·lax·a·tion** [,riːlæk'seɪʃn] *s.* **1.** Entspannung *f* (*a. fig. Erholung*); Lockerung *f* (*a. fig.*); Erschlaffung *f*; **2.** Nachlassen *n*; **3.** Milderung *f e-r Strafe etc.*

re·lay ['riːleɪ] **I** *s.* **1.** a) frisches Gespann, b) Pferdewechsel *m*, c) *fig.* ✝, ✕ Ablösung(smannschaft) *f*: **~ attack** ✕ rollender Angriff; **in ~s** ✕ in rollendem Einsatz; **2.** *sport a.* **~ race** Staffel(lauf *m*, -wettbewerb *f*) *f*: **~ team** Staffel *f*; **3.** a) [,riː'leɪ] ⚡ Re'lais *n*: **~ station** Relais-, Zwischensender *m*, **~ switch** Schaltschütz *n*, b) *Radio*: Über'tragung *f*; **II** *v/t.* **4.** *allg.* weitergeben; **5.** [,riː'leɪ] ⚡ mit Re'lais steuern; *Radio*: (mit Re'lais) über'tragen.

re·lease [rɪ'liːs] **I** *s.* **1.** (Haft)Entlassung *f*, Freilassung *f* (**from** aus); **2.** *fig.* Befreiung *f*, Erlösung *f* (**from** von); **3.** Entlastung *f* (*a. e-s Treuhänders etc.*), Entbindung *f* (**from** von *e-r Pflicht*); **4.** Freigabe *f* (*Buch, Film, Vermögen etc.*): **first ~** *Film*: Uraufführung *f*;

(*press*) ~ (Presse)Verlautbarung *f*; ~ *of energy* Freiwerden *n* von Energie; **5.** ⚖ a) Verzicht(leistung *f*, -urkunde *f*) *m*, b) ('Rechts)Über,tragung *f*, c) Quittung *f*; **6.** ⚙, *phot.* a) Auslöser *m*, b) Auslösung *f*: ~ *of bombs* ✗ Bombenabwurf *m*; **II** *v/t.* **7.** Häftling ent-, freilassen; **8.** *fig.* (*from*) a) befreien, erlösen (von), b) entbinden, -lasten (von *e-r Pflicht, Schuld etc.*); **9.** *Buch, Film, Guthaben* freigeben; **10.** ⚖ verzichten auf (*acc.*), *Recht* aufgeben *od.* über'tragen; *Hypothek* löschen; **11.** 🜔, *phys.* freisetzen; **12.** ⚙ a) auslösen (*a. phot.*); *Bomben* abwerfen; *Gas* abblasen, b) ausschalten: ~ *the clutch* auskuppeln.

rel·e·gate ['relɪgeɪt] *v/t.* **1.** relegieren, verbannen (*out of* aus): *be ~d* *sport* absteigen; **2.** verweisen (*to* an *acc.*); **3.** (*to*) verweisen (in *acc.*), zuschreiben (*dat.*): ~ *to the sphere of legend* in das Reich der Fabel verweisen; *he was ~d to fourth place* *sport* er wurde auf den vierten Platz verwiesen; **rel·e·ga·tion** [,relɪ'geɪʃn] *s.* **1.** Verbannung *f* (*out of* aus); **2.** Verweisung *f* (*to* an *acc.*); **3.** *sport* Abstieg *m*: *in danger of* ~ in Abstiegsgefahr.

re·lent [rɪ'lent] *v/i.* weicher *od.* mitleidig werden, sich erweichen lassen; **re·lent·less** [-lɪs] *adj.* □ unbarmherzig, schonungslos, hart.

rel·e·vance ['relɪvəns], **'rel·e·van·cy** [-sɪ] *s.* Rele'vanz *f*, (*a.* Beweis)Erheblichkeit *f*, Bedeutung *f* (*to* für); **'rel·e·vant** [-nt] *adj.* □ **1.** einschlägig, sachdienlich, anwendbar (*to* auf *acc.*); **2.** (beweis-, rechts- *etc.*)erheblich, belangvoll, von Bedeutung (*to* für).

re·li·a·bil·i·ty [rɪ,laɪə'bɪlətɪ] *s.* Zuverlässigkeit *f*, ⚙ *a.* Betriebssicherheit *f*: ~ *test* Zuverlässigkeitsprüfung *f*; **re·li·a·ble** [rɪ'laɪəbl] *adj.* □ **1.** zuverlässig (*a.* ⚙ *betriebssicher*), verlässlich; **2.** glaubwürdig; **3.** vertrauenswürdig, re'ell (*Firma etc.*); **re·li·ance** [rɪ'laɪəns] *s.* Vertrauen *n*: *in* ~ (*up*)*on* unter Verlass auf (*acc.*), bauend auf; *place* ~ *on* (*od.* *in*) Vertrauen in *j-n* setzen; **re·li·ant** [rɪ'laɪənt] *adj.* **1.** vertrauensvoll; **2.** zuversichtlich.

rel·ic ['relɪk] *s.* **1.** ('Über)Rest *m*, 'Überbleibsel *n*, Re'likt *n*: ~*s of the past* *fig.* Zeugen der Vergangenheit; **2.** *R.C.* Re'liquie *f*.

re·lief¹ [rɪ'liːf] *s.* **1.** Erleichterung *f* (*a.* ⚕, → *sigh* 5; **2.** (angenehme) Unter'brechung, Abwechslung *f*, Wohltat *f* (*to* für *das Auge etc.*); **3.** Trost *m*; **4.** Entlastung *f*; (*Steuer- etc.*)Erleichterung *f*; **5.** a) Unter'stützung *f*, Hilfe *f*, b) *Am.* Sozi'alhilfe *f*: ~ *fund* Unterstützungsfonds *m*, -kasse *f*; *be on* ~ Sozialhilfe beziehen; **6.** ⚖ a) Rechtshilfe *f*: *the* ~ *sought* das Klagebegehren, b) Rechtsbehelf *m*, -mittel *n*; **7.** ✗ a) *allg.* Ablösung *f*, b) Entsatz *m*, Entlastung *f*, c) *in Zssgn* Entlastungs...: ~ *attack* (*road, train*); ~ *driver* *mot.* Beifahrer *m*.

re·lief² [rɪ'liːf] *s.* △ *etc.* Reli'ef *n*; erhabene Arbeit: ~ *map* Relief-, Höhenkarte *f*; *be in* ~ *against* sich (scharf) abheben gegen; *set into vivid* ~ *fig. et.* plastisch schildern; *stand out in* (*bold*) ~ deutlich hervortreten (*a. fig.*); *throw into* ~ hervortreten lassen (*a. fig.*).

re·lieve [rɪ'liːv] *v/t.* **1.** *Schmerzen etc.*, *a. Gewissen* erleichtern: ~ *one's feelings* s-n Gefühlen Luft machen; ~ *s.o.'s mind* j-n beruhigen; → *nature* 7; **2.** j-n entlasten: ~ *s.o. from* (*od. of*) j-m *et.* abnehmen, j-n von *e-r Pflicht etc.* ent-

binden, j-n *e-r Verantwortung etc.* entheben, j-n von *et.* befreien; ~ *s.o. of humor.* j-n um *et.* ,erleichtern', j-m *et.* stehlen; **3.** *j-n* erleichtern, beruhigen, trösten: *I am ~d to hear* es beruhigt mich, zu hören; **4.** ✗ a) *Platz* entsetzen, b) *Kampftruppe* entlasten, c) *Posten, Einheit* ablösen; **5.** *Bedürftige* unter'stützen, *Armen* helfen; **6.** *Eintöniges* beleben, Abwechslung bringen in (*acc.*); **7.** her'vor-, abheben; **8.** *j-m* Recht verschaffen; *e-r Sache* abhelfen; **9.** ⚙ a) entlasten (*a.* △), *Feder* entspannen, b) 'hinterdrehen.

re·lie·vo [rɪ'liːvəʊ] *pl.* **-vos** *s.* Reli'efarbeit *f*.

re·li·gion [rɪ'lɪdʒən] *s.* **1.** Religi'on *f* (*a. iro.*): *get* ~ F fromm werden; **2.** Frömmigkeit *f*; **3.** Ehrensache *f*, Herzenspflicht *f*; **4.** mo'nastisches Leben: *enter* ~ in e-n Orden eintreten; **re'li·gion·ist** [-dʒənɪst] *s.* religi'öser Schwärmer *od.* Eiferer; **re·lig·i·os·i·ty** [rɪ,lɪdʒɪ'ɒsətɪ] *s.* **1.** Religiosi'tät *f*; **2.** Frömme'lei *f*.

re·li·gious [rɪ'lɪdʒəs] *adj.* □ **1.** Religions..., religi'ös (*Buch, Pflicht etc.*); **2.** religi'ös, fromm; **3.** Ordens...: ~ *order* geistlicher Orden; **4.** *fig.* gewissenhaft, peinlich genau; **5.** *fig.* andächtig: ~ *silence*.

re·lin·quish [rɪ'lɪŋkwɪʃ] *v/t.* **1.** *Hoffnung, Idee, Plan etc.* aufgeben; **2.** (*to*) *Besitz, Recht* abtreten (*dat. od.* an *acc.*), preisgeben (*dat.*), über'lassen (*dat.*); **3.** *et.* loslassen, fahren lassen; **4.** verzichten auf (*acc.*); **re'lin·quish·ment** [-mənt] *s.* **1.** Aufgabe *f*; **2.** Über'lassung *f*; **3.** Verzicht *m* (*of* auf *acc.*).

rel·i·quar·y ['relɪkwərɪ] *s.* *R.C.* Re'liquienschrein *m*.

rel·ish ['relɪʃ] **I** *v/t.* **1.** gern essen, sich schmecken lassen; *a. fig.* (mit Behagen) genießen, Geschmack finden an (*dat.*): *I do not much ~ the idea* ich bin nicht gerade begeistert davon (*of doing* zu tun); **2.** *fig.* schmackhaft machen; **II** *v/i.* **3.** schmecken *od.* (*fig.*) riechen (*of* nach); **III** *s.* **4.** (Wohl)Geschmack *m*; **5.** *fig.* a) Kostprobe *f*, b) Beigeschmack *m* (*of* von); **6.** a) Gewürz *n*, Würze *f* (*a. fig.*), b) Horsd'œuvre *n*, Appe'tithappen *m*; **7.** *fig.* (*for*) Geschmack *m* (an *dat.*), Sinn *m* (für): *have no* ~ *for* sich nichts machen aus; *with* (*great*) ~ mit (großem) Behagen, mit Wonne (*a. iro.*).

re·live [,riː'lɪv] *v/t. et.* noch einmal durch'leben *od.* erleben.

re·lo·cate [,riːləʊ'keɪt] **I** *v/t.* **1.** 'umsiedeln, *Betrieb, Werk*: *a.* verlegen; **2.** *Computer*: verschieben; **II** *v/i.* **3.** 'umziehen (*to* nach).

re·luc·tance [rɪ'lʌktəns] *s.* **1.** Wider'streben *n*, Abneigung *f* (*to* gegen, *to do s.th.* et. zu tun): *with* ~ widerstrebend, ungern, zögernd; **2.** *phys.* mag-'netischer Widerstand; **re'luc·tant** [-nt] *adj.* □ widerwillig, wider'strebend, zögernd, ungern: *be* ~ *to do s.th.* sich sträuben, et. zu tun; et. nur ungern tun.

re·ly [rɪ'laɪ] *v/i.* **1.** ~ (*up*)*on* sich verlassen, vertrauen *od.* bauen *od.* zählen auf (*acc.*): ~ *on s.th.* (*for*) auf et. angewiesen sein (hinsichtlich *gen.*), et. (ausschließlich) beziehen (von); **2.** ~ (*up*)*on* sich auf *e-e Quelle etc.* stützen *od.* berufen.

re·main [rɪ'meɪn] **I** *v/i.* **1.** *allg.* bleiben; **2.** (übrig) bleiben (*a. fig. to s.o.* j-m): zu'rück-, verbleiben, noch übrig sein: *it now ~s for me to explain* es bleibt mir nur noch übrig, zu erklären; *nothing* ~*s* (*to us*) *but to* (*inf.*) es bleibt (uns) nichts anderes übrig, als zu (*inf.*); *that*

~*s to be seen* das bleibt abzuwarten; **3.** (bestehen) bleiben: ~ *in force* in Kraft bleiben; **4.** *im Briefschluss*: verbleiben; **II** *s. pl.* **5.** *a. fig.* Reste *pl.*, 'Überreste *pl.*, -bleibsel *pl.*; **6.** *die* sterblichen 'Überreste *pl.*; **7.** *a. literary* ~*s* hinter'lassene Werke *pl.*, lite'rarischer Nachlass; **re'main·der** [-də] **I** *s.* **1.** Rest *m* (*a.* 𝔸), *das* Übrige; **2.** ✝ Restbestand *m*, -betrag *m*: ~ *of a debt* Restschuld *f*; **3.** ⚙ Rückstand *m*; **4.** *Buchhandel*: Restauflage *f*, Remit'tenden *pl.*; **5.** ⚖ a) Anwartschaft *f* (auf Grundeigentum), b) Nacherbenrecht *n*; **II** *v/t.* **6.** *Bücher* billig abgeben; **re-'main·der·man** [-dəmæn] *s.* [*irr.*] ⚖ a) Anwärter *m*, b) Nacherbe *m*; **re'main·ing** [-nɪŋ] *adj.* übrig (geblieben), Rest..., verbleibend, restlich.

re·make [,riː'meɪk] **I** *v/t.* [*irr.* → *make*] wieder *od.* neu machen, *Film*: *a.* neu drehen; **II** *s.* ['riːmeɪk] Neuverfilmung *f*, Re'make *n*.

re·mand [rɪ'mɑːnd] **I** *v/t.* ⚖ a) (in Unter'suchungshaft) zu'rückschicken, b) *Rechtssache* (an die untere In'stanz) zu-'rückverweisen; **II** *s.* (Zu'rücksendung *f* in die) Unter'suchungshaft *f*: ~ *prison* Untersuchungsgefängnis *n*; *prisoner on* ~ Untersuchungsgefangene(r *m*) *f*; *be brought up on* ~ aus der Untersuchungshaft vorgeführt werden; ~ *centre* (*od. home*) Unter'suchungshaftanstalt *f* für Jugendliche.

re·mark [rɪ'mɑːk] **I** *v/t.* **1.** (be)merken, beobachten; **2.** bemerken, äußern (*that* dass); **II** *v/i.* **3.** e-e Bemerkung *od.* Bemerkungen machen, sich äußern ([*up*]*on* über *acc.*, zu); **III** *s.* **4.** Bemerkung *f*, Äußerung *f*: *without* ~ ohne Kommentar; *worthy of* ~ → **re'mark·a·ble** [-kəbl] *adj.* □ bemerkenswert: a) beachtlich, b) ungewöhnlich; **re'mark·a·ble·ness** [-kəblnɪs] *s.* **1.** Ungewöhnlichkeit *f*, Merkwürdigkeit *f*; **2.** Bedeutsamkeit *f*.

re·mar·riage [,riː'mærɪdʒ] *s.* 'Wiederver,heiratung *f*; **re'mar·ry** [-rɪ] *v/i.* wieder heiraten.

re·me·di·a·ble [rɪ'miːdjəbl] *adj.* □ heilbar, abstellbar: *this is* ~ dem ist abzuhelfen; **re'me·di·al** [-jəl] *adj.* □ **1.** heilend, Heil...: ~ *gymnastics* Heilgymnastik *f*; ~ *teaching* Förderunterricht *m* (*für Lernschwache*); **2.** abhelfend: ~ *measure* Abhilfsmaßnahme *f*.

rem·e·dy ['remɪdɪ] **I** *s.* **1.** ⚚ (Heil)Mittel *n*, Arz'nei *f* (*for, against* für, gegen); **2.** *fig.* (Gegen)Mittel *n* (*for, against* gegen); Abhilfe *f*; ⚖ Rechtsmittel *n*, -behelf *m*; **3.** *Münzwesen*: Re'medium *n*, Tole'ranz *f*; **II** *v/t.* **4.** *Mangel, Schaden* beheben; **5.** *Missstand* abstellen, abhelfen (*dat.*), in Ordnung bringen.

re·mem·ber [rɪ'membə] **I** *v/t.* **1.** sich entsinnen (*gen.*) *od.* an (*acc.*), sich besinnen auf (*acc.*), sich erinnern an (*acc.*): *I ~ that* es fällt mir (gerade) ein, dass; **2.** sich et. merken, nicht vergessen; **3.** eingedenk sein (*gen.*), denken an (*acc.*), beherzigen, sich et. vor Augen halten; **4.** j-n mit e-m Geschenk, in s-m Testament bedenken; **5.** empfehlen, grüßen: ~ *me to him* grüßen Sie ihn von mir; **II** *v/i.* **6.** sich erinnern *od.* entsinnen: *not that I* ~ nicht, dass ich wüsste; **re'mem·brance** [-brəns] *s.* **1.** Erinnerung *f*, Gedächtnis *n* (*of* an *acc.*); **2.** Gedächtnis *n*, An-, Gedenken *n*: *in* ~ *of* im Gedenken *od.* zur Erinnerung an (*acc.*); **2** *Day* Volkstrauertag *m* (*11. November*); **3.** Andenken *n* (*Sache*); **4.** *pl.* Grüße *pl.*, Empfehlungen *pl.*

re·mi·gra·tion [ˌriːmaɪˈgreɪʃn] s. Rückwanderung f.

re·mil·i·ta·ri·za·tion [ˈriːˌmɪlɪtəraɪˈzeɪʃn] s. Remilitarisierung f.

re·mind [rɪˈmaɪnd] v/t. j-n erinnern (**of** an acc., **that** dass); **that ~s me** da(bei) fällt mir (et.) ein; **this ~s me of home** das erinnert mich an zu Hause; **re·ˈmind·er** [-də] s. **1.** Mahnung f: **a gentle ~** ein (zarter) Wink; **2.** Erinnerung f (**of** an acc.); **3.** Gedächtnishilfe f.

rem·i·nisce [ˌremɪˈnɪs] v/i. in Erinnerungen schwelgen; **rem·i·ˈnis·cence** [-sns] s. **1.** Erinnerung f; **2.** pl. (Lebens)Erinnerungen pl., Reminis'zenzen pl.; **3.** fig. Anklang m; **rem·i·ˈnis·cent** [-snt] adj. □ **1.** sich erinnernd (**of** an acc.), Erinnerungs...; **2.** Erinnerungen wachrufend (**of** an acc.), erinnerungsträchtig; **3.** sich (gern) erinnernd, in Erinnerungen schwelgend.

re·mise[1] [rɪˈmaɪz] s. ⚖ Aufgabe f e-s Anspruchs, Rechtsverzicht m.

re·mise[2] [rəˈmiːz] s. **1.** obs. a) Re'mise f, Wagenschuppen m, b) Mietkutsche f; **2.** fenc. Ri'messe f.

re·miss [rɪˈmɪs] adj. □ (nach)lässig, säumig; lax, träge: **be ~ in one's duties** s-e Pflichten vernachlässigen; **re·ˈmis·si·ble** [-səbl] adj. **1.** erlässlich; **2.** verzeihlich; R.C. lässlich (Sünde); **re·ˈmis·sion** [-ɪʃn] s. **1.** Vergebung f (der Sünden); **2.** a) (teilweiser) Erlass e-r Strafe, Schuld, Gebühr etc., b) Nachlass m, Ermäßigung f; **3.** Nachlassen n der Intensität etc.; ✚ Remissi'on f; **re·ˈmiss·ness** [-nɪs] s. (Nach)Lässigkeit f.

re·mit [rɪˈmɪt] I v/t. **1.** Sünden vergeben; **2.** Schulden, Strafe (ganz od. teilweise) erlassen; **3.** hin'aus-, verschieben (**till, to** bis, **to** auf acc.); **4.** a) nachlassen in s-n Anstrengungen etc., b) Zorn etc. mäßigen, c) aufhören mit, einstellen; **5.** ✝ Geld etc. über'weisen, -'senden; **6.** bsd. ⚖ a) (Fall etc. zur Entscheidung) über'tragen, b) → **remand** I b; **II** v/i. **7.** ✝ Zahlung leisten, remittieren; **re·ˈmit·tal** [-tl] → **remission**; **re·ˈmit·tance** [-təns] s. **1.** (bsd. Geld)Sendung f, Über'weisung f; **2.** ✝ (Geld-, Wechsel-)Sendung f, Über'weisung f, Ri'messe f: **~ account** Überweisungskonto n; **make ~** remittieren, Deckung anschaffen; **re·ˈmit·tee** [ˌremɪˈtiː] s. ✝ (Zahlungs-, Über'weisungs)Empfänger m; **re·ˈmit·tent** [-tənt] bsd. ✚ I adj. (vo-'rübergehend) nachlassend; remittierend (Fieber); **II** s. remittierendes Fieber; **re·ˈmit·ter** [-tə] s. **1.** ✝ Geldsender m, Über'sender m; Remit'tend m; **2.** ⚖ a) Wieder'einsetzung f (**to** in frühere Rechte etc.), b) Über'weisung f e-s Falles.

rem·nant [ˈremnənt] s. **1.** ('Über)Rest m, 'Überbleibsel n; kläglicher Rest; fig. (letzter) Rest, Spur f; **2.** ✝ (Stoff)Rest m; pl. Reste(r) pl.: **~ sale** Resteverkauf m.

re·mod·el [ˌriːˈmɒdl] v/t. 'umbilden, -bauen, -formen, -gestalten.

re·mon·e·ti·za·tion [riːˌmʌnɪtaɪˈzeɪʃn] s. ✝ Wiederin'kurssetzung f.

re·mon·strance [rɪˈmɒnstrəns] s. (Gegen)Vorstellung f, Vorhaltung f, Einspruch m, Pro'test m; **re·ˈmon·strant** [-nt] I adj. □ protestierend; **II** s. Einspruch erheber m; **re·mon·strate** [ˈremənstreɪt] I v/i. **1.** protestieren (**against** gegen); **2.** Vorhaltungen od. Vorwürfe machen (**on** über acc., **with s.o.** j-m); **II** v/t. **3.** einwenden (**that** dass).

re·morse [rɪˈmɔːs] s. Gewissensbisse pl., Reue f (**at** über acc., **for** wegen): **with-**

out ~ unbarmherzig, kalt; **re·ˈmorse·ful** [-fʊl] adj. □ reumütig, reuevoll; **re·ˈmorse·less** [-lɪs] adj. □ unbarmherzig, hart(herzig).

re·mote [rɪˈməʊt] I adj. □ **1.** räumlich u. zeitlich, a. fig. fern, (weit) entfernt (**from** von), fig. schwach, vage: **~ antiquity** graue Vorzeit; **a ~ chance** e-e winzige Chance; **~ control** ⊛ a) Fernsteuerung f, b) Fernbedienung f; **~~-control(led)** ferngesteuert, -gelenkt, mit Fernbedienung; **~ future** ferne Zukunft; **not the ~st idea** keine blasse Ahnung; **~ pickup** ⊛ Fernabfrage f; **~ possibility** vage Möglichkeit; **~ relation** entfernte(r) od. weitläufige(r) Verwandte(r); **~ resemblance** entfernte od. schwache Ähnlichkeit; **~ sensing** ⊛ Remote Sensing n, Fernerkundung f; **2.** abgelegen, entlegen; **3.** mittelbar, 'indi,rekt: **~ damages** ✝ Folgeschäden; **4.** distan'ziert, unnahbar; **II** s. **5.** Am. TV: 'Außenüber,tragung f; **re·ˈmote·ness** [-nɪs] s. Ferne f, Entlegenheit f.

re·mount [ˌriːˈmaʊnt] I v/t. **1.** Berg, Pferd etc. wieder besteigen; **2.** ✕ neue Pferde beschaffen für; **3.** ⊛ Maschine wieder aufstellen; **II** v/i. **4.** wieder aufsteigen; wieder aufsitzen (Reiter); **5.** fig. zu'rückgehen (**to** auf acc.); **III** s. [ˈriːmaʊnt] **6.** frisches Reitpferd; ✕ Re'monte f.

re·mov·a·ble [rɪˈmuːvəbl] adj. □ **1.** absetzbar; **2.** ⊛ abnehmbar, auswechselbar; **3.** behebbar (Übel); **re·ˈmov·al** [-vl] s. **1.** Fort-, Wegschaffen n, -'räumen n; Entfernen n; Abfuhr f, 'Ab trans,port m; Beseitigung f (a. fig. Behebung von Fehlern, Missständen, e-s Gegners); **2.** 'Umzug m (**to** in acc., nach): **~ of business** Geschäftsverlegung f; **~ man** a) Spediteur m, b) Möbelpacker m; **~ van** Möbelwagen m; **3.** a) Absetzung f, Enthebung f (**from** office) aus dem Amt), b) (Straf)Versetzung f; **4.** ⚖ Verweisung f (**to** an acc.); **re·move** [rɪˈmuːv] I v/t. **1.** allg. (weg-) nehmen, entfernen (**from** aus); ⊛ abnehmen, abmontieren, ausbauen; Kleidungsstück ablegen; Hut abnehmen; Hand zu'rückziehen; fig. Furcht, Zweifel etc. nehmen; **~ from the agenda** von der Tagesordnung absetzen; **~ o.s.** sich entfernen (**from** von); **2.** wegräumen, -rücken, -bringen, fortschaffen, abtransportieren; (a. fig. j-n) aus dem Weg(e) räumen; (a. fig. j-n) 'umziehen: **~ furniture** (Wohnungs)Umzüge besorgen; **~ a prisoner** e-n Gefangenen abführen (lassen); **~ mountains** fig. Berge versetzen; **~ by suction** ⊛ absaugen; **a first cousin once ~d** Kind e-s Vetters od. e-r Kusine; **3.** Fehler, Gegner, Hindernis, Spuren etc. beseitigen; Flecken entfernen; fig. Schwierigkeiten beheben; **4.** wohin bringen, schaffen, verlegen; **5.** Beamten absetzen, entlassen; s-s Amtes entheben; **II** v/i. **6.** (aus-, 'um-, ver)ziehen (**to** nach); **III** v/t. **7.** Entfernung f, Abstand m: **at a ~** fig. mit einigem Abstand; **8.** Schritt m, Stufe f, Grad m; **9.** Brit. nächster Gang (beim Essen); **re·ˈmov·er** [-və] s. **1.** Abbeizmittel n; **2.** ('Möbel)Spedi,teur m.

re·mu·ner·ate [rɪˈmjuːnəreɪt] v/t. **1.** j-n entschädigen, belohnen (**for** für); **2.** entlohnen, vergüten, Entschädigung zahlen für, ersetzen; **re·mu·ner·a·tion** [rɪˌmjuːnəˈreɪʃn] s. **1.** Entschädigung f, Vergütung f; **2.** Belohnung f; **3.** Hono'rar n, Lohn m, Entgelt n; **re·ˈmu·ner·a·tive** [-nərətɪv] adj. □ einträglich, lohnend,

lukra'tiv, vorteilhaft.

Ren·ais·sance [rəˈneɪsəns] (Fr.) s. **1.** Renais'sance f; **2.** ⚲ 'Wiedergeburt f, -erwachen n.

re·nal [ˈriːnl] adj. anat. Nieren...

re·name [ˌriːˈneɪm] v/t. **1.** 'umbenennen; **2.** neu benennen.

re·nas·cence [rɪˈnæsns] s. **1.** 'Wiedergeburt f, Erneuerung f; **2.** ⚲ Renais-'sance f; **re·ˈnas·cent** [-nt] adj. sich erneuernd, wieder auflebend, wieder erwachend.

rend [rend] [irr.] I v/t. **1.** (zer)reißen: **~ from** j-m entreißen; **~ the air** die Luft zerreißen (Schrei etc.); **2.** spalten (a. fig.); **II** v/i. **3.** (zer)reißen.

ren·der [ˈrendə] v/t. **1.** a. **~ back** zu-'rückgeben, -erstatten; **~ up** herausgeben, fig. vergelten (**good for evil** Böses mit Gutem); **2.** (a. ✕ Festung) über'geben, ✝ Rechnung (vor)legen: **per account ~ed** ✝ laut (erteilter) Rechnung; **~ a profit** Gewinn abwerfen; → a. **account** 6 u. 7; **3.** (**to s.o.** j-m) e-n Dienst, Hilfe etc. leisten; Aufmerksamkeit, Ehre, Gehorsam erweisen; Dank abstatten: **for services ~ed** für geleistete Dienste; **4.** Grund angeben; **5.** ⚖ Urteil fällen; **6.** berühmt, schwierig, sichtbar etc. machen: **~ audible** hörbar machen; **~ possible** möglich machen, ermöglichen; **7.** künstlerisch 'wiedergeben, interpretieren; **8.** sprachlich, sinngemäß 'wiedergeben, über'setzen; **9.** ⊛ Fett auslassen; **10.** ⚼ roh bewerfen; **'ren·der·ing** [-dərɪŋ] s. **1.** 'Übergabe f; **~ of account** ✝ Rechnungslegung f; **2.** künstlerische 'Wiedergabe, Interpreta-ti'on f, Gestaltung f, Vortrag m; **3.** Über'setzung f, 'Wiedergabe f; **4.** ⚼ Rohbewurf m.

ren·dez·vous [ˈrɒndɪvuː] pl. **-vous** [-vuːz] (Fr.) s. **1.** a) Rendez'vous n, Verabredung f, Stelldichein n, b) Zs.-kunft f; **2.** Treffpunkt m (a. ✕).

ren·di·tion [renˈdɪʃn] s. **1.** → **rendering** 2 u. 3; **2.** Am. (Urteils)Fällung f, (-)Verkündung f.

ren·e·gade [ˈrenɪgeɪd] I s. Rene'gat(in), Abtrünnige(r m) f, 'Überläufer(in); **II** adj. abtrünnig.

re·nege [rɪˈniːg] I v/i. **1.** sein Wort brechen: **~ on** et. nicht (ein)halten, e-r Sache untreu werden; **2.** Kartenspiel: nicht bedienen; **II** v/t. **3.** ab-, verleugnen.

re·new [rɪˈnjuː] v/t. **1.** allg. erneuern (z.B. Bekanntschaft, Angriff, Autoreifen, Gelöbnis): **~ed** erneut; **2.** Briefwechsel etc. wieder aufnehmen: **~ one's efforts** sich erneut bemühen; **3.** Jugend, Kraft 'wiedererlangen; biol. regenerieren; **4.** ✝ Vertrag etc. erneuern, verlängern; Wechsel prolongieren; **5.** ergänzen, -setzen; sich wieder'holen; **re·ˈnew·a·ble** [-juːəbl] adj. **1.** erneuerbar, zu erneuern(d): **~ resources** erneuerbare Ressourcen od. Energiequellen; **2.** erneuerungs-, verlängerungsfähig; prolongierbar (Wechsel); **re·ˈnew·al** [-juːəl] s. **1.** Erneuerung f; **2.** ✝ a) Erneuerung f, Verlängerung f, b) Prolongati'on f.

ren·i·form [ˈriːnɪfɔːm] adj. nierenförmig.

ren·net[1] [ˈrenɪt] s. ⚘, zo. Lab n.

ren·net[2] [ˈrenɪt] s. ♥ Brit. Re'nette f.

re·nounce [rɪˈnaʊns] I v/t. **1.** verzichten auf (acc.), et. aufgeben; entsagen (dat.); **2.** verleugnen; dem Glauben etc. abschwören; Freundschaft aufsagen; ✝ Vertrag kündigen; et. von sich weisen, ablehnen; sich von j-m lossagen; j-n verstoßen; **3.** *Kartenspiel: Farbe* nicht bedienen (können); **II** *v/i.* **4.** Verzicht leisten; **5.** *Kartenspiel:* nicht bedienen (können), passen.

ren·o·vate ['renəʊveɪt] *v/t.* **1.** erneuern; wieder'herstellen; **2.** renovieren; **ren·o·va·tion** [ˌrenəʊ'veɪʃn] *s.* Renovierung *f*, Erneuerung *f*; '**ren·o·va·tor** [-tə] *s.* Erneuerer *m*.

re·nown [rɪ'naʊn] *s. rhet.* Ruhm *m*, Ruf *m*, Berühmtheit *f*; **re'nowned** [-nd] *adj.* berühmt, namhaft.

rent[1] [rent] **I** *s.* **1.** (Wohnungs)Miete *f*, Mietzins *m*: **for ~** *bsd. Am.* a) zu ver'mieten, b) zu verleihen; **~-controlled** miet(preis)gebunden; **~ tribunal** Mieterschiedsgericht *n*; **2.** Pacht(geld *n*, -zins *m*) *f*; **II** *v/t.* **3.** vermieten; **4.** verpachten; **5.** mieten; **6.** (ab)pachten; **7.** *Am.* a) *et.* ausleihen, b) sich *et.* leihen; **III** *v/i.* **8.** vermietet *od.* verpachtet werden (**at** *od.* **for** zu).

rent[2] [rent] **I** *s.* Riss *m*; Spalt(e *f*) *m*; **II** *pret. u. p.p. von* **rend**.

rent·a·ble ['rentəbl] *adj.* (ver)mietbar.

'**rent-a-'car** (**serv·ice**) *s. mot.* Autoverleih *m*.

ren·tal ['rentl] *s.* **1.** Miet-, Pachtbetrag *m*, -satz *m*: **~ car** Mietwagen *m*; **~ library** *Am.* Leihbücherei *f*: **~ value** Miet-, Pachtwert *m*; **2.** (Brutto)Mietertrag *m*; **3.** Zinsbuch *n*.

rent| boy *s.* Strichjunge *m*; **~ charge** *pl.* **rents charge** *s.* Grundrente *f*; **~ con·trol** *s.* Mietbindung *f*.

rent·er ['rentə] *s. bsd. Am.* **1.** Pächter (-in), Mieter(in); **2.** Verpächter(in), -mieter(in), -leiher(in); '**rent-'free** *adj.* miet-, pachtfrei.

re·nun·ci·a·tion [rɪˌnʌnsɪ'eɪʃn] *s.* **1.** (**of**) Verzicht *m* (auf *acc.*), Aufgabe *f* (*gen.*); **2.** Entsagung *f*; **3.** Ablehnung *f*.

re·o·pen [ˌriː'əʊpən] **I** *v/t.* **1.** wieder eröffnen; **2.** wieder beginnen, wieder aufnehmen; **II** *v/i.* **3.** sich wieder öffnen; **4.** 'wieder eröffnen (*Geschäft etc.*); **5.** wieder beginnen.

re·or·gan·i·za·tion ['riːˌɔːɡənaɪ'zeɪʃn] *s.* **1.** 'Umbildung *f*, Neuordnung *f*, -gestaltung *f*; **2.** ✝ Sanierung *f*; **re·or·gan·ize** [ˌriː'ɔːɡənaɪz] *v/t.* **1.** reorganisieren, neu gestalten, 'umgestalten, 'umgliedern; **2.** ✝ sanieren.

rep[1] [rep] *s.* Rips *m* (*Stoff*).

rep[2] [rep] *s. sl.* **1.** Wüstling *m*; **2.** *Am.* Ruf *m*.

re·pack [ˌriː'pæk] *v/t.* 'umpacken.

re·paint [ˌriː'peɪnt] *v/t.* neu (an)streichen, über'malen.

re·pair[1] [rɪ'peə] **I** *v/t.* **1.** reparieren, (wieder) in'stand setzen; ausbessern, flicken; **2.** wieder'herstellen; **3.** wieder gutmachen; *Verlust* ersetzen; **II** *s.* **4.** Repara'tur *f*, In'standsetzung *f*, Ausbesserung *f*; *pl.* In'standsetzungsarbeit(en *pl.*) *f*: **state of ~** (baulicher *etc.*) Zustand *m*; **in good ~** in gutem Zustand; **in need of ~** reparaturbedürftig; **out of ~** a) betriebsunfähig, b) baufällig; **under ~** a) in Reparatur; **~ kit**, **~ outfit** Reparaturwerkzeug *n*, Flickzeug *n*.

re·pair[2] [rɪ'peə] **I** *v/i.* sich begeben (**to** nach, zu); **II** *s.* Zufluchtsort *m*, (beliebter) Aufenthaltsort.

re·pair·a·ble [rɪ'peərəbl] *adj.* **1.** repara'turbedürftig; **2.** zu reparieren(d), reparierbar; **3. → repairable**.

re'pair|·man [-mæn] *s.* [*irr.*] *bsd. Am.* Me'chaniker *m*, Autoschlosser *m*, (*Fernseh- etc.*)Techniker *m*; **~ shop** *s.* Repara'turwerkstatt *f*.

rep·a·ra·ble ['repərəbl] *adj.* □ wieder gutzumachen(d); ersetzbar (*Verlust*);

rep·a·ra·tion [ˌrepə'reɪʃn] *s.* **1.** Wieder'gutmachung *f*: **make ~** Genugtuung leisten; **2.** Entschädigung *f*, Ersatz *m*; **3.** *pol.* Wieder'gutmachungsleistung *f*; *pl.* Reparati'onen *pl.*

rep·ar·tee [ˌrepɑː'tiː] *s.* schlagfertige Antwort, Schlagfertigkeit *f*: **quick at ~** schlagfertig.

re·par·ti·tion [ˌriːpɑː'tɪʃn] **I** *s.* Aufteilung *f*, (Neu)Verteilung *f*; **II** *v/t.* (neu) auf-, verteilen.

re·pass [ˌriː'pɑːs] *v/i.* (*u. v/t.*) wieder vor'beikommen (**an** *dat.*).

re·past [rɪ'pɑːst] *s.* Mahl(zeit *f*) *n*.

re·pa·tri·ate [riː'pætrieɪt] **I** *v/t.* repatriieren, (in die Heimat) zu'rückführen; **II** *s.* Repatriierte(r *m*) *f*, Heimkehrer (-in); **re·pa·tri·a·tion** [ˌriːpætrɪ'eɪʃn] *s.* Rückführung *f*.

re·pay [*irr.* **→ pay**] **I** *v/t.* [riː'peɪ] **1.** *Geld etc.* zu'rückzahlen, (zu'rück)erstatten; **2.** *fig. Besuch, Gruß, Schlag etc.* erwidern; *Böses* heimzahlen, vergelten (**to** *s.o.* j-m); **3.** *j-n* belohnen, (*a.* ✝) entschädigen (**for** für); **4.** *et.* lohnen, vergelten (**with** mit); **II** *v/i.* [ˌriː'peɪ] **5.** nochmals (be)zahlen; **re'pay·a·ble** [-'peəbl] *adj.* rückzahlbar; **re'pay·ment** [-mənt] *s.* **1.** Rückzahlung *f*; **2.** Erwiderung *f*, **3.** Vergeltung *f*.

re·peal [rɪ'piːl] **I** *v/t.* **1.** *Gesetz etc.* aufheben, außer Kraft setzen; **2.** wider'rufen; **II** *s.* **3.** Aufhebung *f von Gesetzen*; **re'peal·a·ble** [-ləbl] *adj.* 'widerruflich, aufhebbar.

re·peat [rɪ'piːt] **I** *v/t.* **1.** wieder'holen: **~ an experience** *et.* nochmals durchmachen *od.* erleben; **~ an order** (**for** *s.th.*) *et.*) nachbestellen; **2.** nachsprechen, wieder'holen; weitererzählen; **3.** *ped. Gedicht* aufsagen; **II** *v/i.* **4.** sich wieder'holen (*Vorgang*); **5.** repetieren (*Uhr, Gewehr*); **6.** aufstoßen (*Speisen*); **III** *s.* **7.** Wieder'holung *f* (*a. TV etc.*); **8.** *et.* sich wieder'holendes (*z.B. Muster*), *bsd. Stoff, Tapete:* Rap'port *m*; **9.** ♪ a) Wieder'holung *f*, b) Wieder'holungszeichen *n*; **10.** ✝ *oft* **~ order** Nachbestellung *f*; **re'peat·ed** [-tɪd] *adj.* □ wieder'holt, mehrmalig; neuerlich; **re'peat·er** [-tə] *s.* **1.** Wieder'holende(r *m*) *f*; **2.** Repetieruhr *f*; **3.** Repetier-, Mehrladegewehr *n*; **4.** *Am.* Wähler, *der widerrechtlich mehrere Stimmen abgibt*; **5.** ♈ peri'odische Dezi'malzahl *f*; **6.** ☷ Rückfällige(r *m*) *f*; **7.** ♆ Tochterkompass *m*; **8.** ⚡ a) (Leitungs)Verstärker *m*, b) Über'trager *m*; **re'peat·ing** [-tɪŋ] *adj.* wieder'holend: **~ decimal → repeater** 5; **~ rifle → repeater** 3; **~ watch → repeater** 2.

re·pel [rɪ'pel] *v/t.* **1.** *Angreifer* zu'rückschlagen, -treiben; **2.** *Angriff* abschlagen, abweisen, *a. Schlag* abwehren; **3.** *fig.* ab-, zu'rückweisen; **4.** *phys.* abstoßen; **5.** *fig.* j-n abstoßen, anwidern; **re'pel·lent** [-lənt] *adj.* □ **1.** ab-, zu'rückstoßend; **2.** *fig.* abstoßend.

re·pent [rɪ'pent] *v/t.* (*a. v/i.* **of**) *et.* bereuen; **re'pent·ance** [-təns] *s.* Reue *f*; **re'pent·ant** [-tənt] *adj.* □ reuig (**of** über *acc.*), bußfertig.

re·per·cus·sion [ˌriːpə'kʌʃn] *s.* **1.** Rückprall *m*, -stoß *m*; **2.** Widerhall *m*; **3.** *mst pl. fig.* Rück-, Auswirkungen *pl.* (**on** auf *acc.*).

rep·er·toire ['repətwɑː] *s.* **→ repertory** 1.

rep·er·to·ry ['repətərɪ] *s.* **1.** *thea.* Reper'toire *n*, Spielplan *m*: **~ theatre** (*Am. theater*) Repertoirebühne *f*, -theater *n*; **2.** **→ repository**.

rep·e·ti·tion [ˌrepɪ'tɪʃn] *s.* **1.** Wieder'holung *f*: **~ order** ✝ Nachbestellung *f*; **~ work** ☼ Reihenfertigung *f*; **2.** *ped.* (Stück *n* zum) Aufsagen *n*; **3.** Ko'pie *f*, Nachbildung *f*; **rep·e·ti·tious** [ˌrepɪ'tɪʃəs] *adj.* □ sich ständig wieder'holend; ewig gleich bleibend; **re·pet·i·tive** [rɪ'petətɪv] *adj.* □ **1.** sich wieder'holend, wieder'holt; **2. → repetitious**.

re·pine [rɪ'paɪn] *v/i.* murren, 'missvergnügt *od.* unzufrieden sein (**at** über *acc.*); **re'pin·ing** [-nɪŋ] *adj.* □ unzufrieden, murrend, mürrisch.

re·place [rɪ'pleɪs] *v/t.* **1.** wieder hinstellen *od.* -legen; *teleph. Hörer* auflegen; **2.** *et. Verlorenes, Veraltetes* ersetzen, an die Stelle treten von; ☼ austauschen, ersetzen, *a.* wieder einsetzen; **3.** *j-n* ersetzen *od.* ablösen *od.* vertreten, *j-s* Stelle einnehmen; **4.** *Geld* zu'rückstatten, ersetzen; **5.** ♈ vertauschen; **re'place·a·ble** [-səbl] *adj.* ersetzbar; ☼ auswechselbar; **re'place·ment** [-mənt] *s.* **1.** a) Ersetzung *f*, b) Ersatz *m*: **~ engine** ☼ Austauschmotor *m*; **~ part** Ersatzteil *n*; **2.** ✗ a) Ersatzmann *m*, b) Ersatz *m*, Auffüllung *f*: **~ unit** Ersatztruppenteil *m*; **3.** *med.* Pro'these *f*: **~ surgery** Ersatzteilchirurgie *f*.

re·plant [ˌriː'plɑːnt] *v/t.* **1.** 'umpflanzen; **2.** neu pflanzen.

re·play [rɪ'pleɪ] *s. sport* **1.** Wieder'holungsspiel *n*; **2.** *TV:* Wieder'holung *f* e-r *Spielszene*.

re·plen·ish [rɪ'plenɪʃ] *v/t.* (wieder) auffüllen, ergänzen; **re'plen·ish·ment** [-mənt] *s.* **1.** Auffüllung *f*, Ersatz *m*; **2.** Ergänzung *f*.

re·plete [rɪ'pliːt] *adj.* **1.** (**with**) (zum Platzen) voll (von), angefüllt (von); **2.** reichlich versehen (**with** mit); **re'ple·tion** [-iːʃn] *s.* ('Über)Fülle *f*: **full to ~** bis zum Rand(e) voll.

re·plev·in [rɪ'plevɪn] *s.* ☷ **1.** (Klage *f* auf) Her'ausgabe *f gegen* Sicherheitsleistung; **2.** einstweilige Verfügung (auf Herausgabe).

rep·li·ca ['replɪkə] *s.* **1.** *paint.* Re'plik *f*, Origi'nalko,pie *f*; **2.** Ko'pie *f*; **3.** *fig.* Ebenbild *n*.

rep·li·ca·tion [ˌreplɪ'keɪʃn] *s.* **1.** Erwiderung *f*; **2.** Echo *n*; **3.** ☷ Re'plik *f*; **4.** Reprodukti'on *f*, Ko'pie *f*.

re·ply [rɪ'plaɪ] **I** *v/i.* **1.** antworten, erwidern (**to** *s.th.* auf *et.*, **to** *s.o.* j-m) (*a. fig.*); **2.** replizieren; **II** *s.* **3.** Antwort *f*, Erwiderung *f*: **in ~ to** (als Antwort) auf (*acc.*); **in ~ to your letter** in Beantwortung Ihres Schreibens; **~-paid telegram** Telegramm *n* mit bezahlter Rückantwort; **~ (postal) card** Postkarte *f* mit Rückantwort; **~ postage** Rückporto *n*; (**there is**) **no ~** *teleph.* der Teilnehmer meldet sich nicht; **4.** *Funk:* Rückmeldung *f*; **5.** ☷ Re'plik *f*.

re·port [rɪ'pɔːt] **I** *s.* **1.** *allg.* Bericht *m* (**on** über *acc.*); ✝ (Geschäfts-, Sitzungs-, Verhandlungs)Bericht *m*: **month under ~** Berichtsmonat *m*; **~ stage** *parl.* Erörterungsstadium *n* e-r *Vorlage*; **2.** Gutachten *n*, Refe'rat *n*; **3.** ✗ Meldung *f*; **4.** ☷ Anzeige *f*; **5.** Nachricht *f*, (Presse-) Bericht *m*, (-)Meldung *f*; **6.** (Schul-) Zeugnis *n*; **7.** Gerücht *n*; **8.** Ruf *m*, Leumund *m*; **9.** Knall *m*; **II** *v/t.* **10.** berichten (**to** *s.o.* j-m); **2.** Bericht erstatten, berichten über (*acc.*); erzählen: **it is ~ed that** es heißt, dass; **he is ~ed as saying** er soll gesagt haben; **~ed speech** *ling.* indirekte Rede; **11.** *Vorkommnis, Schaden etc.* melden; **12.** *j-n* (*o.s.* sich) melden; anzeigen (**to** bei, **for** wegen); **13.** *parl. Gesetzesvorlage* (wieder) vorlegen (*Ausschuss*); **III** *v/i.* **14.** (e-n) Bericht geben *od.* erstatten, berichten (**on**, **of**

über *acc.*); **15.** als Berichterstatter(in) arbeiten (*for* für *e-e Zeitung*); **16.** (*to*) sich melden (bei); sich stellen (*dat.*): **~ for duty** sich zum Dienst melden; **17. ~ to** Am. *j-m* unter'stellt sein; **re·port·a·ble** [-təbl] *adj.* **1.** ⚕ meldepflichtig (*Krankheit*); **2.** steuerpflichtig (*Einkommen*); **re'port·ed·ly** [-tɪdlɪ] *adv.* wie verlautet; **re'port·er** [-tə] *s.* **1.** Re'porter(in), (Presse)Berichterstatter(in); **2.** Berichterstatter (-in), Refe'rent(in); **3.** Proto'kollführer(in).

re·pose [rɪ'pəʊz] I *s.* **1.** Ruhe *f* (*a. fig.*); Erholung *f* (*from* von): *in ~* in Ruhe, untätig (*a. Vulkan*); **2.** *fig.* Gelassenheit *f*, (Gemüts)Ruhe *f*; II *v/i.* **3.** ruhen (*a. Toter*); (sich) ausruhen, schlafen; **4. ~ on** a) liegen *od.* ruhen auf (*dat.*), b) *fig.* beruhen auf (*dat.*), c) verweilen bei (*Gedanken*); **5. ~ in** *fig.* vertrauen auf (*acc.*); III *v/t.* **6.** *j-m* Ruhe gewähren, *j-n* (sich aus)ruhen lassen: **~ o.s.** sich zur Ruhe legen; **7. ~ on** legen *od.* betten auf (*acc.*); **8. ~ in** *fig. Vertrauen, Hoffnung* setzen auf (*acc.*); **re·pos·i·to·ry** [rɪ'pɒzɪtərɪ] *s.* **1.** Behältnis *n*, Gefäß *n* (*a. fig.*); **2.** Verwahrungsort *m*; ✝ (Waren)Lager *n*, Niederlage *f*; **3.** *fig.* Fundgrube *f*, Quelle *f*; **4.** Vertraute(r *m*) *f.*

re·pos·sess [ˌriːpə'zes] *v/t.* **1.** wieder in Besitz nehmen; **2. ~ of** *j-n* wieder in den Besitz *e-r Sache* setzen.

rep·re·hend [ˌreprɪ'hend] *v/t.* tadeln, rügen; **rep·re'hen·si·ble** [-nsəbl] *adj.* □ tadelnswert, sträflich; **rep·re'hen·sion** [-nʃn] *s.* Tadel *m*, Rüge *f*, Verweis *m*.

rep·re·sent [ˌreprɪ'zent] *v/t.* **1.** *j-n od. j-s Sache* vertreten: **be ~ed at** bei *e-r Sache* vertreten sein; **2.** (bildlich, grafisch) dar-, vorstellen, abbilden; **3.** *thea.* a) *Rolle* darstellen, verkörpern, b) *Stück* aufführen; **4.** *fig.* (*symbolisch*) darstellen, verkörpern, bedeuten, repräsentieren; *e-r Sache* entsprechen; **5.** darlegen, ausführen, schildern, vor Augen führen (*to dat.*): **~ to o.s.** sich *et.* vorstellen; **6.** hin-, darstellen (*as od.* **to be** als); behaupten, vorbringen: **~ that** behaupten, dass; es so hinstellen, als ob; **~ to s.o. that** *j-m* vorhalten, dass; **rep·re·sen·ta·tion** [ˌreprɪzen'teɪʃn] *s.* **1.** ⚖, ✝, *pol.* Vertretung *f*; → **proportional 1;** **2.** (*bildliche, grafische*) Darstellung, Bild *n*; **3.** *thea.* a) Darstellung *f e-r Rolle*, b) Aufführung *f e-s Stückes*; **4.** Schilderung *f*, Darstellung *f des Sachverhalts*: *false* **~s** ⚖ falsche Angaben; **5.** Vorhaltung *f*: *make* **~s** *to* bei *j-m* vorstellig werden, Vorstellungen erheben bei; **6.** ⚖ a) Anzeige *f* von Ge'fahr, umständen (*Versicherung*), b) Rechtsnachfolge *f* (*bsd. Erbrecht*); **7.** *phls.* Vorstellung *f*, Begriff *m*; **rep·re'sent·a·tive** [-tətɪv] I *s.* **1.** Vertreter (-in), Stellvertreter(in), Beauftragte(r *m*) *f*, Repräsen'tant(in): *authorized* **~** Bevollmächtigte(r *m*) *f*; (*commercial*) **~** Handelsvertreter(in); **2.** *parl.* (Volks-) Vertreter(in), Abgeordnete(r *m*) *f*: *House of* **~s** Am. Repräsentantenhaus *n*; **3.** *fig.* typischer Vertreter, Musterbeispiel *n* (*of gen.*); II *adj.* □ **4.** (*of*) vertretend (*acc.*), stellvertretend (für): *in a* **~** *capacity* als Vertreter(in); **5.** *pol.* repräsenta'tiv: **~** *government* parlamentarische Regierung; **6.** darstellend (*of acc.*): **~** *arts*; **7.** (*of*) *fig.* verkörpernd (*acc.*), sym'bolisch (für); **8.** typisch, kennzeichnend (*of* für); *Statistik etc.:* repräsenta'tiv (*Auswahl, Querschnitt*): **~** *sample* ✝ Durchschnittsmuster *n*; **9.** ⚕, *zo.* entspre-

chend (*of dat.*).

re·press [rɪ'pres] *v/t.* **1.** *Gefühle, Tränen etc.* unter'drücken; **2.** *psych.* verdrängen; **re'pres·sion** [-eʃn] *s.* **1.** Unter'drückung *f*; **2.** *psych.* Verdrängung *f*; **re'pres·sive** [-sɪv] *adj.* □ **1.** repres'siv, unter'drückend; **2.** hemmend, Hemmungs...

re·prieve [rɪ'priːv] I *s.* **1.** ⚖ a) Begnadigung *f*, b) (Straf-, Voll'streckungs)Aufschub *m*; **2.** *fig.* (Gnaden)Frist *f*, Atempause *f*; II *v/t.* **3.** ⚖ *j-s* 'Urteilsvoll,streckung aussetzen, (*a. fig.*) *j-m e-e* Gnadenfrist gewähren; **4.** *j-n* begnadigen; **5.** *fig. j-m e-e* Atempause gönnen.

rep·ri·mand ['reprɪmɑːnd] I *s.* Verweis *m*, Rüge *f*, Maßregelung *f*; II *v/t.* *j-m e-n* Verweis erteilen, *j-n* rügen *od.* maßregeln.

re·print [ˌriː'prɪnt] I *v/t.* neu drucken, nachdrucken, neu auflegen; II *s.* ['riːprɪnt] Nach-, Neudruck *m*, Re'print *m*, Neuauflage *f.*

re·pris·al [rɪ'praɪzl] *s.* Repres'salie *f*, Vergeltungsmaßnahme *f*: *make* **~s** (*up*)*on* Repressalien ergreifen gegen.

re·pro ['reprəʊ] *pl.* -**pros** *s.* F **1.** *typ.* ,Repro' *f*, Reprodukti'on(svorlage) *f*; **2.** → *reproduction* 8.

re·proach [rɪ'prəʊtʃ] I *s.* **1.** Vorwurf *m*, Tadel *m*: *without fear or* **~** ohne Furcht u. Tadel; *heap* **~es on** *j-n* mit Vorwürfen überschütten; **2.** *fig.* Schande *f* (*to* für): *bring* **~** (*up*)*on* *j-m* Schande machen; II *v/t.* **3.** vorwerfen, -halten, zum Vorwurf machen (*s.o. with s.th.* *j-m et.*); **4.** *j-m* Vorwürfe machen, *j-n* tadeln (*for* wegen); **5.** *et.* tadeln; **6.** *fig.* ein Vorwurf sein für, *et.* mit Schande bedecken; **re'proach·ful** [-fʊl] *adj.* □ vorwurfsvoll, tadelnd.

rep·ro·bate ['reprəʊbeɪt] I *adj.* **1.** ruchlos, lasterhaft; **2.** *eccl.* verdammt; II *s.* **3.** a) verkommenes Sub'jekt, b) Schurke *m*, c) Taugenichts *m*; **4.** (*von Gott*) Verworfene(r *m*) *f*, Verdammte(r *m*) *f*; III *v/t.* **5.** miss'billigen, verurteilen, verwerfen; verdammen (*Gott*); **rep·ro·ba·tion** [ˌreprəʊ'beɪʃn] *s.* 'Missbilligung *f*, Verurteilung *f.*

re·pro·cess [ˌriː'prəʊses] *v/t.* ⊛ wieder aufbereiten; ,**re'pro·cess·ing** *s.* Wieder'aufbereitung *f*: **~** *plant* Wieder'aufbereitungsanlage *f* (*für Kernbrennstoffe*).

re·pro·duce [ˌriːprə'djuːs] I *v/t.* **1.** *biol. u. fig.* (wieder) erzeugen, (wieder) her'vorbringen; (*o.s.* sich) fortpflanzen; **2.** *biol.* Glied regenerieren, neu bilden; **3.** *Bild etc.* reproduzieren; (*a.* ⊛) nachbilden, kopieren; *typ.* ab-, nachdrucken, vervielfältigen; **4.** *Stimme etc.* reproduzieren, 'wiedergeben; **5.** *Buch, Schauspiel* neu her'ausbringen; **6.** *et.* wieder'holen; II *v/i.* **7.** sich fortpflanzen *od.* vermehren; **re·pro'duc·er** [-sə] *s.* ⚡ a) 'Ton,wiedergabegerät *n*, b) Tonabnehmer *m*; **2.** *Computer:* (Loch)Kartendoppler *m*; ,**re·pro'duc·i·ble** [-səbl] *adj.* reproduzierbar; ,**re·pro'duc·tion** [-'dʌkʃn] *s.* **1.** *allg.* 'Wiedererzeugung *f*; **2.** *biol.* Fortpflanzung *f*; **3.** *typ., phot.* Reprodukti'on *f* (*a. psych.* früherer Erlebnisse); **4.** *typ.* Nachdruck *m*, Vervielfältigung *f*; **5.** ⊛ Nachbildung *f*; **6.** ♪, ⚡ *etc.* 'Wiedergabe *f*; **7.** *ped.* Nacherzählung *f*; **8.** Reprodukti'on *f:* a) Nachbildung *f*, b) *paint.* Ko'pie *f*; ,**re·pro'duc·tive** [-'dʌktɪv] *adj.* □ **1.** sich vermehrend, fruchtbar; **2.** *biol.* Fortpflanzungs...: **~** *organs*; **3.** *psych.* reproduk'tiv, nachschöpferisch.

re·proof [rɪ'pruːf] *s.* Tadel *m*, Rüge *f*,

Verweis *m.*

re·prov·al [rɪ'pruːvl] → *reproof*; **re·prove** [rɪ'pruːv] *v/t.* *j-n* tadeln, rügen; *et.* miss'billigen; **re'prov·ing·ly** [-vɪŋlɪ] *adv.* tadelnd *etc.*

reps [reps] → *rep*[1].

rep·tant ['reptənt] *adj.* ♥, *zo.* kriechend; '**rep·tile** [-taɪl] I *s.* **1.** *zo.* Rep'til *n*, Kriechtier *n*; **2.** *fig.* a) Kriecher(in), b) ,falsche Schlange'; II *adj.* **3.** kriechend, Kriech...; **4.** *fig.* a) kriecherisch, b) gemein, niederträchtig, **rep·til·i·an** [rep'tɪlɪən] I *adj.* **1.** *zo.* Reptilien..., Kriechtier..., *fig. 'kriechend*; **2.** → *reptile* 4 b; II *s.* **3.** → *reptile* 1 *u.* 2.

re·pub·lic [rɪ'pʌblɪk] *s. pol.* Repu'blik *f*: *the* **~** *of letters* *fig.* die Gelehrtenwelt, die literarische Welt; **re'pub·li·can** [-kən] (*USA pol. ⅌*) I *adj.* republi'kanisch; II *s.* Republi'kaner(in); **re'pub·li·can·ism** [-kənɪzəm] *s.* **1.** republi'kanische Staatsform; **2.** republi'kanische Gesinnung.

re·pub·li·ca·tion [ˈriːˌpʌblɪˈkeɪʃn] *s.* **1.** 'Wiederveröffentlichung *f*; **2.** Neuauflage *f* (*a. Erzeugnis*); **re·pub·lish** [ˌriː'pʌblɪʃ] *v/t.* neu veröffentlichen.

re·pu·di·ate [rɪ'pjuːdɪeɪt] I *v/t.* **1.** *Autorität, Schuld etc.* nicht anerkennen; *Vertrag für unverbindlich erklären*; **2.** *als unberechtigt* zu'rückweisen, verwerfen; **3.** *et.* ablehnen, nicht glauben; **4.** *Sohn etc.* verstoßen; II *v/i.* **5.** Staatsschulden nicht anerkennen; **re·pu·di·a·tion** [rɪ,pjuːdɪ'eɪʃn] *s.* **1.** Nichtanerkennung *f* (*bsd. e-r Staatsschuld*); **2.** Ablehnung *f*, Zu'rückweisung *f*, Verwerfung *f*; **3.** Verstoßung *f.*

re·pug·nance [rɪ'pʌgnəns] *s.* **1.** Widerwille *m*, Abneigung *f* (*to, against* gegen); **2.** Unvereinbarkeit *f*, (innerer) Widerspruch (*of gen. od.* von, *to, with* mit); **re'pug·nant** [-nt] *adj.* **1.** widerlich, zu'wider(laufend), widerwärtig (*to dat.*); **2.** unvereinbar (*to, with* mit); **3.** wider'strebend.

re·pulse [rɪ'pʌls] I *v/t.* **1.** *Feind* zu'rückschlagen, -werfen; *Angriff* abschlagen, -weisen; **2.** *fig. j-n* abweisen; *Bitte* abschlagen; II *s.* **3.** Zu'rückschlagen *n*, Abwehr *f*; **4.** *fig.* Zu'rückweisung *f*, Absage *f*: *meet with a* **~** abgewiesen werden (*a. fig.*); **5.** *phys.* Rückstoß *m*; **re'pul·sion** [-lʃn] *s.* **1.** *phys.* Abstoßung *f*, Repulsi'on *f*: **~** *motor* ⚡ Repulsionsmotor *m*; **2.** *fig.* Abscheu *m*, *f*; **re'pul·sive** [-sɪv] *adj.* □ *fig.* abstoßend (*a. phys.*), widerwärtig; **re'pul·sive·ness** [-sɪvnɪs] *s.* Widerwärtigkeit *f.*

re·pur·chase [ˌriː'pɜːtʃəs] I *v/t.* 'wieder-, zu'rückkaufen; II *s.* ✝ Rückkauf *m.*

rep·u·ta·ble ['repjʊtəbl] *adj.* □ **1.** achtbar, geachtet, angesehen, ehrbar; **2.** anständig; **rep·u·ta·tion** [ˌrepjʊ'teɪʃn] *s.* **1.** (guter) Ruf, Name *m*: *a man of* **~** ein Mann von Ruf *od.* Namen; **2.** Ruf *m*: *good* (*bad*) **~**; *have the* **~** *of being* im Ruf stehen, *et.* zu sein; *have a* **~** *for* bekannt sein für *od.* wegen.

re·pute [rɪ'pjuːt] I *s.* **1.** Ruf *m*, Leumund *m*: *by* **~** dem Rufe nach, wie es heißt; *of ill* **~** von schlechtem Ruf, übel beleumdet; *house of ill* **~** Bordell *n*; → *reputation* 1: *be held in high* **~** hohes Ansehen genießen; II *v/t.* **3.** halten für: *be* **~d** (*to be*) gelten als; *be well* (*ill*) **~d** in gutem (üblem) Rufe stehen; **re'put·ed** [-tɪd] *adj.* □ **1.** angeblich; **2.** ungeeicht, landesüblich (*Maß*); **3.** bekannt, berühmt; **re'put·ed·ly** [-tɪdlɪ] *adv.* angeblich, dem Vernehmen nach.

R

re·quest [rɪ'kwest] **I** s. **1.** Bitte f, Wunsch m; (a. formelles) Ersuchen, Gesuch n, Antrag m; (Zahlungs- etc.) Aufforderung f: **at** (od. **by**) **(s.o.'s)** ~ auf (j-s) Ansuchen od. Bitte hin, auf (j-s) Veranlassung; **by** ~ auf Wunsch; **no flowers by** ~ Blumenspenden dankend verbeten; ~ **denied!** a. iro. (Antrag) abgelehnt!; (musical) ~ **program(me)** Wunschkonzert n; ~ **stop** 🚌 etc. Bedarfshaltestelle f; **2.** Nachfrage f (a. ♥): **be in** (**great**) ~ (sehr) gefragt od. begehrt sein; **II** v/t. **3.** bitten od. ersuchen um: ~ **s.th. from s.o.** j-n um et. ersuchen; **it is** ~**ed** es wird gebeten; **4.** j-n (höflich) bitten, j-n (a. amtlich) ersuchen (**to do** zu tun).

re·qui·em ['rekwɪəm] s. Requiem n (a. ♪), Seelen-, Totenmesse f.

re·quire [rɪ'kwaɪə] **I** v/t. **1.** erfordern (Sache): **be** ~**d** erforderlich sein; **if** ~**d** erforderlichenfalls, wenn nötig; **2.** brauchen, nötig haben, e-r Sache bedürfen: **a task which** ~**s to be done** e-e Aufgabe, die noch erledigt werden muss; **3.** verlangen, fordern (**of s.o.** von j-m): ~ (**of**) **s.o. to do s.th.** j-n auffordern, et. zu tun; von j-m verlangen, dass er et. tue; ~**d subject** ped. Am. Pflichtfach n; **4.** Brit. wünschen; **II** v/i. **5.** (es) verlangen; **re·quire·ment** [-mənt] s. **1.** (fig. An)Forderung f; fig. Bedingung f, Vor'aussetzung f: **meet the** ~**s** den Anforderungen entsprechen; **2.** Erfordernis n, Bedürfnis n; mst pl. Bedarf m: ~**s of raw materials** Rohstoffbedarf m.

req·ui·site ['rekwɪzɪt] **I** adj. **1.** erforderlich, notwendig (**for**, **to** für); **II** s. **2.** Erfordernis n, Vor'aussetzung f (**for** für); **3.** (Be'darfs-, Ge'brauchs)Ar,tikel m: **office** ~**s** Büroartikel; **req·ui·si·tion** [,rekwɪ'zɪʃn] **I** s. **1.** Anforderung f (**for** an dat.): ~ **number** Bestellnummer f; **2.** (amtliche) Aufforderung; Völkerrecht: Ersuchen n; **3.** ✕ Requisiti'on f, Beschlagnahme f; In'anspruchnahme f; **4.** Einsatz m, Beanspruchung f; **5.** Erfordernis n; **II** v/t. **6.** verlangen; **7.** in Anspruch nehmen; ✕ requirieren.

re·quit·al [rɪ'kwaɪtl] s. **1.** Belohnung f (**for** für); **2.** Vergeltung f (**of** für); **3.** Vergütung f (**for** für); **re·quite** [rɪ'kwaɪt] v/t. **1.** belohnen; ~ **s.o.** (**for s.th.**); **2.** vergelten.

re·read [,riː'riːd] v/t. [irr. → read] nochmals ('durch)lesen.

re·route [,riː'ruːt] v/t. 'umleiten.

re·run [,riː'rʌn] **I** v/t. [irr. → run] thea. Film: wieder aufführen; Radio, TV, a. Computer: Programm wieder'holen; **II** s. ['riːrʌn] 'Wiederaufführung f; Wieder'holung f; Computer: Wiederholungslauf m.

res [riːz] pl. **res** (Lat.) s. ⚖ Sache f: ~ **judicata** rechtskräftig entschiedene Sache, weitS. (materielle) Rechtskraft; ~ **gestae** (beweiserhebliche) Tatsachen, Tatbestand m.

re·sale ['riːseɪl] s. 'Wieder-, Weiterverkauf m: ~ **price maintenance** Preisbindung f der zweiten Hand.

re·sched·ule [Brit. ,riː'ʃedjuːl; Am. ,riː-'skedʒʊl] v/t. **1.** Termin, Konzert verlegen, verschieben (**for** auf acc.), neu festsetzen; **2.** ♥ die 'Rückzahlungsmodali,täten für ... ändern.

re·scind [rɪ'sɪnd] v/t. Gesetz, Urteil etc. aufheben, für nichtig erklären; Kauf etc. rückgängig machen; von e-m Vertrag zu'rücktreten; **re·scis·sion** [-sɪʒn] s. **1.** Aufhebung f e-s Urteils etc.; **2.** Rücktritt m vom Vertrag.

res·cue ['reskjuː] **I** v/t. **1.** (**from**) retten

(aus), (bsd. ⚖ gewaltsam) befreien (von); (bsd. et.) bergen; ~ **from oblivion** der Vergessenheit entreißen; **2.** (gewaltsam) zu'rückholen; **II** s. **3.** Rettung f (a. fig.); Bergung f: **come to s.o.'s** ~ j-m zu Hilfe kommen; **4.** (gewaltsame) Befreiung; **III** adj. **5.** Rettungs...: ~ **operation** a. fig. Rettungsaktion f; ~ **party** Rettungs-, Bergungsmannschaft f; ~ **vessel** ⚓ Bergungsfahrzeug f; **'res·cu·er** [-juə] s. Befreier(in), Retter(in).

re·search [rɪ'sɜːtʃ] **I** s. **1.** Forschung(sarbeit) f, (wissenschaftliche) Unter'suchung (**on** über acc., auf dem Gebiet gen.); **2.** (genaue) Unter'suchung, (Nach)Forschung f (**after**, **for** nach); **II** v/i. **3.** forschen, Forschungen anstellen, wissenschaftlich arbeiten (**on** über acc.): ~ **into** → 4; **III** v/t. **4.** erforschen, unter'suchen; **IV** adj. **5.** Forschungs...: **re'search·er** [-tʃə] s. Forscher(in).

re·seat [,riː'siːt] v/t. **1.** Saal etc. neu bestuhlen; **2.** j-n 'umsetzen; **3.** ~ **o.s.** sich wieder setzen; **4.** ⚙ Ventile nachschleifen.

re·sect [rɪ'sekt] v/t. 🔪 her'ausschneiden; **re'sec·tion** [-kʃn] s. 🔪 Resekti'on f.

re·se·da ['resɪdə] s. **1.** ♀ Re'seda f; **2.** Re'sedagrün n.

re·sell [,riː'sel] v/t. [irr. → sell] wieder verkaufen, weiterverkaufen; **,re'sell·er** [-lə] s. 'Wiederverkäufer m.

re·sem·blance [rɪ'zembləns] s. Ähnlichkeit f (**to** mit, **between** zwischen dat.): **bear** (od. **have**) ~ **to** → **re·sem·ble** [rɪ'zembl] v/t. (dat.) ähnlich sein od. sehen, gleichen, ähneln.

re·sent [rɪ'zent] v/t. übel nehmen, ver-übeln, sich ärgern über (acc.); **re'sent·ful** [-fʊl] adj. □ **1.** (**against**, **of**) aufgebracht (gegen), ärgerlich od. voller Groll (auf acc.); **2.** übelnehmerisch, reizbar; **re'sent·ment** [-mənt] s. **1.** Ressenti'ment n, Groll m (**against**, **at** gegen); **2.** Verstimmung f, Unmut m, Unwille m.

res·er·va·tion [,rezə'veɪʃn] s. **1.** Vorbehalt m; ⚖ a. Vorbehaltsrecht n: ~-klausel f; **without** ~ ohne Vorbehalt; → **mental** 1; **2.** oft pl. Am. Vorbestellung f, Reservierung f von Zimmern etc.; **3.** Am. Reser'vat n: a) Na'turschutzgebiet n, b) Indi'anerreservati,on f.

re·serve [rɪ'zɜːv] **I** s. **1.** allg. Re'serve f (a. fig.), Vorrat m: **in** ~ in Reserve, vorrätig; ~ **seat** Notsitz m; **2.** † Re'serve f, Rücklage f, -stellung f: ~ **account** Rückstellungskonto n; ~ **currency** Leitwährung f; **3.** ✕ a) Re'serve f: ~ **holdings** pl. † Reserveguthaben n, ~ **officer** Reserveoffizier m; b) pl. taktische Re'serven pl.; **4.** sport Ersatz (-mann) m, Re'servespieler m; **5.** Reser'vat n, Schutzgebiet n: ~ **game** geschützter Wildbestand; **6.** Vorbehalt m (a. ⚖): **without** ~ vorbehalt-, rückhaltlos; **with certain** ~**s** mit gewissen Einschränkungen; ~ **price** † Mindestgebot n (bei Versteigerungen); **7.** fig. Zu'rückhaltung f, Re'serve f, zu'rückhaltendes Wesen: **receive with** ~ e-e Nachricht etc. mit Zurückhaltung aufnehmen; **II** v/t. **8.** (sich) et. aufsparen od. -bewahren, (zu'rück)behalten, in Re'serve halten; ✕ j-n zu'rückstellen; **9.** (sich) zu'rückhalten mit, warten mit, et. verschieben: ~ **judg(e)ment** ⚖ die Urteilsverkündung aussetzen; **10.** reservieren (lassen), vorbestellen, vormerken (**to**, **for** für); **11.** bsd. ⚖ a) vorbe-

---

halten (**to s.o.** j-m), b) sich vorbehalten: ~ **the right to do** (od. **of doing**) **s.th.** sich das Recht vorbehalten, et. zu tun; **all rights** ~**d** alle Rechte vorbehalten; **re'served** [-vd] adj. □ fig. zu-'rückhaltend, reserviert; **re'serv·ist** [-vɪst] s. ✕ Reser'vist m.

res·er·voir ['rezəvwaː] s. **1.** Behälter m für Wasser etc.; Speicher m; **2.** ('Wasser)Reser,voir n: a) Wasserturm m, b) Sammel-, Staubecken n, Bas'sin n; **3.** fig. Reser'voir n (**of** an dat.).

re·set [,riː'set] v/t. [irr. → set] **1.** Edelstein neu fassen; **2.** Messer neu abziehen; **3.** typ. neu setzen; **4.** ⚙ nachrichten, -stellen; Computer: rücksetzen, nullstellen.

re·set·tle [,riː'setl] **I** v/t. **1.** Land wieder besiedeln; **2.** j-n wieder ansiedeln, 'umsiedeln; **3.** wieder in Ordnung bringen; **II** v/i. **4.** sich wieder ansiedeln; **5.** fig. sich wieder setzen od. legen od. beruhigen; **,re'set·tle·ment** [-mənt] s. **1.** 'Wiederansiedlung f, 'Umsiedlung f; **2.** Neuordnung f.

re·shape [,riː'ʃeɪp] v/t. neu formen, 'umgestalten.

re·ship [,riː'ʃɪp] v/t. **1.** Güter wieder verschiffen; **2.** 'umladen; **,re'ship·ment** [-mənt] s. **1.** 'Wiederverladung f; **2.** Rückladung f, -fracht f.

re·shuf·fle [,riː'ʃʌfl] **I** v/t. **1.** Spielkarten neu mischen; **2.** bsd. pol. 'umgruppieren, -bilden; **II** s. **3.** pol. 'Umbildung f, 'Umgruppierung f.

re·side [rɪ'zaɪd] v/i. **1.** wohnen, ansässig sein, s-n (ständigen) Wohnsitz haben (**in**, **at** in dat.); **2.** fig. (**in**) a) wohnen (in dat.), b) innewohnen (dat.), c) zustehen (dat.), liegen, ruhen (bei j-m).

res·i·dence ['rezɪdəns] s. **1.** Wohnsitz m, -ort m; Sitz m e-r Behörde etc.: **take up one's** ~ s-n Wohnsitz nehmen od. aufschlagen, sich niederlassen; **2.** Aufenthalt m: ~ **permit** Aufenthaltsgenehmigung f; **place of** ~ Wohn-, Aufenthaltsort m; **3.** (herrschaftliches) Wohnhaus; **4.** Wohnung f: **official** ~ Dienstwohnung f; **5.** Wohnen n; **6.** Ortsansässigkeit f: ~ **is required** es besteht Residenzpflicht; **be in** ~ am Amtsort ansässig sein; **'res·i·dent** [-nt] **I** adj. **1.** (orts-)ansässig, (ständig) wohnhaft; **2.** im (Schul- od. Kranken- etc.)Haus wohnend: ~ **physician**; **3.** fig. innewohnend (**in** dat.); **4.** zo. sesshaft: ~ **birds** Standvögel; **5.** Computer: resident; **II** s. **6.** Ortsansässige(r m) f, Einwohner(in); mot. Anlieger m; **7.** 🔪 Am. Assis'tenzarzt m, -ärztin f; pol. a. **minister-**~ Mi'nisterresi,dent m (Gesandter); **res·i·den·tial** [,rezɪ'denʃl] adj. **1.** a) Wohn...: ~ **allowance** Ortszulage f; ~ **area** (a. vornehme) Wohngegend; ~ **university** Internatsuniversität f, b) herrschaftlich: ~ Wohnsitz...

re·sid·u·al [rɪ'zɪdjʊəl] **I** adj. **1.** 🜂 'rückbleibend, übrig; **2.** übrig (gebleiben), Rest... (a. phys. etc.): ~ **product** 🜂, ⚙ Nebenprodukt n; ~ **soil** geol. Eluvialboden m; **3.** phys. rema'nent: ~ **magnetism**; **II** s. **4.** Rückstand m, Rest m; **5.** 🜂 Rest(wert) m, Diffe'renz f; **re'sid·u·ar·y** [-əri] adj. restlich, übrig (gebleiben): ~ **estate** ⚖ Reinnachlass m; ~ **legatee** Nachvermächtnisnehmer(in); **res·i·due** ['rezɪdjuː] s. **1.** Rest m (a. 🜂, ♥); **2.** Rückstand m; **3.** ⚖ reiner (Erb)Nachlass; **re'sid·u·um** [-jʊəm] pl. **-u·a** [-jʊə] (Lat.) s. **1.** bsd. 🜂 Rückstand m, (a. 🜂) Re'siduum n; **2.** fig. Bodensatz m, Hefe f e-s Volkes etc.

re·sign [rɪˈzaɪn] **I** *v/t.* **1.** *Besitz, Hoffnung etc.* aufgeben; verzichten auf (*acc.*); *Amt* niederlegen; **2.** überˈlassen (***to*** *dat.*); **3.** **~ *o.s.*** sich anvertrauen *od.* überlassen (***to*** *dat.*); **4.** **~ *o.s.*** (***to***) sich ergeben (in *acc.*), sich abfinden *od.* versöhnen (mit *s-m Schicksal etc.*); **II** *v/i.* **5.** (***to*** in *acc.*) sich ergeben, sich fügen; **6.** (***from***) a) zuˈrücktreten (von *e-m Amt*), abdanken, b) austreten (aus); **res·ig·na·tion** [ˌrezɪɡˈneɪʃn] *s.* **1.** Aufgabe *f*, Verzicht *m*; **2.** Rücktritt(sgesuch *n*) *m*, Amtsniederlegung *f*, Abdankung *f*: ***send in*** (*od.* ***tender***) ***one's ~*** s-n Rücktritt einreichen; **3.** Ergebung *f* (***to*** in *acc.*); **reˈsigned** [-nd] *adj.* □ ergeben: ***he is ~ to his fate*** er hat sich mit s-m Schicksal abgefunden.

re·sil·i·ence [rɪˈzɪlɪəns] *s.* Elastiziˈtät *f*: a) *phys.* Prallkraft *f*, b) *fig.* Spannkraft *f*; **reˈsil·i·ent** [-nt] *adj.* eˈlastisch: a) federnd, b) *fig.* spannkräftig, unverwüstlich.

res·in [ˈrezɪn] **I** *s.* **1.** Harz *n*; **2.** → ***rosin*** I; **II** *v/t.* **3.** harzen, mit Harz behandeln; **ˈres·in·ous** [-nəs] *adj.* harzig, Harz...

re·sist [rɪˈzɪst] **I** *v/t.* **1.** widerˈstehen (*dat.*): ***I cannot ~ doing it*** ich muss es einfach tun; **2.** Widerstand leisten (*dat. od.* gegen), sich widerˈsetzen (*dat.*), sich sträuben gegen: ***~ing a public officer in the excecution of his duty*** ⚖ Widerstand *m* gegen die Staatsgewalt; **II** *v/i.* **3.** Widerstand leisten, sich widerˈsetzen; **III** *s.* **4.** ⚙ Deckmittel *n*, Schutzlack *m*; **reˈsist·ance** [-təns] *s.* **1.** Widerstand *m* (***to*** gegen): ***air ~*** *phys.* Luftwiderstand; ***~ movement*** *pol.* Widerstandsbewegung *f*; ***offer ~*** Widerstand leisten (***to*** *dat.*); ***take the line of least ~*** den Weg des geringsten Widerstandes einschlagen; **2.** Widerstandskraft *f* (*a.* ⚕); ⚙ (*Hitze-, Kälte- etc.*)Beständigkeit *f*, (*Biegungs-, Säure-, Stoß- etc.*)Festigkeit *f*: ***~ to wear*** Verschleißfestigkeit *f*; **3.** ⚡ Widerstand *m*; **reˈsist·ant** [-tənt] *adj.* **1.** widerˈstehend, -ˈstrebend; **2.** ⚙ widerstandsfähig (***to*** gegen), beständig; **re·sis·tiv·i·ty** [ˌriːzɪˈstɪvətɪ] *s.* ⚡ speˈzifischer Widerstand; **reˈsis·tor** [-tə] *s.* ⚡ Widerstand *m* (*Bauteil*).

re·sit **I** *s.* [ˈriːsɪt] *ped.* Wiederˈholungsprüfung *f*; **II** *v/t.* [ˌriːˈsɪt] [*irr.* → ***sit***] *Prüfung* wiederˈholen; **III** *v/i.* [ˌriːˈsɪt] [*irr.* → ***sit***] die Prüfung wiederˈholen.

re·sole [ˌriːˈsəʊl] *v/t.* neu besohlen.

res·o·lu·ble [rɪˈzɒljʊbl] *adj.* **1.** ⚗ auflösbar; **2.** *fig.* lösbar.

res·o·lute [ˈrezəluːt] *adj.* □ entschieden, entschlossen, resoˈlut; **ˈres·o·lute·ness** [-nɪs] *s.* Entschlossenheit *f*; resoˈlute Art.

res·o·lu·tion [ˌrezəˈluːʃn] *s.* **1.** Entschlossenheit *f*, Entschiedenheit *f*; **2.** Entschluss *m*: ***good ~s*** gute Vorsätze; **3.** ☤, *parl.* Beschluss(fassung *f*) *m*, Entschließung *f*, Resolutiˈon *f*; **4.** ⚗, ∡, ♪, *phys.*, *opt.* (*a. Metrik*) Auflösung *f* (***into*** in *acc.*); **5.** ⚙ Rasterung *f* (*Bild*); **6.** ⚕ a) Lösung *f e-r Entzündung etc.*, b) Zerteilung *f e-s Tumors*; **7.** *fig.* Lösung *f e-r Frage*; Behebung *f von Zweifeln.*

re·solv·a·ble [rɪˈzɒlvəbl] *adj.* (auf)lösbar (***into*** in *acc.*); **reˈsolve** [rɪˈzɒlv] **I** *v/t.* **1.** *a. opt.*, ⚗, ♪, ∡ auflösen (***into*** in *acc.*): ***be ~d into*** sich auflösen in (*acc.*); ***~d into dust*** in Staub verwandelt; ***resolving power*** *opt.*, *phot.* Auflösungsvermögen *n*; → ***committee***; **2.** analysieren; **3.** *fig.* zuˈrückführen (***into, to*** auf *acc.*); **4.** *fig. Frage etc.* lösen; **5.** *fig. Bedenken, Zweifel* zerstreuen; **6.** a) beschließen, sich entschließen (***to do*** *et.* zu tun), b) entscheiden; **II** *v/i.* **7.** sich auflösen (***into*** in *acc.*, ***to*** zu); **8.** (***on, upon s.th.***) (et.) beschließen, sich entschließen (zu et.); **III** *s.* **9.** Entschluss *m*, Vorsatz *m*; **10.** *Am.* → ***resolution*** 3; **11.** *rhet.* Entschlossenheit *f*; **reˈsolved** [-vd] *p.p. u. adj.* □ (fest) entschlossen.

res·o·nance [ˈrezənəns] *s.* Resoˈnanz *f* (*a.* ♪, ⚕, *phys.*), Nach-, Widerhall *m*, Mitschwingen *n*: ***~ box*** Resonanzkasten *m*; **ˈres·o·nant** [-nt] *adj.* □ **1.** wider-, nachhallend (***with*** von); **2.** volltönend (*Stimme*); **3.** *phys.* mitschwingend, Resonanz...; **ˈres·o·na·tor** [-neɪtə] *s.* **1.** *phys.* Resoˈnator *m*; **2.** ⚡ Resoˈnanzkreis *m*.

re·sorb [rɪˈsɔːb] *v/t.* (wieder) aufsaugen, resorbieren; **reˈsorb·ence** [-bəns], **reˈsorp·tion** [-ɔːpʃn] *s.* Resorptiˈon *f*.

re·sort [rɪˈzɔːt] **I** *s.* **1.** Zuflucht *f* (***to*** zu); Mittel *n*: ***in the*** (*od.* ***as a***) ***last ~*** als letzter Ausweg, ‚wenn alle Stricke reißen'; ***have ~ to*** → 5; ***without ~ to force*** ohne Gewaltanwendung; **2.** Besuch *m*, Zustrom *m*: ***place of ~*** (beliebter) Treffpunkt; **3.** (Aufenthalts-, Erholungs)Ort *m*: ***health ~*** Kurort; ***summer ~*** Sommerurlaubsort; **II** *v/i.* **4.** **~ *to*** a) sich begeben zu *od.* nach, b) *Ort* oft besuchen; **5.** **~ *to*** s-e Zuflucht nehmen zu, zuˈrückgreifen auf (*acc.*), greifen zu, Gebrauch machen von.

re·sound [rɪˈzaʊnd] **I** *v/i.* **1.** widerhallen (***with, to*** von): ***~ing*** schallend; **2.** erschallen, ertönen (*Klang*); **II** *v/t.* **3.** widerhallen lassen.

re·source [rɪˈsɔːs] *s.* **1.** (Hilfs)Quelle *f*, (-)Mittel *n*; **2.** *pl.* a) Mittel *pl.*, Reichtümer *pl. e-s Landes*: ***natural ~s*** Bodenschätze, b) Geldmittel *pl.*, c) ☤ *Am.* Akˈtiva *pl.*; **3.** → ***resort*** 1; **4.** Findig-, Wendigkeit *f*; Taˈlent *n*: ***he is full of ~*** er weiß sich immer zu helfen; **5.** Entspannung *f*, Unterˈhaltung *f*; **reˈsource·ful** [-fʊl] *adj.* □ **1.** reich an Hilfsquellen; **2.** findig, wendig, einfallsreich.

re·spect [rɪˈspekt] **I** *s.* **1.** Rücksicht *f* (***to, of*** auf *acc.*): ***without ~ to persons*** ohne Ansehen der Person; **2.** Hinsicht *f*, Beziehung *f*: ***in every*** (***some***) ***~*** in jeder (gewisser) Hinsicht; ***in ~ of*** (*od.* ***to***), ***with ~ to*** (*od.* ***of***) hinsichtlich (*gen.*), bezüglich (*gen.*), in Anbetracht (*gen.*); ***have ~ to*** sich beziehen auf (*acc.*); **3.** (Hoch)Achtung *f*, Ehrerbietung *f*, Reˈspekt *m* (***for*** vor *dat.*); **4.** ***one's ~s*** *pl.* s-e Empfehlungen *pl. od.* Grüße *pl.* (***to*** an *acc.*): ***give him my ~s*** grüßen Sie ihn von mir; ***pay one's ~s to*** a) *j-n* bestens grüßen, b) *j-m* s-e Aufwartung machen; **II** *v/t.* **5.** sich beziehen auf (*acc.*), betreffen; **6.** (hoch) achten, ehren; **7.** *Gefühle, Gesetze etc.* respektieren, (be)achten; **~ *o.s.*** etwas auf sich halten; **re·spect·a·bil·i·ty** [rɪˌspektəˈbɪlətɪ] *s.* **1.** Ehrbarkeit *f*, Achtbarkeit *f*; **2.** Ansehen *n*; ☤ Solidiˈtät *f*; **3.** a) *pl.* Reˈspektsperˌsonen *pl.*, Honoratiˈoren *pl.*, b) Reˈspektsperˌson *f*; **4.** *pl.* Anstandsregeln *pl.*; **reˈspect·a·ble** [-təbl] *adj.* □ **1.** ansehnlich, (recht) beachtlich; **2.** acht-, ehrbar; anständig, soˈlide; **3.** angesehen, geachtet; **4.** korˈrekt, konventioˈnell; **reˈspect·er** [-tə] *s.*: ***be no ~ of persons*** ohne Ansehen der Person handeln; **reˈspect·ful** [-fʊl] *adj.* □ reˈspektvoll (*a. iro. Entfernung*), ehrerbietig, höflich: ***Yours ~ly*** mit vorzüglicher Hochachtung (*Briefschluss*); **reˈspect·ing** [-tɪŋ] *prp.* bezüglich (*gen.*), hinsichtlich (*gen.*), über (*acc.*); **reˈspec·tive** [-tɪv] *adj.* □ jeweilig (*jedem einzeln zukommend*), verschieden: ***to our ~ places*** *wir gingen* jeder an s-n Platz; **reˈspec·tive·ly** [-tɪvlɪ] *adv.* a) beziehungsweise, b) in dieser Reihenfolge.

res·pi·ra·tion [ˌrespəˈreɪʃn] *s.* Atmung *f*, Atmen *n*, Atemholen *n*: ***artificial ~*** künstliche Beatmung; **res·pi·ra·tor** [ˈrespəreɪtə] *s.* **1.** *Brit.* Gasmaske *f*; **2.** Atemfilter *m*; **3.** ⚕ Atemgerät *n*, ˈSauerstoffappaˌrat *m*; **re·spir·a·to·ry** [rɪˈspaɪərətərɪ] *adj. anat.* Atmungs...

re·spire [rɪˈspaɪə] **I** *v/i.* **1.** atmen; **2.** *fig.* aufatmen; **II** *v/t.* **3.** (ein)atmen; *poet.* atmen.

res·pite [ˈrespaɪt] **I** *s.* **1.** Frist *f*, (Zahlungs)Aufschub *m*, Stundung *f*; **2.** ⚖ a) Aussetzung *f* des Vollˈzugs (*der Todesstrafe*), b) Strafaufschub *m*; **3.** *fig.* (Atem-, Ruhe)Pause *f*; **II** *v/t.* **4.** auf-, verschieben; **5.** *j-m* Aufschub gewähren, e-e Frist einräumen; **6.** ⚖ die Vollˈstreckung des Urteils an *j-m* aufschieben; **7.** Erleichterung von *Schmerz etc.* verschaffen.

re·splend·ence [rɪˈsplendəns], **reˈsplend·en·cy** [-sɪ] *s.* Glanz *m* (*a. fig. Pracht*); **reˈsplend·ent** [-nt] *adj.* □ glänzend, strahlend, prangend.

re·spond [rɪˈspɒnd] *v/i.* **1.** (***to***) antworten (auf *acc.*) (*a. eccl.*), *Brief etc.* beantworten; **2.** *fig.* antworten, erˈwidern (***with*** mit); **3.** *fig.* (***to***) reagieren *od.* ansprechen (auf *acc.*), empfänglich sein (für), eingehen auf (*acc.*): ***~ to a call*** e-m Ruf(e) folgen; **4.** ⚙ ansprechen (*Motor*), gehorchen; **reˈspond·ent** [-dənt] **I** *adj.* **1.** **~ *to*** reagierend auf (*acc.*), empfänglich für; **2.** ⚖ beklagt; **II** *s.* **3.** ⚖ a) (Scheidungs)Beklagte(r *m*) *f*, b) Berufungsbeklagte(r *m*) *f*.

re·sponse [rɪˈspɒns] *s.* **1.** Antwort *f*, Erwiderung *f*: ***in ~ to*** als Antwort auf (*acc.*), in Erwiderung (*gen.*); ***~ mode*** *Computer*: Antwortmodus *m*; **2.** *fig.* a) Reaktiˈon *f* (*a. biol.*, *psych.*), Antwort *f*, b) Widerhall *m* (*alle*: ***to*** auf *acc.*): ***meet with a good ~*** Widerhall *od.* e-e gute Aufnahme finden; ***receive a positive ~*** e-e gute *od.* positive Resonanz finden; **3.** *eccl.* Antwort(strophe) *f*; **4.** ⚙ Ansprechen *n* (*des Motors etc.*).

re·spon·si·bil·i·ty [rɪˌspɒnsəˈbɪlətɪ] *s.* **1.** Verantwortlichkeit *f*; **2.** Verantwortung *f* (***for, of*** für): ***on one's own ~*** auf eigene Verantwortung; **3.** ⚖ a) Zurechnungsfähigkeit *f*, b) Haftbarkeit *f*; **4.** Vertrauenswürdigkeit *f*; ☤ Zahlungsfähigkeit *f*; **5.** *oft pl.* Verbindlichkeit *f*, Verpflichtung *f*; **re·spon·si·ble** [rɪˈspɒnsəbl] *adj.* □ **1.** verantwortlich (***to*** *dat.*, ***for*** für): ***~ partner*** ☤ persönlich haftender Gesellschafter; **2.** ⚖ a) zurechnungsfähig, b) geschäftsfähig, c) haftbar; **3.** verantwortungsbewusst, zuverlässig; ☤ soˈlide, zahlungsfähig; **4.** verantwortungsvoll, verantwortlich (*Stellung*): ***used to ~ work*** an selbstständiges Arbeiten gewöhnt; **5.** (***for***) a) schuld (an *dat.*), verantwortlich (für), b) die Ursache (*gen. od.* von); **reˈspon·sive** [rɪˈspɒnsɪv] *adj.* □ **1.** Antwort..., antwortend (***to*** auf *acc.*); **2.** (***to***) (leicht) reagierend (auf *acc.*), ansprechbar; *weitS.* empfänglich *od.* zugänglich *od.* aufgeschlossen (für): ***be ~ to*** a) ansprechen *od.* reagieren auf (*acc.*), b) eingehen auf (*j-n*), (*e-m Bedürfnis etc.*) entgegenkommen; **3.** ⚙ eˈlastisch (*Motor*).

rest¹ [rest] **I** *s.* **1.** (*a.* Nacht)Ruhe *f*, Rast

R

f; fig. a) Ruhe *f* (*Frieden, Untätigkeit*), b) Ruhepause *f*, Erholung *f*, c) ewige *od.* letzte Ruhe (*Tod*); *phys.* Ruhe(lage *f*): **at ~** in Ruhe, ruhig; **be at ~** a) ruhen (*Toter*), b) beruhigt sein, c) ❂ sich in Ruhelage befinden; **give a ~ to** a) *Maschine etc.* ruhen lassen, b) F *et.* auf sich beruhen lassen; **have a good night's ~** gut schlafen; **lay to ~** zur letzten Ruhe betten; **set s.o.'s mind at ~** j-n beruhigen; **set a matter at ~** e-e Sache (endgültig) entscheiden *od.* erledigen; **take a ~** sich ausruhen; **2.** Ruheplatz *m* (*a. Grab*), Raststätte *f*; Aufenthalt *m*; Herberge *f*, Heim *n*; **3.** ❂ a) Auflage *f*, Stütze *f*, (Arm)Lehne *f*, (Fuß)Raste *f*, *teleph.* Gabel *f*, b) Sup'port *m* e-r Drehbank, c) ✕ (Gewehr)Auflage *f*; **4.** ♪ Pause *f*; **5.** *Metrik*: Zä'sur *f*; **II** *v/i.* **6.** ruhen, schlafen (*a. Toter*); **7.** (sich aus-)ruhen, rasten, e-e (Ruhe)Pause einlegen: **let a matter ~** *fig.* e-e Sache auf sich beruhen lassen; **the matter cannot ~ there** damit kann es nicht sein Bewenden haben; **8.** sich stützen: **~ against** sich stützen *od.* lehnen gegen, ❂ anliegen an (*acc.*); **~ (up)on** a) ruhen auf (*dat.*) (*a. Last, Blick, Schatten etc.*), b) *fig.* beruhen auf (*dat.*), sich stützen auf (*acc.*), c) *fig.* sich verlassen auf (*acc.*); **9. ~ with** bei j-m liegen (*Entscheidung, Schuld*), in j-s Händen liegen, von j-m abhängen, j-m überlassen bleiben; **10.** ⚖ *Am.* → 16; **III** *v/t.* **11.** (aus)ruhen lassen, j-m Ruhe gönnen: **~ o.s.** sich ausruhen; **God ~ his soul** Gott hab ihn selig; **12.** *Augen, Stimme* schonen; **13.** legen, lagern (**on** auf *acc.*); **14.** *Am.* F *Hut etc.* ablegen; **15. ~ one's case** ⚖ *Am.* den Beweisvortrag abschließen.

rest² [rest] **I** *s.* **1.** Rest *m*; (*das*) Übrige, (*die*) Übrigen: **and all the ~ of it** und alles Übrige; **the ~ of us** wir Übrigen; **for the ~** im Übrigen; **2.** ✝ *Brit.* Re'serve‚fonds *m*; **3.** ✝ *Brit.* a) Bilanzierung *f*, b) Restsaldo *m*; **II** *v/i.* **4.** *in e-m Zustand* bleiben, weiterhin sein: **~ assured that** seien Sie versichert *od.* verlassen Sie sich darauf, dass; **5. ~ with → rest¹** 9.

re·state [‚riː'steɪt] *v/t.* neu (u. besser) formulieren; **'re·state·ment** [-mənt] *s.* neue Darstellung *od.* Formulierung.

res·tau·rant ['restərõːŋ] (*Fr.*) *s.* Restau'rant *n*, Gaststätte *f*: **~ car** Speisewagen *m*.

rest| cure ⚕ Liegekur *f*; **~ home** *s.* Alten- *od.* Pflegeheim *n*.

rest·ed ['restɪd] *p.p. u. adj.* ausgeruht, erholt; **rest·ful** ['restfʊl] *adj.* □ **1.** ruhig, friedlich; **2.** erholsam, gemütlich; **3.** bequem, angenehm.

rest house *s.* Rasthaus *n*.

rest·ing place ['restɪŋ] *s.* **1.** Ruheplatz *m*; **2.** (letzte) Ruhestätte, Grab *n*.

res·ti·tu·tion [‚restɪ'tjuːʃn] *s.* **1.** Restituti'on *f*: a) (Zu)'Rückerstattung *f*, b) Entschädigung *f*, c) Wieder'gutmachung *f*, d) Wieder'herstellung *f* von *Rechten etc.*: **make ~** Ersatz leisten (*of* für); **2.** *phys.* (e'lastische) Rückstellung; **3.** *phot.* Entzerrung *f*.

res·tive ['restɪv] *adj.* □ **1.** unruhig, ner'vös; **2.** störrisch, widerspenstig, bockig (*a. Pferd*); **'res·tive·ness** [-nɪs] *s.* **1.** Unruhe *f*, Ungeduld *f*; **2.** Widerspenstigkeit *f*.

rest·less ['restlɪs] *adj.* □ **1.** ruhe-, rastlos; **2.** unruhig; **3.** schlaflos (*Nacht*); **'rest·less·ness** [-nɪs] *s.* **1.** Ruhe-, Rastlosigkeit *f*; **2.** (ner'vöse) Unruhe, Unrast *f*.

re·stock [‚riː'stɒk] **I** *v/t.* **1.** ✝ a) *Lager* wieder auffüllen, b) *Ware* wieder auf Lager nehmen; **2.** *Gewässer* wieder mit Fischen besetzen; **II** *v/i.* **3.** neuen Vorrat einlagern.

res·to·ra·tion [‚restə'reɪʃn] *s.* **1.** Wieder'herstellung *f* (*e-s Zustandes, der Gesundheit etc.*); **2.** Restaurierung *f* e-s *Kunstwerks etc.*; **3.** Rückerstattung *f*, -gabe *f*; **4.** Wieder'einsetzung *f* (**to** in ein *Amt*); **5. the ~** *hist.* die Restaurati'on; **re·stor·a·tive** [rɪ'stɒrətɪv] ⚕ **I** *adj.* □ **1.** stärkend; **2.** Stärkungsmittel *n*; **3.** 'Wiederbelebungsmittel *n*.

re·store [rɪ'stɔː] *v/t.* **1.** *Einrichtung, Gesundheit, Ordnung etc.* wieder'herstellen (*a. Computer: Datei etc.*); **2.** a) *Kunstwerk etc.* restaurieren, b) ❂ in'stand setzen; **3.** *j-n* wieder einsetzen (**to** in *acc.*); **4.** zu'rückerstatten, -bringen, -geben: **~ s.th. to its place** et. an s-n Platz zurückstellen; **~ the receiver** *teleph.* den Hörer auflegen *od.* einhängen; **~ s.o.** (**to health**) j-n gesund machen *od.* wiederherstellen; **~ s.o. to liberty** j-m die Freiheit wiedergeben; **~ s.o. to life** j-n ins Leben zurückrufen; **~ a king** (**to the throne**) e-n König wieder auf den Thron setzen; **re'stor·er** [-ɔːrə] *s.* **1.** Wieder'hersteller (-in); **2.** Restau'rator *m*, Restaura'torin *f*; **3.** Haarwuchsmittel *n*.

re·strain [rɪ'streɪn] *v/t.* **1.** zu'rückhalten: **~ s.o. from doing s.th.** j-n davon abhalten, et. zu tun; **~ing order** ⚖ Unterlassungsurteil *n*; **2.** a) in Schranken halten, Einhalt gebieten (*dat.*), b) *Pferd* im Zaum halten, zügeln (*a. fig.*); **3.** *Gefühl* unter'drücken, bezähmen; **4.** a) einsperren, -schließen, b) *Geisteskranken* in e-r Anstalt 'unterbringen; **5.** *Macht etc.* be-, einschränken; **6.** ✝ *Produktion etc.* drosseln; **re'strained** [-nd] *adj.* □ **1.** zu'rückhaltend, beherrscht, maßvoll; **2.** verhalten, gedämpft; **re'straint** [-nt] *s.* **1.** Einschränkung *f*, Beschränkung(en *pl.*) *f*; Hemmnis *n*, Zwang *m*: **~ of** (*od.* **upon**) **liberty** Beschränkung der Freiheit; **~ of trade** a) Beschränkung des Handels, b) Einschränkung des freien Wettbewerbs, Konkurrenzverbot *n*; **~ clause** Konkurrenzklausel *f*; **call for ~** Maßhalteappell *m*; **without ~** frei, ungehemmt, offen; **2.** ⚖ Freiheitsbeschränkung *f*, Haft *f*: **place s.o. under ~** j-n in Gewahrsam nehmen; **3.** a) Zu'rückhaltung *f*, Beherrschtheit *f*, b) (künstlerische) Zucht.

re·strict [rɪ'strɪkt] *v/t.* a) einschränken, b) beschränken (**to** auf *acc.*): **be ~ed to doing** sich darauf beschränken müssen, et. zu tun; **re'strict·ed** [-tɪd] *adj.* □ eingeschränkt, beschränkt, begrenzt: **~!** nur für den Dienstgebrauch!; **~ area** Sperrgebiet *n*; **~ district** Gebiet *n* mit bestimmten Baubeschränkungen; **re'stric·tion** [-kʃn] *s.* **1.** Ein-, Beschränkung *f* (*of, on gen.*): **~s on imports** Einfuhrbeschränkungen; **~s of space** räumliche Beschränktheit; **without ~s** uneingeschränkt; **2.** Vorbehalt *m*; **re'stric·tive** [-tɪv] *adj.* □ be-, einschränkend (*of acc.*): **~ clause** a) *ling.* einschränkender Relativsatz, b) ✝ einschränkende Bestimmung; **~ practices** wettbewerbsbeschränkende Praktiken; **II** *s. ling.* Einschränkung *f*.

rest room *s. Am.* Toi'lette *f* (*Hotel etc.*).

re·struc·ture [‚riː'strʌktʃə] *v/t.* 'umstrukturieren.

re·sult [rɪ'zʌlt] **I** *s.* **1.** *a.* ♣ Ergebnis *n*, Resul'tat *n*; (*a. guter*) Erfolg: **without**

~ ergebnislos; 2. Folge *f*, Aus-, Nachwirkung *f*: **as a ~** die Folge war, dass, b) folglich: **get ~s** Erfolge erzielen, et. erreichen; **II** *v/i.* **3.** sich ergeben, resultieren (**from** aus): **~ in** hinauslaufen auf (*acc.*), zur Folge haben (*acc.*), enden mit (*dat.*); **re'sult·ant** [-tənt] **I** *adj.* **1.** sich ergebend, (dabei *od.* daraus) entstehend, resultierend (**from** aus); **II** *s.* **2.** *phys.*, ♣ Resul'tante *f*; **3.** (End)Ergebnis *n*.

re·sume [rɪ'zjuːm] *v/t.* **1.** *Tätigkeit etc.* wieder aufnehmen, wieder anfangen; fortsetzen: **he ~d painting** er begann wieder zu malen, er malte wieder; **2.** 'wiedererlangen; *Platz* wieder einnehmen; *Amt, Kommando* wieder über'nehmen; *Namen* wieder annehmen; **3.** resümieren, zs.-fassen; **II** *v/i.* **4.** s-e Tätigkeit wieder aufnehmen; **5.** *in s-r Rede* fortfahren, wieder beginnen.

ré·su·mé ['rezjuːmeɪ] (*Fr.*) *s.* **1.** Resü'mee *n*, Zs.-fassung *f*; **2.** *bsd. Am.* Lebenslauf *m*.

re·sump·tion [rɪ'zʌmpʃn] *s.* **1.** a) Zu'rücknahme *f*, b) ⚖ Li'zenzentzug *m*; **2.** Wieder'aufnahme *f* e-r *Tätigkeit, von Zahlungen etc.*

re·sur·gence [rɪ'sɜːdʒəns] *s.* Wieder'vorkommen *n*, Wieder'aufleben *n*, -'aufstieg *m*, 'Wiedererweckung *f*; **re'sur·gent** [-nt] *adj.* wieder auflebend, wieder erwachend.

res·ur·rect [‚rezə'rekt] *v/t.* **1.** F wieder zum Leben erwecken; **2.** *fig. Sitte* wieder aufleben lassen; **3.** *Leiche* ausgraben; **‚res·ur'rec·tion** [-kʃn] *s.* **1.** (*eccl.* ♀) Auferstehung *f*; **2.** *fig.* Wieder'aufleben *n*, 'Wiedererwachen *n*; **3.** Leichenraub *m*.

re·sus·ci·tate [rɪ'sʌsɪteɪt] **I** *v/t.* **1.** wieder beleben; **2.** *fig.* wieder erwecken, wieder aufleben lassen; **II** *v/i.* **3.** das Bewusstsein 'wiedererlangen; **4.** wieder aufleben; **re·sus·ci·ta·tion** [rɪ‚sʌsɪ'teɪʃn] *s.* **1.** 'Wiederbelebung *f* (*a. fig. Erneuerung*); **2.** Auferstehung *f*.

ret [ret] **I** *v/t. Flachs etc.* rösten, rötten; **II** *v/i.* verfaulen (*Heu*).

re·tail ['riːteɪl] **I** *s.* Einzel-, Kleinhandel *m*, Kleinverkauf *m*, De'tailgeschäft *n*: **by** (*Am.* **at**) **~** → III; **II** *adj.* Einzel-, Kleinhandels...: **~ bookseller** Sortimentsbuchhändler *m*; **~ dealer** Einzelhändler *m*; **~ price** Einzelhandels-, Ladenpreis *m*; **~ price maintenance** Preisbindung *f*; **~ trade** → I; **III** *adv.* im Einzelhandel, einzeln, en de'tail: **sell ~**; **IV** *v/t.* [riː'teɪl] a) *Waren* im Kleinen *od.* en de'tail verkaufen, b) *Klatsch* weitergeben, (haarklein) weitererzählen; **V** *v/i.* [riː'teɪl] im Einzelhandel verkauft werden (**at** zu 6 Dollar *etc.*); **re·tail·er** [riː'teɪlə] *s.* **1.** ✝ Einzel-, Kleinhändler (-in); **2.** Erzähler(in), Verbreiter(in) von Klatsch *etc.*

re·tain [rɪ'teɪn] *v/t.* **1.** zu'rück(be)halten, einbehalten; **2.** *Eigenschaft, Posten etc., a. im Gedächtnis* behalten; **3.** *Brauch* beibehalten; **4.** j-n in s-n Diensten halten: **~ a lawyer** e-n Anwalt nehmen; **~ing fee** → **retainer** 2 a; **5.** ❂ halten, sichern, stützen; *Wasser* stauen: **~ing nut** Befestigungsmutter *f*; **~ing ring** Sprengring *m*; **~ing wall** Stütz-, Staumauer *f*; **re·tain·er** [-nə] *s.* **1.** *hist.* Gefolgsmann *m*: **old ~** F altes Faktotum; **2.** ⚖ a) Verpflichtung *f* e-s Anwalts, b) Hono'rarvorschuss *m*: **general ~** Pauschalhonorar *n*, c) Pro'zessvollmacht *f*; **3.** ❂ a) Befestigungsteil *n*, b) Käfig *m* e-s Kugellagers.

re·take [ˌriːˈteɪk] **I** v/t. [irr. → **take**] **1.** wieder (an-, ein-, zuˈrück)nehmen; **2.** ✕ wieder einnehmen; **3.** Film: Szene etc. wiederˈholen, nochmals (ab)drehen; **II** s. [ˈriːteɪk] **4.** Film: Reˈtake n, Wiederˈholung f.

re·tal·i·ate [rɪˈtælɪeɪt] **I** v/i. Vergeltung üben, sich rächen (**upon** s.o. an j-m); **II** v/t. vergelten, sich rächen für, heimzahlen; **re·tal·i·a·tion** [rɪˌtælɪˈeɪʃn] s. Vergeltung f; **in** ~ als Vergeltung(smaßnahme); **re·tal·i·a·to·ry** [-ɪətərɪ] adj. Vergeltungs...: ~ **duty** ✝ Kampfzoll m.

re·tard [rɪˈtɑːd] v/t. **1.** verzögern, -langsamen, aufhalten; **2.** phys. retardieren, verzögern; Elektronen bremsen: be ~ed nacheilen; **3.** biol. retardieren; **4.** psych. j-s. Entwicklung hemmen: ~ed **child** zurückgebliebenes Kind; **mentally** ~ed geistig zurückgeblieben; **5.** mot. Zündung nachstellen: ~ed **ignition** a) Spätzündung f, b) verzögerte Zündung; **re·tar·da·tion** [ˌriːtɑːˈdeɪʃn] s. **1.** Verzögerung f (a. phys.), -langsamung f, -spätung f; Aufschub m; **2.** ✏, phys., biol. Retardatiˈon f; phys. (Elektronen-)Bremsung f; **3.** psych. a) Entwicklungshemmung f, b) ˈUnterentwickeltheit f; **4.** ♪ a) Verlangsamung f, b) aufwärts gehender Vorhalt.

retch [retʃ] v/i. würgen (beim Erbrechen).

re·tell [ˌriːˈtel] v/t. [irr. → **tell**] **1.** nochmals erzählen od. sagen, wiederˈholen; **2.** ped. nacherzählen.

re·ten·tion [rɪˈtenʃn] s. **1.** Zuˈrückhalten n; **2.** Einbehaltung f; **3.** Beibehaltung f (a. von Bräuchen etc.), Bewahrung f; **4.** ⚕ Verhalten n; **5.** Festhalten n, Halt m: ~ **pin** ✪ Arretierstift m; **6.** Merken n, Merkfähigkeit f; **re·ten·tive** [-ntɪv] adj. □ **1.** (zuˈrück)haltend (of acc.); **2.** erhaltend, bewahrend; gut (Gedächtnis); **3.** Wasser speichernd.

re·think [ˌriːˈθɪŋk] v/t. [irr. → **think**] et. nochmals überˈdenken; **re·think·ing** [-kɪŋ] s. ˈUmdenken n.

ret·i·cence [ˈretɪsəns] s. **1.** Verschwiegenheit f, Schweigsamkeit f; **2.** Zuˈrückhaltung f; **ret·i·cent** [-nt] adj. □ verschwiegen (about, on über acc.), schweigsam; zuˈrückhaltend.

ret·i·cle [ˈretɪkl] s. opt. Fadenkreuz n.

re·tic·u·lar [rɪˈtɪkjʊlə] adj. □ netzartig, -förmig, Netz...; **re·tic·u·late I** adj. □ [-lət] netzartig, -förmig; **II** v/t. [-leɪt] netzförmig mustern od. bedecken; **III** v/i. [-leɪt] sich verästeln; **re·tic·u·lat·ed** [-leɪtɪd] adj. netzförmig, maschig, Netz...: ~ **glass** Filigranglas n; **re·tic·u·la·tion** [rɪˌtɪkjʊˈleɪʃn] s. Netzwerk n; **ret·i·cule** [ˈretɪkjuːl] s. **1.** → reticle; **2.** Damentasche f; Arbeitsbeutel m; **re·ti·form** [ˈriːtɪfɔːm] adj. netz-, gitterförmig.

ret·i·na [ˈretɪnə] s. anat. Retina f, Netzhaut f.

ret·i·nue [ˈretɪnjuː] s. Gefolge n.

re·tire [rɪˈtaɪə] **I** v/i. **1.** allg. sich zuˈrückziehen (a. ✕): ~ (**from** business) a. sich zur Ruhe setzen; ~ **into** o.s. sich verschließen; ~ (**to rest**) sich zur Ruhe begeben, schlafen gehen; **2.** ab-, zuˈrücktreten; in den Ruhestand treten, in Pensiˈon od. Rente gehen, s-n Abschied nehmen (Beamter); **3.** fig. zuˈrücktreten (Hintergrund, Ufer etc.); **II** v/t. **4.** zuˈrückziehen (a. ✕); **5.** ✝ Noten aus dem Verkehr ziehen; Wechsel einlösen; **6.** bsd. ✕ verabschieden, pensionieren; → **retired** 1; **re·tired** [-əd] p.p. u. adj. □ **1.** pensioniert, im Ruhestand (lebend): ~ **general** Gene-

ral m a.D. od. außer Dienst; ~ **pay** Ruhegeld n, Pension f; **be placed on the** ~ **list** ✕ den Abschied erhalten; **2.** im Ruhestand (lebend); **3.** zuˈrückgezogen (Leben); **4.** abgelegen, einsam (Ort): **re·tire·ment** [-mənt] s. **1.** (Sich-) Zuˈrückziehen n; **2.** Aus-, Rücktritt m, Ausscheiden n; **3.** Ruhestand m: **early** ~ vorzeitiger Ruhestand; ~ **pension** (Alters)Rente f, Ruhegeld n; ~ **sioner** (Alters)Rentner(in), Ruhegeldempfänger(in); **go into** ~ sich ins Privatleben zurückziehen; **4.** j-s Zuˈrückgezogenheit f; **5.** a) Abgeschiedenheit f, b) abgelegener Ort, Zuflucht f; **6.** ✕ (planmäßige) Absetzbewegung, Rückzug m; **7.** ✝ Einziehung f; **re·tir·ing** [-ərɪŋ] adj. □ **1.** Ruhestands...: ~ **age** Renten-, Pensionsalter n; ~ **pension** Ruhegeld n; **2.** fig. zuˈrückhaltend, bescheiden; **3.** unauffällig, deˈzent (Farbe etc.); **4.** ~ **room** a) Privatzimmer n, b) Toilette f.

re·tool [ˌriːˈtuːl] v/t. Fabrik mit neuen Maˈschinen ausrüsten.

re·tort¹ [rɪˈtɔːt] **I** s. **1.** (scharfe od. treffende) Entgegnung, (schlagfertige) Antwort; Erwiderung f; **II** v/t. **2.** (darauf) erwidern; **3.** Beleidigung etc. zuˈrückgeben (on s.o. j-m); **III** v/i. **4.** (scharf od. treffend) erwidern, entgegnen.

re·tort² [rɪˈtɔːt] s. ⚗, ✪ Reˈtorte f.

re·tor·tion [rɪˈtɔːʃn] s. **1.** (Sich-)ˈUmwenden n, Zuˈrückströmen n, -biegen n, -beugen n; **2.** Völkerrecht: Retorsiˈon f (Vergeltungsmaßnahme).

re·touch [ˌriːˈtʌtʃ] **I** v/t. et. überˈarbeiten; phot. retuschieren; **II** s. Reˈtusche f.

re·trace [rɪˈtreɪs] **I** v/t. (a. fig. Stammbaum etc.) zuˈrückverfolgen; fig. zuˈrückführen (to auf acc.): ~ **one's steps** a) (denselben Weg) zurückgehen, b) fig. die Sache ungeschehen machen; **II** s. ⚡ Rücklauf m.

re·tract [rɪˈtrækt] **I** v/t. **1.** Behauptung zuˈrücknehmen, (a. ⚖ Aussage) widerˈrufen; **2.** Haut, Zunge etc., a. ⚖ Anklage zuˈrückziehen; **3.** zo. Klauen etc., a. ✈ Fahrgestell einziehen; **II** v/i. **4.** sich zurückziehen; **5.** widerrufen, es zurücknehmen; **6.** zuˈrücktreten (from von e-m Entschluss, e-m Vertrag etc.); **re·tract·a·ble** [-təbl] adj. **1.** einziehbar: ~ **landing gear** ✈ einziehbares Fahrgestell; ~ **clothes line** ausziehbare Wäscheleine (z. B. über Badewanne); **2.** zuˈrückziehbar; **3.** zuˈrücknehmbar, zu widerˈrufen(d); **re·trac·ta·tion** [ˌriːtrækˈteɪʃn] → retraction 1; **re·trac·tile** [-taɪl] adj. **1.** einziehbar; **2.** a. anat. zuˈrückziehbar; **re·trac·tion** [-kʃn] s. **1.** Zuˈrücknahme f, Widerruf m; **2.** Zuˈrück-, Einziehen n; **3.** ⚕, zo. Retraktiˈon f; **re·trac·tor** [-tə] s. **1.** anat. Retraktiˈonsmuskel m; **2.** ⚖ Reˈtraktor m, Wundhaken m.

re·train [ˌriːˈtreɪn] v/t. j-n ˈumschulen; **re·train·ing** [-nɪŋ] s. a. occupational ˈUmschulung(skurs m) f.

re·trans·late [ˌriːtrænsˈleɪt] v/t. (zu-)ˈrücküber,setzen; **re·trans·la·tion** [-eɪʃn] s. ˈRücküber,setzung f.

re·tread [ˌriːˈtred] **I** v/t. ✪ Reifen runderneuern; **II** [ˈriːtred] s. runderneuerter Reifen.

re·treat [rɪˈtriːt] **I** s. **1.** bsd. ✕ Rückzug m: **beat a** ~ fig. das Feld räumen, klein beigeben; **sound the** (od. **a**) ~ zum Rückzug blasen; **there was no** ~ es gab kein Zurück; **2.** Zufluchtsort m, Schlupfwinkel m; **3.** Anstalt f für Geisteskranke etc.; **4.** Zuˈrückgezogenheit

f, Abgeschiedenheit f; **5.** ✕ Zapfenstreich m; **II** v/i. **6.** a. ✕ sich zuˈrückziehen; **7.** zuˈrücktreten, -weichen (z. B. Meer): ~ing **chin** fliehendes Kinn; **III** v/t. **8.** bsd. Schachfigur zuˈrückziehen.

re·treat [ˌriːˈtriːt] v/t. allg. erneut behandeln.

re·trench [rɪˈtrentʃ] **I** v/t. **1.** Ausgaben etc. einschränken, a. Personal abbauen; **2.** beschneiden, kürzen; **3.** a) Textstelle streichen, b) Buch zs.-streichen; **4.** Festungswerk mit inneren Verschanzungen versehen; **II** v/i. **5.** sich einschränken, Sparmaßnahmen ˈdurchführen, sparen; **re·trench·ment** [-mənt] s. **1.** Einschränkung f, (Kosten-, Personal-) Abbau m; Sparmaßnahme f; (Gehalts-) Kürzung f; **2.** Streichung f, Kürzung f; **3.** ✕ Verschanzung f, innere Verteidigungsstellung.

re·tri·al [ˌriːˈtraɪəl] s. **1.** nochmalige Prüfung; **2.** ⚖ Wiederˈaufnahmeverfahren n.

ret·ri·bu·tion [ˌretrɪˈbjuːʃn] s. Vergeltung f, Strafe f; **re·trib·u·tive** [rɪˈtrɪbjʊtɪv] adj. □ vergeltend, Vergeltungs...

re·triev·a·ble [rɪˈtriːvəbl] adj. □ **1.** ˈwiederzugewinnen(d); **2.** wieder gutzumachen(d), wettzumachen(d); **re·trieve** [rɪˈtriːv] **I** v/t. **1.** hunt. apportieren; **2.** wieder finden, wiederbekommen; **3.** (sich et.) zuˈrückholen; **4.** et. herˈausholen, -fischen (from aus); **5.** fig. ˈwiedergewinnen, -erlangen; Fehler wieder gutmachen; Verlust wettmachen; **6.** j-n retten (from aus); **7.** et. der Vergessenheit entreißen; **II** s. **8.** beyond (od. past) ~ unwiederbringlich dahin; **re·triev·er** [-və] s. hunt. Reˈtriever m, allg. Apportierhund m.

ret·ro- [retrəʊ] in Zssgn zurück..., rück(-wärts)..., Rück..., entgegengesetzt; hinter...; **ret·ro·ac·tive** adj. □ **1.** ⚖ rückwirkend; zuˈrückwirkend; **ret·ro·ces·sion** s. **1.** a) ✈ Zuˈrückgehen n, b) ⚕ Nachˈinnenschlagen n; **2.** ⚖ ˈWieder-, Rückabtretung f; **ret·ro·fit I** s. **1.** nachträglich ausstatten (with mit), nachrüsten, ˈumrüsten; **2.** Gebäude etc. modernisieren; **II** s. **3.** Nachrüstung f, ˈUmrüstung f; **4.** Modernisierung f; **ret·ro·gra·da·tion** s. **1.** → retrogression 1; **2.** Zuˈrückgehen n; **3.** fig. Rück-, Niedergang m; **ret·ro·grade** [ˈretrəʊgreɪd] **I** adj. **1.** ✈, ♪, ast., zo. rückläufig; **2.** fig. rückgängig, -läufig, Rückwärts..., rückschrittlich; **II** v/i. **3.** a) rückläufig sein, b) zuˈrückgehen; **4.** rückwärts gehen; **5.** bsd. biol. entarten.

ret·ro·gres·sion [ˌretrəʊˈɡreʃn] s. **1.** ast. rückläufige Bewegung; **2.** bsd. biol. Rückentwicklung f; **3.** fig. Rückgang m, -schritt m; **ret·ro·gres·sive** [-esɪv] adj. □ **1.** bsd. biol. rückschreitend: ~ **metamorphosis** biol. Rückbildung f; **2.** fig. rückschrittlich; **3.** fig. nieder-, zuˈrückgehend; **ret·ro·rock·et** [ˈretrəʊ,rɒkɪt] s. ˈBremsra,kete f; **ret·ro·spect** [ˈretrəʊspekt] s. Rückblick m, -schau f (of, on auf acc.): **in** (**the**) ~ rückschauend, im Rückblick; **ret·ro·spec·tion** [ˌretrəʊˈspekʃn] s. Erinnerung f; Zuˈrückblicken n; **ret·ro·spec·tive** [ˌretrəʊˈspektɪv] adj. □ **1.** zuˈrückblickend; **2.** nach rückwärts od. hinten (gerichtet); **3.** ⚖ rückwirkend.

ret·rous·sé [rəˈtruːseɪ] (Fr.) adj. nach oben gebogen: ~ **nose** Stupsnase f.

re·try [ˌriːˈtraɪ] v/t. ⚖ a) Prozess wieder aufnehmen, b) neu verhandeln gegen j-n.

R

re·turn [rɪ'tɜːn] **I** v/i. **1.** zu'rückkehren, -kommen (**to** zu); 'wiederkehren (a. fig.); fig. wieder auftreten (*Krankheit etc.*): **~ to** fig. a) auf *ein Thema* zurückkommen, b) zu *e-m Vorhaben* zurückkommen, c) in *e-e Gewohnheit etc.* zurückfallen, d) in *e-n Zustand* zurückkehren; **~ to dust** zu Staub werden; **~ to health** wieder gesund werden; **2.** zu'rückfallen (*Besitz*) (**to** an *acc.*); **3.** erwidern, antworten; **II** v/t. **4.** *Gruß etc.*, *a. Besuch*, ✕ *Feuer*, *Liebe*, *Schlag etc.* erwidern: **~ thanks** danken; **5.** zu'rückgeben, *Geld a.* zu'rückzahlen, -erstatten; **6.** zu'rückschicken, -senden; **~ed empties** ✝ zurückgesandtes Leergut; **~ed letter** unzustellbarer Brief; **7.** (an s-n Platz) zu'rückstellen, -tun; **8.** (ein-)bringen, *Gewinn* abwerfen, *Zinsen* tragen; **9.** *Bericht* erstatten; ⚖ a) 'Voll'zugsbericht erstatten über (*acc.*), b) *Gerichtsbefehl* mit 'Vollzugsbericht rückvorlegen; **10.** ⚖ *Schuldspruch* fällen *od.* aussprechen: **be ~ed guilty** schuldig gesprochen werden; **11.** *Votum* abgeben; **12.** amtlich erklären für *od.* als, *j-n arbeitsunfähig etc.* schreiben; **13.** *Einkommen* zur Steuerveranlagung erklären, angeben (**at** mit); **14.** *amtliche Liste etc.* vorlegen *od.* veröffentlichen; **15.** *parl. Brit. Wahlergebnis* melden; **16.** *parl. Brit.* als Abgeordneten wählen (**to Parliament** ins Parlament); **17.** *sport Ball* zu'rückschlagen; **18.** *Echo, Strahlen* zu'rückwerfen; **19.** ⊚ zu'rückführen, -leiten; **III** s. **20.** Rückkehr f, -kunft f; 'Wiederkehr f (a. fig.): **~ of health** Genesung f; **by ~ of post** *Brit.*, **by ~ mail** *Am.* postwendend, umgehend; **many happy ~s of the day!** herzlichen Glückwunsch zum Geburtstag!; **on my ~** bei m-r Rückkehr; **21.** Wieder'auftreten n (*Krankheit etc.*): **~ of influenza** Gripperückfall m; **~ of cold weather** Kälterückfall m; **22.** ✝ Rückfahrkarte f; **23.** Rück-, Her'ausgabe f: **on sale or ~** ✝ in Kommission; **24.** oft pl. ✝ Rücksendung f (a. Ware): **~s** a) Rückgut, b) Buchhandel: **~ copies** Remittenden; **25.** ✝ Rückzahlung f, (-)Erstattung f; *Versicherung*: **~ (of premium)** Ristorno n; **26.** Entgelt n, Gegenleistung f, Entschädigung f: **in ~** dafür, dagegen; **in ~ for** (als Gegenleistung) für; **without ~** unentgeltlich; **27.** oft pl. ✝ a) (*Kapitaletc.*)'Umsatz m: **quick ~s** schneller Umsatz, b) Ertrag m, Einnahme f, Verzinsung f, Gewinn m: **yield** (*od.* **bring**) **a ~** Nutzen abwerfen, sich rentieren; **28.** Erwiderung f (a. fig. e-s Grußes etc.): **~ of affection** Gegenliebe f; **29.** (amtlicher) Bericht, (sta'tistischer) Ausweis, Aufstellung f; *pol. Brit.* Wahlbericht m, -ergebnis n: **annual ~** Jahresbericht m, -ausweis m; **bank ~** Bankausweis m; **official ~s** amtliche Ziffern; **30.** Steuererklärung f; **31.** ⚖ a) Rückvorlage f (*e-s Vollstreckungsbefehls etc.*) (mit Voll'zugsbericht), b) Voll'zugsbericht m (*des Gerichtsvollziehers etc.*); **32.** a. **~ day** ⚖ Ver'handlungster,min m; **33.** ⊚ a) Rückführung f, -leitung f, b) Rücklauf m, c) ⚡ Rückleitung f, d) *Computer*: Re'turn m (*Betätigen der Rückführtaste*); **34.** Biegung f, Krümmung f; **35.** △ a) 'Wieder'kehr f, b) vorspringender od. zu'rückgesetzter Teil, c) (Seiten)Flügel m; **36.** *Tennis*: Re'turn m, Rückschlag m (a. Ball); **37.** *sport a.* **~ match** Rückspiel n; **38.** (leichter) Feinschnitt (*Tabak*); **IV** adj. **39.** Rück...(-*porto*, -*reise*, -*spiel*

etc.): **~ cable** ⚡ Rückleitung f; **~ cargo** Rückfracht f, -ladung f; **~ current** ⚡ Rück-, Erdstrom m; **~ ticket** a) Rückfahrkarte f, b) ✈ Rückflugkarte f; **~ valve** ⊚ Rückschlagventil n; **~ visit** Gegenbesuch m; **~ wire** ⚡ Nullleiter m; **re'turn·a·ble** [-nəbl] adj. **1.** zu'rückzugeben(d); einzusenden(d): **~ bottle** Mehrwegflasche f; **2.** ✝ rückzahlbar.

re·turn·ing of·fi·cer [rɪ'tɜːnɪŋ] s. pol. Brit. 'Wahlkommis,sar m.

re'turn key s. Computer: **1.** Eingabetaste f; **2.** Rückführtaste f.

re·u·ni·fi·ca·tion [ˌriːˌjuːnɪfɪ'keɪʃn] s. pol. 'Wiedervereinigung f.

re·un·ion [ˌriː'juːnjən] s. **1.** 'Wiedervereinigung f; fig. Versöhnung f; **2.** (Familien-, Klassen- etc.)Treffen n, Zs.-kunft f.

re·u·nite [ˌriːjuː'naɪt] **I** v/t. wieder vereinigen; **II** v/i. sich wieder vereinigen.

re·us·a·ble [ˌriː'juːzəbl] adj. wieder verwendbar od. verwertbar: **~ package** Mehrwegverpackung f.

rev [rev] mot. F **I** s. Umdrehung f: **~s per minute** Dreh-, Tourenzahl f; **II** v/t. mst **~ up** auf Touren bringen; **III** v/i. laufen, auf Touren sein (*Motor*): **~ up** a) auf Touren kommen, b) den Motor ,hochjagen' od. auf Touren bringen.

re·vac·ci·nate [ˌriː'væksɪneɪt] v/t. ⚕ wieder impfen, nachimpfen.

re·val·or·i·za·tion [ˈriːˌvælɔraɪ'zeɪʃn] s. ✝ Aufwertung f; **re·val·or·ize** [ˌriː'vælɔraɪz] v/t. aufwerten.

re·val·u·ate [ˌriː'væljʊeɪt] v/t. ✝ **1.** neu bewerten; **2.** aufwerten; **re·val·u·a·tion** [ˈriːˌvæljʊ'eɪʃn] s. **1.** Neubewertung f; **2.** Aufwertung f.

re·val·ue [ˌriː'væljuː] → **revaluate**.

re·vamp [ˌriː'væmp] v/t. F ,aufpolieren'.

re·vanch·ist [rɪ'væntʃɪst] **I** adj. revan'chistisch; **II** s. Revan'chist m.

re·veal [rɪ'viːl] **I** v/t. (**to**) **1.** eccl., a. fig. offenbaren (dat.); **2.** enthüllen, zeigen (dat.) (a. fig. erkennen lassen), sehen lassen; **3.** fig. Geheimnis etc. enthüllen, verraten, aufdecken; **II** s. **4.** ⊚ a) innere Laibung (Tür etc.), b) Fensterrahmen m (Auto); **re'veal·ing** [-lɪŋ] adj. **1.** enthüllend, aufschlussreich; **2.** ,offenherzig' (Kleid).

rev·eil·le [rɪ'vælɪ] s. ✕ (Si'gnal n zum) Wecken n.

rev·el ['revl] **I** v/i. **1.** (lärmend) feiern, ausgelassen sein; **2.** (**in**) fig. a) schwelgen (in dat.), b) in vollen Zügen genießen, b) sich weiden od. ergötzen (**in** an dat.); **II** s. **3.** oft pl. → **revelry**.

rev·e·la·tion [ˌrevə'leɪʃn] s. **1.** Enthüllung f, Offen'barung f: **it was a ~ to me** es fiel mir wie Schuppen von den Augen; **what a ~!** welch überraschende Entdeckung!, ach so ist das!; **2.** (göttliche) Offen'barung: **the ~** (**of St. John**) bibl. die (Geheime) Offenbarung (des Johannes); **3.** F ,Offen'barung' f (et. Ausgezeichnetes).

rev·el·(l)er ['revlə] s. **1.** Feiernde(r m) f; **2.** Zecher m; **3.** Nachtschwärmer m; **'rev·el·ry** [-lrɪ] s. lärmende Festlichkeit, Rummel m, Trubel m.

re·venge [rɪ'vendʒ] **I** v/t. et., a. j-n rächen ([**up**]**on** dat.): **~ o.s. for s.th.** sich für et. rächen; **be ~d** a) gerächt sein od. werden, b) sich rächen; **2.** sich rächen für, vergelten (**upon**, **on** an dat.); **II** s. **3.** Rache f: **take one's ~** Rache nehmen, sich rächen; **in ~ for it** dafür; **4.** Re'vanche f (beim Spiel): **have one's ~** sich revanchieren; **5.** Rachsucht f, -gier f; **re'venge·ful** [-fʊl] adj. □ rachsüchtig; **re'venge·ful·ness**

[-fʊlnɪs] → **revenge** 5.

rev·e·nue ['revənjuː] s. **1.** a. **public ~** öffentliche Einnahmen pl., Staatseinkünfte pl.; **2.** a) Fi'nanzverwaltung f, b) Fiskus m: **defraud the ~** Steuern hinterziehen; **~ board** → **revenue office**; **3.** pl. Einnahmen pl., Einkünfte pl.; **4.** Ertrag m, Nutzung f; **5.** Einkommensquelle f; **~ cut·ter** s. ⚓ Zollkutter m; **~ of·fice** s. Fi'nanzamt n; **~ of·fi·cer** s. Zollbeamte(r) m; Fi'nanzbeamte(r) m; **~ stamp** s. ✝ Bande'role f, Steuermarke f.

re·ver·ber·ate [rɪ'vɜːbəreɪt] phys. **I** v/i. **1.** zu'rückstrahlen; **2.** (nach-, wider-)hallen; **II** v/t. **3.** Strahlen, Hitze, Klang zu'rückwerfen; von e-m Klange widerhallen; **re·ver·ber·a·tion** [rɪˌvɜːbə'reɪʃn] s. **1.** Zu'rückwerfen n, -strahlen n; **2.** Widerhall(en n) m; Nachhall m; **re'ver·ber·a·tor** [-tə] s. ⊚ **1.** Re'flektor m; **2.** Scheinwerfer m.

re·vere [rɪ'vɪə] v/t. (ver)ehren.

rev·er·ence ['revərəns] **I** s. **1.** Verehrung f (**for** für od. gen.); **2.** Ehrfurcht f (**for** vor dat.); **3.** Ehrerbietung f; **4.** Reve'renz f (Verbeugung od. Knicks); **5.** dial. od. humor. **Your** (**His**) **~** Euer (Seine) Ehrwürden; **II** v/t. **6.** (ver)ehren; **'rev·er·end** [-nd] **I** adj. **1.** ehrwürdig; **2.** ♄ eccl. hochwürdig (Geistlicher): **Very ♄** (im Titel e-s Dekans); **Right ♄** (Bischof); **Most ♄** (Erzbischof): ♄ **Mother** Mutter Oberin f; **II** s. **3.** Geistliche(r) m; **'rev·er·ent** [-nt] adj. □, **rev·er·en·tial** [ˌrevə'renʃl] adj. □ ehrerbietig, ehrfurchtsvoll.

rev·er·ie ['revərɪ] s. Träume'rei f (a. ♪): **be lost in** (a) **~** in Träumen versunken sein.

re·ver·sal [rɪ'vɜːsl] s. **1.** 'Umkehr(ung) f, 'Umschwung m, -schlagen m: **~ film** phot. Umkehrfilm m; **~ of opinion** Meinungsumschwung; **~ process** phot. Umkehrentwicklung f; **2.** ⚖ (Urteils)Aufhebung f, 'Umstoßung f; **3.** ⊚ 'Umsteuerung f; **4.** ⚡ ('Strom),Umkehr f; **5.** ✝ Stornierung f; **re'verse** [rɪ'vɜːs] **I** s. **1.** Gegenteil n, das 'Umgekehrte; **2.** Rückschlag m (a. fig. of fortune Schicksalsschlag m; **3.** ✕ Niederlage f, Schlappe f; **4.** Rückseite f, bsd. fig. Kehrseite f: **~ of a coin** Rückseite od. Revers m e-r Münze; **~ of the medal** fig. Kehrseite der Medaille; **on the ~** umstehend; **take in ~** ✕ im Rücken packen; **5.** mot. Rückwärtsgang m; **6.** ⊚ 'Umsteuerung f; **II** adj. □ **7.** 'umgekehrt, verkehrt, entgegengesetzt (**to** dat.): **~-charge call** teleph. R-Gespräch n; **~ current** ⚡ Gegenstrom m; **~ flying** ✈ Rückenflug m; **~ order** umgekehrte Reihenfolge; **~ side** a) Rückseite f, b) linke (Stoff)Seite; **8.** rückläufig, rückwärts ...: **~ gear** → 5; **III** v/t. **9.** 'umkehren (a. ✕, ♄), 'umdrehen; fig. Politik (ganz) 'umstellen; Meinung völlig ändern: **~ the charge(s)** teleph. ein R-Gespräch führen; **~ the order of things** die Weltordnung auf den Kopf stellen; **10.** ⚖ Urteil aufheben, 'umstoßen; **11.** ✝ stornieren; **12.** ⊚ im Rückwärtsgang od. rückwärts laufen (lassen); **13.** ⚡ a) 'umpolen, b) 'umsteuern; **IV** v/i. **14.** rückwärts fahren; **15.** beim Walzer 'linksher,um tanzen; **re'vers·i·ble** [-səbl] adj. **1.** a. ♄, ➚, phys. 'umkehrbar; **2.** doppelseitig, wendbar (Stoff, Mantel); **3.** ⊚ 'umsteuerbar; **4.** ⚖ 'umstoßbar; **re'vers·ing** [-sɪŋ] adj. ⊚, phys. Umkehr..., Umsteuerungs...: **~ gear** a) Umsteuerung f, b) Wendegetriebe n, c) Rückwärtsgang *m*; ~ *pole* ⚡ Wendepol *m*; ~ *switch* ⚡ Wendeschalter *m*; **re'ver-sion** [-ɜːʃn] *s.* **1.** *a.* ⚐ 'Umkehrung *f*; **2.** ⚖ a) Heim-, Rückfall *m*, b) *a.* *right of* ~ Heimfallsrecht *n*; **3.** ⚖ a) Anwartschaft *f* (*of* auf *acc.*), b) Anwartschaftsrente *f*; **4.** *biol.* a) Rück-artung *f*, b) Ata'vismus *m*; **5.** ⚡ 'Um-polung *f*; **re'ver-sion-ar-y** [-ɜːʃnərɪ] *adj.* **1.** ⚖ anwartschaftlich, Anwart-schafts...: ~ *annuity* Rente *f* auf den Überlebensfall; ~ *heir* Nacherbe *m*; **2.** *biol.* ata'vistisch; **re'ver-sion-er** [-ɜːʃnə] *s.* ⚖ Anwartschaftsberech-tigte(r *m*) *f*, Anwärter(in); **7.** Nach-erbe *m*, -erbin *f*; **re-vert** [rɪ'vɜːt] **I** *v/i.* **1.** zu'rückkehren (*to* zu *s-m Glauben etc.*); **2.** zu'rückkommen (*to* auf *e-n Brief, ein Thema etc.*); **3.** wieder zu-'rückfallen (*to* in *acc.*): ~ *to barbarism*; **4.** ⚖ zu'rück-, heimfallen (*to s.o.* an j-n); **5.** *biol.* zu'rückschlagen (*to* zu); **II** *v/t.* **6.** *Blick* (zu'rück)wenden; **re-'vert-i-ble** [-ɜːtəbl] *adj.* ⚖ heimfällig (*Besitz*).

re-vet-ment [rɪ'vetmənt] *s.* **1.** ⚙ Ver-kleidung *f*, Futtermauer *f* (*Ufer etc.*); **2.** ✗ Splitterschutzwand *f*.

re-view [rɪ'vjuː] **I** *s.* **1.** Nachprüfung *f*, (Über)'Prüfung *f*, Revisi'on *f*: *court of* ~ ⚖ Rechtsmittelgericht *n*; *be under* ~ überprüft werden; **2.** (Buch)Bespre-chung *f*, Rezensi'on *f*, Kri'tik *f*: ~ *copy* Rezensionsexemplar *n*; **3.** Rundschau *f*, kritische Zeitschrift; **4.** ✗ Pa'rade *f*, Truppenschau *f*: *naval* ~ Flottenpara-de; *pass in* ~ a) mustern, b) (vorbei-) defilieren (lassen), c) → **5.** Rückblick *m*, -schau *f* (*of* auf *acc.*): *pass in* ~ a) Rückschau halten über (*acc.*), b) *im Geiste* Revue passieren lassen; **6.** Be-richt *m*, 'Übersicht *f*, -blick *m* (*of* über *acc.*): *market* ~ ✝ Markt-, Börsenbe-richt; *month under* ~ Berichtsmonat *m*; **7.** 'Durchsicht *f*; **8.** → *revue*; **II** *v/t.* **9.** nachprüfen, (über)'prüfen, e-r Revi-si'on unter'ziehen; **10.** ✗ besichtigen, inspizieren; **11.** *fig.* zu'rückblicken auf (*acc.*); **12.** über'blicken, -'schauen: ~ *the situation*; **13.** e-n 'Überblick ge-ben über (*acc.*); **14.** *Buch* besprechen, rezensieren; **III** *v/i.* **15.** (Buch)Bespre-chungen schreiben; **re'view-er** [-juːə] *s.* Kritiker(in), Rezen'sent(in): ~'*s copy* Rezensionsexemplar *n*.

re-vile [rɪ'vaɪl] *v/t. u. v/i.*: ~ (*at od. against*) *s.th.* et. schmähen *od.* verun-glimpfen; **re'vile-ment** [-mənt] *s.* Schmähung *f*, Verunglimpfung *f*.

re-vis-al [rɪ'vaɪzl] *s.* **1.** (Nach)Prüfung *f*; **2.** (nochmalige) 'Durchsicht; **3.** *typ.* zweite Korrek'tur; **re-vise** [rɪ'vaɪz] **I** *v/t.* **1.** revidieren: a) *typ.* in zweiter Korrek'tur lesen, b) *Buch* über'arbei-ten: ~*ed edition* verbesserte Auflage, c) *fig.* Ansicht ändern; *Buch* über'prüfen, (wieder) 'durchsehen; **II** *s.* **3.** *a.* ~ *proof typ.* Revisi'onsbogen *m*, Korrek'turab-zug *m*; **4.** → *revision*; **re'vis-er** [-zə] *s.* **1.** *typ.* Kor'rektor *m*; **2.** Bearbeiter *m*; **re-vi-sion** [rɪ'vɪʒn] *s.* Revisi'on *f*: a) 'Durchsicht *f*, b) Über'arbeitung *f*, c) Korrek'tur *f*; **2.** verbesserte Ausgabe *od.* Auflage.

re-vis-it [,riː'vɪzɪt] *v/t.* nochmals *od.* wie-der besuchen: *London* ~*ed* Wiederse-hen *n* mit London.

re-vi-tal-ize [,riː'vaɪtəlaɪz] *v/t.* neu bele-ben, wieder beleben.

re-viv-al [rɪ'vaɪvl] *s.* **1.** 'Wiederbelebung *f* (*a.* ✝; *a. von Rechten*): ~ *of archi-tecture* Neugotik *f*; ⚖ *of Learning hist.* Renaissance *f*; **2.** Wieder'aufleben *n*,

-'aufblühen *n*, Erneuerung *f*; **3.** *eccl.* a) Erweckung *f*, b) *a.* ~ *meeting* Erwe-ckungsversammlung *f*; **4.** Wieder'auf-greifen *n e-s veralteten Worts etc.*; *thea.* Wieder'aufnahme *f e-s vergessenen Stücks*; **re'viv-al-ism** [-vəlɪzəm] *s. bsd. U.S.A.* a) (religi'öse) Erweckungsbe-wegung, Evangelisati'on *f*, b) Erwe-ckungseifer *m*; **re-vive** [rɪ'vaɪv] **I** *v/t.* **1.** wieder beleben (*a. fig.*); **2.** *Anspruch, Gefühl, Hoffnung, Streit etc.* wieder aufleben lassen; *Gefühle* wieder er-wecken; *Brauch, Gesetz* wieder einfüh-ren; *Vertrag* erneuern; *Gerechtigkeit, Ruf* wieder'herstellen; *Thema* wieder aufgreifen; **3.** *thea. Stück* wieder auf die Bühne bringen; **4.** ⚙ *Metall* frischen; **II** *v/i.* **5.** wieder (zum Leben) erwachen; **6.** das Bewusstsein 'wiedererlangen; **7.** *fig.* wieder aufleben (*a. Rechte*); wieder erwachen (*Hass etc.*); wieder auf-blühen; ✝ sich erholen; **8.** wieder auf-treten; wieder aufkommen (*Brauch etc.*); **re'viv-er** [-və] *s.* **1.** ⚙ Auffri-schungs-, Regenerierungsmittel *n*; **2.** *sl.* (alkoholische) Stärkung; **re'viv-i-fy** [riː'vɪvɪfaɪ] *v/t.* **1.** wieder beleben; **2.** *fig.* wieder aufleben lassen, neu bele-ben.

rev-o-ca-ble ['revəkəbl] *adj.* ⚖ wider-ruflich; **rev-o-ca-tion** [,revə'keɪʃn] *s.* ⚖ Widerruf *m*, Aufhebung *f*; (*Lizenz-etc.*)Entzug *m*.

re-voke [rɪ'vəʊk] **I** *v/t.* wider'rufen, auf-heben, rückgängig machen; **II** *v/i.* Kar-tenspiel: nicht Farbe bekennen, nicht bedienen.

re-volt [rɪ'vəʊlt] **I** *s.* **1.** Re'volte *f*, Auf-ruhr *m*, Aufstand *m*; **II** *v/i.* **2.** a) (*a. fig.*) revoltieren, sich em'pören, sich auflehnen (*against* gegen), b) abfallen (*from* von); **3.** *fig.* Widerwillen emp-finden (*at* über *acc.*), sich sträuben *od.* empören (*against, at, from* gegen); **III** *v/t.* **4.** *fig.* empören, mit Abscheu erfül-len, abstoßen; **re'volt-ing** [-tɪŋ] *adj.* ⚐ em'pörend, abstoßend, widerlich.

rev-o-lu-tion [,revə'luːʃn] *s.* **1.** 'Umwäl-zung *f*, Um'drehung *f*, Rotati'on *f*: ~*s per minute* ⚙ Umdrehungen pro Mi-nute, Dreh-, Tourenzahl *f*; ~ *counter* Drehzahlmesser *m*, Tourenzähler *m*; **2.** *ast.* a) Kreislauf *m* (*a. fig.*), b) Um'dre-hung *f*, c) 'Umlauf(zeit *f*) *m*; **3.** *fig.* Revoluti'on *f*: a) 'Umwälzung *f*, 'Um-schwung *m*, b) *pol.* 'Umsturz *m*; **,rev-o-'lu-tion-ar-y** [-ʃnərɪ] **I** *adj.* revolutio'när: a) *pol.* Revolutions..., Umsturz..., b) *fig.* 'umwälzend, E'poche machend; **II** *s. a.* **,rev-o-'lu-tion-ist** [-ʃnɪst] Revolutio'när (-in) (*a. fig.*); **,rev-o-'lu-tion-ize** [-ʃnaɪz] *v/t.* **1.** aufwiegeln, in Aufruhr bringen; **2.** *Staat* revolutionieren (*a. fig. von Grund auf umgestalten*).

re-volve [rɪ'vɒlv] **I** *v/i.* **1.** *bsd.* ⚐, ⚙, *phys.* rotieren, sich drehen, kreisen (*on, about* um *e-e Achse*, *round* um *e-n Mittelpunkt*); **2.** e-n Kreislauf bil-den, da'hinrollen (*Jahre etc.*); **II** *v/t.* **3.** drehen, rotieren lassen; **4.** *fig.* (hin u. her) über'legen, *Gedanken, Problem* wälzen; **re'volv-er** [-və] *s.* Re'volver *m*; **re'volv-ing** [-vɪŋ] *adj.* a) sich drehend, kreisend, drehbar (*about, round* um), b) Dreh...(-bleistift, -brücke, -bühne, -tür etc.): ~ *credit* ✝ Revolvingkredit *m*; ~ *shutter* Rolladen *m*.

re-vue [rɪ'vjuː] *s. thea.* **1.** Re'vue *f*; **2.** (zeitkritisches) Kaba'rett, sa'tirische Kaba'rettvorführung.

re-vul-sion [rɪ'vʌlʃn] *s.* **1.** ⚕ Ableitung *f*; **2.** *fig.* 'Umschwung *m*; **3.** *fig.* Ab-scheu *m* (*against* vor *dat.*); **re'vul-sive**

[-lsɪv] *adj. u. s.* ableitend(es Mittel).

re-ward [rɪ'wɔːd] **I** *s.* **1.** Entgelt *n*; Be-lohnung *f*, *a.* Finderlohn *m*; **2.** Vergel-tung *f*, (gerechter) Lohn; **II** *v/t.* **3.** j-n *od.* et. belohnen (*a. fig.*); *fig.* j-m ver-gelten (*for s.th.* et.); *j-n od. et.* bestra-fen; **re'ward-ing** [-dɪŋ] *adj.* ☐ lohnend (*a. fig.*); *fig. a.* dankbar (*Aufgabe*).

re-wind [,riː'waɪnd] **I** *v/t.* [*irr.* → *wind*²] *Film, Tonband etc.* (zu')rückspulen, 'umspulen; *Garn etc.* wieder aufspulen; *Uhr* wieder aufziehen; **II** *s.* Rückspu-lung *f etc.*; Rücklauf *m* (*am Tonband-gerät etc.*): ~ *button* Rücklauftaste *f*.

re-word [,riː'wɜːd] *v/t.* neu *od.* anders formulieren.

re-write [,riː'raɪt] **I** *v/t. u. v/i.* [*irr.* → *write*] **1.** nochmals *od.* neu schreiben; **2.** 'umschreiben; *Am.* Pressebericht re-digieren, über'arbeiten; **II** *s.* **3.** *Am.* re-digierter Bericht: ~ *man* Überarbeiter *m*.

Rex [reks] (*Lat.*) *s.* ⚖ *Brit.* der König.

rhap-sod-ic, rhap-sod-i-cal [ræp'sɒ-dɪk(l)] *adj.* ☐ **1.** rhap'sodisch; **2.** *fig.* begeistert, 'überschwänglich, ek'sta-tisch; **rhap-so-dist** ['ræpsədɪst] *s.* **1.** Rhap'sode *m*; **2.** *fig.* begeisterter Schwärmer; **rhap-so-dize** ['ræpsədaɪz] *v/i. fig.* schwärmen (*about, on* von); **rhap-so-dy** ['ræpsədɪ] *s.* **1.** Rhapso'die *f* (*a. ♪*); **2.** *fig.* (Wort)Schwall *m*, Schwärme'rei *f*: *go into rhapsodies over* in Ekstase geraten über (*acc.*).

rhe-o-stat ['rɪəʊstæt] *s.* ⚡ Rheo'stat *m*, 'Regel,widerstand *m*.

rhet-o-ric ['retərɪk] *s.* **1.** Rhe'torik *f*, Re-dekunst *f*; **2.** *fig. contp.* schöne Reden *pl.*, (leere) Phrasen *pl.*, Schwulst *m*; **rhe-tor-i-cal** [rɪ'tɒrɪkl] *adj.* ☐ **1.** rhe-'torisch, Redner...: ~ *question* rhetori-sche Frage; **2.** *contp.* schönrednerisch, phrasenhaft, schwülstig; **rhet-o-ri-cian** [,retə'rɪʃn] *s.* **1.** guter Redner, Rede-künstler *m*; **2.** *contp.* Schönredner *m*, Phrasendrescher *m*.

rheu-mat-ic [ruː'mætɪk] ⚕ **I** *adj.* (☐ ~*ally*) **1.** rheu'matisch: ~ *fever* Ge-lenkrheumatismus *m*; **II** *s.* **2.** Rheu'ma-tiker(in); **3.** *pl. sg. konstr.* F Rheuma *n*; **rheu-ma-tism** ['ruːmətɪzəm] *s.* Rheu-ma'tismus *m*, Rheuma *n*: *articular* ~ Gelenkrheumatismus.

Rhine-land-er ['raɪnlændə] *s.* Rheinlän-der(in).

rhine-stone ['raɪnstəʊn] *s. min.* Rhein-kiesel *m* (*Bergkristall*).

rhi-no¹ ['raɪnəʊ] *s. sl.* 'Kies' *m* (*Geld*).

rhi-no² ['raɪnəʊ] *pl.* **-nos** *s.* F, **rhi-noc-er-os** [raɪ'nɒsərəs] *pl.* **-os-es**, *coll.* **-os** *s. zo.* Rhi'nozeros *n*, Nashorn *n*.

rhi-zoph-a-gous [raɪ'zɒfəgəs] *adj. zo.* wurzelfressend.

Rho-de-si-an [rəʊ'diːzjən] *hist.* **I** *adj.* rho'desisch; **II** *s.* Rho'desier(in).

rho-do-cyte ['rəʊdəsaɪt] *s. physiol.* rotes Blutkörperchen.

rho-do-den-dron [,rəʊdə'dendrən] *s.* ♀ Rhodo'dendron *n*, *m*.

rhomb [rɒm] → *rhombus*; **rhom-bic** ['rɒmbɪk] *adj.* rhombisch, rautenför-mig; **rhom-bo-he-dron** [,rɒmbə'he-drən] *pl.* **-he-dra** [-drə], **-he-drons** *s.* ⚖ Rhombo'eder *n*; **rhom-boid** ['rɒmbɔɪd] **I** *s.* **1.** ⚖ Rhombo'id *n*, Pa-rallelo'gramm *n*; **II** *adj.* **2.** rautenförmig; **3.** → *rhomboidal*; **rhom-boi-dal** [rɒm'bɔɪdl] *adj.* ⚖ rhombo'idförmig, rhombo'idisch; **rhom-bus** ['rɒmbəs] *pl.* **-bus-es, -bi** [-baɪ] *s.* ⚖ Rhombus *m*, Raute *f*.

rhu-barb ['ruːbɑːb] *s.* **1.** ♀ Rha'barber *m*; **2.** *Am. sl.* 'Krach' *m*.

rhumb [rʌm] *s.* **1.** Kompassstrich *m*; **2.** *a.* **~ line** a) ✠ loxo'dromische Linie, b) ⚓ Dwarslinie *f.*

rhyme [raɪm] **I** *s.* **1.** Reim *m* (**to** auf *acc.*): **without ~ or reason** ohne Sinn und Zweck; **2.** *sg. od. pl.* a) Vers *m*, b) Reim *m*, Gedicht *n*, Lied *n*; **II** *v/i.* **3.** reimen, Verse machen; **4.** sich reimen (**with** mit, **to** auf *acc.*); **III** *v/t.* **5.** reimen, in Reime bringen; **6.** *Wort* reimen lassen (**with** auf *acc.*); '**rhyme·less** [-lɪs] *adj.* reimlos; '**rhym·er** [-mə], '**rhyme·ster** [-stə] *s.* Verseschmied *m*; **rhym·ing dic·tion·ar·y** ['raɪmɪŋ] *s.* Reimwörterbuch *n.*

rhythm ['rɪðəm] *s.* ♪ Rhythmus *m* (*a. Metrik u. fig.*); Takt *m*: **three-four ~**; **dance ~s** Tanzrhythmen, beschwingte Weisen; **~ method** Knaus-Ogino-Methode *f* (*Empfängnisverhütung*); **2.** Versmaß *n*; **3.** ✿ Pulsschlag *m*; **rhyth·mic, rhyth·mi·cal** ['rɪðmɪk(l)] *adj.* □ rhythmisch: a) taktmäßig, b) *fig.* regelmäßig (wiederkehrend); **rhyth·mics** ['rɪðmɪks] *s. pl. sg. konstr.* ♪ Rhythmik *f* (*a. Metrik*).

ri·al·to [rɪ'æltəʊ] *pl.* **-tos** *s.* **1.** *Am.* The'aterviertel *n*; **2.** Börse *f*, Markt *m.*

rib [rɪb] **I** *s.* **1.** *anat.* Rippe *f*: **~ cage** Brustkorb *m*; **2.** *Küche:* a) *a.* **~ roast** Rippenstück *n*, b) Rippe(n)speer *m*; **3.** *humor.* 'Ehehälfte' *f*; **4.** ❀ (Blatt)Rippe *f*, (-)Ader *f*; **5.** ⚙ Stab *m*, Stange *f*, (*a. Heiz-, Kühl- etc.*)Rippe *f*; **6.** △ (Gewölbe- etc.)Rippe *f*, Strebe *f*; **7.** ⚓ a) (Schiffs)Rippe *f*, Spant *m*, b) Spiere *f*; **8.** ♪ Zarge *f*; **9.** (*Stoff*)Rippe *f*: **~ stitch** *Stricken:* linke Masche; **II** *v/t.* **10.** mit Rippen versehen; **11.** *Stoff etc.* rippen; **12.** *sl.* 'aufziehen', hänseln.

rib·ald ['rɪbəld] **I** *adj.* **1.** lästerlich, frech; **2.** zotig, 'saftig', ob'szön; **II** *s.* **3.** Spötter(in), Lästermaul *n*; **4.** Zotenreißer *m*; '**rib·ald·ry** [-drɪ] *s.* Zoten(reiße'rei *f*) *pl.*, 'saftige' Späße *pl.*

rib·and ['rɪbənd] *s.* (Zier)Band *n.*

ribbed [rɪbd] *adj.* gerippt, geriffelt, Rippen...: **~ cooler** ⚙ Rippenkühler *m*; **~ glass** Riffelglas *n.*

rib·bon ['rɪbən] *s.* **1.** Band *n*, Borte *f*; **2.** Ordensband *n*; **3.** (schmaler) Streifen; **4.** Fetzen *m*: **tear to ~s** in Fetzen reißen; **5.** Farbband *n* (*Schreibmaschine*); **6.** ⚙ a) (Me'tall)Band *n*, (-)Streifen *m*, b) (Holz)Leiste *f*: **~ cartridge** Farbbandkassette *f*; **~ microphone** Bändchenmikrofon *n*; **~ saw** Bandsäge *f*; **7.** *pl.* Zügel *pl.*; **~ build·ing, ~ de·vel·op·ment** *s. Brit.* Stadtrandsiedlung *f* entlang e-r Ausfallstraße.

rib·bon·ed ['rɪbənd] *adj.* **1.** bebändert; **2.** gestreift.

ri·bo·fla·vin [ˌraɪbəʊ'fleɪvɪn] *s.* ✿ Ribo'fla'vin *n* (*Vitamin B₂*).

ri·bo·nu·cle·ic ac·id [ˌraɪbəʊnjuː'kliː-ɪk] *s.* Ribonukleinsäure *f.*

rice [raɪs] *s.* ❀ Reis *m*; **~ flour** *s.* Reismehl *n*; **~ pad·dy** *s.* Reisfeld *n*; **~ pa·per** *s.* 'Reis·pa₁pier *n*; **~ pud·ding** *s.* Milchreis *m.*

ric·er ['raɪsə] *s. Am.* Kar'toffelpresse *f.*

rich [rɪtʃ] **I** *adj* (□ → **richly**) **1.** reich (**in** an *dat.*) (*a. fig.*), wohlhabend: **~ in cattle** viehreich; **~ in hydrogen** wasserstoffreich; **~ in ideas** ideenreich; **2.** schwer (*Stoff*), prächtig, kostbar (*Seide, Schmuck etc.*); **3.** reich(lich), reichhaltig, ergiebig (*Ernte etc.*); **4.** fruchtbar, fett (*Boden*); **5.** ⚒ geol. (erz)reich, fündig (*Lagerstätte*), b) *min.* reich, fett (*Erz*): **strike it ~** *min.* a) auf Öl *etc.* stoßen, b) *fig.* arrivieren, zu Geld kommen, c) *fig.* das große Los ziehen, e-n

Volltreffer landen; **6.** 🍖 schwer; *mot.* fett, gasreich (*Luftgemisch*); **7.** schwer, fett (*Speise*); **8.** schwer, kräftig (*Wein, Duft etc.*); **9.** satt, voll (*Farbton*); **10.** voll, satt (*Ton*); voll(tönend), klangvoll (*Stimme*); **11.** inhalt(s)reich; **12.** F 'köstlich', 'großartig'; **II** *s.* **13.** *coll.* **the ~** die Reichen *pl.*; **rich·es** ['rɪtʃɪz] *s. pl.* Reichtum *m*, -tümer *pl.*; '**rich·ly** [-lɪ] *adv.* reichlich, in reichem Maße; '**rich·ness** [-nɪs] *s.* **1.** Reichtum *m*, Reichhaltigkeit *f*, Fülle *f*; **2.** Pracht *f*; **3.** Ergiebigkeit *f*; **4.** Nahrhaftigkeit *f*; **5.** (Voll)Gehalt *m*, Schwere *f* (*Wein etc.*); **6.** Sattheit *f* (*Farbton*); **7.** Klangfülle *f.*

rick¹ [rɪk] ⚒ *bsd. Brit.* **I** *s.* (Getreide-, Heu)Schober *m*; **II** *v/t.* schobern.

rick² [rɪk] *v/t. bsd. Brit.* verrenken.

rick·ets ['rɪkɪts] *s. sg. od. pl. konstr.* ✿ Ra'chitis *f*; '**rick·et·y** [-tɪ] *adj.* **1.** ✿ ra'chitisch; **2.** gebrechlich (*Person*), wack(e)lig (*a. Möbel u. fig.*), klapp(e)rig (*Auto etc.*).

ric·o·chet ['rɪkəʃeɪ] **I** *s.* **1.** Abprallen *n*; **2.** ✗ a) Rikoschettieren *n*, b) *a.* **~ shot** Abpraller *m*, Querschläger *m*; **II** *v/i.* **3.** abprallen.

rid [rɪd] *v/t.* [*irr.*] befreien, frei machen (**of** von): **get ~ of** *j-n od. et.* loswerden; **be ~ of** *j-n od. et.* los sein; **rid·dance** ['rɪdəns] *s.* Befreiung *f*, Erlösung *f*: (**he is a**) **good ~!** man ist froh, dass man ihn (wieder) los ist!, den wären wir los!

rid·den ['rɪdn] **I** *p.p. von* **ride**; **II** *adj.* in *Zssgn.* bedrückt, geplagt, gepeinigt von: **fever-~**; **pest-~** von der Pest heimgesucht.

rid·dle¹ ['rɪdl] **I** *s.* **1.** Rätsel *n* (*a. fig.*): **speak in ~s** → 4; **II** *v/t.* **2.** enträtseln: **me** rate mal; **3.** *fig. j-n* vor ein Rätsel stellen; **III** *v/i.* **4.** *fig.* in Rätseln sprechen.

rid·dle² ['rɪdl] **I** *s.* **1.** Schüttelsieb *n*; **II** *v/t.* **2.** ('durch-, aus)sieben; **3.** *fig.* durch'sieben, durch'löchern: **~ s.o. with bullets**; **4.** *fig. Argument etc.* zerpflücken; **5.** *fig.* mit Fragen bestürmen.

ride [raɪd] **I** *s.* **1.** a) Ritt *m*, b) Fahrt *f* (*bsd. auf e-m [Motor]Rad od. in e-m öffentlichen Verkehrsmittel*): **go for a ~**, **take a ~** a) ausreiten, b) ausfahren; **give s.o. a. ~** *j-n* reiten *od.* fahren lassen, *j-n im Auto etc.* mitnehmen; **take s.o. for a ~** F a) *j-n* (im Auto entführen und) umbringen, b) *j-n* 'reinlegen' (be'trügen), c) *j-n* 'auf den Arm nehmen' ('hänseln'); **2.** Reitweg *m*, Schneise *f*; **II** *v/i.* [*irr.*] **3.** reiten (*a. fig. rittlings sitzen*): **~ out** F zusteuern (**for** zustreben (*dat.*), entgegeneilen (*dat.*); **~ for a fall** halsbrecherisch reiten, *fig.* in sein Verderben rennen; **~ up** hochrutschen (*Kragen etc.*); **let it ~!** F lass die Karre laufen!; **he let the remark ~** er ließ die Bemerkung hingehen; **Nixon ~s again!** *iro.* N. ist wieder da!; **4.** fahren: **~ on a bicycle** Rad fahren; **~ in a train** mit e-m Zug fahren; **5.** sich (fort)bewegen, da'hinziehen (*a. Mond, Wolken etc.*); **6.** (auf dem Wasser) treiben, schwimmen; *fig.* schweben: **~ at anchor** ⚓ vor Anker liegen; **~ on the waves of popularity** *fig.* von der Woge der Volksgunst getragen werden; **~ on the wind** sich vom Wind tragen lassen (*Vogel*); **be riding on air** *fig.* selig sein (*vor Glück*); **7.** *fig.* ruhen, liegen, sich drehen (**on** auf *dat.*); **8.** sich über'lagern (*z.B. Knochenfragmente*); ⚓ unklar laufen (*Tau*); **9.** ❀ fahren, laufen, gleiten; **10.** zum Reiten *gut etc.* geeignet sein (*Boden*); **11.** im Reitdress wiegen; **III** *v/t.* [*irr.*] **12.** reiten: **~ at sein Pferd** lenken

nach *od.* auf (*acc.*); **~ to death** zu Tode reiten (*a. fig. Theorie, Witz etc.*); **~ a race** an e-m Rennen teilnehmen; **13.** reiten *od.* rittlings sitzen (lassen) auf (*dat.*); *j-n auf den Schultern* tragen; **14.** *Motorrad etc.* fahren, lenken: **~ over** a) *j-n* überfahren, b) → 17; c) über *e-e Sache* rücksichtslos hinweggehen; **15.** *fig.* reiten *od.* schwimmen *od.* schweben auf (*dat.*): **~ the waves** auf den Wellen reiten; **16.** aufliegen *od.* ruhen auf (*dat.*); **17.** tyrannisieren, beherrschen; *weitS.* heimsuchen, plagen, quälen; *j-m* bös zusetzen (*a. mit Kritik*); *Am.* F *j-n* reizen, hänseln: **the devil ~s him** ihn reitet der Teufel; → **ridden** II; **18.** *Land* durch'reiten; **~ down** *v/t.* **1.** über'holen; **2.** a) niederreiten, b) über'fahren; **~ out** *v/t. Sturm etc.* (gut) über-'stehen (*a. fig.*).

rid·er ['raɪdə] *s.* **1.** Reiter(in); **2.** (Mit-) Fahrer(in); **3.** ⊕ a) Oberteil *n*, b) Laufgewicht *n* (*Waage*); **4.** △ Strebe *f*; **5.** ⚓ Binnenspant *n*; **6.** ✤ a) Zusatz (-klausel *f*) *m*, b) Beiblatt *n*, c) ('Wechsel)Al₁longe *f*, d) zusätzliche Empfehlung; **7.** ✠ Zusatzaufgabe *f*; **8.** ✗ Salband *n.*

ridge [rɪdʒ] **I** *s.* **1.** a) (Gebirgs)Kamm *m*, Grat *m*, Kammlinie *f*, b) Berg-, Hügelkette *f*, c) Wasserscheide *f*; **2.** Kamm *m* e-r Welle; **3.** Rücken *m* der Nase, e-s Tiers; **4.** △ (Dach)First *m*; **5.** ⚒ a) (Furchen)Rain *m*, b) erhöhtes Mistbeet; **6.** ⊕ Wulst *m*; **7.** *meteor.* Hochdruckgürtel *m*; **II** *v/t. u. v/i.* **8.** (sich) furchen; **~ pole** *s.* **1.** △ Firstbalken *m*; **2.** Firststange *f* (*Zelt*); **~ tent** *s.* Hauszelt *n*; **~ tile** *s.* Firstziegel *m*; '**~·way** *s.* Kammlinien-, Gratweg *m.*

rid·i·cule ['rɪdɪkjuːl] **I** *s.* Spott *m*: **hold up to ~** → II; **turn (in)to ~** et. ins Lächerliche ziehen; **II** *v/t.* lächerlich machen, verspotten; **ri·dic·u·lous** [rɪ'dɪkjʊləs] *adj.* □ lächerlich; **ri·dic·u·lous·ness** [rɪ'dɪkjʊləsnɪs] *s.* Lächerlichkeit *f.*

rid·ing ['raɪdɪŋ] *s.* **1.** Reiten *n*; Reitsport *m*; **2.** Fahren *n*; **3.** Reitweg *m*; **4.** *Brit.* Verwaltungsbezirk *m*; **II** *adj.* **5.** Reit...: **~ horse** (**school, whip** *etc.*); **~ breeches** *pl.* Reithose *f*; **~ habit** Reitkleid *n.*

rife [raɪf] *adj. pred.* **1.** weit verbreitet, häufig: **be ~** (vor)herrschen, grassieren; **grow** (*od.* **wax**) **~** überhand nehmen; **2.** (**with**) voll (von), angefüllt (mit).

ri·fle¹ ['raɪfl] **I** *s.* **1.** ⊕ Rille *f*, Riefelung *f*; **2.** *Am.* a) seichter Abschnitt (*Fluss*), b) Stromschnelle *f*; **3.** Stechen *n* (*Mischen von Spielkarten*); **II** *v/t.* **4.** ⊕ riffeln; **5.** *Spielkarten* stechen (*mischen*); **6.** 'durchblättern; *Zettel etc.* durchein'anderbringen.

riff-raff ['rɪfræf] *s.* Pöbel *m*, Gesindel *n*, Pack *n.*

ri·fle¹ ['raɪfl] **I** *s.* **1.** Gewehr *n* (*mit gezogenem Lauf*), Büchse *f*; **2.** *pl.* ✗ Schützen *pl.*; **II** *v/t.* **3.** *Gewehrlauf* ziehen.

ri·fle² ['raɪfl] *v/t.* (aus)plündern, *Haus a.* durch'wühlen.

ri·fle| corps *s.* Schützenkorps *n*; **~ gre·nade** *s.* Ge'wehrgranate *f*; '**~·man** [-mən] *s.* [*irr.*] ✗ Schütze *m*, Jäger *m*; **~ pit** *s.* ✗ Schützenloch *n*; **~ prac·tice** *s.* ✗ Schießübung *f*; **~ range** *s.* **1.** Schießstand *m*; **2.** Schussweite *f*; **~ shot** *s.* **1.** Gewehrschuss *m*; **2.** Schussweite *f.*

ri·fling ['raɪflɪŋ] *s.* **1.** Ziehen *n* e-s Gewehrlaufs *etc.*; **2.** Züge *pl.*

rift [rɪft] **I** *s.* **1.** Spalte *f*, Spalt *m*, Ritze *f*; **2.** Sprung *m*, Riss *m*: **a little ~ within the lute** *fig.* der Anfang vom Ende; **II**

v/t. **3.** (zer)spalten; **~ saw** *s.* ⊛ Gattersäge *f;* **~ val·ley** *s. geol.* Senkungsgraben *m.*

rig¹ [rɪg] **I** *s.* **1.** ⊕ Takelung *f,* Take'lage *f;* ⚲ (Auf)Rüstung *f;* **2.** Ausrüstung *f;* Vorrichtung *f;* **3.** F *fig.* Aufmachung *f* (*Kleidung*): **in full ~** in voller Montur; **4.** *Am.* a) Fuhrwerk *n,* b) Sattelschlepper *m;* **5.** Bohranlage *f;* **II** *v/t.* **6.** ⊕ a) *Schiff* auftakeln, b) *Segel* anschlagen; **7.** ⚲ (auf)rüsten, montieren; **8. ~ out,** **~ up** a) ⊕ *etc.* ausrüsten, -statten, b) F *fig.* j-n ,auftakeln', ausstaffieren; **9.** *oft* **~ up** (behelfsmäßig) zs.-bauen, zs.-basteln.

rig² [rɪg] **I** *v/t.* ⚓ *Markt etc., pol. Wahl* manipulieren; **II** *s.* ('Schwindel)Ma,növer *n,* Schiebung *f.*

rig·ger ['rɪgə] *s.* **1.** ⊕ Takler *m;* **2.** ⚲ Mon'teur *m,* ('Rüst)Me,chaniker *m;* **3.** ⚡ Kabelleger *m;* **4.** △ Schutzgerüst *n;* **5.** ⊕ Schnur-, Riemenscheibe *f;* **6.** ⚓ Kurstreiber *m.*

rig·ging ['rɪgɪŋ] *s.* **1.** ⊕ Take'lage *f,* Takelwerk *n:* **running (standing)** ~ laufendes (stehendes) Gut; **2.** ⚲ Verspannung *f;* **3.** → **rig²** II; **~ loft** *s. thea.* Schnürboden *m.*

right [raɪt] **I** *adj.* □ → **rightly;** **1.** richtig, recht, angemessen: **it is only** ~ es ist nicht mehr als recht und billig; **he is** ~ **to do so** er tut recht daran (, so zu handeln); **the ~ thing** das Richtige; **say the ~ thing** das rechte Wort finden; **2.** richtig: a) kor'rekt, b) wahr(heitsgemäß): **the solution is** ~ die Lösung stimmt *od.* ist richtig; **is your watch** ~? geht Ihre Uhr richtig?; **be** ~ Recht haben; **get s.th.** ~ et. klarlegen, et. in Ordnung bringen; ~? F klar?; **all** ~! a) alles in Ordnung, b) ganz recht!, c) abgemacht!, in Ordnung!, gut!, (na) schön! (→ *a.* 4); **~ you are!** F richtig!, jawohl!; **that's** ~! ganz recht!, stimmt!; **3.** richtig, geeignet: **he is the ~ man** er ist der Richtige; **he is all** ~ F er ist in Ordnung (→ *a.* 4); **the ~ man in the ~ place** der rechte Mann am rechten Platz; **4.** gesund, wohl: **he is all** ~ a) es geht ihm gut, er fühlt sich wohl, b) ihm ist nichts passiert; **out of one's ~ mind, not** ~ **in one's** (*od.* **the**) **head** F nicht ganz bei Trost; **in one's** ~ **mind** bei klarem Verstand; **5.** richtig, in Ordnung: **come** ~ in Ordnung kommen; **put** (*od.* **set**) ~ a) in Ordnung bringen, b) j-n (über e-n Irrtum) aufklären, c) *Irrtum* richtig stellen, d) j-n gesund machen; **put o.s.** ~ **with s.o.** a) sich vor j-m rechtfertigen, b) sich mit j-m gut stellen; **6.** recht, Rechts... (*a. pol.*): ~ **arm** (*od.* **hand**) *fig.* rechte Hand; ~ **side** rechte Seite, Oberseite *f* (*a.* Münze, Stoff *etc.*); **on** (*od.* **to**) **the** ~ **side** rechts, rechter Hand; **on the** ~ **side of 40** noch nicht 40 (Jahre alt); ~ **turn** Rechtswendung *f* (um 90 Grad); ~ **wing** a) *sport u. pol.* rechter Flügel, b) *sport* Rechtsaußen *m* (Spieler); **7.** ⚓ a) recht(er Winkel), b) rechtwink(e)lig (*Dreieck*), c) gerade (*Linie*), d) senkrecht (*Figur*): **at** ~ **angles** rechtwink(e)lig; **8.** *obs.* rechtmäßig (*Erbe*): echt (*Kognak etc.*); **II** *adv.* **9.** richtig, recht: **act** (*od.* **do**) ~; **guess** ~ richtig (er)raten; **10.** recht, richtig, gut: **nothing goes** ~ **with me** (bei mir geht alles schief; **turn out** ~ gut ausgehen; → 5; **11.** rechts (**from** von); nach rechts; auf der rechten Seite: ~ **and left** a) rechts und links, b) *fig. a.* ~ **left and centre** (*Am.* **center**) überall, von *od.* auf *od.* nach allen Seiten; ~ **about face!** ✕

(ganze Abteilung,) kehrt!; **12.** gerade (-wegs), (schnur)stracks, so'fort: ~ **a-head,** ~ **on** geradeaus; ~ **away** (*od.* **off**) *bsd. Am.* sofort, gleich; ~ **now** *Am.* jetzt (gleich); **13.** völlig, ganz (und gar), di'rekt: **rotten ~ through** durch und durch faul; **14.** genau, gerade: ~ **in the middle;** **15.** F ,richtig', ,ordentlich': **I was** ~ **glad;** **he's a big shot all ~** (**but**) er ist schon ein ,großes Tier' (, aber); **16.** *obs.* recht, sehr: **know ~ well** sehr wohl wissen; **17.** ⚖ *in Titeln:* hoch, sehr: → **reverend;** **III** *s.* **18.** Recht *n:* **of** (*od.* **by**) ~s von Rechts wegen, rechtmäßig, eigentlich; **in the** ~ im Recht; ~ **and wrong** Recht und Unrecht; **do s.o.** ~ j-m Gerechtigkeit widerfahren lassen; **give s.o. his** ~s j-m sein Recht geben *od.* lassen; **19.** ⚖ (subjek'tives) Recht, Anrecht *n,* (Rechts)Anspruch *m* (**to** auf *acc.*); Berechtigung *f:* ~**s and duties** Rechte und Pflichten; ~ **of inheritance** Erbschaftsanspruch; ~ **of possession** Eigentumsrecht; ~ **of sale** Verkaufsrecht; ~ **of way** → **right-of-way;** **industrial** ~**s** gewerbliche Schutzrechte; **by** ~ **of** kraft (*gen.*), auf Grund (*gen.*); **in** ~ **of his wife** a) im Namen s-r Frau, b) vonseiten s-r Frau; **in one's own** ~ aus eigenem Recht; **be within one's** ~**s** das Recht auf s-r Seite haben; **20.** *das* Rechte *od.* Richtige: **do the** ~; **21.** *pl.* (richtige) Ordnung: **bring** (*od.* **put** *od.* **set**) **s.th. to** ~**s** et. (wieder) in Ordnung bringen; **22.** wahrer Sachverhalt: **know the** ~**s of a case;** **23.** die Rechte, rechte Seite (*a.* Stoff): **on** (*od.* **to**) **the** ~ rechts, zur Rechten; **on the** ~ **of** rechts von; **keep to the** ~ *mot.* rechts fahren; **turn to the** ~ (sich) nach rechts wenden; **24.** rechte Hand, Rechte *f;* **25.** *Boxen:* Rechte *f* (Faust *od.* Schlag); **26.** ⚖ a) rechter Flügel, b) 'Rechtspar,tei *f;* **IV** *v/t.* **27.** (⊕ auf)richten, ins Gleichgewicht bringen; ⚲ *Maschine* abfangen; **28.** *Fehler, Irrtum* berichtigen: ~ **itself** a) sich wieder ausgleichen, b) (wieder) in Ordnung kommen; **29.** *Unrecht etc.* wieder gutmachen, in Ordnung bringen; **30.** *Zimmer etc.* in Ordnung bringen; **31.** j-m zu s-m Recht verhelfen: ~ **o.s.** sich rehabilitieren; **V** *v/i.* **32.** sich wieder aufrichten.

'right·a·bout *s. a.* ~ **face** (*od.* **turn**) Kehrtwendung *f* (*a. fig.*): **send s.o. to the** ~ j-m ,heimleuchten'; **'~-an·gled** → **right** 7 b; **'~-down** *adj. u. adv.* ,regelrecht', ausgesprochen.

right·eous ['raɪtʃəs] **I** *adj.* □ gerecht (*a.* Sache, Zorn), rechtschaffen; **II** *s. coll.* **the** ~ die Gerechten *pl.;* **'right·eous·ness** [-nɪs] *s.* rechtschaffenheit *f.*

'right·ful [-fʊl] *adj.* □ rechtmäßig; **'~-hand** *adj.* **1.** recht: ~ **bend** Rechtskurve *f;* ~ **man** a) ✕ rechter Nebenmann, b) *fig.* rechte Hand; **2.** ⊕ ~ **blow** *Boxen:* Rechte *f;* **3.** ⊕ ~ **Rechts...;** rechtsgängig (Schraube); rechtsläufig (Motor); ~ **drive** Rechtssteuerung *n;* ~ **thread** Rechtsgewinde *n;* ~**-'hand·ed** *adj.* **1.** rechtshändig; ~ **person** Rechtshänder(in); **2.** → **right-hand** 3; **,~-'hand·er** [-'hændə] *s.* F **1.** Rechtshänder(in); **2.** *Boxen:* Rechte *f* (Schlag).

right·ist ['raɪtɪst] **I** *adj. pol.* rechtsgerichtet, rechts stehend; **II** *s.* 'Rechtspar,teiler *m,* Rechte(r *m*) *f.*

right·ly ['raɪtlɪ] *adv.* **1.** richtig; **2.** mit Recht; **3.** F (*nicht*) genau.

,right-'mind·ed *adj.* rechtschaffen.

right·ness ['raɪtnɪs] *s.* **1.** Richtigkeit *f;* **2.** Rechtmäßigkeit *f;* **3.** Geradheit *f* (Linie).

right·o [,raɪt'əʊ] *int. Brit.* F gut!, schön!, in Ordnung!

,right|-of-'way *pl.* **,rights-of-'way** *s.* **1.** *Verkehr:* a) Vorfahrt(srecht *n*) *f,* b) Vorrang *m* (*e-r Straße, a. fig.*): **yield the** ~ (die) Vorfahrt gewähren (**to** *dat.*); **2.** Wegerecht *n;* **3.** öffentlicher Weg; **4.** *Am.* zu öffentlichen Zwecken beanspruchtes (*z. B.* Bahn)Gelände; ~**-'wing** *adj. pol.* Rechts..., dem rechten Flügel angehörend, rechts stehend: ~ **extremism** Rechtsextremismus *m;* ~ **extremist** Rechtsextremist(in); ~**-'wing·er** *s.* **1.** → **rightist** II; **2.** *sport* Rechtsaußen *m.*

right·oh → **righto.**

rig·id ['rɪdʒɪd] *adj.* □ **1.** starr, steif; **2.** ⊕ a) starr, unbeweglich, b) (stand-, form-)fest, sta'bil: ~ **airship** Starrluftschiff *n;* **3.** *fig.* a) streng (*Disziplin, Glaube, Sparsamkeit etc.*), b) starr (Politik, ⚓ Preise etc.), c) streng, hart, unbeugsam (*Person*); **ri·gid·i·ty** [rɪ'dʒɪdətɪ] *s.* **1.** Starr-, Steifheit *f* (*a. fig.*), Starre *f;* **2.** ⊕ a) Starrheit *f,* Unbeweglichkeit *f,* b) (Stand-, Form)Festigkeit *f,* Stabili'tät *f;* **3.** *fig.* Strenge *f,* Härte *f,* Unnachgiebigkeit *f.*

rig·ma·role ['rɪgmərəʊl] *s.* **1.** Geschwätz *n:* **tell a long** ~ lang u. breit erzählen; **2.** *iro.* Brim'borium *n.*

rig·or¹ ['rɪgə] *Am.* → **rigour.**

rig·or² ['rɪgə] *s.* ⚚ **1.** Schüttel-, Fieberfrost *m;* **2.** Starre *f;* → **ri·gor mor·tis** [,raɪgɔː'mɔːtɪs] *s.* ⚚ Leichenstarre *f.*

rig·or·ous ['rɪgərəs] *adj.* □ **1.** streng, hart, rigo'ros: ~ **measures;** **2.** streng (*Winter*); rau (*Klima etc.*); **3.** (peinlich) genau, strikt, ex'akt.

rig·our ['rɪgə] *s.* **1.** Strenge *f,* Härte *f* (*a. des Winters*); Rauheit *f* (*Klima*): ~**s of the weather** Unbilden der Witterung; **2.** Ex'aktheit *f,* Schärfe *f.*

rile [raɪl] *v/t.* F ärgern: **be** ~**d at** aufgebracht sein über (*acc.*).

rill [rɪl] *s.* Bächlein *n,* Rinnsal *n.*

rim [rɪm] **I** *s.* **1.** *allg.* Rand *m;* **2.** ⊕ a) Felge *f,* b) (Rad)Kranz *m:* ~ **brake** Felgenbremse *f;* **3.** (Brillen)Rand *m,* Fassung *f;* **II** *v/t.* **4.** mit e-m Rand versehen; einfassen; **5.** ⊕ *Rad* befelgen.

rime [raɪm] *s. poet.* (Rau)Reif *m.*

rim·less ['rɪmlɪs] *adj.* randlos.

rim·y ['raɪmɪ] *adj.* bereift, voll Reif.

rind [raɪnd] *s.* **1.** ⚘ (Baum)Rinde *f,* Borke *f;* **2.** (Brot-, Käse)Rinde *f,* Kruste *f;* **3.** (Speck)Schwarte *f;* **4.** (Obst-, Gemüse)Schale *f;* **5.** *fig.* Schale *f,* das Äußere.

ring¹ [rɪŋ] **I** *s.* **1.** *allg.* Ring *m* (*a.* ⚘, ⚛): **form a** ~ *fig.* e-n Kreis bilden (*Personen*); **2.** ⊕ Öse *f;* **3.** *ast.* Hof *m;* **4.** (Zirkus)Ring *m,* Ma'nege *f;* **5.** (Box-)Ring *m,* *weitS.* (*das*) (Berufs)Boxen: **be in the** ~ **for** *fig.* kämpfen um; **6.** *Rennsport:* a) Buchmacherstand *m,* b) *coll.* die Buchmacher *pl.;* **7.** ⚓ Ring *m,* Kar'tell *n;* **8.** (Verbrecher-, Spionage*etc.*)Ring *m,* Organisati'on *f; weitS.* Clique *f;* **II** *v/t.* **9.** beringen; **e-m** *Tier* e-n Ring durch die Nase ziehen; **10.** ⚲ *Baum* ringeln; **11.** in Ringe schneiden: ~ **onions;** **12.** *mst* ~ **in** (*od.* **round** *od.* **about**) um'ringen, -'kreisen, einschließen; *Vieh* um'reiten, zs.-treiben.

ring² [rɪŋ] **I** *s.* **1.** a) Glockenklang *m,* -läuten *n,* b) Glockenspiel *n,* Läutwerk *n* (*Kirche*); **2.** Läut-, Rufzeichen *n,* Klingeln *n;* **3.** *teleph.* Anruf *m:* **give**

me a ~ rufe mich an; **4.** Klang *m*, Schall *m*: **the ~ of truth** der Klang der Wahrheit, der echte Klang; **II** *v/i.* [*irr.*] **5.** läuten (*Glocke*), klingeln (*Glöckchen*): **~ at the door** klingeln; **~ for** nach *j-m* klingeln; **~ off** *teleph.* (den Hörer) auflegen; **6.** klingen (*Münze, Stimme, Ohr etc.*): **~ true** wahr klingen; **7.** *oft* **~ out** erklingen, -schallen (**with** von), ertönen (*a. Schuss*): **~ again** widerhallen; **III** *v/t.* [*irr.*] **8.** *Glocke* läuten: **~ the bell** a) klingeln, läuten, b) *fig.* → **bell**[1]; **~ down (up) the curtain** *thea.* den Vorhang nieder- (hoch)gehen lassen; **~ in the new year** das neue Jahr einläuten; **~ s.o. up** *teleph. bsd. Brit.* j-n *od.* bei j-m anrufen; **9.** erklingen lassen; *fig. j-s Lob* erschallen lassen.

'**ring|-a₁round-a-'ros·y** *s.* ,Ringelreihen' *n* (*Kinderspiel*); '**~·bind·er** *s.* Ringbuch *n*; **~ com·pound** *s.* 🜍 Ringverbindung *f*; '**~·dove** *s. orn.* **1.** Ringeltaube *f*; **2.** Lachtaube *f*.

ringed [rɪŋd] *adj.* **1.** beringt (*Hand etc.*); *fig.* verheiratet; **2.** *zo.* Ringel...

ring·er ['rɪŋə] *s.* **1.** Glöckner *m*; **2.** F a) *Pferderennen*: ,Ringer' *m vertauschtes Pferd*, b) *fig.* a. **dead ~** Doppelgänger(in), Double *n*, (genaues) Ebenbild, ,Zwilling' *m* (**for** von *od. gen.*), c) (gestohlenes) Kfz mit falschem Kennzeichen.

ring| fence [,rɪŋ'fens] *s.* (vollständige) Um'zäunung; '**~-fence** *v/t.* **1.** einzäunen, um'zäunen; **2.** *fig. Geld, Budget etc.* fest einplanen, festlegen; **3.** *fig. berufliche Stellung etc.* fest absichern.

ring·ing[1] ['rɪŋɪŋ] **I** *s.* **1.** (Glocken)Läuten *n*; **2.** Klinge(l)n *n*: **he has a ~ in his ears** ihm klingen die Ohren; **II** *adj.* □ **3.** klinge(l)nd, schallend: **~ cheers** brausende Hochrufe; **~ laugh** schallendes Gelächter; **~ tone** *teleph.* Rufzeichen *n*.

ring·ing[2] ['rɪŋɪŋ] *s. a.* **car ~** F betrügerisches Abändern der Identität e-s Kfz durch Anbringen e-s falschen Kennzeichens.

'**ring₁lead·er** *s.* Rädelsführer *m*.

ring·let ['rɪŋlɪt] *s.* **1.** Ringlein *n*; **2.** (Ringel)Löckchen *n*.

'**ring₁mas·ter** *s.* 'Zirkusdi₁rektor *m*; **~ road** *s. mot. bsd. Brit.* Ring-, Um'gehungsstraße *f*; '**~·side** *s.*: **at the ~** Boxen: am Ring; **~ seat** Ringplatz *m*, *weitS.* guter Platz: **have a ~ seat** *fig.* die Sache aus nächster Nähe verfolgen (können); **~ snake** *s. zo.* Ringelnatter *f*.

ring·ster ['rɪŋstə] *s. Am.* F *bsd. pol.* Mitglied *n* e-s Ringes *od.* e-r Clique.

ring| wall *s.* Ringmauer *f*; '**~·worm** *s.* 🜏 Ringelflechte *f*.

rink [rɪŋk] *s.* **1.** a) (*bsd. Kunst*)Eisbahn *f*, b) Rollschuhbahn *f*; **2.** a) *Bowls*: Spielfeld *n*, b) *Curling*: Rink *m*, Bahn *f*.

rinse [rɪns] **I** *v/t.* **1.** *oft* **~ out** (ab-, aus-, nach)spülen; **2.** *Haare* tönen; **II** *s.* **3.** Spülung *f*: **give s.th. a good ~** et. gut (ab- *od.* aus)spülen; **4.** Spülmittel *n*; **5.** Tönung *f* (*Haar*); '**rins·ing** [-sɪŋ] *s.* **1.** (Aus)Spülen *n*, Spülung *f*; **2.** *mst pl.* Spülwasser *n*.

ri·ot ['raɪət] **I** *s.* **1.** *bsd.* 🜫 Aufruhr *m*, Zs.-rottung *f*; 🜪 *Act hist. Brit.* Aufruhrakte *f*; **read the** 🜪 **Act to** *fig. humor.* j-m (ernstlich) warnen, j-m die Leviten lesen; **~ call** *Am.* Hilfeersuchen *n* (der Polizei bei Aufruhr *etc.*); **~ gun** Straßenkampfwaffe *f*; **~ squad, ~ police** Überfallkommando *n*; **2.** Tu'mult *m*, Aufruhr *m*, (*a. fig. der Gefühle*), Kra'wall *m* (*a. =*

Lärm *m*); **3.** *fig.* Ausschweifung *f*, Orgie *f* (*a. weitS. in Farben etc.*): **run ~** a) (sich aus)toben, b) durchgehen (*Fantasie etc.*), c) *hunt.* e-e falsche Fährte verfolgen (*Hund*), d) 🜔 wuchern; **he** (**it**) **is a ~** F er (es) ist einfach ,toll' *od.* ,zum Schreien' (komisch); **II** *v/i.* **4.** a) an e-m Aufruhr teilnehmen, b) e-n Aufruhr anzetteln; **5.** randalieren, toben; **6.** *a. fig.* schwelgen (**in** in *dat.*); '**ri·ot·er** [-tə] *s.* Aufrührer *m*; Randalierer *m*, Kra'wallmacher *m*; '**ri·ot·ous** [-təs] *adj.* □ **1.** aufrührerisch: **~ assembly** 🜫 Zs.-rottung *f*; **2.** tumultu'arisch, tobend; **3.** ausgelassen, wild (*a. Farbe etc.*); **4.** zügellos, toll.

rip[1] [rɪp] **I** *v/t.* **1.** (zer)reißen, (-)schlitzen; *Naht etc.* (auf-, zer)trennen: **~ off** los-, wegreißen, *fig. sl.* sich et. ,unter den Nagel reißen'; *Bank etc.* ausrauben; *j-n* ,ausnehmen', neppen; **~ up** (*od.* open) aufreißen, -schlitzen, -trennen; **II** *v/i.* **2.** reißen, (auf)platzen; **3.** F sausen: **let her ~!** gib Gas!; **~ into** *fig.* auf *j-n* losgehen; **~ out with** *Fluch etc.* ausstoßen; **III** *s.* **5.** Schlitz *m*, Riss *m*.

ri·par·i·an [raɪ'peərɪən] **I** *adj.* **1.** Ufer...: **~ owner** → 3; **II** *s.* **2.** Uferbewohner (-in); **3.** Uferanlieger *m*.

'**rip·cord** *s.* ✈ Reißleine *f*.

ripe [raɪp] *adj.* □ **1.** reif (*Obst, Ernte etc.*); ausgereift (*Käse, Wein*); schlachtreif (*Tier*); *hunt.* abschussreif; 🜓 operati'onsreif (*Abszess etc.*): **~ beauty** *fig.* reife Schönheit; **2.** körperlich, geistig reif, voll entwickelt; **3.** *fig.* reif, gereift, (*Alter, Urteil etc.*); voll'endet (*Künstler etc.*); ausgereift (*Plan etc.*); **4.** (*zeitlich*) reif (**for** für); **5.** reif, bereit, fertig (**for** für); **6.** F deftig (*Witz etc.*); '**rip·en** [-pən] *v/t.* **1.** *a. fig.* reifen, reif werden; **2.** sich (voll) entwickeln, her'anreifen (**into** zu); **II** *v/t.* **3.** reifen lassen; '**ripe·ness** [-nɪs] *s.* Reife *f* (*a. fig.*).

'**rip-off** *s.* **1.** a) Diebstahl *m*, b) Raub *m*; **2.** ,Nepp' *m*, *allg.* ,Beschiss' *m*.

ri·poste [rɪ'pɒst] **I** *s.* **1.** *fenc.* Ri'poste *f*, Nachstoß *m*; **2.** *fig.* a) schlagfertige Erwiderung, b) scharfe Antwort; **II** *v/i.* **3.** *fenc.* ripostieren; e-n Gegenstoß machen (*a. fig.*); **4.** *fig.* (schlagfertig *od.* hart) kontern.

rip·per ['rɪpə] *s.* **1.** ⊙ a) Trennmesser *n*, b) 'Trennma₁schine *f*, c) → **rip saw**; **2.** *sl.* a) 'Prachtexem₁plar *n*, b) Prachtkerl *m*; **3.** *blutrünstiger Mörder*; '**rip·ping** ['rɪpɪŋ] *obs. Brit. sl. adj.* □ prächtig, ,prima', ,toll'.

rip·ple[1] ['rɪpl] **I** *s.* **1.** kleine Welle(n *pl.*), Kräuselung *f* (*Wasser, Sand etc.*): **~ of laughter** *fig.* leises Lachen; **cause a ~** *fig.* ein kleines Aufsehen erregen; **2.** Rieseln *n*, (Da'hin)Plätschern *n* (*a. fig. Gespräch*); **3.** *fig.* Spiel(en) *n* (*der Muskeln etc.*); **II** *v/i.* **4.** kleine Wellen schlagen, sich kräuseln; **5.** rieseln, (da'hin-)plätschern (*a. fig. Gespräch*); **6.** *fig.* spielen (*Muskeln etc.*); **III** *v/t.* **7.** *Wasser etc.* leicht bewegen, kräuseln.

rip·ple[2] ['rɪpl] ⊙ **I** *s.* Riffelkamm *m*; **II** *v/t. Flachs* riffeln.

rip·ple| cloth *s.* Zibe'line *f* (*Wollstoff*); **~ cur·rent** *s.* ⚡ Brummstrom *m*; **~ fin·ish** *s.* ⊙ Kräusellack *m*.

rip·pling abs ['rɪplɪæbz] *s. pl.* F ,Waschbrettbauch' *m* (*e-s Muskelmannes*).

,**rip|-'roar·ing** *adj.* F ,toll': **~ saw** *s.* ⊙ Spaltsäge *f*; '**~·snort·er** [-₁snɔːtə] *s. sl.* a) ,tolle Sache', b) ,toller Kerl'; '**~·snort·ing** [-'snɔːtɪŋ] *adj. sl.* ,toll'.

rise [raɪz] **I** *v/i.* [*irr.*] **1.** sich erheben, *vom Bett, Tisch etc.* aufstehen: **~ (from**

the dead) *eccl.* (von den Toten) auferstehen; **2.** a) aufbrechen, b) die Sitzung schließen, sich vertagen; **3.** auf-, em'por-, hochsteigen (*Vogel, Rauch etc.; a. Geruch; a. fig. Gedanke, Zorn etc.*): **the curtain ~s** der Vorhang geht auf; **my hair ~s** die Haare stehen mir zu Berge; **her colo(u)r rose** die Röte stieg ihr ins Gesicht; **land ~s to view** Land kommt in Sicht; **spirits rose** die Stimmung hob sich; **the word rose to her lips** das Wort kam ihr auf die Lippen; **4.** steigen, sich bäumen (*Pferd*): **~ to a fence** zum Sprung über ein Hindernis ansetzen; **5.** sich erheben, em'porragen (*Berg etc.*); **6.** aufgehen (*Sonne etc.; a. Saat, Teig*); **7.** (an)steigen (*Gelände etc.; a. Wasser; a. Temperatur etc.*); **8.** (an)steigen, anziehen (*Preise etc.*); **9.** 🜍 sich bilden (*Blasen*); **10.** sich erheben, aufkommen (*Sturm*); **11.** sich erheben *od.* em'pören, revoltieren: **~ in arms** zu den Waffen greifen; **my stomach ~s against** (*od.* **at**) **it** mein Magen sträubt sich dagegen, (*a. fig.*) es ekelt mich an; **12.** beruflich *od.* gesellschaftlich aufsteigen: **~ in the world** vorwärts kommen, es zu et. bringen; **13.** *fig.* sich erheben *od.* erhaben sein (**above** über *acc.*), b) sich em'porschwingen (*Geist*); → **occasion** 3; **14.** ♪ (an)steigen, anschwellen; **II** *v/t.* [*irr.*] **15.** aufsteigen lassen; *Fisch* an die Oberfläche locken; **16.** *Schiff* sichten; **III** *s.* **17.** (Auf)Steigen *n*, Aufstieg *m*; **18.** *ast.* Aufgang *m*; **19.** Auferstehung *f von den Toten*; **20.** Steigen *n* (*Fisch*), Schnappen *n* nach dem Köder: **get** (*od.* **take**) **a ~ out of s.o.** *sl.* j-n ,auf die Palme bringen'; **21.** *fig.* Aufstieg *m* (*Person, Nation etc.*): **a young man on the ~** ein aufstrebender junger Mann; **22.** (An)Steigen *n*, Erhöhung *f* (*Flut, Temperatur etc.*; ♀ *Preise etc.*); *Börse*: Aufschwung *m*, Hausse *f*; *bsd. Brit.* Aufbesserung *f*, Lohn-, Gehaltserhöhung *f*: **buy for a ~** auf Hausse spekulieren; **on the ~** im Steigen (begriffen) (*Preise*); **23.** Zuwachs *m*, -nahme *f*: **~ in population** Bevölkerungszuwachs *m*; **24.** Ursprung *m* (*a. fig. Entstehung*): **take** (*od.* **have**) **its ~** entspringen, entstehen; **25.** Anlass *m*: **give ~ to** verursachen, hervorrufen, erregen; **26.** a) Steigung *f* (*Gelände*), b) Anhöhe *f*, Erhebung *f*; **27.** Höhe *f*; △ Pfeilhöhe *f* (*Bogen*); '**ris·en** [ˈrɪzn] *p.p. von* **rise**.

'**ris·er** [-zə] *s.* **1.** early **~** Frühaufsteher (-in); late **~** Langschläfer(in); **2.** Steigung *f* e-r Treppenstufe; **3.** a) ⊙ Steigrohr *n*, b) ⚡ Steigleitung *f*, c) *Gießerei*: Steiger *m*.

ris·i·bil·i·ty [₁rɪzɪ'bɪlətɪ] *s.* **1.** *a. pl.* Lachlust *f*; **2.** Gelächter *n*; **ris·i·ble** ['rɪzɪbl] *adj.* **1.** lachlustig; **2.** Lach...: **~ muscles**; **3.** lachhaft.

ris·ing ['raɪzɪŋ] **I** *adj.* **1.** (an)steigend (*a. fig.*): **~ ground** (Boden)Erhebung *f*, Anhöhe *f*; **~ gust** Steigböe *f*; **~ main** a) ⊙ Steigrohr *n*, b) ⚡ Steigleitung *f*; **~ rhythm** *Metrik*: steigender Rhythmus; **2.** her'anwachsend, kommend (*Generation*); **3.** aufstrebend: **a ~ lawyer**; **II** *prp.* **4.** *Am.* F **~ of** a) (etwas) mehr als, b) genau; **III** *s.* **5.** Aufstehen *n*; **6.** (An-) Steigen *n* (*a. fig. Preise, Temperatur etc.*); **7.** Steigung *f*, Anhöhe *f*; **8.** *ast.* Aufgehen *n*; **9.** Aufstand *m*, Erhebung *f*; **10.** Steigerung *f*, Zunahme *f*; **11.** Aufbruch *m* e-r Versammlung; **12.** 🜏 ⊙ Geschwulst *f*, Pustel *f*.

risk [rɪsk] **I** *s.* **1.** Wagnis *n*, Gefahr *f*, Risiko *n*: **at one's own ~** auf eigene

Gefahr; *at the ~ of one's life* unter Lebensgefahr; *at the ~ of* (*ger.*) auf die Gefahr hin, zu (*inf.*); *be at ~* gefährdet sein, auf dem Spiel stehen; *put at ~* gefährden; *run the ~ of doing s.th.* Gefahr laufen, et. zu tun; *run* (*od. take*) *a ~* ein Risiko eingehen; **2.** ✝ a) Risiko *n*, Gefahr *f*, b) versichertes Wagnis (*Ware od. Person*): *~ capital* Risikokapital *n*; *~ spreading* Risikostreuung *f*; *security ~ pol.* Sicherheitsrisiko; **II** *v/t.* **3.** riskieren, wagen, aufs Spiel setzen: *~ one's life*; **4.** *Verlust, Verletzung etc.* riskieren; '**risk·y** [-kɪ] *adj.* □ **1.** ris'kant, gewagt, gefährlich; **2.** → *risqué.*

ris·qué ['riːskeɪ] *adj.* gewagt, schlüpfrig: *a ~ story.*

ris·sole ['rɪsəʊl] (*Fr.*) *s.* Küche: Briso-'lett *n.*

rite [raɪt] *s.* **1.** *bsd. eccl.* Ritus *m*, Zeremo'nie *f*, feierliche Handlung: *funeral ~s* Totenfeier *f*, Leichenbegängnis *n*; *last ~s* Sterbesakramente; **2.** *oft 2 eccl.* Ritus *m*: a) Religi'onsform *f*, b) Litur-'gie *f*, **3.** Gepflogenheit *f*, Brauch *m.*

rit·u·al ['rɪtʃʊəl] **I** *s.* **1.** *eccl. etc., a. fig.* Ritu'al *n*; **2.** *eccl.* Ritu'albuch *n*; **II** *adj.* □ **3.** ritu'al, Ritual...: *~ murder* Ritualmord *m*; **4.** ritu'ell, feierlich: *~ dance.*

ritz·y ['rɪtsɪ] *adj. sl.* **1.** ,stinkvornehm', ,feu'dal'; **2.** angeberisch.

ri·val ['raɪvl] **I** *s.* **1.** Ri'vale *m*, Ri'valin *f*, Nebenbuhler(in), Konkur'rent(in): *without a ~ fig.* ohnegleichen, unerreicht; **II** *adj.* **2.** rivalisierend, wetteifernd: *~ firm* ✝ Konkurrenzfirma *f*; **III** *v/t.* **3.** rivalisieren *od.* wetteifern *od.* konkurrieren mit, *j-m* den Rang streitig machen; **4.** *fig.* es aufnehmen mit; gleichkommen (*dat.*); '**ri·val·ry** [-rɪ] *s.* **1.** Rivali'tät *f*, Nebenbuhlerschaft *f*; **2.** Wettstreit *m*, -eifer *m*, Konkur'renz *f*: *enter into ~ with s.o.* j-m Konkurrenz machen.

rive [raɪv] **I** *v/t.* [*irr.*] **1.** (zer)spalten; **2.** *poet.* zerreißen; **II** *v/i.* [*irr.*] **3.** sich spalten; *fig.* brechen (*Herz*); **riv·en** ['rɪvn] *p.p. von rive.*

riv·er ['rɪvə] *s.* **1.** Fluss *m*, Strom *m*: *the ~ Thames* die Themse; *Hudson 2* der Hudson; *down the ~* strom(ab)(wärts); *sell s.o. down the ~* F j-n ,verkaufen'; *up the ~* a) strom(auf)(wärts), b) *Am.* F in den *od.* im ,Knast'; **2.** *fig.* Strom *m*, Flut *f.*

riv·er·ain ['rɪvəreɪn] **I** *adj.* Ufer..., Fluss...; **II** *s.* Ufer- *od.* Flussbewohner(in).

riv·er| ba·sin *s. geol.* Einzugsgebiet *n*; '**~·bed** *s.* Flussbett *n*; *~ dam s.* Staudamm *m*, Talsperre *f*; '**~·front** *s.* (Fluss-) Hafenviertel *n*; '**~·head** *s.* (Fluss)Quelle *f*, Quellfluss *m*; *~ horse s. zo.* Flusspferd *n.*

riv·er·ine ['rɪvəraɪn] *adj.* am Fluss (gelegen *od.* wohnend); Fluss...

riv·er| po·lice *s.* 'Wasserschutzpoli,zei *f*; '**~·side I** *s.* Flussufer *n*; **II** *adj.* am Ufer (gelegen), Ufer...

riv·et ['rɪvɪt] **I** *s.* ⊙ **1.** Niete *f*, Niet *m*: *~ joint* Nietverbindung *f*; **II** *v/t.* **2.** ⊙ (ver)nieten; **3.** befestigen (*to* an *dat.*); **4.** *fig.* a) *Blick, Aufmerksamkeit* heften, richten (*on* auf *acc.*), b) *Aufmerksamkeit, a. j-n* fesseln: *stand ~ed to the spot* wie angewurzelt stehen bleiben; '**riv·et·ing** [-tɪŋ] *s.* ⊙ **1.** Nietnaht *f*; **2.** (Ver)Nieten *n*: *~ hammer* Niethammer *m.*

riv·u·let ['rɪvjʊlɪt] *s.* Flüsschen *n.*

roach¹ [rəʊtʃ] *s. ichth.* Plötze *f*, Rotauge

n: sound as a ~ kerngesund.

roach² [rəʊtʃ] *s.* ♻ Gilling *f.*

roach³ [rəʊtʃ] *bsd. Am.* → *cockroach.*

road [rəʊd] **I** *s.* **1.** a) (Land)Straße *f*, b) Weg *m* (*a. fig.*), c) Strecke *f*, d) Fahrbahn *f*: *by ~* a) auf dem Straßenweg, b) per Achse, mit dem Fahrzeug; *on the ~* a) auf der Straße, b) auf Reisen, unterwegs, c) *thea.* auf Tournee; *hold the ~ well mot.* e-e gute Straßenlage haben; *take* (*sl. hit*) *the ~* aufbrechen; *rule of the ~* Straßenverkehrsordnung *f*; *the ~ to success* fig. der Weg zum Erfolg; *be in s.o.'s ~ fig.* j-m im Wege stehen; *~ up!* Straßenarbeiten!; **2.** *mst pl.* ♻ Reede *f*; **3.** ☒ *Am.* Bahn(strecke) *f*; **4.** ⚒ Förderstrecke *f*; **II** *adj.* **5.** Straßen..., Weg...: *~ conditions* Straßenzustand *m*; *~ junction* Straßenknotenpunkt *m*, -einmündung *f*; *~ sign* Straßenschild *n*, Wegweiser *m.*

road·a·bil·i·ty [,rəʊdə'bɪlətɪ] *s. mot.* Fahreigenschaften *pl.*; *engS.* Straßenlage *f.*

road| ac·ci·dent *s.* Verkehrsunfall *m*; '**~·bed** *s.* a) ☒ Bahnkörper *m*, b) Straßenbettung *f*; '**~·block** *s.* **1.** Straßensperre *f*; **2.** Verkehrshindernis *n*; **3.** *fig.* Hindernis *n*; '**~·book** *s.* Reisehandbuch *n*; *~ haul·age s.* Güterkraftverkehr *m*; *~ hog s.* Verkehrsrowdy *m* (*rücksichtsloser Fahrer*); '**~,hold·ing** *s. mot.* Straßenlage *f*; *~ hole s.* Schlagloch *n*; *~ house s.* Rasthaus *m*; '**~·man** [-mən] *s.* [*irr.*] **1.** Straßenarbeiter *m*; **2.** Straßenhändler *m*; *~ man·ag·er s.* Roadmanager *m* (*e-r Rockgruppe*); *~ map s.* Straßen-, Autokarte *f*; *~ met·al s.* Straßenbeschotterung *f*, -schotter *m*; *~ rage s.* Aggressivi'tät *f* (*od.* aggres'sives Verhalten) im Straßenverkehr; *~ rag·er s.* aggressive(r) Straßenverkehrsteilnehmer(in); *~ roll·er s.* ⊙ Straßenwalze *f*; *~ sense s. mot.* Fahrverstand *m*; '**~·side I** *s.* (*by the ~*) am Straßenrand *m*; **II** *adj.* an der Landstraße (gelegen): *~ inn*; '**~·stead** *s.* ♻ Reede *f.*

road·ster ['rəʊdstə] *s.* **1.** *Am.* Roadster *m*, (offener) Sportzweisitzer; **2.** *sport* (starkes) Tourenrad.

road| tank·er *s. mot.* Tankwagen *m*; *~ tax s. Brit.* Kraftfahrzeugsteuer *f*; *~ test mot. s.* Probefahrt *f*; '**~·test** *v/t.* ein Auto Probe fahren; *~ toll s.* Straßenbenutzungsgebühr *f*, Maut(gebühr) *f*; *~ us·er s.* Verkehrsteilnehmer(in); '**~·way** *s.* Fahrdamm *m*, -bahn *f*; '**~·work** *s. sport* Lauftraining *n*; *~ works s. pl.* Straßenarbeiten *pl.*, Baustelle *f auf e-r Straße*; '**~,wor·thi·ness** *s. mot.* Verkehrssicherheit *f* (*Auto*); '**~,wor·thy** *adj. mot.* verkehrssicher (*Auto*).

roam [rəʊm] **I** *v/i. a. ~ about* (um'her-) streifen, (-)wandern; **II** *v/t.* durch'streifen (*a. fig. Blick etc.*); **III** *s.* Wandern *n*, Um'herstreifen *n.*

roan [rəʊn] **I** *adj.* **1.** rötlich grau; **2.** gefleckt; **II** *s.* **3.** Rotgrau *n*; **4.** *zo.* a) Rotschimmel *m*, b) rotgraue Kuh; **5.** Schafleder *n.*

roar [rɔː] **I** *v/i.* **1.** brüllen: *~ at* j-n anbrüllen, b) über j-n schallend lachen; *~ with* vor *Schmerz, Lachen etc.* brüllen; **2.** *fig.* tosen, toben, brausen (*Wind, Meer*); krachen, (g)rollen (*Donner*); (er)dröhnen, donnern (*Geschütz, Motor etc.*); brausen, donnern (*Fahrzeug*); **3.** *vet.* keuchen (*Pferd*); **II** *v/t.* **4.** *et.* brüllen: *~ out Freude, Schmerz etc.* hinausbrüllen; *~ s.o. down* j-n niederschreien; **III** *s.* **5.** Brüllen *n*, Gebrüll *n* (*a. fig.*): *set the table*

in a ~ (*of laughter*) bei der Gesellschaft schallendes Gelächter hervorrufen; **6.** *fig.* Tosen *n*, Toben *n*, Brausen *n* (*Wind, Meer*); Krachen *n*, Rollen *n* (*Donner*); Donner *m* (*Geschütze*); Dröhnen *n*, Lärm *m* (*Motor, Maschinen etc.*); Getöse *n*; '**roar·ing** [-rɪŋ] **I** *adj.* □ **1.** brüllend (*a. fig. with* vor *dat.*); **2.** lärmend, laut; **3.** tosend (*etc.* → *roar* 2); **4.** brausend, stürmisch (*Nacht, Fest*); **5.** a) großartig, ,fan'tastisch': *a ~ business* (*od. trade*) ein schwunghafter Handel, ein ,Bombengeschäft'; *in ~ health* vor Gesundheit strotzend, b) ,wild', ,fa'natisch': *a ~ Christian*; **II** *s.* **6.** → *roar* 5 u. 6; **7.** *vet.* Keuchen *n* (*Pferd*).

roast [rəʊst] **I** *v/t.* **1.** *Fleisch etc.* braten, rösten; schmoren: *be ~ed alive* a) bei lebendigem Leibe verbrannt werden *od.* verbrennen, b) *fig.* vor Hitze fast umkommen; **2.** *Kaffee etc.* rösten; **3.** *metall.* rösten, abschwelen; **4.** F a) ,durch den Kakao ziehen', b) ,verreißen' (*kritisieren*); **II** *v/i.* **5.** rösten, braten; schmoren (*a. fig. in der Sonne etc.*): *I am simply ~ing fig.* mir ist wahnsinnig heiß; **III** *s.* **6.** Braten *m*; → *rule* 13; **IV** *adj.* **7.** geröstet, gebraten, Röst...: *~ beef* Rinderbraten *m*; *~ meat* Braten *m*; *~ pork* Schweinebraten *m*; '**roast·er** [-tə] *s.* **1.** Röster *m*, 'Röstappa,rat *m*; **2.** *metall.* Röstofen *m*; **3.** Spanferkel *n*, Brathähnchen *n etc.*; '**roast·ing** [-tɪŋ] *s.*: *give s.o. a ~* F a) → *roast* 4, b) j-n ,total niedermachen'.

rob [rɒb] *v/t.* **1.** a) *et.* rauben, stehlen, b) *Haus etc.* ausrauben, (-)plündern, c) *fig.* berauben (*of gen.*); **2.** *j-n* berauben: *~ s.o. of* a) j-n e-r *Sache* berauben (*a. fig.*), b) *fig.* j-n um et. bringen, j-n et. nehmen; **rob·ber** ['rɒbə] *s.* Räuber *m*; **rob·ber·y** ['rɒbərɪ] *s.* **1.** *a.* 🏴 Raub *m* (*from* an *dat.*); 'Raub,überfall *m*; **2.** *fig.* ,Diebstahl' *m*, ,Beschiss' *m.*

robe [rəʊb] **I** *s.* **1.** (Amts)Robe *f*, Ta'lar *m* (*Geistlicher, Richter etc.*): *~s* Amtstracht *f*; *state ~* Staatskleid *n*; (*the gentlemen of*) *the* (*long*) *~ fig.* die Juristen; **2.** Robe *f*: a) wallendes Gewand, b) Festkleid *n*, c) Abendkleid *n*, d) ✝ einteiliges Damenkleid, e) Bademantel *m*; **3.** *bsd.* Taufkleid *n* (*Säugling*); **II** *v/t.* **4.** j-n (feierlich an)kleiden, j-m die Robe anlegen; **5.** *fig.* (ein)hüllen; **III** *v/i.* **6.** die Robe anlegen.

rob·in ['rɒbɪn] *s.* **1.** *a. ~ redbreast orn.* a) Rotkehlchen *n*, b) amer. Wanderdrossel *f*; **2.** → *round robin.*

rob·o·rant ['rɒbərənt] ✚ **I** *adj.* stärkend; **II** *s.* Stärkungsmittel *n*, Roborans *n.*

ro·bot ['rəʊbɒt] *s.* **1.** Roboter *m* (*a. fig.*), ⊙ *a.* Auto'mat *m*; **2.** *a. ~ bomb* ✗ V-Geschoss *n*; **II** *adj.* **3.** auto'matisch: *~ pilot* ✈ Selbststeuergerät *n.*

ro·bot·ics [rəʊ'bɒtɪks] *s. pl. sg. konstr.* Robotertechnik *f.*

ro·bust [rəʊ'bʌst] *adj.* □ **1.** ro'bust: a) kräftig, stark (*Gesundheit, Körper, Person etc.*), b) kernig, gerade (*Geist*), c) derb (*Humor*); **2.** ⊙ sta'bil, widerstandsfähig; **3.** hart, schwer (*Arbeit etc.*); **ro'bust·ness** [-nɪs] *s.* Ro'bustheit *f.*

roc [rɒk] *s. myth.* (Vogel *m*) Rock *m.*

rock¹ [rɒk] *s.* **1.** Fels *m* (*a. fig.*), Felsen *m*; *coll.* Felsen *pl.*, (Fels)Gestein *n*: *the 2 geogr.* Gibraltar; *volcanic ~ geol.* vulkanisches Gestein; (*as*) *firm as a ~ fig.* wie ein Fels, zuverlässig; **2.** Klippe *f* (*a. fig.*): *on the ~s* a) F ,pleite', in Geldnot, b) F ,kaputt', in die Brüche gegangen (*Ehe etc.*), c) on the rocks, mit Eiswürfeln (*Getränk*); *see ~s a-*

head mit Schwierigkeiten rechnen; **3.** *Am.* Stein *m*: *throw* ~*s at s.o.*; **4.** Pfefferminzstange *f*; **5.** *sl.* Stein, *bsd.* Dia-'mant *m, pl.* ‚Klunkern‘ *pl.*; **6.** *Am. sl.* a) Geldstück *n, bsd.* Dollar *m,* b) *pl.* ‚Kies‘ *m* (*Geld*); **7.** *pl.* ∨ ‚Eier‘ *pl.* (*Hoden*).

rock² [rɒk] **I** *v/t.* **1.** wiegen, schaukeln; *Kind* (in den Schlaf) wiegen: ~ *in security fig.* j-n in Sicherheit wiegen; **2.** ins Wanken bringen, erschüttern: ~ *the boat fig.* die Sache gefährden; **3.** *Sieb, Sand etc.* rütteln; **II** *v/i.* **4.** (sich) schaukeln, sich wiegen; **5.** (sich) wanken, wackeln, taumeln (*a. fig.*); **6.** ♪ a) Rock 'n' Roll tanzen, b) ‚rocken‘ (*spielen*); **III** *s.* **7.** → *rock 'n' roll.*

rock| and roll [ˌrɒkən'rəʊl] → *rock 'n' roll;* ~ **bed** Felsengrund *m;* ~ **bot·tom** *s. fig.* Tief-, Nullpunkt *m*: *get down to* ~ der Sache auf den Grund gehen; *his supplies touched* ~ s-e Vorräte waren erschöpft; ‚~'**bot·tom** *adj.* F aller'niedrigst, äußerst (*Preis etc.*); '~-**bound** *adj.* von Felsen um'schlossen; ~ **cake** *s.* hart gebackenes Plätzchen; ~ **can·dy** → *rock¹* 4; ~ **climb·ing** *s.* Felsenklettern *n;* ~ **cork** *s. min.* 'Bergas,best *m,* -kork *m;* ~ **crys·tal** *s. min.* 'Bergkri,stall *m;* ~ **de·bris** *s. geol.* Felsgeröll *n;* ~ **draw·ings** *s. pl.* Felszeichnungen *pl.;* ~ **drill** *s.* ⚙ Steinbohrer *m.*

rock·er ['rɒkə] *s.* **1.** Kufe *f* (*Wiege etc.*): *off one's* ~ *sl.* ‚übergeschnappt‘, verrückt; **2.** a) Schaukelpferd *n,* b) *Am.* Schaukelstuhl *m;* **3.** ⚙ a) Wippe *f,* b) Wiegemesser *n,* c) Schwing-, Kipphebel *m;* **4.** Schwingtrog *m* (*zur Goldwäsche*); **5.** *Eislauf:* a) Holländer(schlittschuh) *m,* b) Kehre *f;* **6.** *pl. Brit.* Rocker *pl.,* ‚Lederjacken‘ *pl.* (*Jugendliche*); ~ **arm** *s.* ⚙ Kipphebel *m;* ~ **switch** *s.* ⚡ Wippschalter *m.*

rock·er·y ['rɒkərɪ] *s.* Steingarten *m.*

rock·et¹ ['rɒkɪt] **I** *s.* **1.** *allg.* Ra'kete *f;* **2.** *fig.* F ‚Zi'garre‘ *f,* Anpfiff *m;* **II** *adj.* **3.** Raketen...: ~ *bomb;* ~ *aircraft,* ~*-driven airplane* Raketenflugzeug *n;* ~*-assisted take-off* ✈ Raketenstart *m;* **III** *v/i.* **4.** (wie e-e Ra'kete) hochschießen; **5.** ♥ hochschnellen (*Preise*); **6.** *fig.* e-n ko'metenhaften Aufstieg nehmen; **IV** *v/t.* **7.** ✕ mit Ra'keten beschießen; **8.** mit e-r Ra'kete *in den Weltraum etc.* befördern.

rock·et² ['rɒkɪt] *s.* ♥ **1.** 'Nachtvi,ole *f;* **2.** Rauke *f;* **3.** *a.* ~ *plant,* *garden* (*od. salad*) ~ Rucola *f;* **4.** *a.* ~ *cress* (echtes) Barbarakraut.

rock·et·eer [ˌrɒkɪ'tɪə] *s.* ✕ **1.** Ra'ketenkano,nier *m od.* -pi,lot *m;* **2.** Ra'ketenforscher *m,* -fachmann *m.*

rock·et| jet *s.* Ra'ketentriebwerk *n;* ~ **launch·er** *s.* ✕ Ra'ketenwerfer *m;* '~-**launch·ing site** *s.* ✕ Ra'ketenabschussbasis *f;* '~-**pow·ered** *adj.* mit Ra'ketenantrieb; ~ **pro·jec·tor** *s.* ✕ (Ra'keten)Werfer *m.*

rock·et·ry ['rɒkɪtrɪ] *s.* **1.** Ra'ketentechnik *f od.* -forschung *f;* **2.** *coll.* Ra'keten *pl.*

rock·et sal·ad *s.* ♥ 'Rucola(sa,lat *m*) *f.*

rock| flour *s. min.* Bergmehl *n;* ~ **gar·den** *s.* Steingarten *m;* ~ **group** *s.* ♪ Rockgruppe *f,* -band *f.*

rock·i·ness ['rɒkɪnɪs] *s.* felsige *od.* steinige Beschaffenheit.

rock·ing| chair ['rɒkɪŋ] *s.* Schaukelstuhl *m;* ~ **horse** *s.* Schaukelpferd *n;* ~ **le·ver** *s.* Schwinghebel *m.*

rock| leath·er → *rock cork;* ~ **lob·ster** *s.* Lan'guste *f;* ~ **'n' roll** [ˌrɒkən'rəʊl] *s.* Rock 'n' Roll *m* (*Musik u. Tanz*); ~ **oil**

---

s. Stein-, Erdöl *n,* Pe'troleum *n;* ~ **plant** *s.* ♥ Felsen-, Alpen-, Steingartenpflanze *f;* '~-**rose** *s.* ♥ Zistrose *f;* ~ **salt** *s.* 🜨 Steinsalz *n;* '~-**slide** *s.* Steinschlag *m,* Felssturz *m;* '~-**wood** *s. min.* 'Holzas,best *m;* '~-**work** *s.* **1.** Gesteinsmasse *f;* **2.** a) Steingarten *m,* b) Grottenwerk *n;* **3.** △ Quaderwerk *n.*

rock·y¹ ['rɒkɪ] *adj.* **1.** felsig; **2.** steinhart (*a. fig.*).

rock·y² ['rɒkɪ] *adj.* □ F wack(e)lig (*a. fig.*), wankend.

ro·co·co [rəʊ'kəʊkəʊ] **I** *s.* **1.** Rokoko *n;* **II** *adj.* **2.** Rokoko...; **3.** verschnörkelt, über'laden.

rod [rɒd] *s.* **1.** Rute *f,* Gerte *f; a. fig. bibl.* Reis *n;* **2.** (Zucht)Rute *f* (*a. fig.*): *have a* ~ *in pickle for s.o.* mit j-m noch ein Hühnchen zu rupfen haben; *kiss the* ~ sich unter die Rute beugen; *make a* ~ *for one's own back fig.* sich die Rute selber flechten; *spare the* ~ *and spoil the child* wer die Rute spart, verzieht das Kind; **3.** a) Zepter *n,* b) Amtsstab *m,* c) *fig.* Amtsgewalt *f,* d) *fig.* Knute *f,* Tyran'nei *f;* → *Black Rod;* **4.** (Holz)Stab *m,* Stock *m;* **5.** ⚙ (Rund-)Stab *m,* (Treib-, Verbindungs- *etc.*) Stange *f:* ~ *aerial* ⚡ Stabantenne *f; Kernkraft:* Brennstab *m;* **6.** a) Angelrute *f,* b) Angler *m;* **7.** Messlatte *f,* -stab *m;* **8.** a) Rute *f* (*Längenmaß*), b) Quad'ratrute *f* (*Flächenmaß*); **9.** *Am. sl.* ‚Ka'none‘ *f* (*Pistole*); **10.** *anat.* Stäbchen *n* (*Netzhaut*); **11.** *biol.* 'Stäbchenbak,terie *f;* **12.** *Am. sl.* → *hot rod.*

rode [rəʊd] *pret. von* **ride.**

ro·dent ['rəʊdənt] *adj.* **1.** *zo.* nagend; Nage...: ~ *teeth;* **2.** 🜆 fressend (*Geschwür*); **II** *s.* **3.** Nagetier *n.*

ro·de·o [rəʊ'deɪəʊ] *pl.* **-os** *s. Am.* Ro-'deo *m, n:* a) Zs.-treiben *n von* Vieh, b) Sammelplatz für diesen Zweck, c) 'Cowboytur,nier *n,* Wild'westvorführung *f,* d) 'Motorrad-, 'Autoro,deo *m, n.*

roe¹ [rəʊ] *s. zo.* **1.** *a. hard* ~ Rogen *m,* Fischlaich *m;* ~ *corn* Fischei *n;* **2.** *a. soft* ~ Milch *f;* **3.** Eier *pl.* (*vom Hummer etc.*).

roe² [rəʊ] *pl.* **roes,** *coll.* **roe** *s. zo.* **1.** Reh *n;* **2.** a) Ricke *f* (*weibliches Reh*), b) Hirschkuh *f;* '~-**buck** *s.* Rehbock *m;* ~ **deer** *s.* Reh *n.*

roent·gen → **röntgen.**

ro·ga·tion [rəʊ'geɪʃn] *s. eccl.* a) (Für-)Bitte *f,* ('Bitt)Lita,nei *f,* b) *mst pl.* Bittgang *m:* ℞ *Sunday* Sonntag *m* Rogate; ℞ *week* Himmelfahrts-, Bittwoche *f.*

rog·a·to·ry ['rɒgətərɪ] *adj.* 🜩 Untersuchungs...: ~ *commission; letters* ~ Amtshilfeersuchen *n.*

rog·er ['rɒdʒə] *int.* **1.** *Funk:* roger!, verstanden!; **2.** F in Ordnung!

rogue [rəʊg] *s.* **1.** Schurke *m,* Gauner *m:* ~*s' gallery* Verbrecheralbum *n;* **2.** *humor.* Schelm *m,* Schlingel *m,* Spitzbube *m;* **3.** ♥ a) aus der Art schlagende Pflanze, b) 'Missbildung *f;* **4.** *zo. a.* ~ *elephant,* ~ *buffalo etc.* bösartiger Einzelgänger; **5.** *Pferderennen:* a) bockendes Pferd, b) Ausreißer *m* (*Pferd*).

'ro·guer·y [-gərɪ] *s.* **1.** Schurke'rei *f,* Gaune'rei *f;* **2.** Spitzbübe'rei *f;* '**ro·guish** [-gɪʃ] *adj.* □ **1.** schurkisch; **2.** schelmisch, schalkhaft, spitzbübisch.

roil [rɔɪl] **I** *v/i.* **1.** tosen, brausen (*Wasser*); **II** *v/t.* **2.** *Wasser etc.* aufwühlen; **3.** *bsd. Am.* ärgern, reizen: *be* ~*ed at* aufgebracht sein über (*acc.*).

roist·er ['rɔɪstə] *v/i.* **1.** kra'keelen; **2.** aufschneiden, prahlen; '**roist·er·er** [-tərə] *s.* **1.** Kra'keeler *m;* **2.** Großmaul *n.*

---

role [rəʊl] *s. thea. u. fig.* Rolle *f:* *play a* ~ e-e Rolle spielen; ~ *play*(*·ing*) *s. ped., psych.* Rollenspiel *n;* ~ *swap·ping s.* Rollentausch *m.*

roll [rəʊl] **I** *s.* **1.** (Haar-, Kragen-, Papier- *etc.*)Rolle *f;* **2.** a) *hist.* Schriftrolle *f,* Perga'ment *n,* b) Urkunde *f,* c) (*bsd.* Namens)Liste *f,* Verzeichnis *n,* d) 🜩 Anwaltsliste *f:* ~ *of hono*(*u*)*r* Ehrenliste, -tafel *f* (*bsd. der Gefallenen*); *the* ℞*s* Staatsarchiv *n* (*Gebäude in London*); *call the* ~ die (Namens- *od.* Anwesenheits)Liste verlesen, Appell abhalten; *strike s.o. off the* ~ j-n von der Anwaltsliste streichen; → *master* 13; **3.** △ a) *a.* ~ *mo*(*u*)*lding* Rundleiste *f,* Wulst *f,* b) *antiq.* Vo'lute *f;* **4.** ⚙ Rolle *f,* Walze *f;* **5.** Brötchen *n,* Semmel *f;* **6.** (*bsd.* 'Fleisch)Rou,lade *f;* **7.** *sport* Rolle *f* (*a.* ✈ *Kunstflug*); **8.** ⚓ Rollen *n,* Schlingern *n* (*Schiff*); **9.** wiegender Gang, Seemannsgang *m;* **10.** Fließen *n,* Fluss *m* (*des Wassers; a. fig. der Rede, von Versen etc.*); **11.** (Orgel- *etc.*)Brausen *n;* (Donner)Rollen *n;* (Trommel-)Wirbel *m;* Dröhnen *n* (*Stimme etc.*); Rollen *n,* Trillern *n* (*Vogel*); **12.** *Am. sl.* a) Geldscheinbündel *n,* b) *fig.* (e-e Masse) Geld *n;* **II** *v/i.* **13.** rollen (*Ball etc.*): *start* ~*ing* ins Rollen kommen; **14.** rollen, fahren (*Fahrzeug*); **15.** *a.* ~ *along* sich (da'hin)wälzen, da'hinströmen (*Fluten*) (*a. fig.*); **16.** da'hinziehen (*Gestirn, Wolken*); **17.** sich wälzen: *be* ~*ing in money* F im Geld schwimmen; **18.** *sport, a.* ✈ e-e Rolle machen; **19.** ⚓ schlingern; **20.** wiegend gehen: ~*ing gait* → 9; **21.** a) grollen (*Donner*); brausen (*Orgel*); dröhnen (*Stimme*); wirbeln (*Trommel*); trillern (*Vogel*); **22.** a) ⚙ sich walzen lassen, b) *typ.* sich verteilen (*Druckfarbe*); **III** *v/t.* **23.** *Fass, Rad etc., a. Augen* rollen, (her'um)wälzen, (-)drehen: ~ *a problem round in one's mind fig.* ein Problem wälzen; *Film:* ~ *film!,* ~ *it Am.* Kamera an!; **24.** *Wagen etc.* rollen, fahren, schieben; **25.** *Wassermassen* wälzen (*Fluss*); **26.** (zs.-, auf-, ein)rollen, (-)wickeln; **27.** *Teig* (aus)rollen; *Zigarette* drehen; *Schneeball etc.* formen: ~*ed ham* Rollschinken *m;* **28.** ⚙ *Metalle* walzen, strecken; *Rasen, Straße* walzen: ~*ed glass* gezogenes Glas; ~*ed gold* Walzgold *n,* Golddublee *n;* ~*ed iron* (*od. products*) Walzeisen *n;* ~ *on et.* aufwalzen; **29.** *typ.* a) *Papier* ka'landern, glätten, b) *Druckfarbe* verteilen; **30.** rollen(d sprechen): ~ *one's r's;* ~*ed r* Zungen-R *n;* **31.** *Trommel* wirbeln; **32.** ⚓ *Schiff* zum Rollen bringen; **33.** *Körper etc. beim Gehen* wiegen; **34.** *Am. sl. Betrunkenen etc.* ausplündern.

Zssgn mit adv.:

roll| back *v/t. fig.* her'unterschrauben, reduzieren; ~ **down I** *v/i.* **1.** her'unterrollen, -kugeln, her'unterrollen: *tears were rolling down his cheeks* Tränen liefen ihm über die Wangen; **II** *v/t.* **2.** hin'unterrollen; **3.** *Autofenster etc.* her'unterkurbeln, *Ärmel* her'unterkrempeln; ~ **in** *v/i.* **1.** *fig.* her'einströmen, eintreffen (*Angebote, Geld etc.*); **2.** F schlafen gehen; ~ **out 1.** *metall.* auswalzen, strecken; **2.** *Teig* ausrollen; **3.** a) *Lied etc.* (hin'aus)schmettern, b) *Verse* deklamieren; ~ **o·ver** *v/t.* (*v/i.* sich) her'umwälzen, -drehen; ~ **up I** *v/t.* **1.** (her)'anrollen, (-)'anfahren; F vorfahren; **2.** F ‚aufkreuzen‘, auftauchen; **3.** sich zs.-rollen; **4.** *fig.* sich ansammeln *od.* (-)häufen; **II** *v/t.* **5.** her'anfahren; **6.** aufrollen, -wickeln: ~ *one's* *sleeves* die Ärmel hochkrempeln (*a. fig.*); **7.** ✕ *gegnerische Front* aufrollen; **8.** *sl.* ansammeln: **~ a fortune**.

'roll·back *s. Am.* **1.** ✕ Zu'rückwerfen *n* (*des Feinds*); **2.** ♈ Zu'rückschrauben *n* (*der Preise*); **3.** *fig.* Rückgang *m*; '~·**bar** *s. mot.* 'Überrollbügel *m*; ~ **call** *s.* **1.** Namensaufruf *m*: ~ (*vote*) *pol.* namentliche Abstimmung; **2.** ✕ 'Anwesenheitsap‚pell *m*.

roll·er ['rəʊlə] *s.* **1.** ⊙ a) Walzwerkarbeiter *m*, b) Fördermann *m*; **2.** (Stoff-, Garn- *etc.*)Rolle *f*; **3.** ⊙ a) (Gleit-, Lauf-, Führungs)Rolle *f*, b) (Gleit)Rolle *f*, Rädchen *n* (*unter Möbeln, an Rollschuhen etc.*); **4.** a) Walze *f*, b) Zy'linder *m*, Trommel *f*; **5.** *typ.* Druckwalze *f*; **6.** Rollstab *m* (*Landkarte etc.*); **7.** ⚓ Roller *m*, Sturzwelle *f*; **8.** *orn.* a) Flug-, Tümmlertaube *f*, b) *e-e* Racke: **common** ~ Blauracke, c) Harzer Roller *m*; ~ **band·age** *s.* ♣ Rollbinde *f*; ~ **bear·ing** *s.* ⊙ Rollen-, Wälzlager *n*; ~ **clutch** *s.* ⊙ Rollen-, Freilaufkupplung *f*; ~ **coast·er** *s.* Achterbahn(wagen *m*) *f*; ~ **mill** *s.* **1.** Mahl-, Quetschwerk *n*; **2.** → *rolling mill*; ~ **skate** *s.* Rollschuh *m*; '~-**skate** *v/i.* Rollschuh laufen; ~ **skating** *s.* Rollschuhlaufen *n*; ~ **tow·el** *s.* Rollhandtuch *n*.

roll| **film** *s. phot.* Rollfilm *m*; '~-**front cab·i·net** *s.* Rollschrank *m*.

rol·lick ['rɒlɪk] *v/i.* **1.** a) ausgelassen *od.* 'übermütig sein, b) her'umtollen; **2.** das Leben genießen; **'rol·lick·ing** [-kɪŋ] *adj.* ausgelassen, 'übermütig.

roll·ing ['rəʊlɪŋ] *I s.* **1.** Rollen *n*; **2.** Da'hinfließen *n* (*Wasser etc.*); **3.** Rollen *n* (*Donner*); Brausen *n* (*Wasser*); **4.** *metall.* Walzen *n*, Strecken *n*; **5.** ⚓ Schlingern *n*; *II adj.* **6.** rollend *etc.*; → *roll* II; ~ **bar·rage** *s.* ✕ Feuerwalze *f*; ~ **cap·i·tal** *s.* ♈ Be'triebskapi‚tal *n*; ~ **chair** *s.* ♣ Rollstuhl *m*; ~ **kitch·en** *s.* ✕ Feldküche *f*; ~ **mill** *s.* ⊙ **1.** Walzwerk *n*, Hütte *f*; **2.** 'Walzma‚schine *f*; **3.** Walz(en)straße *f*; ~ **pin** *s.* Nudel-, Wellholz *n*; ~ **press** *s.* ⊙ **1.** Walzen-, Rotati'onspresse *f*; **2.** Papierfabrikation: Sati'nierma‚schine *f*; ~ **stock** *s.* 🚋 rollendes Materi'al, Betriebsmittel *pl.*; ~ **stone** *s. fig.* Zugvogel *m*: *a* ~ *gathers no moss* wer rastet, der rostet; ~ **ti·tle** *s. Film*: Rolltitel *m*.

roll| **lathe** *s.* ⊙ Walzendrehbank *f*; '~-**mop** *s.* Rollmops *m*; '~-**neck** *s.* 'Rollkragen(pul‚lover) *m*; '~-**on** *s.* **1.** E'lastikschlüpfer *m*; **2.** *a.* ~ **deodorant** Deorollstift *m*, F Deoroller *m*; '~-**out** *s.* **1.** ✈ Ausrollen *n* (*nach der Landung*); **2.** ✈ Roll-out *m* (*Präsentation e-s neuen Flugzeugs*); **3.** Präsentati'on *f od.* Vorstellung *f e-s neuen Produktes*; '**roll·o·ver** *s.* **1.** *Brit. Lotto: das im Jackpot verbliebene Geld*, (aufgestockter) Jackpot; **2.** ♈ Laufzeitverlängerung *f*; '~-**top desk** *s.* Rollpult *n*; ~ **train** *s. metall.* Walzenstrecke *f*.

ro·ly-po·ly [‚rəʊlɪ'pəʊlɪ] *I s.* **1.** *a.* ~ **pudding** Art Pudding *m*; **2.** Pummelchen *n* (*Person*); *II adj.* **3.** mollig, pummelig.

Ro·ma·ic [rəʊ'meɪɪk] *I adj.* ro'maisch, neugriechisch; *II s. ling.* Neugriechisch *n*.

Ro·man ['rəʊmən] *I adj.* **1.** römisch: ~ **arch** △ romanischer Bogen; ~ **candle** Leuchtkugel *f* (*Feuerwerk*); ~ **holiday** *fig.* a) blutrünstiges Vergnügen, b) Vergnügen *n* auf Kosten anderer, c) Riesenskandal *m*; ~ **law** römisches Recht; ~ **nose** Römer-, Adlernase *f*; ~ **numeral** römische Ziffer; **2.** (römisch-)ka'tholisch; **3.** *mst* 𝓁 *typ.* Antiqua...; *II s.* **4.**

Römer(in); **5.** *mst* 𝓁 *typ.* An'tiqua *f*; **6.** *eccl.* Katho'lik(in); **7.** *pl. bibl.* (Brief *m* des Paulus an die) Römer *pl.*

ro·man à clef [rəʊ‚mɑːnɑː'kleɪ] (*Fr.*) *s.* 'Schlüsselro‚man *m*.

Ro·man Cath·o·lic *eccl.* *I adj.* (römisch-)ka'tholisch; *II s.* Katho'lik(in); ~ **Church** *s.* römische *od.* (römisch-)ka'tholische Kirche.

ro·mance [rəʊ'mæns] *I s.* **1.** *hist.* ('Ritter-, 'Vers)Ro‚man *m*; **2.** Ro'manze *f*: a) (ro'mantischer) 'Liebes-, 'Abenteuerro‚man, b) *fig.* 'Liebesaf‚färe *f*, c) ♪ *Lied od. lyrisches Instrumentalstück*; **3.** *fig.* Märchen *n*, Fantaste'rei *f*; **4.** *fig.* Ro'mantik *f*: a) Zauber *m*, b) ro'mantische I'deen *pl.*; *II v/i.* **5.** (Ro'manzen) dichten; **6.** *fig.* a) fabulieren, ‚Ro'mane erzählen', b) ins Schwärmen geraten.

Ro·mance [rəʊ'mæns] *bsd. ling.* *I adj.* ro'manisch: ~ **peoples** Romanen; ~ **philologist** Romanist(in); *II s.* a) Ro'manisch *n*, b) *a.* **the** ~ **languages** die romanischen Sprachen *pl.*

ro·manc·er [rəʊ'mænsə] *s.* **1.** Ro'manzendichter(in); Verfasser(in) *e-s* ('Vers)Ro‚mans; **2.** a) Fan'tast(in), b) Aufschneider(in).

Rom·a·nes ['rɒmənes] *s.* Zi'geunersprache *f*.

Ro·man·esque [‚rəʊmə'nesk] *I adj.* **1.** △, *ling.* ro'manisch; **2.** *ling.* proven'zalisch; **3.** 𝓁 *fig.* ro'mantisch; *II s.* **4.** *a.* ~ **style** romanische (Bau)Stil; *das* Ro'manische; **5.** → *Romance²* II.

ro·man-fleuve [rəʊ‚mãː'ŋ'flɜːv] (*Fr.*) *s.* Fa'milienro‚man *m*.

Ro·man·ic [rəʊ'mænɪk] *adj.* **1.** → *Romance²* I; **2.** römisch (*Kulturform*).

Ro·man·ism ['rəʊmənɪzəm] *s.* **1.** a) Ro'ma'nismus *m*, römisch-ka'tholische Einstellung, b) Poli'tik *f od.* Gebräuche *pl.* der römischen Kirche; **2.** *hist.* das Römertum; **'Ro·man·ist** [-ɪst] *s.* **1.** *ling.*, 🚋 Roma'nist(in); **2.** ('Römisch-)Ka‚tholische(r *m*) *f*.

ro·man·tic [rəʊ'mæntɪk] *I adj.* (□ *~ally*) **1.** *allg.* ro'mantisch: a) *die Romantik betreffend* (*Kunst etc.*): *the* ~ *movement* die Romantik, b) ro'manhaft, fan'tastisch (*a. iro.*): *a* ~ *tale*, c) ro'mantisch veranlagt: *a* ~ *girl*, d) malerisch: *a* ~ *town*, e) gefühlvoll: *a* ~ *scene*; *II s.* **2.** Ro'mantiker(in) (*a. fig.*); **3.** *das* Ro'mantische; **4.** *pl.* ro'mantische I'deen *pl. od.* Gefühle *pl.*; **ro-'man·ti·cism** [-ɪsɪzəm] *s.* **1.** *Kunst*: Ro'mantik *f*; **2.** (Sinn *m* für) Ro'mantik *f*; **ro'man·ti·cist** [-ɪsɪst] *s. Kunst*: Ro'mantiker(in); **ro'man·ti·cize** [-ɪsaɪz] *I v/t.* **1.** romantisieren; **2.** in ro'mantischem Licht sehen; *II v/i.* **3.** *fig.* schwärmen.

Rom·a·ny ['rɒmənɪ] *s.* **1.** Zi'geuner(in); **2.** *coll.* die Zigeuner *pl.*; **3.** Ro'mani *n*, Zi'geunersprache *f*.

Rome [rəʊm] *npr.* Rom *n* (*a. fig. hist.* das Römerreich; *eccl.* die katholische Kirche*)*: ~ *was not built in a day* Rom ist nicht an einem Tag erbaut worden; *do in* ~ *as the Romans do!* man sollte sich immer s-r Umgebung anpassen!

romp [rɒmp] *I v/i.* **1.** um'hertollen, sich balgen, toben; ~ *through fig.* spielend durchkommen; **2.** ‚rasen', flitzen: ~ *away* davonziehen (*Rennpferd etc.*); *II s.* **3.** *obs.* Wildfang *m*, Range *f*; **4.** Tollen *n*, Balge'rei *f*; **5.** F *sport* leichter Sieg; **6.** F ‚(wilde) Schmuse'rei'; '**romp·ers** [-pəz] *s. pl.* Spielanzug *m* (*für Kinder*); '**romp·y** [-pɪ] *adj.* ausgelassen, wild.

ron·deau ['rɒndəʊ] *pl.* -**deaus** [-dəʊz]

s. Metrik: Ron'deau *n*, Ringelgedicht *n*; **ron·del** ['rɒndl] *s.* vierzehnzeiliges Ron'deau.

ron·do ['rɒndəʊ] *s.* ♪ Rondo *n*.

rönt·gen ['rɒntjən] *I s. phys.* Röntgen *n* (*Maßeinheit*); *II adj. mst* 𝓁 Röntgen...: ~ **rays**; *III v/t.* → '**rönt·gen·ize** [-tgənaɪz] *v/t.* röntgen; **rönt·gen·o·gram** [rɒnt'genəgræm] *s.* Röntgenaufnahme *f*; **rönt·gen·og·ra·phy** [‚rɒntgə'nɒgrə-fɪ] *s.* 'Röntgenfotogra‚fie *f* (*Verfahren*); **rönt·gen·ol·o·gist** [‚rɒntgə'nɒlədʒɪst] *s.* Röntgeno'loge *f*; **rönt·gen·os·co·py** [‚rɒntgə'nɒskəpɪ] *s.* 'Röntgendurch‚leuchtung *f*, -unter‚suchung *f*; **rönt·gen·o·ther·a·py** [‚rɒntgənə'θerəpɪ] *s.* 'Röntgenthera‚pie *f*.

rood [ruːd] *I s.* **1.** *eccl.* Kruzi'fix *n*; **2.** Viertelacre *m* (*Flächenmaß*); **3.** Rute *f* (*Längenmaß*); *II adj.* **4.** △ Lettner...: ~ **altar**; ~ **loft** Chorbühne *f*; ~ **screen** Lettner *m*.

roof [ruːf] *I s.* **1.** △ (Haus)Dach *n*: *under my* ~ *fig.* unter m-m Dach, in m-m Haus; *raise the* ~ ♪ Krach schlagen; **2.** *mot.* Verdeck *n*; **3.** *fig.* (Blätter-, Zelt*etc.*)Dach *n*, (Himmels)Gewölbe *n*, (-)Zelt *n*: ~ *of the mouth anat.* Gaumen(dach *n*) *m*; *the* ~ *of the world* das Dach der Welt; **4.** ✕ Hangende(s) *n*; *II v/t.* **5.** bedachen: ~ *in Haus* (ein)decken; ~ *over* überdachen; ~*ed-in* überdacht, umbaut; '**roof·age** [-fɪdʒ] → **roofing** 2; '**roof·er** [-fə] *s.* Dachdecker *m*; **roof gar·den** *s.* **1.** Dachgarten *m*; **2.** *Am.* 'Dachrestau‚rant *n*; '**roof·ing** [-fɪŋ] *I s.* **1.** Bedachen *n*, Dachdeckerarbeit *f*; **2.** a) 'Deckmateri‚alien *pl.*, b) Dachwerk *n*; *II adj.* **3.** Dach...: ~ *felt* Dachpappe *f*; '**roof·less** [-lɪs] *adj.* **1.** ohne Dach, unbedeckt; **2.** *fig.* obdachlos; **roof rack** *s. mot.* Dachgepäckträger *m*; **roof tree** *s.* **1.** △ Firstbalken *m*; **2.** *fig.* Dach *n*.

rook¹ [rʊk] *I s.* **1.** *orn.* Saatkrähe *f*; **2.** *fig.* Gauner *m*, Bauernfänger *m*; *II v/t.* **3.** *j-n* betrügen.

rook² [rʊk] *s.* Schachspiel: Turm *m*.

rook·er·y ['rʊkərɪ] *s.* **1.** a) Krähenhorst *m*, b) 'Krähenkolo‚nie *f*; **2.** *orn., zo.* Brutplatz *m*; **3.** *fig.* a) 'Elendsquar‚tier *n*, -viertel *n*, b) 'Mietska‚serne *f*.

rook·ie ['rʊkɪ] *s. sl.* **1.** ✕ Re'krut *m*; **2.** Neuling *m*, Anfänger *m*.

room [ruːm] *I s.* **1.** Raum *m*, Platz *m*: *make* ~ (*for*) *a. fig.* Platz machen (*dat.*); *no* ~ *to swing a cat (in)* sehr wenig Platz; *in the* ~ *of* anstelle von (*od. gen.*); **2.** Raum *m*, Zimmer *n*, Stube *f*: *next* ~ Nebenzimmer; ~ *heating* Raumheizung *f*; ~ *temperature* (*a. normale*) Raum-, Zimmertemperatur *f*; **3.** *pl. Brit.* Wohnung *f*; **4.** *fig.* (Spiel-)Raum *m*; Gelegenheit *f*, Anlass *m*: ~ *for complaint* Anlass zur Klage; *there is no* ~ *for hope* es besteht keinerlei Hoffnung; *there is* ~ *for improvement* es ließe sich noch manches besser machen; *II v/i.* **5.** *bsd. Am.* wohnen, logieren (*at in dat., with* bei): ~ *together* zs.-wohnen; **-roomed** [ruːmd] *adj. in Zssgn.* ...zimmerig; **room·er** ['ruːmə] *s. bsd. Am.* 'Untermieter(in); **'room·ful** [-fʊl] *pl.* -**fuls** *s.*: *a* ~ *of people* ein Zimmer voll(er) Leute; **room·i·ness** ['ruːmɪnɪs] *s.* Geräumigkeit *f*.

room·ing **house** *s.* 'Untermiete ['ruːmɪŋ] *s. Am.* Fremdenheim *n*, Pensi'on *f*; '~-**in** *n* ♀ Rooming-'in *n* (*gemeinsame Unterbringung von Mutter und Kind*).

'room·mate *s.* 'Stubenkame‚rad(in).

room·y ['ruːmɪ] *adj.* □ geräumig.

roost [ruːst] *I s.* a) Schlafplatz *m*, -sitz *m*

(*Vogel*), b) Hühnerstange *f od.* -stall *m*: **at** ~ auf der Stange; **come home to** ~ *fig.* auf den Urheber zurückfallen; → **rule** 13; **II** *v/i. orn.* a) auf der Stange sitzen, b) sich (zum Schlafen) niederhocken; '**roost·er** [-tə] *s. bsd. Am.* (Haus)Hahn *m*.

root¹ [ru:t] **I** *s.* **1.** ⚘ Wurzel *f* (*a. weitS. Wurzelgemüse, Knolle, Zwiebel*): ~ **and branch** *fig.* mit Stumpf u. Stiel; **pull out by the** ~ mit der Wurzel herausreißen (*a. fig. ausrotten*); **put down** ~**s** *fig.* Wurzel schlagen, sesshaft werden; **strike at the** ~ **of** *fig. et.* an der Wurzel treffen; **strike** (*od.* **take**) ~ Wurzel schlagen (*a. fig.*); ~**s of a mountain** der Fuß e-s Berges; **2.** *anat.* (Haar-, Nagel-, Zahn-, Zungen- *etc.*) Wurzel *f*; **3.** Ⱥ a) Wurzel *f*, b) eingesetzter *od.* gesuchter Wert (*Gleichung*): ~ **extraction** Wurzelziehen *n*; **4.** *ling.* Wurzel(wort *n*) *f*, Stammwort *n*; **5.** ♪ Grundton *m*; **6.** *fig.* a) Quelle *f*, Ursache *f*, Wurzel *f*: ~ **of all evil** Wurzel alles Bösen; **get at the** ~ **of** e-r Sache auf den Grund gehen; **have its** ~ **in**, **take its** ~ **from** → 8, b) *pl.* Wurzeln *pl.*, Ursprung *m*, c) Kern *m*, Wesen *n*, Gehalt *m*: ~ **of the matter** Kern der Sache; ~ **idea** Grundgedanke *m*; **II** *v/i.* **7.** Wurzel fassen *od.* schlagen, (ein)wurzeln (*a. fig.*): **deeply** ~**ed** *fig.* tief verwurzelt; **stand** ~**ed to the ground** wie angewurzelt dastehen; **8.** ~ **in** beruhen auf (*dat.*), s-n Grund *od.* Ursprung haben in (*dat.*); **III** *v/t.* **9.** tief einpflanzen, einwurzeln lassen: **fear** ~**ed him to the ground** *fig.* er stand vor Furcht wie angewurzelt; **10.** ~ **up**, ~ **out**, ~ **away** a) ausreißen, b) *fig.* ausrotten, vertilgen.

root² [ru:t] **I** *v/i.* **1.** wühlen (**for** nach) (*Schwein*); **2.** ~ **about** *fig.* her'umwühlen; **II** *v/t.* **3.** Boden auf-, 'umwühlen; **4.** ~ **out**, ~ **up** *a. fig.* ausgraben, aufstöbern.

root³ [ru:t] *v/i.* ~ **for** *Am. sl.* a) *sport* j-n anfeuern, b) *fig.* Stimmung machen für j-n *od. et.*

,root-and-'branch *adj.* radi'kal, restlos.

root di·rec·to·ry *s. Computer:* Stamm-, Wurzelverzeichnis *n*.

root·ed ['ru:tɪd] *adj.* □ (fest) eingewurzelt (*a. fig.*); '**root·ed·ly** [-lɪ] *adv.* von Grund auf, zu'tiefst; '**root·ed·ness** [-nɪs] *s.* Verwurzelung *f*, Eingewurzeltsein *n*.

root·er ['ru:tə] *s. sport Am.* F begeisterter Anhänger, ,Fa'natiker' *m*.

root·less ['ru:tlɪs] *adj.* wurzellos (*a. fig.*); **root·let** ['ru:tlɪt] *s.* ⚘ Wurzelfaser *f*.

,root|-mean-'square *s.* Ⱥ qua'dratischer Mittelwert; '~**·stock** *s.* **1.** ⚘ Wurzelstock *m*; **2.** *fig.* Wurzel *f*; ~ **treat·ment** *s.* ✷ (Zahn)Wurzelbehandlung *f*.

rope [rəʊp] **I** *s.* **1.** Seil *n*, Tau *n*; Strick *m*, Strang *m* (*beide a. zum Erhängen*); ♻ (Tau)Ende *n*: **the** ~ *fig.* der Strick (*Tod durch den Strang*); **be at the end of one's** ~ mit s-m Latein am Ende sein; **know the** ~**s** sich auskennen, ,den Bogen raushaben'; **learn the** ~**s** sich einarbeiten; **show s.o. the** ~**s** j-m die Kniffe beibringen; **2.** *mount.* (Kletter)Seil *n*: **on the** ~ angeseilt; ~ (**team**) Seilschaft *f*; **3.** (Ar'tisten)Seil *n*: **on the high** ~**s** *fig.* a) hochgestimmt, b) hochmütig; **4.** *Am.* Lasso *n*, *m*; **5.** *pl.* Boxen: (Ring)Seile *pl.*: **be on the** ~**s** a) (angeschlagen) in den Seilen hängen, b) *fig.* am Ende *od.* ,fertig' sein; **have s.o. on the** ~**s** *sl.* j-n ,zur Schnecke'

gemacht haben; **6.** *fig.* Strang *m* Tabak *etc.*; Bund *n* Zwiebeln *etc.*; Schnur *f* Perlen *etc.*: ~ **of sand** *fig.* Illusion *f*; **7.** Faden *m* (*Flüssigkeit*); **8.** *fig.* Spielraum *m*, Handlungsfreiheit *f*: **give s.o.** (**plenty of**) ~; **II** *v/t.* **9.** (mit e-m Seil) zs.-binden; festbinden; **10.** *mst* ~ **in** (*od.* **off** *od.* **out**) Platz (durch ein Seil) absperren *od.* abgrenzen; **11.** *mount.* anseilen: ~ **down** (**up**) j-n ab- (auf)seilen; **12.** *Am.* mit dem Lasso einfangen: ~ **in** *sl.* Wähler, Kunden *etc.* fangen, j-n ,an Land ziehen', sich *ein* Mädchen *etc.* ,anlachen'; **III** *v/i.* **13.** Fäden ziehen (*Flüssigkeit*); **14.** *a.* ~ **up** *mount.* sich anseilen: ~ **down** sich abseilen; ~ **danc·er** *s.* Seiltänzer(in); ~ **lad·der** *s.* **1.** Strickleiter *f*; **2.** ♻ Seefallreep *n*; ~ **mo(u)ld·ing** *s.* △ Seilleiste *f*; ~ **quoit** *s.* ♻, *sport* Seilring *m*; ~ **rail·way** → ropeway.

rop·er·y ['rəʊpərɪ] *s.* Seile'rei *f*.

'rope's-end ♻ **I** *s.* Tauende *n*; **II** *v/t.* mit dem Tauende prügeln.

rope| tow *s.* Skisport: Schlepplift *m*; '~**·walk** *s.* Seiler-, Reeperbahn *f*; '~**,walk·er** *s.* Seiltänzer(in); '~**·way** *s.* (Seil)Schwebebahn *f*; '~**·yard** *s.* Seile'rei *f*; ~ **yarn** *s.* **1.** ⊙ Kabelgarn *n*; **2.** *fig.* Baga'telle *f*.

rop·i·ness ['rəʊpɪnɪs] *s.* Dickflüssigkeit *f*, Klebrigkeit *f*; '**rop·y** [-pɪ] *adj.* □ **1.** klebrig, zäh, fadenziehend: ~ **sirup**; **2.** kahmig: ~ **wine**; **3.** F ,mies'.

ror·qual ['rɔ:kwəl] *s. zo.* Finnwal *m*.

ro·sace ['rəʊzeɪs] (*Fr.*) *s.* △ **1.** Ro'sette *f*; **2.** → rose window.

ro·sa·ceous [rəʊ'zeɪʃəs] *adj.* **1.** ⚘ a) zu den Rosa'zeen gehörig, b) rosenblütig; **2.** Rosen...

ro·sar·i·an [rəʊ'zeərɪən] *s.* **1.** Rosenzüchter *m*; **2.** *R.C.* Mitglied *n* einer Rosenkranzbruderschaft.

ro·sa·ry ['rəʊzərɪ] *s.* **1.** *R.C.* Rosenkranz *m*: **say the** ♻ den Rosenkranz beten; **2.** Rosengarten *m*, -beet *n*.

rose¹ [rəʊz] **I** *s.* **1.** ⚘ Rose *f*: ~ **of Jericho** Jerichorose; ~ **of May** Weiße Narzisse; ~ **of Sharon** a) *bibl.* Sharontulpe *f*, b) Großblumiges Johanniskraut; **the** ~ **of** *fig.* die Rose (*das schönste Mädchen*) von; **gather** (*life's*) ~**s** sein Leben genießen; **on a bed of** ~**s** *fig.* auf Rosen gebettet; **it is no bed of** ~**s** es ist kein Honiglecken; **it is not all** ~**s** es ist nicht so rosig, wie es aussieht; **under the** ~ im Vertrauen; **2.** → rose colo(u)r; **3.** *her. hist.* Rose *f*: **Red** ♻ Rote Rose (*Haus Lancaster*); **White** ♻ Weiße Rose (*Haus York*); **Wars of the** ♻**s** Rosenkriege; **4.** △ Ro'sette *f* (*a. Putz*; *a. Edelstein[schliff]*); **5.** Brause *f* (*Gießkanne etc.*); **6.** *phys.* Kreisskala *f*; **7.** ♻ *etc.* Windrose *f*; **8.** ✳ Wundrose *f*; **II** *adj.* **9.** Rosen...; **10.** rosenfarbig.

rose² [rəʊz] *pret. von* **rise**.

ro·se·ate ['rəʊzɪət] *adj.* □ → rose-colo(u)red.

rose| bit *s.* ⊙ Senkfräser *m*; '~**·bud** *s.* ⚘ Rosenknospe *f* (*a. fig. Mädchen*); '~**·bush** *s.* Rosenstrauch *m*; ~ **col·o(u)r** *s.* Rosa-, Rosenrot *n*: **life is not all** ~ *fig.* das Leben besteht nicht nur aus Annehmlichkeiten; '~**·,col·o(u)red** *adj.* **1.** rosa-, rosenfarbig, rosenrot; **2.** *fig.* rosig, opti'mistisch: **see things through** ~ **spectacles** die Dinge durch e-e rosa (-rote) Brille sehen; '~**·hip** *s.* ⚘ Hagebutte *f*.

rose·mar·y ['rəʊzmərɪ] *s.* ⚘ Rosmarin *m*.

ro·se·o·la [rəʊ'zɪːələ] *s.* ✷ **1.** Rose'ole *f* (*Ausschlag*); **2.** → German measles.

,rose|-'pink I *s.* ⊙ Rosenlack *m*, roter

Farbstoff; **II** *adj.* rosa, rosenrot (*a. fig.*); ~ **rash** → roseola 1; **,~-'red** *adj.* rosenrot.

ro·ser·y → rosary 2.

rose tree *s.* Rosenstock *m*.

ro·sette [rəʊ'zet] *s.* Ro'sette *f* (*a.* △); **ro·set·ted** [-tɪd] *adj.* **1.** mit Ro'setten geschmückt; **2.** ro'settenförmig.

rose| wa·ter *s.* **1.** Rosenwasser *n*; **2.** *fig.* a) Schmeiche'leien *pl.*, b) Gefühlsduse'lei *f*; '~**,wa·ter** *adj. fig.* a) ('über-)fein, (-)zart, b) affek'tiert, c) sentimen'tal; ~ **win·dow** *s.* △ ('Fenster)Ro,sette *f*, (-)Rose *f*; '~**·wood** *s.* Rosenholz *n*.

ros·in ['rɒzɪn] **I** *s.* ♈ (Terpen'tin)Harz *n*, *bsd.* Kolo'phonium *n*, Geigenharz *n*; **II** *v/t.* mit Kolo'phonium einreiben.

ros·i·ness ['rəʊzɪnɪs] *s.* Rosigkeit *f*, rosiges Aussehen.

ros·ter ['rəʊstə] *s.* ✕ **1.** (Dienst-, Namens)Liste *f*; **2.** Dienstplan *m*.

ros·tral ['rɒstrəl] *adj.* (schiffs)schnabelförmig; '**ros·trate(d)** [-reɪt(ɪd)] *adj.* **1.** ♈, *zo.* geschnäbelt; **2.** → rostral.

ros·trum ['rɒstrəm] *pl.* **-tra** [-trə] *s.* **1.** a) Rednerbühne *f*, Podium *n*, b) Kanzel *f*, c) *fig.* Plattform *f*; **2.** ♻ *hist.* Schiffsschnabel *m*; **3.** ♈, *zo.* Schnabel *m*; **4.** *zo.* a) Kopfspitze *f*, b) Rüssel *m* (*Insekt*).

ros·y ['rəʊzɪ] *adj.* □ **1.** rosenrot, -farbig: ~ **red** Rosenrot *n*; **2.** rosig, blühend (*Wangen etc.*); **3.** *fig.* rosig.

rot [rɒt] **I** *v/i.* **1.** (ver)faulen, (-)modern (*a. fig. im Gefängnis*); verrotten, verwesen; *geol.* verwittern; **2.** *fig.* verkommen, verrotten; **3.** *Brit. sl.* ,quatschen', Unsinn reden; **II** *v/t.* **4.** faulen lassen; **5.** *bsd. Flachs* rotten; **6.** *Brit. sl.* Plan *etc.* vermurksen; **7.** *Brit. sl.* j-n ,anpflaumen' (*hänseln*); **III** *s.* **8.** a) Fäulnis *f*, Verwesung *f*, b) Fäule *f*, c) *et.* Verfaultes; → **dry-rot**; **9.** ♈, *zo.* a) Fäule *f*, b) *vet.* Leberfäule *f* (*Schaf*); **10.** *Brit. sl.*, *a. int.* ,Quatsch' *m*, Blödsinn *m*.

ro·ta ['rəʊtə] *s.* **1.** → roster; **2.** *Brit.* a) Dienstturnus *m*, b) *a.* ~ **system** Turnusplan *m*; **3.** *mst* ♻ *R.C.* Rota *f* (*oberster Gerichtshof der römisch-katholischen Kirche*).

Ro·tar·i·an [rəʊ'teərɪən] **I** *s.* Ro'tarier *m*; **II** *adj.* Rotary..., Rotarier...

ro·ta·ry ['rəʊtərɪ] **I** *adj.* **1.** rotierend, kreisend, sich drehend, 'umlaufend; Rotations..., Dreh...: ~ **crane** Dreh-, Schwenkkran *m*; ~ **file** Drehkartei *f*; ~ **pump** Umlaufpumpe *f*; ~ **switch** ⚡ Drehschalter *m*; ~ **traffic** Kreisverkehr *m*; **II** *s.* **2.** ⊙ durch Rotation arbeitende Maschine, *bsd.* a) → **rotary engine**, b) → **rotary machine**, c) → **rotary press**; **3.** *Am. mot.* Kreisverkehr *m* (*Straße*); **4.** ♻ → ♻ **Club** *s.* Rotary Club *m*; ~ **cur·rent** *s.* ⚡ Drehstrom *m*; ~ **en·gine** *s.* Drehkolbenmotor *m*; ~ **hoe** *s.* ♪ Hackfräse *f*; ♻ **In·ter·na·tion·al** *s.* Weltvereinigung *f* der Rotary Clubs; ~ **ma·chine** *s. typ.* Rotati'onsma,schine *f*; ~ **pis·ton en·gine** *s.* → **rotary engine**; ~ **press** *s. typ.* Rotati'ons-(druck)presse *f*.

ro·tate¹ [rəʊ'teɪt] **I** *v/i.* **1.** rotieren, kreisen, sich drehen; **2.** der Reihe nach *od.* turnusmäßig wechseln: ~ **in office**; **II** *v/t.* **3.** rotieren *od.* (um)'kreisen lassen; **4.** *Personal* turnusmäßig *etc.* auswechseln; **5.** ♪ *Frucht* wechseln: ~ **crops** im Fruchtwechsel anbauen.

ro·tate² ['rəʊteɪt] *adj.* ♈, *zo.* radförmig.

ro·ta·tion [rəʊ'teɪʃn] *s.* **1.** ⊙, *phys.* Rotati'on *f*, (Achsen-, 'Um)Drehung *f*, 'Um-, Kreislauf *m*, Drehbewegung *f*: ~ **of the earth** (tägliche) Erdumdrehung (*um die eigene Achse*); **2.** Wechsel *m*, Abwechslung *f*: *in* (*od.* **by**) *~* der Reihe nach, abwechselnd, im Turnus; *~ in office* turnusmäßiger Wechsel im Amt; *~ of crops* ✗ Fruchtwechsel, -folge *f*; **ro·ta·tive** ['rəʊtətɪv] *adj.* **1.** → *rotary* 1; **2.** abwechselnd, regelmäßig 'wiederkehrend; **ro·ta·to·ry** ['rəʊtətərɪ] *adj.* **1.** → *rotary* 1; **2.** *fig.* abwechselnd *od.* turnusmäßig (aufein'ander folgend): *~ assemblies*; **3.** *~ muscle anat.* Dreh-, Rollmuskel *m*.

rote [rəʊt] *s.*: *by ~ fig.* a) (rein) mechanisch, b) auswendig.

'**rot·gut** *s. sl.* Fusel *m*.

ro·ti·fer ['rəʊtɪfə] *s. zo.* Rädertier(chen) *n*; **Ro·tif·er·a** [rəʊ'tɪfərə] *s. pl. zo.* Rädertiere *pl.*

ro·to·gra·vure [ˌrəʊtəʊgrə'vjʊə] *s. typ.* **1.** Kupfer(tief)druck *m*; **2.** → *roto section.*

ro·tor ['rəʊtə] *s.* **1.** ✔ Rotor *m*, Drehflügel *m*; **2.** ⚡ Rotor *m*, Anker *m*; **3.** ⊙ Rotor *m* (*Drehteil e-r Maschine*); **4.** ⚓ (Flettner)Rotor *m*.

ro·to sec·tion ['rəʊtəʊ] *s.* Kupfertiefdruckbeilage *f e-r Zeitung.*

rot·ten ['rɒtn] *adj.* □ **1.** faul, verfault: *~ to the core* a) kernfaul, b) *fig.* durch u. durch korrupt; **2.** morsch, mürbe; **3.** brandig, stockig (*Holz*); **4.** ⚙ faul(ig) (*Zahn*); **5.** *fig.* a) verderbt, kor'rupt, b) niederträchtig, gemein; **6.** *sl.* ('hunds-)mise,rabel': *~ luck* Saupech *m*; *~ weather* Sauwetter *n*; '**rot·ten·ness** [-nɪs] *s.* **1.** Fäule *f*, Fäulnis *f*; **2.** *fig.* Verderbtheit *f*, Kor'ruptheit *f*; **rot·ter** ['rɒtə] *s. Brit. sl.* Schweinehund *m*, ,Scheißkerl' *m*.

ro·tund [rəʊ'tʌnd] *adj.* □ **1.** *obs.* rund, kreisförmig; **2.** rundlich (*Mensch*); **3.** *fig.* a) voll(tönend) (*Stimme*), b) hochtrabend, blumig, pom'pös (*Ausdruck*); **4.** *fig.* ausgewogen (*Stil*); **ro·tun·da** [-də] *s.* △ Rundbau *m*; **ro·tun·date** [-deɪt] *adj. bsd.* ♀ abgerundet; **ro·tun·di·ty** [-dɪtɪ] *s.* **1.** Rundheit *f*; **2.** Rundlichkeit *f*; **3.** Rundung *f*; **4.** *fig.* Ausgewogenheit *f* (*des Stils etc.*).

rou·ble ['ruːbl] *s.* Rubel *m* (*russische Währung*).

rou·é ['ruːeɪ] (*Fr.*) *s. obs.* Rou'é *m*, Lebemann *m*.

rouge [ruːʒ] **I** *s.* Rouge *n*, (rote) Schminke; ⊙ Polierrot *n*; **II** *adj. her.* rot; **III** *v/i.* Rouge auflegen, sich schminken; **IV** *v/t.* (rot) schminken.

rough [rʌf] **I** *adj.* □ → *roughly*; **1.** rau (*Oberfläche, a. Haut, Tuch etc.; a. Stimme*); **2.** rau, struppig (*Fell, Haar*); **3.** holp(e)rig, uneben (*Gelände, Weg*); **4.** rau, unwirtlich, zerklüftet (*Landschaft*); **5.** rau (*Wind etc.*); stürmisch (*See, Überfahrt, Wetter*): *~ sea* ⚓ grobe See; **6.** grob, roh (*Mensch, Manieren etc.*); raubeinig, ungehobelt (*Person*); heftig (*Temperament etc.*): *~ play* rohes *od.* hartes Spiel; *~ stuff* F Gewalttätigkeit(en *pl.*) *f*; **7.** rau, barsch, schroff (*Person od. Redeweise*): *~ words* have a *~ tongue* e-e raue Sprache sprechen; **8.** F rau (*Behandlung, Empfang etc.*), hart (*Leben, Tag etc.*), garstig, böse: *it was:* es war e-e böse Sache; *I had a ~ time* es ist mir ziemlich ,mies' ergangen; *that's ~ luck for him* da hat er aber Pech (gehabt); **9.** roh, grob: a) ohne Feinheit, b) unbearbeitet, im Rohzustand: *~ cloth* ungewalktes Tuch; *~ food* grobe Kost; *~ rice* unpolierter Reis; *~ style* grober *od.* ungeschliffener Stil; *~ stone* a) unbehauener Stein, b) ungeschliffener (Edel-)

Stein; → *diamond* 1, *rough-and-ready*; **10.** ⊙ Grob...; *~ carpenter* Grobtischler *m*; *~ file* Schruppfeile *f*; **11.** unfertig, Roh...: *~ copy* Konzept *n*; *~ draft* (*od.* *sketch*) Faustskizze *f*; → *rohentwurf m*; *in a ~ state* im Rohzustand; **12.** *fig.* grob: a) annähernd (richtig), ungefähr, b) flüchtig, im 'Überschlag: *~ analysis* Rohanalyse *f*; *~ calculation* Überschlag *m*; *~ size* ⊙ Rohmaß *n*; **13.** *typ.* noch nicht beschnitten (*Buchrand*); **14.** herb, sauer (*bsd. Wein*); **15.** stark (wirkend) (*Arznei*); **16.** *Brit. sl.* schlecht, ungenießbar (*Fisch*); **II** *adv.* **17.** rau, hart, roh: *play ~*; *cut up ~* ,massiv' werden; **18.** grob, flüchtig; **III** *s.* **19.** Rauheit *f*, *das* Raue: *over ~ and smooth* über Stock und Stein; *take the ~ with the smooth fig.* das Leben nehmen, wie es ist; → *rough-and-tumble* II; **20.** *bsd. Brit.* ,Schläger' *m*, Rowdy *m*, Rohling *m*; **21.** Rohzustand *m*: *from the ~* aus dem Rohen *arbeiten*; *in the ~* im Groben, im Rohzustand; *take us in the ~* j-n nehmen, wie er ist; **22.** a) holperiger Boden, b) *Golf:* Rough *n*; **23.** Stollen *m* (*am Pferdehufeisen*); **IV** *v/t.* **24.** an-, aufrauen; **25.** *j-n* miss'handeln, übel zurichten; **26.** *mst ~ out* Material roh *od.* grob bearbeiten, vorbearbeiten; *metall.* vorwalzen; *Linse, Edelstein* grob schleifen; **27.** *Pferd* zureiten; **28.** *Pferd*(*ehuf*) mit Stollen versehen; **29.** *~ in, ~ out* entwerfen, flüchtig skizzieren; **30.** *~ up* Haare etc. gegen den Strich streichen; → *the wrong way fig.* j-n reizen *od.* verstimmen; **31.** *sport* Gegner hart ,nehmen'; **V** *v/i.* **32.** rau werden; **33.** *sport* (über'trieben) hart spielen; **34.** *~ it* primi'tiv *od.* anspruchslos leben, ein spar'tanisches Leben führen.

rough·age ['rʌfɪdʒ] *s. a.* ✗ Raufutter *n*, b) grobe Nahrung, c) *biol.* Ballaststoffe *pl.*

,**rough|-and-'read·y** *adj.* **1.** grob (gearbeitet), Not..., Behelfs...: *~ rule* Faustregel *f*; **2.** rau *od.* grob, aber zuverlässig (*Person*); **3.** schludrig: *a ~ worker*; ,**~-and-'tum·ble** **I** *adj.* **1.** wild, heftig, verworren: *a ~ fight*; **II** *s.* **2.** wildes Handgemenge, wüste Keile'rei; **3.** *fig.* Wirren *pl. des Krieges, des Lebens etc.*; '**~·cast** **I** *s.* **1.** *fig.* roher Entwurf; **2.** △ Rohputz *m*, Berapp *m*; **II** *adj.* **3.** im Entwurf, unfertig; **4.** roh verputzt, angeworfen; **III** *v/t.* [*irr.* → *cast*] **5.** im Entwurf anfertigen, roh entwerfen; **6.** △ berappen, (*mit Rohputz*) anwerfen; '**~·dry** *v/t.* Wäsche (nur) trocknen (*ohne sie zu bügeln od. mangeln*).

rough·en ['rʌfən] **I** *v/i.* rau(er) werden; **II** *v/t. a. ~ up* an-, aufrauen, rau machen.

,**rough|-'grind** *v/t.* [*irr.* → *grind*] **1.** ⊙ vorschleifen; **2.** *Korn* schroten; ,**~-'han·dle** *v/t.* grob *od.* bru'tal behandeln; ,**~-'hew** *v/t.* [*irr.* → *hew*] **1.** *Holz, Stein etc.* roh behauen, grob bearbeiten; **2.** *fig.* in groben Zügen entwerfen; ,**~-'hewn** *adj.* **1.** ⊙ roh behauen; **2.** *fig.* in groben Zügen entworfen *od.* gestaltet; **3.** *fig.* grobschlächtig, ungehobelt; '**~·house** *sl.* **I** *s.* a) Ra'dau *m*, b) wüste Keile'rei; **II** *v/t.* → *rough* 25; **III** *v/i.* Ra'dau machen, toben.

rough·ly ['rʌflɪ] *adv.* **1.** rau, roh, grob; **2.** *a.* grob, ungefähr, annähernd: *~ speaking* etwa, ungefähr, b) ganz allgemein (gesagt).

,**rough|-ma'chine** *v/t.* ⊙ grob bearbeiten; '**~·neck** *s. Am. sl.* **1.** Raubein *n*, Grobian *m*; **2.** Rowdy *m*.

rough·ness ['rʌfnɪs] *s.* **1.** Rauheit *f*, Unebenheit *f*; **2.** ⊙ raue Stelle; **3.** *fig.* Rohheit *f*, Grobheit *f*, Ungeschliffenheit *f*; **4.** Wildheit *f*, Heftigkeit *f*; **5.** Herbheit *f* (*Wein*).

,**rough|-'plane** *v/t.* ⊙ vorhobeln; '**~·rid·er** *s.* **1.** Zureiter *m*; **2.** verwegener Reiter; **3.** *Am.* ✗ *hist.* a) 'irregu,lärer Ka-valle'rist, b) ⚔ Angehöriger e-s im spanisch-amer. Krieg aufgestellten Kavalle-rie-Freiwilligenregiments; '**~·shod** *adj.* scharf beschlagen (*Pferd*): *ride ~ over fig.* a) j-n rücksichtslos behandeln, j-n schikanieren, b) rücksichtslos über *et.* hinweggehen.

rou·lade [ruː'lɑːd] (*Fr.*) *s.* **1.** ♪ Rou'lade *f*, Pas'sage *f*; **2.** Küche: Rou'lade *f*.

rou·lette [ruː'let] *s.* **1.** Rou'lett *n* (*Glücksspiel*); **2.** ⊙ Rollrädchen *n*.

Rou·ma·ni·an → *Rumanian.*

round [raʊnd] **I** *adj.* □ → *roundly*; **1.** *allg.* rund: a) kugelrund, b) kreisrund, c) zy'lindrisch, d) abgerundet, e) bogenförmig, f) e-n Kreis beschreibend (*Bewegung, Linie etc.*), g) rundlich, dick (*Arme, Wangen etc.*): *~ round angle* (*hand, robin etc.*); **2.** *ling.* gerundet (*Vokal*); **3.** weich, vollmundig (*Wein*); **4.** ♪ ganz (*ohne Bruch*): *in numbers* a) in ganzen Zahlen, b) aufod. abgerundet; **5.** *fig.* rund, voll: *a ~ dozen*; **6.** rund, annähernd (richtig); **7.** rund, beträchtlich (*Summe*); **8.** (ab)gerundet, flüssig (*Stil*); **9.** voll(tönend) (*Stimme*); **10.** flott, scharf: *at a ~ pace*; **11.** offen, unverblümt: *a ~ answer*; *~ lie* freche Lüge; **12.** kräftig, derb, ,saftig': *in ~ terms* in unmissverständlichen Ausdrücken; **II** *s.* **13.** Rund *n*, Kreis *m*, Ring *m*; **14.** Rund (-teil *n*, -bau *m*) *n*, *et.* Rundes; **15.** a) (runde) Stange, b) ⊙ Rundstab *m*, c) (Leiter)Sprosse *f*; **16.** Rundung *f*: *out of ~* ⊙ unrund; *worked on the ~* über e-n Leisten gearbeitet (*Schuh*); **17.** *Kunst:* Rundplastik *f*: *in the ~* a) plastisch, b) *fig.* vollkommen; **18.** *a. ~ of beef* Rindskeule *f*; **19.** *Brit.* Scheibe *f*, Schnitte *f* (*Brot etc.*); **20.** Kreislauf *m*, Runde *f*: *the ~ of the seasons*; *the daily ~* der tägliche Trott; **21.** a) (Dienst)Runde *f*, Rundgang *m* (*Briefträger, Polizist etc.*), b) ✗ Streife *f*: *make the ~ of* e-n Rundgang machen um; **22.** a) (Inspekti'ons)Rundgang *m*, -fahrt *f*, b) Rundreise *f*, Tour *f*; **23.** *fig.* Reihe *f*, Folge *f von Besuchen, Pflichten etc.*: *a ~ of pleasures*; **24.** a) *Boxen, Golf etc.:* Runde *f*, b) (Verhandlungs- etc.)Runde *f*: *first ~ to him!* die erste Runde geht an ihn!, *fig. humor. a.* eins zu null für ihn!; **25.** Runde *f*, Lage *f* (*Bier etc.*): *stand a ~* (*of drinks*) ,e-n ausgeben' (*für alle*); **26.** Runde *f*, Kreis *m* (*Bewegung*): *go* (*od.* **make**) *the ~* (*of*) die Runde machen, kursieren (bei, in *dat.*) (*Gerücht, Witz etc.*); **27.** a) ✗ Salve *f*, b) Schuss *m*: *20 ~s* (*of cartridge*) 20 Schuss (Patronen); **28.** *fig.* Lach-, Beifallssalve *f*: *~ after ~ of applause* nicht enden wollender Beifall; **29.** ♪ a) Rundgesang *m*, Kanon *m*, b) Rundtanz *m*, Reigen *m*; **III** *adv.* **30.** *a. ~ about* rund-, rings(her)'um; **31.** rund(her)'um, im ganzen 'Umkreis, auf *od.* von allen Seiten: *all ~* a) ringsum, überall, b) *fig.* durch die Bank, auf der ganzen Linie; *for a mile ~* im Umkreis von e-r Meile; **32.** rundher'um, im Kreise: *~ and ~* immer rundherum; *hand s.th. ~* et. herumreichen; *look ~* um sich blicken; *turn ~* (sich) umdrehen; *the wheels go ~* die Räder drehen sich; **33.** außen her'um: *a long way* ~ ein weiter Umweg; **34.** *zeitlich*: her'an: *comes ~ again* der Sommer etc. kehrt wieder; **35.** e-e Zeit lang: *all the year* ~ das ganze Jahr lang *od.* hindurch; *the clock* ~ volle 24 Stunden; **36.** a) hi'nüber, b) he'rüber: *ask s.o.* ~ j-n zu sich bitten; *order one's car* ~ (den Wagen) vorfahren lassen; **IV** *prp.* **37.** (rund) um: *a tour ~ the world*; **38.** um (... her'um): *sail ~ the Cape*; *just ~ the corner* gleich um die Ecke; **39.** in *od.* auf (*dat.*) ... herum: ~ *all the shops* in allen Läden herum; **40.** um (... he'rum), im 'Umkreis von (*od. gen.*); **41.** um (... he'rum): *write a book ~ a story*; *argue ~ and ~ a subject* um ein Thema herumreden; **42.** *zeitlich*: durch, während (*gen.*); **V** *v/t.* **43.** rund machen, (*a. fig.* ab)runden: ~*ed edge* abgerundete Kante; ~*ed number* auf- *od.* abgerundete Zahl; ~*ed teaspoon* gehäufter Teelöffel; ~*ed vowel* *ling.* gerundeter Vokal; **44.** um'kreisen; **45.** um'geben, -'schließen; **46.** *Ecke, Landspitze etc.* um'fahren, -'segeln, her'umfahren *od.* biegen um; **47.** *mot. Kurve* ausfahren; **VI** *v/i.* **48.** rund werden, sich runden; **49.** *fig.* sich abrunden, voll'kommen werden; **50.** ♣ drehen, wenden; **51.** ~ *on* F a) j-n ,anfahren‘, b) über j-n herfallen;

Zssgn mit adv.:

round| off *v/t.* **1.** abrunden (*a. fig.*); **2.** *Fest, Rede etc.* beschließen, krönen; **3.** *Zahlen* auf- *od.* abrunden; **4.** *Schiff* wenden; ~ **out** I *v/t.* **1.** (*v/i.* sich) runden *od.* ausfüllen; **2.** *fig.* abrunden; **II** *v/i.* **3.** rundlich werden (*Person*); ~ **to** *v/i.* ♣ beidrehen; ~ **up** *v/t.* **1.** *Vieh* zs.-treiben; **2.** F a) *Verbrecherbande* ausheben, b) *Leute etc.* zs.-trommeln, *a. et.* auftreiben, c) zs.-klauben; **3.** *Zahl etc.* aufrunden.

'round·a·bout I *adj.* **1.** 'umständlich, weitschweifig (*Erklärung etc.*): ~ *way* Umweg m; **2.** rundlich (*Person*); **II** *s.* **3.** 'Umweg m; **4.** *fig.* 'Umschweife pl.; **5.** *bsd. Brit.* Karus'sell n; → *swing* 24; **6.** *Brit.* Kreisverkehr m.

round| an·gle *s.* ⊾ Vollwinkel m; ~ **arch** *s.* △ (ro'manischer) Rundbogen; ~ **cell** *s. Batterie*: Knopfzelle f; ~ **dance** *s.* Rundtanz m; Dreher m.

roun·del ['raʊndl] *s.* **1.** kleine runde Scheibe; **2.** Medail'lon n (*a. her.*), runde Schmuckplatte; **3.** △ a) rundes Feld *od.* Fenster, b) runde Nische; **4.** *Metrik*: → *rondel*.

roun·de·lay ['raʊndɪleɪ] *s.* **1.** ♪ Re'frainliedchen n, Rundgesang m; **2.** Rundtanz m; **3.** (Vogel)Lied n.

round·er ['raʊndə] *s.* **1.** *Brit. sport* a) *pl. sg. konstr.* Rounders n, Rundball m (*Art Baseball*), b) ganzer 'Umlauf; **2.** *Am. sl.* a) liederlicher Kerl, b) Säufer m.

'round|-eyed *adj.* mit großen Augen, staunend; ~ **hand** *s.* Rundschrift f; '~**-head** *s.* **1.** ♀ *hist.* Rundkopf m (*Puritaner*); **2.** Rundkopf m (*Person*; *a.* ⊛); ~ **screw** Rundkopfschraube f; '~**house** *s.* **1.** ▥ Lokomo'tivschuppen m; **2.** ♣ *hist.* Achterhütte f; **3.** *hist.* Turm m, Gefängnis n; **4.** *Am. sl.* (wilder) Schwinger (*Schlag*).

round·ing ['raʊndɪŋ] *s.* Rundung f (*a. ling.*): ~*off* Abrundung f; **'round·ish** [-ɪʃ] *adj.* rundlich; **'round·ly** [-dlɪ] *adv.* **1.** rund, ungefähr; **2.** rundweg, rundher'aus; **3.** gründlich, gehörig; **'round·ness** [-dnɪs] *s.* **1.** Rundheit f (*a. fig.*); Rundung f; **2.** *fig.* Unverblümtheit f;

'round·nose(d) *adj.* ⊛ Rund...: ~ *pliers* Rundzange f; **round rob·in** *s.* **1.** Petiti'on f, Denkschrift f (*bsd. mit im Kreis herum geschriebenen Unterschriften*); **2.** *sport Am.* Turnier, bei dem jeder gegen jeden antritt; **round shot** *s.* ⚔ *hist.* Ka'nonenkugel f.

rounds·man ['raʊndzmən] *s.* [*irr.*] *Brit.* Austräger m, Laufbursche m: *milk* ~ Milchmann m.

round| steak *s. aus der Keule geschnittenes Beefsteak*; ~ **ta·ble** *s.* **1.** a) runder Tisch, b) Tafelrunde f: *the* ⊘ die Tafelrunde (des König Artus); **2.** *a.* **round-table conference** Konfe'renz f am runden Tisch, 'Round-Table-Konfe,renz f; ~**-the-'clock** *adj.* 24-stündig, rund um die Uhr; '~**top** *s.* ♣ Krähennest n; **tow·el** *s.* Rollhandtuch n; ~ **trip** *s. Am.* Hin- u. Rückfahrt f *od.* -flug m; ~**-'trip** *adj.*: ~ *ticket Am.* a) Rückfahrkarte f, b) ✈ Rückflugticket n; ~ **turn** *s.* ♣ Rundtörn m (*Knoten*): *bring up with a* ~ j-n jäh unterbrechen; '~**up** *s.* **1.** Zs.-treiben n von Vieh; **2.** *fig.* a) Zs.-treiben n, Sammeln n, b) Razzia f, Aushebung f von Verbrechern, c) Zs.-fassung f, 'Übersicht f: *football* ~; ~ *of the news* Nachrichtenüberblick m; '~**worm** *s. zo.*, ⚕ Spulwurm m.

roup [ruːp] *s. vet.* a) Darre f der Hühner, b) Pips m.

rouse [raʊz] I *v/t.* **1.** *oft* ~ *up* wachrütteln, (auf)wecken (*from* aus); **2.** *Wild etc.* aufjagen; **3.** *fig.* j-n auf-, wachrütteln, ermuntern: ~ *o.s.* sich aufraffen; **4.** *fig.* j-n in Wut bringen, aufbringen, reizen; **5.** *fig. Gefühle etc.* erwecken, wachrufen, *Hass* entflammen, *Zorn* erregen; **6.** ⊛ *Bier etc.* ('um)rühren; **II** *v/i.* **7.** *mst* ~ *up* aufwachen (*a. fig.*); **8.** aufschrecken; **III** *s.* **9.** ⚔ *Brit.* Wecken n; **'rous·er** [-zə] *s.* F **1.** Sensati'on f; **2.** faustdicke Lüge, Schwindel m; **'rous·ing** [-zɪŋ] *adj.* □ **1.** *fig.* aufrüttelnd, zündend, mitreißend (*Ansprache, Lied etc.*); **2.** brausend, stürmisch (*Beifall etc.*); **3.** aufregend, spannend; **4.** F ,toll‘.

roust·a·bout ['raʊstəbaʊt] *s.* **1.** *Am.* a) Werft-, Hafenarbeiter m, b) *oft contp.* Gelegenheitsarbeiter m; **2.** Handlanger m, Hilfsarbeiter m.

rout¹ [raʊt] I *s.* **1.** Rotte f, wilder Haufen; **2.** ⚖ Zs.-rottung f, Auflauf m; **3.** *bsd.* ⚔ a) wilde Flucht, b) Schlappe f, Niederlage f: *put to* ~ → 5; **4.** *obs.* (große) Abendgesellschaft f; **II** *v/t.* **5.** ⚔ in die Flucht *od.* vernichtend schlagen.

rout² [raʊt] *v/t.* **1.** → *root²* II; **2.** ~ *out*, ~ *up* aus dem Bett *od.* e-m Versteck etc. (her'aus)treiben, (-)jagen; **3.** vertreiben; **4.** ⊛ ausfräsen (*a. typ.*), ausschweifen.

route [ruːt; ⚔ *a.* raʊt] I *s.* **1.** (Reise-, Fahrt)Route f, (-)Weg m: *en* ~ (*Fr.*) unterwegs; **2.** (Bahn-, Bus-, Flug-) Strecke f, Route f; (Verkehrs)Linie f; ♣ Schifffahrtsweg m; (Fern)Straße f; **3.** ⚡ Leit(ungs)weg m; **4.** ⚔ a) Marschroute f, b) *Brit.* Marschbefehl m: ~ *march Brit.* Übungsmarsch m, *Am.* Marsch m mit Marscherleichterungen; ~ *step, march!* ohne Tritt(, marsch)!; **5.** ✚ *Am.* Versand(art f) m; **II** *v/t.* **6.** *Truppen* in Marsch setzen; *Transportgüter etc.* befördern (*a. weitS.* (*via* über *acc.*); **7.** die Route (*od.* ⊛ den Arbeitsgang) festlegen von (*od. gen.*); **8.** *Anträge etc.* (auf dem Dienstweg) weiterleiten; **9.** *a.* ⚡ legen, führen: ~ *lines*, b) *tel.* leiten.

rou·tine [ruː'tiːn] I *s.* **1.** a) (Ge'schäfts-,

'*Amts-* etc.)Rou,tine f, übliche *od.* gleichbleibende Proze'dur, gewohnter Gang, b) me'chanische Arbeit, (ewiges) Einerlei, c) Rou'tinesache f, d) *contp.* Scha'blone f, e) *contp.* (alter) Trott; **2.** *Am.* a) (Zirkus- *etc.*)Nummer f, b) *contp.* ,Platte‘ f, Geschwätz n; **3.** *Computer etc.*: Rou'tine f, ('Unter)Pro,gramm n; **II** *adj.* **4.** a) all'täglich, immer gleich bleibend, üblich, b) laufend, regel-, rou'tinemäßig: ~ *check*; **5.** *contp.* me'chanisch, scha'blonenhaft; **rou'tine·ly** [-lɪ] *adv.* **1.** rou'tinemäßig; **2.** *contp.* me'chanisch; **rou'tin·ist** [-nɪst] *s.* Gewohnheitsmensch m; **rou'tin·ize** [-naɪz] *v/t.* **1.** e-r Rou'tine *etc.* unter-'werfen; **2.** *et.* zur Rou'tine machen.

roux [ruː] *s. pl.* **roux** [ruːz] Mehlschwitze f, Einbrenne f.

rove¹ [rəʊv] I *v/i. a.* ~ *about* um'herstreifen, -schweifen, -wandern (*a. fig. Augen etc.*); **II** *v/t.* durch'streifen; **III** *s.* (Um'her)Wandern n; Wanderschaft f.

rove² [rəʊv] I *v/t.* **1.** ⊛ vorspinnen; **2.** *Wolle etc.* ausfasern; *Gestricktes etc.* auftrennen, aufräufeln; **II** *s.* **3.** Vorgespinst n; **4.** (*Woll- etc.*)Strähne f.

rov·er¹ ['rəʊvə] *s.* ⊛ 'Vorspinnma,schine f.

rov·er² ['rəʊvə] *s.* **1.** Wanderer m; **2.** Pi'rat(enschiff n) m; **3.** Wandertier n; **4.** *obs. Brit.* Pfadfinder über 17.

rov·ing ['rəʊvɪŋ] *adj.* **1.** um'herziehend, -streifend; **2.** *fig.* ausschweifend: ~ *fancy*; *have a* ~ *eye* gern ein Auge riskieren; **3.** *fig.* ,fliegend‘: ~ *reporter*; ~ *force* (Polizei)Einsatztruppe f.

row¹ [rəʊ] *s.* **1.** *allg.* (*a.* Häuser-, Sitz-) Reihe f: *in* ~*s* in Reihen, reihenweise; *a hard* ~ *to hoe* *fig.* e-e schwierige Sache; **2.** Straße f: *Rochester* ⊘; **3.** △ Baufluchtlinie f.

row² [rəʊ] I *v/i.* **1.** rudern; **II** *v/t.* **2.** *Boot, a. Rennen, a.* j-n rudern: ~ *down* j-n (*beim Rudern*) überholen; **3.** rudern gegen, mit j-m (*wett*)rudern; **III** *s.* **4.** Rudern n; '*Ruderpar,tie* f: *go for a* ~ rudern gehen.

row³ [raʊ] F I *s.* Krach m: a) Kra'wall m, Spek'takel m, b) Streit m, c) Schläge'rei f: *get into a* ~ a) ,eins aufs Dach bekommen‘, b) Krach bekommen (*with* mit); *have a* ~ *with* Krach haben mit; *kick up a* ~ Krach schlagen; *what's the* ~? was ist denn los?; **II** *v/t.* j-n ,zs.--stauchen‘; **III** *v/i.* randalieren.

row·an ['raʊən] *s.* ♀ Eberesche f; '~,**ber·ry** *s.* Vogelbeere f.

row·di·ness ['raʊdɪnɪs] *s.* Pöbelhaftigkeit f, rüpelhaftes Benehmen *od.* Wesen; **row·dy** ['raʊdɪ] I *s.* Rowdy m, Ra'bauke m, Schläger m; **II** *adj.* rüpel-, rowdyhaft, gewalttätig; '**row·dy·ism** [-ɪɪzəm] *s.* **1.** Rowdytum n, rüpelhaftes Benehmen; **2.** Gewalttätigkeit f, Rüpe-'lei f.

row·el ['raʊəl] I *s.* Spornrädchen n; **II** *v/t.* e-m Pferd die Sporen geben.

row·en ['raʊən] *s.* ♪ Grummet n.

row·ing ['rəʊɪŋ] *s.* **1.** Rudern n, Rudersport m; **II** *adj.* Ruder...: ~ *boat*; ~ *machine* Ruderapparat m.

row·lock ['rɒlək] *s.* ♣ Dolle f.

roy·al ['rɔɪəl] I *adj.* □ **1.** königlich, Königs...: *His* ⊘ *Highness* S-e Königliche Hoheit; ~ *prince* Prinz m von königlichem Geblüt; ~ *princess* 1; ⊘ *Academy* Königliche Akademie der Künste (*Großbritanniens*); ~ *blue* Königsblau n; ⊘ *Exchange* die Londoner Börse (*Gebäude*); ~ *flush* Poker: Royal Flush m; ⊘ *Navy* (Königlich-Brit.) Marine f; ~ *paper* → 6; ~ *road* *fig.* leichter *od.*

bequemer Weg (**to** zu); **~ speech** Thronrede f; **2.** fürstlich (*a. fig.*): **the ~ and ancient game** das Golfspiel; **3.** *fig.* (*a.* F) prächtig, großartig: **in ~ spirits** F in glänzender Stimmung; **~ stag** *hunt.* Kapitalhirsch m; **~ tiger** *zo.* Königstiger m; **4.** edel (*a. Gas*); **II** s. **5.** F Mitglied n des Königshauses; **6.** Roy'alpa,pier n (*Format*); **7.** *a.* **~ sail ♣** Ober(bram)segel n; **roy·al·ist** ['rɔɪəlɪst] **I** s. Roya'list(in), Königstreue(r m) f; **II** adj. königstreu; **'roy·al·ty** [-ltɪ] s. **1.** Königtum n: a) Königswürde f, b) Königreich n: **insignia of ~** Kroninsignien pl.; **2.** königliche Abkunft; **3.** a) fürstliche Per'sönlichkeit, b) pl. Fürstlichkeiten pl., c) Königshaus n; **4.** Krongut n; **5.** Re'gal n, königliches Privi'leg; **6.** Abgabe f an die Krone, Pachtgeld n: **mining ~** Bergwerksabgabe f; **7.** mo'narchische Regierung; **8.** ☫ (Autoren- *etc.*)Tanti,eme f, Gewinnanteil m; **9.** ☫ a) Li'zenz f, b) Li'zenzgebühr f: **~ fees** Pa'tentgebühren; **subject to payment of royalties** lizenzpflichtig.
roz·zer ['rɒzə] s. *Br. sl.* Bulle m (*Polizist*).

rub [rʌb] **I** s. **1.** (Ab)Reiben n, Polieren n: **give it a ~** reibe es (doch einmal); **have a ~ with a towel** sich (mit dem Handtuch) abreiben *od.* abtrocknen; **2.** *fig.* Schwierigkeit f, Haken m: **there's the ~!** F da liegt der Hase im Pfeffer!; **there's a ~ in it** F die Sache hat e-n Haken; **3.** Unannehmlichkeit f; **4.** *fig.* Stiche'lei f; **5.** raue *od.* aufgeriebene Stelle; **6.** Unebenheit f; **II** v/t. **7.** reiben: **~ one's hands** sich die Hände reiben (*mst fig.*); **~ shoulders with** *fig.* verkehren mit, (*dat.*) nahe stehen; **~ it in, ~ s.o.'s nose in it** es j-m ,unter die Nase reiben'; → **rub up**; **8.** reiben, (reibend) streichen; massieren; **9.** einreiben (**with** mit e-r Salbe *etc.*); **10.** streifen, reiben an (*dat.*); (wund) scheuern; **11.** a) scheuern, schaben, b) *Tafel etc.* abwischen, c) polieren, d) wichsen, bohnern, e) abreiben, frottieren; **12.** ☼ (ab)schleifen, (ab)feilen: **~ with emery** (**pumice**) abschmirgeln (abbimsen); **13.** *typ.* abklatschen; **III** v/i. **14.** reiben, streifen (**against** *od.* [**up**]**on** an *dat.*, **gegen**); **15.** *fig.* sich schlagen (**through** durch);
Zssgn mit adv.:

rub| a·long v/i. **1.** sich (mühsam) 'durchschlagen; **2.** (gut) auskommen (**with** mit j-m); **~ down** v/t. **1.** abreiben, frottieren; *Pferd* striegeln; **2.** he'runter-, wegreiben; **~ in** v/t. **1.** *a. Zeichnung* einreiben; **2.** *sl.* ,her'umreiten' auf (*dat.*); → **rub** 7; **~ off** **I** v/t. **1.** ab-, wegreiben; abschleifen; **II** v/i. **2.** abgehen (*Lack etc.*); **3.** *fig.* sich abnützen; **4.** *fig.* F abfärben (**onto** auf *acc.*); **~ out** **I** v/t. **1.** ausradieren; **2.** wegwischen, -reiben; **3.** *Am. sl.* ,'umlegen' (*töten*) **II** v/i. **4.** weggehen (*Fleck etc.*); **~ up** v/t. **1.** (auf)polieren; **2.** *fig.* a) *Kenntnisse etc.* auffrischen, b) *Gedächtnis etc.* stärken; **3.** *fig.* F **rub s.o. up the right way** j-n richtig behandeln; **rub s.o. up the wrong way** j-n ,verschnupfen' *od.* verstimmen; **it rubs me up the wrong way** es geht mir gegen den Strich; **4.** *Farben etc.* verreiben.
rub-a-dub ['rʌbədʌb] s. Ta'ramtamtam n, Trommelwirbel m.
rub·ber¹ ['rʌbə] **I** s. **1.** Gummi n, m, (Na'tur)Kautschuk m; **2.** (Radier-) Gummi m; **3.** a. **~ band** Gummiband n, -band n; **4.** **~ tyre** (*od.* bsd. Am. **tire**) Gummireifen m; **5.** pl. a) Am. ('Gum-

mi),Überschuhe pl., b) *Brit.* Turnschuhe pl.; **6.** *sl.* ,Gummi' m, ,Pa'riser' m (*Kondom*); **7.** Reiber m, Polierer m; **8.** Mas'seur(in), Mas'seuse f; **9.** Reibzeug n; **10.** a) Frottier(hand)tuch n, -handschuh m, b) Wischtuch n, c) Polierkissen n, d) *Brit.* Geschirrtuch n; **11.** Reibfläche f; **12.** ☼ a) Schleifstein m, b) Putzfeile f; **13.** *typ.* Farbläufer m; **14.** 'Schmirgelpa,pier n; 'Glaspa,pier n; **15.** (weicher) Formziegel; **16.** F *Eishockey:* Puck m, Scheibe f; **17.** *Baseball:* Platte f; **II** v/t. **18.** → **rubberize**; **III** v/i. **19.** → **rubberneck** 4, 5; **IV** adj. **20.** Gummi...: **~ solution** Gummilösung f.
rub·ber² ['rʌbə] s. *Kartenspiel:* Robber m.
rub·ber| boat s. Gummi-, Schlauchboot n; **~ ce·ment** s. ☼ Gummilösung f; **~ check** s. *Am.,* **cheque** s. *Brit.* F geplatzter Scheck; **~ coat·ing** s. Gummierung f; **~ din·ghi** s. Schlauchboot n; **~ gloves** s. pl. a. **pair of ~** Gummihandschuhe pl.
rub·ber·ize ['rʌbəraɪz] v/t. ☼ mit Gummi imprägnieren, gummieren.
'rub·ber|·neck *Am.* F **I** s. **1.** Gaffer(in), Neugierige(r m) f; **2.** Tou'rist(in); **II** adj. **3.** neugierig, schaulustig; **III** v/i. **4.** neugierig gaffen, ,sich den Hals verrenken'; **5.** die Sehenswürdigkeiten (*e-r Stadt etc.*) ansehen; **IV** v/t. **6.** neugierig betrachten; **~ plant** s. ♣ Kautschukpflanze f, bsd. Gummibaum m; **~ stamp** s. **1.** Gummistempel m; **2.** F a) sturer Beamter, b) bloßes Werkzeug, c) Nachbeter m; **3.** bsd. Am. F (abgedroschene) Phrase; **,~-'stamp** v/t. **1.** abstempeln; **2.** F (rou'tinemäßig) genehmigen; **~ tree** s. ♣ Gummibaum m, b) Kautschukbaum m.
rub·bing ['rʌbɪŋ] s. a) *phys.* Reibung f, b) ☼ Abrieb m; **2.** *typ.* Reiberdruck m; **~ cloth** s. Frottier-, Wisch-, Scheuertuch n; **~ con·tact** s. ⚡ 'Reibe-, 'Schleifkon,takt m; **'~-stone** s. Schleif-, Wetzstein m; **~ var·nish** s. ☼ Schleiflack m.
rub·bish ['rʌbɪʃ] s. *bsd. Brit.* **1.** Abfall m, Kehricht m, Müll m: **~ bin** Abfalleimer m; **~ chute** Müllschlucker m; **2.** (Gesteins)Schutt m (*a. geol.*); **3.** F Schund m, Plunder m; **4.** F *a. int.* Blödsinn m, Quatsch m; **5.** ⚒ a) *über Tage:* Abraum m, b) *unter Tage:* taubes Gestein; **rub·bish tip** s. *bsd. Brit.* 'Mülldepo,nie f, -halde f; **'rub·bish·y** [-ʃɪ] adj. **1.** schuttbedeckt; **2.** F Schund..., wertlos.
rub·ble ['rʌbl] s. **1.** Bruchstein(e pl.) m, Schotter m; **2.** *geol.* (Stein)Schutt m, Geröll n, Geschiebe n; **3.** (rohes) Bruchsteinmauerwerk; **4.** loses Packeis; **~ ma·son·ry** → **rubble** 3; **'~-stone** s. Bruchstein m; **'~-work** → **rubble** 3.
'rub·down s. Abreibung f: **have a ~** sich trockenreiben od. frottieren.
rube [ru:b] s. *Am. sl.* ,Lackel' m.
ru·be·fa·cient [,ru:bɪ'feɪʃənt] **☞ I** adj. (*bsd.* haut)rötend; **II** s. (*bsd.* haut)rötendes Mittel; **ru·be'fac·tion** [-'fækʃn] s. ☞ Hautröte f, -rötung f.
ru·bi·cund ['ru:bɪkənd] adj. rötlich, rot, rosig (*Person*).
ru·bric ['ru:brɪk] **I** s. **1.** *typ.* Ru'brik f ([roter] Titelkopf *od.* Buchstabe; Abschnitt); **2.** *eccl.* Ru'brik f, li'turgische Anweisung; **II** adj. **3.** rot (gedruckt *etc.*), rubriziert; **'ru·bri·cate** [-keɪt] v/t. **1.** rot bezeichnen; **2.** rubrizieren.
'rub·stone s. Schleifstein m.

ru·by ['ru:bɪ] **I** s. **1.** a. **true ~**, **Oriental ~** min. Ru'bin m; **2.** (Ru'bin)Rot n; **3.** *fig.* Rotwein m; **4.** *fig.* roter (Haut)Pickel; **5.** *Uhrmacherei:* Stein m; **6.** *typ.* Pa'riser Schrift f, Fünflein'halbpunktschrift f; **II** adj. **7.** (kar'min-, ru'bin)rot.
ruche [ru:ʃ] s. Rüsche f; **ruched** [-ʃt] adj. mit Rüschen besetzt; **'ruch·ing** [-ʃɪŋ] s. **1.** *coll.* Rüschen(besatz m) pl.; **2.** Rüschenstoff m.
ruck¹ [rʌk] s. **1.** *sport* das (Haupt)Feld; **2. the** (**common**) **~** *fig.* die breite Masse: **rise out of the ~** *fig.* sich über den Durchschnitt erheben.
ruck² [rʌk] **I** s. Falte f; **II** v/t. oft **~ up** hochschieben, zerknüllen, -knittern; **III** v/i. oft **~ up** Falten werfen, hochrutschen.
ruck·sack ['rʌksæk] (*Ger.*) s. Rucksack m.
ruck·us ['rʌkəs] → **ruction**.
ruc·tion ['rʌkʃn] s. oft pl. F a) Tohuwa'bohu n, b) Krach m, Kra'wall m, c) Schläge'rei f.
rud·der ['rʌdə] s. **1.** ♣ (Steuer)Ruder n, Steuer n; **2.** ✈ Seitenruder n, -steuer n: **~ controls** Seitensteuerung f; **3.** *fig.* Richtschnur f; **4.** *Brauerei:* Rührkelle f; **'rud·der·less** [-lɪs] adj. **1.** ohne Ruder; **2.** *fig.* führer-, steuerlos.
rud·di·ness ['rʌdɪnɪs] s. Röte f; **rud·dy** ['rʌdɪ] adj. □ **1.** rot, rötlich, gerötet; gesund (*Gesichtsfarbe*); **2.** *Brit. sl.* verflixt.
rude [ru:d] adj. □ **1.** grob, unverschämt; rüde, ungehobelt; **2.** roh, unsanft (*a. fig. Erwachen*); **3.** wild, heftig (*Kampf, Leidenschaft*); rau (*Klima etc.*); hart (*Los, Zeit etc.*); **4.** wild (*Landschaft*); holp(e)rig (*Weg*); **5.** wirr (*Masse etc.*): **~ chaos** chaotischer Urzustand; **6.** *allg.* primi'tiv: a) unzivilisiert, b) ungebildet, c) kunstlos, d) behelfsmäßig; **7.** ro'bust, unverwüstlich (*Gesundheit*): **be in ~ health** vor Gesundheit strotzen; **8.** roh, unverarbeitet (*Stoff*); **9.** plump, ungeschickt; **10.** a) ungefähr, b) flüchtig, grob: **~ sketch**; **a ~ observer** ein oberflächlicher Beobachter; **'rude·ness** [-nɪs] s. **1.** Grobheit f; **2.** Rohheit f; **3.** Heftigkeit f; **4.** Wild-, Rauheit f; **5.** Primitivi'tät f; **6.** Unebenheit f.
ru·di·ment ['ru:dɪmənt] s. **1.** Rudi'ment n (*a. biol.* rudimentäres Organ), Ansatz m; **2.** pl. Anfangsgründe pl., Grundlagen pl., Rudi'mente pl.; **ru·di·men·tal** [,ru:dɪ'mentl], **ru·di·men·ta·ry** [,ru:dɪ'mentərɪ] adj. □ **1.** elemen'tar, Anfangs...; **2.** rudimen'tär (*a. biol.*).
rue¹ [ru:] s. ♣ Gartenraute f.
rue² [ru:] v/t. bereuen, bedauern; *Ereignis* verwünschen: **he will live to ~ it** er wird es noch bereuen; **'rue·ful** [-fʊl] adj. □ **1.** kläglich, jämmerlich: **the Knight of the ☾ Countenance** der Ritter von der traurigen Gestalt (*Don Quichotte*); **2.** wehmütig; **3.** reumütig; **'rue·ful·ness** [-fʊlnɪs] s. **1.** Gram m, Traurigkeit f; **2.** Jammer m.
ruff¹ [rʌf] s. **1.** Halskrause f (*a. zo., orn.*); **2.** (Pa'pier)Krause f (*Topf etc.*); **3.** Rüsche f; **4.** *orn.* a) Kampfläufer m, b) Haustaube f mit Halskrause.
ruff² [rʌf] **I** s. *Kartenspiel:* Trumpfen n; **II** v/t. u. v/i. mit Trumpf stechen.
ruff(e)³ [rʌf] s. *ichth.* Kaulbarsch m.
ruf·fi·an ['rʌfjən] s. **1.** Rüpel m; **2.** Raufbold m; **'ruf·fi·an·ism** [-nɪzəm] s. Rohheit f, Brutali'tät f; **'ruf·fi·an·ly** [-lɪ] adj. **1.** roh, bru'tal; **2.** wild.
ruf·fle ['rʌfl] **I** v/t. **1.** *Wasser etc., a.* Tuch kräuseln; *Stirn* kraus ziehen; **2.** *Federn,*

Haare sträuben: **~ one's feathers** sich aufplustern (*a. fig.*); **3.** *Papier* zerknittern; **4.** durchein'ander bringen *od.* werfen; **5.** *fig. j-n* aus der Fassung bringen; *j-n* (ver)ärgern: **~ s.o.'s temper** j-n verstimmen; **II** *v/i.* **6.** sich kräuseln; **7.** zerknüllt *od.* zerzaust werden; **8.** *fig.* die Ruhe verlieren; **9.** *fig.* sich aufspielen, anmaßend auftreten; **III** *s.* **10.** Kräuseln *n*; **11.** Rüsche *f*, Krause *f*; **12.** *orn.* Halskrause *f*; **13.** *fig.* Aufregung *f*, Störung *f*: **without ~ or excitement** in aller Ruhe.

ru·fous ['ruːfəs] *adj.* rotbraun.

rug [rʌg] *s.* **1.** (kleiner) Teppich, (Bett-, Ka'min)Vorleger *m*, Brücke *f*: **pull the ~ from under s.o.** *fig.* j-m den Boden unter den Füßen wegziehen; **2.** *bsd. Brit.* dicke wollene (Reise- *etc.*)Decke.

rug·by (foot·ball) ['rʌgbɪ] *s. sport* Rugby *n.*

rug·ged ['rʌgɪd] *adj.* □ **1.** zerklüftet, wild (*Landschaft etc.*), zackig, schroff (*Fels etc.*), felsig; **2.** durch'furcht (*Gesicht etc.*), uneben (*Boden etc.*), holperig (*Weg etc.*), knorrig (*Gestalt*); **3.** rauh (*Rinde, Tuch, a. fig. Manieren, Sport etc.*): **life is ~** das Leben ist hart; **~ individualism** krasser Individualismus; **4.** ruppig, grob; **5.** *bsd. Am. a.* ⚙ ro'bust, stark, sta'bil; **'rug·ged·ize** *v/t.* besonders ro'bust machen: **~d laptop** besonders robuster Laptop; **'rug·ged·ness** [-nɪs] *s.* **1.** Rauheit *f*; **2.** Grobheit *f*; **3.** *Am.* Ro'bustheit *f*.

rug·ger ['rʌgə] *Brit.* F *für* **rugby (football)**.

ru·in ['rʊɪn] **I** *s.* **1.** Ru'ine *f* (*a. fig. Person etc.*); *pl.* Ruine(n *pl.*) *f*, Trümmer *pl.*: **lay in ~s** in Schutt u. Asche legen; **lie in ~s** in Trümmern liegen; **2.** Verfall *m*: **go to ~** verfallen; **3.** Ru'in *m*, 'Untergang *m*, Zs.-bruch *m*, Verderben *n*: **bring to ~** → 5; **the ~ of my hopes (plans)** das Ende m-r Hoffnungen (Pläne); **it will be the ~ of him** es wird sein Untergang sein; **II** *v/t.* **4.** vernichten, zerstören; **5.** *j-n, a. Sache, Gesundheit etc.* ruinieren, zu'grunde richten; *Hoffnungen, Pläne* zu'nichte machen; *Augen, Aussichten etc.* verderben; *Sprache* verhunzen; **6.** *Mädchen* verführen; **ru·in·a·tion** [rʊɪ'neɪʃn] *s.* **1.** Zerstörung *f*, Verwüstung *f*; **2.** F *j-s* Ru'in *m*, Verderben *n*, 'Untergang *m*; **'ru·in·ous** [-nəs] *adj.* □ **1.** verfallen(d), baufällig, ru'inenhaft; **2.** verderblich, mörderisch, ruinierend, rui'nös: **a ~ price** a) ruinöser *od.* enormer Preis, b) Schleuderpreis *m*; **'ru·in·ous·ness** [-nəsnɪs] *s.* **1.** Baufälligkeit *f*; **2.** Verderblichkeit *f*.

rule [ruːl] **I** *s.* **1.** Regel *f*, Nor'malfall *m*: **as a ~** in der Regel; **as is the ~** wie es allgemein üblich ist; **become the ~** zur Regel werden; **make it a ~ to** (*inf.*) es sich zur Regel machen, zu (*inf.*); **by all the ~s** eigentlich; → **exception** 1; **2.** Regel *f*, Richtschnur *f*, Grundsatz *m*; *sport etc.* Spielregel *f* (*a. fig.*): **against the ~s** regelwidrig; **~s of action** (*od.* **conduct**) Verhaltensmaßregeln, Richtlinien; **~ of thumb** Faustregel, praktische Erfahrung; **by ~ of thumb** über den Daumen gepeilt; **serve as a ~** als Richtschnur *od.* Maßstab dienen; **3.** ⚖ a) Vorschrift *f*, (gesetzliche) Bestimmung, Norm *f*, b) gerichtliche Entscheidung, c) Rechtsgrundsatz *m*: **~s of the air** Luftverkehrsregeln; **work to ~** Dienst nach Vorschrift tun (*als Streikmittel*); → **road** 1; **4.** *pl.* (Geschäfts-, Gerichts- *etc.*)Ordnung *f*: **(standing) ~s of court** ⚖ Prozessordnung; **~s of procedure** a) Verfahrensordnung, b) Geschäftsordnung; **5.** *a.* **standing ~** Satzung *f*: **against the ~s** satzungswidrig; **the ~s (and by-laws)** die Satzungen, die Statuten; **6.** *eccl.* Ordensregel *f*; **7.** ✝ U'sance *f*, Handelsbrauch *m*; **8.** 𝔄 Regel *f*, Rechnungsart *f*: **~ of proportion, ~ of three** Regeldetri *f*, Dreisatz *m*; **9.** Herrschaft *f*, Regierung *f*: **during (under) the ~ of** während (unter) der Regierung (*gen.*); **~ of law** Rechtsstaatlichkeit *f*; **10.** a) Line'al *n*, b) *a.* **folding ~** Zollstock *m*; **11.** a) Richtmaß *n*, b) Winkel(eisen *n*, -maß *n*) *m*; **12.** *typ.* a) (Messing)Linie *f*: **~ case** Linienkasten *m*, b) Ko'lumnenmaß *n* (*Satzspiegel*), c) *Brit.* Strich *m*: **em ~** Gedankenstrich; **en ~** Halbgeviert *n*; **II** *v/t.* **13.** *a.* **~ over** *Land, Gefühl etc.* beherrschen, herrschen über (*acc.*), regieren: **~ the roast** (*od.* **roost**) *fig.* das Regiment führen, Herr im Haus sein; **14.** lenken, leiten: **be ~d by** sich leiten lassen von; **15.** *bsd.* ⚖ anordnen, verfügen, entscheiden: **~ out** a) *j-n od. et.* ausschließen (*a. sport*), b) *et.* ablehnen; **~ s.o. out of order** *parl.* j-m das Wort entziehen; **~ s.th. out of order** et. nicht zulassen; **16.** a) *Papier* linieren, b) *Linie* ziehen: **~ s.th. out** et. durchstreichen; **~d paper** liniertes Papier; **III** *v/i.* **17.** herrschen *od.* regieren (**over** über *acc.*); **18.** entscheiden (**that** dass); **19.** ✝ *hoch etc.* stehen, liegen, notieren (*Preise*): **~ high (low)**; weiterhin hoch notieren; **20.** vorherrschen; **21.** gelten, in Kraft sein (*Recht etc.*); **'rul·er** [-lə] *s.* **1.** Herrscher(in); **2.** Line'al *n*; ⚙ Richtscheit *n*; **3.** ⚙ Li'niermaˌschine *f*; **'rul·ing** [-lɪŋ] **I** *s.* **1.** ⚖ (gerichtliche) Entscheidung, Verfügung *f*; **2.** Linie(n *pl.*) *f*; **3.** Herrschaft *f*; **II** *adj.* **4.** herrschend; *fig.* (vor)herrschend: **~ coalition** *pol.* Re'gierungskoalitiˌon *f*; **5.** maßgebend, grundlegend: **~ case**; **6.** ✝ bestehend, laufend: **~ price** Tagespreis *m*.

rum¹ [rʌm] *s.* Rum *m*, *Am. a.* Alkohol *m*.

rum² [rʌm] *adj.* □ *bsd. Brit. sl.* **1.** ‚komisch' (*eigenartig*): **~ customer** komischer Kauz; **~ go** dumme Geschichte; **~ start** (tolle) Überraschung; **2.** ulkig, drollig.

Ru·ma·ni·an [ruː'meɪnjən] **I** *adj.* **1.** ru'mänisch; **II** *s.* **2.** Ru'mäne *m*, Ru'mänin *f*; **3.** *ling.* Ru'mänisch *n*.

rum·ba ['rʌmbə] *s.* Rumba *m, f*.

rum·ble¹ ['rʌmbl] **I** *v/i.* **1.** poltern (*a. Stimme*); rattern (*Gefährt, Zug etc.*), rumpeln, rollen (*Donner*), knurren (*Magen*); **II** *v/t.* **2.** *a.* **~ out** *Worte* he'rauspoltern, *Lied* grölen; **III** *s.* **3.** Gepolter *n*, Rattern *n*, Rumpeln *n*, Rollen *n* (*Donner*); **4.** ⚙ Poliertrommel *f*; **5.** a) Bedientensitz *m*, b) Gepäckraum *m*, c) → **rumble seat**; **6.** *Am.* (Straßen-)Schlacht *f* (*zwischen jugendlichen Banden*).

rum·ble² ['rʌmbl] *v/t. sl.* **1.** *j-n* durch'schauen; **2.** *et.* ‚spitzkriegen'; **3.** *Am. j-n* argwöhnisch machen.

rum·ble seat *s. Am. mot.* Not-, Klappsitz *m*.

rum·bus·tious [rʌm'bʌstɪəs] *adj.* F **1.** laut, lärmend; **2.** wild, ausgelassen.

ru·men ['ruːmen] *pl.* **-mi·na** [-mɪnə] *s. zo.* Pansen *m*; **'ru·mi·nant** [-mɪnənt] **I** *adj.* □ **1.** *zo.* 'wiederkäuend; **2.** *fig.* grübelnd; **II** *s.* **3.** *zo.* 'Wiederkäuer *m*; **'ru·mi·nate** [-mɪneɪt] **I** *v/i.* **1.** 'wiederkäuen; **2.** *fig.* grübeln (**about, over** über *acc., dat.*); **II** *v/t.* **3.** *fig.* grübeln über (*acc., dat.*); **ru·mi·na·tion** [ˌruːmɪ'neɪʃn] *s.* **1.** 'Wiederkäuen *n*; **2.** *fig.* Grübeln *n*; **'ru·mi·na·tive** [-mɪnətɪv] *adj.* □ nachdenklich, grüblerisch.

rum·mage ['rʌmɪdʒ] **I** *v/t.* **1.** durch'stöbern, -'wühlen, wühlen in (*dat.*); **2.** *a.* **~ out, ~ up** aus-, her'vorkramen; **II** *v/i.* **3.** *a.* **~ about** (her'um)stöbern *od.* (-)wühlen (**in** in *dat.*); **III** *s.* **4.** *mst* **~ goods** Ramsch *m*, Ausschuss *m*, Restwaren *pl.*; **~ sale** *s.* **1.** Ramschverkauf *m*; **2.** 'Wohltätigkeitsbaˌzar *m*.

rum·mer ['rʌmə] *s.* Römer *m*, ('Wein-)Poˌkal *m*.

rum·my¹ ['rʌmɪ] *s.* Rommee *n* (*Kartenspiel*).

rum·my² ['rʌmɪ] *adj.* □ → **rum²** 1 *u.* 2.

ru·mo(u)r ['ruːmə] **I** *s.* a) Gerücht *n*, b) Gerede *n*: **~ has it, the ~ runs** es geht das Gerücht; **II** *v/t.* (als Gerücht) verbreiten (*mst pass.*): **it is ~ed that** man sagt *od.* es geht das Gerücht, dass; **he is ~ed to be** man munkelt *od.* es heißt, er sei.

rump [rʌmp] *s.* **1.** *zo.* Steiß *m*, 'Hinterteil *n* (*a. des Menschen*); *orn.* Bürzel *m*; **~ steak** *Küche*: Rumpsteak *n*; **2.** *fig.* Rumpf *m*, kümmerlicher Rest: **the** 𝔑 **(Parliament)** *hist.* das Rumpfparlament.

rum·pie ['rʌmpɪ] *s.* Aufsteiger, der auf dem Land wohnt (= **rural upwardly-mobile professional**).

rum·ple ['rʌmpl] *v/t.* **1.** zerknittern, -knüllen; **2.** *Haar etc.* zerwühlen.

rum·pus ['rʌmpəs] *s.* F **1.** Krach *m*, Kra'wall *m*; **2.** Trubel *m*; **3.** Streit *m*, ‚Krach' *m*; **~ room** *s. Am.* Hobby- *od.* Partyraum *m*.

'rumˌrun·ner *s. Am.* Alkoholschmuggler *m*.

run [rʌn] **I** *s.* **1.** Laufen *n*, Rennen *n*; **2.** Lauf *m* (*a. sport u. fig.*); Lauf-, ⚔ Sturmschritt *m*: **at the ~** im Lauf (-schritt), im Dauerlauf; **in the long ~** *fig.* auf die Dauer, am Ende, schließlich; **in the short ~** fürs Nächste; **on the ~** a) auf der Flucht, b) (immer) auf den Beinen (*tätig*); **be in the ~** *bsd. Am. pol. bei e-r Wahl* infrage kommen *od.* im Rennen liegen, kandidieren; **come down with a ~** schnell *od.* plötzlich fallen (*a. Barometer, Preis*); **go for** (*od.* **take**) **a ~** e-n Lauf machen; **have a ~ for one's money** sich abhetzen müssen; **have s.o. on the ~** j-n herumjagen, -hetzen; **3.** a) Anlauf *m*: **take a ~** (e-n) Anlauf nehmen, b) *Baseball, Kricket*: erfolgreicher Lauf; **4.** *Reiten*: schneller Ga'lopp; **5.** ⚓, *mot.* Fahrt *f*; **6.** *oft* **short ~** Spazierfahrt *f*; **7.** Abstecher *m*, kleine Reise (**to** nach); **8.** ✈ (Bomben)Zielanflug *m*; **9.** ♪ Lauf *m*; **10.** Zulauf *m*, ✝ Ansturm *m*, Run *m* (**on** auf *e-e Bank etc.*); ✝ stürmische Nachfrage (**on** nach *e-r Ware*); **11.** *fig.* Lauf *m*, (Fort)Gang *m*: **the ~ of events**; **12.** *fig.* Verlauf *m*: **the ~ of the hills**; **13.** *fig.* a) Ten'denz *f*, b) Mode *f*; **14.** Folge *f*, (*sport* Erfolgs-, Treffer)Serie *f*: **a ~ of bad (good) luck** e-e Pechsträhne (e-e Glückssträhne); **15.** *Am.* kleiner Wasserlauf; **16.** *bsd. Am.* Laufmasche *f*; **17.** (Bob-, Rodel)Bahn *f*; **18.** ✈ Rollstrecke *f*; **19.** a) (Vieh-)Trift *f*, Weide *f*, b) (Hühner)Hof *m*, Auslauf *m*; **20.** ⚙ a) Bahn *f*, b) Laufschiene *f*, c) Rinne *f*; **21.** Mühl-, Mahlgang *m*; **22.** ⚙ a) Herstellungsgröße *f*, (Rohr- *etc.*)Länge *f*, b) (Betriebs)Leistung *f*, Ausstoß *m*, c) Gang *m*, 'Arbeitsperiˌode *f*, d) 'Durchlauf *m* (*von Beschickungsgut*), e) Charge *f*, Menge

R

f, f) Bedienung f; **23.** Auflage f (*Zeitung*); **24.** *Kartenspiel*: Se'quenz f; **25.** (Amts-, Gültigkeits-, Zeit)Dauer f: ~ *of office*; **26.** *thea.*, *Film*: Laufzeit f: *have a ~ of 20 nights* 20-mal nacheinander gegeben werden; **27.** a) Art f, Schlag m; Sorte f (a. ✝), b) *mst common* (*od.* *general od.* *ordinary*) ~ 'Durchschnitt m, *die* große Masse: ~ *of the mill* Durchschnitt m; **28.** Herde f; **29.** Schwarm m (*Fische*); **30.** ♫ (Achter)Piek f; **31.** (*of*) a) freie Benutzung (*gen.*), b) freier Zutritt (zu); **II** *v/i.* [*irr.*] **32.** laufen, rennen; eilen, stürzen; **33.** da'vonlaufen, Reiß'aus nehmen; **34.** *sport* a) (um die Wette) laufen, b) (an e-m Lauf) teilnehmen, laufen, c) als *Zweiter etc.* einlaufen: *also ran* ferner liefen; **35.** *fig.* laufen (*Blick, Feuer, Finger, Schauer etc.*): *his eyes ran over* ... sein Blick überflog ...; *the tune keeps ~ning through my head* die Melodie geht mir nicht aus dem Kopf; **36.** *pol.* kandidieren (*for* für); **37.** ♫ *etc.* fahren; (*in den Hafen*) einlaufen: ~ *before the wind* vor dem Wind segeln; **38.** wandern (*Fische*); **39.** ☗ *etc.* verkehren, *auf e-r Strecke* fahren, gehen; **40.** fließen, strömen (*beide a. fig. Blut in den Adern, Tränen, a. Verse*): *it ~s in the blood* (*family*) es liegt im Blut (in der Familie); **41.** lauten (*Schriftstück*); **42.** gehen (*Melodie*); **43.** verfließen, -streichen (*Zeit etc.*); **44.** dauern: *three days ~ning* drei Tage hintereinander; **45.** laufen, gegeben werden (*Theaterstück etc.*); **46.** verlaufen (*Straße etc.*, *a. Vorgang*), sich erstrecken; führen, gehen (*Weg etc.*): *my taste* (*talent*) *does not ~ that way* dafür habe ich keinen Sinn (keine Begabung); **47.** ⊙ laufen, gleiten (*Seil etc.*); **48.** ⊙ laufen: a) in Gang sein, arbeiten, b) gehen (*Uhr etc.*), funktionieren; **49.** in Betrieb sein (*Fabrik, Hotel etc.*); **50.** aus-, zerlaufen (*Farbe*); **51.** tropfen, strömen, triefen (*with* vor dat.) (*Gesicht etc.*); laufen (*Nase, Augen*); 'übergehen (*Augen*): ~ *with tears* in Tränen schwimmen; **52.** rinnen, laufen (*Gefäß*); **53.** schmelzen (*Metall*); tauen (*Eis*); **54.** ⚕ eitern, laufen; **55.** fluten, wogen: *a heavy sea was ~ning* es ging e-e schwere See; **56.** *Am.* a) laufen, fallen (*Masche*), b) Laufmaschen bekommen (*Strumpf*); **57.** ⚕ laufen, gelten, in Kraft sein *od.* bleiben: *the period ~s* die Frist läuft; **58.** ✝ sich stellen (*Preis, Ware*); **59.** mit *adj.*: werden, sein: ~ *dry* a) versiegen, b) keine Milch mehr geben, c) erschöpft sein, d) sich ausgeschrieben haben (*Schriftsteller*); → 80; ~ *low* (*od.* *short*) zur Neige gehen, knapp werden; → *high* 22, *riot* 3, *wild* 2; **60.** im Durchschnitt sein, klein *etc.* ausfallen (*Früchte etc.*); **III** *v/t.* [*irr.*] **61.** *Weg etc.* laufen; *Strecke* durch'laufen, zu'rücklegen; *Weg* einschlagen; **62.** fahren (a. ♫); *Strecke* be-, durch'fahren: ~ *a car against a tree* mit e-m Wagen gegen e-n Baum fahren; **63.** *Rennen* austragen, laufen, *Wettlauf* machen; **64.** um die Wette laufen mit: ~ *s.o. close* dicht an j-n herankommen (*a. fig.*); **65.** *Pferd* treiben; **66.** *hunt.* hetzen, *a. Spur* verfolgen (*a. fig.*); **67.** *Botschaften* über'bringen; *Botengänge od. Besorgungen* machen: ~ *errands*; **68.** *Blockade* brechen; **69.** a) *Pferd etc.* laufen lassen, b) *pol.* j-n als Kandi'daten aufstellen (*for* für); **70.** a) *Vieh* treiben, b) weiden lassen; **71.** ☗, ♫ *etc.* fahren

od. verkehren lassen; **72.** *Am. Annonce* veröffentlichen; **73.** transportieren; **74.** *Schnaps etc.* schmuggeln; **75.** *Augen, Finger etc.* gleiten lassen: ~ *one's hand through one's hair* (sich) mit den Fingern durchs Haar fahren; **76.** *Film* laufen lassen; **77.** ⊙ *Maschine etc.* laufen lassen, bedienen; **78.** *Betrieb etc.* führen, leiten, verwalten; *Geschäft etc.* betreiben; *Zeitung* her'ausgeben; **79.** hin'eingeraten (lassen) in (*acc.*): ~ *debts* Schulden machen; ~ *a firm into debt* e-e Firma in Schulden stürzen; ~ *the danger of* (*ger.*) Gefahr laufen zu (*inf.*); → *risk* 1; **80.** ausströmen, fließen lassen; *Wasser etc.* führen (*Leitung*): ~ *dry* leer laufen lassen; → 59; **81.** *Gold etc.* (mit sich) führen (*Fluss*); **82.** *Metall* schmelzen; **83.** *Blei, Kugel* gießen; **84.** *Fieber, Temperatur* haben; **85.** stoßen, stecken, stecken; **86.** *Graben, Linie, Schnur etc.* ziehen; *Straße etc.* anlegen; *Brücke* schlagen; *Leitung* legen; **87.** leicht (ver)nähen, heften; **88.** *j-n* belangen (*for* wegen);

Zssgn mit prp.:

run| a·cross *v/i.* j-n zufällig treffen, stoßen auf (*acc.*); ~ **af·ter** *v/i.* hinter ... (*dat.*) herlaufen *od.* sein, nachlaufen (*dat.*) (*alle a. fig.*); ~ **a·gainst I** *v/i.* **1.** zs.-stoßen mit, laufen *od.* rennen *od.* fahren gegen; **2.** *pol.* kandidieren gegen; **II** *v/t.* **3.** *et.* stoßen gegen: *run one's head against* mit dem Kopf gegen *die Wand etc.* stoßen; ~ **at** *v/i.* losstürzen auf (*acc.*); ~ **for** *v/i.* **1.** auf ... (*acc.*) zulaufen *od.* -rennen; laufen nach; **2.** ~ *it* Reiß'aus nehmen; **3.** *fig.* sich bemühen *od.* bewerben um; *pol.* → *run* 36; ~ **in·to I** *v/i.* **1.** (hin'ein)laufen *od.* (-)rennen in (*acc.*); **2.** ♫ in den Hafen einlaufen; **3.** → *run against* 1; **4.** → *run across*; **5.** geraten *od.* sich stürzen in (*acc.*): ~ *debt*; **6.** werden *od.* sich entwickeln zu; **7.** sich belaufen auf (*acc.*): ~ *four editions* vier Auflagen erleben; ~ *money* ins Geld laufen; **II** *v/t.* **8.** *Messer etc.* stoßen *od.* rennen in (*acc.*); ~ **off** *v/i.* hin'unterfahren *od.* -laufen von: ~ *the rails* entgleisen; ~ **on** *v/i.* **1.** sich drehen um, betreffen; **2.** sich beschäftigen mit; **3.** losfahren auf (*acc.*); **4.** → *run across*; **5.** mit *e-m Treibstoff* fahren, (an)getrieben werden von; ~ **o·ver** *v/i.* **1.** laufen *od.* gleiten über (*acc.*); **2.** über'fahren; **3.** 'durchgehen, -lesen, über'fliegen; ~ **through** *v/i.* **1.** → *run over* 3; **2.** kurz erzählen, streifen; **3.** 'durchmachen, erleben; **4.** sich hin'durchziehen durch; **5.** *Vermögen* 'durchbringen; ~ **to** *v/i.* **1.** sich belaufen auf (*acc.*); **2.** (aus)reichen für (*Geldmittel*); **3.** sich entwickeln zu, neigen zu; **4.** F sich *et.* leisten; **5.** allzu sehr *Blätter etc.* treiben (*Pflanze*); → *fat* 5, *seed* 1; ~ **up·on** → *run on*; ~ **with** *v/i.* über'einstimmen mit;

Zssgn mit adv.:

run| a·way *v/i.* **1.** da'vonlaufen (*from* von *od.* dat.): ~ *from a subject* von einem Thema abschweifen; **2.** 'durchgehen (*Pferd etc.*): ~ *with* a) durchgehen mit j-m (*a. Fantasie, Temperament*); *don't ~ with the idea that* glauben Sie bloß nicht, dass, b) *et.* ,mitgehen lassen', c) *viel Geld* kosten *od.* verschlingen, d) *sport Satz etc.* klar gewinnen; ~ **down I** *v/i.* **1.** hin'unterlaufen (*a. Träne etc.*); **2.** ablaufen (*Uhr*); **3.** *fig.* her'unterkommen; **II** *v/t.* **4.** über'fahren; **5.** ♫ in den Grund bohren; **6.** *j-n* einholen; **7.** *Wild, Verbrecher* zur

Strecke bringen; **8.** aufstöbern, ausfindig machen; **9.** erschöpfen, *Batterie a.* zu stark entladen: *be ~* fig. erschöpft *od.* ab(gearbeitet, -gespannt) sein; **10.** *Betrieb etc.* her'unterwirtschaften; ~ **in** I *v/i.* **1.** hin'ein-, her'einlaufen; **2.** ~ *with* fig. über'einstimmen mit; **II** *v/t.* **3.** hi-'neinlaufen lassen; **4.** einfügen (*a. typ.*); **5.** F *Verbrecher* ,einlochen'; **6.** ⊙ *Maschine* (sich) einlaufen lassen, *Auto etc.* einfahren; ~ **off** I *v/i.* **1.** → *run away*; **2.** ablaufen, -fließen; **II** *v/t.* **3.** *et.* schnell erledigen; *Gedicht etc.* her'unterrasseln; **4.** *typ.* abdrucken, -ziehen; **5.** *Rennen etc.* a) austragen, b) zur Entscheidung bringen; ~ **on** *v/i.* **1.** weiterlaufen; **2.** *fig.* fortlaufen, fortgesetzt werden (*to* bis); **3.** a) (unaufhörlich) reden, fortplappern, b) *in der Rede* fortfahren; **4.** anwachsen (*into* zu); **5.** *typ.* (ohne Absatz) fortlaufen; ~ **out** I *v/i.* **1.** hin'aus-, her'auslaufen; **2.** he-'rausfließen, -laufen; **3.** (aus)laufen (*Gefäß*); **4.** fig. ablaufen, zu Ende gehen; **5.** ausgehen, knapp werden (*Vorrat*): *I have ~ of tobacco* ich habe keinen Tabak mehr; **6.** her'ausragen; sich erstrecken; **II** *v/t.* **7.** hin'ausjagen, -treiben; erschöpfen: *run o.s. out* bis zur Erschöpfung laufen; *be ~* a) vom Laufen ausgepumpt sein, b) ausverkauft sein; ~ **o·ver** I *v/i.* **1.** hin'überlaufen; **2.** 'überlaufen, -fließen; **II** *v/t.* **3.** über'fahren; ~ **through** *v/t.* **1.** durch'bohren, -'stoßen; **2.** *Wort* 'durchstreichen; **3.** *Zug* 'durchfahren lassen; ~ **up** I *v/i.* **1.** hin'auflaufen, -rennen; **2.** zulaufen (*to* auf *acc.*); **3.** schnell anwachsen, hochschießen; **4.** einlaufen, -gehen (*Kleider*); **II** *v/t.* **5.** *Vermögen etc.* anwachsen lassen; **6.** *Rechnung* anwachsen lassen; **7.** *Angebot, Preis* in die Höhe treiben; **8.** *Flagge* hissen; **9.** schnell zs.-zählen; **10.** *Haus etc.* schnell hochziehen; **11.** *Kleid etc.* ,zs.-hauen' (*schnell nähen*).

'run| a·bout s. **1.** Her'umtreiber(in); **2.** a. ~ *car* mot. Kleinwagen m, Stadtauto n; **3.** leichtes Motorboot; '~-**a·round** s. *Am.* F: *give s.o. the ~* a) j-n von Pontius zu Pilatus schicken, b) j-n hinhalten, c) j-n ,an der Nase herumführen'; '~-**a·way** I s. **1.** Ausreißer(in), 'Durchgänger m (a. Pferd); **2.** 'Durchgehen n e-s Atomreaktors; **II** adj. **3.** 'durchgebrannt, flüchtig (*Häftling etc.*): ~ *car* Wagen, der sich selbstständig gemacht hat; ~ *inflation* ✝ galoppierende Inflation; ~ *match* Heirat f e-s durchgebrannten Liebespaares; ~ *victory* sport Kantersieg m; '~-**down** I adj. **1.** erschöpft (a. ⚕ *Batterie*), abgespannt, erledigt'; **2.** her'untergekommen, baufällig; **3.** abgelaufen (*Uhr*); **II** ['rʌndaʊn] s. **4.** F (ausführlicher) Bericht.

rune [ruːn] s. Rune f.

rung[1] [rʌŋ] p.p. *von* ring[2].

rung[2] [rʌŋ] s. **1.** (*bsd.* Leiter)Sprosse f; **2.** fig. Stufe f, Sprosse f; **3.** (Rad)Speiche f; **4.** Runge f.

ru·nic ['ruːnɪk] I adj. **1.** runisch; Runen...; **II** s. **2.** Runeninschrift f; **3.** *typ.* Runenschrift f.

'run-in s. **1.** bsd. Brit. Einlauf m; **2.** *typ.* Einschiebung f; **3.** ⊙ a) Einfahren n (*Auto etc.*), b) Einlaufen n (*Maschine*); **4.** *Am.* F ,Krach' m, Zs.-stoß m (*Streit*); ~ *groove* s. Einlaufrille f (*Schallplatte*).

run·let ['rʌnlɪt] s. Bach m.

run·nel ['rʌnl] s. **1.** Rinnsal n; **2.** Rinne f, Rinnstein m.

run·ner ['rʌnə] s. **1.** (a. Wett)Läufer (-in): *do a ~ Brit.* F a) abhauen, b) die Sache ,sausen' lassen; **2.** Rennpferd n;

3. a) Bote *m*, b) Laufbursche *m*, c) ✕ Melder *m*; **4.** ✝ *Am.* a) Unter'nehmer *m*, b) F Vertreter *m*, c) F ‚Renner' *m*, Verkaufsschlager *m*; **5.** *mst in Zssgn* Schmuggler *m*; **6.** Läufer *m* (*Teppich*); **7.** (*Schlitten- etc.*)Kufe *f*; **8.** ⊛ a) Laufschiene *f*, b) Seilring *m*, c) (*Turbinenetc.*)Laufrad *n*, d) (Gleit-, Lauf)Rolle *f*, e) Rollwalze *f*; **9.** *typ.* Zeilenzähler *m*; **10.** ✓ Drillschar *f*; **11.** ⚓ Drehreep *n*; **12.** ⚘ a) Ausläufer *m*, b) Kletterpflanze *f*, c) Stangenbohne *f*; **13.** *orn.* Ralle *f*; **14.** *ichth.* Goldstöcker *m*; **,~-'up** *s.* (*to* hinter *dat.*) Zweite(r *m*) *f*, *sport a.* Vizemeister(in).

run·ning ['rʌnɪŋ] **I** *s.* **1.** Laufen *n*, Lauf *m* (*a.* ⊛): **~ costs** *pl.* ✝ Betriebskosten *pl.*; *be still in the* **~** noch gut im Rennen liegen (*a. fig. for* um); *be out of the* **~** aus dem Rennen sein (*a. fig. for* um); *make the* **~** a) das Tempo machen, b) das Tempo angeben; *put s.o. out of the* **~** j-n aus dem Rennen werfen (*a. fig.*); *take* (*up*) *the* **~** sich an die Spitze setzen (*a. fig.*); **2.** Schmuggel *m*; **3.** Leitung *f*, Aufsicht *f*; Bedienung *f*, Über'wachung *f e-r Maschine*; **4.** Durch'brechen *n e-r Blockade*; **II** *adj.* **5.** laufend (*a.* ⊛): **~ fight** ✕ a) Rückzugsgefecht *n*, b) laufendes Gefecht (*a. fig.*); **~ gear** ⊛ Laufwerk *n*; **~ glance** *fig.* flüchtiger Blick; **~ jump** Sprung *m* mit Anlauf; **~ knot** laufender Knoten; **~ mate** *pol. Am.* Vizepräsidentschaftsbewerber(in); **~ shot** *Film:* Fahraufnahme *f*; **~ speed** Fahr- *od.* Umlaufgeschwindigkeit *f*; **~ start** *sport* fliegender Start; *in* **~** *order* ⊛ betriebsfähig; **6.** *fig.* laufend (*ständig*), fortlaufend: **~ account** ✝ a) laufende Rechnung, b) Kontokorrent *n*; **~ commentary** a) laufender Kommentar, b) (Funk)Reportage *f*; **~ debts** laufende Schulden; **~ hand** Schreibschrift *f*; **~ head**(*line*) = **~ title** Kolumnentitel *m*; **~ pattern** fortlaufendes Muster; **~ text** fortlaufender Text; **7.** fließend (*Wasser*); **8.** ⚘ laufend, eiternd (*Wunde*); **9.** aufein'ander folgend: *five times* (*for three days*) **~** fünfmal (drei Tage) hintereinander; **~ fire** ✕ Lauffeuer *n*; **10.** line'ar gemessen: *per* **~** *metre* pro laufendem Meter; **11.** ⚘ a) rankend, b) kriechend; **12.** ♪ laufend: **~ passages** Läufe; **~ board** *s. mot.*, 🚢 *etc.* Tritt-, Laufbrett *n*; **,~-'in test** *s.* ⊛ Probelauf *m*.

'run|-off *s. sport* Entscheidungslauf *m*, -rennen *n*; **'~-off vote** *s. pol.* Stichwahl *f*; **,~-of-the-'mill** *adj.* Durchschnitts..., mittelmäßig; **'~-proof** *adj.* maschenfest; **'~-on** *typ.* **I** *adj.* angehängt, fortlaufend gesetzt; **II** *s.* angehängtes Wort.

runs [rʌnz] *s. pl.* F *bsd. Brit.* Durchfall *m*, ‚Scheiße'rei' *f*.

runt [rʌnt] *s.* **1.** *zo.* Zwergrind *n*, -ochse *m*; **2.** *fig.* (*contp.* lächerlicher) Zwerg; **3.** *orn. große kräftige Haustaubenrasse*.

'run|-through *s.* **1.** a) Über'fliegen *n* (*e-s Briefs etc.*), b) kurze Zs.-fassung (*e-s Briefs etc.*); **2.** *thea.* schnelle Probe; **~ time** *s. Computer:* Laufzeit *f*; **'~-up** *s.* **1.** *sport.* Anlauf *m*: *in the* **~** *to fig.* im Vorfeld *der Wahlen etc.*; **2.** ✕ (Ziel)Anflug *m*; **3.** ✈ kurzer Probelauf *der Motoren*; **'~-way** *s.* **1.** ✈ Start-und-'Lande-Bahn *f*, Piste *f*; **2.** *sport* Anlaufbahn *f*; **3.** *hunt.* Wildpfad *m*, (-)Wechsel *m*: **~ watching** Ansitzjagd *f*; **4.** *bsd. Am.* Laufsteg *m*.

ru·pee [ruːˈpiː] *s.* Rupie *f* (*Geld*).

rup·ture ['rʌptʃə] **I** *s.* **1.** Bruch *m* (*a.* ⚘ *u. fig.*), (*a.* ⚘ *Muskel- etc.*)Riss *m*: **dip-**

lomatic **~** Abbruch *m* der diplomatischen Beziehungen; **~ support** ⚕ Bruchband *n*; **2.** Brechen *n* (*a.* ⊛): **~ limit** ⊛ Bruchgrenze *f*; **II** *v/t.* **3.** brechen (*a. fig.*), zersprengen, -reißen (*a.* ⚕): **~** *o.s.* → 6; **4.** *fig.* abbrechen, trennen; **III** *v/i.* **5.** zerspringen, (-)reißen; **6.** ⚕ sich e-n Bruch heben.

ru·ral ['rʊərəl] *adj.* □ **1.** ländlich, Land...; **2.** landwirtschaftlich; **'ru·ral·ize** [-rəlaɪz] **I** *v/t.* **1.** e-n ländlichen Cha'rakter geben (*dat.*); **2.** auf das Landleben 'umstellen; **II** *v/i.* **3.** auf dem Lande leben; **4.** sich auf das Landleben umstellen; **5.** ländlich werden, verbauern.

Ru·ri·ta·ni·an [ˌrʊərɪˈteɪnjən] *adj. fig.* abenteuerlich.

ruse [ruːz] *s.* List *f*, Trick *m*.

rush¹ [rʌʃ] *s.* ⚘ Binse *f*; *coll.* Binsen *pl.*: *not worth a* **~** *fig.* keinen Pfifferling wert.

rush² [rʌʃ] **I** *v/i.* **1.** rasen, stürzen, (da'hin)jagen, stürmen, (he'rum)hetzen: **~** *at s.o.* auf j-n losstürzen; **~** *in* hereinstürzen, -stürmen; **~** *into extremes fig.* ins Extrem verfallen: **~** *through* a) hasten durch, b) *et.* hastig erledigen *etc.*; *an idea* **~***ed into my mind* ein Gedanke schoss mir durch den Kopf; *blood* **~***ed to her face* das Blut schoss ihr ins Gesicht; **2.** (da'hin)brausen (*Wind*); **3.** *fig.* sich (*vorschnell*) stürzen (*into* in *od. dat.*); → *conclusion* 3, *print* 13; **II** *v/t.* **4.** (an)treiben, drängen, hetzen, jagen: *I refuse to be* **~***ed* ich lasse mich nicht drängen; **~** *up prices Am.* die Preise in die Höhe treiben; *be* **~***ed for time* F unter Zeitdruck stehen; **5.** schnell *od.* auf dem schnellsten Wege *wohin* bringen *od.* schaffen: **~** *s.o. to the hospital*; **6.** schnell erledigen, *Arbeit etc.* her'unterhasten, hinhauen: **~** *a bill* (*through*) e-e Gesetzesvorlage durchpeitschen; **7.** über'stürzen, -'eilen; **8.** losstürzen auf (*acc.*), angreifen; **9.** im Sturm nehmen (*a. fig.*), stürmen (*a. fig.*): **~** *s.o. off his feet* j-n in Trab halten; **10.** über *ein Hindernis* hin'wegsetzen; **11.** *Am. sl.* mit Aufmerksamkeiten über'häufen, um'werben; **12.** *Brit. sl.* ‚neppen', ‚bescheißen' (*£5 um* 5 *Pfund*); **III** *s.* **13.** Vorwärtsstürmen *n*, Da'hinschießen *n*; Brausen *n* (*Wind*): *on the* **~** F in aller Eile; *with a* **~** plötzlich; **14.** ✕ a) Sturm *m*, b) Sprung *m*: *by* **~***es* sprungweise; **15.** *American Football:* Vorstoß *m*, 'Durchbruch *m*; **16.** *fig.* a) (An)Sturm *m* (*for* auf *acc.*), b) (Massen)Andrang *m*, c) *a.* ✝ stürmische Nachfrage (*on od.* *for* nach): *make a* **~** *for* losstürzen auf (*acc.*); **17.** ⚕ a) (Blut)Andrang *m*, b) (Adrena'linetc.)Stoß *m*; **18.** *fig.* plötzlicher Ausbruch (*von Tränen etc.*); plötzliche Anwandlung, Anfall *m*: **~** *of pity*; **19.** a) Drang *m* der Geschäfte, ‚Hetze' *f*, b) Hochbetrieb *m*, -druck *m*, c) Über'häufung *f* (*of* mit *Arbeit*); **~** *hour* *s.* Hauptverkehrs-, Stoßzeit *f*; **'~-,hour** *adj.* Hauptverkehrs-, Stoß...: **~** *traffic* Stoßverkehr *m*; **~** *job* *s.* eilige Arbeit, dringende Sache; **~** *or·der* *s.* ✝ Eilauftrag *m*.

rusk [rʌsk] *s.* **1.** Zwieback *m*; **2.** Sandkuchengebäck *n*.

rus·set ['rʌsɪt] **I** *adj.* **1.** a) rostbraun, b) rotgelb, -grau; **2.** *obs.* grob; **II** *s.* **3.** a) Rostbraun *n*, b) Rotgelb *n*, -grau *n*; **4.** grobes handgewebtes Tuch; **5.** Boskop *m* (*rötlicher Winterapfel*).

Rus·sia leath·er ['rʌʃə] *s.* Juchten(leder) *n*; **'Rus·sian** [-ʃn] **I** *s.* **1.** Russe *m*,

Russin *f*; **2.** *ling.* Russisch *n*; **II** *adj.* **3.** russisch; **'Rus·sian·ize** [-ʃənaɪz] *v/t.* russifizieren.

Rus·so- [rʌsəʊ] *in Zssgn* a) russisch, b) russisch-...

rust [rʌst] **I** *s.* **1.** Rost *m* (*a. fig.*): *gather* **~** Rost ansetzen; **2.** Rost- *od.* Moderfleck *m*; **3.** ⚘ a) Rost *m*, Brand *m*, b) *a.* **~** *fungus* Rostpilz *m*; **II** *v/i.* **4.** (ver)rosten, einrosten (*a. fig.*), rostig werden; **5.** moderfleckig werden; **III** *v/t.* **6.** rostig machen; **7.** *fig.* einrosten lassen.

rus·tic ['rʌstɪk] **I** *adj.* □ (**~***ally*) **1.** ländlich, rusti'kal, Land..., Bauern...; **2.** simpel, schlicht, anspruchslos; **3.** grob, ungehobelt, bäurisch; **4.** rusti'kal, roh (gearbeitet): **~** *furniture*; **5.** △ a) Rustika..., b) mit Bossenwerk verziert; **6.** *typ.* unregelmäßig geformt; **II** *s.* **7.** (einfacher) Bauer, Landmann *m*; **8.** *fig.* Bauer *m*; **'rus·ti·cate** [-keɪt] **I** *v/i.* **1.** auf dem Lande leben; **2.** a) ein ländliches Leben führen, b) verbauern; **II** *v/t.* **3.** aufs Land senden; **4.** *Brit. univ.* relegieren, (zeitweilig) von der Universi'tät verweisen; **5.** △ mit Bossenwerk verzieren; **rus·ti·ca·tion** [ˌrʌstɪˈkeɪʃn] *s.* **1.** Landaufenthalt *m*; **2.** Verbauerung *f*; **3.** *Brit. univ.* (zeitweise) Relegati'on; **rus·tic·i·ty** [rʌˈstɪsətɪ] *s.* **1.** ländlicher Cha'rakter; **2.** grobe *od.* bäurische Art; **3.** (ländliche) Einfachheit.

rus·tic| ware *s.* hellbraune Terra'kotta; **~** *work* *s.* **1.** △ Bossenwerk *n*, Rustika *f*; **2.** roh gezimmerte Möbel *etc.*

rust·i·ness ['rʌstɪnɪs] *s.* **1.** Rostigkeit *f*; **2.** *fig.* Eingerostetsein *n*.

rus·tle ['rʌsl] **I** *v/i.* **1.** rascheln (*Blätter etc.*), rauschen, knistern (*Seide etc.*); **2.** *Am. sl.* ‚rangehen', (e'nergisch) zupacken; **II** *v/t.* **3.** rascheln mit (*od.* in *dat.*), rascheln machen; **4.** *Am. sl.* Vieh stehlen; **5.** **~** *up* F a) *et.* ,organisieren', auftreiben, b) *Essen* ,zaubern'; **III** *s.* **6.** Rauschen *n*, Rascheln *n*, Knistern *n*; **'rus·tler** [-lə] *s. Am. sl.* **1.** Viehdieb *m*; **2.** Mordsanstrengung *f*.

rust·less ['rʌstlɪs] *adj.* rostfrei, nicht rostend: **~** *steel*.

rust·y ['rʌstɪ] *adj.* □ **1.** rostig, verrostet; **2.** *fig.* eingerostet (*Kenntnisse etc.*); **3.** rostfarben; **4.** ⚘ vom Rost(pilz) befallen; **5.** schäbig (*Kleidung*); **6.** rau (*Stimme*).

rut¹ [rʌt] **I** *s.* **1.** (Wagen-, Rad)Spur *f*, Furche *f*; **2.** *fig.* altes Geleise, alter Trott *m*: *be in a* **~** sich in ausgefahrenen Gleisen bewegen; *get into a* **~** in e-n (immer gleichen) Trott verfallen; **II** *v/t.* **3.** furchen.

rut² [rʌt] *zo.* **I** *s.* **1.** a) Brunst *f*, b) Brunft *f* (*Hirsch*); **2.** Brunst-, Brunftzeit *f*; **II** *v/i.* **3.** brunften, brunsten.

ru·ta·ba·ga [ˌruːtəˈbeɪgə] *s.* ⚘ *Am.* Gelbe Kohlrübe.

Ruth¹ [ruːθ] *a. Book of* **~** *s. bibl.* (das Buch) Ruth *f*.

ruth² [ruːθ] *s. obs.* Mitleid *n*.

ruth·less ['ruːθlɪs] *adj.* □ **1.** unbarmherzig, mitleidlos; **2.** rücksichts-, skrupellos; **'ruth·less·ness** [-nɪs] *s.* **1.** Unbarmherzigkeit *f*; **2.** Rücksichts-, Skrupellosigkeit *f*.

rut·ting ['rʌtɪŋ] *zo.* **I** *s.* Brunst *f*; **II** *adj.* Brunst..., Brunft...: **~** *time*; **rut·tish** ['rʌtɪʃ] *adj. zo.* brunftig, brünstig.

rut·ty ['rʌtɪ] *adj.* durch'furcht, ausgefahren (*Weg*).

rye [raɪ] *s.* **1.** ⚘ Roggen *m*; **2.** *a.* **~** *whisky* Roggenwhisky *m*.

S, s [es] *s.* S *n*, s *n* (*Buchstabe*).

's [z] **1.** F *für* **is**: *he's here*; **2.** F *für* **has**: *she's just come*; **3.** [s] F *für* **us**: *let's go*; **4.** [s] F *für* **does**: *what's he think about it?*

Sab·bath ['sæbəθ] *s.* Sabbat *m*; *weitS.* ♄ Sonn-, Ruhetag *m*: *break* (*keep*) *the ~* den Sabbat entheiligen (heiligen); *witches' ~* Hexensabbat; **'~‚break·er** *s.* Sabbatschänder(in).

Sab·bat·ic [sə'bætɪk] *adj.* (□ *~ally*) → *sabbatical* I; **sab'bat·i·cal** [-kl] I *adj.* □ ♄ Sabbat...; II *s. a.* **~ year** a) Sabbatjahr *n*, b) *univ.* Ferienjahr *n e-s Professors.*

sa·ber ['seɪbə] *Am.* → *sabre.*

sa·ble ['seɪbl] I *s.* **1.** *zo.* a) Zobel *m*, b) (*bsd.* Fichten)Marder *m*; **2.** Zobelfell *n*, -pelz *m*; **3.** *her.* Schwarz *n*; **4.** *mst pl. poet.* Trauer(kleidung) *f*; II *adj.* **5.** Zobel...; **6.** *her.* schwarz; **7.** *poet.* schwarz, finster.

sa·bot ['sæbəʊ] *s.* **1.** Holzschuh *m*; **2.** ✕ Geschoss-, Führungsring *m.*

sab·o·tage ['sæbətɑːʒ] I *s.* Sabo'tage *f*; II *v/t.* sabotieren; III *v/i.* Sabo'tage treiben; **sa·bo·teur** [‚sæbə'tɜː] (*Fr.*) *s.* Sabo'teur *m.*

sa·bre ['seɪbə] I *s.* **1.** Säbel *m*: *rattle the ~ fig.* mit dem Säbel rasseln; **2.** ✕ *hist.* Kavalle'rist *m*; II *v/t.* **3.** niedersäbeln; **~ rat·tling** *s. fig.* Säbelrasseln *n.*

sab·u·lous ['sæbjʊləs] *adj.* sandig, Sand...: **~ urine** ✿ Harngrieß *m.*

sac [sæk] *s.* **1.** ✿, *anat., zo.* Sack *m*, Beutel *m*; **2.** ⊚ (Tinten)Sack *m* (*Füllhalter*).

sac·cha·rate ['sækəreɪt] *s.* ♔ Sa(c)cha'rat *n*; **sac·char·ic** [sə'kærɪk] *adj.* ♔ Zucker...: **~ acid**; **sac·cha·rif·er·ous** [‚sækə'rɪfərəs] *adj.* ♔ zuckerhaltig *od.* Zucker erzeugend; **sac·char·i·fy** [sə'kærɪfaɪ] *v/t.* **1.** verzuckern, sa(c)charifizieren; **2.** süßen; **sac·cha·rim·e·ter** [‚sækə'rɪmɪtə] *s.* Zuckermesser *m*, Sa(c)chari'meter *n.*

sac·cha·rin(e) ['sækərɪn] *s.* ♔ Sa(c)cha'rin *n* (*Zucker...*, *Süßstoff...*): **2.** *fig.* süßlich: *a ~ smile*; **'sac·cha·roid** [-rɔɪd] *adj.* ♔, *min.* zuckerartig, körnig; **sac·cha·rom·e·ter** [‚sækə'rɒmɪtə] → *saccharimeter*; **'sac·cha·rose** [-rəʊs] *s.* ♔ Rohrzucker *m*, Sa(c)cha'rose *f.*

sac·cule ['sækjuːl] *s. bsd. anat.* Säckchen *n.*

sac·er·do·tal [‚sæsə'dəʊtl] *adj.* □ priesterlich, Priester...; **‚sac·er·do·tal·ism** [-təlɪzəm] *s.* **1.** Priestertum *n*; **2.** *contp.* Pfaffentum *n.*

sa·chem ['seɪtʃəm] *s.* **1.** Indi'anerhäuptling *m*; **2.** *Am. humor.* ‚großes Tier', *bsd. pol.* ‚Par'teiboss' *m.*

sa·chet ['sæʃeɪ] *s.* **1.** Säckchen *n*, Tütchen *n*; **2.** Duftkissen *n.*

sack¹ [sæk] I *s.* **1.** Sack *m*; **2.** F ‚Laufpass' *m*: *get the ~* a) ‚fliegen', ‚an die Luft gesetzt (*entlassen*) werden', b) *von e-m Mädchen* den Laufpass bekommen; *give s.o. the ~* → 7; **3.** *Am.* a) (Ver-

packungs)Beutel *m*, Tüte *f*, b) Beutel (-inhalt) *m*; **4.** a) 'Umhang *m*, b) (kurzer) loser Mantel, c) → *sack coat*, *sack dress*; **5.** *sl.* ‚Falle' *f*, ‚Klappe' *f* (*Bett*): *hit the ~* sich ‚hinhauen'; II *v/t.* **6.** einsacken, in Säcke *od.* Beutel abfüllen; **7.** F a) *j-n* ‚rausschmeißen' (*entlassen*), b) *e-m Liebhaber* den Laufpass geben.

sack² [sæk] I *s.* Plünderung *f*: *put to ~* → II *v/t.* Stadt *etc.* (aus)plündern.

sack³ [sæk] *s.* heller Südwein.

'sack|·but [-bʌt] *s.* ♪ **1.** *hist.* 'Zugpo‚saune *f*; **2.** *bibl.* Harfe *f*; **'~‚cloth** *s.* Sackleinen *n*: *in ~ and ashes fig.* in Sack u. Asche *Buße tun od. trauern*; **~ coat** *s. Am.* Sakko *m, n*; **~ dress** *s.* Sackkleid *n*; **'~·ful** [-fʊl] *pl.* **-fuls** *s.* Sack *m* (voll); **~ race** *s.* Sackhüpfen *n.*

sa·cral ['seɪkrəl] I *adj.* **1.** *eccl.* sa'kral, Sakral...; **2.** *anat.* Sakral..., Kreuz(bein)...; II *s.* **3.** Sa'kralwirbel *m*; **4.** Sa'kralnerv *m.*

sac·ra·ment ['sækrəmənt] *s.* **1.** *eccl.* Sakra'ment *n*: *the* (*Blessed od. Holy*) ~ a) das (heilige) Abendmahl, b) *R.C.* die heilige Kommunion; *the last ~s* die Sterbesakramente; **2.** Sym'bol *n* (*of* für); **3.** My'sterium *n*; **4.** feierlicher Eid; **sac·ra·men·tal** [‚sækrə'mentl] I *adj.* □ sakramen'tal, Sakraments...; *fig.* heilig, weihevoll; II *s. R.C.* heiliger *od.* sakramen'taler Ritus *od.* Gegenstand; *pl.* Sakramen'talien *pl.*

sa·cred ['seɪkrɪd] *adj.* □ **1.** *eccl. u. fig.* heilig (*a. Andenken, Pflicht, Recht etc.*), geheiligt, geweiht (*to dat.*): ~ *cow fig.* ‚heilige Kuh'; **2.** geistlich, kirchlich, Kirchen... (*Dichtung, Musik*); **'sa·cred·ness** [-nɪs] *s.* Heiligkeit *f.*

sac·ri·fice ['sækrɪfaɪs] I *s.* **1.** *eccl. u. fig.* a) Opfer *n* (*Handlung u. Sache*), b) *fig.* Aufopferung *f*; Verzicht *m* (*of* auf *acc.*): ~ *of the Mass* Messopfer *n*; *the great* (*od. last*) ~ das höchste Opfer, *bsd.* der Heldentod; *make a ~ of et.* opfern; *make ~s* → 6; *at some ~ of accuracy* unter einigem Verzicht auf Genauigkeit; **2.** ✝ Verlust *m*: *sell at a ~* → 4; II *v/t.* **3.** *eccl. u. fig., a. Schach:* opfern (*to dat.*): ~ *one's life*; **4.** ✝ mit Verlust verkaufen; III *v/i.* **5.** *eccl.* opfern; **6.** *fig.* Opfer bringen; **sac·ri·fi·cial** [‚sækrɪ'fɪʃl] *adj.* □ **1.** *eccl.* Opfer...; **2.** aufopferungsvoll.

sac·ri·lege ['sækrɪlɪdʒ] *s.* Sakri'leg *n*: a) Kirchenschändung *f*, -raub *m*, b) Entweihung *f*, c) *allg.* Frevel *m*; **sac·ri·le·gious** [‚sækrɪ'lɪdʒəs] *adj.* □ sakri'legisch, *allg.* frevlerisch.

sa·crist ['seɪkrɪst], **sac·ris·tan** ['sækrɪstən] *s. eccl.* Sakri'stan *m*, Mes(s)ner *m*, Küster *m*; **sac·ris·ty** ['sækrɪstɪ] *s. eccl.* Sakri'stei *f.*

sac·ro·sanct ['sækrəʊsæŋkt] *adj.* (*a. iro.*) sakro'sankt, hochheilig.

sa·crum ['seɪkrəm] *s. anat.* Kreuzbein *n*, Sakrum *n.*

sad [sæd] *adj.* □ → *sadly*; **1.** (*at*) traurig (über *acc.*), bekümmert, niedergeschlagen (wegen); melan'cholisch: ~ *der and a wiser man* j-d, der durch Schaden klug geworden ist; **2.** traurig (*Pflicht*), tragisch (*Unfall etc.*): ~ *to say* bedauerlicherweise; **3.** schlimm, arg (*Zustand*); **4.** *contp.* elend, mise'rabel, jämmerlich, F arg, ‚furchtbar': *a ~ dog* ein mieser Kerl; **5.** dunkel, matt (*Farbe*); **6.** teigig, klitschig: ~ *bread*; **sad·den** ['sædn] I *v/t.* traurig machen, betrüben; II *v/i.* traurig werden (*at* über *acc.*).

sad·dle ['sædl] I *s.* **1.** (Pferde-, Fahrrad-*etc.*)Sattel *m*: *in the ~* im Sattel, *fig.* fest im Sattel, im Amt, an der Macht; *put the ~ on the wrong* (*right*) *horse fig.* die Schuld dem Falschen (Richtigen) geben *od.* zuschreiben; **2.** a) (Pferde)Rücken *m*, b) Rücken(stück *n*) *m* (*Schlachtvieh etc.*): ~ *of mutton* Hammelrücken; **3.** (Berg)Sattel *m*; **4.** Buchrücken *m*; **5.** ⊚ a) Querholz *n*, b) Bettschlitten *m*, Sup'port *m* (*Werkzeugmaschine*), c) Lager *n*, d) Türschwelle *f*; II *v/t.* **6.** Pferd satteln; **7.** *bsd. fig.* a) belasten, b) *Aufgabe etc.* aufbürden, -halsen (*on, upon dat.*), c) *et.* zur Last legen (*on, upon dat.*); **'~·back** *s.* **1.** Bergsattel *m*; **2.** ⚠ Satteldach *n*; **3.** *zo.* Tier mit sattelförmiger Rückenzeichnung, *bsd.* a) Nebelkrähe *f*, b) männliche Sattelrobbe; **4.** hohlrückiges Pferd; **'~·backed** *adj.* **1.** hohlrückig (*Pferd etc.*); **2.** sattelförmig; **'~·bag** *s.* Satteltasche *f*; ~ **blan·ket** *s.* Woilach *m*; ~ **horse** *s.* Reitpferd *n*; **'~·nose** *s.* Sattelnase *f.*

sad·dler·y ['sædlərɪ] *s.* **1.** Sattle'rei *f*; **2.** Sattelzeug *n.*

sad·ism ['seɪdɪzəm] *s. psych.* Sa'dismus *m*; **'sad·ist** [-ɪst] *s.* Sa'dist(in); II *adj.* → *sa·dis·tic* [sə'dɪstɪk] *adj.* (□ *~ally*) sa'distisch.

sad·ly ['sædlɪ] *adv.* **1.** traurig, betrübt; **2.** *a. ~ enough* unglücklicherweise, leider; **3.** erbärmlich, arg, schmählich *vernachlässigt etc.*

sad·ness ['sædnɪs] *s.* Traurigkeit *f.*

sa·fa·ri [sə'fɑːrɪ] *s.* (*on ~ auf*) Sa'fari *f.*

safe [seɪf] I *adj.* □ **1.** sicher (*from* vor *dat.*): *we are ~ now* jetzt sind wir in Sicherheit; *keep s.th. ~ et.* sicher aufbewahren; *better to be ~ than sorry!* ‚Vorsicht ist die Mutter der Porzellankiste!'; **2.** sicher, unversehrt, heil; außer Gefahr (*a. Patient*): ~ *and sound* heil u. gesund *ankommen etc.*; **3.** sicher, ungefährlich: ~ *period* ✿ unfruchtbare Tage *pl.* (*der Frau*); ~ *sex* Safer Sex, geschützter Verkehr; ~ (*to operate* ⊚) betriebssicher; ~ ⊚ zulässige Beanspruchung; *the rope is ~* das Seil hält; *is it ~ to go there?* ist es ungefährlich, da hinzugehen?; *in custody* → 7; *as ~ as houses* F absolut sicher; *it is ~ to say* man kann (ruhig) sagen; *to be on the ~ side* um ganz

sicher zu gehen; → **play** 9; **4.** vorsichtig (*Fahrer, Schätzung etc.*); **5.** sicher, zuverlässig: *a ~ leader*; *a ~ method*; **6.** sicher, wahrscheinlich: *a ~ winner*; *he is ~ to be there* er wird sicher *od.* bestimmt da sein; **7.** in sicherem Gewahrsam (*a. Verbrecher*); **II** *s.* **8.** Safe *m*, Tre'sor *m*, Geldschrank *m*; **9.** → *meat safe*; '~,blow·er, '~,crack·er *s.* F Geldschrankknacker *m*; **~ con·duct** *s.* **1.** Geleitbrief *m*; **2.** freies *od.* sicheres Geleit; **~ de·pos·it** *s.* Stahlkammer *f*, Tre'sor(raum) *m*; '~-de,pos·it box *s.* Tre'sor(fach *n*) *m*, Safe *m*; '~-guard **I** *s.* Sicherung *f*: a) Schutz (*against* gegen, vor *dat.*), Vorsichtsmaßnahme *f* (gegen), b) Sicherheitsklausel *f*, c) ⊛ Schutzvorrichtung *f*; **II** *v/t.* sichern, schützen; *Interessen* wahrnehmen: ~*ing duty* Schutzzoll *m*; **~ keep·ing** *s.* sichere Verwahrung, Gewahrsam *m*.
safe·ness ['seɪfnɪs] → **safety** 1–3.
safe·ty ['seɪftɪ] *s.* **1.** Sicherheit *f*: *be in ~*; *jump to ~* sich durch e-n Sprung retten; **2.** Sicherheit *f*, Gefahrlosigkeit *f*: ~ (*of operation*) ⊛ Betriebssicherheit; ~ *glass* Sicherheitsglas *n*; **~ measure** Sicherheitsmaßnahme *f*, -vorkehrung *f*; ~ *in flight* ✈ Flugsicherheit; ~ *on the road* Verkehrssicherheit; *there is ~ in numbers* zu mehreren ist man sicherer; *~ first!* Sicherheit über alles!; ~ *first scheme* Unfallverhütungsprogramm *n*; *play for ~* sichergehen (wollen), Risiken vermeiden; **3.** Sicherheit *f*, Zuverlässigkeit *f*, Verlässlichkeit *f* (*Mechanismus, Verfahren etc.*); **4.** *a. ~ device* ⊛ Sicherung *f*, Schutz-, Sicherheitsvorrichtung *f*; **5.** Sicherung(sflügel *m*) *f* (*Gewehr etc.*): *at ~* gesichert; **~ belt** *s.* **1.** Rettungsgürtel *m*; **2.** ✈, *mot.* Sicherheitsgurt *m*; **~ bolt** *s.* ⊛, ✕ Sicherheitsbolzen *m*; **~ buoy** *s.* Rettungsboje *f*; **~ catch** *s.* **1.** ⊛ Sicherung *f* (*Lift etc.*); **2.** Sicherungsflügel *m* (*Gewehr etc.*): *release the ~* entsichern; **~ curtain** *s. thea.* eiserner Vorhang; **~ fuse** *s.* **1.** ⊛ Sicherheitszünder *m*, -zündschnur *f*; **2.** ⨎ *u.*) Sicherung *f*, b) Sicherheitsausschalter *m*; **~ is·land** *s.* Verkehrsinsel *f*; **~ lamp** *s.* ⚒ Grubenlampe *f*; **~ lock** *s.* **1.** Sicherheitsschloss *n*; **2.** Sicherung *f* (*Gewehr, Mine etc.*); **~ match** *s.* Sicherheitszündholz *n*; **~ net** *s.* Zirkus etc. (*a. fig. soziales*) Netz; **~ pin** *s.* Sicherheitsnadel *f*; **~ razor** *s.* Ra'sierappa,rat *m*; **~ rope** *s.* mount. Sicherungsseil *n*; **~ rules** *pl.* ⊛ Sicherheits-, Unfallverhütungsvorschriften *pl.*; **~ sheet** *s.* Sprungtuch *n* (*Feuerwehr*); **~ valve** *s.* ⊛ 'Überdruck-, 'Sicherheitsven,til *n*; **2.** *fig.* Ven'til *n*: *sit on the ~* Unterdrückungspolitik betreiben; **~ zone** *s.* Verkehrsinsel *f*.
saf·fi·an ['sæfɪən] *s.* Saffian(leder *n*) *m*.
saf·flow·er ['sæflaʊə] *s.* **1.** ⬥ Sa'flor *m*, Färberdistel *f*; **2.** getrockneter Sa'florblüten *pl.*: ~ *oil* Safloröl *n*.
saf·fron ['sæfrən] *s.* **1.** ⬥ echter Safran; **2.** *pharm., Küche*: Safran *m*; **3.** Safrangelb *n*.
sag [sæg] **I** *v/i.* **1.** sich senken, ab-, 'durchsacken; *bsd.* ⊛ 'durchhängen; **2.** (he'rab)hängen (*a. Unterkiefer etc.*): ~*ging shoulders* hängende *od.* abfallende Schultern; **3.** schief hängen (*Rocksaum etc.*); **4.** *fig.* sinken, nachlassen, abfallen; ✝ nachgeben (*Markt, Preise*): ~*ging spirits* sinkender Mut; **5.** ♺ (*mst ~ to leeward* nach Lee) (ab-) treiben; **II** *s.* **1.** 'Durch-, Absacken *n*; **7.** Senkung *f*; ⊛ 'Durchhang *m*; **8.** ✝ (Preis)Abschwächung *f*.

sa·ga ['sɑ:gə] *s.* **1.** Saga *f* (*Heldenerzählung*); **2.** Sage *f*, Erzählung *f*; **3.** *a. ~ novel* Fa'milienro,man *m*.
sa·ga·cious [sə'geɪʃəs] *adj.* ☐ scharfsinnig, klug (*a. Tier*); **sa·gac·i·ty** [sə'gæsɪtɪ] *s.* Scharfsinn *m*.
sage¹ [seɪdʒ] **I** *s.* Weise(r) *m*; **II** *adj.* ☐ weise, klug, verständig.
sage² [seɪdʒ] *s.* ⬥ Salbei *m*, *f*: ~ *tea*.
Sag·it·ta·ri·us [,sædʒɪ'teərɪəs] *s. ast.* Schütze *m*.
sa·go ['seɪgəʊ] *s.* Sago *m*.
said [sed; səd] **I** *pret. u. p.p. von* say: *he is ~ to have been ill* er soll krank gewesen sein; es heißt, er sei krank gewesen; **II** *adj. bsd.* ⛧ vorerwähnt, besagt.
sail [seɪl] **I** *s.* **1.** ♺ a) Segel *n*, b) *coll.* Segel(werk *n*) *pl.*: *make ~* a) die Segel (bei)setzen, b) mehr Segel beisetzen, c) *a. set ~* unter Segel gehen, auslaufen (*for* nach); *take in ~* a) Segel einholen, b) *fig.* zurückstecken; *under ~* unter Segel, auf der Fahrt; *under full ~* mit vollen Segeln; → *trim* 9; **2.** ♺ (Segel-)Schiff(e *pl.*) *n*: *a fleet of 20 ~*; *~ ho!* Schiff ho! (*in Sicht*); **3.** ♺ Fahrt *f*: *have a ~* segeln gehen; **4.** ⊛ a) Segel *n e-s Windmühlenflügels*, b) Flügel *m e-r Windmühle*; **II** *v/i.* **5.** a) *allg.* mit e-m Schiff *od.* zu Schiff fahren *od.* reisen, b) fahren (*Schiff*), c) *bsd. sport* segeln; → *wind¹* 1; **6.** ♺ a) auslaufen (*Schiff*), b) abfahren, -segeln (*for od. to* nach): *ready to ~* seeklar; **7.** a) ✈ fliegen, b) *a. ~ along fig.* da'hinschweben, (-)segeln (*Wolke, Vogel*); **8.** *fig.* (*bsd. stolz*) schweben, 'rauschen', schreiten; **9.** ~ *in* F 'sich ranmachen', zupacken; **10.** ~ *into* F a) j-n *od. et.* attackieren, 'herfallen über (*acc.*), b) 'rangehen' an (*acc.*), *et.* tüchtig anpacken; **III** *v/t.* **11.** durch'segeln, befahren; **12.** *Segelboot* segeln, *allg. Schiff* steuern; **13.** *poet.* durch *die* Luft schweben; '~-boat → *sailing boat.*
sail·er ['seɪlə] *s.* ♺ Segler *m* (*Schiff*).
sail·ing ['seɪlɪŋ] **I** *s.* **1.** ♺ (Segel-) Schifffahrt *f*, Navigati'on *f*: *plain (od. smooth) ~ fig.* ,klare Sache'; *from now on it is all plain ~* von jetzt an geht alles glatt (über die Bühne); **2.** Segelsport *m*, Segeln *n*; **3.** Abfahrt *f* (*for* nach); **4.** ♺ Segel...; ~ *boat* Segelboot *n*; **~ mas·ter** *s.* Navi'gator *m e-r Jacht*; **~ or·ders** *s. pl.* ♺ **1.** Fahrtauftrag *m*; **2.** Befehl *m* zum Auslaufen; **~ ship**, **~ ves·sel** *s.* ♺ Segelschiff *n*.
sail loft *s.* ♺ Segelmacherwerkstatt *f* (*an Bord*).
sail·or ['seɪlə] *s.* **1.** Ma'trose *m*, Seemann *m*: ~ *hat* Matrosenhut *m*; ~*s' home* Seemannsheim *n*; ~*'s knot* Schifferknoten *m*; **2.** *von Seereisenden*: *be a good ~* seefest sein; *be a bad ~* leicht seekrank werden; **3.** Ma'trosenanzug *m od.* -hut *m für Kinder*; '*sail-or·ly* [-lɪ] *adj.* seemännisch.
'sail·plane **I** *s.* Segelflugzeug *n*; **II** *v/i.* segelfliegen.
saint [seɪnt] **I** *s.* (*vor Eigennamen* ⧸, *abbr.* St *od.* S [snt]) *eccl.* (*a. fig., iro. a.* ~ *on wheels*) Heilige(r *m*) *f*: *St Bernard* (*dog*) Bernhardiner *m* (*Hund*); *St Anthony's fire* ☀ die Wundrose; *St Elmo's fire meteor.* das Elmsfeuer; (*the Court of*) *St James('s*) der brit. Hof; *St John's wort* ⬥ das Johanniskraut; *St Monday Brit.* F ‚blauer Montag'; *St Martin's summer* Altweibersommer *m*; *St Paul's* die Paulskathedrale (*in London*); *St Peter's* die Peterskirche (*in Rom*); *St Valentine's Day* der Valentinstag; *St Vitus's dance*

⚡ der Veitstanz; **II** *v/t.* heilig sprechen; **III** *v/i. mst ~ it* a) wie ein Heiliger leben, b) den Heiligen spielen; **'saint·ed** [-tɪd] *p.p. u. adj.* **1.** *eccl.* heilig (gesprochen); **2.** heilig, fromm; **3.** anbetungswürdig; **4.** geheiligt, geweiht (*Ort*); **5.** selig (*Verstorbener*); **'saint·hood** [-hʊd] *s.* (Stand *m* der) Heiligkeit *f*.
'saint·like → *saintly.*
saint·li·ness ['seɪntlɪnɪs] *s.* Heiligkeit *f* (*a. iro.*); **saint·ly** ['seɪntlɪ] *adj.* **1.** heilig; **2.** fromm; **3.** heiligmäßig (*Leben*).
saith [seθ] *obs. od. poet.* 3. *sg. pres. von* say.
sake [seɪk] *s.*: *for the ~ of* um ... (*gen.*) willen, *j-m* zuliebe; wegen (*gen.*), halber (*gen.*): *for heaven's ~* um Himmels willen; *for his ~* ihm zuliebe, seinetwegen; *for my own ~ as well as yours* um meinetwillen ebenso wie um deinetwillen; *for peace(') ~* um des lieben Friedens willen; *for old times' ~, for old ~'s ~* eingedenk alter Zeiten.
sal [sæl] *s.* ☀, *pharm.* Salz *n*: ~ *ammo·niac* Salmiak(salz) *n*.
sa·laam [sə'lɑ:m] **I** *s.* Selam *m* (*orientalischer Gruß*); **II** *v/t. u. v/i.* mit e-m Selam *od.* e-r tiefen Verbeugung (be-) grüßen.
sal·a·bil·i·ty [,seɪlə'bɪlətɪ] *s.* ✝ Verkäuflichkeit *f*, Marktfähigkeit *f*; **sal·a·ble** ['seɪləbl] *adj.* ☐ ✝ **1.** verkäuflich; **2.** marktfähig, gangbar.
sa·la·cious [sə'leɪʃəs] *adj.* ☐ **1.** geil, lüstern; **2.** ob'szön, zotig; **sa·la·cious·ness** [-nɪs], **sa·lac·i·ty** [sə'læsətɪ] *s.* **1.** Geilheit *f*, Wollust *f*; **2.** Obszöni'tät *f*.
sal·ad ['sæləd] *s.* **1.** Sa'lat *m* (*a. fig. Durcheinander*); **2.** ⬥ Sa'lat(gewächs *n*, -pflanze *f*) *m*; **~ cream** *s.* Sa'latmajo,näse *f*; **~ days** *s. pl.*: *in my ~* in m-n wilden Jugendtagen; **~ dress·ing** *s.* Sa'latsoße *f*; **~ oil** *s.* Sa'latöl *n*.
sal·a·man·der ['sælə,mændə] *s.* **1.** *zo.* Sala'mander *m*; **2.** Sala'mander *m* (*Feuergeist*); **3.** *j-d* der große Hitze ertragen *kann*; **4.** a) rot glühendes (Schür)Eisen (*zum Anzünden*), b) glühende Eisenschaufel, die über Gebäck gehalten wird, um es zu bräunen; **5.** *metall.* Ofensau *f*.
sa·la·mi [sə'lɑːmɪ] *s.* Sa'lami *f*; **tac·tics** *s. pl. pol.* Sa'lamitaktik *f*.
sa·lar·i·at [sə'leərɪæt] *s.* (Klasse *f* der) Gehaltsempfänger *pl.*
sal·a·ried ['sælərɪd] *adj.* **1.** (fest) bezahlt, fest angestellt: ~ *employee* Gehaltsempfänger(in), Angestellte(r *m*) *f*; **2.** bezahlt (*Stellung*); **sal·a·ry** ['sælərɪ] **I** *s.* Gehalt *n*, Besoldung *f*; **II** *v/t.* (mit e-m Gehalt) bezahlen, *j-m* ein Gehalt zahlen.
sale [seɪl] *s.* **1.** Verkauf *m*, -äußerung *f*: *by private ~* unter der Hand; *for ~* zu verkaufen; *not for ~* unverkäuflich; *be on ~* angeboten *od.* verkauft werden; *forced ~* Zwangsverkauf *m*; ~ *of work* Basar *m*; **2.** ✝ Verkauf *m*, Vertrieb *m*; → *return* 23; **3.** ✝ Ab-, 'Umsatz *m*, Verkaufsziffer *f*: *slow ~* schleppender Absatz; *meet with a ready ~* schnellen Absatz finden, gut ‚gehen'; **4.** (öffentliche) Versteigerung, Aukti'on *f*: *put up for ~* versteigern, meistbietend verkaufen; **5.** ✝ *a. pl.* (Sai'son)Schlussverkauf *m*; **sale·a·bil·i·ty** *etc. bsd. Brit.* → *sal·ability etc.*; '**sale·room** → *salesroom.*
sales| ac·count [seɪlz] *s.* ✝ Verkaufskonto *n*; **~ a·gent** *s.* (Handels)Vertreter *m*; **~ ap·peal** *s.* Zugkraft *f e-r Ware*; '~-clerk *s.* Am. (Laden)Verkäufer (-in); **~ de·part·ment** *s.* ✝ Verkaufs(s)abteilung *f*) *m*; **~ drive** *s.* ✝ Ver'kaufs-

kam,pagne *f*; **~ en·gi·neer** *s*. ✝ Ver-'kaufsingeni,eur *m*; **~ fi·nance com-pa·ny** *s. Am.* **1.** Absatzfinanzierungs-gesellschaft *f*; **2.** 'Teilzahlungskre,ditin-sti,tut *n*; '**~girl** *s.* (Laden)Verkäuferin *f*; '**~,la·dy** *Am.* → **saleswoman**; '**~man** [-mən] *s.* [*irr.*] **1.** ✝ a) Verkäu-fer *m*, b) *Am.* (Handlungs)Reisende(r) *m*, (Handels)Vertreter *m*; **2.** *fig. Am.* Reisende(r) *m* (**of** in *dat.*); **~ man·ag·er** *s.* ✝ Verkaufsleiter *m*.

sales·man·ship ['seɪlzmənʃɪp] *s.* **1.** a) Verkaufstechnik, b) ✝ Verkaufsge-wandtheit *f*, Geschäftstüchtigkeit *f*; **2.** *fig.* Über'zeugungskunst *f*, wirkungs-volle Art, e-e Idee *etc.* zu 'verkaufen' *od.* 'an den Mann zu bringen'.

sales| pro·mo·tion *s.* ✝ Verkaufsförde-rung *f*; **~ re·sist·ance** *s.* ✝ Kaufabnei-gung *f*, Widerstand *m* (des potenzi'ellen Kunden); '**~room** [-rum] *s.* Ver'kaufs-, *bsd.* Aukti'onsraum *m*, -lo,kal *n*; **~ slip** *s. Am.* Kassenbeleg *m*; **~ talk** *s.* **1.** ✝ Verkaufsgespräch *n*; **2.** anpreisende Worte *pl.*; **~ tax** *s.* ✝ 'Umsatzsteuer *f*; '**~,wom·an** *s.* [*irr.*] ✝ **1.** Verkäuferin *f*; **2.** *Am.* (Handels)Vertreterin *f*.

Sal·ic ['sælɪk] *adj. hist.* salisch: **~ law** Salisches Gesetz.

sal·ic ['sælɪk] *adj. min.* salisch.

sal·i·cyl·ic [,sælɪ'sɪlɪk] *adj.* Salizyl...

sa·li·ence ['seɪljəns], '**sa·li·en·cy** [-sɪ] *s.* **1.** Her'vorspringen *n*, Her'ausragen *n*; **2.** vorspringende Stelle, Vorsprung *m*: **give ~ to** *fig.* e-e Sache herausstellen; '**sa·li·ent** [-nt] **I** *adj.* **1.** (her')vorsprin-gend, her'ausragend: **~ angle** ausprin-gender Winkel; **~ point** *fig.* springen-der Punkt; **2.** *fig.* her'vorstechend, ins Auge springend; **3.** *her. u. humor.* springend; **4.** *poet.* (her'vor)sprudelnd; **II** *s.* **5.** ✕ Frontausbuchtung *f*.

sa·lif·er·ous [sə'lɪfərəs] *adj.* **1.** Salz bil-dend; **2.** *bsd. geol.* salzhaltig.

sa·line [adj. 'seɪlaɪn] **1.** salzig, salzhal-tig, Salz...; **2.** *pharm.* sa'linisch; **II** *s.* [sə'laɪn] **3.** Salzsee *m od.* -sumpf *m od.* -quelle *f*; **4.** Sa'line *f*, Salzwerk *n*; **5.** ▲ a) *pl.* Salze *pl.*, b) Salzlösung *f*; **6.** *pharm.* sa'linisches Mittel; **sa·lin·i·ty** [sə'lɪnətɪ] *s.* **1.** Salzigkeit *f*; **2.** Salzhal-tigkeit *f*, Salzgehalt *m*.

sa·li·va [sə'laɪvə] *s.* Speichel(flüssigkeit *f*) *m*; **sal·i·var·y** ['sælɪvərɪ] *adj.* Spei-chel...; **sal·i·vate** ['sælɪveɪt] **I** *v/t.* **1.** (vermehrten) Speichelfluss her'vorrufen bei *j-m*; **II** *v/i.* **2.** Speichelfluss haben; **3.** Speichel absondern; **sal·i·va·tion** [,sælɪ'veɪʃn] *s.* **1.** Speichelabsonderung *f*; **2.** (vermehrter) Speichelfluss.

sal·low¹ ['sæləʊ] *s.* ♀ (*bsd.* Sal)Weide *f*.

sal·low² ['sæləʊ] *adj.* blässlich, fahl.

sal·ly ['sælɪ] **I** *s.* **1.** ✕ Ausfall *m*: **~ port** *hist.* Ausfalltor *n*; **2.** *fig.* geistreicher Ausspruch *od.* Einfall, Geistesblitz *m*, *a.* (Seiten)Hieb *m*; **3.** (Zornes)Aus-bruch *m*; **II** *v/i.* **4.** *oft* **~ out** ✕ e-n Ausfall machen, her'vorbrechen; **5.** *mst* **~ forth** (*od.* **out**) sich aufmachen, auf-brechen.

Sal·ly Lunn [,sælɪ'lʌn] *s.* leichter Teeku-chen.

sal·ma·gun·di [,sælmə'gʌndɪ] *s.* bun-ter Teller (*Salat, kalter Braten etc.*); **2.** *fig.* Mischmasch *m*.

salm·on ['sæmən] *pl.* **-mons**, *coll.* **-mon I** *s. ichth.* Lachs *m*, Salm *m*: **~ ladder** (*od.* **leap, pass**) Lachsleiter *f*; **~ peal, ~ peel** junger Lachs; **~ trout** Lachsforelle *f*; **2.** *a.* **~ colo(u)r, ~ pink** Lachs(farbe *f*); **II** *adj.* **3.** *a.* **~-col-o(u)red, ~-pink** lachsfarben, -rot.

sal·mo·nel·la [,sælmə'nelə] *s.* **1.** *biol.* a)

---

pl. **-lae** [-liː] Salmo'nelle *f*, b) ◢ *coll.* Salmo'nellen *pl.*; **2.** ◢ *coll. a.* **~ infec-tion** (*od.* **poisoning**) Salmo'nellenver-giftung *f*.

sa·lon ['sælɔ̃ːŋ] (*Fr.*) *s.* Sa'lon *m* (*a. Aus-stellungsraum, vornehmes Geschäft; a. fig.* schöngeistiger Treffpunkt).

sa·loon [sə'luːn] *s.* **1.** Sa'lon *m* (*bsd. in Hotels etc.*), (Gesellschafts)Saal *m*: **~ billiard ~** *Brit.* Billardzimmer *n*; **shaving ~** Rasiersalon; **2.** a) ✓ Sa'lon *m* (*Auf-enthaltsraum*), b) ♣ **~ cabin** Ka'bine *f* erster Klasse, c) → **saloon car**, d) → **saloon bar: sleeping ~** ▥ (Luxus-) Schlafwagen *m*; **3.** *Am.* Kneipe *f*; **4.** *obs.* Sa'lon *m*, Empfangszimmer *n*; **~ bar** *s. Brit.* vornehmerer Teil e-s Lo-kals; **~ car** *s.* **1.** *mot. Brit.* a) Limou'si-ne *f*, b) *sport* Tourenwagen *m*; **2.** → **~ car·riage** *s.* ▥ Sa'lonwagen *m*; **~ deck** *s.* ♣ Sa'londeck *n*; **~ pis·tol** *s. Brit.* 'Übungspi,stole *f*.

sal·sa¹ ['sælsə] ♪ **I** *s.* Salsa *m* (*Musik u. Tanz*); **II** *v/i.* Salsa tanzen.

sal·sa² ['sælsə] *s.* Salsasoße *f*.

salt [sɔːlt] **I** *s.* **1.** (Koch)Salz *n*: **eat s.o.'s ~** *fig.* a) j-s Gast sein, b) von j-m abhängen; **with a grain of ~** *fig.* mit Vorbehalt, cum grano salis; **not to be worth one's ~** keinen Schuss Pulver wert sein; **the ~ of the earth** *bibl. u. fig.* das Salz der Erde; **2.** Salz(fässchen *n*): **above** (**below**) **the ~** am oberen (unteren) Ende der Tafel; **3.** ▲ Salz *n*; **4.** *oft pl. pharm.* a) (*bsd.* Abführ)Salz *n*, b) *mst* **smelling ~s** Riechsalz, c) F → **Epsom salt**; **5.** *fig.* Würze *f*, Salz *n*; **6.** *fig.* Witz *m*, E'sprit *m*; **7.** *bsd.* **old ~** F alter Seebär; **II** *v/t.* **8.** salzen, würzen (*beide a. fig.*); **9.** (ein)salzen, *bsd.* pö-keln: **~ed meat** Pökel-, Salzfleisch *n*; **10.** ✝ F a) *Bücher etc.* ,frisieren', b) *Bohrloch etc.* (betrügerisch) ,anrei-chern'; **11.** *fig.* durch'setzen (**with** mit); **12. ~ away** (*od.* **down**) a) einsalzen, -pökeln, b) F *Geld etc.* ,auf die hohe Kante legen'; **III** *adj.* **13.** salzig, Salz...: **~ spring** Salzquelle *f*; **14.** ♀ halo'phil, Salz...; **15.** → **salted¹**.

sal·tant ['sæltənt] *adj. her.* springend.

sal·ta·tion [sæl'teɪʃn] *s.* **1.** Springen *n*; **2.** Sprung *m*; **3.** plötzlicher 'Um-schwung; **4.** *biol.* Erbsprung *m*; '**sal-ta·to·ry** [-ətərɪ] *adj.* **1.** springend; **2.** Spring..., Sprung...; **3.** Tanz...; **4.** *fig.* sprunghaft.

'**salt,cel·lar** *s.* **1.** Salzfässchen *n*; **2.** *Brit.* F ,Salzfässchen' *n* (*Vertiefung über dem Schlüsselbein*).

salt·ed ['sɔːltɪd] *adj.* **1.** gesalzen; **2.** (ein-) gesalzen, gepökelt: **~ herring** Salzhe-ring *m*; **3.** *sl.* routi'niert, ausgekocht, erfahren; '**salt·ern** [-tən] *s.* ⊙ **1.** Sa'line *f*; **2.** Salzgarten *m* (*Bassins*).

'**salt-free** *adj.* salzlos.

salt·i·ness ['sɔːltɪnɪs] *s.* Salzigkeit *f*.

salt| lick *s.* Salzlecke *f* (*für Wild*); **~ marsh** *s.* **1.** Salzsumpf *m*; **2.** Buten-marsch *f*; **~ mine** *s.* Salzbergwerk *n*.

salt·ness ['sɔːltnɪs] *s.* Salzigkeit *f*.

'**salt·pan** *s.* **1.** ⊙ Salzsiedepfanne *f*; **2.** (*geol.* na'türliches) Ver'dunstungs-bas,sin.

salt·pe·ter *Am.*, **salt·pe·tre** *Brit.* ['sɔːlt,piːtə] *s.* ▲ Sal'peter *m*.

salt| pit *s.* Salzgrube *f*; '**~,wa·ter** *adj.* Salzwasser...; '**~works** *s. pl. oft sg. konstr.* Sa'line *f*.

salt·y ['sɔːltɪ] *adj.* **1.** salzig; **2.** *fig.* gesal-zen, gepfeffert: **~ remarks**.

sa·lu·bri·ous [sə'luːbrɪəs] *adj.* ◻ heil-sam, gesund, zuträglich, bekömmlich;

sa·lu·bri·ty [-rətɪ] *s.* Heilsamkeit *f*, Zu-

---

träglichkeit *f*.

sa·lu·tar·i·ness ['sæljʊtərɪnɪs] → **salu-brity**; **sal·u·tar·y** ['sæljʊtərɪ] *adj.* heil-sam, gesund (*a. fig.*).

sal·u·ta·tion [,sælju:'teɪʃn] *s.* **1.** Begrü-ßung *f*, Gruß *m*: **in ~** zum Gruß; **2.** Anrede *f* (*im Brief*); **sa·lu·ta·to·ry** [sə'lu:tətərɪ] *adj.* Begrüßungs...: **~** (**oration**) *bsd. ped. Am.* Begrüßungsre-de *f*; **sa·lute** [sə'lu:t] **I** *v/t.* **1.** grüßen, begrüßen (*durch e-e Geste etc.*); *weitS.* empfangen, *j-m* begegnen; **~ with a smile**; **2.** (*dem Auge, dem Ohr*) begeg-nen, *j-n* begrüßen (*Anblick, Geräusch etc.*); **3.** ✕, ♣ salutieren vor (*dat.*), grüßen; **4.** *fig.* grüßen, ehren, feiern; **II** *v/i.* **5.** grüßen (**to acc.**); **6.** ✕ (**to**) salu-tieren (vor *dat.*), grüßen (*acc.*); **7.** Sa-'lut schießen; **III** *s.* **8.** Gruß *m* (*a. fenc.*), Begrüßung *f*; **9.** ✕, ♣ a) Gruß *m*, Ehrenbezeigung *f*, b) Sa'lut *m* (*of six guns* von 6 Schuss): **~ of colo(u)rs** ♣ Flaggensalut; **stand at the ~** salutie-ren; **take the ~** a) den Gruß erwidern, b) die Parade abnehmen, c) die Front (der Ehrenkompanie) abschreiten; **10.** *obs.* (Begrüßungs)Kuss *m*; **11.** *Am.* Frosch *m* (*Feuerwerk*).

sal·vage ['sælvɪdʒ] **I** *s.* **1.** a) Bergung *f*, Rettung *f* (*Schiff, Ladung etc.*), b) Bergungsgut *n*, c) *a.* **~ money** Berge-geld *n*: **~ vessel** Bergungs-, *a.* Hebe-schiff *n*, d) *Versicherung:* Wert *m* der geretteten Güter; **2.** *a.* **~ work** Aufräu-mungsarbeiten *pl.*; **3.** ⊙ a) verwertba-res 'Altmateri,al, b) 'Wiederverwertung *f*: **~ value** Schrottwert *m*; **4.** *fig.* (Er-) Rettung *f* (**from** aus); **II** *v/t.* **5.** bergen, retten (*a.* ✕ *u. fig.*); **6.** *Schrott etc.* ver-werten.

sal·va·tion [sæl'veɪʃn] *s.* **1.** (Er)Rettung *f*; **2.** a) Heil *n*, Rettung *f*, b) Retter *m*; **3.** *eccl.* a) (Seelen)Heil *n*, b) Erlösung *f*: ❷ **Army** Heilsarmee *f*; **sal'va·tion·ist** [-nɪst] *s. eccl.* Mitglied *n* der 'Heilsar-,mee.

salve¹ [sælv] **I** *s.* **1.** (Heil)Salbe *f*; **2.** *fig.* Balsam *m*, Pflaster *n*, Trost *m*; **3.** *fig.* Beruhigungsmittel *n* fürs Gewissen *etc.*; **II** *v/t.* **4.** (ein)salben; **5.** *fig. Gewissen etc.* beschwichtigen; **6.** *fig. Mangel* be-schönigen; **7.** *Schaden, Zweifel etc.* be-heben.

salve² [sælv] → **salvage** 5.

sal·ver ['sælvə] *s.* Ta'blett *n*.

sal·vo¹ ['sælvəʊ] *pl.* **-vos, -voes** *s.* **1.** ✕ a) Salve *f*, Lage *f*, b) *a.* ~ **bombing** ✈ Schüttwurf *m*; **~ fire** a) ✕ Laufsalve, b) ♣ Salvenfeuer *n*; **2.** *fig.* (Beifalls)Salve *f*.

sal·vo² ['sælvəʊ] *pl.* **-vos** *s.* **1.** Ausrede *f*; **2.** *bsd.* ⚖ Vorbehalt(sklausel *f*) *m*.

sal·vor ['sælvə] *s.* ♣ **1.** Berger *m*; **2.** Bergungsschiff *n*.

Sa·mar·i·tan [sə'mærɪtən] **I** *s.* Samari'ta-ner(in), Sama'riter(in): **good ~** *bibl. u. fig.* barmherziger Samariter; **II** *adj.* sa-ma'ritisch; *fig.* barmherzig.

sam·ba ['sæmbə] ♪ **I** *s.* Samba *f*, *m* (*Musik u. Tanz*); **II** *v/i.* Samba tanzen.

same [seɪm] **I** *adj.* **1.** selb, gleich, näm-lich: **at the ~ price as** zu demselben Preis wie; **it comes to the ~ thing** es läuft auf dasselbe hinaus; **the very** (*od.* **just the** *od.* **exactly the**) **~ thing** genau dasselbe; **one and the ~ thing** ein u. dasselbe; **he is no longer the ~ man** er ist nicht mehr der Gleiche *od.* der Alte; → **time** 4; **2.** *ohne Artikel fig.* eintönig; **II** *pron.* **3.** der-, die-, dasselbe, der *od.* die *od.* das Gleiche: **it is much the ~** es ist (so) ziemlich das Gleiche; **~ here** F so geht es mir auch, ,ganz meinerseits'; **it is all the ~ to me** es ist mir ganz gleich *od.* einerlei; **4. the ~** a) *a. ɪ̆* der- *od.* dieselbe, die besagte Person, b) *ɪ̆* der- *od.* dieselbe, die erwähnte Person, *a. eccl.* er, sie, es, dieser, diese, dies(es); **5.** *ohne Artikel* ✝ *od.* F der- *od. od.* dasselbe: **£5 for alterations to ~**; **III** *adv.* **6. the ~** in derselben Weise, genauso, ebenso (**as** wie): **all the ~** gleichviel, trotzdem; **just the ~** F a) genau so, b) trotzdem; **(the) ~ to you!** (*danke*,) gleichfalls!; **'same·ness** [-nɪs] *s.* **1.** Gleichheit *f*, Identi'tät *f*; **2.** Einförmigkeit *f*, -tönigkeit *f*.

sam·let ['sæmlɪt] *s.* junger Lachs.

sam·pan ['sæmpæn] *s.* Sampan *m* (*chinesisches* [*Haus*]*Boot*).

sam·ple ['saːmpl] **I** *s.* **1.** ✝ a) (Waren-, Quali'täts-)Probe *f*, (Stück-, Typen-)Muster *n*, b) Probepackung *f*, c) (Ausstellungs)Muster *n*, d) Stichprobe(nmuster *n*): *by ~ post* (als) Muster ohne Wert; *up to ~* dem Muster entsprechend; **~s only** Muster ohne Wert; **2.** *Statistik:* Sample *n*, Stichprobe *f*; **3.** *fig.* Probe *f*: *a ~ of his courage*; *that's a ~ of her behavio(u)r* das ist typisch für sie; **II** *v/t.* **4.** probieren, e-e Probe nehmen von, *bsd. Küche:* kosten; **5.** e-e Stichprobe machen bei; **6.** e-e Probe zeigen von; ✝ *et.* bemustern; **7.** als Muster dienen für; **8.** *Computer:* a) abfragen, b) abtasten; **III** *v/i.* **9. ~ out** ausfallen; **IV** *adj.* **10.** Muster...(-*buch*, -*karte*, -*koffer etc.*), Probe...; **'sam·pler** [-lə] *s.* **1.** Probierer(in), Prüfer *m*; **2.** *Stickerei:* Sticktuch *n*; **3.** *TV* Farbschalter *m*; **4.** *Computer:* Abtaster *m*; **'sam·pling** [-lɪŋ] *s.* **1.** ✝ a) 'Musterkollekti·on *f*, b) Bemusterung *f*; **2.** Stichprobenerhebung *f*.

Sam·son ['sæmsn] *s. fig.* Samson *m*, Herkules *m*.

Sam·u·el ['sæmjʊəl] *npr. u. s.* bibl. (das Buch) Samuel *m*.

san·a·tive ['sænətɪv] *adj.* heilend, heilsam, -kräftig; **san·a·to·ri·um** [ˌsænə'tɔːrɪəm] *pl.* **-ri·ums, -ri·a** [-rɪə] *✱* **1.** Sana'torium *n*, *bsd.* a) Lungenheilstätte *f*, b) Erholungsheim *n*; **2.** (*bsd.* Höhen-)Luftkurort *m*; **3.** *Brit.* (Inter'nats-)Krankenzimmer *n*; **'san·a·to·ry** [-tərɪ] → *sanative*.

sanc·ti·fi·ca·tion [ˌsæŋktɪfɪ'keɪʃn] *s. eccl.* **1.** Heilig(mach)ung *f*; **2.** Weihung *f*, Heiligung *f*; **sanc·ti·fied** ['sæŋktɪfaɪd] *adj.* **1.** geheiligt, geweiht; **2.** heilig u. unverletzlich; **3.** → *sanctimonious*; **sanc·ti·fy** ['sæŋktɪfaɪ] *v/t.* heiligen: a) weihen, b) (von Sünden) reinigen, c) *fig.* rechtfertigen: *the end sanctifies the means* der Zweck heiligt die Mittel.

sanc·ti·mo·ni·ous [ˌsæŋktɪ'məʊnjəs] *adj.* □ frömmelnd, scheinheilig; **sanc·ti·mo·ni·ous·ness** [-nɪs], **sanc·ti·mo·ny** ['sæŋktɪməni] *s.* Scheinheiligkeit *f*, Frömme'lei *f*.

sanc·tion ['sæŋkʃn] **I** *s.* **1.** Sankti'on *f*, (nachträgliche) Billigung *f*, Zustimmung: *give one's ~ to* → 3 a; **2.** *ɪ̆* a) Sanktionierung *f* e-s *Gesetzes etc.*, b) *pol.* Sankti'on *f*, Zwangsmittel *n*, c) *gesetzliche Strafe*, d) *hist.* De'kret *n*; **II** *v/t.* **3.** sanktionieren: a) billigen, gutheißen, b) dulden, c) *Eid etc.* bindend machen, d) Gesetzeskraft verleihen (*dat.*).

sanc·ti·ty ['sæŋktəti] *s.* **1.** Heiligkeit *f* (*a. fig. Unverletzlichkeit*); **2.** *pl.* heilige Ide'ale *pl. od.* Gefühle *pl.*

sanc·tu·ar·y ['sæŋktjʊərɪ] *s.* **1.** Heiligtum *n* (*a. fig.*); **2.** *eccl.* Heiligtum *n*, heilige Stätte; *bsd. bibl.* Aller'heiligste(s) *n*; **3.** Frei- (*fig. a.* Zufluchts)stät-

te *f*, A'syl *n*: (**rights of**) **~** Asylrecht *n*; **break the ~s** das Asylrecht verletzen; **4.** *hunt.* a) Schonzeit *f*, b) Schutzgebiet *n*.

sanc·tum ['sæŋktəm] *s.* Heiligtum *n*: a) heilige Stätte, b) *fig.* Pri'vat-, Studierzimmer *n*, c) innerste Sphäre; **~ sanc·to·rum** [sæŋk'tɔːrəm] *s. eccl., a. humor.* das Aller'heiligste.

sand [sænd] **I** *s.* **1.** Sand *m*: *built on ~ fig.* auf Sand gebaut; *rope of ~ fig.* trügerische Sicherheit; **2.** *oft pl.* a) Sandbank *f*, b) Sand(fläche *f*, -wüste *f*) *m*: *plough the ~*(**s**) *fig.* s-e Zeit verschwenden; **3.** *mst pl.* Sand(körner *pl.*) *m*: *his ~s are running out* s-e Tage sind gezählt; **4.** *Am. sl.* ‚Mumm‘ *m*; **II** *v/t.* **5.** mit Sand bestreuen; **6.** (ab-)schmirgeln.

san·dal[1] ['sændl] *s.* San'dale *f*.

san·dal[2] ['sændl], **'~·wood** *s.* **1.** (rotes) Sandelholz; **2.** Sandelbaum *m*.

'sand|·bag [-ndb-] **I** *s.* **1.** Sandsack *m*; **II** *v/t.* **2.** *bsd.* ✕ mit Sandsäcken befestigen; **3.** mit e-m Sandsack niederschlagen; **'~·bank** [-ndb-] *s.* Sandbank *f*; **'~·blast** [-ndb-] *⊛* **I** *s.* Sandstrahl(gebläse *n*) *m*; **II** *v/t.* sandstrahlen; **'~·blast·er** [-tə] *s.* Sandstrahlgebläse *n*; **'~·box** [-ndb-] *s.* **1.** *hist.* Streusandbüchse *f*; **2.** *Gießerei:* Sandform *f*; **3.** Sandkasten *m*; **'~·boy** [-ndb-] *s.:* (**as**) **happy as a ~** kreuzfidel; **~ drift** *s. geol.* Flugsand *m*.

sand·er ['sændə] *s.* *⊛* **1.** Sandstrahlgebläse *n*; **2.** 'Sandpa,pier,schleifma,schine *f*.

'sand|·fly *s.* a) Sandfliege *f*, b) Gnitze *f*, c) Kriebelmücke *f*; **'~·glass** *s.* Sanduhr *f*, Stundenglas *n*; **'~·grouse** *s. orn.* Flughuhn *n*; **'~·lot** *s. Am.* Sandplatz *m* (*Behelfsspielplatz für Baseball etc.*); **'~·man** [-ndmæn] *s.:* [*irr.*] Sandmann *m*, -männchen *n*; **~ mar·tin** [-nd,m-] *s. orn.* Uferschwalbe *f*; **'~·pa·per** [-nd,p-] **I** *s.* 'Sandpa,pier *n*; **II** *v/t.* (ab)schmirgeln; **'~·pip·er** [-nd,p-] *s. orn.* Flussuferläufer *m*; **'~·pit** [-ndp-] *s.* **1.** Sandgrube *f*; **2.** Sandkasten *m*; **~ shoes** *s. pl.* Strandschuhe *pl.*; **~ spout** *s.* Sandhose *f*; **'~·stone** [-nds-] *s. geol.* Sandstein *m*; **'~·storm** [-nds-] *s.* Sandsturm *m*; **~ ta·ble** *s.* ✕ Sandkasten *m*; **~ trap** *s. Golf:* Sandhindernis *n*.

sand·wich ['sænwɪdʒ] **I** *s.* Sandwich *n* (*belegtes Doppelbrot*): **open ~** belegtes Brot; **sit ~** *fig.* eingezwängt sitzen; **II** *v/t. a.* **~ in** *fig.* einlegen, schieben; einklemmen, -zwängen; *sport* Gegner ‚in die Zange nehmen‘; **~ cake** *s.* Schichttorte *f*; **~ course** *s. ped.* Kurs, bei dem sich theoretische u. praktische Ausbildung abwechseln; **~ man** [-mæn] *s.* [*irr.*] Sandwichman *m*, Pla'katträger *m*.

sand·y ['sændɪ] *adj.* **1.** sandig, Sand...: **~ desert** Sandwüste *f*; **2.** *fig.* sandfarben; rotblond (*Haare*); **3.** sandartig; **4.** *fig.* a) unsicher, b) *Am. sl.* frech.

Sand·y ['sændɪ] *s.* **1.** *bsd. Scot.* Kurzform für *Alexander*; **2.** (*Spitzname für*) Schotte *m*.

sand yacht *s.* Strandsegler *m*.

sane [seɪn] *adj.* □ **1.** geistig gesund *od.* nor'mal; **2.** vernünftig, gescheit.

San·for·ize ['sænfəraɪz] *v/t.* sanforisieren (*Gewebe schrumpffest machen*).

sang [sæŋ] *pret. u. p.p. von sing*.

sang·froid [ˌsɑ̃ːˈfrwɑː] (*Fr.*) *s.* Kaltblütigkeit *f*.

San·grail [sæŋ'greɪl], **San·gre·al** ['sæŋgrɪəl] *s.* der Heilige Gral.

san·gui·nar·y ['sæŋgwɪnərɪ] *adj.* □ **1.** blutig, mörderisch (*Kampf etc.*); **2.** blutdürstig, grausam: *a ~ person*; *~ laws*; **3.** blutig, Blut...; **4.** *Brit.* unflä-

tig; **san·guine** ['sæŋgwɪn] **I** *adj.* □ **1.** heiter, lebhaft, leichtblütig; **2.** 'voll-, heißblütig, hitzig; **3.** zuversichtlich (*a. Bericht, Hoffnung etc.*): *be ~ of success* zuversichtlich auf Erfolg rechnen; **4.** rot, blühend, von gesunder Gesichtsfarbe; **5.** *✱ hist.* sangu'inisch; **6.** (blut-)rot; **II** *s.* **7.** Rötelstift *m*; **8.** Rötelzeichnung *f*; **san·guin·e·ous** [sæŋ'gwɪnɪəs] *adj.* → *sanguine* I.

sa·ni·es ['seɪnɪiːz] *s. ✱* pu'trider Eiter, Jauche *f*.

san·i·tar·i·an [ˌsænɪ'teərɪən] *adj.* **1.** → *sanitary* 1; **II** *s.* **2.** Hygi'eniker *m*; **3.** Ge'sundheitsa,postel *m*; **san·i·tar·i·um** [-rɪəm] *pl.* **-i·ums, -i·a** [-ɪə] *s. bsd. Am. für sanatorium*; **san·i·tar·y** ['sænɪtərɪ] **I** *adj.* □ **1.** hygi'enisch, Gesundheits..., (*a. ⊛*) sani'tär: **~ towel** (*Am. napkin*) Damenbinde *f*; **2.** hygi'enisch (einwandfrei), gesund; **II** *s.* **3.** *Am.* öffentliche Bedürfnisanstalt; **san·i·ta·tion** [-'teɪʃn] *s.* **1.** sani'täre Einrichtungen *pl.* (*in Gebäuden*); **2.** Gesundheitspflege *f*, -wesen *n*, Hygi'ene *f*.

san·i·tize ['sænɪtaɪz] *v/t.* **1.** → *sterilize* a; **2.** *fig. Image etc.* ‚aufpolieren‘.

san·i·ty ['sænətɪ] *s.* **1.** geistige Gesundheit; *bsd. ɪ̆* Zurechnungsfähigkeit *f*; **2.** gesunder Verstand.

sank [sæŋk] *pret. von sink*.

san·se·rif [ˌsæn'serɪf] *s. typ.* Gro'tesk *f*.

San·skrit ['sænskrɪt] *s.* Sanskrit *n*.

San·ta Claus [ˌsæntə'klɔːz] *npr.* der Nikolaus, der Weihnachtsmann.

sap[1] [sæp] **I** *s.* **1.** *♀* Saft *m*; **2.** *fig.* (Lebens)Saft *m*, (-)Kraft *f*, Mark *n*; **3.** *a.* **~ wood** Splint(holz *n*) *m*; **II** *v/t.* **4.** entsaften.

sap[2] [sæp] **I** *s.* **1.** ✕ Sappe *f*, Grabenkopf *m*; **II** *v/t.* **2.** (*a. fig. Gesundheit etc.*) unter'graben, -mi'nieren; **3.** *Kräfte etc.* erschöpfen, schwächen.

sap[3] [sæp] *s.* F Trottel *m*.

sap[4] [sæp] *Am. sl.* **I** *s.* **1.** Totschläger *m* (*Waffe*); **II** *v/t.* *j-n* (mit e-m Totschläger) bewusstlos schlagen.

'sap·head *s.* **1.** ✕ Sappenkopf *m*; **2.** F Trottel *m*.

sap·id ['sæpɪd] *adj.* **1.** e-n Geschmack habend; **2.** schmackhaft; **3.** *fig.* interes'sant; **sa·pid·i·ty** [sə'pɪdətɪ] *s.* Schmackhaftigkeit *f*.

sa·pi·ence ['seɪpjəns] *s. mst iro.* Weisheit *f*; **'sa·pi·ent** [-nt] *adj.* □ *mst iro.* weise.

sap·less ['sæplɪs] *adj.* saftlos (*a. fig.* kraftlos).

sap·ling ['sæplɪŋ] *s.* **1.** junger Baum, Schössling *m*; **2.** *fig.* Grünschnabel *m*, Jüngling *m*.

sap·o·na·ceous [ˌsæpəʊ'neɪʃəs] *adj.* **1.** seifenartig, seifig; **2.** *fig.* glatt.

sa·pon·i·fi·ca·tion [sə,pɒnɪfɪ'keɪʃn] *s. ✍* Verseifung *f*; **sa·pon·i·fy** [sə'pɒnɪfaɪ] *v/t. u. v/i.* verseifen.

sap·per ['sæpə] *s.* ✕ Pio'nier *m*, Sap'peur *m*.

Sap·phic ['sæfɪk] **I** *adj.* **1.** sapphisch; **2** lesbisch; **II** *s.* **3.** sapphischer Vers.

sap·phire ['sæfaɪə] **I** *s.* **1.** *min.* Saphir *m* (*a. am Plattenspieler*); **2.** *a.* **~ blue** Saphirblau *n*; **3.** *orn.* Saphirkolibri *m*; **II** *adj.* **4.** saphirblau; **5.** Saphir...

sap·py ['sæpɪ] *adj.* **1.** saftig; **2.** *fig.* kraftvoll, markig; **3.** *sl.* blöd, doof.

Sar·a·cen ['særəsn] **I** *s.* Sara'zene *m*, Sara'zenin *f*; **II** *adj.* sara'zenisch.

sar·casm ['sɑːkæzəm] *s.* Sar'kasmus *m*: a) beißender Spott, b) sar'kastische Bemerkung; **sar·cas·tic** [sɑː'kæstɪk] *adj.* (□ **~ally**) sarkastisch.

sar·co·ma [sɑː'kəʊmə] *pl.* **-ma·ta** [-mətə] s. ⚑ Sar'kom n (Geschwulst); **sar·'coph·a·gous** [-'kɒfəgəs] adj. zo. Fleisch fressend; **sar'coph·a·gus** [-'kɒfəgəs] pl. **-gi** [-gaɪ] s. Sarko'phag m (Steinsarg).

sard [sɑːd] s. min. Sard(er) m.

sar·dine¹ [sɑː'diːn] pl. **sar·dines** od. coll. **sar·dine** s. ichth. Sar'dine f: **packed like ~s** zs.-gepfercht wie die Heringe.

sar·dine² ['sɑːdaɪn] → **sard**.

sar·don·ic [sɑː'dɒnɪk] adj. (□ ~ally) ⚑ u. fig. sar'donisch.

sa·ri ['sɑːrɪ] s. Sari m.

sark [sɑːk] s. Scot. od. dial. Hemd n.

sark·y ['sɑːkɪ] F für **sarcastic**.

sa·rong [sə'rɒŋ] s. Sarong m.

sar·sen ['sɑːsn] s. geol. großer Sandsteinblock.

sar·to·ri·al [sɑː'tɔːrɪəl] adj. □ **1.** Schneider...; **2.** Kleidung(s)...: ~ **elegance** Eleganz f der Kleidung; **sar'to·ri·us** [-rɪəs] s. anat. Schneidermuskel m.

sash¹ [sæʃ] s. Schärpe f.

sash² [sæʃ] s. **1.** (schiebbarer) Fensterrahmen; **2.** schiebbarer Teil e-s Schiebefensters; **~ saw** s. ⊖ Schlitzsäge f; **~ win·dow** s. Schiebe-, Fallfenster n.

Sas·se·nach ['sæsənæk] Scot. u. Irish I s. ,Sachse' m, Engländer m; II adj. englisch.

sat [sæt] pret. u. p.p. von **sit**.

Sa·tan ['seɪtən] s. Satan m, Teufel m (fig. ☙); **sa·tan·ic** [sə'tænɪk] adj. (□ ~ally) sa'tanisch, teuflisch.

satch·el ['sætʃəl] s. Schultasche f, -mappe f, bsd. Schulranzen m.

sate¹ [seɪt] v/t. über'sättigen: **be ~d with** übersättigt sein von.

sate² [sæt; seɪt] obs. für **sat**.

sa·teen [sæ'tiːn] s. ('Baum)Wolla,tin m.

sat·el·lite ['sætəlaɪt] s. **1.** ast. a) Satel'lit m, Tra'bant m, b) (künstlicher) ('Erd-) Satel,lit m: ~ **dish** Satellitenschüssel f; ~ **picture** Satellitenbild n; ~ **transmission** TV etc. Satellitenübertragung f; ~ **TV** Satellitenfernsehen n; **2.** Tra'bant m, Anhänger m; **3.** fig. a) a. ~ **state** od. **nation** pol. Satel'lit(enstaat) m, b) a. ~ **town** Tra'bantenstadt f, c) a. ~ **airfield** Ausweichflugplatz m, d) ✠ Zweigfirma f.

sa·ti·ate ['seɪʃɪeɪt] v/t. **1.** über'sättigen; **2.** vollauf sättigen od. befriedigen; **sa·ti·a·tion** [,seɪʃɪ'eɪʃn] s. (Über)'Sättigung f; **sa·ti·e·ty** [sə'taɪətɪ] s. **1.** (of) Übersättigung f (mit), 'Überdruss m (an dat.): **to ~** bis zum Überdruss; **2.** Sattheit f.

sat·in ['sætɪn] I s. ⊖ **1.** Sa'tin m, Atlas m (Stoff); **2.** a. **white ~** sl. Gin m; II adj. **3.** Satin...; **4.** a) seidenglatt, b) glänzend; III v/t. **5.** ⊖ satinieren, glätten; **sat·i·net(te)** [,sætɪ'net] s. Halbatlas m.

'sat·in|-,fin·ished adj. ⊖ mattiert; **~ pa·per** s. satiniertes Pa'pier, 'Atlaspa,pier n.

sat·in·y ['sætɪnɪ] adj. seidig.

sat·ire ['sætaɪə] s. **1.** Sa'tire f, bsd. a) Spottgedicht n, -schrift f ([up]on auf acc.), b) sa'tirische Litera'tur, c) Spott m; **2.** fig. Hohn m ([up]on auf acc.); **sa·tir·ic, sa·tir·i·cal** [sə'tɪrɪk(l)] adj. □ sa'tirisch; **sat·i·rist** ['sætərɪst] s. Sa'tiriker(in); **sat·i·rize** ['sætəraɪz] v/t. verspotten, e-e Sa'tire machen auf (acc.).

sat·is·fac·tion [,sætɪs'fækʃn] s. **1.** Befriedigung f, Zu'friedenstellung f: **find ~ in** Befriedigung finden in (dat.); **give ~** befriedigen; **2.** (at, with) Zufriedenheit f (mit), Befriedigung f, Genugtuung f (über acc.): **to the ~ of all** zur

Zufriedenheit aller; **3.** eccl. Sühne f; **4.** Satisfakti'on f, Genugtuung f (Duell etc.); **5.** ✠, ✝ Befriedigung f e-s Anspruchs; Erfüllung f e-r Verpflichtung; (Be)Zahlung f e-r Schuld; **6.** Gewissheit f: **show to the court's ~** ✠ einwandfrei glaubhaft machen; **,sat·is·'fac·to·ri·ness** [-ktərɪnɪs] s. das Befriedigende; **,sat·is·'fac·to·ry** [-ktərɪ] adj. □ **1.** befriedigend, zu'frieden stellend; **2.** eccl. sühnend; **sat·is·fy** ['sætɪsfaɪ] I v/t. **1.** befriedigen, zu'frieden stellen, genügen (dat.): **be satisfied with s.th.** mit et. zufrieden sein; **2.** a) j-n sättigen, b) Hunger etc., a. Neugier stillen, c) fig. Wunsch erfüllen, Bedürfnis, a. Trieb befriedigen; **3.** ✝ Anspruch befriedigen; Schuld begleichen, tilgen; e-r Verpflichtung nachkommen; Bedingungen, ✠ a. Urteil erfüllen; **4.** a) j-n entschädigen, b) Gläubiger befriedigen; **5.** den Anforderungen entsprechen, genügen; **6.** ℞ Bedingung, Gleichung erfüllen; **7.** j-n über'zeugen (of von): **~ o.s. that** sich überzeugen od. vergewissern, dass; **I am satisfied that** ich bin davon (od. habe mich) überzeugt, dass; II v/i. **8.** befriedigen; **sat·is·fy·ing** ['sætɪsfaɪɪŋ] adj. □ **1.** befriedigend, zu'frieden stellend; **2.** sättigend.

sa·trap ['sætrəp] s. hist. Sa'trap m (a. fig.), Statthalter m.

sat·u·rant ['sætʃərənt] I adj. **1.** bsd. ℞ sättigend; II s. **2.** neutralisierender Stoff; **3.** ⚕ Mittel n gegen Magensäure; **sat·u·rate** ['sætʃəreɪt] v/t. **1.** ℞ u. fig. sättigen, saturieren (a. ✠ Markt); **2.** (durch)'tränken, durch'setzen: **be ~d with** fig. erfüllt od. durchdrungen sein von; **3.** ✗ mit Bombenteppichen belegen; **sat·u·rat·ed** ['sætʃəreɪtɪd] adj. **1.** durch'tränkt, -'setzt; **2.** tropfnass: **~ with fig.** satt (Farbe); **4.** ℞ a) a. fig. saturiert, gesättigt, b) reakti'onsträge.

sat·u·ra·tion [,sætʃə'reɪʃn] s. **1.** bsd. ℞, phys. u. fig. Sättigung f, Saturierung f; **2.** (Durch)'Tränkung f, Durch'setzung f; **3.** Sattheit f (Farbe); **~ bomb·ing** s. ✗ Bombenteppich(e pl.) m; **~ point** s. ℞ Sättigungspunkt m.

Sat·ur·day ['sætədɪ] s. Sonnabend m, Samstag m: **on ~** am Sonnabend od. Samstag; **on ~s** sonnabends, samstags.

Sat·urn ['sætən] s. **1.** antiq. Sa'turn(us) m (Gott); **2.** ast. Sa'turn m (Planet); **3.** ℞ hist. Blei n; **4.** her. Schwarz n; **Sat·ur·na·li·a** [,sætə'neɪljə] s. pl. antiq. Sa·tur'nalien pl.; **Sat·ur·na·li·an** [,sætə·'neɪljən] adj. **1.** antiq. satur'nalisch; **2.** ☙ fig. orgi'astisch; **Sa·tur·ni·an** [sæ'tɜːnjən] adj. **1.** antiq.; **2.** myth., a. fig. poet. sa'turnisch: **~ age** fig. goldenes Zeitalter; **'sat·ur·nine** [-naɪn] adj. □ **1.** düster, finster (Person, Gesicht etc.); **2.** ☙ im Zeichen des Sa'turn geboren; **3.** min. Blei...

sat·yr ['sætə] s. **1.** oft ☙ myth. Satyr m (Waldgott); **2.** fig. Satyr m (geiler Mensch); **3.** ⚕ Satyro'mane m; **sa·ty·ri·a·sis** [,sætə'raɪəsɪs] s. ⚕ Saty'riasis f; **sa·tyr·ic** [sə'tɪrɪk] adj. Satyr..., satyrhaft.

sauce [sɔːs] I s. **1.** Sauce f, Soße f, Tunke f: **hunger is the best ~** Hunger ist der beste Koch; **what is ~ for the goose is ~ for the gander** was dem einen recht ist, ist dem andern billig; **2.** fig. Würze f; **3.** Am. Kom'pott n; **4.** F Frechheit f; **5.** ⊖ a) Beize f, b) (Tabak-) Brühe f; II v/t. **6.** mit Soße würzen; **7.** fig. würzen; **8.** F frech sein zu; **'~-boat** s. Sauciere f, Soßenschüssel f; **'~-dish** s. Am. Kom'pottschüssel f, -schale f;

'**~-pan** [-pən] s. Kochtopf m, Kasse'rolle f.

sau·cer ['sɔːsə] s. 'Untertasse f; → **flying saucer**; **~ eye** [-aɪ] s. Glotz-, Kullerauge n; '**~-eyed** [-aɪd] adj. glotzäugig.

sau·ci·ness ['sɔːsɪnɪs] s. **1.** Frechheit f; **2.** Kessheit f; **sau·cy** ['sɔːsɪ] adj. □ **1.** frech, unverschämt; **2.** F kess, flott, fesch: **a ~ hat**.

Sau·di ['saʊdɪ] I s. Saudi m; II adj. ,saudi-a'rabisch; **~ A·ra·bi·an** I s. ,Saudi-'Araber(in); II adj. ,saudi-a'rabisch.

sau·na ['sɔːnə] s. Sauna f.

saun·ter ['sɔːntə] I v/i. schlendern: **~ about** um'herschlendern, (-)bummeln; II s. (Um'her)Schlendern n, Bummel m.

sau·ri·an ['sɔːrɪən] zo. I s. Saurier m; II adj. Saurier..., Echsen...

sau·sage ['sɒsɪdʒ] s. **1.** Wurst f; **2.** a. ~ **balloon** ✗ F 'Fesselbal,lon m; **3.** sl. Deutsche(r m) f; **~ dog** s. Brit. F Dackel m; **~ meat** s. Wurstmasse f, Brät n.

sau·té ['səʊteɪ] (Fr.) I adj. Küche: sau'té, sautiert; II s. Sau'té n.

sav·age ['sævɪdʒ] I adj. □ **1.** allg. wild: a) primi'tiv (Volk etc.), b) ungezähmt (Tier), c) bru'tal, grausam, d) F wütend, e) wüst (Landschaft); II s. **2.** Wilde(r m) f; **3.** Rohling m; **4.** bösartiges Tier, bsd. bissiges Pferd; III v/t. **5.** j-n übel zurichten, a. fig. j-m übel mitspielen; **6.** j-n anfallen, beißen (Pferd etc.); **'sav·age·ness** [-nɪs] s. **1.** Wildheit f, Rohheit f, Grausamkeit f; **2.** Wut f, Bissigkeit f; **'sav·age·ry** [-dʒərɪ] s. **1.** Unzivilisiertheit f, Wildheit f; **2.** Rohheit f, Grausamkeit f.

sa·van·na(h) [sə'vænə] s. geogr. Sa'vanne f.

sa·vant ['sævənt] s. großer Gelehrter.

save¹ [seɪv] I v/t. **1.** (er)retten (from von, vor dat.): **~ s.o.'s life** j-m das Leben retten; **2.** ✞ bergen; schützen, schützen (from vor dat.): **God ~ the Queen** Gott erhalte die Königin; **~ the situation** die Situation retten; → **appearance** 3, **face** 4, **harmless** 2; **4.** Geld etc. sparen, einsparen: **~ time** Zeit gewinnen od. sparen; **5.** (auf)sparen, aufheben, -bewahren: **~ it!** sl. ,geschenkt'!, halts Maul!; → **breath** 1; **6.** a. Augen schonen; schonend od. sparsam 'umgehen mit; **7.** j-m e-e Mühe etc. ersparen: **it ~d me the trouble of going there**; **8.** eccl. erlösen (from aus), erlösen (von); **9.** Brit. ausnehmen: **~ the mark!** verzeihen Sie die Bemerkung!; **~ your presence** (od. **reverence**) mit Verlaub; **10.** F aufsparen; **11.** sport: a) Schuss halten, b) Tor verhindern; **12.** Computer: sichern, (ab)speichern (**onto** auf acc.); II v/i. **13.** sparen; **14.** sport ,retten', halten; **15.** Computer: sich (ab)speichern lassen (Datei); III s. **16.** sport Pa'rade f (Tormann).

save² [seɪv] prp. u. cj. außer (dat.), mit Ausnahme von (od. gen.), ausgenommen (nom.), abgesehen von: **~ for** bis auf (acc.); **~ that** abgesehen davon, dass; nur, dass.

sav·e·loy [,sævə'lɔɪ] s. Zerve'latwurst f.

sav·er ['seɪvə] s. **1.** Retter(in); **2.** Sparer (-in); **3.** sparsames Gerät etc.

sav·ing ['seɪvɪŋ] I adj. □ **1.** sparsam (of mit); **2.** ...sparend: **time-~**; **3.** rettend: **~ grace** eccl. selig machende Gnade; **~ humo(u)r** befreiender Humor; **~ clause** ✠ Vorbehalts...: **~ clause** III s. **5.** (Er-) Rettung f; **6.** a) Sparen n, b) Ersparnis f, Einsparung f: **~ of time** Zeitersparnis; **7.** *pl.* Ersparnis(se *pl.*) *f*; Spargeld (-er *pl.*) *n*; **8.** ⚖ Vorbehalt *m*; **III** *prp. u. cj.* **9.** außer (*dat.*), ausgenommen: ~ **your presence** (*od.* **reverence**) mit Verlaub.

sav·ings| ac·count ['seɪvɪŋz] *s.* Sparkonto *n*; ~ **bank** *s.* Sparkasse *f*; ~ (**deposit**) **book** Spar(kassen)buch *n*; ~ **deposit** *s.* Spareinlage *f*.

sav·io(u)r ['seɪvjə] *s.* (Er)Retter *m*, Erlöser *m*: **the** ℒ *eccl.* der Heiland *od.* Erlöser.

sa·voir| faire [ˌsævwɑːˈfeə] (*Fr.*) *s.* Gewandtheit *f*, Takt(gefühl *n*) *m*, Savoir- -'faire *n*; ~ **vi·vre** [-'viːvr] (*Fr.*) *s.* feine Lebensart, Savoir-'vivre *n*.

sa·vor·y ['seɪvərɪ] *s.* ♀ Bohnenkraut *n*, Kölle *f*.

sa·vo(u)r ['seɪvə] **I** *s.* **1.** (Wohl)Geschmack *m*; **2.** *bsd. fig.* Würze *f*, Reiz *m*; **3.** *fig.* Beigeschmack *m*, Anstrich *m*; **II** *v/t.* **4.** *bsd. fig.* genießen, auskosten; **5.** *bsd. fig.* würzen; **6.** *fig.* e-n Beigeschmack *od.* Anstrich haben von, riechen nach; **III** *v/i.* **7.** ~ **of** a) *a. fig.* schmecken *od.* riechen nach, b) → 6; **'sa·vo(u)r·i·ness** [-vərɪnɪs] *s.* Wohlgeschmack *m*, -geruch *m*, Schmackhaftigkeit *f*; **'sa·vo(u)r·less** [-lɪs] *adj.* geschmack-, geruchlos, fade; **'sa·vo(u)r·y** [-vərɪ] **I** *adj.* □ **1.** wohlschmeckend, -riechend, schmackhaft; **2.** *a. fig.* appe'titlich, angenehm; *a.* würzig, pi'kant (*a. fig.*); **II** *s.* **4.** *Brit.* pi'kante Vor- *od.* Nachspeise.

sa·voy [sə'vɔɪ] *s.* Wirsing(kohl) *m*.

sav·vy ['sævɪ] *sl.* **I** *v/t.* ‚kapieren', verstehen; **II** *s.* ‚Köpfchen' *n*, ‚'Durchblick' *m*, Verstand *m*.

saw¹ [sɔː] *pret. von* **see¹**.

saw² [sɔː] *s.* Sprichwort *n*.

saw³ [sɔː] **I** *s.* ⚙ Säge *f*: **singing** (*od.* **musical**) ~ ♪ singende Säge; **II** *v/t.* **2.** [*irr.*] sägen: ~ **down** *Baum* umsägen; ~ **off** absägen; ~ **out** *Bretter* zuschneiden; ~ **up** zersägen; ~ **the air** (**with one's hands**) (mit den Händen) herumfuchteln; **III** *v/i.* [*irr.*] **3.** sägen; **4.** (auf der Geige) ‚kratzen'.

'saw|·bones *s. pl. sg. konstr. sl.* a) ‚Bauchaufschneider' *m* (*Chirurg*), b) ‚Medi'zinmann' *m* (*Arzt*); **'~·buck** *s. Am.* **1.** Sägebock *m*; **2.** *sl.* 10-Dollar- Note *f*; **'~·dust** *s.* Sägemehl *n*: *let the* ~ *out of fig.* die Hohlheit zeigen von; **'~·fish** *s. ichth.* Sägefisch *m*; **'~·fly** *s. zo.* Blattwespe *f*; ~ **frame**, ~ **gate** *s.* ⚙ Sägegatter *n*; **'~·horse** *s.* Sägebock *m*; **'~·mill** *s.* Sägewerk *n*, -mühle *f*.

sawn [sɔːn] *p.p. von* **saw³**.

Saw·ney ['sɔːnɪ] *s.* F **1.** (*Spitzname für*) Schotte *m*; **2.** ℒ Trottel *m*.

saw| set *s.* ⚙ Schränkeisen *n*; **'~·tooth I** *s.* [*irr.*] **1.** Sägezahn *m*; **II** *adj.* **2.** Sägezahn...: ~ **roof** Säge-, Scheddach *n*; **3.** ♀ Sägezahn..., *Am.* ...(-spannung *etc.*); **'~·wort** *s.* ♀ Färberdistel *f*.

saw·yer ['sɔːjə] *s.* Säger *m*.

Saxe [sæks] *s.* Sächsischblau *n*.

sax·horn ['sæksɔːn] *s.* ♪ Saxhorn *n*.

sax·i·frage ['sæksɪfrɪdʒ] *s.* ♀ Steinbrech *m*.

Sax·on ['sæksn] **I** *s.* Sachse *m*, Sächsin *f*; **2.** *hist.* (Angel)Sachse *m*, (Angel-) Sächsin *f*; **3.** *ling.* Sächsisch *n*; **II** *adj.* **4.** sächsisch; **5.** (alt-, angel)sächsisch, *ling.* oft ger'manisch: ~ **genitive** sächsischer Genitiv; ~ **blue** → **Saxe**; **'Sax·o·ny** [-nɪ] *s.* **1.** *geogr.* Sachsen *n*; **2.** ℒ feiner, glänzender Wollstoff.

sax·o·phone ['sæksəfəʊn] *s.* ♪ Saxo'phon *n*; **sax·o·phon·ist** [sæk'sɒfənɪst] *s.* Saxopho'nist(in).

say [seɪ] **I** *v/t.* [*irr.*] **1.** *et.* sagen, spre-

---

chen; **2.** sagen, äußern, berichten: *he has nothing to* ~ *for himself* a) er ist sehr zurückhaltend, b) *contp.* mit ihm ist nicht viel los; *have you nothing to* ~ *for yourself?* hast du nichts zu deiner Rechtfertigung zu sagen?; *to* ~ *nothing of* ganz zu schweigen von, geschweige; *the Bible* ~*s* die Bibel sagt, in der Bibel heißt es; *people* (*od.* **they**) ~ *he is ill, he is said to be ill* man sagt *od.* es heißt, er sei krank, er soll krank sein; ~ *no more* F schon gut! (*ich habe verstanden*); **3.** sagen, behaupten, versprechen: *you said you would come;* → *soon* **4.** a) *a.* ~ *over Gedicht etc.* auf-, hersagen, b) *Gebet* sprechen, c) *R.C. Messe* lesen; **5.** (be)sagen, bedeuten: *that is to* ~ das heißt; *$500,* ~, *five hundred dollars* $500, in Worten: fünfhundert Dollar; *that is* ~*ing a great deal* das will viel heißen; **6.** annehmen: (*let us*) ~ *it happens* angenommen, es passiert; *a sum of,* ~, *$20* e-e Summe von, sagen wir (mal), *od.* von etwa $20; *I should* ~ ich dächte, ich würde sagen; **II** *v/i.* [*irr.*] **7.** sagen, meinen: *you may well* ~ *so!* das kann man wohl sagen!; *it is hard to* ~ es ist schwer zu sagen; *what do you* ~ (*od.* *what* ~ *you*) *to* ...? was hältst du von ...?, wie wäre es mit ...?; *you don't* ~ (**so**)*!* was Sie nicht sagen!, nicht möglich!; *it* ~*s* es lautet (*Schreiben etc.*); *it* ~*s here* hier steht (*geschrieben*), hier heißt es; **8.** *I* ~*!* *int.* a) hör(en Sie) mal!, sag(en Sie) mal!, b) erstaunt *od.* beifällig: Donnerwetter!; **III** *s.* **9.** *have one's* ~ (*to od.* *on*) s-e Meinung äußern (über *acc. od.* zu); **10.** Mitspracherecht *n*: *have a* (*no*) ~ *in* et. (nichts) zu sagen haben bei; *it is my* ~ *now!* jetzt rede ich!; **11.** *a. final* ~ endgültige Entscheidung: *who has the* ~ *in this matter?* wer hat in dieser Sache zu entscheiden *od.* das letzte Wort zu reden?

say·est ['seɪɪst] *obs. 2. sg. pres. von* **say**: *thou* ~ du sagst.

say·ing ['seɪɪŋ] *s.* **1.** Reden *n*: *it goes without* ~ es ist selbstverständlich; *there is no* ~ man kann nicht sagen *od.* wissen (*ob, wann etc.*); **2.** Ausspruch *m*; **3.** Sprichwort *n*, Redensart *f*: *as the* ~ *goes* (*od.* **is**) wie es (im Sprichwort) heißt, wie man sagt.

says [sez; səz] *3. sg. pres. von* **say**: *he* ~ er sagt.

'say-so *pl.* **-sos** *s.* F **1.** (bloße) Behauptung; **2.** → *say* 11.

scab [skæb] **I** *s.* **1.** ᛉ a) Grind *m*, (Wund)Schorf *m*, b) Krätze *f*; **2.** *vet.* Räude *f*; **3.** ♀ Schorf *m*; **4.** *sl.* Ha'lunke *m*; **5.** *sl.* a) Streikbrecher(in), b) Nichtgewerkschaftler *m*: ~ *work* Schwarzarbeit *f*; *a.* Arbeit unter Tariflohn; **6.** ⚙ Gussfehler *m*; **II** *v/i.* **7.** verschorfen, sich verkrusten; **8.** *a.* ~ *it sl.* als Streikbrecher *od.* unter Ta'riflohn arbeiten.

scab·bard ['skæbəd] *s.* (Schwert- *etc.*) Scheide *f*.

scabbed [skæbd] *adj.* **1.** → **scabby**; **2.** ♀ schorfig.

scab·by ['skæbɪ] *adj.* □ **1.** ᛉ schorfig, grindig; **2.** *vet.* räudig; **3.** F schäbig, schuftig.

sca·bi·es ['skeɪbiːz] → **scab** 1 b *u.* 2.

sca·bi·ous¹ ['skeɪbjəs] *adj.* **1.** ᛉ skabi'ös, krätzig; **2.** *vet.* räudig.

sca·bi·ous² ['skeɪbjəs] *s.* ♀ Skabi'ose *f*.

sca·brous ['skeɪbrəs] *adj.* **1.** rau, schuppig (*Pflanze etc.*); **2.** heikel, kniff(e)lig: *a* ~ *question*; **3.** *fig.* schlüpfrig, anstößig.

scaf·fold ['skæfəld] **I** *s.* **1.** (Bau-, Ar-

---

beits)Gerüst *n*; **2.** Blutgerüst *n*, (*a.* Tod *m* auf dem) Scha'fott *n*; **3.** ('Redner-, 'Zuschauer)Tri,büne *f*; **4.** *anat.* a) Knochengerüst *n*, b) Stützgewebe *n*; **5.** ⚙ Ansatz *m* (*im Hochofen*); **II** *v/t.* **6.** ein Gerüst anbringen an (*dat.*); **7.** auf e-m Gestell aufbauen; **'scaf·fold·ing** [-dɪŋ] *s.* **1.** (Bau)Gerüst *n*; **2.** Ge'rüstmateri,al *n*; **3.** Errichtung *f* des Gerüsts.

scal·a·ble ['skeɪləbl] *adj.* ersteigbar.

scal·age ['skeɪlɪdʒ] *s.* **1.** ♥ *Am.* Schwundgeld *n*; **2.** Holzmaß *n*.

sca·lar ['skeɪlə] A *u* **I** *adj.* ska'lar, ungerichtet; **II** *s.* Ska'lar *m*.

scal·a·wag ['skæləwæg] *s.* **1.** Kümmerling *m* (*Tier*); **2.** F Lump *m*.

scald¹ [skɔːld] *s.* Skalde *m* (*nordischer Sänger*).

scald² [skɔːld] **I** *v/t.* **1.** verbrühen; **2.** *Milch etc.* abkochen: ~*ing hot* a) kochend heiß, b) glühend heiß (*Tag etc.*); ~*ing tears fig.* heiße Tränen; **3.** *Obst etc.* dünsten; **4.** *Geflügel, Schwein etc.* abbrühen; **5.** *a.* ~ *out Gefäß, Instrumente* auskochen; **II** *s.* **6.** Verbrühung *f*.

scale¹ [skeɪl] **I** *s.* **1.** *zo.* Schuppe *f*; *coll.* Schuppen *pl.*; **2.** ⚘ Schuppe *f*: *come off in* ~*s* → 11; *the* ~*s fell from my eyes* es fiel mir wie Schuppen von den Augen; **3.** a) ♀ Schuppenblatt *n*, b) (*Erbsen- etc.*)Hülse *f*, Schale *f*; **4.** (*Messer*)Schale *f*; **5.** Ablagerung *f*, *bsd.* a) Kesselstein *m*, b) ♀ Zahnstein *m*; **6.** *a. pl. metall.* Zunder *m*: *iron* ~ Hammerschlag *m*, Glühspan *m*; **II** *v/t.* **7.** *a.* ~ *off Fisch* (ab)schuppen; *Schicht etc.* ablösen, -schälen, -häuten; **8.** a) abklopfen, den Kesselstein entfernen aus, b) *Zähne* vom Zahnstein befreien; **9.** e-e Kruste *od.* Kesselstein ansetzen an (*dat.*) *od.* an (*dat.*); **10.** *metall.* zunderfrei machen, ausglühen; **III** *v/i.* **11.** *a.* ~ *off* sich abschuppen *od.* -lösen, abblättern; **12.** Kessel- *od.* Zahnstein ansetzen.

scale² [skeɪl] **I** *s.* **1.** Waagschale *f* (*a. fig.*): *hold the* ~*s even fig.* gerecht urteilen; *throw into the* ~ *fig.* Argument, Schwert etc. in die Waagschale werfen; *turn* (*od.* *tip*) *the* ~(**s**) *fig.* den Ausschlag geben; *turn the* ~ *at 55 lbs* 55 Pfund wiegen; → *weight* 4; **2.** *mst pl.* Waage *f*; *a pair of* ~*s* eine Waage; *go to* ~ *sport* gewogen werden (*Jockey, Boxer*); *go to* ~ *at 90 lbs* 90 Pfund auf die Waage bringen; **3.** ~*s pl. ast.* Waage *f*; **II** *v/t.* **4.** wiegen; **5.** F (ab-, aus-) wiegen; **III** *v/i.* **6.** ~ *in* (*out*) vor (nach) dem Rennen gewogen werden (*Jockey*).

scale³ [skeɪl] **I** *s.* **1.** ⚙, *phys.* Skala *f*: ~ *division* Gradeinteilung *f*; ~ *disk* Skalenscheibe *f*; ~ *line* Teilstrich *m*; **2.** a) Stufenleiter *f*, Staffelung *f*, b) Skala *f*, Ta'rif *m*: ~ *of fees* Gebührenordnung *f*; ~ *of wages* Lohnskala, -tabelle *f*; **3.** Stufe *f* (*auf e-r Skala, Tabelle etc.*; *a. fig.*): *social* ~ Gesellschaftsstufe; **4.** A, ⚙ a) Maßstab(zahl *f*) *m*, b) loga'rithmischer Rechenstab: *in* (*od.* *to*) ~ maßstab(s)gerecht: *drawn to a* ~ *of 1:5* im Maßstab 1:5 gezeichnet; ~ *model* maßstab(s)getreues Modell; **5.** *fig.* Maßstab *m*, 'Umfang *m*: *on a large* ~ in großem Umfang, im großen; **6.** A (nu'merische) Zahlenreihe: *decimal* ~ Dezimalreihe *f*; **7.** ♪ a) Tonleiter *f*, b) 'Ton,umfang *m* (*Instrument*): *learn one's* ~*s* Tonleitern üben; **8.** *Am. Börse:* *on a* ~ zu verschiedenen Kurswerten (*Wertpapiere*); **9.** *fig.* Leiter *f*: *a* ~ *to success*; **II** *v/t.* **10.** erklimmen, erklettern (*a. fig.*); **11.** maßstab(s)getreu zeichnen: ~

down (*up*) maßstäblich verkleinern (vergrößern); **12.** einstufen: **~** *down Löhne* herunterschrauben, drücken; **~** *up Preise etc.* hoch schrauben; **III** *v/i.* **13.** *auf e-r Skala od. fig.* klettern, steigen: **~** *down* fallen.

scale| ar·mo(u)r *s.* Schuppenpanzer *m*; **~ beam** *s.* Waagebalken *m*; **~ buy·ing** *s.* † (spekula'tiver) Aufkauf von 'Wertpa‚pieren.

scaled [skeɪld] *adj.* **1.** *zo.* schuppig, Schuppen...; **2.** abgeschuppt: **~** *herring*; **3.** mit e-r Skala (versehen).

'scale-down *s.* maßstab(s)gerechte Verkleinerung.

scale·less ['skeɪllɪs] *adj.* schuppenlos.

sca·lene ['skeɪliːn] *A* **I** *adj.* ungleichseitig (*Figur*), schief (*Körper*); **II** *s.* schiefwinkliges Dreieck.

scal·ing ['skeɪlɪŋ] *s.* **1.** (Ab)Schuppen *n*; **2.** Kesselstein- *od.* Zahnsteinentfernung *f*; **3.** Erklettern *n*, Aufstieg *m* (*a. fig.*); **4.** † (spekula'tiver) Auf- u. Verkauf *m* von 'Wertpa‚pieren.

scall [skɔːl] *s.* ⚕ (Kopf)Grind *m*.

scal·la·wag → *scalawag.*

scal·lion ['skæljən] *s.* ♦ Scha'lotte *f*.

scal·lop ['skɒləp] **I** *s.* **1.** *zo.* Kammmuschel *f*; **2.** *a.* **~** *shell* Muschelschale *f* (*a. aus Porzellan zum Servieren von Speisen*); **3.** *Näherei:* Lan'gette *f*; **II** *v/t.* **4.** ⊙ ausbogen, bogenförmig verzieren; **5.** *Näherei:* langettieren; **6.** *Speisen* in der (Muschel)Schale über'backen.

scalp [skælp] **I** *s.* **1.** *anat.* Kopfhaut *f*; **2.** Skalp *m* (*abgezogene Kopfhaut als Siegeszeichen*): *be out for* **~***s* sich auf dem Kriegspfad befinden, *fig.* kampf-, angriffslustig sein; **3.** *fig.* ('Sieges)Tro‚phäe *f*; **II** *v/t.* **4.** skalpieren; **5.** † *Am.* F *Wertpapiere* mit kleinem Pro'fit weiterverkaufen; **6.** *Am. sl. Eintrittskarten* auf dem schwarzen Markt verkaufen.

scal·pel ['skælpəl] *s.* ⚕ Skal'pell *n*.

scal·y ['skeɪlɪ] *adj.* **1.** schuppig, geschuppt; **2.** Schuppen...; **3.** schuppenförmig; **4.** sich abschuppend, schilferig.

scam [skæm] *s.* F betrügerischer Trick.

scamp [skæmp] **I** *s.* Ha'lunke *m*; *humor. a.* Spitzbube *m*; **II** *v/t. Arbeit etc.* schlud(e)rig ausführen, hinschlampen.

scam·per ['skæmpə] **I** *v/i.* **1.** *a.* **~** *about* (he'rum)tollen, her'umhüpfen; **2.** hasten: **~** *away* (*od.* *off*) sich davonmachen; **II** *s.* **3.** (He'rum)Tollen *n*.

scan [skæn] **I** *v/t.* **1.** genau *od.* kritisch prüfen, forschend *od.* scharf ansehen; **2.** *Horizont etc.* absuchen; **3.** über'fliegen: **~** *the headlines*; **4.** *Vers* skandieren; **5.** ♁, *Radar*, *TV*: abtasten; **6.** *Computer*, ⚕ *etc.*: scannen: **~** *in* einscannen; **II** *v/i.* **7.** *Metrik:* a) skan'dieren, b) *gut etc.* skandieren (lassen); **III** *s.* **8.** genaue Prüfung (*durch Blicke*); **9.** *Radar*, *TV*: Abtastung *f*; **10.** *Computer:* Scan *m*; **11.** ⚕ Scan *m*: a) 'Ultraschalluntersuchung *f*, -aufnahme *f*, b) 'Kernspintomo‚gramm *n*, c) Com'putertomo‚gramm; **12.** *phot.* Scan *m*, Aufnahme *f*, (*durch Überwachungskamera, Satelliten etc.*).

scan·dal ['skændl] *s.* **1.** Skan'dal *m*: a) skanda'löses Ereignis, b) (öffentliches) Ärgernis: *cause* **~** Anstoß erregen, c) Schande *f*, Schmach *f* (*to* für); **2.** Verleumdung *f*, (böswilliger) Klatsch: *talk* **~** klatschen; **~** *sheet* Skandal-, Revolverblatt *n*; **3.** ⚖ üble Nachrede (*im Prozess*); **4.** ‚unmöglicher' Mensch.

scan·dal·ize¹ ['skændəlaɪz] *v/t.* Anstoß erregen bei (*dat.*), j-n schockieren: *be* **~***d at* Anstoß nehmen an (*dat.*), empört

sein über (*acc.*).

scan·dal·ize² ['skændəlaɪz] *v/t.* ⚓ *Segel* verkleinern, ohne zu reffen.

'scan·dal‚mon·ger *s.* Lästermaul *n*, Klatschbase *f*.

scan·dal·ous ['skændələs] *adj.* □ **1.** skanda'lös, anstößig, schockierend; **2.** schändlich, schimpflich; **3.** verleumderisch, Schmäh...: **~** *stories*; **4.** klatschsüchtig (*Person*).

'scan·dal-plagued [-pleɪgd] *adj.* skan-'dalgeplagt.

Scan·di·na·vi·an [‚skændɪ'neɪvjən] **I** *adj.* **1.** skandi'navisch; **II** *s.* **2.** Skandi-'navier(in); **3.** *ling.* a) Skandi'navisch *n*, b) Altnordisch *n*.

scan·ner ['skænə] *s.* **1.** *Computer*, ⚕, ♁: Scanner *m*; **2.** *TV* Bildabtaster *m*; **3.** Ra'dar-, 'Richtan‚tenne *f*.

scan·ning ['skænɪŋ] *s.* **1.** *Computer*, ⚕, ♁: Scannen *n*; **2.** *TV* Bildabtastung *f*; **3.** *Radar etc.:* Abtastung *f*; **~** *disk s. TV* Abtastscheibe *f*; **~** *lines s. pl. TV* Rasterlinien *pl.*

scan·sion ['skænʃn] *s. Metrik:* Skandierung *f*, Skansi'on *f*.

Scan·so·res [skæn'sɔːriːz] *s. pl. orn.* Klettervögel *pl.*; **scan·so·ri·al** [-rɪəl] *adj. orn.* **1.** Kletter...; **2.** zu den Klettervögeln gehörig.

scant [skænt] *adj.* knapp (*of* an *dat.*), spärlich, dürftig, gering: *a* **~** *2 hours* knapp 2 Stunden; **'scant·i·ness** [-tɪz] *s. pl.* Damenslip *m*; **'scant·i·ness** [-tɪnɪs], **'scant·ness** [-nɪs] *s.* **1.** Knappheit *f*, Kargheit *f*; **2.** Unzulänglichkeit *f*; **'scant·y** [-tɪ] *adj.* □ **1.** → *scant*; **2.** unzureichend; **3.** eng, beengt (*Raum etc.*).

scape [skeɪp] *s.* **1.** ♦, *zo.* Schaft *m*; **2.** △ (*Säulen*)Schaft *m*.

'scape·goat *s. fig.* Sündenbock *m*.

'scape·grace *s.* Taugenichts *m*.

scaph·oid ['skæfɔɪd] *anat.* **I** *adj.* scapho-'id, Kahn...; **II** *s. a.* **~** *bone* Kahnbein *n*.

scap·u·la ['skæpjʊlə] *pl.* **-lae** [-liː] *s. anat.* Schulterblatt *n*; **'scap·u·lar** [-lə] **I** *adj.* **1.** *anat.* Schulter(blatt)...; **II** *s.* **2.** → *scapulary*; **3.** ⚕ Schulterbinde *f*; **'scap·u·lar·y** [-lərɪ] *s. eccl.* Skapu'lier *n*.

scar¹ [skaː] **I** *s.* **1.** Narbe *f* (*a.* ♦; *a. fig. u. psych.*); **2.** Schramme *f*, Kratzer *m*; **3.** *fig.* (Schand)Fleck *m*, Makel *m*; **II** *v/t.* **4.** e-e Narbe *od.* Narben hinter'lassen auf (*dat.*); **5.** *fig.* bei *j-m* ein Trauma hinter'lassen; **6.** *fig.* entstellen, verunstalten; **III** *v/i.* **7.** *a.* **~** *over* vernarben (*a. fig.*).

scar² [skaː] *s. Brit.* Klippe *f*, steiler (Felsen)Abhang.

scar·ab ['skærəb] *s.* **1.** *zo.* Skara'bäus *m* (*a. Schmuck etc.*); **2.** *zo.* Mistkäfer *m*.

scarce [skeəs] **I** *adj.* □ **1.** knapp, spärlich: **~** *commodities* † Mangelwaren; **2.** selten, rar: *make o.s.* **~** F a) sich rar machen, b) ‚sich dünnmachen'; **II** *adv.* **3.** *obs.* → **'scarce·ly** [-lɪ] *adv.* **1.** kaum, gerade erst: **~** *anything* kaum etwas, fast nichts; **~** *... when* kaum ... als; **2.** wohl nicht, kaum, schwerlich; **'scarce·ness** [-nɪs], **'scar·ci·ty** [-sətɪ] *s.* **1.** a) Knappheit *f*, Mangel *m* (*of* an *dat.*), b) Verknappung *f* (*Hungers*)Not *f*; **3.** Seltenheit *f*: **~** *value* Seltenheitswert *m*.

scare [skeə] **I** *v/t.* **1.** erschrecken, *j-m* e-n Schrecken einjagen, ängstigen: *be* **~***d of s.th.* sich vor et. fürchten; **2.** *a.* **~** *away* verscheuchen, -jagen; **3.** **~** *up* a) *Wild etc.* aufscheuchen, b) F *Geld etc.* auftreiben, *et.* ‚organisieren'; **II** *v/i.* **4.** erschrecken: *he does not* **~** *easily* er lässt sich nicht leicht ins Bockshorn jagen; **III** *s.* **5.** Schreck(en) *m*, Panik *f*: **~**

buying Angstkäufe *pl.*; **~** *news* Schreckensnachricht(en *pl.*) *f*; **6.** blinder A'larm; '**~-crow** *s.* **1.** Vogelscheuche *f* (*a. fig. Person*); **2.** *fig.* Schreckgespenst *n*; '**~-head** *s.* (riesige) Sensati'onsschlagzeile; '**~‚mon·ger** *s.* Panikmacher(in); '**~‚mon·ger·ing** *s.* Panikmache *f*.

scared·y-cat ['skeə(r)dɪkæt] *s.* Angsthase *m*.

scarf¹ [skaːf] *pl.* **scarfs**, **scarves** [-vz] *s.* **1.** Hals-, Kopf-, Schultertuch *n*, Schal *m*; **2.** (breite) Kra'watte (*für Herren*); **3.** ✕ Schärpe *f*; **4.** *eccl.* Seidenstola *f*; **5.** Tischläufer *m*.

scarf² [skaːf] **I** *s.* ⊙ Laschung *f*, Blatt *n* (*Hölzer*); ⚓ Lasch *m*; **2.** ⊙ → *scarf joint*; **II** *v/t.* **3.** ⊙ zs.-blatten; ⚓ (ver)laschen; **4.** *e-n Wal* aufschneiden.

scarf| joint *s.* ⊙ Blattfuge *f*, Verlaschung *f*; '**~-pin** *s.* Kra'wattennadel *f*; '**~-skin** *s. anat.* Oberhaut *f*.

scar·i·fi·ca·tion [‚skeərɪfɪ'keɪʃn] *s.* ⚕ Hautritzung *f*; **scar·i·fi·ca·tor** ['skeərɪfɪkeɪtə], **scar·i·fi·er** ['skeərɪfaɪə] *s.* **1.** ⚕ Stichelmesser *n*; **2.** ✓ Messeregge *f*; **3.** ⊙ Straßenaufreißer *m*; **scar·i·fy** ['skeərɪfaɪ] *v/t.* **1.** *Haut* ritzen, ⚕ skarifizieren; **2.** ✓ a) *Boden* auflockern, b) *Samen* anritzen; **3.** *fig.* a) *Gefühle etc.* verletzen, b) scharf kritisieren.

scar·la·ti·na [‚skaːlə'tiːnə] *s.* ⚕ Scharlach(fieber *n*) *m*.

scar·let ['skaːlət] **I** *s.* **1.** Scharlach(rot *n*) *m*; **2.** Scharlach(tuch *n*, -gewand *n*) *m*; **II** *adj.* **3.** scharlachrot: *flush* (*od.* *turn*) **~** dunkelrot werden; **4.** *fig.* unzüchtig; **~** *fe·ver* *s.* ⚕ Scharlach(fieber *n*) *m*; **~** *hat* *s.* **1.** Kardi'nalshut *m*; **2.** *fig.* Kardi'nalswürde *f*; **~** *run·ner* *s.* ♦ Scharlach-, Feuerbohne *f*; **♀** *Wom·an* *s.* **1.** *bibl. die* (scharlachrot gekleidete) Hure; **2.** *fig. contp.* (*das heidnische od. päpstliche*) Rom.

scarp [skaːp] **I** *s.* **1.** steile Böschung; **2.** ✕ Es'karpe *f*; **II** *v/t.* **3.** abböschen, abdachen; **scarped** [-pt] *adj.* steil, abschüssig.

scarred [skaːd] *adj.* narbig.

scarves [skaːvz] *pl. von* **scarf¹**.

scar·y ['skeərɪ] *adj.* F **1.** a) grus(e)lig, schaurig, b) unheimlich; **2.** schreckhaft, ängstlich.

scat¹ [skæt] F **I** *int.* **1.** ‚hau ab'!; **2.** Tempo!; **II** *v/i.* **3.** ‚verduften'; **4.** flitzen.

scat² [skæt] *s. Jazz:* Scat *m* (*Singen zs.-hangloser Silben*).

scathe [skeɪð] **I** *v/t.* **1.** *poet.* versengen; **2.** *obs. od. Scot.* verletzen; **3.** *fig.* vernichtend kritisieren; **II** *s.* **4.** Schaden *m*: *without* **~**; **5.** Beleidigung *f*; '**scathe·less** [-lɪs] *adj.* unversehrt; '**scath·ing** [-ðɪŋ] *adj.* □ *fig.* **1.** vernichtend, ätzend (*Kritik etc.*); **2.** verletzend.

sca·tol·o·gy [skæ'tɒlədʒɪ] *s.* ⚕ Skatolo'gie *f*, Kotstudium *n*; **2.** *fig.* Beschäftigung *f* mit dem Ob'szönen (*in der Litera'tur*).

scat·ter ['skætə] **I** *v/t.* **1.** *a.* **~** *about* (aus-, um'her-, ver)streuen; **2.** verbreiten, -teilen; **3.** bestreuen (*with* mit); **4.** *Menge etc.* zerstreuen, *a. Vögel etc.* ausein'anderscheuchen: *be* **~***ed to the four winds* in alle Winde zerstreut werden *od.* sein; **5.** *Geld* verschleudern, verzetteln: **~** *one's strength* *fig.* sich verzetteln; **6.** *phys. Licht etc.* zerstreuen; **II** *v/i.* **7.** sich zerstreuen (*Menge*), ausein'ander stieben (*a. Vögel etc.*), sich zerteilen (*Nebel*); **8.** a) sich verbreiten (*over über acc.*), b) verstreut sein (*von*); **9.** *allg., a. phys. etc.* Streuung *f*; '**~-brain** *s.* Wirrkopf *m*; '**~-brained** *adj.*

wirr, kon'fus.

scat·tered ['skætəd] *adj.* **1.** ver-, zerstreut (liegend *od.* vorkommend *etc.*); **2.** vereinzelt (auftretend): **~ rain showers**; **3.** *fig.* wirr; **4.** *phys.* dif'fus, Streu...

'**scat·ter|·gun** *s. Am.* Schrotflinte *f*; **~ rug** *s. Am.* Brücke *f* (*Teppich*).

scaur [skɔː] *bsd. Scot. für scar².*

scav·enge ['skævɪndʒ] **I** *v/t.* **1.** Straßen *etc.* reinigen, säubern; **2.** *mot.* Zylinder *von Gasen* reinigen, spülen: **~ stroke** Spültakt *m*, Auspuffhub *m*; **3.** *Am.* a) Abfälle *etc.* auflesen, b) *et.* auftreiben, c) *et.* durch'stöbern (**for** nach); **II** *v/i.* **4.** **~ for** (her'um)suchen nach; '**scav·en·ger** [-dʒə] *s.* **1.** Straßenkehrer *m*; **2.** Müllmann *m*; **3.** a) Trödler *m*, b) Lumpensammler *m*; **4.** 🜬 Reinigungsmittel *n*; **5.** *zo.* Aasfresser *m*: **~ beetle** Aas fressender Käfer.

sce·nar·i·o [sɪ'nɑːrɪəʊ] *pl.* **-ri·os** *s.* **1.** a) *thea.* Sze'nar(io) *n*, b) *Film:* Drehbuch *n*; **2.** *fig.* Sze'nario *n*, Plan *m*; **sce·na·rist** ['siːnərɪst] *s.* Drehbuchautor *m*.

scene [siːn] *s.* **1.** *thea., Film, TV:* a) Szene *f*, Auftritt *m*, b) Ort *m* der Handlung, Schauplatz *m* (*a. Roman etc.*); → **lay** 6, c) Ku'lisse *f*, d) → **scenery** b): **behind the ~s** hinter den Kulissen (*a. fig.*); **change of ~** Szenenwechsel *m*, *fig.* ,Tapetenwechsel' *m*; **2.** Szene *f*, Epi'sode *f* (*Roman etc.*); **3.** 'Hintergrund *m* e-r Erzählung *etc.*; **4.** *fig.* Szene *f*, Schauplatz *m*: **~ of accident** (**crime**) Unfallort *m* (Tatort *m*); **5.** Szene *f*, Anblick *m*; *paint.* (Landschafts-) Bild *n*: **~ of destruction** *fig.* Bild der Zerstörung; **6.** Szene *f*: a) Vorgang *m*, b) (heftiger) Auftritt: **make** (**s.o.**) **a. ~** (j-m) eine Szene machen; **7.** *fig.* (Welt-) Bühne *f*: **quit the ~** von der Bühne abtreten, sterben; **8.** *sl.* (Drogen-, Pop- *etc.*)Szene *f*: **that's not my ~** *fig.* das ist nicht mein Fall; **~ dock** *s. thea.* Requi'sitenraum *m*; **~ paint·er** *s.* Bühnenmaler(in).

scen·er·y ['siːnərɪ] *s.* Szene'rie *f*: a) Landschaft *f*, Gegend *f*, b) *thea.* Bühnenbild *n*, -ausstattung *f*.

'**scene,shift·er** *s. thea.* Bühnenarbeiter *m*, Ku'lissenschieber *m*.

sce·nic ['siːnɪk] **I** *adj.* (□ **~ally**) **1.** landschaftlich, Landschafts...; **2.** (landschaftlich) schön, malerisch: **~ railway** (in e-r künstlichen Landschaft angelegte) Liliputbahn; **~ road** landschaftlich schöne Strecke (*Hinweis auf Autokarte*); **3.** *thea.* a) szenisch, Bühnen...: **~ designer** Bühnenbildner(in), b) dra'matisch (*a. Gemälde etc.*), c) Ausstattungs...; **II** *s.* **4.** Na'turfilm *m*.

sce·no·graph·ic, **sce·no·graph·i·cal** [,siːnə'græfɪk(l)] *adj.* □ szeno'graphisch, perspek'tivisch.

scent [sent] **I** *s.* **1.** (*bsd.* Wohl)Geruch *m*, Duft *m*; **2.** Par'füm *n*; **3.** *hunt.* a) Witterung *f*, b) Spur *f*, Fährte *f* (*a. fig.*): **blazing ~** warme Fährte; **on the (wrong) ~** auf der (falschen) Fährte; **put on the ~** auf die Fährte setzen; **put** (*od.* **throw**) **off the ~** von der (richtigen) Spur ablenken; **4.** a) Geruchssinn *m*, b) *zo. u. fig.* Spürsinn *m*, gute *etc.* Nase: **have a ~ for s.th.** *fig.* e-e Nase für et. haben; **II** *v/t.* **5.** *et.* riechen; **6.** a. **~ out** *hunt. u. fig.* wittern, (auf)spüren; **7.** mit Wohlgeruch erfüllen; **8.** parfümieren; **scent bag** *s.* **1.** *zo.* Duftdrüse *f*; **2.** *Fuchsjagd:* künstliche Schleppe; **3.** Duftkissen *n*; **scent bot·tle** *s.* Par'fümfläschchen *n*; '**scent·ed** [-tɪd] *adj.* **1.** duftend; **2.** parfümiert; **scent gland** *s.*

---

zo. Duft-, Moschusdrüse *f*; '**scent·less** [-lɪs] *adj.* **1.** geruchlos; **2.** *hunt.* ohne Witterung (*Boden*).

scep·sis ['skepsɪs] *s.* **1.** Skepsis *f*; **2.** *phls.* Skepti'zismus *m*.

scep·ter ['septə] *etc. Am.* → **sceptre** *etc.*

scep·tic ['skeptɪk] *s.* **1.** (*phls. mst* 𝒮) Skeptiker(in); **2.** *eccl.* Zweifler(in), *allg.* Ungläubige(r *m*); Athe'ist(in); '**scep·ti·cal** [-kl] *adj.* □ skeptisch (*a. phls.*), misstrauisch, ungläubig: **be ~ about** (*od.* **of**) **s.th.** e-r Sache skeptisch gegenüberstehen, et. bezweifeln, an et. zweifeln; '**scep·ti·cism** [-ɪsɪzəm] → **scepsis**.

scep·tre ['septə] *s.* Zepter *n*: **wield the ~** das Zepter führen, herrschen; '**scep·tred** [-əd] *adj.* **1.** zeptertragend, herrschend (*a. fig.*); **2.** *fig.* königlich.

sched·ule [*Brit.* 'ʃedjuːl; *Am.* 'skedʒʊl] **I** *s.* **1.** Liste *f*, Ta'belle *f*, Aufstellung *f*, Verzeichnis *n*; **2.** *bsd.* 🜙 Anhang *m*; **3.** *bsd. Am.* a) (Arbeits-, Lehr-, Stunden-) Plan *m*, b) Fahrplan *m*: **be behind ~** Verspätung haben, *weitS.* im Verzug sein; **on ~** (fahr)planmäßig, pünktlich; **4.** Formblatt *n*, Vordruck *m*, Formu'lar *n*; **5.** Einkommensteuerklasse *f*; **II** *v/t.* **6.** *et.* in e-r Liste *etc. od.* tabel'larisch zs.-stellen; **7.** (in e-e Liste *etc.*) eintragen, -fügen: **~d departure** (fahr)planmäßige Abfahrt; **~d flight** 🛫 Linienflug *m*; **the train is ~d to leave at 6** der Zug fährt fahrplanmäßig um 6; **8.** *bsd.* 🜙 (als Anhang) beifügen (**to** *dat.*); **9.** a) festlegen, b) planen.

sche·mat·ic [skɪ'mætɪk] *adj.* (□ **~ally**) sche'matisch; **sche·ma·tize** ['skiːmətaɪz] *v/t. u. v/i.* schematisieren.

scheme [skiːm] *s.* **1.** Schema *n*, Sys'tem *n*, Anlage *f*: **~ of colo(u)r** Farbenzusammenstellung *f*, -skala *f*; **~ of philosophy** philosophisches System; **2.** a) Schema *n*, Aufstellung *f*, Ta'belle *f*, b) 'Übersicht *f*, c) sche'matische Darstellung; **3.** Plan *m*, Pro'jekt *n*, Pro'gramm *n*: **irrigation ~**; **4.** (dunkler) Plan, In'trige *f*, Kom'plott *n*; **II** *v/t.* **5.** a. **~ out** planen, entwerfen; **6.** Böses planen, aushecken; **7.** in ein Schema *od.* Sy'stem bringen; **III** *v/i.* **8.** Pläne schmieden, *bsd. b.s.* Ränke schmieden, intrigieren; '**schem·er** [-mə] *s.* **1.** Plänemacher *m*; **2.** Ränkeschmied *m*, Intri'gant *m*; '**schem·ing** [-mɪŋ] *adj.* □ ränkevoll, intri'gant.

Schen·gen a·gree·ment ['skeŋən] *s. pol.* Schengener Abkommen *n*.

scher·zan·do [skeət'sændəʊ] (*Ital.*) *adv.* ♪ scher'zando, heiter; **scher·zo** ['skeətsəʊ] *pl.* **-zos** ♪ Scherzo *n*.

schism ['skɪzəm] *s.* **1.** *eccl.* a) Schisma *n*, Kirchenspaltung *f*, b) Lossagung *f*; **2.** *fig.* Spaltung *f*, Riss *m*; **schis·mat·ic** [skɪz'mætɪk] *bsd. eccl.* **I** *adj.* (□ **~ally**) schis'matisch, abtrünnig; **II** *s.* Schis'matiker *m*, Abtrünnige(r) *m*; **schis'mat·i·cal** [skɪz'mætɪkl] *adj.* □ → **schismatic** I.

schist [ʃɪst] *s. geol.* Schiefer *m*.

schiz·oid ['skɪtsɔɪd] *psych.* **I** *adj.* schizo-'id; **II** *s.* Schizo'id(e *r m*) *f*.

schiz·o·my·cete [,skɪtsəʊmaɪ'siːt] *s.* ♀ Spaltpilz *m*, Schizomy'zet *m*.

schiz·o·phrene ['skɪtsəʊfriːn] *s. psych.* Schizo'phrene(r *m*) *f*; **schiz·o·phre·ni·a** [,skɪtsəʊ'friːnjə] *s. psych.* Schizophre'nie *f*; **schiz·o·phren·ic** [,skɪtsəʊ'frenɪk] *psych.* **I** *s.* Schizophrene(r *m*) *f*; **II** *adj.* schizo'phren.

schle·miel, schle·mihl [ʃlə'miːl] *s. Am. sl.* **1.** Pechvogel *m*; **2.** Tollpatsch *m*.

---

schlep(p) [ʃlep] *Am. sl.* **I** *v/t.* **1.** a) schleppen, b) (mit sich) her'umschleppen; **II** *v/i.* **2.** sich schleppen, ,latschen': **~ through the traffic** sich durch den Verkehr quälen; **III** *s.* **3.** Trottel *m*, Tollpatsch *m*, ,Blödmann' *m*; **4.** Umstandskrämer(in); **5.** Langweiler(in); **6.** Gelegenheitsarbeiter(in); **7.** langweilige u. ermüdende Fahrt *od.* Reise *etc.*; '**schlep·per** → **schlep**(p) 3-6.

schmaltz [ʃmɔːlts] (*Ger.*) *s. sl.* **1.** ,Schmalz' *m* (*a. Musik*); **2.** Kitsch *m*; '**schmaltz·y** [-tsɪ] *adj.* ,schmalzig', sentimen'tal.

schmoos(e) [ʃmuːs], **schmooze** [ʃmuːz] *bsd. Am.* F **I** *v/i.* plaudern, schwatzen; **II** *v/t.* beschwatzen; **III** *s.* Schwätzchen *n*, Schwatz *m*, Plauderei *f*.

schnap(p)s [ʃnæps] (*Ger.*) *s.* Schnaps *m*.

schnit·zel ['ʃnɪtsəl] (*Ger.*) *s. Küche:* Wiener Schnitzel *n*.

schnor·kel ['ʃnɔːkəl] → **snorkel**.

schol·ar ['skɒlə] *s.* **1.** a) Gelehrte(r) *m*, *bsd.* Geisteswissenschaftler *m*, b) Gebildete(r) *m*; **2.** Studierende(r *m*) *f*: **he is an apt ~** er lernt gut; **he is a good French ~** er ist im Französischen gut beschlagen; **he is not much of a ~** F mit s-r Bildung ist es nicht weit her; **3.** *ped. univ.* Stipendi'at *m*; **4.** *obs. od. poet.* Schüler(in), Jünger(in); '**schol·ar·ly** [-lɪ] *adj. u. adv.* **1.** gelehrt; **2.** gelehrtenhaft; '**schol·ar·ship** [-ʃɪp] *s.* **1.** Gelehrsamkeit *f*: **classical ~** humanistische Bildung; **2.** *ped.* Sti'pendium *n*.

scho·las·tic [skə'læstɪk] **I** *adj.* (□ **~ally**) **1.** aka'demisch (*Bildung etc.*); **2.** schulisch, Schul..., Schüler...; **3.** erzieherisch: **~ profession** Lehr(er)beruf *m*; **4.** *phls.* scho'lastisch (*a. fig. contp. spitzfindig, pedantisch*); **II** *s. phls.* Scho'lastiker *m*; **6.** *fig.* Schulmeister *m*, Pe'dant *m*; **scho'las·ti·cism** [-ɪsɪzəm] *s.* **1.** *phls.* 𝒜 Scho'lastik *f*; **2.** *fig.* Pedante'rie *f*.

school¹ [skuːl] **I** *s.* **1.** Schule *f* (*Anstalt*): **at ~** auf der Schule; → **high school** *etc.*; **2.** (Schul)Stufe *f*: **lower ~** Unterstufe; **senior** (*od.* **upper**) **~** Oberstufe; **3.** Lehrgang *m*, Kurs(us) *m*; **4.** *mst ohne art.* ('Schul)Unterricht *m*, Schule *f*: **at** (*od.* **in**) **~** in der Schule, im Unterricht; **go to ~** zur Schule gehen; **put to ~** einschulen; → **tale** 5; **5.** Schule *f*, Schulhaus *n*, -gebäude *n*; **6.** *univ.* a) Fakul'tät *f*: **the law ~** die juristische Fakultät, b) Fachbereich *m*, (selbstständige) Ab'teilung innerhalb e-r Fakul'tät; **7.** *Am.* Hochschule *f*; **8.** *pl.* 'Schlussex,amen *n* (*für den Grad e-s* **Bachelor of Arts**; *Oxford*); **9.** *fig.* harte *etc.* Schule, Lehre *f*: **a severe ~**; **10.** *phls., paint. etc.* Schule *f* (*Richtung u. Anhängerschaft*): **~ of thought** (geistige) Richtung; **the Hegelian ~** *phls.* die hegelianische Schule *od.* Richtung, die Hegelianer *pl.*; **a gentleman of the old ~** ein Kavalier der alten Schule; **11.** ♪ Schule *f*: a) Lehrbuch *n*, b) Lehre *f*, Sy'stem *n*; **II** *v/t.* **12.** einschulen; **13.** schulen, unter'richten, ausbilden, trainieren; **14.** *Temperament, Zunge etc.* zügeln; **15.** **~ o.s.** (**to**) sich erziehen (zu), sich üben (in *dat.*); **~ o.s. to do s.th.** lernen *od.* sich daran gewöhnen et. zu tun; **16.** *Pferd* dressieren; **17.** *obs.* tadeln.

school² [skuːl] *s. ichth.* Schwarm *m* (*a. fig.*), Schule *f*, Zug *m* (*Wale etc.*).

school age *s.* schulpflichtiges Alter; '**~-age** *adj.* schulpflichtig; '**~-bag** *s.* Schultasche *f*; **~ board** *s.* (lo'kale) Schulbehörde; '**~·boy** s. Schüler m, Schuljunge m; '**~·bus** s. Schulbus m; **~ days** pl. (alte) Schulzeit; '**~,fel·low** → **schoolmate**; '**~·girl** s. Schülerin f, Schulmädchen n; '**~,girl·ish** adj. schulmädchenhaft; '**~·house** s. 1. (bsd. Dorf)Schulhaus n; 2. Brit. (Wohn)Haus n des Schulleiters.

school·ing ['skuːlɪŋ] s. 1. ('Schul,)Unterricht m; 2. Schulung f, Ausbildung f; 3. Schulgeld n; 4. sport Schulreiten n; 5. obs. Verweis m.

school| leav·er ['liːvə] s. Schulabgänger (-in); **~ leav·ing cer·tif·i·cate** s. Abgangszeugnis n; '**~·ma'am** [-mæm] s. Am. für **schoolmarm**; '**~·man** [-mən] s. [irr.] 1. Päda'goge m; 2. hist. Scho'lastiker m; '**~·marm** [-mɑːm] F 1. Lehrerin f; 2. fig. contp. Schulmeisterin f; '**~,mas·ter** s. 1. Schulleiter m; 2. Lehrer m; 3. fig. contp. Schulmeister m; '**~,mas·ter·ly** adj. schulmeisterlich; '**~·mate** s. 'Schulkame,rad(in); '**~,mis·tress** s. 1. Schulleiterin f; 2. Lehrerin f; **~ re·port** s. Schulzeugnis n; '**~·room** [-rʊm] s. Klassenzimmer n; **~ ship** ⚓ Schulschiff n; **~ tie** s.: old **~** Brit. a) Krawatte f mit den Farben e-r Public School, b) Spitzname für e-n ehemaligen Schüler e-r Public School, c) sentimentale Bindung an die alte Schule, d) der Einfluss der Public Schools auf das öffentliche Leben in England, e) contp. Cliquenwirtschaft f unter ehemaligen Schülern e-r Public School, f) contp. arrogantes Gehabe solcher Schüler; **~ u·ni·form** s. (einheitliche) Schulkleidung; '**~·work** s. (in der Schule zu erledigende) Aufgaben pl.; '**~·yard** s. Am. Schulhof m.

schoon·er ['skuːnə] s. 1. ⚓ Schoner m; 2. bsd. Am. → **prairie schooner**; 3. großes Bierglas.

schorl [ʃɔːl] s. min. Schörl m, (schwarzer) Turma'lin.

schot·tische [ʃɒ'tiːʃ] s. ♪ Schottische(r) m (a. Tanz).

schuss [ʃʊs] (Ger.) Skisport: I s. Schuss (-fahrt f) m; II v/i. Schuss fahren.

schwa [ʃwɑː] s. ling. Schwa n: a) kurzer Vokal von unbestimmter Klangfarbe, b) das phonetische Symbol ə.

sci·a·gram ['skaɪəɡræm], '**sci·a·graph** [-ɡrɑːf] s. ✴ Röntgenbild n; **sci·ag·ra·phy** [skaɪ'æɡrəfɪ] s. 1. ✴ Herstellung f von Röntgenaufnahmen; 2. Schattenmale'rei f, Schattenriss m.

sci·at·ic [saɪ'ætɪk] adj. ✴ 1. Ischias...; 2. an Ischias leidend; **sci·at·i·ca** [-kə] s. ✴ Ischias f.

sci·ence ['saɪəns] s. 1. Wissenschaft f: **man of ~** Wissenschaftler m; **~ park** Technologiezentrum n; 2. a. natural **~** coll. die Na'turwissenschaft(en pl.); 3. fig. Lehre f, Kunde f: **~ of gardening** Gartenbaukunst f; 4. phls., eccl. Erkenntnis f (of von); 5. Kunst (-fertigkeit) f, (gute) Technik (a. sport); 6. 2 → **Christian Science**; **~ fic·tion** s. 'Science-'Fiction f.

sci·en·ter [saɪ'entə] (Lat.) ⚖ adv. wissentlich.

sci·en·tif·ic [saɪən'tɪfɪk] adj. (□ **~ally**) 1. (engS. na'tur)wissenschaftlich; 2. wissenschaftlich, ex'akt, syste'matisch; 3. fig. sport etc. kunstgerecht; **sci·en·tist** ['saɪəntɪst] s. (Na'tur)Wissenschaftler m.

sci-fi [,saɪ'faɪ] F für **science fiction**.

scil·i·cet ['saɪlɪset] adv. (abbr. **scil.** od. **sc.**) nämlich, d. h. (das heißt).

scim·i·tar, **scim·i·ter** ['sɪmɪtə] s. (orien'talischer) Krummsäbel.

scin·til·la [sɪn'tɪlə] s. bsd. fig. Fünkchen

---

n: **not a ~ of truth**; **scin·til·lant** ['sɪntɪlənt] adj. funkelnd, schillernd; **scin·til·late** ['sɪntɪleɪt] I v/i. 1. Funken sprühen; 2. funkeln (a. fig. Augen), sprühen (a. fig. Geist, Witz); II v/t. 3. Funken, fig. Geistesblitze (ver)sprühen; **scin·til·la·tion** [,sɪntɪ'leɪʃn] s. 1. Funkensprühen n, Funkeln n; 2. Schillern n; 3. fig. Geistesblitz m.

sci·o·lism ['saɪəʊlɪzəm] s. Halbwissen n; '**sci·o·list** [-lɪst] s. Halbgebildete(r) m, -wisser m.

sci·on ['saɪən] s. 1. ♣ Ableger m, Steckling m, (Pfropf)Reis n; 2. fig. Spross m, Sprössling m.

scir·rhous ['sɪrəs] adj. ✴ szir'rhös, hart geschwollen; '**scir·rhus** [-rəs] pl. **-rhus·es** s. ✴ Szirrhus m, harte Krebsgeschwulst.

scis·sor ['sɪzə] v/t. 1. (mit der Schere) (zer-, zu-, aus)schneiden; 2. scherenartig bewegen etc.; **~ kick** s. Fußball, Schwimmen: Scherenschlag m.

scis·sors ['sɪzəz] s. pl. 1. a. pair of **~** Schere f; 2. sg. konstr. sport (Hochsprung: a. **~ jump**, Ringen: a. **~ hold**) Schere f.

scis·sure ['sɪʒə] s. bsd. ✴ Fis'sur f, Riss m.

scle·ra ['sklɪərə] s. anat. Sklera f, Lederhaut f des Auges.

scle·ro·ma [,sklɪ'rəʊmə] pl. **-ma·ta** [-mətə] s. ✴ Skle'rom n, Verhärtung f; ,**scle·ro·sis** [-'rəʊsɪs] pl. **-ro·ses** [-siːz] s. 1. ✴ Skle'rose f, Verhärtung f (des Zellgewebes); 2. ♣ Verhärtung f (der Zellwand); **scle·rot·ic** [-'rɒtɪk] I adj. ✴, anat. skle'rotisch; fig. verkalkt; II s. anat. → **sclera**; **scle·rous** ['sklɪərəs] adj. ✴ skle'rös, verhärtet.

scoff [skɒf] I s. 1. Spott m, Hohn m; 2. Zielscheibe f des Spotts; II v/i. 3. spotten (**at** über acc.); '**scoff·er** [-fə] s. Spötter(in).

scold [skəʊld] I v/t. j-n (aus)schelten, auszanken; II s. zänkisches Weib, (Haus)Drachen m; '**scold·ing** [-dɪŋ] s. 1. Schelten n; 2. Schelte f: **get a (good) ~** (tüchtig) ausgeschimpft werden.

scol·lop ['skɒləp] → **scallop**.

sconce¹ [skɒns] s. 1. (Wand-, Kla'vier-) Leuchter m; 2. Kerzenhalter m.

sconce² [skɒns] s. ✕ Schanze f.

sconce³ [skɒns] univ. I v/t. zu e-r Strafe verdonnern; II s. Strafe f.

sconce⁴ [skɒns] s. sl. ,Birne' f, Schädel m.

scone [skɒn] s. weiches Teegebäck.

scoop [skuːp] I s. 1. a) Schöpfkelle f, (a. Wasser)Schöpfer m, b) (a. Zucker- etc.) Schaufel f, Schippe f, c) ⚙ Baggereimer m, -löffel m; 2. (Äpfel-, Käse-)Stecher m; 3. ✴ Spatel m; 4. (Aus)Schöpfen n; 5. Schub m: **in one ~** mit 'einem Schub; 6. sport Schlenzer m; 7. sl. a) ,Schnitt' m, (großer) Fang m, b) Zeitung: sensatio'nelle Erstmeldung, Exklu'sivbericht m, ,Knüller' m; II v/t. 8. schöpfen, schaufeln: **~ out water** Wasser ausschöpfen; **~ up** (auf)schaufeln, fig. Geld scheffeln; 9. mst **~ out** Loch (aus)graben; 10. oft **~ in** sl. Gewinn einstecken, Geld scheffeln; 11. sl. Konkurrenzzeitung durch e-e Erstmeldung ausstechen, j-m zu'vorkommen (**on** bei, mit).

scoot [skuːt] F v/t. 1. rasen, flitzen, ,abhauen'; '**scoot·er** [-tə] s. 1. (Kinder-, a. Motor)Roller m; 2. sport Am. Eisjacht f.

scope [skəʊp] s. 1. Bereich m, Gebiet n; ⚖ Anwendungsbereich m; Reichweite f: **within the ~ of** im Rahmen

---

(gen.); **come within the ~ of** unter ein Gesetz etc. fallen; **an undertaking of wide ~** ein groß angelegtes Unternehmen; 2. Ausmaß n, 'Umfang m: **~ of authority** ⚖ Vollmachtsumfang; 3. (Spiel)Raum m, Bewegungsfreiheit f: **give one's fancy full ~** s-r Fantasie freien Lauf lassen; **have free ~** freie Hand haben (**for** bei); 4. (geistiger) Hori'zont, Gesichtskreis m.

scor·bu·tic [skɔː'bjuːtɪk] ✴ I adj. (□ **~ally**) 1. skor'butisch, Skorbut...; II s. 2. Skor'butkranke(r m) f.

scorch [skɔːtʃ] I v/t. 1. versengen, -brennen; **~ed earth** ✕ verbrannte Erde; 2. (aus)dörren; 3. ⚡ verschmoren; 4. fig. (durch scharfe Kri'tik od. beißenden Spott) verletzen; II v/i. 5. versengt werden; 6. ausdörren; 7. F mot. etc. rasen; '**scorch·er** [-tʃə] s. F et. sehr Heißes, bsd. glühend heißer Tag; 2. sl. ,Ding' n: a) beißende Bemerkung, b) scharfe Kri'tik, c) böser Brief, d) ,tolle' Sache; 3. F mot. ,Raser' m; 4. sport sl. a) ,Bombenschuss' m, b) knallharter Schlag; '**scorch·ing** [-tʃɪŋ] adj. □ 1. sengend, brennend (heiß); 2. vernichtend (Kritik etc.).

score [skɔː] I s. 1. Kerbe f, Rille f; 2. (Markierungs)Linie f, sport Start-, Ziellinie f: **get off at full ~** a) losrasen, b) fig. außer sich geraten; 3. Zeche f, Rechnung f: **run up a ~** Schulden machen; **settle old ~s** fig. e-e alte Rechnung begleichen; **on the ~ of** fig. aufgrund von, wegen; **on that ~** in dieser Hinsicht; **on what ~?** aus welchem Grund?; 4. bsd. sport a) (Spiel)Stand m, b) erzielte Punkt- od. Trefferzahl, (Spiel)Ergebnis n, (Be)Wertung f, c) Punktliste f: **know the ~** F Bescheid wissen; **make a ~ off s.o.** F fig. j-m ,eins auswischen'; **what is the ~?** a) wie steht das Spiel?, b) fig. Am. wie ist die Lage?; **~ one for me!** humor. eins zu null für mich!; 5. (Satz m von) 20, 20 Stück: **four ~ and seven years** 87 Jahre; 6. pl. große (An)Zahl f, Menge f: **~s of times** fig. hundert-, x-mal; 7. ♪ Parti'tur f; II v/t. 8. einkerben; 9. markieren: **~ out** aus-, durchstreichen; 10. oft **~ up** Schulden, Zechen anschreiben, -rechnen: **~ (up) s.th. against** (od. **to**) **s.o.** fig. j-m et. ankreiden; 11. ped. psych. j-s Leistung etc. bewerten; 12. sport a) Punkte, Treffer erzielen, sammeln, Tore schießen, fig. Erfolge, Sieg verzeichnen, erringen, b) Punkte, Spielstand etc. aufschreiben: **~ a hit** a) e-n Treffer erzielen, b) fig. e-n Bombenerfolg haben; **~ s.o.** off F fig. j-m ,eins auswischen'; 13. sport zählen: **a try ~s 6 points**; 14. ♪ a) in Parti'tur setzen, b) instrumentieren; 15. Am. fig. scharf kritisieren od. angreifen; III v/i. 16. sport a) e-n Punkt od. Treffer erzielen, Punkte sammeln, b) die Punkte zählen od. aufschreiben; 17. F Erfolg od. Glück haben, e-n Vorteil erzielen: **~ over** j-n, et. übertreffen; 18. zählen, gezählt werden: **that ~s for us**; '**~·board** s. Anzeigetafel f im Stadion etc.; '**~·card** s. sport 1. Spielberichtsbogen m; 2. Boxen etc.: Punktzettel m; Golf: Zählkarte f.

score·less ['skɔːlɪs] adj. sport torlos; '**score·line** s. Brit. sport Endstand m; '**scor·er** s. sport a) Schreiber m, b) Torschütze m.

sco·ri·a ['skɔːrɪə] pl. **-ri·ae** [-riː] s. (⚙ Me'tall-, geol. Gesteins)Schlacke f; **sco·ri·a·ceous** [,skɔːrɪ'eɪʃəs] adj. schlackig; '**sco·ri·fy** [-ɪfaɪ] v/t. verschlacken.

scorn [skɔːn] **I** s. **1.** Verachtung f: *think ~ of* verachten; **2.** Spott m, Hohn m: *laugh to ~* verlachen; **3.** Zielscheibe f des Spottes, *das* Gespött (*der Leute etc.*); **II** v/t. **4.** verachten: a) gering schätzen, b) verschmähen; **'scorn·ful** [-fʊl] adj. □ **1.** verächtlich; **2.** spöttisch.

Scor·pi·o ['skɔːpɪəʊ] s. ast. Skorpi'on m; **'scor·pi·on** [-pjən] s. zo. Skorpi'on m.

Scot[1] [skɒt] s. Schotte m, Schottin f.

scot[2] [skɒt] s. **1.** (Zahlungs)Beitrag m: *pay (for) one's ~s* s-n Beitrag leisten; **2.** a. *~ and lot* hist. Gemeindeabgabe f: *pay ~ and lot* fig. alles auf Heller u. Pfennig bezahlen.

Scotch [skɒtʃ] **I** adj. **1.** schottisch (*bsd. Whisky etc.*): *~ broth* dicke Rindfleischsuppe mit Gemüse u. Graupen; *~ egg* hart gekochtes Ei in paniertem Wurstbrät; *~ mist* dichter, nasser Nebel; *~ tape TM* (durchsichtiges) Klebeband, (durchsichtiger) Klebestreifen; *~ terrier* Scotchterrier m; *~ woodcock* heißer Toast mit Anchovispaste u. Rührei; **II** s. **2.** Scotch m, schottischer Whisky; **3.** *the ~ coll.* die Schotten pl.; **4.** ling. Schottisch n.

scotch [skɒtʃ] **I** v/t. **1.** (leicht) verwunden, schrammen; **2.** fig. et. im Keim ersticken: *~ s.o.'s plans* j-m e-n Strich durch die Rechnung machen; **3.** Rad etc. mit e-m Bremsklotz blockieren; **II** s. **4.** (Ein)Schnitt m, Kerbe f; **5.** ⊙ Bremsklotz m, Hemmschuh m (a. fig.).

'Scotch·man [-mən] s. [irr.] → **Scotsman**.

,scot-'free [,skɒt-] adj.: *go (od. get off) ~ fig.* ungeschoren davonkommen.

Scot·land Yard ['skɒtlənd] s. Scotland Yard m (*die Londoner Kriminalpolizei*).

Scots [skɒts] **I** s. ling. Schottisch n; **II** adj. schottisch: *~ law;* **'~·man** [-mən] s. [irr.] bsd. Scot. Schotte m; **'~·wom·an** s. [irr.] bsd. Scot. Schottin f.

Scot·ti·cism ['skɒtɪsɪzəm] s. schottische (Sprach)Eigenheit.

Scot·tish ['skɒtɪʃ] adj. schottisch.

scoun·drel ['skaʊndrəl] s. Schurke m, Schuft m, Ha'lunke m; **'scoun·drel·ly** [-rəlɪ] adj. schurkisch, niederträchtig, gemein.

scour[1] ['skaʊə] v/t. **1.** scheuern, schrubben; Messer etc. polieren; **2.** Kleider etc. säubern, reinigen; **3.** Kanal etc. schlämmen, Rohr etc. (aus)spülen; **4.** Pferd etc. putzen, striegeln; **5.** ⊙ Wolle waschen: *~ing mill* Wollwäscherei f; **6.** Darm entschlacken; **7.** a. *~ away, ~ off* Flecken etc. entfernen, Schmutz abreiben.

scour[2] ['skaʊə] **I** v/i. **1.** a. *~ about* (um'her)rennen, (-)jagen; **2.** (suchend) um'herstreifen; **II** v/t. durch'suchen, -'stöbern, Gegend a. -'kämmen, Stadt a. ,abklappern' (*for* nach).

scourge [skɜːdʒ] **I** s. **1.** Geißel f: a) Peitsche f, b) fig. Plage f; **II** v/t. **2.** geißeln, (aus)peitschen; **3.** fig. a) durch Kritik etc. geißeln, b) züchtigen, c) quälen, peinigen.

scouse[1] [skaʊs] s. Labskaus n.

Scouse[2] [skaʊs] s. Brit. F s. **1.** Liverpooler(in); **2.** Liverpooler Jar'gon m.

scout [skaʊt] s. **1.** Kundschafter m, Späher m; **2.** ✕ a) Erkundungsfahrzeug n: *~ car* Spähwagen m, b) ⚓ a. *~ vessel* Aufklärungsfahrzeug n, c) ✈ a. *(air)plane* Aufklärer m; **3.** Kundschaften n; ✕ Erkundung f: *on the ~* auf Erkundung; **4.** Pfadfinder m, Am.

Pfadfinderin f; **5.** *a good ~* F ein feiner Kerl; **6.** univ. Brit. Hausdiener m e-s College (Oxford); **7.** mot. Brit. Straßenwachtfahrer m (Automobilklub); **8.** a) sport ,Späher', Beobachter m (gegnerischer Mannschaften), b) a. *tal·ent ~* Ta'lentsucher m; **II** v/i. **9.** auf Erkundung sein: *~ about (od. around)* sich umsehen (*for* nach); *~ing party* ✕ Spähtrupp m; **III** v/t. **10.** auskundschaften, erkunden; **'~·mas·ter** s. Führer m (e-r Pfadfindergruppe).

scow [skaʊ] s. ⚓ (See)Leichter m.

scowl [skaʊl] **I** v/i. finster blicken: *~ at* finster anblicken; **II** s. finsterer Blick od. (Gesichts)Ausdruck; **'scowl·ing** [-lɪŋ] adj. □ finster.

scrab·ble ['skræbl] **I** v/i. **1.** kratzen, scharren: *~ about* bsd. fig. (herum)suchen (*for* nach); **2.** fig. sich (ab)plagen (*for* für, um); **3.** krabbeln; **4.** kritzeln; **II** v/t. **5.** scharren nach; **6.** bekritzeln.

scrag [skræg] **I** s. **1.** fig. ,Gerippe' n (dürrer Mensch etc.); **2.** mst *~ end (of mutton)* (Hammel)Hals m; **3.** F ,Kragen' m, Hals m; **II** v/t. **4.** sl. a) j-n ,abmurksen', j-m den Hals 'umdrehen; b) j-n aufhängen; **'scrag·gi·ness** [-gɪnɪs] s. Magerkeit f; **'scrag·gy** [-gɪ] adj. □ **1.** dürr, hager, knorrig; **2.** zerklüftet, rau.

scram [skræm] v/i. sl. ,abhauen', verduften: *~! hau ab!, raus!*

scram·ble ['skræmbl] **I** v/i. **1.** krabbeln, klettern: *~ to one's feet* sich aufrappeln; **2.** a. fig. sich raufen od. balgen (*for* um): *~ for a living* sich (um s-n Lebensunterhalt) ,abstrampeln'; **II** v/t. **3.** oft *~ up, ~ together* zs.-scharren, -raffen; **4.** ✄ Funkspruch etc. zerhacken; **5.** Eier verrühren: *~d eggs* Rührei n; **6.** Karten etc. durchein'ander werfen; Flugplan etc. durchein'ander bringen; **III** s. **7.** Krabbe'lei f, Klette'rei f; **8.** a. fig. (for) Balge'rei f (um), Jagd f (nach Geld etc.); **9.** Brit. Moto'crossrennen n; **10.** ✈ a) A'larmstart m, b) Luftkampf m; **'scram·bler** [-lə] s. tel. Zerhacker m.

scrap[1] [skræp] **I** s. **1.** Stück(chen) n, Brocken m, Fetzen m, Schnitzel n, m: *a ~ of paper* ein Fetzen Papier (a. fig.); *not a ~* kein bisschen; **2.** pl. Abfall m, (bsd. Speise)Reste pl.; **3.** (Zeitungs-)Ausschnitt m; ausgeschnittenes Bild etc. zum Einkleben; **4.** mst pl. fig. Bruchstück n, (Gesprächs- etc.)Fetzen m: *~s of conversation;* **5.** mst pl. (Fett)Grieben pl.; **6.** ⊙ a) Schrott m, b) Ausschuss m, c) Abfall m: *~ value* Schrottwert m; **II** v/t. **7.** (als unbrauchbar) ausrangieren; **8.** fig. zum alten Eisen od. über Bord werfen: *~ methods;* **9.** ⊙ verschrotten.

scrap[2] [skræp] sl. **I** s. **1.** Streit m, Ausein'andersetzung f; **2.** Keile'rei f, Prüge'lei f; **3.** (Box)Kampf m; **II** v/i. **4.** streiten; **5.** sich prügeln; kämpfen (*with* mit).

'scrap·book s. Sammelalbum n, Einklebebuch n.

scrape [skreɪp] **I** s. **1.** Kratzen n, Scharren n; **2.** Kratzer m, Schramme f; **3.** obs. Kratzfuß m; **4.** fig. ,Klemme' f: *be in a ~* in der Klemme sein od. sitzen; **5.** *bread and ~* F dünn geschmiertes Butterbrot; **II** v/t. **6.** kratzen, schaben: *~ off* ab-, wegkratzen, *~ together (od. up)* a. fig. Geld etc. zs.-kratzen; *~ (an) acquaintance with* a) oberflächlich bekannt werden mit, b) contp. sich bei j-m anbiedern; *~ a living →* 11; **7.** kratzen od. scharren mit den

Füßen etc.; **III** v/i. **8.** kratzen, schaben, scharren; **9.** scheuern, sich reiben (*against* an dat.); **10.** kratzen (*on* auf e-r Geige etc.); **11.** mst *~ along* fig. sich (mühsam) 'durchschlagen: *~ through (an examination)* mit Ach u. Krach durchkommen (durch e-e Prüfung); **'scrap·er** [-pə] s. **1.** Fußabstreifer m; **2.** ⊙ a) Schaber m, Kratzer m, Streichmesser n, b) ⚒ etc. Schrapper m, c) Planierpflug m.

scrap heap s. Abfall-, Schrotthaufen m: *fit only for the ~* völlig wertlos; *throw on the ~ fig.* j-n zum alten Eisen werfen.

scrap·ing ['skreɪpɪŋ] s. **1.** Kratzen n etc.; **2.** pl. (Ab)Schabsel pl., Späne pl.; **3.** pl. fig. contp. Abschaum m.

scrap| i·ron s., *~ met·al* s. ⊙ (Eisen-)Schrott m, Alteisen n.

scrap·per ['skræpə] s. sl. Raufbold m.

scrap·py[1] ['skræpɪ] adj. □ sl. rauflustig.

scrap·py[2] ['skræpɪ] adj. □ **1.** aus (Speise)Resten (hergestellt): *~ dinner;* **2.** bruchstückhaft; **3.** zs.-gestoppelt.

'scrap·yard s. Schrottplatz m.

scratch [skrætʃ] **I** s. **1.** Kratzer m, Schramme f (beide a. fig. leichte Verwundung), Riss m; **2.** Kratzen n (a. Geräusch): *by the ~ of a pen* mit 'einem Federstrich; **3.** sport a) Startlinie f, b) nor'male Startbedingungen pl.: *come up to (the) ~* a) sich stellen, s-n Mann stehen, b) den Erwartungen entsprechen; *keep s.o. up to (the) ~* j-n bei der Stange halten; *start from ~* a) ohne Vorgabe starten, b) fig. ganz von vorne anfangen; *up to ~* auf der Höhe, in Form; **4.** pl. mst sg. konstr. vet. Mauke f; **II** adj. **5.** Konzept..., Schmier...: *~ paper, ~ pad* a) Notizblock m, b) Computer: Notizblockspeicher m; **6.** sport a) ohne Vorgabe: *~ race,* b) zs.-gewürfelt: *~ team;* **III** v/t. **7.** (zer)kratzen: *~ the surface of fig. et.* (nur) oberflächlich behandeln; **8.** kratzen; Tier kraulen: *~ one's head* sich (aus Verlegenheit etc.) den Kopf kratzen; *~ together (od. up)* bsd. fig. zs.-kratzen, -scharren; **9.** kritzeln; **10.** a. *~ out, ~ through* aus-, 'durchstreichen; **11.** sport Pferd etc. vom Rennen, a. Nennung zu'rückziehen; **12.** pol. Kandidaten streichen; **IV** v/i. **13.** kratzen (a. Schreibfeder etc.); **14.** sich kratzen od. scheuern; **15.** scharren (*for* nach); **16.** *~ along, ~ through → scrape* 11; **17.** sport s-e Meldung zu'rückziehen, ausscheiden; *~ card* s. Rubbelkarte f, -los n; **'scratch·y** [-tʃɪ] adj. □ **1.** kratzend; **2.** zerkratzt; **3.** kritzelig; **4.** sport a) → scratch 6, b) unausgeglichen; **5.** vet. an Mauke erkrankt.

scrawl [skrɔːl] **I** v/t. kritzeln, hinschmieren; **II** v/i. kritzeln; **III** s. Gekritzel n; Geschreibsel n.

scray [skreɪ] s. Brit. Seeschwalbe f.

scream [skriːm] **I** s. **1.** (gellender) Schrei; **2.** Gekreisch(e) n: *~s of laughter* brüllendes Gelächter; *he (it) was a (perfect) ~ sl.* er (es) war zum Schreien (komisch); **3.** Heulen n (Sirene etc.); **II** v/i. **4.** schreien (a. fig. Farben etc.), gellen; kreischen: *~ out* aufschreien; *~ with laughter* vor Lachen brüllen; **5.** heulen (Wind etc.), schrill pfeifen; **III** v/t. **6.** oft *~ out* (her'aus)schreien; **'scream·er** [-mə] s. **1.** Schreiende(r m) f; **2.** sl. a) ,tolle Sache', b) bsd. Am. F Riesenschlagzeile f; **'scream·ing** [-mɪŋ] adj. □ **1.** schrill, gellend; **2.** fig. schreiend, grell: *~ colo(u)rs;* **3.** F a)

,toll', großartig, b) *a.* *~ly funny* zum Schreien (komisch).

scree [skri:] *s. geol. Brit.* **1.** Geröll *n*; **2.** Geröllhalde *f.*

screech [skri:tʃ] **I** *v/i.* (gellend) schreien; kreischen (*a. weitS.* Bremsen *etc.*); **II** *v/t. et.* kreischen; **III** *s.* ('durchdringender) Schrei; **~ owl** *s. orn.* Schreiende Eule, Käuzchen *n.*

screed [skri:d] *s.* **1.** lange Liste; **2.** langatmige Rede *etc.*, Ti'rade *f.*

screen [skri:n] **I** *s.* **1.** (Schutz)Schirm *m*, (-)Wand *f*; **2.** △ a) Zwischenwand *f*, b) *eccl.* Lettner *m*; **3.** a) (Film)Leinwand *f*, b) *coll.* **the ~** der Film, das Kino: **~ star** Filmstar *m*; **on the ~** im Film; **4.** a) *TV*, *Radar*, *Computer:* Bildschirm *m*, b) ⚡ Röntgenschirm *m*: **~ flicker** Bildschirmflimmern *n*; **5.** Drahtgitter *n*, -netz *n*; **6.** Fliegenfenster *n*; **7.** ⊛ Gittersieb *n für Sand etc.*; **8.** ✕ a) *taktische* Abschirmung, (⚓ Geleit-) Schutz *m*, b) (Rauch-, Schützen-) Schleier *m*, Nebelwand *f*, c) Tarnung *f*; **9.** *fig.* a) Schutzwand *f*, b) Tarnung *f*, Maske *f*; **10.** *phys.* a) *a.* **optical ~** Filter *m*, Blende *f*, b) *a.* **electric ~** Abschirmung *f*, c) *a.* **ground ~** Erdungsebene *f*; **11.** *phot.*, *typ.* Raster (-platte *f*) *m*; **12.** *mot.* Windschutzscheibe *f*; **II** *v/i.* **13.** *a.* **~ off** abschirmen, verdecken; *Licht* abblenden; **14.** (be-) schirmen (*from* vor *dat.*); **15.** *fig. j-n* decken; **16.** ✕ a) tarnen (*a. fig.*), b) einnebeln; **17.** ⊛ *Sand etc.* ('durch)sieben: **~ed coal** Würfelkohle *f*; **18.** *phot.* Bild projizieren; **19.** *Film:* a) verfilmen, b) für den Film bearbeiten; **20.** *fig. Personen* (aus)sieben, (über-) 'prüfen; **III** *v/i.* **21.** sich (ver)filmen lassen; sich für den Film eignen (*a. Person*); **~ grid** *s.* ⚡ Schirmgitter *n*; **~ junk·ie** *s.* F Com'putersüchtige(r *m*) *f*, Bildschirm-Junkie *m*; **'~·land** [-lənd] *s. Am.* Filmwelt *f*; **'~·play** *s. Film:* Drehbuch *n*; **'~·print** *s.* **I.** Siebdruck *m*; **II** *v/t.* im Siebdruckverfahren herstellen; **~ sav·er** *s. Computer:* Bildschirmschoner *m*; **~ test** *s. Film:* Probeaufnahme *f*; **'~-test** *v/t. Film:* Probeaufnahmen machen von; **~ wash·er** *s. mot.* Scheibenwaschanlage *f*; **~ wire** *s.* ⊛ Maschendraht *m*; **'~·writ·er** *s.* Drehbuchautor(in).

screw [skru:] **I** *s.* **1.** ⊛ Schraube *f* (*ohne Mutter*): **there is a ~ loose** (*somewhere*) *fig.* da stimmt et. nicht; **he has a ~ loose** F bei ihm ist e-e Schraube locker; **2.** ⊛ Spindel *f* (*Presse*); **3.** (Flugzeug-, Schiffs)Schraube *f*; **4.** ⚓ Schraubendampfer *m*; **5.** F *fig.* Druck *m*: **apply the ~ to**, **put the ~(s) on** *j-n* unter Druck setzen; **give another turn to the ~** *a. fig.* die Schraube anziehen; **6.** *Brit.* Tütchen *n Tabak etc.*; **7.** *bsd.* *sport* Ef'fet *m*; **8.** *Brit.* Geizhals *m*; **9.** *Brit.* alter Klepper (*Pferd*) **10.** *Brit. sl.* Lohn *m*, Gehalt *n*; **11.** Korkenzieher *m*; **12.** *sl.* Gefängniswärter *m*; **13.** V ,Nummer' *f*: **have a ~** ,bumsen'; **be a good ~** gut ,bumsen'; **II** *v/t.* **14.** schrauben: **~ down** ein-, festschrauben; **~ on** an-, aufschrauben; **~ up** a) zuschrauben, b) *Papier* zerknüllen; **his head is ~ed on the right way** F er ist nicht auf den Kopf gefallen; **15.** *fig.* Augen, Körper *etc.* (ver)drehen; *Mund etc.* verziehen; **16.** **~ down** (**up**) ✝ *Preise* her'unterschrauben (hoch schrauben); **~ s.th. out of** et. aus *j-m* herauspressen; **~ up one's courage** Mut fassen; **17.** *sport* dem *Ball* Ef'fet geben; **18.** F *j-n* ,reinlegen'; **19.** **~ up** F ,vermasseln'; **20.** V

,bumsen', ,vögeln': **~ you!**, **get ~ed** *bsd. Am.* geh zum Teufel!; **III** *v/i.* **21.** sich (ein)schrauben lassen; **22.** knausern; **23.** V ,bumsen', ,vögeln'; **24.** **~ around** *Am. sl.* sich he'rumtreiben.

'screw|·ball *Am.* **I** *s.* **1.** *Baseball:* Ef'fetball *m*; **2.** *sl.* ,Spinner' *m*; **II** *adj.* **3.** *sl.* verrückt; **~ bolt** *s.* ⊛ Schraubenbolzen *m*; **~ cap** *s.* Schraubdeckel *m*, Verschlusskappe *f*; **2.** 'Überwurfmutter *f*; **con·vey·er** *s.* Förderschnecke *f*; **~ die** *s.* Gewindeschneideisen *n*; **'~·driv·er** *s.* Schraubenzieher *m*.

screw·ed [skru:d] *adj.* **1.** verschraubt; **2.** mit Gewinde; **3.** verdreht, gewunden; **4.** F ,besoffen'.

screw| gear(·**ing**) *s.* ⊛ **1.** Schneckenrad *n*; **2.** Schneckengetriebe *n*; **~ jack** *s.* **1.** Hebespindel *f*; **2.** Wagenheber *m*; **~ nut** *s.* Mutterschraube *f*; **~ press** *s.* Spindel- *od.* Schraubenpresse *f*; **~ steam·er** → **screw** 4; **~ tap** *s.* ⊛ Gewindebohrer *m*; **~ top** *s.* Schraubverschluss *m*; **~ wrench** *s.* ⊛ Schraubenschlüssel *m*.

screw·y ['skru:ɪ] *adj.* **1.** schraubenartig; **2.** F ,beschwipst'; **3.** *Am. sl.* verrückt; **4.** knickerig.

scrib·ble ['skrɪbl] **I** *v/t.* **1.** *a.* **~ down** (hin)kritzeln, (-)schmieren: **~ over** bekritzeln; **2.** ⊛ *Wolle* krempeln; **II** *v/i.* **3.** kritzeln; **III** *s.* **4.** Gekritzel *n*, Geschreibsel *n*; **'scrib·bler** [-lə] *s.* **1.** Kritzler *m*, Schmierer *m*; **2.** Schreiberling *m*; **3.** ⊛ 'Krempelma,schine *f.*

scrib·bling| block, **~ pad** ['skrɪblɪŋ] *s. Brit.* Schmier-, No'tizblock *m.*

scribe [skraɪb] **I** *s.* **1.** Schreiber *m* (*a. hist.*), Ko'pist *m*; **2.** *bibl.* Schriftgelehrte(r) *m*; **3.** *humor.* a) Schriftsteller *m*, b) Journa'list *m*; **4.** *a.* **~ awl** Reißnadel *f*; **II** *v/t.* **5.** ⊛ anreißen; **'scrib·er** [-bə] → **scribe** 4.

scrim [skrɪm] *s.* leichter Leinen- *od.* Baumwollstoff.

scrim·mage ['skrɪmɪdʒ] *s.* **1.** Handgemenge *n*, Getümmel *n*; **2.** a) *American Football:* Scrimmage *n* (*Rückpass*), b) *Rugby:* Gedränge *n.*

scrimp [skrɪmp] **I** *v/t.* **1.** knausern mit, knapp bemessen; **2.** *j-n* knapp halten (*for* mit); **II** *v/i.* **3.** *a.* **~ and save** knausern (**on** mit); **III** *adj.* **4.** → **'scrimp·y** [-pɪ] knapp, eng.

'scrim·shank *v/i. bsd.* ✕ *Brit. sl.* sich drücken.

scrip[1] [skrɪp] *s. hist.* (Pilger-, Schäfer-) Tasche *f*, Ränzel *n.*

scrip[2] [skrɪp] *s.* **1.** ✝ a) Berechtigungsschein *m*, b) Scrip *m*, Interimsschein *m*, -aktie *f*, *coll.* die Scrips *pl. etc.*; **2.** *a.* **~ money** a) Er'satzpa,piergeldwährung *f*, b) ✕ Besatzungsgeld *n.*

script [skrɪpt] *s.* **1.** Handschrift *f*; **2.** Schrift(art) *f*, *phonetic* ~ Lautschrift; **3.** *typ.* (Schreib)Schrift *f*; **4.** a) Text *m*, b) *thea. etc.* Manu'skript *n*, c) *Film:* Drehbuch *n*; **5.** ✍ Urschrift *f*; **6.** *ped. Brit.* (schriftliche) Prüfungsarbeit; **~ ed·i·tor** *s. Film*, *thea.*, *TV:* Drama'turg *m*; **~ girl** *s. Film:* Scriptgirl *n* (*Ateliersekretärin*).

scrip·tur·al ['skrɪptʃərəl] *adj.* **1.** Schrift...; **2.** *a.* ⳨ biblisch, der Heiligen Schrift; **scrip·ture** ['skrɪptʃə] *s.* **1.** ⳨, *mst* **the ⳨s** die Heilige Schrift, die Bibel; **2.** *obs.* ⳨ Bibelstelle *f*; **3.** heilige (nichtchristliche) Schrift: **Buddhist** ~; **4.** *a.* **~ class** (*od.* **lesson**) *ped.* Religi'onsstunde *f.*

'script,writ·er *s.* **1.** *Film*, *TV:* Drehbuchautor(in). **2.** *Radio:* Hörspielautor(in).

scriv·ener ['skrɪvnə] *s. hist.* **1.** (öffentlicher) Schreiber; **2.** No'tar *m.*

scrof·u·la ['skrɒfjʊlə] *s.* ✽ Skrofu'lose *f*; **'scrof·u·lous** [-ləs] *adj.* □ ✽ skrofu'lös.

scroll [skrəʊl] **I** *s.* **1.** Schriftrolle *f*; **2.** a) △ Vo'lute *f*, b) ♪ Schnecke *f*, c) Schnörkel *m* (*Schrift*); **3.** Liste *f*, Verzeichnis *n*; **4.** ⊛ Triebkranz *m*; **5.** *Computer:* Scrollen *n*, ,Blättern' *n*; **II** *v/i. Computer:* scrollen, ,blättern'; **~ chuck** *s.* ⊛ Univer'salspannfutter *n*; **~ gear** *s.* ⊛ Schneckenrad *n*; **~ saw** *s.* ⊛ Laubsäge *f*; **'~·work** *s.* **1.** Schneckenverzierung *f*; **2.** Laubsägearbeit *f.*

scro·tum ['skrəʊtəm] *pl.* **-ta** [-tə] *s. anat.* Hodensack *m*, Skrotum *n.*

scrounge [skraʊndʒ] F **I** *v/t.* **1.** ,organisieren': a) ,klauen', b) beschaffen; **2.** schnorren; **II** *v/i.* **3.** ,klauen'; **4.** schnorren, nassauern; **'scroung·er** [-dʒə] *s.* F **1.** Dieb *m*; **2.** Schnorrer *m*, Nassauer *m.*

scrub[1] [skrʌb] **I** *v/t.* **1.** schrubben, scheuern; **2.** ⊛ *Gas* reinigen; **3.** F *fig.* streichen, ausfallen lassen; **II** *v/i.* **4.** schrubben, scheuern; **III** *s.* **5.** Schrubben *n*: **that wants a good ~** das muss tüchtig gescheuert werden; **6.** *sport* a) Re'servespieler *m*, b) *a.* **~ team** zweite Mannschaft *od.* ,Garni'tur', c) *a.* **~ game** Spiel *n* der Re'servemannschaften.

scrub[2] [skrʌb] *s.* **1.** Gestrüpp *n*, Buschwerk *n*; **2.** Busch *m* (*Gebiet*); **3.** a) verkümmerter Baum, b) Tier *n* minderwertiger Abstammung, c) Knirps *m*, d) *fig. contp.* ,Null' *f* (*Person*).

'scrub(·bing) brush ['skrʌbɪŋ] *s.* Scheuerbürste *f.*

scrub·by ['skrʌbɪ] *adj.* **1.** verkümmert, -krüppelt; **2.** gestrüppreich; **3.** armselig, schäbig; **4.** stopp(e)lig.

scruff [skrʌf], **~ of the neck** *s.* Genick *n*: **take s.o. by the ~ of the neck** *j-n* beim Kragen packen.

scruff·y ['skrʌfɪ] *adj.* F schmudd(e)lig, dreckig.

scrum·mage ['skrʌmɪdʒ] → **scrimmage.**

scrump·tious ['skrʌmpʃəs] *adj.* F ,toll', ,prima'.

scrunch [skrʌntʃ] **I** *v/t.* **1.** knirschend (zer)kauen; **2.** zermalmen; **II** *v/i.* **3.** knirschen; **4.** knirschend kauen; **III** *s.* **5.** Knirschen *n.*

scru·ple ['skru:pl] **I** *s.* **1.** Skrupel *m*, Zweifel *m*, Bedenken *n* (*alle mst pl.*): **have ~s about doing** Bedenken haben, *et.* zu tun; **without ~** skrupellos; **2.** *pharm.* Skrupel *n* (= 20 Gran *od.* 1,296 Gramm); **II** *v/i.* **3.** Skrupel *od.* Bedenken haben; **'scru·pu·lous** [-pjʊləs] *adj.* □ **1.** voller Skrupel *od.* Bedenken, (allzu) bedenklich (**about** in *dat.*); **2.** ('über)gewissenhaft, peinlich (genau); **3.** ängstlich, vorsichtig.

scru·ti·neer [,skru:tɪ'nɪə] *s. pol.* Wahlprüfer *m*; **scru·ti·nize** ['skru:tɪnaɪz] *v/t.* **1.** (genau) prüfen, unter'suchen; **2.** genau ansehen, studieren; **scru·ti·ny** ['skru:tɪnɪ] *s.* **1.** (genaue) Unter'suchung, *pol.* Wahlprüfung *f*; **2.** prüfender *od.* forschender Blick.

scu·ba ['sku:bə] *s.* (Schwimm)Tauchgerät *n*: **~ diving** Sporttauchen *n.*

scud [skʌd] **I** *v/i.* **1.** eilen, jagen; **2.** ⚓ lenzen; **II** *s.* **3.** (Da'hin)Jagen *n*; **4.** (tief treibende) Wolkenfetzen *pl.*; **5.** (Wind)Bö *f.*

scuff [skʌf] **I** *v/i.* **1.** schlurfen(d gehen); **2.** ab-, aufscharren; **II** *v/t.* **3.** *bsd. Am.* abstoßen, abnutzen; **4.** boxen.

scuf·fle ['skʌfl] **I** *v/i.* **1.** sich balgen, raufen; **2.** → *scuff* 1; **II** *s.* **3.** Balge'rei *f*, Raufe'rei *f*, Handgemenge *n*; **4.** Schlurfen *n*.

scull [skʌl] ♣ **I** *s.* **1.** Heck-, Wriggriemen *m*; **2.** Skullboot *n*; **II** *v/i. u. v/t.* **3.** wriggen; **4.** skullen; **'scul·ler** [-lə] *s.* **1.** Skuller *m* (*Ruderer*); **2.** → *scull* 2.

scul·ler·y ['skʌlərɪ] *s.* Brit. Spülküche *f*: ~ **maid** Spül-, Küchenmädchen *n*; **'scul·lion** [-ljən] *s.* hist. Brit. Küchenjunge *m*.

sculp(t) [skʌlp(t)] F *für sculpture* II u. III.

sculp·tor ['skʌlptə] *s.* Bildhauer *m*; **'sculp·tress** [-trɪs] *s.* Bildhauerin *f*; **'sculp·tur·al** [-tʃərəl] *adj.* □ bildhauerisch, Skulptur...; **'sculp·ture** [-tʃə] **I** *s.* Plastik *f*: a) Bildhauerkunst *f*, b) Skulp'tur *f*, Bildhauerwerk *n*; **II** *v/t.* formen, (her'aus)meißeln *od.* (-)schnitzen; **III** *v/i.* bildhauern.

scum [skʌm] **I** *s.* (℗ *u. fig.* Ab)Schaum *m*: *the ~ of the earth fig.* der Abschaum der Menschheit; **II** *v/t. u. v/i.* abschäumen.

scum·ble ['skʌmbl] *paint.* **I** *v/t.* **1.** Farben, Umrisse vertreiben, dämpfen; **II** *s.* **2.** Gedämpftheit *f*; **3.** La'sur *f*.

scum·my ['skʌmɪ] *adj.* **1.** schaumig; **2.** *fig.* gemein, ,fies'.

scup·per ['skʌpə] **I** *s.* **1.** ♣ Speigatt *n*; **II** *v/t.* ✕ Brit. sl. **2.** niedermetzeln; **3.** *Schiff* versenken; **4.** *fig.* ka'puttmachen.

scurf [skɜːf] *s.* **1.** ✿ a) Schorf *m*, Grind *m*, b) *bsd.* Brit. (Kopf)Schuppen *pl.*; **2.** abblätternde Kruste; **'scurf·y** [-fɪ] *adj.* schorfig, grindig, schuppig.

scur·ril·i·ty [skʌ'rɪlətɪ] *s.* **1.** zotige Scherzhaftigkeit; **2.** Zotigkeit *f*; **3.** Zote *f*; **scur·ril·ous** ['skʌrɪləs] *adj.* □ **1.** ordi'när-scherzhaft, ,frech'; **2.** unflätig, zotig.

scur·ry ['skʌrɪ] **I** *v/i.* **1.** huschen, hasten; **II** *s.* **2.** Hasten *n*; Getrippel *n*; **3.** *sport* a) Sprint *m*, b) Pferdesport: Fliegerrennen *n*; **4.** Schneetreiben *n*.

scur·vy ['skɜːvɪ] **I** *s.* ✿ Skor'but *m*; **II** *adj.* (hunds)gemein, ,fies'.

scut [skʌt] *s.* **1.** *hunt.* Blume *f*, kurzer Schwanz (*Hase*), Wedel *m* (*Rotwild*); **2.** Stutzschwanz *m*.

scu·tage ['skjuːtɪdʒ] *s.* ✕ hist. Schildpfennig *m*, Rittersteuer *f*.

scutch [skʌtʃ] ℗ **I** *v/t.* **1.** *Flachs* schwingen; **2.** *Baumwolle od. Seidenfäden* (durch Schlagen) entwirren; **II** *s.* **3.** (Flachs)Schwingmesser *n*, ('Flachs-) ,Schwingma,schine *f*.

scutch·eon ['skʌtʃən] *s.* **1.** → *escutcheon*; **2.** → *scute*.

scute [skjuːt] *s. zo.* Schuppe *f*.

scu·tel·late(d) ['skjuːtəleɪt(ɪd)] *adj. zo.* schuppig; **scu'tel·lum** [skjuː'teləm] *pl.* **-la** [-lə] *s.* ♀, *zo.* Schildchen *n*.

scut·tle¹ ['skʌtl] *s.* **1.** Kohlenkasten *m*, -eimer *m*; **2.** (flacher) Korb.

scut·tle² ['skʌtl] **I** *v/i.* **1.** hasten, flitzen; **2.** ~ *out of* ✕ *u. fig.* sich hastig zu'rückziehen aus *od.* von; **II** *s.* **3.** hastiger Rückzug.

scut·tle³ ['skʌtl] **I** *s.* **1.** (Dach-, Boden-) Luke *f*; **2.** ♣ (Spring)Luke *f*; **3.** *mot.* Stirnwand *f*, Spritzbrett *n*; **II** *v/t.* **4.** ♣ a) *Schiff* anbohren *od.* die 'Bodenven,tile öffnen, b) (selbst) versenken; **'~·butt** *s.* **1.** ♣ Trinkwassertonne *f od.* -anlage *f*; **2.** *Am.* F Gerücht *n*.

scythe [saɪð] **I** *s.* Sense *f*; **II** *v/t.* **2.** (ab)mähen; **3.** ~ *down* Fußball: ,umsäbeln'.

sea [siː] *s.* **1.** a) See *f*, Meer *n* (*a. fig.*), b) Ozean *m*, Weltmeer *n*: *at ~* auf *od.*

zur See; *mst all at ~ fig.* ratlos, im Dunkeln tappend; *beyond the ~, over ~(s)* nach *od.* in Übersee; *by ~* auf dem Seeweg; *on the ~* a) auf *od.* zur See, b) an der See *od.* Küste (gelegen); *follow the ~* zur See fahren; *put (out) to ~* in See stechen; *the four ~s* die vier (*Großbritannien umgebenden*) Meere; *the high ~s* die hohe See, die Hochsee; **2.** ♣ See(gang *m*) *f*: *heavy ~, long (short) ~* lange (kurze) See; **3.** ♣ See *f*, hohe Welle; → *ship* 7; ~ **an·chor** *s.* **1.** ♣ Treibanker *m*; **2.** ✈ Wasseranker *m*; ~ **bear** *s.* *zo.* **1.** Eisbär *m*; **2.** Seebär *m*; **'~·board I** *s.* (See)Küste *f*; **II** *adj.* Küsten...; **'~·born** *adj.* **1.** aus dem Meer stammend; **2.** *poet.* meergeboren; **'~·borne** *adj.* auf dem Seewege befördert, See...: ~ *goods* Seehandelsgüter; ~ *invasion* ✕ Landungsunternehmen *n* von See aus; ~ *trade* Seehandel *m*; **calf** *s.* [*irr.*] → *sea dog* 1 a; ~ **cap·tain** *s.* ('Schiffs)Kapi,tän *m*; ~ **cock** *s.* ♣ 'Bordven,til *n*; ~ **cow** *s. zo.* **1.** Seekuh *f*, Si'rene *f*; **2.** Walross *n*; ~ **dog** *s.* **1.** *zo.* a) Gemeiner Seehund, Meerkalb *n*, b) → *dogfish*; **2.** *fig.* ♣ (alter) Seebär; **'~·drome** [-drəʊm] *s.* ✈ Wasserflughafen *m*; ~ **el·e·phant** *s. zo.* 'See-Ele,fant *m*; '~·far·er [-,feərə] *s.* Seefahrer *m*, -mann *m*; '~·far·ing [-,feərɪŋ] **I** *adj.* seefahrend: ~ *man* Seemann *m*; ~ *nation* Seefahrernation *f*; **II** *s.* Seefahrt *f*; ~ **farm·ing** *s.* 'Aquakul,tur *f*; '~·food *s.* Meeresfrüchte *pl.*; '~·fowl *s.* Seevogel *m*; ~ **front** *s.* Seeseite *f* (*e-r Stadt etc.*); ~ **ga(u)ge** *s.* ♣ **1.** Tiefgang *m*; **2.** Lotstock *m*; '~·girt *adj. poet.* 'meerum,schlungen; ~ **god** *s.* Meeresgott *m*; '~·go·ing *adj.* ♣ seetüchtig, Hochsee...; ~ **green** *s.* Meergrün *n*; ~ **gull** *s. orn.* Seemöwe *f*; ~ **hog** *s. zo.* Schweinswal *m*, *bsd.* Meerschwein *n*; ~ **horse** *s.* **1.** *zo.* a) Seepferdchen *n*, b) Walross *n*; **2.** *myth.* Seepferd *n*; **3.** große Welle.

seal¹ [siːl] *s.* **1.** *pl.* **seals**, *bsd. coll.* **seal** *zo.* Robbe *f*, *engS.* Seehund *m*; **2.** → *sealskin*; **II** *v/i.* **3.** auf Robbenjagd gehen.

seal² [siːl] **I** *s.* **1.** Siegel *n*: *set one's ~ to* sein Siegel auf *et.* drücken, *bsd. fig. et.* besiegeln (*bekräftigen*); *under the ~ of secrecy fig.* unter dem Siegel der Verschwiegenheit; **2.** Siegel(prägung *f*) *n*; **3.** Siegel(stempel *m*) *n*, Petschaft *n*; → *Great Seal*; **4.** ⚖ *etc.* Siegel *n*, Verschluss *m*; *Zollverkehr etc.*: Plombe *f*: *under* ~ unter Verschluss; **5.** ℗ a) (wasser-, luftdichter) Verschluss, b) (Ab-) Dichtung *f*, c) Versiegelung *f* (*Kunststoff etc.*); **6.** *fig.* Siegel *n*, Besiegelung *f*, Bekräftigung *f*; **7.** Zeichen *n*, Garan'tie *f*; **8.** *fig.* Stempel *m*, Zeichen *n* des Todes *etc.*; **II** *v/t.* **9.** Urkunde siegeln; **10.** *Rechtsgeschäft etc.* besiegeln (*bekräftigen*); **11.** *fig.* besiegeln: *his fate is ~ed*; **12.** *fig.* zeichnen, s-n Stempel aufdrücken (*dat.*); **13.** versiegeln: *~ed offer* ✝ versiegeltes Angebot; *under ~ed orders* ♣ mit versiegelter Order; **14.** *Verschluss etc.* plombieren; **15.** *oft* ~ *up* her'metisch (*od.* ℗ wasser-, vaku'umdicht) abschließen *od.* abdichten, *Holz, Kunststoff etc.* versiegeln, ℗ a) einzementieren, zuschmelzen, *mit Klebestreifen etc.* verschließen: *it is a ~ed book to me fig.* es ist mir ein Buch mit sieben Siegeln; ~ *a letter* e-n Brief zukleben; **16.** ~ *off fig.* a) ✕ *etc.* abriegeln, b) dichtmachen; ~ *off the border*.

sea lane *s.* See-, Schifffahrtsweg *m*.

seal·ant ['siːlənt] *s.* ℗ Dichtungsmittel *n*.

sea| law·yer *s.* ♣ F Queru'lant *m*; ~ **legs** *s. pl.*: *get od. find one's ~* ♣ seefest werden.

seal·er¹ ['siːlə] *s.* ♣ Robbenfänger *m* (*Mann od. Schiff*).

seal·er² ['siːlə] *s.* ℗ a) Versiegler *m*, b) Verschlussvorrichtung *f*, c) Versiegelungsmasse *f*.

'seal·er·y [-ərɪ] *s.* **1.** Robbenfang *m*; **2.** Robbenfangplatz *m*.

sea lev·el *s.* Meeresspiegel *m*, -höhe *f*: *corrected to ~* auf Meereshöhe umgerechnet.

seal fish·er·y → *sealery* 1.

seal·ing ['siːlɪŋ] *s.* **1.** (Be)Siegeln *n*; **2.** Versiegeln *n*, ℗ *a.* (Ab)Dichtung *f*: ~ (*compound*) Dichtungsmasse *f*; ~ *machine* → *sealer²* b; ~ *ring* Dichtungsring *m*; ~ *wax* *s.* Siegellack *m*.

sea| li·on *s. zo.* Seelöwe *m*; **♀ Lord** *s.* ♣ Brit. Seelord *m* (*Amtsleiter in der brit. Admiralität*).

seal| rook·er·y *s. zo.* Brutplatz *m* von Robben; **'~·skin** *s.* **1.** Seal(skin) *m*, *n*, Seehundsfell *n*; **2.** Sealmantel *m*, -cape *n*.

seam [siːm] **I** *s.* **1.** Saum *m*, Naht *f* (*a.* ✈): *burst at the ~s* aus den Nähten platzen (*a. fig.*); **2.** ℗ a) (Guss-, Schweiß)Naht *f*: ~ *welding* Nahtschweißen *n*, b) *bsd.* ♣ Fuge *f*, c) Sprung *m*, d) Falz *m*; **3.** Runzel *f*; **4.** Narbe *f*; **5.** *geol.* (Nutz)Schicht *f*, Flöz *n*; **II** *v/t.* **6.** *a.* ~ *up*, *together* zs.-nähen; **7.** säumen; **8.** *bsd. fig.* (durch-) 'furchen; **9.** (zer)schrammen; **10.** ℗ durch e-e (Guss- *od.* Schweiß)Naht verbinden.

sea·man ['siːmən] *s.* [*irr.*] ♣ **1.** Seemann *m*, Ma'trose *m*; **2.** ✕ *Am.* (Ma'rine)Obergefreite(r) *m*: ~ *recruit* Matrose *m*; **'sea·man·like** *adj. u. adv.* seemännisch; **'sea·man·ship** [-ʃɪp] *s.* Seemannschaft *f*.

sea| mark *s.* Seezeichen *n*; ~ **mew** *s. orn.* Sturmmöwe *f*; ~ **mile** *s.* Seemeile *f*; ~ **mine** *s.* ✕ Seemine *f*.

seam·less ['siːmlɪs] *adj.* □ **1.** naht-, saumlos: ~ *drawn tube* ℗ nahtlos gezogene Röhre; **2.** fugenlos.

sea mon·ster *s.* Meeresungeheuer *n*.

seam·stress ['semstrɪs] *s.* Näherin *f*.

sea mud *s.* Seeschlamm *m*, Schlick *m*.

seam·y ['siːmɪ] *adj.* gesäumt: *the ~ side* a) die linke Seite, b) *fig.* die Kehr- *od.* Schattenseite.

se·ance, sé·ance ['seɪɑ̃ːns] (*Fr.*) *s.* Sé'ance *f*, (spiri'tistische) Sitzung.

'sea·piece *s. paint.* Seestück *n*; '~·plane *s.* See-, Wasserflugzeug *n*; '~·port *s.* Seehafen *m*, Hafenstadt *f*; ~ **pow·er** *s.* Seemacht *f*; '~·quake *s.* Seebeben *n*.

sear¹ [sɪə] **I** *v/t.* **1.** versengen; **2.** ✿ (aus-) brennen; **3.** *Fleisch* anbraten; **4.** *bsd. fig.* brandmarken; **5.** *fig.* abstumpfen: *a ~ed conscience*; **6.** verdorren lassen; **II** *v/i.* **7.** verdorren; **III** *adj.* **8.** *poet.* verdorrt, -welkt: *the ~ and yellow leaf fig.* der Herbst des Lebens.

sear² [sɪə] *s.* ✕ Abzugsstollen *m* (*Gewehr*).

search [sɜːtʃ] **I** *v/t.* **1.** durch'suchen, -'stöbern (*for* nach); **2.** ⚖ Person, Haus *etc.* durch'suchen, visitieren; **3.** unter'suchen; **4.** *fig.* Gewissen *etc.* erforschen, prüfen; **5.** *mst* ~ *out* auskundschaften, ausfindig machen; **6.** durch'dringen (*Wind, Geschosse etc.*); **7.** ✕ mit Tiefenfeuer belegen *od.* bestreichen; **8.** *sl.* ~ *me!* keine Ahnung!; **II** *v/i.* **9.** (*for*) suchen, forschen (nach); ⚖ fahnden (nach): ~ *into* ergründen, untersuchen; **10.** ~ *after* streben nach; **III** *s.* **11.** Suchen *n*, Forschen *n* (*for*, *of* nach): *in* ~ *of* auf der Suche nach; *go in* ~ *of* auf die Suche gehen nach; **12.** ⚎ a) Fahndung *f*, b) Haussuchung *f*, c) ('Leibes)Visitati,on *f*, d) Einsichtnahme *f in öffentliche Bücher*, e) Überprüfung *f*, *Patentwesen*: Re'cherche *f*: *right of* (*visit and*) ~ ⚓ Recht *n* auf Durchsuchung neutraler Schiffe; **search en-gine** *s. Internet*: 'Suchma,schine *f*; **'search·er** [-tʃə] *s.* **1.** Sucher *m*, (Er-)Forscher *m*; **2.** (*Zoll- etc.*)Prüfer *m*; **3.** ⚹ Sonde *f*; **search func·tion** *s. Computer*: 'Suchfunkti,on *f*; **'search·ing** [-tʃɪŋ] *adj.* □ **1.** gründlich, eingehend, tief schürfend; **2.** forschend (*Blick*): durch'dringend (*Wind etc.*): ~ *fire* ✕ Tiefen-, Streufeuer *n*.

'search·light *s.* (Such)Scheinwerfer *m*; ~ **op·er·a·tion** *s. Computer*: Suchlauf *m*; ~ **par·ty** *s.* Suchtrupp *m*; ~ **ra·dar** *s.* ✕ Ra'darsuchgerät *n*; ~ **war·rant** *s.* ⚎ Haussuchungsbefehl *m*; ~ **word** *s. Computer*: Suchwort *n*.

'sea|-,res·cue *adj.* Seenot...; ~ **risk** *s.* ⚎ Seegefahr *f*; ~ **room** *s.* ⚓ Seeräume *f*; ~ **route** *s.* See-, Schifffahrtsweg *m*; **'~·scape** *s.* **1.** *paint.* Seestück *n*; **2.** (Aus)Blick *m* auf das Meer; ~ **ser·pent** *s. zo. u. myth.* Seeschlange *f*; **'~·shore** *s.* Seeküste *f*; **'~·sick** *adj.* seekrank; **'~·sick·ness** *s.* Seekrankheit *f*; **'~·side** **I** *s.* See-, Meeresküste *f*: *go to the* ~ an die See fahren; **II** *adj.* an der See gelegen, See...: ~ *place*, ~ *resort* Seebad *n*.

sea·son ['siːzn] **I** *s.* **1.** (Jahres)Zeit *f*; **2.** a) (Reife- *etc.*)Zeit *f*, rechte Zeit (*für et.*), b) *hunt.* (Paarungs- *etc.*)Zeit *f*: *in* ~ a) (gerade) reif, (günstig auf dem Markt) zu haben (*Frucht*), b) zur rechten Zeit, c) *hunt.* jagdbar, d) brünstig (*Tier*): *out of* ~ a) nicht (auf dem Markt) zu haben, b) *fig.* unpassend; *in and out of* ~ jederzeit; *cherries are now in* ~ jetzt ist Kirschenzeit; *a word in* ~ ein Rat zur rechten Zeit; *for a* ~ e-e Zeit lang; → *close season*; **3.** ✝ Sai'son *f*, Haupt(betriebs-, -geschäfts)zeit *f*: *dull* (*od. slack*) ~ stille Saison, tote Jahreszeit; *height of the* ~ Hochsaison; **4.** (*Veranstaltungs*)Sai'son *f*: *theatrical* ~ Theatersaison, Spielzeit *f*; **5.** (*Bade-, Kur- etc.*)Sai'son *f*: *holiday* ~ Ferienzeit *f*; **6.** Festzeit *f*; → *compliment* 3; **7.** F → *season ticket*; **II** *v/t.* **8.** Speisen würzen (*a. fig.*): *~ed with wit* geistreich; **9.** *Tabak etc.* (aus)reifen lassen: *~ed wine* abgelagerter *od.* ausgereifter Wein; **10.** *Holz* ablagern; **11.** *Pfeife* einrauchen; **12.** gewöhnen (*to an acc.*), abhärten: *be ~ed to* an *ein Klima etc.* gewöhnt sein; *~ed soldiers* fronterfahrene Soldaten; *~ed by battle* kampfgewohnt; **13.** *obs.* mildern; **III** *v/i.* **14.** reifen; **15.** ablagern (*Holz*); **'sea·son·a·ble** [-nəbl] *adj.* □ **1.** rechtzeitig; **2.** jahreszeitlich; **3.** zeitgemäß; **4.** passend, angebracht, oppor'tun, günstig; **'sea·son·al** [-zənl] *adj.* □ **1.** jahreszeitlich; **2.** sai'sonbedingt, -gemäß: ~ *closing-out sale* ✝ Saisonschlussverkauf *m*; ~ *trade* Saisongewerbe *n*; ~ *unemployment* saisonbedingte Arbeitslosigkeit; ~ *work(er)* Saisonarbeit(er *m*) *f*; **sea·son·al·ly** [-nəlɪ] *adv.*: ~ *adjusted* saisonbereinigt; **'sea·son·ing** [-nɪŋ] *s.* Würze *f* (*a. fig.*), Gewürz *n*; **2.** Reifen *n etc.*; **sea·son tick·et** *s.* **1.** ❊ *etc. Brit.* Dauer-, Zeitkarte *f*; **2.** *thea. etc.* Abonne'ment(skarte *f*) *n*.

seat [siːt] **I** *s.* **1.** Sitz(gelegenheit *f*,

-platz *m*) *m*; Stuhl *m*, Sessel *m*, Bank *f*; **2.** (*Stuhl- etc.*)Sitz *m*; **3.** Platz *m bei Tisch etc.*: *take a* ~ Platz nehmen; *take one's* ~ s-n Platz einnehmen; *take your ~s!* ❊ einsteigen!; **4.** *thea. etc.* Platz *m*, Sitz *m*: *book a* ~ e-e (*Theateretc.*)Karte kaufen; **5.** (*Präsi'denten- etc.*) Sitz *m* (*a. fig. Amt*); **6.** (Amts-, Regierungs-, ✝ Geschäfts)Sitz *m*; **7.** *parl. etc.* Sitz *m* (*a. Mitgliedschaft*), *parl. a.* Man'dat *n*: *a* ~ *in parliament*; *have* ~ *and vote* Sitz u. Stimme haben; **8.** Wohn-, Fa'milien-, Landsitz *m*; **9.** *fig.* Sitz *m*: a) Stätte *f*, (Schau)Platz *m*: ~ *of war* Kriegsschauplatz, b) ⚹ Herd *m* e-r Krankheit (*a. fig.*); **10.** Gesäß *n*, Sitzfläche *f*; Hosenboden *m*; **11.** *Reitsport etc.*: Sitz *m* (*Haltung*); **12.** ❊ Auflager *n*, Funda'ment *n*; **II** *v/t.* **13.** *j-n wohin* setzen, *j-m* e-n Sitz anweisen: ~ *o.s.* sich setzen; **14.** Sitzplätze bieten für: *the hall ~s 600 persons*; **15.** Raum bestuhlen, mit Sitzplätzen versehen; **16.** *Stuhl* mit e-m (neuen) Sitz versehen; **17.** ❊ a) auflegen, lagern (*on* auf *dat.*), b) einpassen, *Ventil* einschleifen; **18.** *pass.* sitzen, s-n Sitz haben, liegen (*in* in *dat.*); **seat belt** *s.* ✈, *mot.* Sicherheitsgurt *m*: ~ *tensioner* Gurtstraffer *m*; **'seat·ed** [-tɪd] *adj.* **1.** sitzend: *be* ~ → *seat* 18; *be ~!* nehmen Sie Platz!; *remain* ~ sitzen bleiben, Platz behalten; **2.** *in Zssgn* ...sitzig: *two-~*; **'seat·er** [-tə] *s. in Zssgn* ...sitzer *m*: *two-~*; **'seat·ing** [-tɪŋ] **I** *s.* **1.** a) Anweisen *n* von Sitzplätzen, b) Platznehmen *n*; **2.** Sitzgelegenheit(en *pl.*) *f*, Bestuhlung *f*; **II** *adj.* **3.** Sitz...: ~ *accommodation* Sitzgelegenheiten; **seat mile** *s.* ⚓ Passa'giermeile *f*.

sea| trout *s.* 'Meer-, 'Lachsfo,relle *f*; ~ **ur·chin** *s. zo.* Seeigel *m*; **'~·wall** *s.* Deich *m*; (Hafen)Damm *m*.

sea·ward ['siːwəd] **I** *adj. u. adv.* seewärts; **II** *s.* Seeseite *f*; **'sea·wards** [-dz] *adv.* seewärts.

sea| wa·ter *s.* See-, Meerwasser *n*; **'~·way** *s.* **1.** ⚓ Fahrt *f*; **2.** Seeweg *m*; **3.** Seegang *m*; **'~·weed** *s.* **1.** (See)Tang *m*, Alge *f*; **2.** *allg.* Meerespflanze(n *pl.*) *f*; **'~·wor·thy** *adj.* seetüchtig.

se·ba·ceous [sɪ'beɪʃəs] *adj. physiol.* Talg...

sec [sek] (*Fr.*) *adj.* sec, trocken (*Wein*).

se·cant ['siːkənt] **I** *s.* ⅄ a) Se'kante *f*, b) Schnittlinie *f*; **II** *adj.* schneidend.

sec·a·teur ['sekətɜː] (*Fr.*) *s. mst* (*a pair of*) ~*s pl.* (e-e) Baumschere.

se·cede [sɪ'siːd] *v/i. bsd. eccl., pol.* sich trennen *od.* lossagen, abfallen (*from* von); **se'ced·er** [-də] *s.* Abtrünnige(r *m*) *f*, Separa'tist *m*.

se·ces·sion [sɪ'seʃn] *s.* **1.** Sezessi'on *f* (*USA hist. oft* ⚎), (Ab-, *eccl.* Kirchen-)Spaltung *f*, Abfall *m*, Lossagung *f*; **2.** 'Übertritt *m* (*to zu*); **se'ces·sion·al** [-ʃənl] *adj.* Sonderbunds..., Abfall..., Sezessions...; **se'ces·sion·ist** [-nɪst] *s.* Abtrünnige(r *m*) *f*, Sonderbündler *m*, Sezessio'nist *m* (*Am. hist. oft* ⚎).

se·clude [sɪ'kluːd] *v/t.* (*o.s.* sich) abschließen, absondern (*from* von); **se'clud·ed** [-dɪd] *adj.* □ einsam, abgeschieden: a) zu'rückgezogen (*Lebensweise*), b) abgelegen (*Ort*); **se'clu·sion** [-uːʒn] *s.* **1.** Abschließung *f*; **2.** Zu'rückgezogenheit *f*, Abgeschiedenheit *f*: *live in* ~ zurückgezogen leben.

sec·ond ['sekənd] **I** *adj.* □ → *second-ly*: **1.** zweit; nächst: ~ *Advent* (*od. Coming*) *eccl.* Wiederkunft *f* (Christi); ~ *ballot* Stichwahl *f*; ~ *Chamber parl.* Oberhaus *m*; ~ *floor* a) *Brit.* zweiter

Stock, b) *Am.* erster Stock (*über dem Erdgeschoss*); ~ *home* Zweitwohnung *f*; ~ *in height* zweithöchst; *at* ~ *hand* aus zweiter Hand; *in the* ~ *place* zweitens; *it has become* ~ *nature with him* es ist ihm zur zweiten Natur geworden *od.* in Fleisch u. Blut übergegangen; → *self* 1, *sight* 1, *thought* 3, *wind*[1] 6; **2.** (*to*) 'untergeordnet (*dat.*), geringer (als): ~ *cabin* ⚓ Kabine *f* zweiter Klasse; ~ *cousin* Vetter *m* zweiten Grades; ~ *lieutenant* ✕ Leutnant *m*; *come* ~ *fig.* an zweiter Stelle kommen; ~ *to none* unerreicht; *he is* ~ *to none* er ist unübertroffen; → *fiddle* 1; **II** *s.* **3.** der (die, das) Zweite: ~ *in command* ✕ a) stellvertretender Kommandeur, b) ⚓ erster Offizier; ~ *Zweite(r *m*) *f*, zweiter Sieger: *run* ~ den zweiten Platz belegen; *be a good* ~ nur knapp geschlagen werden; **5.** *univ.* → *second class* 2; **6.** F ❊ *etc.* zweite Klasse; **7.** *Duell, Boxen*: Sekun'dant *m*; *fig.* Beistand *m*; **8.** Se'kunde *f*; *weitS. a.* Augenblick *m*, Mo'ment *m*; **9.** ♩ a) Se'kunde *f*, b) Begleitstimme *f*; **10.** *pl.* ✝ Ware(n *pl.*) *f* zweiter Quali'tät *od.* Wahl; **11.** ~ *of exchange* ✝ Se'kundawechsel *m*; **III** *v/t.* **12.** sekundieren (*dat.*) (*a. fig.*); **13.** *fig.* unter'stützen (*a. parl.*), beistehen (*dat.*); **14.** [sɪ'kɒnd] ✕ *Brit. Offizier* abstellen, abkommandieren.

sec·ond·ar·i·ness ['sekəndərɪnɪs] *s.* das Sekun'däre, Zweitrangigkeit *f*; **sec·ond·ar·y** ['sekəndərɪ] **I** *adj.* □ **1.** se-kun'där, zweitrangig, 'untergeordnet, nebensächlich: *of* ~ *importance*; **2.** ⚡, ⚫, *biol., geol., phys.* sekun'där, Sekun-där...; ~ *electron*; **3.** Neben...: ~ *col-o(u)r*; ~ *effect*; **4.** Neben..., Hilfs...: ~ *line* ❊ Nebenbahn; **5.** *ling.* a) sekun'där, abgeleitet, b) Neben...: ~ *accent* Nebenakzent *m*; ~ *derivative* Sekun-därableitung *f*; ~ *tense* Nebentempus *n*; **6.** *ped.* Oberschul...: ~ *education* höhere Schulbildung; ~ *school* höhere Schule; **II** *s.* **7.** 'Untergeordnete(r *m*) *f*, Stellvertreter(in); **8.** ⚡ a) Sekun'där-(strom)kreis *m*, b) Sekun'därwicklung *f*; **9.** *ast. a.* ~ *planet* Satel'lit *m*; **10.** *orn.* Nebenfeder *f*.

'sec·ond|-best *adj.* zweitbest: *come off* ~ *fig.* den Kürzeren ziehen; ~ *class* *s.* F ❊ *etc.* zweite Klasse; **2.** *univ. Brit.* akademischer Grad zweiter Klasse; **|~-'class** [-nd'k-] *adj.* **1.** zweitklassig, -rangig; **2.** ❊ *etc.* Wagen *etc.* zweiter Klasse: ~ *mail* a) *Am.* Zeitungspost *f*, b) *Brit.* gewöhnliche Inlandspost; **|~-de'gree** *adv.* **1.** zweiten Grades: ~ *burns*; **2.** ~ *murder* ⚎ Totschlag *m*; **|~-'guess** *v/t. Am.* **1.** *im* Nachhinein kritisieren; **2.** a) durch'schauen, b) vor'hersehen; **'~·hand I** *adj.* **1.** über'nommen, *a. Wissen etc.* aus zweiter Hand; **2.** 'indi,rekt: ~ *smoking* passives Rauchen; **3.** gebraucht, alt; anti'quarisch (*Bücher*): ~ *bookshop* Antiquariat *n*; ~ *car* Gebrauchtwagen *m*; ~ *dealer* Altwarenhändler *m*; ~ *shop* Secondhandshop *m*, -laden *m*; **II** *adv.* **4.** gebraucht: *buy s.th.* ~; ~ *hand s.* Se-'kundenzeiger *m*.

sec·ond·ly ['sekəndlɪ] *adv.* zweitens.

se·cond·ment [sɪ'kɒndmənt] *s. Brit.* **1.** ✕ Abkommandierung *f*; **2.** Versetzung *f*.

|sec·ond|-'rate *adj.* zweitrangig, -klassig, mittelmäßig; **|~-'rat·er** *s.* mittelmäßige Per'son *od.* Sache.

se·cre·cy ['siːkrəsɪ] *s.* **1.** Verborgenheit *f*; **2.** Heimlichkeit *f*: *in all* ~, *with absolute* ~ ganz im Geheimen, insgeheim;

3. Verschwiegenheit *f*; Geheimhaltung(spflicht) *f*; (*Wahl- etc.*)Geheimnis *n*: **official** ~ Amtsverschwiegenheit *f*; **professional** ~ Berufsgeheimnis *n*, Schweigepflicht *f*; → **swear** 6; **se·cret** ['siːkrɪt] **I** *adj*. □ **1.** geheim, heimlich, Geheim...(*-dienst, -diplomatie, -tür etc.*): ~ **ballot** geheime Wahl; ~ **police** Geheimpolizei *f*; → **keep** 13; **2.** a) verschwiegen, b) verstohlen (*Person*); **3.** verschwiegen (*Ort*); **4.** unerforschlich, verborgen; **II** *s*. **5.** Geheimnis *n* (*from* vor *dat.*): **the** ~ **of success** *fig.* das Geheimnis des Erfolgs, der Schlüssel zum Erfolg; **in** ~ a) heimlich, im Geheimen, b) im Vertrauen; **be in the** ~ (in das Geheimnis) eingeweiht sein; **let s.o. into the** ~ j-n (in das Geheimnis) einweihen; **make no** ~ **of** kein Geheimnis *od.* Hehl aus et. machen.

se·cre·taire [ˌsekrəˈteə] (*Fr.*) *s.* Sekreˈtär *m*, Schreibschrank *m*.

se·cre·tar·i·al [ˌsekrəˈteərɪəl] *adj.* **1.** Sekretärs...: ~ **help** Schreibkraft *f*; **2.** Schreib..., Büro...; **ˌsec·reˈtar·i·at(e)** [-ɪət] *s.* Sekretariʼat *n*.

sec·re·tar·y ['sekrətrɪ] *s.* **1.** Sekreˈtär (-in): ~ **of embassy** Botschaftsrat *m*; **2.** Schriftführer *m*; **✝** a) Geschäftsführer *m*, b) Syndikus *m*; **3.** *pol. Brit.* a) ~ (**of state**) Miˈnister *m*, b) ˈStaatssekre·ˌtär *m*: **☿ of State for Foreign Affairs**, **Foreign ☿** Außenminister *m*; **☿ of State for Home Affairs, Home ☿** Innenminister; **4.** *pol. Am.* Miˈnister *m*: **☿ of Defense** Verteidigungsminister; **☿ of State** a) Außenminister, b) Staatssekreˈtär *m* e-s *Bundesstaats*; **5.** → **secretaire**; ~ **bird** *s. orn.* Sekreˈtär *m*; **☿ Gen·er·al** *pl.* **Sec·re·tar·ies Gen·er·al** *s.* Gene'ralsekretär *m*.

sec·re·tar·y·ship ['sekrətrɪʃɪp] *s.* **1.** Posten *m od.* Amt *n* e-s Sekreˈtärs *etc.*; **2.** Miˈnisteramt *n*.

se·crete [sɪˈkriːt] *v/t.* **1.** *physiol.* absondern, abscheiden; **2.** verbergen (*from* vor *dat.*); **⚖** *Vermögensstücke* beiˈseite schaffen; **se'cre·tion** [-iːʃn] *s.* **1.** *physiol.* a) Sekretiʼon *f*, Absonderung *f*, b) Seˈkret *n*; **2.** Verheimlichung *f*; **se'cre·tive** [-tɪv] *adj.* □ heimlich, verschlossen, geheimnistuerisch: **be** ~ **about** mit *et.* geheim tun; **se'cre·tive·ness** [-tɪvnɪs] *s.* Heimlichtueˈrei *f*; Verschwiegenheit *f*.

'se·cret·ˌmon·ger *s.* Geheimniskrämer(in).

se·cre·to·ry [sɪˈkriːtərɪ] *physiol.* **I** *adj.* sekreˈtorisch, Sekretions...; **II** *s.* sekreˈtorische Drüse.

sect [sekt] *s.* **1.** Sekte *f*; **2.** Religiʼonsgemeinschaft *f*.

sec·tar·i·an [sekˈteərɪən] **I** *adj.* **1.** sekˈtiererisch; **2.** Konfessions...; **II** *s.* **3.** Anhänger(in) e-r Sekte; **4.** Sekˈtierer (-in); **secˈtar·i·an·ism** [-nɪzəm] *s.* Sekˈtierertum *n*.

sec·tion ['sekʃn] **I** *s.* **1.** a) Durchˈschneidung *f*, b) (*a. mikroskopischer*) Schnitt, c) **✝** Sektiʼon *f*, Schnitt; **2.** Ab-, Ausschnitt *m*, Teil *m* (*a. der Bevölkerung etc.*); **3.** Abschnitt *m*, Absatz *m* (*Buch etc.*); **⚖** (*Gesetzes- etc.*)Paraʼgraph *m*; **4.** a) ~ **mark** Paraʼgraph(enzeichen *n*) *m*; **5.** ☿ Teil *m*, *n*; **6.** ✂, ☿ Schnitt(bild *n*) *m*, Querschnitt, Proˈfil *n*: **horizontal** ~ Horizontalschnitt *m*; **7.** ✂ *Am.* a) Streckenabschnitt *m*, b) Abˈteil *n* e-s *Schlafwagens*; **8.** *Am.* Bezirk *m*; **9.** *Am.* ˈLandparˌzelle *f* von e-r Quadˈratmeile; **10.** ✿, *zo.* ˈUntergruppe *f*, **11.** Abˈteilung *f*, Refeˈrat *n* (*Verwaltung*); **12.** ✂ a) *Brit.* Gruppe *f*, b) *Am.*

Halbzug *m*, c) ✈ Halbstaffel *f*, d) 'Stabsabˌteilung *f*; **II** *v/t.* **13.** (ab-, ein-) teilen, unterˈteilen; **14.** e-n Schnitt machen von; **'sec·tion·al** [-ʃənl] *adj.* □ **1.** Schnitt...(*-fläche, -zeichnung etc.*); **2.** Teil...(*-ansicht, -streik etc.*); **3.** zs.-setzbar, montierbar: ~ **furniture** Anbaumöbel *pl.*; **4.** ☿ Profil..., Form... (*-draht, -stahl*); **5.** regioˈnal, *contp.* partikulaˈristisch: ~ **pride** Lokalpatriotismus *m*; **'sec·tion·al·ism** [-nəlɪzəm] *s.* Partikulaˈrismus *m*.

sec·tor ['sektə] *s.* **1.** ✂ (Kreis- *od.* Kugel)Sektor *m*; **2.** ✂, *ast.* Sektor *m* (*a. fig. Bereich*); **3.** ✂ Sektor *m*, Frontabschnitt *m*.

sec·u·lar ['sekjʊlə] **I** *adj.* □ **1.** weltlich: a) diesseitig, b) proˈfan: ~ **music**, c) nicht kirchlich (*Erziehung etc.*): ~ **arm** weltliche Gerichtsbarkeit; **2.** 'freireligiˌös, -denkerisch; **3.** *eccl.* weltgeistlich, Säkular...: ~ **clergy** Weltgeistlichkeit *f*, **4.** säkuˈlar: a) hundertjährlich, b) hundertjährig, c) säkuˈlar; **5.** jahrˈhundertelang; **6.** *ast., phys.* säkuˈlar; **II** *s.* **7.** *R.C.* Weltgeistliche(r) *m*; **'sec·u·lar·ism** [-ərɪzəm] *s.* **1.** Säkulaˈrismus *m* (*a. phls.*), Weltlichkeit *f*; **2.** Antikleriˈkalismus *m*; **sec·u·lar·i·ty** [ˌsekjʊˈlærətɪ] *s.* **1.** Weltlichkeit *f*; **2.** *pl.* weltliche Dinge *pl.*; **sec·u·lar·i·za·tion** [ˌsekjʊləraɪˈzeɪʃn] *s.* **1.** *eccl.* Säkularisierung *f*, **2.** Verweltlichung *f*; **'sec·u·lar·ize** [-əraɪz] *v/t.* **1.** kirchlichem Einfluss entziehen; **2.** *kirchlichen Besitz, a. Ordensgeistliche* säkularisieren; **3.** verweltlichen; *Sonntag etc.* entheiligen; **4.** mit freidenkerischen I'deen durchˈdringen.

sec·un·dine ['sekəndɪn] *s.* **1.** *mst pl.* ✠ Nachgeburt *f*; **2.** ✿ inneres Integuˈment der Samenanlage.

se·cure [sɪˈkjʊə] **I** *adj.* □ **1.** sicher: a) geschützt (*from* vor *dat.*), b) fest (*Grundlage etc.*), c) gesichert (*Existenz*), d) gewiss (*Hoffnung, Sieg etc.*); **2.** ruhig, sorglos: **a** ~ **life**; **II** *v/t.* **3.** sichern, schützen (*from, against* vor *dat.*); **4.** sichern, garantieren (**s.th. to s.o.** *od.* **s.o. s.th.** j-m et.); **5.** sich *et.* sichern *od.* beschaffen; erreichen, erlangen; *Patent, Urteil etc.* erwirken; **6.** ☿ *etc.* sichern, befestigen; *Türe etc.* (fest) (ver)schließen: ~ **by bolts** festschrauben; **7.** *Wertsachen* sicherstellen; **8.** *Verbrecher* festnehmen; **9.** *bsd.* ✠ sicherstellen: a) *et.* sichern (**on, by** durch *Hypothek etc.*), b) j-m Sicherheit bieten: ~ **a creditor**; **10.** ✠ *Ader* abbinden.

se·cu·ri·ty [sɪˈkjʊərətɪ] *s.* **1.** Sicherheit *f* (*Zustand od. Schutz*) (**against, from** vor *dat.*, gegen): ☿ Sicherheit(sabteilung) *f*; **✝** ✂ Werkspolizei *f*; ~ **agency** Sicherheitsdienst *m*; ☿ **Council** *pol.* Sicherheitsrat *m*; ~ **check** Sicherheitsüberprüfung *f*; ~ **clearance** Unbedenklichkeitsbescheinigung *f*; ☿ **Force** Friedenstruppe *f*; → **risk** 2; **2.** (innere) Sicherheit, Sorglosigkeit *f*; **3.** Gewissheit *f*; **4.** a) ✠ Bürge *m*, b) Sicherheit *f*, Bürgschaft *f*, Kautiʼon *f*: ~ **bond** Bürgschaftswechsel *m*; **give** (*od.* **put up, stand**) ~ Bürgschaft leisten, Kautiʼon stellen; **5.** ✠ a) Schuldverschreibung *f*, b) Aktie *f*, c) *pl.* 'Wertpaˌpiere *pl.*: ~ **market** Effektenmarkt *m*; **public securities** Staatspapiere.

se·dan [sɪˈdæn] *s.* **1.** *mot.* Limouˈsine *f*; **2.** *a.* ~ **chair** Sänfte *f*.

se·date [sɪˈdeɪt] *adj.* □ **1.** ruhig, gelassen; **2.** gesetzt, ernst; **se'date·ness** [-nɪs] *s.* **1.** Gelassenheit *f*; **2.** Gesetztheit *f*; **se'da·tion** [-eɪʃn] *s.* **be under** ~

✱ unter dem Einfluss von Beruhigungsmitteln stehen.

sed·a·tive ['sedətɪv] *bsd.* ✱ **I** *adj.* beruhigend; **II** *s.* Beruhigungsmittel *n*.

sed·en·tar·i·ness ['sedntərɪnɪs] *s.* **1.** sitzende Lebensweise; **2.** Sesshaftigkeit *f*; **sed·en·tar·y** ['sedntərɪ] *adj.* □ **1.** sitzend (*Beschäftigung, Statue etc.*): ~ **life** sitzende Lebensweise; **2.** sesshaft: ~ **birds** Standvögel.

sedge [sedʒ] *s.* ✿ **1.** Segge *f*; **2.** *allg.* Riedgras *n*.

sed·i·ment ['sedɪmənt] *s.* Sediˈment *n*: a) (Boden)Satz *m*, Niederschlag *m*, b) *geol.* Schichtgestein *n*; **sed·i·men·ta·ry** [ˌsedɪˈmentərɪ] *adj.* sedimenˈtär, Sediment...; **sed·i·men·ta·tion** [ˌsedɪmenˈteɪʃn] *s.* Sedimentatiʼon *f*: a) Ablagerung *f*, b) *geol.* Schichtbildung *f*; **2.** *a.* **blood** ~ ✱ Blutsenkung *f*: ~ **rate** Senkungsgeschwindigkeit *f*.

se·di·tion [sɪˈdɪʃn] *s.* **1.** Aufwiegelung *f*, *a.* ✠ Volksverhetzung *f*; **2.** Aufruhr *m*; **se'di·tious** [-ʃəs] *adj.* □ aufrührerisch, 'umstürzlerisch, staatsgefährdend.

se·duce [sɪˈdjuːs] *v/t.* **1.** *Frau etc.* verführen (*a. fig. verleiten*, **into, to** zu: **into doing s.th.** dazu, et. zu tun); **2.** ~ **from** j-n von s-r Pflicht *etc.* abbringen; **se'duc·er** [-sə] *s.* Verführer *m*; **se·duc·tion** [sɪˈdʌkʃn] *s.* **1.** (*a. sexuelle*) Verführung; Verlockung *f*; **2.** *fig.* Versuchung *f*, verführerischer Zauber; **se·duc·tive** [sɪˈdʌktɪv] *adj.* □ verführerisch (*a. fig.*).

se·du·li·ty [sɪˈdjuːlətɪ] *s.* Emsigkeit *f*, (emsiger) Fleiß; **sed·u·lous** ['sedjʊləs] *adj.* □ emsig, fleißig.

see[1] [siː] **I** *v/t.* [*irr.*] **1.** sehen: ~ **page 15** siehe Seite 15; **I** ~ **him come** (*od.* **coming**) ich sehe ihn kommen; **I cannot** ~ **myself doing it** *fig.* ich kann mir nicht vorstellen, dass ich es tue; **I** ~ **things otherwise** *fig.* ich sehe *od.* betrachte die Dinge anders; ~ **o.s. obliged to** *fig.* sich gezwungen sehen zu; **2.** (ab)sehen, erkennen: ~ **danger ahead**; **3.** ersehen, entnehmen (**from** aus *der Zeitung etc.*); **4.** (ein)sehen, verstehen: **as I** ~ **it** wie ich es sehe, in m-n Augen; **I do not** ~ **the use of it** ich weiß nicht, wozu es gut sein soll; → **joke** 2; **5.** (sich) ansehen, besuchen: ~ **a play**; **6.** a) j-n besuchen: **go** (**come**) **to** ~ **s.o.** j-n besuchen (gehen *od.* kommen), b) *Anwalt etc.* aufsuchen, konsultieren (**about** wegen), j-n sprechen (**on business** geschäftlich); **7.** j-n empfangen: **he refused to** ~ **me**; **8.** nachsehen, her'ausfinden; **9.** dafür sorgen (dass): ~ (**to it**) **that it is done!** sorge dafür *od.* sieh zu, dass es geschieht!; ☿ **justice done to s.o.** dafür sorgen, dass j-m Gerechtigkeit widerfährt; **10.** sehen, erleben: **live to** ~ erleben; ~ **action** ✂ im Einsatz sein, Kämpfe mitmachen; **he has seen better days** er hat (schon) bessere Tage gesehen; **11.** j-n begleiten, geleiten, bringen (**to the station** zum Bahnhof); → **see off, see out**; **II** *v/i.* [*irr.*] **12.** sehen; → **fit**[1] 3; **13.** verstehen, einsehen: **I** ~**!** (ich) verstehe!, aha!, ach so!; (**you**) ~ wissen Sie, weißt du; (**you**) ~**?** verstehst du?; **14.** nachsehen; **15.** sehen, sich über'legen: **let me** ~**!** warte mal!, lass mich über'legen!; **we'll** ~ wir werden sehen, mal abwarten.

Zssgn mit prp.:

see| **a·bout** *v/i.* **1.** sich kümmern um; **2.** F sich *et.* über'legen; ~ **af·ter** *v/i.* sehen nach, sich kümmern um; ~ **in·to** *v/i.* e-r Sache auf den Grund gehen; ~

o·ver *v/i.* sich ansehen; **~ through I** *v/i.* j-n *od. et.* durch'schauen; **II** *v/t.* j-m über *et.* hin'weghelfen; **~ to** *v/i.* sich kümmern um; → *see¹* 9.
Zssgn mit adv.:
see| off *v/t.* j-n fortbegleiten, verabschieden; **~ out** *v/t.* **1.** j-n hin'ausbegleiten; **2.** F *et.* bis zum Ende ansehen *od.* mitmachen; **~ through I** *v/t.* **1.** j-m 'durchhelfen (*with* in e-r *Sache*); **2.** *et.* (bis zum Ende) 'durchhalten *od.* -fechten; **II** *v/i.* **3.** F durchhalten.
see² [siː] *s. eccl.* **1.** (Erz)Bischofssitz *m*; → *Holy See*; **2.** (Erz)Bistum *n*.
seed [siːd] **I** *s.* **1.** ♀ a) Same *m*, b) (Obst-)Kern *m*, c) *coll.* Samen *pl.*, d) ✐ Saat (*-gut n*) *f*: **go** (*od.* **run**) **to ~** in Samen schießen, *fig.* herunterkommen; **2.** *zo.* a) Ei *n od.* Eier *pl.* (*des Hummers etc.*), b) Austernbrut *f*; **3.** *physiol.* Samen *m*; *fig.* Nachkommenschaft *f*: *the ~ of A-braham bibl.* der Same Abrahams; **4.** *pl. fig.* Saat *f*, Keim *m*: **sow the ~s of discord** (die Saat der) Zwietracht säen; **II** *v/t.* **5.** entsamen; *Obst* entkernen; **6.** *Acker* besäen; **7.** *sport Spieler* setzen; **III** *v/i.* **8.** ♀ a) Samen tragen, b) in Samen schießen, c) sich aussäen; **'~·bed** *s.* Treibbeet *n*; *fig.* Pflanz-, *contp.* Brutstätte *f*; **'~·cake** *s.* Kümmelkuchen *m*; **'~·case** *s.* ♀ Samenkapsel *f*; **~ corn** *s.* **1.** Saatkorn *n*; **2.** *Am.* Saatmais *m*; **~ drill** → *seeder* 1.
seed·er ['siːdə] *s.* **1.** ✐ 'Säma,schine *f*; **2.** (Frucht)Entkerner *m*.
seed·i·ness ['siːdɪnɪs] *s.* F **1.** Schäbigkeit *f*, Abgerissenheit *f*; verwahrloster Zustand; **2.** ,Flauheit' *f des Befindens*.
seed leaf *s.* [*irr.*] ♀ Keimblatt *n*.
seed·less ['siːdlɪs] *adj.* kernlos; **'seed·ling** [-lɪŋ] *s.* ♀ Sämling *m*.
seed| oys·ter *s. zo.* **1.** Saatauster *f*; **2.** *pl.* Austernlaich *m*; **~ pearl** *s.* Staubperle *f*; **~ plot** *s.* → *seedbed*; **~ po·ta·to** *s.* 'Saatkar,toffel *f*.
seed·y ['siːdɪ] *adj.* **1.** ♀ Samen tragend, samenreich; **2.** F schäbig: a) fadenscheinig, b) her'untergekommen (*Person*); **3.** F ,flau', ,mies' (*Befinden*): **look ~** elend aussehen.
see·ing ['siːɪŋ] **I** *s.* Sehen *n*: **worth ~** sehenswert; **II** *cj.* a. **~ that** da doch; in Anbetracht dessen, dass; **III** *prp.* angesichts (*gen.*), in Anbetracht (*gen.*); **'~·eye dog** *s. Am.* Blindenhund *m*.
seek [siːk] **I** *v/t.* [*irr.*] **1.** suchen; **2.** *Bett, Schatten,* j-n aufsuchen; **3.** (*of*) *Rat, Hilfe etc.* suchen (bei), erbitten (von); **4.** begehren, erstreben, nach *Ruhm etc.* trachten; *⚖ etc.* beantragen, begehren: **~ divorce;** → *life Redew.*; **5.** (ver)suchen, trachten (*et. zu tun*); **6.** zu ergründen suchen; **7.** **be to ~** *obs.* (noch) fehlen, zu wünschen übrig lassen; **8.** *a.* **~ out** her'ausfinden, aufspüren, *fig.* aufs Korn nehmen; **II** *v/i.* [*irr.*] **9.** suchen, fragen, forschen (*for, after* nach): **~ after** *a.* begehren; **'seek·er** [-kə] *s.* **1.** Sucher(in): **~ after truth** Wahrheitssucher; **2.** ✐ Sonde *f*.
seem [siːm] *v/i.* **1.** (zu sein) scheinen, anscheinend sein, erscheinen: **it ~s impossible to me** es (er)scheint mir unmöglich; **2.** *mit inf.* scheinen: **you ~ to believe it** du scheinst es zu glauben; **apples ~ not to grow here** Äpfel wachsen hier anscheinend nicht; **I ~ to hear voices** mir ist, als hörte ich Stimmen; **3.** *impers.* **it ~s that** es scheint, dass; anscheinend; **it ~s as if** (*od. though*) es sieht so aus *od.* es scheint so als ob; **it ~s to me that it will rain** mir

scheint, es wird regnen; **it should** (*od. would*) **~ that** man sollte glauben, dass; **I can't ~ to open this door** ich bringe diese Tür einfach nicht auf; **'seem·ing** [-mɪŋ] *adj.* □ **1.** scheinbar: **a ~ friend**; **2.** anscheinend; **'seem·li·ness** [-lɪnɪs] *s.* Anstand *m*, Schicklichkeit *f*; **'seem·ly** [-lɪ] *adj. u. adv.* geziemend, schicklich.
seen [siːn] *p.p. von see¹.*
seep [siːp] *v/i.* ('durch)sickern (*a. fig.*), tropfen, lecken: **~ away** versickern; **~ in** *a. fig.* einsickern, -dringen; **'seep·age** [-pɪdʒ] *s.* **1.** ('Durch-, Ver)Sickern *n*; **2.** 'Durchgesickertes *n*; **3.** Leck *n*.
se·er ['siːə] *s.* Seher(in).
seer·suck·er ['sɪə,sʌkə] *s.* leichtes, kreppartiges Leinen.
see·saw ['siːsɔː] **I** *s.* **1.** Wippen *n*, Schaukeln *n*; **2.** Wippe *f*, Wippschaukel *f*; *fig.* (ständiges) Auf u. Ab *od.* Hin u. Her; **II** *adj.* **4.** schaukelnd, (*a. fig.*) Schaukel...(*-bewegung, -politik*); **III** *v/i.* **5.** wippen, schaukeln; **6.** sich auf u. ab *od.* hin u. her bewegen; **7.** *fig.* (hin u. her) schwanken.
seethe [siːð] *v/i.* **1.** kochen, sieden, wallen (*alle a. fig. with* vor *dat.*); **2.** *fig.* brodeln, gären (*with* vor *dat.*): **seeth·ing with rage** vor Wut kochend; **3.** wimmeln (*with* von).
'see-through *adj.* **1.** 'durchsichtig: **~ blouse**; **2.** Klarsicht...: **~ package**.
seg·ment ['segmənt] **I** *s.* **1.** Abschnitt *m*, Teil *m*, *n*; **2.** *bsd.* ♈ (*Kreis- etc.*) Seg'ment *n*; **3.** *biol.* a) allg. Glied *n*, Seg'ment *n*, b) 'Körperseg,ment *n*, Ring *m* (*Wurm etc.*); **II** *v/t.* [seg'ment] **4.** (*v/i.* sich) in Seg'mente teilen; **seg·men·tal** [seg'mentl] *adj.* □, **'seg·men·tar·y** [-tərɪ] *adj.* segmen'tär; **seg·men·ta·tion** [,segmən'teɪʃn] *s.* **1.** Segmentati'on *f*; **2.** *biol.* Zellteilung *f*, (Ei)Furchung *f*.
seg·ment| gear *s.* Seg'ment(zahnrad)getriebe *n*; **~ saw** *s.* **1.** Baumsäge *f*; **2.** Bogenschnittsäge *f*.
seg·re·gate ['segrɪgeɪt] **I** *v/t.* **1.** trennen (*a. nach Rassen etc.*), absondern; **2.** ⚗ ausseigern, -scheiden; **II** *v/i.* **3.** sich absondern *od.* abspalten (*a. fig.*); ♈ sich abscheiden; **4.** *biol.* mendeln; **III** *adj.* [-gɪt] **5.** abgesondert, isoliert; **seg·re·ga·tion** [,segrɪ'geɪʃn] *s.* **1.** Absonderung *f*, -trennung *f*; **2.** Rassentrennung *f*; **3.** ♈ Ausscheidung *f*; **4.** abgespaltener Teil *m*; **seg·re·ga·tion·ist** [,segrɪ'geɪʃnɪst] **I** *s.* Verfechter(in) der Rassentrennung; **II** *adj.* die Rassentrennung befürwortend; **'seg·re·ga·tive** [-gətɪv] *adj.* sich absondernd, Trennungs...
sei·gneur [se'njɜː], **sei·gnor** ['seɪnjə] *s.* **1.** *hist.* Lehns-, Feu'dalherr *m*; **2.** Herr *m*; **seign·ior·age** ['seɪnjərɪdʒ] *s.* Re'gal *n*, Vorrecht *n*; **2.** a) *königliche* Münzgebühr, b) Schlagschatz *m*; **sei·'gno·ri·al** [-'njɔːrɪəl] *adj.* feu'dalherrschaftlich; **seign·ior·y** ['seɪnjərɪ] *s.* **1.** Feu'dalrechte *pl.*; **2.** (feu'dal)herrschaftliche Do'mäne.
seine [seɪn] *s.* ⚓ Schlagnetz *n*.
seise [siːz] → *seize 4*; **'sei·sin** [-zɪn] → *seizin*.
seis·mic ['saɪzmɪk] *adj.* seismisch.
seis·mo·graph ['saɪzməgrɑːf] *s.* Seismo'graph *m*, Erdbebenmessgerät *n*; **seis·mol·o·gist** [saɪz'mɒlədʒɪst] *s.* Seismo'loge *m*; **seis·mol·o·gy** [saɪz-'mɒlədʒɪ] *s.* Erdbebenkunde *f*, Seismik *f*; **seis·mom·e·ter** [saɪz'mɒmɪtə] *s.* Seismo'meter *n*; **'seis·mo·scope** [-ə-skəʊp] *s.* Seismo'skop *n*.
seiz·a·ble ['siːzəbl] *adj.* **1.** (er)greifbar; **2.** *⚖* pfändbar; **seize** [siːz] **I** *v/t.* **1.** *et.*

od. j-n (er)greifen, packen, fassen (*alle a. fig. Panik etc.*): **~d with** ♣ von e-r *Krankheit* befallen; **~d with apoplexy** ♣ vom Schlag getroffen; **2.** ✕ (ein-)nehmen, erobern; **3.** sich e-r *Sache* bemächtigen, *Macht etc.* an sich reißen; **4.** *⚖* j-n in den Besitz setzen (*of* von *gen.*): **be ~d with, stand ~d of** im Besitz e-r *Sache* sein; **5.** j-n ergreifen, festnehmen; **6.** beschlagnahmen; **7.** *Gelegenheit* ergreifen, wahrnehmen; **8.** *geistig* erfassen, begreifen; **9.** ⚓ (bei)zeisen, zurren; **II** *v/i.* **10.** **~ (up)on** *Gelegenheit* ergreifen, *Idee* (begierig) aufgreifen, *a.* einhaken bei; **11.** *oft* **~ up** ⚙ sich festfressen; **'sei·zin** [-zɪn] *s.* *⚖* *Am.* (Grund)Besitz *m*, verbunden mit Eigentumsvermutung; **'seiz·ings** [-zɪŋz] *s. pl.* ⚓ Zurrtau *n*; **sei·zure** ['siːʒə] *s.* **1.** Ergreifung *f*; **2.** Inbesitznahme *f*; **3.** *⚖* a) Beschlagnahme *f*, b) Festnahme *f*; **4.** ♣ Anfall *m*.
sel·dom ['seldəm] *adv.* selten.
se·lect [sɪ'lekt] **I** *v/t.* **1.** auswählen, -lesen; **II** *adj.* **2.** ausgewählt: **~ committee** *parl. Brit.* Sonderausschuss *m*; **3.** erlesen (*Buch, Geist, Speise etc.*); exklu'siv (*Gesellschaft etc.*); **4.** wählerisch; **se·lect·ee** [sɪ,lek'tiː] *s.* ✕ *Am.* Einberufene(r) *m*; **se·lec·tion** [-kʃn] *s.* **1.** Wahl *f*; **2.** Auswahl *f*, -lese *f*; **3.** *biol.* Zuchtwahl *f*: **natural ~** natürliche Auslese; **4.** Auswahl *f* (*of* an *dat.*); **se·lec·tive** [-tɪv] *adj.* □ **1.** auswählend, Auswahl...: **~ service** *hist.* ✕ *Am.* Wehrpflicht *f*, -dienst *m*; **~ strike** punktueller Streik, Schwerpunktstreik *m*; **2.** ↯ trennscharf, selek'tiv: **~ circuit** Trennkreis *m*; **se·lec·tiv·i·ty** [,sɪlek'tɪvətɪ] *s.* *Radio, TV:* Trennschärfe *f*; **se'lect·man** [-mən] *s.* [*irr.*] *Am.* Stadtrat *m*; **se'lec·tor** [-tə] *s.* **1.** Auswählende(r *m*) *f*; **2.** Sortierer(in); **3.** ⚙ a) *↯* Wähler *m*, b) Schaltgriff *m*, c) *mot.* Gangwähler *m*, d) *Computer:* Se'lektor *m*.
se·le·nic [sɪ'lenɪk] *adj.* ♣ se'lensauer, Selen...; **se·le·ni·um** [sɪ'liːnjəm] *s.* ♣ Se'len *n*.
sel·e·nog·ra·phy [,selɪ'nɒgrəfɪ] *s.* Mondbeschreibung *f*; **sel·e·nol·o·gy** [-nɒlədʒɪ] *s.* Selenolo'gie *f*, Mondkunde *f*.
self [self] **I** *pl.* **selves** [selvz] *s.* **1.** Selbst *n*, Ich *n*: **my better** (**second**) **~** mein besseres Selbst (mein zweites Ich); **my humble** (*od.* **poor**) **~** meine Wenigkeit; **the study of the ~** *phls.* das Studium des Ich; → *former²* 1; **2.** Selbstsucht *f*, das eigene Ich; **3.** *biol.* a) Tier *n od.* Pflanze *f* von einheitlicher Färbung, b) auto'games Lebewesen; **II** *adj.* **4.** einheitlich, *bsd.* ♀ einfarbig; **III** *pron.* **5.** † *od.* F → *myself etc.*
,self-a'ban·don·ment *s.* (Selbst)Aufopferung *f*, (bedingungslose) Hingabe; **~·a'base·ment** *s.* Selbsterniedrigung *f*; **~·ab'sorbed** *adj.* **1.** mit sich selbst beschäftigt; **2.** ego'zentrisch; **~·a'buse** *s.* Selbstbefleckung *f*; **,~·'act·ing** *adj.* ⚙ selbsttätig; **,~·ad'he·sive** *adj.* selbstklebend; **,~·ad'just·ing** *adj.* ⚙ selbstregelnd, -einstellend; **,~·ap'point·ed** *adj.* selbst ernannt; **,~·as'ser·tion** *s.* **1.** Geltendmachung *f* s-r Rechte, s-s Willens, s-r Meinung *etc.*; **2.** anmaßendes Auftreten; **,~·as'sert·ive** *adj.* **1.** anmaßend, über'heblich; **2.** **~ person** j-d, der sich durchzusetzen weiß; **,~·as·'sur·ance** *s.* Selbstsicherheit *f*, -bewusstsein *n*; **,~·as'sured** *adj.* selbstbewusst; **,~·'ca·ter·ing** *s.* Selbstverpflegung *f*; **II** *adj.* für Selbstversorger, mit Selbstverpflegung; **,~·'cent(e)red**

adj. ichbezogen, ego'zentrisch; ˌ~-'**col·o(u)red** *adj.* **1.** einfarbig; **2.** na'turfarben; ˌ~-**com'mand** *s.* Selbstbeherrschung *f*; ˌ~-**com'pla·cent** *adj.* selbstgefällig, -zufrieden; ˌ~-**con'ceit** *s.* Eigendünkel *m*; ˌ~-**con'fessed** *adj.* selbst erklärt: *a ~ racist* j-d, der zugibt, Rassist zu sein; ˌ~-**con·fi·dence** *s.* Selbstvertrauen *n*, -bewusstsein *n*; ˌ~-**con·fi·dent** *adj.* selbstbewusst; ˌ~-**con·scious** *adj.* befangen, gehemmt; ˌ~-**con·scious·ness** *s.* Befangenheit *f*; ˌ~-**con'tained** *adj.* **1.** *a.* ⊛ (in sich) geschlossen, unabhängig, selbstständig: *~ country* Selbstversorgerland *n*; *~ flat* abgeschlossene Wohnung; *~ house* Einfamilienhaus *n*; **2.** reserviert, zu-'rückhaltend (*Charakter, Person*); **3.** selbstbeherrscht; ˈ~-ˌcon·tra'dic·tion *s.* innerer Widerspruch; ˈ~-ˌcon·tra-'dic·to·ry *adj.* widersprüchlich; ˌ~-**con'trol** *s.* Selbstbeherrschung *f*: *lose one's ~* die Beherrschung verlieren; ˌ~-**de'ceit**, ˌ~-**de'cep·tion** *s.* Selbsttäuschung *f*, -betrug *m*; ˌ~-**de'feat·ing** *adj.* genau das Gegenteil bewirkend, sinn- und zwecklos; ˌ~-**de'fence** *Brit.*, ˌ~-**de'fense** *Am. s.* **1.** Selbstverteidigung *f*; **2.** ⚖ Notwehr *f*; ˌ~-**de'lu·sion** *s.* Selbsttäuschung *f*; ˌ~-**de'ni·al** *s.* Selbstverleugnung *f*; ˌ~-**de'ny·ing** *adj.* selbstverleugnend; ˌ~-**de'spair** *s.* Verzweiflung *f* an sich selbst; ˌ~-**de'struct** *v/i.* sich selbst zerstören (*Maschine etc.*); ˌ~-**de'struc·tion** *s.* **1.** Selbstzerstörung *f*; **2.** Selbstvernichtung *f*, -mord *m*; ˈ~-**de·ter·mi'na·tion** *s.* **1.** *pol. etc.* Selbstbestimmung *f*; **2.** *phls.* freier Wille; ˌ~-**de'vel·op·ment** *s.* Selbstentfaltung *f*; ˌ~-**de'vo·tion** → *self-abandonment*; ˌ~-**dis'trust** *s.* Mangel *m* an Selbstvertrauen; ˌ~-**'doubt** *s.* Selbstzweifel *pl.*; ˌ~-**'ed·u·cat·ed** → *self-taught* 1; ˌ~-**em'ployed** *adj.* ⚕ selbstständig (*Handwerker etc.*); ˌ~-**es'teem** *s.* **1.** Selbstachtung *f*; **2.** Eigendünkel *m*; ˌ~-**'ev·i·dent** *adj.* □ selbstverständlich; ˌ~-**ex'plan·a·to·ry** *adj.* ohne Erläuterung verständlich, für sich (selbst) sprechend; ˌ~-**ex'pres·sion** *s.* Ausdruck *m* der eigenen Per'sönlichkeit; ˌ~-**'feed·ing** *adj.* ⊛ auto'matisch (*Material od. Brennstoff*) zuführend; ˌ~-**for'get·ful** *adj.* □ selbstvergessen, -los; ˌ~-**'ful·fil(l)·ment** *s.* Selbstverwirklichung *f*; ˌ~-**'gov·ern·ing** *adj. pol.* selbst verwaltet, auto'nom, unabhängig; ˌ~-**'gov·ern·ment** *s. pol.* Selbstverwaltung *f*, -regierung *f*, Autono'mie *f*; ˌ~-**'help** *s.* Selbsthilfe *f*: *~ group*; ˌ~-**ig'ni·tion** *s. mot.* Selbstzündung *f*; ˌ~-**'im·age** *s. psych.* Selbstverständnis *n*; ˌ~-**im'por·tance** *s.* 'Selbstüberˌhebung *f*, Wichtigtue'rei *f*; ˌ~-**im'por·tant** *adj.* über'heblich, wichtigtuerisch; ˌ~-**in'duced** *adj.* **1.** ⚡ selbst induziert; **2.** selbst verursacht; ˌ~-**in'dul·gence** *s.* **1.** Sich'gehenlassen *n*; **2.** Zügellosigkeit *f*, Maßlosigkeit *f*; ˌ~-**in'dul·gent** *adj.* **1.** schwach, nachgiebig gegen sich selbst; **2.** zügellos; ˌ~-**in'flict·ed** *adj.* selbst zugefügt: *~ wounds* ✗ Selbstverstümmelung *f*; ˌ~-**in'struc·tion** *s.* 'Selbstˌunterricht *m*; ˌ~-**in'struc·tion·al** *adj.* Selbstlehr..., Selbstunterrichts...: *~ manual*; ˌ~-**'in·ter·est** *s.* Eigennutz *m*, eigenes Inter'esse.

self·ish ['selfɪʃ] *adj.* □ selbstsüchtig, ego'istisch, eigennützig; **'self·ish·ness** [-nɪs] *s.* Selbstsucht *f*, Ego'ismus *m*.

ˌ**self'-knowl·edge** *s.* Selbst(er)kenntnis *f*; ˌ~-**lac·er·a·tion** *s.* Selbstzerfleischung *f*.

self·less ['selflɪs] *adj.* selbstlos; **'self·less·ness** [-nɪs] *s.* Selbstlosigkeit *f*. ˌ**self'-load·ing** *adj.* Selbstlade...; ˌ~-**'love** *s.* Eigenliebe *f*; ˌ~-**'lu·bri·cat·ing** *adj.* ⊛ selbstschmierend; ˌ~-**'made** *adj.* selbst gemacht: *~ man* j-d, der durch eigene Kraft hochgekommen ist, Selfmademan *m*; ˈ~-ˌmed·i'ca·tion *s.* ⚕ 'Selbstmedikatiˌon *f*; ˌ~-**neg'lect** *s.* **1.** Selbstlosigkeit *f*; **2.** Vernachlässigung *f* s-s Äußeren; ˌ~-**o'pin·ion·at·ed** *adj.* **1.** eingebildet; **2.** rechthaberisch; ˌ~-**'pit·y** *s.* Selbstmitleid *n*; ˌ~-**'por·trait** *s.* 'Selbstporˌträt *n*, -bildnis *n*; ˌ~-**pos'ses·sion** *s.* Selbstbeherrschung *f*; ˌ~-**'praise** *s.* Eigenlob *n*; ˈ~-ˌpres·er-'va·tion *s.* Selbsterhaltung *f*: *instinct of ~* Selbsterhaltungstrieb *m*; ˌ~-**pro'pelled** *adj.* ⊛ Selbstfahr..., mit Eigenantrieb; ˈ~-ˌrais·ing flour *s. Brit.* Mehl *n* mit Backpulver; ˈ~-ˌre·al·i'za·tion *s.* Selbstverwirklichung *f*; ˌ~-**re'cord·ing** *adj.* ⊛ selbstschreibend; ˌ~-**re'gard** *s.* **1.** Eigennutz *m*; **2.** Selbstachtung *f*; ˌ~-**re'li·ance** *s.* Selbstvertrauen *n*, -sicherheit *f*; ˌ~-**re'li·ant** *adj.* selbstbewusst, -sicher; ˌ~-**re'proach** *s.* Selbstvorwurf *m*; ˌ~-**re'spect** *s.* Selbstachtung *f*; ˌ~-**re'spect·ing** *adj.*: *every ~ craftsman* jeder Handwerker, der etwas auf sich hält; ˌ~-**re'straint** *s.* Selbstbeherrschung *f*; ˌ~-**'right·eous** *adj.* selbstgerecht; ˈ~-ˌris·ing flour *s. Am.* Mehl *n* mit Backpulver; ˌ~-**'sac·ri·fice** *s.* Selbstaufopferung *f*; ˌ~-**'sac·ri·fic·ing** *adj.* aufopferungsvoll; ˈ~-**same** *adj.* ebenderselbe, -dieselbe, -dasselbe; ˌ~-**'sat·is·fied** *adj.* selbstzufrieden; ˌ~-**'seal·ing** *adj.* **1.** ⊛ selbstdichtend; **2.** selbstklebend (*bsd. Briefumschlag*); **3.** schusssicher; ˌ~-**'seek·er** *s.* Ego'ist(in); ˌ~-**'serv·ice** I *adj.* Selbstbedienungs...: *~ shop*; II *s.* Selbstbedienung *f*; ˌ~-**'start·er** *s. mot.* (Selbst)Anlasser *m*; ˌ~-**'stick notes** *s. pl.* a) 'Haftnoˌtizen *pl.*, b) 'Haftnoˌtizˌzettel *pl.*; ˌ~-**'styled** *adj. iron.* von eigenen Gnaden; ˌ~-**suf'fi·cien·cy** *s.* **1.** Unabhängigkeit *f* (von fremder Hilfe); **2.** ⚕ Autar'kie *f*; **3.** Eigendünkel *m*; ˌ~-**suf'fi·cient** *adj.* **1.** unabhängig, Selbstversorger..., ⚕ au'tark; **2.** dünkelhaft; ˌ~-**sug'ges·tion** *s. psych.* 'Autosuggestiˌon *f*; ˌ~-**sup'pli·er** *s.* Selbstversorger *m*; ˌ~-**sup'port·ing** *adj.* **1.** → *self-sufficient* 1; **2.** ⊛ freitragend (*Brücke etc.*); ˌ~-**'taught** *adj.* **1.** autodi'daktisch: *~ person* Autodidakt *m*; **2.** selbst erlernt; ˌ~-**'tim·er** *s. phot.* Selbstauslöser *m*; ˌ~-**'will** *s.* Eigensinn *m*; ˌ~-**'willed** *adj.* eigensinnig; ˌ~-**'wind·ing** *adj.* auto'matisch (*Uhr*).

sell [sel] I *s.* **1.** F a) Reinfall *m*, b) Schwindel *m*; **2.** ⚕ F (*hard ~* aggres-'sive) Ver'kaufsmeˌthode; → *soft* 1; II *v/t.* [*irr.*] **3.** verkaufen, -äußern (*to an* acc.); **4.** ⚕ Waren führen, handeln mit, vertreiben; **5.** *fig.* verkaufen, e-n guten Absatz sichern (*dat.*): *his name will ~ the book*; **6.** *fig.* verraten: *~ s.o. down the river* j-n ,verraten u. verkaufen'; **7.** *sl.* ,anschmieren'; **8.** F j-m et. ,verkaufen', aufschwatzen, schmackhaft machen: *~ s.o. on* j-m et. andrehen, j-n zu et. überreden: *be sold on fig.* von et. überzeugt od. begeistert sein; III *v/i.* [*irr.*] **9.** verkaufen; **10.** verkauft werden (*at* für); **11.** sich *gut* etc. verkaufen, *gut* etc. gehen, ,ziehen'; ˌ~-**by date** *s.* **1.** (Mindest)Haltbarkeitsdatum *n*; **2.** *he is past his ~* F *fig.* er hat s-e besten Tage hinter sich; *~ off v/t.* ausverkaufen, *Lager* räumen; *~ out v/t.*

1. → *sell off*: *be sold out* ausverkauft sein; **2.** *Wertpapiere* realisieren; **3.** *fig.* → *sell* 6; *~ up v/t.* **1.** (*v/i.* sein) Geschäft etc. verkaufen; **2.** *~ s.o. up* j-n auspfänden.

sell·er ['selə] *s.* **1.** Verkäufer(in); Händler(in): *~s' market* ⚕ Verkäufermarkt *m*; *~'s option* Verkaufsoption *f, Börse*: Rückprämie(ngeschäft *n*) *f*; **2.** *good ~* ⚕ gut gehende Ware, zugkräftiger Artikel.

sell·ing ['selɪŋ] I *adj.* **1.** Verkaufs..., Absatz..., Vertriebs...: *~ area* od. *space* Verkaufsfläche *f*; II *s.* **2.** Verkauf *m*; **3.** → *sell* 2.

Sel·lo·tape ['seləʊteɪp] *TM s. Brit.* (durchsichtiges) Klebeband *n*, Klebestreifen *m*; **'sel·lo·tape** *v/t. Brit.* F **1.** (mit Klebeband) kleben (*to an* acc.); **2.** festkleben (*to an* acc.); **3.** zukleben: *~ a parcel* ein Paket zukleben.

'sell·out *s.* **1.** Ausverkauf *m* (*a. fig. pol.*); **2.** ausverkaufte Veranstaltung, volles Haus; **3.** *fig.* Verrat *m*.

Selt·zer (**wa·ter**) ['seltsə] *s.* Selters (-wasser) *n*.

sel·vage ['selvɪdʒ] *s. Weberei*: Salband *n*.

selves [selvz] *pl. von self.*

se·man·tic [sɪ'mæntɪk] *adj. ling.* se'mantisch; **se'man·tics** [-ks] *s. pl. mst sg. konstr.* Se'mantik *f*, (Wort)Bedeutungslehre *f*.

sem·a·phore ['seməfɔː] I *s.* **1.** ⊛ Sema-'phor *n*: a) 🚩 ('Flügel)Siˌgnalmast *m*, b) optischer Tele'graf; **2.** ✗, ♣ (Flaggen)Winken *n*: *~ message* Winkspruch *m*; II *v/t. u. v/i.* **3.** signalisieren.

sem·blance ['sembləns] *s.* **1.** (äußere) Gestalt, Erscheinung *f*: *in the ~ of* in Gestalt (gen.); **2.** Ähnlichkeit *f* (*to* mit); **3.** (An)Schein *m*: *the ~ of honesty; under the ~ of* unter dem Deckmantel (gen.).

se·mei·ol·o·gy [ˌsemɪ'ɒlədʒɪ] *s.*, **se·mei·ot·ics** [-'ɒtɪks] *s. pl. sg. konstr.* Semi'otik *f*: a) *Lehre von den Zeichen*, b) ⚕ Symptomatolo'gie *f*.

se·men ['siːmen] *s. physiol.* Samen *m* (*a.* ♀), Sperma *n*, Samenflüssigkeit *f*.

se·mes·ter [sɪ'mestə] *s. univ. bsd. Am.* Se'mester *n*, Halbjahr *n*.

sem·i ['semɪ] *s.* F für a) *semidetached* II, b) *semifinal* I, c) *Am. semitrailer*.

sem·i- [semɪ] *in Zssgn* halb..., halb...; ˌ~**an·nu·al** *adj.* □ halbjährlich; ˌ~**au·to'mat·ic** *adj.* (□ *~ally*) 'halbauto,matisch; ˌ~**'bold** *adj. u. s. typ.* halbfett(e Schrift); ˌ~**'breve** *s. ♪* ganze Note: *~ rest* ganze Pause; ˌ~**'cir·cle** *s.* **1.** Halbkreis *m*; **2.** ⚕ Winkelmesser *m*; ˌ~**'cir·cu·lar** *adj.* halbkreisförmig; ˌ~**'co·lon** *s.* Semi'kolon *n*, Strichpunkt *m*; ˌ~**'con·duc·tor** *s.* ⚡ Halbleiter *m*; ˌ~**'con·scious** *adj.* nicht bei vollem Bewusstsein; ˌ~**de'tached** I *adj.*: *~ house* → II *s.* Doppelhaushälfte *f*; ˌ~**'fi·nal** *sport* I *s.* **1.** 'Semi-, 'Halbfiˌnale *n*, Vorschlussrunde *f*; **2.** 'Halbfiˌnalspiel *n*; II *adj.* **3.** Halbfinal...; ˌ~**'fi·nal·ist** *s. sport* 'Halbfinaˌlist(in); ˌ~**'fin·ished** *adj.* ⊛ halb fertig: *~ product* Halbfabrikat *n*; ˌ~**'flu·id** *adj.* halb-, zähflüssig; ˌ~**man·u'fac·tured** → *semifinished*; ˌ~**'month·ly** I *adj. u. adv.* halbmonatlich; II *s.* Halbmonatsschrift *f*.

sem·i·nal ['semɪnl] *adj.* □ **1.** ♀, *physiol.* Samen...: *~ duct* Samengang *m*, -leiter *m*; *~ fluid* Samenflüssigkeit *f*, Sperma *n*; *~ leaf* ♀ Keimblatt *n*; *~ power* Zeugungsfähigkeit *f*; **2.** *fig.* a) zukunftsträchtig, fruchtbar, b) folgenreich; **3.** noch unentwickelt: *in the ~ state* im

Entwicklungsstadium.

sem·i·nar ['semɪnɑː] *s. univ.* Semi'nar *n.*

sem·i·nar·y ['semɪnərɪ] *s.* **1.** (*eccl.* 'Priester)Semi,nar *n*, Bildungsanstalt *f*; **2.** *fig.* Schule *f*, Pflanzstätte *f*, *contp.* Brutstätte *f*.

sem·i·na·tion [,semɪ'neɪʃn] *s.* (Aus)Säen *n.*

,sem·i·of'fi·cial *adj.* □ halbamtlich, offizi'ös.

se·mi·ol·o·gy [,semɪ'ɒlədʒɪ] *s.*, **,se·mi·'ot·ics** [-'ɒtɪks] *s. pl. sg. konstr.* → **se·meiology**.

'sem·i|,pre·cious *adj.* halbedel: **~ stone** Halbedelstein *m*; **'~·pro'fes·sion·al I** *adj.* 'halbprofessio,nell; **II** *s. sport* ,Halbprofi‘ *m*; **'~,qua·ver** *s.* ♪ Sechzehntel(note *f*) *n*; **~ rest** Sechzehntelpause *f*; **,~·re'tire·ment** *s.* Altersteilzeit *f*; **,~'rig·id** *adj.* halbstarr (*Luftschiff*); **,~'skilled** *adj.* angelernt (*Arbeiter*); **,~'skimmed** *adj.*: **~ milk** Halbfettmilch *f*, teilentrahmte Milch.

Sem·ite ['siːmaɪt] **I** *s.* Se'mit(in); **II** *adj.* se'mitisch; **Se·mit·ic** [sɪ'mɪtɪk] **I** *adj.* se'mitisch; **II** *s. ling.* Se'mitisch *n.*

'sem·i|·steel *s.* ⊚ Halb-, *Am.* Puddelstahl *m*; **'~·tone** *s.* ♪ Halbton *m*; **'~,trail·er** *s. mot.* Sattelschlepper(anhänger) *m*; **'~,vow·el** *s. ling.* 'Halbvo,kal *m*; **,~'week·ly I** *adj. u. adv.* halbwöchentlich; **II** *s.* halbwöchentlich erscheinende Veröffentlichung.

sem·o·li·na [,semə'liːnə] *s.* Grieß(mehl *n*) *m.*

sem·pi·ter·nal [,sempɪ'tɜːnl] *adj. rhet.* immer während, ewig.

semp·stress ['sempstrɪs] → **seamstress**.

sen·ate ['senɪt] *s.* **1.** Se'nat *m* (*a. univ.*); **2.** ♀ *parl. Am.* Se'nat *m* (*Oberhaus*); **sen·a·tor** ['senətə] *s.* Se'nator *m*; **sen·a·to·ri·al** [,senə'tɔːrɪəl] *adj.* □ **1.** sena·'torisch, Senats...; **2.** *Am.* zur Wahl von Sena'toren berechtigt.

send [send] [*irr.*] **I** *v/t.* **1.** *j-n*, Brief, Hilfe etc. senden, schicken (**to** *dat.*): **~ s.o. to bed** (**to a school, to prison**) j-n ins Bett (auf e-e Schule, ins Gefängnis) schicken; → **word** 6; **2.** Ball, Kugel etc. wohin senden, schießen, jagen; **3.** *mit adj. od. pres.p.* machen: **~ s.o. mad**; **~ s.o. flying** a) j-n verjagen, b) j-n hinschleudern; **~ s.o. reeling** j-n taumeln machen *od.* lassen; **4.** *sl. Zuhörer etc.* in Ek'stase versetzen, 'hinreißen; **II** *v/i.* **5.** **~ for** a) nach *j-m* schicken, *j-n* kommen lassen, *j-n* holen *od.* rufen (lassen), b) (sich) *et.* kommen lassen, bestellen; **6.** ⚡, *Radio etc.*: senden;

Zssgn mit adv.:

send| a·way I *v/t.* **1.** weg-, fortschicken; **2.** Brief etc. absenden; **II** *v/i.* **3. ~ for** (**to s.o.**) sich (von j-m) *et.* kommen lassen; **~ down** *v/t.* **1.** *fig.* Preise, Temperatur (her'ab)drücken; **2.** *univ.* relegieren; **3.** F *j-n* einsperren; **~ forth** *v/t.* **1.** *j-n, et., a. Licht* aussenden; *Wärme etc.* ausstrahlen; **2.** Laut etc. von sich geben; **3.** her'vorbringen; **4.** *fig.* veröffentlichen, verbreiten; **~ in** *v/t.* **1.** einsenden, -schicken, -reichen; → **name** Redew.; **2.** *sport* Ersatzmann aufs Feld schicken; **~ off** *v/t.* **1.** → *send away* 1; **2.** *j-n* (herzlich) verabschieden; **3.** *sport* vom Platz stellen; **~ on** *v/t.* vor'aus-, nachschicken; **~ out** → *send forth*; **~ up** *v/t.* **1.** *j-n, a.* Ball etc. hin'aufsenden; **2.** Schrei ausstoßen; **3.** *fig.* Preise, Fieber in die Höhe treiben; **4.** *Brit.* F ,durch den Ka'kao‘ ziehen, parodieren; **5.** F ,einlochen‘.

send·er ['sendə] *s.* **1.** Absender(in); **2.**

(Über)'Sender(in); **3.** *tel.* Geber *m* (*Sendegerät*).

'send|·off *s.* F **1.** Abschied *m*, Abschiedsfeier *f*, Geleit(e) *n*; **2.** gute Wünsche *pl.* zum Anfang; **3.** *sport u. fig.* Start *m*; **'~·up** *s. Brit.* F Verulkung *f*, Paro'die *f.*

se·nes·cence [sɪ'nesns] *s.* Altern *n*; **se·'nes·cent** [-nt] *adj.* **1.** alternd; **2.** Alters...

sen·es·chal ['senɪʃl] *s. hist.* Seneschall *m*, Major'domus *m.*

se·nile ['siːnaɪl] *adj.* **1.** se'nil: a) greisenhaft, b) ,verkalkt‘, kindisch; **2.** Alters...: **~ decay** Altersabbau *m*; **~ speckle** 🦋 Altersfleck *m*; **se·nil·i·ty** [sɪ'nɪlətɪ] *s.* Senili'tät *f.*

sen·ior ['siːnjə] **I** *adj.* **1.** (*nachgestellt, abbr. in England sen., in USA Sr.*) se'nior: **Mr. John Smith sen.** (**Sr.**) Herr John Smith sen.; **2.** älter (**to** als): **~ citizen** älterer Mitbürger, Rentner(in); **~ citizens** Senioren *pl.*; **~ partner** ✝ Seniorchef *m*, Hauptteilhaber; **3.** rang-, dienstälter, ranghöher, Ober...: **a ~ man** *Brit.* ein höheres Semester (*Student*); **~ officer** a) höherer Offizier, *mein etc.* Vorgesetzter, b) Rangälteste(r); **~ service** *Brit.* die Kriegsmarine; **4.** *ped.* Ober...: **~ classes** Oberklassen; **5.** *Am.* im letzten Schuljahr (stehend): **the ~ class** die oberste Klasse; **~ high** (**school**) *Am.* die obersten Klassen der High-School; **~ college** College, an dem das 3. und 4. Jahr eines Studiums absolviert wird; **II** *s.* **6.** Ältere(r *m*) *f*; Älteste(r *m*) *f*: **he is my ~ by four years, he is four years my ~** er ist vier Jahre älter als ich; **7.** Rang-, Dienstälteste(r *m*) *f*; **8.** Vorgesetzte(r *m*) *f*; **9.** *Am.* Stu'dent *m od.* Schüler *m* im letzten Studienjahr.

sen·ior·i·ty [,siːnɪ'ɒrətɪ] *s.* **1.** höheres Alter; **2.** höheres Dienstalter: **by ~** Beförderung nach dem Dienstalter.

sen·na ['senə] *s. pharm.* Sennesblätter *pl.*

sen·sate ['senseɪt] *adj.* sinnlich (wahrgenommen).

sen·sa·tion [sen'seɪʃn] *s.* **1.** (Sinnes-)Wahrnehmung *f*, (-)Empfindung *f*, Gefühl *n*: **pleasant ~**; **~ of thirst** Durstgefühl *n*; **3.** Empfindungsvermögen *n*; **4.** Sensati'on *f* (*a. Ereignis*), (großer) Eindruck, Aufsehen *n* (*od. create*) **a ~** großes Aufsehen erregen; **sen·sa·tion·al** [-ʃənl] *adj.* □ **1.** sensatio'nell, Sensations...; **2.** sinnlich, Sinnes...; **3.** *phls.* sensua'listisch; **sen·'sa·tion·al·ism** [-ʃnəlɪzəm] *s.* **1.** Sensati'onsgier *f*, -lust *f*; **2.** ,Sensati'onsmache‘ *f*; **3.** *phls.* Sensua'lismus *m.*

sense [sens] **I** *s.* **1.** Sinn *m*, 'Sinnesor,gan *n*: **the five ~s** die fünf Sinne; **~ of smell** (**touch**) Geruchs- (Tast)sinn; **~ organ** Sinnesorgan *n*; → **sixth** 1; **2.** *pl.* Sinne *pl.*, (klarer) Verstand: **in** (**out of**) **one's ~s** bei (von) Sinnen; **in one's right ~s** bei Verstand; **lose one's ~s** den Verstand verlieren; **bring s.o. to his ~s** j-n zur Besinnung bringen; **3.** *fig.* Vernunft *f*, Verstand *m*: **a man of ~** ein vernünftiger *od.* kluger Mensch; **common** (*od.* **good**) **~** gesunder Menschenverstand; **have the ~ to do s.th.** so klug sein, et. zu tun; **knock some ~ into s.o.** j-m den Kopf zurechtsetzen; **4.** Sinne, Empfindungsvermögen *n*; **5.** Gefühl *n*, Empfindung *f* (**of** für): **~ of pain** Schmerzgefühl, -empfindung; **~ of security** Gefühl der Sicherheit; **6.** Sinn *m*, Gefühl *n* (**of** für): **~ of beauty** Schönheitssinn; **~ of direction** Orientierungssinn *m*; **~ of duty** Pflichtgefühl;

~ of humo(u)r (Sinn für) Humor *m*; **~ of justice** Gerechtigkeitssinn; **~ of locality** Ortssinn; **~ of purpose** Zielstrebigkeit *f*; **7.** Sinn *m*, Bedeutung *f* (*e-s Wortes etc.*): **in a ~** gewissermaßen; **8.** Sinn *m* (*et. Vernünftiges*): **what is the ~ of doing this?** was hat es für e-n Sinn, das zu tun?; **talk ~** vernünftig reden; **it does not make ~** es hat keinen Sinn; **9.** (allgemeine) Ansicht, Meinung *f*: **take the ~ of** die Meinung (*gen.*) einholen; **10.** ⟳ Richtung *f*: **~ of rotation** Drehsinn *m*; **II** *v/t.* **11.** fühlen, spüren, ahnen; **12.** *Am.* F ,begreifen; **13.** *Computer*: a) abtasten, ⚡ *a.* (ab)fühlen, b) abfragen; **'sense·less** [-lɪs] *adj.* □ **1.** a) besinnungslos, b) gefühllos; **2.** unvernünftig, dumm, verrückt (*Mensch*); **3.** sinnlos, unsinnig (*Sache*); **'sense·less·ness** [-lɪsnɪs] *s.* **1.** Unempfindlichkeit *f*; **2.** Bewusstlosigkeit *f*; **3.** Unvernunft *f*; **4.** Sinnlosigkeit *f.*

sen·si·bil·i·ty [,sensɪ'bɪlətɪ] *s.* **1.** Sensibili'tät *f*, Empfindungsvermögen *n*; **2.** *phys. etc.* Empfindlichkeit: **~ to light** Lichtempfindlichkeit; **3.** *fig.* Empfänglichkeit *f* (**to** für); **4.** Sensibili'tät *f*, Empfindsamkeit *f*; **5.** *a. pl.* Fein-, Zartgefühl *n*; **sen·si·ble** ['sensəbl] *adj.* □ **1.** vernünftig (*Person, Sache*); **2.** fühl-, spürbar; **3.** merklich, wahrnehmbar; **4.** bei Bewusstsein; **5.** bewusst (**of** *gen.*): **be ~ of** a) sich *e-r Sache* bewusst sein, b) *et.* empfinden; **sen·si·ble·ness** ['sensəblnɪs] *s.* Vernünftigkeit *f*, Klugheit *f.*

sens·ing| el·e·ment ['sensɪŋ] *s.* ⊚ (Mess)Fühler *m*; **~ head** *s. Computer*: Abtastkopf *m.*

sen·si·tive ['sensɪtɪv] **I** *adj.* □ **1.** fühlend (*Kreatur etc.*); **2.** Empfindungs...: **~ nerves**; **3.** sensi'tiv, ('über)empfindlich (**to** gegen): **be ~ to** empfindlich reagieren auf (*acc.*); **4.** sen'sibel, feinfühlig, empfindsam; **5.** *phys. etc.* (*phot.* licht-)empfindlich: **~ to heat** wärmeempfindlich; **~ plant** ♉ Sinnpflanze *f*; **~ spot** *fig.* empfindliche Stelle, neuralgischer Punkt; **~ subject** *fig.* heikles Thema; **6.** schwankend (*a.* ✝ *Markt*); **7.** ✠ gefährdet; **II** *s.* **8.** sensi'tiver Mensch; **'sen·si·tive·ness** [-nɪs], **sen·si·tiv·i·ty** [,sensɪ'tɪvətɪ] *s.* **1.** → *sensibility* 1 *u.* 2: **~ group** *psych.* Trainingsgruppe *f*; **~ training** *psych.* Sensitivitätstraining *n*; **2.** Sensitivi'tät *f*, Feingefühl *n.*

sen·si·tize ['sensɪtaɪz] *v/t.* sensibilisieren, (*phot.* licht)empfindlich machen.

sen·sor ['sensə] *s.* ⚡, ⊚ Sensor *m.*

sen·so·ri·al [sen'sɔːrɪəl] → **sensory**; **sen·so·ri·um** [-əm] *pl.* **-ri·a** [-rɪə] *s. anat., psych.* **1.** Sen'sorium *f*, 'Sinnesappa,rat *m*; **2.** Sitz *m* des Empfindungsvermögens, Bewusstsein *n*; **sen·so·ry** ['sensərɪ] *adj.* sen'sorisch, Sinnes...: **~ perception**.

sen·su·al ['sensjʊəl] *adj.* □ **1.** sinnlich: a) Sinnes..., b) wollüstig, *bsd. bibl.* fleischlich; **2.** *phls.* sensua'listisch; **'sen·su·al·ism** [-lɪzəm] *s.* **1.** Sinnlichkeit *f*, Lüsternheit *f*; **2.** *phls.* Sensua'lismus *m*; **'sen·su·al·ist** [-lɪst] *s.* **1.** sinnlicher Mensch; **2.** *phls.* Sensua'list *m*; **sen·su·al·i·ty** [,sensjʊ'ælətɪ] *s.* Sinnlichkeit *f*; **'sen·su·al·ize** [-laɪz] *v/t.* **1.** sinnlich machen; **2.** versinnlichen.

sen·su·ous ['sensjʊəs] *adj.* □ sinnlich: a) Sinnes..., b) sinnenfroh; **'sen·su·ous·ness** [-nɪs] *s.* Sinnlichkeit *f.*

sent [sent] *pret. u. p.p. von* **send**.

sen·tence ['sentəns] **I** *s.* **1.** *ling.* Satz (-verbindung *f*) *m*: **complex ~** Satzgefüge n; **~ stress** Satzbetonung f; **2.** ⚖ a) (bsd. Straf)Urteil n: **pass ~ (up)on** das (fig. ein) Urteil fällen über (acc.), verurteilen (a. fig.), b) Strafe f: **under ~ of death** zum Tode verurteilt; **serve a ~ of imprisonment** e-e Freiheitsstrafe verbüßen; **3.** obs. Sen'tenz f, Sinnspruch m; **II** v/t. **4.** ⚖ u. fig. verurteilen (**to** zu).

sen·ten·tious [sen'tenʃəs] adj. □ **1.** sentenzi'ös, präg'nant, kernig; **2.** spruchreich, lehrhaft; contp. aufgeblasen, salbungsvoll; **sen'ten·tious·ness** [-nɪs] s. **1.** Präg'nanz f; **2.** Spruchreichtum m, Lehrhaftigkeit f; **3.** Großspreche'rei f.

sen·ti·ence ['senʃəns] s. **1.** Empfindungsvermögen n; **2.** Empfindung f; **'sen·tient** [-nt] adj. □ **1.** empfindungsfähig; **2.** fühlend.

sen·ti·ment ['sentɪmənt] s. **1.** Empfindung f, (Gefühls)Regung f, Gefühl n (**towards** j-m gegenüber); **2.** pl. Gedanken pl., Meinung f, (Geistes)Haltung f: **noble ~s** edle Gesinnung; **them's my ~s** humor. (so) denke ich; **3.** (Fein)Gefühl n, Innigkeit f (a. Kunst); **4.** contp. Sentimentali'tät f.

sen·ti·men·tal [ˌsentɪ'mentl] adj. □ **1.** sentimen'tal: a) gefühlvoll, empfindsam, b) contp. rührselig; **2.** gefühlsmäßig, Gefühls..., emotio'nal: **~ value** ✝ Liebhaberwert m; **sen·ti'men·tal·ism** [-təlɪzəm] **1.** Empfindsamkeit f; **2.** → **sentimentality**; **sen·ti'men·tal·ist** [-təlɪst] s. Gefühlsmensch m; **sen·ti·men·tal·i·ty** [ˌsentɪmen'tælətɪ] s. contp. Sentimentali'tät f, Rührseligkeit f, Gefühlsduse'lei f; **sen·ti'men·tal·ize** [-təlaɪz] **I** v/t. sentimen'tal gestalten; **II** v/i. (**about**, **over**) in Gefühlen schwelgen (bei), sentimen'tal werden (bei), über dat.).

sen·ti·nel ['sentɪnl] s. **1.** Wächter m: **stand ~ over** bewachen; **2.** → **sentry** 1; **3.** Computer: 'Trennsym·bol n.

sen·try ['sentrɪ] ✗ s. **1.** (Wach)Posten m, Wache f; **2.** Wache f, Wachdienst m; **~ box** s. Wachhäus·chen n; **'~-go** s. Wachdienst m.

se·pal ['sepəl] s. ♀ Kelchblatt n.

sep·a·ra·ble ['sepərəbl] adj. □ (ab-) trennbar; **'sep·a·rate** ['sepəreɪt] **I** v/t. **1.** trennen (**from** von): a) Freunde, a. Kämpfende etc. ausein'ander bringen, ⚖ (ehelich) trennen, b) abtrennen, -schneiden, c) (ab)sondern, (aus)scheiden, d) ausein'ander halten, unterscheiden zwischen (dat.); **2.** (auf-, zer)teilen (**into** in acc.); **3.** 🔥, ⚙ a) scheiden, (ab)spalten, b) sortieren, c) aufbereiten; **4.** Milch zentrifugieren; **5.** ✗ Am. entlassen; **II** v/i. **6.** sich (⚖ ehelich) trennen (**from** von), ausein'ander gehen; **7.** 🔥, ⚙ sich absondern; **III** adj. ['seprət] □ **8.** getrennt, besonder, sepa'rat, Separat..., Sonder...: **~ account** ✝ Sonderkonto n; **~ estate** ⚖ eingebrachtes Sondergut (der Ehefrau); **9.** einzeln, gesondert, getrennt, Einzel...: **~ questions** gesondert zu behandelnde Fragen; **10.** einzeln, isoliert; **IV** s. ['seprət] **11.** typ. Sonder(ab)druck m; **sep·a·rate·ness** ['seprətnɪs] s. **1.** Getrenntheit f; **2.** Besonderheit f; **3.** Abgeschiedenheit f, Isoliertheit f; **sep·a·ra·tion** [ˌsepə'reɪʃn] s. **1.** ⚖ eheliche Trennung, Absonderung f: **judicial ~** (gerichtliche) Aufhebung der ehelichen Gemeinschaft; **~ of powers** pol. Gewaltenteilung f; **~ allowance** Trennungszulage f; **2.** ⚙, 🔥 a) Abscheidung f, -spaltung f, b) Scheidung f,

Klassierung f von Erzen; **3.** ✗ Am. Entlassung f; **'sep·a·ra·tism** [-ətɪzəm] s. Separa'tismus m; **'sep·a·ra·tist** [-ətɪst] **I** s. **1.** Separa'tist(in); **2.** eccl. Sektierer (-in); **II** adj. **3.** separa'tistisch; **'sep·a·ra·tive** [-ətɪv] adj. trennend, Trennungs...; **sep·a·ra·tor** ['sepəreɪtə] s. **1.** ⚙ a) (Ab)Scheider m, b) (bsd. 'Milch-) Zentri·fuge f; **2.** a. **~ stage** ⚡ Trennstufe f; **3.** bsd. 🛠 Spreizvorrichtung f.

Se·phar·dim [se'fɑːdɪm] (Hebrew) s. pl. Se'phardim pl.

se·pi·a ['siːpjə] s. **1.** zo. Sepia f, (Gemeiner) Tintenfisch m; **2.** Sepia f (Sekret od. Farbstoff); **3.** paint. a) Sepia f (Farbe), b) Sepiazeichnung f; **4.** phot. Sepiadruck m.

sep·sis ['sepsɪs] s. 🩺 Sepsis f.

sept- [sept] in Zssgn sieben...

sep·ta ['septə] pl. von **septum**.

sep·tan·gle ['septæŋgl] s. ⟁ Siebeneck n.

Sep·tem·ber [sep'tembə] s. Sep'tember m: **in ~** im September.

sep·te·mi·a [sep'tiːmɪə] → **septic(a)emia**.

sep·te·nar·y [sep'tiːnərɪ] **I** adj. **1.** aus sieben bestehend, Sieben...; **2.** → **septennial**; **II** s. **3.** Satz m von sieben Dingen; **4.** Sieben f.

sep·ten·ni·al [sep'tenjəl] adj. □ **1.** siebenjährlich; **2.** siebenjährig.

sep·tet(te) [sep'tet] s. ♪ Sep'tett n.

sep·tic ['septɪk] adj. (□ **~ally**) 🩺 septisch: **~ sore throat** septische Angina; **II** s. Fäulniserreger m.

sep·ti·c(a)e·mi·a [ˌsepti'siːmɪə] s. 🩺 Blutvergiftung f, Sepsis f.

sep·tu·a·ge·nar·i·an [ˌseptjuədʒɪ'neərɪən] **I** s. Siebzigjährige(r m) f, Siebziger(in); **II** adj. a) siebzigjährig, b) in den Siebzigern; **Sep·tu·a·ges·i·ma** (**Sun·day**) [ˌseptjuə'dʒesɪmə] s. Septua'gesima f (9. Sonntag vor Ostern).

sep·tum ['septəm] pl. **-ta** [-tə] s. ♀, anat., zo. (Scheide)Wand f, Septum n.

sep·tu·ple ['septjupl] **I** adj. siebenfach; **II** s. das Siebenfache; **III** v/t. (v/i. sich) versiebenfachen.

sep·tu·plet ['septjuplɪt] s. **1.** Siebenergruppe f; **2.** mst pl. Siebenling m (Kind).

sep·ul·cher Am. → **sepulchre**; **se·pul·chral** [sɪ'pʌlkrəl] adj. □ **1.** Grab..., Begräbnis...; **2.** fig. düster, Grabes... (-stimme etc.); **sep·ul·chre** ['sepəlkə] s. **1.** Grab(stätte f, -mal n) n; **2.** a. **Easter ~** R.C. Ostergrab n (Schrein).

sep·ul·ture ['sepəltʃə] s. (Toten)Bestattung f.

se·quel ['siːkwəl] s. **1.** (Aufein'ander-) Folge f: **in the ~** in der Folge; **2.** Folge (-erscheinung) f, (Aus)Wirkung f, Konse'quenz f; (gerichtliches etc.) Nachspiel; **3.** (Ro'man- etc.)Fortsetzung f, (a. Hörspiel- etc.)Folge f.

se·quence ['siːkwəns] s. **1.** (Aufein'ander)Folge f: **~ of operations** ⚙ Arbeitsablauf m; **~ of tenses** ling. Zeitenfolge f; **2.** (Reihen)Folge f: **in ~** der Reihe nach; **3.** Folge f, Reihe f, Serie f; **4.** → **sequel** 2; **5.** ♪, eccl., a. Kartenspiel: Se'quenz f; **6.** Film: Szene f; **7.** Folgerichtigkeit f; **8.** fig. Vorgang m; **'se·quent** [-nt] **I** adj. **1.** (aufein'ander) folgend; **2.** (logisch) folgend; **II** s. **3.** (zeitliche od. logische) Folge; **se·quen·tial** [sɪ'kwenʃl] adj. □ **1.** (regelmäßig) (aufein'ander) folgend; **2.** folgend (**to** auf acc.); **3.** folgerichtig, konse'quent; **4.** Computer: sequenti'ell.

se·ques·ter [sɪ'kwestə] v/t. **1.** (o.s. sich) absondern (**from** von); **2.** ⚖ → **se-**

questrate; **se'ques·tered** [-əd] adj. einsam, weltabgeschieden; zu'rückgezogen; **se'ques·trate** [-treɪt] v/t. ⚖ beschlagnahmen: a) unter Treuhänderschaft stellen, b) konfiszieren; **se·ques·tra·tion** [ˌsiːkwe'streɪʃn] s. **1.** Absonderung f; Ausschluss m (**from** von, eccl. aus der Kirche); **2.** ⚖ Beschlagnahme f: a) Zwangsverwaltung f, b) Einziehung f; **3.** Zu'rückgezogenheit f.

se·quin ['siːkwɪn] s. **1.** hist. Ze'chine f (Goldmünze); **2.** Ziermünze f; **3.** Pail'lette f.

se·quoi·a [sɪ'kwɔɪə] s. ♀ Mammutbaum m.

se·ra·glio [se'rɑːlɪəʊ] pl. **-glios** s. Se'rail n.

se·rai [se'raɪ] s. Karawanse'rei f.

ser·aph ['serəf] pl. **'ser·aphs**, **'ser·a·phim** [-fɪm] s. Seraph m (Engel); **se·raph·ic** [se'ræfɪk] adj. (□ **~ally**) se'raphisch, engelhaft, verzückt.

Serb [sɜːb], **'Ser·bian** [-bjən] **I** s. **1.** Serbe m, Serbin f; **2.** ling. Serbisch n; **II** adj. **3.** serbisch.

sere [sɪə] → **sear**[1] 7.

ser·e·nade [ˌserə'neɪd] ♪ **I** s. **1.** Sere'nade f, Ständchen n, 'Nachtmu·sik f; **2.** Sere'nade f (vokale od. instrumentale Abendmusik); **II** v/i. u. v/t. **3.** (j-m) ein Ständchen bringen; **ser·e'nad·er** [-də] s. j-d, der ein Ständchen bringt.

ser·en·dip·i·tous [ˌseren'dɪpɪtəs] adj. **1.** auf Zufallen beruhend, zufällig; **2.** vom Glück begünstigt; **3.** gut, günstig (Wetter etc.); **ser·en'dip·i·ty** s. **1.** a) Glück n, glücklicher Zufall, b) ,mehr Glück als Verstand'; **2.** Geschick n, per Zufall auf wichtige Dinge zu stoßen.

se·rene [sɪ'riːn] adj. □ **1.** heiter, klar (Himmel, Wetter etc.), ruhig (See), friedlich (Natur etc.): **all ~** sl. ,alles in Butter'; **2.** heiter, gelassen (Person, Gemüt etc.); **3.** ♀ durch'lauchtig: **His ♀ Highness** Seine Durchlaucht; **se·ren·i·ty** [sɪ'renətɪ] s. **1.** Heiterkeit f, Klarheit f; **2.** Gelassenheit f, heitere (Gemüts)Ruhe; **3.** (**Your**) ♀ (Eure) 'Durchlaucht f (Titel).

serf [sɜːf] s. **1.** hist. Leibeigene(r m) f; **2.** obs. od. fig. Sklave m; **'serf·age** [-fɪdʒ], **'serf·dom** [-dəm] s. **1.** Leibeigenschaft f; **2.** obs. od. fig. Sklave'rei f.

serge [sɜːdʒ] s. Serge f (Stoff).

ser·geant ['sɑːdʒənt] s. **1.** ✗ Feldwebel m; Artillerie, Kavallerie: Wachtmeister m: **~ first class** Am. Oberfeldwebel; **first ~** Hauptfeldwebel; **2.** (Poli'zei-) Wachtmeister m; **3.** → **serjeant**; **~ major** s. ✗ Hauptfeldwebel m.

se·ri·al ['sɪərɪəl] **I** s. **1.** in Fortsetzungen od. in regelmäßiger Folge erscheinende Veröffentlichung, bsd. 'Fortsetzungsro·,man m; **2.** (Veröffentlichungs)Reihe f, Lieferungswerk n; peri'odische Zeitschrift; **3.** a) Sendereihe f, b) (Hörspiel-, Fernseh)Folge f, Serie f; **II** adj. □ **4.** Serien..., Fortsetzungs...: **~ story**, **~ rights** Copyright n e-s Fortsetzungsromans; **5.** serienmäßig, Serien..., Reihen..., Computer: seri'ell: **~ manufacture**; **~ number** a) laufende Nummer, b) Fabrikationsnummer f; **~ photograph** Reihenbild n; **~ processing** Computer: serielle Verarbeitung; **6.** ♪ Zwölfton...; **'se·ri·al·ize** [-laɪz] v/t. **1.** peri'odisch od. in Fortsetzungen ver'öffentlichen; **2.** reihenweise anordnen; **se·ri·a·tim** [ˌsɪərɪ'eɪtɪm] (Lat.) adv. der Reihe nach.

se·ri·ceous [sɪ'rɪʃəs] adj. **1.** Seiden...; **2.** seidig; **3.** ♀, zo. seidenhaarig; **ser·i·cul·ture** ['serɪˌkʌltʃə] s. Seidenraupenzucht *f.*

se·ries ['sɪəriːz] *pl.* **-ries** *s.* **1.** Serie *f*, Folge *f*, Kette *f*, Reihe *f*: *in ~* der Reihe nach (→ 3 *u.* 9); **2.** (Ar'tikel-, Buch- *etc.*)Serie *f*, Reihe *f*, Folge *f*; **3.** ◉ Serie *f*, Baureihe *f*: *~ production* Reihen-, Serienbau *m*; *in ~* serienmäßig; **4.** (Briefmarken- *etc.*)Serie *f*; **5.** ⚕ Reihe *f*; **6.** ⚘ homo'loge Reihe; **7.** *geol.* Schichtfolge *f*; **8.** *zo.* Ab'teilung *f*; **9.** *a.* **~ connection** ⚡ Serien-, Reihenschaltung *f*: *~ motor* Reihen(schluss)motor *m*; **connect in ~** hintereinander schalten.

ser·if ['serɪf] *s. typ.* Se'rife *f.*

ser·in ['serɪn] *s. orn.* wilder Ka'narienvogel.

se·ri·o-com·ic [ˌsɪərɪəʊ'kɒmɪk] *adj.* (□ **~ally**) ernst-komisch.

se·ri·ous ['sɪərɪəs] *adj.* □ **1.** ernst(haft): a) feierlich, b) von ernstem Cha'rakter, seri'ös, c) schwerwiegend, bedeutend: *~ dress* seriöse Kleidung; *~ music* ernste Musik; *~ problem* ernstes Problem; *~ artist* ernsthafter Künstler; **2.** ernstlich, bedenklich, gefährlich: *~ illness*, *~ rival* ernst zu nehmender Rivale; **3.** ernst(haft, -lich), ernst gemeint (Angebot etc.): *are you ~?* meinst du das im Ernst?; **'se·ri·ous·ly** [-lɪ] *adv.* ernst (-lich); im Ernst: *~ ill* ernstlich krank; *~ wounded* schwer verwundet; *now, ~!* im Ernst!; **'se·ri·ous·ness** [-nɪs] *s.* **1.** Ernst *m*, Ernsthaftigkeit *f*; **2.** Wichtigkeit *f*, Bedeutung *f.*

ser·jeant ['sɑːdʒənt] *s.* ⚖ **1.** Gerichtsdiener *m*; **2.** *Common* ⚖ Stadtsyndikus *m* (London); **3.** *a.* *~ at law* höherer Barrister (des Gemeinen Rechts); *~ at arms* *s. parl.* Ordnungsbeamte(r) *m.*

ser·mon ['sɜːmən] *s.* **1.** Predigt *f*: ⚖ *on the Mount* *bibl.* Bergpredigt; **2.** *iro.* (Mo'ral-, Straf)Predigt *f*; **'ser·mon·ize** [-naɪz] **I** *v/i.* (*a. iro.*) predigen; **II** *v/t.* *j-m* e-e (Mo'ral)Predigt halten.

se·rol·o·gist [sɪə'rɒlədʒɪst] *s.* ⚕ Serolo'ge *m*; **se'rol·o·gy** [-dʒɪ] *s.* Serolo'gie *f*, Serumkunde *f*; **se'ros·i·ty** [-ɒsɪtɪ] *s.* ⚕ **1.** se'röser Zustand; **2.** se'röse Flüssigkeit; **se·rous** ['sɪərəs] *adj.* ⚕ se'rös.

ser·pent ['sɜːpənt] *s.* **1.** (*bsd.* große) Schlange; **2.** *fig.* (Gift)Schlange *f* (Person); **3.** ♪ *ast.* Schlange *f*; **'ser·pen·tine** [-taɪn] **I** *adj.* **1.** schlangenförmig, Schlangen...; **2.** sich schlängelnd od. windend, geschlängelt, Serpentinen...: *~ road*; **3.** *fig.* falsch, tückisch; **II** *s.* **4.** *geol.* Serpen'tin *m*; **5.** *Eislauf:* Schlangenbogen *m*; **6.** ♪ Teich im Hyde Park.

ser·pi·go [sɜː'paɪgəʊ] *s.* ⚕ fressende Flechte.

ser·rate ['serɪt] *, * **ser·rat·ed** [se'reɪtɪd] *adj.* (sägeförmig) gezackt; **'ser·rate·-'den·tate** *adj.* ⚘ gesägt-gezähnt.

ser·ra·tion [se'reɪʃn] *s.* (sägeförmige) Auszackung.

ser·ried ['serɪd] *adj.* dicht geschlossen (Reihen).

se·rum ['sɪərəm] *s.* **1.** *physiol.* (Blut-) Serum *n*; **2.** ⚕ (Heil-, Schutz)Serum *n.*

ser·val ['sɜːvəl] *s. zo.* Serval *m.*

serv·ant ['sɜːvənt] *s.* **1.** Diener *m* (a. fig. Gottes, der Kunst etc.); (domestic) *~* Dienstbote *m*, -mädchen *n*, Hausangestellte(r *m*) *f*; *~s' hall* Gesindestube *f*; *your obedient ~* hochachtungsvoll (Amtsstil); **2.** *bsd.* **public ~** Beamte(r) *m*, Angestellte(r) *m* (im öffentlichen Dienst); → *civil* 2; **3.** ⚖ (Handlungs-) Gehilfe *m*, Angestellte(r) *m* (*Ggs. master* 5 b); *~ girl, ~ maid* *s.* Dienstmädchen *n.*

serve [sɜːv] **I** *v/t.* **1.** *j-m, a.* Gott, *s-m* Land *etc.* dienen; arbeiten für, im Dienst stehen bei; **2.** *j-m* dienlich sein, helfen (a. Sache); **3.** Dienstzeit (a. ✗) ableisten; Lehre 'durchmachen; ⚖ Strafe absitzen, verbüßen; **4.** a) Amt ausüben, innehaben, b) Dienst tun in (dat.), Gebiet, Personenkreis betreuen, versorgen; **5.** e-m Zweck dienen od. entsprechen, e-n Zweck erfüllen, e-r Sache nützen: *it ~s no purpose* es hat keinen Zweck; **6.** genügen (dat.), ausreichen für: *enough to ~ us a month*; **7.** *j-m bei Tisch aufwarten; j-n,* ⛵ Kunden bedienen; **8.** *a.* *~ up* Essen etc. servieren, auftragen, reichen: *dinner is ~d!* es ist serviert *od.* angerichtet!; *~ up* F fig. 'auftischen'; **9.** ✗ Geschütz bedienen; **10.** versorgen (with mit): *~ the town with gas*; **11.** *oft* *~ out* aus-, verteilen; **12.** *mst* F a) *j-n schändlich etc.* behandeln, b) *j-m et.* zufügen: *~ s.o. a trick j-m e-n Streich spielen*; *~ s.o. out* es *j-m* heimzahlen; (*it*) *~s him right* (das) geschieht ihm recht; **13.** Verlangen befriedigen, frönen (dat.); **14.** Stute etc. decken; **15.** ⚖ Vorladung etc. zustellen (dat.): *~ s.o. a writ, ~ a writ on s.o.*; **16.** ◉ um'wickeln; **17.** ⚓ Tau bekleiden; **II** *v/i.* **18.** dienen, Dienst tun (beide a. ✗); in Diensten stehen, angestellt sein (with bei); **19.** servieren, bedienen: *~ at table*; **20.** fungieren, amtieren (as als): *~ on a committee* in e-m Ausschuss tätig sein; **21.** dienen, nützen: *it ~s to inf.* es dient dazu, zu *inf.*; *it ~s to show his cleverness* daran kann man s-e Klugheit erkennen; **22.** dienen (as, for als): a *blanket ~d as a curtain*; **23.** genügen, den Zweck erfüllen; **24.** günstig sein, passen: *as occasion ~s* bei passender Gelegenheit; *the tide ~s* der Wasserstand ist (zum Auslaufen etc.) günstig; **25.** *sport* a) *Tennis etc.:* aufschlagen, b) *Volleyball:* aufgeben: *X to ~!* Aufschlag X; **26.** *R.C.* ministrieren; **III** *s.* **27.** → *service* 20; **'serv·er** [-və] *s.* **1.** *R.C.* Mini'strant *m*; **2.** a) *Tennis:* Aufschläger *m*, b) *Volleyball:* Aufgeber *m*; **3.** a) Tab'lett *n*, b) Warmhalteplatte *f*, c) Serviertischchen *n od.* -wagen *m*, d) Tortenheber *m*; **4.** *Computer:* Server *m.*

serv·ice[1] ['sɜːvɪs] *s.* ⚘ **1.** Spierbaum *m*; **2.** *a.* **wild *~* (tree)** Elsbeerbaum *m.*

serv·ice[2] ['sɜːvɪs] **I** *s.* **1.** Dienst *m*, Stellung *f* (*bsd. v. Hausangestellten*): *be in ~* in Stellung sein; *take s.o. into ~* j-n einstellen; **2.** a) Dienstleistung *f* (*a.* ⛵, ⚖), Dienst *m* (to an dat.), b) (guter) Dienst, Gefälligkeit *f*: *do* (*od. render*) *s.o. a ~* j-m e-n Dienst erweisen; *at your ~* zu Ihren Diensten; *be* (place) *at s.o.'s ~* j-m zur Verfügung stehen (stellen); **3.** ⛵ Bedienung *f*: *prompt ~*; **4.** Nutzen *m*: *be of ~ to* j-m nützen; **5.** (Nacht-, Nachrichten-, Presse-, Telefon- *etc.*)Dienst *m*; **6.** a) Versorgungsdienst *m*, b) Versorgungsbetrieb *m*: *water ~* Wasserversorgung *f*; **7.** Funkti'on *f*, Amt *n* (*e-s Beamten*); **8.** (öffentlicher) Dienst, Staatsdienst *m*: *diplomatic ~*; *on Her Majesty's* ⚖ *Brit.* ♔ Dienstsache *f*; **9.** ⛴ *etc.* Verkehr *m*, Betrieb *m*: *twenty-minute ~* Zwanzigminutentakt *m*; **10.** ◉ Betrieb *m*: *in* (out of) *~* in (außer) Betrieb; *~ conditions* Betriebsbeanspruchung *f*; *~ life* Lebensdauer *f*; **11.** ◉ Wartung *f*, Kundendienst *m*, Service *m*; **12.** ✗ a) (Wehr-) Dienst *m*, b) Waffengattung *f*, c) *pl.* Streitkräfte *pl.*, d) *Brit.* Ma'rine *f*: *be on active ~* aktiv dienen; *~ pistol* Dienstpistole *f*; **13.** ✗ Am. (techni-

sche) Versorgungstruppe; **14.** ✗ Bedienung *f* (Geschütz); **15.** *mst pl.* Hilfsdienst *m*: *medical ~(s)*; **16.** *eccl.* a) *a.* **divine *~*** Gottesdienst *m*, b) Litur'gie *f*; **17.** Ser'vice *n*, Tafelgerät *n*; **18.** ⚖ Zustellung *f*; **19.** ⚓ Bekleidung *f* (Tau); **20.** *sport* a) *Tennis etc.:* Aufschlag *m*, b) *Volleyball:* Aufgabe *f*; **II** *v/t.* **21.** ◉ a) warten, pflegen, b) über'holen; **22.** ⛵ *bsd. Am.* Kundendienst verrichten für *od.* bei; **23.** *zo.* Stute decken; **'serv·ice·a·ble** [-səbl] *adj.* □ **1.** brauch-, verwendbar, nützlich; betriebs-, leistungsfähig; **2.** zweckdienlich; **3.** haltbar, strapazierfähig.

serv·ice| **a·re·a** *s.* **1.** *Radio, TV:* Sendebereich *m*; **2.** *Brit.* (Autobahn)Raststätte *f* (mit Tankstelle); *~* **book** *s. eccl.* Gebet-, Gesangbuch *n*; *~* **box** *s.* ⚡ Anschlusskasten *m*; *~* **brake** *s. mot.* Betriebsbremse *f*; *~* **charge** *s.* **1.** *econ.* Bedienungszuschlag *m*; **2.** ⛵ Bearbeitungsgebühr *f*; *~* **com·pa·ny** *s.* Dienstleistungsbetrieb *m*; *~* **court** *s. Tennis etc.:* Aufschlagfeld *n*; *~* **dress** → *service uniform*; *~* **en·gi·neer** *s.* Kundendiensttechniker *m*; *~* **flat** *s. Brit.* E'tagenwohnung *f* mit Bedienung; *~* **hatch** *s. Brit.* 'Durchreiche *f* (für Speisen); *~* **in·dus·try** *s.* **1.** *mst pl.* Dienstleistungsbetriebe *pl.*, -gewerbe *n*; **2.** 'Zulieferindust,rie *f*; *~* **life** *s.* ◉ Lebensdauer *f*; *~* **line** *s. Tennis etc.:* Aufschlaglinie *f*; **'~·man** [-mən] *s.* [*irr.*] **1.** Sol'dat *m*, Mili'tärangehörige(r) *m*; **2.** ◉ a) 'Kundendienstme,chaniker *m*, b) 'Wartungsmon,teur *m*; *~* **mod·ule** *s.* Versorgungsteil *m* e-s Raumschiffs; *~* **so·ci·e·ty** *s.* Dienstleistungsgesellschaft *f*; *~* **sta·tion** *s.* **1.** Kundendienst- *od.* Repara'turwerkstatt *f*; **2.** (Groß)Tankstelle *f*; *~* **trade** *s.* Dienstleistungsgewerbe *n*; *~* **u·ni·form** *s.* ✗ Dienstanzug *m.*

ser·vi·ette [sɜːvɪ'et] *s.* Servi'ette *f.*

ser·vile ['sɜːvaɪl] *adj.* □ **1.** ser'vil, unter-'würfig, kriecherisch; **2.** *fig.* sklavisch (Gehorsam, Genauigkeit etc.); **ser·vil·i·ty** [sɜː'vɪlətɪ] *s.* Unter'würfigkeit *f*, Krieche'rei *f.*

serv·ing ['sɜːvɪŋ] *s.* Porti'on *f.*

ser·vi·tor ['sɜːvɪtə] *s.* **1.** *obs.* Diener(in) (a. fig.); **2.** *obs. od. poet.* Gefolgsmann *m*; **3.** *univ. hist.* Stipendi'at *m.*

ser·vi·tude ['sɜːvɪtjuːd] *s.* **1.** Sklave'rei *f*, Knechtschaft *f* (a. fig.); **2.** ⚖ Zwangsarbeit *f*: *penal ~* Zuchthausstrafe *f*; **3.** ⚖ Servi'tut *n*, Nutzungsrecht *n.*

'ser·vo-as,sist·ed ['sɜːvəʊ-] *adj.* ◉ Servo...; *~* **brake** *s.* Servobremse *f*; *~* **steer·ing** *s.* Servolenkung *f.*

ses·a·me ['sesəmɪ] *s.* **1.** ⚘ Indischer Sesam; **2.** → *open sesame.*

ses·a·moid ['sesəmɔɪd] *adj. anat.* Sesam...: *~ bones* Sesamknöchelchen.

sesqui- [seskwɪ] *in Zssgn* anderthalb; **,~'al·ter** [-'æltə], **,~'al·ter·al** [-'æltərəl] *adj.* im Verhältnis 3:2 od. 1:1½ stehend; **,~'cen'ten·ni·al** [-ɪəl] *adj.* 150-jährig; **II** *s.* 150-Jahr-Feier *f*; **,~·pe'da·li·an** [-pɪ'deɪljən] *adj.* **1.** anderthalb Fuß lang; **2.** *fig. humor.* sehr lang, monst'rös: *~ word*; **3.** *fig.* vielsilbig; **'~·plane** [-pleɪn] *s.* ✈ 'Andert'halbdecker *m.*

ses·sile ['sesɪl] *adj.* **1.** ⚘ stiellos; **2.** *zo.* ungestielt.

ses·sion ['seʃn] *s.* **1.** *parl.* ⚖ a) Sitzung *f*, b) 'Sitzungsperi,ode *f*: *be in ~* e-e Sitzung abhalten, tagen; **2.** (einzelne) Sitzung (a. ⚕ psych.), Konfe'renz *f*; **3.** *~s pl.* → *magistrates' court, Quarter*

Sessions; **4.** a) *Court of ⚖ oberstes schottisches Zivilgericht,* b) *Court of ⚖s Am.* (einzelstaatliches) *Gericht für Strafsachen;* **5.** *univ.* a) *Brit.* aka'demisches Jahr, b) *Am.* ('Studien)Se‚mester *n;* **'ses·sion·al** [-ʃənl] *adj.* □ **1.** Sitzungs...; **2.** *univ. Brit.* Jahres...: ~ *course.*

ses·tet [ses'tet] *s.* **1.** ♪ Sex'tett *n;* **2.** *Metrik:* sechszeilige Strophe.

set [set] **I** *s.* **1.** Satz *m Briefmarken, Dokumente, Werkzeuge etc.;* (*Möbel-, Toiletten- etc.*)Garni'tur *f;* (*Speise- etc.*) Ser'vice *n,* Besteck *n;* (*Farben- etc.*) Sorti'ment *n;* **2.** ✝ Kollekti'on *f;* **3.** Sammlung *f: a ~ of Shakespeare's works;* **4.** (Schriften)Reihe *f,* (Ar'tikel-)Serie *f;* **5.** ⊙ (Ma'schinen)Anlage *f;* **6.** (Häuser)Gruppe *f;* **7.** (Zimmer)Flucht *f;* **8.** ⊙ a) (Ma'schinen)Satz *m,* Aggre-'gat *n,* b) (*Radio- etc.*)Gerät *n,* Appa-'rat *m;* **9.** a) *thea.* Bühnenausstattung *f,* b) *Film:* Szenenaufbau *m;* **10.** *Tennis etc.:* Satz *m;* **11.** ⋀ a) Zahlenreihe *f,* b) Menge *f;* **12.** ~ *of teeth* Gebiss *n;* **13.** (Per'sonen)Kreis *m:* a) Gesellschaft(sschicht) *f, vornehme, literarische etc.* Welt, b) *contp.* Klüngel *m,* Clique *f: the chic ~* die ‚Schickeria‘; *the fast ~* die Lebewelt; **14.** Sitz *m,* Schnitt *m von Kleidern;* **15.** Haltung *f;* **16.** Richtung *f,* (Ver)Lauf *m e-r Strömung etc.;* **17.** Neigung *f,* Ten'denz *f;* **18.** *poet.* 'Untergang *m der Sonne etc.: the ~ of the day* das Tagesende; **19.** ⊙ → *setting* 10; **20.** *hunt.* Vorstehen *n des Hundes: make a dead ~ at fig.* a) über j-n herfallen, b) es auf *e-n* Mann abgesehen haben (*Frau*); **21.** *hunt.* (*Dachs- etc.*)Bau *m;* **22.** ♀ Setzling *m,* Ableger *m;* **II** *adj.* **23.** starr (*Gesicht, Lächeln*); **24.** fest (*Meinung*); **25.** festgesetzt: *at the ~ day;* **26.** vorgeschrieben, festgelegt: ~ *rules;* ~ *books* od. *reading* Pflichtlektüre *f;* **27.** for'mell, konventio'nell: ~ *party;* **28.** wohl überlegt, einstudiert: ~ *speech;* **29.** a) bereit, b) fest entschlossen (*on doing* zu tun); **30.** zs.-gebissen (*Zähne*); **31.** eingefasst (*Edelstein*); **32.** ~ *piece paint. etc.* Gruppenbild *n;* **33.** ~ *fair* beständig (*Barometer*); **34.** *in Zssgn* ...gebaut; **III** *v/t.* [*irr.*] **35.** setzen, stellen, legen: ~ *the glass to one's lips* das Glas an die Lippen setzen; ~ *a match to* ein Streichholz halten an (*acc.*), *et.* in Brand stecken; → *hand* 7, *sail* 1 *etc.;* **36.** (ein-, her)richten, (an)ordnen, zu'rechtmachen; *thea.* Bühne aufbauen; *Tisch* decken; ⊙ *etc.* (ein)stellen, (-) richten, regulieren; *Uhr, Wecker* stellen; ⊙ *Säge* schränken; *hunt.* Falle (auf-) stellen; ⚒ *Bruch, Knochen* (ein)richten; *Messer* abziehen; *Haar* legen; **37.** ♪ a) vertonen, b) arrangieren; **38.** *typ.* absetzen; **39.** ♪ a) ~ *out* Setzlinge (aus)pflanzen, b) *Boden* bepflanzen; **40.** a) *Bruthenne* setzen, b) *Eier* 'unterlegen; **41.** a) *Edelstein* fassen, b) *mit Edelsteinen etc.* besetzen; **42.** *Wache* (auf)stellen; **43.** *Aufgabe, Frage* stellen; **44.** *j-n* anweisen (*to do s.th. et.* zu tun), *j-n* setzen (*to* an *e-e Sache*): ~ *o.s. to do s.th.* sich daran machen, *et.* zu tun; **45.** vorschreiben; **46.** *Zeitpunkt* festlegen; **47.** *Hund etc.* hetzen (*on* auf *j-n*): ~ *spies on j-n* bespitzeln lassen; **48.** (veran)lassen (*doing* zu tun): ~ *going* in Gang setzen; ~ *s.o. laughing* j-n zum Lachen bringen; ~ *s.o. thinking* j-m zu denken geben; **49.** *in e-n Zustand* versetzen; → *ease* 2; **50.** *Flüssiges* fest werden lassen; *Milch* gerinnen

lassen; **51.** *Zähne* zs.-beißen; **52.** *Wert* bemessen, festsetzen; **53.** *Preis* aussetzen (*on* auf *acc.*); **54.** *Geld, Leben* riskieren; **55.** *Hoffnung, Vertrauen* setzen (*on* auf *acc.;* *in* in *acc.*); **56.** *Grenzen, Schranken etc.* setzen (*to dat.*); **IV** *v/i.* [*irr.*] **57.** 'untergehen (*Sonne etc.*); **58.** a) auswachsen (*Körper*), b) ausreifen (*Charakter*); **59.** fest werden (*Flüssiges*); abbinden (*Zement etc.*); erstarren (*a. Gesicht, Muskel*); gerinnen (*Milch*); ⚒ sich einrenken; **60.** sitzen (*Kleidung*); **61.** fließen, laufen (*Flut etc.*); wehen, kommen (*from* aus, von) (*Wind*); *fig.* sich neigen od. richten (*against* gegen); **62.** ♀ Frucht ansetzen (*Blüte, Baum*); **63.** *hunt.* (vor)stehen (*Hund*);

Zssgn mit prp.:

set| a·bout *v/i.* **1.** sich an *et.* machen, *et.* in Angriff nehmen; **2.** F über *j-n* herfallen; ~ **a·gainst** *v/t.* **1.** entgegenod. gegen'überstellen (*dat.*): *set o.s.* (*od. one's face*) *against* sich *e-r* Sache widersetzen; **2.** *j-n* aufhetzen gegen; ~ (**up-**)**on** *v/i.* herfallen über *j-n.*

Zssgn mit adv.:

set| a·part *v/t.* **1.** *Geld etc.* bei'seite legen; **2.** *set s.o. apart* (*from*) j-n unter'scheiden (von); ~ **a·side** *v/t.* **1.** a) bei'seite legen, b) → *set apart* 1; **2.** *Plan etc.* fallen lassen; **3.** außer Acht lassen, ausklammern; **4.** verwerfen, *bsd.* ⚖ aufheben; ~ **back** I *v/t.* **1.** Uhr zu-'rückstellen; **2.** *Haus etc.* zu'rücksetzen; **3.** *fig. j-n, et.* zu'rückwerfen; **4.** *j-n* ärmer machen (um); **II** *v/i.* **5.** zu'rückfließen (*Flut etc.*); ~ **by** *v/t. Geld etc.* zu-'rücklegen, sparen; ~ **down** *v/t.* **1.** *Last, a. Fahrgast, a. das Flugzeug* absetzen; **2.** (schriftlich) niederlegen, aufzeichnen; **3.** *j-m e-n* ‚Dämpfer‘ aufsetzen; **4.** ~ *as* j-n abtun od. betrachten als; **5.** *et.* zuschreiben (*to dat.*); **6.** *et.* festlegen, -setzen; ~ **forth** I *v/t.* **1.** bekannt machen; **2.** → *set out* 1; **3.** zur Schau stellen; **II** *v/i.* **4.** aufbrechen: ~ *on a journey e-e* Reise antreten; **5.** *fig.* ausgehen (*from* von); ~ **for·ward** I *v/t.* **1.** Uhr vorstellen; **2.** a) *et.* vor'antreiben, b) *j-n od. et.* weiterbringen; **3.** vorbringen, darlegen; **II** *v/i.* **4.** sich auf den Weg machen; ~ **in** *v/i.* einsetzen (*beginnen*); ~ **off** I *v/t.* **1.** her'vortreten lassen, abheben (*from* von); **2.** her'vorheben; **3.** a) *Rakete* abschießen, b) *Sprengladung* zur Explosi'on bringen, c) *Feuerwerk* abbrennen; **4.** *Alarm etc.* auslösen (*a. Streik etc.*), führen zu; **5.** ✝ auf-, anrechnen (*against* gegen); **6.** ⚖ als Ausgleich nehmen (*against* für); **7.** *Verlust etc.* ausgleichen; **II** *v/i.* **8.** → *set forth* 4; **9.** *fig.* anfangen; ~ **on** *v/t.* **1.** a) j-n drängen (*to do* zu tun), b) j-n aufhetzen (*to* zu); **2.** *Hund etc.* hetzen (*to* auf *acc.*); ~ **out** I *v/t.* **1.** (ausführlich) darlegen, aufzeigen; **2.** anordnen, arrangieren; **II** *v/i.* **3.** aufbrechen, sich aufmachen, sich auf den Weg machen (*for* nach); **4.** sich vornehmen, da'rangehen (*to do et.* zu tun); ~ **to** *v/i.* **1.** sich dar'anmachen, sich ‚da'hinter klemmen‘, ‚loslegen‘; **2.** aufein'ander losgehen; ~ **up** I *v/t.* **1.** errichten: ~ *a monument;* **2.** ⊙ *Maschine etc.* aufstellen, montieren; **3.** *Geschäft etc.* gründen; *Regierung* bilden, einsetzen; **4.** *j-m* zu e-m (guten) Start verhelfen, *j-n* etablieren: ~ *s.o. up in business;* ~ *o.s. up* (*as*) → 15; **5.** *Behauptung etc., a. Rekord* aufstellen; ⚖ *Anspruch* geltend machen, *a. Verteidigung* vorbringen; **6.** *Kandidaten* aufstellen; **7.** *j-n* erhöhen

(*over* über *acc.*), *a. j-n* auf den Thron setzen; **8.** *Stimme, Geschrei* erheben; **9.** *a. Krankheit* verursachen; **10.** a) *j-n* kräftigen, b) *gesundheitlich* wieder'herstellen; **11.** *j-m* (finanzi'ell) ‚auf die Beine helfen‘; **12.** *j-n* versehen, -sorgen (*with* mit); **13.** F a) *j-m e-e* Falle stellen, b) *j-m et.* ‚anhängen‘; **14.** *typ.* (ab-) setzen: ~ *in type;* **II** *v/i.* **15.** sich niederlassen od. etablieren (*as* als): ~ *for o.s.* sich selbstständig machen; **16.** ~ *for* sich ausgeben für od. als, sich aufspielen als.

se·ta·ceous [sɪ'teɪʃəs] *adj.* borstig.

'set|·a‚side *s.* **1.** *Am.* Rücklage *f;* **2.** *EU* Flächenstilllegung *f;* '~**·back** *s.* **1.** *fig.* a) Rückschlag *m,* b) ‚Schlappe‘ *f;* **2.** △ a) Rücksprung *m e-r Wand,* b) zu'rückgesetzte Fas'sade; '~**·down** *s.* **1.** Dämpfer *m;* **2.** Rüffel *m;* '~**·off** *s.* **1.** Kon'trast *m;* **2.** ⚖ a) Gegenforderung *f,* b) Ausgleich *m* (*a. fig.* gegen *für*); **3.** ✝ Aufrechnung *f;* '~**·out** *s.* **1.** a) Aufbruch *m,* b) Anfang *m;* **2.** Aufmachung *f;* **3.** F a) Vorführung *f,* b) Party *f;* ~ *piece s.* **1.** *Kunst:* formvollendetes Werk; **2.** ✕ sorgfältig geplante Operati'on; **3.** → *set* 32; ~ *point s.* **1.** *Tennis etc.:* Satzball *m;* **2.** ⊙ Sollwert *m;* '~**·screw** *s.* ⊙ Stellschraube *f;* ~ *square s.* Winkel *m,* Zeichendreieck *n.*

sett [set] *s.* Pflasterstein *m.*

set·tee [se'tiː] *s.* **1.** Sitz-, Polsterbank *f;* **2.** kleineres Sofa: ~ *bed* Bettcouch *f.*

set·ter ['setə] *s.* **1.** *allg.* Setzer(in), Einrichter(in); **2.** *typ.* (Schrift)Setzer *m;* **3.** Setter *m* (*Vorstehhund*); **4.** (Poli'zei-) Spitzel *m;* ‚~·'on [-ər'ɒn] *pl.* ‚s·'on *s.* Aufhetzer(in).

set the·o·ry *s.* ⋀ Mengenlehre *f.*

set·ting ['setɪŋ] *s.* **1.** (*typ.* Schrift)Setzen *n;* Einrichten *n;* (Ein)Fassen *n* (*Edelstein*); **2.** Schärfen *n* (*Messer*); **3.** (*Gold- etc.*)Fassung *f;* **4.** Lage *f,* 'Hintergrund *m e-s Romans etc.;* **5.** Schauplatz *m,* 'Hintergrund *m e-s Romans etc.;* **6.** *thea.* szenischer 'Hintergrund, Bühnenbild *n; a. Film:* Ausstattung *f;* **7.** ♪ a) Vertonung *f,* b) Satz *m;* **8.** (*Sonnen- etc.*)'Untergang *m;* **9.** ⊙ Einstellung *f;* **10.** ⊙ Hartwerden *n,* Abbinden *n von Zement etc.:* ~ *point* Stockpunkt *m;* **11.** ⊙ Schränkung *f* (*Säge*); **12.** Gedeck *n;* ~ *lo·tion* (Haar)Festiger *m;* ~ *rule s. typ.* Setzlinie *f;* ~ *stick s. typ.* Winkelhaken *m;* '~**·up** *s.* **1.** *bsd.* ⊙ Einrichtung *f,* Aufstellung *f;* **2.** ~ *exercises Am.* Gymnastik *f,* Freiübungen *pl.*

set·tle ['setl] I *v/i.* **1.** sich niederlassen od. setzen (*a. Vogel etc.*); **2.** a) sich ansiedeln, b) ~ *in* sich in *e-r* Wohnung *etc.* einrichten, c) ~ *in* sich einleben od. eingewöhnen; **3.** a) *a.* ~ *down* sich *in e-m Ort* niederlassen, b) (häuslich) niederlassen, c) *a. marry and* ~ *down* e-n Hausstand gründen, d) sesshaft werden, zur Ruhe kommen, sich einleben; **4.** ~ *down to* sich widmen (*dat.*), sich *an e-e Arbeit etc.* machen; **5.** sich legen od. beruhigen (*Wut etc.*); **6.** ~ *on* sich zuwenden (*dat.*), fallen auf (*acc.*) (*Zuneigung etc.*); **7.** ⚒ sich festsetzen (*on, in* in *dat.*), sich legen (*on* auf *acc.*) (*Krankheit*); **8.** beständig werden (*Wetter*): *it ~d in for rain* es regnete sich ein; *it is settling for a frost* es wird Frost geben; *the wind has ~d in the west* der Wind steht im Westen; **9.** sich senken (*Mauern etc.*); **10.** langsam absacken (*Schiff*); **11.** sich klären (*Flüssigkeit*); **12.** sich setzen (*Trübstoff*); **13.**

sich legen (*Staub*); **14.** (*upon*) sich entscheiden (für), sich entschließen (zu); **15.** ~ *for* sich begnügen *od.* abfinden mit; **16.** e-e Vereinbarung treffen; **17.** a) ~ *up* zahlen *od.* abrechnen (*with* mit), b) ~ *with* e-n Vergleich schließen mit, *Gläubiger* abfinden; **II** *v/t.* **18.** *Füße, Hut etc.* (fest) setzen (*on* auf *acc.*): ~ *o.s.* sich niederlassen; ~ *o.s. to* sich an *e-e Arbeit etc.* machen, sich anschicken zu; **19.** a) *Menschen* ansiedeln, b) *Land* besiedeln; **20.** *j-n* beruflich, häuslich *etc.* etablieren, 'unterbringen; *Kind etc.* versorgen, ausstatten, *a.* verheiraten; **21.** a) *Flüssigkeit* ablagern lassen, klären, b) *Trübstoff* sich setzen lassen; **22.** *Boden etc., a. fig. Glauben, Ordnung etc.* festigen; **23.** *Institutionen* gründen, aufbauen (*on* auf *dat.*); **24.** *Zimmer etc.* in Ordnung bringen; **25.** *Frage etc.* klären, regeln, erledigen: *that ~s it* a) damit ist der Fall erledigt, b) *iro.* jetzt ist es endgültig aus; **26.** *Streit* schlichten, beilegen; *strittigen Punkt* beseitigen; **27.** *Nachlass* regeln, *s-e Angelegenheiten* in Ordnung bringen: ~ *one's affairs*; **28.** ([*up*]*on*) *Besitz* über'schreiben, -'tragen (auf *acc.*), *letztwillig* vermachen (*dat.*), *Legat, Rente* aussetzen (für); **29.** bestimmen, festlegen, -setzen; **30.** vereinbaren, sich einigen auf (*acc.*); **31.** *a.* ~ *up* † erledigen, in Ordnung bringen: a) *Rechnung* begleichen, b) *Konto* ausgleichen, c) *Anspruch* befriedigen, d) *Geschäft* abwickeln; → *account* 5; **32.** ⚖ *Prozess* durch Vergleich beilegen; **33.** *Magen, Nerven* beruhigen; **34.** *j-n* ‚fertig machen', zum Schweigen bringen (F *a.* töten); **III** *s.* **35.** Sitzbank *f* (mit hoher Lehne); '**set·tled** [-ld] *adj.* **1.** fest, bestimmt; entschieden; feststehend (*Tatsache*); **2.** fest begründet (*Ordnung*); **3.** fest, ständig (*Wohnsitz, Gewohnheit*); **4.** beständig (*Wetter*); **5.** ruhig, gesetzt (*Person, Leben*).

set·tle·ment ['setlmənt] *s.* **1.** Ansied(e)lung *f*; **2.** Besied(e)lung *f e-s Landes*; **3.** Siedlung *f*, Niederlassung *f*; **4.** 'Unterbringung *f*, Versorgung *f* (*Person*); **5.** Regelung *f*, Klärung *f*, Erledigung *f e-r Frage etc.*; **6.** Schlichtung *f*, Beilegung *f e-s Streits*; **7.** Festsetzung *f*; **8.** (endgültige) Entscheidung; **9.** Über'einkommen *n*, Abmachung *f*; **10.** † a) Begleichung *f von Rechnungen*, b) Ausgleich(ung *f*) *m von Konten*, c) *Börse*: Abrechnung *f*, d) Abwicklung *f e-s Geschäfts*, e) Vergleich *m*, Abfindung *f*: ~ *day* Abrechnungstag *m*; *day of* ~ *fig.* Tag *m* der Abrechnung; *in* ~ *of all claims* zum Ausgleich aller Forderungen; **11.** ⚖ a) (*Eigentums*)Über'tragung *f*, b) Vermächtnis *n*, c) Aussetzung *f e-r Rente etc.*, d) Schenkung *f*, Stiftung *f*; **12.** ⚖ Ehevertrag *m*; **13.** a) ständiger Wohnsitz, b) Heimatberechtigung *f*; **14.** sozi'ales Hilfswerk.

set·tler ['setlə] *s.* **1.** (An)Siedler(in), Kolo'nist(in); **2.** F a) entscheidender Schlag, b) *fig.* vernichtendes Argu'ment, c) Abfuhr *f*; '**set·tling** [-lɪŋ] *s.* **1.** Festsetzen *n etc.*; → *settle*; **2.** ⊙ Ablagerung *f*; **3.** *pl.* (Boden)Satz *m*; **4.** † Abrechnung *f*: ~ *day* Abrechnungstag *m*; '**set·tlor** [-lə] *s.* ⚖ Verfügende(r *m*) *f*.

set-to [ˌset'tuː] *pl.* **-tos** *s.* F **1.** Schläge'rei *f*; **2.** (kurzer) heftiger Kampf; **3.** heftiger Wortwechsel.

set-up ['setʌp] *s.* **1.** Aufbau *m*; **2.** Anordnung *f* (*a.* ⊗); **3.** ⊙ Mon'tage *f*: ~ *costs* Rüstkosten *pl.*; ~ *time* Rüstzeit

f; **4.** *Film, TV*: a) (Kamera)Einstellung *f*, b) Bauten *pl.*; **5.** *Am.* Konstituti'on *f*; **6.** F a) Situati'on *f*, b) Pro'jekt *n*; **7.** F ‚Laden' *m*, ‚Verein' *m* (*Firma etc.*), ‚Bude' *f* (*Wohnung etc.*); **8.** F Schwindel *m*, abgekartete Sache; **9.** Ausrüstung *f* (*Geräte*); **10.** *Am.* F a) Schiebung *f*, b) Gimpel *m*, leichtes Opfer.

sev·en ['sevn] **I** *adj.* sieben: ~-*league boots* Siebenmeilenstiefel; *the* ~ *Years' War* der Siebenjährige Krieg; **II** *s.* Sieben *f* (*Zahl, Spielkarte etc.*); '~-*fold* *adj. u. adv.* siebenfach.

sev·en·teen ['sevn'tiːn] **I** *adj.* siebzehn; **II** *s.* Siebzehn *f*: *sweet* ~ ‚göttliche Siebzehn' (*Mädchenalter*); ‚**sev·en-'teenth** [-nθ] **I** *adj.* **1.** siebzehnt; **II** *s.* **2.** der (die, das) Siebzehnte; **3.** Siebzehntel *n*.

sev·enth ['sevnθ] **I** *adj.* **1.** siebent; **II** *s.* **2.** der (die, das) Sieb(en)te: *the* ~ *of May* der 7. Mai; **3.** Sieb(en)tel *n*; **4.** ♪ Sep'time *f*; '**sev·enth·ly** [-lɪ] *adv.* sieb(en)tens.

sev·en·ti·eth ['sevntiːθ] **I** *adj.* **1.** siebzigst; **II** *s.* **2.** der (die, das) Siebzigste; **3.** Siebzigstel *n*; **sev·en·ty** ['sevntɪ] **I** *adj.* siebzig; **II** *s.* Siebzig *f*: *the seventies* a) die Siebzigerjahre (*e-s Jahrhunderts*), b) die Siebziger(jahre) (*Alter*).

sev·er ['sevə] **I** *v/t.* **1.** (ab)trennen (*from* von); **2.** ('durch)trennen; **3.** *fig. Freundschaft etc.* lösen, *Beziehungen* abbrechen; **4.** ~ *o.s.* (*from*) sich trennen *od.* lösen (von), (aus *der Kirche etc.*) austreten; **5.** (vonein'ander) trennen; **6.** ⚖ *Besitz etc.* teilen; **II** *v/i.* **7.** (zer)reißen; **8.** sich trennen (*from* von); **9.** sich (vonein'ander) trennen; **sev·er·al** ['sevrəl] **I** *adj.* □ **1.** mehrere: ~ *people*; **2.** verschieden, getrennt: *three* ~ *occasions*; **3.** einzeln, verschieden: *the* ~ *reasons*; **4.** besonder, eigen: *we went our* ~ *ways* wir gingen jeder seinen (eigenen) Weg; → *joint* 6; **II** *s.* mehrere *pl.*: ~ *of you*; **sev·er·al·ly** ['sevrəlɪ] *adv.* **1.** einzeln, getrennt; **2.** beziehungsweise; '**sev·er·ance** [-ərəns] *s.* **1.** (Ab)Trennung *f*; **2.** Lösung *f e-r Freundschaft etc.*, Abbruch *m von Beziehungen*: ~ *pay* † Entlassungsabfindung *f*.

se·vere [sɪ'vɪə] *adj.* □ **1.** streng: a) hart, scharf (*Kritik, Richter, Strafe etc.*), b) ernst(haft) (*Miene, Person*), c) rau (*Wetter*), hart (*Winter*), d) herb (*Schönheit, Stil*), schmucklos, e) ex'akt, strikt; **2.** schwer, schlimm (*Krankheit, Verlust etc.*); **3.** heftig (*Schmerz, Sturm etc.*); **4.** scharf (*Bemerkung*); **se'vere·ly** [-lɪ] *adv.* **1.** streng, strikt; **2.** schwer, ernstlich: ~ *ill*; **se·ver·i·ty** [sɪ'verətɪ] *s.* **1.** *allg.* Strenge *f*: a) Schärfe *f*, Härte *f*, b) Rauheit *f* (*des Wetters etc.*), c) Ernst *m*, d) (herbe) Schlichtheit *f* (*Stil*), e) Ex'aktheit *f*; **2.** Heftigkeit *f*.

sew [səʊ] *v/t.* [*irr.*] **1.** nähen (*a. v/i.*): ~ *on* annähen; ~ *up* zu-, vernähen (→ 3); **2.** *Bücher* heften, broschieren; **3.** ~ *up* F a) *Brit.* *j-n* ‚restlos fertig machen', b) *Am.* sich *et. od. j-n* sichern, *et.* ‚per-'fekt machen': ~ *up a deal*.

sew·age ['sjuːɪdʒ] *s.* **1.** Abwasser *n*: ~ *farm* Rieselfeld *n*; ~ *sludge* Klärschlamm *m*; ~ *system* Kanalisation *f*; ~ *works* Kläranlage *f*; **2.** → *sewerage*; **sew·er** ['sjʊə] **I** *s.* **1.** 'Abwasserka‚nal *m*, Klo'ake *f*: ~ *gas* Faulschlammgas *n*; ~ *pipe* Abzugrohr *n*; ~ *rat* *zo.* Wanderratte *f*; **2.** Gosse *f*; **II** *v/t.* **3.** kanalisieren; **sew·er·age** ['sjʊərɪdʒ] *s.* **1.** Kanalisati'on *f* (*System u. Vorgang*); **2.** → *sewage* 1.

sew·in ['sjuːɪn] *s.* 'Lachsfo‚relle *f*.

sew·ing ['səʊɪŋ] *s.* Näharbeit *f*; ~ *box* *s.* Nähkasten *m*; ~ *machine* *s.* 'Nähma‚schine *f*; ~ *nee·dle* *s.* Nähnadel *f*.

sex [seks] **I** *s.* **1.** *biol.* Geschlecht *n*; **2.** (*männliches od. weibliches*) Geschlecht (*als Gruppe*): *the* ~ *humor.* die Frauen; *the gentle* (*od. weaker od. softer*) ~ das zarte *od.* schwache Geschlecht; *of both* ~*es* beiderlei Geschlechts; **3.** a) Geschlechtstrieb *m*, b) e'rotische Anziehungskraft, 'Sex(-Ap‚peal) *m*, c) Sexu'al-, Geschlechtsleben *n*, d) Sex(uali-'tät *f*) *m*, e) Geschlechtsteil(e *pl.*) *n*, f) (Geschlechts)Verkehr *m*, ‚Sex' *m*: *have* ~ *with* mit *j-m* schlafen; **II** *v/t.* **4.** das Geschlecht bestimmen von; **5.** ~ *up* F a) *Film etc.* ‚sexy' gestalten, b) *j-n* ‚scharfmachen'; **III** *adj.* **6.** a) Sexual...: ~ *crime* (*education, hygiene etc.*); ~ *appeal* → 3b; ~ *life* → 3c; ~ *object* Lustobjekt *n*, b) Geschlechts...: ~ *act* (*hormone, organ, etc.*), c) Sex...: ~ *film* (*magazine, etc.*).

sex- [seks] *in Zssgn* sechs.

sex·a·ge·nar·i·an [ˌseksədʒɪ'neərɪən] **I** *adj.* a) sechzigjährig, b) in den Sechzigern; **II** *s.* Sechzigjährige(r *m*) *f*; Sechziger(in).

sex·ag·e·nar·y [sek'sædʒənərɪ] **I** *adj.* **1.** sechzigteilig; **2.** → *sexagenarian* I; **II** *s.* **3.** → *sexagenarian* II.

Sex·a·ges·i·ma (**Sun·day**) [ˌseksə'dʒesɪmə] *s.* Sonntag *m* Sexa'gesima (*8. Sonntag vor Ostern*); ‚**sex·a'ges·i·mal** [-məl] **⚚** **I** *adj.* Sexagesimal...; **II** *s.* Sexagesi'malbruch *m*.

sex·an·gu·lar [sek'sæŋɡjʊlə] *adj.* □ sechseckig.

sex·cen·te·nar·y [ˌseksen'tiːnərɪ] **I** *adj.* sechshundertjährig; **II** *s.* Sechshundert'jahrfeier *f*.

sex·en·ni·al [sek'senɪəl] *adj.* □ **1.** sechsjährig; **2.** sechsjährlich.

sex·i·ness ['seksɪnɪs] *s.* F *für* *sex* 3b.

sex·ism ['seksɪzəm] *s.* 'Sexismus *m*; '**sex·ist** [-ɪst] **I** *adj.* se'xistisch; **II** *s.* Se'xist *m*.

sex·less ['sekslɪs] *adj.* *biol.* geschlechtslos (*a. fig.*), a'gamisch.

sex·ol·o·gy [sek'sɒlədʒɪ] *s.* *biol.* Sexu'alwissenschaft *f*.

sex·par·tite [seks'pɑːtaɪt] *adj.* sechsteilig.

'**sex·pot** *s. sl.* a) ‚Sexbombe' *f*, b) ‚Sexbolzen' *m*.

sex·tain ['seksteɪn] *s.* *Metrik*: sechszeilige Strophe.

sex·tant ['sekstənt] *s.* **1.** ⚓, *ast.* Sex'tant *m*; **2.** ✶ Kreissechstel *n*.

sex·tet(te) [seks'tet] *s.* ♪ Sex'tett *n*.

sex·to ['sekstəʊ] *pl.* **-tos** *s. typ.* 'Sexto (-for‚mat) *n*; **sex·to·dec·i·mo** [ˌsekstəʊ'desɪməʊ] *pl.* **-mos** *s.* **1.** Se'dez(for‚mat) *n*; **2.** Se'dezband *m*.

sex·ton ['sekstən] *s.* **1.** Küster *m* (*u.* Totengräber *m*); ~ *bee·tle* *s. zo.* Totengräber *m* (*Käfer*).

sex·tu·ple ['sekstjʊpl] **I** *adj.* sechsfach; **II** *s.* das Sechsfache; **III** *v/t. u. v/i.* (sich) versechsfachen.

sex·u·al ['seksjʊəl] *adj.* □ sexu'ell, geschlechtlich, Geschlechts..., Sexual...: ~ *abuse* sexu'eller Missbrauch; ~ *harassment* sexuelle Belästigung; ~ *intercourse* Geschlechtsverkehr *m*; **sex·u·al·i·ty** [ˌseksjuˈælətɪ] *s.* **1.** Sexuali'tät *f*; **2.** Sexu'al-, Geschlechtsleben *n*; '**sex·y** [-sɪ] *adj.* ‚sexy', ‚scharf'.

shab·bi·ness ['ʃæbɪnɪs] *s.* Schäbigkeit *f* (*a. fig.*).

shab·by ['ʃæbɪ] *adj.* □ *allg.* schäbig: a) fadenscheinig (*Kleider*), b) abgenutzt

(*Sache*), c) ärmlich, her'untergekommen (*Person, Haus, Gegend etc.*), d) niederträchtig, e) geizig; ,**~-gen'teel** *adj.* vornehm, aber arm: *the ~* die verarmten Vornehmen.

shab·rack ['ʃæbræk] *s.* ⚔ Scha'bracke *f*, Satteldecke *f*.

shack [ʃæk] **I** *s.* Hütte *f*, Ba'racke *f* (*a. contp.*); **II** *v/i.* **~ up** *sl.* zs.-leben (**with** mit).

shack·le ['ʃækl] **I** *s.* **1.** *pl.* Fesseln *pl.*, Ketten *pl.* (*a. fig.*); **2.** ⊖ Gelenkstück *n* e-r Kette; Bügel *m*, Lasche *f*; ♣ (Anker)Schäkel *m*; ⚓ Schäkel *m*; **II** *v/t.* **3.** fesseln (*a. fig. hemmen*); **4.** ♣, ⊖ laschen.

'**shack·town** *s. Am.* → shantytown.

shad [ʃæd] *pl.* **shads,** *coll.* **shad** *s. ichth.* Alse *f*.

shade [ʃeɪd] *I s.* **1.** Schatten *m* (*a. paint. u. fig.*): **put** (*od.* **throw**) *into the ~* fig. in den Schatten stellen; (**the**) **~s of Goethe!** *iro.* (das) erinnert doch sehr an Goethe!; **2.** schattiges Plätzchen; **3.** *myth.* a) Schatten *m* (*Seele*), b) *pl.* Schatten(reich *n*) *pl.*; **4.** a) Farbton *m*, Schattierung *f* (*a. fig.*), b) dunkle Tönung; **5.** *fig.* Spur *f*, ,I'dee' *f*: **a ~ better** ein kleines bisschen besser; **6.** (*Schutz-, Lampen-, Sonnen- etc.*)Schirm *m*; **7.** *Am.* Rou'leau *n*; **8.** *pl.* F Sonnenbrille *f*; **II** *v/t.* **9.** beschatten, verdunkeln (*a. fig.*); **10.** *Augen etc.* abschirmen, schützen (**from** gegen); **11.** *paint.* a) schattieren, b) schraffieren; c) dunkel tönen; **12.** *a.* **~ off** a) *fig.* abstufen, b) ✝ *Preise* nach u. nach senken; c) *a.* **~ away** all'mählich 'übergehen lassen (*into* in *acc.*), d) *a.* **~ away** all'mählich verschwinden lassen; **III** *v/i.* **13.** *a.* **~ off** (*od.* **away**) a) all'mählich 'übergehen (*into* in *acc.*), b) nach u. nach verschwinden; '**shade·less** [-lɪs] *adj.* schattenlos; '**shad·i·ness** [-dɪnɪs] *s.* **1.** Schattigkeit *f*; **2.** *fig.* Anrüchigkeit *f*; '**shad·ing** [-dɪŋ] *s. paint. u. fig.* Schattierung *f*.

shad·ow ['ʃædəʊ] **I** *s.* **1.** Schatten *m* (*a. paint. u. fig.*); Schattenbild *n*: **live in the ~** im Verborgenen leben; **worn to a ~** zum Skelett abgemagert; **he is but the ~ of his former self** er ist nur noch ein Schatten s-r selbst; **coming events cast their ~s before** kommende Ereignisse werfen ihre Schatten voraus; **may your ~ never grow less** *fig.* möge es dir immer gut gehen; **2.** Schemen *m*, Phan'tom *n*: **catch** (*od.* **grasp**) **at ~s** Phantomen nachjagen; **3.** *fig.* Spur *f*, Kleinigkeit *f*: **without a ~ of doubt** ohne den leisesten Zweifel; **4.** *fig.* Schatten *m*, Trübung *f* (*e-r Freundschaft etc.*); **5.** *fig.* Schatten *m* (*Begleiter od. Verfolger*); **II** *v/t.* **6.** e-n Schatten werfen auf (*acc.*), verdunkeln (*beide a. fig.*); **7.** *j-n* beschatten, verfolgen; **8.** *mst* **~ forth** (*od.* **out**) a) dunkel andeuten, b) versinnbildlichen; '**~box·ing** *s. sport* Schattenboxen *n*, *fig. a.* Spiegelfechte'rei *f*; **~ cab·i·net** *s. pol.* 'Schattenkabi,nett *n*; **~ fac·to·ry** *s.* Schatten-, Ausweichbetrieb *m*.

shad·ow·less ['ʃædəʊlɪs] *adj.* schattenlos; '**shad·ow·y** [-əʊɪ] *adj.* **1.** schattig: a) dämmerig, düster, b) Schatten spendend; **2.** *fig.* schattenhaft, vage; **3.** *fig.* unwirklich.

shad·y ['ʃeɪdɪ] *adj.* □ **1.** → shadowy 1 *u.* 2: **on the ~ side of forty** *fig.* über die vierzig hinaus; **2.** F anrüchig, zwielichtig, fragwürdig.

shaft [ʃɑːft] *s.* **1.** (*Pfeil- etc.*)Schaft *m*; **2.** *poet.* Pfeil *m* (*a. fig. des Spottes*),

Speer *m*; **3.** (Licht)Strahl *m*; **4.** ⚕ Stamm *m*; **5.** a) Stiel *m* (*Werkzeug etc.*), b) Deichsel(arm *m*) *f*, c) Welle *f*, Spindel *f*; **6.** (Fahnen)Stange *f*; **7.** Säulenschaft *m*, *a.* Säule *f*; **8.** (*Aufzugs-, Bergwerks- etc.*)Schacht *m*; → sink 17.

shag [ʃæg] **I** *s.* **1.** Zotte(l) *f*; zottiges Haar; **2.** a) (lange, grobe) Noppe, b) Plüsch(stoff) *m*; **3.** Shag(tabak) *m*; **4.** *orn.* Krähenscharbe *f*; **II** *v/t.* **5.** zottig machen, aufrauen; **III** *v/i.* **6.** *sl.* ,bumsen'; **shag·gy** ['ʃægɪ] *adj.* □ **1.** zottig, struppig; rauhaarig; **~-dog story** a) surrealistischer Witz, b) kalauerhafte Geschichte; **2.** verwildert, verwahrlost; **3.** *fig.* verschroben.

sha·green [ʃæ'griːn] *s.* Cha'grin *n*, Körnerleder *n*.

shah [ʃɑː] *s.* Schah *m*.

shake [ʃeɪk] **I** *s.* **1.** Schütteln *n*, Rütteln *n*: **~ of the hand** Händeschütteln; **~ of the head** Kopfschütteln; **give s.th. a good ~** et. tüchtig schütteln; **give s.o. the ~** *Am. sl.* j-n ,abwimmeln'; **in two ~s** (**of a lamb's tail**) F im Nu; **2.** (*a. seelische*) Erschütterung; (*Wind- etc.*) Stoß *m*; *Am.* F Erdstoß *m*: **he** (**it**) **is no great ~s** F mit ihm (damit) ist nicht viel los; **3.** Beben *n*: **the ~s** ,Tatterich' *m*; **all of a ~** am ganzen Leibe zitternd; **4.** (Milch- *etc.*)Shake *m*; **5.** ♩ Triller *m*; **6.** Riss *m*, Spalt *m*; **II** *v/i.* [*irr.*] **7.** (sch)wanken; **8.** zittern, beben (*a. Stimme*) (**with** vor *Furcht etc.*); **9.** ♩ trillern; **III** *v/t.* [*irr.*] **10.** schütteln: **one's head** den Kopf schütteln; **~ one's finger at s.o.** j-m mit dem Finger drohen; **be shaken before taken!** vor Gebrauch schütteln!; → hand *Redew.*, **side 4**; **11.** (*a. fig. Entschluss, Gegner, Glauben, Zeugenaussage*) erschüttern; **12.** a) *j-n* (*seelisch*) erschüttern, b) *j-n* aufrütteln; **13.** rütteln an (*dat.*) (*a. fig.*); **14.** ♩ *Ton* trillern; *Zssgn mit adv.* :

shake | **down** *I v/t.* **1.** *Obst etc.* her'unterschütteln; **2.** *Stroh etc.* (zu e-m Nachtlager) ausbreiten; **3.** *Gefäßinhalt* zu'rechtschütteln; **4.** *Am. sl.* a) *j-n* ausplündern (*a. fig.*), b) erpressen, c) ,filzen', durch'suchen; **5.** *bsd. Am.* F *Schiff, Flugzeug* testen; **II** *v/i.* **6.** sich setzen (*Masse*); **7.** a) sich ein (Nacht-) Lager zu'rechtmachen, b) ,sich hinhauen'; **8.** *Am.* F a) sich vor'übergehend niederlassen (*an e-m Ort*), b) sich einleben, -gewöhnen, c) sich ,einpendeln' (*Sache*), d) sich beschränken (**to** auf *acc.*); **~ off** *v/t.* **1.** *Staub etc.*, *a. fig. Joch*, *a. Verfolger etc.* abschütteln; **2.** *fig. j-n od. et.* loswerden; **~ out** *v/t.* **1.** ausschütteln (*a. fig.*); **2.** *Fahne etc.* ausbreiten; **~ up** *v/t.* **1.** *Bett, Kissen* aufschütteln; **2.** *et.* zs.-, 'umschütteln, mischen; **3.** *fig.* a) *j-n* aufrütteln, b) *j-n* arg mitnehmen; **4.** *Betrieb etc.* 'umkrempeln.

'**shake**|**-down** *s.* **1.** (Not)Lager *n*; **2.** *Am. sl.* a) Ausplünderung *f*, b) Erpressung *f*, c) Durch'suchung *f*; **3.** *bsd. Am.* F Testfahrt *f*, -flug *m*; ,**~-'hands** *s.* Händedruck *m*.

shak·en ['ʃeɪkən] **I** *p.p. von* shake; **II** *adj.* **1.** erschüttert, (sch)wankend (*a. fig.*): **badly** ~ arg mitgenommen; **2.** → shaky 5.

'**shake-out** *s.* ✝ Gesundschrumpfung *f*; Perso'nalabbau *m*.

shak·er ['ʃeɪkə] *s.* **1.** Mixbecher *m*, (Cocktail- *etc.*)Shaker *m*; **2.** ⚕ *eccl.* Zitterer *m* (*Sektierer*).

Shake·spear·i·an [ʃeɪk'spɪərɪən] **I** *adj.* shakespearisch; **II** *s.* Shakespeareforscher(in).

'**shake-up** *s.* **1.** F Aufrütt(e)lung *f*; **2.** drastische (*bsd.* perso'nelle) Veränderungen *pl.*, 'Umkrempelung *f*, -gruppierung *f*.

shak·i·ness ['ʃeɪkɪnɪs] *s.* Wack(e)ligkeit *f* (*a. fig.*).

shak·ing ['ʃeɪkɪŋ] **I** *s.* **1.** Schütteln *n*; Erschütterung *f*; **II** *adj.* **2.** Schüttel...; → palsy 1; **3.** zitternd; **4.** wackelnd.

shak·y ['ʃeɪkɪ] *adj.* □ **1.** wack(e)lig (*a. fig. Person, Gesundheit, Kredit, Kenntnisse*): **in rather ~ English** in ziemlich holprigem Englisch; **2.** zitt(e)rig, bebend: **~ hands;** ~ **voice;** **3.** *fig.* (sch)wankend; **4.** *fig.* unsicher, zweifelhaft; **5.** (kern)rissig (*Holz*).

shale [ʃeɪl] *s. geol.* Schiefer(ton) *m*: **~ oil** Schieferöl *n*.

shall [ʃæl; ʃəl] *v/aux.* [*irr.*] **1.** *Futur:* ich werde, wir werden; **2.** *Befehl, Pflicht:* ich, er, sie, es soll; du sollst; ihr sollt, wir, Sie, sie sollen: **~ I come?;** **3.** ⚖ *Mussbestimmung* (*im Deutschen durch Indikativ wiederzugeben*): **any person ~ be liable ...** jede Person ist verpflichtet ...; → should 1.

shal·lop ['ʃæləp] *s.* ♣ Scha'luppe *f*.

shal·lot [ʃə'lɒt] *s.* ♣ Scha'lotte *f*.

shal·low ['ʃæləʊ] **I** *adj.* □ seicht, flach (*beide a. fig. oberflächlich*); **II** *s.* (*a. pl.*) seichte Stelle, Untiefe *f*; **III** *v/t. u. v/i.* (sich) verflachen; '**shal·low·ness** [-nɪs] *s.* Seichtheit *f* (*a. fig.*).

shalt [ʃælt; ʃəlt] *obs.* **2.** *sg. pres. von* shall: **thou ~** du sollst.

sham [ʃæm] **I** *s.* **1.** (Vor)Täuschung *f*, (Be)Trug *m*, Heuche'lei *f*; **2.** Schwindler(in), Scharlatan *m*; **3.** Heuchler(in); **II** *adj.* **4.** vorgetäuscht, fingiert, Schein...: **~ battle** Scheingefecht *n*; **5.** unecht, falsch: **~ diamond; ~ piety;** **III** *v/t.* **6.** vortäuschen, -spiegeln, fingieren, simulieren; **IV** *v/i.* **7.** sich (ver)stellen, heucheln: **~ ill** simulieren, krank spielen.

sha·man ['ʃeɪmən] *s.* Scha'mane *m*.

sham·a·teur ['ʃæmətə] *s.* F *sport* 'Scheinama,teur *m*.

sham·ble ['ʃæmbl] **I** *v/i.* watscheln; **II** *s.* watschelnder Gang.

sham·bles ['ʃæmblz] *s. pl. sg. konstr.* **1.** a) Schlachthaus *n*, b) Fleischbank *f*; **2.** *fig.* a) Schlachtfeld *n* (*a. iro. wüstes Durcheinander*), b) Trümmerfeld *n*, Bild *n* der Verwüstung, c) Scherbenhaufen *m*: **his marriage was a ~.**

shame [ʃeɪm] **I** *s.* **1.** Scham(gefühl *n*) *f*: **for ~!** pfui, schäm dich!; **feel ~ at** sich über et. schämen; **2.** Schande *f*, Schmach *f*: **be a ~ to** → 5; **~ on you!** schäm dich!, pfui!; **put s.o. to ~** a) Schande über j-n bringen, b) j-n beschämen (*übertreffen*); **cry ~ upon s.o.** pfui über j-n rufen; **3.** F Schande *f* (*Gemeinheit*): **what a ~!** a) es ist e-e Schande!, b) es ist ein Jammer!; **II** *v/t.* **4.** *j-n* beschämen, mit Scham erfüllen: **~ s.o. into doing s.th.** j-n so beschämen, dass er et. tut; **5.** *j-m* Schande machen; Schande bringen über (*acc.*); '**~-faced** [-feɪst] *adj.* □ **1.** verschämt, schamhaft; **2.** schüchtern; **3.** schamrot.

shame·ful ['ʃeɪmfʊl] *adj.* □ **1.** schmachvoll, schändlich; **2.** schimpflich; **3.** unanständig, anstößig; '**shame·ful·ness** [-nɪs] *s.* **1.** Schändlichkeit *f*; **2.** Anstößigkeit *f*; '**shame·less** [-lɪs] *adj.* □ schamlos (*a. fig. unverschämt*); '**shame·less·ness** [-lɪsnɪs] *s.* Schamlosigkeit *f* (*a. fig. Unverschämtheit*).

sham·mer ['ʃæmə] *s.* **1.** Schwindler(in); **2.** Heuchler(in); **3.** Simu'lant(in).

sham·my (**leath·er**) [ˈʃæmɪ] s. Sämisch-, Wildleder n.

sham·poo [ʃæmˈpuː] I v/t. **1.** Kopf, Haare schamponieren, waschen; **2.** j-m den Kopf od. das Haar waschen; II s. **3.** Haar-, Kopfwäsche f: ~ and set Waschen u. Legen n; **4.** Sham'poo n, Schampon n (Haarwaschmittel).

sham·rock [ˈʃæmrɒk] s. **1.** ♀ Weißer Feldklee; **2.** Shamrock m (Kleeblatt als Wahrzeichen Irlands).

sham·us [ˈʃeɪməs] s. Am. sl. **1.** ‚Schnüffler' m (Detektiv); **2.** ‚Bulle' m (Polizist).

shan·dy [ˈʃændɪ] s. Mischgetränk aus Bier u. Limonade: a) nordd. Alsterwasser n, b) südd. ‚Radler' m.

shang·hai [ʃæŋˈhaɪ] v/t. F **1.** ♻ schang'haien (gewaltsam anheuern); **2.** fig. j-n zwingen (into doing et. zu tun).

shank [ʃæŋk] s. **1.** a) 'Unterschenkel m, Schienbein n, b) F Bein n, c) Hachse f (vom Schlachttier): go on ♘'s pony (od. mare) auf Schusters Rappen reiten; **2.** (Anker-, Bolzen-, Säulen- etc.) Schaft m; **3.** (Schuh)Gelenk n; **4.** typ. (Schrift)Kegel m; **5.** ♀ Stiel m; **shanked** [-kt] adj. **1.** ...schenk(e)lig; **2.** gestielt.

shan't [ʃɑːnt] F für shall not.

shan·ty¹ [ˈʃæntɪ] s. Shanty n, Seemannslied n.

shan·ty² [ˈʃæntɪ] s. Hütte f, Ba'racke f; '~·town s. Ba'rackensiedlung f, -stadt f.

shape [ʃeɪp] I s. **1.** Gestalt f, Form f (a. fig.): in the ~ of in Form e-s Briefes etc.; in human ~ in Menschengestalt; put od. get into ~ formen, gestalten, s-e Gedanken ordnen; in no ~ in keiner Weise; **2.** Fi'gur f, Gestalt f; **3.** feste Form, Gestalt f: take ~ Gestalt annehmen (a. fig.); → lick 1; **4.** körperliche od. geistige Verfassung, Form f: be in (good) ~ in (guter) Form sein; **5.** ❋ a) Form f, Fas'son f, Mo'dell n, b) Formteil n; **6.** Küche: a) (Pudding- etc.)Form f, b) Stürzpudding m; II v/t. **7.** gestalten, formen, bilden (alle a. fig.), Charakter a. prägen; **8.** anpassen (to dat.); **9.** planen, entwerfen: ~ the course for ♻ u. fig. den Kurs setzen auf (acc.); **10.** ❋ formen; III v/i. **11.** Gestalt od. Form annehmen, sich formen; **12.** sich entwickeln, sich gestalten: ~ (up) well sich ‚machen' od. gut anlassen, viel versprechend sein; ~ up F e-e endgültige Form annehmen, sich (gut) entwickeln; **13.** ~ up to a) Boxstellung einnehmen gegen, b) fig. j-n herausfordern; **shaped** [-pt] adj. geformt, ...gestaltet, ...förmig; '**shape·less** [-lɪs] adj. □ **1.** form-, gestaltlos; **2.** unförmig; '**shape·less·ness** [-lɪsnɪs] s. **1.** Fom-, Gestaltlosigkeit f; **2.** Unförmigkeit f; '**shape·li·ness** [-lɪnɪs] s. Wohlgestalt f, schöne Form; '**shape·ly** [-lɪ] adj. wohlgeformt, schön, hübsch; '**shap·er** [-pə] s. **1.** Former(in), Gestalter(in); **2.** ❋ a) 'Waagrecht-'Stoßma,schine f, b) Schnellhobler m.

shard [ʃɑːd] s. **1.** (Ton)Scherbe f; **2.** zo. (harte) Flügeldecke (Insekt).

share¹ [ʃeə] s. (Pflug)Schar f.

share² [ʃeə] I s. **1.** (An)Teil m (a. fig.): fall to s.o.'s ~ j-m zufallen; go ~s with mit j-m teilen (in s.th. et.); ~ and alike zu gleichen Teilen; **2.** (An)Teil m, Beitrag m; Kontin'gent n: do one's ~ sein(en) Teil leisten; take a ~ in sich beteiligen an (dat.); have (od. take) a large ~ in e-n großen Anteil haben an (dat.); **3.** ♦ Beteiligung f; Geschäftsan-

teil m; Kapi'taleinlage f: ~ in a ship Schiffspart m; **4.** ♦ a) Gewinnanteil m, b) Aktie f, c) ♘ Kux m: hold ~s in Aktionär in e-r Gesellschaft sein; II v/t. **5.** (a. fig. sein Bett, e-e Ansicht, den Ruhm etc.) teilen (with mit); **6.** mst ~ out aus-, verteilen; **7.** teilnehmen, -haben an (dat.); sich an den Kosten etc. beteiligen; III v/i. **8.** ~ in → 7; **9.** sich teilen (in in acc.); ~ cer·tif·i·cate s. ♦ Brit. 'Aktienzertifi,kat n; '~,crop·per s. Am. kleiner Farmpächter (der s-e Pacht mit e-m Teil der Ernte entrichtet); ~ de·nom·i·na·tion s. Aktienstückelung f; '~,hold·er s. ♦ Brit. Aktio'när(in): ~s' meeting Aktionärsversammlung f; ~ list s. ♦ Brit. (Aktien)Kurszettel m; ~ mark·et s. ♦ Brit. Aktienmarkt m; '~-out [-raut] s. Aus-, Verteilung f; '~·ware s. coll. Computer: Shareware f (Computerprogramme, die ausprobiert werden können, bevor man für sie bezahlt).

shark [ʃɑːk] s. **1.** ichth. Hai(fisch) m; **2.** fig. Gauner m, Betrüger m; **3.** fig. Schma'rotzer m; **4.** Am. sl. ‚Ka'none' m (Könner).

sharp [ʃɑːp] I adj. □ **1.** scharf (Messer etc., a. Gesichtszüge, Kurve etc.); **2.** spitz (Giebel etc.); **3.** steil; **4.** fig. allg. scharf: a) deutlich (Gegensatz, Umrisse etc.), b) herb (Geschmack), c) schneidend (Befehl, Stimme), schrill (Schrei, Ton), d) heftig (Schmerz etc.), schneidend (a. Frost, Wind), e) hart (Antwort, Kritik), spitz (Bemerkung, Zunge), f) schnell (Tempo, Spiel etc.): ~'s the word F mach fix!; **5.** scharf, wachsam (Auge, Ohr); angespannt (Aufmerksamkeit); **6.** scharfsinnig, gescheit, aufgeweckt, ‚auf Draht': ~ at figures gut im Rechnen; **7.** gerissen, raffiniert: ~ practice Gaunerei f; **8.** F ele'gant, schick; **9.** ♪ a) (zu) hoch, b) (durch Kreuz um e-n Halbton) erhöht, c) Kreuz...: C ~ Cis n; **10.** ling. stimmlos (Konsonant); II adv. **11.** scharf; **12.** plötzlich; **13.** pünktlich, genau: at 3 o'clock ~ Punkt 3 Uhr, genau um 3 Uhr; **14.** schnell: look ~ mach schnell!; **15.** ♪ zu hoch; III v/i. u. v/t. **16.** ♪ zu hoch singen od. spielen; **17.** betrügen; IV s. **18.** pl. Nadel pl.; **19.** pl. ♦ Brit. grobes Kleienmehl; **20.** ♪ a) Kreuz n, b) Erhöhung f, Halbton m, c) nächsthöhere Taste; **21.** F → sharper; '~·cut adj. **1.** scharf (geschnitten); **2.** fest um'rissen, deutlich; '~-'edged adj. scharfkantig.

sharp·en [ˈʃɑːpən] I v/t. **1.** Messer etc. schärfen, schleifen, wetzen; Bleistift etc. (an)spitzen; **2.** fig. j-n ermuntern od. anspornen; Sinn, Verstand schärfen; Appetit anregen; **3.** Rede etc. verschärfen; s-r Stimme etc. e-n scharfen Klang geben; II v/i. **4.** scharf od. schärfer werden, sich verschärfen (a. fig.); '**sharp·en·er** [-pnə] s. (Bleistift- etc.) Spitzer m.

sharp·er [ˈʃɑːpə] s. **1.** Gauner m, Betrüger m; **2.** Falschspieler m.

'**sharp-'eyed** → sharp-sighted.

sharp·ness [ˈʃɑːpnɪs] s. **1.** Schärfe f, Spitzigkeit f; **2.** fig. Schärfe f (Herbheit, Strenge, Heftigkeit); **3.** (Geistes)Schärfe f, Scharfsinn m; Gerissenheit f; **4.** (phot. Rand)Schärfe f, Deutlichkeit f.

,**sharp|-'set** adj. **1.** (heiß)hungrig; fig. scharf, erpicht (on auf acc.); '~-,shoot·er s. Scharfschütze m; ,~-'sight·ed adj. **1.** scharfsichtig; **2.** fig. scharfsinnig; ,~-'tongued adj. fig. scharfzüngig (Person); ,~-'wit·ted adj. scharf-

sinnig.

shat·ter [ˈʃætə] I v/t. **1.** zerschmettern, -schlagen, -trümmern (alle a. fig.); fig. Hoffnungen zerstören; **2.** Gesundheit, Nerven zerrütten: I was (absolutely) ~ed F ich war ‚am Boden zerstört'; II v/i. **3.** in Stücke brechen, zerspringen; '**shat·ter·ing** [-ərɪŋ] adj. □ **1.** vernichtend (a. fig.); **2.** fig. a) 'umwerfend, e'norm, b) entsetzlich, verheerend; '**shat·ter·proof** adj. ❋ a) bruchsicher, b) splitterfrei, -sicher (Glas).

shave [ʃeɪv] I v/t. **1.** (o.s. sich) rasieren: ~ (off) Bart abrasieren; get ~d rasiert werden; **2.** Rasen etc. (kurz) scheren; Holz (ab)schälen od. glatthobeln; Häute abschaben; **3.** streifen, a. knapp vor'beikommen an (dat.); II v/i. **4.** sich rasieren; **5.** ~ through F (gerade noch) ‚durchrutschen' (in e-r Prüfung); III s. **6.** Ra'sur f, Rasieren n: have (od. get) a ~ sich rasieren (lassen); have a close (od. narrow) ~ fig. mit knapper Not davonkommen; that was a close ~ F ‚das hätte ins Auge gehen können'; by a ~ F um ein Haar; **7.** (Ab)Schabsel n, Span m; **8.** ❋ Schabeisen n; **9.** obs. F Schwindel m, Betrug m; '**shave·ling** [-lɪŋ] s. obs. contp. **1.** Pfaffe m; **2.** Mönch m; '**shav·en** [-vn] adj. **1.** (clean-~ glatt) rasiert; **2.** (kahl) geschoren (Kopf); '**shav·er** [-və] s. **1.** Bar'bier m; **2.** Ra'sierappa,rat m; **3.** mst young ~ F Grünschnabel m.

Sha·vi·an [ˈʃeɪvjən] adj. shawsch, für G. B. Shaw charakte'ristisch: ~ humo(u)r shawscher Humor.

shav·ing [ˈʃeɪvɪŋ] s. **1.** Rasieren n: ~ brush (cream, mirror) Rasierpinsel m (-creme f, -spiegel m); ~ foam Rasierschaum m; ~ head Rasierkopf m; ~ soap, ~ stick Rasierseife f; **2.** mst pl. Schnitzel m, n, (Hobel)Span m.

shawl [ʃɔːl] s. **1.** 'Umhängetuch n; **2.** Kopftuch n.

shawm [ʃɔːm] s. ♪ Schal'mei f.

she [ʃiː; ʃɪ] I pron. **1.** a) sie (3. sg. für alle weiblichen Lebewesen), b) (beim Mond) er, (bei Ländern) es, (bei Schiffen mit Namen) sie, (bei Schiffen ohne Namen) es, (bei Motoren u. Maschinen, wenn personifiziert) er, es; **2.** sie, die (-jenige); II s. **3.** Sie f: a) Mädchen n, Frau f, b) Weibchen n (Tier); III adj. in Zssgn **4.** weiblich: ~-bear Bärin f; ~-dog Hündin f; **5.** contp. Weibs...: ~-devil Weibsteufel m.

sheaf [ʃiːf] I pl. -ves [-vz] s. **1.** ♪ Garbe f; **2.** (Papier-, Pfeil-, phys. Strahlen-) Bündel n: ~ of fire ⚔ Feuer-, Geschossgarbe f; II v/t. **3.** → sheave¹.

shear [ʃɪə] I v/t. [irr.] **1.** scheren: ~ sheep; **2.** a. ~ off (ab)scheren, abschneiden; **3.** fig. berauben; → shorn; **4.** fig. j-n ‚schröpfen'; **5.** poet. mit dem Schwert (ab)hauen; II v/i. [irr.] **6.** ♪ sicheln, mähen; III s. **7.** pl. große Schere; **8.** ❋ Me'tall-, Blechschere f; **8.** → shearing force, shearing stress; '**shear·er** [-rə] s. **1.** (Schaf)Scherer m; **2.** Schnitter m.

shear·ing [ˈʃɪərɪŋ] s. **1.** Schur f (Schafescheren od. Schurertrag); **2.** (Ab)Scherung f; **3.** Scot. od. dial. Mähen n, Mahd f; **3.** ❋ Me'tall-, Blechschere f; ~ force s. phys. Scher-, Schubkraft f; ~ strength s. phys. Scherfestigkeit f; ~ stress s. phys. Scherbeanspruchung f.

shear·ling [ˈʃɪəlɪŋ] s. erst 'einmal geschorenes Schaf.

shear| pin s. ❋ Scherbolzen m; ~ stress → shearing stress; '~,wa·ter s. orn. Sturmtaucher m.

sheath [ʃiːθ] s. **1.** (Schwert- etc.)Scheide f; **2.** Futte'ral n, Hülle f; **3.** ♀, zo. Scheide f; **4.** zo. Flügeldecke f (Käfer); **5.** Kon'dom n, m; **6.** Futte'ralkleid n; **sheathe** [ʃiːð] v/t. **1.** das Schwert in die Scheide stecken; **2.** in e-e Hülle od. ein Futte'ral stecken; **3.** bsd. ⊜ um'hüllen, -'manteln, über'ziehen; Kabel armieren; **sheath-ing** [ʃiːðɪŋ] s. **1.** Verschalung f, -kleidung f; Beschlag m; 'Überzug m, Mantel m; (Kabel)Bewehrung f.

sheave¹ [ʃiːv] v/t. ✔ in Garben binden.

sheave² [ʃiːv] s. ⊜ Scheibe f, Rolle f.

sheaves [ʃiːvz] **1.** pl. von **sheaf**; **2.** pl. von **sheave²**.

she-bang [ʃəˈbæŋ] s. Am. sl. **1.** ‚Bude‘ f, ‚Laden‘ m; **2.** the whole ~ der ganze Plunder od. Kram.

shed¹ [ʃed] s. **1.** Schuppen m; **2.** Stall m; **3.** ✔ kleine Flugzeughalle; **4.** Hütte f.

shed² [ʃed] v/t. [irr.] F **1.** verschütten, a. Blut, Tränen vergießen; **2.** ausstrahlen, -strömen, Duft, Licht, Frieden etc. verbreiten; → **light** 1; **3.** Wasser abstoßen (Stoff); **4.** biol. Laub, Federn etc. abwerfen, Hörner abstoßen, Zähne verlieren: ~ one's skin sich häuten; **5.** Winterkleider etc., a. fig. Gewohnheit, a. iro. Freunde ablegen.

she'd [ʃiːd] F für a) she would, b) she had.

sheen [ʃiːn] s. Glanz m (bsd. von Stoffen), Schimmer m.

sheen-y¹ [ʃiːnɪ] adj. glänzend.

sheen-y² [ʃiːnɪ] s. sl. ‚Itzig‘ m (Jude).

sheep [ʃiːp] pl. **sheep** s. **1.** zo. Schaf n: cast ~'s eyes at s.o. j-m schmachtende Blicke zuwerfen; separate the ~ and the goats bibl. die Schafe von den Böcken trennen; you might as well be hanged for a ~ as (for) a lamb! wennschon, dennschon!; → black sheep; **2.** fig. contp. Schaf n (Person); **3.** pl. fig. Schäflein pl., Herde f (Gemeinde e-s Pfarrers etc.); **4.** Schafleder n; ~ dip s. Desinfekti'onsbad n für Schafe; '~·dog s. Schäferhund m; '~·farm s. Brit. Schaf(zucht)farm f; '~·farm-ing s. Brit. Schafzucht f; '~·fold s. Schafhürde f.

sheep-ish [ʃiːpɪʃ] adj. □ **1.** schüchtern; **2.** einfältig, blöd(e); **3.** verlegen, ‚belämmert‘.

'sheep|-man [-mən] s. [irr.] Am. Schafzüchter m; '~·pen → sheepfold; ~ run → sheepwalk; '~,shear-ing s. Schafschur f; '~·skin s. **1.** Schaffell n; **2.** (a. Perga'ment n aus) Schafleder n; **3.** F a) Urkunde f, b) Di'plom n; '~·walk s. Schafweide f.

sheer¹ [ʃɪə] I adj. □ **1.** bloß, rein, pur, nichts als: ~ nonsense; by ~ force mit bloßer od. nackter Gewalt; **2.** völlig, glatt: ~ impossibility; **3.** rein, unvermischt, pur: ~ ale; **4.** steil, jäh; **5.** hauchdünn (Textilien); II adv. **6.** völlig; **7.** senkrecht; **8.** di'rekt.

sheer² [ʃɪə] I s. **1.** ♣ a) Ausscheren n, b) Sprung m (Deckerhöhung); II v/i. **2.** ♣ abscheren, (ab)gieren (Schiff); **3.** fig. a. ~ away (from) a) abweichen (von), b) sich losmachen (von); ~ off v/i. **1.** → sheer² 2; **2.** abhauen; **3.** ~ from aus dem Wege gehen (dat.).

sheet [ʃiːt] I s. **1.** Betttuch n, (Bett)Laken n; Leintuch n: stand in a white ~ reumütig s-e Sünden bekennen; (as) white as a ~ fig. kreidebleich; **2.** (typ. Druck)Bogen m, Blatt n (Papier): a blank ~ fig. ein unbeschriebenes Blatt; a clean ~ fig. e-e reine Weste; in (the) ~s (noch) nicht gebunden, ungefalzt (Buch); **3.** Bogen m (von Briefmar-

ken); **4.** a) Blatt n, Zeitung f, b) (Flug-) Schrift f; **5.** ⊜ (dünne) (Blech-, Glasetc.)Platte f; **6.** metall. (Fein)Blech n; **7.** weite Fläche (von Wasser etc.); (wogende) Masse; (Feuer-, Regen)Wand f; geol. Schicht f: rain came down in ~s es regnete in Strömen; **8.** ♣ Schot(e) f, Segelleine f: have three ~s in the wind sl. ‚sternhagelvoll‘ sein; **9.** ♣ Vorder- (u. Achter)teil m, n (Boot); II v/t. **10.** Bett beziehen; **11.** (in Laken) (ein)hüllen; **12.** ⊜ mit Blech verkleiden; **13.** a. ~ home Segel anholen; '~·an·chor s. ♣ Notanker m (a. fig.); ~ cop·per s. Kupferblech n; ~ glass s. Tafelglas n.

sheet-ing [ʃiːtɪŋ] s. **1.** Betttuchstoff m; **2.** Blechverkleidung f.

sheet| i·ron s. Eisenblech n; ~ light·ning s. **1.** Wetterleuchten n; **2.** Flächenblitz m; ~ met·al s. (Me'tall)Blech n; ~ mu·sic s. Noten(blätter) pl.; ~ steel s. Stahlblech n.

sheik(h) [ʃeɪk] s. **1.** Scheich m; **2.** fig. F a) ‚Scheich‘ m (Freund), b) Am. ‚Schwarm‘ m (Person); 'sheik(h)·dom [-dəm] s. Scheichtum n.

shek·el [ʃekl] s. **1.** a) S(ch)ekel m (hebräische Gewichts- u. Münzeinheit), b) Schekel m (Münzeinheit in Israel); **2.** pl. F ‚Zaster‘ m (Geld).

shel·drake [ʃeldreɪk] s. orn. Brandente f.

shelf [ʃelf] pl. **shelves** [-vz] s. **1.** (Bücher-, Wand-, Schrank)Brett n; ('Bücher-, 'Waren- etc.)Re,gal n, Bord n, Fach n, Sims m: be put (od. laid) on the ~ fig. a) ausrangiert werden (a. Beamter etc.), b) auf die lange Bank geschoben werden; get on the ~ ,sitzenbleiben‘ (Mädchen); **2.** Riff n, Felsplatte f; **3.** ♣ a) Schelf m, n, Küstensockel m, b) Sandbank f; **4.** geol. Festlandssockel m, Schelf m, n; ~ fill·er s. Re'galauffüller m; ~ life s. ✝ Lagerfähigkeit f; '~·warm·er s. ,Ladenhüter‘ m.

shell [ʃel] I s. **1.** allg. Schale f; **2.** zo. a) Muschelschale f, b) Schneckenhaus n, c) Flügeldecke f (Käfer), d) Rückenschild m (Schildkröte): come out of one's ~ fig. aus sich herausgehen; retire into one's ~ fig. sich in sein Schneckenhaus zurückziehen; **3.** (Eier-) Schale f: in the ~ a) (noch) unausgebrütet, b) fig. noch in der Entwicklung; **4.** a) Muschel f, b) Perlmutt n, c) Schildpatt n; **5.** (Nuss- etc.)Schale f, Hülse f; **6.** ♣, ✔ Schale f, Außenhaut f, (Schiffs)Rumpf m; **7.** Gerippe n, Gerüst n (a. fig.), ⚒ a. Rohbau m; **8.** ⊜ Kapsel f, (Scheinwerfer- etc.)Gehäuse n; **9.** ✕ a) Gra'nate f, b) Hülse f, c) Am. Pa'trone f; **10.** ('Feuerwerks)Ra,kete f; **11.** Küche: (Pa'steten)Hülle f; **12.** phys. (Elek'tronen)Schale f; **13.** sport (leichtes) Renn(ruder)boot; **14.** (Degen- etc.)Korb m; **15.** fig. das (bloße) Äußere; **16.** ped. Brit. Mittelstufe f; II v/t. **17.** schälen; Erbsen etc. enthülsen; Nüsse knacken; Körner von der Ähre, vom Kolben entfernen; **18.** ✕ (mit Gra'naten) beschießen; ~ out v/t. u. v/i. sl. ‚blechen‘ (bezahlen).

shel·lac [ʃəˈlæk] I s. **1.** ♣ Schellack m; II v/t. pret. u. p.p. **shel'lacked** [-kt] **2.** mit Schellack behandeln; **3.** fig. Am. sl. j-n ‚vermöbeln‘.

'shell|·cra·ter s. ✕ Gra'nattrichter m.

shelled [ʃeld] adj. ...schalig.

shell| egg s. Frischei n; '~·fish s. zo. Schalentier m; ~ game s. Am. Falschspielertrick m (a. fig.).

shell·ing [ʃelɪŋ] s. ✕ Beschuss m, (Artille'rie)Feuer n.

shell| shock s. ✕ 'Kriegsneu,rose f; ~ suit s. Brit. Jogginganzug m (aus Ballonseide od. mit Polyesteraußenseite).

shel·ter [ʃeltə] I s. **1.** Schutzhütte f, -dach n; Schuppen m; **2.** Obdach n, Herberge f; **3.** Zuflucht f; **4.** Schutz m: take (od. seek) ~ Schutz suchen (with bei, from vor dat.); **5.** ✕ a) Bunker m, 'Unterstand m, b) Deckung f; II v/t. **6.** (be)schützen, beschirmen (from vor dat.): a ~ed life ein behütetes Leben; **7.** schützen, bedecken, über'dachen; **8.** j-m Schutz od. Zuflucht gewähren: ~ o.s. fig. sich verstecken (behind hinter j-m etc.); ~ed trade ✝ Brit. (durch Zölle) geschützter Handelszweig; ~ed workshop beschützende Werkstatt; **9.** j-n beherbergen; III v/i. **10.** Schutz suchen; sich 'unterstellen; ~ half s. [irr.] ✕ Am. Zeltbahn f.

shelve¹ [ʃelv] v/t. **1.** Bücher (in ein Re'gal) einstellen, auf ein (Bücher)Brett stellen; **2.** fig. a) et. zu den Akten legen, bei'seite legen, b) j-n ausrangieren; **3.** aufschieben; **4.** mit Fächern od. Re'galen versehen.

shelve² [ʃelv] v/i. (sanft) abfallen.

shelves [ʃelvz] pl. von **shelf**.

shelv-ing¹ [ʃelvɪŋ] s. (Bretter pl. für) Fächer pl. od. Re'gale pl.

shelv-ing² [ʃelvɪŋ] adj. schräg, abfallend.

she-nan-i-gan [ʃɪˈnænɪɡən] s. mst pl. F **1.** ,Mumpitz‘ m, ‚fauler Zauber‘; **2.** Trick m; **3.** ‚Blödsinn‘ m, Streich m.

shep·herd [ʃepəd] I s. **1.** (Schaf)Hirt m, Schäfer m; **2.** fig. eccl. (Seelen)Hirt m (Geistlicher): the (good) ᴢ bibl. der Gute Hirte (Christus); II v/t. **3.** Schafe etc. hüten; **4.** fig. Menschenmenge etc. treiben, führen, ,bugsieren‘; 'shep·herd·ess [-dɪs] s. (Schaf)Hirtin f, Schäferin f.

shep·herd's| crook s. Hirtenstab m; ~ dog s. Schäferhund m; ~ pie s. Auflauf m aus Hackfleisch u. Kar'toffelbrei; ~ purse s. ♀ Hirtentäschel n.

sher·bet [ʃɜːbət] s. **1.** Sor'bett n, m (Frucht-, Eisgetränk); **2.** bsd. Am. Fruchteis n; **3.** a. ~ powder Brausepulver n.

sherd [ʃɜːd] → shard.

sher·iff [ʃerɪf] s. ↯ Sheriff m: a) in England, Wales u. Irland der höchste Verwaltungsbeamte e-r Grafschaft, b) in den USA der gewählte höchste Exekutivbeamte e-s Verwaltungsbezirkes, c) in Schottland e-e Art Amtsrichter.

sher·ry [ʃerɪ] s. Sherry m.

she's [ʃiːz, ʃɪz] F für a) she is, b) she has.

shew [ʃəʊ] obs. für show.

shib·bo·leth [ʃɪbəleθ] s. fig. **1.** Schib'boleth n, Erkennungszeichen n, -wort n; **2.** Kastenbrauch m; **3.** Platti'tüde f.

shield [ʃiːld] I s. **1.** Schild m; **2.** Schutzschild m, -schirm m; **3.** fig. a) Schutz m, Schirm m, b) (Be)Schützer(in); **4.** ⚡, ⊜ (Ab)Schirmung f; **5.** Arm-, Schweißblatt n; **6.** zo. (Rücken)Schild m, Panzer m (Insekt etc.); **7.** her. (Wappen)Schild m; II v/t. **8.** (be)schützen, (be-) schirmen (from vor dat.); **9.** bsd. ↯ j-n decken; **10.** ⚡, ⊜ (ab)schirmen; '~·-bear·er s. Schildknappe m; ~ fern s. ♀ Schildfarn m; ~ forc·es s. pl. ✕ Schildstreitkräfte pl.

shiel·ing [ʃiːlɪŋ] s. Scot. **1.** (Vieh)Weide f; **2.** Hütte f.

shift [ʃɪft] I v/i. **1.** den Platz od. die Lage wechseln, sich verlagern; **2.** sich verlagern (a. ↯ Beweislast), sich verwandeln (a. Szene), sich verschieben (a. ling.), wechseln; **3.** ⚓ 'überschießen, sich verlagern (*Ballast, Ladung*); **4.** die Wohnung wechseln; **5.** 'umspringen (*Wind*); **6.** *mot.* schalten: **~** *up* (*down*) hinaufschalten (herunterschalten); **7.** *Kugelstoßen*: angleiten; **8.** **~** *for o.s.* a) auf sich selbst gestellt sein, b) sich selbst (weiter)helfen, sich durchschlagen; **9.** Ausflüchte machen; **10.** *mst* **~** *away* F sich da'vonmachen; **II** *v/t.* **11.** (aus-, 'um)wechseln, (aus)tauschen; → *ground* 2; **12.** (*a. fig.*) verschieben, -lagern, (*a. Schauplatz,* ⚔ *das Feuer*) verlegen, (*a. Betrieb* 'umstellen (*to* auf *acc.*); *thea.* Kulissen schieben; **13.** ⊕ schalten, ausrücken, verstellen, *Hebel* 'umlegen: **~** *gears mot.* schalten; **14.** ⚓ a) *Schiff* verholen, b) *Ladung* 'umstauen; **15.** *Kleidung* wechseln; **16.** *Schuld, Verantwortung* (ab)schieben, abwälzen ([*up*]on auf *acc.*); **17.** *j-n* loswerden; **18.** *Am.* F a) *Essen etc.* 'wegputzen, b) *Schnaps etc.* 'kippen'; **III** *s.* **19.** Verschiebung *f*, -änderung *f*, -lagerung *f*, Wechsel *m*; **20.** ✝ (Arbeits)Schicht *f* (*Arbeiter od. Arbeitszeit*); **21.** Ausweg *m*, Hilfsmittel *n*, Notbehelf *m*: *make* (*a*) **~** a) sich durchschlagen, b) es fertig bringen, es möglich machen (*to do* zu tun), c) sich behelfen (*with* mit, *without* ohne); **22.** Kniff *m*, List *f*, Ausflucht *f*; **23.** **~** *of crop* ✗ *Brit.* Fruchtwechsel *m*; **24.** *geol.* Verwerfung *f*; **25.** ♪ a) Lagenwechsel *m* (*Streichinstrumente*), b) Zugwechsel *m* (*Posaune*), c) Verschiebung *f* (*Klavierpedal etc.*); **26.** *ling.* Lautverschiebung *f*; **27.** *Kugelstoßen*: Angleiten *n*; **28.** *obs.* ('Unter-) Hemd *n der Frau*; **'shift·er** [-tə] *s.* **1.** *thea.* Ku'lissenschieber *m*; **2.** *fig.* schlauer Fuchs; **3.** ⊕ a) Schalter *m*, b) Ausrückvorrichtung *f*; **'shift·i·ness** [-tɪnɪs] *s.* **1.** Gewandtheit *f*; **2.** Verschlagenheit *f*; **3.** Unzuverlässigkeit *f*; **'shift·ing** [-tɪŋ] *adj.* sich verschiebend, veränderlich: **~** *sand* Treib-, Flugsand *m.*

shift key *s.* a) *Computer:* 'Shift-Taste *f*, 'Umschalttaste *f*, b) *Schreibmaschine:* 'Umschalter *m.*

shift·less ['ʃɪftlɪs] *adj.* □ **1.** hilflos (*a. fig. unfähig*); **2.** unbeholfen, einfallslos; **3.** träge, faul.

shift| lock *s. Computer:* Feststelltaste *f*; **~** *work s.* **1.** Schichtarbeit *f*; **2.** *ped.* 'Schicht,unterricht *m*; **~** *work·er s.* Schichtarbeiter(in).

shift·y ['ʃɪftɪ] *adj.* □ **1.** a) wendig, schlau, gerissen, c) verschlagen, falsch; **2.** *fig.* unstet.

shil·ling ['ʃɪlɪŋ] *s. Brit. obs.* Schilling *m*: *a* **~** *in the pound* 5 Prozent; *pay twenty* **~** *s in the pound* s-e Schulden etc. auf Heller u. Pfennig bezahlen; *cut s.o. off with a* **~** j-n enterben; **~** *shock·er s.* 'Schundro,man *m.*

shil·ly-shal·ly ['ʃɪlɪˌʃælɪ] **I** *v/i.* zögern, schwanken; **II** *s.* Schwanken *n*, Zögern *n*; **III** *adj. u. adv.* zögernd, schwankend.

shim [ʃɪm] ⊕ *s.* Keil *m*, Klemmstück *n*, Ausgleichsscheibe *f.*

shim·mer ['ʃɪmə] **I** *v/i.* schimmern; **II** *s.* Schimmer *m*; **'shim·mer·y** [-ərɪ] *adj.* schimmernd.

shim·my ['ʃɪmɪ] **I** *s.* **1.** Shimmy *m* (*Tanz*); **2.** ⊕ Flattern *n* (*der Vorderräder*); **3.** F (Damen)Hemd *n*; **II** *v/i.* **4.** Shimmy tanzen; **5.** ⊕ flattern (*Vorderräder*).

shin [ʃɪn] **I** *s.* **1.** Schienbein *n*; **2.** **~** *of beef* Rinderhachse *f*; **II** *v/i.* **3.** **~** *up* e-n *Baum etc.* hin'aufklettern; **4.** *Am.* ren-

nen; **III** *v/t.* **5.** *j-n* ans Schienbein treten; **6.** **~** *o.s.* sich das Schienbein verletzen; **'~·bone** *s.* Schienbein(knochen *m*) *n.*

shin·dig ['ʃɪndɪg] *s.* **1.** *sl.* 'Schwof' *m*, Tanz(veranstaltung *f*) *m*; *weitS.* (,wilde') Party; **2.** → *shindy.*

shin·dy ['ʃɪndɪ] *s.* F Krach *m*, Ra'dau *m.*

shine [ʃaɪn] **I** *v/i.* [*irr.*] **1.** scheinen; leuchten, strahlen (*a. Augen etc.*; *with joy* vor Freude): **~** *out* hervorleuchten; *fig.* herausragen; **~** (*up*)*on et.* beleuchten; **~** *up to Am. sl.* sich bei *j-m* anbiedern; **2.** glänzen (*a. fig.*); *fig.* sich hervortun *as* als, *at* in *dat.*); **II** *v/t.* [*irr.*] **3.** F *Schuhe etc.* polieren; **III** *v.* **4.** (*Sonnen-etc.*)Schein *m*; → *rain* 1; **5.** Glanz *m*: *take the* **~** *out of* a) *e-r Sache* den Glanz nehmen, b) *et. od. j-n* in den Schatten stellen; **6.** Glanz *m* (*bsd. auf Schuhen*): *have a* **~**? Schuhputzen gefällig?; **7.** *kick up a* **~** F Radau machen; **8.** *take a* **~** *to s.o.* F j-n ins Herz schließen; **'shin·er** [-nə] *s.* **1.** glänzender Gegenstand; **2.** *sl.* a) Goldmünze *f* (*bsd. Sovereign*), b) Dia'mant *m*, c) *pl.* ,Kies' *m* (*Geld*); **3.** *sl.* ,Veilchen' *n*, blaues *od.* blau geschlagenes Auge.

shin·gle¹ ['ʃɪŋgl] **I** *s.* **1.** (Dach)Schindel *f*; **2.** Herrenschnitt *m* (*Damenfrisur*); **3.** *Am.* F (Firmen)Schild *n*: *hang out one's* **~** sich (als Arzt *etc.*) etablieren, ,s-n eigenen Laden aufmachen'; **II** *v/t.* **4.** mit Schindeln decken; **5.** *Haar* (sehr) kurz schneiden; **~***d hair* → 2.

shin·gle² ['ʃɪŋgl] *s. Brit.* **1.** grober Strandkies(el) *m*; **2.** Kiesstrand *m.*

shin·gle³ ['ʃɪŋgl] *v/t. metall.* zängen.

shin·gles ['ʃɪŋglz] *s. pl. sg. konstr.* ✻ Gürtelrose *f.*

shin·gly ['ʃɪŋglɪ] *adj.* kies(el)ig.

shin·ing ['ʃaɪnɪŋ] *adj.* □ leuchtend (*a. fig. Beispiel*), strahlend; glänzend (*a. fig.*): *a* **~** *light* e-e Leuchte (*Person*).

shin·ny ['ʃɪnɪ] *v/i. Am.* F klettern.

shin·y ['ʃaɪnɪ] *adj.* □ glänzend: a) leuchtend (*a. fig.*), funkelnd (*a. Auto etc.*), b) strahlend (*Tag etc.*), c) blank (geputzt), d) abgetragen: *a* **~** *jacket.*

ship [ʃɪp] **I** *s.* **1.** ⚓ *allg.* Schiff *n*: **~'s** *articles* → *shipping articles*; **~'s** *company* Besatzung *f*; **~'s** *husband* Mitreeder *m*; **~'s** *papers* Schiffspapiere; **~** *of the desert fig.* Wüstenschiff (*Kamel*); *take* **~** sich einschiffen (*for* nach); *about* **~**! klar zum Wenden!; *when my* **~** *comes home fig.* wenn ich mein Glück mache; **2.** ✈ Vollschiff *n* (*Segelschiff*); **3.** Boot *n*; **4.** *Am.* a) Luftschiff *n*, b) Flugzeug *n*, c) Raumschiff *n*; **II** *v/t.* **5.** an Bord bringen *od.* (*a. Passagiere*) nehmen, verladen; **6.** ⚓ verschiffen, transportieren; **7.** ✝ a) verladen, b) versenden, -frachten, (aus-) liefern (*a. zu Lande*), c) *Ware zur Verladung* abladen, d) ⚓ *Ladung* über'nehmen: **~** *a sea* e-e See (*Sturzwelle*) übernehmen; **8.** ⚓ *Ruder* einlegen, *Mast* einsetzen: **~** *the oars* die Riemen einlegen; **9.** ⚓ *Matrosen* (an)heuern; **10.** F a. **~** *off* fortschicken; **III** *v/i.* **11.** sich einschiffen; **12.** sich anheuern lassen; **~** *bis·cuit s.* Schiffszwieback *m*; **'~·board** *s.*: *on* **~** an Bord; **'~·borne** *air·craft s.* ✈ Bordflugzeug *n*; **'~·build·er** *s.* ⚓ 'Schiffsarchi,tekt *m*, -bauer *m*; **'~·build·ing** *s.* ⚓ Schiff(s)bau *m*; **~** *ca·nal s.* 'Seeka,nal *m*; **~** *chan·dler s.* Schiffsausrüster *m*; **'~·load** *s.* (volle) Schiffsladung (*als Maß*); **'~·mas·ter** *s.* ⚓ ('Handels)Kapi,tän *m.*

ship·ment ['ʃɪpmənt] *s.* **1.** ⚓ a) Verladung *f*, b) Verschiffung *f*, 'Seetrans,port

m, c) (Schiffs)Ladung *f*; **2.** ✝ (*a. zu Lande*) a) Versand *m*, b) (Waren)Sendung *f*, Lieferung *f.*

'ship,own·er *s.* Reeder *m.*

ship·per ['ʃɪpə] *s.* ✝ **1.** Verschiffer *m*, Ablader *m*; **2.** Spedi'teur *m.*

ship·ping ['ʃɪpɪŋ] *s.* **1.** Verschiffung *f*; **2.** ✝ a) Abladung *f* (*Anbordnahme*), b) Verfrachtung *f*, Versand *m* (*a. zu Lande etc.*); **3.** ⚓ *coll.* Schiffsbestand *m* (*e-s Landes etc.*); **~** *a·gent s.* **1.** 'Schiffs,agent *m*; **2.** Schiffsmakler *m*; **~** *ar·ti·cles s. pl.* ⚓ 'Schiffsar,tikel *pl.*, Heuervertrag *m*; **~** *bill s. Brit.* Mani'fest *n*; **~** *clerk s.* ✝ Leiter *m* der Versandabteilung; **~** *com·pa·ny s.* ⚓ Reede'rei *f*; **~** *fore·cast s.* Seewetterbericht *m.*

'ship|·shape *pred. adj. u. adv.* in tadelloser Ordnung, blitzblank; **'~·to-'ship** *adj.* Bord-Bord-...; **'~·to-'shore** *adj.* Bord-Land-...; **'~·way** *s.* Stapel *m*, Helling *f*; **'~·wreck I** *s.* **1.** ⚓ Wrack *n*; **2.** Schiffbruch *m*, *fig. a.* Scheitern *n von Plänen etc.*: *make* **~** *of* → 4; **II** *v/t.* **3.** scheitern lassen: *be* **~***ed* schiffbrüchig werden *od.* sein; **4.** *fig.* zum Scheitern bringen, vernichten; **III** *v/i.* **5.** Schiffbruch erleiden, scheitern (*beide a. fig.*); **'~·wright** *s.* → *shipbuilder*; **2.** Schiffszimmermann *m*; **'~·yard** *s.* ⚓ (Schiffs)Werft *f.*

shir [ʃɜː] → *shirr.*

shire ['ʃaɪə] *s.* **1.** brit. Grafschaft *f*; **2.** au'stralischer Landkreis; **3.** *a.* **~** *horse ein schweres Zugpferd.*

shirk [ʃɜːk] **I** *v/t.* sich drücken vor (*dat.*); **II** *v/i.* sich drücken (*from* vor *dat.*); **'shirk·er** [-kə] *s.* Drückeberger *m.*

shirr [ʃɜː] **I** *s.* e'lastisches Gewebe, eingewebte Gummischnur, Zugband *n*; **II** *v/t.* Gewebe kräuseln; **shirred** [ʃɜːd] *adj.* e'lastisch, gekräuselt.

shirt [ʃɜːt] *s.* **1.** (Herren-, Ober-, *a.* 'Unter-, Nacht)Hemd *n*: *get s.o.'s* **~** *out* j-n ,auf die Palme bringen'; *give away the* **~** *off one's back* sein letztes Hemd *für* j-n hergeben; *keep one's* **~** *on sl.* sich nicht aufregen; *lose one's* **~** *on sl.* alles auf *ein Pferd etc.* setzen; **2.** *a.* **~** *blouse* Hemdbluse *f*; **~** *front s.* Hemdbrust *f.*

shirt·ing ['ʃɜːtɪŋ] *s.* Hemdenstoff *m.*

'shirt·sleeve I *s.* Hemdsärmel *m*: *in one's* **~***s* in Hemdsärmeln; **II** *adj. fig.* ,hemdsärmelig', ungezwungen, le'ger: **~** *diplomacy* offene Diplomatie.

shirt·y ['ʃɜːtɪ] *adj. sl.* unverschämt, ungehobelt.

shit [ʃɪt] V **I** *s.* **1.** Scheiße *f*: *have a* **~** scheißen; **2.** *fig.* ,Scheiße' *f*, ,Scheiß (-dreck)' *m*; **3.** *fig.* Arschloch *n*; **4.** *pl.* ,Scheiße'rei' *f*; **5.** *sl.* ,Shit' *n* (*Haschisch*); **II** *v/i.* [*irr.*] **6.** scheißen: **~** *on* a) *auf j-n od. et.* scheißen, b) *fig.* j-n ,verpfeifen'; **III** *v/t.* **7.** voll scheißen, scheißen in (*acc.*); **shit·ty** ['ʃɪtɪ] *adj.* ,beschissen'.

shiv·er¹ ['ʃɪvə] **I** *s.* **1.** Splitter *m*, (Bruch-) Stück *n*, Scherbe *f*; **2.** *min.* Dachschiefer *m*; **II** *v/t.* **3.** zersplittern, zerschmettern; **III** *v/i.* **4.** (zer)splittern.

shiv·er² ['ʃɪvə] **I** *v/i.* **1.** (*with* vor *dat.*) zittern, (er)schauern, frösteln; **2.** flattern (*Segel*); **II** *s.* **3.** Schauer *m*, Zittern *n*, Frösteln *n*: *the* **~***s* a) ✻ der Schüttelfrost, b) F *fig.* das kalte Grausen; **'shiv·er·ing** [-vərɪŋ] *s.* Schauer(n *n*) *m*: **~** *fit* Schüttelfrost *m*; **'shiv·er·y** [-ərɪ] *adj.* **1.** fröstelnd; **2.** fiebrig.

shoal¹ [ʃəʊl] **I** *s.* **1.** Schwarm *m*, Zug *m von Fischen*; *fig.* Unmenge *f*, Masse *f*; **II** *v/i.*

in Schwärmen auftreten.

shoal² [ʃəʊl] **I** s. **1.** Untiefe f, seichte Stelle; Sandbank f; **2.** fig. Klippe f; **II** adj. **3.** seicht; **III** v/i. **4.** seicht(er) werden; '**shoal·y** [-lɪ] adj. seicht.

shoat [ʃəʊt] s. Am. gerade entwöhntes Ferkel, junges Schwein.

shock¹ [ʃɒk] **I** s. **1.** Stoß m, Erschütterung f (a. fig. des Vertrauens etc.); **2.** Zs.-stoß m, Zs.-prall m, Anprall m; **3.** ⚕ (Nerven)Schock m, Schreck m, (plötzlicher) Schlag (**to** für), seelische Erschütterung (**to** gen.): **be in** (**a state of**) ~ e-n Schock haben; **get the** ~ **of one's life** a) zu Tode erschrecken, b) sein blaues Wunder erleben; **with a** ~ mit Schrecken; **4.** Schock m, Ärgernis n (**to** für); **5.** ⚡ Schlag m, (a. ⚕ E'lektro-) Schock m; **II** v/t. **6.** erschüttern, erbeben lassen; **7.** fig. schockieren, em'pören: ~ed empört od. entrüstet (**at** über acc., **by** durch); **8.** fig. j-m e-n Schock versetzen, j-n erschüttern: **I was** ~ed **to hear** zu m-m Entsetzen hörte ich; **9.** j-m e-n e'lektrischen Schlag versetzen; ⚕ j-n schocken.

shock² [ʃɒk] ⚐ **I** s. Mandel f, Hocke f; **II** v/t. in Mandeln aufstellen.

shock³ [ʃɒk] **I** s. (~ **of hair** Haar)Schopf m; **II** adj. zottig: ~ **head** Strubbelkopf m.

shock|ab·sorb·er s. ⚙ **1.** Stoßdämpfer m; **2.** 'Schwinge,tall n; ~ **ab·sorp·tion** s. ⚙ Stoßdämpfung f.

shock·er [ʃɒkə] s. **1.** allg. ‚Schocker‘ m; **2.** Elektri'sierappa,rat m.

'**shock-,head·ed** adj. strubb(e)lig: ~ **Peter** (der) Struwwelpeter.

shock·ing [ʃɒkɪŋ] **I** adj. □ **1.** schockierend, em'pörend, unerhört, anstößig; **2.** entsetzlich, haarsträubend; **3.** F scheußlich, schrecklich, mise'rabel; **II** adv. F **4.** schrecklich, unheimlich (groß etc.); ~ **pink I** adj. pink(farben) **II** s. Pink n.

'**shock|,proof** adj. ⚙ stoß-, erschütterungsfest; ~ **tac·tics** s. pl. sg. konstr. ✕ 'Durchbruchs-, Stoßtaktik f; ~ **ther·a·py**, ~ **treat·ment** s. ⚕ 'Schock-thera,pie f, -behandlung f; ~ **troops** s. pl. ✕ Stoßtruppen pl.; ~ **wave** s. Druckwelle f; fig. Erschütterung f, Schock m; ~ **work·er** s. DDR etc.: Stoßarbeiter m.

shod [ʃɒd] **I** pret. u. p.p. von **shoe**; **II** adj. **1.** beschuht; **2.** beschlagen (Pferd, Stock etc.); **3.** bereift.

shod·dy [ʃɒdɪ] **I** s. **1.** Shoddy n (langfaserige) Reißwolle; **2.** Shoddytuch n; **3.** fig. Schund m, Kitsch m; **4.** fig. Protzentum n; **II** adj. **5.** Shoddy...; **6.** fig. a) unecht, falsch: ~ **aristocracy** Talmiaristokratie f, b) kitschig, Schund...: ~ **literature**, c) protzig.

shoe [ʃuː] **I** s. **1.** (bsd. Brit. Halb)Schuh m: **dead men's** ~s fig. ungeduldig erwartetes Erbe; **be in s.o.'s** ~s fig. in j-s Haut stecken; **know where the** ~ **pinches** fig. wissen, wo der Schuh drückt; **shake in one's** ~s fig. vor Angst schlottern; **step into s.o.'s** ~s j-s Stelle einnehmen; **that is another pair of** ~s fig. das sind zwei Paar Stiefel; **now the** ~ **is on the other foot** F jetzt will er etc. (plötzlich) nichts mehr davon wissen; **2.** Hufeisen n; **3.** ⚙ Schuh m, (Schutz)Beschlag m; **4.** ⚙ a) Bremsschuh m, -klotz m, b) Bremsbacke f; **5.** ⚙ (Reifen)Decke f; **6.** ⚡ Gleitschuh m; **II** v/t. [irr.] **7.** a) beschuhen, b) Pferd, a. Stock beschlagen; '~**black** s. Schuhputzer m; '~**horn** s. Schuhlöffel m; '~**lace** s. Schnürsenkel m; '~**mak·er** s. Schuhmacher m; ~'s **thread** Pechdraht

m; '~**shine** s. Am. Schuhputzen n: ~ **boy** Schuhputzer m; '~**string** I s. ~ **shoelace**: **on a** ~ F mit ein paar Groschen, praktisch mit nichts anfangen etc.; **II** adj. F a) fi'nanzschwach, b) ‚klein‘, c) armselig.

shone [ʃɒn] pret. u. p.p. von **shine**.

shoo [ʃuː] **I** int. **1.** husch!, sch!, fort!; **II** v/t. **2.** a. ~ **away** Vögel etc. verscheuchen; **3.** Am. F j-n ‚scheuchen‘; **III** v/i. **4.** husch! od. sch! rufen.

shook¹ [ʃʊk] bsd. Am. s. **1.** Bündel n Fassdauben; **2.** Pack m Kistenbretter; **3.** → **shock²** I.

shook² [ʃʊk] pret. von **shake**.

shoot [ʃuːt] **I** s. **1.** a) (a. Wett)Schießen n, b) Schuss m; **2.** hunt. a) Jagd f, b) 'Jagd(re,vier n) f, c) Jagdgesellschaft f, d) Am. Strecke f; **3.** Am. Ra'ketenabschuss m; **4.** phot. (Film)Aufnahme f; **5.** (Holz- etc.)Rutsche f, Rutschbahn f; **6.** Stromschnelle f; **7.** ♀ Schössling m, Trieb m; **II** v/t. [irr.] **8.** Pfeil, Kugel etc. (ab)schießen, (-)feuern: ~ **questions at s.o.** j-n mit Fragen bombardieren; → **shoot off** I; **9.** a) Wild schießen, erlegen, b) a. j-n anschießen, c) a. ~ **dead** j-n erschießen (**for** wegen); **10.** hunt. in e-m Revier jagen; **11.** sport Ball, Tor schießen; **12.** ♗ Sonne etc. schießen (Höhe messen); → **moon** 1; **13.** fig. Strahl etc. schießen, senden: ~ **a glance at** e-n schnellen Blick werfen auf (acc.); **14.** a) Film, Szene schießen, b) ‚schießen‘, aufnehmen, fotografieren; **15.** fig. stoßen, schleudern, werfen; **16.** fig. unter e-r Brücke etc. hin'durchschießen, über e-e Stromschnelle etc. hin'wegschießen; **17.** Riegel vorschieben; **18.** mit Fäden durch'schie-ßen, -'wirken; **19.** a. ~ **forth** ♀ Knospen etc. treiben; **20.** Müll, Karren etc. abladen, auskippen; **21.** Fass schroten; **22.** ⚕ (ein)spritzen; → **shoot up** 2; **III** v/i. [irr.] **23.** a. sport schießen, feuern (**at** nach, auf acc.): ~! Am. sl. schieß los! (sprich!); **24.** hunt. jagen, schießen: **go** ~**ing** auf die Jagd gehen; **25.** fig. (da-'hin-, vor'bei- etc.)schießen, (-)jagen, (-)rasen: ~ **ahead** nach vorn schießen, voranstürmen; ~ **ahead of** vorbeischie-ßen an (dat.), überholen; **26.** stechen (Schmerz, Glied); **27.** a. ~ **forth** ♀ sprossen, keimen; **28.** a) filmen, b) fo-tografieren; **29.** ♗ 'überschießen (Ballast); **30.** sl. fixen;

Zssgn mit adv.:

shoot| down v/t. **1.** j-n niederschie-ßen; **2.** Flugzeug etc. abschießen; **3.** F ‚abschmettern‘; ~ **off I** v/t. Waffe ab-schießen: ~ **one's mouth** a) ‚blöd da-herreden‘, b) ‚quatschen‘, ‚(weiter-) tratschen‘; **II** v/i. stechen (bei gleicher Trefferzahl); ~ **out I** v/t. **1.** Auge etc. ausschießen; **2. shoot it out** die Sache mit ‚blauen Bohnen‘ entscheiden; **3.** her'ausschleudern, hin'auswerfen; **4.** Faust, Fuß vorschnellen (lassen); Zun-ge her'ausstrecken; **5.** her'ausragen las-sen; **II** v/i. **6.** ♀ her'vorsprießen; **7.** vor-, her'ausschnellen; ~ **up I** v/t. **1.** sl. zs.-schießen; **2.** sl. Heroin etc. ‚drü-cken‘; **II** v/i. **3.** in die Höhe schießen, rasch wachsen (Pflanze, Kind); **4.** em-'porschnellen (a. ♀ Preise); **5.** (jäh) aufragen (Klippe etc.).

shoot·er [ʃuːtə] s. **1.** Schütze m, Schüt-zin f; **2.** F ‚Schießeisen‘ n.

shoot·ing [ʃuːtɪŋ] **I** s. **1.** a) Schießen n, b) Schieße'rei f; **2.** Erschießen n; **3.** fig. Stechen n (Schmerz); **4.** hunt. a) Jagd f, b) Jagdrecht n, c) 'Jagdre,vier n; **5.** Aufnahme(n pl.) f zu e-m Film, Dreh-

arbeiten pl.; **II** adj. **6.** schießend, Schieß...; **7.** fig. stechend (Schmerz); **8.** Jagd...; ~ **box** s. Jagdhütte f; ~ **gal·ler·y** s. **1.** ✕, sport Schießstand m; **2.** Schießbude f; ~ **i·ron** s. sl. ‚Schießei-sen‘ n; ~ **li·cense** s. Jagdschein m; ~ **match** s. Preis-, Wettschießen n: **the whole** ~ F der ganze ‚Kram‘; ~ **range** s. Schießstand m; ~ **star** s. ast. Stern-schnuppe f; ~ **war** s. heißer Krieg, Schießkrieg m.

shoot-out [ʃuːtaʊt] s. **1.** Schießerei f; **2.** Fußball: Elf'meterschießen n (bei unentschiedenem Spielausgang).

shop [ʃɒp] **I** s. **1.** (Kauf)Laden m, Ge-schäft n: **set up** ~ ein Geschäft eröff-nen; **shut up** ~ das Geschäft schließen, den Laden dichtmachen (a. für immer); **come to the wrong** ~ F an die falsche Adresse geraten; **all over the** ~ sl. a) überall verstreut, b) in alle Himmels-richtungen; **2.** ⚙ Werkstatt f; **3.** a) Be-trieb m, Fa'brik f, b) Ab'teilung f in e-r Fabrik: **talk** ~ fachsimpeln; **sink the** ~ F a) nicht vom Geschäft reden, b) s-n Beruf verheimlichen; → **closed shop**, **open shop**; **4.** bsd. Brit. sl. a) ‚Laden‘ m (Institut etc.), ‚Penne‘ f (Schule), ‚Uni‘ f (Universität), b) ‚Kittchen‘ n (Gefängnis); **II** v/i. **5.** einkaufen, Ein-käufe machen: **go** ~**ping**; ~ **around** F a) vor dem Einkauf die Preise vergle-ichen, b) fig. sich umsehen (**for** nach); **III** v/t. **6.** bsd. Brit. sl. a) j-n ‚verpfei-fen‘, b) j-n ‚ins Kittchen bringen‘; ~ **as-sist·ant** s. Brit. Verkäufer(in); ~ **com-mit·tee** s. ✠ Am. Betriebsrat m; '~**fit-ter** s. Ladeneinrichter m, -ausstatter m; ~ **floor** s. **1.** Produkti'onsstätte f; **2.** Arbeiter pl., Belegschaft f; '~**girl** s. Ladenmädchen n; '~**keep·er** s. Laden-besitzer(in): **nation of** ~s fig. contp. Krämervolk n; '~**keep·ing** s. **1.** Klein-handel m; **2.** Betrieb m e-s (Laden)Ge-schäfts; '~**lift·er** s. Ladendieb(in); '~**lift·ing** s. Ladendiebstahl m.

shop·per [ʃɒpə] s. (Ein)Käufer(in); **shop·ping** [ʃɒpɪŋ] s. **1.** Einkauf m, Einkaufen n (in Läden): ~ **basket** Einkaufskorb m; ~ **cart** Am. Einkaufs-wagen m; ~ **centre** Brit., ~ **center** Am. Einkaufszentrum n; ~ **list** Ein-kaufsliste f, -zettel m; ~ **trolley** Brit. Einkaufswagen m; **do one's** ~ (seine) Einkäufe machen; **2.** Einkäufe pl. (Ware).

,**shop|-'soiled** adj. **1.** ✠ angestaubt, be-schädigt; **2.** fig. abgenutzt; ~ **stew·ard** s. ✠ (gewerkschaftlicher) Vertrauens-mann; '~**talk** s. Fachsimpe'lei f; '~**walk·er** s. Brit. (Aufsicht führender) Ab'teilungsleiter (im Kaufhaus); ,~'**win·dow** s. Schaufenster n, Auslage f: **put all one's goods in the** ~ fig. ‚ganz auf Wirkung machen‘; '~**worn** → **shop-soiled**.

shore¹ [ʃɔː] **I** s. **1.** Stütz-, Strebebalken m, Strebe f; **2.** ♗ Schore f (Spreizholz); **II** v/t. **3.** mst ~ **up** a) abstützen, b) fig. (unter)'stützen.

shore² [ʃɔː] **I** s. **1.** Küste f, Strand m, Ufer n, Gestade n: **my native** ~ fig. mein Heimatland; **2.** ♗ Land n: **on** ~ an(s) Land; **in** ~ an Land; **II** adj. **3.** Küsten..., Strand..., Land...: ~ **bat-tery** ✕ Küstenbatterie f; ~ **leave** ♗ Landurlaub m; '**shore·less** [-lɪs] adj. ohne Ufer, uferlos (a. poet. fig.); '**shore·ward** [-wəd] **I** adj. küstenwärts gelegen od. gerichtet etc.; **II** adv. a. ~s küstenwärts, (nach) der Küste zu.

shorn [ʃɔːn] p.p. von **shear**: ~ **of** fig. e-r Sache beraubt.

S

short [ʃɔːt] **I** *adj.* □ → *shortly*; **1.** *räumlich u. zeitlich kurz*: *a ~ life*; *a ~ memory*; *a ~ street*; *a ~ time ago* vor kurzer Zeit, vor kurzem; *~ sight* Kurzsichtigkeit *f* (*a. fig.*); *get the ~ end of the stick Am.* F schlecht wegkommen (*bei e-r Sache*); *have by the ~ hairs Am.* F *j-n od. et.* ,in der Tasche' haben; **2.** kurz, gedrungen, klein; **3.** zu kurz (*for* für): *fall* (*od. come*) *~ of et.* nicht erreichen, *den Erwartungen etc.* nicht entsprechen, hinter (*dat.*) zurückbleiben; **4.** *fig.* kurz, knapp: *a ~ speech*; *be ~ for* die Kurzform sein von; **5.** kurz angebunden, barsch (*with* gegen); **6.** knapp, unzureichend: *~ rations*; *~ weight* Fehlgewicht *n*; *run ~* knapp werden; **7.** knapp (*of* an *dat.*): *~ of breath* kurzatmig; *~ of cash* knapp bei Kasse; *they ran ~ of bread* das Brot ging ihnen aus; **8.** knapp, nicht ganz: *a ~ hour* (*mile*); **9.** geringer, weniger (*of* als): *nothing ~ of* nichts weniger als, geradezu (→ *a.* 17); **10.** mürbe (*Gebäck etc.*): *~ pastry* Mürbeteig *m*; **11.** *metall.* brüchig; **12.** *bsd.* ✝ kurzfristig, *Wechsel etc.* auf kurze Sicht: *at ~ date* kurzfristig; *at ~ notice* a) kurzfristig (kündbar), b) schnell, prompt; **13.** ✝ *Börse*: a) Baisse..., b) ungedeckt, deckungslos: *sell ~*; **14.** a) klein, in e-m Gläs·chen serviert, b) stark (*Getränk*); **II** *adv.* **15.** kurz(erhand), plötzlich, ab'rupt: *cut s.o. ~*, *take s.o. up ~* j-n (jäh) unterbrechen; *be taken ~* F ,dringend (austreten) müssen'; *stop ~* plötzlich innehalten (→ *a.* 17); **16.** zu kurz; **17.** *~ of* a) knapp *od.* kurz vor (*dat.*), b) *fig.* abgesehen von, außer (*dat.*): *anything ~ of murder*; *~ of lying* ehe ich lüge; *stop ~ of* zurückschrecken vor (*dat.*); **III** *s.* **18.** *et.* Kurzes, z. B. Kurzfilm *m*; **19.** *in ~* kurzum; *called Bill for ~* kurz *od.* der Kürze halber Bill genannt; **20.** ⚡ F ,Kurze(r)' *m* (*Kurzschluss*); **21.** ✝ a) 'Baissespeku,lant *m*, b) *pl.* ohne Deckung verkaufte 'Wertpa,piere *pl. od.* Waren *pl.*; **22.** *ling.* a) kurzer Vo'kal, b) kurze Silbe; **23.** *pl.* a) Shorts *pl.* (*kurze Hose*), b) *Am.* kurze 'Unterhose; **IV** *v/t.* **24.** F → *short-cir-cuit* 1, 2; **'short·age** [-tɪdʒ] *s.* **1.** Knappheit *f*, Mangel *m* (*of* an *dat.*); **2.** Fehlbetrag *m*, Defizit *n*.

'short|·bread, **'~·cake** *s.* Mürbe-, Teekuchen *m*; **,~'change** *v/t.* F *j-m* zu wenig (Wechselgeld) her'ausgeben; *fig. j-n* ,übers Ohr hauen'; *~* **cir·cuit** *s.* ⚡ Kurzschluss *m*; **,~'cir·cuit** *v/t.* **1.** ⚡ e-n Kurzschluss verursachen in (*dat.*); **2.** ⚡ kurzschließen; **3.** *fig.* F a) *et.* ,torpedieren', b) um'gehen; **,~'com·ing** *s.* **1.** Unzulänglichkeit *f*; **2.** Fehler *m*, Mangel *m*; **3.** Pflichtversäumnis *n*; **4.** Fehlbetrag *m*; *~* **cut** *s.* Abkürzung *f* (*Weg*); *fig.* abgekürztes Verfahren: *take a ~* (den Weg) abkürzen; **,~'dat·ed** *adj.* ✝ kurzfristig: *~ bond*; **,~'dis·tance** *adj.* Nah...

short·en [ˈʃɔːtn] **I** *v/t.* **1.** (ab-, ver)kürzen, kürzer machen; *Bäume etc.* stutzen; *fig.* vermindern; **2.** ⚓ *Segel* reffen; **3.** *Teig* mürbe machen; **II** *v/i.* **4.** kürzer werden; **5.** fallen (*Preise*); **'short·en·ing** [-nɪŋ] *s.* **1.** (Ab-, Ver)Kürzung *f*; **2.** (Ver)Minderung *f*; **3.** Backfett *n*.

'short|·fall *s.* Fehlbetrag *m*; **'~·hand I** *s.* **1.** Kurzschrift *f*; **II** *adj.* **2.** in Kurzschrift (geschrieben), stenografiert; **3.** Kurzschrift...: *~ typist* Stenotypistin *f*; *~ writer* Stenograf(in); **,~'hand·ed** *adj.* knapp an Arbeitskräften; *~* **haul** *s.* Nahverkehr *m*; **'~·horn** *s. zo.* Short-

horn *n*, Kurzhornrind *n*.
short·ie [ˈʃɔːtɪ] → *shorty*.
short·ish [ˈʃɔːtɪʃ] *adj.* etwas *od.* ziemlich kurz (geraten).
short| list *s.*: *be on the ~* in der engeren Wahl sein; **'~·list** *v/t. j-n* in die engere Wahl ziehen; **,~-'lived** [-'lɪvd] *adj.* kurzlebig, *fig. a.* von kurzer Dauer.
short·ly [ˈʃɔːtlɪ] *adv.* **1.** in Kürze, bald: *~ after* kurz (da)nach; **2.** in kurzen Worten; **3.** kurz (angebunden), schroff; **short·ness** [ˈʃɔːtnɪs] *s.* **1.** Kürze *f*; **2.** Schroffheit *f*; **3.** Knappheit *f*, Mangel *m* (*of* an *dat.*): *~ of breath* Kurzatmigkeit *f*; **4.** Mürbe *f* (*Gebäck etc.*).
'short|-range *adj.* **1.** Kurzstrecken..., Nah..., ✕ *a.* Nahkampf...; **2.** *fig.* kurzfristig; *~* **rib** *s. anat.* falsche Rippe; *~* **sale** *s.* ✝ Leerverkauf *m*; **,~-'sight·ed** [-'saɪtɪd] *adj.* □ kurzsichtig (*a. fig.*); **,~-'sight·ed·ness** [-'saɪtɪdnɪs] *s.* Kurzsichtigkeit *f* (*a. fig.*); **,~-'spo·ken** *adj.* kurz angebunden, schroff; **,~'staffed** *adj.* perso'nell 'unterbesetzt; *~* **sto·ry** *s.* Kurzgeschichte *f*; *~* **tem·per** *s.* Reizbarkeit *f*, Heftigkeit *f*; **,~-'tem·pered** *adj.* reizbar, aufbrausend; **'~-term** *adj. bsd.* ✝ kurzfristig: *~ credit*; *~* **time** *s.* ✝ Kurzarbeit *f*: *work* (*od. be on*) *~* kurzarbeiten; *~* **ton** *s. bsd. Am.* Tonne *f* (2000 *lbs.*); *~* **wave** *s.* ⚡ Kurzwelle *f*; **,~-'wave** *adj.* ⚡ **1.** kurzwellig; **2.** Kurzwellen...; *~* **wind** *s.* Kurzatmigkeit *f* (*a. fig.*); **,~-'wind·ed** *adj.* kurzatmig (*a. fig.*).
short·y [ˈʃɔːtɪ] *s.* F **1.** ,Knirps' *m*; **2.** a) kleines Ding, b) kurze Sache.
shot¹ [ʃɒt] **I** *pret. u. p.p. von shoot*; **II** *adj.* **1.** *a.* *~ through* durch'schossen, gesprenkelt (*Seide etc.*); **2.** changierend, schillernd (*Stoff, Farbe*); **3.** *sl.* ,ka'putt', erschöpft.
shot² [ʃɒt] *s.* **1.** Schuss *m* (*a. Knall*): *by a long ~ fig.* ein kühner Versuch; *by a long ~ sl.* weitaus; *not by a long ~* längst nicht, kein bisschen; *call the ~s fig.* ,am Drücker sein', das Sagen haben; *like a ~* F wie der Blitz, sofort; *take a ~ at* schießen auf (*acc.*); **2.** Schussweite *f*: *out of ~* außer Schussweite; **3.** *a. small ~* a) Schrotkugel *f*, -korn *n*, b) *coll.* Schrot(kugeln *pl.*) *m*; **4.** (Ka'nonen)Kugel *f*, Geschoss, *östr.* Geschoß *n*: *a ~ in the locker* F Geld in der Tasche; **5.** *guter etc.* Schütze: *big ~* F ,großes *od.* hohes Tier'; **6.** *sport* Schuss *m*, Wurf *m*, Stoß *m*, Schlag *m*; **7.** *sport* Kugel *f*: → *shot put*; **8.** a) (Film)Aufnahme *f*, (-)Szene *f*), b) *phot.* F Aufnahme *f*, Schnappschuss *m*; **9.** *fig.* Versuch *m*: *at the third ~* beim dritten Versuch; *have a ~ at et.* (einmal) mit et. versuchen; **10.** *fig.* (Seiten)Hieb *m*; **11.** ✐ Spritze *f* (*Injektion*): *~ in the arm* F *fig.* ,Spritze' *f* (*bsd.* ✝ *finanzielle Hilfe*); **12.** F Schuss *m* Rum *etc.*; *Gläs·chen n Schnaps*: *stand ~* die Zeche (für alle) bezahlen; **13.** ⊕ a) Sprengladung *f*, b) Sprengung *f*; **14.** *Am. sl.* Chance *f*; **'~·gun** *s.* Schrotflinte *f*: *~ wedding* ,Mussheirat' *f*; *~* **put** *s. sport* a) Kugelstoßen *n*, b) Stoß *m*; **'~·put·ter** *s. sport* Kugelstoßer(in).
shot·ten [ˈʃɒtn] *adj. ichth.* gelaicht habend: *~ herring* Laichhering *m*.
shot weld·ing *s.* ⊕ Schussschweißen *n*.
should [ʃʊd; ʃəd] **1.** *pret. von shall, a. konditional futurisch*: *I ~ have gone* ich hätte gehen sollen, *du solltest, wir, Ihr, Sie, sie* sollten: *I ~ have gone* ich hätte gehen sollen; *if he ~ come* falls er kommen sollte; *~ it prove false* sollte es sich als falsch erweisen; **2.** *konditional*: *ich*

würde, *wir* würden: *I ~ go if ...*; *I ~ not have come if* ich wäre nicht gekommen, wenn; *I ~ like to* ich würde *od.* möchte gern; **3.** *nach Ausdrücken des Erstaunens*: *it is incredible that he ~ have failed* es ist unglaublich, dass er versagt hat.
shoul·der [ˈʃəʊldə] **I** *s.* **1.** Schulter *f*, Achsel *f*: *~ to ~ bsd. fig.* Schulter an Schulter; *put one's ~ to the wheel fig.* sich tüchtig ins Zeug legen; (*straight*) *from the ~ fig.* unverblümt, geradeheraus; *give s.o. the cold ~ fig.* j-m die kalte Schulter zeigen; → *rub* 7; *he has broad ~s fig.* er hat e-n breiten Rücken; **2.** Bug *m*, Schulterstück *n* (*von Tieren*): *~ of mutton* Hammelkeule *f*; **3.** *fig.* Schulter *f*, Vorsprung *m*; **4.** *a. hard ~* a) Ban'kett *n*, Seitenstreifen *m*, b) *mot.* Standspur *f*; **5.** ✔ 'Übergangsstreifen *m* (*Flugplatz*); **II** *v/t.* **6.** (mit der Schulter) stoßen *od.* drängen: *~ one's way through the crowd* sich e-n Weg durch die Menge bahnen; **7.** *et.* schultern, auf die Schulter nehmen; ✕ *Gewehr* 'übernehmen; *Aufgabe, Verantwortung etc.* auf sich nehmen; *~ bag s.* 'Umhängetasche *f*; *~ belt s.* **1.** ✕ Schulterriemen *m*; **2.** *mot.* Schultergurt *m*; *~ blade s. anat.* Schulterblatt *n*; *~ strap s.* **1.** Träger *m* (*bsd. an Damenunterwäsche*); **2.** ✕ Schulterstück *n*.
should·n't [ˈʃʊdnt] F *für should not*.
shout [ʃaʊt] **I** *v/i.* **1.** (laut) rufen, schreien (*for* nach): *~ to s.o.* j-m zurufen; **2.** schreien, brüllen (*with* vor *Schmerz, Lachen*): *~ at s.o.* j-n anschreien; **3.** jauchzen (*for, with* vor *dat.*); **II** *v/t.* **4.** (laut) rufen, schreien; *~ disapproval* laut sein Missfallen äußern; *~ s.o. down* j-n niederbrüllen; *~ out* a) herausschreien, b) *Namen etc.* ausrufen; **III** *s.* **5.** Schrei *m*, Ruf *m*; **6.** Geschrei *n*, Gebrüll *n*: *a ~ of laughter* brüllendes Lachen; **7.** *my ~!* F jetzt bin ich dran! (*zum Stiften von Getränken*); **'shout·ing** [-tɪŋ] *s.* Schreien *n*, Geschrei *n*: *all is over but od. bar the ~* es ist so gut wie gelaufen.
shove [ʃʌv] **I** *v/t.* **1.** beiseite *etc.* schieben, stoßen: *~ s.o. around bsd. fig.* F j-n ,herumschubsen'; **2.** (achtlos *od.* rasch) *wohin* schieben, stecken; **II** *v/i.* **3.** schieben, stoßen; **4.** (sich) dränge(l)n; **5.** *~ off* a) vom Ufer abstoßen, b) *sl.* ,abschieben', sich da'vonmachen; **III** *s.* **6.** Stoß *m*, Schubs *m*.
shov·el [ˈʃʌvl] **I** *s.* **1.** Schaufel *f*; **2.** ☉ a) Löffel *m* (*e-s Löffelbaggers*), b) Löffelbagger *m*; **II** *v/t.* **3.** schaufeln: *~ up* (*od. in*) *money* Geld scheffeln; **'shov·el·ful** [-fʊl] *pl.* **-fuls** *s. e-e* Schaufel (voll).
show [ʃəʊ] **I** *s.* **1.** (Her)Zeigen *n*: *vote by ~ of hands* durch Handzeichen wählen; **2.** Schau *f*, Zur'schaustellung *f*: *a ~ of force fig.* e-e Demonstration der Macht; **3.** *künstlerische etc.* Darbietung, Vorführung *f*, -stellung *f*, Show *f*: *put on a ~* F *fig.* ,e-e Schau abziehen'; *steal s.o. the ~* F *fig.* j-m ,die Schau stehlen'; **4.** F (The'ater-, Film)Vorstellung *f*; **5.** Schau *f*, Ausstellung *f*: *flower ~*; *on ~* ausgestellt, zu besichtigen(d); **6.** *prunkvoller* 'Umzug; **7.** Schaubude *f* auf Jahrmärkten; **8.** Anblick *m*: *make a sorry ~* e-n traurigen Eindruck hinterlassen; *make a good ~* (e-e) ,gute Figur' machen; **9.** F *gute etc.* Leistung: *good ~!* gut gemacht!, bravo!; **10.** Protze'rei *f*, Angebe'rei *f*: *for ~* um Eindruck zu machen, (nur) fürs Auge; *be fond of ~* gern großtun; *make a ~ of* mit *et.* protzen (→ *a.* 11); **11.** (leerer)

Schein: *in outward* ~ nach außen hin; *make a* ~ *of rage* sich wütend stellen; **12.** Spur *f*: *no* ~ *of* keine Spur von; **13.** F Chance *f*: *give s.o. a* ~; **14.** F ‚Laden' *m*, ‚Kiste' *f*, ‚Kram' *m*: *run the* ~ *sl.* ‚den Laden schmeißen'; *give the* (*whole*) ~ *away* F den ganzen Schwindel verraten; *a dull* (*poor*) ~ e-e langweilige (armselige) Sache; **II** *v/t.* [*irr.*] **15.** zeigen (*s.o. s.th., s.th. to s.o.* j-m et.), sehen lassen, *Fahrkarten etc. a.* vorzeigen, -weisen: ~ *o.s. od. one's face* sich zeigen *od.* blicken lassen, *fig.* sich *grausam etc.* zeigen, sich erweisen als; ~ *s.o. the door* j-m die Tür weisen; *we had nothing to* ~ *for it* wir hatten nichts vorzuweisen; **16.** ausstellen, (auf e-r Ausstellung) zeigen; **17.** *thea. etc.* zeigen, vorführen; **18.** *j-n ins Zimmer etc.* geleiten, führen: ~ *s.o. over the house* j-n durch das Haus führen; **19.** *Absicht etc.* (auf)zeigen, kundtun, darlegen; **20.** zeigen, beweisen, nachweisen; ɪ̃ʒ *a.* glaubhaft machen: ~ *proof* den Beweis erbringen; *that goes to* ~ *that* das zeigt *od.* beweist, dass; **21.** zeigen, erkennen lassen, verraten: ~ *bad taste*; **22.** *Gunst etc.* erweisen; **23.** j-m zeigen *od.* erklären (*wie et. gemacht wird*): ~ *s.o. how to write* j-m das Schreiben beibringen; **III** *v/i.* [*irr.*] **24.** sich zeigen, sichtbar werden *od.* sein: *it* ~*s* man sieht es; **25.** F sich *in Gesellschaft* zeigen, erscheinen; *Zssgn mit adv.*:

show| forth *v/t.* darlegen, kundtun; ~ **in** *v/t.* j-n her'einführen; ~ **off I** *v/t.* **1.** protzen mit; **2.** *a.* ~ *to advantage* vorteilhaft zur Geltung bringen; **II** *v/i.* **3.** angeben; ~ **out** *v/t.* hin'ausgeleiten, -bringen; ~ **up I** *v/t.* **1.** her'auf-, hin'aufführen; **2.** F a) j-n bloßstellen, entlarven, b) *et.* aufdecken; **II** *v/i.* **3.** F ‚aufkreuzen', -tauchen, erscheinen; **4.** sich abheben (*against* gegen).

show| biz F → **show business**; '~·**boat** *s.* The'aterschiff *n*; ~ **busi·ness** *s.* Showbusiness *n*, Show-, Schaugeschäft *n*; ~ **card** *s.* ✝ **1.** Musterkarte *f*; **2.** 'Werbepla‚kat *n* (*im Schaufenster*); '~·**case** *s.* Schaukasten *m*; '~·**down** *s.* **1.** Aufdecken *n* der Karten (*a. fig.*); **2.** entscheidende Kraftprobe, endgültige Ausein'andersetzung, ‚Show-down' *m*.

show·er ['ʃaʊə] **I** *s.* **1.** (*Regen-*, *Hagel- etc.*)Schauer *m*; **2.** Guss *m*; **3.** *fig.* a) (*Funken-*, *Kugel- etc.*)Regen *m*, (*Geschoss-*, *Stein*)Hagel *m*, b) Schwall *m*, Unmenge *f*; **4.** *Am.* a) Brautgeschenke *pl.*, b) *a.* ~ *party* Party *f* zur Überreichung der Brautgeschenke; **5.** → *shower bath*; **II** *v/t.* **6.** über'schütten, begießen: ~ *gifts etc. upon s.o.* j-n mit Geschenken *etc.* überhäufen; **7.** *j-n* duschen; **8.** niederprasseln lassen; **III** *v/i.* **9.** (~ *down* nieder)prasseln; **10.** (sich) duschen; **show·er bath** *s.* **1.** Dusche *f*: a) Brausebad *n*, b) Brause *f* (*Vorrichtung*); **2.** Duschraum *m*; **show·er·y** ['ʃaʊərɪ] *adj.* **1.** mit einzelnen (Regen-)Schauern; **2.** schauerartig.

show flat *s.* Musterwohnung *f*.

show| girl *s.* Re'vuegirl *n*; ~ **glass** → *showcase*.

show·i·ness ['ʃəʊɪnɪs] *s.* **1.** Prunkhaftigkeit *f*, Gepränge *n*; **2.** Protzigkeit *f*, Auffälligkeit *f*; **3.** pom'pöses Auftreten.

show·ing ['ʃəʊɪŋ] *s.* **1.** Zur'schaustellung *f*; **2.** Ausstellung *f*; **3.** Vorführung *f* (*e-s Films etc.*); **4.** Darlegung *f*, Erklärung *f*; Beweis(*e pl.*) *m*: *on* (*od. by*) *your own* ~ nach Ihrer eigenen Dar-

stellung; *upon proper* ~ ɪ̃ʒ nach erfolgter Glaubhaftmachung; **5.** *gute etc.* Leistung; **6.** Stand *m* der Dinge: *on present* ~ so wie es derzeit aussieht; ‚~-'off *s.* Angebe'rei *f*.

show| jump·er *s.* *sport* **1.** Springreiter(-in); **2.** Springpferd *n*; ~ **jump·ing** *s.* Springreiten *n*.

'**show·man** [-mən] *s.* [*irr.*] **1.** Schausteller *m*; **2.** ‚Showman' *m*: a) j-d der im *Showgeschäft tätig ist*, b) *fig.* geschickter Propagan'dist, wirkungsvoller Redner *etc.*, j-d, der sich gut ‚zu verkaufen' versteht, *contp.* ‚Schauspieler' *m*; '**show·man·ship** [-ʃɪp] *s.* ‚Showmanship' *f*: a) ef'fektvolle Darbietung, b) *die Kunst*, sich in Szene zu setzen, Publikumswirksamkeit *f*.

shown [ʃəʊn] *p.p.* von **show**.

'**show|-off** *s.* F **1.** ‚Angabe' *f*, Protze'rei *f*; **2.** ‚Angeber(in)' *m*; '~·**piece** *s.* Schau-, Pa'radestück *n*; '~·**place** *s.* Ort *m* mit vielen Sehenswürdigkeiten; '~·**room** *s.* **1.** Ausstellungsraum *m*; **2.** Vorführungssaal *m*; ~ **tri·al** *s.* ɪ̃ʒ 'Schaupro‚zess *m*; ~ **win·dow** *s.* Schaufenster *n*.

show·y ['ʃəʊɪ] *adj.* □ **1.** a) prächtig, b) protzig; **2.** auffällig, grell.

shrank [ʃræŋk] *pret.* von **shrink**.

shrap·nel ['ʃræpnl] *s.* ✕ **1.** Schrap'nell *n*; **2.** Schrap'nellladung *f*.

shred [ʃred] **I** *s.* **1.** Fetzen *m* (*a. fig.*), Lappen *m*: *in* ~*s* in Fetzen; *tear to* ~*s* a) → 4, b) *fig.* Argument etc. zerpflücken, -reißen; **2.** Schnitzel *m*, *n*; **3.** *fig.* Spur *f*, A'tom *n*: *not a* ~ *of doubt* nicht der leiseste Zweifel; **II** *v/t.* [*irr.*] **4.** zerfetzen, in Fetzen reißen; **5.** in Streifen schneiden, *Küche*: a. schnetzeln; **III** *v/i.* [*irr.*] **6.** zerreißen, in Fetzen gehen; '**shred·der** [-də] *s.* **1.** ⚙ Reißwolf *m*; **2.** *Küche*: a) 'Schnitzelma‚schine *f*, -einsatz *m*, b) Reibeisen *n*.

shrew¹ [ʃruː] *s.* Xan'thippe *f*, zänkisches Weib.

shrew² [ʃruː] *s. zo.* Spitzmaus *f*.

shrewd [ʃruːd] *adj.* □ **1.** schlau, gerieben; **2.** scharfsinnig, klug, gescheit: *this was a* ~ *guess* das war gut geraten; **3.** *obs.* scharf; '**shrewd·ness** [-nɪs] *s.* **1.** Schlauheit *f*; **2.** Scharfsinn *m*, Klugheit *f*.

shrew·ish ['ʃruːɪʃ] *adj.* □ zänkisch.

shriek [ʃriːk] **I** *s.* **1.** schriller *od.* schriller Schrei; **2.** Kreischen *n* (*a. von Bremsen etc.*): ~*s of laughter* kreischendes Lachen; **II** *v/i.* **3.** schreien, schrille Schreie ausstoßen; **4.** (gellend) aufschreien (*with* vor *Schmerz etc.*): ~ *with laughter* kreischen vor Lachen; **5.** schrill klingen; kreischen (*Bremsen etc.*); **III** *v/t.* **6.** ~ *out et.* kreischen *od.* gellend schreien.

shriev·al·ty ['ʃriːvltɪ] *s.* Amt *n* des Sheriffs.

shrift [ʃrɪft] *s.* **1.** *obs. eccl.* Beichte *f* (u. Absolu'ti'on *f*); **2.** *give s.o. short* ~ *fig.* mit j-m kurzen Prozess machen, j-n kurz abfertigen.

shrike [ʃraɪk] *s. orn.* Würger *m*.

shrill [ʃrɪl] **I** *adj.* □ **1.** schrill, gellend; **2.** *fig.* grell (*Farbe etc.*); **3.** *fig.* heftig; **II** *v/t.* **4.** *et.* kreischen *od.* gellend schreien; **III** *v/i.* **5.** schrillen; '**shrill·ness** [-nɪs] *s.* schriller Klang.

shrimp [ʃrɪmp] **I** *s.* **1.** *pl. coll.* **shrimp** *zo.* Gar'nele *f*; **2.** *fig. contp.* Knirps *m*, ‚Gartenzwerg' *m*; **II** *v/i.* **3.** Gar'nelen fangen.

shrine [ʃraɪn] *s.* **1.** *eccl.* a) (Re'liquien-)Schrein *m*, b) Heiligengrab *n*, c) Al'tar *m*; **2.** *fig.* Heiligtum *n*.

shrink [ʃrɪŋk] **I** *v/i.* [*irr.*] **1.** sich zs.-ziehen, (zs.-, ein)schrumpfen; **2.** einlaufen, -gehen (*Stoff*); **3.** abnehmen, schwinden; **4.** *fig.* zu'rückweichen (*from* vor *dat.*): ~ *from doing s.th.* et. höchst widerwillig tun; **5.** *a.* ~ *back* zu'rückschrecken, -schaudern, -beben (*from*, *at* vor *dat.*); **6.** sich scheuen *od.* fürchten (*from* vor *dat.*); **7.** ~ *away* sich da'vonschleichen; **II** *v/t.* [*irr.*] **8.** (ein-, zs.-)schrumpfen lassen; **9.** *Stoffe* einlaufen lassen, krump(f)en; **10.** *fig.* zum Schwinden bringen; **11.** ~ *on* ⚙ aufschrumpfen: ~ *fit* Schrumpfsitz *m*; **III** *s.* **12.** *sl.* Psychi'ater *m*; '**shrink·age** [-kɪdʒ] *s.* **1.** (Zs.-, Ein-)Schrumpfen *n*; **2.** Schrumpfung *f*; **3.** Verminderung *f*, Schwund *m* (*a.* ✝, ⚙); **4.** Einlaufen *n* (*Textilien*); '**shrink·ing** [-kɪŋ] *adj.* □ **1.** schrumpfend; **2.** abnehmend; **3.** 'widerwillig; **4.** scheu; '**shrink·proof** *adj.* nicht einlaufend (*Gewebe*); '**shrink-wrap** *v/t.* Bücher *etc.* einschweißen.

shriv·el ['ʃrɪvl] **I** *v/t.* **1.** *a.* ~ *up* (ein-, zs.-)schrumpfen lassen; **2.** (ver)welken lassen, ausdörren; **3.** runzeln; **II** *v/i.* **4.** *off* ~ *up* (zs.-, ein)schrumpfen, schrumpeln; **5.** runz(e)lig werden; **6.** (ver)welken; **7.** *fig.* verkümmern.

shroud [ʃraʊd] **I** *s.* **1.** Leichentuch *n*, Totenhemd *n*; **2.** *fig.* Hülle *f*, Schleier *m*; **3.** *pl.* ⚓ Wanten *pl.*; **4.** *a.* ~ *line* Fangleine *f* (*am Fallschirm*); **II** *v/t.* **5.** in ein Leichentuch (ein)hüllen; **6.** *fig. in Nebel, Geheimnis* hüllen; **7.** *fig. et.* verschleiern.

Shrove| Mon·day [ʃraʊv] *s.* Rosen'montag *m*; '~·**tide** *s.* Faschings-, Fastnachtszeit *f*; ~ **Tues·day** *s.* Faschings-, Fastnachts'dienstag *m*.

shrub¹ [ʃrʌb] *s.* Strauch *m*, Busch *m*.

shrub² [ʃrʌb] *s.* A'rt Punsch *m*.

shrub·ber·y ['ʃrʌbərɪ] *s.* ♀ Strauchwerk *n*, Sträucher *pl.*, Gebüsch *n*; '**shrub·by** [-bɪ] *adj.* ♀ strauchig, buschig, Strauch..., Busch...

shrug [ʃrʌg] **I** *v/t.* **1.** *die Achseln* zucken: *she* ~*ged her shoulders*; **2.** ~ *s.th. off fig.* et. mit e-m Achselzucken abtun; **II** *v/i.* **3.** die Achseln zucken; **III** *s.* **4.** *a.* ~ *of the shoulders* Achselzucken *n*.

shrunk [ʃrʌŋk] **I** *p.p.* von **shrink**; **II** *adj.* **1.** (ein-, zs.-)geschrumpft; **2.** eingelaufen, abgemagert (*Stoff*); '**shrunk·en** [-kən] **I** → **shrunk** 1; **II** *adj.* abgemagert, -gezehrt; eingefallen (*Wangen*).

shuck [ʃʌk] *bsd. Am.* **I** *s.* **1.** Hülse *f*, Schote *f* (*von Bohnen etc.*); **2.** grüne Schale (*von Nüssen etc.*), *a.* Austernschale *f*; **3.** *I don't care* ~*s!* F das ist mir völlig ‚schnurz'!; ~*s!* F Quatsch!; **II** *v/t.* **4.** enthülsen, -schoten; schälen.

shud·der ['ʃʌdə] **I** *v/i.* schaudern, (er)zittern (*at* bei, *with* vor *dat.*): *I* ~ *at the thought*, *I* ~ *to think of it* es schaudert mich bei den Gedanken; **II** *s.* Schauder(n *n*) *m*.

shuf·fle ['ʃʌfl] **I** *s.* **1.** Schlurfen *n*, schlurfender Gang; **2.** *Tanz*: a) Schleifschritt *m*, b) Schleifer *m* (*Tanz*); **3.** (Karten-)Mischen *n*; **4.** Ausflucht *f*, Trick *m*; **II** *v/i.* **5.** schlurfen, (mit den Füßen) scharren: ~ *through s.th. fig.* et. flüchtig erledigen; **6.** *fig.* a) Ausflüchte machen, sich her'auszureden suchen, b) sich her'auswinden (*out of* aus); **7.** (die Karten) mischen; **III** *v/t.* **8.** hin u. her schieben, *fig. a.* ‚jonglieren' mit: ~ *one's feet* → 5; **9.** schmuggeln: ~ *away* wegpraktizieren; **10.** ~ *off* a) *Kleider* abstreifen, b) *fig.* abschütteln, sich befreien von, sich *e-r Verpflichtung* entziehen, *Schuld etc.* abwälzen (**on**[**to**] auf *acc.*); **11.** ~ **on** *Kleider* mühsam anziehen; **12.** *Karten* mischen: ~ *together et.* zs.-werfen, -raffen; '**shuffle·board** *s.* a) Beilkespiel *n*), b) ♣ *ein ähnliches Bordspiel*; '**shuf·fler** [-lə] *s.* **1.** Schlurfende(r *m*) *f*; **2.** Ausflüchtemacher *m*; Schwindler(in); '**shuf·fling** [-lɪŋ] *adj.* □ **1.** schlurfend, schleppend; **2.** unaufrichtig, unredlich; **3.** ausweichend: *a* ~ *answer*.

shun [ʃʌn] *v/t.* (ver)meiden, ausweichen (*dat.*), sich fern halten von.

shunt [ʃʌnt] **I** *v/t.* **1.** bei'seite schieben; **2.** 🚋 *Zug etc.* rangieren, auf ein anderes Gleis fahren; **3.** ⚡ nebenschließen, shunten, **4.** *fig. et.* aufschieben; **5.** *fig. j-n* beiseite schieben, *j-n* kaltstellen; **6.** abzweigen; **II** *v/i.* **7.** 🚋 rangieren; **8.** *fig.* von e-m Thema, Vorhaben etc. abkommen, -springen; **III** *s.* **9.** 🚋 a) Rangieren *n*, b) Weiche *f*; **10.** ⚡ a) Nebenschluss *m*, b) 'Neben,widerstand *m*; '**shunt·er** [-tə] *s.* 🚋 a) Weichensteller *m*, b) Rangierer *m*; '**shunt·ing** [-tɪŋ] 🚋 **I** *s.* Rangieren *n*; Weichenstellen *n*; **II** *adj.* Rangier..., Verschiebe...: ~ *engine*.

shush [ʃʌʃ] **I** *int.* sch!, pst!; **II** *v/i.* ‚sch‘ *od.* ‚pst‘ machen; **III** *v/t. j-n* zum Schweigen bringen.

shut [ʃʌt] **I** *v/t.* [*irr.*] **1.** (ver)schließen, zumachen: ~ *one's mind* (*od.* **heart**) *to s.th. fig.* sich gegen et. verschließen; → *Verbindungen mit anderen Substantiven*; **2.** einschließen, -sperren (**into**, **in** in *dat.*, *acc.*); **3.** ausschließen, -sperren (**out of** aus); **4.** *Finger etc.* (ein)klemmen; **5.** *Taschenmesser, Buch etc.* schließen, zs.-, zuklappen; **II** *v/i.* [*irr.*] **6.** sich schließen, zugehen; **7.** schließen (*Fenster etc.*); **III** *p.p. u. adj.* **8.** ge-, verschlossen, zu: *the shops are* ~ die Geschäfte sind geschlossen *od.* zu; *Zssgn mit adv.*:

shut| down I *v/t.* **1.** *Fenster etc.* schließen; **2.** *Fabrik etc.* schließen, stilllegen; **II** *v/i.* **3.** die Arbeit *od.* den Betrieb einstellen, ‚zumachen‘; **4.** ~ (*up*)*on* F ein Ende machen mit; ~ **in** *v/t.* **1.** einschließen (*a. fig.*); **2.** *Aussicht* versperren; ~ **off** *v/t.* **1.** *Wasser, Motor etc.* abstellen; **2.** abschließen (**from** von); ~ **out** *v/t.* **1.** *j-n, a. Licht, Luft etc.* ausschließen, -sperren; **2.** *Landschaft* den Blicken entziehen; **3.** *sport Am. Gegner* (ohne Gegentor *etc.*) besiegen; ~ **to I** *v/t.* → *shut* **1 III** *v/i.* → *shut* **6**; ~ **up I** *v/t.* **1.** *Haus etc.* (fest) verschließen, -riegeln; → *shop* **1**; **2.** *j-n* einsperren, -schließen; **3.** F *j-m* den Mund stopfen; **II** *v/i.* **4.** F die ‚Klappe‘ halten: ~! halts Maul!

'**shut|·down** *s.* **1.** Arbeitsniederlegung *f*; **2.** Schließung *f*, (Betriebs)Stilllegung *f*; **3.** *Radio, TV:* Sendeschluss *m*; '~**eye** *s.:* **catch** *some* ~ *sl.* ein Schläfchen machen; '~**off** *s.* **1.** ⚙ Abstell-, Absperrvorrichtung *f*; **2.** *hunt.* Schonzeit *f*; '~**out** *s.* **1.** Ausschließung *f*; **2.** *sport* Zu-'null-Niederlage *f od.* -Sieg *m*.

shut·ter ['ʃʌtə] **I** *s.* **1.** Fensterladen *m*, Rollladen *m*: *put up the* ~*s fig.* das Geschäft (*am Abend od. für immer*) schließen; **2.** Klappe *f*; Verschluss *m* (*a. phot.*); **3.** △ Schalung *f*; **4.** *Wasserbau:* Schütz(e *f*) *n*; **5.** ♪ Jalou'sie *f* (*Orgel*); **II** *v/t.* **6.** mit Fensterläden versehen *od.* verschließen; '~**bug** *s.* F ‚Fotonarr‘ *m*; ~ **speed** *s. phot.* Belichtung(szeit) *f*.

shut·tle ['ʃʌtl] **I** *s.* **1.** ⚙ a) Weberschiff (-chen) *n*, (Web)Schütze(n) *m*), b)

Schiffchen *n* (*Nähmaschine*); **2.** Schütz (-entor) *n* (*Schleuse*); **3.** Pendelroute *f*; → *a.* **shuttle service**, **shuttle train**; **4.** (Raum)Fähre *f*; **II** *v/t.* **5.** (schnell) hinu. herbewegen *od.* -befördern; **III** *v/i.* **6.** sich (schnell) hin- u. herbewegen; **7.** 🚋 *etc.* pendeln (**between** zwischen *dat.*); '~**cock I** *s. sport* Federball(spiel *n*) *m*; **II** *v/t. fig.* hin u. her jagen; ~ **di·ploma·cy** *s.* 'Reisediploma,tie *f*; ~ **race** *s. sport* Pendelstaffel(lauf *m*) *f*; ~ **service** *s.* Pendelverkehr *m*; ~ **train** *s.* Pendel-, Vorortzug *m*.

shy[1] [ʃaɪ] **I** *adj.* □ **1.** scheu (*Tier*); **2.** scheu, schüchtern; **3.** zu'rückhaltend: *be* (*od.* **fight**) ~ *of s.o.* j-m aus dem Weg gehen; **4.** argwöhnisch; **5.** zaghaft: *be* ~ *of doing s.th.* Hemmungen haben, et. zu tun; **6.** *sl.* knapp (**of** an *dat.*); **7.** *I'm* ~ *of one dollar sl.* mir fehlt (noch) ein Dollar; **II** *v/i.* **8.** scheuen (*Pferd etc.*); **9.** *fig.* zu'rückscheuen, -schrecken (**at** vor *dat.*); **III** *s.* **10.** Scheuen *n* (*Pferd etc.*).

shy[2] [ʃaɪ] **I** *v/t. u. v/i.* **1.** werfen; **II** *s.* **2.** Wurf *m*; **3.** *fig.* Hieb *m*, Stiche'lei *f*; **4.** **have a** ~ **at** (**doing**) **s.th.** F es (mal) mit et. versuchen.

shy·ness ['ʃaɪnɪs] *s.* **1.** Scheu *f*; **2.** Schüchternheit *f*; **3.** Zu'rückhaltung *f*; **4.** 'Misstrauen *n*.

shy·ster ['ʃaɪstə] *s. Am. sl.* **1.** 'Winkeladvo,kat *m*; **2.** *fig.* Gauner *m*.

Si·a·mese [,saɪə'miːz] **I** *adj.* **1.** sia'mesisch; **II** *pl.* ,**Si·a'mese** **2.** Sia'mese *m*, Sia'mesin *f*; **3.** *ling.* Sia'mesisch *n*; ~ **cat** *s. zo.* Siamkatze *f*; ~ **twins** *s. pl.* sia'mesische Zwillinge *pl.* (*a. fig.*).

Si·be·ri·an [saɪ'bɪərɪən] **I** *adj.* si'birisch; **II** *s.* Si'birier(in).

sib·i·lance ['sɪbɪləns] *s.* **1.** Zischen *n*; **2.** *ling.* Zischlaut *m*; '**sib·i·lant** [-nt] **I** *adj.* **1.** zischend; **2.** *ling.* Zisch...: → *sound*; **II** *s.* **3.** *ling.* Zischlaut *m*; '**sib·i·late** [-leɪt] *v/t. u. v/i.* zischen; **sib·i·la·tion** [,sɪbɪ'leɪʃn] *s.* **1.** Zischen *n*; **2.** *ling.* Zischlaut *m*.

sib·ling ['sɪblɪŋ] *s. biol.* Bruder *m*, Schwester *f*; *pl.* Geschwister *pl.*

sib·yl ['sɪbɪl] *s.* **1.** *myth.* Si'bylle *f*; **2.** *fig.* a) Seherin *f*, b) Hexe *f*; **sib·yl·line** [sɪ'bɪlaɪn] *adj.* **1.** sibyl'linisch; **2.** pro'phetisch; geheimnisvoll, dunkel.

sic·ca·tive ['sɪkətɪv] **I** *adj.* trocknend; **II** *s.* Trockenmittel *n*.

Si·cil·ian [sɪ'sɪljən] **I** *adj.* si'zilisch, sizili'anisch; **II** *s.* Si'zilier(in), Sizili'aner(in).

sick[1] [sɪk] **I** *adj.* **1.** (*Brit. nur attr.*) krank (**of** an *dat.*): *fall* ~ krank werden, erkranken; *go* ~ *bsd.* ✕ sich krankmelden; **2.** Brechreiz verspürend: *be* ~ sich erbrechen *od.* übergeben; *I feel* ~ mir ist schlecht *od.* übel; *she turned* ~ ihr wurde übel, sie musste (sich er)brechen; *it makes me* ~ mir wird übel davon, *fig. a.* es widert od. ekelt mich an; **3.** *fig.* krank (**of** vor *dat.*; **for** nach); **4.** *fig.* enttäuscht, ärgerlich (**with** über *j-n*; *at* über *et.*): ~ *at heart* a) todunglücklich, b) angsterfüllt; **5.** F *fig.* (**of**) 'überdrüssig (*gen.*), angewidert (von): *I am* ~ (**and tired**) *of it* ich habe es satt, es hängt mir zum Hals heraus; **6.** fahl (*Farbe, Licht*); **7.** F matt (*Lächeln*); **8.** schlecht (*Nahrungsmittel, Luft*); trüb (*Wein*); **9.** F grausig, ma'kaber: ~ *jokes*; ~ *humo*(*u*)*r* ‚schwarzer‘ Humor; **II** *s.* **10.** *the* ~ *pl.* die Kranken *pl.*

sick[2] [sɪk] *v/t. Hund, Polizei etc.* hetzen (**on** auf *acc.*): ~ *him!* fass!

sick| bay *s.* ♣ ('Schiffs)Laza,rett *n*;

'~·**bed** *s.* Krankenbett *n*; ~ **ben·e·fit** *s. Brit.* Krankengeld *n*; ~ **call** *s.* ✕ Re'vierstunde *f*: *go on* ~ sich krankmelden; ~ **cer·tif·i·cate** *s.* 'Krankheitsat,test *n*.

sick·en ['sɪkn] **I** *v/i.* **1.** erkranken, krank werden: *be* ~*ing for e-e Krankheit* ,ausbrüten‘; **2.** kränkeln; **3.** sich ekeln (*at* vor *dat.*); **4.** 'überdrüssig *od.* müde sein *od.* werden (**of** *gen.*): *be* ~*ed with e-r Sache* überdrüssig sein; **II** *v/t.* **5.** *j-m* Übelkeit verursachen, *j-n* zum Erbrechen reizen; **6.** anekeln, anwidern; '**sick·en·er** [-nə] *s. fig.* Brechmittel *n*; '**sick·en·ing** [-nɪŋ] *adj.* □ **1.** Übelkeit erregend: *this is* ~ dabei kann einem (ja) übel werden; **2.** *fig.* ekelhaft, widerlich.

sick| head·ache *s.* **1.** Kopfschmerz(en *pl.*) *m* mit Übelkeit; **2.** Mi'gräne *f*; ~ **in·sur·ance** *s.* Krankenversicherung *f*, -kasse *f*.

sick·ish ['sɪkɪʃ] *adj.* □ **1.** kränklich, unpässlich, unwohl; **2.** → *sickening*.

sick·le ['sɪkl] *s.* ✎ *u. fig.* Sichel *f*.

sick leave *s.* Fehlen *n* wegen Krankheit: *be on* ~ wegen Krankheit fehlen; *request* ~ sich krankmelden.

sick·li·ness ['sɪklɪnɪs] *s.* **1.** Kränklichkeit *f*; **2.** kränkliches Aussehen; **3.** Unzuträglichkeit *f*.

sick list *s.* ♣, ✕ Krankenliste *f*: *be on the* ~ krank(gemeldet) sein.

sick·ly ['sɪklɪ] *adj. u. adv.* **1.** kränklich, schwächlich; **2.** kränklich, blass (*Aussehen etc.*); matt (*Lächeln*); **3.** ungesund (*Gebiet, Klima*); **4.** 'widerwärtig (*Geruch etc.*); **5.** *fig.* wehleidig, süßlich: ~ *sentimentality*.

sick·ness ['sɪknɪs] *s.* **1.** Krankheit *f*: ~ *insurance → sick insurance*; **2.** Übelkeit *f*, Erbrechen *n*.

sick| nurse *s.* Krankenschwester *f*; ~ **pay** *s.* Krankengeld *n*; ~ **re·port** *s.* ✕ **1.** Krankenbericht *m*, -liste *f*; **2.** Krankmeldung *f*; '~**room** *s.* Krankenzimmer *n*, -stube *f*.

side [saɪd] **I** *s.* **1.** *allg.* Seite *f*: ~ *by* ~ Seite an Seite (**with** mit); *at* (*od.* **by**) *the* ~ *of* an der Seite von (*od. dat.*); *by the* ~ *of fig.* neben (*dat.*), verglichen mit; *stand by s.o.'s* ~ *fig.* j-m zur Seite stehen; *on all* ~*s* überall; *on the* ~ *sl.* nebenbei *verdienen etc.*; *on the* ~ *of a*) auf der Seite von, b) seitens (*gen.*); *on this* (**the other**) ~ *of* diesseits (jenseits) (*gen.*); *this* ~ *up!* Vorsicht, nicht stürzen!; *be on the small* ~ ziemlich klein sein; *keep on the right* ~ *of* sich mit *j-m* gut stellen; *put on one* ~ *Frage etc.* zurückstellen, ausklammern; → *dark* **5**, *right* **6**, *sunny*, *wrong* **2**; **2.** ✦ Seite *f* (*a. Gleichung*); Seitenlinie *f*, -fläche *f*; **3.** (Seiten)Rand *m*; **4.** (Körper)Seite *f*: *shake* (*od.* **split**) *one's* ~*s with laughter* sich schütteln vor Lachen; **5.** (Speck-, Hammel- *etc.*)Seite *f*; **6.** Seite *f*: a) Hang *m*, Flanke *f*, *a.* Wand *f e-s Berges*, b) Ufer(seite *f*) *n*; **7.** Seite *f*, (Abstammungs)Linie *f*: *on one's father's* ~, *on the paternal* ~ väterlicherseits; **8.** *fig.* Seite *f* (Cha'rakter)Zug *m*; **9.** Seite *f*: a) Par'tei *f* (*a.* ♻ *u. sport*), b) *sport* Spielfeld(hälfte *f*) *n*: *be on s.o.'s* ~ auf j-s Seite stehen; *change* ~*s* a) ins andere Lager überwechseln, b) *sport* die Seiten wechseln; *take* ~*s →* **16**; *win s.o. over to one's* ~ j-n auf s-e Seite ziehen; **10.** *sport Brit.* Mannschaft *f*; **11.** *ped. Brit.* Ab'teilung *f*: *classical* ~ humanistische Abteilung; **12.** *Billiard:* Ef'fet *n*; **13.** *put on* ~ *sl.* ‚angeben‘; **II** *adj.* **14.** seitlich (*liegend, stehend etc.*),

S

Seiten...; **15.** Seiten..., Neben...: **~ door**; **III** v/i. **16.** (**with**) Par'tei ergreifen (gen. od. für), es halten (mit); **~ aisle** s. △ Seitenschiff n (Kirche); **~ arms** s. pl. ✕ Seitenwaffen pl.; **~ band** s. ♪, Radio: 'Seiten(fre,quenz)band n; **'~board** s. **1.** Anrichtetisch m; **2.** Sideboard n: a) Bü'fett n, b) Anrichte f; **3.** pl. → **'~burns** s. pl. Kote'letten pl. (Backenbart); **'~car** s. **1.** Beiwagen m; **~ motorcycle** Seitenwagenmaschine f; **2.** → **jaunting-car**; **3.** ein Cocktail.

sid·ed ['saɪdɪd] adj. in Zssgn ...seitig: **four~**.

side| dish s. **1.** Zwischengang m; **2.** Beilage f; **~ ef·fect** s. Nebenwirkung f; **~ face** s. Pro'fil n; **~ glance** s. Seitenblick m (a. fig.); **~ im·pact pro·tec·tion** s. mot. Seitenaufprallschutz m; **~ is·sue** s. Nebenfrage f, -sache f, 'Randpro,blem n; **'~kick** s. Am. sl. Kum'pan m, Kumpel m, 'Spezi' m; **'~light** s. **1.** Seitenleuchte f; ♣ Seitenlampe f; ➤ Positi'onslicht n; mot. Begrenzungslicht n; **2.** Seitenfenster n; **3.** fig. Streiflicht n: **~s** interessante Aufschlüsse (**on** über acc.); **'~line** s. **1.** Seitenlinie f (a. sport): **on the ~s** am Spielfeldrand; **keep on the ~s** fig. sich im Hintergrund halten; **2.** ⛟ Nebenstrecke f; ⛟ Nebenbeschäftigung f, -verdienst m; **4.** ♣ a) Nebenzweig m e-s Gewerbes, b) 'Nebenar,tikel m; **'~long** adj. u. adv. seitlich, seitwärts, schräg: **~ glance** Seitenblick m.

sid·e·re·al [saɪ'dɪərɪəl] adj. ast. si'derisch, Stern(en)...: **~ day** Sterntag m.

sid·er·ite ['saɪdəraɪt] s. ♔, min. **1.** Side'rit m; **2.** Mete'orgestein n.

'side|,sad·dle s. Damensattel m; **'~show** s. **1.** a) Nebenvorstellung f, -ausstellung f, b) kleine Schaubude; **2.** fig. a) Nebensache f, b) Epi'sode f (am Rande); **'~slip** v/i. **1.** seitwärts rutschen; **2.** ➤ seitlich abrutschen; **3.** mot. (seitlich) ausbrechen.

sides·man ['saɪdzmən] s. [irr.] Kirchenrat m.

'side|,split·ting adj. zwerchfellerschütternd; **'~step** I s. **1.** Seit(en)schritt m; **II** v/t. **2.** Boxen: e-m Schlag (durch Seitschritt) ausweichen; **3.** ausweichen (dat.) (a. fig.): **~ a decision**; **III** v/i. **4.** e-n Seit(en)schritt machen; **5.** ausweichen (a. fig.); **'~stroke** s. Seitenschwimmen n; **'~swipe** I v/t. Am. F **1.** j-m e-n ,Wischer' verpassen; **2.** mot. Fahrzeug streifen, a. seitlich abdrängen (beim Überholen); **II** s. **3.** ,Wischer' m (Streifschlag); **4.** fig. Seitenhieb m; **'~track** I s. **1.** → **siding** 1; **II** v/t. **2.** ⛟ Waggon auf ein Nebengleis schieben; **3.** fig. a) et. aufschieben, abbiegen, b) j-n ablenken (a. v/i.), c) j-n kaltstellen; **~ view** s. Seitenansicht f; **'~walk** s. bsd. Am. Bürgersteig m: **~ artist** Pflastermaler m; **~ superintendent** humor. (besserwisserischer) Zuschauer bei Bauarbeiten.

side·ward ['saɪdəwəd] I adj. seitlich; II adv. seitwärts; **'side·wards** [-dz] → **sideward** II; **'side·ways** → **sideward**.

side| whis·kers pl. → **sideburns**; **'~wind·er** [-,waɪndə] s. Am. sl. **1.** (harter) Haken (Schlag); **2.** Art Klapperschlange f.

side·wise ['saɪdwaɪz] → **sideward**.

sid·ing ['saɪdɪŋ] s. **1.** ⛟ Neben-, Anschluss-, Rangiergleis n; **2.** fig. Par'teinahme f.

si·dle ['saɪdl] v/i. sich schlängeln: **~ away** sich davonschleichen; **~ up to** sich an j-n heranmachen.

siege [siːdʒ] s. **1.** ✕ Belagerung f: **state of ~** Belagerungszustand m; **lay ~ to** a) Stadt etc. belagern, b) fig. j-n bestürmen; **2.** fig. a) heftiges Zusetzen, Bestürmen n, b) Zermürbung f; **3.** ❂ a) Werktisch m, b) Glasschmelzofenbank f.

si·es·ta [sɪ'estə] s. Si'esta f, Mittagsruhe f, -schlaf m.

sieve [sɪv] I s. **1.** Sieb n: **have a memory like a ~** ein Gedächtnis wie ein Sieb haben; **2.** fig. Klatschmaul n; **3.** Weidenkorb m (a. Maß); **II** v/t. u. v/i. **4.** ('durch-, aus)sieben.

sift [sɪft] I v/t. **1.** ('durch)sieben: **~ out** a) aussieben, b) erforschen, ausfindig machen; **2.** Zucker etc. streuen; **3.** fig. sichten, sorgfältig (über)'prüfen; **II** v/i. **4.** 'durchrieseln, -dringen (a. Licht etc.); **'sift·er** [-tə] s. Sieb(vorrichtung f) n; **'sift·ing** [-tɪŋ] s. **1.** ('Durch)Sieben n; **2.** Sichten n, (sorgfältige) Unter'suchung; **3.** pl. a) das 'Durchgesiebte, b) Siebabfälle pl.

sigh [saɪ] I v/i. **1.** (auf)seufzen; tief (auf-) atmen; **2.** schmachten, seufzen (**for** nach): **~ed-for** heiß begehrt; **3.** fig. seufzen, ächzen (Wind); **II** v/t. **4.** oft **~ out** seufzen(d äußern); **III** s. **5.** Seufzer m: **a ~ of relief** ein Seufzer der Erleichterung, ein erleichtertes Aufatmen.

sight [saɪt] I s. **1.** Sehvermögen n, -kraft f, Auge(nlicht) n: **good ~** gute Augen; **long (near) ~** Weit- (Kurz)Sichtigkeit f; **second ~** zweites Gesicht; **lose one's ~** das Augenlicht verlieren, erblinden; **2.** fig. Auge n: **in my ~** in m-n Augen; **in the ~ of God** vor Gott; **find favo(u)r in s.o.'s ~** Gnade vor j-s Augen finden; **3.** (An)Blick m, Sicht f: **at** (od. **on**) **~** beim ersten Anblick, auf Anhieb; sofort (er)schießen etc.; **at ~** vom Blatt singen, spielen, übersetzen; **at first ~** auf den ersten Blick; **by ~** vom Sehen kennen; **catch** (od. **get**) **~ of** zu Gesicht bekommen, erblicken; **lose ~ of** a) aus den Augen verlieren (a. fig.), b) et. übersehen; **4.** Sicht(weite) f: (**with**)**in ~** a) in Sicht(weite), b) fig. in Sicht; **within ~ of** kurz vor dem Sieg etc.; **out of ~** außer Sicht; **out of ~, out of mind** aus den Augen, aus dem Sinn; (**get**) **out of my ~!** geh mir aus den Augen!; **come in ~** in Sicht kommen; **put out of ~** wegtun; **5.** ♥ Sicht f: **payable at ~** bei Sicht fällig; **30 days** (**after**) **~** 30 Tage (nach) Sicht; **~ unseen** unbesehen kaufen; **~ bill** (od. **draft**) Sichtwechsel m, -tratte f; **6.** Anblick m: **a sorry ~; a ~ for sore eyes** ein erfreulicher Anblick, eine Augenweide; **be** (od. **look**) **a ~** F grässlich od. ,verboten' aussehen; **I did look a ~!** F ich sah vielleicht aus!; **what a ~ you are!** F wie siehst denn du aus!; → **god** 1; **7.** Sehenswürdigkeit f: **the ~s of a town**; **8.** F Menge f, Masse f Geld etc.: **a long ~ better** zehnmal besser; **not by a long ~** bei weitem nicht; **9.** ✕ etc. Visier n; Zielvorrichtung f: **take ~** (an-) visieren, zielen; **have in one's ~** im Visier haben (a. fig.); **lower one's ~s** fig. zurückstecken; **raise one's ~s** höhere Ziele anstreben; **10.** Am. sl. Aussicht f, Chance f; **II** v/t. **11.** sichten, zu Gesicht bekommen; **12.** ✕ a) anvisieren (a. ♣, ast.), b) Geschütz richten; **13.** Wechsel präsentieren; **II** v/i. **14.** zielen; **'sight·ed** [-tɪd] adj. in Zssgn ...sichtig; **'sight·ing** [-tɪŋ] adj. ✕ Ziel..., Visier...: **~ mech·anism** Zieleinrichtung f, -gerät n; **~ shot** Anschuss m (Probeschuss); **~ tel·escope** Zielfernrohr n; **'sight·less** [-lɪs] adj. □ blind; **'sight·li·ness** [-lɪnɪs] s. Ansehnlichkeit f, Stattlichkeit f; **'sight·ly** [-lɪ] adj. gut aussehend, stattlich.

'sight|-read v/t. u. v/i. [irr. → **read**] **1.** ♪ vom Blatt singen od. spielen; **2.** ling. vom Blatt über'setzen; **'~,see·ing** I s. Besichtigung f von Sehenswürdigkeiten; **II** adj. Besichtigungs...: **~ bus** Rundfahrtautobus m; **~ tour** Stadtrundfahrt f, Besichtigungstour f; **'~,se·er** [-,siːə] s. Tou'rist(in).

sign [saɪn] I s. **1.** (a. Schrift)Zeichen n, Sym'bol n (a. fig.): **~** (**of the cross**) eccl. Kreuzzeichen; **in ~ of** fig. zum Zeichen (gen.); **2.** ♉, ♪ (Vor)Zeichen n; **3.** Zeichen n, Wink m: **give s.o. a ~, make a ~ to s.o.** j-m ein Zeichen geben; **4.** (An)Zeichen n, Sym'ptom n (a. ♪): **no ~ of life** kein Lebenszeichen; **the ~s of the times** die Zeichen der Zeit; **make no ~** sich nicht rühren; **5.** Kennzeichen n; **6.** ast. (Tierkreis)Zeichen n; **7.** (Aushänge-, Wirtshaus-) Schild n: **at the ~ of** im Wirtshaus zum Hirsch etc.; **8.** (Wunder)Zeichen n: **~s and wonders** Zeichen u. Wunder; **9.** hunt. etc. Spur f; **II** v/t. **10.** unter'zeichnen, -'schreiben, (a. typ. u. paint.) signieren; **11.** mit s-m Namen unter'zeichnen: **~ one's name** unterschreiben; **12.** **~ away** Vermögen etc. über'tragen, -'schreiben; **13.** **~ on** (od. **up**) (vertraglich) verpflichten, anstellen, -mustern, ♣ anheuern; **14.** eccl. das Kreuzzeichen machen über (acc. od. dat.); Täufling segnen; **15.** j-m bedeuten (**to do** zu tun), j-m et. (durch Gebärden) zu verstehen geben: **~ one's assent**; **III** v/i. **16.** unter'zeichnen, -'schreiben: **~ in** a) sich eintragen, b) bei Arbeitsbeginn einstempeln; **~ out** a) sich austragen, b) ausstempeln; **17.** **~ on** (**off**) Radio, TV: sein Pro'gramm beginnen (beenden); **~ off** fig. F a. Schluss machen; **~ on** (od. **up**) sich (vertraglich) verpflichten (**for** zu), e-e Arbeit annehmen, b) ♣ anheuern, ✕ sich verpflichten (**for** auf 3 Jahre etc.).

sig·nal ['sɪɡnl] I s. **1.** a. ✕ etc. Si'gnal n, (a. verabredetes) Zeichen: **~ of distress** Notzeichen n; **2.** (Funk)Spruch m: **the ~s** Brit. Fernmeldetruppe f; **3.** fig. Si'gnal n, (auslösendes) Zeichen (**for** für, zu); **4.** Kartenspiel: Si'gnal n; **II** adj. □ **5.** Signal...: **~ beacon**; ⚐ **Corps** Am. Fernmeldetruppe f; **~ communications** ✕ Fernmeldewesen n; **6.** fig. beachtlich, außerordentlich; **III** v/t. **7.** j-m Zeichen geben, winken; **8.** Nachricht signalisieren (a. fig.); et. melden; **IV** v/i. **9.** signalisieren; **~ book** s. ♣ Si'gnalbuch n; **~ box** s. ⛟ Stellwerk n; **~ check** s. Sprechprobe f (Mik'rofon); **~ code** s. Zeichenschlüssel m.

sig·nal·er Am. → **signaller**.

sig·nal·ize ['sɪɡnəlaɪz] v/t. **1.** aus-, kennzeichnen: **~ o.s. by** sich hervortun durch; **2.** her'vorheben; **3.** a. fig. ankündigen, signalisieren.

sig·nal·ler ['sɪɡnələ] s. Si'gnalgeber m, bsd. a) ✕ Blinker m, Melder m, b) ♣ Si'gnalgast m.

'sig·nal·man [-mən] s. [irr.] **1.** ⛟ Stellwärter m; **2.** ♣ Si'gnalgast m; **~ of·fi·cer** s. ✕ Am. **1.** 'Fernmeldeoffi,zier m; **2.** Leiter m des Fernmeldedienstes; **~ rock·et** s. ✕ Leuchtkugel f; **~ tow·er** s. **1.** ❂ Si'gnalturm m; **2.** ⛟ Am. Stellwerk n.

sig·na·ry ['sɪɡnərɪ] s. (Schrift)Zeichensy,stem n.

sig·na·to·ry ['sɪɡnətərɪ] I adj. **1.** unter-

'zeichnend, vertragschließend, Signatar...: **~ powers** → 3 c; **2.** ✝ Zeichnungs...: **~ power** Unterschriftsvollmacht f; **II** s. **3.** a) ('Mit)Unter‚zeichner (-in), b) *pol.* Signa'tar m (*Unterzeichnerstaat*), c) *pl. pol.* Signa'tarmächte *pl.* (**to a treaty** e-s Vertrags).

sig·na·ture ['sɪgnɪtʃə] s. **1.** 'Unterschrift(sleistung) f, Namenszug m; **2.** Signa'tur f (*e-s Buchs etc., a. pharm. Aufschrift*); **3.** ♪ Signa'tur f, Vorzeichnung f; **4.** a. **~ tune** *Radio:* 'Kennmelo‚die f; **5.** *typ.* a) a. **~ mark** Signa'tur f, Bogenzeichen n, b) signierter Druckbogen.

'sign·board s. (*bsd.* Firmen-, Aushänge)Schild n.

sign·er ['saɪnə] s. Unter'zeichner(in).

sig·net ['sɪgnɪt] s. Siegel n, Petschaft n: **privy ~** Privatsiegel des Königs; **~ ring** s. Siegelring m.

sig·nif·i·cance [sɪg'nɪfɪkəns], a. **sig'nif·i·can·cy** [-sɪ] s. **1.** Bedeutung f, (tieferer) Sinn; **2.** Bedeutung f, Wichtigkeit f: **of no ~** nicht von Belang; **sig'nif·i·cant** [-nt] adj. □ **1.** bedeutsam, wichtig, von Bedeutung; **2.** merklich; **3.** bezeichnend (**of** für); **4.** *fig.* viel sagend: **a ~ gesture**; **5.** ☿ geltend; **sig·ni·fi·ca·tion** [‚sɪgnɪfɪ'keɪʃn] s. **1.** (*bestimmte*) Bedeutung, Sinn m; **2.** Bezeichnung f, Bekundung f; **sig'nif·i·ca·tive** [-ətɪv] adj. □ **1.** Bedeutungs..., bedeutsam; **2.** bezeichnend, kennzeichnend (**of** für).

sig·ni·fy ['sɪgnɪfaɪ] **I** v/t. **1.** an-, bedeuten, kundtun, zu verstehen geben; **2.** bedeuten, ankündigen; **3.** bedeuten; **II** v/i. **4.** F wichtig sein: **it does not ~** es hat nichts auf sich.

sign| lan·guage s. Zeichen-, *bsd.* Fingersprache f; **~ man·u·al** s. **1.** (eigenhändige) 'Unterschrift; **2.** Handzeichen n; **~ paint·er** s. Schilder-, Pla'katmaler m; **'~post I** s. **1.** Wegweiser m; **2.** (Straßen)Schild n, (Verkehrs)Zeichen n; **II** v/t. **3.** *Straße etc.* aus-, beschildern.

si·lage ['saɪlɪdʒ] ♪ **I** s. Silofutter n; **II** v/t. *Gärfutter* silieren.

si·lence ['saɪləns] **I** s. **1.** (Still)Schweigen n (a. fig.), Ruhe f, Stille f: **keep ~** a) schweigen, still sein, b) Stillschweigen wahren (**on** über *acc.*); **in ~** (still-) schweigend; **~ gives consent** wer schweigt, scheint zuzustimmen; **~ is golden** Schweigen ist Gold; **~! Ruhe!**; **→ pass over** 4; **2.** Schweigsamkeit f; **3.** Verschwiegenheit f; **4.** Vergessenheit f; **5.** a. ☉ Geräuschlosigkeit f; **II** v/t. **6.** zum Schweigen bringen (a. ✗ u. *fig.*); **'si·lenc·er** [-sə] s. **1.** ✗, ☉ Schalldämpfer m; **2.** *mot.* Auspufftopf m; **'si·lent** [-nt] adj. □ **1.** still, ruhig, schweigsam: **be ~** (sich aus)schweigen (**on** über *acc.*) (a. fig.); **2.** still (*Gebet etc.*), stumm (*Schmerz etc.; a. ling. Buchstabe*): **~ film** Stummfilm m; **~ partner** ✝ stiller Teilhaber (mit unbeschränkter Haftung); **3.** *fig.* stillschweigend: **~ consent**; **~ majority** die schweigende Mehrheit; **4.** a. ☉ geräuschlos, leise.

Si·le·sian [saɪ'li:zjən] **I** adj. schlesisch; **II** s. Schlesier(in).

sil·hou·ette [‚sɪlu:'et] **I** s. **1.** Silhou'ette f: a) Schattenbild n, -riss m, b) 'Umriss m (a. fig.): **~** (**target**) ✗ Kopfscheibe f; **stand out in ~ against** → 4; **2.** Scherenschnitt m; **II** v/t. **3.** silhouettieren; **4.** **be ~d** sich abheben (**against** gegen).

sil·i·ca ['sɪlɪkə] s. 🝆 **1.** Kieselerde f; **2.** Quarz(glas n) m; **'sil·i·cate** [-kɪt] s. 🝆 Sili'kat n; **'sil·i·cat·ed** [-keɪtɪd] adj. siliziert; **si·li·ceous** [sɪ'lɪʃəs] adj. kiesel(erde-, -säure)haltig, -artig, Kiesel...;

---

si·lic·ic [sɪ'lɪsɪk] adj. Kiesel(erde)...; **si·lic·i·fy** [sɪ'lɪsɪfaɪ] v/t. u. v/i. verkieseln; **si·li·cious;** → **siliceous**; **'sil·i·con** [-kən] s. 🝆 Si'lizium n; **'sil·i·cone** [-kəʊn] s. 🝆 Sili'kon n; **sil·i·co·sis** [‚sɪlɪ'kəʊsɪs] s. 🝆 Sili'kose f, Staublunge f.

silk [sɪlk] **I** s. **1.** Seide f: a) Seidenfaser f, b) Seidenfaden m, c) Seidenstoff m, -gewebe n; **2.** Seide(nkleid n) f: **in ~s and satins** in Samt u. Seide; **3.** 🛱 *Brit.* a) → **silk gown**, b) F Kronanwalt m: **take ~** Kronanwalt werden; **4.** *fig.* Seide f, *zo. bsd.* Spinnfäden *pl.*; **5.** Seidenglanz m (*von Edelsteinen*); **II** adj. **6.** seiden, Seiden...: **make a ~ purse out of a sow's ear** *fig.* aus e-m Kieselstein e-n Diamanten schleifen; **~ culture** Seidenraupenzucht f; **'silk·en** [-kən] adj. **1.** *poet.* seiden, Seiden...; **2.** → **silky** 1 u. 2.

silk| gown s. *Brit.* 'Seidenta‚lar m (*e-s King's od. Queen's Counsel*); **~ hat** s. Zy'linder(hut) m.

silk·i·ness ['sɪlkɪnɪs] s. **1.** das Seidige, seidenartige Weichheit; **2.** *fig.* Sanftheit f.

silk| moth s. *zo.* Seidenspinner m; **'~-screen print·ing** s. *typ.* Seidensiebdruck m; **~ stock·ing** s. **1.** Seidenstrumpf m; **2.** *fig. Am.* ele'gante od. vornehme Per'son; **'~worm** s. *zo.* Seidenraupe f.

silk·y ['sɪlkɪ] adj. □ **1.** seidig (glänzend), seidenweich: **~ hair**; **2.** *fig.* sanft, einschmeichelnd, zärtlich (*Person, Stimme etc.*), *contp.* ölig, (aal)glatt; **3.** lieblich (*Wein*).

sill [sɪl] s. **1.** (Tür)Schwelle f; **2.** Fensterbrett n; **3.** ☉ Schwellbalken m; **4.** *geol.* Lagergang m.

sil·la·bub ['sɪləbʌb] s. *Getränk aus Wein, Sahne u. Gewürzen.*

sil·li·ness ['sɪlɪnɪs] s. **1.** Dummheit f, Albernheit f; **2.** Verrücktheit f.

sil·ly ['sɪlɪ] **I** adj. □ **1.** dumm, albern, blöd(e), verrückt (*Person u. Sache*); **2.** dumm, unklug (*Handlungsweise*); **3.** benommen, betäubt; **II** s. **4.** Dummkopf m, Dummerchen n; **~ sea·son** s. ‚Saure-'Gurken-Zeit f.

si·lo ['saɪləʊ] **I** pl. **-los** s. **1.** ♪, ☉ Silo m; **2.** ✗ 'unterirdische Ra'ketenabschussrampe; **II** v/t. **3.** ♪ *Futter* a) in e-m Silo aufbewahren, b) einmieten.

silt [sɪlt] **I** s. Treibsand m, Schlamm m, Schlick m; **II** v/i. u. v/t. *mst* **~ up** verschlammen.

sil·van ['sɪlvən] → **sylvan**.

sil·ver ['sɪlvə] **I** s. **1.** 🝆, *min.* Silber n; **2.** a) Silber(geld) n, b) *allg.* Geld n; **3.** Silber(geschirr m, -zeug n) n; **4.** Silber (-farbe f, -glanz m); **5.** *phot.* 'Silbersalz n, -ni‚trat n; **II** adj. **6.** silbern, Silber...: **~ paper** *phot.* Silberpapier n; **7.** silb(e)rig, silberglänzend; **8.** *fig.* silberhell (*Stimme etc.*); **III** v/t. **9.** versilbern; *Spiegel* belegen; **10.** silbern färben; **IV** v/i. **11.** silberweiß werden (*Haar etc.*); **~ fir** s. ♀ Edel-, Weißtanne f; **~ foil** s. **1.** Silberfolie f; **2.** 'Silberpa‚pier n; **~ fox** s. *zo.* Silberfuchs m; **~ gilt** s. vergoldetes Silber; **~ glance** s. Schwefelsilber n; **‚~'gray** *bsd. Am.*, **‚~'grey** adj. silbergrau; **~ leaf** s. ☉ Blattsilber n; **~ lin·ing** s. *fig.* Silberstreifen m am Hori'zont, Lichtblick m: **every cloud has its ~** jedes Unglück hat auch sein Gutes; **~ med·al** s. 'Silberme‚daille f; **med·al·(l)ist** s. 'Silberme‚daillengewinner(in); **~ ni·trate** s. 🝆, *phot.* 'Silberni‚trat n; *bsd.* ✝ Höllenstein m; **~ plate** s. **1.** Silberauflage f; **2.** Silber(ge-

---

schirr n, -zeug n) n, Tafelsilber n; **'~-plate** v/t. versilbern; **~ point** s. *paint.* Silberstiftzeichnung f; **~ screen** s. **1.** (Film)Leinwand f; **2.** *coll. der* Film; **'~side** s. bester Teil der Rindskeule; **'~-smith** s. Silberschmied m; **~ spoon** s. Silberlöffel m: **be born with a ~ in one's mouth** *fig.* ein Glückskind od. das Kind reicher Eltern sein; **‚~-'tongued** adj. redegewandt; **'~ware** → **silver plate** 2; **~ wed·ding** s. silberne Hochzeit.

sil·ver·y ['sɪlvərɪ] → **silver** 7 u. 8.

sil·vi·cul·ture ['sɪlvɪkʌltʃə] s. Waldbau m, 'Forstkul‚tur f.

sim·i·an ['sɪmɪən] **I** adj. *zo.* affenartig, Affen...; **II** s. (*bsd.* Menschen)Affe m.

sim·i·lar ['sɪmɪlə] **I** adj. □ → **similarly**; **1.** ähnlich (a. 🝆), (annähernd) gleich (**to** *dat.*); **2.** gleichartig, entsprechend; **3.** *phys.,* ☿ gleichnamig; **II** s. **4.** das Ähnliche od. Gleichartige; **5.** *pl.* ähnliche od. gleichartige Dinge *pl.*; **sim·i·lar·i·ty** [‚sɪmɪ'lærətɪ] s. **1.** Ähnlichkeit f (**to** mit), Gleichartigkeit f; **2.** *pl.* Ähnlichkeiten *pl.*; **'sim·i·lar·ly** [-lɪ] adv. ähnlich, entsprechend.

sim·i·le ['sɪmɪlɪ] s. Gleichnis n, Vergleich m; **si·mil·i·tude** [sɪ'mɪlɪtju:d] s. **1.** Ähnlichkeit f (a. 🝆); **2.** Gleichnis n; **3.** (Eben)Bild n.

sim·mer ['sɪmə] **I** v/i. **1.** sieden, wallen, brodeln; **2.** *fig.* kochen (**with** vor *dat.*), gären (*Gefühl, Aufstand*): **~ down** sich ‚abregen od. beruhigen; **II** v/t. **3.** zum Brodeln od. Wallen bringen; **III** s. **4.** **keep at a** (od. **on the**) **~** sieden lassen.

Si·mon ['saɪmən] npr. Simon m: **Simple ~** fig. F Einfaltspinsel m.

si·mo·ny ['saɪmənɪ] s. Simo'nie f, Ämterkauf m.

simp [sɪmp] s. *Am. sl.* Simpel m.

sim·per ['sɪmpə] **I** v/i. albern od. geziert lächeln; **II** s. einfältiges od. geziertes Lächeln.

sim·ple ['sɪmpl] **I** adj. □ → **simply**; **1.** *allg.* einfach: a) simpel, leicht: **a ~ explanation**; **a ~ task**, b) schlicht (*Person, Lebensweise, Stil etc.*): **~ beauty**, c) unkompliziert: **a ~ design**; **~ fracture** ✗ einfacher (Knochen)Bruch, d) nicht zs.-gesetzt, unzerlegbar: **~ equation** 🝆 einfache Gleichung; **~ fraction** 🝆 einfacher od. gemeiner Bruch; **~ fruit** ♀ einfache Frucht; **~ interest** ✝ Kapitalzinsen *pl.*; **~ larceny** einfacher Diebstahl; **~ sentence** *ling.* einfacher Satz, e) niedrig: **of ~ birth**; **2.** ♪ einfach, a) einfältig, simpel, b) na'iv, leichtgläubig; **4.** gering(fügig): **~ efforts**; **5.** rein, glatt: **~ madness**; **II** s. **6.** *pharm.* Heilkraut n, -pflanze f; **‚~-'heart·ed**, **‚~-'mind·ed** adj. **1.** schlicht, einfach; **2.** → **simple** 3; **‚~-'mind·ed·ness** s. **1.** Schlichtheit f; **2.** Einfalt f; **3.** Arglosigkeit f.

sim·ple·ton ['sɪmpltən] s. Einfaltspinsel m.

sim·plex ['sɪmpleks] **I** adj. **1.** ☉, ☿ Simplex...; **II** s. **2.** *ling.* Simplex n; **3.** ☿, *teleph. etc.* Simplex-, Einfachbetrieb m.

sim·plic·i·ty [sɪm'plɪsətɪ] s. **1.** Einfachheit f; **2.** Einfalt f.

sim·pli·fi·ca·tion [‚sɪmplɪfɪ'keɪʃn] s. Vereinfachung f; **sim·pli·fi·ca·tive** ['sɪmplɪfɪkətɪv] adj. vereinfachend; **sim·pli·fy** ['sɪmplɪfaɪ] v/t. **1.** vereinfachen (a. erleichtern, a. als einfach hinstellen); **2.** ☉, ✝ *Am.* normieren.

sim·plis·tic [sɪm'plɪstɪk] adj. (zu) stark vereinfachend.

sim·ply ['sɪmplɪ] adv. **1.** einfach (etc. → **simple**); **2.** bloß, nur; **3.** F einfach (*großartig etc.*).

sim·u·la·crum [ˌsɪmjʊˈleɪkrəm] *pl.* **-cra** [-krə] *s.* **1.** (Ab)Bild *n*; **2.** Scheinbild *n*, Abklatsch *m*; **3.** leerer Schein.

sim·u·lant [ˈsɪmjʊlənt] *adj. bsd. biol.* ähnlich (*of dat.*); **sim·u·late** [ˈsɪmjʊleɪt] *v/t.* **1.** vortäuschen, (-)heucheln, *bsd. Krankheit* simulieren: *~d account* † fingierte Rechnung; **2.** *j-n od. et.* nachahmen; **3.** sich tarnen als; **4.** ähneln (*dat.*); **5.** *ling.* sich angleichen an (*acc.*); **6.** ⊚ simulieren; **sim·u·la·tion** [ˌsɪmjʊˈleɪʃn] *s.* **1.** Vorspiegelung *f*, -täuschung *f*; **2.** Heuche'lei *f*, Verstellung *f*; **3.** Nachahmung *f*; **4.** Simulieren *n*, Krankspielen *n*; **5.** ⊚ Simulierung *f*; **sim·u·la·tor** [ˈsɪmjʊleɪtə] *s.* **1.** Heuchler(in); **2.** Simu'lant(in); **3.** ⊚ *allg.* Simu'lator *m*.

si·mul·ta·ne·i·ty [ˌsɪməltəˈniːɪtɪ] *s.* Gleichzeitigkeit *f*; **si·mul·ta·ne·ous** [ˌsɪməlˈteɪnjəs] *adj.* □ gleichzeitig, simul'tan (*with* mit): *~ translation* Simultandolmetschen *n*.

sin [sɪn] **I** *s.* **1.** *eccl.* Sünde *f*: *cardinal ~* Hauptsünde; *deadly* (*od. mortal*) *~* Todsünde; *original ~* Erbsünde; *like ~* F wie der Teufel; *live in ~ obs. od. humor.* in Sünde leben; **2.** *fig.* (*against*) Sünde *f* (*Verstoß*) (gegen), Versündigung *f* (an *dat.*); **II** *v/i.* **3.** sündigen; **4.** *fig.* (*against*) sündigen, verstoßen (gegen *et.*), sich versündigen (an *j-m*).

sin·a·pism [ˈsɪnəpɪzəm] *s.* ✿ Senfpflaster *n*.

since [sɪns] **I** *adv.* **1.** seit'dem, -'her: *ever ~* seit der Zeit, seitdem; *long ~* seit langem, schon lange; *how long ~?* seit wie langer Zeit?; *a short time ~* vor kurzem; **2.** in'zwischen, mittler'weile; **II** *prp.* **3.** seit: *~ 1945*; *~ Friday*; *~ seeing you* seitdem ich dich sah; **III** *cj.* **4.** seit(dem): *how long is it ~ it happened?* wie lange ist es her, dass das geschah?; **5.** da (ja), weil.

sin·cere [sɪnˈsɪə] *adj.* □ **1.** aufrichtig, ehrlich, offen: *a ~ friend* ein wahrer Freund; **2.** aufrichtig, echt (*Gefühl etc.*); **3.** rein, lauter; **sin'cere·ly** [-lɪ] *adv.* aufrichtig: *Yours ~* Mit freundlichen Grüßen (*Briefschluss*); **sin'cere·ness** [-nɪs], **sin·cer·i·ty** [sɪnˈserətɪ] *s.* **1.** Aufrichtigkeit *f*; **2.** Lauterkeit *f*, Echtheit *f*.

sin·ci·put [ˈsɪnsɪpʌt] *s. anat.* Schädeldach *n*, *bsd.* Vorderhaupt *n*.

sine¹ [saɪn] *s.* Ⓐ Sinus *m*: *~ of angle* Winkelsinus; *~ curve* Sinuskurve *f*; *~ wave phys.* Sinuswelle *f*.

si·ne² [ˈsaɪnɪ] (*Lat.*) *prp.* ohne.

si·ne·cure [ˈsaɪnɪkjʊə] *s.* Sine'kure *f*: a) *eccl. hist.* Pfründe *f* ohne Seelsorge, b) einträglicher Ruheposten.

si·ne di·e [ˌsaɪnɪˈdaɪiː] (*Lat.*) *adv.* ♫ auf unbestimmte Zeit; **si·ne qua non** [ˌsaɪnɪkweɪˈnɒn] (*Lat.*) *s.* unerlässliche Bedingung, Con'ditio *f* sine qua non.

sin·ew [ˈsɪnjuː] *s.* **1.** *anat.* Sehne *f*, Flechse *f*; **2.** *pl.* Muskeln *pl.*, (Muskel-) Kraft *f*: *the ~s of war fig.* das Geld *od.* die Mittel (zur Kriegführung etc.); **'sin·ewed** [-juːd] → *sinewy*; **'sin·ew·less** [-lɪs] *adj. fig.* kraftlos, schwach; **'sin·ew·y** [-juːɪ] *adj.* **1.** sehnig; **2.** zäh (*Fleisch*); **3.** *fig.* a) stark, zäh, b) kräftig, kraftvoll (*a. Stil*).

sin·ful [ˈsɪnfʊl] *adj.* □ sündig, sündhaft.

sing [sɪŋ] **I** *v/i.* [*irr.*] **1.** singen (*a. fig. dichten*): *~ of →* 9; *~ to s.o.* j-m vorsingen; *~ small fig.* F kleinlaut werden, klein beigeben; **2.** summen (*Biene, Wasserkessel etc.*); **3.** krähen (*Hahn*); **4.** *fig.* pfeifen, sausen (*Geschoss*); heulen (*Wind*); **5.** *~ out* F (laut) rufen,

schreien; **6.** *a. ~ out sl.* gestehen, alle(s) verraten, ,singen' (*Verbrecher*); **7.** sich *gut etc.* singen lassen; **II** *v/t.* [*irr.*] **8.** *Lied* singen: *~ a child to sleep* ein Kind in den Schlaf singen; *~ out* ausrufen, schreien; **9.** *poet.* (be)singen; **III** *s.* **10.** *Am.* F (Gemeinschafts)Singen *n*.

singe [sɪndʒ] **I** *v/t.* **1.** ver-, ansengen; → *wing* 1; **2.** *Geflügel, Schwein* sengen; **3.** *a. ~ off Borsten etc.* absengen; **4.** *Haar* sengen (*Friseur*); **II** *v/i.* **5.** versengen; **III** *s.* **6.** Versengung *f*; **7.** versengte Stelle.

sing·er [ˈsɪŋə] *s.* **1.** Sänger(in); **2.** *poet.* Sänger *m* (*Dichter*); ,**~·'song·writ·er** *s.* Liedermacher(in).

sing·ing [ˈsɪŋɪŋ] **I** *adj.* **1.** singend *etc.*; **2.** Sing..., Gesangs...: *~ lesson*; **II** *s.* **3.** Singen *n*, Gesang *m*; **4.** *fig.* Klingen *n*, Summen *n*, Pfeifen *n*, Sausen *n*: *a ~ in the ears* (ein) Ohrensausen; *~ bird s.* Singvogel *m*; *~ voice s.* Singstimme *f*.

sin·gle [ˈsɪŋgl] **I** *adj.* □ → *singly*; **1.** einzig: *not a ~ one* kein *od.* nicht ein Einziger; *~ European currency* gemeinsame europäische Währung, europäische Einheitswährung; *~ (European) market* (europäischer) Binnenmarkt; **2.** einzeln, einfach, Einzel..., Ein(fach)...: *~-decker* ✈ Eindecker *m* (*a. Bus*); *~-stage* einstufig; (*bookkeeping by*) *~ entry* † einfache Buchführung; *~(-trip) ticket →* 10; **3.** einzeln, all'ein, Einzel...: *~ bed* Einzelbett *n*; *~ bill* † Solawechsel *m*; *~ combat* ✗ Einzel-, Zweikampf *m*; *~ game sport* Einzel(spiel) *n*; *~ house* Einfamilienhaus *n*; **4.** a) allein, einsam, für sich (lebend), b) al'lein stehend, ledig, unverheiratet; → *a.* 14; **5.** einmalig: *~ payment*; **6.** ♀ einfach; **7.** *fig.* ungeteilt, einzig: *~ purpose*; *have a ~ eye for* nur Sinn haben für, nur denken an (*acc.*); *with a ~ voice* wie aus 'einem Munde; **8.** *fig.* aufrichtig: *~ mind*; **II** *s.* **9.** *der* (*die, das*) Einzelne *od.* Einzige; Einzelstück *n*; **10.** *Brit.* a) 🚂 einfache Fahrkarte, b) ✈ einfaches (Flug)Ticket *n*; **11.** *pl. sg. konstr. sport* Einzel *n*: *play a ~s*; *men's ~s* Herreneinzel; **12.** Single *f* (*Schallplatte*); **13.** Einbettzimmer *n*; **14.** Single *m*, al'lein stehende Per'son; **III** *v/t.* **15.** *~ out* a) auslesen, -suchen, -wählen (*from* aus), b) bestimmen (*for* für e-n Zweck), c) her'ausheben; *~·'act·ing adj.* ⊚ einfach wirkend; *~·'breast·ed adj.*: *~ suit* Einreiher *m*; *~·'en·gined adj.* ✈ ein,motorig (*Flugzeug*); *~·'eyed → single-minded*; *~·'hand·ed adj. u. adv.* **1.** einhändig; mit 'einer Hand; **2.** *fig.* eigenhändig, al'lein, ohne (fremde) Hilfe; auf eigene Faust; *~·'heart·ed adj.* □ → *single-minded*; *~·'line adj.* 🚂 eingleisig; *~·'mind·ed adj.* **1.** aufrichtig, redlich; **2.** zielbewusst, -strebig.

sin·gle·ness [ˈsɪŋglnɪs] *s.* **1.** Einmaligkeit *f*; **2.** Ehelosigkeit *f*; **3.** *a. ~ of purpose* Zielstrebigkeit *f*; **4.** *fig.* Aufrichtigkeit *f*.

sin·gle par·ent *s.* Al'leinerziehende(r *m*) *f*: *single parents pl.* allein erziehende Eltern *pl.*; '*~·par·ent fam·i·ly s.* Ein'elternfa,milie *f*; ,*~·'phase adj.* ⚡ einphasig, Einphasen...; ,*~·'seat·er bsd.* ✈ **I** *s.* Einsitzer *m*; **II** *adj.* Einsitzer..., einsitzig; '*~·stick s. sport* 'Stockra,pier(fechten) *n*.

sin·glet [ˈsɪŋglɪt] *s.* ärmelloses 'Unterod. Tri'kothemd *n*.

sin·gle·ton [ˈsɪŋgltən] *s.* **1.** *Kartenspiel:* Singleton *m* (*einzige Karte e-r Farbe*); **2.** einziges Kind; **3.** Indi'viduum *n*; **4.**

Einzelgegenstand *m*.

,**sin·gle·'track** *adj.* **1.** einspurig (*Straße*); **2.** 🚂 eingleisig (*a. fig.* F einseitig).

sin·gly [ˈsɪŋglɪ] *adv.* **1.** einzeln, al'lein; **2.** → *single-handed* 2.

'**sing·song I** *s.* **1.** Singsang *m*; **2.** *Brit.* Gemeinschaftssingen *n*; **II** *adj.* **3.** eintönig; **III** *v/t. u. v/i.* **4.** eintönig sprechen *od.* singen.

sin·gu·lar [ˈsɪŋgjʊlə] **I** *adj.* □ **1.** *ling.* singu'larisch: *~ number →* 6; **2.** Ⓐ, *phls.* singu'lär; **3.** *bsd.* ♫ einzeln: *all and ~* jeder (jede, jedes) Einzelne; **4.** *fig.* einzigartig, außer-, ungewöhnlich, einmalig; **5.** *fig.* eigentümlich, seltsam; **II** *s.* **6.** *ling.* Singular *m*, Einzahl *f*; **sin·gu·lar·i·ty** [ˌsɪŋgjʊˈlærətɪ] *s.* **1.** Eigentümlichkeit *f*, Seltsamkeit *f*; **2.** Einzigartigkeit *f*; '**sin·gu·lar·ize** [-əraɪz] *v/t.* **1.** her'ausstellen; **2.** *ling.* in die Einzahl setzen.

sin·is·ter [ˈsɪnɪstə] *adj.* □ **1.** böse, drohend, unheilvoll, schlimm; **2.** finster, unheimlich; **3.** *her.* link.

sink [sɪŋk] **I** *v/i.* [*irr.*] **1.** sinken, 'untergehen (*Schiff, Gestirn etc.*); **2.** (her'ab-, nieder)sinken (*Arm, Kopf, Person etc.*): *~ into a chair*; *~ into the grave* ins Grab sinken; **3.** *im Wasser, Schnee etc.* versinken, ein-, 'untersinken: *~ or swim fig.* egal, was passiert; **4.** sich senken: a) her'absinken (*Dunkelheit, Wolken etc.*), b) abfallen (*Gelände*), c) einsinken (*Haus, Grund*), d) sinken (*Preise, Wasserspiegel, Zahl etc.*); **5.** 'umsinken; **6.** *~ under* erliegen (*dat.*); **7.** (*into*) a) (ein)dringen, (ein)sickern (in *acc.*), b) *fig.* (in *j-s Geist*) eindringen, sich einprägen (*dat.*): *he allowed his words to ~ in* er ließ s-e Worte wirken; **8.** *~ into* in Ohnmacht fallen *od.* sinken, in *Schlaf, Schweigen etc.* versinken; **9.** nachlassen, schwächer werden; **10.** sich dem Ende nähern (*Kranker*): *he is ~ing fast* er verfällt zusehends; **11.** *im Wert, in j-s Achtung etc.* sinken; **12.** *b.s.* (ver)sinken (*into* in *acc.*), in *Armut, Vergessenheit* geraten, *dem Laster etc.* verfallen; **13.** sich senken (*Blick, Stimme*); **14.** sinken (*Mut*): *his heart sank* ihn verließ der Mut; **II** *v/t.* [*irr.*] **15.** *Schiff etc.* versenken; **16.** *bsd. in den Boden* ver-, einsenken; **17.** *Grube etc.* ausheben; *Brunnen, Loch* bohren: *~ a shaft* ✗ e-n Schacht abteufen; **18.** ⊚ a) einlassen, -betten, b) eingravieren, c) *Stempel* schneiden; **19.** *Wasserspiegel etc., a. Preis, Wert* senken; **20.** *Blick, Kopf, Stimme* senken; **21.** *fig. Niveau, Stand* her'abdrücken; **22.** zu'grunde richten: *we are sunk sl.* wir sind ,erledigt'; **23.** *Tatsache* 'drücken, vertuschen; **24.** *et.* ignorieren; *Streit* beilegen; *Ansprüche, Namen etc.* aufgeben; **25.** a) † *Kapital* fest (*bsd.* ungünstig) anlegen, ,stecken' (*into* in *acc.*), b) (*bsd.* durch 'Fehlinvesti,on) verlieren; **26.** † *Schuld* tilgen; **III** *s.* **27.** Ausguss(becken *n*, -loch *n*) *m*, Spülstein *m* (*Küche*); **28.** a) Abfluss *m* (*Rohr*), b) *fig.* Pfuhl *m*: *~ of iniquity fig.* Sündenpfuhl, Lasterhöhle *f*; **29.** *thea.* Versenkung *f*; '**sink·a·ble** [-kəbl] *adj.* zu versenken(d), versenkbar (*bsd. Schiff*); '**sink·er** [-kə] *s.* **1.** ✗ Abteufer *m*; **2.** ⊚ Stempelschneider *m*; **3.** *Weberei:* Pla'tine *f*; **4.** ⚓ a) Senkblei *n* (*Lot*), b) Senkgewicht *n* (*Angelleine, Fischnetz*); **5.** *Am. sl.* Krapfen *m*; '**sink·ing** [-kɪŋ] **I** *s.* **1.** (Ver)Sinken *n*; **2.** Versenken *n*; **3.** ✿ a) Schwächegefühl *n*, b) Senkung *f* e-s Or-gans; **4.** † Tilgung *f*; **II** *adj.* **5.** sinkend (*a. Mut etc.*): **a ~ feeling** Beklommenheit *f*, flaues Gefühl (im Magen); **6.** ✝ Tilgungs...: **~ fund** Amortisationsfonds *m.*

sin·less ['sɪnlɪs] *adj.* □ sünd(en)los, unschuldig, schuldlos.

sin·ner ['sɪnə] *s. eccl.* Sünder(in) (*a. fig.* Übeltäter; *a. humor.* Halunke).

Sinn Fein [ˌʃɪn'feɪn] *s. pol.* Sinn Fein *m* (*nationalistische Bewegung u. Partei in Irland*).

Sino- [sɪnəʊ] *in Zssgn* chi'nesisch, Chinesen..., China...; **si·nol·o·gy** [sɪ'nɒlədʒɪ] *s.* Sinolo'gie *f* (*Erforschung der chinesischen Sprache, Kultur etc.*).

sin·ter ['sɪntə] **I** *s. geol. u. metall.* Sinter *m*; **II** *v/t.* Erz sintern.

sin·u·ate ['sɪnjʊət] *adj.* □ ♀ gebuchtet (*Blatt*); **sin·u·os·i·ty** [ˌsɪnjʊ'ɒsətɪ] *s.* **1.** Biegung *f*, Krümmung *f*; **2.** Gewundenheit *f* (*a. fig.*); **'sin·u·ous** [-jʊəs] *adj.* □ **1.** gewunden, sich schlängelnd: **~ line** Wellen-, Schlangenlinie *f*; **2.** ⚡ sinusförmig gekrümmt; **3.** *fig.* a) verwickelt, b) winkelzügig; **4.** geschmeidig.

si·nus ['saɪnəs] *s.* **1.** Krümmung *f*, Kurve *f*; **2.** Ausbuchtung *f* (*a. ♀, ♣*); **3.** *anat.* Sinus *m*, (Knochen-, Neben)Höhle *f*; **4.** ♣ Fistelgang *m*; **si·nus·i·tis** [ˌsaɪnə'saɪtɪs] *s.* ♣ Sinu'sitis *f*, Nebenhöhlenentzündung *f*; **si·nus·oi·dal** [ˌsaɪnə'sɔɪdl] *adj.* ⚡, ♀, *phys.* sinusförmig: **~ wave** Sinuswelle *f.*

Sioux [suː] *pl.* **Sioux** [suː; suːz] *s.* **1.** 'Sioux(indi,aner[in]) *m*, *f*; **2.** *pl. die* 'Sioux(indi,aner) *pl.*

sip [sɪp] **I** *v/t.* **1.** nippen an (*acc.*) od. von, schlürfen (*a. fig.*); **II** *v/i.* **2.** (*of*) nippen (an *dat. od.* von), schlückchenweise trinken (von); **III** *s.* **3.** Nippen *n*; **4.** Schlückchen *n.*

si·phon ['saɪfn] **I** *s.* **1.** (Saug)Heber *m*; Siphon *m*; **2.** *a.* **~ bottle** Siphonflasche *f*; **3.** *zo.* Sipho *m*; **II** *v/t.* **4. ~ out** (*a. ♣ Magen*) aushebe(r)n; **5. ~ off** a) absaugen, b) *fig.* abziehen, *Gewinne etc.* abschöpfen; **6.** *fig.* (weiter)leiten; **III** *v/i.* **7.** ablaufen.

sip·pet ['sɪpɪt] *s.* **1.** (Brot-, Toast)Brocken *m* (*zum Eintunken*); **2.** geröstete Brotschnitte.

sir [sɜː] *s.* **1.** (mein) Herr! (*respektvolle Anrede*): **yes, ~!** ja(wohl)!; **ℒ(s)** Anrede in (*Leser*)*Briefen* (*unübersetzt*); **Dear ℒs** Sehr geehrte Herren! (*Anrede in Briefen*); **my dear ~!** *iro.* mein Verehrtester!; **2.** ℒ *Brit.* Sir *m* (*Titel e-s baronet od. knight*), **3.** *Brit.* Anrede für den **Speaker** im Unterhaus.

sire ['saɪə] **I** *s.* **1.** *poet.* a) Vater *m*, Erzeuger *m*, b) Vorfahr *m*; **2.** *zo.* Vater (*-tier n*) *m*, *bsd.* Zuchthengst *m*; **3.** ℒ! Sire!, Eure Maje'stät!; **II** *v/t.* **4.** zeugen: **be ~d by** abstammen von (*bsd. Zuchtpferd*).

si·ren ['saɪərən] *s.* **1.** *myth.* Si'rene *f* (*a. fig.* verführerische Frau, bezaubernde Sängerin*); **2.** ⊚ Si'rene *f*; **3.** *zo.* a) Armmolch *m*, b) → **si·re·ni·an** [saɪ'riːnjən] *s. zo.* Seekuh *f*, Si'rene *f.*

sir·loin ['sɜːlɔɪn] *s.* Lendenstück *n.*

si·roc·co [sɪ'rɒkəʊ] *pl.* **-cos** *s.* Schi'rokko *m* (*Wind*).

sir·up ['sɪrəp] → **syrup**.

sis [sɪs] *s.* F Schwester *f.*

si·sal (**hemp**) ['saɪsl] *s.* ♀ Sisal(hanf) *m.*

sis·sy ['sɪsɪ] F **I** *s.* **1.** Weichling *m*, ,Heulsuse' *f*; **2.** ,Waschlappen', Feigling *m*; **II** *adj.* **3.** weibisch, verweichlicht; **4.** feig.

sis·ter ['sɪstə] **I** *s.* **1.** Schwester *f* (*a. fig.* Genossin*): **the three ℒs** *myth.* die drei

Schicksalsschwestern; **Hey, ~!** *Am. sl.* He, Kleine!; **2.** *fig.* Schwester *f* (*Gleichartiges*); **3.** *eccl.* (Ordens)Schwester *f*; **ℒs of Mercy** Barmherzige Schwestern; **4.** ♣ *bsd. Brit.* a) Oberschwester *f*, b) (Kranken)Schwester *f*; **5.** *a.* **~ company** ✝ Schwester(gesellschaft) *f*; **II** *adj.* **6.** Schwester... (*a. fig.*); **'sis·ter·hood** [-hʊd] *s.* **1.** schwesterliches Verhältnis; **2.** *eccl.* Schwesternschaft *f*; **'sis·ter·in-law** [-ərɪn-] *pl.* **'sis·ters-in-law** *s.* Schwägerin *f*; **'sis·ter·ly** [-lɪ] *adj.* schwesterlich.

Sis·tine ['sɪstaɪn] *adj.* six'tinisch: **~ Chapel**; **~ Madonna**.

Sis·y·phe·an [ˌsɪsɪ'fiːən] *adj.*: **~ task** (*od.* **labo[u]r**) Sisyphusarbeit *f.*

sit [sɪt] [*irr.*] **I** *v/i.* **1.** sitzen; **2.** sich setzen; **3.** (*to j-m*) (Por'trät *od.* Mo'dell) sitzen; **4.** sitzen, brüten (*Henne*); **5.** sitzen (*Sache, a. Wind*); **6.** Sitzung (ab)halten, tagen; **7.** (*on*) beraten (über *acc.*), (*in Fall etc.*) unter'suchen; **8.** sitzen, e-n Sitz (inne)haben (*in Parliament* im Parlament): **~ on a committee** e-m Ausschuss angehören; **~ on the bench** Richter sein; **~ on a jury** Geschworener sein; **9.** (*on*) sitzen, passen (*dat.*) (*Kleidung*); *fig.* (*j-m*) gut etc. zu Gesicht stehen; **II** *v/t.* **10.** *~ o.s.* sich setzen; **11.** sitzen auf (*dat.*): **~ a horse well** gut zu Pferde sitzen;

Zssgn mit adv.:

sit| back *v/i.* **1.** sich zu'rücklehnen; **2.** *fig.* die Hände in den Schoß legen; **~ by** *v/i.* untätig zusehen; **~ down I** *v/i.* **1.** sich (hin)setzen, sich niederlassen, Platz nehmen: **~ to work** sich an die Arbeit machen; **2.** **~ under** e-e Beleidigung etc. hinnehmen; **3.** ✔ aufsetzen; **II** *v/t.* **4.** *j-n* (hin)setzen; **~ in** *v/i.* F **1.** babysitten; **2.** F mitmachen (**at,** **on** bei); **3.** **~ for** für *j-n* einspringen; **4.** a) ein Sit-'in veranstalten, b) an e-m Sit-'in teilnehmen; **~ out I** *v/t.* **1.** e-r Vorstellung etc. bis zu Ende beiwohnen; **2.** länger bleiben od. aushalten als; **3.** *Spiel, Tanz* auslassen; **II** *v/i.* **4.** aussetzen, nicht mitmachen (*bei e-m Spiel etc.*); **5.** im Freien sitzen; **~ up** *v/i.* **1.** aufrecht sitzen; **2.** sich aufsetzen; **~ (and beg)** ,schönmachen' (*Hund*); **make s.o. ~** a) *j-n* aufrütteln, b) *j-n* aufhorchen lassen; **~ (and take notice)** F aufhorchen; **3.** sich *im Bett etc.* aufrichten; **4.** aufsitzen, -bleiben; wachen (**with** bei e-m Kranken);

Zssgn mit prp.:

sit| for *v/i.* **1.** e-e Prüfung machen; **2.** *parl.* e-n Wahlkreis vertreten; **3.** **~ one's portrait** sich porträtieren lassen; **~ on** → **sit** 7, 8, 9, **sit upon**; **~ through** → **sit out** 1 (*Zssgn mit adv.*); **~ un·der** *v/i.* **1.** *eccl.* zu *j-s* Gemeinde gehören; **2.** *j-s* Schüler sein; **~ up·on** *v/i.* **1.** lasten auf *j-m*; im Magen liegen; **2.** *sl. j-m* ,aufs Dach steigen'; **3.** F Nachricht etc. zu'rückhalten; auf e-m Antrag ,sitzen'.

sit|·com ['sɪtkɒm] *s. thea.* F Situati'onsko,mödie *f*; **'~-down** *s.* **1.** Verschnaufpause *f*; **2.** a) *a.* **~ strike** ✝ Sitzstreik *m*, b) 'Sitzdemonstrati,on *f.*

site [saɪt] **I** *s.* **1.** Lage *f* (*e-s Gebäudes, e-r Stadt etc.*): **~ plan** Lageplan *m*; **2.** Stelle *f* (*a. ♣*), Örtlichkeit *f*; **3.** Bauplatz *m*, Grundstück *n*; **4.** ✝ *a.*) (Ausstellungs)Gelände *n*, b) Sitz *m* (*e-r Industrie*); **5.** Stätte *f*, Schauplatz *m*; **II** *v/t.* **6.** platzieren, legen, 'unterbringen: **well-~d** gut gelegen, in guter Lage (*Haus*).

'sit-in *s.* Sit-'in *n.*

sit·ter ['sɪtə] *s.* **1.** Sitzende(r *m*) *f*; **2.** a) Glucke *f*: **a good ~** e-e gute Brüterin, b) brütender Vogel; **3.** *paint.* Mo'dell *n*; **4.** *a.* **~-in** Babysitter *m*; **5.** *sl.* a) *hunt.* leichter Schuss, b) *fig.* leichte Beute, c) ,todsichere Sache'.

sit·ting ['sɪtɪŋ] **I** *s.* **1.** Sitzen *n*; **2.** *bsd.* ⚖, *parl.* Sitzung *f*, Tagung *f*; **3.** *paint.*, *phot. etc.* Sitzung *f*: **at a ~** *fig.* in 'einem Zug; **4.** a) Brutzeit *f*, b) Gelege *n*; **5.** *eccl.*, *thea.* Sitz(platz) *m*; **II** *adj.* **6.** sitzend, Sitz...: **~ duck** *fig.* leichtes Opfer; **7.** brütend; **~ room** *s.* **1.** Platz *m* zum Sitzen; **2.** Wohnzimmer *n.*

sit·u·ate ['sɪtjʊeɪt] **I** *v/t.* **1.** aufstellen, *e-r Sache* e-n Platz geben, den Platz festlegen (*gen.*); **2.** in e-e Lage bringen; **II** *adj.* **3.** ⚖ *od. obs.* → **situated** 1; **'sit·u·at·ed** [-tɪd] *adj.* **1.** gelegen: **be ~** liegen *od.* sein (*Haus etc.*); **2.** in e-r schwierigen etc. Lage: **thus ~** in dieser Lage; **well ~** gut situiert, wohlhabend.

sit·u·a·tion [ˌsɪtjʊ'eɪʃn] *s.* **1.** Lage *f e-s Hauses etc.*; **2.** Situati'on *f*: a) Lage *f*, Zustand *m*, b) Sachlage *f*, 'Umstände *pl.*: **difficult ~**; **3.** *thea.* dra'matische Situati'on, Höhepunkt *m*: **~ comedy** Situationskomödie *f*; **4.** Stellung *f*, Stelle *f*, Posten *m*: **~s offered** Stellenangebote; **~s wanted** Stellengesuche.

sit-up ['sɪtʌp] *s.* Gymnastik: Sit-up *n*: **do ten sit-ups** sich zehnmal aufsetzen, zehn Sit-ups machen.

si·tus ['saɪtəs] (*Lat.*) *s.* **1.** ♣ Situs *m*, Lage *f* (*e-s Organs*); **2.** Sitz *m*, Lage *f*: **in situ** an Ort u. Stelle.

six [sɪks] **I** *adj.* **1.** sechs: **it is ~ of one and half a dozen of the other** *fig.* das ist gehupft wie gesprungen; **2.** *in Zssgn* sechs...: **~-cylinder(ed)** sechszylindrig, Sechszylinder... (*Motor*); **II** *s.* **3.** Sechs *f* (*Zahl, Spielkarte etc.*): **at ~es and sevens** a) ganz durcheinander, b) uneins; **4.** *Kricket:* a. **six·er** ['sɪksə] *s.* F Sechserschlag *m*; **'six·fold** [-fəʊld] *adj. u. adv.* sechsfach.

,six·'foot·er *s.* F sechs Fuß langer *od.* ,baumlanger' Mensch; **'~·pence** *s. Brit. obs.* Sixpencestück *n*, ¹⁄₂ Schilling *m*: **it does not matter (a) ~** das ist ganz egal; **,~'shoot·er** *s.* F sechsschüssiger Re'volver.

six·teen [ˌsɪks'tiːn] **I** *s.* Sechzehn *f*; **II** *adj.* sechzehn; **'six'teenth** [-nθ] **I** *adj.* **1.** sechzehnt; **2.** sechzehntel; **II** *s.* **3.** der (die, das) Sechzehnte; **4.** Sechzehntel *n*; **5.** *a.* **~ note** ♩ Sechzehntel(note *f*) *n.*

sixth [sɪksθ] **I** *adj.* **1.** sechst: **~ sense** *fig.* sechster Sinn; **II** *s.* **2.** der (die, das) Sechste; **3.** Sechstel *n*; **4.** ♩ Sext *f*; **5.** *a.* **~ form** *ped. Brit.* Abschlussklasse *f*; **'sixth·ly** [-lɪ] *adv.* sechstens.

six·ti·eth ['sɪkstɪɪθ] **I** *adj.* **1.** sechzigst; **2.** sechzigstel; **II** *s.* **3.** der (die, das) Sechzigste; **4.** Sechzigstel *n.*

Six·tine ['sɪkstaɪn] → **Sistine**.

six·ty ['sɪkstɪ] **I** *adj.* **1.** sechzig; **II** *s.* **2.** Sechzig *f*; **3.** *pl.* a) *die* Sechzigerjahre *pl.* (*e-s Jahrhunderts*), b) *die* Sechziger (*-jahre*) *pl.* (*Alter*).

'six-,wheel·er *s. mot.* Dreiachser *m.*

siz·a·ble ['saɪzəbl] *adj.* (ziemlich) groß, ansehnlich, beträchtlich.

siz·ar ['saɪzə] *s. univ.* Stipendi'at *m* (*in Cambridge od. Dublin*).

size¹ [saɪz] **I** *s.* **1.** Größe *f*, Maß *n*, For'mat *n*, 'Umfang *m*: **all of a ~** (alle) gleich groß; **of all ~s** in allen Größen; **the ~ of** so groß wie; **that's about the ~ of it** F (genau) so ist es; **cut s.o. down to ~** *fig.* j-n in die Schranken verweisen; **2.** (Schuh-, Kleider- etc.) Größe f, Nummer f: **two ~s too big** zwei Nummern zu groß; **what ~ do you take?** welche Größe haben Sie?; **3.** fig. a) Größe f, Ausmaß n, b) geistiges etc. For'mat e-r Person; **II** v/t. **4.** nach Größen ordnen; **5. ~ up** F ab-, einschätzen, taxieren (alle a. fig.); **III** v/i. **6. ~ up** F gleichkommen (**to, with** dat.).

size² [saɪz] **I** s. **1.** (paint. Grundier)Leim m, Kleister m; **2.** a) Weberei: Appre'tur f, b) Hutmacherei: Steife f; **II** v/t. **3.** leimen; **4.** paint. grundieren; **5.** Stoff appretieren; **6.** Hutfilz steifen.

-size [saɪz] → **-sized**.

size·a·ble ['saɪzəbl] → **sizable**.

-sized [saɪzd] adj. in Zssgn ...groß, von od. in ... Größe.

siz·er¹ ['saɪzə] s. **1.** Sortierer(in); **2.** ⊚ a) ('Größen)Sor,tierma,schine f, b) ('Holz),Zuschneidema,schine f.

siz·er² ['saɪzə] s. ⊚ **1.** Leimer m; **2.** Tex-tilindustrie: Schlichter m.

siz·zle ['sɪzl] **I** v/i. zischen; Radio etc.: knistern; **II** s. Zischen n; **'siz·zling** [-lɪŋ] adj. **1.** zischend, brutzelnd; **2.** glühend heiß.

skald [skɔːld] → **scald¹**.

skat [skæt] s. Skat(spiel n) m.

skate¹ [skeɪt] pl. **skates**, bsd. coll. **skate** s. ichth. (Glatt)Rochen m.

skate² [skeɪt] **I** s. a) Schlittschuh m, b) Kufe f; **2.** Rollschuh m; **II** v/i. **3.** Schlittschuh od. Rollschuh laufen: **~ over** fig. Schwierigkeiten etc. überspielen; → **ice** 1; **'skate·board** I s. Skateboard n; **II** v/i. Skateboard fahren; **'skate·board·er** s. Skateboarder(in), Skateboardfahrer (-in); **'skate·board·ing** s. Skateboardfahren n; **'skate·park** s. sport Skateboardanlage f, Skatepark m; **'skat·er** [-tə] s. **1.** Schlittschuh-, Eisläufer(in); **2.** Rollschuhläufer(in); **skate sail·ing** s. Eissegeln n.

skat·ing ['skeɪtɪŋ] s. **1.** Schlittschuhlauf(en n) m, Eislauf(en n) m; **2.** Rollschuhlauf(en n) m; **~ rink** s. **1.** Eisbahn f; **2.** Rollschuhbahn f.

ske·dad·dle [skɪ'dædl] F **I** v/i. ,türmen', ,abhauen'; **II** s. ,Türmen' n.

skeet (**shoot·ing**) [skiːt] s. sport Skeetschießen n.

skein [skeɪn] s. **1.** Strang m, Docke f (Wolle etc.); **2.** Skein n, Warp n (Baumwollmaß); **3.** Kette f, Schwarm m (Wildenten etc.); **4.** fig. Gewirr n.

skel·e·tal ['skelɪtl] adj. **1.** ✷ Skelett...; **2.** ske'lettartig; **skel·e·tol·o·gy** [,skelɪ'tɒlədʒɪ] s. Knochenlehre f.

skel·e·ton ['skelɪtn] **I** s. **1.** Ske'lett n, Knochengerüst n, Gerippe n (alle a. fig.): **~ in the cupboard** (Am. **closet**), **family ~** fig. dunkler Punkt, (düsteres) Familiengeheimnis; **~ at the feast** Gespenst n der Vergangenheit; **2.** ✿ Rippenwerk n (Blatt); **3.** △, ⊚ (Stahl-etc.)Ske'lett n, (a. Schiffs-, Flugzeug-) Gerippe n; (a. Schirm)Gestell n; **4.** fig. a) Entwurf m, Rohbau m, b) Rahmen m; **5.** a) 'Stamm(perso,nal n) m, b) ✕ Kader m, Stammtruppe f; **6.** sport Skeleton m (Schlitten); **II** adj. **7.** Skelett...: **~ construction** △ Skelettbauweise f; **~face type** typ. Skelettschrift f; **8.** ✟, ✄ Rahmen...: **~ agreement; ~ law; ~ bill** Wechselblankett n; **~ wage agreement** Manteltarif(vertrag) m; **9.** ✕ Stamm...: **~ crew** Stamm-, Restmannschaft f, weitS. Notbelegschaft f; **'skel·e·ton·ize** [-tənaɪz] v/t. **1.** skelettieren; **2.** fig. skizzieren, in großen 'Umrissen darstellen; **3.** fig. zahlenmäßig reduzieren.

---

skel·e·ton| key s. Dietrich m, Nachschlüssel m; **~ serv·ice** s. Bereitschaftsdienst m.

skep [skep] s. **1.** (Weiden)Korb m; **2.** Bienenkorb m.

skep·tic ['skeptɪk] etc. Am. → **sceptic** etc.

sker·ry ['skerɪ] s. bsd. Scot. kleine Felseninsel.

sketch [sketʃ] **I** s. **1.** paint. etc. Skizze f, Studie f: **~ block**; **2.** Grundriss m, Schema n, Entwurf m; **3.** fig. (a. literarische) Skizze; **4.** thea. Sketch m; **II** v/t. **5.** oft **~ in** (od. **out**) skizzieren; **6.** fig. skizzieren, in großen Zügen darstellen; **III** v/i. **7.** e-e Skizze od. Skizzen machen; **'sketch·i·ness** [-tʃɪnɪs] s. Skizzenhaftigkeit f, fig. a. Oberflächlichkeit f; **'sketch·y** [-tʃɪ] adj. □ **1.** skizzenhaft, flüchtig; **2.** fig. a) oberflächlich, b) unzureichend: **a ~ meal**; **3.** fig. unklar, vage.

skew [skjuː] **I** adj. **1.** schief, schräg: **~ bridge**; **2.** abschüssig; **3.** Ⓐ 'asym,metrisch; **II** s. **4.** Schiefe f; **5.** Ⓐ Asymmetrie f; **6.** △ a) schräger Kopf (Strebepfeiler), b) 'Untersatzstein m; **'~·back** s. △ schräges 'Widerlager; **'~·bald** I adj. scheckig (bsd. Pferd); **II** s. Schecke m.

skewed [skjuːd] adj. schief, abgeschrägt, verdreht; **skew·er** ['skjuːə] **I** s. **1.** Fleischspieß m; **2.** humor. Schwert n, Dolch m; **II** v/t. **3.** Fleisch spießen, Wurst spießen; **4.** fig. aufspießen.

'skew-,eyed adj. Brit. schielend; **~ gear·ing** s. ⊚ Stirnradgetriebe n.

ski [skiː] **I** pl. **ski**, **skis** s. **1.** sport Ski m; **2.** ✈ (Schnee)Kufe f; **II** v/i. pret. u. p.p. Brit. **ski'd**, Am. **skied 3.** sport Ski laufen od. fahren; **'~·bob** s. Skibob m.

skid [skɪd] **I** s. **1.** Stützbalken m; **2.** Ladebalken m, (Lasten)Rolle f: **put the ~s under** od. **on s.o.** fig. f j-n ,fertig machen' od. ,abschießen'; **he is on the ~s** sl. mit ihm gehts abwärts; **3.** Hemmschuh m, Bremsklotz m; **4.** ✈ (Gleit)Kufe f, Sporn(rad n) m; **5.** a. mot. Rutschen n, Schleudern n: **go into a ~** ins Schleudern geraten (a. fig. F); **~ chain** Schneekette f; **~ mark** Bremsspur f; **II** v/t. **6.** Rad bremsen, hemmen; **III** v/i. **7.** a. mot. etc. a) rutschen, b) schleudern; **'~·lid** s. sl. Sturzhelm m; **'~·proof** adj. rutschfest; **~ row** [rəʊ] s. Am. F a) billiges Vergnügungsviertel, b) ,Pennergegend' f.

ski·er ['skiːə] s. sport Skiläufer(in), -fahrer(in).

skies [skaɪz] pl. von **sky**.

skiff [skɪf] s. Skiff n (Ruderboot).

ski·ing ['skiːɪŋ] s. Skilaufen n, -fahren n, -sport m; **~ gog·gles** s. pl. a. (**a**) **pair of** ~ Skibrille f.

ski|·jor·ing ['skiː,dʒɔːrɪŋ] s. sport Ski-(k)jöring n; **~ jump** s. **1.** Skisprung m; **2.** Sprungschanze f; **~ jump·ing** s. Skispringen n, Sprunglauf m.

skil·ful ['skɪlfʊl] adj. □ geschickt: a) gewandt, b) kunstgerecht (Arbeit, Operation etc.), c) geübt, (sach)kundig (**at, in** in dat.): **be ~ at** sich verstehen auf (acc.); **'skil·ful·ness** [-nɪs] → **skill**.

skill [skɪl] s. **1.** Geschick(lichkeit f) n: a) (Kunst)Fertigkeit f, Können n, b) Gewandtheit f; **2.** (Fach-, Sach-) Kenntnis f (**at, in** in dat.); **skilled** [-ld] adj. **1.** geschickt, gewandt, erfahren (**in** in dat.); **2.** Fach...: **~ labo(u)r** Facharbeiter pl.; **~ trades** Facharbeit f; **~ workman** gelernter Arbeiter, Facharbeiter m.

skil·let ['skɪlɪt] s. **1.** a) Tiegel m, b) Kas-

---

se'rolle f; **2.** Am. Bratpfanne f.

skill·ful(·ness) Am. → **skilful(ness)**.

skil·ly ['skɪlɪ] s. Brit. dünne Hafergrütze.

skim [skɪm] **I** v/t. **1.** (a. fig. ✟ Gewinne) abschöpfen: **~ the cream off** den Rahm abschöpfen (oft fig.); **2.** abschäumen; **3.** Milch entrahmen: **~med milk** → **skim milk; 4.** fig. (hin)gleiten über (acc.); **5.** fig. Buch etc. über'fliegen, flüchtig lesen; **II** v/i. **6.** gleiten, streichen (**over** über acc., **along** entlang); **7. ~ over** → 5; **'skim·mer** [-mə] s. **1.** Schaum-, Rahmkelle f; **2.** ⊚ Abstreicheisen n; **3.** ♫ Brit. leichtes Rennboot; **skim milk** s. entrahmte Milch, Magermilch f; **'skim·ming** [-mɪŋ] s. **1.** mst pl. das Abgeschöpfte; **2.** pl. Schaum m (auf Kochgut etc.); **3.** pl. ⊚ Schlacken pl.; **4.** Abschöpfen n, -schäumen n: **~ of excess profit** ✟ Gewinnabschöpfung f.

skimp [skɪmp] etc. → **scrimp** etc.

skin¹ [skɪn] **I** s. **1.** Haut f (a. biol.): **dark** (**fair**) **~** dunkle (helle) Haut(farbe); **he is mere ~ and bone** er ist nur noch Haut u. Knochen; **be in s.o.'s ~** fig. in j-s Haut stecken; **get under s.o.'s ~** a) j-m ,unter die Haut' gehen, b) j-n ärgern; **have a thick** (**thin**) **~** dickfellig (zart besaitet) sein; **save one's ~** mit heiler Haut davonkommen; **by the ~ of one's teeth** mit knapper Not; **that's no ~ off my nose** F das ,juckt' mich nicht; → **jump** 12; **2.** Fell n, Pelz m, Balg m (von Tieren); **3.** (Obst- etc.) Schale f, Haut f, Hülse f, Rinde f; **4.** ⊚ etc. dünne Schicht, Haut f (auf der Milch etc.); **5.** Oberfläche f, bsd. a) ♫ Außenhaut f, b) ✈ Bespannung f, c) (Ballon)Hülle f; **6.** (Wein- etc.) Schlauch m; **7.** sl. Klepper m (Pferd); **II** v/t. **8.** enthäuten, (ab)häuten, schälen: **keep one's eyes ~ned** F die Augen offen halten; **9.** a. **~ out** Tier abbalgen, -ziehen; **10.** Knie etc. aufschürfen; **11.** sl. j-m das Fell über die Ohren ziehen, j-n ,rupfen' (beim Spiel etc.); **12.** F Strumpf etc. abstreifen; **III** v/i. **13.** **~ over** (zu)heilen (Wunde); **14. ~ out** Am. sl. ,abhauen'.

skin² [skɪn] → **skinhead**.

,skin·|·'deep adj. u. adv. (nur) oberflächlich; **~ dis·ease** s. Hautkrankheit f; **~ div·ing** s. Sporttauchen n; **'~·flicks** s. F Sexfilm m; **'~·flint** s. Knicker m, Geizhals m; **~ food** s. Nährcreme f; **~ fric·tion** s. phys. Oberflächenreibung f; **~ game** s. F Schwindel m, Bauernfänge'rei f; **~ graft** s. ✷ 'Hauttransplan,tat n; **~ graft·ing** s. ✷ 'Hauttransplanti,on f.

skin·head ['skɪnhed] s. F Skinhead m.

skinned [skɪnd] adj. **1.** häutig; **2.** ent-, gehäutet; **3.** in Zssgn ...häutig, ...fellig; **'skin·ner** [-nə] s. **1.** Pelzhändler m, Kürschner m; **2.** Abdecker m; **'skin·ny** [-nɪ] **I** adj. **1.** mager, abgemagert, dünn; **2.** fig. knauserig; **II** s. Am. F 'Insiderinformati,on f.

,skin·|'tight adj. hauteng (Kleidung); **~ wool** s. Schlachtwolle f.

skip¹ [skɪp] **I** v/i. **1.** hüpfen, hopsen, springen; **2.** seilhüpfen; **3.** fig. Sprünge machen, von e-m Thema zum andern springen; ped. Am. e-e Klasse über-'springen; Seiten über'schlagen (in e-m Buch): **~ off** abschweifen; **~ over** et. übergehen; **4.** aussetzen, ein Sprung tun (Herz etc., a. ⊚); **5.** oft **~ out** F ,abhauen'; **~ (over) to** e-n Abstecher nach e-m Ort machen; **II** v/t. **6.** springen gen über (acc.): **~ (a) rope** seilhüpfen; **7.** fig. (ped. Am. a. e-e Klasse) über-

'springen, auslassen, *Buchseite* über-'schlagen: **~ *a lecture*** e-e Vorlesung schwänzen (*od.* ausfallen lassen); **~ *it!*** ‚geschenkt'!; **8.** F a) verschwinden aus e-r *Stadt etc.*, b) sich vor *e-r Verabredung etc.* drücken, *Schule etc.* schwänzen; **9.** F ~ *it* ‚abhauen'; **III** *s.* **10.** Hopser *m*; *Tanzen*: Hüpfschritt *m*.

skip² [skɪp] → **skipper** 2.

skip³ [skɪp] *s.* (Stu'denten)Diener *m*.

skip⁴ [skɪp] *s.* ☉ Förderkorb *m*.

'skip·jack *s.* **1.** *coll. pl. ichth.* a) *ein* T(h)unfisch *m*, b) Blaufisch *m*; **2.** *zo.* Springkäfer *m*; **3.** Stehaufmännchen *n* (*Spielzeug*).

ski plane *s.* Flugzeug *n* mit Schneekufen.

skip·per ['skɪpə] *s.* **1.** ⚓, ✈ Kapi'tän *m*, ⚓ *a.* Schiffer *m*; **2.** *sport* a) 'Mannschaftskapi,tän *m*, b) *Am.* Manager *m* *od.* Trainer *m*.

skip·ping ['skɪpɪŋ] *s.* Hüpfen *n*, (*bsd.* Seil)Springen *n*; **~ rope** *s.* Springseil *n*.

skirl [skɜːl] *dial.* **I** *v/i.* **1.** pfeifen (*bsd. Dudelsack*); **2.** Dudelsack spielen; **II** *s.* **3.** Pfeifen *n* (*des Dudelsacks*).

skir·mish ['skɜːmɪʃ] **I** *s.* ✗ *u. fig.* Geplänkel *n*: **~ line** Schützenlinie *f*; **II** *v/i.* plänkeln; **'skir·mish·er** [-ʃə] *s.* ✗ Plänkler *m* (*a. fig.*).

skirt [skɜːt] **I** *s.* **1.** (Frauen)Rock *m*; **2.** *sl.* ‚Weibsbild' *n*, ‚Schürze' *f*; **3.** (Rock-, Hemd-, *etc.*)Schoß *m*; **4.** Saum *m*, Rand *m* (*fig. oft pl.*); **5.** *pl.* Außenbezirk *m*, Randgebiet *n*; **6.** Kutteln *pl.*: **~ of beef**; **II** *v/t.* **7.** a) (um)'säumen, b) sich entlangziehen an (*dat.*); **8.** entlang·*od.* her'umgehen *od.* -fahren um; **9.** *fig.* um'gehen; **III** *v/i.* **10.** ~ **along** am Rande entlanggehen *od.* -fahren, sich entlangziehen; **'skirt·ed** [-tɪd] *adj.* **1.** e-n Rock tragend; **2.** *in Zssgn* a) mit e-m *langen etc.* Rock: **long-~**, b) *fig.* eingesäumt; **'skirt·ing** [-tɪŋ] *s.* **1.** Rand *m*, Saum *m*; **2.** Rockstoff *m*; **3.** *mst* ~ **board** 🏠 (*bsd.* Fuß-, Scheuer)Leiste *f*.

ski run *s.* Skipiste *f*.

skit [skɪt] *s.* **1.** Stiche'lei *f*, Seitenhieb *m*; **2.** Paro'die *f*, Sa'tire *f* (**on** über, auf *acc.*).

ski tow *s.* Schlepplift *m*.

skit·ter ['skɪtə] *v/i.* **1.** jagen, rennen; **2.** rutschen; **3.** hopsen; **4.** den Angelhaken an der Wasseroberfläche hinziehen.

skit·tish ['skɪtɪʃ] *adj.* □ **1.** ungebärdig, scheu (*Pferd*); **2.** ner'vös, ängstlich; **3.** *fig.* a) lebhaft, wild, b) (kindisch) ausgelassen (*bsd. Frau*), c) fri'vol, d) sprunghaft, kapri'ziös.

skit·tle ['skɪtl] **I** *s.* **1.** *bsd. Brit.* Kegel *m*; **2.** *pl. sg. konstr.* Kegeln *n*, Kegelspiel *n*: **play (at)** ~**s** kegeln; **II** *int.* **3.** ~**s!** F Quatsch!, Unsinn!; **III** *v/t.* **4.** ~ **out** *Kricket: Schläger od. Mannschaft* (rasch) ‚erledigen'; ~ **al·ley** *s.* Kegelbahn *f*.

skive¹ [skaɪv] **I** *v/t.* **1.** *Leder, Fell* spalten; **2.** *Edelstein* abschleifen; **II** *s.* **3.** Dia'mantenschleifscheibe *f*.

skive² [skaɪv] *Brit. sl.* **I** *v/t.* ‚sich drücken' vor (*dat.*); **II** *v/i. a.* ~ **off** sich drücken.

skiv·vy ['skɪvɪ] *s. Brit. contp.* Dienstmagd *f*.

sku·a ['skjuːə] *s. orn.* (**great** ~ Riesen-)Raubmöwe *f*.

skul·dug·ger·y [skʌl'dʌgərɪ] *s.* F Gaune'rei *f*, Schwindel *m*.

skulk [skʌlk] *v/i.* **1.** lauern; **2.** (um'her)schleichen: **~ after s.o.** j-m nachschleichen; **3.** *fig.* sich drücken; **'skulk·er** [-kə] *s.* **1.** Schleicher(in); **2.** Drückeberger(in).

---

skull [skʌl] *s.* **1.** *anat.* Schädel *m*, Hirnschale *f*: **fractured** ~ ⚕ Schädelbruch *m*; **2.** Totenschädel *m*: ~ **and crossbones** a) Totenkopf *m* (*Giftzeichen etc.*), b) *hist.* Totenkopf-, Piratenflagge *f*; **3.** *fig.* Schädel *m* (*Verstand*): **have a thick** ~ ein Brett vor dem Kopf haben; **'~·cap** *s.* **1.** *anat.* Schädeldach *n*; **2.** Käppchen *n*.

skunk [skʌŋk] **I** *s.* **1.** *zo.* Skunk *m*, Stinktier *n*; **2.** Skunk(s)pelz *m*; **3.** *fig. sl.* ‚Scheißkerl' *m*, ‚Schwein' *n*; **II** *v/t.* **4.** *Am.* F a) ‚vermöbeln' (*a. sport*), b) ‚bescheißen'.

sky [skaɪ] **I** *s.* **1.** *oft pl.* (Wolken)Himmel *m*: **in the** ~ am Himmel; **out of a clear** ~ *bsd. fig.* aus heiterem Himmel; **2.** *oft pl.* Himmel *m* (*a. fig.*), Himmelszelt *n*: **under the open** ~ unter freiem Himmel; **praise to the skies** *fig.* in den Himmel heben; **the** ~ **is the limit** F nach oben sind keine Grenzen gesetzt; **3.** a) Klima *n*, b) Himmelsstrich *m*, Gegend *f*, c) ✗, ✈ Luftraum *m*; **II** *v/t.* **4.** *Ball etc.* hoch in die Luft schlagen *od.* werfen; **5.** F *Bild* (zu) hoch aufhängen (*in e-r Ausstellung*); ~ **ad·ver·tis·ing** *s.* ✈ Luftwerbung *f*; ‚~·'blue *adj.* himmelblau; '~·coach *s.* ✈ *Am.* Passagierflugzeug ohne Service; '~,div·er *s. sport* Fallschirmspringer(in); '~,div·ing *s. sport* Fallschirmspringen *n*; ‚~·'high *adj. u. adv.* himmelhoch (*a. fig.*): **blow** ~ a) sprengen, b) *fig. Theorie etc.* über den Haufen werfen; '~·jack *v/t. Flugzeug* entführen; **II** *s.* Flugzeugentführung *f*; '~,jack·er *s.* Flugzeugentführer (-in); '~,jack·ing *s.* → **skyjack** II; '~·lab *s.* 'Raumla,bor *n*; '~·lark **I** *s.* **1.** *orn.* (Feld)Lerche *f*; **2.** Spaß *m*, Ulk *m*; **II** *v/i.* **3.** he'rumtollen, ‚Blödsinn' treiben; um'hertollen; '~·light *s.* Oberlicht *n*, Dachfenster *n*; '~·line *s.* Hori'zont (-linie *f*) *m*, (Stadt- *etc.*)Silhou'ette *f*; '~·lin·er → **airliner**; ~ **mar·shal** *s. Am. Bundespolizist, der zur Verhinderung von Flugzeugentführungen eingesetzt wird*; ~ **pi·lot** *s. sl.* ‚Schwarzrock' *m* (*Geistlicher*); '~,rock·et **I** *s. Feuerwerk*: Ra'kete *f*; **II** *v/i.* in die Höhe schießen (*Preise etc.*), sprunghaft ansteigen; **III** *v/t.* sprunghaft ansteigen lassen; '~·scape [-skeɪp] *s. paint.* Wolkenlandschaft *f* (*Bild*); '~,scrap·er *s.* Wolkenkratzer *m*; ~ **sign** *s.* ✈ 'Leuchtre,klame *f* (*auf Häusern etc.*).

sky·ward ['skaɪwəd] **I** *adv.* himmel'an, -wärts; **II** *adj.* himmelwärts gerichtet; **'sky·wards** [-dz] → **skyward** 1.

'sky|·way *s. bsd. Am.* **1.** ✈ Luftroute *f*; **2.** Hochstraße *f*; '~,writ·er *s.* Himmelsschreiber *m*; '~,writ·ing *s.* Himmelsschrift *f*.

slab [slæb] **I** *s.* **1.** (Me'tall-, Stein-, Holz-*etc.*)Platte *f*, Tafel *f*, Fliese *f*: **on the** ~ F a) auf dem Operationstisch, b) im Leichenschauhaus; **2.** (dicke) Scheibe (*Brot, Fleisch etc.*); **3.** ☉ Schwarten-, Schalbrett *n*; **4.** *metall.* Bramme *f* (*Roheisenblock*); **5.** *Am. sl. Baseball*: Schlagmal *n*; **6.** (*westliche USA*) Be'tonstraße *f*; **II** *v/t.* **7.** ☉ a) *Stamm* abschwarten, b) in Platten *od.* Bretter zersägen.

slack¹ [slæk] **I** *adj.* □ **1.** schlaff, locker, lose (*alle a. fig.*): **keep a** ~ **rein** (*od.* **hand**) die Zügel locker lassen (*a. fig.*); **2.** a) langsam, träge (*Strömung etc.*), b) flau (*Brise*); **3.** ⚓ flau, lustlos; ~ **season** 3; **4.** (nach)lässig, lasch, schlaff: **be** ~ **in one's duties** s-e Pflichten vernachlässigen; ~ **performance** schlappe Leistung; **5.** *ling.* locker: ~ **vowel** offener Vokal; **II** *s.* **6.** ⚓ Lose *n* (*loses Tau-*

---

ende); **7.** ☉ Spiel *n*: **take up the** ~ Druckpunkt nehmen (*beim Schießen*); **8.** ⚓ Stillwasser *n*; **9.** Flaute *f* (*a.* ✝); **10.** F (Ruhe)Pause *f*; **11.** *pl.* Freizeithose *f*; **III** *v/t.* **12.** *a.* ~ **off** → **slacken** 1; **13.** *a.* ~ **up** → **slacken** 2 u. 3; **14.** → **slake** 2; **IV** *v/i.* **15.** → **slacken** 5 u. 6; **16.** *oft* ~ **off** a) nachlassen, b) F trödeln; **17.** ~ **up** langsamer werden *od.* fahren.

slack² [slæk] *s.* ⚒ Kohlengrus *m*.

slack·en ['slækən] **I** *v/t.* **1.** Seil, Muskel *etc.* lockern, locker machen, entspannen; **2.** lösen; ⚓ *Segel* lose machen; (*Tau*)Ende fieren; **3.** *Tempo* verlangsamen, her'absetzen; **4.** nachlassen in (*dat.*); **II** *v/i.* **5.** sich lockern, schlaff werden; **6.** *fig.* erlahmen, nachlassen, nachlässig werden; **7.** langsamer werden; **8.** ✝ stocken; **'slack·er** [-kə] *s.* Bumme'lant *m*, Faulpelz *m*; **'slack·ness** [-knɪs] *s.* **1.** Schlaffheit *f*, Lockerheit *f*; **2.** Flaute *f*, Stille *f* (*a. fig.*); **3.** ✝ Flaute *f*, (Geschäfts)Stockung *f*; Unlust *f*; **4.** *fig.* Schlaffheit *f*, (Nach)Lässigkeit *f*, Trägheit *f*; **5.** ☉ Spiel *n*, toter Gang.

slack| suit *s. Am.* Freizeitanzug *m*; ~ **wa·ter** → **slack¹** 8.

slag [slæg] **I** *s.* **1.** ☉ (*geol.* vul'kanische) Schlacke: ~ **concrete** Schlackenbeton *m*; **2.** *Brit. sl.* Schlampe *f*; **II** *v/t. u. v/i.* **3.** verschlacken; **'slag·gy** [-gɪ] *adj.* schlackig.

slain [sleɪn] *p.p. von* **slay**.

slake [sleɪk] *v/t.* **1.** *Durst, a. fig. Begierde etc.* stillen; **2.** ☉ *Kalk* löschen; ~**d lime** 🔥 Löschkalk *m*.

sla·lom ['slɑːləm] *s. sport* Slalom *m*, Torlauf *m*.

slam¹ [slæm] **I** *v/t.* **1.** *a.* ~ **to** *Tür, Deckel* zuschlagen, zuknallen; **2.** *et. auf den Tisch etc.* knallen: ~ **down** *et.* hinknallen; **3.** *j-n* schlagen; **4.** *sl. sport* ‚überfahren' (*besiegen*); **5.** F *j-n od. et.* ‚in die Pfanne hauen'; **II** *v/i.* **6.** *a.* ~ **to** zuschlagen (*Tür*); **III** *s.* **7.** Knall *m*; **IV** *adv.* **8.** *a. int.* bums(!), peng(!).

slam² [slæm] *s. Kartenspiel*: Schlemm *m*: **grand** ~ Groß-Schlemm.

slan·der ['slɑːndə] **I** *s.* **1.** ⚖ mündliche Verleumdung, üble Nachrede; **2.** *allg.* Verleumdung *f*, Klatsch *m*; **II** *v/t.* **3.** verleumden; **'slan·der·er** [-dərə] *s.* Verleumder(in); **'slan·der·ous** [-dərəs] *adj.* □ verleumderisch.

slang [slæŋ] **I** *s.* Slang *m*, Jar'gon *m*: a) Sonder-, Berufssprache *f*: **schoolboy** ~ Schülersprache; **thieves'** ~ Gaunersprache, *das* Rotwelsch; *b)* sa'loppe 'Umgangssprache; **II** *v/t. j-n* (wüst) beschimpfen: ~**ing match** wüste gegenseitige Beschimpfungen *pl.*; **'slang·y** [-ɪ] *adj.* □ sa'lopp, Slang...

slant [slɑːnt] **I** *s.* **1.** Schräge *f*, schräge Fläche *od.* Richtung *od.* Linie: **on the** (*od.* **on a**) ~ schräg, schief; **2.** Abhang *m*; **3.** *fig. a)* Ten'denz *f*, ‚Färbung' *f* b) Einstellung *f*, Gesichtspunkt *m*: **take a** ~ **at** *Am.* F e-n (Seiten)Blick werfen auf (*acc.*); **II** *adj.* □ **4.** schräg; **III** *v/i.* **5.** schräg liegen; sich neigen, kippen; **6.** *fig.* tendieren (**towards** zu *et.* hin); **IV** *v/t.* **7.** schräg legen, kippen, e-e schräge Richtung geben (*dat.*): ~**ed** schräg; **8.** *fig.* e-e Ten'denz geben, ‚färben'; '~·eye *s.* Schlitzauge *n* (*Asiate etc.*); **'slant-eyed** *adj.* schlitzäugig; **'slant·ing** [-tɪŋ] *adj.* □ schräg; **'slant·wise** *adv. u. adj.* schräg, schief.

slap [slæp] **I** *s.* **1.** Schlag *m*, Klaps *m*: **give s.o. a** ~ **on the back** j-m anerkennend auf den Rücken klopfen; **a** ~ **in the face** e-e Ohrfeige, ein Schlag ins

Gesicht (*a. fig.*); **have a** (*bit of*) ~ **and tickle** F ,knutschen'; **II** *v/t.* **2.** schlagen, e-n Klaps geben (*dat.*): ~ **s.o.'s face** j-n ohrfeigen; **3.** → **slam¹** 2; **4.** scharf tadeln; **5.** ~ **on** F a) *et.* draufklatschen, b) *Zuschlag etc.* ,draufhauen'; **III** *v/i.* **6.** schlagen, klatschen (*a. Regen etc.*); **IV** *adv.* **7.** F genau, bums, ,zack': *I ran into him;* ,~-'**bang** *adv.* **1.** → **slap** 7; **2.** Knall u. Fall; '~-**dash** *I adv.* **1.** blindlings, Hals über Kopf; **2.** hoppla'hopp, ,auf die Schnelle'; **3.** aufs Gerate'wohl; **II** *adj.* **4.** heftig, ungestüm; **5.** schlampig, schlud(e)rig: ~ *work*; '~,**hap·py** *adj.* unbekümmert; '~-**jack** *s. Am.* **1.** Pfannkuchen *m*; **2.** *ein Kinderkartenspiel*; '~-**stick** **I** *s.* **1.** (Narren)Pritsche *f*; **2.** *thea.* a) Slapstick *m*, Kla'mauk *m*, b) 'Slapstickko,mödie *f*; **II** *adj.* **3.** Slapstick..., Klamauk...: ~ *comedy* → 2 b; '~-**up** *adj. sl.* ,todschick', prima, ,toll'.

slash [slæʃ] **I** *v/t.* **1.** (auf)schlitzen; zerfetzen; **2.** *Kleid etc.* schlitzen: ~*ed sleeve* Schlitzärmel *m*; **3.** a) peitschen, b) *Peitsche* knallen lassen; **4.** *Ball etc.* ,dreschen'; **5.** *fig.* geißeln, scharf kritisieren; **6.** *fig.* drastisch kürzen *od.* he'rabsetzen, zs.-streichen; **II** *v/i.* **7.** hauen (*at* nach): ~ *out* um sich hauen (*a. fig.*); **III** *s.* **8.** Hieb *m*, Streich *m*; **9.** Schnitt (-wunde *f*) *m*; **10.** Schlitz *m*; **11.** Holzschlag *m*; **12.** a) drastische Kürzung, b) drastischer Preisnachlass; **13.** *typ.* Schrägstrich *m*; '**slash·ing** [-ʃɪŋ] **I** *s.* **1.** ✕ Verhau *m*; **II** *adj.* **2.** ´schneidend, schlitzend: ~ *weapon* ✕ Hiebwaffe *f*; **3.** *fig.* vernichtend, beißend (*Kritik etc.*); **4.** F ,toll'.

slat [slæt] *s.* **1.** Leiste *f*, (*a.* Jalou'sie'-) Stab *m*; **2.** *pl. sl.* a) Rippen *pl.*, b) ,Arschbacken' *pl.*

slate¹ [sleɪt] *s.* **1.** *geol.* Schiefer *m*; **2.** (Dach)Schiefer *m*, Schieferplatte *f*; **3.** Schiefertafel *f* (*zum Schreiben*): *have a clean* ~ *fig.* e-e reine Weste haben; *clean the* ~ *fig.* reinen Tisch machen; → *wipe off* 2; **4.** *Film:* Klappe *f*; **5.** *pol. etc. Am.* Kandi'datenliste *f*; **6.** Schiefergrau *n* (*Farbe*); **II** *v/t.* **7.** *Dach* mit Schiefer decken; **8.** *Am.* a) Kandidaten (vorläufig) aufstellen, vorschlagen: *be* ~*d for* für e-n Posten vorgesehen sein, b) *zeitlich* ansetzen; **III** *adj.* **9.** schieferartig, -farbig; Schiefer...

slate² [sleɪt] *v/t. sl.* **1.** ,vermöbeln'; **2.** *fig.* a) *et.* ,verreißen' (*kritisieren*), b) *j-n* abkanzeln.

,**slate|-'blue** *adj.* schieferblau; ~ **club** *s. Brit.* Sparverein *m*; ,~-'**gray**, ,~-'**grey** *adj.* schiefergrau; ~ **pen·cil** *s.* Griffel *m*.

slath·er ['slæðə] *Am.* F I *v/t.* **1.** dick schmieren *od.* auftragen; **2.** verschwenden; **II** *s.* **3.** *mst pl.* große Menge.

slat·ing ['sleɪtɪŋ] *s. sl.* **1.** ,Verriss' *m*, beißende Kri'tik; **2.** Standpauke *f*.

slat·tern ['slætɜːn] *s.* **1.** Schlampe *f*; **2.** *Am.* ,Nutte' *f*; '**slat·tern·ly** [-lɪ] *adj. u. adv.* schlampig, schmudd(e)lig.

slat·y ['sleɪtɪ] *adj.* schief(e)rig.

slaugh·ter ['slɔːtə] **I** *s.* **1.** Schlachten *n*; **2.** *fig.* a) Abschlachten *n*, Niedermetzeln *n*, b) Gemetzel *n*, Blutbad *n*; → *innocent* 7; **II** *v/t.* **3.** Vieh schlachten; **4.** *fig.* a) (ab)schlachten, niedermetzeln, b) F *j-n* ,auseinander nehmen' (*a. sport*); '**slaugh·ter·er** [-ərə] *s.* Schlächter *m*; '**slaugh·ter·house** *s.* **1.** Schlachthaus *n*; **2.** *fig.* Schlachtbank *f*.

Slav [slɑːv] **I** *s.* Slawe *m*, Slawin *f*; **II** *adj.* slawisch, Slawen...

slave [sleɪv] **I** *s.* **1.** Sklave *m*, Sklavin *f*; **2.** *fig.* Sklave *m*, Arbeitstier *n*, Kuli *m*:

---

work like a ~ → 4; **3.** *fig.* Sklave *m* (*to, of gen.*): *a* ~ *to one's passions*; *a* ~ *to drink* alkoholsüchtig; **II** *v/i.* **4.** schuften, wie ein Kuli arbeiten; ~ **driv·er** *s.* **1.** Sklavenaufseher *m*; **2.** *fig.* Leuteschinder *m*.

slav·er¹ ['sleɪvə] *s.* **1.** Sklavenschiff *n*; **2.** Sklavenhändler *m*.

slav·er² ['slævə] **I** *v/i.* **1.** geifern, sabbern (*a. fig.*): ~ *for* lechzen nach; **2.** *fig.* katzbuckeln; **II** *v/t.* **3.** *obs.* besabbern; **III** *s.* **4.** Geifer *m*.

slav·er·y ['sleɪvərɪ] *s.* **1.** Sklave'rei *f* (*a. fig.*): ~ *to fig.* sklavische Abhängigkeit von; **2.** Sklavenarbeit *f*; *fig.* Placke'rei *f*, Schinde'rei *f*.

slave| ship *s.* Sklavenschiff *n*; ~ **trade** *s.* Sklavenhandel *m*; ~ **trad·er** *s.* Sklavenhändler *m*.

slav·ey ['sleɪvɪ] *s. Brit.* F ,dienstbarer Geist'.

Slav·ic ['slɑːvɪk] **I** *adj.* slawisch; **II** *s. ling.* Slawisch *n*.

slav·ish ['sleɪvɪʃ] *adj.* **1.** □ sklavisch, Sklaven...; **2.** *fig.* knechtisch, kriecherisch, unter'würfig; **3.** *fig.* sklavisch: ~ *imitation*; '**slav·ish·ness** [-nɪs] *s.* das Sklavische, sklavische Gesinnung.

slaw [slɔː] *s. Am.* 'Krautsa,lat *m*.

slay [sleɪ] [*irr.*] **I** *v/t.* töten, erschlagen, ermorden; **II** *v/i.* morden; **slay·er** ['sleɪə] *s.* Mörder(in).

sleaze [sliːz] *s.* F a) Kunge'lei *f*, b) 'Unmo,ral *f*.

slea·zy ['sliːzɪ] *adj.* **1.** dünn (*a. fig.*), verschlissen (*Gewebe*); **2.** → *shabby*.

sled [sled] → **sledge¹** 1; '**sled·ding** [-dɪŋ] *s. bsd. Am.* 'Schlittenfahren *n*, -trans,port *m*: *hard* (*smooth*) ~ *fig.* schweres (*glattes*) Vorankommen.

sledge¹ [sledʒ] **I** *s.* **1.** a) *a.* ⊙ Schlitten *m*, b) (Rodel)Schlitten *m*; **2.** *bsd. Brit.* (leichterer) Pferdeschlitten; **II** *v/t.* **3.** mit e-m Schlitten befördern *od.* fahren; **III** *v/i.* **4.** Schlitten fahren, rodeln.

sledge² [sledʒ] ⊙ *s.* **1.** Vorschlag-, Schmiedehammer *m*; **2.** schwerer Treibfäustel; **3.** ✕ Schlägel *m*; '~,**ham·mer** **I** *s.* → **sledge²** 1; **II** *adj. fig.* a) Holzhammer...(-*argumente etc.*), b) wuchtig, vernichtend (*Schlag*), c) ungeschlacht (*Stil*).

sleek [sliːk] **I** *adj.* □ **1.** glatt, glänzend (*Haar*); **2.** geschmeidig, glatt (*Körper*; *a. fig. Wesen*); **3.** *fig.* a) gepflegt, elegant, schick, b) schnittig (*Form*); **4.** *fig. b.s.* aalglatt, ölig; **II** *v/t.* **5.** *a.* ⊙ glätten; *Haar* glatt kämmen *od.* bürsten; ⊙ *Leder* schlichten; '**sleek·ness** [-nɪs] *s.* Glätte *f*, Geschmeidigkeit *f* (*a. fig.*).

sleep [sliːp] **I** *v/i.* [*irr.*] **1.** schlafen, ruhen (*beide a. fig. Dorf, Streit, Toter etc.*): ~ *late* lange schlafen; ~ *like a log* (*od. top od. dormouse*) schlafen wie ein Murmeltier; ~ [*up*]*on* (*od. over*) *s.th.* et. überschlafen; **2.** schlafen, über'nachten: ~ *in* (*out*) im (außer) Haus schlafen; **3.** stehen (*Kreisel*); **4.** ~ *with* mit j-m schlafen; ~ *around* mit vielen Männern ins Bett gehen; **II** *v/t.* [*irr.*] **5.** schlafen: ~ *the sleep of the just* den Schlaf des Gerechten schlafen; **6.** ~ *away Zeit* verschlafen; **7.** ~ *off Kopfweh etc.* ausschlafen; ~ *it off* s-n Rausch *etc.* ausschlafen; **8.** Schlafgelegenheit bieten für; *j-n* 'unterbringen; **III** *s.* **9.** Schlaf *m*, Ruhe *f* (*a. fig.*): *in one's* ~ im Schlaf; *the last* ~ *fig.* die letzte Ruhe, der Tod(esschlaf); *get some* ~ ein wenig schlafen; *go to* ~ a) schlafen gehen, b) einschlafen (*a. fig. sterben*); *put to* ~ *allg.*, *a.* ✿ einschläfern; **10.** *zo.*

(Winter)Schlaf *m*; **11.** ♀ Schlafbewegung *f*; '**sleep·er** [-pə] *s.* **1.** Schläfer(in): *be a light* (*sound*) ~ e-n leichten (festen) Schlaf haben; **2.** 🚃 a) Schlafwagen *m*, b) *Brit.* Schwelle *f*; **3.** *Am.* Lastwagen *m* mit Schlafkoje; **4.** *Am.* a) ('Kinder)Py,jama *m*, b) (Baby)Schlafsack *m*; **5.** *Am.* F über'raschender Erfolg; **6.** ✝ *Am.* Ladenhüter *m*; '**sleep-in** *s.* Sleep-in *n*, 'Schlafdemonstrati,on *f*; '**sleep·i·ness** [-pɪnɪs] *s.* **1.** Schläfrigkeit *f*; **2.** *a. fig.* Verschlafenheit *f*.

sleep·ing ['sliːpɪŋ] *adj.* **1.** schlafend; **2.** Schlaf...: ~ *accommodation* Schlafgelegenheit *f*; ~ **bag** *s.* Schlafsack *m*; ⚪ **Beau·ty** *s.* Dorn'rös-chen *n*; ~ **car** 🚃 Schlafwagen *m*; ~ **draught** *s.* Schlaftrunk *m*, -mittel *n*; ~ **part·ner** *s.* ✝ *Brit.* stiller Teilhaber (mit unbeschränkter Haftung); ~ **po·lice·man** *s.* [*irr.*] *Brit.* Rüttelschwelle *f* (*zur Verkehrsberuhigung*); ~ **sick·ness** *s.* 🐛 Schlafkrankheit *f*; ~ **suit** *s.* → *sleeper* 4 a; ~ **tab·let** *s.* 🐛 'Schlafta,blette *f*.

sleep·less ['sliːplɪs] *adj.* □ **1.** schlaflos; **2.** *fig.* a) rast-, ruhelos, b) wachsam; '**sleep·less·ness** [-nɪs] *s.* **1.** Schlaflosigkeit *f*; **2.** *fig.* Rast-, Ruhelosigkeit *f*; **3.** Wachsamkeit *f*.

'**sleep|,walk·er** *s.* Nachtwandler(in); '~,**walk·ing** *s.* **1.** Nacht-, Schlafwandeln *n*; **II** *adj.* schlafwandelnd; nachtwandlerisch.

sleep·y ['sliːpɪ] *adj.* □ **1.** schläfrig, müde; **2.** *fig.* schläfrig, schlafmützig, träge; **3.** *fig.* verschlafen, verträumt (*Dorf etc.*); **4.** teigig (*Obst*); '~-**head** *s. fig.* Schlafmütze *f*.

sleet [sliːt] *meteor.* **I** *s.* **1.** Graupel(n *pl.*) *f*, Schloße(n *pl.*) *f*; **2.** a) *Brit.* Schneeregen *m*, b) *Am.* Graupelschauer *m*; **3.** F 'Eis,überzug *m auf Bäumen etc.*; **II** *v/i.* **4.** graupeln; '**sleet·y** [-tɪ] *adj.* graupelig.

sleeve [sliːv] *s.* **1.** Ärmel *m*: *have s.th. up* (*od. in*) *one's* ~ et. auf Lager *od.* in petto haben, b) et. im Schild führen; *laugh in one's* ~ sich ins Fäustchen lachen; *roll up one's* ~*s* die Ärmel hochkrempeln (*a. fig.*); **2.** ⊙ Muffe *f*, Buchse *f*, Man'schette *f*; **3.** (Schutz-) Hülle *f*; **sleeved** [-vd] *adj.* **1.** mit Ärmeln; **2.** *in Zssgn* ...ärmelig; '**sleeve·less** [-lɪs] *adj.* ärmellos.

sleeve| link *s.* Man'schettenknopf *m*; ~ **note** *s.* Plattencovertext *m*; ~ **tar·get** *s.* ✕ Schleppsack *m*; ~ **valve** *s.* ⊙ 'Muffenven,til *n*.

sleigh [sleɪ] *s.* (Pferde- *od.* Last)Schlitten *m*; **II** *v/i.* (im) Schlitten fahren; ~ **bell** *s.* Schlittenschelle *f*.

sleight [slaɪt] *s.* **1.** Geschicklichkeit *f*; **2.** Trick *m*; ,~-**of-'hand** *s.* (Taschenspieler)Kunststück *n*, (-)Trick *m* (*a. fig.*); **2.** (Finger)Fertigkeit *f*.

slen·der ['slendə] *adj.* □ **1.** schlank; **2.** schmal, schmächtig; **3.** *fig.* a) schmal, dürftig: ~ *income*, b) gering, schwach: *a* ~ *hope*; **4.** mager, karg (*Essen*); '**slen·der·ize** [-əraɪz] *v/t. u. v/i.* schlank (-er) machen *od.* werden; '**slen·der·ness** [-nɪs] *s.* **1.** Schlankheit *f*, Schmalheit *f*; **2.** *fig.* Dürftigkeit *f*; **3.** Kargheit *f* (*des Essens*).

slept [slept] *pret. u. p.p.* von *sleep*.

sleuth [sluːθ] **I** *s. a.* ~*hound* Spürhund *m* (*a. fig. Detektiv*); **II** *v/i.* ,(he'rum-) schnüffeln'; **III** *v/t. j-s* Spur verfolgen.

slew¹ [sluː] *pret.* von *slay*.

slew² [sluː] *s. Am. od. Canad.* Sumpf (-land *n*, -stelle *f*) *m*.

slew³ [sluː] **I** *v/t. a.* ~ *round* her'umdrehen, (-)schwenken; **II** *v/i.* sich her'umdrehen.

slew⁴ [sluː] *s. Am.* F (große) Menge, Haufe(n) *m*: *a ~ of people*.

slice [slaɪs] **I** *s.* **1.** Scheibe *f*, Schnitte *f*, Stück *n*: *a ~ of bread*; **2.** *fig.* Stück *n Land etc.*; (An)Teil *m*: *a ~ of the profits* ein Anteil am Gewinn; *a ~ of luck fig.* e-e Portion Glück; **3.** (*bsd.* Fisch-) Kelle *f*; **4.** ⊗ Spa(ch)tel *m*; **5.** *Golf, Tennis*: Slice *m* (*Schlag u. Ball*); **II** *v/t.* **6.** in Scheiben schneiden, aufschneiden: *~ off* Stück abschneiden; **7.** *a.* Luft, Wellen durch'schneiden; **8.** *fig.* aufteilen; **9.** *Golf, Tennis*: den Ball slicen; **III** *v/i.* **10.** Scheiben schneiden; **11.** *Golf, Tennis*: slicen; **'slic·er** [-sə] *s.* (*Brot-, Gemüse- etc.*)'Schneidema·schine *f*; (*Gurken-, Kraut- etc.*)Hobel *m*.

slick [slɪk] F **I** *adj.* □ **1.** glatt, glitschig; **2.** *Am.* Hochglanz...; → *a.* 8; **3.** F a) geschickt, raffiniert, b) ,schick', ,flott'; **II** *adv.* **4.** geschickt; **5.** flugs; **6.** genau, ,peng': *~ in the eye*; **III** *v/t.* **7.** glätten; **8.** ,auf Hochglanz bringen'; **IV** *s.* **9.** Ölfläche *f*; **10.** F *a. ~ paper Am.* F ele'gante Zeitschrift; **'slick·er** [-kə] *s. Am.* **1.** Regenmantel *m*; **2.** F a) raffinierter Kerl, Schwindler *m*, b) ,Großstadtpinkel' *m*.

slid [slɪd] *pret. u. p.p. von* **slide**.

slide [slaɪd] **I** *v/i.* [*irr.*] **1.** gleiten (*a. Riegel etc.*): *~ down* hinunterrutschen, -gleiten; *~ from* entgleiten (*dat.*); *let things ~ fig.* die Dinge laufen lassen; **2.** auf Eis schlittern; **3.** (aus)rutschen; **4.** *~ over fig.* leicht über *ein Thema* hin'weggehen; **5.** *~ into fig.* in *et.* hin'einschlittern; **II** *v/t.* [*irr.*] **6.** *Gegenstand, s-e Hände etc.* wohin gleiten lassen, schieben: *~ in fig.* Wort einfließen lassen; **III** *s.* **7.** Gleiten *n*; **8.** Schlittern *n auf Eis*; **9.** a) Schlitterbahn *f*, b) Rodelbahn *f*, c) (*a.* Wasser)Rutschbahn *f*; **10.** *geol.* Erd-, Fels-, Schneerutsch *m*; **11.** ⊗ a) Rutsche *f*, b) Schieber *m*, c) Schlitten *m* (*Drehbank etc.*), Führung *f*; **12.** ♪ Zug *m*; **13.** Spange *f*; **14.** *phot.* Dia(posi-'tiv) *n*: *~ lecture* Lichtbildervortrag *m*; **15.** *Mikroskop*: Ob'jektträger *m*; **16.** (*Haar- etc.*)Spange *f*; *~ cal·i·per s.* ⊗ Schieb-, Schublehre *f*; *~ rest s.* ⊗ Sup'port *m*; *~ rule s.* ⊗ Rechenschieber *m*; *~ valve s.* ⊗ 'Schieber(ven‚til *n*) *m*.

slid·ing ['slaɪdɪŋ] *adj.* □ **1.** gleitend; **2.** Schiebe...: *~ door*, *~ fit s.* ⊗ Gleitsitz *m*; *~ roof s. mot.* Schiebedach *n*; *~ rule* → *slide rule*; *~ scale s.* ✝ **1.** gleitende (Lohn- *od.* Preis)Skala; **2.** 'Staffelta‚rif *m*; *~ seat s. Rudern*: Gleit-, Rollsitz *m*; *~ ta·ble s.* Ausziehtisch *m*; *~ time s.* ✝ *Am.* Gleitzeit *f*.

slight [slaɪt] **I** *adj.* □ → *slightly*; **1.** schmächtig, dünn; **2.** schwach (*Konstruktion*); **3.** leicht, schwach (*Geruch etc.*); **4.** leicht, gering(fügig), unbedeutend: *a ~ increase*; *not the ~est doubt* nicht der geringste Zweifel; **5.** schwach, gering (*Intelligenz etc.*); **6.** flüchtig, oberflächlich (*Bekanntschaft etc.*); **II** *v/t.* **7.** j-n kränken; **8.** *et.* auf die leichte Schulter nehmen; **III** *s.* **9.** Kränkung *f*; **'slight·ing** [-tɪŋ] *adj.* □ abschätzig, kränkend; **'slight·ly** [-lɪ] *adv.* leicht, schwach, etwas, ein bisschen; **'slight·ness** [-nɪs] *s.* **1.** Geringfügigkeit *f*; **2.** Schmächtigkeit *f*; **3.** Schwäche *f*.

sli·ly ['slaɪlɪ] *adv. von* **sly**.

slim [slɪm] **I** *adj.* □ **1.** schlank, dünn; **2.** *fig.* gering, dürftig, schwach: *a ~ chance*; **3.** schlau, gerieben; **II** *v/t.* **4.**

---

schlank(er) machen; **5.** *~ down* F *fig.* ,abspecken', *a.* gesundschrumpfen; **III** *v/i.* **6.** schlank(er) werden; **7.** e-e Schlankheitskur machen; **'slim·down** *s. fig.* ,Schlankheitskur' *f*, Gesundschrumpfung *f*.

slime [slaɪm] **I** *s.* **1.** *bsd.* ⍾, *zo.* Schleim *m*; **2.** Schlamm *m*; *fig.* Schmutz *m*; **II** *v/t.* **3.** mit Schlamm *od.* Schleim über'ziehen *od.* bedecken; **'slim·i·ness** [-mɪnɪs] *s.* **1.** Schleimigkeit *f*, das Schleimige; **2.** Schlammigkeit *f*.

'slim·line *v/t.* (*v/i.* sich) gesundschrumpfen.

slim·ming ['slɪmɪŋ] **I** *s.* Abnehmen *n*; Schlankheitskur *f*; **II** *adj.* Schlankheits...: *~ cure*, *~ diet*; **'slim·ness** [-mnɪs] *s.* **1.** Schlankheit *f*; **2.** *fig.* Dürftigkeit *f*.

slim·y ['slaɪmɪ] *adj.* □ **1.** schleimig, glitschig; **2.** schlammig; **3.** *fig.* a) ,schleimig', kriecherisch, b) schmierig, schmutzig, c) widerlich, ,fies'.

sling¹ [slɪŋ] **I** *s.* **1.** Schleuder *f*; **2.** (Schleuder)Wurf *m*; **II** *v/t.* [*irr.*] **3.** schleudern; *~ ink* F schriftstellern.

sling² [slɪŋ] **I** *s.* **1.** Schlinge *f zum Heben von Lasten*; **2.** ✚ (Arm)Schlinge *f*, Binde *f*; **3.** Tragriemen *m*; **4.** *mst pl.* ⚓ Stropp *m*, Tauschlinge *f*; **II** *v/t.* [*irr.*] **5.** a) e-e Schlinge legen um *e-e Last*, b) *Last* hochziehen; **6.** aufhängen: *be slung from* hängen *od.* baumeln von; **7.** ✕ *Gewehr* 'umhängen; **8.** ✚ *Arm* in die Schlinge legen.

sling³ [slɪŋ] *s.* Art Punsch *m*.

'sling·shot *s.* **1.** (Stein)Schleuder *f*; **2.** *Am.* Kata'pult *n, m*.

slink [slɪŋk] **I** *v/i.* [*irr.*] **1.** schleichen, sich *wohin* stehlen: *~ off* wegschleichen, sich fortstehlen; **2.** *zo.* fehlgebären, *bsd.* verkalben (*Kuh*); **II** *v/t.* [*irr.*] **3.** *Junges* vor der Zeit werfen, zu früh zur Welt bringen; **'slink·y** [-kɪ] *adj.* **1.** aufreizend; **2.** geschmeidig; **3.** hauteng (*Kleid*).

slip [slɪp] **I** *s.* **1.** (Aus)Gleiten *n*, (-)Rutschen *n*; Fehltritt *m* (*a. fig.*); **2.** *fig.* (Flüchtigkeits)Fehler *m*, Schnitzer *m*, Lapsus *m*: *~ of the pen* Schreibfehler *m*; *~ of the tongue* ,Versprecher' *m*; *it was a ~ of the tongue* ich habe mich (er hat sich *etc.*) versprochen; **3.** *fig.* ,Panne' *f*: a) Missgeschick *n*, b) Fehler *m*, Fehlleistung *f*; **4.** 'Unterkleid *n*, -rock *m*; **5.** (Kissen)Bezug *m*; **6.** (Hunde)Leine *f*, Koppel *f*: *give s.o. the ~ fig.* j-m entwischen; **7.** ⚓ (Schlipp)Helling *f*; **8.** ⊗ Schlupf *m* (*Nachbleiben der Drehzahl*); **9.** *geol.* Erdrutsch *m*; **10.** ⍾ Pfropfreis *n*, Setzling *m*; **11.** *fig.* Sprössling *m*; **12.** Streifen *m*, Stück *n Holz od.* Papier, Zettel *m*: *a ~ of a boy fig.* ein schmächtiges Bürschchen; *a ~ of a room* ein winziges Zimmer; **13.** (Kon'troll- *etc.*)Abschnitt *m*; **14.** *typ.* Fahne *f*; **15.** *Kricket*: Eckmann *m*; **II** *v/i.* **16.** gleiten, rutschen: *~ from* der Hand, *a.* dem Gedächtnis entgleiten; **17.** sich (hoch- *etc.*)schieben, (ver)rutschen; **18.** sich lösen (*Knoten*); **19.** wohin schlüpfen: *~ away* a) *a. ~ off* entschlüpfen, -wischen, sich davonstehlen, b) *~ by* verstreichen (*Tage, Zeit*); *~ in* sich einschleichen (*a. fig.* Fehler *etc.*), hineinschlüpfen; *~ into* in *ein Kleid, Zimmer etc.* schlüpfen *od.* gleiten; *let an opportunity ~* sich e-e Gelegenheit entgehen lassen; **20.** *a.* F *~ up* e-n Fehler machen, sich vertun: *he is ~ping* F er lässt nach; **III** *v/t.* **21.** *Gegenstand, et.* wohin gleiten lassen, *(bsd.* heimlich) *wohin* stecken *od.* schieben:

~ s.o. s.th. j-m et. zustecken; *~ in* a) *et.* hineingleiten lassen, b) *Bemerkung* einfließen lassen; **22.** *Ring, Kleid etc.* 'über- *od.* abstreifen: *~ on* (*off*); **23.** j-m entwischen; **24.** j-s Aufmerksamkeit entgehen: *have ~ped s.o.'s memory* (*od. mind*) j-m entfallen sein; **25.** *et.* fahren lassen; **26.** a) *Hundehalsband, a. Fessel etc.* abstreifen, b) *Hund etc.* loslassen; **27.** *Knoten* lösen; **28.** → *slink* 3; *~ case s.* **1.** ('Bücher)Kas‚sette *f*; **2.** → *~ cov·er s.* Schutzhülle *f* (*für Bücher*); Schonbezug *m* (*für Möbel*); *~ knot s.* Laufknoten *m*; *~ on* **I** *s.* Kleidungsstück *n* zum 'Überstreifen, *bsd.* a) 'Slip-on *m* (*Mantel*), b) Pull'over *m*, c) Slipper *m*; **II** *adj.* a) Umhänge..., Überzieh..., b) ⊗ Aufsteck...

slip·per ['slɪpə] **I** *s.* **1.** a) Pan'toffel *m*, b) Slipper *m* (*leichter Haus- od. Straßenschuh*); **2.** ⊗ Hemmschuh *m*; **II** *v/t.* **3.** mit e-m Pantoffel schlagen.

slip·per·i·ness ['slɪpərɪnɪs] *s.* **1.** Schlüpfrigkeit *f*; **2.** *fig.* Gerissenheit *f*; **slip·per·y** ['slɪpərɪ] *adj.* □ **1.** schlüpfrig, glatt, glitschig; **2.** *fig.* gerissen (*Person*); **3.** *fig.* zweifelhaft, unsicher; **4.** *fig.* heikel (*Thema*); **slip·py** ['slɪpɪ] *adj.* F **1.** → *slippery* 1; **2.** fix, flink: *look ~!* mach fix!

slip| ring *s.* ⚡ Schleifring *m*; *~ road s. Brit.* (Autobahn)Zubringerstraße *f*; *'~·shod adj.* schlampig, schludrig; *'~·slop s.* F labberiges Zeug (*Getränk*; *a. fig.* leeres Gewäsch); *~ sole s.* Einlegesohle *f*; *'~·stick s. Am.* Rechenschieber *m*; *'~·stream s.* **1.** ✈ Luftschraubenstrahl *m*; **2.** *sport* Windschatten *m*; *'~·up s.* → *slip* 2, 3; *'~·way s.* ⚓ Helling *f*.

slit [slɪt] **I** *v/t.* [*irr.*] **1.** aufschlitzen, -schneiden; **2.** zerschlitzen; **3.** spalten; **4.** ritzen; **II** *v/i.* [*irr.*] **5.** reißen, schlitzen, e-n Riss bekommen; **III** *s.* **6.** Schlitz *m*; *'~·eyed adj.* schlitzäugig.

slith·er ['slɪðə] *v/i.* **1.** schlittern, rutschen, gleiten; **2.** (schlangenartig) gleiten; **'slith·er·y** [-ðərɪ] *adj.* schlüpfrig.

sliv·er ['slɪvə] **I** *s.* **1.** Splitter *m*, Span *m*; **2.** *Spinnerei*: a) Kammzug *m*, b) Florband *n*; **II** *v/t.* **3.** *Span etc.* abspalten; **4.** zersplittern; **III** *v/i.* **5.** zersplittern.

slob [slɒb] *s.* **1.** *bsd. Ir.* Schlamm *m*; **2.** *sl.* a) ,fieser Typ', b) ordi'närer Kerl, c) ,Blödmann' *m*.

slob·ber ['slɒbə] **I** *v/i.* **1.** geifern, sabbern; **2.** *~ over fig.* kindisch schwärmen von; **II** *v/t.* **3.** begeifern, -sabbern; **4.** j-n abküssen; **III** *s.* **5.** Geifer *m*; **6.** *fig.* sentimen'tales Gewäsch; **'slob·ber·y** [-ərɪ] *adj.* **1.** sabbernd; **2.** besabbert; **3.** *fig.* gefühlsduselig; **4.** schlampig.

sloe [sləʊ] *s.* ⍾ **1.** Schlehe *f*; **2.** *a. ~ bush*, *~ tree* Schleh-, Schwarzdorn *m*; *'~·worm* → *slowworm*.

slog [slɒg] F **I** *v/t.* **1.** hart schlagen; **2.** (ver)prügeln; **II** *v/i.* **3.** *~ on*, *~ away* a) sich da'hinschleppen, b) sich ,'durchbeißen'; **4.** *a. ~ away* sich plagen, schuften; **III** *s.* **5.** harter Schlag; **6.** Schinde'rei *f*: *a long ~* e-e ,Durststrecke'.

slo·gan ['sləʊgən] *s.* **1.** *Scot.* Schlachtruf *m*; **2.** Slogan *m*: a) Schlagwort *n*, b) ✝ Werbespruch *m*.

slog·ger ['slɒgə] *s.* **1.** *sport* harter Schläger; **2.** *fig.* ,Arbeitstier' *m*.

sloop [sluːp] *s.* ⚓ Scha'luppe *f*.

slop¹ [slɒp] **I** *s.* **1.** Pfütze *f*; **2.** *pl.* a) Spülwasser *n*, b) Schmutzwasser *n*; **3.** Schweinetrank *m*; **4.** *pl.* a) (Kranken)süppchen *n*, b) ,labberiges Zeug', ,Spülwasser' *n*; **5.** F rührseliges Zeug,

II *v/t.* **6.** (ver)schütten; **7.** *a.* ~ *up* geräuschvoll essen *od.* trinken; **III** *v/i.* **8.** ~ *over* 'überschwappen; **9.** ~ *over* F kindisch schwärmen; **10.** patschen, waten; **11.** *a.* ~ *around* ,her'umhängen, -schlurfen'.

slop² [slɒp] *s.* **1.** Kittel *m*, lose Jacke; **2.** *pl.* (billige) Konfekti'onskleider *pl.*; **3.** ♣ ,Kla'motten' *pl.* (*Kleidung u. Bettzeug*).

slop ba·sin *s.* Schale *f* für Tee- *od.* Kaffeereste.

slope [sləʊp] **I** *s.* **1.** (Ab)Hang *m*; **2.** Böschung *f*; **3.** a) Neigung *f*, Gefälle *n*, b) Schräge *f*, geneigte Ebene: *on the* ~ schräg, abfallend; **4.** *geol.* Senke *f*; **5.** *at the* ~ ✕ mit Gewehr über; **II** *v/i.* **6.** sich neigen; (schräg) abfallen; **III** *v/t.* **7.** neigen, senken; **8.** abschrägen (*a.* ◉); **9.** schräg legen; **10.** (ab)böschen; **11.** ✕ *Gewehr* 'übernehmen; **12.** F a) ~ *off* ,abhauen', b) ~ *around* her'umschlendern; '**slop·ing** [-pɪŋ] *adj.* □ schräg, abfallend; ansteigend.

slop pail *s.* Toi'letteneimer *m*.

slop·pi·ness ['slɒpɪnɪs] *s.* **1.** Matschigkeit *f*; **2.** Matsch *m*; **3.** Schlampigkeit *f*; **4.** F Rührseligkeit *f*; '**slop·py** ['slɒpɪ] *adj.* □ **1.** matschig (*Boden etc.*); **2.** nass, bespritzt (*Tisch etc.*); **3.** *fig.* labberig (*Speisen*); **4.** schlampig, nachlässig (*Arbeit etc.*), sa'lopp (*Sprache*); **5.** rührselig.

'**slop·shop** *s. Laden mit billiger Konfektionsware.*

slosh [slɒʃ] **I** *s.* **1.** → *slush* 1 *u.* 2; **II** *v/i.* **2.** im (Schmutz)Wasser her'umpatschen; **3.** schwappen; **III** *v/t.* **4.** bespritzen: ~ *on Farbe etc.* a) draufklatschen, b) klatschen auf (*acc.*); **5.** *Bier im Glas etc.* schwenken; **6.** *a.* ~ *down* F *Bier etc.* ,hin'unterschütten'; '**sloshed** [-ʃt] *adj. sl.* ,besoffen'.

slot¹ [slɒt] **I** *s.* **1.** Schlitz(einwurf) *m*; Spalte *f*; **2.** ◉ Nut *f*: ~ *and key* Nut u. Feder (*Metall*); **3.** F (freie) Stelle, Platz *m*: *find a* ~ *for* (*in*) → 5; **II** *v/t.* **4.** ◉ nuten, schlitzen: ~*ting machine* Nutenstoßmaschine *f*; **5.** F *j-n od. et.* 'unterbringen (*into* in *dat.*); **III** *v/i.* **6.** ~ *into* F *a. fig.* (hin'ein)passen in (*acc.*).

slot² [slɒt] *s. hunt.* Spur *f*.

sloth [sləʊθ] *s.* **1.** Faulheit *f*; **2.** *zo.* Faultier *n*; '**sloth·ful** [-fʊl] *adj.* □ faul, träge.

slot ma·chine *s.* ('Waren-, 'Spiel)Auto·mat *m*.

slouch [slaʊtʃ] **I** *s.* **1.** krumme, nachlässige Haltung; **2.** latschiger Gang; **3.** a) her'abhängende Hutkrempe, b) → *slouch hat*; **4.** F ,Flasche' *f*, ,Niete' *f* (*Nichtskönner*): *he is no* ~ ,er ist auf Draht'; *the show is no* ~ das Stück ist nicht ohne; **II** *v/i.* **5.** krumm dasitzen *od.* -stehen; **6.** *a.* ~ *along* latschen, latschig gehen; **7.** her'abhängen (*Krempe*); **III** *v/t.* **8.** *Schultern* hängen lassen; **9.** *Krempe* her'unterbiegen; **slouch hat** *s.* Schlapphut *m*; '**slouch·ing** [-tʃɪŋ] *adj.* □, '**slouch·y** [-tʃɪ] *adj.* □ **1.** krumm (*Haltung*); latschig (*Gang, Haltung, Person*); **2.** her'abhängend (*Krempe*); **3.** lax, faul.

slough¹ [slaʊ] *s.* **1.** Sumpf-, Schmutzloch *n*; **2.** Mo'rast *m* (*a. fig.*): ♫ *of Despond* Sumpf *m* der Verzweiflung.

slough² [slʌf] **I** *s.* **1.** abgestreifte Haut (*bsd. Schlange*); **2.** ♣ Schorf *m*; **II** *v/i.* **3.** *oft* ~ *away* (*od.* *off*) sich häuten; **4.** sich ablösen (*Schorf etc.*); **III** *v/t.* **5.** *a.* ~ *off* *Haut etc.* abstreifen, -werfen; *fig. Gewohnheit etc.* ablegen; '**slough·y** [-fɪ] *adj.* ♣ schorfig.

Slo·vak ['sləʊvæk], **Slo'vak·i·an** [-ɪən] **I** *adj.* **1.** slo'wakisch; **II** *s.* **2.** Slo'wake *m*, Slo'wakin *f*; **3.** *ling.* Slo'wakisch *n*, das Slo'wakische.

slov·en ['slʌvn] *s.* a) Schlamper *m*, b) Schlampe *f*.

Slo·ve·ni·an [sləʊ'viːnɪən] **I** *adj.* **1.** slo'wenisch; **II** *s.* **2.** Slo'wene *m*, Slo'wenin *f*; **3.** *ling.* Slo'wenisch *n*, das Slo'wenische.

'**slov·en·ly** ['slʌvnlɪ] *adj. u. adv.* schlampig, schlud(e)rig.

slow [sləʊ] **I** *adj.* □ **1.** *allg.* langsam: ~ *and sure* langsam, aber sicher; ~ *train* 🚆 Personenzug *m*; *be* ~ *in arriving* lange ausbleiben, auf sich warten lassen; *be* ~ *to write* sich mit dem Schreiben Zeit lassen; *be* ~ *to take offence* nicht leicht et. übel nehmen; *not to be* ~ *to do s.th.* et. prompt tun, nicht lange mit et. fackeln; *the clock is 20 minutes* ~ die Uhr geht 20 Minuten nach; **2.** all'mählich, langsam: ~ *growth*; **3.** säumig (*a. Zahler*); unpünktlich; **4.** schwach (*Feuer*); **5.** schleichend (*Fieber, Gift*); **6.** ♥ schleppend, schlecht (*Geschäft*); **7.** schwerfällig, schwer von Begriff, begriffsstutzig: *be* ~ *in learning* et. nur schwer lernen; *be* ~ *of speech* e-e schwere Zunge haben; **8.** langweilig, fad(e), ,müde'; **9.** langsam (*Rennbahn*); schwer (*Boden*); **10.** *mot.* Leerlauf...; **II** *adv.* **11.** langsam: *go* ~ *fig.* a) ,langsam treten', b) ♥ e-n Bummelstreik machen; **III** *v/t.* **12.** *mst* ~ *down* (*od.* *off*, *up*) a) *Geschwindigkeit* verlangsamen, verringern, b) *et.* verzögern; **IV** *v/i.* **13.** ~ *down od. up* sich verlangsamen, langsamer werden, *fig.* ,langsamer tun'; '~-,**burn·ing stove** *s.* Dauerbrandofen *m*; '~-**coach** *s. contp.* ,Schlafmütze' *f*; '~-**down** *s.* **1.** Verlangsamung *f*; **2.** *Am.* Bummelstreik *m*; ~ **lane** *s. mot.* Kriechspur *f*; ~ **march** *s.* ♪ Trauermarsch *m*; ~ **match** *s.* ✕ Zündschnur *f*, Lunte *f*; ~ **mo·tion** *s.* Zeitlupentempo *n*; ,~-'**mo·tion** *adj.* Zeitlupen...: ~ *picture* Zeitlupe(naufnahme) *f*.

slow·ness ['sləʊnɪs] *s.* **1.** Langsamkeit *f*; **2.** Schwerfälligkeit *f*, Begriffsstutzigkeit *f*; **3.** Langweiligkeit *f*, ,Lahmheit' *f*.

'**slow|·poke** *Am.* F Langweiler *m*; ,~-'**speed** *adj.* ◉ langsam (laufend); ~ **train** *s.* Bummel-, Per'sonenzug *m*; ,~--'**wit·ted** *adj.* → *slow* 7; '~-**worm** *s. zo.* Blindschleiche *f*.

sloyd [slɔɪd] *s. ped.* 'Werk,unterricht *m* (*bsd. Schnitzen*).

sludge [slʌdʒ] *s.* **1.** Schlamm *m*, (*a.* Schnee)Matsch *m*; **2.** ◉ Schlamm *m*, Bodensatz *m*; **3.** Klärschlamm *m*; **4.** Treibeis *n*; '**sludg·y** [-dʒɪ] *adj.* schlammig, matschig.

slue [sluː] → *slew³ u. slew⁴*.

slug¹ [slʌg] **I** *s. zo.* **1.** (Weg)Schnecke *f*; **2.** F Faulpelz *m*; **II** *v/i.* **3.** faulenzen.

slug² [slʌg] *s.* **1.** Stück *n* 'Rohme,tall; **2.** a) *hist.* Mus'ketenkugel *f*, b) grobes Schrot, c) (Luftgewehr-, *Am.* Pi'stolen-)Kugel *f*; **3.** *Am.* a) falsche Münze, b) Gläs-chen *n Schnaps etc.*; **4.** *typ.* a) Reglette *f*, b) 'Setzma,schinenzeile *f*, c) Zeilenguss *m*; **5.** *phys.* Masseneinheit *f*.

slug³ [slʌg] **I** *bsd. Am.* harter Schlag **II** *v/t. j-m* ,ein Ding verpassen'.

slug·a·bed ['slʌɡəbed] *s.* Langschläfer(in).

slug·gard ['slʌɡəd] **I** *s.* Faulpelz *m*; **II** *adj.* □ faul.

slug·ger ['slʌɡə] *s. Am.* F *Baseball*, Bo-

---

xen: harter Schläger.

slug·gish ['slʌɡɪʃ] *adj.* □ **1.** träge (*a.* ♣ *Organ*), langsam, schwerfällig; **2.** ✝ *etc.* schleppend; **3.** träge fließend (*Fluss etc.*); '**slug·gish·ness** [-nɪs] *s.* Trägheit *f*, Langsamkeit *f*, Schwerfälligkeit *f*.

sluice [sluːs] **I** *s.* ◉ **1.** Schleuse *f* (*a. fig.*); **2.** Stauwasser *n*; **3.** 'Schleusen·ka,nal *m*; **4.** *min.* (Erz-, Gold)Waschrinne *f*; **II** *v/t.* **5.** *Wasser* ablassen; **6.** *min. Erz etc.* waschen; **7.** (aus)spülen; **III** *v/i.* **8.** (aus)strömen; ~ **gate** *s.* Schleusentor *n*; '~-**way** → *sluice* 3.

slum [slʌm] **I** *s.* **1.** schmutzige Gasse; **2.** *mst pl.* Slums *pl.*, Elendsviertel *n*; **II** *v/i.* **3.** *mst go* ~**ming** die Slums aufsuchen (*bsd. aus Neugierde*); **4.** in primi'tiven Verhältnissen leben; **III** *v/t.* **5.** ~ *it* → 4.

slum·ber ['slʌmbə] **I** *v/i.* **1.** *bsd. poet.* schlummern (*a. fig.*); **2.** da'hindösen; **II** *v/t.* **3.** ~ *away Zeit* verschlafen; **III** *s. mst pl.* **4.** (*fig.* tiefer) Schlummer; '**slum·ber·ous** [-bərəs] *adj.* □ **1.** schläfrig; **2.** einschläfernd.

slump [slʌmp] **I** *v/i.* **1.** (hin'ein)plumpsen; **2.** *mst* ~ *down* (in sich) zs.-sacken (*Person*); **3.** ✝ stürzen (*Preise*); **4.** völlig versagen; **II** *s.* **5.** ✝ a) (Börsen-, Preis)Sturz *m*, Baisse *f*, b) starker Konjunk'turrückgang, Wirtschaftskrise *f*; **6.** *allg.* plötzlicher Rückgang.

slung [slʌŋ] *pret. u. p.p. von* **sling**.

slung shot *s. Am.* Schleudergeschoss, *östr.* -geschoß *n*.

slunk [slʌŋk] *pret. u. p.p. von* **slink**.

slur¹ [slɜː] **I** *v/t.* **1.** verunglimpfen, verleumden; **II** *s.* **2.** Makel *m* (Schand-) Fleck *m*: *put od. cast a* ~ (*up*)*on* a) → 1, b) *j-s Ruf etc.* schädigen; **3.** Verunglimpfung *f*.

slur² [slɜː] **I** *v/t.* **1.** a) undeutlich schreiben, b) *typ.* schmitzen, verwischen; **2.** undeutlich aussprechen; *Silbe etc.* verschleifen, -schlucken; **3.** ♪ a) *Töne* binden, b) *Noten* mit Bindebogen bezeichnen; **4.** *oft* ~ *over* (leicht) über *ein Thema* hin'weggehen; **II** *v/i.* **5.** undeutlich schreiben *od.* sprechen; **6.** ♪ le'gato singen *od.* spielen; **III** *s.* **7.** Undeutlichkeit *f*, ,Genuschel' *n*; **8.** ♪ a) Bindung *f*, b) Bindebogen *m*; **9.** *typ.* Schmitz *m*.

slurp [slɜːp] *v/t. u. v/i.* schlürfen.

slush [slʌʃ] *s.* **1.** Schneematsch *m*; **2.** Schlamm *m*, Matsch *m*; **3.** ◉ Schmiere *f*, Rostschutzmittel *n*; **4.** ◉ Pa'pierbrei *m*; **5.** *fig.* Gefühlsduse'lei *f*; **6.** *fig.* Kitsch *m*, Schund *m*; **II** *v/t.* **7.** bespritzen; **8.** ◉ schmieren; **III** *v/i.* **9.** → *slosh* 2 *u.* 3; **slush fund** *s. pol. Am.* Schmiergelderfonds *m*; '**slush·y** [-ʃɪ] *adj.* **1.** matschig, schlammig; **2.** rührselig, kitschig.

slut [slʌt] *s.* **1.** Schlampe *f*; **2.** Hure *f*, ,Nutte' *f*; **3.** *humor.* ,kleines Luder' (*Mädchen*); **4.** *Am.* Hündin *f*; '**slut·tish** [-tɪʃ] *adj.* □ schlampig, liederlich.

sly [slaɪ] *adj.* □ **1.** schlau, verschlagen, listig; **2.** verstohlen, heimlich, 'hinterhältig: *a* ~ *dog* ein ganz Schlauer; *on the* ~ ,klammheimlich'; **3.** durch'trieben, pfiffig; '**sly·boots** *s. humor.* Pfiffikus *m*, Schlauberger *m*; '**sly·ness** [-nɪs] *s.* Schlauheit *f etc.*

smack¹ [smæk] **I** *s.* **1.** (Bei)Geschmack *m* (*of* von); **2.** Prise *f Salz etc.*; **3.** *fig.* Beigeschmack *m*, Anflug *m* (*of* von); **II** *v/i.* **4.** schmecken (*of* nach); **5.** *fig.* schmecken *od.* riechen (*of* nach).

smack² [smæk] **I** *s.* **1.** Klatsch *m*, Klaps *m*: *a* ~ *in the eye fig.* a) ein Schlag ins Gesicht, b) ein Schlag ins Kontor; **2.** Schmatzen *n*; **3.** (*Peitschen- etc.*)Knall *m*; **4.** Schmatz *m* (*Kuss*); **II** *v/t.* **5.** *et.*

schmatzend genießen; **6.** **~** *one's lips* a) (mit den Lippen) schmatzen, b) sich die Lippen lecken; **7.** *Hände etc.* zs.-schlagen; **8.** mit *der Peitsche* knallen; **9.** *j-m* e-n Klaps geben; **10.** *et.* hinklatschen; **III** *v/i.* **11.** schmatzen; **12.** knallen (*Peitsche etc.*); **13.** (hin)klatschen (*on* auf *acc.*); **IV** *adv. u. int.* **14.** F a) klatsch(!), platsch(!), b) ,zack', di'rekt: *run* **~** *into s.th.*

smack³ [smæk] *s.* ♣ Schmack(e) *f.*

smack·er ['smækə] *s.* **1.** F Schmatz *m* (*Kuss*); **2.** *sl.* a) *Brit.* Pfund *n*, b) *Am.* Dollar *m*; **'smack·ing** [-kɪŋ] *s.* Tracht *f* Prügel.

small [smɔːl] **I** *adj.* **1.** *allg.* klein; **2.** klein, schmächtig; **3.** klein, gering (*Anzahl, Ausdehnung, Grad etc.*): *they came in* **~** *numbers* es kamen nur wenige; **4.** klein, armselig, dürftig; **5.** wenig: **~** *blame to him* das macht ihm kaum Schande; **~** *wonder* kein Wunder; *have* **~** *cause for* kaum Anlass zu *Dankbarkeit etc.* haben; **6.** klein, mit wenig Besitz: **~** *farmer* Kleinbauer *m*; **7.** klein, (sozi'al) niedrig: **~** *people* kleine Leute; **8.** klein, unbedeutend: *a* **~** *man*; *a* **~** *poet*; **9.** trivi'al, klein: *the* **~** *worries* die kleinen Sorgen: *a* **~** *matter* e-e Kleinigkeit; **10.** klein, bescheiden: *a* **~** *beginning*; *in a* **~** *way* a) bescheiden *leben etc.*, b) im Kleinen handeln *etc.*; **11.** *contp.* kleinlich; **12.** *b.s.* niedrig (*Gesinnung etc.*): *feel* **~** sich schämen; *make s.o. feel* **~** *j-n* beschämen; **13.** dünn (*Bier*); **14.** schwach (*Stimme, Puls*); **II** *s.* **15.** schmal(st)er *od.* verjüngter Teil: **~** *of the back anat.* das Kreuz; **16.** *pl. Brit.* F 'Unterwäsche *f*, Taschentücher *pl. etc.*; **~** *arms s. pl.* ✗ Hand(feuer)waffen *pl.*; **~** *beer s.* **1.** *obs.* Dünnbier *n*; **2.** *bsd. Brit.* F a) Lap'palie *f*, b) ,Null' *f*, unbedeutende Per'son: *think no* **·** *of o.s.* F e-e hohe Meinung von sich haben; **~** *cap·i·tals s. pl. typ.* Kapi'tälchen *pl.*; **~** *change s.* **1.** Kleingeld *n*; **2.** → *small beer* 2; **'~·clothes** *s.* **1.** *pl. hist.* Kniehosen *pl.*; **2.** 'Unterwäsche *f*; **3.** Kinderkleidung *f*; **~** *coal s.* Feinkohle *f*, Grus *m*; **~** *fry s.* **1.** junge, kleine Fische *pl.*; **2.** ,junges Gemüse', *die Kleinen pl.*; **3.** → *small beer* 2; **'~·hold·er** *s. Brit.* Kleinbauer *m*; **'~·hold·ing** *s. Brit.* Kleinlandbesitz *m*; **~** *hours s. pl.* die frühen Morgenstunden *pl.*

small·ish ['smɔːlɪʃ] *adj.* ziemlich klein.

small| let·ter *s.* Kleinbuchstabe *m*; **'~--'mind·ed** *adj.* engstirnig, kleinlich, ,kleinkariert'.

small·ness ['smɔːlnɪs] *s.* **1.** Kleinheit *f*; **2.** geringe Anzahl; **3.** Geringfügigkeit *f*; **4.** Kleinlichkeit *f*; **5.** niedrige Gesinnung.

small| pi·ca *s. typ.* kleine Cicero (-schrift); **'~·pox** [-pɒks] *s.* ✿ Pocken *pl.*, Blattern *pl.*; **~** *print s.* das Kleingedruckte *e-s Vertrags*; **~** *shot s.* Schrot *m, n*; **'~·sword** *s. fenc.* Flo'rett *n*; **~** *talk s.* oberflächliche Konversati'on, Geplauder *n*: *he has no* **~** er kann nicht (unverbindlich) plaudern; **'~·time** *adj. Am. sl.* unbedeutend, klein, ,Schmalspur...'; **'~·ware** *s.* Kurzwaren *pl.*

smalt [smɔːlt] *s.* **1.** ✿ S(ch)malte *f*, Kobaltblau *n*; **2.** Kobaltglas *n*.

smar·agd ['smæræɡd] *s. min.* Sma'ragd *m.*

smarm·ball ['smɑːm-] *s.* F Schleimer *m.*

smarm·y ['smɑːmɪ] *adj.* □ *Brit.* F **1.** ölig; **2.** kriecherisch; **3.** kitschig.

smart [smɑːt] **I** *adj.* □ **1.** klug, gescheit, intelli'gent, pa'tent; **2.** geschickt, ge-

wandt; **3.** geschäftstüchtig; **4.** *b.s.* gerissen, raffiniert; **5.** witzig, geistreich; **6.** *contp.* ,superklug', ,klugscheißerisch'; **7.** flink, fix; **8.** schmuck, gepflegt; **9.** a) ele'gant, fesch, schick, b) modisch (*Person, Kleidung, Wort etc.*): *the* **~** *set* die elegante Welt, die ,Schickeria'; **10.** forsch, schneidig: **~** *pace*; *salute* **~***ly* zackig grüßen; **11.** hart, empfindlich (*Schlag, Strafe*); **12.** scharf (*Schmerz, Kritik etc.*); **13.** F beträchtlich; **II** *v/i.* **14.** schmerzen, brennen; **15.** leiden (*from, under* unter *dat.*): *he* **~***ed under the insult* die Kränkung nagte an s-m Herzen; **III** *s.* **16.** Schmerz *m*; **smart al·eck** ['ælɪk] *s.* F ,Klugscheißer' *m*; **'smart-,al·eck·y** [-kɪ] → *smart* 6; **'smart·card** *s.* 'Smartcard *f*, (*intelligente*) 'Chipkarte; **'smart·en** [-tn] **I** *v/t.* **1.** *a.* **~** *up* her'ausputzen; **2.** *fig. j-n* ,auf Zack' bringen; **II** *v/i. mst* **~** *up* **3.** sich schönmachen, sich ,in Schale werfen'; **4.** *fig.* aufwachen; **'smart-,mon·ey** *s.* Schmerzensgeld *n*; **'smart·ness** [-nɪs] *s.* **1.** Klugheit *f*, Gescheitheit *f*; **2.** Gewandtheit *f*; **3.** *b.s.* Gerissenheit *f*; **4.** flotte Ele'ganz, Schick *m*; **5.** Forschheit *f*; **6.** Schärfe *f*, Heftigkeit *f*; **'smart·phone** *s. teleph.* 'Smartphone *n* (*internetfähiges Handy*); **'smart·y** [-tɪ] → *smart aleck.*

smash [smæʃ] **I** *v/t.* **1.** *oft* **~** *up* zertrümmern, -schmettern, -schlagen; **~** *in* einschlagen; **2.** *j-n* (zs.-)schlagen; *Feind* vernichtend schlagen; *fig. Argument* restlos wider'legen, *Gegner* ,fertig machen'; **3.** *j-n* (finanzi'ell) ruinieren; **4.** *Faust, Stein etc. wohin* schmettern; **5.** *Tennis: Ball* schmettern; **II** *v/i.* **6.** zersplittern, in Stücke springen; **7.** krachen, knallen (*against* gegen, *through* durch); **8.** zs.-stoßen, -krachen (*Autos etc.*); ✈ Bruch machen; **9.** a) *oft* **~** *up* ,zs.-krachen', Bank'rott gehen, b) zu-'schanden werden, c) (gesundheitlich) ka'puttgehen; **III** *adv.* (*a. int.*) **10.** krachend, krach(!); **IV** *s.* **11.** Zerkrachen *n*; **12.** Krach *m*; **13.** (*a. finanzi'eller*) Zs.-bruch, Ru'in *m*: *go* **~** a) völlig zs.-brechen, ,kaputtgehen', b) → 9; **14.** F voller Erfolg; **15.** *Tennis:* Schmetterball *m*; **16.** *kaltes Branntweinmischgetränk*; **smash-and-'grab raid** [-ʃn'ɡ-] *s.* Schaufenstereinbruch *m*; **smashed** [-ʃt] *adj. sl.* **1.** ,blau', besoffen; **2.** ,high' (*unter Drogeneinfluss*); **'smasher** [-ʃə] *s. sl.* **1.** schwerer Schlag (*a. fig.*); **2.** vernichtendes Argu'ment; **3.** ,Wucht' *f*: a) ,tolle Sache', b) ,tolle Person': *a* **~** (*of a girl*) ein tolles Mädchen; **smash hit** *s.* F Schlager *m*, Bombenerfolg *m*; **'smash·ing** [-ʃɪŋ] *adj.* **1.** F ,toll', sagenhaft; **2.** vernichtend (*Schlag, Niederlage*); **'smash-up** *s.* **1.** völliger Zs.-bruch; **2.** Bank'rott *m*; **3.** *mot. etc.* Zs.-stoß *m*; **4.** ✈ Bruch(landung *f*) *m.*

smat·ter·er ['smætərə] *s.* Stümper *m*, Halbwisser *m*; Dilet'tant *m*; **'smat·ter·ing** [-tərɪŋ] *s.* oberflächliche Kenntnis: *he has a* **~** *of French* er kann ein bisschen Französisch.

smear [smɪə] **I** *v/t.* **1.** *Fett etc.* schmieren (*on* auf *acc.*); **2.** *et.* beschmieren, bestreichen (*with* mit); **3.** (ein)schmieren; **4.** *Schrift* verschmieren; **5.** beschmieren, besudeln; **6.** *fig.* a) *j-s Ruf etc.* besudeln, b) *j-n* verleumden, ,durch den Dreck ziehen'; **7.** *sport Am.* F ,über'fahren'; **II** *v/i.* **8.** schmieren; **9.** sich verwischen; **III** *s.* **10.** Schmiere *f*; **11.** (Fett-, Schmutz)Fleck *m*; **12.** *fig.* Besudelung *f*; **13.** ✿ Abstrich *m*; *fig.*

cam·paign *s. pol.* Ver'leumdungskam-,pagne *f*; **'~·case** *s. Am.* Quark *m*; **sheet** *s.* Skan'dalblatt *n*; **~** *test s.* ✿ Abstrich *m.*

smear·y ['smɪərɪ] *adj.* □ **1.** schmierig; **2.** verschmiert.

smell [smel] **I** *v/t.* [*irr.*] **1.** *et.* riechen; **2.** *et.* beriechen, riechen an (*dat.*); **3.** *fig. Verrat etc.* wittern; → *rat* 1; **4.** *fig.* sich aufspüren (*a. fig. entdecken, ausschnüffeln*); **II** *v/i.* [*irr.*] **6.** riechen (*at* an *dat.*): **~** *about* (*od. round*) *fig.* herumschnüffeln; **7.** *gut etc.* riechen: *his breath* **~***s* er riecht aus dem Mund; **8.** **~** *of* riechen nach (*a. fig.*); **III** *s.* **9.** Geruch(ssinn) *m*; **10.** Geruch *m*: a) Duft *m*, b) Gestank *m*; **11.** *fig.* Anflug *m*, -strich *m* (*of* von); **12.** *take a* **~** *at s.th. et.* beriechen (*a. fig.*); **'smell·er** [-lə] *s. sl.* **1.** ,Riechkolben' *m* (*Nase*); **2.** Schlag *m* auf die Nase; Sturz *m*; **'smell·y** [-lɪ] *adj.* F übel riechend, muffig: **~** *feet* Schweißfüße.

smelt¹ [smelt] *pl.* **smelts** *coll. a.* **smelt** *s. ichth.* Stint *m.*

smelt² [smelt] *v/t.* **1.** *Erz* (ein)schmelzen, verhütten; **2.** *Kupfer etc.* ausschmelzen.

smelt³ [smelt] *pret. u. p.p. von* **smell.**

smelt·er ['smeltə] *s.* Schmelzer *m*; **'smelt·er·y** [-ərɪ] *s.* Schmelzhütte *f*; **'smelt·ing** [-tɪŋ] *s.* ✿ Verhüttung *f*: **~** *furnace* Schmelzofen *m.*

smile [smaɪl] **I** *v/i.* **1.** lächeln (*a. fig. Sonne etc.*): **~** *at* a) *j-m* zulächeln, b) *et.* belächeln, lächeln über (*acc.*); *come up smiling fig.* die Sache leicht überstehen; **2.** **~** (*up*)*on fig. j-m* lächeln, hold sein: *fortune* **~***d on him*; **II** *v/t.* **3.** **~** *away Tränen etc.* hin'weglächeln; **4.** **~** *approval* (*consent*) beifällig (zustimmend) lächeln; **III** *s.* **5.** Lächeln *n*: *be all* **~***s* (über das ganze Gesicht) strahlen; **6.** *mst pl.* Gunst *f*; **'smil·ing** [-lɪŋ] *adj.* □ **1.** lächelnd (*a. fig. heiter*); **2.** *fig.* huldvoll.

smirch [smɜːtʃ] **I** *v/t.* besudeln (*a. fig.*); **II** *s.* Schmutzfleck *m*; *fig.* Schandfleck *m.*

smirk [smɜːk] **I** *v/i.* affektiert *od.* blöd lächeln, grinsen; **II** *s.* einfältiges Lächeln, Grinsen *n.*

smite [smaɪt] [*irr.*] **I** *v/t.* **1.** *bibl., rhet., a. humor.* schlagen (*a. erschlagen, heimsuchen*): *smitten with the plague* von der Pest befallen; **2.** *j-n* quälen, peinigen (*Gewissen*); **3.** *fig.* packen: *smitten with* von *Begierde etc.* gepackt; **4.** *fig.* hinreißen: *he was smitten with* (*od. by*) *her charms* er war hingerissen von ihrem Charme; *be smitten by* (sinnlos) verliebt sein in (*acc.*); **II** *v/i.* **5.** **~** *upon bsd. fig.* an *das Ohr etc.* schlagen.

smith [smɪθ] *s.* Schmied *m.*

smith·er·eens [,smɪðə'riːnz] *s. pl.* F Fetzen *pl.*, Splitter *pl.*: *smash to* **~** in (tausend) Stücke schlagen.

smith·er·y ['smɪðərɪ] *s.* **1.** Schmiedearbeit *f*; **2.** Schmiedekunst *f.*

smith·y ['smɪðɪ] *s.* Schmiede *f.*

smit·ten ['smɪtn] **I** *p.p. von* **smite**; **II** *adj.* **1.** betroffen, befallen; **2.** (*by*) hingerissen (von), ,verknallt', verliebt (in *acc.*); → *smite* 4.

smock [smɒk] **I** *s.* **1.** (Arbeits)Kittel *m*: **~** *frock Art* Fuhrmannskittel *m*; **2.** Kinderkittel *m*; **II** *v/t.* **3.** *Bluse etc.* smoken, mit Smokarbeit verzieren; **'smock·ing** [-kɪŋ] *s.* Smokarbeit *f* (*Vorgang u. Verzierung*).

smog [smɒɡ] *s.* (*aus* **smoke** *u.* **fog**)

Smog *m*, Dunstglocke *f*; ~ **a·lert** *s.* 'Smoga‚larm *m*; '~·**bound** *adj.* von Smog eingehüllt.

smok·a·ble ['sməʊkəbl] *adj.* rauchbar; **smoke** [sməʊk] **I** *s.* **1.** Rauch *m* (*a.* 🎯, *phys.*): *like* ~ *sl.* wie der Teufel; *no* ~ *without a fire fig.* irgendetwas ist immer dran (*an e-m Gerücht*); **2.** Qualm *m*, Dunst *m*: *end* (*od.* *go up*) *in* ~ *fig.* in nichts zerrinnen, zu Wasser werden; **3.** ⚔ (Tarn)Nebel *m*; **4.** Rauchen *n e-r Zigarre etc.*: *have a* ~ ‚eine' rauchen; **5.** F ‚Glimmstängel' *m*, Zi'garre *f*, Ziga-'rette *f*; **6.** *sl.* a) ‚Hasch' *n*, b) Marihu'ana *n*; **II** *v/i.* **7.** rauchen, qualmen (*Schornstein, Ofen etc.*); **8.** dampfen (*a. Pferd*); **9.** rauchen: *do you* ~?; **III** *v/t.* **10.** *Pfeife etc.* rauchen; **11.** ~ *out* a) ausräuchern (*a. fig.*), b) *fig.* ans Licht bringen; **12.** *Fisch etc.* räuchern; **13.** *Glas etc.* schwärzen; ~ **ball**, ~ **bomb** *s.* Nebel-, Rauchbombe *f*; ~ **con·sum·er** *s. Gerät:* Rauchverzehrer *m*; ~ **de·tec·tor** *s. Gerät:* Rauchmelder *m*; '~·**dried** *adj.* geräuchert; ~ **hel·met** *s.* Rauchmaske *f (Feuerwehr)*.

smoke·less ['sməʊklɪs] *adj.* □ *a.* ⚔ rauchlos.

smok·er ['sməʊkə] *s.* **1.** Raucher(in): ~*'s cough* Raucherhusten *m*; ~*'s heart* ⚕ Nikotinherz *n*; **2.** 🚃 Raucher(abteil *n*) *m*.

smoke| room [rʊm] *s.* Herren-, Rauchzimmer *n*; ~ **screen** *s.* ⚔ Rauch-, Nebelvorhang *m*; *fig.* Tarnung *f*, Nebel *m*; '~·**stack** *s.* ⚓, 🚂, ⚙ Schornstein *m*.

smok·ing ['sməʊkɪŋ] **I** *s.* **1.** Rauchen *n*; **II** *adj.* **2.** Rauch...; **3.** Raucher...; ~ **car**, ~ **com·part·ment** *s.* 🚃 'Raucherab‚teil *n*.

smok·y ['sməʊkɪ] *adj.* □ **1.** qualmend; **2.** dunstig, verräuchert; **3.** rauchig (*a. Stimme*); rauchgrau.

smol·der ['sməʊldə] *Am.* → **smoulder**.

smooch [smuːtʃ] *v/i. sl.* **1.** schmusen, knutschen; **2.** *Brit.* eng um'schlungen tanzen.

smooth [smuːð] **I** *adj.* □ **1.** *allg.* glatt; **2.** glatt, ruhig (*See*): *I am in* ~ *water now fig.* jetzt habe ich es geschafft; **3.** ⚙ ruhig (*Gang*); *mot. a.* zügig (*Fahren, Schalten*); ✈ glatt (*Landung*); **4.** *fig.* glatt, reibungslos: *make things* ~ *for j-m* den Weg ebnen; **5.** fließend, geschliffen (*Rede etc.*); schwungvoll (*Melodie, Stil*); **6.** *fig.* sanft, weich (*Stimme, Ton*); **7.** glatt, gewandt (*Manieren, Person*); *b.s.* aalglatt: *a* ~ *tongue* e-e glatte Zunge; **8.** *Am. sl. a)* fesch, schick, b) ‚sauber', prima; **9.** geschmeidig, nicht klumpig (*Teig etc.*); **10.** lieblich (*Wein*); **II** *adv.* **11.** glatt, ruhig: *things have gone* ~ *with me* bei mir ging alles glatt; **III** *v/t.* **12.** glätten (*a. fig.*): ~ *the way for fig. j-m od. e-r Sache* den Weg ebnen; **13.** besänftigen; **IV** *v/i.* **14.** → **smooth down** 1; *Zssgn mit adv.:*

smooth| a·way *v/t.* Schwierigkeiten *etc.* wegräumen, ‚ausbügeln'; ~ **down I** *v/i.* **1.** sich glätten *od.* beruhigen (*Meer etc.*) (*a. fig.*); **II** *v/t.* **2.** glatt streichen, glätten; **3.** *fig.* besänftigen; **4.** *Streit* schlichten; ~ **out** *v/t.* **1.** *Falte* ausplätten (*from* aus); **2.** → **smooth away**; ~ **o·ver** *v/t.* **1.** *Fehler etc.* bemänteln; **2.** *Streit* schlichten.

'**smooth·|bore** *adj. u. s.* (Gewehr *n*) mit glattem Lauf; '~·**faced** *adj.* **1.** a) bartlos, b) glatt rasiert; **2.** *fig.* glatt, schmeichlerisch; ~ **file** *s.* ⚙ Schlichtfeile *f*.

smooth·ie ['smuːðɪ] *s.* F **1.** ‚dufter Typ';

2. aalglatter Bursche.

smooth·ing| i·ron ['smuːðɪŋ] *s.* Plätt-, Bügeleisen *n*; ~ **plane** *s.* ⚙ Schlichthobel *m*.

smooth·ness ['smuːðnɪs] *s.* **1.** Glätte *f* (*a. fig.*); **2.** Reibungslosigkeit *f* (*a. fig.*); **3.** *fig.* glatter Fluss, Ele'ganz *f e-r Rede etc.*; **4.** Glätte *f*, Gewandtheit *f*; **5.** Sanftheit *f*.

'**smooth-tongued** *adj.* glattzüngig, schmeichlerisch, aalglatt.

smote [sməʊt] *pret. von* **smite**.

smoth·er ['smʌðə] **I** *v/t.* **1.** *j-n, a. Feuer, Rebellion, Ton* ersticken; **2.** *bsd. fig.* über'häufen (*with* mit *Arbeit etc.*): ~ *s.o. with kisses* j-n abküssen; **3.** ~ *in* (*od.* *with*) völlig bedecken mit, einhüllen in (*dat.*); **4.** *oft* ~ *up* Gähnen, Wut *etc., a. Geheimnis etc.* unter'drücken; *Skandal* vertuschen; **II** *v/i.* **5.** ersticken; **6.** *sport* F ‚über'fahren'; **III** *s.* **7.** dicker Qualm; **8.** Dampf-, Dunst-, Staubwolke *f*; **9.** ⚗ (erdrückende) Masse.

smoul·der ['sməʊldə] **I** *v/i.* **1.** glimmen, schwelen (*a. fig. Feindschaft, Rebellion etc.*); **2.** glühen (*a. fig. Augen*); **II** *s.* **3.** schwelendes Feuer.

smudge [smʌdʒ] **I** *s.* **1.** Schmutzfleck *m*, Klecks *m*; **2.** qualmendes Feuer (*gegen Mücken, Frost etc.*); **II** *v/t.* **3.** beschmutzen; **4.** be-, verschmieren, voll klecksen; **5.** *fig. Ruf etc.* besudeln; **III** *v/i.* **6.** schmieren (*Tinte, Papier etc.*); **7.** schmutzig werden; '**smudg·y** [-dʒɪ] *adj.* □ verschmiert, schmierig, schmutzig.

smug [smʌɡ] *adj.* □ **1.** *obs.* schmuck; **2.** geschniegelt u. gebügelt; **3.** selbstgefällig, blasiert.

smug·gle ['smʌɡl] **I** *v/t.* Waren, *a. weitS.* Brief, *j-n etc.* schmuggeln: ~ *in* einschmuggeln; **II** *v/i.* schmuggeln; '**smug·gler** [-lə] *s.* **1.** Schmuggler *m*; **2.** Schmugglerschiff *n*; '**smug·gling** [-lɪŋ] *s.* Schmuggel *m*.

smut [smʌt] **I** *s.* **1.** Ruß-, Schmutzflocke *f od.* -fleck *m*; **2.** *fig.* Zote(n *pl.*) *f*, Schmutz *m*, Schweine'rei(en *pl.*) *f*: *talk* ~ Zoten reißen, ‚schweinigeln'; **3.** ♀ (*bsd.* Getreide)Brand *m*; **II** *v/t.* **4.** beschmutzen; **5.** ♀ brandig machen.

smutch [smʌtʃ] **I** *v/t.* beschmutzen; **II** *s.* schwarzer Fleck.

smut·ty ['smʌtɪ] *adj.* □ **1.** schmutzig, rußig; **2.** *fig.* zotig, ob'szön: ~ *joke* Zote *f*; **3.** ♀ brandig.

snack [snæk] *s.* **1.** a) Imbiss *m*, b) Happen *m*, Bissen *m*; **2.** Anteil *m*: *go* ~*s* teilen; ~ **bar** *s.* Imbissstube *f*.

snaf·fle ['snæfl] **I** *s.* **1.** *a.* ~ *bit* Trense(ngebiss *n*) *f*; **II** *v/t.* **2.** *e-m Pferd* die Trense anlegen; **3.** mit der Trense lenken; **4.** *Brit. sl.* ‚klauen'.

sna·fu [snæ'fuː] *bsd. Am. sl.* **I** *adj.* **1.** a) in heillosem Durchein'ander, b) ‚beschissen'; **II** *s.* **2.** heilloses Durchein'ander; **3.** grober Fehler; **4.** ‚beschissene Lage'; **III** *v/t.* **5.** ‚versauen'.

snag [snæɡ] **I** *s.* **1.** Aststumpf *m*; **2.** Baumstumpf *m* (*in Flüssen*); *fig.* ‚Haken' *m*: *strike a* ~ auf Schwierigkeiten stoßen; **3.** a) Zahnstumpf *m*, b) *Am.* Raffzahn *m*; **II** *v/t.* **4.** *Boot* gegen e-n Stumpf fahren lassen; **5.** *Fluss* von Baumstümpfen befreien; '**snagged** [-ɡd], '**snag·gy** [-ɡɪ] *adj.* **1.** ästig, knorrig; **2.** voller Baumstümpfe (*Fluss*).

snail [sneɪl] *s.* **1.** *zo.* Schnecke *f* (*a. fig. lahmer Kerl*): *at a* ~*'s pace* im Schneckentempo; **2.** → **snail wheel**; ~ **shell** *s.* Schneckenhaus *n*; ~ **wheel** *s.* Schnecke(nrad *n*) *f* (*Uhr*).

snake [sneɪk] **I** *s.* **1.** Schlange *f* (*a. fig.*):

~ *in the grass* a) verborgene Gefahr, b) (falsche) Schlange; *see* ~*s* F weiße Mäuse sehen; **2.** ✝ Währungsschlange *f*; **II** *v/i.* **3.** sich schlängeln (*a. Weg*); ~ **charm·er** *s.* Schlangenbeschwörer *m*; ~ **snake pit** *s.* **1.** Schlangengrube *f*; **2.** Irrenanstalt *f*; **3.** *fig.* Hölle *f*; '**snake·skin** *s.* **1.** Schlangenhaut *f*; **2.** Schlangenleder *n*; **snak·y** ['sneɪkɪ] *adj.* □ **1.** Schlangen...; **2.** schlangenartig, gewunden; **3.** *fig.* 'hinterhältig.

snap [snæp] **I** *s.* **1.** Schnappen *n*, Biss *m*; **2.** Knacken *n*, Knacks *m*, Klicken *n*; **3.** (*Peitschen- etc.*)Knall *m*; **4.** Reißen *n*; **5.** Schnappschloss *n*, Schnapper *m*; **6.** *phot.* Schnappschuss *m*; **7.** *etwa:* Schnipp-Schnapp *n* (*Kartenspiel*); **8.** *fig.* Schwung *m*, Schmiss *m*; **9.** kurze Zeit: *in a* ~ im Nu; *cold* ~ Kältewelle *f*; **10.** (knuspriges) Plätzchen; **11.** *Am.* Kleinigkeit *f*, ‚Kinderspiel' *n*; **II** *adj.* **12.** Schnapp...; **13.** spontan, Schnell...: ~ *decision* rasche Entscheidung; ~ *judgement* (vor)schnelles Urteil; ~ *vote* Blitzabstimmung *f*; **III** *adv. u. int.* **14.** knack(s)(!), krach(!), schnapp(!); **IV** *v/i.* **15.** schnappen (*at* nach *a. fig. e-m Angebot etc.*), zuschnappen: ~ *at the chance* zugreifen, die Gelegenheit beim Schopfe fassen; **16.** *a.* ~ *to* zuschnappen, zuknallen (*Schloss, Tür*); **17.** knacken, klicken; **18.** knallen (*Peitsche etc.*); **19.** (zer)springen, (-)reißen, entzweigehen: *there something* ~*ped in me* da ‚drehte ich durch'; **20.** schnellen: ~ *to attention* ⚔ ‚Männchen bauen'; ~ *to it!* F mach Tempo!; ~ *out of it!* F komm, komm!, lass das (sein)!; **V** *v/t.* **21.** (er-)schnappen; beißen: ~ *off* abbeißen; ~ *s.o.'s head* (*od.* *nose*) *off* → **snap up** 4; **22.** (zu)schnappen lassen; **23.** *phot.* knipsen; **24.** zerknicken, -knacken, -brechen, -reißen: ~ *off* abbrechen; **25.** mit *der Peitsche* knallen; mit *den Fingern* schnalzen: ~ *one's fingers at fig.* auslachen, verhöhnen; **26.** *a.* ~ *out Wort* her'vorstoßen, bellen; ~ *up v/t.* **1.** auf-, wegschnappen; **2.** (gierig) an sich reißen, ‚ergattern': *snap it up!* F mach fix!; **3.** *Häuser etc.* aufkaufen; **4.** a) *j-n* anschnauzen, b) *j-m* das Wort abschneiden.

snap| catch *s.* ⚙ Schnapper *m*; '~·**drag·on** *s.* **1.** ♀ Löwenmaul *n*; **2.** Ro'sinenfischen *n aus brennendem Branntwein* (*Spiel*); ~ **fas·ten·er** *s.* Druckknopf *m*; ~ **hook** *s.* Kara'binerhaken *m*; ~ **lock** *s.* Schnappschloss *n*.

snap·pish ['snæpɪʃ] *adj.* □ **1.** bissig (*Hund, a. Person*); **2.** schnippisch.

snap·py ['snæpɪ] *adj.* □ **1.** → **snappish**; **2.** F a) schnell, fix, b) ‚zackig', forsch, c) schwungvoll, schmissig, d) schick: *make it* ~!, *look* ~! mach mal fix!

snap| shot *s.* ⚔ Schnellschuss *m*; '~·**shot** *phot.* **I** *s.* Schnappschuss *m*; **II** *v/t.* e-n Schnappschuss machen von, *et.* knipsen.

snare [sneə] **I** *s.* **1.** Schlinge (*a.* 🪤), Fallstrick *m*, *fig. a.* Fußangel *f*: *set a* ~ *for s.o.* j-m e-e Falle stellen; **2.** ♪ Schnarrsaite *f*; **II** *v/t.* **3.** mit e-r Schlinge fangen; *fig.* um'stricken, fangen, *j-m* e-e Falle stellen; **4.** sich *et.* ‚angeln' *od.* unter den Nagel reißen; ~ **drum** *s.* ♪ kleine Trommel, Schnarrtrommel *f*.

snarl[1] [snɑːl] *s.* **1.** Knoten *m*, ‚Fitz' *m*; **2.** *fig.* wirres Durchein'ander, Gewirr *n*, *a.* Verwicklung *f*: (*traffic*) ~ Verkehrschaos *n*; **II** *v/t.* **3.** *a.* ~ *up* verwirren, durchein'ander bringen; **III** *v/i.* **4.** *a.* ~ *up* sich verwirren; (völlig) durchein'ander geraten.

snarl² [snɑːl] **I** v/i. wütend knurren, die Zähne fletschen (*Hund, a. Person*): ~ **at** j-n anfauchen; **II** v/t. et. knurren, wütend her'vorstoßen; **III** s. Knurren n, Zähnefletschen n.

'snarl-up s. F → **snarl¹** 2.

snatch [snætʃ] **I** v/t. **1.** et. schnappen, packen, (er)haschen, fangen: ~ **up** aufraffen; **2.** fig. Gelegenheit etc. ergreifen; et., a. Schlaf ergattern: ~ **a hurried meal** rasch et. zu sich nehmen; **3.** et. an sich reißen; a. Kuss rauben; **4.** ~ (**away**) **from** j-m et., a. j-n dem Meer, dem Tod, durch den Tod entreißen: **he was ~ed away from us** er wurde uns durch e-n frühen Tod etc. entrissen; **5.** ~ **off** weg-, her'unterreißen; **6.** Am. sl. Kind rauben; **7.** Gewichtheben: reißen; **II** v/i. **8.** ~ **at** schnappen od. greifen od. haschen nach: ~ **at the offer** fig. mit beiden Händen zugreifen; **III** s. **9.** Schnappen n, schneller Griff: **make a ~ at** → 8; **10.** fig. (kurzer) Augenblick: ~**es of sleep**; **11.** pl. Bruchstücke pl., ,Brocken' pl., Aufgeschnappte(s) n: ~**es of conversation** Gesprächsfetzen pl.; **by** (od. **in**) ~**es** a) hastig, ruckweise, b) ab und zu; **12.** Am. V a) ,Möse' f, b) ,Nummer' f (Koitus); **'snatch·y** [-tʃɪ] adj. □ abgehackt, ruckweise, spo'radisch.

snaz·zy ['snæzɪ] adj. F ,todschick'.

sneak [sniːk] **I** v/i. **1.** (sich wohin) schleichen: ~ **about** herumschleichen, -schnüffeln; ~ **out of** fig. sich von et. drücken, sich aus e-r Sache herauswinden; **2.** ped. Brit. sl. ,petzen': ~ **on s.o.** j-n verpetzen; **II** v/t. **3.** et. (heimlich) wohin schmuggeln; **4.** sl. ,sti'bitzen'; **III** s. **5.** contp. ,Leisetreter' m, Kriecher m; **6.** Brit. F ,Petze' f; ~ **at·tack** s. ✕ Über'raschungsangriff m.

sneak·ers ['sniːkəz] s. pl. bsd. Am. leichte Turnschuhe pl.; **'sneak·ing** [-kɪŋ] adj. □ **1.** verstohlen; **2.** 'hinterlistig, gemein; **3.** fig. heimlich, leise (Verdacht etc.).

sneak| pre·view s. Am. F inoffizielle erste Vorführung e-s neuen Films; ~ **thief** s. [irr.] Einsteig- od. Gelegenheitsdieb m.

sneak·y ['sniːkɪ] → **sneaking**.

sneer [snɪə] **I** v/i. **1.** höhnisch grinsen, ,feixen' (at über acc.); **2.** spötteln (at über acc.); **3.** (höhnisch) äußern); **III** v/t. **4.** Hohnlächeln n; **5.** Hohn m, Spott m, höhnische Bemerkung; **'sneer·er** [-ərə] s. Spötter m, ,Feixer' m; **'sneer·ing** [-ərɪŋ] adj. □ höhnisch, spöttisch, ,feixend'.

sneeze [sniːz] **I** v/i. niesen: **not to be ~d at** F nicht zu verachten(d); **II** s. Niesen n; '~**wort** s. ♀ Sumpfgarbe f.

snick [snɪk] **I** v/t. (ein)kerben; **II** s. Kerbe f.

snick·er ['snɪkə] **I** v/i. **1.** kichern; **2.** wiehern; **II** v/t. **3.** et. kichern; **III** s. **4.** Kichern n; **5.** riechen (d. fig. wittern); **III** s. **7.** Schnüffeln n; **8.** kurzer Atemzug; **9.** Naserümpfen n.

snif·fle ['snɪfl] Am. **I** v/i. **1.** schniefen; **2.** greinen, heulen; **3.** Schnüffeln n; **4. the ~s** pl. F Schnupfen m.

sniff·y ['snɪfɪ] adj. □ F **1.** naserümpfend, hochnäsig, verächtlich; **2.** muffig.

snif·ter ['snɪftə] s. **1.** Schnäps-chen n, ,Gläs-chen' n; **2.** Am. Kognakschwen-

---

ker m.

snift·ing valve ['snɪftɪŋ] s. ☻ 'Schnüffelven,til n.

snig·ger ['snɪgə] → **snicker**.

snip [snɪp] **I** v/t. **1.** schnippeln, schnipseln, schneiden; **2.** Fahrkarte knipsen; **II** s. **3.** Schnitt m: **have the ~** F sich sterilisieren lassen; **4.** Schnippel m, Schnipsel m, n; **5.** Brit. F a) todsichere Sache, b) günstige (Kauf)Gelegenheit, Schnäppchen n: **it's a ~ at £200** für 200 Pfund ist das (aber) günstig; **6.** Am. F (frecher) Knirps.

snipe [snaɪp] **I** s. **1.** orn. Schnepfe f; **II** v/i. **2.** hunt. Schnepfen jagen od. schießen; **3.** ✕ aus dem 'Hinterhalt schießen (at auf acc.); **III** v/t. **4.** ✕ abschießen, ,wegputzen'; **'snip·er** [-pə] s. **1.** ✕ Scharf-, Heckenschütze m: ~**scope** ✕ Infrarotvisier n; **2.** Todesschütze m, Killer m.

snip·pet ['snɪpɪt] s. **1.** (Pa'pier)Schnipsel m, n; **2.** pl. fig. Bruchstücke pl., ,Brocken' pl.

snitch [snɪtʃ] sl. **I** v/t. ,klauen', sti'bitzen; **II** v/i. ~ **on** j-n ,verpfeifen'.

sniv·el ['snɪvl] **I** v/i. **1.** schniefen; **2.** greinen, plärren; **3.** wehleidig tun; **II** v/t. **4.** et. (her'aus)schluchzen; **III** s. **5.** Greinen n, Plärren n; **6.** wehleidiges Getue; **'sniv·el·(l)er** [-lə] s. ,Heulsuse' f; **'sniv·el·(l)ing** [-lɪŋ] **I** adj. **1.** triefnasig; **2.** wehleidig; **II** s. **3.** → **snivel** 5 u. 6.

snob [snɒb] m: ~ **appeal** Snob-Appeal m; **'snob·ber·y** [-bərɪ] s. Sno'bismus m; **'snob·bish** [-bɪʃ] adj. □ sno'bistisch, versnobt.

snog [snɒg] v/i. F knutschen.

snook [snuːk] s.: **cock a ~ at** j-m e-e lange Nase machen, fig. j-n auslachen.

snook·er ['snuːkə] s. a. ~ **pool** Billard: Snooker Pool m; **'snook·ered** [-əd] adj. F ,to'tal erledigt'.

snoop [snuːp] bsd. Am. F **I** v/i. **1.** a. ~ **around** her'umschnüffeln; **II** s. **2.** Schnüffe'lei f; **3.** → **snoop·er** [-pə] ,Schnüffler' m; **'snoop·y** [-pɪ] adj. □ schnüffelnd, neugierig.

snoot [snuːt] s. Am. F **1.** ,Schnauze' f (Nase, Gesicht); **2.** Gri'masse f, Schnaute' f; **'snoot·y** [-tɪ] adj. Am. F ,großkotzig', hochnäsig, patzig.

snooze [snuːz] F **I** v/i. **1.** ein Nickerchen machen; **2.** dösen; **II** v/t. **3.** ~ **away** Zeit vertrödeln; **III** s. **4.** Nickerchen n: **have a ~** → 1.

snore [snɔː] **I** v/i. schnarchen; **II** s. Schnarchen n; **snor·er** ['snɔːrə] s. Schnarcher m.

snor·kel ['snɔːkl] **I** s. ♣, ✕ etc. Schnorchel m; **II** v/i. schnorcheln.

snort [snɔːt] v/i. (a. wütend od. verächtlich) schnauben; prusten; **II** v/t. a. ~ **out** Worte (wütend) schnauben; **III** s. Schnauben n; Prusten n; **'snort·er** [-tə] s. F **1.** heftiger Sturm; **2.** Mordsding n; **3.** Mordskerl m.

snot [snɒt] s. **1.** Rotz m; **2.** ,Schwein' n; **'snot·ty** [-tɪ] adj. □ **1.** V rotzig, Rotz...; **2.** F ,dreckig', gemein; **3.** Am. sl. patzig.

snout [snaʊt] s. **1.** zo. Schnauze f (a. F fig. Nase, Gesicht); **2.** ,Schnauze' f, Vorderteil n (Auto etc.); **3.** ☻ Schnabel m, Tülle f.

snow [snəʊ] **I** s. **1.** Schnee m (a. 🌿 u. Küche; a. TV); **2.** Schneefall m; **3.** pl. Schneemassen pl.; **4.** sl. ,Snow' m, ,Schnee' m (Kokain, Heroin); **II** v/i. **5.** schneien: ~ **in** hereinschneien (a. fig.); ~**ed in** (od. **up, under**) eingeschneit; **be ~ed under** fig. a) mit Arbeit etc. überhäuft sein, von Sorgen etc. er-

---

drückt werden, b) pol. Am. in e-r Wahl vernichtend geschlagen werden; **6.** fig. regnen, hageln; **III** v/t. **7.** her'unterrieseln lassen; '~**ball** s. **1.** Schneeball m (a. ♀): ~ **fight** Schneeballschlacht f; **2.** fig. La'wine f: snow-job; **II** v/t. **4.** Schneebälle werfen auf; **III** v/i. **5.** sich mit Schneebällen bewerfen; **6.** fig. la'winenartig anwachsen; '~**bank** s. Schneewehe f; '~**bird** s. **1.** → **snow bunting**; **2.** sl. ,Kokser', Koka'inschnupfer m; '~**blind** adj. schneeblind; '~**blow·er** s. Schneefräse f; '~**board** s Snowboard n; **II** v/i. snowboarden; '~**board·er** s. Snowboarder(in); '~**board·ing** s. Snowboarden n, Snowboardfahren n; '~**bound** adj. eingeschneit, durch Schnee(massen) abgeschnitten; ~ **bun·ny** s. F ,Skihaserl' n; ~ **bun·ting** s. orn. Schneeammer f; '~**cap** s. orn. ein Kolibri m; '~**capped** adj. schneebedeckt; '~**drift** s. Schneewehe f; '~**drop** s. ♀ Schneeglöckchen n; '~**fall** s. Schneefall m, -menge f; '~**field** s. Schneefeld n; '~**flake** s. Schneeflocke f; ~ **gog·gles** s. pl. Schneebrille f; ~ **line** s. Schneegrenze f; '~**man** s. [irr.] Schneemann m: **Abominable ☃** Schneemensch m, der Yeti; '~**mo·bile** [-məʊ-bɪːl] s. 'Schneemo,bil n; '~**plough**, Am. '~**plow** s. Schneepflug m (a. beim Skifahren); '~**shoe** s. Schneeschuh m; **II** v/i. auf Schneeschuhen gehen; '~**slide**, '~**slip** s. Schneerutsch m; '~**storm** s. Schneesturm m; ~ **tire** (Brit. **tyre**) s. mot. Winterreifen m; ~'**white** adj. schneeweiß; ☃ **White** npr. Schnee'wittchen n.

snow·y ['snəʊɪ] adj. □ **1.** schneeig, Schnee...: ~ **weather**; **2.** schneebedeckt, Schnee...; **3.** schneeweiß.

snub¹ [snʌb] **I** v/t. **1.** j-n brüskieren, vor den Kopf stoßen; **2.** j-n kurz abfertigen; **3.** j-m über den Mund fahren; **II** s. **4.** Brüskierung f.

snub² [snʌb] adj. stumpf: ~ **nose** Stupsnase f; '~**nosed** adj. stupsnasig.

snuff¹ [snʌf] **I** v/t. **1.** a. ~ **up** durch die Nase einziehen; **2.** beschnüffeln; **II** v/i. **3.** schnüffeln (at an dat.); **4.** (Schnupftabak) schnupfen; **III** s. **5.** Atemzug m, Einziehen n; **6.** Schnupftabak m, Prise f: **take ~** schnupfen; **be up to ~** F a) ,schwer auf Draht sein', b) (toll) in Form sein; **give s.o. ~** F j-m ,Saures geben'.

snuff² [snʌf] **I** s. **1.** Schnuppe f e-r Kerze; **II** v/t. **2.** Kerze putzen; **3.** ~ **out** auslöschen (a. fig.); fig. ersticken, vernichten; **4.** ~ **it** Brit. F ,abkratzen' (sterben).

'snuff| box s. Schnupftabaksdose f; '~-**col·o(u)red** adj. gelbbraun, tabakfarben.

snuf·fle ['snʌfl] **I** v/i. **1.** schnüffeln, schnuppern; **2.** schniefen; **3.** näseln; **II** v/t. **4.** mst ~ **out** näseln; **III** s. **5.** Schnüffeln n; **6.** Näseln n; **7. the ~s** pl. Schnupfen m.

'snuff|-,tak·er s. Schnupfer(in); '~-,**tak·ing** s. (Tabak)Schnupfen m.

snug [snʌg] **I** adj. □ **1.** gemütlich, behaglich, traulich; **2.** geborgen, gut versorgt: **as ~ as a bug in a rug** F wie die Made im Speck; **3.** angenehm; **4.** auskömmlich, ,hübsch' (Einkommen etc.); **5.** kom'pakt; **6.** ordentlich; **7.** eng anliegend (Kleid): ~ **fit** a) guter Sitz, b) ☻ Passsitz m; **8.** ♣ schmuck, seetüchtig (Schiff); **9.** verborgen: **keep s.th. ~** et. geheim halten; **lie ~** sich verborgen halten; **II** v/i. **10.** → **snuggle** I; **III** v/t. **11.** oft ~ **down** gemütlich od. bequem machen; **12.** *mst* **~ down** ⚓ *Schiff* auf Sturm vorbereiten; **'snug·ger·y** [-gərı] *s.* **1.** behagliche Bude, warmes Nest (*Zimmer etc.*); **2.** kleines Nebenzimmer; **'snug·gle** [-gl] **I** *v/i.* sich schmiegen *od.* kuscheln ([**up**] *in* in *e-e Decke*, **up to** an *acc.*): **~ down** (*in bed*) sich ins Bett kuscheln; **II** *v/t.* an sich schmiegen, (lieb)'kosen.

so [səʊ] **I** *adv.* **1.** (*mst vor adj. u. adv.*) so, dermaßen: *I was* **~** *surprised*; *not* **~ ...** *as* nicht so ... wie; **~** *great a man* ein so großer Mann; → *far* 3, *much Redew.*; **2.** (*mst exklamatorisch*) (ja) so, 'überaus: *I am* **~** *glad!*; **3.** so, in dieser Weise: *and* **~** *on* (*od. forth*) und so weiter; *is that* **~**? wirklich?; **~** *as to* sodass, um zu; **~** *that* sodass; *or* **~** etwa, oder so; **~** *saying* mit *od.* bei diesen Worten; → *if* 1; **4.** (*als Ersatz für ein Prädikativum od. e-n Satz*) a) es, das: *I hope* **~** ich hoffe (es); *I have never said* **~** das habe ich nie behauptet, b) auch: *you are tired,* **~** *am I* du bist müde, ich (bin es) auch, c) allerdings, ja: *are you tired?* **~** *I am* bist du müde? ja *od.* allerdings; *I am stupid!* **~** *you are* ich bin dumm! allerdings (das bist du); **~** *what?* F na und?; **5.** so ..., dass: *it was* **~** *hot I took my coat off*; **II** *cj.* **6.** daher, folglich, also, und so: *it was necessary* **~** *we did it* es war nötig, und so taten wir es (denn); **~** *you came after all!* du bist also doch (noch) gekommen!

soak [səʊk] **I** *v/i.* **1.** sich voll saugen, durch'tränkt werden: **~***ing wet* tropfnass; **2.** ('durch)sickern; **3.** *fig.* langsam *ins Bewusstsein* einsickern *od.* -dringen; **4.** *sl.* 'saufen; **II** *v/t.* **5.** *et.* einweichen; **6.** durch'tränken, -'nässen, -'feuchten; ⊚ *a.* imprägnieren (*in* mit); **7.** **~** *o.s. in fig.* sich ganz versenken in; **8.** **~** *in* einsaugen; **~** *up* a) aufsaugen, b) *fig. Wissen etc.* in sich aufnehmen; **9.** *sl. et.* 'saufen; **10.** *sl. j-n* 'schröpfen; **11.** *sl. j-n* verdreschen; **III** *s.* **12.** Einweichen *n*, Durch'tränken *n*; ⊚ Imprägnieren *n*; **13.** *sl.* a) Säufer *m*, b) Saufe'rei *f*; **14.** F Regenguss *m*, 'Dusche' *f*; **'soak·age** [-kıdʒ] *s.* **1.** 'Durchsickern *n*; **2.** 'durchgesickerte Flüssigkeit, Sickerwasser *n*; **'soak·er** [-kə] → *soak* 14.

'so-and-so ['səʊənsəʊ] *pl.* **-sos** *s.* **1.** (Herr *etc.*) Soundso: *Mr.* **~**; **2.** F ,(blöder) Hund'.

soap [səʊp] **I** *s.* Seife *f* (*a.* 📷): *no* **~!** *Am.* F nichts zu machen!; **II** *v/t. a.* **~ down** a) (ein-, ab)seifen, b) → *soft-soap*; **'~·box I** *s.* **1.** 'Seifenkiste *f*, -kar,ton *m*; **2.** ,Seifenkiste' *f* (*improvisierte Rednerbühne od. Fahrzeug*); **II** *adj.* Seifenkisten...: **~** *derby* Seifenkistenrennen *n*; **~** *orator* Straßenredner *m*; **~ bub·ble** *s.* Seifenblase *f* (*a. fig.*); **~ dish** *s.* Seifenschale *f*; **~ op·er·a** *s.* Radio, TV: 'Seifenoper' *f* (*rührselige Serie*); **'~·stone** *s. min.* Seifen-, Speckstein *m*; **'~·suds** *s. pl.* Seifenlauge *f*, -wasser *n*; **'~·works** *s. pl. oft sg. konstr.* Seifensiede'rei *f*.

soap·y ['səʊpı] *adj.* □ **1.** seifig, Seifen...; **2.** *fig.* ölig, schmeichlerisch.

soar [sɔː] *v/i.* **1.** (hoch) aufsteigen, sich erheben (*Vogel, Berge etc.*); **2.** in großer Höhe schweben; **3.** ✈ segelfliegen, segeln; **4.** *fig.* sich em'porschwingen (*Geist*): **~***ing thoughts* hochfliegende Gedanken; **5.** 🌡 in die Höhe schnellen (*Preise*); **soar·ing** ['sɔːrıŋ] **I** *adj.* □ **1.** hochfliegend (*a. fig.*); **2.** *fig.* em'por-strebend; **II** *s.* **3.** ✈ Segeln *n*.

sob [sɒb] **I** *v/i.* schluchzen; **II** *v/t. a.* **~ out** *Worte* (her'aus)schluchzen; **III** *s.*

Schluchzen *n*; schluchzender Laut: **~** *sister sl.* a) Briefkastenonkel *m*, -tante *f* (*Frauenzeitschrift*), b) Verfasser(in) rührseliger Romane *etc.*; **~** *stuff sl.* rührseliges Zeug, Schnulze(n *pl.*) *f.*

so·ber ['səʊbə] **I** *adj.* □ **1.** nüchtern: a) nicht betrunken, b) *fig.* sachlich: **~** *facts* nüchterne Tatsachen; *in* **~** *fact* nüchtern betrachtet, c) unauffällig, gedeckt (*Farbe etc.*); **2.** mäßig; **II** *v/t.* **3.** *oft* **~** *up* ernüchtern; **III** *v/i.* **4.** *oft* **~** *down od. up* a) (wieder) nüchtern werden, b) *fig.* vernünftig werden; **~-'mind·ed** *adj.* besonnen, nüchtern; **'~·sides** *s.* fader Kerl, ,Trauerkloß' *m*, Spießer *m*.

so·bri·e·ty [səʊ'braıətı] *s.* **1.** Nüchternheit *f* (*a. fig.*); **2.** Mäßigkeit *f*; **3.** Ernst (-haftigkeit *f*) *m*.

so·bri·quet ['səʊbrıkeı] (*Fr.*) *s.* Spitzname *m*.

soc·age ['sɒkıdʒ] *s.* 🏰 *hist.* **1.** Lehensleistung *f* (*ohne Ritter- u. Heeresdienst*); **2.** Frongut *n*.

,so-'called [,səʊ-] *adj.* so genannt (*a. angeblich*).

soc·cage ['sɒkıdʒ] → *socage*.

soc·cer ['sɒkə] **I** *s. sport* Fußball *m* (*Spiel*); **II** *adj.* Fußball...: **~** *team*; **~** *ball* Fußball *m*.

so·cia·bil·i·ty [,səʊʃə'bılətı] *s.* Geselligkeit *f*, 'Umgänglichkeit *f*; **so·cia·ble** ['səʊʃəbl] **I** *adj.* □ **1.** gesellig (*a. zo. etc.*), 'umgänglich, freundlich; **2.** gesellig, gemütlich, ungezwungen: **~** *evening*; **II** *s.* **3.** Kremser *m* (*Kutschwagen*); **4.** Zweisitzer *m* (*Dreirad etc.*); **5.** Plaudersofa *n*; **6.** *bsd. Am.* → *social* 7.

so·cial ['səʊʃl] **I** *adj.* □ **1.** *zo. etc.* gesellig; **2.** gesellschaftlich, Gesellschafts..., sozi'al, Sozial...: **~** *action* Bürgerinitiative *f*; **~** *climber contp.* gesellschaftlicher ,Aufsteiger'; **~** *contract hist.* Gesellschaftsvertrag *m*; **~** *criticism* Sozialkritik *f*; **~** *engineering* angewandte Sozialwissenschaft; **~** *evil* die Prostitution; **~** *order* Gesellschaftsordnung *f*; **~** *rank* gesellschaftlicher Rang, soziale Stellung; **~** *register* Prominentenliste *f*; **~** *science* Sozialwissenschaft *f*; **3.** sozi'al, Sozial...: **~** *insurance* Sozialversicherung *f*; **~** *insurance contribution* Sozialversicherungsbeitrag *m*; **~** *partner* Sozialpartner *m* (*bsd. bei Tarifverhandlungen*); **~** *policy* Sozialpolitik *f*; **~** *security* a) soziale Sicherheit, b) Sozialversicherung *f*, c) Sozialhilfe *f*; *be on* **~** *security* Sozialhilfe beziehen; **~** *services* a) Sozialeinrichtungen, b) staatliche Sozialleistungen; **~** *spending* Sozialausgaben *pl.*; **~** *studies* Gemeinschaftskunde *f*; **~** *work* Sozialarbeit *f*; **~** *worker* Sozialarbeiter(in); **4.** *pol.* Sozial...: 𝓢 *Democrat* Sozialdemokrat(in); **5.** gesellschaftlich, gesellig: **~** *activities* gesellschaftliche Veranstaltungen; **6.** → *sociable* 1; **II** *s.* **7.** geselliges Bei'sammensein; **'so·cial·ism** [-ʃlızəm] *s. pol.* Sozia'lismus *m*; **'so·cial·ist** [-ʃəlıst] **I** *s.* Sozia'list(in); **II** *adj. a.* **so·cial·is·tic** [,səʊʃə'lıstık] *adj.* (□ **~***ally*) sozia'listisch; **'so·cial·ite** [-ʃəlaıt] *s. Am.* F Angehörige(r *m*) *f* der oberen Zehn'tausend, Promi'nente(r *m*) *f.*

so·cial·i·za·tion [,səʊʃəlaı'zeıʃn] *s.* **1.** *pol.*, 🌱 Sozialisierung *f*; **2.** *sociol. ped.* Sozialisation *f*; **so·cial·ize** ['səʊʃəlaız] **I** *v/i.* **1.** unter die Leute gehen; **2.** (*with*) a) Umgang haben *od.* zs.-sein (mit), b) sich unterhalten (mit); **II** *v/t.* **3.** *pol.*, 🌱 sozialisieren, verstaatlichen, vergesellschaften; **4.** *sociol. ped.* sozia-

lisieren.

so·ci·e·ty [sə'saıətı] *s. allg.* Gesellschaft *f*: a) Gemeinschaft *f*: *human* **~**, b) Kul'turkreis *m*, c) (*die große od.* ele'gante) Welt: **~** *lady* Dame *f* der großen Gesellschaft; *not fit for good* **~** nicht salon*od.* gesellschaftsfähig, d) (gesellschaftlicher) 'Umgang, e) Anwesenheit *f*, f) Verein(igung *f*) *m*: 𝓢 *of Friends* Gesellschaft der Freunde (*die Quäker*); 𝓢 *of Jesus* Gesellschaft Jesu.

socio- [səʊsjəʊ] *in Zssgn* a) Sozial..., b) sozio'logisch: **~***biology* Soziobiologie *f*; **~***critical* sozialkritisch; **~***political* sozialpolitisch; **~***psychology* Sozialpsychologie *f.*

so·ci·og·e·ny [,səʊsı'ɒdʒənı] *s.* Wissenschaft *f* vom Ursprung der menschlichen Gesellschaft; **so·ci·o·gram** ['səʊsjəgræm] *s.* Sozio'gramm *n*; **so·ci·o·log·ic, so·ci·o·log·i·cal** [,səʊsjə'lɒdʒık(l)] *adj.* □ sozio'logisch: **so·ci·o·o·gist** [,səʊsı'ɒlədʒıst] *s.* Sozio'loge *m*; **so·ci·ol·o·gy** [,səʊsı'ɒlədʒı] *s.* Soziolo'gie *f.*

sock¹ [sɒk] *s.* **1.** Socke *f*: *pull up one's* **~***s Brit.* F ,sich am Riemen reißen', sich anstrengen; *put a* **~** *in it! Brit. sl.* hör auf!, halts Maul!; **2.** *Brit.* Einlegesohle *f.*

sock² [sɒk] *sl.* **I** *v/t. j-m* ,eine knallen *od.* reinhauen': **~** *it to s.o.* j-m ,Bescheid stoßen', j-m ,Saures geben'; **II** *s.* (Faust)Schlag *m*; **III** *adj. Am.* ,toll'.

sock·et ['sɒkıt] *s.* **1.** *anat.* a) (Augen-, Zahn)Höhle *f*, b) (Gelenk)Pfanne *f*; **2.** ⊛ Muffe *f*, Rohransatz *m*; **3.** ⚡ a) Steckdose *f*, b) Fassung *f*, c) Sockel *m* (*für Röhren etc.*), d) Anschluss *m*; **~** *joint* *s.* ⊛, *anat.* Kugelgelenk *n*; **~** *wrench* *s.* ⊛ Steckschlüssel *m*.

so·cle ['sɒkl] *s.* △ Sockel *m*.

sod¹ [sɒd] **I** *s.* **1.** Grasnarbe *f*: *under the* **~** unterm Rasen (*tot*); **2.** Rasenstück *n*; **II** *v/t.* **3.** mit Rasen bedecken.

sod² [sɒd] *sl.* **I** *s.* **1.** ,Heini' *m*, Blödmann *m*; **2.** Kerl *m*: *the poor* **~**; **II** *v/t.* **3.** **~** *it!* ,Mist!'

so·da ['səʊdə] *s.* 🔥 **1.** Soda *f, n*, kohlensaures Natrium: (*bicarbonate of*) **~** → *sodium bicarbonate*; **2.** → *sodium hydroxide*; **3.** 'Natriumo,xid *n*; **4.** Soda(wasser) *n*: *whisky and* **~**; **5.** Am. → *soda water* 2; **~** *foun·tain* *s.* **1.** Siphon *m*; **2.** *Am.* Erfrischungshalle *f*, Eisbar *f*; **~** *jerk*(·**er**) *s. Am.* F Verkäufer *m* in e-r Erfrischungshalle *od.* Eisbar; **~** *lye* *s.* Natronlauge *f*; **~** *pop* *s. Am.* ,Limo' *f*; **wa·ter** *s.* **1.** Sodawasser *n*; **2.** Selters (-wasser) *n*, Sprudel *m*.

sod·den ['sɒdn] *adj.* **1.** durch'weicht, -'nässt; **2.** teigig, klitschig (*Brot etc.*); **3.** *fig.* a) ,voll', ,besoffen', b) blöd(e) (*vom Trinken*); **4.** aufgedunsen; **5.** *sl.* a) ,blöd', ,doof', b) fad.

so·di·um ['səʊdjəm] *s.* 🔥 Natrium *n*; **~** *bi·car·bon·ate* *s.* 'Natriumbikarbo,nat *n*, doppeltkohlensaures Natrium; **~** *car·bon·ate* *s.* Soda *f, n*; 'Natriumkarbo,nat *n*; **~** *chlor·ide* *s.* 'Natriumchlo-,rid *n*, Kochsalz *n*; **~** *hy·drox·ide* *s.* 'Natriumhydro,xid *n*, Ätznatron *n*; **~** *ni·trate* *s.* 'Natriumni,trat *n*.

sod·o·my ['sɒdəmı] *s.* **1.** A'nalverkehr *m*; **2.** O'ralverkehr *m*.

Sod's Law [sɒdz] *s. etwa:* Murphy's Gesetz *n* (*nach dem tatsächlich einmal schief geht, was schief gehen kann*).

so·ev·er [səʊ'evə] *adv.* (*mst in Zssgn* wer *etc.*) auch immer.

so·fa ['səʊfə] *s.* Sofa *n*; **~** *bed* *s.* Bettcouch *f.*

sof·fit ['sɒfıt] *s.* △ Laibung *f.*

soft [sɒft] **I** *adj.* □ **1.** *allg.* weich (*a. fig. Person, Charakter etc.*): *as* ~ *as silk* seidenweich; ~ *currency* ✝ weiche Währung; ~ *prices* ✝ nachgiebige Preise; ~ *sell* ✝ weiche Verkaufstaktik, zurückhaltende Verkaufsstrategie; **2.** ⊚ weich, *bsd.* a) ungehärtet (*Eisen*), b) schmiedbar (*Metall*), c) enthärtet (*Wasser*): ~ *coal* ⚒ Weichkohle *f*; ~ *solder* Weichlot *n*; **3.** *fig.* weich, sanft (*Augen, Worte etc.*); → *spot* 5; **4.** mild, sanft (*Klima, Regen, Schlaf, Wind, a. Strafe etc.*): *be* ~ *with* umgehen mit *j-m*; **5.** leise, sacht (*Bewegung, Geräusch, Rede*); **6.** sanft, gedämpft (*Licht, Farbe, Musik*); **7.** schwach, verschwommen: ~ *outlines*; ~ *negative phot.* weiches Negativ; **8.** mild, lieblich (*Wein*); **9.** *Brit.* schwül, feucht, regnerisch; **10.** höflich, ruhig, gewinnend; **11.** zart, zärtlich, verliebt: ~ *nothings* zärtliche Worte; → *sex* 2; **12.** schlaff (*Muskeln*); **13.** *fig.* verweichlicht, schlapp; **14.** angenehm, leicht, ‚gemütlich‘: ~ *job*; *a* ~ *thing* e-e ruhige Sache, e-e ‚Masche‘ (*einträgliches Geschäft*); **15.** *a.* ~ *in the head* F ‚leicht bescheuert‘, ‚doof‘; **16.** a) alkoholfrei: ~ *drinks*, b) weich: ~ *drug* Soft Drug *f*, weiche Droge; **II** *adv.* **17.** sanft, leise; **III** *s.* **18.** F Trottel *m*; '~**ball** *s. Am. sport Form des Baseball mit weicherem Ball u. kleinerem Feld*; '~**-boiled** *adj.* **1.** weich (gekocht) (*Ei*); **2.** F weichherzig; '~-,**cen·tred** *adj. Brit.* mit Cremefüllung.

sof·ten [ˈsɒfn] **I** *v/t.* **1.** weich machen; ⊚ *Wasser* enthärten; **2.** *Ton, Farbe* dämpfen; **3.** *a.* ~ *up* ✕ a) *Gegner* zermürben, b) *Festung etc.* sturmreif schießen; **4.** *fig.* mildern; *j-n* erweichen; *j-s Herz* rühren; *contp.* ‚kleinkriegen‘; **5.** *fig.* verweichlichen; **II** *v/i.* **6.** weich(er) werden, sich erweichen; '**sof·ten·er** [-nə] *s.* ⊚ **1.** Enthärtungsmittel *n*; **2.** Weichmacher *m* (*bei Kunststoff, Öl etc.*); '**sof·ten·ing** [-nɪŋ] *s.* **1.** Erweichen *n*; ~ *of the brain* ⚕ Gehirnerweichung *f*; ~ *point* ⊚ Erweichungspunkt *m*; **2.** *fig.* Besänftigung *f*.

soft| **goods** *s. pl.* Tex'tilien *pl.*; ~ *hail s.* Eisregen *m*; '~**-head** *s.* Schwachkopf *m*; ,~'**heart·ed** *adj.* weichherzig; ,~-'**land** *v/t. u. v/i.* weich landen.

soft·ness [ˈsɒftnɪs] *s.* **1.** Weichheit *f*; **2.** Sanftheit *f*; **3.** Milde *f*; **4.** Zartheit *f*; **5.** *contp.* Weichlichkeit *f*.

soft| **ped·al** *s.* ♪ (Pi'ano)Pe‚dal *n*; ,~-'**ped·al** *v/t.* **1.** (*a. v/i.*) mit dem Pi'anope‚dal spielen; **2.** F *et.* ‚her'unterspielen‘; ~ *re·turn s. Computer:* ‚weiche‘ Zeilenschaltung (*in Textverarbeitung*); ~ *sci·ence s. Ggs. exakte Wissenschaft, z. B. Soziologie, Psychologie etc.*; ~ **soap** *s.* **1.** Schmierseife *f*; **2.** *sl.* ‚Schmus‘ *m*, Schmeiche'lei(en *pl.*) *f*; ,~-'**soap** *v/t. sl. j-m* ‚um den Bart gehen‘, *j-m* Honig ums Maul schmieren; ,~-'**sol·der** *v/t.* ⊚ weichlöten; '~-,**spo·ken** *adj.* **1.** leise sprechend; **2.** *fig.* gewinnend, freundlich; ~ **top** *s. mot.* Kabrio *n*, Kabrio'lett *n*; ~ **toy** *s.* Stofftier *n*; '~**·ware** *s. Computer:* Software *f*; ~ *package* Softwarepaket *n*; ~ *company* (*od. provider*) Softwareanbieter *m*; '~**·wood** *s.* **1.** Weichholz *n*; **2.** Nadelbaumholz *n*; **3.** Baum *m* mit weichem Holz.

soft·y [ˈsɒftɪ] *s.* F **1.** ‚Softie‘ *m*; **2.** ‚Schlappschwanz‘ *m*.

sog·gy [ˈsɒgɪ] *adj.* **1.** feucht, sumpfig (*Land*); **2.** durchnäßt, -'weicht; **3.** klitschig (*Brot etc.*); **4.** F ‚doof‘.

soi-di·sant [ˌswaːdiːˈzãːŋ] (*Fr.*) *adj.* an-

geblich, so genannt.

soil¹ [sɔɪl] **I** *v/t.* **1.** a) schmutzig machen, verunreinigen, b) *bsd. fig.* besudeln, beflecken, beschmutzen; **II** *v/i.* **2.** schmutzig werden, *leicht etc.* schmutzen; **III** *s.* **3.** Verschmutzung *f*; **4.** Schmutzfleck *m*; **5.** Schmutz *m*; **6.** Dung *m*.

soil² [sɔɪl] *s.* **1.** (Erd)Boden *m*, Erde *f*, (Acker)Krume *f*, Grund *m*; **2.** *fig.* (Heimat)Erde *f*, Land *n*: *on British* ~ auf britischem Boden; *one's native* ~ die heimatliche Erde.

soil³ [sɔɪl] *v/t.* ✔ mit Grünfutter füttern; '**soil·age** [-lɪdʒ] *s.* ✔ Grünfutter *n*.

soil pipe *s.* ⊚ Abflussrohr *n*.

soi·rée [ˈswaːreɪ] (*Fr.*) *s.* Soi'ree *f*, Abendgesellschaft *f*.

so·journ [ˈsɒdʒɜːn] **I** *v/i.* sich (vor'übergehend) aufhalten, (ver)weilen (*in* in *od.* an *dat.*, *with* bei); **II** *s.* (vor'übergehender) Aufenthalt; '**so·journ·er** [-nə] *s.* Gast *m*, Besucher(in).

soke [səʊk] *s.* ⚖ *hist. Brit.* Gerichtsbarkeit(sbezirk *m*) *f*.

sol·ace [ˈsɒləs] **I** *s.* Trost *m*: *she found* ~ *in religion*; **II** *v/t.* trösten.

so·la·num [səʊˈleɪnəm] *s.* ❀ Nachtschatten *m*.

so·lar [ˈsəʊlə] *adj.* **1.** *ast.* Sonnen...(*-system, -tag, -zeit etc.*), Solar...: ~ *eclipse* Sonnenfinsternis *f*; ~ *plexus anat.* Solarplexus *m*, F Magengrube *f*; **2.** ⊚ a) Sonnen...: ~ *cell* (*energy etc.*); ~ *collector od. panel* Sonnenkollektor *m*, b) durch 'Sonnenener‚gie angetrieben: ~ *power station* Sonnen-, Solarkraftwerk *n*.

so·lar·i·um [səʊˈleərɪəm] *pl.* **-i·a** [-ɪə], **-i·ums** *s. allg.* So'larium *n*, ❀ *a.* Sonnenliegehalle *f*.

so·lar·ize [ˈsəʊləraɪz] *v/t.* **1.** ❀ *j-n* mit Lichtbädern behandeln; **2.** ⊚ *Haus* auf 'Sonnenener‚gie 'umstellen; **3.** *phot.* solarisieren (*a. v/i.*).

sold [səʊld] *pret. u. p.p. von* **sell**.

sol·der [ˈsɒldə] **I** *s.* ⊚ Lot *n*, 'Lötme‚tall *n*; **II** *v/t.* **2.** (ver)löten; ~*ed joint* Lötstelle *f*; ~*ing iron* Lötkolben *m*; **3.** *fig.* zs.-schweißen; **III** *v/i.* **4.** löten.

sol·dier [ˈsəʊldʒə] **I** *s.* Sol'dat *m* (*a. engS. Feldherr*): ~ *of Christ* Streiter *m* Christi; ~ *of fortune* Glücksritter *m*; *old* ~ a) F ‚alter Hase‘, b) *sl.* leere Flasche; **2.** ✕ (einfacher) Sol'dat, Schütze *m*, Mann *m*; **3.** *fig.* Kämpfer *m*; **4.** *zo.* Krieger *m*, Sol'dat *m* (*bei Ameisen etc.*); **II** *v/i.* **5.** (als Sol'dat) dienen: *go* ~*ing* Soldat werden; ~ *on fig.* (unbeirrt) weitermachen; '**sol·dier·ly** [-lɪ] *adj.* **1.** sol'datisch; **2.** Soldaten...; '**sol·dier·y** [-ərɪ] *s.* **1.** Mili'tär *n*; **2.** Sol'daten *pl.*, *contp.* Solda'teska *f*.

sole¹ [səʊl] **I** *s.* **1.** (Fuß- *od.* Schuh)Sohle *f*: ~ *leather* Sohlleder *n*; **2.** Bodenfläche *f*, Sohle *f*; **II** *v/t.* **3.** besohlen.

sole² [səʊl] *adj.* □ *solely*; **1.** einzig, al'leinig, Allein...: ~ *agency* Alleinvertretung *f*; ~ *bill* ✝ Solawechsel *m*; ~ *heir* Allein-, Universalerbe *m*; **2.** ⚖ unverheiratet.

sole³ [səʊl] *pl.* **soles**, *coll.* **sole** *s. ichth.* Seezunge *f*.

sol·e·cism [ˈsɒlɪsɪzəm] *s.* Schnitzer *m*, Verstoß *m*, ‚Sünde‘ *f*: a) *ling.* Sprachsünde, b) Faux'pas *m*; **sol·e·cis·tic** [ˌsɒlɪˈsɪstɪk] *adj.* **1.** *ling.* 'unkor‚rekt; **2.** ungehörig.

sole·ly [ˈsəʊllɪ] *adv.* (einzig u.) al'lein, ausschließlich, nur.

sol·emn [ˈsɒləm] *adj.* □ **1.** *allg.* feierlich, ernst, so'lenn: ~ *oath* (*Eid etc.*); ⚖ for'mell (*Vertrag*); **3.** gewichtig, ernst: *a* ~ *warning*; **4.** hehr, erha-

ben: ~ *building*; **5.** düster; **so·lem·ni·ty** [səˈlemnətɪ] *s.* **1.** Feierlichkeit *f*, (feierlicher *od.* würdevoller) Ernst; **2.** *oft pl.* feierliches Zeremoni'ell; **3.** *bsd. eccl.* Festlich-, Feierlichkeit *f*; '**sol·em·nize** [-mnaɪz] *v/t.* **1.** feierlich begehen; **2.** *Trauung* (feierlich) voll'ziehen.

so·le·noid [ˈsəʊlənɔɪd] *s.* ⚡, ⊚ Soleno'id *n*, Zy'linderspule *f*: ~ *brake* Solenoidbremse *f*.

sol-fa [ˌsɒlˈfaː] ♪ **I** *s.* **1.** *a.* ~ *syllables* Solmisati'onssilben *pl.*; **2.** Tonleiter *f*; **3.** Solmisati'on(sübung) *f*; **II** *v/t.* **4.** auf Solmisati'onssilben singen; **III** *v/i.* **5.** solmisieren.

so·lic·it [səˈlɪsɪt] **I** *v/t.* **1.** (dringend) bitten, angehen (*s.o.* j-n; *s.th.* um et.; *s.o. for s.th. od. s.th. of s.o.* j-n um et.); **2.** sich um *ein Amt etc.* bemühen; ✝ um *Aufträge, Kundschaft* werben; **3.** *j-n* ansprechen (*Prostituierte*); **4.** ⚖ anstiften; **II** *v/i.* **5.** dringend bitten (*for* um); **6.** ✝ Aufträge sammeln; **7.** sich anbieten (*Prostituierte*); **so·lic·i·ta·tion** [səˌlɪsɪˈteɪʃn] *s.* **1.** dringende Bitte; **2.** ✝ (Auftrags-, Kunden)Werbung *f*; **3.** Ansprechen *n* (*durch Prostituierte*); **4.** ⚖ Anstiftung *f* (*of* zu).

so·lic·i·tor [səˈlɪsɪtə] *s.* **1.** ⚖ *Brit.* So'licitor *m*, Anwalt *m* (*der nur vor niederen Gerichten plädieren darf*); **2.** *Am.* 'Rechtsre‚rent *m e-r Stadt etc.*; **3.** *Am.* ✝ A'gent *m*, Werber *m*; **gen·er·al** *pl.* **so·lic·i·tors gen·er·al** *s.* ⚖ **1.** zweiter Kronanwalt (*in England*); **2.** *USA* a) stellvertretender Ju'stizmi‚nister, b) oberster Ju'stizbeamter (*in einigen Staaten*).

so·lic·i·tous [səˈlɪsɪtəs] *adj.* □ **1.** besorgt (*about* um, *for* um, wegen); **2.** fürsorglich; **3.** (*of*) eifrig bedacht (auf *acc.*), begierig (nach); **4.** bestrebt *od.* eifrig bemüht (*to do* zu tun); **so·lic·i·tude** [-tjuːd] *s.* **1.** Besorgtheit *f*, Sorge *f*; **2.** (über'triebener) Eifer; **3.** *pl.* Sorgen *pl.*

sol·id [ˈsɒlɪd] **I** *adj.* □ **1.** *allg.* fest (*Eis, Kraftstoff, Speise, Wand etc.*): ~ *body* Festkörper *m*; ~ *lubricant* ⊚ Starrschmiere *f*; ~ *state phys.* fester (Aggregat)Zustand; ~ *waste* Festmüll *m*; *on* ~ *ground* auf festem Boden (*a. fig.*); **2.** kräftig, sta'bil, derb, fest: ~ *build* kräftiger Körperbau; ~ *leather* Kernleder *n*; *a* ~ *meal* ein kräftiges Essen; *a* ~ *blow* ein harter Schlag. **3.** mas'siv (*Ggs. hohl*), Voll...(*-gummi, -reifen*); **4.** mas'siv, gediegen: ~ *gold*; **5.** *fig.* so'lid(e), gründlich: ~ *learning*; **6.** *fig.* gewichtig, triftig (*Grund etc.*), stichhaltig, handfest (*Argument etc.*); **7.** so'lid(e), gediegen, zuverlässig (*Person*); **8.** ✝ so'lid(e), gut fundiert; **9.** a) soli'darisch, b) einmütig, geschlossen (*for* für *j-n od. et.*): *be* ~ *for s.o.*; *be* ~*ly behind s.o.* geschlossen hinter j-m stehen; *a* ~ *vote* e-e einstimmige Wahl; **10.** *be* ~ (*with s.o.*) *Am.* F (mit j-m) auf gutem Fuß stehen; **11.** *Am. sl.* ‚prima‘, erstklassig; **12.** A a) körperlich, räumlich, b) Kubik..., Raum...: ~ *capacity*; ~ *geometry* Stereometrie *f*; ~ *measure* Raummaß *n*; **13.** geschlossen: *a* ~ *row of buildings*; **14.** F voll, ‚geschlagen‘: *a* ~ *hour*; **15.** F to'tal: *booked* ~ total ausgebucht; **II** *s.* **16.** A Körper *m*; **17.** *phys.* Festkörper *m*; **18.** *pl.* feste Bestandteile *pl.*: *the* ~*s of milk*.

sol·i·dar·i·ty [ˌsɒlɪˈdærətɪ] *s.* Solidari'tät *f*, Zs.-halt *m*, Zs.-gehörigkeitsgefühl *n*; **sol·i·dar·y** [ˈsɒlɪdərɪ] *adj.* soli'darisch.

'**sol·id|-drawn** *adj.* ⊚ gezogen: ~ *axle*; ~ *tube* nahtlos gezogenes Rohr; '~-

-hoofed adj. zo. einhufig.

so·lid·i·fi·ca·tion [sə‚lɪdɪfɪ'keɪʃn] s. phys. etc. Erstarrung f, Festwerden n; **so·lid·i·fy** [sə'lɪdɪfaɪ] I v/t. **1.** fest werden lassen; **2.** verdichten; **3.** fig. Partei festigen, konsolidieren; II v/i. **4.** fest werden, erstarren.

so·lid·i·ty [sə'lɪdətɪ] s. **1.** Festigkeit f (a. fig.); kom'pakte od. mas'sive Struk'tur; Dichtigkeit f; **2.** fig. Gediegenheit f, Zuverlässigkeit f, Solidi'tät f; ✝ Kre'ditfähigkeit f.

'sol·id-state chem·is·try s. 'Festkörperche‚mie f.

sol·id·un·gu·late [‚sɒlɪd'ʌŋgjʊleɪt] adj. zo. einhufig.

so·lil·o·quize [sə'lɪləkwaɪz] I v/i. Selbstgespräche führen, bsd. thea. monologisieren; II v/t. et. zu sich selbst sagen; **so·lil·o·quy** [-kwɪ] s. Selbstgespräch n, bsd. thea. Mono'log m.

sol·i·ped ['sɒlɪped] zo. I s. Einhufer m; II adj. einhufig.

sol·i·taire ['sɒlɪteə] s. **1.** Soli'tär(spiel) n; **2.** Pa'tience f; **3.** Soli'tär m (einzeln gefasster Edelstein).

sol·i·tar·y ['sɒlɪtərɪ] adj. □ **1.** einsam (Leben, Spaziergang etc.); → confinement 2; **2.** einsam, abgelegen (Ort); **3.** einsam, einzeln (Baum, Reiter etc.); **4.** ♥, zo. soli'tär; **5.** fig. einzig; → exception; **'sol·i·tude** [-tjuːd] s. **1.** Einsamkeit f; **2.** (Ein)Öde f.

sol·mi·za·tion [‚sɒlmɪ'zeɪʃn]s. ♪ a) Solmisati'on f, b) Solmisati'onsübung f.

so·lo ['səʊləʊ] pl. **-los** I s. **1.** bsd. ♪ Solo(gesang m, -spiel n, -tanz m etc.) n; **2.** Kartenspiele: Solo n; **3.** ✈ Al'leinflug m (Flug); **4.** bsd. ♪ Solo...; **5.** Allein...: **~ flight** → 3; **~ run** sport Alleingang m; III adv. **6.** al'lein, 'solo': **fly ~** e-n Alleinflug machen; **'so·lo·ist** [-əʊɪst]s. So'list(in).

sol·stice ['sɒlstɪs] s. ast. Sonnenwende f: **summer ~**; **sol·sti·tial** [sɒl'stɪʃl] adj. Sonnenwende...: **~ point** Umkehrpunkt m.

sol·u·bil·i·ty [‚sɒljʊ'bɪlətɪ] s. **1.** ♠ Löslichkeit f; **2.** fig. Lösbarkeit f; **sol·u·ble** ['sɒljʊbl] adj. **1.** ♠ löslich; **2.** fig. (auf-)lösbar.

so·lu·tion [sə'luːʃn] s. **1.** ♠ a) Auflösung f, b) Lösung f: **aqueous ~** wässerige Lösung; (**rubber**) **~** Gummilösung f; **2.** ♠ etc. (Auf)Lösung f; **3.** fig. Lösung f (e-s Problems etc.); (Er)Klärung f.

solv·a·ble ['sɒlvəbl] → soluble.

solve [sɒlv] v/t. **1.** Aufgabe, Problem lösen; **2.** lösen, (er)klären: **~ a mystery**; **~ a crime** ein Verbrechen aufklären; **'sol·ven·cy** [-vənsɪ] s. ✝ Zahlungsfähigkeit f; **'sol·vent** [-vənt] I adj. **1.** ♠ (auf)lösend; **2.** fig. zersetzend; **3.** fig. erlösend: **the ~ power of laughter**; **4.** ✝ zahlungsfähig, sol'vent, li'quid; II s. **5.** ♠ Lösungsmittel n: **~ abuse** Missbrauch m von Lösungsmitteln, F ‚Schnüffeln'; **~ abuser** ‚Schnüffler(in)'; **6.** fig. zersetzendes Ele'ment; **'solvent-based** adj. lösungsmittelhaltig; **'sol·vent-free** adj. lösungsmittelfrei.

so·mat·ic [səʊ'mætɪk] adj. biol., ✦ **1.** körperlich, physisch; **2.** so'matisch: **cell** Somazelle f.

so·ma·tol·o·gy [‚səʊmə'tɒlədʒɪ] s. ✦ Somatolo'gie f, Körperlehre f; **so·ma·to·psy·chic** [‚səʊmətəʊ'saɪkɪk] adj. ✦ psych. psychoso'matisch.

som·ber Am., **som·bre** Brit. ['sɒmbə] adj. □ **1.** düster, trübe (a. fig.); **2.** dunkel(farbig); **3.** fig. melan'cholisch; **'som·ber·ness** Am., **'som·bre·ness**

Brit. [-nɪs] s. **1.** Düsterkeit f, Trübheit f (a. fig.); **2.** fig. Trübsinnigkeit f.

some [sʌm; səm] I adj. **1.** (vor Substantiven) (irgend)ein: **~ day** eines Tages; **~ day** (**or other**), **~ time** irgendwann (einmal), mal; **2.** (vor pl.) einige, ein paar: **~ few** einige wenige; **3.** manche; **4.** ziemlich (viel), beträchtlich, e-e ganze Menge; **5.** gewiss: **to ~ extent** in gewissem Grade, einigermaßen; **6.** etwas, ein (klein) wenig: **~ bread** (etwas) Brot; **take ~ more!** nimm noch etwas!; **7.** ungefähr, gegen: **a village of ~ 60 houses** ein Dorf von etwa 60 Häusern; **8.** sl. beachtlich, ‚ganz hübsch': **~ race!** das war vielleicht ein Rennen!; **~ teacher!** contp. ein ‚schöner' Lehrer (ist das)!; II adv. **9.** bsd. Am. etwas, ziemlich; **10.** F ‚e'norm', ‚toll'; III pron. **11.** (irgend)ein: **~ of these days** dieser Tage, demnächst; **12.** etwas: **~ of it** etwas davon; **~ of these people** einige dieser Leute; **13.** welche: **will you have ~?**; **14.** Am. sl. dar'über hinaus, noch mehr; **15.** **some ... some** die einen ... die anderen.

some·bod·y ['sʌmbədɪ] I pron. jemand, (irgend)einer; II s. e-e bedeutende Per'sönlichkeit: **he thinks he is ~** er bildet sich ein, er sei jemand; **'~·how** adv. oft **~ or other 1.** irgend'wie, auf irgendeine Weise; **2.** aus irgendeinem Grund(e), ‚irgendwie': **~ (or other) I don't trust him**; **'~·one** I pron. jemand, (irgend)einer: **~ or other** irgendeiner; II s. → **somebody** II; **'~·place** adv. Am. irgendwo('hin).

som·er·sault ['sʌməsɔːlt] I s. a) Salto m, b) Purzelbaum m (a. fig.): **turn od. do a ~** → II v/i. e-n Salto machen od. e-n Purzelbaum schlagen.

Som·er·set House ['sʌməsɪt] s. Verwaltungsgebäude in London mit Personenstandsregister, Notariats- u. Inlandssteuererbehörden etc.

'some·thing ['sʌm-] I s. **1.** (irgend)etwas, was: **~ or other** irgendetwas; **a certain ~** ein gewisses Etwas; **2.** **~ of** so etwas wie: **he is ~ of a mechanic**; **3.** **or ~** oder so (etwas Ähnliches); II adv. **4.** **~ like** a) so etwas wie, so ungefähr, b) F wirklich, mal: **that's ~ like a pudding!**; **that's ~ like!** das lasse ich mir gefallen!; **'~·time** I adv. **1.** irgend(-wann) einmal (bsd. in der Zukunft): **write ~!** schreib (ein)mal!; **2.** früher, ehemals; II adj. **3.** ehemalig, weiland (Professor etc.); **'~·times** adv. manchmal, hie und da, gelegentlich, zu'weilen; **'~·what** adv. u. s. etwas, ein wenig, ein bisschen: **she was ~ puzzled**; **~ of a shock** ein ziemlicher Schock; **'~·where** adv. **1.** irgend'wo; **2.** irgendwo'hin: **~ else** sonst wohin, woandershin; **3.** **~ about** so etwa, um ... her'um.

som·nam·bu·late [sɒm'næmbjʊleɪt] v/i. schlaf-, nachtwandeln; **som'nam·bu·lism** [-lɪzəm] s. Schlaf-, Nachtwandeln n; **som'nam·bu·list** [-lɪst] s. Schlaf-, Nachtwandler(in); **som·nam·bu·lis·tic** [sɒm‚næmbjʊ'lɪstɪk] adj. schlaf-, nachtwandlerisch.

som·nif·er·ous [sɒm'nɪfərəs] adj. einschläfernd.

som·no·lence ['sɒmnələns] s. **1.** Schläfrigkeit f; **2.** ✦ Schlafsucht f; **'som·no·lent** [-nt] adj. □ **1.** schläfrig; **2.** einschläfernd.

son [sʌn] s. **1.** Sohn m: **~ and heir** Stammhalter m; **~ of God** (od. **man**), **the ❷** eccl. Gottes-, Menschensohn (Christus); **2.** fig. Sohn m, Abkomme m: **~ of a bitch** Am. sl. a) ‚Scheißkerl'

---

m, b) ‚Scheißding' n; **~ of a gun** Am. sl. a) ‚toller Hecht', b) ‚(alter) Gauner'; **3.** fig. pl. coll. Schüler pl., Jünger pl.; Söhne pl. (e-s Volks, e-r Gemeinschaft etc.); **4.** → sonny.

so·nance ['səʊnəns] s. **1.** Stimmhaftigkeit f; **2.** Laut m; **'so·nant** [-nt] ling. I adj. stimmhaft; II s. a) So'nant m, b) stimmhafter Laut.

so·nar ['səʊnɑː] s. ♠ Sonar n, S-Gerät n (aus **sound navigation and ranging**).

so·na·ta [sə'nɑːtə] s. ♪ So'nate f; **so·na·ti·na** [‚sɒnə'tiːnə] s. ♪ Sona'tine f.

song [sɒŋ] s. **1.** ♪ Lied n, Gesang m: **~ (and dance)** F fig. Getue n, The'ater n (**about** wegen); **for a ~** fig. für ein Butterbrot; **2.** Song m; **3.** poet. a) Lied n, Gedicht n, b) Dichtung f: **❷ of Solomon**, **❷ of Songs** bibl. das Hohelied (Salomonis); **❷ of the Three Children** bibl. der Gesang der drei Männer od. Jünglinge im Feuerofen; **4.** Singen n, Gesang m: **break** (od. **burst**) **into ~** zu singen anfangen; **'~·bird** s. **1.** Singvogel m; **2.** ‚Nachtigall' f (Sängerin); **'~·book** s. Liederbuch s.

song·ster ['sɒŋstə] s. **1.** ♪ Sänger m; **2.** Singvogel m; **3.** Am. (bsd. volkstümliches) Liederbuch; **'song·stress** [-trɪs] s. Sängerin f.

song thrush s. orn. Singdrossel f.

son·ic ['sɒnɪk] adj. ❷ Schall...; **~ bang** → **sonic boom**; **~ bar·ri·er** → **sound barrier**; **~ boom** ✈ Düsen-, 'Überschallknall m; **~ depth find·er** s. ♠ Echolot n.

'son-in-law pl. **'sons-in-law** s. Schwiegersohn m.

son·net ['sɒnɪt] s. So'nett n.

son·ny ['sʌnɪ] s. Junge m, Kleiner m (Anrede).

son·o·buoy ['səʊnəbɔɪ] s. ♠ Schallboje f.

so·nom·e·ter [səʊ'nɒmɪtə] s. Schallmesser m.

so·nor·i·ty [sə'nɒrətɪ] s. **1.** Klangfülle f, (Wohl)Klang m; **2.** ling. (Ton)Stärke f (e-s Lauts); **so·no·rous** [sə'nɔːrəs] adj. □ **1.** tönend, reso'nant (Holz etc.); **2.** volltönend (a. ling.), klangvoll, so'nor (Stimme, Sprache); **3.** phys. Schall..., Klang...

son·sy ['sɒnsɪ] adj. Scot. **1.** drall (Mädchen); **2.** gutmütig.

soon [suːn] adv. **1.** bald, unverzüglich; **2.** (sehr) bald, (sehr) schnell: **no ~er ... than** kaum ... als; **no ~er said than done** gesagt, getan; **3.** bald, früh: **as ~ as** sobald als od. wie; **~er or later** früher oder später; **the ~er the better** je früher desto besser; **4.** gern: (**just**) **as ~** ebenso gern; **I would ~er ... than** ich möchte lieber ... als; **'soon·er** [-nə] comp. adv. **1.** früher, eher; **2.** schneller; **3.** lieber; → **soon** 2, 3, 4; **'soon·est** [-nɪst] sup. adv. frühestens.

soot [sʊt] I s. Ruß m; II v/t. mit Ruß bedecken, be-, verrußen.

sooth [suːθ] s. Brit. obs.: **in ~**, **to say ~** fürwahr, wahrlich.

soothe [suːð] v/t. **1.** besänftigen, beruhigen, beschwichtigen; **2.** Schmerz etc. mildern, lindern; **'sooth·ing** [-ðɪŋ] adj. □ **1.** besänftigend; **2.** lindernd; **3.** wohltuend, sanft: **~ light**; **~ music**.

sooth·say·er ['suːθ‚seɪə] s. Wahrsager(in).

soot·y ['sʊtɪ] adj. □ **1.** rußig; **2.** geschwärzt; **3.** schwarz.

sop [sɒp] I s. **1.** eingetunkter Bissen (Brot etc.); **2.** fig. Beschwichtigungsmittel n, ‚Schmiergeld' n, ‚Brocken' m; → **Cerberus**; **3.** fig. Weichling m; II

---

v/t. **4.** *Brot etc.*eintunken; **5.** durch'nässen, -'weichen; **6.** ~ *up Wasser* aufwischen.

soph [sɒf] F *für* **sophomore**.

soph·ism ['sɒfɪzəm] *s.* **1.** So'phismus *m*, Spitzfindigkeit *f*, 'Scheinargu,ment *n*; **2.** Trugschluss *m*; '**Soph·ist** [-ɪst] *s. phls.* So'phist *m* (*a. fig. spitzfindiger Mensch*); '**soph·ist·er** [-ɪstə] *s. univ. hist. Student im 2. od. 3. Jahr* (*in Cambridge, Dublin*).

so·phis·tic, so·phis·ti·cal [sə'fɪstɪk(l)] *adj.* □ so'phistisch; **so'phis·ti·cate** [-keɪt] **I** *v/t.* **1.** verfälschen; **2.** *j-n* verbilden; **3.** *j-n* verfeinern; **II** *v/i.* **4.** So'phismen gebrauchen; **III** *s.* **5.** weltkluge (*etc.*) Per'son (→ **sophisticated** 1 *u.* 2); **so'phis·ti·ca·tion** [-keɪtɪd] *adj.* **1.** weltklug, intellektu'ell, (geistig) anspruchsvoll; **2.** *contp.* blasiert, 'auf mo-'dern *od.* intellektuell machend', ,hochgestochen'; **3.** verfeinert, kultiviert, raffiniert (*Stil etc.*); hoch entwickelt (*a.* ⊕ *Maschinen*); **4.** anspruchsvoll, exqui-'sit (*Roman etc.*); **5.** unecht, verfälscht; **so·phis·ti·ca·tion** [sə,fɪstɪ'keɪʃn] *s.* **1.** Intellektua'lismus *m*, Kultiviertheit *f*; **2.** Blasiertheit *f*, hochgestochene Art; **3.** das (geistig) Anspruchsvolle; **4.** ⊕ Ausgereiftheit, (technisches) Raffine-'ment; **5.** (Ver)Fälschung *f*; **6.** → **sophistry**; **soph·ist·ry** ['sɒfɪstrɪ] *s.* **1.** Spitzfindigkeit *f*, Sophiste'rei *f*; **2.** So-'phismus *m*, Trugschluss *m*.

soph·o·more ['sɒfəmɔ:] *s. ped. Am.* 'Collegestu,dent(in) *od.* Schüler(in) e-r **High School** im 2. Jahr.

so·po·rif·ic [,sɒpə'rɪfɪk] **I** *adj.* einschläfernd, schlafförderend; **II** *s. bsd. pharm.* Schlafmittel *n*.

sop·ping ['sɒpɪŋ] *adj. a.* ~ *wet* patschnass, triefend (nass); '**sop·py** [-pɪ] *adj.* □ **1.** durch'weicht (*Boden etc.*); **2.** regnerisch; **3.** F saftlos, fad(e); **4.** F rührselig, ,schmalzig'; **5.** F ,verknallt' (*on s.o.* in j-n).

so·pran·o [sə'prɑ:nəʊ] *pl.* **-nos I** *s.* **1.** So'pran *m* (*Singstimme*); **2.** So'pranstimme *f*, -par,tie *f* (*e-r Komposition*); **3.** Sopra'nist(in); **II** *adj.* **4.** Sopran...

sorb [sɔ:b] *s.* ♥ **1.** Eberesche *f*; **2.** *a.* ~ *apple* Elsbeere *f*.

sor·be·fa·cient [,sɔ:bɪ'feɪʃənt] **I** *adj.* absorbierend, absorpti'onsfördernd; **II** *s.* ♣ Ab'sorbens *n*.

sor·bet ['sɔ:bɪt] *s.* Fruchteis *n*.

sor·cer·er ['sɔ:sərə] *s.* Zauberer *m*; '**sor·cer·ess** [-rɪs] *s.* Zauberin *f*, Hexe *f*; '**sor·cer·ous** [-rəs] *adj.* Zauber..., Hexen...; '**sor·cer·y** [-rɪ] *s.* Zaube'rei *f*, Hexe'rei *f*.

sor·did ['sɔ:dɪd] *adj.* □ *bsd. fig.* schmutzig, schäbig; '**sor·did·ness** [-nɪs] *s.* Schmutzigkeit *f* (*a. fig.*).

sor·dine ['sɔ:di:n], **sor·di·no** [sɔ:'di:nəʊ] *pl.* **-ni** [-ni:] ♪ Dämpfer *m*, Sor'dine *f*.

sore [sɔ:] **I** *adj.* □ → **sorely; 1.** weh(e), wund: ~ *feet*; ~ *heart fig.* wundes Herz, Leid *n*; *like a bear with a* ~ *head* brummig, bärbeißig; → *spot* 5; **2.** entzündet, schlimm, ,böse': ~ *finger*; ~ *throat* Halsentzündung *f*; → *sight* 6; **3.** *fig.* schlimm, arg: ~ *calamity*; **4.** F verärgert, beleidigt, böse (*about* über *acc.*, wegen); **5.** heikel (*Thema*); **II** *s.* Wunde *f*, wunde Stelle, Entzündung *f*: *an open* ~ a) e-e offene Wunde (*a. fig.*), b) *fig.* ein altes Übel, ein ständiges Ärgernis; **III** *adv.* **7.** → **sorely** 1; '**sore·head** *s. Am.* F mürrischer Mensch; '**sore·ly** [-lɪ] *adv.* **1.** arg, ,bös': a) sehr, bitter; b) schlimm; **2.** drin-

gend; **3.** bitterlich *weinen etc.*

so·ror·i·ty [sə'rɒrətɪ] *s.* **1.** *Am.* Verbindung *f* von Stu'dentinnen; **2.** *eccl.* Schwesternschaft *f*.

sorp·tion ['sɔ:pʃn] *s.* 🜛, *phys.* (Ab-) Sorpti'on *f*.

sor·rel¹ ['sɒrəl] **I** *s.* **1.** Rotbraun *n*; **2.** (Rot)Fuchs *m* (*Pferd*); **II** *adj.* **3.** rotbraun.

sor·rel² ['sɒrəl] *s.* ♥ **1.** Sauerampfer *m*; **2.** Sauerklee *m*.

sor·row ['sɒrəʊ] **I** *s.* **1.** Kummer *m*, Leid *n*, Gram *m* (*at* über *acc.*, *for* um): *to my* ~ zu m-m Kummer *od.* Leidwesen; **2.** Leid *n*, Unglück *n*; *pl.* Leid(en *pl.*) *n*; **3.** Reue *f* (*for* über *acc.*); **4.** *bsd. iro.* Bedauern *n*: *without much* ~; **5.** Klage *f*, Jammer *m*; **II** *v/i.* **6.** sich grämen *od.* härmen (*at, over, for* über *acc.*, wegen, um); **7.** klagen, trauern (*after, for* um, über *acc.*); **sor·row·ful** ['sɒrəʊfʊl] *adj.* □ **1.** sorgen-, kummervoll, bekümmert; **2.** klagend, traurig: *a* ~ *song*; traurig, beklagenswert: *a* ~ *accident*.

sor·ry ['sɒrɪ] *adj.* □ **1.** betrübt: *I am* (*od. feel*) ~ *for him* er tut mir Leid; *be* ~ *for o.s.* sich selbst bedauern; (*I am*) (*so*) ~! (es) tut mir (sehr) Leid!, (ich) bedaure!, Verzeihung!; *we are* ~ *to say* wir müssen leider sagen; **2.** reuevoll: *be* ~ *about et.* bereuen *od.* bedauern; **3.** *contp.* traurig, erbärmlich (*Anblick, Zustand etc.*): *a* ~ *excuse* ,e-e faule Ausrede'.

sort [sɔ:t] **I** *s.* **1.** Sorte *f*, Art *f*, Klasse *f*, Gattung *f*; ✝ *a.* Marke *f*, Quali'tät *f*: *all* ~*s of people* allerhand *od.* alle möglichen Leute; *all* ~*s of things* alles Mögliche; **2.** Art *f*: *after a* ~ gewissermaßen; *nothing of the* ~ nichts dergleichen; *something of the* ~ so etwas, et. Derartiges; *he is not my* ~ er ist nicht mein Fall *od.* Typ; *he is not the* ~ *of man who ...* er ist nicht der Mann, der so et. tut; *what* ~ *of a ...?* was für ein ...?; *he is a good* ~ er ist ein guter *od.* anständiger Kerl; (*a*) ~ *of a peace* so etwas wie ein Frieden; *I* ~ *of expected it* F ich habe es irgendwie *od.* halb erwartet; *he* ~ *of hinted* F er machte so eine *od.* e-e vage Andeutung; **3.** *of a* ~, *of* ~*s contp.* so was wie: *a politician of* ~*s*; **4.** *out of* ~*s* a) unwohl, nicht auf der Höhe, b) verstimmt; → 5; **5.** *typ.* 'Schriftgarni,tur *f*: *out of* ~ ausgegangen; **II** *v/t.* **6.** sortieren, (ein)ordnen, sichten; **7.** sondern, trennen (*from* von); **8.** *oft* ~ *out* auslesen, -suchen, -sortieren; **9.** ~ *s.th. out fig.* a) et. ,auseinander klauben', sich Klarheit verschaffen über et., b) e-e Lösung finden für et.; ~ *itself out* sich von selbst erledigen; **10.** ~ *s.o. out* F a) j-m den Kopf zurechtsetzen, b) j-n ,zur Schnecke machen'; ~ *o.s. out* zur Ruhe kommen, mit sich ins Reine kommen; **11.** *a.* ~ *together* zs.-stellen, -tun (*with* mit);

sort code *s.* Bankleitzahl *f*; '**sort·er** [-tə] *s.* Sortierer(in).

sor·tie ['sɔ:ti:] **I** *s.* ✕ a) Ausfall *m*, b) ✈ (Einzel)Einsatz *m*, Feindflug *m*; **II** *v/i.* ✕ a) e-n Ausfall machen, b) ✈ e-n Einsatz fliegen, c) ♣ auslaufen.

sor·ti·lege ['sɔ:tɪlɪdʒ] *s.* Wahrsagen *n* (aus Losen).

so-so, so so ['səʊsəʊ] *adj. u. adv.* F so la'la (*leidlich, mäßig*).

sot [sɒt] **I** *s.* Säufer *m*; **II** *v/i.* (sich be-) saufen; '**sot·tish** ['sɒtɪʃ] *adj.* □ **1.** ,versoffen'; **2.** ,besoffen'; **3.** ,blöd' (*albern*).

sot·to vo·ce [,sɒtəʊ'vəʊtʃɪ] (*Ital.*) *adv.* ♪ *u. fig.* leise, gedämpft.

sou·brette [su:'bret] (*Fr.*) *s. thea.* Soub-

rette *f*.

sou·bri·quet ['su:brɪkeɪ] → **sobriquet**.

souf·fle ['su:fl] *s.* ✗ Geräusch *n*.

souf·flé ['su:fleɪ] (*Fr.*) *s.* Auflauf *m*, Souf'flee *n*.

sough [saʊ] **I** *s.* Rauschen *n* (*des Windes*); **II** *v/i.* rauschen.

sought [sɔ:t] *pret. u. p.p. von* **seek**.

soul [səʊl] *s.* **1.** *eccl., phls.* Seele *f*: *upon my* ~*!* ganz bestimmt!; **2.** Seele *f*, Herz *n*, *das* Innere: *he has a* ~ *above mere money-grubbing* er hat auch noch Sinn für andere Dinge als Geldraffen; **3.** *fig.* Seele *f* (*Triebfeder*): *he was the* ~ *of the enterprise*; **4.** *fig.* Geist *m* (*Person*): *the greatest* ~*s of the past*; **5.** Seele *f*, Mensch *m*: *the ship went down with 300* ~*s*; *a good* ~ e-e gute Seele, e-e Seele von e-m Menschen; *poor* ~ armer Kerl; *not a* ~ keine Menschenseele, niemand; **6.** Inbegriff *m*, ein Muster (*of an dat.*): *the* ~ *of generosity* er ist die Großzügigkeit selbst; **7.** Inbrunst *f*, Kraft *f*, künstlerischer Ausdruck; **8.** *a.* ~ *music* ♪ Soul *m*; **9.** ~ *brother*, ~ *sister Am.* Schwarze(r *m*) *f*; '**soul-de,stroy·ing** *adj.* geisttötend (*Arbeit etc.*); '**soul·ful** [-fʊl] *adj.* □ seelenvoll (*a. fig. u. iro.*); '**soul·less** [-lɪs] *adj.* □ seelenlos (*a. fig. gefühllos, egoistisch, ausdruckslos*); '**soul-,stir·ring** *adj.* ergreifend.

sound¹ [saʊnd] **I** *adj.* □ **1.** gesund: *as* ~ *as a bell* kerngesund; ~ *in mind and body* körperlich u. geistig gesund; *of* ~ *mind* 🜨 voll zurechnungs- *od.* handlungsfähig; **2.** fehlerfrei (*Holz etc.*), tadellos, in'takt: ~ *fruit* unverdorbenes Obst; **3.** gesund, fest (*Schlaf*); **4.** ✝ gesund, so'lide (*Firma, Währung*); sicher (*Kredit*); **5.** gesund, vernünftig (*Urteil etc.*); gut, brauchbar (*Rat, Vorschlag*); kor'rekt, folgerichtig (*Denken etc.*); 🜨 begründet, gültig; **6.** zuverlässig (*Freund etc.*); **7.** gut, tüchtig (*Denker, Schläfer, Stratege etc.*); **8.** tüchtig, kräftig, gehörig: *a* ~ *slap* e-e saftige Ohrfeige; **II** *adv.* **9.** fest, tief *schlafen*.

sound² [saʊnd] *s.* **1.** Sund *m*, Meerenge *f*; **2.** *ichth.* Fischblase *f*.

sound³ [saʊnd] **I** *v/t.* **1.** ♣ (aus)loten, peilen; **2.** *Meeresboden etc.* erforschen (*a. fig.*); **3.** ✗ a) sondieren, b) → **sound⁴** 14; *fig.* a) sondieren, erkunden, b) *j-n* ausholen, *j-m* auf den Zahn fühlen; **II** *v/i.* **5.** ♣ loten; **6.** (weg)tauchen (*Wal*); **7.** *fig.* sondieren; **III** *s.* **8.** ✗ Sonde *f*.

sound⁴ [saʊnd] **I** *s.* **1.** Schall *m*, Laut *m*, Ton *m*: ~ *amplifier* Lautverstärker *m*; *faster than* ~ mit Überschallgeschwindigkeit; ~ *and fury* a) Schall und Rauch, b) hohles Getöse; ♫ *Peter Brown Film, TV*: Ton: Peter Brown; *within* ~ in Hörweite; **2.** Geräusch *n*, Laut *m*: *without a* ~ geräusch-, lautlos; **3.** Ton *m*, Klang *m*, *a. fig.* Tenor *m* (*e-s Briefes, e-r Rede etc.*); **4.** ♪ Klang *m*, *Jazz etc.*: Sound *m*; **5.** *ling.* Laut *m*; **II** *v/i.* **6.** (er)schallen, (-)tönen, (-)klingen; **7.** (*a. fig.* gut, unwahrscheinlich *etc.*) klingen; **8.** ~ *off* F ,tönen' (*about, on* von): ~ *off against* ,herziehen' über (*acc.*); **9.** ~ *in* 🜨 lauten (*Klage*); **III** *v/t.* **10.** *Trompete etc.* erschallen *od.* ertönen *od.* erklingen lassen: ~ *s.o.'s praises fig.* j-s Lob singen; **11.** *durch ein Signal* verkünden; → *alarm* 1; *retreat* 1; **12.** äußern, von sich geben: ~ *a note of fear*; **13.** *ling.* aussprechen; **14.** ✗ abhorchen, -klopfen; ~ *bar·ri·er s.* ✈, *phys.* Schallgrenze *f*, -mauer *f*; ~ *bite s.*

S

mst. pl. Radio, TV: 'Soundbite *n* (*kurzer Ausschnitt aus e-m Interview, e-r Rede etc.*); ~ **board** *s.* ♪ Reso'nanzboden *m*, Schallbrett *n*; ~ **box** *s.* **1.** ♪ Reso'nanzkasten *m*; **2.** *Film etc.:* 'Tonka,bine *f*; ~ **broad·cast·ing** *s.* Hörfunk *m*; ~ **card** *s. Computer:* Soundkarte *f*; ~ **ef·fects** *s. pl. Film, TV:* 'Tonef,fekte *pl.*, Geräusche *pl.*; ~ **en·gi·neer** *s. Film:* Tonmeister *m*.

sound·er ['saʊndə] *s.* **1.** ♫ a) Lot *n*, b) ✕ Lotgast *m*; **2.** *tel.* Klopfer *m*.

sound film *s.* Tonfilm *m*.

sound·ing¹ ['saʊndɪŋ] *adj.* □ **1.** tönend, schallend; **2.** wohlklingend; **3.** *contp.* lautstark, bom'bastisch.

sound·ing² ['saʊndɪŋ] *s.* **1.** Loten *n*; **2.** *pl.* (ausgelotete *od.* auslotbare) Wassertiefe: *take a* ~ loten, *fig.* sondieren.

sound·ing| bal·loon *s.* Ver'suchsbal,lon *m*, Bal'lonsonde *f*; ~ **board 1.** ♪ = *sound board*; **2.** Schallmuschel *f* (*für Orchester etc. im Freien*); **3.** Schalldämpfungsbrett *n*; **4.** *fig.* Podium *n*.

sound in·su·la·tion *s.* Schalldämmung *f.*

sound·less ['saʊndlɪs] *adj.* □ laut-, geräuschlos.

sound mix·er *s. Film etc.:* Tonmeister *m*.

sound·ness ['saʊndnɪs] **1.** Gesundheit *f* (*a. fig.*); **2.** Vernünftigkeit *f*; **3.** Brauchbarkeit *f*; **4.** Folgerichtigkeit *f*; **5.** Zuverlässigkeit *f*; **6.** Tüchtigkeit *f*; **7.** ⚖ Rechtmäßigkeit *f*, Gültigkeit *f*.

'sound|-on film *s.* Tonfilm *m*; '~-**proof** [-ndp-] **I** *adj.* schalldicht; ~ *barrier* Lärmschutzwall *m*; **II** *v/t.* schalldicht machen, isolieren; '~,**proof·ing** [-ndp-] *s.* ⊙ Schalldämpfung *f*, Schallisolierung *f*; ~ **rang·ing I** *s.* ✕ Schallmessen *n*; **II** *adj.* Schallmess...; ~ **re·cord·er** *s.* Tonaufnahmegerät *n*; ~ **shift** *s. ling.* Lautverschiebung *f*; '~-**track** *s. Film:* Soundtrack *m*, Tonstreifen *m*, -spur *f*; ~ **truck** *s. Am.* Lautsprecherwagen *m*; ~ **wave** *s. phys.* Schallwelle *f*.

soup [suːp] **I** *s.* **1.** Suppe *f*, Brühe *f*: *be in the* ~ F ,in der Tinte sitzen'; *from* ~ *to nuts* F von A bis Z; **2.** *fig.* dicker Nebel, ,Waschküche' *f*; **3.** *phot.* F Entwickler *m*; **4.** *mot. sl.* P'S *f*; **II** *v/t.* **5.** *Am. sl.* ~ *up* a) *Motor* ,frisieren', b) *fig. et.* ,aufmöbeln', c) *fig.* Dampf hinter e-e Sache machen.

soup·çon ['suːpsɔ̃:ŋ] *s.* Spur *f* (*of Knoblauch, a. Ironie etc.*).

soup| kitch·en *s.* **1.** Armenküche *f*; **2.** ✕ Feldküche *f*; '~-**mix** *s.* 'Suppenpräpa,rat *n*.

sour ['saʊə] **I** *adj.* □ **1.** sauer (*a. Geruch, Milch*); herb, bitter: ~ *grapes fig.* saure Trauben; *turn od. go* ~ → 8 *u.* 9; **2.** *fig.* sauer (*Gesicht etc.*); **3.** *fig.* sauertöpfisch, mürrisch, bitter; **4.** nasskalt (*Wetter*); **5.** ✓ sauer (*kalkarm, nass*) (*Boden*); **II** *s.* **6.** Säure *f*; **7.** *fig.* Bitternis *f*: *take the sweet with the* ~ das Leben nehmen, wie es (eben) ist; **III** *v/i.* **8.** sauer werden; **9.** *fig.* a) verbittert *od.* ,sauer' werden, b) die Lust verlieren (*on an dat.*), c) ,mies' werden, d) ,ka'puttgehen'; **IV** *v/t.* **10.** sauer machen, säuern; **11.** *fig.* verbittern.

source [sɔːs] *s.* **1.** Quelle *f*, *poet.* Quell *m*; **2.** Quellfluss *m*; **3.** *poet.* Strom *m*; **4.** *fig.* (*Licht-, Strom- etc.*)Quelle *f*: ~ *im·pedance* ⚡ Quellwiderstand *m*; ~ *ma·terial* Ausgangsstoff *m* (→ *a.* 6); **5.** *fig.* Quelle *f*, Ursprung *m*: ~ *of informa·tion* Nachrichtenquelle *f*; *from a relia·ble* ~ aus zuverlässiger Quelle; *have its* ~ *in* s-n Ursprung haben in (*dat.*); *take its* ~ *from* entspringen (*dat.*); **6.** *fig.*

literarische Quelle: ~ *material* Quellenmaterial *n*; **7.** ✝ (*Einnahme-, Kapital- etc.*)Quelle *f*: ~ *of supply* Bezugsquelle; *levy a tax at the* ~ e-e Steuer an der Quelle erheben; ~ *file s. Computer:* 'Quellda,tei *f*; ~ *lan·guage s. ling.* Ausgangssprache *f* (*Übersetzung etc.*).

sour| cream *s. Brit.* Sauerrahm *m*; '~-**dough** *s. Am.* **1.** Sauerteig *m*; **2.** A'laskaschürfer *m*.

sour·ing ['saʊərɪŋ] *s.* 🍏 Säuerung *f*; '**sour·ish** [-ərɪʃ] *adj.* säuerlich, angesäuert; '**sour·ness** [-ənɪs] *s.* **1.** Herbheit *f*; **2.** Säure *f* (*als Eigenschaft*); **3.** *fig.* Bitterkeit *f.*

'**sour·puss** *s.* F ,Sauertopf' *m*.

souse [saʊs] **I** *s.* **1.** Pökelfleisch *n*; **2.** Pökelbrühe *f*, Lake *f*; **3.** Eintauchen *n*; **4.** Sturz *m* ins Wasser; **5.** ,Dusche' *f*, (Regen)Guss *m*; **6.** *sl.* a) Saufe'rei *f*, b) *Am.* Säufer *m*, c) *Am.* ,Suff' *m*; **II** *v/t.* **7.** eintauchen; **8.** durch'tränken, einweichen; **9.** *Wasser etc.* ausgießen (*over* über *acc.*); **10.** (ein)pökeln; **11.** ~*d sl.* ,voll', besoffen.

sou·tane [suːˈtɑːn] *s. R.C.* Sou'tane *f.*

sou·ten·eur [ˌsuːtəˈnɜː] (*Fr.*) *s.* Zuhälter *m*.

south [saʊθ] **I** *s.* **1.** Süden *m*: *in the* ~ *of* im Süden von; *to the* ~ *of* → 6; **2.** *a.* ♌ Süden *m* (*Landesteil*): *from the* ♌ aus dem Süden (*Person, Wind*); *the* ♌ der Süden, die Südstaaten (*der USA*); **3.** *poet.* Südwind *m*; **II** *adj.* **4.** südlich, Süd...: ♌ *Pole* Südpol *m*; ♌ *Sea* Südsee *f*; **III** *adv.* **5.** nach Süden, südwärts; **6.** ~ *of* südlich von; **7.** aus dem Süden (*Wind*); ♌ *Af·ri·can* **I** *adj.* 'südafri'kanisch; **II** *s.* 'Südafri'kaner(in); ~ *Dutch* Afrikaander(in); ~ *by east s.* Südsüd-'ost *m*; ~·**east** [ˌsaʊθˈiːst] **I** *s.* Südosten *m*; **II** *adj.* süd'östlich, Südost...; **III** *adv.* süd'östlich; nach Süd-'osten.

south|-east·er [ˌsaʊθˈiːstə] *s.* Südostwind *m*, -'oststurm *m*; ,~-'**east·er·ly** [-lɪ] **I** *adj.* → *southeast* II; **II** *adv.* von *od.* nach Süd'osten; ,~-'**east·ern** [-ən] → *southeast* II; ,~-'**east·ward** [-stwəd] **I** *adj. u. adv.* nach Süd'osten, süd'östlich; **II** *s.* süd'östliche Richtung; ,~-'**east·wards** [-stwədz] *adv.* nach Süd'osten.

south·er·ly ['sʌðəlɪ] **I** *adj.* südlich, Süd...; **II** *adv.* von *od.* nach Süden.

south·ern ['sʌðən] **I** *adj.* **1.** südlich, Süd...: ♌ *Cross ast.* das Kreuz des Südens; ~ *lights ast.* das Südlicht; **2.** ♌ südstaatlich, ... der Südstaaten (*der USA*); **II** *s.* **3.** → *southerner*; '**south·ern·er** [-nə] *s.* **1.** Bewohner(in) des Südens (*e-s Landes*); **2.** ♌ Südstaatler(in) (*in den USA*); '**south·ern·ly** [-lɪ] → *southerly*; '**south·ern·most** *adj.* südlichst.

south·ing ['saʊθɪŋ] *s.* **1.** ♫ a) Südrichtung *f*, südliche Fahrt, b) 'Breiten,unterschied *m* bei südlicher Fahrt; **2.** *ast.* a) Kulminati'on *f* (*des Mondes etc.*), b) südliche Deklinati'on (*e-s Gestirns*).

'**south|-most** *adj.* südlichst; '~-**paw** *sport* **I** *adj.* linkshändig; **II** *s.* Linkshänder *m*; *Boxen:* Rechtsausleger *m*; ~-**-south·east** [♫,saʊsaʊˈiːst] **I** *adj.* südsüd'östlich, Südsüdost...; **II** *adv.* nach *od.* aus Südsüd'osten; **III** *s.* Südsüd-'osten *m*; '~-**ward** [-wəd] *adj. u. adv.* nach Süden, südwärts.

south|-west [ˌsaʊθˈwest; ♫ saʊˈwest] **I** *adj.* süd'westlich, Südwest...; **II** *adv.* nach *od.* aus Süd'westen; **III** *s.* Süd'westen *m*; ,~-'**west·er** [-tə] *s.* **1.** Süd'westwind *m*; **2.** = *sou'wester* 1; ,~-'**west·er·ly** [-təlɪ] *adj.* nach *od.* aus Süd'wes-

ten; ,~-'**west·ern** [-tən] *adj.* süd'westlich, '~-'**west·ward** [-wəd] *adj. u. adv.* nach Süd'westen.

sou·ve·nir [ˌsuːvəˈnɪə] *s.* Andenken *n*, Souve'nir *n*: ~ *shop*.

sou'west·er [saʊˈwestə] *s.* **1.** Süd'wester *m* (*wasserdichter Hut*); **2.** → *southwester* 1.

sov·er·eign ['sɒvrɪn] **I** *s.* **1.** Souve'rän *m*, Mon'arch(in); **2.** die Macht im Staate (*Person od. Gruppe*); **3.** souve'räner Staat; **4.** ✝ *Brit.* Sovereign *m* (*alte 20-Schilling-Münze aus Gold*); **II** *adj.* **5.** höchst, oberst; **6.** 'unum,schränkt, souve'rän, königlich: ~ *power*; **7.** souve-'rän (*Staat*); **8.** äußerst, größt: ~ *con·tempt* tiefste Verachtung; **9.** 'unüber-,trefflich; '**sov·er·eign·ty** [-rəntɪ] *s.* **1.** höchste (Staats)Gewalt; **2.** Landeshoheit *f*, Souveräni'tät *f*; **3.** Oberherrschaft *f.*

so·vi·et ['saʊvɪət] **I** *s.* *oft* ♎ **1.** So'wjet *m*: *Supreme* ♎ Oberster Sowjet; **2.** ♎ So'wjetsy,stem *n*; **3.** *pl. die* So'wjets; **II** *adj.* **4.** ♎ so'wjetisch, Sowjet...; '**so·vi·et·ize** [-taɪz] *v/t.* sowjetisieren.

sow¹ [saʊ] *s.* **1.** Sau *f*, (Mutter)Schwein *n*: *get the wrong* ~ *by the ear* a) den Falschen erwischen, b) sich gewaltig irren; **2.** *metall.* a) (Ofen)Sau *f*, b) Massel *f* (*Barren*).

sow² [səʊ] [*irr.*] **I** *v/t.* **1.** säen; **2.** *Land* besäen; **3.** *fig.* säen, ausstreuen; → *seed* 4, *wind¹* 1; **4.** *et.* verstreuen; **II** *v/i.* **5.** säen.

sown [səʊn] *p.p. von* **sow².**

soy [sɔɪ] *s.* **1.** Sojabohnenöl *n*; **2.** → '**so·ya** (**bean**) ['sɔɪə], '**soy·bean** *s.* Sojabohne *f.*

soz·zled ['sɒzld] *adj. Brit. sl.* ,blau'.

spa [spɑː] *s.* a) Mine'ralquelle *f*, b) Badekurort *m*, Bad *n*.

space [speɪs] **I** *s.* **1.** Raum *m* (*Ggs. Zeit*): *disappear into* ~ ins Nichts verschwinden; *look into* ~ ins Leere starren; **2.** Raum *m*, Platz *m*: *require much* ~; *for* ~ *reasons* aus Platzgründen; **3.** (Welt)Raum *m*; **4.** (Zwischen-) Raum *m*, Stelle *f*, Lücke *f*; **5.** Zwischenraum *m*, Abstand *m*, Leerzeile *f*; **6.** Zeitraum *m*: *a* ~ *of three hours*; *after a* ~ nach e-r Weile; *for a* ~ e-e Zeit lang; **7.** *typ.* Spatium *n*, Ausschlussstück *n*; **8.** *tel.* Abstand *m*, Pause *f*; **9.** *Am.* a) Raum *m* für Re'klame (*Zeitung*), b) *Radio, TV:* (Werbe)Zeit *f*; **II** *v/t.* **10.** räumlich *od.* zeitlich einteilen: ~*d out over 10 years* auf 10 Jahre verteilt; **11.** in Zwischenräumen anordnen; **12.** *mst* ~ *out typ.* a) ausschließen, b) gesperrt setzen, sperren: ~*d type* Sperrdruck *m*; **13.** gesperrt schreiben (*auf der Schreibmaschine*); ~ *age s.* Weltraumzeitalter *n*; ~ *bar s.* Leertaste *f*; '~-**borne** *adj.* **1.** Weltraum...: ~ *satel·lite*; **2.** über Satel'lit, Satelliten...; ~ *television*; ~ *cap·sule s.* Raumkapsel *f*; '~-**craft** *s.* Raumfahrzeug *n*, -schiff *n*; ~ *de·bris s.* Weltraummüll *m*; ~ *flight s.* Raumflug *m*; ~ *heat·er s.* Raumerhitzer *m*, -strahler *m*; '~-**lab** *s.* 'Raumla,bor *n*; '~-**man** *s.* [*irr.*] **1.** Raumfahrer *m*, Astro'naut *m*; **2.** Außerirdische(r) *m*; ~ *med·i·cine s.* ☇ 'Raumfahrtmedi-,zin *f*; ~ *mod·ule s.* 'Weltraummo,dul *n*; ~ *probe s.* Raumsonde *f.*

spac·er ['speɪsə] *s.* ⊙ **1.** Di'stanzstück *n*; **2.** → *space bar*.

space| race *s.* Wettlauf *m* um die Eroberung des Weltraums; ~ *re·search s.* (Welt)Raumforschung *f*; '~-**sav·ing** *adj.* Raum sparend; '~-**ship** *s.* Raumschiff *n*; ~ *shut·tle s.* Raumfähre *f*; ~

sta·tion *s.* 'Raumstati,on *f*; '**~·suit** *s.* Raumanzug *m*; **,~·'time I** *s.* ✳, *phls.* Zeit-Raum *m*; **II** *adj.* Raum-Zeit-...; **~·trav·el** *s.* (Welt)Raumfahrt *f*; '**~·walk** *s.* Weltraumspaziergang *m*; '**~,wom·an** *s.* [*irr.*] **1.** Raumfahrerin *f*, Astro'nautin *f*; **2.** Außerirdische *f*; **~ writ·er** *s.* (Zeitungs- *etc.*)Schreiber, der nach dem 'Umfang s-s Beitrags bezahlt wird.

spa·cious ['speɪʃəs] *adj.* □ **1.** geräumig, weit, ausgedehnt; **2.** *fig.* weit, 'umfangreich, um'fassend; '**spa·cious·ness** [-nɪs] *s.* **1.** Geräumigkeit *f*; **2.** *fig.* Weite *f*, 'Umfang *m*, Ausmaß *n*.

spade¹ [speɪd] **I** *s.* **1.** Spaten *m*: *call a ~ a ~ fig.* das Kind beim (rechten) Namen nennen; *dig the first ~* den ersten Spatenstich tun; **2.** ✕ La'fettensporn *m*; **II** *v/t.* **3.** 'umgraben, mit e-m Spaten bearbeiten; **III** *v/i.* **4.** graben.

spade² [speɪd] *s.* **1.** Pik(karte *f*) *n*, Schippe *f* (*französisches Blatt*), Grün *n* (*deutsches Blatt*): *seven of ~s* Piksieben *f*; *in ~s Am.* F mit Zins u. Zinseszinsen; **2.** *mst pl.* Pik(farbe *f*) *n*.

spade·ful ['speɪdfʊl] *pl.* **-fuls** *s.* ein Spaten *m* (voll).

'**spade·work** *s. fig.* (mühevolle) Vorarbeit, Kleinarbeit *f*.

spa·dix ['speɪdɪks] *pl.* **spa·di·ces** [speɪ-'daɪsiːz] *s.* ♀ (Blüten)Kolben *m*.

spa·do ['speɪdəʊ] *pl.* **spa·do·nes** [spɑ'dəʊniːz] (*Lat.*) *s.* **1.** Ka'strat *m*; **2.** kastriertes Tier.

spa·ghet·ti [spə'getɪ] (*Ital.*) *s.* **1.** Spa-'g(h)etti *pl.*; **2.** *sl.* 'Filmsa,lat *m*.

spake [speɪk] *obs. pret. von* **speak**.

spall [spɔːl] **I** *s.* (Stein-, Erz)Splitter *m*; **II** *v/t.* ⚙ Erz zerstückeln; **III** *v/i.* zerbröckeln, absplittern.

spam [spæm] **I** *s. coll.* **1.** *Internet:* a) unerwünschte Werbe-E-Mails *pl.* über das Internet, b) unerwünschte u. uninteressante E-Mails *pl.* über das Internet; **2.** ☻ *TM e-e* Art Frühstücksfleisch in Dosen; **II** *v/t. Internet* **3.** *Newsgroups, Mailboxen etc.* mit e-r Nachricht (*od.* mit Nachrichten *pl.*) *od.* mit Werbung über-'frachten *od.* ,bombardieren'; '**spamming** *s. coll. Internet:* Spamming *n:* a) *massenhaftes Versenden unerwünschter Werbe-E-Mails über das Internet,* b) *,Zuschütten' aller möglichen Newsgroups, Mailboxen etc. mit der gleichen Nachricht.*

span [spæn] **I** *s.* **1.** Spanne *f:* a) *gespreizte Hand,* b) *engl. Maß = 9 inches*; **2.** △ a) Spannweite *f* (*Brückenbogen*), b) Stützweite *f* (*e-r Brücke*), c) (einzelner) Brückenbogen, d) ✓ Spannweite *f*; **4.** ♻ Spann *n, m* (*Haltetau, -kette*); **5.** *fig.* Spanne *f*, 'Umfang *m*; **6.** *fig.* (kurze) Zeitspanne *f*; **7.** Lebensspanne *f*, -zeit *f*; **8.** ✷, *psych.* (*Gedächtnis-, Seh- etc.*) Spanne *f*; **9.** Gewächshaus *n*; **10.** *Am.* Gespann *n*; **II** *v/t.* **11.** abmessen; **12.** um'spannen (*a. fig.*); **13.** sich erstrecken über (*acc.*) (*a. fig.*), über'spannen; **14.** *Fluss* über'brücken; **15.** *fig.* über-spannen, bedecken.

span·drel ['spændrəl] *s.* **1.** △ Spand-'rille *f*, (Gewölbe-, Bogen)Zwickel *m*; **2.** ⚙ Hohlkehle *f*.

span·gle ['spæŋgl] **I** *s.* **1.** Flitter(plättchen *n*) *m*, Pail'lette *f*; **2.** ♀ Gallapfel *m*; **II** *v/t.* **3.** mit Flitter besetzen; **4.** *fig.* schmücken, über'säen (*with* mit): *the ~d heavens* der gestirnte Himmel.

Span·iard ['spænjəd] *s.* Spanier(in).

span·iel ['spænjəl] *s. zo.* Spaniel *m*, Wachtelhund *m*: *a* (*tame*) *~ fig.* ein Kriecher.

Span·ish ['spænɪʃ] **I** *adj.* **1.** spanisch; **II**

s. **2.** *coll. die* Spanier; **3.** *ling.* Spanisch *n*; **~ A·mer·i·can I** *adj.* la'teinameri,kanisch; **II** *s.* La'teinameri,kaner(in); **~ chest·nut** *s.* ♀ 'Esska,stanie *f*; **~ pa·pri·ka** *s.* ♀ Spanischer Pfeffer, Paprika *m*.

spank [spæŋk] **F I** *v/t.* **1.** verhauen, *j-m* ,den Hintern versohlen'; **2.** *Pferde etc.* antreiben; **II** *v/i.* **3.** **~ along** da'hinflitzen; **III** *s.* **4.** Schlag *m*, Klaps *m*; '**spank·er** [-kə] *s.* **1.** F Renner *m* (*Pferd*); **2.** ♻ Be'san *m*; **3.** *sl.* a) Prachtkerl *m*, b) 'Prachtexem,plar *n*; '**spank·ing** [-kɪŋ] F **I** *adj.* □ **1.** schnell, tüchtig; **2.** scharf, stark: *~ breeze* steife Brise; **3.** prächtig, ,toll'; **II** *adv.* **4.** prächtig; **III** *s.* **5.** ,Haue' *f*, Schläge *pl.*

span·ner ['spænə] *s.* ⚙ Schraubenschlüssel *m:* *throw a ~ in(to) the works* F ,quer schießen'.

spar¹ [spɑː] *s. min.* Spat *m*.

spar² [spɑː] *s.* **1.** ♻ Rundholz *n*, Spiere *f*; **2.** ✓ Holm *m*.

spar³ [spɑː] **I** *v/i.* **1.** *Boxen:* sparren: *~ for time fig.* Zeit schinden; **2.** (mit Sporen) kämpfen (*Hähne*); **3.** sich streiten (*with* mit), sich in den Haaren liegen; **II** *s.* **4.** *Boxen:* Sparringskampf *m*; **5.** Hahnenkampf *m*; **6.** (Wort)Geplänkel *n*.

spare [speə] **I** *v/t.* **1.** *j-n od. et.* verschonen; *Gegner, j-s Gefühle, j-s Leben etc.* schonen: *if we are ~d* wenn wir verschont *od.* am Leben bleiben; **~** *his blushes!* bring ihn doch nicht in Verlegenheit!; **2.** sparsam 'umgehen mit, schonen; kargen mit: *~ neither trouble nor expense* weder Mühe noch Kosten scheuen: (*not to*) *~ o.s.* sich (nicht) schonen; **3.** *j-m et.* ersparen, *j-n* verschonen mit; **4.** entbehren: *we cannot ~ him just now*; **5.** *et.* erübrigen, übrig haben: *can you ~ me a cigarette (a moment)?* hast du e-e Zigarette (e-n Augenblick Zeit) für mich (übrig)?; *no time to ~* keine Zeit (zu verlieren); *~ enough* II; **II** *v/i.* **6.** sparen; **7.** Gnade walten lassen; **III** *adj.* □ **8.** Ersatz..., Reserve...: *~ part →* 14; *~ tyre* (*od. tire*) a) Ersatzreifen *m*, b) *humor.* ,Rettungsring' *m* (*Fettwulst*); **9.** 'überflüssig, übrig: *~ hours* (*od. time*) Freizeit *f*, Mußestunden *pl.*; *~ moment* freier Augenblick; *~ room* Gästezimmer *n*; *~ money* übriges Geld; **10.** sparsam, kärglich; **11.** → *sparing* 2; **12.** sparsam (*Person*); **13.** hager, dürr (*Person*); **IV** *s.* **14.** ⚙ Ersatzteil *n*; **15.** *Bowling:* Spare *m*; '**spare·ness** [-nɪs] *s.* **1.** Magerkeit *f*; **2.** Kärglichkeit *f*.

'**spare|-part sur·ger·y** *s.* ✷ Er'satzteilchirur,gie *f*; '**~·rib** *s.* Rippe(n)speer *m*.

spar·ing ['speərɪŋ] *adj.* □ **1.** sparsam (*in, of* mit), karg; mäßig: *be ~ of* sparsam umgehen mit, mit *et.*, *a.* Lob kargen; **2.** spärlich, dürftig, knapp, gering; '**spar·ing·ness** [-nɪs] *s.* **1.** Sparsamkeit *f*; **2.** Spärlichkeit *f*, Dürftigkeit *f*.

spark¹ [spɑːk] **I** *s.* **1.** Funke(n) *m* (*a. fig.*): *the vital ~* der Lebensfunke; *strike ~s out of s.o.* j-n in Fahrt bringen; **2.** *fig.* Funke(n) *m*, Spur *f* (*of von Intelligenz, Leben etc.*); **3.** ⚡ a) (e'lektrischer) Funke, b) Entladung *f*, c) (Licht-) Bogen *m*; **4.** *mot.* (Zünd)Funke *m:* *advance* (*retard*) *the ~* die Zündung vor-(zurück)stellen; **5.** → *sparks*; **II** *v/i.* **6.** Funken sprühen, funke(l)n; **7.** ⚙ zünden; **III** *v/t.* **8.** *fig. j-n* befeuern; **9.** *fig. et.* auslösen.

spark² [spɑːk] **I** *s.* **1.** flotter Kerl; **2.** *bright ~ Brit. iro.* ,Intelli'genzbolzen' *m*; **II** *v/t.* **3.** *j-m* den Hof machen.

spark| ad·vance *s. mot.* Vor-, Frühzündung *f*; **~ ar·rest·er** *s.* ⚡ Funkenlöscher *m*; **~ dis·charge** *s.* ⚡ Funkenentladung *f*; **~ gap** *s.* ⚡ (Mess)Funkenstrecke *f*.

spark·ing plug ['spɑːkɪŋ] *s. mot.* Zündkerze *f*.

spar·kle ['spɑːkl] **I** *v/i.* **1.** funkeln (*a. fig. Augen etc.; with* vor *Zorn etc.*); **2.** *fig.* a) funkeln, sprühen (*Geist, Witz*), b) brillieren, glänzen (*Person*): *his conversation ~d with wit* s-e Unterhaltung sprühte vor Witz; **3.** Funken sprühen; **4.** perlen (*Wein*); **II** *v/t.* **5.** *Licht* sprühen; **III** *s.* **6.** Funkeln *n*, Glanz *m*; **7.** Funke(n) *m*; **8.** *fig.* Bril'lanz *f*; '**spar·kler** [-lə] *s.* **1.** *sl.* Dia'mant *m*; **2.** Wunderkerze *f* (*Feuerwerk*); '**spark·let** [-lɪt] *s.* **1.** Fünkchen *n* (*a. fig.*); **2.** Kohlen'dioxidkapsel *f* (*für Siphonflaschen*); '**spar·kling** [-lɪŋ] *adj.* □ **1.** funkelnd, sprühend (*beide a. fig. Witz etc.*); **2.** *fig.* geistsprühend (*Person*); **3.** schäumend, moussierend: *~ wine* Schaumwein *m*, Sekt *m*.

'**spark|,o·ver** ⚡ ('Funken),Überschlag *m*; **~ plug** *s.* **1.** *mot.* Zündkerze *f*; **2.** F ,Motor' *m*, treibende Kraft.

sparks [spɑːks] *s.* F **1.** ♻ Funker *m*; **2.** E'lektriker *m*.

spar·ring ['spɑːrɪŋ] *s.* **1.** *Boxen:* Sparring *n:* *~ partner* Sparringspartner *m*; **2.** *fig.* Wortgefecht *n*.

spar·row ['spærəʊ] *s. orn.* Spatz *m*, Sperling *m*; '**~·grass** *s.* F Spargel *m*; **~ hawk** *s. orn.* Sperber *m*.

sparse [spɑːs] *adj.* □ spärlich, dünn (gesät); '**sparse·ness** [-nɪs], '**spar·si·ty** [-sətɪ] *s.* Spärlichkeit *f*.

Spar·tan ['spɑːtən] **I** *adj. antiq. u. fig.* spar'tanisch; **II** *s.* Spar'taner(in).

spasm ['spæzəm] *s.* **1.** ✷ Krampf *m*, Spasmus *m*, Zuckung *f*; **2.** *a. fig.* Anfall *m*; **spas·mod·ic** [spæz'mɒdɪk] *adj.* (□ *~ally*) **1.** ✷ krampfhaft, -artig, spas'modisch; **2.** *fig.* sprunghaft, vereinzelt; **spas·tic** ['spæstɪk] ✷ **I** *adj.* (□ *~ally*) spastisch, Krampf...; **II** *s.* Spastiker(in).

spat¹ [spæt] *zo.* **I** *s.* **1.** Muschel-, Austernlaich *m*; **2.** a) *coll.* junge Schaltiere *pl.*, b) junge Auster; **II** *v/i.* **3.** laichen (*bsd. Muscheln*).

spat² [spæt] *s.* Ga'masche *f*.

spat³ [spæt] **F I** *s.* **1.** Klaps *m*; **2.** *Am.* Kabbe'lei *f*; **II** *v/i.* **3.** *Am.* sich kabbeln.

spat⁴ [spæt] *pret. u. p.p. von* **spit**.

spatch·cock ['spætʃkɒk] **I** *s.* sofort nach dem Schlachten gegrilltes Huhn *etc.*; **II** *v/t.* F *Worte etc.* einflicken.

spate [speɪt] *s.* **1.** Über'schwemmung *f*, Hochwasser *n*; **2.** *fig.* Flut *f*, (Wort-) Schwall *m*.

spathe [speɪð] *s.* ♀ Blütenscheide *f*.

spa·tial ['speɪʃl] *adj.* □ räumlich, Raum...

spat·ter ['spætə] **I** *v/t.* **1.** bespritzen (*with* mit); **2.** (ver)spritzen; **3.** *fig. j-s* Namen besudeln, *j-n* ,mit Dreck bewerfen'; **II** *v/i.* **4.** spritzen; **5.** prasseln, klatschen (*a.* ✷); **III** *s.* **6.** Spritzen *n*; **7.** Klatschen *n*, Prasseln *n*; **8.** Spritzer *m*, Spritzfleck *m*; '**~·dash** → *spat²*.

spat·u·la ['spætjʊlə] *s.* ⚙, ✷ Spatel *m*, Spachtel *m*, *f*; '**spat·u·late** [-lɪt] *adj.* spatelförmig.

spav·in ['spævɪn] *s. vet.* Spat *m*; '**spav·ined** [-nd] *adj.* spatig, lahm.

spawn [spɔːn] *s.* **1.** *ichth.* Laich *m*; **2.** ♀ My'zel(fäden *pl.*) *n*; **3.** *fig. contp.* Brut *f*; **II** *v/i.* **4.** *ichth.* laichen; **5.** *fig. contp.* a) sich wie Ka'ninchen vermehren, b) wie Pilze aus dem Boden schießen; **III** *v/t.* **6.** *ichth.* Laich ablegen; **7.**

fig. contp. Kinder massenweise in die Welt setzen; **8.** *fig.* ausbrüten, her'vorbringen; **'spawn·er** [-nə] *s. ichth.* Rogener *m*, Fischweibchen *n* zur Laichzeit; **'spawn·ing** [-nɪŋ] **I** *s.* **1.** Laichen *n*; **II** *adj.* **2.** Laich...; **3.** *fig.* sich stark vermehrend.

spay [speɪ] *v/t. vet.* die Eierstöcke (*gen.*) entfernen, kastrieren.

speak [spiːk] [*irr.*] **I** *v/i.* **1.** reden, sprechen (**to** mit, zu, **about**, **of**, **on** über *acc.*): **spoken** *thea.* gesprochen (*Regieanweisung*); **so to ~** sozusagen; **the portrait ~s** *fig.* das Bild ist sprechend ähnlich; **~ speak of** *u.* **to, speaking** I; **2.** (öffentlich) sprechen *od.* reden; **3.** *fig.* ertönen (*Trompete etc.*); **4.** ♣ signalisieren; **II** *v/t.* **5.** sprechen, sagen; **6.** *Gedanken, s-e Meinung etc.* aussprechen, äußern, *die Wahrheit etc.* sagen; **7.** verkünden (*Trompete etc.*); **8.** *Sprache* sprechen (können): **he ~s French** er spricht Französisch; **9.** *fig. Eigenschaft etc.* verraten; **10.** ♣ *Schiff* ansprechen;

Zssgn mit prp.:

speak| for *v/i.* **1.** sprechen *od.* eintreten für: **that speaks well for him** das spricht für ihn; **~ o.s.** a) selbst sprechen, b) s-e eigene Meinung äußern; **that speaks for itself** das spricht für sich selbst; **2.** zeugen von: **~ of** *v/i.* **1.** sprechen von *od.* über (*acc.*): **nothing to ~** nicht der Rede wert; **not to ~** ganz zu schweigen von; **2.** *et.* verraten, zeugen von; **~ to** *v/i.* **1.** *j-n* ansprechen; mit *j-m* reden (*a. mahnend etc.*); **2.** *et.* bestätigen, bezeugen; **3.** zu sprechen kommen auf (*acc.*);

Zssgn mit adv.:

speak| out **I** *v/i.* → **speak up** 1 *u.* 2; **II** *v/t.* aussprechen; **~ up** *v/i.* **1.** laut u. deutlich sprechen: **~!** (sprich) lauter!; **2.** kein Blatt vor den Mund nehmen, frei her'aussprechen: **~!** heraus mit der Sprache!; **3.** sich einsetzen (**for** für).

'speak·eas·y *pl.* **-,eas·ies** *s. Am. sl.* Flüsterkneipe *f* (*ohne Konzession*).

speak·er ['spiːkə] *s.* **1.** Sprecher(in), Redner(in); **2.** ♗ *parl.* Sprecher *m*, Präsi'dent *m*: **the ♗ of the House of Commons**; **Mr ♗!** Herr Vorsitzender!; **3.** ♪ Lautsprecher *m*.

speak·ing ['spiːkɪŋ] **I** *adj.* □ **1.** sprechend (*a. fig. Ähnlichkeit*): **~!** *teleph.* am Apparat!; **Brown ~!** *teleph.* (hier) Brown!; **have a ~ knowledge of** *e-e Sprache* (nur) sprechen können; **~ acquaintance** flüchtige(r) Bekannte(r) → **term** 9; **2.** Sprech..., Sprach...: **a ~ voice** *e-e* (gute) Sprechstimme; **II** *s.* **3.** Sprechen *n*, Reden *n*; **III** (*adverbial*) **4.** **generally ~** allgemein; **legally ~** vom rechtlichen Standpunkt aus (gesehen); **strictly ~** streng genommen; **~ clock** *s. teleph.* Zeitansage *f*; **~ trum·pet** *s.* Sprachrohr *n*; **~ tube** *s.* **1.** Sprechverbindung *f* zwischen zwei Räumen *etc.*; **2.** Sprachrohr *n*.

spear [spɪə] **I** *s.* **1.** (Wurf)Speer *m*, Lanze *f*; Spieß *m*: **~ side** männliche Linie *e-r Familie*; **2.** *poet.* Speerträger *m*; **3.** ♀ Halm *m*, Spross *m*; **II** *v/t.* **4.** durch'bohren, aufspießen; **III** *v/i.* **5.** ♀ (auf-) sprießen; **~ gun** *s.* Har'punenbüchse *f*; **'~·head** *s.* **1.** Lanzenspitze *f*; **2.** ✕ a) Angriffsspitze *f*, b) Stoßkeil *m*; **3.** *fig.* a) Anführer *m*, Vorkämpfer *m*, b) Spitze *f*; **II** *v/t.* **4.** *fig.* an der Spitze (*gen.*) stehen, die Spitze (*gen.*) bilden; **'~·mint** *s.* ♀ Grüne Minze.

spec [spek] *s.* F Spekulati'on *f*: **on ~** auf ,Verdacht', auf gut Glück.

spe·cial ['speʃl] **I** *adj.* □ → **specially**; **1.** spezi'ell: a) (ganz) besonder: **a ~ occasion**; **his ~ charm**; **my ~ friend**; **on ~ days** an bestimmten Tagen, b) spezialisiert, Spezial..., Fach...: **~ knowledge** Fachkenntnis(se *pl.*) *f*; **2.** Sonder...(*-erlaubnis, -fall, -schule, -steuer, -zug etc.*), Extra..., Ausnahme...: **~ area** *Brit.* Notstandsgebiet *n*; **♗ Branch** *Brit.* Staatssicherheitspolizei *f*; **~ character** *Computer:* Sonderzeichen *n*; **~ constable** → 3a; **~ correspondent** → 3b; **~ delivery** ✈ *Am.* Eilzustellung *f*, ,durch Eilboten'; **~ edition** → 3c; **~ levy** *EU* Sonderabschöpfung *f*; **~ offer** ♣ Sonderangebot *n*; **~ waste** Sondermüll *m*; **~ waste dump** Sondermülldeponie *f*; **II** *s.* **3.** a) 'Hilfspoli,zist *m*, b) Sonderberichterstatter *m*, c) Sonderausgabe *f*, d) Sonderzug *m*, e) Sonderprüfung *f*, f) ♣ *Am.* Sonderangebot *n*, g) *Radio, TV:* Sondersendung *f*, h) *Am.* Tagesgericht (*im Restaurant*); **'spe·cial·ist** [-ʃəlɪst] **I** *s.* **1.** Spezia'list *m*: a) Fachmann *m*, b) ♚ Facharzt *m* (**in** für); **2.** *Am. Börse:* Jobber *m* (*der sich auf e-e bestimmte Kategorie von Wertpapieren beschränkt*); **II** *adj.* **3.** → **spe·cial·ist·ic** [,speʃə'lɪstɪk] *adj.* spezialisiert, Fach..., Spezial...; **spe·ci·al·i·ty** [,speʃɪ'ælətɪ] *s. bsd. Brit.* **1.** Besonderheit *f*; **2.** besonderes Merkmal; **3.** Spezi'alfach *n*, -gebiet *n*; **4.** Speziali'tät *f* (*a.* ♥); **5.** ♥ a) Spezi'alar,tikel *m*, b) Neuheit *f*; **spe·cial·i·za·tion** [,speʃəlaɪ'zeɪʃn] *s.* Spezialisierung *f*; **'spe·cial·ize** [-ʃəlaɪz] **I** *v/i.* **1.** sich spezialisieren (**in** auf *acc.*); **II** *v/t.* **2.** spezialisieren; ♗ spezialisiert, Spezial..., Fach...; **3.** näher bezeichnen; **4.** *biol.* *Organe* besonders entwickeln; **'spe·cial·ly** [- ʃəlɪ] *adv.* **1.** besonders, im Besonderen; **2.** eigens, extra, ausdrücklich; **'special·ty** [-tɪ] *s.* **1.** *bsd. Am.* → **speciality**; **2.** ♚ a) besiegelte Urkunde, b) formgebundener Vertrag.

spe·cie ['spiːʃɪ] *s.* **1.** Hartgeld *n*, Münze *f*; **2.** Bargeld *n*: **~ payments** Barzahlung *f*; **in ~** a) in bar, b) in natura, c) *fig.* in gleicher Münze.

spe·cies ['spiːʃiːz] *s. sg. u. pl.* **1.** *allg.* Art *f*, Sorte *f*; **2.** *biol.* Art *f*, Spezies *f*: **our** (*od.* **the**) **~** die Menschheit; **3.** *Logik:* Art *f*, Klasse *f*; **4.** *eccl.* (sichtbare) Gestalt (*von Brot u. Wein*).

spe·cif·ic [spɪ'sɪfɪk] **I** *adj.* (□ **~ally**). spe'zifisch, spezi'ell, bestimmt; **2.** ei-gen(tümlich); **3.** typisch, kennzeichnend, besonder; **4.** wesentlich; **5.** genau, defini'tiv, prä'zis(e), kon'kret: **a ~ statement**; **6.** *biol.* Art...: **~ name**; **7.** ♚ spe'zifisch (*Heilmittel, Krankheit*); **8.** *phys.* spe'zifisch: **~ gravity** spezifisches Gewicht, *die Wichte*; **II** *s.* **9.** ♚ Spe'zifikum *n*.

spec·i·fi·ca·tion [,spesɪfɪ'keɪʃn] *s.* **1.** Spezifizierung *f*; **2.** genaue Aufzählung, Einzelaufstellung *f*; **3.** *mst pl.* Einzelangaben *pl.*, -vorschriften *pl.*, *bsd.* a) △ Baubeschrieb *m*, b) ⚙ (technische) Beschreibung; **4.** ♚ Pa'tentbeschreibung *f*, -schrift *f*; **5.** ♚ Spezifikati'on *f* (*Eigentumserwerb durch Verarbeitung*); **spec·i·fy** ['spesɪfaɪ] **I** *v/t.* **1.** (einzeln) angeben *od.* aufführen, (be)nennen, spezifizieren; **2.** bestimmen, (im Einzelnen) festsetzen; **3.** in e-r Aufstellung besonders anführen; **II** *v/i.* **4.** genaue Angaben machen.

spec·i·men ['spesɪmɪn] *s.* Exem'plar *n*: **a fine ~**; **2.** Muster *n* (*a. typ.*), Probe(stück *n*) *f*, ⚙ Prüfstück *n*: **~ of s.o.'s handwriting** Handschriftenprobe; **3.** *fig.* Probe *f*, Beispiel *n* (**of** gen.); **4.** *fig.*

contp. a) ,Exem'plar' *n*, ,Muster' *n* (**of** an *dat.*), b) ,Type' *f*, komischer Kauz; **~ cop·y** *s.* 'Probeexem,plar *n*; **~ sig·na·ture** *s.* 'Unterschriftsprobe *f*.

spe·cious ['spiːʃəs] *adj.* □ äußerlich blendend, bestechend, trügerisch, Schein...(*Argument etc.*): **~ prosperity** scheinbarer Wohlstand; **'spe·cious·ness** [-nɪs] *s.* **1.** *das* Bestechende; **2.** trügerischer Schein.

speck [spek] **I** *s.* **1.** Fleck(en) *m*, Fleckchen *n*; **2.** Stückchen *n*, *das* bisschen: **a ~ of dust** ein Stäubchen; **3.** faule Stelle (*im Obst*); **4.** *fig.* Pünktchen *n*; **II** *v/t.* sprenkeln; **'speck·le** [-kl] **I** *s.* Fleck (-en) *m*, Sprenkel *m*, Tupfen *m*, Punkt *m*; **II** *v/t.* → **speck** 5; **'speck·led** [-ld] *adj.* **1.** gefleckt, gesprenkelt, getüpfelt; **2.** (bunt)scheckig; **'speck·less** [-lɪs] *adj.* □ fleckenlos, sauber, rein (*a. fig.*).

specs [speks] *s. pl.* F Brille *f*.

spec·ta·cle ['spektəkl] *s.* **1.** Schauspiel *n* (*a. fig.*); **2.** Schaustück *n*: **make a ~ of o.s.** sich zur Schau stellen, (unangenehm) auffallen; **3.** *trauriger etc.* Anblick; **4.** *pl.* **a pair of ~s** e-e Brille; **'spec·ta·cled** [-ld] *adj.* **1.** bebrillt; **2.** *zo.* Brillen...(*-bär etc.*): **~ cobra** Brillenschlange *f*; **spec·tac·u·lar** [spek'tækjulə] **I** *adj.* □ **1.** Schau..., schauspielartig; **2.** spektaku'lär, Aufsehen erregend, sensatio'nell; **II** *s.* **3.** *Am.* große (Fernseh)Schau, 'Galare,vue *f*; **spec·ta·tor** [spek'teɪtə] *s.* Zuschauer(in): **~ sport** Zuschauersport *m*.

spec·ter ['spektə] *Am.* → **spectre**.

spec·tra ['spektrə] *pl. von* **spectrum**; **'spec·tral** [-trəl] *adj.* □ **1.** geisterhaft, gespenstisch; **2.** *phys.* Spektral...: **~ colo(u)r** Spektral-, Regenbogenfarbe *f*; **'spec·tre** [-tə] *s.* **1.** Geist *m*, Gespenst *n*; **2.** *fig.* a) (Schreck)Gespenst *n*, b) *fig.* Hirngespinst *n*.

spec·tro·gram ['spektrəʊgræm] *s. phys.* Spektro'gramm *n*; **'spec·tro·graph** [-grɑːf] *s. phys.* **1.** Spektro'graph *m*; **2.** Spektro'gramm *n*; **spec·tro·scope** ['spektrəskəʊp] *s. phys.* Spektro'skop *n*.

spec·trum ['spektrəm] *pl.* **-tra** [-trə] *s.* **1.** *phys.* Spektrum *n*: **~ analysis** Spektralanalyse *f*; **2.** *a.* **radio ~** ∿ (Fre'quenz)Spektrum *n*; **3.** *a.* **ocular ~** *opt.* Nachbild *n*; **4.** *fig.* Spektrum *n*, Skala *f*: **all across the ~** auf der ganzen Linie.

spec·u·la ['spekjulə] *pl. von* **speculum**; **'spec·u·lar** [-lə] *adj.* **1.** spiegelnd, Spiegel...: **~ iron** *min.* Eisenglanz *m*; **2.** ♚ Spekulum...

spec·u·late ['spekjuleɪt] *v/i.* **1.** nachsinnen, -denken, theoretisieren, Vermutungen anstellen, ,spekulieren' (**on**, **upon**, **about** über *acc.*); **2.** ♣ spekulieren (**for, on** auf *Baisse etc.*, **in** in *Kupfer etc.*); **spec·u·la·tion** [,spekju'leɪʃn] *s.* **1.** Nachdenken *n*, Grübeln *n*; **2.** Betrachtung *f*, Theo'rie *f*, Spekulati'on *f* (*a. phls.*); **3.** Vermutung *f*, Mutmaßung *f*, Rätselraten *n*, Spekulati'on *f*: **mere ~**; **4.** ♣ Spekulati'on *f*; **'spec·u·la·tive** [-lətɪv] *adj.* □ **1.** *phls.* spekula'tiv; **2.** theo'retisch; **3.** nachdenkend, grüblerisch; **4.** forschend, abwägend (*Blick etc.*); **5.** ♣ spekula'tiv, Spekulations...; **'spec·u·la·tor** [-leɪtə] *s.* ♣ Speku'lant *m*.

spec·u·lum ['spekjuləm] *pl.* **-la** [-lə] *s.* **1.** (Me'tall)Spiegel *m* (*bsd. für Teleskope*); **2.** ♚ Spekulum *n*, Spiegel *m*.

sped [sped] *pret. u. p.p. von* **speed**.

speech [spiːtʃ] **I** *s.* **1.** Sprache *f*, Sprechvermögen *n*: **recover one's ~** die Sprache wiedergewinnen; **2.** Reden *n*, Sprechen *n*: *freedom of* ～ Redefreiheit *f*; **3.** Rede *f*, Äußerung *f*: *direct one's* ～ *to* das Wort an *j-n* richten; **4.** Gespräch *n*: *have* ～ *with* mit *j-m* reden; **5.** Rede *f*, Ansprache *f*, Vortrag *m*; ⚖ Plädoy'er *n*; **6.** a) (Landes)Sprache *f*, b) Dia'lekt *m*: *in common* ～ in der Umgangssprache, landläufig; **7.** Sprech-, Ausdrucksweise *f*, Sprache *f* (*e-r Person*); **8.** ♩ Klang *m e-r Orgel etc.*; **II** *adj.* **9.** Sprach..., Sprech...: ～ *area* ling. Sprachraum *m*; ～ *centre* (*Am. center*) *anat.* Sprechzentrum *n*; ～ *clinic* ⚕ Sprachklinik *f*; ～ *day* *ped.* (Jahres-) Schlussfeier *f*; ～ *defect* Sprachfehler *m*; ～ *island* Sprachinsel *f*; ～ *map* Sprachenkarte *f*; ～ *recognition* *Computer, ling.*: Spracherkennung *f*; ～ *record* Sprechplatte *f*; ～ *therapist* Logo'päde *m*, Logo'pädin *f*; ～ *therapy* Logopädie *f*.

speech·i·fi·ca·tion [ˌspiːtʃɪfɪˈkeɪʃn] *s. contp.* Redenschwingen *n*; **speech·i·fi·er** [ˈspiːtʃɪfaɪə] *s.* Viel-, Volksredner *m*; **speech·i·fy** [ˈspiːtʃɪfaɪ] *v/i.* Reden schwingen.

speech·less [ˈspiːtʃlɪs] *adj.* □ **1.** *fig.* sprachlos (*with* vor *Empörung etc.*): *that left him* ～ das verschlug ihm die Sprache; **2.** stumm, wortkarg; **3.** *fig.* unsäglich: ～ *grief*; **'speech·less·ness** [-nɪs] *s.* Sprachlosigkeit *f*.

speed [spiːd] **I** *s.* **1.** Geschwindigkeit *f*, Schnelligkeit *f*, Eile *f*, Tempo *n*: *at a* ～ *of* mit e-r Geschwindigkeit von; *at full* ～ mit Höchstgeschwindigkeit; *at the* ～ *of light* mit Lichtgeschwindigkeit; *full* ～ *ahead* ⚓ volle Kraft voraus; *that's not my* ～*!* *sl.* das ist nicht mein Fall!; **2.** ⚙ a) Drehzahl *f*, b) *mot. etc.* Gang *m*: *three-*～ *bicycle* Fahrrad mit Dreigangschaltung; **3.** *phot.* a) Lichtempfindlichkeit *f*, b) Verschlussgeschwindigkeit *f*; **4.** *obs.*: *good* ～*!* viel Erfolg!, viel Glück!; **5.** *sl.* ,Speed' *m* (*Aufputschmittel*); **II** *adj.* **6.** Schnell..., Geschwindigkeits...; **III** *v/t.* [*irr.*] **7.** Gast (rasch) verabschieden, *j-m* Lebe'wohl sagen; **8.** *j-m* beistehen: *God* ～ *you!* Gott sei mit dir!; **9.** rasch befördern; **10.** *Lauf etc.* beschleunigen; **11.** *mst* ～ *up* (*pret. u. p.p. speeded*) *Maschine* beschleunigen, *fig. Sache* vo'rantreiben; *Produktion* erhöhen; **IV** *v/i.* [*irr.*] **12.** (da'hin-) eilen, rasen; **13.** *mot.* (zu) schnell fahren; → *speeding*; **14.** ～ *up* (*pret. u. p.p. speeded*) die Geschwindigkeit erhöhen; **15.** *obs.* gedeihen, Glück haben; '～·**boat** *s.* **1.** ⚓ Schnellboot *n*; **2.** *sport* Rennboot *n*; ～ *bump* *s. mot.* Fahrbahnschwelle *f*, *offiziell*: Aufpflasterung *f*; ～ *cop* *s.* F motorisierter Ver-'kehrspoli,zist; ～ **count·er** *s.* ⚙ Drehzahlmesser *m*, Tourenzähler *m*.

speed·er [ˈspiːdə] *s.* **1.** ⚙ Geschwindigkeitsregler *m*; **2.** *mot.* ,Raser' *m*.

speed| hump *Brit.* → *speed bump*; ～ **in·di·ca·tor** *s.* **1.** → *speedometer*; **2.** → *speed counter*.

speed·i·ness [ˈspiːdɪnɪs] *s.* Schnelligkeit *f*, Zügigkeit *f*.

speed·ing [ˈspiːdɪŋ] *s. mot.* zu schnelles Fahren, Ge'schwindigkeitsüber,tretung *f*: *no* ～*!* Schnellfahren verboten!

speed| lathe *s.* ⚙ Schnelldrehbank *f*; ～ **lim·it** *s. mot.* Geschwindigkeitsbegrenzung *f*, Tempolimit *n*; ～ **mer·chant** *s. mot. Brit. sl.* ,Raser' *m*.

speed·o [ˈspiːdəʊ] *pl.* -os *s. mot.* F ,Tacho' *m*.

speed·om·e·ter [spɪˈdɒmɪtə] *s. mot.* Tacho'meter *m*, *n*.

speed| ramp *s. mot.* Bodenschwelle *f*;

'～-,**read·ing** *s.* 'Schnelllese,thode *f*; ～ **skat·er** *s. sport* Eisschnellläufer(in); ～ **skat·ing** *s.* Eisschnelllauf *m*.

speed·ster [ˈspiːdstə] *s.* **1.** → *speeder* 2; **2.** ,Flitzer' *m* (*Sportwagen*).

speed| trap *s.* Ra'darfalle *f*; '～·**up** *s.* **1.** Beschleunigung *f*; **2.** Produkti'onserhöhung *f*; '～·**way** *s.* **1.** *sport* a) Speedwayrennen *pl.*, b) a. ～ *track* Speedwaybahn *f*; **2.** *Am.* a) Schnellstraße *f*, b) Autorennstrecke *f*.

speed·well [ˈspiːdwel] *s.* ♣ Ehrenpreis *n*, *m*.

speed·y [ˈspiːdɪ] *adj.* □ schnell, zügig, rasch, prompt: *wish s.o. a* ～ *recovery* *j-m* gute Besserung wünschen.

speiss [spaɪs] *s.* ⛏, *metall.* Speise *f*.

spe·le·ol·o·gist [ˌspelɪˈɒlədʒɪst] *s.* Höhlenforscher *m*; ,**spe·le·ol·o·gy** [-dʒɪ] *s.* Speläolo'gie *f*, Höhlenforschung *f*.

spell¹ [spel] **I** *v/t.* [*a. irr.*] **1.** buchstabieren: ～ *backward* a) rückwärts buchstabieren, b) *fig.* völlig verdrehen; **2.** (ortho'graphisch richtig) schreiben; **3.** *Wort* bilden, ergeben: *l-e-d* ～*s led*; **4.** *fig.* bedeuten: *it* ～*s trouble*; **5.** ～ *out* (*od. over*) (mühsam) entziffern; **6.** *oft* ～ *out* *fig.* a) darlegen, b) (*for s.o.* *j-m*) *et.* ,ausein'ander klauben'; **II** *v/i.* [*a. irr.*] **7.** (richtig) schreiben; **8.** geschrieben werden, sich schreiben.

spell² [spel] **I** *s.* **1.** Arbeit(szeit) *f*: *have a* ～ *at* sich e-e Zeit lang mit *et.* beschäftigen; **2.** (Arbeits)Schicht *f*: *give s.o. a* ～ → 7; **3.** *Am.* (*Husten- etc.*)Anfall *m*, (ner'vöser) Zustand; **4.** a) Zeit(abschnitt *m*) *f*, b) *ein Weilchen n*: *for a* ～; **5.** *Am.* F Katzensprung *m* (*kurze Strecke*); **6.** *meteor.* Peri'ode *f*: *a* ～ *of fine weather* e-e Schönwetterperiode; *hot* ～ Hitzewelle *f*; **II** *v/t.* **7.** *Am. j-n* (bei der Arbeit) ablösen.

spell³ [spel] **I** *s.* **1.** Zauber(wort *n*) *m*; **2.** *fig.* Zauber *m*, Bann *m*, Faszinati'on *f*: *be under a* ～ a) verzaubert sein, b) *fig.* gebannt *od.* fasziniert sein; *break the* ～ den Zauberbann (*fig.* das Eis) brechen; *cast a* ～ *on* → 3; **II** *v/t.* **3.** *j-n* a) verzaubern, b) *fig.* bezaubern, fesseln, faszinieren; '～·**bind** *v/t.* [*irr.*] → *bind*] → *spell³* 3; '～·**bind·er** *s.* faszinierender Redner, fesselnder Ro'man *etc.*; '～·**bound** *adj. u. adv.* (wie) gebannt, fasziniert; ～·**check·er** *s. Computer*: 'Rechtschreib(hilfe)pro,gramm *n*.

spell·er [ˈspelə] *s.* **1.** *he is a good* ～ er ist in der Orthographie gut beschlagen; **2.** Fibel *f*; '**spell·ing** [-lɪŋ] *s.* **1.** Buchstabieren *n*; **2.** Rechtschreibung *f*, Orthogra'phie *f*: ～ *bee* Rechtschreibewettbewerb *m*; ～ *checker* *Computer*: 'Rechtschreib(hilfe)pro,gramm *n*.

spelt¹ [spelt] *s.* ♣ Spelz *m*, Dinkel *m*.

spelt² [spelt] *pret. u. p.p. von* **spell¹**.

spel·ter [ˈspeltə] *s.* **1.** ✝ (Handels-, Roh)Zink *n*; **2.** a. ～ *solder* ⚙ Messingschlaglot *n*.

spe·lunk [spɪˈlʌŋk] *v/i. Am.* Höhlen erforschen (*als Hobby*).

spen·cer¹ [ˈspensə] *s. hist. u. Damenmode*: Spenzer *m* (*kurze Überjacke*).

spen·cer² [ˈspensə] *s.* ⚓ *hist.* Gaffelsegel *n*.

spend [spend] [*irr.*] **I** *v/t.* **1.** verbrauchen, aufwenden, ausgeben (*on* für): ～ *money*, → *penny* 1; **2.** *Geld, Zeit etc.* verwenden, anlegen (*on* für): ～ *time on s.th.* Zeit für et. verwenden; **3.** verschwenden, -geuden, 'durchbringen; **4.** *Zeit* zu-, verbringen; **5.** (*o.s.* sich) erschöpfen, verausgaben: *the storm is spent* der Sturm hat sich gelegt *od.* ausgetobt; **II** *v/i.* **6.** Geld ausgeben,

---

Ausgaben machen; **7.** laichen (*Fische*).

spend·ing [ˈspendɪŋ] *s.* **1.** (*das*) Geldausgeben; **2.** Ausgabe(n *pl.*) *f*; ～ *mon·ey* Taschengeld *n*; ～ *pow·er* *s.* Kaufkraft *f*.

spend·thrift [ˈspendθrɪft] **I** *s.* Verschwender(in); **II** *adj.* verschwenderisch.

Spen·se·ri·an [spenˈsɪərɪən] *adj.* (Edmund) Spenser betreffend: ～ *stanza* Spenserstanze *f*.

spent [spent] **I** *pret. u. p.p. von* **spend**; **II** *adj.* **1.** matt, verausgabt, erschöpft, entkräftet: ～ *bullet* matte Kugel; ～ *liquor* ⊚ Ablauge *f*; **2.** verbraucht; **3.** *zo.* (*von Eiern od. Samen*) entleert (*Insekten, Fische*): ～ *herring* Hering *m* nach dem Laichen.

sperm¹ [spɜːm] *s. physiol.* **1.** Sperma *n*, Samenflüssigkeit *f*; **2.** Samenzelle *f*.

sperm² [spɜːm] *s.* **1.** Walrat *m*, *n*; **2.** → *sperm whale*; **3.** → *sperm oil*.

sper·ma·ce·ti [ˌspɜːməˈsetɪ] *s.* Walrat *m*, *n*.

sper·ma·ry [ˈspɜːmərɪ] *s. physiol.* Keimdrüse *f*; **sper·mat·ic** [spɜːˈmætɪk] *adj. physiol.* sper'matisch, Samen...: ～ *cord* Samenstrang *m*; ～ *filament* Samenfaden *m*; ～ *fluid* → *sperm¹* 1.

sper·ma·to·blast [ˈspɜːmətəʊblæst] *s. biol.* Ursamenzelle *f*; ,**sper·ma·to'gen·e·sis** [-əʊˈdʒenɪsɪs] *s. biol.* Samenbildung *f*; ,**sper·ma·to'zo·on** [-əʊˈzəʊɒn] *pl.* -'**zo·a** [-'zəʊə] *s. biol.* Spermato'zoon *n*, Spermium *n*.

spermo- [spɜːməʊ] *in Zssgn* Samen...

sperm oil *s.* Walratöl *n*.

sper·mo·log·i·cal [ˌspɜːməˈlɒdʒɪkl] *adj.* **1.** ♣ spermato'logisch; **2.** ♣ samenkundlich.

sperm whale *s. zo.* Pottwal *m*.

spew [spjuː] **I** *v/i.* sich erbrechen, ,spucken', ,speien'; **II** *v/t.* (er)brechen: ～ *forth* (*od. out, up*) (aus)speien, (-)spucken, (-)werfen; **III** *s.* das Erbrochene.

sphac·e·la·tion [ˌsfæsɪˈleɪʃn] *s.* ♣ Brandbildung *f*; **sphac·e·lous** [ˈsfæsɪləs] *adj.* ♣ gangrä'nös, ne'krotisch.

sphaero- [sfɪərəʊ] *in Zssgn* Kugel..., Sphäro...

sphe·nog·ra·phy [sfɪˈnɒgrəfɪ] *s.* Keilschriftkunde *f*; **sphe·noid** [ˈsfiːnɔɪd] **I** *adj.* **1.** keilförmig; **2.** *anat.* Keilbein...; **II** *s.* **3.** *min.* Spheno'id *n* (*Kristallform*).

sphere [sfɪə] *s.* **1.** Kugel *f* (*a. ♔; a. sport Ball*), kugelförmiger Körper; Erd-, Himmelskugel *f*; Himmelskörper *m*: *doctrine of the* ～ ♔ Sphärik *f*; **2.** *antiq. ast.* Sphäre *f*: *music of the* ～*s* Sphärenmusik *f*; **3.** *poet.* Himmel *m*, Sphäre *f*; **4.** *fig.* (*Einfluss-, Interessenetc.*)Sphäre *f*, Gebiet *n*, Bereich *m*, Kreis *m*: ～ *of influence*; ～ (*of activity*) Wirkungskreis; **5.** Mili'eu *n*, (gesellschaftliche) Um'gebung; **spher·ic** [ˈsferɪk] **I** *adj.* **1.** *poet.* himmlisch; **2.** kugelförmig; **3.** sphärisch; **II** *s. pl.* **4.** → *spherics¹*; **spher·i·cal** [ˈsferɪkl] *adj.* □ **1.** kugelförmig; **2.** ♔ Kugel... (-ausschnitt, -vieleck *etc.*), sphärisch: ～ *astronomy*; ～ *trigonometry*; **sphe·ric·i·ty** [sfɪˈrɪsətɪ] *s.* Kugelgestalt *f*, sphärische Gestalt.

spher·ics¹ [ˈsferɪks] *s. pl. sg. konstr.* ♔ Sphärik *f*, Kugellehre *f*.

spher·ics² [ˈsferɪks] *s. pl. sg. konstr.* Wetterbeobachtung *f* mit elek'tronischen Geräten.

sphero- → *sphaero-*.

sphe·roid [ˈsfɪərɔɪd] **I** *s.* ♔ Sphäro'id *n*; **II** *adj.* **sphe·roi·dal** [ˌsfɪəˈrɔɪdl] *adj.* □ sphäro'idisch, kugelig; **sphe·roi·dic**,

sphe·roi·di·cal [ˌsfɪəˈrɔɪdɪk(l)] adj. □ → **spheroidal**.

spher·ule [ˈsferjuːl] s. Kügelchen n.

sphinc·ter [ˈsfɪŋktə] s. a. ~ **muscle** anat. Schließmuskel m.

sphinx [sfɪŋks] pl. **ˈsphinx·es** s. 1. mst ♀ myth. u. ♙ Sphinx f (a. fig. rätselhafter Mensch); 2. a) a. ~ **moth** Sphinx f (Nachtfalter), b) a. ~ **baboon** Sphinxpavian m; '~-like adj. sphinxartig (a. fig. rätselhaft).

spi·ca [ˈspaɪkə] pl. **-cae** [-siː] s. 1. ♀ Ähre f; 2. ✿ Kornährenverband m; **ˈspi·cate** [-keɪt] adj. ♀ a) Ähren tragend (Pflanze), b) ährenförmig (angeordnet) (Blüte).

spice [spaɪs] I s. 1. a) Gewürz n, Würze f, b) coll. Gewürze pl.; 2. fig. Würze f; 3. fig. Beigeschmack m, Anflug m; II v/t. 4. würzen (a. fig.); **spiced** [-st] → spicy 1 u. 2; **ˈspic·er·y** [-sərɪ] s. coll. Gewürze pl.; **ˈspic·i·ness** [-sɪnɪs] s. fig. das Würzige, das Piˈkante.

spick-and-span [ˌspɪkənˈspæn] adj. 1. funkelnagelneu; 2. a) blitzsauber, b) ‚wie aus dem Ei gepellt' (Person).

spic·u·lar [ˈspaɪkjʊlə] adj. 1. zo. nadelförmig; 2. ♀ ährchenförmig; **spic·ule** [ˈspaɪkjuːl] s. 1. (Eis- etc.)Nadel f; 2. zo. nadelartiger Fortsatz, bsd. Skeˈlettnadel f (e-s Schwammes etc.); 3. ♀ Ährchen n.

spic·y [ˈspaɪsɪ] adj. □ 1. gewürzt; 2. würzig, aroˈmatisch (Duft etc.); 3. Gewürz...; 4. fig. a) gewürzt, witzig, b) piˈkant, gepfeffert, schlüpfrig; 5. sl. a) ‚gewieft', geschickt, b) schick.

spi·der [ˈspaɪdə] s. 1. zo. Spinne f; 2. ✿ a) Armkreuz n, b) Drehkreuz n, c) Armstern m (Rad); 3. ⚡ Ständerkörper m; 4. Am. Dreifuß m (Untersatz); ~ **catch·er** s. orn. 1. Spinnenfresser m; 2. Mauerspecht m; ~ **line** s. math, opt. Faden(kreuz n) m, Ableselinie f; ~ **web**, a. ~'s web s. Spinn(en)gewebe n (a. fig.).

spi·der·y [ˈspaɪdərɪ] adj. 1. spinnenartig; 2. spinnwebartig; 3. voll von Spinnen.

spiel [spiːl] s. Am. sl. 1. Werbesprüche pl.; 2. ‚Platte' f, Gequassel n.

spiff·ing [ˈspɪfɪŋ] adj. sl. ‚toll', ‚(tod-)schick'.

spif·(f)li·cate [ˈspɪflɪkeɪt] v/t. sl. ‚es j-m besorgen'.

spig·ot [ˈspɪgət] s. ✿ 1. (Fass)Zapfen m; 2. Zapfen m (e-s Hahns); 3. (Fass-, Leitungs)Hahn m; 4. Muffenverbindung f (bei Röhren).

spike¹ [spaɪk] s. ♀ 1. (Gras-, Korn)Ähre f; 2. (Blüten)Ähre f.

spike² [spaɪk] I s. 1. Stift m, Spitze f, Dorn m, Stachel m; 2. ✿ (Haken-, Schienen)Nagel m, Bolzen m; 3. (Zaun-)Eisenspitze f; 4. a) mst pl. Spike m (am Rennschuh etc.), b) pl. mot. Spikes pl. (am Reifen); 5. hunt. Spieß m (e-s Junghirsches); 6. ichth. junge Maˈkrele; II v/t. 7. festnageln; 8. mit (Eisen)Spitzen versehen; 9. aufspießen; 10. sport mit den Spikes verletzen; 11. ✕ Geschütz vernageln; ~ **s.o.'s guns** fig. j-m e-n Strich durch die Rechnung machen; 12. a) e-n Schuss Alkohol geben in ein Getränk, b) fig. ‚pfeffern'.

spiked¹ [spaɪkt] adj. ♀ Ähren tragend.

spiked² [spaɪkt] adj. 1. mit Nägeln od. (Eisen)Spitzen (versehen): ~ **shoes**; ~ **helmet** Pickelhaube f; 2. mit ‚Schuss' (Getränk).

spike·nard [ˈspaɪknɑːd] s. 1. Laˈvendelöl n; 2. ♀ Indische Narde; 3. ♀ Traubige Aˈralie.

spike oil → spikenard 1.

spik·y [ˈspaɪkɪ] adj. 1. spitz, dornenartig, stachelig; 2. Brit. F a) eigensinnig, b) empfindlich.

spile [spaɪl] I s. 1. (Fass)Zapfen m, Spund m; 2. Pflock m, Pfahl m; II v/t. 3. verspunden; 4. anzapfen; '~-hole s. Spundloch n.

spill¹ [spɪl] s. 1. (Holz)Splitter m; 2. Fidibus m.

spill² [spɪl] I v/t. [irr.] 1. aus-, verschütten, überlaufen lassen; 2. Blut vergießen; 3. um'her-, verstreuen; 4. ♻ Segel killen lassen; 5. a) Reiter abwerfen, b) j-n schleudern; 6. sl. auspacken, verraten; → **bean** 1; II v/i. [irr.] 7. 'überlaufen, verschüttet werden; 8. a. ~ **over** sich ergießen (a. fig.); 9. ~ **over with** fig. wimmeln von; 10. sl. ‚auspacken', ‚singen'; III s. 11. F Sturz m (vom Pferd etc.); 12. ♥ Preissturz m.

spil·li·kin [ˈspɪlɪkɪn] s. 1. (bsd. Miˈkado-) Stäbchen n; 2. pl. sg. konstr. Miˈkado n.

ˈspill·way s. ✿ 'Überlauf(rinne f) m, 'Abflusska,nal m.

spilt [spɪlt] pret. u. p.p. von spill²; → milk 1.

spin [spɪn] I v/t. [irr.] 1. Wolle, Flachs etc. (zu Fäden) spinnen; 2. Fäden, Garn spinnen; 3. schnell drehen, (herum)wirbeln; Kreisel treiben; ✈ Flugzeug trudeln lassen; Münze hochwerfen; Wäsche schleudern; Schallplatte ‚laufen lassen'; 4. a) sich erst. ausdenken, Pläne aushecken, b) erzählen; → **yarn** 3; 5. ~ **out** in die Länge ziehen, Geschichte ausspinnen, a. Suppe etc. ‚strecken'; 6. sport Ball mit Efˈfet behandeln; 7. sl. Kandidaten ‚durchrasseln' lassen; II v/i. [irr.] 8. spinnen; 9. a. ~ **round** sich (im Kreis um die eigene Achse) drehen, her'umwirbeln; **s.o.** ~**ning** j-n hinschleudern; **my head** ~**s** mir dreht sich alles; 10. ~ **along** da'hinsausen (fahren); 11. ✈ trudeln; 12. mot. 'durchdrehen (Räder); 13. sl. ‚durchrasseln' (Prüfungskandidat); III s. 14. das Her'umwirbeln; 15. schnelle Drehung, Drall m; 16. phys. Spin m, Drall m (des Elektrons); 17. **go for a** ~ F e-e Spritztour machen; 18. ✈ a) (Ab)Trudeln n, b) 'Sturzspiˌrale f; 19. sport Efˈfet m.

spin·ach [ˈspɪnɪdʒ] s. 1. ♀ Spiˈnat m; 2. Am. sl. ‚Mist' m.

spi·nal [ˈspaɪnl] adj. anat. spiˈnal, Rückgrat..., Rückenmarks...; ~ **col·umn** s. Wirbelsäule f, Rückgrat n; ~ **cord**, ~ **mar·row** s. Rückenmark n; ~ **nerve** s. Spiˈnalnerv m.

spin·dle [ˈspɪndl] I s. 1. ✿ a) (Hand-, a. Drehbank)Spindel f, b) Welle f, Achszapfen m, c) Triebstock m, d) Hydro'meter n; 2. ein Garnmaß; 3. biol. Kernspindel f; 4. ♀ Spindel f; II v/i. 5. (auf)schießen (Pflanze); 6. in die Höhe schießen (Person); '~-legged adj. storchbeinig; '~-legs, '~-shanks s. pl. 1. ‚Storchbeine' pl.; 2. sg. konstr. ‚Storchbein' n (Person).

spin·dling [ˈspɪndlɪŋ], **ˈspin·dly** [-lɪ] adj. lang u. dünn, spindeldürr.

spin doc·tor s. F 1. offiziell eingesetzte(r) schönrednerische(r) Pressesprecher(in), Schönredner(in), F ‚Märchenerzähler(in)'; 2. Imageberater(in); ‚~-'dry v/t. Wäsche schleudern; ‚~-'dry·er, a. ‚~-'dri·er s. Wäscheschleuder f.

spine [spaɪn] s. 1. ♀, zo. Stachel m; 2. anat. Rückgrat n (a. fig. fester Charakter), Wirbelsäule f; 3. (Gebirgs)Grat m; 4. Buchrücken m; **spined** [-nd] adj. 1. bot., zo. stachelig, Stachel...; 2. Rück-

grat..., Wirbel...; **ˈspine·less** [-lɪs] adj. 1. stachellos; 2. rückgratlos (a. fig.).

spin·et [spɪˈnet] s. ♪ Spiˈnett n.

spin·na·ker [ˈspɪnəkə] s. ♻ Spinnaker m (großes Dreieckssegel).

spin·ner [ˈspɪnə] s. 1. poet. od. dial. Spinne f; 2. Spinner(in); 3. ✿ 'Spinnma,schine f; 4. Kreisel m; 5. (Polier-) Scheibe f; 6. → **spin·ner·et** [-əret] s. zo. Spinndrüse f.

spin·ney [ˈspɪnɪ] pl. **-neys** s. Brit. Dickicht n.

spin·ning ~ **jen·ny** [ˈspɪnɪŋ] s. 'Feinspinnma,schine f; ~ **mill** s. Spinneˈrei f; ~ **wheel** s. Spinnrad n.

ˈspin-off s. ✿ 'Nebenpro,dukt n (a. fig.).

spi·nose [ˈspaɪnəʊs], **ˈspi·nous** [-nəs] adj. stach(e)lig.

spin·ster [ˈspɪnstə] s. 1. älteres Fräulein, alte Jungfer; 2. Brit. ♟ a) unverheiratete Frau, b) nach dem Namen: ledig: ~ **aunt** unverheiratete Tante; **ˈspin·ster·hood** [-hʊd] s. 1. Alt'jüngferlichkeit f; 2. Alt'jungfernstand m; 3. lediger Stand; **ˈspin·ster·ish** [-ərɪʃ], **ˈspin·ster·ly** [-lɪ] adj. alt'jüngferlich.

spin·y [ˈspaɪnɪ] adj. 1. ♀, zo. stach(e)lig; 2. fig. heikel (Thema etc.).

spi·ra·cle [ˈspaɪərəkl] s. 1. Atem-, Luftloch n, bsd. zo. Traˈchee f; 2. zo. Spritzloch n (bei Walen etc.).

spi·ral [ˈspaɪərəl] I adj. □ 1. gewunden, schrauben-, schneckenförmig, spiˈral, Spiral...: ~ **balance** ✿ (Spiral)Federwaage f; ~ **staircase** Wendeltreppe f; 2. ⚗ spiˈralig, Spiral...; II s. 3. ⚗ etc. Spiˈrale f; 4. Windung f e-r Spirale; 5. ✿ a) ~ **conveyer** Förderschnecke f, b) a. ~ **spring** Spiˈralfeder f; 6. ⚡ a) Spule f, b) Wendel f (Glühlampe); 7. a. ~ **nebula** ast. Spiˈralnebel m; 8. ✈ Spi'ralflug m, Spi'rale f; 9. ♥ (Preis-, Lohn- etc.)Spiˈrale f: **wage-price** ~ Lohn-Preis-Spirale f; III v/t. 10. spiˈralig machen; 11. ~ **up** (**down**) Preise etc. hin'auf- (her'unter)schrauben; IV v/i. 12. sich spiˈralförmig nach oben od. unten bewegen, a. ✈, ♥ sich hoch schrauben od. niederschrauben.

spi·rant [ˈspaɪərənt] ling. I s. Spirans f, Reibelaut m; II adj. spiˈrantisch.

spire¹ [ˈspaɪə] s. 1. → spiral 4; 2. Spiˈrale f; 3. zo. Gewinde n.

spire² [ˈspaɪə] s. 1. (Dach-, Turm-, Baum-, Berg- etc.)Spitze f; 2. Spitzturm m; 3. Kirchturm(spitze f) m; 4. spitz zulaufender Körper od. Teil, z. B. (Blüten)Ähre f, Grashalm m, (Geweih)Gabel f; II v/i. u. v/t. 5. spitz zulaufen (lassen).

spired¹ [ˈspaɪəd] adj. spiˈralförmig.

spired² [ˈspaɪəd] adj. 1. spitz (zulaufend); 2. spitztürmig.

spir·it [ˈspɪrɪt] I s. 1. allg. Geist m: a) Odem m, Lebenshauch m, b) innere Vorstellung, ~ im Geiste, c) Seele f (a. e-s Toten), d) Gespenst n, e) Gesinnung f, (Gemein- etc.)Sinn m, f) Cha'rakter m, g) Sinn m: **the ~ of the law**; ~ **enter into** 4; 2. Stimmung f, Gemütsverfassung f, pl. a. Lebensgeister pl.: **in high** (**low**) ~**s** gehobener (in gedrückter) Stimmung; 3. Feuer n, Schwung m, E'lan m; Ener'gie f, Mut m; 4. (Mann m von) Geist m, Kopf m, Ge'nie n; 5. Seele f e-s Unternehmens; 6. (Zeit)Geist m: ~ **of the age**; 7. ⚗ Destil'lat n, Geist m, Spiritus m: ~(s) **of hartshorn** Hirschhornspiritus, -geist; ~(s) **of turpentine** Terpentinöl n; ~(s) **of wine** Weingeist; 8. pl. alko'holische od. geistige Getränke pl., Spiritu'osen pl.; 9. a. pl. ⚗ Am. Alkohol m; II v/t.

10. *a.* ~ *up* aufmuntern, anstacheln; **11.** ~ *away*, ~ *off* wegschaffen, -zaubern, verschwinden lassen; **'spir·it·ed** [-tɪd] *adj.* □ **1.** le'bendig, lebhaft, schwungvoll, tempera'mentvoll; **2.** e'nergisch, beherzt; **3.** feurig (*Pferd etc.*); **4.** (geist-) sprühend, le'bendig (*Rede, Buch etc.*). **-spir·it·ed** [spɪrɪtɪd] *adj. in Zssgn* **1.** ...gesinnt: → *public-*~; **2.** ...gestimmt: → *low-*~.

spir·it·ed·ness ['spɪrɪtɪdnɪs] *s.* **1.** Lebhaftigkeit *f*, Le'bendigkeit *f*; **2.** Ener'gie *f*, Beherztheit *f*; **3.** *in Zssgn:* *low-*~ Niedergeschlagenheit *f*; *public-*~ Gemeinsinn *m*.

spir·it·ism ['spɪrɪtɪzəm] *s.* Spiri'tismus *m*; **'spir·it·ist** [-ɪst] *s.* Spiri'tist(in); **spir·it·is·tic** [ˌspɪrɪ'tɪstɪk] *adj.* (□ ~*al·ly*) spiri'tistisch.

spir·it·less ['spɪrɪtlɪs] *adj.* □ **1.** geistlos; **2.** leb-, lust-, schwunglos, schlapp; **3.** niedergeschlagen, mutlos; **'spir·it·less·ness** [-nɪs] *s.* **1.** Geistlosigkeit *f*; **2.** Lust-, Schwunglosigkeit *f*; **3.** Kleinmut *m*.

spir·it | **lev·el** *s.* ⊕ Nivellier-, Wasserwaage *f*; ~ **rap·ping** *s.* Geisterklopfen *n*.

spir·it·u·al ['spɪrɪtjʊəl] **I** *adj.* □ **1.** geistig, unkörperlich; **2.** geistig, innerlich, seelisch: ~ *life* Seelenleben *n*; **3.** vergeistigt (*Person, Gesicht etc.*); **4.** göttlich (inspiriert); **5.** a) religi'ös, b) kirchlich, c) geistlich (*Gericht, Lied etc.*); **6.** geistig, intellektu'ell; **7.** geistreich, -voll; **II** *s.* **8.** ♪ (Neger)Spiritual *n*; **'spir·it·u·al·ism** [-lɪzəm] *s.* **1.** Geisterglaube *m*, Spiri'tismus *m*; **2.** *phls.* a) Spiritua'lismus *m*, b) meta'physischer Idea'lismus *m*; **3.** *das* Geistige; **'spir·it·u·al·ist** [-lɪst] *s.* **1.** Spiritua'list *m*, Idea'list *m*; **2.** Spiri'tist *m*; **spir·it·u·al·i·ty** [ˌspɪrɪtju'ælətɪ] *s.* **1.** *das* Geistige, *das* Geistliche; **2.** Un-körperlichkeit *f*, geistige Na'tur; **3.** *oft pl. hist.* geistliche Rechte *pl. od.* Einkünfte *pl.*; **'spir·it·u·al·ize** [-laɪz] *v/t.* **1.** vergeistigen; **2.** im über'tragenen Sinne deuten.

spir·it·u·ous ['spɪrɪtjuəs] *adj.* **1.** alko'holisch: ~ *liquors* Spirituosen; **2.** destilliert.

spir·y¹ ['spaɪərɪ] → *spired¹*.

spir·y² ['spaɪərɪ] *adj.* **1.** spitz zulaufend; **2.** vieltürmig.

spit¹ [spɪt] **I** *v/i.* [*irr.*] **1.** spucken: ~ *on fig.* auf *et.* spucken; ~ *on* (*od. at*) *s.o.* j-n anspucken; ~ *s.o. in the eye* j-m ins Gesicht spucken (*a. fig.*); **2.** spritzen, klecksen (*Federhalter*); **3.** sprühen (*Regen*); **4.** fauchen, zischen (*Katze etc.*): ~ *at s.o.* j-n anfauchen; **5.** (her'aus)sprudeln, (-)spritzen (*kochendes Wasser etc.*); **II** *v/t.* [*irr.*] **6.** *a.* ~ *out* (aus)spucken; **7.** *Feuer etc.* speien; **8.** *a.* ~ *out fig. Worte* (heftig) her'vorstoßen, zischen: ~ *it out!* F nun sags schon!; **III** *s.* **9.** Spucke *f*, Speichel *m*: ~ *and polish* ♣, ✕ *sl.* a) Putz- u. Flickstunde *f*, b) peinliche Sauberkeit, c) Leuteschinderei *f*; ~*-and-polish* F *attr.* ,wie aus dem Ei gepellt'; **10.** Fauchen *n* (*e-r Katze*); **11.** Sprühregen *m*; **12.** F Eben-, Abbild *n*: *she is the* ~ (*and image*) *of her mother* sie ist ihrer Mutter wie aus dem Gesicht geschnitten.

spit² [spɪt] **I** *s.* **1.** (Brat)Spieß *m*; **2.** *geogr.* Landzunge *f*; **3.** spitz zulaufende Sandbank; **II** *v/t.* **4.** an e-n Bratspieß stecken; **5.** aufspießen.

spit³ [spɪt] *s.* Spatenstich *m*.

spite [spaɪt] **I** *s.* **1.** Boshaftigkeit *f*, Gehässigkeit *f*: *from pure* (*od. in od. out of*) ~ aus reiner Bosheit; **2.** Groll *m*: *have a* ~ *against* j-m grollen; ~ *vote*

---

pol. Protest-, Trotzwahl *f*; **3.** (*in*) ~ *of* trotz, ungeachtet (*gen.*): *in* ~ *of that* dessen ungeachtet; *in* ~ *of o.s.* unwillkürlich; **II** *v/t.* **4.** j-m ,eins auswischen'; → *nose Redew.*; **'spite·ful** [-fʊl] *adj.* □ boshaft, gehässig; **'spite·ful·ness** [-fʊlnɪs] → *spite* 1.

'spit,fire *s.* **1.** Feuer-, Hitzkopf *m*, *bsd.* ,Drachen' *m* (*Frau*); **2.** Feuer speiender Vul'kan.

spit·tle ['spɪtl] *s.* Spucke *f*, Speichel *m*.

spit·toon [spɪ'tuːn] *s.* Spucknapf *m*.

spitz (**dog**) [spɪts] *s. zo.* Spitz *m* (*Hund*).

spiv [spɪv] *s. Brit. sl.* Schieber *m*, Schwarzhändler *m*.

splanch·nic ['splæŋknɪk] *adj. anat.* Eingeweide...

splash [splæʃ] **I** *v/t.* **1.** (mit Wasser *od.* Schmutz *etc.*) bespritzen; **2.** *Wasser etc.* spritzen, gießen, *Farbe etc.* klatschen (*on, over* über *acc. od.* auf *acc.*); **3.** *s-n Weg* patschend bahnen; **4.** *Plakate* anbringen; **5.** F *in der Zeitung* in großer Aufmachung bringen; **II** *v/i.* **6.** spritzen; **7.** platschen: a) plan(t)schen, b) klatschen (*Regen etc.*), c) plumpsen: ~ *down* wassern (*Raumkapsel*); **III** *adv. u. int.* **8.** p(l)atsch(!), klatsch(!); **IV** *s.* **9.** a) Spritzen *n*, b) Platschen *n*, Klatschen *n*, c) Schwapp *m*, Guss *m*; **10.** Spritzer *m*, (Spritz)Fleck *m*; **11.** (Farb-, Licht)Fleck *m*; **12.** F a) Aufsehen *n*, Sensati'on *f*, b) großer Aufwand: *get a* ~ groß herausgestellt werden; *make a* ~ Aufsehen erregen, Furore machen; **13.** *Brit.* F Schuss *m* (Soda)Wasser (*zum Whisky etc.*); **'~·board** *s.* ⊕ Schutzblech *n*; **'~·down** *s.* Wasserung *f*, Eintauchen *n* (*e-r Raumkapsel*).

splash·er ['splæʃə] *s.* **1.** Schutzblech *n*; **2.** Wandschoner *m*.

splash | **guard** *s.* ⊕ Spritzschutz *m*; **'~·proof** *adj.* ⊕ spritzwassergeschützt.

splash·y ['splæʃɪ] *adj.* **1.** spritzend; **2.** klatschend, platschend; **3.** bespritzt, beschmutzt; **4.** matschig; **5.** F sensatio'nell, ,toll'.

splat·ter ['splætə] → *splash* 1, 2, 6, 7.

splay [spleɪ] **I** *v/t.* **1.** ausbreiten, -dehnen; **2.** △ ausschrägen; **3.** (ab)schrägen; **4.** *bsd. vet.* Schulterknochen ausrenken (*bei Pferden*); **II** *v/i.* **5.** ausgeschrägt sein; **III** *adj.* **6.** breit u. flach; **7.** gespreizt, auswärts gebogen (*Fuß*); **8.** schief, schräg; **9.** *fig.* linkisch; **IV** *s.* **10.** △ Ausschrägung *f*; **splayed** [-eɪd] → *splay* 7.

'splay·foot **I** *s.* ✿ Spreiz-, Plattfuß *m*; **II** *adj. a.* ,~**'foot·ed** spreiz- *od.* plattfüßig.

spleen [spliːn] *s.* **1.** *anat.* Milz *f*; **2.** *fig.* schlechte Laune; **3.** *obs.* Hypochondrie *f*, Melancho'lie *f*; **4.** *obs.* Spleen *m*, ,Tick' *m*; **'spleen·ful** [-fʊl], **'spleen·ish** [-nɪʃ] *adj.* □ **1.** mürrisch, übel gelaunt; **2.** hypo'chondrisch.

splen·dent ['splendənt] *adj. min. u. fig.* glänzend, leuchtend.

splen·did ['splendɪd] *adj.* □ **1.** *alle a.* F glänzend, großartig, herrlich, prächtig: ~ *isolation pol. hist.* Splendid Isolation *f*; **2.** glorreich; **3.** wunderbar, her'vorragend: ~ *talents*; **'splen·did·ness** [-nɪs] *s.* **1.** Glanz *m*, Pracht *f*; **2.** Großartigkeit *f*.

splen·dif·er·ous [splen'dɪfərəs] *adj.* F *od. humor.* herrlich, prächtig.

splen·do(u)r ['splendə] *s.* **1.** heller Glanz; **2.** Pracht *f*; **3.** Großartigkeit *f*, Bril'lanz *f*, Größe *f*.

sple·net·ic [splɪ'netɪk] **I** *adj.* (□ ~*al·ly*) **1.** ✿ Milz...; **2.** milzkrank; **3.** →

---

spleen·ish; **II** *s.* **4.** ✿ Milzkranke(r *m*) *f*; **5.** Hypo'chonder *m*.

splen·ic ['splenɪk] *adj.* ✿ Milz...: ~ *fever* Milzbrand *m*.

splice [splaɪs] **I** *v/t.* **1.** spleißen, zs.-splissen; **2.** (ein)falzen; **3.** verbinden, zs.-fügen, *bsd. Filmstreifen, Tonband* (zs.-)kleben; **4.** F verheiraten: *get* ~*d* getraut werden; **II** *s.* **5.** ♣ Spleiß *m*, Splissung *f*; **6.** ⊕ (Ein)Falzung *f*; **7.** Klebestelle *f* (*an Filmen etc.*).

spline [splaɪn] *s.* **1.** längliches, dünnes Stück Holz *od.* Me'tall; **2.** *Art* 'Kurvenline,al *n*; **3.** ⊕ a) Keil *m*, Splint *m*, b) (Längs)Nut *f*.

splint [splɪnt] **I** *s.* **1.** ✿ Schiene *f*: *in* ~*s* geschient; **2.** ⊕ Span *m*; **3.** → *splint bone*; **4.** *vet.* a) → *splint bone* 2, b) Knochenauswuchs *m*, Tumor *m* (*Pferdefuß*); **5.** *a.* ~ *coal* Schieferkohle *f*; **II** *v/t.* **6.** ✿ schienen; ~ *bone s.* **1.** *anat.* Wadenbein *n*; **2.** *vet. Knochen des Pferdefußes hinter dem Schienbein*.

splin·ter ['splɪntə] **I** *s.* **1.** (*a. Bomben-, Knochen- etc.*)Splitter *m*, Span *m*: *go* (*in*)*to* ~*s* → 4; **2.** *fig.* Splitter *m*, Bruchstück *n*; **II** *v/t.* **3.** zersplittern (*a. fig.*); **III** *v/i.* **4.** zersplittern (*a. fig.*): ~ *off* (*fig.* sich) absplittern; ~ *group s.* Splittergruppe *f*; ~ *par·ty s. pol.* 'Splitterpar,tei *f*; '**~·proof** *adj.* splittersicher.

splin·ter·y ['splɪntərɪ] *adj.* **1.** *bsd. min.* splitterig, schieferig; **2.** leicht splitternd; **3.** Splitter...

split [splɪt] **I** *v/t.* [*irr.*] **1.** (zer)spalten, zerteilen, schlitzen; *Holz, fig. Haare* spalten; **2.** zerreißen; → *side* 4; **3.** *fig.* zerstören; **4.** *Gewinn, Flasche Wein etc.* (unterein'ander) teilen, sich in *et.* teilen; ✝ *Aktien* splitten: ~ *the difference* a) ✝ sich in die Differenz teilen, b) sich auf halbem Wege entgegenkommen *od.* einigen; ~ *screen Computer:* geteilter Bildschirm; → *ticket* 7; **5.** trennen, entzweien, *Partei etc.* spalten; **6.** *sl. Plan etc.* verraten; **7.** *Am.* F *Whisky etc.* ,spritzen' (*mit Wasser verdünnen*); **8.** ✿, *phys. Atome etc.* (auf)spalten: ~ *off* abspalten; **II** *v/i.* [*irr.*] **9.** sich aufspalten, reißen; platzen, bersten, zerspringen: *my head is* ~*ing fig.* ich habe rasende Kopfschmerzen; **10.** zerschellen (*Schiff*); **11.** sich spalten (*into* in *acc.*): ~ *off* sich abspalten; ~ *ends* Haarspliss *m*; **12.** sich entzweien *od.* trennen (*over* wegen *e-r Sache*); **13.** sich teilen (*on* in *acc.*); **14.** ~ *on* j-n ,verpfeifen'; **15.** a) F sich schütteln vor Lachen, b) *sl.* ,abhauen'; **16.** *pol. Am.* panaschieren; **III** *s.* **17.** Spalt *m*, Riss *m*, Sprung *m*; **18.** *fig.* Spaltung *f*, Zersplitterung *f* (*e-r Partei etc.*); **19.** *fig.* Entzweiung *f*, Bruch *m*; **20.** *pol.* Splittergruppe *f*; **21.** ⊕ Schicht *f* von *Spaltleder*; **22.** (*bsd. Ba'nanen*)Split *m*; **23.** F a) halbe Flasche (*Mineralwasser etc.*), b) halb gefülltes (*Schnaps- etc.*) Glas; **24.** *pl.* a) Akrobatik: Spa'gat *m*: *do the* ~*s* e-n Spagat machen, b) *sport* Grätsche *f*; **25.** *sl.* Spitzel *m*; **IV** *adj.* **26.** zer-, gespalten, Spalt...: ~ *infinitive ling.* gespaltener Infinitiv; ~*·level house* Halbgeschosshaus *n*; ~ *peas*(e) getrocknete halbe Erbsen (*für Püree etc.*); ~ *personality psych.* gespaltene Persönlichkeit; ~ *second* Bruchteil *m* e-r Sekunde; ~*·second watch* sport Stoppuhr *f*; ~ *ticket Am.* Wahlzettel *m* mit Stimmen für Kandidaten mehrerer Parteien; **'split·ting** [-tɪŋ] **I** *adj.* **1.** (ohren- etc.)zerreißend; **2.** rasend, heftig (*Kopfschmerzen*); **3.** blitzschnell; **4.** zwerchfellerschütternd: *a* ~ *farce*; **II** *s.*

5. Spaltung f; **6.** ✝ Splitting n: a) Aktienteilung f, b) *Besteuerung e-s Ehepartners zur Hälfte des gemeinsamen Einkommens;* '**split-up** s. **1.** → split 17–19; **2.** ✝ (Aktien)Split m.

splodge [splɒdʒ], **splotch** [splɒtʃ] I s. Fleck m, Klecks m; II v/t. beklecksen; **splotch·y** ['splɒtʃɪ] adj. fleckig, schmutzig.

splurge [splɜːdʒ] F I s. **1.** ‚Angabe' f, protziges Getue; **2.** verschwenderischer Aufwand; II v/i. **3.** protzen, angeben; **4.** prassen.

splut·ter ['splʌtə] I v/i. **1.** stottern; **2.** ‚stottern', ‚kotzen' (*Motor*); **3.** zischen (*Braten etc.*); **4.** klecksen (*Schreibfeder*); **5.** spritzen, platschen (*Wasser etc.*); II v/t. **6.** *Worte* her'aussprudeln, -stottern; **7.** verspritzen; **8.** bespritzen; **9.** *j-n (beim Sprechen)* bespucken; III s. **10.** Geplapper m; **11.** Spritzen n; Sprudeln n; Zischen n.

spoil [spɔɪl] I v/t. [*irr.*] **1.** *et.*, a. *Appetit, Spaß* verderben, ruinieren, vernichten; *Plan* vereiteln; **2.** *Charakter etc.* verderben, *Kind* verziehen, -wöhnen: *a **~ed brat** ein verzogener Fratz;* **3.** (*pret. u. p.p. nur ~ed*) berauben, entblößen (*of* gen.); **4.** (*pret. u. p.p. nur ~ed*) obs. (aus)plündern; II v/i. [*irr.*] **5.** verderben, ‚ka'puttgehen', schlecht werden (*Obst etc.*); **6.** *be ~ing for* brennen auf (*acc.*); *~ing for a fight* streitlustig; III s. **7.** *mst pl.* (Sieges)Beute f, Raub m; **8.** Beute(stück n) f; **9.** *mst pl. bsd. Am.* a) Ausbeute f, b) *pol.* Gewinn m, Einkünfte pl. (*e-r Partei nach dem Wahlsieg*); **10.** Errungenschaft f, Gewinn m; **11.** *pl.* 'Überreste pl., -bleibsel pl. (*von Mahlzeiten*); '**spoil·age** [-lɪdʒ] s. **1.** *typ.* Makula'tur f; **2.** ✝ Verderb m *von Waren;* '**spoil·er** [-lə] s. **1.** *mot.* Spoiler m; **2.** ✈ Störklappe f.

spoils·man ['spɔɪlzmən] s. [*irr.*] *pol. Am.* j-d, der nach der ‚Futterkrippe' strebt. '**spoil·sport** s. Spielverderber(in).

'**spoils sys·tem** s. *pol. Am.* 'Futterkrippensy‚stem n.

spoilt [spɔɪlt] *pret. u. p.p. von* spoil.

spoke[1] [spəʊk] s. **1.** (Rad)Speiche f; **2.** (Leiter)Sprosse f; **3.** ⚓ Spake f (*des Steuerrads*); **4.** Bremsvorrichtung f: *put a ~ in s.o.'s wheel fig.* j-m e-n Knüppel zwischen die Beine werfen; II v/t. **5.** *Rad* a) verspeichen, b) (ab)bremsen.

spoke[2] [spəʊk] *pret. u. obs. p.p. von* speak.

spoke bone s. *anat.* Speiche f.

spo·ken ['spəʊkən] I *p.p. von* speak; II adj. **1.** gesprochen, mündlich: *~ English* gesprochenes Englisch; **2.** *in Zssgn* ... sprechend.

spokes·man ['spəʊksmən] s. [*irr.*] Wortführer m, Sprecher m: *government ~ pol.* Regierungssprecher.

spo·li·ate ['spəʊlɪeɪt] v/t. u. v/i. plündern; **spo·li·a·tion** [ˌspəʊlɪ'eɪʃn] s. **1.** Plünderung f, Beraubung f; **2.** ⚓, ✗ *kriegsrechtliche Plünderung neutraler Schiffe;* **3.** ⚖ *unberechtigte Änderung e-s Dokuments.*

spon·da·ic [spɒn'deɪɪk] adj. *Metrik:* spon'deisch; **spon·dee** ['spɒndiː] s. Spon'deus m.

spon·dyl(e) ['spɒndɪl] s. *anat., zo.* Wirbelknochen m.

sponge [spʌndʒ] I s. **1.** *zo. u. weitS.* Schwamm m: *pass the ~ over fig.* aus dem Gedächtnis löschen, vergessen; *throw up the ~ Boxen:* das Handtuch werfen (a. *fig. sich geschlagen geben*); **2.** ✗ Wischer m; **3.** *fig.* Schma'rotzer m, ‚Nassauer' m (*Person*); **4.** *Küche:* a)

---

aufgegangener Teig, b) *lockerer, gekochter Pudding;* II v/t. **5.** a. *~ down* (mit e-m Schwamm) reinigen, abwaschen: *~ off, ~ away* weg-, abwischen; *~ out* auslöschen (a. *fig.*); **6.** *~ up Wasser etc.* (mit e-m Schwamm) aufsaugen, -nehmen; **7.** (kostenlos) ergattern, ‚schnorren'; III v/i. **8.** Schwämme sammeln; **9.** F schma'rotzen, ‚nassauern': *~ on s.o.* auf j-s Kosten leben; *~ bag s.* Kul'turbeutel m; *~ cake s.* Bis'kuitkuchen m; *~ cloth s.* ✝ *Art* Frot'tee n; '*~-down s.* Abreibung f (mit e-m Schwamm).

spong·er ['spʌndʒə] s. **1.** ⊛ Dekatierer m; **2.** ⊛ Deka'tiermaˌschine f; **3.** Schwammtaucher m; **4.** → sponge 3.

sponge rub·ber s. Schaumgummi m.

spon·gi·ness ['spʌndʒɪnɪs] s. Schwammigkeit f; **spon·gy** ['spʌndʒɪ] adj. **1.** schwammig, po'rös, Schwamm...; **2.** *metall.* locker, porös; **3.** sumpfig, matschig.

spon·sal ['spɒnsəl] adj. Hochzeits...

spon·sion ['spɒnʃn] s. **1.** ('Übernahme f e-r) Bürgschaft f; **2.** ⚖, *pol.* (von e-m nicht bsd. bevollmächtigten Vertreter) für e-n Staat übernommene Verpflichtung.

spon·sor ['spɒnsə] I s. **1.** Bürge m, Bürgin f; **2.** (Tauf)Pate m, (-)Patin f: *stand ~ to* (od. for) Pate stehen bei; **3.** Förderer m, Gönner(in); **4.** Schirmherr(in); **5.** Sponsor m, Geldgeber m; II v/t. **6.** bürgen für; **7.** fördern; **8.** die Schirmherrschaft (gen.) über'nehmen; **9.** *Radio, TV, sport etc.* sponsern, (als Sponsor) finanzieren; **spon·so·ri·al** [spɒn'sɔːrɪəl] adj. Paten...; '**spon·sor·ship** [-ʃɪp] s. **1.** Bürgschaft f; **2.** Gönnerschaft f, Schirmherrschaft f; **3.** a. *bsd. sport* finanzielle Förderung, Sponsoring n.

spon·ta·ne·i·ty [ˌspɒntə'neɪətɪ] s. **1.** Spontanei'tät f, Freiwilligkeit f, eigener od. freier Antrieb; **2.** *das* Impul'sive, impul'sives od. spon'tanes Handeln; **3.** Ungezwungenheit f, Na'türlichkeit f; **spon·ta·ne·ous** [spɒn'teɪnjəs] □ adj. **1.** spon'tan: a) plötzlich, impul'siv, b) freiwillig, von innen her'aus (erfolgend), c) ungekünstelt, ungezwungen (*Stil etc.*); **2.** auto'matisch, 'unwill‚kürlich; **3.** ♀ wild wachsend; **4.** selbsttätig, von selbst (entstanden): *~ combustion phys.* Selbstverbrennung f; *~ generation biol.* Urzeugung f; *~ ignition* ⊛ Selbstentzündung f; **spon·ta·ne·ous·ness** [spɒn'teɪnjəsnɪs] → spontaneity.

spoof [spuːf] F I s. **1.** Humbug m, Schwindel m; **2.** Ulk m; II v/t. **3.** beschwindeln; **4.** verulken.

spook [spuːk] I s. F **1.** Spuk m, Gespenst n; **2.** *Am. sl.* Ghostwriter m; II v/i. **3.** (her'um)geistern, spuken; '**spook·ish** [-kɪʃ], '**spook·y** [-kɪ] adj. **1.** gespenstisch, spukhaft, schaurig; **2.** *Am.* schreckhaft.

spool [spuːl] I s. Rolle f, Spule f, Haspel f; II v/t. (auf)spulen.

spoon [spuːn] I s. **1.** Löffel m; **2.** ⚓ Löffelruder(blatt) n; **3.** ⚓, ✗ Führungsschaufel f (*Torpedorohr*); **4.** *spoon bait;* **5.** *sport* Spoon m (*Golfschläger*); **6.** F Einfaltspinsel m; II v/t. **7.** *mst ~ up, ~ out* auslöffeln: *~ out* a. (löffelweise) austeilen; **8.** *sport Ball* schlenzen; III v/i. **9.** mit e-m Blinker angeln; **10.** *sl. obs.* ‚schmusen'; *~ bait s.* Angeln: Blinker m; '*~-bill s. orn.* **1.** Löffelreiher m, Löffelente f.

spoon·er·ism ['spuːnərɪzəm] s. (un)beabsichtigtes Vertauschen von Buchsta-

---

ben od. Silben (*z. B. **queer old dean** statt **dear old queen**).

'**spoon|·feed** v/t. [*irr.* → feed] **1.** mit dem Löffel füttern; **2.** *fig.* j-n auf-, hochpäppeln, a. verwöhnen; **3.** *~ s.th. to s.o. fig.* a) j-m et. ‚vorkauen', b) j-m et. eintrichtern; **4.** *~ s.o. fig.* j-n (geistig) bevormunden; '*~-ful* [-fʊl] *pl.* **-fuls** s. *ein* Löffel m (voll); *~ meat s.* (Kinder-, Kranken)Brei m, ‚Papp' m.

spoor [spʊə] *hunt.* I s. Spur f, Fährte f; II v/t. aufspüren; III v/i. e-e Spur verfolgen.

spo·rad·ic [spə'rædɪk] adj. (□ *~ally*) spo'radisch, vereinzelt (auftretend).

spore [spɔː] s. **1.** *biol.* Spore f, Keimkorn n; **2.** *fig.* Keim(zelle f) m.

spo·rif·er·ous [spɔː'rɪfərəs] adj. Sporen tragend od. bildend.

spo·ro·zo·a [ˌspɔːrə'zəʊə] s. *pl. zo.* Sporentierchen pl., Sporo'zoen pl.

spor·ran ['spɒrən] s. beschlagene Felltasche (*Schottentracht*).

sport [spɔːt] I s. **1.** *oft pl.* Sport m: *go in for ~s* Sport treiben; **2.** 'Sport(art f, -diszi‚plin f) m, *engS.* Jagd-, Angelsport m; **3.** Kurzweil f, Zeitvertreib m; **4.** Spaß m, Scherz m: *in ~* im Spaß, zum Scherz; *make ~ of* sich lustig machen über (acc.); **5.** Zielscheibe f des Spottes; **6.** *fig.* Spielball m (*des Schicksals, der Wellen etc.*); **7.** feiner od. anständiger Kerl: *be a (good) ~* a) sei kein Spielverderber, b) sei ein guter Kerl, nimm es nicht übel; **8.** *Am.* F a) Sportbegeisterte(r m) f, *bsd.* Spieler m, b) Genießer m; **9.** *biol.* Spiel-, Abart f; II adj. **10.** sportlich, Sport...; III v/i. **11.** sich belustigen; **12.** sich tummeln, herumtollen; **13.** sich lustig machen (*at, over, upon* über acc.); IV v/t. **14.** stolz (zur Schau) tragen, protzen mit; '**sport·ing** [-tɪŋ] adj. □ **1.** a) Sport...: *~ editor,* b) Jagd...: *~ gun;* **2.** sportlich (a. *fig. fair, anständig*): *a ~ chance* e-e faire Chance; **3.** unter'nehmungslustig, mutig; '**spor·tive** [-tɪv] adj. □ **1.** a) mutwillig, b) verspielt; **2.** spaßhaft.

sports [spɔːts] adj. □ Sport...: *~ car* Sportwagen m; *~ coat, jacket* Sportsakko m, n; '*~-cast s. Radio, TV:* Am. Sportsendung f; '*~-cast·er s.* Am. 'Sportreˌporter m; *~ cen·ter s.* Am., *~ cen·tre s.* Brit. Sportzentrum n; '*~-man* [-mən] s. [*irr.*] **1.** Sportsmann m, Sportler m; **2.** *fig.* fairer, anständiger Kerl; '*~-man·like* [-mənlaɪk] adj. sportlich, fair; '*~-man·ship* [-mənʃɪp] s. sportliches Benehmen, Fairness f; '*~-wear s.* Sport- od. Freizeitkleidung f; '*~-wom·an s.* [*irr.*] Sportlerin f.

sport·y ['spɔːtɪ] adj. F **1.** angeberisch, auffallend; **2.** sportlich: a) Sport treibend, b) fair, c) schick.

spor·ule ['spɒrjuːl] s. *biol.* (kleine) Spore.

spot [spɒt] I s. **1.** (Schmutz-, Rost- etc.) Fleck(en) m; **2.** *fig.* Schandfleck m, Makel m; **3.** (Farb)Fleck m, Tupfen m (a. zo.); **4.** ✿ a) Leberfleck m, Hautmal n, b) Pustel f, Pickel m; **5.** Stelle f, Ort m, Platz m: *on the ~* a) zur Stelle, da, b) an Ort u. Stelle, ‚vor Ort', c) auf der Stelle, sofort, d) ‚auf Draht', e) *sl.* in der ‚Tinte' od. Klemme; *put on the ~* F a) j-n in Verlegenheit bringen, b) *j-n ,umlegen'* (*töten*); *~ of four* Punkt 4 Uhr; *in ~s* stellenweise; *soft ~ fig.* Schwäche (*for* für); *sore (od. tender) ~ fig.* wunder Punkt, empfindliche Stelle; **6.** Fleckchen n, Stückchen n (*Erde*); **7.** *bsd. Brit.* F a) Bissen m, Häppchen n (*Essen*), b) Tropfen m,

Schluck *m* (*Whisky etc.*); **8.** *Billard*: Point *m*; **9.** *Am.* Auge *n* (*Würfel etc.*); **10.** *pl.* ✝ Lokowaren *pl.*; **11.** ✝, *Radio, TV*: (Werbe)Spot *m*; **12.** *Am.* F Nachtklub *m*; **13.** → *spotlight* I; II *adj.* **14.** ✝ a) so'fort lieferbar, b) so'fort zahlbar (*bei Lieferung*), c) bar, Bar...: ~ *business* Lokogeschäft *n*; ~ *goods* → 10; → *spot cash*; III *v/t.* **15.** beflecken (*a. fig.*); **16.** tüpfeln, sprenkeln; **17.** F entdecken, erspähen, her'ausfinden; **18.** platzieren: ~ *a billiard ball*; **19.** ✕, ✔ (genau) ausmachen; IV *v/i.* **20** e-n Fleck *od.* Flecke machen; **21.** flecken, fleckig werden.

spot| **an·nounce·ment** → *spot* 11; ~ **ball** *s. Billard*: auf dem Point stehender Ball; ~ **cash** *s.* ✝ Barzahlung *f*, so'fortige Kasse; ~ **check** *s.* Stichprobe *f*; ‚~-'**check** *v/t.* stichprobenweise über'prüfen.

spot·less ['spɒtlɪs] *adj.* □ fleckenlos (*a. fig.*); '**spot·less·ness** [-nɪs] *s.* Flecken-, Makellosigkeit *f* (*a. fig.*).

'**spot**|·**light** I *s.* **1.** *thea.* (Punkt)Scheinwerfer(licht *n*) *m*; **2.** *fig.* Rampenlicht *n* (der Öffentlichkeit): *in the* ~ im Brennpunkt des Interesses; **3.** *mot.* Suchscheinwerfer *m*; II *v/t.* **4.** anstrahlen; **5.** *fig.* die Aufmerksamkeit lenken auf (*acc.*); ~ **news** *s. pl.* Kurznachrichten *pl.*; ‚~-'**on** *adj. Brit.* F haargenau; ~ **price** *s.* ✝ Kassapreis *m*; ~ **re·mov·er** *s.* Fleckentferner *m*.

spot·ted ['spɒtɪd] *adj.* **1.** fleckig, gefleckt, getüpfelt, gesprenkelt; **2.** *fig.* besudelt, befleckt; **3.** ✳ Fleck...: ~ **fever** a) Fleckfieber *n*, b) Genickstarre *f*; '**spot·ter** [-tə] *s.* **1.** *Am.* F Detek'tiv *m*; **2.** ✕ a) (Luft)Aufklärer *m*, Artille-'riebeobachter *m*, b) *Luftschutz*: Flugmelder *m*.

spot test → *spot check*.

spot·ty ['spɒtɪ] *adj.* □ **1.** → *spotted* 1; **2.** uneinheitlich; **3.** pickelig.

'**spot-weld** *v/t.* ⊕ punktschweißen.

spous·al ['spauzl] I *adj.* **1.** a) Hochzeits..., b) ehelich; II *s.* **2.** *mst pl.* Hochzeit *f*; **3.** *obs.* Ehe(stand *m*) *f*; **spouse** [spauz] *s.* (*a.* ⚖ Ehe)Gatte *m*, Gattin *f*, Gemahl(in).

spout [spaut] I *v/t.* **1.** *Wasser etc.* (aus-)speien, (her'aus)spritzen; **2.** a) *Gedicht etc.* deklamieren, b) ‚her'unterrasseln‘, c) *Fragen etc.* her'aussprudeln; **3.** *sl.* versetzen, -pfänden; II *v/i.* **4.** *Wasser* speien, spritzen (*a. Wal*); **5.** her'vorsprudeln, her'ausschießen, -spritzen (*Blut, Wasser etc.*); **6.** a) deklamieren, b) *contp.* sal'badern; III *s.* **7.** Tülle *f*, Schnauze *f e-r Kanne*; **8.** Abfluss-, Speirohr *n*; **9.** (kräftiger) Wasserstrahl; **10.** *zo.* a) Fon'täne *f* (*e-s Wals*); b) → *spout hole*; **11.** *up the* ~ *fig.* F a) versetzt, verpfändet, b) ‚im Eimer‘, futsch, c) ‚in Schwulitäten‘ (*Person*): *she's up the* ~ bei ihr ist was ‚unterwegs‘; '**spout·er** [-tə] *s.* **1.** (spritzender) Wal; **2.** Ölquelle *f*; **3.** ‚Redenschwinger‘ *m*.

spout hole *s. zo.* Spritzloch *m* (*Wal*).

sprag¹ [spræg] *s.* **1.** Bremsklotz *m*; **2.** ⊕ Spreizholz *n*.

sprag² [spræg] *s. ichth.* Dorsch *m*.

sprain [spreɪn] I *v/t.* verstauchen; II *s.* ✳ Verstauchung *f*.

sprang [spræŋ] *pret. von* **spring**.

sprat [spræt] *s. ichth.* Sprotte *f*: *throw a* ~ *to catch a whale* (*od. mackerel*) *fig.* mit der Wurst nach der Speckseite werfen.

sprawl [sprɔːl] I *v/i.* **1.** ausgestreckt daliegen: *send s.o.* ~*ing* j-n zu Boden

strecken; **2.** sich spreizen; **3.** sich (hin-)rekeln *od.* (-)lümmeln; **4.** sich ausbreiten: ~*ing town*; ~ *ing hand* ausladende Handschrift; **5.** ♥ wuchern; II *v/t.* **6.** *mst* ~ *out* ausstrecken, -spreizen; III *s.* **7.** Rekeln *n*, Sich-'breit-Machen *n*; **8.** Ausbreitung *f des Stadtgebiets etc.*: *urban* ~.

spray¹ [spreɪ] *s.* **1.** Zweig(chen *n*) *m*, Reis *n*; **2.** *coll.* a) Gezweig *n*, b) Reisig *n*; **3.** Zweigverzierung *f*.

spray² [spreɪ] I *s.* **1.** Gischt *m*, *f*, Schaum *m*; Sprühnebel *m*, -regen *m*, -wasser *n*; **2.** ⊕, *pharm.* a) Spray *m, n*, b) Zerstäuber *m*, Sprüh-, Spraydose *f*; II *v/t.* **3.** zerstäuben, (ver)sprühen; *vom Flugzeug* abregnen; **4.** *a.* ~ *on* ⊕ aufsprühen, -spritzen; **5.** *et.* besprühen, -spritzen, *Haar* sprayen; *mot. etc.* spritzlackieren; ~ **art·ist** *s.* Sprayer(in); '**spray·er** [-erə] → *spray²* 2b.

spray| **gun** *s.* ⊕ 'Spritzpi‚stole *f*; ~ **noz·zle** *s.* **1.** (Gießkannen)Brause *f*; **2.** Brause *f*; **3.** *mot.* Spritzdüse *f*; '~-**paint** *v/t.* parolen etc. sprühen (*on auf acc.*).

spread [spred] I *v/t.* [*irr.*] **1.** *oft* ~ *out Hände, Flügel, Teppich etc.* ausbreiten, *Arme etc. a.* ausstrecken: ~ *the table* den Tisch decken; *the peacock* ~*s its tail* der Pfau schlägt ein Rad; **2.** *oft* ~ *out* ausdehnen; *Beine etc.* spreizen (*a.* ⊕); **3.** bedecken, über'ziehen, -'säen (*with* mit); **4.** *Heu etc.* ausbreiten; **5.** *Butter etc.* aufstreichen, *Farbe, Mörtel etc.* auftragen; **6.** *Brot* streichen, schmieren; **7.** breit schlagen; **8.** *Krankheit, Geruch etc., a. Furcht* verbreiten; **9.** *a.* ~ *abroad Gerücht, Nachricht* verbreiten, aussprengen, -streuen; **10.** *zeitlich* verteilen; **11.** ~ *o.s. sl.* a) sich als Gastgeber etc. mächtig anstrengen, b) ‚angeben‘; II *v/i.* [*irr.*] **12.** *a.* ~ *out* sich ausbreiten *od.* verteilen; **13.** sich ausbreiten (*Fahne etc.; a. Lächeln etc.*); sich spreizen (*Beine etc.*); **14.** sich *vor den Augen* ausbreiten *od.* -dehnen, sich erstrecken (*Landschaft*); **15.** ⊕ sich strecken *od.* dehnen (lassen) (*Werkstoff*); **16.** sich streichen *od.* auftragen lassen (*Butter, Farbe*); **17.** sich ver- *od.* ausbreiten (*Geruch, Pflanze, Krankheit, Gerücht etc.*), ‚übergreifen (*to auf acc.*) (*Feuer, Epidemie etc.*); III *s.* **18.** Ausbreitung *f*, -dehnung *f*; **19.** Aus-, Verbreitung *f* (*e-r Krankheit, von Wissen etc.*); **20.** Ausdehnung *f*, Weite *f*, 'Umfang *m*; **21.** (weite) Fläche *f*; **22.** *orn.*, ✔ (Flügel)Spanne *f*; **23.** ⚕, *phys., a. Ballistik*: Streuung *f*; **24.** (Zwischen)Raum *m*, Abstand *m*, Lücke *f* (*a. fig.*); (*a. Zeit*)Spanne *f*; **25.** Dehnweite *f*; **26.** Körperfülle *f*; **27.** (Bett- *etc.*)Decke *f*; **28.** Brotaufstrich *m*; **29.** F fürstliches Mahl; **30.** *typ.* Doppelseite *f*; **31.** ✝ Stel'lagegeschäft *n*; **32.** ✝ *Am.* Marge *f*, (Verdienst-)Spanne *f*, Differ'enz *f*; IV *adj.* **33.** verbreitet; ausgebreitet; **34.** gespreizt; **35.** Streich...: ~ *cheese*.

spread| **ea·gle** *s.* **1.** *her.* Adler *m*; **2.** *Am.* F Chauvi'nismus *m*; **3.** *Eiskunstlauf*: Mond *m*; ‚~-'**ea·gle** I *adj.* **1.** F angeberisch, bom'bastisch; **2.** F chauvi-'nistisch; II *v/t.* **3.** ausbreiten, spreizen.

spread·er ['spredə] *s.* Streu- *od.* Spritzgerät *n*, *bsd.* a) ('Dünger)Streuma‚schine *f*, b) Abstandsstütze *f*, c) Zerstäuber *m*, d) Spritzdüse *f*, e) Buttermesser *n*.

spread-sheet ['spredʃiːt] *Computer*: Ta'bellenkalkulati‚on(spro‚gramm *n*) *f*.

spree [spriː] F *s.* (*Kauf-*)Orgie *f*: *go on a* ~ a) ‚einen draufmachen‘, b) e-e ‚Sauftour‘ machen; *go on a buying*

(*od. shopping, spending*) ~ wie verrückt einkaufen.

sprig [sprɪg] I *s.* **1.** Zweigchen *n*, Schössling *m*, Reis *n*; **2.** F Sprössling *m*, ‚Ableger‘ *m*; **3.** Bürschchen *n*; **4.** → *spray¹* 3; **5.** ⊕ Zwecke *f*, Stift *m*; II *v/t.* **6.** mit e-m Zweigmuster verzieren; **7.** anheften.

spright·li·ness ['spraɪtlɪnɪs] *s.* Lebhaftigkeit *f*, Munterkeit *f*; '**spright·ly** ['spraɪtlɪ] *adj. u. adv.* lebhaft, munter, ‚spritzig‘,

spring [sprɪŋ] I *v/i.* [*irr.*] **1.** springen: ~ *at* (*od.* [*up*]*on*) auf j-n lossspringen, j-n anfallen; **2.** aufspringen; **3.** springen, schnellen, hüpfen: ~ *open* aufspringen (*Tür*); *the trap sprang* die Falle schnappte zu; **4.** *oft* ~ *forth* (*od. out*) a) her'ausschießen, (-)sprudeln (*Wasser, Blut etc.*), b) (her'aus)sprühen, springen (*Funken etc.*); **5.** (*from*) entspringen (*dat.*): a) quellen (aus), b) *fig.* herkommen, abstammen (von): *be sprung from* entstanden sein aus; **6.** *mst* ~ *up* aufkommen (*Wind*), b) *fig.* plötzlich entstehen *od.* aufkommen (*Ideen, Industrie etc.*): ~ *into existence*; ~ *into fame* plötzlich berühmt werden; **7.** aufschießen (*Pflanzen etc.*); **8.** (hoch) aufragen; **9.** auffliegen (*Rebhühner etc.*); **10.** ⊕ a) sich werfen, b) springen, platzen (*Holz*); **11.** ✕ explodieren (*Mine*); II *v/t.* [*irr.*] **12.** *Falle* zuschnappen lassen, *et.* zu'rückschnellen lassen; **13.** *Riss etc., ⚓ Leck* bekommen; **14.** explodieren lassen; → *mine²* 8; **15.** mit e-r *Neuigkeit etc.* ‚her'ausplatzen‘: ~ *s.th. on s.o.* j-m et. plötzlich eröffnen; **16.** △ *Bogen* wölben; **17.** ⊕ (ab)federn; **18.** *Brit.* F *Geld etc.* springen lassen; **19.** *Brit.* F *j-n* erleichtern (*for* um *Geld etc.*); **20.** *sl. j-n* ‚rausholen‘ (*befreien*); III *s.* **21.** Sprung *m*, Satz *m*; **22.** Frühling *m*, Lenz *m* (*beide a. fig.*); **23.** Elastizi'tät *f*, Sprung-, Schnellkraft *f*; **24.** *fig.* (geistige) Spannkraft; **25.** Sprung *m*, Riss *m im Holz etc.*; Krümmung *f e-s Bretts*; **26.** (*a. Mineral-, Öl*)Quelle *f*, Brunnen *m*: *hot* ~*s* heiße Quellen; **27.** *fig.* Quelle *f*, Ursprung *m*; **28.** *fig.* Triebfeder *f*, Beweggrund *m*; **29.** △ a) (Bogen)Wölbung *f*, b) Gewölbeanfang *m*; **30.** ⊕ (*bsd.* Sprung)Feder *f*, Federung *f*; IV *adj.* **31.** Sprung..., Schwung...; **32.** Feder...; **33.** Frühlings...; ~ **bal·ance** *s.* ⊕ Federwaage *f*; ~ **bed** *s.* 'Sprungfederma‚tratze *f*; '~-**board** *s. sport* Sprungbrett *n* (*a. fig.*): ~ *diving* Kunstspringen *n*; '~-**bok** [-bɒk] *pl.* -**boks**, *bsd. coll.* -**bok** *s. zo.* Springbock *m*; ~ **bows** [bəuz] *s. pl.* ⊕ Federzirkel *m*; ~ **chick·en** *s.* Brathühnchen *n*: *she is no* ~ *fig.* F a) sie ist nicht mehr die Jüngste, b) sie ist nicht von gestern; ~ **clean·ing** *s.* Frühjahrsputz *m*.

springe [sprɪndʒ] I *s.* **1.** *hunt.* Schlinge *f*; **2.** *fig.* Falle *f*; II *v/t.* **3.** *Tier* mit e-r Schlinge fangen.

spring·er ['sprɪŋə] *s.* **1.** *a.* ~ *spaniel hunt.* Springerspaniel *m*; **2.** △ (Bogen-)Kämpfer *m*.

spring| **fe·ver** *s.* **1.** Frühjahrsmüdigkeit *f*; **2.** (*rastlose*) Frühlingsgefühle *pl.*; ~ **gun** *s.* Selbstschuss *m*.

spring·i·ness ['sprɪŋɪnɪs] → *spring* 23.

spring·ing ['sprɪŋɪŋ] *s.* **1.** ⊕ Federung *f*; **2.** △ Kämpferlinie *f*.

spring| **leaf** *s.* [*irr.*] ⊕ Federblatt *n*; ~ **lock** *s.* ⊕ Schnappschloss *n*; ~ **mat·tress** → *spring bed*; ~ **on·ion** *s.* Frühlingszwiebel *f*; ~ **roll** *s.* *Essen*: Frühlingsrolle *f*; ~ **sus·pen·sion** *s.* ⊕

federnde Aufhängung, Federerung *f*; '**~·tide** → *spring* 22; **~ tide** *s.* ♣ Springflut *f*, *fig.* Flut *f*, Über'schwemmung *f*; '**~·time** → *spring* 22; **~ wheat** *s.* ♪ Sommerweizen *m.*

spring·y ['sprɪŋɪ] *adj.* □ **1.** federnd, e'lastisch; **2.** *fig.* schwungvoll.

sprin·kle ['sprɪŋkl] **I** *v/t.* **1.** Wasser etc. sprenkeln, (ver)sprengen (**on** auf *acc.*); **2.** *Salz, Pulver etc.* sprenkeln, streuen; **3.** (ver-, zer)streuen, verteilen; **4.** *et.* besprenkeln, besprengen, bestreuen, (be)netzen (**with** mit); **5.** *Stoff etc.* sprenkeln; **II** *v/i.* **6.** sprenkeln; **7.** (nieder)sprühen; **III** *s.* **8.** Sprühregen *m*; **9.** leichter Schneefall; **10.** Prise *f Salz etc.*; **11.** → *sprinkling* *s.* '**sprin·kler** [-lə] *s.* **1.** a) 'Spreng-, Be'rieselungsappa,rat *m*; **~ system** Sprinkler-, Beregnungsanlage *f*, b) Sprinkler *m*, Rasensprenger *m*, c) Brause *f*, Gießkannenkopf *m*, d) Sprinkler *m* (*e-r Feuerlöschanlage*), e) Sprengwagen *m*, f) Streuer *m*, Streudose *f*; **2.** *R.C.* Weihwasserwedel *m*; '**sprin·kling** [-lɪŋ] *s.* **1.** → *sprinkle* 8–10; **2.** *a.* **~ of** *fig.* ein bisschen, etwas, e-e Spur, ein paar *Leute etc.*, ein wenig *Salz etc.*

sprint [sprɪnt] **I** *v/i.* **1.** rennen; **2.** *sport* sprinten (*Läufer*), *allg.* spurten; **II** *s.* **3.** *sport* a) Sprint *m*, Kurzstreckenlauf *m*, b) *allg.* Spurt *m* (*a. fig.*); c) *Pferde-, Radsport*: Fliegerrennen *n*; '**sprint·er** [-tə] *s. sport* **1.** Sprinter(in), *a. allg.* Spurter(in); **2.** *Radsport*: Flieger *m*.

sprit [sprɪt] *s.* ♣ Spriet *n*.

sprite [spraɪt] *s.* **1.** Elfe *f*, Fee *f*; Kobold *m*; **2.** Geist *m*, Schemen *n*.

sprit·sail ['sprɪtsl] *s.* ♣ Sprietsegel *n*.

spritz·er ['sprɪtsə] *s.* Weinschorle *f*, Gespritzter *m.*

sprock·et ['sprɒkɪt] *s.* ⚙ **1.** Zahn *m* e-s (Ketten)Rades; **2.** *a.* **~ wheel** (Ketten-) Zahnrad *n*, Kettenrad *n*; **3.** 'Filmtransˌporttrommel *f.*

sprout [spraʊt] **I** *v/i.* **1.** *a.* **~ up** sprießen, (auf)schießen, aufgehen; **2.** keimen; **3.** schnell wachsen, sich schnell entwickeln; in die Höhe schießen (*Person*); wie Pilze aus dem Boden schießen (*Gebäude etc.*); **II** *v/t.* **4.** (her'vor)treiben, wachsen od. keimen lassen, entwickeln; **III** *s.* **5.** Spross *m*, Sprössling *m* (*a. fig.*), Schössling *m*; **6.** *pl.* → *Brussels sprouts.*

spruce¹ [spruːs] *s.* ♀ **1.** *a.* **~ fir** Fichte *f*, Rottanne *f*; **2.** Fichte(nholz *n*) *f.*

spruce² [spruːs] **I** *adj.* □ **1.** schmuck, (blitz)sauber, a'drett; **2.** geschniegelt; **II** *v/t.* **3.** *oft* **~ up** j-n fein machen, (heraus)putzen; **~ o.s. up** → 4; **III** *v/i.* **4.** *oft* **~ up** sich fein machen, sich ˌin Schale werfen'; '**spruce·ness** [-nɪs] *s.* A'drettheit *f*; *contp.* Affigkeit *f.*

sprung [sprʌŋ] **I** *pret. u. p.p. von spring*; **II** *adj.* **1.** ⚙ gefedert; **2.** rissig (*Holz*).

spry [spraɪ] *adj.* **1.** flink, hurtig; **2.** lebhaft, munter.

spud [spʌd] **I** *s.* **1.** ♪ a) Jätmesser *n*, Reutspaten *m*, b) Stoßeisen *n*; **2.** Spachtel *m, f*; **3.** F Kar'toffel *f*; **II** *v/t.* **4.** *mst* **~ up**, **~ out** ausgraben, -jäten; **5.** Ölquelle anbohren.

spue [spjuː] → *spew.*

spume [spjuːm] *s.* Schaum *m*, Gischt *m, f*; '**spu·mous** [-məs], '**spu·my** [-mɪ] *adj.* schäumend.

spun [spʌn] **I** *pret. u. p.p. von spin*; **II** *adj.* gesponnen: **~ glass** Glasgespinst *n*; **~ gold** Goldgespinst *n*; **~ silk** Schappseide *f.*

spunk [spʌŋk] *s.* **1.** Zunderholz *n*; **2.**

Zunder *m*, Lunte *f*; **3.** F a) Feuer *n*, Schwung *m*, b) ˌMumm' *m*, Mut *m*; '**spunk·y** [-kɪ] *adj.* **1.** schwungvoll; **2.** mutig, draufgängerisch; **3.** *Am.* reizbar.

spur [spɜː] **I** *s.* **1.** (Reit)Sporn *m*: **~s** Sporen *pl.*; **put** (*od.* **set**) **~s to** → 8; **win one's ~s** *fig.* sich die Sporen verdienen; **2.** *fig.* Ansporn *m*, -reiz *m*: **on the ~ of the moment** der Eingebung des Augenblicks folgend, ohne Überlegung, spontan; **3.** ♀ a) Dorn *m*, Stachel *m* (*kurzer Zweig etc.*), b) Sporn *m* (*Nektarbehälter*); **4.** *zo.* Sporn *m*, Stachel *m* (*des Hahns*); **5.** *geogr.* Ausläufer *m*, (Gebirgs)Vorsprung *m*; **6.** △ a) Strebe *f*, Stütze *f*, b) Strebebalken *m*, c) (Mauer)Vorsprung *m*; **7.** ✕ *hist.* Außen-, Vorwerk *n*; **II** *v/t.* **8.** Pferd spornen, die Sporen geben (*dat.*); **9.** *oft* **~ on** j-n anspornen, -stacheln; **~ s.o. into action**; **10.** mit Sporen versehen, Sporen (an)schnallen an (*acc.*); **III** *v/i.* **11.** (das Pferd) spornen; **12.** a) sprengen, eilen, b) *fig.* (vorwärts) drängen.

spurge [spɜːdʒ] *s.* ♀ Wolfsmilch *f.*

spur| gear *s.* ⚙ **1.** Geradstirnrad *n*; **2.** → **~ gear·ing** *s.* Geradstirnradgetriebe *n.*

spu·ri·ous ['spjʊərɪəs] *adj.* □ **1.** falsch, unecht, Pseudo..., *a.* ♀, *zo.* Schein...: **~ fruit**; **2.** nachgemacht, gefälscht; **3.** unehelich; '**spu·ri·ous·ness** [-nɪs] *s.* Unechtheit *f.*

spurn [spɜːn] *v/t.* **1.** *obs.* mit dem Fuß (weg)stoßen; **2.** verschmähen, verächtlich zu'rückweisen, j-n *a.* abweisen, e-n *Rat* missachten: **~ed lover** abgewiesener Liebhaber.

spurred [spɜːd] *adj.* gespornt; *a.* ♀, *zo.* Sporen tragend.

spurt¹ [spɜːt] **I** *s.* **1.** *sport* (*a.* Zwischen-) Spurt *m*; **2.** plötzliche Aktivi'tät, ruckartige Anstrengung; **3.** ✝ plötzliches Anziehen (*von Preisen etc.*); **II** *v/i.* **4.** *sport* spurten; **5.** plötzlich ak'tiv werden.

spurt² [spɜːt] **I** *v/t. u. v/i.* **1.** (her'aus)spritzen; **II** *s.* (*Wasser- etc.*)Strahl *m.*

spur| track *s.* ⚓ Neben-, Seitengleis *n*; **~ wheel** → *spur gear* 1.

sput·ter ['spʌtə] → *splutter.*

spu·tum ['spjuːtəm] *pl.* **-ta** [-tə] *s.* ⚕ Sputum *n*, Auswurf *m.*

spy [spaɪ] **I** *v/t.* **1.** *a.* **~ out** ausspionieren, -spähen, -kundschaften: **~ out** *a.* herausfinden; **~ the land** *fig.* ˌdie Lage peilen'; **2.** erspähen, entdecken; **II** *v/i.* **3.** ✕ *etc.* spionieren, Spio'nage treiben: **~ (up)on** j-m nachspionieren, j-n bespitzeln, *Gespräch etc.* abhören; **4.** her'umspionieren; **III** *s.* **5.** Späher(in), Kundschafter(in); **6.** ✕, *pol.* Spi'on(in) (*a. fig.* Spitzel); '**~·glass** *s.* Fernglas *n*; '**~·hole** *s.* Guckloch *n*; '**~ ring** *s.* Spio'nagering *m*; **~ sat·el·lite** *s.* ✕ ˌHimmelsspiˌon' *m.*

squab·ble ['skwɒbl] **I** *v/i.* sich zanken *od.* balgen; **II** *v/t. typ.* verquirlen; **III** *s.* Zank *m*, Kabbe'lei *f*; '**squab·bler** [-lə] *s.* ˌStreithammel' *m.*

squab·by ['skwɒbɪ] *adj.* unter'setzt, feist, plump.

squad [skwɒd] *s.* **1.** ✕ Gruppe *f*, Korpo'ralschaft *f*: **awkward ~** a) ˌpatschnasse' Re'kruten, b) *fig.* ˌFlaschenverein' *m*; **2.** (Arbeits- etc.)Trupp *m*; **3.** *Polizei*: a) ('Überfall- *etc.*)Komˌmando *n*, b) ('Raub- *etc.*)Dezerˌnat *n*; → **murder squad** *etc.*; **~ car** *Am.* (Funk-) Streifenwagen *m*; **4.** *sport* Riege *f*, Kader *m.*

squad·ron ['skwɒdrən] *s.* **1.** ✕ a) ('Rei-

---

ter)Schwaˌdron *f*, b) ('Panzer)Batailˌlon *n*; **2.** ♣, ✕ (Flotten)Geschwader *n*; **3.** ✈ Staffel *f*; **4.** *allg.* Gruppe *f*, Ab'teilung *f*, Mannschaft *f*; **~ lead·er** *s.* ('Flieger)Maˌjor *m.*

squail [skweɪl] *s.* **1.** *pl. sg. konstr.* Flohhüpfen *n*; **2.** Spielplättchen *n.*

squal·id ['skwɒlɪd] *adj.* □ schmutzig, verkommen (*beide a. fig.*), verwahrlost; **squa·lid·i·ty** [skwɒ'lɪdətɪ], '**squal·id·ness** [-nɪs] *s.* Schmutz *m*, Verkommenheit *f* (*beide a. fig.*), Verwahrlosung *f.*

squall¹ [skwɔːl] **I** *s.* **1.** *meteor.* Bö *f*, heftiger Windstoß: **white ~** Sturmbö aus heiterem Himmel; **2.** F ˌSturm' *m*, ˌGewitter' *n*: **look out for ~s** die Augen offen halten, auf der Hut sein; **II** *v/i.* **3.** stürmen.

squall² [skwɔːl] **I** *v/i.* kreischen, schreien (*a. Kind*); **II** *v/t. oft* **~ out** *et.* kreischen; **III** *s.* schriller Schrei: **~s** Geschrei *n*; '**squall·er** [-lə] *s.* Schreihals *m.*

squall·y ['skwɔːlɪ] *adj.* böig, stürmisch (*a.* F *fig.*).

squal·or ['skwɒlə] → *squalidity.*

squa·ma ['skweɪmə] *pl.* **-mae** [-miː] *s.* ♀, *anat.*, *zo.* Schuppe *f*, schuppenartige Or'ganbildung; '**squa·mate** [-meɪt], '**squa·mous** [-məs] *adj.* schuppig.

squan·der ['skwɒndə] *v/t. oft* **~ away** *Geld, Zeit etc.* verschwenden, -geuden: **~ o.s. od. one's energies** sich verzetteln *od.* ˌverplempern'; '**squan·der·er** [-dərə] *s.* Verschwender(in); '**squan·der·ing** [-dərɪŋ] **I** *adj.* □ verschwenderisch; **II** *s.* Verschwendung *f*, -geudung *f.*

squan·der·ma·ni·a [ˌskwɒndə'meɪnjə] *s.* Verschwendungssucht *f.*

square [skweə] **I** *s.* **1.** A Qua'drat *n* (*Figur*); **2.** Qua'drat *n*, Viereck *n*, quad'ratisches Stück (*Glas, Stoff etc.*), Karo *n*; **3.** Feld *n* (*Schachbrett etc.*): **be back to ~ one** *fig.* wieder da sein, wo man angefangen hat; **4.** Häuserblock *m*; **5.** (öffentlicher) Platz; **6.** ⚙ a) Winkel(maß *n*) *m*, b) *bsd. Zimmerei*: Geviert *n*: **on the ~** a) rechtwink(e)lig, b) F ehrlich, anständig, in Ordnung; **out of ~** a) nicht rechtwink(e)lig, b) *fig.* nicht in Ordnung; **7.** A Qua'drat(zahl *f*) *n*: **in the ~** im Quadrat; **8.** ✕ *hist.* Kar'ree *n*; **9.** ('Wort-, 'Zahlen)Qua'drat *n*; **10.** △ Säulenplatte *f*; **11.** *sl.* Spießer *m*; **II** *v/t.* **12.** rechtwink(e)lig *od.* quad'ratisch machen; **13.** *a.* **~ off** in Quadrate einteilen, *Papier etc.* karieren: **~d paper** Millimeterpapier *n*; **14.** auf s-e Abweichung vom rechten Winkel prüfen; **15.** A a) den Flächeninhalt berechnen von (*od. gen.*), b) *Zahl* quadrieren, ins Qua'drat erheben, c) *Figur* quadrieren; → **circle** 1; **16.** ⚙ vierkantig behauen; **17.** *Schultern* straffen; **18.** *fig.* in Einklang bringen (**with** mit), anpassen (**to** an *acc.*); **19.** (*a.* ✝ *Konten*) ausgleichen; → **account** 5; **20.** *Schuld* begleichen; **21.** *Gläubiger* befriedigen; **22.** *sl.* j-n ˌschmieren', bestechen; **23.** *sport Kampf* unentschieden beenden; **III** *v/i.* **24.** **~ up** (*Am. a.* **off**) in Boxerstellung od. in Auslage gehen: **~ up to** sich vor j-m aufpflanzen, *fig. Problem* anpacken; **25.** (**with**) über'einstimmen (mit), passen (zu); **26.** **~ up** ✝ *u. fig.* abrechnen (**with** mit); **IV** *adj.* □ **27.** A qua'dratisch, Quadrat...(*-meile, -wurzel, -zahl etc.*); **28.** im Qua'drat: **2 feet ~**; **29.** rechtwink(e)lig, im rechten Winkel (stehend) (**to** zu); **30.** (vier)eckig; **31.** ⚙ Vierkant...; **32.** gerade, gleichmäßig...; **33.** breit(schultrig), stämmig, vierschrötig; **34.** *fig.* in Einklang (stehend) (**with** mit), stimmend, in Ordnung: *get things* ~ die Sache in Ordnung bringen; **35.** ✝ abgeglichen (*Konten*): *get* ~ *with* mit *j-m* quitt werden (*a. fig.*); **36.** F a) re'ell, anständig, b) offen, ehrlich: ~ *deal* a) reeller Handel, b) anständige Behandlung; **37.** klar, deutlich: *a* ~ *refusal*; **38.** F ordentlich, reichlich: *a* ~ *meal*; **39.** *sl.* ,spießig'; **40.** zu viert: ~ *game*; V *adv.* **41.** quadratisch, viereckig; rechtwink(e)lig; **42.** F anständig, ehrlich; **43.** *Am.* di'rekt, gerade; ,~-'built → square 33; ~ dance *s. Am.* Square Dance *m*; '~-head *s. contp.* ,Qua'dratschädel' *m* (*Skandinavier od. Deutscher in U.S.A. od. Kanada*); ~ meas·ure *s.* Flächenmaß *n*.

square·ness ['skweənɪs] *s.* **1.** *das* Quadratische *od.* Viereckige; **2.** Vierschrötigkeit *f*; **3.** F Ehrlichkeit *f*; **4.** *sl.* ,Spießigkeit' *f*.

,square|-'rigged *adj.* ⚓ mit Rahen getakelt; '~-,rig·ger *s.* ⚓ Rahsegler *m*; ~ root *s.* ⅍ (Qua'drat)Wurzel *f*; ~ sail *s.* ⚓ Rahsegel *n*; ~ shoot·er *s. Am.* F ehrlicher *od.* anständiger Kerl; ,~--'shoul·dered *adj.* breitschultrig; ,~--'toed *adj. fig.* a) altmodisch, b) steif.

squash [skwɒʃ] I *v/t.* **1.** (zu Brei) zerquetschen, zs.-drücken; breit schlagen; **2.** *fig. Aufruhr etc.* niederschlagen, im Keim ersticken; **3.** F *j-n* ,fertig machen'; II *v/i.* **4.** zerquetscht werden; **5.** glucksen (*Schuhe im Morast etc.*); III *s.* **6.** Matsch *m*, Brei *m*; **7.** Gedränge *n*; **8.** ⚘ Kürbis *m*; **9.** (Zi'tronen- *etc.*)Saft *m*; **10.** Glucksen *n*, Platsch(en *n*) *m*; **11.** *sport* a) *a.* ~ *tennis* Squash *n*, b) *a.* ~ *rackets ein dem Squash ähnliches Spiel*; ~ court *s. sport* Squashcourt *m*; ~ courts *s. pl. sport* Squashhalle *f*; ~ rack·et *s. sport* Squashschläger *m*; 'squash·y [-ʃɪ] *adj.* □ **1.** weich, breiig; **2.** matschig (*Boden*).

squat [skwɒt] I *v/t.* **1.** hocken, kauern: ~ *down* sich hinhocken; **2.** sich ducken (*Tier*); **3.** F ,hocken' (*sitzen*); **4.** sich ohne Rechtstitel ansiedeln; II *v/t.* **5.** *leer stehendes Haus* besetzen; III *adj.* **6.** unter'setzt, vierschrötig (*Person*); **7.** flach, platt; IV *s.* **8.** Hockstellung *f*, Hocke *f* (*a. sport*); **9.** Sitz *m*, Platz *m*; 'squat·ter [-tə] *s.* **1.** Hockende(r *m*) *f*); **2.** Hausbesetzer *m*; **3.** Squatter *m*, Ansiedler *m* ohne Rechtstitel; **4.** Siedler *m* auf regierungseigenem Land; **5.** *Austral.* Schafzüchter *m*.

squaw [skwɔ:] *s.* **1.** Squaw *f*, Indi'anerfrau *f*; **2.** *Am.* F (Ehe)Frau *f*.

squawk [skwɔ:k] I *v/i.* **1.** *bsd. orn.* kreischen; **2.** *fig.* F zetern, aufbegehren; II *s.* **3.** *bsd. orn.* Kreischen *n*; **4.** F Gezeter *n*.

squeak [skwi:k] I *v/i.* **1.** quiek(s)en, piep(s)en; **2.** quietschen (*Bremsen, Türangel etc.*); **3.** *sl.* → *squeal* 5; II *v/t.* **4.** *et.* quiek(s)en; III *s.* **5.** Gequiek(s)e *n*, Piep(s)en *n*; **6.** Quietschen *n*; **7.** *have a narrow* (*od. close*) ~ F mit knapper Not davonkommen; 'squeak·y [-kɪ] *adj.* □ **1.** quiek(s)end; **2.** quietschend.

squeal [skwi:l] I *v/i.* **1.** kreischen, (auf-) schreien: ~ *with laughter* laut (*od.* schrill) auflachen, F vor Lachen quietschen; **2.** quietschen (*Bremsen etc.*); **3.** quieken, piepsen; **4.** F zetern, schimpfen (*about, against* gegen); **5.** *sl.* ,pfeifen', ,singen' (*verraten*): ~ *on s.o.* j-n verpetzen *od.* ,verpfeifen' (*to* bei); II *v/t.* **6.** *et.* schreien, kreischen; III *s.* **7.** schriller Schrei; **8.** Kreischen *n*,

Quieken *n*; **9.** F *fig.* Aufschrei *m*; 'squeal·er [-lə] *s.* **1.** Schreier *m*; **2.** Täubchen *n, allg.* junger Vogel; **3.** *sl.* Verräter *m*.

squeam·ish ['skwi:mɪʃ] *adj.* □ **1.** ('über)empfindlich, zimperlich; **2.** a) heikel (*im Essen*), b) (leicht) Ekel empfindend; **3.** 'übergewissenhaft, pe'nibel; 'squeam·ish·ness [-nɪs] **1.** 'Überempfindlichkeit *f*, Zimperlichkeit *f*; **2.** 'Übergewissenhaftigkeit *f*; **3.** a) heikle Art, b) Ekel *m*, Übelkeit *f*.

squee·gee [ˌskwi:'dʒi:] *s.* **1.** Gummischrubber *m*; **2.** *phot. etc.* (Gummi-) Quetschwalze *f*.

squeez·a·ble ['skwi:zəbl] *adj.* **1.** zs.-drückbar; **2.** *fig.* gefügig; 'squeeze [skwi:z] I *v/t.* **1.** (zs.-)drücken; **2.** a) *Frucht* auspressen, -quetschen, *Schwamm* ausdrücken, b) F *j-n* ,ausnehmen', ,schröpfen'; **3.** *oft* ~ *out Saft etc.* (her)'auspressen, -quetschen (*from* aus): ~ *a tear fig.* e-e Träne zerdrücken, ein paar Krokodilstränen weinen; **4.** drücken, quetschen, zwängen (*into* in *acc.*); eng (zs.-)packen: ~ *o.s.* (*od. one's way*) *into* (*through*) sich hinein-(hindurch)zwängen; **5.** F fest *od.* innig an sich drücken; **6.** F a) unter Druck setzen, erpressen, b) *Geld etc.* her'auspressen, *Vorteil etc.* her'ausschinden (*out of* aus); **7.** e-n Abdruck machen von (*e-r Münze etc.*); II *v/i.* **8.** quetschen, drücken, pressen; **9.** sich zwängen: ~ *through* (*in*) sich durch- (hinein)zwängen; III *s.* **10.** Druck *m*, Pressen *n*, Quetschen *n*; **11.** Händedruck *m*; **12.** (innige) Um'armung; **13.** Gedränge *n*; **14.** F a) Klemme *f, bsd.* Geldverlegenheit *f*, b) ,Druck' *m*, Erpressung *f*: *put the* ~ *on* j-n unter Druck setzen; **15.** ✝ wirtschaftlicher Engpass, (*a. Geld*)Knappheit *f*; **16.** (*bsd.* Wachs)Abdruck *m*; squeeze bot·tle *s.* (Plastik)Spritzflasche *f*; squeeze box *s.* ♪ F ,'Quetschkom,mode' *f*; 'squeez·er [-zə] *s.* **1.** (Frucht)Presse *f*; **2.** ⊙ a) ('Aus)Pressma,schine *f*, b) Quetschwerk *n, c)* 'Pressformma,schine *f*.

squelch [skweltʃ] I *v/t.* **1.** zermalmen; **2.** *fig.* F *j-n* ,kurz fertig machen', *j-m* den Mund stopfen, *Kritik etc.* abwürgen; II *v/i.* **3.** p(l)atschen; **4.** glucksen (*nasser Schuh etc.*); III *s.* **5.** Matsch *m*; **6.** P(l)atschen *n*, Glucksen *n*; **7.** → 'squelch·er [-tʃə] *s.* F **1.** vernichtender Schlag; **2.** vernichtende Antwort.

squib [skwɪb] *s.* **1.** a) Frosch *m*, (Feuerwerks)Schwärmer *m*, b) *Brit. allg.* (Hand)Feuerwerkskörper *m*: *damp* ~ *fig.* ,Flop' *m*, *Ladung m* ins Wasser; **2.** ✗, *a.* ✗ *hist.* Zündladung *f*; **3.** Spottgedicht *n*, Sa'tire *f*.

squid [skwɪd] *pl.* squids, *bsd. coll.* squid *s.* **1.** *zo.* e-e zehnarmiger Tintenfisch; **2.** künstlicher Köder in Tintenfischform.

squif·fy ['skwɪfɪ] *adj. sl.* beschwipst.

squig·gle ['skwɪgl] I *s.* **1.** Schnörkel *m*; II *v/i.* **2.** kritzeln; **3.** sich winden.

squill [skwɪl] *s.* **1.** ⚘ a) Meerzwiebel *f*, b) Blaustern *m*; **2.** *zo.* Heuschreckenkrebs *m*.

squint [skwɪnt] I *v/i.* **1.** schielen (*a. weitS.*); **2.** ~ *at* a) schielen nach, b) e-n Blick werfen auf (*acc.*), c) scheel *od.* argwöhnisch blicken auf (*acc.*); **3.** blinzeln, zwinkern; II *v/t.* **4.** *Augen* a) verdrehen, b) zs.-kneifen; III *s.* **5.** Schielen *n* (*a. fig.*): *have a* ~ schielen; **6.** F (rascher *od.* verstohlener) Blick: *have a* ~ *at* → 2b; IV *adj.* **7.** schielend; **8.** schief, schräg; '~-eyed *adj.* **1.** schie-

lend; **2.** *fig.* scheel, böse.

squir·arch·y ['skwaɪərɑːkɪ] *s.* → squirearchy.

squire ['skwaɪə] I *s.* **1.** *englischer* Landjunker, *a.* Gutsherr *m*, Großgrundbesitzer *m*; **2.** *bsd.* F (*a. Am.*) a) (Friedens)Richter *m*, b) *andere Person mit lokaler Obrigkeitswürde*; **3.** *hist.* Edelknabe *m*, (Schild)Knappe *m*; **4.** Kava-'lier *m*: a) Begleiter *m* (*e-r Dame*), b) Ga'lan *m*: ~ *of dames* Frauenheld *m*; II *v/t. u. v/i.* **5.** *obs.* a) (e-e Dame) begleiten, b) (e-r Dame) Ritterdienste leisten *od.* den Hof machen; 'squire·arch·y [-ərɑːkɪ] *s.* Junkertum *n*: a) *coll.* die (Land)Junker *pl.*, b) (Land-) Junkerherrschaft *f*; 'squire·ling [-əlɪŋ] *s. contp.* Krautjunker *m*.

squirm [skwɜːm] I *v/i.* **1.** sich krümmen, sich winden (*a. fig.* *with* vor Scham *etc.*): ~ *out of* a) sich (mühsam) aus *e-m Kleid* ,herausschälen', b) *fig.* sich aus *e-r Notlage etc.* (heraus)winden; II *s.* **2.** Krümmen *n*, Sich'winden *n*; **3.** ⚓ Kink *m im Tau*; 'squirm·y [-mɪ] *adj.* **1.** sich windend; **2.** *fig.* eklig.

squir·rel ['skwɪrəl] *s.* **1.** *zo.* Eichhörnchen *n*: *flying* ~ Flughörnchen *n*; **2.** Feh *n* (*Pelzwerk*); ~ *cage s.* **1.** a) Laufradkäfig *m*, b) *fig.* ,Tretmühle' *f*; **2.** ⚡ Käfiganker *m*; '~-cage *adj.* ⚡ Käfig..., Kurzschluss...

squirt [skwɜːt] I *v/i.* **1.** spritzen; **2.** her-'vorspritzen, -sprudeln; II *v/t.* **3.** *Flüssigkeit etc.* her'vor-, her'ausspritzen; **4.** bespritzen; III *s.* **5.** (Wasser- *etc.*)Strahl *m*; **6.** Spritze *f*: ~ *can* ⊙ Spritzkanne *f*; **7.** *a.* ~ *gun* 'Wasserpi,stole *f*; **8.** F ,kleiner Scheißer'.

squish [skwɪʃ] F I *v/t.* zermatschen; II *v/i.* → squelch 4.

stab [stæb] I *v/t.* **1.** *j-n* a) (nieder)stechen, b) erstechen, erdolchen; **2.** *Messer etc.* bohren, stoßen (*into* in *acc.*); **3.** *fig.* verletzen: ~ *s.o. in the back* j-m in den Rücken fallen; ~ *s.o.'s reputation* an j-m Rufmord begehen; **4.** ⊙ *Mauer* rau hauen; II *v/i.* **5.** stechen (*at* nach); **6.** *mit den Fingern etc.* stoßen (*at* nach, *auf acc.*); **7.** stechen (*Schmerz*); III *s.* **8.** (Dolch- *etc.*)Stoß *m*, Stich *m*: ~ *in the back fig.* Dolchstoß; *have* (*od. make*) *a* ~ *at* F *et.* probieren; **9.** Stich (-wunde *f*) *m*; **10.** *fig.* Stich *m* (*Schmerz, jähes Gefühl*); ~ *cell s. biol.* Stabzelle *f*.

sta·bil·i·ty [stə'bɪlətɪ] *s.* **1.** Stabili'tät *f*: a) Standfestigkeit *f*, b) (Wert)Beständigkeit *f*, Festigkeit *f*, Haltbarkeit *f, c)* Unveränderlichkeit *f* (*a.* ⅍), d) ⅋ Resi'stenz *f*: *monetary* ~ ✝ Währungsstabilität; **2.** *fig.* Beständigkeit *f*, Standhaftigkeit *f*, (Cha'rakter)Festigkeit *f*; **3.** a) ⊙ Kippsicherheit *f*, b) ✍ dy'namisches Gleichgewicht, c) ~ *on curves mot.* Kurvenstabilität *f*; sta'bil·i·ty--,or·i·ent·ed *adj.* stabili'tätsorien,tiert (*Politik*).

sta·bi·li·za·tion [ˌsteɪbɪlaɪ'zeɪʃn] *s. allg., bsd.* ⊙, ✝ Stabilisierung *f*; sta·bi·lize ['steɪbɪlaɪz] *v/t.* stabilisieren (*a.* ⊙, ⅍, ✍): a) festigen, stützen, b) kon'stant halten: ~*d warfare* ✗ Stellungskrieg *m*; sta·bi·liz·er ['steɪbɪlaɪzə] *s.* ⊙, ✍, ⅍, ⅋ Stabili'sator *m*.

sta·ble[1] ['steɪbl] *adj.* □ **1.** sta'bil (*a.* ✝): a) standfest, -sicher (*a.* ⊙), b) (wert-) beständig, fest, dauerhaft, haltbar, c) unveränderlich (*a.* ⅍), d) ⅋ resi'stent; **2.** ✝, *pol.* sta'bil: ~ *currency* sta'bile Währung; ~ *exchange rates a.* 'Wechselkursstabili,tät *f*; **3.** *fig.* beständig, (*a.* cha'rakterlich) gefestigt.

sta·ble[2] ['steɪbl] I *s.* **1.** (Pferde-, Kuh-)

Stall *m*; **2.** Stall(bestand) *m*; **3.** Rennstall *m* (*bsd. coll. Pferde, a. Rennfahrer*); **4.** *fig.* ,Stall' *m* (*Mannschaft etc., a. Familie*); **5.** *pl.* ✕ *Brit.* a) Stalldienst *m*, b) → **stable call**; **II** *v/t.* **6.** *Pferd* einstallen; **III** *v/i.* **7.** im Stall stehen (*Pferd*); **8.** *fig.* hausen; **'~boy** *s.* Stalljunge *m*; **~ call** *s.* ✕ Si'gnal *n* zum Stalldienst; **~ com·pan·ion** → **stablemate**; **'~man** [-mən] *s.* [*irr.*] Stallknecht *m*; **'~mate** *s.* Stallgefährte *m* (*a. fig. Radsport etc.*).

sta·ble·ness ['steɪblnɪs] → **stability**.

sta·bling ['steɪblɪŋ] *s.* **1.** Einstallung *f*; **2.** Stallung(en *pl.*) *f*, Ställe *pl.*

stac·ca·to [stəˈkɑːtəʊ] (*Ital.*) *adv.* **1.** ♪ stak'kato; **2.** *fig.* abgehackt.

stack [stæk] **I** *s.* **1.** Schober *m*, Feim *m*; **2.** Stoß *m*, Stapel *m* (*Holz, Bücher etc.*); **3.** *Brit.* Maßeinheit für Holz u. Kohlen (3,05814 m³); **4.** *Am.* ('Bücher-)Re‚gal *n*; *pl.* 'Hauptmaga‚zin *n e-r Bibliothek*; **5.** ✕ (Ge'wehr)Pyra‚mide *f*; **6.** a) *bsd.* 🜄, ♨ Schornstein *m*, Ka'min *m*, b) (Schmiede)Esse *f*, c) *mot.* Auspuffrohr *n*, d) Aggre'gat *n*, Satz *m*, e) (gestockte) An'tennenkombinati‚on, f) *Computer*: Stapelspeicher *m*: **blow one's ~** F ,in die Luft gehen'; **7.** Felssäule *f*; **II** *v/t.* **8.** *Heu etc.* aufschobern; **9.** aufschichten, -stapeln; **10.** *et.* voll stapeln; **11.** ✕ *Gewehre* zs.-setzen: **~ arms**; **12.** **~ the cards** die Karten ‚packen' (*um zu betrügen*): **the cards are ~ed against him** *fig.* er hat kaum e-e Chance; **'stack·er** [-kə] *s.* Stapler *m* (*Person u. Gerät*).

sta·di·a¹ ['steɪdjə] *pl. von* **stadium**.

sta·di·a² ['steɪdjə] *s. a.* **~ rod** *surv.* Messlatte *f*.

sta·di·um ['steɪdjəm] *pl.* **-di·a** [-djə] *s.* **1.** *antiq.* Stadion *n* (*Kampfbahn u. Längenmaß*); **2.** *pl. mst* **'sta·di·ums** *sport* Stadion *n*; **3.** *bsd.* 🜄, *biol.* Stadium *n*.

staff¹ [stɑːf] **I** *s.* **1.** Stock *m*, Stecken *m*; **2.** (*a.* Amts-, Bischofs-, Kom'mando-, Mess-, Wander)Stab *m*; **3.** (Fahnen-)Stange *f*, ♨ Flaggenstock *m*; **4.** *fig.* a) Stütze *f des Alters etc.*, b) *das Nötige od.* Wichtigste: **~ of life** Brot *n*, Nahrung *f*; **5.** Unruhewelle *f* (*Uhr*); **6.** a) (Assi'stenten-, Mitarbeiter)Stab *m*, b) Beamtenkörper *m*, -stab *m*, c) Lehrkörper *m*, 'Lehrerkol‚legium *n*, d) Perso'nal *n*, Belegschaft *f*: **editorial ~** Redaktion(sstab *m*) *f*; **nursing ~** 🜚 Pflegepersonal *n*; **the senior ~** 🜚 die leitenden Angestellten; **be on the ~** (**of**) zum Stab *od.* Lehrkörper *od.* Personal gehören (*gen.*), Mitarbeiter sein (*bei*), fest angestellt sein (*bei*); **7.** ✕ Stab *m*: **~ order** Stabsbefehl *m*; **8.** *pl.* **staves** [steɪvz] ♪ 'Noten(linien)sy‚stem *n*; **II** *adj.* **9.** *bsd.* ✕ Stabs...; **10.** Personal...; **III** *v/t.* **11.** (mit Perso'nal) besetzen: **well ~ed** gut besetzt; **~ing level** Personaldecke *f*; **12.** mit e-m Stab *od.* Lehrkörper *etc.* versehen; **13.** den Lehrkörper *e-r Schule* bilden.

staff² [stɑːf] *s.* 🜚 *Baustoff aus Gips u.* (*Hanf*)*Fasern*.

staff‖ car *s.* ✕ Befehlsfahrzeug *n*; **~ col·lege** *s.* ✕ Gene'ralstabsakade‚mie *f*; **~ man·ag·er** *s.* 🜚 Perso'nalchef *m*; **~ mem·ber** *s.* Mitarbeiter(in); **~ no·ta·tion** *s.* ♪ Liniennotenschrift *f*; **~ of·fi·cer** *s.* ✕ 'Stabsoffi‚zier *m*; **~ re·duc·tions** *pl.* 🜚 Perso'nalabbau *m*; **~ room** *s. ped.* Lehrerzimmer *n*; **~ ser·geant** *s.* ✕ (*Brit.* Ober)Feldwebel *m*; **~ turn·o·ver** *s.* Personalfluktuation *f*.

stag [stæg] **I** *s.* **1.** *hunt., zo.* a) Rothirsch *m*, b) Hirsch *m*; **2.** *zo. bsd. dial.* Männ-

chen *n*; **3.** *nach der Reife kastriertes männliches Tier*; **4.** F a) Herr *m* ohne Damenbegleitung, b) *bsd. Am.* → **stag party**; **5.** ⊤ *Brit.* Kon'zertzeichner *m*; **II** *adj.* **6.** F a) Herren...: **~ dinner**, b) Sex...: **~ film**; **III** *v/i.* **7.** ⊤ *Brit. sl.* in neu ausgegebenen Aktien spekulieren; **8.** *a.* **go ~** F ohne Damenbegleitung *od.* ‚solo' gehen; **~ bee·tle** *s. zo.* Hirschkäfer *m*.

stage [steɪdʒ] **I** *s.* **1.** Bühne *f*, Gerüst *n*; ♨ Landungsbrücke *f*; **2.** *thea.* Bühne *f* (*a. fig. Theaterwelt, Bühnenlaufbahn*): **the ~** *fig.* die Bühne, das Theater; **be on the ~** Schauspieler(in) *od.* beim Theater sein; **bring on the ~** → 11a; **go on the ~** zur Bühne gehen; **hold the ~** sich auf der Bühne halten; **set the ~ for** *fig.* alles vorbereiten für; **3.** *hist.* a) ('Post)Stati‚on *f*, b) Postkutsche *f*; **4.** a) *Brit.* Teilstrecke *f*, Fahrzone *f* (*Bus etc.*), b) (Reise)Abschnitt *m*, E'tappe *f* (*a. fig. u. Radsport*): **by** (*od.* **in**) **(easy) ~s** etappenweise; **5.** 🜘, ⊤, *biol. etc.* Stadium *n*, (Entwicklungs)Stufe *f*, Phase *f*: **at this ~** zum gegenwärtigen Zeitpunkt; **critical** (*experimental, initial*) **~** kritisches (Versuchs-, Anfangs-)Stadium; **~s of appeal** 🜨 Instanzenweg *m*; **6.** 🜚 (Schalt- *etc.*, ↯ Verstärker-, *a.* Ra'keten)Stufe *f*; **7.** *geol.* Stufe *f e-r Formation*; **8.** Ob'jektträger *m* (*am Mikroskop*); **9.** 🜚 Farbläufer *m*; **10.** *Am.* Höhe *f des Spiegels* (*e-s Flusses*); **II** *v/t.* **11.** *Theaterstück* a) auf die Bühne bringen, inszenieren, b) für die Bühne bearbeiten; **12.** *fig.* a) *allg.* veranstalten, b) inszenieren, aufziehen: **~ a demonstration**; **13.** 🜚 berüsten; **14.** ✕ *Am. Personen* 'durchschleusen; **~ box** *s. thea.* Pro'szeniumsloge *f*; **'~coach** *s. hist.* Postkutsche *f*; **'~craft** *s.* drama'turgisches *od.* schauspielerisches Können; **~ de·sign·er** *s.* Bühnenbildner(in); **~ di·rec·tion** *s.* Bühnen-, Re'gieanweisung *f*; **~ di·rec·tor** *s.* Regis'seur *m*; **~ door** *s.* Bühneneingang *m*; **~ ef·fect** *s.* **1.** 'Bühnenwirkung *f*, -ef‚fekt *m*; **2.** *fig.* Thea'tralik *f*; **~ fe·ver** *s.* The'aterbesessenheit *f*; **~ fright** *s.* Lampenfieber *n*; **'~hand** *s.* Bühnenarbeiter *m*; **‚~'man·age** → **stage** 12; **~ man·ag·er** *s.* Inspizi'ent *m*; **~ name** *s.* Bühnen-, Künstlername *m*; **~ play** *s.* Bühnenstück *n*.

stag·er ['steɪdʒə] *s. mst* **old ~** ,alter Hase'.

stage‖ race *s. Radsport*: E'tappennen *n*; **~ rights** *s. pl.* 🜨 Aufführungs-, Bühnenrechte *pl.*; **'~struck** *adj.* the'aterbesessen; **~ ver·sion** *s. thea.* Bühnenfassung *f*; **~ whis·per** *s.* **1.** *thea.* nur für das Publikum bestimmtes Flüstern; **2.** *fig.* weithin hörbares Geflüster; **'‚~worth·y** *adj.* bühnenfähig, -gerecht (*Schauspiel*).

stag·y ['steɪdʒɪ] *adj. Am. für* **stagy**.

stag·fla·tion [stægˈfleɪʃn] *s.* ⊤ Stagflati'on *f*.

stag·ger ['stægə] **I** *v/i.* **1.** (sch)wanken, taumeln, torkeln; **2.** *fig.* wanken (*werden*); **II** *v/t.* **3.** ins Wanken bringen, erschüttern (*a. fig.*); **4.** *fig.* verblüffen, *stärker:* 'umwerfen, über'wältigen; **5.** *gestaffelt od.* versetzt anordnen; (*a. fig. Arbeitszeit*) staffeln; **III** *s.* **6.** Schwanken *n*, Taumeln *n*; **7.** *pl. sg. konstr.*: a) Schwindel *m*, b) *vet.* Schwindel *m* (*von Rindern*), Koller *m* (*von Pferden*), Drehkrankheit *f* (*von Schafen*); **8.** 🜚, ✈ *u. fig.* Staffelung *f*; **9.** *Leichtathletik*: Kurvenvorgabe *f*; **'stag·gered** [-əd] *adj.* **1.** 🜚 versetzt (angeordnet), gestaf-

felt; **2.** gestaffelt (*Arbeitszeit etc.*); **'stag·ger·ing** [-ərɪŋ] *adj.* □ **1.** (sch)wankend, taumelnd; **2.** wuchtig, heftig (*Schlag*); **3.** *fig.* a) 'umwerfend, fan'tastisch, b) Schwindel erregend (*Preise etc.*).

stag·i·ness ['steɪdʒɪnɪs] *s.* Thea'tralik *f*, Effekthasche'rei *f*.

stag·ing ['steɪdʒɪŋ] *s.* **1.** *thea.* a) Inszenierung *f* (*a. fig.*), b) Bühnenbearbeitung *f*; **2.** (Bau)Gerüst *n*; **3.** ♨ Hellinggerüst *n* (*e-r Werft*); **~ a·re·a** *s.* ✕ **1.** Bereitstellungsraum *m*; **2.** Auffangraum *m*.

stag·nan·cy ['stægnənsɪ] *s.* Stagnati'on *f*: a) Stockung *f*, Stillstand *m*, b) *bsd.* ⊤ Flauheit *f*, c) *fig.* Trägheit *f*; **'stag·nant** [-nt] *adj.* □ stagnierend: a) stockend (*a.* ⊤), stillstehend, b) abgestanden (*Wasser*), c) *fig.* träge; **'stag·nate** [-neɪt] *v/i.* stagnieren, stocken; **stag·na·tion** [stægˈneɪʃn] → **stagnancy**.

stag par·ty *s.* F (*bsd. feuchtfröhlicher*) Herrenabend *m*.

stag·y ['steɪdʒɪ] *adj.* □ **1.** bühnenmäßig, Bühnen...; **2.** *fig.* thea'tralisch.

staid [steɪd] *adj.* □ gesetzt, seri'ös; ruhig (*a. Farbe*), gelassen; **'staid·ness** [-nɪs] *s.* Gesetztheit *f*.

stain [steɪn] **I** *s.* **1.** (Schmutz-, *a.* Farb-)Fleck *m*; **~-resistant** Schmutz abweisend; **2.** *fig.* Schandfleck *m*, Makel *m*; **3.** Färbung *f*; **4.** 🜚 Farbe *f*, Färbemittel *n* (*a. beim Mikroskopieren*); **5.** (Holz-)Beize *f*; **II** *v/t.* **6.** beschmutzen, beflecken, besudeln (*alle a. fig.*); **7.** färben; *Holz* beizen; *Glas etc.* bemalen; *Stoff etc.* bedrucken: **~ed glass** buntes (Fenster)Glas; **III** *v/i.* **8.** Flecken verursachen; **9.** Flecken bekommen, schmutzen; **'stain·ing** [-nɪŋ] *s.* **1.** (Ver)Färbung *f*; **2.** Verschmutzung *f*; **3.** 🜚 Färben *n*, Beizen *n*: **~ of glass** Glasmalerei *f*; **II** *adj.* **4.** Färbe...; **'stain·less** [-lɪs] *adj.* □ **1.** *bsd. fig.* fleckenlos, unbefleckt; **2.** rostfrei, nicht rostend (*Stahl*).

stair [steə] *s.* **1.** Treppe *f*, Stiege *f*; **2.** (Treppen)Stufe *f*; **3.** *pl.* Treppe(nhaus *n*) *f*: **below ~s** a) unten, b) *Br. obs.* beim Hauspersonal; **'~case** → **stair** 3; **'~head** *s.* oberster Treppenabsatz; **'~way** → **stair** 3; **'~well** *s.* Treppenhaus *n*.

stake¹ [steɪk] **I** *s.* **1.** (*a.* Grenz)Pfahl *m*, Pfosten *m*: **pull up ~s** *Am.* F *fig.* s-e Zelte abbrechen; **2.** Marter-, Brandpfahl *m*: **the ~** *fig.* der (Tod auf dem) Scheiterhaufen; **3.** Pflock *m* (*zum Anbinden von Tieren*); **4.** (Wagen)Runge *f*; **5.** Absteckpfahl *m*, -pflock *m*; **6.** kleiner (Hand)Amboss; **II** *v/t.* **7.** *oft* **~ off**, **~ out** abstecken (*a. fig.*): **~ out a claim** *fig.* s-e Ansprüche anmelden (**to** auf *acc.*); **~ in** (*od.* **out**) mit Pfählen einzäunen; **8.** *Pflanze* mit e-m Pfahl stützen; **9.** *Tier* anpflocken; **10.** a) mit e-m Pfahl durch'bohren, aufspießen, b) pfählen (*als Strafe*).

stake² [steɪk] **I** *s.* **1.** (Wett-, Spiel)Einsatz *m*: **place one's ~s on** setzen auf (*acc.*); **be at ~** *fig.* auf dem Spiel stehen; **play for high ~s** a) um hohe Einsätze spielen, b) *fig.* ein hohes Spiel spielen, allerhand riskieren; **sweep the ~s** den ganzen Gewinn kassieren; **2.** *fig.* Inter'esse *n*, Anteil *m* (*a.* ⊤): **have a ~ in** interessiert *od.* beteiligt sein an (*dat.*); **3.** *pl. Pferderennen*: a) Dotierung *f*, b) Rennen *n*; **II** *v/t.* **4.** *Geld* setzen (**on** auf *acc.*); **5.** *fig.* (ein)setzen, aufs Spiel setzen, riskieren: **I'd ~ my life on that** darauf gehe ich jede Wette ein; **6.** *Am.* F Geld in *j-n od. et.* investieren.

'stake|,hold·er *s.* 'Unpar,teiische(r), der die Wetteinsätze verwahrt; **~ net** *s.* ♣ Staknetz *n*; **'~·out** *s.* F (poli'zeiliche) Über'wachung (*on gen.*).

Sta·kha·no·vism [stæˈkænəvɪzəm] *s.* Staˈchanowsy,stem *n.*

sta·lac·tic, sta·lac·ti·cal [stəˈlæktɪk(l)] *adj.* → *stalactitic*; **sta·lac·tite** ['stæ-ləktaɪt] *s.* Stalak'tit *m*, hängender Tropfstein; **stal·ac·tit·ic** [ˌstælək'tɪtɪk] *adj.* (□ **~ally**) stalak'titisch, Stalaktiten...

sta·lag·mite ['stæləgmaɪt] *s. min.* Stalag'mit *m*, stehender Tropfstein; **stal·ag·mit·ic** [ˌstæləg'mɪtɪk] *adj.* (□ **~ally**) stalag'mitisch.

stale¹ [steɪl] **I** *adj.* □ **1.** *allg.* alt (*Ggs. frisch*), *bsd.* a) schal, abgestanden (*Wasser, Wein*), b) alt(backen) (*Brot*), c) schlecht, verdorben (*Lebensmittel*); **2.** verbraucht (*Luft*); **3.** schal (*Geruch, Geschmack, fig. Vergnügen*); **4.** fad, abgedroschen, (ur)alt (*Witz*); **5.** a) verbraucht (*Person, Geist*), über'anstrengt, b) ,eingerostet', aus der Übung (gekommen); **6.** ⅋ verjährt (*Scheck, Schuld etc.*), gegenstandslos (geworden); **II** *v/i.* **7.** schal *etc.* werden.

stale² [steɪl] **I** *v/i.* stallen, harnen (*Vieh*); **II** *s.* Harn *m.*

stale·mate ['steɪlmeɪt] **I** *s.* **1.** *Schach:* Patt *n*; **2.** *fig.* 'Patt(situati,on *f*) *n*, Sackgasse *f*; **II** *v/t.* **3.** patt setzen; **4.** *fig.* a) in e-e Sackgasse führen, b) matt setzen.

stale·ness ['steɪlnɪs] *s.* **1.** Schalheit *f* (*a. fig.*); **2.** a) Verbrauchtheit *f*, b) Abgedroschenheit *f.*

Sta·lin·ism ['staːlɪnɪzəm] *s. pol.* Stali'nismus *m*; **'Sta·lin·ist** [-nɪst] **I** *s.* Stali'nist(in); **II** *adj.* stali'nistisch.

stalk¹ [stɔːk] *s.* **1.** ⅋ Stengel *m*, Stiel *m*, Halm *m*; **2.** *biol., zo.* Stiel *m* (*Träger e-s Organs*); **3.** *zo.* Federkiel *m*; **4.** Stiel *m* (*e-s Weinglases etc.*); **5.** (Fa'brik-) Schlot *m.*

stalk² [stɔːk] **I** *v/i.* **1.** *hunt.* (sich an)pirschen; **2.** (ein'her)schreiten, (-)stolzieren; **3.** *fig.* 'umgehen (*Krankheit, Gespenst etc.*); **4.** staken, steifbeinig gehen; **II** *v/t.* **5.** *hunt. u. fig.* sich her'anpirschen an (*acc.*); **6.** *hunt.* durch'jagen; **7.** *fig.* verfolgen, belästigen: **~ one's former boyfriend** (*od.* **girlfriend**) den Exfreund (*od.* die Exfreundin) belästigen (*od.* nicht in Ruhe lassen); **8.** 'umgehen in (*dat.*) (*Gespenst etc.*); **III** *v/t.* **9.** Pirsch(jagd) *f.*

stalked [stɔːkt] *adj.* ⅋, *zo.* gestielt, ...stielig.

stalk·er ['stɔːkə] *s.* Pirschjäger *m.*

'stalk·ing-horse ['stɔːkɪŋ] *s.* **1.** *hunt., hist.* Versteckpferd *n*; **2.** *fig.* Deckmantel *m*; **3.** *pol.* Strohmann *m.*

stalk·less ['stɔːklɪs] *adj.* **1.** ungestielt; **2.** ⅋ stängellos, sitzend.

stalk·y ['stɔːkɪ] *adj.* **1.** stängel-, stielartig; **2.** hoch aufgeschossen.

stall¹ [stɔːl] **I** *s.* **1.** Box *f* (*im Stall*); **2.** (Verkaufs)Stand *m*, (Markt)Bude *f*: **~ money** Standgeld *n*; **3.** Chor-, Kirchenstuhl *m*; **4.** *pl. thea. Brit.* Sperrsitz *m*; **5.** Hülle *f*, Schutz *m*; **6.** ⚒ Arbeitsstand *m*; **7.** ✈ Sackflug *m*; **8.** (markierter) Parkplatz *m*; **II** *v/t.* **9.** Tiere in Boxen 'unterbringen; **10.** im Stall füttern *od.* mästen; **11.** a) Wagen durch ,Abwürgen' des Motors zum Stehen bringen, b) *Motor* abwürgen, c) ✈ über'ziehen: **~ing speed** kritische Geschwindigkeit *f*; **III** *v/i.* **12.** stecken bleiben (*Wagen*); **13.** absterben (*Motor*); **14.** ✈ abrut

schen.

stall² [stɔːl] **I** *s.* **1.** Ausflucht *f*, 'Hinhaltema,növer *n*; **2.** *Am.* Kom'plize *m*; **II** *v/i.* **3.** a) Ausflüchte machen, ausweichen, b) a. **~ for time** Zeit schinden; **4.** *sport* a) auf Zeit spielen, b) ,kurz treten'; **III** *v/t.* **5.** a. **~ off** a) *j-n* hinhalten, b) *et.* hin'ausziehen.

stall·age ['stɔːlɪdʒ] *s. Brit.* Standgeld *n.*

stal·lion ['stæljən] *s. zo.* (Zucht)Hengst *m.*

stal·wart ['stɔːlwət] **I** *adj.* □ **1.** ro'bust, stramm, (hand)fest; **2.** *bsd. pol.* unentwegt, treu; **II** *s.* **3.** strammer Kerl; **4.** *bsd. pol.* treuer Anhänger, Unentwegte(r *m*) *f.*

sta·men ['steɪmən] *s.* ⅋ Staubblatt *n*, -gefäß *n*, -faden *m.*

stam·i·na ['stæmɪnə] *s.* **1.** a) Lebenskraft *f* (*a. fig.*), b) Vitali'tät *f*; **2.** Zähigkeit *f*, Ausdauer *f*, 'Durchhalte-, Stehvermögen *n*; **3.** *a.* ⚔ 'Widerstandskraft *f*; **'stam·i·nal** [-nl] *adj.* **1.** Lebens..., vi'tal; **2.** Widerstands..., Konditions...; **3.** ⅋ Staubblatt...

stam·mer ['stæmə] **I** *v/i.* (*v/t. a.* **~ out**) stottern, stammeln; **II** *s.* Stottern *n* (*a.* ⚕), Gestammel *n*; **'stam·mer·er** [-ərə] *s.* Stotterer *m*, Stotterin *f*; **'stam·mer·ing** [-ərɪŋ] **I** *adj.* □ stotternd; **II** *s.* → **stammer** II.

stamp [stæmp] **I** *v/t.* **1.** stampfen (auf *acc.*): **~ one's foot** → 12; **~ down** a) feststampfen, b) niedertrampeln; **~ out** a) *Feuer* austreten, b) zertrampeln, c) ausmerzen, d) *Aufstand* niederschlagen; **2.** *Geld* prägen; **3.** aufprägen (**on** auf *acc.*); **4.** *Namen etc.* aufstempeln; **5.** *Urkunde etc.* stempeln; **6.** *Gewichte* eichen; **7.** *Brief etc.* frankieren, e-e Brief- *od.* Gebührenmarke (auf)kleben auf (*acc.*): **~ed envelope** Freiumschlag *m*; **~ed addressed envelope** frankierter, mit (eigener) Anschrift versehener Briefumschlag; **8.** kennzeichnen; **9.** *fig.* stempeln, kennzeichnen, charakterisieren (**as** als); **10.** *fig.* (fest) einprägen: **~ed on s.o.'s memory** j-s Gedächtnis eingeprägt, unverrückbar in j-s Erinnerung; **11.** ⚒ a) a. **~ out** (aus)stanzen, b) pressen, c) *Erz* pochen, d) *Lumpen etc.* einstampfen; **II** *v/i.* **12.** (auf)stampfen; **13.** stampfen, trampeln (**upon** auf *acc.*); **III** *s.* **14.** Stempel *m*, (*Dienstetc.*)Siegel *n*; **15.** *fig.* Stempel *m* (*der Wahrheit etc.*), Gepräge *n*: **bear the ~ of** den Stempel *des Genies etc.* tragen, das Gepräge *j-s od. e-r Sache* haben; **16.** (Brief)Marke *f*, (Post)Wertzeichen *n*; **17.** (Stempel-, Steuer-, Gebühren-) Marke *f*; **18.** ⅋ Ra'battmarke *f*; **19.** ⅋ (Firmen)Zeichen *n*, Eti'kett *n*; **20.** *fig.* Art *f*, Schlag *m*: **a man of his ~** ein Mann s-s Schlages; **of a different ~** aus e-m andern Holz geschnitzt; **21.** ⚒ a) Prägestempel *m*, b) Stanze *f*, c) Stampffe *f*, d) Presse *f*, e) Pochstempel *m*, f) Pa'trize *f*; **22.** Prägung *f*; **23.** Aufdruck *m*; **24.** Eindruck *m*, Spur *f*; ⚗ **Act** *s. hist.* Stempelakte *f*; **~ col·lec·tor** *s.* Briefmarkensammler *m*; **~ du·ty** *s.* Stempelgebühr *f.*

stam·pede [stæm'piːd] **I** *s.* **1.** a) wilde, panische Flucht, b) wilder Ansturm; **2.** (Massen)Ansturm *m* (*von Käufern etc.*); **3.** *Am. pol.* a) (krasser) 'Meinungs,umschwung, b) ,Erdrutsch' *m*; b) wilder Flucht) da'vonstürmen, 'durchgehen; **5.** (in Massen) losstürmen; **III** *v/t.* **6.** in wilde Flucht jagen; **7.** a) in Panik versetzen, b) *j-n* treiben (**into doing** dazu, *et.* zu tun), c) über'rumpeln, d) *Am. pol.* e-n Erd

rutsch her'vorrufen bei.

stamp·ing ['stæmpɪŋ] *s.* ⚒ **1.** Ausstanzen *n etc.*; **2.** Stanzstück *n*; **3.** Pressstück *n*; **4.** Prägung *f*; **~ die** *s.* ⚒ 'Schlagmat,rize *f*; **~ ground** *s. zo. u. fig.* Tummelplatz *m*, Re'vier *n.*

stamp(·ing) mill *s.* ⚒ a) Stampfwerk *n*, b) Pochwerk *n.*

stance [stæns] *s.* Stellung *f*, Haltung *f* (*a. sport*).

stanch¹ [stɑːntʃ] *v/t. Blutung* stillen.

stanch² [stɑːntʃ] → **staunch** ².

stan·chion ['stɑːnʃn] **I** *s.* Pfosten *m*, Stütze *f* (*a.* ♣); **II** *v/t.* (ab)stützen, verstärken.

stand [stænd] **I** *s.* **1.** Stillstand *m*, Halt *m*; **2.** Standort *m*, Platz *m*, *fig.* Standpunkt *m*: **take one's** a) sich (auf)stellen (**at** bei, auf *dat.*), b) Stellung beziehen; **3.** *fig.* Eintreten *n*: **make a ~ for** sich einsetzen für; **make a ~ against** sich entgegenstellen *od.* -stemmen (*dat.*); **4.** (Verkaufs-, Messe)Stand *m*; **5.** Stand(platz) *m* für Taxis; **6.** ('Zuschauer)Tri,büne *f*; **7.** Podium *n*; **8.** *Am.* ⅋ Zeugenstand *m*: **take the ~** a) den Zeugenstand betreten, b) als Zeuge aussagen; **9.** (Kleider-, Noten- *etc.*) Ständer *m*; **10.** Gestell *n*; **11.** *phot.* Sta'tiv *n*; **12.** (Baum)Bestand *m*; **13.** ✈ Stand *m* des Getreides *etc.*, (zu erwartende) Ernte: **~ of wheat** stehender Weizen; **14. ~ of arms** ⚔ ('vollständige) Ausrüstung *e-s Soldaten*; **II** *v/i.* [*irr.*] **15.** *allg.* stehen: **~ alone** a) allein (da)stehen *mit e-r Ansicht etc.*, b) unerreicht dastehen *od.* sein; **~ fast** (*od. firm*) hart bleiben (**on** in *e-r Sache*); **~ or fall** siegen oder untergehen; **~s at 78** *das Thermometer* steht auf 78 Grad (Fahrenheit); **the wind ~s in the west** der Wind weht von Westen; **~ well with s.o.** mit j-m gut stehen; **~ to lose** (**win**) (mit Sicherheit) verlieren (gewinnen); **as matters ~** (so) wie die Dinge (jetzt) liegen, nach Lage der Dinge; **I want to know where I ~** ich will wissen, woran ich bin; **16.** aufstehen, sich erheben; **17.** sich *wohin* stellen, treten: **~ back** (*od. clear*) zurücktreten; **18.** sich wo befinden, stehen, liegen (*Sache*); **19.** a. **~ still** stehen bleiben, stillstehen: **~!** halt!; **~ fast!** ⚔ *Brit.* stillgestanden!, *Am.* Abteilung halt!; **20.** bestürzt *etc.* sein: **~ aghast**; **~ convicted** überführt sein; **~ corrected** s-n Irrtum *od.* sein Unrecht zugeben; **~ in need of** benötigen; **21.** groß sein, messen: **he ~s six feet (tall)**; **22.** neutral *etc.* bleiben: **~ unchallenged** unbeanstandet bleiben; **and so it ~s** und dabei bleibt es; **23.** a. **~ good** gültig bleiben, (weiterhin) gelten: **my offer ~s** mein Angebot bleibt bestehen; **24.** bestehen, sich behaupten: **~ through** *et.* überstehen, -dauern; **25.** *a. ~ auf en* Kurs liegen, steuern; **26.** zu'statten kommen (**to** *dat.*); **27.** *hunt.* vorstehen (**upon** *dat.*) (*Hund*); **III** *v/t.* [*irr.*] **28.** *wohin* stellen; **29.** *e-n Angriff etc.* standhalten; **30.** *Beanspruchung, Kälte etc.* aushalten; *Klima, Person* (v)ertragen: **I cannot ~ him** ich kann ihn nicht ausstehen; **31.** sich *et.* gefallen lassen, dulden: **I won't ~ it any longer**; **32.** sich *e-r Sache* unter'ziehen; *Pate* stehen; → **trial** 2; **33.** a) aufkommen für *et.*; Bürgschaft leisten, b) *j-m ein Essen etc.* spendieren: **~ a drink** ,einen ausgeben'; → **treat** 11; **34.** *e-e Chance* haben;
Zssgn mit prp.:

stand| by *v/i.* **1.** *fig.* j-m zur Seite stehen, zu j-m halten *od.* stehen; **2.** s-m

S

Wort, s-n Prinzipien etc. treu bleiben, stehen zu; **~ for** v/i. **1.** stehen für, bedeuten; **2.** eintreten für, vertreten; **3.** bsd. Brit. sich um ein Amt bewerben; **4.** pol. Brit. kandidieren für e-n Sitz im Parlament: **~ election** kandidieren, sich zur Wahl stellen; **5.** → **stand** 31; **~ on** v/i. **1.** bestehen od. halten auf (acc.); → **ceremony** 2; **2.** auf sein Recht etc. pochen; **3.** ♣ Kurs beibehalten; **~ o·ver** v/i. j-m auf die Finger sehen; **~ to** v/i. **1.** → **stand by** 1; **2.** zu s-m Versprechen etc. stehen, bei s-m Wort bleiben: **~ it that** dabei bleiben od. darauf beharren, dass; **~ one's duty** (treu) s-e Pflicht tun; **~ up·on** → **stand on**;

Zssgn mit adv.:

stand| a·loof, ~ a·part v/i. **1.** a) abseits od. für sich stehen, b) sich ausschließen, nicht mitmachen; **2.** fig. sich distanzieren (from von); **~ a·side** v/i. **1.** bei'seite treten; **2.** fig. zu j-s Gunsten verzichten, zu'rücktreten; **3.** tatenlos her'umstehen; **~ by** v/i. **1.** da'bei sein u. zusehen (müssen), (ruhig) zusehen; **2.** a) bsd. ✕ bereitstehen, sich in Bereitschaft halten, b) ✓! Achtung!, ♣ klar zum Manöver!; **3.** Funk: a) auf Empfang stehen, b) seewärts anliegen; **II** v/t. **4.** ✝ j-n (vor'übergehend) entlassen; **5.** sich j-n vom Leibe halten; **~ out** v/i. **1.** (a. fig. deutlich) her'vortreten: **~ against** sich gut abheben von; → 4; **2.** abstehen (Ohren); **3.** fig. herausragen, her'vorstechen; **4.** aus-, 'durchhalten: **~ against** sich hartnäckig wehren gegen; **5.** ✝ for bestehen auf (dat.); **6.** **~ to sea** ♣ in See stechen; **~ o·ver I** v/i. **1.** (to auf acc.) a) sich vertagen, b) verschoben werden; **2.** für später liegen bleiben, warten; **II** v/t. vertagen, verschieben (to auf acc.); **~ to** ✕ **I** v/t. in Bereitschaft versetzen; **II** v/i. in Bereitschaft stehen; **~ up I** v/i. **1.** aufstehen, sich erheben (beide a. fig.); **2.** sich aufrichten (Stachel etc.); **3.** eintreten od. sich einsetzen (for für); **4. ~ to** (mutig) gegen'übertreten (dat.); **5.** (under, to) sich (gut) halten (unter, gegen), standhalten (dat.); **II** v/t. **6.** F j-n ,versetzen'.

stand·ard¹ ['stændəd] **I** s. **1.** Standard m, Norm f; **2.** Muster n, Vorbild n; **3.** Maßstab m: **apply another ~** e-n anderen Maßstab anlegen; **~ of value** Wertmaßstab m; **by present-day ~s** nach heutigen Begriffen; **double** ~ doppelte Moral; **4.** Richt-, Eichmaß n; **5.** Richtlinie f; **6.** (Mindest)Anforderungen pl.: **be up to (below)** ~ den Anforderungen (nicht) genügen od. entsprechen; **set a high** ~ hohe Anforderungen stellen, viel verlangen; **~ of living** Lebensstandard m; **7.** ✝ 'Standard(quali,tät f od. -ausführung f) m; **8.** (Gold- etc.) Währung f, (-)Standard m; **9.** Standard m: a) (gesetzlich vorgeschriebener) Feingehalt m, b) Münzfuß m; **10.** Ni'veau n, Grad m: **be of a high** ~ ein hohes Niveau haben; **~ of knowledge** Bildungsgrad, stand m; **~ of prices** Preisniveau; **11.** ped. bsd. Brit. Stufe f, Klasse f; **II** adj. **12.** nor-

'mal, Normal...(-film, -wert, -zeit etc.); Standard..., Einheits...(-modell etc.); Durchschnitts...(-wert etc.): ~ (class) Brit. 🐾 zweiter Klasse; **~ format** Computer: 'Standardfor,mat n; **~ ga(u)ge** 🐾 Normalspur f; **~ letter** 'Standardbrief m (mit vorformuliertem Inhalt als Antwort auf Anfragen); **~ set** Seriengerät n; **~ size** gängige Größe (Schuhe etc.); **13.** gültig, maßgebend, Standard...(-muster, -werk), ling. hochsprachlich: **~ German** Hochdeutsch n; **14.** klassisch: **~ novel; ~ author** Klassiker m.

stand·ard² ['stændəd] **I** s. a) pol. u. ✕ Stan'darte f, b) Fahne f, Flagge f, c) Wimpel m, d) fig. Banner n: **~-bearer** Fahnen-, a. fig. Bannerträger m; **2.** ❀ a) Ständer m, b) Pfosten m, Pfeiler m, Stütze f; **3.** ✔ Hochstämmchen n, Bäumchen n; **II** adj. **4.** Steh...: **~ lamp; 5.** ✔ hochstämmig: **~ rose.**

stand·i·za·tion [,stændədai'zeiʃn] s. **1.** Normung f, Standardisierung f; **~ committee** Normenausschuss m; **2.** ✝, pol. Homogeni'sierung f, Angleichung f, ♣ Titrierung f; **4.** Eichung f; **stand·ard·ize** ['stændədaiz] v/t. **1.** normen, normieren, standardisieren; **2.** 🍷 einstellen, titrieren; **3.** eichen.

'stand|-by [-nd-] **I** pl. **-bys** s. **1.** Stütze f, Beistand f, Hilfe f: (old) ~ altbewährte Sache; (on ~ in) (A'larm- etc.) Bereitschaft f; **2.** ❀ Hilfs-, Re'servegerät n; **3.** ✔ a) a. ~ ticket 'Stand-by-,Ticket n, b) a. **~ passenger** 'Stand-by-Passa,gier m; **II** adj. **4.** Hilfs..., Ersatz..., Reserve...: **~ unit** ⚡ Notaggregat n; **~ credit** ✝ Beistandskredit m; **5.** bsd. ✕ Bereitschafts...(-dienst etc.); **6.** ✔ 'Stand-by-...; **'~-down** s. Pause f.

stand·ee [stæn'di:] s. Am. F Stehplatzinhaber(in).

'stand-in s. **1.** Film: Double n; **2.** Vertreter(in), Ersatzmann m.

stand·ing ['stændiŋ] **I** s. **1.** Stehen n: **no ~** keine Stehplätze; **2.** a) Stand m, Rang m, Stellung f, b) Ruf m, Ansehen n, c) ✝ Bonität f, Kreditwürdigkeit f: **of high ~** hoch angesehen od. stehend; **3.** Dauer f: **of long ~** alt (Brauch, Freundschaft etc.); **II** adj. **4.** stehend, Steh...: **~ army** stehendes Heer; **~ corn** Getreide n auf dem Halm; **~ jump** Sprung m aus dem Stand; **~ ovation** stürmischer Beifall; **~ rule** stehende Regel; **~ start** stehender Start; **5.** fig. ständig (a. Ausschuss etc.); **6.** ✝ laufend (Unkosten etc.); **7.** üblich, gewohnt: **a ~ dish; 8.** bewährt, alt (Witz etc.); **~ or·der** s. **1.** ✝ Dauerauftrag m; **2.** pl. parl. etc. Geschäftsordnung f; **3.** ✕ Dauerbefehl m; **~ room** s. Platz m zum Stehen: **~ only!** nur Stehplätze!

'stand|-off s. **1.** Am. Distanzierung f; **2.** fig. Sackgasse f; **,~'off-ish** [-'ɒfiʃ] adj. □ reserviert, (sehr) ablehnend, unnahbar; **,~'pat(·ter)** [-nd'pæt(ə)] s. pol. Am. F sturer Konserva'tiver; **'~·pipe** [-ndp-] s. ❀ Standrohr n; **'~·point** [-ndp-] s. Standpunkt m (a. fig.); **'~·still** [-nds-] **I** s. Stillstand m: **be at a ~** stillstehen, stocken, ruhen; **to a ~** zum Stillstand kommen, bringen; **II** adj. stillstehend: **~ agreement** pol. Stillhalteabkommen n; **'~-up** adj. **1.** stehend: **~ collar** Stehkragen m; **2.** F im Stehen eingenommen: **~ meal; 3.** wild, wüst (Schlägerei).

stank [stæŋk] pret. von **stink.**

stan·na·ry ['stænəri] Brit. **I** s. **1.** Zinngrubengebiet n; **2.** Zinngrube f; **II** adj. **3.** Zinn(gruben)...; **'stan·nate** [-nət] s. 🔬 Stan'nat n; **'stan·nic** [-nik] adj. 🔬

Zinn...; **'stan·nite** [-nait] s. **1.** min. Zinnkies m, Stan'nin n; **2.** 🔬 Stan'nit n; **'stan·nous** [-nəs] adj. 🔬 Zinn...

stan·za ['stænzə] pl. **-zas** s. **1.** Strophe f; **2.** Stanze f.

sta·ple¹ [steipl] **I** s. **1.** ✝ Hauptzeugnis n e- Landes etc.; **2.** ✝ Stapelware f: a) 'Hauptar,tikel m, b) Massenware f; **3.** ✝ Rohstoff m; **4.** ❀ Stapel m: a) Fadenlänge od. -qualität: **of short ~** kurzstapelig, b) Büschel Schafwolle; **5.** ❀ a) Rohwolle f, b) Faser f: **~ fibre** (Am. **fiber**) Zellwolle f; **6.** fig. Hauptgegenstand m, -thema n; **7.** ✝ a) Stapelplatz m, b) Handelszentrum n, c) hist. Markt m (mit Stapelrecht); **II** adj. **8.** Stapel...: **~ goods; 9.** Haupt...: **~ food; ~ industry;** ~ **topic** Hauptthema n; **10.** ✝ a) Haupthandels..., b) gängig, c) Massen...; **III** v/t. **11.** Wolle (nach Stapel) sortieren.

sta·ple² [steipl] ❀ **I** s. **1.** (Draht)Öse f; **2.** Krampe f; **3.** Heftdraht m, -klammer f; **II** v/t. **4.** (mit Draht) heften; klammern (to an acc.): **stapling machine** → **stapler¹.**

sta·pler¹ ['steiplə] s. ❀ 'Heftma,schine f.

sta·pler² ['steiplə] s. ✝ **1.** (Baumwoll-) Sortierer m; **2.** Stapelkaufmann m.

star [stɑː] **I** s. **1.** ast. a) Stern m, mst **fixed ~** Fixstern m; **2.** Stern m: a) sternähnliche Figur, b) fig. Größe f, Berühmtheit f (Person), c) Orden m, d) typ. Sternchen n, e) weißer Stirnfleck, bsd. e-s Pferdes: **♀s and Stripes** das Sternenbanner (Nationalflagge der USA); **see ~s** F Sterne sehen (nach e-m Schlag); **3.** a) Stern m (Schicksal), b) a. **lucky ~** Glücksstern m: **un·lucky ~** Unstern m; **his ~ is in the ascendant (is** od. **has set)** sein Stern ist im Aufgehen (ist untergegangen); **my good ~** mein guter Stern; **you may thank your ~s** Sie können von Glück sagen (, dass); **4.** thea. (Bühnen-, bsd. Film)Star m; **5.** sport Star m; **II** adj. **6.** Stern...; **7.** Haupt...: **~ prosecution witness** ✐ Hauptbelastungszeuge m; **8.** thea., sport Star...: **~ performance** Elitevorstellung f; **~ turn** Hauptattraktion f; **9.** Segeln: Star m (Boot); **III** v/t. **10.** mit Sternen schmücken, besternen; **11.** j-n in der Hauptrolle zeigen: **~ring X** mit X in der Hauptrolle; **12.** typ. Wort mit Sternchen versehen; **IV** v/i. **13.** die od. e-e Hauptrolle spielen: **~ in a film.**

star·board ['stɑːbəd] ♣ **I** s. Steuerbord n; **II** adj. Steuerbord...; **III** adv. a) nach Steuerbord, b) steuerbord(s).

starch [stɑːtʃ] **I** s. **1.** Stärke f: a) Stärkemehl n, b) Wäschestärke f, c) Stärkekleister m, d) ❀ A'mylum n; **2.** pl. stärkereiche Nahrungsmittel pl., 'Kohle(n)hy,drate pl.; **3.** fig. Steifheit f, Förmlichkeit f; **4.** Am. F ,Mumm' m: **take the ~ out of s.o.** j-m ,die Gräten ziehen'; **II** v/t. **6.** Wäsche stärken.

Star Cham·ber s. ✐ hist. Sternkammer f (nur dem König verantwortliches Willkürgericht bis 1641).

starched [stɑːtʃt] adj. □ **1.** gestärkt, gesteift; **2.** → **starchy** 4; **'starch·i·ness** [-tʃinis] s. fig. F Steifheit f, Förmlichkeit f; **'starch·y** [-tʃi] adj. □ **1.** stärkehaltig: **~ food; 2.** Stärke..., **3.** gestärkt; **4.** fig. F steif, förmlich.

'star-crossed adj. poet. von e-m Unstern verfolgt, unglückselig.

star·dom ['stɑːdəm] s. **1.** Welt f der Stars; **2.** coll. Stars pl.; **3.** Berühmtheit f: **rise to ~** ein Star werden.

star dust s. ast. **1.** Sternennebel m; **2.** kosmischer Staub.

stare [steə] **I** v/i. **1.** (~ *at* an)starren, (-)stieren; **2.** große Augen machen, erstaunt blicken: ~ *at* anstaunen, angaffen; *make s.o.* ~ j-n in Erstaunen versetzen; **II** v/t. **3.** ~ *s.o. out* (od. *down*) j-n durch Anstarren aus der Fassung bringen; **4.** ~ *s.o. in the face* fig. a) j-m in die Augen springen, b) j-m deutlich od. drohend vor Augen stehen; **III** s. **5.** (starrer od. erstaunter) Blick, Starrblick m, Starren n.

'**star·finch** s. orn. Rotschwänzchen n; '~·**gaz·er** s. humor. **1.** Sterngucker m; **2.** Träumer(in); **3.** ,Anbeter(in)' (von Idolen).

star·ing ['steərɪŋ] **I** adj. □ **1.** stier, starrend: ~ *eyes*; **2.** auffallend: *a* ~ *tie*; **3.** grell (*Farbe*). **4.** to'tal.

stark [stɑːk] **I** adj. □ **1.** steif, starr; **2.** rein, völlig: ~ *folly*; ~ *nonsense* barer Unsinn; **3.** fig. rein sachlich (*Bericht*); **4.** kahl, öde (*Landschaft*); **II** adv. **5.** ganz, völlig: ~ (*staring*) *mad* ,total' verrückt; ~ *naked* → **stark·ers** ['stɑːkəz] adj. F splitternackt.

stark·less [stɑːklɪs] adj. sternlos.

star·let ['stɑːlɪt] s. **1.** Sternchen n; **2.** fig. Starlet(t) n, Filmsternchen n.

'**star·light I** s. Sternenlicht n; **II** adj. → **starlit**.

star·ling¹ ['stɑːlɪŋ] s. orn. Star m.

star·ling² ['stɑːlɪŋ] s. ⊚ Pfeilerkopf m (*Eisbrecher e-r Brücke*).

'**star·lit** adj. sternhell, -klar.

star map s. ast. Sternkarte f, -tafel f.

starred [stɑːd] p.p. u. adj. **1.** gestirnt (*Himmel*); **2.** sternengeschmückt; **3.** typ. etc. mit (e-m) Sternchen bezeichnet.

star·ry ['stɑːrɪ] adj. **1.** Sternen..., Stern...; **2.** → a) **starlit**, b) **starred** 2; **3.** strahlend: ~ *eyes*; **4.** sternförmig; ,~·'**eyed** adj. **1.** mit strahlenden Augen; **2.** fig. a) ,blauäugig', na'iv, b) ro'mantisch.

star shell s. ✕ Leuchtgeschoss, östr. -geschoß n; '~·,**span·gled** adj. sternenbesät: *Star-Spangled Banner* Am. das Sternenbanner (*Nationalflagge od. -hymne der USA*); '~·**struck** adj. 'starbegeistert.

start [stɑːt] **I** s. **1.** sport Start m (a. fig.): *good* ~; ~·*and-finish line* Start u. Ziel; *give s.o. a* ~ (*in life*) j-m zu e-m Start ins Leben verhelfen; **2.** Startzeichen n (a. fig.): *give the* ~; **3.** a) Aufbruch m, b) Abreise f, c) Abfahrt f, d) ✈ Abflug m, Start m, e) Abmarsch m; **4.** Beginn m, Anfang m: *at the* ~ am Anfang; *from the* ~ von Anfang an; *from* ~ *to finish* von Anfang bis Ende; *make a fresh* ~ e-n neuen Anfang machen, noch einmal von vorn anfangen; **5.** sport a) Vorgabe f, b) Vorsprung m (a. fig.): *get* (od. *have*) *the* ~ *of one's rivals* s-n Rivalen zuvorkommen; **6.** Auf-, Zs.-fahren n, -schrecken n; Schreck m: *give a* ~ → 12; *give s.o. a* ~ j-n erschrecken; *with a* ~ jäh, erschrocken; **II** v/i. **7.** aufbrechen, sich aufmachen (*for* nach): ~ *on a journey* e-e Reise antreten; **8.** a) abfahren, abgehen (*Zug etc.*), b) auslaufen (*Schiff*), ✈ abfliegen, starten (*for* nach); **9.** anfangen, beginnen (*on* mit *e-r Arbeit etc.*, *doing* zu tun): ~ *in business* ein Geschäft anfangen od. eröffnen; *to* ~ *with* (*Redew.*) a) erstens, als Erstes, b) zunächst, c) um es gleich zu sagen, d) ... als Vorspeise; **10.** fig. ausgehen (*from* von *e-m Gedanken*); **11.** entstehen, aufkommen; **12.** a) auffahren, -schrecken, b) zs.-fahren, -zucken (*at* vor dat.,

bei *e-m Laut etc.*); **13.** a) aufspringen, b) losstürzen; **14.** stutzen (*at* bei); **15.** aus den Höhlen treten (*Augen*); **16.** sich lockern od. lösen; **17.** ⊚, mot. anspringen, anlaufen, starten (a. *Computer*); **III** v/t. **18.** in Gang od. in Bewegung setzen; ⊚ a. anlassen; *Feuer* anzünden, in Gang bringen, starten (a. *Computer*); **19.** *Brief, Streit etc.* anfangen; *Aktion* starten; *Geschäft, Zeitung* gründen, aufmachen; **20.** *Frage* aufwerfen, *Thema* anschneiden; **21.** *Gerücht* in 'Umlauf setzen; **22.** sport starten (lassen); **23.** *Läufer, Pferd* aufstellen, an den Start bringen; **24.** ⟨Zug abfahren lassen; **25.** fig. j-m zu e-m Start verhelfen: ~ *s.o. in business*; **26.** j-n (veran)lassen (*doing* zu tun); **27.** lockern, lösen; **28.** aufscheuchen; ~ *in* (*Am. a. out*) v/i. F anfangen (*to do* zu tun); ~ *off* → **start** 9, 18; ~ *up* → **start** 12 a, 13 a, 17, 18.

start·er ['stɑːtə] s. **1.** sport a) Starter m (*Kampfrichter u. Wettkampfteilnehmer* [-*in*]); **2.** mot. Starter m, Anlasser m; **3.** fig. Initi'ator m; F bsd. Brit. Vorspeise f; **5.** *for* ~s F a) als Erstes, b) zunächst, c) um es gleich zu sagen.

start·ing ['stɑːtɪŋ] **I** s. **1.** Starten n, Ablauf m; **2.** ⊚ Anlassen n, In'gangsetzen n, Starten n: *cold* ~ mot. Kaltstart m; **II** adj. **3.** Start...(-block, -geld, -linie, -schuss etc.); mot. etc. Anlass...(-kurbel, -motor, -schalter); ~ *gate* s. Pferderennen: 'Startma,schine f; ~ *point* s. Ausgangspunkt m (a. fig.); ~ *price* s. **1.** Pferderennen: Eventu'alquote f; **2.** *Auktion:* Mindestgebot n; ~ *sal·a·ry* s. Anfangsgehalt n; ~ *sig·nal* s. Startzeichen n.

star·tle ['stɑːtl] **I** v/t. **1.** erschrecken; **2.** aufschrecken; **3.** über'raschen: a) bestürzen, b) verblüffen; **II** v/i. **4.** auf-, erschrecken: ~ *easily* sehr schreckhaft sein; '**star·tling** [-lɪŋ] adj. □ **1.** erschreckend, bestürzend; **2.** verblüffend, Aufsehen erregend.

'**start-up** s. **1.** Start m (*e-s Gerätes, e-s Unternehmens*); **2.** Neugründung f.

star·va·tion [stɑː'veɪʃn] s. **1.** Hungern n: ~ *diet* Hungerkur f; ~ *wages* Hungerlohn m, -löhne pl.; **2.** Hungertod m, Verhungern n.

starve [stɑːv] **I** v/i. **1.** a. ~ *to death* verhungern, sl. *I am simply starving* F ich komme fast um vor Hunger; **2.** hungern (a. fig. *for* nach), Hunger (fig. Not) leiden; **3.** fasten; **4.** fig. verkümmern; **II** v/t. **5.** a. ~ *to death* verhungern lassen; **6.** aushungern; **7.** hungern lassen: *be* ~*d* Hunger leiden, ausgehungert sein (a. fig. *for* nach); **8.** darben lassen (a. fig.): *be* ~*d of* od. *for* knapp sein an (*dat.*); '**starve·ling** [-lɪŋ] obs. **I** s. **1.** Hungerleider m; **2.** Kümmerling m; **II** adj. **3.** hungrig; **4.** abgemagert; **5.** kümmerlich.

star wheel s. ⊚ Sternrad n.

stash [stæʃ] v/t. sl. **1.** mst ~ *away* verstecken, bei'seite tun; **2.** aufhören mit.

sta·sis ['steɪsɪs] pl. **-ses** [-siːz] s. ✱ Stase f, (*Blut- etc.*) Stauung f.

state [steɪt] **I** s. **1.** mst ⚳ pol., a. zo. Staat m: *affairs of* ~ Staatsgeschäfte; **2.** pol. Am. (*Bundes-, Einzel*)Staat m: *the* ⚳s die (Vereinigten) Staaten; ~ *law* Rechtsordnung f des Einzelstaates; ⚳'s *attorney* ⚖ Staatsanwalt m; *turn* ~'s *evidence* ⚖ als Kronzeuge auftreten, gegen s-e Komplizen aussagen; **3.** (*Gesundheits-, Geistes- etc.*)Zustand m: ~ *of health*; ~ *of aggregation* phys. Aggregatzustand; ~ *of war* Kriegszustand; *in a* ~ F a) in e-m schrecklichen Zu-

stand, b) ,ganz aus dem Häus-chen'; → *emergency* **I**; **4.** Stand m, Lage f (*of affairs* der Dinge): ~ *of the art* neuester Stand der Technik; ~ *of convergence* EU Konver'genzlage f, -stand m (*bei Vereinheitlichung von Gesetzen mehrerer Staaten etc.*) **5.** (Fa'milien-) Stand m: *married* ~ Ehestand; **6.** ⚥, zo. Stadium n; **7.** (gesellschaftliche) Stellung, Stand m: *in a style befitting one's* ~ standesgemäß; **8.** Pracht f, Staat m: *in* ~ feierlich, mit großem Zeremoniell od. Pomp; *lie in* ~ feierlich aufgebahrt liegen; *live in* ~ großen Aufwand treiben; **9.** pl. pol. hist. (Land-etc.)Stände pl.; **10.** *Kupferstecherei:* (Ab)Druck m; **II** adj. **11.** Staats..., staatlich, po'litisch: ~ *borrowing* staatliche Kreditaufnahme; ~ *capitalism* Staatskapitalismus m; ~ *funeral* Staatsbegräbnis n; ~ *mourning* Staatstrauer f; ~ *prison* staatliche Strafanstalt (*in U.S.A. in e-s Bundesstaates*); ~ *prisoner* politischer Häftling od. Gefangener; **12.** Staats..., Prunk..., Parade..., feierlich: ~ *apartment* → **stateroom** 1; ~ *carriage* Prunk-, Staatskarosse f; **III** v/t. **13.** festsetzen, -legen; *e-e Regel* aufstellen; → **stated** 1; **14.** erklären: a) darlegen, b) a. ⚖ (aus)sagen, *Gründe, Klage etc.* vorbringen, *Tatsachen etc.* anführen; → *case¹* 1, c) *Einzelheiten etc.* angeben; **15.** feststellen, konstatieren; **16.** behaupten; **17.** erwähnen, bemerken; **18.** *Problem etc.* stellen; **19.** Ⱥ (mathe'matisch) ausdrücken.

,**state·con'trolled** adj. staatlich gelenkt, unter staatlicher Aufsicht: ~ *economy* Zwangswirtschaft f; '~·**craft** s. pol. Staatskunst f.

stat·ed ['steɪtɪd] p.p. u. adj. **1.** festgesetzt: *at the* ~ *time; at* ~ *intervals* in regelmäßigen Abständen; ~ *meeting* bsd. Am. ordentliche Versammlung; **2.** festgestellt; **3.** bezeichnet, (a. amtlich) anerkannt; **4.** angegeben: *as* ~ *above*; ~ *case* ⚖ Sachdarstellung f.

State·De·part·ment s. pol. Am. 'Außenmini,sterium n; ⚳·**hood** ['steɪthʊd] s. pol. bsd. Am. Eigenstaatlichkeit f, Souveräni'tät f; ⚳·**house** s. pol. Am. Parla'mentsgebäude n od. Kapi'tol n (*e-s Bundesstaats*).

state·less ['steɪtlɪs] adj. pol. staatenlos: ~ *person* Staatenlose(r m) f.

state·li·ness ['steɪtlɪnɪs] s. **1.** Stattlichkeit f; Vornehmheit f; **2.** Würde f; **3.** Pracht f; '**state·ly** [-lɪ] adj. **1.** stattlich, impo'sant; prächtig; **2.** würdevoll; **3.** erhaben, vornehm.

state·ment ['steɪtmənt] s. **1.** (a. amtliche etc.) Erklärung: *make a* ~ e-e Erklärung abgeben; **2.** a) (*Zeugen- etc.*) Aussage f, b) Angabe(n pl.) f: *false* ~; ~ *of facts* Sachdarstellung f, Tatbestand m; ~ *of contents* Inhaltsangabe; **3.** Behauptung f; **4.** bsd. ⚖ (schriftliche) Darlegung, (Par'tei)Vorbringen n: ~ *of claim* Klageschrift f; ~ *of defence* (*Am. defense*) a) Klagebeantwortung f, b) Verteidigungsschrift f; **5.** bsd. ✝ (*Geschäfts-, Monats-, Rechenschafts-etc.*)Bericht m, (*Bank-, Gewinn-, Jahres- etc.*)Ausweis m, (*statistische etc.*) Aufstellung: ~ *of affairs* Situationsbericht, Status m e-r Firma; ~ *of account* Kontoauszug m; *financial* ~ Gewinn- und Verlustrechnung f; **6.** Am. ✝ Bi'lanz f: ~ *of assets and liabilities*; **7.** Darstellung f, Darlegung f e-s Sachverhalts; **8.** ✝ Lohn m, Ta'rif m; **9.** fig. Aussage f, Statement n e-s Autors etc.

'**state·room** s. **1.** Staats-, Prunkzimmer

n; **2.** ♣ ('Einzel)Ka,bine f; **3.** 🚢 *Am.* Pri'vatabteil n (*mit Betten*).

'**state-side** *oft ☒ Am.* **I** *adj.* ameri'kanisch, Heimat...; **~ duty** *bsd.* ✕ Dienst m in der Heimat; **II** *adv.* in den *od.* in die Staaten (zurück).

states-man ['steɪtsmən] s. [*irr.*] **1.** *pol.* Staatsmann m; **2.** (bedeutender) Po'litiker; '**states-man-like** [-laɪk], '**states-man-ly** [-lɪ] *adj.* staatsmännisch; '**states-man-ship** [-ʃɪp] s. Staatskunst f.

States' rights s. pl. Staatsrechte pl. (*der Einzelstaaten der USA*).

stat-ic ['stætɪk] **I** *adj.* (□ **~ally**) **1.** *phys. u. fig.* statisch: **~ sense** ⚙ Gleichgewichtssinn m; **2.** ⚡ (elektro)'statisch; **3.** *Funk:* a) atmo'sphärisch (*Störung*), b) Störungs...; **II** s. **4.** ⚡ statische *od.* atmo'sphärische Elektrizi'tät; **5.** *pl. sg. konstr. phys.* Statik f; **6.** *pl. Funk:* atmo'sphärische Störung(en pl.).

sta-tion ['steɪʃn] **I** s. **1.** Platz m, Posten m (*a. sport*); **2.** (*Rettungs-, Unfall- etc.*) Stati'on f, (*Beratungs-, Dienst-, Tanketc.*)Stelle f; (Tele'grafen)Amt n; (Tele'fon)Sprechstelle f; ('Wahl)Lo,kal n; (Handels)Niederlassung f; (Feuer)Wache f; **3.** (Poli'zei)Wache f; **4.** 🚂 a) Bahnhof m, b) ('Bahn)Stati,on f; **5.** *Am.* (*Bus- etc.*)Haltestelle f; **6.** (Zweig-)Postamt n; **7.** ('Forschungs)Stati,on f; (Erdbeben)Warte f; **8.** (Rundfunk-)Sender m, Stati'on f; **9.** Kraftwerk n; **10.** ✕ a) Posten m, b) ⚓ Flotten)Stützpunkt m, b) Standort m, c) ✈ *Brit.* Fliegerhorst m; **11.** *biol.* Standort m; **12.** ✕, ✕ Positi'on f; **13.** Stati'on f (*Rastort*); **14.** *R.C.* a) **~ of the cross** ('Kreuzweg)Stati,on f, b) Stati'onskirche f; **15.** *eccl. a.* **~ day** Wochenfasttag m; **16.** *surv.* a) Stati'on f (*Ausgangspunkt*), b) Basismessstrecke f; **17.** *Austral.* (Rinder-, Schafs)Zuchtfarm f; **18.** *fig.* a) gesellschaftliche etc. Stellung: **~ in life**, b) Stand m, Rang m: **below one's ~** nicht standesgemäß heiraten etc.; **men of ~** Leute von Rang; **II** *v/t.* **19.** aufstellen, postieren; **20.** ✕, ⚓ stationieren: **be ~ed** stehen.

sta-tion-ar-y ['steɪʃnərɪ] *adj.* **1.** ⚙ etc. statio'när (*a. ast.,* ⚕), ortsfest, fest(stehend): **~ treatment** ⚕ stationäre Behandlung; **~ warfare** Stellungskrieg m; **2.** sesshaft; **3.** gleich bleibend, stationär, unveränderlich: **remain ~** unverändert sein *od.* bleiben; **4.** (still)stehend: **be ~** stehen; **~ dis-ease** a) ⚕ lo'kal auftretende u. jahreszeitlich bedingte Krankheit.

sta-tion-er ['steɪʃnə] s. Pa'pier-, Schreibwarenhändler m; '**sta-tion-er-y** [-ərɪ] s. **1.** Schreib-, Pa'pierwaren pl.: **office ~** Büromaterial n, -bedarf m; **2.** 'Brief-, 'Schreibpa,pier n.

sta-tion| **hos-pi-tal** s. ✕ 'Standortlaza,rett n; **~ house** s. **1.** a) Poli'zeiwache f, b) Feuerwache f; **2.** 🚂 'Bahnstati,on f; '**~,mas-ter** s. 🚂 Stati'onsvorsteher m; **~ se-lec-tor** s. ⚡ Stati'onswähler m, Sendereinstellung f; **~ wag-on** s. mot. Am. Kombiwagen m.

stat-ism ['steɪtɪzəm] s. ♥, *pol.* Diri'gismus m, Planwirtschaft f; '**stat-ist** [-tɪst] **I** s. **1.** Sta'tistiker m; **2.** Anhänger(in) der Planwirtschaft; **II** *adj.* **3.** *pol.* diri'gistisch.

sta-tis-tic, **sta-tis-ti-cal** [stə'tɪstɪk(l)] *adj.* □ sta'tistisch; **stat-is-ti-ci-an** [,stætɪ'stɪʃn] s. Sta'tistiker m; **sta'tis-tics** [-ks] s. pl. **1.** sg. konstr. allg. Sta'tistik f; **2.** Sta'tistik(en pl.) f.

sta-tor ['steɪtə] s. ⚙, ⚡ Stator m.

stat-u-ar-y ['stætjʊərɪ] **I** s. **1.** Bildhauerkunst f; **2.** (Rund)Plastiken pl., Statuen pl., Skulp'turen pl.; **3.** Bildhauer m; **II** *adj.* **4.** Bildhauer...; **5.** (rund)plastisch; **6.** Statuen...: **~ marble**; **stat-ue** ['stætʃuː] Statue f, Standbild n, Plastik f; **stat-u-esque** [,stætjʊ'esk] *adj.* □ statuenhaft (*a. fig.*); **stat-u-ette** [,stætjʊ'et] s. Statu'ette f.

stat-ure ['stætʃə] s. **1.** Sta'tur f, Wuchs m, Gestalt f; **2.** Größe f; **3.** *fig.* (geistige *etc.*) Größe, For'mat n, Ka'liber n.

sta-tus ['steɪtəs] pl. **-es** [-ɪz] s. **1.** ⚖ a) Status m, Rechtsstellung f, b) a. **legal ~** Rechtsfähigkeit f, c) Ak'tivlegitimati,on f: **~ of ownership** Eigentumsverhältnisse pl.; **equality of ~** (politische) Gleichberechtigung f; **national ~** Staatsangehörigkeit f; **2.** (Fa'milien-, Per'sonen)Stand m; **3.** a. **military ~** (Wehr-)Dienstverhältnis m; **4.** (gesellschaftliche *etc.*) Stellung f, (Sozi'al)Pre,stige n, Status m: **~ symbol** Statussymbol n; **5.** ✝ (geschäftliche) Lage: **financial ~** Vermögenslage; **6.** a. ⚕ Zustand m, Status m; **~ bar** s. Computer: 'Statuszeile f; **~ quo** [kwəʊ] (*Lat.*) s. der Status quo (*der jetzige Zustand*); **~ quo an-te** [kwəʊ'æntɪ] (*Lat.*) s. der Status quo ante (*der vorherige Zustand*).

stat-ute ['stætjuːt] s. **1.** ⚖ a) Gesetz n (*vom Parlament erlassene Rechtsvorschrift*), b) Gesetzesvorschrift f, c) *parl.* Parla'mentsakte f: **~ of bankruptcy** Konkursordnung f; **2.** **~ (of limitations)** ⚖ (Gesetz n über) Verjährung f: **not subject to the ~** unverjährbar; **3.** Sta'tut n, Satzung f; **~-barred** *adj.* ⚖ verjährt; **~ book** s. Gesetzessammlung f; **~ law** s. Gesetzesrecht n (*Ggs.* **common law**); **~ mile** s. (gesetzliche) Meile (*1,60933 km*).

stat-u-to-ry ['stætjʊtərɪ] *adj.* □ **1.** ⚖ gesetzlich (*Erbe, Feiertag, Rücklage etc.*): **~ corporation** Körperschaft f des öffentlichen Rechts; **~ declaration** eidesstattliche Erklärung; **2.** Gesetzes...; **3.** ⚖ (dem Gesetz nach) strafbar; → **rape¹** 1; **4.** ⚖ Verjährungs...; **5.** satzungsgemäß.

staunch¹ [stɔːnʃ] → **stanch¹**.

staunch² [stɔːnʃ] *adj.* □ **1.** (ge)treu, zuverlässig; **2.** standhaft, fest, eisern; '**staunch-ness** [-ʃnɪs] s. Festigkeit f, Zuverlässigkeit f.

stave [steɪv] **I** s. **1.** (Fass)Daube f; **2.** (Leiter)Sprosse f; **3.** Stock m; **4.** Strophe f, Vers m; **5.** 'Noten(linien)sy,stem n; **II** *v/t.* [*irr.*] **6.** *mst* **~ in** a) einschlagen, b) *Loch* schlagen; **7.** **~ off** a) j-n hinhalten *od.* abweisen, b) *Unheil etc.* abwenden, abwehren, c) *et.* aufschieben; **8.** mit Dauben *od.* Sprossen versehen; **~ rhyme** s. Stabreim m.

staves [steɪvz] pl. von **staff ¹** 8.

stay [steɪ] **I** *v/i.* **1.** bleiben (**with** bei j-m): **~ away** fernbleiben (**from** dat.); **~ behind** zurückbleiben; **~ clean** rein bleiben; **come to ~** (für immer) bleiben; **~ in** Hause *od.* drinnen bleiben; **~ on** (noch länger) bleiben; **~ for** (*od.* **to**) **dinner** zum Essen bleiben; **2.** sich (vor'übergehend) aufhalten, verweilen (**at, in** in dat., **with** bei j-m); **3.** stehen bleiben; **4.** (sich) verweilen; **5.** warten (**for s.o.** auf j-n); **6.** *bsd. sport* F a) 'durchhalten, b) **~ with** Am. mithalten (können) mit; **II** *v/t.* **7.** a) aufhalten, hemmen, Halt gebieten (*dat.*), b) zu'rückhalten (**from** von): **~ one's hand** sich zurückhalten; **8.** ⚖ *Urteilsvollstreckung, Verfahren* aussetzen; *Verfahren, Zwangsvollstreckung* einstellen;

9. *Hunger etc.* stillen; **10.** a. **~ up** stützen (a. fig.); **11.** ⚙ a) absteifen, b) abverspannen, c) verankern; **III** s. **12.** (vor'übergehender) Aufenthalt m; **13.** a) Halt m, Stockung f, b) Hemmnis n (**upon** für): **put a ~ on** s-e Gedanken etc. zügeln; **14.** ⚖ Aussetzung f, Einstellung f, (Voll'streckungs)Aufschub m; **15.** F Ausdauer f; **16.** ⚙ a) Stütze f, b) Strebe f, c) Verspannung f, d) Anker m; **17.** ⚓ Stag n, Stütztau n; **18.** pl. Kor'sett n; **19.** *fig.* Stütze f des Alters etc.

stay|-**at-home** ['steɪəθhəʊm] **I** s. Stubenhocker(in); **II** *adj.* stubenhockerisch; '**~-down (strike)** s. ✕ *Brit.* Sitzstreik m.

stay-er ['steɪə] s. **1.** ausdauernder Mensch; **2.** *Pferdesport:* Steher m.

stay-ing pow-er ['steɪɪŋ] s. Stehvermögen n, Ausdauer f.

'**stay-in strike** s. Sitzstreik m.

stead [sted] s. **1.** Stelle f: **in his ~** an s-r statt, statt seiner; **2.** Nutzen m: **stand s.o. in good ~** j-m (gut) zustatten kommen (*Kenntnisse etc.*).

stead-fast ['stedfəst] *adj.* □ fest: a) unverwandt (*Blick*), b) standhaft, unentwegt, treu (*Person*), c) unerschütterlich (*Person, a. Entschluss, Glaube etc.*); '**stead-fast-ness** [-nɪs] s. Standhaftigkeit f, Festigkeit f.

stead-i-ness ['stedɪnɪs] s. **1.** Festigkeit f; **2.** Beständigkeit f, Stetigkeit f; **3.** so'lide Art; **stead-y** ['stedɪ] **I** *adj.* □ **1.** (stand)fest, sta'bil: a **~ ladder**; **not ~ on one's legs** nicht fest auf den Beinen; **2.** gleich bleibend, gleichmäßig, unveränderlich; ausgeglichen (*Klima*); ✝ fest, sta'bil (*Preise*); **3.** stetig, ständig: **~ progress**; **~ work**; **4.** regelmäßig: **~ customer** Stammkunde m; **go ~ with** F mit e-m Mädchen (fest) ,gehen'; **5.** ruhig (*Augen, Nerven*), sicher (*Hand*); **6.** → **steadfast**; **7.** so'lide, ordentlich, zuverlässig (*Person, Lebensweise*); **II** *int.* **8.** sachte!, ruhig Blut!; **9.** **~ on!** halt!; **III** *v/t.* **10.** festigen, fest *od.* sicher etc. machen; **~ o.s.** sich stützen; **11.** *Pferd* zügeln; **12.** *j-n* zur Vernunft bringen; **IV** *v/i.* **13.** fest *od.* ruhig *od.* sicher etc. werden; sich festigen (a. ✝ *Kurse*); **V** s. **14.** Stütze f (*für Hand od. Werkzeug*); **15.** F fester Freund *od.* feste Freundin; **~ state** s. phys. Fließgleichgewicht n.

steak [steɪk] s. **1.** (*bsd.* Beef)Steak n; **2.** ('Fisch)Kote,lett n, (-)Fi,let n; **~ ham-mer** s. Fleischklopfer m.

steal [stiːl] **I** *v/t.* [*irr.*] **1.** (**from s.o.** j-m) stehlen (a. fig. plagiieren); **2.** fig. stehlen, erhaschen, ergattern: **~ a kiss** e-n Kuss rauben; **~ a look** verstohlenen Blick werfen; → **march¹** 10, **show** 3, **thunder** 1; **3.** fig. wohin schmuggeln; **II** *v/i.* [*irr.*] **4.** stehlen; **5.** schleichen: **~ away** sich davonstehlen; **~ into** sich einschleichen *od.* sich stehlen in (*acc.*); **6.** **~ over** *od.* (**up)on** fig. j-n beschleichen, über'kommen (*Gefühl*); **III** s. **7.** F a) Diebstahl m, b) Am. Schiebung f.

stealth [stelθ] s. Heimlichkeit f: **by ~** heimlich: ✕ **~ bomber** Tarnkappenbomber m; '**stealth-i-ness** [-θɪnɪs] s. Heimlichkeit f; '**stealth-y** [-θɪ] *adj.* □ verstohlen, heimlich.

steam [stiːm] **I** s. **1.** (Wasser)Dampf m: **at full ~** mit Volldampf (a. fig.); **get up ~** Dampf aufmachen (a. fig.); **let** (*od.* **blow**) **off ~** Dampf ablassen, fig. a. sich *od.* s-m Zorn Luft machen; **put on ~** a) Dampf anlassen, b) fig. Dampf dahinter machen; **he ran out of ~** ihm ging die Puste aus; **under one's own ~** mit eigener Kraft (*a. fig.*); **2.** Dunst *m*, Dampf *m*, Schwaden *pl.*; **3.** *fig.* Kraft *f*, Wucht *f*; **II** *v/i.* **4.** dampfen (*a. Pferd etc.*); **5.** verdampfen; **6.** ♣, ⛴ dampfen (*fahren*): *~ ahead* F *fig.* a) sich (mächtig) ins Zeug legen, b) gut vorankommen; **7.** *~ over od. up* (sich) beschlagen (*Glas*); **8.** F vor Wut kochen (*about* wegen); **III** *v/t.* **9.** a) Speisen etc. dämpfen, dünsten, b) *Holz etc.* mit Dampf behandeln, dämpfen, *Stoff* dekatieren; **10.** *~ up Glas* beschlagen; **11.** *~ up* F a) ankurbeln, b) *j-n* in Rage bringen: *be ~ed up* → 8; *~* **bath** *s.* Dampfbad *n*; '*~·*boat *s.* Dampfboot *n*; *~* boil·er *s.* Dampfkessel *m*; *~* en·gine *s.* 'Dampfma,schine *f od.* -lokomo,tive *f.*

steam·er ['stiːmə] *s.* **1.** Dampfer *m*, Dampfschiff *n*; **2.** a) Dampfkochtopf *m*, b) 'Dämpfappa,rat *m.*

steam| fit·ter *s.* ('Heizungs)Installa,teur *m*; *~* ga(u)ge *s.* Mano'meter *n*; *~* ham·mer *s.* Dampfhammer *m*; *~* heat *s.* **1.** durch Dampf erzeugte Hitze; **2.** *phys.* spe'zifische Verdampfungswärme; *~* nav·vy *Brit.* → steam shovel; '*~·*roll·er **I** *s.* **1.** Dampfwalze *f* (*a. fig.*); **II** *v/t.* **2.** glatt walzen; **3.** *fig.* a) *Opposition etc.* niederwalzen, 'über'fahren', b) *Antrag etc.* 'durchpeitschen; '*~·*ship *s.* steam·er 1; *~* shov·el *s.* ◉ (Dampf)Löffelbagger *m*; *~* tug *s.* Schleppdampfer *m.*

steam·y ['stiːmɪ] *adj.* ☐ dampfig, dunstig, dampfend, Dampf...

ste·a·rate ['stɪəreɪt] *s.* 🔥 Stea'rat *n.*

ste·ar·ic [stɪ'ærɪk] *adj.* 🔥 Stearin...;

ste·a·rin ['stɪərɪn] *s.* **1.** Stea'rin *n*; **2.** *der feste Bestandteil e-s Fettes.*

ste·a·tite ['stɪətaɪt] *s. min.* Stea'tit *m.*

steed [stiːd] *s. rhet.* (Streit)Ross *n.*

steel [stiːl] **I** *s.* **1.** Stahl *m*: *~s* 🕇 Stahlaktien *pl.*; *of ~* → 3; **2.** Stahl *m*: a) *oft cold ~* kalter Stahl, Schwert *n*, Dolch *m*, b) Wetzstahl *m*, c) Feuerstahl *m*, d) Korsettstäbchen *n*; **II** *adj.* **3.** stählern (*a. fig.*), aus Stahl, Stahl...; **III** *v/t.* **4.** ◉ (ver)stählen; **5.** *fig.* stählen, (ver)härten, wappnen: *~ o.s. for* (*against*) *s.th.* sich für (gegen) et. wappnen; '*~·*clad *adj.* stahlgepanzert; *~* en·grav·ing *s.* Stahlstich *m*; *~* mill *s.* Stahl(walz)werk *n*; *~* wool *s.* Stahlspäne *pl.*, -wolle *f*; *~·*works *s. pl. mst sg. konstr.* Stahlwerk(e *pl.*) *n.*

steel·y ['stiːlɪ] *adj.* → steel 3.

steel·yard ['stiːljɑːd] *s.* Laufgewichtswaage *f.*

steep¹ [stiːp] **I** *adj.* ☐ **1.** steil, jäh; **2.** F *fig.* a) ‚happig‘, ‚gepfeffert‘, unverschämt (*Preis etc.*), b) ‚toll‘, unglaublich; **II** *s.* **3.** steiler Abhang.

steep² [stiːp] **I** *v/t.* **1.** eintauchen, -weichen; **2.** (*in, with*) (durch)'tränken (mit); imprägnieren (mit); **3.** (*in*) *fig.* durch'dringen (mit), versenken (in *acc.*), erfüllen (von): *~ o.s. in* sich in *ein Thema etc.* versenken; *~ed in* versunken in (*dat.*), *b.s.* tief in et. verstrickt; **II** *v/i.* **4.** Einweichen *n*, -tauchen *n*; **5.** (Wasch)Lauge *f.*

steep·en ['stiːpən] *v/t. u. v/i.* steil(er) machen (werden); *fig.* (sich) erhöhen.

stee·ple ['stiːpl] *s.* **1.** Kirchturm(spitze *f*) *m*; **2.** Spitzturm *m*; '*~·*chase *sport s.* **1.** *Pferdesport*: Steeplechase *f*, Hindernis-, Jagdrennen *n*; **2.** Hindernislauf *m*.

stee·pled ['stiːpld] *adj.* **1.** betürmt (*Gebäude*); **2.** vieltürmig (*Stadt*).

'**stee·ple·jack** *s.* Schornstein- *od.* Turmarbeiter *m.*

steep·ness ['stiːpnɪs] *s.* **1.** Steilheit *f*, Steile *f*; **2.** steile Stelle.

---

steer¹ [stɪə] *s.* (*bsd.* junger) Ochse.

steer² [stɪə] **I** *v/t.* **1.** *Schiff, Fahrzeug, a. fig. Staat etc.* steuern, lenken; **2.** *Weg, Kurs* verfolgen, einhalten; **3.** *j-n wohin* lotsen, dirigieren; **II** *v/i.* **4.** steuern: *~ clear of fig.* vermeiden, aus dem Wege gehen (*dat.*); *~ for* lossteuern auf (*acc.*) (*a. fig.*); '**steer·a·ble** [-ərəbl] *adj.* lenkbar; '**steer·age** [-ərɪdʒ] *s. mst* ♣ **1.** Steuerung *f*; **2.** Steuerwirkung *f*: *~way* ♣ Steuerfahrt *f*; **3.** Zwischendeck *n.*

steer·ing ['stɪərɪŋ] **I** *s.* **1.** Steuern *n*; **2.** Steuerung *f*; **II** *adj.* **3.** Steuer...; *~* col·umn *s. mot.* Lenksäule *f*: *~ lock* Lenk(rad)schloss *n*; *~* com·mit·tee *s.* Lenkungsausschuss *m*; (Kon'gress-*etc.*)Leitung *f*; *~* gear *s.* **1.** *mot.*, 🛩 Steuerung *f*, Lenkung *f*; **2.** ♣ Steuergerät *n*, Ruderanlage *f*; *~* lock *s. mot.* Lenkungseinschlag *m*; *~* wheel *s.* ♣ Steuer-, *mot. a.* Lenkrad *n.*

steeve¹ [stiːv] ♣ *v/t.* traven, *Ballenladung* zs.-pressen.

steeve² [stiːv] *s.* ♣ Steigung *f* (*des Bugspriets*).

stein [staɪn] (*Ger.*) *s.* Bier-, Maßkrug *m.*

stel·lar ['stelə] *adj.* stel'lar, Stern(en)...

stel·late ['stelət] *adj.* sternförmig: *~ leaves* ♀ quirlständige Blätter.

stem¹ [stem] **I** *s.* **1.** (Baum)Stamm *m*; **2.** a) Stängel *m*, b) (Blüten-, Blatt-, Frucht)Stiel *m*, c) Halm *m*; **3.** Bündel *n* Bananen; **4.** (Pfeifen-, Weinglas- *etc.*) Stiel *m*; (Lampen)Fuß *m*; (Ven'til-) Schaft *m*; (Thermo'meter)Röhre *f*; **5.** (Aufzieh)Welle *f* (*Uhr*); **6.** Geschlecht *n*, Stamm *m*; **7.** *ling.* (Wort)Stamm *m*; **8.** ♪ (Noten)Hals *m*; **9.** *typ.* Grundstrich *m*; **10.** ♣ (Vorder)Steven *m*: *from ~ to stern* von vorn bis achtern; **II** *v/t.* **11.** entstielen; **III** *v/i.* **12.** stammen (*from* von).

stem² [stem] **I** *v/t.* **1.** *Fluss etc.* eindämmen (*a. fig.*); **2.** *Blutung* stillen; **3.** ♣ ankämpfen gegen *die Strömung etc.*; **4.** *fig.* a) aufhalten, Einhalt gebieten (*dat.*), b) ankämpfen gegen, sich entgegenstemmen (*dat.*); **II** *v/i.* **5.** *Skisport*: stemmen.

stem·less ['stemlɪs] *adj.* stängellos, ungestielt.

stem| turn *s. Skisport*: Stemmbogen *m*; '*~·*wind·er *s.* Remon'toiruhr *f.*

stench [stenʃ] *s.* Gestank *m.*

sten·cil ['stensl] **I** *s.* **1.** *a. ~ plate* ('Maler)Scha,blone *f*, Pa'trone *f*; **2.** *typ.* ('Wachs)Ma,trize *f*; **3.** Scha'blonenzeichnung *f*, -muster *n*; **4.** Ma'trizenabzug *m*; **II** *v/t.* **5.** *Oberfläche, Buchstaben* schablonieren; **6.** auf Matrize(n) schreiben.

Sten gun [sten] *s.* ✕ leichtes Ma'schinengewehr, LMG *n.*

sten·o ['stenəʊ] F → a) *stenograph* 4, b) *Am. stenographer.*

sten·o·graph ['stenəɡrɑːf] **I** *s.* **1.** Steno'gramm *n*; **2.** Kurzschriftzeichen *n*; **3.** Stenogra'fierma,schine *f*; **II** *v/t.* **4.** stenografieren; **ste·nog·ra·pher** [ste-'nɒɡrəfə] *s.* **1.** Steno'graf(in); **2.** *Am.* Stenoty'pistin *f*; **sten·o·graph·ic** [,stenə'ɡræfɪk] *adj.* (☐ *~ally*) steno'grafisch; **ste·nog·ra·phy** [ste'nɒɡrəfɪ] *s.* Stenogra'fie *f*, Kurzschrift *f.*

sten·o·type ['stenəʊtaɪp] → *stenograph* 2 u. 3.

sten·to·ri·an [sten'tɔːrɪən] *adj.* 'überlaut: *~ voice* Stentorstimme *f.*

step [step] **I** *s.* **1.** Schritt *m* (*a. Geräusch, Maß*): *~ by ~* Schritt für Schritt (*a. fig.*); *take a ~* e-n Schritt machen; **2.** Fußstapfen *m*: *tread in s.o.'s ~s fig.* in j-s Fußstapfen treten; **3.** *eiliger etc.*

Schritt, Gang *m*; **4.** (Tanz)Schritt *m*; **5.** (Gleich)Schritt *m*: *in ~* im Gleichschritt; *out of ~* außer Tritt; *out of ~ with fig.* nicht im Einklang mit; *fall in ~* Tritt fassen; *keep ~ (with)* Schritt halten (mit); **6.** ein paar Schritte *pl.*, ein ‚Katzensprung‘ *m*: *it is only a ~ to the inn*; **7.** *fig.* Schritt *m*, Maßnahme *f*: *take ~s* Schritte unternehmen; *take legal ~s against* gegen *j-n* gerichtlich vorgehen; *a false ~* ein Fehler, e-e Dummheit; → *watch* 17; **8.** *fig.* Schritt *m*, Stufe *f*: *a great ~ forward* ein großer Schritt vorwärts; **9.** Stufe *f* (*e-r Treppe etc.*; *a.* ♪ *e-s Verstärkers etc.*); (Leiter)Sprosse *f*, ◉, ♪ Schaltschritt *m*; **10.** (*pair of*) *~s pl.* Trittleiter *f*; **11.** Tritt(brett *n*) *m*; **12.** *geogr.* Stufe *f*, Ter'rasse *f*; Pla'teau *n*; **13.** ♪ a) (Ton-, Inter'vall)Schritt *m*, b) Inter'vall *n*, c) (Tonleiter)Stufe *f*; **14.** *fig.* a) (Rang-) Stufe *f*, Grad *m*, b) ✕ Beförderung *f*; **II** *v/i.* **15.** schreiten, treten: *~ into a fortune fig.* unverhofft zu e-m Vermögen kommen; **16.** *wohin* gehen, treten: *~ in!* herein!; **17.** → *step out* 2; **18.** treten ([*up*]*on* auf *acc.*): *~ on the gas* (*od. ~ on it*) (F *a. fig.*) Gas geben; *~ on it!* F Tempo!; **III** *v/t.* **19.** *Schritt* machen: *~ it* zu Fuß gehen; **20.** *Tanz* tanzen; **21.** *a. ~ off* (*od. out*) *Entfernung etc.* a) abschreiten, b) abstecken; **22.** abstufen;

Zssgn mit adv.:

step| a·side *v/i.* **1.** zur Seite treten; **2.** → *step down* 2; *~* back **I** *v/i. a. fig.* zu'rücktreten; **II** *v/t.* abstufen; *~* down **I** *v/t.* **1.** her'unter-, hin'unterschreiten; **2.** *fig.* zu'rücktreten (*in favo[u]r of* zu'gunsten); **II** *v/t.* **3.** verrringern, verzögern; **4.** ♪ her'untertransformieren; *~* in *v/i.* **1.** eintreten, -steigen; **2.** *fig.* einschreiten, -greifen; *~* out **I** *v/i.* **1.** heraustreten, aussteigen; **2.** (forsch) ausschreiten; **3.** F (viel) ausgehen; **II** *v/t.* **4.** → *step* 21a; *~* up **I** *v/i.* **1.** hin'auf-, her'aufsteigen; **2.** zugehen (*to* auf *acc.*); **II** *v/t.* **3.** *Produktion etc.* steigern, ankurbeln; **4.** ♪ hochtransformieren.

step- [step] *in Zssgn* Stief...; *~child* Stiefkind *n*; *~father* Stiefvater *m.*

step| dance *s.* Stepp(tanz) *m*; '*~·*down *adj.* ♪ Umspann...: *~ transformer* Abwärtstransformator *m*; '*~·*in **I** *adj.* **1.** zum Hin'einschlüpfen, Schlupf...; **II** *s.* **2.** *mst pl.* Schlüpfer *m*; **3.** *pl. a. ~ shoes* Slipper *pl.*; '*~·*lad·der *s.* Trittleiter *f*; '*~·*moth·er·ly *adj. a. fig.* stiefmütterlich.

steppe [step] *s. geogr.* Steppe *f.*

step·ping stone ['stepɪŋ] *s.* **1.** (Tritt-) Stein *m im Wasserlauf etc.*; **2.** *fig.* Sprungbrett *n* (*to* zu).

'**step-up I** *adj.* stufenweise erhöhend: *~ transformer* ♪ Aufwärtstransformator *m*; **II** *s.* Steigerung *f.*

'**step·wise** *adv.* schritt-, stufenweise.

ster·e·o ['sterɪəʊ] F **I** *s.* **1.** a) → *stereotype* 1, b) → *stereoscope*; **2.** a) Stereogerät *n*, b) Stereo(schall)platte *f*; **II** *adj.* **3.** → *stereoscopic*; **4.** stereo, Stereo...: *~ record* → 2b.

stereo- [sterɪəʊ] *in Zssgn* a) starr, fest, b) 'dreidimensio,nal, stereo..., Stereo..., Raum...; **ster·e·o·chem·is·try** [,sterɪəʊ'kemɪstrɪ] *s.* Stereo-, 'Raum,chemie *f*; **ster·e·og·ra·phy** [,sterɪ'ɒɡrəfɪ] *s.* ✏ Stereogra'phie *f*, Körperzeichnung *f*; **ster·e·om·e·try** [,sterɪ'ɒmɪtrɪ] *s.* **1.** *phys.* Stereome'trie *f*; **2.** ✏ Geome'trie *f* des Raumes.

ster·e·o·phon·ic [,sterɪəʊ'fɒnɪk] *adj.* (☐

~ally) stereo'phonisch, Stereoton...: ~ sound Raumton m.

ster·e·o·plate ['steriǝpleit] s. typ. Stereo'typplatte f, Stereo n.

ster·e·o·scope ['steriǝskǝup] s. Stereo'skop n; **ster·e·o·scop·ic** [,steriǝ'skɔpik] adj. (□ **~ally**) stereo'skopisch, Stereo...; **ster·e·os·co·py** [,steri'ɔskǝpi] s. Stereosko'pie f.

ster·e·o·type ['steriǝtaip] **I** s. **1.** typ. a) Steroty'pie f, Plattendruck m, b) Stereo'type f, Druckplatte f; **2.** fig. Kli'schee n, Scha'blone f; **II** v/t. **3.** typ. stereotypieren; **4.** fig. Redensart etc. stereo'typ wieder'holen; **5.** e-e feste Form geben (dat.); **'ster·e·o·typed** [-pt] adj. **1.** typ. stereotypiert; **2.** fig. stereo'typ, scha'blonenhaft; **ster·e·o·ty·pog·ra·phy** [,stiǝriǝʊtai'pɔgrǝfi] s. typ. Stereo'typdruck(verfahren n) m; **'ster·e·o·typ·y** [-pi] s. typ. Stereoty'pie f.

ster·ile ['sterail] adj. **1.** ste'ril: a) keimfrei, b) physiol. unfruchtbar (a. fig. Geist etc.); **2.** fig. fruchtlos (Arbeit, Diskussion etc.); leer, gedankenarm (Stil); **ste·ril·i·ty** [ste'riliti] s. Sterili'tät f (a. fig.).

ster·i·li·za·tion [,sterǝlai'zeiʃn] s. **1.** Sterilisati'on f: a) Entkeimung f, b) Unfruchtbarmachung f; **2.** Sterili'tät f; **ster·i·lize** ['sterǝlaiz] v/t. sterilisieren: a) keimfrei machen, b) unfruchtbar machen; **'ster·i·li·zer** ['sterǝlaizǝ] s. Sterili'sator m (Apparat).

ster·ling ['stɜ:liŋ] **I** adj. **1.** ✝ Sterling(...): ten pounds ~ 10 Pfund Sterling; ~ area Sterlinggebiet n, -block m; **2.** von Standardwert (Gold, Silber); **3.** fig. echt, gediegen, bewährt; **II** s. **4.** ✝ Sterling m.

stern¹ [stɜ:n] adj. □ **1.** streng, hart: ~ discipline; ~ penalty; **2.** unnachgiebig; **3.** streng, finster: a ~ face.

stern² [stɜ:n] **I** s. **1.** ♻ Heck n, Achterschiff n: (down) by the ~ hecklastig; **2.** zo. a) 'Hinterteil n, b) Schwanz m; **3.** allg. hinterer Teil; **II** adj. **4.** ♻ Heck...

ster·nal ['stɜ:nl] adj. anat. Brustbein...

'stern|-,chas·er s. ♻ hist. Heckgeschütz n; **'~-fast** s. ♻ Achtertau n.

stern·ness ['stɜ:nnis] s. Strenge f, Härte f, Düsterkeit f.

'stern·post s. ♻ Achtersteven m.

ster·num ['stɜ:nǝm] pl. **-na** [-nǝ] s. anat. Brustbein n.

ster·oid ['stiǝrɔid] s. biol., ♻, ♻ Stero'id n.

ster·to·rous ['stɜ:tǝrǝs] adj. □ röchelnd.

stet [stet] (Lat.) typ. **I** imp. stehen lassen!, bleibt!; **II** v/t. mit ,stet' markieren.

steth·o·scope ['steθǝskǝup] ♻ **I** s. Stetho'skop n, Hörrohr n; **II** v/t. abhorchen; **steth·o·scop·ic** [,steθǝ'skɔpik] adj. (□ **~ally**) stetho'skopisch.

ste·ve·dore ['sti:vǝdɔ:] s. ♻ **1.** Stauer m, Schauermann m; **2.** Stauer m (Unternehmer).

stew¹ [stju:] **I** v/t. **1.** schmoren, dämpfen, langsam kochen; → stewed 1; **II** v/i. **2.** schmoren; → juice 1; **3.** fig. ,schmoren', vor Hitze (fast) 'umkommen; **4.** F sich aufregen; **III** s. **5.** Schmor-, Eintopfgericht n; **6.** F Aufregung f.

stew² [stju:] s. Brit. a) Fischteich m, b) Fischbehälter m.

stew·ard ['stjuǝd] s. **1.** Verwalter m; **2.** Haushalter m, Haushofmeister m; **3.** Tafelmeister m, Kämmerer m (e-s College, Klubs etc.); **4.** ♻, ♻ Steward m; **5.** (Fest- etc.)Ordner m; mot. 'Renn-

kommis,sar m; → shop steward; **'stew·ard·ess** [-dis] s. ♻, ♻ Stewardess f; **'stew·ard·ship** [-ʃip] s. Verwalteramt n.

stewed [stju:d] adj. **1.** geschmort, gedämpft, gedünstet; **2.** sl. ,besoffen'.

'stew|-pan s. Schmorpfanne f; **'~-pot** s. Schmortopf m.

stick¹ [stik] **I** s. **1.** Stecken m, Stock m, (trockener) Zweig; pl. Klein-, Brennholz n: dry ~s (dürres) Reisig; **2.** Scheit n, Stück n Holz; **3.** Gerte f, Rute f; **4.** Stängel m, Stiel m (Rhabarber, Sellerie); **5.** Stock m (a. fig. Schläge), Stab m: get (give) the ~ e-e Tracht Prügel bekommen (verabreichen); get hold of the wrong end of the ~ fig. die Sache falsch verstehen; **6.** (Besen- etc.)Stiel m; **7.** (Spazier)Stock m; **8.** (Zucker-, Siegellack)Stange f; **9.** a) (Stück n) Rasierseife f, b) (Lippen- etc.)Stift m; **10.** ♪ a) Taktstock m, b) (Trommel)Schlägel m, c) (Geigen)Bogen m; **11.** sport a) Schläger m, Hockey etc.: Stock m, b) Pferdesport: Hürde f; **12.** a) ✗ Steuerknüppel m, b) mot. Schalthebel m; **13.** ✗ Bombenreihe f; **14.** typ. Winkelhaken m; **15.** F a. dry (od. dull) ~ Stockfisch m, allg. Kerl m; **16.** pl. Am. F finsterste Pro'vinz; **II** v/t. **17.** Pflanze mit e-m Stock stützen; **18.** typ. a) setzen, b) in e-m Winkelhaken anein'ander reihen.

stick² [stik] **I** v/t. [irr.] **1.** durch'stechen, -'bohren; Schweine (ab)stechen; **2.** stechen mit e-r Nadel etc. (in, into in acc.); et. stecken, stoßen; **3.** auf e-e Gabel etc. stecken, aufspießen; **4.** Kopf, Hand etc. wohin stecken od. strecken; **5.** F legen, setzen, in die Tasche etc. stecken; **6.** (an)stecken, anheften; **7.** voll stecken (with mit); **8.** Briefmarke, Plakat etc. ankleben, Fotos etc. (ein)kleben: ~ together et. zs.-kleben; **9.** bekleben; **10.** zum Stecken bringen, festfahren: be stuck im Schlamm etc. stecken (bleiben a. fig.), festsitzen (a. fig.): be stuck on F vernarrt sein in (acc.); be stuck with s.th. et. ,am Hals haben'; be stuck for s.th. um et. verlegen sein; **11.** j-n verwirren; **12.** F j-n ,blechen' lassen (for für); **13.** sl. j-n ,leimen' (betrügen); **14.** sl. et. od. j-n aushalten, -stehen, (v)ertragen: I can't ~ him; **15.** ~ it (out) F ,durchhalten', es aushalten; **16.** ~ it on F a) e-n unverschämten Preis verlangen, b) ,dick auftragen', über'treiben; **II** v/i. [irr.] **17.** stecken; **18.** (fest)kleben, haften: ~ together zs.-kleben; **19.** sich festklammern od. heften (to an acc.); **20.** haften, hängen bleiben (a. fig. Spitzname etc.): some of it will ~ et. (von e-r Verleumdung) bleibt immer hängen; ~ in the mind im Gedächtnis haften bleiben; make s.th. ~ dafür sorgen, dass et. ,sitzt'; **21.** ~ to bei j-m od. e-r Sache bleiben, j-m nicht von der Seite weichen: ~ to the point fig. bei der Sache bleiben; ~ to it dranbleiben; → gun 1; **22.** ~ to bleiben (dat.), zu j-m, s-m Wort etc. stehen, bei s-r Ansicht etc. bleiben, sich an e-e Regel etc. halten; ~ together zs.-halten (Freunde); **23.** im Hals, im Schmutz, a. fig. beim Lesen etc. stecken bleiben: I was really stuck F ich war ,to'tal aufgeschmissen' (wusste nicht mehr weiter); → mud 2; **24.** ~ at nothing vor nichts zurückschrecken; **25.** her'vorstehen (from, out of aus); Zssgn mit adv.:

stick| a·round v/i. F in der Nähe bleiben; **~ out I** v/i. **1.** ab-, her'vor-, he-

rausstehen; **2.** fig. auffallen; **3.** bestehen (for auf dat.); **II** v/t. **4.** Arm, Brust, a. Kopf, Zunge her'ausstrecken; **5.** ~ stick² 15; ~ up **I** v/t. **1.** sl. über'fallen, ausrauben; **2.** ~ 'em up! sl. Hände hoch!; **II** v/i. **3.** in die Höhe stehen; **4.** ~ for sich für j-n einsetzen; **5.** ~ to mutig gegen'übertreten (dat.), Pa'roli bieten (dat.).

stick·er ['stikǝ] s. **1.** a) (Schweine-) Schlächter m, b) Schlachtmesser n; **2.** Sticker m, Aufkleber m; **3.** Am. (angeklebter) Strafzettel; **4.** fig. zäher Kerl; **5.** F ,Hocker' m, (zu) lange bleibender Gast; **6.** F ,Ladenhüter' m; **7.** ,harte Nuss'.

stick·i·ness ['stikinis] s. **1.** Klebrigkeit f; **2.** Schwüle f; **3.** F Schwierigkeit f.

stick·ing plas·ter ['stikiŋ] s. Heftpflaster n.

stick-in-the-mud ['stikinðǝmʌd] F **I** adj. rückständig, -schrittlich; **II** s. Rückschrittler m, bsd. pol. Reaktio'när m.

'stick·jaw s. F ,Plombenzieher' m (zäher Bonbon etc.).

stick·le ['stikl] v/i. **1.** harnäckig zanken od. streiten: ~ for s.th. et. hartnäckig verfechten; **2.** Bedenken äußern, Skrupel haben.

stick·le·back ['stiklbæk] s. ichth. Stichling m.

stick·ler ['stiklǝ] s. **1.** Eiferer m; **2.** Verfechter m (for gen.); **3.** Kleinigkeitskrämer m, Pe'dant m, j-d, der es ganz genau nimmt (for mit).

stick-to-it·ive [,stik'tu:ǝtiv] adj. Am. F hartnäckig, zäh.

'stick-up I adj. **1.** ~ collar → 2; **II** s. **2.** F Stehkragen m; **3.** sl. ('Raub),Überfall m.

stick·y ['stiki] adj. □ **1.** klebrig, zäh: ~ charge ✗ Haftladung f; ~ label Brit. Klebezettel m; ~ note a) Haftnotiz f, b) Haftnotizzettel m; **2.** schwül, stickig (Wetter etc.); **3.** F fig. a) klebrig, b) eklig, c) schwierig, heikel (Sache), d) kritisch, e) kitschig: be ~ about doing s.th. et. nur ungern tun.

stiff [stif] **I** adj. □ **1.** allg. steif, starr (a. Gesicht, Person): ~ collar steifer Kragen; ~ neck steifer Hals; → lip 1; **2.** zäh, dick, steif (Teig etc.); **3.** steif (Brise), stark (Wind, Strömung); **4.** stark (Dosis, Getränk), steif (Grog); **5.** fig. starrköpfig; **6.** fig. hart (Gegner, Kampf etc.), scharf (Konkurrenz, Opposition); **7.** schwierig (Aufstieg, Prüfung etc.); **8.** hart (Strafe); **9.** steif, for-'mell, gezwungen (Benehmen, Person etc.); **10.** steif, linkisch (Stil); **11.** F unglaublich: a bit ~ ziemlich stark, allerhand; **12.** F ,zu Tode' gelangweilt, erschrocken; **13.** ✝ a) sta'bil, fest (Preis, Markt), b) hoch, unverschämt (Forderung, Preis); **II** s. sl. **14.** a) Leiche f, b) Besoffene(r) m; **15.** a) Langweiler m, b) Blödmann m; **16.** Am. a) ,Lappen' m (Banknote), b) ,Blüte' f (Falschgeld), c) ,Kas'siber' m (im Gefängnis); **'stiffen** [-fn] **I** v/t. **1.** (ver)steifen, (ver)stärken; Stoff etc. stärken, steifen; **2.** steif od. starr machen (Flüssigkeit, Glieder etc.), verdicken (Flüssiges); **3.** fig. a) et. verschärfen, b) (be)stärken, j-m den Nacken steifen; **II** v/i. **4.** sich versteifen, -stärken; starr werden; **5.** fig. hart werden, sich versteifen; **6.** steif od. förmlich werden; **7.** ✝ sich festigen (Preise etc.); **'stiff·en·er** [-fnǝ] s. **1.** Versteifung f; **2.** F ,Seelenwärmer' m, Stärkung f (Getränk); **'stiff·en·ing** [-fniŋ] s. Versteifung f: a) Steifwerden *n*, b) 'Steifmateri,al *n*.

,**stiff-'necked** *adj. fig.* halsstarrig.

stiff·ness ['stɪfnɪs] *s*. **1.** Steifheit *f* (*a. fig. Förmlichkeit*), Steife *f*, Starrheit *f*; **2.** Zähigkeit *f*, Dickflüssigkeit *f*; **3.** *fig.* Härte *f*, Schärfe *f*.

sti·fle¹ ['staɪfl] **I** *v/t*. **1.** *j-n* ersticken; **2.** *Fluch etc., a. Gefühl, a. Aufstand etc.* ersticken, unter'drücken, *Diskussion etc.* abwürgen; **II** *v/i*. **3.** (*weitS.* schier) ersticken.

sti·fle² ['staɪfl] *s. zo.* **1.** *a.* ~ **joint** Kniegelenk *n* (*Pferd, Hund*); **2.** *vet.* Kniegelenkgalle *f* (*Pferd*); ~ **bone** *s.* Kniescheibe *f* (*Pferd*).

sti·fling ['staɪflɪŋ] *adj.* □ erstickend (*a. fig.*), stickig.

stig·ma ['stɪgmə] *pl.* **-mas**, **-ma·ta** [-mətə] *s*. **1.** *fig.* Brand-, Schandmal *n*, Stigma *n*; **2.** ⚕ Sym'ptom *n*; **3.** ⚕ (*pl. -mata*) Mal *n*, roter Hautfleck; **4.** *stigmata pl. eccl.* Wundmale *pl.*, Stigmata *pl.*; **5.** ♀ Narbe *f* (*Blüte*); **6.** *zo.* Luftloch *n* (*Insekt*); **stig·mat·ic** [stɪg'mætɪk] *adj.* (□ ~*ally*) **1.** stig'matisch (*a. opt.*); **2.** ♀ narbenartig; **3.** *opt.* (ana-) stig'matisch; **'stig·ma·tize** [-ətaɪz] *v/t.* **1.** ⚕, *eccl.* stigmatisieren; **2.** *bsd. fig.* brandmarken.

stile¹ [staɪl] *s.* Zauntritt *m*.

stile² [staɪl] *s.* Seitenstück *n* (*e-r Täfelung*), Höhenfries *m* (*e-r Tür*).

sti·let·to [stɪ'letəʊ] *pl.* **-tos** [-z] *s.* Sti'lett *n:* ~ **heel** Pfennigabsatz *m*.

still¹ [stɪl] **I** *adj.* □ **1.** *allg.* still: a) reglos, unbeweglich, b) ruhig, lautlos, c) leise, gedämpft, d) friedlich, ruhig: **keep** ~*!* sei ruhig!; → **water** 11; **2.** nicht moussierend: ~ **wine** Stillwein *m*; **3.** *phot.* Stand..., Steh..., Einzel(aufnahme)...; **II** *s.* **4.** *poet.* Stille *f*; **5.** *phot.* Standfoto *n*, Einzelaufnahme *f*; **III** *v/t.* **6.** *Geräusche etc.* zum Schweigen bringen; **7.** *j-n* beruhigen, *Verlangen etc.* stillen; **IV** *v/i.* **8.** still werden.

still² [stɪl] **I** *adv.* **1.** (immer) noch, noch immer, bis jetzt; **2.** (*beim comp.*) noch, immer: ~ **higher, higher** ~ noch höher; ~ **more so because** umso mehr als; **3.** dennoch, doch; **II** *cj.* **4.** (und) dennoch, und doch, in'des(sen).

still³ [stɪl] *s.* a) Destillierkolben *m*, b) Destil'lierappa,rat *m*.

stil·lage ['stɪlɪdʒ] *s.* Gestell *n*.

'**still·birth** *s.* Totgeburt *f*; '~**born** *adj.* tot geboren (*a. fig.*); '~**fish** *v/i.* vom verankerten Boot aus angeln; ~ **hunt** *s.* Pirsch(jagd) *f*; '~**hunt** *v/i.* (*v/t.* an)pirschen; ~ **life** *s. paint.* Stilleben *n*.

still·ness ['stɪlnɪs] *s.* Stille *f*.

still room *s. bsd. Brit.* **1.** *hist.* Destillati'onsraum *m*; **2.** a) Vorratskammer *f*, b) Servierraum *m*.

stilt [stɪlt] *s.* **1.** Stelze *f*; **2.** △ Pfahl *m*, Pfeiler *m*; **3.** *a.* ~ **bird** *orn.* Stelzenläufer *m*; '**stilt·ed** [-tɪd] *adj.* □ **1.** gestelzt, gespreizt, geschraubt (*Rede, Stil etc.*); **2.** △ erhöht; '**stilt·ed·ness** [-tɪdnɪs] *s.* Gespreiztheit *f*.

stim·u·lant ['stɪmjʊlənt] **I** *s.* **1.** ⚕ Stimulans *n*, Anregungs-, Weckmittel *n*; **2.** Genussmittel *n, bsd.* Alkohol *m*; **3.** Anreiz *m* (**of** für); **II** *adj.* **4.** → *stimulating* 1; **stim·u·late** ['stɪmjʊleɪt] *v/t.* **1.** ⚕ *etc., a. fig.* stimulieren, anregen (**s.o. into** *j-n* zu *et.*); *fig. a.* ansporen, anstacheln; beleben, ankurbeln; **2.** *Nerv* reizen; '**stim·u·lat·ing** [-leɪtɪŋ] *adj.* **1.** *a. fig.* stimulierend, anregend, belebend; **2.** *fig.* ansporend; **stim·u·la·tion** [,stɪmjʊ'leɪʃn] *s.* **1.** Anreiz *m*, Antrieb *m*, Anregung *f*, Belebung *f*; **2.** ⚕ Reizung *f*, Reiz *m*; '**stim·u·la·tive** [-lətɪv]

→ *stimulating*; '**stim·u·lus** [-ləs] *pl.* **-li** [-laɪ] *s.* **1.** Stimulus *m:* a) (An)Reiz *m*, Antrieb *m*, Ansporn *m* (**to** zu), b) ⚕ Reiz *m:* ~ **threshold** Reizschwelle *f*; **2.** → *stimulant* 1; **3.** ♀ Nesselhaar *n*.

sti·my ['staɪmɪ] → *stymie*.

sting [stɪŋ] **I** *v/t.* [*irr.*] **1.** stechen (*Insekt, Nessel etc.*); **2.** brennen, beißen in *od.* auf (*dat.*); **3.** schmerzen, wehtun (*Schlag etc.*): *stung by remorse fig.* von Reue geplagt; **4.** *fig. j-n* verletzen, kränken; **5.** anstacheln, reizen (**into** zu); **6.** *sl.* ,neppen' (**for** um Geld); **II** *v/i.* [*irr.*] **7.** stechen; **8.** brennen, beißen (*Pfeffer etc.*); **9.** *a. fig.* schmerzen, wehtun; **III** *s.* **10.** Stachel *m* (*Insekt; a. fig. des Todes, der Eifersucht etc.*); **11.** ♀ Brennborste *f*; **12.** Stich *m*, Biss *m:* ~ **of conscience** *fig.* Gewissensbisse *pl.*; **13.** Schärfe *f*; **14.** Pointe *f*, Spitze *f* (*e-s Witzes*); **15.** Schwung *m*, Wucht *f*; '**sting·er** [-ŋə] *s.* **1.** a) stechendes In'sekt, b) stechende Pflanze; **2.** F a) schmerzhafter Schlag, b) beißende Bemerkung.

sting·i·ness ['stɪndʒɪnɪs] *s.* Geiz *m*.

sting·ing ['stɪŋɪŋ] *adj.* □ **1.** ♀, *zo.* stechend; **2.** *fig.* schmerzhaft (*Schlag etc.*); schneidend (*Kälte, Wind*); scharf, beißend, verletzend (*Worte, Tadel*); ~ **net·tle** *s.* ♀ Brennnessel *f*.

stin·gy ['stɪndʒɪ] *adj.* □ **1.** geizig, knickerig: **be** ~ **of s.th.** mit et. knausern; **2.** dürftig, kärglich.

stink [stɪŋk] **I** *v/i.* [*irr.*] **1.** stinken, übel riechen (**of** nach): ~ **of money** *fig.* F vor Geld stinken; **2.** *fig.* verrufen sein, ,stinken': ~ **to high heaven** zum Himmel stinken; → *nostril*; **3.** *fig.* F ('hunds)mise,rabel sein; **II** *v/t.* [*irr.*] **4.** *a.* ~ **out, up** verstänkern; **5.** ~ **out** a) *Höhle, Tiere* ausräuchern, b) *j-n* durch Gestank vertreiben; **6.** *sl.* (den Gestank *gen.*) riechen: **you can** ~ **it a mile off**; **III** *s.* **7.** Gestank *m*; **8.** Stunk *m*, Krach *m:* **raise** (*od.* **kick up**) **a** ~ Stunk machen (**about** wegen); **9.** *pl. Brit.* Che'mie *f*; **10.** *Am.* F (billiges) Par'füm; '**stink·ard** [-kəd] *s.* **1.** *zo.* Stinktier *n*; **2.** → *stinker* 1; '**stink·er** [-kə] *s.* **1.** a) ,Stinker', b) *sl.* Dreckskerl *m*; **2.** a) ,Stinka'dores' *m* (*Käse*), b) ,Stinka'dores' *f* (*Zigarre*); **3.** *sl.* a) gemeiner Brief, b) böse Bemerkung *od.* Kri'tik, c) ,böse' (*schwierige etc.*) Sache, d) ,Mist' *m*; '**stink·ing** [-kɪŋ] **I** *adj.* □ **1.** stinkend; **2.** *sl.* a) widerlich, b) mise'rabel; **3.** ~ **stinko**; **II** *adv.* **4.** ~ **rich** *sl.* ,stinkreich'.

stink·o ['stɪŋkəʊ] *adj. Am. sl.* ,(stink)besoffen', (to'tal) ,blau'.

'**stink·pot** *s.* **1.** ♺ *hist.* Stinktopf *m*; **2.** F → *stinker* 1.

stint [stɪnt] **I** *v/t.* **1.** *j-n od. et.* einschränken, *j-n* kurz *od.* knapp halten (**in, of** mit): ~ **o.s. of** sich einschränken mit, sich et. versagen (*mit*); **2.** knausern *od.* kargen mit (*Geld, Lob etc.*); **II** *s.* **3.** Be-, Einschränkung *f:* **without** ~ ohne Einschränkung, rückhaltlos; **4.** a) (zugewiesene) Arbeit, Pensum *n*, b) (vorgeschriebenes) Maß; **5.** ☒ Schicht *f*; '**stint·ed** [-tɪd] *adj.* □ knapp, karg.

stipe [staɪp] *s., zo.* Stiel *m*.

sti·pend ['staɪpend] *s.* Gehalt *n* (*bsd. e-s Geistlichen*); **sti·pen·di·a·ry** [staɪ'pendjərɪ] **I** *adj.* besoldet: ~ **magistrate** → **II** *s. Brit.* Richter *m* an e-m **magistrates' court**.

stip·ple ['stɪpl] **I** *v/t.* **1.** *paint.* tüpfeln, punktieren; **II** *s.* **2.** Punk'tierma,nier *f*, Pointil'lismus *m*; **3.** Punktierung *f*.

stip·u·late ['stɪpjʊleɪt] *bsd.* ✍, ♀ **I** *v/i.*

1. (**for**) a) e-e Vereinbarung treffen (über *acc.*), b) *et.* zur Bedingung machen; **II** *v/t.* **2.** festsetzen, vereinbaren, ausbedingen; **3.** ✍ *Tatbestand* einverständlich feststellen, außer Streit stellen; **stip·u·la·tion** [,stɪpjʊ'leɪʃn] *s.* **1.** ♀, ✍ (vertragliche) Abmachung, Über'einkunft *f*; **2.** Klausel *f*, Bedingung *f*; **3.** ✍ Par'teienüber,einkunft *f*.

stip·ule ['stɪpjuːl] *s.* ♀ Nebenblatt *n*.

stir¹ [stɜː] **I** *v/t.* **1.** *Kaffee, Teig etc.* rühren: ~ **up** a) (gut) umrühren, b) *Schlamm* aufwühlen; **2.** *Feuer* (an-) schüren; **3.** *Glied etc.* rühren, bewegen: **not to** ~ **a finger** keinen Finger krumm machen; **4.** *Blätter, See etc.* bewegen (*Wind*); **5.** ~ **up** *a. fig. j-n* auf-, wachrütteln; **6.** ~ **up** *fig.* a) *j-n* aufreizen, -hetzen, b) *Neugier etc.* erregen, c) *Streit etc.* entfachen; **7.** *fig.* aufwühlen, bewegen, erregen; *j-s Blut* in Wallung bringen; **II** *v/i.* **8.** sich rühren *od.* regen (*a. fig. geschäftig sein*): **not to** ~ **from the spot** sich nicht von der Stelle rühren; **he never** ~**red abroad** er ging nie aus; **he is not** ~**ring yet** er ist noch nicht auf(gestanden); **9.** a) im Gange *od.* 'Umlauf sein, b) geschehen, sich ereignen; **III** *s.* **10.** Rühren *n*; **11.** Bewegung *f*; **12.** Aufregung *f*; **13.** Aufsehen *n*, Sensati'on *f:* **create** *od.* **make a** ~ Aufsehen erregen.

stir² [stɜː] *s. sl.* ,Kittchen' *n*, ,Knast' *m* (*Gefängnis*): **in** ~ im Knast.

stirps [stɜːps] *pl.* **stir·pes** ['stɜːpiːz] *s.* **1.** Fa'milie(nzweig *m*) *f*; **2.** ✍ a) Stammvater *m*, b) Stamm *m:* **by stirpes** Erbfolge nach Stämmen.

stir·rer ['stɜːrə] *s.* a) Rührlöffel *m*, b) Rührwerk *n*.

stir·ring ['stɜːrɪŋ] *adj.* □ **1.** bewegt; **2.** *fig.* rührig; **3.** erregend, aufwühlend; zündend (*Rede*); bewegt (*Zeiten*).

stir·rup ['stɪrəp] *s.* **1.** Steigbügel *m*; **2.** ⚙ Bügel *m*; **3.** ♞ Springpferd *n* (*Haltetau*); ~ **bone** *s. anat.* Steigbügel *m* (*im Ohr*); ~ **i·ron** *s.* Steigbügel *m* (*ohne Steigriemen*); ~ **leath·er** *s.* Steig(bügel)riemen *m*.

stitch [stɪtʃ] **I** *s.* **1.** *Nähen etc.:* Stich *m:* **a** ~ **in time saves nine** gleich getan ist viel gespart; **put** ~**es in** → 7; **2.** *Stricken, Häkeln etc.:* Masche *f;* → *take up* 14; **3.** Stich(art *f*) *m*, Strick-, Häkelart *f*; **4.** F Faden *m:* **not to have a dry** ~ **on one** keinen trockenen Faden am Leibe haben; **without a** ~ **on** splitternackt; **5.** a) Stich *m*, Stechen *n* (*Schmerz*), b) *pl.* ~**es in the side** Seitenstechen *n:* **be in** ~**es** F sich kaputtlachen; **II** *v/t.* **6.** nähen, steppen, (be)sticken; **7.** ~ **up** vernähen (*a.* ⚕), (zs.-)flicken; **8.** *Buchbinderei:* (zs.-)heften, broschieren.

sto·a ['stəʊə] *pl.* **-ae** [-iː] *s. antiq.* Stoa *f:* a) △ Säulenhalle *f*, b) ✎ stoische Philoso'phie.

stoat [stəʊt] *s. zo.* **1.** Herme'lin *n*; **2.** Wiesel *n*.

stock [stɒk] **I** *s.* **1.** (Baum-, Pflanzen-) Strunk *m*; **2.** *fig.* ,Klotz' *m* (*steifer Mensch*); **3.** ♀ Lev'koje *f*; **4.** ♂ ('Pfropf),Unterlage *f*; **5.** (*Peitschen-, Werkzeug*)Griff *m*; **6.** ✕ a) (Gewehr-) Schaft *m*, b) Schulterstütze *f* (*MG*); **7.** ⚙ 'Unterlage *f*, Block *m*; (Amboss-) Klotz *m*; **8.** ♺ Stapel *m:* **on the** ~**s** im Bau, im Werden (*a. fig.*); **9.** *hist.* Stock *m* (*Strafmittel*); **10.** ⚙ (Drah-, Werk)Stoff *m:* **paper** ~ Papierstoff; **11.** a) ⚙ (*Füll- etc.*)Gut *n*, Materi'al *n*, b) (Fleisch-, Gemüse)Brühe *f* (*als Suppengrundlage*); **12.** steifer Kragen; *bsd.* ✕ Halsbinde *f*; **13.** Stamm *m*, Rasse *f*,

Her-, Abkunft f; **14.** *allg.* Vorrat m; ⚕ (Waren)Lager n, Inven'tar n: ~ (on **hand**) Warenbestand m; *in* (*out of*) ~ (nicht) vorrätig; *take* ~ Inventur machen, a. *fig.* (e-e) Bestandsaufnahme machen; *take* ~ *of fig.* sich klar werden über (*acc.*), j-n od. et. abschätzen; **15.** ⚕ Ware(n *pl.*) f; **16.** *fig.* (*Wissens- etc.*) Schatz m: *a* ~ *of information*; **17.** a) *a.* *live* ~ lebendes Inven'tar, Vieh(bestand m) n, b) *a.* *dead* ~ totes Inventar, Materi'al n: *fat* ~ Schlachtvieh n; **18.** a) ⚕ 'Anleihckapi,tal n, b) 'Grundkapi,tal n, c) 'Aktienkapi,tal n, d) Geschäftsanteil m; **19.** ⚕ a) *Am.* Aktie(n *pl.*) f: *issue* ~ Aktien ausgeben, b) *pl.* Aktien *pl.*, c) *pl.* Ef'fekten *pl.*, 'Wertpa,piere *pl.*: *his* ~ *has gone up* s-e Aktien sind gestiegen (*a. fig.* F); **20.** ⚕ a) Schuldverschreibung f, b) *pl. Brit.* 'Staatspa,piere *pl.*; **21.** *thea.* Reper'toire(the,ater) n; **II** *adj.* **22.** (stets) vorrätig, Lager..., Serien...: ~ *size* Standardgröße f; **23.** *fig.* stehend, stereo'typ: ~ *phrase*; **24.** ✐ Vieh..., Zucht...; **25.** ⚕ *bsd. Am.* Aktien...; **26.** *thea.* Repertoire...; **III** *v/t.* **27.** versehen, -sorgen, ausstatten, füllen (*with* mit); **28.** *a.* ~ *up* auf Lager legen, (auf)speichern; **29.** ⚕ Ware vorrätig haben, führen; **30.** ✐ anpflanzen; **31.** *Gewehr, Werkzeug* schäften; **IV** *v/i.* **32.** *a.* ~ *up* sich eindecken; ~ *account* s. ⚕ *Brit.* Kapi'tal-, Ef'fektenkonto n, -rechnung f.

stock·ade [stɒ'keɪd] **I** s. **1.** Sta'ket n, Einpfählung f; **2.** ✕ a) Pali'sade f, b) *Am.* Mili'tärgefängnis n; **II** *v/t.* **3.** einpfählen, mit Sta'ket um'geben.

stock‌| book s. ⚕ **1.** Lagerbuch n; **2.** *Am.* Aktienbuch n; '~,**breed·er** s. Viehzüchter m; '~,**bro·ker** s. Ef'fekten-, Börsenmakler m; '~**car** s. 🚗 *Am.* Viehwagen m; ~ *car* s. *mot.* Serienwagen m, *sport* Stock-Car m; ~ *certif·i·cate* s. 'Aktienzertifi,kat n; ~ *clear·ance* s. Lagerräumung f; ~ *com·pa·ny* s. **1.** ⚕ *Am.* Aktiengesellschaft f; **2.** *thea.* Reper'toiregruppe f, En'semble n; ~ *cor·po·ra·tion* s. ⚕ *Am.* **1.** Kapi'talgesellschaft f; **2.** Aktiengesellschaft f; ~ *div·i·dend* s. ⚕ *Am.* Divi'dende f in Form von Gratisaktien *pl.*; ~ *ex·change* s. ⚕ (Ef'fekten-, Aktien)Börse f; ~ *farm·er* s. Viehzüchter m; ~ *farm·ing* s. Viehzucht f; '~**fish** s. Stockfisch m; '~,**hold·er** s. ⚕ *bsd. Am.* Aktio'när m; '~,**hold·ing** s. ⚕ *Am.* Aktienbesitz m.

stock·i·net [,stɒkɪ'net] s. Stocki'nett n, Tri'kot m, n.

stock·ing ['stɒkɪŋ] s. **1.** Strumpf m; **2.** *zo.* Färbung f am Fuß; ~ *mask* s. Strumpfmaske f; ~ *weav·er* s. Strumpfwirker m.

,stock-in-'trade s. **1.** ⚕ a) Warenbestand m, b) Betriebsmittel *pl.*, c) 'Arbeitsmateri,al n; **2.** *fig.* a) Rüstzeug n, b) ,Reper'toire' n.

stock·ist [stɒkɪst] s. *Brit.* Fachhändler m, Fachgeschäft n.

'**stock‌|,job·ber** → *jobber* 3, 4; ~ *ledg·er* s. ⚕ *Am.* Aktienbuch n; '~**list** s. (Aktien- *od.* Börsen)Kurszettel m; ~ *mar·ket* s. ⚕ **1.** → *stock exchange*; **2.** Börsenkurse *pl.*; ~ *op·tion* s. ⚕ 'Aktienopti,on f; '~**pile I** s. Vorrat m (*of* an *dat.*); **II** *v/t.* e-n Vorrat anlegen von, aufstapeln; '~**pot** s. Suppentopf m; '~**room** s. Lager(raum m) n; ~ *shot* s. *phot.* Ar'chivaufnahme f; ,~'**still** *adj.* stockstill, -steif; ~ *swap* s. ⚕ Aktientausch m; '~,**tak·ing** s. ⚕ Bestandsaufnahme f (*a. fig.*), Inven'tur f.

stock·y ['stɒkɪ] *adj.* ⬚ stämmig, unter'setzt.

'**stock·yard** s. Viehhof m.

stodge [stɒdʒ] *sl.* **I** *v/i. u. v/t.* sich (*den Magen*) voll stopfen; **II** s. a) dicker Brei, b) schwer verdauliches Zeug (*a. fig.*); '**stodg·y** [-dʒɪ] *adj.* ⬚ **1.** schwer verdaulich (*a. fig. Stil etc.*), *fig. a.* schwerfällig (*a. Person*); langweilig; **2.** *fig.* ‚spießig'.

sto·gie, sto·gy ['stəʊɡɪ] s. *Am.* billige Zi'garre.

Sto·ic ['stəʊɪk] **I** s. *phls.* Stoiker m (*a. fig.* ⚿); **II** *adj.*, *a.* '**Sto·i·cal** [-kl] ⬚ *phls.* stoisch (*a. fig.* ⚿ unerschütterlich, gleichmütig); '**Sto·i·cism** [-ɪsɪzəm] s. Stoi'zismus m: a) *phls.* Stoa f, b) ⚿ *fig.* Gleichmut m.

stoke [stəʊk] **I** *v/t.* **1.** *Feuer etc.* schüren (*a. fig.*); **2.** *Ofen etc.* (an)heizen, beschicken; **3.** F a) voll stopfen, b) *Essen etc.* hin'einstopfen; **II** *v/i.* **4.** schüren, stochern; **5.** heizen, feuern; '~**hold** s. ⚓ Heizraum m; '~**hole 1.** → *stokehold*; **2.** Schürloch n.

stok·er ['stəʊkə] s. **1.** Heizer m; **2.** (auto'matische) Brennstoffzuführung.

stole¹ [stəʊl] s. *eccl. u. Damenkleidung:* Stola f.

stole² [stəʊl] *pret.*, '**sto·len** [-lən] *p.p.* von *steal*.

stol·id ['stɒlɪd] *adj.* ⬚ **1.** stur, stumpf; **2.** gleichmütig, unerschütterlich; **sto·lidi·ty** [stɒ'lɪdətɪ] s. **1.** Gleichmut m, Unerschütterlichkeit f; **2.** Stur-, Stumpfheit f.

sto·ma ['stəʊmə] *pl.* -**ma·ta** ['stəʊmətə] s. **1.** ♀ Stoma n, Spaltöffnung f; **2.** *zo.* Atmungsloch n.

stom·ach ['stʌmək] **I** s. **1.** Magen m: *on an empty* ~ auf leeren Magen, nüchtern; **2.** Bauch m, Leib m; **3.** Appe'tit m (*for* auf *acc.*); **4.** Lust f (*for* zu); **II** *v/t.* **5.** verdauen (*a. fig.*); **6.** *fig.* a) (v)ertragen, b) ‚einstecken', hinnehmen; '~**ache** s. Magenschmerz(en *pl.*) m.

stom·ach·er ['stʌməkə] s. *hist.* Mieder n, Brusttuch n.

sto·mach·ic [stəʊ'mækɪk] **I** *adj.* **1.** Magen...; **2.** magenstärkend; **II** s. **3.** ✚ Magenmittel n.

sto·ma·ti·tis [,stəʊmə'taɪtɪs] s. ✚ Mundschleimhautentzündung f, Stoma'titis f.

stomp [stɒmp] → *stamp* 1, 12, 13.

stone [stəʊn] **I** s. **1.** *allg.* (*a. Grab-, Schleif- etc.*)Stein m: *a* ~*'s throw* ein Steinwurf (weit), (nur) ein ‚Katzensprung'; *leave no* ~ *unturned* nichts unversucht lassen; *throw* ~*s at fig.* mit Steinen nach j-m werfen; → *rolling stone*; **2.** *a. precious* ~ (Edel)Stein m; **3.** (*Obst*)Kern m, Stein m; **4.** ✚ a) (Gallen- *etc.*)Stein m, b) Steinleiden n; **5.** (Hagel)Korn n; **6.** *brit. Gewichtseinheit (= 6,35 kg);* **II** *adj.* **7.** steinern, Stein...; **III** *v/t.* **8.** mit Steinen bewerfen; **9.** *a.* ~ *to death* steinigen; **10.** *Obst* entkernen, -steinen; **11.** ⊕ schleifen, glätten; ⚨ *Age* s. Steinzeit f; ,~'**blind** *adj.* stockblind; ,~'**broke** *adj.* ‚pleite', völlig ‚abgebrannt'; ~ *coal* s. Steinkohle f, *bsd.* Anthra'zit m; '~**crop** s. ♀ Steinkraut n; '~,**cut·ter** s. **1.** Steinmetz m, -schleifer m; **2.** 'Steinschneidema,schine f.

stoned [stəʊnd] *adj.* **1.** entsteint, -kernt; **2.** *sl.* a) ‚(stink)besoffen', b) ‚high' (*im Drogenrausch*).

,**stone·'dead** *adj.* mausetot; ,~'**deaf** *adj.* stocktaub; ~ *e·ro·sion* s. Steinfraß m; ~ *fruit* s. Steinfrucht f; *coll.* Steinobst n.

stone·less ['stəʊnlɪs] *adj.* steinlos (*Obst*).

stone‌| mar·ten s. *zo.* Steinmarder m; '~,**ma·son** s. Steinmetz m; ~ *pit* s. Steinbruch m; ,~'**wall I** *v/i.* **1.** *sport* mauern (*defensiv spielen*); **2.** *pol.* Obstrukti'on treiben (*on* gegen); **II** *v/t.* **3.** *pol.* Antrag durch Obstrukti'on zu Fall bringen; ,~'**wall·ing** s. **1.** *sport* Mauern n; **2.** *pol.* Obstrukti'on f; '~**ware** s. Steinzeug n.

ston·i·ness ['stəʊnɪnɪs] s. **1.** steinige Beschaffenheit; **2.** *fig.* Härte f; **ston·y** ['stəʊnɪ] *adj.* ⬚ **1.** steinig; **2.** steinern (*a. fig. Herz*), Stein...; **3.** starr (*Blick*); **4.** *a.* ~*broke* → *stone-broke*.

stood [stʊd] *pret. u. p.p.* von *stand*.

stooge [stuːdʒ] s. **1.** *thea.* Stichwortgeber m; **2.** *sl.* Handlanger m, Krea'tur f; **3.** *Am. sl.* (Lock)Spitzel m; **4.** *Brit. sl.* ‚Heini' m.

stool [stuːl] s. **1.** Hocker m; (Bü'ro-, Kla'vier)Stuhl m: *fall between two* ~*s* sich zwischen zwei Stühle setzen; **2.** Schemel m; **3.** Nachtstuhl m; **4.** ✚ Stuhl m: a) Kot m, b) Stuhlgang m: *go to* ~ Stuhlgang haben; **5.** ♀ a) Wurzelschössling m, b) Wurzelstock m, c) Baumstumpf m; ~ *pi·geon* s. **1.** Lockvogel m (*a. fig.*); **2.** *bsd. Am. sl.* (Lock-) Spitzel m.

stoop¹ [stuːp] **I** *v/i.* **1.** sich bücken, sich (vorn'über)beugen; **2.** sich krumm halten, gebeugt gehen; **3.** *fig. contp.* a) sich her'ablassen, b) sich erniedrigen, die Hand reichen (*to* zu et., *to do* zu tun); **4.** her'abstoßen (*Vogel*); **II** *v/t.* **5.** neigen, beugen; *Schultern* hängen lassen; **III** s. **6.** (Sich)Beugen n; **7.** gebeugte *od.* krumme Haltung; krummer Rücken; **8.** Niederstoßen n (*Vogel*).

stoop² [stuːp] s. *Am.* kleine Ve'randa (*vor dem Haus*).

stop [stɒp] **I** *v/t.* **1.** aufhören (*doing* zu tun); ~ *it!* hör auf (damit)!; **2.** aufhören mit, *Besuche*, ⚕ *Lieferung, Zahlung, Tätigkeit,* ⚖ *Verfahren* einstellen; *Kampf, Verhandlungen etc.* abbrechen; **3.** ein Ende machen od. bereiten (*dat.*), Einhalt gebieten (*dat.*); **4.** *Angriff, Fortschritt, Gegner, Verkehr etc.* aufhalten, zum Stehen bringen, *Ball* stoppen; *Wagen, Zug, a. Uhr* anhalten, stoppen; *Maschine, a. Gas, Wasser* abstellen; *Fabrik* stillegen; *Lohn, Scheck etc.* sperren; *Redner etc.* unter'brechen; *Lärm etc.* unter'binden; **5.** verhindern, hindern (*from* an *dat.*, *from doing* zu tun); **6.** *Boxen etc.:* a) *Schlag* parieren, b) *Gegner* besiegen, stoppen: ~ *a bullet* e-e (Kugel) ,verpasst' kriegen; **7.** *a.* ~ *up Ohren etc.* verstopfen: ~ *s.o.'s mouth fig.* j-m den Mund stopfen; → *gap* 4; **8.** *Weg* versperren; **9.** *Blut, Wunde* stillen; **10.** *Zahn* plombieren, füllen; **11.** ♪ a) *Saite, Ton* greifen, b) *Griffloch* zuhalten, c) *Instrument, Ton* stopfen; **12.** *ling.* interpunktieren; **13.** ~ *down phot.* Objektiv abblenden; **14.** ~ *out Ätzkunst:* abdecken; **II** *v/i.* **15.** (an)halten, Halt machen, stehen bleiben, stoppen; **16.** aufhören, an-, innehalten, e-e Pause machen: ~ *dead* (*od. short*) jäh aufhören; ~ *at nothing fig.* vor nichts zurückschrecken; **17.** aufhören (*Vorgang, Lärm etc.*); **18.** ~ *for* warten auf (*acc.*); **19.** F *im Bett etc.* bleiben: ~ *away* (*from*) fernbleiben (*dat.*); ~ *by Am.* (rasch) bei j-m ,reinschauen'; ~ *in* zu Hause bleiben; ~ *off od. over* Zwischenstation machen; ~ *out* a) wegbleiben, nicht heimkommen, b) ⚕ wei terstreiken; **III** *s.* **20.** Halt *m*, Stillstand *m*: **come to a ~** anhalten; **come to a full ~** aufhören, zu e-m Ende kommen; **put a ~ to** → 3; **21.** Pause *f*; **22.** ✽ *etc.* Aufenthalt *m*, Halt *m*; **23.** a) Stati'on *f* (*Zug*), b) Haltestelle *f* (*Autobus*), c) Anlegestelle *f* (*Schiff*); **24.** 'Absteigequar‚tier *n*; **25.** ⊙ Anschlag *m*, Sperre *f*, Hemmung *f*; **26.** ✝ Sperrung *f*, Sperrauftrag *m* (*für Scheck etc.*); → *a.* **stop order**; **27.** ♪ a) Griff *m*, Greifen *n* (*e-r Saite etc.*), b) Griffloch *n*, c) Klappe *f*, d) Ven'til *n*, e) Re'gister *n* (*Orgel etc.*), f) *a.* ✝ Re'gisterzug *m*: **pull out all the ~s** *fig.* alle Register ziehen; **pull out the pathetic ~** *fig.* pathetisch werden; **28.** *phot.* f-stop-Blende *f* (*Einstellmarke*); **29.** *ling.* a) Knacklaut *m*, b) Verschlusslaut *m*; **30.** a) Satzzeichen *n*, b) Punkt *m*; ‚**~-and-'go** *adj.* durch Verkehrsampeln geregelt: **~ traffic** Stop-and-go-Verkehr *m*; '**~•cock** *s.* ⊙ Absperrhahn *m*; '**~•gap I** *s.* Lückenbüßer *m*, Notbehelf *m*; ✝ Über'brückung *f*; **II** *adj.* Not...; Behelfs...; ✝ Überbrückungs...(-*hilfe*, -*kredit*); '**~•light** *s.* **1.** *mot.* Bremslicht *n*; **2.** rotes (Verkehrs)Licht; '**~•loss** *adj.* ✝ zur Vermeidung weiterer Verluste: **~ order** → **~ order**; ✝ Stopp-'Loss-Auftrag *m*; '**~,o•ver** *s.* **1.** 'Reise-, 'Fahrtunter‚brechung *f*, (kurzer) Aufenthalt *m*; **2.** 'Zwischenstati‚on *f*.

stop•page ['stɒpɪdʒ] *s.* **1.** a) (An)Halten *n*, b) Stillstand *m*, c) Aufenthalt *m*; **2.** (Verkehrs- *etc.*)Stockung *f*; **3.** ⊙ a) (Betriebs)Störung *f*, Hemmung *f*, b) *a.* ✽ Verstopfung *f*; **4.** Sperrung *f*, (✝ *Kredit- etc.*, ♫ *Strom*)Sperre *f*; **5.** (Arbeits-, Betriebs-, Zahlungs)Einstellung *f*; **work ~**, **~ of work** Arbeitsniederlegung *f*; **6.** (Gehalts)Abzug *m*.

stop pay•ment *s.* ✝ Zahlungssperre *f* (*für Schecks etc.*).

stop•per ['stɒpə] **I** *s.* **1.** a) Stöpsel *m*, Pfropf(en) *m*, b) Stopfer *m*: **put a ~ on** *fig.* e-r Sache ein Ende setzen; **2.** ⊙ Absperrvorrichtung *f*; Hemmer *m*: **~ circuit** ♫ Sperrkreis *m*; **3.** *Werbung*: F Blickfang *m*; **II** *v/t.* **4.** zustöpseln.

stop•ping ['stɒpɪŋ] *s.* ✽ (Zahn)Füllung *f*, Plombe *f*; **~ dis•tance** *s. mot.* Anhalteweg *m*; **~ place** *s.* Haltestelle *f*; **~ train** *s.* ✽ Bummelzug *m*.

stop•ple ['stɒpl] **I** *s.* Stöpsel *m*; **II** *v/t.* zustöpseln.

stop| press *s.* (Spalte *f* für) letzte (nach Redakti'onsschluss eingelaufene) Meldungen *pl.*; **~ screw** *s.* ⊙ Anschlagschraube *f*; **~ sign** *s. mot.* Stoppschild *n*; **~ valve** *s.* ⊙ 'Absperrven‚til *n*; **~ vol•ley** *s. Tennis*: Stoppflugball *m*; '**~•watch** *s.* Stoppuhr *f*.

stor•a•ble ['stɔːrəbl] **I** *adj.* lagerfähig, Lager...; **II** *s.* lagerfähige Ware.

stor•age ['stɔːrɪdʒ] *s.* **1.** (Ein)Lagerung *f*, Lagern *n*; *a.* ♫ *u. Computer*: Speicherung *f*; → **cold storage**; **2.** Lager(raum *m*) *n*, De'pot *n*; **3.** Lagergeld *n*; **~ bat•ter•y** *s.* ♫ Akku(mu'lator) *m*; **~ cam•er•a** *s.* Speicherkamera *f*; **~ heat•er** *s.* (Nacht)Speicherofen *m*.

store [stɔː] **I** *s.* **1.** (Vorrats)Lager *n*, Vorrat *m*: **in ~** vorrätig, auf Lager; **be in ~ for s.o.** *fig.* j-m bevorstehen, auf j-n warten; **have** (*od.* **hold**) **in ~ for** *fig.* Überraschung *etc.* bereithalten für j-n, j-m e-e Enttäuschung *etc.* bringen; **2.** *pl.* a) Vorräte *pl.*, Ausrüstung *f* (*u.* Verpflegung *f*), Provi'ant *m*, b) *a.* **military ~s** Mili'tärbedarf *m*, Versorgungsgüter *pl.*, c) *a.* **naval** (*od.* **ship's**) **~s** Schiffsbedarf *m*; **3.** *a. pl. bsd. Brit.* Kauf-,

Warenhaus *n*; **4.** *Am.* (Kauf)Laden *m*, Geschäft *n*; **5.** *bsd. Brit.* Lagerhaus *n*, Speicher *m* (*a. Computer*); **6.** *a. pl. fig.* (große) Menge, Fülle *f*, Reichtum *m* (*of an dat.*): **a great ~ of knowledge** ein großer Wissensschatz; **7. set great** (**little**) **~ by** *fig.* a) hoch (gering) einschätzen, b) großen (wenig) Wert legen auf (*acc.*); **II** *v/t.* **8.** versorgen, -sehen, eindecken (**with** mit); *Schiff* verproviantieren; *fig. s-n* Kopf mit Wissen *etc.* anfüllen; **9.** *a.* **~ up** einlagern, (auf-) speichern; *fig. im Gedächtnis* bewahren; **10.** *Möbel etc.* einstellen, -lagern; **11.** fassen, aufnehmen, 'unterbringen; **12.** ♫, *phys., a. Computer*: speichern; '**~•card** *s.* 'Kundenkre‚ditkarte *f*; **~ cat•tle** *s.* Mastvieh *n*; '**~•front** *s.* **1.** *bsd. Am.* Ladenfront *f*; **2.** *Internet*: 'Storefront *f* (*Website für elektronisches Einkaufen*); '**~•house** *s.* **1.** Lagerhaus *n*; **2.** *fig.* Fundgrube *f*; '**~,keep•er** *s.* **1.** Lagerverwalter *m*; ✕ Kammer-, Geräteverwalter *m*; *Am.* Ladensitzer(in); '**~•room** *s.* **1.** Lagerraum *m*; **2.** Verkaufsraum *m*.

sto•rey ['stɔːrɪ] → **story²**; '**sto•reyed** [-ɪd] → **storied²**.

sto•ried¹ ['stɔːrɪd] *adj.* **1.** geschichtlich, berühmt; **2.** 'sagenum‚woben; **3.** mit Bildern aus der Geschichte geschmückt: **a ~ frieze**.

sto•ried² ['stɔːrɪd] *adj.* mit Stockwerken: **two-~** zweistöckig (*Haus*).

stork [stɔːk] *s. orn.* Storch *m*; '**~s•bill** *s.* ✿ Storchschnabel *m*.

storm [stɔːm] **I** *s.* **1.** Sturm *m* (*a.* ✕ *u. fig.*), Unwetter *n*: **~ of applause** Beifallssturm *m*; **~ and stress** *hist.* Sturm u. Drang; **~ in a teacup** *fig.* Sturm im Wasserglas; **take by ~** im Sturm erobern (*a. fig.*); **2.** (Hagel-, Schnee-) Sturm *m*, Gewitter *n*; **II** *v/i.* **3.** stürmen, wüten, toben (*Wind etc.*) (*a. fig. at* gegen, über *acc.*); **4.** ✕ stürmen; **5.** *wohin* stürmen, stürzen; **III** *v/t.* **6.** ✕ (er-) stürmen; **7.** *fig.* bestürmen; **8.** *et. wütend ausstoßen*; **~ an•chor** *s. bsd. fig.* Notanker *m*; '**~-,beat•en** *adj.* sturmgepeitscht; '**~•bird** → **stormy petrel** 1; '**~•bound** *adj.* vom Sturm aufgehalten; **~ cen•ter** *Am.*, **~ cen•tre** *Brit. s.* **1.** *meteor.* Sturmzentrum *n*; **2.** *fig.* Unruheherd *m*; **~ cloud** *s.* Gewitterwolke *f* (*a. fig.*); '**~-tossed** *adj.* sturmgepeitscht; **~ troops** *s. pl.* **1.** ✕ Schock-, Sturmtruppe(n *pl.*) *f*; **2.** *hist.* (*Nazi*-)'Sturmab‚teilung *f*, S'A *f*.

storm•y ['stɔːmɪ] *adj.* ☐ stürmisch (*a. fig.*); **~ pet•rel** *s. orn.* Sturmschwalbe *f*; **2.** *fig.* a) Unruhestifter *m*, b) Unglücksbote *m*.

sto•ry¹ ['stɔːrɪ] *s.* **1.** (*a.* amü'sante) Geschichte, Erzählung *f*: **the same old ~** *fig.* das alte Lied; **2.** Fabel *f*, Handlung *f*, Story *f e-s Dramas etc.*; **3.** Bericht *m*, Geschichte *f*: **the ~ goes** man erzählt sich; **to cut** (*od.* **make**) **a long ~ short** (*Redewendung*) um es kurz zu machen, kurz u. gut; **tell the full ~** *fig.* ‚auspacken'; **that's quite another ~** das ist et. ganz anderes; **4.** (Lebens)Geschichte *f*, Story *f*: **the Glenn Miller** ♫; **5.** *bsd. Am.* ('Zeitungs)Ar‚tikel *m*; **6.** F (Lügen-, Ammen)Märchen *n*.

sto•ry² ['stɔːrɪ] *s.* Stock(werk *n*) *m*, Geschoss *n*, *östr.* Geschoß *n*, E'tage *f*; → **upper** I.

'**sto•ry|•book I** *s.* Geschichten-, Märchenbuch *n*; **II** *adj. fig.* ‚Bilderbuch...', märchenhaft; '**~,tell•er** *s.* **1.** (Märchen-, Geschichten)Erzähler(in); **2.** F Lügenbold *m*.

stoup [stuːp] *s.* **1.** *R.C.* Weihwasserbecken *n*; **2.** *Scot.* Eimer *m*; **3.** *dial.* a) Becher *m*, b) Krug *m*.

stout [staʊt] **I** *adj.* ☐ **1.** dick, beleibt; **2.** stämmig, kräftig; **3.** ausdauernd, zäh; **4.** mannhaft, beherzt, tapfer; **5.** heftig (*Angriff, Wind*); **6.** kräftig, ro'bust (*Material etc.*); **II** *s.* **7.** Stout *m* (*dunkles Bier*); '**stout'heart•ed** *adj.* ☐ → **stout** 4; '**stout•ness** [-nɪs] *s.* **1.** Stämmigkeit *f*; **2.** Beleibtheit *f*, Korpu'lenz *f*; **3.** Tapferkeit *f*, Mannhaftigkeit *f*; **4.** Ausdauer *f*.

stove¹ [staʊv] **I** *s.* **1.** Ofen *m*; **2.** (Koch-) Herd *m*; **3.** ⊙ a) Brennofen *m*, b) Trockenraum *m*; **4.** ✿ Treibhaus *n*; **II** *v/t.* **5.** trocknen, erhitzen; **6.** ✿ im Treibhaus ziehen.

stove² [staʊv] *pret. u. p.p. von* **stave**.

stove| en•am•el *s.* ⊙ Einbrennlack *m*; '**~•pipe** *s.* **1.** Ofenrohr *n*; **2.** *a.* **~ hat** *bsd. Am.* F Zy'linder *m*, ‚Angströhre' *f*; **3.** *pl.* F Röhrenhose *f*.

stow [staʊ] **I** *v/t.* **1.** ♣ (ver)stauen; **2.** verstauen, packen; **~ away** a) wegräumen, -stecken, b) F *Essen* ‚verdrücken'; **3.** *sl.* aufhören mit: **~ it!** hör auf (damit)!, halts Maul!; **II** *v/i.* **4.** **~ away** sich an Bord schmuggeln; **stow•age** ['staʊɪdʒ] *s. bsd.* ♣ **1.** Stauen *n*; **2.** Laderaum *m*; **3.** Ladung *f*; **4.** Staugeld *n*; '**stow•a•way** [-əʊə-] *s.* blinder Passa'gier.

stra•bis•mus [strə'bɪzməs] *s.* ✿ Schielen *n*; **stra'bot•o•my** [-'bɒtəmɪ] *s.* ✿ 'Schieloperati‚on *f*.

strad•dle ['strædl] **I** *v/i.* **1.** a) die Beine spreizen, grätschen, b) breitbeinig *od.* mit gespreizten Beinen gehen *od.* stehen *od.* sitzen, c) rittlings sitzen; **2.** sich spreizen; **3.** sich (aus)strecken; **4.** *Am. fig.* schwanken, es mit beiden Par'teien halten; **II** *v/t.* **5.** rittlings sitzen auf (*dat.*); **6.** mit gespreizten Beinen stehen über (*dat.*); **7.** *die Beine* spreizen; **8.** *fig.* sich nicht festlegen wollen bei e-r *Streitfrage etc.*; **9.** ✕ *Ziel* eingabeln; **10.** *Poker*: den Einsatz blind verdoppeln; **III** *s.* **11.** a) (Beine)Spreizen *n*, b) breitbeiniges *od.* ausgreifendes Gehen, c) breitbeiniges (Da)Stehen, d) Rittlingssitzen *n*; **12.** *a.* Turnen: Grätsche *f*, b) *Hochsprung*: Straddle *m*; **13.** ✝ Stel'lage(geschäft *n*) *f*.

strafe [*Brit.* strɑːf; *Am.* streɪf] **I** *v/t.* **1.** ✕, ✈ im Tiefflug mit Bordwaffen angreifen; **2.** *fig.* F j-n anschnauzen; **II** *s.* **3.** → '**straf•ing** [-fɪŋ] *s.* **1.** (Bordwaffen)Beschuss *m*; **2.** *fig.* ‚Anpfiff' *m*.

strag•gle ['strægl] *v/i.* **1.** um'herstreifen; **2.** (hinter'drein- *etc.*)bummeln, (-)zotteln; **3.** ✿ wuchern; **4.** zerstreut liegen *od.* stehen (*Häuser etc.*); sich hinziehen (*Vorstadt etc.*); **5.** *fig.* abschweifen; '**strag•gler** [-lə] *s.* **1.** Bummler(in); **2.** Nachzügler *m* (*a.* ♣); **3.** ✕ Versprengte(r) *m*; **4.** ✿ wilder Schössling; '**strag•gling** [-lɪŋ] *adj.* ☐, '**strag•gly** [-lɪ] *adj.* **1.** *beim Marsch etc.* zu'rückgeblieben; **2.** ausein'ander gezogen (*Kolonne*); **3.** zerstreut (liegend); **4.** weitläufig; **5.** ✿ wuchernd; **6.** lose, 'widerspenstig (*Haar etc.*).

straight [streɪt] **I** *adj.* ☐ **1.** gerade: **~ angle** ♪ gestreckter Winkel; **~ hair** glattes Haar; **~ left** *Boxen*: linke Gerade; **~ line** gerade Linie, ♪ Gerade *f*; **keep a ~ face** das Gesicht nicht verziehen; **2.** ordentlich: **put ~** in Ordnung bringen; **put things ~** Ordnung schaffen; **set s.o. ~ on** j-n berichten hinsichtlich (*gen.*); → **record¹** 4; **3.** gerade, di'rekt; **4.** *fig.* gerade, offen, ehr-

S

lich, re'ell: *as* ~ *as a die* a) grundehrlich, b) kerzengerade; **5.** anständig; **6.**
F zuverlässig: *a* ~ *tip*; **7.** pur: ~ *whis-
k(e)y*; **8.** *pol. Am.* 'hundertpro,zentig:
a ~ *Republican*; → *ticket* 7; **9.** ✝ *Am.
sl.* ohne ('Mengen)Ra,batt; **10.** *thea.* a)
konventio'nell (*Stück*), b) ef'fektlos
(*Spiel*); **11.** nor'mal, konventio'nell
(*Roman etc.*); II *adv.* **12.** gerade('aus);
13. di'rekt, gerade(s)wegs: ~ *from
London*; **14.** anständig, ordentlich:
live ~; **15.** richtig: *get s.o.* ~ j-n richtig
verstehen; *I can't think* ~ ich kann
nicht (richtig) denken; **16.** ~ *away*, ~
off so'fort, auf der Stelle; **17.** ~ *out*
'rundher,aus; III *s.* **18.** Geradheit *f: out
of the* ~ krumm, schief; **19.** *sport* a)
Gerade *f: back* ~ Gegengerade; *home*
~ Zielgerade, b) (Erfolgs-, Treffer- *etc.*)
Serie *f;* **20.** *Poker*: Straight *m;* **21.** *be
on the* ~ *and narrow* auf dem Pfad der
Tugend wandeln; **22.** *the* ~ *of it Am.* F
die (reine) Wahrheit; **23.** *Am.* ‚Spießer'
m; ‚~·a'way I *adv.* → *straight* 16; II *s.
Am.* → *straight* 19a; ~ *edge s.* ⊙ Line'al *n*, Richtscheit *n.*
straight·en ['streɪtn] I *v/t.* **1.** gerade
machen *od.* biegen *od.* (aus)richten; ⤬
Front begradigen: ~ *one's face* e-e
ernste Miene aufsetzen; ~ *o.s. up* sich
aufrichten; **2.** *oft* ~ *out* in Ordnung
bringen: ~ *one's affairs; things will* ~
themselves out das wird von allein
(wieder) in Ordnung kommen; **3.** *oft* ~
out entwirren, klarstellen; **4.** ~ *s.o. out*
j-m den Kopf zurechtsetzen; II *v/i.* **5.**
gerade werden; **6.** ~ *up Am.* a) sich aufrichten, b) F ein anständiges Leben beginnen.
'straight|-faced *adj.* mit unbewegtem
Gesicht; ~ *flush s. Poker*: Straight
Flush *m;* ‚~·'for·ward [-'fɔːwəd] I *adj.* □
1. di'rekt, offen, freimütig; **2.** ehrlich,
redlich, aufrichtig; **3.** einfach, ganz nor-
'mal, unkompliziert (*Aufgabe etc.*); II
adv. **4.** → I; ‚~·'for·ward·ness [-'fɔː-
wədnɪs] *s.* Geradheit *f,* Offenheit *f,*
Ehrlichkeit *f,* Aufrichtigkeit *f;*
‚~-from-the-'shoul·der *adj.* unverblümt; '~-line *adj.* ⅄, ⊙ geradlinig, line'ar (*a.* ✝).
straight·ness ['streɪtnɪs] *s.* Geradheit *f:*
a) Geradlinigkeit *f,* b) *fig.* Offenheit *f,*
Aufrichtigkeit *f.*
'straight-out *adj. Am.* F **1.** rückhaltlos;
2. offen, aufrichtig.
strain¹ [streɪn] I *s.* **1.** Beanspruchung *f,*
Spannung *f,* Zug *m;* **2.** ⊙ (verformende) Spannung, Verdehnung *f;* **3.** ⚒ a)
Zerrung *f,* b) Über'anstrengung *f* (*on
gen.*); **4.** Anstrengung *f,* -spannung *f,*
Kraftaufwand *m;* **5.** (*on*) Anstrengung
f, Stra'paze *f* (für); starke In'anspruchnahme (*gen.*); *nervliche, finanzielle etc.*
Belastung (für); Druck *m* (auf *acc.*);
Last *f* der Verantwortung *etc.: be a* ~
on, put a (*great*) ~ *on* stark beanspruchen *od.* belasten, strapazieren; **6.** *mst
pl.* ♪ Weise *f,* Melo'die *f: to the* ~*s of*
unter den Klängen (*gen.*); **7.** *fig.* Ton
m, Ma'nier *f: a humorous* ~; Laune
f; II *v/t.* **9.** (an)spannen; **10.** ⊙ verformen, -dehnen; **11.** ⚒ *Muskel etc.* zerren; *Handgelenk etc.* verstauchen; *s-e
Augen, das Herz etc.* über'anstrengen;
→ *nerve* 1; **12.** *fig.* über'spannen, strapazieren, *j-s Geduld, Kräfte etc.* über-
'fordern; *Befugnisse* über'schreiten;
Recht, Sinn vergewaltigen, strapazieren: ~ *a point* zu weit gehen; **13.**
('durch)seihen, filtrieren; ~ *off* (*od.
out*) abseihen; **14.** ~ *s.o. to one's
breast* j-n ans Herz drücken; III *v/i.*

15. sich (an)spannen; **16.** ⊙ sich ver-
dehnen, -formen; **17.** ~ *at* zerren an
(*dat.*); → *gnat* 1; **18.** sich anstrengen: ~
after sich abmühen um, streben nach;
→ *effect* 3; **19.** drücken, pressen.
strain² [streɪn] *s.* **1.** Abstammung *f;* **2.**
Linie *f,* Geschlecht *n;* **3.** *biol.* a) Rasse
f, b) (Spiel)Art *f;* **4.** (Rassen)Merkmal
n, Zug *m,* Schuss *m* (*indischen Bluts
etc.*); **5.** (Erb)Anlage *f,* (Cha'rakter-)
Zug *m;* **6.** Anflug *m* (*of* von).
strained [streɪnd] *adj.* □ **1.** gezwungen:
~ *smile;* **2.** gespannt: ~ *relations;*
'strain·er [-nə] *s.* Sieb *n,* Filter *m.*
strait [streɪt] I *s.* **1.** *oft pl.* Straße *f,*
Meerenge *f: the* 2s *of Dover* die Straße
von Dover; 2s *Settlements ehemalige
brit. Kronkolonie* (*Malakka, Penang,
Singapur*); *the* 2s a) (*früher*) die Meerenge von Gibraltar, b) (*heute*) die Ma-
lakkastraße; **2.** *oft pl.* Not *f,* bsd. finanzielle Verlegenheit, Engpass *m: in dire
~s* in e-r ernsten Notlage; II *adj.* □ **3.**
obs. eng, schmal; **4.** streng, hart;
'strait·en [-tn] *v/t.* beschränken, beengen: *in ~ed circumstances* in beschränkten Verhältnissen; ~*ed for* verlegen um.
'strait|,jack·et I *s.* Zwangsjacke *f* (*a.
fig.*); II *v/t.* in e-e Zwangsjacke stecken
(*a. fig.*); '~-laced *adj.* sittenstreng, puri'tanisch, prüde.
strand¹ [strænd] I *s.* **1.** *poet.* Gestade *n,*
Ufer *n;* II *v/t.* **2.** ⚓ auf den Strand
setzen, auf Grund treiben; **3.** *fig.* stranden *od.* scheitern lassen; ~*ed* a) gestrandet (*a. fig.*), b) *mot.* stecken geblieben, c) *fig.* arbeits-, mittellos: *be
(left)* ~*ed* a) auf dem Trockenen sitzen,
b) ‚aufgeschmissen' sein; III *v/i.* **4.**
stranden.
strand² [strænd] *s.* **1.** Strang *m* (*e-s
Taus od. Seils*); **2.** (*Draht-, Seil*)Litze *f;*
3. *biol.* (Gewebe)Faser *f;* **4.** (Haar-)
Strähne *f;* **5.** (Perlen)Schnur *f;* **6.** *fig.*
Faden *m,* Zug *m* (*e-s Ganzen*); II *v/t.* **7.**
⊙ *Seil* drehen; *Kabel* verseilen: ~*ed
wire* Litzendraht *m,* Drahtseil *n;* **8.**
Tau etc. brechen.
strange [streɪndʒ] *adj.* □ **1.** fremd, neu,
unbekannt, ungewohnt (*to* j-m); **2.**
seltsam, sonderbar, merkwürdig: ~ *to
say* seltsamerweise; **3.** (*to*) nicht gewöhnt (an *acc.*), nicht vertraut (mit);
'strange·ness [-nɪs] *s.* **1.** Fremdheit *f,*
Fremdartigkeit *f;* **2.** Seltsamkeit *f,* das
Merkwürdige; **'stran·ger** [-dʒə] *s.* **1.**
Fremde(r *m*) *f,* Unbekannte(r *m*) *f;*
Fremdling *m: I am a* ~ *here* ich bin hier
fremd; *you are quite a* ~ Sie sind ein
seltener Gast; *he is no* ~ *to me* er ist
mir kein Fremder; *I spy* (*od. see*) ~*s
parl. Brit.* ich beantrage die Räumung
der Zuschauertribüne; *the little* ~ der
kleine Neuankömmling (*Kind*); **2.** Neuling *m* (*to* in *dat.*): *be a* ~ *to* nicht
vertraut sein mit; *he is no* ~ *to poverty*
die Armut ist ihm nicht unbekannt.
stran·gle ['stræŋgl] I *v/t.* **1.** erwürgen,
erdrosseln; **2.** *j-n* würgen, *den Hals* einschnüren (*Kragen etc.*); **3.** *fig.* a) *Seufzer etc.* ersticken, b) *et.* abwürgen; II
v/i. **4.** ersticken; '~-hold *s.* Würgegriff
m, fig. a. to'tale Gewalt (*on* über *acc.*).
stran·gu·late ['stræŋgjuleɪt] *v/t.* **1.** ⚒
abschnüren, abbinden; **2.** → *strangle*
1; **stran·gu·la·tion** [ˌstræŋgjʊ'leɪʃn] *s.*
1. Erdrosselung *f,* Strangulierung *f;* **2.**
⚒ Abschnürung *f.*
stran·gu·ry ['stræŋgjʊrɪ] *s.* ⚒ Harn-
zwang *m.*
strap [stræp] I *s.* **1.** (Leder-, *a.* Trag-, ⊙
Treib)Riemen *m,* Gurt *m,* Band *n;* **2.**

a) Halteriemen *m im Bus etc.,* b) (Stiefel)Schlaufe *f;* **3.** a) Träger *m am Kleid,*
b) Steg *m an der Hose;* **4.** Achselklappe
f; **5.** Streichriemen *m;* **6.** ⊙ a) (Me'tall-)
Band *n,* b) Bügel *m* (*a. am Kopfhörer*);
7. ⚓ Stropp *m;* **8.** ♀ Blatthäutchen *n;* II
v/t. **9.** festschnallen (*to an dat.*): ~ *o.s.
in* sich anschnallen; **10.** *Messer* abziehen; **11.** mit e-m Riemen schlagen; **12.**
⚒ (Heft)Pflaster kleben auf *e-e
Wunde;* '~,hang·er *s.* F Stehplatzinha-
ber(in) *im Omnibus etc.;* ~ *i·ron s.* ⊙
Am. Bandeisen *n.*
strap·less ['stræplɪs] *adj.* trägerlos
(*Kleid*); **'strap·per** [-pə] *s.* a) strammer
Bursche, b) strammes *od.* dralles Mädchen; **'strap·ping** [-pɪŋ] I *adj.* **1.**
stramm (*Bursche, Mädchen*), drall
(*Mädchen*); II *s.* **2.** Riemen *pl.;* **3.**
Tracht *f* Prügel; **4.** ⚒ Heftpflaster(verband *m*) *n.*
stra·ta ['strɑːtə] *pl. von* **stratum.**
strat·a·gem ['strætɪdʒəm] *s.* **1.** Kriegs-
list *f;* **2.** List *f,* Kunstgriff *m.*
stra·te·gic [strə'tiːdʒɪk] *adj.* (□ ~ally)
allg. stra'tegisch, *a.* stra'tegisch wichtig,
a. kriegswichtig, *a.* Kriegs...(-*lage,
-plan*): ~ *arms* strategische Waffen;
strat·e·gist ['strætɪdʒɪst] *s.* Stra'tege
m; **strat·e·gy** ['strætɪdʒɪ] *s.* Strate'gie *f:*
a) Kriegskunst *f,* b) (Art *f* der) Kriegs-
führung *f,* c) *fig.* Taktik *f* (*a. sport*), d)
fig. List *f.*
strat·i·fi·ca·tion [ˌstrætɪfɪ'keɪʃn] *s.*
Schichtung *f* (*a. fig. Gliederung*); **strat-
i·fied** ['strætɪfaɪd] *adj.* geschichtet,
schichtenförmig: ~ *rock geol.* Schichtgestein *n;* **strat·i·form** ['strætɪfɔːm]
adj. schichtenförmig; **strat·i·fy** ['strætɪ-
faɪ] I *v/t.* schichten, *fig. a.* gliedern; II
v/i. (*a. fig.* gesellschaftliche) Schichten
bilden, *fig. a.* sich gliedern.
stra·tig·ra·phy [strə'tɪgrəfɪ] *s. geol.* Formati'onskunde *f.*
strat·o·cruis·er ['strætəʊˌkruːzə] *s.* ✈
Strato'sphärenflugzeug *n.*
strat·o·sphere ['strætəʊˌsfɪə] *s.* Strato-
'sphäre *f;* **strat·o·spher·ic** [ˌstrætəʊ-
'sferɪk] *adj.* **1.** strato'sphärisch; **2.** *Am.*
F ‚astro'nomisch', enorm.
stra·tum ['strɑːtəm] *pl.* -**ta** [-tə] *s.* **1.**
allg. (*a.* Gewebe-, Luft)Schicht *f,* Lage
f; **2.** *geol.* (Gesteins- *etc.*)Schicht *f,* Formati'on *f;* **3.** *fig.* (gesellschaftliche *etc.*)
Schicht.
stra·tus ['streɪtəs] *pl.* -**ti** [-taɪ] *s.* Stratus
m, Schichtwolke *f.*
straw [strɔː] I *s.* **1.** Strohhalm *m: draw
~s* Strohhalme ziehen (*als Lose*); *catch
(od. grasp) at a* ~ sich an e-n Strohhalm klammern; *the last* ~ *that
breaks the camel's back* der Tropfen, der das Fass zum Überlaufen
bringt; *that's the last* ~! das hat gerade
noch gefehlt!, jetzt reicht es mir aber!;
he doesn't care a ~ das ist ihm völlig
‚schnurz'; **2.** Stroh *n;* → *man* 3; **3.**
Trinkhalm *m;* **4.** Strohhut *m;* II *adj.* **5.**
Stroh...
straw·ber·ry ['strɔːbərɪ] *s.* **1.** ♀ Erdbeere *f;* **2.** F ‚Knutschfleck' *m;* ~ *mark s.*
⚒ rotes Muttermal; ~ *tongue s.* ⚒
Himbeerzunge *f* (*bei Scharlach*).
straw| bid *s.* ✝ *Am.* Scheingebot *n;* '~-
,col·o(u)red *adj.* strohfarbig, -farben;
~ *hat s.* Strohhut *m;* ~ *mat·tress s.*
Strohsack *m;* ~ *vote s. bsd. Am.* Probe-
abstimmung *f.*
straw·y ['strɔːɪ] *adj.* **1.** strohern; **2.** mit
Stroh bestreut.
stray [streɪ] I *v/i.* **1.** (um'her)streunen
(*a. Tier*): ~ *to* j-m zulaufen; **2.** weglaufen (*from* von); **3.** a) abirren (*from*

von), sich verlaufen, b) her'umirren, c) *fig.* in die Irre gehen, vom rechten Weg abkommen; **4.** *fig.* abirren, -schweifen (*Gedanken etc.*); **5.** ⚡ streuen, vagabundieren; **II** *s.* **6.** verirrtes *od.* streunendes Tier; **7.** Her'umirrende(r *m*) *f*, Heimatlose(r *m*) *f*; **8.** *pl.* ⚡ atmo'sphärische Störungen *pl.*; **III** *adj.* **9.** *a.* **strayed** verirrt (*a. Kugel*), verlaufen, streunend (*Hund, Kind*); **10.** vereinzelt: ~ **customers**; **11.** beiläufig: *a* ~ **remark**; **12.** ⚡ Streu..., vagabundierend (*Strom*).

streak [striːk] **I** *s.* **1.** Streif(en) *m*, Strich *m*; (Licht)Streifen *m*, (-)Strahl *m*: ~ *of lightning* Blitzstrahl; *like a* ~ (*of lightning*) F blitzschnell; **2.** Maser *f*, Ader *f* (*im Holz*); **3.** *fig.* Spur *f*, Anflug *m*; **4.** Anlage *f*, *humoristische etc.* Ader; **5.** ~ *of* (*bad*) *luck* (Pech-)Glückssträhne *f*; **6.** 🏔 Schliere *f*; **7.** ⚕ Aufstreichimpfung *f*: ~ *culture* Strichkultur *f*; **II** *v/t.* **8.** streifen; **9.** adern; **III** *v/i.* **10.** F flitzen; **streaked** [-kt] *adj.*, **'streak·y** [-kɪ] *adj.* □ **1.** gestreift; **2.** gemasert (*Holz*); **3.** durch'wachsen (*Speck*; *a. Am. fig.* F).

stream [striːm] **I** *s.* **1.** Wasserlauf *m*, Flüsschen *n*, Bach *m*; **2.** Strom *m*, Strömung *f*: *against* (*with*) *the* ~ gegen den (mit dem) Strom *schwimmen* (*a. fig.*); *come on* ~ a) ⚙ in Betrieb gehen, b) zu fließen beginnen (*Flüssigkeit*); **3.** (*a. Blut-, Gas-, Menschen- etc.*) Strom *m*, (*Licht-, Tränen- etc.*)Flut *f*: ~ *of words* Wortschwall *m*; ~ *of consciousness* *psych.* Bewusstseinsstrom; **4.** *ped.* Leistungsgruppe *f*; **5.** *fig.* a) Strömung *f*, Richtung *f*; b) Strom *m*, Lauf *m der Zeit etc.*; **II** *v/i.* **6.** strömen, fluten (*a. Licht, Menschen etc.*); **7.** strömen (*Tränen*), tränen (*Augen*): ~ *with* triefen vor (*dat.*); **8.** *im Wind* flattern; **9.** fließen (*langes Haar*); **III** *v/t.* **10.** aus-, verströmen; **'stream·er** [-mə] *s.* **1.** Wimpel *m*; flatternde Fahne; **2.** (langes, flatterndes) Band; Pa'pierschlange *f*; **3.** Lichtstreifen *m* (*bsd. des Nordlichts*); **4.** *a.* ~ *headline* Zeitung: breite Schlagzeile; **5.** *a. tape* ~ Speichermedium: Streamer *m*; **'stream·ing** [-mɪŋ] *s. ped.* Einteilung *f e-r Klasse in Leistungsgruppen*; **'stream·let** [-lɪt] *s.* Bächlein *n*.

'stream|·line **I** *s.* **1.** *phys.* Stromlinie *f*; **2.** *a.* ~ *shape* Stromlinienform *f*, *weitS.* schnittige Form; **II** *adj.* **3.** → **streamlined** 1; **III** *v/t.* **4.** ⚙ stromlinienförmig konstruieren; windschnittig gestalten *od.* verkleiden; **5.** *fig.* a) modernisieren, b) rationalisieren, 'durchorganisieren, c) *pol.* ‚gleichschalten'; **'~·lined** *adj.* **1.** ⚙ stromlinienförmig, windschnittig, Stromlinien...; **2.** schnittig, formschön; **3.** *fig.* a) modernisiert, fortschrittlich, b) ratio'nell, c) *pol.* ‚gleichgeschaltet'; **'~·lin·er** *s. Am.* Stromlinienzug *m*.

street [striːt] *s.* **1.** Straße *f*: *in the* ~ auf der Straße; *~s ahead* F haushoch überlegen (*of dat.*); *~s apart* F völlig verschieden; *not in the same* ~ *as* F nicht zu vergleichen mit; *walk the* ~s ‚auf den Strich' gehen (*Prostituierte*); *that's* (*right*) *up my* ~ das ist genau mein Fall; → *man* 3; **2.** *the* ~ a) Hauptgeschäfts*od.* Börsenviertel *n*, b) *Brit.* → *Fleet Street*, c) *Am.* → *Wall Street*, d) Finanzwelt *f*; **~ Ar·ab** *s.* Gassenjunge *m*; **'~·ball** *s.* 'Streetball *n* (*auf der Straße gespieltes Basketball- od. Fußballspiel*); **'~·car** *s. Am.* Straßenbahn(wagen *m*) *f*; **'~·clean·er** → **streetsweeper**; ~ **cred**

s. F, ~ **cred·i·bil·i·ty** *s.* (gutes) Image, Glaubwürdigkeit *f*; ~ **fur·ni·ture** *s.* ur'banes Mobili'ar, Stadtmöbel *pl.* (*Bänke, Abfallkörbe, Fahrradständer, Sperrpfosten etc.*); ~ **map** *s.* Stadtplan *m*; ~ **mar·ket** *s.* ✝ **1.** Freiverkehrsmarkt *m*; **2.** *Brit.* Nachbörse *f*; **'~·sweep·er** *s. bsd. Brit.* **1.** Straßenkehrer *m*; **2.** Kehrfahrzeug *n*; ~ **the·a·ter** *Am.*, ~ **the·a·tre** *Brit. s.* 'Straßenthe·ater *n*; **'~·walk·er** *s.* Straßen-, Strichmädchen *n*, Prostituierte *f*; **'~·wise** *adj.* F **1.** ‚mit allen Wassern gewaschen', lebenstüchtig, clever, ‚gewitzt'; **2.** ~ *fashion* schicke junge Mode; **'~·work·er** *s.* Streetworker(in).

strength [streŋθ] *s.* **1.** Kraft *f*, Kräfte *pl.*, Stärke *f*: ~ *of body* (*mind, will*) Körper- (Geistes-, Willens)kraft, -stärke: *go from* ~ *to* ~ immer stärker werden; **2.** *fig.* Stärke *f*: *his* ~ *is* (*od. lies*) *in endurance* s-e Stärke ist die Ausdauer; **3.** ⚔ (Truppen)Stärke *f*, Bestand *m*: *actual* ~ Iststärke; *in full* ~ in voller Stärke, vollzählig; *in* (*great*) ~ in großer Zahl; **4.** ⚔ Stärke *f* (*Heeresetc.*)Macht *f*, Schlagkraft *f*; **5.** ⚙ (⚡ Strom-, Feld- *etc.*)Stärke *f*, (Bruch-, Zerreiß- *etc.*)Festigkeit *f*; 🏔, *phys.* Stärke *f* (*a. e-s Getränks*), Wirkungsgrad *m*; **6.** Stärke *f*, Intensi'tät *f* (*Farbe, Gefühl etc.*); **7.** (Beweis-, Über'zeugungs)Kraft *f*: *on the* ~ *of* aufgrund (*gen.*), kraft (*gen.*), auf (*acc.*) ... hin; **'strength·en** [-θn] **I** *v/t.* **1.** stärken; ~ *s.o.'s hand* *fig.* j-m Mut machen; **2.** *fig.* bestärken; **3.** (*zahlenmäßig, a.* ⚙, ⚡) verstärken; **II** *v/i.* **4.** stark *od.* stärker werden, sich verstärken; **'strengthen·er** [-θənə] *s.* **1.** ⚙ Verstärkung *f*; **2.** ⚕ Stärkungsmittel *n*; **3.** *fig.* Stärkung *f*; **'strength·en·ing** [-θənɪŋ] **I** *s.* **1.** Stärkung *f*; **2.** Verstärkung *f* (*a.* ⚙, ⚡); **II** *adj.* **3.** stärkend; **4.** verstärkend; **'strength·less** [-lɪs] *adj.* kraftlos.

stren·u·ous ['strenjʊəs] *adj.* □ **1.** emsig, rührig; **2.** eifrig, tatkräftig; **3.** e'nergisch: ~ *opposition*; **4.** anstrengend, mühsam; **'stren·u·ous·ness** [-nɪs] *s.* **1.** Emsigkeit *f*; **2.** Eifer *m*, Tatkraft *f*; **3.** Ener'gie *f*; **4.** *das Anstrengende*.

stress [stres] **I** *s.* **1.** ♪, *ling.* a) Ton *m*, ('Wort-, 'Satz)Ak‚zent *m*, b) Betonung *f*: *the* ~ *is on ...* der Ton liegt auf *der zweiten Silbe*; **2.** *fig.* Nachdruck *m*: *lay* ~ (*up*)*on* → 7; **3.** ⚙, *phys.* a) Beanspruchung *f*, Druck *m*, b) Spannung *f*, Dehnung *f*: ~ *analyst* Statiker *m*; **4.** *seelische etc.* Belastung, Druck *m*, Stress *m*: ~ *disease* ⚕ Stress-, Managerkrankheit *f*; **5.** Zwang *m*, Druck *m*: *under* (*the*) ~ *of circumstances* unter dem Druck der Umstände; **6.** Ungestüm *n*; Unbilden *pl. der Witterung*; **II** *v/t.* **7.** ♪, *ling., a. fig.* betonen, den Ak'zent legen auf (*acc.*); *fig.* Nachdruck *od.* Gewicht legen auf (*acc.*), her'vorheben; **8.** ⚙, *phys. u. fig.* beanspruchen, belasten; **stressed·'out** *adj.* gestresst, stressgeplagt; **stress·'free** *adj.* stressfrei; **'stress·ful** [-fʊl] *adj.* anstrengend, ‚stressig', Stress...

stretch [stretʃ] **I** *v/t.* **1.** *oft* ~ *out* (aus-) strecken, *bsd. Kopf, Hals* recken: ~ *o.s.* (*out*) → 11; ~ *one's legs* sich die Beine vertreten; **2.** ~ *out Hand etc.* aus-, hinstrecken; **3.** *j-n* niederstrecken; **4.** *Seil, Saite, Tuch etc.* spannen (*over* über *dat. od. acc.*), straff ziehen; *Teppich etc.* ausbreiten; **5.** strecken; *Handschuhe etc.* ausweiten; *Hosen* spannen; **6.** ⚙ spannen, dehnen; **7.** *Nerven, Muskel* anspannen; **8.** *fig.*

über'spannen, -'treiben: ~ *a principle*; **9.** 'überbeanspruchen, *Befugnisse, Kredit etc.* über'schreiten; **10.** *fig.* es mit der Wahrheit, e-r Vorschrift etc. nicht allzu genau nehmen: ~ *a point* fünf gerade sein lassen, ein Auge zudrücken; **II** *v/i.* **11.** sich (aus)strecken; sich dehnen *od.* rekeln; **12.** langen (*for* nach); **13.** sich erstrecken *od.* hinziehen (*to* [bis] *zu*) (*Gebirge etc., a. Zeit*): ~ *down to* zurückreichen *od.* -gehen (bis) zu *od.* in (*acc.*) (*Zeitalter, Erinnerung etc.*); **14.** sich *vor dem Blick* ausbreiten; **15.** sich dehnen (lassen); **16.** *mst* ~ *out* a) *sport* im gestreckten Galopp reiten, b) F sich ins Zeug legen, c) reichen (*Vorrat*); **III** *s.* **17.** *have a* ~, *give o.s. a* ~ sich strecken; **18.** Strecken *n*, (Aus-) Dehnen *n*; **19.** Spannen *n*; **20.** (An-) Spannung *f*, (Über')Anstrengung *f*: *by every* ~ *of the imagination* unter Aufbietung aller Fantasie; *on the* ~ (an-) gespannt (*Nerven etc.*); **21.** Über'treiben *n*; **22.** Über'schreiten *n von Befugnissen, Mitteln etc.*; **23.** (Weg)Strecke *f*; Fläche *f*, Ausdehnung *f*; **24.** *sport:* Gerade *f*; **25.** Zeit(spanne) *f*: *a* ~ *of 10 years*; *at a* ~ ununterbrochen, hintereinander, auf 'einen Sitz; **26.** *do a* ~ *sl.* ‚Knast schieben', ‚sitzen'; **'stretch·er** [-tʃə] *s.* **1.** ⚕ (Kranken)Trage *f*: **~-bearer** Krankenträger *m*; **2.** (*Schuhetc.*)Spanner *m*; **3.** ⚙ Streckvorrichtung *f*; **4.** *paint.* Keilrahmen *m*; **5.** Fußleiste *f im Boot*; **6.** △ Läufer(stein) *m*; **stretch lim·o** ['lɪməʊ] *s. mot.* F 'Stretchlimousine *f* (*extrem lange Luxuslimousine*); **stretch marks** *s. pl.* a) Dehnungsstreifen *pl.* (*bei Fettleibigkeit*), b) Schwangerschaftsstreifen *pl.* (*auf der Haut*); **'stretch·y** [-tʃɪ] *adj.* dehnbar.

strew [struː] *v/t.* [*irr.*] **1.** (aus)streuen; **2.** bestreuen; **strewn** [struːn] *p.p. von* **strew**.

stri·a ['straɪə] *pl.* **stri·ae** ['straɪiː] *s.* **1.** Streifen *m*, Furche *f*, Riefe *f*; **2.** ⚕ Striemen *pl.*, Streifen *pl.*, Striae *pl.*; **3.** *zo.* Stria *f*; **4.** *pl. geol.* (Gletscher-) Schrammen *pl.*; **5.** △ Riffel *m* (*an Säulen*); **stri·ate** **I** *v/t.* [straɪ'eɪt] **1.** streifen, furchen, riefeln; **2.** *geol.* kritzen; **II** *adj.* ['straɪɪt] **3.** → **stri·at·ed** [straɪ'eɪtɪd] *adj.* **1.** gestreift, gerieselt; **2.** *geol.* gekritzt; **stri·a·tion** [straɪ'eɪʃn] *s.* **1.** Streifenbildung *f*, Riefung *f*; **2.** Streifen *m*, *pl.*, Riefe(n *pl.*) *f*; **3.** *geol.* Schramme(n *pl.*) *f*.

strick·en ['strɪkən] **I** *p.p. von* **strike**; **II** *adj.* **1.** *obs.* verwundet; **2.** (*with*) heimgesucht, schwer betroffen (von *Unglück etc.*), befallen (von *Krankheit*), ergriffen (*von Schrecken, Schmerz etc.*); schwer geprüft (*Person*): ~ *in years* hochbetagt, vom Alter gebeugt; ~ *area* Katastrophengebiet *n*; **3.** *fig.* (nieder)geschlagen, (gram)gebeugt; verzweifelt (*Blick*); **4.** *allg.* angeschlagen: *a* ~ *ship*; **5.** gestrichen (voll).

strick·le ['strɪkl] ⚙ **I** *s.* **1.** Abstreichlatte *f*; **2.** Streichmodel *m*; **II** *v/t.* **3.** abstreichen, glatt streichen.

strict [strɪkt] *adj.* □ → **strictly**; **1.** strikt, streng (*Person; Befehl, Befolgung, Diziplin; Wahrheit etc.*); streng (*Gesetz, Moral, Untersuchung*): *be* ~ *with* mit j-m streng sein; *in* ~ *confidence* streng vertraulich; **2.** streng, genau: *in the* ~ *sense* im strengen Sinne; **'strict·ly** [-lɪ] *adv.* **1.** streng *etc.*; **2.** *a.* ~ *speaking* genau genommen; **3.** völlig, ausgesprochen; **4.** ausschließlich, rein; **'strict·ness** [-nɪs] *s.* Strenge *f*: a) Härte *f*, b) Genauigkeit *f*.

S

stric·ture ['strɪktʃə] s. **1.** oft pl. (**on**, **upon**) scharfe Kri'tik (an dat.), kritische Bemerkung (über acc.); **2.** ✳ Strik'tur f, Verengung f.

strid·den ['strɪdn] p.p. von **stride**.

stride [straɪd] **I** v/i. [irr.] **1.** schreiten; **2.** a. ~ **out** ausschreiten; **II** v/t. [irr.] **3.** et. entlang-, abschreiten; **4.** über-, durch'schreiten; **5.** mit gespreizten Beinen stehen über (dat.) od. gehen über (acc.); **6.** rittlings sitzen auf (dat.); **III** s. **7.** (langer od. großer) Schritt: **get into one's ~** fig. (richtig) in Schwung kommen; **take s.th. into** (od. **hit**) **one's ~** fig. et. spielend (leicht) schaffen; **8.** Schritt(weite f) m; **9.** mst pl. fig. Fortschritt(e pl.) m: **with rapid ~s** mit Riesenschritten.

stri·dent ['straɪdnt] adj. ☐ **1.** 'durchdringend, schneidend, grell (Stimme, Laut); **2.** knirschend; **3.** fig. scharf, heftig.

strife [straɪf] s. Streit m: a) Hader m, b) Kampf m: **be at ~** sich streiten, uneins sein.

stri·gose ['straɪgəʊs] adj. **1.** ♀ Borsten...; **2.** zo. fein gestreift.

strike [straɪk] **I** s. **1.** (a. Glocken)Schlag m, Hieb m, Stoß m; **2.** a) Bowling: Strike m (Abräumen beim 1. Wurf), b) Am. Baseball: (Verlustpunkt m bei) Schlagfehler m; **3.** fig. ,Treffer‘ m, Glücksfall m; **4.** ✝ Streik m, Ausstand m: **be on ~** streiken; **go on ~** in (den) Streik od. in den Ausstand treten; **on ~** streikend; **5.** ✕ a) (bsd. Luft)Angriff m, b) A'tomschlag m; **II** v/t. [irr.] **6.** schlagen, Schläge od. e-n Schlag versetzen (dat.); allg. treffen: ~ **off** abschlagen, -hauen; **struck by a stone** von e-m Stein getroffen; **7.** Waffe stoßen (**into** in acc.); **8.** Schlag führen; → **blow²** 1; **9.** ♪ Ton, a. Glocke, Saite, Taste anschlagen; → **note** 8; **10.** Zündholz anzünden, Feuer machen, Funken schlagen; **11.** Kopf, Fuß etc. (an)stoßen, schlagen (**against** gegen); **12.** stoßen od. schlagen gegen od. auf (acc.); zs.-stoßen mit; ♪ auflaufen auf; einschlagen in (acc.) (Geschoss, Blitz); fallen auf (acc.) (Strahl); Auge, Ohr treffen (Lichtstrahl, Laut): ~ **s.o.'s eye** j-m ins Auge fallen; **13.** j-m einfallen, in den Sinn kommen; **14.** j-m auffallen; **15.** j-n beeindrucken, Eindruck machen auf (acc.); **16.** j-m wie vorkommen: **how does it ~ you?** was hältst du davon?; **it ~s me as ridiculous** es kommt mir lächerlich vor; **17.** stoßen auf (acc.): a) (zufällig) treffen od. entdecken, b) Gold etc. finden; → **oil** 2, **rich** 5; **18.** Wurzeln schlagen; **19.** Lager, Zelt abbrechen; **20.** ♪ Flagge, Segel streichen; **21.** Angeln: Fisch mit e-m Ruck auf den Haken spießen; **22.** Giftzähne schlagen in (acc.) (Schlange); **23.** ⊙ glatt streichen; **24.** a) ♭ Durchschnitt, Mittel nehmen, b) ✝ Bilanz: den Saldo ziehen; → **balance** 6; **25.** (**off** von e-r Liste etc.) streichen; **26.** Münze schlagen, prägen; **27.** Stunde schlagen (Uhr); **28.** fig. j-n schlagen, treffen (Unglück etc.), befallen (Krankheit); **29.** (**with** mit Schrecken, Schmerz etc.) erfüllen; **30.** blind etc. machen: → **blind** 1, **dumb** 1; **31.** Haltung, Pose einnehmen; **32.** Handel abschließen; → **bargain** 2; **33.** ~ **work** die Arbeit niederlegen: a) Feierabend machen, b) in Streik treten; **III** v/i. [irr.] **34.** (zu)schlagen, (-)stoßen; **35.** schlagen, treffen: ~ **at** a) j-n od. j-m schlagen, b) fig. zielen auf (acc.);

36. ([**up**]**on**) a) (an)schlagen, stoßen (an acc., gegen), b) ♪ auflaufen (auf acc.), auf Grund stoßen; **37.** fallen (Licht), auftreffen (Lichtstrahl, Schall etc.) ([**up**]**on** auf acc.); **38.** fig. stoßen ([**up**]**on** auf acc.); **39.** schlagen (Uhrzeit): **the hour has struck** die Stunde hat geschlagen (a. fig.); **40.** sich entzünden, angehen (Streichholz); **41.** einschlagen (Geschoss, Blitz); **42.** Wurzel schlagen; **43.** den Weg einschlagen, sich (plötzlich) nach links etc. wenden: ~ **for home** F heimzu gehen; ~ **into** a) einbiegen in (acc.), Weg einschlagen, b) fig. plötzlich verfallen in (acc.), et. beginnen, a. sich e-m Thema zuwenden; **44.** ✝ streiken (**for** für); **45.** ♭ die Flagge streichen (**to** vor dat.) (a. fig.); **46.** (zu)beißen (Schlange); **47.** fig. zuschlagen (Feind etc.);

Zssgn mit adv.:

strike| back v/i. zu'rückschlagen (a. fig.); ~ **down** v/t. niederschlagen, -strecken (a. fig.); ~ **in** v/i. **1.** beginnen, einfallen (a. ♪); **2.** ✳ (sich) nach innen schlagen; **3.** einfallen, unter'brechen (**with** mit e-r Frage etc.); **4.** sich einmischen, -schalten, a. mitmachen: ~ **with** a) sich richten nach, b) mitmachen bei; ~ **in·wards** → **strike in** 2; ~ **off** v/t. **1.** → **strike** 6; **2.** a) Wort etc. ausstreichen, Eintragung löschen, b) j-n von e-r Liste etc. streichen, j-m die Berufserlaubnis etc. entziehen; **3.** typ. abziehen; ~ **out I** v/t. **1.** → **strike off** 2 a; **2.** fig. et. ersinnen, **3.** mst fig. e-n Weg einschlagen; **II** v/i. **4.** a) (los-, zu)schlagen, b) (zum Schlag) ausholen, **5.** (forsch) ausschreiten, a. (los)schwimmen (**for** nach, auf e-n Ort zu); **6.** fig. loslegen; **7.** mit den Armen beim Schwimmen ausgreifen; ~ **through** v/t. Wort etc. 'durchstreichen; ~ **up I** v/i. **1.** ♪ einsetzen (Spieler, Melodie); **II** v/t. **2.** ♪ a) Lied etc. anstimmen, b) Kapelle einsetzen lassen; **3.** Bekanntschaft, Freundschaft schließen (**with** mit), a. Gespräch anknüpfen (**with** mit).

strike| bal·lot s. Urabstimmung f; **'~bound** adj. bestreikt (Fabrik etc.); **'~break·er** s. Streikbrecher m; ~ **call** s. Streikaufruf m; ~ **pay** s. Streikgeld n; **'~prone** adj. streikanfällig.

strik·er ['straɪkə] s. **1.** Schläger(in) f; **2.** Streikende(r m) f, Ausständige(r m) f; **3.** Hammer m, Klöppel m (Uhr); **4.** ✕ Schlagbolzen m; **5.** ♭ Zünder m; **6.** bsd. Fußball: Stürmer m, ,Spitze‘ f: **be ~** Spitze spielen.

strike vote → **strike ballot**.

strik·ing ['straɪkɪŋ] adj. ☐ **1.** schlagend, Schlag...; **2.** fig. a) bemerkenswert, auffallend, eindrucksvoll, b) über'raschend, verblüffend, c) treffend: ~ **example**; **3.** streikend.

strim·mer ['strɪmə] TM s. ,Rasen,trimmer‘ m (mit elektrischem Antrieb).

string [strɪŋ] **I** s. **1.** Schnur f, Bindfaden m; **2.** (Schürzen-, Schuh- etc.)Band n, Kordel f: **have s.o. on a** ~ j-n an Gängelband od. in s-r Gewalt haben; **3.** (Puppen)Draht m: **pull ~s** fig. s-e Beziehungen spielen lassen; **pull the ~s** fig. der Drahtzieher sein; **4.** (Bogen-) Sehne f: **have two ~s to one's bow** fig. zwei Eisen im Feuer haben; **be a second ~** das zweite Eisen im Feuer sein (→ 5); **5.** a) Saite f, b) pl. 'Streichinstru,mente pl., die Streicher pl.; **first (second etc.)** ~ **sport** etc. erste (zweite etc.) ,Garnitur‘: **be a second** ~ zur zweiten Garnitur gehören; **harp on one** ~ fig. immer auf derselben Sache

herumreiten; **6.** Schnur f (Perlen etc.); **7.** fig. Reihe f, Kette f (von Fragen, Fahrzeugen etc.); **8.** Koppel f (Pferde etc.); **9.** ♀ a) Faser f, Fiber f, b) Faden m von Bohnen; **10.** zo. obs. Flechse f; **11.** △ Fries m, Sims m; **12.** F Bedingung f, ,Haken‘ m: **no ~s attached** ohne Bedingungen; **II** v/t. [irr.] **13.** Schnur etc. spannen; **14.** (zu-, ver-) schnüren, zubinden; **15.** Perlen etc. aufreihen; **16.** fig. anein'ander reihen: ~ **s.th. out** et. ,strecken‘, et. ,ausspinnen‘; **17.** Bogen spannen; **18.** ♪ a) besaiten, bespannen (a. Tennisschläger), b) Instrument stimmen; **19.** mit Girlanden etc. behängen; **20.** Bohnen abziehen; **21.** ~ **up** sl. ,aufknüpfen‘, -hängen; **22.** ~ **up** Nerven anspannen: ~ **o.s. up to** a) sich in e-e Erregung etc. hineinsteigern, b) sich aufraffen (**to do** et. zu tun); → **high-strung**; **23.** Am. sl. j-n ,verkohlen‘, aufziehen; **24.** ~ **along** F a) j-n hinhalten, b) j-n ,einwickeln‘; **III** v/i. [irr.] **25.** Fäden ziehen (Flüssigkeit); **26.** ~ **along** mitmachen (**with** mit, bei); ~ **bag** s. Einkaufsnetz n; **band** s. ♪ 'Streichor,chester n; ~ **bean** s. ♀ Gartenbohne f; **'~course** → **string** 11.

stringed [strɪŋd] adj. **1.** ♪ Saiten..., Streich...; ~ **instruments**; ~ **music** Streichmusik f; **2.** ♪ in Zssgn ...saitig; **3.** aufgereiht (Perlen etc.).

strin·gen·cy ['strɪndʒənsɪ] s. **1.** Strenge f, Schärfe f; **2.** Bündigkeit f, zwingende Kraft: **the ~ of an argument**; **3.** ✝ (Geld-, Kre'dit)Verknappung f, Knappheit f; **'strin·gent** [-nt] adj. ☐ **1.** streng, scharf; **2.** zwingend: ~ **necessi·ty**; **3.** zwingend, über'zeugend, bündig: ~ **arguments**; **4.** ✝ knapp (Geld), gedrückt (Geldmarkt).

string·er ['strɪŋə] s. **1.** ♪ Saitenaufzieher m; **2.** ⊙ Längs-, Streckbalken m; △ (Treppen)Wange f; ⚓ Langschwelle f; ⚐ Längsverstei(f)ung f; ♭ Stringer m.

string·i·ness ['strɪŋɪnɪs] s. **1.** Faserigkeit f; **2.** Zähigkeit f.

string| or·ches·tra s. ♪ 'Streichor,chester n; ~ **quar·tet(te)** s. ♪ 'Streichquar,tett n.

string·y ['strɪŋɪ] adj. **1.** faserig, zäh, sehnig; **2.** zäh(flüssig), klebrig, Fäden ziehend.

strip [strɪp] **I** v/t. **1.** Haut etc. abziehen, (-)schälen; Baum abrinden; **2.** Bett abziehen; **3.** a. ~ **off** Kleid etc. ausziehen, abstreifen; **4.** j-n entkleiden, ausziehen (**to the skin** bis auf die Haut): **~ped** a) nackt, entblößt, b) mot. ,nackt‘ (ohne Extras); **5.** fig. entblößen, berauben (**of** gen.), (aus)plündern: ~ **s.o. of his office** j-n s-s Amtes entkleiden; **6.** Haus etc. ausräumen; Fabrik demontieren; **7.** ♭ abtakeln; **8.** ⊙ zerlegen; **9.** ⊙ Gewinde über'drehen; **10.** Kuh ausmelken; **11.** Kohlenlager etc. freilegen; **II** v/i. **12.** a) sich ausziehen, b) ,strippen‘: ~ **to the waist** den Oberkörper freimachen; **III** s. **13.** a) (Sich)Ausziehen n, b) → **striptease**; **14.** ✔ Start- u. Landestreifen m; **15.** sport F Dress m; **16.** Streifen m (Papier etc., a. Land); **17.** ⊙ a) (Bogen-)Sehne f, b) Bandeisen n, -stahl m; **18.** → **car·toon** s. Comic-Strip m.

stripe [straɪp] **I** s. **1.** mst andersfarbiger Streifen (a. zo.), Strich m; **2.** ✕ Tresse f, (Ärmel)Streifen m: **get one's ~s** (zum Unteroffizier) befördert werden; **lose one's ~s** degradiert werden; **3.** Striemen m; **4.** (Peitschen- etc.)Hieb m; **5.** fig. Am. Sorte f, Schlag m; **II** v/t.

6. streifen: **~d** gestreift, streifig.
strip light·ing s. 'Neonlicht n, 'Neon-, Sof'fittenbeleuchtung f.
strip·ling ['strɪplɪŋ] s. Bürschchen n.
strip min·ing s. ⚒ Tagebau m.
'**strip·per** s. **1.** ☉ 'Schälma,schine f, Abstreifer m; **2.** Farblöser m; **3.** F Stripper(in).
'**strip·-tease** s. Striptease m, n; '**~,teas·er** s. Stripteasetänzerin f, ,Stripperin' f.
strive [straɪv] v/i. [irr.] **1.** sich (be)mühen, bestrebt sein (**to do** zu tun); **2.** (**for**, **after**) streben (nach), ringen, sich mühen (um); **3.** (erbittert) kämpfen (**against** gegen, **with** mit), ringen (**with** mit); **striv·en** ['strɪvn] p.p. von **strive**.
strobe [straʊb] s. **1.** phot. Röhrenblitz m; **2.** Radar: Schwelle f; **~ light** s. Strobo'skoplicht n.
strob·o·scope ['straʊbəskəʊp] s. ⚙, phys. Strobo'skop n; ,**strob·o'scop·ic** [-'skɒpɪk] adj. strobo'skopisch.
strode [straʊd] pret. von **stride**.
stroke [straʊk] I s. **1.** (a. Blitz-, Flügel-, Schicksals)Schlag m; Hieb m, Streich m, Stoß m: **at a** (od. **one**) **~** a. fig. mit 'einem Schlag, auf 'einen Streich; **a good ~ of business** ein gutes Geschäft; **~ of luck** Glückstreffer m, -fall m; **not to do a ~ of work** keinen Finger rühren; **2.** (Glocken-, Hammer-, Herz-etc.)Schlag m: **on the ~** pünktlich; **on the ~ of nine** Punkt neun; **3.** ✈ Anfall m, bsd. Schlag(anfall) m; **4.** mot. a) (Kolben)Hub m, b) Hubhöhe f, c) Takt m; **5.** sport a) Schwimmen: Stoß m, (Bein)Schlag m, (Arm)Zug m, b) Golf, Rudern, Tennis etc.: Schlag m, c) Rudern: Schlagzahl f; **6.** Rudern: Schlagmann m: **row ~ → 11**; **7.** (Pinsel-, Feder)Strich m (a. typ.), (Feder)Zug m: **with a ~ of the pen** mit einem Federstrich (a. fig.); **8.** fig. (glänzender) Einfall, Leistung f: **a clever ~** ein geschickter Schachzug; **a ~ of genius** ein Geniestreich; **9.** ♪ a) Bogenstrich m, b) Anschlag m, c) (Noten)Balken m; **10.** Streicheln n; II v/t. **11. ~ a boat** Rudern: am Schlag (e-s Bootes) sitzen; **12.** streichen über (acc.); glatt streichen; **13.** streicheln.
stroll [straʊl] I v/i. **1.** schlendern, (um-'her)bummeln, spazieren (gehen); **2.** um'herziehen: **~ing actor** (od. **player**) → **stroller** 2; II s. **3.** Spaziergang m, Bummel m: **go for a ~**, **take a ~** e-n Bummel machen; '**stroll·er** [-lə] s. **1.** Bummler(in), Spaziergänger(in); **2.** Wanderschauspieler(in); **3.** (Kinder-) Sportwagen m.
stro·ma ['straʊmə] pl. **-ma·ta** [-mətə] s. biol. Stroma n (a. ♀).
strong [strɒŋ] I adj. ☐ → **strongly**; **1.** allg. stark (a. Gift, Kandidat, Licht, Nerven, Schlag, Verdacht, Gefühl etc.); kräftig (a. Farbe, Gesundheit, Stimme, Wort): **~ face** energisches od. markantes Gesicht; **~ man** pol. starker Mann; **have ~ feelings about** sich erregen über (acc.); **use ~ language** Kraftausdrücke gebrauchen; → **point** 24; **2.** stark (an Zahl od. Einfluss), mächtig: **a company 200 ~** e-e 200 Mann starke Kompanie; **3.** fig. scharf (Verstand), klug (Kopf): **~ in** tüchtig in (dat.); **4.** fest (Glaube, Überzeugung); **5.** eifrig, über'zeugt: **a ~ Tory**; **6.** gewichtig, zwingend: **~ arguments**; **7.** stark, gewaltsam, e'nergisch (Anstrengung, Maßnahmen): **with a ~ hand** mit starker Hand; **8.** stark, schwer (Getränk, Speise, Zigarre); **9.** a) stark (Geruch,

Geschmack, Parfüm), b) übel riechend od. schmeckend, a. ranzig; **10.** ling. stark: **~ declination**; **~ verb**; **11.** ✟ a) anziehend (Preis), b) fest (Markt), c) lebhaft (Nachfrage); II adv. **12.** stark, e'nergisch, nachdrücklich; **13.** F tüchtig, mächtig: **be going ~** gut in Schuss od. Form sein; **come** (od. **go**) **it ~** mächtig ,rangehen', auftrumpfen; '**~·arm** F I adj. Gewalt...: **~ methods**; **~ man** Schläger m; II v/t. a) j-n einschüchtern, b) über'fallen, c) zs.-schlagen; '**~·box** s. ('Geld-, 'Stahl)Kas,sette f; Tre'sorfach n; '**~·head·ed** adj. starrköpfig; '**~·hold** s. **1.** ✕ Feste f; **2.** fig. Bollwerk n; **3.** fig. Hochburg f.
strong·ly ['strɒŋlɪ] adv. **1.** kräftig, stark; heftig: **feel ~ about** sich erregen über (acc.); **2.** nachdrücklich, sehr.
,**strong·-'mind·ed** adj. willensstark, e'nergisch; **~ point** s. 24. ✕ Stützpunkt m; **2.** fig. → **point** 24; '**~·room** s. Tre'sor(raum) m; ,**~·'willed** adj. **1.** willensstark; **2.** eigenwillig, -sinnig.
stron·ti·um ['strɒntɪəm] s. ♠ Strontium n.
strop [strɒp] I s. **1.** Streichriemen m (für Rasiermesser); **2.** ♻ Stropp m; II v/t. **3.** Rasiermesser etc. abziehen.
stro·phe ['straʊfɪ] s. Strophe f; **stroph·ic** ['strɒfɪk] adj. strophisch.
strop·py ['strɒpɪ] adj. F 'widerspenstig, -borstig.
strove [straʊv] pret. von **strive**.
struck [strʌk] I pret. u. p.p. von **strike**; II adj. ✟ Am. bestreikt.
struc·tur·al ['strʌktʃərəl] adj. ☐ **1.** struktu'rell (bedingt), Struktur... (a. fig.): **~ change** Struk'turwandel m; **~ crisis** Struk'turkrise f; **~ unemployment** strukturelle Arbeitslosigkeit; **~ly weak** struk'turschwach; **2.** ☉ baulich, Bau... (-stahl, -teil, -technik etc.), Konstruktions...; **3.** biol. a) morpho'logisch, Struktur..., b) or'ganisch (Krankheit etc.); **4.** geol. tek'tonisch; **5.** ♠ Struktur...; '**struc·tur·al·ism** [-lɪzəm] s. ling. phls. Struktura'lismus m.
struc·ture ['strʌktʃə] I s. **1.** Struk'tur f (a. ♠, biol., phys., psych., sociol.); Gefüge n, (Auf)Bau m, Gliederung f (alle a. fig.): **~ of a sentence** Satzbau m; **price ~** ✟ Preisstruktur, -gefüge; **2.** ☉, △ Bau(art f) m, Konstrukti'on f; **3.** Bau(werk n) m, Gebäude n (a. fig.); pl. Bauten pl.; **4.** fig. Gebilde n; II v/t. **5.** strukturieren; '**struc·ture·less** [-tʃəlɪs] adj. struk'turlos; '**struc·tur·ize** [-raɪz] v/t. strukturieren.
stru·del ['struːdl] s. Strudel m (Gebäck).
strug·gle ['strʌgl] I v/i. **1.** (**against**, **with**) kämpfen (gegen, mit), ringen (mit) (**for** um Atem, Macht etc.); **2.** sich winden, zappeln, sich sträuben (**against** gegen); **3.** sich (ab)mühen (**with** mit, **to do** etc. zu tun), sich anstrengen od. quälen: **~ through** sich durchkämpfen, **~ to one's feet** mühsam aufstehen, sich ,hochrappeln'; II s. **4.** Kampf m, Ringen n, Streit m (for um, **with** mit): **~ for existence** a) biol. Kampf ums Dasein, b) Existenzkampf; **5.** Anstrengung(en pl.) f, Streben n; **6.** Zappeln n, Sich'aufbäumen n; '**strug·gler** [-lə] s. Kämpfer m.
strum [strʌm] I v/t. **1.** klimpern auf (dat.): **~ a piano**; **2.** Melodie (her'unter)klimpern od. (-)hämmern; II v/i. **3.** klimpern (**on** auf dat.); III s. **4.** Geklimper n.
stru·ma ['struːmə] pl. **-mae** [-miː] s. ✄ **1.** Struma f, Kropf m; **2.** Skrofu'lose f; '**stru·mose** [-məʊs], '**stru·mous**

[-məs] adj. **1.** ✄ stru'mös; **2.** ✄ skrofu'lös; **3.** ♧ kropfig.
strum·pet ['strʌmpɪt] s. obs. Metze f, Dirne f, Hure f.
strung [strʌŋ] pret. u. p.p. von **string**.
strut¹ [strʌt] I v/i. **1.** (ein'her)stolzieren; **2.** fig. großspurig auftreten, sich spreizen; II s. **3.** Stolzieren n, stolzer Gang; **4.** fig. großspuriges Auftreten.
strut² [strʌt] △, ☉ I s. Strebe f, Stütze f, Spreize f; II v/t. verstreben, abspreizen, -stützen.
strut·ting¹ ['strʌtɪŋ] I adj. ☐ großspurig, -tuerisch; II s. → **strut¹** II.
strut·ting² ['strʌtɪŋ] s. ☉, △ Verstrebung f, Abstützung f.
strych·nic ['strɪknɪk] adj. ♧ Strychnin...; '**strych·nin(e)** [-niːn] s. ♧ Strych'nin n.
stub [stʌb] I s. **1.** (Baum)Stumpf m; **2.** (Kerzen-, Bleistift- etc.)Stummel m, Stumpf m; **3.** Ziga'retten-, Zi'garrenstummel m, ,Kippe' f; **4.** kurzer stumpfer Gegenstand, z. B. Kuppnagel m; **5.** Am. Kon'trollabschnitt m; II v/t. **6.** Land roden; **7.** mst **~ up** Bäume etc. ausroden; **8.** mit der Zehe etc. (an)stoßen; **9.** mst **~ out** Zigarette ausdrücken.
stub·ble ['stʌbl] s. **1.** Stoppel f; **2.** coll. (Getreide-, Bart- etc.)Stoppeln pl.; **3.** a. **~ field** Stoppelfeld n; '**stub·bly** [-lɪ] adj. stopp(e)lig, Stoppel...
stub·born ['stʌbən] adj. ☐ **1.** eigensinnig, halsstarrig, störrisch, stur; 'widerspenstig (a. Sache); **2.** hartnäckig (a. Widerstand etc.); **3.** standhaft, unbeugsam; **4.** spröde, hart; metall. strengflüssig; '**stub·born·ness** [-nɪs] s. **1.** Eigen-, Starrsinn m, Halsstarrigkeit f; **2.** Hartnäckigkeit f; **3.** Standhaftigkeit f.
stub·by ['stʌbɪ] adj. **1.** stummelartig, kurz; **2.** unter'setzt, kurz und dick; **3.** stopp(e)lig.
stuc·co ['stʌkəʊ] △ I pl. **-coes** s. **1.** Stuck m (Gipsmörtel); **2.** Stuck(arbeit f, -verzierung f) m, Stucka'tur f; II v/t. **3.** mit Stuck verzieren, stuckieren; '**~·work → stucco** 2.
stuck [stʌk] pret. u. p.p. von **stick**. ,**stuck·-'up** adj. F hochnäsig.
stud¹ [stʌd] I s. **1.** Beschlagnagel m, Knopf m, Knauf m, Buckel m; **2.** △ (Wand)Pfosten m, Ständer m; **3.** ☉ a) Kettensteg m, b) Stift m, Zapfen m, c) Stiftschraube f, d) Stehbolzen m; **4.** ✕ (Führungs)Warze f (e-s Geschosses); **5.** Kragen- od. Man'schettenknopf m; **6.** ♂ a) Kon'taktbolzen m, b) Brücke f; **7.** Stollen m (am Fußballschuh etc.); II v/t. **8.** (mit Beschlagnägeln etc.) beschlagen od. verzieren; **9.** a. fig. besetzen, über'säen; **10.** verstreut sein über (acc.).
stud² [stʌd] I s. **1.** Gestüt n; **2.** coll. a) Zucht f (Tiere), b) Stall m (Pferde); **3.** a) (Zucht)Hengst m, b) allg. männliches Zuchttier, c) sl. ,Zuchtbulle' m, ,Aufreißer' m; II v/t. **4.** Zucht...; **5.** Stall...; '**~·book** s. **1.** Gestütbuch n für Pferde; **2.** allg. Zuchtstammbuch n.
stu·dent ['stjuːdnt] s. **1.** univ. Stu'dent (-in), b) ped. bsd. Am. u. allg. Schüler (-in), c) Lehrgangs-, Kursteilnehmer(in): **~ adviser** Studienberater(in); **~ driver** Am. Fahrschüler(in); **~ hostel** Studentenwohnheim n; **~ teacher** ped. Praktikant(in); **2.** Gelehrte(r m) f, Forscher (-in); Büchermensch m; **3.** Beobachter(in), Erforscher(in) des Lebens etc.; '**stu·dent·ship** [-ʃɪp] s. **1.** Stu'dentenzeit f; **2.** Brit. Sti'pendium n.
stud farm s. Gestüt n; **~ horse** s. Zuchthengst m.
stud·ied ['stʌdɪd] adj. ☐ **1.** gewollt, ge-

sucht, gekünstelt; **2.** absichtlich, geflissentlich; **3.** wohl überlegt.

stu·di·o ['stjuːdɪəʊ] *pl.* **-os** *s.* **1.** *paint.*, *phot. etc.* Ateli'er *n*, *a. thea. etc.* Studio *n*; **2.** ('Film)Ateli,er *n*: **~** *shot* Atelieraufnahme *f*; **3.** (Fernseh-, Rundfunk-) Studio *n*, Aufnahme-, Senderaum *m*; **~ couch** *s.* Schlafcouch *f*.

stu·di·ous ['stjuːdɪəs] *adj.* □ **1.** gelehrtenhaft; **2.** fleißig, beflissen, lernbegierig; **3.** (eifrig) bedacht (*of* auf *acc.*), bemüht (*to do* zu tun); **4.** sorgfältig, peinlich (gewissenhaft); **5.** → **studied**; **'stu·di·ous·ness** [-nɪs] *s.* **1.** Fleiß *m*, (Studier)Eifer *m*, Beflissenheit *f*; **2.** Sorgfalt *f*.

stud·y ['stʌdɪ] **I** *s.* **1.** Studieren *n*; **2.** Studium *n*: **studies** Studien *pl.*, Studium *n*; **make a ~ of** et. sorgfältig studieren; **make a ~ of doing s.th.** *fig.* bestrebt sein, et. zu tun; **in a** (**brown**) **~** *fig.* in Gedanken versunken, geistesabwesend; **3.** Studie *f*, Unter'suchung *f* (*of, in* über *acc.*, zu); **4.** 'Studienfach *n*, -zweig *m*, -ob,jekt *n*, Studium *n*: **his face was a perfect ~** *fig.* sein Gesicht war sehenswert; **5.** Studier-, Arbeitszimmer *n*; **6.** *Kunst, Literatur:* Studie *f*, Entwurf *m*; **7.** ♪ E'tüde *f*; **8. be a good** (**slow**) **~** *thea.* s-e Rolle leicht (schwer) lernen; **II** *v/t.* **9.** *allg.* studieren: a) *Fach etc.* erlernen, b) unter'suchen, erforschen, genau lesen: **~ out** *sl.* ausknobeln, c) mustern, prüfen(d ansehen), d) *sport etc. Gegner* abschätzen; **10.** *thea. Rolle* einstudieren; **11.** *Brit.* j-m gegenüber aufmerksam *od.* rücksichtsvoll sein; **12.** sich bemühen um et. (*od.* **to do** zu tun), bedacht sein auf (*acc.*): **one's own interests**; **III** *v/i.* **13.** studieren; **~ group** *s.* Arbeitsgruppe *f*, -gemeinschaft *f*.

stuff [stʌf] **I** *s.* **1.** (*a.* Roh)Stoff *m*, Materi'al *n*; **2.** a) (Woll)Stoff *m*, Zeug *n*, b) *Brit.* (*bsd.* Kamm)Wollstoff *m*; **3.** ⊛ Bauholz *n*; **4.** ⊛ Ganzzeug *n* (*Papier*); **5.** Lederschmiere *f*; **6.** *coll.* Zeug *n*, Sachen *pl.* (*Gepäck, Ware etc.*): **green ~** Grünzeug, Gemüse *n*; **7.** *contp.* (wertloses) Zeug, Kram *m* (*a. fig.*): **~** (**and nonsense**) dummes Zeug; **8.** *fig.* Zeug *n*, Stoff *m*: **the ~ that heroes are made of** das Zeug, aus dem Helden gemacht sind; **he is made of sterner ~** er ist aus härterem Holz geschnitzt; **do your ~!** F zeig mal, was du kannst!; **he knows his ~** F er kennt sich aus (*ist gut bewandert*); **good ~!** bravo!, prima!; **that's the ~** (**to give them**)**!** F so ists richtig!; → **rough** 6; **9.** F a) ,Zeug' *n*, ,Stoff' *m* (*Schnaps etc.*), b) ,Stoff' *m* (*Drogen*); **II** *v/t.* **10.** (*a. fig.* sich den *Kopf mit Tatsachen etc.*) voll stopfen; *e-e Pfeife* stopfen: **~ o.s.** (**on**) sich voll stopfen (mit *Essen*); **~ s.o.** (**with lies**) F j-m die Hucke voll lügen; **~ed shirt** *sl.* Fatzke *m*, Wichtigtuer *m*, ,lackierter Affe'; **11.** *a.* **~ up** ver-, zustopfen; **12.** *Sofa etc.* polstern; **13.** *Geflügel* a) stopfen, nudeln, b) *Küche:* füllen; **14.** *Tiere* ausstopfen; **15.** *Am. Wahlurne* mit gefälschten Stimmzetteln füllen; **16.** *Leder* mit Fett imprägnieren; **17.** *et. wohin* stopfen; **18.** V *Frau* ,bumsen': **get ~ed!** leck mich (am Arsch)!; **III** *v/i.* **19.** sich (den Magen) voll stopfen; **'stuff·i·ness** [-fɪnɪs] *s.* **1.** Dumpfheit *f*, Schwüle *f*, Stickigkeit *f*; **2.** Langweiligkeit *f*; **3.** F a) Spießigkeit *f*, b) Steifheit *f*, c) Verstaubtheit *f*, d) ,Muffigkeit' *f*.

stuff·ing ['stʌfɪŋ] *s.* **1.** Füllung *f*, 'Füllmateri,al *n*; Füllhaar *n*, 'Polstermateri,al *n*: **knock the ~ out of** *fig.* a) j-n

,zur Schnecke machen', b) *j-n* fix u. fertig machen, c) *j-n gesundheitlich* kaputtmachen; **2.** *Küche:* Füllung *f*, Farce *f*; **3.** *fig.* Füllsel *n*; **4.** Lederschmiere *f*; **~ box** *s.* ⊛ Stopfbüchse *f*.

stuff·y ['stʌfɪ] *adj.* □ **1.** stickig, dumpf, schwül; **2.** *fig.* langweilig, fad; **3.** F a) beschränkt, spießig, b) pe'dantisch, c) verknöchert, d) F ,muffig', e) prüde.

stul·ti·fi·ca·tion [,stʌltɪfɪ'keɪʃn] *s.* Verdummung *f*; **stul·ti·fy** ['stʌltɪfaɪ] *v/t.* **1.** *a.* **~ the mind** verdummen; **2.** *j-n* veralbern; **3.** wirkungslos *od.* zu'nichte machen.

stum·ble ['stʌmbl] **I** *v/i.* **1.** stolpern, straucheln (**at** *od.* **over** über *acc.*) (*a. fig.*): **~ in(to)** *fig.* in *e-e Sache* (hinein-)stolpern, (-)schlittern; **~ (up)on** (*od.* **across**) *fig.* zufällig stoßen auf (*acc.*); **2.** stolpern, wanken; **3.** *fig.* e-n Fehltritt tun, straucheln; **4.** stottern, stocken: **~ through** *Rede etc.* herunterstottern; **II** *s.* **5.** Stolpern *n*, Straucheln *n*; *fig. a.* Fehltritt *m*; **6.** *fig.* ,Schnitzer' *m*, Fehler *m*; **stum·bling block** ['stʌmblɪŋ] *s. fig.* **1.** Hindernis *n* (**to** für); **2.** Stolperstein *m*.

stu·mer ['stjuːmə] *s. Brit. sl.* **1.** Fälschung *f*; **2.** gefälschter *od.* ungedeckter Scheck.

stump [stʌmp] **I** *s.* **1.** (*Baum-, Kerzen-, Zahn- etc.*)Stumpf *m*, Stummel *m*; (*Ast*)Strunk *m*: **~ foot** ⚕ Klumpfuß *m*; **up a ~** *Am. sl.* in der Klemme; **2.** *a. go on* (*od.* **take**) **the ~** *bsd. Am. pol.* e-e Propagandareise machen, öffentliche Reden halten; **3.** *Kricket:* Torstab *m*: **draw** (**the**) **~s** das Spiel beenden; **4.** *sl.* ,Stelzen' *pl.* (*Beine*): **stir one's ~s** ,Tempo machen', sich beeilen; **5.** *Zeichnen:* Wischer *m*; **II** *v/t.* **6.** *a.* **~ out** *Kricket:* den Schläger ,aus' machen; **7.** F *j-n durch e-e Frage etc.* verblüffen: **he was ~ed** er war verblüfft *od.* aufgeschmissen; **~ed for** verlegen um *e-e Antwort etc.*; **8.** *bsd. Am.* F *Gegend* als Wahlredner bereisen: **~ it** F → 2; **9.** F sta(m)pfen über (*acc.*); **10.** *Zeichnung* abtönen; **11.** *Am.* F *j-n* her'ausfordern (**to do** zu tun); **12.** **~ up** *Brit.* F ,berappen', ,blechen'; **III** *v/i.* **13.** (da'her-) sta(m)pfen; **14.** → 12; **15.** → 2; **'stump·er** [-pə] *s.* **1.** *Kricket:* Torwächter *m*; **2.** F harte Nuss; **3.** *Am.* F a) Wahlredner *m*, b) Agi'tator *m*; **stump speech** *s. Am.* Wahlrede *f*; **'stump·y** [-pɪ] *adj.* □ **1.** stumpfartig; **2.** gedrungen, unter'setzt; **3.** plump.

stun [stʌn] *v/t.* **1.** *durch Schlag etc., a. durch Lärm etc.* betäuben; **2.** *fig.* betäuben: a) verblüffen, b) niederschmettern, c) über'wältigen: **~ned** wie betäubt *od.* gelähmt.

stung [stʌŋ] *pret. u. p.p. von* **sting**.

stunk [stʌŋk] *pret. u. p.p. von* **stink**.

stun·ner ['stʌnə] *s.* F a) ,toller Kerl', b) ,tolle Frau', c) ,tolle Sache'; **'stun·ning** [-nɪŋ] *adj.* □ **1.** betäubend (*a. fig.* niederschmetternd); **2.** *sl.* ,toll', phänome'nal.

stunt¹ [stʌnt] *v/t.* **1.** (im Wachstum, in der Entwicklung *etc.*) hemmen; **2.** verkümmern lassen, verkrüppeln: **~ed** verkümmert, verkrüppelt.

stunt² [stʌnt] **I** *s.* Kunst-, Glanzstück *n*; Kraftakt *m*; **2.** Sensati'on *f*: a) Schaunummer *f*, b) Bra'vourstück *n*, c) Schlager *m*; **3.** ✈ Flugkunststück *n*; *pl. a.* Kunstflug *m*; **4.** (Re'klame- *etc.*)Trick *m*, ,tolle I'dee', *weitS.* ,tolles Ding'; **5.** *Film:* Stunt *m*; **II** *v/i.* **6.** (Flug)Kunststücke machen, kunstfliegen; **'stunt·er** [-tə] *s.* F **1.** Kunstflieger(in); **2.** Akro-

'bat(in).

stunt| fly·ing *s.* ✈ Kunstflug *m*; **'~·man** *s.* [*irr.*] *Film:* Stuntman *m*, Double *n* (*für gefährliche Szenen*); **'~·wo·man** *s.* [*irr.*] *Film:* 'Stunt,woman *f*, Double *n*.

stupe [stjuːp] ⚕ **I** *s.* heißer 'Umschlag *od.* Wickel; **II** *v/t.* heiße 'Umschläge legen auf (*acc.*), *j-m* heiße 'Umschläge machen.

stu·pe·fa·cient [,stjuːpɪ'feɪʃnt] **I** *adj.* betäubend, abstumpfend; **II** *s.* ⚕ Betäubungsmittel *n*; **,stu·pe'fac·tion** [-'fækʃn] *s.* **1.** Betäubung *f*; **2.** Abstumpfung *f*; Abgestumpftheit *f*; **4.** Bestürzung *f*, Verblüffung *f*; **stu·pe·fy** ['stjuːpɪfaɪ] *v/t.* **1.** betäuben; **2.** verdummen; **3.** abstumpfen; **4.** verblüffen, bestürzen.

stu·pen·dous [stjuː'pendəs] *adj.* □ erstaunlich; riesig, gewaltig, e'norm.

stu·pid ['stjuːpɪd] **I** *adj.* □ **1.** dumm; **2.** stumpfsinnig, blöd, fad; **3.** betäubt, benommen; **II** *s.* **4.** Dummkopf *m*; **stu·pid·i·ty** [stjuː'pɪdətɪ] *s.* **1.** Dummheit *f* (*a. Handlung, Idee*); **2.** Stumpfsinn *m*; **stu·por** ['stjuːpə] *s.* **1.** Erstarrung *f*, Betäubung *f*; **2.** Stumpfheit *f*; **3.** ⚕, *psych.* Stupor *m*: a) Benommenheit *f*, b) Stumpfsinn *m*.

stur·di·ness ['stɜːdɪnɪs] *s.* **1.** Ro'bustheit *f*, Kräftigkeit *f*; **2.** Standhaftigkeit *f*; **stur·dy** ['stɜːdɪ] *adj.* □ **1.** ro'bust, kräftig, sta'bil (*a. Material etc.*); **2.** *fig.* standhaft, fest.

stur·geon ['stɜːdʒən] *pl.* 'stur·geons, *coll.* 'stur·geon *s. ichth.* Stör *m*.

stut·ter ['stʌtə] **I** *v/i.* **1.** stottern (*a. Motor*); **2.** keckern (*MG etc.*); **II** *v/t.* **3.** *a.* **~ out** (her'vor)stottern; **III** *s.* **4.** Stottern *n*: **have a ~** stottern; **'stut·ter·er** [-ərə] *s.* Stotterer *m*.

sty¹ [staɪ] *s.* Schweinestall *m* (*a. fig.*).

sty², stye [staɪ] *s.* ⚕ Gerstenkorn *n*.

Styg·i·an ['stɪdʒɪən] *adj.* **1.** stygisch; **2.** finster; **3.** höllisch.

style [staɪl] **I** *s.* **1.** *allg.* Stil *m*: a) Art *f*, Typ *m*, b) Manier *f*, Art *f* u. Weise *f*, *sport* Technik *f*: **~ of singing** Gesangsstil; **in superior ~** in überlegener Manier, souverän; **it cramps my ~** dabei kann ich mich nicht recht entfalten, c) guter Stil: **in ~** stilvoll (→ e, f), d) Lebensart *f*, -stil: **in good** (**bad**) **~** stil-, geschmackvoll (-los), e) vornehme Lebensart, Ele'ganz *f*: **in ~** vornehm; **put on ~** *Am.* F vornehm tun, f) Mode *f*: **in ~** modisch, g) *literarische etc.* Ausdrucksweise *od.* -kraft: **commercial ~** Geschäftsstil, h) Kunst-, Baustil: **in proper ~** stilecht; **2.** (Mach)Art *f*, Ausführung *f*, Fas'son *f*; *Computer:* For'matvorlage *f*, Stilvorlage *f*; **3.** a) Titel *m*, Anrede *f*, b) ✝ (Firmen)Bezeichnung *f*, Firma *f*: **under the ~ of** unter dem Namen ..., ✝ unter der Firma ...; **4.** a) *antiq.* (Schreib)Griffel *m*, b) (Schreib-, Ritz)Stift *m*, c) Radiernadel *f*, d) Feder *f* *e-s Dichters*, e) Nadel *f* (*Plattenspieler*); **5.** ⚕ Sonde *f*; **6.** Zeiger *m* der Sonnenuhr; **7.** Zeitrechnung *f*, Stil *m*: **Old** (**New**) **⚤**; **8.** ♀ Griffel *m*; **9.** *anat.* Griffelfortsatz *m*; **II** *v/t.* **10.** betiteln, benennen, bezeichnen, anreden (**mit** *od.* **als**); **11.** ⊛, ✝ entwerfen, gestalten; b) modisch zuschneiden; **'styl·er** [-lə] *s.* **1.** Modezeichner(in), -schöpfer (-in); **2.** ⊛ (Form)Gestalter *m*, Designer *m*.

sty·let ['staɪlɪt] *s.* **1.** Sti'lett *n* (*Dolch*); **2.** ⚕ Man'drin *m*, Sondenführer *m*.

styl·ing ['staɪlɪŋ] *s.* **1.** Stilisierung *f*; **2.** ✝, ⊛ Styling *n*, (Form)Gestaltung *f*; **~ mousse** [muːs] *s.* Schaumfestiger

m.

styl·ish ['staɪlɪʃ] *adj.* □ **1.** stilvoll; **2.** modisch, ele'gant, flott; **'styl·ish·ness** [-nɪs] *s.* Ele'ganz *f.*

styl·ist ['staɪlɪst] *s.* **1.** Sti'list(in); **2.** → *styler*; **sty·lis·tic** [staɪ'lɪstɪk] *adj.* (□ **~ally**) sti'listisch, Stil...

sty·lite ['staɪlaɪt] *s. eccl.* Sty'lit *m*, Säulenheilige(r) *m.*

styl·ize ['staɪlaɪz] *v/t.* **1.** *allg.* stilisieren; **2.** der Konventi'on unter'werfen.

sty·lo ['staɪləʊ] *pl.* **-los** F, **'sty·lo·graph** [-ləgrɑːf], **sty·lo·graph·ic pen** [ˌstaɪ-ləʊ'græfɪk] *s.* **1.** Tintenkuli *m*; **2.** Füll(feder)halter *m.*

sty·lus ['staɪləs] *s.* **1.** → *style* 4 *a u.* e, 6, 8, 9; **2.** Kopierstift *m*; **3.** Schreibstift *m* *e-s Registriergeräts.*

sty·mie, *a.* **sty·my** ['staɪmɪ] **I** *s. Golf:* **1.** a) *Situation, wenn der gegnerische Ball zwischen dem Ball des Spielers u. dem Loch liegt, auf das er spielt,* b) *Lage des gegnerischen Balles wie in 1a;* **2.** den Gegner *(durch die Balllage von 1)* hindern; **3.** *fig.* a) *Gegner* matt setzen, b) *Plan etc.* vereiteln: *be stymied* ,aufgeschmissen' sein.

styp·tic ['stɪptɪk] *adj. u. s.* ✶ Blut stillend (-es Mittel).

Styr·i·an ['stɪrɪən] **I** *adj.* stei(e)risch, steiermärkisch; **II** *s.* Steiermärker(in).

Sty·ro·foam ['staɪrəfəʊm] *TM s.* Styro-'por *n.*

Sua·bi·an ['sweɪbjən] → *Swabian.*

su·a·ble ['sjuːəbl] *adj.* ⚖ **1.** (ein)klagbar *(Sache);* **2.** (passiv) pro'zessfähig *(Person).*

sua·sion ['sweɪʒn] *s.* **1. (moral ~** gütliches) Zureden; **2.** Über'redung(sversuch *m) f;* **sua·sive** ['sweɪsɪv] *adj.* □ **1.** über'redend, zuredend; **2.** über'zeugend.

suave [swɑːv] *adj.* □ **1.** verbindlich, höflich, zu'vorkommend, sanft; *contp.* ölig; **2.** lieblich, mild *(Wein etc.);* **suav·i·ty** ['swɑːvətɪ] *s.* **1.** Höflichkeit *f,* Verbindlichkeit *f;* **2.** Lieblichkeit *f,* Milde *f;* **3.** *pl.* a) Artigkeiten *pl.,* b) Annehmlichkeiten *pl.*

sub¹ [sʌb] **I** *s.* F *abbr. für submarine, subordinate, subway, subaltern, sublieutenant etc.;* **II** *adj.* Aushilfs..., Not...; **III** *v/i.* F **(for)** einspringen (für), vertreten *(acc.).*

sub² [sʌb] *(Lat.) prp.* unter: **~ finem** am Ende *(e-s zitierten Kapitels);* **~ judice** (noch) anhängig, (noch) nicht entschieden *(Rechtsfall);* **~ rosa** unter dem Siegel der Verschwiegenheit, vertraulich; **~ voce** unter dem angegebenen Wort *(in e-m Wörterbuch etc.).*

sub- [sʌb, -] *in Zssgn* a) Unter..., Grund..., Sub..., b) 'untergeordnet, Neben..., Unter..., c) annähernd, d) 🔊 basisch, e) ⚓ 'umgekehrt.

,sub·ac·e·tate [ˌsʌb-] *s.* 🔊 basisch essigsaures Salz.

,sub·ac·id [ˌsʌb-] *adj.* **1.** säuerlich; **2.** *fig.* bissig, säuerlich.

,sub·a·gent [ˌsʌb-] *s.* **1.** ✝ a) 'Untervertreter *m,* b) 'Zwischenspedi,teur *m;* **2.** ⚖ 'Unterbevollmächtigte(r *m) f.*

,sub·al·pine [ˌsʌb-] ⚘, *zo.* **I** *adj.* subal-'pin(isch); **II** *s.* a) subal'pines Tier, b) subal'pine Pflanze.

sub·al·tern ['sʌbltən] **I** *adj.* **1.** subal-'tern, 'untergeordnet, Unter...; **II** *s.* Subal'terne(r *m) f,* Unter'gebene(r *m) f;* **3.** ✗ *bsd. Brit.* Subal'ternoffi,zier *m.*

sub·a·qua [sʌb'ækwə] *adj.* **1.** Unterwasser...; **2.** (Sport)Taucher...

,sub'arc·tic [ˌsʌb-] *adj. geogr.* sub'ark-

---

tisch.

sub'au·di·ble [səb-] *adj.* **1.** *phys.* unter der Hörbarkeitsgrenze; **2.** kaum hörbar.

sub'cal·i·ber *Am.,* **sub'cal·i·bre** *Brit.* [səb-] *adj.* **1.** Kleinkaliber...; **2.** ✗ *Artillerie:* Abkommkaliber...

'sub·com,mit·tee ['sʌb-] *s.* 'Unterausschuss *m.*

,sub'com·pact (car) [ˌsʌb-] *s. mot.* Kleinwagen *m.*

,sub'con·scious [ˌsʌb-] 🖤, *psych.* **I** *adj.* □ 'unterbewusst; **II** *s.* 'Unterbewusstsein *n, das* 'Unterbewusste.

,sub'con·ti·nent [ˌsʌb-] *s. geogr.* 'Subkonti,nent *m.*

sub'con·tract [səb-] *s.* Nebenvertrag *m;* **,sub'con'trac·tor** [ˌsʌb-] *s.* ✝ 'Subunter,nehmer(in), *a.* Zulieferer *m.*

,sub'cul·ture [ˌsʌb-] *s. sociol.* 'Subkul-,tur *f.*

sub·cu·ta·ne·ous [ˌsʌbkjuː'teɪnjəs] *adj.* □ *anat.* subku'tan, unter der *od.* die Haut.

sub·deb [ˌsʌb'deb] *s. Am.* F **1.** → *subdebutante;* **2.** Teenager *m;* **sub·'deb·u·tante** [ˌsʌb-] *s. Am.* noch nicht in die Gesellschaft eingeführtes junges Mädchen.

,sub·di'vide [ˌsʌb-] *v/t. (v/i.* sich) unter-'teilen; **'sub·di,vi·sion** *s.* **1.** Unter'teilung *f;* **2.** 'Unterab,teilung *f.*

sub·due [səb'djuː] *v/t.* **1.** unter'werfen **(to** *dat.),* unter'jochen; **2.** über'winden, -'wältigen; **3.** *fig.* besiegen, bändigen, zähmen: **~ one's passions; 4.** *Farbe, Licht, Stimme, Wirkung etc., a.* Begeisterung, Stimmung etc. dämpfen; **5.** *fig. j-m* e-n Dämpfer aufsetzen; **sub'dued** [-juːd] *adj.* **1.** unter'worfen, -'jocht; **2.** gebändigt; **3.** gedämpft *(a. fig.).*

,sub'ed·it [ˌsʌb-] *v/t. Zeitung etc.* redigieren; **,sub'ed·i·tor** *s.* Redak'teur *m.*

'sub,head(·ing) ['sʌb-] *s.* **1.** 'Unter-, Zwischentitel *m;* **2.** 'Unterab,teilung *f e-s Buches etc.*

,sub'hu·man [ˌsʌb-] *adj.* **1.** halb tierisch; **2.** unmenschlich.

sub·ja·cent [sʌb'dʒeɪsənt] *adj.* **1.** darunter *od.* tiefer liegend; **2.** *fig.* zu'grunde liegend.

sub·ject ['sʌbʒɪkt] **I** *s.* **1.** *(Gesprächs-etc.)*Gegenstand *m,* Thema *n,* Stoff *m:* **~ of conversation; on the ~ of** über *(acc.),* bezüglich *(gen.);* **2.** *ped.* (Lehr-, Schul-, Studien)Fach *n,* Fachgebiet *n:* **compulsory ~** Pflichtfach; **3.** Grund *m,* Anlass *m* **(for complaint** zur Beschwerde); **4.** Ob'jekt *n,* Gegenstand *m* **(of ridicule** des Spotts); **5.** *paint. etc.* Thema *n (a.* ♪), Su'jet *n,* Vorwurf *m;* **6.** *ling.* Su'bjekt *n,* Satzgegenstand *m;* **7.** 'Untertan(in), *a.* Staatsbürger(in), -angehörige(r *m) f:* **a British ~; 8.** *bsd.* ✗ a) Ver'suchsper,son *f,* -tier *n,* b) Leichnam *m für Sektionszwecke,* c) Pati'ent (-in), *hysterische etc.* Per'son; **9.** *ohne Artikel* die betreffende Person *etc. (in Informationen);* **10.** *phls.* a) Su'bjekt *n,* Ich *n,* b) Sub'stanz *f;* **II** *adj. pred.* **11.** 'untertan, unter'geben **(to** *dat.);* **12.** abhängig **(to** von); **13.** ausgesetzt **(to** *dem Gespött etc.);* **14. (to)** unter'worfen, -'liegend *(dat.),* abhängig (von), vorbehaltlich *(gen.):* **~ to approval** genehmigungspflichtig; **~ to your consent** vorbehaltlich Ihrer Zustimmung; **~ to change without notice** Änderungen vorbehalten; **~ to being unsold,** **to (prior) sale** ✝ freibleibend, Zwischenverkauf vorbehalten; **15. (to)** neigend (zu), anfällig (für): **~ to headaches; III** *v/t.* [səb'dʒekt] **16. (to)** a)

---

unter'werfen *(dat.),* abhängig machen (von), b) *e-r Behandlung, Prüfung etc.* unter'ziehen, c) *dem Gespött, der Hitze etc.* aussetzen; **~ cat·a·logue** *s.* 'Schlagwortkata,log *m;* **~ head·ing** *s.* Ru'brik *f* in e-m 'Sachre,gister; **~ in·dex** *s.* 'Sachre,gister *n.*

sub·jec·tion [səb'dʒekʃn] *s.* **1.** Unter-'werfung *f;* **2.** Unter'worfensein *n;* **3.** Abhängigkeit *f:* **be in ~ to** *s.o.* von j-m abhängig sein.

sub·jec·tive [səb'dʒektɪv] **I** *adj.* □ **1.** *allg., a.* 🖤, *phls.* subjek'tiv; **2.** *ling.* Subjekts...; **II** *s.* **3.** *a.* **~ case** *ling.* Nominativ *m;* **sub'jec·tive·ness** [-nɪs] *s.* Subjektivi'tät *f;* **sub'jec·tiv·ism** [-vɪ-zəm] *s. bsd. phls.* Subjekti'vismus *m.*

sub·jec·tiv·i·ty [ˌsʌbdʒek'tɪvətɪ] *s.* Subjektivi'tät *f.*

sub·ject| mat·ter *s.* **1.** Gegenstand *m (e-r Abhandlung etc., a.* ⚖); **2.** Stoff *m,* Inhalt *m (Ggs. Form);* **~ ref·er·ence** *s.* Sachverweis *m.*

,sub'join [ˌsʌb-] *v/t.* **1.** hin'zufügen, -setzen; **2.** beilegen, -fügen.

sub ju·di·ce [ˌsʌb 'dʒuːdɪsɪ] *s.* ⚖ *be ~* verhandelt werden.

sub·ju·gate ['sʌbdʒʊgeɪt] *v/t.* **1.** unter-'jochen, -'werfen **(to** *dat.);* **2.** *bsd. fig.* bezwingen, bändigen; **sub·ju·ga·tion** [ˌsʌbdʒʊ'geɪʃn] *s.* Unter'werfung *f,* -'jochung *f.*

sub·junc·tive [səb'dʒʌŋktɪv] *ling.* **I** *adj.* □ **1.** konjunk'tivisch; **II** *s.* **2.** *a.* **~ mood** Konjunktiv *m;* **3.** Konjunktivform *f.*

,sub'lease [ˌsʌb-] **I** *s.* 'Untermiete *f,* -pacht *f,* -vermietung *f,* -verpachtung *f;* **II** *v/t.* 'untervermieten, -verpachten; **,sub·les'see** *s.* 'Untermieter(in), -pächter(in); **,sub·les'sor** [-'sɔː] *s.* 'Untervermieter(in), -verpächter(in).

sub·let [ˌsʌb'let] *v/t. [irr. → let¹]* 'unter-, weitervermieten.

sub·lieu·ten·ant [ˌsʌblef'tenənt] *s.* ⚓ *Brit.* Oberleutnant *m* zur See.

sub·li·mate ['sʌblɪmeɪt] **I** *v/t.* **1.** 🔊 sublimieren; **2.** *fig.* sublimieren *(a. psych.),* veredeln, vergeistigen; **II** *s.* [-mɪt] **3.** 🔊 Subli'mat *n;* **sub·li·ma·tion** [ˌsʌblɪ-'meɪʃn] *s.* **1.** 🔊 Sublimati'on *f;* **2.** *fig.* Sublimierung *f (a. psych.).*

sub·lime [sə'blaɪm] **I** *adj.* □ **1.** erhaben, hehr, su'blim; **2.** a) großartig *(a. iro.):* **~ ignorance,** b) *iro.* kom'plett: **a ~ idiot,** c) krass: **~ indifference; II** *s.* **3. the ~** das Erhabene; **III** *v/t.* **4.** → *sublimate* 1 *u.* 2; **IV** *v/i.* **5.** 🔊 sublimiert werden; **6.** *fig.* sich läutern.

sub·lim·i·nal [ˌsʌb'lɪmɪnl] *psych.* **I** *adj.* **1.** 'unterbewusst: **~ self →** 3; **2.** 'unterschwellig *(Reiz etc.,* ✝ *Werbung);* **II** *s.* **3.** *das* 'Unterbewusste.

,sub·ma'chine gun [ˌsʌb-] *s.* ✗ Ma-'schinenpi,stole *f.*

sub·man ['sʌbmæn] *s. [irr.]* **1.** tierischer Kerl; **2.** Idi'ot *m.*

,sub·ma'rine [ˌsʌb-] **I** *s.* **1.** ⚓, ✗ 'Unterseeboot *n,* U-Boot *n;* **II** *adj.* **2.** 'unterseeisch, Untersee..., unter'seeisch; **3.** ⚓, ✗ Unterseeboot..., U-Boot-...: **~ warfare; ~ chaser** U-Boot-Jäger *m;* **~ pen** U-Boot-Bunker *m.*

sub·merge [səb'mɜːdʒ] **I** *v/t.* **1.** ein-, 'untertauchen; **2.** über'schwemmen, unter Wasser setzen; **3.** *fig.* a) unter-'drücken, b) über'tönen; **II** *v/i.* **4.** 'untertauchen, -sinken; **5.** ⚓ tauchen *(U-Boot);* **sub'merged** [-dʒd] *adj.* **1.** untergetaucht; ⚓, ✗ *Angriff etc.* unter Wasser; **2.** über'schwemmt; **3.** *fig.* verelendet, verarmt.

sub·mersed [səb'mɜːst] *adj.* **1.** → *sub-*

merged 1 *u.* 2; **2.** *bsd.* ⚓ Unterwasser...: **~ plants**; **sub'mers·i·ble** [-səbl] **I** *adj.* **1.** 'untertauch-, versenkbar; **2.** über'schwemmbar; **3.** ⚓ tauchfähig; **II** *s.* ⚓ 'Unterseeboot *n*; **sub'mer·sion** [-ɜːʃn] *s.* **1.** Ein-, 'Untertauchen *n*; **2.** Über'schwemmung *f*.

sub·mis·sion [səb'mɪʃn] *s.* **1.** (*to*) Unter'werfung *f* (unter *acc.*), Ergebenheit *f* (in *acc.*), Gehorsam *m* (gegen); **2.** Unter'würfigkeit *f*: **with all due ~** mit allem schuldigen Respekt; **3.** *bsd.* ⚖ Vorlage *f e-s Dokuments etc.*, Unter'breitung *f e-r Frage etc.*; **4.** ⚖ a) Sachvorlage *f*, Behauptung *f*, b) Kompro'miss *m, n*; **sub'mis·sive** [-ɪsɪv] *adj.* □ **1.** ergeben, gehorsam; **2.** unter'würfig; **sub'mis·sive·ness** [-ɪsɪvnɪs] *s.* **1.** Ergebenheit *f*; **2.** Unter'würfigkeit *f*; **sub'mit** [-'mɪt] **I** *v/t.* **1.** unter'werfen, -'ziehen, aussetzen (*to* dat.) **~ o.s.** (*to*) → 4; **2.** *bsd.* ⚖ unter'breiten, vortragen, -legen (*to* dat.); **3.** *bsd.* ⚖ beantragen, behaupten, zu bedenken geben, an'heim stellen (*to* dat.); *bsd. parl.* ergebenst bemerken; **II** *v/i.* **4.** (*to*) gehorchen (*dat.*), sich fügen (*dat. od.* in *acc.*); sich *j-m*, *e-m Urteil etc.* unter'werfen, *e-r Operation etc.* unter'ziehen; **sub'mit·tal** [-'mɪtl] *s.* Vorlage *f*, Unter'breitung *f*.

sub·nor·mal [ˌsʌb-] *adj.* □ **1.** a) 'unter-ˌdurchschnittlich, b) minderbegabt, c) schwachsinnig; **2.** A 'subnorˌmal.

sub·note·book [ˌsʌb-] *s.* *Computer*: Sub-'Notebook *n* (*tragbarer Computer, kleiner als ein Notebook*).

sub·or·der [ˈsʌb-] *s. biol.* 'Unterordnung *f*.

sub·or·di·nate [sə'bɔːdnɪt] **I** *adj.* □ **1.** 'untergeordnet: a) unter'stellt (*to* dat.): **~ position** untergeordnete Stellung, b) zweitrangig, nebensächlich: **~ clause** *ling.* Nebensatz *m*; **be ~ to** *e-r Sache* an Bedeutung nachstehen; **II** *s.* **2.** Unter'gebene(r *m*) *f*; **III** [-dɪneɪt] *v/t.* **3.** *a. ling.* 'unterordnen (*to* dat.); **4.** zu'rückstellen (*to* hinter *acc.*); **sub·or·di·na·tion** [sə‚bɔːdɪ'neɪʃn] *s.* 'Unterordnung *f* (*to* unter *acc.*); **sub'or·di·na·tive** [-dɪnətɪv] *adj. ling.* 'unterordnend: **~ conjunction**.

sub·orn [sʌ'bɔːn] *v/t.* ⚖ (*bsd.* zum Meineid) anstiften; *Zeugen* bestechen; **sub·or·na·tion** [ˌsʌbɔː'neɪʃn] *s.* ⚖ Anstiftung *f*, Verleitung *f* (**of** zum Meineid, zu falscher Zeugenaussage), (Zeugen)Bestechung *f*.

sub·pe·na *Am.* → **subpoena**.

sub·plot ['sʌb-] *s.* Nebenhandlung *f*.

sub·poe·na [səb'piːnə] ⚖ **I** *s.* (Vor)Ladung *f* (unter Strafandrohung); **II** *v/t.* vorladen.

sub·ro·gate ['sʌbrəʊgeɪt] *v/t.* ⚖ einsetzen (**for s.o.** an *j-s* Stelle); **to the rights of** in *j-s* Rechte); **sub·ro·ga·tion** [ˌsʌbrəʊˈgeɪʃn] *s.* ⚖ 'Forderungs‚übergang *m* (kraft Gesetzes); Ersetzung *f e-s Gläubigers durch e-n anderen*: **~ of rights** Rechtseintritt *m*.

sub·scribe [səb'skraɪb] **I** *v/t.* **1.** *Vertrag etc.* unter'zeichnen, ('unterschriftlich) anerkennen; **2.** *et.* mit *s-m Namen etc.* (unter)'zeichnen; **3.** *Geldbetrag* zeichnen (**for** für *Aktien*, **to** für *e-n Fonds*); **II** *v/i.* **4.** *e-n Geldbetrag* zeichnen (**to** für *e-n Fonds*, **for** für *e-e Anleihe etc.*); **5. ~ for** *Buch* vorbestellen; **6. ~ to** *Zeitung etc.* abonnieren; **7.** unter'schreiben, -'zeichnen (**to** acc.); **8. ~ to** *fig. et.* unter'schreiben, gutheißen, billigen; **sub'scrib·er** [-bə] *s.* **1.** Unter'zeichner(-in), -'zeichnete(r *m*) *f* (**to** gen.); **2.**

Befürworter(in) (**to** gen.); **3.** Subskri'bent(in), Abon'nent(in); *teleph.* Teilnehmer(in); **4.** Zeichner *m*, Spender *m* (**to** *e-s Geldbetrages*).

sub·script ['sʌbskrɪpt] *typ., Computer*: **I** *s.* tiefgestelltes Zeichen; **II** *adj.* tiefgestellt.

sub·scrip·tion [səb'skrɪpʃn] *s.* **1.** a) Unter'zeichnung *f*, b) 'Unterschrift *f*; **2.** (**to**) ('unterschriftliche) Einwilligung (in *acc.*), Zustimmung *f* (zu); **3.** (**to**) Beitrag *m* (zu, für), Spende *f* (für), (gezeichneter) Betrag; (*teleph.* Grund)Gebühr *f*; **4.** *Brit.* (Mitglieds)Beitrag *m*; **5.** Abonne'ment *n*, Bezugsrecht *n*, Subskripti'on *f* (**to** auf *acc.*): **by ~** im Abonnement; **take out a ~ to** *Zeitung etc.* abonnieren; **6.** ✝ Zeichnung *f* (**of** *e-r Summe, Anleihe etc.*): **~ for shares** Aktienzeichnung; **open for ~** zur Zeichnung aufgelegt; **invite ~s for a loan** *e-e Anleihe* (zur Zeichnung) auflegen; **~ list** *s.* **1.** ✝ Subskripti'onsliste *f*; **2.** *Zeitung*: Zeichnungsliste *f*; **~ price** *s.* Bezugspreis *m*.

sub·sec·tion ['sʌb-] *s.* 'Unterab‚teilung *f*, -abschnitt *m*.

sub·se·quence ['sʌbsɪkwəns] *s.* **1.** späteres Eintreten; **2.** ⚖ Teilfolge *f*; **sub·se·quent** [-nt] *adj.* □ (nach)folgend, später, nachträglich, Nach...: **~ to** a) später als, b) nach, im Anschluss an (*acc.*), folgend (*dat.*); **~ upon** a) infolge (gen.), b) *nachgestellt*: (daraus) entstehend, (daraufhin) erfolgend; **sub·se·quent·ly** [-ntlɪ] *adv.* **1.** 'hinterher, nachher; **2.** anschließend; **3.** später.

sub·serve [səb'sɜːv] *v/t.* dienlich *od.* förderlich sein (*dat.*); **sub'ser·vi·ence** [-vjəns] *s.* **1.** Dienlich-, Nützlichkeit *f* (**to** für); **2.** Abhängigkeit *f* (**to** von); Unter'würfigkeit *f*; **sub'ser·vi·ent** [-vjənt] *adj.* □ **1.** dienstbar, 'untergeordnet (**to** dat.); **2.** unter'würfig (**to** gegenüber); **3.** dienlich, förderlich (**to** dat.).

sub·side [səb'saɪd] *v/i.* **1.** sich senken: a) sinken (*Flut etc.*), b) (ein)sinken, absacken (*Boden etc.*), sich setzen (*Haus*); **2.** 🜄 sich niederschlagen; **3.** *fig.* abklingen, abflauen, sich legen: **~ into** verfallen in (*acc.*); **4.** *in e-n Sessel etc.* sinken.

sub·sid·i·ar·i·ty [səb‚sɪdɪ'ærətɪ] *s. pol.* Sub‚sidiari'tät(sprinzip *n*) *f*.

sub·sid·i·ar·y [səb'sɪdjərɪ] **I** *adj.* □ **1.** Hilfs..., Unterstützungs..., Subsidien...: **be ~ to** ergänzen, unterstützen; **2.** 'untergeordnet (**to** dat.), Neben...: **~ company** → 4; **~ stream** Nebenfluss *m*; **II** *s.* **3.** (*fig.* Hilfe *f*, Stütze *f*; **4.** ✝ Tochtergesellschaft *f*.

sub·si·dize ['sʌbsɪdaɪz] *v/t.* subventionieren; **sub·si·dy** [-dɪ] *s.* **1.** Beihilfe *f* (aus öffentlichen Mitteln), Subventi'on *f*; **2.** *oft pl. pol.* Sub'sidien *pl.*, Hilfsgelder *pl.*

sub·sist [səb'sɪst] *v/i.* **1.** existieren, bestehen; **2.** weiter bestehen, fortdauern; **3.** sich ernähren *od.* erhalten, leben ([**up**]**on** von *e-r Nahrung*, **by** von *e-m Beruf*); **II** *v/t.* **4.** *j-n* er-, unter'halten; **sub·sist·ence** [-təns] *s.* **1.** Dasein *n*, Exi'stenz *f*; **2.** ('Lebens)Unterhalt *m*, Auskommen *n*, Exi'stenz(möglichkeit) *f*: **~ level** Existenzminimum *n*; **3.** *bsd.* ✕ Verpflegung *f*, -sorgung *f*; **4.** *a.* **~ money** a) (Lohn)Vorschuss *m*, b) 'Unterhaltsbeihilfe *f*, -zuschuss *m*.

sub·soil ['sʌb-] *s.* 'Untergrund *m*.

sub·son·ic [ˌsʌb-] **I** *adj.* Unterschall...; **II** *s.* 'Unterschallflug(zeug *n*) *m*.

sub·spe·cies ['sʌb-] *s. biol.* 'Unterart *f*, Sub'spezies *f*.

sub·stance ['sʌbstəns] *s.* **1.** Sub'stanz *f*, Ma'terie *f*, Stoff *m*, Masse *f*; **2.** feste Konsi'stenz, Körper *m* (*Tuch etc.*); **3.** *fig.* Sub'stanz *f*: a) Wesen *n*, b) *das* Wesentliche, wesentlicher Inhalt *od.* Bestandteil, Kern *m*: **this essay lacks ~**; **in ~** im Wesentlichen *übereinstimmen etc.*, c) Gehalt *m*: **arguments of little ~** wenig stichhaltige Argumente; **4.** *phls.* a) Sub'stanz *f*, b) Wesen *n*, Ding *n*; **5.** Vermögen *n*, Kapi'tal *n*: **a man of ~** ein vermögender Mann.

sub·stand·ard [səb-] *adj.* **1.** unter der Norm, klein..., Klein...; **2.** *ling.* 'umgangssprachlich.

sub·stan·tial [səb'stænʃl] *adj.* □ → **substantially**; **1.** materi'ell, stofflich, wirklich; **2.** fest, kräftig; **3.** nahrhaft, kräftig: **a ~ meal**; **4.** beträchtlich, wesentlich (*Fortschritt, Unterschied etc.*), namhaft (*Summe*); **5.** wesentlich: **in ~ agreement** im Wesentlichen übereinstimmend; **6.** vermögend, kapi'talkräftig; **7.** *phls.* substanzi'ell, wesentlich; **sub·stan·ti·al·i·ty** [səb‚stænʃɪ'ælətɪ] *s.* **1.** Wirklichkeit *f*, Stofflichkeit *f*; **2.** Festigkeit *f*; **3.** Nahrhaftigkeit *f*; **4.** Gediegenheit *f*; **5.** Stichhaltigkeit *f*; **6.** *phls.* Substanziali'tät *f*; **sub·stan·tial·ly** [-ʃəlɪ] *adv.* **1.** dem Wesen nach; **2.** im Wesentlichen, wesentlich; **3.** beträchtlich, wesentlich, in hohem Maße; **4.** wirklich; **sub·stan·ti·ate** [-ʃɪeɪt] *v/t.* **1.** a) begründen, b) erhärten, beweisen, c) glaubhaft machen; **2.** Gestalt *od.* Wirklichkeit verleihen (*dat.*), konkretisieren; **3.** stärken, festigen; **sub·stan·ti·a·tion** [səb‚stænʃɪ'eɪʃn] *s.* **1.** a) Begründung *f*, b) Erhärtung *f*, Beweis *m*, c) Glaubhaftmachung *f*: **in ~ of** zur Erhärtung *od.* zum Beweis von (*od. gen.*); **2.** Verwirklichung *f*.

sub·stan·ti·val [ˌsʌbstən'taɪvl] *adj.* □ *ling.* substantivisch, Substantiv...; **sub·stan·tive** ['sʌbstəntɪv] **I** *s.* **1.** *ling.* a) Substantiv *n*, Hauptwort *n*, b) substantivisch gebrauchte Form; **II** *adj.* □ **2.** *ling.* substantivisch (gebraucht); **3.** selbstständig; **4.** wesentlich; **5.** wirklich, re'al; **6.** fest; **7.** ⚖ materi'ell: **~ law**.

sub·sta·tion ['sʌb-] *s.* **1.** Neben-, Außenstelle *f*: **~ post office** Zweigpostamt *n*; **2.** ⚡ 'Unterwerk *n*; **3.** *teleph.* (Teilnehmer)Sprechstelle *f*.

sub·sti·tute ['sʌbstɪtjuːt] **I** *s.* **1.** Ersatz (-mann: *m*: a) (Stell)Vertreter(in), b) *sport* Auswechselspieler(in): **act as a ~ for** *j-n* vertreten; **~s' bench** Ersatzbank *f*, Auswechselbank *f*, c) *Am.* Aushilfslehrer(in); **2.** Ersatz(stoff *m*), Surro'gat *n* (**for** für); **3.** *ling.* Ersatzwort *n*; **II** *adj.* **4.** Ersatz...: **~ driver**; **~ material** ⊕ Austausch(werk)stoff *m*; **~ power of attorney** ⚖ Untervollmacht *f*; **III** *v/t.* **5.** (**for**) einsetzen (für, an Stelle von), an die Stelle setzen (von *od. gen.*): **~ A for B** B durch A ersetzen, B gegen A austauschen *od.* auswechseln (*alle a. sport*); **6.** ersetzen, an *j-s* Stelle treten; **IV** *v/i.* **7.** (**for**) als Ersatz dienen, als Stellvertreter fungieren (für), vertreten (*acc.*), an die Stelle treten (von *od. gen.*); **sub·sti·tu·tion** [ˌsʌbstɪ'tjuːʃn] *s.* **1.** Einsetzung *f* (⚖ *e-s Ersatzerben, Unterbevollmächtigten*); *bsd. b.s.* (*Kindes etc.*)'Unterschiebung *f*; **2.** Ersatz *m*, Ersetzung *f*; (ersatzweise) Verwendung; **3.** Stellvertretung *f*; **4.** A, 🜄, *ling.* Substituti'on *f*; **sub·sti·tu·tion·al** [ˌsʌbstɪ'tjuːʃənl] *adj.* □ **1.** stellvertretend, Stellvertretungs...; **2.** Ersatz...

,sub'stra·tum [ˌsʌb-] s. [irr.] **1.** 'Unter-, Grundlage f (a. fig.); **2.** geol. 'Unterschicht f; **3.** biol. a) Sub'strat n, Nähr-, Keimboden m, b) a. 🏭 Träger m, Medium n; **4.** phot. Grundschicht f; **5.** ling. Sub'strat n; **6.** phls. Sub'stanz f.

'sub,struc·ture ['sʌb-] s. **1.** △ Funda-'ment n, 'Unterbau m (a. 🛞); **2.** fig. Grundlage f.

sub·sume [səb'sjuːm] v/t. **1.** zs.-fassen, 'unterordnen (under unter dat. od. acc.); **2.** einordnen, -reihen, -schließen (in in acc.); **3.** phls. als Prämisse vor'ausschicken; **sub'sump·tion** [-'sʌmpʃn] s. **1.** Zs.-fassung f (under unter dat. od. acc.); **2.** Einordnung f.

,sub'ten·ant [ˌsʌb-] s. 'Untermieter m, -pächter m.

sub·ter·fuge ['sʌbtəfjuːdʒ] s. **1.** Vorwand m, Ausflucht f; **2.** List f.

sub·ter·ra·ne·an [ˌsʌbtəˈreɪnjən] adj., ,sub·ter·ra·ne·ous [-njəs] adj. □ **1.** 'unterirdisch (a. fig.); **2.** fig. verborgen, heimlich.

sub·tile ['sʌtl], sub·til·i·ty [sʌbˈtɪlətɪ] → subtle, subtlety; sub·til·i·za·tion [ˌsʌtɪlaɪˈzeɪʃn] s. **1.** Verfeinerung f; **2.** Spitzfindigkeit f; **3.** 🏭 Verflüchtigung f; sub·til·ize ['sʌtɪlaɪz] I v/t. **1.** verfeinern; **2.** spitzfindig diskutieren od. erklären; ausklügeln; **3.** 🏭 verflüchtigen, -dünnen; II v/i. **4.** spitzfindig argumentieren.

'sub,ti·tle ['sʌb-] I s. 'Untertitel m (Buch, Film); II v/t. Film unter'titeln.

sub·tle ['sʌtl] adj. □ **1.** allg. fein: ~ delight; ~ odo(u)r; ~ smile; **2.** fein(sinnig), sub'til: ~ distinction; ~ irony; **3.** scharf(sinnig), spitzfindig; **4.** heikel, schwierig: a ~ point; **5.** raffiniert; **6.** schleichend (Gift); 'sub·tle·ty [-tɪ] s. **1.** Feinheit f; sub'tile Art; **2.** Spitzfindigkeit f; **3.** Scharfsinn(igkeit f) m; **4.** Gerissenheit f, Raffi'nesse f; **5.** schlauer Einfall, Fi'nesse f.

sub·to·pi·a [sʌbˈtəʊpɪə] s. Brit. zersiedelte Landschaft.

sub'to·tal [səb-] s. ⅄ Zwischen-, Teilsumme f.

sub·tract [səb'trækt] I v/t. ⅄ abziehen, subtrahieren; II v/i. fig. (from) Abstriche machen (von), schmälern (acc.); sub'trac·tion [-kʃn] s. ⅄ Subtrakti'on f, Abziehen n; **2.** fig. Abzug m.

sub·tra·hend ['sʌbtrəhend] s. ⅄ Subtra-'hend m.

sub·trop·i·cal [ˌsʌbˈtrɒpɪkl] adj. geogr. subtropisch; 'sub'trop·ics [-ks] s. pl. geogr. Subtropen pl.

sub·urb ['sʌbɜːb] s. Vorstadt f, -ort m; sub·ur·ban [səˈbɜːbən] I adj. **1.** vorstädtisch, Vorstadt..., Vororts...; **2.** contp. kleinstädtisch, spießig; **3.** → suburbanite; sub·ur·ban·ite [səˈbɜːbənaɪt] s. Vorstadtbewohner(in); sub·ur·bi·a [səˈbɜːbɪə] s. oft contp. **1.** Vorstadt f; **2.** coll. die Vorstädter pl.

'sub·va,ri·e·ty ['sʌb-] s. ♀, zo. 'untergeordnete Abart.

sub·ven·tion [səbˈvenʃn] s. (staatliche) Subventi'on, (geldliche) Beihilfe, Unter'stützung f; sub'ven·tioned [-nd] adj. subventioniert.

sub·ver·sion [səbˈvɜːʃn] s. **1.** pol. a) 'Umsturz m, Sturz m e-r Regierung, b) Staatsgefährdung f, Verfassungsverrat m; **2.** Unter'grabung f, Zerrüttung f; sub'ver·sive [-ɜːsɪv] adj. **1.** pol. 'umstürzlerisch, staatsgefährdend, Wühl..., subver'siv; **2.** zerstörerisch; **3.** zerrüttend; sub'vert [-ɜːt] v/t. **1.** Regierung stürzen; Gesetz 'umstoßen; Verfassung gewaltsam ändern; **2.** Glauben, Moral,

---

Ordnung etc. unter'graben, zerrütten.

'sub·way ['sʌb-] s. **1.** ('Straßen-, 'Fuß-gänger)Unter,führung f; **2.** Am. U-Bahn f.

,sub'ze·ro [ˌsʌb-] adj. unter dem Gefrierpunkt.

suc·ceed [səkˈsiːd] I v/i. **1.** glücken, gelingen, erfolgreich sein od. verlaufen, Erfolg haben (Sache); **2.** Erfolg haben, erfolgreich sein, sein Ziel erreichen (Person) (as als, in mit et., with bei j-m): he ~ed in doing s.th. es gelang ihm, et. zu tun; ~ in an action 🏛 obsiegen; **3.** (to) a) Nachfolger werden (in e-m Amt etc.), b) erben (acc.): ~ to the throne auf den Thron folgen; ~ to s.o.'s rights in j-s Rechte eintreten; **4.** (to) unmittelbar folgen (dat. od. auf acc.), nachfolgen (dat.); II v/t. **5.** nachfolgen (dat.), folgen (dat. od. auf acc.); j-s (Amts-, Rechts)Nachfolger werden, an j-s Stelle treten; j-n beerben: ~ s.o. in office j-s Amt übernehmen.

suc·cès d'es·time [sʊkˌseɪdesˈtiːm] (Fr.) s. Achtungserfolg m.

suc·cess [səkˈses] s. **1.** (guter) Erfolg, Gelingen n: with ~ erfolgreich; without ~ erfolglos; be a (great) ~ ein (großer) Erfolg sein (Sache u. Person), (gut) einschlagen; crowned with ~ von Erfolg gekrönt (Bemühung); ~ rate Erfolgsquote f; **2.** Erfolg m, Glanzleistung f; **3.** beruflicher etc. Erfolg; suc'cess·ful [-fʊl] adj. □ **1.** erfolgreich: be ~ in doing s.th. et. mit Erfolg tun, Erfolg haben bei od. mit et.; **2.** erfolgreich, glücklich (Sache): be ~ → succeed 1.

suc·ces·sion [səkˈseʃn] s. **1.** (Aufeinander-, Reihen)Folge f: in ~ nach-, auf-, hintereinander; in rapid ~ in rascher Folge; **2.** Reihe f, Kette f, ('ununter,brochene) Folge (of gen. od. von); **3.** Nach-, Erbfolge f, Sukzessi'on f: ~ to the throne Thronfolge f; in ~ to als Nachfolger von; be next in ~ to s.o. als Nächster auf j-n folgen; ~ to an office Übernahme f e-s Amtes, Amtsnachfol-ge; Apostolic 🝊 eccl. apostolische Sukzession; the War of the Spanish 🝊 hist. der Spanische Erbfolgekrieg; **4.** 🏛 a) Rechtsnachfolge f, b) Erbfolge f, c) a. order of ~ Erbfolgeordnung f, d) a. law of ~ objektives Erb(folge)recht, e) ~ to 'Übernahme f e-s Erbes: ~ duties Erbschaftssteuer f (für unbewegliches Vermögen); ~ rights subjektive Erbrechte; **5.** coll. Nachkommenschaft f, Erben pl.; suc'ces·sive [-esɪv] adj. □ (aufein'ander) folgend, sukzes'siv: 3 ~ days 3 Tage hintereinander; suc'ces·sive·ly [-esɪvlɪ] adv. nach-, hintereinander, der Reihe nach; suc'ces·sor [-esə] s. **1.** Nachfolger(in), (to, of j-s, für j-n): ~ in office Amtsnachfolger; ~ to the throne Thronfolger m; **2.** a. ~ in interest (od. title) 🏛 Rechtsnachfolger(in).

suc·cinct [səkˈsɪŋkt] adj. □ kurz (und bündig), knapp, la'konisch, prä'gnant; suc'cinct·ness [-nɪs] s. Kürze f, Bündigkeit f, Prä'gnanz f.

suc·cor ['sʌkə] Am. → succour.

suc·co·ry ['sʌkərɪ] s. ♀ Zi'chorie f.

suc·cour ['sʌkə] I s. Hilfe f, Beistand m; ✗ Entsatz m; II v/t. beistehen (dat.), zu Hilfe kommen (dat.); ✗ entsetzen.

suc·cu·lence ['sʌkjʊləns], 'suc·cu·len·cy [-sɪ] s. Saftigkeit f; 'suc·cu·lent [-nt] adj. □ **1.** saftig, fleischig, sukku-'lent (Frucht etc.); **2.** fig. kraftvoll, saftig.

suc·cumb [səˈkʌm] v/i. **1.** zs.-brechen

(to unter dat.); **2.** (to) (j-m) unterliegen, (e-r Krankheit, s-n Verletzungen etc., a. der Versuchung) erliegen; **3.** (to, under, before) nachgeben (dat.).

such [sʌtʃ; sətʃ] I adj. **1.** solch, derartig: no ~ thing nichts dergleichen; there are ~ things so etwas gibt es od. kommt vor; ~ people as you see here die(jenigen) od. alle Leute, die man hier sieht; ~ a system ein derartiges System; ~ a one ein solcher, eine solche, ein solches; ~ and ~ persons die u. die Personen; **2.** ähnlich, derartig: silk and ~ luxuries; poets ~ as Spenser Dichter wie Spenser; **3.** pred. so (beschaffen), derart(ig) (as to dass): ~ is life so ist das Leben; ~ as it is wie es nun einmal ist; ~ being the case da es sich so verhält; **4.** solch, so (groß od. klein etc.), dermaßen: ~ a fright that e-n derartigen Schrecken, dass...; ~ was the force of the explosion so groß war die Gewalt der Explosion; **5.** F so (gewaltig), solch: we had ~ fun wir hatten e-n Riesenspaß; II adv. **6.** so, derart: ~ a nice day so ein schöner Tag; ~ a long time e-e so lange Zeit; III pron. **7.** solch, der, die das, die pl.: ~ as a) diejenigen welche, alle die, b) wie (zum Beispiel); ~ was not my intention das war nicht meine Absicht; man as ~ der Mensch als solcher; and ~ (like) u. dergleichen; **8.** F u. ✝ der-, die-, das'selbe, die'selben pl.; '~·like adj. u. pron. dergleichen.

suck [sʌk] I v/t. **1.** saugen (from, out of aus dat.); **2.** saugen an (dat.), aussaugen; **3.** a. ~ up ein-, aufsaugen, absorbieren (a. fig.); **4.** ~ in einsaugen, verschlingen; **5.** lutschen (an dat.): ~ one's thumb (am) Daumen lutschen; **6.** schlürfen: ~ soup; **7.** fig. holen, gewinnen, ziehen: ~ advantage out of Vorteil ziehen aus; **8.** fig. aussaugen: ~ s.o.'s brain j-n ausholen, j-m s-e Ideen stehlen; II v/i. **9.** saugen, lutschen (at an dat.); **10.** Luft saugen od. ziehen (Pumpe); **11.** ... sucks Am. sl. ... ist ,echt beschissen'; **12.** ~ up to sl. j-m ,in den Arsch kriechen'; III s. **13.** Saugen n, Lutschen n: give ~ to → suckle 1; **14.** Sog m, Saugkraft f; **15.** saugendes Geräusch; **16.** Strudel m; **17.** F kleiner Schluck; **18.** sl. ,Arschkriecher' m; 'suck·er [-kə] s. **1.** zo. saugendes Jungtier, bsd. Spanferkel n; **2.** zo. a) Saug-rüssel m, b) Saugnapf m; **3.** ichth. a) ein Karpfenfisch m, b) Neunauge n, c) Lumpenfisch m, d) Schildfisch m; **4.** ⊚ 'Saugven,til n od. -kolben m od. -rohr n; **5.** Lutscher m (Bonbon); **6.** ♀ (a. Wurzel)Schössling m; **7.** sl. Dumme(r) m, Gimpel m: be a ~ for a) stets hereinfallen auf (acc.), b) scharf sein auf (acc.); play s.o. for a ~ j-n ,anschmieren'; there's a ~ born every minute die Dummen werden nicht alle.

suck·ing ['sʌkɪŋ] adj. **1.** saugend; Saug...; **2.** fig. angehend, ,grün', Anfänger...; ~ coil s. ⊚ Tauchkernspule f; ~ disk s. zo. Saugnapf m; ~ pig s. zo. (Span)Ferkel n.

suck·le ['sʌkl] v/t. **1.** Kind, a. Jungtier säugen, Kind stillen; **2.** fig. nähren, pflegen; 'suck·ling [-lɪŋ] s. **1.** Säugling m; **2.** zo. (noch nicht entwöhntes) Jungtier.

su·crose ['sjuːkrəʊs] s. Rohr-, Rübenzucker m, Su'crose f.

suc·tion ['sʌkʃn] I s. **1.** (An)Saugen n; ⊚ a. Saugwirkung f; phys. Saugfähigkeit f; **2.** ⊚, phys. Sog m; **3.** mot. Hub (-höhe f, -kraft f) m; II adj. **4.** Saug...

(-*leistung*, -*pumpe etc*.): ~ **cleaner** (*od.* **sweeper**) Staubsauger *m*; ~ **cup** *s.* ⊖ Saugnapf *m*; ~ **pipe** *s.* ⊖ Ansaugrohr *n*; ~ **plate** *s.* ⚕ Saugplatte *f* (*für Zahnprothese*); ~ **stroke** *s. mot.* (An)Saughub *m*.

Su·da·nese [ˌsuːdəˈniːz] **I** *adj.* suda'ne-sisch; **II** *s.* Suda'nese *m*, Suda'nesin *f*; *pl.* Suda'nesen *pl.*

su·dar·i·um [sjuːˈdeərɪəm] *s. eccl.* Schweißtuch *n* (der heiligen Ve'roni-ka); **su·da·to·ri·um** [ˌsjuːdəˈtɔːrɪəm] *pl.* **ri·a** [-rɪə] → *sudatory* 3; **su·da·to·ry** [ˈsjuːdətərɪ] **I** *adj.* **1.** Schwitz(bad)...; **2.** ⚕ schweißtreibend; **II** *s.* **3.** Schwitzbad *n*; **4.** ⚕ schweißtreibendes Mittel.

sud·den [ˈsʌdn] **I** *adj.* □ plötzlich, jäh, unvermutet, ab'rupt, über'stürzt; **II** *s.*: **on a** ~, (**all**) **of a** ~ (ganz) plötzlich; **'sud·den·ness** [-nɪs] *s.* Plötzlichkeit *f*.

su·dor·if·er·ous [ˌsjuːdəˈrɪfərəs] *adj.* Schweiß absondernd; ~ **glands** Schweißdrüsen; **'su·dor·if·ic** [-fɪk] *adj. u. s.* schweißtreibend(es Mittel).

suds [sʌdz] *s. pl.* **1.** Seifenwasser *n*, -lauge *f*; **2.** *Am.* F Bier *n*; **'suds·y** [-zɪ] *adj. Am.* schaumig, seifig.

sue [sjuː] **I** *v/t.* **1.** ⚖ *j-n* (gerichtlich) belangen, verklagen (**for** *auf acc.*, wegen); **2.** ~ **out** Gerichtsbeschluss etc. er-wirken; **3.** *j-n* bitten (**for** um); **4.** *obs.* werben *od.* anhalten um *j-n*; **II** *v/i.* **5.** (**for**) klagen (*auf acc.*), Klage einrei-chen (wegen); (*e-e Schuld*) einklagen: ~ **for a divorce** auf Scheidung klagen; **6.** nachsuchen (**to s.o.** bei *j-m*, **for s.th.** um et.).

suede, **suède** [sweɪd] *s.* Wildleder *n*, Ve'lours(leder) *n*.

su·et [ˈsjuːɪt] *s.* Nierenfett *n*, Talg *m*.

suf·fer [ˈsʌfə] **I** *v/i.* **1.** leiden (**from** an *e-r Krankheit etc.*); **2.** leiden (**under** [*od. from*] unter *dat.*) (*Handel, Ruf, Maschine etc.*), Schaden leiden, zu Schaden kommen (*a. Person*); **3.** ✕ Verluste erleiden; **4.** büßen, bezahlen müssen (**for** für); **5.** hingerichtet wer-den; **II** *v/t.* **6.** *Strafe, Tod, Verlust etc.* erleiden, *Durst etc.* leiden, erdulden; **7.** *et. od. j-n* ertragen *od.* aushalten; **8.** a) dulden, (zu)lassen, b) erlauben, gestat-ten: **he ~ed himself to be cheated** er ließ sich betrügen; **'suf·fer·a·ble** [-fə-rəbl] *adj.* □ erträglich; **'suf·fer·ance** [-fərəns] *s.* **1.** Duldung *f*, Einwilligung *f*: **on** ~ unter stillschweigender Dul-dung, nur geduldet(erweise); **2.** *obs.* a) Ergebung *f*, (Er)Dulden *n*, b) Leiden *n*, Not *f*: **remain in** ~ ✝ weiter Not leiden (*Wechsel*); **'suf·fer·er** [-fərə] *s.* **1.** Leidende(r *m*) *f*, Dulder(in *f*): **be a** ~ **by** (**from**) leiden durch (an *dat.*); **2.** Geschädigte(r *m*) *f*; **3.** Märtyrer(in); **'suf·fer·ing** [-fərɪŋ] **I** *s.* Leiden *n*, Dul-den *n*; **II** *adj.* leidend.

suf·fice [səˈfaɪs] **I** *v/i.* genügen, (aus)rei-chen: ~ **it to say** es genüge zu sagen; **II** *v/t. j-m* genügen.

suf·fi·cien·cy [səˈfɪʃnsɪ] *s.* **1.** Hinläng-lichkeit *f*, Angemessenheit *f*; **2.** hinrei-chende Menge *od.* Zahl: **a** ~ **of money** genug Geld; **3.** hinreichendes Auskom-men, auskömmliches Vermögen; **suf·-'fi·cient** [-nt] **I** *adj.* □ **1.** genügend, genug, aus-, hin-, zureichend (**for** für): **be** ~ genügen, (aus)reichen; ~ **reason** zureichender Grund; **I am not** ~ **of a scientist** ich bin in den Naturwissen-schaften nicht bewandert genug; **2.** *obs.* tauglich, fähig; **II** *s.* **3.** F genügende Menge, genug; **suf'fi·cient·ly** [-ntlɪ] *adv.* genügend, genug, hinlänglich.

suf·fix [ˈsʌfɪks] **I** *s.* **1.** *ling.* Suf'fix *n*,

Nachsilbe *f*; **II** *v/t.* **2.** *ling.* als Nachsilbe anfügen; **3.** anfügen, -hängen.

suf·fo·cate [ˈsʌfəkeɪt] **I** *v/t.* ersticken (*a. fig.*); **II** *v/i.* (**with**) ersticken (an *dat.*), (fast) 'umkommen (vor *dat.*); **'suf·fo·-cat·ing** [-tɪŋ] *adj.* □ erstickend, sti-ckig; **suf·fo·ca·tion** [ˌsʌfəˈkeɪʃn] *s.* Er-sticken *n*, Erstickung *f*.

suf·fra·gan [ˈsʌfrəgən] *eccl.* **I** *adj.* Hilfs..., Suffragan...; **II** *s. a.* ~ **bishop** Weihbischof *m*.

suf·frage [ˈsʌfrɪdʒ] *s.* **1.** *pol.* Wahl-, Stimmrecht *n*: **female** ~ Frauenstimm-recht; **universal** ~ allgemeines Wahl-recht; **2.** (Wahl)Stimme *f*; **3.** Abstim-mung *f*, Wahl *f*; **4.** Zustimmung *f*; **suf·-fra·gette** [ˌsʌfrəˈdʒet] *s.* Suffra'gette *f*, Stimmrechtlerin *f*.

suf·fuse [səˈfjuːz] *v/t.* **1.** über'strömen, benetzen; über'gießen, -'ziehen, bede-cken (**with** mit *e-r Farbe*); durch'fluten (*Licht*): **a face ~d with blushes** ein von Schamröte übergossenes Gesicht; **2.** *fig.* (er)füllen; **suf'fu·sion** [-juːʒn] *s.* **1.** Über'gießen *n*, -'flutung *f*; **2.** 'Über-zug *m*; **3.** ⚕ 'Blutunter,laufung *f*; **4.** *fig.* Schamröte *f*.

sug·ar [ˈʃʊgə] **I** *s.* **1.** Zucker *m* (*a.* 🜪, *physiol.*); **2.** 🜪 'Kohlehy,drat *m*; **3.** *fig.* honigsüße Worte *pl.*; **4.** *sl.* 'Zaster' *m* (*Geld*); **5.** F 'Schätzchen' *n*; **II** *v/t.* **6.** zuckern, süßen; (über)'zuckern; **7.** *a.* ~ **over** *fig.* a) versüßen, b) über'tünchen; ~ **ba·sin** *s. Brit.* Zuckerdose *f*; ~ **beet** *s.* ♠ Zuckerrübe *f*; ~ **bowl** *s. Am.* Zu-ckerdose *f*; ~ **can·dy** *s.* Kandis(zucker) *m*; ~ **cane** *s.* ♠ Zuckerrohr *n*; **'~-coat** *v/t.* mit Zuckerguss über'ziehen; zu-ckern (*a. fig.*): ~**ed pill** Dragee *n*, ver-zuckerte Pille (*a. fig.*); ~ **coat·ing** *s.* **1.** Über'zuckerung *f*, Zuckerguss *m*; **2.** *fig.* Versüßen *n*; Beschönigung *f*; ~ **dad·dy** *s.* alter 'Knacker', der ein jun-ges Mädchen aushält.

sug·ared [ˈʃʊgəd] *adj.* **1.** gezuckert, ge-süßt; **2.** mit Zuckerguss; **3.** *fig.* (ho-nig)süß.

sug·ar| **loaf** *s.* [*irr.*] Zuckerhut *m*; ~ **ma·ple** *s.* ♠ Zuckerahorn *m*; **'~plum** *s.* **1.** Bon'bon *n*, Süßigkeit *f*; **2.** *fig.* Lockspeise *f*, Schmeiche'lei *f*; ~ **re·fin·er·y** *s.* 'Zuckerraffine,rie *f*; ~ **tongs** *s. pl.* Zuckerzange *f*.

sug·ar·y [ˈʃʊgərɪ] *adj.* **1.** zuckerhaltig, zuck(e)rig, süß; **2.** süßlich (*a. fig.*); **3.** *fig.* zuckersüß.

sug·gest [səˈdʒest] *v/t.* **1.** *et. od. j-n* vor-schlagen, empfehlen; *et.* anregen; *et.* nahe legen (**to** *dat.*); **2.** *Idee etc.* einge-ben, -flüstern, suggerieren: **the idea ~s itself** der Gedanke drängt sich auf (**to** *dat.*); **3.** hindeuten, -weisen, schließen lassen auf (*acc.*); **4.** denken lassen *od.* erinnern *od.* gemahnen an (*acc.*); **5.** *et.* andeuten, anspielen auf (*acc.*); zu ver-stehen geben (**that** dass); **6.** behaupten, meinen (**that** dass); **sug'gest·i·ble** [-təbl] *adj.* **1.** beeinflussbar, sugge'sti-bel; **2.** suggerierbar; **sug'ges·tion** [-tʃn] *s.* **1.** Vorschlag *m*, Anregung *f*: **at the** ~ **of** auf Vorschlag von (*od. gen.*); **2.** Wink *m*, Hinweis *m*; **3.** Spur *f*, I'dee *f*: **not even a** ~ **of fatigue** nicht die leiseste Spur von Müdigkeit; **4.** Vermu-tung *f*: **a mere** ~; **5.** Erinnerung *f* (**of** an *acc.*); **6.** Andeutung *f*, Anspielung *f* (**of** auf *acc.*); **7.** Suggesti'on *f*, Beeinflus-sung *f*; **8.** Eingebung *f*, -flüsterung *f*; **sug'ges·tive** [-tɪv] *adj.* □ **1.** anregend, gehaltvoll; **2.** (**of**) andeutend (*acc.*), erinnernd (an *acc.*): **be** ~ **of** → *sug-gest* 3, 4; **3.** viel sagend; *b.s.* zweideu-tig, schlüpfrig; **4.** *psych.* sugge'stiv;

---

sug'ges·tive·ness [-tɪvnɪs] *s.* **1.** das Anregende *od.* Vielsagende, Gedan-ken-, Beziehungsreichtum *m*; **2.** Schlüpfrigkeit *f*, Zweideutigkeit *f*.

su·i·cid·al [sjʊɪˈsaɪdl] *adj.* □ selbstmör-derisch (*a. fig.*); **su·i·cide** [ˈsjʊɪsaɪd] **I** *s.* **1.** Selbstmord *m* (*a. fig.*), Freitod *m*: **commit** ~ Selbstmord begehen; **2.** Selbstmörder(in); **II** *adj.* **3.** Selbstmord...

su·int [swɪnt] *s.* Wollfett *n*.

suit [suːt] **I** *s.* **1.** Satz *m*, Garni'tur *f*: ~ **of armo(u)r** Rüstung *f*; **2.** a) *a.* ~ **of clothes** (Herren)Anzug *m*, b) ('Da-men)Ko,stüm *n*: **cut one's** ~ **accord-ing to one's cloth** *fig.* sich nach der Decke strecken; **3.** *Kartenspiel:* Farbe *f*: **long** ~ lange Hand; **follow** ~ a) Farbe bekennen, b) *fig.* 'nachziehen', dassel-be tun, *j-s* Beispiel folgen; **4.** ⚖ Rechtsstreit *m*, Pro'zess *m*, Klage(sa-che) *f*; **5.** Werbung *f*, (Heirats)Antrag *m*; **6.** Anliegen *n*, Bitte *f*; **II** *v/t.* **7.** (**to**) anpassen (*dat. od. an acc.*), einrichten (nach): ~ **the action to the word** das Wort in die Tat umsetzen; ~ **one's style to** sich im Stil nach *dem Publikum* richten; **a task** ~**ed to his powers** e-e s-n Kräften angemessene Aufgabe; **8.** entsprechen (*dat.*): → **s.o.'s purpose**; **9.** passen zu; *j-m* stehen, *j-n* kleiden; **10.** passen für, sich eignen zu *od.* für; → **suited** 1; **11.** sich schicken *od.* zie-men für *j-n*; **12.** *j-m* bekommen, zusa-gen (*Klima, Speise etc.*); **13.** *j-m* gefal-len, *j-n* zufrieden stellen: **try to** ~ **everybody** es allen Leuten recht ma-chen wollen; ~ **o.s.** nach Belieben han-deln; ~ **yourself** mach, was du willst; **are you** ~**ed?** haben Sie et. Passendes gefunden?; **14.** *j-m* recht sein *od.* pas-sen; **III** *v/i.* **15.** passen, (an)genehm sein; **16.** (**with**, **to**) passen (zu), über-'einstimmen (mit); **suit·a·bil·i·ty** [ˌsuːtə'bɪlətɪ] *s.* **1.** Eignung *f*; **2.** Angemes-senheit *f*; **3.** Schicklichkeit *f*; **'suit·a·ble** [-təbl] *adj.* □ passend, geeignet; ange-messen (**to**, **for** für, zu): **be** ~ a) passen, sich eignen, b) sich schicken; **'suit·a·ble·ness** [-təblnɪs] → *suitability*.

'suit·case *s.* Handkoffer *m*.

suite [swiːt] *s.* **1.** Gefolge *n*; **2.** Folge *f*, Reihe *f*, Serie *f*; **3.** *a.* ~ **of rooms** a) Suite *f*, Zimmerflucht *f*, b) Apparte-'ment *n*; **4.** ('Möbel)Garni,tur *f*, (Zim-mer)Einrichtung *f*; **5.** Fortsetzung *f* (*Roman etc.*); **6.** ♪ Suite *f*.

suit·ed [ˈsuːtɪd] *adj.* **1.** passend, geeig-net (**to**, **for** für): **he is not** ~ **for** (*od. to be*) **a teacher** er eignet sich nicht zum Lehrer; **2.** *in Zssgn:* gekleidet; **'suit·ing** [-ɪŋ] *s.* Anzugstoff *m*.

suit·or [ˈsuːtə] *s.* **1.** Verehrer *m*, Freier *m*; **2.** ⚖ Kläger *m*, (Pro'zess)Par,tei *f*; **3.** Bittsteller *m*; **4.** ✝ Übernahme-interessent *m*.

sulfa drugs, **sul·fate** *etc.* → *sulpha drugs*, *sulphate etc.*

sulk [sʌlk] **I** *v/i.* schmollen (**with** mit), trotzen, schlechter Laune *od.* 'einge-schnappt' sein; **II** *s. mst pl.* Schmollen *n*, (Anfall *m* von) Trotz *m*, schlechte Laune: **be in the** ~**s** → I; **'sulk·i·ness** [-kɪnɪs] *s.* Schmollen *n*, Trotzen *n*, schlechte Laune, mürrisches Wesen; **'sulk·y** [-kɪ] **I** *adj.* □ **1.** mürrisch, lau-nisch; **2.** schmollend, trotzend; **3.** *Am.* für 'eine Per'son (bestimmt): **a** ~ **set of China**; **4.** ✍, ⊖ *Am.* Pflug mit Fahrer-sitz; **II** *s.* **5.** a) zweirädriger, einsitziger Einspänner, b) *sport* Sulky *n*, Traber-wagen *m*.

sul·len [ˈsʌlən] *adj.* □ **1.** mürrisch,

grämlich, verdrossen; **2.** düster (*Miene, Landschaft etc.*); **3.** 'widerspenstig, störrisch (*bsd. Tiere u. Dinge*); **4.** langsam, träge (*Schritt etc.*); '**sul·len·ness** [-nɪs] *s.* **1.** mürrisches Wesen, Verdrossenheit *f*; **2.** Düsterkeit *f*; **3.** 'Widerspenstigkeit *f*; **4.** Trägheit *f*.

sul·ly ['sʌlɪ] *v/t. mst fig.* besudeln, beflecken.

sul·pha drugs ['sʌlfə] *s. pl. pharm.* Sulfona'mide *pl.*

sul·phate ['sʌlfeɪt] 🜍 **I** *s.* schwefelsaures Salz, Sul'fat *n*: ~ **of copper** 'Kupfervitri,ol *n*, -sulfat; **II** *v/t.* sulfatieren; '**sul·phide** [-faɪd] *s.* 🜍 Sul'fid *n*; '**sul·phite** [-faɪt] *s.* 🜍 schwefeligsaures Salz, Sul'fit *n*.

sul·phur ['sʌlfə] *s.* **1.** 🜍 Schwefel *m*: ~ **dioxide** Schwefeldioxid *n*; **2.** *a.* ~ **yellow** Schwefelgelb *n* (*Farbe*); **3.** *zo.* ein Weißling *m* (*Falter*); '**sul·phu·rate** [-fjʊreɪt] → **sulphurize**; **sul·phu·re·ous** [sʌl'fjʊərɪəs] *adj.* **1.** schwef(e)lig, schwefelhaltig, Schwefel...; **2.** schwefelfarben; '**sul·phu·ret** [-fjʊret] 🜍 **I** *s.* Sul'fid *n*; **II** *v/t.* schwefeln: ~**ted** geschwefelt; ~**ted hydrogen** Schwefelwasserstoff *m*; **sul·phu·ric** [sʌl'fjʊərɪk] *adj.* 🜍 Schwefel...; '**sul·phu·rize** [-jʊəraɪz] *v/t.* **1.** schwefeln; **2.** vulkanisieren; '**sul·phu·rous** [-fərəs] *adj.* **1.** 🜍 → **sulphureous**; **2.** *fig.* hitzig, heftig.

sul·tan ['sʌltən] *s.* Sultan *m*; **sul·tan·a** [sʌl'tɑːnə] *s.* **1.** Sultanin *f*; **2.** [sʌl'tɑːnə] *a.* ~ **raisin** ♀ Sulta'nine *f*; '**sul·tan·ate** [-tənɪt] *s.* Sulta'nat *n*.

sul·tri·ness ['sʌltrɪnɪs] *s.* Schwüle *f*; **sul·try** ['sʌltrɪ] *adj.* □ **1.** schwül (*a. fig. erotisch*); **2.** *fig.* heftig, heiß, hitzig (*Temperament etc.*).

sum [sʌm] **I** *s.* **1.** *allg.* Summe *f*: a) *a.* ~ **total** (Gesamt-, End)Betrag *m*, b) (Geld)Betrag *m*, c) *fig.* Ergebnis *n*, d) *fig.* Gesamtheit *f*: **in** ~ insgesamt, *fig.* mit 'einem Wort; **2.** F a) Rechenaufgabe *f*, b) *pl.* Rechnen *n*: **do** ~**s** rechnen; **he is good at** ~**s** er kann gut rechnen; **3.** *fig.* Inbegriff *m*, Kern *m*, Sub'stanz *f*; **4.** Zs.-fassung *f*; **II** *v/t.* **5.** *a.* ~ **up** summieren, zs.-zählen; **6.** ~ **up** Ergebnis ausmachen; **7.** ~ **up** *fig.* (kurz) zs.-fassen, rekapitulieren; **8.** ~ **up** (kurz) ein-, abschätzen, (mit Blicken) messen; **III** *v/i.* **9.** ~ **up** (das Gesagte) zs.-fassen, resümieren.

sum·ma·ri·ness ['sʌmərɪnɪs] *s.* das Sum'marische, Kürze *f*; '**sum·ma·rize** [-raɪz] *v/t. u. v/i.* (kurz) zs.-fassen; '**sum·ma·ry** [-rɪ] **I** *s.* Zs.-fassung *f*, (gedrängte) 'Übersicht, Abriss *m*, (kurze) Inhaltsangabe; **II** *adj.* sum'marisch: a) knapp, gedrängt, b) 🏛 abgekürzt, Schnell...: ~ **procedure**; ~ **offence** Übertretung *f*; ~ **dismissal** fristlose Entlassung; **sum·ma·tion** [sʌ'meɪʃn] *s.* **1.** a) Zs.-zählen *n*, b) Summierung *f*, c) (Gesamt)Summe *f*; **2.** 🏛 Resü'mee *n*.

sum·mer¹ ['sʌmə] **I** *s.* **1.** Sommer *m*: **in (the)** ~ im Sommer; **2.** Lenz *m* (*Lebensjahr*): **a lady of 20** ~**s**; **II** *v/t.* **3.** *Vieh etc.* über'sommern lassen; **III** *v/i.* **4.** den Sommer verbringen; **IV** *adj.* **5.** Sommer...

sum·mer² ['sʌmə] *s.* △ **1.** Oberschwelle *f*; **2.** Trägerbalken *m*; **3.** Tragstein *m* auf Pfeilern.

sum·mer| camp *s.* 'Ferienlager *n* (*für Kinder*); ~ **house** *s.* **1.** Gartenhaus *n*, (-)Laube *f*; **2.** Landhaus *n*; ~ **light·ning** *s.* Wetterleuchten *n*.

'**sum·mer·like** [-laɪk], **sum·mer·ly** ['sʌməlɪ] *adj.* sommerlich.

sum·mer| re·sort *s.* Sommerfrische *f*, -kurort *m*; ~ **sales** *s. pl.* 'Sommerschlussver,kauf *m*; ~ **school** *s. bsd. univ.* Ferien-, Sommerkurs *m*; ~ **term** *s. univ.* 'Sommerse,mester *n*; '~**time** *s.* Sommer *m*, Sommerzeit *f*; ~ **time** *s.* Sommerzeit *f* (*Uhrzeit*).

sum·mer·y ['sʌmərɪ] *adj.* sommerlich.

,**sum·ming-'up** [,sʌmɪŋ-] *s.* (kurze) Zs.-fassung, Resü'mee *n* (*a. 🏛*).

sum·mit ['sʌmɪt] *s.* **1.** Gipfel *m* (*a. fig. pol.*), Kuppe *f* e-s Berges: ~ **confer·ence** *pol.* Gipfelkonferenz *f*; **reach the** ~ den Gipfel erreichen (*a. fig.*); **2.** Scheitel *m* e-r Kurve etc.; Kappe *f*, Krone *f* e-s Dammes etc.; **3.** *fig.* Gipfel *m*, Höhepunkt *m*: **at the** ~ **of power** auf dem Gipfel der Macht; **4.** höchstes Ziel; '**sum·mit·ry** [-trɪ] *s. pol.* 'Gipfelpoli,tik *f*.

sum·mon ['sʌmən] *v/t.* **1.** auffordern, -rufen (**to do** et. zu tun); **2.** rufen, kommen lassen, (her)zitieren; **3.** 🏛 vorladen; **4.** *Konferenz etc.* zs.-rufen, einberufen; **5.** *oft* ~ **up** Kräfte, Mut etc. zs.-nehmen, zs.-raffen, aufbieten; '**sum·mon·er** [-nə] *s.* (*hist.* Gerichts)Bote *m*; '**sum·mons** [-nz] *s.* **1.** Ruf *m*, Berufung *f*; **2.** Aufforderung *f*, Aufruf *m*; **3.** 🏛 (Vor)Ladung *f*: **take out a** ~ **against s.o.** j-n (vor)laden lassen; **4.** Einberufung *f*.

sump [sʌmp] *s.* **1.** Sammelbehälter *m*, Senkgrube *f*, 🔩, *mot.* Ölwanne *f*; **3.** ⚒ (Schacht)Sumpf *m*.

sump·ter ['sʌmptə] **I** *s.* Saumtier *n*; **II** *adj.* Pack...: ~ **horse**; ~ **saddle**.

sump·tion ['sʌmpʃn] *s. phls.* **1.** Prä'misse *f*; **2.** Obersatz *m*.

sump·tu·ar·y ['sʌmptjʊərɪ] *adj.* Aufwands..., Luxus...; '**sump·tu·ous** [-əs] *adj.* □ **1.** kostspielig; **2.** kostbar, prächtig, herrlich; **3.** üppig; '**sump·tu·ous·ness** [-əsnɪs] *s.* **1.** Kostspieligkeit *f*; **2.** Pracht *f*; Aufwand *m*, Luxus *m*.

sun [sʌn] **I** *s.* **1.** Sonne *f*: **a place in the** ~ *fig.* ein Platz an der Sonne; **under the** ~ *fig.* unter der Sonne, auf Erden; **with the** ~ bei Tagesanbruch; **his** ~ **is set** *fig.* sein Stern ist erloschen; **2.** Sonne *f*, Sonnenwärme *f*, -licht *n*, -schein *m*: **have the** ~ **in one's eyes** die Sonne genau im Gesicht haben; **3.** *poet.* a) Jahr *n*, b) Tag *m*; **II** *v/t. u. v/i.* **4.** (sich) sonnen; ,~**-and-'plan·et (gear)** 🔩 Pla'netengetriebe *n*; '~**-baked** *adj.* von der Sonne ausgedörrt *od.* getrocknet; ~ **bath** *s.* Sonnenbad *n*; '~**bathe** *v/i.* Sonnenbäder *od.* ein Sonnenbad nehmen; '~**beam** *s.* Sonnenstrahl *m*; ~ **blind** *s. Brit.* Mar'kise *f*; '~**block** *s.* Sunblocker *m*; '~**burn** *s.* **1.** Sonnenbrand *m*; **2.** Sonnenbräune *f*; '~**burned**, '~**burnt** *adj.* **1.** sonn(en)verbrannt: **be** ~ *a.* e-n Sonnenbrand haben; **2.** sonnengebräunt; '~**burst** *s.* **1.** plötzlicher 'Durchbruch der Sonne; **2.** Sonnenbanner *n* (*Japans*).

sun·dae ['sʌndeɪ] *s.* Eisbecher *m*.

Sun·day ['sʌndɪ] **I** *s.* **1.** Sonntag *m*: **on** ~ (am) Sonntag; **on** ~**(s)** sonntags; ~ **eve·ning**, ~ **night** Sonntagabend *m*; **II** *adj.* **2.** sonntäglich, Sonntags...: ~ **best** F Sonntagsstaat *m*, -kleider *pl.*; ~ **school** *eccl.* Sonntagsschule *f*; **3.** F Sonntags...: ~ **driver**; ~ **painter**.

sun·der ['sʌndə] *poet.* **I** *v/t.* **1.** trennen, sondern (**from** von); **2.** *fig.* entzweien; **II** *v/i.* **3.** sich trennen; **III** *s.* **4.** **in** ~ entzwei, auseinander.

'**sun|·di·al** *s.* Sonnenuhr *f*; '~**·down** → **sunset**; '~,**down·er** *s.* F **1.** *Austral.* Landstreicher *m*; **2.** Dämmerschoppen *m*.

sun·dries ['sʌndrɪz] *s. pl.* Di'verses *n*, Verschiedenes *n*, allerlei Dinge; di'verse Unkosten; **sun·dry** ['sʌndrɪ] *adj.* verschiedene, di'verse, allerlei, -hand: **all and** ~ all u. jeder, alle miteinander.

'**sun|·fast** *adj. Am.* lichtecht; '~,**flow·er** *s.* Sonnenblume *f*.

sung [sʌŋ] *pret. u. p.p. von* **sing**.

'**sun|,glass·es** *s. pl. a.* **pair of** ~ Sonnenbrille *f*; '~·**glow** *s.* **1.** Morgen- *od.* Abendröte *f*; **2.** Sonnenhof *m*; ~ **god** *s.* Sonnengott *m*; ~ **hel·met** *s.* Tropenhelm *m*.

sunk [sʌŋk] **I** *pret. u. p.p. von* **sink**; **II** *adj.* **1.** vertieft; **2.** *bsd.* ⊕ eingelassen, versenkt: ~ **screw**; '**sunk·en** [-kn] **I** *obs. p.p. von* **sink**; **II** *adj.* **1.** versunken; **2.** eingesunken: ~ **rock** blinde Klippe; **3.** tief liegend, vertieft (angelegt); **4.** ⊕ → **sunk** 2; **5.** *fig.* hohl (*Augen, Wangen*), eingefallen (*Gesicht*).

sun| lamp *s.* ☀ Ultravio'lettlampe *f*; **2.** *Film:* Jupiterlampe *f*; '~·**light** *s.* Sonnenschein *m*, -licht *n*; '~·**lit** *adj.* sonnenbeschienen.

sun·ni·ness ['sʌnɪnɪs] *s. fig.* das Sonnige; **sun·ny** ['sʌnɪ] *adj.* □ sonnig (*a. fig. Gemüt, Lächeln etc.*), Sonnen...: ~ **side** Sonnenseite *f* (*a. fig. des Lebens*), *fig. a.* die heitere Seite; **be on the** ~ **side of forty** noch nicht 40 (Jahre alt) sein.

sun| par·lor, ~ **porch** *s. Am.* 'Glaseveranda *f*; ~ **pow·er** *s. phys.* 'Sonnenener,gie *f*; '~·**proof** *adj.* **1.** für Sonnenstrahlen 'un,durchlässig; **2.** lichtfest; '~·**rise** *s.* (**at** ~ bei) Sonnenaufgang *m*; '~·**roof** *s.* **1.** 'Dachter,rasse *f*; **2.** *mot.* Schiebedach *n*; '~·**screen** *s.* Sonnenschutzmittel *n*; '~·**set** *s.* (**at** ~ bei) 'Sonnen,untergang *m*: ~ **of life** *fig.* Lebensabend *m*; '~·**shade** *s.* **1.** Sonnenschirm *m*; **2.** Mar'kise *f*; **3.** *phot.* Gegenlichtblende *f*; **4.** *pl.* Sonnenbrille *f*; '~·**shine** *s.* Sonnenschein *m* (*a. fig.*); sonniges Wetter: ~ **roof** *mot.* Schiebedach *n*; ~ **show·er** *s.* F leichter Schauer bei Sonnenschein; ~ **spot** *s. ast.* Sonnenfleck *m*; **2.** Sommersprosse *f*; **3.** *Brit.* F sonnige Gegend; '~·**stroke** *s.* ☀ Sonnenstich *m*; '~·**struck** *adj.:* **be** ~ e-n Sonnenstich haben; '~·**tan** *s.* (Sonnen-) Bräune *f*: ~ **lotion** Sonnenöl *n*; '~·**trap** *s.* sonniges Plätzchen; '~·**up** *s. dial.* Sonnenaufgang *m*; ~ **vi·sor** *s. mot.* Sonnenblende *f*; ~ **wor·ship·(p)er** *s.* Sonnenanbeter *m*.

sup¹ [sʌp] *v/i. obs.* zu Abend essen (**off** *od.* **on s.th.** et.).

sup² [sʌp] **I** *v/t. a.* ~ **off**, ~ **out** löffeln, schlürfen: ~ **sorrow** *fig.* leiden; **II** *v/i.* nippen, löffeln; **III** *s.* Mund *m* voll, kleiner Schluck: **a bite and a** ~ et. zu essen u. zu trinken; **neither bit** (*od.* **bite**) **nor** ~ nichts zu nagen u. zu beißen.

super- [suːpə] *in Zssgn* a) 'übermäßig, Über..., über..., b) oberhalb (von *od. gen.*) *od.* über (*dat.*) befindlich, c) Super... (*bsd. in wissenschaftlichen Ausdrücken*), d) 'übergeordnet, Ober...

su·per ['suːpə] **I** *s.* **1.** F für *a.* **superin·tendent**, b) **supernumerary**, c) '**superhet(erodyne)**; **2.** ♀ F a) Spitzenklasse *f*, b) Quali'tätsware *f*; **II** *adj.* **3.** *a. iro.* Super..., ('super', ,toll'; **III** *v/i. thea.* als Sta'tist(in) mitspielen.

su·per·a·ble ['suːpərəbl] *adj.* über'windbar, besiegbar.

,**su·per·a'bound** [-ərə-] *v/i.* **1.** im 'Überfluss vor'handen sein; **2.** Überfluss *od.* e-e 'Überfülle haben (**in, with** an *dat.*); ,~·**a'bun·dance** [-ərə-] *s.* 'Überfülle *f*, -fluss *m* (**of** an *dat.*); ,~·**a'bun·dant** [-ərə-] *adj.* □ **1.** 'überreichlich; **2.**

'überschwänglich; ,~'**add** [-ər'æd] *v/t.* noch hin'zufügen (**to** zu): *be* ~*ed* (*to*) noch dazukommen (zu *et.*).

su·per|·an·nu·ate [,su:pə'rænjʊeɪt] *v/t.* **1.** pensionieren, in den Ruhestand versetzen; **2.** (als zu alt *od.* als veraltet) ausscheiden *od.* zurückweisen; ,~'**an·nu·at·ed** [-tɪd] *adj.* **1.** a) pensioniert, b) über'altert (*Person*); **2.** veraltet, über'holt; **3.** ausgedient (*Sache*); ~·**an·nu·a·tion** ['su:pə,rænjʊ'eɪʃn] *s.* **1.** Pensionierung *f*; **2.** Ruhestand *m*; **3.** (Alters)Rente *f*, Ruhegeld *n*, Pensi'on *f*: ~ *fund* Pensionskasse *f*.

su·perb [sjuː'pɜːb] *adj.* □ **1.** herrlich, prächtig; **2.** vor'züglich.

,**su·per|'cal·en·der** ⊘ **I** *s.* 'Hochka,lander *m*; **II** *v/t.* Papier hochsatinieren; ,~'**car·go** *s.* Frachtaufseher *m*, Super-'kargo *m*; '~·**charge** *v/t.* **1.** über'laden; **2.** ⊘, *mot.* vor-, über'laden; ,~**d engine** Lader-, Kompressormotor *m*; '~,**charg·er** *s.* ⊘ Kom'pressor *m*, Gebläse *n*.

su·per·cil·i·ous [,su:pə'sɪlɪəs] *adj.* □ hochmütig, her'ablassend; ,**su·per'cil·i·ous·ness** [-nɪs] *s.* Hochmut *m*, Hochnäsigkeit *f*.

,**su·per|·con'duc·tive** *adj. phys.* supraleitend; ,~·**con'duc·tor** *s. phys.* Supraleiter *m*; ,~·'**du·ty** *adj.* ⊘ Höchstleistungs...; ,~·**el·e·'va·tion** [-əre-] *s.* ⊘ Über'höhung *f*; ,~·'**em·i·nence** [-ər'e-] *s.* **1.** Vorrang(stellung *f*) *m*; **2.** her'ragende Bedeutung *od.* Quali'tät, Vortrefflichkeit *f*.

su·per·er·o·ga·tion ['su:pər,erə'geɪʃn] *s.* Mehrleistung *f*: *works of* ~ *eccl.* überschüssige (gute) Werke; *work of* ~ *fig.* Arbeit über die Pflicht hinaus; **su·per·e·rog·a·to·ry** [,su:pəre'rɒgətərɪ] *adj.* **1.** über das Pflichtmaß hin'ausgehend, 'übergebührlich; **2.** 'überflüssig.

su·per·fi·ci·al [,su:pə'fɪʃl] *adj.* □ **1.** oberflächlich, Oberflächen...; **2.** Flächen..., Quadrat...: ~ *measurement* Flächenmaß *n*; **3.** äußerlich, äußer: ~ *characteristics*; **4.** *fig.* oberflächlich: a) flüchtig, b) *contp.* seicht; **su·per·fi·ci·al·i·ty** ['su:pə,fɪʃɪ'ælətɪ] *s.* **1.** Oberflächenlage *f*; **2.** *fig.* Oberflächlichkeit *f*; **su·per·fi·ci·es** [,su:pə'fɪʃiːz] *s.* **1.** (Ober)Fläche *f*; **2.** *fig.* Oberfläche *f*, äußerer Anschein.

'**su·per|·film** *s.* Monumen'talfilm *m*; ,~'**fine** *adj.* **1.** *bsd.* ♣ extra-, hochfein; **2.** über'feinert.

su·per·flu·i·ty [,su:pə'fluːɪtɪ] *s.* **1.** 'Überfluss *m*, Zu'viel *n* (*of* an *dat.*); **2.** *mst pl.* Entbehrlichkeit *f*, 'Überflüssigkeit *f*; **su·per·flu·ous** [suː'pɜːfluəs] *adj.* □ 'überflüssig.

,**su·per|'heat** *v/t.* ⊘ über'hitzen; '~,**he·ro** *s.* Superheld *m*; '~·**het** [-het], ,~·**het·er·o·dyne** [-'hetərədaɪn] **I** *adj.* Überlagerungs..., Superhet...; **II** *s.* Über'lagerungsempfänger *m*, Super(het) *m*; '~·**high fre·quen·cy** *s.* ♭ 'Höchstfre,quenz(bereich *m*) *f*; ,~·'**high·way** *s. Am.* Autobahn *f*; ,~·'**hu·man** *adj.* 'übermenschlich: ~ *beings*; ~ *efforts*; ,~·**im·'pose** [-ər'-] *v/t.* **1.** dar'auf *od.* dar'über setzen *od.* legen; **2.** setzen, legen, lagern (*on* auf, über *acc.*): *one* ~*d on the other* übereinander gelagert; **3.** (*on*) hin'zufügen (zu), folgen lassen (*dat.*); **4.** ♭, *phys.* über'lagern; **5.** Film *etc.*: 'durch-, einblenden, einkopieren.

su·per·in·tend [,su:pərɪn'tend] *v/t.* die (Ober)Aufsicht haben über (*acc.*), beaufsichtigen, über'wachen, leiten; ,**su·per·in'tend·ence** [-dəns] *s.* (Ober-) Aufsicht *f* (*over* über *acc.*), Leitung *f* (*of gen.*); ,**su·per·in'ten·dent** [-dənt] **I** *s.* **1.** Leiter *m*, Vorsteher *m*, Di'rektor *m*: ~ *of public works*; **2.** Oberaufseher *m*, Aufsichtsbeamte(r) *m*, In'spektor *m*: ~ *of schools*; **3.** a) *Brit. etwa* 'Hauptkommis,sar *m*, b) *Am.* Poli'zeichef *m*; **4.** *eccl.* Superinten'dent *m*; **5.** Hausverwalter *m*; **II** *adj.* **6.** Aufsicht führend, leitend, Aufsichts...

su·pe·ri·or [su:'pɪərɪə] **I** *adj.* □ **1.** höher liegend, ober: ~ *planets ast.* äußere Planeten; ~ *wings zo.* Flügeldecken; **2.** höher (stehend), Ober..., vorgesetzt: ~ *court* ♯♯ höhere Instanz; ~ *officer* vorgesetzter *od.* höherer Beamter *od.* Offizier, Vorgesetzte(r) *m*; **3.** über'legen, -'ragend: ~ *man*; ~ *skill*; → *style* 1 b; **4.** besser (**to** als), her'vorragend, erlesen: ~ *quality*; **5.** (**to**) größer, stärker (als), über'legen (*dat.*): ~ *forces* ⚔ Übermacht *f*; ~ *in number* zahlenmäßig überlegen, in der Überzahl; **6.** *fig.* erhaben (**to** über *acc.*): ~ *to prejudice*; *rise* ~ *to* sich über *et.* erhaben zeigen; **7.** *fig.* über'legen, -'heblich: ~ *smile*; **8.** *iro.* vornehm: ~ *persons* bessere *od.* feine Leute; **9.** *typ.* hochgestellt; **II** *s.* **10.** *be s.o.'s* ~ j-m überlegen sein (*in* im Denken *etc.*, an Mut *etc.*); **11.** Vorgesetzte(r *m*) *f*; **12.** *eccl.* a) Su'perior *m*, b) *mst lady* ~ Oberin *f*; **su·pe·ri·or·i·ty** [su:,pɪərɪ'ɒrɪtɪ] *s.* **1.** Erhabenheit *f* (**to, over** über *acc.*); **2.** Über'legenheit *f*, 'Übermacht *f* (**to, over** über *acc.*, *in* in *od.* an *dat.*); **3.** Vorrecht *n*, -rang *m*, -zug *m*; **4.** Über'heblichkeit *f*: ~ *complex psych.* Superioritätskomplex *m*.

su·per·la·tive [su:'pɜːlətɪv] **I** *adj.* □ **1.** höchst; **2.** über'ragend, 'unüber,trefflich; **3.** *ling.* superlativisch, Superlativ...: ~ *degree* → 5; **II** *s.* **4.** höchster Grad, Gipfel *m*; *contp.* Ausbund *m* (*of* von *od.* an *dat.*); **5.** *ling.* Superlativ *m*: *talk in* ~*s fig.* in Superlativen reden.

'**su·per|·man** [-mæn] *s.* [*irr.*] **1.** 'Übermensch *m*; **2.** a) ♀ *ein Comic-Held*, b) *iro.* Supermann *m*; '~,**mar·ket** *s.* Supermarkt *m*: ~ *trolley* Einkaufswagen *m*; ,~·**nat·u·ral** **I** *adj.* □ 'überna,türlich; **II** *s.* das 'Überna,türliche; ,~·'**nor·mal** *adj.* □ **1.** über,durchschnittlich; **2.** außer-, ungewöhnlich; ,~·'**nu·mer·ar·y** [-'nju:mərərɪ] **I** *adj.* **1.** 'überzählig, außerplanmäßig, extra; **2.** 'überflüssig; **II** *s.* **3.** 'überzählige Per'son *od.* Sache; **4.** außerplanmäßiger Beamter *od.* Offi'zier; **5.** Hilfskraft *f*, -arbeiter(in); **6.** *thea. etc.* Sta'tist(in); ,~·'**ox·ide** [-ər'ɒ-] *s.* 🜍 'Super-, 'Pero,xid *n*; ,~·'**phos·phate** *s.* 🜍 Superphos,phat *n*.

,**su·per·pose** [,su:pə'pəʊz] *v/t.* **1.** (auf)legen, lagern, schichten (**on** über, auf *acc.*); **2.** über'ein'ander legen *od.* lagern (*a.* ♈); ♭ über'lagern; ,**su·per·po·'si·tion** *s.* **1.** Aufschichtung *f*, -lagerung *f*; **2.** Über'ein'andersetzen *n*; **3.** *geol.* Schichtung *f*; **4.** ♀, ♈ Superpositi'on *f*; **5.** ♭ Über'lagerung.

'**su·per|·pow·er** **I** *s. pol.* Supermacht *f*; **II** *adj.* ♭ Groß...: ~ *station* Großkraftwerk *n*; '~·**race** *s.* Herrenvolk *n*; '~,**sav·er** *s.* **1.** 🜒, ✈ (Fahrkarte *f od.* Flugschein *m* zum) Super'sparpreis *m*; **2.** (stark verbilligtes) Angebot (*in* Laden).

'**su·per·script** ['su:pəskrɪpt] *typ.*, *Computer:* **I** *s.* hochgestelltes Zeichen; **II** *adj.* hochgestellt.

su·per·sede [,su:pə'siːd] *v/t.* **1.** *j-n od. et.* ersetzen (**by** durch); **2.** *et.* abschaffen, beseitigen, *Gesetz etc.* aufheben; **3.** *j-n* absetzen, s-s Amtes entheben; **4.** *j-n in der Beförderung etc.* über'gehen; **5.** *et.* verdrängen, ersetzen, 'überflüssig machen; **6.** an die Stelle treten von (*od. gen.*), *j-n od. et.* ablösen: *be* ~*d by* abgelöst werden von; ,**su·per'se·de·as** [-dɪæs] *s.* **1.** ♯♯ Sistierungsbefehl *m*, 'Widerruf *m* e-r Anordnung; **2.** *fig.* aufschiebende Wirkung, Hemmnis *n*; ,**su·per'sed·ence** [,su:pə'siːdəns] → *su·persession*.

,**su·per'sen·si·tive** *adj.* 'überempfindlich.

,**su·per'ses·sion** *s.* **1.** Ersetzung *f* (*by* durch); **2.** Abschaffung *f*, Aufhebung *f*; **3.** Absetzung *f*; **4.** Verdrängung *f*.

,**su·per'son·ic** **I** *adj.* **1.** *phys.* Ultraschall...; **2.** ✈ Überschall...: ~ *boom*, ~ *bang* → *sonic bang*; *at* ~ *speed* mit Überschallgeschwindigkeit; **II** *s.* **3.** ✈, *phys.* 'Überschallflug(zeug *n*) *m*; ,~·'**son·ics** *pl. phys.* a) Ultraschallwellen *pl.*, b) *mst sg. konstr.* Fachgebiet *n* des Ultraschalls; '~·**star** *s.* Superstar *m*; '~·**state** *s. pol.* Supermacht *f*.

su·per·sti·tion [,su:pə'stɪʃn] *s.* Aberglaube(n) *m*; ,**su·per'sti·tious** [-ʃəs] *adj.* □ abergläubisch; ,**su·per'sti·tious·ness** [-ʃəsnɪs] *s. das* Abergläubische, Aberglaube(n) *m*.

,**su·per|'stra·tum** [*s. irr.*] **1.** *geol.* obere Schicht; **2.** *ling.* Super'strat *n*; '~,**struc·ture** *s.* **1.** Ober-, Aufbau *m*: ~ *work* Hochbau *m*; **2.** ⚓ (Decks)Aufbauten *pl.*; **3.** *fig.* Oberbau *m*; '~·**tax** *s.* **1.** → *surtax* I; **2.** *Brit.* Einkommensteuerzuschlag *m*.

,**su·per·vene** [,su:pə'viːn] *v/i.* **1.** (noch) hin'zukommen ([*up*]*on* zu); **2.** (unvermutet) eintreten, da'zwischenkommen; **3.** (unmittelbar) folgen, sich ergeben; ,**su·per'ven·tion** [-'venʃn] *s.* **1.** Hin'zukommen *n* (*on* zu); **2.** Da'zwischenkommen *n*.

su·per·vise [,su:pə'vaɪz] *v/t.* beaufsichtigen, über'wachen, die Aufsicht haben *od.* führen über (*acc.*), kontrollieren; ,**su·per'vi·sion** [-'vɪʒn] *s.* **1.** Beaufsichtigung *f*; **2.** (Ober)Aufsicht *f*, Leitung *f*, Kon'trolle *f* (*of* über *acc.*): *police* ~ Polizeiaufsicht; **3.** *ped.* 'Schulinspekti'on *f*; '**su·per·vi·sor** [-zə] *s.* **1.** Aufseher *m*, Aufsichtführende(r) *m*, In'spektor *m*, Kontrol'leur *m*; **2.** *Am.* (leitender) Beamter e-s Stadt- *od.* Kreisverwaltungsvorstandes; **3.** *univ.* Doktorvater *m*; '**su·per·vi·so·ry** [-zərɪ] *adj.* Aufsichts...: ~ *in a* ~ *capacity* Aufsicht führend; ~ *board* ♣ *coll.* Aufsichtsrat *m* (*e-r AG*).

su·pine[1] ['sju:paɪn] *s. ling.* Su'pinum *n*.

su·pine[2] [sjuː'paɪn] *adj.* □ **1.** auf dem Rücken liegend, aus-, hingestreckt: ~ *position* Rückenlage *f*; **2.** *poet.* zu'rückgelehnt; **3.** *fig.* (nach)lässig, untätig, träge.

sup·per ['sʌpə] *s.* **1.** Abendessen *n*: *have* ~ zu Abend essen; ~ *club Am.* exklusiver Nachtklub; **2.** *the* ♀ *eccl.* a) *a. the Last* ♀ das letzte Abendmahl, b) *a. the Lord's* ♀ das heilige Abendmahl, *R.C.* die heilige Kommunion.

sup·plant [sə'plɑːnt] *v/t. j-n od. et.* verdrängen, *Rivalen etc.* ausstechen.

sup·ple ['sʌpl] **I** *adj.* □ **1.** geschmeidig: a) biegsam, b) *fig.* beweglich (*Geist etc.*); **2.** unter'würfig; **II** *v/t.* **3.** geschmeidig machen.

sup·ple·ment **I** *s.* ['sʌplɪmənt] **1.** (**to**) Ergänzung *f* (*gen. od. zu*), Zusatz *m* (zu); **2.** Nachtrag *m*, Anhang *m* (*zu e-m Buch*), Ergänzungsband *m*; **3.** (Zei-

tungs- etc.)Beilage *f*; **4.** ⚔ Ergänzung *(auf 180 Grad)*; **II** *v/t.* ['sʌplɪment] **5.** ergänzen; **sup·ple·men·tal** [ˌsʌplɪ'mentl] *adj.* □, **sup·ple·men·ta·ry** [ˌsʌplɪ'mentərɪ] *adj.* □ **1.** ergänzend, Ergänzungs..., Zusatz..., Nach(trags)...: *be ~ to et.* ergänzen; *~ agreement pol.* Zusatzabkommen *n*; *~ budget*, *~ estimates* Nachtragshaushalt *m*, -etat *m*; *~ order* Nachbestellung *f*; *~ question* Zusatzfrage *f*; *~ proceedings* ⚖ (Zwangs)Vollstreckungsverfahren *n*; *take a ~ ticket* (e-e Fahrkarte) nachlösen; **2.** ⚔ supplemen'tär; **3.** Hilfs..., Ersatz..., Zusatz...; **sup·ple·men·ta·tion** [ˌsʌplɪmen'teɪʃn] *s.* Ergänzung *f*: a) Nachtragen *n*, b) Nachtrag *m*, Zusatz *m*.

sup·ple·ness ['sʌplnɪs] *s.* Geschmeidigkeit *f (a. fig.)*.

sup·pli·ant ['sʌplɪənt] **I** *s.* (demütiger) Bittsteller; **II** *adj.* □ flehend, demütig (bittend).

sup·pli·cant ['sʌplɪkənt] → *suppliant*; **sup·pli·cate** ['sʌplɪkeɪt] **I** *v/i.* **1.** demütig *od.* dringlich bitten, flehen *(for* um); **II** *v/t.* **2.** anflehen, demütig bitten *(s.o. for s.th.* j-n um et.); **3.** erbitten, erflehen, bitten um; **sup·pli·ca·tion** [ˌsʌplɪ'keɪʃn] *s.* **1.** demütige Bitte *(for* um), Flehen *n*; **2.** (Bitt)Gebet *n*; **3.** Bittschrift *f*, Gesuch *n*; **'sup·pli·ca·to·ry** [-ətərɪ] *adj.* flehend, Bitt...

sup·pli·er [sə'plaɪə] *s.* Liefe'rant(in), *a. pl.* Lieferfirma *f*.

sup·ply[1] [sə'plaɪ] **I** *v/t.* **1.** *Ware*, ⚡ *Strom etc.*, *a. fig. Beweis etc.* liefern; beschaffen, bereitstellen, zuführen; **2.** j-n beliefern, versorgen, -sehen, ausstatten; ☉, ⚡ speisen *(with* mit); **3.** *Fehlendes* ergänzen; *Verlust* ausgleichen, ersetzen; *Defizit* decken; **4.** *Bedürfnis* befriedigen; *Nachfrage* decken: *~ a want* e-m Mangel abhelfen; **5.** *e-e Stelle* ausfüllen, einnehmen; *Amt* vor'übergehend versehen: *the place of* j-n vertreten; **II** *s.* **6.** Lieferung *f (to* an *acc.)*; Beschaffung *f*, Bereitstellung *f*; An-, Zufuhr *f*; **7.** Belieferung *f*, Versorgung *f (of* mit): *~ of power* Energie-, Stromversorgung *f*; **8.** ☉, ⚡ (Netz)Anschluss *m*; **9.** Ergänzung *f*; Beitrag *m*, Zuschuss *m*; **10.** *pl.* ♚ *and demand* Angebot und Nachfrage; *be in short ~* knapp sein; **11.** *pl.* ♚ Ar'tikel *pl.*, Bedarf *m*: *office supplies* Bürobedarf; **12.** *mst pl.* Vorrat *m*, Lager *n*, Bestand *m*; **13.** *mst pl.* ⚔ Nachschub *m*, Ver'sorgung(smateri‚al *n*) *f*, Provi'ant *m*; **14.** *mst pl. parl.* bewilligter E'tat, ('Ausgabe)Bu‚dget *n*: *Committee of* ⚖ Haushaltsausschuss *m*; **15.** (Amts-, Stell)Vertretung *f*: *on ~* in Vertretung, als Ersatz; **16.** (Stell)Vertreter *m (Lehrer etc.)*; **III** *adj.* **17.** Versorgungs..., Liefer(ungs)...: *~ house* Lieferfirma *f*; *~-side economics pl.* angebotsorientierte Wirtschaftspolitik *sg.*; **18.** ⚔ Versorgungs...(-*bombe*, -*gebiet*, -*offizier*, -*schiff*), Nachschub...: *~ base* Versorgungs-, Nachschubbasis *f*; *~ depot* Nachschublager *n*; *~ lines* Nachschubverbindungen *m*; *~ sergeant* Kammerunteroffizier *m*; **19.** ☉, ⚡ Speise...(-*leitung*, -*stromkreis etc.*): *~ pipe* Zuleitung(srohr *n*) *f*; **20.** Hilfs..., Ersatz...: *~ teacher* Aushilfslehrer(in) *m*.

sup·ply[2] ['sʌplɪ] *adv.* → *supple*.

sup·port [sə'pɔːt] **I** *v/t.* **1.** *Gewicht*, *Wand etc.* tragen, (ab)stützen, (aus-)halten; **2.** ertragen, (er)dulden, aushalten; **3.** j-n unter'stützen, stärken, j-m Rückendeckung geben; beistehen, j-m

---

4. *sich*, *e-e Familie etc.* er-, unter'halten, sorgen für, ernähren *(on* von): *~ o.s.* für s-n Lebensunterhalt sorgen; **5.** *et.* finanzieren; **6.** *Debatte etc.* in Gang halten; **7.** eintreten für, unter'stützen, fördern, befürworten; **8.** *Theorie etc.* vertreten; **9.** *Anklage*, *Anspruch etc.* beweisen, erhärten, begründen, rechtfertigen; **10.** ♱ *Währung* decken; **11.** a) *thea.* Rolle spielen, b) als Nebendarsteller auftreten mit *e-m Star etc.*; **II** *s.* **12.** *allg.* Stütze *f*: *walk without ~*; **13.** *bsd.* ☉ Stütze *f*, Träger *m*, Ständer *m*, Strebe *f*, Absteifung *f*, Bettung *f*; Sta'tiv *n*; △ 'Durchzug *m*; ✕ (Gewehr-)Auflage *f*; **14.** *fig. (a.* ✕ taktische) Unter'stützung, Beistand *m*: *~ buying* ♱ Stützungskäufe *pl.*; *give ~ to* → 3; *in ~ of s.o.* zur Unterstützung von j-m; **15.** ('Lebens),Unterhalt *m*; **16.** Unter'haltung *f e-r Einrichtung*; **17.** *fig.* Stütze *f*, (Rück)Halt *m*; **18.** Beweis *m*, Erhärtung *f*: *in ~ of* zur Bestätigung *(gen.)*; **19.** ✕ Re'serve *f*, Verstärkung *f*; **20.** *thea.* a) Partner(in) e-s Stars, b) Unter'stützung *f e-s Stars durch das Ensemble*, c) En'semble *n*; **sup'port·a·ble** [-təbl] *adj.* □ **1.** haltbar, vertretbar *(Ansicht etc.)*; **2.** erträglich, zu ertragen(d); **sup'port·er** [-tə] *s.* **1.** ☉, △ Stütze *f*, Träger *m*; **2.** Stütze *f*, Beistand *m*, Helfer(in), Unter'stützer(in); **3.** Erhalter(in); **4.** Anhänger(in), Verfechter (-in), Vertreter(in); **5.** ♱ Tragbinde *f*, Stütze *f*; **sup'port·ing** [-tɪŋ] *adj.* **1.** tragend, stützend, Stütz..., Trag..., *fig. a.* Unterstützungs...: *~ actor thea.* Nebendarsteller *m*; *~ cast thea. etc.* Ensemble *n*; *~ bout* Boxen: Rahmenkampf *m*; *~ fire* ✕ Unterstützungsfeuer *n*; *~ measures* flankierende Maßnahmen; *~ part* Nebenrolle *f*; *~ program(me)* Film: Beiprogramm *n*; *~ purchases* ♱ Stützungskäufe; *~ surfaces* ✈ Tragwerk *n*; **2.** erhärtend: *~ document* Beleg *m*, Unterlage *f*; *~ evidence* ⚖ zusätzliche Beweise *pl*; **sup'port·ive** [-tɪv] *adj.* **1.** unter'stützend, hilfsbereit: *be very ~ of s.o* j-m e-e große Hilfe sein, j-n sehr unterstützen; **2.** → *supporting* 2.

sup·pose [sə'pəʊz] **I** *v/t.* **1.** (als möglich *od.* gegeben) annehmen, sich vorstellen: *~ (od. supposing od. let us ~)* angenommen, gesetzt den Fall; *it is to be ~d that* es ist anzunehmen, dass; **2.** *imp.* (e-n Vorschlag einleitend) wie wäre es, wenn *wir ~ a Spaziergang machten!*: *~ we went for a walk!*; *~ you meet me at 10 o'clock* ich schlage vor, du triffst mich um 10 Uhr; **3.** vermuten, glauben, meinen: *I don't ~ we shall be back* ich glaube nicht, dass wir zurück sein werden; *they are British, I ~* es sind wohl *od.* vermutlich Briten; *I ~ so* ich nehme an, wahrscheinlich, vermutlich; **4.** (mit acc. u. inf.) halten für: *I ~ him to be a painter*; *he is ~d to be rich* er soll reich sein; **5.** (mit Notwendigkeit) vor'aussetzen: *creation ~s a creator*; **6.** (pass. mit inf.) sollen: *isn't he ~d to be at home?* sollte er nicht eigentlich zu Hause sein?; *he is ~d to do* man erwartet *od.* verlangt von ihm, dass *et.* tut; *what is that ~d to mean (od. mean)* was soll das sein *(od.* heißen)?; **II** *v/i.* **7.** denken, glauben, vermuten; **sup'posed** [-zd] *adj.* □ **1.** angenommen: *a ~ case*; **2.** vermutlich; **3.** vermeintlich, angeblich.

sup·po·si·tion [ˌsʌpə'zɪʃn] *s.* **1.** Vor'aussetzung *f*, Annahme *f*: *on the ~ that* unter der Voraussetzung, dass; **2.** Ver-

---

mutung *f*, Mutmaßung *f*, Annahme *f*; ,**sup·po'si·tion·al** [-'ʃənl] *adj.* □ angenommen, hypo'thetisch; **sup·pos·i·ti·tious** [sə‚pɒzɪ'tɪʃəs] *adj.* □ **1.** unecht, gefälscht; **2.** 'untergeschoben *(Kind, Absicht etc.)*, erdichtet; **3.** → *suppositional*.

sup·pos·i·to·ry [sə'pɒzɪtərɪ] *s.* ♱ Zäpfchen *n*, Supposi'torium *n*.

sup·press [sə'pres] *v/t.* **1.** *Aufstand etc.*, *a. Gefühl*, *Lachen etc.*, *a.* ⚡ unter'drücken; **2.** *et.* abstellen, abschaffen; **3.** *Buch* verbieten *od.* unter'drücken; **4.** *Textstelle* streichen; **5.** *Skandal*, *Wahrheit etc.* verheimlichen, vertuschen, unter'schlagen; **6.** ♱ *Blutung* stillen, *Durchfall* stopfen; **7.** *psych.* verdrängen; **sup'pres·sant** [-sənt] *s. pharm.* Dämpfungsmittel *n*, (Appe'tit- *etc.*) Zügler *m*; **sup'pres·sion** [-eʃn] *s.* **1.** Unter'drückung *f (a. fig. u.* ⚡); **2.** Aufhebung *f*, Abschaffung *f*; **3.** Verheimlichung *f*, Vertuschung *f*; **4.** ♱ (Blut)Stillung *f*; Stopfung *f*, (Harn)Verhaltung *f*; **5.** *psych.* Verdrängung *f*; **sup'pres·sive** [-sɪv] *adj.* unter'drückend, Unterdrückungs...; **sup'pres·sor** [-sə] *s.* ⚡ a) Sperrgerät *n*, b) Entstörer *m*: *~ grid* Bremsgitter *n*.

sup·pu·rate ['sʌpjʊəreɪt] *v/i.* ♱ eitern; **sup·pu·ra·tion** [ˌsʌpjʊə'reɪʃn] *s.* Eiterung *f*; **'sup·pu·ra·tive** [-rətɪv] *adj.* eiternd, eitrig, Eiter...

su·pra ['suːprə] *(Lat.) adv.* oben *(bei Verweisen in e-m Buch etc.)*.

supra- [suːprə] *in Zssgn* über, supra..., Supra...

,**su·pra**|**con'duc·tor** *s. phys.* Supraleiter *m*; *,~'***mun·dane** *adj.* 'überweltlich; *,~'***nas·al** *adj. anat.* über der Nase (befindlich); *,~'***na·tion·al** *adj.* überstaatlich; *,~'***re·nal** *s. anat.* Nebenniere(ndrüse) *f*.

su·prem·a·cy [sʊ'preməsɪ] *s.* **1.** Oberhoheit *f*: a) *pol.* höchste Gewalt, Souveräni'tät *f*, b) Supre'mat *m*, *n (in Kirchensachen)*; **2.** *fig.* Vorherrschaft *f*, Über'legenheit *f*: *air ~* ✕ Luftherrschaft *f*; **3.** Vorrang *m*; **su·preme** [sʊ'priːm] **I** *adj.* □ **1.** höchst, oberst, Ober...: *~ authority* höchste (Regierungs)Gewalt; *~ command* ✕ Oberbefehl *m*, -kommando *n*; *~ commander* ✕ Oberbefehlshaber *m*; ⚖ *Court Am.* a) oberstes Bundesgericht, b) oberstes Gericht *(e-s Bundesstaates)*; ⚖ *Court (of Judicature) Brit.* Oberster Gerichtshof; *reign ~* herrschen *(a. fig.)*; **2.** höchst, größt, äußerst, über'ragend: *~ courage*; ⚖ *Being* → 6; *the ~ good phls.* das höchste Gut; *the ~ punishment* die Todesstrafe; *stand ~ among* den höchsten Rang einnehmen unter *(dat.)*; **3.** letzt: *~ moment* Augenblick *m* des Todes; *~ sacrifice* Hingabe *f* des Lebens; *~* entscheidend, kritisch: *the ~ hour in the history of a nation*; **II** *s.* **5.** *the ~* der *od.* das Höchste; ⚖ *the* ⚖ der Allerhöchste, Gott *m*; **su·preme·ly** [sʊ'priːmlɪ] *adv.* höchst, aufs Äußerste, 'überaus.

su·pre·mo [sʊ'priːməʊ] *s. Brit.* F Oberboss *m*.

sur-[1] [sɜː] *in Zssgn* über, auf.

sur-[2] [sə] → *sub-*.

sur·cease [sɜː'siːs] *obs.* **I** *v/i.* **1.** ablassen *(from* von); **2.** aufhören; **II** *s.* **3.** Ende *n*, Aufhören *n*; **4.** Pause *f*.

sur·charge **I** *s.* ['sɜːtʃɑːdʒ] **1.** *bsd. fig.* Über'lastung *f (a. fig.)*, b) 'Überpreis *m*, (a. Steuer-) Zuschlag *m*, c) Strafporto *n*; **3.** 'Über-,

Aufdruck *m* (*Briefmarke etc.*); **II** *v/t.* [sɜːˈtʃɑːdʒ] **4.** über'lasten, -'fordern; **5.** ⚕ a) e-n Zuschlag *od.* ein Nachporto erheben auf (*acc.*), b) *Konto* zusätzlich belasten; **6.** *Briefmarken etc.* (*mit neuer Wertangabe*) über'drucken; **7.** über'füllen, -'sättigen.

sur·cin·gle [ˈsɜːˌsɪŋgl] *s.* Sattel-, Packgurt *m.*

sur·coat [ˈsɜːkəʊt] *s.* **1.** *hist.* a) Wappenrock *m*, b) 'Überrock *m* (*der Frauen*); **2.** Freizeitjacke *f.*

surd [sɜːd] **I** *adj.* **1.** ⩓ 'irratio,nal (*Zahl*); **2.** *ling.* stimmlos; **II** *s.* **3.** ⩓ 'irratio,nale Größe, *a.* Wurzelausdruck *m*; **4.** *ling.* stimmloser Laut.

sure [ʃʊə] **I** *adj.* □ → **surely**; **1.** *pred.* (**of**) sicher, gewiss (*gen.*), über'zeugt (von): ***I am ~ he is there***; ***are you ~ (about it)?*** bist du (dessen) sicher?; ***he is*** (*od.* ***feels***) ***~ of success*** er ist sich s-s Erfolges sicher; ***I'm ~ I didn't mean to hurt you*** ich wollte Sie ganz gewiss nicht verletzen; ***are you ~ you won't come?*** wollen Sie wirklich nicht kommen?; **2.** *pred.* sicher, gewiss, (ganz) bestimmt, zweifellos (*objektiver Sachverhalt*): ***he is ~ to come*** er kommt sicher *od.* bestimmt; ***man is ~ of death*** dem Menschen ist der Tod gewiss *od.* sicher; ***make ~ that ...*** sich (davon) überzeugen, dass ...; ***make ~ of s.th.*** a) sich von et. überzeugen, sich e-r Sache vergewissern, b) sich et. sichern; ***to make ~*** (*Redewendung*) um sicher zu gehen; ***be ~ to*** (*od.* ***and***) ***shut the window!*** vergiss nicht, das Fenster zu schließen!; ***to be ~*** (*Redewendung*) sicher(lich), natürlich (*a. einschränkend = freilich, allerdings*); ***~ thing*** *Am.* F (tod)sicher, klar; **3.** sicher, fest: ***a ~ footing***; ***~ faith*** *fig.* fester Glaube; **4.** sicher, untrüglich: ***a ~ proof***; **5.** verlässlich, zuverlässig; **6.** sicher, unfehlbar: ***a ~ cure*** (***method***, ***shot***); **II** *adv.* **7.** *obs. od.* F sicher(lich): (***as***) ***~ as eggs*** ‚bombensicher'; ***~ enough*** a) ganz bestimmt, sicher(lich), b) tatsächlich; **8.** F wirklich, ‚echt': ***it ~ was cold***; **9.** ***~!*** *bsd. Am.* F sicher!, klar!; **'~-,fire** *adj.* F (tod)sicher, zuverlässig; **,~-'foot·ed** *adj.* **1.** sicher (auf den Füßen *od.* Beinen; **2.** *fig.* sicher.

sure·ly [ˈʃʊəlɪ] *adv.* **1.** sicher(lich), zweifellos; **2.** (ganz) bestimmt *od.* gewiss, doch (wohl): ***~ something can be done to help him***; **3.** sicher: ***slowly but ~***; **sure·ness** [ˈʃʊənɪs] *s.* Sicherheit *f*: a) Gewissheit *f*, b) feste Über'zeugung, c) Zuverlässigkeit *f*; **sure·ty** [ˈʃʊərətɪ] *s.* **1.** *bsd.* ⚖ a) Bürge *m*, b) Bürgschaft *f*, Sicherheit *f*: ***stand ~ for*** bürgen *od.* Bürgschaft leisten (***for*** für *j-n*); **2.** Gewähr(leistung) *f*, Garan'tie *f*; **3.** *obs.* Sicherheit *f*: ***of a ~*** sicher(lich), ohne Zweifel; **sure·ty·ship** [ˈʃʊərətɪʃɪp] *s. bsd.* ⚖ Bürgschaft(sleistung) *f.*

surf [sɜːf] **I** *s.* Brandung *f*; **II** *v/i. sport* surfen; **III** *v/t. Computer*: surfen: ***~ the Internet*** im Internet surfen.

sur·face [ˈsɜːfɪs] **I** *s.* **1.** *allg.* Oberfläche *f*: ***~ of water*** Wasseroberfläche *f*; ***come*** (*od.* ***rise***) ***to the*** → 13; **2.** *fig.* Oberfläche *f*, *das* Äußere: ***on the ~*** a) äußerlich, b) vordergründig, c) oberflächlich betrachtet; → ***scratch*** 7; **3.** ⩓ a) (Ober)Fläche *f*, b) Flächeninhalt *m*: ***lateral ~*** Seitenfläche; **4.** (Straßen)Belag *m*, (-)Decke *f*; **5.** ✈ (Trag)Fläche *f*; **6.** ⚒ Tag *m*: ***on the ~*** über Tag, im Tagebau; **II** *adj.* **7.** Oberflächen... (*a.* ⚙ *-härtung etc.*); **8.** *fig.* oberflächlich: a) flüchtig, b) vordergründig, äußerlich, Schein...; **III** *v/t.* **9.** ⚙ *allg.* die Oberfläche behandeln von; glätten; *Lackierung* spachteln; *Straße* mit e-m Belag versehen; **10.** ⚙ flach-, plandrehen; **11.** ⚓ *U-Boot* auftauchen lassen; **IV** *v/i.* **12.** ⚓ auftauchen (*U-Boot*); **13.** an die Oberfläche (*fig.* ans Tageslicht) kommen, sich zeigen; ***~ mail*** *s. Brit.* gewöhnliche Post (*Ggs. Luftpost*); **'~·man** [-mən] *s.* [*irr.*] 🚂 Streckenarbeiter *m*; ***~ noise*** *s.* Rauschen *n* (*e-r Schallplatte*); ***~ print·ing*** *s. typ.* Reli'ef-, Hochdruck *m.*

sur·fac·er [ˈsɜːfɪsə] *s.* ⚙ **1.** Spachtelmasse *f*; **2.** 'Plandreh- *od.* -hobelma,schine *f.*

,sur·face|-to-'air mis·sile *s.* ⚔ 'Boden-'Luft-Ra,kete *f*; **~ work** *s.* ⚒ Über'tagearbeit *f.*

sur·fac·tant [sɜːˈfæktənt] *s.* ⚗ Ten'sid *n.*

'surf|·board *sport* **I** *s.* Surfbrett *n*; **II** *v/i.* surfen; **'~·boat** *s.* ⚓ Brandungsboot *n.*

sur·feit [ˈsɜːfɪt] **I** *s.* **1.** 'Übermaß *n* (***of*** an *dat.*); **2.** *a. fig.* Über'sättigung *f* (***of*** mit); **3.** 'Überdruss *m*: ***to*** (***a***) ***~*** bis zum Überdruss; **II** *v/t.* **4.** über'sättigen, -'füttern (***with*** mit); **5.** über'füllen, -'laden; **III** *v/i.* **6.** sich über'sättigen (***of***, ***with*** mit).

surf·er [ˈsɜːfə] *s. sport*, *Internet*: Surfer (-in); **surf·ing** [ˈsɜːfɪŋ] *s. sport*, *Internet*: Surfen *n.*

surge [sɜːdʒ] **I** *s.* **1.** Woge *f*, Welle *f* (*beide a. fig.*); **2.** Brandung *f*; **3.** *a. fig.* Wogen *n*, (An)Branden *n*; Aufwallung *f der Gefühle*; **4.** ⚡ Spannungsstoß *m*; **II** *v/i.* **5.** wogen: a) (hoch)branden (*a. fig.*), b) *fig.* (vorwärts) drängen (*Menge*), c) brausen (*Orgel*, *Verkehr etc.*); **6.** *fig.* (auf)wallen (*Blut*, *Gefühl etc.*); **7.** ⚡ plötzlich ansteigen, heftig schwanken (*Spannung etc.*).

sur·geon [ˈsɜːdʒən] *s.* **1.** Chir'urg *m*; **2.** ⚔ leitender Sani'tätsoffi,zier: ***~ general*** *Brit.* Stabsarzt *m*; ***♀ General*** *Am.* a) General(stabs)arzt *m*, b) ⚓ Marineadmiralarzt *m*; ***~ major*** *Brit.* Oberstabsarzt *m*; **3.** Schiffsarzt *m*; **4.** *hist.* Bader *m*; **'sur·ger·y** [-dʒərɪ] *s.* ⚕ **1.** Chirur'gie *f*; **2.** chir'urgische Behandlung, opera'tiver Eingriff; **3.** Operati'onssaal *m*; **4.** *Brit.* Sprechzimmer *n*: ***~ hours*** Sprechstunden; **'sur·gi·cal** [-dʒɪkl] *adj.* □ ⚕ **1.** chir'urgisch: ***~ cotton*** (Verband)Watte *f*; **2.** Operations...: ***~ wound***; ***~ fever*** septisches Fieber; **3.** medi'zinisch: ***~ boot*** orthopädischer Schuh; ***~ stocking*** Stützstrumpf *m*; ***~ spirit*** Wundbenzin *n*; **sur·gi·cen·ter** [ˈsɜːdʒɪˌsentə] *s. Am.* 'Poli,klinik *f.*

surg·ing [ˈsɜːdʒɪŋ] **I** *s.* **1.** *a. fig.* Wogen *n*, Branden *n*; **2.** ⚡ Pendeln *n* (*der Spannung etc.*); **II** *adj.* **3.** *a.* **'surg·y** [-dʒɪ] *adj.* wogend, brandend (*a. fig.*).

sur·li·ness [ˈsɜːlɪnɪs] *s.* Verdrießlichkeit *f*, mürrisches Wesen; Bärbeißigkeit *f*; **sur·ly** [ˈsɜːlɪ] *adj.* □ **1.** verdrießlich, mürrisch; **2.** grob, bärbeißig; **3.** zäh (*Boden*).

sur·mise **I** *s.* [ˈsɜːmaɪz] Vermutung *f*, Mutmaßung *f*, Einbildung *f*; **II** *v/t.* [sɜːˈmaɪz] mutmaßen, vermuten, sich *et.* einbilden.

sur·mount [sɜːˈmaʊnt] *v/t.* **1.** über'steigen; **2.** *fig.* über'winden; **3.** bedecken, krönen: ***~ed by*** gekrönt *od.* überdeckt *od.* überragt von; **sur'mount·a·ble** [-təbl] *adj.* **1.** über'steigbar, ersteigbar; **2.** *fig.* über'windbar.

sur·name [ˈsɜːneɪm] **I** *s.* **1.** Fa'milien-, Nach-, Zuname *m*; **2.** *obs.* Beiname *m*; **II** *v/t.* **3.** *j-m* den Zu- *od. obs.* Beinamen ... geben: ***~d*** mit Zunamen.

sur·pass [səˈpɑːs] *v/t.* **1.** *j-n od. et.* über'treffen (***in*** an *dat.*): ***~ o.s.*** sich selbst übertreffen; **2.** *et.*, *j-s Kräfte etc.* über'steigen; **sur'pass·ing** [-sɪŋ] *adj.* □ her'vorragend, 'unüber,trefflich, unerreicht.

sur·plice [ˈsɜːplɪs] *s. eccl.* Chorhemd *n*, -rock *m.*

sur·plus [ˈsɜːpləs] **I** *s.* **1.** 'Überschuss *m*, Rest *m*; **2.** ⚕ a) 'Überschuss *m*, Mehr(-betrag *m*) *n*, b) Mehrertrag *m*, 'überschüssiger Gewinn, c) (unverteilter) Reingewinn, d) Mehrwert *m*; **II** *adj.* **3.** 'überschüssig, Über(schuss)..., Mehr...: ***~ population*** Bevölkerungsüberschuss *m*; ***~ weight*** Mehr-, Übergewicht *n*; **'sur·plus·age** [-sɪdʒ] *s.* **1.** 'Überschuss *m*, -fülle *f* (***of*** an *dat.*); **2.** *et.* 'Überflüssiges; **3.** ⚖ unerhebliches Vorbringen.

sur·prise [səˈpraɪz] **I** *v/t.* **1.** über'raschen: a) ertappen, b) verblüffen, in Erstaunen (ver)setzen: ***be ~d at s.th.*** über et. erstaunt sein, sich über et. wundern, c) *bsd.* ⚔ über'rumpeln; **2.** befremden, empören; **3.** ***~ s.o. into*** (***doing***) ***s.th.*** j-n zu et. verleiten, j-n dazu verleiten, et. zu tun; **II** *s.* **4.** Über'raschung *f*: a) Über'rump(e)lung *f*: ***take by ~*** *j-n*, *feindliche Stellung etc.* überrumpeln, *Festung etc.* im Handstreich nehmen, b) *et.* Über'raschendes: ***it came as a great ~*** (***to him***) es kam (ihm) sehr überraschend, c) Verblüffung *f*, Erstaunen *n*, Verwunderung *f*, Bestürzung *f* (***at*** über *acc.*): ***to my ~*** zu m-r Überraschung; ***stare in ~*** große Augen machen; **III** *adj.* **5.** über'raschend, Überraschungs...: ***~ attack***; ***~ visit***; **sur'pris·ed·ly** [-zɪdlɪ] *adv.* über'rascht; **sur'pris·ing** [-zɪŋ] *adj.* □ über'raschend, erstaunlich; **sur'pris·ing·ly** [-zɪŋlɪ] *adv.* über'raschend(erweise), erstaunlich(erweise).

sur·re·al·ism [səˈrɪəlɪzəm] *s.* Surrea'lismus *m*; **sur're·al·ist** [-ɪst] **I** *s.* Surrea'list(in); **II** *adj.* → **sur·re·al·is·tic** [səˌrɪəˈlɪstɪk] *adj.* (□ ***~ally***) surrea'listisch.

sur·re·but [ˌsʌrɪˈbʌt] *v/i.* ⚖ e-e Quintup'lik vorbringen; **,sur·re'but·ter** [-tə] *s.* ⚖ Quintup'lik *f.*

sur·re·join·der [ˌsʌrɪˈdʒɔɪndə] *s.* ⚖ Trip'lik *f.*

sur·ren·der [səˈrendə] **I** *v/t.* **1.** *et.* über'geben, ausliefern, -händigen (***to*** *dat.*): ***~ o.s.*** (***to***) → 5, 6, 7; **2.** *Amt*, *Vorrecht*, *Hoffnung etc.* aufgeben; *et.* abtreten, verzichten auf (*acc.*); **3.** ⚖ a) *Sache*, *Urkunde* her'ausgeben, b) *Verbrecher* ausliefern; **4.** ⚕ *Versicherungspolice* zum Rückkauf bringen; **II** *v/i.* **5.** ⚔ *u. fig.* sich ergeben (***to*** *dat.*), kapitulieren; **6.** sich *der Verzweiflung etc.* hingeben *od.* über'lassen; **7.** ⚖ sich *der Polizei etc.* stellen; **III** *s.* **8.** 'Übergabe *f*, Auslieferung *f*, -händigung *f*; **9.** ⚔ 'Übergabe *f*, Kapitulati'on *f*; **10.** (***of***) Auf-, Preisgabe *f*, Abtretung *f* (*gen.*), Verzicht *m* (auf *acc.*); **11.** Hingabe *f*, Sich'über'lassen *n*; **12.** ⚖ Aufgabe *f* e-r Versicherung: ***~ value*** Rückkaufswert *m*; **13.** ⚖ a) Aufgabe *f e-s Rechts etc.*, b) Her'ausgabe *f*, c) Auslieferung *f e-s Verbrechers.*

sur·rep·ti·tious [ˌsʌrepˈtɪʃəs] *adj.* □ **1.** erschlichen, betrügerisch; **2.** heimlich, verstohlen: ***a ~ glance***; ***~ edition*** unerlaubter Nachdruck.

sur·ro·gate [ˈsʌrəgɪt] *s.* **1.** Stellvertreter *m* (*bsd. e-s Bischofs*); **2.** ⚖ *Am.* Nachlass- u. Vormundschaftsrichter *m*; **3.** Ersatz *m*, Surro'gat *n* (***of***, ***for*** für).

sur·round [səˈraʊnd] **I** *v/t.* **1.** um'geben,

S

-'ringen (*a. fig.*): **~ed by danger** (*luxury*) von Gefahr umringt *od.* mit Gefahr verbunden (von Luxus umgeben); *circumstances* **~ing s.th.** (Begleit)Umstände e-r Sache; **2.** ✗ *etc.* um'zingeln, -'stellen, einkreisen, -schließen; **II** *s.* **3.** Einfassung *f*, *bsd.* Boden(schutz)belag *m* zwischen Wand u. Teppich; **4.** *hunt. Am.* Treibjagd *f*; **sur'round·ing** [-dɪŋ] **I** *adj.* um'gebend, 'umliegend; **II** *s. pl.* Um'gebung *f*: a) 'Umgegend *f*, b) 'Umwelt *f*, c) 'Umfeld *n*.

sur·tax ['sɜːtæks] **I** *s.* (*a.* Einkommen-) Steuerzuschlag *m*; **II** *v/t.* mit e-m Steuerzuschlag belegen.

sur·veil·lance [sɜː'veɪləns] *s.* Über'wachung *f*, (*a.* Poli'zei)Aufsicht *f*: **be under** **~** unter Polizeiaufsicht stehen; **keep under ~** überwachen.

sur·vey **I** *v/t.* [sə'veɪ] **1.** über'blicken, -'schauen; **2.** genau betrachten, (sorgfältig) prüfen, mustern; **3.** abschätzen, begutachten; **4.** besichtigen, inspizieren; **5.** *Land etc.* vermessen, aufnehmen; **6.** *fig.* e-n 'Überblick geben über (*acc.*); **II** *s.* ['sɜːveɪ] **7.** *bsd. fig.* 'Überblick *m*, -sicht *f* (*of* über *acc.*); **8.** Besichtigung *f*, Prüfung *f*; **9.** Schätzung *f*, Begutachtung *f*; **10.** Gutachten *n*, (Prüfungs)Bericht *m*; **11.** (Land)Vermessung *f*, Aufnahme *f*; **12.** (Lage)Plan *m*; **13.** (sta'tistische) Erhebung, 'Umfrage *f*; **14.** ⚘ 'Reihenunter,suchung *f*; **sur·'vey·ing** [-eɪɪŋ] *s.* **1.** (Land-, Feld)Vermessung *f*, Vermessungsurkunde *f*, -wesen *n*; **2.** Vermessen *n*, Aufnehmen *n* (*von Land etc.*); **sur'vey·or** [-erə] *s.* **1.** Landmesser *m*, Geo'meter *m*: **~'s chain** Messkette *f*; **2.** (amtlicher) In'spektor *od.* Verwalter *od.* Aufseher: **~ of highways** Straßenmeister *m*; **Board of ~s** Baubehörde *f*; **3.** *Brit.* (ausführender) Archi'tekt; **4.** Sachverständige(r) *m*, Gutachter *m*.

sur·viv·al [sə'vaɪvl] *s.* **1.** Über'leben *n*: **~ of the fittest** *biol.* Überleben der Tüchtigsten; **~ kit** Überlebensausrüstung *f*; **~ rate** Überlebensquote *f*; **~ shelter** atomsicherer Bunker; **~ time** ✗ Überlebenszeit *f*; **2.** Weiterleben *n*; **3.** Fortbestand *m*; **4.** 'Überbleibsel *n* alten Brauchtums *etc.*; **sur·vive** [sə'vaɪv] **I** *v/t.* **1.** *j-n od. et.* über'leben (*a. fig.* ertragen), über'dauern, länger leben als; **2.** *Unglück etc.* über'leben, -'stehen; **II** *v/i.* **3.** am Leben bleiben, übrig bleiben, über'leben; **4.** noch leben *od.* bestehen; übrig geblieben sein; **5.** weiter-, fortleben *od.* -bestehen; **sur·'viv·ing** [-vɪŋ] *adj.* **1.** über'lebend: **~ wife**; **2.** hinter'blieben: **~ dependents** Hinterbliebene; **3.** übrig bleibend: **~ debts** ✝ Restschulden; **sur'vi·vor** [-və] *s.* **1.** Über'lebende(r *m*) *f*; **2.** ✚ Über'lebender, auf den nach dem Ableben der Miteigentümer das Eigentumsrecht 'übergeht.

sus [sʌs] *Brit.* F **I** *s.* **1. on ~** auf Verdacht hin, unter Verdacht; **2.** Verdächtige(r *m*) *f*, Verdachtsperson *f*; **II** *adj.* **3.** ,abgebrüht', ,gewieft', ,clever'.

sus·cep·ti·bil·i·ty [sə,septə'bɪlətɪ] *s.* **1.** Empfänglichkeit *f*, Anfälligkeit *f* (**to** für); **2.** Empfindlichkeit *f*; **3.** *pl.* (leicht verletzbare) Gefühle *pl.*, Feingefühl *n*; **sus·cep·ti·ble** [sə'septəbl] *adj.* □ **1.** anfällig (**to** für); **2.** empfindlich (**to** gegen); **3.** (**to**) empfänglich (für *Reize, Schmeicheleien etc.*), zugänglich (*dat.*); **4.** (leicht) zu beeindrucken(d); **5. be ~ of** (*od.* **to**) *et.* zulassen.

sus·cep·tive [sə'septɪv] *adj.* **1.** aufnehmend, aufnahmefähig, rezep'tiv; **2.** →

susceptible.

sus·pect [sə'spekt] **I** *v/t.* **1.** *j-n* verdächtigen (*of gen.*), im Verdacht haben (*of doing et.* getan zu haben *od.* dass *j-d et.* tut): **be ~ed of doing s.th.** im Verdacht stehen *od.* verdächtigt werden, *et.* getan zu haben; **2.** argwöhnen, befürchten; **3.** für möglich halten, halb glauben; **4.** vermuten, glauben (**that** dass); **5.** *Echtheit, Wahrheit etc.* anzweifeln, miss'trauen (*dat.*); **II** *v/i.* **6.** (e-n) Verdacht hegen, argwöhnisch sein; **III** *s.* ['sʌspekt] **7.** Verdächtige(r *m*) *f*, verdächtige Per'son, Ver'dachtsper,son *f*: **smallpox ~** ⚕ Pockenverdächtige(r); **IV** *adj.* ['sʌspekt] **8.** verdächtig, suspekt (*a. fig.* fragwürdig).

sus·pend [sə'spend] *v/t.* **1.** *a.* ⚙ aufhängen (**from** an *dat.*); **2.** *bsd.* ⚕ suspendieren, (*in Flüssigkeiten etc.*) schwebend halten; **3.** *Frage etc.* in der Schwebe *od.* unentschieden lassen; **4.** einstweilen auf-, verschieben; ✚ *Verfahren, Vollstreckung* aussetzen: **~ a sentence** ✚ e-e Strafe zur Bewährung aussetzen; **5.** *Verordnung etc.* zeitweilig aufheben *od.* außer Kraft setzen; **6.** *die Arbeit,* ✗ *die Feindseligkeiten,* ✝ *Zahlungen etc.* (zeitweilig) einstellen; **7.** *j-n* (zeitweilig) des Amtes entheben, suspendieren; **8.** *Mitglied* zeitweilig ausschließen; **9.** *Sportler* sperren; **10.** mit *s-r* Meinung *etc.* zu'rückhalten; **11.** ♪ *Ton* vorhalten; **sus'pend·ed** [-dɪd] *adj.* **1.** hängend, Hänge...(*-decke, -lampe etc.*): **be ~** hängen (**by** an *dat.*, **from** von); **2.** schwebend; **3.** unter'brochen, ausgesetzt, zeitweilig eingestellt: **~ animation** ⚘ Scheintod *m*; **4.** ✚ zur Bewährung ausgesetzt (*Strafe*): **~ sentence of two years** zwei Jahre mit Bewährung; **5.** suspendiert (*Beamter*); **sus'pend·er** [-də] *s.* **1.** *pl. bsd. Am.* Hosenträger *pl.*; **2.** *Brit.* Strumpf- *od.* Sockenhalter *m*: **~ belt** Hüftgürtel *m*, Straps *m*; **3.** Aufhängevorrichtung *f*.

sus·pense [sə'spens] *s.* **1.** Spannung *f*, Ungewissheit *f*: **anxious ~** Hangen u. Bangen *n*; **in ~** gespannt, voller Spannung; **be in ~** in der Schwebe sein; **keep in ~** a) *j-n* in Spannung halten, im Ungewissen lassen, b) *et.* in der Schwebe lassen; **~ account** ✝ Interimskonto *n*; **~ entry** ✝ transitorische Buchung; **2.** → **suspension** 6; **sus'pense·ful** [-fʊl] *adj.* spannend; **sus'pen·sion** [-nʃn] *s.* **1.** Aufhängen *n*; **2.** *bsd.* ⚙ Aufhängung *f*: **front-wheel ~;** ⚕ Hängebrücke *f*; **~ file** Hängeordner *m*; **~ railway** Schwebebahn *f*; **3.** ⚙ Federung *f*: **~ spring** Tragfeder *f*; **4.** ⚕, *phys.* Suspensi'on *f*; *pl.* Aufschlämmungen *pl.*; **5.** (einstweilige) Einstellung (*der Feindseligkeiten etc.*): **~ of payment(s)** ✝ Zahlungseinstellung; **6.** ✚ Aufschub *m*, Aussetzung *f*, vor'übergehende Aufhebung *e-s Rechts*; Hemmung *f* der Verjährung; **7.** Aufschub *m*, Verschiebung *f*; **8.** Suspendierung *f* (**from** von), (Dienst-, Amts)Enthebung *f*; **9.** zeitweiliger Ausschluss; **10.** *sport* Sperre *f*; **11.** ♪ Vorhalt *m*; **sus'pen·sive** [-sɪv] *adj.* □ **1.** aufschiebend, suspen'siv: **~ condition; ~ veto**; **2.** unter'brechend, hemmend; **3.** unschlüssig; **4.** unbestimmt; **sus'pen·so·ry** [-sərɪ] **I** *adj.* **1.** hängend, Schwebe..., Hänge...; **2.** *anat.* Aufhänge...; **3.** ✚ suspensive 1; **II** *s.* **4.** *anat.* a) *a.* **~ ligament** Aufhängeband *n*, b) *a.* **~ muscle** Aufhängemuskel *m*; **5.** ⚕ a) *a.* **~ bandage** Suspen'sorium *n*, b) Bruchband *n*.

sus·pi·cion [sə'spɪʃn] *s.* **1.** Argwohn *m*,

'Misstrauen *n* (*of* gegen); **2.** (*of*) Verdacht *m* (gegen *j-n*), Verdächtigung *f* (*gen.*): **above ~** über jeden Verdacht erhaben; **on ~ of murder** unter Mordverdacht *festgenommen werden*; **be under ~** unter Verdacht stehen; **cast a ~ on** e-n Verdacht auf *j-n* werfen; **have a ~ that** e-n Verdacht haben *od.* hegen, dass; **3.** Vermutung *f*: **no ~** keine Ahnung; **4.** *fig.* Spur *f*: **a ~ of brandy** (*arrogance*); **a ~ of a smile** der Anflug e-s Lächelns; **sus'pi·cious** [-ʃəs] *adj.* □ **1.** 'misstrauisch, argwöhnisch (*of* gegen): **be ~ of s.th.** et. befürchten; **2.** verdächtig, Verdacht erregend; **sus'pi·cious·ness** [-ʃəsnɪs] *s.* **1.** Misstrauen *n*, Argwohn *m* (*of* gegen); 'misstrauisches Wesen; **2.** das Verdächtige.

suss [sʌs] *Brit.* F **I** *v/t.* **1.** *a.* **~ out** kommen hinter (*acc.*), dahinter kommen, *et.* ,spitzkriegen': **~ that ...** dahinter kommen, dass ...; **2.** *mst* **~ out** *et.* ausspionieren *od.* he'rauskriegen: **I can't ~ her out** aus der werd ich nicht schlau, bei der ,schau ich nicht mehr durch'; **I've got her ~ed out** die hab ich durchschaut; **II** *s.* **3.** → **sus** 2; **4.** Erfahrung *f*, (Spezi'al)Wissen *n*, 'Ge'wieftheit' *f*; **III** *adj.* **5.** → **sussed**; **sus·sed** [sʌst] *adj. Brit.* F **1.** clever, abgebrüht, ,gewieft'; **2.** gescheit, bewandert, gut informiert; **'suss·y** [-ɪ] *adj. Brit.* F verdächtig.

sus·tain [sə'steɪn] *v/t.* **1.** stützen, tragen: **~ing wall** Stützmauer *f*; **2.** *Last, Druck, fig.* den Vergleich *etc.* aushalten; *e-m Angriff etc.* standhalten; **3.** *Niederlage, Schaden, Verletzungen, Verlust etc.* erleiden, da'vontragen; **4.** *et.* (aufrecht-) erhalten, in Gang halten; *Interesse* wach halten; **~ing program** *Am. Radio, TV:* Programm *n* ohne Reklameeinblendungen; **5.** *j-n* er-, unter'halten, *Familie etc.* ernähren; *Heer* verpflegen; **6.** *Institution* unter'halten, -'stützen; **7.** *j-n, j-s Forderung* unter'stützen; **8.** ✚ als rechtsgültig anerkennen, *e-m Antrag, Einwand etc.* stattgeben; **9.** *Behauptungen etc.* bestätigen, rechtfertigen, erhärten; **10.** *j-n* aufrecht halten; *j-m* Kraft geben; **11.** ♪ *Ton* (aus)halten; **12.** *Rolle* (gut) spielen; **sus,tain·a·'bil·i·ty** *s.* **1.** Umweltverträglichkeit *f*: **~ programme** *etwa:* Entwicklungsplan *m* für umweltverträgliches Wirtschaften; **2.** Tragbarkeit *f*; **3.** Nachhaltigkeit *f*; **sus'tain·a·ble** *adj.* **1.** umweltverträglich; **2.** vernünftig, tragbar; **3.** dauerhaft, nachhaltig; **4.** aufrecht zu erhalten(d), in Gang zu halten(d); **sus'tained** [-nd] *adj.* **1.** anhaltend (*a. Interesse etc.*), Dauer...(*-feuer, -geschwindigkeit etc.*); **2.** ♪ a) (aus)gehalten (*Ton*), b) getragen; **3.** *phys.* ungedämpft.

sus·te·nance ['sʌstɪnəns] *s.* **1.** ('Lebens-) Unterhalt *m*, Auskommen *n*; **2.** Nahrung *f*; **3.** Nährwert *m*; **4.** Erhaltung *f*, Ernährung *f*; **5.** *fig.* Beistand *m*, Stütze *f*; **sus·ten·ta·tion** [,sʌsten'teɪʃn] *s.* **1.** → **sustenance** 1, 2, 4; **2.** Unter'haltung *f e-s Instituts etc.*; **3.** (Aufrecht-) Erhaltung *f*; **4.** Unter'stützung *f*.

su·sur·rant [sjʊ'sʌrənt] *adj.* **1.** flüsternd, säuselnd; **2.** raschelnd.

sut·ler ['sʌtlə] *s.* ✗ *hist.* Marke'tender(in).

su·ture ['sjuːtʃə] **I** *s.* **1.** ⚕, ⚘, *anat.* Naht *f*; **2.** ⚕ (Zs.-)Nähen *n*; **3.** ⚕ 'Nahtmateri,al *n*, Faden *m*; **II** *v/t.* **4.** *bsd.* ⚕ (zu-, ver)nähen.

su·ze·rain ['suːzəreɪn] **I** *s.* **1.** Oberherr *m*, Suze'rän *m*; **2.** *pol.* Pro'tektorstaat *m*; **3.** *hist.* Oberlehensherr *m*; **II** *adj.* **4.** oberhoheitlich; **5.** *hist.* oberlehensherrlich; **'su·ze·rain·ty** [-tɪ] *s.* **1.** Oberhoheit *f*; **2.** *hist.* Oberlehensherrlichkeit *f*.

svelte [svelt] *adj.* schlank, gra'zil.

swab [swɒb] **I** *s.* **1.** a) Scheuerlappen *m*, b) Schrubber *m*, c) Mopp *m*, d) Handfeger *m*, e) ⚓ Schwabber *m*; **2.** ⚕ a) Tupfer *m*, b) Abstrich *m*; **II** *v/t.* **3.** *a.* ~ **down** aufwischen, ⚓ *Deck* schrubben; **4.** ⚕ a) *Blut etc.* abtupfen, b) *Wunde* betupfen.

Swa·bi·an ['sweɪbjən] **I** *s.* Schwabe *m*, Schwäbin *f*; **II** *adj.* schwäbisch.

swad·dle ['swɒdl] **I** *adj.* **1.** *Säugling* wickeln, in Windeln legen; **2.** um'wickeln, einwickeln; **II** *s.* **3.** *Am.* Windel *f*.

swad·dling ['swɒdlɪŋ] *s.* Wickeln *n e-s Babys*; **~ clothes** [kləʊðz] *s. pl.* Windeln *pl.*: *be still in one's* ~ *fig.* ‚noch in den Windeln liegen'.

swag [swæg] *s.* **1.** Gir'lande *f* (*Zierrat*); **2.** *sl.* Beute *f*, Raub *m*.

swage [sweɪdʒ] **I** *s.* ⚙ **1.** Gesenk *n*; **2.** Präge *f*, Stanze *f*; **II** *v/t.* **3.** im Gesenk bearbeiten.

swag·ger ['swægə] **I** *v/i.* **1.** (ein'her)stolzieren; **2.** prahlen, aufschneiden, renommieren (*about* mit); **II** *s.* **3.** stolzer Gang, Stolzieren *n*; **4.** Großtue'rei *f*, Prahle'rei *f*; **III** *adj.* **5.** F (tod)schick: ~ **stick** ✕ Offi'ziersstöckchen *n*; **'swagger·er** [-ərə] *s.* Großtuer *m*, Aufschneider *m*; **'swag·ger·ing** [-ərɪŋ] *adj.* □ **1.** stolzierend; **2.** schwadronierend.

swain [sweɪn] *s.* **1.** *mst poet.* Bauernbursche *m*, Schäfer *m*; **2.** *poet. od. humor.* Liebhaber *m*, Verehrer *m*.

swal·low[1] ['swɒləʊ] **I** *v/t.* **1.** (ver)schlucken, verschlingen: ~ **down** hinunterschlucken; **2.** *fig. Buch etc.* verschlingen, *Ansicht etc.* begierig in sich aufnehmen; **3.** *Gebiet etc.* ‚schlucken', sich einverleiben; **4.** *mst* ~ **up** *fig. j-n, Schiff, Geld, Zeit etc.* verschlingen; **5.** ‚schlucken', für bare Münze nehmen; **6.** *Beleidigung etc.* schlucken, einstecken; **7.** *Tränen, Ärger* hin'unterschlucken; **8.** *Behauptung* zu'rücknehmen: ~ *one's words*; **II** *v/i.* **9.** schlucken (*a. vor Erregung*): ~ *hard fig.* kräftig schlucken; ~ *the wrong way* sich verschlucken; **III** *s.* **10.** Schlund *m*, Kehle *f*; **11.** Schluck *m*.

swal·low[2] ['swɒləʊ] *s. orn.* Schwalbe *f*: *one ~ does not make a summer* eine Schwalbe macht noch keinen Sommer; **'~·tail** *s.* **1.** *orn.* 'Schwalbenschwanz‚kolibri *m*; **2.** *zo.* Schwalbenschwanz *m* (*Schmetterling*); **3.** ⚙ Schwalbenschwanz *m*; **4.** *a. pl.* Frack *m*; **'~·tailed** *adj.* Schwalbenschwanz...: ~ *coat* Frack *m*.

swam [swæm] *pret. von* **swim**.

swa·mi ['swɑːmɪ] *s.* **1.** Meister *m* (*bsd. Brahmane*); **2.** → **pundit** 2.

swamp [swɒmp] **I** *s.* **1.** Sumpf *m*; **2.** (Flach)Moor *n*; **II** *v/t.* **3.** über'schwemmen (*a. fig.*): *be ~ed with* mit *Arbeit, Einladungen etc.* überhäuft werden *od.* sein, sich nicht mehr retten können vor (*dat.*); **4.** ⚓ *Boot* voll laufen lassen, zum Sinken bringen; **5.** *Am. pol. Gesetz* zu Fall bringen; **6.** *sport* ‚über'fahren'; **'swamp·y** [-pɪ] *adj.* sumpfig, mo'rastig, Sumpf...

swan [swɒn] **I** *s.* **1.** *zo.* Schwan *m*: ♪ *of Avon fig.* der Schwan vom Avon (*Shakespeare*); **2.** ♪ *ast.* Schwan *m* (*Sternbild*); **II** *v/i.* **3.** ~ *about* (*od. around*) F her'umgondeln, -ziehen, sich her'umtreiben in (*dat.*); **4.** ~ *along* F entlangziehen, -gondeln; **5.** ~ *off* F abziehen, losziehen.

swank [swæŋk] F **I** *s.* **1.** Protze'rei *f*, ‚Angabe' *f*; **2.** ‚Angeber' *m*; **II** *v/i.* **3.** protzen, ‚angeben'; **III** *adj.* **4.** → **'swank·y** [-kɪ] *adj.* F **1.** protzig; **2.** (tod)schick.

'swan·|like *adj. u. adv.* schwanengleich; **~ maid·en** *s. myth.* Schwan(en)jungfrau *f*; **'~·neck** *s.* ⚙ Schwanenhals *m*.

swan·ner·y ['swɒnərɪ] *s.* Schwanenteich *m*.

swan|song *s. bsd. fig.* Schwanengesang *m*; **'~·,up·ping** *s. Brit.* Einfangen u. Kennzeichnen der jungen Schwäne (*bsd. auf der Themse*).

swap [swɒp] F **I** *v/t.* (aus-, ein)tauschen (*s.th. for et.* für); *Pferde etc.* tauschen, wechseln: ~ *stories fig.* Geschichten austauschen; **II** *v/i.* tauschen; **III** *s.* Tausch(handel) *m*; ♰ Swap(geschäft *n*) *m*; ~ *meet s. bsd. Am.* Tauschbörse *f*, Flohmarkt *m*.

sward [swɔːd] *s.* Rasen *m*, Grasnarbe *f*; **'sward·ed** [-dɪd] *adj.* mit Rasen bedeckt[1].

swarm[1] [swɔːm] **I** *s.* **1.** (Bienen- *etc.*) Schwarm *m*; **2.** Schwarm *m* (*Kinder, Soldaten etc.*); **3.** *fig.* Haufen *m*, Masse *f* (*Briefe etc.*); **II** *v/i.* **4.** schwärmen (*Bienen*); **5.** (um'her)schwärmen, (zs.-)strömen: ~ *out* a) ausschwärmen, b) hinausströmen; ~ *to a place* zu e-m Ort (hin)strömen; *beggars ~ in that town* in dieser Stadt wimmelt es von Bettlern; **6.** (*with*) wimmeln (von); **III** *v/t.* **7.** um'schwärmen, -'drängen; **8.** *Örtlichkeit* in Schwärmen über'fallen; **9.** *Bienen* ausschwärmen lassen.

swarm[2] [swɔːm] **I** *v/t.* a) hochklettern an (*dat.*), b) hin'aufklettern auf (*acc.*); **II** *v/i.* klettern.

swarth·i·ness ['swɔːðɪnɪs] *s.* dunkle Gesichtsfarbe, Schwärze *f*, Dunkelbraun *n*; **swarth·y** ['swɔːðɪ] *adj.* □ dunkel (-häutig), schwärzlich.

swash [swɒʃ] **I** *v/i.* **1.** klatschen, schwappen (*Wasser etc.*); **2.** plan(t)schen (*im Wasser*); **II** *v/t.* **3.** *Wasser etc.* a) spritzen lassen, b) klatschen; **III** *s.* **4.** Platschen *n*, Schwappen *n*; **5.** Platsch *m*, Klatsch *m* (*Geräusch*); **'~·buck·ler** [-ˌbʌklə] *s.* **1.** Schwadro'neur *m*, Bra'marbas *m*; **2.** verwegener Kerl; **3.** historischer 'Abenteuerfilm *m od.* -ro‚man *m*; **'~·buck·ling** [-ˌbʌklɪŋ] **I** *s.* Bramarbasieren *n*, Prahlen *n*; **II** *adj.* schwadronierend, prahlerisch; ~ *plate s.* ⚙ Taumelscheibe *f*.

swas·ti·ka ['swɒstɪkə] *s.* Hakenkreuz *n*.

swat [swɒt] F **I** *v/t.* **1.** schlagen; **2.** *Fliege etc.* totschlagen; **II** *s.* **3.** (wuchtiger) Schlag; **4.** → **swatter**.

swath [swɔːθ] *s.* ✓ Grasnarbe *f*.

swathe[1] [sweɪð] **I** *v/t.* **1.** (um)'wickeln (*with* mit), einwickeln; **2.** (*wie e-n Verband*) her'umwickeln; **3.** einhüllen; **II** *s.* **4.** Binde *f*, Verband *m*; **5.** (Wickel-) Band *n*; **6.** ⚕ 'Umschlag *m*.

swathe[2] [sweɪð] → **swath**.

swat·ter ['swɒtə] *s.* Fliegenklatsche *f*.

sway [sweɪ] **I** *v/i.* **1.** schwanken, schaukeln, sich wiegen; **2.** sich neigen; **3.** (*to*) *fig.* sich zuneigen (*dat.*) (*öffentliche Meinung etc.*); **4.** herrschen; **II** *v/t.* **5.** *et.* schwenken, schaukeln, wiegen; **6.** neigen; **7.** ⚓ *mst* ~ *up Masten etc.* aufheißen; **8.** *fig.* beeinflussen, lenken; **9.** beherrschen, herrschen über (*acc.*); *Publikum* mitreißen; **10.** *rhet.* Zepter *etc.* schwingen; **III** *s.* **11.** Schwanken *n*, Schaukeln *n*, Wiegen *n*; **12.** Schwung *m*, Wucht *f*; **13.** 'Übergewicht *n*, Einfluss *m*: *under the ~ of* unter dem Einfluss *od.* im Banne (*gen.*) (→ 15);

15. Herrschaft *f*, Gewalt *f*, Macht *f*: *hold ~ over* beherrschen, herrschen über (*acc.*); *under the ~ of* in der Gewalt *od.* unter der Herrschaft (*gen.*).

swear [sweə] **I** *v/i.* [*irr.*] **1.** schwören, e-n Eid leisten (*on the Bible* auf die Bibel): ~ *by* a) bei *Gott etc.* schwören, b) F schwören auf (*acc.*), felsenfest glauben an (*acc.*); ~ *by all that's holy* Stein u. Bein schwören; **2.** fluchen (*at* auf *acc.*); **II** *v/t.* [*irr.*] **3.** *Eid* schwören, leisten; **4.** *et.* beschwören, eidlich bekräftigen; ~ *out* ⚖ *Am.* Haftbefehl durch eidliche Strafanzeige erwirken; **5.** *Rache, Treue etc.* schwören; **6.** *a.* ~ *in j-n* vereidigen; ~ *s.o. into an office* j-n in ein Amt einschwören; ~ *s.o. to secrecy* j-n eidlich zur Verschwiegenheit verpflichten; **III** *s.* **7.** F Fluch *m*; **'swearing** [-ərɪŋ] *s.* **1.** Schwören *n*; ~*-in* ⚖ Vereidigung *f*; **2.** Fluchen *n*; **'swearword** *s.* Fluch(wort *n*) *m*.

sweat [swet] **I** *s.* **1.** Schweiß *m*: *cold ~* kalter Schweiß, Angstschweiß; *by the ~ of one's brow* im Schweiße s-s Angesichts; *be in a ~* a) in Schweiß gebadet sein, b) F (vor Angst, Erregung *etc.*) schwitzen; *get into a ~* in Schweiß geraten; *no ~!* F kein Problem!; **2.** Schwitzen *n*, Schweißausbruch *m*; **3.** ⚙ Ausschwitzung *f*, Feuchtigkeit *f*; **4.** F Pla'cke'rei *f*; **5.** *old* ~ ✕ *sl.* alter Haudegen *m*; **II** *v/i.* [*Am. irr.*] **6.** schwitzen (*with* vor *dat.*); **7.** ⚙, *phys. etc.* schwitzen, anlaufen; gären (*Tabak*); **8.** F schwitzen, sich schinden; **9.** ♰ für e-n Hungerlohn arbeiten; **III** *v/t.* [*Am. irr.*] **10.** schwitzen: ~ *blood* Blut schwitzen; ~ *out* a) *Krankheit etc.* (her)ausschwitzen, b) *fig. et.* mühsam hervorbringen; ~ *it out* F durchhalten, es durchstehen; **11.** *Kleidung* 'durchschwitzen; **12.** *j-n* schwitzen lassen (*a.* F *fig. im Verhör etc.*); *fig.* schuften lassen, *Arbeiter* ausbeuten; F *j-n* ‚bluten lassen'; **13.** ⚙ schwitzen *od.* gären lassen; *metall.* (~ *out* aus)seigern; (heiß-, weich)löten; *Kabel* schweißen; ~ *band* ⚙ Schweißleder *n* (*im Hut*); *bsd. sport* Schweißband *n*.

sweat·ed ['swetɪd] *adj.* ♰ **1.** für Hungerlöhne hergestellt; **2.** ausgebeutet, 'unterbezahlt; **'sweat·er** [-tə] *s.* **1.** Sweater *m*, Pull'over *m*; **2.** ♰ Ausbeuter *m*.

sweat gland *s. physiol.* Schweißdrüse *f*.

sweat·i·ness ['swetɪnɪs] *s.* Verschwitztheit *f*, Schweißigkeit *f*.

sweat·ing ['swetɪŋ] *s.* **1.** Schwitzen *n*; **2.** ♰ Ausbeutung *f*; ~ *bath s.* ♰ Schwitzbad *n*; ~ *sys·tem s.* ♰ 'Ausbeutungssystem *n*.

'sweat·|shirt *s.* Sweatshirt *n*; **'~·shop** *s.* ♰ Ausbeutungsbetrieb *m*; **'~·suit** *s.* Trainingsanzug *m*.

sweat·y ['swetɪ] *adj.* □ **1.** schweißig, verschwitzt; **2.** anstrengend.

Swede [swiːd] *s.* **1.** Schwede *m*, Schwedin *f*; **2.** ♪ *Brit.* → **Swedish turnip**.

Swed·ish ['swiːdɪʃ] **I** *adj.* **1.** schwedisch; **II** *s.* **2.** *ling.* Schwedisch *n*; **3.** *the ~ coll.* die Schweden *pl.*; ~ *tur·nip s.* ♀ *Brit.* Schwedische Rübe, Gelbe Kohlrübe.

sweep [swiːp] **I** *v/t.* [*irr.*] **1.** kehren, fegen: ~ *away* (*off, up*) weg-(fort-, auf-)kehren; **2.** freimachen, säubern (*of* von; *a. fig.*); **3.** hin'wegstreichen über (*acc.*) (*Wind etc.*); **4.** *Flut etc.* jagen, treiben: ~ *before one* vor sich hertreiben; ~ *all before one fig.* auf der ganzen Linie siegen; **5.** *a.* ~ *away* (*od. off*) *fig.* fort-, mitreißen (*Flut etc.*): **~ along with one** *Zuhörer* mitreißen; **~ s.o. off his feet** j-s Herz im Sturm erobern; **6.** *a.* **~ away** *Hindernis etc.* (aus dem Weg) räumen, *e-m Übelstand etc.* abhelfen, aufräumen mit: **~ aside** *et.* abtun, beiseite schieben; **~ off** *j-n* hinwegraffen (*Tod, Krankheit*); **7.** *mit der Hand* streichen über (*acc.*); **8.** *Geld* einstreichen: **~ the board** *Kartenspiel u. fig.* alles gewinnen; **9.** a) *Gebiet* durch'streifen, b) *Horizont etc.* absuchen (*a.* ✕ *mit Scheinwerfern, Radar*) (**for** nach), c) hingleiten über (*acc.*) (*Blick etc.*); **10.** ✕ *mit MG-Feuer* bestreichen; **11.** ♪ *Saiten, Tasten* (be)rühren, schlagen, (hin)gleiten über (*acc.*); **II** *v/i.* [*irr.*] **12.** kehren, fegen; **13.** fegen, stürmen, jagen (*Wind, Regen etc.*, *a. Krieg, Heer*), fluten (*Wasser, Truppen etc.*); *durchs Land* gehen (*Epidemie etc.*): **~ along** (**down, over**) entlang- *od.* einherfegen (herniederfegen, darüber hinfegen) *etc.*; **~ down on** sich (herab)stürzen auf (*acc.*); **fear swept over him** Furcht überkam ihn; **14.** maje'stätisch ein'herschreiten: **she swept from the room** sie rauschte aus dem Zimmer; **15.** in weitem Bogen gleiten; **16.** sich da'hinziehen (*Küste, Straße etc.*); **17.** (**for**) ⚓ (nach *et.*) dreggen; ✕ *Minen* suchen, räumen; **III** *s.* **18.** Kehren *n*, Fegen *n*: **give s.th. a** ~ *et.* kehren; **make a clean** ~ (**of**) *fig.* gründlich aufräumen (mit); **19.** *mst pl.* Müll *m*; **20.** *bsd. Brit.* Schornsteinfeger *m*; **21.** Da'hinfegen *n*, (Da'hin)Stürmen *n* (*des Windes etc.*); **22.** schwungvolle (Hand*etc.*)Bewegung; Schwung *m* (*e-r Sense, Waffe etc.*); (Ruder)Schlag *m*; **23.** *fig.* Reichweite *f*, Bereich *m*, Spielraum *m*; weiter (geistiger) Hori'zont; **24.** Schwung *m*, Bogen *m* (*Straße etc.*); **25.** ausgedehnte Strecke, weite Fläche; **26.** Auffahrt *f* zu e-m Haus; **27.** Ziehstange *f*, Schwengel *m* (*Brunnen*); **28.** ⚓ langes Ruder; **29.** ♪ Tusch *m*; **30.** *Radar:* Abtaststrahl *m*; **31.** *Kartenspiel:* Gewinn *m* aller Stiche *od.* Karten; **IV** *adj.* □ **32.** ⚡ Kipp...

'**sweep·back** ✈ **I** *s.* Pfeilform *f*; **II** *adj.* pfeilförmig, Pfeil...

sweep·er ['swiːpə] *s.* **1.** (Straßen-) Kehrer *m*, Feger(in); **2.** 'Kehrma,schine *f*; **3.** ⚓ Such-, Räumboot *n*; **4.** *Fußball:* Ausputzer *m*; '**sweep·ing** [-pɪŋ] **I** *adj.* □ **1.** kehrend, Kehr...; **2.** sausend, stürmisch (*Wind etc.*); **3.** ausgedehnt; **4.** schwungvoll (*a. fig. mitreißend*); **5.** 'durchschlagend, über'wältigend (*Sieg, Erfolg*); **6.** 'durchgreifend, radi'kal: **~ changes; 7.** um'fassend, weit reichend, *a.* (zu) stark verallgemeinernd, summarisch: **~ statement; II** *s.* **8.** *pl.* a) → **sweep** 19, b) *fig. contp.* Abschaum *m.*

sweep| **net** *s.* **1.** ⚓ Schleppnetz *n*; **2.** Schmetterlingsnetz *n*; '**~·stake** *s. sport* **1.** *sg. od. pl.* a) *Pferderennen, dessen Dotierung rein aus Nenngeldern besteht*, b) *aus den Nenngeldern gebildete Dotierung*; **2.** *Lotterie, deren Gewinne sich ausschließlich aus den Einsätzen zs.-setzen*; **3.** *fig.* Rennen *n*, Kampf *m.*

sweet [swiːt] **I** *adj.* □ **1.** süß (*im Geschmack*); **2.** süß, lieblich (duftend): **be ~ with** duften nach; **3.** frisch (*Butter, Fleisch, Milch*); **4.** Frisch..., Süß...: ~ **water; 5.** süß, lieblich (*Musik, Stimme*), **6.** süß, angenehm: **~ dreams; ~ sleep; 7.** süß, lieb: **~ face; at her own ~ will** (ganz) nach ihrem Köpfchen; **~ seventeen** II; **8.** (**to** zu *od.* gegenüber *j-m*) lieb, nett, freundlich, sanft: **~ na-**

ture *od.* temper; be **~ on s.o.** in j-n verliebt sein; **9.** F ,süß', reizend, goldig (*alle a. iro.*): **what a ~ dress!; 10.** leicht, bequem; glatt, ruhig; **11.** ⚛ a) säurefrei (*Mineralien*), b) schwefelfrei, süß (*bsd. Benzin, Rohöl*); **12.** ♪ nicht sauer (*Boden*); **13.** *Jazz:* ,sweet', melodi'ös; **II** *s.* **14.** Süße *f*; **15.** *Brit.* a) Bon-'bon *m, n*, Süßigkeit *f*, b) *oft pl.* Nachtisch *m*, Süßspeise *f*; **16.** *mst pl.* fig. Freude *f*, Annehmlichkeit *f*: **the ~(s) of life**; → **sour** 7; **17.** *mst in der Anrede:* Liebling *m*, Süße(r *m*) *f*; ,**~-and-'sour** *adj.* süßsauer (*Soße etc.*); '**~·bread** *s.* Bries *n*; ~ **chest·nut** *s.* 'Edelka,stanie *f*; ~ **corn** *s.* **1.** ♀ Zuckermais *m*; **2.** grüne Maiskolben *pl.*

sweet·en ['swiːtn] **I** *v/t.* **1.** süßen; **2.** *fig.* versüßen, angenehm(er) machen; **II** *v/i.* **3.** süß(er) werden; **4.** milder *od.* sanfter werden; '**sweet·en·er** [-nə] *s.* Süßstoff *m.*

'**sweet**|**·heart** *s.* Liebste(r *m*) *f*, Schatz *m*; ~ **herbs** *s. pl.* Küchen-, Gewürzkräuter *pl.*

sweet·ie ['swiːtɪ] *s.* **1.** F Schätzchen *n*, ,Süße' *f*; **2.** *Brit.* Bon'bon *m, n, pl. a.* Süßigkeiten *pl.*

sweet·ing ['swiːtɪŋ] *s.* ♀ Jo'hannisapfel *m*, Süßling *m.*

sweet·ish ['swiːtɪʃ] *adj.* süßlich.

'**sweet**|**·meat** *s.* Lecke'rei *f*, Bon'bon *m, n*; ,**~-'na·tured** → **sweet** 8.

sweet·ness ['swiːtnɪs] *s.* **1.** Süße *f*, Süßigkeit *f*; **2.** süßer Duft; **3.** Frische *f*; **4.** *fig. et.* Angenehmes, Annehmlichkeit *f*, das Süße; **5.** Freundlichkeit *f*, Liebenswürdigkeit *f.*

sweet| **oil** *s.* O'livenöl *n*; ~ **pea** *s.* ♀ Gartenwicke *f*; ~ **po·ta·to** *s.* ♀ 'Süßkar,toffel *f*, Ba'tate *f*; ,**~-'scent·ed** *adj. bsd.* ♀ wohlriechend, duftend; '**~·shop** *s. bsd. Brit.* Süßwarengeschäft *n*; '**~·talk** *v/t. Am.* F *j-m* schmeicheln; ,**~-'tempered** *adj.* sanft-, gutmütig; ~ **tooth** *s.* F: **she has a ~** sie ist gern Süßigkeiten; ~ **wil·liam** *s.* ♀ Stu'dentennelke *f.*

sweet·y ['swiːtɪ] → **sweetie**.

swell [swel] **I** *v/i.* [*irr.*] **1.** *a.* **~ up, ~ out** (an-, auf)schwellen (**into, to** zu), dick werden; **2.** sich aufblasen *od.* -blähen (*a. fig.*); **3.** anschwellen, (an)steigen (*Wasser etc., a. fig. Preise, Anzahl etc.*); **4.** sich wölben: a) ansteigen (*Land etc.*), b) sich ausbauchen *od.* bauschen (*Mauerwerk, Möbel etc.*), c) ⚓ sich blähen (*Segel*); **5.** her'vorbrechen (*Quelle, Tränen*); **6.** *bsd.* ♪ a) anschwellen (**into** zu), b) (an- u. ab-) schwellen (*Ton, Orgel etc.*); **7.** *fig.* bersten (wollen) (**with** vor): **his heart ~s with indignation; 8.** aufwallen, sich steigern (**into** zu) (*Gefühl*); **II** *v/t.* [*irr.*] **9.** ~ **up, ~ out** *a.* ♪ *u. fig.* Buch *etc.* anschwellen lassen; **10.** aufblasen, -blähen, -treiben; **11.** *fig.* aufblähen (**with** vor): **~ed (with pride)** stolzgeschwellt; **III** *s.* **12.** (An)Schwellen *n*; **13.** Schwellung *f*; **14.** ⚓ Dünung *f*; **15.** Wölbung *f*, Ausbauchung *f*; **16.** kleine Anhöhe, sanfte Steigung; **17.** *fig.* Anschwellen *n*, -wachsen *n*, (An)Steigen *n*; **18.** ♪ a) An- (u. Ab)Schwellen *n*, b) Schwellzeichen *n*, c) Schwellwerk *n* (*Orgel etc.*); **19.** F a) ,hohes Tier', ,Größe' *f*, b) ,feiner Pinkel', c) ,Ka'none' *f*, ,Mordskerl' *m* (**at** in dat.); **IV** *adj.* **20.** (*a. int.*) F ,prima', ,bombig'; **21.** F (tod)schick, ,piekfein', feu'dal; **swelled** [-ld] *adj.* **1.** (an)geschwollen, aufgebläht: ~ **head** F *fig.* Aufgeblasenheit *f*; **2.** geschweift (*Möbel*); '**swell·ing** [-lɪŋ] **I** *s.* **1.** (*a. fig. u.* ♪

An)Schwellen *n*; **2.** ❀ Schwellung *f*, Geschwulst *f*, *a.* Beule *f*: **hunger ~** Hungerödem *n*; **3.** Wölbung *f*: a) Erhöhung *f*, b) △ Ausbauchung *f*, ⚙ Schweifung *f*; **II** *adj.* □ **4.** (an)schwellend; **5.** ,geschwollen' (*Stil etc.*).

swell| **man·u·al** *s.* ♪ 'Schwellmanu,al *n* (*Orgel*); ~ **mob** *s. sl.* die Hochstapler *pl.*; ~ **or·gan** *s.* ♪ Schwellwerk *n.*

swel·ter ['sweltə] **I** *v/i.* **1.** vor Hitze (fast) 'umkommen *od.* verschmachten; **2.** in Schweiß gebadet sein; **3.** (vor Hitze) kochen (*Stadt etc.*); **II** *s.* **4.** drückende Hitze, Schwüle *f*; **5.** F *fig.* Hexenkessel *m*; '**swel·ter·ing** [-tərɪŋ], '**swel·try** [-trɪ] *adj.* **1.** vor Hitze vergehend, verschmachtend; **2.** in Schweiß gebadet; **3.** drückend, schwül.

swept [swept] *pret. u. p.p. von* **sweep**; '**~-back wing** → **swept wing**; ~ **volume** *s. mot.* Hubraum *m*; ~ **wing** *s.* ✈ Pfeilflügel *m.*

swerve [swɜːv] **I** *v/i.* **1.** ausbrechen (*Auto, Pferd*); **2.** *mot.* das Steuer he-'rumreißen; **3.** ausweichen; **4.** schwenken (*Straße*); **5.** *fig.* abweichen (**from** von); **II** *v/t.* **6.** *sport* Ball anschneiden; **7.** *fig. j-n* abbringen (**from** von); **III** *s.* **8.** Ausweichbewegung *f*, *mot.* Schlenker *m.*

swift [swɪft] **I** *adj.* □ **1.** *allg.* schnell, rasch; **2.** flüchtig (*Zeit, Stunde etc.*); **3.** geschwind, eilig; **4.** flink, hurtig, *a.* geschickt: **a ~ worker; ~ wit** rasche Auffassungsgabe; **5.** rasch, schnell bereit: **~ to anger** jähzornig; **~ to take offence** leicht beleidigt; **II** *adv.* **6.** *mst poet. od.* in *Zssgn* schnell, geschwind, rasch; **III** *s.* **7.** *orn.* (*bsd.* Mauer)Segler *m*; **8.** *e-e brit.* Taubenrasse; **9.** *zo.* → **newt**; **10.** ⚙ Haspel *f*; '**swift-'foot·ed** *adj.* schnellfüßig, flink; '**swift·ness** [-nɪs] *s.* Schnelligkeit *f.*

swig [swɪg] F **I** *v/t.* *Getränk* ,hin'unterkippen'; **II** *v/i.* e-n kräftigen Schluck nehmen (**at** aus); **III** *s.* (kräftiger) Schluck.

swill [swɪl] **I** *v/t.* **1.** *bsd. Brit.* (ab)spülen: ~ **out** ausspülen; **2.** *Bier etc.* ,saufen'; **II** *v/i.* **3.** ,saufen'; **III** *s.* **4.** (Ab)Spülen *n*; **5.** Schweinetrank *m*, -futter *n*; **6.** Spülicht *n* (*a. fig. contp.*); **7.** *fig. contp.* a) ,Gesöff' *n*, b) ,Saufraß' *m.*

swim [swɪm] **I** *v/i.* [*irr.*] **1.** schwimmen; **2.** schwimmen (*Gegenstand*), treiben; **3.** schweben, (sanft) gleiten; **4.** a) schwimmen (**in** in dat.), b) über-'schwemmt sein, 'überfließen (**with** von): **his eyes were ~ming with tears** s-e Augen schwammen in Tränen; ~ **in** *fig.* schwimmen in (*Geld etc.*); **5.** (ver-) schwimmen (**before one's eyes** vor den Augen): **my head ~s** mir ist schwind(e)lig; **II** *v/t.* [*irr.*] **6.** *Strecke etc.* schwimmen, *Gewässer* durch-'schwimmen; **7.** *Person, Pferd etc.* schwimmen lassen; **8.** F mit *j-m* um die Wette schwimmen; **III** *s.* **9.** Schwimmen *n*, Bad *n*: **go for a ~** schwimmen gehen; **be in (out of) the ~** F *fig.* a) (nicht) auf dem Laufenden sein, b) (nicht) mithalten können; **10.** *Angelsport:* tiefe *u.* fischreiche Stelle (*e-s Flusses*); **11.** Schwindel(anfall) *m*; '**swim·mer** [-mə] *s.* **1.** Schwimmer(in); **2.** *zo.* 'Schwimmor,gan *n.*

swim·mer·et ['swɪmərət] *s. zo.* Schwimmfuß *m* (*Krebs*).

swim·ming ['swɪmɪŋ] **I** *s.* **1.** Schwimmen *n*; **2.** ~ **of the head** Schwindelgefühl *n*; **II** *adj.* □ **3.** schwimmend; **~·ly** adv. schwimmend; **3.** Schwimm...; ~ **bath** *s.* Schwimmbad *n*; ~ **blad·der** *s. zo.* Schwimmblase *f.*

swim·ming·ly ['swɪmɪŋlɪ] *adv. fig.* glatt, reibungslos.
swim·ming| pool *s.* **1.** Schwimmbecken *n*, Schwimmingpool *m*; **2.** Schwimmbad *n*: a) Freibad *n*, b) *mst* **indoor** ~ Hallenbad *n*; ~ **trunks** *s. pl.* Badehose *f*.
swin·dle ['swɪndl] **I** *v/i.* **1.** betrügen, mogeln; **II** *v/t.* **2.** *j-n* beschwindeln, betrügen (*out of s.th.* um et.); **3.** *et.* erschwindeln (*out of s.o.* von j-m); **III** *s.* **4.** Schwindel *m*, Betrug *m*; '**swin·dler** [-lə] *s.* Schwindler(in), Betrüger(in).
swine [swaɪn] *pl.* **swine** *s. zo.*, *mst* ♂, *poet. od. obs.* Schwein *n* (*a. fig. contp.*); ~ **fe·ver** *s. vet.* Schweinepest *f*; '**~·herd** *s. poet.* Schweinehirt *m*; '**~·pox** *s.* **1.** ✿ *hist.* Wasserpocken *pl.*; **2.** *vet.* Schweinepocken *pl.*
swing [swɪŋ] **I** *v/t.* [*irr.*] **1.** Stock, Keule, Lasso etc. schwingen; **2.** Glocke etc. schwingen, (hin- u. her)schwenken: ~ **one's arms** mit den Armen schlenkern; ~ **s.th. about** et. (im Kreis) herumschwenken; **3.** Beine etc. baumeln lassen, a. Tür etc. pendeln lassen; Hängematte etc. aufhängen (*from* an dat.): ~ **open** (*to*) Tor auf-(zu)stoßen; **4.** *j-n* in e-r Schaukel schaukeln; **5.** *auf die Schulter etc.* (hoch)schwingen; **6.** ✕ (~ *in od.* **out** ein- od. aus)schwenken lassen; **7.** ♣ (rund)schwojen; **8.** *bsd. Am.* F a) et. ,schaukeln', ,hinkriegen', b) Wähler her'umkriegen; **II** *v/i.* [*irr.*] **9.** (hin- u. her)schwingen, pendeln, ausschlagen (*Pendel, Zeiger*): ~ **into motion** in Schwung *od.* Gang kommen; **10.** schweben, baumeln (*from* an dat.) (*Glocke etc.*); **11.** (sich) schaukeln; **12.** F ,baumeln' (*gehängt werden*): **he must** ~ **for it**; **13.** sich (*in den Angeln*) drehen (*Tür etc.*): ~ **open** (*to*) sich (auf-zu)schlagen); ~ **round** a) sich ruckartig umdrehen, b) sich drehen (*Wind etc.*), c) *fig.* umschlagen (*öffentliche Meinung etc.*); **14.** ♣ schwojen; **15.** schwenken, mit schwungvollen Bewegungen gehen, (flott) marschieren: ~ **into line** ✕ einschwenken; **16.** *a.* ~ **it** *sl.* a) ,toll leben', b) ,auf den Putz hauen'; **17.** schwanken; **18.** (zum Schlag) ausholen: ~ **at** nach *j-m* schlagen; **19.** ♪ swingen; **III** *s.* **20.** (Hin- u. Her)Schwingen *n*, Pendeln *n*, Schwingung *f*; ✿ Ausschlag *m* (*e-s Pendels od. Zeigers*): **the** ~ **of the pendulum** der Pendelschlag (*a. fig. od. pol.*); **free** ~ Bewegungsfreiheit *f*, Spielraum *m* (*a. fig.*); **in full** ~ in vollem Gange, im Schwung; **give full** ~ **to** a) e-r Sache freien Lauf lassen, b) *j-m* freie Hand lassen; **21.** Schaukeln *n*; **22.** a) Schwung *m* beim Gehen, Skilauf etc., schwingender Gang, Schlenkern *n*, b) ♪ etc. Schwung *m*, (schwingender) Rhythmus: **go with a** ~ a) Schwung haben, b) *fig.* wie am Schnürchen gehen; **23.** ♪ Swing *m* (*Jazz*); **24.** Schaukel *f*: **lose on the** ~**s what you make on the roundabouts** *fig.* genau so weit sein wie am Anfang; **you make up on the** ~**s what you lose on the roundabouts** was man hier verliert, macht man dort wieder wett; **25.** ↑ a) Swing *m*, Spielraum *m* für Kre'ditgewährung, b) *Am.* F Konjunk'turperi̯ode *f*; **26.** *Boxen:* Schwinger *m*; **27.** Schwenkung *f*; '**~·back** *s.* **1.** *phot.* Einstellscheibe *f*; **2.** *fig.* (*to*) Rückkehr *f* (zu), Rückfall *m* (in acc.); '**~·boat** *s.* Schiffsschaukel *f*; ~ **bridge** *s.* Drehbrücke *f*; ~ **cred·it** *s.* ↑ 'Swingkre̩dit *m*; ~ **door** *s.* Pendeltür *f*.
swinge [swɪndʒ] *v/t. obs.* 'durchprügeln, (aus)peitschen; '**swinge·ing** [-dʒɪŋ]

adj. fig. drastisch, ex'trem.
swing·er ['swɪŋə] *s. sl.* lebenslustige Per'son.
swing·ing ['swɪŋɪŋ] *adj.* □ **1.** schwingend, schaukelnd, pendelnd, Schwing...; **2.** Schwenk...; **3.** rhythmisch, schwungvoll; **4.** lebenslustig; **5.** schwankend: ~ **temperature** ✗ Temperaturschwankungen *pl.*
swin·gle ['swɪŋgl] **I** *s.* ✿ (Flachs-, Hanf-) Schwinge *f*; **II** *Flachs, Hanf* schwingeln; '**~·tree** *s.* Ortscheit *n*, Wagenschwengel *m*.
'**swing|-out** *adj.* ✿ ausschwenkbar; ~ **seat** *s.* Hollywoodschaukel *f*; ~ **shift** *s. Am.* ↑ Spätschicht *f*; '**~·wing** *s.* ✈ 1. Schwenkflügel *m*; **2.** Schwenkflügler *m*.
swin·ish ['swaɪnɪʃ] *adj.* □ schweinisch, säuisch.
swipe [swaɪp] **I** *v/i.* **1.** dreinschlagen, hauen; *sport* aus vollem Arm schlagen; **II** *v/t.* **2.** (hart) schlagen; **3.** *sl.* ,klauen', stehlen; **III** *s.* **4.** *bsd. sport* harter Schlag, Hieb *m*; **5.** *pl. sl.* Dünnbier *n*.
swirl [swɜːl] **I** *v/i.* **1.** wirbeln (*Wasser, a. fig. Kopf*), e-n Strudel bilden; **2.** (herum)wirbeln; **II** *v/t.* **3.** *et.* her'umwirbeln; **III** *s.* **4.** Wirbel *m*, Strudel *m*; **5.** *Am.* (Haar)Wirbel *m*; **6.** Wirbel(n *n*) *m* (*Drehbewegung*).
swish [swɪʃ] **I** *v/i.* **1.** schwirren, zischen, sausen; **2.** rascheln (*Seide*); **II** *v/t.* **3.** sausen *od.* schwirren lassen; **4.** *Brit.* 'durchprügeln; **III** *s.* **5.** Sausen *n*, Zischen *n*; **6.** Rascheln *n*; **7.** *Brit.* (Ruten-)Streich *m*, Peitschenhieb *m*; **IV** *adj.* **8.** *Brit. sl.* ,(tod)schick'.
Swiss [swɪs] **I** *pl.* **Swiss** *s.* **1.** Schweizer (-in); **2.** ✿ ♀, *a.* ~ **muslin** 'Schweizermusse̩,lin *m* (*Stoff*); **II** *adj.* **3.** schweizerisch, Schweizer: ~ **German** Schweizerdeutsch *n*; ~ **Guard** *R.C.* a) Schweizergarde *f*, b) Schweizer *m*; ~ **roll** Biskuitrolle *f*.
switch [swɪtʃ] **I** *s.* **1.** Gerte *f*, Rute *f*; **2.** (Ruten)Streich *m*; **3.** falscher Zopf; **4.** ⚡, ✿ Schalter *m*; **5.** ☙ Weiche *f*; **6.** (*to*) *fig.* a) 'Umstellung *f* (auf acc.), Wechsel *m* (zu), b) Verwandlung *f* (in acc.), c) Vertauschung *f*; **II** *v/t.* **7.** peitschen; **8.** zucken mit; **9.** ⚡, ✿ ('um)schalten: ~ **on** einschalten, *Licht* anschalten, *teleph. j-n* verbinden; ~ **off** *Gerät etc.* ab-, ausschalten, abstellen, *teleph. j-n* trennen; ~ **to** anschließen an (acc.); **10.** ☙ a) *Zug* rangieren, b) *Waggons* 'umstellen; **11.** *fig.* Produktion etc. 'umstellen, Methode, Thema etc. wechseln, Gedanken, Gespräch 'überleiten (*to* auf acc.); **III** *v/i.* **12.** ☙ rangieren; **13.** ⚡, ✿ (*a.* ~ **over** 'um)schalten; ~ **off** abschalten, *teleph.* trennen; **14.** *fig.* 'umstellen: ~ (**off** *od.* **over**) **to** übergehen zu, sich umstellen auf (acc.), *univ. etc.* umsatteln auf (acc.); ~ **back** *s. Brit.* **1.** a. ~ **road** Serpen'tinenstraße *f*; **2.** Achterbahn *f*; '**~·blade knife** *s.* Schnappmesser *n*; '**~·board** *s.* ⚡ **1.** Schaltbrett *n*, -tafel *f*; ☎ 'Tele'fon̩Zen̩,trale *f*, Vermittlung *f*: ~ **operator** Telefonist(in); ~ **box** *s.* **1.** ⚡ Schaltkasten *m*; **2.** ☙ Stellwerk *n*.
switch·e·roo [,swɪtʃə'ruː] *s. Am. sl.* **1.** unerwartete Wendung; **2.** → **switch** 6 b u. c.
switch·ing ['swɪtʃɪŋ] **I** *s.* **1.** ⚡, ✿ ('Um-) Schalten *n*; ~**on** Einschalten; ~**off** Ab-, Ausschalten; **2.** ☙ Rangieren *n*; **II** *adj.* **3.** ⚡, ✿ (Um)Schalt...; **4.** ☙ Rangier...
'**switch|,o·ver** *s.* 'Umstellung *f* (*to* auf acc.), Wechsel *m* (*to* zu); ~ **plug** *s.* ⚡, ✿ Schaltstöpsel *m*; '**~·yard** *s. Am.*

Rangier-, Verschiebebahnhof *m*.
swiv·el ['swɪvl] **I** *s.* Drehzapfen *m*, -ring *m*, -gelenk *n*, (✿ Ketten)Wirbel *m*; **II** *v/t.* (*auf e-m Zapfen etc.*) drehen *od.* schwenken; **III** *v/i.* sich drehen; **IV** *adj.* dreh-, schwenkbar, Dreh..., Schwenk...; ~ **bridge** *s.* ✿ Drehbrücke *f*; ~ **chair** *s.* Drehstuhl *m*; ~ **joint** *s.* ✿ Drehgelenk *n*.
swiz·zle stick ['swɪzl] *s.* Sektquirl *m*.
swol·len ['swəʊlən] **I** *p.p. von* **swell**; **II** *adj.* ✗ geschwollen (*a. fig.*): ~**headed** aufgeblasen.
swoon [swuːn] **I** *v/i.* **1.** *oft* ~ **away** in Ohnmacht fallen (*with* vor dat.); **2.** schwärmen (*over* für); **II** *s.* **3.** Ohnmacht(sanfall *m*) *f*.
swoop [swuːp] **I** *v/i.* **1.** *oft* ~ **down** (**[up]on**, **at**) her'abstoßen, sich stürzen (auf acc.), *fig.* zuschlagen, herfallen (über acc.); **II** *v/t.* **2.** *mst* ~ **up** F packen, ,schnappen'; **III** *s.* **3.** Her'abstoßen *n* (*Raubvogel*); **4.** *fig.* a) 'Überfall *m*, b) Razzia *f*; **5.** **at one** (**fell**) ~ mit 'einem Schlag.
swop [swɒp] → **swap**.
sword [sɔːd] *s.* Schwert *n* (*a. fig.*); Säbel *m*, Degen *m*; *allg.* Waffe *f*: **draw** (**sheathe**) **the** ~ das Schwert ziehen (in die Scheide stecken), *fig.* den Kampf beginnen (beenden); **put to the** ~ über die Klinge springen lassen; → **cross** 11, **measure** 16; ~ **belt** *s.* **1.** Schwertgehenk *n*; **2.** ✕ Degenkoppel *n*; ~ **cane** *s.* Stockdegen *m*; ~ **dance** *s.* Schwert(er)tanz *m*; '**~·fish** *s.* Schwertfisch *m*; ~ **knot** *s.* ✕ Degen-, Säbelquaste *f*; ~ **lil·y** ♀ Schwertel *m*, Siegwurz *f*; '**~·play** *s.* **1.** (Degen-, Säbel)Kampf *m*; **2.** Fechtkunst *f*; **3.** *fig.* Gefecht *n*, Du'ell *n*.
swords·man ['sɔːdzmən] *s.* [*irr.*] Fechter *m*; Kämpfer *m*; '**swords·man·ship** [-ʃɪp] *s.* Fechtkunst *f*.
'**sword·stick** → **sword cane**.
swore [swɔː] *pret. von* **swear**; **sworn** [swɔːn] **I** *p.p. von* **swear**; **II** *adj.* **1.** ⚖ (gerichtlich) vereidigt, beeidigt: ~ **expert**; **2.** eidlich: ~ **statement**; **3.** geschworen (*Gegner*): ~ **enemies** Todfeinde; **4.** verschworen (*Freunde*).
swot [swɒt] *ped. Brit.* F **I** *v/i.* **1.** büffeln, pauken; **II** *v/t.* **2.** *mst* ~ **up** *Lehrstoff* pauken, büffeln; **III** *s.* **3.** Büffler(in), Streber(in); **4.** Büffe'lei *f*, Pauke'rei *f*; *weitS.* hartes Stück Arbeit.
swum [swʌm] *p.p. von* **swim**.
swung [swʌŋ] *pret. u. p.p. von* **swing**.
syb·a·rite ['sɪbəraɪt] *s. fig.* Syba'rit *m*, Genussmensch *m*; **syb·a·rit·ic** [,sɪbə'rɪtɪk] *adj.* (□ ~**ally**) syba'ritisch, genusssüchtig; '**syb·a·rit·ism** [-rɪtɪzəm] *s.* Genusssucht *f*.
syc·a·more ['sɪkəmɔː] *s.* ♀ **1.** *Am.* Pla'tane *f*; **2.** *a.* ~ **maple** *Brit.* Bergahorn *m*; **3.** Syko'more *f*, Maulbeerfeigenbaum *m*.
syc·o·phan·cy ['sɪkəfənsɪ] *s.* Krieche'rei *f*, Speichellecke'rei *f*; '**syc·o·phant** [-nt] *s.* Schmeichler *m*, Kriecher *m*, Speichellecker *m*; **syc·o·phan·tic** [,sɪkəʊ'fæntɪk] *adj.* (□ ~**ally**) schmeichlerisch, kriecherisch.
syl·la·bar·y ['sɪləbərɪ] *s.* 'Silbenta̩belle *f*; '**syl·la·bi** [-baɪ] *pl. von* **syllabus**.
syl·lab·ic [sɪ'læbɪk] *adj.* (□ ~**ally**) **1.** syl'labisch (*a.* ♪), Silben...: ~ **accent**; **2.** Silben bildend, silbisch; **3.** *in Zssgn* ...silbig; **syl·lab·i·cate** [-keɪt], **syl·lab·i·fy** [-ɪfaɪ], **syl·la·bize** ['sɪləbaɪz] *v/t. ling.* syllabieren, in Silben teilen, Silbe für Silbe (aus)sprechen.
syl·la·ble ['sɪləbl] **I** *s.* **1.** *ling.* Silbe *f*: **not**

S

a ~ *fig.* keine Silbe *od.* kein Sterbenswörtchen *sagen*; **2.** ♪ Tonsilbe *f*; **II** *v/t.* **3.** → *syllabicate*; **'syl·la·bled** [-ld] *adj.* ...silbig.

syl·la·bus ['sɪləbəs] *pl.* **-bi** [-baɪ] *s.* **1.** Auszug *m*, Abriss *m*; zs.-fassende Inhaltsangabe; **2.** (*bsd.* Vorlesungs)Verzeichnis *n*; Lehr-, 'Unterrichtsplan *m*; **3.** ⚖ Kom'pendium *n von richtungweisenden Entscheidungen*; **4.** *R.C.* Syllabus *m*.

syl·lep·sis [sɪ'lepsɪs] *s.* ling. Syl'lepsis, Syl'lepse *f*.

syl·lo·gism ['sɪlədʒɪzəm] *s.* phls. Syllo-'gismus *m*, (Vernunft)Schluss *m*; **'syl·lo·gize** [-dʒaɪz] *v/i.* syllogisieren, folgerichtig denken.

sylph [sɪlf] *s.* **1.** myth. Sylphe *m*, Luftgeist *m*; **2.** fig. Syl'phide *f*, gra'ziles Mädchen; **'sylph·ish** [-fɪʃ], **'sylph·like** [-laɪk], **'sylph·y** [-fɪ] *adj.* sylphenhaft, gra'zil.

syl·van ['sɪlvən] *adj. poet.* waldig, Wald...

sym·bi·o·sis [ˌsɪmbɪ'əʊsɪs] *s.* biol. u. fig. Symbi'ose *f*; **'sym·bi·ot·ic** [-ɪ'ɒtɪk] *adj.* (□ *~ally*) biol. symbi'o(n)tisch.

sym·bol ['sɪmbl] *s.* **1.** Sym'bol *n*, Sinnbild *n*, Zeichen *n*; **2.** typ., Computer: Sonderzeichen *n*; **sym·bol·ic, symbol·i·cal** [sɪm'bɒlɪk(l)] *adj.* □ sym-'bolisch, sinnbildlich (*of* für): *be ~ of s.th.* et. versinnbildlichen; **sym·bol·ics** [sɪm'bɒlɪks] *s. pl. mst sg. konstr.* **1.** Studium *n* alter Sym'bole; **2.** eccl. Sym'bolik *f*; **'sym·bol·ism** [-bəlɪzəm] *s.* **1.** Sym'bolik *f* (*a. eccl.*), sym'bolische Darstellung; ♣ Forma'lismus *m*; sym'bolische Bedeutung; **3.** coll. Sym-'bole *pl.*; **4.** *paint. etc.* Symbo'lismus *m*; **'sym·bol·ize** [-bəlaɪz] *v/t.* **1.** symbolisieren: a) versinnbildlichen, b) sinnbildlich darstellen; **2.** sym'bolisch auffassen.

sym·met·ric, sym·met·ri·cal [sɪ'metrɪk(l)] *adj.* □ sym'metrisch, ebenmäßig; **~ axis** ♣ Symmetrieachse *f*; **sym·me·trize** ['sɪmɪtraɪz] *v/t.* sym'metrisch machen; **sym·me·try** ['sɪmɪtrɪ] *s.* Symme'trie *f* (*a. fig.* Ebenmaß).

sym·pa·thet·ic [ˌsɪmpə'θetɪk] *adj.* (□ *~ally*) **1.** mitfühlend, teilnehmend: *~ strike* Sympathiestreik *m*; **2.** einfühlend, verständnisvoll; **3.** gleich gesinnt, geistesverwandt, kongeni'al; **4.** sym'pathisch; **5.** F wohlwollend (*to[ward]*) gegen['über]); **6.** sympa'thetisch (*Kur, Tinte etc.*); **7.** ✳, physiol. sym'pathisch (*Nervensystem etc.*); → 9a; **8.** ♪, phys. mitschwingend: *~ vibration* Sympathieschwingung *f*; **II** *s.* **9.** a) *a.* ~ *nerve* physiol. Sym'pathikus(nerv) *m*, b) Sym'pathikussys,tem *n*.

sym·pa·thize ['sɪmpəθaɪz] *v/i.* **1.** (*with*) a) sympathisieren (mit), gleich gesinnt sein (*dat.*), b) über'einstimmen (mit), wohlwollend gegen'überstehen (*dat.*), c) mitfühlen (mit); **2.** sein Mitgefühl *od.* Beileid ausdrücken (*with dat.*); **3.** ✳ in Mitleidenschaft gezogen werden (*with* von); **'sym·pa·thiz·er** [-zə] *s.* j-d, der *mit j-m od.* e-r Sache sympathisiert, Anhänger(in), *bsd. pol.* Sympa-thi'sant(in); **'sym·pa·thy** [-θɪ] *s.* **1.** Sympa'thie *f*, Zuneigung *f* (*for* für): ~ *strike* Sympathiestreik *m*; **2.** Gleichgestimmtheit *f*; **3.** Mitleid *n*, -gefühl *n* (*with* mit, *for* für): *feel ~ for* (*od. with*) Mitleid haben mit *j-m*, Anteil nehmen an *e-r* Sache; **4.** *pl.* (An)Teilnahme *f*, Beileid *n*: *letter of ~* Beileidsschreiben *n*; *offer one's sympathies to s.o.* *j-m* sein Beileid bezeigen, j-m kondolieren; **5.** ✳ Mitleidenschaft *f*; **6.** Wohlwollen

n, Zustimmung *f*; **7.** Über'einstimmung *f*, Einklang *m*; **8.** biol., psych. Sympa-'thie *f*, Wechselwirkung *f*.

sym·phon·ic [sɪm'fɒnɪk] *adj.* (□ *~ally*) sin'fonisch, sym'phonisch, Sinfonie..., Symphonie...: ~ *poem* ♪ symphonische Dichtung; **sym'pho·ni·ous** [-'fəʊnjəs] *adj.* har'monisch (*a. fig.*); **sym·pho·nist** ['sɪmfənɪst] *s.* ♪ Sin'foniker *m*, Sym'phoniker *m*; **sym·pho·ny** ['sɪmfənɪ] **I** *s.* **1.** ♪ Sinfo'nie *f*, Sympho'nie *f*; **2.** fig. (Farben- etc.)Sympho'nie *f*, (*a. häusliche etc.*) Harmo'nie, Zs.-klang *m*; **II** *adj.* **3.** Sinfonie..., Symphonie...: ~ *orchestra*.

sym·po·si·um [sɪm'pəʊzjəm] *pl.* **-si·a** [-zjə] *s.* **1.** antiq. Sym'posion *n*: a) Gastmahl *n*, b) *Titel philosophischer Dialoge*; **2.** fig. Sammlung *f* von Beiträgen (*über e-e Streitfrage*); **3.** Sym'posium *n*, (Fach)Tagung *f*.

symp·tom ['sɪmptəm] *s.* ✳ *u. fig.* Symp-'tom *n* (*of* für, von), (An)Zeichen *n*; **symp·to·mat·ic, symp·to·mat·i·cal** [ˌsɪmptə'mætɪk(l)] *adj.* □ *bsd.* ✳ sympto'matisch (*a. fig. bezeichnend*) (*of* für); **symp·tom·a·tol·o·gy** [ˌsɪmptə-mə'tɒlədʒɪ] *s.* ✳ Symptomatolo'gie *f*.

syn- [sɪn] *in Zssgn* mit, zusammen.

syn·a·gogue ['sɪnəgɒg] *s.* eccl. Syna'goge *f*.

syn·a·l(o)e·pha [ˌsɪnə'liːfə] *s.* ling. Syna'löphe *f*, Verschleifung *f*.

syn·an·ther·ous [sɪ'nænθərəs] *adj.* ♀ syn'andrisch: ~ *plant* Korbblüt(l)er *m*, Komposite *f*.

sync [sɪŋk] F *für* a) *synchronization* 1: *in* (*out of*) ~ (nicht) synchron, fig. (nicht) in Einklang, b) *synchronize* 5.

syn·carp ['sɪnkɑːp] *s.* ♀ Sammelfrucht *f*.

syn·chro|'flash [ˌsɪŋkrəʊ-] *s. phot.* Syn-'chronblitz(licht *n*) *m*; **,~'mesh** [-'meʃ] ⊕ **I** *adj.* Synchron...; **II** *s. a.* ~ *gear* Syn'chrongetriebe *n*.

syn·chro·nism ['sɪŋkrənɪzəm] *s.* **1.** Syn-chro'nismus *m*, Gleichzeitigkeit *f*; **2.** Synchronisati'on *f*; **3.** synchro'nistische (Ge'schichts)Ta,belle; **4.** phys. Gleichlauf *m*; **syn·chro·ni·za·tion** [ˌsɪŋkrənaɪ'zeɪʃn] *s.* **1.** *bsd.* Film, TV: Synchronisati'on *f*; **2.** Gleichzeitigkeit *f*, zeitliches Zs.-fallen; **syn·chro·nize** ['sɪŋkrənaɪz] **I** *v/i.* **1.** gleichzeitig sein, zeitlich zs.-fallen, über'einstimmen; **2.** syn'chron gehen (*Uhr*) *od.* laufen (*Maschine*); **3.** synchronisiert sein (*Bild u. Ton e-s Films*); **II** *v/t.* **4.** Uhren, Maschinen synchronisieren; **~d shifting** mot. Synchron(gang)schaltung *f*; **5.** Film, TV: synchronisieren; **6.** *Ereignisse* syn-chro'nistisch darstellen, *Gleichzeitiges* zs.-stellen; **7.** *Geschehnisse* (zeitlich) zs.-fallen lassen *od.* aufein'ander abstimmen: **~d swimming** Synchronschwimmen *n*; **8.** ♪ a) *Ausführende* zum (genauen) Zs.-spiel bringen, b) *Stelle, Bogenstrich etc.* genau zu'sammen ausführen (lassen); **'syn·chro·nous** [-nəs] *adj.* □ **1.** gleichzeitig: *be* ~ (zeitlich) zs.-fallen; **2.** syn'chron: a) ⊕, ⚡ gleichlaufend (*Maschine etc.*), gleichgehend (*Uhr*), b) ⚡, ⊕ von gleicher Phase u. Schwingungsdauer: ~ *motor* Synchronmotor *m*.

syn·co·pal ['sɪŋkəpl] *adj.* **1.** syn'kopisch; **2.** ✳ Ohnmachts...; **'syn·co·pate** [-peɪt] *v/t.* **1.** ling. Wort synkopieren, zs.-ziehen; **2.** ♪ synkopieren; **syn·co·pa·tion** [ˌsɪŋkə'peɪʃn] *s.* **1.** → *syn-cope* 1; **2.** ♪ a) Synkopierung *f*, b) Syn'kope(n) *pl.* od. syn'kopische Mu-'sik; **syn·co·pe** ['sɪŋkəpɪ] *s.* **1.** ling. a) Syn'kope *f*, kontrahiertes Wort, b)

Kontrakti'on *f*; **2.** ♪ Syn'kope *f*; **3.** ✳ Syn'kope *f*, tiefe Ohnmacht.

syn·dic ['sɪndɪk] *s.* **1.** ⚖, ♦ Syndikus *m*, Rechtsberater *m*; **2.** univ. Brit. Se'nats-mitglied *n*; **'syn·di·cal·ism** [-kəlɪzəm] *s.* Syndika'lismus *m* (*radikaler Gewerkschaftssozialismus*); **'syn·di·cate I** *s.* [-kɪt] **1.** ♦, ⚖ Syndi'kat *n*, Kon'sortium *n*; **2.** ♦ a) Ring *m*, Verband *m*, 'Absatzkar,tell *m*, b) 'Zeitungssyndi,kat *n od.* -gruppe *f*; **3.** 'Pressezen,trale *f*; **4.** ,Syndi'kat' *n*, Verbrecherring *m*; **II** *v/t.* [-keɪt] **5.** ♦ zu e-m Syndi'kat vereinigen; **6.** a) *Artikel etc.* in mehreren Zeitungen zu'gleich veröffentlichen, b) über ein Syndi'kat verkaufen, c) *Zeitungen* zu e-m Syndi'kat zs.-schließen; **III** *v/i.* [-keɪt] **7.** ♦ sich zu e-m Syndi'kat zs.-schließen; **IV** *adj.* [-kɪt] **8.** ♦ Konsortial...; **syn·di·ca·tion** [ˌsɪndɪ'keɪʃn] *s.* ♦ Syndi'katsbildung *f*.

syn·drome ['sɪndrəʊm] *s.* ✳ Syn'drom *n* (*a. sociol. etc.*).

syn·ec·do·che [sɪ'nekdəkɪ] *s.* rhet. Syn-'ekdoche *f*.

syn·er·get·ic [sɪnə'dʒetɪk] *adj.* synergetisch; ~ *effect* Synergieeffekt *m*; **syn-er·gy** ['sɪnədʒɪ] *s.* Synergie *f*: ~ *effects pl.* Syner'gieef,fekte *pl.*

syn·od ['sɪnəd] *s.* eccl. Syn'ode *f*; **'syn-od·al** [-dl], **syn·od·ic, syn·od·i·cal** [sɪ'nɒdɪk(l)] *adj.* □ syn'odisch (*a. ast.*), Synoden...

syn·o·nym ['sɪnənɪm] *s.* ling. Syno'nym *n*, bedeutungsgleiches *od.* -ähnliches Wort: *be a ~ for* fig. gleichbedeutend sein mit; **syn·on·y·mous** [sɪ'nɒnɪməs] *adj.* □ **1.** ling. syno'nym(isch), bedeutungsgleich *od.* -ähnlich; **2.** allg. gleichbedeutend (*with* mit).

syn·op·sis [sɪ'nɒpsɪs] *pl.* **-ses** [-siːz] *s.* **1.** Syn'opse *f*: a) Zs.-fassung *f*, 'Übersicht *f*, Abriss *m*, b) eccl. (vergleichende) Zs.-schau; **syn'op·tic** [-ptɪk] *adj.* (□ *~ally*) **1.** syn'optisch, 'übersichtlich, zs.-fassend: ~ *chart* meteor. synoptische Karte; **2.** um'fassend (*Genie*); **3.** oft ☽ eccl. syn'optisch; **Syn'op·tist**, *a.* ☽ [-ptɪst] *s. eccl.* Syn'optiker *m* (*Matthäus, Markus u. Lukas*).

syn·o·vi·a [sɪ'nəʊvɪə] *s. physiol.* Gelenkschmiere *f*; **syn'o·vi·al** [-əl] *adj.* Syno-vi'al...: ~ *fluid* → *synovia*; **syn·o·vi·tis** [ˌsɪnə'vaɪtɪs] *s.* ✳ Gelenkentzündung *f*.

syn·tac·tic, syn·tac·ti·cal [sɪn'tæk-tɪk(l)] *adj.* □ ling. syn'taktisch, Syn-tax...; **syn'tac·ti·cals** [-ɪklz] *s. pl. sg. konstr.* Syn'taktik *f*; **syn·tax** ['sɪntæks] *s.* **1.** ling. Syntax *f*: a) Satzbau *m*, b) Satzlehre *f*; **2.** ♣, phls. Syntax *f*, Be-'weistheo,rie *f*.

syn·the·sis ['sɪnθɪsɪs] *pl.* **-ses** [-siːz] *s. allg.* Syn'these *f*; **'syn·the·size** [-saɪz] *v/t.* **1.** zs.-fügen, (durch Syn'these) aufbauen; **2.** 🜊, ♣ syn'thetisch *od.* künstlich herstellen; **'syn·the·siz·er** [-saɪzə] *s.* ♪ 'Synthesizer *m*; **syn·thet·ic** [sɪn-'θetɪk] **I** *adj.* (□ *~ally*) syn'thetisch: a) *bsd.* ling., phls. syn'thetisch, zs.-fügend: ~ *language*, b) 🜊 künstlich (*a. fig. unecht*), Kunst...: ~ *rubber*; ~ *trainer* ✈ (Flug)Simulator *m*; 🜊 Kunststoff *m*; **II** *s.* **syn·thet·i·cal** [sɪn'θetɪkl] *adj.* □ → *synthetic* I; **'syn·the·tize** [-taɪz] → *synthesize*.

syn·ton·ic [sɪn'tɒnɪk] *adj.* (□ *~ally*) **1.** ⚡ (auf gleiche Fre'quenz) abgestimmt; **2.** psych. extravertiert; **syn·to·nize** ['sɪntənaɪz] *v/t.* ⚡ (*to* auf e-e bestimmte Frequenz) abstimmen *od.* einstellen.

syn·to·ny ['sɪntənɪ] *s.* **1.** ⚡ (Fre'quenz-) Abstimmung *f*, Reso'nanz *f*; **2.** psych.

Extraversi'on *f*.

syph·i·lis ['sıfılıs] *s*. ♣ Syphilis *f*; **syph-i·lit·ic** [sıfı'lıtık] **I** *adj*. syphi'litisch; **II** *s*. Syphi'litiker(in).

sy·phon ['saıfn] → *siphon*.

Syr·i·an ['sırıən] **I** *adj*. syrisch; **II** *s*. Syr(i)er(in).

sy·rin·ga [sı'rıŋgə] *s*. ♀ Sy'ringe *f*, Flieder *m*.

syr·inge ['sırındʒ] **I** *s*. **1.** ♣, ⊕ Spritze *f*; **II** *v/t*. **2.** *Flüssigkeit etc*. (ein)spritzen; **3.** *Ohr* ausspritzen; **4.** *Pflanze etc*. ab-, bespritzen.

syr·inx ['sırıŋks] *s*. **1.** *antiq*. Pan-, Hirtenflöte *f*; **2.** a) *anat*. eu'stachische Röhre, b) ♣ Fistel *f*; **3.** *orn*. Syrinx *f*, unterer Kehlkopf.

Syro- [saıərəʊ] *in Zssgn* Syro..., syrisch.

syr·up ['sırəp] *s*. **1.** Sirup *m*, Zuckersaft *m*; **2.** *fig*. ‚süßliches Zeug', Kitsch *m*; **'syr·up·y** [-pı] *adj*. **1.** sirupartig, dickflüssig, klebrig; **2.** *fig*. süßlich, senti-

men'tal.

sys·tem ['sıstəm] *s*. **1.** *allg*. Sy'stem *n* (*a*. ♣, ♪, ♙, ♀, *zo*.): a) Gefüge *n*, Aufbau *m*, Anordnung *f*, b) Einheit *f*, geordnetes Ganzes, c) *phls*., *eccl*. Lehrgebäude *n*, d) ☉ Anlage *f*, e) Verfahren *n*: ~ *control Computer*: Systemsteuerung *f*; ~ *crash Computer*: Systemausfall *m*; ~ *error* (*od*. *fault*) *Computer*: Systemfehler *m*; ~ *failure Computer*: Systemausfall *m*; ~ *software* Systemsoftware *f*; ~ *of government* Regierungssystem; ~ *of logarithms* ♣ Logarithmensystem; ~ *of references* Bezugssystem *n*, Referenzsystem *n*; *electoral* ~ *pol*. Wahlsystem, -verfahren; *mountain* ~ Gebirgssystem; *savings-bank* ~ Sparkassenwesen *n*; *lack* ~ kein System haben; **2.** *ast*. Sy'stem *n*: *solar* ~; *the* ~ das Weltall; **3.** *geol*. Formati'on *f*; **4.** *physiol*. a) (Or'gan)Sys,tem *n*, b) *the* ~ der Organismus: *digestive* ~ Verdauungssystem;

get s.th. out of one's ~ F et. loswerden; **5.** (*Eisenbahn-*, *Straßen-*, *Verkehrs-etc*.)Netz *n*: ~ *of roads*; **sys·tem·at·ic**, **sys·tem·at·i·cal** [,sıstı'mætık(l)] *adj*. □ syste'matisch: a) plan-, zweckmäßig, -voll, b) me'thodisch (*vorgehend od*. *geordnet*); **'sys·tem·a·tist** [-mətıst] *s*. Syste'matiker *m*; **sys·tem·a·ti·za·tion** [,sıstımətaı'zeıʃn] *s*. Systematisierung *f*; **'sys·tem·a·tize** [-tımətaız] *v/t*. systematisieren, in ein Sy'stem bringen.

sys·tem·ic [sıs'temık] *adj*. (□ ~*ally*) *physiol*. Körper..., Organ...: ~ *circulation* großer Blutkreislauf; ~ *disease* Systemerkrankung *f*.

sys·tems| a·nal·y·sis *s*. *Computer*: Sys'temana,lyse *f*; ~ *an·a·lyst* *s*. Sys'temana,lytiker *m*.

sys·to·le ['sıstəlı] *s*. Sy'stole *f*: a) ♣ Zs.-ziehung *des Herzmuskels*, b) *Metrik*: Verkürzung *e-r langen Silbe*.

T, t [tiː] *pl.* **T's, Ts, t's, ts** *s.* **1.** T *n*, t *n* (*Buchstabe*): **to a T** haargenau; **it suits me to a T** das passt mir ausgezeichnet; **cross the T's** a) peinlich genau sein, b) es klar u. deutlich sagen; **2.** *a.* **flanged T** ⊕ T-Stück *n*.

ta [tɑː] *int. Brit.* F danke.

Taal [tɑːl] *s. ling.* Afri'kaans *n*.

tab [tæb] *s.* **1.** Streifen *m*, *bsd.* a) Schlaufe *f*, (Mantel)Aufhänger *m*, b) Lappen *m*, Zipfel *m*, c) (Schuh)Lasche *f*, (Stiefel)Strippe *f*, d) Dorn *m* *am Schnürsenkel*, e) Ohrklappe *f* (*Mütze*); **2.** ✕ (Kragen)Spiegel *m*; **3.** Schildchen *n*, Anhänger *m*, Eti'kett *n*; (Kar'tei)Reiter *m*; **4.** F a) Rechnung *f*, b) Kon'trolle *f*: **keep ⚊(s) on** *fig.* kontrollieren, beobachten, sich auf dem Laufenden halten über (*acc.*); **pick up the ⚊** *Am.* (die Rechnung) bezahlen; **5.** ⊕ Nase *f*; **6.** ✍ Trimmruder *n*; **7.** *Computer*: Tabu'lator *m*: **⚊ key** Tabulatortaste *f*.

tab·by ['tæbɪ] **I** *s.* **1.** *obs.* Moi'ré *m*, *n* (*Stoff*); **2.** *mst* **⚊ cat** a) getigerte *od.* gescheckte Katze, b) (weibliche) Katze; **3.** F a) alte Jungfer, b) Klatschbase *f*; **II** *adj.* **4.** *obs.* Moiré...; **5.** gestreift; scheckig; **III** *v/t.* **6.** *Seide* moirieren.

tab·er·nac·le ['tæbənækl] *s.* **1.** *bibl.* Zelt *n*, Hütte *f*; **2.** ⚭ *eccl.* Stiftshütte *f der Juden*: **Feast of ⚭s** Laubhüttenfest *n*; **3.** *eccl.* a) (jüdischer) Tempel, b) ⚭ Mor'monentempel *m*, c) Bethaus *n der Dissenter*; **4.** Taber'nakel *n*: a) *R.C.* Sakra'mentshäus-chen *n*, b) △ Statuennische *f*; **5.** *fig.* Leib *m* (*als Wohnsitz der Seele*); **6.** ✍ Mastbock *m*.

tab·la·ture ['tæblətʃə] *s.* **1.** Bild *n*: a) Tafelgemälde *n*, b) bildliche Darstellung (*a. fig.*); **2.** ♪ *hist.* Tabula'tur *f*.

ta·ble ['teɪbl] **I** *s.* **1.** *allg.* Tisch *m*: **lay** (*od.* **put**) **s.th. on the ⚊** → 14 u. 15a; **set** (*od.* **lay, spread**) **the ⚊** den Tisch decken; **lay s.th. on the ⚊** → 15a; **turn the ⚊s** (**on s.o.**) den Spieß umdrehen (gegenüber j-m); **the ⚊s are turned** das Blatt hat sich gewendet; **2.** Tafel *f*, Tisch *m*: a) gedeckter Tisch, b) Kost *f*, Essen *n*: **at ⚊** bei Tisch, beim Essen; **keep** (*od.* **set**) **a good ⚊** e-e gute Küche führen; **the Lord's ⚊** der Tisch des Herrn, das heilige Abendmahl; **3.** (Tisch-, Tafel)Runde *f*; → **round table**; **4.** Komi'tee *n*, Ausschuss *m*; **5.** *geol.* Tafel(land *n*) *f*, Pla'teau *n*: **⚊ mountain** Tafelberg *m*; **6.** △ a) Tafel *f*, Platte *f*, b) Sims *m*, *n*, Fries *m*; **7.** (Holz-, Stein-, *a.* Gedenk- *etc.*)Tafel *f*: **the (two) ⚊s of the law** die Gesetzestafeln, die Zehn Gebote Gottes; **8.** Ta-'belle *f*, Verzeichnis *n*: **⚊ of contents** Inhaltsverzeichnis; **⚊ of wages** Lohntabelle; **9.** ♣ Ta'belle *f*: **⚊ of logarithms** Logarithmentafel *f*; **learn one's ⚊s** rechnen lernen; **10.** *anat.* Tafel *f*, Tabula *f* (ex'terna *od.* in'terna) (*Schädeldach*); **11.** ⊕ (Auflage)Tisch *m*; **12.** *opt.* Bildebene *f*; **13.** *Chiromantie*: Handteller *m*; **II** *v/t.* **14.** auf den Tisch legen (*a. fig.* vorlegen); **15.** *bsd. parl.* a) *Brit.* Antrag *etc.* einbringen, b) *Am.* zu'rückstellen, *bsd. Gesetzesvorlage* ruhen lassen; **16.** in e-e Ta'belle eintragen, tabel'larisch verzeichnen.

ta·bleau ['tæbləʊ] *pl.* **'ta·bleaux** [-əʊz] *s.* **1.** Bild *n*: a) Gemälde *n*, b) anschauliche Darstellung; **2.** *Brit.* dra'matische Situati'on, über'raschende Szene: **⚊!** Tableau!, man stelle sich die Situation vor!; **3.** → **⚊ vivant** [viːˈvɑ̃ːŋ] (*Fr.*) *s.* a) lebendes Bild, b) *fig.* malerische Szene.

'ta·ble|·cloth *s.* Tischtuch *n*, -decke *f*; **'⚊·cut** *adj.* mit Tafelschnitt (versehen) (*Edelstein*).

ta·ble d'hôte [ˌtɑːblˈdəʊt] (*Fr.*) *s. a.* **⚊ meal** Me'nü *n*.

ta·ble| knife *s.* [*irr.*] *Brit.* Tafel-, Tischmesser *n*; **'⚊·land** *s. geogr., geol.* Tafelland *n*, Hochebene *f*; **'⚊·,lift·ing** → **table-turning**; **⚊ light·er** *s.* Tischfeuerzeug *n*; **⚊ lin·en** *s.* Tischwäsche *f*; **⚊ mat** *s.* Set *n*, *m*; **⚊ nap·kin** *s.* Servi'ette *f*; **'⚊·,rap·ping** *s. Spiritismus*: Tischklopfen *n*; **⚊ salt** *s.* Tafelsalz *n*; **⚊ set** *s. Radio, TV*: Tischgerät *n*; **⚊ soc·cer** *s.* Tischfußball *n*, F Kicker *n*. **'⚊·spoon** *s.* Esslöffel *m*; **'⚊·spoon·ful** *s. ein* Esslöffel (voll).

tab·let ['tæblɪt] *s.* **1.** Täfelchen *n*; **2.** (Gedenk-, Wand- *etc.*)Tafel *f*; **3.** *hist.* Schreibtafel *f*; **4.** (No'tiz-, Schreib-, Zeichen)Block *m*; **5.** a) Stück *n* Seife, b) Tafel *f* Schokolade; **6.** *pharm.* Tab-'lette *f*; **7.** △ Kappenstein *m*.

ta·ble| talk *s.* Tischgespräch *n*; **⚊ ten·nis** *s.* Tischtennis *n*; **⚊ top** *s.* Tischplatte *f*; **'⚊·,turn·ing** *s. Spiritismus*: Tischrücken *n*; **'⚊·ware** *s.* Tischgeschirr *n*; **⚊ wa·ter** *s.* Tafel-, Mine'ralwasser *n*.

tab·loid ['tæblɔɪd] **I** *s.* **1.** Bildzeitung *f*, Boule'vard-, Sensati'onsblatt *n*; *pl. a.* Boule'vardpresse *f*; **2.** *Am.* Informati'onsblatt *n*; **⚊** *fig.* Kurzfassung *f*; **II** *adj.* **4.** konzentriert: **in ⚊ form**; **⚊ TV** *s.* Sensati'onsreportagen *pl.* im Fernsehen.

ta·boo [təˈbuː] **I** *adj.* ta'bu: a) unantastbar, b) verboten, c) verpönt; **II** *s.* Ta'bu *n*: **put s.th. under** (**a**) **⚊** → **III** *v/t.* für ta'bu erklären, tabuisieren.

tab·o(u)·ret ['tæbərɪt] *s.* **1.** Hocker *m*, Tabu'rett *n*; **2.** Stickrahmen *m*.

tab·u·lar ['tæbjʊlə] *adj.* □ **1.** tafelförmig, Tafel..., flach; **2.** dünn; **3.** blättrig; **4.** tabel'larisch, Tabellen...: **⚊ standard** ✝ Preisindexwährung *f*.

ta·bu·la ra·sa [ˌtæbjʊləˈrɑːsə] (*Lat.*) *s.* Tabula *f* rasa: a) unbeschriebenes Blatt, völlige Leere, b) reiner Tisch.

tab·u·late ['tæbjʊleɪt] **I** *v/t.* tabellarisieren, tabel'larisch (an)ordnen; **II** *adj.* → **tabular**; **tab·u·la·tion** [ˌtæbjʊˈleɪʃn] *s.* **1.** Tabellarisierung *f*; **2.** Ta'belle *f*; **'tab·u·la·tor** [-tə] *s.* **1.** Tabellarisierer *m*; **2.** *Computer etc.*: Tabu'lator *m*.

tach [tæk] F *für* **tachometer**.

tach·o·graph ['tækəʊɡrɑːf] *s.* ⊕ Tacho-'graph *m*, Fahrtenschreiber *m*.

ta·chom·e·ter [tæˈkɒmɪtə] *s.* ⊕ *mot.* Drehzahlmesser *m*.

tac·it ['tæsɪt] *adj.* □ *bsd.* ⚖ stillschweigend: **⚊ approval**.

tac·i·turn ['tæsɪtɜːn] *adj.* □ schweigsam, wortkarg; **tac·i·tur·ni·ty** [ˌtæsɪˈtɜːnətɪ] *s.* Schweigsamkeit *f*, Verschlossenheit *f*.

tack¹ [tæk] **I** *s.* **1.** (Nagel)Stift *m*, Reißnagel *m*, Zwecke *f*; **2.** *Näherei*: Heftstich *m*; **3.** ✍ a) Halse *f*, b) Haltetau *n*; **4.** ✍ Schlag *m*, Gang *m* (*beim Lavieren od. Kreuzen*): **be on the port ⚊** auf Backbordhalsen liegen; **5.** ✍ Lavieren *n* (*a. fig.*); **6.** *fig.* Kurs *m*, Weg *m*, Richtung *f*: **on the wrong ⚊** auf dem Holzweg; **try another ⚊** es anders versuchen; **7.** *parl. Brit.* 'Zusatzantrag *m*, -ar'tikel *m*; **8.** ⊕ Klebrigkeit *f*; **II** *v/t.* **9.** heften (**to** an *acc.*); **10.** *a.* **⚊ down** festmachen; **11.** *a.* **⚊ together** anein'ander fügen (*a. fig.*); **12.** (**on, to**) anfügen (an *acc.*): **⚊ mortgages** *Brit.* Hypotheken (verschiedenen Ranges) zs.-schreiben; **⚊ securities** ⚖ *Brit.* Sicherheiten zs.-fassen; **⚊ a rider to a bill** *parl. Brit.* e-e Vorlage mit e-m Zusatzantrag koppeln; **13.** ⊕ heftschweißen; **III** *v/i.* **14.** ✍ a) wenden, b) lavieren (*a. fig.*).

tack² [tæk] *s.* F Nahrung *f*, ‚Fraß' *m*.

tack·le ['tækl] **I** *s.* **1.** Gerät *n*, (Werk-)Zeug *n*, Ausrüstung *f*; **2.** (Pferde)Geschirr *n*; **3.** *a.* **block and ⚊** ⊕ Flaschenzug *m*; **4.** ✍ Talje *f*; **5.** ✍ Takel-, Tauwerk *n*; **6.** *Fußball etc.*: Angreifen *n* (*e-s Gegners im Ballbesitz*); **7.** *American Football*: Halbstürmer *m*; **II** *v/t.* **8.** *et. od. j-n* packen; **9.** *Fußball etc.*: Gegner *im Ballbesitz* angreifen, stoppen; **10.** *j-n* angreifen, anein'ander geraten mit; **11.** *fig. j-n* (*mit Fragen etc.*) angehen (**on** wegen); **12.** *fig.* a) *Problem etc.* anpacken, angehen, in Angriff nehmen, b) *Aufgabe etc.* lösen, fertig werden mit.

'tack·weld *v/t.* ⊕ heftschweißen.

tack·y ['tækɪ] *adj.* **1.** klebrig, zäh; **2.** *Am.* F a) schäbig, her'untergekommen, b) 'unmo,dern, c) protzig.

tact [tækt] *s.* **1.** Takt *m*, Takt-, Zartgefühl *n*; **2.** Feingefühl *n* (**of** für); **3.** ♪ Takt(schlag) *m*; **'tact·ful** [-fʊl] *adj.* □ taktvoll; **'tact·ful·ness** [-fʊlnɪs] → **tact** 1.

tac·ti·cal ['tæktɪkl] *adj.* □ ✕ taktisch (*a. fig.* planvoll, *klug*); **tac·ti·cian** [tækˈtɪʃn] *s.* ✕ Taktiker *m* (*a. fig.*); **'tac·tics** [-ks] *s.* **1.** *sg. od. pl. konstr.* ✕ Taktik *f*; **2.** *nur pl. konstr. fig.* Taktik *f*, planvolles Vorgehen.

tac·tile ['tæktaɪl] *adj.* **1.** tak'til, Tast...: **⚊ sense** Tastsinn *m*; **⚊ hair** *zo.*, ♀ Tasthaar *n*; **2.** tast-, greifbar; **tac·til·i·ty** [tækˈtɪlətɪ] *s.* Greif-, Tastbarkeit *f*.

tact·less ['tæktlɪs] *adj.* □ taktlos; **'tact·less·ness** [-nɪs] *s.* Taktlosigkeit *f*.

tac·tu·al ['tæktjʊəl] *adj.* □ tastbar,

Tast...: **~ sense** Tastsinn *m*.

tad·pole ['tædpəʊl] *s. zo.* Kaulquappe *f*.

taf·fe·ta ['tæfɪtə] *s*. Taft *m*.

taf·fy¹ ['tæfɪ] *s*. **1.** *Am.* → **toffee**; **2.** F ‚Schmus' *m*, Schmeiche'lei *f*.

Taf·fy² ['tæfɪ] *s. sl.* Wa'liser *m*.

tag¹ [tæg] **I** *s*. **1.** (loses) Ende, Anhängsel *n*, Zipfel *m*, Fetzen *m*, Lappen *m*; **2.** Eti'kett *n*, Anhänger *m*, Schildchen *n*; Abzeichen *n*, Pla'kette *f*: **~ day** *Am.* Sammeltag *m*; **3.** a) Schlaufe *f am Stiefel*, b) (Schnürsenkel)Stift *m*; **4.** ⊛ a) Lötklemme *f*, b) Lötfahne *f*; **5.** a) Schwanzspitze *f* (*bsd. e-s Fuchses*), b) Wollklunker *f*, *m* (*Schaf*); **6.** (Schrift)Schnörkel *m*; **7.** *ling.* Frageanhängsel *n*; **8.** Re'frain *m*, Kehrreim *m*; **9.** Schlusswort *n*, Po'inte *f*, Mo'ral *f*; **10.** stehende Redensart, bekanntes Zi'tat; **11.** Bezeichnung *f*, Beiname *m*; **12.** *Computer:* Tag *n* (*Markierung*); **13.** *Am.* Strafzettel *m*; **~ragtag** → **ragtag**; **II** *v/t*. **15.** mit e-m Eti'kett *etc.* versehen, etikettieren; *Waren* auszeichnen; *et.* markieren; *Computer: Daten* taggen; **16.** mit e-m Schlusswort *od.* e-r Mo'ral versehen; **17.** *Rede etc.* verbrämen; **18.** *et.* anhängen (**to** an *acc.*); **19.** *Schafen* Klunkerwolle abscheren; **20.** F hinter *j-m* ‚herlatschen'; **III** *v/i.* **21.** **~ along** F hinter'herlaufen; **~ after** → 20.

tag² [tæg] **I** *s*. Fangen *n*, Haschen *n* (*Kinderspiel*); **II** *v/t*. haschen.

tag end *s*. F **1.** ‚Schwanz' *m*, Schluss *m*; **2.** *Am.* a) (letzter) Rest, b) Fetzen *m* (*a. fig.*).

'tag·ging *s. Computer:* Tagging *n* (*Markierung von Daten*).

ta·glia·tel·le [ˌtæljə'telɪ] *s. pl.* Taglia'telle *pl.*, Bandnudeln *pl.*

Ta·hi·ti·an [tɑː'hiːʃn] **I** *s*. **1.** Tahiti'aner (-in); **2.** *ling.* Ta'hitisch *n*; **II** *adj.* **3.** ta'hitisch.

tail¹ [teɪl] **I** *s*. **1.** *zo.* Schwanz *m*, (Pferde-)Schweif *m*: **turn ~** *fig.* ausreißen, davonlaufen; **twist s.o.'s ~** j-n piesacken; **close on s.o.'s ~** j-m dicht auf den Fersen; **~s up** fidel, hochgestimmt; **keep your ~ up!** lass dich nicht unterkriegen!; **with one's ~ between one's legs** fig. mit eingezogenem Schwanz; **the ~ wags the dog** *fig.* der Kleinste hat das Sagen; **2.** F Hinterteil *m*, Steiß *m*; **3.** *fig.* Schwanz *m*, Ende *n*, Schluss *m* (*e-r Marschkolonne, e-s Briefes etc.*): **~ of a comet** *ast.* Kometenschweif *m*; **the ~ of the class** *ped.* der ‚Schwanz' *od.* die Schlechtesten der Klasse; **~ of a note** ♪ Notenhals *m*; **~ of a storm** (ruhigeres) Ende e-s Sturms; **out of the ~ of one's eye** aus den Augenwinkeln; **4.** Haarzopf *m*, -schwanz *m*; **5.** a) Schleppe *f e-s Kleides*, b) (Rock-, Hemd)Schoß *m*, c) *pl.* Gesellschaftsanzug *m*, *bsd.* Frack *m*; **6.** ✈ Schwanz *m*, Heck *n*; **7.** *mst pl.* Rück-, Kehrseite *f e-r Münze*; **8.** a) Gefolge *n*, Anhang *m e-r Partei*, große Masse *e-r Gemeinschaft*; **9.** F ‚Beschatter' *m* (*Detektiv etc.*): **put a ~ on s.o.** j-n beschatten lassen; **10.** ✈ a) Leitwerk *n*, b) Heck *n*, Schwanz *m*; **II** *v/t*. **11.** mit e-m Schwanz versehen; **12.** *Marschkolonne etc.* beschließen; **13.** *a.* **~ on** befestigen, anhängen (**to** an *acc.*); **14.** *Tier* stutzen; **15.** *Beeren* zupfen, entstielen; **16.** F *j-n* ‚beschatten', verfolgen; **III** *v/i.* **17.** sich hinziehen: **~ away** (*od.* **off**) a) abflauen, -nehmen, sich verlieren, b) zurückbleiben, -fallen, c) sich auseinander ziehen (*Marschkolonne etc.*); **18.** F hinter'herlaufen (**after s.o.** j-m); **19.** **~ back** *mot. Brit.* e-n Rückstau bilden; **20.** ⚠

tail² [teɪl] ⚖ **I** *s*. Beschränkung *f* (*der Erbfolge*), beschränktes Erb- *od.* Eigentumsrecht: **heir in ~** Vorerbe *m*; **estate in ~ male** Fideikommiss *m*; **II** *adj.* beschränkt: **estate ~**.

'tail·back *s. mot. Brit.* Rückstau *m*; **'~·board** *s*. Ladeklappe *f* (*a. mot.*); **~ coat** *s*. Frack *m*; **~ comb** *s*. Stielkamm *m*.

tailed [teɪld] *adj.* **1.** geschwänzt; **2.** *in Zssgn* ...schwänzig.

tail\|end *s*. Schluss *m*, Ende *n*; **2.** → *tail¹* 2; **'~'end·er** *s. sport* ‚Schlusslicht' *n*; **~ fin** *s*. **1.** *ichth.* Schwanzflosse *f*; **2.** ✈ Seitenflosse *f*; **~ fly** *s. Am.* (Angel-)Fliege *f*; **'~·gate I** *s*. **1.** a) → *tailboard*, b) *mot.* Hecktür *f*; **2.** Niedertor *n* (*e-r Schleuse*); **II** *v/t. u. v/i. mot.* (zu) dicht auffahren (auf *acc.*); **'~·gun** *s*. ✈ Heckwaffe *f*; **'~·heav·y** *adj.* ✈ schwanzlastig.

tail·ing ['teɪlɪŋ] *s*. **1.** △ eingelassenes Ende; **2.** *pl.* a) (*bsd.* Erz)Abfälle *pl.*, b) Ausschussmehl *n*.

tail lamp *s. mot. etc.* Rück-, Schlusslicht *n*.

tail·less ['teɪllɪs] *adj.* schwanzlos.

'tail·light → **tail lamp**.

tai·lor ['teɪlə] **I** *s*. **1.** Schneider *m*: **the ~ makes the man** Kleider machen Leute; **II** *v/t*. **2.** schneidern; **3.** schneidern für *j-n*; **4.** *j-n* kleiden; **5.** nach Maß arbeiten; **6.** *fig.* zuschneiden (**to** für *j-n*, auf *et.*); **'tai·lored** [-ləd] *adj.* maßgeschneidert, gut sitzend, tadellos gearbeitet: **~ suit** Maßanzug *m*; **~ costume** Schneiderkostüm *n*; **'tai·lor·ess** [-ə'res] *s*. Schneiderin *f*.

'tai·lor-made I *adj.* **1.** → **tailored** 1; **2.** ele'gant gekleidet (*Dame*); **3.** auf Bestellung angefertigt; **4.** *fig.* (genau) zugeschnitten (**for** auf *acc.*); **II** *s*. **5.** 'Schneiderko,stüm *n*.

'tail\|·piece *s*. **1.** ♪ Saitenhalter *m*; **2.** *typ.* 'Schlussvi,gnette *f*; **~ pipe** *s. mot.* Auspuffrohr(ende) *n*; **~ plane** *s*. ✈ Höhenflosse *f*; **~ skid** *s*. ✈ Schwanzsporn *m*; **'~·spin** *s*. **1.** ✈ (Ab)Trudeln *n*; **2.** *fig.* Panik *f*; **'~·stock** *s*. ⊛ Reitstock *m* (*Drehbank*); **~ u·nit** *s*. ✈ (Schwanz)Leitwerk *n*; **~ wind** *s*. ✈ Rückenwind *m*.

taint [teɪnt] **I** *s*. **1.** *bsd. fig.* Fleck *m*, Makel *m*; *fig.* a) *krankhafter etc.* Zug, b) Spur *f*: **a ~ of suspicion** ein Anflug von Misstrauen; **2.** ✿ a) (verborgene) Ansteckung, b) (verborgene) Anlage (**of** zu e-r Krankheit): **hereditary ~** erbliche Belastung; **3.** *fig.* verderblicher Einfluss, Gift *n*; **II** *v/t*. **4.** *a. fig.* verderben, -giften; **5.** anstecken; **6.** *fig.* verderben: **be ~ed with** behaftet sein mit; **7.** *bsd. fig.* beflecken, besudeln; **III** *v/i.* **8.** verderben, schlecht werden; **'taint·less** [-lɪs] *adj.* □ makellos.

take [teɪk] **I** *s*. **1.** a) *Fischerei:* Fang *m*, b) *hunt.* Beute *f* (*beide a.* F *fig.*); **2.** F Einnahme(n *pl.*) *f*; **3.** F Anteil *m* (**of** an *dat.*); **4.** *Film etc.:* Einstellung *f*, Aufnahme *f*: **her ~ on life** *fig.* ihre Lebenseinstellung (*od.* Einstellung dem Leben gegenüber); **5.** *typ.* Porti'on *f* (*Manuskript*); **6.** ✿ Reakti'on *f* (*a. fig.*), b) Anwachsen *n* (*e-s Transplantats*), **7.** *Schach etc.:* Schlagen *n* (*e-r Figur*); **II** *v/t.* [*irr.*] **8.** *allg.*, *a.* Abschied, Partner, Unterricht etc. nehmen: **~ it or leave it** *sl.* mach, was du willst; **~n all in all** im großen Ganzen; **taking one thing with another** eins zum anderen gerechnet; → **account** 9, **action** 8, **aim** 6, **care** 4, **consideration** 1, **effect** 1 *etc.*; **9.** (weg-)nehmen; **10.** nehmen, fassen, packen, ergreifen; **11.** *Fische etc.* fangen; **12.** *Verbrecher etc.* fangen, ergreifen; **13.** ✗ gefangen nehmen, *Gefangene* machen; **14.** ✗ *Stadt, Stellung etc.* (ein)nehmen, *a. Land* erobern; *Schiff* kapern; **15.** *j-n* erwischen, ertappen (**stealing** beim Stehlen, **in a lie** bei e-r Lüge); **16.** nehmen, sich aneignen, Besitz ergreifen von, sich bemächtigen (*gen.*); **17.** *Gabe etc.* (an-, entgegen)nehmen, empfangen; **18.** bekommen, erhalten; *Geld, Steuer etc.* einnehmen; *Preis etc.* gewinnen; **19.** (her'aus)nehmen (**from, out of** aus); *a. fig. Zitat etc.* entnehmen (**from** *dat.*): **I ~ it from s.o. who knows** ich habe (*weiß*) es von j-m, der es genau weiß; **20.** *Speise etc.* zu sich nehmen; *Mahlzeit* einnehmen; *Gift, Medizin etc.* nehmen; **21.** sich *e-e Krankheit* holen *od.* zuziehen: **be ~n ill** krank werden; **22.** nehmen: a) auswählen: **I am not taking any** *sl.* ‚ohne mich'!, b) kaufen, c) mieten, d) *Eintritts-, Fahrkarte* lösen, e) *Frau* heiraten, f) *e-r Frau* beischlafen, g) *Weg* wählen; **23.** mitnehmen: **~ me with you** nimm mich mit; **you can't ~ it with you** *fig.* im Grabe nützt (dir) aller Reichtum nichts mehr; **24.** (hin- *od.* weg)bringen; *j-n wohin* führen: **business took him to London**; **he was ~n to hospital** er wurde in die Klinik gebracht; **25.** *j-n durch den Tod* nehmen, wegraffen; **26.** ⚕ abziehen (**from** von); **27.** *j-n* treffen, erwischen (*Schlag*); **28.** *Hindernis* nehmen; **29.** *j-n* befallen, packen (*Empfindung, Krankheit*): **be ~n with e-e Krankheit** bekommen (→ 42); **~n with fear** von Furcht gepackt; **30.** *Gefühl* haben, bekommen, *Mitleid etc.* empfinden, *Mut* fassen, *Anstoß* nehmen; *Ab-, Zuneigung* fassen (**to** gegen, für): **~ alarm** beunruhigt sein (**at** über *acc.*); **~ comfort** sich trösten; → **fancy** 5, **pride** 1; **31.** *Feuer* fangen; **32.** *Bedeutung, Sinn, Eigenschaft, Gestalt* annehmen, bekommen: **~ a new meaning**; **33.** *Farbe, Geruch, Geschmack* annehmen; **34.** *sport u. Spiele:* a) *Ball, Punkt, Figur, Stein* abnehmen (**from** *dat.*), b) *Stein* schlagen, c) *Karte* stechen, d) *Spiel* gewinnen; **35.** ♟ *etc.* erwerben, *bsd.* erben: **be ~n**. **36.** *Ware, Zeitung* beziehen; ✝ *Auftrag* her'einnehmen; **37.** nehmen, verwenden: **~ 4 eggs** *Küche:* man nehme 4 Eier; **38.** *Zug, Taxi etc.* benutzen; **39.** *Gelegenheit, Vorteil* ergreifen, wahrnehmen; → **chance** 2; **40.** (als *Beispiel*) nehmen; **41.** *Platz* einnehmen; **~n** besetzt; **42.** *fig. j-n, das Auge, den Sinn* gefangen nehmen, fesseln, (für sich) einnehmen: **be ~n with** (*od.* **by**) begeistert *od.* entzückt sein von (→ 29); **43.** *Befehl, Führung, Rolle, Stellung, Vorsitz* über'nehmen; **44.** *Mühe, Verantwortung* auf sich nehmen; **45.** leisten: a) *Arbeit, Dienst* verrichten, b) *Eid, Gelübde* ablegen, c) *Versprechen* (ab)geben; **46.** *Notiz, Aufzeichnung* machen, niederschreiben, *Diktat, Protokoll* aufnehmen; **47.** *phot. et. od. j-n* aufnehmen, *Bild* machen; **48.** *Messung, Zählung etc.* vornehmen, 'durchführen; **49.** *wissenschaftlich* ermitteln, *Größe, Temperatur etc.* messen; *Maß* nehmen; **50.** machen, tun: **~ a look** e-n Blick tun *od.* werfen; **~ a swing** schaukeln; **51.** *Maßnahme* ergreifen, treffen; **52.** *Auswahl* treffen; **53.** *Entschluss* fassen; **54.** *Fahrt, Spaziergang, a. Sprung, Verbeu-*

gung, *Wendung etc.* machen; *Anlauf* nehmen; **55.** *Ansicht* vertreten; → **stand** 2, **view** 11; **56.** a) verstehen, b) auffassen, auslegen, c) *et. gut etc.* aufnehmen: *do you ~ me?* verstehen Sie(, was ich meine)?; *I ~ it that* ich nehme an, dass; ~ *s.th. ill of s.o.* j-m et. übel nehmen; ~ *it seriously* es ernst nehmen; **57.** ansehen *od.* betrachten (*as* als); halten (*for* für): *I took him for an honest man*; **58.** sich *Rechte, Freiheiten* (her'aus)nehmen; **59.** a) *Rat, Auskunft* einholen, b) *Rat* annehmen, befolgen; **60.** *Wette, Angebot* annehmen; **61.** glauben: *you may ~ it from me* verlass dich drauf!; **62.** *Beleidigung, Verlust etc., a.* j-n hinnehmen, *Strafe, Folgen* auf sich nehmen, sich *et.* gefallen lassen: ~ *people as they are* die Leute nehmen, wie sie (eben) sind; **63.** *et.* ertragen, aushalten: *can you ~ it?* kannst du das aushalten?; ~ *it* F es ,kriegen', es ausbaden (müssen); **64.** ☂ sich *e-r Behandlung etc.* unter'ziehen; **65.** *ped.* Prüfung machen, ablegen: ~ *French* Examen im Französischen machen; → **degree** 3; **66.** *Rast, Ferien etc.* machen, *Urlaub, a. Bad* nehmen; **67.** *Platz, Raum* ein-, wegnehmen, beanspruchen; **68.** a) *Zeit, Material etc., a. fig.* Geduld, Mut etc. brauchen, erfordern, kosten, *gewisse Zeit* dauern: *it took a long time* es dauerte *od.* brauchte lange; *it ~s brains and courage* es erfordert Verstand u. Mut; *it ~s a man to do that* das kann nur ein Mann (fertig bringen), b) *j-n et.* kosten, *j-m et.* abverlangen: *it took him* (*od.* *he took*) *3 hours* es kostete *od.* er brauchte 3 Stunden; → **time** 9; **69.** *Kleidergröße, Nummer* haben: *which size in hats do you ~?*; **70.** *ling.* a) *grammatische Form* annehmen, im *Konjunktiv etc.* stehen, b) *Akzent, Endung, Objekt etc.* bekommen; **71.** aufnehmen, fassen, Platz bieten für; **III** *v/i.* [*irr.*] **72.** ♀ *Wurzel* schlagen; **73.** ♀, ✿ anwachsen (*Pfropfreis, Steckling, Transplantat*); **74.** ✿ wirken, anschlagen (*Droge etc.*); **75.** F ,ankommen', ,ziehen', ,einschlagen', Anklang finden (*Buch, Theaterstück etc.*); **76.** ☂☂ das Eigentumsrecht erlangen, *bsd.* erben, (als Erbe) zum Zuge kommen; **77.** sich *gut etc.* fotografieren (lassen); **78.** Feuer fangen; **79.** anbeißen (*Fisch*); **80.** ☉ an-, eingreifen;

Zssgn mit prp.:

take| af·ter *v/i.* j-m nachschlagen, -geraten, ähneln (*dat.*); ~ **for** *v/t.* **1.** halten für; **2.** auf *e-n Spaziergang etc.* mitnehmen; ~ **from** *v/t.* **1.** *j-m* wegnehmen; **2.** ♉ abziehen von; **II** *v/i.* **3.** Abbruch tun (*dat.*), schmälern (*acc.*), her'absetzen (*acc.*); **4.** beeinträchtigen, mindern, (ab)schwächen; ~ **in·to** *v/t.* **1.** (hin)'einführen in (*acc.*); **2.** bringen in (*acc.*); ~ **to** *v/i.* **1.** a) sich begeben in (*acc.*) *od.* nach *od.* zu, b) sich flüchten in (*acc.*) *od.* zu, *fig.* Zuflucht nehmen zu: ~ *the stage* zur Bühne gehen; → **bed** 1, **heel¹** *Redew.*, **road** 1; **2.** a) (her'an)gehen *od.* sich begeben an *e-e Arbeit etc.*, b) sich *e-r Sache* widmen, sich abgeben mit: ~ *doing s.th.* dazu übergehen, et. zu tun; **3.** *et.* anfangen, sich ergeben (*dat.*), sich verlegen auf (*acc.*); *schlechte Gewohnheiten* annehmen: ~ *drink(ing)* sich aufs Trinken verlegen, das Trinken anfangen; **4.** sich hingezogen fühlen zu, Gefallen finden an *j-m*; ~ **up·on** *v/t.*: ~ *o.s. et.* auf sich nehmen: *take it upon o.s. to do s.th.*

a) es auf sich nehmen, et. zu tun, b) sich berufen fühlen, et. zu tun; ~ **with** *v/i.* verfangen bei *j-m*: *that won't ~ me* das ,zieht' bei mir nicht;

Zssgn mit adv.:

take| a·back *v/t.* verblüffen, über'raschen; → **aback** 3; ~ **a·long** *v/t.* mitnehmen; ~ **a·part** *v/t.* (*a.* F *fig. Gegner etc.*) ausein'ander nehmen; ~ **a·side** *v/t.* *j-n* bei'seite nehmen; ~ **a·way** *v/t.* wegnehmen (*from s.o.* j-m, *from s.th.* von et.): *pizzas to ~* (*Schild*) Pizzas zum Mitnehmen; ~ **back** *v/t.* **1.** zu'rücknehmen (*a. fig. sein Wort*); **2.** *j-n im Geist* zu'rückversetzen (*to* in *e-e Zeit*); ~ **down** *v/t.* **1.** her'unter-, abnehmen; **2.** *Gebäude* abreißen, abtragen, *Gerüst* abnehmen; **3.** ☉ *Motor etc.* zerlegen; **4.** *Baum* fällen; **5.** *Arznei etc.* (hin'unter)schlucken; **6.** *j-n* demütigen, ,ducken'; **7.** nieder-, aufschreiben, notieren; ~ **for·ward** *v/t.* weiterführen, -bringen; ~ **in** *v/t.* **1.** *Wasser etc.* (her)'einlassen; **2.** *Gast etc.* einlassen, aufnehmen; **3.** *Heimarbeit* annehmen; **4.** *Geld* einnehmen; **5.** ♉ *Waren* her'einnehmen; **6.** *Zeitung* halten; **7.** *fig.* in sich aufnehmen; *Lage* über'schauen; **8.** für bare Münze nehmen, glauben; **9.** her'einnehmen, einziehen, ⚓ *Segel* einholen; **10.** *Kleider* kürzer *od.* enger machen; **11.** einschließen (*a. fig. umfassen*); **12.** F *j-n* reinlegen: *be taken in* a) reinfallen, b) reingefallen sein; ~ **off** I *v/t.* **1.** wegnehmen, -bringen; -schaffen; fortführen: *take o.s. off* sich fortmachen; **2.** *durch den Tod* hinraffen; **3.** *Verkehrsmittel* einstellen; **4.** *Hut etc.* abnehmen, *Kleidungsstück* ablegen, ausziehen; **5.** ♉ abnehmen, amputieren; **6.** a) *Rabatt* abziehen, b) *Steuer etc.* senken; **7.** hin'unter-, austrinken; **8.** *thea.* Stück absetzen; **9.** *take a day off* sich e-n Tag freinehmen; **10.** *j-n* nachmachen, -äffen, imitieren; **II** *v/i.* **11.** *sport* abspringen; **12.** ✈ aufsteigen, starten; **13.** fortgehen, sich entfernen; ~ **on** I *v/t.* **1.** *Arbeit* annehmen, über'nehmen; **2.** *Arbeiter* ein-, anstellen; *Mitglied* aufnehmen; **3.** a) *j-n* (als Gegner) annehmen, b) es aufnehmen mit *od.* gegen; **4.** *Wette* eingehen; **5.** *Eigenschaft, Gestalt, Farbe* annehmen; **II** *v/i.* **6.** F ,sich haben', großes The'ater machen: *don't ~ so!*; ~ **out** *v/t.* **1.** a) herausnehmen, *a. Geld* abheben, b) wegnehmen, entfernen (*of* von, aus); **2.** *Fleck* entfernen (*of* aus); **3.** ☂, ☂☂ *Patent, Vorladung etc.* erwirken; *Versicherung* abschließen; **4.** *take it out* sich schadlos halten (*in* an *e-r Sache*); *take it out of* a) sich rächen od. schadlos halten für (*Beleidigung etc.*), b) *j-n* ,kaputtmachen', erschöpfen, c) *sl. j-n* ,wegputzen', liquidieren: *take it out on s.o.* s-n Zorn an j-m auslassen; **5.** (*of s.o.* j-m) den *Unsinn etc.* austreiben; **6.** *j-n zum Abendessen etc.* ausführen; *Kinder* spazieren führen; ~ **o·ver** I *v/t.* **1.** *Amt, Aufgabe, die Macht etc., a. Idee etc.* über'nehmen; **II** *v/i.* **2.** die Amtsgewalt, Leitung *etc.* über'nehmen: ~ **for** *s.o.* j-s Stelle einnehmen; **3.** *fig.* in den Vordergrund treten; ~ **up** I *v/t.* **1.** aufheben, -nehmen; **2.** *Pflaster* aufreißen; **3.** *Gerät, Waffe* erheben, ergreifen (*against* gegen); **4.** *Reisende* mitnehmen; **5.** *Flüssigkeit* aufsaugen, -nehmen; **6.** *Tätigkeit* aufnehmen; sich befassen mit, sich verlegen auf (*acc.*); *Beruf* ergreifen; **7.** *Fall, Idee etc.* aufgreifen: *take s.o. up on s.th.* bei j-m we-

gen *e-r Sache* einhaken (→ 17); **8.** *Erzählung etc.* fortführen; **9.** *Platz, Zeit, Gedanken etc.* ausfüllen, beanspruchen, in Anspruch nehmen: *taken up with* in Anspruch genommen von; **10.** *Wohnsitz* aufschlagen; **11.** *Stelle* antreten; **12.** *Posten* einnehmen; **13.** *Verbrecher* aufgreifen, verhaften; **14.** *Masche* aufnehmen; **15.** ♉ *Gefäß* abbinden; **16.** ♀ a) *Anleihe, Kapital* aufnehmen, b) *Aktien* zeichnen, c) *Wechsel* einlösen; **17.** *Wette, Herausforderung* annehmen: *take s.o. up on it* die Herausforderung annehmen; **18.** a) *j-m Redner* ins Wort fallen, b) *j-n* zu'rechtweisen, korrigieren; **II** *v/i.* **19.** ~ **with** anbändeln *od.* sich einlassen mit.

'take|·a·way *Brit.* **I** *adj.* zum Mitnehmen: ~ *meals*; **II** *s.* Restau'rant *n* mit Straßenverkauf; **'~·down I** *adj.* zerlegbar; **II** *s.* Zerlegen *n*; **'~·home pay** *s.* Nettolohn *m*, -gehalt *n*; **'~·in** *s.* F **1.** Schwindel *m*, Betrug *m*; **2.** ,Reinfall' *m*.

tak·en ['teɪkən] *p.p. von* **take**.

'take|·off *s.* **1.** ✈ Start *m* (*a. mot.*), Abflug *m*; → **assist** 1; **2.** *sport* a) Absprung *m*, b) Absprungstelle *f*: ~ *board* Absprungbalken *m*; **3.** *a.* ~ *point fig.* Ausgangspunkt *m*; **4.** Nachahmung *f*, -äffung *f*, Karika'tur *f*; **'~·out** I *s.* **1.** → **takeaway** I; **II** *s.* **2.** → **takeaway** II; **3.** *sl.* Liquidierung *f*; **'~·o·ver** *s.* **1.** ♀ 'Übernahme *f e-r Firma*: ~ *bid* Übernahmeangebot *n*; **2.** *pol.* 'Macht,übernahme *f*.

tak·er ['teɪkə] *s.* **1.** Nehmer(in); **2.** ♀ Käufer(in); **3.** Wettende(r *m*) *f*.

tak·ing ['teɪkɪŋ] I *s.* **1.** (An-, Ab-, Auf-, Ein-, Ent-, Hin-, Weg- *etc.*)Nehmen *n* (*etc.* → **take** II); ☂☂ Wegnahme *f*; **2.** Inbe'sitznahme *f*; **3.** ⚔ Einnahme *f*, Eroberung *f*; **4.** *pl.* ♀ Einnahmen *pl.*; **5.** F Aufregung *f*; **II** *adj.* □ **6.** fesselnd; **7.** anziehend, einnehmend, gewinnend; **8.** F ansteckend.

talc [tælk] *s.* Talk *m*.

tal·cum ['tælkəm] *s.* Talk *m*; ~ **pow·der** *s.* **1.** Talkum(puder *m*) *n*; **2.** Körperpuder *m*.

tale [teɪl] *s.* **1.** Erzählung *f*, Bericht *m*: *it tells its own ~* es spricht für sich selbst; **2.** Erzählung *f*, Geschichte *f*: *old wives' ~* Ammenmärchen *n*; *thereby hangs a ~* damit ist e-e Geschichte verknüpft; **3.** Sage *f*, Märchen *n*; **4.** Lüge(ngeschichte) *f*, Unwahrheit *f*; **5.** Klatschgeschichte *f*: *tell* (*od.* *carry*, *bear*) *~s* klatschen; *tell ~s* (*out of school*) *fig.* aus der Schule plaudern; **'~·bear·er** *s.* Klatschmaul *n*; **'~·bear·ing** *s.* Zuträge'rei *f*, Klatsch(e'rei) *m*.

tal·ent ['tælənt] *s.* **1.** Ta'lent *n*, Begabung *f* (*beide a. Person*): ~ *for languages* Sprachtalent; **2.** *coll.* Ta'lente *pl.* (*Personen*): *engage the best ~* die besten Kräfte verpflichten; ~ *scout* Talentsucher *m*; ~ *show* ,Talentschuppen' *m*; **3.** *bibl.* Pfund *n*; **'tal·ent·ed** [-tɪd] *adj.* talen'tiert, ta'lentvoll, begabt; **'tal·ent·less** [-lɪs] *adj.* 'untalen,tiert, ta'lentlos.

ta·les·man ['teɪliːzmən] *s.* [*irr.*] Ersatzgeschworene(r) *m*.

'tale,tell·er *s.* **1.** Märchen-, Geschichtenerzähler(in); **2.** Flunkerer *m*; **3.** a) Klatschmaul *n*, b) Petzer(in).

tal·is·man ['tælɪzmən] *pl.* **-mans** *s.* Talisman *m*.

talk [tɔːk] I *s.* **1.** Reden *n*; **2.** Gespräch *n*: a) Unter'haltung *f*, Plaude'rei *f*, b) *a. pol.* Unter'redung *f*: *have a ~ with s.o.* mit j-m reden *od.* plaudern, sich mit j-m unterhalten; **3.** Ansprache *f*; **4.**

bsd. Radio: a) Plaude'rei *f*, b) Vortrag *m*; **5.** Gerede *n*, Geschwätz *n*: *he is all ~* er ist ein großer Schwätzer; *end in ~* im Sand verlaufen; *there is ~ of his being bankrupt* es heißt, dass er bank(e)rott ist; → *small talk*; **6.** Gesprächsgegenstand *m*: *be the ~ of the town* Stadtgespräch sein; **7.** Sprache *f*, Art *f* zu reden; → *baby talk*; **II** *v/i.* **8.** reden, sprechen; *~ big* große Reden führen, ,angeben'; *~ round s.th.* um et. herumreden; **9.** reden, sprechen, plaudern, sich unter'halten (*about, on* über *acc., of* von): *~ at j-n* indirekt ansprechen, meinen; *~ to s.o.* a) mit j-m sprechen, b) reden, b) F j-m die Meinung sagen; *~ to o.s.* Selbstgespräche führen; *~ing of* da wir gerade von ... sprechen; *you can ~!* F du hast gut reden!; *now you are ~ing!* sl. das lässt sich eher hören!; **10.** *contp.* reden, schwatzen; **11.** *b.s.* reden, klatschen (*about* über *acc.*); **III** *v/t.* **12.** *et.* reden: *~ nonsense; ~ sense* vernünftig reden; **13.** reden *od.* sprechen über (*acc.*): *~ business (politics);* **14.** *Sprache* sprechen: *~ French;* **15.** reden: *~ o.s. hoarse* sich heiser reden; *~ s.o. into believing s.th.* j-n et. glauben machen; *~ s.o. into (out of) s.th.* j-m et. ein- (aus-) reden;

Zssgn mit adv.:

talk| a·way *v/t.* Zeit verplaudern; *~* **back** *v/i.* e-e freche Antwort geben; *~* **down I** *v/t.* **1.** a) *j-n* unter den Tisch reden, b) niederschreien; **2.** *Flugzeug* ,her'unterschreiben'; **II** *v/i.* **3.** (*to*) sich dem (*niedrigen*) Ni'veau (*e-r Zuhörerschaft*) anpassen; *~* **o·ver** *v/t.* **1.** *j-n* über'reden; **2.** *et.* besprechen, 'durchsprechen; *~* **round** → *talk over* 1; *~* **up I** *v/i.* **1.** laut u. deutlich reden; **II** *v/t. Am.* F **2.** *et.* rühmen, anpreisen; **3.** *et.* freiher'aus sagen.

talk·a·thon ['tɔːkəθɒn] *s. Am.* F Marathonsitzung *f*.

talk·a·tive ['tɔːkətɪv] *adj.* □ geschwätzig, gesprächig, redselig; **'talk·a·tive·ness** [-nɪs] *s.* Geschwätzigkeit *f etc.*

talk·ee-talk·ee [,tɔːkɪ'tɔːkɪ] *s.* F *contp.* Geschwätz *n*.

talk·er ['tɔːkə] *s.* **1.** Schwätzer(in); **2.** Sprecher *m*, Sprechende(r *m*) *f*: *he is a good ~* er kann (gut) reden.

talk·ie ['tɔːkɪ] *s.* F Tonfilm *m*.

talk·ing ['tɔːkɪŋ] **I** *s.* **1.** Sprechen *n*, Reden *n*: *he did all the ~* er führte allein das Wort; *let him do the ~* lass(t) ihn (für uns alle) sprechen; **II** *adj.* **2.** sprechend: *~ doll*; *~ parrot*; **3.** *teleph.* Sprech...: *~ current*; **4.** *fig.* sprechend: *~ eyes*; *~ film*, *~* (**mo·tion**) **pic·ture** *s.* Tonfilm *m*; **'~-to** *pl.* **-tos** *s.* F: *give s.o. a ~* j-m e-e Standpauke halten.

talk show *s. bsd. Am. TV:* Talkshow *f.*

talk·y ['tɔːkɪ] *adj.* F geschwätzig (*a. fig.*); **'~-talk** *s.* F Geschwätz *n.*

tall [tɔːl] **I** *adj.* **1.** groß, hoch gewachsen: *he is six feet ~* er ist sechs Fuß groß; **2.** hoch: *~ house* hohes Haus; **3.** F a) großsprecherisch, b) über'trieben, unglaublich (*Geschichte*): *that's a ~ order* das ist ein bisschen viel verlangt; **II** *adv.* **4.** F prahlerisch: *talk ~* prahlen; **'tall·boy** *s.* hohe Kom'mode; **'tall·ish** [-lɪʃ] *adj.* ziemlich groß; **'tall·ness** [-nɪs] *s.* Größe *f*, Höhe *f*, Länge *f.*

tal·low ['tæləʊ] **I** *s.* **1.** ausgelassener Talg: *vegetable ~* Pflanzenfett *n*; **2.** ◎ Schmiere *f*; **3.** Talg-, Unschlittkerze *f*; **II** *v/t.* **4.** (ein)talgen, schmieren; **5.** *Tiere* mästen; **'~-faced** *adj.* bleich, käsig.

tal·low·y ['tæləʊɪ] *adj.* talgig.

tal·ly¹ ['tælɪ] **I** *s.* **1.** *hist.* Kerbholz *n*, -stock *m*; **2.** ✝ (Ab)Rechnung *f*; **3.** (Gegen)Rechnung *f*; **4.** ✝ Kontogegenbuch *n* (*e-s Kunden*); **5.** Seiten-, Gegenstück *n* (*of* zu); **6.** Zählstrich *m*: *by the ~* nach dem Stück kaufen; **7.** Eti'kett *n*, Marke *f*, Kennzeichen *n* (*auf Kisten etc.*); **8.** Ku'pon *m*; **II** *v/t.* **9.** (stückweise) nachzählen, buchen, kontrollieren; **10.** *oft ~ up* berechnen; **III** *v/i.* **11.** (*with*) über'einstimmen (mit), entsprechen (*dat.*); **12.** stimmen.

tal·ly² ['tælɪ] *v/t.* ♧ *Schoten* beiholen.

tal·ly-ho [,tælɪ'həʊ] *hunt.* **I** *int.* hallo!, ho! (*Jagdruf*); **II** *pl.* **-hos** *s.* Hallo *n*; **III** *v/i.* ,hallo' rufen.

tal·ly| sheet *s.* ✝ Kon'trollliste *f*; *~* **shop** *s.* ✝ *bsd. Brit.* Abzahlungsgeschäft *n*; *~* **sys·tem**, *~* **trade** *s.* ✝ *bsd. Brit.* 'Abzahlungsgeschäft *n*, -sy,stem *n.*

tal·mi gold ['tælmɪ] *s.* Talmigold *n.*

Tal·mud ['tælmʊd] *s.* Talmud *m*; **Tal·mud·ic** [tæl'mʊdɪk] *adj.* tal'mudisch; **'Tal·mud·ist** [-dɪst] *s.* Talmu'dist *m.*

tal·on ['tælən] *s.* **1.** *orn.* Klaue *f*, Kralle *f*; **2.** △ Kehlleiste *f*; **3.** *Kartenspiel:* Ta'lon *m*; **4.** ✝ Ta'lon *m*, 'Zinsku,pon *m.*

ta·lus¹ ['teɪləs] *pl.* **-li** [-laɪ] *s.* **1.** *anat.* Talus *m*, Sprungbein *n*; **2.** Fußgelenk *n*; **3.** ✻ Klumpfuß *m.*

ta·lus² ['teɪləs] *s.* **1.** Böschung *f*; **2.** *geol.* Geröll-, Schutthalde *f.*

tam [tæm] → *tam-o'-shanter.*

tam·a·ble ['teɪməbl] *adj.* (be)zähmbar.

tam·a·rack ['tæməræk] *s.* ♦ **1.** Nordamer. Lärche *f*; **2.** Tamarakholz *n*;

tam·a·rind ['tæmərɪnd] *s.* ♦ Tama'rinde *f*; **tam·a·risk** ['tæmərɪsk] *s.* ♦ Tama'riske *f.*

tam·bour ['tæm,bʊə] **I** *s.* **1.** (große) Trommel; **2.** *a.* *~ frame* Stickrahmen *m*; **3.** △ a) *~ assets* Säulentrommel *f*, b) Tambour *m* (*Unterbau e-r Kuppel*); **5.** *Festungsbau:* Tambour *m*; **II** *v/t.* **6.** *Stoff* tambu'rieren.

tam·bou·rine [,tæmbə'riːn] *s.* ♪ (flaches) Tamb(o)u'rin.

tame [teɪm] **I** *adj.* □ **1.** *allg.* zahm: a) gezähmt (*Tier*), b) friedlich, c) folgsam, d) harmlos (*Witz*), e) lahm, fad(e): *a ~ affair*; **II** *v/t.* **2.** zähmen, bändigen (*a. fig.*); **3.** *Land* urbar machen; **'tame·ness** [-nɪs] *s.* Zahmheit *f* (*a. fig.*); **2.** Unter'würfigkeit *f*; **3.** Harmlosigkeit *f*; **4.** Lahmheit *f*, Langweiligkeit *f*; **'tam·er** [-mə] *s.* (Be)Zähmer(in), Bändiger(in).

Tam·ma·ny ['tæmənɪ] *s. pol. Am.* **1.** a) *Tammany Hall*, b) *Tammany Society*; **2.** *fig.* po'litische Korrupti'on, ,Filz' *m*; *~* **Hall** *s. pol. Am.* **1.** Zentrale *der Tammany Society in New York*; **2.** *fig. a.* *~* **So·ci·e·ty** *s. pol. Am.* organi'sierte demokratische Partei in New York.

tam-o'-shan·ter [,tæmə'ʃæntə] *s.* Schottenmütze *f.*

tamp [tæmp] *v/t.* ◎ **1.** *Bohrloch* besetzen; zustopfen; **2.** *Sprengladung* ver'dämmen; **3.** *Lehm etc.* feststampfen; *Beton* rammen.

tamp·er¹ ['tæmpə] *s.* ◎ Stampfer *m.*

tam·per² ['tæmpə] *v/i.* **1.** *~ with* a) sich (unbefugt) zu schaffen machen mit, her'umbasteln *od.* -pfuschen an (*dat.*), *bsd. Urkunde etc.* verfälschen, ,frisieren'; **2.** sich (ein)mischen in (*acc.*), b) hin'einpfuschen in (*acc.*); **3.** a) mit *j-m* intrigieren, b) *bsd. Zeugen* (zu) bestechen (suchen).

tam·pon ['tæmpən] **I** *s.* **1.** ✻, *a. typ.*

Tam'pon *m*; **2.** *allg.* Pfropfen *m*; **II** *v/t.* **3.** ✻, *typ.* tamponieren.

tan [tæn] **I** *s.* **1.** ◎ Lohe *f*; **2.** ♠ Gerbstoff *m*; **3.** Lohfarbe *f*; **4.** (gelb)braunes Kleidungsstück (*bsd. Schuh*); **5.** (Sonnen)Bräune *f*; **II** *v/t.* **6.** ◎ a) *Leder* gerben (*a. phot.*), b) beizen; **7.** *Haut* bräunen; **8.** F versohlen, *j-m* das Fell gerben; **III** *v/i.* **9.** a) sich bräunen (*Haut*), b) braun werden; **IV** *adj.* **10.** lohfarben, gelbbraun; **11.** Gerb...

tan·dem ['tændəm] **I** *adv.* **1.** hinterei-'nander (angeordnet) (*bsd. Pferde, Maschinen etc.*); **II** *s.* **2.** Tandem *n* (*Gespann, Wagen, Fahrrad*): *work in ~ with fig.* zs.-arbeiten mit; **3.** ◎ Reihe *f*, Tandem *n*; **4.** ⚡ Kas'kade *f*; **III** *adj.* **5.** Tandem..., hinterein'ander angeordnet; *~* **bicycle** Tandem *n*; *~* **connection** ⚡ Kaskadenschaltung *f* *~* **compound** (**engine**) Reihenverbundmaschine *f.*

tang¹ [tæŋ] *s.* **1.** ◎ a) Griffzapfen *m* (*Messer etc.*), b) Angel *f*, c) Dorn *m*; **2.** scharfer Geruch *od.* Geschmack; Beigeschmack *m* (*of* von) (*a. fig.*).

tang² [tæŋ] **I** *s.* (scharfer) Klang; **II** *v/i. u. v/t.* (laut u. scharf) ertönen (lassen).

tang³ [tæŋ] *s.* ♦ Seetang *m.*

tan·gent ['tændʒənt] **I** *s.* ⅄ Tan'gente *f*: *fly* (*od. go*) *off at a ~ fig.* plötzlich (vom Thema) abspringen; **II** *adj.* → *tangential 1*; **tan·gen·tial** [tæn'dʒenʃl] *adj.* □ **1.** ⅄ berührend, tangenti'al, Berührungs..., Tangential...: *~ force* Tangentialkraft *f*; *~ plane* Berührungsebene *f*; *be ~ to et.* berühren; **2.** *fig.* a) sprunghaft, flüchtig, b) ziellos, c) 'untergeordnet, Neben...

tan·ge·rine [,tændʒə'riːn] *s.* ♦ Manda'rine *f.*

tan·gi·ble ['tændʒəbl] *adj.* □ greifbar: a) fühlbar, b) *fig.* handgreiflich, c) ✝ re'al: *~ assets* materielle Vermögenswerte; *~ property* Sachvermögen *n*; **11.** Gerb...

tan·gle ['tæŋgl] **I** *v/t.* **1.** verwirren, -wickeln, durchein'ander bringen (*alle a. fig.*); **2.** verstricken (*a. fig.*); **II** *v/i.* **3.** sich verheddern; **4.** *~ with* sich mit *j-m* (in e-n Kampf *etc.*) einlassen; **III** *s.* **5.** Gewirr *n*, wirrer Knäuel; **6.** Verwirrung *f*, -wicklung *f*, Durchein'ander *n.*

tan·go ['tæŋgəʊ] **I** *pl.* **-gos** *s.* Tango *m* (*Tanz*); **II** *v/i.* *pret. u. p.p.* **-goed** Tango tanzen.

tank [tæŋk] **I** *s.* **1.** *mot. etc.* Tank *m*; **2.** (Wasser)Becken *n*, Zi'sterne *f*; **3.** ⊕ a) Wasserkasten *m*, b) 'Tenderlokomo,tive *f*; **4.** *phot.* Bad *n*; **5.** ✕ Panzer(wagen) *m*, Tank *m*; **6.** *Am. sl.* a) ,Kittchen' *n*, b) (Haft)Zelle *f*; **II** *v/t. u. v/i.* **7.** tanken; **8.** *~ up* a) auftanken, voll tanken, b) *sl.* sich ,voll laufen' lassen: *~ed* besoffen; **'tank·age** [-kɪdʒ] *s.* **1.** Fassungsvermögen *n* e-s Tanks; **2.** (Gebühr *f* für) Aufbewahrung *f* in Tanks; **3.** ✓ Fleischmehl *n* (*Düngemittel*); **'tank·ard** [-kəd] *s.* (*bsd.* Bier)Krug *m*, Humpen *m.*

'tank|,bust·er *s.* ✕ *sl.* **1.** Panzerknacker *m*; **2.** Jagdbomber *m* zur Panzerbekämpfung; *~* **car** *s.* 🚃 Kesselwagen *m*; *~* **de·stroy·er** *s.* ✕ Sturmgeschütz *n*; *~* **dra·ma** *s. thea. Am.* F Sensati'onsstück *n.*

tank·er ['tæŋkə] *s.* **1.** ♧ Tanker *m*, Tankschiff *n*; **2.** *a.* *~ aircraft* ✈ Tankflugzeug *n*; **3.** *mot.* Tankwagen *m.*

tank farm·ing *s.* 'Hydrokul,tur *f.*

tank top *s.* Pull'under *m.*

tan liq·uor *s.* ◎ Beizbrühe *f.*

tanned [tænd] *adj.* braun gebrannt.

tan·ner¹ ['tænə] *s. Brit. obs. sl.* Sixpencestück *n*.

tan·ner² ['tænə] *s.* ◎ (Loh)Gerber *m*; **'tan·ner·y** [-ərɪ] *s.* Gerbe'rei *f*; **'tan·nic** [-nɪk] *adj.* Gerb...: ~ *acid*; **'tan·nin** [-nɪn] *s.* 🍂 Tan'nin *n*.

tan·ning ['tænɪŋ] *s.* **1.** Gerben *n*; **2.** (Tracht *f*) Prügel *pl*.

tan| ooze, ~ **pick·le** → *tan liquor*; ~ **pit** *s.* Gerberei: Lohgrube *f*.

tan·ta·li·za·tion [,tæntəlaɪ'zeɪʃn] *s.* **1.** Quälen *n*, Zappelnlassen *n*; **2.** (Tanta-lus)Qual *f*; **tan·ta·lize** ['tæntəlaɪz] *v/t.* *fig.* peinigen, quälen, zappeln lassen; **tan·ta·liz·ing** ['tæntəlaɪzɪŋ] *adj.* □ quä-lend, aufreizend, verlockend.

tan·ta·mount ['tæntəmaʊnt] *adj.* gleich-bedeutend (**to** mit): **be** ~ **to** a. gleich-kommen (*dat.*).

tan·tiv·y [tæn'tɪvɪ] **I** *s.* **1.** schneller Ga-'lopp; **2.** Hussa *n* (*Jagdruf*); **II** *adv.* **3.** eiligst, spornstreichs.

tan·trum ['tæntrəm] *s.* F **1.** schlechte Laune; **2.** Wut(anfall *m*) *f*, Koller *m*: *fly into a* ~ e-n Koller kriegen.

Taois·each ['ti:ʃəx; -ʃək] *s.* irisch-gäli-sche Bezeichnung für den Premiermi-nister.

tap¹ [tæp] **I** *s.* **1.** Zapfen *m*, Spund *m* (Fass)Hahn *m*: *on* ~ a) angestochen, angezapft (*Fass*), b) vom Fass (*Bier etc.*), c) *fig.* (sofort) verfügbar; **2.** *Brit.* a) (Wasser-, Gas)Hahn *m*, b) Wasser-leitung *f*: *turn on the* ~ F ,losflennen'; **3.** F (Getränke)Sorte *f*; **4.** *Brit.* → *tap-room*; **5.** ◎ a) Gewindebohrer *m*, b) (Ab)Stich *m*, c) Abzweigung *f*; **6.** ⚡ a) Stromabnehmer *m*, b) Zapfstelle *f*; **7.** 🎣 Punkti'on *f*; **II** *v/t.* **8.** mit e-m Zapfen *od.* Hahn versehen; **9.** *Flüssigkeit* ab-zapfen; **10.** *Fass* anstechen; **11.** 🎣 punktieren; **12.** 🎣 *Telefonleitung etc.* anzapfen: ~ *the wire(s)* a) Strom ab-zapfen, b) Telefongespräche *etc.* abhö-ren; **13.** 🎣 a) *Spannung* abgreifen, b) anschließen; **14.** ◎ mit (e-m) Gewinde versehen; **15.** *metall.* *Schlacke* abste-chen; **16.** *fig.* *Hilfsquellen etc.* erschlie-ßen; **17.** *fig.* *Vorräte etc.* angreifen, an-brechen; **18.** *sl.* *j-n* ,anpumpen' (*for* um).

tap² [tæp] **I** *v/t.* **1.** (leicht) klopfen *od.* pochen an (*acc.*) *od.* auf (*acc.*) *od.* ge-gen, *et.* beklopfen; **2.** klopfen mit; **3.** *Schuh* flicken; **II** *v/i.* **4.** klopfen (**on, at** gegen, an *acc.*); **III** *s.* **5.** Klaps *m*, leich-ter Schlag; **6.** *pl.* ✕ *Am.* Zapfenstreich *m*; **7.** Stück *n* Leder *m*, Flicken *m*.

tap| dance *s.* Stepptanz *m*; **'~-dance** *v/i.* steppen; **~ danc·er** *s.* Stepptän-zer(in); **~ danc·ing** *s.* Stepptanz *m*, Steppen *n*.

tape [teɪp] **I** *s.* **1.** schmales (Leinen-) Band, Zwirnband *n*; **2.** (Isolier-, Mess-, Me'tall- *etc.*)Band *n*, (Pa'pier-, Kleb-*etc.*)Streifen *m*; 🎣 Heftpflaster *n*; **3.** a) *Telegrafie:* Pa'pierstreifen *m*, b) *Fern-schreiber, Computer:* Lochstreifen *m*; **4.** 🎣 (Video-, Ton)Band *n*; **5.** *sport* Zielband *n*: *breast the* ~ das Zielband durchreißen; **II** *v/t.* **6.** mit Band verse-hen; (mit Band) um'wickeln *od.* bin-den; **7.** mit Heftpflaster verkleben; **8.** *Buchteile* heften; **9.** mit dem Bandmaß messen: *I've got him* ~*d sl.* ich habe ihn durchschaut, ich weiß genau Be-scheid über ihn; **10.** mitschneiden: a) auf (Ton)Band aufnehmen, b) *TV* auf-zeichnen; ~ **deck** *s.* 🎣 Tapedeck *n*; ~ **li·brar·y** s. 'Bandar,chiv *n*; ~ **line**, ~ **meas·ure** *s.* Maßband *n*, Bandmaß *n*; ~ **play·er** *s.* 🎣 'Band,wiedergabegerät *n*.

ta·per ['teɪpə] **I** *s.* **1.** (dünne) Wachsker-ze; **2.** ◎ Verjüngung *f*; **3.** 🎣 'Wider-

standsverteilung *f*; **II** *adj.* **4.** spitz zulau-fend, verjüngt; **III** *v/t.* **5.** zuspitzen, ver-jüngen; **6.** ~ *off* *fig.* F *Produktion*, *a.* *den Tag etc.* auslaufen lassen; **IV** *v/i.* **7.** *oft* ~ *off* spitz zulaufen, sich verjüngen; all'mählich dünn werden; **8.** ~ *off* F all-'mählich aufhören, auslaufen.

'tape|-re,cord *v/t.* → *tape* 10; ~ **re-cord·er** *s.* 🎣 Tonbandgerät *n*; ~ **re-cord·ing** *s.* **1.** (Ton)Bandaufnahme *f*; **2.** *TV:* Aufzeichnung *f*.

ta·pered ['teɪpəd] *adj.*, **'ta·per·ing** [-ərɪŋ] → *taper* 4.

tap·es·tried ['tæpɪstrɪd] *adj.* gobe'linge-schmückt; **tap·es·try** ['tæpɪstrɪ] *s.* **1.** a) Gobe'lin *m*, Wandteppich *m*, gewirkte Ta'pete, b) Dekorati'onsstoff *m*; **2.** Ta-pisse'rie *f*.

'tape-worm *s.* *zo.* Bandwurm *m*.

tap·pet ['tæpɪt] *s.* ◎ **1.** Daumen *m*, Mit-nehmer *m*; **2.** (Ven'til- *etc.*)Stößel *m*; **3.** (Wellen)Nocke *f*; **4.** (Steuer)Knag-ge *f*.

'tap|·room [-rʊm] *s.* Schankstube *f*; **'~-root** *s.* ⚘ Pfahlwurzel *f*.

tar [tɑː] **I** *s.* **1.** Teer *m*; **2.** F ,Teerjacke' *f* (*Matrose*), **II** *v/t.* **3.** teeren: ~ *and feather* *j-n* teeren u. federn; ~*red with the same brush* (*od.* *stick*) kein Haar besser.

tar·a·did·dle ['tærədɪdl] *s.* F **1.** Flunke-'rei *f*; **2.** Quatsch *m*.

ta·ran·tu·la [tə'ræntjʊlə] *s.* *zo.* Ta'rantel *f*.

'tar|·board *s.* Dach-, Teerpappe *f*; **'~-brush** *s.* Teerpinsel *m*: *he has a touch of the* ~ *Am. sl. contp.* er hat schwarzes Blut in den Adern.

tar·di·ness ['tɑːdɪnɪs] *s.* **1.** Langsamkeit *f*; **2.** Unpünktlichkeit *f*; **3.** Verspätung *f*; **tar·dy** ['tɑːdɪ] *adj.* □ **1.** langsam, träge; **2.** säumig, unpünktlich; **3.** spät, verspätet: *be* ~ (zu) spät kommen.

tare¹ [teə] *s.* **1.** ⚘ (*bsd.* Futter)Wicke *f*; **2.** *bibl.* Unkraut *n*.

tare² [teə] 🍂 **I** *s.* Tara *f*: ~ *and tret* Tara u. Gutgewicht *n*; **II** *v/t.* tarieren.

tar·get ['tɑːgɪt] **I** *s.* **1.** (Schieß-, Ziel-) Scheibe *f*; **2.** ✕, *Radar etc.:* Ziel *n* (*a.* *fig.*): *be off* ~ das Ziel verfehlen, dane-benschießen, *fig.* ,danebenhauen'; *be on* ~ a) das Ziel erfasst haben, *a.* sich eingeschossen haben, *sport* aufs Tor ge-hen (*Schuss*), b) treffen, sitzen (*Schuss etc.*), c) *fig.* richtig geraten haben; **3.** *fig.* Zielscheibe *f des Spottes etc.*; **4.** *fig.* (Leistungs-, Produkti'ons- *etc.*)Ziel *n*, Soll *n*; **5.** 🔔 'Weichensi,gnal *n*; **6.** 🎣 a) 'Fangelek,trode *f*, b) 'Antika,t(h)ode *f* von Röntgenröhren, c) *Kernphysik:* Target *n*; **7.** *her.* runder Schild; **II** *adj.* **8.** Ziel...: ~ *area* ✕ Zielbereich *m*, -raum *m*; ~ *bombing* gezielter Bom-benwurf; ~ *date* Stichtag *m*, Termin *m*; ~ *electrode* → 6 a; ~ *group* ✝ Ziel-gruppe *f*; ~ *language* Zielsprache *f*; ~ *pistol* Übungspistole *f*; ~ *practice* Übungs-, Scheibenschießen *n*; ~-*seek-ing* zielsuchend (*Rakete etc.*).

tar·iff ['tærɪf] **I** *s.* **1.** 'Zollta,rif *m*; **2.** Zoll (-gebühr *f*) *m*; **3.** (Ge'bühren-, 'Kosten-*etc.*)Ta,rif *m*; **4.** Preisverzeichnis *n* (*in e-m Hotel etc.*); **II** *v/t.* **5.** e-n Ta'rif auf-stellen für; **6.** *Ware* mit Zoll belegen; ~ *rate* *s.* **1.** Ta'rifsatz *m*; **2.** Zollsatz *m*; ~ *wall* *s.* Zollschranke *f e-s Staates.*

tar·mac ['tɑːmæk] *s.* *Brit.* 'Teermaka-,dam(straße *f*, ✈ -rollfeld *n*) *m*, ✈ *a.* Hallenvorfeld *n*.

tar·nish ['tɑːnɪʃ] **I** *v/t.* **1.** trüben, matt *od.* blind machen, e-r *Sache* den Glanz nehmen; **2.** *fig.* besudeln, beflecken; **3.** ◎ mattieren; **II** *v/i.* **4.** matt *od.* trübe

werden; **5.** anlaufen (*Metall*); **III** *s.* **6.** Trübung *f*; Beschlag *m*, Anlaufen *n* (*von Metall*); **7.** *fig.* Fleck *m*, Makel *m*.

tar·ot ['tærəʊ] *s.* Ta'rot *n* (*Kartenlegen bzw. -spiel*).

tarp [tɑːp] *abbr.* → **tar·pau·lin** [tɑː'pɔː-lɪn] *s.* **1.** ⚓ a) Per'senning *f* (*geteertes Segeltuch*), b) Ölzeug *n* (*Hose, Mantel*); **2.** Plane *f*, Wagendecke *f*; **3.** Zeltbahn *f*.

tar·ra·did·dle → *taradiddle*.

tar·ry¹ ['tɑːrɪ] *adj.* teerig.

tar·ry² ['tærɪ] **I** *v/i.* **1.** zögern, zaudern, säumen; **2.** (ver)weilen, bleiben; **II** *v/t.* **3.** *obs. et.* abwarten.

tar·sal ['tɑːsl] *anat.* **I** *adj.* **1.** Fußwurzel-zel...; **2.** (Augen)Lidknorpel...; **II** *s.* **3.** *a.* ~ *bone* Fußwurzelknochen *m*; **4.** (Augen)Lidknorpel *m*.

tar·si·a ['tɑːsɪə] *s.* In'tarsia *f*, Einlegear-beit *f* in Holz.

tar·sus ['tɑːsəs] *pl.* **-si** [-saɪ] *s.* **1.** → *tarsal* 3 *u.* 4; **2.** *orn.* Laufknochen *m*; **3.** *zo.* Fußglied *n*.

tart¹ [tɑːt] *adj.* □ **1.** sauer, herb, scharf; **2.** *fig.* scharf, beißend: ~ *reply*.

tart² [tɑːt] **I** *s.* a) (Obst)Torte *f*, Obst-kuchen *m*, b) *bsd. Am.* (Creme-, Obst-) Törtchen *n*; **2.** *sl.* ,Nutte' *f*; **II** *v/t.* ~ *up* *sl.* ,aufputzen', ,aufmotzen'.

tar·tan¹ ['tɑːtən] *s.* Tartan *m*: a) Schot-tentuch *n*, b) Schottenmuster *n*: ~ *plaid* Schottenplaid *n*.

tar·tan² ['tɑːtən] *s.* *sport* Tartan *m* (*Bahnbelag*).

Tar·tar¹ ['tɑːtə] **I** *s.* **1.** Ta'tar(in); **2.** *a.* 🜪 Wüterich *m*, böser Kerl: *catch a* ~ an den Unrechten kommen; **II** *adj.* **3.** ta'tarisch.

tar·tar² ['tɑːtə] *s.* **1.** Weinstein *m*: ~ *emetic* 🜪 Brechweinstein; **2.** Zahn-stein *m*.

tar·tar(e) sauce ['tɑːtə] *s.* *etwa:* Remou-'ladensoße *f*.

tar·tar·ic [tɑː'tærɪk] *adj.*: ~ *acid* 🜪 Weinsäure *f*.

tart·ness ['tɑːtnɪs] *s.* Schärfe *f*: a) Säure *f*, Herbheit *f*, b) *fig.* Schroffheit *f*, Bis-sigkeit *f*.

task [tɑːsk] **I** *s.* **1.** Aufgabe *f*: *take to* ~ *fig.* *j-n* ins Gebet nehmen (*for* wegen); **2.** Pflicht *f*, (auferlegte) Arbeit; **3.** *ped.* (Prüfungs)Aufgabe *f*; **II** *v/t.* **4.** *j-m* Ar-beit zuweisen *od.* aufbürden, *j-n* be-schäftigen; **5.** *fig.* Kräfte etc. stark be-anspruchen, *sein Gedächtnis etc.* an-strengen; ~ *bar* *s.* Computer: Task-Leis-te *f*; ~ *force s.* **1.** ✕ gemischter Kampf-verband (*für Sonderunternehmen*), Task-Force *f*; **2.** Polizei: a) Spezi'aleinheit *f*, Einsatzgruppe *f*, b) 'Sonder-dezer,nat *n*; **3.** 🎣 Pro'jektgruppe *f*; **'~,mas·ter** *s.* **1.** (*bsd.* strenger) Arbeit-geber: *severe* ~ *fig.* strenger Zuchtmeis-ter; **2.** ◎ (Arbeit)Anweiser *m*; ~ **wag-es** *s. pl.* 🎣 Ak'kord-, Stücklohn *m*; **'~-work** *s.* **1.** 🎣 Ak'kordarbeit *f*; **2.** harte Arbeit.

tas·sel ['tæsl] **I** *s.* Quaste *f*, Troddel *f*; **II** *v/t.* mit Quasten schmücken.

taste [teɪst] **I** *v/t.* **1.** *Speisen etc.* kosten, (ab)schmecken, probieren, versuchen (*a. fig.*); **2.** kosten, *Essen* anrühren: *he had not* ~*d food for days*; **3.** *et.* (he-'raus)schmecken; **4.** *fig.* kosten, kennen lernen, erleben; **5.** *fig.* genießen; **II** *v/i.* **6.** schmecken (*of* nach); **7.** kosten, ver-suchen (*of* von *od. acc.*); **8.** ~ *of* → 4; **III** *s.* **9.** Geschmack *m*: *a* ~ *of garlic* ein Knoblauchgeschmack; *leave a bad* ~ *in one's mouth* *bsd. fig.* e-n üblen Nachgeschmack haben; **10.** Ge-schmackssinn *m*; **11.** (Kost)Probe *f* (*of* von *od. gen.*): a) kleiner Bissen, b) Schlückchen *n*; **12.** *fig.* (Kost)Probe *f*, Vorgeschmack *m* (*of gen.*); **13.** *fig.* Beigeschmack *m*, Anflug *m* (*of* von); **14.** *fig.* (künstlerischer *od.* guter) Geschmack: *in bad* ~ geschmacklos (*a. weitS. unfein, taktlos*); *in good* ~ a) geschmackvoll, b) taktvoll; *each to his (own)* ~ jeder nach s-m Geschmack; **15.** Geschmacksrichtung *f*, Mode *f*; **16.** a) Neigung *f*, Sinn *m* (*for* für), b) Geschmack *m*, Gefallen *n* (*for* an *dat.*): *not to my* ~ nicht nach m-m Geschmack; **taste bud** *s. anat.* Geschmacksbecher *m*; '**taste-ful** [-fʊl] *adj.* □ *fig.* geschmackvoll; '**taste-ful-ness** [-fʊlnɪs] *s. fig.* guter Geschmack *e-r Sache, das* Geschmackvolle; '**taste-less** [-lɪs] *adj.* □ **1.** unschmackhaft, fade; **2.** *fig.* geschmacklos; '**taste-less-ness** [-lɪsnɪs] *s.* **1.** Unschmackhaftigkeit *f*; **2.** *fig.* Geschmack-, Taktlosigkeit *f*; '**tast-er** [-tə] *s.* **1.** (berufsmäßiger Tee-, Wein- *etc.*)Koster *m*; **2.** *hist.* Vorkoster *m*; **3.** Pro'biergläs-chen *n* (*für Wein*); **4.** (Käse)Stecher *m*; '**tast-i-ness** [-tɪnɪs] *s.* **1.** Schmackhaftigkeit *f* (*Speise etc.*); **2.** *fig.* → *tastefulness*; '**tast-y** [-tɪ] *adj.* □ **F 1.** schmackhaft; **2.** *fig.* geschmack-, stilvoll.

ta-ta [ˌtæˈtɑː] *int. Brit.* F ˌtschüss'!, auf 'Wiedersehen!

Ta-tar [ˈtɑːtə] I *s.* Ta'tar(in); II *adj.* ta'tarisch; **Ta-tar-i-an** [tɑːˈteərɪən], **Ta-tar-ic** [tɑːˈtærɪk] *adj.* ta'tarisch.

tat-ter [ˈtætə] *s.* Lumpen *m*, Fetzen *m*: *in* ~s zerfetzt; *tear to* ~s (*a. fig. Argument etc.*) zerfetzen, -reißen; '**tat-tered** [-təd] *adj.* **1.** zerlumpt, abgerissen; **2.** zerrissen, zerfetzt; **3.** ramponiert (*Ruf etc.*).

tat-tle [ˈtætl] I *v/i.* klatschen, ˌtratschen'; II *v/t.* ausplaudern; III *s.* Klatsch *m*, ˌTratsch' *m*; '**tat-tler** [-lə] *s.* Klatschbase *f*, -maul *n*.

tat-too[1] [təˈtuː] I *s.* **1.** ✕ a) Zapfenstreich *m* (*Signal*), b) 'Abendpaˌrade *f* mit Mu'sik; **2.** Trommeln *n*, Klopfen *n*: *beat a* (*od. the devil's*) ~ ungeduldig mit den Fingern trommeln; II *v/i.* **3.** den Zapfenstreich blasen *od.* trommeln; **4.** trommeln, klopfen.

tat-too[2] [təˈtuː] I *v/t. pret. u. p.p.* **tat-'tooed** [-uːd] **1.** *Haut* tätowieren; **2.** *Muster* eintätowieren (*on* in *acc.*); II *s.* **3.** Tätowierung *f*.

tat-ty [ˈtætɪ] *adj.* schäbig, schmuddelig, ˌbillig'.

taught [tɔːt] *pret. u. p.p. von teach.*

taunt [tɔːnt] I *v/t.* verhöhnen, -spotten: ~ *s.o. with* j-m *et.* (höhnisch) vorwerfen; II *v/i.* höhnen, spotten; III *s.* Spott *m*, Hohn *m*; '**taunt-ing** [-tɪŋ] *adj.* □ spöttisch, höhnisch.

tau-rine [ˈtɔːraɪn] *adj.* **1.** *zo.* a) rinderartig, b) Rinder..., Stier...; **2.** *ast.* Stier...; **Tau-rus** [ˈtɔːrəs] *s. ast.* Stier *m* (*Sternbild u. Tierkreiszeichen*).

taut [tɔːt] *adj.* □ **1.** straff, stramm (*Seil etc.*), angespannt (*a. Nerven, Gesicht, Person*); **2.** schmuck (*Schiff etc.*); '**taut-en** [-tən] I *v/t.* stramm ziehen, straff anspannen; II *v/i.* sich straffen *od.* spannen.

tau-to-log-ic, tau-to-log-i-cal [ˌtɔːtəˈlɒdʒɪk(l)] *adj.* □ tauto'logisch, unnötig das'selbe wieder'holend; **tau-tol-o-gy** [tɔːˈtɒlədʒɪ] *s.* Tautolo'gie *f*, Doppelaussage *f*.

tav-ern [ˈtævən] *s.* **1.** *obs.* Ta'verne *f*, Schenke *f*; **2.** *Am.* Gasthaus *n*.

taw[1] [tɔː] *v/t.* weißgerben.

taw[2] [tɔː] *s.* **1.** Murmel *f*; **2.** Murmelspiel

n; **3.** Ausgangslinie *f*.

taw-dri-ness [ˈtɔːdrɪnɪs] *s.* **1.** Flitterhaftigkeit *f*, grelle Buntheit, Kitsch *m*; **2.** Wertlosigkeit *f*, Billigkeit *f*; **taw-dry** [ˈtɔːdrɪ] *adj.* □ **1.** flitterhaft, Flitter...; **2.** geschmacklos aufgemacht; **3.** grell, knallig; **4.** kitschig, billig.

tawed [tɔːd] *adj. Gerberei:* a'laungar (*Leder*); **taw-er** [ˈtɔːə] *s.* Weißgerber *m*; **taw-er-y** [ˈtɔːərɪ] *s.* Weißgerbe'rei *f*.

taw-ny [ˈtɔːnɪ] *adj.* lohfarben, gelbbraun: ~ *owl orn.* Waldkauz *m*.

taws(e) [tɔːz] *s. Brit.* Peitsche *f*.

tax [tæks] I *s.* **1.** (Staats)Steuer *f* (*on* auf *acc.*), Abgabe *f*: ~ *on land* Grundsteuer; **2.** Besteuerung *f* (*on gen.*); *after* (*before*) ~ nach (vor) Abzug der Steuern, *a.* netto (brutto); **3.** Taxe *f*, Gebühr *f*; **4.** *fig.* a) Bürde *f*, Last *f*, b) Belastung *f*, Beanspruchung *f* (*on gen. od.* von): *a heavy* ~ *on his time* e-e starke Inanspruchnahme s-r Zeit; II *v/t.* **5.** *j-n od. et.* besteuern, *j-m* e-e Steuer auferlegen; **6.** ⚖ *Kosten etc.* schätzen, taxieren, ansetzen (*at* auf *acc.*); **7.** *fig.* belasten; **8.** *fig.* stark in Anspruch nehmen, anstrengen, strapazieren; **9.** auf e-e harte Probe stellen; **10.** *j-n* zu-'rechtweisen: ~ *s.o. with* j-n e-r Sache beschuldigen *od.* bezichtigen; **tax a-bate-ment** *s.* Steuernachlass *m*; **tax-a-ble** [ˈtæksəbl] I *adj.* □ **1.** besteuerbar; **2.** steuerpflichtig: ~ *income*; **3.** Steuer...: → *value*; ⚖ gebührenpflichtig; II *s. Am.* **5.** steuerpflichtiges Einkommen; **6.** Steuerpflichtige(r *m*) *f*; **tax ad-van-tage** *s.* Steuervorteil *m*; **tax al-low-ance** *s.* Steuerfreibetrag *m*; **tax as-sess-ment** *s.* Steuerveranlagung *f*; **tax-a-tion** [tækˈseɪʃn] *s.* **1.** Besteuerung *f*: *subject to* ~ steuerpflichtig; *exempt from* ~ steuerfrei; ~ *system* Steuersystem *n*; **2.** *coll.* Steuern *pl.*; **3.** ⚖ Schätzung *f*, Taxierung *f*.

tax a-void-ance (le'gale) 'Steuerumˌgehung; ~ **brack-et** *s.* Steuerklasse *f*, -gruppe *f*; ~ **bur-den** *s.* Steuerlast *f*; ~ **col-lec-tor** *s.* Steuereinnehmer *m*; ~ **com-pe-ti-tion** *s.* Steuerwettbewerb *m*; ~ **cut** *s.* Steuersenkung *f*; '~**de-duct-i-ble** *adj.* steuerabzugsfähig; ~ **disc** *s. Brit.* Steuermarke *f* (*hinter der Windschutzscheibe*); ~ **dodg-er**, ~ **e-vad-er** *s.* 'Steuerhinter‚zieher *m*; ~ **e-va-sion** *s.* 'Steuerhinter‚ziehung *f*; ‚~**ex'empt**, ‚~'**free** *adj.* steuerfrei; ~ **fraud** *s.* Steuerbetrug *m*; ~ **har-mo-ni-za-tion** *s.* Steuerharmonisierung *f*; ~ **ha-ven** *s.* 'Steuero‚ase *f*; ~ **hol-i-day** *s.* vor'übergehende Steuerbefreiung.

tax-i [ˈtæksɪ] I *pl.* '**tax-is** *s.* **1.** → *taxicab*; II *v/i.* **2.** mit e-m Taxi fahren; **3.** ✈ rollen; '~**cab** *s.* Taxi *n*; ~ **danc-er** *s. Am.* Taxigirl *n*.

tax-i-der-mal [ˌtæksɪˈdɜːml], **tax-i-der-mic** [-mɪk] *adj.* taxi'dermisch; **tax-i-der-mist** [ˈtæksɪdɜːmɪst] *s.* Präpa'rator *m*, Ausstopfer *m* (*von Tieren*); **tax-i-der-my** [ˈtæksɪdɜːmɪ] *s.* Taxider'mie *f*.

tax-i driv-er *s.* 'Taxichauf‚feur *m*, -fahrer *m*; '~‚**me-ter** *s.* Taxa'meter *n*, Fahrpreisanzeiger *m*

tax in-crease [ˈɪŋkriːs] *s.* Steuererhöhung *f*.

'**tax-i-plane** *s.* Lufttaxi *n*; ~ **rank** *s.* Taxistand *m*; ~ **strip**, '~**way** *s.* ✈ Rollbahn *f*.

tax loop-hole *s.* Steuerschlupfloch *n*; '~‚**pay-er** *s.* Steuerzahler *m*; ~ **pol-i-cy** *s.* 'Steuerpoliˌtik *f*; ~ **priv-i-lege** Steuervorteil *m*; ~ **rate** *s.* Steuersatz *m*; ~ **re-ceipts** *s. pl.* Steuereinnahmen *pl.*, Steueraufkommen *n*; ~ **re-form** *s.* 'Steu-

er‚form *f*; ~ **re-fund** *s.* Steuerrückzahlung *f*; ~ **re-gime** *s.* 'Steuersysˌtem *n*; ~ **re-lief** *s.* a) Steuererleichterung(en *pl.*) *f*, b) Steuerbegünstigung *f*; ~ **re-turn** *s.* Steuererklärung *f*; ~ **rev-e-nue** *s.* → *tax receipts*; ~ **shel-ter** *s.* Steuerbegünstigung *f*.

'**T-bone steak** *s.* T-Bone-Steak *n* (*Steak aus dem Rippenstück des Rinds*).

tea [tiː] *s.* **1.** Tee *m*; **2.** Tee(mahlzeit *f*) *m*: *five-o'clock* ~ Fünfuhrtee; **3.** *Am. sl.* ‚Grass' *n* (*Marihuana*); ~ **bag** *s.* Teebeutel *m*; ~ **ball** *s. Am.* Tee-Ei *n*; ~ **bread** *s.* ein Teekuchen *m*; ~ **cad-dy** *s.* Teebüchse *f*; ~ **cake** *s.* Teekuchen *m*; '~**cart** *s.* Teewagen *m*.

teach [tiːtʃ] *pret. u. p.p.* **taught** [tɔːt] I *v/t.* **1.** *Fach* lehren, 'Unterricht geben in (*dat.*); **2.** *j-n et.* lehren, *j-n* unter'richten, -'weisen in (*dat.*), *j-m* 'Unterricht geben in (*dat.*); **3.** *j-m et.* zeigen, beibringen: ~ *s.o. to whistle* j-m das Pfeifen beibringen; ~ *s.o. better* j-n e-s Besser(e)n belehren; *I will* ~ *you to steal* F dich werd ich das Stehlen lehren!; *that'll* ~ *you!* F a) das wird dir e-e Lehre sein!, b) das kommt davon!; **4.** *Tier* dressieren, abrichten; II *v/i.* **5.** unter'richten, 'Unterricht geben, '**teach-a-ble** [-tʃəbl] *adj.* □ **1.** lehrbar (*Fach etc.*); **2.** gelehrig (*Person*); '**teach-er** [-tʃə] *s.* Lehrer(in): ~s *college Am.* pädagogische Hochschule.

'**teach-in** *s.* Teach-in *n*.

teach-ing [ˈtiːtʃɪŋ] I *s.* **1.** Unter'richten *n*, Lehren *n*; **2.** *oft pl.* Lehre *f*, Lehren *pl.*; **3.** Lehrberuf *m*; II *adj.* **4.** lehrend, unter'richtend: ~ *aid* Lehrmittel *n*; ~ *machine* Lehr-, Lernmaschine *f*; ~ *profession* Lehrberuf *m*; ~ *staff* Lehrkörper *m*.

tea cloth *s.* **1.** kleine Tischdecke; **2.** *Am.* Geschirrtuch *m*; ~ **co-sy** *s.*, *Am.* ~ **co-zy** *s.* Teewärmer *m*; '~**cup** *s.* Teetasse *f*; → *storm* 1; '~**cup-ful** [-ˌfʊl] *pl.* **-fuls** *s. e-e* Teetasse (voll); ~ **dance** *s.* Tanztee *m*; ~ **egg** *s.* Tee-Ei *n*; ~ **gar-den** *s.* 'Gartenrestauˌrant *n*; ~ **gown** *s.* Nachmittagskleid *n*; '~**house** *s.* Teehaus *n* (*in China u. Japan*).

teak [tiːk] *s.* **1.** ♀ Teakholzbaum *m*; **2.** Teak(holz) *n*.

teal [tiːl] *pl.* **teal** *s. orn.* Krickente *f*.

team [tiːm] *s.* **1.** Gespann *n*; **2.** *bsd. sport u. fig.* Mannschaft *f*, Team *n*; **3.** (*Arbeits- etc.*)Gruppe *f*, Team *n*: *by a* ~ *effort* mit vereinten Kräften; **4.** Ab'teilung *f*, Ko'lonne *f* (*von Arbeitern*); **5.** *orn.* Flug *m*, Zug *m*; II *v/t.* **6.** *Zugtiere* zs.-spannen; **7.** F *Arbeit* (an Unter'nehmer) vergeben; III *v/i.* **8.** ~ *up bsd. Am.* sich zs.-tun (*with* mit); ~ **e-vent** *s. sport* Mannschaftswettbewerb *m*; '~**mate** *s.* 'Mannschaftskameˌrad *m*; ~ **spir-it** *s.* **1.** *sport* Mannschaftsgeist *m*; **2.** *fig.* Gemeinschaftsgeist *m*.

team-ster [ˈtiːmstə] *s.* **1.** Fuhrmann *m*; **2.** *Am.* Lastwagenfahrer *m*.

team teach-ing *s. Am.* gemeinsamer 'Unterricht (*Fachlehrer*); '~**work** *s.* **1.** *sport, thea.* Zs.-spiel *n*; **2.** Teamarbeit *f*, Teamwork *n*.

tea par-ty *s.* Teegesellschaft *f*: *the Boston Tea Party hist.* der Teesturm von Boston (*1773*); '~**pot** *s.* Teekanne *f*; → *tempest* 1.

tear[1] [tɪə] *s.* **1.** Träne *f*: *in* ~s in Tränen (aufgelöst), unter Tränen; → *fetch* 3, *squeeze* 3; **2.** ⊙ (*Harz- etc.*)Tropfen *m*; (Glas)Träne *f*.

tear[2] [teə] I *s.* **1.** Riss *m*; **2.** *at full* ~ in vollem Schwung; *in a* ~ in wilder Hast; II *v/t.* [*irr.*] **3.** zerreißen: ~ *in* (*od. to*) *pieces* in Stücke reißen; ~ *open* aufreißen; ~ *out* herausreißen; *torn between hope and despair* *fig.* zwischen Hoffnung u. Verzweiflung hin- u. hergerissen; *a country torn by civil war* ein vom Bürgerkrieg zerrissenes Land; *that's torn it! sl.* jetzt ist es passiert!, damit ist alles ,im Eimer'!; **4.** *Haut etc.* aufreißen; **5.** *Loch* reißen; **6.** zerren, (aus)reißen: ~ *one's hair* sich die Haare (aus)raufen; **7.** *a.* ~ *away*, ~ *off* ab-, wegreißen (*from* von): ~ *o.s. away* sich losreißen (*a. fig.*); ~ *s.th. from s.o.* j-m et. entreißen; **III** *v/i.* [*irr.*] **8.** (zer)reißen; **9.** reißen, zerren (*at* an *dat.*); **10.** F rasen, sausen, ,fegen': ~ *about* herumsausen; ~ *up v/t.* **1.** aufreißen; **2.** *Baum etc.* ausreißen; **3.** zerreißen, in Stücke reißen; **4.** *fig.* unter'graben, zerstören.

tear·a·way ['teərəweɪ] **I** *adj.* ,wild'; **II** *s.* ,wilder' Kerl, Ra'baule *m*.

tear| bomb [tɪə] Tränengasbombe *f*; '~·**drop** *s.* **1.** Träne *f*; **2.** Anhänger *m* (*Ohrring*).

tear·ful ['tɪəfʊl] *adj.* □ **1.** tränenreich; **2.** weinend, in Tränen; **3.** weinerlich; **4.** schmerzlich.

tear| gas [tɪə] *s.* ♠ Tränengas *n*; ~ **gland** *s. anat.* Tränendrüse *f*.

tear·ing ['teərɪŋ] *adj. fig.* F **1.** rasend, toll (*Tempo, Wut etc.*); **2.** ,toll'; ~ **strength** *s.* ⊕ Zerreißfestigkeit *f*.

'**tear|·jerk·er** ['tɪə-] *s. Am.* F ,Schnulze' *f*, ,Schmachtfetzen' *m*.

'**tear-off** ['teərɒf] *adj.* Abreiß...: ~ *calendar*.

'**tea|·room** [-rʊm] *s.* Teestube *f*, Ca'fé *n*; ~ **rose** *s.* ♥ Teerose *f*.

tear sheet [teə] *s. Am.* Belegbogen *m*.

'**tear-stained** ['tɪə-] *adj.* **1.** tränennass; **2.** verweint (*Augen*).

tease [tiːz] **I** *v/t.* **1.** ⊕ a) *Wolle* kämmen, krempeln, b) *Flachs* hecheln, c) *Werg* auszupfen; **2.** ⊕ *Tuch* krempeln, karden; **3.** *fig.* quälen: a) hänseln, aufziehen, b) ärgern, c) bestürmen, belästigen (*for* wegen); **4.** (auf)reizen; **II** *s.* **5.** F a) → *teaser* 1, 2, b) Plage *f*, lästige Sache.

tea·sel ['tiːzl] **I** *s.* **1.** ♥ Karde(ndistel) *f*; **2.** *Weberei:* Karde *f*; **II** *v/t.* **3.** → *tease* 2.

teas·er ['tiːzə] *s.* **1.** Necker *m*; **2.** Quäl-, Plagegeist *m*; **3.** *sl.* Frau, die ,alles verspricht und nichts hält'; **4.** F ,harte Nuss', schwierige Sache; **5.** F et. Verlockendes.

tea| serv·ice, ~ **set** *s.* 'Teeser,vice *n*; '~·**shop** → *tearoom*; '~·**spoon** *s.* Teelöffel *m*; '~·**spoon,ful** [-,fʊl] *pl.* **-fuls** *s.* ein Teelöffel (voll).

teat [tiːt] *s.* **1.** *zo.* Zitze *f*; **2.** *anat.* Brustwarze *f*; **3.** (Gummi)Sauger *m*; **4.** ⊕ Warze *f*.

tea| things *s. pl.* Teegeschirr *n*; '~·**time** *s.* Teestunde *f*; ~ **tow·el** *s.* Geschirrtuch *n*; ~ **urn** *s.* **1.** 'Teema,schine *f*; **2.** Gefäß *n* zum Heißhalten des Teewassers.

tea·zel, **tea·zle** → *teasel*.

tec [tek] *s. sl.* Detek'tiv *m*.

tech·nic ['teknɪk] **I** *adj.* → *technical*; **II** *s. mst pl.* → a) *technics*, b) *technology*, c) *technique*; '**tech·ni·cal** [-kl] *adj.* □ → *technically*; **1.** ⊕ technisch: ~ *bureau* Konstruktionsbüro *n*; **2.** technisch (*a. sport*), fachlich, fachmännisch, Fach..., Spezial...: ~ *book* (technisches) Fachbuch; ~ *dictionary* Fachwörterbuch *n*; ~ *school* Fachhochschule *f*; ~ *skill* a) (technisches) Geschick, b) ♪ Technik *f*; ~ *staff* technisches Per-

sonal; ~ *term* Fachausdruck *m*; **3.** *fig.* technisch: a) sachlich, b) (rein) for'mal, c) theo'retisch: ~ *knockout* Boxen: technischer K. o.; *on* ~ *grounds* ♯ aus formaljuristischen *od.* verfahrenstechnischen Gründen; **tech·ni·cal·i·ty** [,teknɪ'kælətɪ] *s.* **1.** *das* Technische; **2.** technische Besonderheit *od.* Einzelheit; **3.** Fachausdruck *m*; **4.** *bsd.* ♯ (reine) Formsache, (for'male) Spitzfindigkeit; '**tech·ni·cal·ly** [-kəlɪ] *adv.* **1.** technisch *etc.*; **2.** genau genommen, eigentlich; **tech·ni·cian** [tek'nɪʃn] *s.* **1.** Techniker(in) (*a. weitS. Virtuose etc.*), (technischer) Fachmann; **2.** ✕ *Am.* Techniker *m* (*Dienstrang für Spezialisten*).

tech·nics ['teknɪks] *s. pl.* **1.** *mst sg. konstr.* Technik *f*, *bsd.* Ingeni'eurwissenschaft *f*; **2.** technische Einzelheiten *pl.*; **3.** Fachausdrücke *pl.*; **4.** → *technique* [tek'niːk] *s.* **1.** ⊕ (Arbeits)Verfahren *n*, (Schweiß- *etc.*)Technik *f*, ♪, *paint.*, *sport etc.* Technik *f*: a) Me'thode *f*, b) Art *f* der Ausführung, c) Geschicklichkeit *f*; **tech·no** ['teknəʊ] *s.* ♪ Techno *m*, *n*; **tech·noc·ra·cy** [tek'nɒkrəsɪ] *s.* Technokra'tie *f*; **tech·no·crat** ['teknəʊkræt] *s.* Techno'krat *m*.

tech·no·log·ic, **tech·no·log·i·cal** [,teknə'lɒdʒɪk(l)] *adj.* □ **1.** techno'logisch, technisch; **2.** ♣ techno'logisch (bedingt): ~ *unemployment*; **tech·nol·o·gist** [tek'nɒlədʒɪst] *s.* Techno'loge *m*; **tech·nol·o·gy** [tek'nɒlədʒɪ] *s.* **1.** Technolo'gie *f*: ~ *transfer* Technologietransfer *m*; ~ *park* Technologiepark *m*; *school of* ~ technische Universität; **2.** technische 'Fachterminolo,gie.

tech·y ['tetʃɪ] → *testy*.

tec·tol·o·gy [tek'tɒlədʒɪ] *s. biol.* Struk'turlehre *f*.

tec·ton·ic [tek'tɒnɪk] *adj.* (□ ~*ally*) **1.** △, *geol.* tek'tonisch; **2.** *biol.* struktu'rell; **tec·ton·ics** [-ks] *s. pl. mst sg. konstr.* **1.** △ *etc.* Tek'tonik *f*; **2.** *geol.* ('Geo)Tek,tonik *f*.

tec·to·ri·al [tek'tɔːrɪəl] *adj. physiol.* Schutz..., Deck...: ~ *membrane*.

tec·tri·ces [tek'traɪsɪːz] *s. pl. zo.* Deckfedern *pl.*

ted·der ['tedə] *s.* ✗ Heuwender *m*.

Ted·dy bear ['tedɪ] *s.* Teddybär *m*.

te·di·ous ['tiːdjəs] *adj.* □ **1.** langweilig, öde, ermüdend; **2.** weitschweifig; '**te·di·ous·ness** [-nɪs] *s.* **1.** Langweiligkeit *f*, ⊕ Weitschweifigkeit *f*; '**te·di·um** [-jəm] *s.* **1.** Lang(e)weile *f*; **2.** Langweiligkeit *f*.

tee¹ [tiː] **I** *s.* ⊕ T-Stück *n*; **II** *adj.* T-...: ~ *iron*; **III** *v/t.* ⊕ abzweigen: ~ *across* (*together*) in Brücke (parallel) schalten.

tee² [tiː] **I** *s. sport* Tee *n*: a) *Curling:* Mittelpunkt *m* des Zielkreises, b) *Golf:* Abschlag(stelle *f*) *m*: *to a* ~ *fig.* aufs Haar; **II** *v/t. Golf: Ball* auf die Abschlagstelle legen; **III** *v/i.* ~ *off* a) *Golf:* abschlagen, b) *fig.* anfangen.

teem¹ [tiːm] *v/i.* **1.** wimmeln, voll sein (*with* von): *the roads are* ~*ing with people*; *this page* ~*s with mistakes* diese Seite strotzt von Fehlern; **2.** reichlich vor'handen sein: *fish* ~ *in that river* in dem Fluss wimmelt es von Fischen; **3.** *obs.* a) schwanger sein, b) ♥ Früchte tragen, c) *zo.* Junge gebären.

teem² [tiːm] **I** *v/t. bsd.* ⊕ *flüssiges Metall* (aus)gießen; **II** *v/i.* gießen (*a. fig. Regen*).

teen [tiːn] *Am.* → *teenage(r)*; '**teen·age** [-eɪdʒ] **I** *adj. a.* **teenaged 1.** im

Teenageralter; **2.** Teenager...; **II** *s.* **3.** → *teens* 1; '**teen,ag·er** [-,eɪdʒə] *s.* Teenager *m*.

teens [tiːnz] *s. pl.* **1.** Teenageralter *n*: *be in one's* ~ ein Teenager sein; **2.** Teenager *pl.*

tee·ny¹ ['tiːnɪ], *a.* ,~·'**wee·ny** [-'wiːnɪ] *adj.* F klitzeklein.

teen·y² ['tiːnɪ] *s.* F ,Teeny' *m* (*jüngerer Teenager*).

'**tee-shirt** ['tiː-] *s.* T-Shirt *n*.

tee·ter ['tiːtə] *v/i. Am.* F **1.** (*a. v/t.*) schaukeln, wippen; **2.** (sch)wanken.

teeth [tiːθ] *pl. von tooth.*

teethe [tiːð] *v/i.* zahnen, (die) Zähne bekommen: *teething troubles* a) Beschwerden beim Zahnen, b) *fig.* Kinderkrankheiten.

tee·to·tal [tiː'təʊtl] *adj.* absti'nent, Abstinenzler...; **tee·to·tal·(l)er** [-tlə] *s.* Absti'nenzler(in), ,Antialko'holiker (-in); **tee·to·tal·ism** [-tlɪzəm] *s.* **1.** Absti'nenz *f*; **2.** Absti'nenzprin,zip *n*.

tee·to·tum [,tiːtəʊ'tʌm] *s.* Drehwürfel *m*.

teg·u·ment ['tegjʊmənt] *etc.* → *integument etc.*

tele-¹ [telɪ] *in Zssgn* a) Fern..., b) Fernseh...

tele-² [telɪ] *in Zssgn* a) Ziel, b) Ende.

'**tel·e,bank·ing** *s.* 'Tele,banking *n*.

'**tel·e,cam·er·a** *s. TV* Fernsehkamera *f*.

'**tel·e·cast I** *v/t.* [*irr.* → *cast*] im Fernsehen über'tragen *od.* bringen; **II** *s.* Fernsehsendung *f*; '**tel·e,cast·er** *s.* (Fernseh)Ansager(in).

'**tel·e·com,mu·ni·ca·tion I** *s.* **1.** Fernmeldeverbindung *f*, -verkehr *m*, 'Telekommunikati,on *f*; **2.** *pl.* 'Telekommunikati,onen, Fernmeldewesen *n*, -technik *f*; **II** *adj.* **3.** Fernmelde...

tel·e·com·mut·er ['telɪkə,mjuːtə; ,-kə'mjuːtə] *s.* Telearbeiter(in); **tel·e·com·mut·ing** *s.* Telearbeit *f*.

tel·e·con·fer·ence ['telɪ,kɒnfərəns] *s.* Tele'fonkonfe,renz *f*.

'**tel·e·course** *s.* Fernsehlehrgang *m*, -kurs *m*.

tel·e·di·ag·no·sis ['telɪ,daɪəg'nəʊsɪs] *s.* [*irr.*] ♣ 'Ferndiag,nose *f*.

'**tel·e·film** *s.* Fernsehfilm *m*.

tel·e·gen·ic [,telɪ'dʒenɪk] *adj. TV* tele'gen.

tel·e·gram ['telɪgræm] *s.* Tele'gramm *n*: *by* ~ telegrafisch.

tel·e·graph ['telɪgrɑːf; -græf] **I** *s.* **1.** Tele'graf *m*; **2.** Tele'gramm *n*; **3.** → *telegraph board*; **II** *v/t.* **4.** telegrafieren; **5.** *j-n* tele'grafisch benachrichtigen; **6.** (*durch Zeichen*) zu verstehen geben, signalisieren; **7.** *sport Spielstand etc.* auf e-r Tafel anzeigen; **8.** *sl. Boxen: Schlag* ,telegrafieren' (*erkennbar ansetzen*); **III** *v/i.* **9.** telegrafieren (*to dat. od.* an *acc.*); ~ *board s. bsd. sport* Anzeigetafel *f*; ~ *code s.* Tele'grammschlüssel *m*.

te·leg·ra·pher [tɪ'legrəfə] *s.* Telegra'fist(in).

tel·e·graph·ese [,telɪgrə'fiːz] *s.* Tele'grammstil *m*; **tel·e·graph·ic** [,telɪ'græfɪk] *adj.* (□ ~*ally*) **1.** tele'grafisch: ~ *address* Telegrammadresse *f*, Drahtanschrift *f*; **2.** tele'grammartig (*Kürze, Stil*); **te·leg·ra·phist** [tɪ'legrəfɪst] *s.* Telegra'fist(in).

tel·e·graph| line *s.* Tele'grafenleitung *f*; ~ **pole**, ~ **post** *s.* Tele'grafenstange *f*, -mast *m*.

te·leg·ra·phy [tɪ'legrəfɪ] *s.* Telegra'fie *f*.

tel·e·ki·ne·sis [,telɪkɪ'niːsɪs] *s. psych.* Teleki'nese *f*.

tel·e·lens ['telɪlenz] *s. phot.* 'Teleobjek,tiv *n*.

te·lem·e·ter ['telɪmiːtə] *s.* Tele'meter *n*:

a) ☉ Entfernungsmesser *m*, b) ⚡ Fernmessgerät *n*.

tel·e·o·log·ic, tel·e·o·log·i·cal [,teliə'lɒdʒik(l)] *adj.* □ *phls.* teleo'logisch: ~ **argument** teleologischer Gottesbeweis; **tel·e·ol·o·gy** [,teli'ɒlədʒɪ] *s.* Teleolo'gie *f.*

tel·e·path·ic [,telɪ'pæθɪk] *adj.* (□ ~**ally**) tele'pathisch; **te·lep·a·thy** [tɪ'lepəθɪ] *s.* Telepa'thie *f.*, Ge'dankenüber,tragung *f.*

tel·e·phone ['telɪfəʊn] I *s.* **1.** Tele'fon *n*, Fernsprecher *m*: *at the* ~ am Apparat; *by* ~ telefonisch; *on the* ~ telefonisch, durch das *od.* am Telefon; *be on the* ~ a) Telefonanschluss haben, b) am Telefon sein; *over the* ~ durch das *od.* per Telefon; II *v/t.* **2.** *j-n* anrufen, antelefonieren; **3.** *Nachricht etc.* telefonieren, tele'fonisch über'mitteln (*s.th. to s.o.*, *s.o. s.th.* j-m et.); III *v/i.* **4.** telefonieren; ~ **bank·ing** *s.* Tele'fonbanking *n*; ~ **booth**, *Brit.* ~ **box** *s.* Tele'fon-, Fernsprechzelle *f*; ~ **call** *s.* Tele'fongespräch *n*, (Tele'fon)Anruf *m*; ~ **con·nec·tion** *s.* Tele'fonanschluss *m*; ~ **di·rec·to·ry** *s.* Tele'fon-, Fernsprechbuch *n*; ~ **ex·change** *s.* Fernsprechamt *n*, Tele'fonzen,trale *f*; ~ **op·er·a·tor** *s.* Telefo'nist(in); ~ **re·ceiv·er** *s.* (Tele'fon)Hörer *m*; ~ **sales** *s. pl.* Tele'fonverkauf *m*; ~ **sub·scrib·er** *s.* Fernsprechteilnehmer (-in); ~ **sur·vey** *s.* tele'fonische Befragung.

tel·e·phon·ic [,telɪ'fɒnɪk] *adj.* (□ ~**ally**) tele'fonisch, fernmündlich, Telefon...; **te·leph·o·nist** [tɪ'lefənɪst] *s.* Telefo'nist(in); **te·leph·o·ny** [tɪ'lefənɪ] *s.* Telefo'nie *f*, Fernsprechwesen *n*.

,tel·e·pho·to *phot.* I *adj.* **1.** Telefoto(grafie)..., Fernaufnahme...: ~ **lens** → **telelens**; II *s.* **2.** 'Telefoto(gra,fie *f*) *n*, Fernbild *n*; **3.** 'Bildtele,gramm *n*; **4.** Funkbild *n*; **,tel·e·pho·to·graph** → **telephoto** II; **'tel·e,pho·to'graph·ic** *adj.* (□ ~**ally**) **1.** 'fernfoto,grafisch; **2.** 'bildtele,grafisch; **,tel·e·pho'tog·ra·phy** *s.* **1.** 'Tele-, 'Fernfotogra,fie *f*; **2.** 'Bildtelegra,fie *f*.

tel·e·play ['telɪpleɪ] *s.* Fernsehspiel *n*.

'tel·e,print·er *s.* Fernschreiber *m* (*Gerät*): ~ **message** Fernschreiben *n*; ~ **operator** Fernschreiber(in).

'tel·e,proc·ess·ing *s.* Datenfernverarbeitung *f.*

'tel·e·prompt·er ['telɪ,prɒmptə] *s.* TV Teleprompter *m* (*optisches Souffliergerät, Textband*).

'tel·e·re,cord·ing *s.* (Fernseh)Aufzeichnung *f.*

tel·e·scope ['telɪskəʊp] I *s.* Tele'skop *n*, Fernrohr *n*; II *v/t. u. v/i.* a) (sich) inei'nander schieben, b) (sich) verkürzen; III *adj.* → **telescopic**.

tel·e·scop·ic [,telɪ'skɒpɪk] *adj.* (□ ~**ally**) **1.** tele'skopisch, Fernrohr...: ~ **sight** ⚔ Zielfernrohr *n*; **2.** inein'ander schiebbar, ausziehbar, Auszieh..., Teleskop...

'tel·e·screen *s.* TV Bildschirm *m.*

'tel·e,shop·ping *s.* Teleshopping *n.*

tel·e·text ['telɪtekst] *s.* TV Videotext *m.*

,tel·e·ther'mom·e·ter *s. phys.* 'Fern-, 'Teletherm,ometer *n.*

'tel·e·type, **,tel·e'type,writ·er** *Am.* → **teleprinter.**

'tel·e·view I *v/t.* sich (im Fernsehen) ansehen; II *v/i.* fernsehen; **'tel·e,view·er** *s.* Fernsehzuschauer(in).

tel·e·vise ['telɪvaɪz] → **telecast** I; **'tel·e,vi·sion** I *s.* **1.** Fernsehen *n*: *watch* ~ fernsehen; *on* ~ im Fernsehen; ~ **rat·ings** Fernseheinschaltquoten *pl.*; **2.** *a.* ~ **set** Fernsehgerät *n*, Fernseher *m*; II

adj. Fernseh...; **'tel·e·vi·sor** *s.* **1.** → **television** 2; **2.** → **telecaster**; **3.** → **televiewer**; **'tel·e,work·er** *s.* *Computer*: Telearbeiter(in) *m*; **'tel·e,work·ing** *s.* *Computer*: Telearbeit *f.*

tel·ex ['teleks] I *s.* **1.** Telex *n*, Fernschreibernetz *n*: *be on the* ~ Telex- *od.* Fernschreibanschluss haben; **2.** Fernschreiber *m* (*Gerät*): ~ **operator** Fernschreiber(in); **3.** Fernschreiben *n*: *by* ~ per Telex *od.* Fernschreiben; ~ **operator** Fernschreiber(in); II *v/t.* **4.** *j-m* et. telexen *od.* per Fernschreiben mitteilen.

tell [tel] [*irr.*] I *v/t.* **1.** sagen, erzählen (*s.o. s.th.*, *s.th. to s.o.* j-m et): *I can* ~ *you that …* ich kann Sie *od.* Ihnen versichern, dass; *I have been told* mir ist gesagt worden; *I told you so!* ich habe es (dir) ja gleich gesagt!, ,siehste'!; *you are ~ing me!* *sl.* wem sagen Sie das!; ~ *the world* F (es) hinausposaunen; **2.** mitteilen, berichten, *a.* die Wahrheit sagen; *Neuigkeit* verkünden: ~ *a lie* lügen; **3.** *Geheimnis* verraten; **4.** erkennen (*by*, *from* an *dat.*), feststellen, sagen: ~ *by ear* mit dem Gehör feststellen, hören; **5.** (mit Bestimmtheit) sagen: *I cannot* ~ *what it is*; *it is difficult to* ~ es ist schwer zu sagen; **6.** unter'scheiden (*one from the other* eines vom andern): ~ *apart* auseinander halten; **7.** sagen, befehlen: ~ *s.o. to do s.th.* j-m sagen, er solle et. tun; j-n et. tun heißen; *do as you are told* tu wie dir geheißen; **8.** *bsd. pol. Stimmen* zählen: *all told* alles in allem; **9.** ~ *off* a) abzählen, b) ✗ abkommandieren, c) F *j-m* ,Bescheid stoßen'; II *v/i.* **10.** berichten, erzählen (*of* von, *about* über *acc.*); **11.** *fig.* ein Zeichen *od.* Beweis sein (*of* für, von); **12.** *et.* sagen können, wissen: *how can you* ~?, *you never can* ~ man kann nie wissen; **13.** ,petzen': ~ *on s.o.* j-n verpetzen *od.* verraten; *don't* ~! nicht verraten!; **14.** sich auswirken (*on* bei, auf *acc.*): *the hard work began to* ~ *on him*; *his troubles have told on him* s-e Sorgen haben ihn sichtlich mitgenommen; *every blow (word)* ~*s* jeder Schlag (jedes Wort) sitzt; *that* ~*s against you* das spricht gegen Sie; **15.** sich (deutlich) abheben (*against* gegen, von); zur Geltung kommen (*Farbe etc.*); **'tell·er** [-lə] *s.* **1.** Erzähler(in); **2.** Zähler (-in); *bsd. parl.* Stimmenzähler *m*; **3.** Kassierer(in), Schalterbeamte(r) *m* (*Bank*): ~*'s department* Hauptkasse *f*; **4.** *a.* **automated** (*od.* **automatic**) ~ Geldautomat *m*; **'tell·ing** [-lɪŋ] *adj.* □ **1.** wirkungsvoll (*a. Schlag*), wirksam, eindrucksvoll; 'durchschlagend (*Erfolg, Wirkung*); **2.** *fig.* aufschlussreich; **,tell·ing-'off** *s.*: *give s.o. a* ~ j-m ,Bescheid stoßen'; **'tell·tale** I *s.* **1.** Klatschbase *f*, Zuträger (-in), ,Petze' *f*; **2.** verräterisches (Kenn-)Zeichen; **3.** ☉ (selbsttätige) Anzeigevorrichtung; II *adj.* **4.** *fig.* verräterisch: *a* ~ *tear*; **5.** sprechend (*Ähnlichkeit*); **6.** ☉ a) Anzeige..., b) Warnungs...: ~ *clock* Kontrolluhr *f.*

tel·ly ['telɪ] *s. Brit.* F Fernseher *m* (*Gerät*): *on the* ~ im Fernsehen.

tel·o·type ['teləʊtaɪp] *s.* **1.** e'lektrischer 'Schreib- *od.* 'Drucktele,graf; **2.** auto'matisch gedrucktes Tele'gramm.

tel·pher ['telfə] I *s.* Wagen *m* e-r Hängebahn; II *adj.* (Elektro)Hängebahn...; **'tel·pher·age** [-ərɪdʒ] *s.* e'lektrische Lastenbeförderung; **'tel·pher·way** *s.* Telpherbahn *f*, E'lektrohängebahn *f.*

te·mer·i·ty [tɪ'merətɪ] *s.* **1.** (Toll)Kühnheit *f*, Verwegenheit *f*; *b.s.* Frechheit *f.*

temp [temp] *s. Brit.* F 'Zeitsekre,tärin *f.*

tem·per ['tempə] I *s.* **1.** Tempera'ment *n*, Natu'rell *n*, Gemüt(sart *f*) *n*, Cha'rakter *m*, Veranlagung *f*: *even* ~ Gleichmut *m*; *have a quick* ~ ein hitziges Temperament haben; **2.** Stimmung *f*, Laune *f*: *in a bad* ~ (in) schlechter Laune, schlecht gelaunt; **3.** Gereiztheit *f*, Zorn *m*, Wut *f*: *be in a* ~ gereizt *od.* wütend sein; *fly (od. get) into a* ~ in Wut geraten; **4.** Gemütsruhe *f* (*obs. außer in den Redew.*): *keep one's* ~ ruhig bleiben; *lose one's* ~ in Wut geraten, die Geduld verlieren; *out of* ~ übel gelaunt; *put s.o. out of* ~ j-n wütend machen *od.* erzürnen; **5.** Zusatz *m*, Beimischung *f*, *metall.* Härtemittel *n*; **6.** *bsd.* ☉ richtige Mischung; **7.** *metall.* Härte(grad *m*) *f*; II *v/t.* **8.** mildern (*with* durch); **9.** Farbe, Kalk, Mörtel mischen, anmachen; **10.** ☉ a) *Stahl* härten, anlassen, b) *Eisen* ablöschen, c) *Gusseisen* adouzieren, d) *Glas* rasch abkühlen; **11.** ♪ *Klavier etc.* temperieren; III *v/i.* **12.** ☉ den richtigen Härtegrad erreichen *od.* haben.

tem·per·a ['tempərə] *s.* 'Tempera(male,rei) *f.*

tem·per·a·ment ['tempərəmənt] *s.* **1.** → **temper** 1; **2.** Tempera'ment *n*, Lebhaftigkeit *f*; **3.** ♪ Tempera'tur *f*; **tem·per·a·men·tal** [,tempərə'mentl] *adj.* □ **1.** tempera'mentvoll, veranlagungsmäßig, Temperaments...; **2.** a) reizbar, launisch, b) leicht erregbar; **3.** eigenwillig; **4.** *be* ~ F (s-e) ,Mucken' haben (*Gerät etc.*).

tem·per·ance ['tempərəns] *s.* **1.** Mäßigkeit *f*, Enthaltsamkeit *f*; **2.** Mäßigkeit *f* im *od.* Absti'nenz *f* vom Alkoholgenuss; ~ **ho·tel** *s.* alkoholfreies Hotel; ~ **move·ment** *s.* Absti'nenzbewegung *f.*

tem·per·ate ['tempərət] *adj.* □ **1.** gemäßigt, maßvoll; **2.** ~ *language* zu'rückhaltend; **3.** mäßig: ~ *enthusiasm*; **4.** a) mäßig, enthaltsam (*bsd. im Essen u. Trinken*), b) absti'nent (*alkoholische Getränke meidend*); **5.** gemäßigt, mild (*Klima etc.*); **'tem·per·ate·ness** [-nɪs] *s.* **1.** Gemäßigtheit *f*; **2.** Beherrschtheit *f*, Zu'rückhaltung *f*; **3.** geringes Ausmaß, *a.* Mäßigung *f* (*bsd. im Essen u. Trinken*), b) Absti'nenz *f* (*von alkoholischen Getränken*); **5.** Milde *f* (*des Klimas etc.*).

tem·per·a·ture ['temprətʃə] *s.* **1.** *phys.* Tempera'tur *f*: *at a* ~ *of* bei e-r Temperatur von; **2.** *physiol.* ('Körper)Tempera,tur *f*: *take s.o.'s* ~ j-s Temperatur messen; *have (od. run) a* ~ ⚕ F Fieber *od.* (erhöhte) Temperatur haben.

tem·pest ['tempɪst] *s.* **1.** (wilder) Sturm: ~ *in a teapot* *fig.* ,Sturm im Wasserglas'; **2.** *fig.* Sturm *m*, Ausbruch *m*; **3.** Gewitter *n*; **tem·pes·tu·ous** [tem'pestjʊəs] *adj.* □ *a. fig.* stürmisch, ungestüm, heftig; **tem·pes·tu·ous·ness** [tem'pestjʊəsnɪs] *s.* Ungestüm *n*, Heftigkeit *f.*

Tem·plar ['templə] *s.* **1.** *hist.* Templer *m*, Tempelherr *m*, -ritter *m*; **2.** Tempelritter *m* (*Freimaurer*); **3.** *oft* **Good** ⚖ Guttempler *m* (*ein Temperenzler*).

tem·plate ['templɪt] *s.* **1.** ☉ Scha'blone *f*; **2.** △ a) 'Unterleger *m* (*Balken*), b) (Dach)Pfette *f*, c) Kragholz *n*; **3.** ⚓ Mallbrett *n*; **4.** *Computer*: Doku'mentvorlage *f.*

tem·ple¹ ['templ] *s.* **1.** *eccl.* Tempel *m*

(*a. fig.*); **2.** *Am.* Syna'goge *f*; **3.** ♬ ♱ Temple *m* (*in London, Sitz zweier Rechtskollegien*: **the Inner** ♬ *u.* **the Middle** ♬).

tem·ple² ['templ] *s. anat.* Schläfe *f*.

tem·ple³ ['templ] *s. Weberei*: Tömpel *m*.

tem·plet ['templɪt] → **template**.

tem·po ['tempəʊ] *pl.* **-pos, -pi** [-pi:] *s.* ♪ Tempo *n* (*a. fig. Geschwindigkeit*): ~ **turn** *Skisport*: Temposchwung *m*.

tem·po·ral¹ ['tempərəl] *adj.* □ **1.** zeitlich: a) Zeit... (*Ggs. räumlich*), b) irdisch; **2.** weltlich (*Ggs. geistlich*): ~ **courts**; **3.** *ling.* tempo'ral, Zeit...: ~ **adverb** Umstandswort *n* der Zeit; ~ **clause** Temporalsatz *m*.

tem·po·ral² ['tempərəl] *anat.* **I** *adj.* a) Schläfen..., b) Schläfenbein...; **II** *s.* Schläfenbein *n*.

tem·po·rar·i·ness ['tempərərɪnɪs] *s.* Einst-, Zeitweiligkeit *f*; **tem·po·rar·y** ['tempərɪ] *adj.* **1.** provi'sorisch: a) vorläufig, einst-, zeitweilig, vor'übergehend, tempo'rär, b) behelfsmäßig, Not..., Hilfs..., Interims...: ~ **arrangement** Übergangsregelung *f*; ~ **bridge** Behelfs-, Notbrücke *f*; ~ **credit** † Zwischenkredit *m*.

tem·po·rize ['tempəraɪz] *v/i.* **1.** Zeit zu gewinnen suchen, abwarten, sich nicht festlegen, lavieren: ~ **with s.o.** j-n hinhalten; **2.** mit dem Strom schwimmen, s-n Mantel nach dem Wind hängen; **'tem·po·riz·er** [-zə] *s.* **1.** j-d, der Zeit zu gewinnen sucht *od.* sich nicht festlegt; **2.** Opportu'nist(in); **'tem·po·riz·ing** [-zɪŋ] *adj.* □ **1.** hinhaltend, abwartend; **2.** opportu'nistisch.

tempt [tempt] *v/t.* **1.** *eccl., a. allg.* j-n versuchen, in Versuchung führen; **2.** j-n verlocken, -leiten, da'zu bringen (**to do** zu tun): **be** ~**ed to do** versucht *od.* geneigt sein, zu tun; **3.** reizen, locken (*Angebot, Sache*); **4.** *Gott, sein Schicksal* versuchen, her'ausfordern; **temp·ta·tion** [temp'teɪʃn] *s.* Versuchung *f*, -führung *f*, -lockung *f*: **lead into** ~ in Versuchung führen; **'tempt·er** [-tə] *s.* Versucher *m*, -führer *m*: **the** ♬ *eccl.* der Versucher; **'tempt·ing** [-tɪŋ] *adj.* □ verführerisch, -lockend; **'tempt·ing·ness** [-tɪŋnɪs] *s. das* Verführerische; **'tempt·ress** [-trɪs] *s.* Versucherin *f*, Verführerin *f*.

ten [ten] **I** *adj.* **1.** zehn; **II** *s.* **2.** Zehn *f* (*Zahl, Spielkarte*): **the upper** ~ *fig.* die oberen zehntausend; **3.** F Zehner *m* (*Geldschein etc.*); **4.** zehn (Uhr).

ten·a·ble ['tenəbl] *adj.* **1.** haltbar (✗ *Stellung, fig. Behauptung etc.*); **2.** verliehen (**for** für, auf *acc.*): **an office** ~ **for two years**; **'ten·a·ble·ness** [-nɪs] *s.* Haltbarkeit *f* (*a. fig.*).

te·na·cious [tɪ'neɪʃəs] *adj.* □ **1.** zäh(e), klebrig; **2.** *fig.* zäh(e), hartnäckig: **be** ~ **of** zäh an et. festhalten; ~ **of life** zählebig; ~ **ideas** zählebige Ideen; **3.** verlässlich, gut (*Gedächtnis*); **te·na·cious·ness** [-nɪs], **te·nac·i·ty** [tɪ'næsɪtɪ] *s.* **1.** *allg.* Zähigkeit *f*: a) Klebrigkeit *f*, b) *phys.* Zug-, Zähfestigkeit *f*, c) *fig.* Hartnäckigkeit *f*: ~ **of life** zähes Leben; ~ **of purpose** Zielstrebigkeit *f*; **2.** Verlässlichkeit *f* (*des Gedächtnisses*).

ten·an·cy ['tenənsɪ] *s.* ♱ **1.** Pacht-, Mietverhältnis *n*: ~ **at will** jederzeit beiderseits kündbares Pachtverhältnis; **2.** a) Pacht-, Mietbesitz *m*, b) Eigentum *n*: ~ **in common** Miteigentum *n*; **3.** Pacht-, Mietdauer *f*; **'ten·ant** [-nt] **I** *s.* **1.** ♱ Pächter(in), Mieter(in): ~ **farmer** Gutspächter *m*; **2.** ♱ Inhaber(in) (*von Realbesitz, Renten etc.*); **3.** Bewohner

(-in); **4.** *hist.* Lehnsmann *m*; **II** *v/t.* **5.** bewohnen; **6.** *als Mieter etc.* beherbergen; **'ten·ant·a·ble** [-ntəbl] *adj.* **1.** ♱ pacht-, mietbar; **2.** bewohnbar; **'ten·ant·less** *adj.* **1.** unverpachtet; **2.** unvermietet, leer (stehend); **'ten·ant·ry** [-trɪ] *s. coll.* Pächter *pl.*, Mieter *pl.*

tench [tenʃ] *pl.* **'tench·es**, *bsd. coll.* **tench** *s. ichth.* Schleie *f*.

tend¹ [tend] *v/i.* **1.** sich in e-r bestimmten *Richtung* bewegen; (hin)streben (**to** [**-wards**] nach): ~ **from** wegstreben von; **2.** *fig.* a) tendieren, neigen (**to**[**wards**] zu), b) da'zu neigen (**to do** zu tun); **3.** abzielen, gerichtet sein (**to** auf *acc.*); **4.** (da'zu) führen *od.* beitragen (**to** [**do**] zu [tun]); hin'auslaufen (**to** auf *acc.*); **5.** ⚓ schwojen.

tend² [tend] *v/t.* **1.** ⚙ *Maschine* bedienen; **2.** sich kümmern um, sorgen für, *Kranke* pflegen, *Vieh* hüten.

ten·den·cious *etc.* → **tendentious**.

tend·en·cy ['tendənsɪ] *s.* **1.** Ten'denz *f*: a) Richtung *f*, Strömung *f*, Hinstreben *n*, b) (bestimmte) Absicht, Zweck *m*, c) Hang *m* (**to, towards**), Neigung *f* (**to für**); **2.** Gang *m*, Lauf *m*: **the** ~ **of events**.

ten·den·tious [ten'denʃəs] *adj.* □ tendenzi'ös, Tendenz...; **ten·den·tious·ness** [-nɪs] *s.* tendenzi'öser Cha'rakter.

ten·der¹ ['tendə] *adj.* □ **1.** zart, weich, mürbe (*Fleisch etc.*); **2.** *allg.* zart (*a. Alter, Farbe, Gesundheit*): ~ **passion** Liebe *f*; **3.** zart, zärtlich, sanft; **4.** zart, empfindlich (*Körperteil, a. Gewissen*): ~ **spot** *fig.* wunder Punkt; **5.** heikel, kitzlig (*Thema*); **6.** bedacht (**of** auf *acc.*).

ten·der² ['tendə] **I** *v/t.* **1.** (for'mell) anbieten; → **oath** 1, **resignation** 2; **2.** *s-e Dienste etc.* anbieten, zur Verfügung stellen; **3.** *s-n Dank, s-e Entschuldigung* zum Ausdruck bringen; **4.** †, ♱ als Zahlung (*e-r Verpflichtung*) anbieten; **II** *v/i.* **5.** sich an e-r Ausschreibung beteiligen, ein Angebot machen: ~ **and contract for a supply** e-n Lieferungsvertrag abschließen; **III** *s.* **6.** Anerbieten *n*, Angebot *n*: **make a** ~ **of** → 2; **7.** † (*legal*) gesetzliches Zahlungsmittel; **8.** † Angebot *n*, Of'ferte *f* bei Ausschreibung: **invite** ~**s for** ein Projekt ausschreiben; **put to** ~ in freier Ausschreibung vergeben; **by** ~ in Submission; **9.** † Kosten(vor)anschlag *m*; **10.** ♱ Zahlungsangebot *n*; **11.** ~ **of resignation** Rücktrittsgesuch *n*.

tend·er³ ['tendə] *s.* **1.** Pfleger(in); **2.** 🚂 Tender *m*, Kohlewagen *m*; **3.** ⚓ Tender *m*, Begleitschiff *n*.

'ten·der|·foot *pl.* **-feet** *od.* **-foots** *s. Am.* F **1.** Anfänger(in), Greenhorn *n*; **2.** neu aufgenommener Pfadfinder; **,~-'heart·ed** *adj.* □ weichherzig; **'~·loin** *s.* zartes Lendenstück, Fi'let *n*.

ten·der·ness ['tendənɪs] *s.* **1.** Zartheit *f*, Weichheit *f* (*a. fig.*); **2.** Empfindlichkeit *f* (*a. fig. des Gewissens etc.*); **3.** Zärtlichkeit *f*.

ten·di·nous ['tendɪnəs] *adj.* **1.** sehnig, flechsig; **2.** *anat.* Sehnen...; **ten·don** ['tendən] *s. anat.* Sehne *f*, Flechse *f*; **ten·do·vag·i·ni·tis** ['tendəʊ,vædʒɪ'naɪtɪs] *s.* ♨ Sehnenscheidenentzündung *f*.

ten·dril ['tendrɪl] *s.* ♣ Ranke *f*.

ten·e·brous ['tenɪbrəs] *adj.* dunkel, finster, düster.

ten·e·ment ['tenɪmənt] *s.* **1.** Wohnhaus *n*; **2.** *a.* ~ **house** Miet(s)haus *n*, *bsd.* 'Mietska,serne *f*; **3.** Mietwohnung *f*; **4.** Wohnung *f*; **5.** ♱ a) (Pacht)Besitz *m*, b) beständiger Besitz, beständiges Pri'vi'legium.

te·nes·mus [tɪ'nezməs] *s.* ♨ Te'nesmus *m*: **rectal** ~ Stuhldrang *m*; **vesical** ~ Harndrang *m*.

ten·et ['tenɪt] *s.* (Grund-, Lehr)Satz *m*, Lehre *f*.

'ten·fold I *adj. u. adv.* zehnfach; **II** *s. das* Zehnfache.

,ten-'gal·lon hat *s. Am.* breitrandiger Cowboyhut.

ten·ner ['tenə] *s.* F ,Zehner' *m*: a) *Brit.* Zehn'pfundnote *f*, b) *Am.* Zehn'dollarnote *f*.

ten·nis ['tenɪs] *s. sport* Tennis *n*; ~ **arm** *s.* ♨ Tennisarm *m*; ~ **ball** *s.* Tennisball *m*; ~ **court** *s.* Tennisplatz *m*; ~ **rack·et** *s.* Tennisschläger *m*.

ten·on ['tenən] ⚙ **I** *s.* Zapfen *m*; **II** *v/t.* verzapfen; ~ **saw** *s.* ⚙ Ansatzsäge *f*, Fuchsschwanz *m*.

ten·or ['tenə] **I** *s.* **1.** Verlauf *m*; **2.** Te'nor *m*, (wesentlicher) Inhalt, Sinn *m*; **3.** Absicht *f*; **4.** ♱ Laufzeit *f* (*Wechsel etc.*); **5.** ♪ Te'nor(stimme *f*, -par,tie *f*, -sänger *m*, -instru,ment *n*) *m*; **II** *adj.* **6.** ♪ Tenor...

'ten·pin *s. Am.* **1.** Kegel *m*; **2.** *pl. sg. konstr. Am.* Bowling *n*.

tense¹ [tens] *s. ling.* Zeit(form) *f*, Tempus *n*: **simple** (**compound**) ~**s** einfache (zs.-gesetzte) Zeiten.

tense² [tens] **I** *adj.* □ **1.** gespannt (*a. ling. Laut*); **2.** *fig.* a) (an)gespannt (*Person, Nerven*), b) spannungsgeladen: **a** ~ **moment**; **II** *v/t.* **3.** straffen, (an)spannen; **III** *v/i.* **4.** sich straffen *od.* (an)spannen; **5.** *fig.* (vor Nervosi'tät *etc.*) starr werden; **'tense·ness** [-nɪs] *s.* **1.** Straffheit *f*; **2.** *fig.* (ner'vöse) Spannung; **'ten·si·ble** [-səbl] *adj.* dehnbar; **'ten·sile** [-saɪl] *adj.* dehn-, streckbar; *phys.* Dehn(ungs)..., Zug...: ~ **strength** (**stress**) Zugfestigkeit *f* (-beanspruchung *f*); **ten·sim·e·ter** [ten'sɪmɪtə] *s.* ⚙ Gas-, Dampfdruckmesser *m*; **ten·si·om·e·ter** [tensɪ'ɒmɪtə] *s.* ⚙ Zugmesser *m*.

ten·sion ['tenʃn] *s.* **1.** Spannung *f* (*a.* ♃); **2.** ♨, *phys.* Druck *m*; **3.** *phys.* a) Dehnung *f*, b) Zug-, Spannkraft *f*: ~ **spring** ⚙ Zug-, Spannfeder *f*; **4.** (ner'vöse) Spannung; **5.** *fig.* Spannung *f*, gespanntes Verhältnis: **political** ~; **'ten·sion·al** [-ʃənl] *adj.* Dehn..., Spann(ungs)...; **ten·sor** ['tensə] *s. anat.* Tensor *m* (*a.* ♄), Streck-, Spannmuskel *m*.

'ten|-spot *s. Am. sl.* **1.** Kartenspiel: Zehn *f*; **2.** → **tenner** b; **'~·strike** *s.* **1.** → **strike** 2 a; **2.** F *fig.* ,Volltreffer' *m*.

tent¹ [tent] *s.* Zelt *n* (*a.* ♣): **pitch one's** ~**s** s-e Zelte aufschlagen (*a. fig.*).

tent² [tent] ♨ **I** *s.* Tam'pon *m*; **II** *v/t.* durch e-n Tam'pon offen halten.

tent³ [tent] *s. obs.* Tintowein *m*.

ten·ta·cle ['tentəkl] *s. zo.* **1.** Ten'takel *m, n* (*a.* ♀), Fangarm *m e-s Polypen*; **2.** Fangarm *m* (*a.* ♀); **'ten·ta·cled** [-ld] *adj.* ♀, *zo.* mit Ten'takeln versehen; **ten·tac·u·lar** [ten'tækjʊlə] *adj.* Fühler..., Tentakel...

ten·ta·tive ['tentətɪv] **I** *adj.* □ **1.** versuchsweise, Versuchs...; **2.** provi'sorisch; **3.** vorsichtig; **II** *s.* **4.** Versuch *m*; **'ten·ta·tive·ly** [-lɪ] *adv.* versuchsweise.

ten·ter ['tentə] *s.* ⚙ Spannrahmen *m* für Tuch; **'~·hook** *s.* ⚙ Spannhaken *m*: **be on** ~**s** *fig.* auf die Folter gespannt sein, wie auf glühenden Kohlen sitzen; **keep s.o. on** ~**s** *fig.* j-n auf die Folter spannen.

tenth [tenθ] **I** *adj.* □ **1.** zehnt; **II** *s.* **2.** der (die, das) Zehnte; **3.** **3.** Zehntel *n*: **a** ~ **of a second** e-e Zehntelsekunde; **5.** ♪ De'zime *f*; **'tenth·ly** [-lɪ] *adv.* zehntens.

tent| peg *s.* Zeltpflock *m*, Hering *m*; **~ pole** *s.* Zeltstange *f*; **~ stitch** *s.* Sticke- rei: Perlstich *m*.

ten·u·is ['tenjʊɪs] *pl.* **'ten·u·es** [-iːz] *s. ling.* Tenuis *f* (*stimmloser, nicht aspi- rierter Verschlusslaut*).

te·nu·ous ['tenjʊəs] *adj.* **1.** dünn; **2.** zart, fein; **3.** *fig.* dürftig.

ten·ure ['te͟ˌnjʊə] *s.* **1.** (Grund-, *hist.* Le- hens)Besitz *m*; **2.** ⚖ a) Besitzart *f*, b) Besitztitel *m*: **~ by lease** Pachtbesitz *m*; **3.** Besitzdauer *f*; **4.** (feste) Anstel- lung; **5.** Innehaben *n*, Bekleidung *f* (*e-s Amtes*): **~ of office** Amtsdauer *f*; **6.** *fig.* Genuss *m e-r Sache.*

te·pee ['tiːpiː] *s.* Indi'anerzelt *n*, Tipi *n*.

tep·id ['tepɪd] *adj.* □ lauwarm, lau (*a. fig.*); **te·pid·i·ty** [te'pɪdɪtɪ], **'tep·id· ness** [-nɪs] *s.* Lauheit *f* (*a. fig.*).

ter·cen·te·nar·y [ˌtɜːsen'tiːnərɪ], **ˌter· cen'ten·ni·al** [-'tenjəl] **I** *adj.* **1.** drei- hundertjährig; **II** *s.* **2.** dreihundertster Jahrestag; **3.** Dreihundert'jahrfeier *f*.

ter·cet ['tɜːsɪt] *s.* **1.** *Metrik:* Ter'zine *f*; **2.** ♪ Tri'ole *f*.

ter·gi·ver·sate ['tɜːdʒɪvɜːseɪt] *v/i.* Aus- flüchte machen; sich drehen und wen- den; sich wider'sprechen; **ter·gi·ver· sa·tion** [ˌtɜːdʒɪvɜː'seɪʃn] *s.* **1.** Ausflucht *f*, Winkelzug *m*; **2.** Wankelmut *m*.

term [tɜːm] **I** *s.* **1.** *bsd. fachlicher* Aus- druck, Bezeichnung *f*, Wort *n*: *botani- cal* **~s**; **2.** *pl.* a) Ausdrucksweise *f*, b) ('Denk)Katego,rien *pl.*: *in* **~s of** a) in Form von (*od. gen.*), b) im Sinne (*gen.*), als, c) hinsichtlich (*gen.*) von ... her, vom Standpunkt (*gen.*), e) im Vergleich zu; *in* **~s of approval** beifäl- lig; *in* **~s of literature** literarisch (be- trachtet), vom Literarischen her; *in plain* **~s** rundheraus (gesagt); *in the strongest* **~s** schärfstens; *think in* **~s of money** (nur) in Mark u. Pfennig denken; *think in military* **~s** in militäri- schen Kategorien denken; **3.** Wortlaut *m*; **4.** a) Zeit *f*, Dauer *f*: **~ of imprison- ment** Freiheitsstrafe *f*; **~ of office** Amtsdauer *f*, -periode *f*; *on* (*od. in*) *the long* **~** auf lange Sicht, langfristig (betrachtet); *for a* **~ of four years** für die Dauer von vier Jahren, b) (*Zah- lungs- etc.*)Frist *f*: **~ deposit** Termin- geld *n*; **5.** ✝, ⚖ a) Laufzeit *f* (*Vertrag, Wechsel*), b) Ter'min *m*, c) *Brit.* Quar- 'talster,min *m* (*vierteljährlicher Zahltag für Miete etc.*), d) *Brit. hist.* halbjährli- cher Lohn-, Zahltag (*für Dienstboten*), e) ⚖ 'Sitzungsperi,ode *f*; **6.** *ped., univ.* Quar'tal *n*, Tri'mester *n*, Se'mester *n*: *end of* **~** Schul- *od.* Semesterschluss *m*; *keep* **~s** *Brit.* Jura studieren; **7.** *pl.* ✝, ⚖ (*Vertrags- etc.*)Bedingungen *pl.*: **~s of delivery** Lieferungsbedingungen; **~s of trade** Austauschverhältnis *n im* Au- ßenhandel; *on easy* **~s** zu günstigen Bedingungen; *on equal* **~s** unter glei- chen Bedingungen; *come to* **~s** *a. fig.* handelseinig werden, sich einigen, *fig. a.* sich abfinden (*with* mit); *come to* **~s with the past** die Vergangenheit be- wältigen; **8.** *pl.* Preise *pl.*, Hono'rar *n*: *cash* **~s** Barpreis *m*; *inclusive* **~s** Pau- schalpreis *m*; **9.** *pl.* Beziehungen *pl.*: *be on good* (*bad*) **~s with** auf gutem (schlechtem) Fuße stehen mit; *they are not on speaking* **~s** sie sprechen nicht (mehr) miteinander; **10.** *Logik:* Begriff *m*; → *contradiction* 2; **11.** Å a) Glied *n*: **~ of a sum** Summand *m*, b) *Geomet- rie:* Grenze *f*; **12.** △ Terme *m*, Grenz- stein *m*; **13.** *physiol.* a) Menstruati'on

f, b) (nor'male) Schwangerschaftszeit: *carry to* (*full*) **~** *ein Kind* austragen; *she is near her* **~** ihre Niederkunft steht dicht bevor; **II** *v/t.* **14.** (be)nen- nen, bezeichnen als.

ter·ma·gant ['tɜːməgənt] **I** *s.* Zankteu- fel *m*, (Haus)Drachen *m* (*Weib*); **II** *adj.* zänkisch, keifend.

ter·mi·na·ble ['tɜːmɪnəbl] *adj.* □ **1.** be- grenzbar; **2.** befristet, (zeitlich) be- grenzt, kündbar (*Vertrag etc.*).

ter·mi·nal ['tɜːmɪnl] **I** *adj.* □ → *termi- nally*; **1.** letzt, Grenz..., End..., (Ab-) Schluss...: **~ amplifier** ⚡ Endverstärker *m*; **~ station** **~ value** ⚡ Endwert *m*; **~ voltage** ⚡ Klemmenspannung *f*; **2.** *univ.* Semester... *od.* Trimester...; **3.** ⚕ a) unheilbar (*a. fig.*), b) im Endsta- dium: **~ case**, c) Sterbe...: **~ clinic**, d) *fig.* verhängnisvoll (*to* für); **4.** ⚘ gipfel- ständig; **II** *s.* **5.** Endstück *n*, -glied *n*, Spitze *f*; **6.** *ling.* Endsilbe *f od.* -buch- stabe *m od.* -wort *n*; **7.** ⚡ a) (Anschluss-) Klemme *f*, (Plus-, Minus)Pol *m*, b) Klemmschraube *f*, c) Endstecker *m*; **8.** a) 🚂 'Endstati,on *f*, Kopfbahnhof *m*, b) *bsd.* ✈ Terminal *m od. n*, ✈ Flughalle *f* (→ *a.* **air terminal**), c) (zen'traler) 'Umschlagplatz, d) End- *od.* Ausgangs- punkt *m*; **9.** *Computer:* Terminal *n*; **10.** *univ.* Se'mesterprüfung *f*; **'ter·mi·nal· ly** [-nəlɪ] *adv.* **1.** zum Schluss; **2.** ter- 'minweise; **3.** **~ ill** ⚕ unheilbar krank; **4.** *univ.* se'mesterweise; **'ter·mi·nate** [-neɪt] **I** *v/t.* **1.** räumlich begrenzen; **2.** beendigen, *Vertrag a.* aufheben, kündi- gen; **II** *v/i.* **3.** endigen (*in in dat.*); **4.** *ling.* enden (*in auf acc.*); **III** *adj.* [-nət] **5.** begrenzt; **6.** Å endlich; **ter·mi·na- tion** [ˌtɜːmɪ'neɪʃn] *s.* **1.** Aufhören *n*; **2.** Ende *n*, (Ab)Schluss *m*; **3.** Beendi- gung *f*: **~ of pregnancy** ⚕ Schwanger- schaftsunterbrechung *f*; **4.** ⚖ Beendi- gung *f e-s Vertrags etc.*: a) Ablauf *m*, Erlöschen *n*, b) Aufhebung *f*, Kündi- gung *f*; **5.** *ling.* Endung *f*.

ter·mi·no·log·i·cal [ˌtɜːmɪnə'lɒdʒɪkl] *adj.* □ termino'logisch: **~ inexactitude** *humor.* Schwindelei *f*; **ter·mi·nol·o·gy** [ˌtɜːmɪ'nɒlədʒɪ] *s.* Terminolo'gie *f*, Fachsprache *f*, -ausdrücke *pl.*

ter·mi·nus ['tɜːmɪnəs] *pl.* **-ni** [-naɪ], **-nus·es** *s.* **1.** Endpunkt *m*, Ziel *n*, En- de *n*; **2.** → *terminal* 8 a.

ter·mite ['tɜːmaɪt] *s. zo.* Ter'mite *f*.

'term·time *s.* Schul- *od.* Se'mesterzeit *f* (*Ggs. Ferien*).

tern¹ [tɜːn] *s. orn.* Seeschwalbe *f*.

tern² [tɜːn] *s.* Dreiergruppe *f*, -satz *m*; **'ter·na·ry** [-nərɪ] *adj.* **1.** aus (je) drei bestehend, dreifältig; **2.** ⚘ dreizählig; **3.** *metall.* dreistoffig; **4.** Å ter'när; **5.** aus drei A'tomen bestehend; **'ter·nate** [-nɪt] *adj.* → *ternary* 1 u. 2.

ter·ra ['terə] (*Lat. u. Ital.*) *s.* Land *n*, Erde *f*.

ter·race ['terəs] **I** *s.* **1.** Ter'rasse *f* (*a.* △ *u. geol.*); **2.** *bsd. Brit.* Häuserreihe *f* an erhöht gelegener Straße; **3.** *Am.* Grünstreifen *m*, -anlage *f in der* Straßenmitte; **4.** *sport Brit.* (Zu- schauer)Rang *m*: *the* **~s** die Ränge (*a. die Zuschauer*); **II** *v/t.* **5.** ter'rassen- förmig anlegen, terrassieren; **'ter- raced** [-st] *adj.* **1.** terrassenförmig (an- gelegt); **2.** flach (*Dach*); **3.** **~ house** *Brit.* Reihenhaus *n*.

ter·ra·cot·ta [ˌterə'kɒtə] **I** *s.* **1.** Terra- 'kotta *f*; **2.** Terra'kottafi,gur *f*; **II** *adj.* **3.** Terrakotta...; **~ fir·ma** ['fɜːmə] (*Lat.*) *s.* festes Land.

ter·rain [te'reɪn] *bsd.* ✕ **I** *s.* Ter'rain *n*, Gelände *n*; **II** *adj.* Gelände...

ter·ra in·cog·ni·ta [ɪŋ'kɒgnɪtə] (*Lat.*) *s.* unerforschtes Land; *fig.* (völliges) Neu- land.

ter·ra·ne·ous [tə'reɪnjəs] *adj.* ⚘ Land...

ter·ra·pin ['terəpɪn] *s. zo.* Dosenschild- kröte *f*.

ter·raz·zo [te'rætsəʊ] (*Ital.*) *s.* Ter'razzo *m*, Ze'mentmosa,ik *n*.

ter·rene [te'riːn] *adj.* **1.** irdisch, Erd...; **2.** erdig, Erd...

ter·res·tri·al [tɪ'restrɪəl] **I** *adj.* □ **1.** ir- disch; **2.** Erd...: **~ globe** Erdball *m*; **3.** ⚘, *zo., geol.* Land...; **II** *s.* **4.** Erdenbe- wohner(in).

ter·ri·ble ['terəbl] *adj.* □ schrecklich, furchtbar, fürchterlich (*alle a.* F *außer- ordentlich*); **'ter·ri·ble·ness** [-nɪs] *s.* Schrecklichkeit *f etc.*

ter·ri·er¹ ['terɪə] *s.* **1.** *zo.* Terrier *m* (*Hunderasse*); **2.** F → *territorial* 4 a.

ter·ri·er² ['terɪə] *s.* ⚖ Flurbuch *n*.

ter·rif·ic [tə'rɪfɪk] *adj.* (□ **~ally**) **1.** furchtbar, fürchterlich, schrecklich (*alle a.* F *fig.*); **2.** F ,toll', fan'tastisch.

ter·ri·fied ['terɪfaɪd] *adj.* erschrocken, verängstigt, entsetzt: *be* **~ of** schreckli- che Angst haben vor (*dat.*); **ter·ri·fy** ['terɪfaɪ] *v/t.* erschrecken, j-m Angst und Schrecken einjagen; **'ter·ri·fy·ing** [-aɪɪŋ] *adj.* Furcht erregend, erschre- ckend, fürchterlich.

ter·ri·to·ri·al [ˌterɪ'tɔːrɪəl] **I** *adj.* □ **1.** Grund..., Land...: **~ property**; **2.** terri- tori'al, Landes..., Gebiets...: ♀ *Army*, ♀ *Force* ✕ Territorialarmee *f*, Landwehr *f*; **~ waters** *pol.* Hoheitsgewässer *pl.*; **3.** ♀ *pol.* Territorial..., ein Terri'torium (*der USA*) betreffend; **II** *s.* **4.** ♀ ✕ a) Landwehrmann *m*, b) *pl.* Territori'al- truppen *pl.*; **ter·ri·to·ry** ['terɪtərɪ] *s.* **1.** (*a. fig.*) Gebiet *n*, Terri'torium *n*; **2.** *pol.* Hoheits-, Staatsgebiet *n*: *Federal* **~** Bundesgebiet; *on British* **~** auf briti- schem Gebiet; **3.** *pol.* Terri'torium *n* (*Schutzgebiet*); **4.** ✝ (Vertrags-, Ver- treter)Gebiet *n*, (-)Bezirk *m*; **5.** *sport* F (Spielfeld)Hälfte *f*.

ter·ror ['terə] *s.* **1.** Schrecken *m*, Entset- zen *n*, schreckliche Furcht (*of* vor *dat.*); **2.** Schrecken *m* (*of* od. *to gen.*) (*Schrecken einflößende Person od. Sa- che*); **3.** Terror *m*: a) Gewalt-, Schre- ckensherrschaft *f*, b) Terrorakte *pl.*: *political* **~** Politterror; **~ bombing** Bombenterror; **4.** F a) Ekel *n*, ,Land- plage' *f*, b) (schreckliche) Plage (*to* für), c) Albtraum *m*; **'ter·ror·ism** [-ərɪzəm] *s.* **1.** → *terror* 3; **2.** Terro'ris- mus *m*; **3.** Terrorisierung *f*; **'ter·ror·ist** [-ərɪst] *s.* Terro'rist(in); **'ter·ror·ize** [-əraɪz] *v/t.* **1.** terrorisieren; **2.** ein- schüchtern.

'ter·ror|-,strick·en, **'~-struck** *adj.* schreckerfüllt, starr vor Schreck.

ter·ry ['terɪ] *s.* **1.** ungeschnittener Samt *od.* Plüsch; **2.** Frot'tiertuch *n*, Frot'tee (-gewebe) *n*; **3.** Schlinge *f* (*des unge- schnittenen Samtes etc.*).

terse [tɜːs] *adj.* □ knapp, kurz u. bün- dig, markig; **'terse·ness** [-nɪs] *s.* Knappheit *f*, Kürze *f*, Bündigkeit *f*, Prä'gnanz *f*.

ter·tian ['tɜːʃn] ⚕ **I** *adj.* am dritten Tag wiederkehrend, Tertian...: **~ ague**, **~ fever**, **~ malaria** → **II** *s.* Terti'anfieber *n*.

ter·ti·ar·y ['tɜːʃərɪ] **I** *adj. allg.* terti'är, Tertiär...; **II** *s.* ♀ *geol.* Terti'är *n*.

ter·zet·to [tɜːt'setəʊ] *s.* **-tos**, **-ti** [-tɪ] (*Ital.*) *s.* ♪ Ter'zett *n*, Trio *n*.

tes·sel·late ['tesɪleɪt] *v/t.* tessellieren, mit Mosa'iksteinen auslegen; **~d pave- ment** Mosaik(fuß)boden *m*; **tes·sel· la·tion** [ˌtesɪ'leɪʃn] *s.* Mosa'ik(arbeit *f*) *n.*

test [test] **I** *s.* **1.** *allg., a.* ⊗ Test *m*, Probe *f*, Versuch *m*; **2.** a) Prüfung *f*, Unter'suchung *f*, Stichprobe *f*, b) *fig.* Probe *f*, Prüfung *f*: **put to the ~** auf die Probe stellen; **stand the ~** die Probe bestehen, sich bewähren; **~ of strength** Kraftprobe *f*; → **acid test**, **crucial** 1; **3.** *fig.* Prüfstein *m*, Kri'terium *n*: **success is not a fair ~**; **4.** *ped., psych.* (Eignungs-, Leistungs)Prüfung *f*, Test *m*; **5.** *ped.* Klassenarbeit *f*; **6.** ⚕ (Blut-*etc.*)Probe *f*, (Haut- *etc.*)Test *m*; **7.** 🜚 a) Ana'lyse *f*, b) Rea'gens *n*; **8.** *metall.* a) Versuchstiegel *m*, Ka'pelle *f*, b) Treibherd *m*; **9.** F → **test match**; **10.** *hist. Brit.* Testeid *m*; **II** *v/t.* **11.** (**for s.th.** auf et. [hin]) prüfen (*a. ped.*) *od.* unter'suchen, erproben, e-r Prüfung unter'ziehen, testen (*alle a.* ⊗): **~ out** ausprobieren; **12.** *fig.* j-s Geduld *etc.* auf die Probe stellen; **13.** *ped., psych.* j-n testen; **14.** 🜚 analysieren; **15.** ⚡ *Leitung* prüfen *od.* abfragen; **16.** ✕ *Waffe* anschießen; **III** *adj.* **17.** Probe..., Versuchs..., Prüf(ungs)..., Test...; → **test case**, **test flight** *etc.*

tes·ta·cean [te'steɪʃn] *zo.* **I** *adj.* hartschalig, Schal(tier)...; **II** *s.* Schaltier *n*; **tes·ta·ceous** [-ʃəs] *adj. zo.* hartschalig, Schalen...

tes·ta·ment ['testəmənt] *s.* **1.** ⚖ Testa-'ment *n*, letzter Wille; **2.** ⚯ *bibl.* (*Altes od. Neues*) Testa'ment; **3.** *fig.* Zeugnis *n*, Beweis *m* (**to** *gen. od.* für); **tes·ta·men·ta·ry** [ˌtestə'mentərɪ] *adj.* ⚖ ⚖ testamen'tarisch: a) letztwillig, b) durch Testa'ment (vermacht, bestimmt): **~ disposition** letztwillige Verfügung; **~ capacity** Testierfähigkeit *f*.

tes·tate ['testeɪt] *adj.*: **die ~** ⚖ unter Hinterlassung e-s Testaments sterben, ein Testament hinterlassen; **tes·ta·tor** [te'steɪtə] *s.* ⚖ Erb'lasser *m*; **tes·ta·trix** [te'steɪtrɪks] *pl.* **-tri·ces** [-siːz] *s.* Erb'lasserin *f*.

test bed *s.* ⊗ Prüfstand *m*; **~ card** *s.* TV Testbild *n*; **~ case** *s.* **1.** ⚖ a) 'Musterpro,zess *m*, b) Präze'denzfall *m*; **2.** *fig.* Muster-, Schulbeispiel *n*; **~ drive** *s.* ⚡ Messkreis *m*; **~ drive** *s. mot.* Probebefahrt *f*; **'~-drive** *v/t.* [*irr.* → **drive**] *Auto* Probe fahren.

test·ed [ˈtestɪd] *adj.* geprüft; erprobt (*a. weitS.* bewährt).

test·er¹ ['testə] *s.* **1.** Prüfer *m*; **2.** Prüfgerät *n*.

test·er² ['testə] *s.* **1.** △ Baldachin *m*; **2.** (Bett)Himmel *m*.

tes·tes ['testiːz] *pl. von* **testis**.

test flight *s.* ✈ Probeflug *m*; **~ glass** → **test tube**.

tes·ti·cle ['testɪkl] *s. anat.* Hode *m, f*, Hoden *m*; **tes·tic·u·lar** *adj.* Hoden...

tes·ti·fy ['testɪfaɪ] **I** *v/t.* **1.** ⚖ aussagen, bezeugen; **2.** *fig.* bezeugen *od.* zeugen von, b) kundtun; **II** *v/i.* **3.** ⚖ (als Zeuge) aussagen: **~ to** → 2; **refuse to ~** die Aussage verweigern; **tes·ti·mo·ni·al** [ˌtestɪ'məʊnjəl] *s.* **1.** (Führungs- *etc.*) Zeugnis *n*; **2.** Empfehlungsschreiben *n*; **3.** Zeichen *n* der Anerkennung, *bsd.* Ehrengabe *f*; **tes·ti·mo·ny** [-ɪmənɪ] *s.* **1.** Zeugnis *n* (*a.* Zeugen) Aussage *f*, b) Beweis *m*: **in ~ whereof** ⚖ zu Urkund dessen; **bear ~ to** et. bezeugen (*a. fig.*); **call s.o. in ~** ⚖ j-n als Zeugen aufrufen; **have s.o.'s ~ for** j-n zum Zeugen haben für; **2.** *coll. od. pl.* Zeugnis(se *pl.*) *n*: **the ~ of history**; **3.** *bibl.* Zeugnis *n*: a) Gesetzestafeln *pl.*, b) *mst pl.* göttliche Offenbarung, *a.* Heilige Schrift.

tes·ti·ness ['testɪnɪs] *s.* Gereiztheit *f*.

test·ing ['testɪŋ] *adj. bsd.* ⊗ Probe..., Prüf..., Versuchs...: **~ engineer** ⊗ Prüfingenieur *m*; **~ ground** ⊗ a) Prüffeld *n*, b) Versuchsgelände *n*; **~ method** *psych.* Testmethode *f*.

tes·tis ['testɪs] *pl.* **-tes** [-tiːz] (*Lat.*) → **testicle**.

test match *s. Kricket:* internatio'naler Vergleichskampf.

tes·tos·ter·one [te'stɒstərəʊn] *s. physiol.* Testoste'ron *n* (*Sexualhormon*).

test pa·per *s.* **1.** *ped.* a) schriftliche (Klassen)Arbeit, b) Prüfungsbogen *m*; **2.** 🜚 Rea'genzpa,pier *n*; **~ pat·tern** *s. Am.* TV Testbild *n*; **~ pi·lot** *s.* 'Testpi,lot *m*; **~ print** *s. phot.* Probeabzug *m*; **~ run** *s.* ⊗ Probelauf *m*; **~ stand** *s.* ⊗ Prüfstand *m*; **~ tube** [-sɪt-] *s.* 🜚 Rea'genzglas *n*; **'~-tube** *adj.*: **~ baby** ⚕ Retortenbaby *n*.

tes·ty ['testɪ] *adj.* ☐ gereizt, reizbar.

tet·a·nus ['tetənəs] *s.* ⚕ Tetanus *m*, (*bsd.* Wund)Starrkrampf *m*.

tetch·y ['tetʃɪ] *adj.* ☐ reizbar.

tête-à-tête [ˌteɪtɑː'teɪt] (*Fr.*) **I** *adv.* **1.** vertraulich, unter vier Augen; **2.** ganz al'lein (**with** mit); **II** *s.* **3.** Tete-a-'tete *n*.

teth·er ['teðə] **I** *s.* Haltestrick *m*, -seil *n*: **be at the end of one's ~** *fig.* am Ende s-r (*a. finanziellen*) Kräfte sein, sich nicht mehr zu helfen wissen; **II** *v/t.* anbinden (**to** an *acc.*).

tetra- [tetrə] *in Zssgn* vier.

tet·rad ['tetræd] *s.* **1.** Vierzahl *f*; **2.** 🜚 vierwertiges A'tom *od.* Ele'ment; **3.** *biol.* ('Sporen)Te,trade *f*.

tet·ra·gon ['tetrəgɒn] *s.* ♈ Tetra'gon *n*, Viereck *n*; **te·trag·o·nal** [te'trægənl] *adj.* ♈ tetrago'nal.

tet·ra·he·dral [ˌtetrə'hedrəl] *adj.* ♈ vierflächig, tetra'edrisch; **tet·ra·he·dron** [-drən] *pl.* **-'he·drons**, **-'he·dra** [-drə] *s.* ♈ Tetra'eder *n*.

tet·ter ['tetə] *s.* ⚕ (Haut)Flechte *f*.

Teu·ton ['tjuːtɒn] *s.* **1.** Ger'mane *m*, Ger'manin *f*; **2.** Teu'tone *m*, Teu'tonin *f*; **3.** F Deutsche(r *m*) *f*; **II** *adj.* **4.** → **Teutonic** I; **Teu·ton·ic** [tjuː'tɒnɪk] **I** *adj.* **1.** ger'manisch; **2.** teu'tonisch; **3.** Deutschordens...: **~ Order** *hist.* Deutschritterorden *m*; **4.** F (typisch) deutsch; **II** *s.* **5.** *ling.* Ger'manisch *n*; **'Teu·ton·ism** [-tənɪzəm] *s.* **1.** Ger'manentum *n*, ger'manisches Wesen; **2.** *ling.* Germa'nismus *m*.

Tex·an ['teksən] **I** *adj.* te'xanisch, aus Texas; **II** *s.* Te'xaner(in).

text [tekst] *s.* **1.** (Ur)Text *m*, (genauer) Wortlaut; **2.** *typ.* a) Text(abdruck, -teil) *m* (*Ggs. Illustrationen, Vorwort etc.*), b) Text *m* (*Schriftgrad*), c) Frak'turschrift *f*; **3.** (Lied- *etc.*)Text *m*; **4.** a) Bibelspruch *m*, -stelle *f*, b) Bibeltext *m*; **5.** Thema *n*: **stick to one's ~** bei der Sache bleiben; **~ book** → **text book**; **'~-book** *s.* Lehrbuch *n*, Leitfaden *m*: **~ example** *fig.* Paradebeispiel *n*; **~ hand** *s.* große Schreibschrift.

tex·tile ['tekstaɪl] **I** *s.* a) Gewebe *n*, Web-, Faserstoff *m*, b) *pl.* Web-, Tex'tilwaren *pl.*, Tex'tilien *pl.*; **II** *adj.* gewebt; Textil..., Stoff..., Gewebe...: **~ goods** → I b; **~ industry** Textilindustrie *f*.

text proc·ess·ing *s. Computer:* Textverarbeitung *f*.

tex·tu·al ['tekstjʊəl] *adj.* ☐ **1.** textlich, Text...; **2.** wortgetreu.

tex·tur·al ['tekstʃərəl] *adj.* ☐ **1.** Gewebe..., **2.** struktu'rell, Struktur...: **~ changes; tex·ture** ['tekstʃə] *s.* **1.** Gewebe *n*; **2.** *biol.* Tex'tur *f* (*Gewebezu-*

stand); **3.** Maserung *f* (*Holz*); **4.** Struk-'tur *f*, Beschaffenheit *f*; **5.** *geol., a. fig.* Struk'tur *f*, Gefüge *n*.

'T-,gird·er *s.* ⊗ T-Träger *m*.

Thai [taɪ] **I** *pl.* **Thais**, **Thai** *s.* **1.** Thai *m, f*, Thailänder(in); **2.** *ling.* a) Thai *n*, b) Thaisprachen *pl.*; **II** *adj.* **3.** Thai..., thailändisch.

thal·a·mus ['θæləməs] *pl.* **-mi** [-maɪ] *s. anat.* Sehhügel *m*.

tha·lid·o·mide [θə'lɪdəmaɪd] *s. pharm.* Thalido'mid *n*: **~ child** Contergankind *n*.

Thames [temz] *npr.* Themse *f*: **he won't set the ~ on fire** *fig.* er hat das Pulver auch nicht erfunden.

than [ðæn; ðən] *cj.* (*nach e-m Komparativ*) als: **more ~ was necessary** mehr als nötig.

thane [θeɪn] *s.* **1.** *hist.* a) Gefolgsadlige(r) *m*, b) Than *m*, Lehensmann *m* (*der schottischen Könige*); **2.** *allg.* schottischer Adliger.

thank [θæŋk] **I** *v/t.* j-m danken, sich bedanken bei: (**I**) **~ you** danke; **~ you** bitte (*beim Servieren etc.*); (**yes,**) **~ you** ja, bitte; **no, ~ you** nein, danke; **I will ~ you** *oft iro.* ich wäre Ihnen sehr dankbar (**to do, for doing**, wenn Sie täten); **~ you for nothing** *iro.* ich danke (bestens); **he has only himself to ~ for that** das hat er sich selbst zuzuschreiben; **II** *s. pl.* a) Dank *m*, b) Dankesbezeigung(en *pl.*) *f*, Danksagung(en *pl.*) *f*: **letter of ~s** Dankesbrief *m*; **in ~s for** zum Dank für; **with ~s** dankend, mit Dank; **~s to** *a. fig. u. iro.* dank (*gen.*); **small ~s to her** sie hat sich nicht gerade über'anstrengt; (**many**) **~s!** vielen Dank!, danke!; **no, ~s!** nein, danke!; **small ~s I got** schlecht hat man es mir gedankt; **'thank·ful** [-fʊl] *adj.* ☐ dankbar (**to s.o.** j-m): **I am ~ that** ich bin (heil)froh, dass; **'thank·less** [-lɪs] *adj.* ☐ undankbar (*a. fig. Aufgabe etc.*); **'thank·less·ness** [-lɪsnɪs] *s.* Undankbarkeit *f*.

thank of·fer·ing *s. bibl.* Sühneopfer *n der Juden.*

thanks·giv·ing ['θæŋks,gɪvɪŋ] *s.* **1.** Danksagung *f, bsd.* Dankgebet *n*; **2.** ⚯ (**Day**) (Ernte)'Dankfest *n* (*4. Donnerstag im November*).

'thank,wor·thy *adj.* dankenswert; **'~-you** [-jʊ] *s.* F Dankeschön *n*.

that¹ [ðæt] **I** *pron. u. adj.* (*hinweisend*) *pl.* **those** [ðəʊz] **1.** (*ohne pl.*) das: **~'s all** das ist alles; **~'s it!** a) das ist es ja (gerade)!, b) so ists recht!; **~'s what it is** das ist es ja gerade; **~'s that** F das wäre erledigt, damit basta, das wärs; **~ was ...!** F das wars denn wohl!, aus der Traum!; **~ is** (**to say**) das heißt; **and ~** und zwar; **at ~** a) zudem, obendrein, b) F dabei; **for all ~** trotz alledem; **like ~** so; **2.** jener, jene, jenes, der, die, das, der-, die-, dasjenige: **~ car over there** das Auto da drüben; **~ there man** V der Mann da; **those who** diejenigen welche; **~ which** das, was; **those are his friends** das sind seine Freunde; **3.** solch: **to ~ degree that** in solchem Ausmaße *od.* so sehr, dass; **II** *adv.* **4.** F so (sehr), dermaßen: **~ big; not all ~ good** (**much**) so gut (viel) auch wieder nicht.

that² [ðæt; ðət] *adj.* *that rel. pron.* **1.** (*bsd. in einschränkenden Sätzen*) der, die, das, welch: **the book ~ he wanted** das Buch, das er wünschte; **any house ~** jedes Haus, das; **no one ~** keiner, der; **Mrs. Jones, Miss Black ~ was** F Frau J., geborene B.; **Mrs. Quilp ~ is** F

T

die jetzige Frau Q.; **2.** (*nach all*, *everything*, *nothing etc.*) was: *the best ~* das Beste, was.

that³ [ðæt; ðət] *cj.* **1.** (*in Subjekt- u. Objektsätzen*) dass: *it is a pity ~ he is not here* es ist schade, dass er nicht hier ist; *it is 4 years ~ he went away* es sind nun 4 Jahre her, dass *od.* seitdem er fortging; **2.** (*in Konsekutivsätzen*) dass: *so ~* sodass; **3.** (*in Finalsätzen*) da'mit, dass; **4.** (*in Kausalsätzen*) weil, da (ja), dass: *not ~ I have any objection* nicht, dass ich etwas dagegen hätte; *it is rather ~* es ist eher deshalb, weil; *in ~* a) darum, weil, b) insofern als; **5.** (*nach Adverbien der Zeit*) als, da.

thatch [θætʃ] **I** *s.* **1.** Dachstroh *n*; **2.** Strohdach *n*; **3.** F Haarwald *m*; **II** *v/t.* **4.** mit Stroh *od.* Binsen *etc.* decken; *~ed roof* → 2.

thaw [θɔː] **I** *v/i.* **1.** (auf)tauen, schmelzen; **2.** tauen (*Wetter*): *it is ~ing* es taut; **3.** *fig.* auftauen (*Person*); **II** *v/t.* **4.** schmelzen, auftauen; **5.** *a. ~ out fig. j-n* zum Auftauen bringen; **III** *s.* **6.** (Auf-) Tauen *n*; **7.** Tauwetter *n* (*a. fig. pol.*); **8.** *fig.* ‚Auftauen‘ *n*.

the [*unbetont vor Konsonanten*: ðə; *unbetont vor Vokalen*: ði; *betont od. allein stehend*: ðiː] **I** *bestimmter Artikel* **1.** der, die, das, *pl.* die (*u. die entsprechenden Formen im acc. u. dat.*): *~ book on ~ table* das Buch auf dem Tisch; *~ England of today* das England von heute; *~ Browns* die Browns, die Familie Brown; **2.** *vor Maßangaben:* *one dollar ~ pound* einen Dollar das Pfund; *wine at 2 pounds ~ bottle* Wein zu 2 Pfund die Flasche; **3.** [ðiː] ‚der, ‚die, ‚das (*hervorragende od. geeignete etc.*): *he is ~ painter of the century* er ist ‚der Maler des Jahrhunderts; **II** *adv.* **4.** (*vor comp.*) desto, umso: *~ ... ~* je ... desto; *~ sooner ~ better* je eher, desto besser; *so much ~ better* umso besser.

the·a·ter *Am.*, **the·a·tre** *Brit.* [ˈθiːətə] *s.* **1.** The'ater *n* (*Gebäude u. Kunstgattung*); **2.** *coll.* Bühnenwerke *pl*; **3.** Hörsaal *m*: *lecture ~*; (*operating*) *~ #* Operationssaal *m*; *~ nurse* Operationsschwester *f*; **4.** *fig.* (*of war* Kriegs-) Schauplatz *m*; *‚~·go·er s.* The'aterbesucher(in).

the·at·ri·cal [θɪˈætrɪkl] **I** *adj.* □ **1.** Theater..., Bühnen..., bühnenmäßig; **2.** thea'tralisch: *~ gestures*; **II** *s.* **3.** *pl.* The'ater-, *bsd.* Liebhaberaufführungen *pl.*; **the·at·rics** *s. pl.* **1.** *sg. konstr.* The'ater(re‚gie)kunst *f*; **2.** *fig.* Thea'tralik *f*.

thee [ðiː] *pron.* **1.** *obs. od. poet. od. bibl.* a) dich, b) dir: *of ~* dein; **2.** *dial.* (*u. in der Sprache der Quäker*) du.

theft [θeft] *s.* Diebstahl *m* (*from* aus, *from s.o.* an j-m); *‚~·proof adj.* diebstahlsicher.

the·in(e) [ˈθiːiːn; -ɪn] *s. # The'in n*.

their [ðeə; *vor Vokal* ðer] *pron.* (*besitzanzeigendes Fürwort der 3. pl.*) ihr, ihre: *~ books* ihre Bücher.

theirs [ðeəz] *pron.* der *od.* die *od.* das Ihrige *od.* Ihre: *this book is ~* dieses Buch gehört ihnen; *a friend of ~* ein Freund von ihnen.

the·ism¹ [ˈθiːɪzəm] *s. # Teevergiftung f*.

the·ism² [ˈθiːɪzəm] *s. eccl.* The'ismus *m*; **the·is·tic** [θiːˈɪstɪk] *adj.* the'istisch.

them [ðem; ðəm] *pron.* **1.** (*acc. u. dat. von they*) a) sie (*acc.*), b) ihnen: *they looked behind ~* sie blickten hinter sich; **2.** F *od. dial.* sie (*nom.*): *~ as* diejenigen, die; **3.** *dial. od.* V diese: ~

guys; *~ were the days!* das waren (halt) noch Zeiten!

the·mat·ic [θɪˈmætɪk] *adj.* (□ *~ally*) **1.** *bsd.* ♪ the'matisch; **2.** *ling.* Stamm..., Thema...: *~ vowel*.

theme [θiːm] *s.* **1.** Thema *n* (*a. ♪*): *have s.th. for* (*a*) ~ et. zum Thema haben; **2.** *bsd. Am.* (Schul)Aufsatz *m*, (-)Arbeit *f*; **3.** *ling.* (Wort)Stamm *m*; **4.** *Radio, TV:* 'Kennmelo‚die *f*; *~ park s.* Themenpark *m* (*Erlebnispark mit bestimmter einheitlicher Ausrichtung*); *~ song s.* **1.** 'Titelmelo‚die *f* (*Film etc.*); **2.** → **theme** 4.

them·selves [ðəmˈselvz] *pron.* **1.** (*emphatisch*) (sie) selbst: *they ~ said it*; **2.** *refl.* sich (selbst): *the ideas in ~* die Ideen an sich.

then [ðen] **I** *adv.* **1.** damals: *long before* ~ lange vorher; **2.** dann: *~ and there* auf der Stelle, sofort; *by ~* bis dahin, inzwischen; *from ~* von da an; *till ~* bis dahin; **3.** dann, 'darauf, 'hierauf: *what ~?* was dann?; **4.** dann, außerdem: *~* aber andererseits *od.* freilich; **5.** dann, in dem Falle: *if ... ~* wenn ... dann; **6.** denn: *well ~* nun gut (denn); *how ~ did he do it?* wie hat er es denn (dann) getan?; **7.** also, folglich, dann: *~ you did not expect me?* du hast mich also nicht erwartet?; **II** *adj.* **8.** damalig: *the ~ president*.

the·nar [ˈθiːnɑː] *s. anat.* **1.** Handfläche *f*; **2.** Daumenballen *m*; **3.** Fußsohle *f*.

thence [ðens] *adv.* **1.** von da, von dort; **2.** (*zeitlich*) von da an, seit jener Zeit: *a week ~* e-e Woche darauf; **3.** 'daher, deshalb; **4.** 'daraus, aus dieser Tatsache: *~ it follows*, *‚~'forth*, *‚~'for·ward(s) adv.* von da an, seit der Zeit, seit'dem.

the·oc·ra·cy [θɪˈɒkrəsɪ] *s.* Theokra'tie *f*.

the·o·lo·gi·an [θɪəˈlɒdʒən] *s.* Theo'loge *m*; **the·o·log·i·cal** [-ˈlɒdʒɪkl] *adj.* □ theo'logisch; **the·ol·o·gy** [θɪˈɒlədʒɪ] *s.* Theolo'gie *f*.

the·oph·a·ny [θɪˈɒfənɪ] *s.* Theopha'nie *f*, Erscheinung *f* (*e-s*) Gottes.

the·o·rem [ˈθɪərəm] *s. ⅄, phls.* Theo-'rem *n*, (Grund-, Lehr)Satz *m*: *~ of the cosine* Kosinussatz.

the·o·ret·ic, **the·o·ret·i·cal** [θɪəˈret-ɪk(l)] *adj.* □ **1.** theo'retisch; **2.** spekula'tiv; **the·o·rist** [ˈθɪərɪst] *s.* Theo'retiker(in); **the·o·rize** [ˈθɪəraɪz] *I v/i.* theo-retisieren, Theo'rien aufstellen; **II** *v/t.* *~ that* die Theorie aufstellen, dass; annehmen, dass; **the·o·ry** [ˈθɪərɪ] *s.* Theo-'rie *f*: a) Lehre *f*: *~ of chances* Wahrscheinlichkeitsrechnung *f*, *~ of relativity* Relativitätstheorie, b) theo'retischer Teil (*e-r Wissenschaft*): *~ of music* Musiktheorie, c) *Ggs. Praxis:* *in ~* theoretisch, d) Anschauung *f*: *it is his pet ~* es ist s-e Lieblingsidee.

the·o·soph·ic, **the·o·soph·i·cal** [θɪə-ˈsɒfɪk(l)] *adj.* □ *eccl.* theo'sophisch; **the·os·o·phist** [θɪˈɒsəfɪst] *s.* Theo-'soph(in); **the·os·o·phy** [θɪˈɒsəfɪ] *s.* Theoso'phie *f*.

ther·a·peu·tic, **ther·a·peu·ti·cal** [‚θerə'pjuːtɪk(l)] *adj.* □ *thera'peutisch:* *~ exercises* Bewegungstherapie *f*; **‚ther·a'peu·tics** [-ks] *s. pl. mst sg. konstr.* Thera'peutik *f*, Thera'pie(lehre) *f*; **ther·a·pist** [ˈθerəpɪst] *s.* Thera'peut (-in): *mental ~* Psychotherapeut(in); **ther·a·py** [ˈθerəpɪ] *s.* Thera'pie *f*: a) Behandlung *f*, b) Heilverfahren *n*.

there [ðeə; ðə] **I** *adj.* **1.** da, dort: *down* (*up*, *over*, *in*) *~* da *od.* dort unten (oben, drüben, drinnen); *have been ~*

sl. ‚dabei gewesen sein‘, genau Bescheid wissen; *be not all ~ sl.* ‚nicht ganz richtig (im Oberstübchen) sein‘; *~ and then* a) (gerade) hier u. jetzt, b) *fig.* auf der Stelle, sofort; *~ it is!* a) da ist es!, b) *fig.* so steht es!; *~ you are* (*od. go*)*!* siehst du!, da hast dus; *you ~!* (*Anruf*) du da!, he!; **2.** (‚da-, ‚dort)hin: *down* (*up*, *over*, *in*) *~* (‚da- *od.* ‚dort)hinunter (-hinauf, -hinüber, -hinein); *~ and back* hin u. zurück; *get ~* a) hingelangen, -kommen, b) *sl.* ‚es schaffen‘; **3.** ‚darin, in dieser Sache *od.* Hinsicht: *~ I agree with you*; **4.** *fig.* da, an dieser Stelle (*in e-r Rede etc.*); **5.** es: *~ is*, *pl.* *~ are* es gibt, ist, sind; *~ was once a king* es war einmal ein König; *~ is no saying* es lässt sich nicht sagen; *~ was dancing* es wurde getanzt; *~'s a good boy* (*girl*, *fellow*)*!* a) sei doch (so) lieb!, b) so bist du lieb!, brav!; **II** *int.* **6.** da!, schau (her)!, na!: *~, ~!* tröstend: (ganz) ruhig!; *~ now* na, bitte; *'~·a·bout*, *a.* *'~·bouts* [ˈðeərə-] *adv.* **1.** da her'um, etwa da: *somewhere ~* da irgendwo; **2.** *fig.* so ungefähr, so etwa: *500 people or ~s*; *‚~'af·ter* [ðeərˈɑː-] *adv.* **1.** da'nach, später; **2.** seit'her; *‚~·at* [‚ðeərˈæt] *adv. obs. od. ⅄* **1.** da'selbst, dort; **2.** bei der Gelegenheit, ‚dabei; *‚~'by adv.* **1.** ‚dadurch, auf diese Weise; **2.** da'bei, daran, da'von; **3.** nahe da'bei; *‚~'for adv.* 'dafür; *'~·fore adv. u. cj.* **1.** deshalb, -wegen, 'daher, 'darum; **2.** demgemäß, folglich; *‚~'from adv.* da'von, dar'aus, da'her; *‚~·in* [‚ðeərˈɪn] *adv.* **1.** dar'in, da drinnen; **2.** *fig.* 'darin, in dieser Hinsicht; *‚~·in'af·ter* [‚ðeərɪn-] *adv. bsd. ⅄* (*weiter*) unten, später (*in e-r Urkunde etc.*); *‚~·of* [‚ðeərˈɒv] *adv. obs. od. ⅄* **1.** da'von; **2.** dessen, deren; *‚~·on* [‚ðeərˈɒn] *adv.* 'darauf, -über; *‚~'to adv. obs.* **1.** da'zu, dar'an, da'für; **2.** außerdem, noch da'zu; *‚~·un·der* [‚ðeərˈʌndə] *adv.* dar'unter; *‚~·up·on* [‚ðeərəˈpɒn] *adv.* **1.** dar'auf, hier'auf, da'nach; **2.** darauf'hin, demzufolge, 'darum; *‚~'with adv.* **1.** 'damit; **2.** → *thereup·on*; *‚~·with'al adv. obs.* **1.** über'dies, außerdem; **2.** 'damit.

therm [θɜːm] *s. phys.* **1.** unbestimmte Wärmeeinheit; **2.** *Brit.* 100.000 Wärmeeinheiten *pl.* (*zur Messung des Gasverbrauchs*); **'ther·mae** [-miː] *s. pl.* (*Lat.*) *s. pl.* **1.** *antiq.* Thermen *pl.*; **2.** *#* Ther'malquellen *pl.*

ther·mal [ˈθɜːml] **I** *adj.* □ **1.** *phys.* thermisch, Wärme...: *~ barrier ✈* Hitzemauer *f*; *~ breeder* thermischer Brüter; *~ efficiency* Wärmewirkungsgrad *m*; *~ power station* Wärmekraftwerk *n*; *~ printer* Thermodrucker *m*; *~ reactor* thermischer Reaktor; *~ spring* Thermalquelle *f*, *~ value* Heizwert *m*; **2.** warm, heiß: *~ water* heiße Quelle; **3.** *✈* ther'mal, Thermal...; **II** *s.* **4.** *pl. ✈*, *phys.* Thermik *f*; **'ther·mic** [-mɪk] *adj.* (□ *~ally*) thermisch, Wärme..., Hitze...;

ther·mi·on·ic [‚θɜːmɪˈɒnɪk] **I** *adj.* thermi'onisch: *~ valve* (*Am. tube*) Elektronenröhre *f*; **II** *s. pl. sg. konstr.* Thermi'onik *f*, Lehre *f* von den Elekt-'ronenröhren

thermo- [θɜːməʊ] *in Zssgn* a) Wärme, Hitze, Thermo..., b) thermoe'lektrisch; **‚ther·mo'chem·is·try** *s. # Thermo-che'mie f; **‚ther·mo'cou·ple** *s. ⚡* Thermoele'ment *n*; **‚ther·mo'dy'nam·ics** *s. pl. sg. konstr. phys.* Thermody'namik *f*; **‚ther·mo·e'lec·tric** *adj.* thermoe'lektrisch, 'wärme‚lektrisch: *~ couple* → *thermocouple*; **'ther·mo·mat** *s.* Isomatte *f*.

ther·mom·e·ter [θəˈmɒmɪtə] s. phys. Thermoˈmeter n: **clinical ~** ⚕ Fieberthermometer; **~ reading** Thermometerablesung f, -stand m; **ther·mo·met·ric, ther·mo·met·ri·cal** [ˌθɜːməʊˈmetrɪk(l)] adj. □ phys. thermoˈmetrisch, Thermometer...; **ˌther·moˈnu·cle·ar** adj. phys. thermonukleˈar: **~ bomb** a. Fusionsbombe f; **ˈther·mo·pile** s. phys. Thermosäule f; **ˌther·moˈplas·tic** ⚗ I adj. thermoˈplastisch; II s. Thermoˈplast m.

Ther·mos (bot·tle od. flask) [ˈθɜːmɒs] s. Thermosflasche f.

ˌther·moˈset·ting adj. ⚗ ˌthermostatoˈplastisch, hitzehärtbar.

ther·mo·stat [ˈθɜːməʊstæt] s. ⚡, ⚙ Thermoˈstat m; **ther·mo·stat·ic** [ˌθɜːməʊˈstætɪk] adj. (□ **~ally**) thermoˈstatisch.

the·sau·rus [θɪˈsɔːrəs] pl. **-ri** [-raɪ] (Lat.) s. Theˈsaurus m: a) Wörterbuch n, b) (Wort-, Wissens-, Sprach)Schatz m.

these [ðiːz] pl. von **this**.

the·sis [ˈθiːsɪs] pl. **-ses** [-siːz] s. **1.** These f: a) Behauptung f, b) (Streit)Satz m, Postuˈlat n; **2.** univ. Dissertatiˈon f; **3.** [ˈθesɪs] Metrik: unbetonte Silbe; **~ nov·el** s. Tenˈdenzˌroman m; **~ play** s. thea. Proˈblemstück n.

Thes·pi·an [ˈθespɪən] I adj. fig. draˈmatisch, Schauspiel...; II s. oft humor. Thespisjünger(in).

Thes·sa·lo·ni·ans [ˌθesəˈləʊnjənz] s. pl. sg. konstr. bibl. (Brief m des Paulus an die) Thessaˈlonicher pl.

thews [θjuːz] s. pl. **1.** Muskeln pl., Sehnen pl.; **2.** fig. Kraft f.

they [ðeɪ; ðe] pron. **1.** (pl. zu **he, she, it**) sie; **2.** man: **~ say** man sagt; **3.** es: **who are ~?** – **~ are Americans** Wer sind sie? – Es (od. sie) sind Amerikaner; **4.** (auf Kollektiva bezogen) er, sie, es: **the police** ..., **~** ... die Polizei ..., sie (sg.); **5. ~ who** diejenigen, welche.

they'd [ðeɪd] F für a) **they would**, b) **they had**.

thick [θɪk] I adj. □ **1.** allg. dick: **a ~ neck**; **a board 2 inches ~** ein 2 Zoll starkes Brett; **2.** dicht (Wald, Haar, Menschenmenge, a. Nebel etc.); **3. ~ with** über u. über bedeckt von; **4. ~ with** voll von, voller, reich an (dat.): **a tree ~ with leaves**; **the air is ~ with snow** die Luft ist voll(er) Schnee; **5.** dick(flüssig); **6.** neblig, trüb(e) (Wetter); **7.** schlammig, trübe; **8.** dumpf, belegt (Stimme); **9.** dumm; **10.** dicht (aufeinˈander folgend); **11.** F dick (befreundet): **they are as ~ as thieves** sie sind dicke Freunde, sie halten zusammen wie Pech u. Schwefel; **12.** sl. ˌstarkˈ, frech: **that's a bit ~!** das ist ein starkes Stück!; II s. **13.** dickster od. dichtester Teil; **14.** fig. Brennpunkt m: **in the ~ of** mitten in (dat.); **in the ~ of it** mittendrin; **in the ~ of the fight** im dichtesten Kampfgetümmel; **the ~ of the crowd** das dichteste Menschengewühl; **through ~ and thin** durch dick u. dünn; **15.** F Dummkopf m; III adv. **16.** dick: **spread ~** Butter etc. dick aufstreichen; **lay it on ~** F ˌdick auftragenˈ; **17.** dicht od. rasch (aufeinˈander); a. **fast and ~** hageldicht (Schläge); **thick·en** [ˈθɪkən] I v/t. **1.** dick(er) machen, verdicken; **2.** Sauce, Flüssigkeit eindicken, Suppe legieren; **3.** dicht(er) machen, verdichten; **4.** verstärken, -mehren; **5.** trüben; II v/i. **6.** dick(er) werden; **7.** dicht(er) werden; **8.** sich verdichten; **9.** sich trüben; **10.** sich verwirren,

the plot **~s** der Knoten (im Drama etc.) schürzt sich; **11.** zunehmen; **thick·en·er** [ˈθɪknə] ⚗ **1.** Eindicker m; **2.** Verdicker m, Absetzbehälter m; **3.** Verdickungsmittel n; **thick·en·ing** [ˈθɪknɪŋ] s. **1.** Verdickung f; **2.** Eindickung f; **3.** Eindickmittel n; **4.** Verdichtung f; **5.** ⚕ Anschwellung f, Schwarte f.

thick·et [ˈθɪkɪt] s. Dickicht n; **ˈthick·et·ed** [-tɪd] adj. voller Dickicht(e).

ˈthick|·head s. Dummkopf m; **ˌ~ˈhead·ed** adj. **1.** dickköpfig; **2.** fig. dumm.

thick·ness [ˈθɪknɪs] s. **1.** Dicke f, Stärke f; **2.** Dichte f; **3.** Verdickung f; **4.** ✦ Lage f (Seide etc.), Schicht f; **5.** Dickflüssigkeit f; **6.** Trübheit f: **misty ~** undurchdringlicher Nebel; **7.** Heiserkeit f, Undeutlichkeit f: **~ of speech** schwere Zunge.

ˌthick|·set adj. **1.** dicht (gepflanzt): **a ~ hedge**; **2.** untersetzt (Person); **ˌ~ˈskinned** adj. **1.** dickhäutig; **2.** dickschalig; **3.** zo. Dickhäuter...; **4.** fig. dickfellig; **ˌ~ˈskulled** [-ˈskʌld] adj. **1.** dickköpfig; **2.** → **thick-witted**; **ˌ~ˈwit·ted** adj. dumm, begriffsstutzig, schwer von Begriff.

thief [θiːf] pl. **thieves** [θiːvz] s. Dieb (-in): **thieves' Latin** Gaunersprache f; **stop, ~!** haltet den Dieb!; **one ought to set a ~ to catch a ~** wenn man e-n Schlauen fangen will, muss man e-n Schlauen schicken; **thieve** [θiːv] v/t. u. v/i. stehlen; **thiev·er·y** [ˈθiːvərɪ] s. **1.** Diebeˈrei f, Diebstahl m; **2.** Diebesgut n; **thiev·ish** [ˈθiːvɪʃ] adj. □ **1.** diebisch, Dieb(e)s...; **2.** heimlich, verstohlen; **ˈthiev·ish·ness** [-nɪs] s. diebisches Wesen.

thigh [θaɪ] s. anat. (Ober)Schenkel m; **ˈ~·bone** s. anat. (Ober)Schenkelknochen m.

thill [θɪl] s. (Gabel)Deichsel f; **thill·er** [ˈθɪlə], a. **thill horse** s. Deichselpferd n.

thim·ble [ˈθɪmbl] s. **1.** Näherei: a) Fingerhut m, b) Nähring m; **2.** ⊙ a) Meˈtallring m, b) (Stock)Zwinge f; **ˈthim·ble·ful** [-fʊl] pl. **-fuls** s. **1.** Fingerhut m voll, Schlückchen n; **2.** fig. Kleinigkeit f.

ˈthim·ble|·rig I s. Fingerhutspiel n (Bauernfängerspiel); II v/t. a. allg. betrügen; **ˈ~ˌrig·ger** s. **1.** Fingerhutspieler m; **2.** allg. Bauernfänger m.

thin [θɪn] I adj. □ **1.** allg. dünn: **~ air**; **~ blood**; **~ clothes**; **a ~ line** e-e dünne od. schmale od. feine Linie; **2.** dünn, mager, schmächtig: **as ~ as a lath** spindeldürr; **3.** dünn, licht (Wald, Haar etc.): **~ rain** feiner Regen; **4.** dünn, schwach (Getränk etc., a. Stimme, Ton); **5.** ⚜ mager (Boden); **6.** fig. mager, spärlich, dürftig: **a ~ house** thea. e-e schwach besuchte Vorstellung; **he had a ~ time of it** sl. es ging ihm ˌmiesˈ; **7.** fig. fadenscheinig: **a ~ excuse**; **8.** seicht, subˈstanzlos (Buch etc.); II v/t. **9.** oft **~ down**, **~ off**, **~ out** a) dünn(er) machen, b) Flüssigkeit verdünnen (a.) fig. verringern, Bevölkerung dezimieren, Schlachtreihe, Wald etc. lichten; III v/i. **10.** oft **~ down**, **~ off**, **~ out** a) dünn(er) werden, b) sich verringern, c) sich lichten (a. Haar), d) fig. spärlicher werden, abnehmen: **his hair is ~ning** sein Haar lichtet sich.

thine [ðaɪn] pron. obs. od. bibl. od. poet. **1.** (substantivisch) der od. die od. das Dein(ig)e, Dein(e, er) etc.; **2.** (adjektivisch vor Vokalen od. stummem h für **thy**) dein(e): **~ eyes** deine

Augen.

thing [θɪŋ] s. **1.** konkretes Ding, Sache f, Gegenstand m: **the law of ~s** ⚖ das Sachenrecht; **just the ~ I wanted** genau (das), was ich wollte; **2.** fig. Ding n, Sache f, Angelegenheit f: **~s political** politische Dinge, alles Politische; **above all ~s** vor allen Dingen, vor allem; **another ~** etwas anderes; **the best ~ to do** das Beste(, was man tun kann); **a foolish ~ to do** e-e Torheit; **for one ~** (erstens) einmal; **in all ~s** in jeder Hinsicht; **no small ~** keine Kleinigkeit; **no such ~** nichts dergleichen; **not a ~** (rein) gar nichts; **of all ~s** ausgerechnet (dieses etc.); **a pretty ~** iro. e-e schöne Geschichte; **taking one ~ with the other** im Großen u. Ganzen, im großen Ganzen; **do great ~s** große Dinge tun, Großes vollbringen; **get ~s done** et. zuwege bringen; **do one's own ~** F tun, was man will; **know a ~ or two** Bescheid wissen (**about** über acc.); **it's one of those ~s** da kann man (halt) nichts machen; → **first** 1; **3.** pl. Sachen f, Zeug n (Gepäck, Gerät, Kleider etc.): **swimming ~s** Badesachen, -zeug; **put on one's ~s** sich anziehen; **4.** pl. Dinge pl., ˈUmstände pl., (Sach)Lage f: **~s are improving** die Dinge od. Verhältnisse bessern sich; **~s look black for me** es sieht schwarz aus für mich; **5.** Geschöpf n, Wesen n: **dumb ~s**; **6.** a) Ding n (Mädchen etc.), b) Kerl m: (the) **poor ~** das arme Ding, der od. die Ärmste; **poor ~!** du od. Sie Ärmste(r)!; **the dear old ~** die gute alte Haut; **7. the ~** F a) die Hauptsache, b) das Richtige, richtig, c) das Schickliche, schicklich: **the ~ was to** das Wichtigste war zu; **this is not the ~** das ist nicht das Richtige; **not to be** (od. **feel**) **quite the ~** nicht ganz auf dem Posten sein; **that's not all the ~ to do** so etwas tut man nicht; **ˌ~-in-itˈself** s. phls. das Ding an sich.

thing·um·a·bob [ˈθɪŋəmɪbɒb], **thing·um·a·jig** [ˈθɪŋəmɪdʒɪg], **thing·um·my** [ˈθɪŋəmɪ] s. F der (die, das) ˌDings(da)ˈ od. ˌDingsbumsˈ.

think [θɪŋk] [irr.] I v/i. **1.** denken (**of** an acc.): **~ ahead** vorausdenken, a. vorsichtig sein; **~ aloud** laut denken; **2.** (**about, over**) nachdenken (über acc.), sich (e-e Sache) überˈlegen; **3. ~ of** a) sich besinnen auf (acc.), sich erinnern an (acc.): (**now that I**) **come to ~ of it** dabei fällt mir ein; b) et. bedenken: **~ of it!** denke daran!, c) sich et. denken od. vorstellen, d) Plan etc. ersinnen, ausdenken, e) halten von: **~ much** (od. **highly**) **of** viel halten von, e-e hohe Meinung haben von; **~ nothing of** a) wenig halten von, b) nichts dabei finden (**to do s.th.** et. zu tun); → **better**[1] 4; **4.** meinen, denken: **I ~ so** ich glaube (schon), ich denke; **I should ~ so** ich denke doch, das will ich meinen; **5.** gedenken, vorhaben, beabsichtigen (**of doing, to do** zu tun); II v/t. **6.** et. denken: **~ away** et. wegdenken; **~ out** a) sich et. ausdenken, b) Am. a. **~ through** Problem zu Ende denken; **~ s.th. over** sich et. überˈlegen od. durch den Kopf gehen lassen; **~ up** F Plan etc. aushecken, sich ausdenken, sich et. einfallen lassen; **7.** sich et. denken od. vorstellen; **8.** halten für: **~ o.s. clever**; **~ it advisable** es für ratsam halten od. erachten; **I ~ it best to do** ich halte es für das Beste, et. zu tun; **9.** überˈlegen, nachdenken über (acc.); **10.** denken, vermuten: **~ no harm** nichts Böses denken; **III** s. F **11.** *have a* (*fresh*) ~ *a-bout s.th.* et. (noch einmal) überdenken; *he has another ~ coming!* da hat er sich aber schwer getäuscht!; '**think-a·ble** [-kəbl] *adj.* denkbar: a) begreifbar, b) möglich; '**think·er** [-kə] s. Denker(in); '**think·in** s. F Konfe'renz *f*; '**think·ing** [-kɪŋ] **I** *adj.* □ **1.** denkend, vernünftig: *a ~ being* ein denkendes Wesen; *all ~ men* jeder vernünftig Denkende; *put on one's ~ cap* F (mal) nachdenken; **2.** Denk...; **II** s. **3.** Denken *n*: *way of ~* Denkart *f*; *do some hard* (*quick*) ~ scharf nachdenken (schnell ,schalten'); **4.** Meinung *f*: *in* (*od. to*) *my* (*way of*) ~ m-r Meinung nach; '**think-so** s.: *on his* (*etc.*) *mere* ~ auf eine bloße Vermutung hin; ~ **tank** s. F ,'Denkfa,brik' *f*.

thin·ner¹ ['θɪnə] s. **1.** Verdünner *m* (*Arbeiter od. Gerät*); **2.** (*bsd.* Farben)Verdünnungsmittel *n*.

thin·ner² ['θɪnə] *comp. von* **thin**.

thin·ness ['θɪnnɪs] s. **1.** Dünne *f*, Dünnheit *f*; **2.** Magerkeit *f*; **3.** Spärlichkeit *f*; **4.** *fig.* Dürftigkeit *f*, Seichtheit *f*.

,**thin-'skinned** *adj.* **1.** dünnhäutig; **2.** *fig.* ('über)empfindlich.

third [θɜːd] **I** *adj.* □ → **thirdly**; **1.** dritt: ~ *best* der (*die*, *das*) Drittbeste; ~ *cousin* Vetter *m* dritten Grades; ~ *degree* dritter Grad; ~ *estate* *pol. hist.* dritter Stand, Bürgertum *n*; ~ *party* ♉ Dritte(r *m*) *f*; **II** s. **2.** *der* (*die*, *das*) Dritte; **3.** ♪ Terz *f*; **4.** *mot.* F dritter Gang; **5.** Drittel *n*; **6.** *pl.* ✝ Waren *pl.* dritter Quali'tät, dritte Wahl; ~ *class* s. ⛴ *etc.* dritte Klasse; ~-'**class** *adj. u. adv.* **1.** *allg.* drittklassig; **2.** ⛴ *etc.* Abteil *etc.* dritter Klasse: *travel* ~ dritter Klasse reisen.

third·ly ['θɜːdlɪ] *adv.* drittens.

,**third|-'par·ty** *adj.* ♉ Dritt...: ~ *debtor*; ~ *insurance* Haftpflichtversicherung *f*; *insured against ~ risks* haftpflichtversichert; ,~-'**rate** *adj.* **1.** drittrangig; **2.** *fig.* minderwertig; ♃ **World** s. *pol.* die Dritte Welt.

thirst [θɜːst] **I** s. **1.** Durst *m*; **2.** *fig.* Durst *m*, Gier *f*, Verlangen *n*, Sucht *f* (*for*, *of*, *after* nach): ~ *for blood* Blutdurst; ~ *for knowledge* Wissensdurst; ~ *for power* Machtgier; **II** *v/i.* **3.** *bsd. fig.* dürsten, lechzen (*for*, *after* nach *Rache etc.*); '**thirst·i·ness** [-tɪnɪs] s. Durst(igkeit *f*) *m*; '**thirst·y** [-tɪ] *adj.* □ **1.** durstig: *be* ~ Durst haben, durstig sein; **2.** dürr, trocken (*Boden*, *Jahreszeit*); **3.** F ,durstig', Durst verursachend: ~ *work*; **4.** *fig.* begierig, lechzend: *be ~ for* (*od. after*) *s.th.* nach et. lechzen.

thir·teen [,θɜː'tiːn] **I** *adj.* dreizehn; **II** s. Dreizehn *f*; ,**thir'teenth** [-nθ] **I** *adj.* **1.** dreizehnt; **II** s. **2.** *der* (*die*, *das*) Dreizehnte; **3.** Dreizehntel *n*.

thir·ti·eth ['θɜːtɪɪθ] **I** *adj.* **1.** dreißigst; **II** s. **2.** *der* (*die*, *das*) Dreißigste; **3.** Dreißigstel *n*; '**thir·ty** [-tɪ] **I** *adj.* dreißig: ~ *all*, F ~ *up* Tennis: dreißig beide; **II** s. **2.** Dreißig *f*: *the thirties* a) die Dreißiger(jahre) (*des Lebens*): *he is in his thirties* er ist in den Dreißigern, b) die Dreißigerjahre (*e-s Jahrhunderts*); **3.** *Am. sl.* Ende *n* (*e-s Zeitungsartikels etc.*).

this [ðɪs] *pl.* **these** [ðiːz] **I** *pron.* **1.** a) dieser, diese, dieses, b) dies, das: *all* ~ dies alles, all das; *for all* ~ deswegen, darum; *like* ~ so; ~ *is what I expected* (genau) das habe ich erwartet; ~ *is what happened* Folgendes geschah; ~ *is*, *dieses*, dieser Zeitpunkt, dieses Ereig-

nis: *after* ~ danach; *before* ~ zuvor; *by* ~ bis dahin, mittlerweile; **II** *adj.* **3.** dieser, diese, dieses, ✝ *a.* laufend (*Monat*, *Jahr*): ~ *day week* heute in e-r Woche; *in* ~ *country* hierzulande; ~ *morning* heute Morgen; ~ *time* diesmal; *these 3 weeks* die letzten 3 Wochen, seit 3 Wochen; **III** *adv.* **4.** so: ~ *much* so viel.

this·tle ['θɪsl] s. ♣ Distel *f*; '~·**down** s. ♣ Distelwolle *f*.

this·tly ['θɪslɪ] *adj.* **1.** distelig; **2.** distelähnlich, stach(e)lig.

thith·er ['ðɪðə] *obs. od. poet.* **I** *adv.* dort-, dahin; **II** *adj.* jenseitig.

'**thole(·pin)** [θəʊl] s. ⚓ Dolle *f*.

thong [θɒŋ] **I** s. **1.** (Leder)Riemen *m* (*Halfter*, *Zügel*, *Peitschenschnur etc.*); **2.** *Am.* 'Zehensan,dale *f*. **II** *v/t.* **3.** mit Riemen versehen *od.* befestigen; **4.** (mit e-m Riemen) peitschen.

tho·rac·ic [θɔː'ræsɪk] *adj. anat.* Brust...; **tho·rax** ['θɔːræks] *pl.* **-rax·es** [-ræksɪz] s. **1.** *anat.* Brust(korb *m*, -kasten *m*) *f*, Thorax *m*; **2.** *zo.* Mittelleib *m* bei Gliederfüßlern.

thorn [θɔːn] s. **1.** Dorn *m*: *a ~ in the flesh* (*od. side*) *fig.* ein Pfahl im Fleische, ein Dorn im Auge; *be* (*od. sit*) *on ~s* *fig.* (wie) auf glühenden Kohlen sitzen; **2.** *ling.* Dorn *m* (*altenglischer Buchstabe*); ~ *ap·ple* ♣ Stechapfel *m*.

thorn·y ['θɔːnɪ] *adj.* **1.** dornig, stach(e)lig; **2.** *fig.* dornenvoll, mühselig; **3.** *fig.* heikel: *a ~ subject*.

thor·ough ['θʌrə] *adj.* □ → **thoroughly**; **1.** gründlich: a) sorgfältig (*Person u. Sache*), b) genau, eingehend: *a ~ inquiry*; *a ~ knowledge*, c) 'durchgreifend: *a ~ reform*; **2.** voll'endet: a) voll'kommen, meisterhaft, b) völlig, echt, durch u. durch: *a ~ politician*, c) *contp.* ausgemacht: *a ~ rascal*; ~ *bass* [beɪs] s. ♪ Gene'ralbass *m*; '~·**bred I** *adj.* **1.** reinrassig, Vollblut...; **2.** *fig.* a) rassig, b) ele'gant, c) kultiviert, d) schnittig (*Auto*); **II** s. **3.** Vollblut(pferd) *n*; **4.** rassiger *od.* kultivierter Mensch; **5.** *mot.* rassiger *od.* schnittiger Wagen; '~·**fare** s. **1.** Hauptverkehrs-, 'Durchgangsstraße *f*; **2.** 'Durchfahrt *f*: *no ~!*; **3.** Wasserstraße *f*; '~·**go·ing** *adj.* **1.** → *thorough* 1; **2.** ex'trem, kompro'misslos, durch u. durch.

thor·ough·ly ['θʌrəlɪ] *adv.* **1.** gründlich *etc.*; **2.** völlig, gänzlich, abso'lut; '**thor·ough·ness** [-ənɪs] s. **1.** Gründlichkeit *f*; **2.** Voll'endung *f*, Voll'kommenheit *f*.

'**thor·ough-paced** *adj.* **1.** in allen Gangarten geübt (*Pferd*); **2.** *fig.* → *thorough* 2 b.

those [ðəʊz] *pron. pl. von* **that¹**.

thou [ðaʊ] **I** *pron. poet. od. dial. od. bibl.* du; **II** *v/t.* mit ,thou' anreden.

though [ðəʊ] **I** *cj.* **1.** ob'wohl, ob'gleich, ob'schon; **2.** *a.* *even* ~ wenn auch, wenn'gleich, selbst wenn, zwar: *important ~ it is* so wichtig es auch ist; *what ~ the way is long* was macht es schon aus, wenn der Weg (auch) lang ist; **3.** je'doch, doch; **4.** *as* ~ als ob, wie wenn; **II** *adv.* **5.** F (*am Satzende*) aber, aller'dings, dennoch, immer'hin: *I wish you had told me, ~*.

thought [θɔːt] **I** *pret. u. p.p. von* **think**; **II** s. **1.** a) Gedanke *m*, Einfall *m*: *a happy ~*, b) Gedankengang *m*, c) Gedanken *pl.*, Denken *n*: *lost in ~* in Gedanken (verloren); *his one ~ was how to* er dachte nur daran, wie *es tun könnte*; *it never entered my ~s* es kam mir nie in den Sinn; **2.** *nur sg.* Denken *n*, Denkvermögen *n*; **2.** Über'legung *f*: *give ~ to* sich Gedanken machen über

(*acc.*); *take ~ how* sich überlegen, wie *man es tun könnte*; *after serious* ~ nach ernsthafter Erwägung; *on second ~s* a) nach reiflicher Überlegung, b) wenn ich es mir recht überlege; *have second ~s about it* (so seine) Zweifel darüber haben; *without* ~ ohne zu überlegen; **4.** Absicht *f*: *he had no ~ of coming*; *we had* (*some*) ~*s of going* wir trugen uns mit dem Gedanken zu gehen; **5.** *mst pl.* Gedanke *m*, Meinung *f*, Ansicht *f*; **6.** (Für)Sorge *f*, Rücksicht *f*: *give* (*od. have*) *some* ~ *to* Rücksicht nehmen auf (*acc.*); *take* ~ *for* Sorge tragen für *od.* um (*acc.*); *take no* ~ *to* nicht achten auf (*acc.*); **7.** *nur sg.* Denken *n*: a) Denkweise *f*: *scientific* ~, b) Gedankenwelt *f*: *Greek* ~; **8.** *fig.* Spur *f*: *a ~ smaller* e-e ,Idee' kleiner; *a ~ hesitant* etwas zögernd; '**thought·ful** [-fʊl] *adj.* □ **1.** gedankenvoll, nachdenklich, besinnlich (*a. Buch etc.*); **2.** achtsam (*of* auf *acc.*); **3.** rücksichtsvoll, aufmerksam, zu'vorkommend; '**thought·ful·ness** [-fʊlnɪs] s. **1.** Nachdenklichkeit *f*, Besinnlichkeit *f*; **2.** Achtsamkeit *f*; **3.** Rücksichtnahme *f*, Aufmerksamkeit *f*; '**thought·less** [-lɪs] *adj.* □ **1.** gedankenlos, unbesonnen, unbekümmert; **2.** rücksichtslos, unaufmerksam; '**thought·less·ness** [-lɪsnɪs] s. **1.** Gedankenlosigkeit *f*, Unbekümmertheit *f*; **2.** Rücksichtslosigkeit *f*, Unaufmerksamkeit *f*.

,**thought|-'out** *adj.* (*well* ~ wohl) durchdacht; ~ *read·er* s. Gedankenleser(in); ~ *read·ing* s. Gedankenlesen *n*; ~ *trans·fer·ence* s. Ge'dankenüber,tragung *f*.

thou·sand ['θaʊznd] **I** *adj.* **1.** tausend (*a. fig. unzählige*): ~ *and one* *fig.* zahllos, unzählig; *The ♃ and One Nights* Tausendundeine Nacht; *a ~ times* tausendmal; *a ~ thanks* tausend Dank; **II** s. **2.** Tausend *n*, *pl.* Tausende *pl.*: *many ~s of times* vieltausendmal; *in their ~s*, *by the ~* zu Tausenden; **3.** Tausend *f* (*Zahlzeichen*): *one in a ~* eine(r, s) unter tausend, 'eine Ausnahme; '**thou·sand·fold** [-ndf-] **I** *adj.* tausendfach, -fältig; **II** *adv.* *mst a* ~ tausendfach, -mal; '**thou·sandth** [-nθ] **I** s. **1.** der (*die*, *das*) Tausendste; **2.** Tausendstel *n*; **II** *adj.* **3.** tausendst.

thral·dom ['θrɔːldəm] s. **1.** Leibeigenschaft *f*; **2.** *fig.* Knechtschaft *f*, Sklave'rei *f*; **thrall** [θrɔːl] s. **1.** *hist.* Leibeigene(r *m*) *f*, Hörige(r *m*) *f*; **2.** *fig.* Sklave *m*, Knecht *m*; **3.** → *thraldom*; '**thrall·dom** *Am.* → *thraldom*.

thrash [θræʃ] **I** *v/t.* **1.** → *thresh*; **2.** verdreschen, -prügeln; *fig.* (vernichtend) schlagen, ,vermöbeln'; **II** *v/i.* **3.** *a.* ~ *about* a) sich *im Bett etc.* 'hin- u. 'herwerfen, b) um sich schlagen, c) zappeln; **4.** ⚓ sich vorwärts arbeiten; '**thrash·er** [-ʃə] → *thresher*; '**thrash·ing** [-ʃɪŋ] s. Dresche *f*, Prügel *pl.*: *give s.o. a ~* → *thrash* 2.

thread [θred] **I** s. **1.** Faden *m*: a) Zwirn *m*, Garn *n*: *hang by a ~* a) an e-m Faden hängen, b) *weitS.* Faser *f*, Fiber *f*, c) *fig.* (dünner) Strahl, Strich *m*, d) *fig.* Zs.-hang *m*: *lose the ~* (*of one's story*) den Faden verlieren; *resume* (*od. take up*) *the* ~ den Faden wieder aufnehmen; **2.** ⊕ Gewinde(gang *m*) *n*; **II** *v/t.* **3.** *Nadel* einfädeln; **4.** *Perlen etc.* aufreihen; **5.** mit Fäden durch'ziehen; **6.** *fig.* durch'ziehen, -'dringen; **7.** sich winden durch: ~ *one's way* (*through*) sich (hindurch)schlängeln (durch); **8.** ⊕ Gewinde schneiden in (*acc.*): ~ *on* anschrauben; '~·**bare** *adj.* **1.** fadenscheinig, abgetragen; **2.** schäbig (gekleidet); **3.** *fig.* abgedroschen.

thread·ed ['θredɪd] *adj.* ◎ Gewinde...: **~ flange**; '**thread·er** [-də] *s.* **1.** 'Einfädelma,schine *f*; **2.** ◎ Gewindeschneider *m*.

thread·ing lathe ['θredɪŋ] *s.* ◎ Gewindeschneidbank *f*.

thread·y ['θredɪ] *adj.* **1.** fadenartig, faserig; **2.** Fäden ziehend; **3.** *fig.* schwach, dünn.

threat [θret] *s.* **1.** Drohung *f* (*of* mit, *to* gegen); **2.** (*to*) Bedrohung *f* (*gen.*), Gefahr *f* (für): **a ~ to peace**; **there was a ~ of rain** es drohte zu regnen; '**threat·en** [-tn] **I** *v/t.* **1.** (*with*) j-m drohen (mit), j-m androhen (*acc.*), j-n bedrohen (mit); **2.** drohend ankündigen: **the sky ~s a storm**; **3.** (damit) drohen (**to do** zu tun); **4.** bedrohen, gefährden; **II** *v/i.* **5.** drohen; **6.** *fig.* drohen: a) drohend bevorstehen, b) Gefahr laufen (**to do** zu tun); '**threat·en·ing** [-tnɪŋ] *adj.* □ **1.** drohend, Droh...: **~ letter** Drohbrief *m*; **2.** *fig.* bedrohlich.

three [θriː] **I** *adj.* drei; **II** *s.* Drei *f* (*Zahl, Spielkarte etc.*); **~-'col·o(u)r** *adj.* dreifarbig, Dreifarben...: **~ process** Dreifarbendruck(verfahren *n*) *m*; **~-'cornered** *adj.* **1.** dreieckig: **~ hat** Dreispitz *m*; **2.** zu dreien, Dreier...: **a ~ discussion**; **~-'D** *adj.* 'dreidimensio,nal, 3-'D-...; '**~-day e·vent** *s.* Reitsport: Military *f*; '**~-day e·vent·er** *s.* Militaryreiter *m*; **~-'deck·er** *s.* **1.** ⚓ *hist.* Dreidecker *m*; **2.** *et.* Dreiteiliges, *z.B.* F dreibändiger Ro'man; **~-di'men·sion·al** *adj.* 'dreidimensio,nal. '**three·fold I** *adj. u. adv.* dreifach; **II** *s.* das Dreifache.

'**three-lane** *adj.* dreispurig (*Autobahn etc.*); **~-'mast·er** *s.* ⚓ Dreimaster *m*; '**~-mile** *adj.* Dreimeilen...: **~ zone**.

three·pence ['θrepəns] *s.* Brit. **1.** drei Pence *pl.*; **2.** *obs.* Drei'pencestück *n*; **~-'pen·ny** ['θrepənɪ] *adj.* **1.** drei Pence wert, Dreipence...; **2.** *fig.* billig, wertlos.

'**three-phase** *adj.* ≁ dreiphasig, Dreiphasen...: **~ current** Drehstrom *m*, Dreiphasenstrom *m*; '**~-piece** *adj.* dreiteilig (*Anzug etc.*); '**~-ply I** *adj.* **1.** dreifach (*Garn, Seil etc.*); **2.** dreischichtig (*Holz etc.*); **II** *s.* **3.** dreischichtiges Sperrholz; '**~-point land·ing** *s.* ✈ Dreipunktlandung *f*; **~-'quar·ter I** *adj.* drei viertel; **II** *s. a.* **~ back** Rugby: Drei'viertelspieler *m*; **~-'score** *adj. obs.* sechzig.

three·some ['θriːsəm] **I** *adj.* **1.** zu dreien, Dreier...; **II** *s.* **2.** Dreiergruppe *f*, 'Trio *n*; **3.** Golf etc.: Dreier(spiel *n*) *m*.

'**three-speed gear** *s.* ◎ Dreiganggetriebe *n*; '**~-stage** *adj.* ◎ dreistufig (*Rakete, Verstärker etc.*); '**~-way** *adj.* ◎ Dreiwege...

thresh [θreʃ] *v/t. u. v/i.* dreschen: **~ (over old) straw** *fig.* leeres Stroh dreschen; **~ out** *fig. et.* gründlich erörtern, klären; '**thresh·er** [-ʃə] *s.* **1.** Drescher *m*; **2.** 'Dreschma,schine *f*; '**thresh·ing** [-ʃɪŋ] **I** *s.* Dreschen *n*; **II** *adj.* Dresch...: **~ floor** Dreschboden *m*, Tenne *f*.

thresh·old ['θreʃhəʊld] **I** *s.* **1.** (Tür-) Schwelle *f*; **2.** *fig.* Schwelle *f*, Beginn *m*; **3.** *psych.* (Bewusstseins- *etc.*)Schwelle *f*; **II** *adj.* **4.** *bsd.* ◎ Schwellen...: **~ frequency**; **~ value** Grenzwert *m*.

threw [θruː] *pret von* **throw**.

thrice [θraɪs] *adv. obs.* **1.** dreimal; **2.** *fig.* sehr, 'überaus, höchst.

thrift [θrɪft] *s.* **1.** Sparsamkeit *f*: a) Sparsinn *m*, b) Wirtschaftlichkeit *f*; **2.** ♀

Grasnelke *f*; '**thrift·i·ness** [-tɪnɪs] → **thrift** 1; '**thrift·less** [-lɪs] *adj.* □ verschwenderisch; '**thrift·less·ness** [-lɪsnɪs] *s.* Verschwendung *f*; '**thrift·y** [-tɪ] *adj.* □ sparsam (*of, with* mit): a) haushälterisch, b) wirtschaftlich (*a. Sachen*).

thrill [θrɪl] **I** *v/t.* **1.** erschauern lassen, erregen, packen, begeistern, elektrisieren, entzücken; **2.** *j-n* durch'laufen, -'schauern, über'laufen (*Gefühl*); **II** *v/i.* **3.** (er)beben, erschauern, zittern (*with* vor *Freude etc.*); **4.** (*to*) sich begeistern (für), gepackt werden (von); **5.** durch'laufen, -'schauern, -'rieseln (*through acc.*); **III** *s.* **6.** Zittern *n*, Erregung *f*, prickelndes Gefühl: **a ~ of joy** freudige Erregung; **7.** a) *das* Spannende *od.* Erregende, b) Nervenkitzel *m*, c) Sensati'on *f*; '**thrill·er** [-lə] *s.* F ,Reißer' *m*, ,Krimi' *m*, Thriller *m* (*Kriminalroman, -film etc.*); '**thrill·ing** [-lɪŋ] *adj.* □ **1.** erregend, packend, spannend, sensatio'nell; **2.** hinreißend, begeisternd.

thrive [θraɪv] *v/i.* [*irr.*] **1.** gedeihen (*Pflanze, Tier etc.*); **2.** *fig.* gedeihen: a) blühen, Erfolg haben (*Geschäft etc.*), b) reich werden (*Person*), c) sich entwickeln (*Laster etc.*); **thriv·en** ['θrɪvn] *p.p. von* **thrive**; '**thriv·ing** [-vɪŋ] *adj.* □ *fig.* blühend.

thro' [θruː] *poet. für* **through**.

throat [θrəʊt] *s.* **1.** *anat.* Kehle *f*, Gurgel *f*, Rachen *m*, Schlund *m*: **sore ~** Halsschmerzen *pl.*, rauer Hals; **stick in s.o.'s ~** j-m im Hals stecken bleiben (*Worte*); **ram** (*od.* **thrust**) **s.th. down s.o.'s ~** j-m et. aufzwingen; **2.** Hals *m*, Kehle *f*: **cut s.o.'s ~** j-m den Hals abschneiden; **cut one's own ~** *fig.* sich selbst ruinieren; **take s.o. by the ~** j-n an der Gurgel packen; **3.** *fig.* 'Durch-, Eingang *m*, verengte Öffnung, Schlund *m*, *z.B.* Hals *m* e-r Vase, Kehle *f* e-s Kamins, Gicht *f* e-s Hochofens; **4.** ⚓ Hohlkehle *f*; '**throat·y** [-tɪ] *adj.* □ **1.** kehlig, guttu'ral; **2.** rau, heiser.

throb [θrɒb] **I** *v/i.* **1.** pochen, hämmern, klopfen (*Herz etc.*): **~bing pains** klopfende Schmerzen; **II** *s.* **2.** Pochen *n*, Klopfen *n*, Hämmern *n*, (Puls)Schlag *m*; **3.** *fig.* Erregung *f*, Erbeben *n*.

throe [θrəʊ] *s. mst pl.* heftiger Schmerz: a) *pl.* (Geburts)Wehen *pl.*, b) *pl.* Todeskampf *m*, Ago'nie *f*: **in the ~s of** *fig.* mitten in *et. Unangenehmem*, im Kampf(e) mit.

throm·bo·sis [θrɒm'bəʊsɪs] *pl.* **-ses** [-siːz] *s.* ✿ Throm'bose *f*; **throm'bot·ic** [-'bɒtɪk] *adj.* ✿ throm'botisch.

throne [θrəʊn] **I** *s.* **1.** Thron *m* (*König, Prinz*), Stuhl *m* (*Papst, Bischof*); **2.** *fig.* Thron *m*: a) Herrschaft *f*, b) Herrscher (-in) *m*; **II** *v/t.* **3.** auf den Thron setzen; **III** *v/i.* **4.** thronen.

throng [θrɒŋ] **I** *s.* **1.** (Menschen)Menge *f*; **2.** Gedränge *n*, Andrang *m*; **3.** Menge *f*, Masse *f* (*Sachen*); **II** *v/i.* **4.** sich drängen *od.* (zs.-)scharen, (her'bei-, hin'ein- *etc.*)strömen; **III** *v/t.* **5.** sich drängen in (*dat.*): **~ the streets**; **6.** bedrängen, um'drängen.

throt·tle ['θrɒtl] **I** *s.* **1.** F Kehle *f*; **2.** ◎, *mot.* a) *a.* **~ lever** Gashebel *m*, b) *a.* **~ valve** Drosselklappe *f*: **open** (**close**) **the ~** Gas geben (wegnehmen); **II** *v/t.* **3.** erdrosseln; *fig.* ersticken, abwürgen, unter'drücken; **4.** *a.* **~ down** ◎, *mot.* (ab)drosseln; **III** *v/i.* **5.** *a.* **~ back** (*down*) *mot. etc.* drosseln, Gas wegnehmen.

through [θruː] **I** *prp.* **1.** *räumlich u. fig.* durch, durch ... hin'durch; **2.** durch, in

(*überall umher in e-m Gebiet etc.*): **~ all the country**; **3.** a) *e-n* Zeitraum hin'durch, während, b) *Am.* (von ...) bis; **4.** bis zum Ende *od.* ganz durch, fertig (mit): **when will you get ~ your work?**; **5.** durch, mittels; **6.** aus, von, durch, in-, zu'folge, wegen: **~ fear** aus *od.* vor Furcht; **~ neglect** infolge *od.* durch Nachlässigkeit; **II** *adv.* **7.** durch: **~ and ~** durch u. durch (*a. fig.*); **push a needle ~** e-e Nadel durchstechen; **he would not let us ~** er wollte uns nicht durchlassen; **this train goes ~ to Boston** dieser Zug fährt (durch) bis Boston; **you are ~!** *teleph.* Sie sind verbunden!; **8.** (ganz) durch (*von Anfang bis Ende*): **read a letter ~** e-n Brief ganz durchlesen; **carry a matter ~** e-e Sache durchführen; **9.** fertig (*with* mit): **I am ~ with him** F er ist für mich erledigt; **I'm ~ with it!** ich habe es satt!; **III** *adj.* **10.** 'durchgehend, Durchgangs...: **a ~ train**; **~ carriage** (*od.* **coach**) Kurswagen *m*; **~ dialing** *teleph. Am.* Durchwahl *f*; **~ flight** ✈ Direktflug *m*; **~ traffic** Durchgangsverkehr *m*; **~way** *Am.* Durchgangs- *od.* Schnellstraße *f*; '**through-out** [θruː'aʊt] **I** *prp.* **1.** über'all in (*acc. od. dat.*): **~ the country** im ganzen Land; **2.** während (*gen.*): **~ the year** das ganze Jahr hindurch; **II** *adv.* **3.** durch u. durch, ganz u. gar, 'durchweg; **4.** überall; **5.** die ganze Zeit; '**through-put** *s. econ., a.* Computer: 'Durchsatz *m*.

throve [θrəʊv] *pret. von* **thrive**.

throw [θrəʊ] **I** *s.* **1.** Werfen *n*, (*Speer- etc.*)Wurf *m*; **2.** Wurf *m* (*a. Ringkampf, Würfelspiel*), *fig. a.* Coup *m*; **3.** ◎ (Kolben)Hub *m*; **4.** ◎ (Regler- *etc.*)Ausschlag *m*; **5.** ◎ Kröpfung *f* (*Kurbelwelle*); **II** *v/t.* [*irr.*] **6.** werfen, schleudern; (*a. fig. Blick, Kusshand etc.*) zuwerfen (**s.o. s.th., s.th. to s.o.** j-m et.); mit *Steinen etc.* werfen; *Wasser* schütten *od.* gießen: **~ at** werfen nach; **~ o.s. at s.o.** *fig.* sich j-m an den Hals werfen; **~ a shawl over one's shoulders** sich e-n Schal um die Schultern werfen; **~ together** zs.-werfen; **be thrown** (**together**) **with** *fig.* (*zufällig*) zs.-geraten mit; **7.** *Angel, Netz etc.* auswerfen; **8.** a) *Würfel* werfen, b) *Zahl* würfeln, c) *Karten* ausspielen *od.* ablegen; **9.** *Reiter* abwerfen; **10.** *Ringkampf:* Gegner werfen; **11.** *zo.* Junge werfen; **12.** *Brücke* schlagen (**over, across** über *acc.*); **13.** *zo.* Haut abwerfen; **14.** ◎ *Hebel* 'umlegen, *Kupplung od.* Schalter ein-, ausrücken, ein-, ausschalten; **15.** *Töpferei:* formen, drehen; **16.** ◎ *Seide* zwirnen, mulinieren; **17.** *fig.* in *Entzückung, Verwirrung etc.* versetzen; **18.** F *j-n* ,umwerfen' *od.* aus der Fassung bringen; **19.** F *e-e Gesellschaft* geben, *e-e Party* ,schmeißen'; **20.** *Am.* F *Wettkampf* absichtlich verlieren; **21.** *sl. Wutanfall etc.* bekommen: **~ a fit**; **III** *v/i.* [*irr.*] **22.** werfen; **23.** würfeln; *Zssgn mit prp.:*

throw| in·to *v/t.* (hin'ein)werfen in (*acc.*): **~ prison** j-n ins Gefängnis werfen; **~ the bargain** (beim Kauf) dreingeben; **throw o.s. into** *fig.* sich in *die Arbeit, den Kampf etc.* stürzen; **~ (up·)on** *v/t.* **1.** werfen auf (*acc.*): **be thrown upon o.s.** (*od.* **upon one's own resources**) auf sich selbst angewiesen sein; **2. throw o.s.** (**up**)**on** a) sich auf *die Knie etc.* werfen, b) sich anvertrauen (*dat.*);

Zssgn mit adv.:

throw| a·way *v/t.* **1.** wegwerfen; **2.**

Geld etc. verschwenden, -geuden ([*up*]*on* an *acc.*); **3.** *Gelegenheit* verpassen, -schenken; **4.** *et.* verwerfen; ~ **back I** *v/t.* **1.** zu'rückwerfen (*a. fig. hemmen*): *be thrown back upon* angewiesen sein auf (*acc.*); **II** *v/i.* **2.** zu'rückkehren (zu), zu'rückfallen (auf *acc.*, in *acc.*); **3.** nachgeraten (*to dat.*); *biol.* rückarten; ~ **down** *v/t.* **1.** (*o.s.* sich) niederwerfen; **2.** 'umstürzen, vernichten; ~ **in** *v/t.* **1.** (hin)'einwerfen; **2.** *Bemerkung etc.* einwerfen, -schalten; **3.** *et.* mit in den Kauf geben, dreingeben; **4.** ☼ *Gang etc.* einrücken; ~ **off I** *v/t.* **1.** *Kleider, Maske etc., a. fig. Schamgefühl etc.* abwerfen, ablegen; **2.** *Joch etc.* abwerfen, abschütteln, sich freimachen von; **3.** *Bekannte, Krankheit etc.* loswerden; **4.** *Verfolger, a. Hund* von der Fährte abbringen, abschütteln; **5.** *Gedicht etc.* hinwerfen, aus dem Ärmel schütteln; **6.** ☼ a) kippen, 'umlegen, b) auskuppeln, -rücken; **7.** *typ.* abziehen; **8.** *j-n* aus dem Kon'zept *od.* aus der Fassung bringen; **II** *v/i.* **9.** (*hunt.* die Jagd) beginnen; ~ **on** *v/t. Kleider* 'überwerfen, sich *et.* 'umwerfen; ~ **o·pen** *v/t.* **1.** *Tür etc.* aufreißen, -stoßen; **2.** öffentlich zugänglich machen (**to** *dat.* für); ~ **out** *v/t.* **1.** (*a. j-n* hin)'auswerfen; **2.** *bsd. parl.* verwerfen; **3.** ▲ vorbauen; anbauen (**to** an *acc.*); **4.** *Bemerkung* fallen lassen, *Vorschlag etc.* äußern; *e-n Wink* geben; **5.** a) *et.* über den Haufen werfen, b) *j-n* aus dem Kon'zept bringen; **6.** ☼ auskuppeln, -rücken; **7.** *Fühler etc.* ausstrecken: ~ *a chest* F sich in die Brust werfen; ~ **o·ver** *v/t.* **1.** über den Haufen werfen; **2.** *fig. Plan etc.* über Bord werfen, aufgeben; **3.** *Freund etc.* im Stich lassen, fallen lassen; ~ **up** *v/t.* **1.** in die Höhe werfen, hochwerfen; **2.** *et.* hastig errichten, *Schanze etc.* aufwerfen; **3.** *Karten, a. Amt etc.* hinwerfen, -schmeißen; **4.** erbrechen; **II** *v/i.* **5.** (sich er)brechen, sich über'geben.

'**throw**|**·a·way I** *s. et.* zum Wegwerfen, *z.B.* Re'klamezettel *m*; **II** *adj.* Wegwerf...: ~ *package*, ~ *bottle* Einwegflasche *f*; ~ *prices* ✝ Schleuderpreise; '**~·back** *s.* **1.** *bsd. biol.* Ata'vismus *m*, *a. fig.* Rückkehr *f* (**to** zu); **2.** *Film:* Rückblende *f*.

throw·er ['θrəʊə] *s.* **1.** Werfer(in); **2.** *Töpferei:* Dreher(in), Former(in); **3.** → *throwster*.

'**throw·in** *s. sport* Einwurf *m*.

throw·ing ['θrəʊɪŋ] **I** *s.* Werfen *n*, (*Speer- etc.*)Wurf *m*: ~ *the javelin*; **II** *adj.* Wurf...: ~ *knife*.

thrown [θrəʊn] **I** *p.p. von* **throw**; **II** *adj.* gezwirnt: ~ *silk* Seidengarn *n*.

'**throw**|**off** *s.* **1.** Aufbruch *m* (zur Jagd); **2.** *fig.* Beginn *m*; '**~·out** *s.* ☼ **1.** Auswerfer *m*; **2.** Ausschalter *m*; **3.** *mot.* Ausrückvorrichtung *f*: ~ *lever* (Kupplungs)Ausrückhebel *m*.

throw·ster ['θrəʊstə] *s.* Seidenzwirner(in).

thru [θruː] *Am.* F *für* **through**.

thrum¹ [θrʌm] **I** *v/i.* **1.** ♪ klimpern (*on* auf *dat.*); **2.** (mit den Fingern) trommeln; **II** *v/t.* **3.** ♪ klimpern auf (*dat.*); **4.** (mit den Fingern) trommeln auf (*dat.*).

thrum² [θrʌm] **I** *s.* **1.** *Weberei:* a) Trumm, *m* (*am Ende der Kette*), b) *pl.* (Reihe *f* von) Fransen *pl.*, Saum *m*; **2.** Franse *f*; **3.** loser Faden; **4.** *oft pl.* Garnabfall *m*, Fussel *f*; **II** *v/t.* **5.** befransen.

thrush¹ [θrʌʃ] *s. orn.* Drossel *f*.

---

thrush² [θrʌʃ] *s.* **1.** ⚕ Soor *m*; **2.** *vet.* Strahlfäule *f*.

thrust [θrʌst] **I** *v/t.* [*irr.*] **1.** *Waffe etc.* stoßen; **2.** *allg.* stecken, schieben: ~ *o.s.* (*od. one's nose*) *in fig.* s-e Nase stecken *od.* sich einmischen in (*acc.*); ~ *one's hand into one's pocket* die Hand in die Tasche stecken; ~ *on et.* hastig anziehen, (sich) *et.* hastig überwerfen; **3.** stoßen, drängen, treiben, (*a. ins Gefängnis*) werfen: ~ *aside* zur Seite stoßen; ~ *o.s. into* sich werfen *od.* drängen in (*acc.*); ~ *out* a) (heraus-, hinaus)stoßen, ausstoßen, b) *Zunge* herausstrecken, c) *Hand* ausstrecken; ~ *s.th. upon s.o.* j-m et. aufdrängen; **4.** ~ *through* j-n durch'bohren; **5.** ~ *in Wort* einwerfen; **II** *v/i.* [*irr.*] **6.** stoßen (*at* nach); **7.** sich *wohin* drängen *od.* schieben: ~ *into* ✗ hineinstoßen in *e-e Stellung etc.*; *a ~ing politician* ein ehrgeiziger *od.* aufstrebender Politiker; **III** *s.* **8.** Stoß *m*; **9.** Hieb *m* (*a. fig.*); **10.** *allg. u.* ☼ Druck *m*; **11.** ✈, *phys.* Schub(kraft *f*) *m*; **12.** ☼, △ (Seiten)Schub *m*; **13.** *geol.* Schub *m*; **14.** ✗ *u. fig.* a) Vorstoß *m*, b) Stoßrichtung *f*; ~ *bear·ing s.* ☼, ✈ Drucklager *n*; ~ *per·form·ance s.* ☼, ✈ Schubleistung *f*; ~ *weap·on s.* ✗ Stich-, Stoßwaffe *f*.

thud [θʌd] **I** *s.* dumpfer (Auf)Schlag, Bums *m*; **II** *v/i.* dumpf (auf)schlagen, bumsen.

thug [θʌɡ] *s.* **1.** (Gewalt)Verbrecher *m*, Raubmörder *m*; **2.** Rowdy *m*, ‚Schläger' *m*; **3.** *fig.* Gangster *m*, Halsabschneider *m*.

thumb [θʌm] **I** *s.* **1.** Daumen *m*: *his fingers are all ~s, he is all ~s* er hat zwei linke Hände; *turn ~s down on fig. et.* ablehnen, verwerfen; *under s.o.'s* ~ unter j-s Fuchtel; *that sticks out like a sore ~* F a) das sieht ja ein Blinder, b) das fällt entsetzlich auf; → *rule* 2; **II** *v/t.* **2.** *Buchseiten* 'durchblättern; *Buch* abgreifen, beschmutzen: (*well-*)~*ed* abgegriffen; **4.** ~ *a lift* (*od. ride*) F per Anhalter fahren, trampen; ~ *a car* e-n Wagen anhalten, sich mitnehmen lassen; **5.** ~ *one's nose at* j-m e-e lange Nase machen; ~ *in·dex s. typ.* Daumenindex *m*; '**~·mark** *s.* Daumenabdruck *m*; '**~·nail I** *s.* Daumennagel *m*; **II** *adj.* ~ *sketch* kleine (*fig. kurze*) Skizze; ~ *nut s.* ☼ Flügelmutter *f*; '**~·print** *s.* Daumenabdruck *m*; '**~·screw** *s.* **1.** *hist.* Daumenschraube *f*; **2.** ☼ Flügelschraube *f*; '**~·s-down** *s.* F **1.** (reine) Ablehnung: *it's ~ on your offer!* Ihr Angebot ist abgelehnt!; **2.** *fig.* vernichtende Kri'tik; '**~·stall** *s.* Däumling *m* (*Schutzkappe*); '**~·s-up** *s.* F **1.** (reine) Zustimmung; **2.** *fig.* ‚Lobeshymne' *f*; '**~·tack** *s. Am.* Reißnagel *m*.

thump [θʌmp] **I** *s.* **1.** dumpfer Schlag, Bums *m*; **2.** (Faust)Schlag *m*, Puff *m*; **II** *v/t.* **3.** schlagen auf (*acc.*), hämmern *od.* pochen gegen *od.* auf (*acc.*); *Kissen* aufschütteln; **4.** plumpsen gegen *od.* auf (*acc.*); **III** *v/i.* **5.** (auf)schlagen, (-) bumsen (*on* auf *acc.*, *at* gegen); **6.** (laut) pochen (*Herz*); '**thump·er** [-pə] *s.* **1.** *sl.* Mordsding *n*, *e-e* ‚Wucht'; **2.** *sl.* faustdicke Lüge; '**thump·ing** [-pɪŋ] **I** *adj.* kolos'sal, Mords...; **II** *adv.* mordsmäßig.

thun·der ['θʌndə] **I** *s.* **1.** Donner *m* (*a. fig. Getöse*): *steal s.o.'s* ~ j-m den Wind aus den Segeln nehmen; ~*s of applause* donnernder Beifall; **II** *v/i.* **2.** donnern (*a. fig. Kanone, Zug etc.*); **3.** *fig.* wettern; **III** *v/t.* **4.** *et.* donnern; '**~·bolt** *s.* **1.** Blitz *m* (*u. Donnerschlag*

---

m), Blitzstrahl *m* (*a. fig.*); **2.** *myth. u. geol.* Donnerkeil *m*; '**~·clap** *s.* Donnerschlag *m* (*a. fig.*); '**~·cloud** *s.* Gewitterwolke *f*.

thun·der·ing ['θʌndərɪŋ] **I** *adj.* □ **1.** donnernd (*a. fig.*); **2.** F kolos'sal, gewaltig: *a ~ lie* e-e faustdicke Lüge; **II** *adv.* **3.** F riesig, mächtig: ~ *glad*; '**thun·der·ous** [-rəs] *adj.* □ **1.** gewitterschwül; **2.** *fig.* donnernd; **3.** *fig.* gewaltig.

'**thun·der**|**,show·er** *s.* Gewitterschauer *m*; '**~·storm** *s.* Gewitter *n*, Unwetter *n*; '**~·struck** *adj.* (*fig.* wie) vom Blitz getroffen.

thun·der·y ['θʌndərɪ] *adj.* gewitterschwül: ~ *showers* gewittrige Schauer.

Thu·rin·gi·an [θjʊə'rɪndʒɪən] **I** *adj.* Thüringer(...); **II** *s.* Thüringer(in).

Thurs·day ['θɜːzdɪ] *s.* Donnerstag *m*: *on* ~ am Donnerstag; *on* ~*s* donnerstags.

thus [ðʌs] *adv.* **1.** so, folgendermaßen; **2.** so'mit, also, folglich, demgemäß; **3.** so, in diesem Maße: ~ *far* so weit, bis jetzt; ~ *much* so viel.

thwack [θwæk] **I** *v/t.* verprügeln, schlagen; **II** *s.* derber Schlag.

thwart [θwɔːt] **I** *v/t.* **1.** *Pläne etc.* durch'kreuzen, vereiteln, hinter'treiben; **2.** *j-m* entgegenarbeiten, *j-m* e-n Strich durch die Rechnung machen; **II** *s.* **3.** ⚓ Ruderbank *f*.

thy [ðaɪ] *adj. bibl., rhet., poet.* dein.

thyme [taɪm] *s.* ♀ Thymian *m*.

thy·mus ['θaɪməs] *a.* ~ *gland s. anat.* Thymus(drüse *f*) *m*.

thy·roid ['θaɪrɔɪd] **I** *adj.* **1.** Schilddrüsen...; **2.** Schildknorpel...: ~ *cartilage* → 4; **II** *s.* **3.** *a.* ~ *gland* Schilddrüse *f*; **4.** Schildknorpel *m*.

thyr·sus ['θɜːsəs] *pl.* **-si** [-saɪ] *s. antiq. u.* ♀ Thyrsus *m*.

thy·self [ðaɪ'self] *pron. bibl., rhet., poet.* **1.** du (selbst); **2.** *dat.* dir (selbst); **3.** *acc.* dich (selbst).

ti·a·ra [tɪ'ɑːrə] *s.* **1.** Ti'ara *f* (*Papstkrone u. fig. -würde*); **2.** Dia'dem *n*, Stirnreif *m* (*für Damen*).

tib·i·a ['tɪbɪə] *pl.* **-ae** [-iː] *s. anat.* Schienbein *n*, Tibia *f*; '**tib·i·al** [-əl] *adj. anat.* Schienbein..., Unterschenkel...

tic [tɪk] *s.* ⚕ Tic(k) *m*, (ner'vöses) Muskel- *od.* Gesichtszucken.

tich [tɪtʃ] → **titch**.

tick¹ [tɪk] **I** *s.* **1.** Ticken *n*: *to* (*od. on*) *the* ~ (auf die Sekunde) pünktlich; **2.** F Augenblick *m*; **3.** Häkchen *n*, Vermerkzeichen *n*; **II** *v/i.* **4.** ticken: ~ *over* a) *mot.* im Leerlauf sein, b) *fig.* normal *od.* ganz gut laufen; *what makes him ~?* a) was hält ihn (so) in Schwung?, b) wie ‚funktioniert' er?; **III** *v/t.* **5.** *in e-r Liste* anhaken: ~ *off* a) abhaken, b) F *j-n* ‚zs.-stauchen'.

tick² [tɪk] *s. zo.* Zecke *f*.

tick³ [tɪk] *s.* **1.** (Kissen- *etc.*)Bezug *m*; **2.** Inlett *n*, Ma'tratzenbezug *m*; **3.** F Drillich *m*, Drell *m*.

tick⁴ [tɪk] *s.* F Kre'dit *m*, Pump *m*: *buy on* ~ auf Pump *od.* Borg kaufen.

tick·er ['tɪkə] *s.* **1.** *Börse:* Fernschreiber *m*; **2.** *sl.* a) ‚Wecker' *m* (*Uhr*), b) ‚Pumpe' *f* (*Herz*); ~ *tape s. Am.* Lochstreifen *m*: ~ *parade* Konfettiparade *f*.

tick·et ['tɪkɪt] **I** *s.* **1.** (Ausweis-, Eintritts-, Lebensmittel-, Mitglieds- *etc.*) Karte *f*, 🚢 *etc.* Fahrkarte *f*, -schein *m*; ✈ Flugschein *m*, Ticket *n*: *take a* ~ e-e Karte lösen; **2.** (*bsd.* Gepäck-, Pfand-) Schein *m*; **3.** Lotte'rielos *n*; **4.** Eti'kett *n*, (*Preis- etc.*)Zettel *m*; **5.** *mot.* a) Strafzettel *m*, b) gebührenpflichtige

Verwarnung; **6.** ⚓, ✈ Li'zenz *f*; **7.** *pol. bsd. Am.* a) (Wahl-, Kandi'daten)Liste *f*, b) ('Wahl-, Par'tei)Pro,gramm *n*: *split the* ~ panaschieren; *vote a straight* ~ die Liste e-r Partei unverändert wählen; *write one's own* ~ F (ganz) s-e eigenen Bedingungen stellen; **8.** ~ *of leave* ⚖ *Brit.* (Schein *m* über) bedingte Freilassung: *be on* ~ *of leave* bedingt freigelassen sein; **9.** F *das Richtige*: *that's the* ~*!*; **II** *v/t.* **10.** etikettieren, kennzeichnen, *Waren* auszeichnen; ~ **a·gen·cy** *s. thea. etc.* Vorverkaufsstelle *f*; '~-,can·cel·(l)ing ma·chine *s.* (Fahrschein)Entwerter *m*; ~ col·lec·tor *s.* 🚃 Bahnsteigschaffner *m*; ~ day *s. Börse*: Tag *m* vor dem Abrechnungstag; ~ in·spec·tor *s.* 'Fahrkartenkontrol,leur *m*; ~ ma·chine *s.* 'Fahrscheinauto,mat *m*; ~ of·fice *s.* **1.** Fahrkartenschalter *m*; **2.** (The'ater)Kasse *f*; ~ punch *s.* Lochzange *f*; ~ tout *s.* Kartenschwarzhändler *m*.

tick·ing ['tɪkɪŋ] *s.* Drell *m*, Drillich *m*; ,~-'off *s.* F 'Anpfiff' *m*.

tick·le ['tɪkl] **I** *v/t.* **1.** kitzeln (*a. fig.*); **2.** *fig.* j-s *Eitelkeit etc.* schmeicheln; **3.** *fig.* amüsieren: ~*d pink* F 'ganz weg' (vor Freude); *I'm* ~*d to death* ich könnte mich totlachen (*a. iro.*); **4.** ~ *up* (an-)reizen; **II** *v/i.* **5.** kitzeln; **6.** jucken; **III** *s.* **7.** Kitzel *m* (*a. fig.*); **8.** Juckreiz *m*; 'tick·ler [-lə] *s.* **1.** kitzlige Sache, (schwieriges) Pro'blem; **2.** *Am.* No'tizbuch *n*: ~ *file* Wiedervorlagemappe *f*; **3.** *a.* ~ *coil* ϟ Rückkopplungsspule *f*; 'tick·lish [-lɪʃ] *adj.* □ **1.** kitz(e)lig; **2.** *fig.* a) kitzlig, heikel, schwierig, b) empfindlich (*Person*).

tick·tack ['tɪktæk] *s.* **1.** Ticktack *n*; **2.** *sl. Rennsport*: Zeichensprache *f* der Buchmacher: ~ *man* Buchmachergehilfe *m*.

tid·al ['taɪdl] *adj.* **1.** Gezeiten..., den Gezeiten unter'worfen: ~ *basin* ⚓ Tidebecken *n*; ~ *inlet* Priel *m*; ~ *power plant* Gezeitenkraftwerk *n*; **2.** Flut...: ~ *wave* Flutwelle *f*, *fig. a.* Woge *f*.

tid·bit ['tɪdbɪt] *Am.* → **titbit**.

tid·dly ['tɪdlɪ] *adj. Brit.* F **1.** winzig; **2.** ,angesäuselt', beschwipst.

tid·dly·winks ['tɪdlɪwɪŋks] *s. pl. sg. konstr.* Flohhüpfen *n*.

tide [taɪd] **I** *s.* **1.** a) Gezeiten *pl.*, Ebbe *f* u. Flut, b) Flut *f*, Tide *f*: *high* ~ Flut *f*; *low* ~ Ebbe; *the* ~ *is coming in* (*going out*) die Flut kommt (die Ebbe setzt ein); *the* ~ *is out* es ist Ebbe; *turn of the* ~ a) Gezeitenwechsel *m*, b) *fig.* Umschwung *m*; *the* ~ *turns fig.* das Blatt wendet sich; **2.** *fig.* Strom *m*, Strömung *f*: ~ *of events* der Gang der Ereignisse; *swim against* (*with*) *the* ~ gegen den (mit dem) dem Strom schwimmen; **3.** *fig.* die rechte Zeit, günstiger Augenblick; **4.** *in Zssgn* Zeit *f*: *winter*~; **II** *v/i.* **5.** (mit dem Strom) treiben, ⚓ bei Flut ein- *od.* auslaufen; ~ *over fig.* hin'wegkommen über (*acc.*); **III** *v/t.* **7.** ~ *over fig.* j-m hin'weghelfen über (*acc.*): ~ *it over* ,sich über Wasser halten'; ~ gate *s.* Flut(schleusen)tor *n*; ~ ga(u)ge *s.* (Gezeiten)Pegel *m*; '~-land *s.* Watt *n*; '~-mark *s.* **1.** Gezeitenmarke *f*; **2.** Pegelstand *m*; **3.** *bsd. Brit.* F schwarzer Rand (*am Hals etc.*); ~ ta·ble *s.* Gezeitentafel *f*; '~,wait·er *s. hist.* Hafenzollbeamte(r) *m*; '~,wa·ter *s.* Flut-, Gezeitengewässer *n*; ~ *district* Wattengebiet *n*; '~-way *s.* Priel *m*.

ti·di·ness ['taɪdɪnɪs] *s.* **1.** Sauberkeit *f*, Ordnung *f*; **2.** Nettigkeit *f*.

ti·dings ['taɪdɪŋz] *s. pl. sg. od. pl.*

---

konstr. Nachricht(en *pl.*) *f*, Neuigkeit (-en *pl.*) *f*, Kunde *f*.

ti·dy ['taɪdɪ] **I** *adj.* □ **1.** sauber, reinlich, ordentlich (*Zimmer, Person, Aussehen etc.*); **2.** nett, schmuck; **3.** *fig.* F ordentlich, beträchtlich: *a* ~ *penny* e-e Stange Geld; **II** *s.* **4.** (Sofa- *etc.*)Schoner *m*; **5.** (Arbeits-, Flick- *etc.*)Beutel *m*; Fächerkasten *m*; **6.** Abfallkorb *m*; **III** *v/t.* **7.** *a.* ~ *up* in Ordnung bringen, aufräumen, säubern: ~ *out* ,ausmisten'; ~ *o.s. up* sich zurechtmachen; **IV** *v/i.* **8.** ~ *up* aufräumen, sauber machen.

tie [taɪ] **I** *s.* **1.** (Schnür)Band *n*; **2.** a) Kra'watte *f*, b) Halstuch *n*; **3.** Schleife *f*, Masche *f*; **4.** *fig.* a) Band *n*: *the* ~(*s*) *of friendship*, b) *pol., psych.* Bindung *f*: *mother* ~; **5.** *fig.* (lästige) Fessel, Last *f*; **6.** ⚙, △ a) Verbindung(sstück *n*) *f*, b) Anker *m*, c) → *tie beam*; **7.** 🚃 *Am.* Schwelle *f*; **8.** *parl. pol.* Stimmengleichheit *f*: *end in a* ~ stimmengleich enden; **9.** *sport* a) Punktgleichheit *f*, Gleichstand *m*, b) Unentschieden *n*, c) Ausscheidungsspiel *n*, d) Wieder'holung(sspiel *n*) *f*; **10.** ♪ Bindebogen *m*, Liga'tur *f*; **11.** an-, festbinden (*to* an *acc.*); **12.** binden, schnüren; *fig.* fesseln: ~ *s.o.'s hands* (*tongue*) j-m die Hände (Zunge) binden; **13.** *Schleife, Schuhe etc.* binden; **14.** △, ⚙ veran-kern, befestigen; **15.** ♪ *Noten* (anei-nander) binden; **16.** (*to*) *fig.* j-n binden (an *acc.*), verpflichten (zu); **17.** hindern, hemmen; **18.** *j-n* in Anspruch nehmen (*Pflichten etc.*); **III** *v/i.* **19.** *sport* a) gleichstehen, punktgleich sein, b) unentschieden spielen *od.* kämpfen (*with* gegen); **20.** *parl., pol.* gleiche Stimmenzahl haben;

Zssgn mit adv.:

tie| down *v/t.* **1.** festbinden; **2.** niederhalten, fesseln; **3.** (*to*) *fig.* j-n binden (an *Pflichten, Regeln etc.*), j-n festlegen (auf *acc.*): *be tied down* (*by*) angebunden sein (durch *e-e Familie etc.*); ~ in I *v/i.* (*with*) über'einstimmen (mit), passen (zu); **II** *v/t.* (*with*) verbinden *od.* koppeln (mit), einbauen (in *acc.*); ~ up *v/t.* **1.** (an-, ein-, ver-, zs.-, zu)binden; **2.** *fig.* a) hemmen, fesseln, b) festhalten, beschäftigen; **3.** *fig.* lahm legen; *In-dustrie, Produktion* stilllegen; *Vorräte etc.* blockieren; **4.** ✝, ⚖ festlegen: a) *Geld* fest anlegen, b) *bsd. Am.* *Erbgut* e-r Verfügungsbeschränkung unter'wer-fen; **5.** *tie it up Am.* F die Sache erledigen.

tie| bar *s.* **1.** 🚃 a) Verbindungsstange *f* (*Weiche*), b) Spurstange *f*; **2.** *typ.* Bogen *m* über 2 Buchstaben; ~ beam *s.* △ Zugbalken *m*; '~,break·(er) *s. Tennis*: Tie-Break *m*, *n*.

tied [taɪd] *adj.* ✝ zweckgebunden; ~ house *s. Brit.* Braue'reigaststätte *f*.

'tie|-in *s.* **1.** ✝ *Am.* a) Gemeinschaftswerbung *f*, b) ~ *sale* Kopplungsgeschäft *n*, -verkauf *m*; **2.** Zs.-hang *m*, Verbindung *f*; '~-on *adj.* zum Anbin-den, Anhänge...

tier [tɪə] *s.* **1.** Reihe *f*, Lage *f*: *in* ~*s* in Reihen übereinander, lagenweise; **2.** *thea.* a) (Sitz)Reihe *f*, b) Rang *m*; **3.** *fig.* Rang *m*, Stufe *f*.

tierce [tɪəs] *s.* **1.** [Kartenspiel: tɜːs] ♪, *fenc., eccl., Kartenspiel*: Terz *f*; **2.** Weinfass *n* (*mit 42 Gallonen*).

tie rod *s.* ⚙ **1.** Zugstange *f*; **2.** Kuppelstange *f*; **3.** 🚃 Spurstange *f*.

'tie-up *s.* **1.** a) Verbindung *f*, Zs.-hang *m*, b) Koppelung *f*; **2.** *Am.* Still-, Lahmlegung *f*; **3.** *bsd. Am.* (*a.* Ver-kehrs)Stockung *f*, Stillstand *m*.

---

tiff [tɪf] *s.* **1.** kleine Meinungsverschiedenheit, Kabbe'lei *f*; **2.** schlechte Laune: *in a* ~ übel gelaunt.

tif·fin ['tɪfɪn] *s. Brit.* Mittagessen *n* (*in Indien*).

tige [tiːʒ] (*Fr.*) *s.* **1.** △ Säulenschaft *m*; **2.** ⚙ Stängel *m*, Stiel *m*.

ti·ger ['taɪɡə] *s.* **1.** *zo.* Tiger *m* (*a. fig. Wüterich*): *American* ~ Jaguar *m*: *rouse the* ~ *in s.o. fig.* j-n in kalte Wut versetzen; **2.** *hist. Brit. sl.* livrierter Be-diener, Page *m*; ~ cat *s. zo.* **1.** Tiger-katze *f*; **2.** getigerte (Haus)Katze.

ti·ger·ish ['taɪɡərɪʃ] *adj.* **1.** tigerartig; **2.** blutdürstig; **3.** wild, grausam.

tight [taɪt] **I** *adj.* □ **1.** dicht (*nicht leck*): *a* ~ *barrel*; **2.** fest(sitzend) (*Kork, Kno-ten etc.*), stramm (*Schraube etc.*); **3.** straff, (an)gespannt (*Muskel, Seil etc.*); **4.** schmuck; **5.** a) (zu) eng, knapp, b) eng (anliegend) (*Kleid etc.*): ~ *fit* knapper Sitz, ⚙ Feinpassung; **6.** a) eng, dicht (gedrängt), b) *fig.* F kritisch, ,mulmig'; → *corner* 2; **7.** prall (voll); **8.** *fig.* a) komprimiert, straff (*Handlung etc.*), b) gedrängt, knapp (*Stil*), c) hieb-u. stichfest (*Argument*), d) straff, streng (*Sicherheitsmaßnahmen etc.*): *a* ~ *schedule* knappe Termine, *a.* ein voller Terminkalender; **9.** ✝ a) knapp (*Geld*), b) angespannt (*Marktlage*); **10.** F knick(e)rig, geizig; **11.** eng, am Klei-nen klebend (*Kunst etc.*); **12.** *sl.* ,blau', besoffen; **II** *adv.* **13.** eng, knapp; *a.* ⚙ fest: *hold* ~ festhalten; *sit* ~ a) fest im Sattel sitzen, b) sich nicht (vom Fleck) rühren, c) *fig.* sich eisern behaupten, sich nicht beirren lassen, *a.* abwarten; 'tight·en [-tn] **I** *v/t.* **1.** *a.* ~ *up* zs.-zie-hen; **2.** *Schraube, Zügel etc.* fest-, an-ziehen; *Feder, Gurt etc.* spannen; *Gür-tel* enger schnallen; *Muskel, Seil etc.* straffen; ~ *one's grip* fester zupacken, den Druck verstärken (*a. fig.*); **3.** *a.* ~ *up fig.* a) *Manuskript, Handlung etc.* straffen, b) *Sicherheitsmaßnahmen etc.* verschärfen; **4.** (ab)dichten; **II** *v/i.* **5.** sich straffen; **6.** fester werden (*Griff*); **7.** *a.* ~ *up* sich fest zs.-ziehen; **8.** ✝ sich versteifen (*Markt*).

,tight|-'fist·ed → *tight* 10; ,~-'fit·ting *adj.* **1.** → *tight* 5; **2.** ⚙ genau an- *od.* eingepasst, Pass...; ,~-'laced *adj.* sitten-streng, prüde, puri'tanisch; ,~-'lipped *adj.* **1.** schmallippig; **2.** *fig.* ver-schlossen.

tight·ness ['taɪtnɪs] *s.* **1.** Dichtheit *f*; **2.** Festigkeit *f*; fester Sitz; **3.** Straffheit *f*; **4.** Enge *f*; **5.** Gedrängtheit *f*; **6.** Geiz *m*, Knicke'rei *f*; **7.** ✝ a) (Geld)Knapp-heit *f*, b) angespannte Marktlage.

'tight·rope **I** *s.* (Draht)Seil *n* (*Zirkus*); **II** *adj.* (Draht)Seil...: ~ *walker* Seiltän-zer(in).

tights [taɪts] *s. pl.* **1.** ('Tänzer-, Ar'tis-ten)Tri,kot *n*; **2.** *bsd. Brit.* Strumpfho-se *f*.

'tight·wad *s. Am.* F Geizkragen *m*.

ti·gress ['taɪɡrɪs] *s.* **1.** Tigerin *f*; **2.** *fig.* Me'gäre *f*, (Weibs)Teufel *m*.

tike → **tyke**.

til·de ['tɪldə] *s. ling.* Tilde *f*.

tile [taɪl] **I** *s.* **1.** (Dach)Ziegel *m*: *he has a* ~ *loose sl.* bei ihm ist eine Schraube locker; *be* (*out*) *on the* ~*s sl.* ,herum-sumpfen'; **2.** ([Kunst]Stein)Platte *f*, (Fußboden-, Wand-, Teppich)Fliese *f*, (Ofen-, Wand)Kachel *f*; **3.** *coll.* Ziegel *pl.*, Fliesen(fußboden *m*) *pl.*, Fliesen-(ver)täfelung *f*; **4.** △ Hohlstein *m*; **5.** F a) ,Angströhre' *f* (*Zylinder*), b) ,Deckel' *m* (*steifer Hut*); **II** *v/t.* **6.** (mit Ziegeln) decken; **7.** mit Fliesen *od.* Platten auslegen, fliesen, kacheln; **til·er** ['taɪlə] *s.* **1.** Dachdecker *m*; **2.** Fliesen-, Plattenleger *m*; **3.** Ziegelbrenner *m*; **4.** Logenhüter *m* (*Freimaurer*).

till¹ [tɪl] I *prp.* **1.** bis: **~** *now* bis jetzt, bisher; **~** *then* bis dahin *od.* dann *od.* nachher; **2.** bis zu: **~** *death* bis zum Tod, bis in den Tod; **3.** *not* **~** erst: *not* **~** *yesterday;* II *cj.* **4.** bis; **5.** *not* **~** erst als (*od.* wenn).

till² [tɪl] *s.* **1.** Ladenkasse *f:* **~** *money* ✝ Kassenbestand *m*; **2.** Geldkasten *m*.

till³ [tɪl] I *v/t.* Boden bebauen, bestellen, (be)ackern; II *v/i.* ackern, pflügen; **'till·a·ble** [-ləbl] *adj.* anbaufähig; **'till·age** [-lɪdʒ] *s.* **1.** Bodenbestellung *f*; **2.** Ackerbau *m*; **3.** Ackerland *n*.

till·er¹ ['tɪlə] *s.* **1.** (Acker)Bauer *m*; **2.** Ackerfräse *f*.

till·er² ['tɪlə] *s.* **1.** ⚓ Ruderpinne *f*; **2.** ◉ Griff *m*; **~** *rope* *s.* ⚓ Steuerreep *n*.

tilt¹ [tɪlt] I *v/t.* **1.** kippen, neigen, schräg stellen; **2.** 'umkippen, 'umstoßen; **3.** ⚓ *Schiff* krängen; **4.** ◉ recken (*schmieden*); **5.** *hist.* a) (mit eingelegter Lanze) anreiten gegen, b) *Lanze* einlegen; II *v/i.* **6.** *a.* **~** *over* a) sich neigen, kippen, b) ('um)kippen, 'umfallen; **7.** ⚓ krängen; **8.** *hist.* im Tur'nier kämpfen: **~** *at* a) anreiten gegen, b) (mit der Lanze) stechen nach, c) *fig.* losziehen gegen, attackieren; III *s.* **9.** Kippen *n*: *give a* **~** *to* **~** auf die Kippe; **10.** Schräglage *f*, Neigung *f: on the* **~** auf der Kippe; **11.** *hist.* Tur'nier *n*, Lanzenbrechen *n*; **12.** *fig.* Strauß *m*, (Wort)Gefecht *n*; **13.** (Lanzen)Stoß *m*; **14.** (Angriffs)Wucht *f: (at) full* **~** mit voller Wucht *od.* Geschwindigkeit; **15.** *Am.* 'Drall' *m*, Ten'denz *f*.

tilt² [tɪlt] I *s.* **1.** (Wagen- *etc.*)Plane *f*, Verdeck *n*; **2.** ⚓ Sonnensegel *n*; **3.** Sonnendach *n*; II *v/t.* (mit e-r Plane) bedecken.

tilt cart *s.* Kippwagen *m*.

tilt·er ['tɪltə] *s.* **1.** (*Kohlen- etc.*)Kipper *m*, Kippvorrichtung *f*; **2.** ◉ *Walzwerk:* Wipptisch *m*.

tilth [tɪlθ] → *tillage*.

tilt·ing ['tɪltɪŋ] *adj.* **1.** *hist.* Turnier...; **2.** ◉ schwenk-, kippbar, Kipp...

'tilt·yard *s. hist.* Tur'nierplatz *m*.

tim·bal ['tɪmbl] *s.* ♪ *hist.* (Kessel)Pauke *f*.

tim·ber ['tɪmbə] I *s.* **1.** Bau-, Nutzholz *n*; **2.** *coll.* (Nutzholz)Bäume *pl.*, Baumbestand *m*, Wald(bestand) *m*; **3.** *Brit.* a) Bauholz *n*, b) Schnittholz *n*; **4.** ⚓ Inholz *n*; *pl.* Spantenwerk *n*; **5.** *Am. fig.* Holz *n*, Schlag *m*, Ka'liber *n: a man of his* **~**; *he is of presidential* **~** er hat das Zeug zum Präsidenten; II *v/t.* **6.** (ver-) zimmern; **7.** *Holz* abvieren; **8.** *Graben etc.* absteifen; III *adj.* **9.** Holz...; **'timbered** [-əd] *adj.* **1.** gezimmert; **2.** Fachwerk...; **3.** bewaldet.

tim·ber| **for·est** *s.* Hochwald *m*; **~ frame** ◉ Bundsäge *f*; **'~-framed** *adj.* Fachwerk...

tim·ber·ing ['tɪmbərɪŋ] *s.* **1.** Zimmern *n*, Ausbau *m*; **2.** ◉ Verschalung *f*; **3.** Bau-, Zimmerholz *n*; **4.** a) Gebälk *n*, b) Fachwerk *n*.

'tim·ber·land *s. Am.* Waldland *n* (*für Nutzholz*); **~ line** *s.* Baumgrenze *f*; **'~-man** [-mən] *s. [irr.]* **1.** Holzfäller *m*, -arbeiter *m*; **2.** ⚒ Stempelsetzer *m*; **~ tree** *s.* Nutzholzbaum *m*; **'~-work** *s.* ◉ Gebälk *n*; **'~-yard** *s.* Zimmerplatz *m*, Bauhof *m*.

tim·bre ['tɛ̃mbrə] (*Fr.*) *s.* ♪, *ling.* Klangfarbe *f*, Timbre *n*.

tim·brel ['tɪmbrəl] *s.* Tambu'rin *n*.

time [taɪm] I *s.* **1.** Zeit *f:* **~** *past, present, and to come* Vergangenheit, Gegenwart und Zukunft; *for all* **~** für alle Zeiten; **~** *will show* die Zeit wird es lehren; **2.** Zeit *f*, Uhr(zeit) *f: what's the* **~***?, what* **~** *is it?* wie viel Uhr ist es?; *at this* **~** *of day* a) zu dieser (späten) Tageszeit, b) *fig.* so spät, in diesem späten Stadium; *bid* (*od.* *pass*) *s.o. the* **~** *of* (*the*) *day, pass the* **~** *of day with s.o.* j-n grüßen; *know the* **~** *of the day* F wissen, was es geschlagen hat; *some* **~** *about noon* etwa um Mittag; *this* **~** *tomorrow* morgen um diese Zeit; *this* **~** *twelve months* heute übers Jahr; *keep good* **~** richtig gehen (*Uhr*); **3.** Zeit(dauer) *f*, Zeitabschnitt *m*, (*a. phys. Fall-, Schwingungs- etc.*)Dauer *f*; ✝ Laufzeit *f* (*Wechsel- etc.*); Arbeitszeit *f* im Herstellungsprozess *etc.*: *in three weeks'* **~** in drei Wochen; *a long* **~** lange Zeit; *be a long* **~** *in doing s.th.* lange (Zeit) dazu brauchen, et. zu tun; **4.** Zeit (-punkt *m*) *f:* **~** *of arrival* Ankunftszeit; *at the* **~** a) zu dieser Zeit, damals, b) gerade; *at the present* **~** derzeit, gegenwärtig; *at the same* **~** a) zur selben Zeit, gleichzeitig, b) gleichwohl, zugleich, andererseits; (*at*) *any* **~**, *at all* **~***s* zu jeder Zeit; *at no* **~** nie; *at that* **~** zu der Zeit; *at one* **~** einst, früher (einmal); *at some* **~** irgendwann; *for the* **~** für den Augenblick; *for the* **~** *being* a) vorläufig, fürs Erste, b) unter den gegenwärtigen Umständen; **5.** *oft pl.* Zeit(alter *n*) *f*, E'poche *f:* **~** *immemorial,* **~** *out of mind* un(vor)denkliche Zeit; *at* (*od.* *in*) *the* **~** *of Queen Anne* zur Zeit der Königin Anna; *the good old* **~***s* die gute alte Zeit; **6.** *pl.* Zeiten *pl.*, (Zeit)Verhältnisse *pl.*: *hard* **~***s*; **7.** *the* **~***s* die Zeit: *behind the* **~***s* rückständig; *move with the* **~***s* mit der Zeit gehen; **8.** Frist *f*, Ter'min *m:* **~** *for payment* Zahlungsfrist; **~** *of delivery* ✝ Lieferfrist, -zeit *f; ask* (*for a*) **~** ✝ um Frist(verlängerung) bitten; *you must give me* **~** Sie müssen mir Zeit geben *od.* lassen; **9.** (verfügbare) Zeit: *have no* **~** keine Zeit haben; *have no* **~** *for s.o.* *fig.* nichts übrig haben für j-n; *buy a little* **~** etwas Zeit (heraus)schinden; *kill* **~** die Zeit totschlagen; *take* (*the*) **~**, *take out* **~** sich die Zeit nehmen (*to do* zu tun); *take one's* **~** sich Zeit lassen; **~** *is up!* die Zeit ist um!; **~** *gentlemen, please!* (es ist bald) Polizeistunde! (*Lokal*); **~***!* *sport* Zeit!: a) anfangen!, b) aufhören!; **~***!* *parl.* Schluss!; → *forelock;* **10.** Lehr-, Dienstzeit *f: serve one's* **~** s-e Lehre machen; **11.** a) (na-'türliche *od.* nor'male) Zeit, b) Lebenszeit *f:* **~** *of life* Alter *n; ahead of* **~** vorzeitig; *die before one's* **~** vor der Zeit *od.* zu früh sterben; *his* **~** *is drawing near* sein Tod naht heran; **12.** a) Schwangerschaft *f*, b) Entbindung *f*, Niederkunft *f: she is far on in her* **~** sie ist hochschwanger; *she near her* **~** sie steht kurz vor der Entbindung; **13.** (günstige) Zeit: *now is the* **~** nun ist die passende Gelegenheit, jetzt gilt es (*to do* zu tun); *at such* **~***s* bei solchen Gelegenheiten; *bide one's* **~** (s-e Zeit) abwarten; **14.** Mal *n: the first* **~** das erste Mal; *for the last* **~** zum letzten Mal; *till next* **~** bis zum nächsten Mal; *every* **~** jedes Mal; *many* **~***s* viele Male; **~** *and again,* **~** *after* **~** immer wieder; *at some other* **~**, *at other* **~***s* ein anderes Mal; *at a* **~** auf einmal, zusammen, zugleich, jeweils; *one at a* **~** einzeln,

immer nur eine(r, s); *two at a* **~** zu zweit, jeweils zwei; **15.** *pl.* mal, ...mal: *three* **~***s four is twelve* drei mal vier ist zwölf; *twenty* **~***s* zwanzigmal; *four* **~***s the size of yours* viermal so groß wie deines; **16.** *bsd. sport* (erzielte, gestoppte) Zeit; **17.** a) ♪ Tempo *n*, Zeitmaß *n* (*beide a.* ♪), b) ♪ Takt *m: change of* **~** Taktwechsel *m; beat* (*keep*) **~** den Takt schlagen (halten); **18.** ✕ Marschtempo *n*, Schritt *m: mark* **~** a) ✕ auf der Stelle treten (*a. fig.*), b) *fig.* nicht vom Fleck kommen; *Besondere Redewendungen: against* **~** gegen die Zeit *od.* Uhr, mit größter Eile; *ahead of* (*od.* *before*) *one's* **~** s-r Zeit voraus; *all the* **~** a) die ganze Zeit (über), ständig, b) jederzeit; *at* **~***s* zu Zeiten, gelegentlich; *at all* **~***s* stets, zu jeder Zeit; *at any* **~** a) zu irgendeiner Zeit, jemals, b) jederzeit; *behind* **~** zu spät d(a)ran, verspätet; *between* **~***s* in den Zwischenzeiten; *by that* **~** a) bis dahin, unterdessen, b) zu der Zeit; *for a* (*od.* *some*) **~** e-e Zeit lang, einige Zeit; *for a long* **~** *past* schon seit langem; *not for a long* **~** noch lange nicht; *from* **~** *to* **~** von Zeit zu Zeit; *in* **~** a) rechtzeitig (*to do* um zu tun), b) mit der Zeit, c) im (richtigen) Takt; *in due* **~** rechtzeitig, termingerecht; *in good* **~** (gerade) rechtzeitig; *all in good* **~** alles zu s-r Zeit; *in one's own good* **~** wenn es e-m passt; *in no* **~** im Nu, im Handumdrehen; *on* **~** a) pünktlich, rechtzeitig, b) *bsd. Am.* für e-e (bestimmte) Zeit, c) ✝ *Am.* auf Zeit, *bsd. Am.* auf Raten; *out of* **~** a) zur Unzeit, unzeitig, b) vorzeitig, c) zu spät, d) aus dem Takt *od.* Schritt; *till such* **~** *as* so lange bis; *to* **~** pünktlich; *do* **~** F im *Gefängnis* 'sitzen'; *have a good* **~** es schön haben, es sich gut gehen lassen, sich gut amüsieren; *have the* **~** *of one's life* sich großartig amüsieren, leben wie ein Fürst; *have a hard* **~** Schlimmes durchmachen; *he had a hard* **~** *getting up early* es fiel ihm schwer, früh aufzustehen; *with* **~** mit der Zeit; **~** *was, when* die Zeit ist vorüber, als;

II *v/t.* **19.** (mit der Uhr) messen, (ab-) stoppen, die Zeit messen von; **20.** timen (*a. sport*), die Zeit *od.* den richtigen Zeitpunkt wählen *od.* bestimmen für, zur rechten Zeit tun; → *timed;* **21.** zeitlich abstimmen; **22.** die Zeit festsetzen für: *is* **~***d to leave at 7 der* Zug *etc.* soll um 7 abfahren; **23.** ◉ *Zündung etc.* einstellen; *Uhr* stellen; **24.** zeitlich regeln (*to* nach); **25.** das Tempo *od.* den Takt angeben für; III *v/i.* **26.** Takt halten; **27.** zeitlich zs.- *od.* über'einstimmen (*with* mit); **,~-and-'mo·tion stud·y** *s.* ✝ Zeitstudie *f;* **~ bar·gain** *s.* ✝ Ter'mingeschäft *n;* **'~-base** *adj.* ⚡ Kipp...; **~ bill** *s.* ✝ Zeitwechsel *m;* **~ bomb** *s.* Zeitbombe *f* (*a. fig.*); **'~-card** *s.* **1.** Stech-, Stempelkarte *f;* **2.** Fahrplan *m;* **~ clock** *s.* Stechuhr *f;* **~ con·stant** *s. phys.* 'Zeitkon,stante *f;* **'~--con,sum·ing** *adj.* Zeit raubend; **~ cred·it** *s.* gleitende Arbeitszeit: Zeitguthaben *n*.

timed [taɪmd] *adj.* zeitlich (genau) festgelegt *od.* reguliert, getimed: → *ill--timed; well-timed*.

time| **de·pos·its** *s. pl.* ✝ *Am.* Ter'mingelder *pl.;* **~ dif·fer·ence** *s.* 'Zeit,unterschied *m;* **~ draft** *s.* ✝ Zeitwechsel *m;* **'~-ex,pired** *adj.* ✕ *Brit.* ausgedient (*Soldat od. Unteroffizier*); **~ ex·po·sure** *s. phot.* **1.** Zeitbelichtung *f;* **2.** Zeitaufnahme f; ~ **freight** s. ✈ Am. Eilfracht f; ~ **fuse** s. ✕ Zeitzünder m; '~-,hon·o(u)red adj. alt'ehrwürdig; '~,keep·er s. **1.** Zeitmesser m; **2.** sport u. ✈ Zeitnehmer m; '~,keep·ing s. **1.** sport Zeitnahme f; **2.** Arbeitszeiterfassung f; ~ **lag** s. bsd. ◎ Verzögerung f, zeitliche Nacheilung od. Lücke; '~-lapse adj. phot. Zeitraffer...

time·less ['taɪmlɪs] adj. ☐ **1.** ewig; **2.** zeitlos (a. Schönheit etc.).

time lim·it s. Frist f, Ter'min m.

time·li·ness ['taɪmlɪnɪs] s. **1.** Rechtzeitigkeit f; **2.** günstige Zeit; **3.** Aktuali'tät f.

time| loan s. ✈ Darlehen n auf Zeit; ~ **lock** s. ◎ Zeitschloss n.

time·ly ['taɪmlɪ] I adj. **1.** rechtzeitig; **2.** (zeitlich) günstig, angebracht; **3.** aktu'ell.

,**time·'out** pl. -'outs s. **1.** sport Auszeit f; **2.** Am. Pause f; ~ **pay·ment** s. ✈ Am. Ratenzahlung f; '~·piece s. Chro'no'meter n, Uhr f.

tim·er ['taɪmə] s. **1.** Zeitmesser m (Apparat); **2.** ◎ Zeitgeber m, -schalter m; **3.** mot. Zündverteiler m; **4.** Stoppuhr f; **5.** phot. Zeitauslöser m; **6.** ◎ u. sport Zeitnehmer m (Person).

'**time|,sav·er** s. Zeit sparendes Ge'rät od. Ele'ment; '~,sav·ing adj. Zeit (er-)sparend; ~ **sense** s. Zeitgefühl n; '~-,serv·er s. Opportu'nist(in), Gesinnungslump m; '~,serv·ing I adj. opportu'nistisch; II s. Opportu'nismus m, Gesinnungslumpe'rei f; '~-share I s. Ferienwohnung f (od. -haus n) auf Time-Sharing-Basis; II adj. Time-Sharing-...: ~ **home** Ferienhaus od. -wohnung f, an dem/der man für e-e festgelegte Zeit des Jahres ein Nutzungsrecht hat; ~ **shar·ing** s. Time-Sharing n: a) gleichzeitige Nutzung e-r Daten verarbeitenden Anlage durch mehrere Nutzer od. Geräte, b) Miteigentum an Ferienhäusern od. -wohnungen, das für e-e festgelegte Zeit des Jahres gilt; ~ **sheet** s. **1.** Arbeits(zeit)blatt n; **2.** Stechblatt n; ~ **sig·nal** s. Radio: Zeitzeichen n; '~-,stud·y man s. [irr.] ✈, ◎ Zeitstudienfachmann m; ~ **switch** s. Zeitschalter m; '~,ta·ble s. a) Fahrplan m, b) Flugplan m; **2.** Stundenplan m; **3.** ,Fahrplan' m, Zeitplan m; '~-,test·ed adj. (alt)bewährt; '~·work s. ✈ nach Zeit bezahlte Arbeit; '~·worn adj. **1.** abgenutzt (a. fig.); **2.** veraltet; **3.** abgedroschen.

tim·id ['tɪmɪd] adj. ☐ **1.** furchtsam, ängstlich (of vor dat.); **2.** schüchtern, zaghaft; **ti·mid·i·ty** [tɪ'mɪdətɪ], '**tim·id·ness** [-nɪs] s. **1.** Ängstlichkeit f; **2.** Schüchternheit f.

tim·ing ['taɪmɪŋ] s. **1.** Timing n (a. sport), zeitliche Abstimmung od. Berechnung; **2.** Wahl f des richtigen Zeitpunkts; **3.** (gewählter) Zeitpunkt; **4.** ◎, mot. (zeitliche) Steuerung (Ventil-, Zündpunkt- etc.)Einstellung f.

tim·or·ous ['tɪmərəs] adj. ☐ → timid.

Tim·o·thy ['tɪməθɪ] npr. u. s. bibl. (Brief m des Paulus an) Ti'motheus m.

tim·pa·nist ['tɪmpənɪst] s. ♪ Pauker m; **tim·pa·no** ['tɪmpənəʊ] pl. -ni [-nɪ] s. (Kessel)Pauke f.

tin [tɪn] I s. **1.** ⚒, ◎ Zinn n; **2.** (Weiß-) Blech n; **3.** (Blech-, bsd. Brit. Kon'serven)Dose f, (-)Büchse f; **4.** sl. ,Piepen' pl. (Geld); II adj. **5.** zinnern, Zinn...; **6.** Blech..., blechern (a. fig. contp.); III v/t. **7.** verzinnen; **8.** Brit. eindosen, (in Büchsen) einmachen od. packen, konservieren; → tinned 2; ~ **can** s. **1.** Blechdose f; **2.** ⚒ sl. Zerstörer m; '~-

coat v/t. ◎ feuerverzinnen; ~ **cry** s. ◎ Zinngeschrei n.

tinc·ture ['tɪŋktʃə] I s. **1.** pharm. Tink'tur f; **2.** poet. Farbe f; **3.** her. Farbe f, Tink'tur f; **4.** fig. a) Spur f, Beigeschmack m, b) Anstrich m: ~ of education; II v/t. **5.** färben; **6.** fig. a) → tinge 2, b) durch'dringen (with mit).

tin·der ['tɪndə] s. Zunder m; '~·box s. **1.** Zunderbüchse f; **2.** fig. Pulverfass n.

tine [taɪn] s. **1.** Zinke f, Zacke f (Gabel etc.); **2.** hunt. (Geweih)Sprosse f.

tin| fish s. ⚓ sl. ,Aal' m (Torpedo); ~ **foil** s. **1.** Stanni'ol n; **2.** Stanni'olpa,pier n; '~-foil I v/t. **1.** mit Stanni'ol belegen; **2.** in Stanni'ol(pa,pier) verpacken; II adj. **3.** Stanniol...

ting [tɪŋ] I s. Klingeln n; II v/t. klingeln mit; III v/i. klingeln; '~-a-ling [,tɪŋə'lɪŋ] s. Kling'ling n.

tinge [tɪndʒ] I v/t. **1.** tönen, (leicht) färben; **2.** fig. e-n Anstrich geben (dat.): be ~d with e-n Anflug haben von, et. von ... an sich haben; II v/i. **3.** sich färben; III s. **4.** leichter Farbton, Tönung f: have a ~ of red e-n Stich ins Rote haben, ins Rote spielen; **5.** fig. Anstrich m, Anflug m, Spur f.

tin·gle ['tɪŋgl] I v/i. **1.** prickeln, kribbeln, beißen, brennen (Haut, Ohren etc.) (with cold vor Kälte); **2.** klingen, summen (with vor dat.): my ears are tingling mir klingen die Ohren; **3.** ~ with fig. ,knistern' vor Spannung, Erotik etc.: the story ~s with suspense; **4.** flirren (Hitze, Licht); II s. **5.** Prickeln n etc.; **6.** Klingen n in den Ohren; **7.** (ner'vöse) Erregung.

tin| god s. Götze m, Popanz m; ~ **hat** s. ✕ F Stahlhelm m; '~·horn Am. sl. I adj. angeberisch, hochstaplerisch; II s. Hochstapler m, Angeber m.

tink·er ['tɪŋkə] I s. **1.** Kesselflicker m: not worth a ~'s cuss keinen Pfifferling wert; **2.** a) Pfuscher m, Stümper m, b) Bastler m, Tüftler m; **3.** Pfusche'rei f: have a ~ at an et. herumpfuschen; II v/i. **4.** her'umbasteln, -pfuschen (at, with an dat.); III v/t. **5.** mst ~ up (rasch) zs.-flicken; zu'rechtbasteln od. -pfuschen (a. fig.).

tin·kle ['tɪŋkl] I v/i. **1.** klingeln, hell (er-)klingen; II v/t. **2.** klingeln mit; III s. **3.** Klingeln n, (a. fig. Vers-, Wort)Geklingel n: give s.o. a ~ Brit. F j-n ,anklingeln'; **4.** have a ~ F ,pinkeln'.

tin| Liz·zie ['lɪzɪ] s. humor. alter Klapperkasten (Auto); '~·man [-mən] s. [irr.] **1.** Zinngießer m; **2.** → tinsmith.

tinned [tɪnd] adj. **1.** verzinnt; **2.** Brit. konserviert, Dosen..., Büchsen...: ~ fruit Obstkonserven pl.; ~ meat Büchsenfleisch n; ~ music Dosen ,Musik f aus der Konserve'; **tin·ner** ['tɪnə] s. **1.** → tinsmith; **2.** Verzinner m.

tin·ny ['tɪnɪ] adj. **1.** zinnern; **2.** zinnhaltig; **3.** blechern (a. fig. Klang).

tin| o·pen·er s. Brit. Dosen-, Büchsenöffner m; ♀ **Pan Al·ley** [,tɪnpæn'ælɪ] s. (Zentrum n der) 'Schlagerindu,strie f; ~ **plate** s. Weiß-, Zinnblech n; '~-plate v/t. verzinnen; '~·pot I s. Blechtopf m; II adj. sl. ,schäbig', ,billig'.

tin·sel ['tɪnsl] I s. **1.** Flitter-, Rauschgold n, -silber n; **2.** La'metta n; **3.** Glitzerschmuck m; **4.** fig. Flitterkram m, Kitsch m; II adj. **5.** Flitter...; **6.** fig. flitterhaft, kitschig, Flitter-, Schein...; III v/t. **7.** mit Flitterwerk verzieren.

'**tin|·smith** s. Blechschmied m, Klempner m; ~ **sol·der** s. ◎ Weichlot n, Lötzinn n.

tint [tɪnt] I s. **1.** (hell getönte od. zar-

te) Farbe; **2.** (Farb)Ton m, Tönung f: autumnal ~s Herbstfärbung f; have a bluish ~ ins Blaue spielen, e-n Stich ins Blaue haben; **3.** paint. Weißmischung f; II v/t. **4.** (leicht) färben: ~ed glass Rauchglas n; ~ed paper Tonpapier n; **5.** a) (ab)tönen, b) aufhellen.

tin·tin·nab·u·la·tion ['tɪntɪ,næbjʊ'leɪʃn] s. Geklingel n.

ti·ny ['taɪnɪ] I adj. **1.** winzig (a. Geräusch etc.); II s. Kleine(r m) f (Kind).

tip¹ [tɪp] I s. **1.** (Schwanz-, Stock- etc.) Spitze f, (Flügel- etc.)Ende n: ~ of the ear Ohrläppchen n; ~ of the finger (nose, tongue) Finger- (Nasen-, Zungen)spitze f; have s.th. at the ~s of one's fingers et. ,parat' haben, et. aus dem Effeff können; I have it on the ~ of my tongue es liegt mir auf der Zunge; **2.** Gipfel m, (Berg)Spitze f; → iceberg; **3.** ◎ spitzes Endstück, bsd. a) (Stock- etc.)Zwinge f, b) (Schuh) Spitze f, c) Tülle f, d) (Schuh)Kappe f; **4.** Filter m e-r Zigarette; II v/t. **5.** ◎ mit e-r Spitze etc. versehen; beschlagen, bewehren; **6.** Büsche etc. stutzen.

tip² [tɪp] I s. **1.** Neigung f: give s.th. a ~ → 3; **2.** (Schutt- etc.)Abladeplatz m, (a. Kohlen)Halde f; II v/t. **3.** kippen, neigen; → scale² 1; **4.** mst ~ over umkippen; **5.** Hut abnehmen, an den Hut tippen (zum Gruß); **6.** Brit. Müll etc. abladen; III v/i. **7.** sich neigen; **8.** mst ~ over umkippen; ⚓ auf den Kopf gehen (beim Landen); ~ **off** v/t. **1.** abladen; **2.** sl. Glas Bier etc. ,hin'unterkippen'; ~ **out** I v/t. ausschütten; II v/i. her'ausfallen; ~ **o·ver** → tip² 4 u. 8; ~ **up** v/t. u. v/i. **1.** hochkippen, -klappen; **2.** umkippen.

tip³ [tɪp] I s. **1.** Trinkgeld n; **2.** (Wett- etc.)Tipp m; **3.** Tipp m, Wink m, Fingerzeig m, Rat m; II v/t. **4.** j-m ein Trinkgeld geben; **5.** F j-m e-n Tipp od. Wink geben: ~ s.o. off, ~ s.o. the wink j-m (rechtzeitig) e-n Tipp geben, j-n warnen; **6.** sport tippen auf (acc.); III v/i. **7.** Trinkgeld(er) geben.

tip⁴ [tɪp] I s. Klaps m; leichte Berührung; II v/t. leicht schlagen; antippen, antupfen.

tip| and run s. Brit. Art Kricket n; ,~-and-'run adj. fig. Überraschungs..., blitzschnell: ~ **raider** ✕ Einbruchsflieger m; '~·cart s. Kippwagen m.

'**tip-off** s. **1.** Tipp m, Wink m; **2.** sport Sprungball m.

tipped [tɪpt] adj. **1.** mit e-m Endstück od. e-r Zwinge, Spitze etc. versehen; **2.** mit Filter (Zigarette).

tip·per ['tɪpə] s. ◎ Kippwagen m.

tip·pet ['tɪpɪt] s. **1.** Pele'rine f, (her'abhängender) Pelzkragen f; **2.** eccl. (Seiden)Halsband n, (-)Schärpe f.

tip·ple ['tɪpl] I v/t. u. v/i. ,picheln'; II s. (alko'holisches) Getränk; '**tip·pler** [-lə] s. ,Pichler' m, Säufer m.

tip·si·fy ['tɪpsɪfaɪ] v/t. bedudeln; '**tip·si·ness** [-nɪs] s. Beschwipstheit f.

'**tip·staff** pl. -staves s. **1.** hist. Amtsstab m; **2.** Gerichtsdiener m.

tip·ster ['tɪpstə] s. **1.** bsd. Rennsport u. Börse: (berufsmäßiger) Tippgeber; **2.** Infor'mant m.

tip·sy ['tɪpsɪ] adj. ☐ **1.** angeheitert, beschwipst; **2.** wack(e)lig, schief; ~ **cake** s. mit Wein getränkter u. mit Eiercreme servierter Kuchen.

'**tip|-,tilt·ed** adj.: ~ **nose** Stupsnase f; '~·toe I s.: on ~ a) auf den Zehenspitzen, b) fig. neugierig, gespannt (with vor dat.), c) darauf brennend (et. zu *tun*); **II** *adj. u. adv.* → I; **III** *v/i.* auf den Zehenspitzen gehen, schleichen; ~**'top I** *s.* Gipfel *m, fig. a.* Höhepunkt *m*; **II** *adj. u. adv.* F **'tipp'topp**, erstklassig; **'~- -up** *adj.* aufklappbar: ~ **seat** Klappsitz *m*.

ti·rade [taɪ'reɪd] *s.* **1.** Ti'rade *f (a. ♪)*, Wortschwall *m*; **2.** 'Schimpfkano,nade *f*.

tire¹ ['taɪə] **I** *v/t.* ermüden (*a. fig. langweilen*): ~ **out** erschöpfen; ~ **to death** a) todmüde machen, b) *fig.* tödlich langweilen; **II** *v/i.* müde werden: a) ermüden, ermatten, b) *fig.* 'überdrüssig werden (**of** *gen.*, **of doing** zu tun).

tire² ['taɪə] *mot. bsd. Am.* **I** *s.* (Rad-, Auto)Reifen *m*; **II** *v/t.* bereifen.

tire³ ['taɪə] *obs.* **I** *v/t.* schmücken; **II** *s.* a) (Kopf)Putz *m*, Schmuck *m*, b) (schöne) Kleidung, Kleid *n*.

tire| cas·ing *s. mot.* (Reifen)Mantel *m*, (-)Decke *f*; ~ **chain** *s. mot.* Schneekette *f*.

tired¹ ['taɪəd] *adj.* **1.** müde: a) ermüdet (**by, with** von): ~ **to death** todmüde; ~ **and emotional** F *humor.* angeheitert, nicht mehr ganz nüchtern, b) 'überdrüssig (**of** *gen.*); **I am ~ of it** *fig.* ich habe es satt; **2.** erschöpft, verbraucht; **3.** abgenutzt.

tired² ['taɪəd] *adj.* ⊖, *mot.* bereift.

tired·ness ['taɪədnɪs] *s.* **1.** Müdigkeit *f*; **2.** *fig.* 'Überdruss *m*.

tire| ga(u)ge *s. mot.* Reifendruckmesser *m*; ~ **grip** *s.* ⊖ Griffigkeit *f* der Reifen.

tire·less¹ ['taɪəlɪs] *adj.* ⊖ unbereift.

tire·less² ['taɪəlɪs] *adj.* □ unermüdlich; **'tire·less·ness** [-nɪs] *s.* Unermüdlichkeit *f*.

tire| le·ver *s. mot.* ('Reifen)Mon,tierhebel *m*; ~ **marks** *s. pl. mot.* Reifen-, Bremsspur(en *pl.*) *f*; ~ **rim** *s.* Reifenwulst *m*.

tire·some ['taɪəsəm] *adj.* □ **1.** ermüdend (*a. fig.*); **2.** *fig.* unangenehm, lästig.

'tire,wom·an *s.* [*irr.*] *obs.* **1.** Kammerzofe *f*; **2.** *thea.* Garderobi'ere *f*.

ti·ro *s.* → *tyro*.

Tir·o·lese [,tɪrə'liːz] **I** *adj.* ti'rolerisch, ti'rolisch, Tiroler(...); **II** *s.* Ti'roler(in).

'T-,i·ron *s.* ⊖ T-Eisen *n*.

tis·sue ['tɪʃuː; 'tɪsjuː] *s.* **1.** *biol.* (Zell-, Muskel- *etc.*)Gewebe *n*; **2.** ♥ feines Gewebe, Flor *m*; **3.** *a.* ~ **paper** 'Seidenpa,pier *n*; **4.** Pa'pier(taschen)tuch *n*; **5.** *phot.* 'Kohlepa,pier *n*; **6.** *fig.* (Lügen- *etc.*)Gewebe *n*, Netz *n*.

tit¹ [tɪt] *s. orn.* Meise *f*.

tit² [tɪt] *s.*: ~ **for tat** wie du mir, so ich dir; **give s.o.** ~ **for tat** j-m mit gleicher Münze heimzahlen.

tit³ [tɪt] *s.* **1.** → *teat*; **2.** *vulg.* ‚Titte' *f*.

Ti·tan ['taɪtən] *s.* Ti'tan *m*; **'Ti·tan·ess** [-tənɪs] *s.* Ti'tanin *f*; **ti·tan·ic** [taɪ'tænɪk] *adj.* **1.** ti'tanisch, gi'gantisch; **2.** ♐ Titan...: ~ **acid**; **ti·ta·ni·um** [taɪ'teɪnjəm] *s.* Ti'tan *n*.

tit·bit ['tɪtbɪt] *s.* Leckerbissen *m (a. fig.)*.

titch [tɪtʃ] *s. Brit.* F ‚Zwerg' *m*, ‚Drei'käsehoch' *m*.

tith·a·ble ['taɪðəbl] *adj.* zehntpflichtig.

tithe [taɪð] **I** *s.* **1.** *oft pl. bsd. eccl.* Zehnte *m*; **2.** Zehntel *n*: **not a ~ of it** *fig.* nicht ein bisschen davon; **II** *v/t.* **3.** den Zehnten bezahlen von; **4.** den Zehnten erheben von.

tit·il·late ['tɪtɪleɪt] *v/t. u. v/i.* kitzeln (*a. fig. angenehm erregen*); **tit·il·la·tion** [,tɪtɪ'leɪʃn] *s.* **1.** Kitzeln *n*; **2.** *fig.* Kitzel *m*.

tit·i·vate ['tɪtɪveɪt] *v/t. u. v/i. humor.*

(sich) fein machen, (sich) her'ausputzen.

tit·lark ['tɪtlɑːk] *s. orn.* Pieper *m*.

ti·tle ['taɪtl] *s.* **1.** (*Buch- etc.*)Titel *m*; **2.** (Ka'pitel- *etc.*),Überschrift *f*; **3.** (Haupt)Abschnitt *m* e-s Gesetzes *etc.*; **4.** *Film:* 'Untertitel *m*; **5.** Bezeichnung *f*; **6.** (Adels-, Ehren-, Amts)Titel *m*: ~ **of nobility** Adelsprädikat *n*; **7.** *sport* Titel *m*; **8.** ♐ a) Rechtstitel *m*, -anspruch *m*, Recht *n* (**to** auf *acc.*), b) dingliches Eigentum(srecht) (**to** an *dat.*), c) Eigentumsurkunde *f*; **9.** *allg.* Recht *n* (**to** auf *acc.*), Berechtigung *f* (**to do** zu tun); **10.** *typ.* a) → **title page**, b) Buchrücken *m*; **'ti·tled** [-ld] *adj.* **1.** betitelt, tituliert; **2.** ad(e)lig.

ti·tle| deed → *title* 8 c; **'~,hold·er** *s.* **1.** ♐ (Rechts)Titelinhaber(in); **2.** *sport* Titelhalter(in), -verteidiger(in); ~ **page** *s.* Titelblatt *n*; ~ **role** *s. thea.* Titelrolle *f*.

'tit·mouse *s.* [*irr.*] *orn.* Meise *f*.

ti·trate ['taɪtreɪt] *v/t. u. v/i.* ♐ titrieren.

tit·ter ['tɪtə] **I** *v/i.* kichern; **II** *s.* Gekicher *n*, Kichern *n*.

tit·tle ['tɪtl] *s.* **1.** Pünktchen *n*, (*bsd.* i-) Tüpfelchen *n*; **2.** *fig.* Tüttelchen *n, das bisschen*: **to a** ~ aufs i-Tüpfelchen *od.* Haar, ganz genau; **not a** ~ **of it** ein Iota (davon).

'tit·tle-,tat·tle I *s.* **1.** Schnickschnack *m*, Geschwätz *n*; **2.** Klatsch *m*, Tratsch *m*; **II** *v/i.* **3.** schwatzen, schwätzen; **4.** tratschen.

tit·u·lar ['tɪtjʊlə] **I** *adj.* □ **1.** Titel...; **2.** Titular..., nomi'nell: ~ **king** Titularkönig *m*; **II** *s.* **3.** Titu'lar *m*.

Ti·tus ['taɪtəs] *npr. u. s. bibl.* (Brief *m* des Paulus an) Titus *m*.

tiz·zy ['tɪzɪ] *s.* F Aufregung *f*.

to [tuː; *im Satz mst* tu; *vor Konsonanten* tə] **I** *prp.* **1.** *Grundbedeutung:* zu; **2.** *Richtung u. Ziel, räumlich:* zu, nach, an (*acc.*), in (*acc.*), auf (*acc.*): ~ **bed** zu Bett *gehen*; ~ **London** nach London *reisen etc.*; ~ **school** in die Schule *gehen*; ~ **the ground** auf den *od.* zu Boden *fallen, werfen etc.*; ~ **the station** zum Bahnhof; ~ **the wall** an die Wand *nageln etc.*; ~ **the right** auf der rechten Seite, rechts; **back** ~ **back** Rücken an Rücken; **3.** in (*dat.*): **I have never been** ~ **London** ich war noch nie in London; **4.** *Richtung, Ziel, Zweck, Wirkung:* zu, auf (*acc.*), an (*acc.*), in (*acc.*), für, gegen: **pray** ~ **God** zu Gott beten; **our duty** ~ unsere Pflicht *j-m* gegenüber; ~ **dinner** zum Essen *einladen etc.*; ~ **my surprise** zu m-r Überraschung; **pleasant** ~ **the ear** angenehm für das Ohr; **here's** ~ **you!** F (auf) Ihre Gesundheit!, Prosit!; **what is that** ~ **you?** was geht das Sie an?; ~ **a large audience** vor e-m großen Publikum *spielen*; **5.** *Zugehörigkeit:* zu, in (*acc.*), bei *od.* (*acc.*): **cousin** ~ **Vetter** des *Königs etc.*, der *Frau N.*, von *N.*; **he is a brother** ~ **her** er ist ihr Bruder; **secretary** ~ Sekretär des ..., *j-s* Sekretär; **that is all there is** ~ **it** das ist alles; **a cap with a tassel** ~ **it** e-e Mütze mit e-r Troddel (daran); **a room** ~ **myself** ein eigenes Zimmer; **a key** ~ **the trunk** ein Schlüssel für den (*od.* zum) Koffer; **6.** *Gemäßheit:* nach: ~ **my feeling** m-m Gefühl nach; **not** ~ **my taste** nicht nach m-m Geschmack; **7.** (*im Verhältnis od. Vergleich*) zu, gegen, gegen'über, auf (*acc.*), mit: **you are but a child** ~ **him** Sie sind nur ein Kind gegen ihn; **nothing** ~ nichts im Vergleich zu; **five** ~ **one** fünf gegen eins, *sport etc.* fünf zu eins; **three** ~ **the pound** drei aufs Pfund;

---

8. *Ausmaß, Grenze:* bis, (bis) zu, (bis) an (*acc.*), auf (*acc.*), in (*dat.*): ~ **the clouds; goods** ~ **the value of** Waren im Werte von; **love** ~ **craziness** bis zum Wahnsinn lieben; **9.** *zeitliche Ausdehnung od. Grenze:* bis, bis zu, bis gegen, auf (*acc.*), vor (*dat.*): **a quarter** ~ **one** ein Viertel vor eins; **from three** ~ **four** von drei bis vier (Uhr); ~ **this day** bis zum heutigen Tag; ~ **the minute** auf die Minute (genau); **10.** *Begleitung:* zu, nach: ~ **a guitar** zu e-r Gitarre *singen*; ~ **a tune** nach e-r Melodie *tanzen*; **11.** *zur Bildung des (betonten) Dativs:* ~ **me, you** *etc.* mir, dir, Ihnen *etc.*; **it seems** ~ **me** es scheint mir; **she was a good mother** ~ **him** sie war ihm e-e gute Mutter; **12.** *zur Bezeichnung des Infinitivs:* ~ **be or not** ~ **be** sein oder nicht sein; ~ **go** gehen; **I want** ~ **go** ich möchte gehen; **easy** ~ **understand** leicht zu verstehen; **years** ~ **come** künftige Jahre; **I want her** ~ **come** ich will, dass sie kommt; **13.** *Zweck, Absicht:* um zu, zu: **he only does it** ~ **earn money** er tut es nur, um Geld zu verdienen; **14.** *zur Verkürzung des Nebensatzes:* **I weep** ~ **think of it** ich weine, wenn ich daran denke; **he was the first** ~ **arrive** er kam als Erster; ~ **be honest, I should decline** wenn ich ehrlich sein soll, muss ich ablehnen; ~ **hear him talk** wenn man ihn (so) reden hört; **15.** *zur Andeutung e-s dem Vorhergehenden zu ergänzenden Infinitivs:* **I don't go because I don't want** ~ ich gehe nicht, weil ich nicht (gehen) will; **II** *adv.* [tuː] **16.** zu, geschlossen: **pull the door** ~ die Tür zuziehen; **17.** *bei verschiedenen Verben:* dran; → *fall to*, *put to etc.*; **18.** zu Bewusstsein *od.* zu sich *kommen*, *bringen*; **19.** ♣ nahe am Wind: **keep her** ~**!**; **20.** ~ **and fro** a) hin u. her, b) auf u. ab.

toad [təʊd] *s.* **1.** *zo.* Kröte *f*: **a** ~ **under a harrow** *fig.* ein geplagter Mensch; **2.** Ekel *n* (*Person*); **'~,eat·ing I** *s.* Speichellecke'rei *f*; **II** *adj.* speichelleckerisch; **'~-flax** *s.* ♥ Leinkraut *n*; **'~-in- -the-'hole** *s.* in *Pfannkuchenteig gebackene Würste*; **'~-stool** *s. bot.* **1.** (größerer Blätter)Pilz; **2.** Giftpilz *m*.

toad·y ['təʊdɪ] **I** *s.* Speichellecker *m*; **II** *v/i.* (*v/t. vor j-m*) kriechen *od.* schar'wenzeln; **'toad·y·ism** [-ɪɪzəm] *s.* Speichellecke'rei *f*.

to-and-fro [,tuːən'frəʊ] *s.* Hin u. Her *n*; Kommen u. Gehen *n*.

toast¹ [təʊst] **I** *s.* **1.** Toast *m*, geröstete (Weiß)Brotschnitte *f*: **have s.o. on** ~ *Brit. sl.* j-n ganz in der Hand haben; **II** *v/t.* **2.** toasten, rösten; **3.** sich *die Hände etc.* wärmen; **III** *v/i.* **4.** sich rösten *od.* toasten lassen; **5.** F sich *von der Sonne* braten lassen.

toast² [təʊst] **I** *s.* **1.** Trinkspruch *m*, Toast *m*: **propose a** ~ **to s.o.** e-n Toast auf j-n ausbringen; **2.** gefeierte Per'son *od.* Sache; **II** *v/t.* **3.** toasten *od.* trinken auf (*acc.*); **III** *v/i.* **4.** toasten (**to** auf *acc.*).

toast·er ['təʊstə] *s.* Toaster *m*.

to·bac·co [tə'bækəʊ] *pl.* **-cos** *s.* **1.** *a.* ~ **plant** Tabak(pflanze *f*) *m*; **2.** (*Rauch- etc.*)Tabak *m*: ~ **heart** ♐ Nikotinherz *n*; **to'bac·co·nist** [-kənɪst] *s.* Tabak(waren)händler *m*: ~**'s (shop)** Tabak(waren)laden *m*.

to·bog·gan [tə'bɒgən] **I** *s.* **1.** (Rodel-) Schlitten *m*; **2.** *Am.* Rodelhang *m*; **II** *v/i.* **3.** rodeln; ~ **chute**, ~ **slide** *s.* Rodelbahn *f*.

to·by ['təʊbɪ] *s. a.* ~ **jug** Bierkrug *m* in Gestalt e-s dicken, alten Mannes.

toc·sin ['tɒksɪn] s. **1.** A'larm-, Sturm-glocke f; **2.** A'larm-, 'Warni,gnal n.

tod [tɒd] s.: **on one's ~** Brit. sl. allein.

to·day [təˈdeɪ] **I** adv. **1.** heute; **2.** heute, heutzutage; **II** s. **3.** heutiger Tag: **~'s paper** die heutige Zeitung, die Zeitung von heute; **~'s rate** ✝ Tageskurs m; **4.** das Heute, heutige Zeit, Gegenwart f: **of ~, ~'s** von heute, heutig, Tages..., der Gegenwart.

tod·dle ['tɒdl] **I** v/i. **1.** watscheln (bsd. kleine Kinder); **2.** F (da'hin)zotteln: **~ off** sich trollen, ,abhauen'; **II** s. **3.** Wat-scheln n; **4.** F Bummel m; **5.** F → **'tod·dler** [-lə] s. Kleinkind n.

tod·dy ['tɒdɪ] s. Toddy m: a) Art Grog, b) Palmwein m.

to·do [təˈduː] s. F **1.** Lärm m; **2.** Ge'tue n, ,Wirbel' m, ,The'ater' n: **make much ~ about s.th.** viel Wind um e-e Sache machen.

toe [təʊ] **I** s. **1.** anat. Zehe f: **on one's ~s** F ,auf Draht'; **turn one's ~s in** (out) einwärts (auswärts) gehen; **turn up one's ~s** sl. ins Gras beißen; **tread on s.o.'s ~s** F fig. ,j-m auf die Hühnerau-gen treten'; **2.** Vorderhuf m (Pferd); **3.** Spitze f, Kappe f von Schuhen, Strümp-fen etc.; **4.** ⊕ a) (Well)Zapfen m, b) Nocken m, Daumen m, c) 🔩 Keil m (Weiche); **5.** sport Löffel m (Golfschlä-ger); **II** v/t. **6.** a) Strümpfe mit neuen Spitzen versehen, b) Schuhe bekappen; **7.** mit den Zehen berühren: **~ the line** a) a. **~ the mark** in e-r Reihe (sport zum Start) antreten, b) pol. sich der Parteilinie unterwerfen, ,spuren' (a. weitS. gehorchen); **8.** sport den Ball spitzeln; **9.** sl. j-m e-n (Fuß)Tritt verset-zen; **10.** Golf: Ball mit dem Löffel schlagen; **'~·board** s. sport Stoß-, Wurfbalken m; **'~·cap** s. (Schuh)Kap-pe f.

-toed [təʊd] in Zssgn ...zehig.

'toe,danc·er s. Spitzentänzer(in); **'~·hold** s. **1.** Halt m für die Zehen (beim Klettern); **2.** fig. a) Ansatzpunkt m, b) Brückenkopf m, 'Ausgangspositi,on f: **get a ~** Fuß fassen; **3.** Ringen: Zehen-griff m; **'~·nail** s. Zehennagel m; **~ spin** s. 'Spitzenpirou,ette f.

toff [tɒf] s. Brit. sl. ,Fatzke' m.

tof·fee, tof·fy ['tɒfɪ] s. Brit. 'Sahnebon-,bon m, n, Toffee n: **he can't shoot for ~** F vom Schießen hat er keine Ahnung; **not for ~** F nicht für Geld u. gute Wor-te; **'~·nosed** adj. F eingebildet.

to·fu ['təʊfuː] s. Tofu m.

tog [tɒg] F **I** s. pl. **1.** ,Kla'motten' pl: **golf ~s** Golfdress m; **II** v/t.: **~ o.s. up** sich ,in Schale werfen'.

to·geth·er [təˈgeðə] **I** adv. **1.** zu'sam-men: **call** (sew) **~** zs.-rufen (-nähen); **2.** zu-, bei'sammen, mitein'ander, ge-meinsam; **3.** zusammen (genommen); **4.** mitein'ander od. gegenein'ander: **fight ~;** **5.** zu'gleich, gleichzeitig, zu-'sammen; **6.** Tage etc. nach-, hinterei-nander, e-e Zeit lang od. hin'durch: **he talked for hours ~** er sprach stunden-lang; **7. ~ with** zusammen od. gemein-sam mit, mit(samt); **II** adj. **8.** Am. sl. ausgeglichen (Person); **to'geth·er·ness** [-nɪs] s. bsd. Am. Zs.-gehörig-keit(sgefühl n) f; Einheit f; Nähe f.

tog·ger·y ['tɒgərɪ] → **tog** I.

tog·gle ['tɒgl] **I** s. **1.** ⊕, ⚓ Knebel m; **2.** a. **~ joint** ⊕ Knebel-, Kniegelenk m; **II** v/t. **3.** festknebeln; **~ key** s. Computer: 'Umschalttaste f; **~ switch** s. ⚡ Kipp-schalter m.

toil¹ [tɔɪl] s. mst pl. fig. Schlingen pl., Netz n: **in the ~s of** a) in den Schlingen od. Fängen des Satans etc., b) in Schul-den etc. verstrickt.

toil² [tɔɪl] **I** s. (mühselige) Arbeit, Mühe f, Plage f, Placke'rei f; **II** v/i. a. **~ and moil** sich abmühen od. abplacken od. quälen (**at, on** mit): **~ up a hill** e-n Berg mühsam erklimmen; **'toil·er** [-lə] s. fig. Arbeitstier n, Schwerarbeiter m.

toi·let ['tɔɪlɪt] s. **1.** Toi'lette f, Klo'sett n; **2.** Fri'sier-, Toi'lettentisch m; **3.** Toi-'lette f (Ankleiden etc.): **make one's ~** Toilette machen; **4.** Toi'lette f, Klei-dung f, a. (Abend)Kleid n od. (Gesell-schafts)Anzug m; **~ bag** s. Kul'turbeu-tel m; **~ case** s. 'Reiseneces,saire m; **~ pa·per** s. Toi'letten-, Klo'settpa,pier m; **~ pow·der** s. Körperpuder m; **~ roll** s. Rolle f Klo'settpa,pier.

toi·let·ry ['tɔɪlɪtrɪ] s. Toi'lettenar,tikel pl.

toi·let| set s. Toi'lettengarni,tur f; **~ soap** s. Toi'lettenseife f; **~ ta·ble** s. → **toilet** 2.

toil·ful ['tɔɪlfʊl], **'toil·some** [-səm] adj. □ mühsam, -selig; **'toil·some·ness** [-səmnɪs] s. Mühseligkeit f.

'toil·worn adj. abgearbeitet.

To·kay [təʊˈkeɪ] s. To'kaier m (Wein u. Traube).

to·ken ['təʊkən] **I** s. **1.** Zeichen n: a) Anzeichen n, Merkmal n, b) Beweis m: **as a** (od. **in**) **~ of** als od. zum Zeichen (gen.); **by the same ~** a) aus dem glei-chen Grund(e), mit demselben Recht, umgekehrt, b) ferner, überdies; **2.** An-denken n, (Erinnerungs)Geschenk n, ('Unter)Pfand n; **3.** hist. Scheidemünze f; **4.** (Me'tall)Marke f (als Fahraus-weis); **5.** Spielmarke f; **6.** Gutschein m, Bon m; **II** adj. **7.** nomi'nell: **~ money** a) Scheidemünzen pl., b) Not-, Ersatzgeld n; **~ payment** symbolische Zahlung; **~ strike** (kurzer) Warnstreik; **8.** Alibi...: **~ negro; ~ female** (od. **woman**) a. Quotenfrau f; **9.** Schein...: **~ raid** Scheinangriff m; **to·ken·ism** ['təʊkən-izəm] s. 'Alibipoli,tik f.

told [təʊld] pret. u. p.p. von **tell**.

tol·er·a·ble ['tɒlərəbl] adj. □ **1.** erträg-lich; **2.** fig. leidlich, mittelmäßig, er-träglich; **3.** F ,einigermaßen' (gesund), ,so la'la'; **'tol·er·a·ble·ness** [-nɪs] s. Erträglichkeit f; **'tol·er·ance** [-rəns] s. **1.** Tole'ranz f, Duldsamkeit f; **2.** (**of**) a) Duldung f (gen.), b) Nachsicht f (mit); **3.** ⚕ a) Tole'ranz f, 'Widerstandsfähig-keit f (**for** gegen), b) Verträglichkeit f; **4.** ⊕ Tole'ranz f, zulässige Abwei-chung, Spiel n, Fehlergrenze f; **'tol·er-ant** [-rənt] adj. □ **1.** tole'rant, duldsam (**of** gegen); **2.** geduldig, nachsichtig (**of** mit); **3.** ⚕ 'widerstandsfähig (**of** ge-gen); **tol·er·ate** ['tɒləreɪt] v/t. **1.** j-n od. et. dulden, tolerieren, a. zulassen, hinnehmen, a. j-s Gesellschaft ertragen; **2.** duldsam od. tole'rant sein gegen; **3.** bsd. ⚕ vertragen; **tol·er·a·tion** [,tɒlə-'reɪʃn] s. **1.** Duldung f; **2.** → **tolerance** 1.

toll¹ [təʊl] **I** v/t. **1.** bsd. Totenglocke läu-ten, erschallen lassen; **2.** Stunde schla-gen; **3.** (durch Glockengeläut) verkün-den; die Totenglocke läuten für j-n; **II** v/i. **4.** a) läuten, schallen, b) schlagen (Glocke); **III** s. **5.** Geläut n; **6.** Glo-ckenschlag m.

toll² [təʊl] s. **1.** hist. (bsd. Wege-, Brü-cken)Zoll m; **2.** Straßenbenutzungsge-bühr f, Maut f; **3.** Standgeld n auf dem Markt etc.; **4.** Am. Hafengebühr f; **5.** teleph. Am. Gebühr f für ein Fernge-spräch; **6.** fig. Tri'but m an Menschenle-ben etc., (Blut)Zoll m, (Zahl f der) To-desopfer pl.: **the ~ of the road** die Verkehrsopfer od. -unfälle; **take its ~ of** fig. j-n arg mitnehmen, s-n Tribut fordern von j-m od. e-r Sache, Kräfte, Vorräte etc. strapazieren; **take a ~ of 100 lives** 100 Todesopfer fordern (Ka-tastrophe); **~ bar** → **toll gate**; **~ call** s. teleph. **1.** Am. Ferngespräch n; **2.** Brit. obs. Nahverkehrsgespräch n; **~ gate** s. Schlagbaum m e-r Mautstraße; **'~·house** s. Mautstelle f; **~ road** s., **'~·way** s. gebührenpflichtige Straße, Mautstraße f.

tol·u·ene ['tɒljʊiːn], **'tol·u·ol** [-jʊɒl] s. 🜍 Tolu'ol n.

tom [tɒm] s. **1.** Männchen n kleinerer Tiere: **~ turkey** Truthahn m, Puter m; **2.** Kater m; **3.** ♀ abbr. für **Thomas**: ♀ **and Jerry** Am. Eiergrog m; ♀, **Dick, and Harry** Hinz u. Kunz; ♀ **Thumb** Däumling m.

tom·a·hawk ['tɒməhɔːk] **I** s. Tomahawk m, Kriegsbeil n der Indianer: **bury** (**dig up**) **the ~** fig. das Kriegsbeil begraben (ausgraben); **II** v/t. mit dem Tomahawk (er)schlagen.

to·ma·to [təˈmɑːtəʊ] pl. **-toes** ♀ To-'mate f. **~ juice** s. To'matensaft m; **~ ketch·up** s. Ket(s)chup m od. n; **~ pu·rée** s. To'matenmark n.

tomb [tuːm] s. **1.** Grab(stätte f) n; **2.** Grabmal n, Gruft f; **3.** fig. das Grab, der Tod.

tom·bac, tom·bak ['tɒmbæk] s. metall. Tombak m.

tom·bo·la [tɒmˈbəʊlə] s. Tombola f.

tom·boy ['tɒmbɔɪ] s. Wildfang m, Range f (Mädchen); **'tom·boy·ish** [-bɔɪʃ] adj. ausgelassen, wild.

'tomb·stone ['tuːm-] s. Grabstein m.

'tom·cat s. Kater m.

tome [təʊm] s. **1.** Band m e-s Werkes; **2.** (dicker) Wälzer (Buch).

tom·fool [,tɒmˈfuːl] **I** s. Einfaltspinsel m, Narr m; **II** adj. dumm; **III** v/i. (he'rum-) albern; **tom·fool·er·y** [tɒmˈfuːlərɪ] s. Albernheit f, Unsinn m.

tom·my ['tɒmɪ] s. **1.** a) a. ♀ **Atkins** Tom-my m (der brit. Soldat), b) a. ♀ F Tom-my m, brit. Landser m (einfacher Sol-dat); **2.** dial. ,Fres'salien' pl., Verpfle-gung f; **3.** ⊕ a) (verstellbarer) Schrau-benschlüssel, b) a. **~ bar** Knebelgriff m; ♀ **gun** s. ✗ Ma'schinenpi,stole f; **~ rot** s. F (purer) Blödsinn, Quatsch m.

to·mo·gram ['təʊməgræm] s. ⚕ Tomo-'gramm n; Tomographie f; **'to·mo-graph** [-græf] s. ⚕ Tomo'graph m; **to·mog·ra·phy** [təˈmɒgrəfɪ] s. ⚕ Tomo-gra'phie f.

to·mor·row [təˈmɒrəʊ] **I** adv. morgen: **~ week** morgen in e-r Woche od. acht Tagen; **~ morning** morgen früh; **~ night** morgen Abend; **II** s. der morgige Tag, das Morgen: **~'s paper** die morgi-ge Zeitung; **~ never comes** das werden wir nie erleben; **the day after ~** über-morgen.

'tom·tit s. orn. (Blau)Meise f.

ton¹ [tʌn] s. **1.** engl. Tonne f (Gewicht): a) a. **long ~** bsd. Brit. = 2240 lbs. od. 1016,05 kg, b) a. **short ~** bsd. Am. = 2000 lbs. od. 907,18 kg, c) a. **metric ~** metrische Tonne (= 2205 lbs. od. 1000 kg); **2.** ⚓ Tonne f (Raummaß): a) **reg-ister ~** Registertonne (= 100 cubic feet od. 2,83 m³), b) **gross register ~** Brut-toregistertonne (Schiffsgrößenangabe); **3. weigh a ~** F ,wahnsinnig' schwer sein; **4.** pl. e-e Unmenge (**of money** Geld): **~s of times** ,tausendmal'; **5. do the ~** Brit. sl. a) mit 100 Meilen fahren, b) 100 Meilen schaffen (Auto etc.).

ton² [tɔ̃ː] (Fr.) s. **1.** die (herrschende)

Mode; **2.** Ele'ganz *f*: *in the* ~ modisch, elegant.

ton·al ['təunl] *adj.* □ ♪ **1.** Ton..., tonlich; **2.** to'nal; **to·nal·i·ty** [təʊ'nælətɪ] *s.* **1.** ♪ a) Tonali'tät *f*, Tonart *f*, b) 'Ton-, 'Klangcha,rakter *m*; **2.** *paint.* Farbton *m*, Tönung *f*.

tone [təʊn] **I** *s.* **1.** *allg.* Ton *m*, Klang *m*: *heart ~s* ♪ Herztöne; **2.** Ton *m*, Stimme *f*: *in an angry* ~ in ärgerlichem Ton, mit zorniger Stimme; **3.** *ling.* a) Tonfall *m*, b) Tonhöhe *f*, Betonung *f*; **4.** ♪ a) Ton *m*, b) *Am.* Note *f*, c) Klang(farbe *f*) *m*; **5.** *paint.* (Farb)Ton *m*, Tönung *f* (*a. fig.*); **6.** ♪♪ a) Tonus *m der Muskeln*, b) *fig.* Spannkraft *f*; **7.** *fig.* Geist *m*, Haltung *f*; **8.** Stimmung *f* (*a. Börse*); **9.** a) Ton *m*, Note *f*, Stil *m*, b) Ni'veau *n*: *set the ~ of* a) den Ton angeben für, b) den Stil *e-r Sache* bestimmen; *raise* (*lower*) *the* ~ (*of*) das Niveau (*gen.*) heben (senken); *give ~ to* Niveau verleihen (*dat.*); **10.** e-n Ton verleihen (*dat.*), e-e Färbung geben (*dat.*); **11.** *Farbe etc.* abtönen: ~ *down Farbe*, *fig. Zorn etc.* dämpfen, mildern; ~ *up paint. u. fig.* (ver)stärken; **12.** *phot.* tonen; **13.** *fig.* a) 'umformen, -modeln, b) regeln; **III** *v/i.* **14.** *a.* ~ *in* (*with*) a) verschmelzen (mit), b) harmonieren (mit), passen (zu) (*bsd. Farbe*); **15.** ~ *down* sich mildern *od.* abschwächen; **16.** ~ *up* stärker werden; ~ *arm* Tonarm *m am Plattenspieler*; ~ *con·trol s.* ♫ Klangregler *m*.

tone·less ['təʊnlɪs] *adj.* □ **1.** tonlos (*a. Stimme*); **2.** ausdruckslos.

tone pad *s. teleph.* Fernabfrager *m*.

tone po·em *s.* ♪ Tondichtung *f*.

ton·er ['təʊnə] *s.* **1.** *Drucker etc.*: Toner *m*; **2.** *Kosmetik*: Tönung *f*; ~ *car·tridge s.* 'Tonerkas,sette *f*.

tongs [tɒŋz] *s. pl.* Zange *f*: *a pair of* ~ e-e Zange; *I would not touch that with a pair of* ~ a) das würde ich nicht mal mit e-r Zange anfassen, b) *fig.* mit dieser Sache möchte ich nichts zu tun haben.

tongue [tʌŋ] **I** *s.* **1.** *anat.* Zunge *f* (*a. fig. Redeweise*): *malicious* ~*s* böse Zungen; *have a long* (*ready*) ~ geschwätzig (schlagfertig) sein; *find one's* ~ die Sprache wiederfinden; *give* ~ a) sich laut u. deutlich äußern (*to* zu), b) anschlagen (*Hund*), c) Laut geben (*Jagdhund*); *hold one's* ~ den Mund halten; *keep a civil* ~ *in one's head* höflich bleiben; *put one's* ~ *out* (*at s.o.*) (j-m) die Zunge herausstrecken; *with* (*one's*) ~ *in* (*one's*) *cheek* → *tongue--in-cheek*; → *wag* 1; **2.** Sprache *f e-s Volkes*, Zunge *f*; **3.** *fig.* Zunge *f* (*Schuh, Flamme, Klarinette etc.*); **4.** (Glocken)Klöppel *m*; **5.** (Wagen-)Deichsel *f*; **6.** ♫ Feder *f*, Spund *m*: ~ *and groove* Feder u. Nut; **7.** Dorn *m* (*Schnalle*); **8.** Zeiger *m* (*Waage*); **9.** ♭ (Re'lais)Anker *m*; **10.** *geogr.* Landzunge *f*; **II** *v/t.* **11.** ♪ mit Flatterzunge blasen; **12.** ♫ verzapfen; **tongued** [-ŋd] *adj.* **1.** *in Zssgn* ...züngig; **2.** ♫ gefedert, gezapft.

,**tongue**|**-in-'cheek** *adj.* **1.** i'ronisch; **2.** mit Hintergedanken; '~-,lash·ing *s.* F Standpauke *f*; '~-tied *adj.* stumm, sprachlos (*vor Verlegenheit etc.*): *be* ~ keinen Ton herausbringen; ~ *twist·er s.* Zungenbrecher *m*.

ton·ic ['tɒnɪk] **I** *adj.* (□ ~*ally*) **1.** ♪♪ tonisch: ~ *spasm* Starrkrampf *m*; **2.** stärkend, belebend (*a. fig.*): ~ *water* Tonic *n*; **3.** *ling.* Ton...: ~ *accent* musikalischer Akzent; **4.** ♪ Tonika...,

(Grund)Ton...: ~ *chord* Grundakkord *m*; ~ *major* gleichnamige Dur-Tonart; ~ *sol-fa* Tonika-Do-System *n*; **5.** *paint.* Tönungs..., Farbgebungs...; **II** *s.* **6.** ♪♪ Stärkungsmittel *n*, Tonikum *n*; **7.** Tonic *n* (*Getränk*); **8.** *fig.* Stimulans *n*; **9.** ♪ Grundton *m*, Tonika *f*; **10.** *ling.* stimmhafter Laut; **to·nic·i·ty** [təʊ'nɪsətɪ] *s.* **1.** → *tone* 6; **2.** musi'kalischer Ton.

to·night [tə'naɪt] **I** *adv.* **1.** heute Abend; **2.** heute Nacht; **II** *s.* **3.** der heutige Abend; **4.** diese Nacht.

ton·nage ['tʌnɪdʒ] *s.* **1.** ♪ Ton'nage *f*, Tonnengehalt *m*, Schiffsraum *m*; **2.** ♪ Ge'samtton,nage *f e-s Landes*; **3.** ♪ Tonnengeld *n*; **4.** ◎ (Ge'samt)Produkti,on *f* (*Stahl etc.*).

tonne [tʌn] *s.* metrische Tonne.

ton·neau ['tɒnəʊ] *pl.* -**neaus** (*Fr.*) *s.* mot. hinterer Teil (*mit Rücksitzen*) e-s Autos.

ton·ner ['tʌnə] *s.* ♪ *in Zssgn* ...tonner, *ein Schiff von ...* Tonnen.

to·nom·e·ter [təʊ'nɒmɪtə] *s.* **1.** ♪, *phys.* Tonhöhenmesser *m*; **2.** ♯ Blutdruckmesser *m*.

ton·sil ['tɒnsl] *s. anat.* Mandel *f*; '**ton·sil·lar** [-sɪlə] *adj.* Mandel...; **ton·sil·lec·to·my** [,tɒnsɪ'lektəmɪ] *s.* ♯ Mandelentfernung *f*; **ton·sil·li·tis** [,tɒnsɪ'laɪtɪs] *s.* ♯ Mandelentzündung *f*.

ton·so·ri·al [tɒn'sɔːrɪəl] *adj. mst humor.* Barbier...: ~ *artist* ,Figaro' *m*.

ton·sure ['tɒnʃə] *eccl.* **I** *s.* **1.** Tonsurierung *f*; **2.** Ton'sur *f*; **II** *v/t.* **3.** tonsurieren.

to·ny ['təʊnɪ] *adj. Am.* F (tod)schick.

too [tuː] *adv.* **1.** (*vorangestellt*) zu, allzu: *all ~ familiar* allzu vertraut; ~ *fond of comfort* zu sehr auf Bequemlichkeit bedacht; ~ *many* zu viele; *none* ~ *pleasant* nicht gerade angenehm; **2.** F sehr, äußerst: *it is ~ kind of you*; **3.** (*nachgestellt*) auch, ebenfalls.

took [tʊk] *pret. von* **take**.

tool [tuːl] **I** *s.* **1.** Werkzeug *n*, Gerät *n*, Instru'ment *n*; ~*s pl. a.* Handwerkszeug *n*; *gardener's* ~*s* Gartengerät; **2.** ◎ (Bohr-, Schneide- *etc.*)Werkzeug *n e-r Maschine, a.* Arbeits-, Drehstahl *m*; **3.** ◎ a) 'Werkzeugma,schine *f*, b) Drehbank *f*; **4.** *typ.* a) 'Stempelfi,gur *f* (*Punzarbeit*), b) (Präge)Stempel *m*; **5.** *pl. fig.* a) Handwerkszeug *n* (*Bücher etc.*), b) Rüstzeug *n* (*Fachwissen*); **6.** *fig. contp.* Werkzeug *n*, Handlanger *m*, Krea'tur *f e-s anderen*; **7.** V ,Appa'rat' *m* (*Penis*); **II** *v/t.* **8.** ◎ bearbeiten; **9.** *mst* ~ *up* Fabrik (maschi'nell) ausstatten, -rüsten; **10.** Bucheinband punzen; **11.** *sl.* ,kutschieren' (*fahren*); **III** *v/i.* **12.** *mst* ~ *up* ◎ sich (maschi'nell) ausrüsten (*for* für); **13.** *a.* ~ *along sl.* (da'hin-, her'um)gondeln; ~ *bag s.* Werkzeugtasche *f*; '~-bar *s. Computer*: Sym'bolleiste *f*; ~ *bit s.* ◎ Werkzeugspitze *f*; ~ *box s.* **1.** Werkzeugkasten *m*; **2.** *Computer*: Toolbox *f*; ~ *car·ri·er s.* ◎ Werkzeugschlitten *m*; ~ *en·gi·neer·ing s.* Arbeitsvorbereitung *f*.

tool·ing ['tuːlɪŋ] *s.* ◎ **1.** Bearbeitung *f*; **2.** Einrichten *n e-r Werkzeugmaschine*; **3.** maschi'nelle Ausrüstung *f*; **4.** *Buchbinderei*: Punzarbeit *f*.

'**tool**|,**mak·er** *s.* Werkzeugmacher *m*; '~-**post** *s.* Schneidstahlhalter *m*.

toot [tuːt] *v/i.* **1.** (*a. v/t. et.*) tuten, blasen; **2.** hupen (*Auto*).

tooth [tuːθ] **I** *pl.* **teeth** [tiːθ] *s.* **1.** *anat.* Zahn *m*: ~ *and nail fig.* verbissen, erbittert (*be*)*kämpfen*; *armed to the teeth* bis an die Zähne bewaffnet; *in*

the teeth of fig. a) gegen *Widerstand etc.*, b) trotz *od.* ungeachtet *der Gefahr etc.*; *cut one's teeth* zahnen; *draw the teeth of fig.* a) j-n beruhigen, b) j-n ungefährlich machen, c) *e-r Sache* die Spitze nehmen, *et.* entschärfen; *get one's teeth into* sich *an e-e Arbeit etc.* ,ranmachen'; *have a sweet* ~ gerne Süßigkeiten essen *od.* naschen; *put teeth into* (den nötigen) Nachdruck verleihen (*dat.*); *set s.o.'s teeth on edge* j-m auf die Nerven gehen *od.* ,wehtun'; *show one's teeth* (*to*) a) die Zähne fletschen (gegen), b) *fig.* j-m die Zähne zeigen; **2.** Zahn *m e-s Kammes*, *e-r Säge*, *e-s Zahnrads etc.*; **3.** (Gabel)Zinke *f*; **II** *v/t.* **4.** Rad etc. bezahnen; **5.** Brett verzahnen; **III** *v/i.* **6.** in ein'ander greifen (*Zahnräder*); '~·**ache** *s.* Zahnweh *n*; '~·**brush** *s.* Zahnbürste *f*; '~·**comb** *s.* Staubkamm *m*; ~ **de·cay** *s.* Zahnverfall *m*.

toothed [tuːθt] *adj.* **1.** mit Zähnen (versehen), Zahn..., gezahnt: ~ *wheel* Zahnrad *n*; **2.** ♀ gezähnt, gezackt (*Blattrand*); **3.** ◎ verzahnt; '**tooth·less** [-θlɪs] *adj.* zahnlos.

'**tooth**|-**paste** *s.* Zahnpasta *f*; '~-**pick** *s.* Zahnstocher *m*; ~ **pow·der** *s.* Zahnpulver *n*.

tooth·some ['tuːθsəm] *adj.* □ lecker (*a. fig.*).

too·tle ['tuːtl] *v/i.* **1.** tuten, dudeln; **2.** *Am.* F quatschen; **3.** F a) (her'um)gondeln, b) ,(da'hin)zotteln': ~ *off* sich trollen.

toot·sy(-woot·sy) [,tʊtsɪ('wʊtsɪ)] *s.* Kindersprache: Füßchen *n*.

top¹ [tɒp] **I** *s.* **1.** ober(st)es Ende, Oberteil *n*; Spitze *f*, Gipfel *m e-s Berges etc.*; Krone *f*, Wipfel *m des Baumes*; (Haus-) Giebel *m*, Dach(spitze *f*) *n*; Kopf(ende *n*) *m des Tisches*, *e-r Buchseite etc.*: *at the* ~ oben(an); *at the* ~ *of* oben an (*dat.*); *at the* ~ *of one's speed* mit höchster Geschwindigkeit; *at the* ~ *of one's voice* aus vollem Hals(e); *page 20 at the* ~ auf Seite 20 oben; *on* ~ oben(auf); *on* (*the*) ~ *of* oben auf (*dat.*), über (*dat.*); *on* ~ *of each other* auf- *od.* übereinander; *on* (*the*) ~ *of it* obendrein; *over the* ~ *bsd. Brit.* F (maßlos) übertrieben; *go over the* ~ a) ✕ zum Sturmangriff (*aus dem Schützengraben*) antreten, b) *fig.* es maßlos übertreiben; **2.** *fig.* Spitze *f*, erste *od.* höchste Stelle; 'Spitzenpositi,on *f*: ~ *management* Unternehmensführung *f*; *the* ~ *of the class* der Primus der Klasse; *the* ~ *of the tree* (*od. ladder*) *fig.* die höchste Stellung, der Gipfel des Erfolgs; *at the* ~ an der Spitze; *be on* ~ (*of the world*) obenauf sein; *come out on* ~ als Sieger *od.* Bester hervorgehen; *come to the* ~ an die Spitze kommen, sich durchsetzen; *get on* ~ *of s.th.* e-r Sache Herr werden; **3.** *fig.* Gipfel *m*, das Äußerste *od.* Höchste; **4.** Scheitel *m*, Kopf *m*: *from* ~ *to toe* von Kopf bis Fuß; *blow one's* ~ *sl.* ,hochgehen', e-n Wutanfall haben; **5.** Oberfläche *f des Tisches, Wassers etc.*; **6.** *mot. etc.* Verdeck *n*; **7.** (Bett)Himmel *m*; **8.** (Möbel)Aufsatz *m*; **9.** ♪ Mars *m*, f, Topp *m*; **10.** (Schuh)Oberleder *n*; **11.** Stulpe *f* (*Stiefel, Handschuh*); **12.** (Topf *etc.*)Deckel *m*; **13.** ♀ a) (oberer Teil e-r) Pflanze *f* (*Ggs. Wurzel*), b) *mst pl.* (Rüben- *etc.*)Kraut *n*; **14.** Blume *f des Bieres*; **15.** *mot.* → *top gear*; **II** *adj.* **16.** oberst: ~ *line* Kopf-, Titelzeile *f*; *the* ~ *rung fig.* oberste Stelle, höchste Stellung; **17.** höchst: ~ *earner* Spitzenverdiener(in); **~** *efficiency* ◎ Spitzenleistung *f*; **~** *price* Höchstpreis *m*; **~** *quality* Spitzenqualität *f*; **~** *speed* Höchstgeschwindigkeit *f*; **~** *secret* streng geheim; **18.** *der (die, das)* erste; **19.** Haupt...; **III** *v/t.* **20.** (oben) bedecken; krönen; **21.** über'ragen; **22.** *fig.* über-'treffen, -'ragen; **23.** die Spitze (*gen.*) erreichen; **24.** an der Spitze *der Klasse*, *e-r Liste etc.* stehen; **25.** über'steigen; **26.** ⚡ stutzen, kappen; **27.** *Hindernis* nehmen; **28.** *Golf:* Ball oben schlagen; **~** *off* *v/t.* F *et.* abschließen *od.* krönen (*with* mit); **~** *out* **I** *v/i.* Richtfest feiern; **II** *v/t.* das Richtfest (*gen.*) feiern: **~** *a building*; **~** *up* *v/t.* **1.** auf-, nachfüllen; **2.** F *j-m* nachschenken.

top² [tɒp] *s.* Kreisel *m* (*Spielzeug*).

to·paz ['təʊpæz] *s. min.* To'pas *m*.

top| boot *s.* (kniehoher) Stiefel, Stulpenstiefel *m*; **'~·coat** 'Überzieher *m*, Mantel *m*; **~** *dog* *s.* F *fig.* **1.** *der Herr od.* Über'legene; *der Sieger*; **2.** ‚Chef' *m*, *der* Oberste; **3.** *der (die, das)* Beste; **~** *draw·er* *s.* **1.** oberste Schublade; **2.** F *fig.* die oberen zehntausend: *he does not come from the* **~** er kommt nicht aus vornehmster Familie; **‚~·'draw·er** *adj.* F **1.** vornehm; **2.** best; **~** *dress·ing* *s.* **1.** ⚡ Kopfdüngung *f*; **2.** ◎ Oberflächenbeschotterung *f*.

tope¹ [təʊp] *v/t. u. v/i.* ‚saufen'.

tope² [təʊp] *s. ichth.* Glatthai *m*.

to·pee ['təʊpi:] *s.* Tropenhelm *m*.

top·er ['təʊpə] *s.* Säufer *m*, Zecher *m*.

'top|·flight *adj.* F erstklassig, prima; **'~·flight·er** → *topnotcher*; **~·gal·lant** [‚tɒp'gælənt; ⚓ tə'g-] ⚓ **I** *s.* Bramsegel *n*; **II** *adj.* Bram...: **~** *sail*; **~** *gear* *s. mot.* höchster Gang; **'~·grade** *adj.* erstklassig; **~** *hat* *s.* Zy'linder(hut) *m*; **‚~·'heav·y** *adj.* **1.** oberlastig (*Gefäß etc.*); **2.** ⚓ topplastig; **3.** ✈ kopflastig; **4.** ✝ a) 'überbewertet (*Wertpapiere*), b) 'überkapitalisiert (*Unternehmen*); **‚~·'hole** → *topflight*.

top·ic ['tɒpɪk] *s.* **1.** Thema *n*, Gegenstand *m*; **2.** *phls.* Topik *f*; **'top·i·cal** [-kl] **I** *adj.* □ **1.** örtlich, lo'kal (*a.* ⚕): **~** *colo(u)rs* topische Farben; **2.** a) aktu-'ell, b) zeitkritisch: **~** *song* Lied *n* mit aktuellen Anspielungen; **3.** the'matisch; **II** *s.* **4.** aktu'eller Film; **top·i·cal·i·ty** [‚tɒpɪ'kælətɪ] *s.* aktu'elle *od.* lo'kale Bedeutung.

top| kick *Am. sl. für* → *top sergeant*; **'~·knot** *s.* **1.** Haarknoten *m*; **2.** *orn.* (Feder)Haube *f*, Schopf *m*.

top·less ['tɒplɪs] *adj.* **1.** ohne Kopf; Oben-'ohne-...: **~** *dress* (*night club, waitress*).

‚top|·'line *adj.* **1.** promi'nent; **2.** wichtigst: **~** *news*; **‚~·'lin·er** *s.* F Promi'nente(r *m*) *f*; **'~·mast** [-mɑːst; -məst] *s.* ⚓ (Mars)Stenge *f*; **‚~·'most** *adj.* höchst, oberst; **‚~·'notch** *adj.* F prima, erstklassig; **‚~·'notch·er** *s.* F ‚Ka'none' *m* (*Könner*).

to·pog·ra·pher [tə'pɒɡrəfə] *s. geogr.* Topo'graph *m*; **top·o·graph·ic, top·o·graph·i·cal** [‚tɒpə'ɡræfɪk(l)] *adj.* topo'graphisch; **to'pog·ra·phy** [-fɪ] *s.* **1.** *geogr., a.* ⚕ Topogra'phie *f*; **2.** ✕ Geländekunde *f*.

top·per ['tɒpə] *s.* **1.** △ oberer Stein; **2.** ✝ F (oben'auf liegendes) Schaustück (*Obst etc.*); **3.** F Zy'linder *m* (*Hut*); **4.** F a) ‚(tolles) Ding', b) ‚Pfundskerl' *m*; **top·ping** ['tɒpɪŋ] *adj.* □ F prima, fabelhaft.

top·ple ['tɒpl] **I** *v/i.* **1.** wackeln; **2.** kippen, stürzen, purzeln: **~** *down* (*od. over*) umkippen, hinpurzeln, niederstürzen; **II** *v/t.* **3.** ins Wanken bringen, stürzen: **~** *over et.* umstürzen, -kippen; **4.** *fig. Regierung* stürzen.

‚top·'qual·i·ty prod·uct *s.* 'Spitzenpro-‚dukt *n*.

tops [tɒps] *adj.* F prima, erstklassig, ‚super'.

top|·sail ['tɒpsl] *s.* ⚓ Marssegel *n*; **~** *saw·yer* *s.* F *fig.* ‚hohes Tier'; **‚~·'se·cret** *adj.* streng geheim; **‚~·'sell·ing** *adj.* meistverkauft; **~** *ser·geant* *s.* ✕ *Am.* F Hauptfeldwebel *m*, ‚Spieß' *m*; **'~·soil** *s.* ✓ Ackerkrume *f*, Mutterboden *m*.

top·sy-tur·vy [‚tɒpsɪ'tɜːvɪ] **I** *adv.* **1.** das Oberste zu'unterst, auf den Kopf: *turn everything* **~** alles auf den Kopf stellen; **2.** kopf'über kopf'unter *fallen*; **3.** drunter u. drüber; **II** *adj.* **4.** auf den Kopf gestellt, in wildem Durchein'ander, cha'otisch; **III** *s.* **5.** (wildes *od.* heilloses) Durchein'ander, Kuddelmuddel *m*; **‚top·sy-'tur·vy·dom** [-dəm] → *topsy-turvy* 5.

toque [təʊk] *s.* **1.** *hist.* Ba'rett *n*; **2.** Toque *f* (*randloser Damenhut*).

tor [tɔː] *s. Brit.* Felsturm *m*.

to·ra(h) ['tɔːrə] *s.* **1.** ⚛ *das* Gesetz Mosis; **2.** Tho'ra *f*.

torch [tɔːtʃ] *s.* **1.** Fackel *f* (*a. fig. der Wissenschaft etc.*): *carry a* **~** *for Am. fig.* Mädchen (von ferne) verehren; **2.** *a. electric* **~** *Brit.* Taschenlampe *f*; **3.** ◎ a) Schweißbrenner *m*, b) → *torch lamp*; **4.** *Am.* Brandstifter *m*; **'~·bear·er** *s.* Fackelträger *m* (*a. fig.*); **~** *lamp* ◎ Lötlampe *f*; **'~·light** *s.* Fackelschein *m*: **~** *procession* Fackelzug *m*; **~** *pine* *s.* ❀ (*Amer.*) Pechkiefer *f*; **~** *sing·er* *s.*, **~** *song* *s.* ‚Schnulze' *f*, sentimen'tales Liebeslied.

tore [tɔː] *pret. von tear²*.

tor·e·a·dor ['tɒrɪədɔː] (*Span.*) *s.* Torea'dor *m*, berittener Stierkämpfer.

to·re·ro [tɒ'reərəʊ] *pl.* **-ros** (*Span.*) *s.* To'rero *m*, Stierkämpfer *m* (*zu Fuß*).

tor·ment **I** *v/t.* [tɔː'ment] **1.** *bsd. fig.* quälen, peinigen, foltern, plagen (*with* mit): **~ed with** gequält *od.* gepeinigt von *Zweifel etc.*; **II** *s.* ['tɔːment] **2.** Qual *f*, Pein *f*, Marter *f*: *be in* **~** Qualen ausstehen; **3.** Plage *f*; **4.** Quälgeist *m*; **tor·men·tor** [-tə] *s.* **1.** Peiniger *m*; **2.** Quälgeist *m*; **3.** ⚓ lange Fleischgabel; **4.** *thea.* vordere Ku'lisse; **tor'men·tress** [-trɪs] *s.* Peinigerin *f*.

torn [tɔːn] *p.p. von tear²*.

tor·na·do [tɔː'neɪdəʊ] *pl.* **-does** *s.* **1.** Tor'nado *m*: a) *Wirbelsturm in den USA*, b) *tropisches Wärmegewitter*; **2.** *fig.* a) (Beifall-, Pro'test)Sturm *m*, b) Wirbelwind *m* (*Person*).

tor·pe·do [tɔː'piːdəʊ] **I** *pl.* **-does** *s.* **1.** ⚓ Tor'pedo *m*; **2.** *a. aerial* **~** ✈ 'Lufttor-‚pedo *m*; **3.** *a. toy* **~** Knallerbse *f*; **4.** *ichth.* Zitterrochen *m*; **5.** *Am. sl.* ‚Killer' *m*; **II** *v/t.* **6.** torpedieren (*a. fig. vereiteln*): **~** *boat* *s.* ⚓ Tor'pedoboot *n*; **~** *plane* *s.* ✕ Tor'pedoflugzeug *n*; **~** *tube* *s.* Tor'pedorohr *n*.

tor·pid ['tɔːpɪd] **I** *adj.* □ **1.** starr, erstarrt, betäubt; **2.** träge, schlaff; **3.** a'pathisch, stumpf; **II** *s.* **4.** *mst* **tor·pid·i·ty** [tɔː'pɪdətɪ], **'tor·pid·ness** [-nɪs], **'tor·por** [-pə] *s.* **1.** Erstarrung *f*, Betäubung *f*; **2.** Träg-, Schlaffheit *f*, *# a.* Torpor *m*; **3.** Apa'thie *f*, Stumpfheit *f*.

torque [tɔːk] *s.* ◎, *phys.* 'Drehmo‚ment *n*; **~** *shaft* *s.* ◎ Dreh-, Torsi'onsstab *m*.

tor·re·fy ['tɒrɪfaɪ] *v/t.* rösten, darren.

tor·rent ['tɒrənt] *s.* **1.** reißender Strom, *bsd.* Wild-, Sturzbach *m*; **2.** (Lava-) Strom *m*; **3.** **~s** *of rain* sintflutartige

Regenfälle: *it rains in* **~s** es gießt in Strömen; **4.** *fig.* Strom *m*, Schwall *m*, Sturzbach *m* *von Fragen etc.*; **tor·ren·tial** [tə'renʃl] *adj.* □ **1.** reißend, strömend, sturzbachartig; **2.** sintflutartig: **~** *rain(s)*; **3.** *fig.* a) wortreich, b) wild, ungestüm.

tor·rid ['tɒrɪd] *adj.* **1.** sengend, brennend heiß (*a. fig. Leidenschaft etc.*): **~** *zone* *geogr.* heiße Zone; **2.** ausgedörrt, verbrannt: **~** *plain*.

tor·sion ['tɔːʃn] *s.* **1.** *a.* ⚕ Drehung *f*; **2.** ◎, *phys.* Torsi'on *f*, Verdrehung *f*: **~** *balance* Drehwaage *f*; **3.** # Abschnürung *f e-r Arterie*; **'tor·sion·al** [-ʃənl] *adj.* Dreh..., (Ver)Drehungs..., Torsi-ons...: **~** *force*.

tor·so ['tɔːsəʊ] *pl.* **-sos** *s.* Torso *m*: a) Rumpf *m*, b) *fig.* Bruchstück *n*, unvollendetes Werk.

tort [tɔːt] *s.* # unerlaubte Handlung, zi'vilrechtliches De'likt: *law of* **~s** Schadenersatzrecht *n*; **'~·fea·sor** [-‚fiːzə] *s.* # rechtswidrig Handelnde(r) *m*.

tor·til·la [tɔː'tiːə] (*Span.*) *s. Am.* Tor'tilla *f* (*Maiskuchen*).

tor·tious ['tɔːʃəs] *adj.* □ # rechtswidrig: **~** *act* → *tort*.

tor·toise ['tɔːtəs] **I** *s. zo.* Schildkröte *f*: *as slow as a* **~** *fig.* (langsam) wie e-e Schnecke; **II** *adj.* Schildpatt...; **'~·shell** *s.* Schildpatt *n*: **~** *cat* *zo.* Schildpattkatze *f*.

tor·tu·os·i·ty [‚tɔːtjʊ'ɒsɪtɪ] *s.* **1.** Krümmung *f*, Windung *f*; **2.** Gewundenheit *f* (*a. fig.*); **3.** *fig.* 'Umständlichkeit *f*; **tor·tu·ous** ['tɔːtjʊəs] *adj.* □ **1.** gewunden, verschlungen, gekrümmt; **2.** *fig.* gewunden, 'umständlich; **3.** *fig.* ‚krumm', unehrlich.

tor·ture ['tɔːtʃə] **I** *s.* **1.** Folter(ung) *f*: *put to the* **~** foltern; **2.** *fig.* Tor'tur *f*, Marter *f*, (Folter)Qual(en pl.) *f*; **II** *v/t.* **3.** foltern, martern, *fig. a.* quälen, peinigen; **4.** *Text etc.* entstellen; **'tor·tur·er** [-ərə] *s.* **1.** Folterknecht *m*; **2.** *fig.* Peiniger *m*.

to·rus ['tɔːrəs] *pl.* **-ri** [-raɪ] *s.* △, ⚕, ◎, ❀, ✽ Torus *m*.

To·ry ['tɔːrɪ] **I** *s.* **1.** *pol. Brit.* Tory *m*, (*contp.* 'Ultra)Konserva‚tive(r) *m*; **2.** *hist.* Tory *m* (*Loyalist in Amerika*); **II** *adj.* Tory..., konserva'tiv; **'To·ry·ism** [-ɪɪzəm] **1.** To'rysmus *m*; **2.** 'Ultrakonserva‚tismus *m*.

tosh [tɒʃ] *s. Brit. sl.* ‚Quatsch' *m*.

toss [tɒs] **I** *v/t.* **1.** werfen, schleudern: **~** *off* a) *Reiter* abwerfen (*Pferd*), b) *Getränk* hinunterstürzen, c) *Arbeit* ‚hin'hauen'; **~** *up* hochschleudern, *in e-r Decke* prellen; **2.** *a.* **~** *up Münze etc., a. Kopf* hochwerfen: **~** *s.o. for* mit j-m um *et.* losen (*durch Münzwurf*); **3.** *a.* **~** *a·bout* hin u. her schleudern, schütteln; **4.** ⚓ *Riemen* pieken: **~** *oars!* Riemen hoch!; **5.** *Am. sl. j-n* ‚filzen'; **II** *v/i.* **6.** *a.* **~** *about* sich im *Schlaf etc.* hin u. her werfen *od.* wälzen; **7.** *a.* **~** *about* hin u. her geworfen werden, geschüttelt werden; hin und her schwanken; flattern; **8.** rollen (*Schiff*); **9.** schwer gehen (*See*); **10.** *a.* **~** *up* (durch Hochwerfen e-r Münze) losen (*for* um); **III** *s.* **11.** Werfen *n*, Wurf *m*; **12.** Hoch-, Zu'rückwerfen *n des Kopfes*; **13.** a) Hochwerfen *n e-r Münze*, b) → *toss-up*; **14.** Sturz *m vom Pferd etc.*: *take a* **~** stürzen, *bsd.* abgeworfen werden; **'~·up** *s.* **1.** Losen *n* mit e-r Münze, Loswurf *m*; **2.** *fig.* ungewisse Sache: *it is a* **~** *whether* es ist völlig offen, ob.

tot¹ [tɒt] *s.* F **1.** Knirps *m*, Kerlchen *n*; **2.** *Brit.* Schlückchen *n* (*Alkohol*); **3.** *fig.*

Häppchen *n*.

tot² [tɒt] **F I** *s*. **1.** (Gesamt)Summe *f*; **2.** a) Additi'onsaufgabe *f*, b) Additi'on *f*; **II** *v/t*. **3.** ~ *up* zs.-zählen; **III** *v/i*. **4.** ~ *up* sich belaufen (*to* auf *acc.*); sich summieren.

to·tal ['təʊtl] **I** *adj*. □ **1.** ganz, gesamt, Gesamt...; **2.** to'tal, Total..., völlig, gänzlich; **II** *s*. **3.** (Gesamt)Summe *f*, Gesamtbetrag *m*, -menge *f*: *a* ~ *of 20 cases* insgesamt 20 Kisten; **4.** *die* Gesamtheit, *das* Ganze; **III** *v/t*. **5.** zs.-zählen; **6.** insgesamt betragen, sich belaufen auf (*acc.*): *total(l)ing $70* im Gesamtbetrag von 70 Dollar; **7.** *Am*. F *Auto* zu Schrott fahren; **to·tal·i·tar·i·an** [ˌtəʊtælɪ'teərɪən] *adj. pol.* totali'tär; **to·tal·i·tar·i·an·ism** [ˌtəʊtælɪ'teərɪənɪzəm] *s*. totali'täres Sy'stem; **to·tal·i·ty** [təʊ'tælətɪ] *s*. **1.** Gesamtheit *f*; **2.** Vollständigkeit *f*; **3.** *ast*. to'tale Verfinsterung; '**to·tal·i·za·tor** [-təlaɪzeɪtə] *s*. *Pferderennen*: Totali'sator *m*; '**to·tal·ize** [-təlaɪz] *v/t*. **1.** zs.-zählen; **2.** (zu e-m Ganzen) zs.-fassen; '**to·tal·iz·er** [-təlaɪzə] → *totalizator*.

tote¹ [təʊt] *s*. *sl*. → *totalizator*.

tote² [təʊt] *v/t*. **F 1.** tragen (mit sich) schleppen; **2.** transportieren; ~ *bag* *s*. *Am*. Einkaufs-, Tragtasche *f*.

to·tem ['təʊtəm] *s*. Totem *n*; ~ *pole*, ~ *post* *s*. Totempfahl *m*.

tot·ter ['tɒtə] *v/i*. **1.** torkeln, wanken: ~ *to one's grave* *fig*. dem Grabe zuwanken; **2.** (sch)wanken, wackeln: ~ *to its fall* *fig*. (allmählich) zs.-brechen (*Reich etc.*); '**tot·ter·ing** [-ərɪŋ] *adj*. □, '**tot·ter·y** [-ərɪ] *adj*. wack(e)lig, (sch)wankend.

touch [tʌtʃ] **I** *s*. **1.** Berührung *f*: *at a* ~ beim Berühren; *on the slightest* ~ bei der leisesten Berührung; *it has a velvety* ~ es fühlt sich wie Samt an; *that was a (near)* ~ F das hätte ins Auge gehen können; **2.** Tastsinn *m*: *it is soft to the* ~ es fühlt sich weich an; **3.** (*Pinsel- etc.*)Strich *m*: *put the finishing ~es to* letzte Hand legen an (*acc.*), e-r Sache den letzten Schliff geben; **4.** ♪ a) Anschlag *m* des Pianisten *od.* des Pianos, b) Strich *m* des Geigers; **5.** *fig*. Fühlung(nahme) *f*, Verbindung *f*, Kon'takt *m*: *get into* ~ *with* sich in Verbindung setzen mit, Fühlung nehmen mit; *please get in* ~! bitte melden (Sie sich)!; *keep in* ~ *with* in Verbindung bleiben mit; *lose* ~ *with* den Kontakt mit *j-m od.* e-r Sache verlieren; *put s.o. in* ~ *with* j-n in Verbindung setzen mit; *within* ~ in Reichweite; **6.** *fig*. Hand *f* des *Meisters etc.*, Stil *m*; (souve'räne) Ma'nier: *light* ~ leichte Hand; *with sure* ~ mit sicherer Hand; **7.** Einfühlungsvermögen *n*, Feingefühl *n*; **8.** e-e Spur *Pfeffer etc.*: *a* ~ *of red* ein rötlicher Hauch; **9.** Anflug *m* von *Sarkasmus etc.*, Hauch *m* von *Romantik etc.*: *he has a* ~ *of genius* er hat e-e geniale Ader; **10.** ♯ *etc.* (leichter) Anfall: *a* ~ *of flu* e-e leichte Grippe; *a* ~ *of the sun* ein leichter Sonnenstich; **11.** (besondere) Note, Zug *m*: *the personal* ~ die persönliche Note; **12.** *fig*. Stempel *m*, Gepräge *n*; **13.** Probe *f*: *put to the* ~ auf die Probe stellen; **14.** a) *Rugby etc.*: Mark *f*, b) *Fußball*: Seitenaus *n*; **15.** Fangspiel *n*; **16.** *sl*. a) Anpumpen *n*, b) gepumptes Geld: *he is a soft* ~ er lässt sich leicht anpumpen, *weitS.* er ist ein leichtes Opfer; **II** *v/t*. **17.** an-, berühren (*a. weitS. Essen etc. mst neg.*); anfassen, angreifen: ~ *the spot* das Richtige treffen; **18.** befühlen, betas-

ten; **19.** *Hand etc.* legen (*to* an *acc.*, auf *acc.*); **20.** mitein'ander in Berührung bringen; **21.** in Berührung kommen *od.* stehen mit; **22.** drücken auf (*acc.*), (leicht) anstoßen: ~ *the bell* klingeln; ~ *glasses* (mit den Gläsern) anstoßen; **23.** grenzen *od.* stoßen an (*acc.*); **24.** reichen an (*acc.*), erreichen; F *fig*. her'anreichen an (*acc.*), gleichkommen (*dat.*); **25.** erlangen, erreichen; **26.** ♪ *Saiten* rühren; *Ton* anschlagen; **27.** tönen, (leicht) färben, *fig*. färben, beeinflussen; **28.** beeindrucken; rühren, bewegen: *~ed to tears* zu Tränen gerührt; **29.** *fig*. verletzen, treffen; **30.** *fig*. berühren, betreffen; **31.** in Mitleidenschaft ziehen, mitnehmen: *~ed* a) angegangen (*Fleisch*), b) F ‚bekloppt', ‚nicht ganz bei Trost' (*Person*); **32.** *Ort* berühren, Halt machen in (*dat.*); *Hafen* anlaufen; **33.** *sl*. anpumpen (*for* um); **III** *v/i*. **34.** sich berühren; **35.** ~ *at* ⚓ anlegen bei *od.* in (*dat.*), anlaufen (*acc.*); **36.** (*up*)*on* *fig*. berühren: a) (kurz) erwähnen, b) betreffen;

Zssgn mit adv.:

touch| down *v/i*. **1.** *Rugby etc.*: e-n Versuch legen *od.* erzielen; **2.** ✈ aufsetzen; ~ *off* *v/t*. **1.** skizzieren; **2.** *Skizze* flüchtig entwerfen; **3.** e-e *Explosion*, *fig.* e-e *Krise etc.* auslösen, *fig. a.* entfachen; ~ *up* *v/t*. **1.** auffrischen (*a. fig.*), aufpolieren; verbessern; **2.** *phot.* retuschieren.

touch| and go *s*. ris'kante Sache, pre-'käre Situati'on: *it was* ~ es hing an e-m Haar, es stand auf des Messers Schneide; ‚~-and-'go *adj*. **1.** ris'kant; **2.** flüchtig, oberflächlich; '~-landing ✈ Aufsetz- u. Durchstartlandung *f*; '~-down *s*. **1.** *Rugby etc.*: Versuch *m*; **2.** ✈ Aufsetzen *n*.

touch·i·ness ['tʌtʃɪnɪs] *s*. Empfindlichkeit *f*.

touch·ing ['tʌtʃɪŋ] *adj*. □ *fig*. rührend, ergreifend.

'**touch|·line** *s*. a) *Fußball*: Seitenlinie *f*, b) *Rugby*: Marklinie *f*; '~-me-not *s*. ♣ (*fig*. F Blümlein *n*) Rührmichnichtan *n*; '~·pa·per *s*. 'Zündpa,pier *n*; ~ *screen* *s*. Touchscreen *m*, Berührungsbildschirm *m*; '~·stone *s*. **1.** *min.* Probierstein *m*; **2.** *fig*. Prüfstein *m*; ~ *sys·tem* *s*. Zehn-'fingersys,tem *n*; '~-tel·e·phone *s*. Tastentele,fon *n*; '~-type *v/i*. blind schreiben; '~·wood *s*. **1.** Zunder(holz *n*) *n*; **2.** ♣ Feuerschwamm *m*.

touch·y ['tʌtʃɪ] *adj*. □ **1.** empfindlich, reizbar; **2.** a) ris'kant, b) heikel, kitzlig (*Thema*).

tough [tʌf] **I** *adj*. □ **1.** *allg.* zäh: a) hart, 'widerstandsfähig, b) ro'bust, stark (*Person, Körper etc.*), c) hartnäckig (*Kampf, Wille etc.*); **2.** *fig*. schwierig, unangenehm, ‚bös' (*Arbeit etc., a.* F *Person*); F eklig, grob (*Person*): *it was a* ~ *going* es war ein hartes Stück Arbeit; *he is a* ~ *customer* mit ihm ist nicht gut Kirschen essen; *if things get* ~ wenn es ‚mulmig' wird; ~ *luck* F ‚Pech' *n*; **3.** rowdyhaft, bru'tal, übel, Verbrecher...: *get* ~ *with s.o.* j-m gegenüber massiv werden; **II** *s*. **4.** Rowdy *m*, Schläger(typ) *m*, ‚übler Kunde'; **tough·book** ['tʌfbʊk] *s*. *Computer*: Toughbook *n* (*besonders robuster Laptop*); **tough·en** ['tʌfn] *v/t. u. v/i*. zäh(er) *etc.* machen (werden); **tough·ie** ['tʌfɪ] *s*. F **1.** ‚harte Nuss', schwierige Sache, **2.** → *tough* 4; '**tough·ness** [-nɪs] *s*. **1.** Zähigkeit *f*, Härte *f* (*a. fig.*); **2.** Ro'bustheit *f*; **3.** *fig*. Hartnäckigkeit

f; **4.** Schwierigkeit *f*; **5.** Brutali'tät *f*.

tou·pee, *a*. **tou·pet** ['tuːpeɪ] (*Fr.*) *s*. Tou'pet *n* (*Haarersatzstück*).

tour [tʊə] **I** *s*. **1.** Tour *f* (*of* durch): a) (Rund)Reise *f*, (-)Fahrt *f*, b) Ausflug *m*, Wanderung *f*: *conducted* ~ a) Führung *f*, b) Gesellschaftsreise *f*; *the grand* ~ *hist*. (Bildungs)Reise durch Europa; ~ *operator* Reiseveranstalter *m*; **2.** Rundgang *m* (*of* durch): ~ *of inspection* Besichtigungsrundgang *od.* -rundfahrt *f*; **3.** *thea. etc.* Tour'nee *f*, Gastspielreise *f*: *go on* ~ auf Tournee gehen; **4.** ✕ (turnusmäßige) Dienstzeit; **II** *v/t*. **5.** bereisen; **III** *v/i*. **6.** e-e (*thea.* Gastspiel)Reise *od.* (*a. sport*) e-e Tour'nee machen (*through*, *about* durch); ~ *de force* [ˌtʊədə'fɔːs] (*Fr.*) *s*. **1.** Gewaltakt *m*; **2.** Glanzleistung *f*.

tour·ing ['tʊərɪŋ] *adj*. Touren..., Reise...: ~ *car* *mot.* Tourenwagen *m*; ~ *coach* Reisebus *m*; ~ *company* *thea.* Wanderbühne *f*; ~ *exhibition* Wanderausstellung *f*; **tour·ism** ['tʊərɪzəm] *s*. Reise-, Fremdenverkehr *m*, Tou'rismus *m*; **tour·ist** ['tʊərɪst] **I** *s*. Tou'rist(in), (Ferien-, Vergnügungs)Reisende(r *m*) *f*; **II** *adj*. Reise..., Fremden(verkehrs)..., Touristen...: ~ *agency* Reisebüro *n*; ~ *association* Fremdenverkehrsverband *m*; ~ *bureau*, ~ *office* a) Reisebüro *n*, b) Verkehrsamt *n*, -verein *m*; ~ *centre* (*Am.* *center*) Touristenort *m*; ~ *class* ⚓, ✈ Touristenklasse *f*; ~ *industry* Fremdenverkehr(sindustrie *f*) *m*; ~ (*information*) *office* Fremdenverkehrsamt *n*, -büro *n*; ~ *season* Reisezeit *f*; ~ *ticket* Rundreisekarte *f*; ~ *trap* Touristenfalle *f*; '**tour·ist·y** *adj. contp.* tou'ristisch, Touristen...

tour·na·ment ['tʊənəmənt] *s*. (*hist. Ritter-, a.* Tennis- *etc.*)Tur'nier *n*.

tour·ney ['tʊənɪ] *bsd. hist.* **I** *s*. Tur'nier *n*; **II** *v/i*. turnieren.

tour·ni·quet ['tʊənɪkeɪ] *s*. ♯ Aderpresse *f*.

tou·sle ['taʊzl] *v/t*. *Haar etc.* (zer)zausen, verwuscheln.

tout [taʊt] **I** *v/i*. **1.** (*bsd. aufdringliche* Kunden-, Stimmen)Werbung treiben (*for* für); **2.** *Pferderennen*: a) *Brit*. sich *durch Spionieren* gute Renntipps verschaffen, b) Wetttipps geben *od.* verkaufen; **II** *s*. **3.** Kundenschlepper *m*, -werber *m*; **4.** *Pferderennen*: a) *Brit*. ‚Spi'on' *m* beim Pferdetraining, b) Tippgeber *m*; **5.** (Karten)Schwarzhändler *m*.

tow¹ [təʊ] **I** *s*. **1.** a) Schleppen *n*, b) Schlepptau *n*: *have in* ~ im Schlepptau haben (*a. fig.*); *take* ~ sich schleppen lassen; *take in* ~ *bsd. fig*. ins Schlepptau nehmen; **2.** *bsd.* ⚓ Schleppzug *m*; **II** *v/t*. **3.** (ab)schleppen, ins Schlepptau nehmen: ~ *away* *Auto* abschleppen; *~ed flight* (*target*) Schleppflug *m* (-ziel *n*); **4.** *Schiff* treideln; **5.** *fig*. j-n abschleppen, *wohin* bugsieren.

tow² [təʊ] *s*. (Schwing)Werg *n*.

tow·age ['təʊɪdʒ] *s*. **1.** Schleppen *n*, Bugsieren *n*; **2.** Schleppgebühr *f*.

to·ward **1** *adj*. **1.** *obs.* fügsam; **2.** *obs. od. Am.* viel versprechend; **3.** im Gange, am Werk; **4.** bevorstehend; **II** *prp*. [tə'wɔːd] **5.** auf (*acc.*) ... zu, (nach) ... hin, auf ... hin, gegen *od.* zu ... (hin); **6.** *zeitlich*: gegen; **7.** *Gefühle etc.* gegen'über; **8.** *als Beitrag* zu, um e-r *Sache* willen, zum Zweck(e) (*gen.*): *efforts ~ reconciliation* Bemühungen um e-e Versöhnung; **to·wards** [tə'wɔːdz] → *toward* II.

'**tow·a·way** *adj*. Abschlepp...: ~ *zone*; '~-boat *s*. Schleppschiff *n*, Schlepper

m.

tow·el ['tauəl] **I** *s.* Handtuch *n*: *throw in the ~ Boxen*: das Handtuch werfen (*a. fig. sich geschlagen geben*); **II** *v/t.* (mit e-m Handtuch) (ab)trocknen, (-)reiben; **~ horse, ~ rack** *s.* Handtuchständer *m.*

tow·er ['tauə] **I** *s.* **1.** Turm *m*: **~ block** *Brit.* (Büro-, Wohn)Hochhaus *n*; **2.** Feste *f*, Bollwerk *n*: **~ of strength** *fig.* Stütze *f*, Säule *f*; **3.** Zwinger *m*, Festung *f* (*Gefängnis*); **4.** 🌫 Turm *m* (*Reinigungsanlage*); **II** *v/i.* **5.** (hoch)ragen, sich (em'por)türmen (*to* zu): **~ above** *et. od. j-n* (weit) überragen (*a. fig. turmhoch überlegen sein* [*dat.*]); **'tow·ered** [-əd] *adj.* (hoch) getürmt; **'tow·er·ing** [-ərɪŋ] *adj.* **1.** hoch, hoch aufragend; **2.** *fig.* maßlos, gewaltig: **~ ambition**; **~ passion**; **~ rage** rasende Wut.

tow·ing ['təuɪŋ] *adj.* (Ab)Schlepp...; **~ line, ~ path, ~ rope** → **towline, towpath, towrope**.

'tow·line *s.* **1.** ⚓ Treidelleine *f*, Schlepptau *n*; **2.** Abschleppseil *n*.

town [taun] **I** *s.* **1.** Stadt *f* (*unter dem Rang e-r city*); **2. the ~** *fig.* die Stadt: a) die Stadtbevölkerung, die Einwohnerschaft, b) das Stadtleben; **3.** *Brit.* Marktflecken *m*; **4.** *ohne art. die* (nächste) Stadt: a) Stadtzentrum *n*, b) *Brit. bsd.* London: *to ~* nach der *od.* in die Stadt, *Brit. bsd.* nach London; *out of ~* nicht in der Stadt, *Brit. bsd.* nicht in London, auswärts; *go to ~* F ,auf den Putz hauen'; → *paint* 2; **5.** *Brit.* Bürgerschaft *f e-r Universitätsstadt*; → *gown* 3; **II** *adj.* **6.** städtisch, Stadt..., Städte...; **'~-bred** *adj.* in der Stadt aufgewachsen; **~ cen·tre** *s. Brit.* Innenstadt *f*, City *f*; **~ clerk** *s.* 'Stadtdi,rektor *m*; **~ coun·cil** *s.* Stadtrat *m* (*Gremium*); **~ coun·cil·(l)or** *s.* Stadtrat(smitglied *n*) *m*; **~ cri·er** *s.* Ausrufer *m*; **~ hall** *s.* Rathaus *n*; **~ house** *s.* Stadt-, *Am.* Reihenhaus *n*; **~ plan·ning** *s.* Städte-, Stadtplanung *f*; **'~-scape** [-skeɪp] *s.* Stadtbild *n, paint.* -ansicht *f.*

towns·folk ['taunzfəuk] *s. pl.* Stadtleute *pl.*, Städter *pl.*

town·ship ['taunʃɪp] *s.* **1.** *hist.* (Dorf-, Stadt)Gemeinde *f od.* (-)Gebiet *n*; **2.** *Am.* Verwaltungsbezirk *m*; **3.** *surv. Am.* 6 Qua'dratmeilen großes Gebiet.

towns·man ['taunzmən] *s.* [*irr.*] **1.** Städter *m*, Stadtbewohner *m*; **2.** *a.* **fellow ~** Mitbürger *m*; **'~,peo·ple** [-nz-] → *townsfolk*.

'tow·path *s.* Treidelpfad *m*; **'~-rope** → *towline*.

tox·(a)e·mi·a [tɒk'siːmɪə] *s.* 🩸 Blutvergiftung *f.*

tox·ic, tox·i·cal ['tɒksɪk(l)] *adj.* □ giftig, toxisch, Gift...; **'tox·i·cant** [-sɪkənt] **I** *adj.* giftig, toxisch; **II** *s.* Gift (-stoff *m*) *n*; **tox·i·co·log·i·cal** [ˌtɒksɪkə'lɒdʒɪkl] *adj.* □ toxiko'logisch; **tox·i·col·o·gist** [ˌtɒksɪ'kɒlədʒɪst] *s.* 🩸 Toxikolo'gin *f*, Giftkundler *m*; **tox·i·col·o·gy** [ˌtɒksɪ'kɒlədʒɪ] *s.* 🩸 Toxikolo'gie *f*, Giftkunde *f*; **tox·ic waste** *s.* Giftmüll *m*; **'tox·in** [-sɪn] *s.* 🩸 Toxin *n*, Gift(stoff *m*) *n.*

toy [tɔɪ] **I** *s.* **1.** (Kinder)Spielzeug *n* (*a. fig.*); *pl.* Spielwaren *pl.*, -sachen *pl.*; **2.** *fig.* Tand *m*, ,Kinkerlitzchen' *n*; **II** *v/i.* **3.** (*with*) spielen (mit *e-m Gegenstand, fig. mit e-m Gedanken*), *fig. a.* liebäugeln (mit); **III** *adj.* **4.** Spielzeug..., Kinder..., Zwerg...: **~ dog** Schoßhund *m*; **~ train** Miniatur-, Kindereisenbahn *f*; **~ book** *s.* Bilderbuch *n*; **'~-box** *s.* Spielzeugkiste *f*; **'~-shop** *s.* Spielwarenhand-

lung *f.*

trace¹ [treɪs] *s.* Zugriemen *m*, Strang *m* (*Pferdegeschirr*): *in the ~s* angespannt (*a. fig.*); *kick over the ~s* *fig.* über die Stränge schlagen.

trace² [treɪs] **I** *s.* **1.** (Fuß-, Wagen-, Wild- *etc.*)Spur *f*: *hot on s.o.'s ~s* j-m dicht auf den Fersen; *without a ~* spurlos; **~ element** 🐟 Spurenelement *n*; **2.** *fig.* Spur *f*: a) ('Über)Rest *m*: **~s of ancient civilizations**, b) (An)Zeichen *n*: **~s of fatigue**, c) geringe Menge, bisschen: *not a ~ of fear* keine Spur von Angst; *a ~ of a smile* der Anflug e-s Lächelns; **3.** ⚔ a) Leuchtspur *f*, b) *Radar*: Bildspur *f*; **4.** Linie *f*: a) Aufzeichnung *f* (*Messgerät*), b) Zeichnung *f*, Skizze *f*, c) Pauszeichnung *f*, d) Grundriss *m*; **5.** *Am.* (markierter) Weg; **II** *v/t.* **6.** nachspüren (*dat.*), j-s Spur verfolgen; **7.** *Wild, Verbrecher* verfolgen, aufspüren; **8.** *a.* **~ out** *et. od. j-n* ausfindig machen *od.* aufspüren, *et.* auf-, herausfinden; **9.** *fig. e-r Entwicklung etc.* nachgehen, *e-e Sache* 'zu'rückverfolgen (*to* bis zu): **~ back** *et.* zu'rückverfolgen (*to* bis zu); **~ s.th. to** *et.* zu'rückführen auf (*acc.*), *et.* herleiten von; **10.** erkennen; **11.** *Pfad* verfolgen; **12.** *a.* **~ out** (auf)zeichnen, skizzieren, entwerfen; **13.** *Buchstaben* sorgfältig (aus)ziehen, schreiben; **14.** ⚙ a) *a.* **~ over** ('durch)pausen, b) *Bauflucht etc.* abstecken, *et.* Messung aufzeichnen (*Gerät*); **'trace·a·ble** [-səbl] *adj.* □ **1.** auffindbar, nachweisbar; **2.** zu'rückzuführen(d) (*to* auf *acc.*); **'trac·er** [-sə] *s.* **1.** Aufspürer(in); **2.** 🩸 *Am.* Lauf-, Suchzettel *m*; **3.** *Schneiderei*: Kopierrädchen *n*; **4.** ⚙ Punzen *m*; **5.** 🌫 Iso'topenindi,kator *m*; **6.** ⚔ a) *mst* **~ bullet, ~ shell** Leuchtspur-, Rauchspurgeschoss *n*, b) *mst* **~ composition** Leuchtspursatz *m*; **7.** a) technischer Zeichner, b) Pauser *m*; **'trac·er·y** [-sərɪ] *s.* **1.** △ Maßwerk *n an gotischen Fenstern*; **2.** Flechtwerk *n.*

tra·che·a [trə'kiːə] *pl.* **-che·ae** [-'kiːiː] *s.* **1.** *anat.* Tra'chea *f*, Luftröhre *f*; **2.** ⚘, *zo.* Tra'chee *f*; **tra·che·al** [-'kiːəl] *adj.* **1.** *anat.* Luftröhren...; **2.** *zo.* Tracheen...; **3.** ⚘ Gefäß...; **tra·che·i·tis** [ˌtræ-kɪ'aɪtɪs] *s.* 🩹 'Luftröhrenka,tarr(h) *m*; **tra·che·ot·o·my** [ˌtrækɪ'ɒtəmɪ] *s.* 🩹 Luftröhrenschnitt *m.*

trac·ing ['treɪsɪŋ] *s.* **1.** Suchen *n*, Nachforschung *f*; **2.** ⚙ a) (Auf)Zeichnen *n*, b) 'Durchpausen *n*; **3.** ⚙ a) Zeichnung *f*, (Auf)Riss *m*, Plan *m*, b) Pause *f*; **4.** Aufzeichnung *f* (*e-s Kardiographen etc.*); **~ file** *s.* 'Suchkar,tei *f*; **~ op·er·a·tion** *s.* Fahndung *f*; **~ pa·per** *s.* 'Pauspa,pier *n*; **~ serv·ice** *s.* Suchdienst *m.*

track [træk] **I** *s.* **1.** (Fuß-, Wild- *etc.*) Spur *f* (*a. fig.*), Fährte *f*: *on s.o.'s ~s* j-m auf der Spur; *be on the wrong ~* auf der falschen Spur *od.* auf dem Holzweg sein; *cover up one's ~s* s-e Spuren verwischen; *throw s.o. off the ~* j-n von der (richtigen) Spur ablenken; *keep ~ of fig. et.* verfolgen, sich auf dem Laufenden halten über (*acc.*); *lose ~ of* aus den Augen verlieren; *make ~s* *sl.* ,abhauen'; *make ~s for* schnurstracks losgehen auf (*acc.*); *stop in one's ~s* wie festgewurzelt stehen bleiben; *shoot s.o. in his ~s* j-n auf der Stelle niederschießen; **2.** 🛤 Gleis *n*, Geleise *n u. pl.*, Schienenstrang *m*: *off the ~* entgleist, aus den Schienen; *on ~* auf (der) Achse, rollend; *born on the wrong side of the ~s fig. Am.* aus ärmlichen Verhältnissen stammend; **3.** ⚓ Fahrwasser *n*; **4.** ⚓ übliche Route; **5.**

Weg *m*, Pfad *m*; **6.** (Ko'meten- *etc.*) Bahn *f*; **7.** *sport* a) (Renn-, Lauf-) Bahn *f*, b) *mst* **~ events** 'Laufdiszi,plinen *pl.*, c) *a.* **~-and-field sports** 'Leichtath,letik *f*; **8.** (Gleis-, Raupen-) Kette *f e-s Traktors etc.*; **9.** *mot.* a) Spurweite *f*, b) 'Reifenpro,fil *n*; **10.** *Computer, Tonband*: Spur *f*; **11.** *ped. Am.* Leistungsgruppe *f*; **II** *v/t.* **12.** nachspüren (*dat.*), *a. fig.* verfolgen (*acc.*); **13.** aufspüren: a) **~ down** *Wild, Verbrecher* zur Strecke bringen, b) ausfindig machen; **14.** *Weg* kennzeichnen; **15.** durch'queren; **16.** 🛤 *Am.* Gleise verlegen in (*dat.*); **17.** *Am.* (Schmutz)Spuren hinter'lassen auf (*dat.*); **18.** ⚙ mit Raupenketten versehen: **~ed vehicle** Ketten-, Raupenfahrzeug *n*; **III** *v/i.* **19.** Spur halten (*Räder*); **20.** *Film*: (mit der Kamera) fahren: **~ing shot** Fahraufnahme *f*; **IV** *adj.* **21.** 🛤 Gleis..., Schienen...; **22.** *sport* a) (Lauf)Bahn..., Lauf..., b) Leichtathletik...: **'track·age** [-kɪdʒ] *s.* 🛤 **1.** *coll.* Schienen *pl.*; **2.** Schienenlänge *f*; **3.** *Am.* Streckenbenutzungsrecht *n*, -gebühr *f*; **'track-and-'field** *adj.* Leichtathletik...; → *track* 7 c; **'track·ball** [-bɔːl] *s. Computer*: 'Trackball *m* (*Steuerkugel als Mausersatz*); **'track·er** [-kə] *s.* **1.** *bsd. hunt.* Spurenleser *m*: **~ dog** Spürhund *m*; **2.** *fig.* ,Spürhund' *m* (*Person*); **3.** ⚔ Zielgeber *m* (*Gerät*).

'track·lay·er *s.* **1.** 🛤 *Am.* Streckenarbeiter *m*; **2.** Raupenschlepper *m*; **'~·lay·ing** *adj.* ⚙ Raupen..., Gleisketten...: **~ vehicle.**

track·less ['træklɪs] *adj.* □ **1.** unbetreten; **2.** weg-, pfadlos; **3.** schienenlos; **4.** spurlos.

track meet *s. Am.* 'Leichtath,letikveranstaltung *f*; **~ shoe** *s.* Rennschuh *m*; **'~-suit** *s.* Trainingsanzug *m*, Jogginganzug *m*: **~ trousers** *pl.* Jogginghose *f*; **~ walk·ing** *s. sport* Bahngehen *n.*

tract¹ [trækt] *s.* **1.** (ausgedehnte) Fläche, Strecke *f*, (Land)Strich *m*, Gebiet *n*, Gegend *f*; **2.** Zeitraum *m*; **3.** *anat.* Trakt *m*, (Ver'dauungs- *etc.*)Sy,stem *n*: **respiratory ~** Atemwege *pl.*; **4.** *physiol.* (Nerven)Strang *m*: **optic ~** Sehstrang.

tract² [trækt] *s. eccl.* Trak'tat *m, n*; *contp.* Trak'tätchen *n.*

trac·ta·ble ['træktəbl] *adj.* **1.** □ lenk-, folg-, fügsam; **2.** *fig.* gefügig, geschmeidig (*Material*).

trac·tion ['trækʃn] *s.* **1.** Ziehen *n*; **2.** ⚙, *phys.* a) Zug *m*, b) Zugleistung *f*: **~ engine** Zugmaschine *f*; **3.** *phys.* Reibungsdruck *m*; **4.** *mot.* a) Griffigkeit *f* (*Reifen*), b) *a.* **~ of the road** Bodenhaftung *f*; **5.** Trans'port *m*, Fortbewegung *f*; **6.** *physiol.* Zs.-ziehung *f* (*Muskeln*); **'trac·tion·al** [-ʃənl], **'trac·tive** [-ktɪv] *adj.* ⚙ Zug...

trac·tor ['træktə] *s.* **1.** ⚙ 'Zugma,schine *f*, Traktor *m*, Schlepper *m*; **2.** ✈ a) Zugschraube *f*, b) *a.* **~ airplane** Flugzeug *n* mit Zugschraube; **~ truck** *s. Am. mot.* Sattelschlepper *m.*

trade [treɪd] *s.* **I** *s.* **1.** ✝ Handel *m*, (Handels)Verkehr *m*: **foreign ~** a) Außenhandel, b) ⚓ große Fahrt; **home ~** a) Binnenhandel, b) ⚓ kleine Fahrt; → *board* 9; **2.** ✝ Geschäft *n* od. a) Gewerbe *n*, Geschäftszweig *m*, Branche *f*, b) (Einzel-, Groß)Handel *m*, c) Geschäftslage *f*, -gewinn *m*: *be in ~* (Einzel)Händler sein; *do a good ~* gute Geschäfte machen; *sell to the ~* an Wiederverkäufer abgeben; **3.** ✝ *the ~*

a) *coll.* die Geschäftswelt, b) *Brit.* der Spiritu'osenhandel, c) die Kundschaft; **4.** Gewerbe *n*, Beruf *m*, Handwerk *n*: *the ~ coll.* die Zunft *od.* Gilde; **by ~** *Bäcker etc.* von Beruf; **every man to his ~** jeder, wie er es gelernt hat; ***the ~ of war** das Kriegshandwerk; **5.** *mst* **the ~s** *pl.* die Pas'satwinde *pl.*; **II** *v/i.* **6.** Handel treiben, handeln (*in* mit *et.*); in Geschäftsverbindung stehen (**with** mit *j-m*); *Am.* (ein)kaufen (**with** bei *j-m*, **at** in *e-m* Laden); **7. ~** (**up**)**on** *fig.* spekulieren *od.* ,reisen' auf (*acc.*), ausnutzen; **III** *v/t.* **8.** (aus)tauschen (**for** gegen); **9. ~ in** *bsd.* Auto in Zahlung geben; **~ ac·cept·ance** *s.* ✝ 'Handelsak,zept *n*; **~ ac·count** *s.* Bilanz: a) **~s payable** Warenschulden *pl.*, b) **~s receivable** Warenforderungen *pl.*; **~ as·so·ci·a·tion** *s.* **1.** Wirtschaftsverband *m*; **2.** Arbeitgeberverband *m*; **~ bal·ance** *s.* 'Handelsbi,lanz *f*; **~ bar·riers** *s. pl.* Handelsschranken *pl.*; **~ bill** *s.* Warenwechsel *m*; **~ cy·cle** *s.* Konjunk'turzyklus *m*; **~ di·rec·to·ry** *s.* Branchen-, Firmenverzeichnis *n*, 'Handels-a,dressbuch *n*; **~ dis·count** *s.* 'Händlerra,batt *m*; **~ dis·pute** *s.* Handelsstreit *m*; **~ fair** *s.* (Handels)Messe *f*; **~ gap** *s.* 'Handelsbi,lanzdefizit *n*; **~-in** *s.* in Zahlung gegebene Sache (*bsd.* Auto): **~ value** Eintausch-, Verrechnungswert *m*; **'~-mark I** *s.* **1.** Warenzeichen *n*: **registered ~** eingetragenes Warenzeichen; **2.** *fig.* Kennzeichen *n*; **II** *v/t.* **3.** *Ware* gesetzlich schützen lassen: **~ed goods** Markenartikel; **~ mis·sion** *s. pol.* 'Handelsmissi,on *f*; **~ name** *s.* **1.** Handelsbezeichnung *f*, Markenname *m*; **2.** Firmenname *m*, Firma *f*; **~ price** *s.* (Groß)Handelspreis *m*.

trad·er ['treɪdə] *s.* **1.** Händler *m*, Kaufmann *m*; **2.** *Börse:* 'Wertpa,pierhändler *m*; **3.** ♣ Handelsschiff *n*.

trade| school *s.* Gewerbeschule *f*; **~ se·cret** *s.* Geschäftsgeheimnis *n*; **~ show** *s.* Filmvorführung *f* für Verleiher u. Kritiker.

trades·man ['treɪdzmən] *s.* [*irr.*] **1.** (Einzel)Händler *m*; **2.** Ladeninhaber *m*; **3.** Handwerker *m*; **'~,peo·ple** [-z,p-] *s. pl.* Geschäftsleute *pl.*

trade| sym·bol *s.* Bild *n* (*Warenzeichen*); **~ un·ion** *s.* Gewerkschaft *f*; **~ un·ion·ism** *s.* Gewerkschaftswesen *n*; **~ un·ion·ist** *s.* Gewerkschaftler(in); **~ wind** *s.* Pas'satwind *m*.

trad·ing ['treɪdɪŋ] **I** *s.* **1.** Handeln *n*; **2.** Handel *m* (**in** mit *et.*, **with** mit *j-m*); **II** *adj.* **3.** Handels...; **~ a·re·a** *s.* ✝ Absatzgebiet *n*; **~ cap·i·tal** *s.* Be'triebskapi,tal *n*; **~ com·pa·ny** *s.* Handelsgesellschaft *f*; **~ post** *s.* Handelsniederlassung *f*; **~ stamp** *s.* Ra'battmarke *f*.

tra·di·tion [trə'dɪʃn] *s.* **1.** Traditi'on *f*: a) (mündliche) Über'lieferung (*a. eccl.*), b) Herkommen *n*, (alter) Brauch, Brauchtum *n*: **be in the ~** sich im Rahmen der Tradition halten; **2.** ⚖ Auslieferung *f*, 'Übergabe *f*; **tra'di·tion·al** [-ʃənl] *adj.* □ traditio'nell, Traditions...: a) (mündlich) über'liefert, b) herkömmlich, brauchtümlich, (alt)hergebracht, üblich; **tra'di·tion·al·ism** [-ʃnəlɪzəm] *s. bsd. eccl.* Traditiona'lismus *m*, Festhalten *n* an der Über'lieferung.

tra·duce [trə'djuːs] *v/t.* verleumden.

traf·fic ['træfɪk] **I** *s.* **1.** (öffentlicher, Straßen-, Schiffs-, Eisenbahn- *etc.*) Verkehr; **2.** (Per'sonen-, Güter-, Nachrichten-, Fernsprech- *etc.*)Verkehr *m*;

3. a) (Handels)Verkehr *m*, Handel *m* (**in** in *dat.*, mit), b) *b.s.* ('ille,galer) Handel: **drug ~**; **4.** *fig.* a) Verkehr *m*, Geschäft(e *pl.*) *n*), b) Austausch *m* (**in** von): **~ in ideas**; **II** *v/i. pret. u. p.p.* **'traf·ficked** [-kt] **5.** handeln, Handel treiben (**in** in *dat.*, **with** mit); **6.** *fig.* verhandeln (**with** mit).

traf·fi·ca·tor ['træfɪkeɪtə] *s. mot. Brit.* a) Blinker *m*, b) *hist.* Winker *m*.

traf·fic| calm·ing *s.* Verkehrsberuhigung *f*; **~ cen·sus** *s.* Verkehrszählung *f*; **~ cir·cle** *s. mot. Am.* Kreisverkehr *m*; **~ guid·ance sys·tem** *s.* Ver'kehrsleitsys,tem *n*; **~ is·land** *s.* Verkehrsinsel *f*; **~ jam** *s.* Verkehrsstauung *f*, -stockung *f*, (Fahrzeug)Stau *m*.

traf·fick·er ['træfɪkə] *s.* (*a.* 'ille,galer) Händler.

traf·fic| lane *s. mot.* Spur *f*; **~ lights** *s. pl.* Verkehrsampel *f*; **~ man·age·ment** *s.* Verkehrsmanagement *n*; **~ man·ag·er** *s.* ✝ **1.** Versandleiter *m*; **2.** Be'triebsdi,rektor *m*; **~ of·fence** *s. Brit.*, **~ of·fense** *s. Am.* Ver'kehrsde,likt *n*; **~ of·fend·er** *s.* Verkehrssünder *m*; **~ reg·u·la·tions** *s. pl.* Verkehrsvorschriften *pl.*, (Straßen)Verkehrsordnung *f*; **~ sign** *s.* Verkehrszeichen *n*, -schild *n*; **~ ward·en** *s.* Poli'tesse *f*.

tra·ge·di·an [trə'dʒiːdjən] *s.* **1.** Tragiker *m*, Trauerspieldichter *m*; **2.** *thea.* Tra'göde *m*, tragischer Darsteller *m*; **tra·ge·di·enne** [trədʒiː'djen] *s. thea.* Tra'gödin *f*; **trag·e·dy** ['trædʒɪdɪ] *s.* **1.** Tra'gödie *f*: a) *thea.* Trauerspiel *n*, b) *fig.* tragische Begebenheit, *a.* Unglück *n*; **2.** *fig.* das Tragische, Unglück *n*; **trag·ic, trag·i·cal** ['trædʒɪk(l)] *adj.* □ *thea. u. fig.* tragisch: **~ly** tragischerweise; **trag·i·com·e·dy** [,trædʒɪ'kɒmɪdɪ] *s.* Tragiko'mödie *f* (*a. fig.*); **trag·i·com·ic** [,trædʒɪ'kɒmɪk] *adj.* (□ **~ally**) tragi'komisch.

trail [treɪl] **I** *v/t.* **1.** (nach)schleppen, (-) schleifen, hinter sich herziehen: **~ one's coat** *fig.* Streit suchen; **2.** verfolgen (*acc.*), nachspüren (*dat.*), ,beschatten' (*acc.*); **3.** zu'rückbleiben hinter (*dat.*); **II** *v/i.* **4.** schleifen (*Rock etc.*); **5.** wehen, flattern; her'unterhängen; **6.** ♀ kriechen, sich ranken; **7.** (sich da'hin-) ziehen (*Rauch etc.*); **8.** sich da'hinschleppen; **9.** nachhinken (*a. fig.*); **III** *v/i.* **11.** geschleppter Teil, *z.B.* Schleppe *f* (*Kleid*); **12.** *fig.* Schweif *m*, Schwanz *m* (*Meteor etc.*): **~ of smoke** Rauchfahne *f*; **13.** Spur *f*: **~ of blood**; **14.** *hunt. u. fig.* Fährte *f*, Spur *f*: **on s.o.'s ~** j-m auf der Spur *od.* auf den Fersen; **off the ~** von der Spur abgekommen; **15.** (Trampel)Pfad *m*, Weg *m*: **blaze the ~** a) den Weg markieren, b) *fig.* den Weg bahnen (**for** für), bahnbrechend sein; **'~,blaz·er** *s.* **1.** Pistensucher *m*; **2.** *fig.* Bahnbrecher *m*, Pio'nier *m*.

trail·er ['treɪlə] *s.* **1.** ♀ Kriechpflanze *f*; rankender Ausläufer *m*; **2.** *mot.* a) Anhänger *m*, b) *Am.* Wohnwagen *m*, Caravan *m*: **~ camp**, **~ park** Platz *m* für Wohnwagen; **3.** *Film, TV:* Trailer *m* (*Filmausschnitte zu Werbezwecken*); **'trail·er·ite** *s. Am.* Caravaner *m*.

trail·ing| aer·i·al ['treɪlɪŋ] *s.* ⚡ 'Schlepp-an,tenne *f*; **~ ax·le** *s. mot.* nicht angetriebene Achse, Schleppachse *f*.

train [treɪn] **I** *s.* **1.** (Eisenbahn)Zug *m*: **~ journey** Bahnfahrt *f*; **~ staff** Zugpersonal *n*; **by ~** mit der Bahn; **be on the ~** im Zug sein *od.* sitzen; **take a ~ to** mit dem Zug fahren nach; **2.** Zug *m* von *Personen, Wagen etc.*, Kette *f*, Ko'lon-

ne *f*: **~ of barges** Schleppzug (*Kähne*); **3.** Gefolge *n* (*a. fig.*): **have** (*od.* **bring**) **in its ~** *et.* mit sich bringen, zur Folge haben; **4.** *fig.* Folge *f*, Kette *f*, Reihe *f* *von Ereignissen etc.*: **~ of thought** Gedankengang *m*; **in ~** a) im Gang, im Zuge, b) bereit (**for** für); **put in ~** in Gang setzen; **5.** Schleppe *f* am Kleid; **6.** (Ko'meten)Schweif *m*; **7.** ✕, ✕ Zündlinie *f*; **8.** ⚙ ☉ Räder-, Triebwerk *n*; **II** *v/t.* **9.** auf-, erziehen; **10.** ♀ ziehen; **11.** *j-n* ausbilden (*a.* ✕), *a. Auge, Geist etc.* schulen: **→ trained**; **12.** *j-m et.* einexerzieren, beibringen; **13.** a) *Sportler, a.* Pferde trainieren, b) *Tiere* abrichten, dressieren (**to do** zu tun), *Pferd* zureiten; **14.** ✕ *Geschütz* richten (**on** auf *acc.*); **III** *v/i.* **15.** sich ausbilden (**for** zu, als); sich schulen *od.* üben; **16.** *sport* trainieren (**for** für); **17.** *a.* **~ it** F mit der Bahn fahren; **~ down** *v/i. sport* abtrainieren, ,abkochen'.

'train|,bear·er *s.* Schleppenträger *m*; **~ call** *s. teleph.* Zuggespräch *n*.

trained [treɪnd] *adj.* **1.** geübt, geschult (*Auge, Geist etc.*); **2.** (voll) ausgebildet, geschult, Fach...: **~ men** Fachkräfte; **train·ee** [treɪ'niː] *s.* **1.** a) Auszubildende(r *m*) *f*, Lehrling *m*, b) Prakti'kant (-in), c) *Management:* Trai'nee *m*, *f*: **~ nurse** Lernschwester *f*; **2.** ✕ *Am.* Rekrut *m*; **'train·er** [-nə] *s.* **1.** Ausbilder *m*; **2.** *sport* Trainer *m* (*od.* **~'s**) **bench** Trainerbank *f*; **3.** a) Abrichter *m*, ('Hunde- *etc.*)Dres,seur *m*, b) Zureiter *m*; **4.** ✈ a) Schulflugzeug *n*, b) ('Flug)Simu,lator *m*; **5.** *mst. pl.* Turnschuh *m*.

train fer·ry *s.* Eisenbahnfähre *f*.

train·ing ['treɪnɪŋ] **I** *s.* **1.** Schulung *f*, Ausbildung *f*; **2.** Üben *n*; **3.** *sport* Training *n*: **be in ~** a) im Training stehen, b) (gut) in Form sein; **go into ~** das Training aufnehmen; **out of ~** nicht in Form; **4.** a) Abrichten *n* von *Tieren*, b) Zureiten *n*; **II** *adj.* **5.** Ausbildungs..., Schul(ungs)..., Lehr...; **6.** *sport* Trainings...; **~ camp** *s.* **1.** *sport* Trainingslager *n*; **2.** ✕ Ausbildungslager *n*; **~ cen·ter** *Am.*, **~ cen·tre** *Brit.* *s.* Ausbildungszentrum *n*; **~ film** *s.* Lehrfilm *m*; **~ school** *s.* **1.** *ped.* Aufbauschule *f*; **2.** ⚖ Jugendstrafanstalt *f*; **~ ship** *s.* ♣ Schulschiff *n*.

'train|·load *s.* Zugladung *f*; **~ oil** *s.* (Fisch)Tran *m*, *bsd.* Walöl *n*; **'~·sick** *adj.*: **she gets ~** ihr wird beim Zugfahren schlecht.

traipse [treɪps] → **trapse**.

trait [treɪ] *s.* **1.** (Cha'rakter)Zug *m*, Merkmal *n*; **2.** *Am.* Gesichtszug *m*.

trai·tor ['treɪtə] *s.* Verräter *m* (**to** an *dat.*); **'trai·tor·ous** [-tərəs] *adj.* □ ver'räterisch; **'trai·tress** [-trɪs] *s.* Verräterin *f*.

tra·jec·to·ry [trə'dʒektərɪ] *s.* **1.** *phys.* Flugbahn *f*, Fallkurve *f* *e-r Bombe*; **2.** ⚛ Trajekto'rie *f*.

tram [træm] **I** *s.* **1.** *Brit.* (**by ~** mit der) Straßenbahn *f*; **2.** ✕ Förderwagen *m*, Hund *m*; **II** *v/i.* **3.** *a.* **~ it** *Brit.* mit der Straßenbahn fahren; **'~·car** *s. Brit.* Straßenbahnwagen *m*; **'~·line** *s.* **1.** *Brit.* Straßenbahnlinie *f*; **2.** *pl. Tennis etc.*: Seitenlinien *pl.* für Doppel; **3.** *pl. fig.* 'Leitprin,zipien *pl.*

tram·mel ['træml] *s.* **1.** (Schlepp)Netz *n*; **2.** Spannriemen *m* für *Pferde*; **3.** *fig.* Fessel *f*; **4.** Kesselhaken *m*; **5.** ⚛ El'lipsenzirkel *m*; **6.** *a.* **pair of ~s** Stangenzirkel *m*; **II** *v/t.* **7.** *mst fig.* hemmen.

tra·mon·tane [trə'mɒnteɪn] *adj.* **1.** transal'pin(isch); **2.** *fig.* fremd, bar'ba-

risch.
tramp [træmp] **I** *v/i.* **1.** trampeln
([*up*]**on** auf *acc.*); sta(m)pfen; **2.** *mst* ~
it marschieren, wandern, ,tippeln'; **3.**
vagabundieren; **II** *v/t.* **4.** durch'wandern; **5.** ~ *down* niedertrampeln; **III** *s.*
6. Getrampel *n;* **7.** (schwerer) Tritt; **8.**
(Fuß)Marsch *m,* Wanderung *f:* **on the**
~ auf (der) Wanderschaft; **9.** Landstreicher *m;* **10.** F ,Luder' *n,* ,Flittchen' *n;*
11. ⚓ Trampschiff *n;* '**tram·ple** [-pl] **I**
v/i. **1.** (her'um)trampeln ([*up*]**on** auf
dat.); **2.** *fig.* mit Füßen treten ([*up*]**on**
acc.); **II** *v/t.* **3.** (zer)trampeln; ~ *down*
niedertrampeln; ~ *out* Feuer austreten; ~
~ *under foot* herumtrampeln auf
(*dat.*); **III** *s.* **4.** Trampeln *n.*
tram·po·lin(e) ['træmpəlin] *s. sport*
Trampo'lin *n;* '**tram·po·lin·er** *s.* Trampo'linspringer(in), -turner(in).
'**tram·way** *s.* **1.** *Brit.* Straßenbahn(linie)
f; **2.** ⚒ Grubenbahn *f.*
trance [trɑːns] *s.* **1.** Trance(zustand *m)*
f: **go** (*put*) *into a* ~ in Trance fallen
(versetzen); **2.** Verzückung *f,* Ek'stase
f.
trank [træŋk] *s. Am.* F Beruhigungsmittel *n.*
tran·quil ['træŋkwil] *adj.* □ **1.** ruhig,
friedlich; **2.** gelassen, heiter; **tran·quil-
(l)i·ty** [træŋ'kwiləti] *s.* **1.** Ruhe *f,* Frie-
de(n) *m,* Stille *f;* **2.** Gelassenheit *f,* Heiterkeit *f;* '**tran·quil·(l)ize** [-laiz] *v/t.*
(*v/i.* sich) beruhigen; '**tran·quil·(l)iz·er**
[-laizə] *s.* Beruhigungsmittel *n.*
trans·act [træn'zækt] **I** *v/t. Geschäfte
etc.* ('durch)führen, abwickeln; *Handel*
abschließen; **II** *v/i.* ver-, unter'handeln
(*with* mit); **trans'ac·tion** [-kʃn] *s.* **1.**
'Durchführung *f,* Abwicklung *f,* Erledigung *f;* **2.** Ver-, Unter'handlung *f;* **3.** a)
✝ Transakti'on *f,* (Geschäfts)Abschluss
m, Geschäft *n,* b) ⚖ Rechtsgeschäft *n;*
4. *pl.* ✝ (Ge'schäfts),Umsatz *m;* **5.** *pl.*
Proto'koll *n,* Sitzungsbericht *m.*
trans·al·pine [,trænz'ælpain] *adj.* transal'pin(isch).
trans·at·lan·tic [,trænzət'læntik] *adj.* **1.**
transat'lantisch, 'überseeisch; **2.** Übersee...: ~ *liner,* ~ *flight* Ozeanflug *m.*
trans·ceiv·er [træn'siːvə] *s.* ⚡ Sender-
Empfänger *m.*
tran·scend [træn'send] *v/t.* **1.** *bsd. fig.*
über'schreiten, -'steigen; **2.** *fig.* über-
'treffen; **tran'scend·ence** [-dəns],
tran'scend·en·cy [-dənsi] *s.* **1.** Über-
'legenheit *f,* Erhabenheit *f;* **2.** *phls.,
eccl., a.* ✝ Transzen'denz *f;* **tran-
'scend·ent** [-dənt] *adj.* □ **1.** transzen-
'dent: a) *phls.* 'übersinnlich, b) *eccl.*
'überweltlich; **2.** her'vorragend.
tran·scen·den·tal [,trænsen'dentl] *adj.*
□ **1.** *phls.* transzenden'tal: a) meta-
'physisch, b) *bei Kant:* apri'orisch: ~
meditation transzendentale Medita-
tion; **2.** 'überna,türlich; **3.** erhaben; **4.**
ab'strus, verworren; **5.** ⚡ transzen-
'dent; ,**tran·scen'den·tal·ism** [-təli-
zəm] *s.* Transzenden'talphiloso,phie *f.*
tran·scribe [træn'skraib] *v/t.* **1.** abschreiben; **2.** *Stenogramm etc.* über'tragen; **3.** ♪ transkribieren; **4.** *Radio, TV:*
a) aufzeichnen, auf Band aufnehmen,
b) (vom Band) über'tragen; **5.** *Computer:* 'umschreiben; **tran·script** ['træn-
skript] *s.* Abschrift *f,* Ko'pie *f;* **tran-
'scrip·tion** [-ripʃn] *s.* **1.** 'Umschreiben
n; **2.** Abschrift *f;* **3.** 'Umschrift *f;* **4.** ♪
Transkripti'on *f;* **5.** *Radio, TV:* a) Aufnahme *f,* b) Aufzeichnung *f.*
trans·duc·er [trænz'djuːsə] *s.* **1.** ⚡
('Um)Wandler *m;* **2.** ⊙ 'Umformer *m;* **3.**
Computer: Wandler *m.*

tran·sept ['trænsept] *s.* △ Querschiff *n.*
trans·fer [træns'fɜː] **I** *v/t.* **1.** hin'überbringen, -schaffen (*from ... to* von ...
nach *od.* zu); **2.** über'geben (*to dat.*); **3.**
Betrieb, Truppen, Wohnsitz etc. verle-
gen, *Beamten, Schüler in e-e andere
Schule etc.* versetzen (*to* nach, *in, into*
in *acc.*); *Technologie, a. sport Spieler*
transferieren; ✝ *Patienten* über'weisen;
4. ⚖ (*to*) über'tragen (auf *acc.*), abtreten (an *acc.*); **5.** ✝ a) *Summe* vortragen, b) *Posten, Wertpapiere* 'umbuchen, c) *Aktien etc.* über'tragen; **6.**
Geld über'weisen; **7.** *fig. Zuneigung
etc.* über'tragen (*to* auf *acc.*); **8.** *typ.*
Druck, Stich etc. 'umdrucken, über'tra-
gen; **II** *v/i.* **9.** 'übertreten (*to* zu); **10.**
verlegt *od.* versetzt werden (*to* nach);
11. 🚋 *etc.* 'umsteigen; **III** *s.* ['trænsfɜː]
12. (*to*) Über'tragung *f* (auf *acc.*),
'Übergabe *f* (an *acc.*); **13.** Wechsel *m*
(*to* zu); **14.** (*to*) a) Verlegung *f* (nach),
b) Versetzung *f* (nach), c) *sport* Trans-
'fer *m od.* Wechsel *m* (zu); **15.** ⚖ (*to*)
Über'tragung *f* (*to* auf *acc.*), Abtretung
f (an *acc.*); **16.** ('Geld)Über,weisung *f:*
~ *business* ✝ Giroverkehr *m;* ~ *of foreign exchange* Devisentransfer *m;*
17. ✝ ('Wertpa,pier- *etc.*),Umbuchung
f; **18.** ✝ ('Aktien- *etc.*)Über,tragung *f;*
19. *typ.* a) Über'tragung *f,* 'Umdruck
m, b) Abziehen *n,* Abzug *m,* c) Abziehbild *n;* **20.** 🚋 *etc.* a) 'Umsteigen *n,* b)
'Umsteigefahrkarte *f,* c) a. ⚓ 'Umschlagplatz *m,* d) Fährboot *n;* **trans-
'fer·a·ble** [-'fɜːrəbl] *adj. bsd.* ✝, ⚖
über'tragbar (*a. Wahlstimme*).
trans·fer| bank *s.* ✝ Girobank *f;* ~
book *s.* ✝ 'Umschreibungs-, Aktien-
buch *n;* ~ **day** *s.* ✝ 'Umschreibungstag
m; ~ **deed** *s.* Über'tragungsurkunde *f.*
trans·fer·ee [,trænsfɜː'riː] *s.* Zessio'nar
m, Über'nehmer *m;* **trans·fer·ence**
['trænsfərəns] *s.* **1.** → *transfer* 14, 15,
17, 18; **2.** *psych.* Über'tragung *f;* **trans-
fer·en·tial** [,trænsfə'renʃl] *adj.* Über-
tragungs...
trans·fer ink *s. typ.* 'Umdrucktinte *f,*
-farbe *f.*
trans·fer·or [træns'fɜːrə] *s.* ⚖ Ze'dent
m, Abtretende(r *m) f.*
trans·fer| pa·per *s. typ.* 'Umdruckpa-
,pier *n;* ~ **pic·ture** *s.* Abziehbild *n.*
trans·fer·rer [træns'fɜːrə] *s.* **1.** Über-
'trager *m;* **2.** → *transferor.*
trans·fer tick·et → *transfer* 20b.
trans·fig·u·ra·tion [,trænsfigjʊ'reiʃn] *s.*
1. 'Umgestaltung *f,* Verklärung *f;* **2.**
the R a) Verklä-
rung *f,* b) ⚳ Fest *n* der Verklärung (6.
August); **trans·fig·ure** [træns'figə] *v/t.*
1. 'umgestalten; **2.** *eccl. u. fig.* verklären.
trans·fix [træns'fiks] *v/t.* **1.** durch'stechen, -'bohren (*a. fig.*); **2.** *fig.* lähmen:
~*ed* (wie) versteinert, starr (*with* vor
dat.).
trans·form [træns'fɔːm] **I** *v/t.* **1.** 'umgestalten, -wandeln ([*in*]*to* in *acc.,* zu);
'umformen (*a.* A); *a. j-n* verwandeln,
verändern; ⚡ 'umspannen; **II** *v/i.* **3.**
sich verwandeln (*into* zu); **trans·for-
ma·tion** [,trænsfə'meiʃn] *s.* **1.** 'Umgestaltung *f,* -bildung *f;* 'Umwandlung *f,*
-formung *f* (*a.* A); Verwandlung *f,* (*a.* ~ *of
energy phys.* Energieumsetzung *f;* ~
(*scene*) *thea.* Verwandlungsszene *f;* **2.**
⚡ 'Umspannung *f;* **3.** 'Damenpe,rücke
f; **trans·form·er** [-mə] *s.* **1.** 'Umgestal-
ter(in); **2.** ⚡ Transfor'mator *m.*
trans·fuse [træns'fjuːz] *v/t.* **1.** 'umgießen; **2.** ✚ a) *Blut* über'tragen, b) e-e
'Bluttransfusi,on machen bei, c) *Serum*

etc. einspritzen; **3.** *fig.* einflößen (*into*
dat.); **4.** *fig.* durch'dringen, erfüllen
(*with* mit, von); **trans'fu·sion** [-juːʒn]
s. **1.** 'Umgießen *n;* **2.** ✚ ('Blut)Transfu-
si,on *f;* **3.** *fig.* Erfüllung (*with* mit).
trans·gress [træns'gres] **I** *v/t.* **1.** über-
'schreiten (*a. fig.*); **2.** *fig. Gesetze etc.*
über'treten; **II** *v/i.* **3.** (*against* gegen)
sich vergehen, sündigen; **trans'gres-
sion** [-eʃn] *s.* **1.** Über'schreitung *f* (*a.
fig.*); **2.** Über'tretung *f* von *Gesetzen
etc.;* **3.** Vergehen *n,* Missetat *f;* **trans-
'gres·sor** [-sə] *s.* Missetäter(in).
tran·sience ['trænziəns], '**tran·sien·cy**
[-nsi] *s.* Vergänglichkeit *f,* Flüchtigkeit
f; '**tran·sient** [-nt] **I** *adj.* □ **1.** zeitlich
vor'übergehend; **2.** vergänglich, flüch-
tig; **3.** *Am.* Durchgangs...: ~ *camp,* ~
visitor → 5; **4.** ⚡ Einschalt..., Ein-
schwing...; **II** *s.* **5.** *Am.* 'Durchreisen-
de(r *m) f;* **6.** ⚡ a) Einschaltstoß *m,* b)
Einschwingvorgang, c) Wanderwelle *f.*
trans·i·re [trænz'aiəri] *s.* ✝ Zollbegleit-
schein *m.*
tran·sis·tor [træn'sistə] *s.* ⚡ Tran'sistor
m; **tran·sis·tor·ize** [-raiz] *v/t.* ⚡ transis-
torisieren.
trans·it ['trænsit] **I** *s.* **1.** 'Durch-, 'Überfahrt *f;* **2.** *a. ast.* 'Durchgang *m;* **3.** ✝
Tran'sit *m,* 'Durchfuhr *f,* Trans'port *m:
in* ~ unterwegs, auf dem Transport; **4.**
✝ 'Durchgangsverkehr *m;* **5.** 'Durchgangsstraße *f;* **6.** *Am.* öffentliche Verkehrsmittel *pl.;* **7.** *fig.* 'Übergang *m* (*to*
zu); **II** *adj.* **8.** *a.* ✝ Durchgangs...(-*lager, -verkehr etc.*): ~ *visa* Durchreise-,
Transitvisum *n;* **9.** ✝ Durchfuhr...,
Transit...: ~ *trade* Transithandel *m.*
tran·si·tion [træn'siʒn] **I** *s.* **1.** 'Übergang
m (*a.* ♪, *phys.*): ~ *agreements pl.*
'Übergangsregelung(en *pl.*) *f;* ~ *period*
(*od. phase*) 'Übergangszeit *f,* -phase *f;*
2. 'Übergangszeit *f:* (*state of*) ~ Über-
gangsstadium *n;* **II** *adj.* **3.** ~ **tran-
'si·tion·al** [-ʒənl] *adj.* □ Übergangs...,
Überleitungs..., Zwischen...: ~ *period*
Übergangszeit *f.*
tran·si·tive ['trænsitiv] *adj.* □ **1.** *ling.*
transitiv: ~ (*verb*) Transitiv *n,* transitives Verb; **2.** Übergangs...
tran·si·to·ri·ness ['trænsitərinis] *s.*
Flüchtigkeit *f,* Vergänglichkeit *f;* **tran-
si·to·ry** ['trænsitəri] *adj.* □ **1.** zeitlich
vor'übergehend, transi'torisch; **2.** vergänglich, flüchtig.
trans·lat·a·ble [træns'leitəbl] *adj.* über-
'setzbar; **trans·late** [træns'leit] **I** *v/t.* **1.**
Buch etc. über'setzen (*a. Computer*),
-'tragen (*into* in *acc.*); **2.** *fig.* Grundsätze etc. über'tragen (*into* in *acc.,* zu): ~
ideas into action Gedanken in die Tat
umsetzen; **3.** *fig.* a) auslegen, b) ausdrücken (*in* in *dat.*); **4.** *eccl.* a) *Geistlichen* versetzen, b) *Reliquie etc.* 'überführen, verlegen (*to* nach), c) *j-n* entrücken; **5.** *Brit. Schuhe etc.* 'umarbeiten; **6.** ⊙ *Bewegung* über'tragen (*to* auf
acc.); **II** *v/i.* **7.** sich *gut etc.* über'setzen
lassen; **trans·la·tion** [-eiʃn] *s.* **1.** Über-
'setzung *f,* -'tragung *f:* ~ *program(me)*
Computer: Übersetzungsprogramm *n;*
~ *software* Übersetzungssoftware *f;*
2. *fig.* Auslegung *f;* **3.** *eccl.* a) Versetzung *f,* b) Entrückung *f;* **trans·la·tor**
[-tə] *s.* **1.** Über'setzer(in); **2.** *Computer:*
Über'setzer *m.*
trans·lit·er·ate [trænz'litəreit] *v/t.* transkribieren, 'umschreiben; **trans·lit·er·a-
tion** [,trænzlitə'reiʃn] *s.* Transkripti-
ti'on *f.*
trans·lo·cate [,trænzlə'keit] *v/t.* verlagern.
trans·lu·cence [trænz'luːsns], **trans'lu-**

cen·cy [-sɪ] *s.* **1.** 'Durchscheinen *n*; **2.** 'Licht,durchlässigkeit *f*; **trans'lu·cent** *adj.* □ **1.** a) 'licht,durchlässig, b) halb 'durchsichtig; **2.** 'durchscheinend.

trans·ma·rine [,trænzmə'riːn] *adj.* 'überseeisch, Übersee...

trans·mi·grant [trænz'maɪɡrənt] *s.* 'Durchreisende(r *m*) *f*, -wandernde(r *m*) *f*; **trans·mi·grate** [,trænzmaɪ'ɡreɪt] *v/i.* **1.** fortziehen; **2.** 'übersiedeln; **3.** auswandern; **4.** wandern (*Seele*); **trans·mi·gra·tion** [,trænzmaɪ'ɡreɪʃn] *s.* **1.** Auswanderung *f*, 'Übersiedlung *f*; **2.** *a.* ~ **of souls** Seelenwanderung *f*; **3.** ♣ a) 'Überwandern *n* (*Ei-*, *Blutzelle etc.*), b) Diape'dese *f*.

trans·mis·si·ble [trænz'mɪsəbl] *adj.* **1.** über'sendbar; **2.** *a.* ♣ *u. fig.* über'tragbar (**to** auf *acc.*).

trans·mis·sion [trænz'mɪʃn] *s.* **1.** Über'sendung *f*, -'mittlung *f*; ♈ Versand *m*; **2.** Über'mittlung *f von Nachrichten etc.*; **3.** *ling.* ('Text)Über,lieferung *f*; **4.** ⚙ a) Transmissi'on *f*, Über'setzung *f*, -'tragung *f*, b) Triebwelle *f*, -werk *n*, Getriebe *n*: ~ **gear** Wechselgetriebe *n*; **automatic** ~ *mot.* Auto'matik(getriebe *n*) *f*; **5.** Über'tragung *f*: a) *biol.* Vererbung *f*, b) ♣ Ansteckung *f*, c) *Radio, TV*: Sendung *f*, d) ⚡ Über'lassung *f*, e) *phys.* Fortpflanzung *f*, f) 'Datenüber,tragung *f*: ~ **error** *EDV* Übertragungsfehler *m*; ~ **belt** *s.* ⚙ 'Treibriemen *m*; ~ **gear·ing** *s.* ⚙ Über'setzungsgetriebe *n*; ~ **ra·tio** *s.* ⚙ Über'setzungsverhältnis *n*; ~ **shaft** *s.* ⚙ Kar'danwelle *f*.

trans·mit [trænz'mɪt] *v/t.* **1.** (**to**) über'senden, -'mitteln (*dat.*), (ver)senden (**an** *acc.*); *a. Telegramm etc.* weitergeben (**an** *acc.*), befördern; **2.** *Nachrichten etc.* mitteilen (**to** *dat.*); **3.** *fig. Ideen etc.* über'mitteln, weitergeben (**to** an *acc.*); **4.** über'tragen (*a.* ♣): a) *biol.* vererben, b) ⚡ über'schreiben, vermachen; **5.** *phys. Wellen, Wärme etc.* a) (weiter)leiten, b) *a. Kraft* über'tragen, c) *Licht etc.* 'durchlassen; **trans·mit·tal** [-tl] → **transmission** 1–4a; **trans·mit·ter** [-tə] *s.* **1.** Über'sender *m*, -'mittler *m*; **2.** *Radio*: a) Sendegerät *n*, b) Sender *m*; **3.** *teleph.* Mikro'fon *n*; **4.** ⚙ (Messwert)Geber *m*; **trans·mit·ting** [-tɪŋ] *adj.* Sende-(-*antenne*, -*stärke etc.*): ~ **station** Sender *m*.

trans·mog·ri·fy [trænz'mɒɡrɪfaɪ] *v/t. humor.* (gänzlich) 'ummodeln.

trans·mut·a·ble [trænz'mjuːtəbl] *adj.* □ 'umwandelbar; **trans·mu·ta·tion** [,trænzmjuː'teɪʃn] *s.* **1.** 'Umwandlung *f* (*a.* ♈, *phys.*); **2.** *biol.* Transmutati'on *f*, 'Umbildung *f*; **trans·mute** [trænz'mjuːt] *v/t.* 'umwandeln (**into** in *acc.*).

trans·na·tion·al [trænz'næʃənl] *adj.* 'über-, ♈ 'multinatio,nal.

trans·o·ce·an·ic ['trænz,əʊʃɪ'ænɪk] *adj.* **1.** transoze'anisch, 'überseeisch; **2.** a) Übersee..., b) Ozean...

tran·som ['trænsəm] *s.* △ a) Querbalken *m* über e-r *Tür*, b) (Quer)Blende *f* e-s *Fensters*.

tran·son·ic [træn'sɒnɪk] *adj. phys.* Überschall...

trans·par·en·cy [træns'pærənsɪ] *s.* **1.** *a. fig.* 'Durchsichtigkeit *f*, Transpa'renz *f*; **2.** a) 'Folie *f* (*für Tageslichtprojektor*), b) Transpa'rent *n*, Leuchtbild *n*; **3.** *phot.* Dia(posi'tiv) *n*; **trans·par·ent** [-nt] *adj.* □ **1.** 'durchsichtig (*a. fig. offenkundig*): ~ **colo(u)r** ♣ Lasurfarbe; ~ **slide** Diapositiv *n*; **2.** *phys.* transpa'rent, 'licht,durchlässig; **3.** *fig.* a) klar (*Stil etc.*), b) offen, ehrlich.

tran·spi·ra·tion [,trænspɪ'reɪʃn] *s.* **1.**

(*bsd.* Haut)Ausdünstung *f*; **2.** Schweiß *m*; **tran·spire** [træn'spaɪə] I *v/i.* **1.** *physiol.* transpirieren, schwitzen; **2.** ausgedünstet werden; **3.** *fig.* 'durchsickern, bekannt werden; **4.** *fig.* passieren, sich ereignen; II *v/t.* **5.** ausdünsten, ausschwitzen.

trans·plant [træns'plɑːnt] I *v/t.* **1.** ♣ 'umpflanzen; **2.** ♣ transplantieren, verpflanzen; **3.** *fig.* versetzen, -pflanzen (**to** nach, **into** in *acc.*); II *v/i.* **4.** sich verpflanzen lassen; III *s.* ['trænsplɑːnt] **5.** a) → **transplantation**, b) ♣ Transplan'tat *n*; **trans·plan·ta·tion** [,trænsplɑːn'teɪʃn] *s.* Verpflanzung *f*: a) ♣ 'Umpflanzung *f*, b) *fig.* Versetzung *f*, 'Umsiedlung *f*, c) ♣ Transplantati'on *f*.

trans·port I *v/t.* [træn'spɔːt] **1.** transportieren, befördern, versenden; **2.** *mst pass. fig.* a) *j-n* hinreißen, entzücken (**with** vor *dat.*, von), b) heftig erregen: **~ed with joy** außer sich vor Freude; **3.** *bsd. hist.* deportieren; II *s.* ['trænspɔːt] **4.** a) ('Ab-, 'An)Trans,port *m*, Beförderung *f*, b) Versand *m*, c) Verschiffung *f*; **5.** Verkehr *m*; **6.** Beförderungsmittel *n od. pl.*; **7.** *a.* ~ **ship**, ~ **vessel** a) Trans'port-, Frachtschiff *n*, b) ✕ 'Truppentrans,porter *m*; **8.** *a.* ~ **plane** ✈ Trans'portflugzeug *n*; **9.** *fig.* a) Taumel *m der Freude etc.*, b) heftige Erregung: **in a ~ of** außer sich vor *Entzücken, Wut etc.*; **trans·port·a·ble** [-təbl] *adj.* trans'portfähig, versendbar; **trans·por·ta·tion** [,trænspɔː'teɪʃn] *s.* **1.** → **transport** 4; **2.** Trans'portsy,stem *n*; **3.** *bsd. Am.* a) Beförderungsmittel *pl.*, b) Trans'portkosten *pl.*, c) Fahrausweis *m*; **4.** *bsd. hist.* Deportati'on *f*; **trans·port ca·fé** (*od.* caff [kæf]) *s. Brit.* 'Fernfahrerlo,kal *n*, -kneipe *f*; **trans·port·er** [-tə] *s.* **1.** Beförderer *m*; **2.** ⚙ Förder-, Trans'portvorrichtung *f*.

trans·pose [træns'pəʊz] *v/t.* **1.** 'umstellen (*a. ling.*), ver-, 'umsetzen; **2.** ♪, ♮ transponieren; **trans·po·si·tion** [,trænspə'zɪʃn] *s.* **1.** 'Umstellen *n*; **2.** 'Umstellung *f* (*a. ling.*); **3.** ♪, ♮ Transpositi'on *f*; **4.** ⚡, ⚙ Kreuzung *f von Leitungen etc.*

trans·sex·u·al [trænz'seksjʊəl] I *adj.* transsexu'ell; II *s.* Transsexu'elle(r *m*) *f.*

trans·ship [træns'ʃɪp] *v/t.* ♈, ⚓ 'umladen, -schlagen; **trans'ship·ment** [-mənt] *s.* ⚓ 'Umladung *f*, 'Umschlag *m*: ~ **charge** Umladegebühr *f*; ~ **port** Umschlaghafen *m.*

tran·sub·stan·ti·ate [,trænsəb'stænʃɪeɪt] *v/t.* 'umwandeln, (*a. eccl. Brot u. Wein*) verwandeln (**into, to** in *acc.*, zu); **tran·sub·stan·ti·a·tion** ['trænsəb,stænʃɪ'eɪʃn] *s.* **1.** 'Stoff,umwandlung *f*; **2.** *eccl.* Transsubstantiati'on *f.*

tran·sude [træn'sjuːd] *v/i.* **1.** *physiol.* 'durchschwitzen (*Flüssigkeiten*); **2.** ('durch)dringen, (-)sickern (**through** durch); **3.** abgesondert werden.

trans·ver·sal [trænz'vɜːsl] I *adj.* □ → **transverse** 1; II *s.* ♮ Transver'sale *f*; **trans·verse** ['trænzvɜːs] I *adj.* □ **1.** schräg, diago'nal, Quer..., quer (laufend) (**to** zu): ~ **flute** ♪ Querflöte *f*; ~ **section** ♮ Querschnitt *m*; II *s.* **2.** Querstück *n*, -achse *f*, -muskel *m*; **3.** ♮ große Achse e-r El'lipse.

trans·ves·tism [trænz'vestɪzəm] *s. psych.* Transve'stismus *m*; **trans·ves·tite** [-taɪt] *s.* Transve'stit *m.*

trap[1] [træp] I *s.* **1.** *hunt.*, *a.* ✕ *u. fig.* Falle *f*: **lay** (*od.* **set**) **a** ~ **for s.o.** j-m e-e Falle stellen; **walk** (*od.* **fall**) **into a** ~ in e-e Falle gehen; **2.** ♨ Abscheider *m*; **3.**

a) Auffangvorrichtung *f*, b) Dampf-, Wasserverschluss *m*, c) Geruchverschluss *m* (*Klosett*); **4.** ⚡ (Funk)Sperrkreis *m*; **5.** *Tontaubenschießen*: 'Wurfma,schine *f*; **6.** *Golf*: Sandhindernis *n*; **7.** → **trapdoor**; **8.** *Brit.* Gig *n*, zweirädriger Einspänner; **9.** *mot.* offener Zweisitzer; **10.** *pl.* ♪ Schlagzeug *n*; **11.** *sl.* ,Klappe' *f* (*Mund*); II *v/t.* **12.** fangen (*a. fig.*); (*a. phys. Elektronen*) einfangen; **13.** einschließen (*a.* ✕); verschütten; **14.** *fig.* in e-e Falle locken, ,fangen'; **15.** Fallen aufstellen in (*dat.*); **16.** ⚙ a) mit Wasserverschluss *etc.* versehen, verschließen, b) *Gase etc.* abfangen; III *v/i.* **17.** Fallen stellen (**for** *dat.*).

trap[2] [træp] *s. mst pl.* F ,Kla'motten' *pl.*, Siebensachen *pl.*, Gepäck *n.*

trap[3] [træp] *s. min.* Trapp *m.*

,**trap'door** *s.* **1.** Fall-, Klapptür *f*, (✓ Boden)Klappe *f*; **2.** *thea.* Versenkung *f.*

tra·peze [trə'piːz] *s.* Tra'pez *n*; **tra·pe·zi·form** [-zɪfɔːm] *adj.* tra'pezförmig; **tra·pe·zi·um** [-zjəm] *s.* **1.** ♮ Tra'pez *n*, b) *bsd. Am.* Trapezo'id *n*; **2.** *anat.* großes Vieleckbein (*Handwurzel*); **trap·e·zoid** ['træpɪzɔɪd] I *s.* **1.** ♮ a) *Brit.* Trapezo'id *n*, b) *bsd. Am.* Tra'pez *n*; **2.** *anat.* kleines Vieleckbein (*Handwurzel*); II *adj.* **3.** → **trap·e·zoi·dal** [,træpɪ'zɔɪdl] ♮ trapezo'id, *bsd. Am.* tra'pezförmig.

trap·per ['træpə] *s.* Trapper *m*, Pelztierjäger *m.*

trap·pings ['træpɪŋz] *s. pl.* **1.** Staatsgeschirr *n für Pferde*; **2.** *fig.* a) ,Staat' *m*, Schmuck *m*; b) Drum u. Dran *n*, ,Verzierungen' *pl.*

trapse [treɪps] *v/i.* **1.** (da'hin)latschen; **2.** (um'her)schlendern.

trap shoot·ing *s. sport* Trapschießen *n.*

trash [træʃ] *s.* **1.** *bsd. Am.* Abfall *m*, Müll *m*: ~ **can** Abfall-, Mülleimer *m od.* -tonne *f*; **2.** Plunder *m*, Schund *m*; **3.** *fig.* Schund *m*, Kitsch *m* (*Bücher etc.*); **4.** ,Blech' *n*, Unsinn *m*; **5.** Ausschuss *m*, Gesindel *n*; → **white trash**; '**trash·i·ness** [-ʃɪnɪs] *s.* Wertlosigkeit *f*, Minderwertigkeit *f*; '**trash·y** [-ʃɪ] *adj.* □ wertlos, minderwertig, kitschig, Schund..., Kitsch...

trau·ma ['trɔːmə] *s.* Trauma *n*: a) ♣ Wunde *f*, b) *psych.* seelische Erschütterung, (bleibender) Schock; **trau·mat·ic** [trɔː'mætɪk] *adj.* (□ *-ally*) ♣, *psych.* trau'matisch: ~ **medicine** Unfallmedizin *f.*

trav·ail ['træveɪl] I *s.* **1.** *obs. od. rhet.* (mühevolle) Arbeit; **2.** (Geburts)Wehen *pl.*; **3.** *fig.* (Seelen)Qual *f*: **be in** ~ **with** schwer ringen mit; II *v/i.* **4.** sich abrackern; **5.** in den Wehen liegen.

trav·el ['trævl] I *s.* **1.** Reisen *n*: ~ **sickness** Reisekrankheit *f*; **2.** *mst pl.* (längere) Reise: **book of** ~ Reisebeschreibung *f*; **3.** ⚙ Bewegung *f*, Lauf *m*, (Kolben- *etc.*)Hub *m*; II *v/i.* **4.** reisen, e-e Reise machen; ~ **light** mit leichtem Gepäck reisen; **5.** ♈ reisen (**in** in e-r Ware), als (Handels)Vertreter arbeiten (**for** für); **6.** *ast.*, *phys.*, *mot. etc.* sich bewegen; sich fortpflanzen (*Licht etc.*); **7.** ⚙ sich ('hin- u. 'her)bewegen, laufen (*Kolben etc.*); **8.** *bsd. fig.* schweifen, wandern (*Blick etc.*); **9.** F (da'hin)sausen; III *v/t.* **10.** *Land, a.* ♈ Vertreterbezirk bereisen, *Strecke* zu'rücklegen; ~ **a·gen·cy** *s.* 'Reisebü,ro *n*; ~ **al·low·ance** *s.* Reisekostenzuschuss *m.*

trav·el·la·tor ['trævəleɪtə] *s. Brit.* Rollsteig *m.*

trav·el(l)ed ['trævld] *adj.* **1.** (weit, viel)

gereist; **2.** (viel) befahren (*Straße etc.*);
'trav·el·(l)er [-lə] *s.* **1.** Reisende(r *m*)
f; **2.** ✝ *bsd. Brit.* (Handlungs)Reisende(r) *m*, (Handels)Vertreter *m*; **3.** ☻
Laufstück *n*, *bsd.* a) Laufkatze *f*, b)
Hängekran *m*.
trav·el·(l)er's| check (*Brit.* **cheque**) *s.*
Reisescheck *m*; ~ **joy** *s.* ♥ Waldrebe *f*.
trav·el·(l)ing ['trævlɪŋ] *adj.* **1.** Reise...
(*-koffer, -wecker, -kosten etc.*): ~
agent, *bsd. Am.* ~ **salesman** → *travel(l)er* 2; **2.** Wander...(-*ausstellung,
-bücherei, -zirkus etc.*); fahrbar, auf
Rädern: ~ *dental clinic*; ~ *crane* Laufkran *m*.
trav·e·log(ue) ['trævəlɒg] *s.* Reisebericht *m* (*Vortrag, mst mit Lichtbildern*),
Reisefilm *m*.
trav·ers·a·ble ['trævəsəbl] *adj.* **1.**
(leicht) durch- *od.* über'querbar; **2.**
passierbar, befahrbar; **3.** ☻ (aus-)
schwenkbar; **trav·erse** ['trævəs] **I** *v/t.*
1. durch-, über'queren; **2.** durch'ziehen, -'fließen; **3.** *Fluss etc.* über'spannen; **4.** *fig.* 'durchgehen, -sehen; **5.** ☻,
a. ✕ *Geschütz* (seitwärts) schwenken,
6. *Linie etc.* kreuzen, schneiden; **7.**
Plan etc. durch'kreuzen; **8.** ⚓ kreuzen;
9. ✍ a) *Vorbringen* bestreiten, b) gegen *e-e Klage etc.* Einspruch erheben;
10. *mount., Skisport*: Hang queren; **II**
v/i. **11.** ☻ sich drehen; **12.** *fenc., Reitsport*: traversieren; **13.** *mount., Skisport*: queren; **III** *s.* **1.** Durch-, Über
'querung *f*; **15.** ⚔ a) Quergitter *n*, b)
Querwand *f*, c) Quergang *m*, d) Tra
'verse *f*, Querstück *n*; **16.** ⚕ Schnittlinie *f*; **17.** ⚓ Koppelkurs *m*; **18.** ✕ a)
Traverse *f*, Querwall *m*, b) Schulterwehr *f*, **19.** ✕ Schwenken *n* (*Geschütz*); **20.** ☻ a) Schwenkung *f* e-r Maschine, b) schwenkbarer Teil; **21.** *surv.*
Poly'gon(zug *m*) *n*; **22.** ✍ a) Bestreitung *f*, b) Einspruch *m*; **23.** *mount.,
Skisport*: a) Queren *n* e-s Hanges, b)
Quergang *m*; **IV** *adj.* **24.** quer laufend,
Quer...(-*bohrer etc.*): ~ *motion*
Schwenkung *f*; **25.** Zickzack...: ~ *sailing* ⚓ Koppelkurs *m*; **26.** sich kreuzend (*Linien*).
trav·es·ty ['trævɪstɪ] **I** *s.* **1.** Trave'stie *f*;
2. *fig.* Zerrbild *n*, Karika'tur *f*; **II** *v/t.* **3.**
travestieren (*scherzhaft umgestalten*);
4. *fig.* ins Lächerliche ziehen, verzerren.
trawl [trɔːl] ⚓ **I** *s. a.* ~ *net* (Grund-)
Schleppnetz *n*; **II** *v/t. u. v/i.* mit dem
Schleppnetz fischen; **'trawl·er** [-lə] *s.*
(Grund)Schleppnetzfischer *m* (*Boot u.
Person*).
tray [treɪ] *s.* **1.** Ta'blett *n*, (Ser'vier-,
Tee)Brett *n*; **2.** a) Auslagekästchen *n*,
b) ('umgehängtes) Verkaufsbrett *n*,
,Bauchladen' *m*; **3.** flache Schale; **4.**
Ablagekorb *m im Büro*; **5.** (Koffer-)
Einsatz *m*.
treach·er·ous ['tretʃərəs] *adj.* ☐ **1.** verräterisch, treulos (*to* gegen); **2.** (heim-)
tückisch, 'hinterhältig; **3.** *fig.* tückisch,
trügerisch (*Eis, Wetter etc.*), unzuverlässig (*a. Gedächtnis*); **'treach·er·ous·
ness** [-nɪs] *s.* **1.** Treulosigkeit *f*, Verräte'rei *f*; **2.** *a. fig.* Tücke *f*; **'treach·er·y**
[-rɪ] *s.* **1.** Treulosigkeit *f* (*to* an *dat.*), Verräte
'rei *f*, Treulosigkeit *f* (gegen).
trea·cle ['triːkl] *s.* **1.** a) Sirup *m*, b) Me
'lasse *f*; **2.** *fig.* a) Süßlichkeit *f*, b) süßliches Getue; **'trea·cly** [-lɪ] *adj.* **1.** sirupartig, Sirup...; **2.** *fig.* süßlich.
tread [tred] **I** *s.* **1.** Tritt *m*, Schritt *m*; **2.**
a) Tritt(spur *f*) *m*, b) (Rad- *etc.*)Spur *f*;
3. ☻ Lauffläche *f* (*Rad*); *mot.* (Reifen-)
Pro,fil *n*; **4.** Spurweite *f*; **5.** Pe'dalab

---

stand *m* (*Fahrrad*); **6.** a) Fußraste *f*,
Trittbrett *n*, b) (Leiter)Sprosse *f*; **7.**
Auftritt *m* (*Stufe*); **8.** *orn.* a) Treten *n*
(*Begattung*), b) Hahnentritt *m* (*im Ei*);
II *v/t.* [*irr.*] **9.** beschreiten: ~ *the
boards thea.* (als Schauspieler) auftreten; **10.** *rhet.* Zimmer etc. durch'messen; **11.** *a.* ~ *down* zertreten, -trampeln; ~ *out Feuer* austreten, *fig. Aufstand* niederwerfen; ~ *underfoot* niedertreten, *fig.* mit Füßen treten; **12.**
Pedale etc., a. Wasser treten; **13.** *orn.*
treten, begatten; **III** *v/i.* [*irr.*] **14.** treten
(*on* auf *acc.*): ~ *on air* (glück)selig sein;
~ *lightly* leise auftreten, *fig.* vorsichtig
zu Werke gehen; **15.** (ein'her)schreiten; **16.** trampeln; ~ (*up*)*on* zertrampeln; **17.** unmittelbar folgen (*on* auf
acc.); → *heel¹ Redew.*; **18.** *orn.* a) treten (*Hahn*), b) sich paaren; **trea·dle**
['tredl] **I** *s.* ☻ Tretkurbel *f*, Tritt *m*; **II**
v/t. *Fußantrieb m*; **2.** Pe'dal *n*; **II** *v/i.*
3. treten; **'tread·mill** *s.* Tretmühle *f* (*a.
fig.*).
trea·son ['triːzn] *s.* (⚖ Landes)Verrat
m (*to* an *dat.*): *high* ~, *felony* Hochverrat *m*; **'trea·son·a·ble** [-nəbl] *adj.*
☐ (landes- *od.* hoch)verräterisch.
treas·ure ['treʒə] **I** *s.* **1.** Schatz *m* (*a.
fig.*); **2.** Reichtum *m*, Reichtümer *pl.*,
Schätze *pl.*: ~*s of the soil* Bodenschätze; ~ *trove* (herrenloser) Schatzfund,
fig. Fundgrube *f*; **3.** F ,Perle' *f* (*Dienstmädchen etc.*); ~ *Schatz m*, Liebling
m; **II** *v/t.* **5.** *oft* ~ *up Schätze* (an)sammeln, aufhäufen; **6.** a) (hoch) schätzen,
b) hegen, *a. Andenken* in Ehren halten;
~ *house* *s.* Schatzhaus *n*, -kammer *f*;
2. *fig.* Gold-, Fundgrube *f*.
treas·ur·er ['treʒərə] *s.* **1.** Schatzmeister
(-in) (*a.* ✝); Kassenwart *m*; **2.** ✝ Leiter
m der Fi'nanzab,teilung: *city* ~ Stadtkämmerer *m*; **3.** Fis'kalbeamte(r) *m*: ⚖
of the Household Brit. Fiskalbeamte(r) des königlichen Haushalts; **'treas·
ur·er·ship** [-ʃɪp] *s.* Schatzmeisteramt
n, Amt *n* e-s Kassenwarts.
treas·ur·y ['treʒərɪ] *s.* **1.** Schatzkammer
f, -haus *n*; **2.** a) Schatzamt *n*, b) Staatsschatz *m*: *Lords* ⚖ *Commissioners)
of the* ⚖ das brit. Finanzministerium;
First Lord of the ⚖ erster Schatzlord
(*mst der Premierminister*); **3.** Fiskus *m*,
Staatskasse *f*; **4.** Schatz(kästlein *n*)
m, Antholo'gie *f* (*Buchtitel*); ⚖ **bench**
s. parl. Brit. Regierungsbank *f*; ~ **bill** *s.*
✝ (*kurzfristiger*) Schatzwechsel; ~
Board *s. Brit.* Fi'nanzmini,sterium *n*; ~
bond *s. Am.* (*langfristige*) Schatzanweisung; ~ **cer·tif·i·cate** *s. Am.* (*kurzfristiger*) Schatzwechsel; ⚖ **De·part·ment**
s. Am. Fi'nanzmini,sterium *n*; ~ **note** *s.*
Am. (*mittelfristiger*) Schatzwechsel; ⚖
war·rant *s. Brit.* Schatzanweisung *f*.
treat [triːt] **I** *v/t.* **1.** behandeln, 'umgehen mit: ~ *s.o. brutally*; **2.** behandeln,
betrachten (*as* als); **3.** ✖, ⚒, ☻ behandeln (*for* gegen, *with* mit); **4.** *fig. Thema etc.* behandeln; **5.** *j-m* e-n Genuss
bereiten, *bsd. j-n* bewirten (*to* mit): ~
o.s. to sich *et.* gönnen *od.* leisten *od.*
genehmigen; ~ *s.o. to s.th.* j-m et.
spendieren; *be ~ed to s.th.* in den Genuss e-r Sache kommen; **II** *v/i.* **6.** ~ *of*
handeln von, *Thema* behandeln; **7.** ~
with verhandeln mit; **8.** (die Zeche)
bezahlen, e-e Runde ausgeben; **III** *s.* **9.**
(Extra)Vergnügen *n*, *bsd.* (Fest-)
Schmaus *m*: *school* ~ Schulfest *n od.*
-ausflug *m*; **10.** *fig.* (Hoch)Genuss *m*,
Wonne *f*; **11.** (Gratis)Bewirtung *f*:
stand ~ → 8; *it is my* ~ das geht auf
m-e Rechnung, diesmal bezahle ich;

'trea·tise [-tɪz] *s.* (*wissenschaftliche*)
Abhandlung; **'treat·ment** [-mənt] *s.* **1.**
Behandlung *f* (*a.* ✖, ⚒, *a. fig. e-s Themas etc.*): *give s.th. the full* ~ *fig.* et.
gründlich behandeln; *give s.o. the* ~ F
j-n ,in die Mangel nehmen'; **2.** ☻ Bearbeitung *f*; **3.** *Film*: Treatment *n* (*erweitertes Handlungsschema*).
trea·ty ['triːtɪ] *s.* **1.** (*bsd. Staats*)Vertrag
m, Pakt *m*: ~ *powers* Vertragsmächte;
2. *obs.* Verhandlung *f*.
tre·ble ['trebl] **I** *adj.* ☐ **1.** dreifach; **2.** ♪
dreistellig; **3.** ♪ Diskant..., Sopran...;
4. hoch, schrill; **5.** *Radio*: Höhen...: ~
control Höhenregler *m*; **II** *s.* **6.** ♪ *allg.*
Dis'kant *m*; **III** *v/t. u. v/i.* **7.** (sich) verdreifachen.
tree [triː] **I** *s.* **1.** Baum *m*: ~ *of life* a)
bibl. Baum des Lebens, b) ♀ Lebensbaum; *up a* ~ F in der Klemme; → *top¹*
2; **2.** (*Rosen- etc.*)Strauch *m*, (*Bananenetc.*)Staude *f*; **3.** ☻ Baum *m*, Welle *f*,
Schaft *m*; (Holz)Gestell *n*; (Stiefel)Leisten *m*; **4.** → *family tree*; **II** *v/t.* **5.** auf
e-n Baum jagen; **6.** *j-n* in die Enge treiben; ~ *fern s.* ♀ Baumfarn *m*; ~ *frog s.
zo.* Laubfrosch *m*.
tree·less ['triːlɪs] *adj.* baumlos, kahl.
tree| line *s.* Baumgrenze *f*; **'~·nail** *s.* ☻
Holznagel *m*, Dübel *m*; ~ **nurs·er·y** *s.*
Baumschule *f*; ~ **sur·geon** *s.* 'Baumchir,urg *m*; ~ **toad** → *tree frog*; **'~·top**
s. Baumkrone *f*, -wipfel *m*.
tre·foil ['trefɔɪl] *s.* **1.** ♀ Klee *m*; **2.** △
Dreipass *m*; **3.** *bsd. her.* Kleeblatt *n*.
trek [trek] **I** *v/i.* **1.** *Südafrika*: trecken,
(im Ochsenwagen) reisen; **2.** ziehen,
wandern; **II** *s.* **3.** Treck *m*.
trel·lis ['trelɪs] **I** *s.* **1.** Gitter *n*, Gatter *n*;
2. ☻ Gitterwerk *n*; **3.** ✍ Spa'lier *n*; **4.**
Pergola *f*; **II** *v/t.* **5.** vergittern: ~*ed window* Gitterfenster *n*; **6.** ✍ am Spalier
ziehen; **'~·work** *s.* Gitterwerk *n* (*a.* ☻).
trem·ble ['trembl] **I** *v/i.* **1.** (er)zittern, (-)
beben (*at, with* vor *dat.*): ~ *all over*
(*od. in every limb*) am ganzen Leibe
zittern; ~ *at the thought* (*od. to think*)
bei dem Gedanken zittern; → *balance*
2; **2.** zittern, bangen (*for* für, um): *a
trembling uncertainty* e-e bange Ungewissheit; **II** *s.* **3.** Zittern *n*, Beben *n*:
be all of a ~ am ganzen Körper zittern;
4. *pl. sg. konstr. vet.* Milchfieber *n*;
'trem·bler [-lə] *s.* **1.** ∮ ('Selbst)Unter
,brecher *m*; **2.** e'lektrische Glocke *od.*
Klingel; **'trem·bling** [-lɪŋ] *adj.* ☐ zitternd: ~ *grass* ♀ Zittergras *n*; ~ *poplar*
(*od. tree*) ♀ Zitterpappel *f*, Espe *f*.
tre·men·dous [trɪ'mendəs] *adj.* ☐ **1.**
schrecklich, fürchterlich; **2.** F ungeheuer, e'norm, ,toll'.
trem·o·lo ['tremələʊ] *pl.* **-los** ♪ Tremolo *n*.
trem·or ['tremə] *s.* **1.** ✖ Zittern *n*, Zucken *n*: ~ *of the heart* Herzflackern *n*;
2. Zittern *n*, Schau(d)er *m* der Erregung; **3.** Beben *n* der Erde; **4.** Angst
(-gefühl *n*) *f*, Beben *n*.
trem·u·lous ['tremjʊləs] *adj.* ☐ **1.** zitternd, bebend; **2.** (ä'ng)stig, ängstlich.
tre·nail ['trenl] → *treenail*.
trench [trentʃ] **I** *v/t.* **1.** mit Gräben
durch'ziehen *od.* (✕) befestigen; **2.** ✍
tief 'umpflügen, ri'golen; **3.** zerschneiden, durch'furchen; **II** *v/i.* **4.** (✕ Schützen)Gräben ausheben; **5.** *geol.* sich
(ein)graben (*Fluss etc.*); **6.** ~ (*up*)*on* beeinträchtigen, in *j-s* Rechte eingreifen;
7. ~ (*up*)*on fig.* hart grenzen an (*acc.*);
III *s.* **8.** (✕ Schützen)Graben *m*; **9.**
Furche *f*, Rinne *f*; **10.** ✕ Schramm *m*.
trench·an·cy ['trentʃənsɪ] *s.* Schärfe *f*;
'trench·ant [-nt] *adj.* ☐ **1.** scharf,

schneidend (*Witz etc.*); **2.** einschneidend, e'nergisch: *a ~ policy*.

trench coat *s.* Trenchcoat *m*.

trench·er¹ ['trentʃə] *s.* ✗ Schanzarbeiter *m*.

trench·er² ['trentʃə] *s.* **1.** Tranchier-, Schneidebrett *n*; **2.** *obs.* Speise *f*; **~ cap** → **mortarboard** 2; '**~·man** [-mən] *s.* [*irr.*] guter *etc.* Esser.

trench| fe·ver *s.* 🏵 Schützengrabenfieber *n*; **~ foot** *s.* 🏵 Schützengrabenfüße *pl.* (*Fußbrand*); **~ mor·tar** *s.* ✗ Gra'natwerfer *m*; **~ war·fare** *s.* ✗ Stellungskrieg *m*.

trend [trend] **I** *s.* **1.** Richtung *f* (*a. fig.*); **2.** *fig.* Ten'denz *f*, Entwicklung *f*, Trend *m* (*alle a.* †); Neigung *f*, Bestreben *n*: *the ~ of his argument was* s-e Beweisführung lief darauf hinaus; *~ in od. of prices* 🌱 Preistendenz; **3.** *fig.* (Ver-)Lauf *m*: *the ~ of events*; **II** *v/i.* **4.** sich neigen, streben, tendieren (*towards* nach e-r *Richtung*); **5.** sich erstrecken, laufen (*towards* nach *Süden etc.*); **6.** *geol.* streichen (*to* nach); **~ a·nal·y·sis** *s.* [*irr.*] † Konjunk'turana,lyse *f*; '**~·set·ter** *s. Mode etc.*: j-d, der den Ton angibt, Schrittmacher *m*, Trendsetter *m*; '**~·set·ting** *adj.* tonangebend.

trend·y ['trendɪ] **I** *adj.* **1.** ('super)mo,dern; **2.** schick, modebewusst; **3.** schick (*Kleidung*); **4.** F ,in', in Mode: *a ~ place* ein In-Lokal *etc.*; **II** *s.* **5.** *oft contp.* Schicki'micki *m*.

tre·pan [trɪ'pæn] **I** *s.* **1.** 🏵 *hist.* Schädelbohrer *m*; **2.** ⊙ 'Bohrma,schine *f*; **3.** *geol.* Stein-, Erdbohrer *m*; **II** *v/t.* **4.** 🏵 trepanieren.

trep·i·da·tion [,trepɪ'deɪʃn] *s.* **1.** 🏵 (Glieder-, Muskel)Zittern *n*; **2.** Beben *n*; **3.** Angst *f*, Bestürzung *f*.

tres·pass ['trespəs] **I** *s.* **1.** Über'tretung *f*, Vergehen *n*, Verstoß *m*, Sünde *f*; **2.** 'Übergriff *m*; **3.** 'Missbrauch *m* (*on gen.*); **4.** 🏛 *allg.* unerlaubte Handlung (*Zivilrecht*): a) unbefugtes Betreten, b) Besitzstörung *f*, c) 'Übergriff *m* gegen die Per'son (*z.B. Körperverletzung*); **5.** *a.* **action for ~** 🏛 Schadenersatzklage *f* aus unerlaubter Handlung, *z.B.* Besitzstörungsklage *f*; **II** *v/i.* **6.** 🏛 e-e unerlaubte Handlung begehen: **~** (*up*)*on* a) widerrechtlich betreten, b) rechtswidrige Übergriffe gegen *j-s* Eigentum begehen; **7. ~** (*up*)*on fig.* a) 'übergreifen auf (*acc.*), b) hart grenzen an (*acc.*), c) *j-s* Zeit *etc.* über Gebühr in Anspruch nehmen; **8.** (*against*) verstoßen (gegen), sündigen (wider *od.* gegen); '**tres·pass·er** [-sə] *s.* **1.** 🏛 a) Rechtsverletzer *m*, b) Unbefugte(r *m*) *f*: *~s will be prosecuted!* Betreten bei Strafe verboten!; **2.** *obs.* Sünder(in).

tress [tres] *s.* **1.** (Haar)Flechte *f*, Zopf *m*; **2.** Locke *f*; **3.** *pl.* üppiges Haar; **tressed** [-st] *adj.* **1.** geflochten; **2.** gelockt.

tres·tle ['tresl] *s.* **1.** ⊙ Gestell *n*, Gerüst *n*, Bock *m*, Schragen *m*; **2.** ✗ Brückenbock *m*: **~ bridge** Bockbrücke *f*; '**~·work** *s.* **1.** Gerüst *n*; **2.** *Am.* 'Bahnvia,dukt *m*.

trey [treɪ] *s.* Drei *f* im Karten- *od.* Würfelspiel.

tri·a·ble ['traɪəbl] *adj.* 🏛 a) justizi'abel, zu verhandeln(d) (*Sache*), b) belangbar, abzuurteilen(d) (*Person*).

tri·ad ['traɪəd] *s.* **1.** Tri'ade *f*: a) Dreizahl *f*, b) 🜨 dreiwertiges Ele'ment, c) ⚹ Dreiergruppe *f*, Trias *f*; **2.** ♪ Dreiklang *m*.

tri·al ['traɪəl] **I** *s.* **1.** Versuch *m* (*of* mit), Probe *f*, Erprobung *f*, Prüfung *f* (*alle a.*

⊙): *~ and error* a) ⚹ Regula *f* Falsi, b) empirische Methode; *~ of strength* Kraftprobe; *on ~* auf *od.* zur Probe; *give a ~, make a ~ of* e-n Versuch machen mit, erproben; *be on ~* a) erprobt werden, b) e-e Probezeit durchmachen (*Person*), c) *fig.* auf dem Prüfstand sein (→ *a.* 2); **2.** 🏛 ('Straf- *od.* Zi'vil)Pro,zess *m*, (Gerichts)Verfahren *n*, (Haupt)Verhandlung *f*: *~ by jury* Schwurgerichtsverfahren; *be on* (*od. stand*) *~* unter Anklage stehen (*for* wegen); *bring* (*od. put*) *s.o. to ~* vor Gericht bringen; *stand* (*one's*) *~* sich vor Gericht verantworten; **3.** (*to* für) *fig.* a) (Schicksals)Prüfung *f*, Heimsuchung *f*, b) Last *f*, Plage *f*, Stra'paze *f*; **4.** *sport* a) Vorlauf *m*, Ausscheidungsrennen *n*, b) Ausscheidungsspiel *n*; **II** *adj.* **5.** Versuchs..., Probe...: *~ bal·ance* 🌱 Rohbilanz *f*; *~ bal·loon* Versuchsballon *m*; *~ marriage* Ehe *f* auf Probe; *~ match* → 4 b; *~ order* 🌱 Probeauftrag *m*; *~ package* 🌱 Probepackung *f*; *~ period* Probezeit *f*; *~ run* Probefahrt *f*, -lauf *m*, *a.* ⊙ Testlauf *m*; **6.** 🏛 Verhandlungs...: *~ court* erstinstanzliches Gericht; *~ judge* Richter *m* der ersten Instanz; *~ lawyer Am.* Prozessanwalt *m*.

tri·an·gle ['traɪæŋgl] *s.* **1.** ⚹ Dreieck *n*; **2.** ♪ Triangel *m*; **3.** ⊙ a) Reißdreieck *n*, b) Winkel *m*; **4.** *mst eternal ~ fig.* Dreiecksverhältnis *n*; **tri·an·gu·lar** [traɪ'æŋgjʊlə] *adj.* dreieckig, -winkelig; *fig.* dreiseitig, Dreiecks...; **tri·an·gu·la·tion** [traɪ,æŋgjʊ'leɪʃn] *s.* **1.** *surv* Triangulati'on *f*; **2.** 'Dreiecksme,thode *f* (*Umrechnungsverfahren für die Teilnehmerwährungen der Europäischen Währungsunion*).

Tri·as ['traɪəs] → **Tri·as·sic** [traɪ'æsɪk] *geol.* **I** *s.* 'Trias(formati,on) *f*; **II** *adj.* Trias...

tri·ath·lete [traɪ'æθliːt] *s. sport* 'Triath,let(in); **tri·ath·lon** [-lɒn; -lən] *s.* 'Triath,lon *n*.

trib·al ['traɪbl] *adj.* ☐ Stammes...; '**trib·al·ism** [-bəlɪzəm] *s.* 'Stammessy,stem *n od.* -gefühl *n*.

tri·bas·ic [traɪ'beɪsɪk] *adj.* 🜨 drei-, tribasisch.

tribe [traɪb] *s.* **1.** (Volks)Stamm *m*; **2.** ♀, *zo.* Tribus *f*, Klasse *f*; **3.** *humor. u. contp.* Sippschaft *f*, ,Verein' *m*; **tribes·man** ['traɪbzmən] *s.* [*irr.*] Stammesangehörige(r) *m*, -genosse *m*.

trib·u·la·tion [,trɪbjʊ'leɪʃn] *s.* Drangsal *f*, 'Widerwärtigkeit *f*.

tri·bu·nal [traɪ'bjuːnl] *s.* **1.** 🏛 Gericht(shof *m*) *n*, Tribu'nal *n* (*a. fig.*); **2.** Richterstuhl *m* (*a. fig.*); **trib·une** ['trɪbjuːn] *s.* **1.** *antiq.* ('Volks)Tri,bun *m*; **2.** Volksheld *m*; **3.** Tri'büne *f*; **4.** Rednerbühne *f*; **5.** Bischofsthron *m*.

trib·u·tar·y ['trɪbjʊtərɪ] **I** *adj.* ☐ **1.** tri'but-, zinspflichtig (*to dat.*); **2.** 'untergeordnet (*to dat.*); **3.** helfend, beisteuernd (*to zu*); **4.** *geogr.* Neben...: *~ stream*; **II** *s.* **5.** Tri'butpflichtige(r) *m*, *a.* tri'butpflichtiger Staat; **6.** *geogr.* Nebenfluss *m*; **trib·ute** ['trɪbjuːt] *s.* Tri'but *m*: a) Zins *m*, Abgabe *f*, b) *fig.* Zoll *m*, Beitrag *m*, c) *fig.* Huldigung *f*, Achtungsbezeigung *f*, Anerkennung *f*: *~ of admiration* gebührende Bewunderung; *pay ~ to j-m* Hochachtung bezeigen *od.* Anerkennung zollen.

tri·car ['traɪkɑː] *s. Brit.* Dreiradlieferwagen *m*.

trice [traɪs] *s.*: *in a ~* im Nu.

tri·ceps ['traɪseps] *pl.* **tri·ceps·es** *anat.* Trizeps *m* (*Muskel*).

tri·chi·na [trɪ'kaɪnə] *pl.* **-nae** [-niː] *s. zo.* Tri'chine *f*; **trich·i·no·sis** [,trɪkɪ'nəʊsɪs] *s.* 🏵 Trichi'nose *f*.

trich·o·mon·ad [,trɪkəʊ'mɒnæd] *s. zo.* Trichomo'nade *f*.

tri·chord ['traɪkɔːd] *adj. u. s.* ♪ dreisaitig(es Instru'ment).

tri·chot·o·my [traɪ'kɒtəmɪ] *s.* Dreiheit *f*, -teilung *f*.

trick [trɪk] **I** *s.* **1.** Trick *m*, Kunstgriff *m*, Kniff *m*, List *f*; *pl. a.* Schliche *pl.*, Ränke *pl.*, Winkelzüge *pl.*: *full of ~s* raffiniert; **2.** (*dirty ~* gemeiner) Streich: *~s of fortune* Tücken des Schicksals; *the ~s of the memory fig.* die Tücken des Gedächtnisses; *be up to one's ~s* (wieder) Dummheiten machen; *be up to s.o.'s ~s* j-n *od.* j-s Schliche durchschauen; *what ~s have you been up to?* was hast du angestellt?; *play s.o. a ~, play a ~ on s.o.* j-m e-n Streich spielen; *none of your ~s!* keine Mätzchen!; **3.** Trick *m*, (*Karten- etc.*)Kunststück *n*: *do the ~* den Zweck erfüllen; *that did the ~* damit war es geschafft; **4.** (Sinnes)Täuschung *f*; **5.** (*bsd.* üble *od.* dumme) Angewohnheit, Eigenheit *f*; **6.** Kartenspiel: Stich *m*: *take od. win a ~* e-n Stich machen; **7.** ⚓ Rudertörn *m*; **8.** *Am. sl.* ,Mieze' *f* (*Mädchen*); **9.** V ,Nummer' *f* (*Koitus*); **II** *adj.* **10.** Trick...(-*dieb*, -*film*, -*szene*); **11.** Kunst...(-*flug*, -*reiten*); **III** *v/t.* **12.** über'listen, betrügen, prellen (*out of* um); **13.** *j-n* verleiten (*into doing et.* zu tun); **14.** *mst ~ up* (*od. out*) schmücken, (hér'aus)putzen; '**trick·er** [-kə] → **trickster**; '**trick·er·y** [-kərɪ] *s.* **1.** Betrüge'rei(en *pl.*) *f*, Gaune'rei(en *pl.*) *f*; **2.** Kniff *m*; '**trick·i·ness** [-kɪnɪs] *s.* **1.** Verschlagenheit *f*, Durch'triebenheit *f*; **2.** Kitzligkeit *f e-r Situation etc.*; **3.** Kompliziertheit *f*; '**trick·ish** [-kɪʃ] → **tricky**.

trick·le ['trɪkl] **I** *v/i.* **1.** tröpfeln (*a. fig.*); **2.** rieseln, kullern (*Tränen*); **3.** sickern: *~ out fig.* durchsickern; **4.** trudeln (*Ball etc.*); **II** *v/t.* **5.** tröpfeln (lassen), träufeln; **6.** rieseln lassen; **III** *s.* **7.** Tröpfeln *n*; Rieseln *n*, *a. fig.*); **~ charg·er** *s.* ⚡ Kleinlader *m*.

trick·si·ness ['trɪksɪnɪs] *s.* **1.** → **trickiness**; **2.** 'Übermut *m*.

trick·ster ['trɪkstə] *s.* Gauner(in), Schwindler(in).

trick·sy ['trɪksɪ] *adj.* **1.** → **tricky** 1; **2.** 'übermütig.

trick·y ['trɪkɪ] *adj.* ☐ **1.** verschlagen, durch'trieben, raffiniert; **2.** heikel, kitzlig (*Lage, Problem*); **3.** kompliziert, knifflig; **4.** unzuverlässig.

tri·col·o·(u)r ['traɪkələ] *s.* Triko'lore *f*.

tri·cot ['triːkəʊ] *s.* Tri'kot *m* (*Stoff*).

tri·cy·cle ['traɪsɪkl] **I** *s.* Dreirad *n*; **II** *v/i.* Dreirad fahren.

tri·dent ['traɪdnt] *s.* Dreizack *m*.

tried [traɪd] **I** *p.p. von* **try**; **II** *adj.* erprobt, bewährt.

tri·en·ni·al [traɪ'enjəl] *adj.* ☐ **1.** dreijährig; **2.** alle drei Jahre stattfindend, dreijährlich.

tri·er·arch·y ['traɪərɑːkɪ] *s. hist.* Trierar'chie *f*.

tri·fle ['traɪfl] **I** *s.* **1.** Kleinigkeit *f*: a) unbedeutender Gegenstand, b) Baga-'telle *f*, Lap'palie *f*, c) Kinderspiel *n* (*to für j-n*), d) kleine Geldsumme, e) *das* bisschen: *a ~ expensive* etwas *od.* ein bisschen teuer; *not to stick at ~s* sich nicht mit Kleinigkeiten abgeben; *stand upon ~s* ein Kleinigkeitskrämer sein; **2.** a) *Brit.* Trifle *n* (*Biskuitdessert*), b) *Am.* 'Obstdes,sert *n* mit Sahne; **II** *v/i.* **3.**

spielen (**with** mit *dem Bleistift etc.*); **4.** (**with**) *fig.* spielen (mit), sein Spiel treiben *od.* leichtfertig 'umgehen (mit): **he is not to be ~d with** er lässt nicht mit sich spaßen; **5.** tändeln, scherzen; leichtfertig da'herreden; **6.** (her'um-)trödeln; III *v/t.* **7. ~ away** Zeit vertändeln, vertrödeln, *a.* Geld verplempern; '**tri·fler** [-lə] *s.* **1.** oberflächlicher *od.* fri'voler Mensch; **2.** Tändler *m*; **3.** Müßiggänger *m*; '**tri·fling** [-lıŋ] *adj.* □ **1.** oberflächlich, leichtfertig; **2.** tändelnd; **3.** unbedeutend, geringfügig.

tri·fo·li·ate [traɪˈfəʊlɪət] *adj.* ♥ **1.** dreiblätt(e)rig; **2.** → **tri·fo·li·o·late** [traɪˈfəʊlɪəleɪt] *adj.* ♥ **1.** dreizählig (*Blatt*); **2.** mit dreizähligen Blättern (*Pflanze*).

trig [trɪg] F *für* **trigonometry**.

trig·ger [ˈtrɪgə] I *s.* **1.** ⚡, *phot.*, ⊛ Auslöser *m* (*a. fig.*); **2.** Abzug *m* (*Feuerwaffe*), *am Gewehr*: *a.* Drücker *m*, *e-r Bombe*: Zünder *m*: **pull the ~** abdrücken; **quick on the ~** *fig.* ,fix', ,auf Draht' (*reaktionsschnell od. schlagfertig*); II *v/t.* **3.** ⊛ auslösen (*a. fig.*); ~ **guard** *s.* ✗ Abzugsbügel *m*; '**~-,hap·py** *adj.* **1.** schießwütig; **2.** *pol.* kriegslüstern; **3.** *fig.* kampflustig.

trig·o·no·met·ric, trig·o·no·met·ri·cal [ˌtrɪgənəˈmetrɪk(l)] *adj.* □ ♣ trigono'metrisch; **trig·o·nom·e·try** [ˌtrɪgəˈnɒmɪtrɪ] *s.* Trigonome'trie *f.*

tri·he·dral [ˌtraɪˈhedrl] *adj.* ♣ dreiflächig, tri'edrisch.

tri·lat·er·al [ˌtraɪˈlætərəl] *adj.* **1.** ♣ dreiseitig; **2.** *pol.* Dreier...: ~ **talks.**

tril·by [ˈtrɪlbɪ] *s.* **1.** *a.* ~ **hat** Brit. F weicher Filzhut; **2.** *pl. sl.* ,Haxen' *pl.* (*Füße*).

tri·lin·e·ar [ˌtraɪˈlɪnɪə] *adj.* ♣ dreilinig: ~ **coordinates** Dreieckskoordinaten.

tri·lin·gual [ˌtraɪˈlɪŋgwəl] *adj.* dreisprachig.

trill [trɪl] I *v/t. u. v/i.* **1.** ♪ *etc.* trillern, trällern; **2.** *ling.* (*bsd.* das r) rollen; II *s.* **3.** ♪ Triller *m*; **4.** *ling.* gerolltes r, gerollter Konso'nant.

tril·lion [ˈtrɪljən] *s.* **1.** *Brit.* Trilli'on *f*; **2.** *Am.* Billi'on *f.*

tril·o·gy [ˈtrɪlədʒɪ] *s.* Trilo'gie *f.*

trim [trɪm] I *v/t.* **1.** in Ordnung bringen, zu'rechtmachen; **2.** *Feuer* anschüren; **3.** *Haar, Hecken etc.* (be-, zu'recht-) schneiden; stutzen, *bsd. Hundefell* trimmen; **4.** *fig. Budget etc.* stutzen, beschneiden; **5.** ⊛ *Bauholz* behauen, zurichten; **6.** *a.* ~ **up** (her'aus)putzen, schmücken, ausstaffieren, schönmachen; **7.** *Hüte etc.* besetzen, garnieren; **8.** F a) j-n ,zs.-stauchen', b) ,reinlegen', c) ,vertrimmen' (*a. sport schlagen*); **9.** ✈, ⚓ trimmen (*a.*) *Flugzeug, Schiff* in die richtige Lage bringen, b) *Segel* stellen, brassen: ~ **one's sails to every wind** *fig.* sein Mäntelchen nach dem Wind hängen, c) *Kohlen* schaufeln, d) *Ladung* (richtig) verstauen; **10.** ⚡ trimmen, (fein) abgleichen; II *v/i.* **11.** *fig.* e-n Mittelkurs steuern, *bsd. pol.* lavieren: ~ **with the times** sich den Zeiten anpassen, Opportunitätspolitik treiben; III *s.* **12.** Ordnung *f*, (richtiger) Zustand, *a.* richtige (*körperliche od. seelische*) Verfassung *od.* Form: **in good (out of) ~** in guter (schlechter) Verfassung (*a. Person*); **13.** ✈, ⚓ a) Trimm (-lage *f*) *m*, b) richtige Stellung *der Segel*, c) gute Verstauung *der Ladung*; **14.** Putz *m*, Staat *m*, Gala *f*; **15.** *mot.* a) Innenausstattung *f*, b) Zierleiste(n *pl.*) *f*; IV *adj.* **16.** ordentlich; **17.** schmuck, sauber, a'drett; gepflegt (*a. Bart, Rasen etc.*); **18.** (gut) in Schuss.

tri·mes·ter [trɪˈmestə] *s.* **1.** Zeitraum *m* von drei Monaten, Vierteljahr *n*; **2.** *univ.* Tri'mester *n.*

trim·mer [ˈtrɪmə] *s.* **1.** Aufarbeiter(in), Putzmacher(in); **2.** ⚓ a) (Kohlen)Trimmer *m*, b) Stauer *m*; **3.** *Zimmerei*: Wechselbalken *m*; **4.** *fig. bsd. pol.* Opportu'nist(in); '**trim·ming** [-mɪŋ] *s.* **1.** (Auf-, Aus)Putzen *n*, Zurichten *n*; **2.** a) (Hut-, Kleider)Besatz *m*, Borte *f*, b) *pl.* Zutaten *pl.*, Posa'menten *pl.*, c) *fig.* ,Verzierung' *f*, ,Garnierung' *f im Stil etc.*; **3.** *pl.* Garnierung *f*, Zutaten *pl.* (*Speise*); **4.** *pl.* Abfälle *pl.*, Schnipsel *pl.*; **5.** ⚓ a) Trimmen *n*, (Ver)Stauen *n*, b) Staulage *f*; **6.** (Tracht *f*) Prügel *pl.*; **7.** *bsd. sport* (böse) Abfuhr; '**trim·ness** [-mnɪs] *s.* **1.** gute Ordnung; **2.** gutes Aussehen, Gepflegtheit *f.*

trine [traɪn] I *adj.* **1.** dreifach; II *s.* **2.** Dreiheit *f*; **3.** *ast.* Trigo'nala,spekt *m.*

Trin·i·tar·i·an [ˌtrɪnɪˈteərɪən] *eccl.* I *adj.* **1.** Dreieinigkeits...; II *s.* **2.** Bekenner (-in) der Drei'einigkeit; **3.** *hist.* Trinita'rier *m*; '**Trin·i'tar·i·an·ism** [-nɪzəm] *s.* Drei'einigkeitslehre *f.*

tri·ni·tro·tol·u·ene [traɪˌnaɪtrəʊˈtɒljuːiːn] *s.* ⚗ Trinitrotolu'ol *n.*

trin·i·ty [ˈtrɪnɪtɪ] *s.* **1.** Dreiheit *f*; **2.** ♀ *eccl.* Drei'einigkeit *f*; ♀ **House** *s.* Verband *m* zur Aufsicht über See- u. Lotsenzeichen *etc.*; ♀ **Sun·day** *s.* Sonntag *m* Trini'tatis; ♀ **term** *s. univ.* 'Sommer,tri,mester *n.*

trin·ket [ˈtrɪŋkɪt] *s.* **1.** Schmuck *m*; (*bsd.* wertloses) Schmuckstück; **2.** *pl. fig.* Kram *m*, Plunder *m.*

tri·no·mi·al [traɪˈnəʊmjəl] I *adj.* **1.** ♣ tri'nomisch, dreigliedrig, -namig; **2.** *biol., zo.* dreigliedrig (*Artname*); II *s.* **3.** ♣ Tri'nom *n*, dreigliedrige (Zahlen-)Größe.

tri·o [ˈtriːəʊ] *pl.* **-os** *s. ♪ u. fig.* Trio *n.*

tri·ode [ˈtraɪəʊd] *s.* ⚡ Tri'ode *f*, 'Drei,elek,troden,röhre *f.*

tri·o·let [ˈtriːəʊlet] *s.* Trio'lett *n* (*Ringelgedicht*).

trip [trɪp] I *s.* **1.** (*bsd.* kurze, *a.* See)Reise; Ausflug *m*, Spritztour *f* (*to* nach); **2.** *weitS.* Fahrt *f*; **3.** Trippeln *n*; **4.** Stolpern *n*; **5.** Fehltritt *m* (*bsd. fig.*); **6.** *fig.* Fehler *m*; **7.** Beinstellen *n*; **8.** ⊛ Auslösung *f*: ~ **cam** *od.* **dog** Schaltnocken *m*; ~ **lever** Auslöse- *od.* Schalthebel *m*; **9.** *sl.* ,Trip' *m* (*Drogenrausch*); II *v/i.* **10.** trippeln, tänzeln; **11.** stolpern, straucheln (*a. fig.*); **12.** *fig.* (e-n) Fehler machen: **catch s.o. ~ping** j-n bei e-m Fehler ertappen; **13.** über ein Wort stolpern, sich versprechen; III *v/t.* **14.** *oft* ~ **up** j-m ein Bein stellen, *j-n* zu Fall bringen (*beide a. fig.*); **15.** *fig.* vereiteln; **16.** (*in* bei *e-m Fehler etc.*) ertappen; **17.** ⊛ a) auslösen, b) schalten.

tri·par·tite [ˌtraɪˈpɑːtaɪt] *adj.* **1.** ♥ dreiteilig; **2.** Dreier..., Dreimächte... (*Vertrag etc.*)

tripe [traɪp] *s.* **1.** Kal'daunen *pl.*, Kutteln *pl.*; **2.** *sl.* a) Schund *m*, Kitsch *m*, b) Quatsch *m*, Blödsinn *m.*

tri·phase [ˈtraɪfeɪz] → **three-phase.**

tri·phib·i·ous [traɪˈfɪbɪəs] *adj.* ✗ mit Einsatz von Land-, See- u. Luftstreitkräften ('durchgeführt).

triph·thong [ˈtrɪfθɒŋ] *s. ling.* Triph'thong *m*, Dreilaut *m.*

tri·plane [ˈtraɪpleɪn] *s.* ✈ Dreidecker *m.*

tri·ple [ˈtrɪpl] I *adj.* □ **1.** dreifach; **2.** dreimalig; **3.** Drei..., drei...: ♀ **Alliance** *hist.* Tripelallianz *f*, Dreibund *m*; ~ **fugue** ♪ **jump** *sport* Dreisprung *m*; ~ **time** ♪ Tripeltakt *m*; II *s.* **4.** *das* Dreifache; III *v/t. u. v/i.* **5.**

(sich) verdreifachen.

tri·plet [ˈtrɪplɪt] *s.* **1.** *biol.* Drilling *m*; **2.** Dreiergruppe *f*, Trio *n* (*drei Personen etc.*); **3.** ♪ Tri'ole *f*; **4.** Verskunst: Dreireim *m.*

tri·plex [ˈtrɪpleks] I *adj.* **1.** dreifach: ~ **glass** → 3; II *s.* **2.** ♪ Tripeltakt *m*; **3.** ⊛ Triplex-, Sicherheitsglas *n.*

trip·li·cate [ˈtrɪplɪkət] I *adj.* **1.** dreifach; **2.** in dreifacher Ausfertigung (geschrieben *etc.*); II *s.* **3.** *das* Dreifache; **4.** dreifache Ausfertigung: **in ~** in dreifacher Ausfertigung; **5.** dritte Ausfertigung; III *v/t.* [-keɪt] **6.** verdreifachen; **7.** dreifach ausfertigen.

tri·pod [ˈtraɪpɒd] *s.* **1.** Dreifuß *m*; **2.** *bsd. phot.* Sta'tiv *n*; ✗ Dreibein *n.*

tri·pos [ˈtraɪpɒs] *s.* letztes Ex'amen *für* **honours** (*Cambridge*).

trip·per [ˈtrɪpə] *s.* a) Ausflügler(in), b) Tou'rist(in).

trip·ping [ˈtrɪpɪŋ] *adj.* □ **1.** leicht(füßig), flink; **2.** flott, munter; **3.** strauchelnd (*a. fig.*); **4.** ⊛ Auslöse..., Schalt...; II *s.* **5.** Trippeln *n*; **6.** Beinstellen *n.*

trip·tych [ˈtrɪptɪk] *s.* Triptychon *n*, dreiteiliges (Al'tar)Bild.

tri·sect [traɪˈsekt] *v/t.* in drei (gleiche) Teile teilen.

tri·syl·lab·ic [ˌtraɪsɪˈlæbɪk] *adj.* (□ **~al·ly**) dreisilbig; **tri·syl·la·ble** [ˌtraɪˈsɪləbl] *s.* dreisilbiges Wort.

trite [traɪt] *adj.* □ abgedroschen, platt, ba'nal; '**trite·ness** [-nɪs] *s.* Abgedroschenheit *f*, Plattheit *f.*

Tri·ton [ˈtraɪtn] *s.* **1.** *antiq.* Triton *m* (*niederer Meergott*): **a ~ among (the) minnows** ein Riese unter Zwergen; **2.** ♀ *zo.* Tritonshorn *n*; **3.** ♀ *zo.* Molch *m.*

tri·tone [ˈtraɪtəʊn] *s.* ♪ Tritonus *m.*

trit·u·rate [ˈtrɪtjʊreɪt] *v/t.* zerreiben, -mahlen, -stoßen, pulverisieren.

tri·umph [ˈtraɪəmf] I *s.* **1.** Tri'umph *m*: a) Sieg *m* (**over** über *acc.*), b) Siegesfreude *f* (**at** über *acc.*): **in ~** im Triumph, triumphierend; **2.** Tri'umph *m* (*Großtat, Erfolg*): **the ~s of science**; II *v/i.* **3.** triumphieren: a) den Sieg da'vontragen, b) jubeln, froh'locken (*beide over* über *acc.*), c) Erfolg haben; **tri·um·phal** [traɪˈʌmfl] *adj.* Triumph..., Sieges...: ~ **arch** Triumph-bogen *m*; ~ **procession** Triumphzug *m*; **tri·um·phant** [traɪˈʌmfənt] *adj.* □ **1.** triumphierend: a) den Sieg feiernd, b) sieg-, erfolg-, glorreich, c) froh'lockend, jubelnd; **2.** *obs.* herrlich.

tri·um·vir [traɪˈʌmvə] *pl.* **-virs** *od.* **-vi·ri** [traɪˈʌmvɪriː] *s. antiq.* Tri'umvir *m* (*a. fig.*); **tri·um·vi·rate** [traɪˈʌmvɪrət] *s.* **1.** *antiq.* Triumvi'rat *n* (*a. fig.*); **2.** *fig.* Dreigestirn *n.*

tri·une [ˈtraɪjuːn] *adj. bsd. eccl.* drei'einig.

tri·va·lent [ˌtraɪˈveɪlənt] *adj.* ♣ dreiwertig.

triv·et [ˈtrɪvɪt] *s.* Dreifuß *m* (*bsd. für Kochgefäße*): (**as**) **right as a ~** *fig.* bei bester Gesundheit.

triv·i·a [ˈtrɪvɪə] *s. pl.* Baga'tellen *pl.*; '**triv·i·al** [-əl] *adj.* □ **1.** trivi'al, ba'nal, all'täglich; **2.** gering(fügig), unbedeutend; **3.** oberflächlich (*Person*); **4.** volkstümlich (*Ggs. wissenschaftlich*); **triv·i·al·i·ty** [ˌtrɪvɪˈælɪtɪ] *s.* **1.** Triviali'tät *f*, Plattheit *f*, Banali'tät *f* (*a. Ausspruch etc.*); **2.** Geringfügigkeit *f*, Belanglosigkeit *f*; '**triv·i·al·ize** *v/t.* bagatellisieren.

tri·week·ly [ˌtraɪˈwiːklɪ] I *adj.* **1.** dreiwöchentlich; **2.** dreimal wöchentlich erscheinend (*Zeitschrift etc.*); II *adv.* **3.** dreimal in der Woche.

troat [trəʊt] **I** s. Röhren n des Hirsches; **II** v/i. röhren.

tro·cha·ic [trəʊ'keɪɪk] Metrik: **I** adj. tro-'chäisch; **II** s. Tro'chäus m (Vers); **tro·chee** ['trəʊkiː] s. Tro'chäus m (Versfuß).

trod [trɒd] pret. u. p.p. von **tread**.

trod·den ['trɒdn] p.p. von **tread**.

trog·lo·dyte ['trɒɡlədaɪt] s. **1.** Troglo-'dyt m, Höhlenbewohner m; **2.** fig. a) Einsiedler m, b) primi'tiver od. bru'taler Kerl; **trog·lo·dyt·ic** [ˌtrɒɡlə'dɪtɪk] adj. troglo'dytisch.

troi·ka ['trɔɪkə] (Russ.) s. Troika f, Dreigespann n.

Tro·jan ['trəʊdʒən] **I** adj. tro'janisch; **II** s. Tro'janer(in): like a ~ F wie ein Pferd arbeiten.

troll¹ [trəʊl] **I** v/t. u. v/i. **1.** (fröhlich) trällern; **2.** (mit der Schleppangel) fischen (for nach); **II** s. **3.** Schleppangel f, künstlicher Köder.

troll² [trəʊl] s. Troll m, Kobold m.

trol·ley ['trɒlɪ] s. **1.** Brit. Hand-, Gepäck-, Einkaufswagen m; Kofferkuli m; (Schub)Karren m; **2.** ⚙ Förderwagen m; **3.** 🚃 Brit. Drai'sine f; **4.** ⚡ Kon-'taktrolle f bei Oberleitungsfahrzeugen; **5.** Am. Straßenbahn(wagen m) f; **6.** Brit. Tee-, Servierwagen m; ~ **bus** s. O(berleitungs)bus m; ~ **car** s. Am. Straßenbahnwagen m; ~ **pole** s. ⚡ Stromabnehmerstange f; ~ **wire** s. Oberleitung f.

trol·lop ['trɒləp] **I** s. **1.** Schlampe f; **2.** ,Flittchen' n; **II** v/i. **3.** schlampen; **4.** ,latschen'.

trom·bone [trɒm'bəʊn] s. ♪ **1.** Po'saune f; **2.** → **trom'bon·ist** [-nɪst] s. ♪ Posau'nist m.

troop [truːp] **I** s. **1.** Trupp m, Schar f; **2.** pl. ✗ Truppe(n pl.) f; **3.** ✗ a) Schwadron f, b) ('Panzer)Kompa,nie f, c) Batte'rie f; **II** v/i. **4.** oft ~ **up**, ~ **together** sich scharen, sich sammeln; **5.** (in Scharen) wohin ziehen, (her'ein- etc.) strömen, marschieren: ~ **away**, ~ **off** F abziehen, sich da'vonmachen; **III** v/t. **6.** ~ **the colour(s)** Brit. ✗ Fahnenparade abhalten; ~ **car·ri·er** ✗ **1.** ✈, ⚓ 'Truppentrans,porter m; **2.** Mannschaftswagen m; '~-,car·ry·ing adj.: ~ **vehicle** → **troop carrier** 2.

troop·er ['truːpə] s. **1.** ✗ Reiter m, Kavalle'rist m: **swear like a** ~ fluchen wie ein Landsknecht; **2.** 'Staatspoli,zist m; **3.** bsd. Am. berittener Poli'zist; **4.** ✗ Kavalle'riepferd n; **5.** Brit. → **troopship**.

'troop·ship s. ⚓ 'Truppentrans,porter m.

trope [trəʊp] s. Tropus m (a. ♪), bildlicher Ausdruck.

troph·ic ['trɒfɪk] adj. biol. trophisch, Ernährungs...

tro·phy ['trəʊfɪ] **I** s. **1.** Tro'phäe f, Siegeszeichen n, -beute f (alle a. fig.); **2.** Preis m, (Jagd- etc.)Tro'phäe f; **II** v/t. **3.** mit Tro'phäen schmücken.

trop·ic ['trɒpɪk] s. **1.** ast., geogr. Wendekreis m; **2.** pl. geogr. Tropen pl.; **II** adj. **3.** → **tropical¹**.

trop·i·cal¹ ['trɒpɪkl] adj. □ Tropen..., tropisch: ~ **forest** Tropenwald m; ~ **rain forest** tropischer Regenwald.

trop·i·cal² ['trɒpɪkl] → **tropological**.

trop·o·log·i·cal [ˌtrɒpə'lɒdʒɪkl] adj. □ fi'gürlich, meta'phorisch.

trop·o·sphere ['trɒpə,sfɪə] s. meteor. Tropo'sphäre f.

trot [trɒt] **I** v/i. **1.** traben, trotten, im Trab gehen od. reiten: ~ **along** (od. off) F ab-, losziehen; **II** v/t. **2.** Pferd traben lassen, a. j-n in Trab setzen; **3.** ~ **out** a) Pferd vorreiten, -führen, b) fig. et. od. j-n vorführen, renommieren mit, Argumente, Kenntnisse etc., a. Wein etc. auftischen, aufwarten mit; **4.** a. ~ **round** j-n her'umführen; **III** s. **5.** Trott m, Trab m (a. fig.): **at a** ~ im Trab; **keep s.o. on the** ~ j-n in Trab halten; **6.** F ,Taps' m (kleines Kind); **7.** F ,Tante' f (alte Frau); **8. the** ~**s** pl. F ,Dünnpfiff' m; **9.** ped. Am. sl. a) Eselsbrücke f, ,Klatsche' f (Übersetzungshilfe), b) Spickzettel m; **10.** F Trabrennen n.

troth [trəʊθ] s. obs. Treue(gelöbnis n) f: **by my** ~**!, in** ~**!** meiner Treu!, wahrlich!; **pledge one's** ~ sein Wort verpfänden, ewige Treue schwören; **plight one's** ~ sich verloben.

trot·ter ['trɒtə] s. **1.** Traber m (Pferd); **2.** F Fuß m, Bein n von Schlachttieren: **pigs** ~**s** Schweinsfüße pl.; **3.** pl. humor. ,Haxen' pl.; **trot·ting race** ['trɒtɪŋ] s. Trabrennen n.

trou·ble ['trʌbl] **I** v/t. **1.** beunruhigen, stören, ängstigen; **2.** j-n bemühen, bitten (for um): **may I** ~ **you to pass me the salt** darf ich Sie um das Salz bitten; **I will** ~ **you to hold your tongue** iro. würden sie gefälligst den Mund halten; **3.** j-m 'Umstände od. Unannehmlichkeiten bereiten, j-m Mühe machen; j-n behelligen (**about, with** mit); **4.** j-n plagen, quälen: **be** ~**d with** von e-r Krankheit etc. geplagt sein; **5.** j-m Sorge od. Verdruss od. Kummer machen od. bereiten, j-n beunruhigen: **be** ~**d about** wegen Sorgen machen wegen; **don't let it** ~ **you** machen Sie sich deswegen keine Gedanken; ~**d face** sorgenvolles od. gequältes Gesicht; **6.** Wasser trüben: ~**d waters** fig. schwierige Situation, unangenehme Lage; **fish in** ~**d waters** fig. im Trüben fischen; **II** v/i. **7.** sich beunruhigen (**about** über acc.): **I should not** ~ a) ich wäre beruhigt, wenn, b) es wäre mir gleichgültig, wenn; **8.** sich die Mühe machen, sich bemühen (**to do** zu tun); sich 'Umstände machen: **don't** ~ (**yourself**) bemühen Sie sich nicht; **don't** ~ **to write** du brauchst nicht zu schreiben; **III** s. **9.** Mühe f, Plage f, Last f, Belästigung f, Störung f: **give s.o.** ~ j-m Mühe verursachen; **go to much** ~ sich besondere Mühe machen od. geben; **put s.o. to** ~ j-m Umstände bereiten; **save o.s. the** ~ **of doing** sich die Mühe (er)sparen, zu tun; **take (the)** ~ sich (die) Mühe machen; **take** ~ **over** sich Mühe geben mit; (**it is**) **no** ~ (**at all**) (es ist) nicht der Rede wert; **10.** Unannehmlichkeiten pl., Schwierigkeiten pl., Scherereien pl., ,Ärger' m (**with** mit der Polizei etc.): **ask** od. **look for** ~ unbedingt Ärger haben wollen; **be in** ~ in Schwierigkeiten sein; **get into** ~ in Schwierigkeiten geraten, Ärger bekommen; **make** ~ **for s.o.** j-n in Schwierigkeiten bringen; **he is** ~ F er ist gefährlich, mit ihm wird es Ärger geben; **11.** Schwierigkeit f, Pro'blem n: **the** ~ **is** der Haken dabei ist, das Unangenehme ist (**that** dass); **what's the** ~**?** wo(ran) fehlts?, was ist los?; **12.** ✚ Störung f, Leiden n: **heart** ~ Herzleiden n; **13.** a) pol. Unruhe(n pl.) f, Wirren pl., b) allg. Af'färe f, Kon-'flikt m; **14.** ⚙ Störung f, De'fekt m; '~,mak·er s. Unruhestifter m; ~ **man** [mən] s. [irr.] ⚙ Störungssucher m; '~-proof adj. störungsfrei; '~,shoot·er s. bsd. Am. **1.** → **trouble man**; **2.** ⚙, Friedensstifter m, ,Feuerwehrmann' m, Vermittler(in); '~,shoot·ing s. **1.** ⚙,

Computer: Troubleshooting n, Prob-'lembehandlung f; **2.** Krisenmanagement n.

trou·ble·some ['trʌblsəm] adj. □ lästig, beschwerlich, unangenehm; '**trou·ble·some·ness** [-nɪs] s. Lästigkeit f, Beschwerlichkeit f; das Unangenehme.

trouble spot s. **1.** ⚙ Schwachstelle f; **2.** bsd. pol. Unruheherd m.

trou·blous ['trʌbləs] adj. □ obs. unruhig.

trough [trɒf] s. **1.** Trog m, Mulde f; **2.** Wanne f; **3.** Rinne f, Ka'nal m; **4.** Wellental n: ~ **of the sea**; **5.** a. ~ **of low pressure** meteor. Tief(druckrinne f) n; **6.** bsd. ✚ Tiefpunkt m, ,Talsohle' f.

trounce [traʊns] v/t. **1.** verprügeln; **2.** fig. her'untermachen; **3.** sport ,über-'fahren', j-m e-e Abfuhr erteilen.

troupe [truːp] s. (Schauspieler-, Zirkus-) Truppe f.

trou·sered ['traʊzəd] adj. Hosen tragend, behost; '**trou·ser·ing** [-zərɪŋ] s. Hosenstoff m; **trou·sers** ['traʊzəz] s. pl. (**a pair of** ~ e-e) (lange) Hose; Hosen pl.; → **wear¹** 1.

trou·ser suit s. Hosenanzug m.

trousse [truːs] s. 🔪 (chi'rurgisches) Besteck.

trous·seau ['truːsəʊ] pl. **-seaus** (Fr.) s. Aussteuer f.

trout [traʊt] ichth. **I** pl. **-s**, bsd. coll. **trout** s. Fo'relle f; **II** v/i. Fo'rellen fischen; **III** adj. Forellen...

trove [trəʊv] s. Fund m.

tro·ver ['trəʊvə] s. ⚖ **1.** rechtswidrige Aneignung; **2.** a. **action of** ~ Klage f auf Her'ausgabe des Wertes.

trow·el ['traʊəl] **I** s. **1.** (Maurer)Kelle f: **lay it on with a** ~ fig. (zu) dick auftragen; **2.** ✿ Hohlspatel m, Pflanzenheber m; **II** v/t. **3.** mit der Kelle auftragen, glätten.

troy (**weight**) [trɔɪ] s. ✚ Troygewicht n (für Edelmetalle, Edelsteine u. Arzneien; 1 lb. = 373,24 g).

tru·an·cy ['truːənsɪ] s. (Schul)Schwänze-'rei f, unentschuldigtes Fernbleiben; '**tru·ant** [-nt] **I** s. **1.** a) (Schul)Schwänzer(in), b) Bummler(in), Faulenzer (-in): **play** ~ (bsd. die Schule) schwänzen, a. bummeln; **II** adj. **2.** träge, faul, pflichtvergessen; **3.** (schul)schwänzend; **4.** fig. (ab)schweifend (Gedanken).

truce [truːs] s. **1.** ✗ Waffenruhe f, -stillstand m: **flag of** ~ Parlamentärflagge f; ~ **of God** hist. Gottesfriede m; (**political**) ~ Burgfriede m; **a** ~ **to talking!** Schluss mit (dem) Reden!; **2.** fig. (Ruhe-, Atem)Pause f (**from** von).

truck¹ [trʌk] **I** s. **1.** Tausch(handel) m; **2.** Verkehr m: **have no** ~ **with s.o.** mit j-m nichts zu tun haben; **3.** Am. Gemüse f: ~ **farm**, ~ **garden** Am. Gemüsegärtnerei f; ~ **farmer** Am. Gemüsegärtner m; **4.** coll. a) Kram(waren pl.) m, Hausbedarf m, b) contp. Plunder m; **5.** mst ~ **system** ✚ hist. Natu'rallohn-, 'Trucksy,stem n; **II** v/t. **6.** (for) (aus-, ver)tauschen (gegen), eintauschen (für); **7.** verschachern; **III** v/i. **8.** Tauschhandel treiben; **9.** schachern, handeln (for um).

truck² [trʌk] **I** s. **1.** ⚙ Block-, Laufrad n; **2.** Hand-, Gepäck-, Rollwagen m; **3.** Lore f: a) 🚃 Brit. offener Güterwagen, b) 🔧 Kippkarren m, Förderwagen m; **4.** Am. Lastauto n, -(kraft)wagen m: ~ **trailer** a) Lastwagenanhänger m, b) Lastzug m; **5.** 🚃 Dreh-, 'Untergestell n; **6.** ⚓ Flaggenknopf m; **II** v/t. **7.** auf Güter- od. Lastwagen etc. befördern; '**truck·age** [-kɪdʒ] s. **1.** Am. 'Lastwa-

gentrans,port m; **2.** Trans'portkosten pl.
truck·er¹ ['trʌkə] s. Am. **1.** Lastwagen-, Fernlastfahrer m; **2.** 'Autospedi,teur m.
truck·er² ['trʌkə] s. Am. Gemüsegärtner m.
truck·le¹ ['trʌkl] v/i. (zu Kreuze) kriechen (**to** vor dat.).
truck·le² ['trʌkl] s. **1.** (Lauf)Rolle f; **2.** mst ~**bed** (niedriges) Rollbett.
truc·u·lence ['trʌkjʊləns], **'truc·u·len·cy** [-sɪ] s. **1.** Brutalität f; **2.** Aufsässigkeit f; aggressive Ablehnung; **3.** Gehässigkeit f; **'truc·u·lent** [-nt] adj. □ **1.** wild, grausam; **2.** aufsässig; **3.** gehässig.
trudge [trʌdʒ] **I** v/i. (bsd. mühsam) stapfen; sich (mühsam) (fort)schleppen: ~ **along**; **II** v/t. (mühsam) durch'wandern; **III** s. mühseliger Marsch od. Weg.
true [truː] **I** adj. □ → **truly**; **1.** wahr, wahrheitsgetreu: a ~ **story**; be ~ **of** zutreffen auf (acc.), gelten für; **come** ~ sich bewahrheiten, sich erfüllen, eintreffen; **2.** wahr, echt, wirklich, (regel-)recht: a ~ **Christian**; ~ **bill** ✠ begründete (von den Geschworenen bestätigte) Anklage(schrift); ~ **love** wahre Liebe; (**it is**) ~ zwar, allerdings, freilich, zugegeben; **3.** (ge)treu (**to** dat.): a ~ **friend**; (**as**) ~ **as gold** (od. **steel**) treu wie Gold; ~ **to one's principles** (**word**) s-n Grundsätzen (s-m Wort) getreu; **4.** (ge)treu (**to** dat.) (von Sachen): ~ **copy**; ~ **weight** genaues od. richtiges Gewicht; ~ **to life** lebenswahr, -echt; ~ **to nature** naturgetreu; ~ **to size** ⊙ maßgerecht, -haltig; ~ **to type** artgemäß, typisch; **5.** rechtmäßig: ~ **heir** (**owner**); **6.** zuverlässig: a ~ **sign**; **7.** ⊙ genau, richtig eingestellt od. eingepasst; **8.** ⚓, phys. rechtweisend (Kurs, Peilung): ~ **declination** Ortsmissweisung f; ~ **north** geographisch Nord; **9.** ♪ richtig gestimmt, rein; **10.** biol. reinrassig; **II** adv. **11.** wahr('haftig): **speak** ~ die Wahrheit reden; **12.** (ge)treu (**to** dat.); **13.** genau: **shoot** ~; **III** s. **14.** **the** ~ das Wahre; **15. out of** ~ ⊙ unrund; **IV** v/t. **16.** a. ~ **up** ⊙ Lager ausrichten; Werkzeug nachschleifen; Rad zentrieren; ~ **blue** s. getreuer Anhänger (Brit. der Tories); **,~-'blue** adj. waschecht, treu; **'~-born** adj. echt, gebürtig; **'~-bred** adj. reinrassig; **,~-'heart·ed** adj. aufrichtig, ehrlich; **,~-'life** adj. lebenswahr, -echt; **'~-love** s. Geliebte(r m) f.
true·ness ['truːnɪs] s. **1.** Wahrheit f; **2.** Echtheit f; **3.** Treue f; **4.** Richtigkeit f; **5.** Genauigkeit f.
truf·fle ['trʌfl] s. ♣ Trüffel f.
tru·ism ['truːɪzəm] s. Binsenwahrheit f, Gemeinplatz m.
trull [trʌl] s. Dirne f, Hure f.
tru·ly ['truːlɪ] adv. **1.** wahrheitsgemäß; **2.** aufrichtig: **Yours** (**very**) ~ (als Briefschluss) Hochachtungsvoll; **yours** ~ humor. meine Wenigkeit; **3.** wahr'haftig, in der Tat; **4.** genau.
trump¹ [trʌmp] s. obs. od. poet. Trom'pete(nstoß m) f: **the** ~ **of doom** die Posaune des Jüngsten Gerichts.
trump² [trʌmp] **I** s. **1.** a) Trumpf m, b) a. ~ **card** Trumpfkarte f (a. fig.): **play one's** ~ **card** fig. s-n Trumpf ausspielen; **put s.o. to his** ~ fig. j-n bis zum Äußersten treiben; **turn up** ~s a) sich als das Beste erweisen, b) Glück haben; **2.** F fig. feiner Kerl; **II** v/t. **3.** (über-) 'trumpfen; **4.** fig. j-n über'trumpfen (**with** mit); **III** v/i. **5.** Trumpf ausspielen, trumpfen.
trump³ [trʌmp] v/t. ~ **up** contp. erdichten, erfinden, sich aus den Fingern saugen; **,trumped-'up** [,trʌmpt-] adj. erfunden, erlogen, falsch: ~ **charges**.

trump·er·y ['trʌmpərɪ] **I** s. **1.** Plunder m, Schund m; **2.** fig. Gewäsch n, Quatsch m; **II** adj. **3.** Schund..., Kitsch..., kitschig, geschmacklos; **4.** fig. billig, nichts sagend: ~ **arguments**.
trum·pet ['trʌmpɪt] **I** s. **1.** ♪ Trom'pete f: ~ **call** Trompetensignal n; **blow one's own** ~ fig. sein eigenes Lob singen; **the last** ~ die Posaune des Jüngsten Gerichts; **2.** Trom'petenstoß m (a. des Elefanten); **3.** ♪ Trom'pete(nre,gister n) f (Orgel); **4.** Schalltrichter m, Sprachrohr n; **5.** Hörrohr n; **II** v/t. u. v/i. **6.** trom'peten (a. Elefant): ~ (**forth**) fig. ausposaunen; **'trum·pet·er** [-tə] s. **1.** Trom'peter m; fig. a.) 'Auspo,sauner(in), b) Lobredner m, c) ‚Sprachrohr' n; **3.** orn. Trom'petertaube f;
trum·pet ma·jor s. ✕ 'Stabstrom,peter m.
trun·cate [trʌŋ'keɪt] **I** v/t. **1.** a. fig. stutzen, beschneiden; **2.** ⚕ abstumpfen; **3.** ⊙ Gewinde abflachen; **4.** Computer: beenden; **II** adj. **5.** abgestutzt, -stumpft (Blätter, Muscheln); **trun'cat·ed** [-tɪd] adj. **1.** a. fig. gestutzt, beschnitten; **2.** ⚕ abgestumpft: ~ **cone** (**pyramid**) Kegel- (Pyramiden)stumpf m; **3.** ⊙ abgeflacht; **trun·ca·tion** [trʌŋ'keɪʃn] s. **1.** a. fig. Stutzung f; **2.** ⚕ Abstumpfung f; **3.** ⊙ Abflachung f; **4.** Computer: Beendigung f.
trun·cheon ['trʌntʃən] s. **1.** Brit. (Gummi)Knüppel m, Schlagstock m der Polizei; **2.** Kom'mandostab m.
trun·dle ['trʌndl] **I** v/t. Fass etc. trudeln, rollen; Reifen schlagen; j-n im Rollstuhl etc. fahren; **II** v/i. oft ~ **along** rollen, sich wälzen, trudeln; **III** s. Rolle f, Walze f: ~ **bed** → **truckle²** 2.
trunk [trʌŋk] s. **1.** (Baum)Stamm m; **2.** Rumpf m, Leib m, Torso m; **3.** zo. Rüssel m; **4.** (Schrank)Koffer m, Truhe f; **5.** △ (Säulen)Schaft m; **6.** anat. (Nerven- etc.)Strang m, Stamm m; **7.** pl. a) → **trunk hose**, b) Badehose f, c) sport Shorts pl., d) ('Herren),Unterhose f; **8.** ⊙ Rohrleitung f, Schacht m; **9.** teleph. bsd. Brit. a) Fernleitung f, b) Fernverbindung f; **10.** ⟅ → **trunk line** 1; **11.** mot. Am. Kofferraum m; **12.** Computer: Anschlussstelle f; ~ **call** s. teleph. Brit. Ferngespräch n; ~ **hose** s. hist. Kniehose f; ~ **line** s. **1.** ⟅ Hauptstrecke f, -linie f; **2.** → **trunk** 9 a; ~ **road** s. Haupt-, Fernverkehrsstraße f; ~ **route** s. allg. Hauptstrecke f.
trun·nion ['trʌnjən] s. ⊙ (Dreh)Zapfen m.
truss [trʌs] **I** v/t. **1.** oft ~ **up** a) bündeln, (fest)schnüren, zs.-binden, b) j-n fesseln; **2.** Geflügel zum Braten dressieren; **3.** △ absteifen, stützen; **4.** oft ~ **up** obs. Kleider etc. aufschürzen, -stecken; **5.** obs. j-n aufhängen; **II** s. **6.** ✿ Bruchband n; **7.** △ a) Träger m, Binder m, b) Fach-, Gitter-, Hängewerk n, Gerüst n; **8.** ⚓ Rack n; **9.** (Heu-, Stroh)Bündel n, (a. Schlüssel)Bund n; **10.** ♣ Dolde f; ~ **bridge** s. (Gitter)Fachwerkbrücke f.
trust [trʌst] **I** s. **1.** (in) Vertrauen n (auf acc.), Zutrauen n (zu dat.): **place** (od. **put**) **one's** ~ **in** → 13; **position of** ~ Vertrauensposten m; **take s.th. on** ~ et. (einfach) glauben; **2.** Zuversicht f, zuversichtliche Erwartung od. Hoffnung, Glaube m; **3.** Kre'dit m: **on** ~ a) auf Kredit, b) auf Treu u. Glauben; **4.** Pflicht f, Verantwortung f; **5.** Verwahrung f, Obhut f: **in** ~ zu treuen Händen; **6.** Pfand n, anvertrautes Gut; **7.** ✠ a) Treuhand(verhältnis n) f, b) Treuhand-

gut n, -vermögen n: **breach of** ~ Verletzung f der Treupflicht; ~ **territory** pol. Treuhandgebiet n; **hold s.th. in** ~ et. treuhänderisch verwalten; **8.** ✠ a) Trust m, b) Kon'zern m; **9.** Kar'tell n, Ring m; (Familien- etc.)Stiftung f; **II** v/t. **10.** j-m (ver)trauen, glauben, sich auf j-n verlassen: ~ **s.o. to do s.th.** j-m zutrauen, dass er et. tut; ~ **him to do that!** iro. a) das sieht ihm ähnlich!, b) verlass dich drauf, er wird es tun!; **11.** (**s.o. with s.th., s.th. to s.o.**) j-m et. anvertrauen; **12.** (zuversichtlich) hoffen od. erwarten, glauben; **III** v/i. **13.** (**in, to**) vertrauen (auf acc.), sein Vertrauen setzen (auf acc.); **14.** hoffen, glauben, denken; ~ **com·pa·ny** s. Am. Treuhandgesellschaft f od. -bank f; ~ **deed** s. Treuhandvertrag m.
trus·tee [,trʌs'tiː] s. **1.** Sachwalter m (a. fig.), (Vermögens)Verwalter m, Treuhänder m: ~ **in bankruptcy**, **official** ~ Konkurs-, Masseverwalter; **Public** ℒ Brit. öffentlicher Treuhänder; ~ **process** Am. Beschlagnahme f, (bsd. Forderungs)Pfändung f; ~ **securities**, ~ **stock** mündelsichere Wertpapiere; **2.** Ku'rator m, Pfleger m: **board of** ~s Kuratorium n; **trus'tee·ship** [-ʃɪp] s. **1.** Treuhänderschaft f; **2.** Kura'torium n; **3.** pol. a) Treuhandverwaltung f, b) Treuhandgebiet n.
trust·ful ['trʌstfʊl] adj. □ vertrauensvoll, zutraulich.
trust fund s. ✠ Treuhandvermögen n.
trust·i·fi·ca·tion [,trʌstɪfɪ'keɪʃn] s. ✠ Ver'trustung f, Trustbildung f.
trust·ing ['trʌstɪŋ] adj. □ → **trustful**.
'trust,wor·thi·ness [-,wɜːðɪnɪs] s. Vertrauenswürdigkeit f; **'trust,wor·thy** adj. □ vertrauenswürdig, zuverlässig.
trust·y ['trʌstɪ] **I** adj. □ **1.** vertrauensvoll; **2.** treu, zuverlässig; **II** s. **3.** ‚Kal'fakter' m (privilegierter Sträfling).
truth [truːθ] s. **1.** Wahrheit f: **in** ~, obs. **of a** ~ in Wahrheit; **the** ~, **the whole** ~ **and nothing but the** ~ ✠ die reine Wahrheit; **to tell the** ~, **to tell** um die Wahrheit zu sagen, ehrlich gesagt; **there is no** ~ **in it** daran ist nichts Wahres; **the** ~ **is that I forgot it** in Wirklichkeit od. tatsächlich habe ich es vergessen; **2.** allgemein anerkannte Wahrheit: **historical** ~; **3.** Wahr'haftigkeit f; Aufrichtigkeit f; **4.** Wirklichkeit f, Echtheit f, Treue f; **5.** Richtigkeit f, Genauigkeit f: **be out of** ~ ⊙ nicht genau passen; ~ **to life** Lebensechtheit f; ~ **to nature** Naturtreue f.
truth·ful ['truːθfʊl] adj. □ **1.** wahr (-heitsgemäß); **2.** wahrheitsliebend; **3.** echt, genau, getreu; **'truth·ful·ness** [-nɪs] s. **1.** Wahr'haftigkeit f; **2.** Wahrheitsliebe f; **3.** Echtheit f.
try [traɪ] **I** s. **1.** Versuch m: **have a** ~ e-n Versuch machen, es versuchen (**at** mit); **2.** Rugby: Versuch m; **II** v/t. **3.** versuchen, probieren: ~ **one's best** sein Bestes tun; ~ **one's hand at s.th.** sich an e-r Sache versuchen; **4.** a. ~ **out** (aus-, 'durch)probieren, erproben, prüfen: ~ **a new method** (**remedy**, **invention**); ~ **on** Kleid etc. anprobieren, Hut aufprobieren; ~ **it on with s.o.** sl. ‚es bei j-m probieren'; **5.** e-n Versuch machen mit, es versuchen mit: ~ **the door** die Tür zu öffnen suchen; ~ **one's luck** sein Glück versuchen (**with** bei j-m); **6.** ✠ a) verhandeln über e-e Sache, Fall unter'suchen, b) verhandeln gegen j-n, vor Gericht stellen; **7.** Augen etc. angreifen, (über)'anstrengen, Geduld, Mut, Nerven etc. auf e-e harte Probe

stellen; **8.** *j-n* arg mitnehmen, plagen, quälen; **9.** *mst* **~ out** ⊙ a) *Metalle* raffinieren, scheiden, b) *Talg etc.* ausschmelzen, c) *Spiritus* rektifizieren; **III** *v/i.* **10.** versuchen (*at acc.*), sich bemühen *od.* bewerben (*for* um); **11.** versuchen, e-n Versuch machen: **~ again!** (versuch es) noch einmal!; **~ and read!** F versuche zu lesen!; **~ hard** sich große Mühe geben.

try·ing ['traɪɪŋ] *adj.* □ **1.** schwierig, kritisch, unangenehm, nervtötend; **2.** anstrengend, ermüdend (**to** für).

'try|-on *s.* **1.** Anprobe *f*; **2.** F 'Schwindelma,növer *n*; **'~-out** *s.* **1.** Probe *f*, Erprobung *f*; **2.** *sport* Ausscheidungskampf *m*, -spiel *n*; **~·sail** ['traɪsl] *s.* ♣ Gaffelsegel *n*; **~ square** ⊙ Richtscheit *n*.

tryst [trɪst] *obs.* **I** *s.* **1.** Stelldichein *n*, Rendez'vous *n*; **2.** → *trysting place*; **II** *v/t.* **3.** *j-n* (an e-n verabredeten Ort) bestellen; **4.** *Zeit, Ort* verabreden; **tryst·ing place** [-tɪŋ] *s.* Treffpunkt *m*.

tsar [zɑː] *etc.* → *czar etc.*

tset·se (fly) ['tsetsɪ] *s. zo.* Tsetsefliege *f*.

'T-shirt *s.* T-Shirt *n*.

'T-square *s.* ⊙ **1.** Reißschiene *f*; **2.** Anschlagwinkel *m*.

tub [tʌb] **I** *s.* **1.** (Bade)Wanne *f*; **2.** *Brit.* F (Wannen)Bad *n*; **3.** Bottich *m*, Kübel *m*, Wanne *f*; **4.** (*Butter- etc.*)Fass *n*, Tonne *f*; **5.** Fass *n* (*als Maß*): **a ~ of tea**; **6.** ♣ *humor.* ,Kahn' *m*, ,Kasten' *m* (*Schiff*); **7.** *Rudern:* Übungsboot *n*; **8.** ⚒ Förderkorb *m*, -wagen *m*; **9.** *humor.* Kanzel *f*; **II** *v/t.* **10.** *bsd. Butter* in ein Fass tun; **11.** ♀ in e-n Kübel pflanzen; **12.** F baden; **III** *v/i.* **13.** F (sich) baden; **14.** *Rudern:* im Übungsboot trainieren.

tu·ba ['tjuːbə] *s.* ♪ Tuba *f*.

tub·by ['tʌbɪ] **I** *adj.* **1.** fass-, tonnenartig; **2.** F rundlich, klein u. dick; **3.** dumpf, hohl (*klingend*); **II** *s.* **4.** F ,Dickerchen' *n*.

tube [tjuːb] **I** *s.* **1.** Rohr(leitung *f*) *n*, Röhre *f*; (*Glas- etc.*)Röhrchen *n*: **test tube**; **2.** Schlauch *m*: (*inner*) **~** ⊙ (Luft)Schlauch *m*; **3.** (Me'tall)Tube *f*: **~ colo(u)rs** Tubenfarben; **4.** ♪ (Blas-) Rohr *n*; **5.** *anat.* (*Luft- etc.*)Röhre *f*, Ka'nal *m*; **6.** ♀ (Pollen)Schlauch *m*; **7.** ↯ Röhre *f*: **the ~** die ,Röhre' *f* (*Fernseher*); **on the ~** ,in der Glotze'; **8.** a) (U-Bahn)Tunnel *m*, b) *a.* ➁ die Londoner U-Bahn; **II** *v/t.* **9.** ⊙ mit Röhren versehen; **10.** (durch Röhren) befördern; **11.** (in Röhren *od.* Tuben) abfüllen; **'tube-feed** [*irr.* → **feed**] *v/t.* ⚕ künstlich (⚕ zwangs)ernähren; **'tube·less** [-lɪs] *adj.* schlauchlos (*Reifen*).

tu·ber ['tjuːbə] *s.* **1.** ♀ Knolle *f*, Knollen(gewächs *n*) *m*; **2.** ♣ Knoten *m*, Schwellung *f*, Tuber *m*.

tu·ber·cle ['tjuːbəkl] *s.* **1.** *biol.* Knötchen *n*; **2.** ♣ a) Tu'berkel(knötchen *n*) *m*, b) (*bsd.* 'Lungen)Tu,berkel *m*; **3.** ♀ kleine Knolle, Warze *f*; **tu·ber·cu·lar** [tjuː'bɜːkjʊlə] → **tuberculous**; **tu·ber·cu·lo·sis** [tjuːˌbɜːkjʊ'ləʊsɪs] *s.* ♣ Tuberku'lose *f*; **tu·ber·cu·lous** [tjuː'bɜːkjʊləs] *adj.* **1.** ♣ tuberku'lös, Tuberkel...; **2.** knotig.

tube·rose¹ ['tjuːbərəʊz] *s.* ♀ Tube'rose *f*, 'Nachthya,zinthe *f*.

tu·ber·ose² ['tjuːbərəʊs] → **tuberous**.

tu·ber·os·i·ty [ˌtjuːbə'rɒsɪtɪ] → **tuber** 2.

tu·ber·ous ['tjuːbərəs] *adj.* **1.** *anat.*, ♣ knotig, knötchenförmig; **2.** ♀ a) Knollen tragend, b) knollig.

tub·ing ['tjuːbɪŋ] *s.* ⊙ **1.** 'Röhrenmateri,al *n*, Rohr *n*; **2.** *coll.* Röhren *pl.*, Röhrenanlage *f*; **3.** Rohr(stück) *n*.

'tub|-,thump·er *s.* (g)eifernder *od.* schwülstiger Redner; **'~-,thump·ing**

---

adj. (g)eifernd, schwülstig.

tu·bu·lar ['tjuːbjʊlə] *adj.* rohrförmig, Röhren..., Rohr...: **~ boiler** Heizrohrkessel *m*; **~ furniture** Stahlrohrmöbel *pl.*; **tu·bule** ['tjuːbjuːl] *s.* **1.** Röhrchen *n*; **2.** *anat.* Ka'nälchen *n*.

tuck [tʌk] **I** *s.* **1.** Falte *f*, Biese *f*, Einschlag *m*, Saum *m*; Lasche *f*; **2.** ♣ Gilling *f*; **3.** *ped. Brit.* F Süßigkeiten *pl.*; **4.** *sport* Hocke *f*; **II** *v/t.* **5.** *mst* **~ in** a) einnähen, b) *Falte* einschlagen; **6.** Biesen nähen in *ein Kleid*; **7.** *mst* **~ in** (*od.* **up**) ein-, 'umschlagen: **~ up** a) abnähen, b) hochstecken, -schürzen, c) raffen, d) *Ärmel* hochkrempeln; **8.** *et. wohin* stecken, *unter den Arm etc.* klemmen: **~ away** a) wegstecken, verstauen, b) verstecken: **~ed away** versteckt (liegend) (*z.B. Dorf*); **~ in** (*od.* **up**) (*warm*) zudecken, (*behaglich*) einpacken: **~ up in bed** ins Bett stecken; **~ up one's legs** die Beine anziehen; **9.** **~ in** *sl. Essen etc.* ,verdrücken'; **III** *v/i.* **10.** sich falten: **~ away** sich verstauen lassen; **11.** **~ in** F *beim Essen* ,einhauen': **~ into** sich *et.* schmecken lassen.

tuck·er¹ ['tʌkə] *s.* **1.** Faltenleger *m* (*Nähmaschine*); **2.** *hist.* Brusttuch *n*: **best bib and ~** *fig.* Sonntagsstaat *m*.

tuck·er² ['tʌkə] *v/t. mst* **~ out** *Am.* F *j-n* ,fertig machen' (*völlig erschöpfen*): **~ed out** (total) erledigt.

'tuck|-in *s. Brit. sl.* ,Fresse'rei' *f*, Schmaus *m*; **'~-shop** *s. Brit. ped. sl.* Süßwarenladen *m*.

Tues·day ['tjuːzdɪ] *s.* Dienstag *m*: **on ~** am Dienstag; **on ~s** dienstags.

tu·fa ['tjuːfə] *s. geol.* Kalktuff *m*, Tuff(-stein) *m*; **tu·fa·ceous** [tjuː'feɪʃəs] *adj.* (Kalk)Tuff...

tuff [tʌf] → *tufa*.

tuft [tʌft] *s.* **1.** (*Gras-, Haar- etc.*)Büschel *n*, (*Feder- etc.*)Busch *m*, (*Haar-*) Schopf *m*; **2.** Quaste *f*, Troddel *f*; **3.** *anat.* Kapil'largefäßbündel *n*; **'tuft·ed** [-tɪd] *adj.* **1.** büschelig; **2.** *orn.* Hauben...: **~ lark**; **'tuft,hunt·er** *s.* gesellschaftlicher Streber; **'tuft·y** ['tʌftɪ] *adj.* büschelig.

tug [tʌg] **I** *v/t.* **1.** zerren, ziehen an (*dat.*); ♣ schleppen; **II** *v/i.* **2.** **~ at** zerren an (*dat.*); **3.** *fig.* sich (ab)placken; **III** *s.* **4.** Zerren *n*, (heftiger) Zug, Ruck *m*: **give a ~ at** → 2; **~ of war** *sport u. fig.* Tauziehen *n*; **5.** *fig.* a) große Anstrengung, b) schwerer (*a. seelischer*) Kampf; **6.** *a.* **~boat** ♣ Schleppdampfer *m*, Schlepper *m*.

tu·i·tion [tjuː'ɪʃn] *s.* 'Unterricht *m*: **private ~** Privatunterricht, -stunden *pl.*; **tu·i·tion·al** [-ʃənl], **tu·i·tion·ar·y** [-ʃnərɪ] *adj.* Unterrichts..., Studien...

tu·lip ['tjuːlɪp] *s.* ♀ Tulpe *f*; **~ tree** *s.* ♀ Tulpenbaum *m*.

tulle [tjuːl] *s.* Tüll *m*.

tum·ble ['tʌmbl] **I** *s.* **1.** Fall *m*, Sturz *m* (*a.* ↑): **~ in prices** ↑ Preissturz *m*; **2.** Purzelbaum *m*; Salto *m*; **3.** *fig.* Wirrwarr *m*: **all in a ~** kunterbunt durcheinander; **4.** **give s.o. a ~** *sl.* von *j-m* Notiz nehmen; **II** *v/i.* **5.** *a.* **~ down** (ein-, 'um-, hin-, hin'ab)fallen, (-)stürzen, (-)purzeln: **~ over** umkippen, sich überschlagen; **6.** purzeln, stolpern (**over** über *acc.*); **7.** *wohin* stolpern (*eilen*): **~ into** *fig.* a) *j-m* in *die Arme* laufen, b) in *e-n Krieg etc.* ,hineinschlittern'; **~ to** *sl. et.* plötzlich ,kapieren' *od.* ,spitzkriegen'; **8.** Luftsprünge *od.* Saltos *etc.* machen; *sport* Bodenübungen machen; **9.** *sl.* sich wälzen; **10.** ✕ taumeln (*Geschoss*); **11.** ↑ ,purzeln' (*Aktien, Preise*); **III** *v/t.* **12.** zu Fall brin-

---

gen, 'umstürzen, -werfen; **13.** durch'wühlen; **14.** schleudern, schmeißen; **15.** zerknüllen; *Haar* zerzausen; **16.** ⊙ schleudern; **17.** *hunt.* abschießen; **'~-down** *adj.* baufällig; **~ dri·er** *s.* Wäschetrockner *m*.

tum·bler ['tʌmblə] *s.* **1.** Trink-, Wasserglas *n*, Becher *m*; **2.** Par'terreakro,bat (-in); **3.** ⊙ a) Zuhaltung *f* (*Türschloss*), b) Richtwelle *f* (*Übersetzungsmotor*), c) Zahn *m*, d) Nocken, e) (Wasch-, Scheuer)Trommel *f*; **4.** *orn.* Tümmler *m*; **5.** *Am.* Stehaufmännchen *n*; **~ switch** *s.* ↯ Kippschalter *m*.

tum·brel ['tʌmbrəl], **tum·bril** [-rɪl] *s.* **1.** ✗ Mistkarren *m*; **2.** *hist.* Schinderkarren *m*; **3.** ✕ *hist.* Muniti'onskarren *m*.

tu·me·fa·cient [ˌtjuːmɪ'feɪʃnt] *adj.* ♣ Schwellung erzeugend, **tu·me·fac·tion** [-'fækʃn] *s.* ♣ (An)Schwellung *f*, Geschwulst *f*; **tu·me·fy** ['tjuːmɪfaɪ] *v/i. u. v/t.* ♣ (an)schwellen lassen; **tu·mes·cent** [tjuː'mesnt] *adj.* (an)schwellend, geschwollen.

tu·mid ['tjuːmɪd] *adj.* ♣ geschwollen (*a. fig.*); **tu·mid·i·ty** [tjuː'mɪdətɪ] *s.* **1.** ♣ Schwellung *f*; **2.** *fig.* Geschwollenheit *f*.

tum·my ['tʌmɪ] *s. Kindersprache:* Bäuchlein *n*: **~ ache** Bauchweh *n*.

tu·mo(u)r ['tjuːmə] *s.* ♣ Tumor *m*.

tu·mult ['tjuːmʌlt] *s.* Tu'mult *m*: a) Getöse *n*, Lärm *m*, b) (*a. seelischer*) Aufruhr *m*; **tu·mul·tu·ar·y** [tjuː'mʌltjʊərɪ] *adj.* **1.** → **tumultuous**; **2.** verworren; **3.** aufrührerisch; **tu·mul·tu·ous** [tjuː'mʌltjʊəs] *adj.* □ **1.** tumultu'arisch, lärmend; **2.** heftig, stürmisch, turbu'lent.

tu·mu·lus ['tjuːmjʊləs] *s.* (*bsd. alter* Grab)Hügel.

tun [tʌn] *s.* **1.** Fass *n*; **2.** *Brit.* Tonne *f* (*altes Flüssigkeitsmaß*); **3.** *Brauerei:* Maischbottich *m*.

tune [tjuːn] **I** *s.* **1.** ♪ Melo'die *f*; Weise *f*, Lied *n*; *a.* Hymne *f*, Cho'ral *m*: **to the ~ of** a) nach der Melodie von, b) *fig.* in Höhe von, von sage u. schreibe £ 100; **call the ~** *fig.* das Sagen haben; **change one's ~**, **sing another ~** F e-n anderen Ton anschlagen, andere Saiten aufziehen; **2.** ♪ a) (richtige) (Ein)Stimmung e-s Instru'ments, b) richtige Tonhöhe: **in ~** (richtig) gestimmt; **out of ~** verstimmt; **keep ~** a) Stimmung halten (*Instrument*), b) Ton halten; **play out of ~** unrein *od.* falsch spielen; **sing in ~** tonrein *od.* sauber singen; **3.** ↯ Abstimmung *f*, (Scharf)Einstellung *f*; **4.** *fig.* Harmo'nie *f*: **in ~ with** übereinstimmend mit, im Einklang (stehend) mit, harmonierend mit; **be out of ~ with** im Widerspruch stehen zu, nicht übereinstimmen mit; **5.** *fig.* Stimmung *f*: **not in ~ for** nicht aufgelegt zu; **out of ~** verstimmt, missgestimmt; **II** *v/t.* **6.** *a.* **~ up** a) ♪ stimmen, b) *fig.* abstimmen (**to** auf *acc.*); **7.** *Antenne, Radio, Stromkreis* abstimmen, einstellen (**to** auf *acc.*); **8.** *fig.* a) (**to**) anpassen (an *acc.*), b) (**for**) bereitmachen (für); **III** *v/i.* **9.** stimmen; **~ in** *v/i.* (das Radio *etc.*) einschalten: **~ to** a) e-n *Sender, ein Programm* einschalten, b) *fig.* sich einstellen auf (*acc.*); **~ up I** *v/t.* **1.** → **tune** 6; **2.** *mot.*, ✈ a) startbereit machen, b) *Motor* einfahren, c) e-n Motor tunen; **3.** *fig.* a) bereitmachen, b) in Schwung bringen, c) *das Befinden etc.* heben; **II** *v/i.* **4.** ♪ (die Instru'mente) stimmen; **5.** F a) einsetzen, b) F losheulen.

tune·ful ['tjuːnfʊl] *adj.* □ **1.** me'lodisch; **2.** *obs.* sangesfreudig: **~ birds**; **tune·less** [-nlɪs] *adj.* 'unme,lodisch.

tun·er ['tjuːnə] s. **1.** ♪ (Instru'menten-)Stimmer m; **2.** ♪ a) Stimmpfeife f, b) Stimmvorrichtung f (Orgel); **3.** ♫ Abstimmvorrichtung f; **4.** Radio, TV: Tuner m, Ka'nalwähler m.

tune-up ['tjuːnʌp] s. **1.** Am. → warm-up 1 u. 3; **2.** ⊚ leistungsfördernde Maßnahmen pl.

tung·state ['tʌŋsteit] s. ♜ Wolfra'mat n; **'tung·sten** [-stən] s. ♜ Wolfram n: ~ steel ⊚ Wolframstahl m; **'tung·stic** [-stik] adj. ♜ Wolfram...: ~ acid.

tu·nic ['tjuːnik] s. **1.** antiq. Tunika f; **2.** bsd. ✕ Brit. Waffenrock m; **3.** a) 'Überkleid n, b) Kasack m; **4.** → tunicle; **5.** biol. Häutchen n, Hülle f; **'tu·ni·ca** [-kə] pl. -cae [-siː] s. anat. Häutchen n, Mantel m; **'tu·ni·cate** [-kət] s. zo. Manteltier n; **'tu·ni·cle** [-kl] s. R.C. Messgewand n.

tun·ing ['tjuːniŋ] I s. **1.** a) ♪ Stimmen n, b) fig. Ab-, Einstimmung f (to auf acc.); **2.** Anpassung f (to an acc.); **3.** ♫ Abstimmung f, Einstellung f (to auf acc.); II adj. **4.** ♪ Stimm...: ~ fork; **5.** ♫ Abstimm...(-kreis, -skala etc.).

tun·nel ['tʌnl] I s. **1.** Tunnel m, Unter'führung f (Straße, Bahn, Kanal); **2.** a. zo. 'unterirdischer Gang, Tunnel m; **3.** ✕ Stollen m; **4.** ✔ 'Windka,nal m; II v/t. **5.** unter'tunneln, e-n Tunnel bohren od. treiben durch; III v/i. **6.** e-n Tunnel anlegen od. treiben (through durch); **'tun·nel·(l)ing** [-liŋ] s. ⊚ Tunnelanlage f, -bau m.

tun·ny ['tʌni] s. bsd. coll. T(h)unfisch m.

tup [tʌp] I s. **1.** zo. Widder m; **2.** ⊚ Hammerkopf m, Rammklotz m; II v/t. **3.** zo. bespringen, decken.

tup·pence ['tʌpəns], **'tup·pen·ny** [-pni] Brit. F für twopence, twopenny.

tur·ban ['tɜːbən] s. Turban m; **'tur·baned** [-nd] adj. Turban tragend.

tur·bid ['tɜːbid] adj. □ **1.** dick(flüssig), trübe, schlammig; **2.** dick, dicht: ~ fog; **3.** fig. verworren, wirr; **tur·bid·i·ty** [tɜː'bidəti], **'tur·bid·ness** [-nis] s. **1.** Trübheit f; **2.** Dicke f; **3.** fig. Verworrenheit f.

tur·bine ['tɜːbain] I s. Tur'bine f; II adj. Turbinen...: ~ steamer; ~-powered mit Turbinenantrieb.

turbo- [tɜːbəʊ] ⊚ in Zssgn Turbinen..., Turbo...; **'tur·bo,charg·er** s. mot. 'Turbolader m; **,tur·bo'jet** (en·gine) s. ✔ (Flugzeug n mit) Turbostrahltriebwerk n; **,tur·bo'prop(-jet)** (en·gine) s. ✔ (Flugzeug n mit) 'Turbo-Pro'peller-Strahltriebwerk n; **,tur·bo'ram-jet en-gine** s. ✔ Ma'schine f mit Staustrahltriebwerk.

tur·bot ['tɜːbət] s. ichth. Steinbutt m.

tur·bu·lence ['tɜːbjʊləns] s. **1.** Unruhe f, Aufruhr m, Ungestüm n, Sturm m (a. meteor.); **2.** phys. Turbu'lenz f, Wirbelbewegung f; **'tur·bu·lent** [-nt] adj. □ **1.** unruhig, ungestüm, stürmisch, turbu'lent; **2.** aufrührerisch; **3.** phys. verwirbelt, turbu'lent, Wirbel...

turd [tɜːd] s. V **1.** ,Scheißhaufen' m; **2.** ,Scheißer' m.

tu·reen [tə'riːn] s. Ter'rine f.

turf [tɜːf] I s. **1.** Rasen m; **2.** Rasenstück n, -sode f; **3.** Torf(ballen) m; **4.** sport Turf m: a) (Pferde)Rennbahn f, b) the ~ fig. der Pferderennsport; **5.** fig. j-s Re'vier n; II v/t. **6.** mit Rasen bedecken; **7.** ~ out Brit. F j-n ,rausschmeißen'; **'turf·ite** [-fait] s. (Pferde)Rennsportliebhaber m; **'turf·y** [-fi] adj. **1.** rasenbedeckt; **2.** torfartig; **3.** fig. (Pferde)Rennsport...

tur·ges·cence [tɜː'dʒesns] s. **1.** ✵, ♥

Schwellung f, Geschwulst f; **2.** fig. Schwulst m.

tur·gid ['tɜːdʒid] adj. □ **1.** ✵ geschwollen; **2.** fig. schwülstig, ,geschwollen'; **tur·gid·i·ty** [tɜː'dʒidəti], **'tur·gid·ness** [-nis] s. **1.** Geschwollensein n; **2.** fig. Geschwollenheit f, Schwülstigkeit f.

Turk [tɜːk] I s. **1.** Türke m, Türkin f: Young ~s pol. Jungtürken pl.; **2.** obs. Ty'rann m; II adj. **3.** türkisch, Türken...

Tur·key¹ ['tɜːki] I s. Tür'kei f; II adj. türkisch: ~ carpet Orientteppich m; ~ red das Türkischrot.

tur·key² ['tɜːki] s. **1.** orn. Truthahn m, -henne f, Pute(r m) f: talk ~ Am. sl. a) Fraktur reden (with mit), b) offen od. sachlich reden; **2.** Am. sl. thea. etc. ,Pleite' f, ,'Durchfall' m; ~ cock s. **1.** Truthahn m, Puter m: (as) red as a ~ puterrot (im Gesicht); **2.** fig. eingebildeter Fatzke.

Turk·ish ['tɜːkiʃ] I adj. türkisch, Türken...; II s. ling. Türkisch n; ~ bath s. türkisches Bad; ~ de·light s. 'Fruchtge,leekon,fekt n; ~ tow·el s. Frottier-, Frot'tee(hand)tuch n.

Turko- [tɜːkəʊ, -kə] in Zssgn türkisch, Türken...

Tur·ko·man ['tɜːkəmən] pl. -mans s. **1.** Turk'mene m; **2.** ling. Turk'menisch n.

tur·mer·ic ['tɜːmərik] s. **1.** ♥ Gelbwurz f; **2.** pharm. Kurkuma f; **3.** Kurkumagelb n (Farbstoff): ~ paper ♜ Kurkumapapier n.

tur·moil ['tɜːmɔil] s. **1.** a. fig. Aufruhr m, Tu'mult m: in a ~ in Aufruhr; **2.** Getümmel n.

turn [tɜːn] I s. **1.** (Um)'Drehung f: a single ~ of the handle; done to a ~ gerade richtig durchgebraten; to a ~ fig. aufs Haar, vortrefflich; **2.** Turnus m, Reihe(nfolge) f: by (od. in) ~s abwechselnd, wechselweise; in ~ a) der Reihe nach, b) dann wieder; in his ~ seinerseits; speak out of ~ a) unpassende Bemerkungen machen; it is my ~ ich bin an der Reihe od. dran; take ~s (mit)einander od. sich abwechseln (at in dat., bei); take one's ~ handeln, wenn die Reihe an einen kommt; wait your ~! warte, bis du dran bist!; my ~ will come fig. m-e Zeit kommt (auch) noch, ,ich komme schon noch dran'; **3.** a) Drehung f, (~ to the left Links)Wendung f, b) Schwimmen: Wende f, c) Skisport: Wende f, Kehre f, Schwung m, d) Eislauf etc.: Kehre f; **4.** Wendepunkt m (a. fig.); **5.** Biegung f, Kurve f, Kehre f; **6.** Krümmung f (a. Å); **7.** Wendung f: a) 'Umkehr f: be on the ~ ♦ umschlagen (Gezeit) (→ a. 23); ~ tide 1, b) Richtung f, (Ver)Lauf m: take a good (bad) ~ sich zum Guten (Schlechten) wenden; take a ~ for the better (worse) sich bessern (verschlimmern); take an interesting ~ e-e interessante Wendung nehmen (Gespräch etc.), c) (Glücks-, Zeiten- etc.) Wende f, Wechsel m, 'Umschwung m, Krise f: ~ of the century Jahrhundertwende; ~ of the millennium Jahrtausendwende; ~ of life Lebenswende, ♪ Wechseljahre pl. der Frau; **8.** Ausschlag (-en n) m e-r Waage; **9.** (Arbeits-) Schicht f; **10.** Tour f, (einzelne) Windung (Bandage, Kabel etc.); **11.** (Rede-)Wendung f, Formulierung f; **12.** a) (kurzer) Spaziergang: take a ~ e-n Spaziergang machen, b) kurze Fahrt, ,Spritztour'; **13.** (for, to) Neigung f, Hang m, Ta'lent n (zu), Sinn m (für); **14.** a. ~ of mind Denkart f, -weise f;

15. a) (ungewöhnliche od. unerwartete) Tat, b) Dienst m, Gefallen m: a bad ~ e-e schlechte Tat od. ein schlechter Dienst; a friendly ~ ein Freundschaftsdienst; do s.o. a good ~ j-m e-n Gefallen tun; one good ~ deserves another e-e Liebe ist der andern wert; **16.** Anlass m: at every ~ auf Schritt u. Tritt; **17.** (kurze) Beschäftigung: ~ (of work) (Stück n) Arbeit f; take a ~ at rasch mal an e-e Sache gehen, sich kurz mit e-r Sache versuchen; **18.** F Schock m, Schrecken m: give s.o. a. ~ j-n erschrecken; **19.** Zweck m: this won't serve my ~ damit ist mir nicht gedient; **20.** ♪ Doppelschlag m; **21.** (Pro-'gramm)Nummer f; **22.** ✕ (Kehrt-)Wendung f: left (right) ~! links-(rechts)um!; about ~! Brit. ganze Abteilung kehrt!; **23.** on the ~ am Sauerwerden (Milch); II v/t. **24.** (im Kreis od. um e-e Achse) drehen; Hahn, Schlüssel, Schraube, e-n Patienten etc. ('um-, her'um)drehen; **25.** a. Kleider wenden; et. 'umkehren, -stülpen, -drehen; Blatt, Buchseite 'umdrehen, -wenden, Buch 'umblättern; Boden 'umpflügen, -graben; ♞ Weiche, ⊚ Hebel 'umlegen: it ~s my stomach mir dreht sich dabei der Magen um; ~ s.o.'s head fig. a) j-m den Kopf verdrehen, b) j-m zu Kopf steigen; **26.** zuwenden, -drehen, -kehren (to dat.); **27.** Blick, Kamera, Schritte etc. wenden, a. Gedanken, Verlangen richten, lenken (against gegen, on auf acc., to, toward(s) nach, auf acc.): ~ the hose on the fire den (Spritzen)Schlauch auf das Feuer richten; **28.** a) 'um-, ablenken, (-)leiten, (-) wenden, b) abwenden, abhalten, c) j-n 'umstimmen, abbringen (from von), d) Richtung ändern, e) Gesprächsthema wechseln; **29.** a) Waage zum Ausschlagen bringen, b) fig. ausschlaggebend sein bei: ~ an election bei e-r Wahl den Ausschlag geben; → balance 2, scale² 1; **30.** verwandeln (into in acc.): ~ water into wine; ~ love into hate; ~ into cash ✝ flüssig machen, zu Geld machen; **31.** a) machen, werden lassen (into zu): it ~ed her pale es ließ sie erblassen; ~ colo(u)r die Farbe wechseln, b) a. ~ sour Milch sauer werden lassen, c) Laub verfärben; **32.** Text über'tragen, -'setzen (into ins Italienische etc.); **33.** her'umgehen um: ~ the corner um die Ecke biegen, fig. über den Berg kommen; **34.** ✕ a) um'gehen, -'fassen, b) aufrollen: ~ the enemy's flank; **35.** hin'ausgehen od. hinaus sein über ein Alter, e-n Betrag etc.: he is just ~ing (od. has just ~ed) 50 er ist gerade 50 geworden; **36.** ⊚ a) drehen, b) Holzwaren, a. fig. Komplimente, Verse drechseln; **37.** formen, fig. gestalten, bilden: a well-~ed ankle; **38.** fig. Satz formen, (ab)runden: ~ a phrase; **39.** ✝ verdienen, 'umsetzen; **40.** Messerschneide etc. verbiegen, a. stumpf machen: ~ the edge of fig. e-r Bemerkung etc. die Spitze nehmen; **41.** Purzelbaum etc. schlagen; **42.** ~ loose los-, freilassen, -machen; III v/i. **43.** sich drehen (lassen), sich (im Kreis) (her'um)drehen; **44.** sich (ab-, hin-, zu-) wenden; → turn to I; **45.** sich stehend, liegend etc. ('um-, her'um)drehen; ♦, mot. wenden, (♦ ab)drehen, ✔, mot. kurven; **46.** (ab-, ein)biegen: I do not know which way to ~ fig. ich weiß nicht, was ich machen soll; **47.** e-e Biegung machen (Straße, Wasserlauf etc.); **48.** sich krümmen od. winden (Wurm

etc.): **~** *in one's grave* sich im Grabe umdrehen; **49.** sich umdrehen, -stülpen (*Schirm etc.*): *my stomach ~s at this sight* bei diesem Anblick dreht sich mir der Magen um; **50.** schwind(e)lig werden: *my head ~s* mein Kopf dreht sich; **51.** sich (ver)wandeln (*into, to* in *acc.*), 'umschlagen (*bsd. Wetter*): *love has ~ed into hate*; **52.** *Kommunist, Soldat etc.*, *a. blass, kalt etc.* werden: **~** (*sour*) sauer werden (*Milch*); **~** *traitor* zum Verräter werden; **53.** sich verfärben (*Laub*); **54.** sich wenden (*Gezeiten*); → *tide* 1;
Zssgn mit prp.:

turn| a·gainst I *v/i.* **1.** sich (*feindlich etc.*) wenden gegen; **II** *v/t.* **2.** *j-n* aufhetzen *od.* aufbringen gegen; **3.** *Spott etc.* richten gegen; **~** *in·to* → *turn* 30, 31, 32, 51; **~** *on* **I** *v/i.* **1.** sich drehen um *od.* in (*dat.*); **2.** → *turn upon*; **3.** sich wenden *od.* richten gegen; **II** *v/t.* **4.** → *turn* 27; **~** *to* **I** *v/i.* **1.** sich nach *links etc.* wenden (*Person*), nach *links etc.* abbiegen (*a. Fahrzeug, Straße etc.*); **2.** a) sich *der Musik, e-m Thema etc.* zuwenden, b) sich beschäftigen mit, c) sich anschicken (*doing s.th.* et. zu tun); **3.** s-e Zuflucht nehmen zu: **~** *God*; **4.** sich an *j-n* wenden, *j-n od. et.* zurate ziehen; **5.** → *turn* 51; **II** *v/t.* **6.** *Hand* anlegen bei: *turn a* (*od. one's*) *hand to s.th.* et. in Angriff nehmen; *he can turn his hand to anything* er ist zu allem zu gebrauchen; **7.** → *turn* 26, 27; **8.** verwandeln in (*acc.*); **9.** anwenden zu; → *account* 11; **~** *up·on* *v/i.* **1.** *fig.* abhängen von; **2.** *fig.* sich drehen um, handeln von; **3.** → *turn on* 3;
Zssgn mit adv.:

turn| a·bout, ~ a·round I *v/t.* **1.** 'umdrehen; **2.** ⚓ *Heu, Boden* wenden; **II** *v/i.* **3.** sich 'umdrehen; ✗ kehrtmachen; *fig.* 'umschwenken; **~** *a·side* *v/t.* (*v/i.* sich) abwenden; **~** *a·way* **I** *v/t.* **1.** abwenden (*from* von); **2.** abweisen, wegschicken, -jagen; **3.** entlassen; **II** *v/i.* **4.** sich abwenden; **~** *back* **I** *v/t.* **1.** 'umkehren lassen; **2.** → *turn down* 3; **3.** *Uhr* zu'rückdrehen; **II** *v/i.* **4.** zu-'rück-, 'umkehren; **5.** zu'rückgehen; **~** *down* **I** *v/t.* **1.** 'umkehren, -legen, -biegen; *Kragen* 'umschlagen, *Buchseite etc.* 'umknicken; **2.** *Gas, Lampe* kleiner stellen, *Radio etc.* leiser stellen; **3.** *Bett* aufdecken; *Bettdecke* zu'rückschlagen; **4.** *j-n, Vorschlag etc.* ablehnen; *j-m* e-n Korb geben; **II** *v/i.* **5.** abwärts *od.* nach unten gebogen sein; **6.** sich 'umlegen *od.* -schlagen lassen; **~** *in* **I** *v/t.* **1.** a) einreichen, -senden, b) ab-, zu'rückgeben; **2.** *Füße etc.* einwärts *od.* nach innen drehen *od.* biegen *od.* stellen; **3.** F et. zu'stande bringen; **II** *v/i.* **4.** F zu Bett gehen; **5.** einwärts gebogen sein; **~** *off* **I** *v/t.* **1.** *Wasser, Gas* abdrehen; *Licht, Radio etc.* ausschalten, abstellen; **2.** *Schlag etc.* abwenden, ablenken; **3.** F ,rausschmeißen', entlassen; **4.** F a) *j-m* die Lust nehmen, b) *j-n* anwidern; **II** *v/i.* **5.** abbiegen (*Person, a. Straße*); **~** *on* *v/t.* **1.** *Gas, Wasser* aufdrehen, *a. Radio* anstellen; *Licht, Gerät* anmachen, einschalten; **2.** F a) *j-n* ,antörnen', b) *j-n* (*a. sexuell*) ,anmachen', ,in Fahrt' bringen; **~** *out* **I** *v/t.* **1.** hin'auswerfen, wegjagen, vertreiben; **2.** entlassen (*of* aus *e-m Amt etc.*); **3.** *Regierung* stürzen; **4.** *Vieh* auf die Weide treiben; **5.** *Taschen etc.* 'umkehren, -stülpen; **6.** *Zimmer, Möbel* ausräumen; **7.** a) ✝ *Waren* produzieren, herstellen, b) *contp. Bücher etc.* produzie-

ren, c) *fig. Wissenschaftler etc.* her'vorbringen (*Universität etc.*): *Oxford has turned out many statesmen* aus Oxford sind schon viele Staatsmänner hervorgegangen; **8.** → *turn off* 1; **9.** *Füße etc.* auswärts *od.* nach außen drehen *od.* biegen; **10.** ausstatten, herrichten, *bsd.* kleiden: *well turned-out* gut gekleidet; **11.** ✗ antreten *od.* die Wache her'austreten lassen; **II** *v/i.* **12.** auswärts gebogen sein (*Füße etc.*); **13.** a) hin'ausziehen, her'auskommen (*of* aus), b) ✗ ausrücken (*a. Feuerwehr etc.*), c) *zur Wahl etc.* kommen (*Bevölkerung*), d) ✗ antreten, e) in Streik treten, f) F *aus dem Bett* aufstehen; **14.** gut ausfallen, werden; **15.** sich gestalten, *gut etc.* ausgehen, ablaufen; **16.** sich erweisen *od.* entpuppen als, sich her'ausstellen: *he turned out (to be) a good swimmer* er entpuppte sich als guter Schwimmer; *it turned out that he was (had), he turned out to be (have)* es stellte sich heraus, dass er … war (hatte); **~** *o·ver* **I** *v/t.* **1.** ✝ *Geld, Ware* 'umsetzen, e-n 'Umsatz haben von; **2.** 'umdrehen, -wenden, *Buch, Seite a.* 'umblättern: *please ~!* bitte wenden!; → *leaf* 3; **3.** (*to*) a) über'tragen (*dat. od. auf acc.*), über'geben (*dat.*), b) *j-n der Polizei etc.* ausliefern, über'geben; **4.** a. **~** *in one's mind* über-'legen, sich et. durch den Kopf gehen lassen; **II** *v/i.* **5.** *im Bett etc.* 'umdrehen; **6.** 'umkippen, -schlagen; **~** *round* **I** *v/i.* **1.** sich (*im Kreis od.* her'um)drehen; **2.** *fig.* s-n Sinn ändern, 'umschwenken: *but then he turned round and said* doch dann sagte er plötzlich; **II** *v/t.* **3.** (her'um)drehen; **~** *to* *v/i.* sich ,ranmachen' (an die Arbeit), sich ins Zeug legen; **~** *un·der* *v/t.* 'unterpflügen; **~** *up* **I** *v/t.* **1.** nach oben drehen *od.* richten *od.* biegen; *Kragen* hochschlagen, -klappen; → *nose Redew., toe* 1; **2.** aufjagen, zu'tage fördern; **3.** *Spielkarte* aufdecken; **4.** *Hose etc.* 'um-, einschlagen; **5.** *Brit.* a) *Wort* nachschlagen, b) *Buch* zurate ziehen; **6.** *Gas, Licht* groß *od.* größer drehen, *Radio* lauter stellen; **7.** *Kind* übers Knie legen (*züchtigen*); **8.** F *j-m* den Magen 'umdrehen (*vor Ekel*); **9.** *sl. Arbeit* ,aufstecken'; **II** *v/i.* **10.** sich nach oben drehen, nach oben gerichtet *od.* hochgeschlagen sein; **11.** *fig.* auftauchen: a) aufkreuzen, erscheinen (*Person*), b) zum Vorschein kommen, sich (ein)finden (*Sache*); **12.** geschehen, eintreten, passieren.

turn·a·ble ['tɜːnəbl] *adj.* drehbar.

'turn|·a·bout *s.* **1.** *a. fig.* Kehrtwendung *f*; **2.** ⚓ Gegenkurs *m*; **3.** *fig.* 'Umschwung *m*; **4.** *Am.* Karus'sell *n*; **'~·a·round** *s.* **1.** → *turnabout* 1, 3; **2.** *mot. etc.* Wendeplatz *m*; **3.** ⊕ (Gene-'ral)Über,holung *f*; **'~·coat** *s.* Abtrünnige(r *m*) *f*, Rene'gat *m*; **'~·down** **I** *adj.* **1.** 'umlegbar, Umlege...; **II** *s.* **2.** *a.* **~** *collar* Umleg(e)kragen *m*; **3.** *fig.* Ablehnung *f*.

turned [tɜːnd] *adj.* **1.** ⊕ gedreht, gedrechselt; **2.** ('um)gebogen; **~·back** zurückgebogen; **~·down** a) abwärts gebogen, b) Umlege...; **~·in** einwärts gebogen; **3.** *typ.* auf dem Kopf stehend; **'turn·er** [-nə] *s.* **1.** ⊕ a) Dreher *m*, b) Drechsler *m*; **2.** *sport Am.* Turner(in); **'turn·er·y** [-nərɪ] *s.* **1.** *coll.* a) Dreharbeit(en *pl.*) *f*, b) Drechslerarbeit(en *pl.*) *f*; **2.** a) Drehe'rei *f*, b) Drechsle'rei *f* (*Werkstatt*).

turn·ing ['tɜːnɪŋ] *s.* **1.** ⊕ Drehen *n*, Drechseln *n*; **2.** a) (Straßen-, Fluss)Bie-

gung *f*, b) (Straßen)Ecke *f*, c) Querstraße *f*, Abzweigung *f*; **3.** *pl.* ⊕ Drehspäne *pl.*; **~** *cir·cle* *s. mot.* Wendekreis *m*; **~** *lane* *s. mot.* Abbiegespur *f*; **~** *lathe* *s.* ⊕ Drehbank *f*; **~** *ma·chine* *s.* ⊕ 'Drehma,schine *f*; **~** *point* *s.* **1.** ⚲, *sport* Wendemarke *f*; **2.** *fig.* Wendepunkt *m*.

tur·nip ['tɜːnɪp] *s.* **1.** ♦ (*bsd.* Weiße) Rübe; **2.** *sl.* ,Zwiebel' *f* (*Uhr*).

'turn|·key *s.* Gefangenenwärter *m*, Schließer *m*; **'~·off** *s.* **1.** Abzweigung *f*; **2.** Ausfahrt *f* (*Autobahn*); **'~·out** *s.* **1.** ✝ *Brit.* a) Streik *m*, Ausstand *m*, b) Streikende(r *m*) *f*; **2.** a) Besucher(zahl *f*) *pl.*, Zuschauer *pl.*, b) (Wahl- *etc.*) Beteiligung *f*; **3.** (Pferde)Gespann *n*, Kutsche *f*, *bsd.* Ausstattung *f*, *bsd.* Kleidung *f*; **5.** ✝ Ge'samtprodukti,on *f*, Ausstoß *m*; **6.** a) Ausweichstelle *f* (*Autostraße*), b) → *turn-off*; **'~·o·ver** *s.* **1.** 'Umstürzen *n*; **2.** ✝ 'Umsatz *m*: **~** *tax* Umsatzsteuer *f*; **3.** Zu- u. Abgang *m* (*von Patienten in Krankenhäusern etc.*): *labo(u)r ~* Arbeitskräftebewegung *f*; **4.** ✝ 'Umgruppierung *f*, -schichtung *f*; **5.** *Brit.* ('Zeitungs)Ar,tikel, der auf die nächste Seite übergreift; **6.** (Apfel- *etc.*) Tasche *f* (*Gebäck*); **'~·pike** *s.* **1.** Schlagbaum *m* (*Mautstraße*); **2.** *a.* **~** *road* gebührenpflichtige (*Am.* Schnell)Straße *f*, Mautstraße *f*; **'~·round** *s.* **1.** ⚲, ⚓ 'Umschlag *m* (*Schiffsabfertigung*); **2.** Wendestelle *f*; **3.** → *turnabout* 3; **'~·screw** *s.* ⊕ Schraubenzieher *m*; **'~·spit** *s.* Drehspieß *m*; **'~·stile** *s.* Drehkreuz *n* an *Durchgängen etc.*; **'~,ta·ble** *s.* **1.** ⬛ Drehscheibe *f*; **2.** Plattenteller *m* (*Plattenspieler*); **'~·up** **I** *adj.* **1.** hochklappbar; **II** *s.* **2.** ('Hosen- *etc.*),Umschlag *m*; **3.** F Über'raschung *f*, ,Ding' *n*.

tur·pen·tine ['tɜːpəntaɪn] *s.* ♠ **1.** Terpen'tin *n*; **2.** *a.* **~** *oil* (*od.* *spirits*) *of* **~** Terpen'tingeist *m*, -öl *n*.

tur·pi·tude ['tɜːpɪtjuːd] *s.* **1.** *a. moral* **~** Verworfenheit *f*; **2.** Schandtat *f*.

turps [tɜːps] F → *turpentine* 2.

tur·quoise ['tɜːkwɔɪz] *s.* **1.** *min.* Tür'kis *m*; **2.** *a.* **~** *blue* Tür'kisblau *n*: **~** *green* Türkisgrün *n*.

tur·ret ['tʌrɪt] *s.* **1.** △ Türmchen *n*; **2.** ✗, ⚓ Geschütz-, Panzer-, Gefechtsturm *m*: **~** *gun* Turmgeschütz *n*; **3.** ⚲ Kanzel *f*; **4.** Re'volverkopf *m*: **~** *lathe* Revolverdrehbank *f*; **'tur·ret·ed** [-tɪd] *adj.* **1.** mit Türmchen; **2.** *zo.* spi-'ral-, türmchenförmig.

tur·tle[1] ['tɜːtl] *s. zo.* (Wasser)Schildkröte *f*: *turn* **~** a) ⚓ kentern, umschlagen, b) sich überschlagen, c) *Am.* F hilflos *od.* feige sein.

tur·tle[2] ['tɜːtl] *s. obs. für* *turtledove*.

'tur·tle|·dove *s. orn.* Turteltaube *f*; **'~·neck** *s.* 'Rollkragen(pull,over) *m*.

Tus·can ['tʌskən] **I** *adj.* tos'kanisch; **II** *s.* Tos'kaner(in).

tusk [tʌsk] *s. zo.* a) Fangzahn *m*, b) Stoßzahn *m des Elefanten etc.*, c) Hauer *m des Wildschweins*; **tusked** [-kt] *adj. zo.* mit Fangzähnen *etc.* (bewaffnet); **'tusk·er** [-kə] *s. zo.* Ele'fant *m od.* Keiler *m* (*mit ausgebildeten Stoßzähnen*); **'tusk·y** [-kɪ] → *tusked*.

tus·sle ['tʌsl] **I** *s.* **1.** Balge'rei *f*, Raufe-'rei *f* (*a. fig.*); **2.** *fig.* scharfe Kontro'verse; **II** *v/i.* **3.** kämpfen, raufen, sich balgen (*for* um *acc.*).

tus·sock ['tʌsək] *s.* (*bsd.* Gras)Büschel *n*.

tut(-tut) ['tʌt] *int.* **1.** ach was!; **2.** pfui!; **3.** Unsinn!, na, 'na!

tu·te·lage ['tjuːtɪlɪdʒ] *s.* **1.** 🜍 Vormundschaft *f*; **2.** Unmündigkeit *f*; **3.** *fig.* a) Bevormundung *f*, b) Schutz *m*, c) (An-

Leitung *f*; '**tu·te·lar** [-lə], '**tu·te·lar·y** [-lərɪ] *adj.* **1.** schützend, Schutz...; **2.** ♊ Vormunds..., Vormundschafts...

tu·tor ['tjuːtə] I *s.* **1.** Pri'vat-, Hauslehrer *m*; **2.** *ped., univ. Brit.* Tutor *m*, Studienleiter *m*; **3.** *ped., univ. Am.* Assistent *m mit Lehrauftrag*; **4.** (Ein)Pauker *m*, Repe'titor *m*; **5.** ♊ Vormund *m*; II *v/t.* **6.** *ped.* unter'richten, j-m Pri'vat,unterricht geben; **7.** j-n schulen, erziehen; **8.** *fig.* j-n bevormunden; '**tu·tor·ess** *s.* **1.** *ped.* Pri'vatlehrerin *f*; **2.** *univ. Brit.* Tu'torin *f*; **tu·to·ri·al** [tjuː'tɔːrɪəl] *ped.* I *adj.* Tutor...; II *s.* Tu'torenkurs *m*; '**tu·tor·ship** [-ʃɪp] *s.* **1.** Pri'vatlehrerstelle; **2.** *univ. Brit.* Amt *n* e-s Tutors.

tu·tu ['tuːtuː] *s.* (Bal'lett)Röckchen *n*.

tux·e·do [tʌk'siːdəʊ] *pl.* **-dos** *s. Am.* Smoking *m*.

TV [ˌtiː'viː] F I *adj.* Fernseh...; II *s.* a) 'Fernsehappa,rat *m*, b) (**on ~** im) Fernsehen *n*; **~ din·ner** *s.* (tiefgefrorenes) Fertiggericht.

twad·dle ['twɒdl] I *v/i.* **1.** quasseln; II *s.* **2.** Gequassel *n*; **3.** Quatsch *m*.

twain [tweɪn] I *adj. obs.* zwei: **in ~** entzwei; II *s. die* Zwei *pl.*

twang [twæŋ] I *v/i.* **1.** schwirren, (scharf) klingen; **2.** näseln; II *v/t.* **3.** *Saiten etc.* schwirren (lassen), zupfen; klimpern *od.* kratzen auf (*dat.*); **4.** *et.* näseln, durch die Nase sprechen; III *s.* **5.** scharfer Ton *od.* Klang, Schwirren *n*; **6.** Näseln *n*.

tweak [twiːk] I *v/t.* zwicken, kneifen; II *s.* Zwicken *n*.

tweed [twiːd] *s.* **1.** Tweed *m* (*Wollgewebe*); **2.** *pl.* Tweedsachen *pl.*

Twee·dle·dum and Twee·dle·dee [ˌtwiːdl'dʌmən,twiːdl'diː] *s.*: **be** (**alike**) **as ~** a) sich gleichen wie ein Ei dem andern, b) 'Jacke wie Hose' sein.

'**tween** [twiːn] I *adv. u. prp.* → **between**; II *in Zssgn* Zwischen...; **~ deck** *s.* ♻ Zwischendeck *n*.

tween·y ['twiːnɪ] *s. obs.* Hausmagd *f*.

tweet·er ['twiːtə] *s. Radio:* Hochtonlautsprecher *m*.

tweez·ers ['twiːzəz] *s. pl. a.* **pair of ~** Pin'zette *f*.

twelfth [twelfθ] I *adj.* □ **1.** zwölft: **☽ Night** Dreikönigsabend *m*; II *s.* **2.** *der* (*die, das*) Zwölfte; **3.** Zwölftel *n*; '**twelfth·ly** [-lɪ] *adv.* zwölftens.

twelve [twelv] I *adj.* zwölf; II *s.* Zwölf *f*; '**twelve·mo** [-məʊ] *pl.* **-mos** *s. typ.* Duo'dez(for,mat, -band *m*) *n*.

'**twelve-tone** *adj.* ♪ Zwölfton...

twen·ti·eth ['twentɪɪθ] I *adj.* **1.** zwanzigst; II *s.* **2.** *der* (*die, das*) Zwanzigste; **3.** Zwanzigstel *n*.

twen·ty ['twentɪ] I *adj.* **1.** zwanzig; II *s.* **2.** Zwanzig *f*; **3.** *in the twenties* in den Zwanzigerjahren (*e-s Jahrhunderts*); *he is in his twenties* er ist in den Zwanzigern.

twerp [twɜːp] *s. sl.* **1.** '(blöder) Heini'; **2.** 'Niete' *f*, 'Flasche' *f*.

twice [twaɪs] *adv.* zweimal: *think ~ about s.th. fig.* sich e-e Sache gründlich überlegen; *he didn't think ~ about it* er zögerte nicht lange; *~ as much* doppelt so viel, das Doppelte; *~ the sum* die doppelte Summe; '*~·told adj. fig.* alt, abgedroschen: *~ tales*.

twid·dle ['twɪdl] *v/t.* (her'um)spielen mit: *~ one's thumbs fig.* Däumchen drehen, die Hände in den Schoß legen.

twig¹ [twɪg] *s.* **1.** (dünner) Zweig, Rute *f*: *hop the ~* F 'abkratzen' (*sterben*); **2.** Wünschelrute *f*.

twig² [twɪg] *Brit. sl.* I *v/t.* **1.** 'kapieren' (*verstehen*); **2.** 'spitzkriegen'; II *v/i.* **3.**

'kapieren'.

twi·light ['twaɪlaɪt] I *s.* **1.** (*mst* Abend-) Dämmerung *f*: **~ of the gods** *myth.* Götterdämmerung; **2.** Zwielicht *n* (*a. fig.*), Halbdunkel *n*; **3.** *fig. a.* **~ state** Dämmerzustand *m*; II *adj.* **4.** Zwielicht..., dämmerig, schattenhaft (*a. fig.*): **~ sleep** *♯ u. fig.* Dämmerschlaf *m*.

twill [twɪl] I *s.* Köper(stoff) *m*; II *v/t.* köpern.

twin [twɪn] I *s.* **1.** Zwilling *m*: *the ☆s ast.* die Zwillinge; II *adj.* **2.** Zwillings..., Doppel..., doppelt: **~-bedded room** Zweibettzimmer *n*; **~ brother** Zwillingsbruder *m*; **~ engine** ✈ Zwillingstriebwerk *n*; **~-engined** zweimotorig; **~ town** Partnerstadt *f*; **~ track** Doppelspur *f* (*Tonband*); **3.** ♀ gepaart; III *v/t.* **4.** eng verbinden: *Aberdeen is twinned with Regensburg* Aberdeen ist die Partnerstadt von Regensburg; **5.** *Geschäftssparten etc.* zs.-legen, verbinden.

twine [twaɪn] I *s.* **1.** Bindfaden *m*, Schnur *f*; **2.** ♦ Garn *n*, Zwirn *m*; **3.** Wick(e)lung *f*; **4.** Windung *f*; **5.** Geflecht *n*; **6.** ♀ Ranke *f*; II *v/t.* **7.** Fäden *etc.* zs.-drehen, zwirnen; **8.** *Kranz* winden; **9.** *fig.* inein'ander schlingen, verflechten; **10.** schlingen, winden (*about, around* um); **11.** um'schlingen, -'winden, -'ranken (*with* mit); III *v/i.* **12.** sich verflechten (*with* mit); **13.** sich winden *od.* schlingen; sich schlängeln; '**twin·er** [-nə] *s.* **1.** ♀ Kletter-, Schlingpflanze *f*; **2.** ◎ 'Zwirnma,schine *f*.

twinge [twɪndʒ] I *s.* **1.** stechender Schmerz, Zwicken *n*, Stechen *n*, Stich *m* (*a. fig.*): **~ of conscience** Gewissensbisse *pl.*; II *v/t. u. v/i.* **2.** stechen; **3.** zwicken, kneifen.

twin·kle ['twɪŋkl] I *v/i.* **1.** (auf)blitzen, glitzern, funkeln (*Sterne etc.*; *a. Augen*); **2.** huschen; **3.** (verschmitzt) zwinkern, blinzeln; II *s.* **4.** Blinken *n*, Blitzen *n*, Glitzern *n*; **5.** (Augen)Zwinkern *n*, Blinzeln *n*: *a humorous ~*; **6.** → **twinkling** 2; '**twin·kling** [-lɪŋ] *s.* **1.** → **twinkle** 4, 5; **2.** *fig.* Augenblick *m*: *in the ~ of an eye* im Nu, im Handumdrehen.

twin·ning ['twɪnɪŋ] *s.* **1.** *♯* Zwillingsschwangerschaft *f*; **2.** Städtepartnerschaft(en *pl.*) *f*.

twirl [twɜːl] I *v/t.* **1.** (her'um)wirbeln, quirlen; *Daumen, Locke etc.* drehen; *Bart* zwirbeln; → *a. twiddle*; II *v/i.* **2.** (sich her'um)wirbeln; III *s.* **3.** schnelle (Um)'Drehung, Wirbel *m*; **4.** Schnörkel *m*.

twist [twɪst] I *v/t.* **1.** drehen: *~ off* losdrehen, *Deckel* abschrauben; **2.** zs.-drehen, zwirnen; **3.** verflechten, -schlingen; **4.** *Kranz etc.* winden; *Schnur etc.* wickeln: *~ s.o. round one's* (*little*) *finger* j-n um den (kleinen) Finger wickeln; **5.** um'winden; **6.** wringen; **7.** (ver)biegen, (-)krümmen; *Fuß* vertreten; *Gesicht* verzerren: *~ s.o.'s arm* a) j-m den Arm verdrehen, b) F *fig.* j-n (*zu et.*) über'reden; *well, if you ~ my arm* F *fig.* also, bevor ich mich schlagen lasse; *~ed mind fig.* verbogener *od.* krankhafter Geist; *~ed with pain* schmerzverzerrt (*Züge*); **8.** *fig.* Sinn, Bericht verdrehen, entstellen; **9.** *dem Ball* Ef'fet geben; II *v/i.* **10.** sich drehen: *~ round* sich umdrehen; **11.** sich krümmen; **12.** sich winden (*a. fig.*); **13.** sich winden *od.* schlängeln (*Fluss etc.*); **14.** sich verziehen *od.* verzerren

---

(*a. Gesicht*); **15.** sich verschlingen; III *s.* **16.** Drehung *f*, Windung *f*, Biegung *f*, Krümmung *f*; **17.** Drehung *f*, Rotati'on *f*; **18.** Geflecht *n*; **19.** Zwirnung *f*; **20.** Verflechtung *f*, Knäuel *m*, *n*; **21.** (Gesichts)Verzerrung *f*; **22.** *fig.* Verdrehung *f*; **23.** *fig.* Veranlagung *od.* Neigung (*towards* zu); **24.** *fig.* Trick *m*, 'Dreh' *m*; **25.** *fig.* über'raschende Wendung, 'Knallef,fekt' *m*; **26.** ◎ a) Drall *m* (*Schusswaffe, Seil etc.*), b) Torsi'on *f*; **27.** Spi'rale *f*: **~ drill** ◎ Spiralbohrer *m*; **28.** ♪ Twist *m* (*Tanz*); **29.** a) (Seiden-, Baumwoll)Twist *m*, b) Zwirn *m*; **30.** Seil *n*, Schnur *f*; **31.** Rollentabak *m*; **32.** *Bäckerei:* Kringel *m*, Zopf *m*; **33.** *Wasserspringen:* Schraube *f*; '**twist·er** [-tə] *s.* **1.** a) Dreher(in), Zwirner(in), b) Seiler(in); **2.** ◎ 'Zwirn-, 'Drehma,schine *f*; **3.** *sport* Ef'fetball *m*; **4.** F harte Nuss, knifflige Sache; **5.** F Gauner *m*; **6.** *Am.* Tor'nado *m*, Wirbel(wind) *m*; '**twist·y** [-tɪ] *adj.* **1.** gewunden, kurvenreich; **2.** *fig.* falsch, verschlagen.

twit¹ [twɪt] *v/t.* **1.** j-n aufziehen (**with** mit); **2.** j-m Vorwürfe machen (**with** wegen).

twit² [twɪt] *s. Brit.* F Trottel *m*.

twitch [twɪtʃ] I *v/t.* **1.** zupfen, zerren, reißen; **2.** zucken mit; II *v/i.* **3.** zucken (**with** vor); III *s.* **4.** Zucken *n*, Zuckung *f*; **5.** Ruck *m*; **6.** Stich *m* (*Schmerz*); **7.** Nasenbremse *f* (*Pferd*).

twit·ter ['twɪtə] I *v/i.* **1.** zwitschern (*Vogel*), zirpen (*a. Insekt*); **2.** *fig.* a) (aufgeregt) schnattern, b) piepsen, c) kichern; **3.** F (vor Aufregung) zittern; II *v/t.* **4.** *et.* zwitschern; III *s.* **5.** Gezwitscher *n*; **6.** *fig.* Geschnatter *n* (*Person*); **7.** Kichern *n*; **8.** Nervosi'tät *f*: *in a ~* aufgeregt.

two [tuː] I *s.* **1.** Zwei *f* (*Zahl, Spielkarte, Uhrzeit etc.*); **2.** Paar *n*: *the ~* die beiden, beide; *the ~ of us* wir beide; *put ~ and ~ together fig.* es sich zs.-reimen, s-e Schlüsse ziehen; *in* (*od. by*) *~s* zu zweien, paarweise; *~ and ~* paarweise, zwei u. zwei; *~ can play at that game!* das kann ich (*od.* ein anderer) auch! II *adj.* **3.** zwei: *one or ~* einige; *in a day or ~* in ein paar Tagen; *in ~* entzwei; *cut in ~* entzweischneiden; **4.** beide: *the ~ cars*; '**~-bit** *adj. Am.* F **1.** 25-Cent-...; **2.** billig (*a. fig. contp.*); klein, unbedeutend; '**~-,cy·cle** *adj.* ◎ Zweitakt...: **~ engine**; '**~-'edged** *adj.* zweischneidig (*a. fig.*); '**~-'faced** *adj. fig.* falsch, heuchlerisch; '**~-'fist·ed** *adj. Am.* F *fig.* 'knallhart'; handfest; '**~-fold** *adj. u. adv.* zweifach, doppelt; '**~-'four** *adj.* ♪ Zweiviertel...; '**~-'hand·ed** *adj.* **1.** zweihändig; **2.** für zwei Per'sonen (*Spiel etc.*); '**~-horse** *adj.* zweispännig; '**~-,in·come fam·i·ly** *s.* Doppelverdiener *pl.*; '**~-job man** *s.* [*irr.*] Doppelverdiener *m*; '**~-lane** *adj.* zweispurig (*Straße*); **~-pence** ['tʌpəns] *s. Brit.* zwei Pence *pl.*: *not to care ~ for fig.* sich nicht scheren um; *he didn't care ~* es war ihm völlig egal; **~-pen·ny** ['tʌpnɪ] *adj.* **1.** zwei Pence wert *od.* betragend, Zweipenny...; **2.** *fig.* armselig, billig; **~-pen·ny-half·pen·ny** [ˌtʌpnɪ'heɪpnɪ] *adj.* **1.** Zweieinhalbpenny...; **2.** *fig.* mise'rabel, schäbig; '**~-phase** *adj.* ⚡ zweiphasig, Zweiphasen...; '**~-piece** I *adj.* zweiteilig; II *s.* a) **~ dress** Jackenkleid *n*, b) a. **~ swimming suit** Zweiteiler *m*; '**~-ply** *adj.* doppelt (*Stoff etc.*); zweischäftig (*Tau*); zweisträhnig (*Wolle etc.*); ,**~-'seat·er** *s.* ✈, *mot.* Zweisitzer *m*; '**~-some** [-səm] *s.* **1.** *Golf:* Zweier(spiel *n*) *m*; **2.** *bsd.*

humor. ‚Duo' *n*, ‚Pärchen' *n*; '**~-speed** *adj.* ⊙ Zweigang...; '**~-stage** *adj.* ⊙ zweistufig; '**~-step** *s.* Twostepp *m* (*Tanz*); '**~-stroke** *adj. mot.* Zweitakt...; '**~-time** *v/t.* F **1.** *bsd. Ehepartner* betrügen; **2.** *j-n* ‚reinlegen'; '**~-way** *adj.* Zweiweg(e)..., Doppel...: **~** *adapter* (*od. plug*) ⚡ Doppelstecker *m*; **~** *cock* Zweiwegehahn *m*; **~** *communication* ⚡ Doppelverkehr *m*, Gegensprechen *n*; **~** *traffic* Gegenverkehr *m*.

ty·coon [taɪˈkuːn] *s.* F **1.** Indu'striemag·‚nat *m*, -kapi‚tän *m*: *oil* **~** Ölmagnat; **2.** *pol.* ‚Oberbonze' *m*.

ty·ing [ˈtaɪɪŋ] *pres. p. von* **tie.**

tyke [taɪk] *s.* **1.** Köter *m*; **2.** Lümmel *m*, Kerl *m*; **3.** *Am.* F Kindchen *n*.

tym·pan [ˈtɪmpən] *s.* **1.** *typ.* Pressdeckel *m*; **2.** → **tympanum** 2; **tym·pan·ic** [tɪmˈpænɪk] *adj. anat.* Mittelohr..., Trommelfell...: **~** *membrane* Trommelfell *n*; **tym·pa·ni·tis** [ˌtɪmpəˈnaɪtɪs] *s.* ✚ Mittelohrentzündung *f*; '**tym·pa·num** [-nəm] *pl.* **-na** [-nə], **-nums** *s.* **1.** *anat.* a) Mittelohr *n*, b) Trommelfell *n*; **2.** △ Tympanon *n*: a) Giebelfeld *n*, b) Türbogenfeld *n*.

type [taɪp] **I** *s.* **1.** Typ(us) *m*: a) Urform *f*, b) typischer Vertreter, c) charakte'ristische Klasse; **2.** Ur-, Vorbild *n*, Muster *n*; **3.** ⊙ Typ *m*, Mo'dell *n*, Ausführung *f*, Baumuster *n*: **~** *plate* Typenschild *n*; **4.** Art *f*, Schlag *m*, Sorte *f* (*alle a.* F); *out of* **~** atypisch; *he acted out of* **~** das war sonst nicht s-e Art; → *true* 4; **5.** *typ.* a) Letter *f*, (Druck)Type *f*, b) *coll.* Lettern *pl.*, Schrift *f*, Druck *m*: *in* **~** (ab)gesetzt; *set* (*up*) *in* **~** setzen; **6.** *fig.* Sinnbild *n*, Sym'bol *n* (*of gen. od.*

für); **II** *v/t.* **7.** mit der Ma'schine (ab-) schreiben, (ab)tippen; **~d** maschine(n)-geschrieben; *typing pool* Schreibsaal *m*, -büro *n*; **8.** **~** *into* in *e-n* Computer eingeben, -tippen; **III** *v/i.* **9.** Ma'schine schreiben, tippen; **~cast** *v/t.* [*irr.* → **cast**] *thea. etc.* a) *e-m Schauspieler* e-e s-m Typ entsprechende Rolle geben, b) *e-n Schauspieler* auf ein bestimmtes Rollenfach festlegen; '**~-face** *s. typ.* **1.** Schriftbild *n*; **2.** Schriftart *f*; **~** *found·er* *s. typ.* Schriftgießer *m*; **~** *found·ry* *s. typ.* Schriftgieße'rei *f*; **~** *met·al* *s. typ.* 'Letternme‚tall *n*; '**~·o·ver mode** *s.* *Computer:* 'Überschreibemodus *m*; **~** *page* *s. typ.* Satzspiegel *m*; '**~·script** *s.* Ma'schinenschrift(satz *m*) *f*, ma'schine(n)geschriebener Text; '**~·set·ter** *s. typ.* (Schrift)Setzer *m*; **~** *size* *s. typ.* Schriftgrad *m*; '**~·spec·i·men** *s.* **1.** ⊙ 'Musterexem‚plar *n*; **2.** *biol.* Typus *m*, Origi'nal *n*; '**~·write** *v/t. u. v/i.* [*irr.* → **write**] → *type* 7, 9; '**~·writ·er** *s.* **1.** 'Schreibma‚schine *f*; **~** *ribbon* Farbband *n*; **2.** *a.* **~** *face* *typ.* 'Schreibma‚schinenschrift *f*; '**~·writ·ing** *s.* **1.** Ma'schineschreiben *n*; **2.** Ma'schinenschrift *f*; '**~·writ·ten** *adj.* ma'schine(n)-geschrieben, in Ma'schinenschrift.

ty·phoid [ˈtaɪfɔɪd] ✚ **I** *adj.* ty'phös, Typhus...: **~** *fever* → **II** *s.* ('Unterleibs-) Typhus *m*.

ty·phoon [taɪˈfuːn] *s.* Tai'fun *m*.

ty·phus [ˈtaɪfəs] *s.* ✚ Flecktyphus *m*, -fieber *n*.

typ·i·cal [ˈtɪpɪkl] *adj.* □ **1.** typisch: a) repräsenta'tiv, b) charakte'ristisch, bezeichnend, kennzeichnend (*of* für): *be* **~** *of et.* kennzeichnen *od.* charakterisie-

ren; **3.** sym'bolisch, sinnbildlich (*of* für); **4.** a) vorbildlich, echt, b) hinweisend (*of* auf *et. Künftiges*); '**typ·i·cal·ness** [-nɪs] *s.* **1.** *das* Typische; **2.** Sinnbildlichkeit *f*; '**typ·i·fy** [-ɪfaɪ] *v/t.* **1.** typisch *od.* ein typisches Beispiel sein für, verkörpern; **2.** versinnbildlichen.

typ·ist [ˈtaɪpɪst] *s.* **1.** Ma'schinenschreiber(in); **2.** Schreibkraft *f*.

ty·pog·ra·pher [taɪˈpɒɡrəfə] *s.* **1.** (Buch)Drucker *m*; **2.** (Schrift)Setzer *m*; **ty·po·graph·ic**, **ty·po·graph·i·cal** [ˌtaɪpəˈɡræfɪk(l)] *adj.* □ **1.** Druck..., drucktechnisch: **~** *error* Druckfehler *m*; **2.** typo'graphisch, Buchdruck(er)...; **ty·pog·ra·phy** [-fɪ] *s.* **1.** Buchdruckerkunst *f*, Typogra'phie *f*; **2.** (Buch-) Druck *m*; **3.** Druckbild *n*.

ty·po·log·i·cal [ˌtaɪpəˈlɒdʒɪkl] *adj.* typo'logisch; **ty·pol·o·gy** [taɪˈpɒlədʒɪ] *s.* Typolo'gie *f*.

ty·ran·nic, **ty·ran·ni·cal** [tɪˈrænɪk(l)] *adj.* □ ty'rannisch; **ty'ran·ni·cide** [-ɪsaɪd] *s.* **1.** Ty'rannenmord *m*; **2.** Ty'rannenmörder *m*; **tyr·an·nize** [ˈtɪrənaɪz] **I** *v/i.* ty'rannisch sein *od.* herrschen: **~** *over* → **II** *v/t.* tyrannisieren; **tyr·an·nous** [ˈtɪrənəs] *adj.* □ *rhet.* ty'rannisch; **tyr·an·ny** [ˈtɪrənɪ] *s.* **1.** Ty'ran'nei *f*: a) Despo'tismus, b) Gewalt-, Willkürherrschaft *f*; **2.** Tyran'nei *f* (*tyrannische Handlung etc.*); **3.** *antiq.* Ty'rannis *f*; **ty·rant** [ˈtaɪərənt] *s.* Ty'rann(in).

tyre *etc. bsd. Brit.* → **tire²** *etc.*

ty·ro [ˈtaɪərəʊ] *pl.* **-ros** *s.* Anfänger(in), Neuling *m*.

Tyr·o·lese [ˌtɪrəˈliːz] **I** *pl.* **-lese** *s.* Ti'roler(in); **II** *adj.* ti'rol(er)isch, Tiroler(...).

tzar *etc.* → **czar** *etc.*

T

U

U, u [juː] **I** s. **1.** U n, u n (Buchstabe); **2.** U n: *U-bolt* ⊕ U-Bolzen m; **II** adj. **3.** *U Brit.* F vornehm; **4.** *Brit.* jugendfrei: ~ *film.*

u·biq·ui·tous [juːˈbɪkwɪtəs] adj. □ all-'gegenwärtig, (gleichzeitig) 'überall zu finden(d); **u'biq·ui·ty** [-kwətɪ] s. All'gegenwart f.

'U-boat s. ⚓ U-Boot n, (deutsches) 'Unterseeboot.

u·dal [ˈjuːdl] s. ⚖ hist. Al'lod(ium) n, Freigut n.

ud·der [ˈʌdə] s. Euter n.

u·dom·e·ter [juːˈdɒmɪtə] s. meteor. Regenmesser m, Udo'meter n.

ugh [ʌx; ʊh; ɜːh] int. hu!, pfui!

ug·li·fy [ˈʌɡlɪfaɪ] v/t. hässlich machen, entstellen; **'ug·li·ness** [-ɪnɪs] s. Hässlichkeit f; **ug·ly** [ˈʌɡlɪ] **I** adj. □ **1.** hässlich, garstig (beide a. fig.); **2.** fig. gemein, schmutzig; **3.** unangenehm, 'widerwärtig, übel: *an ~ customer* ein unangenehmer Kerl, ,ein übler Kunde'; **4.** bös, schlimm, gefährlich (Situation, Wunde etc.); **II** s. **5.** F hässlicher Mensch; ,Ekel' n.

UHT milk [ˈjuːeɪtʃtiː] s. H-Milch f.

u·kase [juːˈkeɪz] s. hist. u. fig. Ukas m, Erlass m, Befehl m.

U·krain·i·an [juːˈkreɪnjən] **I** adj. **1.** ukra'inisch; **II** s. **2.** Ukra'iner(in); **3.** ling. Ukra'inisch n.

u·ku·le·le [juːkəˈleɪlɪ] s. ♪ Uku'lele f, n.

ul·cer [ˈʌlsə] s. **1.** ♣ (Magen- etc.)Geschwür n; **2.** fig. a) (Eiter)Beule f, b) Schandfleck m; **'ul·cer·ate** [-əreɪt] **I** v/t. schwären lassen, ~d eitrig, vereitert; **II** v/i. geschwürig werden, schwären; **ul·cer·a·tion** [ˌʌlsəˈreɪʃn] s. ♣ Geschwür(bildung f) n; Schwären n, (Ver-)Eiterung f; **ul·cer·ous** [ˈʌlsərəs] adj. □ **1.** ♣ geschwürig, eiternd; Geschwür(s)..., Eiter...; **2.** fig. kor'rupt, giftig.

ul·lage [ˈʌlɪdʒ] s. ♣ Schwund m: a) Leckage f, Flüssigkeitsverlust m, b) Gewichtsverlust m.

ul·na [ˈʌlnə] pl. **-nae** [-niː] s. anat. Elle f.

ul·ster [ˈʌlstə] s. Ulster(mantel) m.

ul·te·ri·or [ʌlˈtɪərɪə] adj. □ **1.** (räumlich) jenseitig; **2.** später (folgend), weiter, anderweitig: ~ *action*; **3.** fig. tiefer (liegend), versteckt: ~ *motives* tiefere Beweggründe, Hintergedanken.

ul·ti·mate [ˈʌltɪmət] **I** adj. □ **1.** äußerst, (aller)letzt, höchst; **2.** entferntest; **3.** endgültig, End...: ~ *consumer* ✝ Endverbraucher m; ~ *result* Endergebnis n; **4.** grundlegend, elemen'tar, Grund...; **5.** ⊕, phys. Höchst..., Grenz...: ~ *strength* Bruchfestigkeit f; **II** s. **6.** das Letzte, das Äußerste; **7.** fig. der Gipfel (*in* an dat.); **'ul·ti·mate·ly** [-lɪ] adv. schließlich, endlich, letzten Endes, im Grunde.

ul·ti·ma·tum [ˌʌltɪˈmeɪtəm] pl. **-tums**, **-ta** [-tə] s. pol. u. fig. Ulti'matum n (*to* an acc.): *deliver an ~ to* j-m ein Ultimatum stellen.

ul·ti·mo [ˈʌltɪməʊ] (Lat.) adv. ✝ letzten od. vorigen Monats.

ul·tra [ˈʌltrə] **I** adj. **1.** ex'trem, radi'kal, Erz..., Ultra...; **2.** 'übermäßig, über-'trieben; ultra..., super...; **II** s. **3.** Ext-re'mist m, Ultra m; **'~-high fre·quen·cy** ⚡ **I** s. Ultra'hochfre,quenz f, Ultra-'hochfrequenz f; **II** adj. Ultrahochfrequenz..., Ultrakurzwellen...

ul·tra·ism [ˈʌltraɪzəm] s. Extre'mismus m.

ul·tra|·ma·rine [ˌʌltrəməˈriːn] **I** adj. **1.** 'überseeisch; **2.** ♣, paint. ultrama'rin; ~ *blue* → **II** s. **3.** Ultrama'rin(blau) n; **~'mod·ern** adj. 'ultra-, 'hypermo,dern; **~'mon·tane** [-ˈmɒnteɪn] **I** adj. **1.** jenseits der Berge (gelegen); **2.** südlich der Alpen (gelegen), itali'enisch; **3.** pol., eccl. ultramon'tan, streng päpstlich; **II** s. **4.** → **~'mon·ta·nist** [-ˈmɒntənɪst] s. Ultramon'tane(r m) f; **~'na·tion·al** adj. 'ultranatio,nal; **~'short wave** s. ⚡ Ultra'kurzwelle f; pl. sg. konstr. Ultraschall...; **II** s. pl. sg. konstr. (Lehre f vom) Ultraschall m; **~'son·ic** phys. **I** adj. Ultraschall...; **II** s. pl. sg. konstr. (Lehre f vom) Ultraschall m; **~-sound** s. phys., ♣ **1.** 'Ultraschall m; **2.** a. ~ *scan* 'Ultraschall,aufnahme f: ~ *scanner* Ultraschallgerät n; **~'vi·o·let** adj. phys. 'ultravio,lett.

ul·u·late [ˈjuːljʊleɪt] v/i. heulen; **ul·u·la·tion** [ˌjuːljʊˈleɪʃn] s. Heulen n, (Weh-)Klagen n.

um·bel [ˈʌmbəl] s. ♣ Dolde f; **'um·bel·late** [-leɪt] adj. doldenblütig, Dolden...; **um·bel·li·fer** [ʌmˈbelɪfə] s. Doldengewächs n; **um·bel·lif·er·ous** [ˌʌmbeˈlɪfərəs] adj. doldenblütig, Dolden tragend.

um·ber [ˈʌmbə] s. **1.** min. Umber(erde f) m, Umbra f; **2.** paint. Erd-, Dunkelbraun n.

um·bil·i·cal [ˌʌmbɪˈlaɪkl] adj. anat. Nabel...: ~ *(cord)* Nabelschnur f; **um·bil·i·cus** [ʌmˈbɪlɪkəs] pl. **-cus·es** s. **1.** anat. Nabel m; **2.** (nabelförmige) Delle; **3.** ♣ (Samen)Nabel m; **4.** ♣ Nabelpunkt m.

um·bra [ˈʌmbrə] pl. **-brae** [-briː], **-bras** s. ast. a) Kernschatten m, b) Umbra f (dunkler Kern e-s Sonnenflecks).

um·brage [ˈʌmbrɪdʒ] s. **1.** Anstoß m, Ärgernis n: *give* ~ Anstoß erregen (*to* bei); *take* ~ *at* Anstoß nehmen an (dat.); **2.** poet. Schatten m von Bäumen; **um·bra·geous** [ʌmˈbreɪdʒəs] adj. □ **1.** schattig, Schatten spendend; **2.** fig. empfindlich, übelnehmerisch.

um·brel·la [ʌmˈbrelə] s. **1.** (bsd. Regen-) Schirm m: ~ *stand* Schirmständer m; *get* (od. *put*) *under one* ~ fig. ,unter 'einen Hut bringen'; **2.** ✈, ✕ a) Jagdschutz m, Abschirmung f, b) a. ~ *barrage* Feuervorhang m, -glocke f; **3.** fig. a) Schutz m, b) Rahmen m, c) Dach...: ~ *organization*.

um·laut [ˈʊmlaʊt] ling. **I** s. 'Umlaut(zei-

chen n) m; **II** v/t. 'umlauten.

um·pire [ˈʌmpaɪə] **I** s. **1.** sport etc. Schiedsrichter m, 'Unpar,teiische(r m) f; **2.** ⚖ Obmann m e-s Schiedsgerichts; **II** v/t. **3.** als Schiedsrichter fungieren bei, sport a. das Spiel leiten.

ump·teen [ˌʌmpˈtiːn] adj. F ,zig' (viele): ~ *times* x-mal; **ump'teenth** [-nθ], **'ump·ti·eth** [-tɪɪθ] adj. F ,zigst', der (die, das) 'soundso'vielte ...: *for the* ~ *time* zum x-ten Mal.

'un [ən] pron. F für one.

un- [ʌn] in Zssgn **1.** Un..., un..., nicht...; **2.** ent..., los..., auf..., ver... (bei Verben).

un·a'bashed adj. **1.** unverfroren; **2.** unerschrocken.

un·a·bat·ed [ˌʌnəˈbeɪtɪd] adj. unvermindert; **un·a·bat·ing** [-tɪŋ] adj. unablässig, anhaltend.

un·ab'bre·vi·at·ed adj. ungekürzt.

un·a·ble adj. **1.** unfähig, außer'stande (*to do* zu tun): *be* ~ *to work* nicht arbeiten können, arbeitsunfähig sein; ~ *to pay* zahlungsunfähig, insolvent; **2.** untauglich, ungeeignet (*for* für).

un·a'bridged adj. ungekürzt.

un·ac'cent·ed adj. unbetont.

un·ac'cept·a·ble adj. **1.** unannehmbar (*to* für); **2.** untragbar, unerwünscht (*to* für).

un·ac'com·mo·dat·ing adj. **1.** ungefällig, **2.** unnachgiebig.

un·ac'com·pa·nied adj. unbegleitet, ohne Begleitung (a. ♪).

un·ac'com·plished adj. **1.** 'unvoll,endet, unfertig; **2.** fig. ungebildet.

un·ac'count·a·ble adj. □ **1.** nicht verantwortlich; **2.** unerklärlich, seltsam; **un·ac'count·a·bly** adv. unerklärlicherweise.

un·ac'count·ed-for adj. **1.** unerklärt (geblieben); **2.** nicht belegt.

un·ac'cus·tomed adj. **1.** ungewohnt; **2.** nicht gewöhnt (*to* an acc.).

un·a·chiev·a·ble [ˌʌnəˈtʃiːvəbl] adj. **1.** unausführbar; **2.** unerreichbar; **un·a-'chieved** [-vd] adj. unerreicht, 'unvoll-,endet.

un·ac'knowl·edged adj. **1.** nicht anerkannt; **2.** uneingestanden; **3.** unbestätigt (Brief etc.).

un·ac'quaint·ed adj. (*with*) unerfahren (in dat.), nicht vertraut (mit), unkundig (gen.): *be* ~ *with* et. nicht kennen.

un·act·a·ble adj. thea. nicht bühnengerecht, unaufführbar.

un·a'dapt·a·ble adj. **1.** nicht anpassungsfähig (*to* an acc.); **2.** nicht anwendbar (*to* auf acc.); **3.** ungeeignet (*for*, *to* für, zu); **un·a'dapt·ed** adj. **1.** nicht angepasst (*to* dat. od. an acc.); **2.** ungeeignet, nicht eingerichtet (*to* für).

un·ad'dressed adj. ohne Anschrift.

un·a'dorned adj. schmucklos.

un·a'dul·ter·at·ed adj. rein, unverfälscht, echt.

un·ad'ven·tur·ous adj. **1.** ohne Unter-

'nehmungsgeist; **2.** ereignislos (*Reise*).

'un·ad͵vis·a'bil·i·ty s. Unratsamkeit f; **͵un·ad'vis·a·ble** adj. □ unratsam, nicht ratsam od. empfehlenswert; **͵un·ad'vised** adj. □ **1.** unberaten; **2.** unbesonnen, 'unüber͵legt.

͵un·af'fect·ed adj. □ **1.** ungekünstelt, nicht affektiert (*Stil, Auftreten etc.*); **2.** echt, aufrichtig; **3.** unberührt, ungerührt, unbeeinflusst (**by** von); **͵un·af'fect·ed·ness** [-nɪs] s. Na'türlichkeit f; Aufrichtigkeit f.

͵un·a'fraid adj. furchtlos: **be ~ of** keine Angst haben vor (*dat.*).

͵un·'aid·ed adj. **1.** ohne Unter'stützung, ohne Hilfe (**by** von); (ganz) al'lein; **2.** unbewaffnet, bloß (*Auge*).

͵un·'al·ien·a·ble adj. □ unveräußerlich (*a. fig. Recht*).

͵un·'al'loyed adj. **1.** ⚒ unvermischt, unlegiert; **2.** fig. ungetrübt, rein: **~ happiness.**

un·'al·ter·a·ble adj. □ unveränderlich, unabänderlich; **͵un·'al·tered** adj. unverändert.

͵un·a'mazed adj. nicht verwundert: **be ~ at** sich nicht wundern über (*acc.*).

un·am·big·u·ous [͵ʌnæmˈbɪgjʊəs] adj. □ unzweideutig; **͵un·am'big·u·ous·ness** [-nɪs] s. Eindeutigkeit f.

͵un·am'bi·tious adj. □ **1.** nicht ehrgeizig, ohne Ehrgeiz; **2.** anspruchslos, schlicht (*Sache*).

͵un·a'me·na·ble adj. **1.** unzugänglich (**to** dat. od. für); **2.** nicht verantwortlich (**to** gegenüber).

͵un·a'mend·ed adj. unverbessert, unabgeändert; nicht ergänzt.

͵un·A'mer·i·can adj. **1.** 'unameri͵kanisch; **2.** **~ activities** pol. Am. staatsfeindliche Umtriebe.

͵un·'a·mi·a·ble adj. □ unliebenswürdig, unfreundlich.

͵un·a'mus·ing adj. □ nicht unter'haltsam, langweilig, unergötzlich.

u·na·nim·i·ty [͵juːnəˈnɪmətɪ] s. **1.** Einstimmigkeit f; **2.** Einmütigkeit f; **u·nan·i·mous** [juːˈnænɪməs] adj. □ **1.** einmütig, einig; **2.** einstimmig (*Beschluss etc.*).

͵un·an'nounced adj. unangemeldet, unangekündigt.

͵un·'an·swer·a·ble adj. □ **1.** nicht zu beantworten(d); unlösbar (*Rätsel*); **2.** 'unwider͵legbar; **3.** nicht verantwortlich od. haftbar; **͵un·'an·swered** adj. **1.** unbeantwortet; **2.** 'unwider͵legt.

un·ap'peal·a·ble [͵ʌnəˈpiːləbl] adj. ⚖ nicht berufungs- od. rechtsmittelfähig, unanfechtbar.

un·ap'peas·a·ble [͵ʌnəˈpiːzəbl] adj. **1.** nicht zu besänftigen(d), unversöhnlich; **2.** nicht zu'frieden zu stellen(d), unersättlich.

͵un·'ap·pe·tiz·ing adj. □ 'unappe͵titlich, fig. a. wenig reizvoll.

͵un·ap'plied adj. nicht angewandt od. gebraucht: **~ funds** totes Kapital.

͵un·ap'pre·ci·at·ed adj. nicht gebührend gewürdigt od. geschätzt, unbeachtet.

͵un·ap'proach·a·ble adj. □ unnahbar.

͵un·ap'pro·pri·at·ed adj. **1.** herrenlos; **2.** nicht verwendet od. gebraucht; **3.** † nicht zugeteilt, keiner bestimmten Verwendung zugeführt.

͵un·ap'proved adj. ungebilligt, nicht genehmigt.

͵un·'apt adj. □ **1.** ungeeignet, untauglich (**for** für, zu); **2.** unangebracht, unpassend; **3.** nicht geeignet (**to do** zu tun); **4.** ungeschickt (**at** bei, in dat.).

͵un·'ar·gued adj. **1.** unbesprochen; **2.**

unbestritten.

͵un·'armed adj. **1.** unbewaffnet; **2.** unscharf (*Munition*).

͵un·'ar·mo(u)red adj. **1.** bsd. ✕, ⚓ ungepanzert; **2.** ⊕ nicht bewehrt.

͵un·as·cer'tain·a·ble adj. nicht feststellbar; **͵un·as·cer'tained** adj. nicht (sicher) festgestellt.

͵un·a'shamed adj. □ **1.** nicht beschämt; **2.** schamlos.

͵un·'asked adj. **1.** ungefragt; **2.** ungebeten, unaufgefordert; **3.** uneingeladen.

͵un·as'pir·ing adj. □ ohne Ehrgeiz, anspruchslos, bescheiden.

͵un·as'sail·a·ble adj. **1.** unangreifbar (a. fig.); **2.** fig. unanfechtbar.

͵un·as'sign·a·ble adj. ⚖ nicht über'tragbar.

͵un·as'sist·ed adj. □ ohne Hilfe od. Unter'stützung (**by** von), (ganz) al'lein.

͵un·as'sum·ing adj. □ anspruchslos, bescheiden.

͵un·at'tached adj. **1.** nicht befestigt (**to** an dat.); **2.** nicht gebunden, unabhängig; **3.** ungebunden, frei, ledig; **4.** ped., univ. ex'tern, keinem College angehörend (*Student*); **5.** ✕ zur Dispo-siti'on stehend; **6.** ⚖ nicht mit Beschlag belegt.

͵un·at'tain·a·ble adj. □ unerreichbar.

͵un·at'tempt·ed adj. unversucht.

͵un·at'tend·ed adj. **1.** unbegleitet; **2.** mst **~ to** a) unbeaufsichtigt, b) vernachlässigt.

͵un·at'test·ed adj. **1.** unbezeugt, unbestätigt; **2.** Brit. (behördlich) nicht über'prüft.

͵un·at'trac·tive adj. □ wenig anziehend, reizlos, 'unattrak͵tiv.

͵un·au·thor·ized adj. **1.** nicht bevollmächtigt, unbefugt: **~ person** Unbefugte(r m) f; **2.** unerlaubt; unberechtigt (*Nachdruck etc.*).

un·a·vail·a·ble [͵ʌnəˈveɪləbl] adj. □ **1.** nicht verfügbar od. vor'handen; **2.** → **͵un·a'vail·ing** [-lɪŋ] adj. □ frucht-, nutzlos, vergeblich.

un·a·void·a·ble [͵ʌnəˈvɔɪdəbl] adj. □ **1.** unvermeidlich, unvermeidbar: **~ cost** notwendige Kosten; **2.** ⚖ unanfechtbar.

un·a·ware [͵ʌnəˈweə] adj. **1.** (**of**) nicht gewahr (gen.), in Unkenntnis (gen.): **be ~ of** sich e-r Sache nicht bewusst sein, et. nicht wissen od. bemerken; **2.** nichts ahnend: **he was ~ that** er ahnte nicht, dass; **͵un·a'wares** [-eəz] adv. **1.** versehentlich, unabsichtlich; **2.** unversehens, unerwartet, unvermutet: **catch** (od. **take**) **s.o. ~** j-n überraschen; **at ~** unverhofft, überraschend.

͵un·'backed adj. **1.** ohne Rückhalt od. Unter'stützung; **2.** **~ horse** Pferd, auf das nicht gesetzt wurde; **3.** † ungedeckt, nicht indossiert.

͵un·'baked adj. **1.** ungebacken; **2.** fig. unreif.

͵un·'bal·ance I v/t. **1.** aus dem Gleichgewicht bringen (a. fig.); **2.** fig. Geist verwirren; II s. **3.** gestörtes Gleichgewicht, fig. a. Unausgeglichenheit f; **4.** ⚡, ⊕ Unwucht f; **͵un·'bal·anced** adj. **1.** aus dem Gleichgewicht gebracht, nicht im Gleichgewicht (befindlich); **2.** fig. unausgeglichen (a. ⚡); **3.** psych. la'bil, ͵gestört'.

͵un·'bap·tized adj. ungetauft.

͵un·'bar v/t. aufriegeln.

͵un·'bear·a·ble adj. □ unerträglich.

͵un·'beat·en adj. **1.** ungeschlagen, unbesiegt; **2.** fig. 'unüber͵troffen; **3.** unerforscht: **~ region.**

͵un·be'com·ing adj. □ **1.** unkleidsam:

this hat is ~ to him dieser Hut steht ihm nicht; **2.** fig. unpassend, unschicklich, ungeziemend (**of, to, for** für j-n).

͵un·be'fit·ting → **unbecoming** 2.

͵un·be'friend·ed adj. ohne Freund(e).

un·be'known(st F) [͵ʌnbɪˈnəʊn(st)] adj. u. adv. **1.** (**to**) ohne j-s Wissen; **2.** unbekannt(erweise).

͵un·be'lief s. Unglaube m, Ungläubigkeit f; **͵un·be'liev·a·ble** adj. □ unglaublich; **͵un·be'liev·er** s. eccl. Ungläubige(r m) f, Glaubenslose(r m) f; **͵un·be'liev·ing** adj. □ ungläubig.

͵un·'bend [irr. → **bend**] I v/t. **1.** Bogen etc., a. fig. Geist entspannen; **2.** ⊕ gerade biegen, glätten; **3.** ⚓ a) Tau etc. losmachen, b) Segel abschlagen; II v/i. **4.** sich entspannen, sich lösen; **5.** fig. auftauen, freundlich(er) werden, s-e Förmlichkeit ablegen; **͵un·'bend·ing** [-dɪŋ] adj. □ **1.** unbiegsam; **2.** fig. unbeugsam, entschlossen; **3.** fig. reserviert, steif.

un·be'seem·ing [͵ʌnbɪˈsiːmɪŋ] → **unbecoming** 2.

͵un·'bi·as(s)ed adj. □ unvoreingenommen, a. ⚖ unbefangen.

͵un·'bid(·den) adj. ungeheißen, unaufgefordert; ungebeten (a. Gast).

͵un·'bind v/t. [irr. → **bind**] **1.** Gefangenen etc. losbinden, befreien; **2.** Haar, Knoten etc. lösen.

͵un·'bleached adj. ungebleicht.

͵un·'blem·ished adj. bsd. fig. unbefleckt, makellos.

͵un·'blink·ing adj. □ **1.** ungerührt; **2.** unerschrocken.

͵un·'blush·ing adj. □ fig. schamlos.

͵un·'bolt v/t. aufriegeln, öffnen.

͵un·'born adj. **1.** (noch) ungeboren; **2.** fig. (zu)künftig, kommend.

͵un·'bos·om v/t. Gedanken, Gefühle etc. enthüllen, offen'baren (**to** dat.): **~ o.s.** (**to s.o.**) sich (j-m) offenbaren, (j-m) sein Herz ausschütten.

͵un·'bound adj. ungebunden: a) broschiert (*Buch*), b) fig. frei.

͵un·'bound·ed adj. □ **1.** unbegrenzt; **2.** fig. grenzen-, schrankenlos.

͵un·'brace v/t. Gurte etc. lösen, losschnallen; **2.** entspannen (a. fig.): **~ o.s.** sich entspannen.

͵un·'break·a·ble adj. unzerbrechlich.

͵un·'brib·a·ble adj. unbestechlich.

͵un·'bri·dled adj. **1.** ab-, ungezäumt; **2.** fig. ungezügelt, zügellos.

͵un·'bro·ken adj. □ **1.** ungebrochen (a. fig. Eid etc.), unzerbrochen, ganz, heil; **2.** 'ununter͵brochen, ungestört; **3.** nicht zugeritten (*Pferd*); **4.** unbeeinträchtigt; **5.** ✏ ungepflügt; **6.** ungebrochen: **~ record.**

͵un·'broth·er·ly adj. unbrüderlich.

͵un·'buck·le v/t. auf-, losschnallen.

͵un·'built adj. **1.** (noch) nicht gebaut; **2.** a. **~-on** unbebaut (*Gelände*).

͵un·'bur·den v/t. **1.** bsd. fig. entlasten, von e-r Last befreien, Gewissen etc. erleichtern: **~ o.s.** (**to s.o.**) (j-m) sein Herz ausschütten; **2.** a) Geheimnis etc. loswerden, b) Sünden bekennen, beichten: **~ one's troubles to s.o.** s-e Sorgen bei j-m abladen.

͵un·'bur·ied adj. unbegraben.

͵un·'burnt adj. **1.** unverbrannt; **2.** ⊕ ungebrannt (*Ziegel etc.*).

͵un·'bur·y v/t. ausgraben (a. fig.).

͵un·'busi·ness·like adj. unkaufmännisch, nicht geschäftsmäßig.

͵un·'but·ton v/t. aufknöpfen; **͵un·'but·toned** adj. aufgeknöpft, fig. a. gelöst, zwanglos.

͵un·'called adj. **1.** unaufgefordert; **2.** ✝

nicht aufgerufen; ˌun'**called-for** *adj.* **1.** ungerufen, unerwünscht; unverlangt (*Sache*); **2.** unangebracht, unpassend: ~ *remarks.*

un'**can·ny** *adj.* □ unheimlich (*a. fig.*).

ˌun'**cared-for** *adj.* **1.** unbeachtet; **2.** vernachlässigt; ungepflegt.

ˌun'**case** *v/t.* auspacken.

un·**ceas·ing** [ʌn'siːsɪŋ] *adj.* □ unaufhörlich.

'un·**cer·e·mo·ni·ous** *adj.* □ **1.** ungezwungen, zwanglos; **2.** a) unsanft, grob, b) unhöflich.

un'**cer·tain** *adj.* □ **1.** unsicher, ungewiss, unbestimmt; **2.** nicht sicher: *be* ~ *of s.th.* e-r Sache nicht sicher *od.* gewiss sein; **3.** zweifelhaft, undeutlich, vage: *an* ~ *answer;* **4.** unzuverlässig; *an* ~ *friend;* **5.** unstet, unbeständig, veränderlich, launenhaft: ~ *temper;* ~ *weather;* **6.** unsicher, verunsichert; un·'**cer·tain·ty** *s.* **1.** Unsicherheit *f,* Ungewissheit *f;* **2.** Zweifelhaftigkeit *f;* **3.** Unzuverlässigkeit *f;* **4.** Unbeständigkeit *f.*

ˌun'**cer·ti·fied** *adj.* nicht bescheinigt, unbeglaubigt.

ˌun'**chain** *v/t.* **1.** losketten; **2.** befreien (*a. fig.*).

ˌun'**chal·lenge·a·ble** *adj.* □ unanfechtbar, unbestreitbar; ˌun'**chal·lenged** *adj.* unbestritten, 'unwiderˌsprochen, unangefochten.

un·**change·a·ble** [ʌn'tʃeɪndʒəbl] *adj.* □ unveränderlich, unwandelbar; un·**changed** [ʌn'tʃeɪndʒd] *adj.* unverändert; ˌun'**chang·ing** [-dʒɪŋ] *adj.* □ unveränderlich.

ˌun'**charged** *adj.* **1.** nicht beladen; **2.** ⚖ nicht angeklagt; **3.** ⚡ nicht (auf)geladen; **4.** ungeladen (*Schusswaffe*); **5.** ♦ a) unbelastet (*Konto*), b) unberechnet.

ˌun'**char·i·ta·ble** *adj.* □ lieblos, hartherzig, unfreundlich.

ˌun'**chart·ed** *adj.* auf keiner (Land)Karte verzeichnet, unbekannt, unerforscht (*a. fig.*).

ˌun'**chaste** *adj.* □ unkeusch; ˌun'**chas·ti·ty** *s.* Unkeuschheit *f.*

ˌun'**checked** *adj.* **1.** ungehindert, ungehemmt; **2.** unkontrolliert, ungeprüft.

ˌun'**chiv·al·rous** *adj.* unritterlich, 'ungaˌlant.

ˌun'**chris·tened** *adj.* ungetauft.

ˌun'**chris·tian** *adj.* □ unchristlich.

un·**ci·al** ['ʌnsɪəl] **I** *adj.* **1.** Unzial...; **II** *s.* **2.** Unzi'ale *f (abgerundeter Großbuchstabe);* **3.** Unzi'alschrift *f.*

un·**ci·form** ['ʌnsɪfɔːm] **I** *adj.* hakenförmig; **II** *s. anat.* Hakenbein *n.*

ˌun'**cir·cum·cised** *adj.* unbeschnitten; 'un·ˌcir·cum'**ci·sion** *s. bibl.* die Unbeschnittenen *pl., die* Heiden *pl.*

ˌun'**civ·il** *adj.* □ **1.** unhöflich, grob; **2.** *obs.* → ˌun'**civ·i·lized** *adj.* unzivilisiert.

ˌun'**claimed** *adj.* **1.** nicht beansprucht, nicht geltend gemacht; **2.** nicht abgeholt *od.* abgehoben.

ˌun'**clasp** *v/t.* **1.** lösen, auf-, loshaken, -schnallen; öffnen; **2.** loslassen.

ˌun'**clas·si·fied** *adj.* **1.** nicht klassifiziert: ~ *road* Landstraße *f;* **2.** ✕ offen, nicht geheim.

un·**cle** ['ʌŋkl] *s.* **1.** Onkel *m: cry* ~ *Am.* F aufgeben; **2.** *sl.* Pfandleiher *m.*

ˌun'**clean** *adj.* □ unrein (*a. fig.*).

ˌun'**clean·li·ness** *s.* **1.** Unreinlichkeit *f,* Unsauberkeit *f;* **2.** *fig.* Unreinheit *f;* ˌun'**clean·ly** *adj.* **1.** unreinlich; **2.** *fig.* unrein, unkeusch; ˌun'**clench I** *v/t.* **1.** *Faust* öffnen; **2.**

Griff lockern; **II** *v/i.* **3.** sich öffnen *od.* lockern.

ˌun'**cloak** *v/t.* **1.** *j-m* den Mantel abnehmen; **2.** *fig.* enthüllen, -larven.

un·**close** [ˌʌn'kləuz] **I** *v/t.* **1.** öffnen; **2.** *fig.* enthüllen; **II** *v/i.* **3.** sich öffnen.

ˌun'**clothe** *v/t.* entkleiden, -blößen, -hüllen (*a. fig.*); ˌun'**clothed** *adj.* unbekleidet.

ˌun'**cloud·ed** *adj.* **1.** unbewölkt, wolkenlos; **2.** *fig.* ungetrübt.

un·**co** ['ʌŋkəu] *Scot. od. dial.* **I** *adj.* ungewöhnlich, seltsam; **II** *adv.* äußerst, höchst: *the* ~ *guid* die ach so guten Menschen.

ˌun'**cock** *v/t. Gewehr(hahn) etc.* entspannen.

ˌun'**coil** *v/t.* (*v/i.* sich) abwickeln *od.* abspulen *od.* aufrollen.

ˌun'**col·lect·ed** *adj.* **1.** nicht (ein)gesammelt; **2.** ♣ (noch) nicht erhoben (*Gebühren*); **3.** *fig.* nicht gefasst *od.* gesammelt.

ˌun'**col·o(u)red** *adj.* **1.** ungefärbt; **2.** *fig.* ungeschminkt, objek'tiv.

un·**come-at-a·ble** [ˌʌnkʌm'ætəbl] *adj.* F unerreichbar; unzugänglich: *it's* ~ ,da ist nicht ranzukommen'.

ˌun'**come·ly** *adj.* **1.** unschön, reizlos; **2.** *obs.* unschicklich.

un'**com·fort·a·ble** *adj.* □ **1.** unangenehm, beunruhigend; **2.** unbehaglich, ungemütlich (*beide a. fig. Gefühl etc.*), unbequem: ~ *silence* peinliche Stille; **3.** *fig.* unangenehm berührt.

ˌun'**com·mit·ted** *adj.* **1.** nicht begangen (*Verbrechen etc.*); **2.** (*to*) nicht verpflichtet (zu), nicht gebunden (an *acc.*); **3.** ⚖ nicht inhaftiert *od.* eingewiesen; **4.** *parl.* nicht an e-n Ausschuss *etc.* verwiesen; **5.** *pol.* neu'tral, blockfrei; **6.** nicht zweckgebunden: ~ *funds.*

un'**com·mon I** *adj.* □ ungewöhnlich: a) selten, b) außergewöhnlich, -ordentlich; **II** *adv. obs.* äußerst, ungewöhnlich; un'**com·mon·ness** *s.* Ungewöhnlichkeit *f.*

ˌun'**com·mu·ni·ca·ble** *adj.* **1.** nicht mitteilbar; **2.** ♣ nicht ansteckend; ˌun·com'**mu·ni·ca·tive** *adj.* □ nicht *od.* wenig mitteilsam, verschlossen.

ˌun'**com·pan·ion·a·ble** *adj.* ungesellig, nicht 'umgänglich.

ˌun'**com·pet·i·tive** *adj.* nicht wettbewerbsfähig.

un·**com·plain·ing** [ˌʌnkəm'pleɪnɪŋ] *adj.* □ klaglos, ohne Murren, geduldig; ˌun·com'**plain·ing·ness** [-nɪs] *s.* Klaglosigkeit *f.*

ˌun·com'**plai·sant** *adj.* □ ungefällig.

ˌun'**com·plet·ed** *adj.* 'unvollˌendet.

ˌun'**com·pli·cat·ed** *adj.* unkompliziert, einfach.

'un·ˌcom·pli'**men·ta·ry** *adj.* **1.** nicht *od.* wenig schmeichelhaft; **2.** unhöflich.

un·**com·pro·mis·ing** [ʌn'kɒmprəmaɪzɪŋ] *adj.* □ **1.** kompro'misslos; **2.** unbeugsam, unnachgiebig; **3.** *fig.* entschieden, eindeutig.

ˌun'**con·cealed** *adj.* unverhohlen.

un·**con·cern** [ˌʌnkən'sɜːn] *s.* **1.** Sorglosigkeit *f,* Unbekümmertheit *f;* **2.** Gleichgültigkeit *f;* ˌun·con'**cerned** [-nd] *adj.* □ **1.** (*in*) unbeteiligt (an *dat.*), nicht verwickelt (in *acc.*); **2.** uninteressiert (*with* an *dat.*), gleichgültig; **3.** unbesorgt, unbekümmert (*about* um, wegen): *be* ~ *about* sich über *et.* keine Gedanken *od.* Sorgen machen; ˌun·con'**cern·ed·ness** [-nɪdnɪs] → *unconcern.*

ˌun·con'**di·tion·al** *adj.* □ **1.** unbedingt, bedingungslos: ~ *surrender* bedin-

gungslose Kapitulation; **2.** uneingeschränkt, vorbehaltlos.

ˌun·con'**di·tioned** *adj.* **1.** → *unconditional;* **2.** unbedingt: a) *phls.* abso'lut, b) *psych.* angeboren: ~ *reflex.*

ˌun·con'**fined** *adj.* □ unbegrenzt, unbeschränkt.

ˌun·con'**firmed** *adj.* **1.** unbestätigt, nicht erhärtet, unverbürgt; **2.** *eccl.* a) nicht konfirmiert (*Protestanten*), b) nicht gefirmt (*Katholiken*).

ˌun·con'**gen·ial** *adj.* □ **1.** ungleichartig, nicht kongeni'al; **2.** nicht zusagend, unangenehm, 'unsymˌpathisch (*to dat.*); **3.** unfreundlich.

ˌun·con'**nect·ed** *adj.* **1.** unverbunden, getrennt; **2.** 'unzuˌsammenhängend; **3.** ungebunden, ohne Anhang; **4.** nicht verwandt.

un·con·quer·a·ble [ˌʌn'kɒŋkərəbl] *adj.* □ 'unüberˌwindlich (*a. fig.*), unbesiegbar; ˌun·con'**quered** [-kəd] unbesiegt, nicht erobert.

'un·ˌcon·sci'**en·tious** *adj.* □ nicht gewissenhaft, nachlässig.

un·con·scion·a·ble [ʌn'kɒnʃnəbl] *adj.* □ **1.** gewissen-, skrupellos; **2.** unvernünftig, nicht zumutbar; **3.** ,unverschämt', unglaublich, e'norm.

un·**con·scious I** *adj.* □ **1.** unbewusst: *be* ~ *of* nichts ahnen von, sich e-r Sache nicht bewusst sein; **2.** ♣ bewusstlos, ohnmächtig; **3.** unbewusst, unwillkürlich; unfreiwillig (*a. Humor*); **4.** unabsichtlich; **5.** *psych.* unbewusst; **II** *s.* **6.** *the* ~ *psych.* das Unbewusste; un·'**con·scious·ness** *s.* **1.** Unbewusstheit *f;* **2.** ♣ Bewusstlosigkeit *f.*

ˌun·**con·se·crat·ed** *adj.* ungeweiht.

ˌun·con'**sid·ered** *adj.* **1.** unberücksichtigt; **2.** unbedacht, 'unüberˌlegt.

ˌun·con·sti'**tu·tion·al** *adj.* □ *pol.* verfassungswidrig.

ˌun·con'**strained** *adj.* □ zwanglos, ungezwungen; ˌun·con'**straint** *s.* Ungezwungenheit *f,* Zwanglosigkeit *f.*

ˌun·con'**test·ed** *adj.* unbestritten, unangefochten: ~ *election pol.* Wahl *f* ohne Gegenkandidaten.

'un·con·tra'**dict·ed** *adj.* 'unwiderˌsprochen, unbestritten.

ˌun·con'**trol·la·ble** *adj.* □ **1.** unkontrollierbar; **2.** unbändig, unbeherrscht: *an* ~ *temper;* ˌun·con'**trolled** *adj.* □ **1.** nicht kontrolliert, unbeaufsichtigt; **2.** unbeherrscht, zügellos.

ˌun·con'**ven·tion·al** *adj.* □ 'unkonventioˌnell: a) unüblich, b) ungezwungen, form-, zwanglos; 'un·conˌven·tion·al·i·ty *s.* Zwanglosigkeit *f,* Ungezwungenheit *f.*

ˌun·con'**vert·ed** *adj.* **1.** unverwandelt; **2.** *eccl.* unbekehrt (*a. fig. nicht überzeugt*); **3.** ♣ nicht konvertiert; ˌun·con'**vert·i·ble** *adj.* **1.** nicht verwandelbar; **2.** nicht vertauschbar; **3.** ♣ nicht konvertierbar.

ˌun·con'**vinced** *adj.* nicht über'zeugt; ˌun·con'**vinc·ing** *adj.* nicht über'zeugend.

ˌun'**cooked** *adj.* ungekocht, roh.

ˌun'**cord** *v/t.* auf-, losbinden.

ˌun'**cork** *v/t.* **1.** entkorken; **2.** *fig.* F Gefühlen *etc.* Luft machen; **3.** *Am.* F *et.* ,vom Stapel lassen'.

ˌun·cor'**rob·o·rat·ed** *adj.* unbestätigt, nicht erhärtet.

un·**count·a·ble** [ˌʌn'kauntəbl] *adj.* **1.** unzählbar; **2.** zahllos; ˌun'**count·ed** [-tɪd] *adj.* **1.** ungezählt; **2.** unzählig.

ˌun'**cou·ple** *v/t.* **1.** *Hunde etc.* aus der Koppel (los)lassen; **2.** loslösen, trennen; **3.** ⊕ aus-, loskuppeln.

U

un·couth [ʌn'kuːθ] *adj.* □ **1.** ungeschlacht, unbeholfen, plump; **2.** grob, ungehobelt; **3.** *poet.* öde, wild (*Gegend*); **4.** *obs.* wunderlich.

ˌun'cov·e·nant·ed *adj.* **1.** nicht vertraglich festgelegt; **2.** nicht vertraglich gebunden.

un'cov·er I *v/t.* **1.** aufdecken, freilegen; *Körperteil, a. Kopf* entblößen: **~** *o.s.* → 5; **2.** *fig.* aufdecken, enthüllen; **3.** ✕ ohne Deckung lassen; ~ *Boxen etc.*: ungedeckt lassen; **II** *v/i.* **5.** den Hut abnehmen; **un'cov·ered** *adj.* **1.** unbedeckt (*a.* barhäuptig); **2.** unbekleidet, nackt; **3.** ✕, *sport etc.* ungedeckt, ungeschützt; **4.** ✝ ungedeckt (*Wechsel etc.*).

ˌun'crit·i·cal *adj.* □ unkritisch, kri'tiklos (*of* gegenüber).

ˌun'cross *v/t.* gekreuzte Arme *od.* Beine gerade legen; **ˌun'crossed** *adj.* nicht gekreuzt: **~** *cheque* (*Am.* check) ✝ Barscheck *m.*

unc·tion ['ʌŋkʃn] *s.* **1.** Salbung *f*, Einreibung *f*; **2.** ✚ Salbe *f*; **3.** *eccl.* a) (heiliges) Öl, b) Salbung *f* (Weihe), c) *a.* *extreme* ~ Letzte Ölung; **4.** *fig.* Balsam *m* (*Linderung, Trost*) (**to** für); **5.** *fig.* Inbrunst *f*, Pathos *n*; **6.** *fig.* Salbung *f*, unechtes Pathos: **with** ~ a) salbungsvoll, b) mit Genuss; **'unc·tu·ous** [-ktjʊəs] *adj.* □ **1.** ölig, fettig: ~ *soil* fetter Boden; **2.** *fig.* salbungsvoll, ölig.

ˌun'cul·ti·vat·ed *adj.* **1.** ⚚ unbebaut, unkultiviert; **2.** *fig.* brachliegend (*Talent etc.*); **3.** *fig.* ungebildet, unkultiviert.

ˌun'cul·tured *adj.* unkultiviert (*a. fig.* ungebildet).

ˌun'curbed *adj.* **1.** abgezäumt; **2.** *fig.* ungezähmt, zügellos.

ˌun'cured *adj.* **1.** ungeheilt; **2.** ungesalzen, ungepökelt.

ˌun'curl *v/t.* (*v/i.* sich) entkräuseln *od.* glätten.

ˌun'cur'tailed *adj.* ungekürzt, unbeschnitten.

ˌun'cut *adj.* **1.** ungeschnitten; **2.** unzerschnitten; **3.** ⚚ ungemäht; **4.** ungeschliffen (*Diamant*); **5.** unbeschnitten (*Buch*); **6.** *fig.* ungekürzt.

ˌun'dam·aged *adj.* unbeschädigt, unversehrt.

ˌun'damped *adj.* **1.** *bsd.* ♪, ⚡, *phys.* ungedämpft; **2.** unangefeuchtet; **3.** *fig.* nicht entmutigt.

un·date ['ʌndeɪt] *adj.* wellig, wellenförmig.

un·dat·ed¹ ['ʌndeɪtɪd] → **undate.**

ˌun'dat·ed² *adj.* **1.** undatiert, ohne Datum; **2.** unbefristet.

un·daunt·ed [ˌʌn'dɔːntɪd] *adj.* □ unerschrocken.

un·dead [ʌn'ded] *s:* *the* ~ *pl.* die Untoten *pl.*

ˌun·de'ceive *v/t.* **1.** *j-m* die Augen öffnen, *j-n* desillusio'nieren; **2.** aufklären (*of* über *acc.*), e-s Besser(e)n belehren; **ˌun·de'ceived** *adj.* **1.** nicht irregeführt; **2.** aufgeklärt, e-s Besser(e)n belehrt.

ˌun·de'cid·ed *adj.* □ **1.** unentschieden, offen: *leave s.th.* ~; **2.** unbestimmt, vage; **3.** unentschlossen; **4.** unbeständig (*Wetter*).

ˌun·de'ci·pher·a·ble *adj.* **1.** nicht zu entziffern(d), nicht entzifferbar; **2.** unerklärlich, nicht enträtselbar.

ˌun·de'clared *adj.* **1.** nicht bekannt gemacht, nicht erklärt: ~ *war* Krieg *m* ohne Kriegserklärung; **2.** ✝ nicht deklariert.

ˌun·de'fend·ed *adj.* **1.** unverteidigt; **2.** ⚖ a) unverteidigt, ohne Verteidiger, b)

'unwider‚sprochen (*Klage*).

ˌun·de'filed *adj.* unbefleckt, rein (*a. fig.*).

ˌun·de'fin·a·ble *adj.* undefinierbar, unbestimmt.

ˌun·de'fined *adj.* **1.** unbegrenzt; **2.** unbestimmt, vage.

'un·de‚lete *v/t.* *Computer:* Datei *etc.* wieder'herstellen.

ˌun·de'mand·ing *adj.* **1.** anspruchslos (*a. fig.*); **2.** leicht: ~ *task.*

ˌun·de'mon·stra·tive *adj.* zu'rückhaltend, reserviert, unaufdringlich.

ˌun·de'ni·a·ble *adj.* □ unleugbar, unbestreitbar.

'un·de‚nom·i'na·tion·al *adj.* **1.** nicht konfessio'nell gebunden; **2.** *ped.* interkonfessio'nell, Gemeinschafts..., Simultan...: ~ *school.*

un·der ['ʌndə] **I** *prp.* **1.** *allg.* unter (*dat. od. acc.*); **2.** *Lage:* unter (*dat.*), 'unterhalb von (*od. gen.*): *from* ~ ... unter dem Tisch *etc.* hervor; *get out from* ~ *Am. sl.* a) sich herauswinden, b) den Verlust wettmachen; **3.** *Richtung:* unter (*acc.*); **4.** unter (*dat.*), am Fuße von (*od. gen.*); **5.** *zeitlich:* unter (*dat.*), während: ~ *his rule*; ~ *the Stuarts* unter den Stuarts; ~ *the date of* unter dem Datum von *1. Januar etc.*; **6.** unter der Autorität, Führung *etc.*: *he fought* ~ *Wellington*; **7.** unter (*dat.*), unter dem Schutz von: ~ *arms* unter Waffen; ~ *darkness* im Schutz der Dunkelheit; **8.** unter (*dat.*), geringer als, weniger als: *persons* ~ *40* (*years of age*) Personen unter 40 (Jahren); *in* ~ *an hour* in weniger als 'einer Stunde; **9.** *fig.* unter (*dat.*): ~ *alcohol* unter Alkohol; ~ *an assumed name* unter e-m angenommenen Namen; ~ *supervision* unter Aufsicht; **10.** gemäß, laut, nach: ~ *the terms of the contract*; *claims* ~ *a contract* Forderungen aus e-m Vertrag; **11.** in (*dat.*): ~ *construction* im Bau; ~ *repair* in Reparatur; ~ *treatment* ✚ in Behandlung; **12.** bei: *he studied physics* ~ *Maxwell*; **13.** mit: ~ *s.o.'s signature* mit j-s Unterschrift, (eigenhändig) unterzeichnet von j-m; ~ *separate cover* mit getrennter Post; **II** *adv.* **14.** dar'unter, unter; → *go* (*keep etc.*) *under*; **15.** unten: *as* ~ wie unten (angeführt); **III** *adj.* **16.** unter, Unter...; **17.** unter, nieder, 'untergeordnet, Unter...; **18.** *nur in Zssgn* ungenügend, zu gering: *an* ~*dose*; ~'act [-ər'æ-] *v/t. u. v/i. thea. etc.* unter'spielen, unter'treiben (*a. fig.*); ~·a'chieve [-ərə-] *v/i.* weniger leisten *od.* schlechter abschneiden als erwartet; ~'age [-ər'eɪ-] *adj.* minderjährig; ~‚a·gent [-ər‚eɪ-] *s.* 'Untervertreter *m*; ~'arm [-ərɑːm] **I** *adj.* **1.** Unterarm...; **2.** → *underhand* 2; **II** *adv.* **3.** mit e-r 'Unterarmbewegung; ~'bid *v/t.* [*irr.* → *bid*] unter'bieten; ~'bred *adj.* unfein, ungebildet; **'~·brush** *s.* 'Unterholz *n*, Ge'strüpp *n*; **'~‚car·riage** *s.* **1.** ✈ Fahrwerk *n*; **2.** *mot. etc.* Fahrgestell *n*; **3.** *typ.* 'Unterla‚fette *f*; ~'charge **I** *v/t.* **1.** *j-m* zu wenig berechnen; **2.** *et.* zu gering berechnen; **3.** *Batterie etc.* unter'laden; **4.** *Geschütz etc.* zu schwach laden; **II** *s.* **5.** zu geringe Berechnung *od.* Belastung; **6.** ungenügende (Auf)Ladung; **'~·clothes** *s. pl.*, **'~‚cloth·ing** *s.* 'Unterkleidung *f*, -wäsche *f*; **'~·coat** *s.* **1.** ⚙, *paint.* Grundierung *f*; **2.** *zo.* Wollhaarkleid *n*; **'~‚cov·er** *adj.* **1.** Geheim...: ~ *agent*, ~ *man* a) (*bsd.* eingeschleuster) Geheimagent, Spitzel *m*, b) verdeckter Ermittler; **'~·croft** *s.* ⛪

'unterirdisches Gewölbe, Krypta *f*; **'~‚cur·rent** *s.* 'Unterströmung *f* (*a. fig.*); ~'cut **I** *v/t.* [*irr.* → *cut*] **1.** unter'höhlen; **2.** (im Preis) unter'bieten; **3.** *Golf, Tennis etc.:* Ball mit 'Unterschnitt spielen; **II** *s.* **'undercut 4.** Unter'höhlung *f*; **5.** *Golf, Tennis etc.:* unter'schnittener Ball; **6.** *Küche: Brit.* Fi'let *n*, zartes Lendenstück; **~·de'vel·oped** *adj. phot. u. fig.* 'unterentwickelt: ~ *child*; ~ *country* Entwicklungsland *n*; **'~·dog** *s. fig.* **1.** Verlierer *m*, Unter'legene(r *m*) *f*; **2.** a) *der* (sozi'al *etc.*) Schwächere *od.* Benachteiligte, b) *der* (zu Unrecht) Verfolgte; ~·'done *adj.* nicht gar, nicht 'durchgebraten; **'~·dose** ☞ **I** *s.* **1.** zu geringe Dosis; **II** *v/t. ‚under'dose:* *j-m* e-e zu geringe Dosis geben; **3.** *et.* 'unterdosieren; ~'dress *v/t.* (*v/i.* sich) zu einfach kleiden; ~'es·ti·mate [-ər'estɪmeɪt] **I** *v/t.* unter'schätzen; **II** *s.* [-mət] *a.* '~‚es·ti'ma·tion [-ər‚e-] Unter'schätzung *f*; 'Unterbewertung *f*; ~·ex'pose [-dərɪ-] *v/t. phot.* 'unterbelichten; ~·ex'po·sure [-dərɪ-] *s. phot.* 'Unterbelichtung *f*; ~'fed *adj.* 'unterernährt; **'~'feed·ing** *s.* 'Unterernährung *f*; ~'foot *adv.* **1.** unter den Füßen, unten, am Boden *zer*trampeln *etc.*; **2.** *fig.* in der Gewalt, unter Kon'trolle; **'~·frame** *s. mot. etc.* 'Untergestell *n*, Rahmen *m*; **'~·gar·ment** *s.* 'Unterkleid(ung *f*) *n*; *pl.* 'Unterwäsche *f*; ~'go *v/t.* [*irr.* → *go*] **1.** e-n Wandel *etc.* erleben, 'durchmachen; **2.** sich e-r Operation *etc.* unter'ziehen; **3.** erdulden; ~'grad·u·ate *univ.* **I** *s.* Stu'dent(in); **II** *adj.* Studenten...; **'~·ground I** *s.* **1.** *bsd. Brit.* 'Untergrundbahn *f*, U-Bahn *f*; **2.** *pol.* 'Untergrund(bewegung *f*) *m*; **3.** *Kunst:* Untergrund *m*; **II** *adj.* **4.** 'unterirdisch: ~ *cable* ⚙ Erdkabel *n*; ~ *car park*, ~ *garage* Tiefgarage *f*; ~ *railway* (*Am. railroad*) → 1; ~ *water* Grundwasser *n*; **5.** ✕ unter Tag(e): ~ *mining* Untertag(e)bau *m*; **6.** ⚙ Tiefbau...: ~ *engineering* Tiefbau *m*; **7.** *fig.* Untergrund..., Geheim..., verborgen: ~ *movement pol.* Untergrundbewegung *f*; **8.** *Kunst:* Underground...: ~ *film*; **III** *adv.* ‚under'ground **9.** unter der *od.* die Erde, 'unterirdisch; **10.** *fig.* im Verborgenen, geheim: *go* ~ a) *pol.* in den Untergrund gehen, b) untertauchen; **'~·growth** *s.* 'Unterholz *n*, Gestrüpp *n*; **'~·hand** *adj. u. adv.* **1.** *fig.* a) heimlich, verstohlen, b) 'hinterlistig; **2.** *sport* mit der Hand unter Schulterhöhe ausgeführt: ~ *service Tennis:* Tiefaufschlag *m*; ~'hand·ed *adj.* □ **1.** → *underhand*; **2.** ✝ knapp an Arbeitskräften, 'unterbelegt; **~·in'sure** [-ərɪ-] *v/t.* (*v/i.* sich) 'unterversichern; ~'lay **I** *v/t.* [*irr.* → *lay¹*] **1.** (dar)'unterlegen; **2.** *et.* unter'legen; **3.** *typ.* Satz zurichten; **II** *v/i.* **4.** ✕ sich neigen, einfallen; **III** *s.* **'underlay 5.** 'Unterlage *f*; **6.** *typ.* Zurichtebogen *m*; **7.** ✕ schräges Flöz; **'~·lease** *s.* 'Unterverpachtung *f*, -miete *f*; ~'let *v/t.* [*irr.* → *let¹*] **1.** unter Wert verpachten *od.* vermieten; **2.** 'unterverpachten, -vermieten; ~'lie *v/t.* [*irr.* → *lie²*] **1.** liegen unter (*dat.*); **2.** zu'grunde liegen (*dat.*); **3.** ✝ unter'liegen (*dat.*), unter'worfen sein (*dat.*); ~'line **I** *v/t.* **1.** unter'streichen (*a. fig.* betonen); **II** *s.* **'underline 2.** Unter'streichung *f*; **3.** *thea.* (Vor)Ankündigung *f* am Ende e-s The'aterpla‚kats; **4.** 'Bild‚unterschrift *f*.

un·der·ling ['ʌndəlɪŋ] *s. contp.* Unter'gebene(r *m*) *f*, (kleiner) Handlanger, ‚Kuli *m*.

‚un·der|'ly·ing *adj.* **1.** dar'unter liegend; **2.** *fig.* zu'grunde liegend; **3.** ✝ *Am.* Vorrangs...; **‚~'manned** [-'mænd] *adj.* a) ♋ 'unterbemannt, b) (perso'nell) 'unterbesetzt; **‚~'men·tioned** *adj.* unten erwähnt; **‚~'mine** *v/t.* **1.** ⚙ untermi'nieren (*a. fig.*); **2.** unter'spülen, auswaschen; **3.** *fig.* unter'graben, (all'mählich) zu'grunde richten; **'~·most I** *adj.* unterst; **II** *adv.* zu'unterst.

un·der·neath [‚ʌndə'niːθ] **I** *prp.* **1.** unter (*dat. od. acc.*), 'unterhalb (*gen.*); **II** *adv.* **2.** unten, dar'unter; **3.** auf der 'Unterseite.

‚un·der|'nour·ished *adj.* 'unterernährt; **'~·pants** *s. pl.* 'Unterhose *f*; **'~·pass** *s.* ('Straßen- *etc.*)Unter‚führung *f*; **‚~'pay** *v/t.* [*irr.* → *pay*] ✝ 'unterbezahlen; **‚~'pin** *v/t.* 🏛 (unter)'stützen, unter'mauern (*beide a. fig.*); **‚~'pin·ning** *s.* **1.** 🏛 Unter'mauerung *f*, 'Unterbau *m* (*a. fig.*); **2.** F ‚Fahrgestell' *n* (*Beine*); **‚~'play** *v/t. u. v/i.* **1.** → *underact*; **2.** **~ one's hand** *fig.* nicht alle Trümpfe ausspielen; **'~·plot** *s.* Nebenhandlung *f*, Epi'sode *f* (*Roman etc.*); **‚~'pop·u·lat·ed** *adj.* 'unterbevölkert; **‚~'print** *v/t.* **1.** *typ.* a) gegendrucken, b) zu schwach drucken; **2.** *phot.* 'unterkopieren; **‚~'priv·i·leged** ✝, *pol.* 'unterprivilegiert, schlechter gestellt; **‚~·pro'duc·tion** *s.* ✝ 'Unterprodukti‚on *f*; **‚~'proof** *adj.* ✝ 'unterpro‚zentig (*Spirituosen*); **‚~'rate** *v/t.* **1.** unter'schätzen, 'unterbewerten (*a. sport*); **2.** ✝ zu niedrig veranschlagen; **‚~·re'ac·tion** *s.* zu schwache Reakti'on; **'~·seal** *mot.* **I** *s.* 'Unterbodenschutz *m*; **II** *v/t.* mit 'Unterbodenschutz versehen; **‚~'score** *v/t.* unter'streichen (*a. fig. betonen*); **‚~'sec·re·tar·y** *s. pol.* 'Staatssekre‚tär *m*; **‚~'sell** *v/t.* [*irr.* → *sell*] ✝ **1.** *j-n* unter'bieten; **2.** *Ware* verschleudern, unter Wert verkaufen; **‚~'sexed** *adj.*: **be ~** e-n unterentwickelten Geschlechtstrieb haben; **'~·shirt** *s.* 'Unterhemd *n*; **‚~'shoot** *v/t.* [*irr.* → *shoot*]: **~ the runway** ✈ vor der Landebahn aufsetzen; **'~·shot** *adj.* **1.** ⚙ 'unterschlächtig (*Wasserrad*); **2.** mit vorstehendem 'Unterkiefer; **'~·signed I** *adj.* unter'zeichnet; **II** *s.*: **the undersigned** a) der (die) Unter'zeichnete, b) die Unter'zeichneten *pl.*; **‚~'size(d)** *adj.* **1.** unter Nor'malgröße; **2.** winzig; **'~·skirt** *s.* 'Unterrock *m*; **‚~'slung** *adj.* ⚙, *mot.* Hänge...(-kühler *etc.*), Unterzug...(-rahmen); unter'baut (*Feder etc.*); **‚~'soil** *s.* 'Untergrund *m*; **‚~'staffed** *adj.* 'unterbesetzt.

un·der·stand [‚ʌndə'stænd] [*irr.* → *stand*] **I** *v/t.* **1.** verstehen: a) begreifen, b) einsehen, c) 'wörtlich *etc.* auffassen, d) Verständnis haben für: **~ each other** *fig.* sich *od.* einander verstehen, *a.* zu e-r Einigung kommen; **give s.o. to ~** *j-m* zu verstehen geben; **make o.s. understood** sich verständlich machen; **do I** (*od.* **am I to**) **~ that ...** soll das etwa heißen, dass ...; **be it understood** wohlverstanden; **what do you ~ by ...?** was verstehen Sie unter (*dat.*)?; **2.** sich verstehen auf (*acc.*), wissen (*how to inf.* wie man *et. macht*): **he ~s horses** er versteht sich auf Pferde; **she ~s children** sie kann mit Kindern umgehen; **3.** (als sicher) annehmen, vor'aussetzen: **an understood thing** e-e ausod. abgemachte Sache; **it is understood** das versteht sich (von selbst); **it is understood that** ✝✝ es gilt als vereinbart, dass; **4.** erfahren, hören: **I ~ ...** wie ich höre; **I ~ that** ich hörte *od.* man sagte mir, dass; **it is understood** es

heißt, wie verlautet; **5.** (*from*) entnehmen (*dat. od.* aus), schließen (aus); **6.** *bsd. ling.* sinngemäß ergänzen, hin'zudenken; **II** *v/i.* **7.** verstehen: a) begreifen, b) *fig.* (volles) Verständnis haben; **8.** Verstand haben; **9.** hören: **..., so I ~** wie ich höre; **un·der'stand·a·ble** [-'dəbl] *adj.* verständlich; **‚un·der'stand·a·bly** [-'dəbli] *adv.* verständlich(erweise); **‚un·der'stand·ing** [-'dɪŋ] **I** *s.* **1.** Verstehen *n*; **2.** Verstand *m*, Intelli'genz *f*; **3.** Verständnis *n* (*of* für); **4.** *gutes etc.* Einvernehmen (*between* zwischen); **5.** Verständigung *f*, Vereinbarung *f*, Über'einkunft *f*, Abmachung *f*: **come to an ~ with s.o.** zu e-r Einigung mit *j-m* kommen; **6.** Bedingung *f*: **on the ~ that** unter der Bedingung *od.* Voraussetzung, dass; **II** *adj.* □ **7.** verständig; **8.** verständnisvoll.

un·der|·state [‚ʌndə'steɪt] *v/t.* **1.** zu gering angeben; **2.** (bewusst) zu'rückhaltend darstellen, unter'treiben; **3.** abschwächen, mildern; **‚~'state·ment** *s.* **1.** zu niedrige Angabe; **2.** Unter'treibung *f*, Under'statement *n*; **‚~'steer** *v/i. Auto* unter'steuern; **'~·strap·per** → *underling*; **‚~'stud·y** *thea.* **I** *v/t.* **1.** *Rolle* als zweite Besetzung einstudieren; **2.** für *e-n Schauspieler* einspringen; **II** *s.* **3.** zweite Besetzung; *fig.* Ersatzmann *m*; **‚~'take** *v/t.* [*irr.* → *take*] **1.** *Aufgabe* über'nehmen, *Sache* auf sich *od.* in die Hand nehmen; **2.** *Reise etc.* unter'nehmen; **3.** *Risiko, Verantwortung etc.* über'nehmen, eingehen; **4.** sich erbieten, sich verpflichten (*to do* zu tun); **5.** garantieren, sich verbürgen (*that* dass); **'~·tak·er** *s.* Leichenbestatter *m*, Be'stattungsinsti‚tut *n*; **‚~'tak·ing** *s.* **1.** 'Übernahme *f e-r Aufgabe*; **2.** Unter'nehmung *f*, -'fangen *n*; **3.** ✝ Unter'nehmen *n*, Betrieb *m*: **industrial ~**; **4.** Verpflichtung *f*; **5.** Garan'tie *f*; **6.** **'un·der‚taking** Leichenbestattung *f*; **‚~'ten·ant** *s.* 'Untermieter(in), -pächter(in); **‚~'tim·ed** *adj. phot.* 'unterbelichtet; **'~·tone** *s.* **1.** gedämpfter Ton, gedämpfte Stimme: **in an ~** halblaut; **2.** *fig.* 'Unterton *m*; *Börse:* Grundton *m*; **3.** gedämpfte Farbe; **'~·tow** *s.* ♋ **1.** Sog *m*; **2.** 'Widersee *f*; **‚~'val·ue** *v/t.* unter'schätzen, 'unterbewerten, zu gering ansetzen; **'~·vest** *s. Brit.* 'Unterhemd *n*; **'~·wear** → *underclothes*; **'~·weight I** *s.* 'Untergewicht *n*; **II** *adj.* ‚under'weight' 'untergewichtig: **be ~** 'Untergewicht haben; **'~·wood** *s.* 'Unterholz *n*, Gestrüpp *n* (*a. fig.*); **‚~'worked** *adj.* unterbeschäftigt, nicht ausgelastet; **'~·world** *s. allg.* 'Unterwelt *f*; **'~·write** *v/t.* [*irr.* → *write*] **1.** a) *et.* da'runter schreiben, b) *fig. et.* unter'schreiben; **2.** ✝ a) *Versicherungspolice* unter'zeichnen, *Versicherung* über'nehmen, b) *et.* versichern, c) die Haftung über'nehmen für; **2.** *Aktienemission etc.* ga‚rantieren; **'~·writ·er** *s.* ✝ **1.** Versicherer *m*, Versicherungs(gesellschaft) *f*; **2.** Mitglied *n e-s* Versiche'onskon‚sortiums; **3.** Ver'sicherungsa‚gent *m*; **'~·writ·ing** *s.* ✝ **1.** (See)Versicherung(sgeschäft *n*) *f*; **2.** Emissi'onsgaran‚tie *f*: **~ syndicate** Emissionskonsortium *n*.

‚un·de'served *adj.* unverdient; **‚un·de'serv·ed·ly** [-ɪdli] *adv.* unverdientermaßen; **‚un·de'serv·ing** *adj.* **1.** unwert, unwürdig (*of gen.*): **be ~ of** kein Mitgefühl *etc.* verdienen.

‚un·de'signed *adj.* □ unbeabsichtigt, unabsichtlich; **‚un·de'sign·ing** *adj.* ehrlich, aufrichtig.

'un·de‚sir·a'bil·i·ty *s.* Unerwünschtheit *f*; **‚un·de'sir·a·ble I** *adj.* □ **1.** nicht wünschenswert; **2.** unerwünscht, lästig: **~ alien**; **II** *s.* **3.** unerwünschte Per'son; **‚un·de'sired** *adj.* unerwünscht, 'unwill‚kommen; **‚un·de'sir·ous** *adj.* nicht begierig (*of nach*): **be ~ of** *et.* nicht wünschen *od.* (haben) wollen.

‚un·de'tach·a·ble *adj.* nicht (ab)trennbar *od.* abnehmbar.

‚un·de'tect·ed *adj.* unentdeckt.

‚un·de'ter·mined *adj.* **1.** unentschieden, schwebend, offen: **an ~ question**; **2.** unbestimmt, vage; **3.** unentschlossen, unschlüssig.

‚un·de'terred *adj.* nicht abgeschreckt, unbeeindruckt (*by* von).

‚un·de'vel·oped *adj.* **1.** unentwickelt; **2.** unerschlossen (*Gebiet*).

un·de·vi·at·ing [ʌn'diːvɪeɪtɪŋ] *adj.* □ **1.** nicht abweichend; **2.** unentwegt, unbeirrbar.

un·dies ['ʌndɪz] *s. pl.* F ('Damen-) ‚Unterwäsche *f*.

'un‚dif·fer·en·ti·at·ed *adj.* undifferenziert.

‚un·di'gest·ed *adj.* unverdaut (*a. fig.*).

un'dig·ni·fied *adj.* würdelos.

‚un·di'lut·ed *adj.* unverdünnt, *a. fig.* unverwässert, unverfälscht.

‚un·di'min·ished *adj.* unvermindert.

‚un·di'rect·ed *adj.* **1.** ungeleitet, führungslos, ungelenkt; **2.** unadressiert; **3.** *phys.* ungerichtet.

‚un·dis'cerned *adj.* □ unbemerkt; **‚un·dis'cern·ing** *adj.* □ urteils-, einsichtslos, unkritisch.

‚un·dis'charged *adj.* **1.** unbezahlt; unbeglichen; **2.** (noch) nicht entlastet: **~ debtor**; **3.** nicht abgeschossen (*Feuerwaffe*); **4.** nicht entladen (*Schiff etc.*).

un'dis·ci·plined *adj.* **1.** undiszipliniert, zuchtlos; **2.** ungeschult.

‚un·dis'closed *adj.* ungenannt, geheim gehalten, nicht bekannt gegeben.

‚un·dis'cour·aged *adj.* nicht entmutigt.

‚un·dis'cov·er·a·ble *adj.* unauffindbar, nicht zu entdecken(d); **‚un·dis'covered** *adj.* **1.** unentdeckt; **2.** unbemerkt.

‚un·dis'crim·i·nat·ing *adj.* □ **1.** unterschiedslos; **2.** urteilslos, unkritisch.

‚un·dis'cussed *adj.* unerörtert.

‚un·dis'guised *adj.* □ **1.** unverkleidet, unmaskiert; **2.** *fig.* unverhüllt.

‚un·dis'mayed *adj.* unerschrocken.

‚un·dis'posed *adj.* **1.** **~ of** nicht verteilt *od.* vergeben, ✝ *a.* unverkauft; **2.** abgeneigt, nicht bereit *od.* (dazu) aufgelegt (*to do* zu tun).

‚un·dis'put·ed *adj.* □ unbestritten.

‚un·dis'tin·guish·a·ble *adj.* □ **1.** nicht erkenn- *od.* wahrnehmbar; **2.** nicht unter'scheidbar, nicht zu unter'scheiden(d) (*from* von); **‚un·dis'tin·guished** *adj.* **1.** sich nicht unter'scheidend (*from* von); **2.** 'durchschnittlich, nor'mal; **3.** → *undistinguishable*.

‚un·dis'turbed *adj.* □ **1.** ungestört, unberührt, gelassen.

‚un·di'vid·ed *adj.* □ **1.** ungeteilt (*a. fig. Aufmerksamkeit etc.*); **2.** ✝ nicht verteilt: **~ profits**.

un·do [‚ʌn'duː] *v/t.* [*irr.* → *do*] **1.** *Paket, Knoten, a. Kragen, Mantel etc.* aufmachen, öffnen; aufknöpfen, -knüpfen, -lösen; losbinden; *j-m* den Reißverschluss *etc.* aufmachen; *Saum etc.* auftrennen; → *undone*; **2.** *fig.* ungeschehen *od.* rückgängig machen, aufheben; **3.** *fig. et. od. j-n* ruinieren, zu'grunde richten; *Hoffnungen etc.* zu'nichte machen; **'un'do·ing** *s.* **1.** *das* Aufmachen *etc.*; **2.** Ungeschehen-, Rückgängigma-

U

chen *n*; **3.** Zu'grunderichtung *f*; **4.** Unglück *n*, Verderben *n*, Ru'in *m*; **,un-'done I** *p.p. von* **undo**; **II** *adj.* **1.** ungetan, unerledigt: *leave s.th.* ~ *et.* unausgeführt lassen, et. unterlassen; *leave nothing* ~ nichts unversucht lassen; **2.** offen: *come* ~ aufgehen; **3.** ruiniert, 'erledigt', ,hin': *he is* ~ es ist aus mit ihm.

un·doubt·ed [ʌn'daʊtɪd] *adj.* □ unbezweifelt, unbestritten; unzweifelhaft; **un'doubt·ed·ly** [-lɪ] *adv.* zweifellos, ohne (jeden) Zweifel.

un·dreamed, *a.* **un·dreamt** [*beide* ʌn'dremt] *adj. oft* ~*-of* ungeahnt, nie erträumt, unerhört.

,un'dress I *v/t.* **1.** (*v/i.* sich) entkleiden *od.* ausziehen; **II** *s.* **2.** Alltagskleid(ung *f*) *n*; **3.** Hauskleid *n*; **4.** *in a state of* ~ a) halb bekleidet, im Negli'gee, b) unbekleidet; **5.** ✕ 'Interimsuni,form *f*; **,un'dressed** *adj.* **1.** unbekleidet; **2.** *Küche:* a) ungarniert, b) unzubereitet; **3.** ⚙ a) ungegerbt (*Leder*), b) unbehauen (*Holz, Stein*); **4.** ⚕ unverbunden (*Wunde etc.*).

,un'drink·a·ble *adj.* nicht trinkbar.

,un'due *adj.* (□ → **unduly**) **1.** 'übermäßig, über'trieben; **2.** ungehörig, unangebracht, unbührlich; **3.** *bsd.* ⚖ unzulässig: ~ *influence* unzulässige Beeinflussung; **4.** ⚕ noch nicht fällig.

un·du·late ['ʌndjʊleɪt] **I** *v/i.* **1.** wogen, wallen, sich wellenförmig (fort)bewegen; **2.** wellenförmig verlaufen; **II** *v/t.* **3.** in wellenförmige Bewegung versetzen, wogen lassen; **4.** wellen; **III** *adj.* □ **5.** → **'un·du·lat·ed** [-tɪd] *adj.* wellenförmig, wellig, Wellen...: ~ *line* Wellenlinie *f*; **'un·du·lat·ing** [-tɪŋ] *adj.* □ **1.** → **undulated**; **2.** wallend, wogend; **un·du·la·tion** [,ʌndjʊ'leɪʃn] *s.* **1.** wellenförmige Bewegung; Wallen *n*, Wogen *n*; **2.** *geol.* Welligkeit *f*; **3.** *phys.* Wellenbewegung *f*, -linie *f*; **4.** *phys.* Schwingung(sbewegung) *f*; **5.** ♬ Undulati'on *f*; **'un·du·la·to·ry** [-lətrɪ] *adj.* wellenförmig, Wellen...

,un'du·ly *adv. von* **undue** 1–3: *not* ~ *worried* nicht übermäßig *od.* über Gebühr besorgt.

,un'du·ti·ful *adj.* □ **1.** pflichtvergessen; **2.** ungehorsam; **3.** unehrerbietig.

un'dy·ing *adj.* □ **1.** unsterblich, unvergänglich (*Liebe, Ruhm etc.*); **2.** unendlich (*Hass etc.*).

,un'earned *adj.* unverdient, nicht erarbeitet: ~ *income* ⚕ Einkommen *n* aus Vermögen, Kapitaleinkommen *n*.

,un'earth *v/t.* **1.** Tier aus der Höhle treiben; **2.** ausgraben (*a. fig.*); **3.** *fig. et.* ans (Tages)Licht bringen, aufstöbern, ausfindig machen.

un'earth·ly *adj.* **1.** 'überirdisch; **2.** unirdisch, 'überna,türlich; **3.** schauerlich, unheimlich; **4.** F unmöglich (*Zeit*): *at an* ~ *hour.*

un'eas·i·ness *s.* **1.** (*körperliches u. geistiges*) Unbehagen; **2.** (*innere*) Unruhe; **3.** Unbehaglichkeit *f e-s Gefühls etc.*; **4.** Unsicherheit *f*; **un'eas·y** *adj.* □ **1.** unruhig, unbehaglich, besorgt, ner'vös: *feel* ~ *about s.th.* über et. beunruhigt sein; **2.** unbehaglich (*Gefühl*), beunruhigend (*Verdacht etc.*); **3.** unruhig: ~ *night*; **4.** unsicher (*im Sattel etc.*); **5.** gezwungen, unsicher (*Benehmen etc.*).

,un'eat·a·ble *adj.* ungenießbar.

'un,e·co'nom·ic, 'un,e·co'nom·i·cal *adj.* □ unwirtschaftlich.

,un'ed·i·fy·ing *adj. fig.* wenig erbaulich, unerquicklich.

,un'ed·u·cat·ed *adj.* ungebildet.

,un·em'bar·rassed *adj.* **1.** nicht verle-

gen, ungeniert; **2.** unbehindert; **3.** von (Geld)Sorgen frei.

,un·e'mo·tion·al *adj.* □ **1.** leidenschaftslos, nüchtern; **2.** teilnahmslos, passiv, kühl; **3.** gelassen.

,un·em'ploy·a·ble I *adj.* **1.** nicht verwendbar, unbrauchbar; **2.** arbeitsunfähig (*Person*); **II** *s.* **3.** Arbeitsunfähige(r *m*) *f*; **,un·em'ployed I** *adj.* **1.** arbeits-, erwerbs-, stellungslos; **2.** ungenützt, brachliegend: ~ *capital* ⚕ totes Kapital; **II** *s.* **3.** *the* ~ *pl.* die Arbeitslosen *pl.*; **,un·em'ploy·ment** *s.* Arbeitslosigkeit *f*: ~ *benefit* Arbeitslosenunterstützung *f*; ~ *insurance* Arbeitslosenversicherung *f*; ~ *rate* Arbeitslosenquote *f*.

,un·en'cum·bered *adj.* **1.** ⚖ unbelastet (*Grundbesitz*); **2.** (*by*) unbehindert (durch), frei (von).

un'end·ing *adj.* □ endlos, nicht enden wollend, unaufhörlich.

,un·en'dowed *adj.* **1.** nicht ausgestattet (*with* mit); **2.** nicht dotiert (*with* mit), ohne Zuschuss; **3.** nicht begabt (*with* mit).

,un·en'dur·a·ble *adj.* □ unerträglich.

,un·en'gaged *adj.* frei: a) nicht gebunden *od.* verpflichtet, b) nicht verlobt, c) unbeschäftigt.

,un·'Eng·lish *adj.* unenglisch.

,un·en'light·ened *adj. fig.* **1.** unerleuchtet; **2.** unaufgeklärt.

,un·en'ter·pris·ing *adj.* □ nicht *od.* wenig unter'nehmungslustig, ohne Unter'nehmungsgeist.

,un·en'vi·a·ble *adj.* □ nicht zu beneiden(d), wenig beneidenswert.

,un·e'qual *adj.* □ **1.** ungleich (*a. Kampf*), 'unterschiedlich; **2.** nicht gewachsen (*to dat.*); **3.** ungleichförmig; **,un·e'qual(l)ed** *adj.* **1.** unerreicht, 'unüber,troffen (*by von, for* in *od.* an *dat.*); **2.** beispiellos, *nachgestellt:* ohne'gleichen: ~ *ignorance.*

,un·e'quiv·o·cal *adj.* □ **1.** unzweideutig, eindeutig; **2.** aufrichtig.

,un'err·ing *adj.* □ unfehlbar, untrüglich.

,un·es'sen·tial I *adj.* unwesentlich, unwichtig; **II** *s.* Nebensache *f*.

,un'e·ven *adj.* □ **1.** uneben: ~ *ground*; **2.** ungerade (*Zahl*); **3.** ungleich(mäßig, -artig); **4.** unausgeglichen (*Charakter etc.*); **,un'e·ven·ness** *s.* Unebenheit *f etc.*

,un·e'vent·ful *adj.* □ ereignislos: *be* ~ *a.* ohne Zwischenfälle verlaufen.

,un·ex'am·pled *adj.* beispiellos, unvergleichlich, *nachgestellt:* ohne'gleichen: *not* ~ nicht ohne Beispiel.

un·ex'celled [,ʌnɪk'seld] *adj.* 'unüber-,troffen.

,un·ex'cep·tion·a·ble *adj.* □ untadelig, einwandfrei.

,un·ex'cep·tion·al *adj.* □ **1.** nicht außergewöhnlich; **2.** ausnahmslos; **3.** → *unexceptionable.*

,un·ex'cit·ing *adj.* nicht *od.* wenig aufregend.

un·ex'pect·ed [,ʌnɪk'spektɪd] *adj.* □ unerwartet, unvermutet.

,un·ex'pired *adj.* (noch) nicht abgelaufen *od.* verfallen (*Frist etc.*), noch in Kraft.

,un·ex'plain·a·ble *adj.* unerklärlich; **,un·ex'plained** *adj.* unerklärt.

,un·ex'plored *adj.* unerforscht.

,un·ex'pressed *adj.* unausgesprochen.

,un·ex'pur·gat·ed *adj.* nicht gereinigt, ungekürzt (*Bücher etc.*).

un'fad·ing *adj.* □ **1.** unverwelklich (*a. fig.*); **2.** *fig.* unvergänglich; **3.** nicht verblassend (*Farbe*).

un'fail·ing *adj.* □ **1.** unfehlbar; **2.** nie versagend; **3.** treu; **4.** unerschöpflich, unversiegbar.

,un'fair *adj.* □ unfair: a) unbillig, ungerecht, b) unehrlich, *bsd.* ✝ unlauter, c) nicht anständig, d) unsportlich (*alle to* gegen'über): ~ *competition* unlauterer Wettbewerb; ~ *dismissal* ungerechtfertigte Entlassung; **,un'fair·ly** *adv.* **1.** unfair, unbillig(erweise) *etc.*; zu Unrecht: *not* ~ nicht zu Unrecht; **2.** 'übermäßig; **,un'fair·ness** *s.* Unfairness *f*, Ungerechtigkeit *f etc.*

,un'faith·ful *adj.* □ **1.** un(ge)treu, treulos; **2.** unaufrichtig; **3.** nicht wortgetreu, ungenau (*Abschrift, Übersetzung*); **,un'faith·ful·ness** *s.* Untreue *f*, Treulosigkeit *f*.

un'fal·ter·ing *adj.* □ **1.** nicht schwankend, sicher (*Schritt etc.*); **2.** fest (*Stimme, Blick*); **3.** *fig.* unbeugsam, entschlossen.

,un·fa'mil·iar *adj.* □ **1.** nicht vertraut, unbekannt (*to dat.*); **2.** ungewohnt, fremd (*to dat. od.* für).

,un'fash·ion·a·ble *adj.* □ 'unmo,dern, altmodisch.

,un'fas·ten I *v/t.* aufmachen, losbinden, lösen, öffnen; **II** *v/i.* sich lösen, aufgehen; **,un'fas·tened** *adj.* unbefestigt, lose.

,un'fa·ther·ly *adj.* unväterlich, lieblos.

un·fath·om·a·ble [ʌn'fæðəməbl] *adj.* □ unergründlich (*a. fig.*); **,un'fath·omed** *adj.* unergründet.

,un'fa·vo(u)r·a·ble *adj.* □ **1.** unvorteilhaft (*a. Aussehen*), ungünstig (*for, to* für); **2.** widrig (*Wetter, Umstände etc.*); **2.** ✝ passiv (*Zahlungsbilanz etc.*); **,un'fa·vo(u)r·a·ble·ness** *s.* Unvorteilhaftigkeit *f*.

,un'fea·si·ble *adj.* unausführbar.

un'feel·ing [ʌn'fiːlɪŋ] *adj.* □ gefühllos; **un'feel·ing·ness** [-nɪs] *s.* Gefühllosigkeit *f*.

un'feigned *adj.* □ **1.** ungeheuchelt, **2.** wahr, echt.

,un'felt *adj.* ungefühlt.

,un·fer'ment·ed *adj.* ungegoren.

un'fet·ter *v/t.* **1.** losketten; **2.** *fig.* befreien; **,un'fet·tered** *adj. fig.* unbehindert, unbeschränkt, frei.

,un'fil·i·al *adj.* □ **1.** lieb-, re'spektlos, pflichtvergessen (*Kind*).

,un'filled *adj.* **1.** un(aus)gefüllt; **2.** unbesetzt (*Posten, Stelle*); **3.** ~ *orders* ✝ nicht ausgeführte Bestellungen, Auftragsbestand *m*.

,un'fin·ished *adj.* **1.** unfertig (*a. fig. Stil etc.*); ⚙ unbearbeitet; **2.** 'unvoll,endet (*Sinfonie etc.*); **3.** unerledigt: ~ *business parl.* unerledigte Punkte *pl.* (*der Geschäftsordnung*).

,un'fit I *adj.* □ **1.** untauglich (*a.* ✕), ungeeignet (*for* für, zu): ~ *for* (*military*) *service* (wehr)dienstuntauglich; **2.** unfähig, unbefähigt (*for* zu et., *to do* zu tun); **II** *v/t.* **3.** ungeeignet *etc.* machen (*for* für); **,un'fit·ness** *s.* Untauglichkeit *f*; **,un'fit·ted** *adj.* **1.** ungeeignet, untauglich; **2.** nicht (gut) ausgerüstet (*with* mit); **,un'fit·ting** *adj.* □ **1.** ungeeignet, unpassend; **2.** unschicklich.

,un'fix *v/t.* losmachen, lösen: ~ *bayonets!* ✕ Seitengewehr an Ort!; **,un-'fixed** *adj.* **1.** unbefestigt, lose; **2.** *fig.* schwankend.

,un'flag·ging *adj.* □ unermüdlich.

,un'flap·pa·ble *adj.* F unerschütterlich, nicht aus der Ruhe zu bringen.

,un'flat·ter·ing *adj.* □ **1.** nicht *od.* wenig schmeichelhaft; **2.** ungeschminkt.

,un'fledged *adj.* **1.** *orn.* ungefiedert, (noch) nicht flügge; **2.** *fig.* unreif.

un·flinch·ing [ʌn'flɪntʃɪŋ] *adj.* □ **1.** unerschütterlich, unerschrocken; **2.** entschlossen, unnachgiebig.

un·fly·a·ble [ˌʌn'flaɪəbl] *adj.* ✈ **1.** fluguntüchtig; **2.** ~ *weather* kein Flugwetter.

,un'fold I *v/t.* **1.** entfalten, ausbreiten, öffnen; **2.** *fig.* a) enthüllen, darlegen, b) entwickeln; II *v/i.* **3.** sich entfalten *od.* öffnen; **4.** *fig.* sich entwickeln.

,un'forced *adj.* □ ungezwungen.

,un·fore'see·a·ble *adj.* 'unvor,hersehbar; ,un·fore'seen *adj.* 'unvor,hergesehen, unerwartet.

un·for·get·ta·ble [ˌʌnfə'getəbl] *adj.* □ unvergesslich: *of ~ beauty.*

un·for·giv·a·ble [ˌʌnfə'gɪvəbl] *adj.* unverzeihlich; ,un·for'giv·en *adj.* unverziehen; ,un·for'giv·ing *adj.* □ unversöhnlich, nachtragend.

,un·for'got·ten *adj.* unvergessen.

,un'formed *adj.* **1.** ungeformt, formlos; **2.** unfertig, unentwickelt; unausgebildet.

un'for·tu·nate I *adj.* □ **1.** unglücklich, Unglücks...; verhängnisvoll, un(glück)selig; **2.** bedauerlich; II *s.* **3.** Unglückliche(r *m*) *f*; un'for·tu·nate·ly *adv.* unglücklicherweise, bedauerlicherweise, leider.

,un'found·ed *adj.* □ unbegründet, grundlos.

,un'freeze *v/t.* **1.** auftauen; **2.** ✝ *Preise etc.* freigeben; **3.** *Gelder* zur Auszahlung freigeben.

,un·fre'quent·ed *adj.* **1.** nicht *od.* wenig besucht; **2.** einsam.

,un'friend·ed *adj.* ohne Freund(e).

,un'friend·li·ness *s.* Unfreundlichkeit *f*; ,un'friend·ly *adj.* unfreundlich (*a. fig. Zimmer etc.*) (*to* zu); **2.** ungünstig (*for, to* für).

,un'frock *v/t. eccl. j-m* das Priesteramt entziehen.

,un'fruit·ful *adj.* □ **1.** unfruchtbar; **2.** *fig.* frucht-, ergebnislos; ,un'fruit·ful·ness *s.* **1.** Unfruchtbarkeit *f*; **2.** *fig.* Fruchtlosigkeit *f.*

,un'fund·ed *adj.* ✝ unfundiert.

,un'furl I *v/t. Fahne etc.* entfalten, -rollen; *Fächer* ausbreiten; ⚓ *Segel* losmachen; II *v/i.* sich entfalten.

,un'fur·nished *adj.* **1.** nicht ausgerüstet *od.* versehen (*with* mit); **2.** unmöbliert: ~ *room.*

un·gain·li·ness [ʌn'geɪnlɪnɪs] *s.* Plumpheit *f*, Unbeholfenheit *f*; un·gain·ly [ʌn'geɪnlɪ] *adj.* unbeholfen, plump, linkisch.

,un'gal·lant *adj.* □ **1.** 'unga,lant (*to* zu, gegenüber); **2.** nicht tapfer.

,un'gear *v/t.* ⚙ auskuppeln.

,un'gen·er·ous *adj.* □ **1.** nicht freigebig, knauserig; **2.** kleinlich.

,un'gen·ial *adj.* unfreundlich.

,un'gen·tle *adj.* □ unsanft, unzart.

un'gen·tle·man·like → *ungentlemanly*; un'gen·tle·man·li·ness *s.* **1.** unfeine Art; **2.** ungebildetes *od.* unfeines Benehmen; un'gen·tle·man·ly *adj.* unfein.

un·get·at·a·ble [ˌʌnget'ætəbl] *adj.* unnahbar.

,un'gird *v/t.* losgürten.

,un'glazed *adj.* **1.** unverglast; **2.** unglasiert.

,un'gloved *adj.* ohne Handschuh(e).

,un'god·li·ness *s.* Gottlosigkeit *f*; ,un'god·ly *adj.* **1.** gottlos (*a. weitS. verrucht*); **2.** F scheußlich, schrecklich, heillos.

un·gov·ern·a·ble [ˌʌn'gʌvənəbl] *adj.* □ **1.** unlenksam; **2.** zügellos, unbändig, wild; ,un'gov·erned *adj.* unbeherrscht.

,un'grace·ful *adj.* □ 'ungrazi,ös, ohne Anmut; plump, ungelenk.

,un'gra·cious *adj.* □ ungnädig.

,un·gram'mat·i·cal *adj.* □ *ling.* 'ungram,matisch.

un'grate·ful *adj.* □ undankbar (*to* gegen) (*a. fig. unangenehm*); un'grateful·ness *s.* Undankbarkeit *f.*

,un'grat·i·fied *adj.* unbefriedigt.

,un'ground·ed *adj.* □ **1.** unbegründet; **2.** a) ungeschult, b) ohne sichere Grundlagen (*Wissen*).

,un'grudg·ing *adj.* □ **1.** bereitwillig; **2.** neidlos, großzügig: *be ~ in* reichlich *Lob etc.* spenden.

un·gual ['ʌŋgwəl] *adj. zo.* Nagel..., Klauen..., Huf...

,un'guard·ed *adj.* □ **1.** unbewacht (*a. fig. Moment etc.*); *a.* ⊕ ungeschützt; *a. sport, Schach:* ungedeckt; **2.** unbedacht.

un·guent ['ʌŋgwənt] *s.* Salbe *f.*

,un'guid·ed *adj.* **1.** ungeleitet, führer-, führungslos; **2.** nicht (fern)gelenkt.

un·gu·late ['ʌŋgjʊlet] *zo.* I *adj.* hufförmig; mit Hufen; Huf...: ~ *animal* → II *s.* Huftier *n.*

,un'hal·lowed *adj.* **1.** nicht geheiligt, ungeweiht; **2.** unheilig, pro'fan.

,un'ham·pered *adj.* ungehindert.

,un'hand *v/t. obs. j-n* loslassen.

,un'hand·i·ness *s.* **1.** Unhandlichkeit *f*; **2.** Ungeschick(lichkeit *f*) *n.*

,un'hand·some *adj.* □ unschön (*a. fig. Benehmen etc.*).

,un'hand·y *adj.* □ **1.** unhandlich (*Sache*); **2.** unbeholfen, ungeschickt.

un'hap·pi·ly *adv.* unglücklicherweise, leider; un'hap·pi·ness *s.* Unglück(seligkeit *f*) *n*, Elend *n*; un'hap·py *adj.* □ unglücklich: a) traurig, elend, b) un(glück)selig, unheilvoll, c) unpassend, ungeschickt (*Bemerkung etc.*).

,un'har·ness *v/t.* Pferd ausspannen.

,un·har'mo·ni·ous *adj.* 'unhar,monisch (*a. fig.*).

un'health·i·ness *s.* Ungesundheit *f*; un'health·y *adj.* □ *allg.* ungesund: a) kränklich (*a. Aussehen etc.*), b) gesundheitsschädlich, c) (*moralisch*) schädlich, d) F gefährlich, e) *fig.* krankhaft.

,un'heard *adj.* **1.** ungehört: *go ~* unbeachtet bleiben; **2.** ⚖ ohne rechtliches Gehör; ,un'heard-of *adj.* unerhört, beispiellos.

un·heed·ed [ˌʌn'hi:dɪd] *adj.* □ unbeachtet: *go ~* unbeachtet bleiben; ,un'heed·ful *adj.* □ unachtsam; nicht achtend (*of* auf *acc.*); ,un'heed·ing [-dɪŋ] *adj.* □ sorglos, unachtsam.

,un'help·ful *adj.* □ **1.** nicht hilfreich, ungefällig; **2.** (*to*) nutzlos (für), wenig dienlich (*dat.*).

un·hes·i·tat·ing [ʌn'hezɪteɪtɪŋ] *adj.* □ **1.** ohne Zaudern *od.* Zögern, unverzüglich; **2.** anstandslos, bereitwillig, *adv. a.* ohne weiteres.

,un'hin·dered *adj.* ungehindert.

,un'hinge *v/t.* **1.** *Tür etc.* aus den Angeln heben (*a. fig.*); **2.** die Angeln entfernen von; **3.** *fig. Nerven, Geist* zerrütten; **4.** *fig. j-n* aus dem Gleichgewicht bringen.

,un·his'tor·ic, ,un·his'tor·i·cal *adj.* □ **1.** 'unhi,storisch; **2.** ungeschichtlich, legen'där.

,un'hitch *v/t.* **1.** loshaken, -machen; **2.** *Pferd* ausspannen.

,un'ho·ly *adj.* □ **1.** unheilig; **2.** ungeheiligt, nicht geweiht; **3.** gott-, ruchlos; **4.**

F a) scheußlich, schrecklich, b) ,unmöglich' (*Zeit*).

,un'hon·o(u)red *adj.* **1.** ungeehrt; unverehrt; **2.** ✝ nicht honoriert.

,un'hook I *v/t.* auf-, loshaken; II *v/i.* sich auf- *od.* loshaken (lassen).

un'hoped, un'hoped-for *adj.* unverhofft, unerwartet.

,un'horse *v/t.* aus dem Sattel heben *od.* werfen.

,un'house *v/t.* **1.** (aus dem Hause) vertreiben; **2.** obdachlos machen.

,un'hur·ried *adj.* □ gemütlich, gemächlich.

,un'hurt *adj.* **1.** unverletzt; **2.** unbeschädigt.

u·ni·cel·lu·lar [ˌju:nɪ'seljʊlə] *adj. biol.* einzellig: ~ *animal*, ~ *plant* Einzeller *m.*

u·ni·col·o(u)r [ˌju:nɪ'kʌlə], u·ni·col·o(u)red [-əd] *adj.* einfarbig.

u·ni·corn ['ju:nɪkɔ:n] *s.* Einhorn *n.*

un·i·de·aed [ˌʌnaɪ'dɪəd] *adj.* i'deenlos.

,un·i'den·ti·fied *adj.* nicht identifiziert, unbekannt: ~ *flying object* unbekanntes Flugobjekt.

u·ni·di·men·sion·al [ˌju:nɪdɪ'menʃənl] *adj.* 'eindimensio,nal.

u·ni·fi·ca·tion [ˌju:nɪfɪ'keɪʃn] *s.* **1.** Vereinigung *f*; **2.** Vereinheitlichung *f.*

u·ni·form ['ju:nɪfɔ:m] I *adj.* □ **1.** gleich (-förmig), uni'form; **2.** gleich bleibend, gleichmäßig, kon'stant; **3.** einheitlich, über'einstimmend, gleich, Einheits...; **4.** einförmig, -tönig; II *s.* **5.** Uni'form *f*, Dienstkleidung *f*; (Schwestern-) Tracht *f*; III *v/t.* **6.** uniformieren (*a.* ✠ *etc.*): ~ed uniformiert, in Uniform; u·ni·form·i·ty [ˌju:nɪ'fɔ:mətɪ] *s.* **1.** Gleichförmigkeit *f*, -mäßigkeit *f*, Gleichheit *f*, Über'einstimmung *f*; **2.** Einheitlichkeit *f*; **3.** Einförmigkeit *f*, -tönigkeit *f.*

u·ni·fy ['ju:nɪfaɪ] *v/t.* **1.** verein(ig)en, zs.-schließen; **2.** vereinheitlichen.

u·ni·lat·er·al [ˌju:nɪ'lætərəl] *adj.* □ einseitig (*a.* ♣ *u.* ⚖).

,un·il'lu·mi·nat·ed *adj.* **1.** unerleuchtet (*a. fig.*); **2.** *fig.* unwissend.

,un·im'ag·i·na·ble *adj.* □ unvorstellbar; ,un·im'ag·i·na·tive *adj.* □ fantasielos, einfallslos; ,un·im'ag·ined *adj.* ungeahnt.

,un·im'paired *adj.* unvermindert, unbeeinträchtigt, ungeschmälert.

,un·im'pas·sioned *adj.* leidenschaftslos.

,un·im'peach·a·ble *adj.* □ **1.** unanfechtbar; **2.** untad(e)lig.

,un·im'ped·ed *adj.* □ ungehindert.

,un·im'por·tant *adj.* unwichtig.

,un·im'pos·ing *adj.* nicht imponierend *od.* impo'sant, eindrucks-los.

,un·im'pres·sion·a·ble *adj.* nicht zu beeindrucken(d), (für Eindrücke) unempfänglich.

,un·im'pres·sive → *unimposing.*

,un·in'flect·ed *adj. ling.* unflektiert.

,un·in'flu·enced *adj.* unbeeinflusst (*by* durch, von); 'un,in·flu'en·tial *adj.* ohne Einfluss, nicht einflussreich.

,un·in'formed *adj.* **1.** (*on*) nicht informiert *od.* unter'richtet (über *acc.*), nicht eingeweiht (in *acc.*); **2.** ungebildet.

,un·in'hab·it·a·ble *adj.* unbewohnbar; ,un·in'hab·it·ed *adj.* unbewohnt.

,un·in'i·ti·at·ed *adj.* uneingeweiht, nicht eingeführt (*into* in *acc.*).

,un·in'jured *adj.* **1.** unverletzt; **2.** unbeschädigt.

,un·in'spired *adj.* schwunglos, ohne Feuer, unbegeistert; ,un·in'spir·ing *adj.* nicht begeisternd, wenig anregend.

U

,un·in'stall *v/t. Computer: Programm* ,deinstal'lieren.

,un·in'struct·ed *adj.* **1.** nicht unter'richtet, unwissend; **2.** nicht instruiert, ohne Verhaltensmaßregeln; ,un·in'struc·tive *adj.* nicht *od.* wenig instruk'tiv *od.* lehrreich.

,un·in'sured *adj.* unversichert.

,un·in'tel·li·gent *adj.* □ 'unintelli,gent, beschränkt, geistlos, dumm.

'un·in,tel·li·gi'bil·i·ty *f.* Unverständlichkeit *f.*; ,un·in'tel·li·gi·ble *adj.* □ unverständlich.

,un·in'tend·ed *adj.,* ,un·in'ten·tion·al *adj.* □ unbeabsichtigt, unabsichtlich, ungewollt.

,un·in·ter·est·ed *adj.* □ inter'esselos, uninteressiert (*in an dat.*), gleichgültig; ,un·in·ter·est·ing *adj.* □ 'uninteres,sant.

'un,in·ter'rupt·ed *adj.* □ 'ununter,brochen: a) ungestört (*by* von), b) kontinuierlich, fortlaufend, anhaltend: ~ *working hours* durchgehende Arbeitszeit.

,un·in'vit·ed *adj.* un(ein)geladen; ,un·in'vit·ing *adj.* □ nicht *od.* wenig einladend *od.* verlockend *od.* anziehend.

un·ion ['juːnjən] *s.* **1.** *allg.* Vereinigung *f,* (*a. eheliche*) Verbindung *f,* Eintracht *f,* Harmo'nie *f;* **3.** *pol.* Zs.-schluss *m;* **4.** *pol. etc.* Uni'on *f:* a) (Staaten-) Bund *m, z. B. die* U.S.A. *pl.,* b) Vereinigung *f,* (Zweck)Verband *m,* Bund *m,* (*a. Post-, Zoll- etc.*)Verein *m,* c) *Brit. Vereinigung unabhängiger Kirchen;* **5.** Gewerkschaft *f:* ~ *dues pl.* Gewerkschaftsbeitrag *m;* **6.** *Brit. hist.* a) *Kirchspielverband zur Armenpflege,* b) Armenhaus *n;* **7.** ⊙ Anschlussstück *n,* (Rohr)Verbindung *f;* **8.** ⊙ Mischgewebe *n;* **9.** ⚓ Gösch *f* (*Flaggenfeld mit Hoheitsabzeichen*): ~ *flag* → *union jack* 1; 'un·ion·ism [-nɪzəm] *s.* **1.** *pol.* Unio'nismus *m,* unio'nistische Bestrebungen *pl.;* **2.** Gewerkschaftswesen *n;* 'un·ion·ist [-nɪst] *s.* **1.** ⚌ *pol. hist.* Unio'nist *m;* **2.** Gewerkschaftler *m;* 'un·ion·ize [-naɪz] *v/t.* gewerkschaftlich organisieren.

un·ion| jack *s.* **1.** *Union Jack* Union Jack *m* (*brit. Nationalflagge*); **2.** ⚓ → *union* 9; ~ *joint s.* Rohrverbindung *f;* ~ *shop s.* ✝ *bsd. Am. Betrieb, der nur Gewerkschaftsmitglieder einstellt od. Arbeitnehmer, die bereit sind, innerhalb von 30 Tagen der Gewerkschaft beizutreten;* ~ *suit s. Am.* Hemdhose *f* mit langem Bein.

u·nip·a·rous [juˈnɪpərəs] *adj.* **1.** ✿ erst einmal geboren habend; **2.** *zo.* nur 'ein Junges gebärend (*bei e-m Wurf*); **2.** ✿ nur 'eine Achse *od.* 'einen Ast treibend.

u·ni·par·tite [ˌjuːnɪˈpɑːtaɪt] *adj.* einteilig.

u·ni·po·lar [ˌjuːnɪˈpəʊlə] *adj.* **1.** *phys.,* ⚡ einpolig, Einpol...; **2.** *anat.* monopo'lar (*Nervenzelle*).

u·nique [juːˈniːk] I *adj.* □ **1.** einzig; **2.** einmalig, einzigartig; unerreicht, *nachgestellt:* ohne'gleichen; **3.** F außer-, ungewöhnlich; großartig; **4.** ⊹ eindeutig; II *s.* **5.** Seltenheit *f,* Unikum *n;* u'nique·ness [-nɪs] *s.* Einzigartig-, Einmaligkeit *f.*

'u·ni·sex *adj.* Unisex...

,u·ni'sex·u·al *adj.* □ **1.** eingeschlechtig; **2.** *zo.,* ✿ getrenntgeschlechtlich.

u·ni·son ['juːnɪzn] *s.* **1.** ♪ Ein-, Gleichklang *m,* Uni'sono *n: in* ~ unisono, einstimmig (*a. fig.*); **2.** *fig.* Einklang *m,*

Über'einstimmung *f: in* ~ *with* in Einklang mit; u·nis·o·nous [juːˈnɪsənəs] *adj.* **1.** ♪ a) gleich klingend, b) einstimmig; **2.** *fig.* über'einstimmend.

u·nit ['juːnɪt] *s.* **1.** *allg.* Einheit *f* (*Einzelding*): ~ *of account* (*trade, value*) ✝ (Ver)Rechnungs- (Handels-, Währungs)einheit; *dwelling* ~ Wohneinheit; ~ *factor biol.* Erbfaktor *m;* ~ *furniture* Anbaumöbel *pl.;* ~ *price* ✝ Einheitspreis *m;* ~ *wages* ✝ Stück-, Akkordlohn *m;* **2.** *phys.* (Grund-, Maß-) Einheit *f:* ~ (*of*) *power* (*time*) Leistungs- (Zeit)einheit; **3.** ⊹ Einer *m,* Einheit *f;* **4.** ✕ Einheit *f,* Verband *m,* Truppenteil *m;* **5.** ⊙ a) (Bau)Einheit *f,* b) Aggre'gat *n,* Anlage *f:* ~ *construction* Baukastenbauweise *f;* **6.** *fig.* Kern *m,* Zelle *f: the family as the* ~ *of society.*

U·ni·tar·i·an [ˌjuːnɪˈteərɪən] I *s. eccl.* Uni'tarier(in); II *adj.* uni'tarisch; ~ 'tar·i·an·ism [-nɪzəm] *s. eccl.* Unita'rismus *m;* u·ni·tar·y ['juːnɪtərɪ] *adj.* Einheits... (*a. ✞*), ⊹ *a.* uni'tär; einheitlich.

u·nite [juːˈnaɪt] I *v/t.* **1.** verbinden (*a.* ✿, ⊙), vereinigen; **2.** (ehelich) verbinden, verheiraten; **3.** *Eigenschaften* in sich vereinigen; II *v/i.* **4.** sich vereinigen; **5.** ✿, ⊙ sich verbinden (*with* mit); **6.** sich zs.-tun: ~ *in doing s.th.* et. geschlossen *od.* vereint tun; **7.** sich anschließen (*with dat. od.* an *acc.*); **8.** sich verheiraten; u'nit·ed [-tɪd] *adj.* vereinigt; vereint (*Kräfte etc.*), gemeinsam: *2 Kingdom* das Vereinigte Königreich (*Großbritannien u. Nordirland*); *2 Nations* Vereinte Nationen; *2 States* die Vereinigten Staaten *von Nordamerika, die* U.S.A. *pl.*

u·nit·ize ['juːnɪtaɪz] *v/t.* **1.** zu e-r Einheit machen; **2.** ⊙ nach dem 'Baukastenprin,zip konstruieren; **3.** in Einheiten verpacken.

u·nit trust *s.* ✝ In'vestmentge,sellschaft *f.*

u·ni·ty ['juːnətɪ] *s.* **1.** Einheit *f* (*a.* ⊹, ⚌): *the dramatic unities thea.* die drei Einheiten; **2.** Einheitlichkeit *f* (*a. e-s Kunstwerks*); **3.** Einigkeit *f,* Eintracht *f:* ~ (*of sentiment*) Einmütigkeit *f: at* ~ in Eintracht, im Einklang; **4.** *nationale etc.* Einheit.

u·ni·va·lent [ˌjuːnɪˈveɪlənt] *adj.* ✿ einwertig.

u·ni·ver·sal [ˌjuːnɪˈvɜːsl] I *adj.* □ **1.** ('all)um,fassend, univer'sal, Universal...(-genie, -erbe etc.), gesamt, glo'bal: ~ *knowledge* umfassendes Wissen; ~ *succession* ⚌ Gesamtnachfolge *f;* **2.** allgemein (*a. Wahlrecht, Wehrpflicht etc.*): ~ *partnership* ⚌ allgemeine Gütergemeinschaft; *the disappointment was* ~ die Enttäuschung war allgemein; **3.** allgemein (gültig), univer'sell: ~ *rule;* ~ *remedy* ✿ Universalmittel *n;* **4.** allgemein, 'überall üblich *od.* anzutreffen(d); **5.** 'weltum,fassend, Welt...: ~ *language* Weltsprache *f; 2 Postal Union* Weltpostverein *m;* ~ *time* Weltzeit *f;* **6.** ⊙ Universal...(-gerät etc.): ~ *current* ⚡ Allstrom *m;* ~ *joint* Universal-, Kardangelenk *n;* II *s.* **7.** *das* Allgemeine; **8.** *Logik:* allgemeine Aussage; **9.** *phls.* Allgemeinbegriff *m;* u·ni'ver·sal·ism [-səlɪzəm] *s. eccl., phls.* Universa'lismus *m;* u·ni·ver·sal·i·ty [ˌjuːnɪvɜːˈsælətɪ] *s.* **1.** *das* 'Allum,fassende, Allgemeinheit *f;* **2.** Universali'tät *f,* Vielseitigkeit *f,* um'fassende Bildung; **3.** Allgemeingültigkeit *f;* ,u·ni'ver·sal·ize [-səlaɪz] *v/t.* allgemein gültig machen; allgemein verbrei-

ten; u·ni·verse ['juːnɪvɜːs] *s.* **1.** Uni'versum *n,* (Welt)All *n,* Kosmos *m;* **2.** Welt *f;* ,u·ni'ver·si·ty [-sətɪ] I *s.* Universi'tät *f,* Hochschule *f: Open 2, 2 of the Air* Fernsehuniversität *f; at the 2 of Oxford, at Oxford 2* auf *od.* an der Universi'tät Oxford; II *adj.* Universitäts..., Hochschul..., aka'demisch: ~ *education* Hochschulbildung *f;* ~ *extension Art* Volkshochschule *f;* ~ *man* Akademiker *m;* ~ *place* Studienplatz *m;* ~ *professor* ordentlicher Professor.

u·ni·vo·cal [ˌjuːnɪˈvəʊkl] I *adj.* □ eindeutig, unzweideutig; II *s.* Wort *n* mit nur 'einer Bedeutung.

,un'just *adj.* □ ungerecht (*to* gegen); ,un'jus·ti·fi·a·ble *adj.* □ nicht zu rechtfertigen(d), unverantwortlich; ,un'jus·ti·fied *adj.* ungerechtfertigt, unberechtigt; ,un'just·ness *s.* Ungerechtigkeit *f.*

un·kempt [ˌʌnˈkempt] *adj.* **1.** *obs.* ungekämmt, zerzaust; **2.** *fig.* ungepflegt, unordentlich, verwahrlost.

un'kind *adj.* □ **1.** unfreundlich (*to* zu); **2.** rücksichtslos, herzlos (*to* gegen); un'kind·li·ness *s.* Unfreundlichkeit *f;* un'kind·ly → *unkind;* un'kind·ness *s.* Unfreundlichkeit *f etc.*

,un'know·ing *adj.* □ **1.** unwissend; **2.** unwissentlich, unbewusst; **3.** nicht wissend, ohne zu wissen (*that* dass, *how* wie *etc.*).

,un'known I *adj.* unbekannt (*to dat.*): → *quantity* 2; **2.** nie gekannt, beispiellos (*Entzücken etc.*); II *adv.* **3.** (*to s.o.*) ohne (j-s) Wissen; III *s.* **4.** der (die, das) Unbekannte; **5.** ⊹ Unbekannte *f.*

,un'la·bel(l)ed *adj.* nicht etikettiert, ohne Eti'kett *od.* Aufschrift.

,un'la·bo(u)red *adj.* mühelos (*a. fig. ungezwungen, leicht*).

,un'lace *v/t.* aufschnüren.

,un'lade *v/t.* [*irr.* → *lade*] **1.** aus-, entladen; **2.** ⚓ *Ladung etc.* löschen; ,un'lad·en *adj.* unbeladen: ~ *weight* Leergewicht *n;* **2.** *fig.* unbelastet (*with* von).

,un'la·dy·like *adj.* nicht damenhaft, unfein.

,un'la'ment·ed *adj.* unbeklagt, unbeweint, unbetrauert.

,un'latch *v/t.* aufklinken.

,un'law·ful *adj.* □ **1.** ⚌ rechtswidrig, 'widerrechtlich, ungesetzlich, 'ille,gal: ~ *assembly* Auflauf *m,* Zs.-rottung *f;* **2.** unerlaubt; **3.** unehelich; ,un'law·ful·ness *s.* Ungesetzlichkeit *f etc.*

un·lead·ed [ˌʌnˈledɪd] I *adj.* unverbleit, bleifrei (*Benzin*); II *s.* bleifreies (*od.* unverbleites) Benzin.

,un'learn [*irr.* → *learn*] I *v/t.* verlernen, vergessen; II *v/i.* 'umlernen.

un·learned[1] [ˌʌnˈlɜːnt] *adj.* nicht er- *od.* gelernt.

un·learn·ed[2] [ˌʌnˈlɜːnɪd] *adj.* ungelehrt.

,un'learnt → *unlearned[1].*

,un'leash *v/t.* **1.** losbinden, *Hund* loskoppeln; **2.** *fig.* entfesseln, auslösen, loslassen.

,un'leav·ened *adj.* ungesäuert (*Brot*).

un·less [ənˈles] I *cj.* wenn ... nicht; so'fern ... nicht; es sei denn (, dass) ...; außer wenn ...; ausgenommen (wenn) ...; vor'ausgesetzt, dass nicht ...; II *prp.* außer.

,un'let·tered *adj.* **1.** analpha'betisch; **2.** ungebildet, ungelehrt; **3.** unbeschriftet, unbedruckt.

,un'li·censed *adj.* **1.** unerlaubt; **2.** nicht konzessioniert, (amtlich) nicht zugelassen, ohne Li'zenz.

,un'licked *adj. fig.* a) ungehobelt, ungeschliffen, roh, b) unreif: **~ cub** grüner Junge.

‚un·lik·a·ble *adj.* 'unsym‚pathisch.

‚un·like I *adj.* **1.** ungleich, (vonein'ander) verschieden; **2.** unähnlich; **II** *prp.* **3.** unähnlich (*s.o.* j-m), verschieden von, anders als: *that is very ~ him* das sieht ihm gar nicht ähnlich; **4.** anders als, nicht wie; **5.** im Gegensatz zu.

‚un·like·a·ble → *unlikable*.

un·like·li·hood, un·like·li·ness *s.* Unwahrscheinlichkeit *f*; **un·like·ly I** *adj.* **1.** unwahrscheinlich; **2.** (ziemlich) unmöglich: **~ place**; **3.** aussichtslos; **II** *adv.* **4.** unwahrscheinlich.

‚un·lim·ber *v/t. u. v/i.* **1.** ✕ abprotzen; **2.** *fig.* (sich) bereitmachen.

un·lim·it·ed *adj.* **1.** unbegrenzt, unbeschränkt (*a. Haftung etc.*): **~ company** ✝ *Brit.* Gesellschaft *f* mit unbeschränkter Haftung; **2.** ✝ *Börse:* nicht limitiert; **3.** *fig.* grenzen-, uferlos.

‚un·lined¹ *adj.* ungefüttert: **~ coat**.

‚un·lined² *adj.* **1.** unliniert, ohne Linien; **2.** faltenlos (*Gesicht*).

‚un·link *v/t.* **1.** losketten; **2.** *Kettenglieder* trennen; **3.** *Kette* ausein'ander nehmen.

‚un·liq·ui·dat·ed *adj.* ✝ **1.** a) ungetilgt (*Schuld etc.*), b) nicht festgestellt (*Betrag etc.*); **2.** unliquidiert: **~ company**.

‚un·list·ed *adj.* **1.** nicht verzeichnet; **2.** *teleph. Am.* Geheim...: **~ number**; **3.** ✝ nicht notiert (*Wertpapier*).

‚un·load I *v/t.* **1.** ab-, aus-, entladen; ⚓ *Ladung* löschen; **2.** *fig.* (von e-r Last) befreien, erleichtern; **3.** *Waffe* entladen; **4.** *Börse:* Aktien (*massenhaft*) abstoßen, auf den Markt werfen; **5.** F (**on**, **onto**) a) j-n, et. ‚abladen' (bei), b) abwälzen (auf *acc.*), c) *Wut etc.* auslassen (an *dat.*); **II** *v/i.* **6.** aus-, abladen; **7.** gelöscht *od.* ausgeladen werden.

‚un·lock *v/t.* **1.** aufschließen, öffnen; **2.** *Waffe* entsichern; **‚un·locked** *adj.* unverschlossen.

un·looked-for *adj.* unerwartet, 'unvor‚hergesehen, über'raschend.

‚un·loose, un·loos·en *v/t.* **1.** *Knoten etc.* lösen; **2.** *Griff etc.* lockern; **3.** losmachen, -lassen.

‚un·lov·a·ble *adj.* nicht *od.* wenig liebenswert; **‚un·loved** *adj.* ungeliebt; **‚un·love·ly** *adj.* unschön, reizlos; **‚un·lov·ing** *adj.* □ kalt, lieblos.

un·luck·i·ly *adv.* unglücklicherweise; **un·luck·y** *adj.* □ unglücklich: a) vom Pech verfolgt: **be ~** Pech *od.* kein Glück haben, b) fruchtlos: **~ effort**, c) ungünstig: **~ moment**, d) unheilvoll, Unglücks...: **~ day**.

‚un·made *adj.* ungemacht.

‚un·make *v/t.* [*irr.* → **make**] **1.** aufheben, 'umstoßen, wider'rufen, rückgängig machen; **2.** j-n absetzen; **3.** vernichten; **4.** 'umbilden.

‚un·man *v/t.* **1.** entmannen; **2.** j-n s-r Kraft berauben; **3.** j-n verzagen lassen, entmutigen; **4.** verrohen (lassen); **5.** *e-m Schiff etc.* die Mannschaft nehmen; **~ned** unbemannt.

un·man·age·a·ble *adj.* □ **1.** schwer zu handhaben(d), unhandlich; **2.** *fig.* unfügsam, unlenksam, 'widerspenstig: **~ child**; **3.** unkontrollierbar (*Lage*).

‚un·man·li·ness *s.* Unmännlichkeit *f*; **‚un·man·ly** *adj.* **1.** unmännlich; **2.** weibisch; **3.** feige.

un·man·ner·li·ness *s.* schlechtes Benehmen; **un·man·ner·ly** *adj.* ungezogen, 'unma‚nierlich.

‚un·marked *adj.* **1.** nicht markiert, unbezeichnet, ungezeichnet (*a. Gesicht*);

---

2. unbemerkt; **3.** *sport* ungedeckt.

‚un·mar·ket·a·ble *adj.* ✝ **1.** nicht marktgängig *od.* -fähig; **2.** unverkäuflich.

‚un·mar·riage·a·ble *adj.* nicht heiratsfähig; **‚un·mar·ried** *adj.* unverheiratet, ledig.

un·mask [‚ʌn'mɑːsk] **I** *v/t.* **1.** *j-m* die Maske abnehmen, *j-n* demaskieren; **2.** *fig. j-n* entlarven, *j-m* die Maske her'unterreißen; **II** *v/i.* **3.** sich demaskieren; **4.** *fig.* die Maske fallen lassen; **‚un·'mask·ing** [-kɪŋ] *s. fig.* Entlarvung *f*.

‚un·matched *adj.* unvergleichlich, unerreicht, 'unüber‚troffen.

‚un·mean·ing *adj.* □ sinn-, bedeutungslos; nichts sagend (*a. Gesicht*); **‚un·'meant** *adj.* unbeabsichtigt.

‚un·meas·ured *adj.* **1.** ungemessen; **2.** unermesslich, grenzenlos, unbegrenzt; **3.** unmäßig.

un·me·lo·di·ous *adj.* □ 'unme‚lodisch.

un·men·tion·a·ble I *adj.* **1.** unaussprechlich, ta'bu: **an ~ topic** ein Thema, über das man nicht spricht; **2.** → **unspeakable; II** *s. pl. humor.* die Unaussprechlichen *pl.* (*Unterwäsche*); **‚un·men·tioned** *adj.* unerwähnt.

‚un·mer·chant·a·ble → *unmarketable*.

un·mer·ci·ful *adj.* □ unbarmherzig.

‚un·mer·it·ed *adj.* □ unverdient(erma-ßen *adv.*).

‚un·me·thod·i·cal *adj.* 'unme‚thodisch, sys'tem-, planlos.

‚un·mil·i·tar·y *adj.* **1.** 'unmili‚tärisch; **2.** nicht mili'tärisch, Zivil...

un·mind·ful *adj.* □ unachtsam; uneingedenk (**of** *gen.*): **be ~ of** nicht achten auf (*acc.*), b) nicht denken an (*acc.*).

‚un·mis·tak·a·ble *adj.* □ **1.** 'un‚missverständlich; **2.** unverkennbar.

un·mit·i·gat·ed *adj.* □ **1.** ungemildert, ganz; **2.** voll'endet, Erz..., *nachgestellt:* durch u. durch: **an ~ liar**.

‚un·mixed *adj.* □ **1.** unvermischt; **2.** *fig.* ungemischt, rein, pur.

‚un·mod·i·fied *adj.* unverändert, nicht abgeändert.

un·mo·lest·ed *adj.* unbelästigt, ungestört: **live ~** in Frieden leben.

‚un·moor ⚓ **I** *v/t.* **1.** abankern, losmachen; **2.** vor 'einem Anker liegen lassen; **II** *v/i.* **3.** den *od.* die Anker lichten.

un·mor·al *adj.* 'amo‚ralisch.

‚un·mort·gaged *adj.* ⚖ **1.** unverpfändet; **2.** hypo'thekenfrei, unbelastet.

‚un·mount·ed *adj.* **1.** unberitten: **~ police**; **2.** nicht aufgezogen (*Bild etc.*); **3.** ⊙, ✕ unmontiert; **4.** nicht gefasst (*Stein*).

‚un·mourned *adj.* unbetrauert.

‚un·mov·a·ble *adj.* □ unbeweglich; **‚un·'moved** *adj.* □ **1.** unbewegt; **2.** *fig.* ungerührt, unbewegt; **3.** *fig.* unerschütterlich, standhaft, gelassen; **‚un·'mov·ing** *adj.* regungslos.

‚un·mur·mur·ing *adj.* □ ohne Murren, klaglos.

‚un·mu·si·cal *adj.* □ **1.** 'unmusi‚kalisch (*Person*); **2.** 'unme‚lodisch.

‚un·muz·zle *v/t.* **1.** *e-m Hund* den Maulkorb abnehmen: **~d** ohne Maulkorb; **2.** *fig. j-m* freie Meinungsäußerung gewähren.

‚un·nam(e)·a·ble *adj.* unsagbar.

‚un·named *adj.* **1.** namenlos; **2.** nicht namentlich genannt, ungenannt.

un·nat·u·ral *adj.* □ **1.** 'unna‚türlich; **2.** künstlich, gekünstelt; **3.** 'widerna‚türlich (*Laster, Verbrechen etc.*); **4.** ungeheuerlich, ab'scheulich; **5.** ungewöhnlich; **6.** ano'mal.

‚un·nav·i·ga·ble *adj.* nicht schiffbar, un-

---

befahrbar.

un·nec·es·sar·i·ly *adv.* unnötigerweise; **un·nec·es·sar·y** *adj.* □ **1.** unnötig, nicht notwendig; **2.** nutzlos, 'überflüssig.

‚un·need·ed *adj.* nicht benötigt, nutzlos; **‚un·need·ful** *adj.* □ unnötig.

‚un·neigh·bo(u)r·ly *adj.* nicht gutnachbarlich, unfreundlich.

‚un·nerve *v/t.* entnerven, zermürben, *j-n* die Nerven *od.* den Mut verlieren lassen.

‚un·not·ed *adj.* **1.** unbeachtet, unberühmt; **2.** → *unnoticed* 1.

‚un·no·ticed *adj.* **1.** unbemerkt, unbeobachtet; **2.** → *unnoted* 1.

‚un·num·bered *adj.* **1.** unnummeriert; **2.** *poet.* ungezählt, zahllos.

‚un·ob·jec·tion·a·ble *adj.* □ einwandfrei.

‚un·ob·lig·ing *adj.* ungefällig.

‚un·ob·serv·ant *adj.* unaufmerksam, unachtsam: **be ~ of** *et.* nicht beachten; **‚un·ob·served** *adj.* □ unbeobachtet, unbemerkt.

‚un·ob·struct·ed *adj.* unversperrt, ungehindert: **~ view**; **2.** *fig.* unbehindert.

‚un·ob·tain·a·ble *adj.* **1.** ✝ nicht erhältlich; **2.** unerreichbar.

‚un·ob·tru·sive *adj.* □ **1.** unaufdringlich: a) zu'rückhaltend, bescheiden, b) unauffällig; **‚un·ob·tru·sive·ness** *s.* Unaufdringlichkeit *f*.

‚un·oc·cu·pied *adj.* frei: a) unbewohnt, leer (stehend), b) unbesetzt, c) unbeschäftigt.

‚un·of·fend·ing *adj.* **1.** nicht beleidigend; **2.** nicht anstößig.

‚un·of·fi·cial *adj.* □ **1.** nichtamtlich, 'inoffizi‚ell; **2.** **~ strike** ✝ wilder Streik.

‚un·o·pened *adj.* **1.** ungeöffnet, verschlossen: **~ letter**; **2.** ✝ unerschlossen: **~ market**.

‚un·op·posed *adj.* **1.** unbehindert; **2.** unbeanstandet: **~ by** ohne Widerstand *od.* Einspruch seitens (*gen.*).

‚un·or·gan·ized *adj.* **1.** 'unor‚ganisch; **2.** unorganisiert, wirr; **3.** nicht organisiert.

‚un·or·tho·dox *adj.* **1.** *eccl.* 'unortho‚dox; **2.** *fig.* 'unortho‚dox, unüblich, 'unkonventio‚nell.

'un‚os·ten·ta·tious *adj.* □ unaufdringlich, unauffällig: a) prunklos, schlicht, b) anspruchslos, zu'rückhaltend, c) de'zent (*Farben etc.*).

‚un·owned *adj.* herrenlos.

‚un·pack *v/t. u. v/i.* auspacken.

‚un·paid *adj.* **1.** a. **~-for** unbezahlt; rückständig (*Zinsen etc.*); **2.** ✝ noch nicht eingezahlt (*Kapital*); **3.** unbesoldet, unbezahlt, ehrenamtlich (*Stellung*).

un·pal·at·a·ble *adj.* □ **1.** unschmackhaft, schlecht (schmeckend); **2.** *fig.* unangenehm, 'widerwärtig.

un·par·al·leled *adj.* einmalig, beispiellos, *nachgestellt:* ohne'gleichen.

un·par·don·a·ble *adj.* □ unverzeihlich.

'un‚par·lia·men·ta·ry *adj. pol.* 'unparla‚men‚tarisch.

un·pat·ent·ed *adj.* nicht patentiert.

'un‚pa·tri·ot·ic *adj.* (□ **~ally**) 'unpatri‚otisch.

‚un·paved *adj.* ungepflastert.

‚un·ped·i·greed *adj.* ohne Stammbaum.

‚un·peo·ple *v/t.* entvölkern.

un·per·ceived *adj.* □ unbemerkt.

‚un·per·formed *adj.* **1.** nicht ausgeführt, ungetan, unverrichtet; **2.** *thea.* nicht aufgeführt (*Stück*).

‚un‚per·son *s. fig.* 'Unper‚son *f*.

‚un·per·turbed *adj.* nicht beunruhigt, gelassen, ruhig.

‚un'pick v/t. Naht etc. (auf)trennen; ‚un-'picked adj. 1. ungepflückt; 2. ✝ unausgesucht, unsortiert (Proben).

‚un'pin v/t. 1. die Nadeln entfernen aus; 2. losstecken, -machen.

‚un'pit·ied adj. unbemitleidet; ‚un'pit·y·ing adj. ☐ mitleid(s)los.

‚un'placed adj. 1. nicht 'untergebracht; nicht angestellt, ohne Stellung; 2. Rennsport: unplatziert.

‚un'plait v/t. 1. glätten; 2. das Haar etc. aufflechten.

‚un'play·a·ble adj. 1. sport unbespielbar (Boden, Platz); 2. ♪ unspielbar; 3. thea. nicht bühnenreif.

un'pleas·ant adj. ☐ allg. unangenehm: a) unerfreulich, b) unfreundlich, c) unwirsch (Person); un'pleas·ant·ness s. 1. das Unangenehme; 2. Unannehmlichkeit f; 3. 'Misshelligkeit f, Unstimmigkeit f.

‚un'pledged adj. 1. nicht verpflichtet; 2. ⚖ unverpfändet.

‚un'plug v/t. den Pflock od. Stöpsel od. Stecker entfernen aus; un'plugged [-'plʌgd] adj. ♪ auf a'kustischen Instrumenten (od. ohne Verstärker) gespielt.

‚un'plumbed adj. fig. unergründet, unergründlich.

‚un·po'et·ic, ‚un·po'et·i·cal adj. ☐ 'unpo‚etisch, undichterisch.

‚un'pol·ished adj. 1. unpoliert (a. Reis), ungeglättet, ungeschliffen; 2. fig. unausgefeilt (Stil etc.); 3. fig. ungeschliffen, ungehobelt.

‚un'pol·i·tic → unpolitical 1; ‚un·po-'lit·i·cal adj. 1. (po'litisch) unklug; 2. 'unpo‚litisch, an Poli'tik uninteressiert; 3. 'unpar‚teiisch.

‚un'polled adj. pol. 1. nicht gewählt habend: ~ elector Nichtwähler m; 2. Am. nicht (in die Wählerliste) eingetragen.

‚un·pol'lut·ed adj. 1. unverschmutzt, unverseucht (Wasser etc.); 2. fig. unbefleckt.

‚un'pop·u·lar adj. ☐ unpopu'lär, unbeliebt; ‚un‚pop·u'lar·i·ty s. 'Unpopulari‚tät f, Unbeliebtheit f.

‚un·pos'sessed adj. 1. herrenlos (Sache); 2. ~ of s.th. nicht im Besitz e-r Sache.

‚un'post·ed adj. 1. nicht informiert, 'ununter‚richtet; 2. Brit. nicht aufgegeben (Brief).

‚un'prac·ti·cal adj. ☐ unpraktisch; un-'prac·ticed Am., un'prac·tised Brit. adj. ungeübt (in in dat.).

un'prec·e·dent·ed adj. ☐ 1. beispiellos, unerhört, noch nie da gewesen; 2. ⚖ ohne Präze'denzfall.

‚un·pre'dict·a·ble adj. unvorhersehbar, unberechenbar (a. Person): he is quite ~ a. er ist sehr schwer auszumachen.

‚un'prej·u·diced adj. 1. unvoreingenommen, vorurteilsfrei, a. ⚖ unbefangen; 2. a. ⚖ unbeeinträchtigt.

‚un·pre'med·i·tat·ed adj. ☐ 1. 'unüber‚legt; 2. unbeabsichtigt; 3. ⚖ ohne Vorsatz.

‚un·pre'pared adj. ☐ 1. unvorbereitet: an ~ speech; 2. (for) nicht vorbereitet od. gefasst (auf acc.), nicht gerüstet (für).

‚un‚pre·pos'sess·ing adj. wenig anziehend, 'unsym‚pathisch.

‚un·pre'sent·a·ble adj. nicht präsen'tabel.

‚un·pre'sum·ing adj. nicht anmaßend od. vermessen, bescheiden.

‚un·pre'tend·ing, ‚un·pre'ten·tious adj. ☐ anspruchslos.

un'prin·ci·pled adj. 1. ohne (feste) Grundsätze, haltlos, cha'rakterlos (Person); 2. gewissenlos, charakterlos (Benehmen).

un'print·a·ble [‚ʌn'prɪntəbl] adj. nicht druckfähig od. druckreif (a. fig. anstößig); ‚un'print·ed [-tɪd] adj. 1. ungedruckt (Schriften); 2. unbedruckt (Stoffe etc.).

‚un'priv·i·leged adj. nicht privilegiert od. bevorrechtigt: ~ creditor ⚖ Massegläubiger m.

‚un·pro'duc·tive adj. ☐ 'unproduk‚tiv (a. fig.), unergiebig (of an dat.), unfruchtbar (a. fig.), 'unren‚tabel: ~ capital ✝ totes Kapital; ‚un·pro'duc·tive·ness s. 'Unproduktivi‚tät f, Unfruchtbarkeit f, Unergiebigkeit f, 'Unrentabili‚tät f.

‚un·pro'fes·sion·al adj. ☐ 1. keiner freien Berufsgruppe zugehörig; 2. nicht berufsmäßig; 3. berufswidrig: ~ conduct; 4. unfachmännisch.

‚un'prof·it·a·ble adj. ☐ 1. nicht einträglich od. Gewinn bringend od. lohnend, 'unren‚tabel; 2. unvorteilhaft; 3. nutz-, zwecklos; ‚un'prof·it·a·ble·ness s. 1. Uneinträglichkeit f; 2. Nutzlosigkeit f.

‚un·pro'gres·sive adj. ☐ 1. nicht fortschrittlich, rückständig; 2. rückschrittlich, konserva'tiv, reaktio'när.

‚un'prom·is·ing adj. ☐ nicht viel versprechend, ziemlich aussichtslos.

‚un'prompt·ed adj. spon'tan.

‚un·pro'nounce·a·ble adj. unaussprechlich.

‚un·pro'pi·tious adj. ☐ ungünstig.

‚un·pro'por·tion·al adj. ☐ unverhältnismäßig, 'unproportio‚nal.

‚un·pro'tect·ed adj. 1. ungeschützt, schutzlos; 2. ungedeckt.

‚un'proved, ‚un'prov·en adj. unerwiesen.

‚un·pro'vid·ed adj. ☐ 1. nicht versehen (with mit): ~ with ohne; 2. unvorbereitet; 3. ~ for unversorgt (Kind); 4. ~ for nicht vorgesehen.

‚un·pro'voked adj. ☐ 1. unprovoziert; 2. grundlos.

‚un'pub·lish·a·ble adj. zur Veröffentlichung ungeeignet; ‚un'pub·lished adj. unveröffentlicht.

‚un'punc·tu·al adj. ☐ unpünktlich; 'un‚punc·tu'al·i·ty s. Unpünktlichkeit f.

‚un'pun·ished adj. unbestraft, ungestraft: go ~ straflos ausgehen.

un·put·down·a·ble [‚ʌnpʊt'daʊnəbl] adj. F so faszinierend, dass man es nicht mehr aus der Hand legen kann (Buch).

‚un'qual·i·fied adj. 1. unqualifiziert: a) unbefähigt, ungeeignet (for für), b) unberechtigt; 2. uneingeschränkt, unbedingt, bedingungslos; 3. F ausgesprochen (Lügner etc.).

un·quench·a·ble [‚ʌn'kwentʃəbl] adj. ☐ 1. unlöschbar; 2. fig. unstillbar.

un·ques·tion·a·ble [ʌn'kwestʃənəbl] adj. ☐ 1. unzweifelhaft, fraglos; 2. unbedenklich; un'ques·tioned [-tʃənd] adj. 1. ungefragt; 2. unbezweifelt, unbestritten; un'ques·tion·ing [-nɪŋ] adj. ☐ bedingungslos, blind: ~ obedience; un'ques·tion·ing·ly [-nɪŋli] adv. ohne zu fragen, ohne Zögern.

‚un'quote v/i.: ~! Ende des Zitats!; ‚un-'quot·ed adj. 1. nicht zitiert; 2. Börse: nicht notiert.

un'rav·el I v/t. 1. Gewebe ausfasern; 2. Gestricktes auftrennen; 3. entwirren; 4. fig. entwirren, enträtseln; II v/i. 5. sich entwirren etc.

un·read [‚ʌn'red] adj. 1. ungelesen; 2. a) unbelesen, ungebildet, b) unbewandert (in in dat.).

‚un'read·a·ble adj. 1. unleserlich (Handschrift etc.); 2. schwer zu lesen(d) (Buch etc.); 3. nicht lesenswert (Buch etc.).

‚un'read·i·ness s. mangelnde Bereitschaft; ‚un'read·y adj. ☐ nicht bereit od. fertig (for zu).

‚un'real adj. ☐ 1. unwirklich; 2. wesenlos; 3. → 'un‚re·al'is·tic adj. (☐ ~ally) wirklichkeitsfremd, 'unrea‚listisch; ‚un·re·al'i·ty s. 1. Unwirklichkeit f; 2. Wesenlosigkeit f.

‚un·re·al·iz·a·ble adj. nicht realisierbar: a) nicht zu verwirklichen(d), b) ✝ nicht verwertbar, unverkäuflich; ‚un're·al·ized adj. 1. nicht verwirklicht od. erfüllt; 2. nicht vergegenwärtigt od. erkannt.

‚un·rea·son s. 1. Unvernunft f; 2. Torheit f; ‚un're·son·a·ble adj. ☐ 1. unvernünftig; 2. unvernünftig, unbillig, unmäßig, 'übermäßig; unzumutbar; un'rea·son·a·ble·ness s. 1. Unvernunft f; 2. Unbilligkeit f, Unmäßigkeit f; Unzumutbarkeit f; un'rea·son·ing adj. ☐ 1. vernunftlos; 2. unvernünftig, blind.

‚un·re'ceipt·ed adj. ✝ unquittiert.

‚un·re'cep·tive adj. nicht aufnahmefähig, unempfänglich (of, to für).

‚un·re'claimed adj. 1. fig. ungebessert; 2. ungezähmt; 3. unkultiviert (Land).

‚un'rec·og·niz·a·ble adj. ☐ nicht 'wieder zu erkennen(d); ‚un'rec·og·nized adj. 1. nicht ('wieder) erkannt; 2. nicht anerkannt.

‚un·rec·on·ciled adj. unversöhnt (to mit).

un·re·cord·ed [‚ʌnrɪ'kɔːdɪd] adj. 1. (geschichtlich) nicht über'liefert od. aufgezeichnet od. belegt; 2. nicht eingetragen od. registriert; 3. ⚖ nicht beurkundet; 4. a) nicht (auf Tonband etc.) aufgenommen, b) Leer...: ~ tape.

‚un·re'deemed adj. 1. eccl. unerlöst; 2. ✝ a) ungetilgt (Schuld), b) uneingelöst (Wechsel); 3. uneingelöst (Pfand, Versprechen); 4. fig. ungemildert (by durch); Erz...: ~ rascal.

‚un·re'dressed adj. 1. nicht wieder gutgemacht; 2. nicht abgestellt (Missstand).

‚un'reel v/t. (v/i. sich) abspulen.

‚un·re'fined adj. 1. ⚙ nicht raffiniert, ungeläutert, roh, Roh...; 2. fig. ungebildet, unfein, unkultiviert.

‚un·re'flect·ing adj. ☐ 1. nicht reflektierend; 2. gedankenlos, 'unüber‚legt.

‚un·re'formed adj. 1. unverbessert; 2. ungebessert (Person).

‚un·re'fut·ed adj. 'unwider‚legt.

‚un·re'gard·ed adj. unberücksichtigt, unbeachtet; ‚un·re'gard·ful adj. unachtsam, ohne Rücksicht (of auf acc.).

un·re·gen·er·a·cy [‚ʌnrɪ'dʒenərəsi] s. eccl. Sündhaftigkeit f; ‚un·re'gen·er·ate [-rət] adj. 1. eccl. nicht 'wieder geboren; 2. nicht gebessert.

‚un'reg·is·tered adj. 1. nicht registriert od. eingetragen (a. ✝, ⚖); 2. (amtlich) nicht zugelassen (Auto etc.); nicht approbiert (Arzt etc.); 3. nicht eingeschrieben (Brief).

‚un·re'gret·ted adj. unbedauert, unbeklagt.

‚un·re'hearsed adj. 1. thea. ungeprobt; 2. über'raschend, spon'tan.

‚un·re'lat·ed adj. 1. ohne Beziehung (to zu); 2. nicht verwandt (to, with mit) (a. fig.); 3. nicht berichtet.

‚un·re'lent·ing adj. ☐ 1. unbeugsam, unerbittlich; 2. unvermindert.

'un·re‚li·a'bil·i·ty s. Unzuverlässigkeit f; ‚un·re'li·a·ble adj. ☐ unzuverlässig.

‚un·re'lieved adj. ☐ 1. ungelindert; 2.

nicht unter'brochen, 'ununter,brochen; **3.** ✕ a) nicht abgelöst (*Wache*), b) nicht entsetzt (*Festung etc.*).

un·re·mit·ting [,ʌnrɪ'mɪtɪŋ] *adj.* □ unablässig, beharrlich.

,un·re'mu·ner·a·tive *adj.* nicht lohnend *od.* einträglich, 'unren,tabel.

,un·re'pair *s.* Baufälligkeit *f,* Verfall *m*: **in** (*a state of*) ~ in baufälligem Zustand.

,un·re'pealed *adj.* **1.** nicht wider'rufen; **2.** nicht aufgehoben.

,un·re'pent·ant *adj.* reuelos, unbußfertig; **,un·re'pent·ed** [-tɪd] *adj.* unbereut.

,un·rep·re'sent·ed *adj.* nicht vertreten.

,un·re'quit·ed *adj.* □ **1.** unerwidert: ~ *love;* **2.** unbelohnt (*Dienste*); **3.** ungesühnt (*Missetat*).

un·re·served [,ʌnrɪ'zɜːvd] *adj.* □ **1.** uneingeschränkt, vorbehalt-, rückhaltlos, völlig; **2.** freimütig, offen(herzig); **3.** nicht reserviert; **,un·re'serv·ed·ness** [-vɪdnɪs] *s.* Offenheit *f,* Freimütigkeit *f.*

,un·re'sist·ed *adj.* ungehindert: **be** ~ keinen Widerstand finden; **,un·re'sist·ing** *adj.* □ 'widerstandslos.

,un·re'solved *adj.* **1.** ungelöst: ~ *problem;* **2.** unschlüssig, unentschlossen; **3.** ♫, ♪ *etc.* unaufgelöst.

,un·re'spon·sive *adj.* □ **1.** unempfänglich (**to** für): **be** ~ (**to**) nicht reagieren *od.* ansprechen (auf *acc.*); **2.** teilnahmslos, kalt.

un·rest [,ʌn'rest] *s.* Unruhe *f, pol. a.* Unruhen *pl.*; **,un'rest·ful** *adj.* □ **1.** ruhelos; **2.** ungemütlich; **3.** unbequem; **,un'rest·ing** *adj.* □ rastlos, unermüdlich.

,un·re'strained *adj.* □ **1.** ungehemmt (*a. fig.* ungezwungen); **2.** hemmungs-, zügellos; **3.** uneingeschränkt; **,un·re'straint** *s.* **1.** Ungehemmtheit *f, fig. a.* Ungezwungenheit *f;* **2.** Hemmungslosigkeit *f.*

,un·re'strict·ed *adj.* □ uneingeschränkt, unbeschränkt.

,un·re'turned *adj.* **1.** nicht zu'rückgegeben; **2.** unerwidert, unvergolten: **be** ~ unerwidert bleiben; **3.** *pol.* nicht (*ins Parlament*) gewählt.

,un·re'vealed *adj.* nicht offen'bart, verborgen, geheim.

,un·re'vised *adj.* nicht revidiert (*a. fig.* Ansicht *etc.*).

,un·re'ward·ed *adj.* unbelohnt.

,un'rhymed *adj.* ungereimt, reimlos.

,un'rid·dle *v/t.* enträtseln.

,un'rig *v/t.* **1.** ♺ abtakeln; **2.** abmontieren.

un'right·eous *adj.* □ **1.** nicht rechtschaffen; **2.** *eccl.* ungerecht, sündig; **un'right·eous·ness** *s.* Ungerechtigkeit *f.*

,un'rip *v/t.* aufreißen, -schlitzen.

,un'ripe *adj. allg.* unreif; **,un'ripe·ness** *s.* Unreife *f.*

un'ri·val(l)ed *adj.* **1.** ohne Ri'valen *od.* Gegenspieler; **2.** unerreicht, unvergleichlich; ♥ konkur'renzlos.

,un'roll I *v/t.* **1.** entrollen, -falten; **2.** abwickeln; II *v/i.* **3.** sich entfalten; sich ausein'ander rollen.

,un·ro'man·tic *adj.* (□ ~ally) *allg.* 'unro,mantisch.

,un'roof *v/t.* Haus abdecken.

,un'rope *v/t.* **1.** losbinden; **2.** *mount.* (*a. v/i.* sich) ausseilen.

,un'round *v/t. ling.* Vokale entrunden.

,un'ruf·fled *adj.* **1.** ungekräuselt, glatt; **2.** *fig.* gelassen, unerschüttert.

,un'ruled *adj.* **1.** *fig.* unbeherrscht; **2.** unliniert (*Papier*).

un·ru·li·ness [ʌn'ruːlɪnɪs] *s.* **1.** Unlenk-

barkeit *f,* 'Widerspenstigkeit *f;* **2.** Ausgelassenheit *f,* Unbändigkeit *f;* **un·ru·ly** [ʌn'ruːlɪ] *adj.* **1.** unlenksam, aufsässig; **2.** ungebärdig; ausgelassen; **3.** ungestüm.

,un'sad·dle I *v/t.* **1.** Pferd absatteln; **2.** *j-n* aus dem Sattel werfen; II *v/i.* **3.** absatteln.

,un'safe *adj.* □ unsicher, gefährlich.

,un'said *adj.* ungesagt, unerwähnt.

,un'sal·a·ble *adj.* **1.** unverkäuflich; **2.** nicht gangbar (*Waren*).

,un'sal·a·ried *adj.* unbezahlt, ehrenamtlich: ~ **clerk** ♥ Volontär *m.*

,un'sale·a·ble → **unsalable**.

,un'sanc·tioned *adj.* nicht sanktioniert, nicht gebilligt *od.* geduldet.

,un'san·i·tar·y *adj.* **1.** ungesund; **2.** 'unhygi,enisch.

'un,sat·is'fac·to·ri·ness *s.* das Unbefriedigende, Unzulänglichkeit *f;* **'un-,sat·is'fac·to·ry** *adj.* □ unbefriedigend, ungenügend, unzulänglich; **,un-'sat·is·fied** *adj.* **1.** unbefriedigt; **2.** unzufrieden; **3.** ♥ a) unbefriedigt (*Anspruch, Gläubiger*), b) unbezahlt, c) unerfüllt (*Bedingung*); **un'sat·is·fy·ing** *adj.* → **unsatisfactory**.

,un'sa·vo(u)r·i·ness *s.* **1.** Unschmackhaftigkeit *f;* **2.** Widerlichkeit *f;* **,un'sa·vo(u)r·y** *adj.* □ **1.** unschmackhaft; **2.** *a. fig.* 'unappe,titlich, unangenehm.

,un'say *v/t.* [*irr.* → **say**] wider'rufen.

,un'scal·a·ble *adj.* unersteigbar.

,un'scathed [-'skeɪðd] *adj.* (völlig) unversehrt, unbeschädigt.

,un'sched·uled *adj.* **1.** nicht pro'grammgemäß; **2.** außerplanmäßig (*Abfahrt etc.*).

,un'schol·ar·ly *adj.* **1.** unwissenschaftlich; **2.** ungelehrt.

,un'schooled *adj.* **1.** ungeschult, nicht ausgebildet; **2.** unverbildet.

'un,sci·en'tif·ic *adj.* (□ ~ally) unwissenschaftlich.

,un'scram·ble *v/t.* **1.** F entwirren; **2.** entschlüsseln, dechiffrieren; **3.** ✂ aussteuern.

,un'screened *adj.* **1.** ungeschützt, *a.* ✂ nicht abgeschirmt; **2.** ungesiebt (*Sand etc.*); **3.** nicht über'prüft.

,un'screw I *v/t.* ⊚ ab-, auf-, losschrauben; II *v/i.* sich her'aus- *od.* losdrehen; sich losschrauben lassen.

,un'script·ed *adj.* improvisiert (*Rede etc.*).

un'scru·pu·lous *adj.* □ skrupel-, bedenken-, gewissenlos.

,un'seal *v/t.* **1.** Brief etc. entsiegeln *od.* öffnen; **2.** *fig. j-m die Augen, Lippen* öffnen; **3.** *fig.* enthüllen; **,un'sealed** *adj.* **1.** a) unversiegelt, b) geöffnet; **2.** *fig.* nicht besiegelt.

,un'search·a·ble *adj.* □ unerforschlich, unergründlich.

un'sea·son·a·ble *adj.* □ **1.** unzeitig; **2.** *fig.* unpassend, ungünstig.

,un'sea·soned *adj.* **1.** nicht (aus)gereift; **2.** nicht abgelagert (*Holz*); **3.** *fig.* nicht abgehärtet (**to** gegen); **4.** *fig.* unerfahren; **5.** ungewürzt.

,un'seat *v/t.* **1.** Reiter abwerfen; **2.** *j-n* absetzen, des Postens entheben; **3.** *pol. j-m* s-n Sitz (im Parla'ment) nehmen; **,un'seat·ed** *adj.* ohne Sitz(gelegenheit): **be** ~ nicht sitzen.

,un'sea,wor·thy *adj.* ♺ seeuntüchtig.

,un·se'cured *adj.* **1.** ungesichert (*a.* ♥ Schuld); **2.** unbefestigt; **3.** ♥ ungedeckt, nicht sichergestellt.

,un'seed·ed *sport* ungesetzt (*Spieler etc.*).

,un'see·ing *adj. fig.* blind: **with** ~ **eyes**

mit leerem Blick, blind.

un'seem·li·ness *s.* Unziemlichkeit *f;* **un'seem·ly** *adj.* unziemlich, ungehörig.

,un'seen I *adj.* **1.** ungesehen, unbemerkt; **2.** unsichtbar; **3.** *ped.* unvorbereitet (*Übersetzungstext*); II *s.* **4. the** ~ die Geisterwelt; **5.** *ped. Brit.* unvorbereitete 'Herüber,setzung *f.*

,un'self·ish *adj.* □ selbstlos, uneigennützig; **,un'self·ish·ness** *s.* Selbstlosigkeit *f,* Uneigennützigkeit *f.*

,un·sen'sa·tion·al *adj.* wenig sensatio-'nell *od.* aufregend.

,un'serv·ice·a·ble *adj.* □ **1.** nicht verwendbar, unbrauchbar (*Gerät etc.*); **2.** betriebsunfähig.

,un'set·tle *v/t.* **1.** *et.* aus s-r (festen) Lage bringen; **2.** *fig.* beunruhigen; *a. j-n, j-s Glauben etc.* erschüttern, ins Wanken bringen; **3.** *fig.* verwirren, durchein'ander bringen; *j-n* aus dem (gewohnten) Gleis werfen; **4.** in Unordnung bringen; **,un'set·tled** *adj.* **1.** ohne festen Wohnsitz; **2.** unbesiedelt (*Land*); **3.** *fig.* unbestimmt, ungewiss, *a. allg.* unsicher (*Zeit etc.*); **4.** unentschieden, unerledigt (*Frage*); **5.** unbeständig, veränderlich (*Wetter;* ♥ *Markt*); **6.** schwankend, unentschlossen (*Person*); **7.** (geistig) gestört, aus dem (seelischen) Gleichgewicht; **8.** unstet (*Charakter, Leben*); **9.** ♥ unbezahlt, unerledigt; **10.** ♫ nicht zugeschrieben; nicht reguliert (*Erbschaft*).

,un'sex *v/t.* Frau vermännlichen: ~ *o.s.* alles Frauliche ablegen.

,un'shack·le *v/t. j-n* befreien (*a. fig.*); **,un'shack·led** *adj.* ungehemmt.

,un'shad·ed *adj.* **1.** unverdunkelt, unbeschattet; **2.** *paint.* nicht schattiert.

un'shak·a·ble *adj.* unerschütterlich; **,un'shak·en** *adj.* □ **1.** unerschüttert, fest; **2.** unerschütterlich.

,un'shape·ly *adj.* unförmig.

,un'shaved, ,un'shav·en *adj.* unrasiert.

,un'sheathe *v/t. das Schwert* aus der Scheide ziehen.

,un'shed *adj.* unvergossen (*Tränen*).

,un'shell *v/t.* (ab)schälen, enthülsen.

,un'shel·tered *adj.* ungeschützt, schutz-, obdachlos.

,un'ship *v/t.* ♺ a) Ladung löschen, ausladen, b) Passagiere ausschiffen, c) Ruder, Mast etc. abbauen.

,un'shod *adj.* **1.** unbeschuht, barfuß; **2.** unbeschlagen (*Pferd*).

,un'shorn *adj.* ungeschoren.

un'shrink·a·ble [,ʌn'ʃrɪŋkəbl] *adj.* nicht einlaufend (*Stoffe*); **un'shrink·ing** *adj.* □ unverzagt, fest.

,un'sift·ed *adj.* **1.** ungesiebt; **2.** *fig.* ungeprüft.

,un'sight *adj.*: **buy s.th.** ~, **unseen** et. unbesehen kaufen; **,un'sight·ed** *adj.* **1.** nicht gesichtet; **2.** ungezielt (*Schuss*); **3.** ohne Vi'sier (*Gewehr etc.*).

un'sight·ly *adj.* unansehnlich, hässlich.

,un'signed *adj.* **1.** unsigniert, nicht unter'zeichnet; **2.** ♪ unbezeichnet.

,un'sized¹ *adj.* nicht nach Größe(n) geordnet *od.* sortiert.

,un'sized² *adj.* ⊚ **1.** ungrundiert; **2.** ungeleimt.

,un'skil·ful *adj.* □ ungeschickt.

,un'skilled *adj.* **1.** unerfahren, ungeschickt; **2.** ♥ ungelernt: ~ **worker;** **the** ~ **labo(u)r** *coll.* die Hilfsarbeiter *pl.*

,un'skill·ful *Am.* → **unskilful**.

,un'skimmed *adj.* nicht entrahmt: ~ **milk** Vollmilch *f.*

,un'slaked *adj.* **1.** ungelöscht (*Kalk; a.* Durst); **2.** *fig.* ungestillt.

,un'sleep·ing *adj.* **1.** schlaflos; **2.** *fig.*

immer wach.

,un'smil·ing *adj.* □ ernst.

,un'smoked *adj.* **1.** ungeräuchert; **2.** nicht aufgeraucht: ~ *cigar*.

,un'snarl *v/t.* entwirren.

un'so·cia·ble *adj.* □ ungesellig, nicht 'umgänglich, reserviert.

,un'so·cial *adj.* □ **1.** 'unsozi,al; **2.** 'aso-zi,al, gesellschaftsfeindlich; **3.** *work ~ hours Brit.* außerhalb der normalen Arbeitszeit arbeiten.

,un'soiled *adj.* rein, sauber, *fig. a.* unbefleckt.

,un'sold *adj.* unverkauft; → *subject* 14.

,un'sol·der *v/t.* ⊚ ab-, loslöten.

UN sol·dier ['ju:en] *s.* U'N-Sol,dat *m*, F Blauhelm *m*.

,un'sol·dier·ly *adj.* 'unsol,datisch.

,un·so'lic·it·ed *adj.* **1.** unaufgefordert, unverlangt; **2.** freiwillig.

,un'solv·a·ble *adj.* unlösbar.

,un'solved *adj.* ungelöst.

,un·so'phis·ti·cat·ed *adj.* **1.** unverfälscht; **2.** lauter, rein; **3.** ungekünstelt, na'türlich, unverbildet; **4.** na'iv, harmlos; **5.** unverdorben.

,un'sought, un'sought-for *adj.* ungesucht, ungewollt.

,un'sound *adj.* □ **1.** ungesund (*a. fig.*): *of ~ mind* geistesgestört, unzurechnungsfähig; **2.** verdorben, schlecht (*Ware etc.*), faul (*Obst*); **3.** morsch, wurmstichig; **4.** brüchig, rissig; **5.** unzuverlässig; 'unso,lide (*a. ✝*); **6.** nicht stichhaltig, anfechtbar: ~ *argument*; **7.** falsch, verkehrt: ~ *doctrine* Irrlehre *f*; ~ *policy* verfehlte Politik; ~**ness** *s.* **1.** Ungesundheit *f* (*a. fig.*); **2.** Verdorbenheit *f*; **3.** *fig.* Unzuverlässigkeit *f*; **4.** Anfechtbarkeit *f*; **5.** Verfehltheit *f, das* Verkehrte.

un'spar·ing *adj.* □ **1.** freigebig, verschwenderisch (*in, of* mit): *be ~ in* nicht kargen mit *Lob etc.*; *be ~ in one's efforts* keine Mühe scheuen; **2.** reichlich, großzügig; **3.** schonungslos (*of* gegen).

un'speak·a·ble *adj.* □ **1.** unsagbar, unsäglich, unbeschreiblich; **2.** F scheußlich, entsetzlich.

,un'spec·i·fied *adj.* nicht (einzeln) angegeben, nicht spezifiziert.

,un'spir·it·u·al *adj.* □ ungeistig.

,un'spoiled, ,un'spoilt *adj.* **1.** *allg.* unverdorben; **2.** unbeschädigt; **3.** nicht verzogen (*Kind*).

,un'spo·ken *adj.* un(aus)gesprochen, ungesagt; stillschweigend: ~*-of* unerwähnt; ~*-to* unangeredet.

,un'sport·ing, ,un'sports·man·like *adj.* unsportlich, unfair.

,un'spot·ted *adj.* **1.** fleckenlos; **2.** *fig.* makellos, unbefleckt; **3.** F unentdeckt.

,un'sprung *adj.* ⊚ ungefedert.

,un'sta·ble *adj.* **1.** *a. fig.* unsicher, nicht fest, schwankend, la'bil; **2.** *fig.* unbeständig, unstet(ig); **3.** 🜍 'insta,bil.

,un'stained *adj.* **1.** → *unspotted* 1, 2; **2.** ungefärbt.

,un'stamped *adj.* ungestempelt; ✍ unfrankiert (*Brief*).

,un'states·man·like *adj.* unstaatsmännisch.

,un'stead·i·ness *s.* **1.** Unsicherheit *f*; **2.** *fig.* Unstetigkeit *f*, Schwanken *n*; **3.** Unzuverlässigkeit *f*; **4.** Unregelmäßigkeit *f*; ,un'stead·y *adj.* □ **1.** unsicher, wack(e)-lig; **2.** *fig.* unstet(ig); unbeständig, schwankend (*beide a. ✝ Kurse, Markt*); **3.** *fig.* 'unso,lide; **4.** unregelmäßig.

,un'stick *v/t.* [*irr.* → *stick²*] lösen, losmachen.

un'stint·ed *adj.* uneingeschränkt, unbegrenzt; un'stint·ing [-tɪŋ] → *unsparing* 1, 2.

,un'stitch *v/t.* auftrennen: ~*ed* a) aufgetrennt, b) ungesteppt (*Falte*): *come* ~*ed* aufgehen (*Naht*).

,un'stop *v/t.* **1.** entstöpseln, -korken, aufmachen; **2.** freimachen.

,un'strained *adj.* **1.** unfiltriert, ungefiltert; **2.** nicht angespannt (*a. fig.*); **3.** *fig.* ungezwungen.

,un'strap *v/t.* ab-, losschnallen.

,un'stressed *adj.* **1.** *ling.* unbetont; **2.** ⊚ unbelastet.

,un'string *v/t.* [*irr.* → *string*] **1.** Perlen *etc.* abfädeln; **2.** ♪ entsaiten; **3.** *Bogen, Saite* entspannen; **4.** *j-s Nerven* ka'puttmachen, *j-n* (nervlich) ,fertig machen', demoralisieren.

,un'strung *adj.* **1.** ♪ a) saitenlos, unbezogen (*Saiteninstrument*), b) entspannt (*Saite, Bogen*); **2.** abgereiht (*Perlen*); **3.** *fig.* entnervt, mit den Nerven am Ende.

,un'stuck *adj.* : *come ~* a) sich lösen, b) *fig.* scheitern.

,un'stud·ied *adj.* ungesucht, ungekünstelt, na'türlich.

,un·sub'mis·sive *adj.* □ nicht unter-'würfig, 'widerspenstig.

,un·sub'stan·tial *adj.* □ **1.** unstofflich, unkörperlich; **2.** unwesentlich; **3.** wenig stichhaltig *od.* fundiert: ~ *arguments*; **4.** gehaltlos (*Essen*).

,un·sub'stan·ti·at·ed *adj.* **1.** unbegründet; **2.** nicht erhärtet.

,un·suc'cess *s.* 'Misserfolg *m*, Fehlschlag *m*; ,un·suc'cess·ful *adj.* □ **1.** erfolglos: a) ohne Erfolg, b) miss-'glückt, miss'lungen: *be ~* keinen Erfolg haben (*in doing s.th.* bei *od.* mit et.); ~ *take-off* ✈ Fehlstart *m*; **2.** 'durchgefallen (*Kandidat*); zu'rückgewiesen (*Bewerber*); ♔ unter'legen (*Partei*); ,un·suc'cess·ful·ness [-sək'sesfʊlnɪs] *s.* Erfolglosigkeit *f*.

,un'suit·a·ble *adj.* □ **1.** unpassend, ungeeignet (*to, for* für); **2.** unangemessen, unschicklich (*to, for* für); ,un-'suit·ed → *unsuitable* 1.

,un'sul·lied *adj.* *mst fig.* unbefleckt.

,un'sung *poet.* **I** *adj.* unbesungen; **II** *adv. fig.* sang- u. klanglos.

,un·sup'port·ed *adj.* **1.** ungestützt; **2.** *fig.* unbestätigt, ohne 'Unterlagen; **3.** *fig.* nicht unter'stützt (*Antrag etc., a. Kinder etc.*).

,un'sure *adj. allg.* unsicher, nicht sicher (*of* gen.).

,un·sur'mount·a·ble *adj.* 'unüber,windlich (*Hindernis etc.*) (*a. fig.*).

,un·sur'pass·a·ble *adj.* □ 'unüber,trefflich; ,un·sur'passed *adj.* 'unüber,troffen.

,un·sus'cep·ti·ble *adj.* **1.** unempfindlich (*to* gegen); **2.** *fig.* unempfänglich (*to* für).

un·sus·pect·ed [,ʌnsə'spektɪd] *adj.* □ **1.** unverdächtig(t); **2.** unvermutet, ungeahnt; ,un·sus'pect·ing [-ɪŋ] *adj.* □ **1.** nichts ahnend, ahnungslos: ~ *of* ohne et. zu ahnen; **2.** → *unsuspicious* 1.

,un·sus'pi·cious *adj.* □ **1.** arglos, nicht argwöhnisch; **2.** unverdächtig, harmlos.

,un'sweet·ened *adj.* **1.** ungesüßt; **2.** *fig.* unversüßt.

un-swerv·ing [ʌn'swɜ:vɪŋ] *adj.* □ unbeirrbar, unerschütterlich.

,un'sworn *adj.* **1.** unbeeidet; **2.** unvereidigt (*Zeuge etc.*).

,un·sym'met·ri·cal *adj.* □ 'unsym,metrisch.

'un,sym·pa'thet·ic *adj.* (□ ~*ally*) teilnahmslos, ohne Mitgefühl.

,un·sys·tem'at·ic *adj.* (□ ~*ally*) 'unsys-te,matisch, planlos.

,un'taint·ed *adj.* □ **1.** fleckenlos (*a. fig.*); **2.** unverdorben: ~ *food*; **3.** *fig.* unbeeinträchtigt (*with* von).

,un'tal·ent·ed *adj.* untalentiert, unbegabt.

,un'tam·a·ble *adj.* □ un(be)zähmbar; ,un'tamed *adj.* ungezähmt.

,un'tan·gle *v/t.* **1.** entwirren (*a. fig.*); **2.** aus einer schwierigen Lage befreien.

,un'tanned *adj.* **1.** ungegerbt (*Leder*); **2.** ungebräunt (*Haut*).

,un'tapped *adj.* unangezapft (*a. fig.*): ~ *resources* ungenützte Hilfsquellen.

,un'tar·nished *adj.* **1.** ungetrübt; **2.** makellos, unbefleckt (*a. fig.*).

,un'tast·ed *adj.* ungekostet (*a. fig.*).

,un'taught *adj.* **1.** ungelehrt, nicht unter'richtet; **2.** unwissend, ungebildet; **3.** ungelernt, selbst entwickelt (*Fähigkeit etc.*).

,un'taxed *adj.* unbesteuert.

,un'teach·a·ble *adj.* **1.** unbelehrbar (*Person*); **2.** unlehrbar (*Sache*).

,un'tem·pered *adj.* **1.** ⊚ ungehärtet, unvergütet (*Stahl*); **2.** *fig.* ungemildert (*with, by* durch).

,un'ten·a·ble *adj. fig.* unhaltbar.

,un'ten·ant·a·ble *adj.* unbewohn-, unvermietbar; ,un'ten·ant·ed *adj.* **1.** unbewohnt, leer (stehend); **2.** ♔ ungemietet, ungepachtet.

,un'tend·ed *adj.* **1.** unbehütet, unbeaufsichtigt; **2.** vernachlässigt.

,un'thank·ful *adj.* □ undankbar.

un'think·a·ble *adj.* undenkbar, unvorstellbar: *the ~* das Undenkbare; ,un-'think·ing *adj.* □ **1.** gedankenlos; **2.** nicht denkend.

,un'thought *adj.* **1.** 'unüber,legt; **2.** *mst* ~*-of* a) unerwartet, unvermutet, b) unvorstellbar.

,un'thread *v/t.* **1.** *Nadel* ausfädeln; den Faden her'ausziehen aus; **2.** *Perlen etc.* abfädeln; **3.** *a. fig.* sich hin'durchfinden durch, her'ausfinden aus; **4.** *mst fig.* entwirren.

,un'thrift·y *adj.* □ **1.** verschwenderisch; **2.** unwirtschaftlich (*a. Sache*).

,un'throne *v/t. a. fig.* entthronen.

un'ti·di·ness *s.* Unordentlichkeit *f*; un-'ti·dy *adj.* □ unordentlich.

,un'tie *v/t.* aufknoten, auf-, losbinden, *Knoten* lösen.

un·til [ən'tɪl] **I** *prp.* bis (*zeitlich*): *not ~ Monday* erst (am) Montag; **II** *cj.* bis: *not ~* erst als *od.* wenn, nicht eher als.

,un'tilled *adj.* ✓ unbebaut.

un'time·li·ness *s.* Unzeit *f*, falscher *od.* verfrühter Zeitpunkt; un'time·ly *adj. u. adv.* unzeitig: a) verfrüht, b) ungelegen, unpassend.

un'tir·ing *adj.* □ unermüdlich.

un·to ['ʌntu] *prp. obs. od. poet. od. bibl.* → *to* I.

,un'told *adj.* **1.** a) unerzählt, b) ungesagt: *leave nothing ~* nichts unerwähnt lassen; **2.** unsäglich (*Leiden etc.*); **3.** ungezählt, zahllos; **4.** unermesslich.

un'touch·a·ble **I** *adj.* **1.** unberührbar; **2.** unantastbar, unangreifbar; **3.** unerreichbar, unnahbar; **II** *s.* **4.** Unberührbare(r *m*) *f* (*bei den Hindus*); ,un-'touched *adj.* **1.** unberührt (*a. Essen*) (*a. fig.*); unangetastet (*a. Vorrat*); **2.** *fig.* ungerührt, unbeeinflusst; nicht zu'rechtgemacht, *fig.* ungeschminkt; **4.** *phot.* unretuschiert; **5.** *fig.* unerreicht.

un·to·ward [,ʌntə'wɔ:d] *adj.* **1.** *obs.* ungefügig, 'widerspenstig; **2.** widrig, ungünstig, unglücklich (*Umstand etc.*);

ˌun·toˈward·ness [-nɪs] *s.* **1.** *obs.* ˈWiderspenstigkeit *f*; **2.** Widrigkeit *f*, Ungunst *f*.

ˌunˈtrace·a·ble *adj.* unauffindbar, nicht ausfindig zu machen(d).

ˌunˈtrained *adj.* **1.** ungeschult (*a. fig.*), *a.* ⚔ unausgebildet; **2.** *sport* untrainiert; **3.** ungeübt; **4.** undressiert (*Tier*).

unˈtram·mel(l)ed *adj. bsd. fig.* ungebunden, ungehindert.

ˌun·transˈlat·a·ble *adj.* □ 'unüberˌsetzbar.

ˌun·travˈel(l)ed *adj.* **1.** unbefahren (*Straße etc.*); **2.** nicht (weit) herˈumgekommen (*Person*).

ˌunˈtreat·ed *adj.* unbehandelt (*Obst, Gemüse etc.*).

ˌunˈtried *adj.* **1.** a) unerprobt, ungeprüft, b) unversucht; **2.** ⚖ a) unerledigt, (noch) nicht verhandelt (*Fall*), b) (noch) nicht vor Gericht gestellt.

ˌunˈtrimmed *adj.* **1.** unbeschnitten (*Bart, Hecke etc.*); **2.** ungepflegt, nicht (ordentlich) zuˈrechtgemacht; **3.** ungeschmückt.

ˌunˈtrod·den *adj.* unberührt (*Wildnis etc.*): **~ paths** *fig.* neue Wege.

ˌunˈtrou·bled *adj.* **1.** ungestört, unbelästigt; **2.** ruhig (*Geist, Zeiten etc.*); **3.** ungetrübt (*a. fig.*).

ˌunˈtrue *adj.* □ **1.** untreu (**to** *dat.*); **2.** unwahr, falsch, irrig; **3.** (**to**) nicht in Überˈeinstimmung (mit), abweichend (von); **4.** ⊙ a) unrund, b) ungenau; **ˌunˈtru·ly** *adv.* fälschlich(erweise).

ˌunˈtrustˌwor·thi·ness *s.* Unzuverlässigkeit *f*; **ˌunˈtrustˌwor·thy** *adj.* □ unzuverlässig, nicht vertrauenswürdig.

ˌunˈtruth *s.* **1.** Unwahrheit *f*; **2.** Falschheit *f*; **ˌunˈtruth·ful** *adj.* □ **1.** unwahr (*Person od. Sache*); unaufrichtig; **2.** falsch, irrig.

ˌunˈtuned *adj.* **1.** ♪ verstimmt; **2.** *fig.* verwirrt; **3.** → **ˌunˈtune·ful** *adj.* □ 'unmeˌlodisch.

ˌunˈturned *adj.* nicht 'umgedreht; → **stone** 1.

ˌunˈtu·tored *adj.* **1.** ungebildet, ungeschult; **2.** unerzogen; **3.** unverbildet, naˈtürlich; **4.** unkultiviert.

ˌunˈtwine, ˌunˈtwist I *v/t.* **1.** aufdrehen, -flechten; **2.** *bsd. fig.* entwirren, lösen; **II** *v/i.* **3.** sich aufdrehen, aufgehen.

ˌunˈused *adj.* **1.** unbenutzt, ungebraucht, nicht verwendet; **2.** a) ungewohnt, nicht gewöhnt (**to** an *acc.*), b) nicht gewohnt (**to doing** zu tun).

unˈu·su·al *adj.* □ un-, außergewöhnlich: **it is ~ for him to** es ist nicht s-e Art zu *inf*.

unˈut·ter·a·ble *adj.* □ **1.** unaussprechlich (*a. fig.*); **2.** → **unspeakable** 1; **3.** unglaublich, Erz...: **~ scoundrel**; **ˌunˈut·tered** *adj.* unausgesprochen, ungesagt.

ˌunˈval·ued *adj.* **1.** nicht (ab)geschätzt, untaxiert; **2.** ✝ nennwertlos (*Aktien*); **3.** nicht geschätzt, wenig geachtet.

unˈvar·ied *adj.* unverändert, unförmig.

ˌunˈvar·nished *adj.* **1.** ungefirnißt; **2.** *fig.* ungeschminkt: **~ truth**; **3.** *fig.* schlicht, einfach.

unˈvar·y·ing *adj.* □ unveränderlich, gleich bleibend.

ˌunˈveil I *v/t.* **1.** *Gesicht etc.* entschleiern, *Denkmal etc.* enthüllen (*a. fig.*): **~ed** a) unverschleiert, b) unverhüllt (*a. fig.*); **2.** sichtbar werden lassen; **II** *v/i.* **3.** den Schleier fallen lassen, sich enthüllen (*a. fig.*).

ˌun·verˈi·fied *adj.* unbelegt, unbewiesen.

ˌunˈversed *adj.* unbewandert (**in** in

dat.).

ˌunˈvoiced *adj.* **1.** unausgesprochen, nicht geäußert; **2.** *ling.* stimmlos.

ˌunˈvouched, *a.* **unˈvouched-for** *adj.* unverbürgt.

ˌunˈvouch·ered *adj.* : **~ fund** *pol. Am.* Reptilienfonds *m*.

ˌunˈwant·ed *adj.* unerwünscht.

unˈwar·i·ness *s.* Unvorsichtigkeit *f*.

ˌunˈwar·like *adj.* unkriegerisch.

ˌunˈwarped *adj.* **1.** nicht verzogen (*Holz*); **2.** *fig.* 'unparˌteiisch.

unˈwar·rant·a·ble *adj.* □ unverantwortlich, ungerechtfertigt, nicht vertretbar, untragbar, unhaltbar; **unˈwar·rant·a·bly** *adv.* in unverantwortlicher *od.* ungerechtfertigter Weise; **unˈwar·rant·ed** *adj.* □ **1.** ungerechtfertigt, unberechtigt, unbefugt; **2.** ˌunˈwarranted unverbürgt, ohne Gewähr.

unˈwar·y *adj.* □ **1.** unvorsichtig; **2.** 'unüberˌlegt.

ˌunˈwashed *adj.* ungewaschen: **the great ~** *fig. contp.* der Pöbel.

ˌunˈwatched *adj.* unbeobachtet.

ˌunˈwa·tered *adj.* **1.** unbewässert; nicht begossen, nicht gesprengt (*Rasen etc.*); **2.** unverwässert (*Milch etc.*; *a.* ✝ Kapital).

unˈwa·ver·ing *adj.* □ unerschütterlich, standhaft, unentwegt.

un·weaˈried [ʌnˈwɪərɪd] *adj.* □ **1.** nicht ermüdet; **2.** unermüdlich; **unˈwea·ry·ing** [-ɪɪŋ] *adj.* □ unermüdlich.

ˌunˈwed(·ded) *adj.* unverheiratet.

ˌunˈweighed *adj.* **1.** ungewogen; **2.** nicht abgewogen, unbedacht.

unˈwel·come *adj.* □ 'unwillˌkommen (*a. fig. unangenehm*).

ˌunˈwell *adj.* unwohl, unpäßlich (*a. euphem.*).

ˌunˈwept *adj.* **1.** unbeweint; **2.** unvergossen (*Tränen*).

ˌunˈwhole·some *adj.* □ *allg.* ungesund (*a. fig.*); **ˌunˈwhole·some·ness** *s.* Ungesundheit *f*.

un·wieldˈi·ness [ʌnˈwiːldɪnɪs] *s.* **1.** Unbeholfenheit *f*, Schwerfälligkeit *f*; **2.** Unhandlichkeit *f*; **unˈwield·y** *adj.* □ **1.** unbeholfen, plump, schwerfällig; **2.** a) unhandlich, b) sperrig.

ˌunˈwill·ing *adj.* □ un-, 'widerwillig: **be ~ to do** abgeneigt sein, et. zu tun, et. nicht tun wollen; **I am ~ to admit it** ich gebe es ungern zu; **unˈwill·ing·ly** *adv.* ungern, 'widerwillig; **unˈwill·ing·ness** *s.* 'Widerwille *m*, Abgeneigtheit *f*.

un·wind [ˌʌnˈwaɪnd] [*irr.* → **wind²**] **I** *v/t.* **1.** ab-, auf-, loswickeln, abspulen; **II** *v/i.* **2.** sich ab- *od.* loswickeln; **3.** F sich entspannen.

un·wink·ing [ˌʌnˈwɪŋkɪŋ] *adj.* □ unverwandt, starr (*Blick*).

ˌunˈwis·dom *s.* Unklugheit *f*; **ˌunˈwise** *adj.* □ unklug, töricht.

ˌunˈwished *adj.* ungewünscht; **2.** *a.* **~-for** unerwünscht.

ˌunˈwit·ting *adj.* □ unwissentlich, unabsichtlich.

unˈwom·an·li·ness *s.* Unweiblichkeit *f*; **unˈwom·an·ly** *adj.* unweiblich, unfraulich.

unˈwont·ed *adj.* □ **1.** nicht gewöhnt (**to** an *acc.*), ungewohnt (**to** *inf.* zu *inf.*); **2.** ungewöhnlich.

ˌunˈwork·a·ble *adj.* **1.** unaus-, 'unˌdurchführbar (*Plan*); **2.** ⊙ nicht bearbeitungsfähig; **3.** ⊙ a) nicht betriebsfähig, b) ⚒ nicht abbauwürdig.

ˌunˈworked *adj.* **1.** unbearbeitet (*Boden etc.*), roh (*a.* ⚒); **2.** ⚒ unverritzt: **~ coal** anstehende Kohle.

ˌunˈwork·man·like *adj.* unfachmän-

nisch, unfachgemäß, stümperhaft.

ˌunˈworld·li·ness *s.* **1.** Weltfremdheit *f*; **2.** Uneigennützigkeit *f*; **3.** Geistigkeit *f*; **ˌunˈworld·ly** *adj.* **1.** unweltlich, nicht weltlich (gesinnt); weltfremd; **2.** uneigennützig; **3.** unirdisch, geistig.

ˌunˈworn *adj.* **1.** ungetragen (*Kleid etc.*); **2.** nicht abgetragen.

unˈwor·thi·ness *s.* Unwürdigkeit *f*; **unˈwor·thy** *adj.* □ unwürdig (**of** *gen.*): **he is ~ of it** er verdient es nicht, er ist es nicht wert; **he is ~ of respect** er verdient keine Achtung.

un·wound [ˌʌnˈwaʊnd] *adj.* **1.** abgewickelt; **2.** abgelaufen, nicht aufgezogen (*Uhr*).

ˌunˈwrap *v/t.* auswickeln, -packen.

ˌunˈwrin·kled *adj.* nicht gerunzelt *od.* zerknittert, faltenlos, glatt.

ˌunˈwrit·ten *adj.* **1.** ungeschrieben: **~ law** a) ⚖ ungeschriebenes Recht, b) *fig.* ungeschriebenes Gesetz; **2.** *a.* **~-on** unbeschrieben.

ˌunˈwrought *adj.* unbe-, unverarbeitet, roh: **~ goods** Rohstoffe.

unˈyield·ing *adj.* □ **1.** nicht nachgebend (**to** *dat.*), fest (*a. fig.*), unbiegsam, starr; **2.** *fig.* unnachgiebig, hart, unbeugsam.

ˌunˈyoke *v/t.* **1.** aus-, losspannen; **2.** *fig.* (los)trennen, lösen.

ˌunˈzip I *v/t.* **1.** den Reißverschluss aufmachen an (*dat.*); **2.** *Computer:* Datei ent'packen, ent'zippen; **II** *v/i.* **3.** aufgehen, sich öffnen (lassen) (*Kleid, Reißverschluss*).

up [ʌp] **I** *adv.* **1.** a) nach oben, hoch, (her-, hin)'auf, aufwärts, in die Höhe, emˈpor, b) oben (*a. fig.*): **... and ~** u. (noch) höher *od.* mehr, von ... aufwärts; **~ and ~** immer höher; **three stor(e)ys ~** drei Stock hoch, oben im dritten Stock(werk); **~ and down** auf u. ab, hin u. her; *fig.* überall; **~ from the country** vom Lande; **~ till now** bis jetzt; **2.** nach *od.* im Norden; **~ from Cuba** von Kuba aus in nördlicher Richtung; **3.** a) in der *od.* in die (*bsd.* Haupt)Stadt, b) *Brit. bsd.* in *od.* nach London; **4.** am *od.* zum Studienort, im College *etc.*: **he stayed ~ for the vacation**; **5.** *Am.* F in (*dat.*): **~ north** im Norden; **6.** aufrecht, gerade: **sit ~**; **7.** her'an, her, auf ... (*acc.*) zu, hin: **he went straight ~ to the door** er ging geradewegs auf die Tür zu *od.* zur Tür; **8.** **~ to** a) hin'auf nach *od.* zu, b) bis (zu), bis an *od.* auf (*acc.*), c) gemäß, entsprechend; → **date²** 5; **~ to town** in die Stadt, *Brit. bsd.* nach London; **~ to the chin** bis ans *od.* zum Kinn; **~ to death** bis zum Tode; **be ~ to** F a) et. vorhaben, et. im Schilde führen, b) gewachsen sein (*dat.*), c) entsprechen (*dat.*), d) j-s Sache sein, abhängen von j-m, e) fähig sein *od.* bereit sein zu, f) vorbereitet *od.* gefasst sein auf (*acc.*), g) vertraut sein mit, bewandert sein in (*dat.*): **what are you ~ to?** was hast du vor?, was machst du (**there** da)?; → **trick** 2; **he is ~ to no good** er führt nichts Gutes im Schilde; **it is ~ to him** es liegt an ihm, es hängt von ihm ab, es ist s-e Sache; **it is not ~ to much** es taugt nicht viel; **he is not ~ to much** mit ihm ist nicht viel los; **9.** *mit Verben* (*siehe jeweils diese*): **sit ~**, ...; add ~ zs.-zählen; **eat ~** aufessen; **II** *adj.* **10.** aufwärts ..., nach oben gerichtet; **11.** im Innern (des Landes); **12.** nach der *od.* zur Stadt: **~ train; ~ platform** Bahnsteig *m* für Stadtzüge; **13.** a) oben (befindlich), b) hoch (*a. fig.*): **be ~** *fig.* an der Spitze sein, obenauf sein; *he is ~ in* (*od.* *on*) *that subject* F in diesem Fach ist er gut beschlagen *od.* weiß er (gut) Bescheid; *prices are ~* die Preise sind hoch *od.* gestiegen; *wheat is ~* ⚚ Weizen steht hoch (im Kurs), der Weizenpreis ist gestiegen; **14.** auf(gestanden), auf den Beinen (*a. fig.*): **~ and about** F (wieder) auf den Beinen; **~ and coming** → **up-and-coming**; **~ and doing** a) auf den Beinen, b) rührig, tüchtig; *be ~ and running* a) einwandfrei funktionieren, b) *weitS* in Gang sein; auf dem Markt sein; sich etablieren; *be ~ late* lange aufbleiben; *be ~ against* F *e-r Schwierigkeit etc.* gegenüberstehen; *be ~ against it* F ‚dran‘ sein, in der Klemme sein *od.* sitzen; *be ~ to* → 8; **15.** *parl. Brit.* geschlossen: *Parliament is ~* das Parlament hat s-e Sitzungen beendet *od.* hat sich vertagt; **16.** (zum Sprechen) aufgestanden: *the Home Secretary is ~* der Innenminister spricht; **17.** (*bei verschiedenen Substantiven*) a) aufgegangen (*Sonne, Samen*), b) hochgeschlagen (*Kragen*), c) hochgekrempelt (*Ärmel etc.*), d) aufgespannt (*Schirm*), e) aufgeschlagen (*Zelt*), f) hoch-, aufgezogen (*Vorhang etc.*), g) aufgestiegen (*Ballon etc.*), h) aufgeflogen (*Vogel*), i) angeschwollen (*Fluss etc.*); **18.** schäumend (*Apfelwein etc.*); **19.** in Aufregung, in Aufruhr: *his temper is ~* er ist aufgebracht; *the whole country was ~* das ganze Land befand sich in Aufruhr; **20.** F ‚los‘, im Gange: *what's ~?* was ist los?; *is anything ~?* ist (irgendet-)was los?; *the hunt is ~* die Jagd ist eröffnet; → *arm²* 1, *blood* 2; **21.** abgelaufen, vor'bei, um (*Zeit*): *the game is ~* *fig.* das Spiel ist aus; *it's all ~* alles ist aus; *it's all ~ with him* es ist aus mit ihm; **22.** *~ with j-m* ebenbürtig *od.* gewachsen; **23.** *~ for* bereit zu: *be ~ for discussion* zur Diskussion stehen; *be ~ for election* auf der Wahlliste stehen; *be ~ for examination* sich e-r Prüfung unterziehen; *be ~ for sale* zum Kauf stehen; *be ~ for trial* ⚖ a) vor Gericht stehen, b) verhandelt werden; *be (had) ~ for* F vorgeladen werden wegen; *the case is ~ before the court* der Fall wird (vor Gericht) verhandelt; **24.** *sport etc.* um e-n Punkt *etc.* vor'aus: *be one ~; one ~ for you!* eins zu null für dich! (*a. fig.*); **25.** *Baseball:* am Schlag; **26.** *sl.* a) hoffnungsvoll, opti'mistisch, b) in Hochstimmung; **III** *int.* **27.** *~!* auf!, hoch!, her'auf!, hin'auf!, her'an!; *~ (with you)!* (steh) auf!; *~ ...! hoch* (lebe) ...!; **IV** *prp.* **28.** auf ... (*acc.*) (hinauf), hinauf, em'por (*a. fig.*): *~ the hill* (*river*) den Berg (Fluss) hinauf, bergauf (flussaufwärts); *~ the street* die Straße hinauf *od.* entlang; *~ yours!* V ‚leck mich‘!; **29.** in das Innere *e-s Landes etc.*: *~ (the) country* landeinwärts; **30.** oben an *od.* auf (*dat.*): *~ the tree* (oben) auf dem Baum; *~ the road* weiter oben an der Straße; **V** *s.* **31.** *the ~s and downs* das Auf u. Ab, die Höhen u. Tiefen *des Lebens; on the ~ and ~* F a) im Steigen (begriffen), im Kommen, b) in Ordnung, ehrlich; **32.** F Preisanstieg *m*; **33.** *sl.* Aufputschmittel *n;* **VII** *v/i.* **35.** *~ with sl. et.* hochreißen; *he ~ped with his gun*; **36.** *Am. sl.* Aufputschmittel nehmen; **VII** *v/t.* **37.** *Preis, Produktion etc.* erhöhen; **38.** *Am.* F *j-n* (im Rang) befördern (*to* zu).

,up-and-'com·ing *adj.* aufstrebend.

,up-and-'down *adj.* auf und ab gehend: *~ looks* kritisch musternde Blicke; *~ motion* Aufundabbewegung *f; ~ stroke* ⊙ Doppelhub *m.*

u·pas ['juːpəs] *s.* **1.** *a. ~ tree* ⚘ Upasbaum *m;* **2.** a) Upassaft *m* (*Pfeilgift*), b) *fig.* Gift, verderblicher Einfluss.

'up·beat I *s.* **1.** ♪ Auftakt *m;* **2.** *on the ~* *fig.* im Aufschwung; **II** *adj.* **3.** F beschwingt.

'up-bow [-bəʊ] *s.* ♪ Aufstrich *m.*

up'braid *v/t. j-m* Vorwürfe machen, *j-n, a. et.* tadeln, rügen; *~ s.o. with* (*od.* *for*) *s.th.* j-m et. vorwerfen, j-m wegen e-r Sache Vorwürfe machen; **up'braid·ing I** *s.* Vorwurf *m*, Tadel *m*, Rüge *f;* **II** *adj.* □ vorwurfsvoll, tadelnd.

'up·cast I *adj.* em'porgerichtet (*Blick etc.*), aufgeschlagen (*Augen*); **II** *s. a. ~ shaft* ⚒ Wetter-, Luftschacht *m.*

'up·chuck *v/i.* (sich er)brechen; **II** *v/t. et.* erbrechen.

'up,com·ing *adj. Am.* kommend, be'vorstehend.

,up'coun·try I *adv.* land'einwärts; **II** *adj.* im Inneren des Landes (gelegen *od.* lebend), binnenländisch; *contp.* bäurisch; **III** *s.* das (Landes)Innere, Binnen-, Hinterland *n.*

'up,cur·rent *s.* ✈ Aufwind *m.*

up'date I *v/t.* **1.** auf den neuesten Stand bringen: *~ a file* (*od.* *one's records*) e-e Da'tei (*od.* s-e Aufzeichnungen) aktualisieren; **II** *s.* **'update 2.** 'Unterlage(n *pl.*) *f etc.* über den neuesten Stand; **3.** auf den neuesten Stand gebrachte Versi'on *etc.*, neuester Bericht (*on* über *acc.*), *Software:* 'Update *m.*

'up·do *s.* F 'Hochfri,sur *f.*

'up·draft *Am.*, **'up·draught** *Brit. s.* Aufwind *m.*

up'end *v/t.* F **1.** hochkant stellen, *Fass etc.* aufrichten; **2.** *Gefäß* 'umstülpen; **3.** *fig.* ‚auf den Kopf stellen‘.

'up·front *adj. Am.* F **1.** freimütig, di'rekt; **2.** vordringlich; **3.** führend; **4.** Voraus...

'up·grade I *s.* **1.** Steigung *f: on the ~ fig.* im (An)Steigen (begriffen); **2.** *Computer:* Aufrüstung *f;* **II** *adj.* **3.** *Am.* ansteigend; **III** *adv.* **4.** *Am.* berg'auf; **IV** *v/t.* up'grade **5.** höher einstufen; **6.** *j-n* (im Rang) befördern; *~ s.o.'s status fig.* j-n ‚aufwerten‘; **7.** ⚚ a) (die Quali'tät *gen.*) verbessern, b) *Produkt* durch ein besseres Erzeugnis ersetzen; **8.** *Computer:* aufrüsten.

up·heav·al [ʌp'hiːvl] *s.* **1.** *geol.* Erhebung *f;* **2.** *fig.* 'Umwälzung *f*, 'Umbruch *m*: *social ~s.*

up'heave *v/t. u. v/i.* [*irr.* → *heave*] (sich) heben.

,up'hill I *adv.* **1.** den Berg hin'auf, berg'auf; **2.** aufwärts; **II** *adj.* **3.** bergauf führend, ansteigend; **4.** hoch gelegen, oben (auf dem Berg) gelegen; **5.** *fig.* mühselig, hart: *~ work.*

up'hold *v/t.* [*irr.* → *hold²*] **1.** hochhalten, aufrecht halten; **2.** halten, stützen (*a. fig.*); **3.** *fig.* aufrechterhalten, unter'stützen; **4.** ⚖ *Urteil* (in zweiter In'stanz) bestätigen; **5.** *fig.* beibehalten; **6.** *Brit.* in'stand halten; **up'hold·er** *s.* Erhalter *m*, Verteidiger *m*, Wahrer *m*: *~ of public order* Hüter *m* der öffentlichen Ordnung.

up·hol·ster [ʌp'həʊlstə] *v/t.* **1.** a) (auf-, aus)polstern, b) beziehen: *~ed goods* Polsterware(n *pl.*) *f;* **2.** *Zimmer* (mit Teppichen, Vorhängen *etc.*) ausstatten; **up'hol·ster·er** [-tərə] *s.* Polsterer *m;* **up'hol·ster·y** [-tərɪ] *s.* **1.** 'Polstermateri,al *n*, Polsterung *f*, (Möbel)Bezugsstoff *m;* **2.** Polstern *n.*

'up·keep *s.* **1.** a) In'standhaltung *f,* b) In'standhaltungskosten *pl.;* **2.** 'Unterhalt(skosten *pl.*) *m.*

up·land ['ʌplənd] *s. mst pl.* Hochland *n;* **II** *adj.* Hochland(s)...

up'lift I *v/t.* **1.** em'porheben; **2.** *Augen, Stimme, a. fig. Stimmung, Niveau* heben; **3.** *fig.* a) aufrichten, Auftrieb verleihen (*dat.*), b) erbauen; **II** *s.* **'uplift 4.** *fig.* a) (innerer) Auftrieb, b) Erbauung *f;* **5.** *fig.* a) Aufschwung *m*, b) Hebung *f*, (Ver)Besserung *f;* **6.** *~ brassiere* Stützbüstenhalter *m.*

'up-light·er *s.* Deckenfluter *m.*

,up-'mar·ket I *adj.* **1.** anspruchsvoll, ex'klusiv (*Produkt, Kundenkreis*); **II** *adv.* **2.** an (*od.* in) exklusivere (*od.* anspruchsvollere) Kreise (*verkaufen, aufsteigen etc.*); **3.** *go ~* Waren für e-n anspruchsvolleren Kundenkreis produzieren *od.* anbieten.

up·on [ə'pɒn] *prp.* → *on* (*upon ist bsd. in der Umgangssprache weniger geläufig als* on, *jedoch in folgenden Fällen üblich*): a) *in verschiedenen Redewendungen: ~ this* hierauf, darauf(hin), b) *in Beteuerungen: ~ my word* (*of hono[u]r*)*!* auf mein Wort!, c) *in kumulativen Wendungen: loss ~ loss* Verlust auf Verlust, dauernde Verluste; *petition ~ petition* ein Gesuch nach dem anderen, d) *als Märchenanfang: once ~ a time there was* es war einmal.

up·per ['ʌpə] **I** *adj.* **1.** ober, höher, Ober...(-*arm*, -*deck*, -*kiefer*, -*leder etc.*): *~ circle thea.* zweiter Rang; *~ class sociol.* Oberschicht *f; ~ crust* F die Spitzen *pl.* der Gesellschaft; *get the ~ hand fig.* die Oberhand gewinnen; *2 House parl.* Oberhaus *n; ~ stor(e)y* oberes Stockwerk; *there is something wrong in his ~ stor(e)y* F *fig.* er ist nicht ganz richtig im Oberstübchen; **II** *s. mst pl.* Oberleder *n* (*Schuh*): *be (down) on one's ~s* F a) die Schuhe durchgelaufen haben, b) *fig.* ‚total abgebrannt‘ *od.* ‚auf dem Hund‘ sein; **3.** F a) Oberzahn *m*, b) obere (‚Zahn)Pro,these, c) (Py'jama- *etc.*)Oberteil *n;* **4.** *sl.* Aufputschmittel *n; ~ case s. typ.* Großbuchstabe(n *pl.* coll.) *m*, Ver'sal *m od.* Ver'salien *pl.* coll.: *set s.th. in ~ et.* in Großbuchstaben setzen; *'~-case adj. typ.* groß, Versal...: *~ letter* Großbuchstabe *m*, Ver'sal *m; '~-cut Boxen:* **I** *s.* Aufwärts-, Kinnhaken *m;* **II** *v/t.* [*irr.* → *cut*] *j-m* e-n Aufwärtshaken versetzen.

'up·per·most I *adj.* oberst, höchst; **II** *adv.* ganz oben, oben'an, zu'oberst; an erster Stelle: *say whatever comes ~* sagen, was e-m gerade einfällt.

up·pish ['ʌpɪʃ] *adj.* □ F **1.** hochnäsig; **2.** anmaßend.

up·pi·ty ['ʌpətɪ] *adj.* → *uppish.*

up'raise *v/t.* erheben: *with hands ~d* mit erhobenen Händen.

up·right I *adj.* □ [,ʌp'raɪt] **1.** auf-, senkrecht, gerade: *~ piano* → 7; *~ size* Hochformat *n;* **2.** aufrecht (sitzend, stehend, gehend); **3.** ['ʌpraɪt] *fig.* aufrecht, rechtschaffen; **II** *adv.* [,ʌp'raɪt] **4.** aufrecht, gerade; **III** *s.* ['ʌpraɪt] **5.** (senkrechte) Stütze, Träger *m*, Ständer *m*, Pfosten *m*, (Treppen)Säule *f;* **6.** *pl. sport* (Tor)Pfosten *pl.;* **7.** ♪ ('Wand-)Kla,vier *n*, Pi'ano *n;* **up·right·ness** ['ʌpraɪtnɪs] *s. fig.* Geradheit *f*, Rechtschaffenheit *f.*

U

'up·ris·ing s. **1.** Aufstehen n; **2.** fig. Aufstand m, (Volks)Erhebung f.

,up'riv·er → upstream.

'up·roar s. fig. Aufruhr m, Tu'mult m, Toben n, Lärm m: **in** (**an**) ~in Aufruhr; up·roar·i·ous [ʌp'rɔːrɪəs] adj. □ **1.** lärmend, laut, stürmisch (Begrüßung etc.), tosend (Beifall), schallend (Gelächter); **2.** tumultu'arisch, tobend; **3.** ‚toll', zum Brüllen (komisch).

up'root v/t. **1.** ausreißen; Baum etc. entwurzeln (a. fig.); **2.** fig. her'ausreißen (from aus); **3.** fig. ausmerzen, -rotten.

up'set¹ I v/t. [irr. → set] **1.** 'umwerfen, -kippen, -stoßen; Boot zum Kentern bringen; **2.** fig. Regierung stürzen; **3.** fig. Plan 'umstoßen, über den Haufen werfen, vereiteln; → apple-cart; **4.** fig. j-n umwerfen, aus der Fassung bringen, bestürzen, durchein'ander bringen; **5.** in Unordnung bringen; Magen verderben; **6.** ☉ stauchen; II v/i. [irr. → set] **7.** 'umkippen, -stürzen; 'umschlagen, kentern (Boot); III s. **8.** 'Umkippen n; ⚓ 'Umschlagen n, Kentern n; **9.** Sturz m, Fall m; **10.** 'Umsturz m; **11.** Unordnung f, Durchein'ander n; **12.** Bestürzung f, Verwirrung f; **13.** Vereitelung f; **14.** (a. ☟ Magen)Verstimmung f, Ärger m; **15.** Streit m, Meinungsverschiedenheit f; **16.** sport Über'raschung f (unerwartete Niederlage etc.).

'up·set² adj. attr. **1.** verdorben (Magen): ~ **stomach** Magenverstimmung f; **2.** ~ **price** Anschlagspreis m (Auktion).

'up·shot s. (End)Ergebnis n, Ende n, Ausgang m, Fazit n: **in the** ~ am Ende, schließlich.

'up·side s. Oberseite f; ~ **down** adv. **1.** das Oberste zu'unterst, mit dem Kopf od. Oberteil nach unten, verkehrt (herum); **2.** fig. drunter u. drüber, vollkommen durchein'ander: **turn everything** ~ alles auf den Kopf stellen; ,~-'**down** adj. auf den Kopf gestellt, 'umgekehrt: ~ **flight** ✈ Rückenflug m; ~ **world** fig. verkehrte Welt.

up·si·lon [ju:p'saɪlən] s. Ypsilon n (Buchstabe).

,up'stage I adv. thea. **1.** im od. in den 'Hintergrund der Bühne; II adj. **2.** zum 'Hintergrund gehörig; **3.** F hochnäsig; III v/t. **4.** fig. j-m ,die Schau stehlen', j-n in den 'Hintergrund drängen; **5.** F j-n hochnäsig behandeln; IV s. **6.** thea. 'Bühnen,hintergrund m.

,up'stairs I adv. **1.** die Treppe hin'auf, nach oben; → kick 9; **2.** e-e Treppe höher; **3.** oben, in e-m oberen Stockwerk: **a bit weak** ~ F leicht ‚behämmert'; **4.** im oberen Stockwerk (gelegen), ober; II s. pl. a. sg. konstr. **5.** oberes Stockwerk, Obergeschoss n.

up'stand·ing adj. **1.** aufrecht (a. fig. ehrlich, tüchtig); **2.** groß gewachsen, (groß u.) kräftig.

'up·start s. Em'porkömmling m, Parve'nü m; II adj. em'porgekommen, Parvenü..., neureich.

'up·state Am. I s. 'Hinterland n e-s Staates; II adj. u. adv. aus dem od. in den od. im ländlichen od. nördlichen Teil des Staates, in od. aus der od. in die Pro'vinz.

,up'stream I adv. strom'aufwärts; **2.** gegen den Strom; II adj. **3.** strom'aufwärts gerichtet; **4.** (weiter) strom'aufwärts gelegen.

'up·stroke s. **1.** Aufstrich m beim Schreiben; **2.** ☉ (Aufwärts)Hub m.

up'surge I v/i. aufwallen; II s. 'upsurge Aufwallung f; fig. a. Aufschwung m.

'up·sweep s. **1.** Schweifung f (Bogen etc.); **2.** 'Hochfri,sur f; up'swept adj. **1.** nach oben gebogen od. gekrümmt; **2.** hochgekämmt (Frisur).

'up·swing s. fig. Aufschwung m.

up·sy-dai·sy [,ʌpsɪ'deɪzɪ] int. F hoppla!

'up·take s. **1.** Auffassungsvermögen n: **be quick on the** ~ schnell begreifen, ‚schnell schalten'; **be slow on the** ~ schwer von Begriff sein, e-e ,lange Leitung' haben; **2.** Aufnahme f; **3.** ☉ a) Steigrohr n, -leitung f, b) 'Fuchs(ka,nal) m.

'up·throw s. **1.** 'Umwälzung f; **2.** geol. Verwerfung f (ins Hangende).

'up·thrust s. **1.** Em'porschleudern n, Stoß m nach oben; **2.** geol. Horstbildung f.

'up·tight adj. **1.** sl. ner'vös (about wegen); **2.** ‚zickig'; **3.** steif, verklemmt; **4.** ‚pleite'.

,up-to-'date adj. **1.** a) mo'dern, neuzeitlich, b) zeitnah, aktu'ell (Thema etc.); **2.** a) auf der Höhe (der Zeit), auf dem Laufenden, auf dem neuesten Stand, b) modisch; ,up-to-'date·ness [-nɪs] s. **1.** Neuzeitlichkeit f, Moderni'tät f; **2.** Aktuali'tät f.

,up-to-the-'min·ute adj. allerneuest, allerletzt.

up'town I adv. **1.** im od. in den oberen Stadtteil; **2.** in den Wohnvierteln, in die Wohnviertel; II adj. **3.** im oberen Stadtteil (gelegen); **4.** in den Wohnvierteln (gelegen od. lebend).

'up·trend s. Aufschwung m, steigende Ten'denz.

up'turn I v/t. **1.** 'umdrehen; **2.** (v/i. sich) nach oben richten od. kehren; Blick in die Höhe richten; II s. 'upturn **3.** (An-) Steigen n (der Kurse etc.); **4.** fig. Aufschwung m; ,up'turned adj. **1.** nach oben gerichtet od. gebogen: ~ **nose** Stupsnase f; **2.** 'umgeworfen, 'umgekippt, ⚓ gekentert.

up·ward ['ʌpwəd] I adv. a. 'up·wards [-dz] **1.** aufwärts (a. fig.): **from five dollars** ~ von 5 Dollar an (aufwärts); **2.** nach oben (a. fig.); **3.** mehr, dar'über (hin'aus): ~ **of 10 years** mehr als od. über 10 Jahre; II adj. **4.** nach oben gerichtet; (an)steigend (Tendenz etc.): ~ **glance** Blick m nach oben; ~ **movement** ✈ Aufwärtsbewegung f.

u·rae·mi·a [,jʊə'riːmjə] s. ☟ Urä'mie f; u·ra·nal·y·sis [,jʊərɪ'næləsɪs] s. ☟ U'rin-, 'Harnunter,suchung f.

u·ra·nite ['jʊərənaɪt] s. min. Ura'nit n, U'ranglimmer m.

u·ra·ni·um [jʊ'reɪnjəm] s. U'ran n.

u·ra·nog·ra·phy [,jʊərə'nɒgrəfɪ] s. Himmelsbeschreibung f.

u·ra·nous ['jʊərənəs] adj. 🜍 Uran..., u'ranhaltig.

U·ra·nus ['jʊərənəs] s. ast. Uranus m (Planet).

ur·ban ['ɜːbən] adj. städtisch, Stadt...: ~ **decay** Verslummung f; ~ **district** Stadtbezirk m; ~ **guerilla** Stadtguerilla m; ~ **planning** Stadtplanung f; ~ **renewal** Stadtsanierung f; ~ **sprawl**, ~ **spread** unkontrollierte Ausdehnung e-r Stadt; ur·bane [ɜː'beɪn] adj. □ **1.** ur'ban: a) weltgewandt, -männisch, b) kulti'viert, gebildet, **2.** höflich, liebenswürdig; ur·ban·e·ness [ɜː'beɪnɪs] s. **1.** (Welt)Gewandtheit f; Bildung f; **2.** Höflichkeit f, Liebenswürdigkeit f; 'ur·ban·ism [-nɪzəm] s. Am. **1.** Stadtleben n; **2.** Urba'nistik f; **3.** → urbanization; 'ur·ban·ite [-naɪt] s. Am. Städter(in); ur·ban·i·ty [ɜː'bænətɪ] → urbane-

ness; ur·ban·i·za·tion [,ɜːbənaɪ'zeɪʃn] s. **1.** Verstädterung f; **2.** Verfeinerung f; 'ur·ban·ize [-naɪz] v/t. urbanisieren: a) verstädtern, städtischen Cha'rakter verleihen (dat.), b) verfeinern.

ur·chin ['ɜːtʃɪn] s. **1.** Bengel m, Balg m, n; **2.** zo. a) dial. Igel m, b) mst **sea** ~ Seeigel m.

u·re·a ['jʊərɪə] s. 🜍, biol. Harnstoff m, Karba'mid n; 'ure·al [-əl] adj. Harnstoff...

u·re·mi·a → uraemia.

u·re·ter [jʊə'riːtə] s. anat. Harnleiter m; ,u're·thra [-'riːθrə] s. anat. Harnröhre f; ,u'ret·ic [-'retɪk] adj. physiol. **1.** harntreibend, diu'retisch; **2.** Harn...

urge [ɜːdʒ] I v/t. **1.** a. ~ **on** (od. **forward**) antreiben, (vorwärts) treiben, ansporen (a. fig.); **2.** fig. j-n drängen, dringend bitten od. auffordern, dringen in j-n, j-m (heftig) zusetzen: **be** ~**d to do** sich genötigt sehen zu tun; ~**d by necessity** der Not gehorchend; **3.** drängen od. dringen auf (acc.); (hartnäckig) bestehen auf (dat.); Nachdruck legen auf (acc.): ~ **s.th. on s.o.** j-m et. eindringlich vorstellen od. vor Augen führen, j-m et. einschärfen; **he** ~**d the necessity for immediate action** er drängte auf sofortige Maßnahmen; **4.** als Grund geltend machen, Einwand etc. ins Feld führen; **5.** Sache vor'an-, betreiben, beschleunigen; II v/i. **6.** drängen: ~ **against** sich nachdrücklich aussprechen gegen; III s. **7.** Drang m, (An)Trieb m: **creative** ~ Schaffensdrang; **sexual** ~ Geschlechtstrieb; **8.** Inbrunst f: **religious** ~; 'ur·gen·cy [-dʒənsɪ] s. **1.** Dringlichkeit f; **2.** (dringende) Not, Druck m; **3.** Drängen n; **4.** parl. Brit. Dringlichkeitsantrag m; **5.** Eindringlichkeit f; 'ur·gent [-dʒənt] adj. □ **1.** dringend (a. Mangel; a. teleph. Gespräch), dringlich, eilig: **the matter is** ~ die Sache eilt; **be in** ~ **need of** et. dringend brauchen; **2.** drängend: **be** ~ **about** (od. **for**) **s.th.** zu et. drängen, auf et. dringen; **be** ~ **with s.o.** j-n drängen, in j-n dringen (for wegen, to do zu tun); **3.** zu-, aufdringlich; **4.** hartnäckig.

u·ric ['jʊərɪk] adj. Urin..., Harn...: ~ **acid** Harnsäure f.

u·ri·nal ['jʊərɪnl] s. **1.** U'rinflasche f (für Kranke); **2.** Harnglas n; **3.** a) U'rinbecken n (in Toiletten), b) Pis'soir n; u·ri·nal·y·sis [,jʊərɪ'næləsɪs] pl. -ses [-siːz] → uranalysis; u·ri·nar·y ['jʊərɪnərɪ] adj. Harn..., Urin...: ~ **bladder** Harnblase f; ~ **calculus** ☟ Blasenstein m; u·ri·nate ['jʊərɪneɪt] v/i. urinieren; u·rine ['jʊərɪn] s. U'rin m, Harn m: ~ **sample** (od. **specimen**) ☟ U'rinprobe f.

urn [ɜːn] s. **1.** Urne f; **2.** 'Tee- od. 'Kaffeema,schine f.

u·ro·gen·i·tal [,jʊərəʊ'dʒenɪtl] adj. ☟ urogeni'tal.

u·rol·o·gy [jʊə'rɒlədʒɪ] s. ☟ Urolo'gie f.

ur·sine ['ɜːsaɪn] adj. zo. bärenartig, Bären...

U·ru·guay·an [,jʊərə'gwaɪən] I adj. uruguay'aisch; II s. Urugu'ayer(in).

us [ʌs; əs] pron. **1.** uns (dat. od. acc.): **all of** ~ wir alle; **both of** ~ wir beide; **2.** dial. wir: ~ **poor people**.

us·a·ble ['juːzəbl] adj. brauch-, verwendbar.

us·age ['juːsɪdʒ] s. **1.** Brauch m, Gepflogenheit f, Usus m: (**commercial**) ~ Handelsbrauch, Usance f; **2.** übliches Verfahren, Praxis f; **3.** Sprachgebrauch m: **English** ~; **4.** Gebrauch m, Verwendung f; **5.** Behandlung(sweise) f.

us·ance ['juːzns] s. ✝ **1.** (übliche) Wechselfrist, Uso m: **at ~** nach Uso; **bill at ~** Usowechsel m; **2.** Uso m, U'sance f, Handelsbrauch m.

use I s. [juːs] **1.** Gebrauch m, Benutzung f, Benützung f, An-, Verwendung f: **for ~** zum Gebrauch; **for ~ in schools** für den Schulgebrauch; **directions for ~** Gebrauchsanweisung f; **in ~** in Gebrauch, gebräuchlich; **be in daily ~** täglich gebraucht werden; **in common ~** allgemein gebräuchlich; **come into ~** in Gebrauch kommen; **out of ~** nicht in Gebrauch; **fall** (od. **go** od. **pass**) **out of ~** außer Gebrauch kommen, ungebräuchlich werden; **with ~** durch (ständigen) Gebrauch; **make ~ of** Gebrauch machen von, benutzen; **make** (**a**) **bad ~ of** (e-n) schlechten Gebrauch machen von; **2.** a) Verwendung(szweck m) f, b) Brauchbarkeit f, Verwendbarkeit f, c) Zweck m, Sinn m, Nutzen m, Nützlichkeit f: **of ~** (**to**) brauchbar (für), nützlich (dat.), von Nutzen (für); **it is of no ~ doing od. to do** es ist unnütz od. nutz- od. zwecklos zu tun, es hat keinen Zweck zu tun; **is this of ~ to you?** können Sie das (ge-) brauchen?; **crying is no ~** Weinen führt zu nichts; **what is the ~ (of it)?** was hat es (überhaupt) für einen Zweck?; **put to** (**good**) **~** (gut) an- od. verwenden; **have no ~ for** a) nicht brauchen können, mit et. od. j-m nichts anfangen können, b) bsd. Am. F nichts übrig haben für; **3.** Fähigkeit f, et. zu gebrauchen, Gebrauch m: **he lost the ~ of his right eye** er kann auf dem rechten Auge nicht mehr sehen; **have the ~ of one's limbs** sich bewegen können; **4.** Gewohnheit f, Brauch m, Übung f, Praxis f: **once a ~ and ever a custom** jung gewohnt, alt getan; **5.** Benutzungsrecht n; **6.** ✝✝ a) Nutznießung f, b) Nutzen m; II v/t. [juːz] **7.** gebrauchen, Gebrauch machen von (a. von e-m Recht etc.), benutzen, benützen, a. Gewalt anwenden, a. Sorgfalt verwenden, sich bedienen (gen.), Gelegenheit etc. nutzen, sich zu'nutze machen: **~ one's brains** den Verstand gebrauchen, s-n Kopf anstrengen; **~ one's legs** zu Fuß gehen; **8. ~ up** a) et. auf-, verbrauchen, b) F j-n erschöpfen, ‚fertig machen'; → **used** 2; **9.** behandeln, verfahren mit: **~ s.o. ill** j-n schlecht behandeln; **how has the world ~d you?** wie ist es dir ergangen?; III v/i. **10.** nur pret. [juːst] pflegte (**to do** zu tun): **it ~d to be said** man pflegte zu sagen; **he ~d to live here** er wohnte früher hier; **he does not come as often as he ~d** (**to**) er kommt nicht mehr so oft wie früher od. sonst; **use·a·ble** ['juːzəbl] → **usable**; **used** [juːzd] adj. **1.** gebraucht, getragen (Kleidung): **~ car** mot. Gebrauchtwagen m; **2. ~ up** a) aufgebraucht, verbraucht (a. Luft), b) F ‚erledigt', ‚fertig', erschöpft; **3.** [juːst] a) gewohnt (**to** zu od. acc.), b) gewöhnt (**to an** acc.): **he is ~ to working late** er ist gewohnt, lange zu arbeiten; **get ~ to** sich gewöhnen an (acc.); **use·ful** ['juːsfʊl] adj. □ **1.** nützlich, brauchbar, (zweck)dienlich, (gut) verwendbar: **~ tools**; **a ~ man** ein brauchbarer Mann; **~ talks** nützliche Gespräche; **make o.s. ~** sich nützlich machen; **2.** bsd. ⊗ nutzbar, Nutz...: **~ ef-**

ficiency Nutzleistung f; **~ life** (**expectancy**) gewöhnliche Nutzungsdauer; **~ load** Nutzlast f; **~ plant** Nutzpflanze f; **use·less** ['juːslɪs] adj. □ **1.** nutz-, sinn-, zwecklos, unnütz, vergeblich: **it is ~ to** es erübrigt sich zu; **2.** unbrauchbar; **'use·less·ness** [-lɪsnɪs] s. Nutz-, Zwecklosigkeit f, Unbrauchbarkeit f; **us·er** ['juːzə] s. **1.** Benutzer(in), Computer, Software: User m, Anwender m: **~-defined** be'nutzerdefi,niert; **~ friendliness** Be'nutzerfreundlichkeit f; **~-friendly** benutzerfreundlich, anwenderfreundlich; **~ interface** Be'nutzer,oberfläche f; **~ program** Computer: Anwenderprogramm n; **~ prompting** Computer: Benutzerführung f; **2.** ✝ Verbraucher(in); **3.** ✝✝ Nießbrauch m, Benutzungsrecht n.

'U-shaped adj. U-förmig: **~ iron** ⊗ U-Eisen n.

ush·er ['ʌʃə] I s. **1.** Türhüter m; **2.** Platzanweiser(in); **3.** a) ✝✝ Gerichtsdiener m, b) allg. 'Aufsichtsper,son f; **4.** Zere'monienmeister m; **5.** Brit. obs. Hilfslehrer m; II v/t. **6.** (mst **~ in**) her'ein-, hin'ein)führen, (-)geleiten; **7. ~ in** a. fig. ankündigen, e-e Epoche etc. einleiten; **ush·er·ette** [,ʌʃə'ret] s. Platzanweiserin f.

u·su·al ['juːʒʊəl] adj. □ üblich, gewöhnlich, gebräuchlich: **as ~** wie gewöhnlich, wie sonst; **the ~ thing** das Übliche; **it has become the ~ thing** (**with us**) es ist (bei uns) gang u. gäbe geworden; **it is ~ for shops to close at 6 o'clock** die Geschäfte schließen gewöhnlich um 6 Uhr; **the ~ pride with her** ihr üblicher Stolz; **'u·su·al·ly** [-əlɪ] adv. (für) gewöhnlich, in der Regel, meist(ens).

u·su·fruct ['juːsjuːfrʌkt] s. ✝✝ Nießbrauch m, Nutznießung f; **u·su·fruc·tu·ar·y** [,juːsjuː'frʌktjʊərɪ] I s. Nießbraucher(in); II adj. Nutzungs...: **~ right**.

u·su·rer ['juːʒərə] s. Wucherer m; **u·su·ri·ous** [juː'zjʊərɪəs] adj. □ wucherisch, Wucher...: **~ interest → usury** (**2**); **u·su·ri·ous·ness** [juː'zjʊərɪəsnɪs] s. Wuche'rei f.

u·surp [juː'zɜːp] v/t. **1.** an sich reißen, sich 'widerrechtlich aneignen, sich bemächtigen (gen.); **2.** sich ('widerrechtlich) anmaßen; **3.** Aufmerksamkeit etc. mit Beschlag belegen; **u·sur·pa·tion** [,juːzɜː'peɪʃn] s. **1.** Usurpati'on f: a) 'widerrechtliche Machtergreifung od. An-eignung, Anmaßung f e-s Rechts etc., b) **~ of the throne** Thronraub m; **2.** unberechtigter Eingriff (**on** in acc.); **u'surp·er** [-pə] s. **1.** Usur'pator m, unrechtmäßiger Machthaber, Thronräuber m; **2.** unberechtigter Besitzergreifer; **3.** Eindringling m (**on** in acc.); **u'surp·ing** [-pɪŋ] adj. □ usurpa'torisch.

u·su·ry ['juːʒʊrɪ] s. **1.** (Zins)Wucher m: **practise ~** Wucher treiben; **2.** Wucherzinsen pl. (**at** auf acc.): **return s.th. with ~** fig. et. mit Zins u. Zinseszins heimzahlen.

u·ten·sil [juː'tensl] s. **1.** (a. Schreib- etc.) Gerät n, Werkzeug n; Gebrauchs-, Haushaltsgegenstand m: (**kitchen**) **~** Küchengerät n; **2.** Geschirr n, Gefäß n; **3.** pl. Uten'silien pl., Geräte pl.; (Küchen)Geschirr n.

u·ter·ine ['juːtəraɪn] adj. **1.** anat. Gebärmutter..., Uterus...; **2.** von der'selben Mutter stammend: **~ brother** Halbbruder mütterlicherseits; **u·ter·us** ['juːtərəs] pl. **-ter·i** [-tərai] s. anat. Uterus m, Gebärmutter f.

u·til·i·tar·i·an [,juːtɪlɪ'teərɪən] I adj. **1.** utilita'ristisch, Nützlichkeits...; **2.** praktisch, zweckmäßig; **3.** contp. gemein; II s. **4.** Utilita'rist(in); **u·til·i'tar·i·an·ism** [-nɪzəm] s. Utilita'rismus m.

u·til·i·ty [juː'tɪlətɪ] I s. **1.** a. ✝ Nutzen m (**to** für), Nützlichkeit f; **2.** et. Nützliches, nützliche Einrichtung; **3.** a) a. **public ~** (**company** od. **corporation**) öffentlicher Versorgungsbetrieb, pl. a. Stadtwerke pl., b) pl. Leistungen pl. der öffentlichen Versorgungsbetriebe, bsd. Strom-, Gas- u. Wasserversorgung f; **4.** ⊗ Zusatzgerät n; II adj. **5.** ✝, ⊗ Gebrauchs...(-güter, -möbel, -wagen etc.); **6.** Mehrzweck...; **~ man** s. [irr.] **1.** bsd. Am. Fak'totum n; **2.** thea. vielseitig einsetzbarer Chargenspieler.

u·til·iz·a·ble ['juːtɪlaɪzəbl] adj. verwendbar, verwertbar, nutzbar; **u·til·i·za·tion** [,juːtɪlaɪ'zeɪʃn] s. Nutzbarmachung f, Verwertung f, (Aus)Nutzung f, An-, Verwendung f; **u·ti·lize** ['juːtɪlaɪz] v/t. **1.** (aus)nutzen, verwerten, sich et. nutzbar od. zu'nutze machen; **2.** verwenden.

ut·most ['ʌtməʊst] I adj. äußerst: a) entlegenst, fernst, b) fig. höchst, größt; II s. das Äußerste: **the ~ that I can do**; **do one's ~** sein Äußerstes od. Möglichstes tun; **at the ~** allerhöchstens; **to the ~** aufs Äußerste; **to the ~ of my powers** nach besten Kräften.

U·to·pi·a [juː'təʊpjə] s. **1.** U'topia n (Idealstaat); **2.** oft ⚨ fig. Uto'pie f; **U'to·pi·an** [-jən], a. ⚨ I adj. u'topisch, fan'tastisch; II s. Uto'pist(in), Fan'tast (-in); **U'to·pi·an·ism** [-jənɪzəm], a. ⚨ s. Uto'pismus m; **U'to·pi·an·ist** [-jənɪst] s. Utopist m.

u·tri·cle ['juːtrɪkl] s. **1.** zo., ♀ Schlauch m, bläs-chenförmiges Luft- od. Saftgefäß; **2.** ⚕ U'triculus m (Säckchen im Ohrlabyrinth).

ut·ter ['ʌtə] I adj. □ → **utterly**; **1.** äußerst, höchst, völlig; **2.** endgültig, entschieden: **~ denial**; **3.** contp. ausgesprochen, voll'endet (Schurke, Unsinn etc.); II v/t. **4.** Gedanken, Gefühle äußern, ausdrücken, aussprechen; **5.** Laute etc. ausstoßen, von sich geben, hervorbringen; **6.** Falschgeld etc. in 'Umlauf setzen, verbreiten; **ut·ter·ance** ['ʌtərəns] s. **1.** (stimmlicher) Ausdruck, Äußerung f: **give ~ to** e-m Gefühl etc. Ausdruck verleihen; **2.** Sprechweise f, Aussprache f, Vortrag m; **3.** a. pl. Äußerung f, Aussage f, Worte pl.; **'ut·ter·er** [-ərə] s. **1.** Äußernde(r m) f; **2.** Verbreiter(in); **'ut·ter·ly** [-lɪ] adv. äußerst, abso'lut, völlig, ganz, to'tal; **'ut·ter·most** [-məʊst] → **utmost**.

'U-turn s. **1.** mot. Wende f; **2.** fig. Kehrtwende f.

u·vu·la ['juːvjʊlə] pl. **-lae** [-liː] s. anat. Zäpfchen n; **'u·vu·lar** [-lə] I adj. Zäpfchen..., ling. a. uvu'lar; II s. ling. Zäpfchenlaut m, Uvu'lar m.

ux·o·ri·ous [ʌk'sɔːrɪəs] adj. □ treu liebend od. ergeben; **ux'o·ri·ous·ness** [-nɪs] s. treue Ergebenheit (des Gatten).

U

V, v [viː] s. V n, v n (*Buchstabe*).
vac [væk] *Brit.* F *für* **vacation.**
va·can·cy ['veɪkənsɪ] s. **1.** Leere f (a. *fig.*): *stare into* ~ ins Leere starren; **2.** leerer od. freier Platz; Lücke f (a. *fig.*); **3.** leeres od. leer stehendes od. unbewohntes Haus; **4.** freie od. offene Stelle, unbesetztes Amt, Va'kanz f; *univ.* freier Studienplatz m; pl. *Zeitung*: Stellenangebote pl.; **5.** a) Geistesabwesenheit f, b) geistige Leere, c) Geistlosigkeit f; **6.** Untätigkeit f, Muße f; **'va·cant** [-nt] adj. □ **1.** leer, frei, unbesetzt (*Sitz, Zimmer, Zeit etc.*); **2.** leer (stehend), unbewohnt, unvermietet (*Haus*): unbebaut (*Grundstück*): ~ *possession* sofort beziehbar; **3.** frei, offen (*Stelle*), va'kant, unbesetzt (*Amt*); **4.** a) geistesabwesend, b) leer: ~ *mind*; ~ *stare*, va'kant, unbesetzt.
va·cate [və'keɪt] v/t. **1.** Wohnung etc., ✕ *Stellung etc.* räumen; *Sitz etc.* freimachen; **2.** *Stelle* aufgeben, aus e-m Amt scheiden: *be* ~*d* frei werden (*Stelle*); **3.** *Truppen etc.* evakuieren; **4.** ✭ *Vertrag, Urteil etc.* aufheben; **va'ca·tion** [-eɪʃn] I s. **1.** Räumung f; **2.** Niederlegung f od. Erledigung f e-s Amtes; **3.** (Gerichts-, *univ.* Se'mester-, *Am.* Schul)Ferien pl.: *the long* ~ die großen Ferien, die Sommerferien; **4.** bsd. Am. Urlaub m: *on* ~ *im od. in Urlaub; ~shut-down* Betriebsferien pl.; II v/i. **5.** bsd. Am. in Ferien sein, Urlaub machen; **va'ca·tion·ist** [-eɪʃnɪst] s. Am. Urlauber(in).
vac·ci·nal ['væksɪnl] adj. ⚕ Impf...; **vac·ci·nate** ['væksɪneɪt] v/t. u. v/i. impfen (*against* gegen); **vac·ci·na·tion** [ˌvæksɪ'neɪʃn] s. (Schutz)Impfung f; **'vac·ci·na·tor** [-neɪtə] s. **1.** Impfarzt m; **2.** Impfnadel f; **'vac·cine** [-siːn] ⚕ I adj. Impf..., Kuhpocken...: ~ *matter* → II; II s. Impfstoff m, Vak'zine f; ~ *bovine* ~ Kuhlymphe f; **vac·cin·i·a** [væk'sɪnɪə] s. ⚕ Kuhpocken pl.
vac·il·late ['væsɪleɪt] v/i. mst fig. schwanken; **'vac·il·lat·ing** [-tɪŋ] adj. □ schwankend (*mst fig. unschlüssig*); **vac·il·la·tion** [ˌvæsɪ'leɪʃn] s. Schwanken n (*mst fig. Unschlüssigkeit, Wankelmut*).
va·cu·i·ty [væ'kjuːətɪ] s. **1.** → **vacancy** 1, 5; **2.** fig. Nichtigkeit f, Plattheit f; **vac·u·ous** ['vækjʊəs] adj. □ **1.** → *vacant* 4; **2.** nichts sagend (*Redensart*); **3.** müßig (*Leben*); **vac·u·um** ['vækjʊəm] I pl. **-ums** [-z] s. **1.** ❂, phys. Vakuum n, (bsd. luft)leerer Raum; **2.** fig. Vakuum n, Leere f, Lücke f; II adj. **3.** Vakuum...: ~ *bottle* (od. *flask*) Thermosflasche f; ~ *brake* ⊖ Unterdruckbremse f; ~ *can*, ~ *tin* Vakuumdose f; ~ *cleaner* Staubsauger m; ~ *drier* Vakuumtrockner m; ~ *ga(u)ge* Unterdruckmesser m; ~*packed* vakuumverpackt; ~*-sealed* vakuumdicht; ~ *tube*, ~ *valve* ⚡ Vakuumröhre f; III v/t. **4.** (mit dem Staubsauger) saugen od. reinigen.

va·de me·cum [ˌveɪdɪ'miːkəm] s. Vade-'mekum n, Handbuch n.
vag·a·bond ['vægəbɒnd] I adj. **1.** vagabundierend (a. ♫); **2.** Vagabunden..., vaga'bundenhaft; **3.** nomadisierend; **4.** Wander..., unstet: *a* ~ *life*; II s. **5.** Vaga'bund(in), Landstreicher(in); **6.** F Strolch m; III v/i. **7.** vagabundieren; **'vag·a·bond·age** [-dɪdʒ] s. **1.** Landstreiche'rei f, Vaga'bundenleben n; **2.** coll. Vaga'bunden pl.; **'vag·a·bond·ism** [-dɪzəm] → **vagabondage** 1; **'vag·a·bond·ize** [-daɪz] → **vagabond** 7.
va·gar·y ['veɪɡərɪ] s. **1.** wunderlicher Einfall; pl. a. Fantaste'reien pl.; **2.** Ka'price f, Grille f, Laune f; **3.** mst pl. Extrava'ganzen pl.: *the vagaries of fashion*.
va·gi·na [və'dʒaɪnə] pl. **-nas** s. **1.** anat. Va'gina f, Scheide f; **2.** ♀ Blattscheide f; **vag·i·nal** [-nl] adj. vagi'nal, Vagi'nal..., Scheiden...: ~ *spray* Intimspray n.
va·gran·cy ['veɪɡrənsɪ] s. **1.** Landstreiche'rei f (a. ✭); **2.** coll. Landstreicher pl.; **'va·grant** [-nt] I adj. □ **1.** wandernd (a. weitS. Zelle etc.), vagabundierend; **2.** → **vagabond** 3 u. 4; **3.** fig. kapri'ziös, launisch; II s. **4.** → **vagabond** 5.
vague [veɪɡ] adj. □ **1.** vage: a) undeutlich, nebelhaft, verschwommen (alle a. fig.), b) unbestimmt (*Gefühl, Verdacht, Versprechen etc.*), dunkel (*Ahnung, Gerücht etc.*), c) unklar (*Antwort etc.*): ~ *hope* vage Hoffnung; *not the* ~*st idea* nicht die leiseste Ahnung; *be* ~ *about s.th.* sich unklar ausdrücken über (acc.); **2.** → *vacant* 4a; **'vague·ness** [-nɪs] s. Unbestimmtheit f, Verschwommenheit f.
vain [veɪn] adj. □ **1.** eitel, eingebildet (*of* auf acc.); **2.** fig. eitel, leer (*Vergnügen etc.*; a. Drohung, Hoffnung etc.), nichtig; **3.** vergeblich, fruchtlos: ~ *efforts*; **4.** *in* ~ vergeblich: a) vergebens, um'sonst, b) unnütz; **~'glo·ri·ous** adj. □ prahlerisch, großsprecherisch, -spurig.
vain·ness ['veɪnnɪs] s. **1.** Vergeblichkeit f; **2.** Hohl-, Leerheit f.
vale[1] [veɪl] s. poet. od. in Namen: Tal n: ~ *of tears* Jammertal n.
va·le[2] ['veɪlɪ] (*Lat.*) I int. lebe wohl!; II s. Lebe'wohl n.
val·e·dic·tion [ˌvælɪ'dɪkʃn] s. **1.** Abschied(nehmen n) m; **2.** Abschiedsworte pl.; **val·e·dic·to·ri·an** [ˌvælɪdɪk'tɔːrɪən] s. Am. ped., univ. Abschiedsredner m; **val·e·dic·to·ry** [-ktərɪ] Am. I adj. Abschieds...: ~ *address* → II; II s. bsd. Am. ped., univ. Abschiedsrede f.
va·lence ['veɪləns], **'va·len·cy** [-sɪ] ♫, ✭, biol., phys. Wertigkeit f, Va'lenz f.
val·en·tine ['væləntaɪn] s. **1.** Valentinsgruß m (*zum Valentinstag, 14. Februar, dem od. der Liebsten gesandt*); **2.** am Valentinstag erwählte(r) Liebste(r), a. allg. Schatz m.

va·le·ri·an [və'lɪərɪən] s. ♣, pharm. Baldrian m; **va·le·ri·an·ic** [və'lɪərɪ'ænɪk], **va'ler·ic** [-'lerɪk] adj. ♣ Baldrian..., Valerian...
val·et ['vælɪt] I s. a) (Kammer)Diener m, b) Hausdiener m im Hotel: ~ *parking* 'Parkservice m (*durch Hotelangestellte*); II v/t. j-n bedienen, versorgen; III v/i. Diener sein.
val·e·tu·di·nar·i·an [ˌvælɪtjuːdɪ'neərɪən] I adj. **1.** kränklich, kränkelnd; **2.** rekonvales'zent; **3.** a) ge'sundheitsfa,natisch, b) hypo'chondrisch; II s. **4.** kränkliche Per'son; **5.** Rekonvales-'zent(in); **6.** ,Ge'sundheitsa,postel' m; **7.** Hypo'chonder m; **val·e·tu·di·nar·i·an·ism** [-nɪzəm] s. **1.** Kränklichkeit f; **2.** Hypochon'drie f; **val·e·tu·di·nar·y** [-nərɪ] → **valetudinarian**.
Val·hal·la [væl'hælə], **Val'hall** [-'hæl] s. myth. Wal'halla f.
val·iant ['væljənt] adj. □ tapfer, mutig, heldenhaft, he'roisch.
val·id ['vælɪd] adj. □ **1.** gültig: a) stichhaltig, triftig (*Beweis, Grund*), b) begründet, berechtigt (*Anspruch, Argument etc.*), c) richtig (*Entscheidung etc.*); **2.** ✭ (rechts)gültig, rechtskräftig; **3.** wirksam (*Methode etc.*); **'val·i·date** [-deɪt] v/t. ✭ a) für (rechts)gültig erklären, rechtswirksam machen, b) bestätigen; **val·i·da·tion** [ˌvælɪ'deɪʃn] s. Gültigkeit(serklärung) f; **va·lid·i·ty** [və'lɪdətɪ] s. **1.** Gültigkeit f: a) Triftigkeit f, Stichhaltigkeit f, b) Richtigkeit f; **2.** ✭ Rechtsgültigkeit f, -kraft f; **3.** Gültigkeit(sdauer) f.
va·lise [və'liːz] s. Reisetasche f.
Val·kyr ['vælkɪə], **Val·kyr·i·a** [væl'kɪərjə], **Val·kyr·ie** [-'kɪərɪ] s. myth. Walküre f.
val·ley ['vælɪ] s. **1.** Tal n: *down the* ~ talabwärts; **2.** △ Dachkehle f.
val·or Am. → **valour.**
val·or·i·za·tion [ˌvælɔːraɪ'zeɪʃn] s. ✭ Valorisati'on f, Aufwertung f; **val·or·ize** ['vælɔːraɪz] v/t. ✭ valorisieren, aufwerten, den Preis e-r Ware heben od. stützen.
val·or·ous ['vælərəs] adj. □ rhet. tapfer, mutig, heldenhaft, -mütig; **val·our** ['vælə] s. Tapferkeit f, Heldenmut m.
val·u·a·ble ['væljʊəbl] I adj. □ **1.** wertvoll: a) kostbar, teuer, b) fig. nützlich: *for* ~ *consideration* ✭ entgeltlich; **2.** abschätzbar; II s. **3.** pl. Wertsachen pl., -gegenstände pl.
val·u·a·tion [ˌvælju'eɪʃn] s. **1.** Bewertung f, (Ab)Schätzung f, Wertbestimmung f, Taxierung f, Veranschlagung f; **2.** a) Schätzungswert m (festgesetzter) Wert od. Preis, Taxe f, b) Gegenwartswert m e-r 'Lebensver,sicherungspo,li,ce; **3.** Wertschätzung f, Würdigung f: *we take him at his own* ~ wir beurteilen ihn so, wie er sich selbst sieht; **val·u·a·tor** ['væljʊeɪtə] s. ✭ (Ab)Schätzer m, Ta'xator m.
val·ue ['væljuː] I s. **1.** allg. Wert m (a.

Å, ♏, *phys. u. fig.*): **moral** ⁓**s** *fig.* sittliche Werte; **be of** ⁓ **to** *j-m* wertvoll *od.* nützlich sein; **2.** Wert *m*, Einschätzung *f*: **set a high** ⁓ (**up**)**on** a) großen Wert legen auf (*acc.*), b) *et.* hoch einschätzen; **3.** ♱ Wert *m*: **assessed** ⁓ Taxwert; ⁓ **added** Wertschöpfung *f*; **at** ⁓ zum Tageskurs; **book** ⁓ Buchwert; **commercial** ⁓ Handelswert; **4.** ♱ a) (Verkehrs)Wert *m*, Kaufkraft *f*, Preis *m*, b) Gegenwert *m*, -leistung *f*, c) Währung *f*, Va'luta *f*, d) *a.* **good** ⁓ re'elle Ware, Quali'tätsware *f*, e) → **valuation** 1 *u.* 2, f) Wert *m*, Preis *m*, Betrag *m*: ⁓ **date** Wertstellung *f*; **for** ⁓ **received** Betrag erhalten; **to the** ⁓ **of** im *od.* bis zum Betrag von; **give** (**get**) **good** ⁓ (**for one's money**) reell bedienen (bedient werden); **it is excellent** ⁓ **for money** es ist äußerst preiswert, es ist ausgezeichnet; **5.** *fig.* Wert *m*, Gewicht *n e-s Wortes etc.*; **6.** *paint.* Verhältnis *n* von Licht u. Schatten, Farb-, Grauwert *m*; **7.** ♪ Noten-, Zeitwert *m*; **8.** *ling.* Lautwert *m*; **II** *v/t.* **9.** a) den Wert *od.* Preis *e-r Sache* bestimmen *od.* festsetzen, b) (ab-)schätzen, veranschlagen, taxieren (**at** auf *acc.*); **10.** ♱ Wechsel ziehen ([*up*]*on* auf *j-n*); **11.** *Wert, Nutzen, Bedeutung* schätzen, (*vergleichend*) bewerten; **12.** (hoch) schätzen, achten; ‚⁓-'**add·ed tax** *s.* ♱ Mehrwertsteuer *f*.

val·ued ['vælju:d] *adj.* **1.** (hoch) geschätzt; **2.** taxiert, veranschlagt (**at** auf *acc.*): ⁓ **at £100** £100 wert.

'**val·ue**|**-free** *adj.* wertfrei; ⁓ **judg(e)·ment** *s.* Werturteil *n*. **val·ue·less** ['væljuls] *adj.* wertlos; '**val·u·er** [-juə] → **valuator**.

val·ue stress *s. Phonetik*: Sinnbetonung *f*.

va·lu·ta [və'lu:tə] (*Ital.*) *s.* ♱ Va'luta *f*.

valve [vælv] *s.* **1.** ⊙ Ven'til *n*, Absperrvorrichtung *f*, Klappe *f*, Hahn *m*, Regu'lieror‚gan *n*: ⁓ **gear** Ventilsteuerung *f*; ⁓**-in-head engine** kopfgesteuerter Motor; **2.** ♪ Klappe *f* (*Blasinstrument*); **3.** ♣ (*Herz- etc.*)Klappe *f*; **cardiac** ⁓; **4.** *zo.* (Muschel)Klappe *f*; **5.** ♀ a) Klappe *f*, b) Kammer *f* (*beide e-r Fruchtkapsel*); **6.** ♭ *Brit.* (Elek'tronen-, Fernseh-, Radio)Röhre *f*: ⁓ **amplifier** Röhrenverstärker *m*; **7.** ⊙ Schleusentor *n*; **8.** *obs.* Türflügel *m*; '**valve·less** [-lɪs] *adj.* ven'tillos; '**val·vu·lar** [-vjulə] *adj.* **1.** klappenförmig, Klappen...: ⁓ **defect** ♣ Klappenfehler *m*; **2.** mit Klappe(n) *od.* Ven'til(en) (versehen); **3.** ♣ klappig; '**val·vule** [-vju:l] *s.* kleine Klappe; **val·vu·li·tis** [‚vælvju'laɪtɪs] *s.* ♣ (Herz-) Klappenentzündung *f*.

va·moose [və'mu:s], **va'mose** [-'məʊs] *Am. sl.* **I** *v/i.* ‚verduften', ‚Leine ziehen'; **II** *v/t.* fluchtartig verlassen.

vamp¹ [væmp] **I** *s.* **1.** a) Oberleder *n*, b) (Vorder)Klappe *f* (*Schuh*), c) (aufgesetzter) Flicken; **2.** ♪ (improvisierte) Begleitung; **3.** *fig.* Flickwerk *n*; **II** *v/t.* **4.** *mst* ⁓ **up** a) flicken, reparieren, b) vorschuhen; **5.** ⁓ **up** F a) *et.* ‚aufpolieren', ‚aufmotzen', b) *Zeitungsartikel etc.* zs.-stoppeln; **6.** ♪ (aus dem Stegreif) begleiten; **III** *v/i.* **7.** ♪ improvisieren.

vamp² [væmp] F **I** *s.* Vamp *m*; **II** *v/t.* a) *Männer* verführen, ‚ausnehmen', b) *j-n* bezirzen.

vam·pire ['væmpaɪə] *s.* **1.** Vampir *m*: a) *Blut saugendes Gespenst*, b) *fig.* Erpresser(in), Blutsauger(in); **2.** *a.* ⁓ **bat** *zo.* Vampir *m*, Blattnase *f*; **3.** *thea.* kleine Falltür auf der Bühne; '**vam·pir·ism**

[-ərɪzəm] *s.* **1.** Vampirglaube *m*; **2.** Blutsaugen *n* (*e-s Vampirs*); **3.** *fig.* Ausbeutung *f*.

van¹ [væn] *s.* **1.** ✕ Vorhut *f*, Vor'ausab‚teilung *f*, Spitze *f*; **2.** ⚓ Vorgeschwader *n*; **3.** *fig.* vorderste Reihe, Spitze *f*.

van² [væn] *s.* **1.** Last-, Lieferwagen *m*; **2.** Gefangenenwagen *m* (*Polizei*); **3.** F a) Wohnwagen *m*: **gipsy's** ⁓ Zigeunerwagen *m*, b) *Am.* 'Wohnmo‚bil *n*; **4.** ⚙ *Brit.* (geschlossener) Güterwagen/ Dienst-, Gepäckwagen *m*.

van³ [væn] *s.* **1.** *obs. od. poet.* Schwinge *f*, Fittich *m*; **2.** *Brit.* Getreideschwinge *f*; **3.** ⚒ *Brit.* Schwingschaufel *od.* -probe *f*.

va·na·di·um [və'neɪdjəm] *s.* ♏ Va'nadium *n*.

Van·dal ['vændl] **I** *s.* **1.** *hist.* Wan'dale *m*, Wan'dalin *f*; **2.** ⚹ *fig.* Wan'dale *m*; **II** *adj. a.* **Van·dal·ic** [væn'dælɪk] **3.** *hist.* wan'dalisch, Wandalen...; **4.** ⚹ *fig.* wan'dalenhaft, zerstörungswütig; '**van·dal·ism** [-dəlɪzəm] *s. fig.* Wanda'lismus *m*: a) Zerstörungswut *f*, b) *a.* **act**(**s**) **of** ⁓ mutwillige Zerstörung; '**van·dal·ize** *v/t.* **1.** mutwillig zerstören, verwüsten; **2.** wie die Wan'dalen hausen in (*dat.*).

Van·dyke [‚væn'daɪk] **I** *adj.* **1.** von Van Dyck, in van-dyckscher Ma'nier; **II** *s.* **2.** *oft* ⚹ *abbr. für* a) ⁓ **beard**, b) ⁓ **collar**; **3.** Zackenmuster *n*; ⁓ **beard** *s.* Spitz-, Knebelbart *m*; ⁓ **col·lar** *s.* Van'dyckkragen *m*.

vane [veɪn] *s.* **1.** Wetterfahne *f*, -hahn *m*; **2.** Windmühlenflügel *m*; **3.** (Pro'peller-, Venti'lator- *etc.*)Flügel *m*; (Tur'binen-, ⚓ Leit)Schaufel *f*; **4.** *surv.* Di'opter *n*; **5.** *zo.* Fahne *f* (*Feder*); **6.** (Pfeil)Fiederung *f*.

van·guard ['vænga:d] → **van¹**.

va·nil·la [və'nɪlə] *s.* ♀, ♱ Va'nille *f*.

van·ish ['vænɪʃ] *v/i.* **1.** (plötzlich) verschwinden; **2.** (langsam) (ver-, ent-) schwinden, da'hinschwinden, sich verlieren (**from** von, aus); **3.** (spurlos) verschwinden: ⁓ **into** (**thin**) **air** sich in Luft auflösen; **4.** Å verschwinden, null werden.

van·ish·ing | **cream** ['vænɪʃɪŋ] *s.* (*rasch eindringende*) Tagescreme; ⁓ **line** *s.* Fluchtlinie *f*; ⁓ **point** *s.* **1.** Fluchtpunkt *m* (*Perspektive*); **2.** *fig.* Nullpunkt *m*.

van·i·ty ['vænətɪ] *s.* **1.** *persönliche* Eitelkeit; **2.** *j-s* Stolz *m* (*Sache*); **3.** Leer-, Hohlheit *f*, Eitel-, Nichtigkeit *f*: ⚹ **Fair** *fig.* Jahrmarkt *m* der Eitelkeit; **4.** *Am.* Toi'lettentisch *m*; **5.** *a.* ⁓ **bag** (*od.* **box**, **case**) Hand-, Kos'metiktäschchen *n*, -koffer *m*.

van·quish ['væŋkwɪʃ] **I** *v/t.* besiegen, über'wältigen, *a. fig. Stolz etc.* über'winden, bezwingen; **II** *v/i.* siegreich sein, siegen; '**van·quish·er** [-ʃə] *s.* Sieger *m*, Bezwinger *m*.

van·tage ['va:ntɪdʒ] *s.* **1.** *Tennis*: Vorteil *m*; **2.** **coign** (*od.* **point**) **of** ⁓ günstiger (Angriffs- *od.* Ausgangs)Punkt; ⁓ **ground** *s.* günstige Lage *od.* Stellung (*a. fig.*); ⁓ **point** *s.* **1.** Aussichtspunkt *m*; **2.** günstiger (Ausgangs)Punkt; **3.** → **vantage ground**.

vap·id ['væpɪd] *adj.* □ **1.** *schal*: ⁓ **beer**; **2.** *fig.* a) schal, seicht, leer, b) öd(e), fad(e); **va·pid·i·ty** [væ'pɪdətɪ], '**vap·id·ness** [-nɪs] *s.* **1.** Schalheit *f* (*a. fig.*); **2.** *fig.* a) Fadheit, b) Leere *f*.

va·por *Am.* → **vapour**.

va·por·i·za·tion [‚veɪpəraɪ'zeɪʃn] *s. phys.* Verdampfung *f*, -dunstung *f*.

va·por·ize ['veɪpəraɪz] **I** *v/t.* **1.** ♏, *phys.* ver-, eindampfen, verdunsten (lassen); **2.** ⊙ vergasen; **II** *v/i.* **3.** verdampfen,

verdunsten; '**va·por·iz·er** [-zə] *s.* ⊙ **1.** Ver'dampfungsappa‚rat *m*, Zerstäuber *m*; **2.** Vergaser *m*; '**va·por·ous** [-rəs] *adj.* □ **1.** dampfig, dunstig; **2.** *fig.* nebelhaft; **3.** duftig (*Gewebe*).

va·pour ['veɪpə] **I** *s.* **1.** Dampf *m* (*a. phys.*), Dunst *m* (*a. fig.*): ⁓ **bath** Dampfbad *n*; ⁓ **trail** ✈ Kondensstreifen; **2.** a) ⊙ Gas *n*, b) *mot.* Gemisch *n*: ⁓ **motor** Gasmotor *m*; **3.** ♰ a) (Inhalati'ons)Dampf *m*, b) *obs.* (*innere*) Blähung; **4.** *fig.* Phan'tom *n*, Hirngespinst *n*; **5.** *pl. obs.* Schwermut *f*; **II** *v/i.* **6.** (ver)dampfen; **7.** *fig.* schwadronieren, prahlen.

var·an ['værən] *s. zo.* Wa'ran *m*.

var·ec ['værek] *s.* **1.** Seetang *m*; **2.** ♏ Varek *m*, Seetangasche *f*.

var·i·a·bil·i·ty [‚veərɪə'bɪlətɪ] *s.* **1.** Veränderlichkeit *f*, Schwanken *n*, Unbeständigkeit *f* (*a. fig.*); **2.** Å, *phys.*, *a. biol.* Variabili'tät *f*.

var·i·a·ble ['veərɪəbl] **I** *adj.* □ **1.** veränderlich, 'unterschiedlich, wechselnd; schwankend (*a. Person*): ⁓ **cost** ♱ bewegliche Kosten *pl.*; ⁓ **wind** *meteor.* Wind aus wechselnder Richtung; **2.** *bsd.* Å, *ast.*, *biol.*, *phys.* vari'abel, wandelbar, Å, *phys. a.* ungleichförmig; **3.** ⊙ regelbar, ver-, einstellbar: ⁓ **capacitor** Drehkondensator *m*; ⁓ **gear** Wechselgetriebe *n*; **infinitely** ⁓ stufenlos regelbar; ⁓**-speed** mit veränderlicher Drehzahl; **II** *s.* **4.** veränderliche Größe, *bsd.* Å Vari'able *f*, Veränderliche *f*; **5.** *ast.* vari'abler Stern; '**var·i·a·ble·ness** [-nɪs] → **variability**; '**var·i·ance** [-ɪəns] *s.* **1.** Veränderung *f*; **2.** Abweichung *f* (*a. ⚖ zwischen Klage u. Beweisergebnis*); **3.** Uneinigkeit *f*, Meinungsverschiedenheit *f*, Streit *m*: **be at** ⁓ (**with**) uneinig sein (mit *j-m*); → 4; **set at** ⁓ entzweien; **4.** *fig.* 'Widerstreit *m*, -spruch *m*, Unvereinbarkeit *f*: **be at** ⁓ (**with**) unvereinbar sein (mit *et.*), im Widerspruch stehen (zu); → 3; '**var·i·ant** [-ɪənt] **I** *adj.* abweichend, verschieden; 'unterschiedlich; **II** *s.* Vari'ante *f*: a) abweichende Lesart; **var·i·a·tion** [‚veərɪ'eɪʃn] *s.* **1.** Veränderung *f*, Wechsel *m*, Schwankung *f*; **2.** Abweichung *f*; **3.** ♪, Å, *ast.*, *biol. etc.* Variati'on *f*; **4.** ('Orts‚)Missweisung *f*, mag'netische Deklinati'on *f* (*Kompass*).

var·i·col·o(u)red ['veərɪkʌləd] *adj.* bunt: a) vielfarbig, b) *fig.* mannigfaltig.

var·i·cose ['værɪkəʊs] *adj.* ♣ krampfad(e)rig, vari'kös: ⁓ **vein** Krampfader *f*; ⁓ **bandage** Krampfaderbinde *f*; **var·i·co·sis** [‚værɪ'kəʊsɪs], **var·i·cos·i·ty** [‚værɪ'kɒsətɪ] *s.* Krampfaderleiden *n*, Krampfader(n *pl.*) *f*.

var·ied ['veərɪd] *adj.* □ verschieden(artig); mannigfaltig, abwechslungsreich, bunt.

var·i·e·gate ['veərɪgeɪt] *v/t.* **1.** bunt gestalten (*a. fig.*); **2.** *fig.* (durch Abwechslung) beleben, variieren; '**var·i·e·gat·ed** [-tɪd] *adj.* **1.** bunt(scheckig), bunt gefleckt, vielfarbig, mit bunter Musterung, ♀ panaschiert; **2.** → **varied**; **var·i·e·ga·tion** [‚veərɪ'geɪʃn] *s.* Buntheit *f*.

va·ri·e·ty [və'raɪətɪ] *s.* **1.** Verschieden-, Buntheit *f*, Mannigfaltigkeit *f*, Vielseitigkeit *f*, Abwechslung *f*; **2.** Vielfalt *f*, Reihe *f*, Anzahl *f*, *bsd.* ♱ Auswahl *f*: **owing to a** ⁓ **of causes** aus verschiedenen Gründen; **3.** Sorte *f*, Art *f*; **4.** *allg.*, *a. ⊙ Ab-*, Spielart *f*; **5.** ♀, *zo.* a) Varie'tät *f* (*Unterabteilung e-r Art*), b) Vari'ante *f*; **6.** Varie'té *n*: ⁓ **artist**

Varie'teekünstler *m*; ~ **meat** *s. Am.* Inne'reien *pl.*; ~ **show** *s.* Varie'tee(vorstellung *f*) *n*; ~ **store** *s.* ✝ *Am.* Kleinkaufhaus *n*; ~ **the·a·tre** *s.* Varie'tee (-the,ater) *n*.

var·i·form ['veərɪfɔːm] *adj.* vielgestaltig (*a. fig.*).

va·ri·o·la [və'raɪələ] *s.* ✷ Pocken *pl.*

var·i·om·e·ter [,veərɪ'ɒmɪtə] *s.* ◎, ⚡, *phys.* Vario'meter *n*.

var·i·o·rum [,veərɪ'ɔːrəm] I *adj.* ~ *edition* → II *s.* Ausgabe *f* mit Anmerkungen verschiedener Kommenta'toren *od.* mit verschiedenen Lesarten.

var·i·ous ['veərɪəs] *adj.* □ **1.** verschieden(artig); **2.** mehrere, verschiedene; **3.** → *varied*.

var·ix ['veərɪks] *pl.* **-i·ces** ['værɪsiːz] *s.* ✷ Krampfader(knoten *m*) *f.*

var·let ['vɑːlɪt] *s.* **1.** *hist.* Knappe *m*, Page *m*; **2.** *obs.* Schelm *m*, Schuft *m*.

var·mint ['vɑːmɪnt] *s.* **1.** *zo.* Schädling *m*; **2.** F Ha'lunke *m*.

var·nish ['vɑːnɪʃ] I *s.* ◎ **1.** Lack *m*: *oil* ~ Öllack *m*; **2.** *a.* *clear* ~ Klarlack *m*, Firnis *m*; **3.** ('Möbel)Poli,tur *f*; **4.** *Töpferei*: Gla'sur *f*; **5.** *fig.* Firnis *m*, Tünche *f*, äußerer Anstrich; II *v/t. a.* ~ *over* **6.** a) lackieren, firnissen, b) glasieren; **7.** *Möbel* (auf)polieren; **8.** *fig.* über'tünchen, beschönigen.

var·si·ty ['vɑːsətɪ] *s.* F **1.** ,Uni' *f* (*Universität*); **2.** *a.* ~ *team* *sport Am.* Universi'täts- *od.* College- *od.* Schulmannschaft *f.*

var·y ['veərɪ] I *v/t.* **1.** (ver-, *a.* ♫ ab)ändern; **2.** variieren, 'unterschiedlich gestalten, Abwechslung bringen in (*acc.*), wechseln mit *et., a.* ♪ abwandeln; II *v/i.* **3.** sich (ver)ändern, variieren (*a. biol.*), wechseln, schwanken; **4.** verschieden sein, abweichen (*from* von); **'var·y·ing** [-ɪɪŋ] *adj.* wechselnd, 'unterschiedlich, verschieden.

vas·cu·lar ['væskjʊlə] *adj.* ♀, *physiol.* Gefäß...(-*pflanzen, -system etc.*): ~ *tissue* ♀ Stranggewebe *n.*

vase [vɑːz] *s.* Vase *f.*

vas·ec·to·my [væ'sektəmɪ] *s.* ✷ Vasekto'mie *f.*

vas·e·line ['væsɪliːn] *s.* 🔥 Vase'lin *n.*

vas·sal ['væsl] I *s.* **1.** Va'sall(in), Lehnsmann *m*; **2.** *fig.* 'Untertan *m*, Unter'gebene(r *m*) *f*; **3.** *fig.* Sklave *m* (*to gen.*); II *adj.* **4.** Vasallen...; **'vas·sal·age** [-səlɪdʒ] *s.* **1.** *hist.* Va'sallentum *n*, Lehnspflicht *f*, (*to* gegenüber); **2.** *coll.* Va'sallen *pl.*; **3.** *fig.* a) Abhängigkeit *f* (*to* von), b) 'Unterwürfigkeit *f.*

vast [vɑːst] I *adj.* □ **1.** weit, ausgedehnt, unermesslich; **2.** *a. fig.* ungeheuer, (riesen)groß, riesig, gewaltig: ~ *difference*; ~ *quantity*; II *s.* **3.** *poet.* Weite *f*; **'vast·ly** [-lɪ] *adv.* gewaltig, in hohem Maße; ungemein, äußerst: ~ *superior* haushoch überlegen, weitaus besser; **'vast·ness** [-nɪs] *s.* **1.** Weite *f*, Unermesslichkeit *f* (*a. fig.*); **2.** ungeheure Größe, riesige Zahl, Unmenge *f.*

vat [væt] I *s.* ◎ **1.** großes Fass, Bottich *m*, Kufe *f*; **2.** a) *Färberei*: Küpe *f*, b) *a.* *tan* ~ *Gerberei*: Lohgrube *f*; II *v/t.* **3.** (ver)küpen, in ein Fass *etc.* füllen; **4.** in e-m Fass *etc.* behandeln; ~*ted* fassreif (*Wein etc.*).

Vat·i·can ['vætɪkən] *s.* Vati'kan *m*: ~ *council* Vatikanisches Konzil.

vaude·ville ['vəʊdəvɪl] *s.* **1.** *Brit.* heiteres Singspiel (mit Tanzeinlagen); **2.** *Am.* Varie'tee *n.*

vault¹ [vɔːlt] I *s.* **1.** △ (*a. poet.* Himmels)Gewölbe *n*, Wölbung *f*; **2.** Kellergewölbe *n*; **3.** Grabgewölbe *n*, Gruft *f*;

family ~; **4.** Tre'sorraum *m*; **5.** *anat.* Wölbung *f*, (Schädel)Dach *n*; (Gaumen)Bogen *m*; (Zwerchfell)Kuppel *f*; II *v/t.* **6.** (über)'wölben; III *v/i.* **7.** sich wölben.

vault² [vɔːlt] I *v/i.* **1.** springen, sich schwingen, setzen (*over* über *acc.*); **2.** *Reitsport*: kurbettieren; II *v/t.* **3.** über'springen; III *s.* **4.** *bsd. sport* Sprung *m*; **5.** *Reitsport*: Kur'bette *f.*

vault·ed ['vɔːltɪd] *adj.* **1.** gewölbt, Gewölbe...; **2.** über'wölbt.

vault·er ['vɔːltə] *s.* Springer *m.*

vault·ing¹ ['vɔːltɪŋ] *s.* △ **1.** Spannen *n* e-s Gewölbes; **2.** Wölbung *f*; **3.** Gewölbe *n* (*od. pl. coll.*).

vault·ing² ['vɔːltɪŋ] *s.* Springen *n*; ~ *horse* *s. Turnen*: (Lang-, Sprung)Pferd *n*; ~ *pole* *s. sport* Sprungstab *m.*

vaunt [vɔːnt] I *v/t.* sich rühmen (*gen.*), sich brüsten mit; II *v/i.* (*of*) sich rühmen (*gen.*), sich brüsten (mit); III *s.* Prahle'rei *f*; **'vaunt·er** [-tə] *s.* Prahler(in); **'vaunt·ing** [-tɪŋ] *adj.* □ prahlerisch.

'V-Day *s.* Tag *m* des Sieges (*im 2. Weltkrieg*; *8. 5. 1945*).

've [v] F *abbr. für* **have.**

veal [viːl] *s.* Kalbfleisch *n*: ~ *chop* Kalbskotelett *n*; ~ *cutlet* Kalbsschnitzel *n.*

vec·tor ['vektə] I *s.* **1.** A, *a.* ✈ Vektor *m*; **2.** ✷, *vet.* Bak'terienüber,träger *m*; II *v/t.* **3.** *Flugzeug* (mittels Funk *od.* Ra'dar) leiten, (auf Ziel) einweisen.

V-E Day → *V-Day*.

vee [viː] I *s.* V *n*, v *n*, Vau *n* (*Buchstabe*), II *adj.* V-förmig, V-...: ~ *belt* Keilriemen *m*; ~ *engine* V-Motor *m.*

veep [viːp] *s. Am.* F ,Vize' *m* (*Vizepräsident*).

veer [vɪə] *v/i. a.* ~ *round* **1.** sich ('um-) drehen; 'umspringen, sich drehen (*Wind*), *fig.* 'umschwenken (*to* zu); **2.** ⚓ (ab)drehen, wenden; II *v/t.* **3.** *a.* ~ *round* *Schiff etc.* wenden, drehen, schwenken; **4.** ⚓ *Tauwerk* fieren, abschießen: ~ *and haul* fieren u. holen; III *s.* **5.** Wendung *f*, Drehung *f*, Richtungswechsel *m.*

Veg·e·burg·er ['vedʒɪ,bɜːgə] *TM s.* Ge-'müse,burger *m.*

veg·e·ta·ble ['vedʒtəbl] I *s.* **1.** *allg.* (*bsd.* Gemüse-, Futter)Pflanze *f*: *be a mere* ~, *live like a* ~ *fig.* (nur noch) dahinvegetieren; **2.** *a. pl.* Gemüse *n*; **3.** ♪ Grünfutter *n*; II *adj.* **4.** pflanzlich, vegeta'bilisch, Pflanzen...: ~ *diet* Pflanzenkost *f*; ~ *kingdom* Pflanzenreich *n*; ~ *marrow* Kürbis(frucht *f*) *m*; **5.** Gemüse...: ~ *garden*; ~ *soup*.

veg·e·tal ['vedʒɪtl] *adj.* **1.** ♀ → *vegetable* 4 u. 5; **2.** *physiol.* vegeta'tiv; **veg·e·tar·i·an** [,vedʒɪ'teərɪən] I *s.* **1.** Vege'tarier(in); II *adj.* **2.** vege'tarisch; **3.** Vegetarier...; **veg·e·tar·i·an·ism** [,vedʒɪ-'teərɪənɪzəm] *s.* Vegeta'rismus *m*, vege-'tarische Lebensweise; **'veg·e·tate** [-teɪt] *v/i.* **1.** (*wie e-e Pflanze*) wachsen, vegetieren; **2.** *contp.* (da'hin)vegetieren; **veg·e·ta·tion** [,vedʒɪ'teɪʃn] *s.* **1.** Vegetati'on *f*, Pflanzenwelt *f*, -decke *f*: *luxuriant* ~; **2.** *a.* Pflanzenwuchs *m*; **3.** *fig.* (Da'hin)Vegetieren *n*; **4.** ✷ Wucherung *f*; **'veg·e·ta·tive** [-tə-tɪv] *adj.* □ *biol.* **1.** vegeta'tiv: a) wie Pflanzen wachsend, b) wachstumsfördernd, c) Wachstums...; **2.** Vegetations..., pflanzlich.

veg·gie ['vedʒɪ] F → *vegetarian*; ~ **burg·er** *s.* Ge'müse,burger *m.*

ve·he·mence ['viːɪməns] *s.* **1.** *a. fig.* Heftigkeit *f*, Vehe'menz *f*, Gewalt *f*,

Wucht *f*; **2.** *fig.* Ungestüm *n*, Leidenschaft *f*; **'ve·he·ment** [-nt] *adj.* □ *a. fig.* heftig, gewaltig, vehe'ment, *fig. a.* ungestüm, leidenschaftlich, hitzig.

ve·hi·cle ['viːɪkl] *s.* **1.** Fahrzeug *n*, Beförderungsmittel *n*, *engS.* Wagen *m*: ~ *excise duty* Kf'z-Steuer *f*; **2.** a) *a.* **space** ~ Raumfahrzeug *n*, b) 'Trägerra,kete *f*; **3.** *fig.* a) Ausdrucksmittel *n*, Medium *n*, Ve'hikel *n*, b) Träger *m*, Vermittler *m*; **4.** 🔥, *biol.* Trägerflüssigkeit *f*; **5.** *pharm.*, 🔥, ◎ Bindemittel *n*; **ve·hic·u·lar** [vɪ'hɪkjʊlə] *adj.* Fahrzeug..., Wagen...: ~ *traffic*.

veil [veɪl] I *s.* **1.** (Gesichts- *etc.*)Schleier *m*: *take the* ~ *eccl.* den Schleier nehmen (*Nonne werden*); **2.** *phot.* (*a.* Nebel-, Dunst)Schleier *m*; **3.** *fig.* Schleier *m*, Maske *f*, Deckmantel *m*: *draw a* ~ *over* den Schleier des Vergessens breiten über (*acc.*); *under the* ~ *of darkness* im Schutze der Dunkelheit; *under the* ~ *of charity* unter dem Deckmantel der Nächstenliebe; **4.** ♀, *anat.* → *velum*; **5.** *eccl.* a) (Tempel)Vorhang *m*, b) Velum *n* (*Kelchtuch*); **6.** Verschleierung *f der Stimme*; II *v/t.* **7.** verschleiern, -hüllen (*a. fig.*); III *v/i.* **8.** sich verschleiern; **veiled** [-ld] *adj.* verschleiert (*a. phot.*, *fig.*) (*a.* Stimme); **'veil·ing** [-lɪŋ] *s.* **1.** Verschleierung *f* (*a. phot. u. fig.*); **2.** ✝ Schleier(stoff) *m.*

vein [veɪn] *s.* **1.** *anat.* Vene *f*; **2.** *allg.* Ader *f*; *anat.* Blutgefäß *n*, ♀ Blattnerv *m*, c) Maser *f* (*Holz, Marmor*), d) *geol.* (Erz)Gang *m*, e) Wasserader *f*; **3.** *fig.* a) poetische *etc.* Ader, Veranlagung *f*, Hang *m* (*of* zu), b) (Ton)Art *f*, c) Stimmung *f*: *be in the* ~ *for* in Stimmung sein zu; **veined** [-nd] *adj.* **1.** *allg.* geädert; **2.** gemasert; **'vein·ing** [-nɪŋ] *s.* **1.** *allg.* Äderung *f*, Maserung *f*; **'vein·let** [-lɪt] *s.* **1.** Äderchen *n*; **2.** ♀ Seitenrippe *f.*

ve·la ['viːlə] *pl. von* **velum.**

ve·lar ['viːlə] I *adj. anat., ling.* ve'lar, Gaumensegel..., Velar...; II *s. ling.* Gaumensegellaut *m*, Ve'lar(laut) *m*; **'ve·lar·ize** [-əraɪz] *v/t. ling.* Laut velarisieren.

Vel·cro ['velkrəʊ] *TM s. a.* ~ *fastening* Klettverschluss *m.*

veld(t) [velt] *s. geogr.* Gras- *od.* Buschland *n* (*Südafrika*).

vel·le·i·ty [ve'liːətɪ] *s.* kraftloses, zögerndes Wollen.

vel·lum ['veləm] *s.* **1.** ('Kalbs-, 'Schreib-) Perga,ment *n*, Ve'lin *n*: ~ *cloth* Pausleinen *n*; **2.** *a.* ~ *paper* Ve'linpa,pier *n.*

ve·loc·i·pede [vɪ'lɒsɪpiːd] *s.* **1.** *hist.* Velozi'ped *n* (*Lauf-, Fahrrad*); **2.** *Am.* (Kinder)Dreirad *n.*

ve·loc·i·ty [vɪ'lɒsətɪ] *s. bsd.* ◎, *phys.* Geschwindigkeit *f*: *at a* ~ *of* mit e-r Geschwindigkeit von; *initial* ~ Anfangsgeschwindigkeit.

ve·lour(s) [və'lʊə] *s.* ✝ Ve'lours *m.*

ve·lum ['viːləm] *pl.* **-la** [-lə] *s.* **1.** ♀, *anat.* Hülle *f*, Segel *n*; **2.** *anat.* Gaumensegel *n*, weicher Gaumen; **3.** ♀ Schleier *m* an *Hutpilzen*.

vel·vet ['velvɪt] I *s.* **1.** Samt *m*: *be on* ~ *sl.* glänzend dastehen; **2.** *zo.* Bast *m* an *jungen Geweihen etc.*; II *adj.* **3.** samten, aus Samt, Samt...; **4.** samtartig, -weich, samten (*a. fig.*): *an iron hand in a* ~ *glove fig.* e-e eiserne Faust unter dem Samthandschuh; *handle s.o. with* ~ *gloves fig.* j-n mit Samthandschuhen anfassen; **vel·vet·een** [,velvɪ'tiːn] *s.* Man'(s)chester *m*, Baumwollsamt *m*; **'vel·vet·y** [-tɪ] → *velvet* 4.

ve·nal ['viːnl] *adj.* □ käuflich, bestechlich, kor'rupt; **ve·nal·i·ty** [viː'nælətɪ] *s.*

Käuflichkeit f, Kor'ruptheit f, Bestechlichkeit f.

ve·na·tion [viːˈneɪʃn] s. ♀, zo. Geäder n.

vend [vend] v/t. a) bsd. ⚖ verkaufen, b) zum Verkauf anbieten, c) hausieren mit; **vend·ee** [venˈdiː] s. ⚖ Käufer m; '**vend·er** [-də] s. **1.** (Straßen)Verkäufer m, (-)Händler m; **2.** → vendor.

ven·det·ta [venˈdetə] s. Blutrache f.

vend·i·ble [ˈvendəbl] adj. □ verkäuflich.

vend·ing ma·chine [ˈvendɪŋ] s. (Ver'kaufs)Auto,mat m.

ven·dor [ˈvendɔː] s. **1.** ⚖ Verkäufer(in); **2.** (Ver'kaufs)Auto,mat m.

ven·due [ˈvendjuː] s. bsd. Am. Aukti'on f, Versteigerung f.

ve·neer [vəˈnɪə] I v/t. **1.** ⊛ a) Holz furnieren, einlegen, b) Stein auslegen, c) Töpferei: (mit dünner Schicht) über'ziehen; **2.** fig. um'kleiden, e-n äußeren Anstrich geben; **3.** fig. Eigenschaften etc. über'tünchen, verdecken; II s. **4.** ⊛ Fur'nier(holz, -blatt) n; **5.** fig. Tünche f, äußerer Anstrich; **ve'neer·ing** [-ərɪŋ] s. **1.** ⊛ a) Furnierholz n, b) Furnierung f, c) Fur'nierarbeit f; **2.** fig. → veneer 5.

ven·er·a·bil·i·ty [ˌvenərəˈbɪlətɪ] s. Ehrwürdigkeit f; **ven·er·a·ble** [ˈvenərəbl] adj. □ **1.** ehrwürdig (a. R.C.) (a. fig. Bauwerk etc.), verehrungswürdig; **2.** anglikanische Kirche: Hoch(ehr)würden m (Archidiakon): ♫ Sir; **ven·er·a·ble·ness** [ˈvenərəblnɪs] s. Ehrwürdigkeit f.

ven·er·ate [ˈvenəreɪt] v/t. **1.** verehren; **2.** in Ehren halten; **ven·er·a·tion** [ˌvenəˈreɪʃn] s. (of) a) Verehrung f (gen.), b) Ehrfurcht f (vor dat.); '**ven·er·a·tor** [-tə] s. Verehrer(in).

ve·ne·re·al [vəˈnɪərɪəl] adj. **1.** geschlechtlich, Geschlechts..., Sexual...; **2.** ♂ a) ve'nerisch, Geschlechts..., b) geschlechtskrank: ~ disease Geschlechtskrankheit f; **ve·ne·re·ol·o·gist** [vəˌnɪərɪˈɒlədʒɪst] s. ♂ Venero'loge m, Facharzt m für Geschlechtskrankheiten.

Ve·ne·tian [vəˈniːʃn] I adj. venezi'anisch: ~ blind (Stab)Jalousie f; ~ glass Muranoglas n; II s. Venezi'aner(in).

Ven·e·zue·lan [ˌveneˈzweɪlən] I adj. venezo'lanisch; II s. Venezo'laner(in).

venge·ance [ˈvendʒəns] s. Rache f, Vergeltung f: take ~ (up)on Vergeltung üben od. sich rächen an (dat.); with a ~ F a) mächtig, mit Macht, wie besessen, wie der Teufel, b) jetzt erst recht, c) im Exzess, übertrieben; '**venge·ful** [-fʊl] adj. □ rhet. rachsüchtig, -gierig.

ve·ni·al [ˈviːnjəl] adj. □ verzeihlich: ~ sin R.C. lässliche Sünde.

ven·i·son [ˈvenɪzn] s. Wildbret n.

ven·om [ˈvenəm] s. **1.** zo. (Schlangen- etc.)Gift n; **2.** fig. Gift n, Gehässigkeit f; '**ven·omed** [-md], '**ven·om·ous** [-məs] adj. □ **1.** giftig: ~ snake Giftschlange f; **2.** fig. giftig, gehässig; '**ven·om·ous·ness** [-məsnɪs] s. Giftigkeit f, fig. a. Gehässigkeit f.

ve·nose [ˈviːnəʊs] → venous; **ve·nos·i·ty** [vɪˈnɒsətɪ] s. biol. **1.** Äderung f; **2.** ♂ Venosi'tät f; **ve·nous** [ˈviːnəs] adj. □ biol. **1.** Venen..., Adern...; **2.** ve'nös: ~ blood; **3.** ♀ geädert.

vent [vent] I s. **1.** (Luft)Loch n, (Abzugs)Öffnung f, Schlitz m, ⊛ a. Entlüfter(stutzen) m: ~ window → ventipane; **2.** Spundloch n (Fass); **3.** ✗ hist. Schießscharte f; **4.** Fingerloch n (Flöte etc.); **5.** (Vul'kan)Schlot m; **6.** orn., ichth. After

m; **7.** zo. Aufstoßen n zum Luftholen (Otter etc.); **8.** Auslass m (a. fig.): find (a) ~ fig. sich entladen (Gefühl); give to → 9; II v/t. **9.** fig. e-m Gefühl Luft machen, Wut etc. auslassen (on an dat.); **10.** ⊛ a) e-e Abzugsöffnung etc. anbringen an (dat.), b) Rauch etc. abziehen lassen, c) ventilieren; III v/i. **11.** hunt. aufstoßen (zum Luftholen) (Otter etc.); '**vent·age** [-tɪdʒ] → vent 1, 4, 8.

ven·ter [ˈventə] s. **1.** anat. a) Bauch (-höhle f) m, b) (Muskel- etc.)Bauch m; **2.** zo. (In'sekten)Magen m; **3.** ⚖ Mutter(leib m) f: child of a second ~ Kind n von e-r zweiten Frau.

'**vent·hole** → vent 1.

ven·ti·late [ˈventɪleɪt] v/t. **1.** ventilieren, (be-, ent-, 'durch)lüften; **2.** physiol. Sauerstoff zuführen (dat.); **3.** fig. ventilieren: a) zur Sprache bringen, erörtern, b) Meinung etc. äußern; **4.** → vent 9; '**ven·ti·lat·ing** [-tɪŋ] adj. Ventilations..., Lüftungs....; **ven·ti·la·tion** [ˌventɪˈleɪʃn] s. **1.** Ventilati'on f, (Be-, Ent)Lüftung f (beide a. Anlage), Luftzufuhr f; ✗ Bewetterung f; **2.** a) (freie) Erörterung, öffentliche Diskussi'on b) Äußerung f e-s Gefühls etc., Entladung f; '**ven·ti·la·tor** [-tə] s. Venti'lator m, Entlüfter m, Lüftungsanlage f.

ven·ti·pane [ˈventɪpeɪn] s. mot. Ausstellfenster n.

ven·tral [ˈventrəl] adj. □ biol. ven'tral, Bauch...

ven·tri·cle [ˈventrɪkl] s. anat. Ven'trikel m, (Körper)Höhle f, bsd. (Herz-, Hirn-) Kammer f; **ven·tric·u·lar** [venˈtrɪkjʊlə] adj. anat. ventriku'lär, Kammer...

ven·tril·o·qui·al [ˌventrɪˈləʊkwɪəl] adj. bauchrednerisch, Bauchrede...

ven·tril·o·quism [venˈtrɪləkwɪzəm] s. Bauchreden n; **ven'tril·o·quist** [-ɪst] s. Bauchredner(in); **ven'tril·o·quize** [-kwaɪz] I v/i. bauchreden; II v/t. et. bauchrednerisch sagen; **ven'tril·o·quy** [-kwɪ] s. Bauchreden n.

ven·ture [ˈventʃə] I s. **1.** Wagnis n: a) Risiko n, b) (gewagtes) Unter'nehmen; **2.** ♥ a) (geschäftliches) Unter'nehmen, Operati'on f, b) Spekulati'on f; ~ capital Risikokapital n; ~ capitalist 'Risikokapital,geber(in); **3.** Spekulati'onsob,jekt n, Einsatz m: at a ~ aufs Geratewohl, auf gut Glück; II v/t. **5.** et. riskieren, wagen, aufs Spiel setzen: nothing ~ nothing have (od. gain[ed]) wer nicht wagt, der nicht gewinnt; **6.** Bemerkung etc. (zu äußern) wagen; III v/i. **7.** (es) wagen, sich erlauben (to do zu tun); **8.** ~ (up)on sich an e-e Sache wagen; **9.** sich wohin wagen; '**ven·ture·some** [-səm] adj. □ waghalsig: a) kühn, verwegen (Person), b) gewagt, ris'kant (Tat); '**ven·ture·someness** [-sənnɪs] s. Waghalsigkeit f; '**ven·tur·ous** [-ərəs] adj. □ → venturesome.

ven·ue [ˈvenjuː] s. **1.** ⚖ a) Gerichtsstand m, zuständiger Verhandlungsort m, Brit. a. zuständige Grafschaft, b) örtliche Zuständigkeit; **2.** a) Schauplatz m, b) Treffpunkt m, Tagungsort m, c) sport Austragungsort m.

Ve·nus [ˈviːnəs] s. allg. Venus f.

ve·ra·cious [vəˈreɪʃəs] adj. □ **1.** wahr'haftig, wahrheitsliebend; **2.** wahr (-heitsgetreu): ~ account; **ve·rac·i·ty** [vəˈræsɪtɪ] s. **1.** Wahr'haftigkeit f, Wahrheitsliebe f; **2.** Richtigkeit f; **3.** Wahrheit f.

ve·ran·da(h) [vəˈrændə] s. Ve'randa f.

verb [vɜːb] s. ling. Zeitwort n, Verb(um) n; '**ver·bal** [-bl] I adj. □ **1.** Wort...

(-fehler, -gedächtnis, -kritik etc.); **2.** mündlich (a. Vertrag etc.); **3.** (wort)wörtlich: ~ copy; ~ translation; **4.** wörtlich, Verbal...: ~ note pol. Verbalnote f; **5.** ling. ver'bal, Verbal..., Zeitwort...: ~ noun → 6; II s. **6.** ling. Ver'bal,substantiv n; '**ver·bal·ism** [-bəlɪzəm] s. **1.** Ausdruck m; **2.** Verba'lismus m, Wortemache'rei f; **3.** Wortklaube'rei f; '**ver·bal·ist** [-bəlɪst] s. **1.** bsd. ped. Verba'list(in); **2.** wortgewandte Per'son; '**ver·bal·ize** [-bəlaɪz] I v/t. **1.** in Worte fassen, formulieren; **2.** ling. in ein Verb verwandeln; II v/i. **3.** viele Worte machen; **ver·ba·tim** [vɜːˈbeɪtɪm] I adv. ver'batim, (wort-) wörtlich, Wort für Wort; II adj. → verbal 3; III s. wortgetreuer Bericht; '**ver·bi·age** [-bɪɪdʒ] s. **1.** Wortschwall m; **2.** Dikti'on f; **ver·bose** [vɜːˈbəʊs] adj. □ wortreich, weitschweifig; **ver·bos·i·ty** [vɜːˈbɒsətɪ] s. Wortreichtum m.

ver·dan·cy [ˈvɜːdənsɪ] s. **1.** (frisches) Grün; **2.** fig. Unerfahrenheit f, Unreife f; '**ver·dant** [-nt] adj. □ **1.** grün, grünend; **2.** fig. grün, unreif.

ver·dict [ˈvɜːdɪkt] s. **1.** ⚖ (Wahr)Spruch m der Geschworenen, Ver'dikt n: ~ of not guilty Erkennen n auf „nicht schuldig"; bring in (od. return) a ~ of guilty auf schuldig erkennen; **2.** fig. Urteil n (on über acc.).

ver·di·gris [ˈvɜːdɪgrɪs] s. Grünspan m.

ver·dure [ˈvɜːdʒə] s. **1.** (frisches) Grün; **2.** Vegetati'on f, saftiger Pflanzenwuchs; **3.** fig. Frische f, Kraft f.

verge [vɜːdʒ] I s. **1.** mst fig. Rand m, Grenze f: on the ~ of am Rande der Verzweiflung etc., dicht vor (dat.); on the ~ of tears den Tränen nahe; on the ~ of doing nahe daran, zu tun; **2.** ♪ (Beet)Einfassung f, (Gras)Streifen m; **3.** ⚖ Brit. hist. Gerichtsbezirk m rund um den Königshof; **4.** ⊛ a) 'überstehende Dachkante; b) Säulenschaft m, c) Schwungstift m (Uhrhemmung), d) Zugstab m (Setzmaschine); **5.** a) bsd. eccl. Amtsstab m, b) hist. Belehnungsstab m; II v/i. **6.** mst fig. grenzen od. streifen (on an acc.); **7.** (on, into) sich nähern (dat.), (in e-e Farbe etc.) 'übergehen; **8.** sich (hin)neigen (to[wards] nach); '**ver·ger** [-dʒə] s. **1.** Kirchendiener m, Küster m; **2.** bsd. Brit. eccl. (Amts)Stabträger m.

ver·i·est [ˈverɪɪst] adj. (sup. von very II) obs. äußerst: the ~ child (selbst) das kleinste Kind; the ~ nonsense der reinste Unsinn; the ~ rascal der ärgste od. größte Schuft.

ver·i·fi·a·ble [ˈverɪfaɪəbl] adj. nachweis-, nachprüfbar, verifizierbar; **ver·i·fi·ca·tion** [ˌverɪfɪˈkeɪʃn] s. **1.** Nachprüfung f; **2.** Echtheitsnachweis m, Richtigbefund m; **3.** Beglaubigung f, Beurkundung f; (⚖ eidliche) Bestätigung; **ver·i·fy** [ˈverɪfaɪ] v/t. **1.** auf die Richtigkeit hin (nach)prüfen; **2.** die Richtigkeit od. Echtheit e-r Angabe etc. feststellen od. nachweisen, verifizieren; **3.** Urkunde etc. beglaubigen; beweisen, belegen; **4.** ⚖ eidlich beteuern; **5.** bestätigen; **6.** Versprechen etc. erfüllen, wahr machen.

ver·i·ly [ˈverəlɪ] adv. bibl. wahrlich.

ver·i·si·mil·i·tude [ˌverɪsɪˈmɪljtjuːd] s. Wahr'scheinlichkeit f.

ver·i·ta·ble [ˈverɪtəbl] adj. □ wahr (-haft), wirklich, echt.

ver·i·ty [ˈverɪtɪ] s. **1.** (Grund)Wahrheit f: of a ~ wahr'haftig; eternal verities ewige Wahrheiten; **2.** Wahrheit f; **3.** (j-s) Wahr'haftigkeit f.

ver·juice ['vɜːdʒuːs] s. **1.** Obst-, Traubensaft m (bsd. von unreifen Früchten); **2.** Essig m (a. fig.).

ver·meil ['vɜːmeɪl] **I** s. **1.** bsd. poet. für **vermilion**; **2.** ☉ Ver'meil n: a) feuervergoldetes Silber od. Kupfer, vergoldete Bronze, b) hochroter Gra'nat; **II** adj. **3.** poet. purpur-, scharlachrot.

ver·mi·cel·li [ˌvɜːmɪˈselɪ] (Ital.) s. pl. Fadennudeln pl.

ver·mi·cide ['vɜːmɪsaɪd] s. pharm. Wurmmittel n; **ver·mic·u·lat·ed** [vɜːˈmɪkjʊleɪtɪd] adj. **1.** wurmstichig; **2.** △ geschlängelt; **ver·mi·form** ['vɜːmɪfɔːm] adj. biol. wurmförmig; ~ **appendix** anat. Wurmfortsatz m; **ver·mi·fuge** ['vɜːmɪfjuːdʒ] → **vermicide**.

ver·mil·ion [vəˈmɪljən] **I** s. **1.** Zin'nober m; **2.** Zin'noberrot n; **II** adj. **3.** zin'noberrot; **III** v/t. **4.** mit Zin'nober od. zin'noberrot färben.

ver·min ['vɜːmɪn] s. mst pl. konstr. **1.** zo. coll. a) Ungeziefer n, b) Schädlinge pl., Para'siten pl., c) hunt. Raubzeug n; **2.** fig. contp. Geschmeiß n, Pack m; '**~-ˌkill·er** s. **1.** Kammerjäger m; **2.** Ungeziefervertilgungsmittel n.

ver·min·ous ['vɜːmɪnəs] adj. □ **1.** voller Ungeziefer; verlaust, verwanzt, verseucht; **2.** durch Ungeziefer verursacht: ~ **disease**; **3.** fig. a) schädlich, b) niedrig, gemein.

ver·mo(u)th ['vɜːməθ] s. Wermut(wein) m.

ver·nac·u·lar [vəˈnækjʊlə] **I** adj. □ **1.** einheimisch, Landes...(-sprache); **2.** mundartlich, Volks..., Heimat...: ~ **poetry**; **3.** ✶ en'demisch, lo'kal: ~ **disease**; **II** s. **4.** Landes-, Mutter-, Volkssprache f; **5.** Mundart f, Dia'lekt m; **6.** Jar'gon m, Fachsprache f; **8.** → **ver-'nac·u·lar·ism** [-ərɪzəm] s. volkstümlicher od. mundartlicher Ausdruck; **ver-'nac·u·lar·ize** [-əraɪz] v/t. **1.** Ausdrücke etc. einbürgern; **2.** in Volkssprache od. Mundart über'tragen, mundartlich ausdrücken.

ver·nal ['vɜːnl] adj. □ **1.** Frühlings...; **2.** fig. frühlingshaft, Jugend...; ~ **e·qui·nox** s. ast. 'Frühlingsäqui,noktium n (21. März).

ver·ni·er ['vɜːnjə] s. ☉ **1.** Nonius m (Gradteiler); **2.** Fein(ein)steller m, Verni'er m; **3.** ⬡ (a. ~ **cal·(l)i·per(s)** s. ☉) Schublehre f mit Nonius.

Ver·o·nese [ˌverəˈniːz] **I** adj. vero'nesisch, aus Ve'rona; **II** s. Vero'neser(in).

ve·ron·i·ca [vɪˈrɒnɪkə] s. **1.** ♀ Ve'ronika f, Ehrenpreis m; **2.** R.C. u. paint. Schweißtuch n der Ve'ronika.

ver·sa·tile ['vɜːsətaɪl] adj. □ **1.** vielseitig (begabt od. gebildet); gewandt, wendig, beweglich; **2.** unbeständig, wandelbar; **3.** ♀, zo. (frei) beweglich; **ver·sa·til·i·ty** [ˌvɜːsəˈtɪlətɪ] s. **1.** Vielseitigkeit f, Gewandtheit f, Wendigkeit f, geistige Beweglichkeit f; **2.** Unbeständigkeit f.

verse [vɜːs] **I** s. **1.** a) Vers(zeile f) m, b) (Gedicht)Zeile f, c) allg. Vers m, Strophe f; → **drama** Versdrama n; → **chapter** 1; **2.** coll. ohne art. a) Verse pl., b) Poe'sie f, Dichtung f; **3.** Vers (-maß n) m: **blank** ~ a) Blankvers, b) reimloser Vers; **II** v/t. **4.** in Verse bringen; **III** v/i. **5.** dichten, Verse machen.

versed[1] [vɜːst] adj. bewandert, beschlagen, versiert (in in dat.).

versed[2] [vɜːst] adj. ✶ 'umgekehrt: ~ **sine** Sinusversus m.

ver·si·fi·ca·tion [ˌvɜːsɪfɪˈkeɪʃn] s. **1.** Verskunst f, Versemachen n; **2.** Versbau m; **ver·si·fi·er** ['vɜːsɪfaɪə] s. Verse-

schmied m, Dichterling m; **ver·si·fy** ['vɜːsɪfaɪ] → **verse** 4 u. 5.

ver·sion ['vɜːʃn] s. **1.** (a. 'Bibel)Über-,setzung f; **2.** thea. etc. (Bühnen- etc.) Fassung f; **3.** Darstellung f, Fassung f, Lesart f, Versi'on f; **4.** Spielart f, Vari'ante f; **5.** ☉ (Export- etc.)Ausführung f, Mo'dell n.

ver·sus ['vɜːsəs] prp. ✝, a. sport u. fig. gegen, kontra.

vert [vɜːt] eccl. F **I** v/i. 'übertreten, konvertieren; **II** s. Konver'tit(in).

ver·te·bra ['vɜːtɪbrə] pl. **-brae** [-briː] s. anat. **1.** (Rücken)Wirbel m; **2.** pl. Wirbelsäule f; **'ver·te·bral** [-rəl] adj. □ verte'bral, Wirbel(säulen)...: ~ **column** Wirbelsäule f; **'ver·te·brate** [-rɪt] **I** adj. **1.** mit e-r Wirbelsäule (versehen), Wirbel...(-tier); **2.** zo. zu den Wirbeltieren gehörig; **II** s. **3.** Wirbeltier n; **'ver·te·brat·ed** [-reɪtɪd] → **vertebrate** I.

ver·tex ['vɜːteks] pl. mst **-ti·ces** [-tɪsiːz] s. **1.** biol. Scheitel m; **2.** ✠ Scheitelpunkt m, Spitze f (beide a. fig.); **3.** ast. a) Ze'nit m, b) Vertex m; **4.** fig. Gipfel m; **'ver·ti·cal** [-tɪkl] **I** adj. □ **1.** senk-, lotrecht, verti'kal: ~ **clearance** ⬡ lichte Höhe; ~ **engine** ⬡ stehender Motor; ~ **section** △ Aufriss m; ~ **take-off** ✈ Senkrechtstart m; ~ **take-off plane** od. **aircraft** ✈ Senkrechtstarter m; **2.** ast. ✠ Scheitel..., Höhen..., Vertikal...: ~ **angle** Scheitelwinkel m; ~ **circle** ast. Vertikalkreis m; **II** s. **3.** Senkrechte f.

ver·tig·i·nous [vɜːˈtɪdʒɪnəs] adj. □ **1.** wirbelnd; **2.** schwindlig, Schwindel...; **3.** Schwindel erregend, schwindelnd: ~ **height**; **ver·ti·go** ['vɜːtɪɡəʊ] pl. **-goes** s. ✶ Schwindel(gefühl n, -anfall m) m.

ver·tu [vɜːˈtuː] → **virtu**.

ver·vain ['vɜːveɪn] s. ♀ Eisenkraut n.

verve [vɜːv] s. (künstlerische) Begeisterung, Schwung m, Feuer n, Verve f.

ver·y ['verɪ] **I** adv. **1.** sehr, äußerst, außerordentlich: ~ **good** a) sehr gut, b) einverstanden, sehr wohl; ~ **well** a) sehr gut, b) meinetwegen, na schön; **not** ~ **good** nicht sehr od. besonders od. gerade gut; **2.** ~ **much** (in Verbindung mit Verben) sehr, außerordentlich: **he was** ~ **much pleased**; **3.** (vor sup.) aller...: **the** ~ **last drop** der allerletzte Tropfen; **4.** völlig, ganz; **II** adj. **5.** gerade, genau: **the** ~ **opposite** genau das Gegenteil; **the** ~ **thing** genau od. gerade das (Richtige); **at the** ~ **edge** ganz am Rand, am äußersten Rand; **6.** bloß: **the** ~ **fact of his presence**; **the** ~ **thought** der bloße Gedanke, schon der Gedanke; **7.** rein, pur, schier: **from** ~ **egoism**; **the** ~ **truth** die reine Wahrheit; **8.** frisch: **in the** ~ **act** auf frischer Tat; **9.** wahr, wirklich: ~ **God of** ~ **God** bibl. wahrer Gott vom wahren Gott; **the** ~ **heart of the matter** der Kern der Sache; **in** ~ **deed** (**truth**) tatsächlich (wahrhaftig); **10.** (nach this, that, the) (der-, die-, das)'selbe, (der, die, das) gleiche ... od. nämliche ...: **that** ~ **afternoon**; **the** ~ **same words**; **11.** selbst, so'gar: **his** ~ **servants**; **12.** → **veriest**.

ver·y| high fre·quen·cy ['verɪ] s. ⚡ 'Hochfre,quenz f, Ultra'kurzwelle f.

Ver·y| light ['vɪərɪ; 'verɪ] s. ✕ 'Leuchtpa,trone f; ~ **pis·tol** s. ✕ 'Leuchtpi,stole f; ~**'s night sig·nals** s. ✕ Si'gnalschießen n mit 'Leuchtmuniti,on.

ves·i·ca ['vesɪkə] pl. **-cas** (Lat.) s. **1.** biol. Blase f, Zyste f; anat., zo. (Harn-, Gallen-, ichth. Schwimm)Blase f; '**ves·i·cal** [-kl] adj. Blasen...; '**ves·i-**

cant [-kənt] **I** adj. **1.** ✶ Blasen ziehend; **II** s. **2.** ✶ Blasen ziehendes Mittel, Zugpflaster n; **3.** ✕ ätzender Kampfstoff; '**ves·i·cate** [-keɪt] **I** v/i. Blasen ziehen; **II** v/t. Blasen ziehen auf (dat.); **ves·i·ca·tion** [ˌvesɪˈkeɪʃn] s. Blasenbildung f; '**ves·i·ca·to·ry** [-keɪtərɪ] → **vesicant**; '**ves·i·cle** [-kl] s. Bläs·chen n; **ve·sic·u·lar** [vɪˈsɪkjʊlə] adj. **1.** Bläs·chen..., Blasen...; **2.** blasenförmig, blasig; **3.** blasig, Bläs·chen aufweisend.

ves·per ['vespə] s. **1.** ⚹ ast. Abendstern m; **2.** poet. Abend m; **3.** pl. eccl. Vesper f, Abendgottesdienst m, -andacht f; **4.** a. ~ **bell** Abendglocke f, -läuten n.

ves·sel ['vesl] s. **1.** Gefäß n (a. anat., ♀ u. fig.); **2.** ♪ (a. ✈ Luft)Schiff n, (Wasser)Fahrzeug n.

vest [vest] **I** s. **1.** Brit. 'Unterhemd n; **2.** Brit. ✝ od. Am. Weste f; **3.** a) Damenweste f, b) Einsatzweste f; **4.** poet. Gewand n; **II** v/t. **5.** bsd. eccl. bekleiden; **6.** (with) fig. j-n bekleiden, ausstatten (mit Befugnissen etc.), bevollmächtigen; j-n einsetzen (in Eigentum, Rechte etc.); **7.** Recht etc. über'tragen, verleihen (in s.o. j-m): ~**ed interest**, ~**ed right** sicher begründetes Anrecht, unabdingbares Recht; ~**ed interests** die maßgeblichen Kreise (e-r Stadt etc.); **8.** Am. Feindvermögen mit Beschlag belegen: ~**ing order** Beschlagnahmeverfügung f; **III** v/i. **9.** bsd. eccl. sich bekleiden; **10.** 'übergehen (in auf acc.) (Vermögen etc.); **11.** (in) zustehen (dat.), liegen (bei) (Recht etc.).

ves·ta ['vestə] s. Brit. a. ~ **match** kurzes Streichholz.

ves·tal ['vestl] **I** adj. **1.** antiq. ve'stalisch; **2.** fig. keusch, rein; **II** s. **3.** antiq. Ves'talin f; **4.** Jungfrau f; **5.** Nonne f.

ves·ti·bule ['vestɪbjuːl] s. **1.** (Vor)Halle f, Vorplatz m, Vesti'bül n; **2.** 🜂 Am. (Har'monika)Verbindungsgang m zwischen zwei D-Zug-Wagen; ~ Am. Vorhof m; ~ **school** s. Am. Lehrwerkstatt f (e-s Industriebetriebs); ~ **train** s. bsd. Am. D-Zug m.

ves·tige ['vestɪdʒ] s. **1.** obs. od. poet. Spur f; **2.** bsd. fig. Spur f, 'Überrest m, -bleibsel n; **3.** fig. Spur f, ein bisschen: **4.** biol. Rudi'ment n, verkümmertes Or'gan od. Glied; **ves·tig·i·al** [ve'stɪdʒɪəl] adj. **1.** spurenhaft, restlich; **2.** biol. rudimen'tär, verkümmert.

vest·ment ['vestmənt] s. **1.** Amtstracht f, Robe f, a. eccl. Or'nat m; **2.** eccl. Messgewand n; **3.** Gewand n, Kleid n (beide a. fig.).

'**vest-ˌpock·et** adj. fig. im 'Westentaschenfor,mat, Westentaschen..., Klein..., Miniatur...

ves·try ['vestrɪ] s. eccl. **1.** Sakri'stei f; **2.** Bet-, Gemeindesaal m; **3.** Brit. a) a. **common** ~, **general** ~, **ordinary** ~ Gemeindesteuerpflichtige pl., b) a. **select** ~ Kirchenvorstand m; ~ **clerk** s. Brit. Rechnungsführer m der Kirchengemeinde; '~·**man** [-mən] s. [irr.] Gemeindevertreter m.

ves·ture ['vestʃə] s. obs. od. poet. a) Gewand n, Kleid(ung f) n, b) Hülle f (a. fig.), Mantel m.

ve·su·vi·an [vɪˈsuːvjən] **I** adj. **1.** ⚹ geogr. ve'suvisch; **2.** vul'kanisch; **II** s. **3.** obs. Windstreichhölzchen n.

vet[1] [vet] F **I** s. **1.** Tierarzt m; **II** v/t. **2.** Tier unter'suchen od. behandeln; **3.** humor. a) j-n verarzten, b) j-n auf Herz u. Nieren prüfen, (a. po'litisch) über'prüfen.

vet[2] [vet] Am. F für **veteran**.

vetch [vetʃ] *s.* ♀ Wicke *f*; **'vetch·ling** [-lɪŋ] *s.* ♀ Platterbse *f*.

vet·er·an ['vetərən] **I** *s.* **1.** Vete'ran *m* (*alter Soldat od. Beamter*); **2.** ✗ *Am.* ehemaliger Kriegsteilnehmer; **3.** *fig.* ,alter Hase'; **II** *adj.* **4.** alt-, ausgedient; **5.** kampferprobt: ~ *troops*; **6.** *fig.* erfahren: ~ *golfer*; **7.** ~ *car mot.* Oldtimer *m* (*vor 1917 hergestellt*).

vet·er·i·nar·i·an [ˌvetərɪ'neərɪən] → **vet·er·i·nar·y** ['vetərɪnərɪ] **I** *s.* Tierarzt *m*, Veteri'när *m*; **II** *adj.* tierärztlich: ~ *medicine* Tiermedizin *f*; ~ *surgeon* → I.

ve·to ['viːtəʊ] *pol.* **I** *pl.* **-toes** *s.* **1.** Veto *n*, Einspruch *m*: *put a* (*od.* one's) (*up*)*on* → 3; **2.** *a.* ~ *power* Veto-, Einspruchsrecht *n*; **II** *v/t.* **3.** sein Veto einlegen gegen, Einspruch erheben gegen; **4.** unter'sagen, verbieten.

vet·ting ['vetɪŋ] *s. pol.* F 'Sicherheitsüber‚prüfung *f*.

vex [veks] *v/t.* **1.** j-n ärgern, belästigen, aufbringen, irritieren; → *vexed*; **2.** quälen, bedrücken, beunruhigen; **3.** schikanieren; **4.** j-n verwirren, j-m ein Rätsel sein; **5.** *obs. od. poet. Meer* aufwühlen.

vex·a·tion [vek'seɪʃn] *s.* **1.** Ärger *m*, Verdruss *m*; **2.** Plage *f*, Qual *f*; **3.** Belästigung *f*; **4.** Schi'kane *f*; **5.** Beunruhigung *f*, Sorge *f*; **vex·a·tious** [vek'seɪʃəs] *adj.* □ **1.** lästig, verdrießlich, ärgerlich, leidig; **2.** ⬚ schika'nös: *a ~ suit*; **vex·a·tious·ness** [vek'seɪʃəsnɪs] *s.* Ärgerlich-, Verdrießlich-, Lästigkeit *f*; **vexed** [vekst] *adj.* □ **1.** ärgerlich (*at s.th., with s.o.* über *acc.*); **2.** beunruhigt (*with* durch, von); **3.** (viel) umstritten, strittig: ~ *question*; **vex·ing** ['veksɪŋ] → *vexatious* 1.

vi·a ['vaɪə] (*Lat.*) **I** *prp.* via, über (*acc.*): ~ *London*; ~ *air mail* per Luftpost; **II** *s.* Weg *m*: ~ *media fig.* Mittelding *od.* -weg.

vi·a·ble ['vaɪəbl] *adj. a. fig.* lebensfähig: ~ *child*; ~ *industry*.

vi·a·duct ['vaɪədʌkt] *s.* Via'dukt *m*.

vi·al ['vaɪəl] *s.* (Glas)Fläschchen *n*, Phi'ole *f*: *pour out the ~s of one's wrath bibl. u. fig.* die Schalen s-s Zornes ausgießen (*upon* über *acc.*).

vi·and ['vaɪənd] *s. pl.* **1.** Lebensmittel *pl.*; **2.** ('Reise)Provi‚ant *m*.

vi·at·i·cum [vaɪ'ætɪkəm] *pl.* **-cums** *s. eccl.* Vi'atikum *n* (*bei der Letzten Ölung gereichte Eucharistie*).

vibes [vaɪbz] *s. pl.* F **1.** *mst sg konstr.* ♪ Vibra'phon *n*; **2.** Ausstrahlung *f* (*e-r Person*); **3.** Schwingungen, „Vibrations".

vi·bran·cy ['vaɪbrənsɪ] *s.* Reso'nanz *f*, Schwingen *n*; **vi·brant** ['vaɪbrənt] *adj.* **1.** vibrierend: a) schwingend (*Saite etc.*), b) laut schallend (*Ton*); **2.** zitternd, bebend (*with* vor *dat.*): ~ *with energy*; **3.** pulsierend (*with* von): ~ *cities*; **4.** kraftvoll, lebensprühend: *a ~ personality*; **5.** erregt; **6.** *ling.* stimmhaft (*Laut*).

vi·bra·phone ['vaɪbrəfəʊn] *s.* ♪ Vibra'phon *n*.

vi·brate [vaɪ'breɪt] **I** *v/i.* **1.** vibrieren: a) zittern (*a. phys.*), b) (nach)klingen, (-)schwingen (*Töne*); **2.** pulsieren (*with* von); **3.** zittern, beben (*with* vor *Erregung etc.*); **II** *v/t.* **4.** in Schwingungen versetzen; **5.** vibrieren *od.* schwingen *od.* zittern lassen, rütteln; **vi·bra·tion** [-eɪʃn] *s.* **1.** Schwingung *f*, Vibrieren *n*, Zittern *n*: *~proof* erschütterungsfrei; **2.** *phys.* Vibrati'on *f*: a) Schwingung *f*, b) Oszillati'on *f*; **3.** *fig.* a) Pulsieren *n*,

b) *pl.* Ausstrahlung *f e-r Person*; **vi·bra·tion·al** [-eɪʃənl] *adj.* Schwingungs...; **vi·bra·tor** [-eɪtə] *s.* **1.** ⊗ Vib'rator *m* (*a.* ⚡), 'Rüttelappa‚rat *m*; **2.** ⚡ Oszil'lator *m*: a) Summer *m*, b) Zerhacker *m*; **3.** ♪ Zunge *f*, Blatt *n*; **vi·bra·to·ry** ['vaɪbrətərɪ] *adj.* **1.** schwingungsfähig; **2.** vibrierend; **3.** Vibrations..., Schwingungs...

vic·ar ['vɪkə] *s. eccl.* **1.** *Brit.* Vi'kar *m*, ('Unter)Pfarrer *m*; **2.** *protestantische Episkopalkirche in den USA:* a) ('Unter)Pfarrer *m*, b) Stellvertreter *m* des Bischofs; **3.** *R.C.* a) *cardinal ~* Kardinalvikar *m*, b) *~ of* (*Jesus*) *Christ* Statthalter *m* Christi (*Papst*); **4.** Ersatz *m*; **vic·ar·age** [-ərɪdʒ] *s.* **1.** Pfarrhaus *n*; **2.** Vikari'at *n* (*Amt des Vikars*); **vic·ar gen·er·al** *s. eccl.* Gene'ralvi‚kar *m*.

vi·car·i·ous [vaɪ'keərɪəs] *adj.* □ **1.** stellvertretend; **2.** *fig.* mit-, nachempfunden, *Erlebnis etc.* aus zweiter Hand: ~ *pleasure*.

vice[1] [vaɪs] *s.* **1.** Laster *n*: a) Untugend *f*, b) schlechte (An)Gewohnheit; **2.** Lasterhaftigkeit *f*, Verderbtheit *f*: ~ *squad* Sittenpolizei *f*, 'Sittendezer‚nat *n*; **3.** körperlicher Fehler, Gebrechen *n*; **4.** *fig., a.* ⬚ Mangel *m*, Fehler *m*; **5.** Verirrung *f*, Auswuchs *m*; **6.** Unart *f* (*Pferd*).

vice[2] [vaɪs] *s.* ⊗ Schraubstock *m* (*a. fig.*).

vi·ce[3] ['vaɪsɪ] *prp.* anstelle von.

vice[4] [vaɪs] *s.* F ,Vize' *m* (*abbr. für vice admiral etc.*).

vice- [vaɪs] *in Zssgn* stellvertretend, Vize...

vice ad·mi·ral ⚓ 'Vizeadmi‚ral *m*; **,~-'chair·man** *s.* [*irr.*] stellvertretender Vorsitzender, 'Vizepräsi‚dent *m*; **,~-'chan·cel·lor** *s.* **1.** 'Vizekanzler *m*; **2.** *Brit. univ.* (geschäftsführender) Rektor; **,~-'con·sul** *s.* 'Vize‚konsul *m*; **,~-'ge·rent** [-'dʒerənt] **I** *s.* Stellvertreter *m*, Statthalter *m*; **II** *adj.* stellvertretend; **,~-'pres·i·dent** *s.* 'Vizepräsi‚dent *m*: a) stellvertretender Vorsitzende, b) ⟊ *Am.* Di'rektor *m*, Vorstandsmitglied *n*; **,~'re·gal** *adj.* vizeköniglich; **,~reine** [ˌvaɪs'reɪn] *s.* Gemahlin *f* des Vizekönigs; **,~roy** ['vaɪsrɔɪ] *s.* Vizekönig *m*; **,~'roy·al** *adj.* vizeköniglich.

vi·ce ver·sa [ˌvaɪsɪ'vɜːsə] (*Lat.*) *adv.* 'umgekehrt, vice versa.

vic·i·nage ['vɪsɪnɪdʒ] → *vicinity*; **'vic·i·nal** [-nl] *adj.* benachbart, 'umliegend, nah; **vi·cin·i·ty** [vɪ'sɪnətɪ] *s.* **1.** Nähe *f*, Nachbarschaft *f*: *in close ~ to* in unmittelbarer Nähe von; *in the ~ of 40 fig.* um (die) 40 herum; **2.** Nachbarschaft *f*, (nähere) Um'gebung: *the ~ of London*.

vi·cious ['vɪʃəs] *adj.* □ **1.** lasterhaft, verderbt, 'unmo‚ralisch; **2.** verwerflich: ~ *habit*; **3.** bösartig, boshaft, gemein: ~ *attack*; **4.** bös-, unartig (*Tier*); **5.** heftig, ,bös': *a ~ blow*; **6.** F scheußlich, schlimm: ~ *headache*; **7.** *a.* ⬚ fehler-, mangelhaft; **8.** *obs.* schädlich: ~ *air*; ~ *cir·cle* *s.* **1.** Circulus *m* viti'osus, Teufelskreis *m*; **2.** *phls.* Zirkel-, Trugschluss *m*.

vi·cious·ness ['vɪʃəsnɪs] *s.* **1.** Lasterhaftigkeit *f*, Verderbtheit *f*; **2.** Verwerflichkeit *f*; **3.** Bösartigkeit *f*, Gemeinheit *f*; **4.** Fehlerhaftigkeit *f*.

vi·cis·si·tude [vɪ'sɪsɪtjuːd] *s.* **1.** Wandel *m*, Wechsel *m*; **2.** *pl.* Wechselfälle *pl.*, das Auf u. Ab: *the ~s of life*; **3.** *pl.* Schicksalsschläge *pl.*; **vi·cis·si·tu·di·nous** [vɪˌsɪsɪ'tjuːdɪnəs] *adj.* wechselvoll.

vic·tim ['vɪktɪm] *s.* **1.** Opfer *n*: a) (Unfall- *etc.*)Tote(r *m*) *f*), b) Leidtragende(r *m*) *f*, c) Betrogene(r *m*) *f*: *fall a ~ to* zum Opfer fallen (*dat.*); **2.** Opfer(tier) *n*; **'vic·tim·ize** [-maɪz] *v/t.* **1.** j-n (auf-)opfern; **2.** quälen, schikanieren, belästigen; **3.** prellen, betrügen.

vic·tor ['vɪktə] **I** *s.* Sieger(in); **II** *adj.* siegreich, Sieger...

vic·to·ri·a [vɪk'tɔːrɪə] *s.* Vik'toria *f* (*zweisitziger Einspänner*); ≗ *Cross* *s.* Vik'toriakreuz *n* (*brit. Tapferkeitsauszeichnung*).

Vic·to·ri·an [vɪk'tɔːrɪən] **I** *adj.* **1.** Viktori'anisch: ~ *Period*; **2.** viktori'anisch: ~ *habits*; **II** *s.* **3.** Viktori'aner(in).

vic·to·ri·ous [vɪk'tɔːrɪəs] *adj.* □ **1.** siegreich (*over* über *acc.*): *be ~* den Sieg davontragen, siegen; **2.** Sieges...; **vic·to·ry** ['vɪktərɪ] *s.* **1.** Sieg *m* (*a. fig.*): ~ *ceremony* Siegerehrung *f*; ~ *rostrum* Siegespodest *n*; **2.** *fig.* Tri'umph *m*, Erfolg *m*, Sieg *m*: *moral ~*.

vict·ual ['vɪtl] **I** *s. mst pl.* Esswaren *pl.*, Lebensmittel *pl.*, Provi'ant *m*; **II** *v/t.* (*v/i.* sich) verpflegen *od.* verproviantieren *od.* mit Lebensmitteln versorgen; **'vict·ual·(l)er** [-lə] *s.* **1.** ('Lebensmittel-)Liefe‚rant *m*; **2.** *a. licensed ~* *Brit.* Schankwirt *m*; **3.** ⚓ Provi'antschiff *n*; **'vict·ual·(l)ing** [-lɪŋ] *s.* Verproviantierung *f*: ~ *ship* Proviantschiff *n*.

vi·de ['vaɪdiː] (*Lat.*) *int.* siehe!

vi·de·li·cet [vɪ'diːlɪset] (*Lat.*) *adv.* nämlich, das heißt (*abbr. viz; lies: namely, that is*).

vid·e·o ['vɪdɪəʊ] **I** *pl.* **-os** *s.* **1.** 'Video *n* (*Videotechnik*); **2.** *Computer:* Bildschirm-, Datensichtgerät *n*; **3.** *Am.* (*on im*) Fernsehen *n*; **II** *adj.* **4.** 'Video...: ~ *cassette* (*recorder*); ~ *clip* Videoclip *m*; ~ *conference* 'Videokonfe‚renz *f*; ~ *disc* Bildplatte *f*; ~ *library* Video'thek *f*; ~ *nasty* F Videoschocker *m*; ~ *recording* Videoaufnahme *f*; **5.** *Computer:* Bildschirm...: ~ *terminal* 2; **6.** *Am.* F Fernseh...: ~ *program* 'Fernsehpro‚gramm *n*; ~ *con·fer·enc·ing* *s. Computer:* ‚Videokonfe'renzschaltung *f*: ~ *over the Internet* Videokonferenzschaltung via Internet; '~·phone F *für* *videotelephone*; '~·tape **I** *s.* Videoband *n*; **II** *v/t.* auf Videoband aufnehmen, aufzeichnen; '~‚tel·e·phone *s.* 'Bildtele‚fon *n*.

vie [vaɪ] *v/i.* wetteifern: ~ *with s.o. in* (*od. for*) *s.th.* mit j-m in *od.* um et. wetteifern.

Vi·en·nese [ˌvɪə'niːz] **I** *s. sg. u. pl.* **1.** a) Wiener(in), b) Wiener(innen) *pl.*; **2.** *ling.* Wienerisch *n*; **II** *adj.* **3.** wienerisch, Wiener(...).

view [vjuː] **I** *v/t.* **1.** (sich) ansehen, betrachten, besichtigen, in Augenschein nehmen, prüfen: *~ing figures TV* Sehbeteiligung *f*, Einschaltquote *f*; **2.** *fig.* ansehen, auffassen, betrachten, beurteilen; **3.** über'blicken, -'schauen; **4.** *obs.* sehen; **II** *s.* **5.** (An-, Hin)Sehen *n*, Besichtigung *f*: *at first ~* auf den ersten Blick; *on nearer ~* bei näherer Betrachtung; **6.** Sicht *f* (*a. fig.*): *in ~* a) in Sicht, sichtbar, b) *fig.* in (Aus)Sicht; *in ~ of fig.* im Hinblick auf (*acc.*), in Anbetracht *od.* angesichts (*gen.*); *in full ~ of* direkt vor j-s Augen; *on ~* zu besichtigen(d), ausgestellt; *on the long ~ fig.* auf weite Sicht; *out of ~* außer Sicht, nicht zu sehen; *come in ~* in Sicht kommen, sichtbar werden; *have in ~ fig.* im Auge haben, beabsichtigen; *keep in ~ fig.* im Auge behalten; **7.** Aussicht *f*, (Aus)Blick *m* (*of, over* auf *acc.*); Sze-

V

ne'rie *f*; **8.** *paint., phot.* Ansicht *f*, Bild *n*: **~s of London**; **sectional ~** ⊕ Ansicht im Schnitt; **9.** *fig.* 'Überblick *m* (**of** über *acc.*); **10.** Absicht *f*: **with a ~ to** a) (*ger.*) mit *od.* in der Absicht zu (*tun*), zu dem Zweck (*gen.*), b) im Hinblick auf (*acc.*); **11.** *fig.* Ansicht *f*, Auffassung *f*, Urteil *n* (**of, on** über *acc.*): **in my ~** in m-n Augen, m-s Erachtens; **form a ~ on** sich ein Urteil bilden über (*acc.*); **take the ~ that** die Ansicht *od.* den Standpunkt vertreten, dass; **take a bright** (**dim, grave**) **~ of** *et.* optimistisch (pessimistisch, ernst) beurteilen; **12.** Vorführung *f*: **private ~ of a film**; **view·a·ble** ['vjuːəbl] *adj.* **1.** sichtbar; **2.** *fig.* sehenswert; **view da·ta** *s. pl.* Bildschirmtext *m*; **view·er** ['vjuːə] *s.* **1.** Betrachter(in); **2.** Fernsehzuschauer (-in); **'view·er·ship** *s.* Fernsehpublikum *n*.

'view‚find·er *s. phot.* (Bild)Sucher *m*; **~hal·loo** *s. hunt.* Hal'lo(ruf *m*) *n* (*beim Erscheinen des Fuchses*).

'view‚phone *s.* 'Bildtele‚fon *n*; **'~‚point** *s. fig.* Gesichts-, Standpunkt *m*.

view·y ['vjuːɪ] *adj.* F verstiegen, über'spannt, ‚fimmelig'.

vig·il ['vɪdʒɪl] *s.* **1.** Wachsein *n*, Wachen *n* (*zur Nachtzeit*); **2.** Nachtwache *f*: **keep ~** wachen (**over** bei); **3.** *eccl.* a) *mst pl.* Vi'gilie(n *pl.*) *f*, Nachtwache *f* (*vor Kirchenfesten*), b) Vi'gil *f* (*Vortag e-s Kirchenfests*): **on the ~ of** am Vorabend von (*od. gen.*); **'vig·i·lance** [-ləns] *s.* **1.** Wachsamkeit *f*: **~ committee** *od.* **group** *bsd. Am.* Bürgerwehr *f*, Selbstschutzgruppe *f*; **2.** ✄ Schlaflosigkeit *f*; **'vig·i·lant** [-lənt] *adj.* □ wachsam, 'umsichtig, aufmerksam; **vig·i·lan·te** [‚vɪdʒɪ'læntɪ] *s.* Mitglied *n* e-s **vigilance committee.**

vi·gnette [vɪ'njet] I *s. typ., phot. etc.* Vig'nette *f*; II *v/t.* vignettieren.

vig·or *Am. →* **vigour.**

vig·or·ous ['vɪɡərəs] *adj.* □ **1.** *allg.* kräftig; **2.** kraftvoll, vi'tal; **3.** lebhaft, ak'tiv, tatkräftig; **4.** e'nergisch, nachdrücklich; wirksam; **vig·our** ['vɪɡə] *s.* **1.** (Körper-, Geistes)Kraft *f*, Vitali'tät *f*; **2.** Ener'gie *f*; **3.** *biol.* Lebenskraft *f*; **4.** *fig.* Nachdruck *m*, Wirkung *f*.

Vi·king [--] *s.* ['vaɪkɪŋ] *hist.* I *s.* Wiking (-er) *m*; II *adj.* Wikinger-.

vile [vaɪl] *adj.* □ **1.** *obs.* wertlos; **2.** gemein, schändlich, abstoßend, schmutzig; **3.** F scheußlich, ab'scheulich, mise'rabel: **a ~ hat; ~ weather;** **'vile·ness** [-nɪs] *s.* **1.** Gemeinheit *f*, Schändlichkeit *f*; **2.** F Scheußlichkeit *f*.

vil·i·fi·ca·tion [‚vɪlɪfɪ'keɪʃn] *s.* **1.** Schmähung *f*, Verleumdung *f*, -unglimpfung *f*; **2.** Her'absetzung *f*; **vil·i·fi·er** ['vɪlɪfaɪə] *s.* Verleumder(in); **vil·i·fy** ['vɪlɪfaɪ] *v/t.* **1.** schmähen, verleumden, verunglimpfen; **2.** her'absetzen.

vil·la ['vɪlə] *s.* **1.** Villa *f*, Landhaus *n*; **2.** *Brit.* a) Doppelhaushälfte *f*, b) 'Einfa‚milienhaus *n*.

vil·lage ['vɪlɪdʒ] I *s.* Dorf *n*; II *adj.* dörflich, Dorf...; **'vil·lag·er** [-dʒə] *s.* Dorfbewohner(in), Dörfler(in).

vil·lain ['vɪlən] *s.* **1.** *a. thea. u. humor.* Schurke *m*, Bösewicht *m*; **2.** *humor.* Schlingel *m*; **3.** → **villein;** **vil·lain·age** ['vɪlɪnɪdʒ] → **villeinage;** **'vil·lain·ous** [-nəs] *adj.* □ **1.** schurkisch, Schurken..., schändlich; **2.** F → **vile** 2, 3; **'vil·lain·y** [-nɪ] *s.* **1.** Schurke'rei *f*; **2.** → **vileness.**

vil·lein ['vɪlɪn] *s. hist.* **1.** Leibeigene(r) *m*; **2.** *später:* Zinsbauer *m*; **'vil·lein·age** [-nɪdʒ] *s.* **1.** Leibeigenschaft *f*; **2.** 'Hin-

tersassengut *n*.

vil·li·form ['vɪlɪfɔːm] *adj. biol.* zottenförmig; **vil·lose** ['vɪləʊs], **vil·lous** ['vɪləs] *adj. biol.* zottig; **'vil·lus** [-ləs] *pl.* **-li** [-laɪ] *s.* **1.** *anat.* (Darm)Zotte *f*; **2.** ♀ Zottenhaar *n*.

vim [vɪm] *s.* F Schwung *m*, ‚Schmiss' *m*: **full of ~** ‚toll in Form'.

vin·ai·grette [‚vɪneɪ'ɡret] *s.* **1.** Riechfläschchen *n*, -dose *f*; **2.** *a.* **~ sauce** *Küche:* Vinai'grette *f* (*Soße*).

vin·ci·ble ['vɪnsɪbl] *adj.* besiegbar, über'windbar.

vin·cu·lum ['vɪŋkjʊləm] *pl.* **-la** [-lə] *s.* **1.** ₳ Strich *m* (*über mehreren Zahlen*), Über'streichung *f* (*an Stelle von Klammern*); **2.** *bsd. fig.* Band *n*.

vin de pays [‚vændəpeɪ'iː] *s.* Landwein *m*.

vin·di·ca·ble ['vɪndɪkəbl] *adj.* haltbar, zu rechtfertigen(d); **vin·di·cate** ['vɪndɪkeɪt] *v/t.* **1.** in Schutz nehmen, verteidigen (**from** vor *dat.*, gegen); **2.** rechtfertigen (**o.s.** sich), bestätigen; **3.** ⚖ a) Anspruch erheben auf (*acc.*), beanspruchen, b) *Recht, Anspruch* geltend machen, c) *Recht etc.* behaupten; **vin·di·ca·tion** [‚vɪndɪ'keɪʃn] *s.* **1.** Verteidigung *f*, Rechtfertigung *f*: **in ~ of** zur Rechtfertigung von (*od. gen.*); **2.** ⚖ a) Behauptung *f*, b) Geltendmachung *f*; **'vin·di·ca·to·ry** [-keɪtərɪ] *adj.* □ **1.** rechtfertigend, Rechtfertigungs...; **2.** rächend, Straf...

vin·dic·tive [vɪn'dɪktɪv] *adj.* □ **1.** rachsüchtig; **2.** als Strafe: **~ damages** ⚖ tatsächlicher Schadenersatz zuzüglich e-r Buße; **vin'dic·tive·ness** [-nɪs] *s.* Rachsucht *f*.

vin du pays [‚vændʊeɪ'iː] *s.* Landwein *m*.

vine [vaɪn] ♀ I *s.* **1.** (*Hopfen- etc.*)Rebe *f*, Kletterpflanze *f*; **2.** Wein(stock) *m*, (Wein)Rebe *f*; II *adj.* **3.** Wein..., Reb (-en)...; **'~-clad** *adj. poet.* weinlaubbekränzt; **'~‚dress·er** *s.* Winzer *m*; **~ fret·ter** *s.* Reblaus *f*.

vin·e·gar ['vɪnɪɡə] I *s.* **1.** (Wein)Essig *m*: **aromatic ~** aromatischer Essig, Gewürzessig; **2.** *pharm.* Essig *m*; **3.** *fig.* Verdrießlichkeit *f*; **4.** *Am.* F → **vim;** II *v/t.* **5.** Essig tun an (*acc.*); **'vin·e·gar·y** [-ərɪ] *adj.* **1.** (essig)sauer (*a. fig.*); **2.** a) griesgrämig, b) ätzend.

'vine‚grow·er *s.* Weinbauer *m*, Winzer *m*; **'~‚grow·ing** *s.* Weinbau *m*; **~ leaf** *s.* [*irr.*] Wein-, Rebenblatt *n*: **vine leaves** Weinlaub *n*; **~ louse** *s.* [*irr.*] Reblaus *f*; **~ mil·dew** *s.* ♀ Traubenfäule *f*.

vin·er·y ['vaɪnərɪ] *s.* **1.** Treibhaus *n* für Reben; **2.** → **vine·yard** ['vɪnjəd] *s.* Weinberg *m od.* -garten *m*.

vin·i·cul·tur·al [‚vɪnɪ'kʌltʃərəl] *adj.* weinbaukundlich; **vin·i·cul·ture** ['vɪnɪkʌltʃə] *s.* Weinbau *m* (*Fach*).

vi·nos·i·ty [vaɪ'nɒsɪtɪ] *s.* **1.** Weinartigkeit *f*; **2.** Weinseligkeit *f*; **vi·nous** ['vaɪnəs] *adj.* **1.** weinartig, Wein...; **2.** weinhaltig; **3.** weinselig; **4.** weingerötet: **~ face;** **5.** weinrot.

vin·tage ['vɪntɪdʒ] *s.* **1.** Weinertrag *m*, -ernte *f*; **2.** Weinlese(zeit) *f*; **3.** (guter) Wein, (her'vorragender) Jahrgang: **~ wine** Spitzenwein *m*; **4.** F a) Jahrgang *m*, b) Herstellung *f*, *mot. etc. a.* Baujahr *n*: **~ car** *mot.* Oldtimer *m* (*zwischen 1917 u. 1930 hergestellt*); **'vin·tager** [-dʒə] *s.* Weinleser(in).

vint·ner ['vɪntnə] *s.* Weinhändler *m*.

vi·nyl ['vaɪnɪl] ₪ I *s.* Vi'nyl *n*; II *adj.* Vinyl...: **~ polymers** Vinylpolymere *pl.*

vi·ol ['vaɪəl] *s.* ♪ *hist.* Vi'ole *f*: **bass ~**

Viola *f* da Gamba, Gambe *f*.

vi·o·la¹ [vɪ'əʊlə] *s.* ♪ **1.** Vi'ola *f*, Bratsche *f*; **2.** → **viol.**

vi·o·la² ['vaɪələ] *s.* ♀ Veilchen *n*, Stiefmütterchen *n*.

vi·o·la·ble ['vaɪələbl] *adj.* □ verletzbar (*bsd. Gesetz, Vertrag*); **vi·o·late** ['vaɪəleɪt] *v/t.* **1.** *Eid, Vertrag, Grenze etc.* verletzen, *Gesetz* über'treten, *bsd. Versprechen* brechen, *e-m Gebot, dem Gewissen* zu'widerhandeln; **2.** *Frieden, Stille, Schlaf* (grob) stören; **3.** *a. fig.* Gewalt antun (*dat.*); **4.** *Frau* schänden, vergewaltigen; **5.** *Heiligtum etc.* entweihen, schänden; **vi·o·la·tion** [‚vaɪə'leɪʃn] *s.* **1.** Verletzung *f*, Über'tretung *f*, Bruch *m e-s Eides, Gesetzes*; Zu'widerhandlung *f*: **in ~ of** unter Verletzung von; **2.** (grobe) Störung *f*; **3.** Vergewaltigung *f* (*a. fig.*), Schändung *f e-r Frau*; **4.** Entweihung *f*, Schändung *f*; **'vi·o·la·tor** [-leɪtə] *s.* **1.** Verletzer(in), Über'treter (-in); **2.** Schänder(in).

vi·o·lence ['vaɪələns] *s.* **1.** Gewalt(tätigkeit) *f*; **2.** ⚖ Gewalt(tat, -anwendung) *f*: **by ~** gewaltsam; **crimes of ~** Gewaltverbrechen *pl.*; **3.** Verletzung *f*, Unrecht *n*, Schändung *f*: **do ~ to** Gewalt antun (*dat.*), *Gefühle etc.* verletzen, *Heiliges* entweihen; **4.** *bsd. fig.* Heftigkeit *f*, Ungestüm *n*; **'vi·o·lent** [-nt] *adj.* □ **1.** heftig, gewaltig, stark: **~ blow; ~ tempest;** **2.** gewaltsam, -tätig (*Person od. Handlung*), Gewalt...: **~ death** gewaltsamer Tod; **~ interpretation** *fig.* gewaltsame Auslegung; **~ measures** Gewaltmaßnahmen *pl.*; **lay ~ hands on** Gewalt antun (*dat.*); **3.** *fig.* heftig, ungestüm, hitzig; **4.** grell, laut (*Farben, Töne*).

vi·o·let ['vaɪəlɪt] I *s.* **1.** ♀ Veilchen *n*: **shrinking ~** F scheues Wesen (*Person*); **2.** Veilchenblau *n*, Vio'lett *n*; II *adj.* **3.** veilchenblau, vio'lett.

vi·o·lin [‚vaɪə'lɪn] *s.* ♪ Vio'line *f*, Geige *f*: **play the ~** Geige spielen, geigen; **first ~** erste(r) Geige(r); **~ case** Geigenkasten *m*; **~ clef** Violinschlüssel *m*; **vi·o·lin·ist** ['vaɪəlɪnɪst] *s.* Violi'nist(in), Geiger(in).

vi·ol·ist ['vaɪəlɪst] *s.* ♪ **1.** *hist.* Vi'olenspieler(in); **2.** [vɪ'əʊlɪst] Brat'schist(in).

vi·o·lon·cel·list [‚vaɪələn'tʃelɪst] *s.* ♪ (Violon)Cel'list(in); **vi·o·lon'cel·lo** [-ləʊ] *pl.* **-los** *s.* (Violon)'Cello *n*.

VIP [‚viːaɪ'piː] *s. sl.* ‚hohes' *od.* ‚großes Tier' (*aus Very Important Person*).

vi·per ['vaɪpə] *s.* **1.** *zo.* Viper *f*, Otter *f*, Natter *f*; **2.** *zo. a.* **common ~** Kreuzotter *f*; **3.** *allg.* Giftschlange *f* (*a. fig.*): **cherish a ~ in one's bosom** *fig.* e-e Schlange an s-m Busen nähren; **generation of ~s** *bibl.* Natterngezücht *n*; **'vi·per·ine** [-əraɪn] *adj. zo.* a) vipernartig, b) Vipern...; **'vi·per·ish** [-ərɪʃ] *adj.*; **'vi·per·ous** [-ərəs] *adj.* □ **1.** → **viperine;** **2.** *fig.* giftig, tückisch.

vi·per's grass *s.* ♀ Schwarzwurzel *f*.

vi·ra·go [vɪ'rɑːɡəʊ] *pl.* **-gos** *s.* **1.** Mannweib *n*; **2.** Zankteufel *m*, ‚Drachen' *m*, Xan'thippe *f*.

vi·res ['vaɪəriːz] *pl. von* **vis.**

vir·gin ['vɜːdʒɪn] I *s.* **1.** a) Jungfrau *f* (*a. ast.*), b) ‚Jungfrau' *f* (*Mann*); **2.** a) *eccl.* **the** (**Blessed**) **⚹** (**Mary**) die Heilige Jungfrau, b) *Kunst:* Ma'donna *f*; II *adj.* **3.** jungfräulich, unberührt (*beide a. fig. Schnee etc.*): **~ forest** Urwald *m*; **⚹ Mother** *eccl.* Mutter *f* Gottes; **the ⚹ Queen** *hist.* die jungfräuliche Königin (*Elisabeth I von England*); **~ queen** *zo.* unbefruchtete (Bienen)Königin; **~ soil** a) jungfräulicher Boden, ungepflügtes

Land, b) *fig.* Neuland *n*, c) *fig.* unberührter Geist; **4.** rein, keusch, jungfräulich: ~ *modesty*; **5.** ⊕ a) rein, unvermischt (*Stoffe etc.*), b) jungfräulich, gediegen (*Metalle*): ~ *gold* (*oil*) Jungferngold *n* (-öl *n*); ~ *wool* Schurwolle *f*; **6.** *fig.* Jungfern...: ~ *cruise* Jungfernfahrt *f*; '**vir·gin·al** [-nl] *adj.* □ **1.** jungfräulich, Jungfern...: ~ *membrane anat.* Jungfernhäutchen *n*; **2.** → *virgin* 4; **3.** *zo.* unbefruchtet; '**vir·gin·hood** [-hʊd] *s.* Jungfräulichkeit *f*, Jungfernschaft *f*.

Vir·gin·i·a [vəˈdʒɪnjə] *s. a.* ~ *tobacco* Virginia(tabak) *m*; ~ *creep·er s.* ♀ Wilder Wein, Jungfernrebe *f*.

Vir·gin·i·an [vəˈdʒɪnjən] **I** *adj.* Virginia...; **II** *s.* Vir'ginier(in).

vir·gin·i·ty [vəˈdʒɪnətɪ] *s.* **1.** Jungfräulichkeit *f*, Jungfernschaft *f*; **2.** Reinheit *f*, Keuschheit *f*, Unberührtheit *f* (*a. fig.*).

Vir·go [ˈvɜːgəʊ] *s. ast.* Jungfrau *f*.

vir·i·des·cent [ˌvɪrɪˈdesnt] *adj.* grün(-lich); **vi·rid·i·ty** [vɪˈrɪdətɪ] *s.* **1.** *biol.* grünes Aussehen; **2.** *fig.* Frische *f*.

vir·ile [ˈvɪraɪl] *adj.* **1.** männlich, kräftig (*beide a. fig. Stil etc.*), Männer..., Mannes...: ~ *voice*; **2.** *physiol.* po'tent: ~ *member* männliches Glied; **vi·ril·i·ty** [vɪˈrɪlətɪ] *s.* **1.** Männlichkeit *f*; **2.** Mannesalter *n*, -jahre *pl.*; **3.** *physiol.* Po'tenz *f*, Zeugungskraft *f*; **4.** *fig.* Kraft *f*.

vi·rol·o·gy [ˌvaɪəˈrɒlədʒɪ] *s.* ✹ Virolo'gie *f*, Virusforschung *f*.

vir·tu [vɜːˈtuː] *s.* **1.** Kunst-, Liebhaberwert *m*: *article of* ~ Kunstgegenstand *m*; **2.** *coll.* Kunstgegenstände *pl.*; **3.** → *virtuosity* 2.

vir·tu·al [ˈvɜːtʃʊəl] *adj.* □ **1.** tatsächlich, praktisch, eigentlich; **2.** ⊕, *phys.*, *Computer*: virtu'ell: ~ *memory* virtueller (Arbeits)Speicher; ~ *reality* virtu'elle Reali'tät; '**vir·tu·al·ly** [-əlɪ] *adv.* eigentlich, praktisch, im Grunde (genommen).

vir·tue [ˈvɜːtjuː] *s.* **1.** Tugend(haftigkeit) *f*: *woman of* ~ tugendhafte Frau; *lady of easy* ~ leichtes Mädchen; **2.** Rechtschaffenheit *f*; **3.** Tugend *f*: *make a* ~ *of necessity* aus der Not e-e Tugend machen; **4.** Wirksamkeit *f*, Wirkung *f*, Erfolg *m*; **5.** (gute) Eigenschaft, Vorzug *m*; (hoher) Wert; **6.** *by* (*od. in*) ~ *of* kraft *e-s Gesetzes, e-r Vollmacht etc.*, aufgrund von (*od. gen.*), vermöge (*gen.*).

vir·tu·os·i·ty [ˌvɜːtjʊˈɒsɪtɪ] *s.* **1.** Virtuosi'tät *f*, blendende Technik, meisterhaftes Können; **2.** Kunstsinn *m*, -liebhabe-'rei *f*; **vir·tu·o·so** [ˌvɜːtjʊˈəʊzəʊ] **I** *pl.* **-si** [-siː] *s.* **1.** Virtu'ose *m*; **2.** Kunstkenner *m*; **II** *adj.* **3.** virtu'os, meisterhaft.

vir·tu·ous [ˈvɜːtʃʊəs] *adj.* □ **1.** tugendhaft; **2.** rechtschaffen.

vir·u·lence [ˈvɪrʊləns], '**vir·u·len·cy** [-sɪ] *s.* ✹ *u. fig.* Viru'lenz *f*, Giftigkeit *f*, Bösartigkeit *f*; '**vir·u·lent** [-nt] *adj.* □ **1.** giftig, bösartig (*Gift, Krankheit*) (*a. fig.*); **2.** ✹ viru'lent (*a. fig.*), sehr ansteckend.

vi·rus [ˈvaɪərəs] *s.* **1.** ✹ Virus *n*: a) Krankheitserreger *m*, b) Gift-, Impfstoff *m*; **2.** *fig.* Gift *n*, Ba'zillus *m*: *the* ~ *of hatred*; **3.** *Computer*: Virus *m*, *n*: ~ *detection* Viruserkennung *f*; ~ *scanner* Virensuchprogramm *n*.

vis [vɪs] *pl.* **vi·res** [ˈvaɪəriːz] (*Lat.*) *s. bsd. phys.* Kraft *f*: ~ *inertiae* Trägheitskraft; ~ *mortua* tote Kraft; ~ *viva* kinetische Energie; ~ *major* ☆ höhere Gewalt.

vi·sa [ˈviːzə] **I** *s.* Visum *n*: a) Sichtvermerk *m* (*im Pass etc.*), b) Einreisebewil-

ligung *f*; **II** *v/t.* ein Visum eintragen in (*acc.*).

vis·age [ˈvɪzɪdʒ] *s. poet.* Antlitz *n*.

vis-à-vis [ˈviːzɑːviː; vizaˈvi] (*Fr.*) **I** *adv.* gegen'über (*to, with* von); **II** *s.* Gegen'über *n*: a) Visa'vis *n*, b) *fig.* ('Amts-) Kol,lege *m*.

vis·cer·a [ˈvɪsərə] *s. pl. anat.* Eingeweide *pl.*: *abdominal* ~ Bauchorgane *pl.*; '**vis·cer·al** [-rəl] *adj. anat.* Eingeweide...

vis·cid [ˈvɪsɪd] *adj.* **1.** klebrig (*a.* ♀); **2.** *bsd. phys.* vis'kos, dick-, zähflüssig; **vis·cid·i·ty** [vɪˈsɪdətɪ] *s.* **1.** Klebrigkeit *f*; **2.** → *viscosity*.

vis·cose [ˈvɪskəʊs] *s.* ⊕ Vis'kose *f* (*Art Zellulose*): ~ *silk* Viskose-, Zellstoffseide *f*; **vis·cos·i·ty** [vɪsˈkɒsətɪ] *s. phys.* Viskosi'tät *f*, (Grad *m* der) Zähflüssigkeit *f*, Konsi'stenz *f*.

vis·count [ˈvaɪkaʊnt] *s.* Vi'comte *m* (*brit. Adelstitel zwischen baron u. earl*); '**vis·count·cy** [-sɪ] *s.* Rang *m od.* Würde *f e-s* Vi'comte; '**vis·count·ess** [-tɪs] *s.* Vi'comtesse *f*; '**vis·count·y** [-tɪ] → *viscountcy*.

vis·cous [ˈvɪskəs] → *viscid*.

vi·sé [ˈviːzeɪ] **I** *s.* → *visa* I; **II** *v/t. pret. u. p.p.* **-séd** → *visa* II.

vise [vaɪs] *Am.* → *vice²*.

vis·i·bil·i·ty [ˌvɪzɪˈbɪlətɪ] *s.* **1.** Sichtbarkeit *f*; **2.** *meteor.* Sicht(weite) *f*: *high* (*low*) ~ gute (schlechte) Sicht; ~ (*conditions*) Sichtverhältnisse *pl.*; **vis·i·ble** [ˈvɪzəbl] *adj.* □ **1.** sichtbar; **2.** *fig.* (er-, offen-) sichtlich, merklich, deutlich, erkennbar; **3.** ⊕ sichtbar (gemacht), grafisch dargestellt; **4.** *pred.* a) zu sehen (*Sache*), b) zu sprechen (*Person*).

Vis·i·goth [ˈvɪzɪgɒθ] *s. hist.* Westgote *m*, -gotin *f*.

vi·sion [ˈvɪʒn] **I** *s.* **1.** Sehkraft *f*, -vermögen *n*: *field of* ~ Blickfeld *n*; **2.** *fig.* a) visio'näre Kraft, (Seher-, Weit)Blick *m*, b) Fanta'sie *f*, Vorstellungsvermögen *n*, Einsicht *f*: *bold* ~ kühne (Zukunfts)Ideen; **3.** Visi'on *f*: a) Traum-, Wunschbild *n*, b) *oft pl. psych.* Halluzinati'onen *pl.*, Gesichte *pl.*; **4.** a) Anblick *m*, Bild *n*, b) Traum *m*, et. Schönes; **II** *adj.* **5.** *TV* Bild...: ~ *mixer*; ~ *control* Bildregie *f*; **III** *v/t.* **6.** *fig.* (er-) schauen; '**vi·sion·ar·y** [-nərɪ] **I** *adj.* **1.** visio'när, (hell)seherisch; **2.** fan'tastisch, verstiegen, ,traumtänzerisch': *a* ~ *scheme*; **3.** unwirklich, eingebildet; **4.** Visions...; **II** *s.* **5.** Visio'när *m*, Hellseher *m*; **6.** Fan'tast *m*, Träumer *m*, Schwärmer *m*, ,Traumtänzer' *m*.

vis·it [ˈvɪzɪt] **I** *v/t.* **1.** besuchen: a) *j-n, Arzt, Kranke, Lokal etc.* aufsuchen, b) inspizieren, in Augenschein nehmen, c) *Stadt, Museum etc.* besichtigen; **2.** ☆ durch'suchen; **3.** heimsuchen (*s.th. upon j-n* mit et.): a) befallen (*Krankheit, Unglück*), b) *bibl. u. fig.* (be-) strafen, *Sünden* vergelten (*upon* an *dat.*); **4.** *bibl.* belohnen, segnen; **II** *v/i.* **5.** e-n Besuch *od.* Besuche machen; **6.** *Am.* F plaudern; **III** *s.* **7.** Besuch *m*: *on a* ~ auf Besuch (*to* bei *j-m, in e-r Stadt etc.*); *make* (*od. pay*) *a* ~ e-n Besuch machen; ~ *to the doctor* Konsultation *f* beim Arzt, Arztbesuch *m*; **8.** (for'mel-ler) Besuch, *bsd.* Inspekti'on *f*; **9.** ☆, ☆ Durch'suchung *f*; **10.** *Am.* F Plausch *m*; '**vis·it·ant** [-tənt] **I** *s.* **1.** *rhet.* Besucher (-in); **2.** *orn.* Strichvogel *m*; **II** *adj.* **3.** *rhet.* auf Besuch; **vis·it·a·tion** [ˌvɪzɪˈteɪʃn] *s.* **1.** Besuchen *n*; **2.** offizi'eller Besuch, Besichtigung *f*, Visita-ti'on *f*: *right of* ~ ☆ Durchsuchungs-recht *n* (*auf See*); ~ (*of the sick*) *eccl.*

Krankenbesuch; **3.** *fig.* Heimsuchung: a) (gottgesandte) Prüfung *f*, Strafe *f* (Gottes), b) himmlischer Beistand: ⒉ *of our Lady R.C.* Heimsuchung Mariae; **4.** *zo.* massenhaftes Auftreten; **5.** F langer Besuch; **vis·it·a·to·ri·al** [ˌvɪzɪtə-ˈtɔːrɪəl] *adj.* Visitations..., Überwachungs..., Aufsichts...: ~ *power* Aufsichtsbefugnis *f*; '**vis·it·ing** [-tɪŋ] *adj.* Besuchs..., Besucher...: ~ *book* Besuchsliste *f*; ~ *card* Visitenkarte *f*; ~ *hours* Besuchszeit *f*; ~ *nurse Am.* Gemeindeschwester *f*; ~ *professor univ.* Gastprofessor *m*; ~ *team sport* Gastmannschaft *f*; *be on* ~ *terms with s.o.* j-n so gut kennen, dass man ihn besucht; '**vis·i·tor** [-tə] *s.* **1.** Besucher(in) (*to gen.*), (*a.* Kur)Gast *m*; *pl.* Besuch *m*: *summer* ~s Sommergäste *pl.*; ~s' *book* a) Fremdenbuch *n*, b) Gästebuch *n*; **2.** Visi'tator *m*, In'spektor *m*; **vis·i·to·ri·al** [ˌvɪzɪˈtɔːrɪəl] → *visitatorial*.

vi·sor [ˈvaɪzə] *s.* **1.** *hist. u. fig.* Vi'sier *n*; **2.** (Mützen)Schirm *m*; **3.** *mot.* Sonnenblende *f*.

vis·ta [ˈvɪstə] *s.* **1.** (Aus-, 'Durch)Blick *m*, Aussicht *f*; **2.** Al'lee *f*; **3.** △ Gale'rie *f*, Korridor *m*; **4.** (lange) Reihe, Kette *f*: *a* ~ *of years*; **5.** *fig.* Ausblick *m*, -sicht *f* (*of* auf *acc.*), Möglichkeit *f*, Perspek'tive *f*: *his words opened up new* ~s.

vis·u·al [ˈvɪzjʊəl] **I** *adj.* □ **1.** Seh..., Gesichts...: ~ *acuity* Sehschärfe *f*; ~ *angle* Gesichtswinkel *m*; ~ *nerve* Sehnerv *m*; ~ *test* Augentest *m*; **2.** visu'ell (*Eindruck, Gedächtnis etc.*): ~ *aid*(*s*) *ped.* Anschauungsmaterial *n*; ~ *arts* bildende Künste; ~ *display unit Computer*: Datensichtgerät *n*; ~ *instruction ped.* Anschauungsunterricht *m*; **3.** sichtbar: ~ *objects*; **4.** optisch, Sicht...(-*anzeige, -bereich, -zeichen etc.*); **II** *s.* **5.** *typ.*, ✹ a) (Roh)Skizze *f e-s* Layouts, b) 'Bildele,ment *n e-r* Anzeige; **vis·u·al·i·za·tion** [ˌvɪzjʊəlaɪˈzeɪʃn] *s.* Vergegenwärtigung *f*; '**vis·u·al·ize** [-laɪz] *v/t.* sich vergegenwärtigen *od.* vor Augen stellen, sich vorstellen, sich ein Bild machen von; '**vis·u·al·iz·er** [-laɪzə] *s.* ✹ grafischer I'deengestalter.

vi·ta [ˈviːtə] (*Lat.*) *pl.* **-tae** [-taɪ] *s. Am.* Lebenslauf *m*.

vi·tal [ˈvaɪtl] **I** *adj.* **1.** Lebens...(-*frage, -funktion, -funke etc.*): ~ *energy* (*od. power*) Lebenskraft *f*; ~ *statistics* a) Bevölkerungsstatistik *f*, b) *humor.* Körpermaße *pl.*: *Bureau of* ⒉ *Statistics Am.* Personenstandsregister *n*; **2.** lebenswichtig (*Industrie, Organ etc.*): ~ *parts* → 8; **3.** (hoch)wichtig, entscheidend (*to* für): ~ *problems*; *of* ~ *importance* von entscheidender Bedeutung; **4.** wesentlich, grundlegend; **5.** *mst fig.* le'bendig: ~ *style*; **6.** vi'tal, lebensprühend; **7.** lebensgefährlich: ~ *wound*; **II** *s.* **8.** *pl.* a) *anat.* ,edle Teile' *pl.*, lebenswichtige Or'gane *pl.*, b) *fig. das* Wesentliche, wichtige Bestandteile *pl.*; **vi·tal·i·ty** [vaɪˈtælətɪ] *s.* **1.** Vitali'tät *f*, Lebenskraft *f*; **2.** Lebensfähigkeit *f*, -dauer *f* (*a. fig.*); **vi·tal·i·za·tion** [ˌvaɪtəlaɪ-ˈzeɪʃn] *s.* Belebung *f*, Aktivierung *f*; '**vi·tal·ize** [-təlaɪz] *v/t.* **1.** beleben, kräftigen; **2.** mit Lebenskraft erfüllen; **3.** *fig.* a) verle'bendigen, b) le'bendig gestalten.

vi·ta·min(**e**) [ˈvɪtəmɪn] *s.* Vita'min *n*.

vi·ti·ate [ˈvɪʃɪeɪt] *v/t.* **1.** *allg.* verderben; **2.** beeinträchtigen; **3.** a) *Luft etc.* verunreinigen, b) *fig. Atmosphäre* vergiften; **4.** *Argument etc.* wider'legen; **5.**

bsd. ☙ ungültig machen, aufheben; **vi-ti-a-tion** [ˌvɪʃɪˈeɪʃn] *s.* **1.** Verderben *n*, Verderbnis *f*; **2.** Beeinträchtigung *f*; **3.** Verunreinigung *f*; **4.** Wider'legung *f*; **5.** ☙ Aufhebung *f*.

vit-i-cul-ture [ˈvɪtɪkʌltʃə] *s.* Weinbau *m*.

vit-re-ous [ˈvɪtrɪəs] *adj.* **1.** Glas..., aus Glas, gläsern; **2.** glasartig, glasig: **~ body** *anat.* Glaskörper *m des Auges*; **~ electricity** positive Elektrizität; **3.** *geol.* glasig; **vi-tres-cent** [vɪˈtresnt] *adj.* **1.** verglasend; **2.** verglasbar.

vit-ri-fac-tion [ˌvɪtrɪˈfækʃn], **vit-ri-fi-ca-tion** [ˌvɪtrɪfɪˈkeɪʃn] *s.* ⊙ Ver-, Über'gla-sung *f*, Sinterung *f*; **vit-ri-fy** [ˈvɪtrɪfaɪ] ⊙ **I** *v/t.* ver-, über'glasen, glasieren, sin-tern; *Keramik:* dicht brennen; **II** *v/i.* (sich) verglasen.

vit-ri-ol [ˈvɪtrɪəl] *s.* **1.** ⚗ Vitri'ol *n*: **blue ~**, **copper ~** Kupfervitriol, -sulfat *n*; **green ~** Eisenvitriol, Ferrosulfat *n*; **white ~** Zinksulfat *n*; **2.** ⚗ a) Vitri'ol-säure *f*, b) **oil of ~** Vitriolöl *n*, rauchen-de Schwefelsäure; **3.** *fig.* a) Gift *n*, Säure *f*, b) Giftigkeit *f*, Schärfe *f*; **vit-ri-ol-ic** [ˌvɪtrɪˈɒlɪk] *adj.* **1.** vitri'olisch, Vitriol...: **~ acid** → **vitriol** 2b; **2.** *fig.* ätzend, beißend: **~ remark**; **'vit-ri-ol-ize** [-laɪz] *v/t.* **1.** ⚗ vitriolisieren; **2.** *j-n* mit Vitriol bespritzen *od.* verletzen.

vi-tu-per-ate [vɪˈtjuːpəreɪt] *v/t.* **1.** be-schimpfen, schmähen; **2.** scharf tadeln; **vi-tu-per-a-tion** [vɪˌtjuːpəˈreɪʃn] *s.* **1.** Schmähung *f*, (wüste) Beschimpfung; *pl.* Schimpfworte *pl.*; **2.** scharfer Tadel *m*; **vi'tu-per-a-tive** [-pərətɪv] *adj.* □ **1.** schmähend, Schmäh...; **2.** tadelnd.

vi-va¹ [ˈviːvə] (*Ital.*) **I** *int.* Hoch!; **II** *s.* Hoch(ruf *m*) *n*.

vi-va² [ˈvaɪvə] → **viva voce**.

vi-va-cious [vɪˈveɪʃəs] *adj.* □ lebhaft, munter; **vi-vac-i-ty** [vɪˈvæsətɪ] *s.* Leb-haftigkeit *f*, Munterkeit *f*.

vi-var-i-um [vaɪˈveərɪəm] *pl.* **-i-a** [-ɪə] *s.* Vi'varium *n* (*Aquarium, Terrarium etc.*).

vi-va vo-ce [ˌvaɪvəˈvəʊsɪ] **I** *adj. u. adv.* mündlich; **II** *s.* mündliche Prüfung; **vi-va-vo-ce** [ˌvaɪvəˈvəʊsɪ] *v/t.* mündlich prüfen.

viv-id [ˈvɪvɪd] *adj.* □ **1.** *allg.* lebhaft: a) impul'siv (*Mensch*), b) inten'siv (*Ge-fühle, Fantasie*), c) leuchtend (*Farbe etc.*), d) deutlich, klar (*Schilderung etc.*); **2.** le'bendig (*Porträt etc.*); **'viv-id-ness** [-nɪs] *s.* **1.** Lebhaftigkeit *f*; **2.** Le-'bendigkeit *f*.

viv-i-fy [ˈvɪvɪfaɪ] *v/t.* **1.** 'wieder beleben; **2.** *fig.* Leben geben (*dat.*), beleben, an-regen; **3.** *fig.* intensivieren; **4.** *biol.* in lebendes Gewebe verwandeln; **vi-vip-a-rous** [vɪˈvɪpərəs] *adj.* □ **1.** *zo.* le-bend gebärend; **2.** ♀ noch an der Mut-terpflanze keimend (*Samen*); **viv-i-sect** [ˌvɪvɪˈsekt] *v/t. u. v/i.* vivisezieren, le-bend sezieren; **viv-i-sec-tion** [ˌvɪvɪ-ˈsekʃn] *s.* Vivisekti'on *f*.

vix-en [ˈvɪksn] *s.* **1.** *zo.* Füchsin *f*; **2.** *fig.* ‚Drachen', Xan'thippe *f*; **'vix-en-ish** [-nɪʃ] *adj.* zänkisch.

vi-zier [vɪˈzɪə] *s.* We'sir *m*.

vi-zor → **visor**.

V-J Day *s.* Tag *m* des Sieges der Alli'ier-ten über Japan (*im 2. Weltkrieg; 2. 9. 1945*).

vo-ca-ble [ˈvəʊkəbl] *s.* Vo'kabel *f*.

vo-cab-u-lar-y [vəʊˈkæbjʊlərɪ] *s.* Voka-bu'lar *n*: a) Wörterverzeichnis *n*, b) Wortschatz *m*.

vo-cal [ˈvəʊkl] **I** *adj.* □ → **vocally**; **1.** stimmlich, mündlich, Stimm..., Sprech...: **~ c(h)ords** Stimmbänder *pl.*; **2.** ♪ Vokal..., Gesang(s)..., ge-

sanglich: **~ music** Vokalmusik *f*; **~ part** Singstimme *f*; **~ recital** Liederabend *m*; **3.** klingend, 'widerhallend (**with** von); **4.** stimmbegabt, der Sprache mächtig; **5.** laut, vernehmbar, *a.* gesprächig: **be-come ~** *fig.* laut werden, sich verneh-men lassen; **6.** *ling.* a) vo'kalisch, b) stimmhaft; **II** *s.* **7.** (gesungener) Schla-ger; **vo-cal-ic** [vəʊˈkælɪk] *adj.* vo'ka-lisch; **'vo-cal-ism** [-kəlɪzəm] *s.* **1.** Vo-kalisati'on *f* (*Vokalbildung u. -ausspra-che*); **2.** Vo'kalsy₁stem *n e-r Sprache*; **'vo-cal-ist** [-kəlɪst] *s.* ♪ Sänger(in); **vo-cal-i-za-tion** [ˌvəʊkəlaɪˈzeɪʃn] *s.* **1.** *bsd.* ♪ Stimmgebung *f*; **2.** *ling.* a) Vokalisa-ti'on *f*, b) stimmhafte Aussprache; **'vo-cal-ize** [-kəlaɪz] **I** *v/t.* **1.** *Laut* ausspre-chen, *a.* singen; **2.** *ling.* a) *Konsonanten* vokalisieren, b) stimmhaft ausspre-chen; **3.** → **vowelize** 1; **II** *v/i.* **4.** (*beim Singen*) vokalisieren.

vo-ca-tion [vəʊˈkeɪʃn] *s.* **1.** (*eccl.* göttli-che, *allg.* innere) Berufung (**for** zu); **2.** Begabung *f*, Eignung *f* (**for** für); **3.** Be-ruf *m*, Beschäftigung *f*; **vo-ca-tion-al** [-ʃənl] *adj.* □ beruflich, Berufs... (*-aus-bildung, -krankheit, -schule etc.*): **~ guidance** Berufsberatung *f*; **~ retrain-ing** berufliche 'Umschulung; **~ training** Be'rufs₁ausbildung *f*, berufliche Bildung.

voc-a-tive [ˈvɒkətɪv] **I** *adj.* *ling.* vokati-visch, Anrede...: **~ case** → **II** *s.* Vokati-v *m*.

vo-cif-er-ate [vəʊˈsɪfəreɪt] *v/i.* schreien, brüllen; **vo-cif-er-a-tion** [vəʊˌsɪfə-ˈreɪʃn] *s. a. pl.* Schreien *n*, Brüllen *n*, Geschrei *n*; **vo'cif-er-ous** [-fərəs] *adj.* □ **1.** laut schreiend, brüllend; **2.** lär-mend, laut; **3.** lautstark: **~ protest**.

vod-ka [ˈvɒdkə] *s.* Wodka *m*.

vogue [vəʊg] *s.* **1.** *allg.* (herrschende) Mode: **all the ~** (die) große Mode, der letzte Schrei; **be in ~** (in) Mode sein; **come into ~** in Mode kommen; **2.** Be-liebtheit *f*: **be in full ~** großen Anklang finden, sehr beliebt sein; **have a short-lived ~** sich e-r kurzen Beliebtheit er-freuen; **~ word** *s.* Modewort *n*.

voice [vɔɪs] **I** *s.* **1.** Stimme *f* (*a. fig. des Gewissens etc.*): **the still, small ~** (*within*) *fig.* die leise Stimme des Ge-wissens; **in** (**good**) **~** ♪ (gut) bei Stim-me; **in a low ~** mit leiser Stimme; **~ box** Kehlkopf *m*; **~ off** *TV etc:* Offstimme *f*; **~ on** *TV etc:* Onstimme *f*; **~ recog-nition** *Computer:* Spracherkennung *f*; **~ radio** ♫ Sprechfunk *m*; **~ range** ♪ Stimmumfang *m*; **2.** *fig.* Ausdruck *m*, Äußerung *f:* **find ~ in** Ausdruck finden in (*dat.*); **give ~ to** → 7; **3.** *fig. allg.* Stimme *f:* a) Entscheidung *f:* **give one's ~ for** stimmen für; **with one ~** einstimmig, b) Stimmrecht *n:* **have a** (**no**) **~ in** et. (nichts) zu sagen haben bei *od.* in (*dat.*), c) Sprecher(in), Sprach-rohr *n*; **4.** ♪ a) **~ quality** Stimmton *m*, b) (Orgel)Stimme *f*; **5.** *ling.* a) stimmhafter Laut, b) Stimmton *m*; **6.** *ling. Gra. des Verbs:* **active ~** Aktiv *n*; **passive ~** Passiv *n*; **II** *v/t.* **7.** Aus-druck geben *od.* verleihen (*dat.*), Mei-nung etc. äußern, in Worte fassen; **8.** ♪ *Orgelpfeife etc.* regulieren; **9.** *ling.* (stimmhaft) (aus)sprechen; **voiced** [-st] *adj.* **1.** *in Zssgn mit leiser etc.* Stim-me: **low-~**; **2.** *ling.* stimmhaft; **'voice-less** [-lɪs] *adj.* **1.** ohne Stimme, stumm; **2.** sprachlos; **3.** *parl.* nicht stimmfähig; **4.** *ling.* stimmlos; **voice mail** *s. teleph.* Voice-Mail *f*; **'voice-₁o-ver** *s. Film, TV:* 'Offkommen₁tar *m*.

void [vɔɪd] **I** *adj.* □ **1.** leer; **2.** **~ of** ohne, bar (*gen.*), arm an (*dat.*), frei von; **3.**

unbewohnt; **4.** unbesetzt, frei (*Amt*); **5.** ☙ nichtig, ungültig, -wirksam; → **null** 1; **II** *s.* **6.** (*fig.* Gefühl *n* der) Leere *f*, leerer Raum; **7.** *fig.* Lücke *f:* **fill the ~** die Lücke schließen; **8.** ☙ unbewohn-tes Gebäude; **III** *v/t.* **9.** räumen (**of** von); **10.** ☙ a) aufheben, b) anfechten; **11.** *physiol.* Urin etc. ausscheiden; **'void-a-ble** [-dəbl] *adj.* ☙ aufheb- *od.* anfechtbar; **'void-ance** [-dəns] *s.* Räu-mung *f*; **'void-ness** [-nɪs] *s.* **1.** Leere *f*; **2.** ☙ Nichtigkeit *f*, Ungültigkeit *f*.

voile [vɔɪl] *s.* Voile *m*, Schleierstoff *m*.

vo-lant [ˈvəʊlənt] *adj.* **1.** *zo.* fliegend (*a. her.*); **2.** *poet.* flüchtig.

vol-a-tile [ˈvɒlətaɪl] *adj.* **1.** *phys.* ver-dampfbar, (leicht) flüchtig, vola'til, ä'therisch (*Öl etc.*); **2.** *fig.* flüchtig, ver-gänglich; **3.** *fig.* a) le'bendig, lebhaft, b) launisch, unbeständig, flatterhaft; **vol-a-til-i-ty** [ˌvɒləˈtɪlətɪ] *s.* **1.** *phys.* Ver-dampfbarkeit *f*, Flüchtigkeit *f* (*a. fig.*); **2.** *fig.* a) Lebhaftigkeit *f*, b) Unbestän-dig-, Flatterhaftigkeit *f*; **vol-a-til-i-za-tion** [vɒˌlætɪlaɪˈzeɪʃn] *s. phys.* Verflüch-tigung *f*, Verdampfung *f*; **vol-a-til-ize** [vɒˈlætɪlaɪz] *v/t.* (*v/i.* sich) verflüchtigen, verdunsten, verdampfen.

vol-au-vent [ˈvɒləʊvɑ̃; vɒlovɑ̃] (*Fr.*) *s.* Vol-au-'Vent *m* (*gefüllte Blätterteigpas-tete*).

vol-can-ic [vɒlˈkænɪk] *adj.* (□ **~ally**) **1.** *geol.* vul'kanisch, Vulkan...; **2.** *fig.* un-gestüm, explo'siv; **vol-ca-no** [vɒlˈkeɪ-nəʊ] *pl.* **-no(e)s** *s.* **1.** *geol.* Vul'kan *m*; **2.** *fig.* Vul'kan *m*, Pulverfass *n:* **sit on the top of a ~** (wie) auf e-m Pulverfass sitzen; **vol-can-ol-o-gy** [ˌvɒlkəˈnɒlədʒɪ] *s.* Vulkanolo'gie *f*.

vole¹ [vəʊl] *s. zo.* Wühlmaus *f*.

vole² [vəʊl] *s. Kartenspiel:* Gewinn *m* aller Stiche.

vo-li-tion [vəʊˈlɪʃn] *s.* **1.** Willensäuße-rung *f*, -akt *m*, (Willens)Entschluss *m:* **on one's own ~** aus eigenem Ent-schluss; **2.** Wille *m*, Wollen *n*, Willens-kraft *f*; **vo'li-tion-al** [-ʃənl] *adj.* □ Wil-lens..., willensmäßig; **vol-i-tive** [ˈvɒlɪ-tɪv] *adj.* **1.** Willens...; **2.** *ling.* voli'tiv.

vol-ley [ˈvɒlɪ] **I** *s.* **1.** (Gewehr-, Ge-schütz)Salve *f*; (Pfeil-, Stein- *etc.*)Hagel *m*; *Artillerie, Flak:* Gruppe *f:* **~ bomb-ing** ✈ Reihenwurf *m*; **2.** *fig.* Schwall *m*, Strom, Flut *f:* **a ~ of oaths**; **3.** *sport:* a) *Tennis:* Volley *m* (*Schlag*), (*Ball a.*) Flugball *m*, b) *Fußball:* Vol-leyschuss *m:* **take a ball at od. on the ~** → 6; **4.** *Badminton:* Ballwechsel *m*; **II** *v/t.* **5.** in e-r Salve abschießen; **6.** *sport:* den Ball volley nehmen, (*Fußball a.*) (di'rekt) aus der Luft nehmen; **7.** *mst* **~ out od. forth** e-n Schwall von Worten etc. von sich geben; **III** *v/i.* **8.** e-e Salve *od.* Salven abgeben; **9.** hageln (*Ge-schosse*), krachen (*Geschütze*); **10.** *sport:* a) *Tennis:* volieren, b) *Fußball:* volley schießen; **'~ball** *s. sport* **1.** Vol-leyball(spiel *n*) *m*; **2.** Volleyball *m*.

vol-plane [ˈvɒlpleɪn] ✈ **I** *s.* Gleitflug *m*; **II** *v/i.* im Gleitflug niedergehen.

volt¹ [vɒlt] *s. fenc. u. Reitsport:* Volte *f*.

volt² [vəʊlt] *s.* ⚡ Volt *n*; **'volt-age** [-tɪdʒ] *s.* ⚡ (Volt)Spannung *f*; **vol-ta-ic** [vɒl-ˈteɪɪk] *adj.* ⚡ vol'taisch, gal'vanisch (*Batterie, Element, Strom etc.*): **~ cou-ple** Elektrodenmetalle *pl*.

volte-face [ˌvɒltˈfɑːs; vɒltfas] (*Fr.*) *s. fig.* (to'tale) (Kehrt)Wendung.

volt-me-ter [ˈvəʊltˌmiːtə] *s.* ⚡ Voltmeter *m*, Spannungsmesser *m*.

vol-u-bil-i-ty [ˌvɒljʊˈbɪlətɪ] *s. fig.* a) glat-ter Fluss (*der Rede*), b) Zungenfertig-keit *f*, Redegewandtheit *f*, c) Redseligkeit *f*, d) Wortreichtum *m*; **vol·u·ble** ['vɒljʊbl] *adj.* □ **1.** a) geläufig (*Zunge*), fließend (*Rede*), b) zungenfertig, (rede)gewandt, c) redselig, d) wortreich; **2.** ♀ windend.

vol·ume ['vɒljuːm] *s.* **1.** Band *m* e-s Buches; Buch *n* (*a. fig.*): *a three-~ novel* ein dreibändiger Roman; *speak ~s (for) fig.* Bände sprechen (für); **2.** ⚹, ♠, *phys. etc.* Vo'lumen *n*, (Raum)Inhalt *m*; **3.** *fig.* 'Umfang *m*, Vo'lumen *n*: *~ of imports; ~ of traffic* Verkehrsaufkommen *n*; **4.** *fig.* Masse *f*, Schwall *m*; **5.** ♪ Klangfülle *f*, 'Stimmvo,lumen *n*, -,umfang *m*; **6.** ♮ Lautstärke *f*: *~ control* Lautstärkeregler *m*; **'vol·umed** [-md] *adj. in Zssgn* ...bändig; **'vol·u·met·ric** [,vɒljʊ'metrɪk] *adj.* (□ *~ally*) ⚹, ♠ volu'metrisch: *~ analysis* ♠ volumetrische Analyse, Maßanalyse *f*; *~ density* Raumdichte *f*; **vol·u·met·ri·cal** [,vɒljʊ'metrɪkl] *adj.* □ → **volumetric; vo·lu·mi·nous** [və'ljuːmɪnəs] *adj.* □ **1.** vielbändig (*literarisches Werk*); **2.** produk'tiv: *a ~ author*; **3.** massig, 'umfangreich, volumi'nös: *~ correspondence*; **4.** bauschig; **5.** ♪ voll: *~ voice*.

vol·un·tar·i·ness ['vɒləntərɪnɪs] *s.* **1.** Freiwilligkeit *f*; **2.** (Willens)Freiheit *f*; **vol·un·tar·y** ['vɒləntərɪ] **I** *adj.* □ **1.** freiwillig, spon'tan: *~ contribution; ~ death* Freitod *m*; **2.** frei, unabhängig; **3.** ½ a) vorsätzlich, schuldhaft, b) freiwillig, unentgeltlich, c) außergerichtlich, gütlich: *~ settlement; ~ jurisdiction* freiwillige Gerichtsbarkeit; **4.** durch freiwillige Spenden unter'halten (*Schule etc.*); **5.** *physiol.* willkürlich: *~ muscles*; **6.** *psych.* volunta'ristisch; **II** *s.* **7.** a) freiwillige od. wahlweise Arbeit, b) *a. ~ exercise sport* Kür(übung) *f*; **8.** ♪ Orgelsolo *n*.

vol·un·teer [,vɒlən'tɪə] **I** *s.* **1.** Freiwillige(r *m*) *f* (*a.* ✕); **2.** ½ unentgeltlicher Rechtsnachfolger; **II** *adj.* **3.** freiwillig, Freiwilligen...; **4.** ♀ wild wachsend; **III** *v/i.* **5.** sich freiwillig melden *od.* erbieten (*for* für, zu), als Freiwilliger eintreten *od.* dienen; **IV** *v/t.* **6.** *Dienste etc.* freiwillig anbieten *od.* leisten; **7.** sich *e-e Bemerkung* erlauben; **8.** (freiwillig) zum Besten geben: *he ~ed a song*.

vo·lup·tu·ar·y [və'lʌptjʊərɪ] *s.* Lüstling *m*, sinnlicher Mensch; **vo'lup·tu·ous** [-tʃʊəs] *adj.* □ **1.** wollüstig, sinnlich; geil, lüstern; **2.** üppig, sinnlich: *~ body*; **vo'lup·tu·ous·ness** [-tʃʊəsnɪs] *s.* **1.** Wollust *f*, Sinnlichkeit *f*, Geilheit *f*, Lüsternheit *f*; **2.** Üppigkeit *f*.

vo·lute [və'ljuːt] *s.* **1.** Schnörkel *m*, Spi'rale *f*; **2.** △ Vo'lute *f*, Schnecke *f*; **3.** *zo.* Windung *f* (*Schneckengehäuse*); **vo'lut·ed** [-tɪd] *adj.* **1.** gewunden, spi'ral-, schneckenförmig; **2.** △ mit Vo'luten (versehen); **vo'lu·tion** [-juːʃn] *s.* **1.** Drehung *f*; **2.** *anat., zo.* Windung *f*.

vom·it ['vɒmɪt] **I** *v/t.* **1.** (er)brechen; **2.** *fig. Feuer etc.* (aus)speien; *Rauch, a. Flüche etc.* ausstoßen; **II** *v/i.* **3.** (sich er)brechen, sich über'geben; **4.** Rauch ausstoßen; Lava auswerfen, Feuer speien (*Vulkan*); **III** *s.* **5.** Erbrechen *n*; **6.** das Erbrochene; **7.** ☀ Brechmittel *n*; **8.** *fig.* Unflat *m*; **'vom·i·tive** [-tɪv], **'vom·i·to·ry** [-tərɪ] **I** *s.* ☀ Brechmittel *n*; **II** *adj.* Erbrechen verursachend, Brech...

voo·doo ['vuːduː] **I** *s.* **1.** Wodu *m*, Voo-

doo *m*, Zauberkult *m*; **2.** Zauber *m*, Hexe'rei *f*; **3.** *a. ~ doctor, ~ priest* (Wodu)Zauberer *m*, Medi'zinmann *m*; **4.** Fetisch *m*, Götze *m*; **II** *v/t.* **5.** behexen; **'voo·doo·ism** *s.* Wodukult *m*.

vo·ra·cious [və'reɪʃəs] *adj.* □ gefräßig, gierig, unersättlich (*a. fig.*); **vo'ra·cious·ness** [-nɪs], **vo·rac·i·ty** [vɒ'ræsətɪ] *s.* Gefräßigkeit *f*, Unersättlichkeit *f*, Gier *f* (*of* nach).

vor·tex ['vɔːteks] *pl.* **-ti·ces** [-tɪsiːz] *s.* Wirbel *m*, Strudel *m* (*a. phys. fig.*); **'vor·ti·cal** [-tɪkl] *adj.* □ **1.** wirbelnd, kreisend, Wirbel...; **2.** wirbel-, strudelartig.

vo·ta·ress ['vəʊtərɪs] *s.* Geweihte *f* (*etc.*, → *votary*); **vo·ta·ry** ['vəʊtərɪ] *s. eccl.* Geweihte(r *m*) *f*; **2.** *fig.* Verfechter(in), (Vor)Kämpfer(in); **3.** *fig.* Anhänger(-in), Verehrer(in), Jünger(in), Enthusi'ast(in).

vote [vəʊt] **I** *s.* **1.** (Wahl)Stimme *f*, Votum *n*: *~ of censure, ~ of no confidence parl.* Misstrauensvotum; *~ of confidence parl.* Vertrauensvotum; *give one's ~ to (od. for)* s-e Stimme geben (*dat.*), stimmen für; **2.** Abstimmung *f*, Wahl *f*: *put s.th. to the ~, take a ~ on s.th.* über e-e Sache abstimmen lassen; *take the ~* abstimmen; **3.** Stimmzettel *m*, Stimme *f*: *cast one's ~* s-e Stimme abgeben; **4.** *the ~* das Stimm-, Wahlrecht; **5.** a) Stimme *f*, Stimmzettel *m*, b) *the ~ coll.* die Stimmen *pl.*: *the Labour ~*, c) Wahlergebnis *n*; **6.** Beschluss *m*: *a unanimous ~*; **7.** (Geld)Bewilligung *f*; **II** *v/i.* **8.** (ab)stimmen, wählen, s-e Stimme abgeben: *~ against* stimmen gegen; *~ for* stimmen für (*a.* F *für et. sein*); **III** *v/t.* **9.** abstimmen über (*acc.*), wählen, stimmen für: *~ down* niederstimmen; *~ s.o. in* j-n wählen; *~ s.o. out (of office)* j-n abwählen; *~ s.th. through* et. durchbringen; *~ that* dafür sein, dass, vorschlagen, dass; **10.** (durch Abstimmung) wählen *od.* beschließen *od.* Geld bewilligen; **11.** allgemein erklären für *od.* halten für: *~ s.th. a bore*; **'vote-,catch·er** *s.*, **'vote-,get·ter** *s.* ,'Wahllokomo,tive' *f*, Stimmenfänger *m*; **'vote·less** [-lɪs] *adj.* ohne Stimmrecht *od.* Stimme; **'vot·er** [-tə] *s.* Wähler(in), Wahl-, Stimmberechtigte(r *m*) *f*; **'vote-,rig·ging** *s.* Wahlschwindel *m*, -manipulation *f*.

vot·ing ['vəʊtɪŋ] **I** *s.* (Ab)Stimmen *n*, Abstimmung *f*; **II** *adj.* Stimm..., Wahl...; *~ age* Wahlalter *n*; *~ machine s.* 'Wahlma,schine *f*; *~ pa·per s.* Stimmzettel *m*; *~ share s.* ☀ Stimmrechtaktie *f*; *~ stock s.* ☀ stimmberechtigtes 'Aktienkapi,tal; **2.** *bsd. Am.* 'Stimmrechts,aktie *f*; *~ pow·er s.* ☀ Stimmrecht *n*.

vo·tive ['vəʊtɪv] *adj.* Weih..., Votiv..., Denk...: *~ medal* (Ge)Denkmünze *f*; *~ tablet* Votivtafel *f*.

vouch [vaʊtʃ] **I** *v/i.* **1.** *~ for* (sich ver-) bürgen für; **2.** *~ that* dafür bürgen, dass; **II** *v/t.* **3.** bezeugen; bestätigen, (urkundlich) belegen; **4.** (sich ver)bürgen für; **'vouch·er** [-tʃə] *s.* **1.** Zeuge *m*, Bürge *m*; **2.** 'Unterlage *f*, Doku'ment *n*: *support by ~* dokumentarisch belegen; **3.** (Rechnungs)Beleg *m*, Quittung *f*: *~ check* ☀ *Am.* Verrechnungsscheck; *~ copy* Belegdoppel *n*; **4.** Gutschein *m*; **5.** Eintrittskarte *f*; **vouch'safe** [-'seɪf] *v/t.* **1.** (gnädig) gewähren; **2.** geruhen

zu *tun*; **3.** sich her'ablassen zu: *he ~d me no answer* er würdigte mich keiner Antwort.

vow [vaʊ] **I** *s.* **1.** Gelübde *n* (*a. eccl.*); *oft pl.* (feierliches) Versprechen, (Treue-)Schwur *m*: *be under a ~* ein Gelübde abgelegt haben, versprochen haben (*to do* zu tun); *take (od. make) a ~* ein Gelübde ablegen; *take ~s eccl.* Profess ablegen, in ein Kloster eintreten; **II** *v/t.* **2.** geloben; **3.** (sich) schwören, (sich) geloben, hoch u. heilig versprechen (*to do* zu tun); **4.** feierlich erklären.

vow·el ['vaʊəl] **I** *s. ling.* **1.** Vo'kal *m*, Selbstlaut *m*; **II** *adj.* **2.** vo'kalisch; **3.** Vokal..., Selbstlaut...: *~ gradation* Ablaut *m*; *~ mutation* Umlaut *m*; **vow·el·ize** ['vaʊəlaɪz] *v/t.* **1.** hebräischen *od. kurzschriftlichen Text* mit Vo'kalzeichen versehen; **2.** *Laut* vokalisieren.

voy·age ['vɔɪɪdʒ] **I** *s.* längere (See-, Flug-) Reise: *~ home* Rück-, Heimreise; *~ out* Hinreise *f*; **II** *v/i.* (*bsd.* zur See) reisen; **III** *v/t.* reisen durch, bereisen; **voy·ag·er** ['vɔɪədʒə] *s.* (See)Reisende(r *m*) *f*.

vo·yeur·ism [vwɑː'jɜːrɪzəm] *s.* Voy'eurtum *n*.

'V|-sign *s.* **1.** Siegeszeichen *n* (*mit gespreizten Fingern*), *Am. a.* Zeichen der Zustimmung; **2.** *Brit.* ,Vogel' *m*; **'~-type en·gine** *s. mot.* V-Motor *m*.

vul·can·ite ['vʌlkənaɪt] *s.* Ebo'nit *n*, Vulka'nit *n* (*Hartgummi*); **'vul·can·ize** [-aɪz] *v/t. Kautschuk* vulkanisieren: *~d fibre* (*Am. fiber*) ⚹ Vulkanfiber *f*.

vul·gar ['vʌlgə] **I** *adj.* □ → *vulgarly*; **1.** (all)gemein, Volks...: *~ herd die* Masse, *das gemeine Volk*; ♀ *Era die* christlichen Jahrhunderte; **2.** volkstümlich: *~ superstitions*; **3.** vul'gärsprachlich, in der Volkssprache (verfasst *etc.*): *~ tongue* Volkssprache *f*; ♀ *Latin* Vulgärlatein *n*; **4.** ungebildet, ungehobelt; **5.** vul'gär, unfein, ordi'när, gewöhnlich, unanständig, pöbelhaft; **6.** ⚹ gemein, gewöhnlich: *~ fraction*; **7.** *the ~ pl.* das (gemeine) Volk; **vul·gar·i·an** [vʌl'geərɪən] *s.* **1.** vul'gärer Mensch, Ple'bejer *m*; **2.** Parve'nü *m*, Protz *m*; **'vul·gar·ism** [-ərɪzəm] *s.* **1.** Unfeinheit *f*, vul'gäres Benehmen; **2.** Gemeinheit *f*, Unanständigkeit *f*; **3.** *ling.* Vulga'rismus *m*, vul'gärer Ausdruck; **vul·gar·i·ty** [vʌl'gærətɪ] *s.* **1.** ungehobeltes Wesen, vul'gäre Art; **2.** Gewöhnlichkeit *f*, Pöbelhaftigkeit *f*; **3.** Unsitte *f*, Ungezogenheit *f*; **'vul·gar·ize** [-əraɪz] *v/t.* **1.** popularisieren, verbreiten; **2.** her'abwürdigen, vulgarisieren; **'vul·gar·ly** [-lɪ] *adv.* **1.** allgemein, gemeinhin, landläufig; **2.** → *vulgar* 4, 5.

vul·ner·a·bil·i·ty [,vʌlnərə'bɪlətɪ] *s.* Verwundbarkeit *f*; **vul·ner·a·ble** ['vʌlnərəbl] *adj.* **1.** verwundbar (*a. fig.*); **2.** angreifbar; **3.** anfällig (*to* für); **4.** ✕, *sport* ungeschützt, offen; **vul·ner·ar·y** ['vʌlnərərɪ] **I** *adj.* Wund..., Heil...; **II** *s.* Wundmittel *n*.

vul·pine ['vʌlpaɪn] *adj.* **1.** fuchsartig, Fuchs...; **2.** *fig.* füchsisch, verschlagen.

vul·ture ['vʌltʃə] *s. zo.* Geier *m* (*a. fig.*).

vul·va ['vʌlvə] *pl.* **-vae** [-viː] *s. anat.* Vulva *f*, (äußere) weibliche Scham.

vy·ing ['vaɪɪŋ] *adj.* □ wetteifernd.

V

W, w [ˈdʌbljuː] s. W n, w n (*Buchstabe*).

Waac [wæk] s. ✕ F *Brit.* Ar'meehelferin f (*aus Women's Army Auxiliary Corps*).

Waaf [wæf] s. ✕ F *Brit.* Luftwaffenhelferin f (*aus Women's Auxiliary Air Force*).

WAC, Wac [wæk] s. ✕ F *Am.* Ar'meehelferin f (*aus Women's Army Corps*).

wack·y [ˈwækɪ] adj. ˌblöd'.

wad [wɒd] I s. 1. Pfropf(en) m, (*Watte- etc.*)Bausch m, Polster n; 2. Pa'pierknäuel m, n; 3. a) (Banknoten)Bündel n, (-)Rolle f, b) *Am.* F Haufen m Geld, c) Stoß m Pa'piere; 4. ✕ *hist.* Ladepfropf m; II v/t. 5. zu e-m Bausch *etc.* zs.-pressen; 6. ~ **up** *Am.* fest zs.-rollen; 7. *Öffnung* ver-, zustopfen; 8. *Kleidungsstück etc.* wattieren, auspolstern, füttern; **wad·ding** [ˈwɒdɪŋ] I s. 1. Einlage f (*zum Polstern od. Verpacken*); 2. Watte f; 3. Wattierung f; II adj. 4. Wattier...

wad·dle [ˈwɒdl] I v/i. watscheln; II s. watschelnder Gang.

wade [weɪd] I v/i. waten: ~ **through** F *fig.* sich durchkämpfen durch; ~ **in(to)** F *fig.* a) ˌhin'einsteigen', sich einmischen (in *acc.*), b) sich ˌreinknien' (in *e-e Arbeit etc.*); ~ **into a problem** ein Problem anpacken *od.* angehen; II v/t. durch'waten; III s. Waten n; **'wad·er** [-də] s. 1. *orn.* Wat-, Stelzvogel m; 2. pl. (hohe) Wasserstiefel pl.

wa·fer [ˈweɪfə] s. 1. Ob'late f (a. ✿ u. *Siegelmarke*); 2. (*bsd.* Eis)Waffel f: **as thin as a ~, ~-thin** hauchdünn (a. *fig.*); 3. a. consecrated ~ *eccl.* Hostie f, Ob'late f; 4. ✄ Mikroplättchen n.

waf·fle [ˈwɒfl] I s. Waffel f; II v/i. F ˌquasseln'; **'~·i·ron** s. Waffeleisen n.

waft [wɑːft] I v/t. 1. wohin wehen, tragen; II v/i. 2. (her'an)getragen werden, schweben; III s. 3. Flügelschlag m; 4. Wehen n; 5. (Duft)Hauch m, (-)Welle f; 6. *fig.* Welle f (*von Freude, Neid etc.*); 7. ⚓ Flagge f im Schau (*Notsignal*).

wag [wæg] I v/i. 1. wackeln; wedeln, wippen (*Schwanz*): ~ **one's tongue** tratschen; **set tongues ~ging** viel Gerede verursachen; → **tail** 1; II v/t. 2. wackeln *od.* wedeln *od.* wippen mit *dem Schwanz etc.*; *den Kopf* schütteln *od.* wiegen: ~ **one's finger at** j-m mit dem Finger drohen; 3. (hin- u. her)bewegen, schwenken; III s. 4. Wackeln n; Wedeln n, (Kopf)Schütteln n; 5. Witzbold m, Spaßvogel m.

wage¹ [weɪdʒ] v/t. *Krieg* führen, *Feldzug* unter'nehmen (**on, against** gegen): ~ **effective war on** *fig.* e-r Sache wirksam zu Leibe gehen.

wage² [weɪdʒ] s. 1. *mst pl.* ✝ (Arbeits-) Lohn m: **~s per hour** Stundenlohn m; 2. pl. ✝ Lohnanteil m (*an der Produktion*); 3. pl. sg. konstr. fig. Lohn m: **the ~s of sin** *bibl.* der Sünde Sold; ~

a·gree·ment s. ✝ Ta'rifvertrag m; ~ **bill** s. (aus)bezahlte (Gesamt)Löhne pl.; ~ **claim** s. Lohnforderung f; ~ **dispute** s. Lohnkampf m; ~ **earn·er** s. Lohnempfänger(in); ~ **freeze** s. Lohnstopp m; ~ **fund** s. Lohnfonds m; ~ **in·cen·tive** s. Lohnanreiz m; **~·in·ci·den·tals** s. pl. Lohn'nebenkosten pl.; '**~·in·ten·sive** adj. 'lohninten·siv; ~ **lev·el** s. 'Lohnni·veau n; ~ **pack·et** s. Lohntüte f.

wa·ger [ˈweɪdʒə] I s. 1. Wette f; II v/t. 2. wetten um, setzen auf (*acc.*); wetten mit (**that** dass); 3. *fig. Ehre etc.* aufs Spiel setzen; III v/i. 4. wetten, e-e Wette eingehen.

wage| **rate** s. Lohnsatz m; ~ **scale** s. ✝ 1. Lohnskala f; 2. ('Lohn)Ta,rif m; ~ **set·tle·ment** s. Lohnabschluss m; ~ **slave** s. Lohnsklave m; ~ **slip** s. Lohnstreifen m, -zettel m.

wag·ger·y [ˈwægərɪ] s. Schelme'rei f, Schalkhaftigkeit f; **wag·gish** [ˈwægɪʃ] adj. □ schalkhaft, schelmisch, spaßig, lose; **wag·gish·ness** [ˈwægɪʃnɪs] → **waggery**.

wag·gle [ˈwægl] → **wag** I u. II.

wag·gon [ˈwægən] s. 1. (Last-, Roll-) Wagen m; 2. 🚋 *Brit.* (offener) Güterwagen, Wag'gon m: **by ~** ✝ per Achse; 3. *Am.* a) (Liefer-, Transport-, Poli'zei- etc.)Wagen m, b) *mot.* Kombi(wagen) m; 4. **the 2** *ast.* der Große Wagen; 5. F *fig.* → **water wag(g)on**.

wag·gon·er [ˈwægənə] s. 1. (Fracht-) Fuhrmann m; 2. **2** *ast.* Fuhrmann m.

'**wag·gon**|**·load** s. 1. Wagenladung f, Fuhre f; 2. Wag'gonladung f: **by the ~** wag'gonweise; ~ **train** s. ✕ Ar'meetrain m; 2. 🚋 *Am.* Güterzug m; ~ **vault** s. △ Tonnengewölbe n.

Wag·ne·ri·an [vɑːgˈnɪərɪən] ♪ I adj. wagnerisch, wagneri'anisch, Wagner...; II s. a. **Wag·ner·ite** [ˈvɑːgnəraɪt] Wagneri'aner(in).

wag·on etc. bsd. *Am.* → **waggon** etc.

wa·gon-lit [ˈvægɒnˈliː; vagˈli] (*Fr.*) s. 🚋 Schlafwagen(abteil n) m.

'**wag·tail** s. orn. Bachstelze f.

waif [weɪf] s. 1. ♃ a) *Brit.* weggeworfenes Diebesgut, b) herrenloses Gut, bsd. Strandgut n (a. fig.); 2. a) Heimatlose(r m) f, b) verlassenes od. verwahrlostes Kind: **~s and strays** verwahrloste Kinder, c) streunendes od. verwahrlostes Tier; 3. fig. 'Überrest m.

wail [weɪl] I v/i. (weh)klagen, jammern (**for** um, **over** über *acc.*); schreien, wimmern, heulen (a. *Sirene, Wind*) (**with** vor *Schmerz etc.*); II v/t. bejammern; III s. (Weh)Klagen n, Jammern n; (Weh)Geschrei n, Wimmern n; '**wail·ing** [-lɪŋ] I s. → **wail** III; II adj. □ (weh)klagend etc.; Klage...: **2 Wall** Klagemauer f.

wain [weɪn] s. 1. poet. Karren m, Wagen m; 2. **2** → **Charles's Wain**.

wain·scot [ˈweɪnskət] I s. (*bsd. untere*) (Wand)Täfelung, Tafelwerk n, Holz-

verkleidung f; II v/t. *Wand etc.* verkleiden, (ver)täfeln; '**wain·scot·ing** [-tɪŋ] s. 1. → **wainscot** I; 2. Täfelholz n.

waist [weɪst] s. 1. Taille f; 2. a) Mieder n, b) *bsd. Am.* Bluse f; 3. Mittelstück n, schmalste Stelle (*e-s Dinges*), Schweifung f (*e-r Glocke etc.*); 4. ⚓ Mitteldeck n, Kuhl f; '**~·band** [-stb-] s. (Hosen-, Rock)Bund m; **~·coat** [ˈweɪskəʊt] s. (a. Damen)Weste f, (ärmellose) Jacke; *hist.* Wams n; '**~·deep** adj. u. adv. bis zur Taille *od.* Hüfte, hüfthoch.

waist·ed [ˈweɪstɪd] adj. mit e-r ... Taille: **short-~**.

ˌwaist|**-ˈhigh** → **waist-deep**; '**~-line** s. 1. Gürtellinie f, Taille f; 2. 'Taille(n·umfang m) f: **watch one's ~** auf s-e Linie achten.

wait [weɪt] I v/i. 1. warten (**for** auf *acc.*): ~ **for s.o. to come** warten, dass *od.* bis j-d kommt; ~ **up for s.o.** aufbleiben u. auf j-n warten; **keep s.o. ~ing** j-n warten lassen; **that can ~** fig. das kann warten, das hat Zeit; **dinner is ~ing** das Essen wartet *od.* ist bereit; **you just ~!** F na warte!; **~ for it!** F *Brit.* a) immer mit der Ruhe, b) du wirsts kaum glauben!; 2. (ab)warten, sich gedulden: ~ **and see!** ˌabwarten u. Tee trinken'!; **I can't ~ to see him** ich kann es kaum noch erwarten, bis ich ihn sehe; 3. ~ (**up)on** a) j-m dienen, b) j-m aufwarten, j-n bedienen, c) j-m e-e Aufwartung machen, d) fig. e-r Sache folgen, et. begleiten (*Umstand*); 4. a. ~ **at table** (bei Tisch) bedienen; II v/t. 5. warten auf (*acc.*), abwarten: ~ **one's opportunity** e-e günstige Gelegenheit abwarten; ~ **out** das Ende (*gen.*) abwarten; 6. F aufschieben, mit *dem Essen etc.* warten (**for s.o.** auf j-n); III s. 7. a) Warten n, b) Wartezeit f: **have a long ~** lange warten müssen; 8. Lauer f: **lay a ~ for** j-m e-n Hinterhalt legen; **lie in ~** im Hinterhalt liegen; **lie in ~ for** j-m auflauern; 9. pl. a) Weihnachtssänger pl., b) *hist.* 'Stadtmusi,kanten pl.; '**wait·er** [-tə] s. 1. Kellner m, in der Anrede: (Herr) Ober m; 2. Servier-, Präsentierteller m.

wait·ing [ˈweɪtɪŋ] I s. 1. → **wait** 7; 2. Dienst m bei Hofe etc., Aufwarten n: **in ~** a) Dienst tuend; → **lady-in-waiting** etc., b) ✕ *Brit.* in Bereitschaft; II adj. 3. (ab)wartend; → **game** 4; 4. Warte...: ~ **list, ~ period** allg. Wartezeit f; ~ **room** a) 🚋 Wartesaal m, b) ♣ etc. Wartezimmer n; ~ **girl** s., ~ **maid** s. Kammerzofe f.

wait·ress [ˈweɪtrɪs] s. Kellnerin f; in der Anrede: Fräulein n.

waive [weɪv] v/t. bsd. ♃ 1. verzichten auf (*acc.*), sich e-s Rechtes,Vorteils begeben; 2. *Frage* zu'rückstellen; '**waiv·er** [-və] s. ♃ 1. Verzicht m (**of** auf *acc.*), Verzicht(leistung) f; 2. Verzichterklärung f; 3. Ausnahmegenehmigung f.

wake¹ [weɪk] s. 1. ⚓ Kielwasser n (a.

fig.): *in the ~ of* a) im Kielwasser *e-s Schiffes*, b) *fig.* im Gefolge (*gen.*); *follow in s.o.'s ~ fig.* in j-s Kielwasser segeln; *bring s.th. in its ~* et. nach sich ziehen, et. zur Folge haben; **2.** ✓ Luftschraubenstrahl *m*; **3.** Sog *m*.

wake² [weɪk] **I** *v/i.* [*irr.*] **1.** *oft ~ up* auf-, erwachen, wach werden (*alle a. fig. Person, Gefühl etc.*); **2.** wachen, wach sein *od.* bleiben; **3.** *~ to* sich *e-r Gefahr etc.* bewusst werden; **4.** vom Tode *od.* von den Toten auferstehen; **II** *v/t.* [*irr.*] **5.** *a. ~ up* (auf)wecken, wachrütteln (*a. fig.*); **6.** *fig.* erwecken, *Erinnerungen, Gefühle* wachrufen, *Streit etc.* erregen; **7.** *fig.* j-n, *j-s Geist etc.* aufrütteln; **8.** (*von den Toten*) auferwecken; **III** *s.* **9.** *bsd. Irish* a) Totenwache *f*, b) Leichenschmaus *m*; **10.** *hist.* Kirchweih(fest *n*) *f*, Kirmes *f*; **11.** *Brit.* Betriebsferien *pl.*; '**wake·ful** [-fʊl] *adj.* □ **1.** wachend; **2.** schlaflos; **3.** *fig.* wachsam; '**wak·en** [-kən] → *wake²* 1, 3, 5, 6 *u.* 7; '**wak·ing** [-kɪŋ] **I** *s.* **1.** (Er)Wachen *n*; **2.** (Nacht-)Wache *f*; **II** *adj.* **3.** wach: *~ dream* Tagtraum *m*; *in his ~ hours* in s-n wachen Stunden, *a.* von früh bis spät.

wale [weɪl] *s.* **1.** → *weal²*; **2.** *Weberei:* a) Rippe *f* (*e-s Gewebes*), b) Salleiste *f*, feste Webkante; **3.** ☉ a) Verbindungsstück *n*, b) Gurtholz *n*; **4.** ♣ a) Berg-, Krummholz *n*, b) Dollbord *m* (*e-s Boots*).

walk [wɔːk] **I** *s.* **1.** Gehen *n*: *go at a ~* im Schritt gehen; **2.** Gang(art *f*) *m*, Schritt *m*: *a dignified ~*; **3.** Spaziergang *m*: *go for* (*od. take*) *a ~* e-n Spaziergang machen; *take s.o. for a ~* j-n spazieren führen, mit j-m spazieren gehen; **4.** (Spazier)Weg *m*: *a)* Prome'nade *f*, b) Strecke *f*: *a ten minutes' ~ to the station* zehn (Geh)Minuten zum Bahnhof; *quite a ~* ein gutes Stück zu gehen; **5.** Al'lee *f*; **6.** (Geflügel)Auslauf *m*; → *sheepwalk*; **7.** Route *f e-s Hausierers etc.*, Runde *f e-s Polizisten etc.*; **8.** *fig.* a) (Arbeits)Gebiet *n*, b) *mst ~ of life* (sozi'ale) Schicht *od.* Stellung, *a.* Beruf *m*; **II** *v/i.* **9.** gehen (*a. sport*), zu Fuß gehen; **10.** im Schritt gehen (*a. Pferd*); **11.** spazieren gehen, wandern; **12.** 'umgehen (*Geist*): *~ in one's sleep* nachtwandeln; **III** *v/t.* **13.** *Strecke* zu'rücklegen, (zu Fuß) gehen; **14.** *Bezirk* durch'wandern, *Raum* durch'schreiten; **15.** auf u. ab (*od.* um'her)gehen in *od.* auf (*dat.*); **16.** *Pferd* a) führen, b) im Schritt gehen lassen; **17.** j-n wohin führen: *~ s.o. off his feet* j-n abhetzen; **18.** spazieren führen; **19.** um die Wette gehen mit;

Zssgn mit adv. u. prp.:

walk a·bout, *~ a·round* **I** *v/i.* um'hergehen, -wandern; **II** *v/t.* j-n um'herführen; *~ a·way v/i.* **1.** weg-, fortgehen: *~ from sport* j-m (einfach) davonlaufen, j-n ,stehen lassen'; **2.** *~ with* a) mit et. durchbrennen, b) et. ,mitgehen' lassen, c) e-n Kampf etc. spielend gewinnen; *~ off* **I** *v/i.* **1.** da'von-, fortgehen; **2.** → *walk away* 2; **II** *v/t.* **3.** j-n abführen; **4.** *s-n Rausch, Zorn etc.* durch e-n Spaziergang vertreiben; *~ out* **I** *v/i.* **1.** hinausgehen: *~ on* **I** j-n im Stich lassen, verlassen; **2.** *~ with s.o.* **F** mit j-m ,gehen' *od.* ein Verhältnis haben; **3.** ✝ in (den) Streik treten; **4.** *pol.* zu'rücktreten; **II** *v/t.* **5.** *Hund etc.* ausführen; **6.** j-n auf e-n Spaziergang mitnehmen; *~ o·ver v/i. fig.* spielend gewinnen; *~ up v/i.* **1.** hin'aufgehen, her'aufkommen: *~ to s.o.* auf j-n zugehen; **2.** *Straße* entlanggehen.

'**walk·a·bout** *s.* **1.** Wanderung *f*; **2.** ,Bad *n* in der Menge' (*e-s Politikers etc.*).

walk·a·thon ['wɔːkəθɒn] **1.** *sport* Marathongehen *n*; **2.** 'Dauertanztur,nier *n*.

'**walk·a·way** → *walkover* 2.

walk·er ['wɔːkə] *s.* **1.** Spaziergänger(in): *be a good ~* gut zu Fuß sein; **2.** *sport* Geher *m*; **3.** *orn. Brit.* Laufvogel *m*; *,~-'on* [-ər'ɒn] *s.* → *walk-on* 1.

walk·ie-talk·ie [,wɔːkɪ'tɔːkɪ] *s.* tragbares Funksprechgerät, Walkie-Talkie *n*.

'**walk-in I** *adj.* **1.** begehbar: *~ closet* → 2; **II** *s.* **2.** begehbarer Schrank; **3.** Kühlraum *m*; **4.** *Am.* **F** leichter Wahlsieg.

walk·ing ['wɔːkɪŋ] **I** *adj.* **1.** gehend, wandernd; *bsd. fig.* wandelnd (*Leiche, Lexikon*): *~ wounded* ✗ Leichtverwundete *pl.*; **2.** Geh..., Marsch..., Spazier...: *drive at a ~ speed mot.* (im) Schritt fahren; *within ~ distance* zu Fuß erreichbar; **II** *s.* **3.** (Spazieren)Gehen *n*; Wandern *n*; **4.** *sport* Gehen *n*; *~ boots s. pl.* Wanderstiefel *pl.*; *~ chair* → *gocart* 1; *~ del·e·gate s.* Gewerkschaftsbeauftragte(r) *m*; *~ gen·tle·man s.* [*irr.*], *~ la·dy* → *walk-on* 1; *~ pa·pers s. pl. sl.* **1.** Ent'lassung(spa,piere *pl.*) *f*; **2.** ,Laufpass' *m*; *~ part s. thea.* Sta'tistenrolle *f*; *~ shoes s. pl.* Wanderschuhe *pl.*; *~ stick s.* Spazierstock *m*; *~ tick·et* → *walking papers*; *~ tour s.* Wanderung *f*.

'**walk·on** *s. Film, thea.* **1.** Sta'tist(in), Kom'parse *m*, Kom'parsin *f*; **2.** *a. ~ part* Sta'tisten-, Kom'parsenrolle *f*; *'~-out s.* **1.** ✝ Ausstand *m*, Streik *m*; **2.** Auszug *m*; *'~·o·ver s. sport* **1.** einseitiger Wettbewerb; **2.** ,Spaziergang' *m*, leichter Sieg (*a. fig.*); *'~-up Am.* **F I** *adj.* ohne Fahrstuhl (*Haus*); **II** *s.* (Wohnung *f* in e-m) Haus ohne Fahrstuhl; *'~·way s.* **1.** Laufgang *m*; **2.** *Am.* Gehweg *m*.

wall [wɔːl] **I** *s.* **1.** Wand *f* (*a. fig.*): *up against the ~, with one's back to the ~* in e-r aussichtslosen Lage; *drive* (*od. push*) *s.o. to the ~ fig.* a) j-n an die Wand drücken, b) j-n in die Enge treiben; *go to the ~* a) an die Wand gedrückt werden, b) ✝ Konkurs machen; *drive* (*od. send*) *s.o. up the ~* **F** j-n ,auf die Palme bringen'; *run* (*od. bang*) *one's head against a ~* **F** mit dem Kopf durch die Wand wollen; **2.** ☉ (Innen)Wand *f*; **3.** Mauer *f* (*a. fig.*): *a ~ of silence*; *the ♄* a) die (Berliner) Mauer, b) die Klagemauer (*in Jerusalem*); **4.** Wall *m* (*a. fig.*), (Stadt-, Schutz)Mauer *f*: *within the ~s* in den Mauern (e-r Stadt); **5.** *anat.* (Brust-, Zell- etc.)Wand *f*; **6.** Häuserseite *f*: *give s.o. the ~* j-n auf der Häuserseite gehen lassen (*aus Höflichkeit*), b) fig. j-m den Vorrang lassen; **7.** ⚒ (Abbau-, Orts)Stoß *m*; **II** *v/t.* **8.** *a. ~ in* mit e-r Mauer *od.* e-m Wall um'geben, *um'mauern: ~ in* (*od. up*) einmauern; **9.** *a. ~ up* a) ver-, zumauern, b) (aus)mauern, um'wanden; **10.** *fig.* ab-, einschließen, *den Geist* verschließen (*against gegen*).

wal·la·by ['wɒləbɪ] *pl.* **-bies** [-bɪz] *s. zo.* Wallaby *n* (*kleineres Känguru*).

wal·lah ['wɒlə] *s.* **F** ,Knülch' *m*.

wall bars *s. pl. sport* Sprossenwand *f*; *~ brack·et s.* 'Wandarm *m*, -kon,sole *f*; *~ creep·er s. orn.* Mauerläufer *m*; *~ cress s.* ♀ Acker-, *Brit. a.* Gänsekresse *f*.

wal·let ['wɒlɪt] *s.* **1.** kleine Werkzeugtasche; **2.** a) Brieftasche *f*, b) (flache) Geldtasche.

wall eye *s.* **1.** *vet.* Glasauge *n*; **2.** ✗ a) Hornhautfleck *m*, b) auswärts schielendes Auge; '**wall-eyed** *adj.* **1.** *vet.* glasäugig (*Pferd etc.*); **2.** ✗ a) mit Hornhautflecken, b) (auswärts) schielend.

'**wall,flow·er** *s.* **1.** ♀ Goldlack *m*; **2.** **F** *fig.* ,Mauerblümchen' *n* (*Mädchen*); *~ fruit s.* Spa'lierobst *n*; *~ map s.* Wandkarte *f*.

Wal·loon [wɒ'luːn] **I** *s.* **1.** Wal'lone *m*, Wal'lonin *f*; **2.** *ling.* Wal'lonisch *n*; **II** *adj.* **3.** wal'lonisch.

wal·lop ['wɒləp] **I** *v/t.* **1.** **F** a) (ver)prügeln, verdreschen, b) j-m eine ,knallen', c) *sport* ,über'fahren' (*besiegen*); **II** *v/i.* **2.** **F** rasen, sausen; **3.** brodeln; **III** *s.* **4.** **F** a) wuchtiger Schlag, b) Schlagkraft *f*, c) *Am.* Mordsspaß *m*; '**wal·lop·ing** [-pɪŋ] **I** *adj.* **F** riesig, Mords...; **II** *s.* **F** ,Dresche' *f*, Tracht *f* Prügel.

wal·low ['wɒləʊ] **I** *v/i.* **1.** sich wälzen *od.* suhlen (*Schweine etc.*) (*a. fig.*): *~ in money fig.* in Geld schwimmen; *~ in pleasure* im Vergnügen schwelgen; *~ in vice* dem Laster frönen; **II** *s.* **2.** Sich-'wälzen *n*; **3.** Schwelgen *n*; **4.** *hunt.* Suhle *f*; **5.** *fig.* Sumpf *m*.

wall paint·ing *s.* Wandgemälde *n*; *'~,pa·per I s.* Ta'pete *f*; **II** *v/t. u. v/i.* tapezieren; *~ plug s.* ⚡ Netzstecker *m*; *~ sock·et s.* ⚡ (Wand)Steckdose *f*; ⚡ **Street** *s.* Wall Street *f*: a) *Bank- u. Börsenstraße in New York*, b) *fig.* der amer. Geld- u. Kapi'talmarkt, c) *fig.* die amer. 'Hochfi,nanz; *~ tent s.* Steilwandzelt *n*; *,~-to-' adj.: ~ carpet* Spannteppich *m*; *~ carpeting* Teppichboden *m*; *~ tree s.* Spa'lierbaum *m*.

wal·nut ['wɔːlnʌt] *s.* ♀ **1.** Walnuss *f* (*Frucht*); **2.** Walnuss(baum *m*) *f*; **3.** Nussbaumholz *n*.

wal·rus ['wɔːlrəs] *s.* **1.** *zo.* Walross *n*; **2.** *a. ~ m(o)ustache* Schnauzbart *m*.

waltz [wɔːls] **I** *s.* **1.** Walzer *m*; **II** *v/i.* **2.** (*v/t.* mit j-m) Walzer tanzen, walzen; **3.** *vor Freude etc.* her'umtanzen; *~ time s.* ♪ Walzertakt *m*.

wan [wɒn] *adj.* □ **1.** bleich, blass, fahl; **2.** schwach, matt (*Lächeln etc.*).

wand [wɒnd] *s.* **1.** Rute *f*; **2.** Zauberstab *m*; **3.** (Amts-, Kom'mando)Stab *m*; **4.** ♪ Taktstock *m*.

wan·der ['wɒndə] *v/i.* **1.** wandern: a) ziehen, streifen, b) schlendern, bummeln, c) *fig.* schweifen, irren, gleiten (*Auge, Gedanken etc.*): *~ in* hereinschneien (*Besucher*); *~ off* a) davonziehen-hen, b) sich verlieren (*into in acc.*) (*a. fig.*); **2.** *a. ~ about* um'herwandern, -ziehen, -irren, -schweifen (*a. fig.*); **3.** *a. ~ away* irregehen, sich verirren (*a. fig.*); **4.** abirren, -weichen (*from von*) (*a. fig.*): *~ from the subject* vom Thema abschweifen; **5.** fantasieren: a) irrereden, faseln, b) im Fieber reden; **6.** geistesabwesend sein; '**wan·der·ing** [-dərɪŋ] **I** *s.* **1.** Wandern *n*; **2.** He'rumziehen *n*; **3.** *mst pl.* a) Wanderung(en *pl.*) *f*, b) Wanderschaft *f*; **4.** *mst pl.* Fantasieren *n*: a) Irrereden *n*, Faseln *n*, b) Fieberwahn *m*; **II** *adj.* □ **5.** wandernd, Wander...; **6.** um'herschweifend, Nomaden...; **7.** unstet: *the ♄ Jew* der Ewige Jude; **8.** irregehend, abirrend (*a. fig.*): *~ bullet* verirrte Kugel; **9.** ✗ Kriech..., Schling...; **10.** ✗ Wander...(-niere, -zelle).

wan·der·lust ['wɒndəlʌst] (*Ger.*) *s.* Wanderlust *f*, Fernweh *n*.

wane [weɪn] *v/i.* **1.** abnehmen (*a. Mond*), nachlassen, schwinden (*Einfluss, Kräfte, Interesse etc.*); **2.** schwächer werden, verblassen (*Licht, Farben* *etc.*); **3.** zu Ende gehen; **II** *s.* **4.** Abnehmen *n*, Abnahme *f*, Schwinden *n*: **be on the ~ → 1** *u.* **3**; **in the ~ of the moon** bei abnehmendem Mond.

wan·gle ['wæŋgl] *sl.* **I** *v/t.* **1.** *et.* ‚drehen' *od.* ‚deichseln' *od.* ‚schaukeln'; **2.** *et.* ‚organisieren' (*beschaffen*): **~ o.s. s.th.** et. für sich ‚herausschlagen'; **3.** ergaunern: **~ s.th. out of s.o.** j-m et. abluchsen; **~ s.o. into doing s.th.** j-n dazu bringen, et. zu tun; **4.** ‚frisieren' (*fälschen*); **II** *v/i.* **5.** mogeln, ‚schieben'; **6.** sich her'auswinden (**out of** aus *dat.*); **III** *s.* **7.** Kniff *m*, Trick *m*; **8.** Schiebung *f*, Moge'lei *f*; **'wan·gler** [-lə] *s.* Gauner *m*, Schieber *m*, Mogler *m*.

wank [wæŋk] *v/i. Brit.* V ‚wichsen' (*masturbieren*).

wan·na ['wɒnə] F *für* **want to:** *I* **~** *go*.

wan·na·be ['wɒnəbiː] *s.* F *contp.* ‚Möchtegern' *m*: ‚Möchtegern-autor(in)'; **~ rock star** 'Möchtegern-,Rockstar *m*; **~ starlet** 'Möchtegern-Star *m*, -,Starlet *n*.

want [wɒnt] **I** *v/t.* **1.** wünschen: a) (haben) wollen, b) *vor inf.* (*et. tun*) wollen: *I* **~** *to go* ich möchte gehen; *I* **~ed to go** ich wollte gehen; **what do you ~** (**with me**)? was hab ich damit zu tun?; *I* **~ you to try** ich möchte, dass du es versuchst; *I* **~** *it done* ich wünsche *od.* möchte, dass es getan wird; **~ed** gesucht (*in Annoncen*; *a.* von der Polizei); **you are ~ed** du wirst gewünscht *od.* gesucht, man will dich sprechen; **2.** ermangeln (*gen.*), nicht (genug) haben, es fehlen lassen an (*dat.*): *obs.* **he ~s judg(e)ment** es fehlt ihm an Urteilsvermögen; **3.** a) brauchen, nötig haben, erfordern, benötigen, bedürfen (*gen.*), b) müssen, sollen: **you ~ some rest** du hast etwas Ruhe nötig; **this clock ~s repairing** (*od.* **to be repaired**) diese Uhr müsste *od.* sollte repariert werden; **it ~s doing** es muss getan werden; **you don't ~ to be rude** Sie brauchen nicht grob zu werden; **you ~ to see a doctor** du solltest e-n Arzt aufsuchen; **II** *v/i.* **4.** ermangeln (**for** *gen.*): **he does not ~ for talent** es fehlt ihm nicht an Begabung; **he ~s for nothing** es fehlt ihm an nichts; **5.** (**in**) es fehlen lassen (an *dat.*), ermangeln (*gen.*); **→ wanting 2**; **6.** Not leiden; **III** *s.* **7.** *pl.* Bedürfnisse *pl.*, Wünsche *pl.*: **a man of few ~s** ein Mann mit geringen Bedürfnissen *od.* Ansprüchen; **8.** Notwendigkeit *f*, Bedürfnis *n*, Erfordernis *n*; Bedarf *m*; **9.** Mangel *m*, Ermangelung *f*: *a* (**long-**)**felt ~ → feel 2**; **~ of care** Achtlosigkeit *f*; **~ of sense** Unvernunft *f*; **from** (*od.* **for**) **~ of** aus Mangel an (*dat.*), in Ermang(e)lung (*gen.*); **be in** (**great**) **~ of s.th.** et. (dringend) brauchen *od.* benötigen; **in ~ of repair** reparaturbedürftig; **10.** Bedürftigkeit *f*, Armut *f*, Not *f*: **be in ~** Not leiden; **want ad** *s.* F **1.** Stellengesuch *n*; **2.** Stellenangebot *n*; **want·age** ['wɒntɪdʒ] ✝ Fehlbetrag *m*, Defizit *n*; **'want·ing** [-tɪŋ] **I** *adj.* **1.** fehlend, mangelnd; **2.** ermangelnd (**in** *gen.*): **be ~ in** es fehlen lassen an (*dat.*); **be ~ to** j-m im Stich lassen, e-r Erwartung nicht gerecht werden, e-r Lage nicht gewachsen sein; **he is never found ~** auf ihn ist immer Verlass; **3.** nachlässig (**in** in *dat.*); **II** *prp.* **4.** ohne: *a book* **~** *a cover*.

wan·ton ['wɒntən] **I** *adj.* □ **1.** mutwillig: a) ausgelassen, wild, b) leichtfertig, c) böswillig (*a.* ✝), d) rücksichtslos: **~ negligence** ✝ grobe Fahrlässigkeit; **2.** liederlich, ausschweifend; **3.** wollüstig,

geil; **4.** üppig (*Haar*, *Fantasie etc.*); **II** *s.* **5.** *obs.* a) Buhlerin *f*, Dirne *f*, b) Wüstling *m*; **III** *v/i.* **6.** um'hertollen; **7.** ⚕ wuchern; **'wan·ton·ness** [-nɪs] *s.* **1.** Mutwille *m*; **2.** Böswilligkeit *f*; **3.** Liederlichkeit *f*; **4.** Geilheit *f*, Lüsternheit *f*.

wap·en·take ['wæpənteɪk] *s.* Hundertschaft *f*, Bezirk *m* (*Unterteilung der nördlichen Grafschaften Englands*).

war [wɔː] **I** *s.* **1.** Krieg *m*: **~ of aggression** (**attrition**, **independence**, **nerves**, **succession**) Angriffs- (Zermürbungs-, Unabhängigkeits-, Nerven-, Erbfolge)krieg; **be at ~** (**with**) a) Krieg führen (gegen *od.* mit), b) *fig.* im Streit liegen *od.* auf (dem) Kriegsfuß stehen (mit); **make ~** Krieg führen, kämpfen (**on**, **upon**, **against** gegen, **with** mit); **go to ~** (**with**) Krieg beginnen (mit); **carry the ~ into the enemy's country** (*od.* **camp**) a) den Krieg ins feindliche Land *od.* Lager tragen, b) *fig.* zum Gegenangriff 'übergehen; **he has been in the ~s** *fig. Brit.* es hat ihn arg mitgenommen; **~ declare 1**; **2.** Kampf *m*, Streit *m* (*a. fig.*); **3.** Feindseligkeit *f*; **II** *v/i.* **4.** kämpfen, streiten (**against** gegen, **with** mit); **5. → warring 2**; **III** *adj.* **6.** Kriegs...

war·ble ['wɔːbl] **I** *v/t. u. v/i.* trillern, schmettern (*Singvögel od. Person*); **II** *s.* Trillern *n*; **'war·bler** [-lə] *s.* **1.** trillernder Vogel; **2.** a) Grasmücke *f*, b) Teichrohrsänger *m*.

'war|-,blind·ed *adj.* kriegsblind; **~ bond** *s.* Kriegsschuldverschreibung *f*; **~ cloud** *s. mst pl.* (drohende) Kriegsgefahr; **~ crime** *s.* Kriegsverbrechen *n*; **~ crim·i·nal** *s.* Kriegsverbrecher *m*; **~ cry** *s.* Schlachtruf *m* (*der Soldaten*) (*a. fig.*), Kriegsruf *m* (*der Indianer*).

ward [wɔːd] **I** *s.* **1.** (Stadt-, Wahl)Bezirk *m*: **~ heeler** *pol. Am.* F (Wahl)Bezirksleiter *m* (*e-r Partei*); **2.** a) (Kranken)Stati,on *f*: **~ sister** Stationsschwester *f*, b) (Kranken)Saal *m od.* (-)Zimmer *n*; **3.** a) (Gefängnis)Trakt *m*, b) Zelle *f*; **4.** *obs.* Gewahrsam *m*, Haft *f*; **5.** ⚖ a) Mündel *n*: **~ of court**, **~ in chancery** Mündel unter Amtsvormundschaft, b) Vormundschaft *f*: **in ~** unter Vormundschaft (stehend); **6.** Schützling *m*; **7.** ⚙ a) Gewirre *n* (*e-s Schlosses*), b) (Einschnitt *m* im) Schlüsselbart *m*; **8. keep watch and ~** Wache halten; **II** *v/t.* **9. ~ off** Schlag etc. parieren, abwehren, Gefahr abwenden.

war| dance *s.* Kriegstanz *m*; **~ debt** *s.* Kriegsschuld *f*.

ward·en ['wɔːdn] *s.* **1.** *obs.* Wächter *m*; **2.** Aufseher *m*, (*bsd.* Luftschutz)Wart *m*; Herbergsvater *m*; **→ game warden**; **3.** *mst hist.* Gouver'neur *m*; **4.** (*Brit.* 'Anstalts-, *Am.* Ge'fängnis)Di,rektor *m*, (*a.* Kirchen)Vorsteher *m*; *Brit. univ.* Rektor *m e-s College*: **⚖ of the Mint** *Brit.* Münzwardein *m*.

ward·er ['wɔːdə] *s.* **1.** *obs.* Wächter *m*; **2.** *Brit.* a) (Mu'seums- etc.)Wärter *m*, b) Aufsichtsbeamte(r) *m* (*Strafanstalt*); **'ward·ress** [-drɪs] *s. Brit.* Aufsichtsbeamtin *f*.

ward·robe ['wɔːdrəʊb] *s.* **1.** Garde'robe *f*, Kleiderbestand *m*; **2.** Kleiderschrank *m*; **3.** Garde'robe *f* (*a. thea.*): a) Kleiderkammer *f*, b) Ankleidezimmer *n*; **~ bed** *s.* Schrankbett *n*; **~ trunk** *s.* Schrankkoffer *m*.

ward·room ['wɔːdrʊm] *s.* ⚓ Offi'ziersmesse *f*.

ward·ship ['wɔːdʃɪp] *s.* Vormundschaft *f* (**of**, **over** über *acc.*).

ware¹ [weə] *s.* **1.** *mst pl.* Ware(n *pl.*) *f*,

Ar'tikel *m* (*od. pl.*), Erzeugnis(se *pl.*) *n*: **peddle one's ~s** *fig. contp.* mit s-m Kram hausieren gehen; **2.** Geschirr *n*, Porzel'lan *n*, Töpferware *f*.

ware² [weə] *v/i. u. v/t. obs.* sich vorsehen (*vor dat.*): **~!** Vorsicht!

'ware·house I *s.* [-haʊs] **1.** Lagerhaus *n*, Speicher *m*: **customs ~** ✝ Zollniederlage *f*; **2.** (Waren)Lager *n*, Niederlage *f*; **3.** *bsd. Brit.* Großhandelsgeschäft *n*; **4.** *Am. contp.* ‚Bude' *f*, ‚Schuppen' *m*; **II** *v/t.* [-haʊz] **5.** auf Lager nehmen, (ein)lagern; **6.** Möbel etc. zur Aufbewahrung geben *od.* nehmen; **7.** unter Zollverschluss bringen; **~ ac·count** *s.* Lagerkonto *n*; **~ bond** *s.* **1.** Lagerschein *m*; **2.** Zollverschlussbescheinigung *f*; **'~·man** [-mən] *s.* [*irr.*] ✝ **1.** Lage'rist *m*, Lagerverwalter *m*; **2.** Lagerarbeiter *m*; **3.** *Brit.* Großhändler *m*.

'war·fare *s.* **1.** Kriegführung *f*; **2.** (*a. Wirtschafts- etc.*)Krieg *m*; **3.** *fig.* Kampf *m*, Fehde *f*, Streit *m*.

war| game *s.* ⚔ **1.** Kriegs-, Planspiel *n*; **2.** Ma'növer *n*; **~ god** *s.* Kriegsgott *m*; **~ grave** *s.* Kriegs-, Sol'datengrab *n*; **~ guilt** *s.* Kriegsschuld *f*; **'~·head** *s.* ⚔ Spreng-, Gefechtskopf *m* (*e-s Torpedos etc.*); **'~·horse** *s. poet.* Schlachtross *n* (*a. fig.* F); **2.** F alter Haudegen *od.* Kämpe (*a. fig.*).

war·i·ness ['weərɪnɪs] *s.* Vorsicht *f*, Behutsamkeit *f*.

'war·like *adj.* **1.** kriegerisch; **2.** Kriegs...

war·lock ['wɔːlɒk] *s. obs.* Zauberer *m*.

'war·lord *s. rhet.* Kriegsherr *m*.

warm [wɔːm] **I** *adj.* □ **1.** *allg.* warm (*a. Farbe etc.*; *a. fig.* Herz, Interesse *etc.*): *a* **~ corner** *fig.* e-e ‚ungemütliche Ecke' (*gefährlicher Ort*); *a* **~ reception** ein warmer Empfang (*a. iro. von Gegnern*); **~ work** a) schwere Arbeit, b) gefährliche Sache, c) heißer Kampf; **keep s.th. ~** (F *fig.* sich) et. warm halten; **make it** (*od.* **things**) **~ for s.o.** j-m die Hölle heiß machen; **this place is too ~ for me** *fig.* hier brennt mir der Boden unter den Füßen; **2.** erhitzt, heiß; **3.** a) glühend, leidenschaftlich, eifrig, b) herzlich; **4.** erregt, hitzig; **5.** *hunt.* frisch (*Fährte etc.*); **6.** F ‚warm', nahe (dran) (*im Suchspiel*): **you are getting ~** *fig.* du kommst der Sache (schon) näher; **II** *s.* **7.** *et.* Warmes, warmes Zimmer *etc.*; **8. give** (**have**) **a ~** et. (sich) (auf)wärmen; **III** *v/t.* **9.** a. **~ up** (an-, auf-, er)wärmen, Milch etc. warm machen: **~ over** *Am.* Speisen etc., *a. fig.* alte Geschichten etc. aufwärmen; **~ one's feet** sich die Füße wärmen; **10.** *fig.* Herz etc. (er)wärmen; **11.** a. **~ up** *fig.* a) Schwung bringen in (*acc.*), b) Zuschauer etc. einstimmen; **12.** F verprügeln, -sohlen; **IV** *v/i.* **13.** a. **~ up** warm werden, sich erwärmen; *Motor etc.* warm laufen; **14. ~ up** *fig.* in Schwung kommen (*Party etc.*); **15.** *fig.* (**to**) a) sich erwärmen (für), b) warm werden (mit *j-m*); **16.** (**for**) a) *sport* sich aufwärmen (für), b) sich vorbereiten (auf *acc.*); **,~·'blood·ed** *adj.* **1.** *zo.* warmblütig: **~ animals** Warmblüter *pl.*; **2.** *fig.* heißblütig; **~ boot** *s. Computer:* Warmstart *m*; **,~·'heart·ed** *adj.* □ warmherzig.

warm·ing ['wɔːmɪŋ] *s.* **1.** (Auf-, An-) Wärmen *n*, Erwärmung *f*; **2.** F Tracht *f* Prügel, ‚Senge' *f*; **~ pad** *s.* ⚡ Heizkissen *n*.

warm·ish ['wɔːmɪʃ] *adj.* lauwarm.

war|·mon·ger ['wɔːˌmʌŋgə] *s.* Kriegshetzer *m*; **'~·mon·ger·ing** [-ərɪŋ] *s.* Kriegshetze *f*, -treibe'rei *f*.

warm start s. *Computer*: Warmstart m.
warmth [wɔːmθ] s. **1.** Wärme f; **2.** fig. Wärme f: a) Herzlichkeit f, b) Eifer m, Begeisterung f; **3.** Heftigkeit f, Erregtheit f.
'warm·up s. **1.** a) *sport* Aufwärmen n, b) fig. Vorbereitung (**for** auf acc.); **2.** Warmlaufen n (*des Motors etc.*); **3.** TV etc.: Einstimmung f (*des Publikums*).
warn [wɔːn] v/t. **1.** warnen (**of**, **against** vor dat.): **~ s.o. against doing s.th.** j-n davor warnen, et. zu tun; **2.** j-n (warnend) hinweisen, aufmerksam machen (**of** auf acc., **that** dass); **3.** ermahnen od. auffordern (**to do** zu tun); **4.** j-m (dringend) raten, nahe legen (**to do** zu tun); **5.** (**of**) j-n in Kenntnis setzen od. verständigen (von), j-n wissen lassen (acc.), j-m ankündigen (acc.); **6.** verwarnen; **7.** **~ off** (**from**) a) abweisen, -halten (von), b) hin'ausweisen (aus);
'warn·ing [-nɪŋ] **I** s. **1.** Warnen n, Warnung f: **give s.o.** (**fair**) **~**, **give** (**fair**) **~ to s.o.** j-n (rechtzeitig) warnen (**of** vor dat.); **take ~ by** (od. **from**) sich et. zur Warnung dienen lassen; **2.** a) Verwarnung f, b) (Er)Mahnung f; **3.** fig. Warnung f, warnendes Beispiel; **4.** warnendes An- od. Vorzeichen (**of** für); **5.** 'Warnsi,gnal n; **6.** Benachrichtigung f, (Vor)Anzeige f, Ankündigung f: **give ~** (**of**) j-m ankündigen (acc.), Bescheid geben (über acc.); **without any ~** völlig unerwartet; **7.** a) Kündigung f, b) (Kündigungs)Frist f: **give ~** (**to**) (j-m) kündigen; **at a minute's ~** a) ✝ auf jederzeitige Kündigung, b) ♣ fristlos, c) in kürzester Frist, jeden Augenblick; **II** adj. □ **8.** warnend, Warn...(-*glocke, -meldung, etc.*): **~ col·o(u)r, ~ coloration** zo. Warn-, Trutzfarbe f; **~ light** a) ◎ Warnlicht n, b) ♣ Warn-, Signalfeuer n; **~ shot** Warnschuss m; **~ strike** ✝ Warnstreik m; **~ triangle** mot. Warndreieck n.
warn't [wɑːnt] dial. für a) **wasn't**, b) **weren't**.
War| Of·fice s. *Brit. hist.* 'Kriegsminis,terium n; **~ or·phan** s. Kriegswaise f.
warp [wɔːp] **I** v/t. **1.** *Holz etc.* verziehen, werfen, krümmen; ✈ *Tragflächen* verwinden; **2.** j-n, j-s *Geist* nachteilig beeinflussen, verschroben machen; j-s *Urteil* verfälschen; → **warped** 3; **3.** a) verleiten (**into** zu), b) abbringen (**from** von); **4.** *Tatsache etc.* entstellen, verdrehen, -zerren; **5.** ♣ *Schiff* bugsieren, verholen; **6.** *Weberei*: *Kette* anscheren, anzetteln; **7.** ✎ a) mit Schlamm düngen, b) a. **~ up** verschlammen; **II** v/i. **8.** sich werfen od. verziehen od. krümmen, krumm werden (*Holz etc.*); **9.** entstellt od. verdreht werden; **III** s. **10.** Verziehen n, Verkrümmung f, -werfung f (*von Holz etc.*); **11.** fig. Neigung f; **12.** fig. a) Entstellung f, Verzerrung f, b) Verschrobenheit f; **13.** *Weberei*: Kette(nfäden pl.) f, Zettel m: **~ and woof** Kette u. Schuss; **14.** ♣ Bugsiertau n, Warpleine f; **15.** ✎, *geol.* Schlamm(-ablagerung f) m, Schlick m.
war| paint s. **1.** Kriegsbemalung f (*der Indianer*); **2.** F a) 'volle Kriegsbemalung', b) große Gala; **~ path** s. Kriegspfad m (*der Indianer*): **be on the ~** a) auf dem Kriegspfad sein (a. fig.), b) fig. kampflustig sein.
warped [wɔːpt] adj. **1.** verzogen (*Holz etc.*), krumm (a. ✗); **2.** fig. verzerrt, verfälscht; **3.** fig. 'verbogen', verschroben: **~ mind** pej. per'teiisch.
war plane s. Kampfflugzeug n.
war·rant ['wɒrənt] **I** s. **1.** a. **~ of attor-**

ney Vollmacht f; Befugnis f, Berechtigung f; **2.** Rechtfertigung f: **not without ~** nicht ohne gewisse Berechtigung; **3.** Garan'tie f, Gewähr f (a. fig.); **4.** Berechtigungsschein m: **dividend ~** ✝ Dividenden-, Gewinnanteilschein m; **5.** ⚖ (Voll'ziehungs- etc.)Befehl m: **~ of apprehension** a) Steckbrief m, b) a. **~ of arrest** Haftbefehl m; **~ of attachment** Beschlagnahmeverfügung f; **a ~ is out against him** er wird steckbrieflich gesucht; **6.** ✗ Pa'tent n, Beförderungsurkunde f: **~** (**officer**) a) ♣ (Ober)Stabsbootsmann m, Deckoffizier m, b) ✗ etwa: (Ober)Stabsfeldwebel m; **7.** ✝ (Lager-, Waren)Schein m: **bond ~** Zollgeleitschein; **8.** ✝ (Rück-) Zahlungsanweisung f; **II** v/t. **9.** bsd. ⚖ bevollmächtigen, autorisieren; **10.** rechtfertigen, berechtigen zu; **11.** a. ✝ garantieren, zusichern, haften für, gewährleisten: **I can't ~ that** das kann ich nicht garantieren; **~ed for three years** drei Jahre Garantie; **I'll ~** (**you**) F a) mein Wort darauf, b) ich könnte schwören; **12.** bestätigen, erweisen; **'war·rant·a·ble** [-təbl] adj. □ **1.** vertretbar, gerechtfertigt, berechtigt; **2.** hunt. jagdbar (*Hirsch*); **'war·rant·a·bly** [-təblɪ] adv. mit Recht, berechtigterweise; **war·ran·tee** [,wɒrən'tiː] s. ✝, ⚖ Sicherheitsempfänger m; **'war·rant·er, 'war·ran·tor** [-tə] s. ✝, ⚖ Sicherheitsgeber m; **'war·ran·ty** [-tɪ] s. **1.** ✝, ⚖ Ermächtigung f, Vollmacht f (**for** zu); **2.** Rechtfertigung f; **3.** bsd. ⚖ Bürgschaft f, Garan'tie f; **4.** a. **~ deed** ⚖ a) 'Rechtsgaran,tie f, b) Am. 'Grundstücksüber,tragungsurkunde f.
war·ren ['wɒrən] s. **1.** Ka'ninchengehege n; **2.** hist. Brit. Wildgehege n; **3.** fig. Laby'rinth n, bsd. a) 'Mietska,serne f, b) enges Straßengewirr.
war·ring ['wɔːrɪŋ] adj. **1.** sich bekriegend, streitend: **~ factions** Kriegsparteien pl; **2.** fig. 'widerstreitend, entgegengesetzt.
war·ri·or ['wɒrɪə] s. poet. Krieger m.
war| risk in·sur·ance s. ✝ Kriegsversicherung f; **'~·ship** s. Kriegsschiff n.
wart [wɔːt] s. **1.** ✗, ♀, zo. Warze f: **~s and all** fig. mit all s-n Fehlern u. Schwächen; **2.** ♀ Auswuchs m; **'wart·ed** [-tɪd] adj. warzig.
'war·time I s. Kriegszeit f; **II** adj. Kriegs...
wart·y ['wɔːtɪ] adj. warzig.
war|-wea·ry ['wɔː,wɪərɪ] adj. kriegsmüde; **~ whoop** s. Kriegsgeheul n (*der Indianer*); **~ wid·ow** s. Kriegerwitwe f; **'~-worn** adj. **1.** kriegszerstört, vom Krieg verwüstet; **2.** kriegsmüde.
war·y ['weərɪ] adj. □ vorsichtig: a) wachsam, a. argwöhnisch, b) 'umsichtig, c) mistrauisch: **be ~** sich hüten (**of** vor dat., **of doing** et. zu tun).
was [wɒz; wəz] 1. u. 3. sg. pret. ind. von **be**; im pass. wurde: **he ~ killed**; **he ~ to have come** er hätte kommen sollen; **he didn't know what ~ to come** er ahnte nicht, was noch kommen sollte; **he ~ never to see his mother again** er sollte seine Mutter nie mehr wiedersehen.
wash [wɒʃ] **I** s. **1.** Waschen n, Wäsche f: **at the ~** in der Wäsche(rei); **give s.th. a ~** et. (ab)waschen; **have a ~** sich waschen; **come out in the ~** a) herausgehen (*Flecken*), b) fig. F in Ordnung kommen, c) fig. F sich zeigen; **2.** (*zu waschende od. gewaschene*) Wäsche: **in the ~** in der Wäsche; **3.** Spülwasser n (a. fig. dünne Suppe etc.); **4.** Spülicht n,

Küchenabfälle pl.; **5.** fig. contp. Gewäsch n, leeres Gerede; **6.** ✈ Waschung f; **7.** (Augen-, Haar- etc.)Wasser n; **8.** Wellenschlag m, (Tosen n der) Brandung f; **9.** ♣ Kielwasser n (a. fig.); **10.** ✈ a) Luftstrudel m, b) glatte Strömung; **11.** geol. a) (Alluvi'al)Schutt m, b) Schwemmland n; **12.** seichtes Gewässer; **13.** 'Farb,überzug m: a) dünn aufgetragene (Wasser)Farbe, b) △ Tünche f; **14.** ◎ a) Bad n, Abspritzung f, b) Plattierung f; **II** adj. **15.** waschbar, -echt, Wasch...: **~ glove** Waschlederhandschuh m; **~ silk** Waschseide f; **III** v/t. **16.** waschen: **~** (**up**) **dishes** Geschirr (ab)spülen; → **hand** Redew.; **17.** (ab)spülen; **18.** be-, um-, über'spülen (*Fluten*); **19.** (fort-, weg-) spülen, (-)schwemmen: **~ ashore**; **20.** geol. graben (*Wasser*); → **wash away** 2, **wash out** 1; **21.** a) tünchen, b) dünn anstreichen, c) tuschen; **22.** Erze waschen, schlämmen; **23.** ◎ plattieren; **IV** v/i. **24.** sich waschen; waschen (*Wäscherin etc.*); **25.** sich gut etc. waschen (lassen), waschecht sein; **26.** bsd. Brit. F a) standhalten, b) 'ziehen', stichhaltig sein: **that won't ~** (**with me**) das zieht nicht (bei mir); **27.** (vom Wasser) gespült od. geschwemmt werden; **28.** fluten, spülen (**over** über acc.); branden, schlagen (**against** gegen), plätschern; Zssgn mit adv.:
wash| a·way I v/t. **1.** ab-, wegwaschen; **2.** weg-, fortspülen, -schwemmen; **II** v/i. **3.** weggeschwemmt werden; **~ down** v/t. **1.** abwaschen, -spritzen; **2.** hin'unterspülen (a. Essen mit e-m Getränk); **~ off** → **wash away**; **~ out I** v/t. **1.** auswaschen, ausspülen, unter'spülen (a. geol. etc.); **2.** F Plan etc. fallen lassen, aufgeben; **3.** **washed out** a) → **washed-out**, b) wegen Regens abgesagt od. abgebrochen (*Veranstaltung*); **II** v/i. **4.** sich auswaschen, verblassen; **5.** sich wegwaschen lassen (*Farbe*); **~ up I** v/t. **1.** Geschirr spülen; **2.** → **washed-up**; **II** v/i. **3.** F sich (Gesicht u. Hände) waschen; **4.** Geschirr spülen.
wash·a·ble ['wɒʃəbl] adj. waschecht, -bar; *Tapete*: abwaschbar.
'wash|·bag s. Brit. Kul'turbeutel m; **~·ba·sin** ['wɒʃ,beɪsn] s. Waschbecken n, -schüssel f; **'~·board** s. **1.** Waschbrett n; **~ belly** F (od. **stomach**) Waschbrettbauch m; **2.** Fuß-, Scheuerleiste f (*an der Wand*); **~ bot·tle** s. ↑ **1.** Spritzflasche f; **2.** (Gas)Waschflasche f; **'~·bowl** → **washbasin**; **'~·cloth** s. Am. Waschlappen m.
washed|-out [,wɒʃt'aut] adj. **1.** verwaschen, verblasst; **2.** F ,fertig', ,erledigt' (*erschöpft*); **,~·'up** adj. F ,erledigt', ,fertig': a) erschöpft, b) völlig ruiniert.
wash·er ['wɒʃə] s. **1.** Wäscher(in); **2.** 'Waschma,schine f; **3.** (Ge'schirr)Spülma,schine f; **4.** Papierherstellung: Halb(zeug)holländer m; **5.** ◎ 'Unterlegscheibe f, Dichtungsring m; '~·wom·an s. [irr.] Waschfrau f, Wäscherin f.
wash·e·te·ri·a [,wɒʃə'tɪərɪə] s. Brit. **1.** 'Waschsa,lon m; **2.** (Auto)Waschanlage f.
'wash·hand adj. Brit. Handwasch...: **~ basin** (Hand)Waschbecken n; **~ stand** (Hand)Waschständer m.
wash·i·ness ['wɒʃɪnɪs] s. **1.** Wässerigkeit f (a. fig.); **2.** Verwaschenheit f.
wash·ing ['wɒʃɪŋ] **I** s. **1.** → **wash** 1, 2; **2.** oft pl. Spülwasser n; **3.** ◎ nasse Aufbereitung, Erzwäsche f; **4.** 'Farb,überzug m; **II** adj. **5.** Wasch...; Wäsche...; **ma·chine** s. 'Waschma,schine f; **~ so-**

da *s.* (Bleich)Soda *f, n*; ˌ͜ˈup *s.* Abwasch *m* (*a. Geschirr*): **do the** ͜ Geschirr spülen; ͜ **liquid** Spülmittel *n*.

wash| leath·er *s.* **1.** Waschleder *n*; **2.** Fenster(putz)leder *n*; '͜·**out** *s.* **1.** *geol.* Auswaschung *f*; **2.** Unter¹spülung *f* (*e-r Straße etc.*); **3.** *sl.* a) ‚Niete' *f*, Versager *m* (*Person*), b) ‚Pleite' *f*, ‚Reinfall' *m*, c) ⚔ ‚Fahrkarte' *f* (*Fehlschuss*); '͜·**rag** *s. Am.* Waschlappen *m*; '͜·**room** *s. Am.* (öffentliche) Toi¹lette; ͜ **sale** *s.* ✝ *Börse*: Scheinverkauf *m*; '͜·**stand** *s.* **1.** Waschständer *m*; **2.** Waschbecken *n* (*mit fließendem Wasser*); '͜·**tub** *s.* Waschwanne *f*.

wash·y ['wɒʃɪ] *adj.* □ **1.** verwässert, wässerig (*beide a. fig. kraftlos, seicht*); **2.** verwaschen, blass (*Farbe*).

WASP [wɒsp] *s. Am.* prote¹stantischer weißer Angelsachse (*aus White Anglo-Saxon Protestant*).

wasp [wɒsp] *s. zo.* Wespe *f*; '**wasp·ish** [-pɪʃ] *adj.* □ *fig.* a) reizbar, b) gereizt, giftig.

was·sail ['wɒseɪl] *s. obs.* **1.** (Trink)Gelage *n*; **2.** Würzbier *n*.

wast [wɒst; wəst] *obs. 2. sg. pret. ind. von* **be**: **thou** ͜ du warst.

wast·age ['weɪstɪdʒ] *s.* **1.** Verlust *m*, Abgang *m*, Verschleiß *m*; **2.** Vergeudung *f*: ͜ **of energy** a) Energieverschwendung *f*, b) *fig.* Leerlauf *m*.

waste [weɪst] **I** *adj.* **1.** öde, wüst, unfruchtbar, unbebaut (*Land*): **lie** ͜ brachliegen; **lay** ͜ verwüsten; **2.** a) nutzlos, ¹überflüssig, b) ungenutzt, ¹überschüssig: ͜ **energy**; **3.** unbrauchbar, Abfall...; **4.** ⊙ a) abgängig, Abgangs..., Ab...(-*gas etc.*), b) Abfluss..., Ablauf...; **II** *s.* **5.** Verschwendung *f*, Vergeudung *f*: ͜ **of energy** (*money, time*) Kraft- (Geld-, Zeit)verschwendung; **go** (*od.* **run**) **to** ͜ a) brachliegen, verwildern, b) vergeudet werden, c) verlottern, -fallen; **6.** Verfall *m*, Verschleiß *m*, Abgang *m*, Verlust *m*; **7.** Wüste *f*, (Ein)Öde *f*: ͜ **of water** Wasserwüste *f*; **8.** Abfall *m*; ⊙ *a.* Abgänge *pl., bsd.* a) Ausschuss *m*, b) Putzbaumwolle *f*, c) Wollabfälle *pl.*, d) Werg *n*, e) *typ.* Makula¹tur *f*, f) Gekrätz *n*; **9.** ⚒ Abraum *m*; **10.** ⚖ Wertminderung *f* (*e-s Grundstücks durch Vernachlässigung*); **III** *v/t.* **11.** Geld, Worte, Zeit etc. verschwenden, vergeuden (**on** an *acc.*): **you are wasting your breath** du kannst dir deine Worte sparen; **a** ͜**d talent** ein ungenutztes Talent; **12. be** ͜**d** nutzlos sein, ohne Wirkung bleiben (**on** auf *acc.*), am falschen Platz stehen; **13.** zehren an (*dat.*), aufzehren, schwächen; **14.** verwüsten, verheeren; **15.** ⚖ Vermögensschaden verursachen bei, *Besitztum* verkommen lassen; **16.** a) F *Sportler etc.* ‚verheizen', b) *Am. sl.* j-n ‚umlegen'; **IV** *v/i.* **17.** *fig.* vergeudet *od.* verschwendet werden; **18.** sich verzetteln (**in** in *dat.*); **19.** vergehen, (un)genutzt) verstreichen (*Zeit, Gelegenheit etc.*); **20.** *a.* ͜ **away** a) abnehmen, schwinden, b) da¹hinsiechen, verfallen; **21.** verschwenderisch sein: ͜ **not, want not** spare in der Zeit, so hast du in der Not; ͜ **a·void·ance** *s.* Abfallvermeidung *f*; '͜·**bas·ket** *s.* Abfall-, *bsd.* Pa¹pierkorb *m*; ͜ **dis·pos·al** *s.* Müllbeseitigung *f*.

waste·ful ['weɪstfʊl] *adj.* □ **1.** kostspielig, unwirtschaftlich, verschwenderisch; **2.** verschwenderisch (**of** mit): **be** ͜ **of** verschwenderisch umgehen mit; **3.** *poet.* wüst, öde; '**waste·ful·ness** [-nɪs] *s.* Verschwendung(ssucht) *f*.

waste| gas *s.* ⊙ Abgas *n*; ͜ **gas clean·ing** *s.* Abgasentgiftung *f*; ͜ **heat** *s.* ⊙ Abwärme *f*; ͜ **in·cin·er·a·tion** *s.* Müllverbrennung *f*; ͜ **in·cin·er·a·tion plant** *s.* Müllverbrennungsanlage *f*; ͜ **in·dus·try** *s.* Entsorgungswirtschaft *f*; '͜·**land** *s.* Ödland *n* (*a. fig.*); ͜ **oil** *s.* Altöl *n*; ˌ͜ˈ**pa·per** *s.* **1.** 'Abfallpa,pier *n*, Makula¹tur *f* (*a. fig.*); **2.** 'Altpa,pier *n*; ˌ͜ˈ**pa·per bas·ket** *s.* Pa¹pierkorb *m*; ͜ **pipe** *s.* ⊙ Abfluss-, Abzugsrohr *n*; ͜ **prod·uct** *s.* **1.** ⊙ 'Abfallpro,dukt *n*; **2.** *biol.* Ausscheidungsstoff *m*.

wast·er ['weɪstə] *s.* **1.** → **wastrel** 1 *u.* 3; **2.** *metall.* a) Fehlguss *m*, b) Schrottstück *n*.

waste| re·cov·er·y *s.* Abfallverwertung *f*; ͜ **sep·a·ra·tion** *s.* Mülltrennung *f*; ͜ **steam** *s.* ⊙ Abdampf *m*; ͜ **water** *s.* Abwasser *n*; ͜ **wool** *s.* Twist *m*.

wast·ing ['weɪstɪŋ] *adj.* **1.** zehrend, schwächend: ͜ **disease**; → **palsy** 1; **2.** schwindend, abnehmend.

wast·rel ['weɪstrəl] *s.* **1.** a) Verschwender *m*, b) Taugenichts *m*; **2.** He¹rumtreiber *m*; **3.** ✝ 'Ausschuss(ar,tikel *m*, -ware *f*) *m*, fehlerhaftes Exem¹plar.

watch [wɒtʃ] **I** *s.* **1.** Wache *f*, Wacht *f*: **be** (**up**)**on the** ͜ a) wachsam *od.* auf der Hut sein, b) (**for**) Ausschau halten (nach), lauern (auf *acc.*), Acht haben (auf *acc.*); **keep** (**a**) ͜ (**on** *od.* **over**) Wache halten, wachen (über *acc.*), aufpassen (auf *acc.*); → **ward** 8; **2.** (Schild)Wache *f*, Wachtposten *m*; **3.** *mst pl. hist.* (Nacht)Wache *f* (*Zeiteinteilung*): **in the silent** ͜**es of the night** in den stillen Stunden der Nacht; **4.** ♣ (Schiffs)Wache *f* (*Zeitabschnitt u. Mannschaft*); **5.** *hist.* Nachtwächter *m*; **6.** *obs.* a) Wachen *n*, wache Stunden *pl.*, b) Totenwache *f*; **7.** (Taschen-, Armband)Uhr *f*; **II** *v/i.* **8.** zusehen, zuschauen; **9.** (**for**) warten, lauern (auf *acc.*), Ausschau halten (nach); **10.** wachen (**with** bei), wach sein; **11.** ͜ **over** wachen über (*acc.*), bewachen, aufpassen auf (*acc.*); **12.** ⚔ Posten stehen, Wache halten; **13.** ͜ **out** (**for** a) → 9, b) aufpassen, Acht geben: ͜ **out!** Vorsicht!, pass auf!; **III** *v/t.* **14.** beobachten: a) j-m zuschauen (**working** bei der Arbeit), b) ein wachsames Auge halten auf (*acc.*), *a. Verdächtigen* über¹wachen, c) *Vorgang etc.* verfolgen, im Auge behalten, d) ⚖ *den Verlauf e-s Prozesses* verfolgen; **15.** *Vieh* hüten, bewachen; **16.** *Gelegenheit* abwarten, abpassen, wahrnehmen: ͜ **one's time**; **17.** Acht haben auf (*acc.*) (*od.* **that** dass): ͜ **one's step** a) vorsichtig gehen, b) F sich vorsehen; ͜ **your step!** Vorsicht!; '͜·**boat** *s.* ♣ Wach(t)boot *n*; ͜ **box** *s.* **1.** ⚔ Schilderhaus *n*; **2.** 'Unterstand *m* (*für Wachmänner etc.*); ͜ **case** *s.* Uhrgehäuse *n*; '͜·**dog** *s.* Wachhund *m* (*a. fig.*): ͜ **committee** Überwachungsausschuss *m*.

watch·er ['wɒtʃə] *s.* **1.** Wächter *m*; **2.** Beobachter(in); **3.** j-d, der Kranken- *od.* Totenwache hält.

watch·ful ['wɒtʃfʊl] *adj.* □ wachsam, aufmerksam, *a.* lauernd (**of** auf *acc.*); '**watch·ful·ness** [-nɪs] *s.* **1.** Wachsamkeit *f*; **2.** Vorsicht *f*; **3.** Wachen *n* (**over** über *dat.*).

watch| house ['wɒtʃhaʊs] *s.* (Poli¹zei)Wache *f*; '͜·**mak·er** *s.* Uhrmacher *m*; '͜·**mak·ing** *s.* Uhrmache¹rei *f*; '͜·**man** [-mən] *s.* [*irr.*] **1.** (Nacht)Wächter *m*; **2.** *hist.* Nachtwächter *m* (*e-r Stadt etc.*); ͜ **night** *s. eccl.* Sil¹vestergottesdienst *m*; ͜ **of·fi·cer** *s.* ♣ 'Wachoffi,zier *m*; ͜

pock·et *s.* Uhrtasche *f*; ͜ **spring** *s.* Uhrfeder *f*; '͜·**strap** *s.* Uhr(arm)band *n*; '͜·**tow·er** *s.* ⚔ Wach(t)turm *m*; '͜·**word** *s.* **1.** Losung *f*, Pa¹role *f* (*a. fig. e-r Partei etc.*); **2.** *fig.* Schlagwort *n*.

wa·ter ['wɔːtə] **I** *v/t.* **1.** bewässern, *Rasen, Straße etc.* sprengen, *Pflanzen* (be-) gießen; **2.** *Vieh* tränken; **3.** mit Wasser versorgen; **4.** *oft* ͜ **down** verwässern: a) verdünnen, *Wein* pan(t)schen) *fig. Erklärung etc.* abschwächen, c) *fig.* mundgerecht machen: **a** ͜**ed-down liberalism** ein verwässerter Liberalismus; **5.** ✝ *Aktienkapital* verwässern; **6.** ⊙ *Stoff* wässern, moirieren; **II** *v/i.* **7.** wässern (*Mund*), tränen (*Augen*): **his mouth** ͜**ed** das Wasser lief ihm im Mund zusammen (**for, after** nach); **make s.o.'s mouth** ͜ j-m den Mund wässerig machen; **8.** ♣ Wasser einnehmen; **9.** trinken, zur Tränke gehen (*Vieh*); **10.** ✈ wassern; **III** *s.* **11.** Wasser *n*: **in deep** ͜(**s**) *fig.* in Schwierigkeiten, in der Klemme; **hold** ͜ *fig.* stichhaltig sein; **keep one's head above** ͜ *fig.* sich (gerade noch) über Wasser halten; **make the** ͜ ♣ vom Stapel laufen; **throw cold** ͜ **on** *fig.* e-r Sache e-n Dämpfer aufsetzen, wie e-e kalte Dusche wirken auf (*acc.*); **still** ͜**s run deep** stille Wasser sind tief; → **hot** 13, **oil** 1, **trouble** 6; **12.** *oft pl.* Brunnen *m*, Wasser *n* (*e-r Heilquelle*): **drink** (*od.* **take**) **the** ͜**s** (**at**) e-e Kur machen (in *dat.*); **13.** *oft pl.* Wasser *n od. pl.*, Gewässer *n od. pl.*, *a.* Fluten *pl.*: **by** ͜ zu Wasser, auf dem Wasserweg; **on the** ͜ a) zur See, b) zu Schiff; **the** ͜**s** *poet.* das Meer, die See; **14.** Wasserstand *m*; → **low water**; **15.** (Toi¹letten)Wasser *n*; **16.** Wasserlösung *f*; **17.** *physiol.* Wasser *n* (*Sekret, z. B. Speichel, a. Urin*): **the** ͜(**s**) das Fruchtwasser; **make** (*od.* **pass**) ͜ Wasser lassen, urinieren; ͜ **on the brain** Wasserkopf *m*; ͜ **on the knee** Kniegelenkerguss *m*; **18.** Wasser *n* (*reiner Glanz e-s Edelsteins*): **of the first** ͜ reinsten Wassers (*a. fig.*); **19.** Wasser(glanz *m*) *n*, Moi¹ré *n* (*Stoff*); ͜ **bath** *s.* Wasserbad *n* (*a.* 🍳); ͜ **bed** *s.* 🛏 Wasserbett *n*, -kissen *n*; ͜ **bird** *s. zo. allg.* Wasservogel *m*; ͜ **blis·ter** *s.* 🩸 Wasserblase *f*; '͜·**borne** *adj.* **1.** auf dem Wasser schwimmend; **2.** zu Wasser befördert (*Ware*), auf dem Wasser stattfindend (*Verkehr*), Wasser...; ͜ **bot·tle** *s.* **1.** Wasserflasche *f*; **2.** Feldflasche *f*; '͜·**bound** *adj.* vom Wasser eingeschlossen *od.* abgeschnitten; ͜ **bus** *s.* (Linien)Flussboot *n*; ͜ **butt** *s.* Wasserfass *n*, Regentonne *f*; ͜ **can·non** *s.* Wasserwerfer *m*; ͜ **car·riage** *s.* Trans¹port *m* zu Wasser, 'Wassertrans,port *m*; ♀ **Car·ri·er** → **Aquarius**; '͜·**cart** *s.* Wasserwagen *m, bsd.* Sprengwagen *m*; ͜ **chute** *s.* Wasserrutschbahn *f*; ͜ **clock** *s.* ⊙ Wasseruhr *f*; ͜ **clos·et** *s.* ('Wasser)Klo,sett *n*; '͜·**col·o(u)r I** *s.* **1.** Wasser-, Aqua¹rellfarbe *f*; **2.** Aqua-¹rellmale,rei *f*; **3.** Aqua¹rell *n* (*Bild*); **II** *adj.* **4.** Aquarell...; '͜·**col·o(u)r·ist** *s.* Aqua¹rellmaler(in); '͜·**cooled** *adj.* ⊙ wassergekühlt; ͜ **cool·ing** *s.* ⊙ Wasserkühlung *f*; '͜·**course** *s.* **1.** Wasserlauf *m*; **2.** Fluss-, Strombett *n*; **3.** Ka¹nal *m*; '͜·**craft** *s.* Wasserfahrzeug(*e pl.*) *n*; '͜·**cress** *s. oft pl.* 🌿 Brunnenkresse *f*; ͜ **cure** *s.* 🩺 **1.** Wasserkur *f*; **2.** Wasserheilkunde *f*; '͜·**fall** *s.* Wasserfall *m*; '͜·**find·er** *s.* (Wünschel)Rutengänger *m*; '͜·**fog** *s.* Tröpfchennebel *m*; '͜·**fowl** *s. zo.* **1.** Wasservogel *m*; **2.** *coll.* Wasservögel *pl.*; '͜·**front** *s.* Hafengebiet *n*,

-viertel *n*; an ein Gewässer grenzendes (Stadt)Gebiet; ~ **gage** *Am.* → *water gauge*; ~ **gate** *s.* **1.** Schleuse *f*; **2.** Fluttor *n*; ~ **gauge** *s.* ◎ **1.** Wasserstands(an)zeiger *m*; **2.** Pegel *m*, Peil *m*, hydraulischer Wasserdruckmesser; **3.** *Wasserdruck, gemessen in inches Wassersäule*; ~ **glass** *s.* Wasserglas *n* (*a.* 🐟): ~ **egg** Kalkei *n*; ~ **gru·el** *s.* (dünner) Haferschleim; ~ **heat·er** *s.* Warmwasserbereiter *m*; ~ **hose** *s.* Wasserschlauch *m*; ~ **ice** *s.* Fruchteis *n*.

wa·ter·i·ness ['wɔːtərɪnɪs] *s.* Wässrigkeit *f*.

wa·ter·ing ['wɔːtərɪŋ] **I** *s.* **1.** (Be)Wässern *n etc.*; **II** *adj.* **2.** Bewässerungs...; **3.** Kur..., Bade...; ~ **can** *s.* Gießkanne *f*; ~ **cart** *s.* Sprengwagen *m*; ~ **place** *s.* **1.** *bsd. Brit.* a) Bade-, Kurort *m*, Bad *n*, b) (See)Bad *n*; **2.** (Vieh)Tränke *f*, Wasserstelle *f*; ~ **pot** *s. Am.* Gießkanne *f*.

wa·ter| jack·et *s.* ◎ (Wasser)Kühlmantel *m*; ~ **jump** *s. sport* Wassergraben *m*; ~ **lev·el** *s.* **1.** Wasserstand *m*, -spiegel *m*; **2.** ◎ a) Pegelstand *m*, b) Wasserwaage *f*; **3.** *geol.* (Grund)Wasserspiegel *m*; ~ **lil·y** *s.* ♀ Seerose *f*, Wasserlilie *f*; '~**line** *s.* ⚓ Wasserlinie *f e-s Schiffs od. als Wasserzeichen*; '~**logged** *adj.* **1.** voll Wasser (*Boot etc.*); **2.** voll gesogen (*Holz etc.*).

Wa·ter·loo [ˌwɔːtə'luː] *s.*: *meet one's ~ fig.* sein Waterloo erleben.

wa·ter| main *s.* Haupt(wasser)rohr *n*; '~**man** [-mən] *s.* [*irr.*] **1.** ⚓ Fährmann *m*; **2.** *sport* Ruderer *m*; **3.** *myth.* Wassergeist *m*; '~**mark** *s.* **1.** Wasserzeichen *n* (*in Papier*); **2.** ⚓ Wassermarke *f, bsd.* Flutzeichen *n*; → *high* (*low*) *watermark*; **II** *v/t.* **3.** *Papier* mit Wasserzeichen versehen; '~**mel·on** *s.* ♀ 'Wasserme,lone *f*; ~ **me·ter** *s.* Wasserzähler *m*, -uhr *f*; ~ **pipe** *s.* **1.** ◎ Wasser(leitungs)rohr *n*; **2.** orien'talische Wasserpfeife; ~ **pis·tol** *s.* 'Wasserpis,tole *f*; ~ **plane** *s.* Wasserflugzeug *n*; ~ **plate** *s.* Wärmeteller *m*; ~ **po·lo** *s. sport* Wasserballspiel *n*; '~**proof I** *adj.* wasserdicht; **II** *s.* wasserdichter Stoff *od.* Mantel *etc.*, Regenmantel *m*; **III** *v/t.* imprägnieren; ~ **re·cy·cling** *s.* Wasseraufbereitung *f*; ,~**re'pel·lent** *adj.* Wasser abstoßend; '~**scape** -skeɪp] *s. paint.* Seestück *n*; ~ **seal** *s.* ◎ Wasserverschluss *m*; '~**shed** *s. geogr.* **1.** *Brit.* Wasserscheide *f*; **2.** Einzugs-, Stromgebiet *n*; **3.** *fig.* a) Trennungslinie *f*, b) Wendepunkt *m*; '~**side I** *s.* Küste *f*, See-, Flussufer *n*; **II** *adj.* Küsten..., (Fluss)Ufer...; '~**ski** *v/i.* Wasserski laufen; ,~**'sol·u·ble** *adj.* 🐟 wasserlöslich; '~**spout** *s.* **1.** Abtraufe *f*; **2.** *meteor.* Wasserhose *f*; ~ **sup·ply** *s.* **1.** Wasserversorgung *f*; **2.** Wasserreserven *pl.*; ~ **ta·ble** *s.* **1.** △ Wasserabflussleiste *f*; **2.** *geol.* Grundwasserspiegel *m*; '~**tight** *adj.* **1.** wasserdicht: *keep s.th. in ~ compartments fig.* et. isoliert halten *od.* betrachten; **2.** *fig.* a) unanfechtbar, b) sicher, c) stichhaltig (*Argument*); ~ **vole** *s. zo.* Wasserratte *f*; ~ **wag·(g)on** *s.* Wasser(versorgungs)wagen *m*: *be on* (*off*) *the ~* F nicht mehr (wieder) trinken; *go on the ~* F das Trinken sein lassen; ~ **wag·tail** *s. orn.* Bachstelze *f*; '~**wave I** *s.* Wasserwelle *f* (*im Haar*); **II** *v/t.* in Wasserwellen legen; '~**way** *s.* **1.** Wasserstraße *f*, Schifffahrtsweg *m*; **2.** ⚓ Wassergang *m* (*Decksrinne*); ~ **wings** *s. pl.* Schwimmflügel *pl.*; '~**works** *s. pl. oft sg. konstr.* **1.** Wasserwerk *n*; **2.** a) Fon'täne(n *pl.*) *f*, b) Wasserspiel *n*: *turn on the ~* F (los-)

heulen; **3.** F (Harn)Blase *f*.

wa·ter·y ['wɔːtərɪ] *adj.* **1.** Wasser...: *a ~ grave* ein nasses Grab; **2.** wässerig: a) feucht (*Boden*), b) Regen verkündend (*Sonne etc.*): ~ *sky* Regenhimmel *m*; **3.** triefend: a) *allg.* voll Wasser, nass (*Klei*der), b) tränend (*Auge*); **4.** verwässert: a) fad(e) (*Speise*), b) wässerig, blass (*Farbe*), c) *fig.* seicht (*Stil*).

watt [wɒt] *s.* ⚡ Watt *n*; **watt·age** ['wɒtɪdʒ] *s.* ⚡ Wattleistung *f*.

wat·tle ['wɒtl] **I** *s.* **1.** *Brit. dial.* Hürde *f*; **2.** *a. pl.* Flecht-, Gitterwerk *n*: ~ *and daub* △ mit Lehm beworfenes Flechtwerk; **3.** ♀ (au'stralische) A'kazie; **4.** a) *orn.* Kehllappen *pl.*, b) *ichth.* Bartfäden *pl.*; **II** *v/t.* **5.** aus Flechtwerk herstellen; **6.** *Ruten* zs.-flechten; '**wat·tling** [-lɪŋ] *s.* Flechtwerk *n*.

waul [wɔːl] *v/i.* jämmerlich schreien, jaulen.

wave [weɪv] **I** *s.* **1.** Welle *f* (*a. phys.*; *a. im Haar etc.*), Woge *f* (*beide a. fig. von Gefühl etc.*): *the ~s* poet. die See; ~ *of indignation* Woge der Entrüstung; *make ~s fig. Am.* 'Wellen schlagen'; **2.** (*Angriffs-, Einwanderer- etc.*)Welle *f*: *in ~s* in aufeinander folgenden Wellen; **3.** ◎ a) Flamme *f* (*im Stoff*), b) *typ.* Guil'loche *f* (*Zierlinie auf Wertpapieren etc.*); **4.** Wink(en *n*) *m*, Schwenken *n*; **II** *v/i.* **5.** wogen (*a. Kornfeld etc.*); **6.** wehen, flattern, wallen; **7.** (*to s.o.* j-m zu)winken, Zeichen geben; **8.** sich wellen (*Haar*); **III** *v/t.* **9.** *Fahne, Waffe etc.* schwenken, schwingen, hin u. her bewegen: ~ *one's arms* mit den Armen fuchteln; ~ *one's hand* (mit der Hand) winken (*to* j-m); **10.** *Haar etc.* wellen, in Wellen legen; **11.** ◎ a) *Stoff* flammen, b) *Wertpapiere etc.* guillochieren; **12.** j-m zuwinken: ~ *aside* j-n beiseite winken, *fig.* j-n *od. et.* mit e-r Handbewegung abtun; **13.** *et.* zuwinken: ~ *a farewell* nachwinken (*to s.o.* j-m); ~ **band** *s.* ⚡ Wellenband *n*; '~**length** *s.* ⚡, *phys.* Wellenlänge *f*: *be on the same ~ fig.* auf der gleichen Wellenlänge liegen.

wa·ver ['weɪvə] *v/i.* **1.** (sch)wanken, taumeln; flackern (*Licht*); zittern (*Hände, Stimme etc.*); **2.** *fig.* wanken: a) unschlüssig sein, schwanken (*between* zwischen), b) zu weichen beginnen.

wa·ver·er ['weɪvərə] *s. fig.* Unentschlossene(r *m*) *f*; '**wa·ver·ing** [-vərɪŋ] *adj.* □ **1.** flackernd; **2.** zitternd; **3.** (sch)wankend (*a. fig.*).

wave trap *s.* ⚡ Sperrkreis *m*.

wav·y ['weɪvɪ] *adj.* □ **1.** wellig, gewellt (*Haar, Linie etc.*); **2.** wogend.

wax¹ [wæks] **I** *v/i.* **1.** wachsen, zunehmen (*bsd. Mond*) (*a. fig. rhet.*): ~ *and wane* zu- u. abnehmen; **2.** *vor ad.*: alt, frech, laut *etc.* werden; **II** *s.* **3.** *be in a ~* F e-e Stinkwut haben.

wax² [wæks] **I** *s.* **1.** (Bienen-, Pflanzenetc.)Wachs *n*: *like ~ fig.* (wie) Wachs in j-s Händen; **2.** Siegellack *m*; **3.** *a. cob·bler's ~* Schusterpech *n*; **4.** Ohrenschmalz *n*; **II** *v/t.* **5.** (ein)wachsen, bohnern; **6.** verpichen; **7.** (auf Schallplatte) aufnehmen; '~**cloth** *s.* **1.** Wachstuch *n*; **2.** Bohnertuch *n*; ~ **doll** *s.* Wachspuppe *f*.

wax·en ['wæksən] → *waxy*.

wax·ing¹ ['wæksɪŋ] **I** *adj.* zunehmend, wachsend (*a. Mond*); **II** *s.* Zunahme *f*, (An)Wachsen *n*.

wax·ing² ['wæksɪŋ] *s.* **1.** (Ein)Wachsen *n* (*Behandlung mit Wachs*); **2.** Kosmetik: Epilati'on *f*, Depilati'on *f*, Enfer-

nung *f* von Körperhaaren.

wax| light *s.* Wachskerze *f*; ~ **pa·per** *s.* 'Wachspa,pier *n*; '~**work** *s.* **1.** 'Wachsfi,gur *f*; **2.** *a. pl. sg. konstr.* 'Wachsfi,gurenkabi,nett *n*.

wax·y ['wæksɪ] *adj.* □ **1.** wächsern (*a. Gesichtsfarbe*), wie Wachs; **2.** *fig.* weich (wie Wachs), nachgiebig; **3.** 🐟 Wachs...: ~ *liver*.

way¹ [weɪ] *s.* **1.** Weg *m*, Pfad *m*, Straße *f*, Bahn *f* (*a. fig.*): ~ *back* Rückweg; ~ *home* Heimweg; ~ *in* Eingang *m*; ~ *out bsd. fig.* Ausweg; ~ *through* Durchfahrt *f*, -reise *f*; ~*s and means* Mittel u. Wege, *bsd. pol.* Geldbeschaffung(smaßnahmen) *f*; *Committee of ≈s and Means parl.* Finanz-, Haushaltsausschuss *m*; *the ~ of the Cross R.C.* der Kreuzweg; *over* (*od. across*) *the ~* gegenüber; *ask the* (*od. one's*) *~* nach dem Weg fragen; *find a ~ fig.* e-n (Aus-)Weg finden; *lose one's ~* sich verirren *od.* verlaufen; *take one's ~* sich aufmachen (*to* nach); **2.** *fig.* Gang *m*, (üblicher) Weg: *that is the ~ of the world* das ist der Lauf der Welt; *go the ~ of all flesh* den Weg allen Fleisches gehen (*sterben*); **3.** Richtung *f*, Seite *f*: *which ~ is he looking?* wohin schaut er?; *this ~* a) hierher, b) hier entlang, c) → 6; *the other ~ round* umgekehrt; **4.** Weg *m*, Entfernung *f*, Strecke *f*: *a long ~ off* weit (von hier) entfernt; *a long ~ off perfection* alles andere als vollkommen; *a little ~* ein kleines Stück (Wegs); **5.** (freie) Bahn, Platz *m*: *be* (*od. stand*) *in s.o.'s ~* j-m im Weg sein (*a. fig.*); *give ~* a) nachgeben, b) (zurück)weichen, c) sich *der Verzweiflung etc.* hingeben; **6.** Art *f* u. Weise *f*, Weg *m*, Me'thode *f*: *any ~* auf jede *od.* irgendeine Art; *any ~ you please* ganz wie Sie wollen; *in a big* (*small*) *~* im Großen (Kleinen); *one ~ or another* irgendwie, so oder so; *some ~ or other* auf die eine oder andere Weise, irgendwie; ~ *of living* (*thinking*) Lebens-(Denk)weise; *to my ~ of thinking* nach m-r Meinung; *in a polite* (*friendly*) ~ höflich (freundlich); *in its ~* auf s-e Art; *in what* (*od. which*) ~ inwiefern, wieso; *the right* (*wrong*) ~ (*to do it*) richtig (falsch); *the same ~* genauso; *the ~ he does it* so wie er es macht; *this* (*od. that*) ~ so; *that's the ~ to do it* so macht man das; **7.** Brauch *m*, Sitte *f*: *the good old ~* die guten alten Bräuche; **8.** Eigenart *f*: *funny ~s* komische Manieren; *it is not his ~* es ist nicht s-e Art *od.* Gewohnheit; *she has a winning ~ with her* sie hat e-e gewinnende Art; *that is always the ~ with him* so macht er es (*od.* geht es ihm) immer; **9.** Hinsicht *f*, Beziehung *f*: *in a ~* in gewisser Hinsicht; *in one ~* in 'einer Beziehung; *in some ~s* in mancher Hinsicht; *in the ~ of food* an Lebensmitteln, was Nahrung anbelangt; *no ~* keineswegs; **10.** (*bsd.* Gesundheits)Zustand *m*, Lage *f*: *in a bad ~* in e-r schlimmen Lage; *live in a great* (*small*) ~ auf großem Fuß (in kleinen Verhältnissen *od.* sehr bescheiden) leben; **11.** Berufszweig *m*, Fach *n*: *it is not in his ~* es schlägt nicht in sein Fach; *he is in the oil ~* er ist im Ölhandel (beschäftigt); **12.** F Um'gebung *f*, Gegend *f*: *somewhere London ~* irgendwo in der Gegend von London; **13.** ◎ a) (Hahn)Weg *m*, Bohrung *f*, b) *pl.* Führungen *pl.* (*bei Maschinen*); **14.** Fahrt(geschwindigkeit) *f*: *gather* (*lose*) ~ Fahrt vergrößern (verlieren); **15.** *pl. Schiffbau:* a) Helling *f*,

b) Stapelblöcke *pl.*;

Besondere Redewendungen: **by the ~** a) im Vorbeigehen, unterwegs; b) am Weg(esrand), an der Straße, c) *fig.* übrigens, nebenbei (bemerkt); **but that is by the ~!** doch dies nur nebenbei; **by ~ of** a) (auf dem Weg) über (*acc.*), durch, b) *fig.* in der Absicht zu, um ... zu, c) als *Entschuldigung etc.*; **by ~ of example** beispielsweise; **by ~ of exchange** auf dem Tauschwege; **be by ~ of being angry** im Begriff sein aufzubrausen; **be by ~ of doing (s.th.)** a) dabei sein(, et.) zu tun, b) pflegen *od.* gewohnt sein *od.* die Aufgabe haben(, et.) zu tun; → **family** 5; **in the ~ of** a) auf dem Weg. dabei zu, b) hinsichtlich (*gen.*); **in the ~ of business** auf dem üblichen Geschäftsweg; **put s.o. in the ~ (of doing)** j-m die Möglichkeit geben (zu tun); **no ~!** F nichts da!; **on the** (*od.* **one's**) **~** unterwegs, auf dem Wege; **be well on one's ~** im Gange sein, schon weit vorangekommen sein (*a. fig.*); **out of the ~** a) abgelegen, b) *fig.* ungewöhnlich, ausgefallen, c) *fig.* abwegig; **nothing out of the ~** nichts Ungewöhnliches; **go out of one's ~** ein Übriges tun, sich besonders anstrengen; **put s.o. out of the ~** *fig.* j-n aus dem Wege räumen (*töten*); → **harm** 1; **under ~** a) ⚓ in Fahrt, unterwegs, b) *fig.* im *od.* in Gang; **be in a fair** (*od.* **good**) **~** auf dem besten Wege sein, die besten Möglichkeiten haben; **come (in) s.o.'s ~** *bsd. fig.* j-m über den Weg laufen, j-n begegnen; **go a long ~ to(wards)** viel dazu beitragen zu, ein gutes Stück weiterhelfen bei; **go s.o.'s ~** a) den gleichen Weg gehen wie j-d, b) j-n begleiten; **go one's ~(s)** seinen Weg gehen, *fig.* s-n Lauf nehmen; **have a ~ with** mit *j-m* umzugehen wissen; **have one's own ~** s-n Willen durchsetzen; **if I had my (own) ~** wenn es nach mir ginge; **have it your ~!** du sollst Recht haben!; **you can't have it both ~s** du kannst nicht beides haben; **know one's ~ about** sich auskennen (*fig.* **in** mit); **lead the ~** (*a. fig.* mit gutem Beispiel) vorangehen; **learn the hard ~** Lehrgeld bezahlen müssen; **make** a) Platz machen (**for** für), b) vorwärts kommen (*a. fig. Fortschritte machen*); **make one's ~** sich durchsetzen, s-n Weg machen; → **mend** 2, **pave**, **pay** 3; **see one's ~ to do s.th.** e-e Möglichkeit sehen, et. zu tun; **work one's ~ through college** sich sein Studium durch Nebenarbeit verdienen, Werkstudent sein; **work one's ~ up** *a. fig.* sich hocharbeiten.

way² [weɪ] *adv.* F weit *oben, unten etc.*: **~ back** weit entfernt; **~ back in 1902** (schon) damals im Jahre 1902.

'way|·bill *s.* **1.** Passa'gierliste *f*; **2.** ✝ Frachtbrief *m*, Begleitschein *m*; **'~·far·er** [-ˌfeərə] *s. obs.* Reisende(r) *m*, Wandersmann *m*; **'~·far·ing** [-ˌfeərɪŋ] *adj.* reisend, wandernd; **~·lay** *v/t.* [*irr.* → **lay¹**] *j-m* auflauern; **'~·leave** *s.* ⚒ *Brit.* Wegerecht *n*; **~·'out** *adj.* F **1.** ex'zentrisch, ausgefallen, 'irr(e)'; **2.** 'toll', ,super'; **'~·side** I *s.* Straßen-, Wegrand *m*: **by the ~** am Wege, am Straßenrand; **fall by the ~** *fig.* auf der Strecke bleiben; II *adj.* am Wege (stehend), an der Straße (gelegen): **a ~ inn**.

way| sta·tion *s.* 🚉 *Am.* 'Zwischenstati,on *f*; **~ train** *s. Am.* Bummelzug *m*.

way·ward ['weɪwəd] *adj.* □ **1.** launisch, unberechenbar; **2.** eigensinnig, 'wider-

spenstig; 🚸 verwahrlost (*Jugendliche[r]*); **3.** ungeraten: **a ~ son**; **'way·ward·ness** [-nɪs] *s.* **1.** 'Widerspenstigkeit *f*, Eigensinn *m*; **2.** Launenhaftigkeit *f*.

'way·worn *adj.* reisemüde.

we [wiː; wɪ] *pron. pl.* wir *pl.*

weak [wiːk] *adj.* □ **1.** *allg.* schwach (*a. zahlenmäßig*) (*a. fig. Argument, Spieler, Stil, Stimme etc.*; *a. ling.*): **~ in Latin** *fig.* schwach in Latein; → **sex** 2; **2.** ♣ schwach: a) empfindlich, b) kränklich; **3.** (cha'rakter)schwach, la'bil, schwächlich: **~ point** (*od.* **side**) schwacher Punkt, schwache Seite, Schwäche *f*; **4.** schwach, dünn (*Tee etc.*); **5.** ✝ schwach, flau (*Markt*); **'weak·en** [-kən] I *v/t.* **1.** *j-n od. et.* schwächen; **2.** *Getränk etc.* verdünnen; **3.** *fig. Beweis etc.* abschwächen, entkräften; II *v/i.* **4.** schwach *od.* schwächer werden, nachlassen, erlahmen; **'weak·en·ing** [-knɪŋ] *s.* (Ab)Schwächung *f*.

weak·'kneed *adj.* F **1.** feig; **2.** → **weak-minded**.

weak·ling ['wiːklɪŋ] *s.* Schwächling *m*; **'weak·ly** [-lɪ] I *adj.* schwächlich; II *adv.* von **weak**; **weak·'mind·ed** *adj.* **1.** schwachsinnig; **2.** cha'rakterschwach.

weak·ness ['wiːknɪs] *s.* **1.** *allg.* (*a.* Cha'rakter)Schwäche *f*; **2.** Schwächlichkeit *f*, Kränklichkeit *f*; **3.** schwache Seite, schwacher Punkt; **4.** Nachteil *m*, Schwäche *f*, Mangel *m*; **5.** F Schwäche *f*, Vorliebe *f* (**for** für); **6.** ✝ Flauheit *f*.

weak·'sight·ed *adj.* 🚸 schwachsichtig; **~·'spir·it·ed** *adj.* kleinmütig.

weal¹ [wiːl] *s.* Wohl *n*: **~ and woe** das Wohl u. Wehe, gute u. schlechte Tage; **the public** (*od.* **common** *od.* **general**) **~** das Allgemeine.

weal² [wiːl] *s.* Schwiele *f*, Strieme(n *m*) *f* (*auf der Haut*).

wealth [welθ] *s.* **1.** Reichtum *m* (*a. fig. Fülle*) (**of** an *dat.*, von); **2.** Reichtümer *pl.*; **3.** ✝ a) Besitz *m*, Vermögen *n*: **~ tax** Vermögenssteuer *f*, b) *a.* **personal ~** Wohlstand *m*; **'wealth·y** [-θɪ] *adj.* □ reich (*a. fig. an od. dat.*), wohlhabend.

wean [wiːn] *v/t.* **1.** *Kind, junges Tier* entwöhnen; **2.** *a.* **~ away from** *fig. j-n* abbringen von, *j-m et.* abgewöhnen.

weap·on ['wepən] *s.* Waffe *f* (*a.* ♀, *zo. u. fig.*); **'weap·on·less** [-lɪs] *adj.* wehrlos, unbewaffnet; **'weap·on·ry** [-rɪ] *s.* Waffen *pl*; **'weap·ons-grade** *adj.* waffenfähig (*Plutonium*).

wear¹ [weə] I *v/t.* [*irr.*] **1.** am Körper tragen (*a. Bart, Brille, a. Trauer*), Kleidungsstück *a.* anhaben, Hut *a.* aufhaben: **~ the breeches** (*od.* **trousers** *od.* **pants**) F *fig.* die Hosen anhaben (*Ehefrau*); **she ~s her years well** *fig.* sie sieht jung aus für ihr Alter; **~ one's hair long** das Haar lang tragen; **~ a smile** *Lächeln, Miene etc.* zur Schau tragen, zeigen; **3.** **~ away** (*od.* **down**, **off**, **out**) *Kleid etc.* abnutzen, abtragen, *Absätze* abtreten, *Stufen etc.* austreten; *Löcher* reißen (**in** in *acc.*): **~ into holes** ganz abtragen, *Schuhe* durchlaufen; **4.** eingraben, nagen: **a groove worn by water**; **5.** **~ away** *Gestein etc.* auswaschen, -höhlen; *Farbe etc.* verwischen; **6.** *a.* **~ out** ermüden, *a. Geduld* erschöpfen; → **welcome** 1; **7.** *a.* **~ down** zermürben: a) entkräften, b) *fig.* niederringen, *Widerstand* brechen: **worn to a shadow** nur noch ein Schatten (*Person*); II *v/i.* [*irr.*] **8.** halten, haltbar sein: **~ well** a) sehr haltbar sein (*Stoff etc.*), sich gut tragen (*Kleid etc.*), b) *fig.* sich gut halten, wenig altern (*Person*);

9. *a.* **~ away** (*od.* **down**, **off**, **out**) sich abtragen *od.* abnutzen, verschleißen: **~ away** *a.* sich verwischen; **~ off** *fig.* sich verlieren (*Eindruck, Wirkung*); **~ out** *fig.* sich erschöpfen; **~ thin** a) fadenscheinig werden, b) sich erschöpfen (*Geduld etc.*); **10.** *a.* **~ away** langsam vergehen, da'hinschleichen (*Zeit*): **~ to an end** schleppend zu Ende gehen; **11.** **~ on** sich da'hinschleppen (*Zeit, Geschichte etc.*); **III** *s.* **12.** Tragen *n*: **clothes for everyday ~** Alltagskleidung *f*; **have in constant ~** ständig tragen; **13.** (Be)Kleidung *f*, Mode *f*: **be the ~** Mode sein, getragen werden; **14.** Abnutzung *f*, Verschleiß *m*: **~ and tear** a) ☉ Abnutzung, Verschleiß (*a. fig.*), b) ✝ Abschreibung *f* für Wertminderung; **for hard ~** strapazierfähig; **the worse for ~** abgetragen, mitgenommen (*a. fig.*); **15.** Haltbarkeit *f*: **there is still a great deal of ~ in it** das lässt sich noch gut tragen.

wear² [weə] ⚓ I *v/t.* [*irr.*] *Schiff* halsen; II *v/i.* [*irr.*] vor dem Wind drehen (*Schiff*).

wear·a·ble ['weərəbl] *adj.* tragbar (*Kleid*).

wea·ri·ness ['wɪərɪnɪs] *s.* **1.** Müdigkeit *f*; **2.** *fig.* 'Überdruss *m*.

wear·ing ['weərɪŋ] *adj.* **1.** Kleidungs...; **2.** abnützend; **3.** ermüdend, zermürbend.

wea·ri·some ['wɪərɪsəm] *adj.* □ ermüdend (*mst fig.* langweilig).

wear-re'sist·ant *adj.* strapa'zierfähig.

wea·ry ['wɪərɪ] I *adj.* □ **1.** müde, matt (**with** von, vor *dat.*); **2.** müde, 'überdrüssig (**of** *gen.*): **~ of life** lebensmüde; **3.** ermüdend: a) beschwerlich, b) langweilig; II *v/t.* **4.** ermüden (*a. fig.* langweilen); III *v/i.* **5.** überdrüssig *od.* müde werden (**of** *gen.*).

wea·sel ['wiːzl] *s.* **1.** *zo.* Wiesel *n*; **2.** F *contp.* ,Schlange' *f*, ,Ratte' *f*.

weath·er ['weðə] I *s.* **1.** a) Wetter *n*, Witterung *f*, b) Unwetter *n*: **in fine ~** bei schönem Wetter; **make good** (*od.* **bad**) **~** ⚓ auf gutes (schlechtes) Wetter stoßen; **make heavy ~ of s.th.** *fig.* ,viel Wind machen' um et.; **under the ~** F a) nicht in Form (*unpässlich*), b) e-n Katzenjammer habend, c) ,angesäuselt'; **2.** ⚓ Luv-, Windseite *f*; II *v/t.* **3.** dem Wetter aussetzen, *Holz etc.* auswittern; *geol.* verwittern (lassen); **4.** a) ⚓ *den Sturm* abwettern, b) *a. fig. Sturm, Krise etc.* über'stehen; **5.** ⚓ luvwärts um'schiffen; III *v/i.* **6.** *geol.* verwittern; **'~·,beat·en** *adj.* **1.** vom Wetter mitgenommen; **2.** verwittert; **3.** wetterhart; **'~·board** *s.* **1.** ☉ a) Wasserschenkel *m*, b) Schal-, Schindelbrett *n*, c) *pl.* Verschalung *f*; **2.** ⚓ Waschbord *n*; **'~·board·ing** *s.* Verschalung *f*; **'~·bound** *adj.* schlechtwetterbehindert; **~ bureau** *s.* Wetteramt *n*; **~ chart** *s.* Wetterkarte *f*; **'~·cock** *s.* **1.** Wetterhahn *m*; **2.** *fig.* wetterwendische Per'son; **'~·eye** [-əraɪ] *s.*: **keep one's ~ open** *fig.* gut aufpassen; **~ fore·cast** *s.* 'Wetterbericht *m*, -vor,hersage *f*; **'~·man** [-mæn] *s.* [*irr.*] F **1.** Meteoro'loge *m*; **2.** Wetteransager *m*; **'~·proof** *adj.* wetterfest; **~ sat·el·lite** *s.* 'Wettersatel,lit *m*; **~ side** *s.* **1.** → **weather** 2; **2.** Wetterseite *f*; **~ sta·tion** *s.* Wetterwarte *f*; **~ strip** *s.* Dichtungsleiste *f*; **~ vane** *s.* Wetterfahne *f*; **'~·worn** → **weather-beaten**.

weave [wiːv] I *v/t.* [*irr.*] **1.** weben, wirken; **2.** zs.-weben, flechten; **3.** (ein-) flechten (**into** in *acc.*), verweben,

-flechten (**with** mit, **into** zu) (a. fig.); **4.** fig. ersinnen, erfinden; **II** v/i. [irr.] **5.** weben; **6.** hin- u. herpendeln (a. Boxer), sich schlängeln od. winden; **7. get weaving** Brit. F ‚sich ranhalten'; **III** s. **8.** Gewebe n; **9.** Webart f; **'weav·er** [-və] s. **1.** Weber(in); Wirker(in); **2.** a. **~bird** orn. Webervogel m; **'weav·ing** [-vɪŋ] **I** s. Weben n, Webe'rei f; **II** adj. Web...: **~ loom** Webstuhl m; **~ mill** Weberei f.

wea·zen ['wiːzn] → **wizen**.

web [web] s. **1.** a) Gewebe n, Gespinst n, b) Netz n (der Spinne etc.) (alle a. fig.): **a ~ of lies** ein Lügengewebe; **2.** Gurt(band n) m; **3.** zo. a) Schwimm-, Flughaut f, b) Bart m e-r Feder; **4.** ⊗ Sägeblatt n; **5.** (Pa'pier- etc.)Bahn f, (-)Rolle f; **6. the ℒ** das (World Wide) Web (Internet); **webbed** [webd] adj. zo. schwimmhäutig: **~ foot** Schwimmfuß m; **web·bing** ['webɪŋ] s. **1.** Gewebe n; **2.** → **web** 2.

Web| brows·er s. Internet: 'Webbrowser m (Programm für die Suche im Internet); **'℥·foot** s. [irr.] zo. Schwimmfuß m; **'℥-,foot·ed** adj. schwimmfüßig; **~ page** s. Internet: 'Webseite f; **~ serv·er** s. Internet: 'Webserver m; **~ site** s. Internet: 'Website f (zs.-hängende Webseiten, die mit e-r Homepage beginnen); **~ space** s. Internet: 'Webspace m: a) Speicherplatz, den ein Internet-Provider auf e-m Server für e-n Kunden zur Verfügung stellt , b) Platz, den das World Wide Web im Cyberspace einnimmt; **'~-toed** → **web-footed**.

wed [wed] **I** v/t. **1.** rhet. ehelichen, heiraten: **~ded bliss** eheliches Glück; **2.** vermählen (**to** mit); **3.** fig. eng verbinden (**with**, **to** mit): **be ~ded to s.th.** a) an et. fest gebunden od. gekettet sein, b) sich e-r Sache verschrieben haben; **II** v/i. **4.** sich vermählen.

we'd [wiːd; wɪd] F für a) **we would**, **we should**, b) **we had**.

wed·ding ['wedɪŋ] s. Hochzeit f, Trauung f; **~ an·ni·ver·sa·ry** s. (dritter etc.) Hochzeitstag m; **~ break·fast** s. Hochzeitsessen n; **~ cake** s. Hochzeitskuchen m; **~ day** s. Hochzeitstag m; **~ dress** s. Hochzeits-, Brautkleid n; **~ ring** s. Trauring m.

we·del ['wedl] v/i. Skisport: wedeln.

wedge [wedʒ] **I** s. **1.** ⊗ Keil m (a. fig.): **~ writing** Keilschrift f; **the thin end of the ~** fig. ein erster kleiner Anfang; **2.** a) keilförmiges Stück (Land etc.), b) Ecke f (Käse etc.), c) Stück n (Kuchen); **3.** ✕ 'Keil(formati,on f) m; **4.** Golf: Wedge m (Schläger); **II** v/t. **5.** ⊗ a) verkeilen, festklemmen, b) (mit e-m Keil) spalten: **~ off** abspalten; **6.** (ein-) keilen, (-)zwängen (**in** in acc.): **~ o.s. in** sich hineinzwängen; **~ (fric·tion) gear** s. ⊗ Keilrädergetriebe n; **~ heel** s. (Schuh m mit) Keilabsatz m; **'~-shaped** adj. keilförmig.

wed·lock ['wedlɒk] s. Ehe(stand m) f: **born in lawful (out of) ~** ehelich (unehelich) geboren.

Wednes·day ['wenzdɪ] s. Mittwoch m: **on ~** am Mittwoch; **on ~s** mittwochs.

wee¹ [wiː] adj. klein, winzig: **a ~ bit** ein klein wenig; **the ~ hours** die frühen Morgenstunden.

wee² [wiː] F **I** s. ‚Pi'pi' n; **II** v/i. ‚Pi'pi machen'.

weed [wiːd] **I** s. **1.** Unkraut n: **ill ~s grow apace** Unkraut verdirbt nicht; **~ killer** Unkrautvertilgungsmittel n; **2.** F a) ‚Glimmstängel' m (Zigarre, Zigarette), b) ‚Kraut' n (Tabak), c) ‚Grass' n

(Marihuana); **3.** sl. Kümmerling m (schwächliches Tier, a. Person); **II** v/t. **4.** Unkraut od. Garten etc. jäten; **5. ~ out**, **~ up** fig. aussondern, -merzen; **6.** fig. säubern; **III** v/i. **7.** (Unkraut) jäten; **'weed·er** [-də] s. **1.** Jäter m; **2.** ⊗ Jätwerkzeug n; **weed kil·ler** s. Unkrautvertilgungsmittel n.

weeds [wiːdz] s. pl. mst **widow's ~** Witwen-, Trauerkleidung f.

weed·y ['wiːdɪ] adj. **1.** voll Unkraut; **2.** unkrautartig; **3.** F a) schmächtig, b) schlaksig, c) klapperig.

week [wiːk] s. Woche f: **by the ~** wochenweise; **for ~s** wochenlang; **today ~**, **this day ~** a) heute in 8 Tagen, b) heute vor 8 Tagen; **'~·day** s. Wochen-, Werktag m: **on ~s** werktags; **II** adj. Werktags...; **,~'end I** s. Wochenende n; **II** adj. Wochenend...: **~ speech** Sonntagsrede f; **~ ticket** Sonntags(rückfahr)karte f; **III** v/i. das Wochenende verbringen; **,~'end·er** [-'endə] s. Wochenendausflügler(in); **'~-ends** adv. Am. an Wochenenden.

week·ly ['wiːklɪ] **I** adj. u. adv. wöchentlich; **II** s. a. **~ paper** Wochenzeitung f, -(zeit)schrift f.

wee·ny ['wiːnɪ] adj. F winzig.

weep [wiːp] **I** v/i. [irr.] **1.** weinen, Tränen vergießen (**for** vor Freude etc., um j-n): **~ at** (od. **over**) weinen über (acc.); **2.** a) (Blut) tröpfeln, c) ⚕ nässen (Wunde etc.); **3.** trauern (Baum); **II** v/t. [irr.] **4.** Tränen vergießen, weinen; **5.** beweinen; **III** s. **6. have a good ~** F sich tüchtig ausweinen; **'weep·er** [-pə] s. **1.** Weinende(r m) f, bsd. Klageweib n; **2.** a) Trauerbinde f od. -flor m, b) pl. Witwenschleier m; **'weep·ie** → **weepy** 3; **'weep·ing** [-pɪŋ] **I** adj. □ **1.** weinend; **2.** ⚘ Trauer...: **~ willow** Trauerweide f; **3.** triefend, tropfend; **4.** ⚕ nässend; **II** s. **5.** Weinen n; **'wee·py** ['wiːpɪ] F **I** adj. **1.** weinerlich; **2.** rührselig; **II** s. ‚Schnulze' f.

wee·vil ['wiːvɪl] s. zo. **1.** Rüsselkäfer m; **2.** allg. Getreidekäfer m.

'wee-wee → **wee²**.

weft [weft] s. Webe'rei: a) Einschlag(faden) m, Schuss(faden) m, b) Gewebe n (a. poet.).

weigh¹ [weɪ] **I** s. **1.** Wiegen n; **II** v/t. **2.** (ab)wiegen (**by** nach); **3.** (in der Hand) wiegen; **4.** fig. (sorgsam) er-, abwägen (**with**, **against** gegen): **~ one's words** s-e Worte abwägen; **5. ~ anchor** ⚓ u) den Anker lichten, b) auslaufen (Schiff); **6.** (nieder)drücken; **III** v/i. **7.** wiegen, 2 Kilo etc. schwer sein; **8.** fig. schwer etc. wiegen, ins Gewicht fallen, ausschlaggebend sein (**with s.o.** bei j-m): **~ against s.o.** a) gegen j-n sprechen, b) gegen j-n ins Feld geführt werden; **9.** fig. lasten (**on**, **upon** auf dat.); Zssgn mit adv.:

weigh| down v/t. niederdrücken (a. fig.); **~ in I** v/t. **1.** ⚞ sein Gepäck wiegen lassen; **2.** sport a) Jockei nach dem Rennen wiegen, b) Boxer, Gewichtheber etc. vor dem Kampf wiegen; **II** v/i. **3.** ⚞ sein Gepäck wiegen lassen; **4.** sport gewogen werden: **he ~ed in at 200 pounds** er brachte 200 Pfund auf die Waage; **5.** a) eingreifen, sich einschalten, b) **~ with Argument etc.** vorbringen; **~ out I** v/t. **1.** Ware auswiegen; **2.** sport Jockei vor dem Rennen wiegen; **II** v/i. **3.** sport gewogen werden.

weigh² [weɪ] s.: **get under ~** ⚓ unter Segel gehen.

'weigh·bridge s. Brückenwaage f.

weigh·er ['weɪə] s. **1.** Wäger m, Waagemeister m; **2.** → **weigh·ing ma·chine** ['weɪɪŋ] s. ⊗ Waage f.

weight [weɪt] **I** s. **1.** Gewicht n (a. Maß u. Gegenstand): **~s and measures** Maße u. Gewichte; **by ~** nach Gewicht; **under ~** ⚓ untergewichtig, zu leicht; **lose (put on) ~** an Körpergewicht ab-(zu)nehmen; **pull one's ~** fig. sein(en) Teil leisten; **throw one's ~ about** F sich aufspielen od. ‚breit machen'; **that takes a ~ off my mind** da fällt mir ein Stein vom Herzen; **2.** fig. Gewicht n: a) Last f, Wucht f, b) (Sorgen- etc.)Last f, Bürde f, c) Bedeutung f, d) Einfluss m, Geltung f: **of ~** gewichtig, schwerwiegend; **men of ~** bedeutende od. einflussreiche Leute; **the ~ of evidence** die Last des Beweismaterials; **add ~ to** e-r Sache Gewicht verleihen; **carry** (od. **have**) **~ with** viel gelten bei; **give ~ to** e-r Sache große Bedeutung beimessen; **3.** sport a) a. **~ category** Gewichtsklasse f, b) Gewicht n (Gerät), c) (Stoß)Kugel f; **II** v/t. **4.** a) beschweren, b) belasten (a. fig.): **~ the scales in favo(u)r of s.o.** j-m e-n (unerlaubten) Vorteil verschaffen; **5.** ⚕ Stoffe etc. durch Beimischung von Mineralien etc. schwerer machen; **'weight·i·ness** [-tɪnɪs] s. Gewicht n, fig. a. (Ge)Wichtigkeit f.

weight·less ['weɪtlɪs] adj. schwerelos; **'weight·less·ness** [-nɪs] s. Schwerelosigkeit f.

'weight|,lift·er s. sport Gewichtheber m; **'~,lift·ing** s. sport Gewichtheben n; **~ watch·er** s. j-d, der auf sein Gewicht achtet.

weight·y ['weɪtɪ] adj. □ **1.** schwer, gewichtig, fig. a. schwerwiegend; **2.** fig. einflussreich, gewichtig (Person).

weir [wɪə] s. **1.** (Stau)Wehr n; **2.** Fischreuse f.

weird [wɪəd] adj. □ **1.** poet. Schicksals...: **~ sisters** Schicksalsschwestern, Nornen; **2.** unheimlich; **3.** F ulkig, ‚verrückt'; **weir·do** ['wɪədəʊ] pl. **-dos** s. F ‚irrer Typ'.

welch [welʃ] → **welsh²**.

wel·come ['welkəm] **I** s. **1.** Willkomm (-en n) m, Empfang m (a. iro.): **bid s.o. ~** → 2; **outstay** (od. **overstay** od. **wear out) one's ~** länger bleiben als man erwünscht ist; **II** v/t. **2.** bewillkommnen, will'kommen heißen; **3.** fig. begrüßen: a) et. gutheißen, b) gern annehmen; **III** adj. **4.** will'kommen, angenehm (Gast, a. Nachricht etc.): **make s.o. ~** j-n herzlich empfangen od. aufnehmen; **5. you are ~ to it** Sie können es gerne behalten od. nehmen, es steht zu Ihrer Verfügung; **you are ~ to do it** es steht Ihnen frei, es zu tun; das können Sie gerne tun; **you are ~ to your own opinion** iro. meinetwegen können Sie denken, was Sie wollen; **(you are) ~!** nichts zu danken!, keine Ursache!, bitte (sehr)!; **and ~** iro. meinetwegen, wenns Ihnen Spaß macht; **IV** int. **6.** will'kommen (**to** in England etc.).

weld [weld] **I** v/t. ⊗ (ver-, zs.-)schweißen: **~ on** anschweißen (**to** an acc.); **~ together** zs.-schweißen, fig. a. zs.-schmieden; **II** v/i. ⊗ sich schweißen lassen; **III** s. ⊗ Schweißstelle f, -naht f; **'weld·a·ble** [-dbl] adj. schweißbar; **'weld·ed** [-dɪd] adj. geschweißt, Schweiß...: **~ joint** Schweißverbindung f; **'weld·er** [-də] s. ⊗ **1.** Schweißer m; **2.** Schweißbrenner m, -gerät n; **'weld·ing** [-dɪŋ] adj. Schweiß...

wel·fare ['welfeə] s. **1.** Wohl n, e-r Person: a. Wohlergehen n; **2.** a) (public) ~

(öffentliche) Wohlfahrt, b) *Am.* So-zi'alhilfe *f*: *be on* ~ Sozialhilfe bezie-hen; ~ **state** *s. pol.* Wohlfahrtsstaat *m*; ~ **stat·ism** ['steɪtɪzəm] → *welfarism*; ~ **work** *s. Am.* Sozi'alarbeit *f*; ~ **sys·tem** *s. pol.* Sozi'alsys,tem *n*; ~ **work·er** *s. Am.* Sozi'alarbeiter(in).

wel·far·ism ['welfeərɪzəm] *s.* wohl-fahrtsstaatliche Poli'tik.

wel·kin ['welkɪn] *s. poet.* Himmelszelt *n*: *make the* ~ *ring with shouts* die Luft mit Geschrei erfüllen.

well¹ [wel] **I** *adv.* **1.** gut, wohl: *be* ~ *off* a) gut versehen sein (*for* mit), b) wohl-habend *od.* gut daran sein; *do o.s.* (*od. live*) ~ gut leben, es sich wohl sein las-sen; *be* ~ *up in* bewandert sein in *e-m Fach etc.*; **2.** gut, recht, geschickt: *do* ~ gut *od.* recht daran tun (*to do* zu tun); *sing* ~ gut singen; ~ *done!* gut ge-macht!, bravo!; ~ *roared, lion!* gut ge-brüllt, Löwe!; **3.** gut, freundschaftlich: *think* (*od. speak*) ~ *of* gut denken (*od.* sprechen) über (*acc.*); **4.** gut, sehr: *love s.o.* ~ j-n sehr lieben; *it speaks* ~ *for him* es spricht sehr für ihn; **5.** wohl, mit gutem Grund: *one may* ~ *ask this question* man kann wohl *od.* mit gu-tem Grund so fragen; *you cannot very* ~ *do that* das kannst du nicht gut tun; *not very* ~ wohl kaum; **6.** recht, eigent-lich: *he does not know* ~ *how* er weiß nicht recht wie; **7.** gut, genau, gründ-lich: *know s.o.* ~ j-n gut kennen; *he knows only too* ~ er weiß nur zu gut; **8.** gut, ganz, völlig: *he is* ~ *out of sight* er ist völlig außer Sicht; **9.** gut, be-trächtlich, weit: ~ *away* weit weg; *he walked* ~ *ahead of them* er ging ihnen ein gutes Stück voraus; *until* ~ *past midnight* bis lange nach Mitternacht; **10.** gut, tüchtig, gründlich: *stir* ~; **11.** gut, mit Leichtigkeit: *you could* ~ *have done it* du hättest es leicht tun können; *it is very* ~ *possible* es ist durchaus *od.* sehr wohl möglich; *as* ~ ebenso, außerdem; (*just*) *as* ~ ebenso (gut), genauso (gut); *as* ~ ... *as* sowohl ... als auch, nicht nur ... sondern auch; *as* ~ *as* ebenso gut wie; **II** *adj.* **12.** wohl, gesund: *be* (*od. feel*) ~ sich wohl fühlen; **13.** in Ordnung, richtig, gut: *I am very* ~ *where I am* ich fühle mich hier sehr wohl; *it is all very* ~ *but iro.* das ist ja alles schön u. gut, aber; **14.** gut, günstig: *that is just as* ~ das ist schon gut so; *very* ~ sehr wohl, nun gut; ~ *and good* schön und gut; **15.** ratsam, richtig, gut: *it would be* ~ es wäre an-gebracht *od.* ratsam; **III** *int.* **16.** nun, na, schön: ~*!* (*empört*) na, hör mal!; ~ *then* nun (also); ~ *then?* (*erwartend*) na, und?; ~, ~*!* so, so!, (*beruhigend*) schon gut; **17.** (*überlegend*) (t)ja, hm; **IV** *s.* **18.** *das Gute*: *let* ~ *alone!* lass gut sein!, lass die Finger davon!)

well² [wel] **I** *s.* **1.** (*gegrabener*) Brunnen, Ziehbrunnen *m*; **2.** *a. fig.* Quelle *f*; **3.** a) Mine'ralbrunnen *m*, b) *pl.* (*in Orts-namen*) Bad *n*; **4.** *fig.* (Ur)Quell *m*; **5.** ☉ a) (Senk-, Öl- *etc.*)Schacht *m*, b) Bohrloch *n*; **6.** ⚒ a) Fahrstuhl-, Luft-, Lichtschacht *m*, b) (Raum *m* für das) Treppenhaus *n*; **7.** ⚓ a) Pumpensod *m*, b) Fischbehälter *m*; **8.** ☉ eingelassener Behälter: a) *mot.* Kofferraum *m*, b) Tintenbehälter *m*; **9.** ⚖ *Brit.* eingefrie-digter Platz für Anwälte; **II** *v/i.* **10.** quellen (*from* aus): ~ *up* (*od. forth, out*) hervorquellen; ~ *over* über-fließen.

,well·ad'vised *adj.* wohl überlegt, klug; ,~-**ap'point·ed** *adj.* gut ausgestattet;

,~-'**bal·anced** *adj. fig.* **1.** ausgewogen: ~ *diet*; **2.** (*innerlich*) ausgeglichen; ,~-**be'haved** *adj.* wohlerzogen, artig; ,~-'**be·ing** *s.* **1.** Wohl(ergehen) *n*; **2.** *mst sense of* ~ Wohlgefühl *n*; ,~-**be-** '**lov·ed** *adj.* viel geliebt; ,~-'**born** *adj.* von vornehmer Herkunft, aus guter Fa-'milie; ,~-'**bred** *adj.* **1.** wohlerzogen; **2.** gebildet, fein; ,~-'**cho·sen** *adj.* (gut) gewählt, treffend: ~ *words*; ,~-con-'**nect·ed** *adj.* mit guten Beziehungen *od.* mit vornehmer Verwandtschaft; ,~- -**di'rect·ed** *adj.* wohl *od.* gut gezielt (*Schlag etc.*); ,~-'**dis'posed** *adj.* wohl-gesinnt; ,~-'**done** *adj.* **1.** gut gemacht; **2.** 'durchgebraten (*Fleisch*); ,~-'**earned** *adj.* wohlverdient; ,~-'**fa·vo(u)red** *adj. obs.* gut aussehend, hübsch; ,~-'**fed** *adj.* gut genährt, wohlgenährt; ,~-'**found·ed** *adj.* wohl begründet; ,~-'**groomed** *adj.* gepflegt; ,~-'**ground·ed** *adj.* **1.** → *well- -founded*; **2.** mit guter Vorbildung (*in e-m Fach*).

'**well·head** *s.* **1.** → *wellspring*; **2.** Brun-neneinfassung *f*.

,**well·**-'**heeled** *adj.* F ,(gut) betucht'; ,~- -in'**formed** *adj.* **1.** gut unterrichtet; **2.** (vielseitig) gebildet.

Wel·ling·ton (**boot**) ['welɪŋtən] *s.* Schaft-, Gummi-, Wasserstiefel *m*.

,**well·in·ten·tioned** [,welɪn'tenʃnd] *adj.* **1.** gut *od.* wohl gemeint; **2.** wohlmei-nend (*Person*); ,~-'**judged** *adj.* wohl berechnet, angebracht; ,~-'**kept** *adj.* **1.** gepflegt; **2.** streng gehütet: ~ *secret*; ,~-'**knit** *adj.* **1.** drahtig (*Figur, Person*); **2.** gut durchdacht; ,~-'**known** *adj.* **1.** weithin bekannt; **2.** wohl bekannt; ,~- -'**made** *adj.* **1.** gut gemacht; **2.** gut ge-wachsen, gut gebaut (*Person od. Tier*); ,~-'**man·nered** *adj.* wohlerzogen, mit guten Ma'nieren; ,~-'**matched** *adj.* **1.** *sport* gleich stark; **2.** *a* ~ *couple* ein Paar, das gut zs.-passt; ,~-'**mean·ing** → *well-intentioned*; ,~-'**meant** *adj.* gut gemeint; '~**·ness** *s.* Wellness *f* (*Wohl-befinden durch Entspannungsübungen, leichte sportliche Betätigung etc.*); '~- -**nigh** *adv.* fast, so gut wie: ~ *impossi-ble*; ,~-'**off** *adj.* wohlhabend, gut si-tuiert; ,~-'**oiled** *adj. fig.* F **1.** gut funk-tionierend; **2.** ziemlich ,angesäuselt'; ,~-**pro'por·tioned** *adj.* wohlproportio-niert, gut gebaut; ,~-'**read** [-'red] *adj.* (sehr) belesen; ,~-'**reg·u·lat·ed** *adj.* wohl geregelt, wohl geordnet; ,~- -'**round·ed** *adj.* **1.** (wohl)beleibt; **2.** *fig.* a) abgerundet, ele'gant (*Stil, Form etc.*), b) ausgeglichen, c) vielseitig (*Bil-dung etc.*); ,~-'**spent** *adj.* **1.** gut genützt (*Zeit*); **2.** sinnvoll ausgegeben (*Geld*); ,~-'**spo·ken** *adj.* **1.** redegewandt; **2.** höflich im Ausdruck.

'**well·spring** *s.* Quelle *f*, *fig. a.* (Ur-) Quell *m*.

,**well·**-'**tem·pered** *adj.* **1.** gutmütig; **2.** ♪ wohltemperiert (*Klavier, Stimmung*); '~-,**thought-'out** *adj.* 'wohlerwogen, wohl durchdacht; ,~-'**timed** *adj.* (zeit-lich) wohl berechnet; *sport* gut getimed; ,~-**to-'do** *adj.* wohlhabend; ,~-'**tried** *adj.* (wohl) erprobt, bewährt; ,~- -'**turned** *adj. fig.* wohlgesetzt, ele'gant (*Worte*); '~-,**wish·er** *s.* **1.** Gönner(in); **2.** Befürworter(in); **3.** *pl.* jubelnde Menge; ,~-'**worn** *adj.* **1.** abgetragen, abgenutzt; **2.** *fig.* abgedroschen.

Welsh¹ [welʃ] **I** *adj.* **1.** wa'lisisch; **II** *s.* **2.** *the* ~ die Wa'liser *pl.*; **3.** *ling.* Wa'li-sisch *n*.

welsh² [welʃ] *v/i.* F **1.** mit den (Wett-) Gewinn 'durchgehen (*Buchmacher*): ~ *on* a) j-n um s-n (Wett)Gewinn betrü-

gen, b) j-n ,verschaukeln'; **2.** sich ,drücken' (*on* vor *dat.*).

Welsh cor·gy *s.* Welsh Corgi *m* (*walisi-sche Hunderasse*).

welsh·er ['welʃə] *s.* F **1.** betrügerischer Buchmacher; **2.** ,falscher Hund'.

Welsh|·man ['welʃmən] *s.* [*irr.*] Wa'liser *m*; ~ **rab·bit**, ~ **rare·bit** *s.* über'backe-ne Käseschnitte.

welt [welt] **I** *s.* **1.** Einfassung *f*, Rand *m*; **2.** *Schneiderei*: a) (Zier)Borte *f*, b) Rollsaum *m*, c) Stoßkante *f*; **3.** Rah-men *m* (*Schuh*); **4.** a) Strieme(n *m*) *f*, b) F (heftiger) Schlag; **II** *v/t.* **5.** a) *Kleid etc.* einfassen, b) *Schuh* auf Rahmen arbeiten, c) *Blech* falzen: ~*ed* randge-näht (*Schuh*); **6.** F ,verdreschen'.

wel·ter ['weltə] *v/i.* **1.** *poet.* sich wälzen (*in* in *s-m Blut etc.*) (*a. fig.*); **II** *s.* **2.** Wogen *n*, Toben *n* (*Wellen etc.*); **3.** *fig.* Tu'mult *m*, Durchein'ander *n*, Wirr-warr *m*, Chaos *n*.

'**wel·ter·weight** *s. sport* Weltergewicht (-ler *m*) *n*.

wen [wen] *s.* ✶ (Balg)Geschwulst *f*, *bsd.* Grützbeutel *m am Kopf*: *the great* ~ *fig.* London *n*.

wench [wentʃ] **I** *s.* **1.** *obs. od. humor.* (*bsd.* Bauern)Mädchen *n*, Weibsbild *n*; **2.** *obs.* Hure *f*, Dirne *f*; **II** *v/i.* **3.** huren.

wend [wend] *v/t.* ~ *one's way* sich wen-den, s-n Weg nehmen (*to* nach, zu).

Wen·dy house ['wendɪ] *s. Brit.* Spiel-haus *n* (*für Kinder*).

went [went] *pret. von go.*

wept [wept] *pret u. p.p. von weep.*

were [wɜː; wə] **1.** *pret. von be*: *du warst, Sie waren*; *wir, sie waren*, *ihr wart*; **2.** *pret. pass.*: wurde(n); **3.** *subj. pret.* wäre(n).

were·wolf ['wɪəwʊlf] *s.* [*irr.*] Werwolf *m*.

west [west] **I** *s.* **1.** Westen *m*: *the wind is coming from the* ~ der Wind kommt von Westen; **2.** Westen *m* (*Landesteil*); **3.** *the* ⒉ *geogr.* der Westen: a) West-england *n*, b) die *amer.* Weststaaten *pl.*, c) das Abendland; **4.** *poet.* West (-wind) *m*; **II** *adj.* **5.** westlich, West...; **III** *adv.* **6.** westwärts, nach Westen: *go* ~ a) nach Westen *od.* westwärts gehen *od.* ziehen, b) *sl.* ,draufgehen' (*sterben, kaputtgehen od. verloren gehen*); **7.** ~ *of* westlich von; '**west·er·ly** [-təlɪ] **I** *adj.* westlich, West...; **II** *adv.* westwärts, ge-gen Westen.

west·ern ['westən] **I** *adj.* **1.** westlich, West...: *the* ⒉ *Empire hist.* das weströ-mische Reich; **2.** *oft* ⒉ westlich, abend-ländisch; **3.** ⒉ 'westameri,kanisch, (Wild)West...; **II** *s.* **4.** → *westerner*; **5.** Western *m*: a) Wild'westfilm *m*, b) Wild'westro,man *m*; '**west·ern·er** [-nə] *s.* **1.** Westländer *m*; **2.** *a.* ⒉ *Am.* West-staatler *m*; **3.** *oft* ⒉ Abendländer *m*; '**west·ern·ize** [-naɪz] *v/t.* verwestli-chen; '**west·ern·most** [-məʊst] *adj.* westlichst.

West In·di·an I *adj.* west'indisch; **II** *s.* West'indier(in).

West·pha·li·an [west'feɪljən] **I** *adj.* west'fälisch; **II** *s.* West'fale *m*, West'fä-lin *f*.

west·ward ['westwəd] *adj. u. adv.* west-lich, westwärts, nach Westen; '**west-wards** [-dz] *adv.* → *westward.*

wet [wet] **I** *adj.* **1.** nass, durch'nässt (*with* von): ~ *through* durchnässt; ~ *to the skin* nass bis auf die Haut; ~ *blanket fig.* a) Dämpfer *m*, kalte Du-sche, b) Störenfried *m*, Spielverder-ber(in); fader Kerl; *throw a* ~ *blanket on e-r Sache* e-n Dämpfer aufsetzen; ~

W

paint! frisch gestrichen!; **~ steam** ◎ Nassdampf *m*; **2.** regnerisch, feucht (*Klima*); **3.** ◎ nass, Nass...(*-gewinnung etc.*); **4.** *Am.* ‚feucht‘ (*nicht unter Alkoholverbot stehend*); **5.** F feuchtfröhlich; **6.** a) blöd, ‚doof‘, b) *all* ~ falsch, verkehrt: **you are all ~!** du irrst dich gewaltig!; **II** *s.* **7.** Flüssigkeit *f*, Feuchtigkeit *f*, Nässe *f*; **8.** Regen(wetter *n*) *m*; **9.** F Drink *m*: **have a ~** ‚einen heben‘; **10.** *Am.* F Gegner *m* der Prohibiti'on; **11.** F a) Blödmann *m*, b) *Brit.* Weichling *m*; **III** *v/t.* [*irr.*] **12.** benetzen, anfeuchten, nass machen, nässen: **~ through** durchnässen; → **whistle** 7; **13.** F *ein Ereignis etc.* ‚begießen‘: **~ a bargain**; '**~·back** *s. Am. sl.* illegaler Einwanderer aus Mexiko; **~ cell** *s.* ⚡ 'Nasse‚ment *n*; **~ dock** *s.* ⚓ Flutbecken *n*.

weth·er ['weðə] *s. zo.* Hammel *m*.

wet·ness ['wetnɪs] *s.* Nässe *f*, Feuchtigkeit *f*.

'**wet| nurse** *s.* (Säug)Amme *f*; '**~-nurse** *v/t.* **1.** säugen; **2.** *fig.* verhätscheln; **~ pack** *s.* 💉 feuchter 'Umschlag; **~ suit** *s. sport* Kälteschutzanzug *m*.

wey [weɪ] *s. obs.* ein Trockengewicht.

whack [wæk] F **I** *v/t.* **1.** a) *j-m* e-n (knallenden) Schlag versetzen, b) *sport* F haushoch schlagen: **~ed** F ‚fertig‘, geschafft‘; **2. ~ up** F (auf)teilen; **3. ~ up** *Am.* F a) et. organisieren, b) *j-n* antreiben; **II** *s.* **4.** (knallender) Schlag; **5.** (An)Teil *m* (*of* an *dat.*); **6.** Versuch *m*: **take a ~ at** e-n Versuch machen mit; **7.** **out of ~** nicht in Ordnung; '**whack·er** [-kə] *s. sl.* **1.** Mordsding *n*; **2.** faustdicke Lüge; '**whack·ing** [-kɪŋ] **I** *adj. u. adv.* F Mords...; **II** *s.* F (Tracht *f*) Prügel *pl.*

whale [weɪl] **I** *pl.* **whales** *bsd. coll.* **whale** *s. zo.* Wal *m*: **a ~ of** F Riesen..., Mords...; **a ~ of a lot** e-e Riesenmenge; **a ~ of a fellow** F ein Riesenkerl; **be a ~ for** (*od.* **on**) F ganz versessen sein auf (*acc.*); **be a ~ at** F e-e ‚Kanone‘ sein in (*dat.*); **we had a ~ of a time** wir hatten e-n Mordsspaß; **II** *v/i.* Walfang treiben; **III** *v/t.* F ‚verdreschen‘; '**~·bone** *s.* Fischbein(stab *m*) *n*; **~ calf** *s.* [*irr.*] *zo.* junger Wal; **~ fish·er·y** *s.* **1.** Walfang *m*; **2.** Walfanggebiet *n*; **~ oil** *s.* Walfischtran *m*.

whal·er ['weɪlə] *s.* Walfänger *m* (*Person u. Boot*).

whal·ing[1] ['weɪlɪŋ] **I** *s.* Walfang *m*; **II** *adj.* Walfang...: **~ gun** Harpunengeschütz *n*.

whal·ing[2] ['weɪlɪŋ] F **I** *adj. u. adv.* e'norm, Mords...; **II** *s.* (Tracht *f*) Prügel *pl.*

wham·my ['wæmɪ] *s.* F **1.** böser Blick; **2.** ‚Hammer‘ *m*: a) böse Sache, b) (knallharter) Schlag (*Unglück*), ‚dicker Brocken‘: **a double ~** ein doppelter ‚Schlag‘.

whang [wæŋ] F **I** *s.* Knall *m*, Krach *m*, Bums *m*; **II** *v/t.* knallen, hauen; **III** *v/i.* knallen (*a. schießen*), krachen, bumsen; **IV** *int.* krach!, bums!

wharf [wɔːf] ⚓ **I** *pl.* **wharves** [-vz] *od.* **wharfs** *s.* **1.** Kai *m*; **II** *v/t.* **2.** *Waren* löschen; **3.** *Schiff* am Kai festmachen; '**wharf·age** [-fɪdʒ] *s.* **1.** Kaianlage(n *pl.*) *f*, **2.** Kaigeld *n*; '**wharf·in·ger** [-fɪndʒə] *s.* ⚓ **1.** Kaimeister *m*; **2.** Kaibesitzer *m*.

what [wɒt] **I** *pron. interrog.* **1.** was, wie: **~ is her name?** wie ist ihr Name?; **~ did he do?** was hat er getan?; **~ is he?** was ist er (von Beruf)?; **~'s for lunch?** was gibts zum Mittagessen?; **2.** was für ein, welcher, *vor pl.* was für: **~ an idea!** was für e-e Idee!; **~ book?** was für ein Buch?; **~ luck!** welch ein Glück!; **3.** was (*um Wiederholung e-s Wortes bittend*): **he claims to be ~?** was will er sein?; **II** *pron. rel.* **4.** (das) was: **this is ~ we hoped for** (gerade) das erhofften wir; **I don't know ~ he said** ich weiß nicht, was er sagte; **it is nothing compared to ~ ...** es ist nichts im Vergleich zu dem, was ...; **5.** was (auch immer); **III** *adj.* **6.** was für ein, welch: **I don't know ~ decision you have taken** ich weiß nicht, was für e-n Entschluss du gefasst hast; **7.** alle *od.* jede die, alles was: **~ money I had** was ich an Geld hatte, all mein Geld; **8.** so viel(e) ... wie;

Besondere Redewendungen:

and ~ not, and ~ have you F und was nicht sonst noch alles; **~ about?** wie wärs mit *od.* wenn?, wie stehts mit?; **~ for?** wozu?, wofür?; **~ if?** und wenn nun?, (und) was geschieht, wenn?; **~ next?** a) was sonst noch?, b) *iro.* sonst noch was?, das fehlte noch!; **~ news?** was gibt es Neues?; **(well,) ~ of it?, so ~?** na und?, na wennschon?; **~ though?** was tuts, wenn?; **~ with** infolge, durch, in Anbetracht (*gen.*); **~ with ..., ~ with ...** teils durch ..., teils durch ...; **but ~** F dass (*nicht*); **I know ~** F ich weiß was, ich habe e-e Idee; **she knows ~'s ~** F sie weiß Bescheid; sie weiß, was los ist; **I'll tell you ~** ich will dir (mal) was sagen.

what|·cha·ma·call·it ['wɒtʃəməˌkɔːlɪt], **~-d'you-call-it** ['wɒdʒuˌkɔːlɪt] (*od.* -'em [-əm] *od.* -him *od.* -her), '**~-d'ye·call-it** [-dʒəˌkɔːlɪt] (*od.* -'em [-əm] *od.* -him *od.* -her) *s.* F Dings(da, -bums) *m*, *f*, *n*; '**~e'er** *poet.* → **whatev·er**, **~'ev·er** I *pron.* **1.** was (auch immer), alles was: **take ~ you like!**; **~ you do** was du auch tust; **2.** was auch; trotz allem, was: **do it ~ happens!**; **3.** F was denn, was in aller Welt: **~ do you want?** was willst du denn?; **II** *adj.* **4.** welch ... auch (immer): **for ~ reasons he is angry** aus welchen Gründen er auch immer ärgerlich ist; **5.** *mit neg.*: über'haupt, gar *nichts, niemand etc.*: **no doubt ~** überhaupt *od.* gar kein Zweifel; '**~·not** *s.* Eta'gere *f*.

what's [wɒts] F *für* **what is**; '**~-her-name** [-sənem], '**~-his-name** [-sɪzneɪm], *s.* F Dings(da) *m*, *f*, *n*: **Mr. what's-his-name** Herr Dingsda, Herr Soundso.

whats·it ['wɒtsɪt] *s.* F Dingsda *m*, *f*, *n*, -bums *m*, *f*, *n*.

,**what·so'ev·er** → **whatever**.

wheal [wiːl] → **wale**.

wheat [wiːt] *s.* 🌾 Weizen *m*: **~ belt** *geogr. Am.* Weizengürtel *m*.

whee·dle ['wiːdl] **I** *v/t.* **1.** *j-n* um'schmeicheln; **2.** *j-n* beschwatzen, über'reden (*into doing s.th.* et. zu tun); **3. ~ s.th. out of s.o.** *j-m* et. abschwatzen *od.* abschmeicheln; **II** *v/i.* **4.** schmeicheln; '**whee·dling** [-lɪŋ] *adj.* □ schmeichlerisch.

wheel [wiːl] **I** *s.* **1.** *allg.* Rad *n* (*a.* ◎): **the ~s of government** die Regierungsmaschinerie; **the ~ of Fortune** *fig.* das Glücksrad; **~s within ~s** *fig.* a) ein kompliziertes Räderwerk, b) e-e äußerst komplizierte *od.* schwer durchschaubare Sache; **a big ~** *Am.* F ein ‚großes Tier‘; → **fifth wheel, shoulder** 1, **spoke**[1] 4; **2.** ◎ Scheibe *f*; **3.** Lenkrad *n*: **at the ~** a) am Steuer, b) *fig.* am Ruder; **4.** F a) (Fahr)Rad *n*, b) Auto *n*, ‚fahrbarer 'Untersatz‘; **5.** *hist.* Rad *n* (*Folterinstrument*): **break s.o. on the ~** j-n rädern *od.* aufs Rad flechten; **break a (butter)fly (up)on the ~** *fig.* mit Kanonen nach Spatzen schießen; **6.** *pl. fig.* Räder(werk *n*) *pl.*, Getriebe *n*; **7.** Drehung *f*, Kreis(bewegung *f*) *m*; ✕ Schwenkung *f*: **right (left) ~!** rechts (links) schwenkt!; **II** *v/t.* **8.** *j-n od. et.* fahren, schieben, *et. a.* rollen; **9.** ✕ schwenken lassen; **III** *v/i.* **10.** sich (im Kreis) drehen; **11.** *a.* **~ about** *od.* **(a)round** sich (rasch) 'umwenden *od.* -drehen; **12.** ✕ schwenken; **13.** rollen, fahren; **14.** F radeln; '**~·bar·row** *s.* Schubkarre(n *m*) *f*; '**~·base** *s.* ◎ Radstand *m*; **~ brace** *s.* ◎, *mot.* Kreuzschlüssel *m*; **~ brake** *s.* Radbremse *f*; '**~·chair** *s.* Rollstuhl *m*: **~ user** Rollstuhlfahrer *m*; **~ clamp** *s.* Parkkralle *f*.

wheeled [wiːld] *adj.* **1.** fahrbar, Roll..., Räder...: **~ bed** 🛏 Rollbett *n*; **2.** *in Zssgn* ...räd(e)rig: **three-~**.

wheel·er ['wiːlə] *s.* **1.** *in Zssgn* Fahrzeug *n* mit ... Rädern: **four-~** Vierradwagen *m*, Zweiachser *m*; **2.** → **wheel horse**; **3.** **~** ,**deal·er** *s. Am.* F ,ausgekochter‘ Bursche, *a.* (raffinierter) Geschäftemacher; **~-'deal·ing** *s.* F **1.** Machenschaften *pl.*; **2.** Geschäftemache'rei *f*.

wheel horse *s.* Stangen-, Deichselpferd *n*.

wheel·ie ['wiːlɪ] *s.* F (Motor)Radfahren) Wheelie *n* (*Manöver, bei dem das Vorderrad abrupt angehoben wird*): **do a ~** ein Wheelie machen; **~ bin** *s. Brit.* F (große) Mülltonne auf Rädern.

wheel·ing and deal·ing ['wiːlɪŋ] → **wheeler-dealing**.

'**wheel·wright** [-raɪt] *s.* ◎ Stellmacher *m*.

wheeze [wiːz] **I** *v/i.* **1.** keuchen, schnaufen; **II** *v/t.* **2. ~ out** *et.* keuchen(d her'vorstoßen); **III** *s.* **3.** Keuchen *n*, Schnaufen *n*, pfeifendes Atmen *od.* Geräusch; **4.** *sl.* a) *thea.* (improvisierter) Scherz, Gag *m*, b) Jux *m*, Ulk *m*, c) alter Witz; '**wheez·y** [-zɪ] *adj.* □ keuchend, asth'matisch (*a. humor.* Orgel *etc.*).

whelk[1] [welk] *s. zo.* Wellhorn(schnecke *f*) *n*.

whelk[2] [welk] *s.* 💉 Pustel *f*.

whelm [welm] *v/t. poet.* **1.** ver-, über'schütten, versenken, -schlingen; **2.** *fig.* a) über'schütten *od.* ·'häufen (*in, with* mit), b) über'wältigen.

whelp [welp] **I** *s.* **1.** *zo.* a) Welpe *m* (*junger Hund, Fuchs od. Wolf*), b) *allg.* Junge(s) *n*; **2.** Balg *m*, *n* (*ungezogenes Kind*); **II** *v/t. u. v/i.* **3.** (Junge) werfen.

when [wen] **I** *adv.* **1.** *fragend:* wann; **2.** *relativ:* also, wo, da: **the years ~ we were poor** die Jahre, als wir arm waren; **the day ~** der Tag, an dem *od.* als; **II** *cj.* **3.** wann: **she doesn't know ~ to be silent** sie weiß nicht, wann sie schweigen muss; **4.** zu der Zeit *od.* in dem Augenblick, als: **~ (he was) young, he lived in M.** als er noch jung war, wohnte er in M.; **we were about to start ~ it began to rain** wir wollten gerade fortgehen, als es anfing zu regnen *od.* da fing es an zu regnen; **say ~!** F sag halt!, sag, wenn du genug hast! (*bsd. beim Eingießen*); **5.** (dann,) wenn; **6.** (immer) wenn, so'bald, so'oft; **7.** worauf'hin, und dann; **8.** ob'wohl, wo ... (doch), da ... doch; **III** *pron.* **9.** wann, welche Zeit: **from ~ does it date?** aus welcher Zeit stammt es?; **since ~?** seit wann?; **till ~?** bis wann?; **10.** *relativ: since* **~** und seitdem; **till ~** und bis dahin; **IV** *s.* **11. the ~ and**

where of s.th. das Wann und Wo e-r Sache.

whence [wens] *bsd. poet.* **I** *adv.* **1.** wo'her: a) von wo(her), *obs.* von wannen, b) *fig.* wo'von, wo'durch, wie: ~ *comes it that* wie kommt es, dass; **II** *cj.* **2.** von wo'her; **3.** *fig.* wes'halb, und deshalb.

‚when(·so)'ev·er I *cj.* wann (auch) immer, einerlei wann, (immer) wenn, so'oft, jedes Mal wenn; **II** *adv. fragend:* wann denn (nur).

where [weə] **I** *adv. (fragend u. relativ)* **1.** wo; **2.** wo'hin; **3.** wor'in, inwie'fern, in welcher Hinsicht; **II** *cj.* **4.** (da) wo; **5.** da'hin *od.* irgendwo'hin wo, wo'hin; **III** *pron.* **6.** *(relativ)* (da *od.* dort,) wo: *he lives not far from ~ it happened* er wohnt nicht weit von dort, wo es geschah; **7.** *(fragend)* wo: ~ *... from?* woher?, von wo?; ~ *... to?* wohin?; **~·a·bouts I** *adv. od. cj.* [‚weərə'baʊts] wo ungefähr *od.* etwa; **II** *s. pl.* ['weərə-baʊts] *sg. konstr.* Aufenthalt(sort) *m*, Verbleib *m*; **~·as** [weər'æz] *cj.* **1.** wo-hin'gegen, während, wo ... doch; **2.** ʦʦ da; in Anbetracht dessen, dass *(im Deutschen mst unübersetzt);* **~·at** [weər-'æt] *adv. u. cj.* **1.** wor'an, wo'bei, worauf; **2.** *(relativ)* an welchem (welcher) *od.* dem (der), wo; **~·by** *adv. u. cj.* **1.** wo'durch, wo'mit; **2.** *(relativ)* durch welchen (welche[s]); **~·fore I** *adv. od. cj.* **1.** wes'halb, wo'zu, war'um; **2.** *(relativ)* wes'wegen, und deshalb; **II** *s. oft pl.* **3.** *das* Weshalb, *die* Gründe *pl.;* **~·from** *adv. u. cj.* wo'her, von wo; **~·in** [weər'ɪn] *adv.* wor'in, in welchem (welcher); **~·of** [weər'ɒv] *adv. u. cj.* wo'von; **~·on** [weər'ɒn] *adv. od. cj.* **1.** wor'auf; **2.** *(relativ)* auf dem (der) *od.* den (die, das), auf welchem (welcher) *od.* welchen (welche, welches); **~·so'ev·er → wher·ever** 1; **~·to** *adv. od. cj.* wo'hin; **~·up·on** [‚weərə'pɒn] *adv. od. cj.* **1.** worauf('hin); **2.** *(als Satzanfang)* darauf'hin.

wher·ev·er [‚weər'evə] *adv. od. cj.* **1.** wo (-'hin) auch immer; ganz gleich, wo (-hin); **2.** F wo(hin) denn (nur)?

‚where'with *adv. od. cj.* wo'mit; **~·with·al** *s.* Mittel *pl., das* Nötige, *das* nötige (Klein)Geld.

wher·ry ['werɪ] ♄ *s.* **1.** Jolle *f;* **2.** Skullboot *n;* **3.** Fährboot *n;* **4.** *Brit.* Frachtsegler *m.*

whet [wet] **I** *v/t.* wetzen, schärfen, schleifen; **2.** *fig. Appetit* anregen; *Neugierde etc.* anstacheln; **II** *s.* **3.** Wetzen *n,* Schärfen *n;* **4.** *fig.* Ansporn *m,* Anreiz *m;* **5.** (Appe'tit)Anreger *m,* Aperi-'tif *m.*

wheth·er ['weðə] *cj.* **1.** ob (**or not** oder nicht); ~ *or no* auf jeden Fall, so oder so; **2.** ~ *... or* entweder ... oder sei es, dass ... oder.

'whet·stone *s.* **1.** Wetz-, Schleifstein *m;* **2.** *fig.* Anreiz *m,* Ansporn *m.*

whew [hwuː] *int.* **1.** erstaunt: (h)ui!, Mann!; **2.** angeekelt, erleichtert, erschöpft: puh!

whey [weɪ] *s.* Molke *f;* **'~-faced** *adj.* käsig, käseweiß.

which [wɪtʃ] **I** *interrog.* **1.** welch (aus e-r bestimmten Gruppe od. Anzahl): ~ *of you?* welcher *od.* wer von euch?; **II** *pron. (relativ)* **2.** welch, der (die, das) *(bezogen auf Dinge, Tiere od. obs. Personen);* **3.** *(auf den vorhergehenden Satz bezüglich)* was; **4.** *(in eingeschobenen Sätzen)* (etwas,) was; **III** *adj.* **5.** *(fragend od. relativ)* welch: ~ *place will you take?;* **~'ev·er, ‚~·so'ev·er** *pron. u. adj.* welch (auch) immer; ganz gleich, welch.

---

whiff [wɪf] **I** *s.* **1.** Luftzug *m,* Hauch *m;* **2.** Duftwolke *f (a.* übler) Geruch; **3.** Zug *m (beim Rauchen);* **4.** Schuss *m Chloroform etc.;* **5.** *fig.* Anflug *m;* **6.** F Ziga'rillo *n, m;* **II** *v/i. u. v/t.* **7.** blasen, wehen; **8.** paffen, rauchen; **9.** *(nur v/i.)* ‚duften', (unangenehm) riechen.

whif·fle ['wɪfl] *v/i. u. v/t.* wehen.

whiff·y ['wɪfɪ] *adj. Brit.* F übel riechend, stinkend, stinkig.

Whig [wɪg] *pol. hist.* **I** *s.* **1.** *Brit.* Whig *m (Liberaler);* **2.** *Am.* Whig *m:* a) Natio-'nal(republi‚kan)er *m (Unterstützer der amer. Revolution),* b) Anhänger e-r Oppositionspartei gegen die Demokraten um 1840); **II** *adj.* **3.** Whig..., whig'gistisch; **Whig·gism** ['wɪgɪzəm] *s. pol.* Whig'gismus *m.*

while [waɪl] **I** *s.* **1.** Weile *f,* Zeit(spanne) *f: a long ~ ago* vor e-r ganzen Weile; *(for) a ~* e-e Zeit lang; *for a long ~* lange (Zeit), seit langem; *in a little ~* bald, binnen kurzem; *the ~* derweil, währenddessen; *between ~s* zwischendurch; *worth (one's) ~* der Mühe wert, (sich) lohnend; *it is not worth (one's) ~* es ist nicht der Mühe wert, es lohnt sich nicht; → *once* 1; **II** *cj.* **2.** *(zeitlich)* während; **3.** so'lange; **4.** während, wo(hin)'gegen; **5.** wenn auch, ob'wohl, zwar; **III** *v/t.* **6.** *mst ~ away* sich *die Zeit* vertreiben; **whilst** [waɪlst] → *while* II.

whim [wɪm] *s.* **1.** Laune *f,* Grille *f,* wunderlicher Einfall, Ma'rotte *f: at one's own ~* ganz nach Laune; **2.** ⚒ Göpel *m.*

whim·per ['wɪmpə] **I** *v/t. u. v/i.* wimmern, winseln; **II** *s.* Wimmern *n,* Winseln *n.*

whim·sey → whimsy.

whim·si·cal ['wɪmzɪkl] *adj.* □ **1.** launen-, grillenhaft, wunderlich; **2.** schrullig, ab'sonderlich, seltsam; **3.** hu'morig, launig; **whim·si·cal·i·ty** [‚wɪmzɪ'kælətɪ], **'whim·si·cal·ness** [-nɪs] *s.* **1.** Grillenhaftigkeit *f,* Wunderlichkeit *f;* **2.** → *whim* 1; **whim·sy** ['wɪmzɪ] **I** *s.* Laune *f,* Grille *f,* Schrulle *f;* **II** *adj.* → *whim-sical.*

whin¹ [wɪn] *s.* ♄ *bsd. Brit.* Stechginster *m.*

whin² [wɪn] → *whinstone.*

whine [waɪn] **I** *v/i.* **1.** winseln, wimmern; **2.** greinen, quengeln, jammern; **II** *v/t.* **3.** *et.* weinerlich sagen, winseln; **III** *s.* **4.** Gewinsel *n;* **5.** Gejammer *n,* Gequengel *n;* **'whin·ing** [-nɪŋ] *adj.* □ weinerlich, greinend; winselnd.

whin·ny ['wɪnɪ] **I** *v/i.* wiehern; **II** *s.* Wiehern *n.*

whin·stone ['wɪnstəʊn] *s. geol.* Ba'salt (-tuff) *m,* Trapp *m.*

whip [wɪp] **I** *s.* **1.** Peitsche *f,* Geißel *f;* **2.** *be a good* (*poor*) ~ gut (schlecht) kutschieren; **3.** *hunt.* Pi'kör *m;* **4.** *parl.* a) Einpeitscher *m,* b) parlamen'tarischer Geschäftsführer, c) Rundschreiben *n,* Aufforderung(sschreiben *n) f (bei e-r Versammlung etc. zu erscheinen):* *three-line ~* a) Aufforderung, unbedingt zu erscheinen, b) (abso'luter) Fraktionszwang (*on a vote* bei e-r Abstimmung); **5.** ⊚ a) Wippe *f (a. ⚡),* b) *a. ~-and-derry* Flaschenzug *m;* **6.** *Näherei:* über'wendliche Naht; **7.** *Küche:* Creme(speise) *f;* **II** *v/t.* **8.** peitschen; **9.** (aus)peitschen, geißeln *(a. fig.);* **10.** *a.* ~ *on* antreiben; **11.** schlagen: a) ver'prügeln: ~ *s.th. into* (*out of*) *s.o.* j-m et. einbläuen (mit Schlägen austreiben), b) *bsd. sport* F besiegen, 'über-'fahren'; **12.** reißen, raffen: ~ *away* wegreißen; ~ *from* wegreißen *od.* fegen

---

von; ~ *off* a) weg-, herunterreißen, b) *j-n* entführen; ~ *out* (plötzlich) zücken, (schnell) *aus der Tasche* ziehen; **13.** *Gewässer* abfischen; **14.** a) *Schnur etc.* um'wickeln, ♄ *Tau* betakeln, b) *Schnur* wickeln (**about** um *acc.*); **15.** über'wendlich nähen, über'nähen, um'säumen; **16.** *Eier, Sahne* (schaumig) schlagen: **~ped cream** Schlagsahne *f;* **~ped eggs** Eischnee *m;* **17.** *Brit.* F ‚klauen'; **III** *v/i.* **18.** sausen, flitzen, schnellen; ~ *in v/t.* **1.** *hunt. Hunde* zs.-treiben; **2.** *parl.* zs.-trommeln; ~ *round v/i.* **1.** sich ruckartig 'umdrehen; **2.** F den Hut herumgehen lassen; ~ *up v/t.* **1.** antreiben; **2.** *fig.* aufpeitschen; **3.** a) *Leute* zs.-trommeln, b) *Essen etc.* ‚herzaubern'.

whip| aer·i·al (*bsd. Am.* **an·ten·na**) *s.* ⚡ 'Staban‚tenne *f;* **'~·cord** *s.* **1.** Peitschenschnur *f;* **2.** Whipcord *m (schräg geripptes Kammgarn);* ~ **hand** *s.* rechte Hand *des Reiters etc.: get the ~ of s.o.* die Oberhand gewinnen über j-n; *have the ~ of j-n* an der Kandare *od.* in der Gewalt haben; '~·**lash** *s.* **1.** → *whip-cord* 1; **2.** *a.* ~ *injury* ✈ 'Peitschen-schlagsyn‚drom *n.*

whip·per ['wɪpə] *s.* Peitschende(r *m) f;* '~·**in,** *pl.* '~·**s-'in** → *whip* 3; **4.** '~·**snap·per** *s.* **1.** Drei'käsehoch *m;* **2.** Gernegroß *m,* Gelbschnabel *m,* Springinsfeld *m.*

whip·pet ['wɪpɪt] *s.* **1.** *zo.* Whippet *m (kleiner englischer Rennhund);* **2.** ✖ *hist. leichter* Panzerkampfwagen.

whip·ping ['wɪpɪŋ] *s.* **1.** (Aus)Peitschen *n;* **2.** (Tracht *f)* Prügel *pl.,* Hiebe *pl.* (*a. fig.* F *Niederlage);* **3.** 'Garnum‚wick(e)-lung *f;* ~ **boy** *s. hist.* Prügelknabe *m,* *fig. a.* Sündenbock *m;* ~ **cream** *s.* Schlagsahne *f;* ~ **post** *s. hist.* Schandpfahl *m;* ~ **top** *s.* Kreisel *m (der mit Peitsche getrieben wird).*

whip·ple·tree ['wɪpltriː] *s.* Ortscheit *n,* Wagenschwengel *m.*

whip| ray *s. ichth.* Stechrochen *m;* '~·**round** *s. Brit.* F spon'tane (Geld-) Sammlung: *have a ~* → *whip round* 2; '~·**saw** *s.* (zweihändige) Schrotsäge; **II** *v/t.* mit der Schrotsäge sägen; **III** *v/i. bsd. Poker: Am.* zs.-spielen mit.

whir → *whirr.*

whirl [wɜːl] **I** *v/i.* **1.** wirbeln, sich drehen: ~ *about* (*od.* *round*) a) herumwirbeln, b) sich rasch umdrehen; **2.** sausen, hetzen, eilen; **3.** wirbeln, sich drehen (*Kopf*): *my head ~s* mir ist schwindelig; **II** *v/t.* **4.** *allg.* wirbeln: ~ *up dust* Staub aufwirbeln; **III** *s.* **5.** Wirbeln *n;* **6.** Wirbel *m:* a) schnelle Kreisbewegung, b) Strudel *m: give s.th. a ~* a) et. herumwirbeln, b) F et. (aus)probieren; **7.** *fig.* Wirbel *m:* a) Trubel *m,* wirres Treiben, b) Schwindel *m (der Sinne etc.): a ~ of passion: her thoughts were in a ~* ihre Gedanken wirbelten durcheinander; '~·**blast** *s.* Wirbelsturm *m.*

whirl·i·gig ['wɜːlɪgɪg] *s.* **1.** a) Windrädchen *n,* b) Kreisel *m* (*a. Spielzeug*); **2.** Karus'sell *n (a. fig. der Zeit);* **3.** *fig.* Wirbel *m der Ereignisse etc.*

'whirl|·pool *s.* **1.** Strudel *m (a. fig.);* **2.** 'Whirlpool *m;* '~·**wind** *s.* Wirbelwind *m (a. fig. Person): a ~ romance* e-e stürmische Romanze.

'whirl·y·bird ['wɜːlɪ-] *s. Am.* F Hubschrauber *m.*

whirr [wɜː] **I** *v/i.* schwirren, surren; **II** *v/t.* schwirren lassen; **III** *s.* Schwirren *n,* Surren *n.*

whisk [wɪsk] **I** *s.* **1.** Wischen *n,* Fegen *n;* **2.** Wischer *m:* a) leichter Schlag, b) schnelle Bewegung (*bsd. Tierschwanz*); **3.** Husch *m*: *in a ~* im Nu; **4.** (*Stroh- etc.*)Wisch *m*, Büschel *n*; **5.** (Staub-, Fliegen)Wedel *m*; **6.** *Küche:* Schneebesen *m*; **II** *v/t.* **7.** *Staub etc.* (weg)wischen, (-)fegen; **8.** fegen, *mit dem Schwanz schlagen;* **9.** *~ away* (*od. off*) schnell verschwinden lassen, wegzaubern, -nehmen; *j-n* schnellstens wegbringen, entführen; **10.** *Sahne, Eischnee schlagen;* **III** *v/i.* **11.** wischen, huschen, flitzen; *~ away* forthuschen; '**whisk·er** [-kə] *s.* **1.** *pl.* Backenbart *m*; **2.** a) Barthaar *n*, b) F Schnurrbart *m*; **3.** *zo.* Schnurr-, Barthaar *n* (*von Katzen etc.*); '**whisk·ered** [-kəd] *adj.* **1.** e-n Backenbart tragend; **2.** *zo.* mit Schnurrhaaren versehen.

whis·key ['wɪskɪ] *s.* **1.** (*bsd. in den USA u. Irland hergestellter*) Whisky; **2.** → **whis·ky** *s.* Whisky *m*: *~ and soda* Whisky Soda *m*; *~ sour* Whisky mit Zitrone.

whis·per ['wɪspə] **I** *v/i. u. v/t.* **1.** wispern, flüstern, raunen (*alle a. poet. Baum, Wind etc.*): *~ s.th. to s.o.* j-m et. zuflüstern; **2.** *fig. b.s.* flüstern, tuscheln, munkeln; **II** *s.* **3.** Flüstern *n*, Wispern *n*, Geflüster *n*: *in a ~, in ~s* im Flüsterton; **4.** Getuschel *n*; **5.** a) geflüsterte *od.* heimliche Bemerkung, b) Gerücht *n*; **6.** Raunen *n*; '**whis·per·er** [-ərə] *s.* **1.** Flüsternde(r *m*) *f*; **2.** Zuträger(in), Ohrenbläser(in); '**whis·per·ing** [-pərɪŋ] **I** *adj.* □ **1.** flüsternd; **2.** Flüster...: *~ baritone*; *~ campaign* Flüsterkampagne *f*; *~ gallery* Flüstergalerie *f*; **II** *s.* **3.** *~ whisper* 3.

whist¹ [wɪst] *int. dial.* pst!, st!, still!

whist² [wɪst] *s.* Whist *n* (*Kartenspiel*): *~ drive* Whistrunde *f*.

whis·tle ['wɪsl] **I** *v/i.* **1.** pfeifen (*Person, Vogel, Lokomotive etc.; a. Kugel, Wind etc.*) (*to s.o.* j-m); *~ for* j-m, s-m Hund etc. pfeifen; *he may ~ for it* F darauf kann er lange warten, das kann er sich in den Kamin schreiben; *~ in the dark fig.* den Mutigen markieren; **II** *v/t.* **2.** *Melodie etc.* pfeifen; **3.** *~ back Hund etc.* zurückpfeifen; *~ up fig.* a) herbeordern, b) ins Spiel bringen; **III** *s.* **4.** Pfeife *f*: *blow the ~ on* F a) *j-n, et.* ,verpfeifen‘, b) *et.* ausplaudern, c) *j-n, et.* stoppen; *pay for one's ~* den Spaß teuer bezahlen; **5.** (*sport a.* Ab)Pfiff *m*; Pfeifton *m*; **6.** Pfeifen *n* (*des Windes etc.*); **7.** F Kehle *f*: *wet one's ~* ,einen heben‘; '**~·stop** *s. Am.* **1.** 🚉 Bedarfshaltestelle *f*; **2.** *fig.* Kleinstadt *f*, ,Kaff‘ *n*; **3.** *pol.* kurzer Besuch (*e-s Kandidaten*); '**~-stop** *v/i. Am. pol.* von Ort zu Ort reisen u. Wahlreden halten.

whis·tling ['wɪslɪŋ] *s.* Pfeifen *n*; *~ buoy s.* ⚓ Pfeifboje *f*; *~ thrush s. orn.* Singdrossel *f*.

whit [wɪt] *s.* (*ein*) bisschen: *no ~, not a ~* keinen Deut, kein Jota, kein bisschen.

white [waɪt] **I** *adj.* **1.** *allg.* weiß: *as ~ as snow* schneeweiß; **2.** blass, bleich: *as ~ as a sheet* leichenblass; → *bleed* 10; **3.** weiß(rassig): *~ supremacy* Vorherrschaft der Weißen; **4.** *fig.* a) rechtschaffen, b) harmlos, c) *Am.* F anständig: *that's ~ of you;* **II** *s.* **5.** Weiß *n*, weiße Farbe: *dressed in ~* weiß *od.* in Weiß gekleidet; **6.** Weiße *f*, weiße Beschaffenheit; **7.** Weiße(r *m*) *f*, Angehörige(r *m*) *f* der weißen Rasse; **8.** a. *~ of egg* Eiweiß *n*; **9.** a. *~ of the eye* das Weiße im Auge; **10.** *typ.* Lücke *f*; **11.** *zo.* Weißling *m*; **12.** *pl.* 🦠 Weißfluss *m*, Leukor'rhö(e) *f*; *~ ant s. zo.* Ter'mite *f*; '**~·bait** *s.* ein Weißfisch *m*, Breitling *m*;

~ bear s. zo. Eisbär *m*; '**~·board** *s.* Weißwandtafel *f* (*für Präsentationen*); ⚘ **Book** *s. pol.* Weißbuch *n*; *~ bronze s.* 'Weißme,tall *n*; '**~·cap** *s.* schaumgekrönte Welle; *~ coal s.* ⚙ weiße Kohle, Wasserkraft *f*; '**~·col·lar** *adj.* Büro...: *~ worker* (Büro)Angestellte(r *m*) *f*; *~ crime* Weiße-Kragen-Kriminalität *f*; *~ el·e·phant s.* **1.** *zo.* weißer Ele'fant; **2.** F lästiger Besitz; ⚘ **En·sign** *s.* ⚓ *Brit.* Kriegsflagge *f*; '**~-faced** *adj.* blass: *~ horse* Blesse *f*; *~ feath·er s.: show the ~* sich feige zeigen, ‚kneifen‘; ⚘ **Fri·ar** *s. R.C.* Karme'liter(mönch) *m*; *~ frost s.* (Rau)Reif *m*; *~ goods s. pl.* **1.** Weißwaren *pl.;* **2.** Haushaltswäsche *f*; '**~-haired** *adj.* weiß- *od.* hellhaarig: *~ boy Am.* F Liebling *m* (*des Chefs etc.*). **White'hall** *s. Brit.* Whitehall *n*: a) *Straße in Westminster, London, Sitz der Ministerien,* b) *fig.* die brit. Regierung *od.* ihre Politik.

white| **heat** *s.* Weißglut *f* (*a. fig. Zorn*): *work at a ~* mit fieberhaftem Eifer arbeiten; *~ hope s.* **1.** *Am. sl.* weißer Boxer, der Aussicht auf den Meistertitel hat; **2.** F ‚die große Hoffnung‘ (*Person*); *~ horse s.* **1.** *zo.* Schimmel *m*, weißes Pferd; **2.** → *whitecap;* '**~·hot** *adj.* **1.** weiß glühend (*a. fig. vor Zorn etc.*); **2.** *fig.* rasend (*Eile etc.*); ⚘ **House** *s.* das Weiße Haus (*Regierungssitz des Präsidenten der USA in Washington*); *~ lie s.* Notlüge *f*; *~ line s.* weiße Linie, Fahrbahnbegrenzung *f*; '**~·,liv·ered** *adj.* feig(e); *~ mag·ic s.* weiße Ma'gie (*Gutes bewirkende Zauberkunst*); *~ man s.* [*irr.*] **1.** → *white* 7; **2.** F ‚feiner Kerl‘; *~ man's bur·den s. fig.* die Bürde des weißen Mannes; *~ meat s.* weißes Fleisch (*vom Geflügel, Kalb etc.*); *~ met·al s.* ⚙ a) Neusilber *n*, b) 'Weißme,tall *n*.

whit·en ['waɪtn] **I** *v/i.* weiß (*od.* blass, bleich) werden; **II** *v/t.* weiß machen, bleichen; '**whit·en·er** *s.* **1.** Weißmacher *m* (*in Waschmittel*); **2.** a. *coffee ~* Kaffeeweißer *m* (*laktosefreier Milchersatz*); '**white·ness** [-nɪs] *s.* **1.** Weiße *f*; **2.** Helligkeit *f*; **3.** Blässe *f*; '**whit·en·ing** [-nɪŋ] *s.* **1.** Weißen *n*; **2.** Bleichen *n*; **3.** Weißwerden *n*; **4.** Schlämmkreide *f*.

white| **noise** *s.* 🅕 weißes Rauschen; '**~-out** *s.* **1.** heftiger Schneesturm; **2.** 'White-out *m* (*Schneeblindheit od. zeitweiliger Verlust des Sehvermögens wegen Blendung durch Schnee u. Wolken*); **3.** Korrek'turflüssigkeit *f* (*bei Tippfehlern*); *~ sale s.* ⚑ Weiße Woche; *~ sauce s.* helle Sauce; *~ sheet s.* Büßerhemd *n*: *stand in a ~ fig.* s-e Sünden bekennen; '**~-'slave** *s.: ~ agent* *~* **~ slav·er** *s.* Mädchenhändler *m*; '**~·smith** *s.* ⚙ **1.** Klempner *m*; **2.** *metall.* Feinschmied *m*; '**~·thorn** *s.* 🌿 Weißdorn *m*; '**~·throat** *s. orn.* (Dorn)Grasmücke *f*; *~ tie s.* **1.** weiße Fliege; **2.** Abendanzug *m*; *~ trash s. Am.* F **1.** arme weiße Bevölkerung; **2.** arme(r) Weiße(r) (*in den amer. Südstaaten*); *~ wash I v/t.* **1.** Tünche *f*, **2.** flüssiges Hautbleichmittel; **3.** *fig.* F a) Tünche *f*, Beschönigung *f*, b) Ehrenrettung *f*, *contp.* ‚Mohrenwäsche‘ *f*, c) ⚑ *Brit.* Schuldentlastung *f*; **4.** *sport* F ‚Zu-'null-Niederlage‘ *f*; **II** *v/t.* **5.** a) tünchen, b) weißen, kalken; **6.** *fig.* a) über'tünchen, b) rein waschen, rehabilitieren, c) ⚑ *Brit.* Bankrotteur wieder zahlungsfähig erklären; **7.** *sport* F Gegner zu null schlagen; *~ wa·ter s. bsd. Am.* F schäumendes Wasser; **2.** Wildwasser *n*; '**~·wa·ter raft·ing** *s. sport* 'Wildwasser-,Rafting *n*; *~ wine s.*

Weißwein *m*.

whit·ey ['waɪtɪ] *s. Am. contp.* **1.** Weiße(r) *m*; **2.** *oft* ⚘ *coll.* die Weißen.

whith·er ['wɪðə] *adv. poet.* **1.** (*fragend*) wo'hin: *~ England?* (*Schlagzeile*) England, wohin *od.* was nun?; **2.** (*relativ*) wohin: a) (*verbunden*) in welchen *etc.*, zu welchem *etc.*, b) (*unverbunden*) da'hin, wo.

whit·ing¹ ['waɪtɪŋ] *s. ichth.* Weißfisch *m*, Mer'lan *m*.

whit·ing² ['waɪtɪŋ] *s.* Schlämmkreide *f*.

whit·ish ['waɪtɪʃ] *adj.* weißlich.

whit·low ['wɪtləʊ] *s.* 🦠 'Umlauf *m*, Nagelgeschwür *n*.

Whit [wɪt] *in Zssgn* Pfingst...: *~ Mon·day;* *~ Sunday.*

Whit·sun ['wɪtsn] **I** *adj.* Pfingst..., pfingstlich; **II** *s.* → '**~·tide** *s.* Pfingsten *n od. pl.*, Pfingstfest *n.*

whit·tle ['wɪtl] *v/t.* **1.** (zu'recht)schnitzen; **2.** *~ away, ~ off* wegschnitze(l)n, -schnippeln; **3.** *~ down, ~ away, ~ off fig.* a) (Stück für Stück) beschneiden, stutzen, verringern, b) *Gesundheit etc.* schwächen.

whiz(z) [wɪz] **I** *v/i.* **1.** zischen, schwirren, sausen (*Geschoss etc.*); **II** *s.* **2.** Zischen *n*, Sausen *n*; **3.** *Am.* F a) ‚Ka'none‘ *f* (*Könner*), b) tolles Ding; **III** *adj.* **4.** F ‚toll‘, ,super‘; *~ kid s.* F ‚Wunderkind‘ *n*, Ge'nie *n*, a. ,Senkrechtstarter‘ *m.*

who [hu:; hʊ] **I** *interrog.* **1.** wer: ⚘*'s* ⚘ Wer ist Wer? (*Verzeichnis prominenter Persönlichkeiten*); *~ goes there?* ✗ (halt,) wer da?; **2.** F (*für whom*) wen, wem; **II** *pron.* (*relativ*) **3.** (*unverbunden*) wer: *I know ~ has done it;* **4.** (*verbunden*) welch, der (die, das): *the man ~ arrived yesterday.*

whoa [wəʊ] *int.* brr!, halt!

who·dun·(n)it [,hu:'dʌnɪt] *s.* F ,Krimi‘ *m* (*Kriminalroman etc.*).

who·ev·er [hu:'evə] **I** *pron.* (*relativ*) wer (auch) immer, jeder der; **II** *interrog.* F (*für who ever*) wer denn nur.

whole [həʊl] **I** *adj.* □ → *wholly;* **1.** ganz, voll(kommen, -ständig): *~ num·ber* ⚘ ganze Zahl; *a ~ lot of* F e-e ganze Menge; **2.** heil: a) unversehrt: *with a ~ skin* mit heiler Haut, b) unbeschädigt, ,ganz‘; **3.** Voll(wert)...: *~ food;* *~ meal* Vollweizenmehl *n*; *~ milk* Vollmilch *f*; (*made*) *out of ~ cloth Am.* F völlig aus der Luft gegriffen, frei erfunden; **II** *s.* **4.** das Ganze, Gesamtheit *f*: *the ~ of London* ganz London; *the ~ of my property* mein ganzes Vermögen; **5.** Ganze(s) *n*, Einheit *f*: *in ~ or in part* ganz oder teilweise; *on the ~* im (Großen u.) Ganzen, alles in allem; '**~-bound** *adj.* in Ganzleder (gebunden); ,**~-'col·o(u)red** *adj.* einfarbig; '**~·food** *Brit.* **I** *s.* Vollwertkost *f*; **II** *adj.* Vollwert..., Bio...: *~ shop* Bioladen *m*; '**~·foods** *s. pl.* → *wholefood* I; '**~-'heart·ed** *adj.* □ aufrichtig, rückhaltlos, voll, von ganzem Herzen; ,**~-'hog·ger** [-'hɒgə] *s. sl.* kompro'missloser Mensch; *pol.* ,'Hundert-('fünfzig)pro,zentige(r)‘ *m*; ,**~-'length** *adj.* Ganz..., Voll...: *~ portrait* Vollporträt *n*, Ganzbild *n*; **II** *s.* Por'trät *n od.* Statue *f* in voller Größe; *~ life in·sur·ance s.* Erlebensfallversicherung *f*; '**~·meal** *adj. Brit.* Vollkorn...: *~ pasta* sg. Vollkornnudeln *pl.*

whole·ness ['həʊlnɪs] *s.* **1.** Ganzheit *f*; **2.** Vollständigkeit *f.*

'**whole·sale I** *s.* **1.** ⚑ Großhandel *m*: *by ~* → 4; **II** *adj.* **2.** ⚑ Großhandels..., Engros...: *~ dealer* → *wholesaler;* *~ purchase* Einkauf *m* im Großen, Engroseinkauf *m*; **~ trade** Großhandel *m*; **3.** *fig.* a) Massen..., b) 'unterschiedslos, pau'schal: **~ slaughter** Massenmord *m*; **III** *adv.* **4. ✝** im Großen, en gros; **5.** a) *fig.* in Bausch u. Bogen, 'unterschiedslos, b) massenhaft; '**whole,sal·er** [-,seɪlə] *s.* ✝ Großhändler *m*; Gros'sist *m*.

whole·some ['həʊlsəm] *adj.* □ **1.** gesund (*bsd. heilsam, bekömmlich*) (*a. fig. Humor, Strafe etc.*); **2.** gut, nützlich, zuträglich; '**whole·some·ness** [-nɪs] *s.* **1.** Gesundheit *f*, Bekömmlichkeit *f*; **2.** Nützlichkeit *f*.

,**whole|-'time** → **full-time**; **~ tone** *s.* ♪ Ganzton *m*; '**~-wheat** *adj.* Vollkorn...

whol·ly ['həʊllɪ] *adv.* ganz, gänzlich, völlig.

whom [huːm] **I** *pron.* (*interrog.*) **1.** wen; **2.** (*Objekt-Kasus von* **who**): **of ~** von wem; **to ~** wem; **II** *pron.* (*relativ*) **3.** (*verbunden*) welchen, welche, welches, den (die, das); **4.** (*unverbunden*) wen; den(jenigen), welchen; die(jenige), welche; *pl.* die(jenigen), welche; **5.** (*Objekt-Kasus von* **who**): **of ~** von welchem *etc.*, dessen, deren; **to ~** dem (der, denen); **all of ~ were dead** welche alle tot waren; **6.** welchem, welcher, welchen, dem (der, denen): **the master ~ she serves** der Herr, dem sie dient.

whoop [huːp] **I** *s.* **1.** a) Schlachtruf *m*, b) (*bsd. Freuden*)Schrei *m*: **not worth a ~** F keinen Pfifferling wert; **2.** ⚕ Keuchen *n* (*bei Keuchhusten*); **II** *v/i.* **3.** schreien, brüllen, *a.* jauchzen; **4.** ⚕ keuchen; **III** *v/t.* **5.** *et.* brüllen; **6. ~ it up** *Am. sl.* a) 'auf den Putz hauen', 'toll feiern'; b) die Trommel rühren (**for** für).

whoop·ee ['wʊpiː] *Am.* F **I** *s.:* **make ~** 'auf den Putz hauen', 'toll feiern', a. Sauf- *od.* Sexparties feiern'; **II** *int.* [wʊ'piː] juch'hu!

whoop·ing cough ['huːpɪŋ] *s.* ⚕ Keuchhusten *m*.

whoops [wʊps] *int.* hoppla!

woosh [wʊʃ; wuːʃ] *v/i.* zischen, sausen.

whop [wɒp] *v/t.* F vertrimmen (*a. fig. besiegen*); **whop·per** ['wɒpə] *s. sl.* **1.** Mordsding *n*; **2.** (faust)dicke Lüge; **whop·ping** ['wɒpɪŋ] *adj. u. adv.* F e'norm, Mords...

whore [hɔː] **I** *s.* Hure *f*; **II** *v/i.* huren; '**~·house** *s.* Bor'dell *n*.

whorl [wɜːl] *s.* **1.** ♀ Quirl *m*; **2.** *anat., zo.* Windung *f*; **3.** ⚙ Wirtel *m*.

whor·tle·ber·ry ['wɜːtl,berɪ] *s.* **1.** ♀ Heidelbeere *f*: **red ~** Preiselbeere *f*; **2.** → **huckleberry**.

whose [huːz] *pron.* **1.** (*fragend*) wessen: **~ is it?** wem gehört es?; **2.** (*relativ*) dessen, deren.

who·sit ['huːzɪt] *s.* F 'Dingsda' *m, f, n.*

,**who·so·ev·er** → **whoever**.

whunk [wʌŋk] F **I** *int.* bumm!, peng!, bäng!; **II** *v/t.* anstoßen (*acc.* mit), sich den Kopf *etc.* anstoßen; **III** *v/i.* knallen (*od.* bumsen) (**against** gegen).

why [waɪ] **I** *adv.* (*fragend u. relativ*) war'um, wes'halb, wo'zu: **~ so?** wieso?, warum das?; **the reason ~** (der Grund) weshalb; **that is ~** deshalb; **II** *int.* **2.** nun (gut); **3.** (ja) na'türlich; **4.** ja na'türlich; **5.** na'nu; aber (... doch): **~, that's Peter!** aber das ist ja *od.* doch Peter!; **III** *s.* **6.** *das* War'um, Grund *m*: **the ~ and wherefore** das Warum u. Weshalb.

wick [wɪk] *s.* Docht *m*.

wick·ed ['wɪkɪd] *adj.* □ **1.** böse, gottlos, schlecht, sündhaft, verrucht: **the ~ one** *bibl.* der Böse, Satan *m*; **2.** böse, schlimm (*ungezogen, a. humor. schalk-*

haft) (*a.* F *Schmerz, Wunde etc.*); **3.** boshaft, bösartig (*a. Tier*); **4.** gemein; **5.** *sl.* ,toll', großartig; '**wick·ed·ness** [-nɪs] *s.* Gottlosigkeit *f*; Schlechtigkeit *f*, Verruchtheit *f*; Bosheit *f*.

wick·er ['wɪkə] **I** *s.* a) Weidenrute *f*, b) Korbweide *f*, c) → **wickerwork**; **II** *adj.* aus Weiden geflochten, Weiden..., Korb..., Flecht...: **~ basket** Weidenkorb *m*; **~ chair** Rohrstuhl *m*; **~ furniture** Korbmöbel *pl.*; '**~·work** *s.* **1.** Flechtwerk *n*; **2.** Korbwaren *pl.*

wick·et ['wɪkɪt] *s.* **1.** Pförtchen *n*; **2.** (*Tür f* mit) Drehkreuz *n*; **3.** (*mst vergittertes*) Schalterfenster; **4.** *Kricket:* a) Dreistab *m*, Tor *n*, b) Spielfeld *n*: **be on a good** (**sticky**) **~** gut (schlecht) stehen (*a. fig.*); **take a ~** e-n Schläger ausmachen; **keep ~** Torwart sein; **win by 2 ~s** das Spiel gewinnen, obwohl 2 Schläger noch nicht geschlagen haben; **first** (**second etc.**) **~ down** nachdem der erste (zweite *etc.*) Schläger ausgeschieden ist; '**~,keep·er** *s.* Torhüter *m.*

wide [waɪd] **I** *adj.* □ **~ widely**: **1.** breit (*a. bei Maßangaben*): **a ~ forehead** (**ribbon**, **street**); **~ screen** (*Film*) Breitwand *f*; **5 feet ~** 5 Fuß breit; **2.** weit, ausgedehnt: **~ distribution**; **~ difference** großer Unterschied; **a ~ public** ein breites Publikum; **the ~ world** die weite Welt; **3.** *fig.* a) ausgedehnt, um'fassend, 'umfangreich, weit reichend, b) reich (*Erfahrung, Wissen etc.*): **~ culture** umfassende Bildung; **~ reading** große Belesenheit; **4.** a) weit (-gehend, -läufig), b) weitherzig, großzügig: **take ~ views** weitherzig *od.* großzügig sein; **5.** weit offen, aufgerissen: **~ eyes**; **6.** weit, lose, nicht anliegend: **~ clothes**; **7.** weit entfernt (**of** von *der Wahrheit etc.*), weit'ab vom Ziel; → **mark¹** 11; **II** *adv.* **8.** weit: **~ apart** weit auseinander; **~ open** a) weit offen, b) völlig ungedeckt (*Boxer etc.*), c) *fig.* schutzlos, d) → **wide-open** 2; **far and ~** weit u. breit; **9.** weit'ab (*vom Ziel, der Wahrheit etc.*): **go ~** weit danebengehen; ,**~·'an·gle** *adj. phot.* Weitwinkel...: **~ lens**; ,**~-'a·wake I** *adj.* **1.** hellwach (*a. fig.*); **2.** *fig.* aufgeweckt, ,hell'; **3.** *fig.* wachsam, aufmerksam, voll bewusst (**to** *gen.*); **II** *s.* '**wide-awake** 4. Kala'braser *m* (*Schlapphut*); ,**~-,bod·ied jet** *s.* ✈ Großraumflugzeug *n*; ,**~-,bod·y ✈ I** *s.* Großraumflugzeug *n*; **II** *adj.* Großraum...: **~ jet** → **I**; **~ boy** *s. Brit.* F (gerissener) kleiner Gauner; ,**~-'eyed** *adj.* **1.** mit (weit) aufgerissenen Augen; **2.** *fig.* na'iv, kindlich.

wide·ly ['waɪdlɪ] *adv.* weit: **~ scattered** weit verstreut; **~ known** weit u. breit *od.* in weiten Kreisen bekannt; **~ discussed** viel diskutiert; **be ~ read** sehr belesen sein; **differ ~** a) sehr verschieden sein, b) sehr unterschiedlicher Meinung sein.

wid·en ['waɪdn] *v/t. u. v/i.* **1.** breiter machen (werden); **2.** (sich) erweitern (*a. fig.*); **3.** (sich) vertiefen (*Kluft, Zwist*); '**wide·ness** [-nɪs] *s.* **1.** Breite *f*; **2.** Ausdehnung *f* (*a. fig.*).

,**wide|-'o·pen** *adj.* **1.** weit geöffnet; **2.** *Am.* äußerst ,großzügig' (*Stadt etc., bezüglich Glücksspiel etc.*); '**~-spread** *adj.* **1.** weit ausgebreitet, ausgedehnt; **2.** weit verbreitet.

widg·eon ['wɪdʒən] *pl.* **-eons**, *coll.* **-eon** *s. orn.* Pfeifente *f.*

wid·get ['wɪdʒɪt] *s.* F **1.** ,Ding' *n*, ,Dingsda' *n*; **2.** Einheit *f*, ,Ding' (*einzelnes Produkt aus e-r größeren Anzahl*):

5,000 ~s a day 5000 Dinger pro Tag.

wid·ow ['wɪdəʊ] *s.* Witwe *f*: **~'s mite** *bibl.* Scherflein *n* der (armen) Witwe; '**wid·owed** [-əʊd] *adj.* **1.** verwitwet; **2.** verwaist, verlassen; '**wid·ow·er** [-əʊə] *s.* Witwer *m*; '**wid·ow·hood** [-əʊhʊd] *s.* Witwenstand *m.*

width [wɪdθ] *s.* **1.** Breite *f*, Weite *f*: **2 feet in ~** 2 Fuß breit; **2.** (Stoff-, Ta'peten-, Rock)Bahn *f.*

wield [wiːld] *v/t.* **1.** Macht, Einfluss *etc.* ausüben (**over** über *acc.*); **2.** *rhet.* Werkzeug, Waffe handhaben, führen, schwingen: **~ the pen** die Feder führen, schreiben; → **sceptre**.

wie·ner ['wiːnə] *s. Am.*, **wie·nie** ['wiːnɪ] *s.* F Wiener Würstchen *n.*

wife [waɪf] *pl.* **wives** [waɪvz] *s.* **1.** (Ehe-)Frau *f*, Gattin *f*: **wedded ~** angetraute Gattin; **take to ~** zur Frau nehmen; **2.** Weib *n*; '**wife·hood** [-hʊd] *s.* Ehestand *m* e-r Frau; '**wife·like** [-laɪk], '**wife·ly** [-lɪ] *adj.* (haus)fraulich; **wife swapping** *s.* F Partnertausch *m*; **wif·ie** ['waɪfɪ] *s.* F Frauchen *n.*

wig [wɪg] *s.* Pe'rücke *f*; **wigged** [wɪgd] *adj.* mit Perücke (versehen); **wig·ging** ['wɪgɪŋ] *s. Brit.* F Standpauke *f.*

wig·gle ['wɪgl] **I** *v/i.* 1; **2.** → **wriggle** 1; **2.** wackeln, schwänzeln; **II** *v/t.* **3.** wackeln mit.

wight [waɪt] *s. obs. od. humor.* Wicht *m*, Kerl *m.*

wig·wam ['wɪgwæm] *s.* Wigwam *m*, Indi'anerzelt *n*, -hütte *f.*

wild [waɪld] **I** *adj.* □ **1.** *allg.* wild: a) *zo.* ungezähmt, in Freiheit lebend, gefährlich, b) ♀ wild wachsend, c) verwildert, 'wildro,mantisch, verlassen (*Land*), d) unzivilisiert, bar'barisch (*Volk, Stamm*), e) stürmisch: **a ~ coast**, f) wütend, heftig (*Sturm, Streit etc.*), g) irr, verstört: **a ~ look**, h) scheu (*Tier*), i) rasend (**with** vor *dat.*): **~ with fear**, j) F wütend (**about** *acc.*): **drive s.o. ~** j-n wild machen, j-n ,auf die Palme bringen', k) ungezügelt (*Person, Gefühl*), l) unbändig: **~ delight**, m) F toll, verrückt, n) ausschweifend, o) (**about**) versessen *od.* scharf (auf *acc.*), wild (nach), p) hirnverbrannt, unsinnig, abenteuerlich: **~ plan**, q) plan-, ziellos: **a ~ guess** e-e wilde Vermutung; **a ~ shot** ein Schuss ins Blaue, r) wirr, wüst: **~ disorder**; **II** *adv.* **2.** aufs Gerate'wohl: **run ~** a) ♀ ins Kraut schießen, b) verwildern (*Garten etc., a. fig.*); **shoot ~** ins Blaue schießen; **talk ~** a) (wild) drauflosreden, b) sinnloses Zeug reden; **III** *s. rhet.* **3.** *a. pl.* Wüste *f*; **4.** *a. pl.* Wildnis *f*; **~ boar** *s. zo.* Wildschwein *n*; '**~-card** *s. Computer:* 'Wildcard *f*, Jokerzeichen *n*; '**~-cat I** *s.* **1.** *zo.* Wildkatze *f*; **2.** *fig.* Wilde(r *m*) *f*; **3.** → **wildcatting** 2; **4.** ✝ 'Schwindelunter,nehmen *n*; **5.** ✝ wilder Streik; **II** *adj.* **6.** ✝ a) unsicher, spekula'tiv, b) Schwindel...: **~ company**, c) ungesetzlich, wild: **~ strike**; '**~,cat·ting** [-,kætɪŋ] *s.* **1.** wildes Spekulieren (*-gehend etc.*); **2.** wildes *od.* spekula'tive Ölbohrung.

wil·der·ness ['wɪldənɪs] *s.* **1.** Wildnis *f*, Wüste *f* (*a. fig.*): **voice** (**crying**) **in the ~** a) *bibl.* Stimme des Predigers in der Wüste, b) *fig.* Rufer *m* in der Wüste; **be sent into the ~** *fig. pol.* in die Wüste geschickt werden; **2.** wild wachsendes Gartenstück; **3.** *fig.* Masse *f*, Gewirr *n.*

,**wild|-'eyed** *adj.* mit wildem Blick; '**~-fire** *s.* **1.** verheerendes Feuer: **spread like ~** sich wie ein Lauffeuer verbreiten (*Nachricht etc.*); **2.** ⚔ *hist.* griechisches Feuer; '**~·fowl** *s. coll.* Wildvögel *pl.*; **~**

goose s. [irr.] Wildgans f; ˌ~-'**goose chase** s. fig. vergebliche Mühe, fruchtloses Unterfangen.

wild·ing ['waɪldɪŋ] s. ♀ a) Wildling m (unveredelte Pflanze), bsd. Holzapfelbaum m, b) Frucht e-r solchen Pflanze.

'**wild·life** s. coll. wild lebende Tiere pl.: ~ **park** Naturpark m.

wild·ness ['waɪldnɪs] s. allg. Wildheit f.

'**wild·wa·ter** s. Wildwasser n: ~ **sport**.

wile [waɪl] I s. 1. mst pl. List f, Trick m; pl. Kniffe pl., Schliche pl., Ränke pl.; II v/t. 2. verlocken, j-n wohin locken; 3. → **while** 6.

wil·ful ['wɪlfʊl] adj. □ 1. bsd. ⚖ vorsätzlich: ~ **deceit** arglistige Täuschung; ~ **murder** Mord m; 2. eigenwillig, -sinnig, halsstarrig; '**wil·ful·ness** [-nɪs] s. 1. Vorsätzlichkeit f; 2. Eigenwille m, -sinn m, Halsstarrigkeit f.

wil·i·ness ['waɪlɪnɪs] s. (Arg)List f, Verschlagenheit f, Gerissenheit f.

will¹ [wɪl] I v/aux. [irr.] 1. (zur Bezeichnung des Futurs, Brit. mst nur 2. u. 3. sg. u. pl.) werden: **he** ~ **come** er wird kommen; 2. wollen, werden, willens sein zu: ~ **you pass me the bread, please?** reichen Sie mir doch bitte das Brot!; ~ **do!** sl. wird gemacht!; 3. (immer, bestimmt, unbedingt) werden (oft a. unübersetzt): **birds** ~ **sing** Vögel singen; **boys** ~ **be boys** Jungen sind nun einmal so; **accidents** ~ **happen** Unfälle wird es immer geben; **you** ~ **get in my light!** du musst mir natürlich (immer) im Licht stehen!; 4. Erwartung, Vermutung od. Annahme: werden: **they** ~ **have gone now** sie werden od. dürften jetzt (wohl) gegangen sein; **this** ~ **be your train, I suppose** das ist wohl dein Zug, das dürfte dein Zug sein; 5. → **would**; II v/i. u. v/t. 6. wollen, wünschen: **as you** ~**!** wie du willst!; → **would** 3, **will²** II.

will² [wɪl] I s. 1. Wille m (a. phls.): a) Wollen n, b) Wunsch m, Befehl m, c) (Be)Streben n, d) Willenskraft f: **an iron** ~ ein eiserner Wille; **good** ~ guter Wille (→ a. **goodwill**); ~ **to peace** Friedenswille; ~ **to power** Machtwille, -streben; **at** ~ nach Wunsch od. Belieben od. Laune; **of one's own (free)** ~ aus freien Stücken; **with a** ~ mit Lust u. Liebe, mit Macht; **have one's** ~ s-n Willen haben od. durchsetzen; 2. a. **last** ~ **and testament** ⚖ letzter Wille, Testa'ment n; II v/t. 3. wollen, entscheiden; 4. ernstlich od. fest wollen; 5. j-n (durch Willenskraft) zwingen (**to do** zu tun): ~ **o.s. (in)to** sich zwingen zu; 6. ⚖ (letzt)willig a) verfügen, b) vermachen (**to** dat.); III v/i. 7. wollen.

willed [wɪld] adj. ...willig, mit e-m ... Willen; → **strong-willed** etc.

will·ful, will·ful·ness bsd. Am. → **wilful, wilfulness**.

wil·lie ['wɪlɪ] Brit. F → **willy**.

wil·lies ['wɪlɪz] s. pl. F: **get the** ~ ‚Zustände' bekommen; **it gives me the** ~ dabei wird mir ganz anders, dabei läuft es mir eiskalt den Rücken runter.

will·ing ['wɪlɪŋ] adj. □ 1. pred. gewillt, willens, bereit: **I am** ~ **to believe** ich glaube gern; 2. (bereit)willig; 3. gern geschehen od. geleistet: **a** ~ **gift** ein gern gegebenes Geschenk; '**will·ing·ly** [-lɪ] adv. bereitwillig, gern; '**will·ing·ness** [-nɪs] s. (Bereit)Willigkeit f, Bereitschaft f, Geneigtheit f.

will·less ['wɪllɪs] adj. willenlos.

will-o'-the-wisp [ˌwɪləðəˈwɪsp] s. 1. Irrlicht n (a. fig.); 2. fig. Illusi'on f, Phan'tom n.

wil·low¹ ['wɪləʊ] s. 1. ♀ Weide f: **wear the** ~ fig. um den Geliebten trauern; 2. F Kricket: Schlagholz n.

wil·low² ['wɪləʊ] I s. Spinnerei: Reißwolf m; II v/t. Baumwolle etc. wolfen, reißen.

wil·low·y ['wɪləʊɪ] adj. 1. weidenbestanden od. -artig; 2. fig. a) biegsam, geschmeidig, b) gertenschlank.

'**will·pow·er** s. Willenskraft f.

wil·ly ['wɪlɪ] s. Brit. F Pimmel m (Penis).

wil·ly-nil·ly [ˌwɪlɪˈnɪlɪ] adv. wohl oder übel, nolens volens.

wilt¹ [wɪlt] obs. od. poet. du willst.

wilt² [wɪlt] v/i. 1. (ver)welken, welk od. schlaff werden; 2. F fig. a) schlappmachen, ‚eingehen', b) nachlassen.

wil·y ['waɪlɪ] adj. □ gerissen.

wimp [wɪmp] I s. 1. F Schwächling m; 2. Schlappschwanz m, Niete f, Versager m; II v/i. 4. ~ **out** F kneifen (**of s.th.** bei et.), sich drücken (**of s.th.** vor et. dat.); '**wimp·ish** adj. □ 1. schwächlich; 2. F schlapp, lahmarschig; 3. feige.

wim·ple ['wɪmpl] s. 1. hist. Rise f; 2. (Nonnen)Schleier m.

win [wɪn] I v/t. [irr.] 1. Kampf, Spiel etc., a. Sieg, Preis gewinnen: ~ **s.th. from** (od. **of**) s.o. j-m et. abgewinnen; ~ **one's way** fig. s-n Weg machen; → **day** 5, **field** 6; 2. Reichtum, Ruhm etc. erlangen, (sich) erwerben: → **spur** 1; 3. j-m Lob etc. einbringen, -tragen; 4. Liebe, Sympathie, a. e-n Freund, j-s Unterstützung gewinnen; 5. a. ~ **over** j-n für sich gewinnen, auf s-e Seite ziehen, a. j-s Herz erobern; 6. j-n dazu bringen (**to do** zu tun): ~ **s.o. round** j-n ‚rumkriegen'; 7. Stelle, Ziel erreichen: ~ **the shore**; 8. sein Brot, s-n Lebensunterhalt verdienen; 9. ✕ sl. ‚organisieren'; 10. ✕, min. a) Erz, Kohle gewinnen, b) erschließen; II v/i. [irr.] 11. gewinnen, siegen: ~ **hands down** F spielend gewinnen; ~ **out** F sich durchsetzen (**over** gegen); ~ **through** a) durchkommen, b) ans Ziel gelangen (a. fig.), c) fig. sich durchsetzen; III s. 12. bsd. sport Sieg m.

wince [wɪns] I v/i. (zs.-)zucken, zs.-, zu-'rückfahren (**at** bei, **under** unter dat.); II s. (Zs.-)Zucken n.

winch [wɪntʃ] ⊚ I s. 1. Winde f, Haspel f; 2. Kurbel f; II v/t. 3. hochwinden.

wind¹ [wɪnd; poet. a. waɪnd] I s. 1. Wind m: **before the** ~ vor dem od. im Wind; **between** ~ **and water** a) ⚓ zwischen Wind u. Wasser, b) in der od. die Magengrube, c) fig. an e-r empfindlichen Stelle; **in(to) the** ~'s **eye** gegen den Wind; **like the** ~ wie der Wind (schnell); **to the four** ~s in alle (vier) Winde, in alle (Himmels)Richtungen; **under the** ~ ⚓ in Lee; **be in the** ~ fig. (heimlich) im Gange sein, in der Luft liegen; **cast** (od. **fling**, **throw**) **to the** ~s fig. in den Wind schlagen, Klugheit etc. außer Acht lassen; **get (have) the** ~ **up** sl. ‚Manschetten' od. ‚Schiss' kriegen (haben); **know how the** ~ **blows** wissen, woher der Wind weht; **put the** ~ **up s.o.** F j-n ins Bockshorn jagen; **raise the** ~ F (das nötige) Geld auftreiben; **sail close to the** ~ a) ⚓ hart am Wind segeln, b) fig. mit e-m Fuß im Zuchthaus stehen, sich hart an der Grenze des Erlaubten bewegen; **sow the** ~ **and reap the whirlwind** den Wind säen u. Sturm ernten; **have** (od. **take**) **the** ~ **of** a) e-m Schiff den Wind abgewinnen, b) fig. e-n Vorteil

od. die Oberhand haben über (acc.); **take the** ~ **out of s.o.'s sails** fig. j-m den Wind aus den Segeln nehmen; ~ **and weather permitting** bei gutem Wetter; → **ill** 4; 2. ⊚ (Gebläse- etc.) Wind m, b) Luft f in e-m Reifen etc.; 3. ♫ (Darm)Wind(e pl.) m, Blähung(en pl.) f: **break** ~ e-n Wind abgehen lassen; 4. ♪ the ~ coll. die Blasinstrumente pl., a. die Bläser pl.; 5. hunt. Wind m, Witterung f (a. fig.): **get** ~ **of** a) wittern, b) fig. Wind bekommen von; 6. Atem m: **have a good** ~ e-e gute Lunge haben; **have a long** ~ e-n langen Atem haben (a. fig.); **get one's second** ~ den zweiten Wind bekommen, den toten Punkt überwunden haben; **sound in** ~ **and limb** kerngesund; **have lost one's** ~ außer Atem sein; 7. Wind m, leeres Geschwätz; II v/t. 8. hunt. wittern; **be** ~**ed** außer Atem od. erschöpft sein; 10. verschnaufen lassen.

wind² [waɪnd] I s. 1. Windung f, Biegung f; 2. Um'drehung f; II v/t. [irr.] 3. winden, wickeln, schlingen (**round** um acc.): ~ **off** (**on to**) **a reel** et. ab- (auf-) spulen; 4. oft ~ **up** a) auf-, hochwinden, b) Garn etc. aufwickeln, -spulen, c) Uhr etc. aufziehen, d) Saite etc. spannen; 5. a) Kurbel drehen, a. kurbeln: ~ **forward** od. **on (back)** Kassette etc. vor- (zurück)spulen; ~ **up (down)** Autofenster hoch- (herunter)kurbeln; 6. ⚓ Schiff wenden; 7. (sich) wohin schlängeln: ~ **o.s.** (od. **one's way**) **into s.o.'s affection** fig. sich j-s Zuneigung erschleichen; III v/i. [irr.] 8. sich winden od. schlängeln (a. Straße etc.); 9. sich winden od. wickeln od. schlingen (**round** um acc.); ~ **off** v/t. abwickeln, -spulen; ~ **up** I v/t. 1. → **wind²** 4, 5; 2. fig. anspannen, erregen, (hin'ein)steigern; 3. bsd. Rede (ab-) schließen; 4. ♥ a) Geschäft abwickeln, b) Unternehmen auflösen, liquidieren; II v/i. 5. (bsd. s-e Rede) schließen (**by saying** mit den Worten); 6. F wo enden, ‚landen': **he'll** ~ **in prison**; 7. ♥ Kon'kurs machen; 8. **wind s.o. up** a) Brit. F j-n ‚aufziehen', b) j-n (ver)ärgern; **be wound up** verärgert sein, sich aufregen (**about** über acc.).

wind·bag ['wɪndbæg] s. F contp. Schwätzer m, Schaumschläger m.

'**wind·blown** ['wɪnd-] adj. 1. windig; 2. windschief; 3. (vom Wind) zerzaust; 4. Windstoß...: ~ **hairdo**; '~**break** s. Windschutz m (Hecke etc.); 2. Windbruch m; '~**bro·ken** adj. vet. kurzatmig (Pferd); '~**cheat·er** s. Brit. Windjacke f; ~ **cone** s. ✈ Luftsack m.

wind·ed ['wɪndɪd] adj. 1. außer Atem; 2. in Zssgn ...atmig: **short-**~.

wind| egg [wɪnd] s. Windei n; ~ **en·er·gy** s. 'Windener,gie f, -kraft f.

wind·er ['waɪndə] s. 1. Spuler(in) f; 2. ⊚ Winde f; 3. ♀ Schlingpflanze f; 4. a) Schlüssel m (zum Aufziehen), b) Kurbel f.

'**wind·fall** ['wɪnd-] s. 1. Fallobst n; 2. Windbruch m; 3. fig. (unverhoffter) Glücksfall od. Gewinn: ~ **profit** ♥ Marktlagengewinn m, Q-Gewinn; ~ **tax** a) ♥ Zufallsgewinnsteuer f, b) Spekulati'ons(gewinn)steuer f; ~ **farm** s. Windpark m; '~**flow·er** s. ♀ Ane'mone f; ~ **force** s. Windstärke f; ~ **ga(u)ge** s. Wind(stärke-, -geschwindigkeits)messer m, Anemo'meter n.

wind·i·ness ['wɪndɪnɪs] s. Windigkeit f (a. fig. contp.).

wind·ing ['waɪndɪŋ] I s. 1. Winden n, Spulen n; 2. (Ein-, Auf)Wickeln n,

(Um)'Wickeln *n*; **3.** Windung *f*, Biegung *f*; **4.** Wind(e)lung *f*; **5.** ⚡ Wicklung *f*; **II** *adj.* □ **6.** gewunden: a) sich windend *od.* schlängelnd, b) Wendel...(-*treppe*); **7.** krumm, schief (*a. fig.*); ~ **sheet** *s.* Leichentuch *n*; **tack·le** *s.* ⚓ Gien *n* (*Flaschenzug*); '~-**·up** *s.* **1.** Aufziehen *n* (*Uhr etc.*): ~ **mechanism** Aufziehwerk *n*; **2.** ⚕ a) Abwicklung *f*, Erledigung *f* (*e-s Geschäfts*), b) Liquidati'on *f*, Auflösung *f* (*e-r Firma*); ~ **order** Liquidationsbeschluss *m*; ~ **sale** (Total)Ausverkauf *m*.

wind| in·stru·ment [wind] *s.* ♪ Blasinstru,ment *n*; '~-**jam·mer** [-,dʒæmə] *s.* **1.** ⚓ Windjammer *m* (*Schiff*); **2.** *Am. sl.* → **windbag.**

wind·lass ['windləs] **I** *s.* **1.** ⚙ Winde *f*; **2.** ⚒ Förderhaspel *f*; **3.** ⚓ Ankerspill *n*; **II** *v/t.* hochwinden.

wind·less ['windlis] *adj.* windstill.

wind·mill ['windmil] *s.* **1.** Windmühle *f*: *tilt at* (*od.* *fight*) ~*s* *fig.* gegen Windmühlen kämpfen; *throw one's cap over the* ~ a) Luftschlösser bauen, b) jede Vorsicht außer Acht lassen; **2.** Windrädchen *n*.

win·dow ['windəʊ] *s.* **1.** Fenster *n* (*a. Computer*, ⚙, *geol.*; *a. im Briefumschlag*): *look out of* (*od.* *at*) *the* ~ zum Fenster hinaussehen; **2.** Fensterscheibe *f*; **3.** Schaufenster *n*, Auslage *f*; **4.** (*Bank- etc.*)Schalter *m*; **5.** ✕ *Radar*: Störfolie *f*.

win·dow| box *s.* Blumenkasten *m*; ~ **clean·er** *s.* Fensterputzer *m*; ~ **dis·play** *s.* 'Schaufensterauslage *f*, -re,klame *f*; '~-**dress** *v/t.* **1.** ⚕ *Bilanz* verschleiern, ,frisieren'; **2.** ,aufputzen'; ~ **dress·er** *s.* 'Schaufensterdeko,rateur *m*; ~ **dress·ing** *s.* **1.** 'Schaufensterdekorati,on *f*; **2.** *fig.* Aufmachung *f*, Mache *f*; **3.** ⚕ Bi'lanzverschleierung *f*, ,Frisieren' *n*.

win·dowed ['windəʊd] *adj.* mit Fenster(n) (versehen).

win·dow| en·ve·lope *s.* 'Fenster,briefumschlag *m*; ~ **gar·den·ing** *s.* Blumenzucht *f* am Fenster; ~ **jam·ming** *s.* ✕ *Radar*: Folienstörung *f*; '~-**pane** *s.* Fensterscheibe *f*; '~-**screen** *s.* **1.** Fliegenfenster *n*; **2.** Zierfüllung *f* e-s Fensters (*aus Buntglas, Gitter etc.*); ~ **seat** *s.* Fensterplatz *m*; ~ **shade** *s.* *Am.* Rou'leau *n*, Jalou'sie *f*; '~-**shop·per** *s.* j-d, der e-n Schaufensterbummel macht; '~-**shop·ping** *s.* Schaufensterbummel *m*: *go* ~ e-n Schaufensterbummel machen; ~ **shut·ter** *s.* Fensterladen *m*; '~-**sill** *s.* Fensterbrett *n*, -bank *f*; ~ **tech·nol·o·gy** *s.* *Computer*: Fenstertechnik *f*.

'**wind|-pipe** ['wind-] *s.* *anat.* Luftröhre *f*.

wind| pow·er [wind] *s.* Windkraft *f*: ~ **plant** Windkraftanlage *f* (*zur Stromerzeugung*); ~ **rose** *s. meteor.* Windrose *f*; '~-**sail** *s.* **1.** Windflügel *m*; **2.** ⚓ Windsack *m*; '~-**screen** *s.* *Brit.*, '~-**shield** *s. Am. mot.* Windschutzscheibe *f*: ~ **wash·er** Scheibenwaschanlage *f*; ~ **wiper** Scheibenwischer *m*; '~-**sleeve** *s.*, '~-**sock** *s.* ✈ Luftsack *m*; '~-**swept** ['wind-] *adj.* **1.** vom Wind gepeitscht; **2.** *fig.* Windstoß...(-*frisur*): '~-**surf·ing** *s.* Windsurfen *n*; ~ **tun·nel** *s.* ✈, *phys.* 'Windka,nal *m*; '~-**up** ['waind-] *s.* **1.** → **winding-up** 2; **2.** Schluss *m*, Ende *n*.

wind·ward ['windwəd] **I** *adv.* wind-, luvwärts; **II** *adj.* windwärts, Luv..., Wind...; **III** *s.* Windseite *f*, Luv(seite) *f*.

wind·y ['windi] *adj.* □ **1.** windig: a) stürmisch (*Wetter*), b) zugig (*Ort*); **2.** *fig.* a) windig, hohl, leer, b) geschwätzig; **3.** ⚒

blähend; **4.** *Brit. sl.* ner'vös, ängstlich.

wine [wain] **I** *s.* **1.** Wein *m*: *new* ~ *in old bottles* *bibl.* junger Wein in alten Schläuchen (*a. fig.*); **2.** *Brit. univ.* Weinabend *m*; **II** *v/t.*: ~ *and dine s.o.* j-n fürstlich bewirten; '~-**bib·ber** [-,bibə] *s.* Weinsäufer(in); ~ **bot·tle** *s.* Weinflasche *f*; ~ **cool·er** *s.* Weinkühler *m*; ~ **cra·dle** *s.* Weinkorb *f*; '~-**glass** *s.* Weinglas *n*; '~-**grow·er** *s.* Weinbauer *m*; '~-**grow·ing** *s.* Wein(an)bau *m*: ~ **area** Weinbaugebiet *n*; ~ **list** *s.* Weinkarte *f*; ~ **mer·chant** *s.* Weinhändler *m*; '~-**press** *s.* Weinpresse *f*, -kelter *f*.

win·er·y ['wainəri] *s.* Weinkelle'rei *f*, -gut *n*.

'**wine|-skin** *s.* Weinschlauch *m*; ~ **stone** *s.* 🜌 Weinstein *m*; '~-**tast·er** *s.* Weinprüfer *m*; '~-**tast·ing** *s.* Weinprobe *f*.

wing [wiŋ] **I** *s.* **1.** *orn.* Flügel *m* (*a.* ⚘, *zo.*, *a.* ⚙, △, *a. pol.*); *rhet.* Schwinge *f*, Fittich *m* (*a. fig.*): *on the* ~ a) im Fluge, b) *fig.* auf Reisen; *on the* ~*s of the wind* mit Windeseile; *on a* ~ *and a prayer* mit wenig Aussichten auf Erfolg, ,auf gut Glück'; *under s.o.'s* ~(*s*) *fig.* unter j-s Fittichen *od.* Schutz; *clip s.o.'s* ~*s* j-m die Flügel stutzen; *lend* ~*s to* a) *Hoffnung etc.* beflügeln, b) j-m Beine machen; *spread* (*od.* *try*) *one's* ~*s* versuchen, auf eigenen Beinen zu stehen *od.* sich durchzusetzen; *singe one's* ~*s* *fig.* sich die Finger verbrennen; *take* ~ a) aufsteigen, davonfliegen, b) aufbrechen, c) *fig.* beflügelt werden; **2.** Federfahne *f* (*Pfeil*); **3.** *humor.* Arm *m*; **4.** (Tür-, Fenster- *etc.*) Flügel *m*; **5.** *mst pl. thea.* ('Seiten)Ku,lisse *f*: *wait in the* ~*s* *fig.* sich bereithalten; **6.** ✈ Tragfläche *f*; **7.** *mot.* Kotflügel *m*; **8.** ✕, ⚓ Flügel *m* (*Aufstellung*); **9.** ✈ *brit. Luftwaffe:* Gruppe *f*, b) *amer. Luftwaffe:* Geschwader *n*, c) *pl.* F ,Schwinge' *f* (*Pilotenabzeichen*); **10.** *sport* a) Flügel *m* (*Spielfeldteil*), b) → **winger**; **11.** mit Flügeln *etc.* versehen; **12.** *fig.* beflügeln (*beschleunigen*); **13.** *Strecke* (durch)'fliegen; **14.** a) *Vogel* anschießen, flügeln, b) F *j-n* (*bsd. am Arm*) verwunden; **III** *v/i.* **15.** fliegen; ~ **as·sem·bly** *s.* ✈ Tragwerk *n*; '~-**beat** *s.* Flügelschlag *m*; ~ **case** *s. zo.* Flügeldecke *f*; ~ **chair** *s.* Ohrensessel *m*; ~ **com·mand·er** *s.* ✈, ✕ *Brit.* Oberst'leutnant *m* der Luftwaffe; **2.** *Am.* Ge'schwaderkommo,dore *m*; ~ **cov·ert** *s. zo.* Deckfeder *f*.

wing-ding ['wiŋdiŋ] *s. sl.* **1.** (*a.* Wut-) Anfall *m*; **2.** ,tolles Ding'.

winged [wiŋd] *adj.* □ **1.** *orn., a.* ⚘ geflügelt; Flügel...; *in Zssgn* ...flügelig: *the* ~ *horse fig.* der Pegasus; ~ **screw** ⚙ Flügelschraube *f*; ~ **words** *fig.* geflügelte Worte; **2.** *fig.* a) beflügelt, schnell, b) beschwingt.

wing·er ['wiŋə] *s. sport* Außen-, Flügelstürmer *m*.

wing| feath·er *s. orn.* Schwungfeder *f*; '~-**heav·y** *adj.* ✈ querlastig; ~ **nut** *s.* ⚙ Flügelmutter *f*; ~ **o·ver** *s.* ✈ Immelmann-Turn *m*; ~ **sheath** *s.* → **wing case**; '~-**span** ✈, '~-**spread** *s. orn.*, ✈ Spannweite *f*.

wink [wiŋk] **I** *v/i.* **1.** blinzeln, zwinkern: ~ *at* a) j-m zublinzeln, b) *fig.* ein Auge zudrücken bei, *et.* ignorieren; *as easy as* ~*ing Brit.* F kinderleicht; *like* ~*ing* F wie der Blitz; **2.** blinken, flimmern (*Licht*); **II** *v/t.* **3.** mit *den Augen* blinzeln *od.* zwinkern; **III** *s.* **4.** Blinzeln *n*, Zwinkern *n*, Wink *m* (*mit den Augen*): *forty* ~*s* Nickerchen *n*; *not to sleep a* ~, *not to get a* ~ *of sleep* kein Auge

zutun; → *tip³* 5; *in a* ~ im Nu.

win·kle ['wiŋkl] **I** *s. zo.* (essbare) Strandschnecke; **II** *v/t.* ~ *out* a) her'ausziehen (*a. fig.* F), b) F j-n aussieben, -sondern.

win·ner ['winə] *s.* **1.** Gewinner(in), *sport a.* Sieger(in); **2.** sicherer Gewinner; **3.** ,todsichere' Sache; **4.** ,Schlager' *m*.

win·ning ['winiŋ] **I** *adj.* □ **1.** *bsd. sport* siegreich, Sieger..., Sieges...; **2.** entscheidend: ~ *hit* entscheidender Treffer; **3.** *fig.* gewinnend, einnehmend; **II** *s.* **4.** ⚒ Abbau *m*, Gewinnung *f*; **5.** *pl.* Gewinn *m* (*bsd. im Spiel*); **6.** Gewinnen *n*, Sieg *m*; ~ **post** *s. sport* Zielpfosten *m*.

win·now ['winəʊ] **I** *v/t.* **1.** a) *Getreide* schwingen, b) *Spreu* trennen (*from* von); **2.** *fig.* sichten; **3.** *fig.* trennen, (unter)'scheiden (*from* von); **4.** aussortieren; **5.** herausfinden; **II** *s.* **6.** Wanne *f*, Futterschwinge *f*.

wi·no ['wainəʊ] *pl.* -**nos** *s.* F Saufbruder *m*, (Wein)Säufer(in).

win·some ['winsəm] *adj.* □ **1.** gewinnend: ~ *smile*; **2.** (lieb)reizend.

win·ter ['wintə] **I** *s.* **1.** Winter *m*; **2.** *poet.* Lenz *m*, (Lebens)Jahr *n*: *a man of fifty* ~*s*; **II** *v/i.* **3.** (*a. v/t.* *Tiere, Pflanzen*) über'wintern; **III** *adj.* **4.** winterlich; Winter...: ~ *crop* ✦ Winterfrucht *f*; ~ *garden* Wintergarten *m*; ~ *resort* 'Winterurlaubsort *m*, -,kurort *m*; ~ *sleep* Winterschlaf *m*; ~ *sports* Wintersport *m*; **win·ter·ize** ['wintəraiz] *v/t.* auf den Winter vorbereiten, *bsd.* ⚙ winterfest machen; '**win·ter·tide** *s.* Winter(zeit *f*) *m*; '~-**weight** *adj.* Winter...: ~ *clothes*.

win·tri·ness ['wintrinis] *s.* Kälte *f*, Frostigkeit *f*; **win·try** ['wintri] *adj.* **1.** winterlich, frostig; **2.** *fig.* a) trüb(e), b) alt, c) frostig: ~ *smile*.

wipe [waip] **I** *s.* **1.** (Ab)Wischen *n*: *give s.th. a* ~ et. abwischen; **2.** F a) (harter) Schlag, b) *fig.* Seitenhieb *m*; **II** *v/t.* **3.** (ab-, trocken)wischen, sauber wischen, abreiben, reinigen: ~ *s.o.'s eye* (*for him*) *sl.* j-n ausstechen; ~ *one's lips* sich den Mund wischen; → *floor* 1; ~ *off* *v/t.* **1.** ab-, wegwischen; **2.** *fig.* bereinigen, auslöschen; *Rechnung* begleichen: *wipe s.th. off the slate* et. begraben *od.* vergessen; ~ *out* *v/t.* **1.** auswischen; **2.** wegwischen, (aus)löschen, tilgen (*a. fig.*): ~ *a disgrace* e-n Schandfleck tilgen, e-e Scharte auswetzen; **3.** *Armee, Stadt etc.* vernichten, ,ausradieren'; *Rasse etc.* ausrotten; ~ *up* *v/t.* **1.** aufwischen; **2.** (ab)trocknen.

wip·er ['waipə] *s.* **1.** Wischer *m* (*Person od. Vorrichtung*); **2.** Wischtuch *n*; **3.** ⚙ a) Hebedaumen *m*, b) Abstreifring *m*, c) ⚡ Kon'takt-, Schleifarm *m*; **4.** → *wipe* 2.

wire ['waiə] **I** *s.* **1.** Draht *m*; **2.** ⚡ Leitung(sdraht *m*) *f*; → *live²* 3; ⚡ (Kabel)Ader *f*; **4.** F Tele'gramm *n*: *by* ~ telegrafisch; **5.** *pl.* a) Drähte *pl.* e-s Marionettenspiels, b) *fig.* geheime Fäden *pl.*, Beziehungen *pl.*: *pull the* ~*s* a) der Drahtzieher sein, b) s-e Beziehungen spielen lassen; **6.** *opt.* Faden *m* im Okular; **7.** ♪ Drahtsaite(n *pl.*) *f*; **II** *adj.* **8.** Draht...: ~ *brush*; **III** *v/t.* **9.** mit Draht(geflecht) versehen; **10.** mit Draht zs.-binden *od.* befestigen; **11.** ⚡ Leitungen legen in (*dat.*), verdrahten: ~ *to* anschließen an (*acc.*); **12.** F e-e Nachricht *od.* j-m telegrafieren; **13.** *hunt.* mit Drahtschlingen fangen; **IV** *v/i.* **14.** F telegrafieren: ~ *away od. in sl.* loslegen, sich ins Zeug legen; ~ *cloth* → *wire gauze*; ~ *cut·ter* *s.* ⚙

W

Drahtschere f; '**~·draw** v/t. [irr. → draw] **1.** ⊙ Metall drahtziehen; **2.** fig. a) in die Länge ziehen, b) Argument über'spitzen; '**~·drawn** adj. fig. a) langatmig, b) über'spitzt; **~ en·tan·gle·ment** s. ✕ Drahtverhau m; **~ ga(u)ge** s. ⊙ Drahtlehre f; **~ gauze** s. Drahtgaze f, -gewebe n, -netz n; '**~·haired** adj. zo. Drahthaar...: **~ terrier**. **wire·less** ['waɪəlɪs] ⚡ I adj. **1.** drahtlos, Funk...: **~ message** Funkspruch m; **2.** Brit. Radio..., Rundfunk...: **~ set** → 3; **II** s. **3.** Brit. 'Radio(appa,rat m) n: **on the ~** im Radio od. Rundfunk; **4.** abbr. für **~ telegraphy**, **~ telephony** etc.; **III** v/t. Brit. **5.** Nachricht etc. funken; **~ car** s. Brit. Funkstreifenwagen m; **~ op·er·a·tor** s. ✈ (Bord)Funker m; **~ pirate** s. Schwarzhörer m; **~ (re·ceiving) set** s. (Funk)Empfänger m; **~ station** s. (a. 'Rund)Funkstati,on f; **~ te·leg·ra·phy** s. drahtlose Telegra'fie, 'Funktelegra,fie f; **~ te·leph·o·ny** s. drahtlose Telefo'nie, Sprechfunk m. **'wire|·man** [-mən] s. [irr.] ⚡ F **1.** Am. 'Abhörspezialist m; **2.** bsd. Am. E'lektroinstalla,teur m, E'lektriker m; **3.** Journalist, der für e-e Nachrichtenagentur arbeitet; **~ net·ting** s. ⊙ **1.** Drahtnetz n; **2.** pl. Maschendraht m; **~ ·pho·to** s. 'Bildtele,gramm n; '**~,pull·er** s. fig. ,Drahtzieher' m; '**~,pull·ing** s. bsd. pol. ,Drahtziehe'rei f; **~ rod** s. ⊙ Walz-, Stabdraht m; **~ rope** s. Drahtseil n; **~ ·rope·way** s. Drahtseilbahn f; **~ serv·ice** s. Am. 'Nachrichtenagen,tur f; '**~·tap** v/t. u. v/i. (j-s) Tele'fongespräche abhören, (j-s) Leitung(en) anzapfen; '**~,tap·ping** s. Abhören n, Anzapfen n (von Tele'fonleitungen); '**~,walk·er** s. 'Drahtseilakro,bat(in), Seiltänzer(in); '**~·worm** s. zo. Drahtwurm m; '**~·wove** adj. **1.** Velin...(-papier); **2.** aus Draht geflochten.

wir·ing ['waɪərɪŋ] s. ⚡ **1.** Verdrahtung f (a. ⚡); **2.** ⚡ a) (Be)Schaltung f b) Leitungsnetz n: **~ diagram** Schaltplan m, -schema n.

wir·y ['waɪərɪ] adj. **1.** Draht...; **2.** drahtig (Haar, Muskeln, Person etc.); **3.** a) vibrierend, b) me'tallisch (Ton).

wis·dom ['wɪzdəm] s. Weisheit f, Klugheit f; **~ tooth** s. [irr.] Weisheitszahn m: **cut one's ~ teeth** fig. vernünftig werden.

wise¹ [waɪz] **I** adj. □ → **wisely**; **1.** weise, klug, erfahren, einsichtig; **2.** gescheit, verständig; **3.** wissend, unter'richtet: **be none the ~r** (for it) nicht klüger sein als zuvor; **without anybody being the ~r for it** ohne dass es j-d gemerkt hätte; **~ after the event** um e-e Erfahrung klüger; **be ~ to** F Bescheid wissen über (acc.); **get ~ to** F et. ,spitzkriegen', j-n od. et. durch'schauen; **put s.o. ~ to** F j-m et. ,stecken'; **4.** schlau, gerissen; **5.** F neunmalklug: **~ guy** ,Klugscheißer' m; **6.** obs. **~ man** Zauberer m; **~ woman** a) Hexe f, b) Wahrsagerin f, c) weise Frau (Hebamme); **II** v/t. **7.** **~ up** Am. F j-n informieren (to über acc.); **III** v/i. **8.** **~ up** Am. F a) ,schlau' werden, b) **~ up to** et. ,spitzkriegen'.

wise² [waɪz] s. obs. Art f, Weise f: **in any ~** auf irgendeine Weise; **in no ~** in keiner Weise, keineswegs; **in this ~** auf diese Art u. Weise.

-wise [waɪz] in Zssgn a) ...artig, nach Art von, b) ...weise, c) F ...mäßig.

'wise|,a·cre [-,eɪkə] s. Neunmalkluge(r) m, Besserwisser m; '**~·crack** F **I** s. witzige od. treffende Bemerkung; Witze-

'lei f; **II** v/i. witzeln, ,flachsen'; '**~·,crack·er** s. F Witzbold m.

wise·ly ['waɪzlɪ] adv. **1.** weise (etc.; → **wise¹** 1 u. 2); **2.** klug, kluger-, vernünftigerweise; **3.** (wohl)weislich.

wish [wɪʃ] **I** v/t. **1.** (sich) wünschen; **2.** wollen, wünschen: **I ~ I were rich** ich wollte, ich wäre reich; **I ~ you to come** ich möchte, dass du kommst; **~ s.o. further** (od. **at the devil**) j-n zum Teufel wünschen; **~ o.s. home** sich nach Hause sehnen; **3.** hoffen: **I ~ it may prove true**; **it is to be ~ed** es ist zu hoffen od. wünschen; **4.** j-m Glück, Spaß etc. wünschen: **~ s.o. well** (ill) j-m wohl (übel) wollen; **~ s.th. on s.o.** j-m et. (Böses) wünschen, j-m et. aufhalsen; → **joy** 1; **5.** j-m guten Morgen etc. wünschen; j-m Adieu etc. sagen: **~ s.o. farewell**; **II** v/i. **6.** wünschen: **~ for** sich et. wünschen, sich sehnen nach; **he cannot ~ for anything better** er kann sich nichts Besseres wünschen; **III** s. **7.** Wunsch m: a) Verlangen n (for nach), b) Bitte f (for um acc.), c) das Gewünschte: **you shall have your ~** du sollst haben, was du dir wünschst; → **father** 5; **8.** pl. gute Wünsche pl., Glückwünsche pl.: **good ~es; 'wish·bone** s. orn. Brust-, Gabelbein n; **2.** mot. Dreieckslenker m: **~ suspension** Schwingarmfederung f; **wish·ful** ['wɪʃʊl] adj. □ **1.** vom Wunsch erfüllt, begierig (to do zu tun); **2.** sehnsüchtig: **~ thinking** Wunschdenken n.

wish·ing| bone ['wɪʃɪŋ] → **wishbone** 1; **~ cap** s. Zauber-, Wunschkappe f.

wish-wash ['wɪʃwɒʃ] s. **1.** labberiges Zeug (a. fig. Geschreibsel); **2.** fig. Geschwätz n; **wish·y-wash·y** ['wɪʃɪ,wɒʃɪ] adj. labberig: a) wässrig, b) fig. saft- u. kraftlos, seicht.

wisp [wɪsp] s. **1.** (Stroh- etc.)Wisch m, (Heu-, Haar)Büschel n; (Haar)Strähne f; **2.** Handfeger m; **3.** Strich m, Zug m (Vögel); **4.** Fetzen m, Streifen m: **~ of smoke** Rauchfetzen m; **a ~ of a boy** ein schmächtiges Bürschchen; '**wisp·y** [-pɪ] adj. **1.** büschelig (Haar etc.); **2.** dünn, schmächtig.

wist·ful ['wɪstʊl] adj. □ **1.** sehnsüchtig, wehmütig; **2.** nachdenklich, versonnen.

wit¹ [wɪt] s. **1.** oft pl. geistige Fähigkeiten pl., Intelli'genz f; **2.** oft pl. Verstand m: **be at one's ~s' end** mit s-r Weisheit zu Ende sein; **have one's ~s about one** s-e fünf Sinne beisammen haben; **keep one's ~s about one** e-n klaren Kopf behalten; **live by one's ~s** sich mehr oder weniger ehrlich durchs Leben schlagen; **out of one's ~s** von Sinnen, verrückt; **frighten s.o out of his ~s** j-n zu Tode erschrecken; **3.** Witz m, Geist m, Es'prit m; **4.** witziger Kopf, geistreicher Mensch; **5.** obs. Witz m, witziger Einfall.

wit² [wɪt] v/t. u. v/i. [irr.] obs. wissen: **to ~** bsd. ⚡ das heißt, nämlich.

witch [wɪtʃ] **I** s. **1.** Hexe f, Zauberin f: **~es' sabbath** Hexensabbat m; **2.** fig. alte Hexe; **3.** F betörendes Wesen, bezaubernde Frau; **II** v/t. **4.** be-, verhexen; '**~·craft** s. **1.** Hexe'rei f, Zaube'rei f; **2.** Zauber(kraft f) m; **~ doc·tor** s. Medi'zinmann m.

witch·er·y ['wɪtʃərɪ] s. **1.** → **witchcraft**; **2.** fig. Zauber m.

witch hunt s. bsd. pol. Hexenjagd f (for, against auf acc.).

witch·ing ['wɪtʃɪŋ] adj. □ **1.** Hexen...: **~ hour** Geisterstunde f; **2.** → **bewitching**.

wit·e·na·ge·mot [,wɪtɪnəgɪ'məʊt] s. hist.

gesetzgebende Versammlung im Angelsachsenreich.

with [wɪð] prp. **1.** mit (vermittels): **cut ~ a knife**; **fill ~ water**; **2.** (zs.) mit: **he went ~ his friends**; **3.** nebst, samt: **~ all expenses**; **4.** mit (besitzend): **a coat ~ three pockets**; **~ no hat** ohne Hut; **5.** mit (Art u. Weise): **~ care**; **~ a smile**; **~ the door open** bei offener Tür; **6.** in Über'einstimmung mit: **I am quite ~ you** ich bin ganz Ihrer Ansicht od. ganz auf Ihrer Seite; **7.** mit (in derselben Weise, im gleichen Grad, zur selben Zeit): **the sun changes ~ the seasons**; **rise ~ the sun**; **8.** bei: **sit** (**sleep**) **~ s.o.**; **work ~ a firm**; **I have no money ~ me**; **9.** (kausal) durch, vor (dat.), von, an (dat.): **die ~ cancer** an Krebs sterben; **stiff ~ cold** steif vor Kälte; **wet ~ tears** von Tränen nass, tränennass; **tremble ~ fear** vor Furcht zittern; **10.** bei, für: **~ God all things are possible** bei Gott ist kein Ding unmöglich; **11.** gegen, mit: **fight ~ s.o.**; **12.** bei, aufseiten (von): **it rests ~ you to decide** die Entscheidung liegt bei dir; **13.** trotz, bei: **~ all her brains** bei all ihrer Klugheit; **14.** angesichts; in Anbetracht der Tatsache, dass: **you can't leave ~ your mother so ill** du kannst nicht weggehen, wenn deine Mutter so krank ist; **15.** **~ it** sl. a) ,auf Draht', ,schwer auf der Höhe', b) modebewusst, c) up to date; **get ~ it!** mach mit!, sei kein Frosch!

with·al [wɪ'ðɔ:l] obs. **I** adv. außerdem, 'oben'drein, da'bei; **II** prp. (nachgestellt) mit.

with·draw [wɪð'drɔ:] [irr. → draw] **I** v/t. **1.** (from) zu'rückziehen, -nehmen (von, aus): a) wegnehmen, entfernen (von, aus), Schlüssel etc., a. ✕ Truppen abziehen, her'ausziehen (aus), b) entziehen (dat.), c) einziehen, d) fig. Auftrag, Aussage etc. wider'rufen, Wort etc. zu'rücknehmen: **~ a motion** Antrag zurückziehen; **2.** ✝ a) Geld abheben, a. Kapital entnehmen, b) Kredit kündigen; **II** v/i. **3.** (from) sich zu'rückziehen (von, aus): a) sich entfernen, b) zu'rückgehen, ✕ a. sich absetzen, c) zu'rücktreten (von e-m Posten, Vertrag), d) austreten (aus e-r Gesellschaft), e) fig. sich distanzieren (von j-m, e-r Sache): **~ within o.s.** fig. sich in sich selbst zurückziehen; **with·draw·al** [-ɔ:əl] s. **1.** Zu'rückziehung f, -nahme f (a. fig. Widerrufung) (a. ✕ von Truppen): **~ (from circulation)** Einziehung, Außerkurssetzung f; **2.** ✝ (Geld)Abhebung f, Entnahme f; **3.** bsd. ✕ Ab-, Rückzug m; **4.** (from) Rücktritt m (von e-m Amt, Vertrag etc.), Ausscheiden n (aus); **5.** 🕮 Entzug m: **~ symptoms** Entzugs-, Ausfallserscheinungen pl.; **6.** 🕮 Entziehung f: **~ cure**; **7.** sport Startverzicht m; **with'drawn** [-ɔ:n] **I** pp von **withdraw**; **II** adj. **1.** psych. in sich gekehrt; **2.** zu'rückgezogen.

with·er ['wɪðə] **I** v/i. **1.** oft **~ up** (ver)welken, verdorren, austrocknen; **2.** fig. a) vergehen (Schönheit etc.), b) ,eingehen' (Firma etc.), c) oft **~ away** schwinden (Hoffnung etc.); **II** v/t. **3.** (ver)welken lassen, ausdörren, -trocknen; **~ed** fig. verhutzelt; **4.** fig. j-n mit e-m Blick etc., a. j-s Ruf vernichten; **with·er·ing** ['wɪðərɪŋ] adj. □ **1.** ausdörrend; **2.** fig. vernichtend: **a ~ look** (**remark**).

with·ers ['wɪðəz] s. pl. zo. 'Widerrist m (Pferd etc.): **my ~ are unwrung** fig. das trifft mich nicht.

with'hold v/t. [irr. → hold²] **1.** zu'rück-,

abhalten (**s.o. from** j-n von *et.*): **~ o.s. from s.th.** sich e-r Sache enthalten; **~ing tax** Quellensteuer *f*; **2.** vorenthalten, versagen (**s.th. from s.o.** j-m *et.*).

with·in [wɪ'ðɪn] **I** *prp.* **1.** innerhalb von (*od. gen.*), in (*dat.*) (*beide a. zeitlich binnen*): **~ 3 hours** binnen *od.* in nicht mehr als 3 Stunden; **~ a week of his arrival** e-e Woche nach *od.* vor s-r Ankunft; **2.** im *od.* in den Bereich von: **~ call** (**hearing**, **reach**, **sight**) in Ruf- (Hör-, Reich-, Sicht)weite; **~ the meaning of the Act** im Rahmen des Gesetzes; **~ my powers** a) im Rahmen m-r Befugnisse, b) soweit es in m-n Kräften steht; **~ o.s.** *sport* ohne sich zu verausgaben (*laufen etc.*); **live ~ one's income** nicht über s-e Verhältnisse leben; **3.** im 'Umkreis von, nicht weiter (entfernt) als: **~ a mile of** bis auf e-e Meile von; → **ace** 3; **II** *adv.* **4.** (dr)innen, drin, im Innern: **~ and without** innen u. außen; **from ~** von innen; **5.** a) im *od.* zu Hause, drinnen, b) ins Haus, hi'nein; **6.** *fig.* innerlich, im Innern; **III** *s.* **7.** *das* Innere.

with·out [wɪ'ðaʊt] **I** *prp.* **1.** ohne (**doing** zu tun): **~ difficulty**; **~ his finding me** ohne dass er mich fand *od.* findet; **~ doubt** zweifellos; → **do without**, **go without**; **2.** außerhalb, jenseits, vor (*dat.*); **II** *adv.* **3.** (dr)außen, äußerlich; **4.** ohne: **go ~** leer ausgehen; **III** *s.* **5.** *das* Äußere: **from ~** von außen; **IV** *cj.* **6.** *a.* **~ that** *obs. od.* F a) wenn nicht, außer wenn, b) ohne dass.

with'stand *v/t.* [*irr.* → **stand**] wider'stehen (*dat.*): a) sich wider'setzen (*dat.*), b) aushalten (*acc.*), standhalten (*dat.*).

wit·less ['wɪtlɪs] *adj.* □ **1.** geist-, witzlos; **2.** dumm, einfältig; **3.** verrückt; **4.** ahnungslos.

wit·ness ['wɪtnɪs] **I** *s.* **1.** Zeuge *m*, Zeugin *f* (*a.* ✝ *u. fig.*): **be a ~ of s.th.** Zeuge von et. sein; **call s.o. to ~** j-n als Zeugen anrufen; **a living ~ to** ein lebender Zeuge (*gen.*); **~ for the prosecution** (*Brit. a.* **for the Crown**) Belastungszeuge; **prosecuting ~** a) Nebenkläger(in), b) Belastungszeuge; **~ for the defence** (*Am.* **defense**) Entlastungszeuge; *✎ eccl.* Zeuge Je'hovas; **2.** Zeugnis *n*, Bestätigung *f*, Beweis *m* (**of**, **to** *gen.* für): **bear ~ to** (*od.* **of**) Zeugnis ablegen von, et. bestätigen; **in ~ whereof** zum Zeugnis *od.* urkundlich dessen; **II** *v/t.* **3.** bezeugen, beweisen: **~ Shakespeare** als Beweis dient Shakespeare; **4.** Zeuge sein von, zu'gegen sein bei, (mit)erleben (*a. fig.*); **5.** *fig.* zeugen von, Zeuge sein von; **6.** ✝ *✎* j-s Unterschrift beglaubigen, *Dokument* als Zeuge unter'schreiben; **III** *v/i.* **7.** zeugen, Zeuge sein, Zeugnis ablegen, ✝ *a.* aussagen (**against** gegen, **for**, **to** für): **~ to s.th.** *fig.* et. bezeugen; **this agreement ~eth** ✝ dieser Vertrag be-inhal-tet; **~ box** *bsd. Brit.*, **~ stand** *Am. s.* ✝ Zeugenstand *m*.

wit·ted ['wɪtɪd] *adj. in Zssgn* ...denkend, ...sinnig; → **half-witted** *etc.*

wit·ti·cism ['wɪtɪsɪzəm] *s.* witzige Bemerkung.

wit·ti·ness ['wɪtɪnɪs] *s.* Witzigkeit *f*.

wit·ting·ly ['wɪtɪŋlɪ] *adv.* wissentlich.

wit·ty ['wɪtɪ] *adj.* □ witzig, geistreich.

wives [waɪvz] *pl. von* **wife**.

wiz [wɪz] F *für* **wizard** 2.

wiz·ard ['wɪzəd] **I** *s.* **1.** Zauberer *m*, Hexenmeister *m* (*beide a. fig.*); **2.** *fig.* Ge-'nie *n*, Leuchte *f*, ,Ka'nonè *f*; **II** *adj.* **3.** magisch, Zauber...; **4.** F ,fan'tas-

tisch'; **'wiz·ard·ry** [-drɪ] *s.* Zaube'rei *f*, Hexe'rei *f* (*a. fig.*).

wiz·en ['wɪzn], **'wiz·ened** [-nd] *adj.* verhutzelt, schrump(e)lig.

wo, **woa** [wəʊ] *int.* brr! (*zum Pferd*).

wob·ble ['wɒbl] **I** *v/i.* **1.** wackeln, schwabbeln; schwanken (*a. fig. between* zwischen); **2.** schlottern (*Knie etc.*); **3.** ⚙ a) flattern (*Rad*), b) ,eiern' (*Schallplatte*); **II** *s.* **4.** Wackeln *n*; Schwanken *n* (*a. fig.*); ⚙ Flattern *n*; **'wob·bler** [-lə] → **wobbly** II; **'wob·bly** [-lɪ] **I** *adj.* **1.** wack(e)lig; **2.** zitt(e)rig (*Stimme*, *Schrift*); **3.** eiernd (*Rad*); **4.** unsicher, ungewiss; **II** *s. Brit.* F **5.** Wutanfall *m*: **throw a ~** e-n Wutanfall kriegen, ,ausrasten'; **6.** *a.* **the wobblies** *pl.* 'Panikanfall *m*, -at,tacke *f*: **throw a ~** in Panik geraten.

woe [wəʊ] **I** *int.* wehe!, ach!; **II** *s.* Weh *n*, Leid *n*, Kummer *m*, Not *f*: **face of ~** jämmerliche Miene; **tale of ~** Leidensgeschichte *f*; **~ is me!** wehe mir!; **~** (**be**) **to ...!**, **~ betide ...!** wehe (*dat.*)!, verflucht sei(en) ...!; → **weal'**; **woe·be·gone** ['wəʊbɪ,gɒn] *adj.* **1.** leid-, jammervoll, vergrämt; **2.** verwahrlost; **woe·ful** ['wəʊfʊl] *adj.* □ *rhet. od. humor.* **1.** kummer-, sorgenvoll; **2.** elend, jammervoll; **3.** *contp.* erbärmlich, jämmerlich.

wog [wɒg] *s. sl. contp.* Ka'nake *m*, ,Ka-'meltreiber' *m* (*farbiger Ausländer*).

wok [wɒk] *s.* Wok *m* (*ostasiatischer schüsselförmiger Kochtopf*).

woke [wəʊk] *pret. von* **wake²**.

wold [wəʊld] *s.* **1.** hügeliges Land; **2.** Hochebene *f*.

wolf [wʊlf] **I** *pl.* **wolves** [-vz] *s.* **1.** *zo.* Wolf *m*: **a ~ in sheep's clothing** *fig.* ein Wolf im Schafspelz; **lone ~** *fig.* Einzelgänger *m*; **cry ~** *fig.* blinden Alarm schlagen; **keep the ~ from the door** *fig.* sich über Wasser halten; **2.** *fig.* a) Wolf *m*, räuberische *od.* gierige Per'son, b) F ,Casa'novà *m*, Schürzenjäger *m*; **3.** ♪ Disso'nanz *f*; **II** *v/t.* **4.** *a.* **~ down** Speisen (gierig) verschlingen; **~ call** *s. Am.* F bewundernder Pfiff *od.* Ausruf (*beim Anblick e-r attraktiven Frau*); **~ cub** *s. zo.* junger Wolf.

wolf·ish ['wʊlfɪʃ] *adj.* □ **1.** wölfisch (*a. fig.*), Wolfs...; **2.** *fig.* wild, gefräßig: **~ appetite** Wolfshunger *m*.

wolf pack *s.* **1.** Wolfsrudel *n*; **2.** ⚓, ✕ Rudel *n* U-Boote.

wolf·ram ['wʊlfrəm] *s.* **1.** 🜍 Wolfram *n*; **2.** → **'wolf·ram·ite** [-maɪt] *s. min.* Wolfra'mit *m*.

wol·ver·ine ['wʊlvəriːn] *s. zo.* (*Amer.*) Vielfraß *m*.

wolves [wʊlvz] *pl. von* **wolf**.

wom·an ['wʊmən] **I** *pl.* **wom·en** ['wɪmɪn] *s.* **1.** Frau *f*, Weib *n*: **~ of the world** Frau von Welt; **play the ~** empfindsam *od.* ängstlich sein; → **women**; **2.** a) Hausangestellte *f*, b) Zofe *f*; **3.** (*ohne Artikel*) das weibliche Geschlecht, die Frauen *pl.*, das Weib: **born of ~** vom Weibe geboren (*sterblich*); **~'s reason** weibliche Logik; **4.** **the ~** *fig.* das Weib, die Frau, das typisch Weibliche; **5.** F a) (Ehe)Frau *f*, b) Freundin *f*, Geliebte *f*; **II** *adj.* **6.** weiblich, Frauen...: **~ doctor** Ärztin *f*; **~ student** Studentin *f*.

wom·an·hood ['wʊmənhʊd] *s.* **1.** Stellung *f* der (erwachsenen) Frau: **reach ~** e-e Frau werden; **2.** Weiblich-, Fraulichkeit *f*; **3.** → **womankind** 1; **'woman·ish** [-nɪʃ] *adj.* □ **1.** *contp.* weibisch; **2.** → **womanly**; **'wom·an·ize** [-naɪz] **I** *v/t.* weibisch machen; **II** *v/i.*

F hinter den Weibern her sein; **'wom·an·iz·er** [-naɪzə] *s.* F Schürzenjäger *m*.

'wom·an|·kind *s.* **1.** *coll.* Frauen(welt *f*) *pl.*, Weiblichkeit *f*; **2.** → **womenfolk** 2; **'~·like** *adj.* wie e-e Frau, fraulich, weiblich.

wom·an·li·ness ['wʊmənlɪnɪs] *s.* Fraulich-, Weiblichkeit *f*; **wom·an·ly** ['wʊmənlɪ] *adj.* fraulich, weiblich (*a. weitS.*).

womb [wuːm] *s. anat.* Gebärmutter *f*; *weitS.* (Mutter)Leib *m*, Schoß *m* (*a. fig. der Erde*, *der Zukunft etc.*); **~ en·vy** *s. psych.* Gebärneid *m*; **'~-to-'tomb** *adj.* von der Wiege bis zur Bahre.

wom·en ['wɪmɪn] *pl. von* **woman**: **~'s rights** Frauenrechte; **~'s team** *sport* Damenmannschaft *f*; **'~·folk** *s. pl.* **1.** → **womankind** 1; **2.** *die* Frauen *pl.* (*in e-r Familie*), mein *etc.* ,Weibervolk' *n* (da-'heim).

Wom·en's| Lib [lɪb] F, **~ Lib·e·ra·tion** (**Move·ment**) *s.* 'Frauenemanzipati,onsbewegung *f*; **~ Lib·ber** ['lɪbə] *s.* F Anhängerin *f* der Emanzipati'onsbewegung, *contp.* ,E'manzè *f*.

won [wʌn] *pret. u. p.p. von* **win**.

won·der ['wʌndə] **I** *s.* **1.** Wunder *n*, et. Wunderbares, Wundertat *f*, -werk *n*: **a ~ of skill** ein (wahres) Wunder an Geschicklichkeit (*Person*); **the 7 ~s of the world** die 7 Weltwunder; **work** (*od.* **do**) **~s** Wunder wirken; **promise ~s** j-m goldene Berge versprechen; (**it is**) **no** (*od.* **small**) **~ that** kein Wunder, dass; **~s will never cease** es gibt immer noch Wunder; → **nine** 1, **sign** 8; **2.** Verwunderung *f*, (Er)Staunen *n*: **filled with ~** von Staunen erfüllt; **for a ~** a) erstaunlicherweise, b) ausnahmsweise; **in ~** erstaunt, verwundert; **II** *v/i.* **3.** sich (ver)wundern, erstaunt sein (**at**, **about** über *acc.*): **not to be ~ed at** nicht zu verwundern; **4.** a) neugierig *od.* gespannt sein, gern wissen mögen (**if**, **whether**, **what** *etc.*), b) sich fragen *od.* über'legen: **I ~ whether I might ...?** dürfte ich vielleicht ...?, ob ich wohl ... kann?; **I ~ if you could help me** vielleicht können Sie mir helfen; **well, I ~!** na, ich weiß nicht (recht)!; **~ boy** *s.* ,Wunderknabe' *m*; **~ child** *s.* [*irr.*] *Am.* Wunderkind *n*; **~ drug** *s.* Wunderdroge *f*, -mittel *n*.

won·der·ful ['wʌndəfʊl] *adj.* □ wunderbar, -voll, herrlich: **not so ~** F nicht so toll.

won·der·ing ['wʌndərɪŋ] *adj.* □ verwundert, erstaunt, staunend.

'won·der·land *s.* Wunder-, Märchenland *n* (*a. fig.*).

won·der·ment ['wʌndəmənt] *s.* Verwunderung *f*, Staunen *n*.

'won·der|·struck *adj.* von Staunen ergriffen (**at** über *acc.*); **'~·,work·er** *s.* Wundertäter(in); **'~·,work·ing** *adj.* wundertätig.

won·drous ['wʌndrəs] *rhet.* **I** *adj.* □ wundersam, -bar; **II** *adv.* a) wunderbar(erweise), b) außerordentlich.

won·ky ['wɒŋkɪ] *adj. Brit. sl.* wack(e)lig (*a. fig.*).

won't [wəʊnt] F *für* **will not**.

wont [wəʊnt] **I** *adj.*: **be ~ to do** gewohnt sein *od.* pflegen zu tun; **II** *s.* Gewohnheit *f*, Brauch *m*; **'wont·ed** [-tɪd] *adj.* **1.** *obs.* gewohnt; **2.** gewöhnlich, üblich; *Am.* eingewöhnt (**to** in *dat.*).

woo [wuː] *v/t.* **1.** werben *od.* freien um, j-m den Hof machen; **2.** *fig.* trachten nach, buhlen um; **3.** *fig.* a) j-n um'werben, b) locken, drängen (**to** zu).

wood [wʊd] **I** s. **1.** oft pl. Wald m, Waldung f, Gehölz n: **be out of the ~** (Am. **~s**) F über den Berg sein; **he cannot see the ~ for the trees** er sieht den Wald vor lauter Bäumen nicht; → **halloo** III; **2.** Holz n: **touch ~!** unberufen!; **3.** (Holz)Fass n: **wine from the ~** Wein (direkt) vom Fass; **4. the ~ ♪** → **woodwind** 2; **5.** → **wood block** 2; **6.** Bowling: (bsd. abgeräumter) Kegel; **7.** pl. Skisport: ‚Bretter' pl.; **8.** Golf: Holz (-schläger m) n; **II** adj. **9.** hölzern, Holz...; **10.** Wald...; ~ **al·co·hol** s. 🜍 Holzgeist m; ~ **a·nem·o·ne** s. ♀ Buschwindrös·chen n; '~**bind**, '~**bine** s. **1.** ♀ Geißblatt n; **2.** Am. wilder Wein; ~ **block** s. **1.** Par'kettbrettchen n; **2.** typ. a) Druckstock m, b) Holzschnitt m; ~ **carv·er** s. Holzschnitzer m; ~ **carv·ing** s. Holzschnitze'rei f (a. Schnitzwerk); '~**chuck** s. zo. (amer.) Waldmurmeltier n; ~ **coal** s. **1.** min. Braunkohle f; **2.** Holzkohle f; '~**cock** s. orn. Waldschnepfe f; '~**craft** s. **1.** die Fähigkeit, im Wald zu (über)leben; **2.** Holzschnitze'rei f; '~**cut** s. typ. **1.** Holzstock m (Druckform); **2.** Holzschnitt m (Druckerzeugnis); '~**cut·ter** s. **1.** Holzfäller m; **2.** Kunst: Holzschneider m.

wood·ed [ˈwʊdɪd] adj. bewaldet, waldig, Wald...

wood·en [ˈwʊdn] adj. ☐ **1.** hölzern, Holz...: **2 Horse** die Trojanische Pferd; ~ **spoon** a) Holzlöffel m, b) bsd. sport Trostpreis m; **2.** fig. hölzern, steif (a. Person); **3.** fig. ausdruckslos (Gesicht etc.); **4.** stumpf(sinnig).

wood| en·grav·er s. Holzschneider m; ~ **en·grav·ing** s. **1.** Holzschneiden n; **2.** Holzschnitt m.

'**wood·en-|head·ed** adj. F dumm.

wood| gas s. 🜍 Holzgas n; ~ **grouse** s. orn. Auerhahn m.

wood·i·ness [ˈwʊdɪnɪs] s. **1.** Waldreichtum m; **2.** Holzigkeit f.

wood| king·fish·er s. orn. Königsfischer m; '~**land** s. **I** s. Waldland n, Waldung f; **II** adj. Wald...; ~ **lark** s. orn. Heidelerche f; ~ **louse** s. [irr.] zo. Bohrassel f; '~**man** [-mən] s. [irr.] **1.** Brit. Förster m; **2.** Holzfäller m; **3.** Jäger m; **4.** Waldbewohner m; ~ **naph·tha** s. 🜍 Holzgeist m; ~ **nymph** s. **1.** myth. Waldnymphe f; **2.** zo. eine Motte; **3.** orn. ein Kolibri m; '~**peck·er** s. orn. Specht m; ~ **pi·geon** s. orn. Ringeltaube f; '~**pile** s. Holzhaufen m, -stoß m; ~ **pulp** s. 🜍 Holz(zell)stoff m, Holzschliff m; '~**ruff** s. ♀ Waldmeister m; ~**print** → **woodcut** 2; '~**shav·ings** s. pl. Hobelspäne pl.; '~**shed** s. Holzschuppen m.

woods·man [ˈwʊdzmən] s. [irr.] **1.** Waldbewohner m.

wood| sor·rel s. ♀ Sauerklee m; ~ **spir·it** s. 🜍 Holzgeist m; ~ **tar** s. 🜍 Holzteer m; ~ **tick** s. zo. Holzbock m; '~**wind** [-wɪnd] ♪ **I** s. **1.** 'Holzblasinstru,ment n; **2.** oft pl. 'Holzblasinstru,mente pl. (e-s Orchesters), Holz(bläser pl.) n; **II** adj. **3.** Holzblas...; ~ **wool** s. 🜍 Zellstoffwatte f; '~**work** s. △ **1.** Holz-, Balkenwerk n; **2.** Holzarbeit(en pl.) f; '~**work·ing I** s. Holzbearbeitung f; **II** adj. Holz bearbeitend, Holzbearbeitungs...: **machine**; '~**worm** s. zo. Holzwurm m.

wood·y [ˈwʊdɪ] adj. **1.** a) waldig, Wald..., b) waldreich; **2.** holzig, Holz...

'**wood·yard** s. Holzplatz m.

woo·er [ˈwuːə] s. Freier m, Anbeter m.

woof¹ [wuːf] s. **1.** Weberei: a) Einschlag m, (Ein)Schuss m, b) Schussgarn n; **2.** Gewebe n.

woof² [wʊf] v/i. bellen.

woof·er [ˈwuːfə] s. ♫ Tieftonlautsprecher m.

woo·ing [ˈwuːɪŋ] s. (a. fig. Liebes)Werben n, Freien n, Werbung f.

wool [wʊl] **I** s. **1.** Wolle f: **dyed in the ~** in der Wolle gefärbt, bsd. fig. waschecht; → **cry** 2; **2.** Wollfaden m, -garn n; **3.** Wollstoff m, -tuch n; **4.** Zell-, Pflanzenwolle f; **5.** (Baum-, Glas- etc.)Wolle f; **6.** F ‚Wolle' f, (kurzes) wolliges Kopfhaar: **lose one's ~** ärgerlich werden; **pull the ~ over s.o.'s eyes** F j-n hinters Licht führen; **II** adj. **7.** wollen, Woll...; ~ **card** s. Wollkrempel m, -kratze f; ~ **clip** s. ✝ (jährlicher) Wollertrag; ~ **comb·ing** s. Wollkämmen n; '~**dyed** adj. in der Wolle gefärbt.

wool·en Am. → **woollen**.

'**wool|gath·er·ing I** s. fig. Verträumtheit f, Spintisieren n; **II** adj. verträumt, spintisierend; '~**grow·er** s. Schafzüchter m; ~ **hall** s. ✝ Brit. Wollbörse f.

wool·i·ness Am. → **woolliness**.

wool·len [ˈwʊlən] **I** s. **1.** Wollstoff m; **2.** pl. Wollsachen pl. (a. wollene Unterwäsche), Wollkleidung f; **II** adj. **3.** wollen, Woll...: ~ **goods** Wollwaren; ~ **drap·er** s. Wollwarenhändler m.

wool·li·ness [ˈwʊlɪnɪs] s. **1.** Wolligkeit f; **2.** paint. u. fig. Verschwommenheit f; **wool·ly** [ˈwʊlɪ] **I** adj. **1.** wollig, weich, flaumig; **2.** Wolle tragend, Woll...; **3.** paint. u. fig. verschwommen; belegt (Stimme); **II** s. **4.** wollenes Kleidungsstück, bsd. Wolljacke f; pl. → **woollen** 2.

'**wool·pack** s. **1.** Wollsack m (Verpackung); **2.** Wollballen m (240 englische Pfund); **3.** meteor. Haufenwolke f; '~**sack** s. pol. a) Wollsack m (Sitz des Lordkanzlers im englischen Oberhaus), b) fig. Amt n des Lordkanzlers; '~**sort·er** s. Wollsortierer m (Person od. Maschine): ~'**s disease** s. Lungenmilzbrand; '~**sta·pler** s. ✝ **1.** Woll(groß)händler m; **2.** Wollsortierer m; '~**work** s. Wollsticke'rei f.

wool·y Am. → **woolly**.

woo·pies [ˈwuːpɪz] s. pl. wohlhabende Seni'oren pl. (= **well-off older people**).

wooz·y [ˈwuːzɪ] adj. Am. sl. **1.** (von Alkohol etc.) benebelt; **2.** a) wirr (im Kopf), b) ‚komisch' (im Magen).

wop [wɒp] s. sl. contp. ‚Itaker' m, ‚Spa'g(h)etti(fresser)' m.

word [wɜːd] **I** s. **1.** Wort n: ~s a) Worte, b) ling. Wörter; ~ **for** Wort für Wort, (wort)wörtlich; **at a** ~ sofort, aufs Wort; **in a** ~ mit 'einem Wort, kurz (-um); **in other ~s** mit anderen Worten; **in so many ~s** wörtlich, ausdrücklich; **the last** ~ a) das letzte Wort (**on** in e-r Sache), b) das Allerneueste od. -beste (**in** an dat.); **have the last** ~ das letzte Wort haben; **have no ~s for** nicht wissen, was man zu e-r Sache sagen soll; **put into** ~s in Worte fassen; **too silly for ~s** unsagbar dumm; **cold's not the ~ for it!** F kalt ist gar kein Ausdruck!; **he is a man of few ~s** er macht nicht viele Worte, er ist ein schweigsamer Mensch; **he hasn't a ~ to throw at a dog** er macht den Mund nicht auf; **2.** Wort n, Ausspruch m: ~s Worte, Rede, Äußerung; **by ~ of mouth** mündlich; **have a ~ with s.o.** (kurz) mit j-m sprechen; **have a ~ to say** et. (Wichtiges) zu sagen haben; **put in** (od. **say**) **a** (**good**) ~ **for** ein (gutes) Wort einlegen für; **I take your ~ for it** ich glaube es dir; **3.** pl. Text m e-s Lieds etc.; **4.** pl. Wortwechsel m, Streit m:

have ~s (**with**) sich streiten od. zanken mit; **5.** a) Befehl m, Kom'mando n, b) Losung f, Pa'role f, c) Zeichen n, Signal n: **give the ~** (**to do**); **pass the ~** durch-, weitersagen; **sharp's the ~!** (jetzt aber) dalli!; **6.** Bescheid m, Nachricht f: **leave ~** Bescheid hinterlassen (**with** bei); **send ~ to** j-m Nachricht geben; **7.** Wort n, Versprechen n: ~ **of hono(u)r** Ehrenwort; **break** (**give** od. **pass, keep**) **one's** ~ sein Wort brechen (geben, halten); **take s.o. at his** ~ j-n beim Wort nehmen; **he is as good as his** ~ er ist ein Mann von Wort; er hält, was er verspricht; (**up**)**on my** ~**!** auf mein Wort!; **8. the 2** eccl. das Wort Gottes, das Evan'gelium; **II** v/t. **9.** in Worte fassen, (in Worten) ausdrücken, formulieren: ~**ed as follows** mit folgendem Wortlaut; ~ **ac·cent** s. ling. 'Wortak,zent m; '~**blind** adj. ✝ wortblind; '~**book** s. **1.** Vokabu'lar n; **2.** Wörterbuch n; **3.** ♪ Textbuch n, Lib'retto n; '~**catch·er** s. contp. Wortklauber m; '~**deaf** adj. psych. worttaub; ~ **for·ma·tion** s. ling. Wortbildung f; ‚~**for·'word** adj. (wort)wörtlich.

word·i·ness [ˈwɜːdɪnɪs] s. Wortreichtum m, Langatmigkeit f; '**word·ing** [-ɪŋ] s. Fassung f, Formulierung f, Wortlaut m.

word·less [ˈwɜːdlɪs] adj. **1.** wortlos, stumm; **2.** schweigsam.

‚**word|-of-'mouth** adj. mündlich: ~ **ad·vertising** Mundwerbung f; ~ **or·der** s. ling. Wortstellung f (im Satz); ~ **paint·ing** s. anschauliche Schilderung; ‚~'**per·fect** adj. **1.** thea. etc. textsicher; **2.** per'fekt auswendig gelernt: ~ **text**; ~ **pic·ture** → **word painting**; '~**play** s. Wortspiel n; ~ **pow·er** s. Wortschatz m; ~ **proc·ess·ing** s. Computer: Textverarbeitung f; ~ **proc·es·sor** s. Computer: **1.** 'Textverarbeitungspro,gramm n; **2.** 'Textverarbeitungssys,tem n; ~ **split·ting** s. Wortklaube'rei f; ~ **wrap** [ræp] s. Computer: 'Text,umbruch m.

word·y [ˈwɜːdɪ] adj. ☐ **1.** Wort...: ~ **warfare** Wortkrieg m; **2.** wortreich, langatmig.

wore [wɔː] pret. von **wear¹**, pret. u. p.p. von **wear²**.

work [wɜːk] **I** s. **1.** Arbeit f: a) Tätigkeit f, Beschäftigung f, b) Aufgabe f, c) Hand-, Nadelarbeit f, Sticke'rei f, Nähe'rei f, d) Leistung f, e) Erzeugnis n: ~ **done** geleistete Arbeit; **a beautiful piece of** ~ e-e schöne Arbeit; **good ~!** gut gemacht!; **total** ~ **in hand** ✝ Gesamtaufträge pl.; ~ **in process material** ✝ Material in Fabrikation; **at** ~ bei der Arbeit, in Tätigkeit, in Betrieb; **be at** ~ **on** arbeiten an (dat.); **do** ~ arbeiten; **be in** (**out of**) ~ (keine) Arbeit haben; (**put**) **out of** ~ arbeitslos (machen); **set to** ~ an die Arbeit gehen; **have one's** ~ **cut out** (**for one**) (,schwer) zu tun' haben; **make** ~ Arbeit verursachen; **make sad** ~ **of** arg wirtschaften mit; **make short** ~ **of** kurzen Prozess od. nicht viel Federlesens machen mit; **it's all in the day's** ~ das ist nichts Besonderes, das gehört alles (mit) dazu; **2.** phys. Arbeit f: **convert heat into** ~; **3.** künstlerisches etc. Werk n (a. coll.): **the** ~(**s**) **of Bach**; **4.** a) Werk n (Tat u. Resultat): **the** ~ **of a moment** es war das Werk e-s Augenblicks, b) bsd. pl. eccl. (gutes) Werk; **5.** 🜍 → **workpiece**; **6.** pl. a) (bsd. öffentliche) Bauten pl. (Anlagen pl.), b) ⚔ Befestigungen pl., (Festungs)Werk n; **7.** pl. sg. konstr. Werk n, Fa'brik(anlagen pl.)

f, Betrieb *m*: **iron**~**s** Eisenhütte *f*; ~**s council** (*engineer*, *outing*, *superintendent*) Betriebsrat (-ingenieur, -ausflug, -direktor) *m*; ~**s manager** Werkleiter *m*; **8.** *pl*. (Trieb-, Uhr- *etc*.)Werk *n*, Getriebe *n*; **9.** *the* ~**s** *sl*. alles, der ganze Krempel; *give s.o. the* ~**s** j-n ,fertig machen'; *shoot the* ~**s** *Kartenspiel od. fig*. aufs Ganze gehen; **II** *v/i*. **10.** (*at*) arbeiten (an *dat*.), sich beschäftigen (mit): ~ *on commission* auf Provisi'ons,basis arbeiten; ~ *to rule* Dienst nach Vorschrift tun; **11.** arbeiten (*fig. kämpfen against* gegen, *for* für *e-e Sache*), sich anstrengen; **12.** ⚙ a) funktionieren, gehen (*beide a. fig*.), b) in Betrieb od. in Gang sein; **13.** *fig*. ,klappen', gehen, gelingen, sich machen lassen: *it won't* ~ es geht nicht; **14.** (*p.p. oft wrought*) wirken (*a. Gift etc*.), sich auswirken (*[up]on*, *with* auf *acc.*, bei); **15.** sich bearbeiten lassen; **16.** sich (*hindurch-*, *hoch- etc*.)arbeiten: ~ *into* eindringen in (*acc.*); ~ *loose* sich losarbeiten, sich lockern; **17.** in (heftiger) Bewegung sein; **18.** arbeiten, zucken (*Gesichtszüge etc*.), mahlen (*Kiefer*) (*with* vor *Erregung etc*.); **19.** ⚓ *gegen den Wind etc*. fahren, segeln; **20.** gären; arbeiten (*a. fig. Gedanken etc.*); **21.** (hand)arbeiten, stricken, nähen; **III** *v/t*. **22.** *a*. ⚙ a) bearbeiten, *Teig* kneten, b) verarbeiten, (ver)formen, gestalten (*into* zu); **23.** *Maschine etc*. bedienen, *Wagen* führen, lenken; **24.** ⚙ (an-, be)treiben; ~*ed by electricity*; **25.** ⚒ *Boden* bearbeiten, bestellen; **26.** *Betrieb* leiten, *Fabrik etc*. betreiben, *Gut etc*. bewirtschaften; **27.** ⚒ *Grube* abbauen, ausbeuten; **28.** *geschäftlich* bereisen, bearbeiten; **29.** *j-n*, *Tiere tüchtig* arbeiten lassen, antreiben; **30.** *fig. j-n* bearbeiten, *j-m* zusetzen; **31.** arbeiten mit, bewegen: *he* ~*ed his jaws* s-e Kiefer mahlten; **32.** a) ~ *one's way* sich (*hindurch- etc*.)arbeiten, b) verdienen, erarbeiten; → *passage* 6; **33.** sticken, nähen, machen; **34.** gären lassen; **35.** errechnen, lösen; **36.** (*p.p. oft wrought*) her'vorbringen, -rufen, *Veränderung etc*. bewirken, *Wunder* wirken od. tun, führen zu, verursachen: ~ *hardship*; **37.** (*p.p. oft wrought*) fertig bringen, zu'stande bringen: ~ *it* F es ,deichseln'; **38.** *sl. et.* ,her'ausschlagen', ,organisieren'; **39.** *in e-n Zustand* versetzen, erregen: ~ *o.s. into a rage* sich in e-e Wut hineinsteigern;

Zssgn mit adv.:

work| a·round → *work round*; ~ **a·way** *v/i*. (flott) arbeiten (*at* an *dat*.); ~ **in I** *v/t*. einarbeiten, -flechten, -fügen; **II** *v/i*. ~ *with* harmonieren mit, passen zu; ~ **off** *v/t*. **1.** weg-, aufarbeiten; **2.** *überflüssige Energie* loswerden; **3.** *Gefühl* abreagieren (*on* an *dat*.); **4.** *typ*. abdrucken, -ziehen; **5.** *Ware etc*. loswerden, abstoßen (*on* an *acc.*); **6.** *Schuld* abarbeiten; ~ **out I** *v/t*. **1.** ausrechnen, *Aufgabe* lösen; **2.** *Plan* ausarbeiten; **3.** bewerkstelligen; **4.** ⚒ abbauen, (*a. fig. Thema etc*.) erschöpfen; **II** *v/i*. **1.** sich her'ausarbeiten, zum Vorschein kommen (*from* aus); **6.** ~ *at* sich belaufen auf (*acc.*); **7.** ,klappen', *gut etc*. gehen, sich *gut etc*. anlassen: ~ *well* (*badly*); **8.** *sport* trainieren; ~ **o·ver** *v/t*. **1.** über'arbeiten; **2.** *sl. j-n* ,in die Mache nehmen'; ~ **round** *v/i*. **1.** ~ *to* a) *ein Problem etc*. angehen, b) sich ,durchringen zu; **2.** ~ *to* kommen zu, Zeit finden für; **3.** drehen (*Wind*); ~ **to·geth·er** *v/i*. **1.** zs.-arbeiten; **2.** inein'ander

greifen (*Zahnräder*); ~ **up I** *v/t*. **1.** verarbeiten (*into* zu); **2.** ausarbeiten, entwickeln; **3.** *Thema* bearbeiten; sich einarbeiten in (*acc.*), gründlich studieren; **4.** *Geschäft etc*. auf- od. ausbauen; **5.** a) *Interesse etc*. entwickeln, b) sich *Appetit etc*. holen; **6.** *Gefühl*, *Nerven*, *a. Zuhörer etc*. aufpeitschen, -wühlen, *Interesse* wecken: *work s.o. up* sich aufregen; ~ *a rage*, *work o.s. up into a rage* sich in e-e Wut hineinsteigern; *worked up* aufgebracht; **II** *v/i*. **7.** *fig*. sich steigern (*to* zu).

work·a·ble ['wɜːkəbl] *adj*. ☐ **1.** bearbeitungsfähig, (ver)formbar; **2.** betriebsfähig; **3.** 'durch-, ausführbar (*Plan etc*.); **4.** ⚒ abbauwürdig.

work·a·day ['wɜːkədeɪ] *adj*. **1.** Alltags...; **2.** *fig*. all'täglich.

work·a·hol·ic [ˌwɜːkə'hɒlɪk] *s*. Arbeitssüchtige(r *m*) *f*; Arbeitstier *n*.

'work| bench *s*. ⚙ Werkbank *f*; **'~book** *s*. **1.** ⚙ Betriebsanleitung *f*; **2.** *ped*. Arbeitsheft *n*; **'~box** *s*. Nähkasten *m*; ~ **camp** *s*. Arbeitslager *n*; **5.** a) Arbeits-, Werktag *m*: *on* ~**s** werktags.

work·er ['wɜːkə] *s*. **1.** a) Arbeiter(in), b) Angestellte(r *m*) *f*, c) Fachmann *m*, d) *allg*. Arbeitskraft *f*: ~**s** Belegschaft *f*, Arbeiterschaft *f*; **2.** *fig*. Urheber(in); **3.** *a*. ~ **ant**, ~ **bee** *zo*. Arbeiterin *f* (*Ameise*, *Biene*); ~ **di·rec·tor** *s*. ♣ 'Arbeitsdi,rektor *m*; ~ **par·tic·i·pa·tion** *s*. ♣ Mitbestimmung *f*.

'work| fel·low *s*. 'Arbeitskame,rad *m*; **'~flow** *s*. Arbeitsfluss *m*; **'~flow chart** *s*. Arbeitsablaufplan *m*; **'~force** *s*. ♣ **1.** Belegschaft *f*, **2.** 'Arbeitskräftepotenzi,al *n*; **'~girl** *s*. Fa'brikarbeiterin *f*; **'~horse** *s*. Arbeitspferd *n* (*a. fig*.); **'~house** *s*. **1.** *Brit. obs*. Armenhaus *n* (mit Arbeitszwang); **2.** ⚖ *Am*. Arbeitshaus *n*.

work·ing ['wɜːkɪŋ] **I** *s*. **1.** Arbeiten *n*; **2.** *a. pl*. Tätigkeit *f*, Wirken *n*; **3.** ⚙ Be-, Verarbeitung *f*; **4.** ⚙ a) Funktionieren *n*, b) Arbeitsweise *f*; **5.** Lösen *n e-s Problems*; **6.** mühsame Arbeit, Kampf *m*; **7.** Gärung *f*; **8.** *mst pl*. ⚒, *min*. a) Abbau *m*, b) Grube *f*; **II** *adj*. **9.** arbeitend, berufs-, werktätig: ~ *population*; ~ *student* Werkstudent *m*; **10.** Arbeits...: ~ *method* Arbeitsverfahren *n*; ~ *week* Arbeitswoche *f*; **11.** ⚙, ♣ Betriebs...(-kapital, -kosten, ⚡ -spannung *etc*.); **12.** grundlegend, Ausgangs..., Arbeits...: ~ *hypothesis*; ~ *title* Arbeitstitel *m* (*e-s Buchs etc*.); **13.** brauchbar, praktisch: ~ *knowledge* ausreichende Kenntnisse; ~ *class s*. Arbeiterklasse *f*; ~**'class** *adj*. der Arbeiterklasse, Arbeiter...; ~ **con·di·tion** *s*. **1.** ⚙ a) Betriebszustand *m*, b) *pl*. Betriebsbedingungen *pl*.; **2.** Arbeitsverhältnis *n*; ~ **day** → *workday*; ~ **draw·ing** *s*. ⚙ Werk(statt)zeichnung *f*; ~ **hour** *s*. Arbeitsstunde *f*; *pl*. Arbeitszeit *f*; ~ **load** *s*. **1.** ⚡ Betriebsbelastung *f*; **2.** ⚙ Nutzlast *f*; ~ **lunch** *s*. Arbeitsessen *n*; ~ **ma·jor·i·ty** *s*. *pol*. arbeitsfähige Mehrheit; **'~man** *s*. [*irr*.] → *workman*; ~ **mod·el** *s*. ⚙ Ver'suchsmo,dell *n*; ~ **or·der** *s*. ⚙ Betriebszustand *m*: *in* ~ in betriebsfähigem Zustand; ~**'out** *s*. **1.** Ausarbeitung *f*; **2.** Lösung *f* (*e-r Aufgabe*); ~ **stroke** *s*. *mot*. Arbeitstakt *m*; ~ **sur·face** *s*. ⚙ Arbeits-, Lauffläche *f*.

work·less ['wɜːklɪs] *adj*. arbeitslos.

'work| load *s*. Arbeitspensum *f*; **'~man** [-mən] *s*. [*irr*.] **1.** Arbeiter *m*; **2.** Handwerker *m*; **'~man·like** [-laɪk], **'~man·ly** [-lɪ] *adj*. kunstgerecht, fach-

männisch; **'~man·ship** [-ʃɪp] *s*. **1.** *j-s* Werk *n*; **2.** Kunst(fertigkeit) *f*; **3.** *gute etc*. Ausführung; Verarbeitungsgüte *f*; Quali'tätsarbeit *f*; **'~mate** *s. bsd. Brit*. 'Arbeitskol,lege *m*, -kol,legin *f*; **'~men's com·pen·sa·tion act** [-mənz] *s*. Arbeiterunfallversicherungsgesetz *n*; **'~out** *s*. **1.** F *sport* (Konditi'ons)Training *n*; **2.** Versuch *m*, Erprobung *f*; **'~peo·ple** *s. pl*. Belegschaft *f*; ~ **per·mit** *s*. Arbeitserlaubnis *f*; **'~piece** *s*. ⚙ Arbeits-, Werkstück *n*; **'~place** *s. Am*. Arbeitsplatz *m*; ~ **shar·ing** *s*. ♣ Arbeitsaufteilung *f*; ~ **sheet** *s*. **1.** 'Arbeitsbogen *m*, -,unterlage *f*; **2.** *Am*. ♣ 'Rohbi,lanz *f*; **'~shop** *s*. **1.** Werkstatt *f*; ~ **drawing** ⚙ Werkstatt-, Konstruktionszeichnung *f*; **2.** *ped*. Werkraum *m*; **3.** *fig*. a) Werkstatt *f* (*e-r Künstlergruppe etc*.): ~ *theatre* (*Am. theater*) Werkstatttheater *n*, b) Workshop *m*, Kurs *m*, Semi'nar *n*; **'~shy** *adj*. arbeitsscheu; **'~sta·tion** *s*. **1.** Computer: 'Workstation *f*; **2.** Arbeitsbereich *m*, -platz *m*; ~ **stop·page** *s*. Arbeitsniederlegung *f*; **'~ta·ble** *s*. Werktisch *m*; **'~to·'rule** *s*. Dienst *m* nach Vorschrift; **'~wear** *s*. Arbeitskleidung *f*; **'~,wom·an** *s*. [*irr*.] Arbeiterin *f*.

world [wɜːld] **I** *s*. **1.** *allg*. Welt *f*: a) Erde *f*, b) Himmelskörper *m*, c) (Welt)All *n*, d) *fig. die* Menschen *pl*., *die* Leute *pl*., e) Sphäre *f*, Mili'eu *n*, f) (Na'tur)Reich *n*: (*animal*) *vegetable* ~ (Tier-) Pflanzenreich, -welt; *lower* ~ Unterwelt; *the commercial* ~, *the* ~ *of commerce* die Handelswelt; *the* ~ *of letters* die gelehrte Welt; *a* ~ *of difference* ein himmelweiter Unterschied; *other* ~**s** andere Welten; *all the* ~ die ganze Welt, jedermann; *all the* ~ *over* in der ganzen Welt; *all the* ~ *and his wife* F Gott u. die Welt; alles, was Beine hatte; *for all the* ~ in jeder Hinsicht; *for all the* ~ *like* (*od. as if*) genauso wie (*od. als ob*); *for all the* ~ *to see* vor aller Augen; *from all over the* ~ aus aller Herren Länder; *not for the* ~ nicht um die (*od.* alles in der) Welt; *in the* ~ (auf) der Welt; *out of this* (*od. the*) ~ *sl*. fantastisch; *bring* (*come*) *into the* ~ zur Welt bringen (kommen); *carry the* ~ *before one* glänzenden Erfolg haben; *have the best of both* ~**s** die Vorteile beider Seiten genießen; *put into the* ~ in die Welt setzen; *think the* ~ *of* große Stücke halten auf (*acc.*); *she is all the* ~ *to him* sie ist sein Ein u. Alles; *how goes the* ~ *with you?* wie gehts, wie stehts?; *what* (*who*) *in the* ~? was (wer) in aller Welt?; *it's a small* ~! die Welt ist ein Dorf!; **2.** *a* ~ *of* e-e Welt von, e-e Unmenge *Schwierigkeiten etc*.; **II** *adj*. **3.** Welt...: ~ *champion* (*language*, *literature*, *politics*, *record etc*.); ♀ **Court** *s*. Internationaler Ständiger Gerichtshof; ♀ **Cup** *s*. **1.** *Skisport etc*.: Weltcup *m*; **2.** Fußballweltmeisterschaft *f*; **'~,fa·mous** *adj*. weltberühmt.

world·li·ness ['wɜːldlɪnɪs] *s*. Weltlichkeit *f*, weltlicher Sinn.

world·ling ['wɜːldlɪŋ] *s*. Weltkind *n*.

world·ly ['wɜːldlɪ] *adj. u. adv*. **1.** weltlich, irdisch, zeitlich: ~ *goods* irdische Güter; **2.** weltlich (gesinnt): ~ *innocence* Weltfremdheit *f*; ~ *wisdom* Weltklugheit *f*; **'~·wise** *adj*. weltklug.

world| pow·er *s. pol*. Weltmacht *f*; ~ **se·ries** *s. Baseball*: US-Meisterschaftsspiele *pl*.; **'~,shak·ing** *adj. a. iro*. welterschütternd: *it isn't* ~ *after all*; ~ **view** *s*. Weltanschauung *f*; ♀ **War** *s*. Welt-

krieg *m*: **~ I** (**II**) erster (zweiter) Weltkrieg; '~-,**wea·ry** *adj.* weltverdrossen; '**~·wide** *adj.* weltweit, auf der ganzen Welt: **~ reputation** Weltruf *m*; **~ strategy** ✕ Großraumstrategie *f*; ♀ **Wide Web** *s.* World Wide Web *n* (*im Internet*).
worm [wɜːm] **I** *s.* **1.** *zo.* Wurm *m* (*a. fig. contp. Person*): **even a ~ will turn** *fig.* auch der Wurm krümmt sich, wenn er getreten wird; **2.** *pl.* ✵ Würmer *pl.*; **3.** ✿ a) (Schrauben-, Schnecken)Gewinde *n*, b) (Förder-, Steuer- *etc.*)Schnecke *f*, c) (Rohr-, Kühl)Schlange *f*; **II** *v/t.* **4. ~ one's way** (*od. o.s.*) a) sich *wohin* schlängeln, b) *fig.* sich einschleichen (**into** in *j-s Vertrauen etc.*); **5. ~ a secret out of s.o.** j-m ein Geheimnis entlocken; **6.** ✵ von Würmern befreien; **III** *v/i.* **7.** sich schlängeln, kriechen; **8.** sich winden; **~ drive** *s.* ✿ Schneckenantrieb *m*; '~-,**eat·en** *adj.* **1.** wurmstichig; **2.** *fig.* veraltet; **~ gear** *s.* ✿ **1.** Schneckengetriebe *n*; **2.** → **worm wheel**; '**~'s-eye view** *s.* 'Froschperspek,tive *f*; **~ thread** *s.* ✿ Schneckengewinde *n*; **~ wheel** *s.* ✿ Schneckenrad *n*; '~·**wood** *s.* **1.** ♀ Wermut *m*; **2.** *fig.* Bitterkeit *f*: **be** (**gall and**) **~ to** j-n bitter ankommen.
worm·y ['wɜːmɪ] *adj.* **1.** wurmig, voller Würmer; **2.** wurmstichig; **3.** wurmartig; **4.** *fig.* kriecherisch.
worn [wɔːn] **I** *p.p. von* **wear¹**; **II** *adj.* **1.** getragen (*Kleider*); **2.** → **worn-out** 1; **3.** erschöpft, abgespannt; **4.** *fig.* abgedroschen: **~ joke**; ,~-'**out** *adj.* **1.** abgetragen, -genutzt; **2.** völlig erschöpft, todmüde, zermürbt; **3.** → **worn** 4.
wor·ried ['wʌrɪd] *adj.* **1.** gequält; **2.** sorgenvoll, besorgt; **3.** beunruhigt, ängstlich; '**wor·ri·er** [-ɪə] *s.* j-d, der sich ständig Sorgen macht; '**wor·ri·ment** [-ɪmənt] *s.* F **1.** Plage *f*, Quäle'rei *f*; **2.** Angst *f*, Sorge *f*; '**wor·ri·some** [-ɪsəm] *adj.* **1.** quälend; **2.** lästig; **3.** beunruhigend; **4.** unruhig.
wor·ry ['wʌrɪ] **I** *v/t.* **1.** a) zausen, schütteln, beuteln, b) *Tier* (ab)würgen (*Hund etc.*); **2.** quälen, plagen (*a. j-n belästigen*); *fig.* j-m zusetzen: **~ s.o. into a decision** j-n so lange quälen, bis er e-e Entscheidung trifft; **~ s.o. out of s.th.** a) j-n mühsam von et. abbringen, b) j-n durch unablässiges Quälen um et. bringen; **3.** a) ärgern, b) beunruhigen, quälen, *j-m* Sorgen machen: **~ o.s.** → 7; **4.** ~ **out** *Plan etc.* ausknobeln; **II** *v/i.* **5.** zerren, reißen (**at** an *dat.*); **6.** sich quälen *od.* plagen; **7.** sich beunruhigen, sich Gedanken *od.* Sorgen machen (**about, over** um, wegen); **8.** ~ **along** sich mühsam *od.* mit knapper Not durchschlagen; **~ through s.th.** sich durch et. hindurchquälen; **III** *s.* **9.** Kummer *m*, Besorgnis *f*, Sorge *f*, (innere) Unruhe; **10.** (Ursache *f* von) Ärger *m*, Aufregung *f*; **11.** Quälgeist *m*; **12.** a) Schütteln *n*, Beuteln *n*, b) Abwürgen *n* (*bsd. vom Hund*); '**wor·ry·ing** [-ɪŋ] *adj.* □ beunruhigend, quälend.
worse [wɜːs] **I** *adj.* (*comp. von* **bad, evil, ill**) **1.** schlechter, schlimmer (*beide a.* ✵), übler, ärger: **~ and ~** immer schlechter *od.* schlimmer; **the ~** desto schlimmer; **so much** (*od.* **all**) **the ~** umso schlimmer; **~ luck!** leider!, unglücklicherweise!, umso schlimmer!; **to make it ~** (*Redew.*) um das Unglück voll zu machen; → **wear¹** 14; **he is ~ than yesterday** es geht ihm schlechter als gestern; **2.** schlechter gestellt: (**not**) **to be the ~ for** (keinen) Schaden gelitten haben durch, (nicht) schlechter ge-

stellt sein wegen; **he is none the ~** (**for it**) er ist darum nicht übler dran; **you would be none the ~ for a walk** ein Spaziergang würde dir gar nichts schaden; **be** (**none**) **the ~ for drink** (nicht) betrunken sein; **II** *adv.* **3.** schlechter, schlimmer, ärger: **none the ~** nicht schlechter; **be ~ off** schlechter daran sein; **you could do ~ than ...** du könntest ruhig ...; **III** *s.* **4.** Schlechtere(s) *n*, Schlimmere(s) *n*: **~ followed** Schlimmeres folgte; → **better¹** 2; **from bad to ~** vom Regen in die Traufe; **a change for the ~** e-e Wendung zum Schlechten; '**wors·en** [-sn] **I** *v/t.* **1.** schlechter machen, verschlechtern; **2.** *Unglück etc.* verschlimmern; **3.** *j-n* schlechter stellen; **II** *v/i.* **4.** sich verschlechtern; verschlimmern; '**wors·en·ing** [-snɪŋ] *s.* Verschlechterung *f*, -schlimmerung *f*.
wor·ship ['wɜːʃɪp] *s.* **1.** *eccl.* a) (*a. fig.*) Anbetung *f*, Verehrung *f*, Kult(us) *m*, b) (**public ~** öffentlicher) Gottesdienst, Ritus *m*: **place of ~** Kultstätte *f*, Gotteshaus *n*; **the ~ of wealth** *fig.* die Anbetung des Reichtums; **2.** (*der, die, das*) Angebetete; **3. his** (**your**) ♀ *bsd. Brit.* Seiner (Euer) Hochwürden (*Anrede, jetzt bsd. für Bürgermeister u. Richter*); **II** *v/t.* **4.** anbeten, verehren, huldigen (*dat.*) (*alle a. fig. vergöttern*); **III** *v/i.* **5.** beten, s-e Andacht verrichten; **wor·ship·er** *Am.* → **worshipper**; '**wor·ship·ful** [-fʊl] *adj.* □ **1.** verehrend, anbetend (*Blick etc.*); **2.** *obs.* (ehr)würdig, achtbar; **3.** (*in der Anrede*) hochwohllöblich, hochverehrt; '**wor·ship·per** [-pə] *s.* **1.** Anbeter(in), Verehrer(in): **~ of idols** Götzendiener *m*; **2.** Beter(in): **the ~s** die Andächtigen, die Kirchgänger.
worst [wɜːst] **I** *adj.* (*sup. von* **bad, evil, ill**) schlechtest, schlimmst, übelst, ärgst: **and, which is ~** und, was das Schlimmste ist; **II** *adv.* am schlechtesten *od.* übelsten, am schlimmsten *od.* ärgsten; **III** *s.* der (die, das) Schlechteste *od.* Schlimmste *od.* Ärgste: **at** (**the**) **~** schlimmstenfalls; **be prepared for the ~** aufs Schlimmste gefasst sein; **do one's ~** es so schlecht *od.* schlimm wie möglich machen; **do your ~!** mach, was du willst!; **let him do his ~!** soll er nur!; **get the ~ of it** den Kürzeren ziehen; **if** (*od.* **when**) **the ~ comes to the ~** wenn es zum Schlimmsten kommt, wenn alle Stricke reißen; **he was at his ~** er zeigte sich von seiner schlechtesten Seite, er war in denkbar schlechter Form; **see s.o.** (**s.th.**) **at his** (**its**) **~** j-n (et.) von der schlechtesten *od.* schwächsten Seite sehen; **the illness is at its ~** die Krankheit ist auf ihrem Höhepunkt; **the ~ of it is** das Schlimmste daran ist; **IV** *v/t.* übel'wältigen, schlagen.
worst case *s.* schlimmster (*od.* ungünstigster*) Fall; ,~-'**case** *adj.*: **~ scenario** schlimmster Fall; **in the ~ scenario** schlimmstenfalls.
wor·sted ['wʊstɪd] ✿ **I** *s.* **1.** Kammgarn *n*, -wolle *f*; **2.** Kammgarnstoff *m*; **II** *adj.* **3.** wollen, Woll...: **~ wool** Kammwolle *f*; **~ yarn** Kammgarn *n*; **4.** Kammgarn...
wort¹ [wɜːt] *in Zssgn* ...kraut *n*, ...wurz *f*.
wort² [wɜːt] *s.* (Bier)Würze *f*: **original ~** Stammwürze.
worth [wɜːθ] **I** *adj.* **1.** (*e-n bestimmten Betrag*) wert (*to dat. od.* für): **he is ~ a million** er besitzt *od.* verdient e-e Million, er ist e-e Million wert; **for all you are ~** F so sehr du kannst, ,auf Teufel

komm raus'; **my opinion for what it may be ~** m-e unmaßgebliche Meinung; **take it for what it is ~!** *fig.* nimm es für das, was es wirklich ist!; **2.** *fig.* würdig, wert (*gen.*): **~ doing** wert getan zu werden; **~ mentioning** (**reading, seeing**) erwähnens- (lesens-, sehens-)wert; **be ~ the trouble, be ~ it** F sich lohnen, der Mühe wert sein; → **powder** 1, **while** 1; **II** *s.* **3.** Wert *m* (*a. fig. Bedeutung, Verdienst*): **of no ~** wertlos; **get the ~ of one's money** für sein Geld et. (Gleichwertiges) bekommen; **20 pence's ~ of stamps** Briefmarken im Wert von 20 Pence, für 20 Pence Briefmarken; **men of ~** verdiente *od.* verdienstvolle Leute.
wor·thi·ly ['wɜːðɪlɪ] *adv.* **1.** nach Verdienst, angemessen; **2.** mit Recht; **3.** würdig; '**wor·thi·ness** [-ɪnɪs] *s.* Wert *m*; **worth·less** ['wɜːθlɪs] *adj.* □ **1.** wertlos; **2.** *fig.* un-, nichtswürdig.
,**worth'while** *adj.* lohnend, der Mühe wert.
wor·thy ['wɜːðɪ] **I** *adj.* □ → **worthily**; **1.** würdig, achtbar, angesehen; **2.** würdig, wert (**of** *gen.*): **be ~ of** e-r Sache wert *od.* würdig sein, *et.* verdienen; **he is not ~ of her** er ist ihrer nicht wert *od.* würdig; **~ of credit** a) glaubwürdig, b) ✝ kreditwürdig; **~ of a better cause** e-r besseren Sache würdig; **3.** würdig (*Gegner, Nachfolger etc.*), angemessen (*Belohnung*); **4.** *humor.* trefflich, wacker (*Person*); **II** *s.* **5.** große Per'sönlichkeit, Größe *f*, Held(in) (*mst pl.*); **6.** *humor. der* Wackere.
would [wʊd; wəd] **1.** *pret. von* **will¹** I: a) wollte(st), wollten: **he ~ not go** er wollte durchaus nicht gehen, b) pflegte(st), pflegten zu (*oft unübersetzt*): **he ~ take a walk every day** er pflegte täglich e-n Spaziergang zu machen; **now and then a bird ~ call** ab u. zu ertönte ein Vogelruf; **you ~ do that!** du musstest das natürlich tun!, das sieht dir ähnlich!, c) *fragend:* würdest *du*?, würden *Sie*?: **~ you pass me the salt, please?**, d) *vermutend:* **that ~ be 3 dollars** das wären (dann) 3 Dollar; **it ~ seem that** es scheint fast, dass; **2.** *konditional:* würde(st), würden: **she ~ do it if she could**; **he ~ have come if** ... er wäre gekommen, wenn ...; **3.** *pret. von* **will¹** II: *ich wollte od. wünschte od. möchte:* **I ~ it were otherwise**; **~** (**to**) **God** wollte Gott; **I ~ have you know** ich muss Ihnen (schon) sagen.
would-be ['wʊdbiː] *adj.* **1.** Möchtegern...: **~ critic** Kritikaster *m*; **~ painter** Farbenkleckser *m*; **~ poet** Dichterling *m*; **~ huntsman** Sonntagsjäger *m*; **~ witty** geistreich sein sollend (*Bemerkung etc.*); **2.** angehend, zukünftig: **~ author**, **~ wife**; **II** *s.* **3.** Gernegroß *m*, Möchtegern *m*.
wound¹ [waʊnd] *pret. u. p.p. von* **wind²** *u.* **wind³**.
wound² [wuːnd] **I** *s.* **1.** Wunde *f* (*a. fig.*), Verletzung *f*, -wundung *f*: **~ of entry** (**exit**) ✕ Einschuss *m* (Ausschuss *m*); **2.** *fig.* Verletzung *f*, Kränkung *f*; **II** *v/t.* **3.** verwunden, ver'letzen (*beide a. fig. kränken*); '**wound·ed** [-dɪd] *adj.* verwundet, verletzt (*beide a. fig. gekränkt*): **~ veteran** Kriegsversehrte(r) *m*; **the ~** die Verwundeten; **~ vanity** gekränkte Eitelkeit.
wove [wəʊv] *pret. u. obs. p.p. von* **weave**; '**wo·ven** [-vən] *p.p. von* **weave**: **~ goods** Web-, Wirkwaren.
wove pa·per *s.* ✿ Ve'linpa,pier *n*.
wow [waʊ] **I** *int.* Mann!, toll!; **II** *s. bsd.*

Am. sl. a) Bombenerfolg *m*, b) ‚tolles Ding‘, c) ‚toller Kerl‘, ‚tolle Frau‘ *etc.*: **he** (**it**) **is a ~** er (es) ist ’ne Wucht; **III** *v/t.* *j-n* hinreißen.

wrack[1] [ræk] *s.* **1.** → **wreck** 1 *u.* 2; **2. ~ and ruin** Untergang *u.* Verderben; **go to ~** untergehen; **3.** Seetang *m.*

wrack[2] → **rack**[4] I.

wraith [reɪθ] *s.* **1.** Geistererscheinung *f* (*bsd. von gerade Gestorbenen*); **2.** Geist *m*, Gespenst *n.*

wran·gle [ˈræŋgl] **I** *v/i.* (sich) zanken *od.* streiten, sich in den Haaren liegen; **II** *s.* Streit *m*, Zank *m*; **'wran·gler** [-lə] *s.* **1.** Zänker(in), streitsüchtige Per'son; **2.** *univ. Brit.* Student in Cambridge, der bei der höchsten mathematischen Abschlussprüfung den 1. Grad erhalten hat; **3.** guter Debattierer; **4.** *Am.* Cowboy *m.*

wrap [ræp] **I** *v/t.* [*irr.*] **1.** wickeln, hüllen; *a.* *Arme* schlingen (**round** um *acc.*); **2.** *mst* **~ up** (ein)wickeln, (-)packen, (-)hüllen, (-)schlagen (**in** in *acc.*): **~ o.s. up** (**well**) sich warm anziehen; **3. ~ up** F a) *et.* glücklich ‚über die Bühne‘ bringen, b) abschließen, beenden; **~ it up** die Sache (erfolgreich) zu Ende führen; **that ~s it up** (**for today**)*!* das wärs (für heute)!; **4.** *oft* **~ up** *fig.* (ein)hüllen, verbergen, *Tadel etc.* (ver)kleiden (**in** in *acc.*): **~ped up in mystery** *fig.* geheimnisvoll, rätselhaft; **~ped** (*od.* **wrapt**) **in silence** in Schweigen gehüllt; **be ~ped up in** a) völlig in Anspruch genommen sein von (*e-r Arbeit etc.*), ganz aufgehen in (*s-r Arbeit, s-n Kindern etc.*), b) versunken sein in (*acc.*); **5.** *fig.* verwickeln, -stricken (**in** in *acc.*); **II** *v/i.* [*irr.*] **6.** sich einhüllen: **~ up well!** zieh dich warm an!; **7.** sich legen *od.* wickeln *od.* schlingen (**round** um); **8.** sich legen (**over** um) (*Kleider*); **9. ~ up!** *sl.* halts Maul!; **III** *s.* **10.** Hülle *f*, *bsd.* a) Decke *f*, Schal *m*, Pelz *m*, c) 'Umhang *m*, Mantel *m*: **keep s.th. under ~s** *fig.* et. geheim halten; **'~·a·round I** *adj.* ❂ Rundum..., Vollsicht...(-*verglasung*): **~ windshield** (*Brit.* **windscreen**) *mot.* Panoramascheibe *f*; **II** *s.* Wickelbluse *f*, -kleid *n.*

wrap·per [ˈræpə] *s.* **1.** (Ein)Packer(in); **2.** Hülle *f*, Decke *f*, 'Überzug *m*, Verpackung *f*; **3.** ('Buch),Umschlag *m*, Schutzhülle *f*; **4.** *a.* **postal ~** ✉ Kreuz-, Streifband *n*; **5.** a) Schal *m*, b) 'Überwurf *m*, c) Morgenrock *m*; **6.** Deckblatt *n* (*der Zigarre*); **'wrap·ping** [-pɪŋ] *s.* **1.** *mst pl.* Um'hüllung *f*, Hülle *f*, Verpackung *f*; **2.** Ein-, Verpacken *n*: **~ paper** Einwickel-, Packpapier *n.*

wrapt [ræpt] *pret. u. p.p. von* **wrap**.

wrath [rɒθ] *s.* Zorn *m*, Wut *f*: **the ~ of God** der Zorn Gottes; **he looked like the ~ of God** F er sah grässlich aus; **'wrath·ful** [-fʊl] *adj.* □ zornig, grimmig, wutentbrannt; **'wrath·y** [-θɪ] *adj.* □ *bsd.* F → **wrathful**.

wreak [riːk] *v/t.* **1.** *Schäden etc.* anrichten, *Chaos etc.* verursachen, stiften; **2.** *Rache* (aus)üben, *Wut etc.* auslassen ([**up**]**on** an *dat.*).

wreath [riːθ] *pl.* **wreaths** [-ðz] *s.* **1.** Kranz *m* (*a. fig.*), Gir'lande *f*, (Blumen-)Gewinde *n*; **2.** (*Rauch- etc.*)Ring *m*; **3.** Windung *f* (*e-s Seiles etc.*); **4.** (Schnee-*etc.*)Wehe *f*; **wreathe** [riːð] **I** *v/t.* **1.** winden, wickeln (**round**, **about** um); **2.** a) *Kranz etc.* flechten, winden, b) (zu Kränzen) flechten; **3.** um'kränzen, -'geben, -'winden; **4.** bekränzen, schmücken; **5.** kräuseln: **~d in smiles** lächelnd; **II** *v/i.* **6.** sich winden *od.* wi-

ckeln; **7.** sich ringeln *od.* kräuseln (*Rauchwolke etc.*).

wreck [rek] **I** *s.* **1.** ⚓ a) (Schiffs)Wrack *n*, b) Schiffbruch *m*, Schiffsunglück *n*, c) ⚖ Strandgut *n*; **2.** Wrack *n* (*mot. etc.*, *a. fig. bsd. Person*), Ru'ine *f*, Trümmerhaufen *m* (*a. fig.*): **nervous ~** *fig.* Nervenbündel *n*; **she is the ~ of her former self** sie ist nur (noch) ein Schatten ihrer selbst; **3.** *pl.* Trümmer *pl.* (*oft fig.*); **4.** *fig.* a) Ru'in *m*, 'Untergang *m*, b) Zerstörung *f*, Vernichtung *f* von *Hoffnungen etc.*; **II** *v/t.* **5.** *allg.* zertrümmern, -stören, *Schiff* zum Scheitern bringen (*a. fig.*): **be ~ed** a) → 8, b) in Trümmer gehen, c) entgleisen (*Zug*); **6.** *fig.* zu'grunde richten, ruinieren, ka'puttmachen, *Gesundheit a.* zerrütten, *Pläne, Hoffnungen etc.* vernichten, zerstören; **7.** ⚓, ❂ abwracken; **III** *v/i.* **8.** Schiffbruch erleiden, scheitern (*a. fig.*); **9.** verunglücken; **10.** zerstört *od.* vernichtet werden (*mst fig.*); **'wreck·age** [-kɪdʒ] *s.* **1.** Wrack(teile *pl.*) *n*, (Schiffs-, *allg.* Unfall)Trümmer *pl.*; **2.** *fig.* Strandgut *n* (*des Lebens*); **3.** → **wreck** 4; **wrecked** [-kt] *adj.* **1.** gestrandet, gescheitert (*a. fig.*); **2.** schiffbrüchig (*Person*); **3.** zertrümmert, zerstört, vernichtet (*alle a. fig.*); zerrüttet (*Gesundheit etc.*): **~ car** Schrottauto *n*; **'wreck·er** [-kə] *s.* **1.** Strandräuber *m*; **2.** Sabo'teur *m*, Zerstörer *m* (*beide a. fig.*); **3.** ⚓ a) Bergungsschiff *n*, b) Bergungsarbeiter *m*; **4.** ❂ Abbrucharbeiter *m*; **5.** *mot. Am.* Abschleppwagen *m*; **'wreck·ing** [-kɪŋ] *adj.* **1.** *Am.* Bergungs...: **~ crew** od. **service** (**truck**) *mot.* Abschleppdienst *m* (-wagen *m*); **2.** *Am.* Abbruch...: **~ company** Abbruchfirma *f.*

wren [ren] *s. orn.* Zaunkönig *m.*

Wren [ren] *s.* ✕ *Brit.* F Angehörige *f* des **Women's Royal Naval Service**, Ma'rinehelferin *f.*

wrench [rentʃ] **I** *s.* **1.** (drehender *od.* heftiger) Ruck, heftige Drehung; **2.** ✚ Verzerrung *f*, -renkung *f*, -stauchung *f*: **give a ~ to** → 7; **3.** *fig.* Verdrehung *f*, -zerrung *f*; **4.** *fig.* (Trennungs)Schmerz *m*: **it was a great ~** der Abschied tat sehr weh; **5.** ❂ Schraubenschlüssel *m*; **II** *v/t.* **6.** (mit e-m Ruck) reißen, zerren, ziehen: **~ s.th.** (**away**) **from s.o.** j-m et. entwinden *od.* -reißen (*a. fig.*); **~ open** *Tür etc.* aufreißen; **7.** ✚ verrenken, verstauchen; **8.** verdrehen, verzerren (*a. fig. entstellen*).

wrest [rest] **I** *v/t.* **1.** (gewaltsam) reißen: **~ from** *j-m et.* entreißen, -winden, *fig.* a. abringen; **2.** *fig. Sinn, Gesetz etc.* verdrehen; **II** *s.* **3.** Ruck *m*, Reißen *n*; **4.** ♪ Stimmhammer *m.*

wres·tle [ˈresl] **I** *v/i.* **1.** *a. sport* ringen (*a. fig.* **for** um, **with** God mit Gott); **2.** *fig.* sich abmühen, kämpfen (**with** mit); **II** *v/t.* **3.** ringen *od.* kämpfen mit; **III** *s.* **4.** → **wrestling** I; **5.** *fig.* Ringen *n*, schwerer Kampf; **'wres·tler** [-lə] *s. sport* Ringer *m*, Ringkämpfer *m*; **'wres·tling** [-lɪŋ] **I** *s. bsd. sport u. fig.* Ringen *n*; **II** *adj.* Ring...: **~ match** Ringkampf *m.*

wretch [retʃ] **1.** *a. poor* **~** armes Wesen, armer Kerl *od.* Teufel (*a. iro.*); **2.** Schuft *m*; **3.** *iro.* Wicht *m*, ‚Tropf‘ *m*; **wretch·ed** [ˈretʃɪd] *adj.* □ **1.** elend, unglücklich, *a.* deprimiert (*Person*); **2.** erbärmlich, mise'rabel, schlecht, dürftig; **3.** scheußlich, ekelhaft, unangenehm; *a.* **gesundheitlich** elend: **feel ~** sich elend *od.* schlecht fühlen; **wretch·ed·ness** [ˈretʃɪdnɪs] *s.* **1.** Elend *n*, Un-

glück *n*; **2.** Erbärmlichkeit *f*, Gemeinheit *f.*

wrig·gle [ˈrɪgl] **I** *v/i.* **1.** sich winden (*a. fig.* verlegen *od.* listig), sich schlängeln, zappeln; **~ out** sich herauswinden (**of s.th.** aus e-r Sache) (*a. fig.*); **II** *v/t.* **2.** wackeln *od.* zappeln mit; mit *den Hüften* schaukeln; **3.** schlängeln, winden, ringeln: **~ o.s.** (**along**, **through**) sich (entlang-, hindurch)winden; **~ o.s. into** *fig.* sich einschleichen in (*acc.*); **~ o.s. out of** sich herauswinden aus; **III** *s.* **4.** Windung *f*, Krümmung *f*; **5.** schlängelnde Bewegung, Schlängeln *n*, Ringeln *n*, Wackeln *n*; **'wrig·gler** [-lə] *s.* **1.** Ringeltier *n*, Wurm *m*; **2.** *fig.* aalglatter Kerl.

wright [raɪt] *s. in Zssgn* ...verfertiger *m*, ...macher *m*, ...bauer *m.*

wring [rɪŋ] *v/t.* [*irr.*] **1. ~ out** Wäsche *etc.* (aus)wringen, auswinden; **2.** a) *e-m Tier* den Hals abdrehen, b) *j-m* den Hals 'umdrehen: **I'll ~ your neck**; **3.** verdrehen, -zerren (*a. fig.*); **4.** a) *Hände* (*verzweifelt*) ringen, b) *j-m* die Hand (*kräftig*) drücken, pressen; **5.** *j-n* drücken (*Schuh etc.*); **6. ~ s.o.'s heart** *fig.* j-m sehr zu Herzen gehen, j-m ans Herz greifen; **7.** abringen, entreißen, -winden (**from s.o.** j-m): **~ admiration from** *j-m* Bewunderung abnötigen; **8.** *fig.* Geld, Zustimmung erpressen (**from, out of** von); **II** *s.* **9.** Wringen *n*, (Aus)Winden *n*; Pressen *n*, Druck *m*: **give s.th. a ~** → 1 *u.* 4b; **wring·er** [ˈrɪŋə] *s.* 'Wringma,schine *f*: **go through the ~** F ‚durch den Wolf gedreht werden‘; **wring·ing** [ˈrɪŋɪŋ] *adj.* **1.** Wring...: **~ machine** → **wringer**; **2.** *a.* **~ wet** F klatschnass.

wrin·kle[1] [ˈrɪŋkl] **I** *s.* **1.** Runzel *f*, Falte *f* (*im Gesicht*); *a.* Kniff *m* (*in Papier etc.*); **2.** Unebenheit *f*, Vertiefung *f*, Furche *f*; **II** *v/t.* **3.** *oft* **~ up** a) *Stirn, Augenbrauen* runzeln, b) *Nase* rümpfen; **4.** *Stoff, Papier etc.* falten, kniffen, zerknittern; **III** *v/i.* **5.** Falten werfen, Runzeln bekommen, sich runzeln, runz(e)lig werden, knittern.

wrin·kle[2] [ˈrɪŋkl] *s.* F **1.** Kniff *m*, Trick *m*; **2.** Wink *m*, Tipp *m*; **3.** Neuheit *f*; **4.** Fehler *m.*

wrin·kly [ˈrɪŋklɪ] **I** *adj.* **1.** faltig, runz(e)lig (*Gesicht etc.*); **2.** leicht knitternd (*Stoff*); **3.** gekräuselt; **II** *s.* **4.** *Brit. sl.* ‚Grufti‘ *m.*

wrist [rɪst] *s.* **1.** Handgelenk *n*; **2.** ❂ → **wrist pin**; **'~·band** [-stb-] *s.* **1.** Bündchen *n*, ('Hemd)Man,schette *f*; **2.** Armband *n*; **'~·drop** *s.* ✚ Handgelenkslähmung *f.*

wrist·let [ˈrɪstlɪt] *s.* **1.** Pulswärmer *m*; **2.** Armband *n*: **~ watch** → **wristwatch**; **3.** *sport* Schweißband *n*; **4.** *humor. od. sl.* Handschelle *f.*

wrist pin *s.* ❂ Zapfen *m*, *bsd.* Kolbenbolzen *m*; **'~·watch** *s.* Armbanduhr *f.*

writ [rɪt] *s.* **1.** ⚖ a) behördlicher Erlass, b) gerichtlicher Befehl, c) *a.* **~ of summons** (Vor)Ladung *f*: **~ of attachment** a) Haftbefehl *m*, b) dinglicher Arrest(befehl); **~ of execution** Vollstreckungsbefehl *m*; **take out a ~ against s.o.**, **serve a ~ on s.o.** j-n vorladen (lassen); **2.** ⚖ *hist. Brit.* Urkunde *f*; **3.** *pol. Brit.* Wahlausschreibung *f* für das Parla'ment; **4. Holy** (*od.* **Sacred**) 𝔚 die Heilige Schrift.

write [raɪt] [*irr.*] **I** *v/t.* **1.** *et.* schreiben: **writ(ten) large** *fig.* deutlich, leicht erkennbar; **2.** (auf-, nieder)schreiben, schriftlich niederlegen, notieren, auf-

zeichnen: *it is written that* es steht geschrieben, dass; *it is written on* (*od. all over*) *his face* es steht ihm im Gesicht geschrieben; **3.** *Scheck etc.* ausschreiben, -füllen; **4.** *Papier etc.* voll schreiben; **5.** *j-m et.* schreiben, schriftlich mitteilen: ~ *s.o. s.th.*; **6.** *Buch etc.* verfassen, *a. Musik* schreiben: ~ *poetry* dichten, Gedichte schreiben; **7. ⊗** *e-e CD* brennen (*im CD-Brenner*); **8.** ~ *o.s.* sich bezeichnen als; **II** *v/i.* **9.** schreiben; **10.** schreiben, schriftstellern; **11.** schreiben, schriftliche Mitteilung machen: *it's nothing to* ~ *home about fig.* das ist nichts Besonderes, darauf brauchst du dir (braucht er sich *etc.*) nichts einzubilden; ~ *to ask* schriftlich anfragen; ~ *for s.th.* et. anfordern, sich et. kommen lassen; *Zssgn mit adv.:*
write| down *v/t.* **1.** → *write* 2; **2.** *fig.* a) (schriftlich) her'absetzen, herziehen über (*acc.*), b) nennen, bezeichnen *od.* hinstellen als; **3.** ✝ abschreiben; ~ **in** *v/t.* einfügen, -tragen; ~ **off** *v/t.* **1.** (schnell) her'unterschreiben, ‚hinhauen'; **2.** ✝ (vollständig) abschreiben (*a. fig.*); ~ **out** *v/t.* **1.** *Namen etc.* ausschreiben; **2.** abschreiben; ~ *fair* ins Reine schreiben; **3.** *write o.s. out* sich ausschreiben (*Autor*); ~ **up** *v/t.* **1.** ausführlich darstellen *od.* beschreiben; **2.** *ergänzend* nachtragen, *Text* weiterführen; **3.** loben(d erwähnen), her'ausstreichen, anpreisen; **4.** ✝ e-n zu hohen Buchwert angeben für.
'write|-down *s.* ✝ Abschreibung *f:* '~**-off** *s.* a) ✝ (gänzliche) Abschreibung, b) *mot.* F To'talschaden: *it's a* ~ F das können wir abschreiben; '~-**pro**‚**tected** *adj. Computer:* schreibgeschützt.
writ·er ['raɪtə] *s.* **1.** Schreiber(in): ~'*s cramp* (*od. palsy*) Schreibkrampf *m*; **2.** Schriftsteller(in), Verfasser(in), Autor *m*, Au'torin *f: the* ~ der Verfasser (= *ich*); ~ *for the press* Journalist(in); **3.** ~ *to the signet Scot.* No'tar *m*, Rechtsanwalt *m*; '**writ·er·ship** [-ʃɪp] *s. Brit.* Schreiberstelle *f.*
'write-up *s.* **1.** lobender Pressebericht *od.* Ar'tikel; **2.** ✝ zu hohe Buchwertangabe.
writhe [raɪð] *v/i.* **1.** sich krümmen, sich winden (*with* vor *dat.*); **2.** *fig.* sich winden, leiden (*under, at* unter e-r Krän-

kung *etc.*).
writ·ing ['raɪtɪŋ] **I** *s.* **1.** Schreiben *n* (*Tätigkeit*); **2.** Schriftstelle'rei *f;* **3.** schriftliche Ausfertigung *od.* Abfassung; **4.** Schreiben *n*, Schriftstück *n*, et. Geschriebenes, *a.* Urkunde *f: in* ~ schriftlich; *the* ~ *on the wall fig.* die Schrift an der Wand, das Menetekel; **5.** Schrift *f, literarisches* Werk; Aufsatz *m*, Ar'tikel *m*; **6.** Brief *m*; **7.** Inschrift *f;* **8.** Schreibweise *f*, Stil *m*; **9.** (Hand)Schrift *f;* **II** *adj.* **10.** schreibend, *bsd.* schriftstellernd: ~ *man* Schriftsteller *m*; **11.** Schreib...; ~ *book s.* Schreibheft *n*; ~ *case s.* Schreibmappe *f;* ~ *desk s.* Schreibtisch *m*; ~ *pad s.* 'Schreibblock *m*; ~ *pa·per s.* 'Schreib-, 'Briefpa‚pier *n*; ~ *ta·ble s.* Schreibtisch *m*.
writ·ten ['rɪtn] **I** *p.p. von write;* **II** *adj.* **1.** schriftlich; ~ *evidence* ✄ Urkundenbeweis *m*; ~ *language* Schriftsprache *f;* **2.** geschrieben: ~ *law;* ~ *question parl.* kleine Anfrage.
wrong [rɒŋ] **I** *adj.* □ → *wrongly;* **1.** falsch, unrichtig, verkehrt, irrig: *be* ~ *a.* a) Unrecht haben, sich irren (*Person*), b) falsch gehen (*Uhr*); *you are* ~ *in believing* du irrst dich, wenn du glaubst; *prove s.o.* ~ beweisen, dass j-d im Irrtum ist; **2.** verkehrt, falsch: *bring the* ~ *book; do the* ~ *thing* das Falsche tun, es verkehrt machen; *get hold of the* ~ *end of the stick fig.* es völlig missverstehen, es verkehrt ansehen; *the* ~ *side* die verkehrte *od.* falsche (*von Stoff:* linke) Seite; (*the*) ~ *side out* das Innere nach außen (gekehrt) (*Kleidungsstück etc.*); *be on the* ~ *side of 40* über 40 (Jahre alt) sein; *he will laugh on the* ~ *side of his mouth* das Lachen wird ihm schon vergehen; *have got out of bed* (*on*) *the* ~ *side* F mit dem linken Bein zuerst aufgestanden sein; → *blanket* 1; **3.** nicht in Ordnung: *s.th. is* ~ *with it* es stimmt et. daran nicht; *what is* ~ *with you?* was ist los mit dir?, was hast du?; *what's* ~ *with ...?* a) was gibt es auszusetzen an (*dat.*)?, b) F wie wärs mit ...?; **4.** unrecht: *it is* ~ *of you to laugh;* **II** *adv.* **5.** falsch, unrichtig, verkehrt: *get it* ~ es ganz falsch verstehen; *go* ~ a) nicht richtig funktionieren *od.* gehen (*Uhr etc.*), b) schief gehen (*Vorhaben etc.*), c)

auf Abwege *od.* die schiefe Bahn geraten (*bsd. Frau*), d) fehlgehen; *where did we go* ~? was haben wir falsch gemacht?; *get in* ~ *with s.o. Am.* F es mit j-m verderben; *get s.o. in* ~ *Am.* F j-n in Misskredit bringen (*with* bei); *take s.th.* ~ et. übel nehmen; **III** *s.* **6.** Unrecht *n: do s.o.* ~ j-m ein Unrecht zufügen; **7.** Irrtum *m*, Unrecht *n: be in the* ~ Unrecht haben; *put s.o. in the* ~ j-n ins Unrecht setzen; **8.** Kränkung *f*, Beleidigung *f;* **9.** ✄ Rechtsverletzung *f: private* ~ Privatdelikt *n; public* ~ öffentliches Delikt; **IV** *v/t.* **10.** *j-m* Unrecht tun (*a. in Gedanken etc.*), *j-n* ungerecht behandeln: *I am* ~*ed* mir geschieht Unrecht; **11.** *j-m* schaden, Schaden zufügen, *j-n* benachteiligen; '~‚**do·er** *s.* Übel-, Missetäter(in), Sünder(in); '~‚**do·ing** *s.* **1.** Missetat *f*, Sünde *f;* **2.** Vergehen *n*, Verbrechen *n*.
wrong·ful ['rɒŋfʊl] *adj.* □ **1.** ungerecht; **2.** beleidigend, kränkend; **3.** ✄ unrechtmäßig, 'widerrechtlich, ungesetzlich.
‚**wrong'head·ed** *adj.* □ **1.** querköpfig, verbohrt (*Person*); **2.** verschroben, verdreht, hirnverbrannt.
wrong·ly ['rɒŋlɪ] *adv.* **1.** → *wrong* II; **2.** ungerechterweise, zu *od.* mit Unrecht; **3.** irrtümlicher-, fälschlicherweise; **wrong·ness** ['rɒŋnɪs] *s.* **1.** Unrichtigkeit *f*, Verkehrtheit *f*, Fehlerhaftigkeit *f;* **2.** Unrechtmäßigkeit *f;* **3.** Ungerechtigkeit *f.*
wrote [rəʊt] *pret. u. obs. p.p. von write.*
wroth [rəʊθ] *adj.* zornig, erzürnt.
wrought [rɔːt] **I** *pret. u. p.p. von work;* **II** *adj.* **1.** be-, ge-, verarbeitet: ~ *goods* Fertigwaren; **2.** a) gehämmert, geschmiedet, b) geschmiedeeisern; **3.** gewirkt; ~ *i·ron s.* Schmiedeeisen *n*; ‚~-'**i·ron** *adj.* schmiedeeisern; ~ *steel s.* Schmiede-, Schweißstahl *m*; ‚~-'**up** *adj.* aufgebracht, erregt.
wrung [rʌŋ] *pret. u. p.p. von wring.*
wry [raɪ] *adj.* □ **1.** schief, krumm, verzerrt: *make* (*od. pull*) *a* ~ *face* e-e Grimasse schneiden; **2.** *fig.* a) verschroben: ~ *notion*, b) gequält: ~ *smile*, c) sar'kastisch: ~ *humo(u)r*; '~**-mouthed** *adj.* **1.** schiefmäulig; **2.** *fig.* a) wenig schmeichelhaft, b) sar'kastisch; '~**-neck** *s. orn.* Wendehals *m*.

X, x [eks] **I** pl. **X's, x's, Xs, xs** ['eksɪz] s.
1. X n, x n (Buchstabe); **2.** ≯ a) x n (1.
unbekannte Größe od. abhängige Variable), b) x-Achse f, Ab'szisse f (im
Koordinatensystem); **3.** fig. X n, unbekannte Größe; **4.** → 6; **II** adj. **5.** X-...,
x-förmig; **6.** ~ **film** nicht jugendfreier
Film (ab 18).

Xan·thip·pe [zæn'θɪpɪ] s. fig. Xan'thippe
f, Hausdrachen m.

xe·nog·a·my [ziː'nɒgəmɪ] s. ♀ Fremdbe-
stäubung f.

xen·o·pho·bi·a [ˌzenə'fəʊbjə] s. Xeno-
pho'bie f, Fremden- od. Ausländerfeindlichkeit f; **xen·o·pho·bic** [-bɪk]

adj. xeno'phob, fremden- od. ausländerfeindlich.

xe·ra·si·a [zɪ'reɪzɪə] s. ✣ Trockenheit f
des Haares.

xe·ro·phyte ['zɪərəʊfaɪt] s. ♀ Trocken-
heitspflanze f.

xiph·oid ['zɪfɔɪd] adj. anat. **1.** schwertförmig; **2.** Schwertfortsatz...: ~ **appendage, ~ process** Schwertfortsatz m.

Xmas ['krɪsməs] F für **Christmas**.

X-ray [ˌeks'reɪ] **I** s. ✣, phys. **1.** X-Strahl
m, Röntgenstrahl m; **2.** Röntgenauf-
nahme f, -bild n; **II** v/t. **3.** röntgen: a) ein
Röntgenbild machen von, b) durch-
'leuchten; **4.** bestrahlen; **III** adj. **5.**

Röntgen...

xy·lene ['zaɪliːn] s. ✣ Xy'lol n.

xy·lo·graph ['zaɪləgrɑːf] s. Holzschnitt
m; **xy·log·ra·pher** [zaɪ'lɒgrəfə] s. Holzschneider m; **xy·lo·graph·ic** [ˌzaɪlə-
'græfɪk] adj. Holzschnitt...; **xy·log·ra·
phy** [zaɪ'lɒgrəfɪ] s. Xylogra'phie f,
Holzschneidekunst f.

xy·lo·phone ['zaɪləfəʊn] s. ♪ Xylo'phon
n.

xy·lose ['zaɪləʊs] s. ✣ Xy'lose f, Holz-
zucker m.

Y, y [waɪ] **I** pl. **Y's, y's, Ys, ys** [waɪz] s.
1. Y n, y n, Ypsilon n (Buchstabe); **2.**
⅍ a) y n (2. unbekannte Größe od. abhängige Variable), b) y-Achse f, Ordi-
'nate f (im Koordinatensystem); **II** adj.
3. Y-..., y-förmig, gabelförmig.

y- [ɪ] obs. Präfix zur Bildung des p.p.,
entsprechend dem deutschen ge-.

yacht [jɒt] ⚓ **I** s. **1.** (Segel-, Motor-)
Jacht f: **~ club** Jachtklub m; **2.** (Renn-)
Segler m; **II** v/i. **3.** auf e-r Jacht fahren;
4. (sport)segeln; **yacht·er** ['jɒtə] →
yachtsman; yacht·ing ['jɒtɪŋ] **I** s. **1.**
Jacht-, Segelsport m; **2.** (Sport)Segeln
n; **II** adj. **3.** Segel..., Jacht...

yachts·man ['jɒtsmən] s. [irr.] **1.** Jacht-
fahrer m; **2.** (Sport)Segler m; **'yachts-
man·ship** [-ʃɪp] s. Segelkunst f.

yah [jɑː] **I** int. a) puh!, b) ätsch!

ya·hoo [jə'huː] **I** s. **1.** bru'taler Kerl;
2. Saukerl m; **II** int. **3.** hurra!

yak¹ [jæk] v/i. F quasseln.

yak² [jæk] s. Yak m, Grunzochs m.

yank [jæŋk] F **I** v/t. (mit e-m Ruck heraus)ziehen, (hoch- etc.)reißen; **II** v/i.
reißen, heftig ziehen; **III** s. (heftiger)
Ruck.

Yank [jæŋk] F für **Yankee**.

Yan·kee ['jæŋkɪ] s. Yankee m (Spitzna-
me): a) Neu'engländer(in), b) Nord-
staatler(in) (der USA), c) (allg., von
Nichtamerikanern gebraucht) ('Nord-)
Ameri,kaner(in): **~ Doodle** amer.
Volkslied.

yap [jæp] **I** s. **1.** Kläffen n, Gekläff n; **2.**
F a) Gequassel n, b) ,Schnauze' f
(Mund); **II** v/i. **3.** kläffen; **4.** F a) quas-
seln, b) ,meckern'.

yard¹ [jɑːd] s. **1.** Yard n (= 0,914 m); **2.**
→ **yardstick** 1: **by the ~** yardweise; **~
goods** Kurzwaren; **3.** ⚓ Rah(e) f.

yard² [jɑːd] s. **1.** Hof(raum) m; **2.** Ar-
beits-, Bau-, Stapel)Platz m; **3.** 🚂 Brit.
Rangier-, Verschiebebahnhof m; **4. the
⅏** → **Scotland Yard**; **5.** ✗ Hof m, Gehege n: **poultry ~**; **6.** Am. Winterwei-
deplatz m (für Elche u. Rotwild).

yard·age ['jɑːdɪdʒ] s. in Yards angegebene Zahl od. Länge, Yards pl.

'yard·man [-mən] s. [irr.] **1.** 🚂 Rangier-,
Bahnhofsarbeiter m; **2.** ⚓ Werftarbei-
ter m; **3.** ✗ Stall-, Viehhofarbeiter m; **~
mas·ter** s. 🚂 Rangiermeister m;
'~·stick s. **1.** Yard-, Maßstock m; **2.**
fig. Maßstab m.

yarn [jɑːn] **I** s. **1.** Garn n; **2.** ⚓ Kabelgarn n; **3.** F abenteuerliche (a. weitS.
erlogene) Geschichte, (Seemanns)Garn
n: **spin a ~** e-e Abenteuergeschichte
erzählen, ein (Seemanns)Garn spin-
nen; **II** v/i. **4.** F (Geschichten) erzählen,
ein Garn spinnen, (mitein'ander)
klönen.

yar·row ['jærəʊ] s. ♣ Schafgarbe f.

yaw [jɔː] v/i. **1.** ⚓ gieren (vom Kurs
abkommen); **2.** ✈ (um Hochachse) gieren, scheren; **3.** fig. schwanken.

yawl [jɔːl] s. ⚓ **1.** Segeljolle f; **2.** Be'san-
kutter m.

yawn [jɔːn] **I** v/i. **1.** gähnen (a. fig. Abgrund etc.); **2.** fig. a) sich weit u. tief
auftun, b) weit offen stehen; **II** v/t. **3.**
gähnen(d sagen); **III** s. **4.** Gähnen n;
'yawn·ing [-nɪŋ] adj. □ gähnend (a.
fig.).

y·clept [ɪ'klept] adj. obs. od. humor. genannt, namens.

ye¹ [jiː] pron. obs. od. bibl. od. humor.
1. ihr, Ihr; **2.** euch, Euch, dir, Dir; **3.**
du, Du; **4.** F für **you: how d'ye do?**

ye² [jiː] archaisierend für **the.**

yea [jeɪ] **I** adv. **1.** ja; **2.** für'wahr, wahr-
'haftig; **3.** obs. ja so'gar; **II** s. **4.** Ja n; **5.**
parl. etc. Ja(stimme f) n: **~s and nays**
Stimmen für u. wider; **the ~s have it!**
der Antrag ist angenommen!

yean [jiːn] zo. **I** v/t. werfen (Lamm,
Zicklein); **II** v/i. a) lammen (Schaf), b)
zickeln (Ziege); **'yean·ling** [-lɪŋ] s. a)
Lamm n, b) Zicklein n.

year [jɪə] s. **1.** Jahr n: **~ of grace** Jahr
des Heils; **for ~s** jahrelang, seit Jahren,
auf Jahre hinaus; **~ in, ~ out** jahrein,
jahraus; **~ by ~, from ~ to ~, ~ after ~**
Jahr für Jahr; **in the ~ one** humor. vor
undenklichen Zeiten; **take ~s off s.o.**
j-n um Jahre jünger machen; **2.** pl. Alter n: **~s of discretion** gesetztes od.
vernünftiges Alter; **well on in ~s** hochbetagt; **be getting on in ~s** in die Jahre
kommen; **he bears his ~s well** er ist
für sein Alter noch recht rüstig; **3.** ped.
univ. Jahrgang m; **'~·book** s. Jahrbuch
n.

year·ling ['jɪəlɪŋ] **I** s. **1.** Jährling m: a)
einjähriges Tier, b) einjährige Pflanze;
2. Pferdesport: Einjährige(s) n; **II** adj.
3. einjährig.

'year·long adj. einjährig.

year·ly ['jɪəlɪ] **I** adj. jährlich, Jahres...; **II**
adv. jährlich, jedes Jahr (einmal).

yearn [jɜːn] v/i. **1.** sich sehnen, Sehnsucht haben (**for, after** nach, **to do** danach, zu tun); **2.** (bsd. Mitleid, Zuneigung) empfinden (**to[wards]** für, mit);
'yearn·ing [-nɪŋ] **I** s. Sehnsucht f, Sehnen n, Verlangen n; **II** adj. □ sehnsüchtig, sehnend, verlangend.

year 2000| com·pat·i·bil·i·ty [,jɪətuː-
'θaʊznd] s. Jahr-2000-Kompatibilität f,
-tauglichkeit f; **~ com·pat·i·ble** adj.
Jahr-2000-kompatibel, -tauglich; **~
com·pli·ance** Jahr-2000-Fähigkeit f;
~ com·pli·ant adj. Jahr-2000-fähig,
-tauglich; **~ con·form·i·ty** s. Jahr-2000-
-Fähigkeit f, -Tauglichkeit f; **~ con·ver-
sion** s. Jahr-2000-'Umstellung f; **~ sur-
viv·al plan·ning** s. Über'lebenspla-
nung f für das Jahr 2000.

yeast [jiːst] **I** s. **1.** (Bier-, Back)Hefe f;
2. Gischt f, Schaum m; **3.** fig. Triebkraft f; **II** v/i. **4.** gären; **~ pow·der** s.
Backpulver n.

yeast·y ['jiːstɪ] adj. **1.** heftig; **2.** gärend;
3. schäumend; **4.** fig. contp. leer, hohl;
5. fig. a) unstet, b) überschäumend.

yegg(·man) ['jeg(mən)] s. [irr.] Am. sl.
,Schränker' m, Geldschrankknacker m.

yell [jel] **I** v/i. **1.** schreien, brüllen (**with**
vor dat.); **II** v/t. **2.** gellen(d ausstoßen),
schreien; **III** s. **3.** gellender (Auf-)
Schrei; **4.** Am. univ. (rhythmischer)
Anfeuerungs- od. Schlachtruf.

yel·low ['jeləʊ] **I** adj. **1.** gelb (a. Rasse):
~-haired flachshaarig; **the ~ peril** die
gelbe Gefahr; **2.** fig. a) obs. neidisch,
missgünstig, b) F feig: **~ streak** feiger
Zug; **3.** sensati'onslüstern; → **yellow
paper, yellow press; II** s. **4.** Gelb n:
at ~ Am. bei (od. auf) Gelb (Verkehrsampel); **5.** Eigelb n; **6.** ♣, ⚕ od. vet.
Gelbsucht f; **III** v/t. **7.** gelb färben; **IV**
v/i. **8.** sich gelb färben, vergilben; **~
card** s.: **be shown the ~** Fußball: die
gelbe Karte (gezeigt) bekommen; **~
dog** s. **1.** Köter m, ,Prome'nadenmischung' f; **2.** fig. gemeiner od. feiger
Kerl; **II** adj. **3.** a) hundsgemein, b) feig;
4. Am. gewerkschaftsfeindlich; **~ earth**
s. min. **1.** Gelberde f; **2.** → **yellow
ochre; ~ fe·ver** s. ⚕ Gelbfieber n;
'~,ham·mer s. orn. Goldammer f.

yel·low·ish ['jeləʊɪʃ] adj. gelblich.

yel·low jack s. **1.** ⚕ Gelbfieber n; **2.** ⚓
Quaran'täneflagge f; **~ met·al** s.
'Muntzme,tall n; **~ o·chre** (Am.
o·cher) s. min. gelber Ocker, Gelberde f; **~ pag·es** s. pl. teleph. (die) gelben Seiten, Branchenverzeichnis n; **~
pa·per** s. Sensati'ons-, Re'volverblatt
n; **~ press** s. Sensati'ons-, Boule'vardpresse f; **~ soap** s. Schmierseife f.

yelp [jelp] **I** v/i. **1.** a) (auf)jaulen, b)
aufschreien; **2.** (a. v/t.) kreischen; **II** s.
3. a) (Auf)Jaulen n, b) Aufschrei m.

yen¹ [jen] s. Yen m (japanische Münzeinheit).

yen² [jen] F für **yearning** I.

yeo·man ['jəʊmən] s. [irr.] **1.** Brit. hist.
a) Freisasse m, b) ✗ berittener Mi'liz-
sol,dat: **~ service** fig. treue Dienste pl.;
2. a. **⅏ of the Guard** 'Leibgar,dist m; **3.**
⚓ Ver'waltungs,unteroffi,zier m; **'yeo-
man·ry** [-rɪ] s. coll. hist. **1.** Freisassen
pl.; **2.** ✗ berittene Mi'liz.

yep [jep] adv. F ja.

yes [jes] **I** adv. **1.** ja, ja'wohl: **say ~ (to)**
a) Ja sagen (zu), (e-e Sache) bejahen
(beide a. fig.), b) einwilligen (in acc.);
2. ja, gewiss, aller'dings; **3.** (ja) doch;
4. ja so'gar; **5.** fragend od. anzweifelnd:
ja?, wirklich?; **II** s. **6.** Ja n; **7.** fig. Ja
(-wort) n; **8.** parl. Ja(stimme f) n; **~
man** s. [irr.] F Jasager m.

yes·ter ['jestə] adj. **1.** obs. od. poet. gestrig; **2.** in Zssgn → **yesterday** 2;
'~·day [-dɪ] **I** adv. **1.** gestern: **I was not
born ~** fig. ich bin (doch) nicht von
gestern; **II** adj. **2.** gestrig, vergangen,
letzt: **~ morning** gestern früh; **III** s. **3.**
der gestrige Tag: **the day before ~** vorgestern; **~'s paper** die gestrige Zeitung; **of ~** von gestern; **~s** vergangene
Tage, alte Zeiten; **4.** fig. das Gestern;
,~'year adv. u. s. obs. od. poet. voriges

Jahr.

yet [jet] **I** *adv.* **1.** (immer) noch, jetzt noch: *not* ~ noch nicht; *nothing* ~ noch nichts; ~ *a moment* (nur) noch einen Augenblick; **2.** schon (jetzt), jetzt: (*as*) ~ bis jetzt, bisher; *have you finished* ~? bist du schon fertig?; *not just* ~ nicht gerade jetzt; **3.** (doch) noch, schon (noch): *he will win* ~; **4.** noch, so'gar (*beim Komparativ*): ~ *better* noch besser; ~ *more important* sogar noch wichtiger; **5.** noch (da'zu), außerdem: *another and* ~ *another* noch einer u. noch einer dazu; ~ *again* immer wieder; *nor* ~ (und) auch nicht; **6.** dennoch, trotzdem, je'doch, aber: *but* ~ aber doch *od.* trotzdem; **II** *cj.* **7.** aber (dennoch *od.* zu'gleich), doch.

yew [juː] ♀ **I** *s.* **1.** *a.* ~ *tree* Eibe *f*; **2.** Eibenholz *n*; **II** *adj.* **3.** Eiben...

Y-fronts ['waɪfrʌnts] *TM s. pl. Herrenunterhose in der Form e-s umgekehrten Ypsilons.*

Yid [jɪd] *s. sl.* Jude *m*; **Yid-dish** ['jɪdɪʃ] *ling.* **I** *s.* Jiddisch *n*; **II** *adj.* jiddisch.

yield [jiːld] **I** *v/t.* **1.** *als Ertrag* ergeben, (ein-, her'vor)bringen, *a. Ernte* erbringen, *bsd. Gewinn* abwerfen, *Früchte, a. Zinsen etc.* tragen, *Produkte etc.* liefern: ~ *6 %* ♱ *6 %* (Rendite) abwerfen; **2.** *Resultat* ergeben, liefern; **3.** *fig.* gewähren, zugestehen, einräumen (*s.th. to s.o.* j-m et.): ~ *consent* einwilligen; ~ *the point* sich (*in e-r Debatte*) geschlagen geben; ~ *precedence to* j-m den Vorrang einräumen; **4.** *a.* ~ *up* a) auf-, hergeben, b) (*to*) abtreten (an *acc.*), über'lassen, -'geben (*dat.*), ausliefern (*dat. od.* an *acc.*): ~ *o.s. to fig.* sich *e-r Sache* überlassen; ~ *a secret* ein Geheimnis preisgeben; ~ *the palm* (*to s.o.*) sich (j-m) geschlagen geben; ~ *place to* Platz machen (*dat.*); → *ghost* 2; **II** *v/i.* **5.** guten *etc.* Ertrag geben *od.* liefern, *bsd.* ♪ tragen; **6.** nachgeben, weichen (*Sache u. Person*): ~ *to despair* sich der Verzweiflung hingeben; ~ *to force* der Gewalt weichen; *I* ~ *to none* ich stehe keinem nach (*in in dat.*); **7.** sich fügen (*to dat.*); **8.** einwilligen (*to in acc.*); **III** *s.* **9.** Ertrag *m*: a) Ernte *f*, b) Ausbeute *f* (*a.* ☉, *phys.*), Gewinn *m*: ~ *of tax(es)* Steueraufkommen *n*, -ertrag *m*; **10.** ♱ a) Zinsertrag *m*, b) Ren'dite *f*; **11.** ☉ a) Me'tallgehalt *m von Erz*, b) Ausgiebigkeit *f von Farben etc.*, c) Nachgiebigkeit *f von Material*; **'yield·ing** [-dɪŋ] *adj.* □ **1.** ergiebig, einträglich: ~ *interest* ♱ verzinslich; **2.** nachgebend, dehnbar, biegsam; **3.** *fig.* nachgiebig, gefügig; **yield point** *s.* ☉ Fließ-, Streckgrenze *f*, -punkt *m*.

yip [jɪp] *Am.* F *für* **yelp**; **yip·pee** [jɪ'piː; 'jɪpɪ] *int.* hur'ra!

yob [jɒb] *s. Brit.* F Rowdy *m*.

yo·del ['jəʊdl] **I** *v/t. u. v/i.* jodeln; **II** *s.* Jodler *m* (*Gesang*).

yo·ga ['jəʊgə] *s.* Joga *m, n*, Yoga *m, n*.

yo·gh(o)urt ['jɒgət] *s.* Joghurt *m, n*.

yo·gi ['jəʊgɪ] *s.* Jogi *m*, Yogi *m*.

yo-heave-ho [ˌjəʊhiːv'həʊ], **yo-ho** [jəʊ'həʊ] *int.* ♱ hau 'ruck!

yoicks [jɔɪks] *hunt.* **I** *int.* hussa!; **II** *s.* Hussa(ruf *m*) *n*.

yoke [jəʊk] **I** *s.* **1.** ✐, *antiq. u. fig.* Joch *n*: ~ *of matrimony* Joch der Ehe; *pass under the* ~ sich unter das Joch beugen; **2.** *sg. od. pl.* Paar *n*, Gespann *n*: *two* ~ *of oxen*; **3.** ☉ a) Schultertrage *f* (*für Eimer etc.*), b) Glockengerüst *n*, c) Bügel *m*, d) ♫ (Ma'gnet-, Pol)Joch *n*, e) *mot.* Gabelgelenk *n*, f) doppeltes Achslager, g) ♱ Ruderjoch *n*; **4.** Passe *f*, Sattel *m* (*an Kleidern*); **II** *v/t.* **5.** *Tiere* anschirren, anjochen; **6.** *fig.* paaren, verbinden (*with, to* mit); **III** *v/i.* **7.** verbunden sein (*with* mit *j-m*): ~ *together* zs.-arbeiten; ~ *bone* *s. anat.* Jochbein *n*; '~·fel·low *s. obs.* **1.** Mitarbeiter *m*; **2.** (Lebens)Gefährte *m*, (-)Gefährtin *f*.

yo·kel ['jəʊkl] *s.* Bauer(ntrampel) *m*.

'yoke·mate → **yokefellow**.

yolk [jəʊk] *s.* **1.** *zo.* Eidotter *m, n*, Eigelb *n*; **2.** Woll-, Fettschweiß *m* (*der Schafwolle*).

yon [jɒn] *obs. od. dial.* **I** *adj. u. pron.* jene(r, s) dort (drüben); **II** *adv.* → **yonder** I; **'yon·der** [-də] **I** *adv.* **1.** da *od.* dort drüben; **2.** *obs.* da drüben hin; **II** *adj. u. pron.* **3.** → **yon** I.

yore [jɔː] *s.:* *of* ~ vorzeiten, ehedem, vormals; *in days of* ~ in alten Zeiten.

York·shire ['jɔːkʃə] *adj.* aus der Grafschaft Yorkshire, Yorkshire...: ~ *flannel* ♱ feiner Flanell aus ungefärbter Wolle; ~ *pudding* gebackener Eierteig, der zum Rinderbraten gegessen wird.

you [juː; jʊ; jə] *pron.* **1.** a) (*nom.*) du, ihr, Sie, b) (*dat.*) dir, euch, Ihnen, c) (*acc.*) dich, euch, Sie: *don't* ~ *do that!* tu das ja nicht!; *that's a wine for* ~! das ist vielleicht ein (gutes) Weinchen!; **2.** man: *that does* ~ *good* das tut einem gut; *what should* ~ *do?* was soll man tun?

you'd [juːd; jʊd; jəd] F *für* a) *you would*, b) *you had*.

young [jʌŋ] **I** *adj.* jung (*a. fig.* frisch, neu, *unerfahren*): ~ *ambition* jugendlicher Ehrgeiz; ~ *animal* Jungtier *n*; ~ *children* kleine Kinder; ~ *love* junge Liebe; *her* ~ *man* F ihr Schatz; ~ *Smith* Smith junior; *a* ~ *state* ein junger Staat; ~ *person* ♊ Jugendliche(r), Heranwachsende(r) (*14 bis 17 Jahre alt*); *the* ~ *person fig.* die (unverdorbene) Jugend; ~ *in one's job* unerfahren

in s-r Arbeit; **II** *s. coll.* (Tier)Junge *pl.*: *with* ~ trächtig; **young·ish** ['jʌŋɪʃ] *adj.* ziemlich jung; **'young·ster** [-stə] *s.* **1.** Bursch(e) *m*, Junge *m*; Kleine(r *m*) *f*; **2.** *sport* Youngster *m*.

your [jɔː] *pron. u. adj.* **1.** a) *sg.* dein(e), b) *pl.* euer, eure, c) *sg. od. pl.* Ihr(e); **2.** *impers.* F a) so ein(e), b) der (die, das) viel gepriesene ... *od.* gerühmte ...

yours [jɔːz] *pron.* **1.** a) *sg.* dein, der (die, das) Dein(ig)e, die Dein(ig)en, b) *pl.* euer, eure(s), der (die, das) Eur(ig)e, die Eur(ig)en, c) *Höflichkeitsform*, *sg. od. pl.* Ihr, der (die, das) Ihr(ig)e, die Ihr(ig)en: *this is* ~ das gehört dir (euch, Ihnen); *what is mine is* ~ was mein ist, ist (auch) dein; *my sister and* ~ meine u. deine Schwester; → *truly* 2; **2.** a) die Dein(ig)en (Euren, Ihren), b) das Dein(ig)e, deine Habe: *you and* ~; **3.** ♱ Ihr Schreiben.

your'self *pl.* **-'selves** [-vz] *pron.* (*in Verbindung mit you od. e-m Imperativ*) **1.** a) *sg.* (du, Sie) selbst, b) *pl.* (ihr, Sie) selbst: *by* ~ a) selbst, selber, selbstständig, allein, b) allein, für sich; *be* ~! F nimm dich zusammen!; *you are not* ~ *today* du bist (Sie sind) heute ganz anders als sonst *od.* nicht auf der Höhe; *what will you do with* ~ *today?* was wirst du (werden Sie) heute anfangen?; **2.** *refl.* a) *sg.* dir, dich, sich, b) *pl.* euch, sich: *did you hurt* ~? hast du dich (haben Sie sich) verletzt?

youth [juːθ] **I** *s.* **1.** *allg.* Jugend *f*: a) Jungsein *n*, b) Jugendfrische *f*, c) Jugendzeit *f*, d) *coll. sg. od. pl. konstr.* junge Leute *pl. od.* Menschen *pl.*; **2.** Frühstadium *n*; **3.** *pl.* youths [-ðz] junger Mann, Jüngling *m*; **II** *adj.* **4.** Jugend...: ~ *centre* (*Am. center*) Jugendzentrum *n*; ~ *club* Jugendklub *m*; ~ *hostel* Jugendherberge *f*; **'youth·ful** [-fʊl] *adj.* □ **1.** jung (*a. fig.*); **2.** jugendlich; **3.** Jugend...: ~ *days*; **'youth·ful·ness** [-fʊlnɪs] *s.* Jugend(lichkeit) *f*.

yowl [jaʊl] **I** *v/t. u. v/i.* jaulen, heulen; **II** *s.* Jaulen *n*, Heulen *n*.

yuck [jʌk] *int. sl.* pfui Teufel!; **yuck·y** ['jʌkɪ] *adj.* F ätzend.

Yu·go·slav → **Jugoslav**.

yule [juːl] *s.* Weihnachts-, Julfest *n*; ~ *log* *s.* Weihnachtsscheit *n im Kamin*; '~·tide *s.* Weihnachtszeit *f*.

yum·my ['jʌmɪ] F **I** *adj.* a) *allg.* 'prima', 'toll', b) lecker (*Mahlzeit etc.*); **II** *int.* → *yum-yum*.

yum-yum [ˌjʌm'jʌm] *int.* F mm!, lecker!

yup·pie ['jʌpɪ] *s.* Yuppie *m* (*junger karrierebewusster und ausgabefreudiger Mensch mit urbanem Lebensstil, häufig bestimmten Modetrends folgend*) (= *young urban od. upwardly mobile professional*).

Zz

Z, z [*Brit.* zed; *Am.* zi:] *s.* Z *n*, z *n* (*Buchstabe*).

za·ny ['zeɪnɪ] **I** *s.* **1.** *hist.* Hans'wurst *m*; **2.** *fig. contp.* Blödmann *m*; **II** *adj.* **3.** verrückt; **4.** schrullig komisch; **5.** *fig.* ‚blöd'.

zap [zæp] F **I** *v/t.* **1.** *et.* ka'puttmachen, zerstören, *j-n* abknallen, *j-n* ‚erledigen'; **2.** *j-m* ein Ding verpassen (*Kugel, Schlag etc.*); **3.** *Computer:* löschen; **4.** *Am.* im Mikrowellenherd garen; **5.** in rasender Geschwindigkeit *irgendwohin* bringen; **II** *v/i.* **6.** ‚düsen', zischen: ~ *off* ‚abdüsen', ‚abschwirren'; **7.** *TV* ‚zappen'; **III** *int.* **8.** ‚zack!'; **IV** *s.* **9.** Schwung *m*, E'lan *m*, ‚Pep' *m*; **10.** Dy'namik *f*; **zapped** [zæpt] *adj.* F ‚fertig', (to'tal) ‚erledigt'; **'zap·per** *s.* F **1.** *TV etc.:* Fernbedienung *f*; **2.** *Am. elektronischer Insektenkiller.* **'zap·pi·ness** [-pɪnəs] *s.* F **1.** Fetzigkeit *f*, Spritzigkeit *f*; **2.** → *zap* IV; **'zap·py** [-pɪ] *adj.* F **1.** fetzig, spritzig; **2.** dy'namisch.

zeal [ziːl] *s.* **1.** (Dienst-, Arbeits-, Glaubens- *etc.*)Eifer *m*: *full of* ~ (dienst*etc.*)eifrig; **2.** Begeisterung *f*, Hingabe *f*, Inbrunst *f*.

zeal·ot ['zelət] *s.* (*bsd.* Glaubens)Eiferer *m*, Ze'lot *m*, Fa'natiker(in); **'zeal·ot·ry** [-trɪ] *s.* Zelo'tismus *m*, fa'natischer (Glaubens- *etc.*)Eifer.

zeal·ous ['zeləs] *adj.* □ **1.** (dienst)eifrig; **2.** eifernd, fa'natisch; **3.** eifrig bedacht (*to do* darauf, zu tun, *for* auf *acc.*); **4.** heiß, innig; **5.** begeistert; **'zeal·ous·ness** [-nɪs] → *zeal.*

ze·bra ['ziːbrə] *pl.* **-bras** *od. coll.* **-bra** *s. zo.* Zebra *n*; ~ *cross·ing s.* Verkehr: Zebrastreifen *m*.

zed [zed] *s. Brit.* **1.** Zet *n* (*Buchstabe*). **2.** ◉ Z-Eisen *n*.

Zen (**Bud·dhism**) [zen] *s.* 'Zen(-Bud·,dhismus *m*) *n*.

ze·ner di·ode ['ziːnə] *s.* ⚡ 'Zenerdi,ode *f*.

ze·nith ['zenɪθ] *s.* **1.** *ast.* Scheitelpunkt *m* (*a. Ballistik*), b) *fig.* Höhe-, Gipfelpunkt *m*: *be at one's* (*od.* *the*) ~ den Zenit erreicht haben, im Zenit stehen.

Zeph·a·ni·ah [,zefə'naɪə] *npr. u. s. bibl.* (das Buch) Ze'phanja *m*.

zeph·yr ['zefə] *s.* **1.** *poet.* Zephir *m*, Westwind *m*, laues Lüftchen; **2.** sehr leichtes Gewebe, *a.* leichter Schal *etc.*: **3.** ✝ a) *a.* ~ *cloth* Zephir *m* (*Gewebe*), b) *a.* ~ *worsted* Zephirwolle *f*, c) *a.* ~ *yarn* Zephirgarn *n*.

zep·pe·lin ['zepəlɪn] *s.* 'Zeppelin *m*.

ze·ro ['zɪərəʊ] **I** *pl.* **-ros** *s.* **1.** Null *f* (*Zahl od. Zeichen*); **2.** *phys.* Null (-punkt *m*) *f*, Ausgangspunkt *m* (*Skala*), *bsd.* Gefrierpunkt *m*; **3.** ✠ Null (-punkt *m*, -stelle) *f*; **4.** *fig.* Null-, Tiefpunkt *m*: *at* ~ auf dem Nullpunkt (angelangt); **5.** *fig.* Null *f*, Nichts *n*; **6.** ✗ → *zero hour*; **7.** ✔ Höhe *f* unter 1000 Fuß: *at* ~ in Bodennähe; **II** *v/t.* **8.** ◉ auf null (ein)stellen; **III** *v/i.* **9.** ~ *in on* a) ✗ sich einschießen auf (*acc.*) (*a. fig.*),

b) *a. fig.* immer dichter her'ankommen an (*acc.*), einkreisen, c) *fig.* sich konzentrieren auf (*acc.*); **IV** *adj.* **10.** *bsd. Am.* F null; ~ *option* *pol.* Nulllösung *f*; ~ **con·duc·tor** *s.* ⚡ Nullleiter *m*; ~ **-e'mis·sion** *adj.* schadstofffrei, abgasfrei; ~ **grav·i·ty** *s. phys.* (Zustand *m* der) Schwerelosigkeit *f*; ~ **growth** *s.* **1.** ✝ Nullwachstum *m*; **2.** *a.* **zero population growth** Bevölkerungsstillstand *m*; ~ **hour** *s.* **1.** ✗ X-Zeit *f*, Stunde *f* X (*festgelegter Zeitpunkt des Beginns e-r Operation*); **2.** *fig.* genauer Zeitpunkt, kritischer Augenblick; **'~-,rat·ed** *adj* ✝ mehrwertsteuerfrei.

zest [zest] **I** *s.* **1.** Würze *f* (*a. fig. Reiz*): *add* ~ *to* e-r *Sache* Würze *od.* Reiz verleihen; **2.** *fig.* (*for*) Genuss *m*, Lust *f*, Freude *f* (an *dat.*), Begeisterung *f* (für), Schwung *m*: ~ *for life* Lebenshunger *m*; **II** *v/t.* **3.** würzen (*a. fig.*); **'zest·ful** [-fʊl] *adj.* □ **1.** reizvoll; **2.** schwungvoll, begeistert.

zig·zag ['zɪgzæg] **I** *s.* **1.** Zickzack *m*; **2.** Zickzacklinie *f*, -bewegung *f*, -kurs *m* (*a. fig.*); **3.** Zickzackweg *m*, Serpen'tine(nstraße) *f*; **II** *adj.* **4.** zickzackförmig, Zickzack...; **III** *adv.* **5.** im Zickzack; **IV** *v/i.* **6.** im Zickzack fahren, laufen *etc.*, *a.* verlaufen (*Weg etc.*).

zilch [zɪltʃ] *s. Am. sl.* Null *f*, Nichts *n*.

Zim·mer ['zɪmə] *s. TM*, ~ **frame** *s.* Laufgestell *n* (*für Kranke*).

zinc [zɪŋk] **I** *s.* 🜛 Zink *n*; **II** *v/t. pret. u. p.p.* **zinc(k)ed** [-kt] verzinken; **zin·cog·ra·pher** [zɪŋ'kɒgrəfə] *s.* Zinko'graph *m*, Zinkstecher *m*; **'zinc·ous** [-kəs] *adj.* 🜛 Zink...; **zinc white** *s.* Zinkweiß *n*.

zing [zɪŋ] F **I** *s.* → *zip* 1 *u.* 2; **II** *v/i.* → *zip* 4; **III** *v/t.* → *zip* 8.

Zi·on ['zaɪən] *s. bibl.* Zion *m*; **'Zi·on·ism** [-nɪzəm] *s.* Zio'nismus *m*; **'Zi·on·ist** [-nɪst] **I** *s.* Zio'nist(in); **II** *adj.* zio'nistisch, Zionisten...

zip [zɪp] **I** *s.* **1.** Schwirren *n*, Zischen *n*; **2.** F ‚Schmiss' *m*, Schwung *m*; **3.** F → *zip fastener*; **II** *v/i.* **4.** schwirren, zischen, flitzen; **5.** F ‚Schmiss' haben; **III** *v/t.* **6.** schwirren lassen; **7.** mit e-m Reißverschluss schließen *od.* öffnen; **8.** *Computer: Daten* zippen, packen (*komprimieren*); **9.** *a.* ~ *up* F a) ‚schmissig' machen, b) Schwung bringen in (*acc.*); ~ **ar·e·a** *s. Am.* Postleitzone *f*; ~ **code** *s. Am.* Postleitzahl *f*; ~ **fas·ten·er** *s.* Reißverschluss *m*.

zip·per ['zɪpə] **I** *s.* Reißverschluss *m*: ~ *bag* Reißverschlusstasche *f*; **II** *v/t.* mit Reißverschluss versehen; **'zip·ping** [-pɪŋ] *s. Computer:* Zippen *n*, Packen *n* (*Datenkomprimierung*); **zip·py** ['zɪpɪ] *adj.* F **1.** schwungvoll, ‚schmissig'; **2.** flott, flink.

zith·er ['zɪθə] *s.* ♪ Zither *f*; **'zith·er·ist** [-ərɪst] *s.* Zitherspieler(in).

zizz [zɪz] *bsd. Brit.* F **I** *s.* F Schläfchen *n*, Nickerchen *n*; **2.** Zischen *n* (*e-s Feuerwerkskörpers etc.*), (helles) Brummen

(*e-s Motors etc.*); **II** *v/i.* **3.** F ein Nickerchen machen: ~ *off* einschlafen; **4.** zischen, (hell) brummen.

zo·di·ac ['zəʊdɪæk] *s. ast.* Tierkreis *m*: *signs of the* ~ Tierkreiszeichen *pl.*; **zo·di·a·cal** [zəʊ'daɪəkl] *adj.* Tierkreis..., Zodiakal...

zom·bi(e) ['zɒmbɪ] *s.* **1.** Schlangengottheit *f*; **2.** Zombie *m* (*wieder beseelte Leiche*); **3.** F a) ‚Monster' *n*, b) ‚Roboter' *m*, c) Trottel *m*; **4.** *Am.* (*ein*) Cocktail *m*.

zon·al ['zəʊnl] *adj.* □ **1.** zonenförmig; **2.** Zonen...; **zone** [zəʊn] **I** *s.* **1.** *allg.* Zone *f*: a) *geogr.* (Erd)Gürtel *m*, b) Gebietsstreifen *m*, Gürtel *m*, c) *fig.* Bereich *m*, (*a.* Körper)Gegend *f*, d) *poet.* Gürtel *m*: *torrid* ~ heiße Zone; *wheat* ~ Weizengürtel; ~ *of occupation* Besatzungszone; **2.** a) (Verkehrs)Zone *f*, *a.* Teilstrecke *f*, b) 🚃, 🚋 *Am.* (Gebühren)Zone *f*, c) 📮 Post(zustell)bezirk *m*; **II** *v/t.* **3.** in Zonen aufteilen.

zonked [zɒŋkt] *adj. sl.* **1.** ‚high' (*im Drogenrausch*); **2.** ‚stinkbesoffen'.

zoo [zuː] *s.* Zoo *m*.

zo·o·blast ['zəʊəblæst] *s. zo.* tierische Zelle.

zo·o·chem·is·try [,zəʊə'kemɪstrɪ] *s. zo.* Zooche'mie *f*.

zo·og·a·my [zəʊ'ɒgəmɪ] *s. zo.* geschlechtliche Fortpflanzung.

zo·og·e·ny [zəʊ'ɒdʒənɪ] *s. zo.* Zooge'nese *f*, Entstehung *f* der Tierarten.

zo·og·ra·phy [zəʊ'ɒgrəfɪ] *s.* beschreibende Zoolo'gie.

zo·o·lite ['zəʊəlaɪt] *s.* fos'siles Tier.

zo·o·log·i·cal [,zəʊə'lɒdʒɪkl] *adj.* □ zoo'logisch: ~ *garden(s)* [zʊ'lɒdʒɪk] zoo'logischer Garten; **zo·ol·o·gist** [zəʊ'ɒlədʒɪst] *s.* Zoo'loge *m*, Zoo'login *f*; **zo·ol·o·gy** [-dʒɪ] *s.* Zoolo'gie *f*, Tierkunde *f*.

zoom [zuːm] **I** *v/i.* **1.** surren; **2.** sausen; **3.** ✔ steil hochziehen; **4.** *phot.*, *Film:* zoomen: ~ *in on s.th.* a) *et.* heranholen, b) *fig. et.* ‚einkreisen'; **II** *v/t.* **5.** surren; **6.** *Flugzeug* hochreißen; **III** *s.* **7.** ✔ Steilflug *m*; **8.** *fig.* Hochschnellen *n*; **9.** *phot.*, *Film:* a) *a.* ~ *lens* 'Zoom (-objek,tiv) *n*, b) *a.* ~ *travel* Zoomfahrt *f*; **10.** *Am.* (*ein*) Cocktail *m*; **'zoom·er** [-mə] *s.* → *zoom* 9a.

zo·o·phyte ['zəʊəfaɪt] *s. zo.* Zoo'phyt *m*, Pflanzentier *n*.

zo·ot·o·my [zəʊ'ɒtəmɪ] *s.* Zooto'mie *f*, 'Tieranato,mie *f*.

zos·ter ['zɒstə] *s.* ⚕ Gürtelrose *f*.

zounds [zaʊndz] *int. obs.* sapper'lot!

zuc·chi·ni [zuː'kiːnɪ] *pl.* **-ni(s)** *s. bsd. Am.* Zuc'chini *f*.

zy·go·ma [zaɪ'gəʊmə] *pl.* **-ma·ta** [-mətə] *s. anat.* **1.** Jochbogen *m*; **2.** Jochbein(fortsatz *m*) *n*.

zy·mo·sis [zaɪ'məʊsɪs] *pl.* **-ses** [-siːz] *s.* **1.** 🜛 Gärung *f*; **2.** ⚕ Infekti'onskrankheit *f*; **zy'mot·ic** [-'mɒtɪk] *adj.* (□ ~*al·ly*); **1.** 🜛 gärend, Gärungs...; **2.** ⚕ Infektions...

Anhänge

Britische und amerikanische Abkürzungen

A

a *acre* Acre *m*.

AA *anti-aircraft* Fla, Flugabwehr *f*; *Brit. Automobile Association* Automo'bilklub *m*; *Alcoholics Anonymous* Ano-'nyme Alko'holiker *pl*.

AAA *Brit. Amateur Athletic Association* 'Leichtath,letikverband *m*; *American Automobile Association* Amer. Automo'bilklub *m*.

a.a.r. *against all risks* gegen jede Gefahr.

AB *able(-bodied) seaman* 'Vollma,trose *m*; *Am. Bachelor of Arts* (*siehe* BA).

abbr., **abbrev.** *abbreviated* abgekürzt; *abbreviation* Abk., Abkürzung *f*.

ABC *American Broadcasting Company* Amer. Rundfunkgesellschaft *f*.

abr. *abridged* (ab)gekürzt; *abridg(e)ment* (Ab-, Ver)Kürzung *f*.

AC *alternating current* Wechselstrom *m*.

a/c *account current* Kontokor'rent *n*; *account* Kto., Konto *n*; Rechnung *f*.

acc. *according to* gem., gemäß, entspr., entsprechend; *account* Kto., Konto *n*; Rechnung *f*.

acct. *account* Kto., Konto *n*; Rechnung *f*.

AD *Anno Domini* im Jahre des Herrn.

add(r). *address* Adr., A'dresse *f*.

Adm. *Admiral* Adm., Admi'ral *m*.

addnl. *additional* zusätzlich.

advt. *advertisement* Anz., Anzeige *f*, Ankündigung *f*.

AEC *Am. Atomic Energy Commission* A'tomener,gie-Kommissi,on *f*.

AFC *automatic frequency control* auto'matische Fre'quenz(fein)abstimmung *f*.

AFEX ['eɪfeks] *Air Force Exchange* (*Verkaufsläden für Angehörige der amer. Luftstreitkräfte*).

AFL-CIO *American Federation of Labor & Congress of Industrial Organizations* (*größter amer. Gewerkschaftsverband*).

AFN *American Forces Network* (*Rundfunkanstalt der amer. Streitkräfte*).

aft(n). *afternoon* Nachmittag *m*.

AGM *annual general meeting* ✝(ordentliche) Jahres'hauptver,sammlung.

AI *artificial intelligence* *Computer:* K'I *f*, Künstliche Intelligenz.

AIDS [eɪdz] *Acquired Immune Deficiency Syndrome* Aids *n*, Im'munschwächekrankheit *f*.

AK *Alaska* (*Staat der USA*).

AL, **Ala.** *Alabama* (*Staat der USA*).

ALA *in Annoncen:* *all letters* (*will be*) *answered* beantworte jede Zuschrift.

Alas. *Alaska* (*Staat der USA*).

Alta. *Alberta* (*Kanad. Provinz*).

AM *amplitude modulation* (*Frequenzbereich der Kurz-, Mittel- u. Langwellen*); *Am. Master of Arts* (*siehe* MA).

Am. *America* A'merika *n*; *American* ameri'kanisch.

a.m. *ante meridiem* (*Lat.* = *before noon*) morgens, vormittags.

AMA *American Medical Association* Amer. Ärzteverband *m*.

amp. *ampere* A, Am'pere *n*.

AOB *any other business* ✝ Sonstiges *n* (*Tagesordnungspunkt*).

AP *Associated Press* (*amer. Nachrichtenagentur*).

approx. *approximate(ly)* annähernd, etwa.

appx. *appendix* Anh., Anhang *m*.

APR *annual(ized) percentage rate* Jahreszinssatz *m*, effek'tiver Jahreszins.

Apr. *April* A'pril *m*.

APT *Brit. Advanced Passenger Train* (*Hochgeschwindigkeitszug*).

AR *Arkansas* (*Staat der USA*).

ARC *American Red Cross* das Amer. Rote Kreuz.

Ariz. *Arizona* (*Staat der USA*).

Ark. *Arkansas* (*Staat der USA*).

ARP *Air-Raid Precautions* Luftschutz *m*.

arr. *arrival* Ank., Ankunft *f*.

art. *article* Art., Ar'tikel *m*; *artificial* künstlich.

AS *Anglo-Saxon* Angelsächsisch *n*, angelsächsisch; *anti-submarine* U-Boot-Abwehr ...

ASA *American Standards Association* Amer. 'Normungs-Organisati,on *f*.

ASCII ['æskiː] *American Standard Code for Information Interchange* (*standardisierter Code zur Darstellung alphanumerischer Zeichen*).

asst. *assistant* Asst., Assi'stent(in).

asst'd *assorted* assortiert, gem., gemischt.

ATC *air traffic control* Flugsicherung *f*.

ATM *automated teller machine* 'Geldauto,mat *m*.

Aug. *August* Aug., Au'gust *m*.

auth. *author(ess)* Verfasser(in).

av. *average* Durchschnitt *m*; Hava'rie *f*.

avdp. *avoirdupois* Handelsgewicht *n*.

Ave. *Avenue* Al'lee *f*, Straße *f*.

AVI *automatic vehicle identification* auto'matische Fahrzeugidentifizierung.

AWACS ['eɪwæks] *Airborne Warning and Control System* (*luftgestütztes Frühwarn- und Überwachungssystem*).

AWOL *absence without leave* unerlaubte Entfernung von der Truppe.

AZ *Arizona* (*Staat der USA*).

B

b. *born* geboren.

BA *Bachelor of Arts* Bakka'laureus *m* der Philoso'phie; *British Academy* Brit. Akade'mie *f*; *British Airways* Brit. Luftverkehrsgesellschaft *f*.

BAgr(ic) *Bachelor of Agriculture* Bakka'laureus *m* der Landwirtschaft.

B&B, **b&b** *bed and breakfast* Über'nachtung *f* mit Frühstück.

BAOR *British Army of the Rhine* Brit. 'Rheinar,mee *f*.

Bart. *Baronet* Baronet *m*.

BBC *British Broadcasting Corporation* Brit. Rundfunkgesellschaft *f*.

bbl. *barrel* Fass *n*.

BC *before Christ* vor Christus; *British Columbia* (*Kanad. Provinz*).

BCom(m) *Bachelor of Commerce* Bakka'laureus *m* der Wirtschaftswissenschaften.

BD *Bachelor of Divinity* Bakka'laureus *m* der Theolo'gie.

bd. *bound* gebunden (*Buchbinderei*).

BDS *Bachelor of Dental Surgery* Bakka'laureus *m* der 'Zahnmedi,zin.

bds. *boards* kartoniert (*Buchbinderei*).

BE *Bachelor of Education* Bakka'laureus *m* der Erziehungswissenschaft; *Bachelor of Engineering* Bakka'laureus *m* der Ingeni'eurwissenschaft(en); *siehe* B/E.

B/E *bill of exchange* Wechsel *m*.

Beds. *Bedfordshire* (*engl. Grafschaft*).

Berks. *Berkshire* (*engl. Grafschaft*).

b/f *brought forward* 'Übertrag *m*.

BFBS *British Forces Broadcasting Service* (*Rundfunkanstalt der brit. Streitkräfte*).

B'ham *Birmingham* (*Stadt in England*).

b.h.p. *brake horse-power* Brems-PS *f* *od. pl.*, Bremsleistung *f* in PS.

BIF *British Industries Fair* Brit. Indust-'riemesse *f*.

BIS *Bank for International Settlements* BIZ, Bank *f* für internatio'nalen Zahlungsausgleich.

bk. *book* Buch *n*.

BL *Bachelor of Law* Bakka'laureus *m* des Rechts.

B/L *bill of lading* (See)Frachtbrief *m*.

bl. *barrel* Fass *n*.

bldg. *building* Geb., Gebäude *n*.

BLit(t) *Bachelor of Literature* Bakka-'laureus *m* der Litera'tur.

bls. *bales* Ballen *pl.*; *barrels* Fass *pl.* (*bei Mengenangaben*).

Blvd. *Boulevard* Boule'vard *m*.

BM *Bachelor of Medicine* Bakka'laureus *m* der Medi'zin; *British Museum* Britisches Mu'seum.

BMA *British Medical Association* Brit. Ärzteverband *m*.

BMus *Bachelor of Music* Bakka'laureus *m* der Mu'sik.

b.o. *branch office* Zweigstelle *f*, Fili'ale *f*; *body odo(u)r* Körpergeruch *m*; *buyer's option* 'Kaufopti,on *f*; *box office* (The'ater)Kasse *f*.

B.o.T. *Board of Trade* Brit. 'Handelsmini,sterium *n*.

bot. *bought* gekauft; *bottle* Flasche *f*.

BPharm *Bachelor of Pharmacy* Bakka'laureus *m* der Pharma'zie.

BPhil *Bachelor of Philosophy* Bakka-'laureus *m* der Philoso'phie.

BR *British Rail* (*Eisenbahn in Großbritannien*).

B/R *bills receivable* Wechselforderungen *pl.*

BRCS *British Red Cross Society* das Brit. Rote Kreuz.

Brit. *Britain* Großbri'tannien *n*; *British* britisch.

Bros. *brothers* Gebr., Gebrüder *pl.* (*in Firmenbezeichnungen*).

BS *Am. Bachelor of Science* Bakka-

'laureus *m* der Na'turwissenschaften;
British Standard Brit. Norm *f.*

B/S *bill of sale* Über'eignungsvertrag *m.*

BSc *Brit.* **Bachelor of Science** Bakka-
'laureus *m* der Na'turwissenschaften.

BSE *bovine spongiform encephalopathy* BSE, Rinderwahn(sinn).

BSG *British Standard Gauge* (*brit.
Norm*).

B.S.I. *British Standards Institution*
Brit. 'Normungs-Organisati,on *f.*

BST *British Summer Time* Brit. Sommerzeit *f.*

Bt. *Baronet* Baronet *m.*

BTA *British Tourist Authority* Brit.
Fremdenverkehrsbehörde *f.*

bt. fwd. *brought forward* 'Übertrag *m.*

B.th.u, **Btu** *British Thermal Unit*(*s*)
Brit. Wärmeeinheit(en *pl.*) *f.*

bu. *bushel* Scheffel *m.*

Bucks. *Buckinghamshire* (*engl. Grafschaft*).

bus. *Am.* *business* Arbeit *f, die* Geschäfte *pl.*

C

C *Celsius*, *centigrade* Celsius, hundert-
gradig (*Thermometer*).

c *cent*(*s*) Cent *m* (*amer. Münze*); *century* Jahr'hundert *n*; *circa* ca., circa,
ungefähr; *cubic* Kubik...

CA *California* (*Staat der USA*); *chartered account* Frachtrechnung *f*; *Brit.
chartered accountant* beeidigter 'Bücherre,visor *od.* Wirtschaftsprüfer;
current account Girokonto *n.*

CAB *Brit.* *Citizens' Advice Bureau*
(*Bürgerberatungsorganisation auf freiwilliger Basis*).

CAD *computer-aided design* CAD *n*
com'putergestütztes Design.

c.a.d. *cash against documents*
Zahlung *f* gegen Doku'mentaushän-
digung.

CAI *computer-assisted* (*od. -aided*)
instruction com'putergestütztes Lernen.

Cal(*if*). *California* (*Staat der USA*).

CALL *computer-assisted language
learning* CALL *n*, com'putergestütztes
Sprachenlernen.

Cambs. *Cambridgeshire* (*engl. Grafschaft*).

Can. *Canada* Kanada *n*; *Canadian* ka-
'nadisch.

C & W *country and western* (*Musik*).

Cantab. *Cantabrigiensis* (*Titel etc.*)
der Universi'tät Cambridge.

Capt. *Captain* Kapi'tän *m*, Hauptmann
m, Rittmeister *m.*

Card. *Cardinal* Kardi'nal *m.*

CARE [keə] *Cooperative for American
Relief Everywhere* (*amer. Organisation, die Hilfsmittel an Bedürftige in aller Welt versendet*).

CAT ✓ *clear air turbulence* CAT *n*,
Turbulenzen *pl.* bei klarer Sicht; *computer-assisted* (*od. -aided*) *testing*
com'puterunterstütztes Testverfahren;
✝ *computer-assisted trading* Com-
'puterhandel *m.*

Cath. *Catholic* kath., ka'tholisch.

CB *Citizens' Band* C'B-Funk *m* (*Wel-
lenbereich für privaten Funkverkehr*);
Companion of (*the Order of*) *the
Bath* Ritter *m* des Bath-Ordens; (*a.
C/B*) *cash book* Kassabuch *n.*

CBA *cost/benefit analysis* ✝ Kosten-
'Nutzen-Ana,lyse *f.*

CBC *Canadian Broadcasting Corpo-*

ration Ka'nadische Rundfunkgesellschaft.

CBS *Columbia Broadcasting System*
(*amer. Rundfunkgesellschaft*).

CC *City Council* Stadtrat *m*; *Brit.
County Council* Grafschaftsrat *m.*

cc *Brit.* *cubic centimetre*(*s*), *Am. cubic centimeter*(*s*) ccm, Ku'bikzenti-
,meter *m*, *n od. pl.*

CD *compact disc* CD *f*; *Corps Diplo-
matique* (*Fr. = Diplomatic Corps*) CD
n, Diplo'matisches Korps.

CE *Church of England* angli'kanische
Kirche; *civil engineer* 'Bauingeni,eur *m.*

CEO *Chief Executive Officer* ✝ Hauptge'schäftsführer(in), Vorstandsvorsit-
zende(r *m*) *f.*

cert. *certificate* Bescheinigung *f.*

CET *Central European Time* MEZ,
'mitteleuro,päische Zeit.

cf. *confer* vgl., vergleiche.

CFC *chlorofluorocarbon* 🔬 FCK'W *n*,
,Fluorchlorkohlen'wasserstoff *m.*

Ch. *chapter* Kap., Ka'pitel *n.*

ch. *chain* (*Länge einer*) Messkette *f*;
chapter Kap., Ka'pitel *n*; *chief* ltd.,
leitende(r) ..., oberste(r) ...

c.h. *central heating* ZH, Zen'tralheizung *f.*

ChB *Chirurgiae Baccalaureus* (*Lat. =
Bachelor of Surgery*) Bakka'laureus
m der Chirur'gie.

Ches. *Cheshire* (*engl. Grafschaft*).

C.I. *Channel Islands* Ka'nalinseln *pl.*

C/I *certificate of insurance* Ver'sicherungspo,lice *f.*

CIA *Central Intelligence Agency* (*Geheimdienst der USA*).

CID *Criminal Investigation Department* (*brit. Kriminalpolizei*).

c.i.f. *cost, insurance, freight* Kosten,
Versicherung und Fracht einbegriffen.

C.-in-C. *Commander-in-Chief* Ober-
kommandierende(r) *m* (*dem Land-,
Luft- und Seestreitkräfte unterstehen*).

cir(**c**). *circa* ca., circa, ungefähr; *circular* Rundschreiben *n*; *circulation* 'Umlauf *m*, Auflage *f* (*Zeitung etc.*).

CIS *Commonwealth of Independent
States* GUS, Gemeinschaft unabhängiger Staaten.

CJD *Creutzfeld*(*t*)*-Jakob disease*
Creutzfeld(t)-Jakob(sche) Krankheit.

ck(**s**). *cask* Fass *n*; *casks* Fässer *pl.*

cl. *class* Klasse *f.*

cm *Brit.* *centimetre*(*s*), *Am.* *centimeter*(*s*) cm, Zenti'meter *m*, *n od. pl.*

CO *Colorado* (*Staat der USA*); *Commanding Officer* Komman'deur *m.*

Co. *Company* Gesellschaft *f*; *county
Brit.* Grafschaft *f*, (*Verwaltungs*)Bezirk
m.

c/o *care of* p. A., per A'dresse, bei.

COD, c.o.d. *cash* (*Am.* *collect*) *on delivery* zahlbar bei Lieferung, per Nachnahme.

C. of E. *Church of England* angli'kanische Kirche; *Council of Europe* ER,
Eu'roparat *m.*

COI *Brit.* *Central Office of Information*
(*staatliches Auskunftsbüro zur Verbreitung amtlicher Publikationen etc.*).

Col. *Colorado* (*Staat der USA*); *Colonel* Oberst *m.*

Colo. *Colorado* (*Staat der USA*).

conc. *concerning* betr., betreffend, betrifft.

Conn. *Connecticut* (*Staat der USA*).

Cons. *Conservative* konserva'tiv (*Brit.
pol.*); *Consul* Konsul *m.*

cont., contd *continued* fortgesetzt.

Corn. *Cornwall* (*engl. Grafschaft*).

Corp. *Corporal* Korpo'ral *m*, 'Unteroffi,zier *m*; *Corporation* (*siehe Wörterverzeichnis*).

corr. *corresponding* entspr., entsprechend.

cp. *compare* vgl., vergleiche.

CPA *Am.* *certified public accountant*
beeidigter 'Bücherre,visor *od.* Wirtschaftsprüfer.

CPR *cardiopulmonary resuscitation*
e-e Wiederbelebungstechnik für die
Herz- u. Lungenfunktion.

c.p.s. *cycles per second* Hertz *pl.*

CPU *central processing unit* Computer: Zent'raleinheit *f.*

CT *Connecticut* (*Staat der USA*).

ct(**s**) *cent*(**s**) (*amer. Münze*).

CTT *capital transfer tax* Erbschafts-
und Schenkungssteuer *f.*

cu(**b**). *cubic* Kubik...

cu.ft. *cubic foot* Ku'bikfuß *m.*

cu.in. *cubic inch* Ku'bikzoll *m.*

Cumb. *Cumberland* (*ehemal. engl.
Grafschaft*).

cum d(**iv**). *cum dividend* mit Divi-
'dende.

CUP *Cambridge University Press* Verlag *m* der Universi'tät Cambridge.

CV, cv *curriculum vitae* Lebenslauf *m.*

CWIS *campus-wide information system* Computer: Campusnetz *n.*

c.w.o. *cash with order* Barzahlung bei
Bestellung.

cwt *hundredweight* (*etwa 1*) Zentner *m.*

D

d. *Brit.* *penny, pence* (*bis 1971 verwen-
dete Abkürzung*); *died* gest., gestorben.

DA *deposit account* Depo'sitenkonto
n; *Am.* *district attorney* Staatsanwalt
m.

DAR *Am.* *Daughters of the American
Revolution* Töchter *pl.* der amer. Revoluti'on (*patriotische Frauenvereini-
gung*).

DAT *digital audio tape* (*in Kassetten be-
findliches Tonband für Digitalaufnahmen mit DAT-Rekordern*).

DB *daybook* Jour'nal *n.*

d.b.a. *doing business as* ✝ fir'mierend
unter ...

DC *direct current* Gleichstrom *m*; *District of Columbia* Di'strikt Columbia
(*mit der amer. Hauptstadt Washington*).

DCL *Doctor of Civil Law* Doktor *m* des
Zi'vilrechts.

DD *Doctor of Divinity* Dr. theol., Doktor *m* der Theolo'gie.

d-d *euphem. für damned* verdammt.

DDS *Doctor of Dental Surgery* Dr.
med. dent., Doktor *m* der 'Zahnmedi,zin.

DDT *dichlorodiphenyltrichloroethane*
DDT, Di'chlordiphe'nyltrichlorä,than *n*
(*Insekten- u. Seuchenbekämpfungsmit-
tel*).

DE *Delaware* (*Staat der USA*).

Dec. *December* Dez., De'zember *m.*

dec. *deceased* gest., gestorben.

DEd *Doctor of Education* Dr. paed.,
Doktor *m* der Päda'gogik.

def. *defendant* Beklagte(r *m*) *f.*

deg. *degree*(**s**) Grad *m od. pl.*

Del. *Delaware* (*Staat der USA*).

DEng *Doctor of Engineering* Dr.-Ing.,
Doktor *m* der Ingeni'eurwissenschaf-
ten.

dep. *departure* Abf., Abfahrt *f*.

Dept. *Department* Ab'teilung *f*.

Derby. *Derbyshire* (*engl. Grafschaft*).

dft. *draft* Tratte *f*.

diff. *different* versch., verschieden; *difference* 'Unterschied *m*.

Dir. *Director* Dir., Di'rektor *m*.

disc. *discount* Dis'kont *m*, Abzug *m*.

dist. *distance* Entfernung *f*; *district* Bez., Bezirk *m*.

div. *dividend* Divi'dende *f*; *divorced* gesch., geschieden.

DIY *do-it-yourself* „mach es selber!"; (*in Zssgn*) Heimwerker ...

DJ *disc jockey* Diskjockey *m*; *dinner jacket* Smoking(jacke *f*) *m*.

DLit(t) *Doctor of Letters, Doctor of Literature* Doktor *m* der Litera'turwissenschaft.

DNA *deoxyribonucleic acid* DNS *f*.

do. *ditto* do., dito; dgl., desgleichen.

doc. *document* Doku'ment *n*, Urkunde *f*.

dol. *dollar(s)* Dollar *m* (*od. pl.*).

Dors. *Dorsetshire* (*engl. Grafschaft*).

doz. *dozen(s)* Dutzend *n od. pl.*

DP *displaced person* Verschleppte(r *m*) *f*; *data processing* DV, Datenverarbeitung *f*.

d/p *documents against payment* Doku'mente *pl.* gegen Zahlung.

DPh(il) *Doctor of Philosophy* Dr. phil., Doktor *m* der Philoso'phie.

Dpt. *Department* Abteilung *f*.

Dr. *Doctor* Dr., Doktor *m*; *debtor* Schuldner *m*.

dr. *dra(ch)m* Dram *n*, Drachme *f* (*Handelsgewicht*); *drawer* Tras'sant *m*.

d.s., d/s *days after sight* Tage nach Sicht (*bei Wechseln*).

DSc *Doctor of Science* Dr. rer. nat., Doktor *m* der Na'turwissenschaften.

DST *Daylight-Saving Time* Sommerzeit *f*.

DTh(eol) *Doctor of Theology* Dr. theol., Doktor *m* der Theolo'gie.

DTP *desktop publishing* *Computer*: DT'P *n*, ‚Desktop-'Publishing *n*.

Dur. *Durham* (*engl. Grafschaft*).

DVD *digital versatile* (*od. video*) *disk* digi'tale, vielseitig verwendbare (*od.* Video-)Disk.

dwt. *pennyweight* Pennygewicht *n*.

dz. *dozen(s)* Dutzend *n* (*od. pl.*).

E

E *east* O, Ost(en *m*); *east(ern)* ö, östlich; *English* engl., englisch.

E. & O. E. *errors and omissions excepted* Irrtümer und Auslassungen vorbehalten.

EC *European Community* EG, Euro'päische Gemeinschaft; *East Central* London Mitte-Ost (*Postbezirk*).

ECB *European Central Bank* EZ'B *f*, Euro'päische Zent'ralbank.

ECE *Economic Commission for Europe* 'Wirtschaftskommissi,on *f* für Eu'ropa (*des Wirtschafts- u. Sozialrates der UN*).

ECG *electrocardiogram* EKG, E'lektrokardio,gramm *n*.

ECOSOC *Economic and Social Council* Wirtschafts- und Sozi'alrat *m* (*der UN*).

ECSC *European Coal and Steel Community* EGKS, Euro'päische Gemeinschaft für Kohle und Stahl.

ECU *European Currency Unit(s)* Euro'päische Währungseinheit(en *pl.*) *f*.

Ed., ed. *edition* Aufl., Auflage *f*; *edited* hrsg., her'ausgegeben; *editor* Hrsg., Her'ausgeber *m*.

EDP *electronic data processing* EDV, elek'tronische Datenverarbeitung.

E.E., E./E. *errors excepted* Irrtümer vorbehalten.

EEC *hist. European Economic Community* EWG, Euro'päische Wirtschaftsgemeinschaft.

EEG *electroencephalogram* EEG *n*, Elektroenzephalo'gramm *n*.

EFL *English as a Foreign Language* English *n* als Fremdsprache.

EFTA ['eftə] *European Free Trade Association* EFTA, Euro'päische Freihandelsgemeinschaft.

Eftpos *electronic funds transfer at point of sale* Zahlungsart „ec-Kasse".

e.g. *exempli gratia* (*Lat. = for instance*) z. B., zum Beispiel.

EIB *European Investment Bank* EI'B *f*, Euro'päische In'vestmentbank.

ELT *English language teaching* Englischunterricht *m* für Ausländer.

EMS *European Monetary System* EWS, Euro'päisches 'Währungssy,stem.

EMU *European Monetary Union* EW'U *f*, Euro'päische 'Währungsunion.

enc(l). *enclosure(s)* Anl., Anlage(n *pl.*) *f*.

Eng(l). *England* Engl., England *n*; *English* engl., englisch.

ENT *ear, nose, and throat* HNO..., Hals-Nasen-Ohren-....

EP *European Parliament* Euro'päisches Parla'ment.

EPOS *electronic point of sale* elekt'ronische Verkaufsstelle.

ESA *European Space Agency* Euro'päische Weltraumbehörde.

ESL *English as a second language* Englisch *n* als Zweitsprache *od.* Fremdsprache.

ESP *extrasensory perception* außersinnliche Wahrnehmung.

Esq(r). *Esquire* (*in Briefadressen, nachgestellt*) Herrn.

ESRO *European Space Research Organization* ESRO, Euro'päische Organisati'on für Weltraumforschung.

Ess. *Essex* (*engl. Grafschaft*).

est. *established* gegr., gegründet; *estimated* gesch., geschätzt.

E Sx *East Sussex* (*engl. Grafschaft*).

ETA *estimated time of arrival* vo'raussichtliche Ankunft(szeit).

etc., &c. *et cetera, and the rest, and so on* etc., usw., und so weiter.

ETD *estimated time of departure* vo'raussichtliche Abflugzeit *bzw.* Abfahrtszeit.

EU *European Union* EU *f*, Euro'päische Uni'on.

EURATOM [juər'ætəm] *European Atomic Energy Community* Eura'tom *f*, Euro'päische A'tomgemeinschaft.

excl. *exclusive, excluding* ausschl., ausschließlich, ohne.

ex div. *ex dividend* ohne (*od.* ausschließlich) Divi'dende.

ex int. *ex interest* ohne (*od.* ausschließlich) Zinsen.

F

F *Fahrenheit* (*Thermometereinteilung*); *univ. Fellow* (*siehe Wörterverzeichnis fellow* 6).

f. *farthing* (*ehemalige brit. Münze*); *fathom* Faden *m*, Klafter *m*, *n*, *f*; *feminine* w., weiblich; *foot, feet* Fuß *m od. pl.*; *following* folgend.

FA *Brit. Football Association* Fußballverband *m*.

f.a.a. *free of all average* frei von Beschädigung.

Fah(r). *Fahrenheit* (*Thermometereinteilung*).

FAO *Food and Agriculture Organization* Organisati'on *f* für Ernährung und Landwirtschaft (*der UN*).

FAQ, pl. a. FAQs *frequently asked question(s)* häufig gestellte Frage(n).

f.a.s. *free alongside ship* frei Längsseite (See)Schiff.

FBI *Federal Bureau of Investigation* Amer. Bundeskrimi'nalamt *n*; *Federation of British Industries* Brit. Indust'rieverband *m*.

FCC *Federal Communications Commission* Amer. 'Bundeskommissi,on *f* für das Nachrichtenwesen.

Feb. *February* Febr., Februar *m*.

fig. *figure(s)* Abb., Abbildung(en *pl.*) *f*.

f.i.t. *free of income tax* einkommensteuerfrei.

FL, Fla. *Florida* (*Staat der USA*).

FM *frequency modulation* UKW (*Frequenzbereich der Ultrakurzwellen*).

fm *fathom(s)* Faden *m od. pl.*, Klafter *m*, *n*, *f od. pl.*

FO *Brit. Foreign Office* Auswärtiges Amt.

fo(l). *folio* Folio *n*, Seite *f*.

f.o.b. *free on board* frei Schiff.

f.o.d. *free of damage* unbeschädigt, schadenfrei.

f.o.r. *free on rail* frei Wag'gon.

FP *freezing point* Gefrierpunkt *m*; *fireplug* Hy'drant *m*.

Fr. *France* Frankreich *n*; *French* franz., fran'zösisch.

fr. *franc(s)* Franc(s *pl.*) *m*, Franken *m od. pl.*

Fri. *Friday* Fr., Freitag *m*.

ft *foot, feet* Fuß *m od. pl.*

FTC *Federal Trade Commission* Amer. Bundes'handelskommissi,on *f* (*zur Verhinderung unlauteren Wettbewerbs*).

fur. *furlong(s)* (*Längenmaß*).

f.w.h. *flexible working hours* gleitende Arbeitszeit.

FX, f/x *effects pl. TV, Film*: Ef'fekte *pl.*

f.y.i. *for your information* zur Kenntnis(nahme).

G

g *gram(s), gramme(s)* g, Gramm *n od. pl.*; *gallon(s)* Gal'lone(n *pl.*) *f*.

g. *ga(u)ge* Nor'malmaß *n*; 🚆 Spur *f*; *guinea* Gui'nee *f* (*105 p*).

GA *general agent* Gene'ralvertreter *m*; *general assembly* Hauptversammlung *f*; *siehe* **Ga.**

Ga. *Georgia* (*Staat der USA*).

gal(l). *gallon(s)* Gal'lone(n *pl.*) *f*.

GATT [gæt] *General Agreement on Tariffs and Trade* Allgemeines Zoll- und Handelsabkommen.

GB *Great Britain* GB, Großbri'tannien *n*; *gigabyte(s pl.)* GB, 'Gigabyte *n od. pl.*

G.B.S. *George Bernard Shaw* (*irischer Dramatiker*).

GCB *(Knight) Grand Cross of the Bath* (Ritter *m* des) Großkreuz(es) *n* des Bath-Ordens.

GCE *General Certificate of Education* (*siehe Wörterverzeichnis*).

GCSE *General Certificate of Secondary Education* (*schulische Abschlussprüfung, die seit 1988 u. a. die "O-levels" des* **GCE** *ersetzt*).

GDP *gross domestic product* ₸ BIP *n*, Brutto'inlandspro,dukt *n*.

Gen. *General* Gene'ral *m*.

gen. *general(ly)* allgemein.

Ger. *German* deutsch, Deutsche(r *m*) *f*; *Germany* Deutschland *n*.

GI *government issue* von der Regierung ausgegeben, Staatseigentum *n*; *der* amer. Sol'dat.

gi. *gil(s)* Viertelpinte(n *pl.*) *f*.

GLC *Greater London Council* (*ehemaliger*) Stadtrat *m* von Groß-London.

Glos. *Gloucestershire* (*engl. Grafschaft*).

GM ₸ *General Manager* (Gene'ral)Direktor(in), Hauptge'schäftsführer(in); Inten'dant(in); *Lebensmittel etc.*: *genetically modified* gentechnisch verändert, F genmanipuliert.

GMT *Greenwich Mean Time* WEZ, 'westeuro,päische Zeit.

GNP *gross national product* ₸ Bruttosozi'alpro,dukt *n*.

gns. *guineas* Gui'neen *pl.*

GOP *Am.* *Grand Old Party* Republi'kanische Par'tei.

Gov. *Government* Regierung *f*; *Governor* Gouver'neur *m*.

Govt, govt *government* Regierung *f*.

GP *general practitioner* Arzt *m* (Ärztin *f*) für Allge'meinmedi,zin; *Gallup Poll* 'Meinungs,umfrage *f* (*insbes. zum Wählerverhalten*).

GPO *General Post Office* Hauptpostamt *n*.

GPS *global positioning system* GP'S-Sys,tem *n* (*Standortermittlung via Satellitenpeilung*).

gr. *grain(s)* Gran *n* (*od. pl.*); *gross* brutto; Gros *n od. pl.* (*12 Dutzend*).

gr.wt *gross weight* Bruttogewicht *n*.

gs *guineas* Gui'neen *pl.*

GSM *General Sales Manager* Ver'kaufsleiter(in).

gtd, guar. *guaranteed* garantiert.

GUI *graphical user interface* Computer: grafische Be'nutzeroberfläche.

H

h. *hour(s)* Std., Stunde(n *pl.*) *f*, Uhr (*bei Zeitangaben*); *height* Höhe *f*.

h&c *hot and cold* warm u. kalt (*Wasser*).

Hants. *Hampshire* (*engl. Grafschaft*).

HBM *His* (*Her*) *Britannic Majesty* Seine (Ihre) Bri'tannische Maje'stät.

HC *Brit.* *House of Commons* 'Unterhaus *n*; *Holy Communion* heiliges Abendmahl, heilige Kommuni'on.

hdbk *handbook* Handbuch *n*.

HE *high explosive* hochexplo'siv; *His Eminence* Seine Emi'nenz *f*; *His* (*Her*) *Excellency* Seine (Ihre) Exzel'lenz *f*.

Heref. *Herefordshire* (*ehemal. engl. Grafschaft*).

Herts. *Hertfordshire* (*engl. Grafschaft*).

HF *high frequency* 'Hochfre,quenz *f*; *Brit.* *Home Fleet* Flotte *f* in den Heimatgewässern.

hf *half* halb.

hf.bd *half bound* in Halbfranz gebunden (*Halbleder*).

HGV *Brit.* *heavy goods vehicle* Schwerlastkraftwagen *m*, F Schwerlaster *m*.

hhd *hogshead* (*Hohlmaß, etwa 240 Liter*); großes Fass.

HI *Hawaii* (*Staat der USA*).

HIV *human immunodeficiency virus* HIV *n*.

HL *Brit.* *House of Lords* Oberhaus *n*.

HM *His* (*Her*) *Majesty* Seine (Ihre) Maje'stät.

HMS *His* (*Her*) *Majesty's Service* Dienst *m*, ⚓ Dienstsache *f*; *His* (*Her*) *Majesty's Ship* (*Steamer*) Seiner (Ihrer) Maje'stät Schiff *n* (Dampfschiff *n*).

HMSO *His* (*Her*) *Majesty's Stationery Office* (*Brit. Staatsdruckerei*).

HO *Head Office* Hauptge'schäftsstelle *f*, Zen'trale *f*; *Brit.* *Home Office* 'Innenmini,sterium *n*.

Hon. *Honorary* ehrenamtlich; *Hono(u)rable* (*der od. die*) Ehrenwerte (*Anrede und Titel*).

HP, hp *horsepower* PS, Pferdestärke *f*; *high pressure* Hochdruck *m*; *hire purchase* Ratenkauf *m*.

HQ, Hq. *Headquarters* Stab(squartier *n*) *m*, Hauptquartier *n*.

HR *Am.* *House of Representatives* Repräsen'tantenhaus *n*.

hr *hour(s)* Stunde(n *pl.*) *f*.

HRH *His* (*Her*) *Royal Highness* Seine (Ihre) Königliche Hoheit.

hrs *hours* Std., Stunden *pl.*

HT, h.t. *high tension* Hochspannung *f*.

ht *height* H., Höhe *f*.

Hunts. *Huntingdonshire* (*ehemal. engl. Grafschaft*).

HWM *high-water mark* Hochwasserstandsmarke *f*.

I

I. *island(s)*, *isle(s)* Insel(n *pl.*) *f*.

IA, Ia. *Iowa* (*Staat der USA*).

IATA [aɪˈɑːtə] *International Air Transport Association* Internatio'naler Luftverkehrsverband.

IBA *Independent Broadcasting Authority* (*Dachorganisation der brit. privaten Fernseh- u. Rundfunkanstalten*).

ib(id). *ibidem* (*Lat. = in the same place*) ebd., ebenda.

IBRD *International Bank for Reconstruction and Development* Internatio'nale Bank für Wieder'aufbau und Entwicklung, Weltbank *f*.

IC *integrated circuit* inte'grierter Schaltkreis.

ICAO *International Civil Aviation Organization* Internatio'nale Zi'villuftfahrt-Organisati,on.

ICBM *intercontinental ballistic missile* interkontinen'taler bal'listischer Flugkörper, Interkontinen'talra,kete *f*.

ICFTU *International Confederation of Free Trade Unions* Internatio'naler Bund Freier Gewerkschaften.

ICJ *International Court of Justice* IG, Internatio'naler Gerichtshof.

ICU *intensive care unit* Inten'sivstati,on *f*.

ID *Idaho* (*Staat der USA*); *identity* Identi'tät *f*; *Intelligence Department* Nachrichtenamt *n*.

Id(a). *Idaho* (*Staat der USA*).

IDP *international driving permit* internatio'naler Führerschein.

i.e. *id est* (*Lat. = that is to say*) d. h., das heißt.

IHP, ihp *indicated horsepower* i. PS, indizierte Pferdestärke.

IL, Ill. *Illinois* (*Staat der USA*).

ILO *International Labo(u)r Organization* Internatio'nale 'Arbeitsorganisati,on.

ILS *instrument landing system* Instru'menten,landesy,stem *n*.

IMF *International Monetary Fund* IWF, Internatio'naler Währungsfonds.

Imp. *Imperial* Reichs..., Empire...

IN *Indiana* (*Staat der USA*).

in. *inch(es)* Zoll *m* (*od. pl.*).

Inc. *Incorporated* (amtlich) eingetragen.

incl. *inclusive*, *including* einschl., einschließlich.

incog. *incognito* in'kognito (*unter anderem Namen*).

Ind. *Indiana* (*Staat der USA*).

inst. *instant* d. M., dieses Monats.

I/O *input/output* 'Input *m*/'Output *m* (*-Ana,lyse etc.*).

IOC *International Olympic Committee* Internatio'nales O'lympisches Komi'tee.

I. of M. *Isle of Man* (*engl. Insel*).

I. of W. *Isle of Wight* (*engl. Insel*; *Grafschaft*).

IOM *siehe* **I. of M.**

IOU *I owe you* Schuldschein *m*.

IOW *siehe* **I. of W.**

IPA *International Phonetic Association* Internatio'nale Pho'netische Gesellschaft.

IPO *initial public offer(ing)* Börse: 'Erstno,tiz *f* (*e-r Aktie*).

IQ *intelligence quotient* Intelli'genzquoti,ent *m*.

Ir. *Ireland* Irland *n*; *Irish* irisch.

IRA *Irish Republican Army* IRA, 'Irisch-Republi'kanische Ar'mee.

IRBM *intermediate-range ballistic missile* 'Mittelstreckenra,kete *f*.

IRS *Am.* *Internal Revenue Service* Finanzamt *n*.

ISBN *international standard book number* ISB'N-Nummer *f*.

ISDN *integrated services digital network* Dienste integrierendes digi'tales Fernmeldenetz.

ISO *International Organization for Standardization* IOS, Internatio'nale Organisati'on für Standardisierung, Internatio'nale 'Normenorganisati,on.

ISP *Internet service provider* 'Internet-Service-Pro,vider *m od.* -,Anbieter *m*.

IT *information technology* I'T *f*, Informati'onstechnolo,gie *f*.

ITV *Independent Television* (*unabhängige brit. kommerzielle Fernsehanstalten*).

IUD *intrauterine device* Intraute'rinpes,sar *n*, -spi,rale *f*.

IYHF *International Youth Hostel Federation* Internatio'naler Jugendherbergsverband.

J

J. *judge* Richter *m*; *justice* Ju'stiz *f*; Richter *m*.

Jan. *January* Jan., Januar *m*.

JATO ['dʒeɪtəʊ] *jet-assisted takeoff* Start *m* mit 'Startra,kete.

JC *Jesus Christ* Jesus Christus *m*.

JCB *Juris Civilis Baccalaureus* (*Lat. = Bachelor of Civil Law*) Bakka'laureus *m* des Zi'vilrechts.

JCD *Juris Civilis Doctor* (*Lat. = Doctor of Civil Law*) Doktor *m* des Zi'vilrechts.

Jnr *junior siehe* **Jr**, *jun(r)*.

JP *Justice of the Peace* Friedensrichter *m*.

Jr *junior* (*Lat. = the younger*) jr., jun., der Jüngere.

JUD *Juris Utriusque Doctor* (*Lat. = Doctor of Civil and Canon Law*) Doktor *m* beider Rechte.

Jul. *July* Jul., Juli *m.*
Jun. *June* Jun., Juni *m.*
jun(r). *junior* (*Lat.* = *the younger*) jr., jun., der Jüngere.

K

Kan(s). *Kansas* (*Staat der USA*).
KB *kilobyte(s pl.*) KB, 'Kilobyte *n od. pl.*
KC *Knight Commander* Kom'tur *m*, Großmeister *m*; *Brit.* *King's Counsel* Kronanwalt *m.*
KCB *Knight Commander of the Bath* Großmeister *m* des Bath-Ordens.
Ken. *Kentucky* (*Staat der USA*).
kg *kilogram(me)(s)* kg, Kilogramm *n* (*od. pl.*).
kHz *kilohertz* kHz, Kilo'hertz *n od. pl.*
KIA *killed in action* gefallen.
KKK *Ku Klux Klan* (*geheime Terrororganisation in den USA*).
km *Brit.* *kilometre(s)*, *Am.* *kilometer(s)* km, Kilo'meter *m* (*od. pl.*).
KO, **k.o.** *knockout* K.o., Knock-out *m.*
KP *kitchen police Am.* ✕ *sl.* Küchendienst *m* (*Personen*).
k.p.h. *Brit.* *kilometre(s) per hour*, *Am.* *kilometer(s) per hour* 'Stundenkilo,meter *m* (*od. pl.*).
KS *Kansas* (*Staat der USA*).
kV *kilovolt(s)* kV, Kilo'volt *n* (*od. pl.*).
kW *kilowatt(s)* kW, Kilo'watt *n* (*od. pl.*).
KY, **Ky** *Kentucky* (*Staat der USA*).

L

L *Brit.* *learner* (*driver*) Fahrschüler(in) (*Plakette an Kraftfahrzeugen*).
l. *left* l., links; *length* Länge *f*; *line* Z., Zeile *f*; Lin., Linie *f*; (*meist* **l**) *Brit.* *litre(s)*, *Am.* *liter(s)* l, Liter *m*, *n* (*od. pl.*).
£ *pound(s) sterling* Pfund *n* (*od. pl.*) Sterling (*Währung*).
LA *Los Angeles* (*Stadt in Kalifornien*); *Louisiana* (*Staat der USA*).
La. *Louisiana* (*Staat der USA*).
£A *Australian pound* au'stralisches Pfund (*Währung*).
Lab. *Labrador* (*Kanad. Halbinsel*).
LAN *local area network* *Computer*: lo-'kales (*Rechner*)Netz.
Lancs. *Lancashire* (*engl. Grafschaft*).
lang. *language* Spr., Sprache *f.*
lat. *latitude* geo'graphische Breite.
lb. *pound(s)* Pfund *n* (*od. pl.*) (*Gewicht*).
l.c. *lower case typ.* Kleinbuchstabe(n *pl.*) *m.*
L/C *letter of credit* Kre'ditbrief *m.*
LCD *liquid crystal display* *Computer etc.*: LC'D-Anzeige *f*, 'Flüssigkristall,anzeige *f.*
LCJ *Brit.* *Lord Chief Justice* Lord-'oberrichter *m.*
Ld. *Lord* Lord *m.*
£E *Egyptian pound* ä'gyptisches Pfund (*Währung*).
LED ⊕ *light-emitting diode* 'Leuchtdi,ode *f.*
Leics. *Leicestershire* (*engl. Grafschaft*).
lf *linefeed* *Computer, Drucker*: Zeilenvorschub *m.*
Lincs. *Lincolnshire* (*engl. Grafschaft*).
LJ *Brit.* *Lord Justice* Lordrichter *m.*
ll. *lines* Zeilen *pl.*; Linien *pl.*
LL D *Legum Doctor* (*Lat.* = *Doctor of Laws*) Dr. jur., Doktor *m* der Rechte.

LMT *local mean time* mittlere Ortszeit (*in USA*).
loc. cit. *loco citato* (*Lat.* = *in the place cited*) a. a. O., am angeführten Ort.
lon(g). *longitude* geo'graphische Länge.
LP *long-playing record* LP, Langspielplatte *f*; *Labour Party* (*brit. Linkspartei*); *siehe* **l.p.**
l.p. *low pressure* Tiefdruck *m.*
LPG *liquefied petroleum gas* Flüssiggas *n.*
LPO *London Philharmonic Orchestra* das Londoner Philhar'monische Or-'chester.
L'pool *Liverpool* *n.*
LSD *lysergic acid diethylamide* LSD, Lysergsäurediäthylamid *n.*
LSE *London School of Economics* (*renommierte Londoner Wirtschaftshochschule*).
LSO *London Symphony Orchestra* das Londoner Sinfo'nie-Or,chester.
Lt. *Lieutenant* Leutnant *m.*
l.t. *low tension* Niederspannung *f.*
Lt.-Col. *Lieutenant-Colonel* Oberst-'leutnant *m.*
Ltd. *limited* mit beschränkter Haftung.
Lt.-Gen. *Lieutenant-General* Gene'ralleutnant *m.*

M

m *male* m, männlich; *masculine* m, männlich; *married* verh., verheiratet; *Brit.* *metre(s)*, *Am.* *meter(s)* m, 0Meter *m*, *n od. pl.*; *mile(s)* M., Meile(n *pl.*) *f*; *minute(s)* min., Min., Mi'nute(n *pl.*) *f.*
MA *Master of Arts* Ma'gister *m* der Philoso'phie; *Massachusetts* (*Staat der USA*); *military academy* Mili'täraka-de,mie *f.*
Maj. *Major* Ma'jor *m.*
Maj.-Gen. *Major-General* Gene'ralma,jor *m.*
Man. *Manitoba* (*Kanad. Provinz*).
Mar. *March* März *m.*
Mass. *Massachusetts* (*Staat der USA*).
max. *maximum* Max., Maximum *n.*
MB *Medicinae Baccalaureus* (*Lat.* = *Bachelor of Medicine*) Bakka'laureus *m* der Medi'zin; *megabyte(s pl.*) MB, 'Megabyte *n. od. pl.*
MBO ✝ *management buyout* Management Buy-out *n*; *management by objectives* Führen *n* durch Zielvereinbarung.
MC *Master of Ceremonies* Zere'monienmeister *m*; *Am.* Conférencier *m*; *Am.* *Member of Congress* Parla-'mentsmitglied *n.*
MCA *maximum credible accident* GAU *m*, größter anzunehmender Störfall.
MD *Maryland* (*Staat der USA*); *Managing Director* geschäftsführender Di-'rektor; *Medicinae Doctor* (*Lat.* = *Doctor of Medicine*) Dr. med., Doktor *m* der Medi'zin.
M/D *months' date* Monate nach heute.
Md. *Maryland* (*Staat der USA*).
MDS *Master of Dental Surgery* Ma-'gister *m* der 'Zahnmedi,zin.
ME, **Me.** *Maine* (*Staat der USA*).
med. *medical* med., medi'zinisch; *medicine* Med., Medi'zin *f*; *medieval* mittelalterlich.
MEP *Member of the European Parliament* Mitglied *n* des Euro'päischen Parlaments, Eu'ropaabgeordnete(r *m*) *f.*

mg *milligram(me)(s)* mg, Milligramm *n od. pl.*
MI *Michigan* (*Staat der USA*).
mi. *mile(s)* M., Meile(n *pl.*) *f.*
Mich. *Michigan* (*Staat der USA*).
Middx. *Middlesex* (*ehemal. engl. Grafschaft*).
min. *minute(s)* min., Min., Mi'nute(n *pl.*) *f*; *minimum* Min., Minimum *n.*
Minn. *Minnesota* (*Staat der USA*).
Miss. *Mississippi* (*Staat der USA*).
mm *Brit.* *millimetre(s)*, *Am.* *millimeter(s)* mm, Milli'meter *m*, *n od. pl.*
MN *Minnesota* (*Staat der USA*).
MO *Missouri* (*Staat der USA*); *mail order siehe Wörterverzeichnis*; *money order* Postanweisung *f*, Zahlungsanweisung *f.*
Mo. *Missouri* (*Staat der USA*).
Mon. *Monday* Mo., Montag *m.*
Mont. *Montana* (*Staat der USA*).
MOR *middle-of-the-road siehe Wörterverzeichnis.*
MP *Brit.* *Member of Parliament* Abgeordnete(r) *m* des 'Unterhauses; *Military Police* Mili'tärpoli,zei *f.*
mpg *miles per gallon* Meilen *pl.* pro Gal'lone (*Maß für Benzinverbrauch*).
mph *miles per hour* Stundenmeilen *pl.*
MPharm *Master of Pharmacy* Ma-'gister *m* der Pharma'zie.
MPV *multi-purpose vehicle* Mehrzweckfahrzeug *n.*
Mr ['mıstə] *Mister* Herr *m.*
MRI ✻ *magnetic resonance imaging* ,Kernspintomogra'phie *f.*
MRP *manufacturer's recommended price* unverbindliche Preisempfehlung (*des Herstellers*).
Mrs ['mısız] *ursprünglich* **Mistress** Frau *f.* **MS** *Mississippi* (*Staat der USA*); *manuscript* Mskr(pt).., Manu'skript *n*; *motorship* Motorschiff *n.*
Ms [mız] Frau *f* (*neutrale Anredeform für unverheiratete und verheiratete Frauen*).
MSc *Master of Science* Ma'gister *m* der Na'turwissenschaften.
MSL *mean sea level* mittlere (See)Höhe, Nor'malnull *n.*
MSS *manuscripts* Manu'skripte *pl.*
MT *Montana* (*Staat der USA*).
Mt *Mount* Berg *m.*
mt *megaton* Megatonne *f.*
M'ter *Manchester n.*
MTh *Master of Theology* Ma'gister *m* der Theolo'gie.
Mx *Middlesex* (*ehemal. engl. Grafschaft*).

N

N *north* N, Nord(en *m*); *north(ern)* n, nördlich.
n *neuter* n, Neutrum *n*, neu'tral; *noun* Subst., Substantiv *n*; *noon* Mittag *m.*
n/a *not applicable* nicht zutreffend.
NAAFI ['næfı] *Brit.* *Navy, Army and Air Force Institutes* (*Truppenbetreuungsinstitution der brit. Streitkräfte, u. a. für Kantinen u. Geschäfte zuständig*).
NASA ['næsə] *Am.* *National Aeronautics and Space Administration* Natio-'nale Luft- u. Raumfahrtbehörde *f.*
nat. *national* nat., natio'nal; *natural* nat., na'türlich.
NATO ['neıtəʊ] *North Atlantic Treaty Organization* Nordat'lantikpakt-Organisati,on *f.*
NB *New Brunswick* (*Kanad. Provinz*).
NBC *Am.* *National Broadcasting*

Company Natio'nale Rundfunkgesell-schaft.

NBG F *no bloody good* nicht zu gebrau-chen, (völlig) wertlos.

NC *North Carolina* (*Staat der USA*).

NCB *Brit.* *National Coal Board* Na-tio'nale Kohlenbehörde; *no claims bonus* 'Schadenfreiheitsra,batt *m*.

n.d. *no date* ohne Datum.

ND, N Dak. *North Dakota* (*Staat der USA*).

NE *Nebraska* (*Staat der USA*); *north-east* NO, Nord'ost(en *m*); *north-east(ern)* nö, nord'östlich.

Neb(r). *Nebraska* (*Staat der USA*).

neg. *negative* neg., negativ.

Nev. *Nevada* (*Staat der USA*).

NF *Newfoundland* (*Kanad. Provinz*).

N/F *no funds* keine Deckung.

Nf(l)d *Newfoundland* (*Kanad. Provinz*).

NH *New Hampshire* (*Staat der USA*).

NHS *Brit.* *National Health Service* Staatlicher Gesundheitsdienst.

NJ *New Jersey* (*Staat der USA*).

NM, N Mex. *New Mexico* (*Staat der USA*).

No. *North* N, Nord(en *m*); *numero* Nr., Nummer *f*; *number* Zahl *f*.

Norf. *Norfolk* (*engl. Grafschaft*).

Northants. *Northamptonshire* (*engl. Grafschaft*).

Northd., Northumb. *Northumberland* (*engl. Grafschaft*).

Notts. *Nottinghamshire* (*engl. Graf-schaft*).

Nov. *November* Nov., No'vember *m*.

n.p. or d. *no place or date* ohne Ort oder Datum.

NPV *net present value* Tageswert *m*, Barwert *m* (*e-r Summe*).

NS *Nova Scotia* (*Kanad. Provinz*).

NSB *Brit.* *National Savings Bank* etwa Postsparkasse *f*.

NSPCC *National Society for the Pre-vention of Cruelty to Children* (*brit. Kinderschutzverein*).

NSW *New South Wales* (*Bundesstaat Australiens*).

NT *New Testament* NT, Neues Testa-'ment; *Northern Territory* (*Verwal-tungsbezirk Australiens*).

nt.wt. *net weight* Nettogewicht *n*.

NV *Nevada* (*Staat der USA*).

NW *northwest* NW, Nord'west(en *m*); *northwest(ern)* nw, nord'westlich.

NWT *Northwest Territories* (*N-Kanada östl. des Yukon Territory*).

NY *New York* (*Staat der USA*).

NYC *New York City* (die Stadt) New York.

N Yorks. *North Yorkshire* (*engl. Graf-schaft*).

O

O. *Ohio* (*Staat der USA*); *order* Auftr., Auftrag *m*.

o/a *on account of* auf Rechnung von.

OAP *old-age pensioner* (Alters)Rent-ner(in), 'Ruhegeldm,pfänger(in).

OAS *Organization of American States* Organisati'on *f* ameri'kanischer Staa-ten.

OAU *Organization of African Unity* Or-ganisati'on *f* für Afri'kanische Einheit.

ob. *obiit* (*Lat. = died*) gest., gestorben.

OC ✕ *officer commanding* befehlsha-bende(r) Offi'zier.

Oct. *October* Okt., Ok'tober *m*.

OECD *Organization for Economic Cooperation and Development* Or-

ganisati'on *f* für wirtschaftliche Zu'sam-menarbeit und Entwicklung.

OH *Ohio* (*Staat der USA*).

OHMS *On His (Her) Majesty's Service* im Dienste Seiner (Ihrer) Maje'stät; ⅋ Dienstsache *f*.

OHP *overhead projector* 'Overhead-pro,jektor *m*.

OK *Oklahoma* (*Staat der USA*); *siehe O.K.*

O.K. (*möglicherweise aus:*) *all correct* in Ordnung.

Okla. *Oklahoma* (*Staat der USA*).

o.n.o. *or near(est) offer* VB, Verhand-lungsbasis *f*.

Ont. *Ontario* (*Kanad. Provinz*).

OPAC *online public access catalogue* elektronischer Bibliothekskatalog.

OPEC ['əʊpek] *Organization of Petro-leum Exporting Countries* Organisa-ti'on *f* der Erdöl exportierenden Länder.

OR *Oregon* (*Staat der USA*).

o.r. *owner's risk* auf Gefahr des Eigen-tümers.

Ore(g). *Oregon* (*Staat der USA*).

OT *Old Testament* AT, Altes Testa-'ment.

OTT *Brit.* F *over the top* (maßlos) über-'trieben

OUP *Oxford University Press* Verlag *m* der Universi'tät Oxford.

Oxon. *Oxfordshire* (*engl. Grafschaft*); *Oxoniensis* (*Titel etc.*) der Universi'tät Oxford.

oz. *ounce(s)* Unze(n *pl.*) *f*.

P

p *penny, pence* (*brit. Münze*).

p. *page* S., Seite *f*; *part* T., Teil *m*.

PA, Pa. *Pennsylvania* (*Staat der USA*).

p.a. *per annum* (*Lat. = yearly*) jähr-lich.

par(a). *paragraph* Par., Para'graph *m*, Abschnitt *m*.

PAS *mot.* *power-assisted steering* 'Servolenkung *f*.

PAYE *pay as you earn* (*Brit.* Quellen-abzugsverfahren. *Arbeitgeber zieht Lohn- bzw. Einkommensteuer direkt vom Lohn bzw. Gehalt ab*).

PC *Brit.* *police constable* Schutzmann *m*; *Personal Computer* PC, Perso'nal-com,puter *m*; *Am.* *Peace Corps* Frie-denscorps *n*.

p.c. *per cent* %, Pro'zent *n* od. *pl.*; *postcard* Postkarte *f*.

p/c *price current* Preisliste *f*.

pcl. *parcel* Pa'ket *n*.

pcs. *pieces* Stück(e) *pl.*

PD *Police Department* Poli'zeibehörde *f*; *per diem* (*Lat. = by the day*) pro Tag.

pd. *paid* bez., bezahlt.

PDA *personal digital assistant* (*Palm-top-Computer als elektronisches Notiz-buch*).

PE *physical education* Sport *m* (*Schul-fach*).

PEI *Prince Edward Island* (*Kanad. Provinz*).

PEN [pen], *mst* **PEN Club** (*Internation-al Association of*) *Poets, Play-wrights, Editors, Essayists and Novelists* PEN-Club *m* (*Internationa-ler Verband von Dichtern, Dramati-kern, Redakteuren, Essayisten und Ro-manschriftstellern*).

Penn(a). *Pennsylvania* (*Staat der USA*).

per pro(c). *per procurationem* (*Lat. =*

by proxy) pp., ppa., per Pro'kura.

PhD *Philosophiae Doctor* (*Lat. = Doctor of Philosophy*) Dr. phil., Dok-tor *m* der Philoso'phie.

PIN *personal identification number* PIN *m*, *f*, Geheimzahl *f*.

Pk. *Park* Park *m*; *Peak* Spitze *f*, (Berg-)Gipfel *m*.

Pl. *Place* Platz *m*.

PLC, Plc, plc *Brit.* *public limited com-pany* AG, Aktiengesellschaft *f*.

PM *bsd.* *Brit.* *Prime Minister* Premi'er-minister(in).

p.m. *post meridiem* (*Lat. = after noon*) nachm., nachmittags, ab., abends.

PMS *premenstrual syndrome* ♂ ,prä-menstru'elles Syn'drom.

PO *post office* Postamt *n*; *postal order* Postanweisung *f*.

POB *post-office box* Postschließfach *n*.

p.o.d. *pay on delivery* Nachnahme *f*.

POO *post-office order* Postanweisung *f*.

pos(it). *positive* pos., positiv.

POW *prisoner of war* Kriegsgefange-ne(r) *m*.

p.p. *per procurationem* (*Lat. = by proxy*) pp., ppa., per Pro'kura.

pp. *pages* Seiten *pl.*

PR *public relations* PR, Öffentlich-keitsarbeit *f*.

pref. *preface* Vw., Vorwort *n*.

Pres. *President* Präsi'dent *m*.

pro. *professional* professio'nell, Be-rufs...

Prof. *Professor* Pro'fessor *m*.

prol. *prologue* Pro'log *m*.

Prot. *Protestant* Prot., Prote'stant *m*.

prox. *proximo* (*Lat. = next month*) n. M., nächsten Monats.

PS *postscript* PS, Post'skript *n*, Nach-schrift *f*.

PT *physical training* Leibeserziehung *f*.

pt. *part* Teil *m*; *payment* Zahlung *f*; *pint* (*Brit. 0,57 l, Am. 0,47 l*); *point* siehe Wörterverzeichnis.

PTA *Parent-Teacher Association* El-tern-Lehrer-Vereinigung *f*.

Pte. *Brit.* *Private* Sol'dat *m* (*Dienst-grad*).

PTO, p.t.o. *please turn over* b.w., bitte wenden.

Pvt. *Am.* *Private* Sol'dat *m* (*Dienst-grad*).

PW *prisoner of war* Kriegsgefangene(r) *m*.

PX *Post Exchange* (*Verkaufsläden für Angehörige der amer. Streitkräfte*).

Q

QC *Brit.* *Queen's Counsel* Kronanwalt *m*.

Qld. *Queensland* (*Bundesstaat Austra-liens*).

qr *quarter* (*etwa 1*) Viertel'zentner *m* (*Handelsgewicht*).

qt *quart* Quart *n* (*Brit. 1,14 l, Am. 0,95 l*).

Que. *Quebec* (*Kanad. Provinz*).

quot. *quotation* Kurs-, Preisnotierung *f*.

R

R. *Réaumur* (*Thermometereinteilung*); *River* Strom *m*, Fluss *m*.

r. *right* r., rechts.

RA *Brit.* *Royal Academy* Königliche

Akade'mie.

RAC *Brit.* **Royal Automobile Club** Königlicher Automo'bilklub.

RAF **Royal Air Force** Königlich-Brit. Luftwaffe *f.*

RAM *Computer:* **random access memory** Speicher *m* mit wahlfreiem Zugriff, Direktzugriffsspeicher *m.*

RC **Roman Catholic** r.-k., römisch-ka-'tholisch.

Rd **Road** Str., Straße *f.*

recd **received** erhalten.

ref(c). *(in)* **reference (to)** (mit) Bezug *m* (auf); Empf., Empfehlung *f.*

regd **registered** eingetragen; ✎ eingeschrieben.

reg. tn **register ton** RT, Re'gistertonne *f.*

res. **residence** Wohnsitz, -ort *m*; **research** Forschung *f*; **reserve** Re'serve *f*, Reserve...

ret(d). **retired** i. R., im Ruhestand.

Rev(d). **Reverend** Ehrwürden (*Titel u. Anrede*).

RI **Rhode Island** (*Staat der USA*).

RLO *Brit.* **Returned Letter Office** Bü'ro *n* für unzustellbare Briefe.

rm **room** Zi., Zimmer *n.*

RMA *Brit.* **Royal Military Academy** Königliche Mili'tärakade,mie (*Sandhurst*).

RN **Royal Navy** Königlich-Brit. Ma'rine *f.*

RNA **ribonucleic acid** RN'S *f*, ,Ribonukle'insäure *f.*

ROM *Computer:* **read only memory** Nur-Lese-Speicher *m*, Fest(wert)speicher *m.*

RP **received pronunciation** Standardaussprache *f* (*des Englischen in Südengland*); **reply paid** Rückantwort bezahlt (*bei Telegrammen*).

r.p.m. **revolutions per minute** U/min., Um'drehungen *pl.* pro Mi'nute.

RR *Am.* **Railroad** Eisenbahn *f.*

RRP **recommended retail price** unverbindlicher (Einzelhandels-)Richtpreis, empfohlener Endverkaufspreis.

RS *Brit.* **Royal Society** Königliche Gesellschaft (*traditionsreicher u. bedeutendster naturwissenschaftlicher Verein Großbritanniens*).

RSPCA **Royal Society for the Prevention of Cruelty to Animals** (*brit. Tierschutzverein*).

RSVP **répondez s'il vous plaît** (*Fr.* = **please reply**) u. A. w. g., um Antwort wird gebeten; Antwort erbeten.

rt **right** r., rechts.

RTC **real-time clock** Echtzeituhr *f.*

Rt Hon. **Right Honourable** (*der od. die*) Sehr Ehrenwerte (*Titel u. Anrede*).

RU **Rugby Union** 'Rugby-Uni,on *f.*

RV *Am.* **recreational vehicle** Wohnmobil *n*; **rendezvous point** Treffpunkt *m*; **revised version** revi'dierte Über-'setzung (*der Bibel*); **rat(e)able value** Be'messungs,grundlage *f* (*für Steuer*).

Ry *Brit.* **Railway** Eisenbahn *f.*

S

S **south** S, Süd(en *m*); **south(ern)** s, südlich.

s **second(s)** s, sec, sek., Sek., Se'kunde(n *pl.*) *f*; **shilling(s)** Schilling(e *pl.*) *m.*

SA **South Africa** Süd'afrika *n*; **South America** S.A., Süda'merika *n*; **South Australia** (*Bundesstaat Australiens*); **Salvation Army** H.A., 'Heilsar,mee *f.*

s.a.e. **stamped addressed envelope**

frankierter, mit (eigener) Anschrift versehener Briefumschlag.

Salop **Shropshire** (*engl. Grafschaft*).

SALT [sɔːlt] **Strategic Arms Limitation Talks** (*Verhandlungen zwischen der Sowjetunion und den USA über einen Vertrag zur Begrenzung und zum Abbau strategischer Waffensysteme*).

SASE *bsd.* *Am.* **self-addressed stamped envelope** frankierter, mit eigener Anschrift versehener Briefumschlag.

Sask. **Saskatchewan** (*Kanad. Provinz*).

SAT *Am.* **scholastic aptitude test** *ped.* Aufnahmeprüfung *f*; *Brit.* **standard assessment task** Einstufungstest *m.*

Sat. **Saturday** Sa., Samstag *m*; Sonnabend *m.*

S Aus(tr). **South Australia** (*Bundesstaat Australiens*).

SAYE *Brit.* **save as you earn** steuerbegünstigtes Sparen durch Lohnabzug.

SB **sales book** Verkaufsbuch *n.*

Sch. **school** Sch., Schule *f.*

SD, S Dak. **South Dakota** (*Staat der USA*).

SDP *Brit.* **Social Democratic Party** Sozi'aldemo,kratische Par'tei.

SE **southeast** SO, Süd'ost(en *m*); **southeast(ern)** sö, süd'östlich; **Stock Exchange** Börse *f.*

SEATO ['siːtəʊ] **South-East Asia Treaty Organization** Südost'asienpakt-Organisati,on *f* (*1977 aufgelöst*).

Sec. **Secretary** Sekr., Sekre'tär *m*; Mi'nister *m.*

sec. **second(s)** s, sec, sek., Sek., Se-'kunde(n *pl.*) *f*; **secondary** siehe Wörterverzeichnis.

sen(r). **senior** (*Lat.* = **the elder**) sen., der Ältere.

Sep(t). **September** Sep(t)., Sep'tember *m.*

Serg(t). **Sergeant** Fw, Feldwebel *m*; Wachtmeister *m.*

SF **science fiction** Science'fiction *f* (*Literatur*).

Sgt. siehe **Serg(t)**.

sh **share** Aktie *f*; **sheet** Druckbogen *m* (*Buchdruck*); **shilling(s)** Schilling(e *pl.*) *m.*

SHAPE [ʃeip] **Supreme Headquarters Allied Powers Europe** 'Oberkom-,mando *n* der Alliierten Streitkräfte in Eu'ropa.

SIC **standard industrial classification** entspricht etwa unserer *DIN* (*Industrienorm*).

SM **Sergeant-Major** Oberfeldwebel *m*; Oberwachtmeister *m.*

SMS **short message service** *teleph.* Kurzmitteilungsdienst *m.*

S/N **shipping note** Frachtannahmeschein *m*, Schiffszettel *m.*

s.o. **seller's option** Börse: Ver'kaufsopti,on *f.*

Soc. **Society** Gesellschaft *f*; Verein *m.*

Som(s). **Somerset(shire)** (*engl. Grafschaft*).

s.o.r. **sale or return** auf Kommissi'on(s-,basis) *f.*

SOS SOS (*Internationales Seenotzeichen*).

sp.gr. **specific gravity** sp.G., spe'zifisches Gewicht.

S.P.Q.R. **small profits, quick returns** kleine Gewinne, rasche Umsätze.

Sq. **Square** Platz *m.*

sq. **square** Quadrat...

sq.ft **square foot** Qua'dratfuß *m.*

sq.in. **square inch** Qua'dratzoll *m.*

Sr **senior** (*Lat.* = **the elder**) sen., der Ältere.

SS **steamship** Dampfer *m*; **saints** die Heiligen *pl.*

SSP **statutory sick pay** Lohnfortzahlung *f* (im Krankheitsfall).

St. **Saint** ... St., Sankt ...; **Street** Str., Straße *f*; **Station** B(h)f., Bahnhof *m.*

st. **stone** (*Gewicht*).

STA **scheduled time of arrival** planmäßige Ankunft(szeit).

Sta. **Station** B(h)f., Bahnhof *m.*

Staffs. **Staffordshire** (*engl. Grafschaft*).

STD *Brit.* **subscriber trunk dialling** Selbstwählfernverkehr *m*; **scheduled time of departure** planmäßige Abflugzeit *bzw.* Abfahrtszeit; **sexually transmitted disease** Geschlechtskrankheit *f.*

stg **sterling** Sterling *m* (*brit. Währungseinheit*).

STOL [stɒl] **short takeoff and landing** (*aircraft*) STOL-, Kurzstart(-Flugzeug *n*) *m.*

Str. **Strait** Straße *f* (*Meerenge*).

sub. **substitute** Ersatz *m.*

Suff. **Suffolk** (*engl. Grafschaft*).

Sun. **Sunday** So., Sonntag *m.*

supp(l). **supplement** Nachtrag *m.*

Suss. **Sussex** (*ehemal. engl. Grafschaft*).

SW **southwest** SW, Süd'west(en *m*).

Sy **Surrey** (*engl. Grafschaft*).

S Yorks. **South Yorkshire** (*engl. Grafschaft*).

Sx **Sussex** (*ehemal. engl. Grafschaft*).

T

t **ton(s)** Tonne(n *pl.*) *f* (*Handelsgewicht*).

T&E F *humor.* **tired and emotional** angeheitert, nicht mehr ganz nüchtern.

Tas. **Tasmania** (*Bundesstaat Australiens*).

TB **tuberculosis** Tb, Tbc, Tuberkulose *f.*

tbsp **tablespoon(ful[s** *pl.***])** Esslöffel *m* (*od. pl.*) (voll).

TC **Trusteeship Council** Treuhandschaftsrat *m* (*der UN*).

TD **Treasury Department** Fi'nanzmini,sterium *n* der USA.

tel. **telephone** Tel., Tele'fon *n.*

Tenn. **Tennessee** (*Staat der USA*).

TEOTWAWKI **the end of the world as we know it** das Ende der Welt, wie wir sie kennen.

Ter(r). **Terrace** (*in Straßennamen*) Häuserreihe *f* (*in Hanglage od. über einem Hang gelegen*); **Territory** (Hoheits)Gebiet *n*, Terri'torium *n.*

Tex. **Texas** (*Staat der USA*).

tgm. **telegram** Tele'gramm *n.*

TGWU **Transport and General Workers' Union** Trans'portarbeitergewerkschaft *f.*

Th., Thu(r)., Thurs. **Thursday** Do., Donnerstag *m.*

TLC F **tender loving care** liebevolle Zuwendung.

TMO **telegraph money order** tele'grafische Geldanweisung.

TN **Tennessee** (*Staat der USA*).

tn **ton(s)** Tonne(n *pl.*) *f* (*Handelsgewicht*).

TO **Telegraph (Telephone) Office** Tele'grafen- (Fernsprech)amt *n*; **turnover** 'Umsatz *m.*

TRH *Brit.* **Their Royal Highnesses** Ihre Königlichen Hoheiten.

tsp **teaspoon(ful[s** *pl.***])** Teelöffel *m* (*od. pl.*) (voll).

TU *Trade*(*s*) *Union*(*s*) Gew., Gewerk-schaft(en *pl.*) *f.*
Tu. *Tuesday* Di., Dienstag *m.*
TUC *Brit.* *Trades Union Congress* Gewerkschaftsverband *m.*
Tue(*s*). *Tuesday* Di., Dienstag *m.*
TV *television* FS, Fernsehen *n*; Fernseh...
TX *Texas* (*Staat der USA*).

U

U *universal* allgemein (*zugelassen*) (*Kinoprogramm ohne Jugendverbot*).
UEFA [juːˈeɪfə; -ˈiːfə] *Union of European Football Associations* UˈEFA *f.*
UFO *unidentified flying object* Ufo *n.*
UHF *ultrahigh frequency* UHF, Ultra-'hochfrequenz(bereich *m*) *f,* Dezi'meterwellenbereich *m.*
UHT *ultra-heat-treated* ultrahoch erhitzt (*Milch*).
UK *United Kingdom* Vereinigtes Königreich (*England, Schottland, Wales u. Nordirland*).
ult(**o**). *ultimo* (*Lat.* = *in the last* [*month*]) v. Mts., vorigen Monats.
UMTS *universal mobile telecommunications system*(*s*) *teleph.* *Übertragungsstandard für drahtlose Kommunikation.*
UMW *United Mine Workers* Vereinigte Bergarbeiter *pl.* (*amer. Gewerkschaftsverband*).
UN *United Nations* Vereinte Nati'onen *pl.*
UNESCO [juːˈneskəʊ] *United Nations Eductional, Scientific, and Cultural Organization* Organisati'on *f* der Vereinten Nati'onen für Wissenschaft, Erziehung und Kul'tur.
UNICEF [ˈjuːnɪsef] *United Nations Children's Fund* (*früher United Nations International Children's Emergency Fund*) Kinderhilfswerk *n* der Vereinten Nati'onen.
UNO *United Nations Organization* UNO *f.*
UNSC *United Nations Security Council* Sicherheitsrat *m* der Vereinten Nati'onen.
UPI *United Press International* (*amer. Nachrichtenagentur*).
URL *uniform resource locator* UR'L *f,* einheitlicher Quellenlokalisierer,'Interneta,dresse *f.*
US *United States* Vereinigte Staaten *pl.*
u/s *unserviceable* nicht verwendbar, unbrauchbar (*Gerät etc.*); betriebsunfähig.
USA *United States of America* Vereinigte Staaten *pl.* von A'merika; *United States Army* Heer *n* der Vereinigten Staaten.
USAF(**E**) *United States Air Force* (*Europe*) Luftwaffe *f* der Vereinigten Staaten (in Eu'ropa).
USN *United States Navy* Ma'rine *f* der Vereinigten Staaten.
USP ✝ *unique selling proposition* einmaliges Verkaufsargument; *unique selling point* einzigartiger Verkaufsanreiz.
USS *United States Senate* Se'nat *m* der Vereinigten Staaten; *United States Ship* (Kriegs)Schiff *n* der Vereinigten Staaten.

USSR *hist.* *Union of Soviet Socialist Republics* UdSSR, Uni'on *f* der Sozia-'listischen Sow'jetrepu,bliken.
UT, **Ut.** *Utah* (*Staat der USA*).
UV *ultraviolet* UV, 'ultravio,lett.

V

V *Volt*(*s*) V, Volt *n* (*od. pl.*).
v. *very* sehr; *verse* V., Vers *m*; *versus* (*Lat.* = *against*) gegen; *vide* (*Lat.* = *see*) s., siehe; *volt*(*s*) V, Volt *n* (*od. pl.*).
VA, **Va.** *Virginia* (*Staat der USA*).
VAT *value added tax* MwSt., Mehrwertsteuer *f.*
VCR *video cassette recorder* 'Video-re,korder *m.*
VD *venereal disease* Geschlechtskrankheit *f.*
VDU *visual display unit* Bildschirm *m,* Datensichtgerät *n.*
VHF *very high frequency* VHF, UKW, Ultrakurzwelle(n *pl.*) *f,* Meterwellenbereich *m.*
Vic. *Victoria* (*Bundesstaat Australiens*).
VIN *vehicle identification number* Kfz-Kennzeichen *n.*
VIP *very important person* VIP *m,* ,hohes Tier'.
Vis(**c**). *Viscount*(*ess*) Vi'comte *m* (Vi-com'tesse *f*).
viz. *videlicet* (*Lat.* = *namely*) nämlich.
vol. *volume* Bd., Band *m* (*eines Buches*).
vols. *volumes* Bde., Bände *pl.*
VP(**res.**) *Vice President* 'Vizepräsi,dent *m* (*stellvertretender Vorsitzender, Vorstandsmitglied etc.*).
VR *virtual reality* *Computer:* virtu'elle Reali'tät.
vs. *versus* (*Lat.* = *against*) gegen.
VSOP *very superior old pale* (*Bezeichnung für 20–25 Jahre alten Branntwein, Portwein etc.*).
VT, **Vt.** *Vermont* (*Staat der USA*).
VTOL [ˈviːtɒl] *vertical takeoff and landing* (*aircraft*) Senkrechtstarter *m.*
v.v. *vice versa* (*Lat.* = *conversely*) 'umgekehrt.

W

W *west* West(en *m*); *west*(*ern*) w, westlich; *watt*(*s*) W, Watt *n* (*od. pl.*).
w *watt*(*s*) W, Watt *n* (*od. pl.*); *week* Wo., Woche *f*; *width* Weite *f,* Breite *f*; *wife* (Ehe)Frau *f*; *with* mit.
WA *Washington* (*Staat der USA*); *siehe* *W Aus*(*tr*).
WAP *wireless application protocol* *teleph.* *Übertragungsstandard für drahtlose Kommunikation.*
War(**ks**). *Warwickshire* (*engl. Grafschaft*).
Wash. *Washington* (*Staat der USA*).
WASP [wɒsp] *White Anglo-Saxon Protestant* (*protestantischer Amerikaner britischer od. nordeuropäischer Abstammung*).
W Aus(**tr**). *Western Australia* (*Bundesstaat Australiens*).
WC *West Central* London Mitte-West (*Postbezirk*); *water closet* WC, 'Wasserklo,sett *n.*
Wed(**s**). *Wednesday* Mi., Mittwoch *m.*

w.e.f. *with effect from* mit Wirkung vom.
WEU *Western European Union* 'West-euro,päische Uni'on.
WFTU *World Federation of Trade Unions* Weltgewerkschaftsbund *m.*
WHO *World Health Organization* Weltge'sundheitsorganisati,on *f* (*der UN*).
WI *West Indies* 'West'indien *n*; *siehe* *Wis*(*c*).
Wilts. *Wiltshire* (*engl. Grafschaft*).
Wis(**c**). *Wisconsin* (*Staat der USA*).
wk *week* Wo., Woche *f*; *work* Arbeit *f.*
wkly *weekly* wöchentlich.
wks *weeks* Wo., Wochen *pl.*
w/o *without* o., ohne.
Worcs. *Worcestershire* (*ehemal. engl. Grafschaft*).
WP, **w.p.** *weather permitting* (nur) bei gutem Wetter.
w.p.a. *with particular average* mit Teilschaden (*Versicherung inklusive Teilschaden*).
w.p.m. *words per minute* Wörter *pl.* pro Mi'nute.
w.r.t. *with reference to* bezüglich.
W Sx *West Sussex* (*engl. Grafschaft*).
W/T *wireless telegraphy* (*telephony*) drahtlose Telegra'fie (Telefo'nie).
wt *weight* Gewicht *n.*
WV, **W Va.** *West Virginia* (*Staat der USA*).
WW I (*od.* **II**) *World War I* (*od. II*) der Erste (*od.* Zweite) Weltkrieg.
WYSIWYG [ˈwɪzɪwɪg] *what you see is what you get* 'WYSIWIG *n* (*Bildschirmdarstellung der Daten, die dem entspricht, was auf dem Ausdruck erscheint*).
WY, **Wyo.** *Wyoming* (*Staat der USA*).
W Yorks. *West Yorkshire* (*engl. Grafschaft*).
WWW *World Wide Web* *n* (*wichtigster Teil des Internets*).

X

x-d. *ex dividend* ohne Divi'dende.
x-i. *ex interest* ohne Zinsen.
Xm., **Xmas** [ˈkrɪsməs; ˈeksməs] *Christmas* Weihnacht(en *n*) *f.*
Xn *Christian* christlich.
Xroads *crossroads* Straßenkreuzung *f.*
Xt *Christ* Christus *m.*
Xtian *Christian* christlich.

Y

yd(**s**) *yard*(*s*) Elle(n *pl.*) *f* (*Längenmaß*).
YHA *Youth Hostels Association* Jugendherbergsverband *m.*
YMCA *Young Men's Christian Association* CVJM, Christlicher Verein junger Männer.
Yorks. *Yorkshire* (*ehemal. engl. Grafschaft*).
yr, *year* Jahr *n*; *your siehe Wörterverzeichnis*; *younger* jünger(e, -es); junior.
yrs *years* Jahre *pl.*; *yours siehe Wörterverzeichnis.*
Y2K *year 2000* Jahr *n* 2000.
YWCA *Young Women's Christian Association* Christlicher Verein junger Frauen und Mädchen.

Eigennamen

A

Ab·er·deen [ˌæbəˈdiːn] *Stadt in Schottland*; **ˌAb·er·deenˈshire** [-ʃə] *schottische Grafschaft (bis 1975).*

Ab·er·ystˈwyth [ˌæbəˈrɪstwɪθ] *Stadt in Wales.*

A·bra·ham [ˈeɪbrəhæm] Abraham *m.*

A·chil·les [əˈkɪliːz] Aˈchilles *m.*

A·da [ˈeɪdə] Ada *f*, Adda *f.*

Ad·am [ˈædəm] Adam *m.*

Ad·di·son [ˈædɪsn] *englischer Autor.*

Ad·e·laide [ˈædəleɪd] *Stadt in Australien*; Adelheid *f.*

A·den [ˈeɪdn] Aden *n (Hauptstadt des Südjemen).*

Ad·i·ron·dacks [ˌædɪˈrɒndæks] *pl. Gebirgszug im Staat New York (USA).*

Ad·olf [ˈædɒlf], **A·dol·phus** [əˈdɒlfəs] Adolf *m.*

A·dri·an [ˈeɪdrɪən] Adrian *m*, Adriˈane *f.*

A·dri·at·ic Sea [ˌeɪdrɪˈætɪk ˈsiː] *das* Adriˈatische Meer.

Ae·ge·an Sea [iːˈdʒiːən ˈsiː] *das* Äˈgäische Meer, *die* Äˈgäis.

Aes·chy·lus [ˈiːskɪləs] Äschylus *m.*

Ae·sop [ˈiːsɒp] Äˈsop *m.*

Af·ghan·i·stan [æfˈgænɪstæn] Afˈghanistan *n.*

Af·ri·ca [ˈæfrɪkə] Afrika *n.*

Ag·a·tha [ˈægəθə] Aˈgathe *f.*

Ag·gie [ˈægɪ] *Koseform für* **Agatha**, **Agnes**.

Ag·nes [ˈægnɪs] Agnes *f.*

Aix-la-Cha·pelle [ˌeɪkslɑːʃæˈpel] Aachen *n.*

Al·a·bam·a [ˌæləˈbæmə] *Staat der USA.*

Al·an [ˈælən] *m.*

A·las·ka [əˈlæskə] *Staat der USA.*

Al·ba·ni·a [ælˈbeɪnjə] Alˈbanien *n.*

Al·ba·ny [ˈɔːlbənɪ] *Hauptstadt des Staates New York (USA).*

Al·bert [ˈælbət] Albert *m.*

Al·ber·ta [ælˈbɜːtə] *Provinz in Kanada.*

Al·bu·quer·que [ˈælbəkɜːkɪ] *Stadt in New Mexiko (USA).*

Al·der·ney [ˈɔːldənɪ] *brit. Kanalinsel.*

Al·der·shot [ˈɔːldəʃɒt] *Stadt in Südengland.*

A·leu·tian Is·lands [əˌluːʃjənˈaɪlənds] *pl. die* Aleˈuten *pl.*

Al·ex [ˈælɪks] *abbr. für* **Alexander**.

Al·ex·an·der [ˌælɪgˈzɑːndə] Alexˈander *m.*

Al·ex·an·dra [ˌælɪgˈzɑːndrə] Alexˈandra *f.*

Alf [ælf] *abbr. für* **Alfred**.

Al·fred [ˈælfrɪd] Alfred *m.*

Al·ge·ri·a [ælˈdʒɪərɪə] Alˈgerien *n.*

Al·ger·non [ˈældʒənən] *m.*

Al·giers [ælˈdʒɪəz] Algier *n.*

Al·ice [ˈælɪs] Aˈlice *f*, Else *f.*

Al·i·son [ˈælɪsn] *f.*

Al·lan [ˈælən] *m.*

Al·le·ghe·nies [ˈælɪgeɪnɪz; *Am.* ˌælɪˈgeɪnɪz] *pl. Gebirge im Osten der USA.*

Al·le·ghe·ny [ˈælɪgeɪnɪ; *Am.* ˌælɪˈgeɪnɪ] *Fluss in Pennsylvania (USA);* ~ **Moun·tains** *siehe* **Alleghenies**.

Al·len [ˈælən] *m.*

Al·sace [ælˈsæs], **Al·sa·ti·a** [ælˈseɪʃjə] *das* Elsass.

A·man·da [əˈmændə] Aˈmanda *f.*

Am·a·zon [ˈæməzən] Amaˈzonas *m.*

A·me·lia [əˈmiːljə] Aˈmalie *f.*

A·mer·i·ca [əˈmerɪkə] Aˈmerika *n.*

A·my [ˈeɪmɪ] *f.*

An·chor·age [ˈæŋkərɪdʒ] *Stadt in Alaska (USA).*

An·des [ˈændiːz] *pl. die* Anden *pl.*

An·dor·ra [ænˈdɔːrə] Anˈdorra *n.*

An·drew [ˈændruː] Anˈdreas *m.*

An·dy [ˈændɪ] *abbr. für* **Andrew**.

An·ge·la [ˈændʒələ] Angela *f.*

An·gle·sey [ˈæŋglsɪ] *walisische Grafschaft (bis 1974).*

An·gli·a [ˈæŋglɪə] *lateinischer Name für* England.

An·go·la [æŋˈgəʊlə] Anˈgola *n.*

An·gus [ˈæŋgəs] *schottische Grafschaft (bis 1975);* Vorname *m.*

A·ni·ta [əˈniːtə] Aˈnita *f.*

Ann [æn], **An·na** [ˈænə] Anna *f*, Anne *f.*

An·na·bel(le) [ˈænəbel] Annaˈbella *f.*

An·nap·o·lis [əˈnæpəlɪs] *Hauptstadt von Maryland (USA).*

Anne [æn] Anna *f*, Anne *f.*

Ant·arc·ti·ca [æntˈɑːktɪkə] *die* Antˈarktis.

An·the·a [ˈænθɪə; ænˈθɪə] *f.*

An·tho·ny [ˈæntənɪ, ˈænθənɪ] Anton *m.*

An·til·les [ænˈtɪliːz] *pl. die* Anˈtillen *pl.*

An·to·ny [ˈæntənɪ] Anton *m.*

An·trim [ˈæntrɪm] *nordirische Grafschaft.*

Ant·werp [ˈæntwɜːp] Antˈwerpen *n.*

Ap·en·nines [ˈæpɪnaɪnz] *pl. der* Apenˈnin, *die* Apenˈninen *pl.*

Ap·pa·la·chians [ˌæpəˈleɪtʃjənz] *pl. die* Appaˈlachen *pl.*

A·ra·bi·a [əˈreɪbjə] Aˈrabien *n.*

Ar·chi·bald [ˈɑːtʃɪbəld] Archibald *m.*

Ar·chi·me·des [ˌɑːkɪˈmiːdiːz] Archiˈmedes *m.*

Arc·tic [ˈɑːktɪk] *die* Arktis.

Ar·den [ˈɑːdn] *Familienname.*

Ar·gen·ti·na [ˌɑːdʒənˈtiːnə] Argenˈtinien *n.*

Ar·gen·tine [ˈɑːdʒəntaɪn] *the* ~ Argenˈtinien *n.*

Ar·gyll(·shire) [ɑːˈgaɪl(ʃə)] *schottische Grafschaft (bis 1975).*

Ar·is·toph·an·es [ˌærɪˈstɒfəniːz] Ariˈstophanes *m.*

Ar·is·tot·le [ˈærɪstɒtl] Ariˈstoteles *m.*

Ar·i·zo·na [ˌærɪˈzəʊnə] *Staat der USA.*

Ar·kan·sas [ˈɑːkənsɔː] *Fluss in USA; Staat der USA.*

Ar·ling·ton [ˈɑːlɪŋtən] *Ehrenfriedhof bei Washington DC (USA).*

Ar·magh [ɑːˈmɑː] *nordirische Grafschaft.*

Ar·me·ni·a [ɑːˈmiːnjə] Arˈmenien *n.*

Ar·nold [ˈɑːnəld] Arnold *m.*

Art [ɑːt] *abbr. für* **Arthur**.

Ar·thur [ˈɑːθə] Art(h)ur *m; King* ~ König Artus.

As·cot [ˈæskət] *Ort in Südengland (Pferderennen).*

A·sia [ˈeɪʃə] Asien *n;* ~ *Minor* Kleinasi-

As·syr·i·a [əˈsɪrɪə] Asˈsyrien *n.*

Ath·ens [ˈæθɪnz] Aˈthen *n.*

At·lan·ta [ətˈlæntə] *Hauptstadt von Georgia (USA).*

At·lan·tic (**O·cean**) [ətˈlæntɪk (ətˌlæntɪkˈəʊʃn)] *der* Atˈlantik, *der* Atˈlantische Ozean.

Auck·land [ˈɔːklənd] *Hafenstadt in Neuseeland.*

Au·den [ˈɔːdn] *englischer Dichter.*

Au·drey [ˈɔːdrɪ] *f.*

Au·gus·ta [ɔːˈgʌstə] *Hauptstadt von Maine (USA).*

Au·gus·tus [ɔːˈgʌstəs] August *m.*

Aus·ten [ˈɒstɪn] *Familienname.*

Aus·tin [ˈɒstɪn] *Hauptstadt von Texas (USA).*

Aus·tra·lia [ɒˈstreɪljə] Auˈstralien *n.*

Aus·tri·a [ˈɒstrɪə] Österreich *n.*

A·von [ˈeɪvən] *Fluss in Mittelengland; englische Grafschaft.*

Ax·min·ster [ˈæksmɪnstə] *Stadt in Südwest-England.*

Ayr(·shire) [ˈeə(ʃə)] *schottische Grafschaft (bis 1975).*

A·zores [əˈzɔːz] *pl. die* Aˈzoren *pl.*

B

Bab·y·lon [ˈbæbɪlən] Babylon *n.*

Ba·con [ˈbeɪkən] *englischer Philosoph.*

Ba·den-Pow·ell [ˌbeɪdnˈpəʊəl] *Gründer der Boy Scouts.*

Ba·ha·mas [bəˈhɑːməz] *pl. die* Baˈhamas *pl.*

Bah·rain [bɑːˈreɪn] Bahˈrain *n.*

Bai·le A·tha Cli·ath [ˌblɔːˈkliː] *gälischer Name für* **Dublin**.

Bal·dwin [ˈbɔːldwɪn] Balduin *m; amer. Autor.*

Bâle [bɑːl] Basel *n.*

Bal·four [ˈbælfə] *brit. Staatsmann.*

Bal·kans [ˈbɔːlkənz] *pl. der* Balkan.

Bal·mor·al [bælˈmɒrəl] *Residenz des englischen Königshauses in Schottland.*

Bal·tic Sea [ˌbɔːltɪkˈsiː] *die* Ostsee.

Bal·ti·more [ˈbɔːltɪmɔː] *Hafenstadt in Maryland (USA).*

Banff(·shire) [ˈbænf(ʃə)] *schottische Grafschaft (bis 1975).*

Ban·gla·desh [ˌbæŋgləˈdeʃ] Banglaˈdesch *n.*

Bar·ba·dos [bɑːˈbeɪdəʊz] Barˈbados *n.*

Bar·ba·ra [ˈbɑːbərə] Barbara *f.*

Bark·ing [ˈbɑːkɪŋ] *Stadtbezirk von Groß-London.*

Bar·net [ˈbɑːnɪt] *Stadtbezirk von Groß-London.*

Bar·ry [ˈbærɪ] *m.*

Bart [bɑːt] *abbr. für* **Bartholomew**.

Bar·thol·o·mew [bɑːˈθɒləmjuː] Bartholoˈmäus *m.*

Bas·il [ˈbæzl] Baˈsilius *m.*

Bath [bɑːθ] *Badeort in Südengland.*

Bat·on Rouge [ˌbætnˈruːʒ] *Hauptstadt von Louisiana (USA).*

Bat·ter·sea [ˈbætəsɪ] *Stadtteil von London.*

Ba·var·i·a [bə'veərɪə] Bayern n.

Bea·cons·field ['biːkənzfiːld] Adelsname Disraelis.

Beards·ley ['bɪədzlɪ] engl. Zeichner u. Illustrator.

Be·a·trice ['bɪətrɪs] Bea'trice f.

Bea·ver·brook ['biːvəbrʊk] brit. Zeitungsverleger.

Beck·et ['bekɪt]: **Saint Thomas à** ~ der heilige Thomas Becket.

Beck·ett ['bekɪt] irischer Dichter u. Dramatiker.

Beck·y ['bekɪ] f.

Bed·ford ['bedfəd] Stadt in Mittelengland; a. **'Bed·ford·shire** [-ʃə] englische Grafschaft.

Beer·bohm ['bɪəbəʊm] engl. Kritiker u. Karikaturist.

Bei·jing [ˌbeɪ'dʒɪŋ] Peking n.

Bel·fast [ˌbel'fɑːst; 'belfɑːst] Belfast n.

Bel·gium ['beldʒəm] Belgien n.

Bel·grade [ˌbel'greɪd] Belgrad n.

Bel·gra·vi·a [bel'greɪvjə] Stadtteil von London.

Be·lin·da [bɪ'lɪndə; bə-] Be'linda f.

Be·lize [be'liːz] Be'lize n.

Bell, Bel·la ['bel(ə)] abbr. für **Isabel**.

Ben [ben] abbr. für **Benjamin**.

Ben·e·dict ['benɪdɪkt, 'benɪt] Benedikt m.

Ben·gal [ˌbeŋ'gɔːl] Ben'galen n.

Be·nin [be'nɪn] Be'nin n.

Ben·ja·min ['bendʒəmɪn] Benjamin m.

Ben Nev·is [ˌben'nevɪs] höchster Berg Schottlands u. Großbritanniens.

Berke·ley ['bɑːklɪ] Stadt in Kalifornien; ['bɑːklɪ] irischer Bischof u. Philosoph.

Berk·shire ['bɑːkʃə] englische Grafschaft; ~ **Hills** [ˌbɜːkʃɪə'hɪlz] pl. Gebirgszug in Massachusetts (USA).

Ber·lin [bɜː'lɪn] Ber'lin n.

Ber·mu·das [bə'mjuːdəz] pl. die Ber'mudas pl., die Ber'mudainseln pl.

Ber·nard ['bɜːnəd] Bernhard m.

Bern(e) [bɜːn] Bern n.

Ber·nie ['bɜːnɪ] abbr. für **Bernard**.

Bern·stein ['bɜːnstaɪn; -stiːn] amer. Dirigent u. Komponist.

Bert [bɜːt] abbr. für **Albert, Bertram, Bertrand, Gilbert, Hubert**.

Ber·tha ['bɜːθə] Berta f.

Ber·tram ['bɜːtrəm], **Ber·trand** ['bɜːtrənd] Bertram m.

Ber·wick(·shire) ['berɪk(ʃə)] schottische Grafschaft (bis 1975).

Ber·yl ['berɪl] f.

Bess, Bes·sy ['bes(ɪ)], **Bet·s(e)y** ['betsɪ], **Bet·ty** ['betɪ] abbr. für **Elizabeth**.

Bex·ley ['bekslɪ] Stadtbezirk von Groß-London.

Bhu·tan [buː'tɑːn] Bhu'tan n.

Bill, Bil·ly ['bɪl(ɪ)] Willi m.

Bir·ken·head ['bɜːkənhed] Hafenstadt in Nordwest-England.

Bir·ming·ham ['bɜːmɪŋəm] Industriestadt in Mittelengland; Stadt in Alabama (USA).

Bis·cay ['bɪskeɪ; -kɪ]: **Bay of** ~ der Golf von Bis'caya.

Bis·marck ['bɪzmɑːk] Hauptstadt von North Dakota (USA).

Blooms·bur·y ['bluːmzbərɪ] Stadtteil von London.

Bo·ad·i·cea [ˌbəʊədɪ'sɪə] Königin in Britannien.

Bob [bɒb] abbr. für **Robert**.

Bo·he·mi·a [bəʊ'hiːmjə] Böhmen n.

Boi·se ['bɔɪzɪ; -sɪ] Hauptstadt von Idaho

(USA).

Bol·eyn ['bʊlɪn]: **Anne** ~ zweite Frau Heinrichs VIII. von England.

Bo·liv·i·a [bə'lɪvjə] Bo'livien n.

Bom·bay [ˌbɒm'beɪ] Bombay n.

Bo·na·parte ['bəʊnəpɑːt] Bona'parte (Familienname zweier französischer Kaiser).

Booth [buːð] Gründer der Heilsarmee.

Bor·ders ['bɔːdəz] Verwaltungsregion in Schottland.

Bos·ni·a ['bɒznɪə] Bosnien n.

Bos·ton ['bɒstən] Hauptstadt von Massachusetts (USA).

Bo·tswa·na [bɒ'tswɑːnə] Bo'tswana n.

Bourne·mouth ['bɔːnməθ] Seebad in Südengland.

Brad·ford ['brædfəd] Industriestadt in Nordengland.

Bra·zil [brə'zɪl] Bra'silien n.

Breck·nock(·shire) ['breknɒk(ʃə)], **Brec·on(·shire)** ['brekən(ʃə)] walisische Grafschaft (bis 1974).

Bren·da ['brendə] f.

Brent [brent] Stadtbezirk von Groß-London.

Bri·an ['braɪən] m.

Bridg·et ['brɪdʒɪt] Bri'gitte f.

Brigh·ton ['braɪtn] Seebad in Südengland.

Bris·bane ['brɪzbən] Hauptstadt von Queensland (Australien).

Bris·tol ['brɪstl] Hafenstadt in Südengland.

Bri·tain ['brɪtn] Bri'tannien n.

Bri·tan·ni·a [brɪ'tænjə] poet. Bri'tannien n.

Brit·ish Co·lum·bi·a [ˌbrɪtɪʃkə'lʌmbɪə] Provinz in Kanada.

Brit·ta·ny ['brɪtənɪ] die Bre'tagne.

Brit·ten ['brɪtn] englischer Komponist.

Broad·way ['brɔːdweɪ] Straße in Manhattan, New York City (USA). Zentrum des amer. kommerziellen Theaters.

Brom·ley ['brɒmlɪ] Stadtbezirk von Groß-London.

Bron·të ['brɒntɪ] Name dreier englischer Autorinnen.

Bronx [brɒŋks] Stadtbezirk von New York (USA).

Brook·lyn ['brʊklɪn] Stadtbezirk von New York (USA).

Brow·ning ['braʊnɪŋ] englischer Dichter.

Bruce [bruːs] m.

Bruges [bruːʒ] Brügge n.

Bru·nei ['bruːnaɪ] Brunei n.

Bruns·wick ['brʌnzwɪk] Braunschweig n.

Brus·sels ['brʌslz] Brüssel n.

Bry·an ['braɪən] m.

Bu·chan·an [bjuː'kænən] Familienname.

Bu·cha·rest [ˌbjuːkə'rest] Bukarest n.

Buck·ing·ham(·shire) ['bʌkɪŋəm(ʃə)] englische Grafschaft.

Bu·da·pest [ˌbjuːdə'pest] Budapest n.

Bud·dha ['bʊdə] Buddha m.

Bul·gar·i·a [bʌl'geərɪə] Bul'garien n.

Bur·gun·dy ['bɜːgəndɪ] Bur'gund n.

Bur·ki·na Fas·o [bʊəˌkiːnə'fæsəʊ] Bur'kina Faso n (Staat in Westafrika, frühere Bezeichnung: Obervolta).

Bur·ma ['bɜːmə] Birma n.

Burns [bɜːnz] schottischer Dichter.

Bu·run·di [bʊ'rʊndɪ] Bu'rundi n.

Bute(·shire) ['bjuːt(ʃə)] schottische Grafschaft (bis 1975).

By·ron ['baɪərən] englischer Dichter.

C

Caer·nar·von(·shire) [kə'nɑːvən(ʃə)] walisische Grafschaft (bis 1974).

Cae·sar ['siːzə] Cäsar m.

Cain [keɪn] Kain m.

Cai·ro ['kaɪərəʊ] Kairo n.

Caith·ness ['keɪθnes] schottische Grafschaft (bis 1975).

Ca·lais ['kæleɪ] Ca'lais n.

Cal·cut·ta [kæl'kʌtə] Kal'kutta n.

Cal·e·do·nia [ˌkælɪ'dəʊnjə] Kale'donien n (poet. für Schottland).

Cal·ga·ry ['kælgərɪ] Stadt in Alberta (Kanada).

Cal·i·for·nia [ˌkælɪ'fɔːnjə] Kali'fornien n (Staat der USA).

Cam·bo·dia [kæm'bəʊdjə] Kam'bodscha n.

Cam·bridge ['keɪmbrɪdʒ] englische Universitätsstadt; Stadt in Massachusetts (USA), Sitz der Harvard University; a. **'Cam·bridge·shire** [-ʃə] englische Grafschaft.

Cam·den ['kæmdən] Stadtbezirk von Groß-London.

Cam·er·oon ['kæməruːn; bsd. Am. ˌkæmə'ruːn] Kamerun n.

Camp·bell ['kæmbl] Familienname.

Can·a·da ['kænədə] Kanada n.

Ca·nar·y Is·lands [kəˌneərɪ'aɪləndz] pl. die Ka'narischen Inseln pl.

Can·ber·ra ['kænbərə] Hauptstadt von Australien.

Can·ter·bury ['kæntəbərɪ] Stadt in Südengland.

Cape Ca·nav·er·al [ˌkeɪpkə'nævərəl] Raketenversuchszentrum in Florida (USA).

Cape Town ['keɪptaʊn] Kapstadt n.

Cape Verde Is·lands [ˌkeɪp'vɜːd 'aɪləndz] pl. die Kap'verden pl.

Ca·pri ['kæprɪ; 'kɑː-; Am. a. kæ'priː] Ca·pri n.

Car·diff ['kɑːdɪf] Hauptstadt von Wales.

Car·di·gan(·shire) ['kɑːdɪgən(ʃə)] walisische Grafschaft (bis 1974).

Ca·rin·thi·a [kə'rɪnθɪə] Kärnten n.

Carl [kɑːl] Karl m, Carl n.

Car·lisle [kɑː'laɪl] Stadt in Nordwestengland.

Car·low ['kɑːləʊ] Grafschaft in der Provinz Leinster (Irland); Hauptstadt dieser Grafschaft.

Car·lyle [kɑː'laɪl] schottischer Autor.

Car·mar·then(·shire) [kə'mɑːðn(ʃə)] walisische Grafschaft (bis 1974).

Car·ne·gie [kɑː'negɪ] amer. Industrieller.

Car·ol(e) ['kærəl] Ka'rola f.

Car·o·line ['kærəlaɪn], **Car·o·lyn** ['kærəlɪn] Karo'line f.

Car·pa·thi·ans [kɑː'peɪθjənz] pl. die Kar'paten pl.

Car·rie ['kærɪ] abbr. für **Caroline**.

Car·son Cit·y [ˌkɑːsn'sɪtɪ] Hauptstadt von Nevada (USA).

Car·ter ['kɑːtə] 39. Präsident der USA.

Cath·er·ine ['kæθərɪn] Katha'rina f, Kat(h)rin f.

Cath·y ['kæθɪ] abbr. für **Catherine**.

Ca·van ['kævən] Grafschaft im der Republik Irland zugehörigen Teil der Provinz Ulster; Hauptstadt dieser Grafschaft.

Cax·ton ['kækstən] erster englischer Buchdrucker.

Ce·cil ['sesl, 'sɪsl] m.

Ce·cile ['sesɪl; Am. sɪ'siːl], **Ce·cil·ia** [sɪ'sɪljə; sɪ'siːljə], **Cec·i·ly** ['sɪsɪlɪ; 'sesɪlɪ] Cä'cilie f.

Ced·ric ['siːdrɪk; 'sedrɪk] m.

Cel·ia ['siːljə] f.

Cen·tral ['sentrəl] Verwaltungsregion in Schottland.

Cen·tral Af·ri·can Re·pub·lic ['sentrəl-
ˌæfrɪkənrɪ'pʌblɪk] *die* Zen'tralafri,kani-
sche Repu'blik.
Cey·lon [sɪ'lɒn] Ceylon *n.*
Chad [tʃæd] *der* Tschad.
Cham·ber·lain ['tʃeɪmbəlɪn] *Name meh-
rerer brit. Staatsmänner.*
Char·ing Cross [ˌtʃærɪŋ'krɒs] *Stadtteil
von London.*
Char·le·magne [ʃɑːləmeɪn] Karl der
Große.
Charles [tʃɑːlz] Karl *m.*
Charles·ton ['tʃɑːlstən] *Hauptstadt von
West Virginia (USA).*
Char·lotte ['tʃɑːlət] Char'lotte *f.*
Chau·cer ['tʃɔːsə] *englischer Dichter.*
Che·che·nia [tʃe'tʃiːnjə] *siehe* **Chech-
nya.**
Chech·ny·a ['tʃetʃnɪə] Tsche'tschenien *n.*
Chel·sea ['tʃelsɪ] *Stadtteil von London.*
Chel·ten·ham ['tʃeltnəm] *Stadt in Süd-
england.*
Chesh·ire ['tʃeʃə] *englische Grafschaft.*
Ches·ter·field ['tʃestəfiːld] *Industrie-
stadt in Mittelengland.*
Chev·i·ot Hills [ˌtʃevɪət'hɪlz] *pl. Grenz-
gebirge zwischen England u. Schott-
land.*
Chey·enne [ʃaɪ'æn] *Hauptstadt von Wy-
oming (USA).*
Chi·ca·go [ʃɪ'kɑːgəʊ; *bsd. Am.*
ʃɪ'kɔːgəʊ] *Industriestadt in USA.*
Chil·e ['tʃɪlɪ] Chile *n.*
Chi·na ['tʃaɪnə] China *n;* **Republic of ~**
die Repu'blik China; **People's Repub-
lic of ~** *die* Volksrepublik China.
Chip·pen·dale ['tʃɪpəndeɪl] *englischer
Kunsttischler.*
Chris [krɪs] *abbr. für* **Christina, Chris-
tine, Christian, Christopher.**
Christ·church ['kraɪstʃɜːtʃ] *Stadt in
Neuseeland; Stadt in Hampshire (Eng-
land).*
Chlo·e ['kləʊɪ] Chloe *f.*
Chris·tian ['krɪstjən] Christian *m.*
Chris·ti·na [krɪ'stiːnə], **Chris·tine**
['krɪstiːn, krɪ'stiːn] Chri'stine *f.*
Chris·to·pher ['krɪstəfə] Christoph(er)
m.
Chrys·ler ['kraɪzlə] *amer. Industrieller.*
Church·ill ['tʃɜːtʃɪl] *brit. Staatsmann.*
Cin·cin·nat·i [ˌsɪnsɪ'nætɪ] *Stadt in Ohio
(USA).*
Cis·sie ['sɪsɪ] *abbr. für* **Cecily.**
Clack·man·nan(·shire) [klæk'mænən
(-ʃə)] *schottische Grafschaft (bis 1975).*
Clap·ham ['klæpəm] *Stadtteil von Groß-
London.*
Clar·a ['kleərə], **Clare** [kleə] Klara *f.*
Clare [kleə] *Grafschaft in der Provinz
Munster (Irland).*
Clar·en·don ['klærəndən] *Name mehre-
rer englischer Staatsmänner.*
Claud(e) [klɔːd] Claudius *m.*
Clem·ent ['klemənt] Klemens *m,* Cle-
mens *m.*
Cle·o·pat·ra [klɪə'pætrə] Kle'opatra *f.*
Cleve·land ['kliːvlənd] *Industriestadt in
USA; englische Grafschaft.*
Clif·ford ['klɪfəd] *m.*
Clive [klaɪv] *Begründer der brit. Herr-
schaft in Indien; Vorname m.*
Clwyd ['kluːɪd] *walisische Grafschaft.*
Clyde [klaɪd] *Fluß in Schottland.*
Cole·ridge ['kəʊlərɪdʒ] *englischer
Dichter.*
Col·in ['kɒlɪn] *m.*
Co·logne [kə'ləʊn] Köln *n.*
Co·lom·bi·a [kə'lombɪə] Ko'lumbien *n.*
Co·lom·bo [kə'lʌmbəʊ] *Hauptstadt von
Sri Lanka.*

Col·o·ra·do [ˌkɒlə'rɑːdəʊ] *Staat der
USA; Name zweier Flüsse in USA.*
Co·lum·bi·a [kə'lʌmbɪə] *Fluß in USA;
Hauptstadt von South Carolina (USA);
District of ~ (DC) Bundesdistrikt (mit
der Hauptstadt Washington) der USA.*
Co·lum·bus [kə'lʌmbəs] *Entdecker
Amerikas; Hauptstadt von Ohio (USA).*
Com·o·ro Is·lands [ˌkɒmərəʊ'aɪləndz]
pl. die Ko'moren *pl.*
Con·cord ['kɒŋkəd] *Hauptstadt von
New Hampshire (USA).*
Con·fu·cius [kən'fjuːʃjəs, -ʃəs] Kon'fu-
zius *m (chinesischer Philosoph).*
Con·go ['kɒŋgəʊ] *der* Kongo.
Con·nacht ['kɒnət], *früher* **Con·naught**
['kɒnɔːt] *Provinz in Irland.*
Con·nect·i·cut [kə'netɪkət] *USA-Staat.*
Con·nie ['kɒnɪ] *abbr. für* **Conrad,
Constance, Cornelia.**
Con·rad ['kɒnræd] Konrad *m.*
Con·stance ['kɒnstəns] Kon'stanze *f;*
Lake ~ *der* Bodensee.
Con·stan·ti·no·ple [ˌkɒnstæntɪ'nəʊpl]
Konstanti'nopel *n.*
Cook [kʊk] *englischer Weltumsegler.*
Coo·per ['kuːpə] *amer. Autor.*
Co·pen·ha·gen [ˌkəʊpn'heɪgən] Kopen-
'hagen *n.*
Cor·dil·le·ras [ˌkɔːdɪ'ljeərəs] *pl. die*
Kordil'leren *pl.*
Cor·inth ['kɒrɪnθ] Ko'rinth *n.*
Cork [kɔːk] *Grafschaft in der Provinz
Munster (Irland); Hauptstadt dieser
Grafschaft u. der Provinz Munster.*
Cor·ne·lia [kɔː'niːljə] Cor'nelia *f.*
Corn·wall ['kɔːnwəl] *englische Graf-
schaft.*
Cos·ta Ri·ca [ˌkɒstə'riːkə] Costa Rica *n.*
Cov·ent Gar·den [ˌkɒvənt'gɑːdn] *die
Londoner Oper.*
Cov·en·try ['kɒvəntrɪ] *Industriestadt in
Mittelengland.*
Crete [kriːt] Kreta *n.*
Cri·me·a [kraɪ'mɪə] *die* Krim.
Cro·a·tia [krəʊ'eɪʃə] Kroatien *n.*
Crom·well ['krɒmwəl] *englischer Staats-
mann.*
Croy·don ['krɔɪdn] *Stadtbezirk von
Groß-London.*
Cru·soe ['kruːsəʊ]: **Robinson ~** *Ro-
manheld.*
Cu·ba ['kjuːbə] Kuba *n.*
Cum·ber·land ['kʌmbələnd] *englische
Grafschaft (bis 1974).*
Cum·bri·a ['kʌmbrɪə] *englische Graf-
schaft.*
Cyn·thi·a ['sɪnθɪə] *f.*
Cy·prus ['saɪprəs] Zypern *n.*
Cy·rus ['saɪərəs] Cyrus *m.*
Czech·i·a ['tʃekɪə] 'Tschechien *n.*
Czech Re·pub·lic [ˌtʃekrɪ'pʌblɪk] 'Tsche-
chien *n.*

D

Dag·en·ham ['dægənəm] *Stadtteil von
London.*
Da·ho·mey [də'həʊmɪ] Da'home *n (frü-
herer Name von* **Benin**).
Dai·sy ['deɪzɪ] *Koseform von* **Margaret.**
Dal·las ['dæləs] *Stadt in Texas (USA).*
Dal·ma·ti·a [dæl'meɪʃjə] Dal'matien *n.*
Dam·o·cles ['dæməkliːz] Damokles
m.
Dan [dæn] *abbr. für* **Daniel.**
Dan·iel ['dænjəl] Daniel *m.*
Dan·ube ['dænjuːb] Donau *f.*
Daph·ne ['dæfnɪ] Daphne *f.*
Dar·da·nelles [ˌdɑːdə'nelz] *pl. die* Dar-
da'nellen *pl.*

Dar·jee·ling [dɑː'dʒiːlɪŋ] *Stadt in Indien.*
Dart·moor ['dɑːt,mʊə] *Landstrich in
Südwest-England.*
Dart·mouth ['dɑːtməθ] *Stadt in Devon
(England).*
Dar·win ['dɑːwɪn] *englischer Naturfor-
scher.*
Dave [deɪv] *abbr. für* **David.**
Da·vid ['deɪvɪd] David *m.*
Dawn [dɔːn] *f.*
Dean [diːn] *m.*
Deb·by ['debɪ] *abbr. für* **Deborah.**
Deb·o·rah ['debərə] *f.*
Dee [diː] *Fluss in England; Fluss in
Schottland.*
De·foe [dɪ'fəʊ] *englischer Autor.*
Deir·dre ['dɪədrɪ] *(Ir.) f.*
Del·a·ware ['deləweə] *Staat der USA;
Fluss in USA.*
Den·bigh(·shire) ['denbɪ(ʃə)] *walisische
Grafschaft (bis 1974).*
Den·is ['denɪs] *m.*
De·nise [də'niːz; də'niːs] De'nise *f.*
Den·mark ['denmɑːk] Dänemark *n.*
Den·nis ['denɪs] *m.*
Den·ver ['denvə] *Hauptstadt von Colo-
rado (USA).*
Dept·ford ['detfəd] *Stadtteil von Groß-
London.*
Der·by(·shire) ['dɑːbɪ(ʃə)] *englische
Grafschaft.*
Der·ek, Der·rick ['derɪk] *m.*
Des [dez] *abbr. für* **Desmond.**
Des Moines [dɪ'mɔɪn] *Hauptstadt von
Iowa (USA).*
Des·mond ['dezmənd] *m.*
De·troit [də'trɔɪt] *Industriestadt in
Michigan (USA).*
De·viz·es [dɪ'vaɪzɪz] *Stadt in Wiltshire
(England).*
Dev·on(·shire) ['devn(ʃə)] *englische
Grafschaft.*
Dew·ey ['djuːɪ] *amer. Philosoph.*
Di·an·a [daɪ'ænə] Di'ana *f.*
Dick [dɪk] *abbr. für* **Richard.**
Dick·ens ['dɪkɪnz] *englischer Autor.*
Dis·rae·li [dɪs'reɪlɪ] *brit. Staatsmann.*
Dol·ly ['dɒlɪ] *abbr. für* **Dorothy.**
Do·lo·mites ['dɒləmaɪts] *pl. die* Dolo-
'miten *pl. (Teil der Ostalpen).*
Dom·i·nic ['dɒmɪnɪk] Domi'nik *m.*
Do·min·i·can Re·pub·lic [dəˌmɪnɪkən-
rɪ'pʌblɪk] *die* Domini'kanische Re-
pu'blik.
Don [dɒn] *abbr. für* **Donald.**
Don·ald ['dɒnld] *m.*
Don·cas·ter ['dɒŋkəstə] *Stadt in South
Yorkshire (England).*
Don·e·gal ['dɒnɪgɔːl; *Ir.* ˌdʌnɪ'gɔːl] *Graf-
schaft im der Republik Irland zugehöri-
gen Teil der Provinz Ulster.*
Don Juan [ˌdɒn'dʒuːən] Don Ju'an *m.*
Donne [dʌn, dɒn] *englischer Dichter.*
Don Quix·ote [ˌdɒn'kwɪksət] Don Qui-
'chotte *m.*
Do·reen [dɔː'riːn; 'dɔːriːn] *f.*
Dor·is ['dɒrɪs] Doris *f.*
Dor·o·thy ['dɒrəθɪ] Doro'thea *f.*
Dor·set(·shire) ['dɔːsɪt(ʃə)] *englische
Grafschaft.*
Dos Pas·sos [ˌdɒs'pæsɒs] *amer. Autor.*
Doug [dʌg] *abbr. für* **Douglas.**
Doug·las ['dʌgləs] *Vorname m; schotti-
sche Adelsfamilie.*
Do·ra ['dɔːrə] Dora *f.*
Do·ver ['dəʊvə] *Hafenstadt in Südeng-
land; Hauptstadt von Delaware (USA).*
Down [daʊn] *nordirische Grafschaft.*
Down·ing Street ['daʊnɪŋstriːt] *Straße
in London mit der Amtswohnung des
Premierministers.*

Drei·ser ['draɪsə; -zə] *amer. Autor.*
Dry·den ['draɪdn] *englischer Dichter.*
Dub·lin ['dʌblɪn] *Hauptstadt von Irland; Grafschaft in der Provinz Leinster (Irland).*
Du·luth [dju:'lu:θ; *Am.* də'lu:θ] *Stadt in Minnesota (USA).*
Dul·wich ['dʌlɪdʒ] *Stadtteil von Groß-London.*
Dum·bar·ton(·shire) [dʌm'bɑ:tn(ʃə)] *schottische Grafschaft (bis 1975).*
Dum·fries and Gal·lo·way [dʌm,fri:sən'gæləweɪ] *Verwaltungsregion in Schottland;* **Dum'fries·shire** [-ʃə] *schottische Grafschaft (bis 1975).*
Dun·can ['dʌŋkən] *m.*
Dun·e·din [dʌ'ni:dɪn] *Hafenstadt in Neuseeland.*
Dun·ge·ness [,dʌndʒɪ'nes; dʌndʒ'nes] *Landspitze in Kent (England).*
Dun·kirk [dʌn'kɜ:k] *Dün'kirchen n.*
Dur·ban ['dɜ:bən] *Hafenstadt in Südafrika.*
Dur·ham ['dʌrəm] *englische Grafschaft.*
Dyf·ed ['dʌvɪd] *walisische Grafschaft.*

E

Ea·ling ['i:lɪŋ] *Stadtbezirk von Groß-London.*
East Lo·thi·an [,i:st'ləʊðjən] *schottische Grafschaft (bis 1975).*
East Sus·sex [,i:st'sʌsɪks] *englische Grafschaft.*
Ec·ua·dor ['ekwədɔ:] *Ecua'dor n.*
Ed·die ['edɪ] *abbr. für Edward.*
Ed·gar ['edgə] *Edgar m.*
Ed·in·burgh ['edɪnbərə] *Edinburg n.*
Ed·i·son ['edɪsn] *amer. Erfinder.*
E·dith ['i:dɪθ] *Edith f.*
Ed·mon·ton ['edməntən] *Hauptstadt von Alberta (Kanada).*
Ed·mund ['edmənd] *Edmund m.*
Ed·ward ['edwəd] *Eduard m.*
E·gypt ['i:dʒɪpt] *Ä'gypten n.*
Ei·leen ['aɪli:n; *Am.* aɪ'li:n] *f.*
Ei·re ['eərə] *Name der Republik Irland.*
Ei·sen·how·er ['aɪzn,haʊə] *34. Präsident der USA.*
E·laine [e'leɪn; ɪ'leɪn] *siehe Helen.*
El·ea·nor ['elɪnə] *Eleo'nore f.*
E·li·jah [ɪ'laɪdʒə] *E'lias m.*
El·i·nor ['elɪnə] *Eleo'nore f.*
El·i·ot ['eljət] *englischer Dichter.*
E·li·za [ɪ'laɪzə] *abbr. für Elizabeth.*
E·liz·a·beth [ɪ'lɪzəbəθ] *E'lisabeth f.*
El·len ['elɪn] *siehe Helen.*
El·lis Is·land [,elɪs'aɪlənd] *Insel im Hafen von New York (USA).*
El Sal·va·dor [el'sælvədɔ:] *El Salva'dor n.*
El·sa ['elsə], **El·sie** ['elsɪ] *Elsa f, Else f.*
Em·er·son ['eməsn] *amer. Dichter u. Philosoph.*
Em·i·ly ['emɪlɪ] *E'milie f.*
Em·ma ['emə] *Emma f.*
Em·mie, Em·my ['emɪ] *Koseform für Emma.*
En·field ['enfi:ld] *Stadtbezirk von Groß-London.*
Eng·land ['ɪŋglənd] *England n.*
E·nid ['i:nɪd] *f.*
E·noch ['i:nɒk] *m.*
Ep·som ['epsəm] *Stadt in Südengland (Pferderennen).*
Equa·to·ri·al Guin·ea [,ekwə'tɔ:rɪəl'gɪnɪ] *Äquatori'algui,nea n.*
Er·ic ['erɪk] *Erich m.*
Er·i·ca ['erɪkə] *Erika f.*

E·rie ['ɪərɪ] *Hafenstadt in Pennsylvania (USA);* **Lake ~** *der Eriesee (in Nordamerika).*
Er·nest ['ɜ:nɪst] *Ernst m.*
Er·nie ['ɜ:nɪ] *abbr. für Ernest.*
Es·sex ['esɪks] *englische Grafschaft.*
Es·t(h)o·nia [e'stəʊnjə] *Estland n.*
Eth·el ['eθl] *f.*
E·thi·o·pi·a [,i:θɪ'əʊpjə] *Äthi'opien n.*
E·ton ['i:tn] *Stadt in Berkshire (England) mit berühmter Public School.*
Eu·gene ['ju:dʒi:n] *Eugen m.*
Eu·ge·ni·a [ju:'dʒi:njə] *Eu'genie f.*
Eu·nice ['ju:nɪs] *Eu'nice f.*
Eu·phra·tes [ju:'freɪti:z] *Euphrat m.*
Eur·a·sia [jʊə'reɪʒə; -ʒə] *Eu'rasien n.*
Eu·rip·i·des [jʊə'rɪpɪdi:z] *Eu'ripides m.*
Eu·rope ['jʊərəp] *Eu'ropa n.*
Eus·tace ['ju:stəs] *Eu'stachius m.*
E·va ['i:və] *Eva f.*
Ev·ans ['evənz] *Familienname.*
Eve [i:v] *Eva f.*
Ev·e·lyn ['i:vlɪn; 'evlɪn] *m, f.*
Ev·er·glades ['evəgleɪdz] *pl. Sumpfgebiet in Florida (USA).*
Ex·e·ter ['eksɪtə] *Hauptstadt von Devonshire (England).*

F

Faer·oes ['feərəʊz] *pl. die Färöer pl.*
Falk·land Is·lands [,fɔ:(l)klənd'aɪləndz] *pl. die Falklandinseln pl.*
Fal·staff ['fɔ:lstɑ:f] *Bühnenfigur bei Shakespeare.*
Fan·ny ['fænɪ] *abbr. für Frances.*
Far·a·day ['færədɪ] *englischer Chemiker u. Physiker.*
Farn·bor·ough ['fɑ:nbərə] *Stadt in Hampshire (England).*
Far·oes ['feərəʊz] *siehe Faeroes.*
Faulk·ner ['fɔ:knə] *amer. Autor.*
Fawkes [fɔ:ks] *Haupt der Pulververschwörung (1605).*
Fed·er·al Re·pub·lic of Ger·ma·ny ['fedərəlrɪ,pʌblɪkəv'dʒɜ:mənɪ] *die 'Bundesrepu,blik Deutschland.*
Fe·li·ci·a [fə'lɪsɪə] *Fe'lizia f.*
Fe·lic·i·ty [fə'lɪsətɪ] *Fe'lizitas f.*
Fe·lix ['fi:lɪks] *Felix m.*
Fe·lix·stowe ['fi:lɪkstəʊ] *Stadt in Suffolk (England).*
Felt·ham ['feltəm] *Stadtteil von Groß-London.*
Fer·man·agh [fə'mænə] *nordirische Grafschaft.*
Fiel·ding ['fi:ldɪŋ] *englischer Autor.*
Fife [faɪf] *Verwaltungsregion in Schottland; a.* **'Fife·shire** [-ʃə] *schottische Grafschaft (bis 1975).*
Fi·ji [,fi:'dʒi:; *bsd. Am.* 'fi:dʒi:] *Fidschi n.*
Finch·ley ['fɪntʃlɪ] *Stadtteil von London.*
Fin·land ['fɪnlənd] *Finnland n.*
Fi·o·na [fɪ'əʊnə] *f.*
Firth of Forth [,fɜ:θəv'fɔ:θ] *Meeresbucht an der schottischen Ostküste.*
Fitz·ger·ald [fɪts'dʒerəld] *Familienname.*
Flan·ders ['flɑ:ndəz] *Flandern n.*
Flem·ing ['flemɪŋ] *brit. Bakteriologe.*
Flint(·shire) ['flɪnt(ʃə)] *walisische Grafschaft (bis 1974).*
Flo·ra ['flɔ:rə] *Flora f.*
Flor·ence ['flɒrəns] *Flo'renz n; Floren-'tine f.*
Flor·i·da ['flɒrɪdə] *Staat der USA.*
Flush·ing ['flʌʃɪŋ] *Stadtteil von New York; Vlissingen n.*
Folke·stone ['fəʊkstən] *Seebad in Süd-*

england.
Ford [fɔ:d] *amer. Industrieller; 38. Präsident der USA.*
For·syth [fɔ:'saɪθ] *Familienname.*
Fort Lau·der·dale [,fɔ:t'lɔ:dədeɪl] *Stadt in Florida (USA).*
Fort Worth [,fɔ:t'wɜ:θ] *Stadt in Texas (USA).*
Foth·er·in·ghay ['fɒðərɪŋgeɪ] *Schloss in Nordengland.*
Fow·ler ['faʊlə] *Familienname.*
France [frɑ:ns] *Frankreich n.*
Fran·ces ['frɑ:nsɪs] *Fran'ziska f.*
Fran·cis ['frɑ:nsɪs] *Franz m.*
Frank [fræŋk] *Frank m.*
Frank·fort ['fræŋkfət] *Hauptstadt von Kentucky (USA); seltene englische Schreibweise für Frankfurt.*
Frank·lin ['fræŋklɪn] *amer. Staatsmann; Verwaltungsbezirk der Northwest Territories (Kanada).*
Fred [fred] *abbr. für Alfred, Frede-ric(k).*
Fre·da ['fri:də] *Frieda f.*
Fred·die, Fred·dy ['fredɪ] *Koseformen für Frederic(k), Alfred.*
Fred·er·ic(k) ['fredrɪk] *Friedrich m.*
Fres·no ['freznəʊ] *Stadt in Kalifornien (USA).*
Fris·co ['frɪskəʊ] *umgangssprachliche Bezeichnung für San Francisco.*
Frost [frɒst] *amer. Dichter.*
Ful·bright ['fʊlbraɪt] *amer. Politiker.*
Ful·ham ['fʊləm] *Stadtteil von London.*
Ful·ton ['fʊltən] *amer. Erfinder.*

G

Ga·bon ['gæbɒn] *Ga'bun n.*
Gains·bor·ough ['geɪnzbərə] *englischer Maler.*
Gal·la·gher ['gæləhə] *Familienname.*
Gal·lup ['gæləp] *amer. Statistiker.*
Gals·wor·thy ['gɔ:lzwɜ:ðɪ] *englischer Autor.*
Gal·way ['gɔ:lweɪ] *Grafschaft in der Provinz Connacht (Irland); Hauptstadt dieser Grafschaft.*
Gam·bia ['gæmbɪə] *Gambia n.*
Gan·ges ['gændʒi:z] *Ganges m.*
Gar·eth ['gæreθ] *m.*
Gar·ry, Gar·y ['gærɪ] *m.*
Gaul [gɔ:l] *Gallien n.*
Ga·vin ['gævɪn] *m.*
Ga·za Strip ['gɑ:zəstrɪp] *der Gazastreifen.*
Gene [dʒi:n] *abbr. für Eugene, Eugenia.*
Ge·ne·va [dʒɪ'ni:və] *Genf n.*
Gen·o·a ['dʒenəʊə] *Genua n.*
Geoff [dʒef] *abbr. für Geoffr(e)y.*
Geof·fr(e)y ['dʒefrɪ] *Gottfried m.*
George [dʒɔ:dʒ] *Georg m.*
Geor·gia ['dʒɔ:dʒə] *Staat der USA.*
Ger·ald ['dʒerəld] *Gerald m, Gerold m.*
Ger·al·dine ['dʒerəldi:n] *Geral'dine f.*
Ger·ard ['dʒerɑ:d; *bsd. Am.* dʒe'rɑ:d] *Gerhard m.*
Ger·man Dem·o·crat·ic Re·pub·lic ['dʒɜ:məndemə,krætɪk'rɪpʌblɪk] *hist. die Deutsche Demo'kratische Repu'blik.*
Ger·ma·ny ['dʒɜ:mənɪ] *Deutschland n.*
Ger·ry ['dʒerɪ] *abbr. für Gerald, Geraldine.*
Gersh·win ['gɜ:ʃwɪn] *amer. Komponist.*
Ger·tie ['gɜ:tɪ] *Gertie f.*
Ger·trude ['gɜ:tru:d] *Gertrud f.*
Get·tys·burg ['getɪzbɜ:g] *Stadt in Pennsylvania (USA).*
Gha·na ['gɑ:nə] *Ghana n.*

Ghent [gent] Gent *n*.
Gi·bral·tar [dʒɪ'brɔːltə] Gi'braltar *n*.
Giel·gud ['giːlgʊd]: *Sir John* ~ *berühmter englischer Schauspieler.*
Gil·bert ['gɪlbət] Gilbert *m*.
Giles [dʒaɪlz] Julius *m*.
Gill [dʒɪl; gɪl] *abbr. für* **Gillian**.
Gil·li·an ['dʒɪlɪən; 'gɪlɪən] *f*.
Glad·stone ['glædstən] *brit. Staatsmann.*
Glad·ys ['glædɪs] *f*.
Gla·mor·gan·shire [glə'mɔːgənʃə] *walisische Grafschaft* (*bis 1974*).
Glas·gow ['glɑːsgəʊ] *Stadt in Schottland.*
Glen [glen] *m*.
Glo·ri·a ['glɔːrɪə] Gloria *f*.
Glouces·ter ['glɒstə] *Stadt in Südengland; a.* '**Glouces·ter·shire** [-ʃə] *englische Grafschaft.*
Glynde·bourne ['glaɪndbɔːn] *kleiner Ort in East Sussex* (*England*) *mit Opernfestspielen.*
God·frey ['gɒdfrɪ] Gottfried *m*.
Go·li·ath [gəʊ'laɪəθ] Goliath *m*.
Gor·don ['gɔːdn] *Familienname; Vorname m*.
Go·tham ['gəʊtəm] *Ortsname; fig.* ,Schilda' *n*.
Grace [greɪs] Gracia *f*, Grazia *f*.
Gra·ham ['greɪəm] *Familienname; Vorname m*.
Gram·pi·an ['græmpɪən] *Verwaltungsregion in Schottland.*
Grand Can·yon [ˌgrænd'kænjən] *Durchbruchstal des Colorado in Arizona* (*USA*).
Great Brit·ain [ˌgreɪt'brɪtn] Großbri'tannien *n*.
Great·er Lon·don [ˌgreɪtə'lʌndən] *Stadtgrafschaft, bestehend aus der City of London u. 32 Stadtbezirken.*
Great·er Man·ches·ter [ˌgreɪtə'mænʧɪstə] *Stadtgrafschaft in Nordengland.*
Greece [griːs] Griechenland *n*.
Greene [griːn] *englischer Autor.*
Green·land ['griːnlənd] Grönland *n*.
Green·wich ['grenɪʧ] *Stadtbezirk Groß-Londons;* ~ *Village Stadtteil von New York* (*USA*).
Greg [greg] *abbr. für Gregory.*
Greg·o·ry ['gregərɪ] Gregor *m*.
Gre·na·da [gre'neɪdə] Gre'nada *n*.
Gre·ta ['griːtə, 'gretə] *abbr. für Margaret.*
Grims·by ['grɪmzbɪ] *Hafenstadt in Humberside* (*England*).
Gri·sons ['griːzɔ̃:ŋ] Grau'bünden *n*.
Gros·ve·nor ['grəʊvnə] *Platz u. Straße in London.*
Gua·te·ma·la [ˌgwætɪ'mɑːlə] Guate'mala *n*.
Guern·sey ['gɜːnzɪ] *brit. Kanalinsel.*
Guin·ea ['gɪnɪ] Gui'nea *n*; **Guin·ea-Bis·sau** [ˌgɪnɪbɪ'saʊ] Guinea-Bis'sau *n*.
Guin·e·vere ['gwɪnɪˌvɪə] *Gemahlin des Königs Artus.*
Guin·ness ['gɪnɪs, gɪ'nes] *Familienname.*
Gul·li·ver ['gʌlɪvə] *Romanheld.*
Guy [gaɪ] Guido *m*.
Guy·ana [gaɪ'ænə] Gu'yana *n*.
Gwen [gwen] *abbr. für Gwendolen,* **Gwendoline**, **Gwendolyn**.
Gwen·do·len, Gwen·do·line, Gwen·do·lyn ['gwendəlɪn] *f*.
Gwent [gwent] *walisische Grafschaft.*
Gwy·nedd ['gwɪnəð, -eð] *walisische Grafschaft.*

H

Hack·ney ['hæknɪ] *Stadtbezirk von Groß-London.*
Hague [heɪg]: *the* ~ Den Haag.
Hai·ti ['heɪtɪ] Ha'iti *n*.
Hal [hæl] *abbr. für Harold*, *Henry*.
Hal·i·fax ['hælɪfæks] *Hauptstadt von Neuschottland* (*Kanada*); *Stadt in West Yorkshire* (*England*).
Hal·ley ['hælɪ] *englischer Astronom.*
Ham·il·ton ['hæmltən] *Familienname; Stadt in der Provinz Ontario* (*Kanada*).
Ham·let ['hæmlɪt] *Bühnenfigur bei Shakespeare.*
Ham·mer·smith ['hæməsmɪθ] *Stadtbezirk von Groß-London.*
Hamp·shire ['hæmpʃə] *englische Grafschaft.*
Hamp·stead ['hæmpstɪd] *Stadtteil von Groß-London.*
Han·o·ver ['hænəʊvə] Han'nover *n*.
Ha·ra·re [hə'rɑːreɪ] *Hauptstadt von Simbabwe.*
Har·dy ['hɑːdɪ] *englischer Autor.*
Ha·rin·gey ['hærɪŋgeɪ] *Stadtbezirk von Groß-London.*
Har·lem ['hɑːləm] *Stadtteil von New York.*
Har·old ['hærəld] Harald *m*.
Har·ri·et, Har·ri·ot ['hærɪət] *f*.
Har·ris·burg ['hærɪsbɜːg] *Hauptstadt von Pennsylvania* (*USA*).
Har·row ['hærəʊ] *Stadtbezirk Groß-Londons mit berühmter Public School.*
Har·ry ['hærɪ] *abbr. für Harold*, *Henry.*
Hart·ford ['hɑːtfəd] *Hauptstadt von Connecticut* (*USA*).
Har·tle·pool ['hɑːtlɪpuːl] *Hafenstadt in Cleveland* (*England*).
Har·vard U·ni·ver·si·ty ['hɑːvədˌjuːnɪ'vɜːsətɪ] *Universität in Cambridge, Massachusetts* (*USA*).
Har·vey ['hɑːvɪ] *Vorname m; Familienname.*
Har·wich ['hærɪʤ] *Hafenstadt in Südost-England.*
Has·tings ['heɪstɪŋz] *Stadt in Südengland.*
Ha·van·a [hə'vænə] Ha'vanna *n*.
Ha·ver·ing ['heɪvərɪŋ] *Stadtbezirk von Groß-London.*
Ha·wai·i [hə'waɪiː] *Staat der USA.*
Haw·thorne ['hɔːθɔːn] *amer. Schriftsteller.*
Ha·zel ['heɪzl] *f*.
Heath·row ['hiːθrəʊ] *Großflughafen von London.*
Heb·ri·des ['hebrɪdiːz] *pl. die* He'briden *pl*.
Hel·en ['helɪn] He'lene *f*.
Hel·e·na ['helɪnə] *Hauptstadt von Montana* (*USA*).
Hel·i·go·land ['helɪgəʊlænd] Helgoland *n*.
Hel·sin·ki ['helsɪŋkɪ] Helsinki *n*.
Hem·ing·way ['hemɪŋweɪ] *amer. Autor.*
Hen·ley ['henlɪ] *Stadt an der Themse* (*Ruderregatta*).
Hen·ry ['henrɪ] Heinrich *m*.
Hep·burn ['hebɜːn; 'hepbɜːn] *amer. Filmschauspielerin.*
Her·bert ['hɜːbət] Herbert *m*.
Her·e·ford and Worces·ter [ˌherɪfədn'wʊstə] *englische Grafschaft;* '**Her·e·ford·shire** [-ʃə] *englische Grafschaft* (*bis 1974*).
Hert·ford(·shire) ['hɑːfəd(ʃə)] *englische Grafschaft.*
Hesse ['hesɪ] Hessen *n*.
High·land ['haɪlənd] *Verwaltungsregion*

in Schottland.
Hil·a·ry ['hɪlərɪ] Hi'laria *f*; Hi'larius *m*.
Hil·da ['hɪldə] Hilda *f*, Hilde *f*.
Hil·ling·don ['hɪlɪŋdən] *Stadtbezirk von Groß-London.*
Hi·ma·la·ya [ˌhɪmə'leɪə] *der* Hi'malaja.
Hi·ro·shi·ma [hɪ'rɒʃɪmə] *Hafenstadt in Japan.*
Ho·bart ['həʊbɑːt] *Hauptstadt des australischen Bundesstaates Tasmanien.*
Ho·garth ['həʊgɑːθ] *englischer Maler.*
Hol·born ['həʊbən] *Stadtteil von London.*
Hol·land ['hɒlənd] Holland *n*.
Hol·ly·wood ['hɒlɪwʊd] *Filmstadt in Kalifornien* (*USA*).
Holmes [həʊmz] *Familienname.*
Ho·mer ['həʊmə] Ho'mer *m*.
Hon·du·ras [hɒn'djʊərəs] Hon'duras *n*.
Hong Kong [ˌhɒŋ'kɒŋ] Hongkong *n*.
Ho·no·lu·lu [ˌhɒnə'luːluː] *Hauptstadt von Hawaii* (*USA*).
Hor·ace ['hɒrəs] Ho'raz *m* (*römischer Dichter u. Satiriker*); *Vorname m*.
Houns·low ['haʊnzləʊ] *Stadtbezirk von Groß-London.*
Hous·ton ['hjuːstən; 'juːstən] *Stadt in Texas* (*USA*).
How·ard ['haʊəd] *m*.
Hu·bert ['hjuːbət] Hubert *m*, Hu'bertus *m*.
Hud·son ['hʌdsn] *Familienname; Fluss im Staat New York* (*USA*).
Hugh [hjuː] Hugo *m*.
Hughes [hjuːz] *Familienname.*
Hull [hʌl] *Hafenstadt in Humberside* (*England*).
Hum·ber ['hʌmbə] *Fluss in England;* '**Hum·ber·side** [-saɪd] *englische Grafschaft.*
Hume [hjuːm] *englischer Philosoph.*
Hum·phr(e)y ['hʌmfrɪ] *m*.
Hun·ga·ry ['hʌŋgərɪ] Ungarn *n*.
Hun·ting·don(·shire) ['hʌntɪŋdən(ʃə)] *englische Grafschaft* (*bis 1974*).
Hux·ley ['hʌkslɪ] *englischer Autor; englischer Biologe.*
Hyde Park [ˌhaɪd'pɑːk] *Park in London.*

I

I·an [ɪən; 'iːən] Jan *m*.
I·be·ri·an Pen·in·su·la [aɪˌbɪərɪənpɪ'nɪnsjʊlə] *die* I'berische Halbinsel.
Ice·land ['aɪslənd] Island *n*.
I·da ['aɪdə] Ida *f*.
I·da·ho ['aɪdəhəʊ] *Staat der USA.*
Il·ford ['ɪlfəd] *Stadtteil von Groß-London.*
Il·li·nois [ˌɪlɪ'nɔɪ] *Staat der USA; Fluss in USA.*
In·di·a ['ɪndjə] Indien *n*.
In·di·an·a [ˌɪndɪ'ænə] *Staat der USA.*
In·di·an·ap·o·lis [ˌɪndɪə'næpəlɪs] *Hauptstadt von Indiana* (*USA*).
In·do·ne·sia [ˌɪndəʊ'niːzjə] Indo'nesien *n*.
In·dus ['ɪndəs] Indus *m*.
In·gu·she·tia [ˌɪŋgʊ'ʃiːʃ(j)ə] Ingu'schetien *n*.
In·ver·ness(·shire) [ˌɪnvə'nes(ʃə)] *schottische Grafschaft* (*bis 1975*).
I·o·wa ['aɪəʊə; 'aɪəwə] *Staat der USA.*
Ips·wich ['ɪpswɪʧ] *Hauptstadt von Suffolk* (*England*).
I·ran [ɪ'rɑːn] I'ran *m*.
I·raq [ɪ'rɑːk] I'rak *m*.
Ire·land ['aɪələnd] Irland *n*.
I·rene [aɪ'riːnɪ; 'aɪrɪn] I'rene *f*.
I·ris ['aɪərɪs] Iris *f*.
Ir·ving ['ɜːvɪŋ] *amer. Autor.*
I·saac ['aɪzək] Isaak *m*.
Is·a·bel ['ɪzəbel] Isa'bella *f*.

Is·lam·a·bad [ɪz'lɑːməbɑːd] *Hauptstadt von Pakistan.*

Isle of Man [ˌaɪləv'mæn] *Insel in der Irischen See, die unmittelbar der englischen Krone untersteht, aber nicht zum Vereinigten Königreich gehört.*

Isle of Wight [ˌaɪləv'waɪt] *englische Grafschaft, Insel im Ärmelkanal.*

I·sle·worth ['aɪzlwəθ] *Stadtteil von Groß-London.*

Is·ling·ton ['ɪzlɪŋtən] *Stadtbezirk von Groß-London.*

Is·o·bel ['ɪzəbel] *Isa'bella f.*

Is·ra·el ['ɪzreɪəl] *Israel n.*

Is·tan·bul [ˌɪstən'buːl] *Istanbul n.*

It·a·ly ['ɪtəlɪ] *I'talien n.*

I·van ['aɪvən] *Iwan m.*

I·vor ['aɪvə] *m.*

I·vo·ry Coast ['aɪvərɪkəʊst] *die Elfenbeinküste.*

I·vy ['aɪvɪ] *f.*

J

Jack [dʒæk] *Hans m.*

Jack·ie ['dʒækɪ] *abbr. für Jacqueline.*

Jack·son ['dʒæksn] *Hauptstadt von Mississippi (USA).*

Jack·son·ville ['dʒæksnvɪl] *Hafenstadt in Florida (USA).*

Ja·cob ['dʒeɪkəb] *Jakob m.*

Jac·que·line ['dʒækliːn] *f.*

Jaf·fa ['dʒæfə] *Hafenstadt in Israel.*

Ja·mai·ca [dʒə'meɪkə] *Ja'maika n.*

James [dʒeɪmz] *Jakob m.*

Jane [dʒeɪn] *Jo'hanna f.*

Jan·et ['dʒænɪt] *Jo'hanna f.*

Jan·ice ['dʒænɪs] *f.*

Ja·pan [dʒə'pæn] *Japan n.*

Ja·son ['dʒeɪsn] *m.*

Jas·per ['dʒæspə] *Kaspar m.*

Ja·va ['dʒɑːvə] *Java n.*

Jean [dʒiːn] *Jo'hanna f.*

Jeff [dʒef] *abbr. für Jeffrey.*

Jef·fer·son ['dʒefəsn] *3. Präsident der USA.*

Jef·fer·son Cit·y [ˌdʒefəsn'sɪtɪ] *Hauptstadt von Missouri (USA).*

Jef·frey ['dʒefrɪ] *Gottfried m.*

Je·ho·vah [dʒɪ'həʊvə] *Je'hova m.*

Jen·ni·fer ['dʒenɪfə] *f.*

Jen·ny ['dʒenɪ; 'dʒɪnɪ] *Koseform für Jane.*

Jer·e·my ['dʒerɪmɪ] *Jere'mias m.*

Je·rome [dʒə'rəʊm] *Hie'ronymus m.*

Jer·ry ['dʒerɪ] *abbr. für Jeremy, Jerome, Gerald, Gerard.*

Jer·sey ['dʒɜːsɪ] *brit. Kanalinsel.*

Je·ru·sa·lem [dʒə'ruːsələm] *Je'rusalem n.*

Jes·si·ca ['dʒesɪkə] *f.*

Je·sus ['dʒiːzəs] *Jesus m.*

Jill [dʒɪl] *abbr. für Gillian.*

Jim(·my) ['dʒɪm(ɪ)] *abbr. für James.*

Jo [dʒəʊ] *abbr. für Joanna, Joseph, Josephine.*

Joan [dʒəʊn], **Jo·an·na** [dʒəʊ'ænə] *Jo'hanna f.*

Job [dʒəʊb] *Hiob m.*

Joc·e·lin(e), **Joc·e·lyn** ['dʒɒslɪn] *f.*

Joe [dʒəʊ] *abbr. für Joseph, Josephine.*

Jo·han·nes·burg [dʒəʊ'hænɪsbɜːg] *Stadt in Südafrika.*

John [dʒɒn] *Jo'hannes m, Johann m.*

John·ny ['dʒɒnɪ] *Häns-chen n.*

John o' Groats [ˌdʒɒnə'grəʊts] *Dorf an der Nordostspitze des schottischen Festlandes. Gilt volkstümlich als nördlichster Punkt des festländischen Großbritannien.*

John·son ['dʒɒnsn] *36. Präsident der*

USA; englischer Lexikograph.

Jon·a·than ['dʒɒnəθən] *Jonathan m.*

Jon·son ['dʒɒnsn] *englischer Dichter.*

Jor·dan ['dʒɔːdn] *Jor'danien n.*

Jo·seph ['dʒəʊzɪf] *Joseph m.*

Jo·se·phine ['dʒəʊzɪfiːn] *Jose'phine f.*

Josh·u·a ['dʒɒʃwə] *Josua m.*

Joule [dʒuːl] *englischer Physiker.*

Joy [dʒɔɪ] *f.*

Joyce [dʒɔɪs] *irischer Autor; Vorname f.*

Ju·dith ['dʒuːdɪθ] *Judith f.*

Ju·dy ['dʒuːdɪ] *abbr. für Judith.*

Jul·ia ['dʒuːljə] *Julia f.*

Jul·ian ['dʒuːljən] *Juli'an(us) m.*

Ju·li·et ['dʒuːljət; -ljet] *Julia f, Juli'ette f.*

Jul·ius ['dʒuːljəs] *Julius m.*

June [dʒuːn] *f.*

Ju·neau ['dʒuːnəʊ] *Hauptstadt von Alaska (USA).*

Jus·tin ['dʒʌstɪn] *Ju'stin(us) m.*

K

Kam·pu·che·a [ˌkæmpu'tʃɪə] *hist. Kam'bodscha n.*

Kan·sas ['kænzəs] *Staat der USA; Fluss in USA.*

Kan·sas Cit·y [ˌkænzəs'sɪtɪ] *Stadt in Missouri (USA); Stadt in Kansas (USA).*

Ka·ra·chi [kə'rɑːtʃɪ] *Ka'ratschi n.*

Kar·en ['kɑːrən; 'kærən] *Karin f.*

Kash·mir [ˌkæʃ'mɪə] *Kaschmir n.*

Ka·tar [kæ'tɑː] *Katar n (Scheichtum am Persischen Golf).*

Kate [keɪt] *Käthe f.*

Kath·a·rine, **Kath·er·ine** ['kæθərɪn] *Katha'rina f, Kat(h)rin f.*

Kath·leen ['kæθliːn] *f.*

Kath·y ['kæθɪ] *abbr. für Katharine, Katherine.*

Kay [keɪ] *Kai m, f, Kay m, f.*

Keats [kiːts] *englischer Dichter.*

Kee·wa·tin [kiː'wɒtɪn; *Am.* kiː'weɪtn] *Verwaltungsbezirk der Northwest Territories (Kanada).*

Keith [kiːθ] *m.*

Kel·vin ['kelvɪn] *brit. Mathematiker u. Physiker.*

Ken [ken] *abbr. für Kenneth.*

Ken·ne·dy ['kenɪdɪ] *35. Präsident der USA; ~ International Airport Großflughafen von New York (USA).*

Ken·neth ['kenɪθ] *m.*

Ken·sing·ton ['kenzɪŋtən] *Stadtteil von London.*

Ken·sing·ton and Chel·sea [ˌkenzɪŋtənən'tʃelsɪ] *Stadtbezirk von Groß-London.*

Kent [kent] *englische Grafschaft.*

Ken·tuck·y [ken'tʌkɪ] *Staat der USA; Fluss in USA.*

Ken·ya ['kenjə] *Kenia n.*

Ker·ry ['kerɪ] *Grafschaft in der Provinz Munster (Irland).*

Kev·in ['kevɪn] *m.*

Kew [kjuː] *Stadtteil von Groß-London. Botanischer Garten.*

Keynes [keɪnz] *englischer Wirtschaftswissenschaftler.*

Kil·dare [kɪl'deə] *Grafschaft in der Provinz Leinster (Irland).*

Kil·ken·ny [kɪl'kenɪ] *Grafschaft in der Provinz Leinster (Irland); Hauptstadt dieser Grafschaft.*

Kin·car·dine(·shire) [kɪn'kɑːdɪn(ʃə)] *schottische Grafschaft (bis 1975).*

Kings·ton up·on Hull [ˌkɪŋstənəpɒn'hʌl] *offizielle Bezeichnung für Hull.*

Kings·ton up·on Thames [ˌkɪŋstənəpɒn'temz] *Stadtbezirk von Groß-London; Hauptstadt von Surrey (England).*

Kin·ross(·shire) [kɪn'rɒs(ʃə)] *schottische Grafschaft (bis 1975).*

Kirk·cud·bright(·shire) [kɜː'kuːbrɪ(ʃə)] *schottische Grafschaft (bis 1975).*

Kit(·ty) ['kɪt(ɪ)] *abbr. für Catherine, Katherine.*

Klon·dyke ['klɒndaɪk] *Fluss in Kanada; Landschaft in Kanada.*

Knox [nɒks] *schottischer Reformator.*

Knox·ville ['nɒksvɪl] *Stadt in Tennessee (USA).*

Ko·re·a [kə'rɪə] *Ko'rea n; Democratic People's Republic of ~ die Demo'kratische 'Volksrepu,blik Ko'rea; Republic of ~ die Repu'blik Ko'rea.*

Kos·ci·us·ko [ˌkɒsɪ'ʌskəʊ]: *Mount ~ höchster Berg Australiens, im Bundesstaat New South Wales.*

Kos·o·vo ['kɒsəvəʊ] *der 'Kosovo.*

Krem·lin ['kremlɪn] *der Kreml.*

Ku·wait [kʊ'weɪt] *Ku'wait n.*

L

Lab·ra·dor ['læbrədɔː] *Provinz in Kanada.*

La Guar·dia [lə'gwɑːdɪə; lə'gɑːdɪə] *ehemaliger Bürgermeister von New York; ~ Airport Flughafen in New York.*

Laing [læŋ; leɪŋ] *Familienname.*

Lake Con·stance [ˌleɪk'kɒnstəns] *der Bodensee.*

Lake Hu·ron [ˌleɪk'hjʊərən] *der Huronsee (in Nordamerika).*

Lake Su·pe·ri·or [ˌleɪksuː'pɪərɪə] *der Obere See (in Nordamerika).*

Lam·beth ['læmbəθ] *Stadtbezirk von Groß-London; ~ Palace Londoner Residenz des Erzbischofs von Canterbury.*

Lan·ark(·shire) ['lænək(ʃə)] *schottische Grafschaft (bis 1975).*

Lan·ca·shire ['læŋkəʃə] *englische Grafschaft.*

Lan·cas·ter ['læŋkəstə] *Stadt in Nordwest-England; Stadt in USA.*

Land's End [ˌlændz'end] *westlichster Punkt Englands, in Cornwall.*

La·nier [lə'nɪə] *amer. Dichter.*

Lan·sing ['lænsɪŋ] *Hauptstadt von Michigan (USA).*

Laoigh·is [liːʃ; 'leɪʃ] *siehe Leix.*

La·os ['lɑːɒs; laʊs] *Laos n.*

Lar·ry ['lærɪ] *abbr. für Laurence, Lawrence.*

La·tham ['leɪθəm; 'leɪðəm] *Familienname.*

Lat·in A·mer·i·ca [ˌlætɪnə'merɪkə] *La'teina,merika n.*

Lat·via ['lætvɪə] *Lettland n.*

Laugh·ton ['lɔːtn] *Familienname.*

Lau·ra ['lɔːrə] *Laura f.*

Lau·rence ['lɒrəns] *Lorenz m.*

Law·rence ['lɒrəns] *Lorenz m; Familienname.*

Lear [lɪə] *Bühnenfigur bei Shakespeare.*

Leb·a·non ['lebənən] *der Libanon.*

Leeds [liːdz] *Industriestadt in Ostengland.*

Le·fe·vre [lə'fiːvə; lə'feɪvə] *Familienname.*

Legge [leg] *Familienname.*

Leices·ter ['lestə] *Hauptstadt der englischen Grafschaft 'Leices·ter·shire [-ʃə].*

Leigh [liː] *Familienname; Vorname m.*

Lein·ster ['lenstə] *Provinz in Irland.*

Lei·trim ['liːtrɪm] *Grafschaft in der Provinz Connaught* (*Irland*).

Leix [liːʃ] *Grafschaft in der Provinz Leinster* (*Irland*).

Le·o ['liːəʊ] Leo *m*.

Leon·ard ['lenəd] Leonhard *m*.

Les·ley ['lezlɪ; *Am.* 'leslɪ] *f*.

Les·lie ['lezlɪ; *Am.* 'leslɪ] *m*.

Le·so·tho [ləˈsuːtuː; ləˈsəʊtəʊ] Le'sotho *n*.

Lew·is ['luːɪs] Ludwig *m*; *amer. Autor.*

Lew·i·sham ['luːɪʃəm] *Stadtbezirk von Groß-London.*

Lex·ing·ton ['leksɪŋtən] *Stadt in Massachusetts* (*USA*).

Li·be·ria [laɪˈbɪərɪə] Li'beria *n*.

Lib·y·a ['lɪbɪə] Libyen *n*.

Liech·ten·stein ['lɪktənstaɪn] Liechtenstein *n*.

Lil·i·an ['lɪlɪən] *f*.

Lil·y ['lɪlɪ] Lilli *f*, Lili *f*, Lilly *f*, Lily *f*.

Lim·er·ick ['lɪmərɪk] *Grafschaft in der Provinz Munster* (*Irland*); *Hauptstadt dieser Grafschaft.*

Lin·coln ['lɪŋkən] *16. Präsident der USA; Hauptstadt von Nebraska* (*USA*); *Stadt in der englischen Grafschaft* '**Lincoln·shire** [-ʃə].

Lin·da ['lɪndə] Linda *f*.

Lind·bergh ['lɪndbɜːg] *amer. Flieger.*

Li·o·nel ['laɪənl] *m*.

Li·sa ['liːzə; 'laɪzə] Lisa *f*.

Lis·bon ['lɪzbən] Lissabon *n*.

Lith·u·a·nia [ˌlɪθjuːˈeɪnjə] Litauen *n*.

Lit·tle Rock ['lɪtlrɒk] *Hauptstadt von Arkansas* (*USA*).

Liv·er·pool ['lɪvəpuːl] *Hafenstadt in Nordwest-England; Verwaltungszentrum von* **Merseyside**.

Live·sey ['lɪvsɪ; -zɪ] *Familienname.*

Liv·ing·stone ['lɪvɪŋstən] *englischer Afrikaforscher.*

Li·vo·nia [lɪˈvəʊnjə] Livland *n*.

Liv·y ['lɪvɪ] Livius *m*.

Liz [lɪz] *abbr. für* **Elizabeth**.

Li·za ['laɪzə] Lisa *f*.

Lloyd [lɔɪd] *Familienname; Vorname m.*

Loch Lo·mond [ˌlɒkˈləʊmənd], **Loch Ness** [ˌlɒkˈnes] *Seen in Schottland.*

Locke [lɒk] *englischer Philosoph.*

Lo·is ['ləʊɪs] *f*.

Lom·bar·dy ['lɒmbədɪ] *die* Lombar'dei.

Lon·don ['lʌndən] London *n*; *City of* ~ *London im engeren Sinn. Zentraler Stadtbezirk von Groß-London u. eines der größten Finanzzentren der Welt.*

Lon·don·der·ry [ˌlʌndənˈderɪ] *nordirische Grafschaft.*

Long·ford ['lɒŋfəd] *Grafschaft in der Provinz Leinster* (*Irland*).

Lor·na ['lɔːnə] *f*.

Lor·raine [lɒˈreɪn] Lothringen *n*.

Los Al·a·mos [ˌlɒsˈæləmɒs] *Stadt in New Mexico* (*USA*); *Atomforschungszentrum.*

Los An·ge·les [lɒsˈændʒɪliːz] *Stadt in Kalifornien* (*USA*).

Lo·thi·an ['ləʊðjən] *Verwaltungsregion in Schottland.*

Lou [luː] *abbr. für* **Louis, Louisa, Louise.**

Lou·is ['luːɪ; 'luɪ; *bsd. Am.* 'luːɪs] Ludwig *m*.

Lou·i·sa [luːˈiːzə] Lu'ise *f*.

Lou·ise [luːˈiːz] Lu'ise *f*.

Lou·i·si·a·na [luːˌiːzɪˈænə] *Staat der USA.*

Lou·is·ville ['luːɪvɪl] *Stadt in Kentucky* (*USA*).

Louth [laʊð] *Grafschaft in der Provinz Leinster* (*Irland*).

Lowes [ləʊz] *Familienname.*

Lowes·toft ['ləʊstɒft] *Hafenstadt in Suffolk* (*England*).

Low·ry ['laʊərɪ; 'laʊrɪ] *Familienname.*

Lu·cia ['luːsjə] Lucia *f*, Luzia *f*.

Lu·cius ['luːsjəs] *m*.

Lu·cy ['luːsɪ] *abbr. für* **Lucia**.

Lud·gate ['lʌdgɪt; -geɪt] *Familienname.*

Luke [luːk] Lukas *m*.

Lux·em·bourg ['lʌksəmbɜːg] Luxemburg *n*.

Lyd·i·a ['lɪdɪə] Lydia *f*.

Lynn [lɪn] *f*.

Ly·ons ['laɪənz] Lyon *n*; *Familienname.*

M

Ma·bel ['meɪbl] *f*.

Ma·cau·lay [məˈkɔːlɪ] *englischer Historiker.*

Mac·beth [məkˈbeθ] *Bühnenfigur bei Shakespeare.*

Mac·Car·thy [məˈkɑːθɪ] *Familienname.*

Mac·e·do·ni·a [ˌmæsɪˈdəʊnɪə] Mazedonien *n*.

Mac·Gee [məˈgiː] *Familienname.*

Mac·ken·zie [məˈkenzɪ] *Strom in Nordwestkanada; Verwaltungsbezirk der Northwest Territories* (*Kanada*).

Mac·Leish [məˈkliːʃ] *amer. Dichter.*

Mac·leod [məˈklaʊd] *Familienname.*

Mad·a·gas·car [ˌmædəˈgæskə] Mada'gaskar *n*.

Mad·e·leine ['mædlɪn; -leɪn] Magda'lena *f*, Magda'lene *f*.

Ma·dei·ra [məˈdɪərə] Ma'deira *n*.

Madge [mædʒ] *abbr. für* **Margaret**.

Mad·i·son ['mædɪsn] *4. Präsident der USA; Hauptstadt von Wisconsin* (*USA*).

Ma·dras [məˈdrɑːs] Madras *n*.

Mag·da·len ['mægdəlɪn] Magda'lena *f*, Magda'lene *f*; ~ **College** ['mɔːdlɪn] *College in Oxford.*

Mag·da·lene ['mægdəlɪn] Magda'lena *f*, Magda'lene *f*; ~ **College** ['mɔːdlɪn] *College in Cambridge.*

Mag·gie ['mægɪ] *abbr. für* **Margaret**.

Ma·ho·met [məˈhɒmɪt] Mohammed *m*.

Maine [meɪn] *Staat der USA.*

Ma·jor·ca [məˈdʒɔːkə] Mal'lorca *n.* (*Baleareninsel*).

Ma·la·wi [məˈlɑːwɪ] Ma'lawi *n*.

Ma·lay·sia [məˈleɪzɪə] Ma'laysia *n*.

Mal·colm ['mælkəm] *m*.

Mal·dives ['mɔːldɪvz] *pl. die* Male'diven *pl.*

Ma·li ['mɑːlɪ] Mali *n*.

Mal·ta ['mɔːltə] Malta *n*.

Ma·mie ['meɪmɪ] *abbr. für* **Mary, Margaret**.

Man·ches·ter ['mæntʃɪstə] *Industriestadt in Nordwest-England; Verwaltungszentrum von* **Greater Manchester**.

Man·chu·ri·a [mænˈtʃʊərɪə] *die* Mandschu'rei.

Man·dy ['mændɪ] *abbr. für* **Amanda**.

Man·hat·tan [mænˈhætn] *Stadtbezirk von New York* (*USA*).

Man·i·to·ba [ˌmænɪˈtəʊbə] *Provinz in Kanada.*

Mar·ga·ret ['mɑːgərɪt] Marga'reta *f*, Marga'rete *f*.

Mar·ge·ry ['mɑːdʒərɪ] *siehe* **Margaret**.

Mar·gie ['mɑːdʒɪ] *abbr. für* **Margaret**.

Ma·ri·a [məˈraɪə; məˈrɪə] Ma'ria *f*.

Mar·i·an ['meərɪən; 'mærɪən] Mari'anne *f*.

Ma·rie ['mɑːrɪ; məˈriː] Ma'rie *f*.

Mar·i·lyn ['mærɪlɪn] *f*.

Mar·i·on ['mærɪən; 'meərɪən] Marion *f*.

Mar·jo·rie, Mar·jo·ry ['mɑːdʒərɪ] *f*.

Mar·lowe ['mɑːləʊ] *englischer Dichter.*

Mar·tha ['mɑːθə] Mart(h)a *f*.

Mar·tin ['mɑːtɪn; *Am.* 'mɑːrtn] Martin *m*.

Mar·y ['meərɪ] Ma'ria *f*, Ma'rie *f*.

Mar·y·land ['meərɪlænd; *bsd. Am.* 'merɪlənd] *Staat der USA.*

Mar·y·le·bone ['mærələbən] *Stadtteil von London.*

Mas·sa·chu·setts [ˌmæsəˈtʃuːsɪts] *Staat der USA.*

Ma(t)·thew ['mæθjuː] Mat'thäus *m*.

Maud [mɔːd] *abbr. für* **Magdalen(e)**.

Maugham [mɔːm] *englischer Autor.*

Mau·reen ['mɔːriːn; *bsd. Am.* mɔːˈriːn] *f*.

Mau·rice ['mɒrɪs] Moritz *m*.

Mau·ri·ta·nia [ˌmɒrɪˈteɪnjə] Maure'tanien *n*.

Mau·ri·ti·us [məˈrɪʃəs] Mau'ritius *n*.

Ma·vis ['meɪvɪs] *f*.

Max [mæks] Max *m*.

Max·ine ['mæksiːn; *bsd. Am.* mækˈsiːn] *f*.

May [meɪ] *abbr. für* **Mary**.

May·o ['meɪəʊ] *Name zweier amer. Chirurgen; Grafschaft in der Provinz Connacht* (*Irland*).

Mc·Cart·ney [məˈkɑːtnɪ] *englischer Musiker u. Komponist. Mitglied der „Beatles".*

Meath [miːð; miːθ] *Grafschaft in der Provinz Leinster* (*Irland*).

Med·i·ter·ra·ne·an (Sea) [ˌmedɪtəˈreɪnjən('siː)] *das* Mittelmeer.

Meg [meg] *abbr. für* **Margaret**.

Mel·bourne ['melbən] *Stadt in Australien.*

Mel·ville ['melvɪl] *amer. Autor.*

Mem·phis ['memfɪs] *Stadt in Tennessee* (*USA*); *antike Ruinenstadt am Nil, Nordägypten.*

Mer·i·on·eth(·shire) [ˌmerɪˈɒnɪθ(ʃə)] *walisische Grafschaft* (*bis 1974*).

Mer·sey·side ['mɜːzɪsaɪd] *Stadtgrafschaft in Nordwest-England.*

Mer·ton ['mɜːtn] *Stadtbezirk von Groß-London.*

Me·thu·en ['meθjuɪn] *Familienname.*

Mex·i·co ['meksɪkəʊ] Mexiko *n*.

Mi·am·i [maɪˈæmɪ] *Badeort in Florida* (*USA*).

Mi·chael ['maɪkl] Michael *m*.

Mi·chelle [miːˈʃel; mɪˈʃel] Mi'chèle *f*, Mi'chelle *f*.

Mich·i·gan ['mɪʃɪgən] *Staat der USA;* **Lake** ~ *der* Michigansee (*in Nordamerika*).

Mick [mɪk] *abbr. für* **Michael**.

Mid·dles·brough ['mɪdlzbrə] *Hauptstadt von Cleveland* (*England*).

Mid·dle·sex ['mɪdlseks] *englische Grafschaft* (*bis 1974*).

Mid Gla·mor·gan [ˌmɪdgləˈmɔːgən] *walisische Grafschaft.*

Mid·lands ['mɪdləndz] *pl. die* Midlands *pl.* (*die zentral gelegenen Grafschaften Mittelenglands:* Warwickshire, Northamptonshire, Leicestershire, Nottinghamshire, Derbyshire, Staffordshire, West Midlands *u. der Ostteil von* Hereford *and* Worcester).

Mid·lo·thi·an [mɪdˈləʊðjən] *schottische Grafschaft* (*bis 1975*).

Mid·west [ˌmɪdˈwest] *der* Mittlere Westen (*USA*).

Mi·ers ['maɪəz] *Familienname.*

Mike [maɪk] *abbr. für* **Michael**.

Mi·lan [mɪˈlæn] Mailand *n*.

Mil·dred ['mɪldrɪd] Miltraud *f*, Miltrud *f*.

Miles [maɪlz] *m*.

Mil·li·cent ['mɪlɪsnt] *f*.

Mil·lie, Mil·ly ['mɪlɪ] *abbr. für* **Amelia, Emily, Mildred, Millicent.**

Mil·ton ['mɪltən] *englischer Dichter.*

Mil·wau·kee [mɪl'wɔːkiː] *Industriestadt in Wisconsin (USA).*

Min·ne·ap·o·lis [ˌmɪnɪ'æpəlɪs] *Stadt in Minnesota (USA).*

Min·ne·so·ta [ˌmɪnɪ'səʊtə] *Staat der USA.*

Mi·ran·da [mɪ'rændə] Mi'randa *f.*

Mir·i·am ['mɪrɪəm] *f.*

Mis·sis·sip·pi [ˌmɪsɪ'sɪpɪ] *Staat der USA; Fluss in USA.*

Mis·sou·ri [mɪ'zʊərɪ] *Staat der USA; Fluss in USA.*

Mitch·ell ['mɪtʃl] *Familienname; Vorname m.*

Moi·ra ['mɔɪərə] *f.*

Moll [mɒl], **Mol·ly** ['mɒlɪ] *Koseformen für Mary.*

Mo·na·co ['mɒnəkəʊ] Mo'naco *n.*

Mon·a·ghan ['mɒnəhən] *Grafschaft im der Republik Irland zugehörigen Teil der Provinz Ulster.*

Mon·go·lia [mɒŋ'gəʊljə] *die Mongo-'lei.*

Mon·go·li·an Peo·ple's Re·pub·lic [mɒŋ'gəʊljən,piːplzrɪ'pʌblɪk] *die Mon-'golische 'Volksrepu,blik.*

Mon·i·ca ['mɒnɪkə] Monika *f.*

Mon·mouth(·shire) ['mɒnməθ(ʃə)] *walisische Grafschaft (bis 1974).*

Mon·roe [mən'rəʊ] *5. Präsident der USA; amer. Filmschauspielerin.*

Mon·tan·a [mɒn'tænə] *Staat der USA.*

Mont·gom·er·y [mənt'gʌmərɪ] *brit. Feldmarschall; Hauptstadt von Alabama (USA); a.* **Mont'gom·er·y·shire** [-ʃə] *walisische Grafschaft (bis 1974).*

Mont·pe·lier [mɒnt'piːljə] *Hauptstadt von Vermont (USA).*

Mont·re·al [ˌmɒntrɪ'ɔːl] *Stadt in Kanada.*

Mo·ra·vi·a [mə'reɪvjə] Mähren *n.*

Mor·ay(·shire) ['mʌrɪ(ʃə)] *schottische Grafschaft (bis 1975).*

More [mɔː]: *Thomas ~* Thomas Morus.

Mo·roc·co [mə'rɒkəʊ] Ma'rokko *n.*

Mos·cow ['mɒskəʊ] Moskau *n.*

Mo·selle [məʊ'zel] Mosel *f.*

Mount Ev·er·est [ˌmaʊnt'evərɪst] *höchster Berg der Erde.*

Mount Mc·Kin·ley [ˌmaʊntmə'kɪnlɪ] *höchster Berg der USA, in Alaska.*

Mo·zam·bique [ˌməʊzəm'biːk] Moçam-'bique *n*, Mosam'bik *n.*

Mu·nich ['mjuːnɪk] München *n.*

Mun·ster ['mʌnstə] *Provinz in Irland.*

Mu·ri·el ['mjʊərɪəl] *f.*

Mur·ray ['mʌrɪ] *Familienname; Fluss in Australien.*

My·an·mar ['mjænmɑː, ˌmaɪæn'mɑː] Myan'mar *n (Birma).*

My·ra ['maɪərə] *f.*

N

Nab·o·kov [nə'bəʊkɒf] *amer. Schriftsteller russischer Herkunft.*

Nairn(·shire) ['neən(ʃə)] *schottische Grafschaft (bis 1975).*

Na·mib·ia [nə'mɪbɪə] Na'mibia *n.*

Nan·cy ['nænsɪ] *f.*

Nan·ga Par·bat [ˌnʌŋgə'pɑːbət] *Berg im Himalaya.*

Na·o·mi ['neɪəmɪ] *f.*

Na·ples ['neɪplz] Ne'apel *n.*

Na·po·le·on [nə'pəʊljən] Na'poleon *m.*

Nash·ville ['næʃvɪl] *Hauptstadt von Tennessee (USA).*

Na·tal [nə'tæl] Natal *n.*

Nat·a·lie ['nætəlɪ] Na'talia *f*, 'Natalie *f.*

Na·than·iel [nə'θænjəl] Na't(h)anael *m.*

Na·u·ru [nɑː'uːruː] Na'uru *n.*

Naz·a·reth ['næzərɪθ] Nazareth *n.*

Neal [niːl] *m.*

Ne·bras·ka [nɪ'bræskə] *Staat der USA.*

Ned [ned] *abbr. für Edmund, Edward.*

Neil(l) [niːl] *Vorname m; Familienname.*

Nell, **Nel·ly** ['nel(ɪ)] *abbr. für Eleanor, Ellen, Helen.*

Nel·son ['nelsn] *brit. Admiral.*

Ne·pal [nɪ'pɔːl] Nepal *n.*

Neth·er·lands ['neðələndz] *pl. die Niederlande pl.*

Ne·va·da [ne'vɑːdə] *Staat der USA.*

Nev·il, **Nev·ille** ['nevɪl] *m.*

New·ark ['njuːək; Am. 'nuːərk] *Stadt in New Jersey (USA).*

New Bruns·wick [ˌnjuː'brʌnzwɪk] *Provinz in Kanada.*

New·bury ['njuːbərɪ] *Stadt in Berkshire (England).*

New·cas·tle ['njuːˌkɑːsl] *siehe* **Newcastle-upon-Tyne**; *Stadt in New South Wales (Australien).*

New·cas·tle-up·on-Tyne ['njuːˌkɑːslə-ˌpɒn'taɪn] *Hauptstadt von Tyne and Wear (England).*

New Del·hi [ˌnjuː'delɪ] *Hauptstadt von Indien.*

New Eng·land [ˌnjuː'ɪŋglənd] Neu-'England *n (USA).*

New·found·land ['njuːfəndlənd] Neu-'fundland *n (Provinz in Kanada).*

New Guin·ea [ˌnjuː'gɪnɪ] Neugui'nea *n.*

New·ham ['njuːəm] *Stadtbezirk von Groß-London.*

New Hamp·shire [ˌnjuː'hæmpʃə] *Staat der USA.*

New Jer·sey [ˌnjuː'dʒɜːzɪ] *Staat der USA.*

New Mex·i·co [ˌnjuː'meksɪkəʊ] *Staat der USA.*

New Or·le·ans [ˌnjuː'ɔːlɪənz] *Hafenstadt in Louisiana (USA).*

New South Wales [ˌnjuːsaʊθ'weɪlz] Neusüd'wales *n (Bundesstaat Australiens).*

New·ton ['njuːtn] *englischer Physiker.*

New York [ˌnjuː'jɔːk; Am. ˌnuː'jɔːk] *Staat der USA; größte Stadt der USA.*

New Zea·land [ˌnjuː'ziːlənd] Neu'seeland *n.*

Ni·ag·a·ra [naɪ'ægərə] Nia'gara *m.*

Nic·a·ra·gua [ˌnɪkə'rægjʊə] Nica'ragua *n.*

Nich·o·las ['nɪkələs] Nikolaus *m.*

Nick [nɪk] *abbr. für Nicholas.*

Ni·gel ['naɪdʒəl] *m.*

Ni·ger ['naɪdʒə] Niger *m (Fluss in Westafrika)*; [niː'ʒeə] Niger *n (Republik in Westafrika).*

Ni·ge·ri·a [naɪ'dʒɪərɪə] Ni'geria *n.*

Nile [naɪl] Nil *m.*

Nix·on ['nɪksən] *37. Präsident der USA.*

No·bel [nəʊ'bel] *schwedischer Industrieller, Stifter des Nobelpreises.*

No·el ['nəʊəl] *m.*

No·ra ['nɔːrə] Nora *f.*

Nor·folk ['nɔːfək] *englische Grafschaft; Hafenstadt in Virginia (USA) u. Hauptstützpunkt der US-Atlantikflotte.*

Nor·man ['nɔːmən] *m.*

Nor·man·dy ['nɔːməndɪ] *die Nor-man'die.*

North·amp·ton [nɔː'θæmptən] *Stadt in Mittelengland; a.* **North'amp·ton·shire** [-ʃə] *englische Grafschaft.*

North Cape [ˌnɔːθ'keɪp] *das Nordkap.*

North Car·o·li·na [ˌnɔːθkærə'laɪnə] *Staat der USA.*

North Da·ko·ta [ˌnɔːθdə'kəʊtə] *Staat der USA.*

North·ern Ire·land [ˌnɔːðn'aɪələnd] Nord'irland *n.*

North·ern Ter·ri·to·ry [ˌnɔːðn'terɪtərɪ] 'Nordterri,torium *n (Australien).*

North Sea [ˌnɔːθ'siː] *die Nordsee.*

North·um·ber·land [nɔː'θʌmbələnd] *englische Grafschaft.*

North·west Ter·ri·tor·ies [ˌnɔːθ'west 'terɪtərɪz] Nord'westterri,torien *pl. (Kanada).*

North York·shire [ˌnɔːθ'jɔːkʃə] *englische Grafschaft.*

Nor·way ['nɔːweɪ] Norwegen *n.*

Nor·wich ['nɒrɪdʒ] *Stadt in Ostengland.*

Not·ting·ham ['nɒtɪŋəm] *Industriestadt in Mittelengland; a.* **'Not·ting·ham·shire** [-ʃə] *englische Grafschaft.*

No·va Sco·tia [ˌnəʊvə'skəʊʃə] Neu-'schottland *n (Provinz in Kanada).*

Nu·rem·berg ['njʊərəmbɜːg] Nürnberg *n.*

O

Oak·land ['əʊklənd] *Hafenstadt in Kalifornien (USA).*

O'Ca·sey [əʊ'keɪsɪ] *irischer Dramatiker.*

O'Con·nor [əʊ'kɒnə] *Familienname.*

O·ce·an·i·a [ˌəʊʃɪ'eɪnjə] Oze'anien *n.*

O·dets [əʊ'dets] *amer. Dramatiker.*

Of·fa·ly ['ɒfəlɪ] *Grafschaft in der Provinz Leinster (Irland).*

O'Fla·her·ty [əʊ'fleətɪ; əʊ'flæhətɪ] *irischer Romanschriftsteller.*

O'Har·a [əʊ'hɑːrə; Am. əʊ'hærə] *Familienname.*

O·hi·o [əʊ'haɪəʊ] *Staat der USA; Fluss in den USA.*

O·kla·ho·ma [ˌəʊklə'həʊmə] *Staat der USA; ~ Cit·y Hauptstadt von Oklahoma (USA).*

O'Lear·y [əʊ'lɪərɪ] *Familienname.*

Ol·ive ['ɒlɪv] O'livia *f.*

Ol·i·ver ['ɒlɪvə] Oliver *m.*

O·liv·i·a [ɒ'lɪvɪə] *f.*

O·liv·i·er [ə'lɪvɪeɪ]: *Sir Laurence ~ berühmter englischer Schauspieler.*

O·lym·pia [əʊ'lɪmpɪə] *Hauptstadt von Washington (USA).*

O·ma·ha ['əʊməhɑː; Am. a. -hɔː] *Stadt in Nebraska (USA).*

O·man [əʊ'mɑːn] O'man *n.*

O'Neill [əʊ'niːl] *amer. Dramatiker.*

On·ta·ri·o [ɒn'teərɪəʊ] *Provinz in Kanada; Lake ~ der Ontariosee (in Nordamerika).*

Or·ange ['ɒrɪndʒ] O'ranien *n (Herrscherfamilie)*; O'ranje *m (Fluss in Südafrika).*

Or·e·gon ['ɒrɪgən] *Staat der USA.*

Ork·ney ['ɔːknɪ] *insulare Verwaltungsregion Schottlands (bis 1975 schottische Grafschaft); ~ Is·lands* [ˌɔːknɪ'aɪləndz] *pl. die Orkneyinseln pl.*

Or·well ['ɔːwəl] *englischer Autor.*

Os·borne ['ɒzbən] *englischer Dramatiker.*

Os·car ['ɒskə] Oskar *m.*

O'Shea [əʊ'ʃeɪ] *Familienname.*

Ost·end [ɒ'stend] Ost'ende *n.*

O'Sul·li·van [əʊ'sʌlɪvən] *Familienname.*

Os·wald ['ɒzwəld] Oswald *m.*

Ot·ta·wa ['ɒtəwə] *Hauptstadt von Kanada.*

Ouach·i·ta ['wɒʃɪtɔː] *Fluss in Arkansas u. Louisiana (USA).*

Oug·ham ['əʊkəm] *Familienname.*

Ouse [uːz] *englischer Flussname.*

Ow·en ['əʊɪn] *Familienname.*

Ow·ens ['əʊɪnz] *amer. Leichtathlet.*

Ox·ford ['ɒksfəd] *englische Universitäts-*

stadt; a. **'Ox·ford·shire** [-ʃə] *englische Grafschaft.*

O·zark Moun·tains [ˌəʊzɑːkˈmaʊntɪnz] *pl.*, **O·zark Pla·teau** [ˌəʊzɑːkˈplætəʊ] *Plateau westlich des Mississippi in Missouri, Arkansas u. Oklahoma (USA).*

P

Pa·cif·ic (**O·cean**) [pəˈsɪfɪk (pəˌsɪfɪk-ˈəʊʃn)] *der* Pa'zifik, *der* Pa'zifische Ozean.

Pad·ding·ton [ˈpædɪŋtən] *Stadtteil von London.*

Pad·dy [ˈpædɪ] *abbr. für* **Patricia, Patrick**.

Paign·ton [ˈpeɪntən] *Teilstadt von Torbay in Devon (England).*

Paine [peɪn] *amer. Staatstheoretiker englischer Herkunft.*

Pais·ley [ˈpeɪzlɪ] *radikaler nordirischer protestantischer Politiker; Industriestadt in Schottland.*

Pak·i·stan [ˌpɑːkɪsˈtɑːn] *Pakistan n.*

Pal·es·tine [ˈpæləstaɪn] *Palä'stina n.*

Pall Mall [ˌpælˈmæl] *Straße in London.*

Palm Beach [ˌpɑːmˈbiːtʃ; *Am. a.* ˌpɑːlm-] *Seebad in Florida (USA).*

Pal·mer [ˈpɑːmə; *Am. a.* ˈpɑːl-] *Familienname.*

Pam [pæm] *abbr. für* **Pamela**.

Pam·e·la [ˈpæmələ] *Pa'mela f.*

Pan·a·ma [ˌpænəˈmɑː; ˈpænəmɑː] *Panama n.*

Pa·pua New Gui·nea [ˈpɑːpʊəˌnjuː-ˈgɪnɪ; ˈpæpjʊə-] *Papua-Neugui'nea n.*

Par·a·guay [ˈpærəgwaɪ] *Para'guay n.*

Par·is [ˈpærɪs] *Pa'ris n.*

Pat [pæt] *abbr. für* **Patricia, Patrick**.

Pa·tience [ˈpeɪʃns] *f.*

Pa·tri·cia [pəˈtrɪʃə] *Pa'trizia f.*

Pat·rick [ˈpætrɪk] *Pa'trizius m.*

Paul [pɔːl] *Paul m.*

Pau·la [ˈpɔːlə] *Paula f.*

Pau·line [ˈpɔːliːn; ˈpɒːliːn] *Pau'line f.*

Pearl [pɜːl] *f.*

Pearl Har·bor [ˌpɜːlˈhɑːbə] *Hafenstadt auf Hawaii (USA).*

Pears [pɪəz; peəz] *Familienname.*

Pear·sall [ˈpɪəsɔːl; -səl] *Familienname.*

Pear·son [ˈpɪəsn] *Familienname.*

Peart [pɪət] *Familienname.*

Pee·bles(·shire) [ˈpiːblz(ʃə)] *schottische Grafschaft (bis 1975).*

Peg(·gy) [ˈpeg(ɪ)] *abbr. für* **Margaret**.

Pe·king [ˌpiːˈkɪŋ] *Peking n.*

Pem·broke(·shire) [ˈpembrʊk(ʃə)] *walisische Grafschaft (bis 1974).*

Pe·nel·o·pe [pɪˈneləpɪ] *Pe'nelope f.*

Penn·syl·va·nia [ˌpensɪlˈveɪnjə] *Staat der USA.*

Pen·ny [ˈpenɪ] *abbr. für* **Penelope**.

Pen·zance [penˈzæns] *westlichste Stadt Englands, in Cornwall.*

Pepys [piːps] *Verfasser berühmter Tagebücher.*

Per·cy [ˈpɜːsɪ] *f.*

Per·sia [ˈpɜːʃə; *Am.* ˈpɜːrʒə] *Persien n.*

Per·sian Gulf [ˌpɜːʃnˈgʌlf] *der Persische Golf.*

Perth [pɜːθ] *Hauptstadt von West-Australien; Stadt in Tayside (Schottland); siehe* **Perthshire**.

Perth·shire [ˈpɜːθʃə] *schottische Grafschaft (bis 1975).*

Pe·ru [pəˈruː] *Pe'ru n.*

Pete [piːt] *abbr. für* **Peter**.

Pe·ter [ˈpiːtə] *Peter m*, Petrus *m.*

Pe·ter·bor·ough [ˈpiːtəbrə] *Stadt in Cambridgeshire (England).*

Phil·a·del·phia [ˌfɪləˈdelfjə] *Stadt in*

Pennsylvania (USA).

Phil·ip [ˈfɪlɪp] *Philipp m.*

Phi·lip·pa [ˈfɪlɪpə] *Phi'lippa f.*

Phil·ip·pines [ˈfɪlɪpiːnz] *pl. die* Philip'pinen *pl.*

Phoe·be [ˈfiːbɪ] *Phöbe f.*

Phoe·nix [ˈfiːnɪks] *Hauptstadt von Arizona (USA).*

Phyl·lis [ˈfɪlɪs] *Phyllis f.*

Pic·ca·dil·ly [ˌpɪkəˈdɪlɪ] *Straße in London.*

Pied·mont [ˈpiːdmənt] *Pie'mont n.*

Pierce [pɪəs] *Familienname; Vorname m.*

Pierre [pɪə; *Am.* pɪər] *Hauptstadt von South Dakota (USA).*

Pin·ter [ˈpɪntə] *englischer Dramatiker.*

Pitts·burgh [ˈpɪtsbɜːg] *Stadt in Pennsylvania (USA).*

Plan·tag·e·net [plænˈtædʒənɪt] *englisches Herrschergeschlecht.*

Pla·to [ˈpleɪtəʊ] *Plato(n) m.*

Plym·outh [ˈplɪməθ] *Hafenstadt in Südengland.*

Poe [pəʊ] *amer. Dichter u. Schriftsteller.*

Po·land [ˈpəʊlənd] *Polen n.*

Pol·ly [ˈpɒlɪ] *Koseform von* **Mary**.

Pol·y·ne·sia [ˌpɒlɪˈniːzjə; *Am.* -ˈniːʒə] *Poly'nesien n.*

Pom·er·a·nia [ˌpɒməˈreɪnjə] *Pommern n.*

Pope [pəʊp] *englischer Dichter.*

Port-au-Prince [ˌpɔːtəʊˈprɪns] *Hauptstadt von Haiti.*

Port E·liz·a·beth [ˌpɔːtɪˈlɪzəbəθ] *Hafenstadt in Südafrika.*

Port·land [ˈpɔːtlənd] *Hafenstadt in Maine (USA); Stadt in Oregon (USA).*

Ports·mouth [ˈpɔːtsməθ] *Hafenstadt in Südengland; Hafenstadt in Virginia (USA).*

Por·tu·gal [ˈpɔːtjʊgl; ˈpɔːtʃʊgl] *Portugal n.*

Po·to·mac [pəˈtəʊmək] *Fluss in USA.*

Pound [paʊnd] *amer. Dichter.*

Pow·ell [ˈpəʊəl; ˈpaʊəl] *Familienname.*

Pow·lett [ˈpɔːlɪt] *Familienname.*

Pow·ys [ˈpəʊɪs; ˈpaʊɪs] *walisische Grafschaft; Familienname.*

Prague [prɑːg] *Prag n.*

Pre·to·ria [prɪˈtɔːrɪə] *Hauptstadt von Südafrika.*

Priest·ley [ˈpriːstlɪ] *englischer Romanschriftsteller.*

Prince Ed·ward Is·land [prɪnsˌedwəd-ˈaɪlənd] *Provinz in Kanada.*

Prince·ton [ˈprɪnstən] *Universitätsstadt in New Jersey (USA).*

Pris·cil·la [prɪˈsɪlə] *Pris'cilla f.*

Prit·chard [ˈprɪtʃəd] *Familienname.*

Prov·i·dence [ˈprɒvɪdəns] *Hauptstadt von Rhode Island (USA).*

Pru·dence [ˈpruːdns] *Pru'dentia f.*

Prus·sia [ˈprʌʃə] *Preußen n.*

Puer·to Ri·co [ˌpwɜːtəʊˈriːkəʊ] *Puerto Rico n.*

Pugh [pjuː] *Familienname.*

Pul·itz·er [ˈpʊlɪtsə; ˈpjuː-] *amer. Journalist, Stifter des Pulitzerpreises.*

Pun·jab [ˌpʌnˈdʒɑːb] *Pan'dschab n.*

Pur·cell [ˈpɜːsl] *englischer Komponist.*

Pyr·e·nees [ˌpɪrəˈniːz; *Am.* ˈpɪrəniːz] *pl. die* Pyre'näen *pl.*

Q

Qa·tar [kæˈtɑː; *Am.* ˈkɑːtər] *Quatar n.*

Que·bec [kwɪˈbek] *Provinz u. Stadt in Kanada.*

Queen·ie [ˈkwiːnɪ] *f.*

Queens [kwiːnz] *Stadtbezirk von New York (USA).*

Queens·land [ˈkwiːnzlənd] *Bundesstaat Australiens.*

Quen·tin [ˈkwentɪn; *Am.* -tn] *Quin'tin (-us) m.*

Qui·nault [ˈkwɪnlt] *Familienname.*

Quin·c(e)y [ˈkwɪnsɪ] *Familienname; Vorname m, f.*

R

Ra·chel [ˈreɪtʃəl] *Ra(c)hel f.*

Rad·nor(·shire) [ˈrædnə(ʃə)] *walisische Grafschaft (bis 1974).*

Rae [reɪ] *Familienname; Vorname m, f.*

Ra·leigh [ˈrɔːlɪ; ˈrɑːlɪ] *englischer Seefahrer; Hauptstadt von North Carolina (USA).*

Ralph [reɪf; rælf] *Ralf m.*

Ran·dolph [ˈrændɒlf] *m.*

Ran·dy [ˈrændɪ] *abbr. für* **Randolph**.

Rat·is·bon [ˈrætɪzbɒn] *Regensburg n.*

Ra·wal·pin·di [ˌrɑːwəlˈpɪndɪ] *Stadt in Pakistan.*

Ray [reɪ] *m, f.*

Ray·mond [ˈreɪmənd] *Raimund m.*

Read·ing [ˈredɪŋ] *Stadt in Südengland.*

Rea·gan [ˈreɪgən] *40. Präsident der USA.*

Re·bec·ca [rɪˈbekə] *Re'bekka f.*

Red·bridge [ˈredbrɪdʒ] *Stadtbezirk von Groß-London.*

Reg [redʒ] *abbr. für* **Reginald**.

Re·gi·na [rɪˈdʒaɪnə] *Re'gina f*, Re'gine *f; Hauptstadt von Saskatchewan (Kanada).*

Reg·i·nald [ˈredʒɪnld] *Re(g)inald m.*

Reid [riːd] *Familienname.*

Ren·frew(·shire) [ˈrenfruː(ʃə)] *schottische Grafschaft (bis 1975).*

Rhine [raɪn] *Rhein m.*

Rhode Is·land [ˌrəʊdˈaɪlənd] *Staat der USA.*

Rhodes [rəʊdz] *brit.-südafrikan. Staatsmann; Rhodos n.*

Rho·de·sia [rəʊˈdiːzjə; *Am.* -ʒə] *Rho'desien n (heutiger Name:* **Zimbabwe**).

Rhon·dda [ˈrɒndə] *Stadt in Mid Glamorgan (Wales).*

Rich·ard [ˈrɪtʃəd] *Richard m.*

Rich·ard·son [ˈrɪtʃədsn] *englischer Autor.*

Rich·mond [ˈrɪtʃmənd] *Hauptstadt von Virginia (USA); Stadtbezirk von New York (USA), heute üblicherweise* **Staten Island** *genannt; siehe* **Richmond-upon-Thames**.

Rich·mond-up·on-Thames [ˈrɪtʃmənd-əˌpɒnˈtemz] *Stadtbezirk von Groß-London.*

Ri·ta [ˈriːtə] *Rita f.*

Ro·a·noke [ˌrəʊəˈnəʊk] *Fluss in Virginia u. North Carolina (USA); Stadt in Virginia (USA);* ~ **Island** *Insel vor der Küste von North Carolina (USA).*

Rob·ert [ˈrɒbət] *Robert m.*

Rob·in [ˈrɒbɪn] *abbr. für* **Robert**.

Rob·in Hood [ˌrɒbɪnˈhʊd] *legendärer englischer Geächteter, Bandenführer u. Wohltäter der Armen zur Zeit Richards I.*

Roch·es·ter [ˈrɒtʃɪstə] *Stadt im Staat New York (USA); Stadt in Kent (England).*

Rock·e·fel·ler [ˈrɒkɪfelə] *amer. Industrieller.*

Rock·y Moun·tains [ˌrɒkɪˈmaʊntɪnz] *pl. Gebirge in USA.*

Rod [rɒd] *abbr. für* **Rodney**.

Rod·ney [ˈrɒdnɪ] *m.*

Rog·er [ˈrɒdʒə] *Rüdiger m;* Roger *m.*

Ro·ma·nia [ruːˈmeɪnjə; rʊ-; *Am.* rəʊ-] Ru'mänien *n*.

Rome [rəʊm] Rom *n*.

Ro·me·o [ˈrəʊmɪəʊ] *Bühnenfigur bei Shakespeare.*

Ron [rɒn] *abbr. für* **Ronald**.

Ron·ald [ˈrɒnld] Ronald *m*.

Roo·se·velt [ˈrəʊzəvelt] *Name zweier Präsidenten der USA.*

Ros·a·lie [ˈrəʊzəlɪ; ˈrɒz-] Ro'salia *f*, Ro'salie *f*.

Ros·a·lind [ˈrɒzəlɪnd] Rosa'linde *f*.

Ros·com·mon [rɒsˈkɒmən] *Grafschaft in der Provinz Connaught (Irland); Hauptstadt dieser Grafschaft.*

Rose [rəʊz] Rosa *f*.

Rose·mar·y [ˈrəʊzmərɪ; *Am.* -merɪ] 'Rosema,rie *f*.

Ross and Cro·mar·ty [ˌrɒsənˈkrɒmətɪ] *schottische Grafschaft (bis 1975).*

Rouse [raʊs; ruːs] *Familienname.*

Routh [raʊθ] *Familienname.*

Rox·burgh(·shire) [ˈrɒksbərə(ʃə)] *schottische Grafschaft (bis 1975).*

Roy [rɔɪ] *m*.

Ru·dolf, Ru·dolph [ˈruːdɒlf] Rudolf *m*, Rudolph *m*.

Rud·yard [ˈrʌdjəd] *m*.

Rug·by [ˈrʌɡbɪ] *berühmte Public School.*

Ru·pert [ˈruːpət] Rupert *m*.

Rus·sell [ˈrʌsl] *englischer Philosoph.*

Rus·sia [ˈrʌʃə] Russland *n*.

Ruth [ruːθ] Ruth *f*.

Rut·land(·shire) [ˈrʌtlənd(ʃə)] *englische Grafschaft (bis 1974).*

Rwan·da [rʊˈændə] Ru'anda n.

S

Sac·ra·men·to [ˌsækrəˈmentəʊ] *Hauptstadt von Kalifornien (USA).*

Sa·ha·ra [səˈhɑːrə; *Am. a.* səˈhærə; səˈheərə] Sa'hara *f*.

Sa·lem [ˈseɪləm] *Hauptstadt von Oregon (USA).*

Salis·bu·ry [ˈsɔːlzbərɪ] *früherer Name von Harare; Stadt in Südengland.*

Sal·ly [ˈsælɪ] *abbr. für* **Sara(h)**.

Salt Lake Cit·y [ˌsɔːltleɪkˈsɪtɪ] *Hauptstadt von Utah (USA).*

Sa·man·tha [səˈmænθə] *f*.

Sa·moa [səˈməʊə] Sa'moa *n (Inselgruppe im Pazifik);* **Western ~** West-Sa'moa *n (unabhängiger Inselstaat).*

Sam·son [ˈsæmsn] Samson *m*, Simson *m*.

Sam·u·el [ˈsæmjʊəl] Samuel *m*.

San An·to·nio [ˌsænænˈtəʊnɪəʊ] *Stadt in Texas (USA).*

San Ber·nar·di·no [ˌsæn,bɜːnəˈdiːnəʊ] *Stadt in Kalifornien (USA).*

Sand·hurst [ˈsændhɜːst] *Ort in Berkshire (England) mit berühmter Militärakademie.*

San Di·e·go [ˌsændɪˈeɪɡəʊ] *Hafenstadt u. Flottenstützpunkt in Kalifornien (USA).*

San·dra [ˈsændrə] *abbr. für* **Alexandra**.

San·dy [ˈsændɪ] *abbr. für* **Alexander**, **Alexandra**.

San Fran·cis·co [ˌsænfrənˈsɪskəʊ] San Fran'zisko *n (USA).*

San Ma·ri·no [ˌsænməˈriːnəʊ] San Ma'rino *n*.

San·ta Fe [ˌsæntəˈfeɪ] *Hauptstadt von New Mexico (USA).*

Sar·a(h) [ˈseərə] Sara *f*.

Sar·di·nia [sɑːˈdɪnjə] Sar'dinien *n*.

Sas·katch·e·wan [səsˈkætʃɪwən] *Provinz in Kanada.*

Sas·ka·toon [ˌsæskəˈtuːn] *Stadt in Saskatchewan (Kanada).*

Sau·di A·ra·bi·a [ˌsaʊdɪəˈreɪbɪə] Saudi-A'rabien *n*.

Sa·voy [səˈvɔɪ] Sa'voyen *n*.

Saw·yer [ˈsɔːjə] *Familienname.*

Sax·o·ny [ˈsæksnɪ] Sachsen *n*.

Scan·di·na·vi·a [ˌskændɪˈneɪvjə] Skandi'navien *n*.

Sche·nec·ta·dy [skɪˈnektədɪ] *Stadt im Staat New York (USA).*

Scot·land [ˈskɒtlənd] Schottland *n*.

Scott [skɒt] *schottischer Autor; englischer Polarforscher.*

Seam·us [ˈʃeɪməs] *siehe* **James**.

Sean [ʃɔːn] *siehe* **John**.

Searle [sɜːl] *Familienname.*

Se·at·tle [sɪˈætl] *Hafenstadt im Staat Washington (USA).*

Sedg·wick [ˈsedʒwɪk] *Familienname.*

Sel·kirk(·shire) [ˈselkɜːk(ʃə)] *schottische Grafschaft (bis 1975).*

Sen·e·gal [ˌsenɪˈɡɔːl] Senegal *n*.

Seoul [səʊl] Se'oul *n*.

Ser·bi·a [ˈsɜːbɪə] Serbien *n*.

Sev·ern [ˈsevən] *Fluss in Wales u. West-England.*

Sew·ell [ˈsjuːəl; *Am.* ˈsuːəl] *Familienname.*

Sey·chelles [seɪˈʃelz] *pl. die* Sey'chellen(-Inseln) *pl.*

Sey·mour [ˈsiːmɔː; *schottisch* ˈseɪmɔː] *m*.

Shake·speare [ˈʃeɪk,spɪə] *englischer Dichter u. Dramatiker.*

Shar·jah [ˈʃɑːdʒə] Schardscha *n (Mitglied der Vereinigten Arabischen Emirate).*

Shaw [ʃɔː] *irischer Dramatiker.*

Shef·field [ˈʃefiːld] *Industriestadt in Mittelengland.*

Shei·la [ˈʃiːlə] *siehe* **Celia**.

Shel·ley [ˈʃelɪ] *englischer Dichter.*

Sher·lock [ˈʃɜːlɒk] *m*.

Shet·land [ˈʃetlənd] *insulare Verwaltungsregion Schottlands;* **~ Is·lands** [ˌʃetləndˈaɪləndz] *pl. die* Shetlandinseln *pl.*

Shir·ley [ˈʃɜːlɪ] *f*.

Shrop·shire [ˈʃrɒpʃə] *englische Grafschaft.*

Shy·lock [ˈʃaɪlɒk] *Bühnenfigur bei Shakespeare.*

Si·am [ˌsaɪˈæm; ˈsaɪæm] Siam *n (früherer Name Thailands).*

Si·be·ri·a [saɪˈbɪərɪə] Si'birien *n*.

Sib·yl [ˈsɪbɪl] Si'bylle *f*.

Sic·i·ly [ˈsɪsɪlɪ] Si'zilien *n*.

Sid [sɪd] *abbr. für* **Sidney** (*Vorname*).

Sid·ney [ˈsɪdnɪ] *Familienname; Vorname m, f.*

Si·er·ra Le·one [sɪˌerəlɪˈəʊn] Sierra Le'one *n*.

Sik·kim [ˈsɪkɪm] Sikkim *n*.

Si·le·sia [saɪˈliːzjə] Schlesien *n*.

Sil·vi·a [ˈsɪlvɪə] Silvia *f*.

Si·mon [ˈsaɪmən] Simon *m*.

Si·nai (Pen·in·su·la) [ˈsaɪnaɪ (ˌ-pɪˈnɪnsjʊlə)] Sinai(halbinsel *f*) *n*.

Sin·clair [ˈsɪŋkleə] *amer. Autor; Vorname m*.

Sin·ga·pore [ˌsɪŋɡəˈpɔː] Singapur *n*.

Sing Sing [ˈsɪŋsɪŋ] *Staatsgefängnis von New York (USA).*

Sli·go [ˈslaɪɡəʊ] *Grafschaft in der Provinz Connaught (Irland); Hauptstadt dieser Grafschaft.*

Sloan [sləʊn] *amer. Maler.*

Slough [slaʊ] *Stadt in Berkshire (England).*

Slo·vak·i·a [sləʊˈvækɪə] Slowakei *f*.

Slo·ve·ni·a [sləʊˈviːnɪə] Slowenien *n*.

Snow·don [ˈsnəʊdn] *Berg in Wales.*

Soc·ra·tes [ˈsɒkrətiːz] Sokrates *m*.

Sol·o·mon [ˈsɒləmən] Salomo *m*.

So·ma·lia [səʊˈmɑːlɪə] So'malia *n*.

So·mers [ˈsʌməz] *Familienname.*

Som·er·set(·shire) [ˈsʌməsɪt(ʃə)] *englische Grafschaft.*

So·nia [ˈsɒnɪə] Sonja *f*.

So·phi·a [səʊˈfaɪə] So'phia *f*, So'fia *f*.

Soph·o·cles [ˈsɒfəkliːz] Sophokles *m*.

South Af·ri·ca [ˌsaʊθˈæfrɪkə] Süd'afrika *n*.

South·amp·ton [saʊθˈæmptən] *Hafenstadt in Südengland.*

South Aus·tra·lia [ˌsaʊθɒˈstreɪljə] Süd-au'stralien *n (Bundesstaat Australiens).*

South Car·o·li·na [ˌsaʊθkærəˈlaɪnə] *Staat der USA.*

South Da·ko·ta [ˌsaʊθdəˈkəʊtə] *Staat der USA.*

South Gla·mor·gan [ˌsaʊθɡləˈmɔːɡən] *walisische Grafschaft.*

Sou·they [ˈsaʊθɪ; ˈsʌðɪ] *englischer Dichter.*

South·wark [ˈsʌðək; ˈsaʊθwək] *Stadtbezirk von Groß-London.*

South York·shire [ˌsaʊθˈjɔːkʃə] *Stadtgrafschaft in Nordengland.*

So·viet Un·ion [ˌsəʊvɪətˈjuːnjən] *hist.; die* So'wjetuni,on.

Spain [speɪn] Spanien *n*.

Spring·field [ˈsprɪŋfiːld] *Hauptstadt von Illinois (USA); Stadt in Massachusetts (USA); Stadt in Missouri (USA).*

Sri Lan·ka [ˌsriːˈlæŋkə] Sri Lanka *n*.

Staf·ford(·shire) [ˈstæfəd(ʃə)] *englische Grafschaft.*

Stan [stæn] *abbr. für* **Stanley** (*Vorname*).

Stan·ley [ˈstænlɪ] *englischer Afrikaforscher; Vorname m*.

Stat·en Is·land [ˌstætnˈaɪlənd] *Insel an der Mündung des Hudson River in New York; Stadtbezirk von New York.*

Stein·beck [ˈstaɪnbek] *amer. Autor.*

Stel·la [ˈstelə] Stella *f*.

Steph·a·nie [ˈstefənɪ] Stephanie *f*, Stefanie *f*.

Ste·phen [ˈstiːvn] Stephan *m*, Stefan *m*.

Ste·phen·son [ˈstiːvnsn] *englischer Erfinder.*

Steu·ben [ˈstjuːbən; ˈstuː-; ˈʃtɔɪ-] *amer. General preußischer Herkunft im amer. Unabhängigkeitskrieg.*

Steve [stiːv] *abbr. für* **Stephen**, **Steven**.

Ste·ven [ˈstiːvn] *siehe* **Stephen**.

Ste·ven·son [ˈstiːvnsn] *englischer Autor.*

Stew·art [stjʊət; ˈstjuːət; *Am.* ˈstuːət] *Familienname; Vorname m*.

Stir·ling(·shire) [ˈstɜːlɪŋ(ʃə)] *schottische Grafschaft (bis 1975).*

St. John [sntˈdʒɒn] *Hafenstadt an der Mündung des gleichnamigen Flusses in New Brunswick (Kanada);* [ˈsɪndʒən] *Familienname.*

St. John's [sntˈdʒɒnz] *Hauptstadt von Neufundland (Kanada).*

St. Law·rence [sntˈlɒrəns] Sankt-'Lorenz-Strom *m*.

St. Louis [sntˈlʊɪs; *Am.* ˌseɪntˈluːɪs] *Industriestadt in Missouri (USA).*

Stone·henge [ˌstəʊnˈhendʒ] *prähistorisches megalithisches Bauwerk bei Salisbury in Wiltshire (England).*

St. Pan·cras [sntˈpæŋkrəs] *Stadtteil von London.*

St. Paul [sntˈpɔːl; *Am.* ˌseɪnt-] *Hauptstadt von Minnesota (USA).*

Stra·chey [ˈstreɪtʃɪ] *englischer Biograph.*

Strat·ford on A·von [ˌstrætfədɒnˈeɪvn] *Stadt in Mittelengland.*
Strath·clyde [stræθˈklaɪd] *Verwaltungsregion in Schottland.*
Stu·art [stjʊət; ˈstjuːət; *Am.* ˈstuːərt] *schottisch-englisches Herrschergeschlecht; Vorname m.*
Styr·i·a [ˈstɪrɪə] *die Steiermark.*
Su·dan [suːˈdɑːn] *der Su'dan.*
Sud·bur·y [ˈsʌdbərɪ] *Stadt in Ontario (Kanada); Ort in Suffolk (England).*
Sue [sjuː; suː] *abbr. für* **Susan.**
Su·ez [ˈsuɪz; *Am.* suːˈez; ˈsuːez] *Suez n.*
Suf·folk [ˈsʌfək] *englische Grafschaft.*
Sul·li·van [ˈsʌlɪvən] *Familienname.*
Su·ri·nam [ˌsʊərɪˈnæm] *Suri'nam n.*
Su·ri·na·me [ˌsʊərɪˈnæm] *Suri'nam n.*
Sur·rey [ˈsʌrɪ] *englische Grafschaft.*
Su·san [ˈsuːzn] *Su'sanne f.*
Su·sie [ˈsuːzɪ] *Susi f.*
Sus·que·han·na [ˌsʌskwɪˈhænə] *Fluss im Osten der USA.*
Sus·sex [ˈsʌsɪks] *englische Grafschaft.*
Suth·er·land [ˈsʌðələnd] *schottische Grafschaft (bis 1975).*
Sut·ton [ˈsʌtn] *Stadtbezirk von Groß-London.*
Su·zanne [suːˈzæn] *Su'sanne f, Su'sanna f.*
Swan·sea [ˈswɒnzɪ] *Hafenstadt in Wales.*
Swa·zi·land [ˈswɑːzɪlænd] *Swasiland n.*
Swe·den [ˈswiːdn] *Schweden n.*
Swift [swɪft] *irischer Autor.*
Swit·zer·land [ˈswɪtsələnd] *die Schweiz.*
Syd·ney [ˈsɪdnɪ] *Hauptstadt von New South Wales (Australien) u. größte Stadt Australiens.*
Syl·vi·a [ˈsɪlvɪə] *Silvia f, Sylvia f.*
Synge [sɪŋ] *irischer Dichter u. Dramatiker.*
Syr·a·cuse [ˈsɪrəkjuːs] *Stadt im Staat New York (USA); [Brit.* ˈsaɪərəkjuːz] *Syrakus n (Stadt auf Sizilien).*
Syr·ia [ˈsɪrɪə] *Syrien n.*

T

Ta·hi·ti [tɑːˈhiːtɪ; tə-] *Ta'hiti n.*
Tai·wan [ˌtaɪˈwɑːn] *Taiwan n.*
Tal·la·has·see [ˌtæləˈhæsɪ] *Hauptstadt von Florida (USA).*
Tam·pa [ˈtæmpə] *Stadt in Florida (USA).*
Tan·gier [tænˈdʒɪə] *Tanger n.*
Tan·za·nia [ˌtænzəˈnɪə] *Tansa'nia n.*
Tas·ma·nia [tæzˈmeɪnjə] *Tas'manien n (Insel u. Bundesstaat Australiens).*
Tay·lor [ˈteɪlə] *Familienname.*
Tay·side [ˈteɪsaɪd] *Verwaltungsregion in Schottland.*
Ted(·dy) [ˈted(ɪ)] *abbr. für* **Edward, Theodore.**
Tees·side [ˈtiːzsaɪd] *frühere Bezeichnung der Industrieregion um Middlesbrough (Nordengland), heute zu* **Cleveland** *gehörig.*
Teign·mouth [ˈtɪnməθ] *Stadt in Devon (England).*
Ten·e·rife, *früher* **Ten·e·riffe** [ˌtenəˈriːf] *Tene'riffa n.*
Ten·nes·see [ˌtenəˈsiː] *Staat der USA; Fluss in USA.*
Ten·ny·son [ˈtenɪsn] *englischer Dichter.*
Ter·ence [ˈterəns] *m.*
Te·re·sa [təˈriːzə] *Te'resa f, Te'rese f.*
Ter·ry [ˈterɪ] *abbr. für* **Terence,** *T*(*h*)*e-resa.*
Tess, Tes·sa [ˈtes(ə)] *abbr. für* *T*(*h*)*e-resa.*
Tex·as [ˈteksəs] *Staat der USA.*

Thack·er·ay [ˈθækərɪ] *englischer Romanschriftsteller.*
Thai·land [ˈtaɪlænd] *Thailand n.*
Thames [temz] *Themse f (Fluss in Südengland).*
That·cher [ˈθætʃə] *englische Premierministerin.*
The·a [θɪə; ˈθiːə] *Thea f.*
The·o [ˈθiːəʊ; ˈθɪəʊ] *Theo m.*
The·o·bald [ˈθɪəʊbɔːld] *Theobald m.*
The·o·dore [ˈθɪədɔː] *Theodor m.*
The·re·sa [tɪˈriːzə] *The'resa f, The'rese f.*
Tho·mas [ˈtɒməs] *Thomas m.*
Tho·reau [ˈθɔːrəʊ; *Am.* θəˈrəʊ] *amer. Schriftsteller, Philosoph u. Sozialkritiker.*
Thu·rin·gi·a [θjʊəˈrɪndʒɪə] *Thüringen n.*
Thu·ron [tʊˈrɒn] *Familienname.*
Ti·bet [tɪˈbet] *Tibet n.*
Ti·gris [ˈtaɪgrɪs] *Tigris m.*
Tim [tɪm] *abbr. für* **Timothy.**
Tim·o·thy [ˈtɪməθɪ] *Ti'motheus m.*
Ti·na [ˈtiːnə] *abbr. für* **Christina, Christine.**
Tin·dale [ˈtɪndl] *Familienname.*
Tip·per·ary [ˌtɪpəˈreərɪ] *Grafschaft in der Provinz Munster (Irland).*
To·bi·as [təˈbaɪəs] *To'bias m.*
To·by [ˈtəʊbɪ] *abbr. für* **Tobias.**
To·go [ˈtəʊgəʊ] *Togo n.*
To·kyo [ˈtəʊkjəʊ] *Tokio n.*
To·le·do [təˈliːdəʊ] *Stadt in Ohio (USA); [Brit.* tɒˈleɪdəʊ] *Stadt u. Provinz in Zentralspanien.*
Tol·kien [ˈtɒlkiːn] *englischer Schriftsteller u. Philologe.*
Tom(·my) [ˈtɒm(ɪ)] *abbr. für* **Thomas.**
Ton·ga [ˈtɒŋə] *Tonga n (Inselgruppe u. Königreich im südwestl. Pazifik).*
To·ny [ˈtəʊnɪ] *Toni m.*
To·pe·ka [təʊˈpiːkə] *Hauptstadt von Kansas (USA).*
Tor·bay [ˌtɔːˈbeɪ] *Stadt in Devon (England); a.* **Tor Bay** *Bucht des Ärmelkanals an der Küste von Devon.*
To·ron·to [təˈrɒntəʊ] *Stadt in Kanada.*
Tor·quay [ˌtɔːˈkiː] *Teilstadt von* **Torbay** *in Devon (England).*
Tot·ten·ham [ˈtɒtnəm] *Stadtteil von Groß-London.*
Tour·neur [ˈtɜːnə] *Familienname.*
Tow·er Ham·lets [ˈtaʊəˌhæmlɪts] *Stadtbezirk von Groß-London.*
Toyn·bee [ˈtɔɪnbɪ] *englischer Historiker.*
Tra·cy [ˈtreɪsɪ] *amer. Filmschauspieler; Vorname m, (seltener) m.*
Tra·fal·gar [trəˈfælgə]: **Cape ~** *Kap n* Tra'falgar *(an der Südwestküste Spaniens);* **~ Square** *Platz in London.*
Trans·vaal [ˈtrænzvɑːl] *Trans'vaal n.*
Tran·syl·va·nia [ˌtrænsɪlˈveɪnjə] *Siebenbürgen n.*
Trent [trent] *Fluss in Mittelengland;* Tri'ent *n.*
Tren·ton [ˈtrentən] *Hauptstadt von New Jersey (USA).*
Tre·vel·yan [trɪˈveljən; -ˈvɪl-] *Name zweier englischer Historiker.*
Treves [triːvz] *Trier n.*
Trev·or [ˈtrevə] *m.*
Tri·e·ste [triːˈest] *Tri'est n.*
Trin·i·dad and To·ba·go [ˌtrɪnɪdædntəʊˈbeɪgəʊ] *Trinidad und To'bago n.*
Trol·lope [ˈtrɒləp] *englischer Romanschriftsteller.*
Troy [trɔɪ] *Troja n (antike Stadt in Kleinasien am Eingang der Dardanellen); Name mehrerer Städte in USA (im Staat New York; in Michigan; in Ohio).*
Tru·man [ˈtruːmən] *33. Präsident der USA.*

Tuc·son [tuːˈsɒn; ˈtuːsɒn] *Stadt in Arizona (USA).*
Tu·dor [ˈtjuːdə] *englisches Herrschergeschlecht.*
Tu·ni·sia [tjuːˈnɪzɪə; *Am.* tuːˈniːʒə; -ˈnɪʒə] *Tu'nesien n.*
Tur·key [ˈtɜːkɪ] *die Tür'kei.*
Tur·ner [ˈtɜːnə] *englischer Landschaftsmaler.*
Tus·ca·ny [ˈtʌskənɪ] *die Tos'kana.*
Twain [tweɪn] *amer. Autor.*
Twick·en·ham [ˈtwɪknəm] *Stadtteil von Groß-London.*
Tyn·dale [ˈtɪndl] *englischer Bibelübersetzer.*
Tyne and Wear [ˌtaɪnəndˈwɪə] *Stadtgrafschaft in Nordengland.*
Ty·rol [ˈtɪrəl; tɪˈrəʊl] *Ti'rol n.*
Ty·rone [tɪˈrəʊn] *nordirische Grafschaft.*

U

U·gan·da [juːˈgændə] *U'ganda n.*
U·ist [ˈjuːɪst]: **North ~, South ~** *zwei Inseln der Äußeren Hebriden (Schottland).*
U·kraine [juːˈkreɪn] *die Ukra'ine.*
Ul·ster [ˈʌlstə] *Provinz im Norden Irlands, seit 1921 zweigeteilt. 3 Grafschaften gehören heute zur Republik Irland, die restlichen 6 bilden das heutige Nordirland, Teil des Vereinigten Königreichs von Großbritannien u. Nordirland.*
U·lys·ses [juːˈlɪsiːz] *m.*
Un·ion of So·viet So·cial·ist Re·pub·lics [ˌjuːnjənəvˌsəʊvɪətˌsəʊʃəlɪstrɪˈpʌblɪks] *hist. die* Uni'on der Sozia'listischen So'wjetrepu₂bliken.
U·nit·ed Ar·ab E·mir·ates [juːˈnaɪtɪdˌærəbˈmɪərəts] *pl. die Vereinigten* A'rabischen Emi'rate *pl.*
U·nit·ed King·dom [juːˌnaɪtɪdˈkɪŋdəm] *das Vereinigte Königreich (Großbritannien u. Nordirland).*
U·nit·ed States of A·mer·i·ca [juːˌnaɪtɪdˌsteɪtsəvəˈmerɪkə] *pl. die Vereinigten Staaten von* A'merika *pl.*
Up·dike [ˈʌpdaɪk] *amer. Schriftsteller.*
Up·per Vol·ta [ˌʌpəˈvɒltə] *Ober'volta n (ehemalige Bezeichnung für* **Burkina Faso**).
U·ri·ah [ˌjʊəˈraɪə] *U'ria(s) m, Uriel m.*
Ur·quhart [ˈɜːkət] *schottischer Schriftsteller u. Übersetzer.*
Ur·su·la [ˈɜːsjʊlə] *Ursula f.*
U·ru·guay [ˈjʊərʊgwaɪ; ˈʊrə-] *Uruguay n.*
U·tah [ˈjuːtɑː; -tɔː] *Staat der USA.*
Ut·tox·e·ter [juːˈtɒksɪtə; ʌˈtɒksɪtə] *Ort in Staffordshire (England).*

V

Val·en·tine [ˈvæləntaɪn] *Valentin m; Va*len'tine *f.*
Va(l)·let·ta [vəˈletə] *Hauptstadt von Malta.*
Van·brugh [ˈvænbrə; vænˈbruː] *englischer Dramatiker u. Baumeister.*
Van·cou·ver [vænˈkuːvə] *Hafenstadt in Kanada.*
Van·der·bilt [ˈvændəbɪlt] *amer. Finanzier.*
Va·nes·sa [vəˈnesə] *f.*
Vat·i·can [ˈvætɪkən] *der Vati'kan;* **~ Cit·y** [ˌvætɪkənˈsɪtɪ] *Vati'kanstadt f.*
Vaughan [vɔːn] *Familienname;* **~ Wil·liams** [ˌvɔːnˈwɪljəmz] *englischer Komponist.*
Vaux [vɔːz; vɒks; vɔːks; vəʊks] *Familienname;* **de ~** [dɪˈvəʊ] *Familienname.*

Vaux·hall [‚vɒks'hɔːl] *Stadtteil von London.*

Ven·e·zu·e·la [‚vene'zweɪlə] Venezu'ela *n.*

Ven·ice ['venɪs] Ve'nedig *n.*

Ve·ra ['vɪərə] Vera *f.*

Ver·gil ['vɜːdʒɪl] *siehe* **Virgil.**

Ver·mont [vɜː'mɒnt] *Staat der USA.*

Ver·ner ['vɜːnə] *Familienname.*

Ver·non ['vɜːnən] *m.*

Ve·ron·i·ca [vɪ'rɒnɪkə; və-] Ve'ronika *f.*

Vick·y ['vɪkɪ] *abbr. für* **Victoria.**

Vic·tor ['vɪktə] Viktor *m.*

Vic·to·ri·a [vɪk'tɔːrɪə] Vik'toria *f; Bundesstaat Australiens; Hauptstadt von British Columbia (Kanada); Hauptstadt der ehemaligen brit. Kronkolonie Hongkong.*

Vi·en·na [vɪ'enə] Wien *n.*

Viet·nam, Viet Nam [‚vjet'næm] Viet'nam *n.*

Vi·o·la ['vaɪələ; 'vɪəʊlə] Vi'ola *f.*

Vi·o·let ['vaɪələt] Vio'letta *f,* Vio'lette *f.*

Vir·gil ['vɜːdʒɪl] Ver'gil *m (römischer Dichter).*

Vir·gin·ia [və'dʒɪnjə] *Staat der USA;* Vorname *f.*

Vis·tu·la ['vɪstjʊlə] Weichsel *f (Fluss).*

Viv·i·an ['vɪvɪən] *m, (seltener) f.*

Viv·i·en ['vɪvɪən] *f.*

Viv·i·enne ['vɪvɪən; ‚vɪvɪ'en] *f.*

Vol·ga ['vɒlgə] Wolga *f.*

Vosges [vəʊʒ] *pl. die* Vo'gesen *pl.*

W

Wa·bash ['wɔːbæʃ] *Nebenfluss des Ohio in Indiana u. Illinois (USA).*

Wad·dell [wɒ'del; 'wɒdl] *Familienname.*

Wad·ham ['wɒdəm] *Familienname.*

Wales [weɪlz] Wales *n.*

Wal·lace ['wɒlɪs] *englischer Autor.*

Wal·la·sey ['wɒləsɪ] *Stadt in Merseyside (England).*

Wal·pole ['wɔːlpəʊl] *Name zweier englischer Schriftsteller.*

Wal·ter ['wɔːltə] Walter *m.*

Wal·tham For·est [‚wɔːlθəm'fɒrɪst] *Stadtbezirk von Groß-London.*

Wands·worth ['wɒndzwəθ] *Stadtbezirk von Groß-London.*

War·hol ['wɔːhɔːl; 'wɔːhəʊl] *amer. Pop-Art-Künstler u. Filmregisseur.*

War·saw ['wɔːsɔː] Warschau *n.*

War·wick(·shire) ['wɒrɪk(ʃə)] *englische Grafschaft.*

Wash·ing·ton ['wɒʃɪŋtən] *1. Präsident der USA; Staat der USA; a.* ~ **DC** *Bundeshauptstadt der USA.*

Wa·ter·ford ['wɔːtəfəd] *Grafschaft in der Provinz Munster (Irland); Hauptstadt dieser Grafschaft.*

Wa·ter·loo [‚wɔːtə'luː] *Ort in Belgien.*

Wat·son ['wɒtsn] *Familienname.*

Watt [wɒt] *schottischer Erfinder.*

Waugh [wɔː] *englischer Romanschriftsteller.*

Wayne [weɪn] *amer. Filmschauspieler.*

Weald [wiːld]: *the* ~ *Landschaft im südöstlichen England. Früher ausgedehntes Waldgebiet.*

Web·ster ['webstə] *amer. Lexikograph.*

Wedg·wood ['wedʒwʊd] *englischer Keramiker.*

Wel·ling·ton ['welɪŋtən] *brit. Feldherr; Hauptstadt von Neuseeland.*

Wem·bley ['wemblɪ] *Stadtteil von Groß-London.*

Wen·dy ['wendɪ] *f.*

Went·worth ['wentwəθ] *Familienname.*

West Brom·wich [‚west'brɒmɪdʒ] *Stadt in West Midlands (England).*

West·ern Aus·tra·lia [‚westənɒ'streɪljə] 'Westau‚stralien.

West·ern Isles [‚westən'aɪlz] *Insulare Verwaltungsregion Schottlands.*

West·ern Sa·moa [‚westənsə'məʊə] Westsa'moa *n.*

West Gla·mor·gan [‚westglə'mɔːgən] *walisische Grafschaft.*

West In·dies [‚west'ɪndɪz] *pl.: the* ~ *die* West'indischen Inseln *pl.*

West Lo·thi·an [‚west'ləʊðjən] *schottische Grafschaft (bis 1975).*

West·meath [west'miːð] *Grafschaft in der Provinz Leinster (Irland).*

West Mid·lands [‚west'mɪdləndz] *pl. Stadtgrafschaft in Mittelengland.*

West·min·ster ['westmɪnstə] *a.* **City of** ~ *Stadtbezirk von Groß-London.*

West·mor·land ['westmələnd] *englische Grafschaft (bis 1974).*

West·pha·lia [west'feɪljə] West'falen *n.*

West Vir·gin·ia [‚westvə'dʒɪnjə] *Staat der USA.*

West York·shire [‚west'jɔːkʃə] *Stadtgrafschaft in Nordengland.*

Wex·ford ['weksfəd] *Grafschaft in der Provinz Leinster (Irland); Hauptstadt dieser Grafschaft.*

Wey·mouth ['weɪməθ] *Badeort in Dorset (Südengland); Stadt in Massachusetts (USA).*

Whal·ley ['weɪlɪ; 'wɔːlɪ] *Familienname.*

Whar·am ['weərəm] *Familienname.*

Whar·ton ['wɔːtn] *amer. Romanschriftstellerin.*

Whi·tack·er ['wɪtəkə] *Familienname.*

Whit·a·ker ['wɪtəkə] *Familienname.*

Whit·by ['wɪtbɪ] *Fischereihafen in North Yorkshire (England); Stadt in Ontario (Kanada).*

White·hall [‚waɪt'hɔːl] *Straße in London.*

Whit·man ['wɪtmən] *amer. Dichter.*

Whit·ta·ker ['wɪtəkə] *Familienname.*

Wick·low ['wɪkləʊ] *Grafschaft in der Provinz Leinster (Irland).*

Wig·town(·shire) ['wɪgtən(ʃə)] *schottische Grafschaft (bis 1975).*

Wilde [waɪld] *englischer Dichter.*

Wil·der ['waɪldə] *amer. Autor.*

Wil·fred ['wɪlfrɪd] Wilfried *m.*

Will [wɪl] *abbr. für* **William.**

Wil·liam ['wɪljəm] Wilhelm *m.*

Wil·ming·ton ['wɪlmɪŋtən] *Hafenstadt in Delaware (USA); Hafenstadt in North Carolina (USA).*

Wil·son ['wɪlsn] *Familienname.*

Wilt·shire ['wɪltʃə] *englische Grafschaft.*

Wim·ble·don ['wɪmbldən] *Stadtteil von Groß-London (Tennisturniere).*

Win·ches·ter ['wɪntʃɪstə] *Hauptstadt von Hampshire (England) mit berühmter Public School.*

Wind·sor ['wɪnzə] *Stadt in Berkshire (England); Stadt in Ontario (Kanada).*

Win·i·fred ['wɪnɪfrɪd] *f.*

Win·nie ['wɪnɪ] *abbr. für* **Winifred.**

Win·ni·peg ['wɪnɪpeg] *Hauptstadt von Manitoba (Kanada).*

Win·ston ['wɪnstən] *m.*

Wis·con·sin [wɪs'kɒnsɪn] *Staat der USA; Fluss in Wisconsin (USA).*

Wi·tham ['wɪðəm] *Familienname; Fluss in Lincolnshire (England).*

Wit·ham ['wɪtəm] *Stadt in Essex (England).*

Wolds [wəʊldz]: *the* ~ *Höhenzug in Nordostengland.*

Wolfe [wʊlf] *amer. Autor.*

Wol·lon·gong ['wʊləŋgɒŋ] *Industrie- u. Hafenstadt in New South Wales (Australien).*

Wol·sey ['wʊlzɪ] *englischer Kardinal u. Staatsmann.*

Wol·ver·hamp·ton ['wʊlvə‚hæmptən] *Industriestadt in West Midlands (England).*

Woolf [wʊlf] *englische Autorin.*

Wool·wich ['wʊlɪdʒ] *Stadtteil von Groß-London.*

Wor·ces·ter ['wʊstə] *Industriestadt in Mittelengland; a.* '**Wor·ces·ter·shire** [-ʃə] *englische Grafschaft (bis 1974).*

Words·worth ['wɜːdzwəθ] *englischer Dichter.*

Wren [ren] *englischer Architekt.*

Wright [raɪt] *Name zweier amer. Flugpioniere.*

Wyc·liffe ['wɪklɪf] *englischer Reformator u. Bibelübersetzer.*

Wy·man ['waɪmən] *Familienname.*

Wy·o·ming [waɪ'əʊmɪŋ] *Staat der USA.*

X

Xan·thip·pe [zæn'θɪpɪ] Xan'thippe *f.*

Y

Yale [jeɪl] *hoher britischer Kolonialbeamter u. Förderer der Yale University in New Haven, Connecticut (USA).*

Yeat·man ['jiːtmən; 'jeɪt- 'jet-] *Familienname.*

Yeats [jeɪts] *irischer Dichter u. Dramatiker.*

Yel·low·stone ['jeləʊstəʊn] *Fluss im Nordwesten der USA; Nationalpark in Wyoming, Montana u. Idaho (USA).*

Ye·men ['jemən] *der* Jemen.

Yeo·vil ['jəʊvɪl] *Stadt in Somersetshire (England).*

Yonge [jʌŋ] *Familienname.*

Yon·kers ['jɒŋkəz; Am.* 'jɑːŋkərz] *Stadt im Staat New York (USA).*

York [jɔːk] *Stadt in Nordost-England;* '**York·shire** [-ʃə]: (**North, South, West**) ~ *Grafschaften in England.*

Yo·sem·i·te Na·tion·al Park [jəʊ'semɪ‚tɪ‚næʃənl'pɑːk] *Nationalpark in Kalifornien (USA).*

Yu·go·sla·via [‚juːgəʊ'slɑːvjə] Jugo'slawien *n.*

Yu·ill ['juːɪl] *Familienname.*

Yu·kon ['juːkɒn] *Strom im nordwestlichen Nordamerika; a. the* ~ *siehe* **Yukon Territory;** ~ **Ter·ri·tor·y** [‚juːkɒn'terɪtərɪ] *Territorium im äußersten Nordwesten Kanadas.*

Y·vonne [ɪ'vɒn] I'vonne *f,* Y'vonne *f.*

Z

Zach·a·ri·ah [‚zækə'raɪə], **Zach·a·ry** ['zækərɪ] Zacha'rias *m.*

Za·ire [zɑː'ɪə] *hist.* Za'ire *n.*

Zam·bia ['zæmbɪə] Sambia *n.*

Zan·zi·bar [‚zænzɪ'bɑː; *Am.* 'zænzəbɑːr] Sansibar *n (zu Tansania gehörige Insel vor der Ostküste Afrikas).*

Zel·da ['zeldə] *f.*

Zet·land ['zetlənd] *schottische Grafschaft (bis 1975).*

Zim·ba·bwe [zɪm'bɑːbwɪ; -bweɪ] Sim'babwe *n (seit 1980 Name für* **Rhodesia**).

Zo·e ['zəʊɪ] Zoe *f.*

Zu·rich ['zjʊərɪk] Zürich *n.*

Unregelmäßige Verben

Die an erster Stelle stehende Form bezeichnet den Infinitiv (infinitive). Nach dem ersten Gedankenstrich steht das Präteritum (past), nach dem zweiten das Partizip Perfekt (past participle).

abide – abode, abided – abode, abided
arise – arose – arisen
awake – awoke, awaked – awoken, awaked

backbite – backbit – backbitten, backbit
backslide – backslid – backslid, backslidden
be – was, were – been
bear – bore – borne
beat – beat – beaten, beat
become – became – become
befall – befell – befallen
beget – begot – begotten
begin – began – begun
behold – beheld – beheld
bend – bent – bent
bereave – bereft, bereaved – bereft, bereaved
beseech – besought, beseeched – besought, beseeched
beset – beset – beset
bespeak – bespoke – bespoken
bestrew – bestrewed – bestrewed, bestrewn
bestride – bestrode – bestridden, bestrid
bet – bet, betted – bet, betted
betake – betook – betaken
bethink – bethought – bethought
bid – bad(e), bid – bade, bid, bidden
bide – bode, bided – bided
bind – bound – bound
bite – bit – bitten, bit
bleed – bled – bled
blow – blew – blown
break – broke – broken
breed – bred – bred
bring – brought – brought
broadcast – broadcast, broadcasted – broadcast, broadcasted
browbeat – browbeat – browbeaten
build – built – built
burn – burnt, burned – burnt, burned
burst – burst – burst
buy – bought – bought

cast – cast – cast
catch – caught – caught
chide – chid, chided – chidden, chid, chided
choose – chose – chosen
cleave – cleft, clove, cleaved – cleft, cloven, cleaved
cling – clung – clung
come – came – come
cost – cost – cost
creep – crept – crept
cut – cut – cut

deal – dealt – dealt
deepfreeze – deepfroze, -freezed – deepfrozen, -freezed
dig – dug – dug
dive – dived, Am. dove – dived
do – did – done
draw – drew – drawn

dream – dreamt, dreamed – dreamt, dreamed
drink – drank – drunk
drive – drove – driven
dwell – dwelt, dwelled – dwelt, dwelled

eat – ate – eaten

fall – fell – fallen
feed – fed – fed
feel – felt – felt
fight – fought – fought
find – found – found
flee – fled – fled
fling – flung – flung
fly – flew – flown
forbear – forebore – foreborne
forbid – forbade, forbad – forbidden
forecast – forecast, forecasted – forecast, forecasted
forego – forewent – foregone
foreknow – foreknew – foreknown
foresee – foresaw – foreseen
foretell – foretold – foretold
forget – forgot – forgotten, forgot
forgive – forgave – forgiven
forgo – forwent – forgone
forsake – forsook – forsaken
forswear – forswore – forsworn
freeze – froze – frozen

gainsay – gainsaid – gainsaid
get – got – got, Am. gotten
gild – gilded, gilt – gilded, gilt
gird – girded, girt – girded, girt
give – gave – given
go – went – gone
grind – ground – ground
grow – grew – grown

hamstring – hamstrung – hamstrung
hang – hung, hanged – hung, hanged
have – had – had
hear – heard – heard
heave – heaved, hove – heaved, hove
hew – hewed – hewn, hewed
hide – hid – hidden, hid
hit – hit – hit
hold – held – held
hurt – hurt – hurt

inlay – inlaid – inlaid
inset – inset – inset

keep – kept – kept
kneel – knelt, kneeled – knelt, kneeled
knit – knitted, knit – knitted, knit
know – knew – known

lade – laded – laded, laden
lay – laid – laid
lead – led – led
lean – leant, leaned – leant, leaned
leap – leapt, leaped – leapt, leaped
learn – learnt, learned – learnt, learned
leave – left – left
lend – lent – lent

let – let – let
lie – lay – lain
light – lit, lighted – lit, lighted
lose – lost – lost

make – made – made
mean – meant – meant
meet – met – met
misbecome – misbecame – misbecome
miscast – miscast – miscast
misdeal – misdealt – misdealt
misgive – misgave – misgiven
mishear – misheard – misheard
mislay – mislaid – mislaid
mislead – misled – misled
misread – misread – misread
misspell – misspelt, misspelled – misspelt, misspelled
misspend – misspent – misspent
mistake – mistook – mistaken
misunderstand – misunderstood – misunderstood
mow – mowed – mown, mowed

offset – offset – offset
outbid – outbid – outbid, outbidden
outdo – outdid – outdone
outgo – outwent – outgone
outgrow – outgrew – outgrown
outride – outrode – outridden
outrun – outran – outrun
outsell – outsold – outsold
outshine – outshone – outshone
outsit – outsat – outsat
outspeed – outspeed, outspeeded – outsped, outspeeded
outswim – outswam – outswum
outwear – outwore – outworn
overbear – overbore – overborne
overbid – overbid, overbade – overbid, overbidden
overbuild – overbuilt – overbuilt
overbuy – overbought – overbought
overcast – overcast – overcast
overcome – overcame – overcome
overdo – overdid – overdone
overdraw – overdrew – overdrawn
overdrive – overdrove – overdriven
overeat – overate – overeaten
overfeed – overfed – overfed
overgrow – overgrew – overgrown
overhang – overhung – overhung
overhear – overheard – overheard
overlay – overlaid – overlaid
overlie – overlay – overlain
overpay – overpaid – overpaid
override – overrode – overridden
overrun – overran – overrun
oversee – oversaw – overseen
overset – overset – overset
oversew – oversewed – oversewed, oversewn
overshoot – overshot – overshot
oversleep – overslept – overslept
overspeed – oversped, overspeeded – oversped, overspeeded
overspend – overspent – overspent

overspread – overspread – overspread
overtake – overtook – overtaken
overthrow – overthrew – overthrown
overwind – overwound – overwound

partake – partook – partaken
pay – paid – paid
put – put – put

read – read – read
rebroadcast – rebroadcast, rebroadcasted – rebroadcast, rebroadcasted
rebuild – rebuilt – rebuilt
recast – recast – recast
redo – redid – redone
redraw – redrew – redrawn
regrind – reground – reground
remake – remade – remade
rend – rent – rent
repay – repaid – repaid
reread – reread – reread
resell – resold – resold
reset – reset – reset
retake – retook – retaken
retell – retold – retold
rethink – rethought – rethought
rewrite – rewrote – rewritten
rid – rid, ridded – rid, ridded
ride – rode – ridden
ring – rang, rung – rung
rise – rose – risen
rive – rived – rived, riven
run – ran – run

saw – sawed – sawn, sawed
say – said – said
see – saw – seen
seek – sought – sought
sell – sold – sold
send – sent – sent
set – set – set
sew – sewed – sewn, sewed
shake – shook – shaken
shave – shaved – shaved, shaven
shed – shed – shed
shine – shone, shined – shone, shined
shit – shit, shat – shit
shoe – shod, shoed – shod, shoed
shoot – shot – shot

show – showed – shown, showed
shrink – shrank, shrunk – shrunk
shut – shut – shut
sing – sang, sung – sung
sink – sank, sunk – sunk
sit – sat – sat
slay – slew – slain
sleep – slept – slept
slide – slid – slid, slidden
sling – slung – slung
slink – slunk – slunk
slit – slit – slit
smell – smelt, smelled – smelt, smelled
smite – smote – smitten
sow – sowed – sown, sowed
speak – spoke – spoken
speed – sped, speeded – sped, speeded
spell – spelt, spelled – spelt, spelled
spend – spent – spent
spill – spilt, spilled – spilt, spilled
spin – spun, span – spun
spit – spat, spit – spat, spit
split – split – split
spoil – spoilt, spoiled – spoilt, spoiled
spoonfeed – spoonfed – spoonfed
spread – spread – spread
spring – sprang, sprung – sprung
stand – stood – stood
stave – staved, stove – staved, stove
steal – stole – stolen
stick – stuck – stuck
sting – stung – stung
stink – stank, stunk – stunk
strew – strewed – strewn, strewed
stride – strode – stridden, strid, strode
strike – struck – struck
string – strung – strung
strive – strove, strived – striven, strived
sublet – sublet – sublet
swear – swore – sworn
sweat – sweat, sweated – sweat, sweated
sweep – swept – swept
swell – swelled – swollen, swelled
swim – swam, swum – swum
swing – swung – swung

take – took – taken
teach – taught – taught
tear – tore – torn

telecast – telecast – telecast
tell – told – told
think – thought – thought
thrive – thrived, throve – thrived, thriven
throw – threw – thrown
thrust – thrust – thrust
tread – trod – trodden, trod
typecast – typecast – typecast

unbend – unbent – unbent
unbind – unbound – unbound
underbid – underbid – underbid, underbidden
undercut – undercut – undercut
undergo – underwent – undergone
underlay – underlaid – underlaid
underlet – underlet – underlet
underlie – underlay – underlain
underpay – underpaid – underpaid
undersell – undersold – undersold
understand – understood – understood
undertake – undertook – undertaken
underwrite – underwrote – underwritten
undo – undid – undone
unlade – unladed – unladen, unladed
unlearn – unlearned, unlearnt – unlearned, unlearnt
unmake – unmade – unmade
unsay – unsaid – unsaid
unstick – unstuck – unstuck
unstring – unstrung – unstrung
unwind – unwound – unwound
uphold – upheld – upheld
upset – upset – upset

wake – woke, waked – woken, waked
wear – wore – worn
weave – wove – woven
wed – wedded, wed – wedded, wed
weep – wept – wept
wet – wetted, wet – wetted, wet
win – won – won
wind – wound – wound
withdraw – withdrew – withdrawn
withhold – withheld – withheld
withstand – withstood – withstood
wring – wrung – wrung
write – wrote – written

Kennzeichnung der Kinofilme

(in Großbritannien)

U   Universal. Suitable for all ages.
     Für alle Altersstufen geeignet.

PG   Parental Guidance. Some scenes may be unsuitable for young children.
     Einige Szenen ungeeignet für Kinder. Erklärung und Orientierung durch Eltern sinnvoll.

15   No person under 15 years admitted when a "15" film is in the programme.
     Nicht freigegeben für Jugendliche unter 15 Jahren.

18   No person under 18 years admitted when an "18" film is in the programme.
     Nicht freigegeben für Jugendliche unter 18 Jahren.

Kennzeichnung der Kinofilme

(in USA)

G   General audiences. All ages admitted.
     Für alle Altersstufen geeignet.

PG   Parental guidance suggested. Some material may not be suitable for children.
     Einige Szenen ungeeignet für Kinder. Erklärung und Orientierung durch Eltern sinnvoll.

R   Restricted. Under 17 requires accompanying parent or adult guardian.
     Für Jugendliche unter 17 Jahren nur in Begleitung eines Erziehungsberechtigten.

X   No one under 17 admitted.
     Nicht freigegeben für Jugendliche unter 17 Jahren.

Zahlwörter

Grundzahlen
Cardinal Numbers

0 nought, zero, cipher; *teleph.* 0 [əʊ]
null
1 one *eins*
2 two *zwei*
3 three *drei*
4 four *vier*
5 five *fünf*
6 six *sechs*
7 seven *sieben*
8 eight *acht*
9 nine *neun*
10 ten *zehn*
11 eleven *elf*
12 twelve *zwölf*
13 thirteen *dreizehn*
14 fourteen *vierzehn*
15 fifteen *fünfzehn*
16 sixteen *sechzehn*
17 seventeen *siebzehn*
18 eighteen *achtzehn*
19 nineteen *neunzehn*
20 twenty *zwanzig*
21 twenty-one *einundzwanzig*
22 twenty-two *zweiundzwanzig*
30 thirty *dreißig*
31 thirty-one *einunddreißig*
40 forty *vierzig*
41 forty-one *einundvierzig*
50 fifty *fünfzig*
51 fifty-one *einundfünfzig*
60 sixty *sechzig*
61 sixty-one *einundsechzig*
70 seventy *siebzig*
71 seventy-one *einundsiebzig*
80 eighty *achtzig*
81 eighty-one *einundachtzig*
90 ninety *neunzig*
91 ninety-one *einundneunzig*
100 a *od.* one hundred *hundert*
101 hundred and one *hundert(und)-
eins*
200 two hundred *zweihundert*
300 three hundred *dreihundert*
572 five hundred and seventy-two
fünfhundert(und)zweiundsiebzig
1,000 a *od.* one thousand *(ein)tausend*
1066 *Jahreszahl:* ten sixty-six *tausend-
sechsundsechzig*
1992 *Jahreszahl:* nineteen (hundred
and) ninety-two *neunzehnhundert-
zweiundneunzig*
2,000 two thousand *zweitausend*

5044 *teleph.* five 0 double four *fünfzig
vierundvierzig*
1,000,000 a *od.* one million *eine Million*
2,000,000 two million *zwei Millionen*
1,000,000,000 a *od.* one billion *eine Milliarde*

Ordnungszahlen
Ordinal Numbers

1st first *erste*
2nd second *zweite*
3rd third *dritte*
4th fourth *vierte*
5th fifth *fünfte*
6th sixth *sechste*
7th seventh *siebente*
8th eighth *achte*
9th ninth *neunte*
10th tenth *zehnte*
11th eleventh *elfte*
12th twelfth *zwölfte*
13th thirteenth *dreizehnte*
14th fourteenth *vierzehnte*
15th fifteenth *fünfzehnte*
16th sixteenth *sechzehnte*
17th seventeenth *siebzehnte*
18th eighteenth *achtzehnte*
19th nineteenth *neunzehnte*
20th twentieth *zwanzigste*
21st twenty-first *einundzwanzigste*
22nd twenty-second *zweiundzwanzigste*
23rd twenty-third *dreiundzwanzigste*
30th thirtieth *dreißigste*
31st thirty-first *einunddreißigste*
40th fortieth *vierzigste*
41st forty-first *einundvierzigste*
50th fiftieth *fünfzigste*
51st fifty-first *einundfünfzigste*
60th sixtieth *sechzigste*
61st sixty-first *einundsechzigste*
70th seventieth *siebzigste*
71st seventy-first *einundsiebzigste*
80th eightieth *achtzigste*
81st eighty-first *einundachtzigste*
90th ninetieth *neunzigste*
100th (one) hundredth *hundertste*
101st hundred and first *hundertund-
erste*
200th two hundredth *zweihundertste*
300th three hundredth *dreihundertste*
572nd five hundred and seventy-
-second *fünfhundertundzwei-
undsiebzigste*
1000th (one) thousandth *tausendste*

1950th nineteen hundred and fiftieth
neunzehnhundertfünfzigste
2000th two thousandth *zweitausendste*
1,000,000th millionth *millionste*
2,000,000th two millionth *zweimillionste*

Bruchzahlen und andere Zahlenwerte
Fractions and Other Numerical Values

¹/₂ one *od.* a half *ein halb*
1¹/₂ one and a half *anderthalb*
2¹/₂ two and a half *zweieinhalb*
¹/₃ one *od.* a third *ein Drittel*
²/₃ two thirds *zwei Drittel*
¹/₄ one *od.* a quarter, one fourth *ein
Viertel*
³/₄ three quarters, three fourths
drei Viertel
¹/₅ one *od.* a fifth *ein Fünftel*
3⁴/₅ three and four fifths *drei vier
Fünftel*
⁵/₈ five eighths *fünf Achtel*
¹²/₂₀ twelve twentieths *zwölf
Zwanzigstel*
⁷⁵/₁₀₀ seventy-five hundredths
fünfundsiebzig Hundertstel

0.45 (nought [nɔːt]) point four five
null Komma vier fünf
2.5 two point five *zwei Komma fünf*
once *einmal*
twice *zweimal*
three (**four**) **times** *drei-
(vier)mal*
twice as much (**many**) *zweimal od.
doppelt so viel(e)*
firstly (**secondly, thirdly**), **in the first**
(**second, third**) **place** *erstens
(zweitens, drittens)*

7 + 8 = 15 seven and *od.* plus eight are
fifteen *sieben und od. plus acht
ist fünfzehn*
9 − 4 = 5 nine minus *od.* less four is
five *neun minus od. weniger vier
ist fünf*
2 × 3 = 6 twice three is *od.* makes six
zweimal drei ist sechs
20 ÷ 5 = 4 twenty divided by five is
four *zwanzig dividiert od. geteilt
durch fünf ist vier*

Britische und amerikanische Maße und Gewichte

Längenmaße
Linear Measures

1 inch	= 2,54 cm
1 foot	= 12 inches = 30,48 cm
1 yard	= 3 feet = 91,44 cm
1 (statute) mile	
	= 1760 yards = 1,609 km
1 hand	= 4 inches = 10,16 cm
1 rod (perch, pole)	
	= 5¹/₂ yards = 5,029 m
1 chain	= 4 rods = 20,117 m
1 furlong	= 10 chains
	= 201,168 m

Nautische Maße
Nautical Measures

1 fathom	= 6 feet = 1,829 m
1 cable's length	
	= 100 fathoms = 182,9 m
	⚓ ✗ *Brit.* = 608 feet
	= 185,3 m
	⚓ ✗ *Am.* = 720 feet
	= 219,5 m
1 nautical mile	
	= 10 cables' length
	= 1,852 km

Flächenmaße
Square Measures

1 square inch	= 6,452 cm²
1 square foot	= 144 square inches
	= 929,029 cm²
1 square yard	= 9 square feet
	= 8361,26 cm²

1 acre	= 4840 square yards	
	= 4046,8 m²	
1 square mile	= 640 acres	
	= 259 ha = 2,59 km²	
1 square rod (square pole,		
square perch)	= 30¹/₄ square yards	
	= 25,293 m²	
1 rood	= 40 square rods	
	= 1011,72 m²	
1 acre	= 4 roods = 4046,8 m²	

Raummaße
Cubic Measures

1 cubic inch	= 16,387 cm³	
1 cubic foot	= 1728 cubic inches	
	= 0,02832 m³	
1 cubic yard	= 27 cubic feet	
	= 0,7646 m³	

Britische Hohlmaße

British Measures
of Capacity

Trocken- und Flüssigkeitsmaße
Dry and Liquid Measures

1 gill	= 0,142 l	
1 pint	= 4 gills	= 0,568 l
1 quart	= 2 pints	= 1,136 l
1 gallon	= 4 quarts	= 4,5459 l
1 quarter	= 64 gallons	= 290,935 l

Trockenmaße – Dry Measures

1 peck	= 2 gallons	= 9,092 l

1 bushel	= 4 pecks	= 36,368 l

Flüssigkeitsmaß – Liquid Measure

1 barrel	= 36 gallons	= 163,656 l

Amerikanische Hohlmaße

American Measures
of Capacity

Trockenmaße – Dry Measure

1 pint	= 0,5506 l	
1 quart	= 2 pints	= 1,1012 l
1 gallon	= 4 quarts	= 4,405 l
1 peck	= 2 gallons	= 8,8096 l
1 bushel	= 4 pecks	= 35,2383 l

Flüssigkeitsmaße – Liquid Measure

1 gill	= 0,1183 l	
1 pint	= 4 gills	= 0,4732 l
1 quart	= 2 pints	= 0,9464 l
1 gallon	= 4 quarts	= 3,7853 l
1 barrel	= 31.5 gallons	
	= 119,228 l	
1 hogshead	= 2 barrels	= 238,456 l
1 barrel petroleum		
	= 42 gallons	= 158,97 l

Apothekermaße
(Flüssigkeiten)

Apothecaries'
Fluid Measures

1 minim *Brit.*	= 0,0592 ml	
Am.	= 0,0616 ml	
1 fluid dram	= 60 minims	
Brit.	= 3,5515 ml	
Am.	= 3,6966 ml	

Maße und Gewichte

1 fluid ounce	= 8 drams	
Brit.	= 0,0284 l	
Am.	= 0,0296 l	
1 pint *Brit.*	= 20 fluid ounces	
	= 0,5683 l	
Am.	= 16 fluid ounces	
	= 0,4732 l	

Handelsgewichte
Avoirdupois Weights

1 grain	= 0,0648 g
1 dram	= 27.3438 grains
	= 1,772 g

1 ounce	= 16 drams	= 28,35 g
1 pound	= 16 ounces	= 453,59 g
1 hundredweight	= 1 quintal	
Brit.	= 112 pounds	
	= 50,802 kg	
Am.	= 100 pounds	
	= 45,359 kg	

1 long ton

Brit.	= 20 hundredweights
	= 1016,05 kg

1 short ton

Am.	= 20 hundredweights
	= 907,185 kg
1 stone	= 14 pounds = 6,35 kg
1 quarter	
Brit.	= 28 pounds

	= 12,701 kg
Am.	= 25 pounds
	= 11,339 kg

Troygewichte
Troy Weights

1 grain	= 0,0648 g
1 pennyweight	
	= 24 grains = 1,5552 g
1 ounce	= 20 pennyweights
	= 31,1035 g
1 pound	= 12 ounces
	= 373,2418 g

Langenscheidt

Handwörterbuch Englisch

Teil II
Deutsch–Englisch

Völlige Neubearbeitung

Herausgegeben von der
Langenscheidt-Redaktion

Langenscheidt

Berlin · München · Wien · Zürich · New York

Redaktion:
Martin Fellermayer, Dorothée Ronge, Wolfgang Worsch

In der neuen deutschen Rechtschreibung

Ergänzende Hinweise, für die wir jederzeit dankbar sind, bitten wir zu richten an:
Langenscheidt Verlag, Postfach 40 11 20, 80711 München

© 2005 Langenscheidt KG, Berlin und München
Druck: La Tipografica Varese S.p.A.
Printed in Italy · ISBN 3-468-05127-1

Vorwort

Neubearbeitung

Langenscheidt-Wörterbücher sind auf die Wünsche und Bedürfnisse ihrer Benutzer zugeschnitten. Hinter ihnen steht eine lange Tradition, die geprägt ist von der sprachlichen und fachlichen Kompetenz erfahrener Wörterbuchmacher. Sie berücksichtigen gleichermaßen die Anforderungen der modernen Lexikographie wie die Entwicklung der jeweiligen Sprache. Dies gilt auch für die vorliegende völlige Neubearbeitung des *Handwörterbuches Deutsch-Englisch*, deren wichtigste Merkmale wir hier kurz vorstellen:

Aktualität

In dieser Neubearbeitung wurden tausende hochaktuelle Neuwörter ergänzt, sodass der Wortschatz den augenblicklichen Stand der deutschen Sprache in ihrer ganzen Vielfalt widerspiegelt. Die Auswahl reicht dabei von allgemeinsprachlichen Begriffen wie *ablösefrei, Arbeitsfluss, Ärztehaus, bio, Drückerkolonne, Erziehungsgeld, Fettabsaugung, Freilandhaltung, Haushaltsloch, Kinderschänder, Rathausfraktion, Verpackungsindustrie* und der gehobenen Schriftsprache mit Wörtern wie *fakturieren, multikulturell, Pädiatrie, Selbstmedikation* über Umgangssprachliches wie *abzocken, anbaggern, cool, Hype, Muckis, relaxen, Selbstläufer, Weichei* und Slangbegriffe wie *Junkie, Kid, koksen* oder *bekifft sein* bis hin zur Vulgärsprache, wie z. B. *Arsch-und-Titten-Presse.* Selbstverständlich wurden dabei auch regionale Begriffe und Dialekte berücksichtigt, z. B. *Bazi, Grant, Tandler, zündeln.* Natürlich folgen alle deutschen Stichwörter und Wendungen den Regeln der neuen deutschen Rechtschreibung gemäß DUDEN.

Noch mehr Inhalt

Erweitert auf rund 165.000 Stichwörter und Wendungen mit rund 250.000 Übersetzungen, bietet Ihnen Ihr *Handwörterbuch Deutsch-Englisch* mehr Inhalt als je zuvor.

Großes Buchformat

Zusätzliche Attraktivität, Übersichtlichkeit und Bedeutung auf dem Schreibtisch gewinnt das Werk durch das große Format.

Fachwortschatz

Hier haben wir uns auf besonders auf die folgenden Bereiche konzentriert: Computer und Internet, z. B. *Absatzmarke, Benutzeroberfläche, computergesteuert, computerunterstützt, Dokumentvorlage, Echtzeit, Einfügetaste, Großbildschirm, Hyperlink, Internetcafé, Multitasking, Netikette, Quellcode, Suchmaschine,* neue Technologien, z. B. *Biotechnik, genmanipuliert, Gentest, klonen, Mobilfunk, Multiplex, Schlüsseltechnologie, simsen,* Gesellschaft und Politik, z. B. *Altersteilzeit, Atomausstieg, Bildungsnotstand, Designerdroge, medienwirksam, Multikulti, Reformstau, Singledasein, Solidarpakt, Quotenfrau,* Wirtschaft und Börse z. B. *Börsengang, Existenzgründer, Initiativbewerbung, kundenfreundlich, Leiharbeit, Maschinenlaufzeit, Mehrwegverpackung, Produktpiraterie, Schwellenland, Standortdebatte, Wertzuwachs,* EU-

Wortschatz, z. B. *Beitrittsverhandlungen, Euroland, Euronorm, Eurozone, Osterweiterung, Währungsumstellung*, Ökologie und Umwelt, z. B. *Abwasseraufbereitung, Biobauer, Elektrosmog, erbgutschädigend, gentechnikfrei, gentechnisch verändert, Ökobilanz, Raumklima*, und nicht zuletzt Sport, z. B. *Canyoning, Halfpipe, Inline Skates, Snowboarding.*

Austriazismen und Helvetismen

Eine Vielzahl zusätzlicher österreichischer und schweizerischer Begriffe wurde in das Wörterbuch eingearbeitet.

Beispiele für Austriazismen: *Eierschwamm(erl), Feber, sei fesch, Fleischhauer, Häuptelsalat, Janker, Kohlsprossen, Laiberl, Lungenbraten, Mandatar(in), Melanzani, Mistkübel, pfuschen (= schwarzarbeiten), Pickerl, Präsenzdiener, Primarius, Ribisel, Schlag (= Schlagsahne), Stockerl, Wachzimmer, Zwetschke.*

Beispiele für Helvetismen: *Ablage (= Annahme-, Verkaufsstelle; Zweigstelle), Abwart, ausschaffen, Depot (= Pfand), Dole, fegen (= scheuern, schrubben), innert, Jupe, Lavabo, Lehrtochter, Morgenessen, Perron, Plättli, Pneu, Thon, Velo, Visum (= Unterschrift; Zeichen), zügeln (= umziehen*, österreichisch *übersiedeln).*

Kontext

Wörter werden meist in einem typischen sprachlichen Zusammenhang verwendet. Damit die Benutzer des *Handwörterbuches Deutsch-Englisch* stets die treffende Übersetzung der verschiedenen Bedeutungen eines Wortes finden, bietet es eine Vielzahl von illustrierenden Beispielsätzen und typischen Wortverbindungen, z. B. *ein runder Geburtstag, nahtlose Bräune, eingefleischter Junggeselle*, bzw. Redewendungen, z. B. *es ist etwas im Gange* oder *ich bin auch nur ein Mensch.*

Nützliche Extras in den Anhängen

In den Anhängen findet man zusätzlich deutsche Abkürzungen, geographische Namen, historische, biblische und mythologische Namen, musikalische Werkbezeichnungen, Zahlwörter, Maße und Gewichte sowie Temperaturumrechnungstabellen.

Mit seinem aktuellen Inhalt und der besonders übersichtlichen Struktur bietet das neu bearbeitete *Handwörterbuch Deutsch-Englisch* seinen Benutzern also echte Langenscheidt-Qualität für alle Übersetzungen, sei es im Studium oder im Beruf.

LANGENSCHEIDT VERLAG

Inhaltsverzeichnis

Hinweise für die Benutzer

A. Allgemeines

I. Schriftarten

Die verschiedenen Elemente eines Wörterbucheintrags sind durch vier Schriftarten gekennzeichnet:

halbfett für die deutschen Stichwörter,

halbfett-kursiv für die deutschen Wendungen und Anwendungsbeispiele,

Grundschrift für die englischen Übersetzungen und

kursiv für Angaben zur Wortart und Grammatik, zu Sachgebieten, zum Sprachregister, zur regionalen Zuordnung sowie für bedeutungsdifferenzierende Zusätze und sonstige Erläuterungen.

II. Anordnung der Stichwörter

1. Alphabetische Reihenfolge

Die **halbfetten** Stichwörter sind streng alphabetisch geordnet. Wichtige unregelmäßige Formen und orthographische Varianten, die alphabetisch nicht direkt an das Stichwort anschließen, stehen an ihrem alphabetischen Ort mit einem Verweis auf das Stichwort, unter dem sie dargestellt werden. Die Umlaute (ä, ö, ü) werden wie a, o und u behandelt.

Aufgrund der Rechtschreibreform nun getrennt zu schreibende Wendungen, die früher zusammengeschriebene Stichwörter waren, stehen getrennt geschrieben an ihrem alphabetischen Ort mit einem Verweis auf das Stichwort, unter dem die Übersetzung zu finden ist:

> **schwer|verdaulich** → *schwer* II 5; ~
> **verdient** → *schwer* II 3; ~ **verkäuflich**
> → *schwer* II 5

Eine Ausnahme bilden die ehemaligen Verbverbindungen mit **-sein**, die jetzt ebenfalls getrennt geschrieben werden. (Beispiel: **aus sein**). Sie werden als Wendung im Eintrag zum ersten Wort behandelt, ohne dass an ihrer alten alphabetischen Stelle ein Verweis erfolgt.

2. Wortbildungselemente

Wortbildungselemente werden wie Stichwörter an ihrem alphabetischen Ort eingeordnet. In der Regel folgen ihnen Komposita, die selbst nicht als Stichwörter in der Wortliste vorkommen:

> **...bändig** *im Adj.:* ***e-e mehr~e/fünf~e***
> ***Ausgabe*** a multi-volume/five-volume
> edition

sau... *im Adj. umg., verstärkend:* **~gut** damn good; **~schlecht** really lousy, *Brit. auch* bloody awful

Riesen|... *im Subst. umg.* giant ..., gigantic, mammoth ..., colossal; *weitS.* Anstrengung *etc.:* tremendous, superhuman ...; **~appetit** *m* huge (*od.* tremendous, voracious) appetite; **~arbeit** *f* mammoth task; [...]

3. Abkürzungen

Wichtige Abkürzungen sind ebenfalls alphabetisch eingeordnet:

Büx *f*; -, *-en*, **Buxe** *f*; -, *-n*; *nordd.* (pair of) trousers (*Am. auch* pants, slacks) *Pl.*
b.w. *Abk.* (**bitte wenden**) PTO, pto (= please turn over)
BWL (*f*) *Abk.* → **Betriebswirtschafts-lehre**
BWV (*n*) *Abk.* (**Bach-Werke-Verzeichnis**) *list of J. S. Bach's works*
Bypass ['baipas] *m*; *-es*, *Bypässe* (heart) bypass; [...]

4. Femininformen

Femininformen wurden, soweit sie nachweisbar sind, generell in die Wortliste aufgenommen; entweder als eigener Eintrag:

Autor *m*; *-s*, *-en* author, writer

[...]

Autorin *f*; -, *-nen* author; authoress *altm.*

oder als Variante zum Stichwort unter Anhängung von **~in**:

Automobilist *m*; *-en*, *-en*, **~in** *f*; -, *-nen*; *altm. od. schw.* motorist, (car-)driver

oder in Nestern am alphabetischen Ort:

Verlags|anstalt *f* publishing house (*od.* company); [...] **~leiter** *m*, **~leiterin** *f* publishing director; [...]

B. Aufbau eines Wörterbucheintrags

I. Stichwörter

Stichwörter erscheinen in **halbfetter** Schrift. Hauptstichwörter sind in der Wörterbuchspalte ausgerückt:

Riecher *m*; *-s*, -; *umg.* nose; *e-n guten ~ haben für* fig. have a (good) nose for; *ich habe den richtigen ~ gehabt* I read the signs right

Zusammengesetzte Stichwörter sind in so genannten „Nestern" aufgenommen. Aus Platzgründen wird deren erster Wortbestandteil, der dem am Anfang des Eintrags ausgerückten Hauptstichwort entspricht, im Nest durch die Tilde (~) ersetzt:

Geisel *f*; -, *-n* hostage; [...] **~drama** *n* hostage drama (*od.* crisis), kidnapping drama; [...]

Ist das Hauptstichwort selbst ein zusammengesetztes Wort, ersetzt die Tilde bei den Stichwörtern im Eintrag den im Hauptstichwort links vom senkrechten Strich (|) stehenden Wortteil, bei Wendungen das direkt vorhergehende Stichwort:

Tafel|obst *n* dessert fruit; **~öl** *n* salad oil; **~runde** *f* (company at) (the) table; *König Artus und die ~* King Arthur and the Knights of the Round Table; **~salz** *n* table salt; [...]

In Nestern mit semantisch sehr eng verbundenen Stichwörtern werden diese aus Gründen der Klarheit ausgeschrieben:

> **Hypochonder** *m*; *-s*, - hypochondriac;
> **Hypochondrie** *f*; *-*, *-n* hypochondria;
> **hypochondrisch** *Adj.* hypochondriac

Die Kreistilde (⊋) wird sehr selten und nur in kurzen Einträgen verwendet. Sie signalisiert den Wechsel von Groß- zu Kleinschreibung bzw. umgekehrt:

> **Abwehr|fehler** ... **⁓haltung** *f* [...];
> ⊋**schwach** [...]; **⁓schwäche** [...]

Wörter mit gleicher Schreibweise, aber grundsätzlich verschiedener Bedeutung oder auch von anderer Wortart werden mit Hochzahlen unterschieden:

> **Band**[1] *n*; *-es*, *Bänder* **1.** (*Mess-*, *Zielband*) tape; *von Schürze etc.*: string; *am Hut*: band; (*Farb-*, *Schmuck-*, *Ordensband*) ribbon [...]
> **Band**[2] *n*; *-es*, *-e* **1.** *fig.* (*Bindung*) bond(s *Pl.*), ties *Pl.*; *das* **⁓** *der Ehe* the bond of marriage; *familiäre* **⁓e** family ties; [...]
> **Band**[3] *m*; *-es*, *Bände*; *Buch*: volume; *das spricht Bände* that speaks volumes, that's very revealing
> **Band**[4] [bɛnt] *f*; *-*, *-s*; (*Musikgruppe*) band

Besteht ein Stichwort aus der substantivierten Form eines Verbs oder Adjektivs, ist in kurzen Einträgen auch folgende Darstellung möglich:

> **halbrund** *Adj.* semicircular; **Halbrund** *n* semicircle

II. Lautschrift, Betonungszeichen

Zu Stichwörtern, bei denen in der Aussprache Unklarheiten auftreten könnten, z. B. bei aus dem Französischen entlehnten Fremdwörtern, wird die Aussprache mithilfe der IPA-Lautschrift angegeben:

> **Entrecote** [ãtrə'koːt] *n*; *-s*, *-s*; *Gastr.* entrecote, (sirloin) steak
> **Entree** [ã'treː] *n*; *-s*, *-s* **1.** *Gastr.* first course, appetizer, *bes. Brit. auch* starter; *Mus.* opening music **2.** *bes. österr.* (*Eintritt*) admission, entry **3.** *altm.* (*Eingangshalle*) entrance hall, foyer

Betonungszeichen im Stichwort erscheinen nur dort, wo der wechselnde Akzent mit einem Bedeutungswandel zusammenhängt:

> **'Tenor**[1] *m*; *-s*, *kein Pl.* **1.** (*allgemeine Tendenz*, *Einstellung*) tenor, [...]
> **Te'nor**[2] *m*; *-s*, *Tenöre*; *Mus.* **1.** tenor (voice *od.* part); [...]

III. Grammatikalische Angaben

Alle grammatikalischen Angaben erscheinen in *kursiver* Schrift.

1. bei Substantiven

Bei substantivischen Stichwörtern werden das Genus, der Genitiv Singular und der Nominativ Plural angegeben. Diese Deklinationsangaben entfallen bei zusammengesetzten Substantiven, deren zweiter Teil selbst ein Hauptstichwort ist, unter dem diese Angaben aufgeführt sind.

> **Wink** *m*; *-(e)s*, *-e* **1.** sign; *mit der Hand*: wave **2.** *fig.* hint, tip; *warnender*: tip-off; *ein* **⁓** *des Schicksals* a sign from above; *ein* **⁓** *mit dem Zaunpfahl* a broad hint

> **Wonne** *f*; *-*, *-n* delight, bliss; [...] **⁓monat** *m lit.*: *im* **⁓** *Mai* in the merry month of May; **⁓proppen** *m*; *-s*, *-*; *umg.*, *hum.* bundle of joy; **⁓schauer** *m geh.* frisson of pleasure

Auftretende Besonderheiten bei Singular und Plural werden wie folgt vermerkt:

> **Mathematik** *f; -, kein Pl.* mathematics
> *Pl. (V. im Sg.)*, maths *Pl. (V. im Sg.)*
> [...]
>
> **Tapezierarbeiten** *Pl.* wallpapering *Sg.;*
> *österr. (Polstern)* upholstering *Sg.*

2. bei Verben

Bei regelmäßig gebeugten Verben steht nach dem Stichwort die Angabe, ob es sich dabei um ein transitives, intransitives etc. Verb handelt:...

> **wimmeln** *v/i. oft unpers.:* **~ von** be
> swarming *(od.* teeming, *umg.* crawling)
> with; *fig., von Fehlern etc.:* be teeming
> *(od.* bristling) with; *es wimmelte nur*
> *so von ...* the place was teeming with ...
> [...]

Bestehen unterschiedliche Verbklassen, werden diese durch römische Ziffern unterschieden. Die Bildung des Partizips mit *sein* oder *haben* wird wie im folgenden Artikel angegeben:

> **wirbeln I** *v/i.* **1.** *(ist gewirbelt) Schnee,*
> *Staub etc.:* whirl, swirl; *Tänzer, Wasser*
> *etc.:* whirl **2.** *(hat) Trommeln:* roll **3.**
> *(hat) fig.:* **mir wirbelt der Kopf** my
> head's spinning
> **II** *v/t. (hat):* **durch die Luft gewirbelt**
> **werden** be whirled through the air

Unregelmäßig gebeugte Verbformen starker Verben werden bei Hauptstichwörtern folgendermaßen aufgeführt:

> **singen;** *singt, sang, hat gesungen* **I** *vt/i.*
> sing; *(Liturgie etc.)* chant; **richtig/falsch**
> **~** sing in/out of tune; [...]

Wichtige unregelmäßige Verbformen erscheinen als Hauptstichwort an alphabetischer Stelle, mit einem Verweis auf den Eintrag zur Infinitiv-Form:

> **warb** *Imperf.* → **werben**

Bei Verben mit Präfixen werden deren regel- bzw. unregelmäßige Beugung, die Trenn- bzw. Untrennbarkeit, das dazugehörige Hilfsverb und der Gebrauch des Präfix *ge-* bzw. des Infix *-ge-* wie folgt dargestellt:

> **umspringen** *v/i. (unreg., trennb., ist -ge-)*
> **1.** *Wind:* veer **2.** *Ampel:* [...]
>
> **vorhersehbar** *Adj.* foreseeable; **nicht ~**
> unforeseeable; **vorhersehen** *v/t.*
> *(unreg., trennb., hat -ge-)* foresee; [...]
>
> **wallfahren** *v/i. (untr., ist ge-)* go on a pil-
> grimage; [...]

In den Stichworteinträgen werden, wo erforderlich, weitere Hilfen zur Grammatik gegeben, z. B. betreffend den Anschluss an Präpositionen:

> **heften I** *v/t.* **1.** *(an + Akk. to);* fix, attach;
> *mit Stecknadeln, Reißzwecken etc.:* pin;
> *mit Klammern:* staple; *Näherei:* baste,
> tack; *(auch Buch)* stitch, sew; [...] **2.**
> *fig.:* **s-e Augen/s-n Blick ~ auf** *(+*
> *Akk.)* fix one's eyes/gaze on; [...]
> **II** *v/refl. fig.:* **sich ~ auf** *(+ Akk.) Augen:*
> fix (themselves) on; *stärker:* be glued to;
> **sich an j-s Fersen ~** stick hard on s.o.'s
> heels
>
> **laben I** *v/refl.* refresh o.s., revive o.s. **(an**
> **+ Dat. with);** **sich ~ an** *(+ Dat.) fig.* rel-
> ish; *mit Schadenfreude:* gloat over; **sich**
> **an e-m Anblick ~** *fig.* feast one's eyes on
> [...]

3. bei Adjektiven

Zu unregelmäßig gesteigerten Adjektiven werden Komparativ und Superlativ angegeben:

> **gut;** *besser, am besten* **I** *Adj.* **1.** good;
> *Wetter: auch* fine; [...]

Bei Identität von Adjektiv und Partizip gilt Folgendes:

> **gereift I** *P.P.* → **reifen II** *Adj. fig.* mature

> **hoch|fahren** [...]; **~fahrend I** *Part. Präs.*
> → **hochfahren II** *Adj.* (*überheblich*)
> overbearing, arrogant

Ebenso erhalten die Benutzer Informationen zum attributiven und prädikativen Gebrauch von Adjektiven:

> [...] **weihnachtlich I** *Adj. attr.* Christ-
> mas ..., *auch präd.* Christmassy; [...]

IV. Kollokationen, Wendungen und Anwendungsbeispiele

Das Wörterbuch bietet eine Fülle von typischen Wortverbindungen (Kollokationen) und Wendungen. Kollokationen werden entweder *kursiv* als Übersetzungshilfen angegeben oder **halbfett-kursiv** in Form einer Wendung mit der entsprechenden Übersetzung:

> **einhalten** (*unreg., trennb., hat -ge-*) **I**
> *v/t.* (*Vereinbarung etc.*) keep to, comply
> with; (*Diät, Regeln*) *auch* stick to; (*Ver-*
> *sprechen*) keep, stick to; (*Verpflichtung*)
> meet; (*Verabredung*) keep; [...]

> **Mut** *m*; *-(e)s, kein Pl.* **1.** (*Tapferkeit*) cour-
> age, bravery; (*Schneid*) pluck; *umg.* guts
> *Pl.*; (*Verwegenheit*) daring; **~ fassen** take
> heart; *für etw.*: pluck up courage; [...]

Wendungen und Anwendungsbeispiele zeigen den Gebrauch eines Wortes im Sinn- und Satzzusammenhang und sind sämtlich mit der idiomatisch treffenden Übersetzung aufgeführt:

> **spätestens** *Adv.* at the latest (*nachge-*
> *stellt*); not later than; **du kriegst sie ~ am**
> **Freitag** you'll have them by Friday at the
> latest; **~ da wurde mir klar, dass ...** it
> was then (if not before) that I realized ...

V. Übersetzungen

Der einfachste Fall liegt vor, wenn ein deutsches Wort im Englischen nur eine Übersetzung hat:

> **teilbar** *Adj.* divisible; **Teilbarkeit** *f* divi-
> sibility

Liegt eine bedeutungsidentische (synonyme) zusätzliche Übersetzung vor, steht sie ohne weitere Angabe nach einem Komma:

> **teilnahmsvoll I** *Adj.* sympathetic, con-
> cerned **II** *Adv.* sympathetically, in a
> concerned way

In allen anderen Fällen, d. h. bei mehr oder weniger starken Bedeutungsunterschieden, werden zu den Übersetzungen zusätzliche, bedeutungsdifferenzierende Hilfen in *kursiver* Schrift gegeben. Dies kann sich auf ein Sachgebiet (z. B. *Med., Phys., Tech., TV*) beziehen, auf die Stilebene (z. B. *fig., iro., pej., vulg.*) oder auf den regionalen Sprachgebrauch (z. B. *österr., schw., südd.;* siehe Liste der Abkürzungen, S. 734 ff.):

> **saldieren** *v/t. Wirts.* balance, settle; *ös-*
> *terr.* confirm payment

> **Schiff** *n*; *-(e)s, -e* **1.** *Naut.* ship; *kleineres*
> *auch*: boat; **auf dem ~** on board ship; **mit**
> **dem ~** by ship; **klar ~ machen** *Naut.*
> clear the decks; *umg., fig.* clear the
> air; **~e Versenken** (*Spiel*) (game of)
> battleships **2.** *Archit.* (*Mittelschiff*) nave;
> (*Seitenschiff*) aisle

> **Tabatiere** [taba'te:rə] *f*; *-, -n* **1.** *bes. österr.*
> (*Tabaksdose*) tobacco tin **2.** *bes. österr.*
> (*Zigarettenetui*) cigarette case **3.** *altm.*
> *für Schnupftabaksdose*: snuffbox

Die Bedeutungsdifferenzierung kann auch durch die Angabe von Synonymen oder andere Erläuterungen in *kursiver* Schrift erfolgen:

> **geben;** *gibt, gab, hat gegeben* **I** *v/t.* **1.** give (*j-m etw.* s.o. s.th., s.th. to s.o.); (*reichen*) *auch* hand; (*schenken*) *auch* present (with); (*verleihen*) *auch* lend; (*Ball etc.*) (*weitergeben*) pass; **etw. nicht aus der Hand geben** (*nicht hergeben*) not let go of s.th., not part with s.th.; *fig.* (*Leitung, Verantwortung*) refuse to give up s.th. (*od.* relinquish s.th.); **j-m zu trinken/essen ~** give s.o. *s.th.* to drink/eat; [...]

Bei transitiven Verben stehen zur Bedeutungsdifferenzierung Objektangaben in Klammern:

> **füllen I** *v/t.* **1.** (*Behälter, Torte, Zahn*) fill; (*Loch*) *auch* stop; (*Braten, Kissen etc.*) stuff; **den Eimer mit Wasser ~** fill (up) the bucket with water; [...]

Die Bedeutung von intransitiven Verben wird durch die Angabe von Subjekten eingegrenzt:

> **fauchen** *v/i.* **1.** *Katze:* hiss; *Tiger etc.:* snarl **2.** *fig. Dampflok etc.:* let off steam; *Wind:* whoosh **3.** *fig. Person, gereizt:* snarl

Entsprechendes gilt, wenn Wendungen unterschiedlich übersetzt werden können:

> **Nase¹** *f; -, -n* **1.** *Anat.* nose (*auch Naut., Flug. etc.*); (*Schnauze*) *auch* snout; [...] **eins auf die ~ kriegen** *umg.* get a punch on the nose; *fig.* get a rap over (*Am.* on) the knuckles; [...]
>
> **gehen** [...] **j-n ~ lassen** let s.o. go; *ungestraft:* let s.o. off; **~ lassen** *umg., fig.* (*Seil etc.*) (*loslassen*) let go; (*j-n, etw.*) (*in Ruhe lassen*) leave alone; **sich ~ lassen** *fig. unmanierlich:* let o.s. go; (*die Beherrschung verlieren*) lose one's temper; [...]

Hat ein Wort oder eine Wendung im Englischen keine direkte Übersetzung, werden in *kursiver* Schrift Definitionen angegeben:

> **Weißwurst** *f Gastr.* veal sausage; **~äquator** *m umg., hum.* the River Main, thought of in Bavaria as the border between the authentic southlands of Germany and the Prussified north

VI. Verweise

Das Verweiszeichen steht bei direkten Verweisen von einem Stichwort zu einem Synonym, unter dem seine Übersetzung zu finden ist:

> **abbummeln** *v/t.* → **abfeiern**

Es verweist außerdem von einem Stichwort zu einem anderen, in dem das Stichwort in Wendungen vorkommt:

> **gehorchen** *v/i.* **1.** **j-m** (**nicht**) **~** (dis)obey s.o.; **du musst d-r Mutter ~** you must do as your mother tells you; → **Wort** [...]

Von Stichwörtern, die eine flektierte Wortform, z. B. ein Partizip darstellen, wird auf das Grundwort verwiesen:

> **anerkennend I** *Part. Präs.* → **anerkennen** [...]
>
> **geholfen** *P.P.* → **helfen**

VII. Britisches und amerikanisches Englisch

Die Unterschiede in der Schreibweise von britischem und amerikanischem Englisch werden wie folgt dargestellt:

Farbe *f*; -, -*n* **1.** colour, *Am.* color; [...]

Lizenz *f*; -, -*en* **1.** licen|ce (*Am.* -se); [...]

Unterschiedliche Übersetzungen im britischen bzw. amerikanischen Englisch werden so wiedergegeben:

Aufzug *m* **1.** (*Fahrstuhl*) lift, *Am.* elevator; [...]

Typ *m*; -*s*, *umg. auch* -*en*, -*en* [...] (*Mann*) guy, bloke, *Am.* dude; (*Freund*) bloke, *Am.* guy; [...]

Erläuterung der Lautschrift

Symbol	Beispiel	Beispiel in Laut-schrift	Symbol	Beispiel	Beispiel in Laut-schrift
a	hat	hat	n̩	reden	'reːdn̩
aː	Tag	taːk	ŋ	lang, Mangan	laŋ, maŋˈgaːn
ɐ	Theater	teˈaːtɐ	o	Poesie	poeˈziː
ɐ̯	leer	leːɐ̯	oː	rot	roːt
ã	balancieren	balãˈsiːrən	ɔ	Toilette	tɔaˈlɛtə
ãː	Balance	baˈlãːs(ə)	õ	Fondue	fõˈdyː
a͜i	steil	ʃtai̯l	õː	Fonds	fõː
aɪ	Midlife-Crisis	ˈmɪdlaɪfˈkraɪsɪs	ɔ	toll	tɔl
au̯	Laut	lau̯t	ø	ökonomisch	økoˈnoːmɪʃ
aʊ	Tower	ˈtaʊɐ	øː	hören	ˈhøːrən
b	Ball	bal	œ	spöttisch	ˈʃpœtɪʃ
ç	ich	ɪç	œ̃ː	Parfum	parˈfœ̃ː
d	du	duː	ou̯	Know-how	nou̯ˈhau̯
dʒ	Gin	dʒɪn	oʊ	Show	ʃoʊ
e	Tenor	teˈnoːɐ̯	ɔy	heute	ˈhɔytə
eː	sehen	ˈzeːən	ɔɪ	Joint	dʒɔɪnt
ɛ	hätte	ˈhɛtə	p	Pelz	pɛlt͜s
ɛː	wählen	ˈvɛːlən	r	Ring	rɪŋ
ɛ̃	Interieur	ɛ̃teˈri̯øːɐ̯	s	Nest, Ruß, besser	nɛst, ruːs, ˈbɛsɐ
ɛ̃ː	Satin	zaˈtɛ̃ː			
ɛə	Jobsharing	ˈdʒɔbʃɛərɪŋ	ʃ	Schotte	ˈʃɔtə
eɪ	Aids	eɪdz	t	Tag	taːk
ə	Affe	ˈafə	t͜s	Zunge, Benzin	ˈt͜suŋə, bɛnˈt͜siːn
f	Fenster, Vater	ˈfɛnstɐ, ˈfaːtɐ	tʃ	Putsch	pʊtʃ
g	gern	gɛrn	θ	Thriller	ˈθrɪlɐ
h	Hut	huːt	u	kulant	kuˈlant
i	Triumph	triˈʊmf	uː	Schuhe	ˈʃuːə
iː	viel	fiːl	u̯	aktuell	akˈtu̯ɛl
i̯	Podium	ˈpoːdi̯ʊm	ʊ	null	nʊl
ɪ	bitte	ˈbɪtə	v	Wasser, Vase	ˈvasɐ, ˈvaːzə
j	ja	jaː	x	achten	ˈaxtn̩
k	Kunst	kʊnst	y	dynamisch	dyˈnaːmɪʃ
l	Lust	lʊst	yː	über, Mühe	ˈyːbɐ, ˈmyːə
l̩	Nebel	ˈneːbl̩	ỹ	Nuance	ˈnỹãːsə
m	Moment	moˈmɛnt	ʏ	synchron	zʏnˈkroːn
m̩	großem	ˈgroːsm̩	z	sagen, Reise	ˈzaːgn̩, ˈraɪzə
n	nett	nɛt	ʒ	Manege	maˈneːʒə

Im Wörterbuch verwendete Abkürzungen

abgek.	abgekürzt, *abbreviated*
Abk.	Abkürzung, *abbreviation*
Adj.	Adjektiv, *adjective*
Adv.	Adverb, *adverb*
Agr.	Landwirtschaft, *agriculture*
Akk.	Akkusativ, *accusative*
allg.	allgemein, *generally*
altm.	altmodisch, veraltet, obsolet, *old-fashioned, dated, obsolete*
Am.	Amerikanisches Englisch, *American English*
Amtsspr.	Amtssprache, *officialese*
Anat.	Anatomie, *anatomy*
Archäol.	Archäologie, *archeology*
Archit.	Architektur, *architecture*
Art.	Artikel, *article*
Astrol.	Astrologie, *astrology*
Astron.	Astronomie, *astronomy*
attr.	attributiv, *attributively*
Bergb.	Bergbau, *mining*
bes.	besonders, *especially*
best.	bestimmt, *definite*
bibl.	biblisch, *biblical*
Bio.	Biologie, *biology*
Bot.	Botanik, *botany*
BRD	Bundesrepublik Deutschland, *Federal Republic of Germany*
Brit.	Britisches Englisch, *British English*
bzw.	beziehungsweise, *or*
Chem.	Chemie, *chemistry*
Dat.	Dativ, *dative*
d-e	deine, *your*
Dem.	Demonstrativ…, *demonstrative*
Dent.	Zahnmedizin, *dentistry*
Dial.	Dialekt, *dialect*
Dim.	Diminutivform, *diminutive*
d-m	deinem, *your, of yours*
d-n	deinen, *your, of yours*
d-r	deiner, *your, of yours*
Druck.	Druckereiwesen, *printing*
d-s	deines, *your*
EDV	elektronische Datenverarbeitung, Computer, *electronic data processing, computing*

e-e	eine, *a (an)*
ehem. DDR	ehemalige DDR, *former GDR*
Eisenb.	Eisenbahn, *railway*
Elektr.	Elektrizität, *electricity*
e-m	einem, *to a (an)*
e-n	einen, *a (an)*
engS.	im engeren Sinne, *in the narrower sense*
e-r	einer, *of a (an), to a (an)*
e-s	eines, *of a (an)*
etc.	et cetera, *et cetera*
Etech.	Elektrotechnik, *electrical engineering*
Etron.	Elektronik, *electronics*
etw.	etwas, *something, s. th.*
EU	Europäische Union, *European Union*
euph.	euphemistisch, *euphemistically*
ev.	evangelisch, *Protestant*
f	feminin, *feminine*
fachspr.	fachsprachlich, *technical term*
fig.	figurativ, im übertragenen Sinne, *figuratively*
Fin.	Finanzwesen, *finances*
Flug.	Flugwesen, Luftfahrt, *aviation*
förm.	förmlich, formell, *formal*
Fot.	Fotografie, *photography*
frz.	französisch, *French*
Funk.	Rundfunk, *radio*
Gastr.	Gastronomie, *gastronomy*
GB	Großbritannien, *Great Britain*
geh.	gehobener Sprachgebrauch, Schriftsprache, *elevated style*
Gen.	Genitiv, *genitive*
Geog.	Geographie, *geography*
Geol.	Geologie, *geology*
Ger.	Gerundium, *gerund*
gespr.	gesprochen, *spoken*
Ggs.	Gegensatz, *antonym*
Gnt.	Genetik, *genetics*
Gram.	Grammatik, *grammar*
Her.	Heraldik, *heraldry*
Hilfsv.	Hilfsverb, *auxiliary verb*
hist.	historisch, *historical*
hum.	scherzhaft, *humerously*
i-e	ihre, *her, Pl. their*
i-m	ihrem, *her, Pl. their*
Imperf.	Imperfekt, *imperfect*
i-n	ihren, *her, Pl. their*
indekl.	indeklinabel, *indeclinable*
Inf.	Infinitiv, *infinitive*
Interj.	Interjektion, *interjection*
Interr.	Interrogativ..., *interrogative*
intr.	intransitiv, *intransitive*
i-r	ihrer, *her, Pl. their*
iro.	ironisch, *ironically*
i-s	ihres, *of her, Pl. of their*
ital.	italienisch, *Italian*
Jägerspr.	Jägersprache, *hunter's jargon*

j-d	jemand, *someone*
j-m	jemandem, *(to) someone*
j-n	jemanden, *someone*
j-s	jemandes, *someone's*
Jugendspr.	Jugendsprache, *teenage slang*
Jur.	Juristik, Rechtswesen, *legal term*
kath.	katholisch, *Catholic*
Kinderspr.	Kindersprache, *children's language*
kirchl.	kirchlich, *church*
Koll.	Kollektivum, Sammelwort, *collective noun*
Komp.	Komparativ, *comparative*
Konj.	Konjunktion, *conjunction*
konstr.	konstruiert, *construed*
Kurzf.	Kurzform, *short form*
Ling.	Linguistik, *linguistics*
Lit.	Literatur, Literaturwissenschaft, *literature, literary studies*
lit.	literarisch, *literary*
m	maskulin, *masculine*
Math.	Mathematik, *mathematics*
m-e	meine, *my*
Mech.	Mechanik, *mechanics*
Med.	Medizin, *medicine*
Met.	Meteorologie, *meteorology*
Metall.	Metallurgie, *metallurgy*
Mil.	Militär, *military*
Min.	Mineralogie, *mineralogy*
m-m	meinem, *(to) my*
m-n	meinen, *my*
Modalv.	Modalverb, *modal verb*
Mot.	Motorwesen, Auto, *motoring*
m-r	meiner, *(of) my*
m-s	meines, *of my*
mst	meist(ens), *mostly, usually*
Mus.	Musik, *music*
Myth.	Mythologie, *mythology*
n	Neutrum, sächlich, *neuter*
Naut.	Schiffahrt, Seefahrt, *nautical term*
neg!	kann als beleidigend empfunden werden, *negative connotation, can be interpreted as an offensive term*
neg.	negativ, *negative*
Nom.	Nominativ, *nominative*
nordd.	norddeutsch, *North German*
o.s.	selbst, *oneself*
Obj.	Objekt, *object*
od.	oder, *or*
Öko.	Ökologie, *ecology*
Opt.	Optik, *optics*
Orn.	Ornithologie, *ornithology*
ostd.	ostdeutsch, *East German*
österr.	österreichischer Sprachgebrauch, *Austrian usage*
Österr.	Österreich, *Austria*
P.P.	Partizip Perfekt, *past participle*
Päd.	Pädagogik, Schule, *didactics, school*
Parl.	Parlamentssprache, *parliamentary term*

Part.	Partizip, *participle*
pej.	pejorativ, *pejoratively*
Perf.	Perfekt, *perfect (tense)*
pers.	persönlich, *personal*
Pharm.	Pharmazie, *pharmacy*
Philos.	Philosophie, *philosophy*
Phon.	Phonetik, *phonetics*
Phys.	Physik, *physics*
Physiol.	Physiologie, *physiology*
Pl.	Plural, *plural*
poet.	poetisch, *poetically*
Pol.	Politik, *politics*
Poss.	Possessiv…, *possessive*
Post.	Postwesen, *postal system*
präd.	prädikativ, *predicatively*
Präp.	Präposition, *preposition*
Präs.	Präsens, *present (tense)*
Pron.	Pronomen, *pronoun*
Psych.	Psychologie, *psychology*
®	eingetragene Marke, *Registered Trademark*
Raumf.	Raumfahrt, *space travel*
refl.	reflexiv, *reflexive*
reg.	regelmäßig, *regular*
Rel.	Relativ…, *relative*
Reli.	Religion, *religion*
Rhet.	Rhetorik, *rhetoric*
schw.	schweizerischer Sprachgebrauch, *Swiss usage*
s-e	seine, *his, one's*
Sg.	Singular, *singular*
Sl.	Slang, *slang*
s-m	seinem, *(to) his, (to) one's*
s-n	seinen, *his, one's*
s.o.	jemand(en, -em), *someone*
Soziol.	Soziologie, *sociology*
Sprichw.	Sprichwort, *proverb*
s-r	seiner, *(of, to) his, (of, to) one's*
s-s	seines, *of his, of one's*
s.th.	something
Subst., subst.	Substantiv, substantivisch, *noun, nominal*
südd.	süddeutsch, *South German*
Sup.	Superlativ, *superlative*
Tech.	Technik, *engineering*
Telef.	Telefon, *telephone*
Telek.	Telekommunikation, *telecommunications*
Theat.	Theater, *theatre*
trennb.	trennbar, *separable*
TV	Fernsehen, *television*
umg.	umgangssprachlich, *colloquial*
unbest.	unbestimmt, *indefinite*
undekl.	undekliniert, undeklinierbar, *not declined, indeclinable*
Univ.	Universität, *university*
unpers.	unpersönlich, *impersonal*
unreg.	unregelmäßig, *irregular*
untr.	untrennbar, *inseparable*

USA	USA, *USA, US*
V.	Verb, *verb*
Verk.	Verkehr, Verkehrswesen, *public transport*
Vet.	Tiermedizin, *veterinary medicine*
vgl.	vergleiche, *compare*
v/i.	intransitives Verb, *intransitive verb*
v/refl.	reflexives Verb, *reflexive verb*
v/t.	transitives Verb, *transitive verb*
vt/i.	transitives und intransitives Verb, *transitive and intransitive verb*
vulg.	vulgär, *vulgar*
weitS.	im weiteren Sinne, *in a wider sense*
Wirts.	Wirtschaft und Handel, *commercial term*
wörtl.	wörtlich, *literally*
Zahlw.	Zahlwort, *numeral*
z. B.	zum Beispiel, *for example*
Zool.	Zoologie, *zoology*

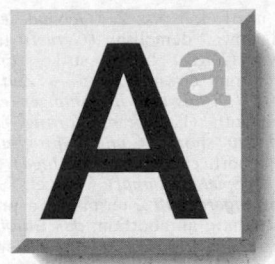

A, a n; -, - od. umg. -s **1.** A, a; **A wie Anton** Buchstabieren: "a" for (od. as in) "Alpha"; **das A und O** the most important thing; (Grundkenntnisse) the basics, the alpha and the omega; **wer A sagt, muss auch B sagen** in for a penny, in for a pound, Am. auch in for a dime, in for a dollar; **von A bis Z** right down the line; **das ist von A bis Z erlogen** there's not a word of truth in it; it's a pack of lies umg.; **2.** Mus. A; **3.** Wirts.: **Güteklasse A** grade (od. quality category) A; → **eins** I

Ä, ä n; -, - od. umg. -s a umlaut, ae

à Präp. at ... each (od. a piece)

Aa [a'a:] n; -, kein Pl.; Kinderspr. pooh, poop, number two; ~ **machen** have a pooh (od. poop), do number two

AA Abk. **1.** (Auswärtiges Amt) → auswärtig 2, Außenministerium; **2.** (Anonyme Alkoholiker) → Alkoholiker

Aachen (n); -s; Geog. Aachen (od. Aix-la-Chapelle)

Aachener¹ m; -s, -, **~in** f; -, -nen inhabitant of Aachen

Aachener² Adj. (from) Aachen; ~ **Printen** special(i)ty shortbread from Aachen

Aal m; -(e)s, -e; Zool. eel; → **winden¹** II

aalen v/refl. umg. laze around; **sich in der Sonne** ~ bask in the sun allg.

Aal|fang m eel fishing

aalglatt Adj. fig. (as) slippery as an eel; **~er Typ** smoothie umg., a slippery customer

Aal|korb m, **~reuse** f eelpot, eel trap (od. basket)

Aalsuppe f Gastr. eel soup

a.a.O. Abk. (am angegebenen Ort) loc. cit.

Aar m; -(e)s, -e; Orn., lit. altm. (Adler) eagle

Aas n; -es, -e und Äser, mst. Sg. **1.** Pl. Aase carcass, carrion kein Pl.; ~ **fressend** Zool. scavenging; **2.** Pl. Äser, umg. fig., mst. pej. swine Sl.; **faules** ~ (Mann) lazy sod (Am. bum) (od. bugger Sl.); (Frau) lazy cow (od. bitch Sl.); **kein** ~ not a sod (od. soul allg.)

aasen v/i. umg.: ~ **mit** (Vorräten) squander; (Geld) auch splash about, throw around; (Butter etc.) waste

Aas|fliege f Zool. carrion fly; **~fresser** m scavenger; **~geier** m Orn. vulture (auch fig.); **~vogel** m Orn. carrion-devouring (od. scavenging) bird

ab I. Präp. **1.** räumlich: from; ~ **Brüssel** from Brussels; Wirts. ~ **Berlin/Werk** etc. ex Berlin/works etc.; **2.** zeitlich: from ... (on[wards]); amtlich: as of, with effect from; ~ **heute** starting today, from today (onwards); ~ **erstem** od. **ersten Mai** from the first of May; ~ **18** Film, Lokal etc.: no admittance to persons under 18; **3.** Reihenfolge etc.: from ... (on[wards]); Menge: from ... (up[wards]); ~ **30 Leute(n)** auch 30 people and up, for groups of 30 and

more; **II.** Adv. **1.** zeitlich: from; **von heute** ~ starting today, from today; **von jetzt** ~ from now on, in future (Am. the future); ~ **und zu** now and then, from time to time, occasionally; **2.** räumlich: **von hier** ~ from here on(wards); ~ **mit dir!** umg. off you go now; ~ **ins Bett!** umg. off to bed (with you)!; **3.** umg.: ~ **sein** (abgegangen sein) have come (od. fallen) off allg.; (erschöpft sein) be knackered (Am. wiped out) umg.; **4.** Eisenb. **Hamburg** ~ **20.15** dep. (= departure) Hamburg 20.15; **5.** Film: ~**!** go ahead; **Kamera** ~**!** roll it!, camera!; **Ton** ~**!** sound!; **6.** Mil.: **Gewehr/Helm** ~**!** order arms / helmet(s) off!

Ab n → **Auf**

Abakus m; -, -; Math. hist. abacus

abänderbar Adj. open to change etc.; **es ist noch** ~ it can still be changed etc.; → **abändern**; **abändern** v/t. (trennb., hat -ge-) change, alter; (Plan etc.) revise, modify; Parl. amend; Jur. commute; **Abänderung** f alteration, change; modification, revision; Parl. amendment; Jur. commutation; → **abändern**

Abänderungs|antrag m Parl. motion for amendment; **~vorschlag** m proposed amendment

abarbeiten (trennb., hat -ge-) **I.** v/t. (Schulden) work off; **s-e Überfahrt** ~ work one's passage; **II.** v/refl. slave (away); work one's fingers to the bone umg.; → **abgearbeitet** II

Abart f **1.** Bot., Zool. variety, species; (Unterart) auch subspecies; **2.** fig. variation (+ Gen. of, on); **abartig I.** Adj. abnormal; Verhalten: auch perverse; **II.** Adv. umg. (~ **kalt**) incredibly; (~ **wehtun**) like hell; **Abartigkeit** f abnormality; perverseness, perversity

abästen v/t. (Baum) prune, trim; (Äste) cut away, lop off

abätzen v/t. (trennb., hat -ge-); Med. cauterize

Abb. Abk. → **Abbildung**

abbalgen v/t. (trennb., hat -ge-); (abhäuten) skin, flay

Abbau m; -(e)s, kein Pl. **1.** e-r Anlage, e-r Maschine, e-s Gerüstes: dismantling, disassembly; e-s Standes: dismantling e-s Zeltes, e-s Lagers: striking; (Abbruch) demolition; **2.** (Reduzierung) (Stellen-, Personalabbau) reduction, cutback (Gen. in), laying off (Gen. of); von Missständen: (gradual) removal, diminution; von Vorurteilen: breaking down; **3.** Chem., Biol. decomposition, disintegration; von radioaktiven Substanzen: decay; im Körper: auch breakdown, catabolism; **4.** Bergb. a) von Kohle etc.: mining; e-r Mine: working, exploiting (of a mine), b) allg. Gewinnung von Bodenschätzen: extracting, extraction, winning; **5.** (Kräfte-, Leistungsabbau) decline

abbaubar Adj.: **biologisch** ~ biodegra-

dable

abbauen (trennb., hat -ge-) **I.** vt/i. (Baracke, Kulissen, Lager, Stand) dismantle, disassemble, strike; (Maschine) dismantle, strip (down); (Zelt) strike; (Gerüst) take down; pull down; **II.** v/t. **1.** (verringern) reduce; (Bestände) run down; (Missstände) remedy; (Vorurteile etc.) get rid of, break down; (Defizit, Löhne, Preise) reduce, cut; (Personal, Stellen, Privilegien) cut (back), streamline euph.; **Arbeitskräfte** ~ cut down on manpower (od. the workforce), lay off workers; **2.** Chem., Biol. (Giftstoffe, Kohlehydrate, Alkohol etc.) break down; **3.** Bergb. (Kohle etc.) über Tage: quarry; unter Tage: mine; (ausbeuten) work, exploit; **III.** v/i. Mensch: go downhill (auch geistig); (nachlassen) flag, lose it umg.; **die Schüler bauen in der 6. Stunde stark ab** the pupils switch off (od. lose concentration) in the 6th lesson (Am. period); **IV.** v/refl. **1.** Vorurteile etc.: break down; **2.** Chem., Biol.; Gift etc. im Körper: break down, decompose; **3.** Met. break up

Abbau|feld n Bergb. district, field, set; **~produkt** n Chem., Biol. degradation product; **~rechte** Pl. Jur. mining (od. mineral) rights; **~strecke** f Bergb. gate

abbauwürdig Adj. Bergb. workable

abbeißen vt/i. (unreg., trennb., hat -ge-) bite off (von etw. from s.th.); **willst du mal** ~**?** do you want a bite?; **sich** (Dat.) **die Nägel** ~ bite (od. chew) one's nails; → **Maus** 1

abbeizen v/t. (trennb., hat -ge-) **1.** (Holz) strip; **2.** (Lack) strip (von etw. from od. off s.th.)

Abbeizmittel n (paint) stripper, paint remover

abbekommen v/t. (unreg., trennb., hat) **1.** (losbekommen) get off; **2.** (e-n Teil bekommen) get; **etwas** ~ get one's share; **3.** (verletzt od. beschädigt werden) be hit, get hurt; Sache: be damaged; **das meiste** ~ an Vorwürfen etc.: bear (od. take) the brunt

abberufen v/t. (unreg., trennb., hat) **1.** (Gesandte etc.) recall; von e-m Amt: relieve from office; **2.** euph.: ~ **werden** pass away, be called home; **Abberufung** f recall; euph. decease, passing away

abbestellen v/t. (trennb., hat); (Zeitung etc.) cancel (the order for); Telefon get (od. have) the line disconnected; **j-n** ~ ask (od. tell) s.o. not to come; **Abbestellung** f cancel(l)ation; Telefon disconnection; von Handwerkern etc.: cancel(l)ing

abbetteln v/t. (trennb., hat -ge-); umg.: **j-m etw.** ~ wheedle s.th. out of s.o.

abbezahlen v/t. (trennb., hat) pay off; **Abbezahlung** f; mst. Sg. repayment

abbiegen (unreg., trennb., -ge-) **I.** v/i. (ist) **1.** Auto, Straße etc.: turn (off);

(*abzweigen*) branch off; **nach rechts (links)** ~ turn right (left); **von der Hauptstraße** ~ turn off the main road; **2.** *Geol.* warp down(ward); **II.** *v/t.* (*hat*) **1.** bend; **2.** *umg. fig.* (*Sache, Gefahr, Gespräch*) head off, stave off; **Abbieger** *m*; *-s*, *-*, **Abbiegerin** *f*; *-*, *-nen* car *etc.* turning off

Abbiege|spur *f* filter lane; **~verbot** *n* turn ban; (*Schild*) no turning, no turns permitted

Abbiegung *f* (*Abzweigung*) junction, branch, fork

Abbild *n* **1.** (*Kopie, Nachbildung*) reproduction, copy; *e-r Person*: image, portrayal; **2.** (*Ebenbild*) image (*od.* likeness); **3.** (*Widerspiegelung*) image, reflection; **abbilden** *v/t.* (*trennb., hat -ge-*) portray, depict; **oben abgebildet** *nachgestellt*: shown above; **Abbildung** *f* (*abgek.* **Abb.**) **1.** picture, illustration; (*Diagramm, Grafik*) diagram, chart; **2.** *nur Sg.* (*das Abbilden*) reproduction, portrayal

abbinden (*unreg., trennb., hat -ge-*) **I.** *v/t.* **1.** untie, undo; (*Krawatte etc.*) take off; **2.** *Med.* ligature; **3.** (*Soße etc.*) bind; **II.** *v/i.* Leim, Zement: set

Abbitte *f* apology; **~ leisten** apologize, make (*od.* offer) one's apologies (*bei j-m für od.* **wegen etw.** to s.o. for s.th.)

abblasen I. *v/t.* (*trennb., hat -ge-*) **1.** (*entfernen*) blow off; **den Staub von e-m Buch** ~ blow the dust from a book; **2.** *umg. fig.* call off; **die ganze Angelegenheit ist abgeblasen** the whole thing's off; **3.** *Tech.* (*entweichen lassen*) (*Dampf*) release, discharge, blow off; **4.** *Tech.* (*Gussstücke etc.*) (sand)blast; **5.** *Tech.* (*Hochofen*) let burn down; **II.** *v/i.* *Tech.* Hochofen: burn down

abblättern *v/i.* (*trennb., ist -ge-*) peel off, *Farbe: auch* flake off

abbleiben *v/i.* (*unreg., trennb., ist -ge-*); *umg.*: **wo ist sie** *etc.* **abgeblieben?** where has she *etc.* got to?; **es muss irgendwo abgeblieben sein** it must be somewhere

Abblende *f Film*: fade-out; **abblenden** (*trennb., hat -ge-*) **I.** *v/t.* (*Licht*) dim; (*Scheinwerfer*) dip, *Am.* dim; **II.** *v/i.* **1.** *Mot.* dip (*Am.* dim) one's headlights; **2.** *Fot.* stop down; **3.** *Film*: fade(-out); **Abblendlicht** *n* anti-dazzle light, dipped beam, *Am.* low beam; **mit ~ fahren** drive with dipped (*od.* dimmed *Am.*) headlights

abblitzen *v/i.* (*trennb., ist -ge-*); *umg.* be sent packing, be told where to go *allg.*; *j-n* **~ lassen** send s.o. packing; **er ist bei ihr abgeblitzt** he was given the brush-off, she gave him the brush-off

abblocken *v/t.* (*trennb., hat -ge-*) **1.** *Sport* block; **2.** *fig.* block; *bes. Pol. auch* stonewall

Abbrand *m* **1.** *Tech.* im Reaktor: burn-up; *in der Rakete*: combustion; **2.** *Metall.* (*Abfall, Verlust*) melting loss; *Elektroden*: consumption; *Chem.* roasting residue

abbrausen (*trennb., -ge-*) **I.** *v/t.* (*hat*); (*Körperteil, Gegenstand*) rinse (off); (*Schmutz*) shower down (*od.* off), rinse off (*von* from); **II.** *v/refl.* (*hat*) have (*od.* take) a shower; **III.** *v/i.* (*ist*); *umg.* roar (*od.* zoom) off

abbrechen (*unreg., trennb., -ge-*) **I.** *v/t.* (*hat*) **1.** (*Stücke*) break off (**von etw.** from s.th.); (*Zweig auch*) snap; (*Blumen*) pluck, pick; (*Bleistift*) break; **sich** (*Dat.*) **e-n Fingernagel** ~ break a (finger)nail; **sich** (*Dat.*) **einen** ~ *umg.*

fig. nearly kill o.s.; **2.** (*Gebäude etc.*) pull down, demolish; (*Gerüst*) take down; (*Lager*) break, strike *camp*; (*Zelt*) put down, strike; **→ Zelt** 1; **3.** *fig.* (*Diskussion, Beziehungen etc.*) break off; (*Verfahren, Vortrag etc.*) *auch* cut short; (*Computerprogramm etc.*) abort, cancel; (*Streik, Jagd*) call off; (*Spiel, Kampf*) cancel; **e-e Schwangerschaft** ~ terminate a pregnancy, have an abortion; **das Studium** ~ drop out of university (*Am.* college); **II.** *v/i.* **1.** (*ist*); *Stück*: break off; *Zweig, Blume auch*: snap (off); *Stück Kreide etc.*: snap (in half); *Bleistift, Fingernagel etc.*: break; **2.** (*hat*); *fig.* (*enden*) break off, stop

Abbrecher *m*; *-s*, *-*, **~in** *f*; *-*, *-nen* von Ausbildung, Studium etc.: dropout

abbremsen (*trennb., hat -ge-*) **I.** *v/i.* brake, slow down, apply the brakes, decelerate; **stark ~ müssen** have to brake hard (*od.* sharply); **II.** *v/t.* (*Auto etc.*) brake, slow down; (*Raumfahrzeug*) deboost, decelerate; (*auffangen*) cushion, absorb

abbrennen (*unreg., trennb., -ge-*) **I.** *v/i.* (*ist*) **1.** *Haus, Dorf*: burn down; be destroyed by fire; **2.** *Kerze, Streichholz*: burn down (*od.* away); **abgebranntes Streichholz** used (*od.* burnt) match; **→ abgebrannt** II; **II.** *v/t.* (*hat*) **1.** (*Dorf etc.*) burn down; (*Unkraut, Stoppeln*) burn off; (*Federn, Haare*) sear, singe; (*Feuerwerk*) let (*od.* set) off; (*Wunde*) cauterize; **2.** *Tech.* (*Porzellan*) give the final firing to; (*Metall*) refine; (*Stahl*) temper

abbringen *v/t.* (*unreg., trennb., hat -ge-*) **1.** *j-n von etw.* ~ *fig.* put s.o. off doing s.th., *Person: auch* talk s.o. out of (*od.* dissuade s.o. from) doing s.th.; **ich habe versucht, sie davon abzubringen** I tried to talk her out of it; *j-n von ein-em Thema* ~ get s.o. off a subject; *j-n vom* (*rechten*) *Weg* ~ lead s.o. astray; **der Wind hat uns vom Kurs abgebracht** the wind put us off course; **2.** *umg.* (*abmachen können*) get off

abbröckeln *v/i.* (*trennb., ist -ge-*) crumble away (*od.* off); *Wirts. fig.*; *Kurse*: drop off, fall

Abbruch *m* **1.** *e-s Gebäudes etc.*: demolition; **reif für den** ~ fit (only) (*od.* due) for demolition; *auch* condemned; **2.** (*Abbau*) *e-s Gerüstes*: dismantling; *e-s Lagers*: striking; **3.** *fig. von Beziehungen etc.*: breaking off; **4.** *e-s Computerprogramms*: abortion; *ungewollt*: crash; **5.** *e-s Experiments*: abortion; **6.** *e-s Kampfes, e-s Spiels, e-s Streiks*: calling off, halting, stopping, abandoning; **Sieg durch** ~ Boxen: win on a technical knockout; **7.** *e-r Schwangerschaft*: termination, abortion; **8.** *e-s Studiums*: breaking off; **9.** *Mil., von Kampfhandlungen*: cessation; **10.** *fig.*: *e-r Sache* (*Dat.*) ~ **tun** impair, detract from, be detrimental to, do any harm to

Abbruch|arbeiten *Pl.* demolition work *Sg.*; **~arbeiter** *m* demolition worker; **~firma** *f* → **Abbruchunternehmen**; **~haus** *n* condemned building

abbruchreif *Adj.* derelict, dilapidated; (*für ... erklärt*) due for demolition, condemned; *Tech.* due to be scrapped

Abbruch|sieger *m* Boxen: winner on a technical knockout; **~unternehmen** *n* demolition contractors *Pl.*, *Am.* wrecking company

abbrühen *v/t.* (*trennb., hat -ge-*); (*Man-*

deln) scald; *fig.* → **abgebrüht**

abbrummen *v/t.* (*trennb., hat -ge-*); *umg.*: **e-e Strafe** ~ do time

abbuchen *v/t.* (*trennb., hat -ge-*); *Wirts.* debit *a sum from an account*; **Abbuchung** *f* charge, debit (entry), debiting; **e-e ~ vornehmen** debit (*od.* charge) an account

Abbuchungs|auftrag *m Wirts.* (direct) debit order; *ständiger*: standing (*od.* debiting) order; **~konto** *n* debiting (*Am.* charge) account; **~verfahren** *n* direct debiting (service, *Am.* automatic payment system)

abbummeln *v/t.* (*trennb., hat -ge-*); *umg.* → **abfeiern**

abbürsten (*trennb., hat -ge-*) **I.** *v/t.* **1.** (*Kleider*) brush (down); **2.** (*Staub*) brush off (**von etw.** s.th.); **II.** *v/refl.* brush one's clothes

abbüßen *v/t.* (*trennb., hat -ge-*) expiate, atone for; **e-e Strafe** ~ serve a sentence

Abc *n*; *-*, *-*, *mst.Sg.* **1.** ABC, alphabet; **nach dem** ~ alphabetically, in alphabetical order; **2.** *fig.*: **das** ~ (+ *Gen.*) the basics *Pl.* of, the ABC(s) of

abchecken *v/t.* (*trennb., hat -ge-*); *umg.* **1.** (*überprüfen*) check; **2.** (*abhaken*) tick (*Am.* check) off

Abc-Schütze *m* school beginner; *formell*: reception child (*od.* pupil)

ABC-Waffen *Pl. Mil.* NBC weapons (= nuclear/atomic, biological and chemical weapons)

abdämmen *v/t.* (*trennb., hat -ge-*) (*Fluss, See etc.*) dam (up); (*tief liegendes Land*) dam off (up); *fig.* (*etwas Unerwünschtes*) curb, (keep in) check; **Abdämmung** *f von Flüss etc.* dam, damming (up); *von tief liegendem Land*: dam, damming off; *fig.* curb, check

Abdampf *m Tech.* exhaust steam; **abdampfen** (*trennb., -ge-*) **I.** *v/i.* (*ist*) **1.** *umg. fig.* clear off; **2.** *Chem.* (*verdicken*) evaporate; **3.** *Gastr.* (*Schnellkochtopf, Kartoffeln etc.*) ~ **lassen** allow the steam to evaporate; **II.** *v/t.* (*hat*); *Chem.* evaporate, vaporize, volatilize

abdämpfen *v/t.* (*trennb., hat -ge-*) → **dämpfen**

Abdampf|gefäß *Tech.* evaporating basin (*od.* dish *od.* pan); **~heizung** *f Tech.* waste-steam heating; **~turbine** *f Tech.* waste-steam turbine; **~wärme** *f* (latent) heat of vaporization

abdanken *v/i.* (*trennb., hat -ge-*) resign; *Herrscher*: abdicate; **Edward VIII. hat zugunsten s-s Bruders abgedankt** Edward VIII renounced his throne in favo(u)r of his brother; **Abdankung** *f* **1.** resignation; abdication, renunciation, renouncement; **2.** *schw.* (*Trauerfeier*) funeral (ceremony)

Abdeck|blech *n* metal cover; **~creme** *f* cover-up (*od.* blemish) cream

abdecken (*trennb., hat -ge-*) *v/t.* **1.** (*Ggs. decken, bedecken*) uncover; (*Haus*) unroof, untile; (*Bett*) strip; (*den Tisch*) clear; **2.** (*entfernen*) (*Bettdecke, Dach, Tuch*) take off; **3.** (*verdecken, auch Tech.*) cover (up); *mit Holz*: plank; *Fot. mit Tusche*: block out; *Opt.* stop out; **4.** (*berücksichtigen*) (*Fälle, Möglichkeiten*) cover; (*befriedigen*) (*Bedarf etc.*) meet, cover, satisfy; **5.** *Wirts.* (*Schuld*) repay; **6.** *Sport* mark, cover

Abdecker *m*; *-s*, *-* knacker; **Abdeckerei** *f*; *-*, *-en* knacker's yard, *Am.* rendering works

Abdeck|folie *f* dustsheet, dust cover;

⁓**haube** f cover(ing); ⁓**plane** f tarpaulin

Abdeckung f (etw. Abdeckendes) cover(ing); Wirtsch. cover

abdichten v/t. (trennb., hat -ge-) seal (up); (Boiler, Schiff) caulk; Tech. auch (stopfen) pack; **gegen Luft (Wasser)** ⁓ make airtight (watertight); **gegen Lärm** ⁓ (make) soundproof; **Abdichtung** f von Loch, Naht etc.: sealing etc.; damp-proofing; → **Dichtung²** 2

abdienen v/t. (trennb., hat -ge-); Mil.: **s-e Zeit** ⁓ serve one's time

abdingbar Adj. Jur. modifiable

abdonnern v/i. (trennb., ist -ge-); umg. roar (zoom) off

abdrängen v/t. (trennb., hat -ge-) push (od. force) aside; Mot. force off the road

abdrehen (trennb., -ge-) **I.** v/t. (hat) **1.** (Gas, Wasser etc.) turn off; Etech. auch switch off; **2.** (Knopf, Stiel etc.) twist off (**von etw.** from s.th.); **3.** (abwenden) turn away; **4.** (Film) finish (shooting); → **abgedreht** II; **II.** v/i. (ist) Naut., Flug. change course; (ausscheren) veer off; **III.** v/refl. turn away (od. aside)

Abdrift f Naut. drift; **abdriften** v/i. (trennb., ist -ge-) drift (off course)

abdrosseln v/t. (trennb., hat -ge-); Mot. (use the) throttle, choke (auch fig.); **Abdross(e)lung** f throttling, choking

Abdruck¹ m; Pl. Abdrücke impression, imprint; (Abguss) cast; (Zahn꜒) impression; ⁓ **in Wachs** wax impression; → auch **Fußabdruck, Fingerabdruck**

Abdruck² m; Pl. Abdrucke; Druck. copy; (Nachdruck) reprint; (Verfahren) (re)printing

abdrucken v/t. (trennb., hat -ge-); Druck. print; **wieder** ⁓ reprint

abdrücken (trennb., hat -ge-) **I.** v/t. **1.** (Ader, Finger) squeeze off; **j-m die Luft** ⁓ choke s.o.; **2.** (abformen) make an impression (od. a mo[u]ld) of; **II.** v/i. fire, pull the trigger; **III.** v/refl. **1.** leave an impression (od. a mark); **2.** (abstoßen) push o.s. away (**von etw.** from s.th.)

abducken v/i. (trennb., ist -ge-) Boxen: duck

abdunkeln v/t. (trennb., hat -ge-); (Licht, Zimmer) darken, dim, vollständig: black out; (Farben) darken

abduschen (trennb., hat -ge-) **I.** v/t. (Kind etc.) shower (off); (Schmutz etc.) spray (od. hose) down, rinse off; **II.** v/refl. have (od. take) a shower

abebben v/i. (trennb., ist -ge-) **1.** ebb away; **2.** fig. die down (od. away)

Abend m; -s, -e **1.** evening; **am** ⁓ in the evening; **am** ⁓ **des 2. Mai** on the evening of May 2nd; **gegen** ⁓ toward(s) (-the) evening; **heute** ⁓ this evening, tonight; **morgen** ⁓ tomorrow evening (od. night); **gestern** ⁓ yesterday evening, last night; **vom Morgen bis zum** ⁓ from morning till night; ⁓ **für** ⁓ every (single) evening, auch night after night; **es wird** ⁓ it's getting dark; **Guten/guten** ⁓**!** good evening!; **zu** ⁓ **essen** have supper (od. dinner), sup altm.; **sie hat heute i-n freien** ⁓ today she has her night out; **man soll den Tag nicht vor dem** ⁓ **loben** Sprichw. don't count your chickens before they're hatched; **2.** (⁓veranstaltung) literarischer, musikalischer soirée, evening; **bunter** ⁓ social (evening), variety show; **3.** (Vorabend) eve; **am** ⁓ **vor dem großen Ereignis** on the eve of the big event; **Heiliger** ⁓ Christmas

Eve; → **Tag¹** 4, **Dienstagabend** usw.

Abend|andacht f evening prayer(s Pl.), evensong; ⁓**anzug** m evening dress (od. suit); ⁓**blatt** n evening paper; ⁓**brot** n; nur Sg.; bes. nordd. supper, tea; ⁓**dämmerung** f twilight, dusk

abendelang I. Adj.: ⁓**e Gespräche** etc. discussions etc. that go (od. went) on for evenings on end; **II.** Adv. for evenings on end, night after night

Abendessen n dinner, supper

abendfüllend Adj. Film etc.: full-length ...

Abend|gebet n evening prayers; Kinderspr. bedtime prayers; ⁓**gesellschaft** f (evening) party; ⁓**gymnasium** n evening classes Pl., night school (leading to Abitur); ⁓**himmel** m (sky at) sunset; ⁓**kasse** f Theat. box office; **Karten an der** ⁓ **bekommen** get tickets on the night; ⁓**kleid** n evening dress (Am. gown); ⁓**kurs** m evening classes Pl., night school

Abendland n: **das** (christliche) ⁓ the Occident, the West; Western civilization; **abendländisch** Adj. Western, formell: occidental

abendlich I. Adj. evening ...; ⁓**e Kühle/Stille** the cool/quiet (od. peace) of the evening; **II.** Adv. in the evening(s)

Abend|mahl n kirchl. **1.** (Holy) Communion; **das** ⁓ **empfangen/reichen** receive/administer Holy Communion; **2. das Letzte** ⁓ the Lord's Supper; ⁓**mahlskelch** m kirchl. Communion chalice; ⁓**nachrichten** Pl. evening news Sg.; ⁓**programm** n: **das heutige** ⁓ tonight's (od. this evening's) program(me)s; ⁓**rot** n sunset; ⁓**röte** f lit. sunset (glow)

abends Adv. in the evening(s); ⁓ **um 7** at 7 in the evening, at 7 p.m.; ⁓ **spät** late in the evening, late at night: → **dienstagabends** usw.

Abend|schule f evening classes Pl., night school; ⁓**sonne** f evening (od. late afternoon) sun; ⁓**spaziergang** m evening walk; ⁓**stern** m evening star; ⁓**stunde** f: **in den** ⁓**n** in the evening(s); **zu später** ⁓ late at night, at a late hour; ⁓**toilette** f (Kleidung) evening dress; ⁓**veranstaltung** f evening event; ⁓**vorstellung** f evening performance; ⁓**wind** m evening breeze; ⁓**zeit** f evening (hours Pl.); ⁓**zeitung** f evening paper

Abenteuer n; -s, - adventure; (Liebesaffäre) affair; **auf** ⁓ **ausgehen** od. ⁓ **suchen** go out in search of adventure

Abenteuer|film m adventure film, Am. action movie; ⁓**geist** m adventurous spirit; ⁓**geschichte** f adventure story

abenteuerlich Adj. adventurous; fig. (riskant) risky; (absonderlich) odd, curious; Plan, Idee etc.: wild, fantastic; **Abenteuerlichkeit** f **1.** nur Sg. riskiness, hazardousness; **2.** mst Pl., Handlung, Erlebnis: bizarreness, curious adventure, odd happening

Abenteuerlust f love of (od. thirst for) adventure, venturesomeness; **abenteuerlustig** Adj. adventurous, venturesome

Abenteuer|roman m adventure story (od. novel); ⁓**spielplatz** m adventure playground; ⁓**urlaub** m adventure holiday (Am. vacation)

Abenteurer m; -s, -, ⁓**in** f; -, -nen adventurer; ⁓**leben** n adventurer's life, life of an adventurer; ⁓**natur** f **1.** adventurous spirit; **2.** Person: adventurer

aber Konj. **1.** but; **oder** ⁓ or alternative-

ly; **2.** verstärkend: ⁓, ⁓**!** now, now!; come, come!; ⁓ **ja!, ⁓ sicher!** (but) of course; ⁓ **nein!** oh no, versichernd: auch of course not; **ist das** ⁓ **schön!** (well) isn't that nice!; **das ist** ⁓ **nett von dir** that's really nice of you; drohend: **mach jetzt,** ⁓ **ein bisschen plötzlich!** umg. come on, get your skates on!

Aber n; -s, - od. umg. -s but; **ich will kein** ⁓ **hören!** I don't want to hear any excuses (od. buts); → **Wenn**

Aberglaube(n) m superstition; **abergläubisch** Adj. superstitious

aberhundert Zahlw., **Aberhundert** (n): ⁓ (+ Nom.) od. ⁓**e** (+ Gen. od. **von**) hundreds of, hundreds and (od. upon) hundreds of

aberkennen v/t. (unreg., trennb., selten auch untr., hat) mst Jur. **j-m etw.** ⁓ deny s.o. s.th., deprive s.o. of s.th.; **Aberkennung** f denial; Jur. deprivation, dispossession

abermalig... Adj. Versuche etc.: further, renewed; **abermals** Adv. (once) again, once more

Abermillionen Pl. millions of, millions and (od. upon) millions of

abernten v/t. (trennb., hat -ge-); (Getreide, Feld) harvest; (Obst) pick

abertausend Zahlw., **Abertausend** (n): ⁓ (+ Nom.) od. ⁓**e** (+ Gen. od. **von**) thousands of, thousands and (od. upon) thousands of

Aberwitz m madness, lunacy; **aberwitzig** Adj. insane, crazy

aberziehen v/t. (unreg., trennb., hat): **j-m etw.** ⁓ get s.o. out of the habit of doing etc. s.th., break s.o. of doing etc. s.th.

abessen (unreg., trennb., hat -ge-) **I.** v/t. **1.** (herunteressen) eat off; **2.** umg.: **den Teller** ⁓ lick the plate clean; **II.** v/i. eat up; **die Kinder hatten abgegessen** the children had finished their meal

Abessinien (n); -s; hist. Abysinnia

abfackeln v/t. (trennb., hat -ge-) **1.** (Erdgas) burn off; **2.** Sl. (Haus etc.) torch

abfahrbereit Adj. ready to leave (od. go) präd.

abfahren (unreg., trennb., -ge-) **I.** v/i. (ist) **1.** leave, set out od. off (**nach** for); **der Zug ist abgefahren** konkret: the train has left (od. gone); umg. fig. you, we etc. have missed the boat; **2. mit Skiern:** ski downhill; **3.** Film etc.: start, run; **4.** umg.: **auf** j-n od. etw. ⁓ be wild about, be really into; **da fahr ich echt drauf ab** that really does things to me; → **abgefahren** II 2; **II.** v/t. **1.** (hat) (beseitigen) cart off, remove; **2.** (hat/ist) (e-e Strecke) cover; do umg.; überwachend: patrol; **3.** (hat); (Reifen etc. abnutzen) wear down; → **abgefahren** II 1; **4.** (hat): **ihm wurde ein Bein abgefahren** he was run over and lost a leg

Abfahrt f **1.** departure; **2.** Ski: downhill run; (Hang) slope; **3.** (Autobahnausfahrt) exit

Abfahrts|lauf m Skisport: downhill (race); ⁓**läufer** m, ⁓**läuferin** f downhill racer, downhiller; ⁓**rennen** n downhill (racing)

Abfahrtszeit f von Zug etc.: departure time

Abfall m **1.** (Hausmüll) auch Pl. rubbish, bes. Am. garbage, trash; formell: refuse; (Müll als Masse) waste; radioaktiv: waste; **Abfälle auf der Straße:** litter; **2.** nur Sg.; (Hang) drop, decline, fall, (steep) slope; **3.** *nur Sg.*; *fig.* (*Abnahme*) decrease, deterioration; drop (*auch Etech.*); **4.** *nur Sg.*; *von e-r Partei*: defection; *von e-m Glauben*: *auch* falling away, apostasy

Abfall... *im Subst. siehe auch Müll...*

Abfall|aufbereitung *f* waste treatment; **~beseitigung** *f* waste disposal; **~eimer** *m* rubbish bin, *Am.* trashcan, garbage can

abfallen *v/i.* (*unreg., trennb., ist -ge-*) **1.** (*herunterfallen*) fall (*od.* drop) off; *alle Angst fiel von ihm ab fig.* his fears left him; **2.** *Gelände*: fall away, drop (*steil* steeply); **3.** *Zahlen, Leistung etc.*: fall off, drop; *Sport, Person*: fall behind; *gegen den Koreaner fiel er stark ab* he was no match for the Korean; **4.** *von e-r Partei*: break away, defect; *von e-m Glauben*: fall away; **5.** *umg.*: *und was fällt* (*dabei*) *für mich ab?* what's in it for me

abfallend I. *Part. Präs.* → *abfallen*; **II.** *Adj. Gelände*: sloping; *steil ~* steep, precipitous

Abfall|entsorgung *f* waste disposal; **~haufen** *m* rubbish (*Am.* trash) heap

abfällig I. *Adj. Bemerkung*: disparaging, deprecating, snide *umg.*; *Kritik*: adverse; *auch Meinung, Urteil*: unfavo(u)rable; **II.** *Adv.* disparagingly *etc.*; *~ sprechen über j-n auch* run s.o. down

Abfall|korb *m* wastepaper basket; **~kübel** *m* → *Abfalleimer*; **~produkt** *n* **1.** waste product; **2.** (*Nebenprodukt*) by-product, spin-off; **~stoffe** *Pl.* waste products; **~tonne** *f* dustbin, *Am.* trash can; **~vermeidung** *f* waste avoidance; **~verwertung** *f* waste recovery; **~wirtschaft** *f*; *nur Sg.* waste management

abfälschen *v/t.* (*trennb., hat -ge-*); (*Ball*) deflect

abfangen *v/t.* (*unreg., trennb., hat -ge-*) **1.** (*nicht durchlassen*) (*Ball, Brief, Spion etc.*) intercept; (*Person*) *auch* catch; (*j-n nach der Arbeit etc.*) waylay; **2.** (*abwehren*) (*Angriff, Feind*) intercept; (*Boxhieb etc.*) parry; **3.** (*bremsen*) (*Auto*) bring under control; *Flug. auch* pull out (of a dive); (*Aufprall, Fall*) absorb; (*Tendenz*) check; **4.** *Sport* (*einholen*) (*Läufer*) catch up with; **5.** *Tech.* (*Mauer etc.*) shore (*od.* prop) up, stay; *mit Pfosten*: timber; (*Flüssigkeit*) collect, recover; (*Stöße*) absorb, cushion; *Phys.* (*Atome*) capture

Abfang|jäger *m Mil.* interceptor; **~satellit** *m* hunter-killer satellite

abfärben *v/i.* (*trennb., hat -ge-*) **1.** lose colo(u)r; *dieses Hemd färbt ab* (*überträgt Farbe*) the dye comes off this shirt; *beim Waschen*: this shirt runs; **2.** *fig.*: *~ auf* (+ *Akk.*) rub off on

abfassen *v/t.* (*trennb., hat -ge-*); (*verfassen*) write (up); (*aufsetzen*) draft; *bes. amtlich*: draw up; (*formulieren*) word, formulate; **Abfassung** *f* **1.** *nur Sg.*; *Vorgang*: writing; (*Aufsetzen*) drafting; **2.** *Ergebnis*: report, letter, draft *etc.*

abfaulen *v/i.* (*trennb., ist -ge-*) rot off (*od.* away), disintegrate

abfedern (*trennb., hat -ge-*) **I.** *v/t.* **1.** *Tech.* spring(-load); (*Auto*) suspend; *gegen Stöße*: cushion; **2.** *fig.* (*Maßnahme*) moderate, mitigate; **II.** *v/i.* **1.** *Tech.* absorb the shock(s); *gut/schlecht abgefedert* (*Fahrzeug*) with a good/bad suspension; **2.** *Sport beim Absprung*: push off; *mit den Knien ~* bend at the knees

abfegen *v/t.* (*trennb., hat -ge-*);

(*Schnee, Schmutz etc.*) sweep off (*od.* away)

abfeiern *v/t.* (*trennb., hat -ge-*); *umg.*: *Überstunden ~* use up one's overtime, take time off in lieu

abfeilen *v/t.* (*trennb., hat -ge-*) (*sich die Fingernägel*) file one's (finger)nails; (*Unebenheiten*) file off (*von etw.* [from] s.th.); (*glätten*) file down

abfertigen *v/t.* (*trennb., hat -ge-*) **1.** (*Sendungen*) get ready for dispatch; *beim Zoll*: clear; (*Auftrag etc.*) deal with; (*Flugpassagier*) check in; (*Zug*) start; *wir wurden an der Grenze sehr schnell abgefertigt* we got through customs very quickly; **2.** *j-n kurz ~* give s.o. short shrift, snub s.o.; *j-n* (*schon*) *an der Tür ~* turn s.o. away without (even) letting him, her *etc.* in

Abfertigung *f* **1.** dispatch; *Zoll*: (*customs*) clearance; *von Kunden*: service; **2.** *fig.* rebuff; **3.** → *Abfertigungsschalter*

Abfertigungs|gebäude *n*, **~halle** *f Flug.* terminal; **~schalter** *m* dispatch counter; *Zoll* customs clearance; *Flug.* check-in desk (*od.* counter)

abfeuern *v/t.* (*trennb., hat -ge-*) **1.** (*Schuss*) fire; (*Rakete*) fire, let off, release; **2.** *Fußball*: *e-n Schuss aufs Tor ~* take a shot at goal, shoot

abfinden (*unreg., trennb., hat -ge-*) **I.** *v/t.* pay off; (*entschädigen*) indemnify, compensate; **II.** *v/refl.*: *sich mit j-m/etw. ~* come to terms with s.o./s.th.; *sich mit etw. ~ auch* resign o.s. to; *sich ~ müssen mit* have to face up to

Abfindung *f* settlement, arrangement; (*Entschädigung*) compensation; *von Angestellten*: severance (*od. Brit.* redundancy) pay, lump sum settlement, golden handshake *umg.*; *von Gläubigern*: paying-off

abfischen *v/t.* (*trennb., hat -ge-*); (*leer fischen*) overfish, fish dry

abflachen (*trennb., -ge-*) **I.** *v/t.* (*hat*) flatten (*od.* level) out; **II.** *v/i.* (*ist*) **1.** *Ufer etc.*: flatten (*od.* level) out, become flatter; **2.** *Unterhaltung etc.*: go flat, flag; **3.** *Zuwachsraten*: level off (*od.* out); **III.** *v/refl.* (*hat*) flatten (*od.* level) out; → *abgeflacht*

abflauen *v/i.* (*trennb., ist -ge-*) **1.** *Wind*: die down, drop, diminish; **2.** *fig. Begeisterung, Wut etc.*: ebb, subside; *Eifer, Interesse*: flag, wane, fall off; **3.** *Wirts. Preise*: sag; *Kurse*: ease off; *Geschäft*: slack(en) (off)

abfliegen (*unreg., trennb., -ge-*) **I.** *v/i.* (*ist*) *Vögel*: fly off; *Person*: fly; *Flugzeug*: take off; **II.** *v/t.* (*hat, bes. südd. und österr. auch ist*) (*Strecke*) patrol

abfließen *v/i.* (*unreg., trennb., ist -ge-*) **1.** run off; *Badewasser*: drain (*in* e-n See etc.): drain (*in* into); **2.** *fig. Gelder*: flow off, drain (*nach* into)

Abflug *m Flug.* takeoff; *auf dem Flugplan etc.*: departure

abflugbereit *Adj. Flug.* ready for take-off *präd.*

Abflug|hafen *m Flug.* departure airport; **~halle** *f* departure lounge; **~zeit** *f* departure (time)

Abfluss *m* **1.** *nur Sg.* (*Abfließen*) flowing off, draining off; **2.** (*~stelle, ~loch*) outlet, drain; *aus e-m See*: effluent; **3.** *nur Sg.*; *von Geld*: outflow; **~graben** *m* drain(age ditch); **~hahn** *m* drain cock; **~reiniger** *m* drain cleaner; **~rinne** *f* (*Strasse*) gutter; *auch* drainage channel (*od.* trench); **~rohr** *n* waste pipe; *außen*: drainpipe

Abfolge *f* succession; (*Reihenfolge*) sequence; *in rascher ~* in quick succession

abfordern *v/t.* (*trennb., hat -ge-*): *j-m etw. ~ auch fig.* demand s.th. of (*od.* from) s.o.; *j-m viel ~ fig.* make high demands on s.o.; *j-m alles ~* push s.o. to the limit

abformen *v/t.* (*trennb., hat -ge-*) mo(u)ld, model

abfotografieren *v/t.* (*trennb., hat*) take a photo of, photograph

Abfrage *f EDV* query, polling, interrogation; **abfragen** *v/t.* (*trennb., hat -ge-*) **1.** *j-n etw. ~* test (*Am.* quiz) s.o. on s.th.; → *auch abhören* 5; **2.** *EDV* query, poll, interrogate

abfressen *v/t.* (*trennb., hat -ge-*); *Tier*: (*Gras*) graze (down), crop; *völlig*: eat (*od.* strip) bare

abfrieren (*unreg., trennb., -ge-*) **I.** *v/i.* (*ist*) be frostbitten; *ihm sind drei Zehen abgefroren* he lost three toes through frostbite; **II.** *v/t.* (*hat*); *umg.*: *ich hab mir die Füße abgefroren* my feet were (absolutely) frozen

abfrottieren (*trennb., hat*) **I.** *v/t.* rub down; **II.** *v/refl.* rub o.s. down

Abfuhr *f*; *-, -en* **1.** (*Abtransport*) removal; **2.** *Sport und fig.*: defeat, beating; (*Abweisung*) rebuff, brush-off, snub; *j-m e-e ~ erteilen fig.* give s.o. the brush-off; *Sport* trounce s.o., thrash s.o., beat s.o. hollow *umg.*; *sich* (*Dat.*) *e-e ~ holen* be snubbed; *Sport* get a thrashing (*od.* get thrashed)

abführen (*trennb., hat -ge-*) **I.** *v/t.* **1.** lead off (*od.* away); (*Häftling*) take into custody; **2.** (*Wasser etc.*) drain off; (*Wärme*) carry off; (*Gas*) draw off; **3.** (*Geldbetrag, Steuer*) pay over (*an* to); **II.** *v/i.* **1.** *Med.* act as a laxative, have a purgative effect; **2.** (*wegführen*) lead away (*von* from); *das führt vom Thema ab* that takes me, us *etc.* off (*od.* away from) the subject; **abführend I.** *Part. Präs.* → *abführen*; **II.** *Adj. Med.* laxative; *der Tee wirkt ~* this tea has a laxative effect

Abführ|mittel *n Med.* laxative; **~tee** *m Med.* (herbal) laxative tea

Abfüll|anlage *f* bottling plant; **~datum** *n* bottling date

abfüllen *v/t.* (*trennb., hat -ge-*) **1.** fill; (*abziehen*) (*Wein*) rack, draw off (*in* into); *in Flaschen*: bottle; *in Tüten*: bag; **2.** *umg. pej.* (*betrunken machen*) get (s.o.) sloshed (*od.* drunk *allg.*)

Abfüllung *f* filling, bottling; *Wein etc.* *aus eigener ~* bottled by the grower, bottled on site

abfüttern *v/t.* (*trennb., hat -ge-*) **1.** (*Vieh, auch umg. Gäste etc.*) feed; **2.** (*Kleidungsstück*) line

Abgabe *f* **1.** (*Ablieferung*) delivery; (*Übergabe, auch fig.*) handing over; (*Einreichung*) handing in; **2.** (*Verkauf*) sale; **3.** *Sport* (*Pass*) pass; (*Punktverlust*) drop; *e-s Schusses*: firing; **4.** *von Strahlungen etc.*: emission; *von Energie*: release; **5.** *e-r Erklärung*: giving, making; *e-s Urteils*: passing, pronouncement; (*Stimmabgabe*) casting; **6.** (*Tribut*) tribute; (*bes. Zoll*) duty; (*Steuer*) tax; → *Kommunalabgaben*, *Sozialabgaben*

abgabenfrei *Adj.* (*zollfrei*) duty-free; (*steuerfrei*) tax-exempt

Abgabenlast *f* tax burden, burden of deductions for tax and social welfare

abgabenpflichtig *Adj. Zoll*: dutiable; *Steuern*: taxable

Abgabetermin *m* deadline; *Ausschrei-*

bung: *auch* closing date

Abgang *m* **1.** *e-r Person, auch fig.*: departure; *auch Theat.* exit; *von e-r Stellung*: retirement; *von der Schule etc.*: leaving, finishing, *Am. auch* graduation; (*Abfahrt*) departure; *Naut.* sailing; **sich e-n guten** ~ **verschaffen** *fig.* make a graceful exit; **mach e-n** ~**!** *umg.* go away!, bugger (*od.* piss) off! *Sl.*; **2.** *vom Turngerät*: dismount; **3.** *Wirts.* (*Warenversand*) dispatch; *Bankbilanz*: items *Pl.* disposed of; → *Absatz* 3; **4.** *Med.* discharge; *e-s Steins*: passing; (*Fehlgeburt*) miscarriage; **5.** (*Tod*) decease, demise

abgängig *Adj. österr.* (*vermisst*) missing

Abgangszeugnis *n* school-leaving certificate, *Am.* diploma

Abgas *n* waste gas; *Mot.* exhaust fumes *Pl.*

abgasarm *Adj. Mot.* low-emission, clean *umg.*

Abgasentgiftung *f* waste gas cleaning

abgasfrei *Adj.* emission-free

Abgas|katalysator *m Mot.* catalytic converter, catalyst; ~**norm** *f* (exhaust) emission standard; ~**sonderuntersuchung** *f* (*abgek. ASU*), ~**untersuchung** *f* (*abgek. AU*) (exhaust) emission test; ~**turbine** *f* exhaust(-gas) turbine; ~**werte** *Pl.* exhaust pollution standards

abgaunern *v/t.* (*trennb., hat -ge-*); *umg.*: *j-m etw.* ~ swindle (*od.* con *od.* trick) s.o. out of s.th.

abgearbeitet **I.** *P.P.* → *abarbeiten*; **II.** *Adj.* **1.** *Person*: exhausted, worn-out ..., *präd.* worn out; run-down; **2.** *Hände*: work-worn; *auch* call(o)used

abgeben (*unreg., trennb., hat -ge-*) **I.** *v/t.* **1.** (*einreichen*) hand in; (*Sendung etc.*) deliver; (*Fahrkarte*) surrender; hand over *umg.*; (*Gepäck*) hand in; *Flug.* check in; ~ **bei** (*Gepäck*) leave with; **2.** (*verschenken*) give away; (*verkaufen*) sell; *in der Zeitung*: **kostenlos/günstig abzugeben** available (for) free / at a bargain price; **3.** *j-m etw.* ~ give s.o. s.th. (**von** of); *auch* share s.th. with s.o.; **4.** (*übergeben*) (*Vorsitz, Macht etc.*) hand over; (*Geschäft etc.*) give up, pass on (**an** to); **5.** (*Strahlung, Wärme etc.*) radiate, emit; **6.** (*Schuss*) *auch Sport* fire; **7.** *Sport* (*Ball*) pass; (*Punkte etc.*) concede, lose; **8.** (*aussprechen*) (*e-e Erklärung etc.*) make ; (*ein Urteil*) pass; **9.** **e-e Stimme** ~ cast a vote; **abgegebene Stimmen** votes cast; **10.** *umg.* (*darstellen*) make; **e-n guten Polizisten** ~ make a good policeman; **II.** *v/refl.*: **sich mit etw./j-m** ~ concern o.s. with s.th./s.o.; **mit ihm gebe ich mich nicht ab** I don't associate (*od.* have anything to do) with him; **III.** *v/i.* **1.** share (things); **2.** *Sport* pass the ball

abgebrannt **I.** *P.P.* → *abbrennen*; **II.** *Adj. umg. fig.* (*pleite*) broke, *Brit. auch* skint; **völlig** ~ stony broke, *Am.* flat broke, busted

abgebrüht **I.** *P.P.* → *abbrühen*; **II.** *Adj. fig.* hard-boiled, tough; (*unempfindlich*) hardened, callous; **Abgebrühtheit** *f; nur Sg.* toughness, callousness

abgedreht **I.** *P.P.* → *abdrehen*; **II.** *Adj.* **1.** *Film*: wrapped up; **2.** *Sl.* (*verrückt*) crazy, wild, spaced out *umg.*

abgedroschen *Adj. umg.* hackneyed, trite, banal *allg.*, corny *umg.*; **Abgedroschenheit** *f* triteness, banality

abgefahren **I.** *P.P.* → *abfahren*;

II. *Adj.* **1.** *Reifen*: worn; **2.** *Jugendspr.* (*super*) excellent, wicked *umg.*

abgefeimt *Adj.* crafty, cunning, wily

abgeflacht **I.** *P.P.* → *abflachen*; **II.** *Adj. Berg, Schädel*: flattened

abgefuckt ['apgəfakt] *Adj. Jugendspr. Sl.* fucked up *vulg.*, wrecked *umg.*

abgegessen *P.P.* → *abessen*

abgegriffen **I.** *P.P.* → *abgreifen*; **II.** *Adj.* (*well-*)worn; *Buch*: well-thumbed; *fig.* → *abgedroschen*

abgehackt **I.** *P.P.* → *abhacken*; **II.** *Adj. fig. Redeweise*: disjointed, choppy

abgehangen *Adj. Fleisch, bes. Wildbret*: seasoned, *Brit. auch* well-hung

abgehängt **I.** *P.P.* → *abhängen*[1], *abhängen*[2]; **II.** *Adj.*: ~**e Decke** suspended ceiling

abgehärmt *Adj. Gesicht*: drawn, care-worn, haggard

abgehärtet **I.** *P.P.* → *abhärten*; **II.** *Adj. körperlich*: tough, hardy; *psychisch*: hardened (**gegen** against), inured (to)

abgehen (*unreg., trennb., -ge-*) **I.** *v/i.* (*ist*) **1.** *Eisenb., Flug.* leave; *Schiff: auch* sail; *Post*: go; **das Schreiben geht mit der nächsten Post ab** the letter will go out with the next post; **und ab geht die Post!** *umg. fig.* here we go!, get a move on!; **da geht was ab!** *Jugendspr.* (*ist viel los*) it's a really cool (*od.* wild) place; **2.** *von der Bühne*: make one's exit (*auch fig.*); *Anweisung*: **... geht** (*gehen*) **ab** exit (exeunt) ...; *von der Schule*: leave *school*; *mit Abschluss Am. auch*: graduate; **3.** (*sich lösen*) *Knopf etc.*: come off; *Farbe auch*: come out (**von etw.** of s.th.); *Schuss*: go off, be fired; **4.** *Sport, vom Barren, Reck etc.*: jump down; **5.** (*abzweigen*) branch off (**nach** towards); (*sich gabeln*) *auch* fork; **6.** *Med.* (*abgesondert werden*) *Fötus*: be aborted; *Stein*: pass; *Würmer*: be discharged; **7.** (*abgezogen werden*) *von e-m Betrag etc.*: be deducted, be taken off (**von etw.** from s.th.); **8.** *umg.* (*fehlen*): **er geht mir sehr ab** I miss him a lot; **mir geht jegliches Verständnis dafür ab** I simply fail to understand that; **9.** (*abweichen*): **von e-m Vorhaben** ~ give up a plan; **davon gehe ich nicht ab** nothing's going to change my mind about that; **10.** (*verlaufen*) go; **das wird nicht ohne Probleme** ~ that won't be straightforward (*od.* so easy); *auch umg.* it won't be a bed of roses; **es ging alles gut ab** everything went (*od.* passed off) well *od.* smoothly; **II.** *v/t.* (*hat, bes. südd., österr., schw. auch ist*) **1.** (*abmessen*) pace out; **2.** (*überwachen*) patrol; **3.** *Blähungen* ~ *lassen* break wind

abgehetzt **I.** *P.P.* → *abhetzen*; **II.** *Adj.* **1.** (*erschöpft*) exhausted; *umg.* shattered, wiped out *präd.*; **2.** (*sehr in Eile*) rushed off one's feet *präd.*; **3.** (*atemlos*) breathless, out of breath *präd.*

abgekämpft *Adj.* worn-out, exhausted

abgekapselt **I.** *P.P.* → *abkapseln*; **II.** *Adj. Person*: cut off; *Staat*: cocooned

abgekartet **I.** *P.P.* → *abkarten*; **II.** *Adj.*: ~**es Spiel** *umg.* put-up job *nur Sg.*

abgeklärt **I.** *P.P.* → *abklären*; **II.** *Adj. fig.* mellow, serene; **Abgeklärtheit** *f; nur Sg.* serenity, tranquil(l)ity

abgelagert **I.** *P.P.* → *ablagern*; **II.** *Adj. Wein*: matured, aged; *Holz*: seasoned; *Tabak*: well-seasoned

abgelatscht *Adj. umg. pej., Schuhe*:

---

worn-out, scuffed

abgelegen **I.** *P.P.* → *abliegen*; **II.** *Adj. präd.* off the beaten track; (*weit entlegen*) remote, faraway ..., *präd.* far away; (*abgeschieden*) secluded, isolated, out-of-the-way; **Abgelegenheit** *f; nur Sg.* remoteness; (*Abgeschiedenheit*) isolation

abgelegt **I.** *P.P.* → *ablegen*; **II.** *Adj.*: ~**e Kleider** cast(-)offs

abgelten *v/t.* (*Schuld*) pay off, settle; (*Verlust*) compensate for; **Abgeltung** *f* payment, compensation

abgemacht *P.P.* → *abmachen*

abgemagert *P.P.* → *abmagern*

abgemessen *P.P.* → *abmessen*

abgeneigt *Adj.*: ~ **sein, etw. zu tun** be loath (*od.* disinclined) to do s.th.; *stärker*: be reluctant (*od.* unwilling) to do s.th.; **e-r Sache** ~ **sein** be averse to s.th., dislike s.th.

abgenutzt, abgenützt **I.** *P.P.* → *abnutzen*, *abnützen*; **II.** *Adj.* worn, a bit frayed around the edges *umg.*

Abgeordnete *m, f; -n, -n; Pol.* (*Delegierter*) delegate, representative; *im Parlament*: member of parliament; *des britischen Unterhauses*: Member of Parliament (*Abk.* MP); *des amerikanischen Repräsentantenhauses*: Representative, Congressman (*f* Congresswoman); **der Herr / die Frau** ~ the Hono(u)rable Member; **Abgeordnetenhaus** *n* parliament; *in GB*: House of Commons; *in den USA*: House of Representatives

abgepackt **I.** *P.P.* → *abpacken*; **II.** *Adj. Lebensmittel*: prepacked, packaged

abgeraten *v/i.* (*unreg., trennb., ist*): **vom Weg** ~ lose one's way, stray (away)

abgerissen **I.** *P.P.* → *abreißen*; **II.** *Adj.* **1.** (*zerlumpt*) ragged, tattered, shabby; *Person*: down-at-(the-)heel; **2.** *fig. Sprache, Gedanken etc.*: disjointed, incoherent

abgerundet **I.** *P.P.* → *abrunden*; **II.** *Adj.* **1.** *Kanten, Ecken etc.*: rounded; **2.** *Erzählung*: well-rounded; **3.** *Zahl*: round

Abgesandte *m, f* envoy, emissary; → *Gesandte*

Abgesang *m* **1.** *Mus.* abgesang; **2.** *Lit. fig.* (*letztes Werk*) swansong, farewell

abgeschabt **I.** *P.P.* → *abschaben*; **II.** *Adj.* (*abgewetzt*) shabby, worn; *Kleidung*: threadbare

abgeschieden **I.** *P.P.* → *abscheiden*; **II.** *Adj.* solitary, secluded; **III.** *Adv.*: ~ *leben* live in seclusion (*od.* isolation); **Abgeschiedenheit** *f; nur Sg.* seclusion

abgeschlafft **I.** *P.P.* → *abschlaffen*; **II.** *Adj. umg.* shattered, whacked, wiped out; **ein** ~**er Typ** a real drip

abgeschlagen **I.** *P.P.* → *abschlagen*; **II.** *Adj.* **1.** *Sport* far behind, defeated, out of the running; **2.** (*erschöpft*) exhausted, shattered

abgeschlossen **I.** *P.P.* → *abschließen*; **II.** *Adj.* **1.** *Wohnung*: self-contained; **2.** (*beendet*) completed; ~**es Studium** degree; **e-e** ~**e Ausbildung haben** be fully qualified (for a job), **als Sekretärin** etc.: be a (fully) qualified secretary etc.; **Abgeschlossenheit** *f; nur Sg.* seclusion, isolation

abgeschmackt *Adj. fig.* (*geschmacklos*) in bad (*od.* poor) taste, tasteless; (*taktlos*) tactless; (*albern*) fatuous, corny *umg.*; **Abgeschmacktheit** *f* **1.** *nur Sg.*; *Zustand*: bad taste; **2.** *Äuße-*

rung: platitude

abgeschnitten *P.P.* → *abschneiden*

abgeschrägt I. *P. P.* → *abschrägen*; II. *Adj. Brett, Wand etc.*: bevel(l)ed

abgesehen I. *P.P.* → *absehen*; II. *Adv.*: ~ *von* apart (*bes. Am.* aside) from, excepting; ~ *davon, dass er krank ist* apart (*Am.* aside) from his being ill, apart (*Am.* aside) from the fact that he's ill

abgesondert *P.P.* → *absondern*

abgespannt I. *P.P.* → *abspannen*; II. *Adj. fig.* (*erschöpft*) exhausted, worn-out ..., *präd.* worn out; *Gesicht*: drawn; **Abgespanntheit** *f*; *nur Sg.* exhaustion, fatigue

abgestanden I. *P.P.* → *abstehen*; II. *Adj. Luft*: stale (*auch fig.*); *Bier etc.*: flat

abgestorben I. *P.P.* → *absterben*; II. *Adj. Glieder*: numb; *Nerv, Gewebe, Pflanze etc.*: dead

abgestumpft I. *P.P.* → *abstumpfen*; II. *Adj. Person*: insensitive (*gegen* to), hardened; **Abgestumpftheit** *f*; *nur Sg.* apathy, indifference (*gegen* towards)

abgetakelt I. *P.P.* → *abtakeln*; II. *Adj. fig. pej.* down-at-(the-)heel

abgetan *P.P.* → *abtun*

abgetragen I. *P.P.* → *abtragen*; II. *Adj. Kleider*: worn, *stärker*: shabby, threadbare; *Schuhe*: worn-down ..., *präd.* worn down

abgetreten I. *P.P.* → *abtreten*; II. *Adj. Schuhe*: worn out (*od.* down)

abgewetzt I. *P.P.* → *abwetzen*; II. *Adj. Hose etc.*: well-worn; *Sofa etc.*: battered

abgewinnen *v/t.* (*unreg., trennb., hat -ge-*) **1.** (*Geld etc.*) *j-m etw.* ~ win s.th. from s.o.; **2.** (*ein Lächeln etc.*) get s.th. out of s.o.; *dem Meer Land* ~ reclaim land from the sea; **3.** *e-r Sache Geschmack* ~ acquire a taste for s.th.; *ich kann dem Buch nichts* ~ I can't get anything out of the book

abgewirtschaftet I. *P.P.* → *abwirtschaften*; II. *Adj. Unternehmen, Land etc.*: run-down

abgewogen I. *P.P.* → *abwägen, abwiegen*; II. *Adj.* (*Urteil, Worte*) balanced, (carefully) considered; **Abgewogenheit** *f*; *nur Sg.* balance, equilibrium

abgewöhnen *v/t.* (*trennb., hat -ge-*): *j-m etw.* ~ break (*od.* cure) s.o. of s.th.; *sich* (*Dat.*) *das Rauchen etc.* ~ give up smoking *etc.*; *das muss er sich langsam* ~ it's time he gave that up; *zum Abgewöhnen sein umg. Film, Spiel etc.*: be enough to make you weep, be enough to put anyone off; *Getränk, Essen*: be awful (*od.* diabolical); *Person*: be a (real) creep

abgewohnt I. *P.P.* → *abwohnen*; II. *Adj. Haus, Wohnung*: shabby; *Möbel*: worn-out

abgewrackt I. *P.P.* → *abwracken*; II. *Adj. umg. fig.* shattered, *Am.* wiped out

abgezehrt *P.P.* → *abzehren*

abgezirkelt *Adj. Bewegungen*: precise, calculated; → *abzirkeln*

abgießen *v/t.* (*unreg., trennb., hat -ge-*) **1.** (*Flüssigkeit*) pour away; (*Kartoffeln, Nudeln*) strain; **2.** (*Metall, Form*) cast

Abglanz *m*; *nur Sg.* **1.** reflection; **2.** *fig.*: *ein schwacher* ~ a pale reflection (+ *Gen.* of)

Abgleich *m*; *-(e)s, -e* → **Abgleichung**; **abgleichen** *v/t.* (*unreg., trennb., hat -ge-*) **1.** *Tech.* (*justieren*) adjust; (*Brücke*) balance; (*Empfänger*) align;

2. (*Einträge*) compare (*miteinander* with each other); **Abgleichung** *f Tech., Etech.* adjustment, balance, alignment

abgleiten *v/i.* (*unreg., trennb., ist -ge-*) **1.** slip (off) (*von etw.* off s.th.); *Kritik etc. gleitet von ihm ab fig.* he's deaf to criticism *etc.*; **2.** (*schlechter werden*) drop, slip; *Wirts. Kurse*: fall; **3.** *fig.* (*abschweifen*) lapse (*in* into)

Abgott *m* idol; *j-n zu s-m* ~ *machen* idolize, make an idol of; **abgöttisch** I. *Adj.* idolatrous; II. *Adv. fig.*: ~ *lieben* idolize, adore; (*bes. Kind, Ehepartner*) *auch* dote on

abgraben *v/t.* (*unreg., trennb., hat -ge-*) dig away; level; (*Wasserlauf*) drain (*od.* draw) off; *j-m das Wasser* ~ *fig.* pull the rug from under s.o.'s feet, pull the plug on s.o. *umg.*

abgrasen *v/t.* (*trennb., hat -ge-*) **1.** (*Wiese, Gras*) graze; **2.** *fig.* scour, comb

abgreifen *v/t.* (*unreg., trennb., hat -ge-*) (*Körperstelle*) feel; (*Entfernung*) measure out (with one's hands); → *abgegriffen*

abgrenzbar *Adj. räumlich*: separable, divisible; *zeitlich*: estimable; *begrifflich*: definable; *schwer* ~ difficult to define (*od.* differentiate); **abgrenzen** (*trennb., hat -ge-*) I. *v/t.* **1.** (*trennen*) divide; (*Grundstück*) mark off; (*Territorium*) demarcate; **2.** *fig.* (*unterscheiden*) differentiate; (*Begriffe*) define; *gegeneinander* ~ draw a clear dividing line between; II. *v/refl. fig.*: *sich* ~ *von Person*: distance (*od.* dissociate) o.s. from; **Abgrenzung** *f nur Sg.* **1.** fencing (*od.* roping) off; (*Umzäunung*) fencing; **2.** *fig.* demarcation; *begriffliche*: definition, delimitation; **3.** (*Distanzierung*) dissociation, separation (*gegen-* [*über*] from)

Abgrund *m* **1.** abyss, chasm; (*steiler* ~) precipice; *die Abgründe der menschlichen Seele fig.* the unplumbed depths of the human soul; **2.** *nur Sg.*; *fig.* (*Ruin*) downfall, ruin; *am Rande des* ~*s stehen* be on the brink of ruin (*od.* disaster), *auch* be staring disaster in the face; **3.** *fig.* (*Kluft*) gulf, chasm, great divide; *zwischen ihnen tun sich Abgründe auf* there is a growing divide between them

abgründig *Adj. bes. fig.* (*rätselhaft*) mysterious; *Geheimnis*: unfathomable; *Humor etc.*: cryptic

abgrundtief I. *Adj.bes. fig. Geheimnis*: unfathomable; *Hass etc.*: all-consuming; II. *Adv.*: **1.** ~ *hassen* hate with every fib|re (*Am.* -er) of one's being; **2.** *etc.* unbelievably ugly *etc.*, ugly as hell *umg.*

abgucken *vt/i.* (*trennb., hat -ge-*); *umg.* copy *allg.*; *j-m etw. od. etw. bei od. von j-m* ~ learn (*unerlaubt*: copy) s.th. from s.o. *allg.*

Abguss *m* **1.** cast, mo(u)ld; **2.** *nur Sg.*; *Vorgang*: casting

abhaben *v/t.* (*unreg., trennb., hat -ge-*); *umg.* **1.** *willst du etwas* (*davon*) ~? do you want some (of it)?; **2.** (*abgemacht haben*) have got (*bes. Am.* gotten) off (*od.* taken off)

abhacken *v/t.* (*trennb., hat -ge-*) chop (*od.* hack) off (*von etw.* (from) s.th.); → *abgehackt*

abhaken *v/t.* (*trennb., hat -ge-*) **1.** (*Geschriebenes*) tick (*Am.* check) off; *fig.* cross off one's list; (*Sehenswürdigkeiten etc.*) *auch umg. pej.* knock off; *fig.* forget; **2.** (*losmachen*) unhook

abhalten *v/t.* (*unreg., trennb., hat -ge-*)

1. keep away (*von* from), keep off (*von etw.* s.th.); (*draußen halten*) keep out; (*abwehren*) ward off; *davon* ~ *zu* (+ *Inf.*) keep (*od.* prevent, stop) from (+ *Ger.*); (*abbringen*) deter from (+ *Ger.*); **2.** (*Prüfung, Versammlung, Parteitag etc.*) hold; (*Lehrstunde, Vorlesung*) give; *abgehalten werden* be held, take place; **3.** (*Kind*) hold out (*od.* over the pot)

abhandeln *v/t.* (*trennb., hat -ge-*) **1.** *j-m etw.* ~ *durch Feilschen*: get s.o. to sell one s.th. cheaply, strike a deal with s.o.; **2.** (*herunterhandeln*) *etwas vom Preis* ~ beat (*od.* knock) the price down, haggle; **3.** (*erörtern*) deal with, treat, discuss

abhanden *Adv.*: ~ *kommen* go astray, get lost, be mislaid; *mir sind m-e Schlüssel* ~ *gekommen* I've lost my keys

Abhandlung *f* treatise, paper (*über* on); (*kurze* ~) essay; (*Artikel*) article

Abhang *m* slope, decline; hillside; *steiler/sanfter* ~ steep/gentle slope

abhängen¹ *v/i.* (*unreg., trennb., ist -ge-*); *fig.* ~ *von* depend on; *auch finanziell etc.*: be dependent on, rely on; *es hängt davon ab, ob* it depends (on) whether; *das hängt von dir ab auch* it's up to you

abhängen² *v/t.* (*trennb., hat -ge-*) **1.** (*Bild, Wäsche*) take down; **2.** (*Anhänger, Waggon*) uncouple, unhitch; **3.** *umg. fig.* (*Konkurrenten*) shake off, leave *s.o.* trailing; (*Verfolger*) shake off, give *s.o.* the slip; → *abgehängt* II

abhängig *Adj.* **1.** dependent (*von* [up]on); ~ *sein von* → *abhängen¹*; *voneinander* ~ interdependent; *etw. von etw.* ~ *machen* make s.th. conditional (up)on s.th.; **2.** *Ling.*: ~*er Satz* subordinate (*od.* dependent) clause; **3.** *von Drogen*: dependent (*von* on), addicted (*von* to); **4.** *Pol. Gebiet*: dependent, satellite

Abhängige *m, f*; *-n, -n* **1.** dependent; **2.** *von Drogen*: addict, dependent

Abhängigkeit *f* **1.** dependence, *auch* reliance (*von* [up]on); *gegenseitige* ~ interdependence, mutual dependence; **2.** *von Drogen etc.*: *auch* addiction (*von* to); **3.** *Ling.* subordination

Abhängigkeitsverhältnis *n* dependent relationship (*zu* to); *gegenseitiges*: interdependence, mutual dependence, codependence

abhärten (*trennb., hat -ge-*) I. *vt/i.* harden, toughen (*gegen* against); II. *v/refl.* become hardened (*gegen* against); *bes. gesundheitlich*: build up one's resistance (to), toughen o.s. up *umg.*; → *abgehärtet*; **Abhärtung** *f*; *nur Sg.* hardening; toughening up *umg.*

abhauen¹ *v/i.* (*unreg., trennb., ist -ge-*); *umg.* (*weggehen*) clear off, decamp; (*türmen*) do a bunk, scarper, *Am.* vamoose, scamper; *hau ab!* push off!, get lost!, beat it!, piss off! *Sl.*, sod off! *Sl.*; *von zu Hause* ~ run away from home *allg.*

abhauen² *v/t.* (*unreg., trennb., hat -ge-*) chop (*od.* cut *od.* knock) off, chop (*od.* cut *od.* knock) down

abhäuten *v/t.* (*trennb., hat -ge-*) skin

abheben (*trennb., -ge-*) I. *v/t.* (*hat*) **1.** (*Deckel, Hörer*) lift (off), take off; (*Karte*) cut; **2.** (*Masche*) slip; **3.** (*Geld*) draw (*von* from); **4.** (*unterstreichen*) set apart (*von* from); II. *v/i.* **1.** (*ist*) *Flug.* take off; **2.** (*hat*) *Telefon*: answer the phone; **3.** (*hat*); *beim Karten-*

spiel: cut the cards; **4.** (*hat*) (*hinweisen*): **~** *auf etw. Jur. auch fig.* point to (*od.* emphasize) s.th.; **III.** *v/refl.* (*hat*): **sich ~ von** contrast with, stand out from; **sich gegen etw. ~** stand out (*od.* be set off) against s.th.; **Abhebung** *f von Geld*: withdrawal

abheften *v/t.* (*trennb., hat -ge-*) **1.** (*Papiere*) file (away); **2.** (*Saum, Falte*) tack, baste

abheilen *v/i.* (*trennb., ist -ge-*) heal (up)

abhelfen *v/i.* (*unreg., trennb., hat -ge-*) remedy; (*e-r Beschwerde, e-m Übel*) redress; (*e-m Mangel*) supply, meet; **dem ist leicht abzuhelfen** that's no problem (at all)

abhetzen (*trennb., hat -ge-*) **I.** *v/refl.* wear (*od.* tire) o.s. out; **II.** *v/t.* (*Hund, Pferd*) tire out, exhaust; → **abgehetzt** II

Abhilfe *f; nur Sg.* remedy; **~ schaffen** put things right

abhobeln *v/t.* (*trennb., hat -ge-*); (*Brett*) plane; (*Unebenheiten*) plane off (*od.* down); (*Parkett*) dress

abhold *Adj. geh.*: **j-m/etw. ~ sein** be averse to s.o./s.th.

Abholdienst *m* pickup service

abholen *v/t.* (*trennb., hat -ge-*) **1.** fetch; (*j-n, Brief etc.*) *auch* call for, come for, pick up, collect; **j-n vom Bahnhof ~** meet s.o. at the station; **~ lassen** send for; **2.** *umg. euph.* (*verhaften*) take away, *bes. Brit.* nick

Abhol|markt *m* cash-and-carry (store); **~preis** *m* → **Mitnahmepreis**

Abholung *f* collection

abholzen *v/t.* (*trennb., hat -ge-*); (*Bäume*) cut down; (*Gebiet*) clear (of trees), *mst pass.* deforest; **Abholzung** *f* deforestation; *e-s Walds*: clearing, chopping down

Abhör|affäre *f* bugging affair (*od.* scandal); **~anlage** *f* bugging system (*od.* device)

abhorchen *v/t.* (*trennb., hat -ge-*); *Med.* sound; *fachspr.* auscultate; **j-m die Brust ~** listen to s.o.'s chest

abhören *v/t.* (*trennb., hat -ge-*) **1.** *Med.* → **abhorchen**; **2.** (*Funksprüche*) intercept; ([*Telefon*]*Gespräch*) bug, listen in on; **3.** (*Tonband etc.*) listen to, play back; **4.** (*überwachen*) monitor; **5.** *Päd.* **j-m ein Gedicht** *etc.* **~** listen to s.o. recite a poem *etc.*; → *auch* **abfragen** 1

Abhör|gerät *n* (*Wanze*) bugging device; (*Überwachungsgerät*) monitor; **~sicher** *Adj.* bug-proof

Abhub *m; nur Sg. bei Erdarbeiten*: removed (*od.* excavated) earth

abhungern (*trennb., hat -ge-*) **I.** *v/refl.* starve (o.s.); **II.** *v/t.*: **sich** (*Dat.*) **etw. ~** scrimp and save to be able to afford s.th.; **sich** (*Dat.*) **zehn Pfund ~** starve off ten pounds, lose ten pounds on a starvation (*od.* crash) diet

abhusten (*trennb., hat -ge-*) **I.** *v/t.* cough up, bring up; **II.** *v/i.* clear one's lungs

Abi *n; -s, -s; umg. Abk.* → **Abitur**

abirren *v/i.* (*trennb., ist -ge-*) stray; **vom Weg ~** lose one's way

abisolieren *v/t.* (*trennb., hat*); *Etech.* strip; **Abisolierzange** *f*: (*e-e ~* a pair of) wire strippers *Pl.*

Abitur *n; -s, -e Qualifikation*: university entry qualification; *Prüfung*: school-leaving exam; *Brit. etwa* A-levels; *Zeugnis*: school-leaving certificate, *Am.* high-school diploma; **das ~ machen** (*die Prüfung machen*) take one's

school-leaving exam, *Brit.* take one's A-levels, *Am.* graduate from high school; *weitS.* get one's school-leaving certificate (*od. Am.* high-school diploma), *Brit.* be taking one's A levels; **Abiturfeier** *f* school-leaving ceremony, *Am.* high-school graduation; school-leavers'(*Am.* graduation) party, ball

Abiturient *m; -en, -en,* **~in** *f; -, -nen vor der Prüfung*: candidate for the school-leaving exam, *Am.* graduating senior, *Brit. etwa* sixth-former; *nach der Prüfung*: school-leaver with the(*od.* who has done the) 'Abitur', *Am. etwa* high-school graduate

Abitur|klasse *f* class of pupils in last year at grammar or high school; *Brit. etwa*: upper sixth (form), *Am.* senior (*od.* graduating) class; **~zeugnis** *n* school-leaving certificate, *Brit. etwa* A-levels, *Am.* high-school diploma

abjagen *v/t.* (*trennb., hat -ge-*): **j-m etw. ~** get s.th. off s.o.; **j-m die Kunden ~** steal s.o.'s customers

Abk. *Abk.* (**Abkürzung**) abbr., abbrev.

abkämmen *v/t.* (*trennb., hat -ge-*) **1.** (*Wolle*) comb; **2.** *fig.* (*absuchen*) comb, scour (**nach** for)

abkanzeln *v/t.* (*trennb., hat -ge-*) *umg.*: **j-n ~** give s.o. a dressing-down *allg.* (*od. umg.* telling-off *od. Brit. Sl.* bollocking)

abkapseln *v/refl.* (*trennb., hat -ge-*) cut o.s. off; *Med. Bazillus etc*: encapsulate; → **abgekapselt**; **Abkapselung** *f; nur Sg.* isolation; *Med.* encapsulation

abkarten *v/t.* (*trennb., hat -ge-*) fix, rig; **abgekartetes Spiel** *umg.* put-up job *nur Sg.*

abkassieren (*trennb., hat*) **I.** *v/i.* **1. bei j-m ~** give s.o. their bill, cash up; **2.** *fig.* (*sich bereichern*) cash in (**bei** on); **II.** *v/t.*: **j-n ~** (*Fahrgast*) take s.o.'s fare

abkauen *v/t.* (*trennb., hat -ge-*) chew off; **sich** (*Dat.*) **die Fingernägel ~** bite one's nails

abkaufen *v/t.* (*trennb., hat -ge-*): **j-m etw. ~** buy s.th. from s.o.; **das kauf ich dir nicht ab!** *umg. fig.* tell me another; you don't expect me to believe that, do you?; **diese Geschichte kauft uns keiner ab** *umg.* nobody will believe that story (in a million years)

Abkehr *f; -, kein Pl.* turning away (**von** from); *fig. auch* break (**von** with); renunciation (**von** of); **abkehren** (*trennb., hat -ge-*) **I.** *v/t.* **1.** → **abfegen**; **2.** (*Augen etc.*) turn away, avert (**von** from); **II.** *v/refl.* **1.** turn away (**von** from); **2.** *fig.* turn one's back on; **sich von e-r Politik etc. ~** abandon, give up

abketten (*trennb., hat -ge-*) **I.** *v/t.* (*Hund etc.*) unchain; **II.** *vt/i. beim Stricken*: cast off

abkippen (*trennb., -ge-*) **I.** *v/t.* (*hat*) (*Kies, Müll*) tip (out), dump; **II.** *v/i.* (*ist*) tilt, tip (over); *Flug.* nosedive

abklappern *v/t.* (*trennb., hat -ge-*); *umg.* (*Sehenswürdigkeiten*) do; knock off; (*suchen*) scour, comb; **ich hab alle Läden abgeklappert** I've been in and out of all the shops *od. Am.* stores

abklären *v/t.* (*trennb., hat -ge-*) (*sich setzen lassen*) clarify; *fig.* (*klären*) clarify, clear; → **abgeklärt**

Abklatsch *m pej.*: (*schwacher ~* poor) imitation; **abklatschen** *vt/i.* (*trennb., hat -ge-*) *beim Tanzen, Spielen*: cut in to dance with s.o. (by clapping hands)

abklemmen *v/t.* (*trennb., hat -ge-*) **1.** (*abtrennen*) (*Draht, Kabel*) pinch off; (*Batterie, Telefon*) disconnect;

2. (*zusammenpressen*) (*Ader etc.*) clamp

Abklingbecken *n e-s Reaktors*: cooling chamber; *fachspr.* neutralization pond

abklingen *v/i.* (*unreg., trennb., hat -ge-*) **1.** (*nachlassen*) *Schmerz*: ease; *Wirkung*: wear off; *Sturm*: subside, abate; *Fieber, Schwellung*: subside; *Begeisterung*: fade; *Erregung*: die away, fade; *Boom etc.*: taper off; **2.** *Phys. Schwingung*: die away (*od.* out), get damped; *Atomstrahlung*: decay; **3.** (*leiser werden*) die (*od.* fade) away

abklopfen *v/t.* (*trennb., hat -ge-*) **1.** (*entfernen*) knock off (**von etw.** from s.th.); (*abstauben*) dust off; **2.** (*säubern*) (*Teppich etc.*) beat; (*Kleider*) brush down; **3.** *Med.* tap; *fachspr.* percuss; **die Argumente auf ihre Stichhaltigkeit hin ~** *fig.* see whether the arguments hold water

abknabbern *v/t.* (*trennb., hat -ge-*) (*Fleisch etc.*) nibble (*od.* gnaw) off (**von etw.** (from) s.th.); (*Knochen*) pick clean

abknallen *v/t.* (*trennb., hat -ge-*): **j-n ~** *umg.* put a bullet through s.o.'s head *allg.*, bump s.o. off; (*Tiere*) gun (*od.* shoot) down *allg.*

abkneifen *v/t.* (*unreg., trennb., hat -ge-*) nip off

abknicken (*trennb., -ge-*) **I.** *v/t.* (*hat*) **1.** (*abtrennen*) snap (*od.* break) off; **2.** (*knicken*) bend; **II.** *v/i.* (*ist*) **1.** (*abbrechen*) snap off; **2.** (*e-n Knick haben*) bend (over); **~de Vorfahrtstraße** street with priority for turning traffic

abknipsen *v/t.* (*trennb., hat -ge-*) *umg.* clip off; (*Blüte*) nip off

abknöpfen *v/t.* (*trennb., hat -ge-*) **1.** unbutton; **2.** *umg. fig.*: **j-m etw. ~** wangle (*od.* wheedle) s.th. out of s.o.

abknutschen *v/t.* (*trennb., hat -ge-*); *umg.* canoodle, have a (good old) snog with *s.o.*, smooch, *bes. Am.* neck

abkochen (*trennb., hat -ge-*) **I.** *v/t.* **1.** (*keimfrei machen*) boil; *Med.* sterilize; **2.** (*Heilkräuter*) make an infusion; *fachspr.* decoct; **II.** *vt/i. beim Boxen etc.*: **einige Pfunde ~** sweat off a few pounds (to make the weight); **III.** *v/i.* cook out in the open, *bes. Am.* have a cookout

abkommandieren *v/t.* (*trennb., hat*); *Mil.* detach, detail, assign (**zu** to)

abkommen *v/i.* (*unreg., trennb., ist -ge-*) **1. vom Weg ~** lose one's way; **vom Kurs ~** drift off course; **von der Fahrbahn ~** get (*rutschen*: skid) off the road; **vom Thema ~** *fig.* stray from the point; **vom rechten Weg ~** *fig.* stray from the straight and narrow; **2. von etw. ~** (*aufgeben*) give up; **von e-r Ansicht ~** change one's views; **von e-m Plan ~** abandon (*od.* give up) a plan

Abkommen *n; -s, -; auch Pol.* agreement, settlement; **ein ~ treffen** conclude an agreement

abkömmlich *Adj.* dispensable; (*verfügbar*) available, free; **er ist zur Zeit nicht ~** he can't get away (*od.* he's very much in demand) at the moment

Abkömmling *m; -s, -e* **1.** (*Nachkomme*) descendant; **2.** *Chem.* derivative

abkönnen *v/t.* (*trennb., hat -ge-*); *nordd. umg.*: **j-n/etw. nicht ~** (*nicht mögen*) not be able to stand (the sight of) s.o./s.th.

abkoppeln (*trennb., hat -ge-*) **I.** *v/t.* **1.** (*Waggon etc.*) uncouple; (*Raumkapsel etc.*) undock; **2.** *fig.* get rid of (**von** from); **II.** *v/refl. fig.* get away

abkratzen (*trennb.*, *-ge-*) **I.** *v/t.* (*hat*) **1.** (*entfernen*) scrape (*od.* scratch) off (*von etw.* (from) s.th.); **2.** (*säubern*) (*Schuhe etc.*) scrape (clean); **II.** *v/i.* (*ist*); *vulg.* (*sterben*) kick the bucket *umg. hum.*, snuff it *Brit. umg.*, buy the farm *Am. umg.*

abkriegen *v/t.* (*trennb.*, *hat -ge-*); *umg.* → **abbekommen**

abkühlen *v/t.*, *v/i. und v/refl.* (*trennb.*, *hat -ge-*) cool (off *od.* down) (*auch fig.*); *über Nacht hat es* (*sich*) *stark abgekühlt* it has become a lot cooler overnight; **Abkühlung** *f*; *mst. Sg.* **1.** cooling; **2.** *Wetter*: drop (*od.* fall) in temperature

Abkunft *f*; *-*, *kein Pl.* descent, origin; (*Geburt*) birth; *von hoher ~* of noble descent; *von niedriger ~* of humble (*od.* low) birth

abkupfern *v/t./i.* (*trennb.*, *hat -ge-*); *umg. pej.*: *bei/von j-m ~* crib (from *od.* off s.o.), lift (from s.o.)

abkuppeln *v/t./i.* (*trennb.*, *hat -ge-*) uncouple, disconnect

abkürzen (*trennb.*, *hat -ge-*) **I.** *v/t./i.* (*e-n Weg*) *~* take a short cut; **II.** *v/t.* **1.** (*Vorgang*) shorten; **2.** (*Aufenthalt*) cut short, shorten; **3.** (*Wort etc.*) abbreviate, shorten

Abkürzung *f* **1.** (*abgek. Abk.*) *e-s Wortes etc.*: abbreviation (*abgek. abbr.*); **2.** *e-s Weges*: short cut (*auch fig.*); **Abkürzungsverzeichnis** *n* list of abbreviations

abküssen *v/t.* (*trennb.*, *hat -ge-*) smother with kisses

abladen *v/t.* (*unreg.*, *trennb.*, *hat -ge-*) **1.** (*Waren, Lastwagen*) unload; (*Schiff*) off-load; (*Müll*) dump; *Müll ~ verboten* no tipping (*Am.* dumping); **2.** *fig.*: *etw. auf j-n ~* unload s.th. on(to) s.o.; *s-e Sorgen bei j-m ~* cry on s.o.'s shoulder, unburden o.s. to s.o.

Ablage *f* **1.** place to put s.th.; (*für Kleider*) coat-stand; (*für Hüte*) hat-stand; *für Akten etc.*: file; (*~korb*) filing (*od.* letter) tray; (*Aktenschrank*) filing cabinet; **2.** *nur Sg.*; (*das Ablegen*) filing; **3.** *mst. Pl.*; (*abgelegte Akten*) files *Pl.*, records *Pl.*; **4.** *schw.* (*Agentur*) depot, agency; (*Zweigstelle*) branch office; *~fach* *n* pigeonhole

ablagern (*trennb.*, *hat -ge-*) **I.** *v/t.* **1.** (*Güter*) store; (*Müll*) deposit; **2.** *Geol.*, *Med.*, *Chem.* deposit; **3.** (*Wein*) store, mature; (*Holz, Tabak*) season; **II.** *v/i. Wein*: mature; *Holz, Tabak*: season; **III.** *v/refl. Geol.*, *Med.*, *Chem.* settle, form a deposit; **Ablagerung** *f* **1.** *nur Sg.* storage, maturing; *von Holz, Tabak*: seasoning; **2.** *von Müll*: dumping; *Geol.*, *Med.*, *Chem. Vorgang*: settling; deposition, alluviation, sedimentation; (*Abgelagertes*) deposit, sediment, alluvium

ablandig *Adj. Naut.* offshore

Ablass *m*; *-es*, *Ablässe* **1.** drain; **2.** *kath.* indulgence; *~brief* *m kirchl. hist.* letter of indulgence

ablassen (*unreg.*, *trennb.*, *hat -ge-*) **I.** *v/t.* **1.** (*Wasser, Motoröl*) drain off; (*Luft*) let out; (*Dampf*) let off; *Luft aus den Reifen ~* let the tyres (*Am.* tires) down; → *Dampf*, **2.** (*Teich etc.*) drain, empty; (*Fass*) broach; **3.** *etw. vom Preis ~* knock s.th. off the price; **4.** *umg.* (*Ggs. aufsetzen, festmachen*) leave off, not put on *allg.*; **II.** *v/i.*: *von etw. ~* stop doing s.th., give s.th. up; *von j-m ~* leave s.o. alone

Ablasshahn *m Tech.* drain (*od.* outlet) cock, *Am.* faucet, tap; *Heizanlage*:

bleeder (valve)

Ablasshandel *m kirchl. hist.* selling of indulgences

Ablassventil *n* drain valve

Ablativ *m*; *-s*, *-e*; *Ling.* ablative (case)

Ablauf *m* **1.** (*Abfluss*) flowing, outflow, discharge; (*Vorrichtung*) outlet, drain; (*~rohr*) waste pipe; **2.** (*Verlauf*) *e-r Sitzung etc.*: order of events; *der ~ der Ereignisse* the course (*od.* sequence) of events; **3.** *e-r Frist etc.*: expiry; *mit ~ des Jahres* at the end of the year; *nach ~ von zwei Wochen* at the end of two weeks, after two weeks; *noch vor ~ e-r Stunde* in less than an hour, before an hour has passed; *~berg* *m Eisenb.* double incline, *Am.* hump

ablaufen (*unreg.*, *trennb.*, *-ge-*) **I.** *v/i.* (*ist*) **1.** run (*od.* flow) off; *auch Badewasser*: drain off; *Flut*: subside; *~ lassen* (*Wasser etc.*) run off, drain off; (*Geschirr etc.*) drain, dry off; *im Bad läuft das Wasser schlecht ab* the bath(tub) isn't draining properly; **2.** (*vonstatten gehen*) go, pass off; *planmäßig ~* go according to plan; *reibungslos ~* go without a hitch; *das Programm läuft automatisch ab* the program runs automatically; **3.** (*ausgehen*) turn out; *für j-n gut/schlecht ~* turn out well/badly for s.o.; *wenn das nur gut abläuft!* here's hoping it'll all work out alright (*od.* OK)!; *es lief nicht so ab wie erhofft* it didn't turn out (quite) as hoped; **4.** (*enden*) *Frist, Pass etc.*: run out, expire; *Amtszeit etc.*: wind down; *Vertrag*: expire, be up; *Wechsel*: become due, mature; **5.** *Uhr*: run down; *d-e Zeit ist abgelaufen fig.* your hour is come; **6.** *Film*: run; *Tonband, CD*: play; *Faden*: unreel, unwind; *~ lassen* (*Film*) run, show; (*Tonband etc.*) play; **7.** *Naut.* (*abdrehen*) launch; **8.** *Naut.*: *~ lassen* give command to launch; *Sport* (*starten*) start; **II.** *v/t.* **1.** (*hat*); (*Schuhe*) wear out; (*Absätze*) wear down; *sich* (*Dat.*) *die Hacken ~ umg. fig.* walk one's legs off (*nach* trying to find); **2.** (*hat/ist*); (*Strecke*) cover; *suchend*: scour; *Sport* (*Bahn*) check out; → *Rang* 3

Ablauffrist *f* time limit; *Wirts. e-s Wechsels*: (date of) maturity, due date; *e-s Abkommens*: date of expiration; *~plan* *m* sequence, order of events *etc.*; *TV etc.* running order

Ablaufrohr *n* outlet tube; *e-r Dachrinne*: downpipe, *bes. Am.* downspout

Ablaut *m*; *mst. Sg.*; *Ling.* vowel gradation, ablaut; **ablauten** *v/i.* (*trennb.*, *hat -ge-*) undergo ablaut

abläuten (*trennb.*, *hat -ge-*); *Sport*: *e-e Runde ~* ring the bell (to end a round)

Ablautreihe *f Ling.* ablaut (*od.* gradation) series

Ableben *n*; *nur Sg.*; *geh. euph.* demise; *auch Jur.* decease

ablecken *v/t.* (*trennb.*, *hat -ge-*) **1.** *den Teller ~* lick the plate clean; *sich* (*Dat.*) *die Lippen/Finger ~* lick one's lips/fingers; *Hund*: *j-n ~* lick s.o. all over; *sich die Zunge nach etw. ~ umg. fig.* want s.th. like mad (*od.* cracy); **2.** (*entfernen*) lick off (*von etw.* (from) s.th.)

abledern *v/t.* (*trennb.*, *hat -ge-*) polish with a chamois (leather)

ablegen (*trennb.*, *hat -ge-*) **I.** *vt/i.* **1.** (*Hut, Kleider*) take *one's* coat etc. off; *bitte legen Sie doch ab* please make yourself comfortable, may I take your coat?; → *abgelegt*; **2.** *Kartenspiel*:

(*auflegen*) put down, play; (*abwerfen*) discard, throw away; **II.** *v/t.* **1.** (*weglegen*) (*Tasche etc.*) put down; (*Akten etc.*) file; *e-e Maske ~* throw (*od.* take) off a mask; *die Waffen od. die Rüstung ~* lay down one's arms; **2.** *fig.* (*aufgeben*) (*Gewohnheit, Namen etc.*) give up, drop; (*Titel etc.*) give up; *s-e Fehler ~* mend one's ways; *sie hat ihre Scheu ihm gegenüber abgelegt* she lost (*od.* has overcome) her shyness toward(s) him; **3.** *fig.* (*Eid, Gelübde, Prüfung etc.*) take; (*Prüfung erfolgreich auch*) pass; (*Beichte, Geständnis etc.*) make; → *Beichte* 1, *Rechenschaft*, *Zeugnis* 2; **III.** *v/i. Schiff*: (set) sail, cast off

Ableger *m*; *-s*, *-* **1.** *Agr.*, *Bot.* shoot; (*Absenker*) layer; (*Steckling*) cutting; *~ ziehen* take cuttings; **2.** (*Zweigunternehmen*) subsidiary; **3.** *umg. hum.* (*Sohn*) offspring *kein Pl. allg.*

ablehnen (*trennb.*, *hat -ge-*) **I.** *v/t.* **1.** (*Antrag, Bitte, Einladung etc.*) turn down; *höflich*: decline; (*Einladung*) *auch* refuse; (*Angebot*) *auch* reject; (*Vorschlag, Gesetzesentwurf*) reject; *sie lehnte es ab, mit ihm zu sprechen* she wouldn't talk to him; **2.** (*nicht gutheißen*) reject; (*gefühlsmäßig ~*) dislike; (*missbilligen*) disapprove of; *er wird von s-n Klassenkameraden abgelehnt* his schoolmates won't (*od.* don't want to) have anything to do with him; *Lügen lehnt er ab* he scorns lying (*od.* to lie *od.* lies); **3.** (*Bewerber*) turn down; (*Richter, Zeugen etc.*) object to s.o. (*wegen Befangenheit* on grounds of interest); **II.** *v/i.* refuse, decline

ablehnend I. *P.P.* → **ablehnen**; **II.** *Adj.* (*Bescheid, Haltung etc.*) negative; **III.** *Adv.*: *~ gegenüberstehen* (+ *Dat.*) disapprove of

Ablehnung *f* **1.** refusal; rejection; **2.** (*Missbilligung*) dislike; disapproval (+ *Gen.* of); *auf ~ stoßen* meet with disapproval; **3.** *Jur. e-s Antrags etc.*: rejection, refusal; *e-s Richters etc.*: objection (*wegen Befangenheit* on grounds of interest)

ableisten *v/t.* (*trennb.*, *hat -ge-*) fulfil(l), perform, complete; *s-n Militärdienst ~* do (*od.* complete) one's military service

ableiten (*trennb.*, *hat -ge-*) **I.** *v/t.* **1.** (*Wasser etc.*) draw off, drain off; (*Wärme*) abduct; (*Dampf, Rauch*) draw off (*od.* out); (*Strom*) divert; **2.** (*umleiten*) (*Bach etc.*) divert; (*ablenken*) (*Blitz*) conduct; **3.** (*folgern*) deduce; *Ling.*, *Math.*, *Philos.* derive (*aus, von* from) (*auch Ansprüche*); **4.** *s-e Herkunft ~ von* trace one's descent from; **II.** *v/refl.* derive, be derived (*von* from); **Ableitung** *f* **1.** (*Umleitung*) diversion; **2.** *Wasser*: drainage; **3.** *Ling.*, *Philos.*, *Math.* (*das Ableiten*) derivation; (*das Abgeleitete*) derivative; (*Folgerung*) deduction, inference

ablenkbar *Adj. Person*: *leicht ~* easily distracted

ablenken (*trennb.*, *hat -ge-*) **I.** *v/t.* **1.** *von e-r Richtung*: divert; **2.** *fig.* (*Gefahr, Verdacht etc.*) avert, ward off; *den Verdacht von sich ~* avert suspicion, divert suspicion (away) from o.s.; **3.** *fig. von der Arbeit etc.*: distract; (*zerstreuen*) divert; *j-s Aufmerksamkeit von etw. ~* take s.o.'s attention off s.th.; *sich leicht / durch nichts ~ lassen* be easily distracted / be oblivious to all distractions; *j-n von s-n Sorgen* *etc.* ~ take s.o.'s mind off his (*od.* her) worries *etc.*; **4.** *Sport:* (*Schlag*) parry; (*Ball*) deflect; *Ball am Tor:* turn away; **5.** *Phys.* (*Strahlen etc.*) deflect; (*Licht*) diffract; (*Magnet*) deviate; **II.** *v/i.* **1.** *Fahrzeug:* turn (off); **2.** *fig.* (*zerstreuen*) *Sache:* create a distraction; **3.** *Person:* change the subject, digress, sidetrack; *lenk nicht ab!* don't change the subject!; **4.** *Phys. Strahlen etc.:* deviate. diverge; **III.** *v/refl. fig.* take one's mind off things

Ablenkung *f* **1.** diversion, deflection *etc.*; → *ablenken*; **2.** (*Zerstreuung*) diversion, distraction

Ablenkungsmanöver *n* diversionary man|oeuvre (*Am.* -euver) (*od.* tactic); *das ist ein* ~ that's a red herring

ablesbar *Adj. bes. Tech.* readable, detectable

ablesen¹ (*unreg., trennb., hat -ge*) **I.** *v/t/i.* (*Rede*) read (from notes); (*j-m etw.*) *von den Lippen* ~ lip(-)read, read lips; **II.** *v/t.* **1.** (*Skala, Instrument*) read; *Gas* (*Strom*) ~ read the gas (electricity) meter; **2.** (*erkennen*) *etw. aus od. von etw.* ~ tell (*od.* see s.th.) from s.th.; *man konnte ihm s-e Enttäuschung etc. vom Gesicht* ~ his disappointment *etc.* showed in his face; *j-m jeden Wunsch von den Augen* ~ anticipate s.o.'s every wish

ablesen² *v/t.* (*unreg., trennb., hat -ge*); (*Beeren, Raupen etc.*) pick (off) (*von etw.* from s.th.)

Ableser *m; -s, -,* ~*in* *f; -, -nen*; (*Gas-, Stromableser*) meter-reader; **Ablesung** *f Tech.* reading

ableuchten *v/t.* (*trennb., hat -ge*) search *s.th.* with a lamp (*od.* torch, *Am.* flashlight); *Scheinwerfer:* sweep

ableugnen *v/t.* (*trennb., hat -ge*) deny; (*von sich weisen*) repudiate

ablichten *v/t.* (*trennb., hat -ge*) **1.** *geh.* (*fotokopieren*) (photo)copy; **2.** *umg.* (*fotografieren*) (take a) photograph; **Ablichtung** *f* **1.** photocopy; **2.** photograph, exposure

abliefern *v/t.* (*trennb., hat -ge*); (*Waren*) deliver (*bei* to); (*Arbeit, Aufsatz etc.*) hand in (+ *Dat.* to); *in Eile:* dash off; (*Waffen*) hand over, surrender; *ich habe die Kinder zu Hause abgeliefert umg.* I took the kids home; **Ablieferung** *f* (*Lieferung*) delivery; (*Abgabe*) handing in; (*Übergabe*) handing over; **Ablieferungstermin** *m* delivery date

abliegen *v/i.* (*unreg., trennb., ist -ge*) be quite a way off; *weit* ~ be a long way away; → *abgelegen* II

ablisten *v/t.* (*trennb., hat -ge*): *j-m etw.* ~ trick s.o. out of s.th.

ablocken *v/t.* (*trennb., hat -ge*): *j-m etw.* ~ wheedle (*od.* coax) s.th. out of s.o.

ablöschen *v/t.* (*trennb., hat -ge*) **1.** (*Brand*) put out, extinguish; **2.** (*abwischen*) (*Schrift*) wipe off; (*Tafel*) clean; **3.** (*Tinte*) *mit Löschpapier:* blot; **4.** *Gastr.* add water (*od.* wine *etc.*) to; **5.** *Tech.* extinguish, quench; (*Kalk*) slake

ablösbar *Adj.* removable, detachable; *leicht/schwer* ~ easy/hard to remove

Ablöse *f; -, -n* **1.** *Sport:* transfer fee; **2.** *österr. Wohnung: etwa* key money; *in Annoncen:* furnishings (and fittings) *Pl.*

ablösefrei *Adj. Sport* (*Vereinswechsel*) on a free transfer *präd.*

ablösen (*trennb., hat -ge*) **I.** *v/t.* **1.** (*entfernen*) remove (*von* from), take (*od.*

get) off (*von etw.* s.th.); (*Rinde, Tapete*) *auch* peel off; **2.** (*Wache, Posten*) relieve; (*j-n im Amt*) replace; *euph.* (*entlassen*) relieve s.o. of their duties; (*Kollegen etc.*) take over from; *sich* ~ take turns (*bei* at), *bei der Arbeit: auch* work in shifts; **3.** *fig.* (*darauf folgen*) take the place of, supersede, replace; *der Winter löst den Sommer ab* summer gives way to winter; **4.** (*Anleihe, Schuld etc.*) pay off, redeem; **II.** *v/refl.:* **1.** *Farbe, Haut etc.:* come (*od.* flake) off (*von etw.* s.th.); **2.** *sich mit j-m* ~ take it in turns (*Am.* take turns) with s.o., rotate with s.o.

Ablösesumme *f Sport* transfer fee

Ablösung *f* **1.** *nur Sg.* detachment, removal; **2.** *von Wache etc.:* relief; *im Amt etc.:* replacement; *euph.* (*Entlassung*) removal; **3.** *nur Sg.; fig.* (*Aufeinanderfolge*) succession, sequence; **4.** *Wirts. Schuld:* discharge; *Anleihe:* redemption; *Kapital:* withdrawal

abluchsen *v/t.* (*trennb., hat -ge*); *umg.: j-m etw.* ~ wangle s.th. out of s.o., bamboozle s.o. out of s.th.

Abluft *f Tech.* used (*od.* waste *od.* outgoing) air; ~*anlage* *f e-s Kernkaftwerks* upward ventilator; ~*rohr* *n* air outlet

ablutschen *v/t.* (*trennb., hat -ge*); *umg.* **1.** (*Blut, Saft etc.*) suck off (*von etw.* (from) s.th.) *allg.*; **2.** (*Löffel, Kern etc.*) lick (clean)

ABM *Abk.* → *Arbeitsbeschaffungsmaßnahme*

abmachen *v/t.* (*trennb., hat -ge*) **1.** *umg.* (*lösen*) take (*od.* get) off (*von etw.* s.th.), remove (*von* from); (*Strick etc.*) *auch* undo *allg.*; **2.** *fig.* (*vereinbaren*) arrange, agree (on), sort (out); (*regeln*) settle, decide; *abgemacht!* done, okay, that's settled; *beim Kauf:* it's a deal; *gespr.* it's sorted; *das ist so gut wie abgemacht* it's as good as fixed; **3.** (*bereinigen*) settle, sort out; *das müsst ihr unter euch* ~ that's for you to sort out (for yourselves); **Abmachung** *f* agreement; arrangement, settlement; *e-e* ~ *treffen* come to an agreement (*über* on); *sich an e-e* ~ *halten* keep (*od.* stick) to an agreement

abmagern *v/i.* (*trennb., ist -ge*) become (*od.* get) (very) thin; *sie sieht furchtbar abgemagert aus* she's just skin and bones; **Abmagerung** *f* emaciation; **Abmagerungskur** *f* (slimming, *Am.* reducing) diet; *e-e* ~ *machen* be on a (strict *od.* crash) diet, be slimming (*Am.* reducing)

abmähen *v/t.* (*trennb., hat -ge*) **1.** mow; *e-e abgemähte Wiese* a lawn; **2.** *umg. fig.* → *abrasieren* 2

abmahnen *v/t.* (*trennb., hat -ge*); *Jur., Wirts.* give s.o. a (written) warning; **Abmahnung** *f* (written) warning

abmalen (*trennb., hat -ge*) *v/t.* paint; (*kopieren*) copy

Abmarsch *m; mst. Sg.* marching off; *fig.* start; ~ *um 8 Uhr* moving off at 8 a.m., *fig.* we leave at 8 o'clock

abmarschbereit *Adj.* ready to march (*fig.* set off)

abmarschieren (*trennb.*) **I.** *v/i.* (*ist*) (*Soldaten*) march (*od.* move) off; (*Gruppe*) depart; **II.** *v/t.* (*hat/ist*) (*Grenze, Gebiet*) march through (*od.* over)

abmeißeln *v/t.* (*trennb., hat -ge*); (*entfernen*) chisel off (*von etw.* (from) s.th.)

Abmelde|bestätigung *f document*

confirming that one has notified the authorities that one intends to move from an address; ~*formular* *n* form to notify the authorities that one intends to move from an address, *Am. etwa* change-of-address kit

abmelden (*trennb., hat -ge*) **I.** *v/t.* **1.** *j-n* ~ take s.o.'s name off the list; *als Mitglied:* cancel s.o.'s membership; *als Teilnehmer:* cancel registration; *bei der Gemeinde:* give notification that s.o. is moving; *ein Kind von der Schule* ~ take a child out of (*od.* away from) school; *bei mir ist er abgemeldet umg. fig.* I want nothing more to do with him *allg., bes. Am.* I'm through with him; **2.** (*Auto, Radio etc.*) cancel registration (*od.* licen|ce [*Am.* -se]); *sein Telefon* ~ have one's (tele)phone disconnected; **3.** *Sport umg.* (*wirkungsvoll decken*) *auch* mark s.o. out of the game; **4.** (*Besuch*) cancel; **II.** *v/refl.* **1.** *bei e-r Institution etc.:* sign out; *im Hotel:* check out; → I 1; **2.** *sich bei j-m* ~ report to s.o. that one is leaving; *beim Vorgesetzten:* report absent (from duty) (*bei j-m* to s.o.); **3.** *EDV* (*Computer*) log out

Abmeldung *f* **1.** *als Einwohner:* cancel(l)ation of one's registration (*bei* at); *als Mitglied:* cancel(l)ation (of membership); *als Teilnehmer:* cancel(-l)ation of subscription (*von* from); **2.** cancel(l)ation; *e-s Autos, Radios etc.:* cancel(l)ation of registration; **3.** *vor dem Weggehen:* notice (of departure)

abmessen *v/t.* (*unreg., trennb., hat -ge*) **1.** (*Entfernung, Größe*) measure; (*1 Meter, 1 Liter etc.*) measure off (*von* from); (*Mehl, Zucker*) weigh; **2.** *fig.* (*Ausmaß, Schaden etc.*) assess

Abmessung *f* **1.** (*das Abmessen*) measurement; **2.** *nur Pl.*; (*Maße*) dimensions

abmildern *v/t.* (*trennb., hat -ge*) **1.** (*Aussage etc.*) moderate; (*Strafe*) reduce, lighten; (*Geschmack, Gegensatz*) tone down; **2.** (*Aufprall, Sturz*) cushion, soften, (*Schock*) lessen

abmontieren *v/t.* (*trennb., hat*) **1.** (*Räder, Teile*) (*entfernen*) take off (*von etw.* (from) s.th.), remove (*von* from); **2.** (*zerlegen*) dismantle

ABM-Stelle *f* job created by a government job creation scheme (*Am.* program); → *Arbeitsbeschaffungsmaßnahme*

abmühen *v/refl.* (*trennb., hat -ge*) struggle (*od.* slave) away; *sich* ~, *etw. zu tun* take great pains to do s.th.; *sich* ~ *mit* struggle (*od.* wrestle) with

abmurksen *v/t.* (*trennb., hat -ge*); *umg.* **1.** (*Person*) do in, bump off; **2.** (*Motor*) stall

abmustern (*trennb., hat -ge*); *Naut.* **I.** *v/t.* pay off; **II.** *v/i.* sign off

abnabeln (*trennb., hat -ge*) **I.** *v/t.:* *ein Kind* ~ cut the umbilical cord; **II.** *v/refl. umg. fig.* cut the cord (*von j-m* between s.o. and s.o.); **Abnabelung** *f* cutting the cord; *fig.* leaving the nest

abnagen *v/t.* (*trennb., hat -ge*); (*Fleisch etc.*) gnaw off (*od.* away) (*von etw.* from s.th.); (*Knochen*) gnaw

abnähen *v/t.* (*trennb., hat -ge*) take in; **Abnäher** *m; -s, -* dart

Abnahme *f; -, -n* **1.** taking down (*od.* off); (*Wegnahme*) removal; *Med.* amputation; **2.** *Wirts.* (*Kauf*) purchase; *bei* ~ *von* on orders of; **3.** (*Verminderung*) decrease (+ *Gen.* in) decline;

von Zahlen etc.: auch drop (+ *Gen.* in); *des Mondes:* waning; *an Gewicht:* loss; ~ *der Kräfte* weakening; **4.** (*Überprüfung*): **technische** ~ (final) inspection; ~ *des TÜV etwa* carrying out (of) the MOT (*Am.* of a state vehicle inspection); ~ *e-s Manuskripts etc.* acceptance of a manuscript *etc.*; **5.** (*Durchführung etc.*) ~ *e-r Prüfung* holding of an exam; ~ *der Parade* review of the troops; ~ *der Fingerabdrücke* taking of s.o.'s fingerprints

Abnahme|garantie *f Wirts.* guaranteed purchase, firm order; **~protokoll** *n Tech.* acceptance (*od.* test) certificate; **~prüfung** *f Tech.* specification test; *werkseigene:* inspection test; **~verweigerung** *f Wirts.* rejection, refusal (of acceptance); **~vorschriften** *Pl. Tech.* quality specifications

abnehmbar *Adj.* removable, detachable

abnehmen (*unreg., trennb., hat -ge-*) **I.** *v/t.* **1.** (*herunternehmen*) take off (*von etw.* (from) s.th.); remove (*von* from) (*beide auch Tech.*); (*Hut, Mantel*) *auch* take off; (*Bild, Wäsche, Vorhang*) *auch* take down; (*Obst, Strauchfrüchte*) pick; **2.** (*Bein etc.*) amputate, take off; (*Bart*) shave off; *j-m Blut* ~ take a blood sample (from s.o.); **3.** *j-m etw.* ~ (*wegnehmen*) take s.th. away from s.o.; *j-m den Führerschein* ~ take s.o.'s driving licen|ce (*Am.* –se) away (from them); **4.** *umg.* (*verlangen*) charge s.o. s.th. *allg.*; *j-m zu viel* ~ overcharge s.o.; **5.** (*von etw. befreien*) (*Aufgabe, Last, Sorge etc.*) relieve s.o. of s.th.; *darf ich Ihnen Ihre Tasche* ~? can I carry your bag for you?, may I help you with your bag?; *kann ich dir etwas* ~? can I give you a hand with anything?; **6.** *Wirts.* (*Ware*) buy (*Dat.* from); (*Lieferung*) take delivery of; *das nimmt ihm keiner ab umg. fig.* (*glaubt ihm keiner*) nobody will buy that; **7.** (*prüfen*) inspect, test; *Tech.* accept; (*Prüfung*) hold; (*Parade*) take the salute (at a parade); → *Beichte* 1, *Eid, Fingerabdruck usw.*; **II.** *vt/i.* **1.** (*Gewicht verlieren*) lose weight; *durch Diät:* be slimming (*Am.* dieting, reducing); *10 Pfund etc.* ~ lose 10 pounds *etc.*; **2.** (*Maschen*) decrease; **3.** (*den Hörer*) ~ pick up the receiver, answer (the phone); *nimmst du mal ab?* can you get it?; **III.** *v/i.* decrease, decline, diminish, grow less; *Kräfte, Leistungsvermögen:* diminish, *langsam:* dwindle; *Geschwindigkeit:* slacken (off), slow down; *Sturm:* abate, subside; *Macht, Begeisterung, Nachfrage, Anzahl etc.:* decline, wane; *Mond:* (be on the) wane; *Temperatur, Fieber, Todesfälle:* drop, fall, subside; *Druck, Erregung, Schwellung, Schmerzen, Spannung:* subside, lessen, fall off; *Helligkeit:* fade, diminish; *Kälte, Niveau:* drop

abnehmend I. *Part. Präs.* → *abnehmen;* **II.** *Adj.* **1.** *Mond:* waning; **2.** *in* **~em Maße** to a decreasing extent

Abnehmer *m; -s, -,* **~in** *f; -, -nen; Wirts.* buyer, purchaser, taker; (*Kunde*) customer; (*Verbraucher*) consumer; *die* ~ *Pl.* the market; *keine* ~ *finden* find no market

Abnehmerland *n* importing country

Abneigung *f* dislike (*gegen* of, for), disinclination (*gegen* towards, *Am. bes.* toward); *stärker:* aversion (*to, Am. bes.* toward); *ich habe e-e ausgesprochene* ~ *dagegen* I real-

ly can't stand it

abnorm *Adj.* abnormal; (*außergewöhnlich*) exceptional, unusual; **abnormal** *Adj.; bes. österr.* abnormal; **Abnormität** *f; -, -en* **1.** *nur Sg.;* (*Zustand*) abnormality; **2.** (*etw. Abnormes*) freak

abnötigen *v/t.* (*trennb., hat -ge-*): *j-m etw.* ~ wring s.th. from s.o.; *j-m Respekt* ~ command s.o.'s respect; *er nötigt mir Bewunderung ab* I can't help admiring him

abnutzen, abnützen (*trennb., hat -ge-*) **I.** *v/t.* wear out; **II.** *v/refl.* wear (out), get worn out; → *abgenutzt*

Abnutzung *f* wear (and tear); **Abnutzungserscheinung** *f auch Med.* sign of wear (and tear)

Abo *n; -s, -s; umg.* → *Abonnement*

Abonnement [abɔnə'mãː] *n; -s, -s* subscription (*für od. von* for); *Theat. auch* season ticket (*bei* for); *e-e Zeitschrift im* ~ *beziehen* subscribe to a magazine

Abonnement(s)|fernsehen *n* pay TV; **~karte** *f* subscription (*od.* season) ticket; **~preis** *m* subscription price; **~vorstellung** *f* subscription performance

Abonnent *m; -en, -en,* **~in** *f; -, -nen* (*Theat.* ticket) subscriber

Abonnentenwerbung *f* attraction of (new) subscribers, campaigning for new subscribers

abonnieren *v/t.* subscribe to; (*Konzertreihe etc.*) have a season ticket for; *er scheint das Glück* (*Pech*) *abonniert zu haben fig.* he seems to have a monopoly on (bad) luck; **abonniert I.** *P.P.* → *abonnieren;* **II.** *Adj. fig.: sie scheint auf den dritten Platz etc.* ~ *zu sein* they seem to have reserved third place *etc.* just for her; *er scheint auf Autounfälle etc.* ~ *zu sein* he seems to have a standing order for car accidents *etc.*

abordnen *v/t.* (*trennb., hat -ge-*) delegate, *Am. auch* deputize; **Abordnung** *f* delegation

Abort[1] [a'bɔrt] *m; -(e)s, -e; altm.* (*Toilette*) toilet, lavatory, *Am. auch* bathroom

Abort[2] *m; -s, -e* **1.** *Med.* miscarriage; **2.** *Raumf.* abort

abpacken *v/t.* (*trennb., hat -ge-*) pack; → *abgepackt*

abpassen *v/t.* (*trennb., hat -ge-*); (*Gelegenheit*) wait for; (*j-n*) *auch* be on the lookout for; (*abfangen*) waylay; *e-n günstigen Moment* ~ wait for the right moment

abpatrouillieren *v/t.* (*trennb., hat*) patrol

abpausen *v/t.* (*trennb., hat -ge-*) trace; make a tracing of

abpellen *v/t.* (*trennb., hat -ge-*); *nordd.* **1.** (*Schale etc.*) peel (*von etw.* off s.th.); **2.** (*Ei, Kartoffel*) peel

abperlen *v/i.* (*trennb., ist -ge-*) trickle down, drip off (*von + Dat.* from)

abpfeifen *vt/i.* (*unreg., trennb., hat -ge-*); *Sport:* (*das Spiel*) ~ stop the game; *bei Spielende:* blow the final whistle; **Abpfiff** *m* final whistle

abpflücken *v/t.* (*trennb., hat -ge-*) **1.** (*Blumen etc.*) pick; **2.** (*leer pflücken*) pick clean (*od.* bare)

abplagen *v/refl.* (*trennb., hat -ge-*) struggle (away); *stärker:* slave away, tire o.s. out; *sich ~ mit* struggle (*od.* grapple) with, bother o.s. with

abplatzen *v/i.* (*trennb., ist -ge-*) *Knopf:* pop off (*von etw.* s.th.); *Metall, Farbe etc.:* flake off (*von etw.* [from] s.th.); *Gestein:* spall

abprägen *v/refl.* (*trennb., hat -ge-*) leave an impression (*auf + Dat.* on); *fig.* leave its mark (*auf, in + Dat.* on)

Abprall *m; -(e)s, -e, mst. Sg.* rebound; *Geschoss:* ricochet; **abprallen** *v/i.* (*trennb., ist -ge-*) **1.** rebound, bounce off; ricochet; *Schall:* reverberate; **2.** *fig.: an od. von j-m* ~ make no impression on s.o.; *Kritik, Beleidigungen etc.:* bounce off s.o.; **Abpraller** *m; -s, -;* (*Geschoss*) ricochet; *Sport* rebound

abpressen *v/t.* (*trennb., hat -ge-*) **1.** squeeze; *es presste ihm die Luft ab* it took his breath away; *fig.* his heart almost stopped; **2.** *j-m etw.* ~ force (*od.* wrest) s.th. out of s.o.; (*Geld*) extort s.th. from s.o.

abpumpen *v/t.* (*trennb., hat -ge-*) **1.** (*Wasser etc.*) pump (off) (*aus* out); (*Muttermilch*) express (by breast-pump); **2.** (*Teich etc.*) drain, empty, pump dry

abputzen *v/t.* (*trennb., hat -ge-*) **1.** (*säubern*) clean (up); *j-m/sich den Hintern etc.* ~ wipe s.o.'s/one's bottom *etc.*; *sich* (*Dat.*) *die Schuhe* ~ wipe one's shoes; **2.** (*entfernen*) wipe off (*od.* up)

abquälen (*trennb., hat -ge-*) **I.** *v/refl. seelisch:* worry (o.s.), fret; *körperlich:* sweat away; *sich ~ mit* have a hard time with; **II.** *v/t.: sich* (*Dat.*) *e-e Antwort etc.* ~ force o.s. to answer *etc.*

abqualifizieren *v/t.* (*trennb., hat*) write off (completely), dismiss; (*schlecht machen*) denigrate; **Abqualifizierung** *f* dismissal, denigration

abquetschen *v/t.* (*trennb., hat -ge-*) crush; *j-m e-n Finger etc.* ~ crush s.o.'s finger *etc.*; *sich* (*Dat.*) *ein paar Tränen* ~ *fig.* squeeze out a few tears

abrackern *v/refl.* (*trennb., hat -ge-*) sweat (*od.* slave) away (*für j-n* for s.o.)

Abraham (*m*): (*so sicher*) *wie in* **~s Schoß** *umg.* safe and sound, safe as houses

abrahmen *v/t.* (*trennb., hat -ge-*); (*Milch*) skim

Abrakadabra *n; -s, kein Pl.* **1.** *ohne Art.:* (*Zauberformel*) abracadabra; **2.** (*unsinniges Gerede*) drivel

abrasieren *v/t.* (*trennb., hat -ge-*) **1.** shave off; *sich* (*Dat.*) *den Bart* ~ shave off one's beard; **2.** *umg. fig.* (*Gebäude etc.*) raze (to the ground); → *rasieren*

Abrasion *f; -, -en* **1.** *Med.* abrasion; **2.** *Geol.* abrasion, attrition, degradation

abraten *v/i.* (*unreg., trennb., hat -ge-*): *j-m* (*von etw.*) ~ advise (*od.* warn) s.o. against (doing) s.th.; *ich rate Ihnen davon ab* I advise you not to (*od.* against it)

Abraum *m; nur Sg.; Bergb.* overburden (*od.* overlay shelf)

abräumen (*trennb., hat -ge-*) **I.** *v/t.* (*Essen, Geschirr etc.*) clear up (*od.* away); **II.** *vt/i.* **1.** (*den Tisch*) ~ clear the table; **2.** *Sport; Kegeln:* score a strike; **3.** *umg. fig.:* (*alle Preise etc.*) ~ cream (*Am.* siphon) off the profits, *bei Turnier etc.:* sweep the board

Abraumhalde *f Bergb.* slag heap, overburden dump, waste pile, *Am. auch* tailings *Pl.*

abrauschen *v/i.* (*trennb., ist -ge-*); *umg.* (*schnell*) zoom off; *mit dem Auto: auch* roar off; *beleidigt:* stalk off (in a temper)

abreagieren (*trennb., hat*) **I.** *v/t.* (*Ärger etc.*) work off (*an + Dat.* on); *Psych.* abreact; **II.** *v/refl.* get rid of one's aggressions, let off steam *umg.; sich ~ an*

(+ *Dat*) let (*Am.* take) one's aggressions (*od.* anger *etc.*) out on

abrechnen (*trennb.*, hat -ge-) **I.** *v/t.* **1.** (*abziehen*) deduct, subtract; **2.** (*Spesen*) account for; (*Kasse*) reckon up, cash up, *bes. Am.* total; **II.** *v/i.* do the accounts; settle accounts (*mit j-m* with s.o.); *fig. auch* get even (with s.o.)

Abrechnung *f* **1.** *nur Sg.*; (*Abzug*) deduction; **nach ~ der Unkosten** after deducting expenses; **2.** *Wirts.* (*Schlussrechnung*) settlement of accounts; (*Rechnung*) account; (*Abrechnen*) accounting, invoicing, *Am.* billing; (*an der Börse*) contract note; **e-n Betrag in ~ bringen** debit (*od.* credit) a sum; **laut ~** as per account rendered; **3.** *fig.* (*Vergeltung*) requital; **Tag der ~** day of reckoning

Abrechnungs|beleg *m Wirts.* voucher; **~takt** *m Telef.* billing unit; **~zeitraum** *m* accounting period

Abrede *f* **1.** *geh.*: **in ~ stellen** deny; (*bestreiten*) contest; **2.** agreement; **e-e ~ treffen** come to an agreement

abregen *v/refl.* (*trennb.*, hat -ge-): **reg dich ab!** *umg.* cool it!, take it easy!

abreiben (*unreg.*, *trennb.*, hat -ge-) **I.** *v/t.* **1.** (*Schmutz etc.*) rub off (**von etw.** (from) s.th.); (*Zitronenschale etc.*) grate; **2.** (*frottieren*) rub down (*auch Pferd*); **3.** (*säubern*) (*Hände etc.*) rub (clean); (*polieren*) polish; **4.** (*abschleifen*) rub down; **II.** *v/refl.* **1.** *Person*: rub o.s. down; (*abnutzen*) wear down; *völlig*: wear off; *Tech.* wear down

Abreibung *f* **1.** (*Frottieren*) rubbing--down; *nasse*: sponge-down; **2.** *umg.* (*Prügel*) thrashing; **j-m e-e ~ verpassen** give s.o. a (good) thrashing, beat the living daylights (*od.* shit *Sl.*) out of s.o.

Abreise *f*; *mst.Sg.* departure (**nach** for) (**aus** *od.* **von** from); **abreisen** *v/i.* (*trennb.*, *ist -ge-*) leave (**nach** for) (**aus** *od.* **von** from)

Abreißblock *m*; *Pl.* -blöcke und -blocks tear-off pad

abreißen (*unreg.*, *trennb.*, -ge-) **I.** *v/t.* (*hat*) **1.** tear off, pull off, rip off (*alle* **von etw.** (from) s.th.); tear down; **er wird dir schon nicht gleich den Kopf ~** he won't bite your head off; **2.** (*Gebäude*) pull (*Am. auch* tear, knock) down; **3.** *umg. fig.* (*Zeit im Gefängnis etc.*) do; **II.** *v/i.* (*ist*) **1.** come off, tear off; (*auseinander reißen*) break, snap; **2.** *fig.* (*plötzlich aufhören*) break off; **die Arbeit reißt nicht ab** the work never lets up; → **abgerissen** II

Abreiß|kalender *m* sheet (*Am.* pad) calendar; **~schiene** *f Tapezieren*: cutter

abreiten (*unreg.*, *trennb.*, -ge-) **I.** *v/i.* (*ist*) (*losreiten*) ride off (*od.* away); **II.** *v/t.* **1.** (*hat/ist*) (*Feld etc.*) ride along; (*Strecke*) (*testen*) have a trial run of, test-drive; **2.** (*hat*); (*Pferd*) train; ride to exhaustion, override; **3.** (*hat*); *Naut.* (*Sturm*) ride out

abrennen (*unreg.*, *trennb.*, hat -ge-); *umg.* **I.** *v/t.* **1.** *sich* (*Dat.*) **die Beine u. Hacken ~** run one's legs off (**nach** for); **2.** *alle Geschäfte ~* run (a)round all the shops (*Am.* stores) *allg.*; **II.** *v/refl.* → I 1

abrichten *v/t.* (*trennb.*, hat -ge-) **1.** (*Tier*) train; *weitS. auch* teach *an animal* tricks; (*Pferd*) break in; **ein Tier** (*darauf*) **~ zu** (+ *Inf.*) train an animal to (+ *Inf.*); **2.** *Tech.* (*Werkstück etc.*) true (off *od.* up), dress, justify;

(*Blech*) pare, plane, straighten; (*Mauer*) level

Abrichtung *f* **1.** training; breaking-in; **2.** *Tech.* adjustment, fit

Abrieb *m*; -(*e*)*s*, -*e*; *Tech. Vorgang*: abrasion, wear; *Produkt*: grindings *Pl.*, dust; *Geol.* attrition; degradation; **abriebfest** *Adj.* non-abrasive; **Abriebfestigkeit** *f* abrasion strength

abriegeln *v/t.* (*trennb.*, hat -ge-) **1.** (*Tür*) bolt; **2.** (*Straße*) durch Barrieren: block; *durch Polizisten etc.*: cordon off; *auch Mil.* seal off; **hermetisch ~** hermetically sealed; **Abriegelung** *f* sealing (*od.* cordoning) off

abringen *v/t.* (*unreg.*, *trennb.*, hat -ge-); (*j-m*) *etw.* **~** wring (*od.* force) s.th. from; (*auch e-r Sache*) wrest s.th. from *lit.*; *sich* (*Dat.*) *e-e Entschuldigung* **~** force o.s. into making an apology

abrinnen *v/i.* (*unreg.*, *trennb.*, *ist -ge-*) run off (*od.* down) (**an** *od.* **von etw.** (from) s.th.)

Abriss *m* **1.** *nur Sg.*; *von Gebäuden*: demolition; **2.** (*kurze Darstellung*) sketch, brief outline (*od.* summary); (*Übersicht*) survey (*auch in Buchform*); **~arbeiten** *Pl.* demolition work *kein Pl.*; **~birne** *f* demolition (*od.* wrecking) ball; **~unternehmen** *n* demolition firm, *Am.* wrecking company (*od.* contractor)

abrollen (*trennb.*, -ge-) **I.** *v/i.* (*ist*) **1.** (*Kabel etc.*) unroll (*od.* uncoil, unwind); **2.** *fig.* (*vonstatten gehen*) pass; **reibungslos ~** go without a hitch; *ihr ganzes Leben rollte noch einmal vor ihren Augen ab* her whole life flashed before her eyes; **3.** *Sport* (*Rolle machen*) roll over; **4.** *Fuß*: roll; *über den ganzen Fuß* **~** roll from heel to toe; **II.** *v/t.* (*hat*) unroll; (*Film, Faden*) unwind; (*Kabel*) pay (*Am. auch* reel) out; **Abroller** *m*; -*s*, - *für Klebestreifen etc.*: dispenser

abrubbeln (*trennb.*, hat -ge-) **I.** *v/t.* **1.** (*entfernen*) rub off (**von etw.** s.th.); **2.** (*frottieren*) rub down; **II.** *v/refl.* rub o.s. down

abrücken (*trennb.*, -ge-) **I.** *v/t.* (*hat*) move away (**von** from); **s-n Stuhl vom Tisch ~** move one's chair back from the table; **II.** *v/i.* (*ist*) **1.** *bes. Mil. Fahrzeuge*: move off; *Truppen*: march off; *umg. fig. Personen*: clear out *allg.*; **2. ~ von** move away; *fig.* dissociate (*od.* distance) o.s. from

Abruf *m*; *mst. Sg.* **1.** *Wirts.* (*von Waren, Geldern*) call (**von** for); **auf ~ bestellen** order on call; **2.** (*Abberufung*) recall; **auf ~** subject to recall; **sich auf ~ bereithalten** be on call (*od.* ready); **3.** *EDV von Daten*: access (**von** to), retrieval

abruf|bar *Adj. EDV Daten*: (readily) retrievable; **alle Daten sind ~** all data can be accessed; **~bereit** *Adj.* on call

abrufen *v/t.* (*unreg.*, *trennb.*, hat -ge-) **1.** (*j-n*) call away; *offiziell*: recall; **2.** *Wirts.* (*Waren*) call; (*Geld*) withdraw; **3.** *EDV* (*Daten, Informationen*) call up, retrieve; **4.** *Flug.* (*zur Landung auffordern*) order to land

abrunden (*trennb.*, hat -ge-) **I.** *v/t.* **1.** (*Kanten etc.*) round off; **2.** *fig.* (*Zahl*) round off; **nach oben** (**unten**) **~** round up (down); → **abgerundet** II; **3.** *fig.* (*Feier, Geschichte, Geschmack etc.*) polish (up *od.* off), complete; **II.** *v/refl. fig.* round o.s. *od.* itself off;

Abrundung *f* rounding off

abrupfen *v/t.* (*trennb.*, hat -ge-) pluck (off)

abrupt *Adj.* abrupt, sudden; **Abruptheit** *f nur Sg.* abruptness

abrüsten (*trennb.*, hat -ge-) **I.** *v/i. Pol.* disarm; **II.** *v/t.* (*Gebäude*) take the scaffolding down from; **Abrüstung** *f* disarmament

Abrüstungs| konferenz *f* disarmament conference (*od.* summit); **~verhandlungen** *Pl.* arms (limitation *od.* reduction *od.* control) talks

abrutschen *v/i.* (*trennb.*, *ist -ge-*) **1.** slip off (*od.* down); *Messer etc.*: slip; *Mot.* skid; *Ski, Flug. seitlich*: sideslip; **2.** *fig. Person in den Leistungen*: slip; *moralisch*: go downhill, backslide; **3.** *fig. Leistungen*: drop (off), go downhill

Abruzzen *Pl. Geog.* Abruzzi

ABS *Abk.* → *Antiblockiersystem*

Abs. *Abk.* → *Absatz* 1, *Absender*, *Absenderin*

absäbeln *v/t.* (*trennb.*, hat -ge-); *umg. mit Messer*: cut off

absacken *v/i.* (*trennb.*, *ist -ge-*) **1.** *Boden etc.*: sag; *auch Schiff*: sink; *Flugzeug*: pitch down, lose altitude; *bei der Landung*: make a pancake landing; *Boden*: sag (downward); **2.** *fig. in der Schule*: slip; *moralisch*: go to seed (*od.* pot *od.* downhill)

Absage *f* **1.** *e-r Veranstaltung, e-s Fluges*: cancel(l)ation; **2.** (*Ggs. Zusage*) refusal, negative reply; **3.** *fig.*: **~ an** renunciation of; **dem Rassismus e-e ~ erteilen** reject racism; *od.* strike a blow against racism); **4.** *TV, Radio*; *am Ende*: signing-off

absagen (*trennb.*, hat -ge-) **I.** *v/t.* **1.** (*Veranstaltung, Flug*) cancel, call off; **2.** (*Einladung*) turn down; **II.** *vt/i.* **1.** *auch als Künstler*: (*nach vorheriger Zusage*) cry (*od.* beg) off; **2.** *TV, Radio*; *am Ende der Sendung*: sign off, make the closing announcement; **III.** *v/i.* **1.** *j-m* **~** (*Veranstaltung, Termin*) tell s.o. s.th. is off; (*j-n ausladen*) tell s.o. not to come; (*wenn man selbst verhindert ist*) tell s.o. one can't come, cancel; **ich muss leider ~** I'm afraid I can't come (after all); **2.** *geh. fig.*: **e-r Sache ~** renounce s.th., break with s.th.

absägen *v/t.* (*trennb.*, hat -ge-) **1.** saw off (**von etw.** from s.th.); **2.** *umg. fig.* (give *s.o.* the) axe (*Am.* ax)

absahnen (*trennb.*, hat -ge-) **I.** *v/t.* **1.** (*entrahmen*) skim, cream; **2.** *umg. fig.* cream off; **II.** *v/i. umg. fig.* cream (*od.* siphon) off the profits *allg.*, **bei etw. ordentlich ~** (really) make a killing

absatteln *vt/i.* (*trennb.*, hat -ge-); (*Pferd*) unsaddle

Absatz *m* **1.** (*abgek. Abs.*) (*Abschnitt*) paragraph (*auch Jur.*); (*Sprechpause*) break; *Druck.* break; **e-n ~ machen** make a break, start a new paragraph; **er bezog sich auf Paragraph 5, ~ 2** he referred to Section 5, paragraph 2; **2.** *an Schuh*: heel; **mit hohen/niedrigen Absätzen** with high/low heels; **auf dem ~ kehrtmachen** *fig.* turn on one's heel; **3.** *Wirts.* sales *Pl.*, turnover; **~ finden** be marketable, find a ready market; **reißenden ~ finden** sell like hot cakes *umg.*; **der ~ stockt** turnover slackens (*od.* is slack); **4.** *an Treppe*: landing; *in der Mauer*: ledge; *im Gelände*: terrace, bench, step; *im Gestein*: overhang, deposition

Absatz|chancen *Pl.* sales prospects; **~einbruch** *m* slump (in sales *od.* the market); **~flaute** *f* slackness (in sales *od.* the market); **~förderung** *f* sales promotion; **~garantie** f guaranteed sales Pl.; **~gebiet** n market(ing area); **~krise** f slump in sales

absatzlos Adj. Schuhe: flat

Absatzmarke f Tastatur: (line) return od. enter key

Absatz|markt m Wirts. market, outlet; **~möglichkeiten** Pl. sales potential Sg.; **~rückgang** m decline in sales; **~schwierigkeiten** Pl. marketing problems; **~steigerung** f increase in sales; **~strategie** f marketing strategy; **~volumen** n sales volume

absatzweise Adv. by (od. in) paragraphs

Absatzzeichen n Druck. break mark

absaufen v/i. (unreg., trennb., ist -ge-); umg. Schiff: sink, go down allg.; Person: drown allg.; Mot. be flooded

Absauganlage f Tech. air extraction system; e-s Z ahnarztes: suction apparatus

absaugen v/t. (trennb., hat -ge-) **1.** (Teppich etc.) vacuum (od. Hoover ® Brit.); **2.** bes. Tech. (Gas, Staub etc.) suck out (**von etw.** from s.th.); (Flüssigkeit) suck off (**von etw.** from s.th.); **3.** Med. aspirate; **Flüssigkeit aus der Lunge** ~ aspirate the lung(s), remove liquid from the lung(s)

Absaugpumpe f Tech. exhaust pump

abschaben v/t. (trennb., hat -ge-) **1.** (entfernen) scrape off (**von etw.** s.th.); **2.** (von etw. befreien) scrape; → **abgeschabt**

abschaffen (trennb., hat -ge-) **I.** v/t. **1.** abolish, do away (with); (Gesetz) repeal; **2.** (Ggs. anschaffen) get rid of; (Auto etc.) auch give up; **3.** umg. (j-s Stelle streichen, etw. einsparen) axe (Am. ax); **II.** v/refl. südd., schw. (abarbeiten) slave away; **Abschaffung** f; nur Sg. abolition; e-s Gesetzes: repeal

abschälen (trennb., hat -ge-) **I.** v/t. **1.** (Rinde etc.) peel off (**von etw.** s.th.); **2.** (Apfel) peel; (Baum etc.) strip (od. peel) bark off a tree; **II.** v/refl. peel off

Abschaltautomatik f automatic shut-off

abschalten (trennb., hat -ge-) **I.** v/t. (Licht, Motor, Radio etc.) switch (od. turn) off (Licht: auch out); (Strom) cut off, disconnect; (Reaktor) shut down; **II.** v/i. umg. fig. switch off; (sich erholen) relax, forget about everything (for a while); **Abschaltung** f von Strom: switching off

abschattieren v/t. (trennb., hat) shade

abschätzbar Adj. Folgen etc.: foreseeable; **abschätzen** v/t. (trennb., hat -ge-); (Zahl, Größe, Entfernung) estimate; (Qualität, Situation, Zustand) assess; (Folgen etc.) anticipate, foresee; fig. (j-n ~d betrachten) size up

abschätzend I. Part.Präs. → **abschätzen**; **II.** Adj. (prüfend) speculative; **ein ~er Blick** an appraising look

abschätzig Adj. Bemerkung etc.: disparaging, derogatory

Abschätzung f estimation (od. assessment)

abschauen v/t. (trennb., hat -ge-); bes. südd., österr., schw. → **abgucken**

Abschaum m pej. scum; fig. (auch ~ der Menschheit) scum of the earth

abschäumen v/t. (trennb., hat -ge-); Gastr. skim off; (Schmutz etc.) scum, skim

abscheiden I. v/t. (unreg., trennb., hat -ge-); **1.** Chem. eliminate; precipitate; **2.** Physiol. in flüssiger Form: secrete, in fester Form: deposit; **3.** Metall. re-

fine; → **abgeschieden** II, III; **II.** v/refl. **1.** Flüssigkeiten: be given off; Eiter etc.: be secreted; **2.** Chem. be precipitated, separate down, be deposited, settle; **Abscheider** m Tech. separator; **Abscheidung** f **1.** elimination; precipitation; Physiol. secretion; Metall. refining; **2.** (Produkt) Chem. precipitate; Geol. deposit; Physiol. secretion

abscheren v/t. (unreg., trennb., hat -ge-); (Haare, Wolle) shear off (**von etw.** from s.th.); **sich** (Dat.) **den Bart** etc. ~ shave off one's beard etc.

Abscheu m; -s und f; -, kein Pl. horror (**vor** of), disgust (for, at), loathing (for); ~ **erregend** repulsive; ~ **haben vor** detest, loathe

abscheuern (trennb., hat -ge-) **I.** v/t. **1.** (entfernen) scrub off, scour off (**beide von etw.** s.th.); **2.** (reinigen) scrub, scour; **3.** (Kleidung) wear thin; (Haut) scrape, rub off; **sich** (Dat.) **die Haut** ~ scrape one's skin off; **II.** v/refl. Kleidung: wear thin

abscheuerregend Adj.: **äußerst** ~ thoroughly repulsive

abscheulich I. Adj. **1.** (sehr böse) Tat: despicable; (grauenhaft) dreadful; Verbrechen: heinous, atrocious; **2.** (sehr schlecht) dreadful, awful; Wetter auch: atrocious; **es war einfach** ~ it was ghastly; **3.** (sehr hässlich) Kröte etc.: hideous, repulsive; **II.** Adv. **1.** umg. (sehr) ~ **kalt** hideously cold; ~ **wehtun** hurt like hell umg.; **2. sich** ~ **benehmen** behave disgracefully; ~ **riechen** etc. smell disgusting; **Abscheulichkeit** f **1.** nur Sg. (Zustand) repulsiveness, awfulness; **2.** (Tat) atrocity, abomination

abschicken v/t. (trennb., hat -ge-) send off, dispatch; (Brief etc.) post, bes. Am. mail

Abschiebehaft f custody prior to deportation, remand pending deportation

abschieben (unreg., trennb., -ge-) **I.** v/t. (hat) **1.** push away (**von** from); **2.** (ausweisen) deport (**nach** to); **3.** umg. fig. (j-n, loswerden) get rid of allg., shunt off umg.; **4. die Schuld auf j-n** ~ put the blame on s.o., push the blame onto s.o.; **II.** v/i. (ist) umg. (weggehen) push off; **Abschiebung** f deportation

Abschiebungshaft f → **Abschiebehaft**

Abschied m; -(e)s, -e **1.** leave-taking geh., farewell, goodbye(s Pl.); **beim** (od. **zum**) ~ on (od. at) parting; ~ **nehmen** say goodbye (**von** to); **2.** altm. (Entlassung) dismissal; Mil. discharge; freiwilliger: resignation

Abschieds|brief m farewell letter; **~feier** f farewell (od. going-away) party; **~gesuch** n altm. letter of resignation; **~gruß** m goodbye, farewell; **~kuss** m goodbye (od. parting od. farewell) kiss; **j-m e-n** ~ **geben** kiss s.o. goodbye; **~rede** f farewell speech; **~schmerz** m pain of parting, wrench; **~spiel** n Sport testimonial (match); **~stunde** f hour of parting; **~vorstellung** f Theat. farewell (od. final) performance; **~wort** n; Pl. Abschiedsworte word of farewell

abschießen v/t. (unreg., trennb., hat -ge-) **1.** (Waffe) fire, discharge fachspr.; (Kugel, Pfeil) shoot, (**auf +** Akk. at); (Rakete, Torpedo) launch; **hasserfüllte Blicke auf j-n** ~ fig. shoot (od. look) daggers at s.o.; **2.** (töten) shoot down; (Vogel) bring down; →

Vogel 2; **3.** (Ast, Hand etc.) shoot off (j-m s.o. od. **von etw.** (from) s.th.); **4.** Mil. (Flugzeug) shoot (od. bring) down; (Panzer) knock out; **5.** umg. fig.: **j-n** ~ (s-e Entlassung etc. bewirken) put the skids under s.o.

abschinden v/refl. (unreg., trennb., hat -ge-); umg. work one's fingers to the bone (**für** for)

Abschirmdienst m: **Militärischer** ~ (abgek. MAD) Military Intelligence Service

abschirmen v/t. (trennb., hat -ge-) guard (**gegen** against); auch Etech. shield (from); **Abschirmung** f **1.** Vorgang: screening, shielding; **2.** bes. Etech. (Schirm) shield, screen

abschirren vt/i. (trennb., hat -ge-) unharness, unyoke

abschlachten v/t. (trennb., hat -ge-) slaughter, butcher (beide auch fig.); **Abschlachtung** f slaughter, butchering kein Pl.

abschlaffen (trennb., -ge-); umg. **I.** v/i. (nachlassen) flag; nach der Arbeit etc.: flake out; → **abgeschlafft** II; **II.** v/t. take it out of s.o.

Abschlag m **1.** Wirts. (Preisrückgang) drop in prices; (Preisnachlass) reduction, discount; (Disagio) mark-down, discount; **e-n** ~ **gewähren** make an allowance, allow a rebate (od. discount); **mit 5 %** ~ less 5 %; **2.** (Anzahlung) payment on account; **Lieferung auf** ~ on account; **e-n** ~ **zahlen auf** (+ Akk.) make a (part) payment of, pay an instal(l)ment; **3.** Fußball: kickoff ; Golf: tee, tee-off

abschlagen (unreg., trennb., hat -ge-) **I.** v/t. **1.** (Ast, Putz etc.) knock off (**von etw.** s.th.); (Kopf) cut off; (Baum) cut down; **2.** (Ball) Fußball: kick out; Golf: tee off; **3.** (Angriff) beat off, repulse; **4.** (ablehnen) turn down; **j-m e-n Wunsch** ~ deny s.o. a wish; **das dürfen Sie mir nicht** ~ you can't refuse me that; **5.** (abbauen) (Gerüst) dismantle (od. take down); (Lager) strike (Zelt) take down (od. dismantle); **6.** beim Fangenspielen etc.: play twos and threes; **II.** v/i. Fußball: kick the ball out (od. kick off); Golf: tee off; **III.** v/refl. (niederschlagen) Dampf etc.: condense; → **abgeschlagen** II

abschlägig Adj. Amtspr. negative; **~e Antwort** negative reply; **e-e ~e Antwort erhalten** be turned down

Abschlagssumme f instal(l)ment

Abschlagszahlung f Wirts. payment on account; (Teilzahlung) part payment

abschlecken v/t. (trennb., hat -ge-); südd., österr., schweiz. umg. → **ablecken**

abschleifen (unreg., trennb., hat -ge-) **I.** v/t. Tech. **1.** (entfernen) grind off (**von etw.** s.th.), grind down (**von** from); (Holz) sand off (od. down); **2.** (glätten etc.) polish, smooth off; **3.** fig. polish, refine; **II.** v/refl. fig. Angewohnheit: wear off

Abschleppdienst m breakdown (Am. towing) service; konkret: breakdown men Pl., Am. wreckers Pl.

abschleppen (trennb., hat -ge-) **I.** v/t. **1.** (Auto, Schiff) (take in) tow, tow off; **2.** umg. (j-n) drag off; mit sexuellen Absichten: pick up; **II.** v/refl.: **sich** ~ **mit** struggle with

Abschlepp|kosten Pl. towing charges; **~seil** n towrope; **~stange** f tow bar; **~wagen** m breakdown truck (od. lorry), *Am.* tow truck, wrecker

abschließbar *Adj.* lockable

abschließen (*unreg.*, *trennb.*, *hat -ge-*) **I.** *v/t.* **1.** lock (up); (*Wertsachen*) lock up (*od.* away); **2.** *bes. Tech.* seal; **luftdicht/hermetisch ~** make *s.th.* airtight / seal *s.th.* hermetically; → **abgeschlossen** II 1; **3.** (*beenden*) end, (bring to a) close, conclude, wind up (**mit** on *od.* with); (*abrunden*) top off; *endgültig*: settle; (*fertigstellen*) complete; *Ausbildung, Lehre etc.*: finish, complete; → **abgeschlossen** II 2; **4.** *Wirts.* (*Bücher*) close, balance; (*Konten, Rechnungen*) settle; **5.** (*vereinbaren*): **e-n Handel ~** make a bargain, close (*od.* do *od.* make *od.* secure) a deal; **e-n Vertrag ~** conclude (*od.* sign *od.* sign) a treaty; **e-e Versicherung ~** take out (*od.* effect *förm.*) insurance (*od.* an insurance policy); **e-e Wette ~** make a bet (**mit** with) (**über** + *Akk.* on *od.* that *something happens etc.*); *Rennsport*: place a bet (**auf** + *Akk.* on); **e-n Vergleich ~** make a comparison; **II.** *v/i.* **1.** end, close, conclude; **2. mit etw. abgeschlossen haben** be done (*Am.* through) with s.th.; **er hat mit dem Leben abgeschlossen** he's ready to die; *lit.* he's prepared to meet his Maker; **3.** *Wirts.* (*sich einigen*) close the deal; sign (the contract); **mit j-m ~** *auch* come to terms with s.o.; (*Bilanz ziehen*) close **mit Gewinn/Verlust** close on (*od.* show) a profit / with a loss

abschließend I. *Part. Präs.* → **abschließen**; **II.** *Adj.* *Worte etc.*: concluding, closing, final; (*endgültig*) final, definitive; **III.** *Adv.* in conclusion; finally; **~ sagte er …** he wound up by saying …

Abschluss *m* **1.** (*Beendigung*) conclusion, end(ing), close; (*endgültiger ~, Bereinigung*) settlement; **krönender ~** culmination; **vor dem ~ stehen** be drawing to a close; **zum ~** in conclusion, finally; **zum ~ bringen/kommen** bring/come to a close; **2.** *Wirts.* a) (*das Abschließen*) *e-s Handels, Vertrags*: conclusion, completion; *e-r Versicherung*: taking out (a policy), b) *Ergebnis*: (*Geschäft*) business deal, transaction; (*Verkauf*) sale, commitment; (*Vertrag*) contract; **e-n ~ tätigen** conclude a transaction; **vor dem ~ stehen** be in the final stages (*od.* almost finished); **3.** *Wirts. der Bücher etc.*: closing, settlement; *Rechnungssumme*: balance; (*Jahresabschluss etc.*) financial statement; **4.** (*Schulabschluss etc.*) qualifications *Pl.*; **keinen ~ haben** be unqualified (*od.* have no qualifications); **5.** *Tech.* (*Abschließen*) shutting off, closing; *luftdichter etc.*: seal

Abschluss|ball *m* end-of-course dance; *Schule*: school leavers' (*Am.* graduation) ball; *Univ.* finalists' (*bes. Am.* graduation) ball; **~bilanz** *f Wirts.* final (*od.* closing) balance (sheet); **~examen** *n* → **Abschlussprüfung**; **~klasse** *f* final-year class; **~kommunikee, ~kommuniqué** *n Pol.* final communiqué; **~prüfung** *f* school-leaving (*Am. und Weiterbildung*: final) examination (*od.* exam); **~zeugnis** *n* (school-)leaving certificate, *Am.* (high-school *od.* graduation) diploma

abschmälzen *v/t.* (*trennb.*, *hat -ge-*) *Gastr.* gratinate

abschmecken *v/t.* (*trennb.*, *hat -ge-*) **1.** (*prüfen*) taste; **2.** (*würzen*) season (to taste) (**mit** with *od.* using)

abschmeicheln *v/t.* (*trennb.*, *hat -ge-*) **j-m etw. ~** wheedle s.th. out of s.o.

abschmelzen (*unreg.*, *trennb.*, *-ge-*) **I.** *v/t.* (*hat*) melt off (**von etw.** s.th.); (*Metall*) fuse; (*Erz*) smelt; **II.** *v/i.* (*ist*) *Eis, Schnee, Gletscher*: melt (away); *Tech.* fuse

abschmettern *v/t.* (*trennb.*, *hat -ge-*); *umg.* (*etw.*) reject out of hand; (*Argumente etc.*) shoot down; (*j-n*) give *s.o.* the brush-off; (*auch Beschwerde etc.*) refuse to listen to *allg.*

abschmieren (*trennb.*, *-ge-*) **I.** *v/t.* (*hat*) **1.** *Tech.* lubricate, grease; **2.** *umg.* (*unsauber abschreiben*) scribble down; (*unerlaubt abschreiben*) copy *allg.*; **II.** *v/i.* (*ist*); *Flug. umg.* (do a) nose--dive

Abschmier|fett *n Tech.* (lubricating) grease; **~presse** *f* grease gun

Abschminkcreme *f* cleanser, makeup remover; **abschminken** (*trennb.*, *hat -ge-*) **I.** *v/t.* take off *s.o.*'s makeup; **das kannst du dir ~!** *umg.* you can forget about that; **II.** *v/refl.* take one's make-up off

abschmirgeln *v/t.* (*trennb.*, *hat -ge-*) **1.** (*glätten*) (*Holz*) sand down, sandpaper; grind with emery, burnish; **2.** (*entfernen*) sand down (*od.* off)

abschmücken *v/t.* (*trennb.*, *hat -ge-*) **den Weihnachtsbaum ~** take the decorations down from the Christmas tree

abschnallen (*trennb.*, *hat -ge-*) **I.** *v/t.* (*Gürtel etc.*) unbuckle, unstrap; (*Ski etc.*) take off; **II.** *v/refl.* take one's seatbelt off; *Flug. auch* unfasten one's seatbelt; **III.** *v/i.*: **da schnallst du ab** *umg.* it's absolutely incredible *allg.*; *stärker*: it's mind-boggling

abschneiden (*unreg.*, *trennb.*, *hat -ge-*) **I.** *v/t.* **1.** cut off (**von etw.** from s.th.); *in Scheiben*: slice; (*Nägel, Haar*) cut; *Agr.* prune, trim; → **Scheibe** 2; **2.** *fig.* (*Verbindung, Zufuhr*) cut off, isolate; **j-m den Weg ~** block s.o.'s path; **von der Außenwelt abgeschnitten** cut off from the outside world; **3.** *fig.*: **j-m das Wort ~** cut s.o. short; **II.** *v/t/i.* (**den Weg**) **~** take a short cut; **III.** *v/i. umg.*: **gut** (**schlecht**) **~** do (*od.* come off *od.* fare) well (badly) (**bei** in); **am besten ~** come out on top

abschnellen (*trennb.*, *-ge-*) **I.** *v/t.* (*hat*) jerk off, flip off; (*Pfeil etc.*) let fly, shoot; **II.** *v/i.* (*ist*) shoot off, fly (*od.* spring) off, snap; **III.** *v/refl.* (*hat*) propel o.s. off, bounce off

abschnippeln *v/t.* (*trennb.*, *hat -ge-*); *umg.* snip off *allg.*

Abschnitt *m* **1.** section; *Math.* segment; *Mil. im Gelände*: sector; *e-r Straße etc.*: section; *e-s Buches*: paragraph, section, passage; *e-s Musikstückes*: section, passage; *e-r Reise etc.*: stage, leg; *e-r Entwicklung, Krankheit etc.*: phase; (*Zeitraum*) period; **ein neuer ~ in j-s Leben** a new chapter (*od.* phase) of s.o.'s life; **2.** (*abtrennbarer Teil*) stub, *e-s Schecks etc.*: *auch* counterfoil

abschnüren *v/t.* (*trennb.*, *hat -ge-*) **1.** (*Blutgefäß, Tumor etc.*) strangulate; (*Glied*) apply a tourniquet to; (*abbinden, trennen*) tie up (*od.* off); (*Schnüre losmachen*) untie; **2. j-m die Luft ~** choke s.o.; *fig.* have a stranglehold on s.o.; (*ruinieren*) ruin s.o.

abschöpfen *v/t.* (*trennb.*, *hat -ge-*) **1.** (*Schaum, Sahne*) skim off (**von etw.** s.th.); **2.** *Wirts. fig.* (*Gewinne etc.*) skim off, siphon off; (*das Beste*) cream

off

abschotten (*trennb.*, *hat -ge-*) **I.** *v/refl.* cut o.s. off; **II.** *v/t.* separate (with *od.* by a bulkhead); **Abschottung** *f* separation

abschrägen *v/t.* (*trennb.*, *hat -ge-*) slope, slant; *Tech.* bevel, chamfer

abschrammen *v/t.* (*trennb.*, *hat -ge-*); *umg.*: **sich** (*Dat.*) **die Haut ~** graze o.s.

abschrauben *v/t.* (*trennb.*, *hat -ge-*) unscrew

abschrecken *v/t.* (*trennb.*, *hat -ge-*) **1.** scare off; *weitS.* put off; **lass dich nicht ~** don't let it (*od.* them etc.) put you off; **2.** (*mit kaltem Wasser*) (*gekochte Eier*) put into cold water, rinse with cold water ; (*Nudeln*) rinse; *Metall.* chill, quench

abschreckend I. *Part.Präs* → **abschrecken**; **II.** *Adj.* off-putting; (*einschüchternd*) forbidding; *Maßnahmen etc.*: deterrent; **~es Beispiel** warning, deterrent; **~e Strafe** exemplary punishment; **III.** *Adv.*: **~ wirken** act as a deterrent (**auf** + *Akk.* to)

Abschreckung *f* **1.** deterrence; **2.** → **Abschreckungsmittel**

Abschreckungs|mittel *n* deterrent; **~strategie** *f Mil.* strategy of deterrence; **~waffe** *f Mil.* deterrent weapon

abschreiben (*unreg.*, *trennb.*, *hat -ge-*) **I.** *vt/i.* *unerlaubt von Mitschülern*, *umg. auch als Autor*: copy, crib *umg.* (**bei** *od.* **von** from); (*Ideen*) plagiarize; **II.** *v/t.* **1.** (*Text*) copy; (*übertragen, bes. von Kurzschrift*) transcribe; **2.** *Wirts.* (*Forderungen*) gänzlich: write off; *teilweise*: write down; *steuerlich*: deduct, write off; (*Wert*) depreciate; (*Summe*) deduct; **3.** *umg. fig.* (*j-n od. etw. aufgeben*) write off; **den kannst du ~** *auch* you can forget about him, you can count him out; **mich kannst du als Freund ~** you can write me off as a friend; **ich hatte dich schon ganz abgeschrieben** (*hatte schon geglaubt, du kommst/lebst nicht mehr*) I'd already given up on you; **dein Auto kannst du ~** your car is finished; **III.** *v/i. j-m ~* write (to s.o.) to say one can't come (*od.* that the party *etc.* is off); **IV.** *v/refl. Bleistift*: wear down; *Farbband*: wear out, *Farbstift*: run out

Abschreibung *f Wirts.* writing off; (*Wertminderung*) depreciation

Abschreibungs|betrag *m Wirts.* depreciation (allowance); **~betrug** *m* tax deduction fraud; **~fonds** *m* depreciation fund; **~gesellschaft** *f* tax-loss company

abschreiten *v/t.* (*unreg.*, *trennb.*, *-ge-*) **1.** (*hat*) (*abmessen*) pace off (*od.* out); **2.** (*hat/ist*) **die Front ~** inspect the troops

Abschrift *f* copy, duplicate; **beglaubigte ~** authenticated copy

abschrubben *v/t.* (*trennb.*, *hat -ge-*); *umg.* **1.** (*säubern*) scrub, scour *allg.*; **2.** (*entfernen*) scrub away *allg.*(**von etw.** from s.th.), scrub off (**von etw.** s.th.) *allg.*

abschuften *v/refl.* (*trennb.*, *hat -ge-*) *umg.* slave away

abschuppen (*trennb.*, *hat -ge-*) **I.** *v/t.* scale; **II.** *v/i. und v/refl.* peel (off)

abschürfen *v/t.* (*trennb.*, *hat -ge-*) **sich** (*Dat.*) **die Haut ~** graze o.s. (**am Knie** etc.) scrape (*od.* graze) one's knee *etc.*; **Abschürfung** *f* graze

Abschuss *m* **1.** *e-r Waffe*: firing, discharge; *Rakete, Torpedo*: launching; **2.** *von Wild*: shooting; **zum ~ freigeben** permit the shooting of animals; **j-n zum ~ freigeben** *umg.*, *fig.* throw s.o.to the wolves; **3.** (*das Abschießen*) *Flugzeug*: downing; *Panzer*: knocking out; **4.** (*Treffer*) hit, strike; **drei Abschüsse wurden gemeldet** three planes were reported shot down; **~basis** *f* launching pad (*od.* site)

abschüssig *Adj.* sloping, sloped, slanting, *stärker*: steep; *fachspr.* declivate, decliv(it)ous

Abschuss|liste *f*: **auf der ~ stehen** *umg.* be on the blacklist, be (in) for the chop; **~prämie** *f Jagd*: bounty; **~rampe** *f Mil.* launching pad

abschussreif *Adj. umg. fig. Politiker etc.*: ready for the boot; **er ist ~ auch** he's on his way out

Abschusssilo *m, n Mil.* silo

abschütteln *v/t.* (*trennb., hat -ge-*) shake off (*auch fig.*)

abschütten *v/t.* (*trennb., hat -ge-*) pour off (*od.* out)

abschwächen (*trennb., hat -ge-*) **I.** *v/t.* **1.** (*Aufprall, Schlag*) cushion, lessen; **2.** (*Wirkung etc.*) weaken, reduce; (*mildern*) mitigate; (*beschönigen*) extenuate; (*Aussage, Farben*) tone down; **3.** *Fot.* (*Negativ*) reduce; **II.** *v/refl.* (*Einfluss, Macht, Wirkung*) weaken, wane; (*abnehmen*) diminish; (*Lärm, Sturm*) abate; **Abschwächung** *f* weakening; reduction; suppression; mitigation; extenuation; toning down, fading; → **abschwächen**

abschwatzen *v/t.* (*trennb., hat -ge-*): **j-m etw. ~** wheedle s.th. out of s.o.

abschweifen *v/i.* (*trennb., ist -ge-*) **1.** *vom Thema*: digress; **nicht ~!** keep (*od.* stick) to the point!; **2. sein Blick schweifte wiederholt ab** his eyes kept wandering; **3.** *vom Weg*: deviate, *versehentlich*: stray; **Abschweifung** *f* deviation; digression

abschwellen *v/i.* (*unreg., trennb., ist -ge-*); *Med.* go down; *Geräusch*: die away; *Sturm*: die down; *Flut*: subside, ebb away

abschwemmen *v/t.* (*trennb., hat -ge-*) wash away, float off; *Chem.* elutriate; *Geol. auch* erode; **Abschwemmung** *f durch Regen*: rainwash

abschwenken *v/i.* (*trennb., ist -ge-*) **1.** swerve, veer (off); *Mil.* wheel (off); **2.** *fig.*: **~ von** switch (*od.* veer) from

abschwindeln *v/t.* (*trennb., hat -ge-*): **j-m etw. ~** swindle s.o. out of s.th.

abschwirren *v/i.* (*trennb., ist -ge-*); *umg.* buzz off *gespr.*

abschwitzen *v/t.* (*trennb., hat -ge-*); (*Gewicht*) sweat off

abschwören *v/i.* (*unreg., trennb., hat -ge-*); *geh.* (*dem Glauben etc.*) renounce; **dem Alkohol ~** give up drinking, swear off drink(ing), forswear drinking

Abschwung *m* **1.** *Turnen*: dismount; **2.** *Wirts.* downswing, downturn

absegeln (*trennb., -ge-*) **I.** *v/i.* a) (*ist*) set sail (**nach** for), sail away, b) (*hat*) finish the sailing (*od.* yachting) season, have one's last sail *umg.*; **II.** *v/t.* (*hat*); (*Strecke*) sail (through); (*Gebiet*) cruise (around *od.* through)

absegnen *v/t.* (*trennb., hat -ge-*); *umg. fig.* give one's blessing to; **es muss noch vom Chef abgesegnet werden** it still has to have the boss's blessing, it still has to be okayed by the boss

absehbar *Adj.* foreseeable; **in ~er Zeit** in the foreseeable future; **nicht ~ zeitlich**: unforeseeable; **der Schaden ist nicht ~** the extent of the damage is not yet known

absehen (*unreg., trennb., hat -ge-*)

I. *v/t.* **1.** (*fore*)see; **es ist kein Ende abzusehen** there's no end in sight; **die Folgen sind nicht abzusehen** there's no telling how things will turn out, the results are unpredictable; **2.** (*ablesen*) see (**an** from, by); **3.** (*abgucken*): **j-m etw. ~** learn s.th. by watching s.o.; **4. es abgesehen haben auf** *umg.* be out for (*od.* to + *Inf.*); (*j-n*) have it in for; **II.** *v/i.* **1. von etw. ~** (*nicht tun*) refrain from; **von e-m Plan ~** abandon, drop; → **Beileidsbezeigung**; **2.** (*unbeachtet lassen*) disregard; → **abgesehen** II; **III.** *vt/i.* (*unerlaubt abschreiben*): (**etw. bei j-m**) **~** copy, crib *umg.* (s.th. from s.o.)

abseifen *v/t.* (*trennb., hat -ge-*) soap (down)

abseihen *v/t.* (*trennb., hat -ge-*) strain

abseilen (*trennb., hat -ge-*) **I.** *v/t.* lower (on a rope); **II.** *v/refl.* **1.** *Bergsteiger*: abseil, *Am. auch* rappel; **2.** *umg. fig.* take o.s. off, make a getaway

abseits I. *Adv.*: **1. ~ stehen** stand apart; *Sport* be offside; **etwas ~ liegen** be a bit out of the way; **~ vom Trubel** away from the action, out of the thick of things; **2.** *fig.*: **sich ~ halten** keep one's distance; **II.** *Präp.* off; **~ der Hauptstraße** off the main road

Abseits *n*; -, - **1.** *Sport* offside; **im ~ stehen** be offside; **nicht im ~ stehen** be onside; **2.** *weitS.* **ins ~ gedrängt werden** be pushed onto the sidelines, be edged out; (*Land, Gesellschaftsschicht etc.*) *auch* be marginalized

Abseits|falle *f Sport* offside trap; **~regel** *f* offside rule; **~stellung** *f*: **in ~ in** an offside position; **~tor** *n* offside goal

abseitsverdächtig *Adj. Sport* possibly offside *präd.*; **ein Tor aus ~er Position** a goal scored from a position which may have been offside

absenden *v/t.* (*auch unreg., trennb., hat -ge-*) send (off); *Wirts. auch* forward, dispatch; (*Postsendung*) send, post, *bes. Am.* mail; **Absender** *m*; -s, - (*abgek.* Abs.) **1.** sender, *Wirts. auch* consignor, consigner; **zurück an ~** return to sender; **2.** (*Adresse des ~s*) return address; **Absenderangabe** *f* sender's address; **Absenderin** *f*; -, -nen (*abgek.* Abs.) → **Absender** 1; **Absendung** *f* dispatch

absengen *v/t.* (*trennb., hat -ge-*) **1.** (*Geflügel*) singe; **2.** (*Federn, Haare*) singe off

absenken (*trennb., hat -ge-*) **I.** *v/t.* **1.** (*Wasserspiegel*) lower; **2.** *Agr.* (*Ableger*) layer; **3.** *Bergb.* (*Schacht*) sink; **II.** *v/refl.* (*Boden, Gelände*) slope, subside; *Gestein*: settle; **Absenkung** *f* **1.** (*Senken*) *Wasser*: lowering; *Gestein*; settling; (*Absinken*) slope, incline; **2.** *Agr.* layering; **3.** *Bergb.* sinking

Absenz *f*; -, -en **1.** *geh.* (*Fehlen*) absence *allg.*; **2.** *österr., schw.* (*in der Schule*) absence

abservieren (*trennb., hat*) **I.** *v/i.* clear the table; **II.** *v/t.*: **j-n ~** *umg.* give s.o. the boot; (*ermorden*) bump s.o. off; **den Gegner ~** thrash one's opponent(s)

absetzbar *Adj.*: (**steuerlich ~** tax-)deductible; *Wirts.* marketable; **leicht/schwer ~** easy/hard to sell

absetzen (*trennb., hat -ge-*) **I.** *v/t.* **1.** (*Gegenstand*) set (*od.* put) down; (*Brille, Hut*) take off; **2.** (*Ggs. ansetzen*) (*Glas, Feder, Gewehr*) put down; **er trank, ohne das Glas einmal abzusetzen** *auch* he downed his pint etc. in one *umg.*, *Am.* he chug-a-lugged it

(*od.* drank it chug-a-lug) *Sl.*; **ohne den Stift abzusetzen** without lifting pen from (the) paper; **3.** (*Mitreisenden, Fallschirmspringer*) drop (off) (**an, bei** at); **4.** *Druck.* (*Text*) set (in type), set up, compose; **die Zeile ~** begin a new line; **5.** (*streichen*) drop; **von der Tagesordnung** etc. **~** take off the agenda etc.; **6.** *Wirts.* write off (*steuerlich*: against tax); (*abziehen*) deduct; **7.** *vom Amt*: dismiss; (*Herrscher etc.*) depose; **8.** *Wirts.* sell; **sich leicht** (*schwer*) **~ lassen** (not) sell well; **9.** *Med.* (*Arznei*) stop taking; (*Drogen*) come off; (*Therapie*) break off; **10.** *mit e-r Borte etc.*: trim; **11.** *bes. Geol., Chem.* deposit, precipitate; **12.** *Pferd*: (*den Reiter*) throw; **13.** *Naut.* (*abstoßen*) push off; **II.** *v/refl.* **1.** *auch Geol., Chem.* (*liegen bleiben*) settle, deposit; **2.** *umg.* (*weggehen*) clear out (*od.* off), make off, leave (**nach** for); **sich ins Ausland ~** leave the country; **3.** *Mil.* withdraw, retreat; **4.** *Sport* pull ahead, leave the others behind; **III.** *v/i.* (*unterbrechen*) stop, break off; **ohne abzusetzen** without a break; *auch beim Trinken*: in one go, *Am.* chug-a-lug *Sl.*; *beim Schreiben*: straight off

Absetzung *f* **1.** *e-s Ministers etc.*: dismissal; *e-s Herrschers*: deposition; **2.** *e-s Theaterstücks*: withdrawal; *e-r Veranstaltung*: cancel(l)ation; **3.** *e-r Arznei*: discontinuation; **4.** *Geol., Chem.* deposition, precipitation; **5.** *Druck.* line *od.* paragraph break

absichern (*trennb., hat -ge-*) **I.** *v/t.* **1.** (*Gefahrenstelle*) make s.th. safe; (*Unfallstelle etc.*) cordon off; **die Decke ~** support the ceiling; **2.** (*Investitionen*) hedge; **II.** *v/refl.* cover o.s. (**gegen** against); **sich vertraglich ~** protect o.s. by contract; **Absicherung** *f* protection; (*Gefahrenstelle*) making safe; *e-s* (*Forschungs- etc.*) *Ergebnisses*: validation

Absicht *f*; -, -en intention; (*Ziel*) aim, object; *bes. Jur.* intent; **in der ~ zu** (+ *Inf.*) with the intention of (+ *Ger.*), with a view to (+ *Ger.*); **in betrügerischer/guter ~** with intent to deceive (*od.* defraud) / with good intentions; **ohne böse ~** not meaning to hurt (you, him etc.); **mit ~** on purpose, deliberately; **mit der festen ~ zu** (+ *Inf.*) determined to (+ *Inf.*); **ohne ~** unintentionally; **nicht ohne ~** not entirely unintentionally; **ich habe die ~ zu** (+ *Inf.*) I intend to (+ *Inf.*), I'm planning to (+ *Inf.*); **es war nicht m-e ~ zu** (+ *Inf.*) I didn't mean to (+ *Inf.*); **das liegt nicht in m-r ~** that isn't my intention; **die ~ war zu** (+ *Inf.*) the idea was to (+ *Inf.*); **j-s ~en durchschauen** see through s.o.'s plans; **~en auf j-n haben** *umg. altm.* have designs on s.o.

absichtlich I. *Adj.* intentional, deliberate; *Jur.* wil(l)ful; **II.** *Adv.* intentionally *etc.*; on purpose

Absichtserklärung *f bes. Pol.* declaration of intent

absichtslos *Adj.* unintentional

absingen *v/t.* (*unreg., trennb., hat -ge-*) (*Lied*) sing (through); *vom Blatt*: sing at sight

absinken *v/i.* (*unreg., trennb., ist -ge-*) **1.** (*Schiff*) sink; **auf den Grund ~** sink to the bottom; **2.** (*sich senken*) *Wasserstand*: drop; *Land, Ufer*: subside; **3.** *fig. Niveau etc.*: drop, sink; *Blutdruck, Fieber*: go down; *Interesse*: flag; **s-e Leistungen sinken ab** he's not doing as well as he used to; **4.** (*Person*) (*verkommen*) degenerate (*in* into)

Absinth *m*; -(*e*)*s*, -*e* absinth(e)

absitzen (*unreg.*, *trennb.*, -*ge*-) **I.** *v/i.* (*ist*); (*auch* **vom Pferd** ~) dismount, get off one's horse; (*auch* **vom Motorrad** *etc.* ~) get off (one's motorbike *etc.*); **II.** *v/t.* (*hat*); (*Zeit*) sit out; *e-e Strafe* ~ serve a sentence; *s-e Strafe* ~ do time (*wegen* for), do a spell inside (for)

absolut I. *Adj. alle Bedeutungen:* absolute; *umg.* (*völlig*) *auch* complete, total; ~*es Gehör auch* perfect pitch; *es ist sein* ~*es Recht zu* (+ *Inf.*) he has every right to (+ *Inf.*); **II.** *Adv.* absolutely; *ich sehe* ~ *keinen Sinn darin* I just don't see the point of it; *er hat* ~ *keine Skrupel* he has no scruples whatsoever; *wenn du* ~ *gehen willst* if you really have to go; ~ *nicht!* not at all

Absolutheit *f*; *nur Sg.* absoluteness, perfection

Absolution *f*; -, -*en*; *kath.* absolution; *j-m die* ~ *erteilen* give (*od.* grant) s.o. absolution, forgive s.o. *umg.*

Absolutismus *m*; -, *kein Pl*; *hist.* absolutism; **absolutistisch** *Adj.* absolutist

Absolvent *m*; -*en*, -*en*, ~*in* *f*; -, -*nen* school-leaver, *Am.* (high-school) graduate; *e-r Hochschule:* graduate

absolvieren *v/t.* (*trennb.*, *hat*); (*Studium*, *Diplom*) finish, complete; (*Schule*, *Hochschule*) finish, *Am.* graduate from; (*Prüfung*) pass; (*Pensum*) do; *mit Mühe:* get through; **Absolvierung** *f*; *nur Sg.* graduation, completion

absonderlich *Adj.* peculiar, strange, odd; **Absonderlichkeit** *f* **1.** *nur Sg.*; *Zustand:* strangeness, oddness; **2.** *Eigenschaft:* peculiarity

absondern (*trennb.*, *hat* -*ge*-) **I.** *v/t.* **1.** separate, segregate; (*isolieren*) isolate; *abgesondert auch* separate; **2.** *Bot.*, *Physiol.* secrete; **3.** *Chem.* separate, isolate; **II.** *v/refl.*; *fig. Person:* isolate o.s., cut o.s. off (*von* from); **Absonderung** *f* separation; isolation; *Physiol.* secretion; *Geol.* detachment, parting

Absorbens *n*; -, *Absorbenzien und Absorbentia*; *Chem.* absorbent

Absorber *m*; -*s*, - absorber

absorbieren *v/t.* (*trennb.*, *hat*) absorb (*auch fig.*); **absorbierend** *Adj.* absorbent

Absorption *f*; -, -*en* absorption

absorptionsfähig *Adj.* absorptive

Absorptionsspektrum *n Phys.* absorption spectrum

abspalten (*trennb.*, *hat* -*ge*-) **I.** *v/t. auch fig.*, *Chem.*, *Phys.* split(*od.* wedge) off (*von* from); (*Stein*) spall; (*Kristall*) cleave; **II.** *v/refl. von Partei etc.:* splinter off, form a splinter group

Abspann *m Film:* credits *Pl.*

abspannen (*trennb.*, *hat* -*ge*-) **I.** *vt/i.* (*Pferd*, *Wagen*) unhitch (*von* from); (*Geschirr abnehmen*) unharness; (*Ochsen*) unyoke; *Tech.* (*strecken*) straighten, stretch; (*schlaff machen*) (*Feder etc.*) relax, unbend, dismount; **II.** *v/t. Tech.* (*Mast etc.*) rig; → *abgespannt* II; **Abspannung** *f* **1.** *Tech.* anchoring; **2.** *fig.* exhaustion, fatigue

absparen *v/t.* (*trennb.*, *hat* -*ge*-): *sich* (*Dat.*) *etw.* (*vom Munde*) ~ scrimp and save for s.th.

abspecken *v/i.* (*trennb.*, *hat* -*ge*-); *umg.* slim, *Am.* reduce

abspeichern *v/t.* (*trennb.*, *hat* -*ge*-); *EDV* save, make a backup (of)

abspeisen *v/t.* (*trennb.*, *hat* -*ge*-) **1.** *pej.*

feed; **2.** *fig. j-n* ~ fob s.o. off (*mit* with)

abspenstig *Adj.*: *j-m j-n / die Freundin* ~ *machen* turn s.o. against s.o. / take s.o.'s girlfriend away (from him)

absperren *v/t.* (*trennb.*, *hat* -*ge*-) **1.** *bes. südd.*, *österr.* lock (up); **2.** (*Straße*) *durch Barrieren:* block, barricade; *durch Polizisten etc.:* cordon off; **3.** (*Wasser*, *Gas etc.*) cut off

Absperr|gitter *n* crowd barrier; ~**hahn** *m* stopcock; ~**kette** *f* cordon

Absperrung *f* **1.** *e-r Straße durch Barrieren:* roadblock; *durch Polizisten:* cordon; **2.** *von Strom etc.:* cutting off

Absperrventil *n* stop (*od.* check *od.* shut-off) valve

Abspiel *n Sport* pass(ing)

abspielen (*trennb.*, *hat* -*ge*-) **I.** *v/t.* **1.** (*Platte*, *CD etc.*) play; (*Tonband etc.*) *bes. zur Überprüfung:* auch play back; **2.** *Mus. vom Blatt:* play at sight; **II.** *vt/i. Sport:* (*den Ball*) ~ pass the ball (*an* + *Akk.* to); **III.** *v/refl.* (*geschehen*) happen, take place; (*los sein*) be going on; *wie/wo hat sich der Unfall abgespielt?* how did the accident happen (*od.* occur *förm.*)? / where did the accident take place?; *da spielt sich nichts ab umg.* nothing doing

absplittern (*trennb.*, -*ge*-) **I.** *v/i.* (*ist*) chip off (*von etw.* s.th.), splinter (*von* off), come (*od.* fly) off in splinters; *Farbe*, *Lack:* flake (*od.* peel) off (*von etw.* s.th.); **II.** *v/t.* (*hat*) splinter (*od.* split) (*von* off); (*auch Farbe*, *Lack*) chip off (*von etw.* (from) s.th.); **III.** *v/refl.* (*hat*) → *abspalten* II; **Absplitterung** *f* **1.** (*das Absplittern*) chipping off, splintering off; **2.** (*Splittergruppe*) splinter group

Absprache *f* arrangement; *mündliche* ~ verbal agreement; *laut* ~ according to the agreement (*od.* arrangement); *in* ~ *mit* in consultation (*od.* arrangement) with; **absprachegemäß** *Adv.* as agreed; *Wirt.* as per agreement (*od.* arrangement)

absprechen (*unreg.*, *trennb.*, *hat* -*ge*-) **I.** *v/t.* **1.** (*abmachen*) arrange; *hast du es mit ihm schon abgesprochen?* have you spoken to him about it?; *das war so abgesprochen* it was planned like that; **2.** (*in Abrede stellen*) deny, dispute; *Talent kann man ihm nicht* ~ there's no denying his talent, he's certainly got talent; **3.** *Jur.* (*j-m etw.*) dispossess of, deprive of; **II.** *v/refl.*: *sich* ~ *über* (+ *Akk.*) agree about, plan

abspreizen *v/t.* (*trennb.*, *hat* -*ge*-) **1.** (*Finger etc.*) stretch out; **2.** *Archit.* (*abstützen*) brace, prop, stay

absprengen *v/t.* (*trennb.*, *hat* -*ge*-) *mit Sprengstoff:* blow up; (*Felsen etc.*) blast (*od.* shoot) off (*von etw.* [from] s.th.); (*Glas*) crack

abspringen *v/i.* (*unreg.*, *trennb.*, *ist* -*ge*-) **1.** jump off (*od.* down); *Sport* take (*od.* jump) off; *Flug.* jump; *im Notfall:* bale out; *vom Pferd* ~ jump off one's horse; **2.** (*abprallen*) bounce off (*von etw.* s.th.); **3.** *Knopf:* fall (*od.* come) off; *Farbe*, *Fahrradkette etc.:* come off; *Splitter:* auch chip off (*beide von etw.* s.th.); **4.** *fig. von e-m Kurs etc.:* drop out (*von* of); *von e-r Verpflichtung:* back out (of); ~ *von e-r Partei etc.:* leave

abspritzen (*trennb.*, *hat* -*ge*-) **I.** *v/t.* (*hat*) **1.** (*bespritzen*) (*Pflanzen*) spray; **2.** (*Schmutz*) hose (*od.* wash) down; **II.** *v/i.* **1.** (*ist*) (*wegspritzen*) spray off; splash off; **2.** (*hat*) *vulg.* come, spurt,

shoot one's wad

Absprung *m* **1.** jump; *Sport Stabhoch-*, *Hoch-*,*Weitsprung:* take-off; **2.** *fig.:* *den* ~ *wagen* take the plunge; *den* ~ *schaffen/verpassen* make it / miss the boat; ~**balken** *m Sport* takeoff board; ~**höhe** *f* drop altitude; ~**stelle** *f* jumping-off point

abspulen *v/t.* (*trennb.*, *hat* -*ge*-) **1.** unwind; (*Film*) run *a* film through; **2.** *umg. fig.* (*ableiern*) reel off

abspülen *v/t.* (*trennb.*, *hat* -*ge*-) **1.** (*spülen*, *ab-*, *aufwaschen*) wash up, do the washing up (*Am.* the dishes); **2.** (*wegspülen*) rinse (*od.* wash) (off), (*sauber spülen*) (*Wäsche etc.*) give *s.th.* a rinse; *Geog.* wash down; erode

abstammen *v/i.* (*trennb.*, *ist* -*ge*-): ~ *von* be descended from; *Ling.* derive from; **Abstammung** *f* **1.** descent, origin; (*Geburt*) birth; *italienischer etc.* ~ of Italian *etc.* descent (*od.* extraction); **2.** *Ling.* derivation, origin

Abstammungslehre *f* theory of evolution

Abstand *m* **1.** *räumlich:* distance (*von/ zu* from); (*Zwischenraum*) space; *zwischen Zeilen:* spacing; *seismischer:* offset; *in gleichmäßigen Abständen* at regular intervals; ~ *halten* keep one's distance; *großen* ~ *halten* keep plenty of distance; *in gleichem* ~ at an equal distance; **2.** *zeitlich:* interval, gap; *zwischen zwei Daten:* span, period (*auf* + *Akk. od.* *zu* to *od.* between); *in Abständen von zwei Stunden* at two-hour intervals; *zehn Sekunden* ~ *zum od. auf den Sieger haben* be ten seconds behind the winner; **3.** *nur Sg.*; *fig.* (*Zurückhaltung*) distance; ~ *halten od. wahren* keep one's distance (*zu* to *od.* towards); ~ *von etw. gewinnen* get s.th. in(to) perspective; (*etw. seelisch überwinden*) get over s.th.; **4.** *fig.* (*großer Unterschied*) *mit* ~ *der Beste* by far (*od.* far and away) the best, the best by miles *umg.*; *mit* ~ *gewinnen:* by a wide margin, by a long chalk (*Am.* a long shot) *umg.*; **5.** *fig.:* ~ *von etw. nehmen* refrain (*od.* desist) from *Ger.*; **6.** *umg.* → *Abstandssumme*

Abstandhalter *m Tech.* spacer, distant-piece

Abstandssumme *f* **1.** (*Abfindung*) indemnity; compensation, indemnification (*an j-n* for s.o); *für Angestellte:* severance pay; **2.** *für Wohnung etwa:* key money

abstatten *v/t.* (*trennb.*, *hat* -*ge*-); *geh.:* *j-m e-n Besuch* ~ pay s.o. a visit; *j-m s-n Dank* ~ thank s.o.

abstauben (*trennb.*, *hat* -*ge*-) **I.** *v/t.* **1.** *im Haushalt etc.:* dust; **2.** *umg.* (*mitgehen lassen*) swipe, lift, snitch, *Brit.* nick; (*ergattern*) cadge, sponge; **II.** *v/i. Sport umg.* tap the ball in; **Abstauber** *m*; -*s*, -, **Abstauberin** *f*; -, -*nen*; *umg.* **1.** *oft pej.* sponge(r); **2.** *Sport* goal-hanger

Abstaubertor *n Sport* tap-in

abstechen (*unreg.*, *trennb.*, *hat* -*ge*-) **I.** *v/t.* **1.** (*Schwein*) stick; *umg.* (*Person*) slit (*od.* cut) s.o.'s throat; **2.** (*abtrennen*) (*Torf*, *Teig*, *Rasen*) cut; **3.** *fachspr.* (*abfließen lassen*) (*Bier*, *Wein*) draw off; (*Stahl etc.*) cut off; **II.** *v/i.* stand out (*von* against), compare (*gegen/vor* with)

Abstecher *m* **1.** detour; *e-n kurzen* ~ *nach X machen* take the trip to X along the way, make a quick trip to X; **2.** *fig.* digression; *e-n* ~ *machen in* (+ *Akk.*) *fig.* digress briefly on

abstecken v/t. (trennb., hat -ge-)
1. (Kleid) fit; **2.** (Land) mark out; mit
Pfählen: stake out; mit Pflöcken: peg
out; (Grundriss) trace (od. lay) out;
(Grenzen) demarcate, mark out;
3. fig. (Thema, Pläne etc.) outline;
(Standpunkt) make clear; **die Fronten
~** lay down the battle-lines; **4.** (Naht,
Saum) pin (out od. up); (Rock) mark
(the hemline [of]); **5.** Naut. (Kurs)
plot; **6.** (Ggs. anstecken) unpin
Absteck|fähnchen n surveyor's flag,
surveying rod; **~pflock** m peg, stake
abstehen v/i. (trennb., hat / südd., österr., schw. ist -ge-) **1.** stand away (von
from); (herausragen) stick out (of);
2. ~ von (verzichten auf) renounce, refrain; → **abgestanden**; **abstehend
I.** Part. Präs. → **abstehen**; **II.** Adj.: **~e
Ohren** bat (od. protruding od. umg.
jug) ears; **er hat ~e Ohren** auch his
ears stick out
absteifen v/t. (trennb., hat -ge-); Archit.
shore (od. prop od. bear) up, under-
prop, support; **Absteifung** f shoring
up, propping up, support
Absteige f umg. pej. dosshouse, dive,
Am. flophouse; (Stundenhotel) transient (od. sleazy) hotel
absteigen v/i. (unreg., trennb., ist -ge-)
1. vom Berg: descend, climb down;
vom Pferd: get off (one's horse), dismount; vom Fahrrad: get off (one's bicycle); **2.** fig. Sportklub: be relegated,
go down; **3. wo seid ihr abgestiegen?**
where did you spend the night?, which
hotel etc. did you stay at?; **absteigend I.** Part. Präs. → **absteigen**;
II. Adj. Kurve: downward, falling, des-
cending; (Rohr) down; Tonleiter: des-
cending; **auf dem ~en Ast sein** fig. be
on the way down; **Absteiger** m Sport
relegated team; **~ des Jahres** umg.
flop of the year
abstellen v/t. (trennb., hat -ge-) **1.** (absetzen) put down; **2.** (wegräumen) put
away; (Auto etc.) park; (Zug, Waggons) shunt, sidetrack; **Fahrräder ~
verboten!** no bicycles; **3.** (Maschine,
Gas, Wasser) turn off; bes. Radio und
Etech.: switch off (auch Motor); (Reaktor) shut down; (Blinker) turn off;
4. fig. (Missstand, Fehler) remedy, correct; (Unarten) eliminate, correct;
(Korruption) abolish; **5.** (abkommandieren) detail, assign (für for); **6. ~ auf**
gear to; **die Kampagne ist darauf abgestellt zu** (+ Inf.) the campaign is intended to (+ Inf.)
Abstell|fläche f storage surface; für
Autos: parking space; **~gleis** n **1.** siding; **2.** fig.: **aufs ~ schieben** put on the
shelf, sideline; (entlassen) throw on
the scrapheap umg., put out to pasture
umg; **~hahn** m stopcock; **~platte** f (im
Kühlschrank) shelf; **~raum** m backroom, lumber room, Am. storeroom,
storage room; **~rost** m grating, grill;
~taste Wecker etc.: stop button;
~tisch m für Speisen und Getränke:
dumb waiter; bei der Arbeit: stand
Abstellung f **1.** von Personen: second-
ment, Am. (temporary) assignment;
bes. Mil. assignment; **2.** von Gas,
Strom: disconnection; **3.** fig. (Beseitigung) elimination, abolition
abstemmen (trennb., hat -ge-) **I.** v/refl.
push o.s.off (od. up) (von from);
II. v/t. (entfernen) chisel off (von etw.
s.th.)
abstempeln v/t. (trennb., hat -ge-)
1. stamp; Post. postmark; (Briefmarke)
auch cancel, deface; (Metall) hallmark;

2. fig. label (als, zu etw. [as] s.th.),
dub ([as] s.th.); (abtun) write s.o. off
(as)
absteppen v/t. (trennb., hat -ge-);
(Naht, Saum) stitch; (Decke) quilt
absterben v/i. (unreg., trennb., ist -ge-)
1. Pflanzen, Zellen: die (off); Blätter,
Zweige etc.: wither; Gewebe, Nerven:
necrotize; **2.** umg. (gefühllos werden)
go numb (od. dead); **3.** umg. fig. Motor: die, stall allg.; **4.** fig. Gefühle, Liebe: die; (allmählich) peter out; → **ab-
gestorben**
Abstich m **1.** (das Abstechen 2) cutting; (Abgestochenes) cuttings Pl.;
2. fachspr. von Stahl: tap(ping), run-
n(ing)-off; von Wein etc.: racking
Abstieg m; -(e)s, -e **1.** descent, way
down; **2.** fig. decline; **3.** Sport relegation
abstiegsgefährdet Adj. threatened by
(od. in danger of) relegation; **Ab-
stiegskandidat** m candidate for relegation
abstillen vt/i. (trennb., hat -ge-); (Kind)
wean
abstimmen (trennb., hat -ge-) **I.** v/i.
Parl. etc. vote (über + Akk. on); **~ lassen über** take a vote on; **II.** v/t. Mus.
(und Radio) tune (auf + Akk. to);
Tech. und fig. (aufeinander ~) coordinate; (anpassen) adjust (to); (Farben)
match; zeitlich: time; **III.** v/refl. Pl.
come to an agreement (od. arrangement); agree to stick to the same version; **sich mit j-m ~ bei** Urlaub etc.: arrange things with s.o., coordinate with
s.o.
Abstimm|knopf m Radio: tuning (con-
trol) knob, tuner; **~schärfe** f selectivity; **~skala** f tuning dial (od. scale)
Abstimmung f **1.** voting, vote (über +
Akk. on); (Volksabstimmung) referendum; **~ durch Handzeichen** vote by
show of hands; **~ durch Zuruf** vote by
acclamation; **geheime ~** (voting by)
ballot; **offene ~** vote by open ballot;
namentliche ~ vote by roll call; **zur ~
kommen** be put to the vote; **2.** coordination (auf + Akk., mit with); zeitliche: timing; Radio: tuning
Abstimmungs|ergebnis n results Pl.
of the poll; **~niederlage** f defeat in
the vote; **~verfahren** n voting procedure
abstinent Adj. abstinent, abstemious
förm. od. hum.; **Abstinenz** f; -, kein
Pl. (total) abstinence; **Abstinenzler**
m; -s, -, **Abstinenzlerin** f; -, -nen tee-
total(l)er
abstoppen (trennb., hat -ge-) **I.** v/t.
1. (anhalten) stop; **2.** mit Stoppuhr:
clock, time, take the time of; **II.** v/i.
stop; (die Geschwindigkeit vermindern) reduce speed
Abstoß m Fußball: goal kick
abstoßen (unreg., trennb., hat -ge-)
I. v/t. **1.** (Boot etc.) push off; Magnet:
repel; **2.** (Geweih, Haut) shed; (Organe) nach Transplantation: reject;
3. (Porzellan) chip; (abbrechen) break
off; (Ecke) knock off; (Wand, Decke)
scrape off; (Schuhe) scuff; (Möbel)
knock, batter; → **Horn¹** 1; **4.** fig. (anwidern) repel, disgust, revolt; **5.** umg.
fig. (loswerden) get rid of; (verkaufen)
sell off, unload; **II.** v/refl. push o.s. off
(von etw. from s.th.); rub off; **sich gegenseitig ~** repel mutually; **III.** v/i.
Fußball: take a goal kick; **abstoßend
I.** Part. Präs. → **abstoßen**; **II.** Adj. repulsive, disgusting, revolting; **Abstoßung** f e-s Organs: rejection

abstottern v/t. (trennb., hat -ge-); umg.
pay for s.th. in instal(l)ments allg.,
Brit. buy s.th. on the never-never; **er
stottert monatlich 100 Mark ab** he
pays 100 marks a month (od. a
monthly instal[l]ment of 100 marks)
abstrafen v/t. (trennb., hat -ge-); geh.
punish; **Abstrafung** f punishment
abstrahieren (trennb., hat) **I.** v/t. (Prinzip etc.) derive, deduce; (das Wesentliche) abstract, distil(l); (in Begriffe fassen) conceptualize, abstract; **II.** v/i.
consider s.th. abstractly (od. in abstraction); in der Kunst etc.: be abstract; **~ von** (absehen von) abstain
from, renounce
abstrahlen v/t. (trennb., hat -ge-)
1. (Wärme etc.) emit, radiate; **2.** Tech.
(sandstrahlen) sandblast
abstrakt I. Adj. abstract (auch Kunst);
II. Adv. in the abstract, abstractly;
Abstraktheit f; mst Sg. abstractness
Abstraktion f; -, -en abstraction; **Abs-
traktionsvermögen** n capacity for
abstract thinking, ability to think in
abstract terms
abstrampeln (trennb., hat -ge-); umg.
I. v/t. (Decke) kick off (od. away)
allg.; **II.** v/refl. (hart arbeiten) slave
away; beim Radfahren: pedal away
(like mad)
abstreichen (unreg., trennb., -ge-)
I. v/t. (hat) **1.** (abwischen) wipe off;
(abkratzen) scrape off; (Schaum) take
off (alle von etw. from s.th.); **2.** (säubern) (Schuhe etc.) wipe; (schärfen)
(Rasiermesser) strap; **3.** (abziehen) deduct; (kürzen) cut; **4.** (Gebiet) scour,
search (nach for); **II.** v/i. (ist); Jägerspr. (Enten, Gänse etc.) fly off (od.
away)
abstreifen (trennb., -ge-) **I.** v/t. (hat)
1. (Kleidung, Ring) slip off; (Halsband, Zaumzeug) slip; **2.** (Beeren etc.)
strip (od. pick) off; (Asche) knock off;
(Schmutz) wipe off (alle von etw. from
s.th.); **3.** (säubern) (Schuhe) wipe;
4. fig. (Hemmungen etc.) cast off, free
o.s. of; (Maske) shed; **5.** (Gelände)
search, scour (nach for); Mil. patrol;
II. v/i. (ist) stray (auch fig.) (von
from)
abstreiten v/t. (unreg., trennb., hat
-ge-) **1.** (aberkennen) dispute; **j-m das
Recht ~ zu** (+ Inf.) deny s.o. the right
to (+ Inf.); **2.** (leugnen) deny; **es lässt
sich nicht ~, dass ...** there's no denying that ...
Abstrich m **1.** (Abzug) deduction;
(Kürzung) curtailment, cut; **~e machen** fig. (Erwartungen senken) lower
one's sights; **~e machen an** e-m Etat
etc. cut back on a budget etc.; **2.** Med.
smear; von den Mandeln: swab; (Untersuchung) smear test; **e-n ~ machen**
take a smear (od. swab); **3.** (Ggs. Aufstrich) beim Schreiben: downward
stroke; beim Geigenspiel etc.: down-
-stroke, down-bow
abstrus Adj. abstruse
abstufen v/t. (trennb., hat -ge-) **1.** (Gelände etc.) terrace, step, arrange in
steps; (Mauer) slope; (Haare) layer;
2. (Löhne, Steuern etc.) grade,
scale; (staffeln) auch graduate; (Farben) shade, tone, tint; (Klangfarbe)
shade; **3.** (herunterstufen) demote, put
in a lower class (od. category); **Abstufung** f **1.** im Gelände: terrace; **2.** (Staffelung) gradation, stepping; **3.** (Nuance) von Farben etc.: shade, tint; auch
fig. nuance
abstumpfen (trennb., -ge-) **I.** v/t. (hat)

1. (*Spitze*) blunt; (*Kristall*) truncate; **2.** (*Gefühle etc.*) dull; (*j-n*) deaden; **II.** *v/i.* (*ist*) *und v/refl.* (*hat*) **1.** *Gefühle etc.*: become dulled; *Person*: become hardened (*od.* insensible *to s.th.*); → *abgestumpft* II

Absturz *m* **1.** fall; *Flug.* crash; **2.** *Computer*: system crash; **3.** (*Abgrund*) precipice

abstürzen *v/i.* (*trennb., ist -ge-*) **1.** fall; *Flug.* brennend: crash (in flames); (*herabfallen*) fall down, dive; **2.** *Computer*: crash; **3.** (*abschüssig sein*) drop (*od.* descend) steeply

absturzgefährdet *Adj.* in danger of falling *präd.*

Absturz|stelle *f* site (*od.* scene) of the (*od.* a) crash; **~ursache** *f* cause of the *od.* a crash

abstützen *v/t.* (*trennb., hat -ge-*) support, prop up; *Tech. auch* shore; **Abstützung** *f* support

absuchen *v/t.* (*trennb., hat -ge-*) search (*nach* for); (*Gelände*) *auch* scour, comb (for); *mit Scheinwerfer, Radar*: sweep (in search of); *mit den Augen*: scan

Absud *m von Kräutern*: decoction, *fachspr.* extract

absurd *Adj.* absurd; (*lächerlich*) *auch* ridiculous; **~es Theater** theat|re (*Am. auch* -er) of the absurd; **Absurdität** *f*; -, *-en* absurdity

Abszess *m*; *-es, -e*; *Med.* abscess

Abszisse *f*; -, *-n*; *Math.* abscissa; **Abszissenachse** *f* axis of abscissae (*od.* abscissas), x-axis

Abt *m*; *-(e)s, Äbte* abbot

Abt. *Abk.* → *Abteilung²*

abtakeln *v/t.* (*trennb., hat -ge-*); *Naut.* unrig; (*außer Dienst stellen*) lay up; → *abgetakelt*

abtanzen *v/i.* (*trennb., hat -ge-*); *umg.* (*austoben*) have a really good dance (*od.* rave-up), *Am.* really cut up the floor

abtasten *v/t.* (*trennb., hat -ge-*) **1.** feel (*nach* for); *nach Waffen etc.*: frisk (for); *Med.* palpate; **2.** *TV, Radar etc.*: scan; *EDV auch* sample

Abtaster *m*; *-s, -*; *Tech.* scanner

Abtast|fehler *m Tech.* reading error; **~intervall** *n EDV* sample period; **~kopf** *m Fot., Druck.* scanning head

Abtauautomatik *f* automatic defroster

abtauchen *v/i.* (*trennb., ist -ge-*) **1.** *U-Boot*: submerge, go down; **2.** *umg. fig. Person*: go underground; **3.** *Boxen*: duck

abtauen (*trennb., -ge-*) **I.** *v/i.* (*ist*); *Schnee etc.*: thaw; *Fenster etc.*: clear; **II.** *v/t.* (*hat*) thaw; (*Kühlschrank etc.*) defrost

Abtausch *m* **1.** (*Schlagabtausch*) exchange (of blows); **2.** *Schach*: exchange; **3.** *schw.* → *Tausch*; **abtauschen** *v/t.* (*trennb., hat -ge-*) **1.** *Schach*: exchange; **2.** *umg.*: *j-m etw.* ~ swap s.th. with s.o., *Am. auch* trade s.o. s.th. (*for s.th. else*); **3.** *schw.* → *tauschen*

Abtei *f*; -, *-en* abbey

Abteil *n* **1.** *Eisenb.* compartment; **2.** *e-s Schranks etc.*: section

abteilen *v/t.* (*trennb., hat -ge-*) divide, split up; *in Fächer etc.*: partition (off)

Abteilung¹ *f* (*das Abteilen*) division

Abteilung² *f* (*abgek. Abt.*) *in Betrieb, Kaufhaus etc.*: department; *Verwaltung*: division; *Strafanstalt, Krankenhaus*: ward; *Mil.* detachment, unit; (*Bataillon*) battalion

Abteilungsleiter *m*, **~in** *f* department

head; *Wirts.* departmental manager; *im Kaufhaus*: floor manager

abtelefonieren, abtelegrafieren *v/i.* (*trennb., hat*); *umg.* → *absagen* I, II 1, III

abtippen *v/t.* (*trennb., hat -ge-*); *umg.* type up, get *s.th.* typed

Äbtissin *f*; -, *-nen* abbess

abtönen *v/t.* (*trennb., hat -ge-*) tone down (*auch Fot.*); **Abtönung** *f* shade

abtöten *v/t.* (*trennb., hat -ge-*) kill (*auch Nerv*); (*Bakterien*) *auch* destroy; *fig.* (*Gefühl*) deaden; **Abtötung** *f* destruction, deadening

Abtrag *m*; *-(e)s, Abträge*; *bes. schw. und Geol.* (*Abtragung*) excavation; erosion, denudation

abtragen (*unreg., trennb., hat -ge-*) **I.** *vt/i. geh.* (*Geschirr, Speisen*) clear away; **II.** *v/t.* **1.** (*Mauer etc.*) pull down (bit by bit, *Am. auch* part by part); (*Erde*) clear away, remove; (*Erhebung*) level; *Med.* (*Warze etc.*) remove; **2.** (*Schuld*) pay off, discharge (*Hypothek*) *auch* amort|ize; **3.** (*abnutzen*) wear out; (*abkratzen*) abrade; **4.** *Math.* (*Strecke*) lay (*od.* mark) off; (*Kurve*) plot; → *abgetragen* II

abträglich *Adj.* inimical (+ *Dat.* to); (*nachteilig*) detrimental (to), not beneficial, harmful; *Äußerung*: adverse, unfavo(u)rable

Abtragung *f* **1.** *Geol.* erosion, denudation; **2.** *e-r Schuld*: paying off, clearing; *e-r Hypothek*: redemption, amortization; **3.** *Math.* laying (*od.* marking) off, plotting; **4.** *Med.* removal, ablation *fachspr.*; **5.** *e-s Hauses*: demolition

abtrainieren *v/t.* (*trennb., hat*) (*Pfunde etc.*) work off

Abtransport *m* transport(ation) away: removal; *von Geschädigten*: evacuation; **abtransportieren** *v/t.* (*trennb., hat*) take away; (*Waren*) carry away; (*Verletzte*) *auch* take to hospital (*Am.* the *od.* a hospital)

abtreiben (*unreg., trennb., -ge-*) **I.** *v/t.* (*hat*) **1.** *Strömung etc.*: carry (*od.* sweep) off (*od.* away); **2.** *Med.* (*Embryo*) abort, get rid of *umg.*; **3.** (*Vieh*) *von der Alm*: drive (*od.* bring) down; **II.** *v/i.* **1.** (*ist*); *Boot etc.*: drift off (course); **2.** (*hat*); *Med. als Frau*: have an abortion; *als Arzt*: carry out (*od.* induce) an abortion; **Abtreibung** *f Med.* abortion

Abtreibungs|gegner *m*, **~gegnerin** *f* anti-abortionist, anti-abortion campaigner; **~gesetz** *n* abortion law(s *Pl.*); **~klinik** *f* abortion clinic; **~pille** *f* abortion pill; **~tourismus** *m* travel(-l)ing to another place or country in order to have a legal abortion; **~verbot** *n* abortion ban, ban on abortions

abtrennbar *Adj.* detachable; **abtrennen** (*trennb., hat -ge-*) **I.** *v/t.* **1.** (*abreißen*) tear off (*von etw.* s.th.); (*Coupon*) *auch* tear off, detach; (*Bein etc.*) *beim Unfall*: sever; **2.** (*abschneiden*) (*Ärmel etc.*) take off; (*Futter*) take out; (*Bein etc.*) operativ: amputate; **3.** (*Gebiet, Fläche etc.*) separate *auch Chem.*; (*Raum*) *auch* separate, partition (*od.* divide) off; **4.** *Jur.* (*Verfahren*) sever, handle separately; **5.** *Etech.* disconnect, isolate; *Metall.* (*Silber*) cupel; **II.** *v/refl.* separate; **Abtrennung** *f* separation; *e-s Beins etc.*: severing; operative: amputation, removal

abtreten (*unreg., trennb., -ge-*) **I.** *v/t.* (*hat*) **1.** (*Schuhe, Stufen*) wear down; **2.** *sich* (*Dat.*) *die Schuhe* ~ wipe one's

feet; **3.** *j-m etw. od. etw. an j-n* ~ hand s.th. over to s.o.; *Jur.* cede s.th. to s.o. (*auch Gebiet*), make s.th. over to s.o.; **II.** *v/i.* (*ist*) withdraw; *vom Amt*: *auch* retire; (*Herrscher*) abdicate; *Theat.* go off, exit; *Mil.* break ranks; *fig.* (*von der Bildfläche* ~, *auch* sterben) make one's exit

Abtreter *m* doormat; (*Gitterrost*) scraper

Abtretung *f* cession (*auch e-s Gebiets*), transfer, assignment (*an* + *Akk.* to)

Abtretungsurkunde *f* transfer deed; *Grundstück*: (deed of) conveyance; *Konkurs*: (deed of) assignment

Abtrieb *m* (*Almabtrieb*) bringing down of cattle (from pasture)

abtrinken *vt/i.* (*unreg., trennb., hat -ge-*) (*Flüssigkeit*) *von Glas*: (take a) sip, drink (*od.* sip) the top off

Abtritt *m* **1.** *Theat.* exit; **2.** *e-s Beamten etc.*: retirement; **3.** *altm.* (*Toilette*) privy

Abtrockentuch *n* tea (*Am. auch* dish) towel

abtrocknen (*trennb., -ge-*) **I.** *vt/i.* (*hat*) (*das Geschirr*) ~ dry up, dry the dishes, do the drying-up; **II.** *v/t.* (*hat*) dry; *sich* (*Dat.*) *die Hände* ~ dry one's hands (*an* + *Dat.* on); *j-m/sich die Tränen* ~ dry (*od.* wipe away) one's/-s.o.'s tears; **III.** *v/i.* (*ist*); (*trocken werden*) (*Straße*) dry off (*od.* up); **IV.** *v/refl.* (*hat*) dry o.s. (off)

Abtropfbrett *n* draining-board, *Am.* drainboard; **abtropfen** *v/i.* (*trennb., ist -ge-*) **1.** *Wasser*: drip; **2.** *Geschirr etc.*: ~ lassen drain, let drain; **Abtropfgestell** *n*, **Abtropfständer** *m* plate (*od.* draining) rack, dish drainer, *Am.* drain rack

abtrotten *v/i.* (*trennb., ist -ge-*); *umg.* creep (*od.* slink) off

abtrotzen *v/t.* (*trennb., hat -ge-*): *j-m etw.* ~ persist in getting s.th. from s.th.; *sie hat es ihm abgetrotzt* she just persisted until he let her have it (*od.* until she got what she wanted); *sie trotzten dem Meer ein Stück Land ab* they wrested (*od.* reclaimed) a piece of land from the sea

abtrünnig *Adj.* unfaithful, disloyal; *Gruppe*: breakaway ...; *kirchl.* lapsed ...; *formell*: apostate; **~ werden von** leave; *e-m Glauben*: *auch* fall away from; **Abtrünnige** *m*, *f*; *-n, -n* defector; *stärker*: renegade; *kirchl.* defector, backslider, lapsed Catholic *etc.*; *formell*: apostate

abtun *v/t.* (*unreg., trennb., hat -ge-*) **1.** *umg.* (*Brille, Schürze*) take off *allg.*; **2.** (*Argumente etc.*) brush aside, pooh--pooh *umg.*; (*auch j-n*) dismiss; pass off (*als* as); *etw. mit e-m Achselzucken* ~ shrug s.th. off

abtupfen *v/t.* (*trennb., hat -ge-*) **1.** (*Stirn etc.*) dab; (*Wunde*) swab; **2.** (*entfernen*) dab off (*von etw.* s.th.)

aburteilen *v/t.* (*trennb., hat -ge-*) pass sentence on; *fig.* condemn (out of hand); **Aburteilung** *f* sentencing; *fig.* condemnation

abverlangen *v/t.* (*trennb., hat*) demand (+ *Dat.* of)

abwägen *v/t.* (*unreg., trennb., hat -ge-*) weigh, consider (carefully); *gegeneinander* ~ weigh up; *fachspr.* counter(-)balance; → *abgewogen*; **Abwägung** *f* consideration

Abwahl *f*; *nur Sg.* voting out (of office); **abwählbar** *Adj.* **1.** *Fach*: optional; **2.** *Politiker*: elected, able to be voted out (of office) *präd.*; **abwählen**

v/t. (trennb., hat -ge-) **1.** *(j-n)* vote s.o. out of office; **2.** *(Fach)* drop, opt out of

abwälzen *v/t. (trennb., hat -ge-)* **1.** roll (off); **2.** shift *(auf* on to); *die Verantwortung auf e-n anderen ~* pass the buck (to someone else)

abwandeln *v/t. (trennb., hat -ge-)* **1.** modify, adapt; **2.** *Ling. altm. (flektieren)* inflect

abwandern *v/i. (trennb., ist -ge-)* Bevölkerung: migrate, move; *Zuschauer, Arbeiter:* drift off; *Sport* leave the club etc.; *Wirts. Kapital:* flow (out); *Met.* move *(nach Osten etc.* east etc.); **Abwanderung** *f* migration; exodus *(aus* from); *Sport* move, transfer; *von Kapital:* outflow; *~ von Wissenschaftlern* (academic) brain drain; → *auch abwandern*

Abwandlung *f* **1.** variation, modification; **2.** *Ling. altm.* inflection

Abwärme *f* waste *(od.* lost) heat; *~verwertung* *f* waste heat recovery

Abwart *m schw.* caretaker, janitor

abwarten *(trennb., hat -ge-)* **I.** *v/t.* wait for; *j-n ~* wait till s.o. comes; *das Gewitter ~* wait till the storm is over; *das bleibt abzuwarten* that remains to be seen; → *abpassen;* **II.** *v/i.* wait (and see); *~ und Tee trinken umg.* wait and see (what happens) *allg.;* **abwartend I.** *Part. Präs.* → *abwarten;* **II.** *Adj. Verhalten:* cautious; *e-e ~e Haltung einnehmen* decide to wait and see, *Pol.* adopt a wait-and-see policy, play a waiting game; **III.** *Adv.: sich ~ verhalten* adopt a wait-and-see attitude

abwärts *Adv.* **1.** down(wards); *den Fluss ~* down the river, downstream; **2.** *von j-m (an) ~* from s.o. down(wards); **3.** *mit ihm / den Geschäften etc. geht es ~* he's / business etc. is going downhill

Abwärts|bewegung *f,* *~trend* *m* **1.** downward movement; downstroke; **2.** *Wirts.* downward trend, downturn

Abwasch *m; -(e)s, Abwäsche* **1.** *(Geschirr)* dirty dishes *Pl.;* **2.** *(Spülen)* washing-up; *den ~ machen* do the dishes *(od.* washing-up); *das geht in einem ~ fig. you, we etc.* can kill two birds with one stone

abwaschbar *Adj.* washable

Abwaschbecken *n* sink

abwaschen *(unreg., trennb., hat -ge-)* **I.** *v/t.* **1.** *(Schmutz)* wash off *(auch ~ von);* **2.** *(Auto, Körper etc.)* wash down; *(das Geschirr)* wash up; *sich (Dat.) die Hände / das Gesicht etc. ~* wash one's hands/face etc.; **II.** *v/i.* do the dishes *(od.* washing-up)

Abwasch|lappen *m* washing-up cloth, dishcloth; *~schüssel* *f* washing-up bowl, *Am.* dishpan

Abwaschwasser *n* dishwater

Abwasser *n; -s, Abwässer auch Pl.:* waste *(od.* residual, foul, used) water, sewage (water), (industrial) effluent; *Pl. auch* sullage, sewage; *~aufbereitung* *f* sewage treatment *(od.* (re)processing); *~beseitigung* *f* sewage *(od.* effluent) disposal; *~kanal* *m* sewer; *~kläranlage* *f* sewage (disposal) plant, clarification plant; *~leitung* *f* sewage pipe, sewer; *~reinigung* *f* sewage treatment

abwechseln *(trennb., hat -ge-)* **I.** *v/i. (und v/t. sich ~) mst zwei:* alternate, *Personen:* take turns *(bei* with, [in] doing s.th.); *sich am Steuer ~* take turns driving *(od.* at the wheel); *Regen und Sonnenschein wechselten (sich) ab*

one minute it was raining, the next the sun was shining; **II.** *v/refl.: sich ~ mit* take turns with; *sich mit j-m beim Fahren etc. ~* take turns driving *(od.* at the wheel) *etc.* with s.o.; *wir bleiben abwechselnd zu Hause* we take turns staying at home; **abwechselnd I.** *Part. Präs.* → *abwechseln;* **II.** *Adj.* alternate, alternating; **III.** *Adv.* alternately; *(der Reihe nach)* by turns; *~ rot und blass werden* change colo(u)r several times

Abwechslung *f* **1.** *vom Alltag:* change; *(Mannigfaltigkeit)* variety; *(Zerstreuung)* change; *~ brauchen* need a change; *~ bringen in* liven up; *zur ~* for a change; **2.** *(Aufeinanderfolge)* succession, alternation

abwechslungs|los *Adj. (eintönig)* monotonous; *(ereignislos)* uneventful; *~reich* *Adj.* varied; *(ereignisreich)* eventful

Abweg *m; meist Pl.; fig.: auf ~e geraten* go astray, stray from the straight and narrow

abwegig *Adj. (sonderbar)* bizarre, outlandish, off-beat *umg.; (unangebracht)* inept, out of place; *(seltsam)* weird, peculiar; *(grundlos)* unfounded, mistaken, groundless; **Abwegigkeit** *f* bizarreness, weirdness, mistakenness, groundlessness

Abwehr *f; -, kein Pl.* **1.** *(Verteidigung)* auch *Sport* defen|ce *(Am.* -se); *(Widerstand)* resistance; *auf ~ stoßen* meet with resistance, *stärker:* be repulsed; **2.** *e-s Angriffs, des Feindes:* repulse; *e-s Balles:* defen|ce *(Am.* -se); *(Torwart)* save; *(Feldspieler)* clearance; *(Abwendung)* auch *e-r Krankheit:* warding off; *Fechten etc.:* parrying; **3.** *Mil. (Spionageabwehr)* counter(-)intelligence; *(Abwehrdienst)* counter(-)intelligence (service)

abwehrbereit ready to take defensive action *präd.; ~ sein Armee etc.:* be on standby; **Abwehrbereitschaft** *f; nur Sg.* readiness to take defensive action

Abwehrdienst *m Mil.* counter(-)intelligence (service)

abwehren *(trennb., hat -ge-)* **I.** *v/t.* **1.** *(Angriff, Feind)* beat back, repulse; *Fechten:* parry; *Boxen, Fußball:* block; *(klären)* clear; **2.** *(zurückweisen) (Einmischung, Hilfe, Vorwurf etc.)* reject; **3.** *(vertreiben) (Besucher, Neugierige)* deter *(od.* drive away); *(Fliegen, Mücken)* repel; **4.** *fig. (abwenden) (Gefahr, Unglück)* ward off, avert; **II.** *v/i.* demur, *(stärker)* protest, dismiss, refuse; **abwehrend I.** *Part. Präs.* → *abwehren;* **II.** *Adj.: ~e Geste* dismissive *(od.* deprecatory) gesture; **III.** *Adv.: ~ die Hand heben* make a dismissive *(od.* deprecatory) gesture (with one's hand)

Abwehr|fehler *m Sport* defensive error; *~haltung* *f auch Psych.* defensiveness; *sich in ~ befinden* be on the defensive; *~kampf* *m Mil.* defensive battle; *~kräfte* *Pl. Med.* resistance *Sg.;* *~mechanismus* *m Bio., Psych.* defen|ce *(Am.* -se) mechanism; *~reaktion* *f* defensive reaction; *~schwach* *Adj. Sport* weak in defen|ce *(Am.* -se) *präd.,* with a poor defen|ce *(Am.* -se) *präd.; das ist e-e ~e Mannschaft* that's a team with a poor defen|ce *(Am.* -se); *~schwäche* *f* **1.** *Med.* lowered resistance; **2.** *Sport* weakness in defen|ce *(Am.* -se); *~spiel* *n Sport* defensive play; *~spieler* *m, ~spielerin* *f* defender; *Pl. auch* defen|ce *(Am.* -se)

Sg., blocker, back

abwehrstark *Adj. Sport* strong in defen|ce *(Am.* -se); *das ist e-e ~e Mannschaft* they're a good defensive team

Abwehr|stoff *m Physiol., Med.* antibody; *~waffe* *f Mil.* defensive weapon

abweichen[1] *v/i. (unreg., trennb., ist -ge-)* **1.** *(sich entfernen)* deviate *(von* from); *vom Kurs ~* get off course, deviate from the course *förm.; vom rechten Weg ~ fig.* stray *(od.* wander) from the straight and narrow; *vom Thema ~* get off the subject, go off on a tangent, digress; **2.** *(differieren)* vary; *(stark) voneinander ~* differ (widely *od.* considerably); **3.** *Naut. Kompassnadel:* deviate *(um* by)

abweichen[2] *v/t. (trennb., hat -ge-); (Briefmarke)* soak off

abweichend I. *Part. Präs.* deviating, differing; **II.** *Adj.* divergent; *(voneinander ~)* varying, differing

Abweichler *m; -s, -, ~in* *f; -, -nen; Pol.* deviationist; **abweichlerisch** *Adj.* deviationist; **Abweichlertum** *n; -s, kein Pl.* deviationism

Abweichung *f* divergence, deviation; *vom Thema:* digression; *von e-r Regel etc.:* departure *(von* from); *(Toleranz)* tolerance, allowance

abweiden *v/t. (trennb., hat -ge-); (Gras, Wiese)* graze

abweisen *v/t. (unreg., trennb., hat -ge-)* **1.** *(Angebot, Antrag etc.)* reject, turn down; **2.** *(j-m den Eintritt verwehren)* send *(od.* turn) away; *(j-n nicht zu sich hereinlassen)* refuse to see; *(Freier)* reject, turn away; *j-n schroff ~* snub s.o.; *er lässt sich nicht ~* he won't take no for an answer; **3.** *Jur.* dismiss; **4.** *Wirts. (Wechsel)* refuse; **5.** *Mil. (Angriff)* repulse; **6.** *(Wasser)* repel; **abweisend I.** *Part. Präs.* → *abweisen;* **II.** *Adj.* unfriendly, cool, off-putting; *Antwort:* dismissive; *Wasser ~* water-repellent; **III.** *Adv.: ~ ansehen* give s.o. a cold look *(od.* stare), look at s.o. in an unfriendly way; *sich ~ verhalten* behave in an unfriendly manner *(od.* way); **Abweisung** *f* rejection; *Jur.* dismissal; *Mil.* repulse; *e-r Person:* snub, rebuff

abwenden *(auch unreg., trennb., hat -ge-)* **I.** *v/t.* **1.** *(Augen, Kopf)* turn away *(von* from); *ich konnte den Blick nicht von ihr ~* I couldn't take my eyes off *(od.* away from) her; **2.** *(Schlag)* ward off; *(Gefahr, Unheil, Krise etc.)* head off, avert; **II.** *v/refl.* **1.** → I 1; **2.** *fig.: sich (innerlich) von j-m ~* become (emotionally) alienated *(od.* estranged) from s.o.; **3.** → *abkehren* II; **Abwendung** *f; nur Sg. e-r Gefahr:* averting; *(Abkehr)* abandonment *(von* of)

abwerben *v/t. (unreg., trennb., hat -ge-); (Kunden)* poach, steal *umg.; (Arbeitskräfte)* auch headhunt; *(auch Wähler)* woo away; **Abwerber** *m,* **Abwerberin** *f* headhunter; **Abwerbeversuch** *m Wirts.* head-hunting; **Abwerbung** *f* poaching, stealing *umg.; von Arbeitskräften:* auch headhunting; *auch von Wählern:* wooing away

abwerfen *(unreg., trennb., hat -ge-)* **I.** *v/t.* **1.** *(Bomben, Ballast etc.)* drop; **2.** *(Decke, Kleidung)* throw off; *(Reiter)* throw; *(Geweih)* cast, shed; *(Blätter)* drop *(od.* shed); *(Haar)* shed; *Zool. (Haare, Federn)* mo(u)lt; **3.** *fig. (Bürde, Joch)* shake off; **4.** *Sport (Hindernis, Latte)* knock down; **5.** *Ballspiele:* get s.o. out; **6.** *Wirts. fig. (Gewinn)* yield, bring in; *(Zinsen)* bear, return, bring in; (*Nebenprodukte*) spin off; **7.** *Sport* (*Ball*) throw out; (*Speer*) throw; **II.** *v/i.* (*Spielkarte*) throw *s.th.* away, discard *s.th.*

abwerten *v/t.* (*trennb.*, *hat* -ge-) **1.** *Wirts.* devalue; **2.** *fig.* disparage, derogate, belittle; (*Person*) run down; **~ als** dismiss as; **abwertend I.** *Part. Präs.* → **abwerten**; **II.** *Adj. fig.* depreciatory, disparaging; **Abwertung** *f* devaluation; *fig.* depreciation

abwesend I. *Adj.* **1.** absent, away; (*nicht da*) not here; (*nicht zu Hause*) präd. out, not in (*od.* at home); **2.** *fig.* (*zerstreut*) lost in thought; *ein ~er Blick* a faraway look; **II.** *Adv.* absently; **Abwesende** *m, f; -n, -n* absentee; *die Abwesenden* those absent; *in Rede*: those who cannot be with us today

Abwesenheit *f; nur Sg.* **1.** absence; *in ~ von* in the absence of; *in/während j-s ~* in/during s.o.'s absence; *durch ~ glänzen iro.* be conspicuous by one's absence; **2.** *Jur.*: *in ~ verurteilt werden Strafrecht*: be sentenced in one's absence; *Zivilrecht*: be sentenced by default; **3.** *fig.* (*Geistesabwesenheit*) abstraction; (*Träumerei*) daydreaming

abwetzen (*trennb.*, -*ge-*) **I.** *v/t.* (*hat*); (*abnutzen*) wear *s.th.* smooth; → *abgewetzt*; **II.** *v/i.* (*ist*); *umg.* (*weglaufen*) zoom off; (*Tier*) bolt *allg.*

abwichsen *v/t.* (*trennb.*, *hat* -ge-): *sich* (*Dat.*) *einen ~ Brit. vulg.* wank off, have a wank, *Am.* jerk (*od.* jack) off

abwickeln (*trennb.*, *hat* -ge-) **I.** *v/t.* **1.** (*Faden etc.*) unwind; (*Verband*) take off; **2.** (*durchführen*) handle; (*erledigen*) settle; (*Verkehr*) regulate; **3.** *Wirts. euph.* (*liquidieren*) wind up; (*Einrichtung*) *auch Univ.* phase out; **II.** *v/refl.*; *Faden etc.*: unwind; **Abwicklung** *f* (*Durchführung*) handling, processing; *e-s Geschäfts*: settlement; *euph.* (*Liquidation*) winding up, phasing out

abwiegeln (*trennb.*, *hat* -ge-) **I.** *v/t.* **1.** (*beruhigen*) calm down, appease; **2.** (*abweisen*) turn away, dismiss; **II.** *v/i.* smooth over the difficulties (*od.* ill feelings *etc.*); play down the issue

abwiegen *v/t.* (*unreg.*, *trennb.*, *hat* -ge-) weigh (out)

abwimmeln *v/t.* (*trennb.*, *hat* -ge-); *umg.* shake off *allg.*; (*Arbeit*) get out of (doing) *allg.*

Abwind *m Flug.* downward current, downwash, *Am.* downdraft

abwinkeln *v/t.* (*trennb.*, *hat* -ge-); (*Arme etc.*) bend; *mit abgewinkelten Armen* with arms akimbo

abwinken (*umg. auch unreg.*, *trennb.*, *hat* -ge-) **I.** *v/t.* (*Fahrzeug*) flag down; (*Rennen*) stop; **II.** *v/i.* **1.** give a dismissive gesture; (*Angebotenes zurückweisen*) make a gesture of refusal; *als ich mit m-m Vorschlag kam, hat er gleich abgewinkt* he wouldn't even listen to my suggestion; **2.** *Dirigent*: stop the orchestra; **3.** *umg.*: *bis zum Abwinken* (*im Überfluss*) in abundance, galore präd.

abwirtschaften (*trennb.*, *hat* -ge-) **I.** *v/i. und v/refl.*; *Firma etc.*: go to ruin; *völlig*: run itself into the ground, go to the wall, *Am.* go bust; *Partei etc.*: be on the road to ruin, collapse; *er hat abgewirtschaftet Politiker etc.*: he's come to the end of the road; **II.** *v/t.* (*Firma etc.*) run down; *völlig*: run into the ground; (*Partei etc.*) bring

to ruin (*od.* to the point of collapse); → *abgewirtschaftet Adj.*

abwischen *v/t.* (*trennb.*, *hat* -ge-) **1.** (*Schmutz etc.*) wipe off (*von etw.* s.th.); *sich die Tränen ~* wipe away one's tears; **2.** (*Tisch etc.*) wipe; *sich den Mund / die Stirn ~* wipe one's mouth / mop one's brow

abwohnen *v/t.* (*trennb.*, *hat* -ge-); *umg.*: *wir haben unsere Wohnung ziemlich abgewohnt* our flat (*Am.* apartment) has a lived-in look; → *abgewohnt*

abwracken *v/t.* (*trennb.*, *hat* -ge-); (*Auto, Schiff*) break up, scrap; → *abgewrackt*

Abwurf *m Flug.* dropping; *Sport* throw-out; *Reiten*: knock-down

abwürgen *v/t.* (*trennb.*, *hat* -ge-) **1.** *umg.* (*Motor*) stall *allg.*; **2.** *fig.* (*Initiative etc.*) quash, scotch; (*Diskussion*) stifle; **3.** (*töten*) strangle

abzahlen *v/t.* (*trennb.*, *hat* -ge-) *vollständig*: pay *s.th.* off, settle; *in Raten*: pay for *s.th.* by instal(l)ments

abzählen (*trennb.*, *hat* -ge-) **I.** *v/t.* count; (*Geld*) count (out); *das kannst du dir an den od. fünf od. zehn Fingern ~ umg. fig.* any fool can see that, it's as clear as day(light) *allg.*; **II.** *v/i.* *beim Kinderspiel*: count out

Abzählreim *m* counting-out rhyme

Abzahlung *f vollständig*: (re)payment, paying off; (*Rate*) instal(l)ment; *Fin. von Anteilen*: redemption; *auf ~ kaufen* buy on hire purchase (*od.* credit), *bes. Am.* buy on the instal(l)ment plan, *Brit.* buy on the never-never *umg.*

Abzahlungs|geschäft *n*, **~kauf** *m* hire purchase (sale), H.P.

Abzählvers *m* counting-out rhyme

abzapfen *v/t.* (*trennb.*, *hat* -ge-); (*Bier, Wein*) tap, draw off; *Med.* (*Blut*) draw; *j-m Geld etc. ~ umg. fig.* scrounge money *etc.* off s.o.

abzäumen *v/t.* (*trennb.*, *hat* -ge-); (*Pferd*) take the bridle off, unbridle

abzäunen *v/t.* (*trennb.*, *hat* -ge-) fence off (*od.* in)

abzehren *v/t.* (*trennb.*, *hat* -ge-) *Krankheit etc.*: emaciate, waste away

Abzeichen *n* **1.** badge; *Mil.* insignia, (*Streifen*) stripe; (*Auszeichnung*) decoration; *Pol.*, *Sport* (*Fanabzeichen*) favo(u)r; **2.** *Zool.* mark(ing), macula *fachspr.*

abzeichnen (*trennb.*, *hat* -ge-) **I.** *v/t.* **1.** (*abbilden*) copy, draw (*von* from); **2.** (*Schriftstück*) initial; **II.** *v/refl.* **1.** (*sich abheben*) stand out; (*sich spiegeln*) be reflected; **2.** *fig.* (*entstehen*) be emerging, be evolving; *Gefahr*: loom on the horizon; *e-e neue Entwicklung etc. zeichnete sich ab* could be seen to emerge; **abzeichnend I.** *Part. Präs.* → **abzeichnen**; **II.** *Adj.*: *sich ~* emerging, emergent, evolving

abzgl. *Abk.* → *abzüglich*

Abziehbild *n* transfer, *Am.* decal

abziehen (*unreg.*, *trennb.*, -ge-) **I.** *v/t.* (*hat*) **1.** (*entfernen*) (*Bettbezug, Hut, Reifen etc.*) take off; (*Ring, Handschuhe*) pull (*od.* slip) off; (*Folie*) take off, peel back (*Fell, Haut*) peel off (*alle von etw.* s.th.); (*Schlüssel*) take out, remove (*von* from); *fig.* (*Hilfe, Truppen etc.*) withdraw (*von* from); **2.** (*von etw. befreien*) (*Bett*) strip; (*Tier*) skin, flay, (*Tomate etc.*) skin; (*Bohnen*) string; **3.** (*vervielfältigen*) make a copy (*od.* copies) of; *Druck.* (*Fahne etc.*) pull (*od.* strike) off; *Fot.* make a print (*od.* prints) of; **4.** *Tech.* (*schleifen*)

smooth, (*Messer*) grind, sharpen; **5.** (*Parkett*) surface; (*Tennisplatz*) brush; **6.** (*abrechnen*) subtract, deduct; *etwas vom Preis ~* deduct something from (*umg.* knock something off) the price; *j-m e-n Punkt* (*wegen unsportlichen Verhaltens*) ~ *Sport* (*Tennis*) dock s.o. (for unsportsmanlike behavio[u]r); **7.** (*abfüllen*) bottle; (*Flüssigkeit von Satz*) decant, pour off; **8.** *Chem.* abstract, extract; **9.** *umg.* (*Party*) have *allg.*, throw; *e-e Schau od. Show ~* make a scene (*od.* fuss); **10.** (*Handgranate*) pull the pin of; **II.** *v/i.* **1.** (*ist*) *Rauch*: escape, (*sich auflösen*) clear, disappear; *Nebel*: clear, disperse; *Wolken*: move off, blow away; *Gewitter*: pass; **2.** (*ist*) *Mil.* withdraw; **3.** (*ist*) *Zugvögel*: head south, migrate; *umg.* (*weggehen*) push off; **4.** (*hat*) *Sport* let fly; **5.** (*abdrücken*) pull (*od.* squeeze) the trigger, fire

Abzieh|presse *f Druck.* proof press; **~riemen** *m* (razor) strop; **~stein** *m* whetstone, hone

abzielen *v/i.* (*trennb.*, *hat* -ge-): *auf etw. ~* aim at; *Maßnahme, Bemerkung etc.*: be designed to *Inf.*; *worauf zielte er ab?* what was he driving (*od.* getting) at?

abzirkeln *v/t.* (*trennb.*, *hat* -ge-) measure out with compasses (*Am. auch* with a compass); *s-e Worte genau ~ fig.* weigh one's words carefully

abzischen *v/i.* (*trennb.*, *ist* -ge-); *umg.* zoom off

abzocken *v/t.* (*trennb.*, *hat* -ge-); *umg. pej.* rip s.o. off, fleece

Abzug *m* **1.** *Mil.* withdrawal, retreat; **2.** *Wirts.* deduction; *vom Preis*: discount; *in ~ bringen* deduct; *nach ~ der Kosten* charges deducted; *nach ~ der Steuer(n)* after tax; **3.** *für Dämpfe etc.*: outlet, escape; *für Flüssigkeit*: drain; **4.** *am Gewehr etc.*: trigger; **5.** *Druck.* proof, (*Vervielfältigung*) copy; *Fot.* print

abzüglich *Adv.* (*abgek. abzgl.*) less, minus; *~ der Kosten* charges deducted

abzugs|fähig *Adj.* deductible; **~frei** *Adj.* tax-free

Abzugs|haube *f* cooker (*Am.* range) hood; **~graben** *m* drainage ditch; **~kanal** *m* sewer, culvert; *für Rauch, Luftstrom*: offtake; **~rohr** *n* waste pipe; *für Gase, Dämpfe*: escape (*od.* outlet *od.* exhaust) pipe, flue; **~schach** *n* discovered check; **~schacht** *m* escape shaft

abzupfen *v/t.* (*trennb.*, *hat* -ge-) pluck off

abzwacken *v/t.* (*trennb.*, *hat* -ge-) **1.** (*abkneifen*) pinch off; **2.** *umg. fig.* (*Geld*) (*abzweigen*) scrape *s.th.* together (*von* from) (*für* for)

Abzweig *m* **1.** (*Straße*) junction, turn (*od.* branch) off; **2.** *Tech.* connection

Abzweigdose *f Tech.* junction (*od.* distribution) box

abzweigen (*trennb.*, -ge-) **I.** *v/i.* (*ist*) branch off, bifurcate *förm.*; **II.** *v/t.* (*hat*); (*Geld etc.*, bestimmen *für*) earmark, set aside (*von* from) (*für* for)

Abzweig|kasten *m* junction box; **~klemme** *f* branch terminal

Abzweigung *f Eisenb.* junction; *e-r Straße*: turning, turnoff, junction; (*Gabelung*) fork, bifurcation *förm.*

abzwicken *v/t.* (*trennb.*, *hat* -ge-) nip off (*von etw.* from s.th.)

abzwitschern *v/i.* (*trennb.*, *ist* –ge-); *umg.* buzz off

Accessoire [aksɛ'soaʀə] *n; -s, -s* accessory

Acetat n; -(e)s, -e; Chem. acetate; ~seide f acetate rayon

Aceton n; -s, kein Pl.; Chem. acetone

Acetylen n; -s, kein Pl.; Chem. acetylene

Acetylsalicylsäure f; nur Sg., Chem. acetylsalicylic acid, aspirin

ach Interj. **1.** bedauernd: oh; ~, wie schade / du lieber Himmel etc.! what a shame / good grief etc.!; **2.** sehnsüchtig: ~, wäre es doch schon morgen! oh if only it were tomorrow; **3.** bittend: ~, komm! oh come on!; ~, sei doch so lieb! do me, us etc. a favo(u)r, come on; **4.** erstaunt, erfreut: ~, wie schön/ nett! etc. oh how lovely/nice!; ~ ja? oh really?; ~ wirklich? you don't say!; **5.** ablehnend: ~ was! od. ~ wo! oh no, of course not!; **6.** ~ ja! (ich erinnere mich) oh yes (od. that's right); ~ ja od. so! (jetzt verstehe ich) oh, I see; **7.** lit.: das ~ so kurze Glück joy which is but short-lived; der ~ so liebe Besuch iro. the oh-so-welcome visitors

Ach n: ~ und Weh schreien wail; mit ~ und Krach by the skin of one's teeth, barely, with great difficulty; mit ~ und Krach e-e Prüfung bestehen scrape through an exam

Achat m; -(e)s, -e agate

Achilles|ferse fig. f Achilles' heel, weak spot; ~sehne f Anat. Achilles' tendon

Achlaut m; nur Sg; Ling. (Ggs. Ichlaut) ach-laut, voiceless velar fricative fachspr.

achromatisch Adj. achromatic

Achs|... im Subst. siehe auch Achsen...; ~abstand m Mot. wheel base; ~antrieb m Mot. final drive; ~aufhängung f Mot. axle suspension; ~bruch m → Achsenbruch

Achse f; -, -n **1.** Math., Archit., Anat., Bot. etc. axis, Pl. axes; sich um die eigene ~ drehen turn (od. rotate) on one's/its own axis; **2.** Tech. axle; **3.** umg. fig.: auf ~ sein (unterwegs sein) be on the move allg. (od. road od. go umg.); (auf den Beinen sein) be (back) on one's feet (od. in action)

Achsel f; -, -n **1.** (Schulter) auch Kleidung: shoulder; die ~ (od. mit den ~n) zucken shrug one's shoulders; über die ~ ansehen fig. look down on; **2.** (~höhle) armpit; **3.** Bot. (Blattachsel) axil(la)

Achsel|... im Subst. siehe auch Schulter...; ~drüse f axillary gland; ~haar n; mst Pl. hair Sg. under one's arms, underarm hair Sg., hairy armpits umg.; ~griff m Med. zur Rettung: chest (od. towing) grip; ~höhle f armpit; ~klappe f → Schulterklappe; ~schweiß m underarm perspiration

Achselzucken n shrug (of the shoulders); mit e-m ~ abtun shrug s.th. off; **achselzuckend** Adv. shrugging one's shoulders, with a shrug; ~ über etw. hinweggehen shrug s.th. off

Achsen|bruch m Mot. **1.** breaking of an axle; **2.** broken axle; ~drehung f Tech. (axial) rotation; ~kreuz n Math. axes Pl. of coordinates, coordinate system; ~mächte Pl. hist. Pol. hist. Axis powers; ~symmetrie f Math. axial symmetry

Achs|lager n Mot. axle bearing; ~last f axle load; ~schenkel m Tech. (axle) journal; Mot. stub axle, Am. steering knuckle; ~stand m Mot. wheel base; ~welle f Tech. axle shaft

acht¹ Zahlw. eight; in ~ Tagen in a week('s time); vor ~ Tagen a week ago; alle ~ Tage every week, once a week; um ~ (Uhr) at eight (o'clock); ich komme gegen ~ Uhr I'll come around eight (o'clock); 10 Minuten vor/ nach ~ Uhr ten (minutes) to/past eight (o'clock); kurz vor/nach ~ shortly (od. just) before/after eight; sie ist ~ (Jahre alt) she's eight (years old); → Acht¹

acht² Adv.: zu ~ eight of ...; wir waren zu ~ there were eight of us; wir gingen zu ~ hin eight of us went (there)

acht|... Zahlw. eighth; ~es Kapitel chapter eight; am ~en April on the eighth of April, on April the eighth; 8. April 8th April, April 8(th); der ~e Teil the eighth part (von of)

Acht¹ f; -, -en **1.** Zahl: (number) eight; **2.** umg. Nummer: (Buslinie etc.) (number) eight; **3.** Form, beim Eislauf: figure (of) eight; am Rad: buckled tyre (Am. tire); **4.** Spielkarte: eight

Acht² f; -, kein Pl.; hist. (Bann) outlawry; über j-n die ~ verhängen od. j-n in ~ und Bann tun outlaw s.o., geh. fig. gesellschaftlich: ostracize s.o.

Acht³ (f): ~ geben be careful; ~ geben auf (+ Akk.) watch, keep an eye on umg.; gib ~! look out!, (be) careful!; habt ~! Mil. attention!; außer ~ lassen disregard, ignore, pay no attention to; sich in ~ nehmen watch out (vor for)

achtbändig Adj. eight-volume ..., in eight volumes

achtbar Adj. geh. respectable; Firma: reputable; **Achtbarkeit** f; -, kein Pl. respectability

Achte m, f, -n -n (the) eighth; er war Achter he was (od. came) eighth; Heinrich VIII. Henry VIII (= Henry the Eighth); heute ist der ~ it's the eighth today

Achteck n; -s, -e; Math. octagon; **achteckig** Adj. octagonal

achteinhalb Zahlw. eight and a half

achtel Adj.: ein ~ Liter an eighth of a liter; **Achtel** n; -s, - eighth

Achtel|finale n Sport last sixteen, round before the quarter-finals; ~liter m eighth of a lit|re (Am. –er)

achteln v/t. divide (od. split) into eighths

Achtel|note f Mus. quaver, Am. eighth note; ~pause f quaver (Am. eighth note) rest

achten I. v/t. **1.** (j-n) respect, have a high opinion of; (Gesetze) observe, abide by; (Rechte, Gefühle etc.) respect; nicht ~ not value very highly,; **2.** geh. altm. (Gefahr) ignore; (erachten) regard (für as), consider (to be); **II.** v/i.: ~ auf pay attention to, mind; (aufpassen auf) watch, keep an eye on; (Ausschau halten nach) watch out for; darauf ~, dass ... see to it that ...

ächten v/t. **1.** hist. (Person) outlaw; (etw.) ban; **2.** fig. gesellschaftlich: ostracize; (verbieten) ban

achtens Adv. eighth(ly), eight, in eighth place

achtenswert Adj. commendable; Person: highly respectable

Achter m; -s, - **1.** Boot: eight; **2.** umg. → Acht¹ 1, 2; **3.** umg., in Fahrradfelge: (number) eight; ~bahn f roller coaster; ~deck n Naut. quarterdeck, Am. auch afterdeck

achterlei Adj. indekl. eight (different) kinds präd., eight (different) sorts of ...

achtern Adv. Naut. astern

Achterschiff n Naut. stern

achtfach I. Adj. eightfold; die ~e Menge eight times the amount; ~er Sieger eight-time winner (od. champion); **II.** Adv.: ~ ausfertigen/vergrößern draw up in eight copies / enlarge (od. blow up) by eight (od. 8X); **Achtfache** n; -n, kein Pl. the eightfold amount; 16 ist das ~ von 2 16 is 8 times 2; um das ~ vergrößern etc. enlarge etc. s.th. by eight (od. 8X)

Acht|flach n, ~flächner m; -s, - octahedron

Achtfüßler m; -s, -; Zool. octopod

achthundert Zahlw. eight hundred

achtjährig Adj. **1.** eight-year-old ...; **2.** (acht Jahre dauernd) eight-year ...; ein ~es ... auch eight years of ...; **Achtjährige** m, f; -n, -n eight-year-old

Achtkampf m Sport octathlon

Achtkant n, m → Achteck; **achtkantig** Adj. eight-sided; j-n ~ hinauswerfen umg. turn (od. kick) s.o. out on his (od. her) ear, boot s.o. out

achtlos Adj. careless; **Achtlosigkeit** f; -, kein Pl. carelessness

achtmal Adv. eight times; **achtmalig** Adj. repeated eight times präd.

acht|minütig Adj. eight-minute attr.; ~monatig Adj. **1.** (8 Monate alt) eight-month-old attr., eight months old präd.; **2.** (8 Monate dauernd) lasting eight months (od. of eight months duration) präd.

Achtmonatskind n Med. eight-month baby

achtprozentig Adj. eight per cent

achtsam Adj. careful, attentive; **Achtsamkeit** f; -, kein Pl. care, attentiveness

achtseitig Adj. **1.** (achtflächig) eight-sided, octagonal; **2.** (8 Seiten lang) eight-page attr., of eight pages präd.; **achtspurig** Adj. eight-lane...; **achtstellig** Adj. Zahl: eight-digit ...; **achtstöckig** Adj. eight-stor(e)y ...

Achtstundentag m eight-hour day

acht|stündig Adj. eight-hour(-long) ...; ~tägig Adj. **1.** eight-day(-long) ..., week-long ...; **2.** (acht Tage alt) eight-day-old ...

achttausend Zahlw. eight thousand

Achttausender m 8000 met|re (Am. -er) peak

achtteilig Adj. eight-part ..., in eight parts

Achttonner m; -s, -; (Lastwagen) eight-tonner

Achtuhr... im Subst. eight o'clock ...

Achtundsechziger m; -s, -, ~in f; -, -nen; hist. sixty-eighter

Achtung f; -, kein Pl. **1.** (Respekt) respect, esteem, regard (vor for); (Rücksicht) consideration (gegenüber for, to); (Ehrerbietung) deference (gegenüber, vor to); alle ~! hats off!, my compliments!, congratulations!, well done!, you've got to hand it to him etc.; ~ genießen be highly respected; sich allgemeiner/hoher ~ erfreuen enjoy widespread/high respect, be held in general/high esteem; in j-s ~ steigen rise in s.o.'s esteem; j-m ~ entgegenbringen show consideration to s.o.; ~ gebietend impressive; **2.** ~! (Vorsicht!) look out!, Am. auch watch out!; Mil. attention!; auf Schild: danger!, caution!, warning!; ~, ~, e-e wichtige Durchsage! (your) attention please, there follows an important announcement; ~, Stufe! mind the step; ~, fertig, los! on your mark(s), get set, go!

Ächtung f; -, -en **1.** hist. outlawing;

2. *fig. gesellschaftliche*: ostracism

Achtungserfolg *m* hollow victory, critical success *iro.*

achtungsvoll *Adj.* respectful

achtwöchig *Adj.* **1.** eight-week ...; **2.** (*acht Wochen alt*) eight-week-old ...

achtzehn *Zahlw.* eighteen

achtzehnhundert *Zahlw.* eighteen hundred

achtzehnjährig *Adj.* (*18 Jahre alt*) eighteen-year-old *attr.*, eighteen years old *präd.*; (*18 Jahre dauernd*) eighteen-year; **Achtzehnjährige** *m, f; -n -n* eighteen-year-old

achtzehnt... *Zahlw.* eighteenth

Achtzehntel *n* eighteenth (part)

achtzig *Zahlw.* eighty; **Anfang/Mitte/ Ende ~ sein** be in one's early/mid/late eighties; **auf ~ sein** *umg.* be having a (blue) fit, be freaking out, *Am. auch* be having kittens; → *auch* **acht**[1]

Achtzig *f; -, -en, mst. Sg. Zahl:* (number) eighty; → *auch* **Acht**[1] 1, 2

achtziger *Adj.*: **in den ~ Jahren** in the eighties; **er ist in den Achtzigern** he's in his eighties

Achtziger *m; -s, -, ~in f; -, -nen* man/ woman in his/her eighties; *förm.* octogenarian; eightysomething *umg.*

Achtzigerjahre *Pl.*: **in den ~n** in the eighties

achtzigjährig *Adj. Person:* eighty-year- -old ...; *Zeitraum:* eighty-year(-long) ...; **Achtzigjährige** *m, f; -n -n* eighty- -year-old, octogenarian

achtzigst... *Zahlw.* eightieth; **sie hat heute ihren Achtzigsten** she's eighty today, it's her eightieth birthday today

achtzigstel *Adj.* eightieth; **Achtzigstel** *n; -s, -* eightieth (part)

Achtzylinder *m* (*Auto*) eight-cylinder (car); (*Motor*) eight-cylinder engine; **achtzylindrig** *Adj.* eight-cylinder *attr.*, with eight cylinders *präd.*

ächzen *v/i.* groan, moan (*vor* with; *fig. unter* under); **Ächzer** *m; -s, -; umg.* groan

Acker *m; -s, Äcker* field(s *Pl.*); (*~land*) farmland; (*Boden*) soil; (*Flächenmaß*) acre; **mach dich vom ~!** *umg.* get lost!, beat it!; **~bau** *m* agriculture, farming; *altm.* tillage; **~ treiben** farm the land, *altm.* till the soil; **~bestellung** *f* cultivation of the soil; **~boden** *m* arable land; **~fläche** *f* area of arable land, acreage; **~gaul** *m* farm horse; **~land** *n* arable land

ackern **I.** *vt/i.* plough, *Am.* plow; **II.** *v/i. umg. fig.* slog (away)

Acker|schlepper *m* field tractor; **~walze** *f* land roller; **~winde** *f Bot.* (field) bindweed

a conto *Adv. Wirts.* on account (= A/C, a/c)

Acryl *n; -s, kein Pl.; Chem.* acryl; **~farbe** *f* acrylic paint; **~faser** *f* acrylic fi-b|re (*Am.* -er); **~lack** *m* acrylic varnish (*od.* lacquer)

Action ['ɛkʃən] *f; -, kein Pl.* **1.** *im Film:* action; **2.** *bes. Jugendspr.:* **das ist mir zu viel ~** it's too much hassle for me; **komm, mach doch nicht so viel ~!** come on, don't make such a fuss!; **~film** *m* action-packed film (*Am. auch* movie)

a.D. *Abk.* (*außer Dienst*) → *Dienst* 3

A.D. *Abk.* (*Anno Domini*) A.D., AD

ad absurdum *Adv.:* **etw. ~ führen** show how absurd (*od.* ridiculous) s.th. is, reduce s.th. to absurdity

ADAC *m; -, kein Pl.; Abk.* (*Allgemeiner Deutscher Automobil-Club*) *General German Automobile Association, etwa*

AA, RAC, *Am.* AAA

ad acta *Adv. fig.:* **~ legen** file away; *fig. Brit.* shelve, *Am.* table; **die Angelegenheit** *etc.* **~ legen** consider the matter *etc.* closed; *fig.* forget about it *etc.*

adagio [a'da: dʒo] *Adv.,Adj. Mus.* adagio; **Adagio** [a'da: dʒo] *n Mus.* adagio

Adam *m; -s, -s* **1.** *nur Sg.; bibl.* Adam; **seit ~s Zeiten** *umg.* since the year dot, *Am.* since day one; **bei ~ und Eva anfangen** *hum.* start from square one (*od.* scratch); **2.** *fig.* (*Mann*) Adam, man; **der alte ~** *altm. hum.* the old Adam (*od.* man); **3. nach ~ Riese** according to Cocker; *auch* by my reckoning

Adams|apfel *m Anat.* (*der ~* one's) Adam's apple; **~kostüm** *n:* **im ~** *umg.* in one's birthday suit *hum.*, in the buff *altm., Am.* in the raw

Adaptation *f; -, -en; Bio., Lit., Soziol.* adaptation (*an + Akk.* to)

Adapter *m; -s, -; Etech.* adapter

adaptieren *v/t. und v/refl. Bio., Lit., Soziol.* adapt; **Adaption** *f; -, kein Pl.* adaptation (*an + Akk.* to)

adäquat *Adj. geh., fachspr.* adequate; (*geeignet*) suitable; (*wirksam*) effectual; **Adäquatheit** *f; -, kein Pl.* adequacy, suitability

addieren *v/t.* add (up)

Addis Abeba (*n*); *-s* Addis Ababa

Addition *f; -, -en; Math.* addition; (*Summe*) sum

Additiv *n; -s, -e; Chem.* additive

ade **I.** *Adv. südd.* (good)bye; **II. Ade** *n; -s, -s* goodbye, farewell, adieu

Adebar *m; -s, -e; lit. od. umg. hum.:* (*Meister*) **~** stork

Adel *m; -s, kein Pl.* **1.** nobility, aristocracy; (*Titel*) title; **die Familie ist alter ~** it is an old aristocratic family; **~ verpflichtet** *Sprichw.* noblesse oblige; **2.** *fig.* nobility (of mind); **ad(e)lig** *Adj.* noble (*auch fig.*), titled; **Ad(e)lige** *m, f; -n, -n* aristocrat *m* nobleman, *f* noblewoman; **die Ad(e)ligen** the nobility, the aristocracy (*V. im Sg. od. Pl.*)

adeln *v/t.* **1.** make *s.o.* a peer, raise *s.o.* to the peerage; **2.** *geh. fig.* ennoble

Adels|brief *m* patent of nobility; **~herrschaft** *f* aristocratic rule; **~krone** *f Her.* baronet's coronet; **~prädikat** *n* title of nobility; **~stand** *m* nobility; *in GB:* peerage; **in den ~ erheben** bestow a title on s.o., raise s.o. to the peerage; **~titel** *m* title (of nobility)

Adept *m; -en, -en; hist. od. geh. hum.* (*Jünger*) disciple *allg.*

Ader *f; -, -n* **1.** *Anat.* (*Vene*) vein; (*Puls-, Schlagader, Arterie*) artery; **j-n zur ~ lassen** *auch fig.* bleed s.o. (white *od.* dry); **2.** *fig.* (*Begabung*) vein, bent; (*Wesenszug*) streak; **dichterische ~** poetic vein; **sie hat e-e leichte ~** there is a frivolous streak in her; **3.** (*Gold-, Gesteinsader etc.*) vein, lode; **4.** *Etech.* wire, core, conductor; **5.** *Bot.* (*Blattader*) vein; **6.** *Zool. im Insektenflügel:* vein; **...aderig, ...adrig** *im Adj. Etech.* -wire, -core; **dreiaderig** three-wire; **zweiaderig** double-wire, two-core, double-conductor; **Aderlass** *m* bloodletting (*auch fig.*); **Aderung, Äderung** *f* veining

Adhäsion *f; -, -en; Phys.* adhesion; **Adhäsionsverschluss** *m* adhesion flap

ad hoc *Adv.* ad hoc; **etw. ~ entscheiden** make an ad hoc decision on s.th.

Ad-hoc-Bildung *f* ad hoc formulation; (*einzelnes Wort*) nonce word

adieu [a'dʲøː] **I.** *Interj.* goodbye, *lit.*

farewell; **II. Adieu** *n; -s, -s* adieu, farewell

Adj. *Abk.* → *Adjektiv*

Adjektiv *n; -s, -e; Ling.* (*abgek. Adj.*) adjective; **substantiviertes ~** substantival adjective, adjectival noun; **adjektivisch** *Adj.* adjectival

Adjutant *m; -en, -en; Mil.* aide-de- -camp

Adler *m; -s, -* eagle; *Astron.* Aquila, *the* Eagle; **~auge** *n fig.* eagle eye; **~n haben** *auch* have eyes like a hawk; **~blick** *m* eagle eye; **~horst** *m* eyrie; **~nase** *f* aquiline nose

adlig *Adj.*, **Adlige** *m, f* → *ad(e)lig, Ad(e)lige*

Administration *f; -, -en* administration; **administrativ** *Adj.* administrative

Admiral *m; -s, -e und Admiräle* **1.** *Mil.* admiral; **2.** *Pl. nur -e; Zool.* (*Schmetterling*) red admiral; **Admiralität** *f; -, -en; Mil.* admiralty; **Admiralitätsinseln** *Pl.* Admiralty Islands; **Admiralsrang** *m; nur Sg.* rank of admiral; **Admiralsschiff** *n* flagship; **Admiralstab** *m* naval staff

Adoleszenz *f; -, kein Pl.; Med.* adolescence

Adonis *m; -, -se; geh. fig.* good-looker *umg.*; **er ist nicht gerade ein ~** he's no Adonis

adoptieren *v/t.* adopt; **Adoption** *f; -, -en* adoption

Adoptiv|eltern *Pl.* adoptive parents; **~kind** *n* adopted (*od.* adoptive) child; **~sohn** *m* adopted son; **~tochter** *f* adopted daughter

Adrenalin *n; -s, kein Pl.; Med.* adrenalin; **~spiegel** *m* adrenalin level; **~stoß** *m* surge of adrenalin

Adressat *m; -en, -en, ~in f; -, -nen; altm. od. fachspr.* addressee

Adressbuch *n* directory

Adresse *f; -, -n* **1.** address (*auch EDV*); **per ~** care of (*Abk.* c/o); **an die falsche ~ geraten sein** *od.* **an der falschen ~ sein** come to the wrong place; *umg. fig.* (*anecken*) go to the wrong shop, be knocking at the wrong door (*Am. auch* barking up the wrong tree) (**bei j-m mit etw.** to s.o. with s.th.); *diese Bemerkung war an d-e ~ gerichtet* was directed at (*od.* meant for) you; *die Opposition richtete eine eindringliche Warnung an die Adresse der Regierung* the opposition addressed an urgent warning to the government; **2.** (*Dank-, Grußadresse*) (formal) address; **3.** *Wirts.* house, firm; **zu den ersten ~n gehören** be a top (*od.* first-class) firm (*od.* business)

Adressen|aufkleber *m* address label; **~verwaltung** *f EDV* address database; **~verzeichnis** *n* directory of addresses

adressieren *v/t.* address (*an* to); *Wirts.* (*Güter*) consign; **Adressiermaschine** *f* addressing machine

adrett **I.** *Adj.* smart, neat, trim; **II.** *Adv.:* **~ gekleidet** smartly dressed

Adria *f; -* - Adriatic (Sea)

...adrig *im Adj.* → *...aderig*

adsorbieren *v/t. Chem., Phys.* adsorb; **Adsorption** *f; -, -en* adsorption

Adstringens *n; -, Adstringentia und Adstringenzien; Med.* astringent

A-Dur *n; -, kein Pl.; Mus.* A major; **A-Dur-Tonleiter** *f* A major scale

Adv. *Abk.* → *Adverb*; **adv.** *Abk.* → *adverbiell*

Advent *m; -(e)s, -e, mst. Sg.* **1.** Advent; **2. der erste** *etc.* **~** the first *etc.* Sunday of (*od.* in) Advent

Adventist *m; -en, -en, ~in f; -, -nen* Re-

li. (Second) Adventist

Advents|kalender *m* Advent calendar; **~kranz** *m* Advent wreath; **~sonntag** *m* Sunday in Advent; → **Advent** 2; **~zeit** *f* Advent season

Adverb *n*; *-s*, *-ien*; *Ling.* (*abgek.* **Adv.**) adverb; **adverbial** *Adj.* (*abgek.* **adv.**) adverbial; **~e Bestimmung** adverbial qualification; **Adverbialsatz** *m* adverbial clause; **adverbiell** *Adj.* (*abgek.* **adv.**) adverbial

Advokat *m*; *-en*, *-en*, **~in** *f*; *-*, *-nen* **1.** *schw. od. altm. od. pej.* lawyer *allg.*; **2.** *fig.* advocate, champion

Aerobic [ɛ'roːbɪk] (*n*); *-s*, *kein Pl.* aerobics *Pl.* (*V. im Sg.*)

Aerodynamik [aerody'naːmɪk] *f Phys.* aerodynamics *Pl.* (*V. im Sg.*); **aerodynamisch** *Adj.* aerodynamic(ally *Adv.*); *Form: auch* streamlined

Aerosol [aero'zoːl] *n*; *-s*, *-e*; *fachspr., bes. Med.* aerosol

Aerostatik [aero'staːtɪk] *f Phys.* aerostatics *Pl.* (*V. im Sg.*)

Affäre *f*; *-*, *-n* **1.** (*Liebesaffaire, Spionageaffaire etc.*) affair (*mit/um* with/ about); (*Vorfall*) incident; *sich* (*geschickt*) *aus der* ~ *ziehen umg.* get out of it (nicely); **2.** *umg.* (*Angelegenheit*) matter, business; *das ist doch keine* ~ it's no trouble (*od.* problem); *jetzt mach doch keine solche* ~ *daraus!* don't make such heavy weather (*od.* a fuss) about it!

Äffchen *n* little monkey (*od.* ape)

Affe *m*; *-n*, *-n* **1.** monkey; (*Menschenaffe*) ape; **2.** *umg. fig.*: *e-n* ~*n* (*sitzen*) *haben* be plastered; *ich dachte, mich laust der* ~ I thought I was seeing (*od.* hearing) things *allg.*; *mich laust der* ~*!* well, I'll be blowed (*od.* hanged, *Am.* danged!); *s-m* ~*n Zucker geben* a) be onto one's favo(u)rite topic again,, b) indulge one's vice(s) *allg.*; **3.** *umg. fig. pej.* (*eitler* ~) dandy *allg.*; (*blöder* ~) twit; **4.** *Mil. umg.* (*Tornister*) knapsack, pack *allg.*

Affekt *m*; *-(e)s*, *-e*; *Psych.* emotion; *im* ~ *in the heat of the moment*; *Mord im* ~ crime of passion

affektgeladen *Adj. Diskussion etc.*: very emotional; *Person:* very excited; *es war e-e* ~*e Atmosphäre auch* feelings were running high, the situation was fraught

Affekthandlung *f Psych.* impulsive act; *Jur.* crime of passion

affektiert *Adj.* affected, artificial; **Affektiertheit** *f*; *-*, *-en* affectation

affektiv *Adj. Psych.* affective

Affekt|stau *m Psych.* emotional block, pent-up emotions *Pl.*; **~störung** *f* emotional disturbance

affenartig *Adj.* **1.** *Zool.* apelike, simian *fachspr.*; **2.** *umg.*: *mit* ~*er Geschwindigkeit* like greased lightning

Affenbrotbaum *m Bot.* baobab (tree), monkey bread tree

affengeil *Adj. Sl.* (*toll*) wicked, brill, fab, groovy, cool

Affen|haus *n im Zoo:* monkey-house; **~hitze** *f umg.* scorching (*od. bes. Am.* sizzling) heat *allg.*; *hier drinnen ist ja e-e* ~*!* it's simply baking (*od.* like an oven) in here; **~liebe** *f* doting affection; **~mensch** *m* apeman; **~schande** *f umg.* absolute scandal *allg.*; *das war e-e* ~ it was a crying shame; **~stall** *m umg.* madhouse; *wie im* ~ like (in) a madhouse; **~tempo** *n umg.*: *in e-m* ~ like the clappers, *Am.* like mad, *in e-m* ~ *fahren: auch* belt (along); **~theater** *n*; *nur Sg.*; *umg.* farce; *das ist ja*

ein ~ *auch* it's crazy; *er hat ein* ~ *deswegen veranstaltet* he made such a fuss about it; **~zahn** *m umg.*: *e-n* ~ *draufhaben* be going at some lick, scorch along; *mit e-m* ~ at a spanking rate, like a bat out of hell

affig *Adj. umg.* foppish; (*albern*) silly *gespr.*

Äffin *f*; *-*, *-nen* she-ape; she-monkey; female ape (*od.* monkey)

Affinität *f*; *-*, *-en*; *geh., fachspr.* affinity (*zu/zwischen* towards/between)

Affirmation *f*; *-*, *-en*; *fachspr.* affirmation; **affirmativ** *Adj.* affirmative

Affix *n*; *-es*, *-e*; *Ling.* affix

Affront [a'frõː] *m*; *-s*, *-s* affront (*gegen* to), insult (*to*)

Afghane *m*; *-n*, *-n* **1.** Afghan; **2.** (*Hund*) Afghan hound; **Afghanin** *f*; *-*, *-nen* Afghan (girl *od.* woman); **afghanisch** *Adj.* Afghan

Afrika (*n*); *-s* Africa; *im tiefsten* ~ in darkest Africa; **Afrikaner** *m*; *-s*, *-*, **Afrikanerin** *f*; *-*, *-nen* African, *weibl. auch* African girl (*od.* woman); **afrikanisch** *Adj.* African

Afrikanistik *f*; *-*, *kein Pl.* African studies *Pl.*

Afro-Amerikaner *m*, **~in** *f* African--American; **afro-amerikanisch** *Adj.* African-American

Afro-Look *m*: (*im* ~ with an) Afro hairstyle

After *m*; *-s*, *-*; *Anat.* anus; *Med. euph.* back passage

Aftershave ['aːftɐʃeːv] *n*; *-s*, *-s* aftershave (lotion)

AG *Abk.* → *Aktiengesellschaft, Arbeitsgemeinschaft*

Ägäis *f*; *-* Aegean; **ägäisch** *Adj.*: *das Ägäische Meer* the Aegean (Sea); *die Ägäischen Inseln* the Aegean Islands

Agave *f*; *-*, *-n*; *Bot.* agave

Agens *n*; *-*, *Agenzien und Agentia* **1.** *Chem.* agent; **2.** *nur Sg.*; *Ling.* agent; **3.** *Pl. nur Agenzien*; *Philos.*, *fig.* driving force

Agent *m*; *-en*, *-en* agent; (*Zirkusagent*) (artiste) agent

Agenten|austausch *m* spy swap; **~netz** *n* spy ring; **~ring** *m* spy ring; **~tätigkeit** *f* espionage

Agentin *f*; *-*, *-nen* (female) agent

Agentur *f*; *-*, *-en* agency

Agglomerat *n*; *-(e)s*, *-e*; *Geol., Metall. od. geh.* agglomerate; **agglomerieren** *vt/i.* agglomerate, nodulize

Agglutination *f*; *-*, *-en*; *Med. und Ling.* agglutination; **agglutinieren** *v/i.* agglutinate

Aggregat *n*; *-(e)s*, *-e* **1.** *Tech.* (*Stromaggregat*) unit; **2.** *Phys., Bio., Math.* aggregate; **~zustand** *m Chem.* physical state

Aggression *f*; *-*, *-en* aggression

Aggressions|krieg *m* war of aggression; **~lust** *f*; *nur Sg.* belligerence; **~politik** *f* policy of aggression; **~stau** *m* build-up of aggression; **~trieb** *m*; *nur Sg.* aggressive instinct (*od.* impulse)

aggressiv *Adj.* aggressive; *Mittel: auch* abrasive; *Attacke etc.: auch* hard-hitting; **Aggressivität** *f*; *-*, *kein Pl.* aggressiveness

Aggressor *m*; *-s*, *-en*; *Pol.* aggressor

Ägide *f*: *unter der* ~ *von* under the aegis (*od.* auspices) of

agieren *v/i.* act (*auch Theat.*); (*gestikulieren*) gesticulate

agil *Adj.* agile; *geistig* ~ mentally alert; **Agilität** *f*; *-*, *kein Pl.* agility

Agio ['aː dʒo] *n*; *-s*, *-s und Agien*;

Wirts. premium; **~papier** *n* premium bond

Agitation *f*; *-*, *-en*; *Pol. pej. od. marxistisch:* political agitation (*für/gegen* in support of / against); **Agitator** *m*; *-s*, *-en*, **Agitatorin** *f*; *-*, *-nen* political agitator; rabble-rouser *pej.*; **agitatorisch** *Adj.* inflammatory; (*aufrührerisch*) rabble-rousing, seditious; **agitieren** *v/i.* canvass, campaign (*für* for); ~ *gegen* campaign against

Agitprop *f*; *-*, *kein Pl.*, **~theater** *n Theat.* agitprop (theat|re [*Am. auch* -er])

Agnostiker *m*; *-s*, *-*, **~in** *f*; *-*, *-nen* agnostic; **agnostisch** *Adj.* agnostic

Agonie *f*; *-*, *-n*; *geh. od. Med.* death throes *Pl.*

Agoraphobie *f*; *nur Sg.*; *Psych.* agoraphobia

Agrar|... *im Subst.* agrarian, farm ..., agricultural, agro...: **~exporte** agricultural (*od.* farm) exports; **~gesellschaft** agrarian society; **~importe** agricultural (*od.* farm) imports

Agrar|ausgaben *Pl.* agricultural spending *Sg.*; **~fabrik** *f* factory farm

agrarisch *Adj.* agrarian

Agrar|land *n* agrarian country; **~markt** *m* agricultural commodities market; **~politik** *f* agricultural policy; **~preise** *Pl.* farm prices; **~produkt** *n* agricultural (*od.* farm) product; **~reform** *f* agricultural reform; **~staat** *m* agrarian state; **~subventionen** *Pl.* farm subsidies; **~wirtschaft** *f* farming; **~wissenschaft** *f* agronomy; **~wissenschaftler** *m*, **~wissenschaftlerin** *f* agronomist; **~zoll** *m* import tariff (on produce)

Agreement [ə'griːmənt] *n*; *-s*, *-s*; *Pol.* agreement

Agrément [agre'mãː] *n*; *-s*, *-s*; *Pol.* agrément

Agrikultur *f* agriculture, husbandry, farming

Agronom *m*; *-en*, *-en*, **~in** *f*; *-*, *-nen* agronomist; **Agronomie** *f*; *-*, *kein Pl.* agronomy; **agronomisch** *Adj.* agronomic(al)

Ägypten (*n*); *-s* Egypt; **Ägypter** *m*; *-s*, *-*, **Ägypterin** *f*; *-*, *-nen* Egyptian; **ägyptisch** *Adj.* Egyptian; → **Finsternis**

ah I. *Interj. überrascht:* ah, oh; *verächtlich:* pooh; **II. Ah** *n*; *-s*, *-s* oh, ah

äh *Interj. gespr.* **1.** *Pausen füllend:* er, um; **2.** *umg.* (*igitt*) ugh, pooh, *Am.* phew

aha *Interj.* I see; (*Ausdruck der Genugtuung*) aha, oh, I see; there you are; **Aha-Erlebnis** *n* aha experience, sudden realization

Ahle *f*; *-*, *-n* awl; *Druck.* point, bodkin; *Tech.* reamer, broach

Ahn *m*; *-s und -en*, *-en* ancestor, forefather

ahnden *v/t. geh.* (*strafen, rächen*) punish; *ein Foul mit e-m Elfmeter* ~ award a penalty for a foul; **Ahndung** *f* revenge; punishment

Ahne *m*; *-n*, *-n und f*; *-*, *-n*; *geh.* forebear, ancestor

ähneln *v/i.* **1.** look (*od.* be) like, resemble; *Dinge: auch* be similar (*Dat.* to); *von Kindern:* take after; *sie ähnelt ihrem Vater* she takes after her father; **2.** *sich* (*Dat.*) ~ be (*od.* look) alike; *Dinge: auch* be similar

ahnen I. *v/t.* (*vorhersehen*) foresee; (*vermuten*) suspect; (*Böses*) have a presentiment (*od.* foreboding) of; *ich hab's geahnt!* I had a funny feeling, I knew it; *ich konnte doch nicht* ~ ... I had no way of knowing ...; (*ach,*) *du*

ahnst es nicht! *umg.* blow me (down)!; *das lässt ~, ...* it makes one suspect ...; *als ob er es geahnt hätte* as if he had known it (in advance); *nichts ~d* unsuspecting; **II.** *v/i.*: *was s-e Zukunft betrifft, ahnt mir nichts Gutes* geh. I have grave misgivings as to his future

Ahnen|bild *n* ancestral portrait; *~forschung* *f* genealogy, ancestor research; *~galerie* *f* ancestral halls *Pl.*; *weitS.* the family portraits *Pl.*; *~kult* *m* ancestral worship; *~reihe* *f* line of ancestors; *~tafel* *f* genealogical table, family tree

Ahn|frau *f* (female) ancestor, ancestress *förm.*; (*Stammmutter*) progenitor, progenitrix *förm.*; *~herr* *m* ancestor; (*Stammvater*) progenitor

ähnlich I. *Adj.* similar (*Dat.* to), (a)like; *in ~er Weise* in like manner; *ein ~er Fall* a similar case; *so etwas Ähnliches wie* something like; *... oder so ~* umg. something like that; *j-m ~ sehen* look (*od.* be) like s.o.; *ärgerlich*: *das sieht ihm etc. ~* that's him *etc.* all over, he *etc.* would; *das sieht ihm etc. aber gar nicht ~* that's not like him *etc.* at all!; *sie sieht i-r Mutter ~* she resembles her mother; *das Foto ist nicht sehr ~* the photo is not a good likeness; *oder Ähnliches* (*abgek. o. Ä.*) or the like; *und Ähnliche(s)* (*abgek. u. Ä.*) and the like; **II.** *Adv.* similarly; **Ähnlichkeit** *f* resemblance (*mit* to), likeness; *fig.* similarity (with); *verblüffende ~* remarkable (*od.* deceptive) resemblance; *viel ~ haben mit* look very much like, *fig.* be very similar to

Ahnung *f* **1.** (*Vorgefühl*) presentiment; (*schlimme ~*) *auch* foreboding; (*Vermutung*) suspicion, hunch; *ich habe so e-e ~* I have a kind of hunch, I have a funny feeling; *m-e ~ hat nicht getrogen* my hunch was right; **2.** (*Vorstellung*) idea (*von* of); *hast du e-e ~, was das kostet?* do you have any idea how much that costs?; *keine ~!* no idea; *ich habe keine blasse / nicht die geringste od. leiseste etc. ~ davon* I haven't the faintest (*od.* foggiest) idea / a clue *umg.*; *er hat von Tuten und Blasen keine ~* umg. he doesn't know the first thing about it *allg.*, he doesn't have a (bloody) clue; *hast du e-e ~!* that's what you think

ahnungslos *Adj.* **1.** unsuspecting, unsuspicious; **2.** (*unwissend*) ignorant, innocent; **Ahnungslosigkeit** *f; nur Sg.* cluelessness, ignorance, innocence

ahnungsvoll *Adj. Person*: full of foreboding; apprehensive, fearful; *Lit. Ereignis*: ominous, mysterious

ahoi *Interj. Naut.* ahoy!; *Boot/Schiff ~!* boat/ship ahoy!

Ahorn *m*; *-s, -e*; *Bot.* **1.** *Baum*: maple (tree); **2.** *nur Sg., Holz*: maple (wood); *~blatt* *n* maple leaf; *~holz* *n* maple (wood); *~sirup* *m* maple syrup

Ähre *f*; *-, -n*; *Bot.* ear (of corn *etc.*); **Ährenlese** *f* gleaning

Ai *n*; *-s, -s*; *Zool.* ai, three-toed sloth

Aids *n*; *-, kein Pl.*; *Med.* AIDS, Aids; *~infektion* *f* AIDS infection

aidsinfiziert *Adj.* infected with AIDS *nur präd.*; **Aidsinfizierte** *m, f* person infected with AIDS, *Am. auch* PWA (= person with AIDS)

aidskrank *Adj.*: *~ sein* have AIDS; **Aidskranke** *m, f* AIDS sufferer (*od.* patient, victim),, *Am. auch* PWA

Aids|test *m* AIDS test; *e-n ~ machen lassen* have (*od.* go for) an AIDS

test; *~tote* *m, f* AIDS fatality

Airbag ['ɛːɐ̯bɛk] *m*; *-s, -s*; *Mot.* airbag

ais, Ais *n*; *-, -*; *Mus.* A sharp

Ajatollah *m*; *-(s), -s* ayatollah

Akademie *f*; *-, -n* **1.** (*Fachhochschule*) academy (*Fachschule*) college; **2.** (*Gelehrtengesellschaft*) (learned) society; *~ der Künste/Wissenschaften* Academy of Arts/Sciences; *~mitglied* *n* academician, member of an (*od.* the) academy

Akademiker *m*; *-s, -*, *~in* *f*; *-, -nen* (university) graduate; university man (*f* woman), academic

akademisch I. *Adj.* **1.** academic; *~e Bildung* university education; *~er Grad* academic qualification; *~es Viertel* the quarter of an hour between the official and actual start of a lecture or event; **2.** *fig. pej.* (*weltfremd, trocken*) learned; **II.** *Adv.* academically

Akazie *f*; *-, -n* **1.** *Bot.* acacia; **2.** *umg.* (*Robinie, Scheinakazie*) robinia, false acacia; **Akazienholz** *n* acacia

Akk. *Abk.* → *Akkusativ*

Akklamation *f*; *-, -en* **1.** *Pol.*: *durch* (*od. per*) *~ wählen* elect by acclamation; **2.** *geh.* (*Beifall*) acclamation; (*Anerkennung*) acclaim

Akklimatisation *f*; *-, -en* acclimatization; **akklimatisieren I.** *v/t.* acclimatize (*auch fig.*); **II.** *v/refl.* become acclimatized (*auch fig.*); **Akklimatisierung** *f* acclimatization

Akkord *m*; *-(e)s, -e* **1.** *Mus.* chord; **2.** *Wirts.* piecework; *im ~ arbeiten* do piecework; **3.** *Jur.* settlement; *~arbeit* *f* piecework; *~arbeiter* *m*, *~arbeiterin* *f* pieceworker

Akkordeon *n*; *-s, -s* accordion; *~spieler* *m*, *~spielerin* *f* accordionist, accordion player

Akkord|lohn *m* piecework wage; *~ verdienen* earn piece rate; *~satz* *m* piece rate

akkreditieren *v/t.* **1.** (*Gesandten*) accredit (*bei* to); **2.** *Wirts.* open a credit in favo(u)r of *s.o.*

Akkreditiv *n*; *-s, -e* **1.** *Wirts.* letter of credit (*Abk.* L/C); *j-m ein ~ eröffnen* open a credit in favo(u)r of s.o.; **2.** *Pol.* (*Beglaubigunsschreiben*) credentials *Pl.*

Akku *m*; *-s, -s*; *umg.* → *Akkumulator*

Akkumulation *f*; *-, -en*; *geh.* accumulation

Akkumulator *m*; *-s, -en*; *Tech.* accumulator, storage battery

akkumulieren *v/t. und v/refl. geh. und fachspr.* accumulate

akkurat I. *Adj.* meticulous; *Dial. südd.* (*exakt*) precise, exact; *Handschrift*: neat; **II.** *Adv. südd., österr.* precisely, exactly; (*tatsächlich*) naturally, of course; **Akkuratesse** [akura'tɛsə] *f*; *-, kein Pl.* meticulousness; (*Präzision*) precision

Akkusativ *m*; *-s, -e*; *Ling.* (*abgek.* **Akk.**) accusative (case); *~objekt* *n* direct object

Akne *f*; *-, -n*; *Med.* acne

Akontozahlung *f Wirts.* payment on account

akquirieren *v/i. Wirts.* attract (new) business

Akquisiteur [akvizi'tøːɐ̯] *m*; *-s, -e*, *~in* *f*; *-, -nen*; *Wirts.* agent, canvasser

Akribie *f*; *-, kein Pl.* meticulousness; **akribisch** *Adj.* meticulous, painstaking

Akrobat *m*; *-en, -en* acrobat; **Akrobatik** *f*; *-, kein Pl.* acrobatics *Pl.*; **Akrobatin** *f*; *-, -nen* acrobat; **akrobatisch** *Adj.*

acrobatic

Akronym *n*; *-s, -e*; *Ling.* acronym

Akt[1] *m*; *-(e)s, -e* **1.** *geh.* (*Tat*) act, action; *symbolischer ~* symbolic action; **2.** (*Zeremonie*) (ceremonial) act; (*Festakt*) ceremony; **3.** (*Geschlechtsakt*) sexual act, coitus; **4.** *Theat.* act; **5.** *Fot., Kunst*: nude; **6.** *im Zirkus etc.*: act

Akt[2] *m*; *-(e)s, -en*; *südd., österr.* → *Akte*

Akt|aufnahme *f*, *~bild* *n* nude (photograph)

Akte *f*; *-, -n* file, record, (official) document; *Jur.* (legal) instrument, deed; *e-e ~ anlegen über* (+ *Akk.*) open a file on; *e-e ~ ablegen von etw.* file s.th.; *die ~n einsehen* look at (*od.* consult) a file; *die ~(n) schließen über* (+ *Akk.*) close the file(s) on; *zu den ~n legen* file away, put on file; *Brit. fig.* shelve, *Am.* table; *in den ~n findet sich dazu nichts* there is nothing on file about it

Akten|deckel *m* folder; *~einsicht* *f* inspection of records; *~ erhalten* be given access to (the) records (*od.* files); *~koffer* *m* attaché case

aktenkundig *Adj.* on record, on file; *Person*: known to the police

Akten|mappe *f* **1.** folder; **2.** → *Aktentasche*; *~notiz* *f* memo(randum); *~ordner* *m* (document) file; *~schrank* *m* filing cabinet; *~stoß* *m* pile (*od.* bundle) of documents; *~tasche* *f* briefcase; *~vermerk* *m* memo(randum); *~wolf* *m* shredder; *~zeichen* *n* file number; *auf Brief*: reference (number)

Akteur [ak'tøːɐ̯] *m*; *-s, -e* **1.** (*Handelnder*) protagonist; **2.** *Film etc.*: actor; **3.** *Sport*: (*Spieler*) player, (*Wettkämpfer*) competitor,; **4.** *förm.* (*Hauptvertreter*) protagonist

Akt|foto *n* nude (photograph); *~fotografie* *f* **1.** nude photography; **2.** (*Bild*) nude photograph

Aktie *f*; *-, -n* **1.** *Wirts.* share (of stock); *e-e ~ steigt/fällt* a share price is rising/falling; **2.** *umg. fig.*: *wie stehen die ~n?* how are things?, how's tricks?; *s-e ~n steigen* things are looking up for him

Aktien|anlage *f*; *meist Pl.*; *Fin.* equity investing; *~börse* *f* stock exchange; *~fonds* *m* share (*Am.* stock) fund; *~gesellschaft* *f* (*abgek.* **AG**) public limited company (*abgek.* plc), joint-stock company, *Am.* (stock) corporation (*abgek.* Inc.); *~index* *m* share index; *~kapital* *n* (*Pl. selten*) share (*od.* equity) capital, *Am.* capital stock; *nur der Aktionäre*: shareholder's (*Am.* stockholder's) equity; *~kurs* *m* share (*Am. auch* stock) price; *~markt* *m* stock (*Brit. auch* share) market; *~mehrheit* *f* majority holding; *die ~ besitzen* hold the controlling interest; *~notierung* *f* share (*Am.* stock) quotation (*od.* listing); *~paket* *n* block (*od.* parcel) of shares (*Am.* stock); *~spekulation* *f* speculation on the stock market

Aktion *f*; *-, -en* **1.** (*Handlung*) action; *Pl. auch* activities; *in ~ sein* in action; *in ~ treten* take action, act; *sie sind voll in ~* umg. it's all stations go (with them); **2.** (*Unternehmung, Werbeaktion etc.*) drive, campaign; (*Maßnahme*) measures *Pl.*; (*Hilfsaktion*) operation; *künstlerische*: happening; *Pol.* action; *konzertierte ~* concerted action; *groß angelegte ~* large-scale project

Aktionär *m*; *-s, -e*, *~in* *f*; *-, -nen* shareholder, *Am. auch* stockholder; **Aktio-närsversammlung** *f* shareholders' (*Am. auch* stockholders') meeting

Aktionismus *m*; -, *kein Pl.* **1.** *Kunstform*: action painting, tachism(e); **2.** *pej.*: (*blinder*) ~ doing things for the sake of doing things

Aktions|art *f* *Ling.* manner of action; **~bereich** *m* sphere of action; **~freiheit** *f* freedom of action; **~gemeinschaft** *f* *Pol.* action group; **~herd** *m* *Met. e-s Vulkans*: focus of activity; **~komitee** *n* action (*od.* acting) committee; **~maler** *m*, **~malerin** *f* action painter; **~malerei** *f* action painting; **~preis** *m* *Wirts.* sale price; **~programm** *n* program(me) of action; **~radius** *m* radius (of action); *fig.* sphere of action; **~woche** *f* (special) campaign week; *Wirt.* (one-)week sale

aktiv I. *Adj.* **1.** (*Ggs. passiv*) *Mitglied, Sportler, Leben, Mitarbeit etc.*: active; *politisch/sexuell* ~ politically/sexually active; ~ *sein* be active; **~es Wahlrecht** right to vote, suffrage; **~er Wortschatz** active vocabulary; *er ist ~es Mitglied der Church of England* a practi|sing (*Am.* -cing) member of the Church of England; **2.** *Bio., Chem., Med., Phys.* active, *Chem. auch* activated; **3.** *Wirts. Bilanz*: favo(u)rable; **4.** *Soldat, Truppe*: regular; **~er Dienst** active duty; **5.** *Ling. Verb*: active; **II.** *Adv.* actively; *sich ~ beteiligen an* (+ *Dat.*) take an active part in s.th.

Aktiv *n*; -s, -s/-e **1.** *nur Sg.*; *Ling.* active (voice); **2.** *hist., ehem. DDR* special (work) team; *Pol.* selected group (of party activists); (*~tagung*) (special) meeting (of activists)

Aktiva *Pl. Wirts.* assets; ~ *und Passiva* assets and liabilities

Aktivbestand *m Wirts.* assets *Pl.*

Aktive *m*, *f*; -n, -n **1.** *Sport* active player (*od.* runner *etc.*); **2.** *Mil.* regular

Aktiv|forderung *f Wirts.* active debt, account receivable; **~geschäft** *n* credit transaction(s *Pl.*)

aktivieren *v/t.* **1.** activate, get *s.th.* (*od. s.o.*) going; **2.** *Phys. etc.* activate; **3.** *Wirts.* carry as an asset; **Aktivierung** *f auch fig.* activation

Aktivismus *m*; -, *kein Pl.* activism

aktivisch *Adj. Ling.* active

Aktivist *m*; -en, -en, **~in** *f*; -, -nen; *Pol.* activist, militant; *ehem. DDR Wirts.* (*Bestarbeiter*) activist

Aktivität *f*; -, -en activity; *schöpferische* ~ *entfalten* become very creative

Aktiv|kohle *f Chem.* activated carbon; **~posten** *m Wirts. und fig.* credit item, asset; **~saldo** *m Wirts.* credit balance; **~seite** *f Wirts.* asset side; **~urlaub** *m* activity (*od.* active) holiday; **~zinsen** *m*; *Pl.* interest receivable (*od.* to be received)

Akt|malerei *f* nude painting; **~modell** *n* nude model; **~studie** *f* nude study; **~zeichnung** *f* nude drawing

aktualisieren *v/t.* update, bring *s.th.* up to date; **Aktualisierung** *f* updating

Aktualität *f*; -, -en topicality, relevance to the present

aktuell *Adj.* (*zeitgemäß*) topical, of current interest; (*Problem*: present-day ...; (*modern*) up-to-date ..., *präd.* up to date; *Computer*: current; *ein ~er Bericht* a report on current affairs; *ein ~er Vortrag* a current-events lecture; *das ist nicht mehr* ~ we've crossed that off the agenda, that's not happening; *wieder* ~ *werden Buch, Stil etc.*: come back into fashion, *Frage etc.*: be-

come a burning issue again; *Pol.* ~*e Stunde* special session; *Aktuelles aus der Literatur, Filmbranche etc.* the latest from the literary world, the movie world *etc.*

Akupressur *f*; -, -en; *Med.* acupressure

Akupunkteur [akupʊŋk'tøːɐ̯] *m*; -s, -e, **~in** *f*; -, -nen; *Med.* acupuncturist; **akupunktieren** *v/t.* give *s.o.* acupuncture treatment; **Akupunktur** *f*; -, -en acupuncture

Akustik *f*; -, *kein Pl.* acoustics *Pl.* (*Lehre*: *V. im Sg.*); **akustisch I.** *Adj.* acoustic(al); ~*es Signal* acoustic (*od.* sound) signal; **II.** *Adv.* acoustically; *ich habe Sie* ~ *nicht verstanden* I didn't quite catch what you said

akut *Adj. Med.* acute, *Schmerzen: auch* severe (*beide auch fig.*); (*Problem, Angelenheit etc.*) pressing; **Akut** *m*; -(e)s, -e; *Phon.* acute accent; **Akutkrankenhaus** *n* emergency hospital

AKW *n*; -(s), -s; *Abk. umg.* → *Atomkraftwerk*; **AKW-Gegner** *m*, **AKW-Gegnerin** *f* anti-nuclear protest|er (*od.* –or)

Akzent *m*; -(e)s, -e **1.** *amerikanischer, bayrischer etc.*: accent; **2.** *Ling.* (*Betonung*) accent, stress; (*Betonungszeichen*) accent; *der* ~ *liegt auf der ersten Silbe* the stress is on the first syllable; **3.** *fig.* stress; ~*e setzen* set a course, indicate directions; *neue ~e setzen* point the way to the future, set new trends

akzent|frei, **~los** *Adj. und Adv.* without (an *od.* any) accent

akzentuieren *v/t. auch fig.* accentuate

Akzentverschiebung *f* shift of stress (*od. fig.* emphasis)

Akzept *n Fin.* (*Annahmevermerk e-s Wechsels*) acceptance; (*angenommener Wechsel*) accepted bill

akzeptabel *Adj.* acceptable (*für* to)

Akzeptanz *f*; -, -en; *geh. und fachspr.* acceptance; *Wirts.* market acceptance

akzeptierbar *Adj* acceptable; **akzeptieren** *v/t.* accept; **Akzeptierung** *f* acceptance

Akzidenzdruck *m*; *Pl.* -drucke job printing

Alabaster *m*; -s, - alabaster

à la carte *Adv.*: ~ *bestellen* (*essen*) order (eat) à la carte

Alarm *m*; -(e)s, -e alarm, alert; (*Fliegeralarm*) air-raid warning, alert; *blinder od. falscher* ~ false alarm; ~ *schlagen* sound (*od.* raise) the alarm; **~anlage** *f* alarm system

alarmbereit *Adj.* on alert, *Mil. auch* on standby *präd.*; **Alarmbereitschaft** *f*: *in* ~ on alert, *Mil. auch* on standby; *in höchster* ~ in a high state of alert; *in* ~ *versetzen* put on alert (*Mil. auch* standby)

Alarm|geber *m Tech.* alarm annunciator; **~glocke** *f* alarm bell, tocsin; **alarmieren** *v/t.* alarm (*auch fig.*), alert; **alarmierend I.** *Part.Präs.* → *alarmieren*; **II.** *Adj. fig.* alarming; **Alarmierung** *f* alarming, alerting

Alarm|signal *n* alarm signal; **~sirene** *f* (fire) alarm siren; **~stufe** *f* alert phase; *höchste* ~ high state of alert; **~zeichen** *n* danger signal (*auch fig.*); **~zustand** *m* state of alert; *im* ~ on alert

Alaun *m*; -s, -e; *Chem.* alum; **~stift** *m* styptic (pencil)

Alb *m*; -(e)s, -e; (*Beklemmung*) (spiritual) burden

Albaner *m*; -s, -, **~in** *f*; -, -nen Albanian; **Albanien** (*n*); -s Albania; **alba-**

nisch **I.** *Adj.* Albanian; **II. Albanisch** *n*; -en; *Ling.* Albanian; *das Albanische* Albanian, the Albanian language

Albatros *m*; -, -se; *Orn.* albatross

Albdruck *m*; *Pl.* -drücke, **Albdrücken** *n*; -s nightmare(s *Pl.*), oppressive thought

Alberei *f*; -, -en fooling (*od.* messing) around; (*Tat*) prank; (*Bermerkung*) inanity

albern[1] *Adj.* silly; ~*es Zeug* rubbish, nonsense

albern[2] *v/i. umg.* fool around *allg.*; **Albernheit** *f* silly behavio(u)r

Albino *m*; -s, -s albino

Albtraum *m auch fig.* nightmare

Album *n*; -s, *Alben*; (*früher auch LP*) album

Albumen *n*; -s, *kein Pl.*; *Bio.* albumen

Albumin *n*; -s, -e; *Bio., Tech.* albumin

Alchemie *f hist.* alchemy; **Alchemist** *m*; -en, -en alchemist; **alchemistisch** *Adj.* alchemic(al), alchemistic

Alchimie *etc.* → *Alchemie etc.*

Aldehyd *n*; -s, -e; *Chem.* aldehyde

Alemanne *m*; -n, -n, **Alemannin** *f*; -, -nen; *auch hist.* Alemannian; *hist. die Alemannen* the Alemanni; **alemannisch I.** *Adj.*; Alemannic; **II. Alemannisch** *n*; -en; *Ling.* Alemannic; *das Alemannische* Alemannic, the Alemannic language

Aleuten *Pl. Geog.*: *die* ~ the Aleutian Islands

Alexandriner *m*; -s, -; (*Vers*) Alexandrine (verse)

Alge *f*; -, -n alga; *Pl.* algae, seaweed *Sg.*

Algebra *f* -, *kein Pl.*; *Math.* algebra; **algebraisch** *Adj.* algebraic

Algen|pest *f* algal bloom, proliferation of algae; **~teppich** *m* layer (*od.* tide) of algae

Algerien (*n*); -s Algeria; **Algerier** *m*; -s, -, **Algerierin** *f*; -, -nen Algerian; **algerisch** *Adj.* Algerian; **Algier** ['alʒiːɐ̯] (*n*); -s Algiers

Algorithmus *m*; -, *Algorithmen*; *Math.* algorithm

alias *Adv.* alias, also known as, *Abk.* aka

Alibi *n*; -s, -s; *Jur.* alibi (*auch fig.*); **~frau** *f* token woman; **~funktion** *f*: *das* (*od. sie*) *hat nur e-e* ~ it's just a cover-up (she's just a token); **~schwarze** *m*, *f* token black

Alimente *Pl.* maintenance *Sg.*, child support *Sg.*

aliphatisch *Adj. Chem.* aliphatic

Alk *m*; -(e)s *od.* -en, -e(n); *Orn.* auk

Alkali *n*; -s, -en; *Chem.* alkali

Alkali|metall *n Chem.* alkali metal; **~salz** *n* alkali salt

alkalisch *Adj. Chem.* alkaline

Alkaloid *n*; -(e)s, -e; *Chem.* alkaloid

Alkohol *m*; -s, -e alcohol, liquor; *als Getränk auch*: drink; *der Verkauf von* ~ the sale of spirits (*od.* liquor); *er steht unter* ~ he's been drinking

alkoholabhängig *Adj.*: ~ *sein* be an alcoholic; **Alkoholabhängige** *m*, *f* alcoholic

alkoholarm *Adj.* low in alcohol *präd.*, low-alcohol ...

Alkohol|ausschank *m* sale of alcohol(ic drinks); **~einfluss** *m*: *er stand unter* ~ he had been drinking; *Fahren unter* ~ drink-driving, *Am.* drunk-driving, DUI (= driving under the influence), DWI (= driving while intoxicated)

alkoholfrei *Adj.* non-alcoholic, alcohol-free; ~*e Getränke* soft drinks (and

ˈbeverages)

Alkohol|gehalt *m* alcoholic content; **~genuss** *m* consumption of alcohol, drinking

alkoholhaltig *Adj.* alcoholic

Alkoholika *Pl.* alcohol *Sg.*, alcoholic drinks

Alkoholiker *m; -s, -,* **~in** *f; -, -nen* alcoholic; **Anonyme ~** (*abgek.* **AA**) Alcoholics Anonymous (*abgek.* AA)

alkoholisch *Adj.* alcoholic; (**starke**) **~e Getränke** spirits

alkoholisieren *v/t.* **1.** *Chem.* alcoholize; **2.** *j-n* **~** get s.o. drunk; **alkoholisiert I.** *P.P.* → *alkoholisieren*; **II.** *Adj. Person:* drunk; **in ~em Zustand** (while) under the influence of alcohol

Alkoholismus *m; -, kein Pl.* alcoholism

Alkohol|konsum *m* consumption of alcohol

alkoholkrank *Adj.* alcoholic; **Alkoholkranke** *m, f* alcoholic

Alkoholmissbrauch *m* alcohol abuse

alkoholreich *Adj.* high in alcohol, high-alcohol …

Alkohol|schmuggel *m* liquor smuggling, bootlegging *umg.*; **~spiegel** *m* blood-alcohol level

Alkoholsucht *f* alcoholism, alcohol dependence; **alkoholsüchtig** *Adj.*: **~ sein** be an alcoholic

Alkohol|sünder *m* drunk(en) driver; **~test** *m* breathalyser (*Am.* breath) test; **~verbot** *n* ban on alcohol; *USA hist.* Prohibition; **~vergiftung** *f* alcohol poisoning

Alkoven *m; -s, -* **1.** alcove, recess; **2.** windowless room

all *unbest. Pron.* **1.** *adjektivisch* all (of); all the (+ *Pl.*); (*jeder*) every; each; **~e anderen** all the others, all the rest; **~es andere** all else; **das ~es** all that; **~es andere als** (*nützlich etc.*) anything but (useful *etc.*); **~e Menschen** everyone, everybody; **~e Welt** the whole world, all the world; **~es Amerikanische** all things American; **~es Gute** all the best; **~es Übrige** all the rest; **Sachen ~er Art** all kinds of things; **~en Ernstes** in all seriousness; **auf ~e Fälle** in any case (*od.* event); **in ~er Deutlichkeit** quite distinctly; **in ~er Form** in good and due form; **mit ~er Kraft** with all one's strength; **trotz ~er Anstrengungen** despite all efforts; **vor ~en Leuten** in front of everybody, in public; **sie hat ~ ihr Geld verloren** she lost all her money; **2.** *in Zeit- und Mengenangaben:* **~e** (**zwei**) **Tage** every (other) day; **~e acht Tage** once a week; **~e Jahre wieder** year after year; **~e drei Schritte/Meter** every couple of (*od.* few) feet/yards *umg.*; **3.** *substantivisch* a) **alle** all; **~e beide** both of them; **~e drei** all three (of them); **sie/wir ~e** all of them/us; **~e außer mir** *etc.* everyone except me *etc.*; **fast ~e** almost everyone; **sind ~e da?** is everyone (*od.* everybody) here?; **~e und jeder** all and sundry, everyone (and his dog *umg.*); **~e, die …** all who (*od.* that), whoever; *Amtsspr.* any persons who (*od.* being *od.* having) …; **~e, die ein Visum benötigen** anyone (*od.* those) requiring a visa; **das wollen nicht ~e** not everyone wants that, b) **alles** everything; **~es lachte** everybody laughed; **~es außer …** all but …; **~es auf einmal** all at once; **das ist ~es** that is (*od.* will be) all; **er kann ~es** he can do anything; **~es oder nichts!** it's all or nothing; **~es in allem** all in all,

overall, on balance, (*letztendlich*) *auch* when all is said and done; *trotz* **~em** despite everything; *vor* **~em** above all; **sie ist gut in ~em** she is good at everything; **was soll das ~es?** what's the meaning of all that?; **damit ist ~es gesagt** I need say no more; **~es zu s-r Zeit** all in good time; **auf ~es gefasst sein** be prepared for the worst; **~es hat zwei Seiten** there are two sides to everything; **es geht ihr über ~es** she values that more than anything, c) *verstärkend:* **Geschwindigkeit ist ~es** speed is everything; **sie ist ~es für mich** she is evrything to me; **wer war denn ~es da?** who all was there?; **um ~es in der Welt** for anything in the world; **da war** (**aber**) **~es dran** *umg.* it was just perfect; *pej.* it was the limit, it couldn't have been worse, d) **ihr Ein und** (**ihr**) **Alles** her all in all, her little all; → **ein¹** II 1, **Mädchen** 2

All *n; -s, kein Pl.* universe; (*Weltraum*) (outer) space; **ins ~ schicken** send into space

allabendlich I. *Adj. Bad, Besuch etc.:* regular evening … (*nur attrib.*); **II.** *Adv.* every (*od.* each) evening

allbekannt *Adj.* well-known; *pej.* notorious

alldem → *alledem*

alldieweil *altm. od. hum.* **I.** *Konj.* → *weil*; **II.** *Adv.* → *währenddessen*

alle¹ *Adj. präd. und Adv. umg.* **1.** (*aufgebraucht*) finished, all gone; **mein Geld ist ~** I've run out of money, I'm broke *allg.*; **der Zucker ist ~** we've *etc.* run out of sugar, there's no sugar left *allg.*; **allmählich ~ werden** run out; **Dumme werden nie ~** fools will never die out *allg., Am.* there's a sucker born every minute; **2.** (*erschöpft*) whacked, bushed; **3.** *j-n* **~** **machen** *umg.* (*ruinieren, fertig machen*) finish s.o. off *allg.*; (*umbringen*) do s.o. in

alle² *unbest. Pron.* → **all**

alledem *Pron.*: **bei** *od.* **mit ~** with all that; **trotz ~** despite everything; **nichts von ~ ist wahr** not a word of it is true, there's no truth in any of it

Allee *f; -, -n* avenue, boulevard

Allegorie *f; -, -n* allegory; **allegorisch** *Adj.* allegorical

allein I. *Adj. präd. und Adv.* **1.** (*ohne andere Personen*) alone, on one's own, (all) by oneself; **ganz ~** all alone; **kann ich dich ~ lassen?** will you be all right (*Am. umg.* alright) on your own?; **kann ich mal mit dir ~ sprechen?** could I have a word with you in private?; **~ leben** live alone, live on one's own; **~ reisende Kinder** unaccompanied minors; **das kann ich nicht ~ entscheiden** I can't make that decision on my own; **~ stehend** (*ledig*) single, unmarried, unattached; **~ stehend sein** (*keine Verwandten haben*) live alone; **~ stehendes Haus** detached house; **2.** (*ohne Hilfe*) alone, by oneself; **~ erziehend** single (*od.* lone) parent *etc.*; **ich kann das schon ~** I can manage on my own; **das hat sie alles ~ geschafft** she did everything (by) herself; **das Kind kann schon** (**ganz**) **~ gehen** the child can walk (completely) independently (*od.* on his/her own); **3.** (*einsam*) lonely; **sich sehr ~ fühlen** feel very lonely; **4.** (*nur*) only; **er kann das entscheiden** he's the only one who can decide that; **das gehört mir ganz ~** it's (mine) all mine; **Mut ~ genügt nicht** courage alone is not

enough; **die ~ selig machende Kirche** the only true redeeming church; **5.** (*bereits*) just, mere(ly), already; **~ schon ihre Stimme regt mich auf** just the sound of her voice is enough to get me going; (**schon**) **~ der Gedanke** the mere thought (of it); **6.** *von* **~** by itself, (*aus freien Stücken*) of one's own accord; **II.** *Konj.; geh.* (*jedoch*) but, however

Alleinbesitz *m* sole ownership

alleine *Adj. präd. und Adv. umg.* → *allein* I

Allein|erbe *m,* **~erbin** *f* sole heir(ess *f*); **~erziehende** *m, f* single (*od.* lone) parent; **~flug** *m* solo flight; **im ~ den Atlantik überqueren** fly solo across the Atlantic; **~gang** *m* single-handed effort, independent initiative; **im ~** single-handedly, solo; **~herrschaft** *f* autocracy, dictatorship; **~herrscher** *m,* **~herrscherin** *f* autocrat, absolute ruler, dictator

alleinig… *Adj.* only, sole, exclusive, unique

Allein|inhaber *m,* **~inhaberin** *f* sole owner; **~recht** *n* exclusive right; **~reisende** *m, f* unaccompanied passenger (*od.* travel[l]er); **~schuld** *f* sole responsibility; **~sein** *n* loneliness, solitude; **Angst vor dem ~ haben** be afraid of being alone; **~stehende** *m, f* single person; **~unterhalter** *m,* **~unterhalterin** *f* *Theat.* solo entertainer, *umg.* one-man (*od.* woman) show; **~verdiener** *m,* **~verdienerin** sole (wage) earner; **~verkauf** *m* exclusive distribution (*od.* selling rights *Pl.*), monopoly

Alleinvertreter *m,* **~in** *f* sole agent; **Alleinvertretungsrecht** *n* right of exclusive representation

Alleinvertrieb *m* → *Alleinverkauf*

allemal *Adv. umg.*: **wir schaffen das** (**noch**) **~** we'll manage it, no problem (*od.* bother); → *auch Mal¹*

allenfalls *Adv.* (*höchstens*) at most, at best; (*vielleicht*) perhaps, possibly; (*auf alle Fälle*) in any event; (*zur Not*) if need be

allenthalben *Adv. lit.* everywhere

aller|äußerst… *Adj.* outermost; *fig.* utmost; *Preis:* rock-bottom *price*; **~best… I.** *Adj.* very best; **II.** *Adv.*: **am ~en** best of all

allerdings *Adv.* **1.** *war es ein gutes Konzert? - ~!* it certainly was, indeed it was; **2.** *einschränkend:* though, but, however; **sie sagte ~ …** she did say, however (*od.* though), …

aller|erst… *Adj.* very first; → *auch zuallererst*; **~frühestens** *Adv.*: **~ um zwei** (at) two at the very earliest

Allergen *n; -s, -e; Med.* allergen

Allergie *f; -, -n Med.* allergy; *fig.* (*Abneigung*) aversion; **e-e ~ gegen etw. haben** be allergic to s.th.; *fig.* have an aversion to s.th.

allergieauslösend *Adj. Med. Substanz:* allergenic

Allergie|pass *m Med.* allergy ID; **~schock** *m* anaphylactic shock

Allergiker *m; -s, -,* **~in** *f; -, -nen* allergy sufferer; **er ist Allergiker** he suffers from an allergy (*od.* from allergies)

allergisch I. *Adj. auch fig.* allergic (**gegen** to); **II.** *Adv.*: **~ reagieren auf** have an allergic reaction to, *generell, auch fig.*: be allergic to

Allergologe *m; -n,-n,* **Allergologin** *f; -, -nen* allergist

allerhand *Adj. und unbest. Pron. umg.* → *allerlei* I, II; **das ist ~!** *lobend:* not bad; *tadelnd*: that's a bit thick, that takes the biscuit (*Am.* cake) *umg.*

Allerheiligen (*n*); -(*s*), - All Saints' Day

Allerheiligste *n*; -*n*, -*n* **1.** holy of holies; *auch fig.* inner sanctum; *R.C.* sanctuary; **2.** (*Hostie*) Blessed Sacrament

aller|höchst... **I.** *Adj.* highest ... of all; very highest; *es wird ~e Zeit* it's high time; **II.** *Adv.*: *am ~en* highest of all; **~höchstens** *Adv.* at the very most

allerlei I. *Adj.* all kinds (*od.* sorts) of; **II.** *Pron.* all sorts of things; *wir hatten uns ~ zu erzählen* we had a lot to tell each other; **III. Allerlei** *n*; -*s*, -*s*, *mst. Sg.* (*Musik etc.*) medley, potpourri; (*bunte Mischung*) *pej.* jumble; (*Gericht*) hotchpotch, *Am.* hodgepodge; *Leipziger Allerlei* mixed vegetables

aller|letzt... *Adj.* **1.** very last; *er kam als Allerletzter an* he was the last to arrive; **2.** *umg.* (*unmöglich*) incredible, dreadful; *das ist das Allerletzte! pej.* that really is the limit!; → *auch* **zualerletzt**, **~liebst I.** *Adj.* (*reizend*) lovely, sweet; (*Lieblings...*) favo(u)rite ... of all; **II.** *Adv.*: *am ~en* best of all; **~meist... I.** *Adj.* (very) most; **II.** *Adv.*: *am ~en* most of all; **~modernst...** *Adj.* the very latest; *Tech. auch* state-of-the-art ...; **~nächst...** *Adj.* very next; *räumlich*: (very) nearest; *aus ~er Nähe* at close quarters; *die ~e Mode* the latest fashion (*od.* thing *umg.*); **~nötigst...** *Adj.* most necessary; *nur das Allernötigste* only what is (*od.* was) absolutely necessary

allerorten *altm.*, **allerorts** *geh. Adv.* everywhere

allerschlimmst... I. *Adj.* worst ... of all; **II.** *Adv.*: *am ~en* worst of all

Allerseelen (*n*); -*s*, *kein Pl.*; *kirchl.* All Souls' Day

allerseits *Adv.* on all sides; *gute Nacht ~!* good night everybody

allerspätestens *Adv.*: *~ um 10 Uhr* (at) 10 o'clock at the very latest

Allerwelts|... *im Subst.* (very) common; (*Nullachtfünfzehn...*) run-of-the-mill; **~gesicht** *n* nondescript face; **~wort** *n*; *Pl.* -*wörter* everyday word; *pej.* meaningless (*od.* hackneyed) word

allerwenigst|... I. *Adj.*: least ... of all; *die ~en Leute* very few people; **II.** *Adv.*: *am ~en* least of all; **allerwenigstens** *Adv.* at the very least

Allerwerteste *m*; -*n*, -*n*; *umg. euph. hum.* posterior

allerwichtigst|... I. *Adj.* most important; *das Allerwichtigste ist jetzt ...* the most important thing now is ...; **II.** *Adv.*: *am ~en* most importantly

alles *unbest. Pron.* → *all*

allesamt *unbest. Pron. und Zahlw.* all of them (*od.* us); *sie kamen ~* they all came

Alles|fresser *m*; -*s*, -; *Zool.* omnivore; **~kleber** *m* all-purpose glue (*od.* adhesive); **~könner** *m* man (*od.* woman) of many talents; *er ist ein ~ auch* there's nothing (*od.* very little) he can't do; **~schneider** *m* food-slicer

allg. *Abk.* → *allgemein*

allgegenwärtig *Adj.* (all-)pervasive, omnipresent *förm.*

allgemein (*abgek.* **allg.**) **I.** *Adj.* **1.** (*alle[s] betreffend*) general; (*üblich*) common; (*umfassend*) overall; *stärker*: universal; *von ~em Interesse* of general

interest; *auf ~en Wunsch* by popular request (*od.* demand); *~e Zustimmung finden* meet with general approval; *~e Redensart* generality; *~e Wahlen* general election(s); *~es Wahlrecht* universal suffrage; *~e Wehrpflicht* universal conscription, compulsory military service; *~e Schulpflicht* compusory education; *Allgemeine Ortskrankenkasse* (*abgek.* **AOK**) statutory health insurance company; **2.** (*öffentlich*) public; *das ~e Wohl* the common good, the public welfare; **3.** (*ohne Details*) *Frage, Darstellung*: general, generic; *im Allgemeinen* generally, in general; (*im Ganzen*) on the whole; *vom Allgemeinen auf das Besondere schließen* infer the particular from the general, instantiate (s. th. [general] in s.th. [special]).; *das ist mir viel zu ~* that's much too general for my taste; **II.** *Adv.* **1.** in general, generally; *es ist ~ bekannt, dass ...* it's a well-known fact that..., it is common knowledge that ...; *~ bildende Schulen etwa* comprehensive schools, *Am.* ordinary public schools; *~ gültig* universally applicable (*od.* valid), general *rule*; *es ist ~ üblich, dass man ...* it's (*od.* that's) common practi|ce (*Am.* -se) to ...; *~ verbindlich* generally binding; *~ verständlich* comprehensible, simple; **2.** (*Ggs. konkret, detailliert*) generally; (*oberbegrifflich*) generically; *~ anerkannt* generally accepted; *~ gehalten* general

Allgemein|arzt *m*, **~ärztin** *f Med. etwa* general practitioner, *Am. auch* family practitioner; **~befinden** *n* general (state of) health; **~bildung** *f*; *nur Sg.* general education; *e-e gute ~* a good, all-round education; **~gültigkeit** *f*: *~ haben* be universally applicable, be generally valid; **~gut** *n fig.*: *~ sein* be part of everyday life, (*Traditionelles*) be part of our *etc.* common heritage

Allgemeinheit *f* **1.** *nur Sg.*; (*Öffentlichkeit*) general public, public at large; **2.** *nur Sg.* (*Unbestimmtheit*) *e-r Aussage etc.*: generality; **3.** *nur Pl.*; (*Allgemeinplätze*) generalities

Allgemein|medizin *f Med. nur Sg.* general medicine; *Arzt für ~ etwa* general practitioner; **~mediziner** *m*, **medizinerin** *f* → *Allgemeinarzt*, **~platz** *m* commonplace, platitude; **~verständlichkeit** *f* general intelligibility (*od.* comprehensibility); **~wissen** *n* general knowledge; **~wohl** *n* public welfare (*od.* weal); **~zustand** *m* general condition; (*Lage*) general situation; *gesundheitliche*: general well-being (*od.* health)

Allgewalt *f*; *mst Sg. geh.* omnipotence *förm.*; **allgewaltig** *Adj geh.* omnipotent *förm.*; *auch fig.* all-powerful *allg.*

Allheilmittel *n* panacea, cure-all (*beide auch fig.*)

Allianz *f*; -, -*en* alliance

Alligator *m*; -*s*, -*en Zool.* alligator

alliieren *v/refl. Pl.* form an alliance; **alliiert I.** *P.P.* → *alliieren*; **II.** *Adj.*: *~e Streitkräfte* allied forces; **Alliierte** *m*; -*n*, -*n*, *mst Pl.* ally; *die ~n hist.* the Allies

Alliteration *f*; -, -*en Lit.* alliteration

alljährlich I. *Adj.* yearly, annual; **II.** *Adv.* annually, every year

Allmacht *f*; *nur Sg.*; *geh.* omnipotence; **allmächtig** *Adj. geh.* omnipotent; *der Allmächtige* God Almighty; *Allmächtiger!* good lord!

allmählich I. *Adj.* gradual; **II.** *Adv.*

gradually, by degrees, bit by bit, *Am.* little by little; *~ müsstest du das können* it's time you knew how to do that, you should be able to do that by now; *er müsste ~ kommen* he should be here any minute; *~ reicht's mir umg.* I'm beginning to get fed up with it

Allmende *f*; -, -*n*; *hist.* common land

all|monatlich I. *Adj.* monthly; **II.** *Adv.* every month; **~morgendlich** *Adj.* regular (*od.* every) morning *präd.*; **~nächtlich** *Adj.* nightly

Allmutter *f*; *kein Pl.*; *poet.*: (*die*) *~ Natur* Mother Nature

Allopath *m*; -*en*, -*en*; *Med.* allopath; **Allopathie** *f*; -, *kein Pl.* allopathy; **Allopathin** *f*; -, -*nen* allopath; **allopathisch** *Adj.* allopathic(ally *Adv.*)

Allotria *n*; -(*s*), -, *Pl. altm.* larking about, fooling around *allg.*; *~ treiben* lark about, fool around, mess around *umg.*

Allparteien... *im Subst.* all-party

Allradantrieb *m Mot.* all-wheel drive; *Wagen mit ~* all-wheel drive vehicle

Allrounder [ɔːl'raʊndɐ] *m*; -*s*, - all-rounder

Allround... [ɔːl'raʊnd...] *im Subst.* (*Allroundsportler*, *Allroundwissenschaftler etc.*) all-rounder, all-round ...

allseitig *Adj.* general, all-round ...

allseits *Adv.* on all sides; *~ bekannt* generally known; *~ geachtet* universally respected; *er war ~ beliebt* he was very popular; *stärker*: everybody loved him

Alltag *m* **1.** (ordinary) weekday; **2.** *nur Sg.*; (*Tagesablauf*) daily routine (*pej.* grind); *der graue ~* the daily grind, mundane everyday routines

alltäglich *Adj.* **1.** (*durchschnittlich*) ordinary; (*fad*) humdrum; **2.** (*täglich*) daily; **3.** (*Ggs. sonntäglich*) everyday ...; **Alltäglichkeit** *f* **1.** everyday occurrence; **2.** *Beschaffenheit*: ordinariness

Alltags|... *im Subst. mst* everyday; **~leben** *n* day-to-day life, everyday (*od.* workaday) life; **~trott** *m* daily grind (*od.* treadmill)

allüberall *Adv. geh.* everywhere *allg.*

allumfassend *Adj.* all-embracing

Allüren *Pl. pej.* airs and graces; *die ~ e-r Diva* the grand airs of a prima donna

Allwetter|... *im Subst.* all-weather; **~platz** *m Tennis*: all-weather court

allwissend *Adj.* omniscient *allg.*, all-knowing; *ich bin doch nicht ~!* you can't expect me to know everything!; **Allwissenheit** *f*; *nur Sg.* omniscience

allwöchentlich I. *Adj.* weekly; **II.** *Adv.* every week, weekly

allzu *Adv.* far (*od.* much) too; over...; *nicht ~ gut, lang(e), schnell, sehr, weit etc.* not too; *ich wäre ~ gern gekommen* I would love to have come, I would have loved to come; (*nur*) *~ gut* only too well; *~ sehr auch* excessively; *~ viel ist ungesund Sprichw.* enough is as good as a feast

Allzweck|... *im Subst.* all-purpose, general-purpose, universal; **~reiniger** *m* general-purpose cleaner

Alm *f*; -, -*en* alpine pasture; **~abtrieb** *m* driving of cattle from alpine pastures, *Am. etwa* fall roundup

Alma Mater *f*; - -; *geh.*, *oft hum.* alma mater

Almanach *m*; -*s*, -*e* almanac

Almauftrieb *m* driving of cattle to alpine pastures

Almenrausch *m südd.*, *österr.*, *Bot.* alpine rose

Almhütte f alpine hut

Almosen n; -s, - alms Pl.; pej. pittance, handout; **~empfänger** m, **~empfängerin** f receiver of alms

Aloe f; -, -n; Bot. aloe

Alp¹ m → **Alb**

Alp² f; -, -en; bes. schw. alpine pasture

Alpaka n; -s, -s Zool. alpaca; **~wolle** f alpaca

al pari Adv. Wirts. at par

Alp|druck m, **~drücken** n → **Albdruck**

Alpen Pl.: **die ~** the Alps; **~glühen** n alpenglow

Alpenländer Pl. Geog. Alpine countries; **alpenländisch** Adj. Alpine, alpine

Alpen|pass m Alpine pass; **~republik** f Alpine republic; **~rose** f Bot. alpine rose; **~veilchen** n Bot. cyclamen; **~verein** m Alpine Club; **~vorland** n; kein Pl.: **das ~** the foothills Pl. of the Alps, the Alpine piedmont

Alphabet n; -(e)s, -e alphabet; **alphabetisch** I. Adj. alphabetic(al); II. Adv.: **~ (ein)ordnen** arrange (od. put) in(to) alphabetic(al) order; **alphabetisieren** v/t. 1. alphabetize, put into alphabetical order; 2. teach s.o. to read and write; **Alphabetisierung** f alphabetization

alphamerisch, alphanumerisch EDV I. Adj. alphanumeric; II. Adv. alphanumerically

Alpha|männchen n Zool. alpha male; **~strahlen** Pl. Phys. alpha rays; **~teilchen** n alpha particle; **~weibchen** n Zool. alpha female; **~zähler** Phys. alpha meter

Alphorn n alpenhorn, alphorn; **~bläser** m, **~bläserin** f alpenhorn (od. alphorn) player

alpin Adj. alpine; **~e Ausrüstung** mountaineering (od. climbing) equipment; **~e Disziplinen** Sport Alpine disciplines; **Alpinismus** m; -, kein Pl. alpinism; **Alpinist** m; -en, -en, **Alpinistin** f; -, -nen alpinist, mountaineer; **alpinistisch** Adj. mountaineering attr.

Alptraum m → **Albtraum**

Alraun m; -(e)s, -e, **Alraune** f; -, -n; Bot. mandrake

als Konj. 1. zeitlich: when, (während) as, while; **damals, ~ ...** back then, when ..., in the days, when ...; **~ ich kam, war er nicht mehr da** he had already left by the time I arrived; **ich kam erst, ~ er schon weg war** I didn't arrive until after he had left; 2. vergleichend; nach Komp.: than; nach Negation: but, except; **er ist älter ~ du** he's older than you; **alles andere ~ (hübsch** etc.) anything but (pretty etc.); **wer sonst ~ er** etc. who else but him etc.; **nichts ~ (Unsinn** etc.) nothing but (rubbish etc.); **mehr ~ genug** more than enough; **so bald ~ möglich** as soon (od. quickly) as possible; **~ ob** as if, as though; **mir war, ~ wenn es geklingelt hätte** I thought the doorbell had rung; **er ist zu anständig, ~ dass er das tun könnte** he's too decent to do a thing like that; 3. erläuternd: as; (in der Eigenschaft von) auch in one's capacity as.; **~ Lehrer/Künstler** etc. as a critic / an artist etc.; **als Deutscher/ Franzose** etc. being a German/Frenchman.; **~ Entschuldigung** by way of an excuse; **~ Geschenk** as a present; **das erwies sich ~ Fehler/richtig** that turned out to be a mistake/right; **du ~ Ältester** you as the eldest; **er starb ~ Held** he died (as) a hero; **sie kam ~**

Letzte herein she was the last to come in; **~ Kind war ich oft krank** I was often ill as a child; → **insofern** II, **solch, sowohl, umso**

als|bald Adv. altm. forthwith, immediately allg.; **~baldig...** Adj. geh. immediate attr. allg.

also Adv. 1. (folglich) so, therefore, consequently; **~ blieb er zu Hause** so he stayed at home; **ich denke, ~ bin ich** I think, therefore I am; 2. zusammenfassend: **lassen wir's ~** let's leave it then; **du kommst ~ nicht?** you're not coming then?; **es ist ~ wahr?** it's true then (, is it)?; 3. umg.; empört: **~ bitte!** well really!; nachgebend: **~ gut!** all right (then), Am. umg. alright (then), okay (then); **~, wenn du mich fragst** (well,) if you ask me; **na ~!** what did I say?; anerkennend: **auch** there you go; 4. altm. (so) thus, so allg.

Alsterwasser n nordd. shandy, beer and lemonade (Am. lemon soda) mixed

alt Adj.; älter, am ältesten 1. neutral in Bezug auf Lebensalter: old; **ein sechs Jahre ~er Junge** a six-year-old boy, a boy, aged six; **wie ~ bist du?** how old are you?; **er ist (doppelt) so ~ wie ich** he's (twice) my age; **er sieht gar nicht so ~ aus** he doesn't look it, he looks much younger, he doesn't look his age; **sie ist zwei Jahre älter als ich** she's two years older than I am (od. me); **als ich so ~ war wie du ...** when I was your age ...; 2. (bejahrt, Ggs. jung) old; **ihr ~er Großvater** her aged grandfather; **Alt und Jung** young and old; **~ werden** get old, age; **mein ~er Herr** umg. (Vater) my old man; **der ~e Goethe** Goethe in his old age; **sie ist** (äußerlich) **ganz schön ~ geworden** she really has aged; **es macht dich ~** it makes you look old, it ages you; **hier werde ich nicht ~** umg. hum. I won't be sticking around here for very long; **dann siehst du ~ aus!** umg. fig. (dann stehst du dumm da) then you'll look really stupid; (dann geht es dir schlecht) then you'll be in a bad way; 3. (Ggs. neu) old; (geschichtlich **~**) auch ancient; (gebraucht) used, second-hand; (altertümlich, aus alter Zeit) antique; (langjährig) auch long-standing; (erfahren) experienced; **die ~en Griechen/Römer** the ancient Greeks/ Romans; **Alte Geschichte** (Ggs. Moderne) Ancient history; **~e Bräuche** old (od. ancient) customs; **~e Kunst** ancient art; **e-e ~e Vase** an antique vase; **~e Zeitungen** auch back numbers (Am. issues) of a newspaper; **~e Sprachen** the classics; **die Alte Welt** the Old World, the ancient world; **noch im ~en Jahr** by (od. before) the end of the year; **in ~en Zeiten** in times of yore, in the old(en altm., lit.) days; **die gute ~e Zeit** the good old days (od. times); **e-r m-r ältesten Freunde** one of my oldest friends; **aus Alt mach Neu** make s.th. new out of the old; 4. (längst bekannt) Fehler, Problem etc.: familiar, well-known; Trick, Witz: old, stale; **es ist wieder die ~e Geschichte mit ihr** etc. it's the same old story with her; 5. (unverändert): **am Alten festhalten** cling to the old ways; **alles bleibt beim Alten** nothing's changed; **sie ist immer noch die Alte** she is still the same; **Peter ist nicht mehr der Alte** he's not the Peter I used to know; **er ist wieder ganz der**

Alte he's back to his usual self, he is quite himself again; 6. (Ggs. frisch) old; Brot etc.: stale; Blumen: wilted, faded; Hemd etc.: worn, old; Wunde: old, healed; Spur: cold, old; 7. (ehemalig) Lehrer, Schüler etc.: former; 8. umg., verstärkend: **~er Angeber** etc. the old poser etc.; **ein ~er Säufer** a confirmed drunkard; **na, ~er Freund** etc., **wie geht's?** well old boy, how's it going?; → **älter, ältest..., Eisen** 3, **Hase** 4

Alt¹ m; -s, -e; Mus. alto

Alt² f; -s, - → **Altbier**

Altan m; -(e)s, -e; Archit. balcony, gallery, platform

alt|angesehen Adj. old-established; **~angestammt** Adj. Recht: inherited

Altanlage f Tech. old plant (od. unit)

Altar m; -(e)s, Altäre kirchl. altar; **vor den ~ treten** marry; **e-e Frau zum ~ führen** lead a woman to the altar; **etw. auf dem ~ ...** (+ Gen.) **opfern** geh. fig. sacrifice s.th. on the altar of ...; **~aufsatz** m reredos; **~bild** n altarpiece; **~decke** f altar cloth; **~nische** f apsis; **~raum** m chancel; **~tuch** n altar cloth, vesperal; **~wein** m communion wine

Altauto n: **das Recycling von ~s** the recycling of scrap(ped) (Am. auch junk) cars

altbacken Adj. 1. Brot: stale; 2. umg. fig. old-fashioned allg.; Ideen: stale, outdated, antiquated allg.

Altbau m; Pl. Altbauten old building

Altbau|modernisierung f modernization of an old building; **~sanierung** f refurbishment of old buildings; **~wohnung** f old flat (Am. apartment), flat (Am. apartment) in an old building

altbekannt Adj. old familiar ...

Altbestand m (Alt-, Baumholz) standing timber; Wirts. stock, stocks Pl.

altbewährt Adj. well-tried; Freundschaft etc.: longstanding; **in ~er Manier** the tried and tested way

Altbier n top-fermented dark beer

Altblockflöte f alto (Brit. treble) recorder

Alt|bundeskanzler m, **~bundeskanzlerin** f ex-chancellor; ex-German (od. -Austrian) chancellor; **~bundesland** n land (od. auch state) of the former FRG; **~bundespräsident** m, **~bundespräsidentin** f ex-president, former president; ex-German (od. -Austrian) president; **~bürgermeister** m, **~bürgermeisterin** f ex-mayor, former mayor; **2christlich** Adj. early Christian

altdeutsch Adj.: **~e Möbel** old-style German furniture

Alte m, f; -n, -n 1. männlich: old man; weiblich: old woman; Pl. (alte Menschen) old people, senior citizens; **die ~n und Kranken** the aged and the infirm; 2. umg. (Vater, Ehemann) the old man; (Mutter) the old woman; (Ehefrau) auch the missus, her indoors, the little lady hum.; Pl. (Eltern) the folks, the Aged Parents hum.; 3. umg. (Chef) the boss; männlich auch: the guv gesproch. (meist von Männern); 4. Zool.; weiblich: (Muttertier) mother, (the) old one; Pl. (Elterntiere) (the) parents; → **alt**

alt|ehrwürdig Adj. time-hono(u)red; **~eingesessen** Adj. old-established

Alteisen n scrap metal (od. iron)

altenglisch Adj Old English; **Altenglisch** n Ling. Old English; **das ~e** Old English

Alten|arbeit f, **~betreuung** f care of old people, work with senior citizens;

~club *m* senior citizens' club

altengerecht *Adj.* suitable for old(er) people *präd.*

Alten|heim *n* old people's (*od.* retirement) home, home for senior citizens; **~hilfe** *f* (financial) assistance for old people (*od.* senior citizens); **~nachmittag** *m* senior citizens' afternoon (*od.* club); **~pflege** *f* geriatric care, care of the elderly; **~pfleger** *m*, **~pflegerin** *f* geriatric (*od.* old people's) nurse; **~tagesstätte** *f* geriatric day-care cent|re (*Am.* -er); **~teil** *n* part of a farm retained by a retired farmer; *sich aufs* **~** *zurückziehen fig.* withdraw from active life; **~wohnheim** *n* → *Altenheim, Altersheim*

Alter *n*; *-s*, - **1.** (*auch von Tieren und Dingen*) age; *er ist in m-m* **~** *he's* (about) my age; *im* **~** *von 20 Jahren* at the age of twenty; *darf ich Sie nach Ihrem* **~** *fragen?* may I ask how old you are?; *mittleren* **~s** middle-aged; *im besten* **~** in the prime of life; *in hohem* **~** at a ripe old age; *ein biblisches* **~** *erreichen* reach a venerable old age; *im zarten* **~** *von* at the tender age of; *ins schulpflichtige* **~** *kommen* reach school age; *sich s-m* **~** *entsprechend benehmen* act one's age; *man sieht ihm sein* **~** *nicht an* he doesn't look his age; *aus dem* **~** *müsstest du heraus sein* you should have grown out of that by now; **2.** (*Greisenalter*) (old) age; *im* **~** *lässt das Gehör nach* (one's) hearing diminishes in later years; *vom* **~** *gebeugt* bent by age; *fürs* **~** *sparen* put s.th. by for one's old age; **~** *schützt vor Torheit nicht Sprichw.* there's no fool like an old fool; **3.** (*Dienstalter*) seniority

älter I. *Komp.* → *alt*; *der* **~***e Bruder* her etc. elder brother; *Breughel der Ältere* (*abgek.* **d. Ä.**) Breughel the Elder; **II.** *Adj.* **1.** *euph.* (*alt*) elderly; **2.** *Jur. Anspruch*: prior

Alter Ego *n*; - -, *kein Pl.*; *Psych.* alter ego (*auch fig.*)

alterfahren *Adj.* seasoned

altern I. *v/i.* (*ist*) **1.** grow old, age, advance in years *lit.*; **2.** *Wein*: mature; *Käse*: ripen, mature; **II.** *v/t.* (*hat*); *Tech.* age; (*Holz*) season

alternativ I. *Adj.* **1.** alternative, New Age; *Energien*: alternative, non-nuclear; **2.** *Gruppe, Zeitung etc.*: fringe ...; **~es Theater** fringe (*od.* alternative) theat|re (*Am.* –er); **II.** *Adv.*: **~ denken** have an alternative way of thinking; **~ leben** have opted out of society, lead an alternative (*od.* New Age) lifestyle; **Alternativbewegung** *f* alternative (*od.* fringe) movement

Alternative¹ *f*; -, -*n* alternative; *keine* **~** *haben* have no alternative; *sich vor e-e* **~** *gestellt sehen* be confronted with an alternative, be left with two options (open)

Alternative² *m*, *f*; -*n*, -*n* person with alternative views

Alternativ|energie *f* alternative energy; **~kultur** *f* counter-culture, alternative culture; **~medizin** *f* alternative medicine; **~szene** *f*: *die* **~** alternative society, the fringe

alternieren *v/i. geh.* alternate (*mit* with) *allg.*

alterprobt *Adj.* well-tried

alters *Adv. geh.*: *von* **~** *her, seit* **~** from (*od.* since) time immemorial

altersabhängig *Adj.* dependent on age *präd.*

Alters|abstand *m* age difference; **~an-**

gabe *f*: *ohne* **~** without age details

altersbedingt *Adj.* age-related; (*im hohen Alter*) geriatric, related to old age *präd.*; *es ist* **~** it's old age

Alters|begrenzung *f*: *ohne* **~** without age limit; **~beschwerden** *Pl.* aches and pains of old age; **~bestimmung** *f* *Bio.*, *Geol.* age determination (*od.* assignment); **~durchschnitt** *m* average age; **~erscheinung** *f* sign of old age; **~fleck** *m* age spot; **~folge** *f* order of age, age sequence; **~forscher** *m* gerontologist; **~forschung** *f* gerontology; **~fürsorge** *f* welfare for the elderly

altersgemäß *Adj. Benehmen, Entwicklung*: appropriate to one's/its age

Alters|genosse *m*, **~genossin** *f* person of the same age, contemporary

altersgerecht *Adj.* suitable for one's/its age

Alters|grenze *f* **1.** *Sportler etc.*: age limit; **2.** retirement age; **~gründe** *Pl.*: *aus* **~n** on grounds of age; **~gruppe** *f* age group (*od.* bracket); **~heilkunde** *f* *Med.* geriatrics *Pl.* (*V. im Sg.*); **~heim** *n altm.* old people's home; **~klasse** *f* **1.** (*Altersgruppe*) age category; **2.** *Sport*: age-group; *von Holz*: age class, cutting cycle; **~leiden** *n* complaint of old age

alterslos *Adj.* ageless

Alters|präsident *m*, **~präsidentin** *f* chairman by seniority; **~pyramide** *f* population pyramid; **~rente** *f*, retirement (*od.* old-age) pension; **~ruhegeld** *n* → *Altersrente*

altersschwach *Adj.* **1.** *Person*: infirm, (old and) frail; **2.** *Gebäude*: dilapidated; *Möbel etc.*: rickety; *Auto etc.*: shaky; **Altersschwäche** *f* debility (of old age); *an* **~** *sterben* die of old age

Alters|schwerhörigkeit *f* age-related hearing loss, presbycusia *fachspr.*; **~sicherung** *f* provision for one's old age; **~sitz** *m*: *wir wollen unseren* **~** *am Bodensee nehmen* we want to retire to Lake Constance

altersspezifisch *Adj.* age-specific

Alters|starrsinn *m* stubbornness (*od.* obstinacy) of old age; **~struktur** *f* age distribution; **~stufe** *f* age (group), stage of life; **~teilzeit** *f* semi-retirement; **~unterschied** *m* age difference; **~versicherung** *f* old-age insurance; **~versorgung** *f* old-age pension (scheme, *Am.* plan); **~vorsorge** *f* provision for one's old age; **~werk** *n* *Kunst*: late work; **~zuschlag** *m* age bonus

Altertum *n*; *-s*, *Altertümer Zeit und Fundstück*: antiquity; **altertümelnd** *Adj. oft pej.* archaic; **altertümlich** *Adj.* ancient; (*veraltet*) antiquated

Altertums|forscher *m* **1.** arch(a)eologist; **2.** classical scholar; **~forschung** *f*, *-; nur Sg.* arch(a)eology; **2.** study of classical antiquity; **~wert** *m*: **~** *haben* have antique value

Alterung *f* ageing (*Am. auch* aging); *Geol.* age hardening; *von Käse, Wein, Whisky*: maturing; *von Holz, Metall*: seasoning; **Alterungsprozess** *m* ageing (*Am. auch* aging) process

ältest... *Sup.* → *alt*; *in der Familie*: eldest; **Älteste** *m*, *f*; -*n*, -*n* elder; senior; *unser* **~***r* / *unsere* **~** our eldest son/daughter

Ältesten|rat *m* council of elders; *Pol.* parliamentary advisory committee, think-tank; **~recht** *n* (right of) primogeniture

Altflöte *f* alto flute

altgedient *Adj. Mil.* long-serving

Alt|gerät *n*: *ein* **~** *in Zahlung nehmen* take an old appliance in part-exchange; **~geselle** *m altm.* senior journeyman

altgewohnt *Adj.* (long-)familiar

Altglas *n*; *nur Sg.* used glass, *auch* empty bottles *Pl.*; *Tech.* cullet; **~container** *m* bottle bank; **~verwertung** *f* recycling of used glass

Altgold *n* **1.** (*dunkles Gold*) artificially darkened gold; **2.** *altm.* old gold, previously worked gold

altgriechisch I. *Adj.* Ancient Greek; **II. Altgriechisch** *n Ling.* Ancient Greek; *das Altgriechische* Ancient Greek, the Ancient Greek language

althergebracht *Adj.* traditional, old

Altherrenmannschaft *f* team of players over thirty(-two); *Fußball*: *auch* veterans' eleven; old crocks (*od.* fogies) *Pl. umg.*

althochdeutsch I. *Adj.* Old High German; **II. Althochdeutsch** *n Ling.* Old High German; *das Althochdeutsche* Old High German, the Old High German language

Altist *m*; -*en*, -*en*; *Mus.* (male) alto; **Altistin** *f*; -, -*nen* (contr)alto

altjüngferlich *Adj.*; *pej.* old-maidish, spinsterish *pej.*

Altklarinette *f Mus.* alto clarinet

Altkleidersammlung *f* old clothes collection

altklug *Adj.* precocious *oft gespr.*; **Altklugheit** *f*; *nur Sg.* precociousness, precocity

Altlage *f Mus.* alto range

Altlast *f*; *mst Pl.* **1.** *Öko.* residual pollution *Sg.*; contaminated soil *Sg.*; abandoned (*od.* disused) waste dump (*od.* landfill); **2.** *fig.* burden *Sg.* (*od.* burdens, *umg.* sins) of the past, inherited problem; *umg.* past sins that come back to haunt one; **Altlastensanierung** *f Öko.* redevelopment of hazardous waste sites

ältlich *Adj.* oldish

Alt|material *n* scrap (material); **~meister** *m* (past) master; *Sport*: ex-champion; **~metall** *n* scrap metal

altmodisch *Adj.* old-fashioned

Altoboe *f Mus.* alto oboe

Altöl *n* used oil

Altpapier *n*; *nur Sg.* waste (*od.* used) paper; *aus* **~** made of recycled paper; **~container** *m* paper bank; **~sammlung** *f* (news)paper (*od.* wastepaper) collection; **~verwertung** *f* waste-paper recycling

Altphilologe *m* classicist, classical philologist; **Altphilologie** *f* (the) classics *Pl.*; **Altphilologin** *f* classicist, classical philologist

Altposaune *f Mus.* alto trombone

Alt|reifen *m* used tyre (*Am.* tire); **♀römisch** *Adj.* ancient Roman, of ancient Rome *präd.*

altrosa I. *Adj.* dusky pink; **II. Altrosa** *n* dusky pink

Alt|sänger *m*, **~sängerin** *f Mus.* (*von einem Mann*) alto; (*von einer Frau*) (contr)alto; **~saxofon**, **~saxophon** *n Mus.* alto sax(ophone); **~schlüssel** *m Mus.* alto clef

Altschnee *m* old snow

Altsilber *n* **1.** (*dunkles Silber*) oxidized silver, artificially darkened silver; **2.** *altm.* old silver(ware)

altsprachlich *Adj.* classical; **~es Gymnasium** *etwa* grammar school (*teaching Latin and Greek*)

Altstadt *f* old (part of) town (*od.* city); *engS.* medi(a)eval cent|re (*Am.* -er);

~fest n street party in the old (part of) town; **~sanierung** f urban renewal

Altsteinzeit f; nur Sg. Old Stone Age, Paleolithic Age

Altstimme f Mus. (bei einem Mann) alto (voice); (bei einer Frau) (contr)alto voice

Altstoff m; mst Pl. waste material mst Sg.

alt|testamentarisch Adj. Old Testament ...; **~väterlich** Adj. patriarchal; **~vertraut** Adj. old familiar attr., very familiar präd.

Altvorder(e)n Pl.; lit. forebears, forefathers

Altwaren Pl. second-hand goods; **~handel** m second-hand goods trade, Am. resale business; **~händler** m junk dealer

Altwasser n; Pl. -; Geog. dead arm of a river, oxbow (od. abandoned) (stream) channnel, loop lake

Altweiber|fas(t)nacht f südd. Thursday prior to Ash Wednesday; **~geschwätz** n pej. idle gossip, silly chatter umg.; **~sommer** m 1. Indian summer; 2. (Sommerfäden) gossamer

Alu n; -s, kein Pl.; Abk. alumin(i)um; **~dose** f alumin(i)um can; **~felge** f alloy wheel; **~folie** f alumin(i)um foil; **~koffer** m alumin(i)um case

Aluminium n; -s, kein Pl.; Chem. aluminium, Am. aluminum

Alzheimer (f); -; Med. Sl., **~krankheit** f Med.: **die Alzheimerkrankheit** Alzheimer's disease

am Präp. + Art. 1. → an I; 2. im Sup.: **~ besten, schnellsten** etc. the best, fastest etc.; 3. im Datum: **~** 1. März on March 1st; **~ Tage** (+ Gen.) on the day of; bei Wochentagen: **~ Sonntag** on Sunday, bes. Am. Sunday; bei Tageszeiten: **~ Abend/Morgen** in the evening/morning; **~ Mittag** at midday (od. lunchtime); **~ Tage** during the day; 4. in geografischen Bezeichnungen: **Frankfurt ~ Main** Frankfurt/Main, Frankfurt on Main; **~ Äquator** at (od. on) the equator; **~ Meer** by the sea(side), on the coast; **~ Nordpol** at the North Pole; 5. in Wendungen: **~ Ball sein/bleiben** be/keep on the ball; **~ Ende** at the end; in the end; **~ Leben sein** be alive; **~ Lager** in stock; **~ Rande** (erwähnen) in passing; (sich befinden) on the sidelines; **~ Stück** unsliced; **~ Werk sein** be at work; **~ Ziel** have reached one's destination; (fig.) have reached (od. achieved) one's goal; **du bist ~ Zug** it's your turn; 6. umg.: **~ Arbeiten** etc. **sein** be (busy) working etc.

Amalgam n; -s, -e; Chem. und fig. amalgam; **~füllung** f amalgam filling

amalgamieren v/t. amalgamate; fig. auch merge (**mit** with)

Amaryllis f; -, Amarillen; Bot. amaryllis

Amateur m; -s, -e, **~in** f; -, -nen 1. amateur; 2. pej. (Dilettant) dilettante, dabbler

Amateur|... im Subst. amateur ...; **~bestimmungen** Pl. amateur rules; **~funk** m amateur radio; **~funker** m, **~funkerin** f radio ham; **~haft** Adj. amateurish; **~liga** f amateur league; **~sportler** m, **~sportlerin** f amateur sportsperson (oder player, runner etc.)

Amazonas m; -; the Amazon

Amazone f; -, -n 1. Myth. Amazon; 2. fig. amazon; 3. Sport: (Rennfahrerin) woman racing driver; (Turnierreiterin) woman show-jumper; 4. Orn.

amazon (parrot)

Ambiente n; -, kein Pl.;. ambience; (Atmosphäre) atmosphere, air

Ambition f; -, -en ambition; **~en auf etw.** (Akk.) **haben** have set one's sights on s.th.; **ambitioniert** Adj. (strebsam) aspiring, ambitious

ambivalent Adj. geh., fachspr. ambivalent; **Ambivalenz** f; -, -en ambivalence

Amboss m; -es, -e anvil; Anat. auch incus

ambulant I. Adj. Med. outpatient ...; 1. ambulatory, itinerant förm.; **~es Gewerbe** street-trading, door-to-door trading (Am. selling), itinerant trade, Am. traveling sales förm.; **~er Händler, ~e Händlerin** street-trader, door-to-door trading (Am. selling), hawker umg.; **II.** Adv. Med.: **~ behandelt werden** get outpatient treatment, be treated as an outpatient; **~ behandelter Patient** outpatient; **Ambulanz** f; -, -en Med. 1. Klinik: outpatient department; (Unfallstation) casualty ward, Am. emergency room; 2. (Krankenwagen) ambulance

Ameise f; -, -n Zool. ant

Ameisen|bär m Zool. anteater; größer: aardvark, giant anteater, ant bear; **~ei** n ant egg; umg. (fälschlich) ant pupa; **~haufen** m anthill; fig. bedlam, madhouse; **~säure** f Chem. formic acid; **~staat** m ant colony; **~straße** f ant(s') trail

amen Interj. amen; **zu allem ja** (od. **Ja**) **und ~** (od. **Amen**) **sagen** say yes to everything; **Amen** n; -s, -, mst. Sg. amen; **sein ~** (**zu etw.**) **geben** give (s.th.) one's blessing; **so sicher wie das ~ in der Kirche** umg. as sure as hell

Amerika (n); -s America; **Amerikaner** m; -s, -, **Amerikanerin** f; -, -nen American; **amerikanisch I.** Adj. American; **II. Amerikanisch** n; -(s); Ling. American (English); **das Amerikanische** American (English), the American English language; **Amerikanismus** m; -, Amerikanismen; Ling. Americanism; **amerikanisieren** v/t. Americanize; **Amerikanisierung** f Americanization; **Amerikanist** m, **Amerikanistin** f 1. student of American English, literature and culture; 2. specialist in Amerindian culture and languages; **Amerikanistik** f; -, kein Pl. 1. (North) American studies Pl.; 2. study of Amerindian culture and languages

Amethyst m; -(e)s, -e; Min. amethyst

Ami m; -s, -s; umg. Yank

Amino|gruppe f Chem. amino group; **~säure** f amino acid

Amische Pl.: **die ~n** the Amish

Ammann m; Pl. Ammänner; schw. etwa mayor

Amme f; -, -n; (engS. wet) nurse; Zool. nurse

Ammenmärchen n pej. fairytale allg., fable

Ammer f; -, -n; Zool. bunting

Ammersee n Lake Ammer

Ammoniak n; -s, kein Pl.; Chem. ammonia; **~dämpfe** Pl. ammonia fumes (od. vapo[u]rs); **₂haltig** Adj. ammoniac; **~lösung** f ammonia solution; **~salz** n ammonia salt

Ammonit m; -en, -en; Zool. ammonite

Ammonium n; -s, kein Pl.; Chem. ammonium; **~sulfat** n ammonium sul|phate (Am. –fate)

Amnesie f; -, -n; Med. amnesia

Amnestie f; -, -n Pol. amnesty; **e-e ~**

erlassen declare an amnesty; **amnestieren** v/t. grant an amnesty to

Amniozentese f; -, -n; Med., bei Fruchtwasseruntersuchung: amniocentesis, amniotic puncture

Amöbe f; -, -n Bio. am(o)eba; **Amöbenruhr** f Med. am(o)ebic dysentery

Amok m: **~ laufen** run amok; **~fahrer** m, **~fahrerin** f maniac driver; Autobahn: motorway maniac, Am. speed demon, deranged driver; **~läufer** m, **~läuferin** f lunatic, maniac; **~schütze** m, **~schützin** f mad (od. crazed) gunman (f gunwoman)

a-Moll n; -, kein Pl.; Mus. A minor; **a-Moll-Tonleiter** f A minor scale

Amor m; -s, kein Pl.; Myth. Cupid; **von ~s Pfeil getroffen** poet. be struck by Cupid's arrow, be smitten hum.

amoralisch Adj. geh. (jenseits von Moral) amoral; (unmoralisch) immoral; **Amoralität** f; -, kein Pl. immorality

amorph Adj. Phys., Bio., geh. amorphous

Amortisation f; -, -en 1. Wirts. amortization, repayment; e-r Anleihe: redemption; 2. Jur. e-r Urkunde: invalidation; **amortisieren** Wirts. **I.** v/t. amortize, pay off; (Anleihe) redeem; **II.** v/refl. amortize, pay itself off

Amouren [a'mu:rən] Pl. altm. od. hum. amours

amourös [amu'rø:s] Adj. amorous; **ein ~es Abenteuer** iro. an affair, a little (od. love) affair, a romance

Ampel f; -, -n 1. traffic lights Pl., Am. auch traffic light, stoplight; in Südafrika: robot; **fahren Sie bei der ersten ~ rechts** turn right at the first set of traffic lights (Am. at the first traffic light od. stoplight); 2. (Hängelampe) hanging lamp; 3. (Blumenampel) hanging basket; **~anlage** f (set of) traffic lights Pl., Am. traffic light, stoplight; in Südafrika: robot; **~koalition** f Pol. coalition formed by the SPD, the FDP and the Green Party

Ampere [am'pe:r] n; -(s), -; Etech. ampere, amp; **~meter** n ammeter; **~stunde** f ampere-hour

Ampfer m; -s, -; Bot. sorrel

Amphetamin n; -s, -e; Chem., Med. amphetamine

Amphibie f; -, -n; Zool. amphibian

Amphibien... im Subst. Tech. amphibian plane, tank etc.; **Amphibienfahrzeug** n amphibious vehicle; **amphibisch** Adj. Zool. amphibious, auch Tech. amphibian

Amphitheater n amphitheat|re (Am. auch -er); (Kampfplatz) arena

Amphore f; -, -n amphora

Amplitude f; -, -n; Math., Phys. amplitude

Ampulle f; -, -n; Med. ampulla (auch Anat.); Pharm. ampoule

Amputation f; -, -en; Med. amputation; **amputieren** v/t. amputate; **Amputierte** m, f; -n, -n amputee

Amsel f; -, -n Zool. blackbird

Amt n; -(e)s, Ämter 1. (Posten) post, position; (Aufgabe, Pflicht) (official) duty, function; (noch) **im ~ sein** (still) hold (od. be in) office; **in ~ und Würden** oft iro. in a position of authority, in an exalted position iro.; **in Ausübung s-s ~es** in carrying out his duty; **kraft m-s ~es** by virtue of my office; **s-s ~es walten** carry out one's duties; **von ~s wegen** (dienstlich) because of one's job; Jur., förm. ex officio; 2. (Behörde) office, department; **von ~s wegen** (amtlich) officially; →

auswärtig 2; **3.** *Telef.* exchange; *das Fräulein vom ~ altm.* the operator *allg.*; **4.** *kirchl.* service, *kath.* mass

Ämter|häufung f accumulation of offices, concentration of posts; **~trennung** f division of offices, separation of posts

Amtfrau f *Titel, Rang:* (woman) senior clerk (*in the middle grade of the German civil service*)

amtieren *v/i.* hold office; *kirchl. und fig.* officiate; *als Vizepräsident etc. ~* be acting vice-president *etc.*; **amtierend I.** *Part.Präs.* → *amtieren;* **II.** *Adj.* incumbent; *stellvertretend:* acting; **~er Meister** *umg.* reigning champion(s)

amtlich *Adj.* official; *umg.* (*ganz sicher*) official, authentic *allg.*; **amtlicherseits** *Adv.* officially

Amtmann m; *Pl.* *Amtmänner und Amtleute,* **Amtmännin** f, -, -nen **1.** senior clerk (*in the middle grade of the German civil service*); **2.** *hist.* bailiff

Amts|anmaßung f (unlawful *od.* false) assumption of authority; **~antritt** m assumption of office (*od.* of one's post); **~arzt** m, **~ärztin** f public health officer; **²ärztlich** *Adj. Attest, Untersuchung:* from, by *etc.* the medical officer *präd.*; **~befugnis** f (official) authority; competence; **~bereich** m jurisdiction, competence; **~bezirk** m administrative district, area of jurisdiction; **~blatt** n official gazette; **~dauer** f term of office; **~deutsch** n officialese; **~eid** m oath of office; *den ~ ablegen* be sworn in; **~einführung** f inauguration (into office); **~enthebung** f removal from office, dismissal; **~führung** f administration (of [an] office); **~geheimnis** n **1.** official secret; **2.** *nur Sg.* (*Geheimhaltung*) official secrecy; **~gericht** n county (*od. Am.* district) court; **~geschäfte** *Pl.* official business *Sg.*; **~gewalt** f (official) authority; **~handlung** f official act; *e-e ~ ausführen* perform an official function (*od.* duty); **~hilfe** f support (*od.* cooperation) through official channels; **~inhaber** m, **~inhaberin** f holder of an (*od.* the) office, incumbent; **~kette** f chain of office; **~kirche** f church hierarchy; **~kollege** m, **~kollegin** f **1.** colleague; **2.** *Pol.* opposite number, counterpart; **~leitung** f *Telef.* exchange line; **~miene** f solemn air; **~missbrauch** m abuse of office (*od.* authority *od.* power)

amtsmüde *Adj.* weary of office *präd.*; **Amtsmüdigkeit** f weariness of (*od.* jadedness from) holding office

Amts|niederlegung f resignation; **~periode** f term of office; **~person** f *altm.* official, functionary *allg.*; **~rat** m, **~rätin** f senior administrative officer (*in the civil service*); **~räume** *Pl.* official chambers; **~richter** m, **~richterin** f district court judge; **~schimmel** m *hum. od. pej.* red tape; *der ~ wiehert* it's red tape all the way; **~sitz** m **1.** official residence; **2.** *e-r Behörde:* office(s *Pl.*); **~sprache** f **1.** official language; **2.** *oft pej.* officialese; **~stunden** *Pl.* office hours; **~tracht** f official dress (*od.* robes *Pl.*); **~träger** m, **~trägerin** f office-bearer; **~übergabe** f handing-over of office (*od.* one's duties); **~übernahme** f assumption of office (*od.* a post); **~vergehen** n misconduct, malfeasance (in office), malpractice, malversation *Jur.*; **~vorgänger** m, **~vorgängerin** f predecessor (in office); **~vorstand** m, **~vorsteher**

m, **~vorsteherin** f head of an office; **~zeichen** n *Telef.* dialling (*Am.* dial) tone; **~zeit** f term of office; *zurückblickend:* term in office; *nach dreijähriger ~* after three years in office

Amulett n; -(e)s, -e amulet, charm

amüsant *Adj.* entertaining; (*lustig*) amusing; **Amüsement** [amyzə'mã:] n; -s, -s amusement, entertainment

Amüsierbetrieb m (*Tanzbar,* -*lokal*) nightclub; (*Spielhalle*) amusement (*od.* gaming) arcade

amüsieren I. *v/t.* entertain; (*belustigen*) amuse; *die Bemerkung amüsierte ihn* he was amused by the remark; **II.** *v/refl.* (*sich die Zeit vertreiben*) amuse o.s. (*mit* with); (*sich gut unterhalten*) enjoy o.s., have fun, have a good/grand time; *sich ~ über* (+ *Akk.*) be amused at (*od.* by), (*sich lustig machen*) make fun of; *schadenfroh:* gloat over; **amüsiert I.** *P.P.* → *amüsieren;* **II.** *Adj. Blick etc.:* amused, entertained; **III.** *Adv.:* ~ *lächeln* smile in amusement

Amüsierviertel n nightclub district; (*Bordellviertel*) red-light district

amusisch *Adj. geh.:* ~ *sein* have no appreciation for the arts (*od.* no artistic sensitivity *od.* no (a)esthetic sensibility)

an I. *Präp.* **1.** (+ *Dat.*); *zeitlich:* on; ~ *Ostern/Weihnachten* at Easter/Christmas; ~ *e-m schönen Sonntagabend* on a pleasant Sunday evening; ~ *jenem Morgen* on that morning; *es ist ~ der Zeit* it's about time; **2.** (+ *Dat.*); *örtlich:* at, on; (+ *Akk.*); *Richtung:* to; ~ *der Grenze* at the border; *am Himmel* in the sky; ~ *e-m Ort* in a place; ~ *s-m Platz* in its place; ~ *der Themse* on the Thames; ~ *erster Stelle* in the first place; *am/ans Fenster* at/to the window; ~ *der/die Wand* (*lehnen[d]*) against the wall; (*hängen[d]*) on the wall; *e-e Lampe ~ die Decke hängen* hang a lamp (from the ceiling); ~ *der Decke hängen* hang from the ceiling; *Schaden am Dach* damage to the roof; *den Hund ~ den Zaun binden* tie the dog to the fence; *j-n ~ sich drücken/ziehen* embrace s.o. / pull s.o. to one('s breast); *er ging an i-r rechten Seite* he was walking on her right (side); ~ *die frische Luft gehen* get a breath of fresh air; *es am Herzen etc. haben* have heart *etc.* trouble; **3.** (+ *Akk. bzw. Dat.*); (*neben*) by, next to; (*nahe*) by, near; *am Wald* by the woods; *am Kamin* (*Tisch*) *sitzen* sit by the fire (at the table); *sich* (*nahe*) ~ *die Tür setzen* take a seat next to the door; *etw. ~ den Eingang stellen* place s.th. near the entrance; ~ *j-m vorbeifahren* drive past s.o., pass s.o. in the car; *Kopf ~ Kopf* neck and neck; *Tür ~ Tür* door to door; **4.** (+ *Dat.*); (*bei*) at, by; ~ *e-r Schule* at a school; *j-n ~ der Hand führen* lead s.o. by the hand; **5.** (+ *Dat.*); (*bezüglich, hinsichtlich*) in; *arm/reich ~* poor/rich in; *jung ~ Jahren* young in years; *drei etc. ~ der Zahl* three in number; **6.** *fig.:* das Leben *etc.* ~ *sich* as such, per se; *e-e ~ sich praktikable Lösung* a solution, practicable in itself; ~ (*und für*) *sich* (*genau genommen*) properly speaking; (*im Grunde*) basically, actually; *e-e ~* (*und für*) *sich gute Idee* a basically good (*od.* sound) idea; *etw. Seltsames etc. ~ sich* (*Dat.*) *haben* have s.th. odd, *etc.* about it, him *etc.*; *ist etwas ~ der Sache?* is there something to it?; *was*

gefällt dir ~ ihm? what do you like about him?; *es ist nicht ~ mir etc. zu* (+ *Inf.*) it is not for me (*od.* my place) to (+ *Inf.*); **7.** *ein Brief ~ j-n* for (*od.* to) s.o.; *e-e Bitte ~ j-n* to s.o.; *e-e Frage ~ j-n* for (*od.* to) you; *der Glaube(n)* ~ (+ *Akk.*) faith (*od.* belief) in; *die Schuld ~* (+ *Dat.*) the blame for; *arbeiten ~* work on; *denken ~* think of; *leiden ~* suffer from; → *auch am, bis I und die mit an verbundenen Adjektive, Substantive, Verben etc.;* **II.** *Adv.* **1.** *von ... ~* from ... (on[wards]); *von da/nun ~* from then/now on; *von heute ~* from today (on); **2.** *London 19.05* arr. (= arrival) London 19:05 (*Am.* 7:05 p.m.); **3.** *das Gas ist ~* the gas is on; ~ - *aus* - off; **4.** ~ *die 50 Leute* about (*od.* roughly) 50 people

Anabolika *Pl.; Pharm., Sport:* anabolic steroids

Anachronismus m; -, *Anachronismen; geh.* anachronism; **anachronistisch I.** *Adj.* anachronistic; **II.** *Adv.* anachronistically

Anagramm n; -s, -e *Lit.* anagram

Anakonda f; -, -s; *Zool.* anaconda

anal *Adj.* anal; **~e Phase** *Psych.* anal stage

Anal... *im Subst.* anal

Analgetikum n; -s, *Analgetika; Pharm.* analgesic; **analgetisch** *Adj.* analgesic

analog I. *Adj.* **1.** analogous (+ *Dat. od. mit od. zu* to); *ein ~er Fall Jur.* a precedent; **2.** (*Ggs. digital*) *Uhr, Waage:* analog(ue); *Aufnahme:* analog(ue); **II.** *Adv.* **1.** by analogy (*zu* with); **2.** ~ *aufgenommen* analogically; **Analogie** f; -, -n analogy (*zu* to; *zwischen* between); **Analogieschluss** m analogism, argument by analogy; **Analogrechner** m analog computer

Analphabet m; -en, -en, **~in** f; -, -nen illiterate (person); **Analphabetentum** n; -s, *kein Pl.,* **Analphabetismus** m; -, *kein Pl.* illiteracy

Analverkehr m anal intercourse; *Jur.* buggery, sodomy *oft altm.*

Analysator m; -s, -en; *Phys., Computer:* analy|ser (*Am.* -zer); **Analyse** f; -, -n analysis; **analysieren** *v/t.* analy|se (*Am.* -ze); **Analysis** f; -, *kein Pl.; Math.* analysis; **Analytiker** m; -s, -, **Analytikerin** f; -, -nen analyst; **analytisch I.** *Adj.* analytical; **II.** *Adv.* analytically; *sie denkt sehr ~* she's got a very analytical mind

Anämie f; -, -n; *Med.* an(a)emia; **anämisch** *Adj.* an(a)emic

Anamnese f; -, -n; *Med.* case (*od.* medical) history

Ananas f; -, -(se) *Bot.* pineapple

Anapher f; -, -n *Lit.* anaphora

anaphylaktisch *Adj. Med.:* **~er Schock** anaphylactic shock

Anarchie f; -, -n anarchy; **anarchisch** *Adj.* anarchic(al); **Anarchismus** m; -, *kein Pl.* anarchism; **Anarchist** m; -en, -en, **Anarchistin** f; -, -nen anarchist; **anarchistisch** *Adj.* anarchist; **Anarcho** m; -s, -s; *Sl.* anarchist; **~szene** f *etwa* young radicals *Pl.*

Anästhesie f; -, -n; *Med.* an(a)esthesia; **anästhesieren** *v/t.* an(a)esthetize; **Anästhesist** m; -en, -en, **Anästhesistin** f; -, -nen an(a)esthetist, *Am.* anesthesiologist; **Anästheti|kum** n; -kum, -ka an(a)esthetic

Anatolien (n); -s *Geog.* Anatolia; **anatolisch** *Adj.* Anatolian

Anatom m; -en, -en, **~in** f; -, -nen; *Med.* anatomist; **Anatomie** f; -, -n **1.** *nur Sg.* (*Wissenschaft, Körperbau*) anatomy; **2.** *Abteilung*: institute of anatomy; *Raum*: dissecting room; **Anatomiesaal** *m* dissecting room; **anatomisch** *Adj.* anatomical

anbaggern *v/t.* (*trennb., hat -ge-*); *umg.* chat up, pull, score with

anbahnen (*trennb., hat -ge-*) **I.** *v/t.* pave the way for, prepare the ground for; (*Gespräche*) initiate, open up; **II.** *v/refl.* be in the offing, *auch Schlimmes*: be coming, be on the way, be in store (**für** for); **Anbahnung** *f* initiation; *e-r Ehe etc.*: arrangement of introductions, smoothing the way to, facilitation of

anbandeln *südd., österr.,* **anbändeln** *v/i.* (*trennb., hat -ge-*); *umg.*: **mit** *j-m* ~ *Beziehung*: try to get friendly with s.o. *allg.*; *Streit*: start an argument, pick a fight (*od.* quarrel) *allg.*

Anbau *m*; *Pl. -ten* **1.** *nur Sg.*; *Agr.* cultivation; **2.** *Archit.* annex(e), extension, wing; **3.** *nur Sg.*; *Archit.* (*das Anbauen*) extension, enlargement; **anbauen** (*trennb., hat -ge-*) **I.** *v/t.* **1.** *Agr.* grow; **2.** *Archit.* add, join (**an** to), build (**an** against), annex; *Tech.* attach; **II.** *v/i. Archit., Tech.* build an extension

anbaufähig *Adj.* **1.** *Agr.* arable; **2.** *Archit.* suitable for extension

Anbau|fläche *f Agr.* (arable) acreage; *genutzte*: area under cultivation; **~gebiet** *n* area of cultivation; **~küche** *f* kitchen unit; **~methode** *f* method of cultivation; **~möbel** *Pl.* sectional (*od.* unit, modular) furniture *Sg.*; **~schrank** *m* cupboard unit; **~wand** *f* wall unit

Anbeginn *m*; *geh.*: **von** ~ (**an**) from the very start *allg.*

anbehalten *v/t.* (*unreg., trennb., hat*) keep on

anbei *Adv.* enclosed, attached, herewith *altm., förm.*; ~ (**sende ich** *od.* **senden wir Ihnen**) enclosed please find

anbeißen (*unreg., trennb., hat -ge-*) **I.** *v/t.* bite into; *ein angebissenes Brot* a half-eaten piece of bread; **II.** *v/i.* bite; *auch fig.* take the bait; *du siehst ja zum Anbeißen aus umg.* you look good enough to eat

anbekommen *v/t.* (*unreg., trennb., hat*), *mst. verneint*; (*Schuhe etc.*) manage to get on; (*Feuer etc.*) manage to get ... going; (*Motor*) manage to start (*od.* get it going)

anbelangen *v/t.* (*trennb., hat*): *was mich anbelangt* as far as I am concerned

anbellen *v/t.* (*trennb., hat -ge-*) bark at (*auch fig.*)

anberaumen *v/t.* (*trennb., hat*); *Amtsspr.* (*Sitzung*) call *allg., Am.* schedule; *e-n Termin* ~ *für* fix a date for

anbeten *v/t.* (*trennb., hat -ge-*) worship; *fig. auch* adore, idolize; → **Angebetete**; **Anbeter** *m; -s, -,* **Anbeterin** *f; -, -nen* worship(p)er; *fig.* admirer

Anbetracht *m*: **in** ~ (+ *Gen.*) considering, taking ... into consideration; **in** ~ *der Tatsache* in view of the fact

anbetreffen *v/t.* (*unreg., trennb., hat*); *geh.*: *was ... anbetrifft* in terms of ..., as far as ... is (*od.* are) concerned

anbetteln *v/t.* (*trennb., hat -ge-*): *j-n* ~ beg from s.o.; *j-n um etw.* ~ beg for s.th. from s.o.

Anbetung *f* worship; *fig.* devotion; **anbetungswürdig** *Adj. fig.* adorable; *Reli.* worthy of adoration

anbiedern *v/refl.* (*trennb., hat -ge-*);

pej.: **sich** (**bei**) *j-m* ~ toady to s.o. *umg.*, ingratiate o.s. with s.o., suck up to s.o. *umg.*; **Anbiederung** *f pej.* ingratiation, currying favo(u)r, brown-nosing *umg.*; **Anbiederungsversuch** *m pej.* attempt to ingratiate o.s. (*od.* curry favo[u]r)

anbieten (*unreg., trennb., hat -ge-*) **I. 1.** *v/t.* offer; *j-m etw.* ~ offer s.o. s.th.; *s-n Rücktritt* ~ offer to resign, tender one's resignation; *j-m das Du* ~ suggest to s.o. that they use the familiar form of address; *er bot* (*ihr*) *an, sie zu begleiten* he offered to accompany her; *darf ich Ihnen etwas* (*zum Trinken*) ~**?** can I get you something to drink?; **2.** *Wirts.* tender, bid; **II.** *v/refl. Person*: offer one's services; *Gelegenheit*: present itself; *Sache*: suggest itself; *sich* ~ *für Sache*: lend itself to; *es bietet sich doch an zu* (+ *Inf.*) the obvious thing (to do) would be to (+ *Inf.*); **Anbieter** *m; -s, -,* **Anbieterin** *f; -, -nen*; *Wirts.* person making an offer, bidder; *bei Dienstleistungen*: provider, supplier

anbinden *v/t.* (*unreg., trennb., hat -ge-*) tie up, fasten (**an** + *Dat. od. Akk.* to); (*Boot*) moor; (*Hund*) put on a (*od.* the) leash (*od.* lead); (*Pferd*) tether; *umg. fig.* put into the context (**bei** of); → **angebunden**; **Anbindung** *f*; (*Stadtanbindung, Autobahnanbindung*) connection, linking

anblasen *v/t.* (*unreg., trennb., hat -ge-*) **1.** blow at; **2.** (*Feuer*) blow on, fan; **3.** (*Jagd*) sound the horn (for the hunt to begin); **4.** *umg.* (*zurechtweisen*) yell at *allg.*, blow up at, *Brit.* give s.o. a rocket; **5.** *Mus.* (*leicht blasen*) (start to) blow

anblenden *v/t.* (*trennb., hat -ge-*): *j-n mit der Taschenlampe* ~ shine one's torch (*Am.* flashlight) on s.o. (*od.* into s.o.'s face)

Anblick *m* sight; *ein trauriger* ~ a sorry sight; *beim* ~ *der Wunde wurde mir schlecht*: when I saw the wound ...; *in den* ~ *versunken* absorbed in contemplation; *ein Anblick für* (*die*) *Götter sein* be a real sight; **anblicken** *v/t.* (*trennb., hat -ge-*) look at; *flüchtig*: glance at; *finster*: glare at; *missbilligend*: frown at

anblinzeln *v/t.* (*trennb., hat -ge-*) *unwillkürlich*: blink at; (*zuzwinkern*) wink at

anbohren *v/t.* (*trennb., hat -ge-*) **1.** *Tech.* bore, spot-drill, drill into; (*Zahn*) (drill) open; **2.** *umg. fig.*: *j-n* ~ sound s.o. out (**ob** as to whether) *allg.*

anbranden *v/i.* (*trennb., hat -ge-*) surge (**gegen** against)

anbraten (*unreg., trennb., hat -ge-*) **I.** *v/t.* sear, brown; **II.** *v/i.*: *etw. kurz* ~ *lassen* brown s.th. a little

anbräunen *v/t.* (*trennb., hat -ge-*); *Gastr.* brown

anbrausen *v/i.* (*trennb., ist -ge-*) *Zug etc.*: roar in (*od.* up); *angebraust kommen umg.* come roaring up

anbrechen (*unreg., trennb., -ge-*) **I.** *v/t.* (*hat*) (*Vorräte*) break into; (*Dose, Packung etc.*) start on; (*Flasche*) open; *angebrochene Tafel Schokolade* started (*od.* opened) bar of chocolate; **II.** *v/i.* (*ist*) begin; *Tag, auch Zeit*: dawn; *Nacht*: fall

anbrennen (*unreg., trennb., -ge-*) **I.** *v/i.* (*ist*) **1.** (*zu brennen beginnen*) catch fire, (start to) burn; **2.** *Speisen*: (*auch* ~ *lassen*) burn; *Milch, Soße etc.*: scorch; *angebrannt schmecken* taste

burnt; have a burnt taste; *nichts* ~ *lassen umg. fig.* not miss a thing, not just hang about (*Am.* around); *auch Sport*: watch out; **II.** *v/t.* (*hat*) kindle, burn; (*Zigarre etc.*) light

anbringen *v/t.* (*unreg., trennb., hat -ge-*) **1.** (*herbeibringen*) bring; **2.** (*befestigen*) (**an** + *Dat.*) fix (to), fasten (to); *Tech. und Am.* attach (to); (*Schilder etc.*) put up, mount (on); **3.** *Wirts.* (*Ware*) sell; **4.** (*Gründe etc.*) present; *gesprächsweise*: mention; (*Wort, Witz etc.*) get in; (*sein Wissen*) display, show off; (*Verbesserungen etc.*) make, carry out; → **angebracht** II

Anbruch *m*; *nur Sg.* **1.** (**bei**) ~ *des Tages* (at) daybreak; (**bei**) ~ *der Nacht* (at) nightfall; **2.** *fig. e-r neuen Zeit etc.*: dawning

anbrüllen *v/t.* (*trennb., hat -ge-*) *Person*: scream at, yell at, bellow at, bawl at; *Löwe*: roar; *Rind* bellow

Anchovis [an'çoːvɪs] *f; -, -; Gastr.* anchovy

Andacht *f; -, -en* **1.** *nur Sg.* devotion; *mit* ~ (*intensiv*) intently, raptly; (*andächtig*) reverently; *in* ~ *versunken* sunk in silent prayer (*od.* worship *od.* devotion); **2.** *Reli.* (*Gebet*) prayers *Pl.*, devotions *Pl.*; (*Gottesdienst*) (short) service; **andächtig I.** *Adj.* **1.** *religiös*: devout, pious, reverent; **2.** *fig.* (*aufmerksam*) absorbed, rapt; **3.** *fig. Stille*: enraptured, spellbound; **II.** *Adv.* **1.** devoutly, piously, reverently; **2.** ~ *zuhören* listen in rapt attention, listen intently

Andachts|buch *n* manual of devotion, devotional book; **~raum** *f auf Flughafen*: chapel

andachtsvoll *Adj. geh.* reverent

Andalusien (*n*); *-s; Geog.* Andalusia; **Andalusier** *m; -s, -,* **Andalusierin** *f; -, -nen* Andalusian

andampfen *v/i.* (*trennb., ist -ge-*); *umg.*: *mst angedampft kommen* come steaming (*od.* charging *od.* puffing) up (*od.* along)

andante I. *Adv. Mus.* andante; **II. Andante** *n; -(s), -s* andante

andauern *v/i.* (*trennb., hat -ge-*) continue, go on; (*anhalten*) last; *hartnäckig*: persist; *der Regen dauert an* it's still raining; *im Wetterbericht*: it will continue to rain; **andauernd I.** *Part. Präs.* → **andauern**; **II.** *Adj.* continual; (*unaufhörlich*) continuous, incessant; (*hartnäckig*) persistent; *ich hasse diese* ~*en Unterbrechungen!* I hate (*od.* can't stand) these constant interruptions!; **III.** *Adv.* **1.** → II; **2.** (*immer wieder*) repeatedly; *sie stört mich* ~*!* she (just) keeps interrupting me!

Anden *Pl.*: *die* ~ the Andes *Pl.*

andenken *v/t.* (*unreg., trennb., hat -ge-*) *umg.* start thinking about

Andenken *n; -s, -;* (**an** + *Akk.*) **1.** *nur Sg.* memory (of); (**an** ~ **an** (+ *Akk.*) in memory (*od.* remembrance) of; *j-m ein freundliches* ~ *bewahren* have fond memories of s.o.; **2.** (*Gegenstand*) keepsake, token (of); (*Souvenir*) souvenir (of); *ein* ~ *an unsere Hochzeit* a memento of our wedding; **~laden** *m* souvenir shop

ander|... *unbest. Pron.* **1.** (*Ggs. dies...*) other; (*folgend*) next, following; (*weiter...*) further; *ein* ~*er, eine* ~*e* someone else; *die* ~*en* the others; ~*es* other things; *alles* ~*e* everything else; *der eine oder* ~*e* someone or other; *der eine oder* ~*e* someone or other; *bei Sachen*: one or the other; *noch viele* ~*e* many (*od.* plenty) more; **manch ~er** many another (*od.* other); **kein ~er als** nobody but; *rühmend*: no less than; **unter ~em** (*abgek.* **u.a.**) among other things; **und ~es** (*abgek.* **u.a.**) and other things, and so on, and so forth; **und ~es mehr** (*abgek.* **u.a.m.**) and more besides, and more of the same; **am ~en Tag** the next (*od.* following) day; **die ~en Bücher** (*die übrigen*) the rest of the books; **eins/einer nach dem ~en!** one (thing) after another; **es kommt eins zum ~en** it's just one thing after another; **zum einen ..., zum ~en ...** on the one hand ..., on the other hand ...; **von einem zum ~en gehen** from one to the other; **ein Tag wie jeder ~e** a perfectly ordinary day, a day like any other; **von denen ist einer wie der ~e** they're all much of a muchness, *Am.* they're six of one, half-dozen of the other; *pej. Personen*: they're (all) as bad as each other; **2.** (*komplementär*) opposite; **das ~e Geschlecht** the opposite sex; **wo ist der ~e Schuh?** Where's the other shoe (*od.* pair to this shoe)?; **3.** (*verschieden*) different; **das ist was ganz ~es** that's a completely different matter; **alles ~e als** anything but, far from; **mit ~en Worten** in other words; **da bin ich ~er Meinung** I disagree (with you *etc.*) about that; **dem hätte ich aber was ~es erzählt!** *umg.* I would have given him a piece of my mind!; **da müssen wir uns etwas ~es einfallen lassen** we'll have to think up s.th. else; → **anders**, **Land** 5, **Umstand** 1

änderbar *Adj.* changeable, alterable
anderen|falls *Adv.* otherwise; **~orts** *Adv. geh.* in another place *allg.*; **~tags** *Adv. geh.* on the following day, on the day after *allg.*
andererseits *Adv.* on the other hand
andermal *Adv.*: **ein ~** some other time
ändern I. *v/t.* change, (*auch Kleidungsstück*) alter; (*variieren*) vary; *teilweise*: modify; **ich kann es nicht ~** I can't help it; **das ist nicht zu ~** that can't be helped; **es ändert nichts an der Tatsache, dass ...** it doesn't alter the fact that ...; **II.** *v/refl.* change; (*variieren*) vary; *Wind*: shift
andernfalls *etc.* → **anderenfalls** *etc.*
anders I. *präd. Adj. und Adv.* (*verschieden*) different(ly *Adv.*); **~ werden** change; **sie ist ~ als ihre Schwester** she's not like her sister; **~ als s-e Freunde** unlike his friends; **er denkt ~ als wir** he doesn't see it the same way as we (*od.* us); **~ ausgedrückt** to put it another way; **~ denkend** *od.* **gesinnt** of a different way of thinking; *Pol.* dissenting; **~ geartet** different, of a different nature; **~ lautend** different, differing; **~ lautende Berichte** reports to the contrary; **ich kann nicht ~** I can't help it; (*bin gezwungen*) I've got no choice; **es kam ganz ~** things turned out very differently; **er ist heute so ~** he's changed so much; **ich hab's mir ~ überlegt** I've changed my mind; (*ich werde doch nicht ...*) I've decided not to; **~** (*verhielt sich*) **Herr X** not so Mr(.) X; *drohend*: **ich kann auch ~!** you, he *etc.* had better watch out!, I can easily change my tune!; **Urlaub mal ~** a holiday (*Am.* vacation) with a difference; **II.** *Adv.*; *mit Pron. od. Adv.*; (*sonst*) else; **jemand ~** somebody (*od.* anybody) else; **niemand ~** nobody else; **niemand ~ als er** nobody but him; **wer ~ (als er)?** who else (but him)?; *ir-*

gendwo **~** somewhere else, some other place *umg.*; *nirgendwo* **~** nowhere else; *nirgendwo* **~ als** nowhere but, no place other than
andersartig *Adj.* different; **Andersartigkeit** *f*; *nur Sg.* different nature (*od.* quality)
Andersdenkende *m*, *f*; *-n*, *-n*; *Pol.* dissenter
anderseits *Adv.* on the other hand
andersfarbig *Adj.* of a different colo(u)r; allochromatic *fachspr.*
Andersgesinnte *m*, *f*; *-n*, *-n* person of a different opinion
andersherum I. *Adv.* the other way (a)round; **II.** *Adj. umg.*: **er ist ~** (*homosexuell*) he's queer, he's gay *allg.*; **andersrum** *umg.* → **andersherum**
Anderssein *n geh.* alterity, otherness *allg.*
anderssprachig *Adj. Texte etc.*: foreign-language ...
anders|wo *Adv.* somewhere else, elsewhere, *Am. umg.* some place else; **~woher** *Adv.* from somewhere (*Am. umg.* some place) else, from elsewhere; **~wohin** *Adv.* (to) somewhere else, elsewhere
anderthalb *Adj.* one and a half; **~ Pfund** a pound and a half (of ...); **~fach** *Adj.* one and a half times; **~fache** *n*; *-n*, *kein Pl.* one and a half times the amount, half as much again; **~jährig** *Adj.* eighteen-month-old, eighteen months old *präd.*; **~mal** *Adv.* one and a half times; **~ so viel** half as much again
Änderung *f* change; *gewollte*: *auch* alteration; *teilweise*: modification; **e-e ~ vornehmen** make a change; **~en vorbehalten** subject to alteration
Änderungs|antrag *m Parl.* amendment; **~kündigung** *f Wirts., Jur.* notification of a change (in the terms of employment); **~vorschlag** *m*: **e-n ~ machen** suggest a change; **s-e Änderungsvorschläge wurden akzeptiert** the changes he suggested (*od.* proposed) were accepted; **~wunsch** *m*; *mst. Pl.* request for changes (*od.* alterations)
anderweitig I. *Adj.* other, further; **wegen ~er Verpflichtungen** due to prior engagements (*od.* commitments); **II.** *Adv.* otherwise; (*anderswo*) elsewhere; **die Stelle wurde ~ vergeben** the job went (*od.* was given) to someone else
andeuten (*trennb., hat -ge-*) **I.** *v/t.* **1.** (*zu verstehen geben*) hint at, intimate, give to understand; *negativ*: insinuate; (*hinweisen auf*) indicate; **was willst du damit ~?** what are you getting (*od.* driving) at?, what are you trying to tell me?; **die angedeuteten Änderungen** the intimated changes; *auch* the changes you *etc.* hinted at; **2.** *Kunst*: suggest; **der Hintergrund war nur angedeutet** the background was only sketched out (*od.* outlined); **II.** *v/refl. Verbesserung etc.*: be on the way
Andeutung *f* **1.** suggestion, hint (**auf +** *Akk.* of) (*beide auch fig.*); *versteckte*: insinuation; (*Hinweis*) indication; **e-e ~ machen** drop a hint; **nicht die ~ eines Lächelns** without a shimmer (*od.* trace) of a smile; **2.** (*Spur*) sign, trace, hint (**+** *Gen.* of); *Kunst*: suggestion; **andeutungsweise** *Adv.* allusively; **etw. ~ mitteilen** hint at s.th.; **man sieht ~ ein Haus dahinter** you can just (about) make out a house behind it

andichten *v/t.* (*trennb., hat -ge-*): **j-m etw. ~** impute s.th. to s.o.
andicken *v/t.* (*trennb., hat -ge-*); *Gastr.* thicken
andiskutieren *v/t.* (*trennb., hat*) (*Thema etc.*) broach, discuss briefly
andocken *v/t. und v/i.* (*trennb., hat -ge-*) *Raumfahrt*: dock (**an +** *Akk.* with)
andonnern (*trennb., -ge-*); *umg. fig.* **I.** *v/i.* (*ist*): **angedonnert kommen** come thundering up (*od.* along); **II.** *v/t.* (*hat*): **j-n ~** roar at s.o. *allg.*
Andorraner *m*; *-s, -*, **~in** *f*; *-, -nen* Andorran; **andorranisch** *Adj.* Andorran
Andrang *m*; *nur Sg.* **1.** (*Gedränge*) crush; (*Ansturm*) rush; (*große Nachfrage*) run (**auf +** *Akk.* on); **in den Freibädern herrschte großer ~** the swimming pools were crowded; **2.** *Med.* (*Blut♀*) rush; **3.** *Wasserbau*: strain; **andrängen** *v/i.* (*trennb., ist -ge-*): **die ~den Wassermassen** the mass of water
andre *unbest. Pron.* → **ander...**
Andreaskreuz *n*: (*auch das ~*) *St.*(.) Andrew's Cross
andrehen *v/t.* (*trennb., hat -ge-*) **1.** (*Gas etc.*) turn on; *Etech. auch* switch (*od.* turn *od.* put) on; *Mot.* (*ankurbeln*) crank, start; **2.** (*Schraube*) tighten; **3.** *umg.*: **j-m etw. ~** palm (*od.* fob) s.th. off on s.o.; (*Arbeit etc.*) land s.o. with s.th., pass s.th. on to s.o. *allg.*
andrerseits *Adv.* on the other hand
andressieren *v/t.* (*trennb., hat*) train, drill
Androide *m*; *-n, -n Sciencefiction*: android
Androgen *n*; *-s, -e*; *Med.* androgen
androgyn *Adj. Bio.* androgynous
androhen *v/t.* (*trennb., hat -ge-*): **j-m etw. ~** threaten s.o. with s.th.; **Androhung** *f* threat; *Jur.* **unter ~ von** *od.* (**+** *Gen.*) under penalty of
Andromeda *f*; *-, kein Pl.*; *Astron.* Andromeda; **~nebel** *m*; *nur Sg.*; Andromeda Galaxy
Andruck *m*; *Pl. -e*; *Druck.* proof; **andrucken** *vt/i.* (*trennb., hat -ge-*) **1.** (pull a) proof; **2.** start printing
andrücken (*trennb., hat -ge-*) **I.** *v/t.* press (down on) (**an +** *Akk.* against, on to); **II.** *v/refl.*: **sich (fest) ~ an** (**+** *Akk.*) press (hard) against; (*e-e Person*) cling (*od.* hold on) (tightly) to
andudeln *v/t.* (*trennb., hat -ge-*); *umg.*: **sich (Dat.) einen ~** get merry (*od.* tiddly, tipsy, tight, plastered); **er ist angedudelt** he's had one too many
andünsten *v/t.* (*trennb., hat -ge-*); *Gastr.* steam
anecken *v/i.* (*trennb., ist -ge-*); *umg.*: **bei j-m / überall ~** rub s.o. / everyone up the wrong way; **mit s-r Offenheit ist er bei den Kollegen angeeckt** his colleagues didn't take to his openness *allg.*
aneignen *v/t.* (*trennb., hat -ge-*): **sich (Dat.) ~** acquire; *widerrechtlich*: *auch* (mis)appropriate; (*Fähigkeiten*) learn; (*Kenntnisse*) acquire; (*Stil etc.*) develop; (*Gewohnheit*) *auch* pick up; **Aneignung** *f*; *nur Sg.* (**+** *Gen.*) acquisition (of); (mis)appropriation (of); development (of); learning (**e-r Sprache** a language)
aneinander *Adv.* (to, of *etc.*) each other; **~ binden** tie together; **~ denken** think of each other (*od.* one another); **~ fügen** join (together); abut (on) *fachspr.*; **sie gerieten heftig ~** *fig.* they came to blows (*od.* quarrel(l)ed); *die*

Grundstücke **grenzen** ~ border on each other; *Bilder zum Vergleich* ~ **halten** hold ... next to each other (*od.* one another); *sie hängen sehr* ~ *fig.* they are very attached to each other; *Waggons* ~ **hängen** couple (... together); *sie klammerten sich ängstlich* ~ they clung to each other in terror; *Schnüre* ~ **knoten** knot (*od.* tie) ... together; ~ **reihen** (*Perlen*) line up; *fig.* (*Argumente*) string together; *sich* ~ **schmiegen** huddle together; ~ **stoßen** (*Autos*) collide (with each other); (*Grundstücke*) border on each other; (*Streit bekommen*) clash; ~ **vorbeigehen** walk past each other; ~ **vorbeireden** talk at cross purposes

Aneinanderreihung *f* lining up, stringing together(+ *Gen.* of)

Anekdote *f*; -, -*n* anecdote; **anekdotenhaft** *Adj.* anecdotal

anekeln *v/t.* (*trennb., hat -ge-*): *j-n* ~ *Essen, Geruch etc.*: make s.o. feel sick, nauseate s.o.; *Benehmen, Person etc.*: make s.o. sick, revolt s.o., turn s.o. off

Anemone *f*; -, -*n Bot.* anemone

Anerbieten *n*; -*s*, - offer, tender

anerkannt I. *P.P.* → **anerkennen**; **II.** *Adj.* recognized; (*allgemein* ~) accepted; ~*e Tatsache* established fact; *ein international* ~*er Schriftsteller etc.* an internationally recognized writer (*od.* author *etc.*), a writer *etc.* of international repute (*od.* standing); → **staatlich** II; **anerkanntermaßen** *Adv.*: *er ist* ~ ... he is acknowledged to be ...

anerkennen *v/t.* (*unreg., trennb. od. untrennb., hat*) **1.** (*hoch schätzen*) acknowledge; (*würdigen*) appreciate; (*billigen*) approve; *man muss* ~, *dass er sich bemüht hat* all credit to him for trying (*od.* doing his best); **2.** *auch Jur.* (*akzeptieren, bestätigen, eingestehen*) acknowledge; (*Staat, Vertrag etc.*) recognize (*als* as); *als gültig*: *auch* accept; (*e-n Anspruch*) allow; (*Schuld, Verpflichtung etc.*) admit, acknowledge; *das erkenne ich an* I will admit that; *nicht* ~ (*Staat, Vertrag etc.*) refuse to recognize; *ein Tor* (*nicht*) ~ signal, allow (disallow); *die Vaterschaft* (*nicht*) ~ (not) acknowledge paternity; **3.** *Wirts.* (*Wechsel*) hono(u)r, accept; → **anerkannt** II

anerkennend I. *Part. Präs.* → **anerkennen**; **II.** *Adj.* appreciative; ~*e Worte* words of appreciation (*Lob*: praise); **III.** *Adv.*: *sich* ~ *äußern über* (+ *Akk.*) praise

anerkennenswert *Adj.* laudable, commendable; **Anerkenntnis** *f bes. Jur.* (*e-r Schuld*) admission

Anerkennung *f* **1.** (*Würdigung, Lob etc.*) acknowledg(e)ment, appreciation, respect, approval; ~ *finden* win recognition; ~ *verdienen* deserve credit; *j-m wird* ~ *zuteil* s.o. is granted recognition; *als* ~ *für* in appreciation of; *in* ~ (+ *Gen.*) in recognition of; *bei großen Leistungen*: *auch* in tribute to; **2.** *bes. Jur.* acknowledg(e)ment; *e-s Staates, Vertrages*: recognition; *e-s Kindes*: legitimation; *von Urkunden*: legalization; *e-r Schuld*: admission; *e-s Wechsels*: acceptance; **Anerkennungsurkunde** *f* citation

anerziehen *v/t.* (*unreg., trennb., hat*): *j-m etw.* ~ instil(l) (*od.* drill) s.th. into s.o.; **anerzogen I.** *P.P.* → **anerziehen**; **II.** *Adj.* acquired; *das ist* ~ I *etc.* was brought up that way

anessen *v/t.* (*unreg., trennb., hat -ge-*):

du hast dir ein ganz schönes Bäuchlein angegessen you're developing a nice little paunch

anfachen *v/t.* (*trennb., hat -ge-*) **1.** (*Feuer*) fan; **2.** *fig.* arouse, stir up; (*Emotionen*) inspire; (*Kontroverse etc.*) stoke up, fan the flames of.

anfahren (*unreg., trennb., -ge-*) **I.** *v/t.* (*hat*) **1.** (*herbeibringen*) deliver; **2.** (*rammen*) run into, hit; (*Fußgänger*) *auch* knock down, run over; **3.** *fig.* (*anschreien*) (*j-n*) snap at; **4.** (*e-n Hafen etc.*) call at; **5.** *Tech.* (*Reaktor, Computer*) start up; **6.** *Hund*: (*j-n*) go for *s.o.*, make a rush for *s.o.*; **II.** *v/i.* (*ist*) **1.** start; **2.** *angefahren kommen* drive up; **3.** *Reaktor*: start up; **Anfahrt** *f* **1.** (*Fahrt*) journey, ride; *e-e weite* ~ *haben zu* have a long journey (*od.* way to go) to; **2.** (*Zufahrt*) approach; *vor e-m Haus*: drive; **3.** *von Waren*: transport, conveyance *förm.*; **4.** (*Start*) start(ing); **5.** (*Näherkommen*) approach

Anfall *m* **1.** *Med.* attack; *plötzlicher, bes.* epileptischer: fit, seizure; *von Grippe*: bout; *leichter*: touch; *krampfartiger*: paroxism *oft Pl.* (*von* of); → **Schwindelanfall, Tobsuchtsanfall** *etc.*; *ein* ~ *von Eifersucht etc. fig.* a fit of jealousy *etc.*; *e-n* ~ *bekommen od. haben* have (*od.* throw) a fit *od. Brit.* wobbly *umg.*; **2.** (*Ertrag*) yield; (*Menge*) amount produced *etc.*; (*Arbeits*∫) volume; **anfallartig** *Adj. Schmerzen*: in fits (*od.* spasms) *präd.*

anfallen (*unreg., trennb., -ge-*) **I.** *v/t.* (*hat*); (*angreifen*) attack; **II.** *v/i.* (*ist*); *Arbeit*: come up; *Gewinn, Zinsen*: accumulate; *Kosten*: arise; *im Herbst fällt immer viel Arbeit an* the work always piles up in (the) autumn (*Am. auch* fall); *alle* ~*den Reparaturen muss ich übernehmen* I'm responsible for any repairs that crop up

anfällig *Adj.* **1.** susceptible (*für* to); *für Krankheiten*: *auch* prone (to), liable (to); **2.** *Gesundheit*: delicate

Anfang *m* **1.** beginning, start, outset; commencement *geh.*; *am od. zu* ~ (*anfangs*) at first; at (*od.* in) the beginning, at the start (*od.* outset) (+ *Gen.* of); *von* ~ *an* (right) from the start, from the outset, from the word go *umg.*; *von* ~ *bis Ende* from start to finish, from beginning to end; ~ *Januar* early in January, in early January; ~ *2001* early in 2001; (*am*) ~ *der dreißiger Jahre* in the early thirties; *er ist* ~ *dreißig etc.* he's in his early thirties *etc.*; *den* ~ *machen* start, make a start; *auch Sport*: lead off; *e-n neuen* ~ *machen* make a fresh start, start all over again; *sich verbessernd*: turn over a new leaf; *s-n* ~ *nehmen geh.* commence, begin *allg.*; *für den* ~ *wollen wir erst einmal* ... to start (off) with we want to ...; *und das ist erst der* ~*!* and that's just the start of it!; *das ist der* ~ *vom Ende* it's the beginning of the end; *aller* ~ *ist schwer Sprichw.* nothing's easy to start off with; *bei Projekt etc.*: *auch* you'll *etc.* get into it; **2.** (*Kopf*) head, top, beginning; *am* ~ *der Seite* at the top of the page; *am* ~ *des Festzuges* at the head of the procession; **3.** *mst Pl.* (*Ursprung*) origin; *noch in den Anfängen stecken* be in its (*od.* their) infancy

anfangen (*unreg., trennb., hat -ge-*) **I.** *vt/i.* start (*mit* with), begin, commence (with) *geh.*; ~ *zu* (+ *Inf.*) start (+ *Ger. od. Inf.*), begin (+ *Ger. od.*

Inf.); *zu rauchen od. mit dem Rauchen* ~ start smoking (*od.* to smoke), take up smoking; *fängst du schon wieder an?* are you at it again?; *beim Streiten*: *er etc.* hat (*damit*) *angefangen!* he *etc.* started (it)!; *lass uns von vorn* ~ let us make a fresh start; *das fängt ja gut an iro.* that's a great (way to) start; *jetzt fängt alles wieder von vorn an!* now it's going to start all over again!; **II.** *v/i.* (*etw. ansprechen*): *immer wieder von etw.* ~ keep harping on about s.th.; *jetzt fang nicht schon wieder damit od. davon an* don't start going on about (*od.* bring that up) that again; **III.** *v/t.* **1.** *umg.* (*tun*) do; *etw. schlau* ~ set (*od.* go) about s.th. cleverly (*od.* well); *das musst du anders* ~ you have to do it (*od.* go about it) in a different way; *was wollen wir mit dem freien Tag* ~*?* what shall we do on our day off?; **2.** *umg.*: *ich weiß nichts damit / mit ihm etc. anzufangen* I don't know what to do with it/him *etc.*; (*verstehe es nicht*) I can't make heads or tails of it; (*mag es/ihn etc. nicht*) it's not my cup of tea / we have absolutely nothing in common, he's *etc.* not my type; *mit dir ist heute ja nichts anzufangen umg.* you're a dead loss today, you're just not with it today

Anfänger *m*, ~*in f* **1.** beginner, novice (*bei* in + *Dat.* at); → *blutig* 4; **2.** *Archit. hist* (*Keilstein*) springer; ~*kurs* *m* beginners' course

anfänglich I. *Adj.* initial; (*früh*) *auch* early; *nach* ~*em Zögern* after initial hestitation; **II.** *Adv.* at first

anfangs I. *Adv.* at first, initially; **II.** *Präp.* (+ *Gen.*); *umg.* at the beginning of, early on in

Anfangs|buchstabe *m* first (*od.* initial) letter; *Pl. e-s Namens*: initials; *großer/kleiner* ~ capital/small letter; ~*erfolg* *m* initial success; ~*gehalt* *n* starting (*od.* initial) salary; ~*geschwindigkeit* *f* starting speed; *Phys.* initial velocity; ~*gründe* *Pl.* rudiments, elements *Pl.* (+ *Gen.* of); ~*kapital* *n* starting capital; ~*schwierigkeiten* *Pl.* initial difficulties; ~*stadium* *n* initial stage(s); ~*unterricht* *m* first years *Pl.* of teaching, early lessons *Pl.*, elementary instruction, beginners' class; ~*zeile* *f* first line; ~*zeit* *f* starting time, time of commencement *geh.*; *e-r Sendung*: broadcasting time, *auch* scheduled start; *was hat das Kino für* ~*en?* when does the film (*Am. auch* movie) start?; *in der* ~ at the start, in the beginning

anfassen (*trennb., hat -ge-*) **I.** *v/t.* **1.** (*berühren*) touch, feel; (*ergreifen*) take hold of (*auch bei der Hand nehmen*); *er fasste sie am Arm* he seized her by the arm, he grabbed her arm; *fass mich nicht an!* get your hands off (me)!; *zum Anfassen fig. Politiker etc.*: for (*od.* of) the people, accessible; *Kunst etc.*: hands-on *art etc.*; *Ausstellung*: *auch* tactile *exhibition*; **2.** *fig.* (*behandeln*) deal with, treat; (*Aufgabe*) *auch* approach, tackle; *j-n hart/sanft* ~ be firm (*od.* strict) / gentle with s.o.; **II.** *v/i.* (*helfen*) (*mit*) ~ lend (*od.* give *s.o.*) a hand, help out; **III.** *v/refl.*: *sich rau* ~ be rough to the touch; *sich weich etc.* ~ feel soft *etc.*

anfauchen *v/t.* (*trennb., hat -ge-*) spit at; *fig.* snap at

anfechtbar *Adj.* contestable; *Wirts.* voidable; *Behauptung etc.*: *auch* disputable; **Anfechtbarkeit** *f*; *nur Sg.* contestability; **anfechten** *v/t.* (*unreg.*, *trennb.*, *hat -ge-*) **1.** contest; (*Urteil*) appeal against; (*Zeugen[beweis]*) challenge; **2.** *geh.* (*beunruhigen*) worry, bother; **was ficht dich an?** what's on your mind (*od.* getting you down)?; **Anfechtung** *f* **1.** *Jur.* challenge; appeal (+ *Gen.* against); *Wirts.* avoidance, recission *förm.*; **2.** *mst Pl.*; *geh.* (*Versuchung*) temptation *allg.*; (*Selbstzweifel*) doubt

anfegen *v/i.* (*trennb.*, *ist -ge-*); *umg.*: *mst* **angefegt kommen** come belting up (*od.* along)

anfeinden *v/t.* (*trennb.*, *hat -ge-*) be hostile to(wards); **angefeindet werden** become (*od.* make o.s.) unpopular (**wegen** because of); *stärker*: make a lot of enemies; **Anfeindung** *f* hostility (+ *Gen.* toward[s])

anfertigen *v/t.* (*trennb.*, *hat -ge-*) make; *in der Fabrik auch*: manufacture; *schriftlich*: draw up; (*Übersetzung, Zeichnung*) do, produce; **Anfertigung** *f* making; *Wirts.* manufacture; drawing up; production; **die ~ e-r Übersetzung** producing a translation.

anfeuchten *v/t.* (*trennb.*, *hat -ge-*) moisten; (*lecken*) lick; → **angefeuchtet**; **Anfeuchter** *m* (*Büroutensil*) moistener

anfeuern *v/t.* (*trennb.*, *hat -ge-*) **1.** (*Ofen, Kessel*) fire; **2.** *fig.* encourage, spur on; *durch Zurufe*: cheer (on), *Am.* root for *umg.*; **Anfeuerung** *f* spurring on; **Anfeuerungsrufe** *Pl.* cheers of encouragement

anflachsen *v/t.* (*trennb.*, *hat -ge-*); *umg.* (*veralbern*) make fun of, tease *allg.*, take the piss out of s.o. *Brit. gespr.*

anflattern *v/i.* (*trennb.*, *ist -ge-*) flutter up; **angeflattert kommen** come fluttering up (*od.* along)

anflehen *v/t.* (*trennb.*, *hat -ge-*) implore, beseech

anfliegen (*unreg.*, *trennb.*, *-ge-*) **I.** *v/t.* (*hat*) *Flug.* approach; (*landen auf*) land at; *linienmäßig*: fly to, make a stop at; *die Fluggesellschaft* **fliegt Funchal (direkt) an** has a service (a direct flight) to Funchal,; **II.** *v/i.* (*ist*) **1.** approach, come in to land; **angeflogen kommen** *auch umg. fig.* come flying up (*od.* along); **2.** *Bergb.* Staub etc.: settle, effloresce

anflitzen *v/i.* (*trennb.*, *ist -ge-*): **angeflitzt kommen** *umg.* come racing up (*od.* along) *allg.*

Anflug *m* **1.** *Flug.* approach; **im ~ auf Wien sein** be approaching Vienna Airport; **beim ~ auf** (+ *Akk.*) while approaching, during the approach to; **2.** (*Spur*) touch, trace, hint, dash, tinge, streak; **3.** *Bergb.* slight coat, efflorescence; **~höhe** *f* approach altitude; **~schneise** *f*, **~weg** *m Flug.* approach corridor

anflunkern *v/t.* (*trennb.*, *hat -ge-*); *umg.* → **anschwindeln**

anfordern *v/t.* (*trennb.*, *hat -ge-*) request, ask for; *stärker*: demand; **Anforderung** *f* demand (+ *Gen.* for); *Pl.* (*Leistungs♀, Niveau♀*) standard *Sg.*, demands; **hohe ~en stellen** make high demands (**an** + *Akk.* on); **den ~en genügen** satisfy (*od.* meet) the demands; **Anforderungsprofil** *n* job profile

Anfrage *f* in|quiry(*od.* en-); question (*auch Parl.*); **anfragen** *v/i.* (*trennb.*, *hat -ge-*) in|quire (*od.* en-), ask; (**bei** *j-m*) **wegen etw. ~** ask (s.o.) about s.th.

anfressen *v/t.* (*unreg.*, *trennb.*, *hat -ge-*) **1.** *Maus etc.*: nibble at; *Raupe*: eat; *Motte*: eat holes into; *Vogel*: peck at; **2.** *Chem.* corrode, eat into, pit, score, attack; **3.** *umg. pej.*: *sich* (*Dat.*) **e-n Bauch** *etc.* ~ develop a paunch (*od.* gut); → **angefressen** II

anfreunden *v/refl.* (*trennb.*, *hat -ge-*) **1.** become (*od.* make) friends (**mit** with *s.o.*); **2.** *fig.*: *sich mit dem Gedanken etc.* ~ get used to the idea *etc.*, reconcile o.s. to the idea *etc.*; *sich mit etw.* ~ get to like s.th., acquire a taste for s.th.

anfrieren *v/i.* (*unreg.*, *trennb.*, *ist -ge-*) **1.** ~ **an** (+ *Dat.*) freeze (on)to; **2.** → **angefroren** II

anfügen *v/t.* (*trennb.*, *hat -ge-*) add, append; *Tech.* attach; (*falzen, anfugen*) join (on), join end to end; (*anstücken*) piece (to)

anfühlen (*trennb.*, *hat -ge-*) **I.** *v/t.* feel; (*berühren*) touch; **II.** *v/refl.*: *sich weich etc.* ~ feel soft *etc.*; *sich kalt* ~ be cold to the touch

Anfuhr *f*; -, -en delivery, transport(ation); (*Zufuhr*) supply

anführen *v/t.* (*trennb.*, *hat -ge-*) **1.** lead; *Mil. auch* command; (*Bewegung, Entwicklung etc.*) head, spearhead; (*Tabelle etc.*) be at the head of; **2.** (*erwähnen, sagen*) state, say; (*Gründe*) put forward, state; (*zitieren*) quote, cite *a law etc.*; (*Beweise, Zeugen*) produce; *zur Verteidigung, Entschuldigung*: state (in *s.o.'s* defen|ce [*Am.* -se]), plead (as an excuse); **3.** *umg.* (*foppen*) have (*Am.* put) s.o. on, take s.o. for a ride; **Anführer** *m*, **Anführerin** *f* leader; *Mil.* commander; (*Rädelsführer*) ringleader; **Anführung** *f* **1.** (*Leitung*) leadership, command; **2.** (*Erwähnung*) citation, quotation, statement; (*Zitierung*) quotation

Anführungs|striche *Pl.*, **~zeichen** *Pl.* quotation marks, *Brit. auch* inverted commas; **einfache/doppelte ~** single/ double quotation marks; **~ Anfang/Ende** *beim Diktieren*: quote/unquote; *beim Zitieren*: (I) quote / end of quote

anfüllen *v/t. und v/refl.* (*trennb.*, *hat -ge-*) fill (up) (**mit** with)

anfunkeln *v/t.* (*trennb.*, *hat -ge-*) dart a glance at) *s.o.*, *umg.* give *s.o.* a dirty look

Angabe *f* **1.** (*Aussage*) statement; (*Auskunft*) information; (*Beschreibung*) description; (*Nennung*) giving; *Pl.* information *Sg.*, data; *Wirts.* specifications; *bewusst falsche* ~ misrepresentation; *genauere* **~n** particulars, details; *zweckdienliche* **~n** relevant information (*od.* details); **~n** *zur Person* personal data, particulars; **~ des Inhalts** declaration of contents; *ohne* **~** *von Gründen* without giving any reasons; *ohne* **~ des Absenders** without a return address, with no return address; *keine* **~n** *zum Tathergang machen können* not be able to give any details about the (course *od.* sequence of) events; **2.** *Sport*: (*Aufschlag*) service; **3.** *umg.* showing-off, bragging; *das ist doch alles* **~** that's all just a lot of hot air

angaffen *v/t.* (*trennb.*, *hat -ge-*); *umg.* gawk at

angaloppieren *v/i.* (*trennb.*, *ist*) **1.** *mst* **angaloppiert kommen** gallop up, come galloping up; **2.** (*zu galoppieren beginnen*) start to (*od.* move into) gallop

angeben (*unreg.*, *trennb.*, *hat -ge-*)

I. *v/t.* **1.** (*Namen, Grund etc.*) give; (*erklären*) declare (*auch Zollware*); (*Kurse, Preise*) quote; (*zeigen*) show, indicate, point out; *zu hoch* (*niedrig*) ~ overstate (understate); *falsch* ~ misstate; *sie gab an, ihn noch nie gesehen zu haben* she claimed never to have seen (*od.* set eyes on) him before; **2.** (*festlegen*) (*Tempo, Takt*) set, determine; → **Ton¹** 2, 3; **3.** (*behaupten*) claim; (*vorgeben*) pretend; (*anzeigen*) denounce, inform against; **II.** *v/i.* **1.** *Sport*: (*anspielen*) serve; **2.** *umg.* (*prahlen*) brag (**mit** with), show off ([with] *s.th. od. s.o.*), pose; *der gibt aber an!* he's such a poser!; **Angeber** *m*, **Angeberin** *f umg.* show-off; (*Prahler*) braggart *allg.*, big mouth, poser; **Angeberei** *f*; -, -en; *umg.* showing-off, posing; **angeberisch** *Adj. umg.* bragging *allg.*; (*protzig*) showy *allg.*

angebetet *P.P.* → **anbeten**; **Angebetete** *m*, *f*; -n, -n; *oft iro.* beloved *allg.*; (*Idol*) idol

angebissen *P.P.* → **anbeißen**

angeblich I. *Adj.* alleged, supposed; ostensible; *pej. Künstler etc.*: would-be; *der* **~e Arzt** the self-styled doctor; **II.** *Adv.*: ~ *ist er ...* he's supposed to be ..., they say he's ...; *sie hat* ~ *nichts davon gewusst* supposedly she knew nothing about it

angeboren *Adj.* inborn, innate (+ *Dat.* in); *Med. auch* congenital, hereditary

Angebot *n* **1.** (*Vorschlag*) offer, proposal, proposition; **2.** (*Offerte*) offer; (*Kostenvoranschlag*) quotation; *auf e-e Ausschreibung hin*: tender; *ein günstiges/unverbindliches* ~ a fair/non-binding offer; *j-m ein* ~ *machen od.* unterbreiten make s.o. (*od.* submit) a proposal; **3.** *nur Sg.*; *Wirts.* (*Warenangebot*) *auch Börse*: supply (**an** + *Dat.* of); ~ *und Nachfrage* supply and demand; *ein reichhaltiges* ~ an extensive range (*od.* selection); *heute haben wir ... im* ~ our special offers today are ..., *Am.* ...is/are on sale today; **4.** *Auktion*: bid

Angebots|lücke *f* gap in supply; **~überhang** *m* excess of supply over demand

angebracht I. *P.P.* → **anbringen**; **II.** *Adj.* appropriate; (*ratsam*) advisable; *Bemerkung*: apt; *nicht* ~ inappropriate; *Bemerkung*: out of place, uncalled-for, ill-timed; *er hielt es für* ~ *zu* (+ *Inf.*) he thought it would be appropriate to (+ *Inf.*)

angebrannt *P.P.* → **anbrennen**

angebraust *P.P.* → **anbrausen**

angebrochen *P.P.* → **anbrechen**

angebrütet *Adj. Ei*: half-hatched, partially incubated

angebunden I. *P.P.* → **anbinden**; **II.** *Adj.* **1.** *fig. durch Kinder etc.*: tied down; **2.** *kurz* ~ curt, abrupt

angedampft *P.P.* → **andampfen**

angedeihen *v/i.*: *j-m etw.* ~ *lassen geh. od. iro.* grant (*od.* afford) s.o. s.th.,bestow (*od.* confer) s.th. on s.o.

angedeutet *P.P.* → **andeuten**

angedonnert *P.P.* → **andonnern**

angedudelt *P.P.* → **andudeln**

angeduselt *Adj. umg.* (slightly) merry *od.* tiddly, tipsy

angefahren *P.P.* → **anfahren**

angefault *Adj.* rotting, mo(u)ldering

angefegt *P.P.* → **anfegen**

angefeuchtet I. *P.P.* → **anfeuchten**; **II.** *Adj.* moist, moistened

angeflattert *P.P.* → **anflattern**

angeflitzt *P.P.* → **anflitzen**

angeflogen *P.P.* → *anfliegen*

angefressen I. *P.P.* → *anfressen*; **II.** *Adj. von Motten*: moth-eaten; *von Rost*: rusty, corroded

angefroren I. *P.P.* → *anfrieren*; **II.** *Adj.*: ~ *sein Blumen etc.*: have gotten) a touch of frost

angegangen *P.P.* → *angehen*

angegilbt *Adj.* yellowing, yellowed

angegossen *Adj. umg.*: **wie** ~ **passen** *od. sitzen* fit like a glove, be a perfect fit

angegraut *Adj.* greying (*Am.* gray-)

angegriffen I. *P.P.* → *angreifen*; **II.** *Adj. Person*: exhausted, weary, worn-out ..., *präd.* worn out; *Gesundheit*: bad; *Nerven*: strained; *stärker Organ*: affected; ~ *aussehen* look unwell

angegurtet *P.P.* → *angurten*

angehaucht I. *P.P.* → *anhauchen*; **II.** *Adj.*: **kommunistisch** ~ **sein** have communist leanings; **künstlerisch** ~ **sein** have an artistic bent

angehäuft *P.P.* → *anhäufen*

angeheiratet *Adj.* (related) by marriage; ~*e Verwandte* in-laws

angeheitert *Adj. umg.* (slightly) merry *od.* tiddly, a little high, tipsy

angehen (*unreg.*, *trennb.*, *-ge-*) **I.** *v/t.* (*hat* / *südd.*, *österr.*, *schw. ist*) **1.** (*betreffen*) concern; **was ihn angeht** as far as he's concerned, as for him; **was geht das mich an?** what's that got to do with me?; **das geht dich nichts an** that's none of your business; **das geht niemanden etwas an** that's my business, that's nobody's business but my own; **2.** (*Problem etc.*) tackle; *Pferd*: (*Hindernis*) approach; **sie ist die Kurve zu schnell angegangen** she took (*od.* approached) the bend (*od.* curve) too fast; **3.** *j-n um etw.* ~ (*bitten*) approach s.o. with a request, ask s.o. for s.th.; **4.** (*Gegner*) *auch Sport*: attack; **II.** *v/i.* (*ist*) **1.** ~ *gegen* resist, fight (against); **2.** (*möglich, zulässig sein*) **es geht nicht an, dass ...** there's no excuse for (+ *Ger.*); **das mag (noch)** ~ one can (just about) overlook (*od.* excuse) that; **das kann nicht** ~ (*darf nicht sein*) that cannot be tolerated (*od.* allowed); (*glaube ich nicht*) it can't be true; **3.** *umg.* (*anfangen*) get going, start *allg.*; **4.** (*funktionieren*) work; *Motor*, *Auto*: start; *Licht*: go on; *Feuer*: start burning, catch; *Ofen*: turn on; *Radio etc.*: come on; **5.** (*anwachsen*) (*Ableger*) take root; *Med.*, *Bio.* (*Bakterien*, *Pilze*) grow; → *angegangen*; **angehend I.** *Part. Präs.* → *angehen*; **II.** *Adj.* beginning, incipient *förm.*; (*künftig*) future; *Künstler*, *Schönheit*: budding; *beruflich*: *auch* trainee; ~*er Arzt etc.* doctor-to-be *etc.*; ~*e Lehrer* prospective teachers

angehetzt *P.P.* → *anhetzen*

angehören *v/i.* (*trennb.*, *hat*) belong (+ *Dat.* to); *als Mitglied*: *auch* be a member (of); *der Vergangenheit* ~ be a thing of the past; **angehörig** *Adj.* belonging (+ *Dat.* to); **Angehörige** *m*, *f*; *-n*, *-n*; (*Mitglied*) member; *e-s Staates*: national (+ *Gen.* of); (*Verwandter*) relative; *der/die nächste* ~ the next of kin; *m-e* ~*n* my family (*od.* relatives)

angejahrt *Adj.* ag(e)ing, getting on (in years) *präd.*

angekettet I. *P.P.* → *anketten*; **II.** *Adj. Hund*: on a (*od.* the) chain; chained up

angekeucht *P.P.* → *ankeuchen*

Angeklagte *m*, *f*; *-n*, *-n* defendant, (the

od. an) accused

angeknackst *Adj. umg.* slightly damaged *allg.*, in a bad way; *Knochen*: chipped; *Rippe*, *Ei*: cracked; *Gesundheit*, *Beziehung*: shaky; *Stolz*, *Selbstbewusstsein*: dented; **sein Selbstbewusstsein ist** ~ his self-confidence has been dented (*od.* has taken a beating)

angekränkelt *Adj.* **1.** sickly, frail; **2.** *fig.* afflicted (*von* by)

angekratzt *Adj. umg. Stolz*, *Selbstbewusstsein*: dented

angekrochen *P.P.* → *ankriechen*

angekündigt I. *P.P.* → *ankündigen*; **II.** *Adj. Sitzung*, *Vortrag etc.*: planned, scheduled; *Besucher etc.*: expected; *der* ~*e Wechsel etc.* the change *etc.* that was announced, the announced (*od.* promised) change *etc.*

Angel¹ *f*; *-*, *-n* fishing rod (*Am. auch* pole); (*e-n Fisch*) *an der* ~ *haben* (a fish) hooked; *auch* be able to reel (a fish) in; *j-m an die* ~ *gehen Fisch*: swallow the bait; *fig. Person*: fall for (*od.* swallow) s.o.'s line, fall for s.o. hook, line and sinker

Angel² *f*; *-*, *-n* **1.** *von Tür*: hinge; (*etw.*) *aus den* ~*n heben* lift (s.th.) out of its hinges, unhinge ; *fig.* revolutionize (s.th.) (*completely*); → *Tür* 2; **2.** *Tech. e-s Bohrers*: shank; *e-r Feile*: tang

angelatscht *P.P.* → *anlatschen*

angelaufen *P.P.* → *anlaufen*

angelegen I. *P.P.* → *anliegen*; **II.** *Adj. geh.*: *sich* (*Dat.*) *etw. sehr* ~ *sein lassen* make s.th. one's concern; **Angelegenheit** *f* matter, concern, affair; *in e-r dienstlichen* ~ on official business; *e-e* ~ *in Ordnung bringen* settle (*od.* sort out) a matter; *sich in j-s* ~*en* (*ein*)*mischen* meddle in (*od.* with) s.o. else's business; *das ist s-e* ~ that's his problem; *kümmere dich um d-e eigenen* ~*en!* mind your own business

angelegentlich *Adv. geh.* (*eingehend*) thoroughly, (*very*) closely; (*nachdrücklich*) particularly

angelegt I. *P.P.* → *anlegen*; **II.** *Adj.*: *fest* ~*es Geld* permanent investment(s), money on time deposit

angelehnt *P.P.* → *anlehnen*

angeleint I. *P.P.* → *anleinen*; **II.** *Adj. Hund*: on a lead (*od.* leash)

angelernt I. *P.P.* → *anlernen*; **II.** *Adj.* **1.** (mechanically) acquired; *Kenntnisse*: just for show; *Höflichkeit etc.*: put-on; **2.** ~*er Arbeiter* semi-skilled worker

angelesen I. *P.P.* → *anlesen*; **II.** *Adj.* **1.** *Buch*: started *book*; *lauter* ~*e Bücher* books started and never finished; **2.** ~*es Wissen* knowledge out of books, book knowledge

Angel|fischerei *f* angling; ~*gerät n* fishing tackle; (*Angelrute*) fishing rod; ~*haken m* fishhook; ~*karte f* → *Angelschein*; ~*leine f* fishing line

angeln I. *vt/i.* fish, angle (*auf* + *Akk. od. nach* for); **II.** *v/t. umg. fig.*, oft *pej.*: *sich* (*Dat.*) *j-n/etw.* ~ hook (*od.* land) o.s. s.o./s.th.; **III.** *v/i. umg.*: ~ *nach dem Schlüssel* / *fig. Komplimenten* fish (*od.* angle) for

Angelplatz *m* fishing ground

Angelpunkt *m* pivot; *fig.* pivotal point; (*Kernfrage*) central issue; (*Mittelpunkt*) hub; (*Kern*) linchpin

Angelrute *f* fishing rod

Angelsachse *m*, **Angelsächsin** *f* Anglo-Saxon; **angelsächsisch** *Adj.* Anglo-Saxon

Angel|schein *m* fishing *od.* angler's licen|ce (*Am.* -se); ~*schnur f* → ~*leine*; ~*sport m* fishing, angling

angemacht *P.P.* → *anmachen*

angemessen *Adj.* appropriate (+ *Dat.* to); *Preis etc.*: reasonable; (*ausreichend*) adequate; *Benehmen*: proper, fitting; **Angemessenheit** *f*; *nur Sg.* appropriateness, suitability

angenagelt *P.P.* ~ *kommen mit Boot*: approach (in a canoe, small boat *etc.*); *Tier*: come (dog[gy])paddling up (*od.* along) *umg.*

angenehm I. *Adj.* (+ *Dat. od. für*) pleasant (for); agreeable (to); (~ *wirkend*) pleasing; (*befriedigend*) gratifying; (*behaglich*) comfortable, co|sy (*Am. mst* -zy); (*willkommen*) welcome; ~*e Fahrt/Musik* restful trip/music; ~*es Wesen* engaging manners; ~*en Aufenthalt!* have a good (*od.* pleasant) stay; ~*e Reise!* have a good journey!, bon voyage!; (*sehr*) ~*!* altm. delighted (to meet you) *förm.*, glad to meet you *allg.*; *es wäre mir sehr* ~, *wenn ...* I would really appreciate it if ...; *das Angenehme mit dem Nützlichen verbinden* combine business with pleasure; **II.** *Adv.*: ~ *überrascht* pleasantly surprised; ~ *weich etc.* nice and soft *etc.*

angenommen *P.P.* → *annehmen*

angepaddelt *P.P.* → *anpaddeln*

angepasst I. *P.P.* → *anpassen*; **II.** *Adj.* conformist; *Psych.* (well-)adjusted (*an* + *Akk.* to); **Angepasstheit** *f*; *nur Sg.* conformism

angepeilt I. *P.P.* → *anpeilen*; **II.** *Adj. Ergebnisse etc.*: targeted, aimed-for

angeprescht *P.P.* → *anpreschen*

Anger *m*; *-s*, *-* meadow, pasture; (*Dorf*~) (village) green, common

angeradelt *P.P.* → *anradeln*

angerannt *P.P.* → *anrennen*

angerast *P.P.* → *anrasen*

angeraucht *Adj. Zigarette etc.*: lit; burning *umg.*

angeraut *Adj. Stoff etc.*: roughened

angeregt I. *P.P.* → *anregen*; **II.** *Adj. Gespräch*: lively, animated; **III.** *Adv.*: *sich* ~ *unterhalten* have a lively conversation

angereichert *P.P.* → *anreichern*

angeritten *P.P.* → *anreiten*

angerostet I. *P.P.* → *anrosten*; **II.** *Adj.* (slightly) rusty

angerußt *Adj.* (slightly) sooty

angesagt I. *P.P.* → *ansagen*; **II.** *Adj.*: ~ *sein* (*vorgesehen*) be on the agenda; *umg.* (*in Mode*) be in; *Fitness ist* ~*!* fitness is the order of the day

angesammelt *P.P.* → *ansammeln*

angesaust *P.P.* → *ansausen*

angesäuselt *Adj. umg.* (slightly) merry *od.* tiddly, tipsy

angeschimmelt *Adj. Brot*: slightly mo(u)ldy; ~ *sein auch* have a touch of mo(u)ld

angeschissen *P.P.* → *anscheißen*

angeschlagen I. *P.P.* → *anschlagen*; **II.** *Adj.* **1.** *Glas*, *Möbel etc.*: chipped; **2.** *fig. Person*: groggy; *seelisch*: shaken; *Gesundheit*: shaky; (*schwer*) ~ *sein* (*von etw.*) have taken a (real) beating by s.th., be (absolutely) shattered (by s.th.)

angeschlendert *P.P.* → *anschlendern*

angeschlichen *P.P.* → *anschleichen*

angeschlossen *P.P.* → *anschließen*

angeschmutzt *Adj.* slightly dirty, soiled; *Wirts.* shopsoiled

angeschnitten I. *P.P.* → *anschneiden*; **II.** *Adj.* **1.** *ein* ~*es Brot* a started loaf; **2.** ~*er Ärmel* dolman (*od.* tapering) sleeve; **3.** ~*er Ball* ball with a spin on it, spin ball

angeschossen P.P. → *anschießen*

angeschrieben I. P.P. → *anschreiben*; II. Adj.: *er ist bei ihr gut/schlecht ~* she thinks a lot of him, he is in her good book(s) / he doesn't rate very highly with her, he is in her bad book(s)

Angeschuldigte m, f; -n, -n; Jur. accused

angeschwärmt P.P. → *anschwärmen*

angeschwemmt P.P. → *anschwemmen*

angeschwirrt P.P. → *anschwirren*

angeschwollen P.P. → *anschwellen*

angeschwommen P.P. → *anschwimmen*

angesegelt P.P. → *ansegeln*

angesehen I. P.P. → *ansehen*; II. Adj. respected; Firma etc.: reputable; Persönlichkeit: distinguished

Angesicht n geh. face, countenance; *von ~ zu ~* face to face; *im ~* (+ Gen.) in the face of allg.; → *Schweiß 1*

angesichts Präp. (+ Gen. od. von) geh. 1. at the sight of; 2. fig. given, in view of, considering; *~ des Todes* etc. in the face of death etc.

angesoffen P.P. → *ansaufen*

angespannt I. P.P. → *anspannen*; II. Adj. Nerven, Person: tense(d up), taut; Phys. intense; Aufmerksamkeit: rapt; politische Lage etc.: tense; (Lage auf dem) Arbeitsmarkt etc.: tight; (knapp) Mittel etc.: strained, overstretched; *~e Finanzlage* financial stringency; III. Adv. intensely; *~ arbeiten* work at full stretch (od. all out)

angesprungen P.P. → *anspringen*

angestammt Adj. 1. Rechte: hereditary; 2. umg. fig. Platz: accustomed, usual allg.

angestapft P.P. → *anstapfen*

angestaubt Adj. 1. Buch etc.: dusty; 2. fig. Ideen etc.: stale

angestaut P.P. → *anstauen*

angestellt P.P. → *anstellen*

Angestellte m, f; -n, -n (salaried) employee, white-collar worker umg.; in Büro: office worker; Pl. (Personal) personnel, staff (Verb im Pl. od. Sg.); *alle ~n streiken* all personnel are on strike; *etwa 25 ~ wurden entlassen* about 25 staff (Am. employees) were made redundant (Am. were laid off)

Angestellten|... im Subst. (salaried) employees' insurance etc.; *~gewerkschaft* f weitS. white-collar union; *~verhältnis* n: *im ~ stehen* be employed, be in salaried employment (bei with); *~versicherung* f weitS. (salaried) employees' insurance (scheme)

angestiefelt P.P. → *anstiefeln*

angestiegen P.P. → *ansteigen*

angestochen I. P.P. → *anstechen*; II. Adj. Apfel etc.: bad, rotten

angestrahlt I. P.P. → *anstrahlen*; II. Adj. Gebäude: floodlit, illuminated

angestrengt I. P.P. → *anstrengen*; II. Adj. Arbeit, Nachdenken etc.: concentrated; *~e Miene* look of concentration; III. Adv.: *~ nachdenken* etc. think etc. hard; *~ zuhören* listen intently; **Angestrengtheit** f; nur Sg. concentration; pej. forcedness

angestürmt P.P. → *anstürmen*

angestürzt P.P. → *anstürzen*

angetan I. P.P. → *antun*; II. präd. Adj. 1. *~ sein von* (beeindruckt) be taken with, be impressed by; (erfreut) be pleased with, have a liking for; 2. (ganz) *dazu ~ zu* (+ Inf.) (very) likely (od. apt) to (+ Inf.); 3. geh. (ge-

kleidet) attired präd., clad (mit in)

angetanzt P.P. → *antanzen*

angetaut P.P. → *antauen*

angetrabt P.P. → *antraben*

Angetraute m, f; -n -n; hum. better half

angetrunken I. P.P. → *antrinken*; II. Adj. slightly drunk, inebriated; *er war in ~em Zustand* he had been drinking; III. Adv.: *~ Auto fahren* drive while drunk, drink and drive: förm. drive while under the influence

angeturnt ['aŋətœrnt] P.P. → *anturnen*

angewandt P.P. → *anwenden*

angewatschelt P.P. → *anwatscheln*

angewetzt P.P. → *anwetzen*

angewiesen I. P.P. → *anweisen*; II. präd. Adj.: *~ sein auf* (+ Akk.) be dependent on, depend on; *darauf bin ich nicht ~* I can manage without it, I don't need that; *auf sich* (Akk.) *allein ~ sein* have to look after o.s.

angewöhnen v/t. (trennb., hat): *j-m etw. ~* get s.o. used to s.th., teach s.o. s.th.; *sich* (Dat.) *etw. / das Rauchen etc. ~* get into the habit of (od. take up, take to) s.th. / smoking etc.; *sich* (Dat.) *~ zu* (+ Inf.) make it a habit to (+ Inf.), make a habit of (+ Ger.)

Angewohnheit f habit; *aus ~* from habit

angewurzelt I. P.P. → *anwurzeln*; II. Adj.: *wie ~ dastehen* stand rooted to the spot

angezeigt I. P.P. → *anzeigen*; II. Adj. (ratsam) advisable; *es für ~ halten zu* (+ Inf.) consider it appropriate (od. advisable) to (+ Inf.)

angezischt P.P. → *anzischen*

angiften v/t. (trennb., hat -ge-); umg. get nasty with, snap at, lay into allg.

Angina f; -, Anginen; Med. tonsil(l)itis

Angina Pectoris f; - -, kein Pl.; Med. angina pectoris

angleichen v/t. und v/refl. (unreg., trennb., hat -ge-) adapt, adjust (+ Dat. od. an + Akk. to); *sich aneinander ~* Personen: become like one another (od. increasingly similar); Kulturen etc.: grow more similiar (od. closer together), assimilate; **Angleichung** f adaptation, adjustment (an + Akk. to)

Angler m; -s, -, *~in* f; -, -nen angler, Mann auch: fisherman, Frau auch: fisherwoman

angliedern v/t. (trennb., hat -ge-) join, attach (+ Dat. od. an + Akk. to); (Organisation) affiliate (with), incorporate (into); (Gebiet, Staat) annex (to); (eingliedern) integrate (into); **Angliederung** f attachment, affiliation, integration

Anglikaner m; -s, -, *~in* f; -, -nen Reli. Anglican; *~ sein* auch be Anglican; **anglikanisch** Adj. Anglican; *die Anglikanische Kirche* the Church of England, the Anglican Church; in USA: the Episcopal Church

anglisieren v/t. Anglicize, anglicize

Anglist m; -en, -en, *~in* f; -, -nen Ling. English student (Dozent: lecturer), student (bzw. professor) of English, English philologist; **Anglistik** f; -, kein Pl. English language and literature, English studies Pl. (od. philology); **anglistisch** Adj. English, related to English studies präd.

Anglizismus m; -, Anglizismen Ling. Anglicism

anglo... im Adj., **Anglo...** im Subst. Anglo-...

anglo|phil Adj. Anglophile; *~phob*

Adj. Anglophobe; *~phon* Adj. Anglophone

anglotzen v/t. (trennb., hat -ge-); umg. gawk at allg.

Angolaner m; -s, -, *~in* f; -, -nen Angolan; **angolanisch** Adj. Angolan

Angora|katze f Zool. Angora cat; *~wolle* f angora (wool); *~ziege* f Angora goat

angreifbar Adj. open to attack; auch fig. vulnerable

angreifen (unreg., trennb., hat -ge-) I. vt/i. 1. attack (auch Sport und fig.); ungestüm: assail; Jur. (tätlich ~) assault; *angegriffen werden* auch fig. be attacked, come under attack; 2. (Aufgabe) tackle; II. v/t. 1. fig. → I 1; 2. (schwächen) weaken; (Augen etc.) strain; (Gesundheit) affect; → angegriffen II; 3. Chem. corrode; 4. (Vorräte, Ersparnisse) break into; 5. südd. umg. (berühren) touch; III. v/i. Phys. (Kraft) act (in e-m Punkt on a point); **Angreifer** m, **Angreiferin** f attacker, assailant; Pol. aggressor

angrenzen v/i. (trennb., ist -ge-): *~ an* (+ Akk.) border on; abut on; **angrenzend** I. Part. Präs. → *angrenzen*; II. Adj. 1. adjacent (an + Akk. to), adjoining; neighbo(u)ring; 2. fig. Fachgebiet: related

Angriff m (auf + Akk. od. gegen) attack (on) (auch Sport und fig.), assault (on); strategisch: offensive (on); tätlicher ~ Jur. assault (and battery); *etw. in ~ nehmen* (handhaben) tackle, (beginnen) get started (od. cracking umg.) on s.th., get down to s.th.; *zum ~ blasen* Mil. sound the charge (od. attack); fig. sound the attack; *zum ~ übergehen* take the (od. mount an) offensive

Angriffs|drittel n Eishockey: attack zone; *~fläche* f fig. point of attack; *keine ~ bieten* lay o.s. open to attack (+ Dat. from); *~fußball* m attacking football; *~krieg* m Mil. offensive warfare; Pol. war of aggression

Angriffslust f aggressiveness, belligerence; **angriffslustig** Adj. aggressive, belligerent

Angriffs|reihe f Sport: forwards Pl.; *~spiel* n attacking play; *~spieler* m, *~spielerin* f 1. striker; 2. Tischtennis: attacking player; Volleyball; front-line player; Faustball: forward; *~spitze* f Mil. spearhead; *~waffe* f offensive weapon

angrinsen v/t. (trennb., hat -ge-) umg. grin at allg.

Angst f; -, Ängste fear (vor + Dat. of); auch Psych. anxiety (um about od. over); große: dread, terror; (Lebens-, Existenzangst) angst lit.; *aus ~* out of fear; *vor ~ zittern* etc. tremble (od. shake) with fear; *~ haben vor* be afraid (od. scared, frightened) of; *um etw./j-n ~ haben* be worried (od. scared) about s.th./ for (od. about) s.o.; *j-m ~ (und Bange) machen* od. *j-n in ~ (und Schrecken) versetzen* od. *j-m ~ einjagen* frighten, scare s.o., Am. put the fear (of God) into s.o. umg.;; *keine ~!* no need to be frightened, don't worry; *schreckliche Ängste ausstehen* be frightened out of one's mind (od. wits); *es mit der ~ zu tun bekommen* (od. kriegen umg.) get scared (get the wind up)

angst Adj.; nur präd.: *mir ist* od. *wird ~ (und bange)* I'm worried (od. scared) to death, I'm scared stiff (od. out of my wits) umg.

angst|erfüllt *Adj.* terrified, fearful; **~frei I.** *Adj.* free from fear, anxiety--free; **II.** *Adv.* without fear

Angst|gefühl *n* frightened feeling; *stärker*: sense of fear (*od.* anxiety); *tiefes*: angst *lit.*; **~gegner** *m*, **~gegnerin** *f Sport*: dreaded opponent; bogey team *umg.*; **~hase** *m umg. pej.* scaredy-cat, chicken

ängstigen I. *v/t.* alarm, frighten; (*besorgt machen*) get *s.o.* worried; **II.** *v/refl.* be afraid (**vor** + *Dat.* of); *stärker*: be alarmed (by); (*sich sorgen*) be worried (**um** about)

Angstkäufe *Pl.* panic buying *Sg.*

ängstlich I. *Adj.* nervous; (*schüchtern*) timid; (*besorgt*) anxious; (*unruhig*) uneasy, jittery *umg.*; (*peinlich*) scrupulous; **II.** *Adv.*: **~** **bemüht zu** (+ *Inf.*) anxious to (+ *Inf.*); **~** **gehütetes Geheimnis** jealously guarded secret; **Ängstlichkeit** *f* nervousness, anxiety; timidness, timidity; scrupulousness

Angst|macher *m pej.* alarmist, fearmonger; **~neurose** *f Psych.* anxiety psychosis; **~psychose** *f Psych.* anxiety psychosis, hysteria

Ångström *n*; -(s), -; *Phys. altm.* angstrom

Angst|schrei *m* frightened scream; *stärker*: scream of terror; **~schweiß** *m* cold sweat; **~traum** *m* nightmare; *Psych.* anxiety dream

angst|verzerrt *Adj. Gesicht*: contorted with fear; *Stimme*: trembling with fear (*od.* fright); **~voll** *Adj.* fearful, apprehensive, frightened; *stärker*: terrified

Angstzustand *m* state of anxiety; **Angstzustände bekommen** get into a panic

angucken *v/t.* (*trennb., hat -ge-*); *umg.* look at *allg.*

angurten *v/t. und v/refl.* (*trennb., hat -ge-*): **j-n ~** fasten s.o.'s seatbelt; **sich ~** fasten one's seatbelt, do one's seatbelt up *umg.*; **angegurtet sein** *auch* have one's seatbelt on, be belted up *umg.*

anhaben *v/t.* (*unreg., trennb., hat -ge-*) **1.** (*Kleider*) have on, wear, be wearing; **2.** (*Licht etc.*) have on; **3.** *j-m etwas/nichts ~ können* (*beweisen können*) be able/unable to get at (*od.* touch) *s.o.*; (*schaden können*) be able/unable to harm *s.o.*, have nothing on *s.o. umg.*; **das kann mir nichts ~** that doesn't worry me

anhaften *v/i.* (*trennb., hat -ge-*); *auch fig.* cling, stick (+ *Dat. od.* **an** + *Dat.* to); *fig.* (*j-m od. e-r Sache*) *Mängel etc.*: be inherent in; **ihm haftete etwas Eigentümliches an** there was something peculiar about him

Anhalt *m fig.*: **e-n ~ gewähren** give a clue (**für** to); → **Anhaltspunkt**

anhalten (*unreg., trennb., hat -ge-*) **I.** *v/t.* **1.** stop, bring to a halt (*od.* stop); *Tech. auch* bring to rest; (*Pferd*) pull up; **den Atem** *od.* **die Luft ~** hold one's breath; **j-n zu etw. ~** urge s.o. to do s.th.; **II.** *v/i.* **1.** stop, come to a stop (*od.* standstill); *Auto: auch* pull up; **2.** (*andauern*) last, continue; *Wetter*: hold; *beharrlich*: persist; **3. er hielt um die Hand i-r Tochter an** *altm.* he asked her for her daughter's hand (in marriage) *allg.*

anhaltend I. *Part. Präs.* → **anhalten**; **II.** *Adj.* continuous, lasting; (*stetig*) sustained; (*beharrlich*) persistent; **~e Bemühungen** prolonged efforts; **~e Nachfrage** persistent demand

Anhalter *m*, **~in** *f* hitchhiker; **per Anhalter fahren** hitchhike, hitch (a lift)

umg., thumb a ride (*od.* lift) *umg.*

Anhaltspunkt *m* lead, clue; *auch Pl.* something to go by; indication (**für** of); (*Grundlage*) basis

anhand *Präp.* (+ *Gen. od. von*) with the help (of), on the basis (of)

Anhang *m* **1.** *allg.* (*auch Anhängsel*) appendage; *e-s Buchs*: appendix; (*Ergänzung*) supplement; *e-s Schriftstücks*: annex, addendum; *e-s Briefes*: enclosure; *e-s Testaments*: codicil; **2.** *nur Sg.*; (*Gefolgschaft*) followers *Pl.*, following, adherents *Pl.*, hangers--on *Pl. pej.*; *umg.* fan club, fans *Pl.*; (*Angehörige*) dependents *Pl.*, family; *umg.* (*Begleiter*) companion, escort *hum.*

anhängen¹ (*trennb., hat -ge-*) **I.** *v/t.* **1.** (*aufhängen*) (*Bild, Mantel, Vorhang etc.*) hang up (**an** + *Akk.* on); (*Zettel etc.*) pin (**an** + *Akk.* on, onto); **2.** (*Waggon etc.*) couple on, attach (**an** + *Akk.* to); (*Anhänger, Wohnwagen etc.*) hook up (to); **3.** (*hinzufügen*) add (**an** + *Akk.* to); *umg.* tag on(to); **4.** *umg fig.*: **j-m etw. ~** frame s.o up; (*in die Schuhe schieben*) pin s.th. on s.o.; (*andrehen*) fob s.th. off on s.o., palm s.th. off with s.th.; **j-m e-n Prozess ~** take s.o. to court *allg.*; **II.** *v/refl.*: **sich ~ an** (+ *Akk.*) **1.** (*festhalten*) hang on; **2.** *umg. fig.* (*an j-n, e-e Gruppe*) latch onto, tag along with; *Sport*: tuck o.s. in behind

anhängen² *v/i.* (*unreg., trennb., hat -ge-*); *fig.* **1.** *e-r Mode, Partei etc.*: follow; *e-r Idee*: believe in, subscribe to; **2.** *geh.* (*anhaften*) *j-m* stick with *s.o. allg.*; **der Ruf hängt ihm immer noch an** he just can't shake off that reputation

Anhänger¹ *m* , **~in** *f*; -, -nen follower; (*Jünger*) disciple; *e-r Partei*: supporter, adherent; *streitbarer*: partisan; *Film etc.*: fan; *Sport auch* supporter; *Rel.*, *Kunst*: devotee

Anhänger² *m* **1.** (*Schmuck*) pendant; **2.** (*Schild*) label, tag; **3.** *Mot.* (drawbar) trailer

Anhängerschaft *f*; *nur Sg.* following, supporters, hangers-on *pej. Pl.*; *umg.* fan club, fans *Pl.*

Anhängerkupplung *f Mot.* trailer coupling

Anhängeschild *n* address tag

anhängig *Adj. Jur.* pending; **e-n Prozess gegen j-n ~ machen** bring an action against s.o., take legal proceedings against s.o.

anhänglich *Adj.* devoted, doting; *Kind, Tier: auch* affectionate; *pej.* clinging, over-dependent; **Anhänglichkeit** *f*; *nur Sg.* devotion, affection; *pej.* dependence

Anhängsel *n*; -s, -; *fig.* appendage (*auch umg. Person*)

anhauchen *v/t.* (*trennb., hat -ge-*) breathe on; (*die Finger*) blow on; **hauch mich mal an!** let me smell your breath; → **angehaucht** II

anhauen (*trennb., hat -ge-*); *umg. v/t.* **1.** (*belästigen*) (*Frau*) molest *allg.*; **2.** (*anbetteln*): **j-n um etw. ~** tap(*od.* touch) s.o. for s.th., scrounge s.th. from s.o.

anhäufen (*trennb., hat -ge-*) **I.** *v/t.* pile up, accumulate; (*Geld*) amass; (*hamstern*) hoard, squirrel away; (*Waffen*) stockpile; **II.** *v/refl.* pile up, accumulate (*auch Kapital*); *Geol. Vulkangestein*: agglomerate; **Anhäufung** *f* accumulation; accretion, acervation *fachspr.*

anheben (*unreg., trennb., hat -ge-*) **I.** *v/t.* **1.** lift, raise; *schnell*: hike (up) *umg.*; **2.** (*erhöhen*) (*Preis, Standard etc.*) raise, hike (up) *umg.*; **3.** *Phys.* (*Frequenzkurve*) accentuate; **II.** *v/i.* (*Imperf. altm.* **hub an**) *geh.* commence, begin *allg.* (**zu** + *Inf.* to + *Inf. od. Ger.*); **Anhebung** *f* increase (+ *Gen.* in)

anheften *v/t.* (*trennb., hat -ge-*) fasten (**an** + *Akk. od. Dat.* to); *mit Nadel*: pin (**an** + *Akk. od. Dat.* to); *mit Heftfäden*: tack (**an** +*Akk. od. Dat.* on *od.* up), baste (**an** + *Akk. od. Dat.* on)

anheim *Adv. geh.*: **~ fallen** (+ *Dat.*) fall prey to *allg.*; **der Vergessenheit ~ fallen** sink into oblivion; **~ geben** (+ *Dat.*) commit (*od.* entrust) to; **j-m etw. ~ stellen** leave s.th. up to s.o. *allg.*

anheimeln *v/t.* (*trennb., hat -ge-*) (*j-n*) remind *s.o.* of home; **es heimelt mich an** it makes me feel at (*od.* like) home; **anheimelnd** *Adj.* homely, *Am.* homey; (*gemütlich*) co|sy (*Am.* -zy); (*vertraut*) familiar

anheischig *Adj. geh.*: **sich ~ machen zu** (+ *Inf.*) offer (*od.* volunteer *od.* pledge o.s.) to (+ *Inf.*) *allg.*

anheizen *v/t.* (*trennb., hat -ge-*) **1.** (*Ofen etc.*) fire; **2.** *umg. fig.* (*Inflation*) heat up, kindle *allg.*; (*Streit etc.*) fuel; (*Gespräch*) liven up; **die Stimmung ~** liven things up (a bit)

Anheizer *m*, **~in** *f Pol.* agitator

anherrschen *v/t.* (*trennb., hat -ge-*) bark at

anhetzen *v/i.* (*trennb., ist -ge-*); *umg.*: **angehetzt kommen** come rushing up (*od.* along)

anheuern (*trennb., hat -ge-*) **I.** *v/t.* **1.** *Naut.* sign on, bes. *Am.* sign up; **2.** *umg.* (*Killer etc.*) hire *allg*; **II.** *v/i.* *Naut.* sign on, bes. *Am.* sign up (**auf** + *Dat.* on)

anheulen *v/t.* (*trennb., hat -ge-*); *Hund*: (*Mond*) wail (*od.* yowl) at

Anhieb *m*: **auf ~** straightaway, right off (the bat) *umg.*; **auf ~ sagen können** be able to say offhand; **auf ~** (*nicht*) **mögen** take an instant liking (dislike) to

anhimmeln *v/t.* (*trennb., hat -ge-*); *umg.*, *oft pej.* idolize; **er himmelte sie den ganzen Abend an** he just couldn't take his eyes off her all evening

Anhöhe *f* rise, elevation; (*Hügel*) (little) hill, hillock, mound

anhören I. *v/t.* **1.** (*sich* [*Dat.*]) **~** (*Musik etc.*) listen to, hear; **etw. mit ~** listen in on s.th.; **hör dir das mal an!** just listen to this!, *weitS.* just listen to him *etc.* talking; **das Gericht will noch e-n Gutachter ~** the court wants to consult an expert witness; **2. man hört ihm an, dass er erkältet ist** you can tell (by his voice) that he's got a cold; **II.** *v/refl.*: **sich gut** (**schlecht**) **~** sound good (bad)

Anhörung *f Parl.*, *Jur.* hearing; **Anhörungsverfahren** *n* hearing procedure

anhusten *v/t.* (*trennb., hat -ge-*): **j-n ~** cough at s.o., cough in(to) s.o.'s face

Anhydrid *n Chem.* anhydride

Anilin *n*; -s, *kein Pl.*; *Chem.* aniline, *seltener*: anilin

animalisch *Adj. auch fig.* animal ...; *fig. pej.* brutish

Animateur [anima'tøːɐ] *m*; -s, -e, **~in** *f*; -, -nen guest host, entertainment officer, GO (= Gentil Organisateur *od.* Gracious Organizer)

Animation *f*; -, -en **1.** (*Zeichentrick*) animation; (*Film*) (animated) cartoon(s); **2.** *im Urlaub*: organized entertainment (*od.* activities *etc.*); **Animator** *m*; *-s*, *-en*, **Animatorin** *f*; *-*, *-nen* animator

Animierdame *f* hostess *euph.*, *Am.* B-girl *umg.*; **animieren** *v/t.*: ~ (**zu**) encourage (to); *stärker*: urge (to); (*anregen*) stimulate (to); **sich animiert fühlen zu** (+ *Inf.*) feel prompted to do *s.th.*; **Animiermädchen** *n* → **Animierdame**

Animosität *f*; *-*, *-en* animosity (**gegen** towards)

Anion *n Phys.*, *Chem.* anion

Anis *m*; *-(es)*, *-e*; *Bot.* anise; (*Gewürz*) aniseed; **~likör** *m* anisette; **~plätzchen** *n* aniseed biscuits; **~schnaps** *m* aniseed brandy

ankämpfen *v/i.* (*trennb.*, *hat -ge-*): ~ **gegen** fight with; (*Wellen*, *Schicksal*) battle with; (*Wind*) struggle against; **gegen den Schlaf ~** fight (*od.* struggle) to keep awake

ankarren *v/t.* (*trennb.*, *hat -ge-*); *umg.* cart along

Ankauf *m* buying, purchase; (*Erwerb*) acquisition; **An- und Verkauf von Schild**: we buy and sell; **ankaufen** (*trennb.*, *hat -ge-*) **I.** *v/t.* buy, purchase; **II.** *v/refl.*: **sie hat sich in der Toskana angekauft** she has bought (herself) some land in Tuscany

ankeifen *v/t.* (*trennb.*, *hat -ge-*); *pej.* scream at

Anker *m*; *-s*, *-* **1.** a) *Naut.* anchor; ~ **werfen** *od.* **vor ~ gehen** drop anchor; **vor ~ liegen** ride at anchor, **den ~ lichten** weigh anchor, b) *umg. fig.*: **bei j-m vor ~ gehen** stop by at s.o.'s house *etc.*, drop in on s.o.; **2.** *Etech.* armature; (*Relais*) pallet; **3.** *Archit.* anchor; **~boje** *f* anchor buoy; **~kette** *f* (anchor) cable, chain cable, mooring chain; **~klüse** *f Naut.* hawsehole; (*Rohr*) hawsepipe

ankern *v/i.* (drop) anchor

Anker|platz *m* anchoring ground; **~spill** *n* capstan; **~winde** *f* windlass

anketten *v/t.* (*trennb.*, *hat -ge-*) chain (**an** + *Dat.* to); (*Hund etc.*) put on a (*od.* the) chain; → **angekettet** II

ankeuchen *v/i.* (*trennb.*, *ist -ge-*); *umg.*: **angekeucht kommen** come panting up (*od.* along)

ankläffen *v/t.* (*trennb.*, *hat -ge-*) bark at; *schrill*: yelp at

Anklage *f* **1.** *Jur.* charge (**gegen** against); *bes. Am.* indictment; *wegen Amtsvergehens*: *bes. Am.* impeachment (of); ~ **erheben** bring (*od.* prefer) a charge; **die ~ fallen lassen** quash (*od.* dismiss) the charge(s); **unter ~ stehen** be on (*od.* stand) trial (**wegen** for); **die ~ lautet auf** (+ *Akk.*) the charge is (as follows), you, they *etc.* are charged with; **2.** *Jur.* (*~vertretung*) the prosecution; **die ~ vertreten** be counsel for the prosecution; **3.** (*Vorwurf*) accusation (**gegen** against); **~bank** *f*: (**auf der ~** in the) dock; **~erhebung** *f* preferment (*od.* preferral) of a charge (*od.* charges)

anklagen *v/t.* (*trennb.*, *hat -ge-*) **1.** (*j-n*) *allg.* accuse (+*Gen. od. wegen* of); *Jur.* charge (with); *des Hochverrats etc.*: impeach; *vor s-m Schwurgericht*: indict; **2.** (*anprangern*) (*Misstände etc.*) protest; *stärker* cry out in protest (*od.* accusation); **anklagend I.** *Part. Präs.* → **anklagen**; **II.** *Adj.* (*Ton*) accusing; (*Blick*) reproachful; **III.** *Adv.*: **j-n ~ ansehen** look at s.o. reproachfully

Anklagepunkt *m Jur.* charge, count (of an indictment)

Ankläger *m*, **~in** *f* accuser; *Jur.* prosecutor; *Am. e-s Bundesgerichts*: D.A. (= district attorney); **öffentlicher ~** public prosecutor

Anklage|schrift *f Jur.* (bill of) indictment; **~vertreter** *m*, **~vertreterin** *f*, **~vertretung** *f* counsel for the prosecution

anklammern (*trennb.*, *hat -ge-*) **I.** *v/t.* fasten, cramp (**an** + *Dat. od. Akk.* to); *mit Büroklammer*: clip on(to); **II.** *v/refl.* **1.** cling (**an** + *Dat. od. Akk.* to); **2.** *fig.* cling (**an** + *Akk.* to)

Anklang *m* **1.** *mst Pl.*; (*Ähnlichkeit*) reminiscence, echo, suggestion (**an** + *Akk.* of); **2.** ~ **finden** strike a chord (**bei** with); *weitS.* go down well (with), get a good response; (*befürwortet werden*) meet with approval (from), find favo(u)r (with); (*sich verbreiten*) catch on (among)

anklatschen *v/t.* (*trennb.*, *hat -ge-*); *umg.* **1.** (*Farbe etc.*) slap on; **2.** (*Haare*) sleek down; *mit Haarcreme*: *auch* plaster down

ankleben (*trennb.*, *-ge-*) **I.** *v/t.* (*hat*) stick on(to **an** + *Akk. od. Dat.*); **II.** *v/i.* (*ist*) stick, cling (**an** + *Dat.* to)

Ankleidekabine *f* cubicle; *im Geschäft*: fitting room, changing-room; **ankleiden** *v/t. und v/refl.* (*trennb.*, *hat -ge-*) dress

Ankleide|puppe *f* **1.** dummy, mannequin; **2.** *für Kinder*: dress-up doll; **~zimmer** *n* changing room

anklicken *v/t.* (*trennb.*, *hat -ge-*); *EDV* (*Menüpunkt etc.*) click

anklingen *v/i.* (*unreg.*, *trennb.*, *hat -ge-*) **1.** be heard; **2.** *fig.*: ~ **an** (+ *Akk.*) (*erinnern an*) be reminiscent of; ~ **lassen** evoke, suggest; **in s-n Worten klang ein wenig Resignation an** there was a hint of resignation in what he said

anklopfen *v/i.* (*trennb.*, *hat -ge-*) **1.** knock (**an** + *Dat.* at, on); (*vorbeigehen*) **bei j-m** ~ drop in on s.o., call by at s.o.'s house; **2.** *fig.*: **bei j-m ~** approach s.o. (**wegen** about); (*bitten um*) touch (*od.* tap) s.o. for *umg.*

anknabbern *v/t.* (*trennb.*, *hat -ge-*) nibble at

anknipsen *v/t.* (*trennb.*, *hat -ge-*) switch on

anknoten *v/t.* (*trennb.*, *hat -ge-*) tie (*od.* fasten) on (*od.* to) (with a knot)

anknüpfen (*trennb.*, *hat -ge-*) **I.** *v/t.* **1.** tie, fasten (**an** + *Akk.* to); **2.** *fig.* start; **ein Gespräch ~** *auch* strike up a conversation (**mit** with); **Beziehungen** ~ establish contacts; **II.** *v/i.*; *fig.*: ~ **an** (+ *Akk.*) go on from, pick up the thread of; *j-s Worte etc.*: go back to; *e-e Tradition*: continue; **Anknüpfungspunkt** *m* **1.** point of contact; **2.** (*Ausgangspunkt*) starting point

anknurren *v/t.* (*trennb.*, *hat -ge-*) **1.** *Hund*: growl at; **2.** *umg. Person*: growl (*od.* snarl) at

ankohlen (*trennb.*, *hat -ge-*) **I.** *v/t.* *umg.*: **j-n ~** pull s.o.'s leg, yank s.o.'s chain, have s.o. on; **II.** *v/i.* char; **ein angekohlter Balken** a charred log (*od.* beam)

ankommen (*unreg.*, *trennb.*, *ist -ge-*) **I.** *v/i.* **1.** arrive (**in** + *Dat.* at, in); ~ **in** (+ *Dat.*) *auch* reach, get (to); **gut ~** *Person*: arrive safely; *Paket*: get there all right (*Am. umg.* alright); **am Ende/ Ziel ~** get to the end/destination; **zu Hause ~** arrive (*od.* get) home; **der Zug soll um zehn Uhr ~** the train is

due (to arrive) at ten o'clock; **2.** *umg.* come (along *od.* up), turn up, intrude, *Am.* butt in; **da kommt sie schon 'wieder an!** here she comes again! *allg.*; **dauernd kommt er mit s-n Fragen an** *umg. fig.* he keeps coming (*od.* intruding) with all these questions *allg.*; **3.** *umg.* (*angestellt werden*) get a job (**bei** with); **4.** *umg.* (*Anklang finden*) go down well (**bei** with); **nicht ~** be a flop, go down badly; **damit kommt er bei mir nicht an** that cuts no ice with me; → **Publikum** 2; **5.** ~ **gegen** be able to cope with, (*j-n*) get the better of; **gegen sie kommt er nicht an** he's no match for her, he can't compete with her, he hasn't got a chance with her; **6.** *unpers.*; (*abhängen von*): **es kommt** (**ganz**) **darauf an** it (all) depends (on) (**ob** whether); **darauf soll es** (**mir**) **nicht ~** that's not the problem, that doesn't matter to me; **das käme auf e-n Versuch an** we'd have to give it a try; **7.** *unpers.*; (*wichtig sein*): **worauf es ankommt, ist ...** the important thing is ...; **es kommt** (**ihm**) **nicht auf den Preis an** it doesn't matter how much it costs (money is no object for him); **wenn es darauf ankommt**, ist er immer da: when it comes to the crunch, when it really matters, when the going gets tough; **jetzt kommt es auf jede Sekunde an** every second counts (now); **darauf kommt es jetzt auch nicht mehr an** that doesn't matter any more now, that won't make any difference now; **8.** *unpers.*; (*riskieren*): **es auf etw. lassen** (be prepared to) risk s.th.; **ich lasse es darauf ~** I'll wait and see what happens; **II.** *vt/i.*: **sich zu entschuldigen kam sie hart an** she found it hard (*od.* it was hard on her) to apologize; **III.**; *v/t. geh.* befall, come over *s.o.*; **es kam ihn die Lust an zu** (+ *Inf.*) he suddenly had the urge to (+ *Inf.*)

Ankömmling *m*; *-s*, *-e* newcomer; (*Kind*) new arrival *umg.*

ankoppeln (*trennb.*, *hat -ge-*) **I.** *v/t.* (**an** + *Akk.*) **1.** (*Waggon etc.*) couple up (to); *Raumf.* dock (with); **2.** *fig.* add (on), join, hook up (to); **II.** *v/i.* *Raumf.* dock (with); **Ankopp(e)lung** *f* connection (**an** + *Akk.* to), linking up (to, with); *Raumf.* docking (with); **Ankopp(e)lungsmanöver** *n Raumf.* docking man|oeuvre (*Am.* -euver)

ankotzen *v/t.* (*trennb.*, *hat -ge-*); *vulg. fig.* make *s.o.* sick; *Person*: *auch Sl.* make *s.o.* (want to) puke

ankrallen *v/refl.* (*trennb.*, *hat -ge-*): **sich ~ an** (+ *Dat.*) clutch at, cling to; *Tier*: dig its claws into

ankreiden *v/t.* (*trennb.*, *hat -ge-*): **j-m etw. ~** fault s.o. with s.th.; (*übel nehmen*) hold s.th. against s.o.; **j-m angekreidet werden** count against s.o.

ankreuzen *v/t.* (*trennb.*, *hat -ge-*) put a cross next to, mark with a cross; (*Kästchen*) put a tick in, tick off

ankriechen *v/i.* (*unreg.*, *trennb.*, *ist -ge-*): **angekrochen kommen** *umg.* come creeping (*od.* crawling) up (*od.* along)

ankriegen *v/t.* (*trennb.*, *hat -ge-*); *umg.* → **anbekommen**

ankündigen (*trennb.*, *hat -ge-*) **I.** *v/t.* **1.** *allg.*: announce (+ *Dat.* to); give *s.o.* notice of *geh.*; *öffentlich*: proclaim; (*einleiten*) herald; (*Veranstaltung*) advertise, publicize; *in der Zeitung*: announce, advertise, publish.; → **ange-**

kündigt II; **2.** *fig.*: *etw. kündigt etw. an indirekt*: s.th. is a sign that s.th. is on its way; *direkt*: s.th. heralds (*od.* presages) s.th., s.th. heralds (*od.* ushers) s.th. in *lit.*; **II.** *v/refl.* tell s.o. that one is coming; *bes. iro.* announce one's arrival; *fig. Sturm, Frühling etc.*: be on its way; *bei mir kündigt sich e-e Grippe an* I think I'm due (*od.* in) for a bout of flu, I think I'm coming down with flu; **Ankündigung** *f* announcement, notification; *feierliche*: proclamation; (*e-s Buches*) prospectus; *Änderung ohne vorherige / nach vorheriger ~* alteration with/without prior (*od.* previous) notice

Ankunft *f*; -, *Ankünfte*, *mst Sg.* arrival; *fig. auch* advent; *bei ~, nach ~* on arrival

Ankunfts|halle *f* arrival lounge; **~tafel** *f* arrivals board, arrival timetable (*Am.* schedule); **~zeit** *f* arrival time, time of arrival

ankuppeln *v/t.* (*trennb., hat -ge-*) connect, couple (*an + Akk.* to); → *auch* **ankoppeln** I 1, II

ankurbeln *v/t.* (*trennb., hat -ge-*) **1.** *Mot.* start, crank; **2.** *fig.* stimulate; (*Wirtschaft*) *auch* boost; (*Produktion*) step up, boost; **Ankurbelung** *f fig.* boost, stimulation

ankuscheln *v/refl.* (*trennb., hat -ge-*): *sich an j-n ~* snuggle up to s.o.

anlächeln *v/t.* (*trennb., hat -ge-*) **1.** smile at, give s.o. a smile; *einladend*: give s.o. a come hither look; **2.** *fig. Glück etc.*: smile (up)on

anlabern *v/t.* (*trennb., hat -ge-*) *umg.* **1.** (*anmachen*) chat s.o. up; **2.** (*dumm anreden*) j-n sidle up to s.o. and make a stupid remark

anlachen *v/t.* (*trennb., hat -ge-*) **1.** laugh at; **2.** *fig. Sonne etc.*: smile (up)on; *das Stück Kuchen da lacht mich an* that piece of cake looks very tempting (*od.* is just asking to be eaten); **3.** *umg. fig.*: *sich* (*Dat.*) *j-n ~* pick s.o. up

Anlage *f* **1.** *nur Sg.*; (*Anlegen*) *e-s Parks etc.*: laying out; *e-r Kartei etc.*: design; (*Bau*) construction; **2.** *nur Sg.*; (*Art der ~*) arrangement, layout; **3.** (*Entwurf*) design; *e-s Romans etc.*: structure; **4.** (*Gelände*) (*Fabrik*) plant; (*Garten*) gardens *Pl.*, grounds *Pl.*, lawn and flowerbeds *Pl.*; (*Grünanlage*) park; (*Sportanlage*) sports complex ; (*im Freien*) sports (*od.* playing) field(s); (*Freizeitanlage*) recreation area (*od.* park); *militärische ~* military installations *Pl.*; *öffentliche ~* public gardens *Pl.*; **5.** (*Vor-, Einrichtung*) installation; (*Alarmanlage, EDV-Anlage etc.*) system; *umg.* (*Stereoanlage*) stereo, hi-fi; *sanitäre ~n* sanitary facilities *förm.*, bathroom fixtures (and fittings); **6.** *~* (*zu*) (*Fähigkeit*) talent, aptitude, gift (for); (*Veranlagung*) (natural) tendency (to + *Inf.*), bent (for); *auch Med.* (pre)disposition (to[wards]); *die ~ zum Musiker etc. haben auch* have the makings of a musician etc.; **7.** *Wirts.* (*das Anlegen*) investment; (*das Angelegte*) invested capital; *feste ~* fixed investment; **8.** (*Beilage*) enclosure; *in der* (*od.* *als*) *~ senden wir Ihnen* enclosed please find, enclosed you will find, we enclose

Anlage... *im Subst. Wirts.* investment ...

anlagebedingt *Adj. Gnt.* constitutional; (*angeboren*) congenital, hereditary; *die Allergien sind bei ihm ~* he has a

natural tendency towards allergies

Anlage|berater *m*, **~beraterin** *f Wirts.* investment consultant; **~betrag** *m* amount to be invested; **~dauer** *f* investment period; **~kapital** *n* invested capital; (*Fonds*) capital assets *Pl.*; **~papier** *n* (investment) security; → *festverzinslich*; **~vermögen** *n* **1.** fixed assets *Pl.*; **2.** invested capital

anlagern *v/refl.* (*trennb., hat -ge-*); *Med., Chem.* be taken up (*an + Akk.* by)

anlanden (*trennb., -ge-*) **I.** *v/t.* (*hat*); (*Fische, Fracht, Truppen*) land; (*Passagiere*) disembark; **II.** *v/i.* (*hat/ist*); *Geol. Insel etc.*: (*sich vebreitern*) accrete; **Anlandung** *f Geol. von Sand etc.*: alluvial deposit, alluviation; alluvium; (*Verbreiterung*) lateral spread

anlangen (*trennb., -ge-*) **I.** *v/i.* (*ist*); *mst angelangt sein* have arrived (*an, bei, in + Dat.* at, in); (*erreichen*) *auch* have reached; **II.** *v/t.* (*hat*) **1.** concern; *was ... anlangt* as for, as far as ... is (*od.* are) concerned; **2.** *bes. südd. umg.* (*anfassen*) touch

Anlass *m*; -es, *Anlässe* **1.** (*Gelegenheit, Ereignis*) occasion; (*Vorkommnis*) incident; *ein besonderer ~* a special occasion; *festlicher ~* festive occasion, special celebration; *dem ~ entsprechend* to suit (*od.* fit) the occasion; *aus ~* (+ *Gen.*) on the occasion of; **2.** (*Grund, Ursache*) motive, reason, cause, grounds *Pl.* (*für od. zu* for; *zu + Inf.* for + *Ger.*); *der äußere ~* the apparent (*od.* supposed) reason; *aus diesem ~* for this reason, on these grounds; *aus gegebenem ~* because of the circumstances, for the reason given; (*den*) *~ geben zu* give rise (*od.* occasion) to; *ohne jeden ~* for no reason at all; *allen ~ haben zu* (+ *Inf.*) / *zu etw.* have every reason to (+ *Inf.*) / for s.th; *etw. zum ~ nehmen zu* (+ *Inf.*) use s.th. as an opportunity (*pej.* excuse) to (+ *Inf.*); *er beschwert sich beim geringsten ~* he complains about every little thing

anlassen (*unreg., trennb., hat -ge-*) **I.** *v/t.* **1.** (*Mantel*) keep on; **2.** (*nicht ausmachen*) leave on; (*Motor*) leave running; **3.** (*starten*) (*Motor*) start (up); (*Maschine*) put in(to) operation; **II.** *v/refl.* start; *die Sache lässt sich gut an* it's a good start, things look promising; *die Woche lässt sich gut an* it's a good start to the week, the week has got(ten) off to a good start; *wie lässt er sich an?* how's he making out?; *er lässt sich gut an* he's doing quite nicely

Anlasser *m*; -s, -; *Mot.* starter

anlässlich *Präp.* on the occasion of; *~ ihres 50. Geburtstags auch* to celebrate her 50th birthday

anlasten *v/t.* (*trennb., hat -ge-*): *j-m etw. ~* blame s.o. for s.th., put the blame on s.o. for s.th.

anlatschen *v/i.* (*trennb., ist -ge-*); *umg.*: *angelatscht kommen* come slouching (*od.* skulking) up (*od.* along) *allg.*

Anlauf *m* **1.** *Sport*: approach; approach path; *Skisprung*: approach; slope; *e-n ~ nehmen* take a run-up; *ein Sprung mit/ohne ~* a jump with/without a run-up, a running/standing jump; **2.** *fig.* attempt; *im ersten ~* on the first go (*od.* attempt); *im zweiten ~* the second time round; *e-n neuen ~ machen* try again, have another go (*Am.* try); **3.** *Tech.* start; **~adresse** *f* → *Anlaufstelle*

anlaufen (*unreg., trennb., -ge-*) **I.** *v/i.* (*ist*) **1.** *angelaufen kommen* come running along; **2.** *Sport*: run up (for the jump); **3.** *~ gegen* → *anrennen* 1; **4.** (*Motor, Maschine*) start (up) (*auch ~ lassen*); **5.** *fig.* (*beginnen*) start, get under way, get going; *der Film läuft nächste Woche an* the film (*bes. Am.* movie) will be (showing) in cinemas (*Am.* theaters) next week, the film opens next week; **6.** (*beschlagen*) steam up; (*sich verfärben*) (*Silber etc.*) tarnish; **7.** *blau/rot ~* go blue/red (in the face); **8.** *Zinsen, Kosten*: accumulate; **II.** *v/t.* (*hat*) (*Hafen*) call at

Anlauf|kosten *Pl. Wirts.* initial (*od.* startup) cost *Sg.*; **~phase** *f* initial phase; **~stelle** *f* place to go; drop-in cent|re (*Am.* -er); (*kriminelle Kontaktadresse*) contact address; **~zeit** *f* **1.** *Tech.* starting-up time; **2.** *fig.* warm-up period; *für Person*: *auch* period of adjustment; *e-e ~ von 6 Wochen brauchen Projekt etc.*: need 6 weeks to get started (*od.* to take off); *Person*: need 6 weeks to get going (*od.* to get into it)

Anlaut *m Ling.* initial sound, anlaut; *im ~* initial ..., in initial position; **anlauten** *v/i.* (*trennb., hat -ge-*) begin (*mit* with)

anläuten *vt/i.* (*trennb., hat -ge-*); *südd., österr., schw.* → *anrufen* I

anlautend *Adj. Ling.* initial

Anlegebrücke *f Naut.* landing stage, jetty; (*Hafendamm*) pier

anlegen (*trennb., hat -ge-*) **I.** *v/t.* **1.** (*Lineal*) set, position; (*die Arme*) put by one's sides; (*die Ohren*) put (*od.* lay) back; (*Säugling*) put to the breast; (*Holz, Kohle*) put (*od.* lay) on; → *auch* II, III 1; **2.** *~ an* (+ *Akk.od. Dat.*) put against, (*Leiter*) lean against; **3.** (*anbringen*) *j-m/e-m Tier* (*Halfter, Halsband, Handschellen*) apply (to), put on; *e-n Verband ~ auch* bandage s.o. up; *j-m Fesseln ~ auch* put s.o. in chains; **4.** *geh.* (*Kleid, Schmuck etc.*) put on; *förm.* don; **5.** (*entwerfen*) design; (*Garten, Straße etc.*) lay out; (*Roman etc.*) structure; (*Kanal*) cut, dig; (*errichten*) (*Lager*) pitch, make; *eine breit angelegte Kampagne* a broad (*od.* widely-pitched) campaign,; **6.** (*beginnen*) (*Akte, Sammlung etc.*) start; (*Kartei*) set up; (*Konto*) open; (*Vorrat*) get in; **7.** (*Geld*) invest (*in + Dat.* in), sink into *umg.*; *mit Zinsen ~* put out at interest; (*ausgeben*) spend (*für* on); → *angelegt* II; **8.** *Etech.* (*Spannung*) feed; **9.** *unpers.*: *es ~ auf* (+ *Akk.*) be out for (*od.* to + *Inf.*); **II.** *vt/i.*: (*das Gewehr*) *~* aim, take aim, point at; (*Karte, Dominostein*) lay (*od.* put) down; **III.** *v/i.* **1.** *~ auf* (+ *Akk.*) *Schütze*: (take) aim at; **2.** *Naut.* land, put in, moor, (take) berth; *längsseits*: lie alongside; *in e-m Hafen ~* call (*od.* dock) at; **IV.** *v/refl.* start a fight (*od.* an argument) (*mit* with); → *Hand*[1] 1, *Maßstab* 1

Anleger *m*; -s, -, **~in** *f*; -, -nen; *Wirts.* investor

Anlege|steg *m für Boot*: jetty; **~stelle** *f Naut.* landing place, moorings *Pl.*; → *Anlegebrücke*

anlehnen (*trennb., hat -ge-*) **I.** *v/t.* **1.** (*Tür*) lean *the door* to; leave *the door* open a crack *od.* an inch; *angelehnt* ajar (*präd.*); **2.** (*Fahrrad, Leiter*) *~ an* (+ *Akk.*) lean against; **II.** *v/refl.* **1.** *sich ~* (*an + Akk.*) lean on; *mit* *dem Kopf*: rest one's head on; **2.** *fig.* **sich (stark) ~ an** (+ *Akk.*) follow (closely); (*Autor etc.*) *auch* lean (heavily) on; **Anlehnung** *f Pol.* dependence (*an* + *Akk.* on); **in ~ an** following (the example of); *Kunst etc.*: in the style of; **Anlehnungsbedürfnis** *n*; *nur Sg.* need for love and affection (*od.* support); **anlehnungsbedürftig** *Adj.*: ~ **sein** need to feel protected, need a lot of support and affection

anleiern *v/t.* (*trennb., hat -ge-*); *umg.* get *s.o. od. s.th.* going, make a start on *s.th. allg.*

Anleihe *f*; *-, -n*; *Wirts.* loan, credit; (*Staatsanleihe*) *auch* bond; (*Schuldverschreibung*) debenture (bond); **e-e ~ aufnehmen /zeichnen** take out / subscribe to a loan; **e-e ~ bei j-m machen** borrow money from s.o.; *fig., oft pej.* plagiarize; **~kapital** *n* loan capital; **~papier** *n* bond; **~schuld** *f* bonded debt

anleimen *v/t.* (*trennb., hat -ge-*) glue on; **~ an** (+ *Akk. od. Dat.*) glue (on)to

anleinen *v/t.* (*trennb., hat -ge-*); (*Hund*) put on a lead (*od.* leash); → **angeleint**

anleiten *v/t.* (*trennb., hat -ge-*) guide; **Anleitung** *f* **1.** *nur Sg.* direction, guidance; **2.** (*Betriebs-, Gebrauchsanleitung*) instructions (for use) *Pl.*, directions *Pl.*; *als Buch*: manual

Anlernberuf *m* semi(-)skilled job; **anlernen** *v/t.* (*trennb., hat -ge-*) train, show *s.o.* the ropes; → **angelernt** II; **Anlernling** *m*; *-s, -e* trainee

anlesen *v/t.* (*unreg., trennb., hat -ge-*) **1.** (*Buch*) dip into; **2.** **sich** (*Dat.*) **etw. ~** get s.th. out of a book (*od.* magazine *etc.*), *gezielt*: read up on s.th.; → **angelesen** II

anleuchten *v/t.* (*trennb., hat -ge-*): **j-n/etw. anleuchten** shine a light on (*od.* at) s.o./s.th.

anliefern *v/t.* (*trennb., hat -ge-*) deliver; **Anlieferung** *f* delivery

anliegen (*unreg., trennb., hat / südd., österr., schw. ist -ge-*) *v/i.* **1.** *Kleidung*: fit, sit; **eng ~** fit tightly (*od.* snugly); **2.** *umg.*: **was liegt heute an?** what's on the agenda today?, what's got to be done today?; **3.** *Ohren*: lie flat; → **angelegen** II

Anliegen *n*; *-s, -*; (*Wunsch*) request; *weitS.* concern, preoccupation; (*Sache*) matter; **ein ~ vorbringen** put forward (*od.* make) a request; **ich habe ein ~ an Sie** I want to ask you a favo(u)r; **anliegend I.** *Part. Präs.* → **anliegen**; **II.** *Adj.* **1.** *Kleidung*: (*eng ~*) close-fitting, snug; *Kleid* figure-hugging; **2.** → **angrenzend** II; **3.** *auch Adv.* (*beiliegend*) enclosed, attached

Anlieger *m*; *-s, -*, **~in** *f*; *-, -nen* resident; **~ frei** (access to) residents only; **~staat** *m* neighbo(u)ring (*od.* bordering) state, littoral state; *an e-m Gewässer*: riparian state *förm.*; *im Pazifik*: (Pacific) rim nation (*od.* country)

anlocken *v/t.* (*trennb., hat -ge-*); (*Tiere*) lure; *durch Köder*: bait; *durch Rufe*: call; (*Menschen*) attract; *stärker*: lure, entice, (*Vögel*) decoy

anlöten *v/t.* (*trennb., hat -ge-*) solder on(to **an** + *Akk. od. Dat.*)

anlügen *v/t.* (*unreg., trennb., hat -ge-*) lie to (*s.o.'s face*)

Anm. *Abk.* → **Anmerkung**

Anmache *f*; *-, -n*; *umg. pej.* → **Anmachtour**

anmachen *v/t.* (*trennb., hat -ge-*) **1.** (*einschalten*) switch on, turn on; **2.** (*anzünden*) light; (*Feuer*) *auch*

make; (*Streichholz*) *auch* strike; **3.** (*befestigen*) attach; *mit Nadel etc.*: fasten, sew on (**an** + *Dat.* to); **4.** (*mischen*) prepare; (*Salat*) dress, toss; (*Mörtel*) temper, mix; **5.** *umg.* a) **j-n ~** (*j-m gefallen*) *auch sexuell*: turn s.o. on; **diese Musik macht mich nicht an** this music doesn't do anything (*od.* it) for me, b) *oft pej.* (*Kontakt suchen*) chat s.o. up *allg.*, (*try to*) get off with s.o. *Sl.*, c) *pej.* (*Streit suchen*) hassle; *stärker*: provoke; **mach mich nicht an!** leave me alone (*od.* in peace)!, stop pestering me!

Anmachtour *f umg. pej.*: **ich mag diese ~ nicht** I don't like the way he sets to work on women

anmahnen *v/t.* (*trennb., hat -ge-*): **etw.** (**bei j-m**) **~** *Wirts.* ask (s.o.) for payment (*od.* delivery *etc.*) of s.th.; *fig.* remind (*od.* warn) s.o. about s.th.

anmalen (*trennb., hat -ge-*) **I.** *v/t.* (*anstreichen*) paint; (*bekritzeln*) draw, scribble; *an die Tafel*: paint s.th. on the board; *im Malbuch*: colo(u)r in; **sich** (*Dat.*) **die Lippen ~** paint one's lips *altm.*, put on (*od.* apply) lipstick; **II.** *v/refl. umg., oft pej.* (*sich schminken*) put one's face (*od.* war paint) on

Anmarsch *m* **1.** *der Truppen*: approach, advance; **der Feind befindet sich im ~** the enemy is advancing (**auf** + *Akk.* towards); **2.** *fig.*: **im ~ sein** *Person, Gewitter, Grippe etc.*: be on the way; **3.** *umg.* (*Weg*) march; **anmarschieren** *v/i.* (*trennb., ist*) march up; **anmarschiert kommen** *umg.* come marching up (*od.* along); **Anmarschweg** *m* approach (route); *umg. zur Arbeit*: way

anmaßen *v/t.* (*trennb., hat -ge-*): **sich** (*Dat.*) **Rechte etc. ~** claim; **sich** (*Dat.*) **~ zu** (+ *Inf.*) take it upon o.s. to (+ *Inf.*); **ich maße mir kein Urteil darüber an** who am I to judge?, far be it from me to pass judg(e)ment on it *geh.*; **was maßt du dir eigentlich an!** what gives you the right?, who do you think you are?; **anmaßend I.** *Part. Präs.* → **anmaßen**; **II.** *Adj.* arrogant, presumptuous; (*herrisch*) overbearing; **Anmaßung** *f* **1.** (*Überheblichkeit*) arrogance, impudence; presumption; *plus* **~!** what a cheek!, *Am.* what nerve!; **2.** (*Amtsanmaßung*) assumption, arrogation; *widerrechtliche*: usurpation

Anmelde|bescheinigung *f* confirmation (*od.* acknowledgement) of registration; **~formular** *n* registration (*od.* entry) form; (*Antrag*) application form; **~frist** *f* registration period; **~gebühr** *f* registration fee

anmelden (*trennb., hat -ge-*) **I.** *v/t.* **1.** *j-n* put *s.o.'s* name on the list, sign *s.o.* up; *als Mitglied*: join (up), subscribe; *als Teilnehmer, Schüler*: enrol(l) (*zu* for); *Sport*: enter *s.o.'s* name (for); *im Hotel*: book in, *Am.* register; *bei der Gemeinde*: register; *beim Arzt etc.*: make an appointment (**bei** with); **2.** (*ankündigen*) (*Gäste*) announce; *bei j-m*: let *s.o.* know *s.o.* has arrived; **s-n Besuch ~** announce one's arrival; **sich ~ lassen** (*als Besucher*) have o.s. announced, send in one's card *förm.*; **3.** (*Auto, Radio, Fernseher*) get a licen|ce (*Am. -se*); (*Telefon*) get a (line) connected; (*Patent*) apply for, take out; (*Gewerbe, Wohnsitz*) register; (*Waren*) *beim Zoll*, (*Vermögen*): declare; **ein Ferngespräch ~** *Brit.* make a trunk call *altm.*, *Am.* make an operator-assisted call; **Konkurs ~** declare

o.s. bankrupt; **4.** *fig.* (*Einwand, Zweifel*) raise; (*Wunsch*) make ; *Ansprüche*: assert, put forward; **II.** *v/refl.* **1.** *Person*: → I 1; *Baby*: be on the way; **2.** *fig.* announce itself

Anmeldepflicht *f* compulsory registration; **anmeldepflichtig** *Adj.* subject to registration; *Med.* notifiable

Anmelde|schluss *m* deadline (*od.* closing date) for registration(s); **~termin** *m* deadline for registration(s); **~verfahren** *n* registration procedure

Anmeldung *f* **1.** *behördlich*: registration; (*Ankündigung*) announcement; (*Reservierung*) booking; (*Einschreibung*) enrol(l)ment; (*Eintritt*) entry; *Zoll*: declaration; **nach vorheriger ~** *Sprechstunde*: by appointment (only); → **anmelden**; **2.** (*Empfangsbüro, -stelle*) reception (desk), registration

anmerken *v/t.* (*trennb., hat -ge-*) **1.** (*anstreichen*) mark; (*notieren*) make a note of; **als Fußnote ~** make an annotation (*od.* footnote); **2.** **j-m etwas ~** notice (*od.* observe *od.* perceive) s.th. in s.o.; **j-m s-n Ärger etc. ~** be able to tell that s.o. is annoyed *etc.* (**an** + *Dat.* by); **sich** (*Dat.*) **nichts ~ lassen** not show (*od.* betray) a thing (*od.* one's feelings), not give o.s. away; **man merkt ihm sofort an, dass ...** you just have to look at him to see that ..., it's written all over his face that ...; **lass dir nichts ~!** don't let on!; **3.** *geh.* (*sagen*) remark

Anmerkung *f* remark (**zu** *od.* **über** + *Akk.* on); *kritische*: comment (on), remark (on); *schriftliche*: note (on); *erklärende*: (foot)note, annotation (on); **~ der Redaktion** (*abgek.* Anm. d. Red.) editor's comment (*od.* postscript) (*Abk.* ed.); **etw. mit ~en versehen** annotate s.th.

anmieten *v/t.* (*trennb., hat -ge-*) rent; *Brit.* (*Auto*) hire; **Anmietung** *f* rental, *Brit. auch* hire

anmontieren *v/t.* (*trennb., hat*) fix (*od.* put) on, attach to (**an** + *Dat. od. Akk.* to), fit, mount (**an** + *Dat. od. Akk.* in, onto)

anmosern *v/t.* (*trennb., hat -ge-*); *umg.* have a (real) go at, tear into

anmotzen *v/t.* (*trennb., hat -ge-*); *umg.* have a (real) go at, tear into, yell at *allg.*

anmustern *v/t. und v/i.* (*trennb., hat -ge-*); *Mil.* sign on (*Am.* up)

Anmut *f*, *-, kein Pl.* grace(fulness), elegance; (*Liebreiz*) charm, loveliness, sweetness; **sich voll ~ bewegen** move gracefully

anmuten (*trennb., hat -ge-*) **I.** *v/t.*: **j-n seltsam etc. ~** strike s.o. as strange *etc.*; **II.** *v/i.*: **wie ein Traum ~** seem like a dream

anmutig I. *Adj.* charming, elegant; *Gegend*: pleasant; **II.** *Adv.*: **sich ~ bewegen** move gracefully

annageln *v/t.* (*trennb., hat -ge-*) nail on(to **an** + *Dat.*)

annagen *v/t.* (*trennb., hat -ge-*) gnaw at

annähen *v/t.* (*trennb., hat -ge-*) sew on(to **an** + *Dat.*)

annähern (*trennb., hat -ge-*) **I.** *v/t. an die Wirklichkeit*: approximate (**an** + *Akk.* to); (*Standpunkte*) *einander*: reconcile; **II.** *v/refl.* **1.** approach (+ *Dat. s.th.*) (*auch fig. ähnlich sein*); **2.** *fig.*: **sich j-m ~** make contact with s.o.; *stärker*: get friendly with s.o.

annähernd I. *Part. Präs.* → **annähern**, **II.** *Adj.* approximate, rough; **III.** *Adv.* roughly; **nicht ~** not nearly, nowhere near; ~ *gleich auch Math.* approximately equal to; ~ *zwei Stunden dauern* last almost (*od.* coming up for *umg.*) two hours; **Annäherung** *f* approach; *von Ansichten:* reconciliation; *Pol.* rapprochement

Annäherungs|politik *f* policy of rapprochement; **~versuch** *m* **1.** advances *Pl.*, pass *umg.*; *e-n ~ bei j-m machen* make a pass at s.o. *allg.*; **2.** *Pol.* attempt at rapprochement, overtures *Pl.*

annäherungsweise *Adv.* approximately

Annahme *f*; -, *-n* **1.** (*Ggs. Ablehnung*) acceptance (*auch fig.*); *e-s Antrags:* adoption; *e-s Gesetzes:* passing (*Am. auch* passage) ; *von Schülern:* employment; *von Schülern:* admission; *die ~* (+ *Gen.*) *verweigern* refuse to accept; *Post.* ~ *verweigert!* refused; **2.** (*Vermutung*) assumption, supposition; *fachspr.* hypothesis; *in der ~, dass ...* on the assumption that ..., assuming that ...; *ich war der ~, dass ...* I was under the impression that ..., I had assumed that ...; *wir haben Grund zur ~, dass ...* we have reason to assume that ...; *gehe ich recht in der ~, dass ...?* am I right to assume (*od.* in assuming) that ...?; **3.** *nur Sg.*; (*das Annehmen*) *e-s Glaubens, Kindes, Namens:* adoption; *e-r Gewohnheit:* taking up, adoption; *e-r Form, Gestalt:* taking on, assumption

Annahme|bestätigung *f* acknowledg(e)ment of receipt; **~frist** *f* period of acceptance; *die ~ ist abgelaufen* the deadline is past, applications *etc.* can no longer be accepted; **~schluss** *m* deadline, closing date; **~stelle** *f* counter; *für Lotto etc.:* agency; *Mil.* recruiting office; **~vermerk** *f Fin.* (*Akzept*) acceptance;: **~verweigerung** *f* non-acceptance, refusal of delivery

Annalen *Pl.* annals; *in die ~ eingehen* go down in history

annehmbar I. *Adj.* acceptable (*für* to); *Preis, Bedingung:* auch reasonable, fair; *umg.* (*leidlich*) passable, tolerable *allg.*; **II.** *Adv.: das schmeckt ganz ~* that doesn't taste (half) bad *umg.*

annehmen (*unreg., trennb., hat -ge-*) **I.** *vt/i.* **1.** (*Ggs. ablehnen*) (*Einladung, Entschuldigung, Geschenk, Hilfe, Vorschlag, Wahl*) accept; (*Arbeit, Auftrag, Wette*) *auch* take on; (*Angebot, Herausforderung*) *auch* take up; *Parl.* (*Antrag*) carry, adopt; (*Gesetzesvorschlag*) pass; (*j-s Rat*) take s.o.'s advice, agree; *Wirts.* (*e-n Wechsel*) ~ / *nicht ~* hono(u)r (*od.* accept) / dishonono(u)r (a draft), accept / not accept; *dankend ~* accept with thanks; *einstimmig ~* accept unanimously; **2.** (*vermuten*) assume, suppose, *bes. Am.* guess; (*glauben*) presume, believe; (*erwarten*) suppose, expect; (*voraussetzen*) assume; *nehmen wir (einmal) an od. angenommen* (let's) suppose, supposing, (let's) say *umg.*; *das ist kaum anzunehmen* that cannot be assumed (*od.* taken for granted); *es ist anzunehmen, dass ...* it can be taken as read that ..., we *etc.* assume that; *das kannst du aber ~!* you can count (*od.* bet) on it!; **II.** *v/t.* **1.** (*entgegennehmen*) (*Bestellung*) take; (*Lieferung*) take; *Sport:* (*Ball*) take; (*Telefongespräch*) take; **2.** (*Bewerber*) take on, accept; (*Schüler*) *auch:* admit; (*Mitarbeiter*) *auch:* hire, employ; (*Besucher*) receive; *wir nehmen keine neuen Patienten mehr an* we are not accepting

(*od.* taking on) any more (*od.* new) patients; **3.** (*Gewohnheit*) take up, *schlechte:* fall into; (*Brauch*) adopt; (*Namen, Titel*) *auch* assume; *Haltung ~ Mil.* stand at (*od.* come to) attention; *Form(en) od. Gestalt ~ Plan etc.:* take shape; **4.** (*adoptieren*) adopt; *an Kindes statt ~* adopt (as one's own); **5.** (*Farbe, Geruch*) take on; *Stoff:* take; *du hast im Urlaub ja richtig Farbe angenommen* you've really caught the sun on holiday (*Am.* vacation); **III.** *v/refl.: sich ~ e-r Sache ~* take care of s.th., see about s.th., attend to the matter; *sich j-s Sache ~* take up the cause of; *sich j-s ~* take care of s.o., take s.o. under one's wing, look after s.o.

Annehmlichkeiten *Pl.* comforts, amenities

annektieren *v/t.* (*trennb., hat*) *Pol.* annex; **Annektierung** *f* annexation

Annex *m*; -*s*, -*e* **1.** *Jur.* annex, appendix; **2.** *Archit.* annex(e)

Annexion *f*; -, -*en*; *Pol.* annexation

anno *Adv.* in the year (of); ~ (*in älteren Dokumenten:* **Anno**) **Domini** (*abgek. a./A. D.*) *förm.* in the year of our Lord; ~ *dazumal umg.* in the olden days (*od.* times) *lit*; *von ~ dazumal umg.* of yore *lit.*; ~ *Tobak umg. hum.* donkey's years ago, yonks ago, *Am.* ages ago

Annonce [a'nõːsə] *f*; -, -*n* advertisement, *Brit. auch* advert; ad *umg.*; → *Anzeige* 2; **annoncieren** [anõ'siːrən] **I.** *v/t.* advertise; **II.** *v/i.* place an ad (*od.* advertisement) in a newspaper; **Annoncenteil** *m* *e-r Zeitung:* advertisements, classified advertisements, classified section

annullieren *v/t.* annul, *Jur. auch* declare null and void; (*Auftrag*) cancel; (*Tor*) disallow; **Annullierung** *f* annulment; cancellation

Anode *f*; -, -*n*; *Phys.* anode, positive pole

anöden *v/t.* (*trennb., hat -ge-*); *umg.* bore to tears; *sich gegenseitig ~* be sick to death of each other, be sick to the back teeth of each other

Anoden|spannung *f* anode (*od.* plate) voltage, anode potential; **~strahlen** *Pl.* anode rays *Pl.*; **~strom** *m* anode (*od.* plate) current

anodisch *Adj. Phys.* anodal, anodic, positive

anomal *Adj.* (*regelwidrig*) abnormal, anomalous, unusual; (*unregelmäßig, nicht normal*) odd, strange; **Anomalie** *f*; -, -*n*; *Bio., Phys. etc.* anomaly, *Med. auch* abnormality

anonym *Adj.* anonymous; → *Alkoholiker*; **anonymisieren** *v/t.* (*Daten*) make anonymous, anonymize; **Anonymität** *f*; -, *kein Pl.* anonymity

Anorak *m*; -*s*, -*s* anorak, *bes. Am.* parka

anordnen *v/t.* (*trennb., hat -ge-*) **1.** arrange, order; *nach Sachgebieten angeordnet* arranged according to subject; **2.** (*befehlen*) order

Anordnung *f* **1.** arrangement; (*Gruppierung*) grouping; (*Anlage*) *auch* design, layout; (*Aufbau*) structure, (*System*) pattern, scheme; **2.** (*Anweisung*) order, instruction; (*Vorschrift*) regulation, rule; **~en treffen** give orders (*od.* instructions); make arrangements, arrange (that); *auf ~ von* by order of, at the instance of *förm.*

Anorexie *f*; -, -*n*; *Med.* anorexia (nervosa); **anorexisch** *Adj.* anorexic

anorganisch *Adj. Chem., Bio.* inor-

ganic

anormal *Adj.* abnormal; *das ist ~ auch* that's not normal

anpacken (*trennb., hat -ge-*) **I.** *v/t.* **1.** (*fest fassen*) grab (*od.* lay) hold (*an* + *Dat.* of), seize, grasp; *j-n am Arm ~* grab (hold of) s.o. by the arm; **2.** *fig.* (*j-n*) hart treat, handle ; (*Arbeit, Problem etc.*) *entschlossen:* tackle, deal with, set about; *etw. anders ~* approach (*od.* set about) s.th. differently; *packen wir's an! umg.* let's get down to business, then; **II.** *v/i.: mit ~* lend a (helping) hand

anpaddeln *v/i.* (*trennb., ist -ge-*): *angepaddelt kommen mit Boot:* approach (in a canoe, small boat *etc.*); *Tier:* come (dog[gy])paddling up (*od.* along) *umg.*

anpassen (*trennb., hat -ge-*) **I.** *v/t.* **1.** (*Kleidung, Bauteile etc.*) fit (+ *Dat.* to); **2.** *fig.* (*Löhne, Renten etc.*) adapt, adjust (+ *Dat. od. an* + *Akk.* to); *Pol.* align (to); *farblich etc.:* match (with); *sich der veränderten Situation ~* adapt o.s. to the new situation; **II.** *v/refl.* **1.** adapt (o.s.), adjust (o.s.) (+ *Dat. od. an* + *Akk.* to); *Pol.* align (to); (*Norm etc.*) conform to *s.th.*; *er kann sich einfach nicht ~* he just won't fit in; → *angepasst* II; **2.** *Augen:* accommodate; **Anpassung** *f* adaptation, adjustment; *kulturelle:* acculturation

anpassungsfähig *Adj.* adaptable; flexible; **Anpassungsfähigkeit** *f* adaptability, flexibility

Anpassungs|schwierigkeiten *Pl.* difficulties in adapting; *Psych.* maladjustment; **~vermögen** *n* → *Anpassungsfähigkeit*

anpeilen *v/t.* (*trennb., hat -ge-*) **1.** (*orten*) take a bearing on; (*ansteuern*) head for; **2.** *umg. fig.* (*j-n*) make for; (*etw.*) (*anstreben*) aim at; (*anvisieren*) have one's sights set on; → *angepeilt*

anpeitschen *v/t.* (*trennb., hat -ge-*) spur on

anpfeifen *v/t.* (*trennb., hat -ge-*) **1.** *Sport: das Spiel ~* start the game; **2.** *umg.: j-n ~* (*zurechtweisen*) give s.o. a roasting, dress s.o. down, *Am.* chew s.o. out

Anpfiff *m* **1.** *Fußball:* kick(-)off; **2.** *umg. fig.: e-n ~ bekommen* be hauled (*od.* raked) over the coals, get a roasting (*od.* dressing down), *Am.* get chewed out

anpflanzen *v/t.* (*trennb., hat -ge-*); (*Baum etc.*) plant; (*anbauen*) cultivate; (*Beet, Garten*) lay out; **Anpflanzung** *f* **1.** *nur Sg.; Handlung:* planting, cultivation; **2.** *Fläche:* cultivated area

anpflaumen *v/t.* (*trennb., hat -ge-*); *umg.* (*anpöbeln*) insult *allg.*

anpflocken *v/t.* (*trennb., hat -ge-*); (*Ziege etc.*) tether, tie up

anpicken *vt/i.* (*trennb., hat -ge-*); *österr.* → *festkleben* I, II

anpiepsen *v/t.* (*trennb., hat -ge-*); *umg. über Funk:* bleep

anpinseln *v/t.* (*trennb., hat -ge-*); *umg., mst pej* → *anmalen* I

anpirschen *v/refl.* (*trennb., hat -ge-*): *sich ~* (*an* + *Akk.*) creep up to, stalk

anpöbeln *v/t.* (*trennb., hat -ge-*); *pej.* (*verbally*) accost, shout (*od.* hurl) abuse at

Anprall *m*; -*(e)s, kein Pl.* impact (*auf* on), collision (*auf* with); **anprallen** *v/i.* (*trennb., ist -ge-*) crash (*an* + *Akk.* into, *gegen* against), collide (with)

anprangern *v/t.* (*trennb., hat -ge-*)

(*Missstände etc.*) denounce, brand (*als* as); *durch die Medien etc.*: pillory, smear; **Anprangerung** *f* denunciation

anpreisen *v/t.* (*unreg., trennb., hat -ge-*) recommend; push *umg.*; talk *s.th.* up *umg.*; (*eigene Ware*) plug, boost; (*loben*) praise, extol

anpreschen *v/i.* (*trennb., ist -ge-*): **angeprescht kommen** *umg.* come hurrying (*od.* rushing) up (*od.* along) *allg.*

anpressen *v/t.* (*trennb., hat -ge-*): **fest ~ press** (on) (**an** + *Akk.* to), squeeze (**an** against)

Anprobe *f* fitting; **zur ~ gehen** go for a fitting; **anprobieren** *v/t.* (*trennb., hat*) try on

anpumpen *v/t.* (*trennb., hat -ge-*); *umg.* tap, pump; **~ um** *auch* touch (*Am.* tap) *s.o.* for

anquatschen *v/t.* (*trennb., hat -ge-*); *umg.* (start to) talk; (*anmachen*) chat up

anradeln *v/i.* (*trennb., ist -ge-*): **angeradelt kommen** *umg.* come cycling up (*od.* along), approach on a bicycle *allg.*

Anrainer *m*; *-s, -* **1.** (*Nachbar*) neighbo(u)r; **2.** → **Anliegerstaat**, **~grundstück** *n* neighbo(u)ring property; **~staat** → **Anliegerstaat**

anrasen *v/i.* (*trennb., ist -ge-*): **angerast kommen** *umg.* come racing (*od.* rushing) up (*od.* along) *allg.*

anraten (*unreg., trennb., hat -ge-*) *v/t.*: **j-m ~, etw. zu tun** advise s.o. to do s.th.; **Anraten** *n*: **auf ~ des Arztes** on the doctor's advice

anrechnen *v/t.* (*trennb., hat -ge-*) **1.** (*gutschreiben*) **~** (**auf** + *Akk.*) credit (**für** for); (*zählen*) count; (*berücksichtigen, abziehen*) take into account, allow for; **j-m etw. ~** (*in Rechnung stellen*) charge s.o. with s.th., charge s.th. to s.o.'s account; (**j-m**) **etw. als Fehler/Pluspunkt ~** *auch* fig. count s.th. against s.o. / count s.th. in s.o.'s favo(u)r; (**j-m**) **das Praktikum** (**auf die Ausbildungszeit**) **~** count (a period of) work experience toward(s) the period of training; **sie haben mir die alte Kamera** (**auf den Preis**) **angerechnet** they knocked something off (the price) for my old camera; **2.** fig.: **j-m etw. als Verdienst ~** give s.o. credit for s.th.; **j-m s-e Hilfe etc. hoch ~** greatly appreciate s.o.'s help *etc.*

Anrechnung *f* **1.** (*Gutschrift*) credit; **2.** (*Abzug*) discount; **3.** (*Berechnung*) charge; **anrechnungsfähig** *Adj.* **1.** *Versicherungszeiten*: creditable, countable; **2.** *Leistungen*: chargeable

Anrecht *n* **1.** right, title, claim (**auf** + *Akk.* on); (**ein**) **~ haben auf** have a right to, be entitled to; **2.** (*Konzert-, Theaterabonnement*) subscription

Anrede *f* address; *im Brief*: opening, salutation *förm.*

anreden *v/t.* (*trennb., hat -ge-*) **1.** address (**als** as; **mit** with); **j-n mit du/Sie ~** call s.o. du/Sie, use the familiar/polite form of address with s.o.; **2.** (*ansprechen*) approach (**auf** + *Akk.* **etw. hin** about *od.* on s.th.); **3.** (*ankämpfen*): **gegen den Lärm etc. ~** compete against the noise *etc.*

anregen (*trennb., hat -ge-*) **I.** *v/t.* **1.** (*vorschlagen*) suggest; (*veranlassen*) elicit, prompt; (*Diskussion*) start; **2.** *Chem., Etech.* excite; **II.** *vt/i.* (*beleben*) (*j-n geistig, Fantasie, Herz, Kreislauf*) stimulate (*j-n Appetit*) *auch* whet; **j-n zum Nachdenken ~** set (*od.* get) s.o. thinking, make s.o. think; →

angeregt II, III

anregend I. *Part. Präs.* → **anregen**; **II.** *Adj.* stimulating, inspiring, exciting; **III.** *Adv.*: **~ wirken** have a stimulating effect

Anregung *f* **1.** stimulation; *fig. auch* encouragement; (*Anreiz*) impulse; *auch Med.* stimulus; **zur ~ des Kreislaufs** to get one's circulation going; **2.** (*Vorschlag*) suggestion; **auf ~ von** at the suggestion of; **wir sind für jede ~ dankbar** all suggestions will be gratefully received; **3.** *Etech.* excitation; **Anregungsmittel** *n Med.* stimulant

anreichern (*trennb., hat -ge-*) **I.** *v/t.* **~** (*mit*) (*verbessern*) *mit Vitaminen etc.*: enrich (with); *mit Sauerstoff*: oxygenate; **mit Uran angereichert** uranium-enriched; **II.** *v/refl.* accumulate (**in** + *Dat.* in); **mit Abgasen angereicherte Luft** fume-filled air; **Anreicherung** *f* enrichment; (*Ansammlung*) accumulation, concentration

Anreicherungsverfahren *n Bergb., Chem.* concentration (*od.* enrichment) method (*od.* process)

anreihen (*trennb., hat -ge-*) **I.** *v/t.* add (**an** + *Akk.* to); (*Perlen etc.*) string; **II.** *v/refl.* line up (**an** + *Akk.* next to); (*sich anschließen*) follow on

Anreise *f* **1.** (*Anfahrt*) journey; **2.** (*Ankunft*) arrival; **anreisen** *v/i.* (*trennb., ist -ge-*) travel; (*ankommen*) arrive, come; **Anreisetag** *m* day of arrival

anreißen *v/t.* (*unreg., trennb., hat -ge-*) **1.** (*beschädigen*) tear (slightly); **2.** *umg. fig.* (*Packung etc.*) start on; (*Vorräte, Gespartes*) break into; **3.** *fig.* (*Frage*) raise, touch on; (*Thema*) broach; **4.** (*Motor*) start up; **5.** *Dial.* (*Streichholz*) strike; **6.** *Tech.* (*vorzeichnen*) trace, mark out; **7.** *umg.* (*Kunden, Käufer*) draw, attract; **Anreißer** *m*; *-s, -*, **Anreißerin** *f*; *-, -nen*; *umg.* (*Kundenfänger*) tout; **anreißerisch** *Adj.* loud

anreiten (*unreg., trennb. -ge-*) **I.** *v/i.* (*ist angeritten*) **1.** **angeritten kommen** come riding up, approach (on horseback); **2.** *Mil. Kavallerie*: charge (**gegen** against); **II.** *v/t.* (*hat*) **1.** (*Hindernis. Ziel etc.*) ride toward(s); **2.** (*Pferd*) warm up

Anreiz *m* **1.** incentive (**zu** to); **2.** **j-m e-n ~ geben** (**zu** + *Inf.*) stimulate s.o. (**to** + *Inf.*); *fig. auch* encourage s.o. (**to** + *Inf.*); (*verlocken*) tempt s.o. (**to** + *Inf.*), spur s.o. on (**to** + *Inf.*); **anreizen** *v/t.* (*trennb., hat -ge-*) → **Anreiz 2**

anrempeln *v/t.* (*trennb., hat -ge-*); *umg.* **1.** jostle (against), bump (*heftiger*: barge) into; **2.** *umg. fig.* (*beschimpfen*) get a dig in at *s.o.* (*wegen* about); *wiederholt*: keep on at (*od.* keep pestering) *s.o.* (about)

anrennen *v/i.* (*unreg., trennb., ist -ge-*) **1.** *fig.*: **~ gegen** (*bekämpfen*) struggle against; *Mil.* charge; *Sport*: throw everything at; **2.** *umg.*: **angerannt kommen** come running (along *od.* up); **ständig kommt er mit etwas anderem angerannt** he is always pestering us *etc.* with something else

Anrichte *f*; *-, -n* sideboard

anrichten *v/t.* (*trennb., hat -ge-*) **1.** (*Salat etc.*) prepare; (*zusammenstellen*) arrange; (*servieren*) serve; **es ist angerichtet!** dinner etc. is served!; **2.** (*Unheil etc.*) cause; **Schaden ~** do damage; **Verwüstungen ~** wreak havoc; **da hast du was Schönes angerichtet** (*angestellt*) *umg. iro.* now you've (gone and) done it, now you've put your

foot in it, you've really made a mess there (*od.* of it); → **Blutbad**

Anriss *m* **1.** (superficial *od.* hairline) fissure; *in Stein*: slight break; **2.** *Tech.* (*Vorzeichnung*) tracing

anrollen (*trennb., -ge-*) **I.** *v/i.* (*ist*) **1.** *auch* **angerollt kommen** roll up; *weitS.* be under way; **2.** (*zu rollen beginnen*) (*Zug*) start moving; *Flug. auch* start taxiing; **II.** *v/t.* (*hat*); (*Fass*) roll up

anrosten *v/i.* (*trennb., ist -ge-*) start to rust; → **angerostet**

anrösten *v/t.* (*trennb., hat -ge-*); *Gastr.* brown

anrüchig *Adj.* **1.** disreputable, of ill repute, notorious; shady *umg.*; *stärker*: infamous; **2.** (*anstößig*) indecent; **Anrüchigkeit** *f*; *nur Sg.* **1.** disreputableness, bad reputation; **2.** indecency

anrucken *v/i.* (*trennb., ist -ge-*) *Zug*: start with a jerk

anrücken *v/i.* (*trennb., ist -ge-*) **1.** *Feuerwehr*: turn up, move in; *Truppen*: advance; **2.** *umg. iro.* show up

Anruf *m* **1.** (phone) call; **e-n ~ entgegennehmen** take a call; **2.** *Mil. e-s Wachpostens*: challenge; **~beantworter** *m* (telephone) answering machine, answerphone

anrufen (*unreg., trennb., hat -ge-*) **I.** *vt/i.* **j-n od. bei j-m** ring (up), call (up); make a phone call; **rufen Sie einfach an** *auch* just give us *etc.* a call; **II.** *v/t.* **1.** (*anflehen*) implore, invoke; **2.** (*Gericht etc.*) appeal to; **Anrufer** *m*; *-s, -*, **Anruferin** *f*; *-, -nen* caller

anrühren *v/t.* (*trennb., hat -ge-*) **1.** (*Alkohol, Essen, Geld etc.*) touch; **sie rührt keinen Alkohol an** she won't touch a drop of alcohol; **2.** *fig.* (*Thema*) touch (on); **3.** (*mischen*) (*Brei, Kleister etc.*) mix (**mit** with); (*Teig*) beat, stir; (*Soße*) blend, stir; **4.** *fig. lit. gefühlsmäßig*: touch, move

ans *Präp.* + *Art.* **1.** → **an** I; **2.** *in Wendungen*: **er ist mir ~ Herz gewachsen** I have grown very fond of him; **j-m ~ Leben wollen** want to kill s.o.; **3.** *mit substantiviertem Inf.*: **~ Nachhausegehen denken** think about going home; **sich ~ Aufräumen machen** start (*od.* set about) tidying (*Am.* cleaning) up

Ansage *f* **1.** *im Fernsehen, Radio, Stadion etc.* announcement; *e-s Künstlers, e-r Darbietung*: introduction; **2.** *Kartenspiel*: bid(ding)

ansagen (*trennb., hat -ge-*) **I.** *v/t.* **1.** (*s-n Besuch, ein Programm*) announce; (*Künstler, Nummer*) introduce, present; (*Zeit*) give, announce; **2.** (*diktieren*) dictate; **II.** *vt/i. Kartenspiel*: bid; **Trumpf ~** declare trumps; **du musst ~** it's your bid; **III.** *v/refl. Person*: say that one is coming; *bes. iro.* announce one's arrival; *Baby, Wetter etc.*: announce o.s.; → **angesagt** II, **Kampf**

Ansager *m*; *-s, -*, **~in** *f*; *-, -nen* announcer

ansammeln (*trennb., hat -ge-*) **I.** *v/t.* (*anhäufen*) *allmählich*: accumulate; *schneller*: amass, pile up; (*Vorräte*) stockpile, build up; **II.** *v/refl.* accumulate, gather (together) (*auch Personen*); *Staub, Wasser auch*: collect; *Zinsen*: build up; accrue *förm.*; *Wut*: build up; **auf den Büchern sammelte sich Staub an** the books accumulated dust; **Ansammlung** *f* **1.** collection; accumulation, concentration; pile; → **ansammeln**; **2.** *von Verschiedenem*: array; *von Menschen*: crowd, gathering, assembly

ansässig *Adj. attr.* resident; ~ **werden** take up residence, settle (*in* in); ~ **sein in** *Völker*: have settled in; **er ist seit 30 Jahren hier** ~ he's lived here for 30 years

Ansatz *m* **1.** *des Halses, der Nase*: base; (*Haaransatz*) *an der Stirn*: hairline; *an den Haarwurzeln*: roots; (*Blüten-, Blattansatz*) stipule; **2.** *Tech.* → **Ansatzstück**; **3.** *fig.* (*Anzeichen*) first sign(s *Pl.*), beginning(s *Pl.*); **etw. schon im** ~ **ersticken** nip s.th. in the bud; **er zeigt den** ~ **zum Bauch** he's starting to get a paunch; **gute Ansätze zeigen** show promise; **er zeigt Ansätze zur Besserung** *leistungsmäßig*: he's slowly beginning to improve; *moralisch*: it looks as if he's turning over a new leaf; **4.** *fig.* (*Versuch*) attempt; (*Methode*) **das ist im** ~ **richtig, aber** ... you've got the right idea, but ...; **5.** *Mus. e-s Bläsers*: lip(ping); *e-s Sängers*: intonation; **6.** *Wirts.* (*Voranschlag*) estimate; *e-s Preises*: fixing, quotation; *im Budget*: appropriation, estimate; **die Kosten mit 10 Millionen Mark in** ~ **bringen** estimate the costs at 10 million marks; **7.** *Bio.* (*Anlage*) tendency, disposition; *zu e-m Organ*: rudiment; **8.** *Chem.* (*Präparat*) setting up; **9.** *von Kalk, Rost etc.*: (*das Ansetzen*) coating; (*Schicht*) coating; **10.** *Chem., Geol.* deposit, sediment

Ansatz|punkt *m* **1.** *fig.* start; (*Ausgangspunkt*) point of departure; **2.** *e-r Bohrung*: location; **~stück** *n Tech.* **1.** attachment; **2.** (*Verlängerung*) extension (piece)

ansatzweise *Adv.*: ~ **zeigen** *etc.* show *etc.* the beginnings of

ansäuern *v/t.* (*trennb., hat -ge-*) acidify

ansaufen *v/t.* (*unreg., trennb., hat -ge-*) *Sl., oft pej.*: **sich** (*Dat.*) **einen** ~ get plastered, go out on the piss *Brit. vulg.*

ansaugen *v/t.* (*trennb., hat -ge-*) suck in (*od.* up); (*Luft*) suck in, draw in

Ansaug|gebläse *n Tech.* suction fan; **~rohr** *n* intake (*od.* induction) pipe; **~stutzen** *m* intake socket; *e-s Motors*: intake manifold; **~takt** *m* suction (*od.* intake) stroke

ansausen *v/i.* (*trennb., ist -ge-*): **angesaust kommen** *umg.* come rushing up (*od.* along) *allg.*

Anschaffe *f umg.*: **auf** ~ **gehen** (*sich prostituieren*) go (*od.* be) on the game, *Am.* be a working girl; (*auf Raubzug gehen*) commit a series of robberies

anschaffen (*trennb., hat -ge-*) **I.** *v/t.* **sich** (*Dat.*) **etw.** ~ (*kaufen*) buy (*od.* purchase) s.th. for o.s., invest in s.th.; (*zulegen*) get (o.s.) s.th.; **sich** (*Dat.*) **Kinder** ~ have children; **II.** *v/i. umg.*: ~ **gehen 1.** (*sich prostituieren*) *Sl.* go (*od.* be) on the game, *Am.* go hustling, be working; **2.** *Sl.* (*ein Dieb sein*) pinch, nick; **III.** *vt/i. südd., österr.* (*befehlen*) give orders (+ *Dat.* to); **j-m etw.** ~ tell s.o. what to do

Anschaffung *f* (*das Anschaffen*) purchase, purchasing (+ *Gen.* of), investment (in); (*Gegenstand*) acquisition, object; **die** ~ **e-s Autos** buying a car

Anschaffungs|darlehen *n* consumer (*od.* personal) loan; **~kosten** *Pl.*; **~preis** *m* cost price; **~wert** *m* cost (*od.* acquisition) value

anschalten *v/t.* (*trennb., hat -ge-*) switch on, turn on

anschauen *v/t.* (*trennb., hat -ge-*); *bes.*

südd., österr., schw., sonst geh., auch fig. → **ansehen** 1, 2

anschaulich I. *Adj.* (*bildhaft*) graphic; (*klar, deutlich*) clear; ~ **machen** illustrate, explain *s.th.*; ~ **schildern** give a graphic description of; ~ **vermittelt werden** come across vividly; **Anschaulichkeit** *f; nur Sg.*; (*Klarheit*) clarity; (*Lebendigkeit*) graphic nature (+ *Gen.* of)

Anschauung *f* **1.** (*Ansicht*) view, opinion; (*Einstellung*) approach, point of view; (*Vorstellung*) idea, notion, perception; (*Auffassung*) conception; **zu der** ~ **gelangen, dass** ... come to the conclusion that ...; **2.** (*intensive Betrachtung*) contemplation; **3.** (*Erleben*) visual perception; **aus eigener** ~ **kennen** know from one's own (*od.* personal) experience; **4.** *Philos.* (*Erkenntnis*) intuition

Anschauungs|material *n* illustrative material; *Ton- und Bildgerät*: audiovisual aids *Pl.*; **~unterricht** *m* visual instruction; *fig.* object lesson; **~vermögen** *n* intuitive faculty; **~weise** *f* approach, point of view; (*Denkweise*) mentality

Anschein *m* appearance, semblance; **den** ~ **erwecken** (+ *Gen.*) give the impression of (being); **es hat den** ~**, als ob** it looks (very much) as if; **sich** (*Dat.*) **den** ~ **geben zu** (+ *Inf.*) / **etw. zu sein** pretend to (+ *Inf.*) / make o.s. out to be s.th.; **dem** *od.* **allem** ~ **nach** to all appearances

anscheinend I. *Adv.* apparently, seemingly; **er ist** ~ **krank** *auch* he seems to be ill; **II.** *Adj.* apparent, seeming

anscheißen (*unreg., trennb. -ge-*); *Sl. v/t.* (*hat angeschissen*) **1.** (*beschimpfen*) give *s.o.* a (good) talking-to (*od.* bollocking *Brit. Sl.*), tell *s.o.* off *umg.*; **2.** (*betrügen*) do; **man hat dich angeschissen** you've been done (*Am.* had)

anschicken *v/refl.* (*trennb., hat -ge-*): **sich zu etw.** ~ get ready for; (*sich machen an*) set about (+ *Ger.*); **sich** ~ **zu** (+ *Inf.*) get ready to (+ *Inf.*); *gerade*: be about to (+ *Inf.*), be on the point of (+ *Ger.*)

anschieben *v/t.* (*unreg., trennb., hat -ge-*) **1.** *Stuhl an den Tisch*: push (**an** + *Akk.* against); **2.** give *s.th.* a push (*Auto*: *auch* a bump-start)

anschielen *v/t.* (*trennb., hat -ge-*) look at *s.o.* (*od. s.th.*) from the corner of one's eye; *mit Mühe*: squint at

anschießen I. *v/t.* (*unreg., trennb., hat -ge-*) **1.** shoot at (and wound), hit; **angeschossen werden** *auch* be hit by a bullet (*od.* several bullets); **angeschossen** *auch* slightly wounded (by bullet-fire); **2.** *Sport*: (*j-n*) hit *s.o.* with the ball; **3.** *umg. fig.* (*kritisieren*) get at *s.o.*; **4.** (*Gewehr etc.*) test-fire; **II.** *v/i. umg. fig.* (*sich schnell nähern*) shoot up; **angeschossen kommen** come shooting along

anschirren *vt/i.* (*trennb., hat -ge-*); (*Pferd etc.*) harness

Anschiss *m*; *-es, -e*; *umg.* bollocking *Sl., Am.* dressing-down; **e-n** ~ **bekommen** be given (*od.* get) a bollocking (*Am.* dressing-down)

Anschlag *m* **1.** (*Plakat*) poster; (*Bekanntmachung*) notice; **e-n** ~ **machen** put a notice up; **durch** ~ **bekannt machen** announce s.th. by putting up a notice (*od.* poster), post s.th.; **2.** (*Überfall*) attack; **ein** ~ **auf j-n** (*j-s Leben*) an attempt on s.o.'s life; **ich habe e-n**

~ **auf dich vor** *umg. fig.* I wanted to ask you (for) something, I have a favo(u)r to ask of you; **3.** *Schreibmaschine*: stroke; (*Raum e-s Buchstabens*) space; **220 Anschläge pro Minute** 220 strokes a minute; **die Tastatur hat e-n sehr leichten** ~ the keyboard has a very light touch; **4.** *Mus. etc.* touch; **5.** *Schwimmen*: touch; *Versteckspiel*: home; **6.** *Gewehr*: firing position; **liegender/stehender** ~ prone/standing position; (*ein Gewehr*) **im** ~ **haben** have (a rifle) at the ready (*od.* level[l]ed); **7.** *Jagd*: aiming position; **8.** *Tech.* (*Sperre*) stop; (*Anschlagplatte*) stop plate; **bis zum** ~ **aufdrehen** turn *s.th.* as far as it will go, open *s.th.* up completely; **9.** *Telef.* (dial) finger position; **10.** *Wirts.* (*Schätzung*) estimate; **11.** *Bergb.* (shaft) landing; **12.** *von Maschen*: casting on

Anschlagbrett *n* notice (*od.* bulletin) board

anschlagen (*unreg., trennb., -ge-*) **I.** *v/t.* (*hat*) **1.** hit, knock (**an** + *Dat.* against); **sich** (*Dat.*) **den Ellbogen** *etc.* (**an etw.**) ~ knock one's elbow *etc.* on (*od.* against) s.th.; → **angeschlagen** II 1; **2.** (*befestigen*) (**an** + *Dat.*) fasten (to), fix (onto), nail (to); (*Zettel etc.*) stick up (to), put up (on), post (on); **die Öffnungszeiten sind am Tor angeschlagen** the opening times are posted on the door; **3.** (*Tasten, Saiten*) hit, strike, touch; (*Glocke*) sound, ring; (*Stunden*) strike; **den Ton** ~ give the note; *fig.* set the tone; **e-n frechen Ton** ~ *fig.* start to get cheeky; **4.** *beim Versteckspiel*: tag *s.o.*, make *s.o.* "it"; **5. e-e schnellere Gangart** ~ quicken one's pace, speed up; **5.** (*befestigen*) *Naut.* (*Leine, Segel*) bend (*od.* bring to); *Bergb.* fasten (*od.* secure) before hoisting; **7.** *geh.* (*einschätzen*) estimate, assess; **8.** *Sport*: (*Ball*) hit; **II.** *v/i.* **1.** (*ist*): ~ **an** (+ *Akk.*) hit (*Wellen*: break) against; **mit dem Kopf an die Wand** ~ hit one's head against the wall; **2.** (*hat*); *Hund*: bark; **3.** (*hat*); *Schwimmen*: touch; **am Beckenrand** ~ touch the edge of the pool; **4.** (*hat*); *Arznei*: take effect; **5.** (*hat*); (*das Gewicht erhöhen*) make *s.o.* put on weight, be fattening; **bei mir schlägt jedes Stück Kuchen an** every little piece of cake tells with me; **6.** (*hat*); *südd., österr.* (*Bierfass anstechen*) tap (*od.* broach) the (first) barrel; → **angeschlagen** II 2

Anschlag|säule *f* advertising pillar (*Am.* kiosk); **~tafel** *f* → **Anschlagbrett**

anschleichen (*unreg., trennb., -ge-*) **I.** *v/t. und v/refl.* (*hat*) creep up (**an** + *Akk.* on); (*Wild*) *auch* stalk; **II.** *v/i.* (*ist*); *mst* **angeschlichen kommen** *heimlich*: come sneaking up; *umg. reumütig etc.*: turn up on the doorstep (with one's tail between one's legs)

anschleifen *v/t.* (*trennb., hat -ge-*) *umg.* → **anschleppen** 1

anschlendern *v/i.* (*trennb., ist -ge-*): **angeschlendert kommen** *umg.* come strolling up (*od.* along) *allg.*

anschleppen *v/t.* (*trennb., hat -ge-*) **1.** (*auch angeschleppt bringen*) drag along; (*Person*) *auch* have in tow *umg.*; **2.** *Mot.*: **ein Auto** ~ give a car a tow, tow a car

anschließen (*unreg., trennb. -ge-*) **I.** *v/t.* **1.** (**an** + *Dat. od. Akk.*) *mit Schloss*: padlock (to); *mit Kette*: chain (to); **2.** (**an** + *Akk. od. Dat.*)

(*Schlauch etc.*) attach, join; *Tech.* connect (to), *Etech. auch* hook up (to); *mit Stecker:* plug in(to); **angeschlossen werden an** *das Kabelnetz etc.:* be connected to, get plugged into, get hooked up to; **angeschlossen sein** *Sender:* be linked up (with); **3.** (*hinzufügen*) add (**an** + *Akk.* to); **II.** *v/refl.* **1.** (*nachfolgen*) follow; **an den Vortrag schloss sich e-e Diskussion an** the lecture was followed by a discussion; **2.** (*sich anreihen*) follow (**an** + *Akk.* on); (*angrenzen*) border (on), be adjacent (to); **3.** (*j-m*) (*mitgehen mit*) join, attach *o.s.* to *s.o.*; *unterstützend:* take *s.o.'s* side; (*sich anfreunden*) make friends, grow close *to s.o.*; (*e-r Ansicht*) support, endorse; (*e-m Beispiel*) follow; (*das Gleiche tun*) follow suit; *Jur.* (*e-m Urteil*) concur with; **der Meinung schließe ich mich an** I'd like to support that view; **III.** *v/i.* → II 1, 2

anschließend I. *Part. Präs.* → **anschließen; II.** *Adv.* afterwards; subsequently *förm.;* **III.** *Adj. zeitlich:* following, ensuing; subsequent *förm.; nachgestellt:* that followed, subsequent (**an** +*Akk.* to); *räumlich:* next, bordering, adjacent

Anschluss *m* **1.** *Telef. etc.:* connection; (*Apparat*) (tele)phone; (*Zweit-, Zusatzanschluss*) extension; (*Leitung*) line; **e-n ~ beantragen** apply for (*od.* order) a (tele)phone line (*od.* connection); **der ~ ist besetzt** the line (*od.* it) is engaged (*Am.* busy); **kein ~ unter dieser Nummer** number unobtainable (*Am.* not in service); **2.** *für Gas, Wasser etc.:* supply; (*Anschlussstelle*) supply point; **~ an die Kanalisation** connection to the sewer system; **3.** *im Verkehr:* connection; **der Bus mit ~ an den Zug nach ...** the bus which connects with the train to ...; **~ haben** have a connection (**nach** to *od.* for); **den ~ erreichen** make (*od.* manage) one's connection; **den ~ verpassen** miss one's connection; *umg. fig. beruflich:* miss the boat; (*keinen Ehepartner finden*) be left on the shelf; **4.** *fig.* (*Kontakt*): **~ finden** make contact (*od.* friends) (**bei** with); **~ suchen** look for company; **5.** *Sport:* **den ~ an** (*die Spitze etc.*) **finden** catch up with; *Fußball etc.:* get back into the game; *in der Tabelle:* narrow the gap; **den ~ verlieren** be left (*od.* fall) behind; **6.** **im ~ an** (+ *Akk.*) after, following; subsequent to *geh.;* **7.** *e-s Staates:* union; *hist.* Anschluss

Anschluss|auftrag *m Wirts.* continuation (*od.* follow-up) order; **~bahn** *f Eisenb.* branch (*od.* feeder) line; **~dose** *f Etech.* (wall) socket, junction box; **~flug** *m* connecting flight, connection; **~gleis** *n Eisenb.* siding; **~kabel** *n Etech.* connecting lead; *Telef.* subscriber's cable; **~karte** *f im Atlas:* connecting map; **~rohr** *n* service pipe; **~stelle** *f* **1.** *Mot.* (motorway) junction; **2.** *Etech.* (*Steckdose*) connection point; **~stutzen** *m Chem.* pipe union; **~tor** *n*, **~treffer** *m Sport:* **Bayern erzielte den Anschlusstreffer zum 3:2** Bayern pulled one back to narrow the score to 3-2; **~zug** *m* connecting train, connection

anschmachten *v/t.* (*trennb., hat -ge-*) drool over

anschmeißen *v/t.* (*unreg., trennb., hat -ge-*); *umg.* (*Motor, Maschine etc.*) get *s.th.* going

anschmieden *v/t.* (*trennb., hat -ge-*) **1.** (*etw.*) forge on; **2.** *hist.* (*j-n*) fetter, put in irons, chain up

anschmiegen *v/refl.* (*trennb., hat -ge-*) **1.** *Kleid:* fit snugly; **2.** **sich ~ an** (+ *Akk.*) snuggle up to; **anschmiegsam** *Adj.* **1.** *Kleid:* soft and smooth; **ein ~er Stoff** a clingy (*od.* figure-hugging) material; **2.** *Person:* affectionate; **Anschmiegsamkeit** *f; nur Sg.* affection

anschmieren (*trennb., hat -ge-*) **I.** *v/t.* **1.** (*Wand etc.*) smear; **2.** *fig., umg.: j-n ~* take *s.o.* for a ride, con *s.o.;* **II.** *v/refl.* **1.** dirty *o.s.;* **2.** *umg. pej. Frau:* put one's face (*od.* war paint) on

anschmoren *v/t.* (*trennb., hat -ge-*); *Gastr.* braise

anschnallen (*trennb., hat -ge-*) **I.** *v/t.* **1.** (*etw.*) strap on; (*Skier*) put on; **2.** (*j-n*) *Flug. etc.* fasten *s.o.'s* seatbelt; *Mot. auch* belt up, buckle up; **II.** *v/refl.* → I 2; *gewohnheitsmäßig:* wear a seatbelt

Anschnall|gurt *m Flug., Mot.* seatbelt; **~pflicht** *f* compulsory wearing of seatbelts; **es besteht ~** it's compulsory to wear seatbelts

anschnauzen *v/t.* (*trennb., hat -ge-*); *umg.* snarl at

anschneiden *v/t.* (*unreg., trennb., hat -ge-*) **1.** (*Brot, Kuchen*) (start to) cut; (*Blumenstiele*) cut, trim; **2.** (*Ball*) put a spin on; **3.** *fig.* (*Thema, Frage*) broach, touch on, raise; **4.** *Mot.* (*Kurve*) cut; *Ski:* (*Tor*) cut, touch; → **angeschnitten** II

Anschnitt *m* **1.** first slice; end bit (*Am.* piece) *umg.;* **2.** (*Schnittfläche*) cutting face

anschnorren *v/t.* (*trennb., hat -ge-*); *umg.: j-n* (**um etw.**) **~** scrounge (*s.th.*) off *s.o.*

Anschovis *f; -, -; Gastr.* anchovy

anschrauben *v/t.* (*trennb., hat -ge-*) screw on(to **an** + *Dat. od. Akk.*)

anschreiben (*unreg., trennb., hat -ge-*) **I.** *v/t.* **1.** write; **an die Tafel ~** write *s.th.* up on the (black)board (*Am. auch* chalkboard); **2.** (*j-n*) write to; **3.** *fig.* → **angeschrieben** II; **II.** *v/t./i.* **1.** (*j-m*) *etw.* **~** charge *s.th.* to *s.o.'s* account; (*etw.*) **~ lassen** take *s.th.* on credit; **2.** (*Spielstand, Punkte*) (keep) score

Anschreiben *n Wirts.* cover note, covering letter

Anschreibetafel *f beim Billard:* billiard marker

anschreien *v/t.* (*unreg., trennb., hat -ge-*) shout at; *stärker:* scream at

Anschrift *f* address

Anschriftenänderung *f* change of address

anschuldigen *v/t.* (*trennb., hat -ge-*) accuse (+ *Gen. od.* **wegen** of); **Anschuldigung** *f* accusation, charge; **schwere ~en erheben** make (*od.* bring) serious accusations (**gegen** against)

anschüren *vt/i.* (*trennb., hat -ge-*) poke up, kindle

anschwärmen (*trennb., -ge-*) **I.** *v/t.* (*hat*) idolize; be crazy about *umg.;* **II.** *v/i.* (*ist*); (*auch* **angeschwärmt kommen**) come swarming along

anschwärzen *v/t.* (*trennb., hat -ge-*) **1.** blacken; **2.** *fig.: j-n ~* (*schlecht machen*) run *s.o.* down; *stärker:* blacken *s.o.'s* name; (*denunzieren*) denounce *s.o.*

anschweigen *v/t.* (*unreg., trennb., hat -ge-*) not say a word to *s.o.,* say nothing; **sie haben sich** (**gegenseitig**) **angeschwiegen** they didn't say a word to each other, they just sat there *etc.* in silence

anschweißen *v/t.* (*trennb., hat -ge-*) weld on(to)

anschwellen *v/i.* (*unreg., trennb., ist -ge-*) **1.** *Backe, Knospen, Lymphknoten etc.:* swell; **2.** *Fluss:* swell, rise; **3.** *Musik:* swell; *Lärm:* grow louder; **4.** *Arbeit:* mount, pile up; **anschwellend I.** *Part. Präs.* → **anschwellen; II.** *Adv. Mus.* crescendo; **Anschwellung** *f* swelling

anschwemmen *v/t.* (*trennb., hat -ge-*) wash ashore (*od.* up); (*Erde etc.*) deposit

Anschwemmung *f Geol.* alluvial deposits *Pl.,* alluvium; (*Vorgang*) alluviation, aggradation, *Am. auch* filling up with alluvium

Anschwemmungsküste *f Geol.* alluvial coast

anschwimmen (*unreg., trennb., -ge-*) **I.** *v/i.* (*ist*) **1.** (*auch* **angeschwommen kommen**) come swimming along (*od.* up); **2.** **~ gegen den Strom, die Strömung** swim against; **II.** *v/t.* (*hat*); (*Ziel*) swim towards

anschwindeln *v/t.* (*trennb., hat -ge-*): *j-n* **~** lie to *s.o.,* tell *s.o.* a lie (*od.* fib)

anschwirren (*unreg., trennb., ist -ge-*) (*auch* **angeschwirrt kommen**) come flying along; *umg. fig. Person:* come breezing along

anschwitzen *v/t.* (*trennb., hat -ge-*); *Gastr.* (*Mehl, Zwiebeln*) brown

ansegeln (*trennb., -ge-*) **I.** *v/i.* **1.** (*ist angesegelt*); (*auch* **angesegelt kommen**) come sailing along (*auch umg. fig.*); **2.** (*hat*) open the sailing season; **II.** *v/t.* (*hat*); (*Hafen*) make for

ansehen *v/t.* (*unreg., trennb., hat -ge-*) **1.** look at; *aufmerksam:* watch, stare; *flüchtig:* glance; *finster:* scowl; *missbilligend:* frown; *prüfend:* examine; *j-n* **von oben herab ~** look down (one's nose) on *s.o.;* **sich** (*Dat.*) *etw.* (**genau**) **~** take (*od.* have) a (close *od.* good) look at; **sich e-n Film / ein Rennen ~** *außer Haus:* go and (*od.* to) see a film / go to the races; *im Fernsehen:* watch a film / the racing; **hübsch** *etc.* **anzusehen sein** be pretty *etc.* to look at; **sieh mich nicht so an!** don't look at me like that!; **sieh** (**mal einer**) **an!** *umg.* well, what do you know!; **2.** *etw.* **mit ~** see; *tatenlos:* stand by and watch; **die Kinder mussten alles mit ~** the children watched it all happen; **3.** *j-m etw.* **~** see (*od.* tell) *s.th.* by looking at *s.o.;* **man sieht ihm sein Alter nicht an** he doesn't look his age; **4.** *fig.* (*beurteilen*) consider, regard, look upon; **~ für** *od.* **als** regard as, consider (to be); **wie ich die Sache ansehe** as I see it; **5.** (*berücksichtigen*) pay regard to, respect; **ohne Ansehen der Person** without respect of persons; → **angesehen** II

Ansehen *n; -s, kein Pl.* respect; **in hohem ~ stehen** be held in great esteem (**bei** by); **großes ~ genießen** enjoy a high standing; **in j-s ~ steigen** rise in *s.o.'s* estimation; **an ~ verlieren** fall (*od.* sink) in *s.o.'s* estimation

ansehnlich *Adj.* **1.** (*beträchtlich*) considerable, important; (*ziemlich groß*) sizable; (*reichlich*) ample; (*großzügig*) handsome; **e-e ~e Summe** a tidy little sum; **2.** *Person:* handsome, goodlooking; *Gestalt: auch* stately; (*eindrucksvoll*) imposing

anseilen *v/t. und v/refl.* (*trennb., hat -ge-*) rope (up)

an sein → *an* II 3

ansengen *v/t.* (*trennb., hat -ge-*) singe

ansetzen (*trennb., hat -ge-*) **I.** *v/t.* **1.** (*in Stellung bringen*) (put into) position; (*aufsetzen*) put on; (*Wagenheber*) put, place; (*Hebel, Meißel*) apply, place; (*Leiter*) put (in position), prop (**an** + *Akk.* against); (*Becher, Flöte etc.*) put to one's lips; (*annähen*) sew on(to); **2.** (*Bowle, Teig etc.*) make, prepare, mix; **3.** (*Frist, Zeitpunkt*) fix, appoint; **e-n Termin ~** set a date; (*Theaterstück, Veranstaltung*) schedule, set; **4.** (*Preis*) fix; (*Kosten etc.*) assess; **zu hoch/niedrig ~** overestimate/underestimate; **5.** (*entwickeln*) (*Knospen, Früchte etc.*) develop, produce, form; (*Kalk, Zahnstein, Rost etc.*) become covered with (*od.* develop a layer of); *Rost auch*: start to rust; **Fett ~** put on weight; **6.** (*j-n / e-n Hund*) *auf j-n/etw. ~* put (s.o. / a dog) onto s.o./s.th.; **II.** *v/i.* **1.** (make a) start; **zum Sprechen etc. ~** be about to speak *etc.*; **zur Landung ~** come in (to land); **zum Sprung ~** get ready to jump (*od.* for a jump); **zum Endspurt ~** make a final spurt (*od.* push); **2.** (*an e-r Stelle wirken*) *Kraft, Hebel*: act; *fig. Kritik etc.*: set in; **3.** *umg.* (*dick werden*) put on weight; **4.** (*anbrennen*) burn, stick to the bottom of the pan; **5.** *gut angesetzt haben Erdbeeren etc.*: be coming up nicely, promise to crop well; **III.** *v/refl. Schmutz etc.*: accumulate; *Chem. auch* be deposited; *in Kristallen*: crystallize; **am Wagen hat sich Rost angesetzt** the car's starting to rust

Ansicht *f; -, -en* **1.** **~** (**von** *od.* **über** + *Akk.*) (*Meinung*) opinion (on *od.* of), view (on); **nach ~** (+ *Gen.*) in the opinion of, according to; **m-r ~ nach** *od.* **nach m-r ~** in my opinion (*od.* view); **ich bin** (**da**) **anderer ~** I don't see it that way; **ich bin da ganz Ihrer ~** in this point I entirely agree with you; *umg.* I'm right with you there; **die ~en sind geteilt** opinion is divided; **der ~ sein** *od.* **die ~ vertreten**, **dass ...** take the view that ...; **zu der ~ kommen, dass ...** come to the conclusion that, decide that ...; **2.** (*Bild, Foto*) view; **mit ~ des Doms** with a view of (*od.* showing) the cathedral; **3.** *Tech.* (*Blickwinkel*) view; **~ von vorne/hinten** front/rear view; **~ von oben/unten** view from above/below; top/bottom view *fachspr.*; **4.** *Wirts. zur ~ schicken* send on approval

Ansichts|exemplar *n* specimen (*od.* inspection) copy; **~karte** *f* picture postcard; **~sache** *f*: **das ist ~** that's a matter of opinion; **~sendung** *f* sample on approval

ansiedeln (*trennb., hat -ge-*) **I.** *v/refl.* settle; **sich wieder ~** *Tierart*: repopulate, (re)colonize, become (re)established; **II.** *v/t.* **1.** (*Siedler*) settle; (*Tierart*) repopulate, colonize; **2.** *fig.* place; *das Manuskript etc.* **ist im 9. Jahrhundert anzusiedeln** goes back to (*od.* belongs to) the 9th century; **Ansiedler** *m*, **Ansiedlerin** *f* settler, colonist; **Ansiedlung** *f* **1.** *Vorgang*: settlement, colonization; **2.** *Ortschaft*: settlement, colony

Ansinnen *n; -s, - mst unzumutbares od. seltsames*: unfair (*od.* strange) demand; **an j-n das ~ stellen zu** (+ *Inf.*) expect s.o. to (+ *Inf.*); **welch ein ~!** what cheek (*od.* nerve) (to expect anyone to do that)

Ansitz *m* **1.** *Jägerspr.* hide, *Am.* blind; **2.** *österr. auch* residence

ansonsten *Adv. umg.* **1.** (*im Übrigen*) otherwise, apart from that; **2.** (*anderenfalls*) otherwise

anspannen (*trennb., hat -ge-*) **I.** *vt/i.* **1.** (*Pferde etc.*) harness; (*Kutsche etc.*) hitch up; **~ lassen** have the carriage made (*od.* got) ready; **II.** *v/t.* **1.** (*Seil etc.*) pull s.th. taut, stretch s.th. out, extend; (*Muskeln*) flex, tense; (*festziehen*) tighten; **2.** *fig.* (*j-n, das Gehirn etc.*) exert; *übermäßig*: strain; **alle Kräfte ~** strain every nerve; → **angespannt** II, III; **III.** *v/refl.* tense up

Anspannung *f* **1.** (*Belastung*) strain, exertion; (*Stress*) tension; **unter ~ aller Kräfte** by exerting all one's energies; **2.** *der Muskeln*: tension

ansparen *v/t.* (*trennb., hat -ge-*) save

anspazieren *v/i.* (*trennb., ist*) *mst* **anspaziert kommen** come walking along (*od.* up)

anspeien *v/t.* (*unreg., trennb., hat -ge-*) spit at

Anspiel *n* **1.** *Sport* a) (*Spielbeginn*) start of play; *Fußball*: kick-off, b) (*Zuspiel*) pass; **2.** *Kartenspiel*: lead

anspielbar *Adj. Sport, Spieler*: playable, free, available; **anspielen** (*trennb., hat -ge-*) **I.** *v/i.* **1.** *Sport*: lead off; *Fußball*: kick off; *Tennis*: serve; **2.** *fig.* **~ auf** (*auf + Akk.*) allude to, hint at, get at; **II.** *v/t. Sport*: **j-n ~** pass (the ball) to s.o.; **III.** *vt/i. Kartenspiel*: lead; *intr. auch* have the lead

Anspielung *f* allusion (**auf** + *Akk.* to), hint (at); **versteckte ~** innuendo

anspinnen (*unreg., trennb., hat -ge-*) **I.** *v/t.* **1.** (*Faden*) join; **2.** *fig.* (*Gespräch*) enter into; **II.** *v/refl.* develop, arise

anspitzen *v/t.* (*trennb., hat -ge-*) **1.** (*Bleistift etc.*) sharpen, point; **2.** *umg. fig.* (*anstacheln*) have a go at, *Am.* spur on; **j-n ~ etw. zu tun** have a go at s.o. (*Am.* spur s.o.) to do s.th.; **Anspitzer** *m* sharpener

Ansporn *m; -(e)s, kein Pl.* incentive (**zu** to); **für j-n ein ~ sein** be an incentive to s.o.; **anspornen** *v/t.* (*trennb., hat -ge-*); (*Pferd etc.*) spur; *fig.* spur on, incite, stimulate

Ansprache *f* **1.** address, speech (**an** + *Akk.* to); **e-e ~ halten** give an address, make a speech; **2.** *umg.*: **keine ~ haben** have no one to talk to

ansprechbar *Adj. Med.* responsive; (*bei Bewusstsein*) conscious; **er ist nicht ~** (*ist weggetreten*) he's dead to the world; *wegen Krankheit*: he's unable to communicate; *fig.* (*ist zu beschäftigt*) he's too busy to see anyone; (*ist schlecht gelaunt*) he's not talking to anyone (*od.* today)

ansprechen (*unreg., trennb., hat -ge-*) **I.** *v/t.* **1.** (*j-n*) speak to (**auf** + *Akk.* about); **mit Vornamen / s-m Titel ~** address s.o. by their first name/title; **~ als** address as; (*herantreten an, auch e-n Fremden*) approach (**wegen, bezüglich** about, on); *in sexueller Absicht*: accost, solicit; **ich habe ihn einfach angesprochen** (*ein Gespräch angefangen*) I just started talking to him; **ich fühle mich nicht angesprochen** it's got nothing to do with me; **keiner fühlt sich angesprochen** nobody wants anything to do with it (*od.* wants to know); **2.** (*e-e Zielgruppe*) appeal to, target; (*erreichen*) reach; **3.** (*Fragen, Probleme*) touch (up)on; **II.** *v/i.* **1.** (**auf** + *Akk.*) (*reagieren*) Pati-

ent *etc.*: respond (to); *Messgerät*: react; *Bremse, Lenkung*: **gut/schlecht ~** respond well/poorly; **2.** (*wirken*) *Medizin*: have the desired effect (**bei** on), work; **III.** *vt/i. Sache*: (*gefallen*) appeal to s.o.; go down well (**bei** with); **e-n breiten Kreis ~** have wide appeal, be very popular

ansprechend I. *Part. Präs.* → **ansprechen**; **II.** *Adj.* pleasing, pleasant, appealing; *auch Erscheinung*: attractive; (*sympathisch*) engaging, winning; *Leistung*: considerable, impressive; *Wein*: pleasant, appealing

Ansprech|partner *m*, **~partnerin** *f* **1.** *geschäftlich*: contact; **2.** *privat*: somebody to talk to

anspringen (*unreg., trennb., -ge-*) **I.** *v/t.* (*hat*) jump at; **II.** *v/i.* (*ist*) **1.** *Motor*: start (up); **2.** *umg.*: **angesprungen kommen** come bounding along (*od.* up); **3.** *umg. fig.*: **~ auf** (*e-n Vorschlag etc.*) jump at

anspritzen *v/t.* (*trennb., hat -ge-*) *mit Schlauch etc.*: spray; *indem man ins Wasser springt etc.*: splash; *mit Schmutz*: sp(l)atter, splash

Anspruch *m* **1.** *auch Jur.* (*Anrecht, Forderung*) claim (**auf** + *Akk.* to); (*Forderung*) *auch* demand (for); (*Anrecht*) *auch* right; *Jur.* title; *Pl.* (*Anforderungen*) demands; **große Ansprüche stellen** be very demanding; **hohe Ansprüche an j-n stellen** *Person und Aufgabe*: make great demands on s.o.; *Person auch*: expect (*od.* demand) a great deal of s.o., be very exacting (*od.* demanding); *Aufgabe auch*: take a lot out of s.o., be very demanding; **~ erheben auf** *od.* **für sich in ~ nehmen** claim, lay claim to; **~ haben auf** (+ *Akk.*) be entitled to; *Jur.* have a legitimate claim to; **der Film erhebt keinen ~ auf historische Genauigkeit** *fig.* the film doesn't claim to be historically accurate; **2.** (*Beschlag*) **in ~ nehmen** *Person*: (*j-s Hilfe*) call on; (*Kredit, j-s Zeit*) take (up); (*Angebot, Möglichkeit*) make use of, take advantage of; *Aufgabe etc.*: (*j-n*) keep s.o. busy, take a lot out of s.o.; (*Platz, Zeit*) take (up); (*j-s Aufmerksamkeit*) engross (*od.* preoccupy); (*j-s Kräfte, Mittel*) make demands; **i-e Arbeit nimmt sie stark in ~** her work keeps her very busy (*od.* takes up most of her time [and energy])

Anspruchsdenken *n* high material expectations *Pl.*; *gegenüber dem Staat*: entitlement mentality

anspruchslos *Adj.* **1.** (*bescheiden*) modest, easily satisfied, unpretentious; (*wenig Pflege etc. brauchend*) undemanding; **2.** (*schlicht*) plain, simple, unassuming; *Roman etc.*: lowbrow, light; **das Stück war ziemlich ~** there wasn't much to the play; **Anspruchslosigkeit** *f; nur Sg.* **1.** (*Bescheidenheit*) modesty; **2.** simplicity; *e-s Romans etc.*: lack of sophistication

anspruchsvoll *Adj.* **1.** *Person*: demanding, exacting; (*wählerisch*) particular; (*kritisch*) critical; (*übertrieben*) fussy; *Vorhaben*: ambitious; **2.** *geistig etc.*: demanding, highbrow; *Ware, Zeitung etc.*: upmarket

anspucken *v/t.* (*trennb., hat -ge-*) spit at

anspülen *v/t.* (*trennb., hat -ge-*) → **anschwemmen**

anstacheln *v/t.* (*trennb., hat -ge-*) spur on, goad on, prod; (*aufhetzen*) incite

Anstalt *f; -, -en* **1.** (*öffentliche ~* public)

institution, establishment; (*Schule*) institute, school; (*Heim*) home; *für schwer Erziehbare*: reform school; (*Sanatorium*) sanatorium, *Am.* sanitarium; *umg.* (*Nervenheilanstalt*) asylum; (*Gefängnis*) penal institution *förm.*; prison, *Am. auch* penitentiary; **~ des öffentlichen Rechts** institution incorporated under public law; **in e-e (geschlossene) ~ kommen** enter a (secure) clinic; **2.** *Pl.*; *fig.*: **~en machen zu** (+ *Inf.*) get ready to (+ *Inf.*); **keine ~en machen zu** (+ *Inf.*) make no move to (+ *Inf.*), show no sign(s) of (+ *Ger.*); **er machte keine ~en zu gehen** he wouldn't budge; **~en zu etw. treffen** make arrangements for s.th.

Anstalts|arzt *m*, **~ärztin** *f* resident physician; **~kleidung** *f* institutional clothing (*od.* dress); **~leiter** *m*, **~leiterin** *f* director of the (*od.* an) institution; **~zögling** *m* child from an institution, child with an institutional upbringing

Anstand¹ *m*; -(e)s, kein Pl. (sense of) decency; (*Benehmen*) manners *Pl.*; **mit ~ verlieren können** be a good loser; **den ~ wahren** preserve a sense of decency (*od.* decorum)

Anstand² *m*; -(e)s, Anstände; *Jägerspr.* hide, *Am.* blind

anständig I. *Adj.* **1.** *Sache*: (*schicklich*) decent, proper; *Witz*: clean; *Leistung etc.*: respectable; **das war sehr ~ von ihr** that was very decent of her; **2.** *Person*: (*ehrbar*) respectable, decent; *altm.* (*keusch, treu*) chaste; **bleib ~!** *umg. hum* be good!, behave yourself!; **3.** *umg.* (*zufrieden stellend*) decent, reasonable, respectable; **e-e ~e Tracht Prügel** a good hiding; **e-e ~e Portion** a sizable piece, quite a hunk; **II.** *Adv.* decently; properly (*auch umg. tüchtig*); **sich ~ benehmen** behave (o.s.) (well); **benimm dich jetzt ~!** *zu Kind*: (you) behave yourself!; **j-n ~ behandeln** treat s.o. like a human being; **j-m ~ die Meinung sagen** *umg.* give s.o. a piece of one's mind

Anstands|besuch *m* courtesy (*od.* duty) call; **~dame** *f* chaperon(e); **~gefühl** *n* sense of decency, tact

anstandshalber *Adv.* for decency's sake

anstandslos *Adv.* without further ado, no bother *umg.*; (*ungehindert*) freely

Anstands|regel *f* rule of etiquette; *Pl. auch* social conventions; **~wauwau** *m umg.* chaperon(e), *Brit. auch* gooseberry, *Am. auch* third wheel

anstapfen *v/i.* (*trennb.*, ist -ge-) *mst* **angestapft kommen** *umg.* come tramping up (*od.* along)

anstarren *v/t.* (*trennb.*, hat -ge-) stare at

anstatt I. *Präp.* (+ *Gen.*) instead of; **II.** *Konj.*: **~ dass er kam** *od.* **~ zu kommen** instead of coming; **~ im Weg zu stehen könntest du mir auch helfen** you could actually help me instead of just getting in the way

anstauen (*trennb.*, hat -ge-) **I.** *v/t. und v/refl.* → **stauen I, aufstauen I**; **II.** *v/refl. fig. Wut etc.*: build up, accumulate (*bei* in); **angestaute Gefühle** pent-up emotions

anstaunen *v/t.* (*trennb.*, hat -ge-) gaze at s.th. in amazement (*od.* wonder); *mit offenem Mund*: gape at

anstechen *v/t.* (*trennb.*, hat -ge-); (*Kuchen, Braten*) prick; (*Blase*) lance, pierce; (*Reifen*) puncture, slit; (*Fass*) tap; → **angestochen**

anstecken (*trennb.*, hat -ge-) **I.** *v/t.* **1.** *mit e-r Nadel*: pin on; (*Ring*) put (*od.* slip) on; **sich** (*Dat.*) **e-e Blume ~** pin a flower on; **2.** (*anzünden*) set on fire, set *s.th.* alight; (*Kerze, Zigarre etc.*) light (up); **3.** *Med.* infect (*mit* with); **von j-m angesteckt werden** catch *a cold etc.* from s.o.; **er hat mich mit s-r Erkältung angesteckt** he's given me his cold, he's passed his cold on to me; **sie hat uns alle mit ihrem Lachen angesteckt** *fig.* she had us all laughing too, her laughter was contagious; **II.** *v/refl.* catch *a cold* (*od. the measles etc.*) (*bei* from); **III.** *v/i. Med. und fig.* be catching (*od.* infectious, contagious)

ansteckend I. *Part. Präs.* → **anstecken**; **II.** *Adj.* infectious, catching; *durch Kontakt übertragbar*: contagious, communicable; *Substanz*: infective (*alle auch fig.*)

Anstecknadel *f* pin; (*Abzeichen*) badge

Ansteckung *f Med.* infection

Ansteckungs|gefahr *f* danger of infection; **~herd** *m* focus (*od.* cent|re [*Am.* -er]) (of infection)

anstehen *v/i.* (*unreg.*, trennb., hat / südd., österr., schw. ist -ge-) **1.** *in e-r Reihe*: stand in a queue (*Am.* line); (*sich anstellen*) queue up, *auch Am.* line up, stand in line (*nach od. um* for) (*an od.* vor der Kasse at the [cash]till *od.* to pay); **2.** *Sache*: be waiting (*zur Diskussion* for discussion); *Arbeit*: be waiting to be done; *Termin*: be fixed (*auf* + *Akk.* for); **was steht an?** what's next on the agenda?; **~ lassen** put off, leave *s.th.* up in the air; (*Rechnung etc.*) put off paying, defer (payment); **3.** *geh.*: **j-m** (*schlecht/ wohl*) **~** (ill/well) befit s.o.; **es steht ihm nicht an zu** (+ *Inf.*) it's not for him to (+ *Inf.*)

ansteigen *v/i.* (*unreg.*, trennb., ist -ge-) *Gelände*: rise; *fig. auch* go up, increase; **leicht ~** be slightly uphill; **jäh ~** rise steeply (*fig. auch* sharply); *fig. Preise etc.*: *auch* escalate; **stark angestiegene Preise** sharp price rises (*od.* increases); **gewaltig ~de Kosten** spiral(l)ing costs

anstelle *Präp.* (+ *Gen. od. von*) instead of, in place of

anstellen (*trennb.*, hat -ge-) **I.** *v/t.* **1.** (*Gas, Wasser etc.*) turn on; (*Radio, Licht etc.*) *auch* switch on; (*Motor*) start; **2.** (*j-n*) (*einstellen*) employ, take on, *bes. Am.* hire; **j-n fest / zur Probe ~** employ s.o. permanently / on a trial basis / temporarily; **angestellt sein bei** work for, be employed by (*od.* with); **wo sind Sie angestellt?** where do you work?; **j-n zu etw. ~** *umg. fig.* rope s.o. in to do s.th. (*od.* into doing s.th.); **3.** *umg.* (*tun*) do (*mit* with); (*bewerkstelligen*) manage; **was soll ich nur mit dir ~?** you're a hopeless (*Sl.* right) case, you are; **wie hast du das nur angestellt?** how on earth did you manage that?; **wie soll ich es nur ~, diesen Job zu bekommen?** what's the best way of making sure I get that job?; **4.** *umg.* (*Dummheiten etc.*) be up to; **etwas ~** get (*od.* be) up to mischief; **5.** (*anlehnen*) put, lean (*an* + *Akk. od. Dat.* against); *an e-e Reihe*: add; **6.** (*vornehmen*): **Experimente ~** conduct (*od.* carry out) experiments; **Nachforschungen ~** make enquiries; **Überlegungen ~** make observations; **Vergleiche ~** make (*od.* draw) compar-

isons, compare; **Vermutungen ~** make assumptions (*od.* suppositions); **II.** *v/refl.* **1.** queue up, *auch Am.* line up, get in line; **2. sich ~, als ob ...** act as if ...; pretend to (+ *Inf.*); **er hat sich sehr geschickt angestellt** he tackled it very well, he made a good job of it, *Am.* he did a good job; **er hat sich sehr ungeschickt angestellt** he made a really bad job of it, he made a real hash of it, *Am. auch* he did a really bad job; **wie kann man sich so dumm ~!** how can anyone be (*od.* do s.th.) so stupid!; **stell dich nicht so an!** *umg.* stop making such a fuss; *weitS.* stop acting stupid

anstellig *Adj. altm.* deft, skil(l)ful, able

Anstellung *f* (*das Anstellen*) employment; (*Stelle*) post, job

Anstellungsvertrag *m* employment contract

anstemmen *v/refl.* (*trennb.*, hat -ge-): **sich** (*mit der Schulter etc.*) **~ gegen** press o.s. (one's shoulder *etc.*) against

ansteuern *v/t.* (*trennb.*, hat -ge-) **1.** *Naut., Flug.* steer (*od.* head, make) for; **2.** *fig.* head for; (*Posten etc.*) have one's sights set on

Anstich *m Fass*: tap

anstiefeln *v/i.* (*trennb.*, ist -ge-); *umg.*: **angestiefelt kommen** come wandering up (*od.* along) *allg.*

Anstieg *m*; -(e)s, -e **1.** *des Geländes*: ascent; *der Straße*: gradient, *Am.* grade; **steiler ~** steep incline; **2.** *Flut, Wasser*: rise; *fig. auch* increase (+ *Gen.* in); **3.** *Bergsteiger, Ballon*: ascent

anstieren *v/t.* (*trennb.*, hat -ge-); *umg. pej.* stare at

anstiften *v/t.* (*trennb.*, hat -ge-); (*verursachen*) cause; (*anzetteln*) stir up; (*anreizen*) incite, instigate; **j-n zu etw. ~** put s.o. up (*od.* set s.o. on) to s.th.; **j-n zu e-m Verbrechen ~** incite s.o. to commit a crime; **Anstifter** *m*, **Anstifterin** *f* instigator; (*Rädelsführer*) ringleader; **Anstiftung** *f* instigation; incitement

anstimmen *v/t.* (*trennb.*, hat -ge-); (*Lied*) start singing, launch into *umg.*; (*Instrument*) start playing; **e-e Melodie ~** strike up a tune; **ein Geschrei ~** start screaming; **Klagelieder ~** *fig.* break out into lamentations

anstinken *v/i.* (*unreg.*, trennb., hat -ge-); *Sl.*: **gegen die kannst du doch nicht ~** you're not in their league, you haven't got a hope in hell against them

Anstoß *m* **1.** *Fußball*: kick(-)off; **2.** *fig.* (*Antrieb*) impulse, impetus; **den (ersten) ~ geben zu** set off, initiate; **der Wirtschaft Anstöße geben** fire up the economy; **3.** (*Ärgernis*) offen|ce (*Am.* -se); **~ erregen** cause (*od.* give) offen|ce (*Am.* -se) (*bei* to); **~ nehmen** (*an* + *Dat.*) take offen|ce (*Am.* -se) (at), take exception (to) → **Stein 1**

anstoßen (*unreg.*, trennb., -ge-) **I.** *v/t.* (*hat*) **1.** (*in Bewegung setzen*) give *s.th.* a push; *mit dem Fuß*: kick; **2.** (*stoßen*) knock, bump; **sich den Kopf an etw. ~** knock (*od.* bump) one's head against s.th.; **3.** *mit dem Ellbogen*: nudge; **II.** *v/i.* **1.** (*ist*): **~ an** (+ *Akk.*) *od.* **gegen** bump (*od.* knock) against; **2.** (*hat*); *mit Gläsern*: clink glasses; **auf etw.** (*j-s Wohl*) **~** drink to s.th. (s.o.'s health); **3.** (*ist*): **bei j-m ~** offend s.o. (*mit* with); **4.** (*hat*): **mit der Zunge ~** lisp; **5.** (*hat*); *Fußball*: kick off; **6.** (*ist*); (*angrenzen*) border, abut (*an* + *Akk.* on); **anstoßend I.** *Part. Präs.* → **an-**

stoßen; **II.** *Adj. Zimmer etc.*: adjacent, adjoining (*an* to)

Anstößer *m*; *-s*, *-*, **⁓in** *f*; *-*, *-nen schw.* resident; (*Nachbar*) neighbo(u)r

anstößig *Adj.* objectionable; *stärker*: offensive, shocking; (*unanständig*) indecent, improper; **Anstößigkeit** *f* **1.** *nur Sg.*; *Zustand*: offensiveness, offensive nature; **2.** *Bemerkung, Handlung*: indecency; impropriety *förm.*

anstrahlen *v/t.* (*trennb., hat -ge-*) **1.** shine a light *etc.* on; *auf der Bühne*: spotlight, turn the spotlight on; (*Gebäude etc.*) illuminate, light up, floodlight; **2.** *fig.* (*j-n*) beam at; → **angestrahlt**

anstreben *v/t.* (*trennb., hat -ge-*) strive for, aim at, aspire to (*od.* after)

anstreichen *v/t.* (*unreg., trennb., hat -ge-*) **1.** paint; (*tünchen*) whitewash; **2.** (*Textstelle*) mark; (*unterstreichen*) underline; (*Fehler*) mark *s.th.* wrong; (*ankreuzen*) mark *s.th.* with a cross; **3.** (*Streichholz*) strike, light; **4.** *Mus.* (*Saite*) bow; **Anstreicher** *m*, **Anstreicherin** *f* painter

anstrengen (*trennb., hat -ge-*) **I.** *v/refl.* make an effort, try (hard); *stärker*: exert o.s.; **streng dich doch mal an!** *umg.* you could try a bit harder; don't strain yourself *iro.*; → **angestrengt** II, III; **II.** *v/t.* **1.** *sein Gedächtnis* ⁓ rack one's brains; *alle Kräfte* ⁓ use all one's strength, strain every muscle; **2.** *Jur.*: *e-n Prozess* ⁓ (*gegen j-n*) initiate (*od.* commence) proceedings (against s.o.), bring an action (against s.o.); **III.** *vt/i.* exert, strain, be a strain on; (*ermüden*) tire (out); (*erschöpfen*) exhaust; **übermäßig** ⁓ overtax, overexert; *das strengt an* it's hard work; *das schlechte Licht strengt die Augen an* the poor light puts a strain on (*od.* is bad for) the eyes

anstrengend I. *Part. Präs.* → **anstrengen**; **II.** *Adj.* hard (*für die Augen etc.* on the eyes *etc.*); *körperlich*: *auch* strenuous

Anstrengung *f* **1.** (*Strapaze*) strain, stress; *die Reise war mit großen körperlichen* ⁓*en verbunden* the journey (*od.* trip) involved severe physical exertion (*od.* hardship); **2.** (*Bemühung*) effort; *weitS. auch* endeavo(u)r; *mit äußerster* ⁓ by a supreme effort; ⁓*en machen* make efforts

Anstrich *m* **1.** (*das Anstreichen*) painting; **2.** (*Farbschicht*) coat(ing); (*Farbe*) paint; *sehr dünn*: film; **3.** *fig.* (*Anschein, Note*) air, look; (*Anflug*) tinge; *Pol. etc.* complexion; *sich* (*Dat.*) *den* ⁓ *geben* (+ *Gen. od. von*) give o.s. the air of (being)

anströmen *v/i.* (*trennb., ist -ge-*) (*auch angeströmt kommen*) come streaming along

anstücke(l)n *v/t.* (*trennb., hat -ge-*) **1.** ⁓ (*an* + *Akk.*) (*anfügen*) piece on(to), add (onto); (*flicken*) patch (on to); **2.** (*verlängern*) add to (*auch fig.*)

Ansturm *m* **1.** assault (*auf* + *Akk.* on); onslaught (on); *Sport*: attack; **2.** *fig. der Gefühle*: rush, onslaught; **3.** *fig.*: ~ *auf* (+ *Akk.*) rush for; (*e-e Bank*) run on; **anstürmen** *v/i.* (*trennb., ist -ge-*) **1.** *Truppe*: ~ (*gegen*) charge; **2.** *Wind*: storm, rage (*gegen* against); *Wellen*: pound (*gegen etw.* against s.th.); **3.** *umg.*: *mst angestürmt kommen* come charging along

anstürzen *v/i.* (*trennb., ist -ge-*): *angestürzt kommen umg.* come pelting up (*od.* along)

ansuchen I. *v/i.* (*trennb., hat -ge-*); *österr. od. altm. Amtsspr.*: *bei j-m um etw.* ⁓ request s.th. of s.o.; (*e-n Antrag stellen*) apply to s.o. for s.th.; **II. Ansuchen** *n*; *-s*, *-* request; application

Antagonismus *m*; *-*, *Antagonismen* antagonism; **Antagonist** *m*; *-en*, *-en*, **Antagonistin** *f*; *-*, *-nen* antagonist; **antagonistisch I.** *Adj.* antagonistic; **II.** *Adv.* antagonistically

antanzen *v/i.* (*trennb., ist -ge-*); *umg.* (*auch angetanzt kommen*) turn (*od.* show) up, waltz in

Antarktika *f Geog.* (*Kontinent*): Antarctica; **Antarktis** *f Geog.* (*Gebiet*) the Antarctic (*Zone*); **antarktisch** *Adj.* Antarctic, South-polar

antasten *v/t.* (*trennb., hat -ge-*) **1.** (*Ersparnisse etc.*) touch; (*Vorräte*) break into; **2.** *fig.* (*j-s Rechte*) infringe on, encroach on; (*j-s Ehre, Würde*) offend; **3.** (*Thema*) broach, touch on, bring up

antauen *v/i.* (*trennb., ist -ge-*) start to thaw; *Lebensmittel* ⁓ *lassen* leave to defrost for a while; *angetaut sein* have started to thaw

antäuschen *v/t.* (*trennb., hat -ge-*); *Sport*: *rechts/links* ⁓ *beim Fußball etc.*: dummy (*od.* fake) to the right/ left; *e-n Schuss* ⁓ fake a shot

Anteil *m* **1.** share (*an* + *Dat.* of); *Jur. Erbe*: (legal) portion; *j-m s-n* ⁓ *ausbezahlen* pay s.o. their share; *prozentualer* ⁓ percentage; ⁓ *an etw.* (*Dat.*) *haben fig.* have a part in s.th.; **2.** (*Teil*) part (+ *Gen.* of); **3.** *Wirts.* (*Beteiligung*) interest; *s-e* ⁓*e verkaufen* sell one's share(s) (*od.* interest); **4.** *fig.* (*Interesse*) interest; (*Mitgefühl*) sympathy; ⁓ *nehmen an* (+ *Dat.*) take an interest in; *mitfühlend*: sympathize with

anteilig *Adj.* (*und Adv.*) proportionate(ly)

Anteilnahme *f* **1.** interest; **2.** (*Mitgefühl*) sympathy; *j-m s-e* ⁓ *aussprechen* express one's condolences to s.o.; *im Brief*: *mit aufrichtiger* ⁓ with sincere sympathy (*od.* heartfelt condolences)

Anteilschein *m Wirts.* share (*Am.* stock) certificate

Anteilseigner *m*, **⁓in** *f Wirts.* share (certificate) holder, *Am.* stockholder

Antenne *f*; *-*, *-n* **1.** aerial, *bes. Am.* antenna; **2.** *Zool.* antenna, feeler; **3.** *umg. fig.*: *e-e* ⁓ *für etw. haben* have a way with (*od.* feeling for) s.th.

Antennen|kabel *n* aerial (*od. bes. Am.* antenna) cable; **⁓mast** *m* radio mast; **⁓steckdose** *f* aerial (*od. bes. Am.* antenna) socket; **⁓stecker** *m* aerial (*od. bes. Am.* antenna) plug; **⁓verstärker** *m* (aerial *od. bes. Am.* antenna) booster

Anthologie *f*; *-*, *-n Lit.* anthology

anthrazit *Adj. präd.* → **anthrazitgrau**; **Anthrazit** *m*; *-s*, *-e*, *mst Sg.* anthracite; **anthrazitgrau** *Adj. Stoff*: charcoal grey (*Am.* gray)

anthropogen *Adj. geh.* anthropogenic

Anthropologe *m*; *-n*, *-n* anthropologist; **Anthropologie** *f*; *-*, *kein Pl.* anthropology; **Anthropologin** *f*; *-*, *-nen* anthropologist; **anthropologisch** *Adj.* anthropological

Anthroposoph *m*; *-en*, *-en* anthroposophist; **Anthroposophie** *f* anthroposophy; **Anthroposophin** *f*; *-*, *-nen* anthroposophist; **anthroposophisch** *Adj.* anthroposophical

Anti..., **anti...** *im Subst. und Adj.* anti(-)...

Antialkoholiker *m*, **⁓in** *f* teetotal(l)er

Antiatomkraftbewegung *f* anti-nuclear movement, movement against nuclear energy

antiautoritär *Adj.* anti-authoritarian

Antibabypille *f umg.* birth control (*od.* contraceptive) pill; *the* Pill *umg.*

antibakteriell *Adj.* bactericidal, anti-bacterial

Antibeschlagtuch *n Mot.* anti-mist cloth

Antibiotikum *n*; *-s*, *Antibiotika*; *Med., Pharm.* antibiotic; **antibiotisch** *Adj.* antibiotic

Antiblockiersystem *n Mot.* (*abgek.* **ABS**) anti-lock braking system

Antichrist *m*; *nur Sg. Reli.* Antichrist

antidemokratisch *Adj.* antidemocratic

Antidepressivum *n*; *-s*, *Antidepressiva*; *Med., Pharm.* antidepressant

Antifaschismus *m Pol.* anti-Fascism; **Antifaschist** *m*, **Antifaschistin** *f* anti-Fascist; **antifaschistisch** *Adj.* anti-Fascist

Antigen *n*; *-s*, *-e*; *Med., Bio.* antigen

Antihaftbeschichtung *f*: *mit* ⁓ *Pfanne etc.*: nonstick

Antiheld *m*, **⁓in** *f* antihero

Antihistamin *n Pharm.* antihistamine

antik *Adj.* **1.** *hist.* ancient, classical; *die* ⁓*en Völker* the peoples of the Ancient World; *das* ⁓*e Rom* Ancient Rome; **2.** *Möbel etc.*: antique, period ...; *nachgemacht*: reproduction ...; ⁓*e Kostüme* period costumes; *auf* ⁓ *gemacht* done up to look old, *Am.* antiqued

Antike *f*; *-*, *-n* **1.** *hist. nur Sg.* (classical) antiquity; *the* Classical (*od.* Ancient) World; *das Griechenland der* ⁓ Ancient Greece; **2.** (*Kunstwerk*) antiquity, antique (*od.* ancient) work of art; **Antikensammlung** *f* collection of antiques

antikisierend *Adj. Dichtung etc.*: in classical style; *Stil*: in a classical vein

antiklerikal *Adj.* anticlerical

Antiklopfmittel *n Mot.* anti-knock agent

Antikommunist *m*, **⁓in** *f Pol.* anti-Communist; **antikommunistisch** *Adj.* anti-Communist

Antikörper *m*; *mst Pl.*; *Med.* antibody

Antillen *Pl. Geog.*: *die Großen/Kleinen* ⁓ the Greater/Lesser Antilles

Antilope *f*; *-*, *-n*; *Zool.* antelope

Antimaterie *f Phys.* antimatter

Antimilitarismus *m Pol.* antimilitarism; **antimilitaristisch** *Adj.* antimilitaristic

Antimon *n*, *-s*, *kein Pl.*; *Chem.* antimony

Antinomie *f*, *-*, *-n*; *Philos.* antinomy

Antioxidationsmittel *m Chem.* antioxidant

Antipathie *f*, *-*, *-n* antipathy (*gegen* toward[s], to), dislike (of, for)

Antipode *m*; *-n*, *-n*, **Antipodin** *f*; *-*, *-nen*; *Geog. und geh. fig.* antipode

antippen *v/t. und v/i.* (*trennb., hat -ge-*); *umg.* **1.** tap, touch lightly; **2.** *fig.* touch (on)

Antiqua *f*; *-*, *kein Pl.*; *Druck.* roman (type)

Antiquar *m*; *-s*, *-e* **1.** second-hand bookseller; *wertvolle Bücher*: antiquarian bookseller; **2.** → **Antiquitätenhändler**; **Antiquariat** *n*; *-(e)s*, *-e* **1.** second-hand book|shop (*Am.* –store); *wertvolle Bücher*: antiquarian book|shop (*Am.* –store); **2.** (*Handel*) second-hand (*od.* antiquarian) book trade; **Antiquarin** *f*; *-*, *-nen* → **Antiquar** 1, 2; **antiquarisch** *Adj.* second-

hand; *wertvolle Bücher*: antiquarian; ~
bekommen get (*od.* buy) *s.th.* second-
-hand
antiquiert *Adj. pej.* antiquated
Antiquität *f*; -, *-en* antique
Antiquitäten|händler *m*, **~händlerin** *f*
antique dealer; **~laden** *m* antique
shop; *Ladenschild*: Antiques; **~samm-**
ler *m*, **~sammlerin** *f* antique collector
Antisemit *m*, **~in** *f Pol.* anti-Semite;
antisemitisch *Adj.* anti-Semitic; **Anti-**
semitismus *m* anti-Semitism
Antiseptikum *n*; *-s*, *Antiseptika*; *Med.*,
Pharm. antiseptic; **antiseptisch** *Med.*
I. *Adj.* antiseptic; **II.** *Adv.* antisepti-
cally
antistatisch *Adj. Phys.* antistatic
Antiteilchen *n Phys.* antiparticle
Antiterror|einheit *f Pol.* anti-terrorist
squad; **~kampf** *m* fight (*od.* struggle)
against terrorism, fighting terrorism
Antithese *f Philos.*, *Lit.* antithesis; **an-**
tithetisch *Adj.* antithetical
Antitoxin *n Physiol.* antitoxin
Antitranspirant *n*; *-s*, *-e od.* *-s* antiper-
spirant
Antivirenprogramm *n EDV* virus
checker, anti-virus program
Antizipation *f*; -, *-en*; *geh.* anticipation;
antizipieren *v/t.* anticipate
antizyklisch *Adj.* anticyclical
Antizyklone *f*; -, *-n*; *Met.* anticyclone
Antlitz *n*; *-es*, *-e*; *geh.* face; *poet.* countenance
Antonym *n*; *-s*, *-e*; *Ling.* antonym (**zu**
of); **antonymisch** *Adj.* antonymous
antörnen *v/t.* → **anturnen**
antraben *v/i.* (*trennb.*, *ist -ge-*) **1.** (*hat*);
(*zu traben beginnen*) start trotting
(on), break into a trot; **2.** (*ist*); (*auch
angetrabt kommen*) *Pferd*, *Reiter*: trot
up (*od.* along); *umg. fig.* trot (*od.*
turn) up
Antrag *m*; *-(e)s*, *Anträge* **1.** ~ (**auf** +
Akk.) application (for), proposal (of);
(*Gesuch*) request (for); *Parl.*, *in e-r
Sitzung*: motion (for); (*Gesetzesantrag*)
bill (on); *Jur.* petition (for); **e-n ~ stel-**
len file an application; *Parl.* propose a
motion; *Jur.* file (*od.* enter) a petition
(*od.* claim); **e-n ~ ablehnen** reject a
application; **e-n ~ im Parlament ein-**
bringen table (*od.* put forward) a motion in Parliament; **über e-n ~ abstim-**
men vote on a motion; **auf ~** (+ *Gen.*
od. **von**) at the request (of); **2.** (*Heiratsantrag*) proposal; **j-m e-n ~ machen**
propose to s.o.
antragen (*unreg.*, *trennb.*, *hat -ge-*);
geh. **I.** *v/t.*: **j-m etw. ~** offer s.o. s.th.;
II. *v/refl.*: **sich ~ zu** (+ *Inf.*) offer to (+
Inf.)
Antragsformular *n* application form
Antragsteller *m*, **~in** *f* applicant; *Jur.*
petitioner; *Parl.* mover
antrainieren *v/t.* (*trennb.*, *hat*): **j-m/sich**
Ausdauer ~ build up s.o.'s/one's stami-
na; **e-m Hund Gehorsam ~** teach a
dog obedience, teach (*od.* train) a dog
to be obedient (*od.* to follow commands)
antreffen *v/t.* (*unreg.*, *trennb.*, *hat -ge-*)
1. (*j-n*) find, catch; *zufällig*: meet; **ich
hoffe Sie bei bester Gesundheit anzu-**
treffen *geh.* I hope to find you in the
best of health; **2.** (*etw.*) find; *zufällig*:
come across
antreiben (*unreg.*, *trennb.*, *-ge-*) **I.** *v/t.*
(*hat*) **1.** (*Tiere*) drive; **2.** *fig.* (*j-n*) urge
on, harry; **j-n zur Arbeit ~** make s.o.
work; **Eifersucht hat ihn dazu ange-**
trieben it was jealousy that made him
do it (*od.* drove him to it), he did it

out of jealousy; **3.** (*Maschine*, *Fahrzeug*) drive; (*mit starkem Motor*,
Schiff etc.) power; **4.** *ans Land*: wash
ashore; **II.** *v/i.* (*ist*); *ans Land*: wash
(*od.* float) ashore; *Ballon*, *Wolken
etc.*: drift inland
Antreiber *m*, **~in** *f pej.* slave driver
antreten (*unreg.*, *trennb.*, *-ge-*) **I.** *v/i.*
1. (*ist*); (*sich aufstellen*) line up (**zu**
for); *umg. fig. zur Arbeit*: turn up (**zu**
for); *beim Chef*: report (**bei** to); *Mil.*
fall in; **der Größe nach ~** line up according to size; **2.** (*ist*); *zum Wettkampf*: enter (**bei**, **zu** for), participate
(in); *auch zum Kampf*: compete (**gegen** with, against); **~ gegen** *auch* challenge; **3.** (*ist*); *Sport*: (*beschleunigen*)
accelerate; **4.** (*ist*); *Ling.* (*hinzukommen*) *Endung etc.*: be added (**an** +
Akk. to); **II.** *v/t.* (*hat*) **1. den Dienst ~**
report for work/duty; **sein Amt ~** take
up office; **j-s Nachfolge ~** succeed s.o.;
die Regierung ~ take up office, come
into power; **das Studium ~** take up
one's studies, start (at) university, **e-e
Erbschaft ~** enter on (*od.* come into)
an inheritance; **e-e Strafe ~** begin
serving a sentence; **e-e Reise ~** set out
(*od.* off) on a journey; **die Heimreise
~** set off (for) home; **den Beweis für
etw. ~** offer proof (*od.* evidence) of
s.th.; **2.** (*Moped etc.*) start up; **3.** (*festtreten*) (*Erde*) tread (*od.* stamp) down
Antrieb *m* **1.** *fig.*, *auch Psych.* (*Beweggrund*) motive; (*Anreiz*) incentive;
(*Drang*) urge; (*Triebkraft*) drive, propulsion; (*Schwung*) impetus; **j-m
neuen ~ geben** give s.o. the motivation he (*od.* she) needs; **aus eigenem
~** of one's own accord, off one's own
bat *umg.*; **2.** *Tech.* drive, propulsion;
→ **Raketenantrieb**
Antriebs|achse *f Tech.* driving axle;
~aggregat *n* engine unit, prime mov-
er; **~kraft** *f* **1.** *Tech.* power; **2.** *fig.* motive power, driving force; **~rad** *n* driving gear; **~riemen** *m* drive belt;
~scheibe *f* drive (*od.* driving) pulley
antriebsschwach *Adj. Psych.* lacking
in drive; abulic *fachspr.*; **Antriebs-**
schwäche *f*; *nur Sg.* lack of drive
Antriebs|stufe *f Rakete*: propulsion
stage; **~welle** *f Mot.* drive (*od.* propeller) shaft
antrinken *v/t.* (*unreg.*, *trennb.*, *hat -ge-*):
sich (*Dat.*) **e-n Rausch** *od. umg.* **einen
~** get (o.s.) drunk (*od.* pissed *umg.*);
sich Mut ~ give o.s. Dutch courage; →
angetrunken II, III
Antritt *m* **1.** *e-r Reise*: start; *e-s Amtes*:
taking up *of office*; *e-r Erbschaft*: accession (+ *Gen.* to); *e-r Regierung*:
coming into power; **bei ~ der Reise**
when we *etc.* set out (*od.* off) on the
journey (*od.* trip); **bei ~ s-s Amtes**
when he took up office, upon taking
up office; **2.** *Sport*: acceleration
Antritts|besuch *m* first visit; **heute
macht X s-n ~** *Botschafter etc.*: today
X will be presenting his credentials
(**bei** to); **~rede** *f* inaugural address;
Parl. maiden speech
antrittsschnell *Adj. Sport*: quick off
the mark
Antrittsvorlesung *f Univ.* inaugural
lecture
antrocknen *v/i.* (*trennb.*, *ist -ge-*) **1.** *Wäsche etc.*: begin to dry; **2.** (*festtrocknen*)
dry on (**an** + *Dat.* to); **angetrocknete
Speisereste abkratzen** scratch (*od.*
scrape) off dried-on food stains
antun *v/t.* (*unreg.*, *trennb.*, *hat -ge-*)
1. j-m etw. ~ do s.th. to s.o.; **j-m/sich**

etw. Gutes ~ do s.th. nice for s.o./o.s.;
j-m Gewalt ~ do violence to s.o.; *e-r
Frau*: *altm.* ravish, violate *s.o.*; **er würde niemandem etwas ~** he wouldn't
hurt (*od.* harm) a fly; **sich** (*Dat.*) **etwas ~** lay hands upon o.s., do away
with o.s.; → **Zwang** 2; **2. es j-m ~** take
s.o.'s fancy; **sie hat's ihm angetan** he's
quite taken by her, he's fallen for her,
he is smitten with her *umg.*, *Am.* he's
got her under his skin; **3.** *geh.* (*anziehen*) put on; **sie war mit e-r Robe angetan** she was clad in a long gown; →
angetan II
anturnen ['antœrnən] *v/t.* (*trennb.*, *hat
-ge-*); *umg.* turn s.o. on; *Drogen*: *auch*
get *s.o.* high
Antwerpen (*n*); *-s*; *Geog.* Antwerp
Antwort *f*; -, *-en*: ~ (**auf** + *Akk.*) answer
(to), reply (to); *fig.* response (to),
echo; **abschlägige ~** negative reply, refusal; **ausweichende ~** evasive (*od.* ca-
gey *umg.*) answer; **schlagfertige ~** repartee, *Am.* comeback; **in ~ auf** (+
Akk.) in answer to; **j-m e-e ~ geben**
(**auf** + *Akk.*) give s.o. an answer (to),
reply to s.o. (about); **j-m etw. zur ~
geben** respond to s.o. with s.th., give
s.o. s.th. as a response; **j-m die ~
schuldig bleiben** owe s.o. an answer;
j-n keiner ~ würdigen *geh.* consider
s.o. unworthy of an answer; **er weiß
auf alles e-e ~** he's got an answer for
everything; **keine ~ ist auch e-e ~** silence gives consent; *iro.* enough said;
auf Einladung: **um ~ wird gebeten**
RSVP (*Abk.* des französischen „*répondez s'il vous plaît*"); **um umgehen-
de ~ wird gebeten** *förm.* please reply
at your earliest convenience; **als ~
drehte sie ihm nur den Rücken zu** in
reponse she simply turned her back
on him; → **Rede** 5
antworten (*trennb.*, *hat -ge-*) **I.** *vt/i.* answer (**j-m** s.o.), reply (to s.o.); *scharf*:
retort; **auf etw.** (*Akk.*) **~** answer s.th.,
reply to s.th.; **mit Ja/Nein ~** reply with
yes/no; answer in the affirmative/nega-
tive *förm.*; **der Wahrheit gemäß ~** answer truthfully; **was hat sie geantwortet?** what did she say (to that)?;
II. *v/i.* (*reagieren*) respond (to) (**mit**
with)
Antwort|karte *f* reply card; **~schein** *m*
Post. (international) reply coupon
anvertrauen (*trennb.*, *hat*) **I.** *v/t.* **j-m
etw. ~** (en)trust s.o. with s.th., place
s.th. in s.o.'s hands; **j-m ein Geheimnis
etc. ~** confide a secret *etc.* to s.o.;
II. *v/refl.* **1. sich j-m ~** confide in s.o.;
2. *j-s Führung* / **j-m ~** entrust o.s.
to s.o.'s guidance / put one's trust in
s.o.; **anvertraut I.** *P.P.* → **anvertrauen**;
II. *Adj.* entrusted; **die ihm ~en Aufgaben** the tasks he has been entrusted
with, the tasks assigned to him
Anverwandte *m*, *f* relative, relation
anvisieren *v/t.* (*trennb.*, *hat*) **1.** (*Ziel*)
take aim at; **2.** *fig.* aim for (*od.* at),
set one's sights on
anwachsen *v/i.* (*unreg.*, *trennb.*, *ist
-ge-*) **1.** (*Wurzeln schlagen*) take root;
(*festwachsen*) grow on (**an** + *Dat.* to),
graft; **2.** (*zunehmen*) grow, increase,
swell, *auch Fluss*: rise; *Arbeit*, *Zinsen*:
accumulate; **~ auf** (+ *Akk.*) *Betrag*:
run up to, amount to
anwählen *v/t.* (*trennb.*, *hat -ge-*) dial
(up), call (a number)
Anwalt *m*; *-(e)s*, *Anwälte*, **Anwältin** *f*;
-, *-nen* **1.** *Jur.* lawyer, solicitor, *Am.* attorney, counselor; *in Schottland*: advocate; *plädierender*: *Brit.* barrister; *vor*

Gericht: counsel (*des Angeklagten* for the defen|ce [*Am.* -se]); ~ *des Klägers* plaintiff's counsel(l)or; *e-n* ~ *nehmen* get a solicitor (*Am.* an attorney *od.* a lawyer); **2.** *fig.* champion, advocate (+ *Gen.* of); **anwaltlich I.** *Adj.* legal; **II.** *Adv.*: ~ *vertreten* (*durch*) legally represented (by)

Anwaltsbüro *n* **1.** *Räume*: lawyer's (*Am. auch* attorney's) office; *Firma*: firm of lawyers (*od. Brit.* solicitors), *bes. Am.* law firm

Anwaltschaft *f*; -, *-en Jur.* **1.** *Beruf*: legal profession, the bar; (*Vertretung*): *j-s* ~ *übernehmen* take on a case; **2.** *Personen*: the Bar, the legal profession

Anwalts|kammer *f Jur.* Bar Council (*Am.* Association); **~kanzlei** *f* → *Anwaltsbüro* 1, 2; **~praxis** legal practice, *bes. Am.* law firm; **~zwang** *m*; *nur Sg.* obligation to be legally represented in court

anwandeln *v/t.* (*trennb.*, *hat -ge-*); *geh.* befall, come over *allg.*; **Anwandlung** *f* feeling, mood; *plötzliche*: (sudden) impulse, fit; *in e-r* ~ *von Großzügigkeit* in a fit of generosity; *aus e-r* ~ *heraus* on (a sudden) impulse; *seltsame* ~*en haben* have strange (*od.* peculiar) moods

anwärmen *v/t.* (*trennb.*, *hat -ge-*) warm (up); *Mot.* warm up; (*Bier etc.*) take the chill off

Anwärter *m*, **~in** *f auf ein Amt*: candidate (*auf* + *Akk.* for); *Sport*: *auch* contender (for)

Anwartschaft *f Versicherung*: claim, right, entitlement; ~ *auf Leistungen* right to (future) benefits; *die* ~ *auf ein Amt haben* be the number one candidate for a post (*od.* position)

anwatscheln *v/i.* (*trennb.*, *ist -ge-*): *angewatschelt kommen umg.* come waddling up (*od.* along) *allg.*

anwehen (*trennb.*, *-ge-*) **I.** *v/t.* (*hat*) **1.** *geh.*: *j-n* ~ *Wind*: blow at s.o.; *Duft*: waft towards s.o.; *e-e leichte Brise wehte uns an* there was a gentle breeze (blowing); **2.** *geh. fig.*: *j-n* ~ *Gefühl*: befall (*od.* come over *allg.*) s.o.; *Erinnerung*: come back to s.o.; **3.** (*Schnee*) drift up to; (*Blätter*) blow up to; **II.** *v/i.* (*ist*); *Schnee*: drift up to; *Blätter*: be blown up to

anweisen *v/t.* (*unreg.*, *trennb.*, *hat -ge-*) **1.** *j-n* ~ *zu* (+ *Inf.*) give s.o. instructions to (+ *Inf.*), tell (*od.* ask) s.o. to (+ *Inf.*); *angewiesen sein zu* (+ *Inf.*) have instructions to (+ *Inf.*); **2.** *j-n* ~ *bei der Arbeit*: give s.o. directions, show s.o. what to do; **3.** (*zuweisen*) assign, allot, allocate; *Zimmer*: *auch* give; *j-m e-n Platz* ~ show s.o. to his, their *etc.* place(s) (*od.* seat[s]); **4.** *Wirts.* (*j-m e-n Betrag*) remit, transfer; → *angewiesen* II

Anweisung *f* **1.** (*Befehl*) order, instruction; *EDV* command, instruction; *auf* ~ (+ *Gen.*) on the instructions of; *strenge* ~ *haben zu* (+ *Inf.*) have strict instructions to (+ *Inf.*); **2.** (*Anleitung*) instructions *Pl.*, set of instructions; **3.** (*Zuweisung*) assignment, allotment, allocation; **4.** (*Zahlung*) remittance, payment; (*Überweisung*) transfer; (*Geld-, Zahlungsanweisung*) (money) order; (*Formular*) payment slip (*od.* order)

anwendbar *Adj.* applicable (*auf* + *Akk.* to); (*durchführbar*) practicable; *leicht* ~ easy to apply; **Anwendbarkeit** *f* applicability; (*Durchführbarkeit*)

practicability

anwenden *v/t.* (*auch unreg.*, *trennb.*, *hat -ge-*) apply (*auf* + *Akk.* to); (*gebrauchen*) use (*bei* for); make use of; *angewandte Wissenschaft* applied science; *etw. gut od. nutzbringend* ~ make good use of s.th., put s.th. to good use; *Gewalt* ~ use (*od.* resort to) force; *große Sorgfalt* ~ take great care

Anwender *m*; *-s*, -, **~in** *f*; -, *-nen*; *EDV* user

Anwendung *f* **1.** application; (*Gebrauch*) use, employment; *unter* ~ *von* (by) using; *e-r List etc.*: (by) resorting to; *zur* ~ *kommen* be used (*od.* applied), be applicable (*in* + *Dat. od. bei* in *od.* for); **2.** *EDV* (*Programm*) application, program

Anwendungs|bereich *m*, **~gebiet** *n* field of application; **~möglichkeit** *f* **1.** *nur Sg.* (*Anwendbarkeit*) applicability; **2.** possible use(s *Pl.*)

anwerben *v/t.* (*unreg.*, *trennb.*, *hat -ge-*) recruit; *bes. Mil.* enlist; *sich* ~ *lassen Mil.* enlist; *für e-e Tätigkeit*: sign on

anwerfen (*unreg.*, *trennb.*, *hat -ge-*) **I.** *v/i. Sport*: have the first throw; **II.** *v/t.* **1.** *Mot.* start (up); (*Gerät*) switch on; **2.** *Archit.* roughcast, throw (*an* + *Akk.* to)

Anwesen *n*; *-s*, - property, estate

anwesend *Adj.* present (*bei* at); *bei etw.* ~ *sein auch* attend s.th.; *er war nicht* ~ he wasn't there; (*war geistesabwesend*) he was away with the fairies *umg.*, he was miles away *umg.*; *die Anwesenden* those present; *Anwesende natürlich ausgenommen* present company excepted(, of course); *verehrte Anwesende!* Anrede: Ladies and Gentlemen!

Anwesenheit *f*; *nur Sg.* presence (*bei* at) (*auch Vorhandensein*); *in der Schule etc.*: attendance; *in* ~ (+ *Gen.*) in the presence of

Anwesenheits|kontrolle *f* roll call; **~liste** *f* attendance list; *Schule*: register; **~pflicht** *f* obligation to attend

anwetzen *v/i.* (*trennb.*, *ist -ge-*): *angewetzt kommen umg.* come rushing (*od.* tearing) up (*od.* along) *allg.*

anwidern *v/t.* (*trennb.*, *hat -ge-*) → *anekeln*

anwinkeln *v/t.* (*trennb.*, *hat -ge-*) bend

Anwohner *m*; *-s*, -, **~in** *f*; -, *-nen* resident, neighbo(u)r; *nur für* ~ (for) residents only; **~schaft** *f* residents *Pl.*, neighbo(u)rhood

Anwurf *m* **1.** *Sport*: first throw, throw-off; **2.** *mst Pl.*; *fig.* accusation

anwurzeln *v/i.* (*trennb.*, *ist -ge-*) *Pflanzen*: take root; *wie angewurzelt dastehen fig.* stand rooted to the spot

Anzahl *f* number, quantity

anzahlen *v/t.* (*trennb.*, *hat -ge-*) (*Betrag*) make a down payment (*od.* deposit) of ... (*für* for, on); **Anzahlung** *f* deposit; *bei Ratenzahlung*: down payment, (first) instal(l)ment

anzapfen *v/t.* (*trennb.*, *hat -ge-*) **1.** (*Fass, Leitung, Telefon etc.*) tap; (*Fass*) *auch* start; **2.** *umg. fig.* (*anpumpen*) *j-n* ~ tap (*od.* pump) s.o. (for money); **3.** *umg.* (*j-m Blut abnehmen*) take some blood from s.o.

Anzeichen *n* sign, indication; *Med.* symptom; *alle* ~ *sprechen dafür, dass* ... everything seems to indicate that ..., all the signs (seem to) show that ...

anzeichnen *v/t.* (*trennb.*, *hat -ge-*) **1.** *Tafel*: draw (*an* + *Akk.* on); **2.** (*markieren*) mark, note, index

Anzeige *f*; -, *-n* **1.** *bei Polizei*: charge(s); *bei Gericht*: information, denunciation; ~ *erstatten* bring (*od.* press) charges *Pl.*, institute legal proceedings *Pl.* (*gegen* against); ~ *gegen Unbekannt* charge(s) against person or persons unknown; *werden Sie den Fall zur* ~ *bringen?* will you report the matter (to the police)?, will you press charges?; **2.** (*Inserat*) advertisement, ad *umg.*, *Brit. auch* advert; *e-e* ~ *aufgeben od. schalten* place (*od.* put in) an ad(vertisement) (*bei od. in* + *Dat.* in); *doppelseitige* ~ double(-page) spread; **3.** (*Bekanntgabe*) announcement; *amtlich*: advice; **4.** *Tech.* indication; *digitales Gerät, Computer*: display; *optische*: visual display; (*Ablesung*) reading

anzeigen (*trennb.*, *hat -ge-*) **I.** *v/t. und v/refl. bei der Polizei etc.*: (*Person und Sache*) report (to the police); (*Person*) *auch* bring a charge (*od.* charges) against; *sich selbst* ~ give o.s.up (to the police), voluntarily admit (*od.* report) an offen|ce (*Am.* -se); **II.** *v/t.* **1.** (*bekannt geben*) notify (*j-m etw.* s.o. of s.th.), announce (s.th. to s.o.); *Wirts.* advise, notify (s.o. of s.th.); *in der Zeitung*: *die Geburt e-r Tochter zeigen an* ... ... are proud to announce the birth of a daughter; **2.** *Messgerät etc.*: indicate; *auf Skala*: read; *digital und auf Bildschirm*: display; *schreibend*: record, register; *Radargerät*: (re)present; **3.** (*wissen lassen*) signal, indicate, notify; **4.** *fig.* (*deuten auf*) indicate, be indicative of, point to; **III.** *v/refl.* (*sich zeigen*) *Entwicklung, Erkrankung etc.*: show, be noted (*od.* perceptible); → *angezeigt* II

Anzeigen| ... *im Subst. siehe auch Werbe...*; **~abteilung** *f* advertising department; **~annahme** *f* advertising office; **~blatt** *n* free paper; **~preise** *Pl.* advertising rates *Pl.*; **~schluss** *m* deadline (for advertisements); (*Tag*) *auch* closing date (for advertisements); **~teil** *m Zeitung*: advertisements *Pl.*, advertisement (*od. Am.* classified) section, ads *Pl. umg.*; *für Kleinanzeigen*: classified advertising; **~werbung** *f*; *nur Sg.* **1.** *durch Anzeigen*: press advertising; **2.** *von Anzeigenkunden*: canvassing for advertisers

Anzeigepflicht *f obligation to report an illness, event etc.*; **anzeigepflichtig** *Adj.* notifiable

Anzeiger *m* **1.** *Tech.* indicator; **2.** (*Amtsblatt*) gazette, journal; *im Namen lokaler Zeitung*: advertiser

Anzeigetafel *f* indicator board; *Sport, für Resultate*: scoreboard; (*Hinweisschild*) notice board, bulletin board

anzetteln *v/t.* (*trennb.*, *hat -ge-*) (*Komplott etc.*) hatch, instigate; engineer *umg.*; *e-e Verschwörung* ~ *gegen* plot against; *er hat das alles angezettelt* it's all his doing

anziehen (*unreg.*, *trennb.*, *hat -ge-*) **I.** *v/t. und v/refl.* (*Kleidung*) put on; (*j-n, sich*) dress; (*sich*) *auch* get dressed; *sich Handschuhe* ~ put (*od.* pull) on one's gloves; **II.** *v/t.* **1.** (*Schnur, Tuch*) stretch, pull (tight); (*Bremse*) apply, put on; (*Handbremse*) *auch* pull on, set; (*Schraube, Saite*) tighten; (*Zügel*) pull, draw in; **2.** (*Bein, Knie*) draw up; **3.** *Phys.* (*Feuchtigkeit etc.*) absorb, take up; *Magnet*: attract; **4.** *fig.* attract, draw, appeal to; *ich fühlte mich von ihm angezogen* I felt attracted (*od.*

drawn) to him; **III.** v/i. **1.** (zu ziehen beginnen) Pferd, Auto: pull away; Schach etc.: move first, make the first move; **Weiß zieht an** white to play; **2.** Wirts. Preise, Aktien etc.: advance, rise, stiffen

anziehend I. Part. Präs. → **anziehen**; **II.** Adj. fig. engaging; stärker: charming; (attraktiv) attractive

Anziehung f auch Phys. attraction

Anziehungs|kraft f **1.** Phys. force of attraction, attractive force; des Mondes etc.: pull; der Erde: gravitational force, power of gravitation; **2.** fig. attraction (**für** for), appeal (to od. for); sexuelle: sex appeal; **~punkt** m (Attraktion) draw, cent|re (Am. -er) of attraction

anzischen (trennb., -ge-) **I.** v/t. (hat) **1.** Schlange, Schwan: hiss at; **2.** fig. böse: snarl at; **3.** umg. fig.: sich einen ~ get a bit merry; **II.** v/i. (ist); umg. (auch **angezischt kommen**) come whizzing along

Anzucht f von Pflanzen: growing, cultivation; von Sämlingen: (plant) propagation, raising of seedlings; von Tieren: rearing, raising

Anzug m **1.** für Männer: suit; für Frauen (Hosenanzug) trousersuit, Am. pantsuit; **2.** (Anrücken) approach, advance; **im ~ sein** be in the offing; Feind: be on the advance, be approaching; Gewitter: be brewing, be coming up; Gefahr: be looming (od. imminent); Grippe: be coming on; **3.** Schach etc.: opening (od. first) move; **4.** Mot. pull, acceleration, Am. pickup; **5.** schw. Pol. (Antrag) motion

anzüglich Adj. Bemerkung: suggestive; Witz: risqué, near the knuckle umg., bes. Am. off-colo(u)r; Lächeln: salacious; ~ **werden** get personal; **Anzüglichkeit** f **1.** nur Sg.; Art: suggestiveness, offensiveness; **2.** (Anspielung) (offensively) suggestive remark

Anzug|hose f suit trousers (Am. pants) Pl.; **~stoff** m suit material (od. cloth), suiting

Anzugsvermögen n Mot. pull, acceleration, Am. pickup

anzünden v/t. (trennb., hat -ge-) light; (Zigarre, Pfeife) auch light up; (Haus, Stroh etc.) set fire to; **Anzünder** m lighter

anzweifeln v/t. (trennb., hat -ge-) doubt; (Zweifel aussprechen über) (call in) question, dispute; **Anzweifelung** f doubt, calling into question

anzwitschern (trennb., -ge-); umg. **I.** v/i. (ist); (auch **angezwitschert kommen**) roll up, come strolling (od. toddling) along; **II.** v/t. (hat) **sich e-n ~** umg. get tipsy (od. sloshed)

AOK Abk. (Allgemeine Ortskrankenkasse) → **allgemein** I 1

Äonen Pl. (a)eons

Aorta f; -, Aorten; Anat. aorta; **Aortenklappe** f aortic valve

Apache [a'pat∫ə] m; -n, -n, **Apachin** [-ɪn] f; -, -nen Apache, weiblich auch: Apache woman (od. girl etc.)

Apanage [apa'na:ʒə] f; -, -n allowance

apart Adj. striking, unusual, individual; Kleidung: stylish

Apartheid f; -, kein Pl. apartheid; **~politik** f policy of apartheid, apartheid policy (od. politics Pl.)

Aparthotel n apartment hotel

Apartment n; -s, -s flat; (Einzimmerwohnung) one-room (Am. efficiency) apartment, Am. auch efficiency, studio, Brit. auch one-room flat, studio

flat, flatlet; **~haus** n block of flats, Am. studio apartment building, apartment house

Apathie f; -, -n apathy; Psych. listlessness; **apathisch** Adj. apathetic(ally Adv.); Psych. listless

Apennin m; -s; Geog.: **der ~** → **Apenninen**; **Apenninen** Pl. Geog.: **die ~** the Apennines; **Apenninenhalbinsel** f; nur Sg.; Geog. Apennine peninsula

aper Adj. südd., österr., schw. snow-free, free from snow präd.

Aperçu [aper'sy:] n; -s, -s witticism, aperçu

Aperitif m; -s, -e od. -s aperitif

apern v/i.; südd., österr., schw. Straßen, Hänge: become clear of snow, **es apert** it's thawing, the snow is going

Apfel m; -s, Äpfel **1.** apple; **2.** fig.: **in den sauren ~ beißen** grasp the nettle, bite the bullet; **der ~ fällt nicht weit vom Stamm** Sprichw. like father like son, Am. the apple never falls far from the tree, he etc. is a chip off the old block, it's in the blood; **für e-n ~ und ein Ei** umg. (arbeiten) for a song (od. peanuts); (bekommen) auch dirt cheap, for next to nothing; **~baum** m Bot. apple tree; **~blüte** f Bot. **1.** apple blossom; **2.** Zeit: apple blossom season (od. time), blossoming of the apple trees

Apfel|essig m Gastr. apple cider vinegar; **~gelee** n od. m Gastr. apple jelly; **~kern** m pip, Am. auch appleseed; **~kuchen** m Gastr. apple flan (Am. cake); **~gedecker** ~ (covered) apple pie; **~küchle** n; -s, -; Gastr. südd. pancake filled with apples; **~most** m Gastr. **1.** (Saft) apple juice; **2.** südd. (alkoholisch) cider, Am. hard cider; **~mus** n Gastr. apple purée; zum Braten: apple sauce; **~quitte** f Bot. apple-shaped quince; **~saft** m apple juice; **~schale** f apple skin (od. peel); **~scheibe** f slice of apple; **~schimmel** m Zool. (Pferd) dapple grey (Am. gray); **~schorle** f: (saure/süße) ~ apple-juice spritzer (with mineral water / lemonade)

Apfelsine f; -, -n Bot. **1.** orange; **2.** orange tree

Apfelsinen|baum m Bot. orange tree; **~blüte** f orange blossom; **~saft** m orange juice; **~schale** f orange peel; **~scheibe** f orange slice, slice of orange

Apfel|sorte f type (od. sort) of apple; **~strudel** m Gastr. apple strudel; **~tasche** f Gastr. apple Danish (pastry), apple turnover; **~wein** m (Am. hard) cider; **~wickler** m; -s, -; Zool. (Kleinschmetterling) codling moth

Aphorismus m; -, Aphorismen; Lit., geh. aphorism; **aphoristisch I.** Adj. aphoristic; **II.** Adv. aphoristically

Aphrodisiakum n; -s, Aphrodisiaka; Med. aphrodisiac

Aplomb m; -s, kein Pl.; geh. aplomb, self-confidence

Apnoe f; -, -n; Med. (sleep) apn(o)ea

Apo f; -, kein Pl.; Abk. Pol. hist. (außerparlamentarische Opposition) extra-parliamentary opposition (anti-authoritarian and non-parliamentary reform movement, particularly during the West-German Grand Coalition of 1966-1969)

apodiktisch Adj. Philos. od. geh. apodictic; weitS. dogmatic

Apogäum n; -s, Apogäen; Astron., Raumf. apogee

Apokalypse f; -, -n; Reli. od. geh.

apocalypse; **apokalyptisch** Adj. apocalyptic; **die ~en Reiter** the Four Horsemen of the Apocalypse

apolitisch Adj. apolitical

Apoll m; -s, **Apollo** m; -s; Myth. Apollo; **Apollofalter** m Zool. apollo (butterfly)

Apologet m; -en, -en, **~in** f; -, -nen; geh. apologist; **Apologetik** f; -, -en **1.** (Verteidigung) apology, apologia; **2.** (Disziplin) apologetics Pl. (V. im Sg.); **apologetisch I.** Adj. apologetic; **II.** Adv. apologetically; **Apologie** f; -, -n apology, apologia

Apostel m; -s, -; Reli. und fig. apostle (+ Gen. of); **~brief** m epistle; **~geschichte** f: **die ~** Acts Pl., the Acts of the Apostles Pl.

...apostel im Subst. mst iro. apostle of ...; **ein Frischluftapostel** a fresh air fanatic (od. enthusiast)

a posteriori Adv. und Adj. geh. a posteriori

apostolisch Adj. Reli. apostolic; **das Apostolische Glaubensbekenntnis** the Apostles' Creed; **~er Segen** apostolic blessing; **der Apostolische Stuhl** the Apostolic See

Apostroph m; -s, -e apostrophe; **apostrophieren** v/t. **1.** apostrophize; **2.** fig. j-n etw. ~ mention (od. refer to) s.o. (**als** as)

Apotheke f; -, -n chemist's (shop), Am. pharmacy, drugstore; **dieses Geschäft ist ja e-e ~** (ist sehr teuer) this shop (Am. auch store) is exorbitant; the prices here are a bit steep umg.

Apothekenhelfer m, **~in** f chemist's (Am. pharmacist's) assistant

apothekenpflichtig Adj. obtainable in a chemist's shop (Am. in a pharmacy) only

Apotheker m; -s, - (dispensing) chemist, bes. Am. pharmacist, Am. druggist

Apothekergewicht n apothecaries' weight

Apothekerin f; -, -nen (dispensing) chemist, bes. Am. pharmacist; **Apothekerwaage** f apothecary's scales

Apotheose f; -, -n; geh. apotheosis

Appalachen Pl. Geog.: **die ~** the Appalachians, the Appalachian Mountains

Apparat m; -(e)s, -e **1.** apparatus; (Gerät) device, appliance, machine; kleiner, auch iro.: gadget; feinmechanischer: instrument; **2.** Bio. (System) apparatus; **3.** umg. a) Funk. radio, b) TV set, c) Fot. camera, d) (Rasierer) shaver, e) Telef. phone; (Nebenstelle) extension; **am ~!** Speaking; **am ~ bleiben** hold the line; **wer ist am ~?** who is speaking (please)?; **4.** fig. organization, apparatus; Pol. auch political (od. party od. propaganda) machine; **5.** umg. fig. Ding, Baby, Fisch: whopper; Person: (great) hulk; **6.** Lit.: (kritischer) ~ critical apparatus; **7.** Päd., Univ. (Semesterapparat) (reference collection of) course material

Apparate|bau m; nur Sg. apparatus engineering, design and manufacture of apparatus; **~medizin** f high-tech(nology) medicine

apparativ Adj. fachspr.: **~e Diagnostik** machine-aided diagnosis

Apparatur f; -, -en equipment kein Pl., apparatus kein Pl.; (Maschinen) machinery kein Pl.

Appartement [apartə'mã:] n; -s, -s **1.** → **Apartment**; **2.** im Hotel: suite

Appell m; -s, -e **1.** Mil. roll call; **zum ~ antreten** line up (od. fall in) for roll call (inspection); **e-n ~ abhalten** call the roll, take the call-over, hold an inspection; **2.** *fig.* appeal (**an** + *Akk.* to)

Appellation *f*; *-, -en*; *Jur. schw., sonst altm.* (*Berufung*) appeal; **Appellationsgericht** *n Jur., altm.* court of appeal, appellate court

Appellativ *n*; *-s, -e*; *Gram.* appellative, common noun

appellieren *v/i.*: **~ an** (+ *Akk.*) (make an) appeal to

Appendix *m*; *-(es)*, *Appendizes od. -e*; *Anat.* appendix (*auch Anhang und fig.*); **Appendizitis** *f*; *-, Appendizitiden*; *Med.* appendicitis

Appetit *m*; *-(e)s, -e, mst Sg.* appetite (*auch fig.*) (**auf** + *Akk.* for); **~ haben** *od.* **bekommen auf etw.** feel like s.th.; **ich hätte richtig ~ auf …** I could just (*od.* really) fancy (*Am.* could really go for) …; **etw. mit ~ verzehren** really enjoy (eating) s.th., tuck into s.th. with relish *umg.*; **j-m ~ machen** give s.o. an appetite (**auf** for); **es macht ~** it really gives you an appetite; **das regt den ~ an** it gives you an appetite (*od.* makes you hungry); **j-m den ~ verderben** spoil s.o.'s appetite; *fig.* put s.o. off; **mir ist der ~ vergangen!** I've lost my appetite!; **dabei kann einem ja der ~ vergehen!** it's enough to put you off your food!; *fig. auch*: it's enough to put you off, (*Am. auch* turn your stomach); **guten ~!** bon appetit!, enjoy! *umg.*, tuck in! *umg. hum.*; **der ~ kommt beim Essen** *Sprichw.* appetite comes with the eating; *fig.* the more you have, the more you want

appetitanregend *Adj.* appetizing; **~es Mittel** appetite stimulant

Appetit|happen *m* canapé; **~hemmer** *m*; *-s, -* appetite suppressant

appetitlich I. *Adj.* **1.** appetizing; **2.** *fig. Person*: attractive; **nicht besonders ~** not very inviting; **II.** *Adv.* **~ verpackt** appetizingly presented (*od.* packed)

Appetitlosigkeit *f*; *nur Sg.* loss of appetite

Appetit|mangel *m*; *nur Sg.* lack (*od.* loss) of appetite; anepithymia *fachspr.*; **~zügler** *m*; *-s, -* appetite suppressant

applaudieren *v/i. geh.* applaud, cheer (+ *Dat.* s.o.); **Applaus** *m*; *-es, -e, mst Sg.* applause; → **Beifall**

Applikation *f*; *-, -en* **1.** *Med. und geh.* application, administration; **2.** **~en** *Mode*: trimmings, appliqué; **Applikator** *m*; *-s, -en* applicator; **applizieren** *v/t.* **1.** (*Stoff*) sew on; **2.** *Med.* administer; **3.** *geh.* (*anwenden*) apply (**auf** + *Akk.* to)

apportieren *v/t.* retrieve, fetch; **Apportierhund** *m* retriever

Apposition *f*; *-, -en*; *Ling.* apposition

appretieren *v/t. fachspr.* finish; (*Textilien stärken*) *auch* starch; (*imprägnieren*) waterproof; (*Holz*) *auch* dress; (*Papier*) *auch* glaze; **Appretur** *f*; *-, -en* finish, dressing, waterproofing

Approbation *f*; *-, -en*; *Med., Pharm.* licen|ce (*Am.* -se) to practi|se (*Am.* -ce) medicine; **approbiert** *Adj.* qualified

Après-Ski [aprɛˈʃiː] *n*; *-, kein Pl.* après-ski (*auch Kleidung*)

Aprikose *f*; *-, -n Bot.* **1.** apricot; **2.** apricot tree; **Aprikosenkonfitüre** *f Gastr.* apricot jam (*od. Am.* preserves *Pl.*)

April *m*; *-, -e, mst Sg.*; (*abgek.* **Apr.**) April; **der erste ~** the first of April, April the first, April first *Am.*; hum. April Fool's (*od.* All Fools') Day; **am 28. ~** on the 28th of April; **am Mon-**

tag, dem 28. ~ on Monday the 28th of April; **München, den 28. ~ 2001** Munich, 28th April 2001, Munich, April 28th, 2001; **im ~** in April; **im Monat ~** in the month of April; **in diesem ~** this April; **im Laufe des ~** during April; **Anfang/Mitte/Ende ~** start (*od.* beginning) of April, early April / middle of April, mid-April / end of April; **j-n in den ~ schicken** make an April fool of s.o.; **~, ~!** April fool!; **~, der tut, was er will** *Sprichw.* April weather, rain and sunshine both together; **~schauer** *m* April shower; **~scherz** *m* April-fool joke; **~wetter** *n* April showers *Pl.*

a priori *Adv. und Adj. geh.* a priori

apropos *Adv.* by the way; talking about …, apropos

Apsis *f*; *-, Apsiden*; *Archit.* apse; *von Zelt*: bell end

Apulien (*n*); *-s Geog.* Apulia; **apulisch** *Adj.* Apulian

Aquädukt *m*; *-(e)s, -e*; *Archit.* aqueduct

Aquakultur *f* aquaculture

aquamarin I. *Adj.* aquamarine; **II. Aquamarin** *m*; *-s, -e*; *Min.* aquamarine

Aquanaut *m*; *-en, -en, ~in* *f*; *-, -nen* aquanaut

Aquaplaning *n*; *-(s), kein Pl.*; *Mot.* aquaplaning, *bes. Am.* hydroplaning

Aquarell *n*; *-s, -e Kunst* watercolo(u)r; **~farbe** *f* watercolo(u)r; **~maler** *m* watercolo(u)rist; **~malerei** *f* watercolo(u)r (painting); **~malerin** *f* watercolo(u)rist

Aquarien|fisch *m* aquarium fish; **~kunde** *f*; *nur Sg.* theory of aquarium care (*od.* good management)

Aquarium *n*; *-s, Aquarien* aquarium

Äquator *m*; *-s, Äquatoren, mst Sg. Geog.* equator; **den ~ überqueren** cross the line; **äquatorial** *Adj.* equatorial; **Äquatortaufe** *f* crossing-the-line ceremony

Aquavit *m*; *-s,-e* aquavit, akvavit

Aquitanien (*n*); *-s; hist.* Aquitania; *Geog.* Aquitaine

äquivalent I. *Adj.* equivalent; **II. Äquivalent** *n*; *-(e)s, -e* **1.** (*Ersatz*) recompense; **2.** (*Entsprechung*) equivalent; **Äquivalenz** *f*; *-, -en* equivalence

Ar *n*; *-s, -e Flächenmaß*: are

Ara *m*; *-s, -s*; *Orn.* Buffon's (*od.* Great Green) macaw

Ära *f*; *-, Ären* era

Araber *m*; *-s, -* Arab (*auch Pferd*); (*Bewohner Arabiens*) Arabian; **Araberin** *f*; *-, -nen* Arab (*od.* Arabian) woman (*od.* girl)

Arabeske *f*; *-, -n*; *Kunst* arabesque

Arabien (*n*); *-s; Geog.* Arabia

arabisch I. *Adj.* **1.** Arab; **die ~e Liga** *Pol.* the Arab League; **~e Ziffern** Arabic numerals; **die ~e Sprache** the Arabic language; **2.** *bes. Geog.* Arabian, of Arabia; **der Arabische Golf** the Arabian Gulf; **die Arabische Halbinsel** the Arabian Peninsula; **II. Arabisch** *n*; *-(s)*; *Ling.* Arabic; **das Arabische** the Arabic language; **Arabistik** *f*; *-, kein Pl.* Arabic studies

Aragonien (*n*); *-s; Geog.* Aragon

Aralsee *m*; *Geog.*: **der ~** the Aral Sea

Arbeit *f*; *-, -en* **1.** *allg.*: work; (*schwere Arbeit*) hard work; **geistige ~** brainwork; **körperliche ~** physical work (*od.* labo[u]r); **~en** work *Sing.* (**an** + *Dat.* on); (*Aufgabe*) task, job; **e-e undankbare ~** a thankless task; **an od. bei der ~** at work; **an die ~ gehen, sich an die ~ machen** start work, get (down) to

work; **los, an die ~!** right, (get) to work!; **s-e ~ tun** *od.* **s-r ~ nachgehen** go about one's work; **ich hab mit dem Garten viel ~** the garden's a lot of work; **ganze** *od.* **gute etc. ~ leisten** do a good job (*auch fig.*); **immer nur halbe ~ machen** never do things (*od.* finish things off) properly; **etw. in ~ haben** be working on s.th.; **etw. in ~ geben** have s.th. done (*od.* made); **etw. ist in ~** work has started (*od.* is in progress) on s.th.; **erst die ~, dann das Vergnügen!** business before pleasure; **er hat die ~ nicht erfunden** *iro.* he's a born skiver (*Am.* slacker) *umg.*; → **getan** II, **Hand**[1] 3; **2.** (*Mühe*) trouble; (*Anstrengung*) effort, exertion; **er lebt von s-r Hände ~** he lives by the labo(u)r of his hands; **unsere ganze ~ war umsonst** all our labo(u)r has been in vain; **viel ~ kosten** be (*od.* create) a lot of work; **die tägliche ~ im Haus** the household chores; **ich hoffe, es macht Ihnen nicht zu viel ~** I hope it's not too much trouble for you; **es war viel ~, sie zu überzeugen** convincing her was hard work; **3.** *nur Sg.* (*bezahlte Arbeit, Beschäftigung*) work, employment; **~ haben** have a job; **ohne ~** unemployed, out of work, jobless; **~ suchen** look for a job, seek employment *geh.*; **~ Suchende** *Pl.* job seekers; **die ~ verlieren** lose one's job; **zur** (*umg. auf*) **~ gehen** go to work; (**bei j-m) in ~ stehen** be employed by s.o., be in the employ of s.o. *förm.*; **e-r** (**geregelten) ~ nachgehen** be in (steady) employment, have a (steady) job; **sie versteht i-e ~** she knows her job; **4.** *Produkt*: (piece of) work; (*schriftliche, wissenschaftliche Arbeit*) paper; *längere*: treatise; **künstlerische ~** work of art; **gute ~! als Lob**: good work!; **5.** (*schriftliche Prüfung*) test, exam; **e-e ~ schreiben** sit (*od.* take) a test; **~en korrigieren** mark (*od.* grade) test papers; **6.** *Pol.* labo(u)r; **Tag der ~** Labo(u)r Day (*GB: 1. Mai; USA, Kanada*: erster Montag im September; *Neuseeland*: erster Montag im Oktober; *Australien*: unterschiedlich je nach *Bundesstaat*); **7.** *Phys.* work; **8.** *Sport*: (*Training*) training (**an** + *Dat. od.* **mit** on *od.* with)

arbeiten I. *v/i.* **1.** *Person*: work; (*berufstätig sein*) *auch* be in work; **geistig/körperlich ~** do mental/phsyical work; **~ als Gärtner etc.** work as a gardener etc.; **~ an** be working on; **~ bei** *od.* **für** (*angestellt sein*) work for; **für Geld ~** work for money; **für** (*sich einsetzen*) work for; **~ für zwei** do the work of two; **die Zeit arbeitet für/gegen uns** *fig.* we've got time on our side / against us; **~ mit e-m Werkzeug, Material**: work with; **e-r Firma**: deal with, do business with; **~ über** (+ *Akk.*) (*schreiben*) work (*od.* write) on; **~ wie ein Wilder** *umg.* work like mad; **2.** (*funktionieren*) work; *Organ auch*: function; *Maschine etc. auch*: operate, run; **3.** *Holz etc.*: expand and contract; *Teig*: rise; *Wein etc.*: work; **4.** *Wirts. Kapital etc.*: work (**mit Gewinn** at a profit); **sein Geld ~ lassen** invest; **5.** *Sport*: (*trainieren*) train (**an** + *Dat. od.* **mit** on *od.* with); **~ mit e-m Pferd, Hund** (*dressieren*) train; **6.** **an sich** (*Dat.*) **~** (work to) improve o.s.; **man sah, wie es in ihm arbeitete** you could almost see it churning around inside him; **II.** *v/refl.* **1.** (*sich mühen*): **sich durch den Schnee / e-n Roman ~**

work (*od.* plough, *Am.* plow) one's way through the snow / a novel; **sich nach oben** ~ work one's way up to the top; **sich müde/krank** *etc.* ~ work until one is tired/ill, work o.s. into the ground; **sich zu Tode** ~ work o.s to death / ruin o.s.; **2.** *unpers.*: **hier arbeitet es sich schlecht** it's difficult to work here; **III.** *v/t.* **1.** (*anfertigen*) make, fashion; **e-e Statue in** *od.* **aus Bronze** ~ make (*od.* work) a statue in bronze; **das Kleid ist sorgfältig gearbeitet** the dress is beautifully made (*od.* finished); **2.** (*tun*) do; **was arbeitet er?** what is he doing?; **höchste Zeit, dass du mal was arbeitest!** it's high time for you to get to work (*od.* do something *od.* do some work)!; **3.** sich (*Dat.*) **die Hände wund** ~ *umg.* work one's hands raw

Arbeiter *m*; *-s, -* worker, working man, worker; *bes. beim Straßenbau*: workman, worker; (*Ggs. Angestellter*) blue--collar worker; *für Schwerarbeit*: labo(u)rer; ~ **und Arbeiterinnen** male and female workers; **die** ~ **als Klasse**: the working classes; ~**ameise** *f Zool.* worker ant; ~**aufstand** *m* workers' revolt; ~**bewegung** *f hist.* Labo(u)r movement; ~**dichtung** *f Lit.* working--class literature; ~**familie** *f* working--class family

arbeiterfeindlich *Adj.* anti-labo(u)r, anti-workers

Arbeiterfrage *f hist.* labo(u)r question

arbeiterfreundlich *Adj.* pro-labo(u)r, pro-workers

Arbeiterführer *m*, ~**in** *f* labo(u)r leader, workers' leader

Arbeitergewerkschaft *f* trade (*Am.* labor) union, workers' union

Arbeiterin *f* **1.** (female) worker, working woman; **2.** *Zool.* (*Biene*) worker bee; (*Ameise*) worker ant

Arbeiter|jugend *f* young workers *Pl.*; ~**kammer** *f österr.*; *etwa* workers' and employees' professional association; ~**kind** *n* working-class boy (*od.* girl); *Pl.* working-class children (*umg.* kids); ~**klasse** *f* working class(es *Pl.*); ~**lied** *n* workers' song; ~**literatur** *f Lit.* working-class literature; ~**milieu** *n* working-class background (*od.* environment); ~**organisation** *f* labo(u)r organization; ~**partei** *f Pol.* workers' party

Arbeiterschaft *f* labo(u)r force, workforce, (the) workers

Arbeiter|siedlung *f* working-class estate; ~**stadt** *f* working-class town; ~**und-Bauern-Staat** *m; nur Sg.*; *hist.*, *ehem. DDR*: workers' and peasants' state; ~**unruhen** *Pl.* unrest *Sg.* among(st) the workers, industrial unrest; ~**verein** *m* workers' association; ~**viertel** *n* working-class area; ~**wohlfahrt** *f* (*abgek. AWO*) workers' welfare association

Arbeitgeber *m* employer; ~**anteil** *m Sozialversicherung*: employer's contribution

Arbeitgeberin *f* (female) employer

Arbeitgeber|seite *f* employers' side; ~**verband** *m* employers' association

Arbeitnehmer *m* employee; ~**anteil** *m Sozialversicherung*: employee's contribution; ~**freibetrag** *m* earned-income allowance

Arbeitnehmerin *f* (female) employee

Arbeitnehmer|seite *f* employees' side; ~**vertretung** *f* employee representatives *Pl.*

Arbeitsablauf *m* flow of work, work

---

routine, work flow; (*Arbeitsfolge*) sequence of operations

arbeitsam *Adj. geh. altm.* industrious, hardworking

Arbeits|amt *n in GB*: job centre; *altm.* employment exchange; *in USA*: employment office; ~**anfall** *m* workload; ~**angebot** *n* vacancies *Pl.*; ~**anleitung** *f* instructions *Pl.*, set of instructions; ~**antritt** *m*: **bei** (**vor**) ~ on (before) taking up work (*od.* one's job); ~**anweisung** *f* working instructions *Pl.*; ~**anzug** *m* (*Overall*) overalls *Pl.*; ~**atmosphäre** *f* work atmosphere, atmosphere at work (*od.* in the workplace); ~**auffassung** *f* attitude toward(s) work; ~**aufwand** *m* amount of work involved (**für** in); *etw.* **mit großem** ~ **erreichen** (have to) put a lot of work into s.th.

arbeitsaufwändig, **arbeitsaufwendig** *Adj.* labo(u)r-intensive; (*kompliziert*) complicated; ~ **sein** *auch* be a lot of work

Arbeits|ausfall *m* loss of working hours; ~**ausschuss** *m* working committee, study group; ~**bedingungen** *Pl.* working (*Tech.* operating) conditions; *im Vertrag*: conditions of employment; ~**beginn** *m* start of work; ~**belastung** *f* work pressure; pressures *Pl.* of work; ~**bereich** *m* **1.** (*Tätigkeitsbereich*) scope (of work); **2.** *Tech.* range of operation; *von Kran, Bagger etc.*: operating radius; **3.** (*Umfeld*) work surroundings, workplace

Arbeitsbeschaffung *f* job creation

Arbeitsbeschaffungs|maßnahme *f* (*abgek. ABM*) job-creating (*od.* -generating) measure(s); ~**programm** *n* job-creation scheme (*Am.* program)

Arbeits|bescheinigung *f* certificate of employment, worksheet; ~**besuch** *m* working visit; ~**biene** *f* **1.** *Zool.* worker bee; **2.** *fig.* busy bee; *Frau*: *auch* busy Lizzie *umg.*; ~**blatt** *n* worksheet; ~**buch** *n Päd.* exercise book, workbook; ~**bühne** *f* work(ing) platform; ~**dienst** *m* community-service (work); *hist.* (*Reichsarbeitsdienst*) (Reich) Labo(u)r Service; ~**eifer** *m* eagerness to work, zeal; ~**einsparung** *f* saving on working hours; ~**einstellung** *f* **1.** work stoppage; *e-s Betriebs*: shutdown; (*Streik*) strike, walkout; **2.** → **Arbeitsauffassung**; ~**emigrant** *m*, ~**emigrantin** *f* economic migrant; ~**ende** *n* end of work, time when one finishes work; ~**erlaubnis** *f* work permit; ~**erleichterung** *f*: **e-e** ~ **darstellen** (**für** *j-n*) save (s.o.) a lot of work; ~**ersparnis** *f* labo(u)r saving; ~**essen** *n* working lunch (*od.* dinner); ~**ethos** *n* work ethic

arbeitsfähig *Adj.* **1.** (*gesund*) fit for (*od.* to) work; *grundsätzlich*: able to work; **2.** *Pol. Regierung*: viable; ~**e Mehrheit** working majority; **Arbeitsfähigkeit** *f; nur Sg.* **1.** *e-r Person*: fitness for work, ability to work; **2.** *Pol.* viability

Arbeitsfläche *f* work(ing) surface; *bes. in der Küche*: worktop, *Am. auch* countertop

Arbeitsfluss *m* work flow

arbeitsfrei *Adj.*: ~**er Tag** day off; (*Feiertag*) public (*Am. auch* legal) holiday; ~**er Nachmittag** afternoon off

arbeitsfreudig *Adj.* eager to work, willing to work

Arbeits|frieden *m* industrial peace; ~**gang** *m* work cycle, (working) process; **in einem** ~ in one process (*od.* go

---

umg.); ~**gebiet** *n* scope of work (*od.* activity); ~**gemeinschaft** *f* **1.** *Wirts.* joint venture; **2.** *internationale etc.*: work(ing) group; syndicate; **3.** *Päd. etc.* project group (*od.* team), working team, study group; ~**genehmigung** *f* work permit; ~**gerät** *n* tool, implement; *als Koll. auch* tools *Pl.*; ~**gericht** *n Jur.* industrial tribunal, *Am.* labor court; ~**gespräch** *n* discussion about work; ~**grube** *f Mot.* inspection (*od.* working) pit; ~**grundlage** *f* working basis; ~**gruppe** *f* working team; *Päd.* study group; ~**haus** *n hist.* correctional institution, *Am.* workhouse; ~**heft** *n Päd.* workbook; ~**hilfe** *f* working aid; ~**hose** *f* work(ing) trousers (*Am.* pants); ~**hygiene** *f* work hygiene; ~**hypothese** *f* working hypothesis; ~**immigrant** *m*, ~**immigrantin** *f* economic migrant

arbeitsintensiv *Adj.* labo(u)r-intensive

Arbeitskampf *m* labo(u)r (*od.* industrial) dispute; ~**maßnahmen** *Pl.* industrial action *Sg.*

Arbeits|kittel *m* overall, *Am.* overalls *Pl.*; ~**kleidung** *f* work(ing) clothes *Pl.*; ~**klima** *n* work climate, working atmosphere; ~**kluft** *f umg.* work gear *Pl.*; ~**kollege** *m*, ~**kollegin** *f* colleague (from work), workmate *umg.*; ~**kopie** *f Film*: studio print; ~**kosten** *Pl.* labo(u)r cost *Sg.*

Arbeitskraft *f* **1.** (*Fähigkeit*) capacity for work; **s-e** ~ **verkaufen** sell one's labo(u)r; **2.** (*Person*) worker; employee; *Pl. Koll.* manpower *Sg.*; *the* workforce *Sg.*; **billige Arbeitskräfte** cheap labo(u)r *Sg.*

Arbeitskräfte|abbau *m* reduction (*od.* cuts *Pl.*) in manpower, downsizing; ~**mangel** *m* manpower shortage

Arbeits|kreis *m* working (*Päd.* study) group; ~**lager** *n hist.* labo(u)r camp; ~**lampe** *f* workbench lamp; ~**leben** *n* working life

Arbeits|leistung *f* efficiency; *Tech. und e-r Person*: *auch* performance; *e-r Fabrik etc.*: output, productivity; ~**lohn** *m* wage(s *Pl.*), pay

arbeitslos *Adj.* unemployed, out of work, jobless; **die** ~**en Jugendlichen** the young jobless (*Pl.*); ~ **werden** lose one's job; *umg.* go on (*od.* join) the dole, *Am.* get the pink slip; *umg.* get the sack, get fired, be given one's marching orders; *euph.* be made redundant; ~ **sein** be unemployed; *Brit. umg.* be on the dole; **Arbeitslose** *m*, *f*; *-n, -n* unemployed person; *Pl. Koll.* the unemployed (*Pl.*), the jobless (*Pl.*); **er ist** (**ein**) ~**r** he is jobless (*od.* unemployed)

Arbeitslosen|geld *n* unemployment benefit, *Brit.* dole *umg.*; ~ **beziehen** be on the dole, *Am.* be collecting unemployment; ~**hilfe** *f* unemployment assistance; ~**initiative** *f* unemployed (persons') action (*od.* campaign) group; ~**quote** *f*, ~**rate** *f* unemployment rate; ~**versicherung** *f* unemployment insurance; ~**zahl** *f* unemployment (*od.* jobless) figures *Pl.*

Arbeitslosigkeit *f; nur Sg.* unemployment, joblessness

Arbeits|lust *f; nur Sg.* enthusiasm for work; ~**mangel** *m; nur Sg.* shortage of work; ~**markt** *m* labo(u)r (*od.* job) market; **die Lage auf dem** ~ the job situation; ~**maschine** *f* **1.** machine; *maschinelles Werkzeug*: machine tool; **2.** *fig. pej.* (*Person*) workhorse

Arbeits|material *n* working material;

~**medizin** f; nur Sg. industrial medicine; ~**mediziner** m, ~**medizinerin** f occupational health specialist (od. practitioner); ~**methode** f working method, approach

Arbeits|minister m, ~**ministerin** f Pol. employment minister, minister for employment, Am. labor secretary; in GB: Secretary of State for Employment, Employment Secretary; in den USA: Secretary of Labor; ~**ministerium** n department of employment (Am. labor); in GB: Department of Employment (in den USA: Labor)

Arbeits|mittel n tool, Pl. auch materials; ~**modell** n working model; ~**möglichkeiten** Pl. job opportunities; ~**moral** f (working) morale, work ethos; ~**motivation** f motivation to work, work motivation; ~**nachweis** m certificate of employment; ~**niederlegung** f strike, walkout, stoppage; ~**norm** f 1. work norm; (Ziel) target; 2. ehem. DDR: stipulated work rate; ~**ordnung** f work regulations (Am. rules) Pl.; ~**organisation** f organization of the (od. one's) work; ~**ort** m workplace, place of work; ~**papier** n 1. (Arbeitsvorlage) working paper; 2. ~e (Unterlagen) Brit. cards, employment papers; ~**pause** f break; ~**pensum** n work load; ~**pferd** n workhorse (auch fig.); ~**plan** m work schedule, work(ing) plan; in Fabrik: production schedule; ~**platte** f work surface, workbench; Einbauküche: work top, Am. auch countertop; ~**plattform** f auf Bohrinsel: drilling platform

Arbeitsplatz m 1. (Stelle) job; freier ~ vacancy; sicherer ~ (nicht gefährdet) secure (od. steady) job; Sicherheit des ~es job security; die Arbeitsplätze sichern safeguard employment; Schaffung von Arbeitsplätzen job creation; 2. Ort: workplace; (Computer) workstation; (Betrieb) place of work; Diskriminierung am ~ discrimination at work; Sicherheit am ~ workplace (Am. auch occupational) safety

Arbeitsplatz|abbau m job cutback(s); ~**angebot** n job offer; ~**beschreibung** f job specification (od. description); ~**garantie** f job protection; ~**gestaltung** f workplace design; ~**sicherung** f; nur Sg. safeguarding of jobs; ~**studie** f workplace study; ~**teilung** f job sharing; ~**verlust** m job loss; ~**vernichtung** f destruction of jobs (od. workplaces); ~**wechsel** m change of job

Arbeits|probe f sample of one's work; ~**programm** n work program(me); ~**prozess** m work process; ~**psychologe** m industrial psychologist; ~**psychologie** f industrial psychology; ~**psychologin** f industrial psychologist; ~**raum** m workroom

Arbeits|recht n; nur Sg. Jur. industrial (Am. labor) law; ~**rechtler** m; -s, -, ~**rechtlerin** f; -, -nen industrial (Am. labor) lawyer; 2**rechtlich** Adj. relating to labo(u)r law präd.

arbeitsreich Adj. Zeit: busy

Arbeits|richter m, ~**richterin** f Jur. judge on an industrial tribunal; ~**sachen** Pl. umg. Dinge: work things; Kleidung: work clothes

arbeitsscheu I. Adj. work-shy; II. **Arbeitsscheu** f aversion to work

Arbeits|schluss m end of work, finishing-time, leaving-time, Am. quitting time; bei/nach/vor ~ at leaving-time / after work / before leaving work; ~ ist

um sechs (Uhr) work finishes at six (o'clock), we knock off at six umg.; ~**schritt** m stage (of work)

Arbeitsschutz m industrial safety; ~**bestimmung** f occupational (od. industrial) health and safety regulation

Arbeits|sieg m Sport uninspired victory; ~**sitzung** f working session; ~**sklave** m, ~**sklavin** f hist. und fig. work slave

arbeitssparend Adj. labo(u)r-saving

Arbeits|speicher m Computer: working (od. internal) memory; ~**stab** m (working) team; ~**stätte** f workplace; ~**stelle** f 1. (Beschäftigung) job; 2. Ort: place of work; ~**studie** f time (and motion) study; ~**stunde** f working hour; Wirts. manhour, personhour

Arbeitssuche f: job-hunting; auf ~ sein auch be looking for a job; **Arbeitssuchende** m, f; -n, -n job-seeker

Arbeitssucht f; -, kein Pl. workaholism; **arbeitssüchtig** Adj.: ~ sein be a workaholic; **Arbeitssüchtige** m, f workaholic

Arbeits|tag m working day, workday; ~**takt** m Maschine: power stroke; am Fließband: phase time; ~**technik** f work(ing) technique; ~**teilung** f division of labo(u)r; ~**tempo** n rate of work, work rate; ~**therapie** f work (Am. occupational) therapy; ~**tier** n 1. work(ing) animal; 2. fig. workhorse; ~**tisch** m work-table, desk; e-s Handwerkers: workbench; ~**titel** m für Buch etc.: working title; ~**überlastung** f overwork

Arbeitssuche etc. → **Arbeitssuche** etc.

arbeitsunfähig Adj. 1. unfit for work präd.; ständig: disabled; 2. Pol. Regierung: non-viable; **Arbeitsunfähigkeit** f; nur Sg. 1. unfitness for work; ständige: disablement; 2. Pol. non-viability

Arbeits|unfall m work (od. industrial) accident (od. injury); ~**verbot** n ban from working, prohibition from employment; ~**verfahren** n working method, technique; ~**verhältnis** n 1. employer-employee relationship; in e-m ~ stehen bei be employed by (od. with); 2. Pl. working conditions; ~**vermittlung** f employment agency; ~**vertrag** m employment contract; ~**verweigerung** f refusal to work; ~**vorbereitung** f job planning (od. scheduling od. routing); ~**vorgang** m working procedure; Tech. operation; ~**weise** f working method; Tech. e-s Geräts: functioning; ~**welt** f world of employment; ~**wille** m: ihm fehlt der ~ he's not willing to work

arbeitswillig Adj. willing to work; **Arbeitswillige** m, f; -n, -n person (od. people) willing to work

Arbeits|wissenschaften Pl. ergonomics, work sciences Pl.; ~**woche** f work week

Arbeitswut f work mania; **arbeitswütig** Adj. umg. work-crazy, work-happy

Arbeitszeit f 1. working hours Pl.; gleitende ~ flex(i)time; benötigte ~ für ... (work) time required for ...; 2. Tech. operating time; 3. (Fertigungszeit) production time; ~**konto** n flex(i)time account; ~**regelung** f (Regulierung) regulation of working hours; (Vorschrift) regulation concerning working hours; ~**verkürzung** f reduction in working hours

Arbeits|zeug n umg. Kleidung: work-clothes; Werkzeug: tools Pl.; ~**zeugnis** n reference from one's employer; ~**zimmer** n study

arbiträr Adj. geh. arbitrary

archaisch Adj. archaic; **Archaismus** m; -, Archaismen; fachspr. archaism

Archäologe m; -n, -n arch(a)eologist; **Archäologie** f; -, kein Pl. arch(a)eology; **Archäologin** f; -, -nen arch(a)eologist; **archäologisch** Adj. arch(a)eological

Archäopteryx m od. f; -, -e od. Archäopteryges Zool. archaeopteryx

Arche f; -, -n bibl. ark; die ~ Noah Noah's ark

Arche|typ m; -s, -en, ~**typus** m; -, -typen archetype; **archetypisch** Adj. archetypal

archimedisch Adj. Math. Archimedean

Archipel m; -s, -e Geog. archipelago

Architekt m; -en, -en, ~**in** f; -, -nen architect; **architektonisch** Adj. architectural

Architektur f; -, -en architecture; ~**büro** n architect's office

Archiv n; -s, -e archives Pl.; staatliches: record-office, Am. bureau of statistics; **Archivar** m; -s, -e, **Archivarin** f; -, -nen archivist

Archiv|aufnahmen Pl. TV etc.: library pictures, Am. file footage; ~**bild** n Fot. library photo(graph); ~**exemplar** n archive copy; Wirts. file copy

archivieren v/t. put into (the) archives; **Archivierung** f archiving, putting into (the) archives

ARD f; -, kein Pl.; Abk. (Arbeitsgemeinschaft der öffentlich-rechtlichen Rundfunkanstalten Deutschlands) German network of TV and radio stations which is run by the Bundesländer

Ardennen Pl. Geog.: die ~ the Ardennes

Areal n; -s, -e area

areligiös Adj. areligious

Arena f; -, Arenen arena (auch fig.); (Stierkampf-, Zirkusarena) ring

arg; ärger, am ärgsten I. Adj. bad; Fehler: grave, gross; (moralisch schlecht) auch wicked, evil; ~e Enttäuschung great disappointment; mach es nicht noch ärger don't make it any worse (than it already is); sein ärgster Feind his worst enemy; im Argen liegen be in a bad way; → auch böse, schlimm; **II.** Adv. 1. badly, severely; j-n ~ mitnehmen (really) take it out of s.o.; 2. umg. (sehr) terribly; das ist ~ wenig that's not a lot

Arg n geh. altm.: an ihr ist kein ~ there's no guile in her, there's not a bad bone in her body

Argentinien (n); -s Geog. Argentina, the Argentine; **Argentinier** m; -s, -, **Argentinierin** f; -, -nen Argentine, Argentinian, weiblich auch: Argentinian woman (od. girl etc.); **argentinisch** Adj. Argentine, Argentinian

Ärger m; -s, kein Pl. 1. (über + Akk.) (Zorn) anger (about s.th., with s.o.); (Verdruss) annoyance, irritation (at s.th., with s.o.); j-s ~ erregen annoy s.o., make s.o. angry; zu m-m großen ~ to my great annoyance; 2. (mit) (Schererei) trouble, strife umg., auch hassle; ~ bekommen get into trouble; j-m ~ machen cause s.o. trouble; das gibt ~ there'll be trouble; mit ihm hatte sie viel ~ she had a great deal of trouble with him; mach keinen ~! umg. don't make trouble!, take it easy!

ärger Komp. worse; → arg

ärgerlich Adj. 1. Person: annoyed,

cross (*auf, über j-n* with s.o.; *über, we-gen etw.* at, about s.th.); **2.** *Sache*: annoying; **~e Sache** nuisance; *das ist ~* that's annoying, that's a (real) nuisance

ärgern I. *v/t.* annoy; (*Kind, Tier*) tease; *j-n bis aufs Blut ~* umg. make s.o. wild; *ärgere mich nicht!* don't make (*od.* get) me angry!; **II.** *v/refl.*: be (*od.* get) annoyed (*über* + *Akk.* at, about *s.th.*, with *s.o.*); *ärgere dich nicht* don't get annoyed (*od.* upset); *sich schwarz od. gelb und grün etc. ~* umg. be (*od.* get) really mad

Ärgernis *n*; *-ses, -se*; (*etw. Lästiges*) nuisance; (*Anstoß*) offen|ce (*Am.* -se); *öffentliches ~ Jur.* public nuisance; *~ erregen* cause offen|ce (*Am.* -se)

Arglist *f*; *nur Sg.*; *geh.* deceitfulness, guile; *Jur.* malice, malicious intent; **arglistig** *Adj.* deceitful; *Jur.* fraudulent; *~e Täuschung Jur.* wil(l)ful deceit

arglos *Adj.* guileless; (*naiv, harmlos*) artless, innocent; (*nichts ahnend*) unsuspecting; **Arglosigkeit** *f*; *nur Sg.* guilelessness; lack of guile; innocence; unawareness

ärgst... *Sup.* worst; → *arg*

Argument *n*; *-(e)s, -e* argument; *ein ~ vorbringen* make a point; *das ist kein ~* that's no(t a) good reason

Argumentation *f*; *-, -en* argumentation; *das ist keine stichhaltige ~* you can't argue like that

Argumentationshilfe *f* support for an argument

argumentativ *Adj.* argumentative; **argumentieren** *v/i.* argue, reason; *...,* (*so*) *wird argumentiert* ..., so the argument goes

Argusaugen *Pl.* eagle-eyes; *etw. mit ~ beobachten* watch s.th. like a hawk

Argwohn *m*; *-(e)s, kein Pl.* suspicion, mistrust (*gegen* of); *~ erregen* arouse suspicion; *~ hegen* be suspicious (*gegen* of), *auch* suspect s.o. (*od. s.th.*); **argwöhnen** *v/t.* (*untr., hat ge-*) suspect; **argwöhnisch** *Adj.* suspicious, distrustful (*gegen* of)

arid *Adj. Geog.* arid

Arie *f*; *-, -n*; *Mus.* aria

Arier *m*; *-s, -, ~in* *f*; *-, -nen* Aryan; **arisch** *Adj.* Aryan; **arisieren** *v/t. hist., im Nationalsozialismus*: Aryanize; **Arisierung** *f* hist., im Nationalsozialismus*: Aryanization

Aristokrat *m*; *-en, -en* aristocrat; **Aristokratie** *f*; *-, -n* aristocracy; **Aristokratin** *f*; *-, -nen* aristocrat; **aristokratisch** *Adj.* aristocratic

aristotelisch *Adj. Philos.* Aristotelian

Arithmetik *f*; *-, kein Pl. Math.* arithmetic; **arithmetisch** *Adj.* arithmetical

Arkade *f*; *-, -n*; *Archit. auch Pl.*: arcade

Arktis *f*; *-, kein Pl. Geog.* the Arctic; **arktisch** *Adj.* arctic (*auch fig.*)

arm; *ärmer, am ärmsten; Adj.* **1.** (*mittellos*) poor; (*bedürftig*) needy; *um 100 Euro ärmer sein* be 100 euros worse off; *um e-e Hoffnung etc. ärmer sein* fig. have one hope etc. less; *Arm und Reich* rich and poor; **2.** *~ an* (+ *Dat.*) poor in, lacking in; *~ an Vitaminen* low on vitamins; **3.** (*bedauernswert*) poor; *~ dran sein* have nothing to laugh about; *ach, du Ärmste(r)!* oh you poor thing!

Arm *m*; *-(e)s, -e* **1.** arm; *ein/zwei ~ voll Bücher* an armful / two armfuls of books; *am ~ führen* lead s.o. by the arm; *auf den ~ nehmen* (*Kind*) (*hoch-heben*) pick up; (*tragen*) carry; *fig. j-n*

---

auf den ~ nehmen pull s.o.'s leg; *j-n im ~ od. in den ~en halten* embrace s.o., hold s.o. in one's arms; *in die ~e nehmen* hug, embrace; *den ~ um j-n legen* put one's arm (a)round s.o.; *j-m in die ~e laufen* fig. bump (*od.* run) into s.o.; *j-m in den ~ fallen* hold s.o. back, stop s.o.; *sich j-m in die ~e werfen* throw o.s. into s.o.'s arms; *j-n j-m/etw. in die ~e treiben* fig.: drive s.o. into s.o.'s arms / drive s.o. to s.th.; *j-m unter die ~e greifen* fig. help s.o. out (with with); *j-n mit offenen ~en empfangen* fig. welcome s.o. with open arms; *j-n am ausgestreckten ~ verhungern lassen* fig. put the screws (*od.* squeeze) on s.o. umg.; *e-n langen ~ haben* fig. have a lot of pull (*od.* clout); *j-s verlängerter ~* fig. the tool (*od.* instrument) of s.o.; *der ~ des Gesetzes* fig. the (long) arm of the law; **2.** (*Ärmel*) sleeve; **3.** *Zool.* (*Fangarm*) tentacle; **4.** *e-s Flusses*: tributary; *toter*: backwater, dead branch; *e-s Leuchters*: branch

...arm *im Adj.* lacking in ..., short of ... *präd.*; *fantasie~* lacking in imagination; *regen~* with (*od.* of) low rainfall *präd.*; *sorgen~* without (many) worries (*od.* cares) *präd.*

Armada *f*; *-, -s od. Armaden* **1.** *hist.* (Spanish) Armada; **2.** *fig.* armada

armamputiert *Adj.* with an arm / both arms amputated

Armaturen *Pl.* **1.** *Bad etc.*: fittings; **2.** *Mot. etc.* instruments, controls; *~brett* *n* dashboard

Armband *n*; *Pl. Armbänder* bracelet; *e-r Uhr*: watchstrap; *~uhr* *f* wristwatch

Arm|beuge *f* **1.** crook of one's arm, inside of one's elbow; **2.** *Sport* arm bend; *~binde* *f* **1.** armband; **2.** *Med.* (*Schlinge*) sling; *~bruch* *m Med.* fracture of the arm, fractured (*od.* broken) arm; *~brust* *f hist.* crossbow

Ärmchen *n Dim.* little (*od.* small) arm

armdick *Adj. Schlange*: (as) thick as one's arm

Armdrücken *n* arm wrestling

Arme *m, f*; *-n, -n*: *ein ~r* a poor man; *altm.* a pauper; *e-e ~* a poor woman; *altm.* a pauper; *die ~n* the poor (*Pl.*); *die Ärmsten der ~n* the poorest of the poor

Armee *f*; *-, -n* **1.** *Mil.* army; *die Rote ~* the Red Army; *bei der ~ sein* be in the army (*od.* forces); **2.** *fig.* army, masses *Pl.* (*von* of); *~führung* *f Mil.* leadership of the army, army leaders; *~korps* *n Mil.* (army) corps

Ärmel *m*; *-s, -* sleeve; *mit kurzen ~n* short-sleeved, with short sleeves *präd.*; *ohne ~* sleeveless; *die ~ hochkrempeln* auch fig.: roll up one's sleeves; *etw. aus dem ~ schütteln* fig. pull s.th. out of a hat, come up with s.th. just like that, give an off-the-cuff answer (*od.* speech etc.); *~aufschlag* *m* cuff

Armeleute... *im Subst.* poor man's; **Armeleutegeruch** *m pej.* smell (*od.* stench) of poverty

Ärmelhalter *m* sleeve band

Ärmelkanal *m*: *Geog.: der ~* the English Channel

ärmellos *Adj.* sleeveless

Ärmel|schoner *m*, *~schützer* *m* oversleeve

Armenhaus *n hist. und fig.* poorhouse

Armenien (*n*); *-s; Geog.* Armenia; **Armenier** *m*; *-s, -*, **Armenierin** *f*; *-, -nen* Armenian, *weiblich auch*: Armenian woman (*od.* girl etc.); **armenisch I.** *Adj.* Armenian; **II. Armenisch** *n*;

-en; Ling. Armenian; *das Armenische* (the) Armenian (language)

Armen|recht *n*; *nur Sg.*; *Jur. hist.* right to legal aid, forma pauperis; *~viertel* *n* poor part of town; *weitS.* slums *Pl.*

ärmer *Komp.* poorer; → *arm*

Armesünder|bank *f hum. bei Prüfung, Prozess etc.*: hot seat; *beim Essen*: children's table; *~glocke* *f hist.* executioner's bell; *~miene* *f* hangdog look

Armhebel *m Sport, Ringen*: arm bar, bararm

armieren *v/t. Archit.* (*Beton*) reinforce; *Tech.* (*Kabel*) armo(u)r, sheathe; **Armierung** *f* reinforcement

...armig *im Adj.* ...-armed, ...-branched; *fünf~ Leuchter*: five-armed; *Flussmündung*: with five branches *präd.*; *mehr~* multi-armed; *viel~* many-armed

armlang *Adj.* arm-length

Arm|länge *f* arm's length; *~lehne* *f* armrest; *~leuchter* *m* **1.** candelabra; **2.** umg. fig. pej. twit, dope

ärmlich I. *Adj.* poor; (*schäbig*) auch shabby(-looking); (*dürftig*) auch paltry, meag|re (*Am.* -er); (*kläglich*) auch wretched, miserable; *Verhältnisse*: poor, impoverished; *aus ~en Verhältnissen* of (*od.* from) impoverished circumstances; **II.** *Adv.* cheaply; *~ leben* live in impoverished circumstances; *~ gekleidet* shabbily dressed; **Ärmlichkeit** *f*; *nur Sg.* poverty; (*schäbig*) auch cheapness, shabbiness

Arm|loch *n* **1.** armhole, sleeve-hole; **2.** umg. euph. swine, jerk *Sl.*; *~manschette* *f Med.* inflatable cuff; *~muskel* *m* arm muscle; (*Bizeps*) biceps; *~prothese* *f* artificial arm, arm prosthesis; *~reif(en)* *m* bangle; *~schiene* *f Med.* splint; *~schlinge* *f* (arm) sling

armselig *Adj.* **1.** *Bettler, Hütte, Leben*: wretched, miserable; *Einrichtung, Mahlzeit*: poor, paltry, meag|re (*Am.* -er); (*Mitleid erregend*) pitiful, piteous; **2.** *pej.* pathetic; *Ausrede*: pathetic, ridiculous; *Gehalt*: miserable, paltry; *Geschenk*: miserable; *Versuch*: pathetic, wretched; *Feigling, Lügner, Stümper*: wretched; *für ~e zehn Minuten* for ten lousy minutes; **Armseligkeit** *f* **1.** *nur Sg.*; *Zustand*: misery, wretchedness; **2.** *Sache*: pathetic (*od.* miserable) thing

Armsessel *m* armchair, easy chair

ärmst... *Sup.* poorest ...; → *arm*

Arm|stumpf *m* stump of an (*od.* one's) arm; *~stütze* *f* armrest

Armut *f*; *-, kein Pl.* **1.** poverty; *stärker*: destitution; *in ~ geraten* be reduced to poverty; **2.** *fig. an Ideen etc.*: poverty (*an* + *Dat.* of); *an Rohstoffen etc.*: lack; *stärker*: dearth (of)

Armuts|flüchtling *m* economic refugee; *~grenze* *f* poverty line; *~zeugnis* *n* **1.** *Jur., hist.* certificate of poverty; **2.** *fig. ~* (*für j-n*) *geistig*: sign of inadequacy; *moralisch*: sign of moral poverty (*od.* cowardice); *sich* (*Dat.*) *ein ~ ausstellen* shame o.s., expose own's inadequacy

Arnika *f*; *-, -s; Bot.* arnica

Aroma *n*; *-s, -, Aromen und geh. altm. Aromata*; (*Duft*) fragrance; *Getränke, Speisen*: aroma; (*Wohlgeschmack, auch Würzstoff*) flavo(u)r; (*Essenz*) essence; *~stoff* *m*; *mst Pl.* flavo(u)r-ing(s); *~therapie* *f* aromatherapy

aromatisch I. *Adj.* **1.** (*wohlriechend*) aromatic; (*wohlschmeckend*) tasty, with a distinctive taste *präd.*; **2.** *Chem.* *Kohlenwasserstoffe*: aromatic; **II.** *Adv.*

etw. **~** *verfeinern* round off the flavo(u)r (of s.th.); **aromatisieren** *v/t.* flavo(u)r

Arpeggio [ar'pɛdʒo] *n; -s, -s od. Arpeggien; Mus.* arpeggio

Arrak *m; -s, -e od. -s* arra(c)k

Arrangement [arãʒə'mã:] *n; -s, -s* **1.** *von Blumen etc., auch Mus.:* arrangement; **2.** (*Übereinkunft*) agreement; **ein ~ treffen** come to an arrangement (*od.* agreement), come to terms; **3.** *Wirts.* package deal

Arrangeur [arã'ʒø:ɐ̯] *m; -s, -e,* **~in** *f; -, -nen* arranger

arrangieren [arã'ʒi:rən] (*untr., hat*) **I.** *v/t.* arrange; **II.** *v/refl.:* **sich ~ mit** *j-m* come to an arrangement with; *etw.* come to terms with s.th.

Arrest *m; -(e)s, -e* **1.** detention (*auch Schule*), confinement; **mit ~ bestrafen** put in confinement; **~ bekommen** be given detention; **2.** *Jur.* (*Beschlagnahme*) seizure, impounding; **~zelle** *f* detention cell

arretieren *v/t.* **1.** *Tech.* arrest, stop, lock; **2.** *altm.* (*verhaften*) arrest, detain; **Arretierung** *f* **1.** *Tech.* locking, stop; **2.** *altm.* (*verhaften*) arrest, detention

Arrhythmie *f; -, -n; allg.* arrhythmia; *Med. auch* irregular heart rate; **arrhythmisch** *Adj.* arrhythmical

arrivieren [ari'vi:rən] *v/i.* (*ist*); *geh.* succeed, make it; *er ist zur Nummer 1 der Modebranche arriviert* he's made it No. 1 in fashion; **arriviert I.** *P. P.* → *arrivieren*; **II.** *Adj.* successful, established; *pej.* upstart ..., parvenu ...; *er gehört jetzt zu den Arrivierten* he's made it *umg.*; *ein ~er Autor* a successful author (*od.* writer)

arrogant *Adj. pej.* arrogant; **Arroganz** *f; -, kein Pl.* arrogance

Arrondierung *f Grundstücke:* consolidation; *Kanten:* rounding off

Arsch *m; -(e)s, Ärsche; vulg.* **1.** arse, *Am.* ass; *j-m geht der ~ auf Grundeis fig.* s.o. is scared witless (*od.* shitless *vulg.*); *der hat doch den ~ offen fig.* he must be crazy, *Brit.* he's round the bloody twist; *j-n am ~ haben fig.* have (hold of) s.o. by the balls *vulg.*, have s.o. by the short and curlies; *j-m in den ~ kriechen fig.* suck up to s.o. *umg.*; *es ist am od. im ~ fig.* it's had it; *leck mich am ~! fig.* get stuffed *Sl.*, go to hell *Sl.*; *zu sich selbst:* bugger (it); *am ~ der Welt fig. iro.* at (*od.* in) the back of beyond *umg.*, in the middle of nowhere, out in the sticks (*Am. auch* boondocks) *umg.*; *sich* (*Dat.*) *den ~ aufreißen (für) fig.* sweat blood (for); *sie hat ihm anständig den ~ aufgerissen* she really put him through it; *ich könnte mich in den ~ beißen* I could kick myself; *den ~ zukneifen* (*sterben*) kick the bucket; → *auch Hintern, Popo;* **2.** *fig. pej.* (*Idiot*) arse(hole), *Am.* asshole, silly bugger; *er ist ein ~ mit Ohren* he's as thick as two short planks, (*Am.* as a board)

Arsch|backe *f vulg.* **1.** bumcheek, *Am.* cheek of one's ass; **2.** *pej. Person:* bastard; **~ficker** *m; -s, -; vulg. pej.* arse bandit, bumfucker, bugger; **~geige** *f vulg. pej.* bastard

arsch|kalt *Adj. vulg. pej.* bloody cold; **~klar** *Adj. vulg.* bloody obvious

Arsch|kriecher *m,* **~kriecherin** *f vulg. pej.* arse-licker; **~loch** *n vulg.* **1.** arsehole; **2.** *pej. Person:* arsehole, *Am.* asshole, bastard; **~tritt** *m vulg.:* *j-m e-n ~ geben* give s.o. a kick in (*od.* up) the

arse (*Am.* ass); **~und-Titten-Presse** *f vulg. pej.* tits-and-ass (*od.* tits-and-bums) press, girlie magazines (*Pl.*)

Arsen *n; -s, kein Pl; Chem.* (*abgek.* **As**) arsenic

Arsenal *n; -s, -e* **1.** (*Lager*) arsenal; (*Waffenarsenal*) weaponry, (weapons) stockpile, armo(u)ry; **2.** *fig.* (*Lager*) repository; (*Reihe, Ansammlung*) battery

arsenhaltig *Adj.* arsenical; **~ sein** contain arsenic; **arsenig** *Adj.* arsenious; **~e Säure** arsenious acid

Arsenvergiftung *f* arsenic poisoning

Art *f; -, -en* **1.** *nur Sg.* (*Eigenart, Wesen*) nature, kind, way; *Fragen allgemeiner ~* questions of a general nature; (*in*) *dieser ~* of this nature (*od.* kind); *einzig in s-r ~* unique; *e-e angenehme/ gewinnende ~ haben* have a pleasant manner / winning way; *sie hat e-e nette ~ zu lachen / mit Kindern umzugehen* she has a nice laugh / she has a nice way with children; *es ist nicht s-e ~ zu* (+ *Inf.*) he's not the sort to (+ *Inf.*); *das ist eigentlich nicht i-e ~* that's not like her (at all); *das ist nun mal s-e ~* that's the way he is; **2. ~** (*und Weise*) way, manner; (*Verfahren*) method; (*Stil*) style; *auf diese ~* (in) this way (*od.* manner); *auf irgendeine ~* somehow or other; *auf welche ~?* in which way?; *auf keine ~* in no way, *auf verschiedene ~en* in different ways; *auf freundliche/ruhige ~* kindly/quietly; *das wäre die einfachste/geschickteste ~ zu* (+ *Inf.*) that would be the easiest / most elegant way to (+ *Inf.*); *in der ~ Haydns* in the style of Haydn; *nach* (*der*) ~ (+ *Gen. od. von*) along the lines of, after the fashion of; *Gastr.* in the style of ..., ... style; *nach ~ des Hauses Gastr.* à la maison; **3.** *nur Sg.; umg.* (*gutes Benehmen*) behavio(u)r, manners *Pl.; ist das denn e-e ~* (*sich zu benehmen*)*?* is that any way to behave?; *das ist* (*doch*) *keine ~!* that's no way to behave; *die feine englische ~ umg.* the proper way to behave; **4.** (*Sorte, Qualität*) kind, sort, type; *Geräte etc. aller ~ auch tools etc.* of every description; *was für e-e ~ Mensch ist er?* what sort of person is he?; *e-e ~ ...* a kind (*od.* sort, type) of ...; *e-e ~ Künstler etc. iro.* an artist of sorts; *jede ~ von Gewalt ablehnen* reject all forms of violence; **5.** *Bio.* species; *umg.* (*Rasse*) race; (*Sorte*) breed, sort; *sie ist völlig aus der ~ geschlagen fig.* she's not like anyone else in the family

Art. *Abk.* → *Artikel*

Artangabe *f Ling.* adverb of manner; *Phrase:* adverbial phrase of manner

Artefakt *n; -(e)s, -e; Archäol., geh.* artefact, *bes. Am.* artifact

arteigen *Adj.* characteristic, true to type

arten *v/i.:* *nach j-m ~* take after s.o.; → *geartet*

Artengemeinschaft *f* biological community

artenreich *Adj. Pflanzenfamilie etc.:* biodiverse, with a large number of species; *Gebiet:* with a rich animal and plant life (*od.* flora and fauna); **Artenreichtum** *m; nur Sg.* species-richness, rich animal and plant life, rich flora and fauna; *fachspr.* biodiversity

Artenschutz *m* protection of endangered species; **~abkommen** *n* agreement on the protection of endangered

species

Artenvielfalt *f* → *Artenreichtum*

arterhaltend *Adj. Bio.* species-preserving; **Arterhaltung** *f* preservation of the species

Arterie *f; -, -n; Med.* artery; **arteriell** *Adj.* arterial

Arterien|erweiterung *f Med.* aneurysm (*od.* aneurism); **~verkalkung** *f* → *Arteriosklerose*

Arteriosklerose *f; -,-n; Med.* hardening of the arteries, arteriosclerosis

artesisch *Adj.:* **~er Brunnen** artesian well

artfremd *Adj.* alien, foreign

Artgenosse *m,* **Artgenossin** *f* member of the same species

art|gerecht *Adj.:* **~e Tierhaltung** keeping animals in their natural environment; **~gleich** *Adj.:* **~ sein** belong to the same species; *sie sind ~* they're (of) the same species

Arthritis *f; -, Arthritiden* arthritis; **arthritisch** *Adj.* arthritic

Arthrose *f; -, -n; Med.* arthrosis

artifiziell *Adj. geh.* artificial

artig I. *Adj.* **1.** well-behaved; good; *sei ~!* be good!, be a good boy (*od.* girl)!; **2.** *geh. altm.* (*galant*) courteous; **II.** *Adv.* **1.** *sich ~ benehmen* behave well, be good; **2.** *geh. altm.* courteously

...artig *im Adj. und Adv.* ...-like; *apfel~ Geschmack:* apple-flavo(u)r; *chamäleon~ Anpassung:* like a chameleon; *schachbrett~ gemustert* like a chess board; *turban~ Frisur:* like a turban

Artigkeit *f* **1.** *nur Sg.;* good behavio(u)r; **2.** *mst Pl.;* (*höfliche Handlung*) courteousness; **3.** *nur Sg.; geh. altm.* politeness, courteousness; (*Redensart*) pleasantry; (*Kompliment*) compliment

Artikel *m; -s, -; (abgek.* **Art.**) **1.** (*Aufsatz*) article, essay (*über* + *Akk. od.* **zu** about *od.* on); **2.** *bes. Jur.* (*Abschnitt*) article; *Reli.* article (of faith); **3.** *Wirts.* article, item, commodity; **4.** *Ling.:* (*un*)*bestimmter ~* (in)definite article; **~reihe** *f,* **~serie** *f* series of articles

Artikulation *f; -, -en* articulation; **Artikulationsvermögen** *n* powers *Pl.* of articulation; **artikulieren I.** *v/t.* express, put into words; articulate; **II.** *v/refl.:* express o.s.

Artillerie *f; -, -n; Mil.* artillery; **~beschuss** *m,* **~feuer** *n* artillery fire; **~gefecht** *n* artillery fighting (*od.* engagement)

Artillerist *m; -en, -en; Mil.* artilleryman, gunner

Artischocke *f; -, -n; Bot.* artichoke

Artischocken|boden *m* artichoke base; **~herz** *n* artichoke heart

Artist *m; -en, -en* acrobat, (variety) artiste, *Am. auch* performer; **Artistik** *f; -, kein Pl.* **1.** acrobatics *Pl.* (*V. oft im Sg.*); **2.** (*Geschicklichkeit*) skill; **Artistin** *f; -, -nen* acrobat, (variety) artiste, *Am. auch* performer; **artistisch** *Adj.* **1.** acrobatic(ally *Adv.*); **2.** (*geschickt*) skil(l)ful

art|spezifisch *Adj.* characteristic of (*od.* specific to) the species; **~verschieden** *Adj.* **1.** **~ sein** belong to a different species; *sie sind ~* they're different species; **2.** (*grundverschieden*) completely different; **~verwandt** *Adj.* related; *nur attr.* kindred

Arznei *f; -, -en* (*Medikament*) medicine, medicament, drug; (*Heilmittel*) remedy; **~buch** *n* pharmacop(o)eia; **~kunde** *f* pharmaceutics *Pl.* (*V. im Sg.*), pharmacy

Arzneimittel n → **Arznei**; ~**forschung** f pharmaceutical(s) research; ~**gesetz** n law concerning the manufacture and distribution of medicines; ~**hersteller** m drug manufacturer, pharmaceutical producer; ~**missbrauch** m drug abuse

Arznei|pflanze f medicinal plant (od. herb); ~**schrank** m medicine cabinet

Arzt m doctor, Am. auch physician geh.; **der behandelnde ~** the attending physician, the doctor in attendance; **der operierende ~** the surgeon operating on the patient; **zum ~ gehen** go to the doctor's; ~**beruf** m medical profession; **der ~ weitS.** a doctor's life, being a doctor; ~**besuch** m in der Praxis: visit to the doctor's; zu Hause: doctor's visit (od. call)

Ärzte|blatt n etwa British Medical Journal, Am. etwa JAMA (= Journal of the American Medical Association); ~**haus** n health clinic; ~**kammer** f General Medical Council, Am. State Medical Board of Registration; ~**muster** n drug sample

Ärzteschaft f medical profession

Ärzte|schwemme f glut (od. surfeit) of doctors; ~**vertreter** m, ~**vertreterin** f pharmaceutical representative

Arzthelfer m, ~**in** f (doctor's) assistant (od. receptionist)

Ärztin f; -, -nen (lady) doctor (od. physician)

Arzt|kittel m (doctor's) white coat; ~**kosten** Pl. doctor's (od. medical) fees

ärztlich I. Adj. medical; **in ~er Behandlung** under medical care, under medical supervision; ~**e Hilfe** medical assistance; **auf ~en Rat** on doctor's orders; → **Attest**; **II.** Adv. medically; ~ **behandeln** treat medically

Arzt|praxis f medical practice, Brit. auch (doctor's) surgery; ~**rechnung** f doctor's bill; ~**roman** m hospital romance; ~**termin** m doctor's (od. medical) appointment; ~**wahl** f: **freie ~** right to go to the doctor of one's choice (od. to choose one's own doctor)

as, As¹ n; -, -; Mus. (Note) A flat

As² n → **Ass**

A-Saite f Mus. A-string

Asbest m; -(e)s, -e asbestos; ~**belastung** f asbestos pollution

asbest|frei Adj. free from (od. of) asbestos; ~**haltig** Adj. containing asbestos präd.

Asbestose f; -, -n; Med. asbestosis

Asbest|staub m asbestos particles Pl.; ♀**verseucht** Adj. contaminated with asbestos präd.

aschblond Adj. ash blonde

Asche f; -, -n **1.** ash, mst ashes Pl.; von Kohlen: cinders Pl.; -e-s Verstorbenen: ashes; **glühende ~** embers Pl.; **zu ~ verbrennen** turn to ashes; **sich** (Dat.) **~ aufs Haupt streuen** fig. put on (od. wear) sackcloth and ashes; → **Friede**, **Phönix**, **2.** nur Sg.; umg. (Geld) dosh, dough

Äsche f; -,-n; Zool. grayling

Aschen|bahn f cinder track; Mot. dirt track; ~**becher** m ashtray

Aschenbrödel n; -s, - Cinderella (auch fig.); ~**dasein** n → **Aschenputteldasein**

Aschenplatz m Tennis: ash court

Aschenputtel n; -s, - Cinderella (auch fig.); ~**dasein** n: **ein ~ führen** lead a Cinderella-like existence

Ascher m; -s, -; umg. ashtray

Ascheregen m ashfall, shower of ash

Aschermittwoch m Ash Wednesday

asch|fahl Adj. Gesicht: ashen; ~**grau** Adj. ash-grey (Am. -gray)

Aschkenasim Pl. Ashkenazim; **aschkenasisch** Adj. Ashkenazic

Aschram m; -s, -s ashram

ASCII-Code ['aski:-] m EDV ASCII-code

Ascorbinsäure f Chem. ascorbic acid

As-Dur n Mus. A flat major; ~**Tonleiter** f A flat major scale

Ase m; -n, -n; Myth. one of the Aesir; **die ~n** the Aesir

A-Seite f Schallplatte etc.: A side

äsen v/i. Jägerspr. graze

Asepsis f Med. asepsis; **aseptisch** Adj. aseptic

Aserbaidschan (n); -s Geog. Azerbaijan; **Aserbaidschaner** m; -s, -, **Aserbaidschanerin** f; -, -nen Azerbaijani, Azeri, weiblich auch: Azerbaijani woman (od. girl etc.); **aserbaidschanisch** Adj. Azerbaijani

asexual, asexuell Adj. Bio., Med. asexual

Asiat m; -en, -en, **Asiate** m; -n,-n, **Asiatin** f; -, -nen Asian; **asiatisch** Adj. Asian; Sachen, Völker: auch Asiatic; **Asiatika** Pl. Oriental art Sg.; ältere: auch Oriental antiquities; **Asien** (n);-s; Geog. Asia

Askese f; -, -n asceticism; **Asket** m; -en, -en, **Asketin** f; -, -nen ascetic; **asketisch** Adj. ascetic(ally Adv.)

Askorbinsäure f Chem. ascorbic acid

Äskulap|natter f Zool. Aesculapian snake; ~**stab** m staff of Aesculapius

as-Moll n Mus. A flat minor; ~**Tonleiter** f A flat minor scale

asozial Adj. Verhalten, Familie etc.: antisocial; (Aussteiger) dropout; Pl. auch antisocial elements

Aspekt m; -(e)s, -e aspect (auch Astrol., Astron., Ling.); **unter diesem ~ betrachtet** seen from this angle (od. point of view); **das ist ein neuer ~** that's a new (od. different) way of looking at it

Asphalt m; -s, -e asphalt, mineral pitch; ~**bahn** f Kegeln: skittle alley with asphalt surface; ~**beton** m asphaltic concrete; ~**decke** f asphalt surface

asphaltieren v/t. (surface with) asphalt

Asphalt|lack m asphalt varnish; ~**platz** m Tennis: asphalt court; ~**straße** f asphalt road

Aspik m od. n; -s, -e; Gastr. aspic; **Aal in ~** jellied eel

Aspirant m; -en, -en, ~**in** f; -, -nen candidate

aspirieren v/t. Ling. aspirate

Aspirin® n; -s, -; Med. aspirin; **Aspirintablette** f aspirin tablet (od. pill)

Ass n; -es, -e **1.** (Spielkarte) ace; **2.** umg. fig. Person: ace (**in** + Dat. at); **3.** Tennis: (clean) ace; Golf: hole in one

aß Prät. → **essen**

Assekuranz f; -, -en; altm. od. als Teil von Namen: insurance

Assel f; -, -n; Zool. woodlouse, slater

Assembler m; -s, -; EDV assembler

Asservat n; -(e)s, -e; Amtsspr. exhibit; **Asservatenkammer** f exhibit room

Assessmentcenter n Wirts. assessment cent|re (Am. -er)

Assessor m; -s, -en, ~**in** f; -, -nen **1.** civil servant who has completed his/her second state examination; **2.** Jur. assistant judge

Assimilation f; -, -en; fachspr. assimila-

tion; **assimilieren** v/t. assimilate; **Assimilierung** f assimilation

Assistent m; -en, -en, ~**in** f; -, -nen assistant

Assistenz f; -, -en, mst Sg. assistance; **unter ~ von** with the assistance of; ~**arzt** m, ~**ärztin** f junior doctor, medical assistant, Am. intern

assistieren v/i. assist (**bei** in)

Assoziation f; -, -en **1.** association; **2.** Wirts. partnership; **Assoziationskette** f chain of association; **assoziativ** Adj. associative; **assoziieren I.** v/t. associate (**mit** with); **II.** v/i.: make associations; **III.** v/refl. Pol. associate (o.s.) (**mit** with); Wirts. enter into a partnership (with)

Assyrer m, ~**in** f hist. Assyrian, weiblich auch: Assyrian woman (od. girl etc.); **Assyrien** (n) Assyria; **assyrisch** Adj. Assyrian

Ast m; -(e)s, Äste **1.** branch; bes. lit. bough; im Holz: knot; **den ~ absägen, auf dem man sitzt** fig. saw off one's own branch, dig one's own grave, shoot o.s. in the foot; → **absteigend** II; **2.** umg. (Rücken, Buckel) hump; **sich** (Dat.) **e-n ~ lachen** fig. split one's sides (laughing)

AStA m; -(s), -s od. Asten; Abk. (**A**llgemeiner **S**tudentenaus**s**chuss) Univ. etwa Student('s) Union

asten v/t. umg. (schleppen) lug, schlepp (along, around etc.)

Aster f; -, -n; Bot. aster, Brit. auch Michaelmas daisy

Asteroid m; -en, -en; Astron. asteroid

Astgabel f fork (in od. of a branch)

Asthenie f; -, -n; Med. asthenia; **Astheniker** m; -s, -, **Asthenikerin** f; -, -nen asthenic (person)

Ästhet m; -en, -en aesthete, Am. auch esthete; **Ästhetik** f; -, -en **1.** (Lehre) (a)esthetics Pl. (V. im Sg.); **2.** nur Sg.; (Schönheit) beauty, (a)esthetic appeal (+ Gen. of); e-s Stils etc.: (a)esthetic; **3.** nur Sg.; (Schönheitssinn) (a)esthetic sense; **Ästhetin** f; -, -nen aesthete, Am. auch esthete; **ästhetisch** Adj. (a)esthetic

Asthma n; -s, kein Pl.; Med. asthma; **Asthmaanfall** m asthma attack; **asthmakrank** Adj. suffering from asthma präd.; **Asthmatiker** m, ~**in** f; -, -nen asthmatic; **asthmatisch** Adj. asthmatic

astigmatisch Adj. Opt., Med. astigmatic; **Astigmatismus** m; -, nur Sg. astigmatism

Astloch n knothole

Astralleib m **1.** astral body; **2.** umg. iro. divine frame

astrein Adj. **1.** Holz: free of knots; **2.** umg. fig. (legal) above-board, on the level, genuine; **die Sache ist nicht ganz ~** there's something fishy (od. dodgy umg.) about the business; **3.** umg. fig. (ausgezeichnet) great, fantastic; **das war ein ~es Tor** schön erzielt: that was a stunning goal; gültig: that goal was 100% valid

Astrologe m; -n, -n astrologer; **Astrologie** f; -, kein Pl. astrology; **Astrologin** f; -, -nen astrologer; **astrologisch** Adj. astrological

Astronaut m; -en, -en astronaut; **Astronautik** f; -, kein Pl. astronautics Pl. (V. im Sg.); **Astronautin** f; -, -nen astronaut

Astronom m; -en, -en astronomer; **Astronomie** f; -, kein Pl. astronomy; **Astronomin** f; -, -nen astronomer; **astronomisch** Adj. astronomic(al) (auch *fig.*)

Astrophysik *f* astrophysics *Pl.* (*V. im Sg.*); **Astrophysiker** *m*, **Astrophysikerin** *f* astrophysicist

Ast|schere *f* tree pruner; **~werk** *n* branches *Pl.*

ASU *f; -, -s; Abk. Mot.* → **Abgassonderuntersuchung**

Asyl *n; -s, -e* **1.** (*Schutz*) sanctuary; *Pol.* asylum; **~ gewähren** grant asylum; **um** (*politisches*) **~ bitten** ask for (political) asylum; **2.** (*Obdachlosenasyl*) home; **Asylant** *m; -en, -en*, **Asylantin** *f; -, -nen* → **Asylbewerber**

Asylantenwohnheim *n* asylum-seekers' hostel

Asyl|antrag *m* application for political asylum; **♀berechtigt** *Adj.* entitled to political asylum; **~bewerber** *m*, **~bewerberin** *f* asylumseeker, (political) refugee; **~gewährung** *f* granting of asylum; **~recht** *n* **1.** *nur Sg.* (*Rechtsanspruch*) right of asylum; **2.** (*Gesetzgebung*) asylum laws *Pl.*; **~suchende** *m, f; -n, -n* asylumseeker; **~verfahren** *n* procedure for seeking asylum

Asymmetrie *f* asymmetry, lack of symmetry; **asymmetrisch** *Adj.* asymmetrical

Asymptote *f; -, -n; Math.* asymptote; **asymptotisch** *Adj.* asymptotic

asynchron *Adj. fachspr.* asynchronous

Aszendent *m; -en, -en; Astrol., Astron.* ascendant

A.T. *Abk.* (**Altes Testament**) OT

Atavismus *m; -, Atavismen; fachspr.* atavism; **atavistisch** *Adj.* atavistic

Atelier [ate'lieː] *n; -s, -s* studio; **~aufnahme** *f* studio shot; **~kamera** *f* studio camera; **~wohnung** *f* studio flat, *Am.* studio (apartment); *unterm Dachboden:* loft

Atem *m; -s, kein Pl.* breath; (*das Atmen*) breathing; **außer ~** out of breath; **~ holen** take a breath; *fig.* (*auch* **~ schöpfen**) get one's breath back; **den ~ anhalten** hold one's breath; **mit angehaltenem ~** with bated breath; **außer ~ kommen** get out of breath; **wieder zu ~ kommen** *auch fig.* get one's breath back; **j-n in ~ halten** *fig.* keep s.o. on his (*od.* her) toes (*in Spannung:* on tenterhooks); **e-n langen / den längeren ~ haben** *fig.* have a lot of / more staying power (*od.* stamina); **das verschlug ihm den ~** *fig.* his jaw just dropped; **ihnen geht der ~ aus** *fig.* they're running dry (*od.* out of resources)

atemberaubend *Adj. fig.* breathtaking

Atem|beschwerden *Pl.* difficulty *Sg.* in breathing; **~ haben** have difficulty breathing; **~frequenz** *f* respiratory rate; **~gerät** *n* breathing apparatus; *Med.* respirator; **~geräusch** *n* respiratory sounds *Pl.*; **~gift** *n* breathing poison; **~gymnastik** *f* breathing exercises *Pl.*; **~holen** *n; -s, kein Pl.* breathing; **~lähmung** *f* respiratory standstill; **~loch** *n Wal:* blowhole; **~luft** *n the* air one breathes

atemlos *Adj.* breathless (*auch fig.*); out of breath; **Atemlosigkeit** *f; nur Sg.* breathlessness

Atem|maske *f* breathing mask, small oxygen mask; **~not** *f; nur Sg.* shortness of breath; **an ~ leiden** have difficulty breathing; **~pause** *f umg.* breather; *auch fig.* breathing space; **~schutzgerät** *n*, **~schutzmaske** *f* breathing apparatus; **~stillstand** *m* respiratory standstill; **~technik** *f* breathing technique; **~übungen** *Pl.* breathing exer-

cises; **~wege** *Pl.* respiratory tract *Sg.*; **~wegserkrankung** *f* respiratory disease; **~zentrum** *n* respiratory cent|re (*Am.* -er); **~zug** *m* breath; **bis zum letzten ~** to the last gasp; **den letzten ~ tun** breathe one's last; **in einem** *od.* **im selben ~** in one breath; **im nächsten ~** the next moment

Äthanol *n; -s, kein Pl. Chem.* ethyl alcohol, ethanol

Atheismus *m; nur Sg.* atheism; **Atheist** *m; -en, -en*, **Atheistin** *f; -, -nen* atheist; **atheistisch** *Adj.* atheistic(ally *Adv.*)

Athen (*n*); *-s; Geog.* Athens

Athener *m; -s, -*, **~in** *f; -, -nen* Athenian, *weiblich auch:* Athenian woman (*od.* girl *etc.*); **athenisch** *Adj.* Athenian

Äther *m; -s, kein Pl.* **1.** *Phys. und Chem.* ether; **2.** *Radio:* air (waves *Pl.*); **3.** *poet.* ether, firmament

ätherisch *Adj.* **1.** (*himmlisch*) *auch fig.* ethereal; **2.** *Chem.* (*ätherhaltig*) ethereal; (*flüchtig*) ethereal, fleeting; **~e Öle** ethereal (*od.* essential *od.* volatile) oils

Äthernarkose *f* etherization

Äthiopien (*n*); *-s Geog.* Ethiopia; **Äthiopier** *m; -s, -*, **Äthiopierin** *f; -, -nen* Ethiopian, *weiblich auch:* Ethiopian woman (*od.* girl *etc.*); **äthiopisch** *Adj.* Ethiopian

Athlet *m; -en, -en; Sport* athlete; **Athletin** *f; -, -nen* athlete; **athletisch** *Adj.* athletic

Äthyl *n; -s, kein Pl; Chem.* ethyl; **~alkohol** *m Chem.* ethyl alcohol

Äthylen *n; -s, kein Pl.; Chem.* ethylene, ethene *fachspr.*

Ätiologie *f; -, -n Med.* (a)etiology

Atlant *m; -en, -en; Archit.* atlas, male caryatid

Atlantik *m; -s Geog.: der ~* the Atlantic (Ocean); **~küste** *f* Atlantic coast

atlantisch *Adj.* Atlantic; **der Atlantische Ozean** the Atlantic (Ocean); **~es Tief** *Met.* depression over the Atlantic

Atlas *m; -(ses), -se od. Atlanten* **1.** atlas; **2.** *Pl. nur -se; Anat.* atlas; **3.** *Pl. nur -se;* (*Seidenatlas*) satin

atmen I. *v/i.* breathe; *Med. auch:* respire; **schwer ~** gasp for breath; **tief ~** breathe deeply, draw a deep breath; **wieder frei ~ können** *auch fig.* be able to breathe freely (*od.* easy) again; **solange ich atme** (for) as long as I live; **II.** *v/t. auch lit. fig.* breathe

Atmosphäre *f; -, -n* atmosphere (*auch fig.*)

Atmosphären|druck *m; Pl. -drücke* atmospheric pressure; **~überdruck** *m* (*abgek.* **atü**) (atmospheric) excess pressure

atmosphärisch I. *Adj.* atmospheric; **II.** *Adv.* atmospherically; **~e Störungen** *Radio:* static *Sg.*, atmospheric disturbance *Sg.*

Atmung *f* breathing; **künstliche ~** artificial respiration

atmungsaktiv *Adj. Stoffe:* cellular, breathing ...

Atmungsorgan *n* respiratory organ; **Erkrankungen der ~e** respiratory diseases

Ätna *m; -(s); Geog.: der ~* Mount Etna

Atoll *n; -s, -e; Geog.* atoll

Atom *n; -s, -e; Phys., Chem.* atom; **~angriff** *m* nuclear attack; **~antrieb** *m* atomic propulsion

atomar *Adj.* atomic, nuclear; **~e Streitkräfte** nuclear powers

Atomausstieg *m; nur Sg.* abandon-

ment of nuclear energy

atombetrieben *Adj.* nuclear-powered

Atombombe *f Mil.* atom(ic) bomb, A-bomb, nuclear bomb; *the* bomb *umg.*

Atombombentest *m* nuclear (weapons) test

Atombunker *m* atomic (*od.* nuclear) shelter

Atombusen *m umg. hum.* big boobs *Pl.*

Atomenergie *f; nur Sg.* atomic (*od.* nuclear) energy; **~kommission** *f* Atomic Energy Commission

Atom|explosion *f* atomic (*od.* nuclear) explosion; **~forscher** *m*, **~forscherin** *f* nuclear scientist; **~forschung** *f* nuclear research; **~gegner** *m*, **~gegnerin** *f* anti-nuclear protester

atomgetrieben *Adj.* nuclear-powered

Atom|gewicht *n Chem., Phys.* atomic weight; **~hülle** *f Chem., Phys.* atomic shell; **~industrie** *f* nuclear industry

atomisieren *v/t.* atomize

Atom|katastrophe *f* nuclear disaster; **~kern** *m Chem., Phys.* atomic nucleus

Atomkraft *f; nur Sg.* atomic (*od.* nuclear) power; **~gegner** *m*, **~gegnerin** *f* anti-nuclear (power) protester

Atom|kraftwerk *n* nuclear power station; **~krieg** *m* atomic (*od.* nuclear) war(fare); **~lobby** *f* nuclear power lobby; **~macht** *f* nuclear power; **~masse** *f Chem., Phys.* atomic mass; **~meiler** *m* (nuclear) reactor, atomic pile; **~modell** *n Chem., Phys.* model of the (*od.* an) atom

Atommüll *m* nuclear (*od.* radioactive) waste; **~endlager** *n* (final) disposal (*od.* dumping *pej.*) site for nuclear (*od.* radioactive) waste; **~transport** *m* transport of nuclear (*od.* radioactive) waste; **~zwischenlager** *n* temporary storage site for nuclear (*od.* radioactive) waste

Atom|physik *f* nuclear physics *Pl.* (*V. im Sg.*); **~physiker** *m*, **~physikerin** *f* nuclear physicist; **~reaktor** *m* nuclear reactor; **~spaltung** *f* nuclear fission; **~sperrvertrag** *m Pol.* non-proliferation treaty; **~sprengkopf** *m Mil.* nuclear warhead; **~stopp** *m* nuclear ban; **~strahlen** *Pl. Chem., Phys.* nuclear radiation, radioactive rays; **~streitmacht** *f Mil.* nuclear force (*od.* capability); **~strom** *m* nuclear energy, electricity generated by nuclear power

Atomtest *m* nuclear (weapons) test; **~stopp** *m* (nuclear) test ban; **~stoppabkommen** *n Pol.* test ban treaty

Atom|tod *m* nuclear death; **~transport** *m* transport of nuclear (*od.* radioactive) waste; **~-U-Boot** *n* nuclear (--powered) submarine; **~uhr** *f* atomic clock; **~umwandlung** *f Chem., Phys.* atomic disintegration; **~waffe** *f Mil.* atomic (*od.* nuclear) weapon

atomwaffenfrei *Adj.* nuclear-free; **die Stadt erklärte sich zur ~en Zone** the town declared itself a nuclear-free zone

Atomwaffen|gegner *m*, **~gegnerin** *f* anti-nuclear protester; **~sperrvertrag** *m Pol.* (nuclear weapons) non-proliferation treaty; **~test** *m* nuclear weapons test; **~verzicht** *m* relinquishment of nuclear weapons

Atom|wirtschaft *f* nuclear industry; **~wissenschaftler** *m*, **~wissenschaftlerin** *f* nuclear scientist; **~wärme** *f Chem., Phys.* atomic heat; **~zeitalter** *n* nuclear age; **~zerfall** *m Chem., Phys.* atomic disintegration

atonal *Adj. Mus.* atonal; **Atonalität** *f;* -, *kein Pl.* atonality

atoxisch *Adj. fachspr.* non-toxic

Atrium *n; -s, Atrien; Archit.* atrium; **~haus** *n* atrium house (*od.* building), house built around a courtyard

Atrophie *f;* -, -*n; Med.* atrophy; **atrophieren** *v/i.* atrophy

Atropin *n; -s, kein Pl.; Chem., Pharm.* atropin(e)

ätsch *Interj. Kinderspr. (da hast du's!)* see!, told you so!; *schadenfroh:* serves you right!

Attaché [ata'ʃeː] *m; -s, -s; Pol.* attaché

Attacke *f;* -, -*n* attack (*auch Med. und fig.*) (**gegen** *od.* **auf** + *Akk.* on); **zur ~ blasen** *Mil.* sound the charge; *fig.* sound the attack; **e-e ~ reiten** *Mil.* (make an) attack; *fig.* mount an attack; **attackieren** *v/t/i.* attack (*auch fig.*), charge

Attentat *n; -(e)s, -e* assassination attempt (**auf** + *Akk.* on), attempted assassination; *geglücktes:* assassination; **ein ~ auf j-n verüben** make an attempt on s.o.'s life; *erfolgreich:* assassinate s.o.; **e-m ~ zum Opfer fallen** fall victim to an assassination; **ich habe ein ~ auf dich vor** *umg. fig. hum.* I've got a big favo(u)r to ask of you (*od.* a job lined up for you); **Attentäter** *m; -s, -,* **Attentäterin** *f;* -, -*nen* assassin

Attest *n; -(e)s, -e; Med.:* (**ärztliches ~** medical *od.* doctor's certificate; **ein ~ ausstellen** make out a medical certificate; **attestieren** *v/t.* certify

Attitüde *f;* -, -*n; geh.* posture; *gekünstelt: bes. Brit.* pose; **es ist bloße ~** it's just a pose

Attraktion *f;* -, -*en* attraction; (*Hauptattraktion*) *auch* draw; (*Ware*) winner; **attraktiv** *Adj.* attractive; **Attraktivität** *f;* -, *kein Pl.* attractiveness, attraction; *weitS.: e-r Stadt etc.: auch* desirability

Attrappe *f;* -, -*n* dummy; *Wirts. auch* display package; *Tech.* mock-up; **das ist alles nur ~** *fig.* it's all show, none of it is real

Attribut *n; -(e)s, -e* **1.** attribute, characteristic; **2.** *Ling.* (*Beifügung*) attribute, (attributive) adjunct; **attributiv** *Adj.* attributive; **Attributsatz** *m Ling.* (*Gliedsatz*) dependent clause

atü *Abk.* → **Atmosphärenüberdruck**

atypisch *Adj.* atypical

Ätzalkali *n Chem.* caustic alkali

Ätzbad *n* etching bath

at-Zeichen ['ɛt-] *n EDV, bei E-Mail--Adresse (= @):* at-sign

ätzen *v/t/i.* **1.** *Säure etc.:* corrode, eat into; **2.** *auf Kupfer etc.:* etch; **3.** *Med.* cauterize; **ätzend I.** *Part. Präs.* → **ätzen**; **II.** *Adj.* **1.** caustic, corrosive; **2.** *fig. Kritik, Spott:* caustic, vitriolic; *Geruch:* pungent; *Rauch:* acrid; **3.** *Sl. fig.* (*fürchterlich*) (really) crappy; (**das ist**) **echt ~** it's the pits; *Mathe etc.* **ist echt ~** maths sucks

Ätz|kalk *m Chem.* unhydrated (*od.* quick *od.* unslaked) lime; **~mittel** *n* corrosive (*od.* corroding) agent; **~stift** *m Med.* cautery, cauterant

Ätzung *f* **1.** corrosion; **2.** *Med.* cauterization; **3.** (*Zeichnung*) etching

au *Interj.* **1.** ouch!; **~ Backe!** (*oje*) ouch!, ow!; **2. ~ ja!** oh yes!; **~ fein** oh great

Au *f;* -, -*en; südd., österr.* → **Aue**

AU *f;* -, -*s; Abk. Mot. siehe* **Abgasuntersuchung**; **AU-Plakette** *f Mot.* exhaust emission check (*od.* test) disc (*Am.* certificate)

aua *Interj.* ouch!

aubergine [obɛr'ʒiːnə] *indekl. Adj.* → **auberginefarben**

Aubergine *f;* -, -*n Bot.* aubergine, *Am.* eggplant; **auberginefarben** *Adj.* aubergine, *Am.* eggplant(-colo[u]red)

auch *Adv.* **1.** (*ebenfalls*) also, too, as well; **das kann ich ~** I can do that too; **kommst du ~ mit?** are you coming too?; **ich habe Durst - ich ~** I'm thirsty – me (*od.* I am) too; **ich glaube es - ich ~** I believe it - so do I; **ich habe sie gesehen - ich ~** I saw her - I did too; **ich kann es nicht - ich ~ nicht** I can't do it - nor (*od.* neither) can I, I can't either; **nicht nur ..., sondern ~** not only ..., but also; **sowohl ... als ~ ...** both ... and ..., ... as well as ...; **~ das noch!** that too!; **2.** (*selbst, sogar*) even; **wenn ~** even if; **ohne ~ nur zu fragen** without even (*od.* so much as) asking; **3.** (*gleich*) **was/wer/wo** *etc.* **~** (*immer*) whatever/whoever/wherever *etc.*; **wer es ~ sei** whoever it is; **mag er ~ noch so unfreundlich sein** however unpleasant he is (*od.* may be); **sosehr ich es ~ bedaure** much as I regret it; **4.** *erklärend:* **sie ist krank, deshalb ist sie ~ nicht gekommen** she's ill, and that's why she hasn't come; **er hat ja ~ schwer gearbeitet** he has been working hard(, after all); **das hab ich ~ nicht gesagt** that's not what I said(, is it?); **5.** *zustimmend:* **so ist es ~** absolutely, that's (exactly) it; **so sieht er ~ aus** *umg.* he looks it; **vom Typ her: ~** auch he looks the sort; **6.** *ermahnend:* **ich gebe dir das Buch, nun lies es aber ~** now mind you read it though; **dass du ~ ja vorsichtig bist!** you make sure to (*od.* and) be careful!; **7.** *in Fragen, sich vergewissernd:* **wirst du es ~ (wirklich) tun?** are you really going to do it?; **ist es ~ wahr?** is it really true?; **haben Sie ihn ~ (wirklich) gesehen?** are you sure you saw him?; **8.** *in rhetorischen Fragen:* **warum hab ich ~ nicht besser aufgepasst?** why ever (*od.* why on earth) did I not pay more attention?; **wie konntest du ~ nur so dumm sein?** how on earth could you have been so stupid?; **wozu ~?** what's the point?; **9.** *verstärkend:* **du bist aber ~ stur!** talk about stubborn *umg.*; **so was aber ~!** that of all things!; **dass ich aber ~ gerade jetzt krank werden muss!** why do I have to get ill right now, of all times?; **so schlimm ist es ~ wieder nicht** it isn't that (*od.* so) bad, after all; **da können wir ~ (genauso gut) zu Hause bleiben** we may as well stay at home

Audienz *f;* -, -*en* audience (**bei** with); **in ~ von j-m empfangen werden** be given an audience by s.o.

Audimax *n;* -, *kein Pl.; Univ., Sl.* main auditorium

Audiometer *n Med.* audiometer; **Audiometrie** *f;* -, *kein Pl.* audiometry

audiovisuell *Adj.* audio-visual; **~e Hilfsmittel** audio-visual aids

Audit *n; -s, -s; Wirts.* (voluntary) audit

Auditorium *n; -s, Auditorien* **1.** *Päd., Univ.* (*Hörsaal*) auditorium, lecture hall (*od.* theat|re, *Am.* -er); **~ maximum** main auditorium; **2.** *geh.* (*Zuhörerschaft*) audience

Aue *f;* -, -*n* (rich) pasture; (*Wiese*) meadow; *lea poet.*

Auenwald *m* riverside forest

Auer|hahn *m Orn.* capercaillie (cock), wood grouse; **~henne** *f,* **~huhn** *n Orn.* capercaillie (hen), wood grouse; **~ochse** *m Zool.* aurochs

auf I. *Präp.* **1.** (+ *Dat.*); *räumlich, als Ortsangabe:* on, in; **~ dem Tisch** on the table; **~ der Welt** in the world; **~ der Straße** in (*Am. auch* on) the street; (*Fahrbahn*) on the road; **auf dem Feld** in the field; **~ See** at sea; **~ Malta** in Malta; **~ der Insel** on the island; **~ dem Rücken liegen** *etc.* on one's back; **~ s-r Seite** at (*od.* by) his side; *liegen etc.:* on his side; **~ Seite 15** on page 15; **er ist ~ s-m Zimmer** he is in his room; (*etw.*) **~ der Geige** *etc.* **spielen** play (s.th. on) the violin *etc.*; **~ einem Auge blind** blind in one eye; **das Wort endet ~ t** the word ends with (*od.* in) a t; **~ der Stelle** *fig.* on the spot; **2.** (+ *Akk.*); *räumlich, als Richtungsangabe:* (on) to; towards; up; **~ den Tisch legen** *etc.* on the table; **~ die Post® etc. gehen** go to the post office *etc.*; **~ sein Zimmer gehen** go to one's room; **~ die Straße gehen** go (out) into the street; **~ e-n Berg klettern** climb up a mountain; **ein Fenster ~ die Straße** a window (giving on, *Am.* looking on) to the street; **sie ging ~ ihn zu** she walked toward(s) him; **3.** (+ *Dat.*); *Aufenthalt:* at, by; (*während*) during, on; **~ der Ausstellung** (**Post**) at the exhibition (post office); **~ e-r Party** at a party (school, university); **~ dem Markt** at the market; **~ Reisen** (**sein**) (be) travel(l)ing, on a trip; **~ Besuch sein** be visiting; **4.** (+ *Akk.*); *Aufenthalt* (*beginnen*): **~ e-e höhere Schule gehen** go up to a secondary (*Am. auch* high) school; **sie geht ~s Gymnasium** etwa she goes to grammar (*Am. auch* grade, high) school; **~ Reisen gehen** go travel(l)ing; **~ die Jagd gehen** go hunting,; **5.** (+ *Akk.*); *Zeitraum:* (*für*) for; **~ Jahre hinaus** for years to come; **~ Monate** (**hinaus**) **ausgebucht** booked (*od.* sold) out (for) months ahead (*od.* in advance); **~ (immer und) ewig** for ever (and ever); **~ Zeit** for a period (*od.* time); **~ vier Jahre gewählt** elected for four years; **ich bleibe noch ~ e-e Tasse Tee** I'll stay for a cup of tea; **6.** (+ *Akk.*); *Reihenfolge:* **er macht Fehler ~ Fehler** he makes one mistake after the other; **in der Nacht vom 1. ~ den 2. Mai** in the night from the 1st to the 2nd of May (*Am. auch* from May 1 to 2); **sie hat es von einem Tag ~ den anderen vergessen** she forgot (about) it from one day to the next; **7.** (+ *Akk.*); *Zeitpunkt:* **es geht ~ neun** (**Uhr**) it's getting on for (*Am.* getting close to) nine; **er geht ~ die Siebzig zu** he's getting on for (*Am.* getting close to, *umg.* pushing) seventy; **den Wecker ~ 7** (**Uhr**) **stellen** set the alarm for 7 (o'clock); **bis ~ den heutigen Tag** until today (*od.* the present day); **~ bald!** see you soon!; **8.** (+ *Akk.*); *Entfernung:* **~ e-e Entfernung von ...** from a distance of ...; (**noch**) **~ 100 Meter zu erkennen sein** be recognizable from (*od.* at a distance of) 100 met|res (*Am.* –ers); **sie kam** (**bis**) **~ zwei Schritte heran** she came up (to) within a yard; **9.** (+ *Dat. bzw. Akk.*); *Art und Weise:* **~ direktem Wege** directly; **~ dem Seeweg** by sea; **~ Englisch** in English; **~ diese Weise** in this way; **~ m-e Kosten** on me; **j-n ~s Äußerste reizen** push s.o. to the limit; **er hat sie ~ das** *od.* **~s Übelste betrogen** he deceived her in the most despicable way; **10.** (+ *Akk.*); *Folge:* **~ s-n Antrag** (**hin**) following his application; **~ ihren Rat** (**hin**) following her advice; **~ vielfachen Wunsch** upon repeated request; **den Ausweis ~ Verlangen vorzeigen** show identification upon request (*od.* when requested); **auch ~ die Gefahr** (**hin**), **dass ...** even if it means risking that ...; **11.** (+ *Akk.*); (*hinsichtlich*) **~ Mängel** (**hin**) **überprüfen** inspect for faults; **12.** (+ *Akk.*); *Ziel, Zweck*: **~ Zeit spielen** play for time; **~ dein Wohl!** (here's) to you (*od.* your health)!; **~ ein gutes Gelingen!** (here's) to our, your *etc.* success (*od.* a successful outcome)!; **~ j-n/etw. aus sein** be out for (*od.* to get) s.th.; **13.** (+ *Akk.*); (*im Verhältnis zu*) to, per, for; **drei Eier ~ ein Pfund Mehl** three eggs to one (*od.* for every) pound of flour; **durchschnittlich ein Fehler ~ zehn Zeilen** on average one mistake (in) every ten lines; **14. er kam um 6, ~ die Minute genau** he came at 6 o'clock on the dot; **das stimmt ~ den Cent** (**genau**) that's right down to the last cent; **15. es hat was ~ sich** there's something to it; **ich frage mich, was es mit ... ~ sich hat** I wonder what's behind ...; **16.** a) (+ *Akk.*): **eifersüchtig ~** jealous of; **sich freuen ~** look forward to; **hoffen ~** hope for; **mit Rücksicht ~ ...** in consideration of ..., taking ... into consideration; **stolz sein ~** be proud of; **es besteht Verdacht ~ Schädelbruch** *etc.* there is a suspected skull fracture; **im Vertrauen ~ s-e Pünktlichkeit** *etc.* counting on (*od.* trusting [to]) his punctuality; **das Bier geht ~ mich** *fig.* the beer's on me (*od.* my treat); I'll get this *umg.*, b) (+ *Dat.*): **beruhen ~** be based on; **~ dem Fuße folgen** follow at s.o.'s heels; → **Anhieb, bis** I 1, 4 - 6, **einmal** 4 *und die mit „auf" verbundenen Adjektive, Verben and Substantive*; **II.** *Adv.* **1.** *umg.* (*offen*) open; **Mund ~!** open wide!; **Tür ~!** open the door!; **ist die Bank schon ~?** is the bank open yet (*od.* already open)?; **komm rein, die Tür ist ~** come (on) in, the door's open (*od.* not locked); **2.** *umg.*: **~ sein** (*nicht im Bett sein*) be up; **~!** (get) up!; **3.** (*los*) **~** (**geht's**)! antreibend: up!, get up!, let's go going!; anfeuernd: come on!; auffordernd: let's go!; **Glück ~!** f (*Bergmannsgruß*) good luck!; **4. ~ und ab** up and down, back and forth; *im Zimmer etc.* **~ und ab gehen** walk (*od.* pace) up and down (*od.* to and fro, *Am.* back and forth); **5. sich ~ und davon machen** clear off; bugger off *umg.*; **und schon war sie ~ und davon** and she'd already taken off (*od.* disappeared); **III.** *Konj.* altm., noch hum.: **~ dass** (in order) that

Auf *n*: **das ~ und Ab des Lebens** the ups and downs of life; **das ~ und Ab der Preise** the ups and downs of prices

aufarbeiten (*trennb., hat -ge-*) **I.** *v/t.* **1.** (*Angesammeltes*) get through, get *s.th.* out of the way; **e-n Rückstand ~** clear a backlog; **ich muss noch viel ~** I have a lot to catch up on; **2.** (*aufbrauchen*) use up; **3.** (*Kleider, Möbel etc.*) do up *umg.*; **4.** (*Wissensbereich*) get a solid grounding in; (*Erkenntnisse*) consolidate; **5.** (*Erlebnis*) digest, review, reappraise; (*Problem*) come to terms with; **II.** *v/refl.* pull o.s. together; **Aufarbeitung** f **1.** *e-s Rückstands etc.*: catching up; **2.** *von Erlebnissen*: reviewing, reappraising; **3.** *von Möbeln etc.*: refurbishing

aufatmen *v/i.* (*trennb., hat -ge-*) **1.** draw a deep breath; **2.** *fig.* heave a sigh of relief

aufbacken *v/t.* (*unreg., trennb., hat -ge-*); (*Brötchen etc.*) warm (*od.* crisp) up

aufbahren *v/t.* (*trennb., hat -ge-*); (*Leiche*) lay out; **Aufbahrung** f laying out; feierlich: lying in state

Aufbau *m*; *Pl. -ten* **1.** *nur Sg.*; (*das Aufbauen*) *e-s Lagers, Zeltes etc.*: erection; (*Wiederaufbau*) rebuilding, (re)construction; *Tech.* (*Montage*) assembly, mounting; *Chem.* synthesis; → **Ost** 4; **2.** *nur Sg.*; *e-r Organisation, e-s Unternehmens etc.*: building, development, system; *der Wirtschaft etc.*: building up; **im ~** under development; **im ~ begriffen** in the process of organization, in the initial stages; **3.** *nur Sg*; (*Struktur, Gliederung*) structure; *e-s Bilds*: composition; *e-s Dramas*: structure; *e-s Kunstwerks*: composition, make-up; **4.** *mst Pl.*; *e-s Schiffes*: superstructure *Sg.*; *auf der Bühne*: stage set; *Film*: set *Sg.*; **5.** (*Karosserie*) (car) body

aufbauen (*trennb., hat -ge-*) **I.** *v/t.* **1.** (*Zelt*) put up; (*Lager*) set up; (*Bude, Bühne, Kamera etc.*) set (*od.* put) up, erect; (*Ausstellung, Schaubild*) mount; (*Gerüst*) assemble; (*Häuser, Stadt etc.*) neu *od.* wieder ~ rebuild; **2.** (*anordnen*) (*Büffet, Geschenke, Waren*) arrange; **3.** (*Unternehmen, Organisation*) (*gründen*) set up, found; (*weiter ~*) build up; **sich** (*Dat.*) **e-e Existenz ~** build a life for o.s.; **4.** (*Drama, Aufsatz*) structure; **5.** **j-n** (*Mut machen*) build s.o. up; kurzfristig: auch give s.o. a pep talk; **6.** (*Politiker, Sportler*) karrieremäßig: build up; **II.** *vt/i.* *fig.*: **~ auf** (+ *Akk.*) build on; **III.** *v/i.*: **~ auf** (+ *Dat.*) *Theorie, Kurs etc.*: be based on; **IV.** *v/refl.*: **1.** *Wolken, Aggressionen etc.*: build up; **2.** **sich ~ auf** (+ *Dat.*) *Stoff etc.*: be made up (*od.* composed) of; **3.** **sich ~ auf** (+ *Dat.*) *Theorie etc.*: be based on; **4. er baute sich vor mir auf** he planted himself in front of me

Aufbau|gymnasium *n* school at which pupils can gain A-levels (*Am.* can graduate) in three years; **~hilfe** f developmental aid (*od.* assistance); **~kurs** *m* continuation course

aufbäumen *v/refl.* (*trennb., hat -ge-*) **1.** *Pferd*: rear (up); *Person*: writhe (**unter** + *Dat.* under); *Flug.* buck; **2.** *fig.* rebel, rise in protest (**gegen** against)

Aufbau|phase f development(al) phase; **~präparat** *n* regenerative preparation

aufbauschen *v/t.* (*trennb., hat -ge-*) **1.** (*auch v/refl.*) swell (out), puff up; **2.** *fig.* exaggerate, play up

Aufbaustudium *n* postgraduate course (*od.* studies *Pl.*)

Aufbauten → **Aufbau** 4, 5

Aufbautraining *n* *Sport* stamina training

aufbegehren *v/i.* (*trennb., hat*) rebel (**gegen j-n** against s.o), protest, be up in arms (**gegen etw.** against s.th.)

aufbehalten *v/t.* (*unreg., trennb., hat*); *umg.*: **den Hut** *etc.* **~** keep one's hat etc. on

aufbeißen *v/t.* (*unreg., trennb., hat -ge-*) bite open; (*Nüsse*) crack with one's teeth; **sich** (*Dat.*) **die Lippen ~** bite one's lips

aufbekommen *v/t.* (*unreg., trennb.,*

hat) **1.** (*Tür etc.*) get open; (*Knoten*) untangle, get undone; **2.** (*Hausaufgabe*) be given, get; **viel ~** get a lot of homework

aufbereiten *v/t.* (*trennb., hat*) **1.** (*Erze, Rohstoffe*) process, separate, dress, wash; (*Trinkwasser*) purify, treat, cleanse; (*Atommüll, Brennstäbe*) **wieder ~** reprocess; **2.** (*auswerten*) (*Statistiken etc.*) process; (*bearbeiten*) (*Daten, Text*) edit; **Aufbereitung** f **1.** processing; concentration, separation; (wet) dressing; trockene: mechanical dressing; **2.** *von Daten, Texten*: editing

Aufbereitungsanlage f (re)processing plant

aufbessern *v/t.* (*trennb., hat -ge-*); (*Verpflegung*) improve; (*Gehalt*) increase; (*Kenntnisse*) improve, better; **j-n ~** *umg.* give s.o. a rise (*Am.* raise) allg.; **Aufbesserung** f improvement; des Gehalts: (salary) increase, *Am.* raise (in salary)

aufbewahren *v/t.* (*trennb., hat*) keep (**für** for); für später: save, preserve; (*Vorräte*) store; **bitte kühl ~** please store in a cool place; **Aufbewahrung** f **1.** keeping, storage; **sichere ~** safekeeping; **j-m etw. zur ~ geben** leave s.th. with s.o. (for safekeeping); **2.** (*Gepäckaufbewahrung*) left-luggage (office), *Am.* baggage check (room); **etw. in ~ geben** hand s.th. in at the left-luggage office (*Am.* baggage check)

Aufbewahrungs|ort *m*: **sicherer ~** safe place (to keep s.th.); **~schein** *m* left-luggage (*Am.* baggage check) ticket (*od.* slip)

aufbieten *v/t.* (*unreg., trennb., hat -ge-*) **1.** (*Kräfte, Mittel, Mut etc.*) muster, summon (up); **alles ~** do one's utmost; **s-n** (*ganzen*) **Einfluss ~** bring (all) one's influence to bear; **2.** (*Truppen*) mobilize; **Aufbietung** f **1.** *von Einfluss etc.*: exertion; **unter ~ aller Kräfte** with all one's might, by mustering all one's strength; **2.** *Mil.* mobilization

aufbinden *v/t.* (*unreg., trennb., hat -ge-*) **1.** (*lösen*) untie, undo; **2.** (*hochbinden*) tie up; **sich die Haare ~** put up one's hair; **3.** (*festbinden auf*) tie (on) (**auf** + *Akk.* to); **j-m e-n Bären ~** *umg.* *fig.* take s.o. for a ride, have (*Am.* put) s.o. on; **4. sich** (*Dat.*) **e-e Verpflichtung** etc. **~** get landed (*od.* saddled) with (*doing*) s.th.

aufblähen (*trennb., hat -ge-*) **I.** *v/t.* **1.** (*Backen*) blow out, puff out; (*Nasenflügel*) flare; (*Bauch etc.*) puff up; *Med.* distend; (*Segel*) billow, fill, below out; (*Gefieder*) ruffle up; **2.** *fig.* (*Verwaltungsapparat, Preise, Währung*) inflate; **ein aufgeblähter Beamtenapparat** an overblown bureaucracy; **II.** *v/refl.* **1.** *Backen*: balloon, puff out; *Bauch*: swell; *Med.* distend; *Frosch*: puff itself up; *Segel*: fill, belly out; *Med.*. tumefy, tumesce; **2.** *fig.* puff o.s. up, make o.s. important

aufblasbar *Adj.* inflatable; **aufblasen** **I.** *v/t.* blow (*od.* pump) up, inflate; **II.** *v/refl.* *fig.* puff o.s. up; → **aufgeblasen** II

aufblättern (*trennb., -ge-*) **I.** *v/t.* (*hat*); (*Buch etc.*) open (up); **II.** *v/i.* (*ist*) *Min.* exfoliate

aufbleiben *v/i.* (*unreg., trennb., ist -ge-*) **1.** *Tür etc.*: stay open; **2.** *Person*: (*wach bleiben*) stay up (**lang** late)

aufblenden (*trennb., hat -ge-*) **I.** *vt/i.* **1.** (*Filmszene*) fade in; **2.** *Mot.* (*Scheinwerfer*) turn the headlights on high beam, turn up the headlights,

Am. put on the brights; **II.** *v/i. Fot.* open (the lens) up

aufblicken *v/i.* (*trennb., hat -ge-*) **1.** look up, glance up (*von etw.* from s.th.; *zu* at); **2.** *fig.:* (*bewundernd*) *zu j-m ~* look up to s.o. (with admiration)

aufblitzen *v/i.* (*trennb., hat -ge-*) **1.** flash, flare (up); *schwach:* flicker; **2.** *fig.* pop up; (*in*) *j-m ~ Gedanke:* flash through s.o.'s mind

aufblühen *v/i.* (*trennb., ist -ge-*) **1.** blossom, open; **2.** *fig. Mädchen:* blossom; **3.** (*aufleben*) blossom (out); *wirtschaftlich etc.:* begin to flourish (*od.* prosper)

aufbocken *v/t.* (*trennb., hat -ge-*); *Mot.* jack up

aufbohren *v/t.* (*trennb., hat -ge-*) bore (open); (*Zahn*) drill

aufbranden *v/i.* (*trennb., ist -ge-*); *geh. Wellen:* surge, break; *Beifall:* burst out (*od.* forth)

aufbraten *v/t.* (*unreg., trennb., hat -ge-*) fry up

aufbrauchen *v/t.* (*trennb., hat -ge-*) use up

aufbrausen *v/i.* (*trennb., ist -ge-*) **1.** *Getränk:* fizz; *Meer:* surge; *Chem.* effervesce; **2.** *fig. Person:* fly off the handle; *Beifall brauste auf* there was a surge of applause / roar of laughter; **aufbrausend I.** *Part. Präs. → aufbrausen;* **II.** *Adj. fig.* quick-tempered

aufbrechen (*unreg., trennb., -ge-*) **I.** *v/t.* (*hat*) **1.** (*Schloss, Siegel, Tür etc.*) break open, force; (*Kiste*) break into; (*Pflaster, Straße*) break up; (*Erde etc.*) *mit Pflug: auch* break ground, turn over; (*Brief*) tear open; **2.** *Jägerspr.* (*ausweiden*) gut; **3.** *geh.* (*Brief*) open *allg.;* **II.** *v/i.* (*ist*) **1.** *Blüten etc.:* open; *Geschwür:* (burst) open; *Eisdecke, Asphalt:* crack; **2.** (*weggehen*) leave, set off, start out (*nach* for); *zu e-m Ausflug ~* set off on an excursion

aufbrennen *v/t.* (*unreg., trennb., hat -ge-*): *Kälbern ein Zeichen ~* brand calves; *j-m eins ~ umg.* (*anschießen*) give s.o. some stick *auch hum.;* (*schlagen*) let s.o. have it

aufbringen *v/t.* (*unreg., trennb., hat -ge-*) **1.** (*öffnen*) get open; (*Knoten*) untangle, get undone; **2.** (*beschaffen*) find; (*Geld*) raise; (*Kosten*) meet; (*Mut, Energie etc.*) summon up, muster; **3.** (*Mode, Gerücht*) start; **4.** *fig.* (*j-n*) make s.o. angry, get s.o.'s goat *umg.;* *~ gegen* set s.o. against; *→ aufgebracht* II; **5.** *Naut.* (*Schiff*) seize; (*in den Hafen bringen*) bring in; **6.** (*Creme, Farbe etc.*) apply, put on

Aufbruch *m* **1.** departure (*nach, zu* for); *fig. Pol.* awakening; *im ~ sein* just be getting ready to go (*od.* leave), be on the point of departure; *zum ~ drängen* be keen (*Am.* eager) to get going; *das Zeichen zum ~ geben umg.* say it's time to go; **2.** (*offene Stelle*) crack; **3.** *Jägerspr.* bowels, entrails *Pl.;* **Aufbruchsstimmung** *f:* *es herrschte ~ bei Fest etc.:* everyone was getting ready to go; *Pol. etc.* there was the sense of a new era about to dawn

aufbrühen *v/t.* (*trennb., hat -ge-*) *auch Gastr.* boil (up); (*Tee, Kaffee*) make, brew

aufbrummen *v/t.* (*trennb., hat -ge-*); *umg.: j-m e-e Strafe etc. ~* land (*od.* lumber *od. Am.* penalize) s.o. with s.th.; *er bekam 4 Monate aufgebrummt* they sent him up for 4 months

Aufbügelmuster *n Sticken:* transfer pattern; **aufbügeln** *v/t.* (*trennb., hat*

-ge-) **1.** (*bügeln*) iron, press; **2.** (*Flicken*) iron *a patch* (*auf* + *Akk.* on)

aufbürden *v/t.* (*trennb., hat -ge-*): *j-m etw. ~* saddle s.o. with s.th.; *j-m e-e Last ~* place a burden on s.o.('s shoulders)

aufdecken (*trennb., hat -ge-*) **I.** *v/t.* **1.** uncover; (*Spielkarte*) show; *seine Karten ~ fig.* lay one's cards on the table; *das Bett ~* turn the bedclothes (*Am.* covers) down; **2.** *fig.* (*Missstände, Verschwörung*) expose, reveal; **3.** (*Tischtuch*) put on; **II.** *v/i.* lay the table; **III.** *v/refl.:* *sich* (*im Schlaf*) *~* throw (*od.* kick) off the covers (in one's sleep)

Aufdeckung *f e-s Skandals etc.:* disclosure, revelation, uncovering, bringing *s.th.* out into the open

aufdonnern *v/refl.* (*trennb., hat -ge-*); *umg.* get (all) dolled up; *aufgedonnert auch* all dressed up, dressed (up) to the nines

aufdrängen (*trennb., hat -ge-*) **I.** *v/t.:* *j-m etw. ~* force s.th. on s.o.; *j-m e-e Meinung ~* force an opinion down s.o.'s throat; **II.** *v/refl.* **1.** *Gedanke:* suggest itself; **2.** *sich j-m ~* force o.s. on s.o.; *ich will mich nicht ~* I don't want to intrude

aufdrehen (*trennb., hat -ge-*) **I.** *v/t.* **1.** (*Gas, Hahn, Wasser etc.*) turn on; (*Schraube*) loosen; *völlig:* unscrew; (*Deckel etc.*) screw off; **2.** (*lauter stellen*) (*Radio*) turn up; **3.** *die Haare ~* put curlers in one's hair, put one's hair in curlers; **4.** *→ aufgedreht* II, III; **II.** *v/i. umg.* **1.** (*beschleunigen*) step on it; *Mot.* step on the gas; *Sport* open up; **2.** (*in Stimmung kommen*) get into the mood (*od.* going); **3.** *südd., österr.* (*wütend werden*) get worked up

aufdringlich *Adj.* **1.** *Person:* obtrusive, importunate, insistent, pushy; *diese ~en Leute!* these people just won't go away; **2.** *Sache:* obtrusive; *Frage:* intrusive, pestering; *Farben etc.:* loud, showy; *Parfüm:* strong; *stärker:* overpowering; **Aufdringlichkeit** *f* **1.** *nur Sg.; Art:* obtrusiveness; *von Personen: auch* importunity, pushiness; *von Parfüm:* strong (*od.* overpowering) smell; *von Farben:* loudness, gaudiness, garishness; **2.** *Handlung:* pushy behavio(u)r

aufdröseln *v/t.* (*trennb., hat -ge-*); *Dial.* **1.** (*Genähtes, Gestricktes*) undo; (*Strick*) unravel, take apart; **2.** *fig.* (*Handlung, Geheimnis etc.*) unravel; (*Satz*) break down, analy|se (*Am.* -ze)

Aufdruck *m; Pl. Aufdrucke; Druck.* imprint; (*Firmenlogo*) company name; *auf Briefmarke:* legend, print; **aufdrucken** *v/t.* (*trennb., hat -ge-*) print (*auf* + *Akk.* on)

aufdrücken (*trennb., hat -ge-*) **I.** *v/t.* **1.** (*öffnen*) (*Tür etc.*) push open; (*Verschluss*) press open; (*Pickel etc.*) squeeze; **2.** (*Stempel etc.*) (*auch ~ auf* + *Akk.*) put on; *j-m e-n Kuss ~* plant a kiss on s.o.; **II.** *v/i. beim Schreiben:* (*zu*) *fest ~* press (too) hard

aufeinander *Adv.* (*übereinander*) on top of each other; (*gegeneinander*) against each other; (*nacheinander*) one after the other, one by one; *~ abgestimmt* coordinated; *Farben etc.:* matching, in harmony; *~ angewiesen sein* be dependent on each other, rely on each other; *die Zähne ~ beißen* press one's teeth together; *bei Schmerzen etc.:* grit one's teeth; *Teile ~ drücken* press parts together; *~ einschla-*

gen smash into each other; *~ folgen* follow each other; *im Abstand von fünf Minuten ~ folgen* occur (*Busse etc.:* run) every five minutes; *~ folgend* successive, consecutive; *~ hetzen* (*Hunde*) set at (*od.* on) each other; *Bücher etc. ~ legen* lay on top of each other, put in a pile; *~ liegen* lie on top of each other; lie in a pile; *~ losgehen* go for each other; *~ prallen* collide, crash; *fig. Personen, Meinungen:* clash; *Dinge ~ schichten/türmen* put in layers / pile one on top of the other; *~ treffen* meet; (*Meinungen*) clash, come into conflict; *~ zugehen* walk towards (*od.* approach) each other (*od.* one another)

Aufeinanderfolge *f; nur Sg.* succession; *von Ereignissen:* series, round

Aufenthalt *m; -(e)s, -e* **1.** stay; *im Urlaubsort: auch* visit, sojourn *geh.;* *der ~ im Maschinenraum ist verboten* entry to the engine-room is forbidden; **2.** *während der Fahrt: Eisenb.* stop; *Flug.* stopover; *unvorhergesehen:* stoppage; *ohne ~ Zug etc.:* nonstop; *wie lange haben wir hier ~?* how long do we stop here?; *wir hatten zwei Stunden ~* we had a two-hour wait; **3.** *geh. → Aufenthaltsort;* **4.** (*Verzögerung*) delay, wait; *ohne ~* without delay

Aufenthalts|dauer *f* (duration of) stay; *~erlaubnis f, ~genehmigung f* residen|ce (*od. ~cy*) permit; *~ort m zum Zeitpunkt des Verbrechens etc.:* whereabouts; *ständiger:* place of residence; *~raum m* lounge; *Schule etc.:* common room, *Am.* teachers' lounge

auferlegen *v/t.* (*trennb. od. untr., hat*); (*Strafe*) impose, inflict (*j-m* on s.o.); *j-m Schweigen ~* constrain s.o. to silence; *j-m Verantwortung ~* place responsibility on s.o.('s shoulders); *sich* (*Dat.*) *Zwang ~* exercise (some) self-restraint

auferstehen *v/i.* (*unreg., trennb., ist*) rise from the dead; *fig.* rise from the ashes; **Auferstehung** *f* resurrection; (*fröhliche*) *~ feiern fig. hum. od. iro.* have been resurrected (*od.* brought back from the dead), make a comeback

auferwecken *v/t.* (*untr., hat*): *j-n* (*von den Toten*) *~* bring s.o. back to life (from the dead); *mit dem Kaffee kannst du Tote ~ fig.* you could raise the dead with this coffee; **Auferweckung** *f* raising from the dead

aufessen *v/t.* (*unreg., trennb., hat -ge-*) eat up, finish; *es war im Nu aufgegessen* it went (down) in no time

auffächern (*trennb., hat -ge-*) **I.** *v/t.* **1.** (*Karten*) fan out; **2.** *fig.* break down (*in* + *Akk.* into); *in dem Film wird die ganze Pracht der Epoche aufgefächert* this film (*Am. auch* movie) shows the era in all its glory; **II.** *v/refl. Straße etc.:* fan out

auffädeln *v/t.* (*trennb., hat -ge-*) thread (*auf* + *Akk.* onto)

auffahren (*unreg., trennb., -ge-*) **I.** *v/i.* (*ist*) **1.** (*prallen*): *~ auf* (+ *Akk.*) crash (*od.* drive) into, ram; *Naut.* ram; *der Radfahrer fuhr auf das geparkte Auto auf* the cyclist rode into the parking car; *die Fähre ist auf ein Riff aufgefahren* the ferry has run aground on a reef; **2.** *Mot.* (*aufschließen*): (*zu*) *dicht auf den Vordermann ~* tailgate the car in front; **3.** (*vorfahren*) drive up, pull up; **4.** *erschreckt:* (give a) start, jump; *aus dem Schlaf ~* waken with a start; **5.** *zornig:* flare up; **6.** *mit Fahrstuhl:*

go up; *auf Berg*: go/come up; *in den Himmel* ~ *Reli.* ascend to heaven; **II.** *v/t.* (*hat*) **1.** (*Speisen etc.*) bring on, serve (up); ~ *lassen* have served; **2.** *Mil.* bring up, deploy; → *Geschütz*; **3.** (*aufwühlen*) (*Weg*) churn (*od.* cut) up; **auffahrend I.** *Part. Präs.* → *auffahren*; **II.** *Adj. fig.* (*erregbar*) quick--tempered; irascible *förm.*

Auffahrrampe *f auch Naut.* ramp

Auffahrt *f* **1.** *zu e-m Haus*: drive(way *Am.*); **2.** *zur Autobahn*: slip road, *Am.* (entrance *od.* on) ramp, access road; **3.** *zum Gipfel*: climb (*od.* drive up) to the summit; *Bergb.* ascent; **4.** *nur Sg.*; (*das Vorfahren*) driving (*od.* pulling) up

Auffahrunfall *m* rear-end collision, ramming

auffallen *v/i.* (*unreg., trennb., ist -ge-*) **1.** (*sich hervorheben*) be conspicuous, attract attention (*durch* through *od.* by); (*bemerkt werden*) stand out; (*un*)*angenehm* ~ make a good (bad) impression (*durch* by *od.* for); *j-m* ~ *auch* strike s.o.; *engS.* catch s.o.'s eye; *fällt es auf?* it is noticeable?; *fällt der Fleck auf?* does the stain show?; *es fällt nicht auf* nobody will notice; *es fällt auf, dass ...* it is (really) obvious that ...; *mir ist es gar nicht aufgefallen* I never noticed; *nicht ~ wollen* keep one's head down, keep a low profile; *bloß nicht ~!* don't make yourself conspicuous!; **2.** ~ *auf* (+ *Akk.*) fall on(to), hit; *Phys. Strahlen*: strike

auffallend I. *Part. Präs.* → *auffallen*; **II.** *Adj.* noticeable, conspicuous; *Schönheit, Erscheinung etc.*: striking; *Benehmen*: odd, weird; blatant *pej.*; *das Auffallendste daran ist ...* the odd(est) thing about it is ..., the (most) peculiar thing about it is ...; **III.** *Adv.*: ~ *schön* extraordinarily (*od.* strikingly) beautiful, ~ *tüchtig* incredibly efficient; ~ *ähnlich sein* *j-m/etw.*: have a striking resemblance to; *einander*: be remarkably alike; *stimmt* ~*!* *umg. hum.* how right you are!, (it's only) too true!

auffällig I. *Adj.* conspicuous; *Kleider, Farben*: loud, flashy *umg.*; *Benehmen*: odd, peculiar; **II.** *Adv.*: ~ *oft* conspicuously often; *sich* ~ *benehmen* behave oddly; ~ *gekleidet* showily dressed; *~er hätten sie es wohl nicht machen können* they couldn't have made it any more obvious (if they had tried); **Auffälligkeit** *f* **1.** *nur Sg.*; *Eigenschaft*: conspicuousness; (*Grellheit*) garishness, loudness; **2.** *Merkmal*: distinctive feature

auffalten (*trennb., hat -ge-*) **I.** *v/t.* open up, unfold; **II.** *v/refl.* **1.** *Blume, Fallschirm etc.* open up; **2.** *Geol. Gebirge*: fold upwards

Auffangbecken *n* **1.** *für Regenwasser*: (rainwater) collecting tank, *Brit.* water butt; *größer*: reservoir; **2.** *fig.* rallying (*od.* assembly) point, gathering place

auffangen *v/t.* (*unreg., trennb., hat -ge-*) **1.** (*Ball etc.*) catch; (*Funksignal, Gesprächsfetzen, Masche*) pick up; *j-s Blick* ~ catch s.o.'s eye; **2.** (*Fall, Stoß*) cushion; (*Angriff, Schlag*) parry; (*Auto, Flugzeug*) get (*od.* bring) under control, regain control of; (*Flugzeug*) *auch* pull out (of a dive); *fig.* (*Preissteigerungen etc.*) cushion (the impact of); **3.** (*sammeln*) (*Wasser*) collect; *fig.* (*Flüchtlinge*) assemble

Auffanglager *n für Flüchtlinge*: transit (*od.* reception) camp

auffassen (*trennb., hat -ge-*) **I.** *vt/i.* (*begreifen*) understand, grasp; *leicht* (*schwer*) ~ be quick (slow) on the uptake; **II.** *v/t.* (*deuten*) interpret, understand; take (*als* as); *falsch* ~ misunderstand, misinterpret; *etw. als Vorwurf/Scherz* ~ take s.th. as an accusation/joke; *wie soll ich deine Worte* ~*?* what's that supposed to mean?

Auffassung *f* **1.** ~ (*von*) (*Meinung*) opinion (of), view (on); (*Vorstellung*) idea (about), conception (of); *der* ~ *sein, dass ...* be of the opinion that ...; *zu der* ~ *gelangen, dass ...* reach the conclusion that ...; *die* ~ *vertreten, dass ...* take the view that ...; *nach m-r* ~ as I see it; *wir haben unterschiedliche* ~*en darüber, wie das zu tun ist* we disagree (*od.* have different views) how it should be gone about; **2.** → *Auffassungsgabe*

Auffassungs\|gabe *f* perceptive faculty, intellectual grasp, perception; *eine schnelle* ~ *haben* be quick on the uptake; *~sache f: das ist* ~ that's a matter of opinion

auffegen *vt/i.* (*trennb., hat -ge-*) *bes. nordd.* sweep up

auffindbar *Adj.*: *nicht* ~ not to be found; **auffinden** *v/t.* (*unreg., trennb., hat -ge-*) find; (*Person*) *auch* trace; *tot aufgefunden werden* be found dead

auffischen *v/t.* (*trennb., hat -ge-*) **1.** fish out of the water; **2.** *fig.* pick up

aufflackern *v/i.* (*trennb., ist -ge-*) **1.** *Feuer*: flicker; **2.** *fig.* flare up

aufflammen *v/i.* (*trennb., ist -ge-*) flare up (*auch fig.*); *Gegenstand*: *auch* burst into flames; *Streichholz*: light up

aufflattern *v/i.* (*trennb., ist -ge-*) **1.** *Vogel*: flutter up; **2.** *Buch*: rustle

auffliegen *v/i.* (*unreg., trennb., ist -ge-*) **1.** fly up; *Vogel*: *auch* soar up; **2.** *Tür etc.*: fly open; **3.** *umg. fig. Unternehmen, Plan etc.*: blow up (*auch* ~ *lassen*); (*entdeckt werden*) be exposed; *Verbrecherring etc.*: be smashed

auffordern *v/t.* (*trennb., hat -ge-*) call (up)on *s.o.* (*zu* + *Inf.* to + *Inf.*); *bittend*: ask, request; *anordnend*: order, bid, summon; *eindringlich*: urge, exhort; *ermunternd*: encourage; (*einladen*) invite, ask; (*herausfordern*) defy, challenge (*alle* + *Inf.*); *zur Zahlung* ~ demand (*od.* call for) payment; *zum Kampf* ~ challenge to a fight; *j-n* (*zum Tanz*) ~ ask s.o. for a (*od.* the next) dance; *ich fordere Sie zum letzten Mal auf, ...* I am asking you for the last time ...; *die Bevölkerung wird aufgefordert zu ...* (+ *Inf.*) the public is requested to ... (+ *Inf.*); *die Polizei forderte ihn auf, sich zu ergeben* the police asked him to give himself up (*od.* surrender)

auffordernd I. *Part. Präs.* → *auffordern*; **II.** *Adj. Blick*: encouraging, inviting; *stärker*: provocative; *in e-r* ~*en Haltung* in a challenging pose; (*sexuell*) ~*e Blicke* come-hither look; **III.** *Adv.*: *j-n* ~ *ansehen* look at s.o. encouragingly

Aufforderung *f* **1.** ~ (*zu*) (*Aufruf, Bitte*) call, request; (*Befehl*) order; (*Ermahnung*) exhortation; (*Einladung*) *auch zum Tanz*: invitation; *zum Kampf*: challenge; (*Anstiftung*) *Jur.* incitement; *j-s* ~ *nachkommen* comply with a request; *an j-n ergeht die* ~ *zu ...* (+ *Inf.*) s.o. is requested (*od.* called upon) to ... (+ *Inf.*); **2.** *Ling.* imperative

Aufforderungssatz *m Ling.* imperative sentence (*od.* clause), sentence

(*od.* clause) expressing a wish or command

aufforsten *v/t.* (*trennb., hat -ge-*) reafforest, *Am.* reforest; **Aufforstung** *f* reafforestation, *Am.* reforestation

auffressen *v/t.* (*trennb., hat -ge-*) eat up; (*Beute*) devour; *er wird dich schon nicht* ~ *umg.* he won't eat you (*od.* bite your head off); *die Arbeit frisst mich auf umg. fig.* I'm drowning in work

auffrischen (*trennb., hat -ge-*) **I.** *v/t.* **1.** *allg.* freshen up, refresh; (*Gemälde, Farben etc.*) touch up, restore; (*Möbel*) varnish; do up *umg.*; (*erneuern*) renew, regenerate; (*Kenntnisse*) brush up; (*Bekanntschaft*) revive; (*Impfung*) boost, get a booster; **2.** (*Lager, Vorräte*) replenish, restock; **II.** *v/refl. und v/i. Wind*: freshen up; **Auffrischung** *f* **1.** (*Erneuerung*) refreshing, restoring, regeneration; **2.** (*Ergänzung*) replenishing, restocking

Auffrischungs\|impfung *f* booster (vaccination *od.* jab *Brit umg.*, shot *Am. umg.*); *~kurs m* refresher course

auffrisieren *v/t.* (*trennb., hat -ge-*) **1.** (*Haar*) touch up; **2.** *umg.* (*Tisch, Auto etc.*) do up; (*Motor*) soup up

aufführbar *Adj.* stageable, performable; *das Stück ist nicht* ~ *auch* the play can't be performed (*od.* put on the stage)

aufführen (*trennb., hat -ge-*) **I.** *v/t.* **1.** (*Stück etc.*) perform, put on; *wieder* ~ stage a repeat performance, perform again; **2.** (*Beispiel, Belege*) cite, quote; *in e-r Liste*: list; *einzeln* ~ (*Posten*) specify, itemize; **3.** *Jur.* (*Zeugen*) produce, cite; **4.** *geh.* (*bauen*) erect, build; **II.** *v/refl. gut, schlecht etc.*: behave (well, badly *etc.*); *sich wie ein Verrückter* ~ act (*od.* behave) like a madman; *führ dich nicht so auf! umg.* don't make such a fuss!, keep your hat on!

Aufführung *f* **1.** *Theat.* performance; *Film*: showing; *zur* ~ *kommen* (*Stück*) be staged, be put on; (*Film*) be screened; (*Musik*) be performed; *zur* ~ *bringen geh.* (*Stück*) stage, put on; (*Film*) screen; (*Musik*) perform; **2.** (*Nennung*) citation, quotation, listing; **3.** *nur Sg.*; *geh.* (*das Bauen*) erection, building

Aufführungsrecht *n Theat.* performing rights *Pl.*

auffüllen (*trennb., hat -ge-*) **I.** *v/t.* **1.** (*leeren Behälter*) fill up; (*nachfüllen*) top up; **2.** (*ergänzen*) (*Vorräte*) replenish; (*Lager*) restock; **3.** (*aufschütten*) (*Grube*) fill in, infill (*mst* be infilled); (*Ufer*) build up, raise; **II.** *vt/i. Gastr. mit Brühe etc.*: top up (with stock); **Auffüllung** *f* **1.** *von leerem Behälter etc.*: filling (*od.* topping) up; **2.** *von Vorräten*: replenishing; *von Lager*: restocking; **3.** *e-r Grube etc.*: filling in

auffuttern *v/t.* (*trennb., hat -ge-*); *umg.* tuck away, polish off

Aufgabe *f* **1.** *j-s* (*Arbeit*) job, assignment; (*Pflicht*) duty; (*Auftrag, Mission*) task, mission; *j-m e-e* ~ *übertragen* give (*od.* assign) s.o. a job (*od.* task); *etw. als s-e* ~ *ansehen* consider s.th. one's duty; *er machte es sich zur* ~ *umg.* (+ *Inf.*) he made it his business to (+ *Inf.*); *es ist nicht m-e* ~ it's not my job (*od.* responsibility); **2.** (*Zweck, Funktion*) function; **3.** *bes. Päd.* (*Denkaufgabe*) question, exercise; (*Rechenaufgabe*) problem; (*Übung*) exercise; (*Hausausgabe*) *auch Pl.* homework; *j-m e-e ~ stellen* set s.o. an exercise; *e-e ~ lösen* solve a problem; *s-e ~n machen* do one's homework; **4.** *nur Sg.*; *e-s Briefes*: posting, *Am.* mailing; *von Gepäck*: registration, checking-in, depositing, *Am.* checking; *von Telegrammen*: sending, handing in; *e-s Auftrags, e-r Anzeige*: placing, insertion; **5.** *nur Sg.*; *e-r Wohnung, e-s Geschäfts*: giving up; *e-s Geschäfts*: *auch* quitting; *e-s Plans*: abandonment, relinquishment; *Rennen etc.*: dropping out; *Sieg durch ~* Sport win through concession (*od.* by default); *Boxkampf auch*: technical knockout; **6.** *Sport* (*Aufschlag*) service

aufgabeln *v/t.* (*trennb., hat -ge-*); *umg.* pick up, get hold of; *wo hast du den bloß aufgegabelt?* where on earth did you find him (*od.* dig him up)?

Aufgaben|bereich *m*, *~gebiet n* (area of) responsibility, (scope of) duties, field of activity; *~heft n* homework book; *~stellung f* terms *Pl.* of reference, nature of the task, type of problem; (*Formulierung*) formulation; *~verteilung f* allocation of duties (*od.* tasks), dividing up of responsibilities; *in Ehe etc.*: sharing of tasks

Aufgabe|ort *m* place of posting (*bes. Am.* mailing); *~schein m* (luggage) receipt, *Am.* baggage check

Aufgalopp *m* trial gallop; *fig.* curtain raiser

Aufgang *m* **1.** (*Ggs. Untergang*) ascent, rising; **2.** (*Treppe*) staircase, stairs *Pl.*; (*Stufen*) steps *Pl.*; *Naut.* companionway

aufgeben (*unreg., trennb., hat -ge-*) **I.** *vt/i.* (*Kampf, Widerstand*) give up (*od.* in), abandon; *Sport, als Läufer, Teilnehmer*: *auch* drop out, concede (defeat); *Schach* resign; *Boxen und fig.*: throw in the towel; *~ müssen* be forced to give up (*od.* admit defeat); *sie gibt nicht so leicht auf* she doesn't give up that easily; → II 3.; **II.** *v/t.* **1.** (*Brief*) post, *Am.* mail; (*Gepäck*) register, *Am.* check; (*Luftgepäck*) check in, baggage check; (*Telegramm*) send; (*Bestellung*) place; (*Anzeige*) place (an ad in the newspaper); **2.** (*Aufgabe*) set, assign; (*Frage, Problem*) pose, ask; (*Rätsel*) ask (*od.* pose); *sie gibt immer sehr viel auf* she always sets (*Am.* gives) a lot of homework; → *Rätsel*; **3.** (*verzichten auf*) *allg.* give up; (*Amt*) resign; (*Beruf*) retire; (*Stelle*) leave; (*Geschäft*) give up (*od.* retire from); (*Gewohnheit*) give up; (*das Rauchen, Trinken*) stop; (*Hoffnung, Plan*) abandon, relinquish; (*Anspruch, Recht*) relinquish; *es ~ zu* (+ *Inf.*) give up (+ *Ger.*); *ich geb's auf* I give up; **4.** *j-n* (*Kranken, Vermissten*) give up (hope for); (*Schüler, Kind*) give up on (*od.* with); **III.** *v/refl.*: *du darfst dich nicht ~!* you must not give up (*od.* resign); **IV.** *v/i.* *Ballspiele*: serve

aufgebläht *P.P.* → *aufblähen*

aufgeblasen I. *P.P.* → *aufblasen*; **II.** *Adj. fig. pej.* conceited, self-important, puffed up; *so ein ~er Kerl!* *umg.* what a conceited jerk (*od.* pompous ass); **Aufgeblasenheit** *f; nur Sg.* conceitedness, pomposity

Aufgebot *n* **1.** *vor Hochzeit*: official wedding notice; *in GB kirchlich*: *etwa* (calling) the banns *Pl.*; *das ~ bestellen* announce a wedding; *kirchlich*: call the banns; **2.** *an Fahrzeugen*: array; *an*

Menschen: crowd; (*an Polizisten etc.*) contingent; *Mil.* (military) force, body (of men); *Sport* (*die Spieler*) pool (of players); (*Mannschaft*) squad; *mit starkem ~ erscheinen* turn out in full force; *das beste* (*stärkste*) *~ Sport* the best (strongest) side; *letztes ~* last--ditch stand; **3.** *Jur.* public notice; **4.** *schw.* (*Stellungsbefehl*) call-up papers *Pl., Am.* draft card

aufgebracht I. *P.P.* → *aufbringen*; **II.** *Adj.* angry, *Am.* mad *umg.* (*gegen* with; *über* + *Akk.* at, about)

aufgedonnert *P.P.* → *aufdonnern*

aufgedreht I. *P.P.* → *aufdrehen*; **II.** *Adj. umg.* in high spirits, *bes. Am.* psyched (up); (*überreizt*) (too) wound (*od.* worked) up *präd.*, over-excited; **III.** *Adv. umg.*; *reden etc.*: excitedly

aufgedunsen *Adj.* bloated; *Gesicht*: *auch* puffy, puffed-up ...; *präd.* puffed up

aufgehen *v/i.* (*unreg., trennb., ist -ge-*) **1.** *Gestirn*: rise; *Tag*: break, dawn; **2.** (*sich öffnen*) open; *Vorhang*: *auch* go up; *Blume, Fallschirm*: *auch* open, unfold; *Knospen*: bud; *Knoten etc.*: come undone; *Naht*: come open; *Geschwür etc.*: burst; **3.** *Saat, Samen*: come up, sprout; **4.** *Kuchen, Teig*: rise; *Hefeteig*: *auch* prove; *~ wie ein Pfannkuchen umg. fig.* get as fat as a barrel, balloon (out); **5.** *Rechnung*: divide exactly, leave no remainder, work out; *fig.* come off, prove right; *Patience*: come out; *diesmal ging s-e Rechnung nicht auf fig.* he miscalculated this time; **6.** *~ in* (+ *Dat.*) *in der Arbeit etc.*: be totally wrapped up in, be absorbed by, be deeply engrossed in; *in e-m anderen Volk*: be assimilated by; *in Flammen/Rauch ~* go up in flames/ smoke; *in der Masse ~* disappear in the crowd; **7.** *j-m ~* become clear to s.o., dawn on s.o.; *j-m geht ein Licht auf* the penny finally drops, it (finally) dawns on s.o.; **8.** (*beginnen*) *die Jagd geht im August auf* the hunting season starts in August

aufgehoben I. *P.P.* → *aufheben*; **II.** *Adj.*: *gut/schlecht ~ sein* be / not be in good hands (*od.* keeping) (*bei* with)

aufgeilen (*trennb., hat -ge-*); *vulg.* **I.** *v/t.* turn s.o. on (*auch fig.*) *umg.*, get s.o. worked up; **II.** *v/refl.*: *sich ~ an* (+ *Dat.*) be turned on by *umg.*, get o.s. worked up with; *fig. an e-m Auto etc.*: go bananas over *umg.*; *an j-s Missgeschick etc.*: get a kick out of *umg.*, gloat over *allg.*

aufgeklärt I. *P.P.* → *aufklären*; **Aufgeklärtheit** *f; nur Sg.* enlightened attitude (*od.* views *Pl.*)

aufgeknöpft I. *P.P.* → *aufknöpfen*; **II.** *Adj. umg.* chatty, open, communicative

aufgekratzt I. *P.P.* → *aufkratzen*; **II.** *Adj. umg. Brit.* chirpy, *Am.* chipper

aufgelaufen *P.P.* → *auflaufen*

Aufgeld *n Wirts.* **1.** (*Agio*) premium, agio, commission; **2.** (*Aufpreis*) surcharge, extra charge; **3.** *auf Lohn*: bonus

aufgelegt I. *P.P.* → *auflegen*; **II.** *Adj.*: *zu etw. ~ sein* (*in Stimmung sein*) feel like (doing) s.th.; *ich bin heute nicht dazu ~* I'm not in the mood for it today; *gut/schlecht ~* in a good/bad mood

aufgelockert *P.P.* → *auflockern*

aufgelöst I. *P.P.* → *auflösen*; **II.** *Adj.* **1.** *Haare*: loose; (*unordentlich*) untidy,

messy; all over the place *umg.*; **2.** *Person*: beside o.s., distraught; (*verzweifelt*) desperate; *vor Sorge*: sick with worry; *er war in Tränen ~* he was crying his eyes (*od.* heart) out, he was all tears

aufgeräumt I. *P.P.* → *aufräumen*; **II.** *Adj. fig.* jovial, cheerful

aufgeraut *P.P.* → *aufrauen*

aufgeregt I. *P.P.* → *aufregen*; **II.** *Adj.* excited; (*nervös*) nervous; (*mitgenommen*) upset; **Aufgeregtheit** *f; nur Sg.* excitement, agitation, (*Nervosität*) agitation

aufgeschlossen I. *P.P.* → *aufschließen*; **II.** *Adj. fig.* open, receptive (*gegenüber od. für* to); open-minded, broad-minded; *j-m/etw. ~ gegenüberstehen* be open-minded about (*od.* as regards) s.o./s.th.; **Aufgeschlossenheit** *f; nur Sg.* open-mindedness

aufgeschmissen *Adj. umg.*: *~ sein* be stuck, be in a fix, be up a creek *Sl.*

aufgeschossen I. *P.P.* → *aufschießen*; **II.** *Adj.* (*hoch ~*) lanky

aufgeschwemmt I. *P.P.* → *aufschwemmen*; **II.** *Adj. Bauch, Körper, Leiche etc.*: bloated, swollen; *Gesicht*: *auch* puffed-up ..., *präd.* puffed up

aufgesetzt I. *P.P.* → *aufsetzen*; **II.** *Adj.* **1.** *~e Tasche* patch pocket; **2.** *Benehmen*: artificial, put-on ..., *präd.* put on

aufgesprungen *P.P.* → *aufspringen*

aufgestaut I. *P.P.* → *aufstauen*; **II.** *Adj. Gefühle*: pent-up

aufgetakelt I. *P.P.* → *auftakeln*; **II.** *Adj. umg.* dolled up, dressed to kill (*od.* to the nines)

aufgetrieben *P.P.* → *auftreiben*

aufgeweckt I. *P.P.* → *aufwecken*; **II.** *Adj. Kind*: very bright; **Aufgewecktheit** *f; nur Sg.* brightness, sharpness

aufgeweicht I. *P.P.* → *aufweichen*; **II.** *Adj. Boden*: sodden, soaked

aufgeworfen I. *P.P.* → *aufwerfen*; **II.** *Adj. Lippen*: pouting

aufgewühlt I. *P.P.* → *aufwühlen*; **II.** *Adj.* **1.** *~e See* stormy sea(s); **2.** *fig.*: *ganz ~ sein Person*: be all churned up inside

aufgezogen *P.P.* → *aufziehen*

aufgießen *v/t.* (*unreg., trennb., hat -ge-*) **1.** (*Wasser etc.*) pour (*auf* + *Akk.* on); **2.** (*Braten etc.*) add water *etc.* to; (*Tee*) pour water on; *weitS.* make

aufgliedern *v/t.* (*trennb., hat -ge-*) split up; *in Klassen*: classify; (*Satz etc.*) analy|se (*Am.* -ze); (*Zahlen*) break down; **Aufgliederung** *f* classification; analysis; breakdown

aufglimmen *v/i.* (*mst unreg., trennb., ist -ge-*); *geh. Glut, Zigarette*: glimmer, flicker (up); *fig. Hoffnung etc.*: glimmer, arise

aufglühen *v/i.* (*trennb., hat od. ist -ge-*) (begin to) glow

aufgraben *v/t.* (*unreg., trennb., hat -ge-*); (*freilegen*) excavate; (*Erde*) dig up

aufgreifen *v/t.* (*unreg., trennb., hat -ge-*) **1.** (*j-n*) snatch (*od.* pick up), seize; (*Verdächtige*) pick up; **2.** *fig.* (*Thema etc.*) take up; (*vorangegangenen Punkt etc.*) *auch* come back to

aufgrund, auf Grund *Präp.* (+ *Gen. od. von*) on account of

Aufguss *m* **1.** infusion; **2.** *fig.*: *schlechter ~* poor imitation; **3.** *in der Sauna*: pouring on of water; *~beutel m* teabag

aufhaben (*unreg., trennb., hat -ge-*);

umg. **I.** *v/t.* **1.** (*Hut etc.*) have on, be wearing; **er hatte die Brille nicht auf** he wasn't wearing his glasses; **2.** (*Augen, Tür etc.*) have open; **immer ~** keep open (all the time); (*Reißverschluß*) have undone; **3.** (*Aufgabe*) have to do; **viel/wenig ~** have a lot of / very little homework; **II.** *v/i. umg. Geschäft etc.*: be open

aufhacken *v/t.* (*trennb., hat -ge-*); (*Boden, Straße*) break up; (*öffnen*) break (*od.* crack) open; **mit Schnabel**: *auch* peck open

aufhaken *v/t.* (*trennb., hat -ge-*) undo

aufhalsen *v/t.* (*trennb., hat -ge-*): **j-m etw. ~** saddle (*od.* lump *umg.*) s.o. with s.th.; **sich etw. ~** get (o.s.) saddled with s.th., get lumped with s.th. *umg.*

aufhalten (*unreg., trennb., hat -ge-*) **I.** *v/t.* **1.** (*stoppen*) (*Fahrzeug, Entwicklung etc.*) stop, halt; (*verlangsamen*) check, hold up, arrest; (*abwenden*) ward off; (*verzögern, behindern*) delay; (*zurückhalten*) (*j-n*) hold up, keep (back); detain *geh.*; detain *geh.*; **ich werde Sie nicht lange ~** this will only take a minute; I will not detain you long *geh.*; **ich will Sie nicht länger ~** don't let me keep you; **du hältst mich bei der Arbeit auf** you hinder me from work; **er hält den ganzen Betrieb auf** he's stopping everyone from working; **Entschuldigung, ich bin aufgehalten worden** sorry, I was (*od.* got) held up; **2.** (*Tasche, Tür etc.*) hold open; (*Augen, Laden*); **die Hand ~** *konkret*: hold out one's hand; *fig. pej.* beg, sponge; **die Augen ~ nach** *fig.* keep a lookout (*od.* one's eyes peeled); **II.** *v/refl.* **1.** (*irgendwo sein*) stay; **sich viel im Freien (in Bibliotheken etc.) ~** spend a lot of time outside (in libraries etc.); **ich kann mich nicht lange ~** I can't stay long; **2.** *fig., oft pej.* (*sich befassen*) **sich ~ mit** spend (*unnütz*: waste) one's time on, linger over, dwell on

aufhängen (*trennb., hat -ge-*) **I.** *v/t.* **1.** (*Lampe, Vorhang, Wäsche etc.*) hang (up) (**an +** *Dat.* on); *Tech.* suspend (from); **2.** **j-n ~** hang s.o. (**an +** *Dat.* from); **3.** *umg. fig. pej.*: **j-m etw. ~** (*Ware etc.*) fob (*od.* palm) s.th. off on s.o.; (*Arbeit*) saddle (*od.* lumber) s.o. with s.th.; **j-m e-e Lüge / ein Märchen ~** tell s.o. lies/stories; **4.** *fig.*: **e-n Artikel an e-m Fall ~** *etc.* use a case as a peg to hang an article on; **II.** *vt/i.* (**den Hörer**) **~** put the phone down, hang up; **III.** *v/refl.* hang o.s.; **Aufhänger** *m* **1.** *an Jacke etc.*: tab, loop; **2.** *fig. pej.* (**für e-e Geschichte** *etc.* to hang a story etc. on), gimmick, hook; *für die Vermarktung e-s Buchs, Films etc.*: plug *umg.*; **e-n ~ für e-e Story finden** find a story a plug; **Aufhängevorrichtung** *f* hanger, suspender; *Tech.* suspension device; **Aufhängung** *f Mot.* suspension

aufhauen *v/t.* (*trennb., hat -ge-*) **1.** (*Imperf. auch hieb auf*); (*Eis, Straße etc.*) break up; (*Mauer*) knock a hole in; (*Nuss*) crack open; **2.** *umg.*: **sich** (*Dat.*) **das Knie ~** cut (*od.* gash) one's knee (open)

aufhäufen *v/t. und v/refl.* (*trennb., hat -ge-*) pile up; (*[sich] sammeln*) accumulate; (*Schätze etc.*) amass

aufhebeln *v/t.* (*trennb., hat -ge-*); (*Tür*) lever up

aufheben (*unreg., trennb., hat -ge-*) *v/t.* **1.** *vom Boden etc.*: pick (*od.* lift) up; (*j-d Liegenden*) help up; **2.** (*hochhe-*

ben) lift, raise; (*etw. Schweres etc.*) *auch*: lift up; **3.** (*aufbewahren*) keep, hold on to; **dein Geheimnis ist bei mir gut aufgehoben** your secret is safe with me; **ich hebe die Reste für später auf** I'll save the leftovers for later; → **aufgehoben** II; **4.** (*beenden*) (*Belagerung*) raise; (*Blockade, Verbot*) lift, abolish; (*Boykott, Streik*) call off, lift; (*Sitzung*) close; (*Vertrag*) cancel, revoke; (*Parlament*) dissolve; (*für ungültig erklären*) (*Ehe*) annul, dissolve; (*Gesetz*) repeal, revoke; abrogate *geh.*; *Jur.* (*Urteil*) quash, rescind, reverse; (*Haftbefehl*) withdraw, cancel; (*abschaffen*) abolish; → **aufschieben** 2, **Tafel** 7; **5.** (*ausgleichen*) compensate, offset; (*e-e Wirkung*) cancel, neutralize

Aufheben *n*: **viel ~(s) machen von** make a big thing out of; **ohne großes ~** quietly, without any fuss

Aufhebung *f e-r Belagerung*: raising; (*Abschaffen*) abolition; *e-s Boykotts, Streiks etc.*: calling off; *e-r Ehe*: annulment; *e-s Gesetzes*: annulment, repeal; *e-s Haftbefehls*: withdrawal; *e-s Urteils*: quashing, reversal; *e-s Vertrags*: cancel(l)ation; (*Abschaffung*) abolition, revocation

aufheitern (*trennb., hat -ge-*) **I.** *v/t.* (*j-n*) cheer s.o. up; **II.** *v/refl.* **1.** *Wetter*: clear up; *Himmel*: clear; **2.** *Stimmung, Gesicht*: brighten; **Aufheiterung** *f* **1.** *e-r Person*: cheering up; **2.** *Pl.; Met.* clearing up, brightening; **zeitweise ~en** sunny spells, bright periods

aufheizen (*trennb., hat -ge-*) *v/t.* **1.** (*Erde, Luft, Wasser*) heat (up); **2.** *fig.* (*Hass, Misstrauen etc.*) stir up; (*auch Inflation etc.*) stoke up; **II.** *v/refl.* **1.** *Klima, Luft*: heat (*od.* build) up; **2.** *Stimmung*: hot up *umg.*

aufhelfen *v/t.* (*unreg., trennb., hat -ge-*) help s.o. up (**von** *od.* **aus** from *od.* out of); *fig.* **j-m ~** help s.o. (to get) back on his, her *etc.* feet again

aufhellen (*trennb., hat -ge-*) **I.** *v/t.* **1.** (*Farbe, Haar*) lighten, make s.th. lighter; *Fot.* (*Schatten*) light(en) up; **2.** *fig.* (*Motive, Zusammenhänge etc.*) shed (*od.* throw) light on; *völlig*: clear up; **II.** *v/refl.* **1.** *Farbe, Haar*: get (*od.* turn) lighter; *Miene*: brighten; *Himmel*: brighten up, clear (up); cheer up *umg.*; **2.** *fig. Problem etc.*: be cleared up, become clear; **III.** *v/i. Fot.* light(en) up the shadows

Aufheller *m*; *-s, -* **1.** *Fot.* fill-in lamp; **2.** *für Textilien*: whitener; *für Papier*: brightening agent

aufhetzen *v/t.* (*trennb., hat -ge-*) stir s.o. up (**gegen** against); **zu etw. ~** incite to s.th.; **j-n ~ etw. zu tun** incite (*od.* get) s.o. to do s.th.; **Aufhetzung** *f* agitation

aufheulen *v/i.* (*trennb., hat -ge-*) **1.** (give a) howl; **2.** *Mot.* (give a) roar; *Sirene*: begin to wail; **den Motor ~ lassen** rev up the engine

aufholen (*trennb., hat -ge-*) **I.** *v/t.* **1.** (*Zeit, Verspätung, Vorsprung*) make up (for); (*Rückstand*) catch up with (*od.* on); (*Lernstoff*) catch up (on); **Versäumtes ~** make up for lost time; **zehn Sekunden ~** make up (*od.* win, pull back) ten seconds; **2.** *Naut.* (*Anker, Segel*) raise, haul up; **II.** *v/i.* **1.** *Person*: catch up; *Läufer etc.*: *auch* make up ground; *Zug*: make up the delay (*od.* time); **2.** *Wirts. Preise etc.*: pick up; *Kurse*: rally; **Aufholjagd** *f; Sport* pursuit race; *fig.* race to catch up

aufhorchen *v/i.* (*trennb., hat -ge-*) prick (up) one's ears; *bes. fig.* sit up and take notice

aufhören *v/i.* (*trennb., hat -ge-*) stop; (*ein Ende nehmen*) (come to an) end; *allmählich*: cease; (*nachlassen*) *Wind, Sturm*: subside; **~ zu** (**+** *Inf.*) stop (**+** *Ger.*), *Am. auch* quit (**+** *Ger.*); desist (from **+** *Ger.*) *förm.*; **nicht ~ zu** (**+** *Inf.*) keep (*od.* carry) on (**+** *Inf.*); **~ mit** (**+** *Akk.*) discontinue; **s-e Besuche hörten auf** he discontinued his visits; **ohne aufzuhören** continuously, nonstop, without stopping; **da hört (sich) doch alles auf!** *umg.* that really is the limit (beats everything *od.* takes the biscuit); **hör auf damit!** stop it!, cut it out!; **das muss ~** this has got to stop!; → **Spaß** 4

aufjagen *v/t.* (*trennb., hat -ge-*) (*Wild*) raise, start; *fig.* (*j-n*) hunt up

aufjauchzen *v/i.* (*trennb., hat -ge-*) shout (out) for joy (*od.* with delight)

aufjubeln *v/i.* (*trennb., hat -ge-*) give a shout of triumph, cheer

aufkanten (*trennb., hat -ge-*) **I.** *v/t.* (*kippen*) tilt; (*hochkant stellen*) upend; **II.** *vt/i.* (*Skier*) carve

Aufkauf *m Wirts.* buy-up, takeover, buyout; **aufkaufen** *v/t.* (*trennb., hat -ge-*) buy up (*od.* out), take over; **Aufkäufer** *m*, **Aufkäuferin** *f* (wholesale) buyer, purchaser, buying agent; (*Spekulant*) speculative buyer; forestaller *hist.*

aufkehren *vt/i.* (*trennb., hat -ge-*); *bes. südd.* sweep up

aufkeimen *v/i.* (*trennb., ist -ge-*) **1.** *Saat*: germinate; *Knospe, Blatt*: sprout; **2.** *fig. Gefühle etc.*: begin to grow; *Liebe, Hoffnung*: *auch* begin to blossom, burgeon

aufklappbar *Adj.* hinged; *Sitz etc.*: folding, fold-out, that folds open *präd.*; **~es Verdeck** folding roof, **Auto mit ~em Verdeck** convertible (car); **aufklappen** (*trennb., -ge-*) **I.** *v/t.* (*hat*) **1.** open (up) (*auch Klappstuhl*); (*Kinositz etc.*) pull down; (*Klappe*) let down; (*Verdeck*) fold back; **2.** (*Kragen etc.*) turn up; **II.** *v/i.* (*ist*) (snap) open

aufklaren (*trennb., hat -ge-*) **I.** *v/i. Himmel, Wetter*: clear (up), brighten up; **es klart auf** it's clearing up; **II.** *v/t. Naut.* tidy, clean

aufklären (*trennb., hat -ge-*) **I.** *v/t.* **1.** (*Missverständnis etc.*) clear up; (*Verbrechen*) solve, *Am.* crack *umg.*; (*Streit*) resolve; (*Ereignis, Sachverhalt*) explain, elucidate, illuminate, shed (*od.* throw) light on; (*Flüssigkeit*) clarify; **2.** (*j-n*) inform (**über +** *Akk.* of), enlighten (about, on); *sexuell*: explain the facts of life (*od. umg.* the birds and the bees) to); *in der Schule*: *auch* give s.o. sex education; **aufgeklärt sein** *auch* be well-informed; *sexuell*: know the facts of life; **II.** *v/refl.* **1.** *Himmel, Wetter*: clear (up), brighten up; cheer up *umg.*; **2.** *fig. Miene*: brighten (up); **3.** *Verbrechen etc.*: be cleared up, be solved; **III.** *vt/i. Mil.* reconnoit|re (*Am.* -er), scout

Aufklärer *m*; *-s, -* **1.** *Mil.* → **Aufklärungsflugzeug**; **2.** *hist.* philosopher, thinker etc. of the Enlightment; **aufklärerisch** *Adj.* **1.** **in ~er Absicht** with (the) intent to enlighten *präd.*; **2.** *Schriften*: informative, educational, of the Enlightenment

Aufklärung *f* **1.** *e-s Verbrechens*: clearing up, solving; **an der ~ e-s Verbrechens etc. arbeiten** be trying to solve (*od.* clear up) a crime *etc.*; **2.** (*Belehrung*) enlightenment; (*Klarstellung*) clarification; *sexuelle* ~ sex education; ~ *verlangen* demand an explanation (*über* + *Akk.* of); *zur* ~ *e-r Sache beitragen* throw light on s.th. (*od.* on the matter); **3.** *Mil.* reconnaissance; **4.** *nur Sg.*; *hist.* (the) Enlightenment, (the) Age of Enlightenment

Aufklärungs|arbeit *f* educational work; *politische* ~ political education; ~**buch** *n* sex education book; ~**flug** *m* *Mil.* reconnaissance flight (*od.* mission); ~**flugzeug** *n* *Mil.* reconnaissance plane, air scout; ~**kampagne** *f* information (*od.* education) campaign; ~**pflicht** *f*; *nur Sg.* **1.** *Jur.* judge's duty to ensure that all people involved in the case present all relevant facts clearly; **2.** *Med.* doctor's duty to inform patient about all possible risks; ~**quote** *f* clear-up (*od.* success) rate; ~**satellit** *m* observation (*od.* spy) satellite; ~**schrift** *f* informative pamphlet; *zur sexuellen Aufklärung*: sex education pamphlet; ~**unterricht** *m* *Päd.* sex education (classes *Pl.*); ~**zeitalter** *n* *hist.* Age of (the) Enlightenment

Aufklebeadresse *f* (gummed *od.* stick-on) address label; **aufkleben** *v/t.* (*trennb., hat -ge-*) stick on; *mit Klebstoff: auch* glue (*od.* paste) on; (*Briefmarken*) stick on, put on; **Aufkleber** *m* sticker; adhesive label *geh.*; *Mot.* bumper sticker

aufklinken *v/t.* (*trennb., hat -ge-*); (*Tür*) open (by the handle), unlatch

aufklopfen *v/t.* (*trennb., hat -ge-*) **1.** (*Ei, Nuss*) crack open; **2.** (*Kissen*) plump up

aufknacken *v/t.* (*trennb., hat -ge-*) **1.** (*Nuss*) crack; **2.** (*Safe*) crack; (*Auto*) break into; (*Tür*) break down

aufknallen *v/i.* (*trennb., ist -ge-*); *umg.* → **aufschlagen** II 1

aufknöpfen *v/t.* (*trennb., hat -ge-*) unbutton, undo

aufknoten *v/t.* (*trennb., hat -ge-*) undo, untie

aufknüpfen (*trennb., hat -ge-*) **I.** *v/t.* **1.** (*lösen*) untie, undo; **2.** (*j-n*) hang; string *s.o.* up *umg.*; **II.** *v/refl.* hang o.s.; string o.s. up *umg.*

aufkochen (*trennb., -ge-*) *v/t.* (*hat*) *und* *v/i.* (*ist*) boil (up); *etw.* ~ (*lassen*) bring to the (*Am.* a) boil

aufkommen *v/i.* (*unreg., trennb., ist -ge-*) **1.** (*entstehen*) arise (*auch Gedanke, Verdacht*); *Mode etc.*: come in(to fashion); *Langeweile*: set in; *Gerücht*: start; *Gewitter*: come (*od.* blow) up; *Wind*: spring up; *Nebel*: come down; *Zweifel/Misstrauen* ~ *lassen* give rise to doubt/suspicion; *um keine Zweifel* ~ *zu lassen* to make things absolutely clear; *Zweifel kamen in ihm auf* he began to be haunted (*od.* niggled) by doubts; *da kommt Freude auf* one can really get into it (*od.* the swing of it) *umg.*; **2.** ~ *für etw.* answer (*od.* be responsible) for; (*bezahlen*) pay for; (*Kosten*) pay, bear; defray; (*Schaden*) compensate for; *für j-n* ~ pay for s.o.'s upkeep, cover s.o.'s costs; **3.** ~ *gegen* assert o.s. against; prevail against; *ich komme nicht gegen ihn / dagegen auf* I'm no match for him / I'm not up to that; *er lässt niemanden neben sich* ~ he won't stand for any competition; he brooks no rivals *geh.*; **4.** *bes. südd.* (*bekannt werden*) get out, leak (out); **5.** (*aufstehen können*) get up (off the ground *od.* floor); **6.** (*landen*)

land; *Ball etc.: auch* hit the ground; **7.** *Läufer etc.*: catch up; **8.** *Naut. Schiff*: appear on the horizon, approach

Aufkommen *n*; *-s, -* **1.** *das* ~ *an* (+ *Dat. Pl.*) the amount of; *das* ~ *an Steuereinnahmen* (*aus*) (tax) revenue (from); *das* ~ *an Anzeigen/Fahrgästen* the number of adverts (*Am.* ads) / the volume of passengers; **2.** *nur Sg.*; (*Entstehung*) emergence, advent; *e-s Gewitters*: formation; *von Wind*: getting up, rise

aufkratzen (*trennb., hat -ge-*) **I.** *v/t.* **1.** scratch; (*Wunde*) scratch open; **2.** *fig.*: *j-n* ~ cheer s.o. up; → *aufgekratzt*; **II.** *v/refl.* scratch o.s. sore

aufkrempeln *v/t.* (*trennb., hat -ge-*); (*Hose*) turn up; (*Ärmel*) roll up

aufkreuzen *v/i.* (*trennb., ist -ge-*); *umg. fig.* turn up, show up

aufkriegen *v/t.* (*trennb., hat -ge-*); *umg.* → *aufbekommen*

aufkündigen *v/t.* (*trennb., hat -ge-*); (*Vertrag etc.*) → *kündigen* II; *den Dienst* ~ *Person*: hand in one's notice (to s.o.); *fig. Auto, Beine*: give up the ghost, jack (*Am.* pack) it in *umg.*; *j-m die Freundschaft* ~ break off one's friendship with s.o.

auflachen *v/i.* (*trennb., hat -ge-*) laugh out loud; *schallend*: burst out laughing; *spöttisch etc.* ~ give a sneering *etc.* laugh

aufladbar *Adj. Batterie*: rechargeable

aufladen (*unreg., trennb., hat -ge-*) **I.** *vt/i.* (*Last*) load (*auf* + *Akk.* onto); (*Fahrzeug*) load (up); **II.** *v/t.* **1.** *Etech.* (*Batterie, Akku*) charge; *wieder* ~ recharge; **2.** *fig.*: *j-m etw.* ~ saddle (*od.* lumber) s.o. with s.th.; *sich* (*Dat.*) *etw.* ~ get o.s. saddled (*od.* lumbered) with s.th.; **III.** *v/refl.*: *sich elektrostatisch* ~ become (electrostatically) charged

Auflader *m*; *-s, -,* ~**in** *f*; *-, -nen* loader, packer

Aufladung *f* *Etech.* **1.** *nur Sg.*; *Vorgang*: charging; **2.** (*Ladung*) charge

Auflage *f* **1.** *e-s Buches*: edition; (*Auflageziffer*) print run; *e-r Zeitung*: circulation; *verbesserte* ~ revised edition; *die Zeitung hat eine hohe* ~ the (news)paper has a wide circulation; **2.** *Wirts.* (*Stückzahl*) target; (*Serie*) series production; **3.** *Jur.* (*Bedingung*) condition, stipulation; *etw. zur* ~ *machen* make s.th. a condition (*j-m* for s.o.); **4.** *auf Schreibtisch etc.*: cover(ing); *e-r Matratze etc.*: overlay; **5.** (*Gold-, Silberschicht*) *auf Besteck*: plating; *eine* ~ *aus Silber haben* be silver-plated

Auflage(n)höhe *f* print run; *e-r Zeitung*: circulation; **auflagenstark** *Adj. Zeitung*: high-circulation ...

auflandig *Adj. Naut. Wind*: onshore

auflassen *v/t.* (*unreg., trennb., hat -ge-*) **1.** *umg.* (*Fenster, Tür etc.*) leave (*od.* keep) open; **2.** *umg.* (*Hut, Mütze*) leave (*od.* keep) on; **3.** *umg.* (*Kind*) let *s.o.* stay up; **4.** (*fliegen lassen*) (*Ballons, Brieftauben*) release; **5.** *Jur.* (*überschreiben*) (*Grundstücke*) convey; **6.** *südd., österr.* (*stilllegen*) (*Betrieb, Werk*) shut (*od.* close) down, shutter; *Bergb.* (*Grube etc.*) abandon, give up; (*Friedhof*) abandon; *ein aufgelassener Schacht* a disused (*od.* abandoned) shaft

Auflassung *f* **1.** *Jur.* conveyance; **2.** (*Stilllegung*) *südd., österr. e-s Betriebes*: shutting (*od.* closing) down; *Bergb.*: abandoning

auflauern *v/i.* (*trennb., hat -ge-*): *j-m* ~ (*auch fig.*) lie in wait for s.o.; (*überfallen*) (*auch fig.*) waylay s.o.

Auflauf *m* **1.** crowd; *stürmischer*: tumult; *Jur.* unlawful assembly, commotion, riot; **2.** *Gastr. mit Kartoffeln etc.*: bake; *mit Eiern*: souffle; **Auflaufbremse** *f* *Mot.* overrunning (*od.* coaster) brake; **auflaufen** (*unreg., trennb., -ge-*) **I.** *v/i.* (*ist*) **1.** *Gelder*: accumulate; *Zinsen*: accrue; *Unkosten*: mount (up); **2.** *Naut.* run aground; *auf ein Riff aufgelaufenes Schiff* a ship run aground on a reef; **3.** (*aufprallen*) run into; *j-n* ~ *lassen Sport* obstruct (*Am.* block) s.o., bodycheck s.o.; *fig.* put s.o. in his (*od.* her) place; **4.** *Gewässer*: rise; **5.** *Saat*: germinate, sprout; **6.** *Sport* (*aufholen*) catch up (*zu* with); **II.** *v/t.* (*hat*): *sich* (*Dat.*) *die Füße* ~ walk (*od.* run) one's feet sore; **Auflaufform** *f* oven(proof) dish, ramekin

aufleben *v/i.* (*trennb., ist -ge-*) *Natur, Person etc.*: (*auch wieder* ~) come to life again, revive; *Diskussion, alte Rechte etc.*: come to life; *auch Verkehr etc.*: liven up; *Hass, Kampf etc.*: be stirred up; *Bräuche*: be revived; *etw. wieder* ~ *lassen* revive s.th.

auflecken *v/t.* (*trennb., hat -ge-*) lick (*Katze*: lap) up

auflegen (*trennb., hat -ge-*) **I.** *v/t.* **1.** (*Schallplatte, Kohle, Tischtuch etc.*) put on; (*Make-up*) apply, put on; (*Gewehr*) rest (*auf* + *Akk.* on); *j-m die Hand* ~ *zum Heilen, Segnen*: lay on one's hands *Pl.*; *e-m Pferd den Sattel* ~ saddle (up) a horse; *ein Pflaster* ~ put on a plaster (*Am.* Band-aid); **2.** (*Buch*) publish, print; *wieder* ~ reprint; **3.** *Wirts.* (*Produkt*) launch, start; *neu od. wieder* ~ re-launch; (*Aktien*) issue, float; **4.** (*auslegen*) *zur Ansicht*: display, exhibit; **5.** *j-m etw.* ~ burden s.o. with s.th.; **6.** *Naut.* (*Schiff*) lay up; **II.** *vt/i.* (*den Hörer*) ~ put the phone (*od.* receiver) down, hang up, ring off

auflehnen (*trennb., hat -ge-*) **I.** *v/refl. fig.*: *sich* ~ *gegen* oppose; *stärker*: rebel (*od.* revolt) against; **II.** *v/t. und* *v/refl. Dial.*: *die Arme auf etw.* (*Dat.*) ~ lean (*od.* rest) one's arms on (*od.* against s.th.); **Auflehnung** *f* opposition (*gegen* to), resistance (to); *stärker*: rebellion (against)

auflesen *v/t.* (*unreg., trennb., hat -ge-*) pick up (*auch fig.*); (*Krankheit*) catch, pick up

aufleuchten *v/i.* (*trennb., hat od. ist -ge-*) light up (*auch Augen*); *Gesicht*: *auch* brighten up; *Blitz etc.*: flash; *Licht*: come on

auflichten (*trennb., hat -ge-*) **I.** *v/t.* **1.** (*Wald etc.*) thin out; **2.** (*Raum, Bild, Farben*) make lighter, brighten (up); **3.** *fig.* (*Geheimnis etc.*) shed light on; *völlig*: clear up; get to the bottom of *umg.*; **II.** *v/refl.* **1.** *Himmel*: brighten up, clear; **2.** *fig. Umstände etc.*: become clear

aufliegen (*unreg., trennb., -ge-*) **I.** *v/i.* (*ist*) **1.** lie (*auf* + *Dat.* on); (*sich stützen*) *auch* rest (on); *Schallplatte*: be on the turntable; *Tischdecke*: be on the table; *Telef. Hörer*: be on the hook; *der Deckel liegt nicht richtig auf* the lid isn't on properly; **2.** *Zeitschriften etc.*: be available (for reference *od.* to the public); *Wahllisten*: be available for inspection; be out *umg.*; **3.** *Naut.* be laid up; **II.** *v/t. und v/refl.* (*hat*) *umg.*: *sich* (*Dat.*) *den Rücken / sich* ~

get bedsores

auflisten *v/t.* (*trennb.*, *hat -ge-*) make a list of, list; **Auflistung** *f* **1.** *nur Sg.*; *Handlung*: listing; **2.** (*Liste*) list

auflockern (*trennb.*, *hat -ge-*) **I.** *v/t.* **1.** (*Erde*) dig up, (*Boden*) loosen; (*Kissen*) plump up; **2.** *fig.* (*Atmosphäre*) relax; (*lebhafter gestalten*) liven up (*auch Vortrag etc.*); (*Monotonie*) relieve, break up, ease; (*Wohngegend etc.*) brighten up; **aufgelockerte Bauweise** open construction; **in aufgelockerter Stimmung** in a relaxed mood; **II.** *v/refl.* **1.** *Bewölkung*: break up, disperse; **aufgelockerte Bewölkung** broken clouds; **2.** *fig. Atmosphäre*: relax, become relaxed, ease up; *Vortrag etc.*: liven up; **3.** *Sport* loosen (*od.* limber) up; **Auflockerung** *f* **1.** *des Erdreichs*: digging up, loosening (+ *Gen.* of); **2.** *von Wolken*: breaking up; **3.** *fig. des Unterrichts etc.*: livening up; **zur ~ der Atmosphäre beitragen** liven things up (a bit)

auflodern *v/i.* (*trennb.*, *ist -ge-*) flare up (*auch fig.*); *Flammen*: leap up

auflösbar *Adj. Math.* solvable; *Rätsel*, *Problem*: *auch* soluble *förm.*; *Chem.* soluble; *Jur.* dissolvable; (*Ehe*) dissoluble

auflösen (*trennb.*, *hat -ge-*) **I.** *v/t.* **1.** (*Pulver*, *Tablette etc.*) dissolve; **etw. in s-e Bestandteile ~** separate s.th. into its (constituent) parts; **2.** (*Rätsel*, *Aufgabe*) solve; *Math.* (*Gleichung*) solve; (*Bruch*) disintegrate; (*Klammern*) remove, take away; (*Widerspruch*) clear up; (*Missverständnis*) resolve; **3.** (*Vertrag*) cancel; (*Verlobung*) break off; (*Ehe*) (*annullieren*) annul; (*scheiden*) dissolve; (*Versammlung*) break off; *von außen*: break up; (*Menge*) break up, disperse; (*Firma*, *Lager*) close down; (*Geschäft*) wind up; (*Konto*) close; (*Haushalt*, *Parlament*, *Verein*) dissolve; (*Gruppe*) disband; **4.** (*Schleife*) close; (*Haare*) let down (*od.* loose); (*Knoten*) undo, untie; → **aufgelöst** II 1; **5.** *Mus.* (*Dissonanz etc.*) resolve; (*Vorzeichen*) cancel; **6.** *Opt.*, *Fot.* resolve; **II.** *v/refl.* **1.** *Tablette*, *Zucker etc.*: dissolve; **sich in s-e Bestandteile ~** disintegrate, separate into its (constituent) parts; **2.** *Nebel*, *Wolken*: disperse, disappear, lift; *Menge*: break up, disperse; *Versammlung*: break up; *Parlament*, *Verein*: dissolve; **der Stau hat sich aufgelöst** the traffic is flowing normally again; **3.** **sich ~ in** (+ *Akk.*) turn into; **sich in nichts ~** disappear (*od.* vanish) into thin air; *Hoffnungen etc.*: come to nothing; *Pläne etc.*: go up in smoke *umg.*; → **aufgelöst** II 2, **Wohlgefallen**

Auflösung *f* **1.** *auch Chem.* dissolving; **2.** (*Zerfall*) fragmentation, disintegration; **sich in ~ befinden** be in the process of disintegration; **3.** *des Nebels etc.*: dispersal; **4.** *e-s Vertrags*: cancel(l)ation, cancel(l)ing; *e-r Verlobung*: breaking off; *e-r Ehe*: (*Annullierung*) annulment; (*Scheidung*) divorce; *e-r Firma etc.*: closing down; *e-s Geschäfts*: winding up, dissolving; *e-s Kontos*: closing; *e-s Parlaments*, *Vereins*: dissolution, dissolving; **5.** *e-s Rätsels etc.*: solution (+ *Gen.* to); *Math. e-r Gleichung*: solution (of); *e-s Bruchs*: disintegration; *von Klammern*: removal; *e-s Widerspruchs*: resolution, clearing up; **6.** *Mus. e-r Dissonanz etc.*: resolution; *e-s Vorzeichens*: cancel(l)ation, cancel(l)ing; **7.** *Opt.*, *Fot.*

resolution; *TV auch* definition; **8.** *fig.*: **in e-m Zustand völliger ~** (*Aufgeregtheit*) completely beside o.s.

Auflösungs|erscheinungen *Pl.* signs of disintegration; **~vermögen** *n* **1.** *Opt.*, *Fot.* resolution; *TV* number of lines, line rate; **2.** *Chem.* solvent power, solvency; **~vertrag** *m Wirts.*, *Jur.* cancel(l)ation (*od.* termination) contract; **~zeichen** *n Mus.* natural

auflöten *v/t.* (*trennb.*, *hat -ge-*) solder on (*auf + Akk.* to)

aufmachen (*trennb.*, *hat -ge-*) **I.** *v/t.* **1.** (*öffnen*) *allg.* open; (*aufschrauben*) unscrew, undo (the top of); (*Schloss*) unlock; (*Weinflasche etc.*) uncork; (*Kleid*, *Knoten*) undo; (*aufschnüren*) unlace; (*aufknöpfen*) unbutton; (*Schirm*, *Vorhang*) put up; (*Vorhang*) draw, pull open; (*Haare*) loosen, undo; (*Hahn*) turn on; *fig.* → *Auge* 2, *Fass* 2, *Mund*, *Ohr* 2; **2.** (*eröffnen*) (*Konto*) open; (*Geschäft*) open up, set (*od.* start) up, establish; (*Rechnung*) draw up, make out; **3.** (*zurechtmachen*) make (*od.* get) up, do; (*gestalten*) design; **hübsch aufgemachte Artikel** attractively packaged articles; **4.** **groß ~** *umg. fig.* go to town (on); **II.** *vt/i.*: **j-m die Tür ~** open the door for s.o., let s.o. in; *auf Klingeln*: answer the door; **III.** *v/i.* **1.** *umg. Bank*, *Geschäft etc.*: (*öffnen*) open (up); (*eröffnet werden*) be opened; **2.** (*Zeitung*) feature; **die AZ macht heute mit folgender Schlagzeile auf: ...** the Evening News leads (*od.* opens) with the following headline: ...; **IV.** *v/refl.*: **1.** **sich ~** (*weggehen*) set out (*od.* off), start; take off *umg.* (*nach* for); **sich zu e-m Ausflug ~** set off on an excursion; **2.** **sich ~ zu** (+ *Inf.*) make the effort to (+ *Inf.*); **3.** *umg.* (*zurechtmachen*) get (*od.* make) o.s. up

Aufmacher *m umg. Zeitung*: front-page story, lead headline

Aufmachung *f* **1.** (*Ausstattung*) presentation, packaging; get-up *umg.*; **2.** *e-r Ware*: packaging; **3.** *e-r Seite*: layout; *Zeitung*: **in großer ~ herausbringen** feature prominently; **4.** *umg.* (*Kleidung*) getup, outfit

aufmalen *v/t.* (*trennb.*, *hat -ge-*) **1.** (*Bild*, *Zeichen etc.*) paint on (*auf + Akk. od. Dat.* [to]); **2.** *umg.* (*aufschreiben*) write down (*auf + Akk. od. Dat.* on)

Aufmarsch *m* **1.** marching up; *von Demonstranten etc.*: march; *feierlicher*: rally; (*Parade*) parade, march-past; **2.** (*Truppenmassierung*) (military) buildup, concentration; *zum Gefecht*: deployment; **aufmarschieren** *v/i.* (*trennb.*, *ist*) **1.** march up; **2.** *Truppen*: mass; **Truppen sind an der Grenze aufmarschiert** troops were deployed along the border

aufmerken *v/i.* (*trennb.*, *hat -ge-*) **1.** pay attention (*auf + Akk.* to); **2.** → **aufhorchen**

aufmerksam I. *Adj.* **1.** attentive (*auf + Akk.* to); **~ sein in der Schule etc.*: pay attention; **j-n ~ machen auf** (+ *Akk.*) call (*od.* draw) s.o.'s attention to, point *s.th.* out to s.o., bring s.th. to s.o.'s notice; **auf etw.** (*Akk.*) **~ werden** become aware of s.th., notice s.th.; **2.** (*höflich*) attentive; (*rücksichtsvoll*) *auch* considerate; **das war sehr ~ von ihr** that was very thoughtful of her; **II.** *Adv.*: **~ verfolgen** follow closely; **~ zuhören** listen attentively

Aufmerksamkeit *f* **1.** *nur Sg.* (*Konzentration*, *Interesse*) attention; **~ erregen**

attract (*od.* draw) attention; **s-e ~ richten auf** focus one's attention on; *j-m od. e-r Sache* **~ schenken** pay attention to; **j-s ~ entgehen** escape s.o.'s attention (*od.* notice); **2.** *nur Sg.* (*Höflichkeit*) attentiveness; **3.** (*Geschenk*) little present, token (gift); (*freundliche Handlung*) kindness

aufmischen *v/t.* (*trennb.*, *hat -ge-*); *umg.* (*verprügeln*) beat up, do *s.o.* over; (*anzetteln*) instigate a fight, stir up

aufmöbeln *v/t.* (*trennb.*, *hat -ge-*); *umg.* **1.** (*Sache*) do up; (*Ruf etc.*) polish up; **2.** (*beleben*) buck up; (*auch aufmuntern*) pep up

aufmontieren *v/t.* (*trennb.*, *hat*) mount (*auf + Akk. od. Dat.* onto), attach (to)

aufmotzen (*trennb.*, *hat -ge-*); *umg.* **I.** *v/t.* (*Sofa etc.*) do up; (*Show etc.*) hype up; **II.** *v/refl.* (*auftakeln*) get (o.s.) tarted (*Am. auch* hussied) up

aufmuck(s)en *v/i.* (*trennb.*, *hat -ge-*); *umg.* be up in arms (*gegen e-e Sache*: against); **~ gegen** (*e-e Autorität etc.*) kick against

aufmuntern *v/t.* (*trennb.*, *hat -ge-*) **1.** (*ermutigen*) encourage (*zu etw.* to do s.th.); **2.** (*aufheitern*) cheer up; **3.** (*aufputschen*) *Kaffee etc.*: pep up *umg.*; get s.o. going; **aufmunternd I.** *Part. Präs.* → **aufmuntern**; **II.** *Adj. Blick*, *Worte*: encouraging; **III.** *Adv.*: **j-n ~ ansehen** look at s.o. encouragingly; **Aufmunterung** *f* encouragement; (*Aufheiterung*) cheering up

aufmüpfig *Adj. Dial.*, *umg.* (*aufsässig*) rebellious; **Aufmüpfigkeit** *f*; *nur Sg.*; *Dial.*, *umg.* → **Aufsässigkeit**

aufnähen *v/t.* (*trennb.*, *hat -ge-*) sew on(to *auf + Akk.*)

Aufnahme *f*; -, -*n* **1.** *e-r Tätigkeit*: taking up; *von Beziehungen*: establishing; *von Gesprächen*: start; *e-s Studiums*: taking up; commencement *förm.*; **2.** *von Nahrung*: intake; *von Gas*, *Flüssigkeit*: absorption; (*Assimilation*) assimilation (*auch von Wissen etc.*); *fig. von Eindrücken etc.*: taking in; **3.** (*Empfang*) reception (*auch fig.*, *e-s Theaterstücks etc.*); *Med.* (*Annahme*) reception; **j-m e-e freundliche ~ bereiten** give s.o. a warm welcome; **4.** *von Gästen*: reception, taking in; *von Flüchtlingen*: taking in; *Naut. von Passagieren*, *Ladung*: taking on board; **5.** (*in + Akk.*) (*Zulassung*) *als Mitglied*: admission ([in]to); *als Schüler*: admission, enrol(l)ment; (*Einschreibung*) enrol(l)ment, registration; *als Patient*: admission (into); **~ finden** be accepted (*od.* admitted) (*bei* [in]to); **6.** (*in + Akk.*) (*Eingliederung*) integration (within), incorporation (into); (*Einbeziehung*) inclusion (in); *in Liste*: incorporation, inclusion; *e-s Wortes in e-e Sprache*: adoption, incorporation; **7.** *Wirts. von Kapital*: taking in, borrowing; *e-r Anleihe*: raising; *e-r Hypothek*: taking up, raising (*auf + Akk.* on); **8.** *e-r Aussage*, *Bestellung*: taking down; *von Inventar*: taking (of the inventory), stocktaking; *e-s Protokolls*: drawing up; *e-s Schadens*, *e-s Unfalls*: accident *etc.* report; **9.** *e-s Films*: shooting, filming; *einzelne*: shot, take; *e-s Fotos*: taking (*od.* shooting) (a picture); (*Foto*) photo(graph), shot; *von Musik*, *Videofilm etc.*: recording; **Achtung ~!** *Film*: action, camera!

Aufnahme|antrag *m* membership application, application for admission (*od.* membership); **e-n ~ stellen** apply for membership (*od.* admission); **~bedingungen** *Pl.* terms of admission

aufnahmebereit *Adj.* **1.** *Kamera*: ready to shoot; **2.** *fig. Person, Geist*: receptive (**für** to); **Aufnahmebereitschaft** *f*; *nur Sg.* receptiveness, receptivity

aufnahmefähig *Adj. geistig*: receptive (**für** to); *Wirts. Markt*: active; **abends bin ich nicht mehr ~** in the evening(s) I can't take any more in; **Aufnahmefähigkeit** *f*; *nur Sg.* receptiveness, receptivity, ability to take things in

Aufnahme|gebühr *f* admission fee; **~gerät** *n* recording equipment *Sg.*, recorder; *Fot.* camera; **~geschwindigkeit** *f* Tech. speed (of exposure); **~kapazität** *f* intake capacity; **~kopf** *m* Etech. recording head; **~leiter** *m*, **~leiterin** *f* **1.** *Film* (*Produktionsleiter*[*in*]): production (*TV* floor) manager; *in Tonstudio*: recording (*od.* studio) manager; **2.** *Film, TV, der Kameraleute*: director of photography; **~prüfung** *f* entrance exam(ination); **~quote** *f für Asylbewerber etc.*: admissions quota; **~studio** *n* (recording) studio; **~taste** *f* Etech. record button; *Tonfilmprojektor*: automatic-threading button; **~technik** *f* **1.** *Etech.* recording method; **2.** *Fot., Film*: shooting technique; **~verfahren** *n Schule, Verein etc.*: admission procedure; **~wagen** *m* recording van; **~zeit** *f* recording time

aufnehmen (*unreg., trennb., hat -ge-*) **I.** *v/t.* **1.** (*fotografieren*) photograph, take a picture (*od.* photo[graph]) of; (*Film*) shoot; *auf Band, Schallplatte*: record, *auf* (*Video*)*Band*: *auch* tape; **wo ist das Bild aufgenommen?** where was this picture (*od.* photo) taken?, where did you take this picture (*od.* photo)?; **2.** (*Fährte, Witterung, Fahrgäste*) pick up; **3.** (*Nahrung*) take in, digest; (*Gas, Flüssigkeit*) absorb; (*Kraft*) resist; (*assimilieren*) assimilate; *geistig*: (*auch* **in sich ~**) assimilate, take in; (*erfassen*) grasp; *sinnlich: auch* perceive; **4.** *vom Boden auch*: pick (*od.* lift) up; (*fassen*) hold, take; **5.** (*empfangen*) (*Gast*) receive (*auch fig. Nachricht etc.*); **j-n freundlich ~** give s.o. a warm welcome; **begeistert/zurückhaltend ~** *fig.* welcome with open arms / with reservations; **wie hat er es aufgenommen?** how did he take it (*od.* the news)?; **die Dunkelheit nahm ihn auf** *lit.* he was swallowed (*od.* enveloped) by darkness; **6.** (*unterbringen*) accommodate; (*Flüchtlinge*) take in, offer refuge; **j-n bei sich ~** take s.o. in, offer s.o. hospitality; **7.** (*in* + *Akk.*) in e-n *Verein etc.*: admit (to); *als Schüler*: enrol(l), take on, *Am. auch* accept; *als Patienten*: admit; *österr. als Angestellte*(*n*): take on, *Am.* hire; **8.** (*in* + *Akk.*) (*Liste, Spielplan, Tagesordnung etc.*) include (in), incorporate (in); **ins Protokoll ~** record in the minutes; **9.** (*Tätigkeit*) take up; (*Betrieb*) start, open up; (*Verhandlungen*) start; (*Beziehungen*) enter into *relations*, establish *contacts*; **Fühlung od. Kontakt ~** contact (**mit** s.o.); **ein Studium ~** start to study; commence a course of study *geh.*; **die Verfolgung ~** take up pursuit; **wieder ~** (*Tätigkeit, Verhandlungen, Studium etc.*) take up again, start to *study etc.* again; (*Beziehungen*) re-establish; (*unterbrochenen Prozess*) continue, resume; **den Kampf ~** start fighting, **mit j-m**: take s.o. on; **sie kann es mit jedem ~** *fig.* she can take any-

one on; **10.** *fig.* (*aufgreifen*) (*Thema etc.*) take up; **11.** (*Geld*) borrow; (*Kapital*) *auch* take up (*Kredit*) take out a *loan*; (*Hypothek*) raise, *Am. auch* take out (*auf* + *Akk.* on); **12.** *schriftlich*: (*Tatbestand etc.*) take down; (*Diktat*) take (down); (*Telegramm*) take; (*Aussage, Bestellung*) take (down); (*katalogisieren*) catalog(ue); (*Inventar*) take (inventory), stocktake; **j-s Personalien ~** take (down) s.o.'s details; **e-n Unfall ~** take (down) details of an accident, make an accident report; **das Protokoll ~** take (down) (*od.* write *od.* draw up) the minutes; **Messdaten ~** log (*od.* pick up) (measuring) data; **13.** *Sport* (*Ball, Flanke*) take, pick up; **14.** *Reiten*: (*Pferd*) collect; **II.** *vt/i. Stricken*: (*Masche*) cast on, increase; → **Fahrt** 2

Aufnehmer *m*; *-s, -; nordd.* floor cloth

aufnotieren *v/t.* (*trennb., hat*) make a note of, jot down

aufnötigen *v/t.* (*trennb., hat -ge-*): **j-m etw. ~** force s.th. on s.o.

aufoktroyieren *v/t.* (*trennb., hat*): **j-m etw. ~** force (*od.* impose) s.th. on s.o.

aufopfern *v/t. und v/refl.* (*trennb., hat -ge-*) sacrifice (**sich** o.s.) (**für** *od. Dat.* for); **aufopfernd I.** *Part. Präs.* → **aufopfern**; **II.** *Adj.* self-sacrificing; **~e Hingabe** self-sacrificing devotion; **Aufopferung** *f*; *mst Sg.* self-sacrifice

aufopferungsbereit *Adj.* ready (*od.* willing) to sacrifice o.s., devoted; **Aufopferungsbereitschaft** *f*; *nur Sg.* readiness (*od.* willingness) to sacrifice o.s., devotion; **aufopferungsvoll** *Adj.* self-sacrificing

aufpacken *v/t. und v/refl.* (*trennb., hat -ge-*) load (*Dat. od.* **auf** + *Akk.* on [to]); *fig.* burden, lumber *umg.*

aufpäppeln *v/t.* (*trennb., hat -ge-*) feed up, spoonfeed, bring up by hand; (*Kranken*) get s.o. on his (*od.* her) feet again

aufpassen *v/i.* (*trennb., hat -ge-*) (*aufmerksam sein*) pay attention; (*vorsichtig sein*) take care; **~ auf** (+ *Akk.*) take care of, look after; *nebenbei*: keep an eye on; *bei Examen* invigilate, *Am.* proctor; **aufgepasst!** *od.* **pass auf!** look out!, watch out!; **~ wie ein Luchs** watch like a hawk; **da muss man höllisch ~** you have to be really (*od.* terribly) careful; **Aufpasser** *m*; *-s, -*, **Aufpasserin** *f*; *-, -nen*; *umg.* watchdog; (*Spitzel*) spy; (*Wachtposten*) lookout

aufpeitschen *v/t.* (*trennb., hat -ge-*) **1.** *Wind*: (*Wellen*) lash; (*Meer*) churn up; **2.** *Musik, Rede*: (*j-n*) get going; (*Emotionen*) inflame, churn up

aufpeppen *v/t.* (*trennb., hat -ge-*); *umg.* pep up

aufpflanzen (*trennb., hat -ge-*) **I.** *v/t.* (*Fahne etc.*) set up; *Mil.* (*Seitengewehr*) fix; **II.** *v/refl. umg.*: **sich vor j-m ~** plant o.s. in front of s.o.

aufpfropfen *v/t.* (*trennb., hat -ge-*) **1.** graft (**auf** + *Akk.* onto); **2.** *fig.* (*aufzwingen*) (super)impose (on)

aufpicken *v/t.* (*trennb., hat -ge-*) *Vogel*: (*Körner*) peck up; (*Ei*) peck open

aufplatzen *v/i.* (*trennb., ist -ge-*) burst (open); *Wunde*: (split) open, rupture; *Lippen*: chap; *Knopf*: pop open

aufplustern (*trennb., hat -ge-*) **I.** *v/refl.* **1.** *Vogel*: ruffle (up) its feathers; **2.** *umg. fig.* act the big shot, puff o.s. up; **II.** *v/t.*: **sein Gefieder ~** ruffle (up) its feathers

aufpolieren *v/t.* (*trennb., hat*) **1.** polish

up; **2.** *umg. fig.* (*Image etc.*) *auch* refurbish; (*Kenntnisse*) brush up

aufprägen *v/t.* (*trennb., hat -ge-*); (*Stempel etc.*) emboss, stamp

Aufprall *m*; *-(e)s, -e, mst Sg.* impact; **aufprallen** *v/i.* (*trennb., ist -ge-*): **~ auf** (*mst* + *Akk.*) hit, strike; *krachend*: crash into (*od.* against, *Boden etc.*: onto), collide with

Aufpreis *m Wirts.* extra (*od.* additional) charge; **gegen e-n ~ von tausend Euro** for an extra thousand euros, for a thousand euros extra (*od.* more)

aufprobieren *v/t.* (*trennb., hat*) try on

aufpulvern *v/t. und v/refl.* (*trennb., hat -ge-*) *umg.*: **j-n/sich** (**mit Kaffee**) **~** pep o.s. up with coffee

aufpumpen (*trennb., hat -ge-*) **I.** *v/t.* pump (*od.* blow) up, inflate; **II.** *v/refl. umg. fig.* (*wichtig tun*) act important, act big; (*wütend werden*) work o.s. up, get o.s. worked up

aufputschen (*trennb., hat -ge-*) **I.** *v/t.* **1.** (*die Massen*) stir up, incite (**gegen** against); **2.** *Kaffee etc.*: get *s.o.* going, buck (*od.* pep up) *s.o.* up *umg.*; *Drogen*: get *s.o.* high; **II.** *v/refl.* get o.s. going, buck o.s. up *umg.*; *mit Drogen*: get high (**mit** on); **Aufputschmittel** *n* stimulant; (*Tablette*) *auch* pep pill *umg.*; *Sport: auch Pl.* dope

aufputzen (*trennb., hat -ge-*); *umg.* **I.** *v/t.* **1.** (*schmücken*) decorate, deck out; **2.** *umg.* (*j-n*) get up; **3.** *mst pej.* (*Image etc.*) hype up; **4.** *umg.* (*aufwischen*) wipe (*od.* mop) up; **II.** *v/refl. Frau, Mädchen*: get dolled up

aufquellen *v/i.* (*unreg., trennb., ist -ge-*) **1.** *Hülsenfrüchte*: swell; *Teig*: rise; *Gesicht*: swell (up), become bloated; *Hülsenfrüchte* **~ lassen** soak; **2.** *Tränen, auch fig. Gefühle*: well up; *Rauch*: rise (up)

aufraffen (*trennb., hat -ge-*) **I.** *v/refl. fig.*: **sich zu etw. ~** bring (*od.* rouse) o.s. to do s.th.; **ich kann mich dazu einfach nicht ~** I just can't be bothered; **II.** *v/t.* **1.** (*aufsammeln*) pick (*od.* gather) up; *schnell: auch* snatch up; **2.** (*Rock, Schürze*) gather (up)

aufragen *v/i.* (*trennb., hat -ge-*) rise (on high), loom (up), tower (up); *Felsen*: jut (up)

aufrappeln *v/refl.* (*trennb., hat -ge-*); *umg.* **1.** (*mühsam aufstehen*) struggle to one's feet; **2.** *nach Krankheit*: get back on one's feet again, recover; **3.** → **aufraffen** I

aufrauchen *v/t.* (*trennb., hat -ge-*); (*Zigarette etc.*) finish (off); (*ganze Schachtel etc.*) get through, smoke

aufrauen *v/t.* (*trennb., hat -ge-*) roughen

Aufräumarbeiten *Pl.* clearing (*od.* clearance) work *Sg.*

aufräumen (*trennb., hat -ge-*) **I.** *vt/i.* (*Zimmer etc.*) tidy (*Am.* clean) up; (*ordnen*) put in order; **II.** *v/t.* (*wegräumen*) put away; **III.** *v/i. fig. in e-r Organisation etc.*: make a clean sweep; (*wüten*) wreak havoc (**unter** among); **~ mit** (*beseitigen*) get rid of, do away with; → **aufgeräumt**; **Aufräumungsarbeiten** *Pl.* clearing work *Sg.*; (*Bergung*) salvage work (*od.* operation)

aufrechnen *v/t.* (*trennb., hat -ge-*) **1.** **j-m etw. ~** charge s.o. for s.th.; **2.** **etw. gegen etw. ~** set s.th. off (*od.* offset s.th.) against s.th.; **die Kosten gegeneinander ~** balance the costs against each other; **Aufrechnung** *f* compensation

aufrecht *Adj.* **1.** *auch Adv.* upright, erect; ~ *sitzen* sit up (straight); ~ *stehen* stand erect; *sich* ~ *halten* hold o.s. up straight; *sich kaum noch / nicht mehr* ~ *halten können* hardly/ not be able to stand up straight any more; **2.** *fig.* (*ehrlich*) upright, honest

aufrechterhalten *v/t.* (*unreg., trennb., hat*) maintain, perpetuate; (*Meinung*) stand by, adhere to; (*Kontakt etc.*) keep up, keep *s.th.* going; (*Angebot*) stand by; (*Entschluss*) keep (*od.* adhere) to, stand by; **Aufrechterhaltung** *f; nur Sg.* maintenance, keeping up; *e-r Meinung*: adherence (+ *Gen.* to)

aufrecken (*trennb., hat -ge-*) **I.** *v/t.* (*Arm, Kopf*) stretch up; (*Hals*) crane; **II.** *v/refl.* stretch up, draw o.s. up (to one's full height)

aufregen (*trennb., hat -ge-*) **I.** *v/t.* **1.** excite, get *s.o.* excited; *sexuell: auch* arouse, turn on *umg.*; **2.** (*beunruhigen*) worry; *stärker:* upset; **3.** (*ärgern*) annoy, irritate; *er regt mich auf* he gets on my nerves; **II.** *v/refl.* get worked up (*über* + *Akk.* about); *reg dich nicht auf!* don't get worked up (about it)!

aufregend I. *Part. Präs.* → *aufregen*; **II.** *Adj.* **1.** exciting; **2.** (*beunruhigend*) upsetting; **3.** *umg.* (*toll*) great, *Am. auch* wild; *nicht sehr* ~ nothing to write home about

Aufregung *f* **1.** excitement; **2.** (*Beunruhigung*) upset; (*allgemeine Erregung*) stir; (*Nervosität*) nervousness; *heftige, oft schmerzliche:* agitation; *unnötige:* fuss; *in heller* ~ in utter (*od.* complete) confusion; *in* ~ *geraten* get excited (*über* about); *vor* (*lauter*) ~ *vergaß sie alles* she was so excited (*od.* upset) that she forgot everything; *es herrschte große* ~ it was bedlam; *kein Grund zur* ~ it's nothing to worry about; *nur keine* ~! don't get into a state; *zur Menge:* don't panic!

aufreiben (*unreg., trennb., hat -ge-*) **I.** *v/t.* **1.** *wund:* rub *s.th.* sore, chafe; **2.** (*verschleißen*) wear away; (*zermürben*) wear down; **3.** *fig.* exhaust, wear out; **4.** *Mil.* (*völlig vernichten*) wipe out, annihilate; **II.** *v/refl. fig.* wear o.s. out; **aufreibend I.** *Part. Präs.* → *aufreiben*; **II.** *Adj.* exhausting; *nervlich:* ennervating

aufreihen (*trennb., hat -ge-*) **I.** *v/t.* **1.** (*Dinge*) put *s.th.* in a row; (*Menschen*) line up; (*Perlen etc.*) thread, string; **2.** *fig.* (*Argumente etc.*) list, enumerate; **II.** *v/refl.* line up; (*hintereinander*) queue, *Am.* get (*od.* stand) in line

aufreißen (*unreg., trennb., hat -ge-*) **I.** *v/t.* **1.** tear (*od.* rip) open; (*Kleid etc.*) tear; (*Straße*) tear up; (*Boden*) remove; *die Abwehr* ~ *Sport fig.* rip open the defen|ce (*Am.* -se); *alte Wunden* ~ *fig.* open up (*od.* reopen) old wounds; → *Arsch* 1; **2.** (*Tür*) fling open; (*Augen, Mund*) open wide; *er riss die Augen auf auch* his eyes nearly popped out of his head; *Mund und Augen* ~ (*staunen*) gape, look aghast; → *Klappe* 4; **3.** (*e-n Aufriss zeichnen von*) draw an elevation of; **4.** (*Thema, Problem*) give a rough idea of; **5.** *umg.* (*Job etc.*) get (*od.* land) o.s.; (*Partner*) pick up; **II.** *v/i.* **1.** *Naht, Papiertüte:* burst, *Plastiktüte: auch* split open; *Haut:* chap; *Holz:* crack; **2.** *Wolken:* break up, disperse; *es reißt auf* it's clearing up; **3.** *Fot. umg.* (*die Blende* ~) open up; **Aufreißer** *m; -s, -* **1.** *Sport, Ringen:* turnover; **2.** *umg.* womanizer

aufreizen *v/t.* (*trennb., hat -ge-*) **1.** stimulate (*zu* to); *stärker:* excite, rouse; *sexuell:* turn *s.o.* on, arouse; **2.** (*aufhetzen*) stir up; *j-m zum Widerstand* ~ incite *s.o.* to resist; **aufreizend I.** *Part. Präs.* → *aufreizen*; **II.** *Adj.* provocative (*auch sexuell*)

aufrichten (*trennb., hat -ge-*) **I.** *v/t.* **1.** (*Oberkörper*) straighten up; (*Pfahl, Zaun etc.*) *wieder* ~ set *s.th.* straight again; **2.** (*aufhelfen*) help *s.o.* up; (*kranke Person etc.*) sit *s.o.* up; **3.** *fig.* (*ermutigen*) set *s.o.* up, comfort, console; *j-n wieder* ~ give fresh heart to *s.o.*; **4.** (*errichten*) put up, erect; *wieder* ~ put *s.th.* up again; **II.** *v/refl.* **1.** get up; *im Bett:* sit up; *aus gebückter Haltung:* straighten up, straighten o.s.; *sich zu voller Größe* ~ draw o.s. up to one's full height; **2.** *sich* (*wieder*) ~ *Gras, Blumen:* straighten up, revive; *Segelboot:* right (up); **3.** *fig.: sich* (*wieder*) ~ pick o.s. up, take heart; *sich an j-m/etw.* (*wieder*) ~ take heart from *s.o./s.th.*

aufrichtig I. *Adj.* sincere, (*Bedauern*) *auch* heartfelt; (*ehrlich*) honest, upright; (*offen*) open, frank, candid; **II.** *Adv.:* ~ *bedauern* sincerely regret; *es tut mir* ~ *Leid* I really am sorry; **Aufrichtigkeit** *f; nur Sg.* sincerity, honesty, uprightness; frankness, cando(u)r

aufriegeln *v/t.* (*trennb., hat -ge-*) unbolt, unbar, open

Aufriss *m* **1.** *Archit.* elevation; (*Vorderansicht*) front elevation (*od.* view), vertical plan; **2.** *fig.* outline

aufritzen *v/t.* (*trennb., hat -ge-*) slit open; (*Haut*) scratch

aufrollen (*trennb., hat -ge-*) **1.** (*zusammenrollen*) (*auch Ärmel*) roll up; (*Garn etc.*) wind up; (*Seil etc.*) coil (*od.* roll) up *sich* (*Dat.*) *die Haare* ~ put curlers in one's hair, put one's hair in curlers; **2.** (*auseinander rollen*) unroll; (*Garn etc.*) unwind; (*Fahne*) unfurl; **3.** *fig.:* (*wieder*) ~ (*Thema etc.*) go into (again); (*Prozess*) retry, reopen; (*Fall*) reopen; **4.** *Mil., Sport* turn, roll up; *das Feld von hinten* ~ *Läufer, Rennfahrer etc.:* storm the field from the back (*od.* behind)

aufrücken *v/i.* (*trennb., ist -ge-*) **1.** move up; *bitte* ~! please move up (*od.* further along)!; **2.** *im Rang:* be promoted (*zu* to *od.* in *e-e höhere Stellung* to a higher position)

Aufruf *m* **1.** call (*auch EDV und Mil.*); (*Befehl, Vorladung*) summons; *öffentlicher:* appeal (*an j-n zu etw.* to s.o. for s.th.); *letzter* ~ *Flug.* last call; *e-n* ~ *an die Bevölkerung richten* (make an) appeal to the public, make a public appeal; **2.** *Wirts. von Banknoten:* calling-in; *von Obligationen:* calling (in); **3.** *von Namen:* calling out (by name)

aufrufen (*trennb., hat -ge-*) **I.** *v/t.* **1.** *beim Arzt etc.:* call up (*auch Mil.*); (*Schüler*) call on (to answer); (*Namen[sliste]*) call out; *Jur.* (*Zeugen, Sache*) call; *j-n als Zeugen* ~ call *s.o.* as a witness; *du wirst aufgerufen* your name will be called; *zum Kauf von Aktien* ~ make a call on shares (*Am.* stock); **2.** *j-n* ~ *zu* (*auffordern*) call (up)on s.o. to (+ *Inf.*); **3.** *EDV* call up; **4.** *Wirts.* (*Banknoten*) call in; (*Obligationen*) call; **II.** *v/i.:* ~ *zu* appeal for; *zum Streik* ~ call a strike

Aufruhr *m; -s, -e, mst Sg.* commotion, turmoil; (*Tumult*) riot, tumult, fracas; (*Rebellion*) uprising, revolt; *innerlicher:* turmoil, conflict; *öffentlicher* ~ public clamo(u)r; *in* ~ in a state of turmoil; *Menge, Volk etc.:* up in arms; *j-n in* ~ *versetzen* stir *s.o.* up, throw (*od.* plunge *poet.*) *s.o.* into turmoil

aufrühren *v/t.* (*trennb., hat -ge-*) stir up (*auch fig. Gefühle, j-n*); (*alte Geschichten*) dig (*od.* rake) up

Aufrührer *m; -s, -, ~in* *f; -, -nen* rebel, insurgent; *Pol.* agitator; rabble-rouser *pej.*; fomenter *förm.*; **aufrührerisch** *Adj.* rebellious; *Reden etc.:* inflammatory, seditious; rabble-rousing

aufrunden *v/t.* (*trennb., hat -ge-*) round up (*auf + Akk.* to)

aufrüsten *vt/i.* (*trennb., hat -ge-*) **1.** *Mil.:* (*wieder*) ~ (re)arm; **2.** (*Computer*) upgrade; **Aufrüstung** *f* **1.** (military) buildup; (re)armament; **2.** *e-s Computers:* upgrading

aufrütteln *v/t.* (*trennb., hat -ge-*) **1.** *aus dem Schlaf:* shake *s.o.* awake; **2.** *fig.* shake *s.o.* up; ~ *aus* rouse from; *j-s Gewissen* ~ *fig.* stir *s.o.'s* conscience; **aufrüttelnd I.** *Part. Präs.* → *aufrütteln*; **II.** *Adj.* rousing

aufs *Präp. + Art.* **1.** → *auf* I; **2.** *in Fügungen: jeden Tag aufs Neue* afresh, anew, once more; ~ *Klo gehen umg.* go to the loo (*Am.* john)

aufsagen *v/t.* (*trennb., hat -ge-*) **1.** (*Gedicht etc.*) recite; *etw. vorwärts und rückwärts* ~ *können* know s.th. inside out (*od.* backwards and forwards); **2.** *geh.* → *aufkündigen*

aufsammeln *v/t.* (*trennb., hat -ge-*) pick up (*auch umg. j-n*)

aufsässig *Adj.* rebellious, refractory; *Kind: auch* recalcitrant, obstreperous; **Aufsässigkeit** **1.** *nur Sg.* rebelliousness, rebellious attitude; *Kind: auch* recalcitrance; **2.** *Handlung, Äußerung:* piece (*od.* act) of rebelliousness

Aufsatz *m* **1.** (*über + Akk.*) essay (on *od.* about); *Päd. auch* composition (on); (*Abhandlung*) paper (on *od.* about); *in Zeitung:* article (on *od.* about); **2.** (*Oberteil*) top (part), upper part; **3.** *Golf:* tee; **4.** *Archit.* cap, crest, crown; **5.** *Mil. Geschütz:* telescopic sight; ~*thema* *n* essay topic

aufsaugen *v/t.* (*auch unreg., trennb., hat -ge-*) **1.** soak (*od.* suck) up; *Chem.* absorb; **2.** *fig.* assimilate, absorb

aufschauen *v/i.* (*trennb., hat -ge-*); *bes. südd., österr., schw.* → *aufblicken*

aufschaukeln (*trennb., hat -ge-*) **I.** *v/refl.* **1.** *Schwingungen:* start rocking (violently); **2.** *Erregung etc.:* build up, mount; **II.** *v/t.* **1.** (*Schwingungen*) build up, amplify; **2.** *fig.: sich gegenseitig* ~ get each other going

aufschäumen (*trennb., -ge-*) **I.** *v/i.* (*ist od. hat*) **1.** *Meer, Sekt etc.:* froth up; **2.** *Schaumstoff:* foam (up), expand; **II.** *v/t.* (*hat*) (*Schaumstoff*) foam (on), apply as foam

aufscheuchen *v/t.* (*trennb., hat -ge-*) **1.** (*erschrecken*) startle; (*wegjagen*) *auch* frighten away; (*stören*) disturb; **2.** *fig. aus der Lethargie etc.:* rouse (*aus* from)

aufscheuern (*trennb., hat -ge-*) **I.** *v/t.* (*die Haut*) rub sore, chafe; *sich* (*Dat.*) *die Haut* ~ rub o.s. (*od.* one's skin) sore, chafe o.s.; **II.** *v/refl.* graze, scrape

aufschichten *v/t.* (*trennb., hat -ge-*) **1.** stack up, pile up; **2.** *Geol.* stratify

aufschiebbar *Adj.* postponable

aufschieben *v/t.* (*unreg., trennb., hat -ge-*) **1.** slide (*od.* push) open; *Bolzen: auch* draw back; **2.** *fig.* postpone, put off; defer *förm.* (*auf, bis* until, till); (*verzögern*) delay; *auf e-n anderen Tag*: adjourn; *er schiebt es immer wieder auf* he keeps putting it off; *aufgeschoben ist nicht aufgehoben* we'll make up for it (another time); **aufschieben I.** *Part. Präs.* → *aufschieben*; **II.** *Adj. Jur.* suspensive

aufschießen (*trennb., -ge-*) **I.** *v/i.* (*ist*); *allg.* shoot up; *Flammen: auch* leap up; *Wasserstrahl: auch* spurt (*od.* gush) up; *Person vom Stuhl: auch* spring (*od.* jump) up; (*entstehen*) *auch* (a)rise; *wie Pilze ~* spring up like mushrooms (*od.* weeds); → *aufgeschossen*; **II.** *v/t.* (*hat*) **1.** *Naut.* (*Segelboot*) luff head to wind, shoot up; (*Tau*) coil (up); **2.** (*schießend öffnen*) shoot open

Aufschlag *m* **1.** *am Ärmel*: cuff; *an der Hose*: turn-up, *Am.* cuff; (*Revers*) lapel; **2.** *~* (*auf + Dat. od. Akk.*) (*Auftreffen*) impact; *dumpfer ~* (dull) thud; *beim ~ auf die od. der Erde zerbrach das Flugzeug* the plane broke up on impact; **3.** *Wirts.* markup; **4.** *Tennis etc.*: service; (*~art*) serve; *sie hat e-n harten ~* she has a tough serve; *wer hat ~?* who's to serve?, who's serve is it?; *~ball m Sport* service

aufschlagen (*unreg., trennb., -ge-*) **I.** *v/t.* (*hat*) **1.** (*Eisdecke, Nuss etc.*) break open; (*Ei*) crack; **2.** (*Augen, Buch*) open; *Seite 3 ~* turn to page 3; **3.** *sich* (*Dat.*) *das Knie ~* cut one's knee; **4.** (*Zelt*) pitch, fix (up) (tent); (*Lager*) set up (camp); (*Quartier, Wohnsitz*) take up; → *Zelt* 1; **5.** (*Maschen*) cast on (a stitch); **6.** *Gastr.* (*Eiweiß, Sahne*) whip (up); **II.** *v/i.* **1.** (*ist*); *~* (*auf + Dat. od. Akk.*) hit (*od.* bang); *mit dem Kopf hart ~* hit (*od.* knock) one's head hard; **2.** (*ist*) *Tür, Buch etc.*: open; *Bettwäsche etc.*: turn back; **3.** (*mst hat*) *Wirts. Waren*: go up (in price); **III.** *vt/i.* (*hat*) **1.** *Händler*: increase (*od.* raise) the price (*um* by); *5% auf den Preis ~* put 5% on the price, increase the price by 5%; **2.** *Sport, bes. Tennis*: serve (the ball)

Aufschläger *m*, *~in f Sport* server

Aufschlag|fehler *m Sport, bes. Tennis*: (service) fault; *~feld n Tennis*: service court; *~linie f* service line

aufschließen (*unreg., trennb., hat -ge-*) **I.** *vt/i.* open up, open (*od.* unlock) the door *etc.*; *schließt du mir bitte auf?* would you please let me in (*od.* open up)?; **II.** *v/i.* (*aufrücken*) move up; *zu Sport* catch up with; **III.** *v/t.* **1.** *Chem.* disintegrate, dissolve, break up (*od.* down); *Bio.* digest, break up (*od.* down); **2.** (*aufbereiten*) *Metall.* treat, prepare; *Papierherstellung*: pulp, treat; **3.** → *erschließen* I 1; **IV.** *v/refl. geh.*: *sich j-m ~ Person*: open one's heart to s.o., confide in s.o.; *Sache*: become obvious (*j-m* to s.o.)

aufschlitzen *v/t.* (*trennb., hat -ge-*) slit; (*Umschlag*) slit open; (*Reifen etc.*) slash

aufschluchzen *v/i.* (*trennb., hat -ge-*) give a loud sob

Aufschluss *m* **1.** (*über + Akk.*) (*Erkenntnis*) insight(s *Pl.*) (into); (*Erklärung*) explanation (of); (*Auskunft*) information *kein Pl.*, data *Sg.* (beide about); *sich ~ verschaffen über* inform o.s. about, gain an (*od.* some) insight into; **2.** *Chem.* breaking down; *Bio.* digestion; **3.** *Geol.* exposure, (natural) section; outcrop; **4.** (*Aufbereitung*) *Metall.* treatment; *Papierherstel-*

lung: pulping; **5.** *Bergb.* (*Erschließung*) development, opening up

aufschlüsseln *v/t.* (*trennb., hat -ge-*) break down (*nach* into); *in Kategorien*: classify (according to); **Aufschlüsselung** *f* breaking down, breakdown; categorization

aufschlussreich *Adj.* informative, instructive; *weitS.* revealing; *das war sehr ~ auch* that was very interesting

aufschmieren *v/t.* (*trennb., hat -ge-*) *umg.* **1.** (*Butter etc.*) spread (on), put on; (*Farbe*) daub on; **2.** *pej.* (*aufschreiben*) scribble down

aufschnallen *v/t.* (*trennb., hat -ge-*) **1.** (*festschnallen*) strap on(to *auf +* *Akk.*); **2.** (*öffnen*) unstrap; (*Gürtel*) undo, unbuckle

aufschnappen (*trennb., -ge-*) **I.** *v/t.* (*hat*) **1.** (*Bissen*) catch; **2.** *umg. fig.* pick up; **II.** *v/i.* (*ist*) *Schloss*: snap (*od.* spring) open

aufschneiden (*unreg., trennb., hat -ge-*) **I.** *v/t.* **1.** (*öffnen*) cut open; *Med.* open; (*Geschwür*) *auch* lance; (*operieren*) cut open; (*sezieren*) dissect; *sich* (*Dat.*) *die Pulsadern ~* slit one's wrists; **2.** (*Braten, Brot etc.*) cut up; *in Scheiben*: slice; **II.** *v/i. umg. pej.* (*prahlen*) boast, show off; (*übertreiben*) lay it on thick; **Aufschneider** *m*; *-s, -; umg. pej.* show-off, poser; **Aufschneiderei** *f umg. pej.* boasting, bragging; **Aufschneiderin** *f*; *-, -nen; umg. pej.* show-off, poser; **aufschneiderisch** *Adj. umg pej.* boastful

aufschnellen *v/i.* (*trennb., ist -ge-*); (*aufspringen*) leap up

Aufschnitt *m* **1.** *Gastr.* (assorted) cold meat(s), *bes. Am.* cold cuts *Pl.*; **2.** *Mus. Orgelpfeife*: mouth, cutup; *~platte f* (slices of) cold meat, *bes. Am.* cold cut platter *Pl.*

aufschnüren *v/t.* (*trennb., hat -ge-*); (*lösen*) untie; (*Knoten*) *auch* undo; (*Schuh*) unlace

aufschrammen *v/t.* (*trennb., hat -ge-*) graze

aufschrauben *v/t.* (*trennb., hat -ge-*) **1.** (*öffnen*) (*Glas, Füller*) open; (*lösen*) (*Schraube*) unscrew; (*Deckel*) take the top (*od.* screw) off; **2.** (*befestigen*) screw on(to *auf + Akk.*)

aufschrecken¹ *v/t.* (*trennb., hat -ge-*) startle; *aus Gedanken, Schlaf*: rouse (*aus* from)

aufschrecken² *v/i.* (*unreg., trennb., ist -ge-*) give a start, jump; *aus dem Schlaf ~* wake (up) with a start

Aufschrei *m*: *~* (*+ Gen.*) cry; *schrill*: scream; *hell und kurz*: shriek; *fig.* outcry; *~ des Entsetzens* scream of horror

aufschreiben *v/t.* (*unreg., trennb., hat -ge-*) **1.** write (*od.* put) down; (*notieren*) make a note of; **2.** *Polizist*: *j-n ~* take down s.o.'s particulars (*od.* details); (*die Autonummer notieren*) take down s.o.'s car (*Am.* license plate) number; *ich bin dreimal wegen Falschparkens aufgeschrieben worden* I've had three parking tickets; **3.** *umg.*: *j-m etw. ~* (*verschreiben*) prescribe s.o. s.th.

aufschreien *v/i.* (*unreg., trennb., hat -ge-*) cry out; *schrill*: (give a) scream; *vor Schmerz ~* cry out with pain

Aufschrift *f* lettering, writing; (*Name*) name; *auf Brief*: address, direction; (*Etikett*) label; (*Inschrift*) inscription, *Am. auch* legend

Aufschub *m* deferment; (*Verzögerung*) delay; *auf bestimmte Zeit*: postpone-

ment; (*Vertagung*) adjournment; *Wirts.* (*Stundung*) respite, grace; *Jur. des Todesurteils*: reprieve; *ohne ~* without delay; *die Sache duldet keinen ~* the matter is extremely urgent (*od.* brooks no further delay *geh.*); *j-m e-n ~ gewähren* give (*od.* allow *od.* grant) s.o. an extension (*od.* period of grace)

aufschürfen *v/t.* (*trennb., hat -ge-*): *sich* (*Dat.*) *die Haut / das Knie ~* graze o.s. (*od.* one's skin) / one's knee

aufschütteln *v/t.* (*trennb., hat -ge-*) shake up; (*Kissen*) *auch* plump up

aufschütten *v/t.* (*trennb., hat -ge-*) **1.** pile up; (*Kies*) scatter; (*Damm*) throw up, raise; *Geol.* (*Erde*) deposit; **2.** (*nachfüllen*) (*Wasser etc.*) pour on; (*Kohlen etc.*) put on (the fire); **Aufschüttung** *f* bank of earth; *Geol.* deposit

aufschwatzen *v/t.* (*trennb., hat -ge-*); *umg.*: *j-m etw. ~* talk s.o. into s.th., palm off s.th. on s.o.

aufschweißen *v/t.* (*trennb., hat -ge-*) **1.** (*befestigen*) weld on(to *auf + Akk.*); **2.** (*Unfallauto etc.*) weld open, *Am.* cut open with a torch

aufschwellen *v/i.* (*unreg., trennb., ist -ge-*) swell (up)

aufschwemmen *vt/i.* (*trennb., hat -ge-*) bloat; → *aufgeschwemmt* II

aufschwindeln *v/t.* (*trennb., hat -ge-*): *j-m etw. ~* trick s.o. into buying s.th.

aufschwingen (*trennb., hat -ge-*) **I.** *v/refl.* **1.** *Vogel*: soar (*up*); **2.** *fig.* *sich zu etw. ~* (*sich überwinden*) bring o.s. to do s.th.; *sich zum Direktor ~* work one's way up to the position of director; *sich zum Richter über j-n ~* set o.s. up as (*od.* appoint o.s.) a judge; **II.** *v/i.* **1.** *Tür*: swing open; **2.** *Sport, Turnen*: swing (*auf + Akk.* on[to])

Aufschwung *m* **1.** *Turnen*: upward circle; **2.** *fig.* (*Antrieb*) impetus; (*Fortschritt*) progress; *Wirts.* upturn, upswing; *e-n ~ nehmen Wirts.* see (*od.* experience) a revival

aufsehen *v/i.* (*trennb., hat -ge-*) → *aufblicken*

Aufsehen *n*; *-s, kein Pl.*: *~ erregen* cause (quite) a stir (*stärker*: sensation); *ohne ~* discreetly, quietly; *um ~ zu vermeiden* (in order) to avoid attracting attention, *in der Öffentlichkeit*: *auch* to avoid (any) publicity; (*großes*) *~ erregend Nachricht, Foto, Entdeckung*: (really) sensational; *Kleidung*: outrageous; *Frisur*: *auch* extravagant; *Idee, Rede*: (*kontrovers*) controversial; *stärker*: provocative; **aufsehenerregend** *Adj.*: *äußerst ~* sensational; *~ sein auch* cause (quite) a stir; → *Aufsehen*

Aufseher *m*; *-s, -*, *~in f*; *-, -nen Museum, Parkplatz etc.*: attendant; *in e-r Fabrik*: foreman; *im Gefängnis*: guard, *Brit.* warder; *während einer Prüfung*: invigilator, *Am.* proctor

aufseiten, **auf Seiten** *Präp.* (+ *Gen. od. von*) on the part of

aufsetzen (*trennb., hat -ge-*) **I.** *v/t.* **1.** (*Brille, Hut, Lächeln, Miene etc.*) put on; → *aufgesetzt* II, *Dämpfer* 4, *Glanzlicht* 2, *Horn¹* 1, *Krone* 2; **2.** (*Essen, Topf*) put on the stove; *Wasser ~* put some water on (to boil); **3.** (*auf + Akk.*) (*Tonarm*) lower; *die Füße (auf den Boden) ~* place (*od.* put) one's feet (on the ground); **4.** (*auf + Akk.*) (*Stockwerk etc.*) add (to), build (on); (*Flicken, Tasche*) put (*od.* sew) on; **5.** (*Brief, Vertrag etc.*) (*entwerfen*) draft; (*Aufsatz*) *auch* make a draft of; (*abfassen*) draw up; **6.** (*kranke Person im Bett etc.*) sit up; **7.** *Naut.* (*Boot*) absichtlich: pull up, beach; *versehentlich*: ground, run aground; **II.** *v/refl.* sit (o.s.) up; **III.** *v/i.* **1.** (*landen*) *Flugzeug, Springer*: touch down, land; **2.** *Ball*: bounce

Aufsetzer *m*; *-s*, *-*; *Sport versehentlich*: awkward bouncing shot (*od.* ball); *absichtlich*: bounce shot

aufseufzen *v/i.* (*trennb., hat -ge-*): (*tief* ~) heave a (deep) sigh

Aufsicht *f*; *-*, *-en* **1.** *nur Sg.*; supervision, control; *polizeilich*: surveillance; *ärztlich*: supervision, observation; *bei Kindern, Entmündigten*: guardianship, care; *während einer Prüfung*: invigilation, *Am.* proctoring; **die ~ führen** *od.* **haben** be in charge (**über** + *Akk.* of); **unter ~ stehen** be under supervision; *Gefangener*: be in (police) custody; **die Kinder ohne ~ lassen** leave the children unattended; **der ~ führende Techniker/Lehrer** the technician on duty / the teacher in charge; **der/die ~ Führende** the supervisor, the person in charge; *während einer Prüfung*: *Brit.* the invigilator, *Am.* the proctor; **2.** *nur Sg.*; (*Person*) supervisor, person in charge; *im Museum etc.*: attendant; **3.** *Math., Tech.* top view; **Aufsichtführende** *m,f* → *Aufsicht* 1

Aufsichts|amt *n* board of control, inspectorate; **~beamte** *m*, **~beamtin** *f* supervisor; *im Gefängnis*: guard, *Brit.* warder; *Eisenb.* stationmaster; *im Museum etc.*: attendant; *während einer Prüfung*: invigilator, *Am.* proctor; *bei Lotto, Lotterie etc.*: supervisor, supervising notary; **~behörde** *f* board of control, inspectorate; **~person** *f* supervisor, person in charge; **~personal** *n* supervisory staff (*mst V. im Pl.*); *im Gefängnis*: prison wardens (*Am.* guards) *Pl.*; **~pflicht** *f* legal responsibility

Aufsichts|rat *m Wirts.* **1.** supervisory board; *etwa* board of directors; **2.** (*Person; f Aufsichtsrätin*) member of the supervisory board (*od.* board of directors), *Am. auch* board member

Aufsichtsrats|mitglied *n Wirts.* member of the board, board member; **~posten** *m* position on the board; **~sitzung** *f* board meeting; **~vorsitzende** *m*, *f*; *Mann*: *etwa* chairman of the board; *Frau*: chairwoman of the board; *neutral*: chair(person)

aufsitzen *v/i.* (*unreg., trennb., -ge-*) **1.** (*ist*); *auf ein Pferd*: mount, get on; *auf ein Motorrad etc.*: get on, hop on; **2.** (*hat / südd., österr., schw. ist*) *umg. im Bett etc.*: sit up; **3.** (*hat / südd., österr., schw. ist*); *umg.* (*aufbleiben*) stay up (late); **4.** (*hat / südd., österr., schw. ist*); *Tech.* rest (**auf** + *Dat.* on); **5.** (*hat / südd., österr., schw. ist*); *Naut. Schiff*: run aground (**auf** + *Dat.* on); **6.** (*ist*); *umg. fig.* (*hereingelegt werden*) be taken in (*od.* tricked) (+ *Dat.* by); **wir sind e-m Schwindel aufgesessen** we were taken in (*od.* fooled) by a fraud; **7.** (*hat*) **j-n ~ lassen** *umg.* (*in Stich lassen*) let s.o. down, leave s.o. in the lurch; *bei Verabredung*: stand s.o. up

aufspalten *v/t. und v/refl.* (*trennb., hat -ge-*); (*Holz, Partei etc.*) split; (*Gruppe, Klasse*) divide, split up; *Chem.* break up, split; **Aufspaltung** *f* splitting; *auch* cleavage *fachspr.*; *e-r Zelle*: fission; *fig.* split

aufspannen *v/t.* (*trennb., hat -ge-*)

1. (*Netz, Plane*) stretch, spread (out); (*Schirm, Zelt*) put up: (*Schirm*) *auch* open; (*Sprungtuch*) open up, spread out; (*Segel, Flügel*) spread; **2.** ~ (**auf** + *Akk.*) (*Leinwand, Zeichenblatt*) mount (on)

aufsparen *v/t.* (*trennb., hat -ge-*) save (up), keep (**für** for); **sich** (*Dat.*) **die Bonbons für später ~** keep the sweets for later

aufspeichern *v/t.* (*trennb., hat -ge-*) store up, accumulate; (*einlagern*) warehouse; (*horten*) hoard

aufsperren *v/t.* (*trennb., hat -ge-*) **1.** *umg.* (*weit öffnen*) open wide; **sperr deine Ohren auf!** prick up your ears!, listen up!; **2.** *bes. südd., österr., schw.* (*aufschließen*) unlock

aufspielen (*trennb., hat -ge-*) **I.** *v/i.* **1.** play; **zum Tanz ~** play dance music; **2.** *Sport*: **groß ~** play brilliantly, give an impressive display; **II.** *v/refl. umg., pej.* throw one's weight around, act the big shot; **sich als Held** etc. ~ play the hero etc.; **spiel dich nicht so auf!** stop putting on airs!, stop showing off!

aufspießen *v/t.* (*trennb., hat -ge-*) **1.** spear; *mit Hörnern*: gore; *mit e-m Pfahl*: impale; *mit e-r Gabel*: prong, put on one's fork; *zum Grillen*: skewer; (*Olive etc.*) spike; (*Insekten etc.*) mount, pin; ~ **auf** (+ *Akk.*) (*Insekten*) mount on[to], pin on(to); **2.** *fig.* (*Missstände etc.*) pillory, denounce

aufsplitten *v/t.* (*trennb., hat -ge-*) → *splitten*

aufsplittern (*trennb., -ge-*) **I.** *v/t.* (*hat*) *und v/i.* (*ist*) splinter; **II.** *v/refl.* (*hat*); *fig.* split up, splinter; **Aufsplitterung** *f*; *nur Sg.* splintering, splitting up

aufsprengen *v/t.* (*trennb., hat -ge-*) **1.** force (*od.* break) open; *mit Sprengstoff*: blast open; **2.** *Jägerspr.* (*aufschrecken*) put up, startle

aufspringen *v/i.* (*unreg., trennb., ist -ge-*) **1.** *vom Stuhl etc.*: jump up, leap up; *fig. Wind*: blow (*od.* come) up; **2. auf e-n Zug ~** jump onto a train; **auf den fahrenden Zug ~** *fig.* jump (*od.* climb) on(to) the bandwagon; **3.** *Tür*: fly (*od.* burst) open; *Koffer*: burst open; *Schloss*: spring open; *Knospe*: burst (open); *Knopf*: pop open; **4.** (*rissig werden*) *Haut*: crack; *Lippen*: crack, chap; **5.** (*landen*) land; *Ball*: bounce

aufspritzen (*trennb., -ge-*) **I.** *v/t.* (*hat*); ~ (**auf** + *Akk.*) (*Farbe*) spray on; **II.** *v/i.* (*ist*) spray (*auch Blut*: spurt) into the air; (*Dreck, Matsch*) splatter, splash

aufsprühen (*trennb., -ge-*) **I.** *v/t.* (*hat*); ~ (**auf** + *Akk.*) spray on; **II.** *v/i.* (*ist*) *Flammen etc.*: shoot up; *Funken etc.*: fly up; *Wasser*: spray up

Aufsprung *m bes. Sport* **1.** (*Landung*) landing; *des Balls*: bounce; **2.** *auf ein Gerät*: mount(ing)

aufspulen *v/t.* (*trennb., hat -ge-*) wind up, wind onto a spool

aufspüren *v/t.* (*trennb., hat -ge-*) **1.** (*Wild*) track (*od.* hunt) down; *Hund etc.*: *auch* scent, smell out; *auch Chem.* trace; **2.** *fig.* track down; (*Geheimnis, Manuskript etc.*) unearth, uncover

aufstacheln *v/t.* (*trennb., hat -ge-*) **1.** (*anspornen*) spur on; (*j-s Ehrgeiz, Leidenschaft*) fire; **j-n zu etw. ~** encourage s.o. to do s.th., goad s.o. into (doing) s.th.; **2.** (*aufwiegeln*) incite, stir up (**gegen** against; **zu** to); **Aufstach(e)lung** *f* **1.** (*Ansporn*) spurring on

(**zu** to); **2.** (*Aufwiegelei*) incitement (**gegen** against; **zu** to)

aufstampfen *v/i.* (*trennb., hat -ge-*): (**mit dem Fuß**) ~ stamp one's foot, stamp on the ground

Aufstand *m* (*Revolution*) revolution; (*Revolte*) revolt, rebellion; *e-r Gruppe, Klasse etc.*: uprising, insurrection; (*Putsch*) putsch; *bes. von Soldaten, Matrosen*: mutiny; (*Ausschreitung*) riot; **e-n ~ machen**; *umg. fig.* make (*od.* kick up) a fuss; **mach hier keinen ~!** don't get all het up (*od.* aerated)!;

aufständisch *Adj.* rebellious, insurgent; **Aufständische** *m*, *f*; *-n*, *-n* rebel, insurgent

aufstapeln *v/t.* (*trennb., hat -ge-*) pile (*od.* stack) up

aufstauen (*trennb., hat -ge-*) **I.** *v/t.* dam up; *fig.* (*Gefühle*) bottle up (inside); **II.** *v/refl.* **1.** pile up, accumulate; *Wasser*: collect; *durch Damm*: dam up, impound, pond back; **2.** *fig.* build up, be bottled (*od.* pent) up; → *aufgestaut*

aufstechen *v/t.* (*unreg., trennb., hat -ge-*) pierce; *Med.* (*Geschwür*) lance, prick; (*Erde*) dig up

aufstecken (*trennb., hat -ge-*) **I.** *v/t.* **1.** (*feststecken*) put on (*auch* ~ **auf** + *Akk.*); *mit e-r Nadel*: pin (**auf** + *Akk.* on[to]); **2.** (*hochstecken*) (*Saum*) pin up; (*Gardinen, Haar*) put up; **3.** *umg.* (*aufgeben*) pack (*od.* chuck) in; **II.** *v/i. umg.* (*aufgeben*) pack (*od.* chuck) in; *beim Sport*: retire, withdraw

aufstehen *v/i.* (*unreg., trennb., -ge-*) **1.** (*ist*); (*sich erheben*) stand (*od.* get) up; *aus dem Bett*: get up, rise; **vom Tisch ~** get up from (*od.* leave) the table; **für j-n ~** *von e-m Stuhl etc.*: stand up for s.o.; **früh/spät ~** get up early/ late; **als Kranker noch nicht ~ dürfen** not be allowed to get up (*od.* out of bed) yet; **da musst du schon früher ~!** *umg.* you'll have to do better than that (to catch me out, *Am.* trip me up)!, you won't catch me out (*Am.* trip me up) that easily!; → *link...* 1; **2.** (*hat / südd., österr., schw. ist*) (*offen stehen*) *Mund, Schrank, Tür*: be open; **3.** (*ist*); (*rebellieren*) revolt, rise up (**gegen** against)

aufsteigen *v/i.* (*unreg., trennb., ist -ge-*) **1.** (**auf** + *Akk.*) ~ *auf ein Fahrrad, Pferd etc.*: get on(to), mount; **j-n ~ lassen** (*mitnehmen*) give s.o. a ride (*od.* lift); **2.** *Flammen, Nebel, Pflanzensäfte, Sonne etc.*: rise, go up; (**auf e-n Berg**) ~ climb; **zum Gipfel ~** climb to the summit (*od.* top); *Flugzeug, Hubschrauber*: (*starten*) take off, become airborne; *höher*: climb; **in** *od.* **mit e-m Ballon ~** go up in a balloon; **e-n Ballon ~ lassen** release a balloon; *Vogel*: (*losfliegen*) fly away; (*hoch* ~) soar; **3.** (*entstehen*) *Gewitter*: come up; *Gefühle, Tränen*: rise; *stärker*: well up *lit.*; *Verdacht, Wunsch*: be roused; **ein Gedanke stieg in mir auf** a thought struck me; **4.** (*aufragen*) tower, rise up; **5.** *fig. beruflich*: be promoted (**zu** to); *gesellschaftlich*: climb (socially), climb the ladder; **6.** *österr. auch Päd.* (*versetzt werden*) be moved (*od.* put) up; **7.** *Sport, in e-e höhere Liga*: be promoted; go up *umg.*; *österr.* (*die nächste Pokalrunde erreichen*) reach the next round; go (*od.* get) through *umg.*; **in die 1. Bundesliga** etc. ~ *etwa* be promoted to (*od.* get into) the Premier League

aufsteigend I. *Part. Präs.* → *aufsteigen*; **II.** *Adj. Tendenz*: rising; **in ~er**

Reihenfolge in ascending order; *Verwandte in ~er Linie* ascendants

Aufsteiger *m*, *~in f*; *-*, *-nen* **1.** *Sport* (newly-)promoted team; **2.** *gesellschaftlich*: social climber; *~ des Jahres* man of the year; **3.** *Hitparade*: chart climber

aufstellen (*trennb., hat -ge-*) **I.** *v/t.* **1.** (*hinstellen*) set up, put up; (*anordnen*); *in e-r Reihe*: line up; (*stapeln*) stack; (*Wachposten*) post, station; **2.** (*aufrichten*) (*Umgefallenes*) (*wieder*) *~* stand up (again); (*Kragen*) turn up (one's collar); (*Ohren, Stacheln*) prick up; (*Fell*) bristle; **3.** (*aufbauen*) (*Falle*) set; (*Leiter*) stand up; (*montieren*) assemble, mount; (*Gerät, Maschine*) install, put in (*od.* up), fit; (*Baracke*) construct, set up; (*Gerüst*) erect, put (*od.* set) up; (*Zelt*) pitch; (*Denkmal, Schild etc.*) erect, put up; *Mil.* (*Raketen etc.*) deploy; **4.** (*zusammenstellen*) (*Mannschaft*) pick, select, put together; (*Truppen*) raise; **5.** (*benennen*) (*Kandidaten*) put forward, field; *j-n als Kandidaten ~* nominate s.o. as a candidate; *sich für e-e Wahl ~ lassen* run (*od. Brit.* stand) (as a candidate) for election; **6.** (*ausarbeiten*) (*Liste, Tabelle, Bilanz*) draw up; **7.** (*formulieren*) (*Grundsatz*) lay down, establish; (*Regel*) make, put forward; (*Theorie*) propose, advance; *Math.* (*Problem*) state, pose; (*Gleichung*) form, set up; *e-e Behauptung ~* make an assertion, claim (*od.* maintain) s.th.; *e-e Forderung ~* put forward a claim, make a demand; **8.** *Wirts.* *die Kosten ~* state the charges, itemize the costs; *e-e Statistik ~* draw up statistics *Pl.*; *e-e Rechnung ~* draw (*od.* make) up a bill; **9.** *Sport*: (*Rekord*) set (up), establish; **10.** *Dial.* (*Essen auf den Herd*) put on; **II.** *v/refl.* **1.** *Person*: position o.s., take one's stand (*vor* in front of); *in Reihen*: get into line; *Pl.* line up; *Mil.* fall in; (*hintereinander*) form a queue (*Am.* line); *sich im Kreis ~* form a circle; **2.** *Fell, Haare*: bristle, rise; *Ohren, Stacheln*: prick up

Aufstellung *f* **1.** *nur Sg.*; (*das Aufstellen*) setting up; *Tech.* installation; *Montage*: assembly; *von Wachen*: posting, stationing; *von Baracken, Gerüsten etc.*: building, constructing; *von Denkmälern, Schildern*: erection; *Mil. von Geschützen etc.*: deployment, emplacement; **2.** *nur Sg.*; (*Anordnung*) arrangement; *Mil.* formation; *~ nehmen* take up position; **3.** *Sport, e-r Mannschaft*: selection; (*aufgestellte Mannschaft*) (team) line-up, team; **4.** *nur Sg.*; (*Nominierung*) nomination; **5.** (*Liste*) list; (*Tabelle*) table; (*Übersicht*) survey; *monatliche ~* monthly statement; **6.** *nur Sg.*; *e-r Bilanz, Liste etc.*: drawing up; *e-r Theorie*: proposition; *e-r Gleichung*: formation, setting up; *e-r Behauptung*: putting forward, claim; **7.** *nur Sg.*; *Mil. von neuen Truppen*: raising

aufstemmen (*trennb., hat -ge-*) **I.** *v/t.* prise (*od.* prize, *Am.* pry) open; *mit Gewalt*: force open; **II.** *v/refl.*: *sich* (*mit den Ellbogen etc.*) *auf den Tisch ~* prop o.s. (up) on the table (on one's elbows *etc.*)

aufstieben *v/i.* (*unreg., trennb., ist -ge-*) *Funken, Schneeflocken*: fly up

Aufstieg *m*; *-(e)s, -e* **1.** *in die Luft, zum Gipfel*: ascent; *zum Gipfel*: auch climb(ing); *Flug.* (*Abheben*) takeoff; **2.** (*Weg*) way (*od.* path) up; **3.** *fig.*

rise; beruflicher, sozialer: ascent, advancement, ascension (*zu* to); *Sport* promotion; (*kometenhafter*) *~ zum Ruhm* (meteoric) rise to fame

Aufstiegs|chancen *Pl.* promotion prospects; *Sport* chances of being promoted; *~kandidat m Sport* promotion candidate; *~möglichkeiten Pl.* → **Aufstiegschancen**; *~runde f Sport* qualifying round deciding promotion; *zur obersten Liga*: first division qualifying round; *~spiel n Sport* promotion decider (*od.* tie); *zur obersten Liga*: first division qualifier

aufstöbern *v/t.* (*trennb., hat -ge-*) **1.** (*Wild*) rouse; **2.** *fig.* hunt (*od.* track) down, run to earth (*Am.* ground); (*Geheimnis, Manuskript etc.*) unearth

aufstocken *vt/i.* (*trennb., hat -ge-*) **1.** *Archit.* raise; add a floor (*od.* storey, *Am.* story); **2.** *Wirts.* (*Kapital*) increase, accumulate; (*Einkünfte*) top up; (*Vorräte*) stock up on; *Quoten ~* increase quotas; **Aufstockung** *f* **1.** *Archit.* addition of another stor(e)y; **2.** *Wirts.* accumulation of capital

aufstöhnen *v/i.* (*trennb., hat -ge-*) give a (loud) groan

aufstoßen (*unreg., trennb., -ge-*) **I.** *v/t.* (*hat aufgestoßen*) **1.** (*Tür etc.*) push open; **2.** *sich* (*Dat.*) *den Kopf / das Knie etc. ~* cut one's head/knee; **3.** *etw. ~* (*auf + Akk.*) bang (*od.* bump) s.th. on(to) *s.th.*; **II.** *v/i.* **1.** (*ist*): (*mit dem Kopf auf etw.* (*Akk.*) *~* bump (one's head on) s.th.; **2.** (*hat*); (*rülpsen*) burp, belch; *das Baby ~ lassen* make the baby bring up wind (*Am.* gas), burp the baby; **3.** (*ist/hat*) *j-m ~ Essen*: repeat on s.o.; → *sauer* II 1

aufstrebend *Adj.* **1.** (*hoch*) *~ Berg, Gebäude etc.*: soaring (high); **2.** *Person*: aspiring; (*erfolgssicher*) up-and-coming; (*Stadt, Land*) emergent, rising

aufstreichen *v/t.* (*unreg., trennb., hat -ge-*); (*Farbe*) apply (*auf + Akk.* to); (*Butter etc.*) spread (on); **Aufstrich** *m* **1.** → **Brotaufstrich**; **2.** *Mus. und Schrift*: upstroke

aufstülpen *v/t.* (*trennb., hat -ge-*) **1.** (*Hut*) pop on *umg.*; **2.** (*Kragen, Krempe, Manschette*) turn up; **3.** *fig. pej.* → *aufpfropfen* 2

aufstützen (*trennb., hat -ge-*) **I.** *v/t.* prop up; **II.** *v/refl.* prop o.s. up; *sich* (*mit den Ellbogen etc.*) *~ auf* (*+ Akk. od. Dat.*) prop o.s. up (on one's elbows *etc.*) on

aufsuchen *v/t.* (*trennb., hat -ge-*); (*besuchen*) visit (*auch an e-m Ort*), call on; *bei der Durchreise etc.*: look up; (*e-n Arzt*) (go and) see; (*Toilette*) go to

auftafeln (*trennb., hat -ge-*) **I.** *v/t.* serve (up); **II.** *v/i.* give a huge spread

auftakeln (*trennb., hat -ge-*) **I.** *v/t. Naut.* rig up; **II.** *v/refl. umg. fig. Frau*: get dolled (*pej. od. hum.* tarted, *Am.* hussied) up; *auch Mann*: dressed to the nines; → *aufgetakelt*

Auftakt *m* **1.** *mst Sg.*; *fig.*: *~* (*+ Gen. od. zu*) prelude (to); lead-up *umg.* (to); (*Beginn*) start (of); *e-s Projekts, e-r Saison etc.*: send-off *umg.* (of); (*Eröffnung*) curtain-raiser (to); *zum ~ des Festivals* to start the festival off, to launch the festival, to get the festival under way; **2.** *Mus.* upbeat

auftanken (*trennb., hat -ge-*) **I.** *vt/i.* fill up; *Flug.* refuel; **II.** *v/t. fig., umg.* (*Energie*) recharge one's batteries; *ich will ein bisschen Sonne ~* I want to

catch some sun(shine)

auftauchen *v/i.* (*trennb., ist -ge-*) **1.** come up, emerge; *U-Boot*: surface; **2.** *fig.* (*erscheinen*) turn up; *Frage etc.*: come up; *bes. Problem etc.*: *auch* crop up, arise; *Verschwunde(s)*: *wieder ~* turn up again; **Auftauchen** *n aus dem Wasser*: (*auch fig.*) emergence

auftauen (*trennb., -ge-*) **I.** *v/i.* (*ist*) *und v/t.* (*hat*) thaw; *Mot., auch Tiefkühlkost*: defrost; **II.** *v/t.* (*hat*); *fig.* thaw, come out of one's shell

aufteilen *v/t.* (*trennb., hat -ge-*) divide (up), split up; (*verteilen*) distribute, share out; (*Raum*) divide, partition; (*bes. Land*) parcel out; **Aufteilung** *f* division; (*Verteilung*) distribution, sharing out

auftischen *v/t.* (*trennb., hat -ge-*) serve (up), dish up; *umg. fig.* dish up; *j-m Lügen ~* tell s.o. a pack of lies

Auftrag *m*; *-(e)s, Aufträge* **1.** (*zu*) (*Anweisung*) directions *Pl.*, instructions *Pl.*, orders *Pl.*; (*Aufgabe*) assignment; (*Pflicht*) task, job; (*Besorgung*) errand; *Mil. und diplomatischer*: mission; *im ~ von* on behalf of, on s.o.'s instructions; *in j-s ~ handeln* act on s.o.'s behalf; *ich komme im ~ von ...* I have been sent by ...; *im ~* (*abgek. i.A.*) pp, P.P. (= per procurationem); *j-m e-n ~ erteilen* instruct s.o. to do s.th., give s.o. the job of doing s.th.; *e-n ~ ausführen* carry out an instruction; *ich habe den ~ zu* (*+ Inf.*) I have been instructed to (*+ Inf.*); **2.** *Wirts.* (*Bestellung*) order; (*Bauauftrag, Liefervertrag*) contract; *laut ~* according to order (*od.* the contract); *j-m e-n geben* place an order with s.o., commission s.th. from s.o.; *e-n ~ vergeben* place an order; *bei Ausschreibungen*: award a contract; *etw. bei j-m in ~ geben* commission s.o. to do s.th.; place an order with s.o. for s.th.; *in ~ gegeben* on order; **3.** *mst Sg.*; (*Aufgabe*) job; (*Mission*) purpose, mission; *die Kirche hat den ~ zu* (*+ Inf.*) it's the job of the Church (*od.* the Church's job) to (*+ Inf.*); **4.** *mst Sg.*; *von Farbe etc.*: application

auftragen (*unreg., trennb., hat -ge-*) **I.** *v/t.* **1.** (*Speisen*) serve (up); *es ist aufgetragen!* dinner is served (*od.* on the table *umg.*)!; **2.** (*Farbe etc.*) apply, put on (*auf + Akk. od. Dat.* to); **3.** (*Kleidung, Schuhe*) (*verschleißen*) wear out; *sie musste immer die Kleider i-r großen Schwester ~* she always had to wear (out) her older sister's cast-offs (*bes. Am.* hand-me-downs); **4.** *j-m etw. ~* assign s.o. with s.th.; *j-m ~ zu* (*+ Inf.*) instruct s.o. to (*+ Inf.*); *er trug mir Grüße an dich auf* he asked me to give you his regards; **II.** *v/i.* **1.** *Stoff etc.*: be bulky; **2.** *umg. fig.* *dick ~* (*übertreiben*) lay it on (a bit) thick (*od.* with a trowel)

Auftrag|geber *m*, *~geberin f* (*Kunde*) customer, client; *e-s Künstlers*: patron; *~nehmer m*; *-s, -*, *~nehmerin f*; *-*, *-nen* contractor, supplier

Auftrags|abwicklung *f Wirts.* order processing; *~arbeit f* commissioned work; *~bestände Pl.* backlog *Sg.* of orders; *~bestätigung f* confirmation (*vom Verkäufer*: acknowledg[e]ment) of order; *~buch n* order book; *~dienst m Telef.* etwa telephone services *Pl.*; *ich möchte mich vom ~ wecken lassen* I'd like to book (*Am.* schedule *od.* request) an alarm call; *~eingang m* **1.** incoming orders *Pl.*;

2. (*Vorgang*) intake of orders; **~erteilung** *f* placing of orders; *bei e-r Ausschreibung*: award; **≗gemäß** *Adv.* as per order; **~lage** *f* orders situation; *die ~ ist gut* the order books are well filled; **~polster** *n* full order books *Pl.*; **~rückgang** *m* drop in orders; **~vergabe** *f*; *nur Sg.* placing of orders; *bei Ausschreibungen*: award of contract

Auftragswerk *n* commissioned work (*od.* piece)

auftreffen *v/i.* (*unreg., trennb., ist -ge-*): **~ auf** (+ *Dat.*) hit

auftreiben *v/t.* (*unreg., trennb., hat -ge-*) **1.** *umg.* (*finden, auch Geld*) get hold of, come by, stump up; **2.** (*aufblähen*) swell (*od.* blow up), distend; (*Teig*) make … rise; (*Bauch, Kadaver*) bloat; **3.** (*aufwirbeln*) swirl up; **4.** (*j-n*) (*hochtreiben*) force *s.o.* up; **5.** (*Vieh*) **auf den Markt ~** drive to market; **auf die Alm ~** drive to the high (*od.* summer) pastures *Pl.*

auftrennen *v/t.* (*trennb., hat -ge-*); (*Saum*) undo, rip open; (*Gestricktes*) undo, unravel

auftreten (*unreg., trennb., -ge-*) **I.** *v/i.* (*ist*) **1.** *mit dem Fuß*: step, tread; **vorsichtig ~** tread (*Am.* walk) carefully (*leise*: softly); **ich kann mit dem linken Fuß nicht ~** I can't stand on my left foot; **2.** (*sich verhalten*) act, conduct *o.s.*; **sicher/energisch ~** have a confident/energetic manner, appear confident/energetic; **3.** (*eintreten*) occur; *Schwierigkeiten, Probleme etc.*: crop up; *Zweifel etc.*: arise; *Folgeerscheinungen*: appear, develop; *Krankheit*: develop, show itself; (*anzutreffen sein*) be found; **4.** *Theat.* appear (on stage); *auch Musiker etc.*: perform; (*auf die Bühne kommen*) enter; *als Redner etc.*: *auch* (stand up to) speak; **zum ersten Mal ~** *auch fig.* make one's debut; **5.** (*erscheinen*) appear; **öffentlich ~** appear in public; **als Zeuge ~** appear as (a) witness; **~ gegen etw.** appear (*od.* speak) in opposition to *s.th.*; **er trat als Kaufinteressent auf** he acted (*od.* presented himself) as a prospective customer; *fälschlich*: he pretended to be a prospective customer; **als Zeuge/Kläger ~** appear as a witness/plaintiff (*od.* claimant); **II.** *v/t.* (*hat*); (*Tür etc.*) kick open; (*Kastanie etc.*) tread (*od.* stamp) open

Auftreten *n*; *-s, kein Pl.* **1.** (*Verhalten*) manner; **2.** (*Erscheinen*) appearance; (*Vorkommen*) occurrence; *auch e-r Krankheit*: incidence

Auftrieb *m* **1.** *nur Sg.*; *Phys.* buoyancy; *Flug.* lift; **2.** *nur Sg.*; *fig.* (*Schwung*) impetus, stimulus, boost *umg., Am.* lift; *j-m ~ geben* buoy *s.o.* up; *neuen ~ geben* (+ *Dat.*). give (a) fresh impetus (to); *j-m wieder ~ geben* get *s.o.* going again, give *s.o.* a new lease of life; **3.** *des Viehs auf die Alm*: driving (of cattle to the Alpine pastures); **Auftriebskraft** *f*; *nur Sg. Phys.* buoyancy, lifting force

Auftritt *m Theat., auch fig.* **1.** appearance; (*Betreten der Bühne*) entry; *sie hat erst im 4. Akt i-n ~* she doesn't make her (first) entrance until the fourth act; **2.** (*Szene*) scene; *fig.* big day, moment of glory

auftrumpfen *v/i.* (*trennb., hat -ge-*); *fig.* **1.** (*mit etw.*) **~** play one's trumps; **2.** (*herrisch auftreten*) show one's superiority, put one's foot down; come on strong *umg.*

auftun (*unreg., trennb., hat -ge-*) **I.** *v/t.*

1. *umg.*: **sich** (*Dat.*) **etw. ~ auf den Teller**: help *o.s.* to *s.th.*, take *s.th.*; *j-m etw. ~* give *s.o.* (a helping of) *s.th.*; **2.** *umg.* (*finden*) find, discover, dig up; **3.** *geh. altm.* (*Fenster, Mund*) open; **4.** *Dial.* (*Brille etc.*) put on; **II.** *v/refl. geh.* **1.** *Tür*: open (up); **2.** *fig.* (*Abgrund, neue Welt*) open up (**vor** before)

auftupfen *v/t.* (*trennb., hat -ge-*) **1.** (*durch Tupfen entfernen*) dab off; **2.** (*durch Tupfen auftragen*) apply, put on (**auf** + *Akk.* to)

auftürmen (*trennb., hat -ge-*) **I.** *v/t.* pile up; **II.** *v/refl. Geschirr, Arbeit etc.*: pile up; *Berge etc.*: tower (**vor j-m** before *od.* in front of *s.o.*)

aufwachen *v/i.* (*trennb., ist -ge-*); *auch fig.* wake up (**aus** + *Dat.* from); *aus der Bewusstlosigkeit*: come (a)round; *fig. Gefühle etc.*: be roused; *er ist endlich aufgewacht* he's finally woken up to the truth (*od.* to reality)

aufwachsen *v/i.* (*unreg., trennb., ist -ge-*) grow up

aufwallen *v/i.* (*trennb., ist -ge-*) **1.** *kochend*: boil up, come to the (*Am.* a) boil; *Wasser etc.*: *auch* bubble (up), well (up); *brausend*: effervesce *fachspr.*; *Meer*: seethe, swell; *Dunst, Nebel*: rise (up); **2.** *fig. Blut*: surge, boil; *Gefühle*: surge up (**in j-m** inside *s.o.*); *Wut*: *auch* seethe; **Aufwallung** *f* **1.** upwelling, effervescence *fachspr.*; **2.** *fig.* (*Gefühlsaufwallung*) surge; *von Wut etc.*: *auch* fit, outburst; *bei Kindern*: tantrum

aufwalzen *v/t.* (*trennb., hat -ge-*); *Tech.* roll on

Aufwand *m*; *-(e)s, kein Pl.* **1.** (*Ausgabe, Aufwendung*) cost, expense; (*Anstrengung*) effort; *der ~ an Zeit* (*Kraft etc.*) the time (energy *etc.*) involved; *mit e-m ~ von finanziell*: at a cost of; *das erfordert e-n großen ~ an …* (+ *Dat.*) it requires a lot (*od.* a huge amount) of …; *der ~ lohnt sich nicht* it's not worth the effort (*od.* candle *umg.*), it's not worth bothering with; → **Aufwendung** 2; **2.** (*Verschwendung*) luxury, extravagance; *großen ~* (*be*)*treiben* live in grand style, be extravagant; **aufwändig** *Adj.* → **aufwendig**, **Aufwandsentschädigung** *f* expense allowance

aufwärmen (*trennb., hat -ge-*) **I.** *v/t.* **1.** warm up; (*Essen*) *auch* heat up; **2.** *fig.* (*alte Geschichten*) rehash; **II.** *v/refl. Person*: warm *o.s.* up; *Sportler, Erdatmosphäre etc.*: warm up

Aufwärmübungen *Pl.* warm(ing)-up (*od.* limbering-up) exercises

Aufwartefrau *f* cleaning lady (*od.* woman), domestic help

aufwarten *v/i.* (*trennb., hat -ge-*) **1.** *fig.* **~** (*können*) come up with, offer; *der Tag wartete mit e-r Überraschung auf* the day held a surprise in store; **2.** *geh.*: *j-m ~ mit Getränken, Speisen* (*anbieten*) offer (*od.* serve) *s.o. s.th.*

aufwärts *Adv.* **1.** upward(s); (*bergan*) uphill; *den Fluss ~* upstream, upriver; **2.** *von j-m* (*an*) **~** in e-r Rangfolge: from *s.o.* up(wards); **3.** *mit ihm / dem Geschäft geht es ~* *fig.* things are looking up for him / business is looking up

Aufwärts|bewegung *f* upward movement; *fig.* upward trend, rise; **~entwicklung** *f* upward trend; **~haken** *m Boxen*: uppercut; **~trend** *m* upward trend, upswing

Aufwartung *f*: *j-m s-e ~ machen* pay

one's respects to *s.o.*; (*besuchen*) pay *s.o.* a courtesy visit

Aufwasch *m*; *-(e)s, kein Pl.* **1.** → **Abwasch**; **2.** *umg. fig.*: *in einem ~* in one go; *das ist 'ein ~* we can kill two birds with one stone; **aufwaschen** *v/i.* (*unreg., trennb., hat -ge-*) do the dishes (*od. Brit.* washing-up)

aufwecken *v/t.* (*trennb., hat -ge-*) wake (up); → **aufgeweckt**

aufweichen (*trennb., -ge-*) **I.** *v/t.* (*hat*) **1.** *durch Feuchtigkeit*: soak; (*Boden*) make … soggy; **2.** *durch Wärme*: soften; (*schmelzen*) melt; **3.** *fig.* undermine; (*schwächen*) weaken; **II.** *v/i.* (*ist*) **1.** soak; *Boden*: become soggy; **2.** *durch Wärme*: soften; (*schmelzen*) melt; **3.** *fig.* become undermined

aufweisen *v/t.* (*unreg., trennb., hat -ge-*) **1.** (*erkennen lassen, haben*) show, exhibit; (*Erfolge etc.*) boast, crow; *etwas aufzuweisen haben* have something to show (for *o.s.*); **2.** → **aufzeigen**

aufwenden *v/t.* (*auch unreg., trennb., hat -ge-*); (*ausgeben*) spend (**für** on); (*Zeit*) *auch* devote (to); (*Energie*) *auch* expend (on); (**viel**) **Mühe ~** take (great) pains (**auf** + *Akk.* over); **viel Geld ~** go to great expense

aufwendig *Adj.* costly, expensive; *Lebensweise etc.*: extravagant; **~e Inszenierung** lavish production; **Aufwendung** *f* **1.** **~en** (*Ausgaben*) expenditure *Sg.*, expense *Sg.*, expenses; **2.** *nur Sg.*: *unter ~ aller zur Verfügung stehenden Mittel* by using all available means (*od.* all means at one's disposal)

aufwerfen (*unreg., trennb., hat -ge-*) **I.** *v/t.* **1.** (*Damm etc.*) throw up; **2.** (*hochwerfen*) throw up; (*Kopf*) toss one's head; **3.** *fig.* (*Frage, Problem*) raise; **4.** (*Tür etc.*) throw (*od.* fling) open; **5.** **~ auf** (+ *Akk.*) throw on(to); **6.** (*schürzen*) *die Lippen ~* purse one's lips; → **aufgeworfen**; **II.** *v/refl.*: **sich zu etw. ~** set *o.s.* up as *s.th.*, appoint *o.s. s.th.*

aufwerten *v/t.* (*trennb., hat -ge-*) *Fin.* revalue, upvalue; *fig.* upgrade; **Aufwertung** *f Fin.* revaluation, upvaluation; *fig.* upgrading

aufwickeln *v/t.* (*trennb., hat -ge-*) **1.** wind up (*auch Film*), roll up; **sich** (*Dat.*) **die Haare ~** put one's hair in curlers; **2.** (*loswickeln*) unwind; (*Päckchen*) unwrap; (*entflechten*) untwist, unbraid, untwine

Aufwiegelei *f*; *-, -en*; *pej.* incitement (to revolt); **aufwiegeln** *v/t.* (*trennb., hat -ge-*) stir up, incite

aufwiegen *v/t.* (*unreg., trennb., hat -ge-*) counterbalance; *fig.* compensate for, make up for, offset, balance out

Aufwiegler *m*; *-s, ~*, **~in** *f*; *-, -nen* agitator, fomenter; (*Anstifter*) instigator; **aufwieglerisch** *Adj.* seditious; *Rede*: inflammatory

Aufwind *m* **1.** *Flug.* upward (*od.* anabatic) wind; *thermischer*: thermal; (*Gegenwind*) upwind; **2.** *fig.*: *im ~ sein* be on the up and up

aufwirbeln (*trennb., -ge-*) **I.** *v/t.* (*hat*) whirl up, swirl up, agitate; (*Staub*) raise; *fig.*: *viel Staub ~* kick up a lot of dust, cause quite a stir; **II.** *v/i.* (*ist*) whirl up, swirl up

aufwischen *v/t.* (*trennb., hat -ge-*) **1.** (*wegwischen*) wipe up; **2.** (*Fußboden*) wipe, mop

Aufwisch|lappen *m*, **~tuch** *n* cleaning cloth (*od.* rag)

aufwölben *v/refl.* (*trennb., hat -ge-*)

swell, buckle

aufwühlen v/t. (trennb., hat -ge-) **1.** (Erde) throw up; (See, Schlamm) churn up; **2.** fig. stir s.o. up, move; agitate förm.; **ein ~des Erlebnis** a deeply moving experience; → **aufgewühlt** II

aufzählen v/t. (trennb., hat -ge-) enumerate; (nennen) name, tell; in e-r Liste: list, itemize; **Aufzählung** f enumeration; (Liste) list

aufzäumen v/t. (trennb., hat -ge-); (Pferd) bridle, put a bridle on; **das Pferd verkehrt ~** umg. fig. put the cart before the horse, go about s.th. the wrong way

aufzehren (trennb., hat -ge-) **I.** v/t. **1.** eat up; **2.** fig. use up; (Vermögen) spend; (Energie) sap, consume; **3.** fig. (Person) drain, exhaust; **II.** v/refl.: wear o.s. out; **er zehrt sich vor Sorgen auf** he's eaten up with worry, his worries are eating away at him

aufzeichnen v/t. (trennb., hat -ge-) **1.** draw, sketch (**auf** + Akk. on); **2.** (schriftlich festhalten) record; (schreiben) auch write down; auf Band: auch tape; **Aufzeichnung** f **1.** (Aufnahme) recording; **2.** ~en Pl. notes; (Dokumente) papers, documents; **sich ~en machen** make (od. take) notes

aufzeigen v/t. (trennb., hat -ge-) show; (klar machen) auch demonstrate; (Fehler etc.) point out

aufziehen (unreg., trennb., -ge-) **I.** v/t. (hat) **1.** (hochziehen) draw up, pull up; (etw. Schweres) haul up; (Fahne, Segel) hoist; (Anker) weigh; (Zugbrücke) raise; **2.** (öffnen) (Gardine) open; (Schublade) (pull) open; (Reißverschluss) undo, pull open; (Schleife) untie, undo; (Flasche) open; Theat. (Vorhang) raise; **3.** (Uhr, Spielzeug) wind up; **Spielzeug zum Aufziehen** clockwork toys; reden etc. **wie aufgezogen** like clockwork; **4.** (spannen) (Reifen, Saiten) put on; (Bild) mount (**auf** + Akk. on); fig. → **Saite; 5.** (Kind, Tier) rear, raise; (Kind) auch bring up; (Pflanze) raise, grow; **6.** (organisieren) organize; (Party etc.) arrange; (Unternehmen, Vorhaben etc.) set up, stage; **die Sache ganz groß ~** plan (od. set up) the affair (od. thing) in grand style; **7.** umg.: **j-n ~** (etwas vormachen) pull s.o.'s leg, have s.o. on, wind s.o. up; (hänseln) tease s.o. (**wegen** about); **du ziehst mich (doch) bloß auf** you're kidding (me); **8.** Med. (Spritze) draw up; **etw. auf e-e Spritze ~** draw s.th. into a syringe, fill a syringe with s.th.; **II.** v/i. (ist) **1.** Gewitter: come up; Wolken: gather; **2.** Mil. march up; Wache: come on duty

Aufzucht f von Tieren: breeding, rearing; von Pflanzen: raising, cultivation

Aufzug m **1.** (Fahrstuhl) lift, Am. elevator; beim Bau: hoist; (Speisenaufzug) dumb waiter; **2.** (Festzug) parade, pageant; (Pomp) pomp, show; feierlicher: procession; **3.** umg. (Aufmachung) getup; **in diesem ~ gehst du nicht aus dem Haus!** you're not leaving the house dressed (od. looking) like that!; **4.** Theat. act; **5.** Turnen: pull-up; **6.** (das Aufziehen) der Wache: mounting guard (od. of the guard); von Wolken: gathering; **Aufzug(s)schacht** m lift (Am. elevator) shaft

aufzüngeln v/i. (trennb., ist -ge-); geh. Flammen: leap (od. dart) up

aufzwingen (unreg., trennb., hat -ge-) **I.** v/t.: **j-m etw. ~** force (od. foist) s.th.

on s.o.; (Handlungsweise etc.) force s.o. into (doing) s.th., impose s.th. on s.o.; **II.** v/refl.: **sich j-m ~** Gedanke etc.: impinge (od. force o.s.) on s.o.

aufzwirbeln v/t. (trennb., hat -ge-); (Bart) twirl (od. twist) up; (Garn) twist up, roll between one's fingers

Augapfel m eyeball; **wie s-n ~ hüten** guard with one's life

Auge n **1.** Anat. eye; **sie hat blaue ~n** she has (got) blue eyes; **gute/schlechte ~n haben** have good/bad eyesight (od. eyes); **auf einem ~ blind sein** be blind in one eye; **mit bloßem ~** with the naked eye; **mit geschlossenen** od. **verbundenen ~n** blindfold(ed); **j-m in die ~n sehen** look into s.o.'s eyes; **ihr fallen die ~n zu** her eyelids are drooping; **ganz kleine ~n haben** fig. be all sleepy; **sich die ~n verderben** ruin one's eyes (od. eyesight); **~n haben wie ein Luchs** be sharp-eyed (od. eagle-eyed) auch fig.; **2.** in Wendungen, oft fig.: **mit eigenen ~n** with one's own eyes; **ich hab's mit eigenen ~n gesehen** auch it happened before my very eyes (od. right under my nose); **vor allen ~n** in front of everyone, in full view (of everyone); **es geschah vor m-n** etc. **~n** right in front of me etc.; **hast du keine ~n im Kopf?** are you blind?; **ich hab doch hinten keine ~n!** I haven't got eyes in the back of my head!; **ich habe schließlich ~n im Kopf!** (ich hab's wirklich gesehen!) I'm not blind you know!; **etwas fürs ~** a feast for the eyes; **etwas fürs ~ sein** have visual appeal; **so weit das ~ reicht** as far as the eye can see; **er konnte mir nicht in die ~n sehen** he couldn't look me in the eye; **~ in ~** face to face (**mit** with); **vier ~n sehen mehr als zwei** Sprichw. two pairs of eyes are better than one; **die ~n aufmachen** open one's eyes; fig. keep one's eyes open; **im ~ behalten/haben** keep/have an eye on; fig. bear/have in mind; (Ziel) auch keep sight of; **ein ~ haben auf** (+ Akk.) have one's eye on; **aus den ~n verlieren** lose sight of; fig. lose touch with; **nicht aus den ~n lassen** not let s.o. (od. s.th.) out of one's sight; **kein ~ lassen von** not let s.o.. (od. s.th.) out of one's sight; **geh mir aus den ~n!** get out of my sight!; **komm mir nicht wieder unter die ~n!** I don't ever want to see you again!, don't darken my doorstep again!; **unter vier ~n** in private; **Gespräch unter vier ~n** private conversation; **sie hat ihre ~n überall** she's got eyes like a hawk; **die ~n offen halten (nach)** keep one's eyes open (for), keep a look-out (for); **mit offenen ~n durch die Welt gehen** walk about with one's eyes open; **ein ~ riskieren** steal a glance; **ein ~ haben** have s.th. in mind; **sich** (Dat.) **etw. vor ~n halten** keep (od. bear) s.th. in mind; **j-m etw. vor ~n führen** make s.th. clear to s.o.; **e-r Gefahr / den Tatsachen ins ~ sehen** face (up to) (a) danger / the facts, look danger / the facts in the face; **sehenden ~s** (ins Verderben rennen etc.) with one's eyes wide open; **vor etw. die ~n verschließen** refuse to see s.th.; **j-m die ~n öffnen** Person: enlighten s.o., open s.o.'s eyes to the truth; etw.: be an eye-opener (for s.o.); **mir gingen plötzlich die ~n auf** suddenly I saw the light; **ein ~** od. **beide ~n zudrücken** turn a blind eye (bei to); **kein ~ zutun** not sleep a wink (all night); **kaum noch aus den ~n sehen**

können not be able to see straight any more; **mit offenen ~n schlafen** daydream, be daydreaming; **s-n ~n nicht trauen** not be able to believe (od. trust) one's eyes; **ins ~ fassen** consider, contemplate (doing s.th.); **ins ~ gefasst haben** be considering; (planen) be planning; **vor m-m geistigen ~** in my mind's eye; **in m-n ~n** as I see it; **sie hat kein ~ dafür** she hasn't got an eye for that; **etw. mit anderen ~n ansehen** see s.th. in a different light; (einem) **ins ~ fallen** od. **springen** catch one's eye, stick out a mile; (überdeutlich sein) hit one in the eye; **einem in die ~n stechen** (gefallen) take one's fancy; Fehler etc.: glare at one; **das ~ beleidigen** offend the eye; **die Dummheit / der Neid** etc. **schaut j-m aus den Augen** you can see the stupidity/jealousy in s.o.'s eyes, stupidity/jealousy is written all over s.o.'s face; **da blieb kein ~ trocken** auch iro. there wasn't a dry eye in the place; **mit e-m lachenden und e-m weinenden ~** with mixed feelings; **sich** (Dat.) **die ~n ausweinen** cry one's eyes out; **j-m gehen die ~n über** s.o. is overwhelmed; geh. (j-d weint) s.o. is moved to tears; **j-n mit den ~n verschlingen** devour s.o. with one's eyes; lüstern: ogle s.o.; **er wird** (große) **~n machen!** he's in for a surprise; **s-e ~n sind größer als sein Magen** his eyes are bigger than his stomach; **er hat ein ~ auf sie geworfen** (findet sie sympathisch) he has his eye on her; **j-m** (schöne) **~n machen** make eyes at s.o.; **j-m j-n/etw. aufs ~ drücken** foist (od. fob) s.o./s.th. off on s.o.; **das hätte leicht ins ~ gehen können** that was close (od. a close one umg.), it could easily have backfired; **j-m die ~n auskratzen** (wollen) (want to) scratch s.o.'s eyes out; **ihre ~n brachen** geh. (sie starb) she passed away; **das ~ des Gesetzes** the (sharp) eye of the law; **aus den ~n, aus dem Sinn** Sprichw. out of sight, out of mind; **~ um ~(, Zahn um Zahn)** bibl. an eye for an eye(, a tooth for a tooth); → **blau** 1, **Dorn**[1] 1, **Faust, schwarz** I 1; **3.** auf Domino, Würfel: pip; beim Kartenspiel: point; **4.** (Keim, Knospe) e-r Kartoffel: eye; e-s Zweiges: bud, axil; **5.** e-s Sturms: eye; **6.** (Fettauge) globule of fat; **7.** Naut. eye; **8.** magisches ~ magic eye

äugeln v/i.: **nach j-m ~** cast (secret) glances at s.o.

äugen v/i.: peer, look

Augenabstand m distance between the (od. one's) eyes; interocular distance fachspr.; zwischen den Pupillen: interpupillary distance fachspr.

Augen|arzt m, **~ärztin** f eye specialist, Brit. oculist; ophthalmologist fachspr.; **augenärztlich** Adj. Untersuchung: opthalmologic(al)

Augen|aufschlag m blink; **~bad** n eye bath; **~binde** f (eye) bandage; (Augenklappe) eye patch

Augenblick m moment; (Zeitpunkt, bestimmter Augenblick) instant; (einen) **~!** one moment (od. just a minute), please; **im ~** at the moment; **für den ~** for the time being; **im letzten ~** at the last minute; (gerade rechtzeitig) auch just in time, at the eleventh hour; **im entscheidenen ~** at the crucial moment, when it comes to the crunch; **im ersten ~** (anfangs) for a moment; (sofort) immediately, right away; **im richtigen ~** at the right moment; **in e-m**

unbeobachteten ~ in a quiet moment, when no one was (*bzw.* is) paying attention; *in diesem* ~ at this moment (in time); *im selben* ~ ... at the same instant ...; *im nächsten* ~ *passierte es* the next instant it happened; *ich erwarte ihn jeden* ~ he should be here any minute, I'm expecting him any minute; *alle* ~*e umg.* constantly; (*immer wieder*) every now and then; → *auch* **Moment**[1]

augenblicklich I. *Adj.* immediate; (*gegenwärtig*) present; *die* ~*e Lage* the situation at present (*od.* at the moment); **II.** *Adv.* **1.** (*momentan*) at the moment, just now; **2.** (*sofort*) immediately

Augenblickserfolg *m* short-lived (*od.* fleeting) success

Augenbraue *f* eyebrow; **Augenbrauenstift** *m* eyebrow pencil

Augen|brennen *n* stinging of (*od.* in) the eyes; *ich habe* ~ my eyes are stinging (*od.* sore); ~**deckel** *m Anat.* eyelid; ~**druck** *m*; *Pl. Augendrücke* → **Augeninnendruck**

augenfällig *Adj.* conspicuous, eye--catching; (*frappierend*) striking; (*offensichtlich*) obvious, evident

Augen|fältchen *Pl.* wrinkles around the eyes; ~**farbe** *f* colo(u)r of *s.o.'s* eyes; *was hat sie für e-e* ~*?* what colo(u)r are her eyes?; ~**fehler** *m* eye defect; ~**heilkunde** *f Med.* ophthalmology; ~**hintergrund** *m Anat.* back of the eye; fundus oculi *fachspr.*; ~**höhe** *f*: *in* ~ at eye level; ~**höhle** *f Anat.* eye socket; orbit(al cavity) *fachspr.*; ~**innendruck** *m*; *Pl. -innendrücke*; *Med.* intraocular pressure; ~**klappe** *f* eye patch; ~**klinik** *f* eye clinic

Augenkrankheit *f* eye disease; (*Sehschwäche*) eye complaint

Augen|leiden *n* eye complaint; *ein* ~ *haben auch* have something wrong with one's eyes; ~**licht** *n*; *nur Sg.* eyesight; *das* ~ *verlieren* lose the sight of one's eyes, lose one's sight; ~**lid** *n* eyelid

Augenmaß *n*; *nur Sg.* sense of distance; *ein gutes* ~ *haben* have a good eye for distances, have a sure (*od.* accurate) eye; *fig.* be good at sizing things up; *nach dem* ~ *zeichnen* draw by eye (*od.* free-hand); ~ *beweisen od.* *zeigen fig.* demonstrate sound judgment; *Politik mit* ~ *fig.* policy of moderation; *etw. nach* ~ *einschätzen* guess (at) the distance (length, width, *etc.*) of s.th.

Augen|mensch *m* visual(ly oriented) person (od. type); ~**merk** *n*; -(e)s, kein *Pl.*: *j-s* ~ *gilt j-m/etw. od. j-d richtet sein* ~ *auf j-n/etw.* s.o. turns his (od. her) attention to s.o./s.th; ~**muskel** *m Anat.* eye muscle; ~**nerv** *m Anat.* optic nerve; ~**optiker** *m*, ~**optikerin** *f* ophthalmic optician, *Am. auch* optometrist; ~**paar** *n* pair of eyes; ~**pflaster** *n zur Behandlung des Schielens etc.*: eye patch; ~**pflege** *f* **1.** eyecare; **2.** *umg.*: ~ *machen* (*schlafen*) get a bit of shuteye; ~**pulver** *n Druck., umg. fig.* miscroscopic print; *das ist ja das reinste* ~ you'd go blind trying to read that; ~**rand** *m* **1.** rim of the (*od.* one's) eye; *gerötete Augenränder* red--rimmed eyes; **2.** *Pl.* rings under one's eyes

Augen|ringe *Pl.* rings (*od.* bags *umg.*) under one's eyes; ~**salbe** *f Med.* eye ointment; ~**schatten** *Pl.* shadows under one's eyes

Augenschein *m*; *nur Sg.*; *geh.* **1.** (*Anschein*) appearance; *dem* ~ *nach* to all appearances; *der* ~ *trügt* appearances are deceptive, don't be (*od.* we mustn't be) deceived by appearances; *nur dem* ~ *nach* (*scheinbar*) seemingly; **2.** (*Besichtigung*) examination, inspection, *Jur.* (judicial) inspection; *in* ~ *nehmen* examine, inspect, take a close look at, view; **augenscheinlich** *Adj. geh.* (*scheinbar*) apparent, evident; (*sichtbar*) obvious, evident

Augen|schirm *m* eyeshade, *bes. Am.* visor; ~**schmaus** *m hum.* feast for the eyes; *weitS.* a sight for sore eyes; ~**spiegel** *m Med.* ophthalmoscope; ~**sprache** *f* visual communication, eye talk *umg.*; ~**steckling** *m Bot.* Pflanze: bud cutting; ~**täuschung** *f* optical illusion; ~**tropfen** *Pl. Med.* eye drops; ~**trost** *m Bot.* eyebright; ~**verletzung** *f* eye injury (*od.* damage); ~**weide** *f*: *e-e* ~ a feast for the eyes, a pleasure to look at; *weitS.* a sight for sore eyes; *keine* ~ an eyesore; ~**wimper** *f* eyelash; ~**winkel** *m* corner of the (*od.* one's) eye; *j-n/etw. aus den* ~*n beobachten* watch s.o./s.th. out of the corner of one's eye; ~**wischerei** *f*; -, -en; *umg., pej.* eyewash, *bes. Am.* baloney; ~**zahl** *f beim Karten-, Würfelspiel*: number (of points); ~**zahn** *m Anat.* eye-tooth

Augenzeuge *m* eyewitness; **Augenzeugenbericht** *m* eyewitness account (*od.* report); **Augenzeugin** *f* eyewitness

Augenzwinkern *n* wink(ing); **augenzwinkernd** *Adv.* with a wink; (*schalkhaft*) with a twinkle in one's eye

Augiasstall *m Myth.* Augean stables *Pl.*; *den* ~ *ausmisten Myth.* clean(se) the Augean stables; *fig.* create order out of chaos, tidy up a terrible mess

...äugig *im Adj.* ...-eyed

Äuglein *n* little (*od.* small) eye

Augsburger *Adj.*: *der* ~ *Religionsfriede hist.* the (Religious) Peace of Augsburg; *das* ~ *Bekenntnis Reli., hist.* the Augustan (*od.* Augsburg) Confession

Augur *m*; -s *od.* -en, -en; *bes. Pol.* pundit

Au'gust[1] *m*; - *od.* -(e)s, -e, mst *Sg.*; (*abgek.* Aug.) August; → **April**

'August[2] *m*; - *od.* -(e)s, -e, mst *Sg.*: *dummer August* clown; *pej.* idiot

Augustiner *m*; -s, ~; *mönch m kath.* Augustinian (monk), *Brit. auch* Austin friar; ~**orden** *m* Augustininan order

Auktion *f*; -, -en auction; *in die* ~ *geben* put up for auction; *zur* ~ *kommen* be auctioned, come under the hammer; **Auktionator** *m*; -s, -en auctioneer; **auktionieren** *v/t.* auction

Auktions|halle *f* auction room; ~**haus** *n* auctioneers *Pl.*

Aula *f*; -, -s *od. Aulen* assembly hall, *Am.* auditorium

Aupairmädchen, Au-pair-Mädchen *n* au pair (girl)

Aura *f*; -, kein *Pl.*; *Astron., Med. und fig.* aura

Aureole *f*; -, -n; *Astron., Reli.* aureole, halo

Aurikel *f*; -, -n; *Bot.* auricula

aus I. *Präp.* (+ *Dat.*) **1.** *räumlich*: out of; from; ~ *dem Fenster* out of (*Am. auch* out) the window; ~ *e-m Glas trinken* drink out of (*od.* from) a glass; ~ *der Ferne/Nähe betrachtet* viewed from a distance / close up; **2.** *Herkunft*: from; ~ *Berlin* from Berlin; *j-d* ~ *der*

Nachbarschaft somebody from the neighbo(u)rhood; ~ *ganz Europa* from all over Europe; ~ *unserer Mitte* from amongst us, from our midst; *Kinder* ~ *dieser Ehe* children from this marriage; *ein Mann* ~ *dem Volke* a man of the people; ~ *zuverlässiger Quelle* on good authority; ~ *dem Jahr 1900* from the year 1900; ~ *der Zeit Cromwells* from the time of Cromwell; ~ *dem Rokoko* from the rococo period; ~ *dem Gedächtnis* from memory; ~ *der Zeitung* from the newspaper; ~ *dem Englischen* present (from (the) English; ~ *dem Englischen übersetzt*: translated from the English (original); **3.** *Ursache, Grund*: out of; ~ *Achtung/Angst/ Hass/Mitleid/Neugier* out of respect/ fear/hatred/pity/curiosity; ~ *Angst vor* for fear of; ~ *Liebe/Spaß* for love/fun; ~ *Liebe zu* out of love for; ~ *Erfahrung* from experience; ~ *Not* through necessity; ~ *Unwissenheit* out of ignorance; ~*Versehen* by mistake (*od.* accident), inadvertently; ~ *Prinzip* on principle; ~ (*genau*) *diesem Grund* for this (very) reason; ~ *e-r Laune* (*heraus*) on impulse, on the spur of the moment; **4.** *Veränderung*: out of, of; ~ *dem Gleichgewicht* out of (*od.* off) balance; ~ *dem Projekt ist nichts geworden* nothing came of the project; ~ *dem Ton e-e Vase formen* create (*od.* make) a vase from the clay; ~ *j-m e-n guten Musiker machen* make a good musician (out) of s.o.; *was ist* ~ *ihr geworden?* what(ever) became of her?; *etwas* ~ *sich machen* make something of o.s.; ~ *ihm ist nichts geworden* he never made anything of himself (*od.* his life); **5.** *Beschaffenheit*: made of; ~ *etw. bestehen* consist of s.th.; ~ *Holz* made (out) of wood, wooden ...; *Schuhe* ~ *Leder* shoes made of leather, leather shoes; **II.** *Adv.* **1.** (*Ggs. an*) *ein* - ~ - on - off; *Licht* ~*!* lights out!; ~ *sein Gerät*: be (switched) off, *Licht: auch* be out; *Feuer*: be out, have gone out; **2.** *umg.* (*vorbei*) ~ (*und vorbei*) *sein* be over; *damit ist es* (*jetzt*) ~ it's all over now, that's the end of that; *es ist* ~ *mit ihm* (*er ist tot*) he's had it; it's curtains for him; (*wir haben uns* / *sie haben sich getrennt*) I'm (*od.* she's) not going out with him any more, I've (*od.* she's) finished with him; *zwischen den beiden ist es* ~ they've split up, they've finished, they're not going out with each other any more; **3.** (*Ggs. drin*) a) *Sport* ~*!* out!; ~ *sein Sport* be out, b) (*außer Haus sein*) be out, c) *umg.* (*ausgegangen*) out, away; *ich war gestern mit ihm* ~ I was (*od.* went) out with him yesterday; **4.** *von* ... ~ from; *von Zypern* ~ from Cyprus; *besuchen wir einige andere Länder*: using Cyprus as a base; *von Natur* ~ by nature; *von sich* ~ of one's own accord; off one's own bat *umg.*, *Am.* on one's own; *von mir* ~ I don't mind, I'm not bothered; *von mir* ~ *könnt ihr gehen* (*ich erlaube es*) you can go as far as I'm concerned; (*es stört mich nicht*) I don't mind (*od.* it doesn't bother me) if you go; *ärgerlich*: go, then, for all I care!; **5.** *auf etw.* (*Akk.*) ~ *sein* be out for s.th., be out to get s.th. → *ein*[2] 1, 2, **Traum**

Aus *n*; -, - **1.** *Sport*: *im od.* *ins* ~ out; *der Ball ging ins* ~ the ball went out; *bei Fußball*: the ball went out of play; **2.** *umg.* (*Ende*) end, curtains *Pl.*; *das* bedeutet das ~ für sie / das Projekt that means it's all over for her / the project, it's curtains for her / the project

ausarbeiten (trennb., hat -ge-) **I.** v/t. **1.** (Plan etc.) gedanklich: conceive, develop, formulate; schriftlich: draw up; **2.** (vervollkommnen) complete; (Schriftliches) finish, write up; **II.** v/refl.: **sich** (körperlich) ~ (have a) work out; **Ausarbeitung** f drawing up; (Vervollständigung) completion

ausarten v/i. (trennb., ist -ge-) **1.** ~ **in** turn into; **das artet ja in Arbeit aus** that looks like work (to me); **2.** (aus dem Rahmen fallen) go too far, get out of control, degenerate; **die Party artete aus** the party got out of hand

ausästen v/t. (trennb., hat -ge-) cut (od. lop) away branches

ausatmen vt/i. (trennb., hat -ge-) breathe out; fachspr. exhale; **Ausatmung** f exhalation

ausbacken (trennb., hat -ge-) v/t. **1.** (Brot) bake through (od. thoroughly); **gut ausgebackenes Brot** well-baked bread; **2.** in Fett: deep-fry

ausbaden v/t. (trennb., hat -ge-); umg. fig. take the rap for, be left holding the baby (Am. auch bag); **die Sache ~** (müssen) (have to) carry the can (od. take the heat)

ausbaggern v/t. (trennb., hat -ge-) **1.** (Grube etc.) dig out, excavate; (Kanal etc.) dredge out; **2.** (Schlamm) dredge up

ausbalancieren v/t. (trennb., hat) balance (out); fig. balance out

ausbaldowern v/t. (trennb., hat); umg. nose out, suss out, scope out

Ausbau m **1.** Tech. removal, disassembly, dismounting; **2.** (Erweiterung) extension, expansion; (Umbau) conversion, alteration; **3.** (Fertigstellung) completion; (Innenausbau) interior works Pl. (of the building); **4.** Bergb. (Grubenausbau) timbering, lining, complete tubing; **5.** fig. (Weiterentwicklung) development, improvement

ausbauen v/t. (trennb., hat -ge-) **1.** Tech. remove, disassemble, dismount; **2.** (erweitern) (Flughafen, Haus etc.) extend; (Straße) improve; (umbauen) convert (**zu** to); **den Dachboden/Keller ~** convert the loft/cellar (Am. basement); **ein gut ausgebautes Straßennetz** a well-developed road network; **3.** fig. (weiterentwickeln) develop, improve; **den Vorsprung /** Sport increase (od. consolidate) one's lead; **seine Position ~** fig. consolidate (od. strengthen) one's position; **4.** (Wein) in Eichenfass etc.: etwa (further) improve; **ausbaufähig** Adj. Haus, Wohnung: extendable; Politik, Beziehungen etc.: capable of development (od. expansion); berufliche Stellung: with good prospects; Markt: expandable

Ausbau|strecke f section of improved road; Schild: **Ende der ~** etwa road narrows; **~stufe** f von Kraftwerk, Flughafen etc.: stage of further development

ausbedingen v/refl. (unreg., trennb., hat): **sich** (Dat.) **etw.** ~ insist on s.th.; **sich ~, dass ...** stipulate that ..., make it a condition that ...; **sich das Recht ~, etw. zu tun** reserve the right to do s.th.

ausbeißen v/t. (unreg., trennb., hat -ge-): **sich** (Dat.) **e-n Zahn ~** break a tooth (**an** + Dat. on); **sich** (Dat.) **die Zähne an j-m/etw. ~** fig. find s.o./s.th. a tough nut to crack; **sich** (Dat.) **an e-nem Problem die Zähne ~** fig. sweat (od. agonize) over a problem

ausbekommen v/t. (unreg., trennb., hat -ge-); mst verneint; umg. (Schuhe) get off

ausbessern v/t. (trennb., hat -ge-) **1.** (Beschädigtes) mend, repair, fix; (Bild etc.) touch up; (Gemälde) restore; **2.** (Fehler etc.) correct; (Schaden) repair; **Ausbesserung** f (Korrektur) correction; (Reparatur) repair; **Ausbesserungsarbeiten** Pl. repairs, repair work Sg.; **ausbesserungsbedürftig** Adj. in need of repair, run-down

ausbetonieren v/t. (trennb., hat) concrete (s.th. over)

ausbeulen (trennb., hat -ge-) **I.** v/t. **1.** **du hast d-e Hose ganz ausgebeult** your trousers have gone all baggy; → **ausgebeult; 2.** Tech., Mot. beat out; **II.** v/refl. Kleidung: go baggy

Ausbeute f (Gewinn) gain(s Pl.), profit; (Ertrag) yield, output (auch Tech. und Bergb.); fig. (Ergebnisse) results Pl.; **e-e reiche ~** rich pickings

ausbeuten v/t. (trennb., hat -ge-) exploit (auch Rohstoffe etc.); **Ausbeuter** m; -s, -, **Ausbeuterin** f; -, -nen exploiter, slave-driver; **Ausbeuterbetrieb** m sweatshop; **ausbeuterisch** Adj. exploitative; **Ausbeutung** f exploitation (auch von Rohstoffen etc.)

ausbezahlen v/t. (trennb., hat) (etw.) pay out; (j-n) pay off

ausbilden (trennb., hat -ge-) **I.** v/t. **1.** (bilden) educate; (schulen) instruct, train (**in** in, **als** od. **zu** as); Mil. train, drill; Sport train, coach; **sich ~ lassen** train (**in** in, **als** od. **zu** as); (studieren) study (to be s.th.); **2.** (entwickeln) develop; (gestalten) design; (formen) shape, form; (Fähigkeiten) cultivate; **3.** Bio. grow, develop; **II.** v/refl. **1.** train; (studieren) study (**zu** to be); **sich ~ in** (+ Dat.) learn about, study, train in; (sich qualifizieren) qualify in od. as s.th.; → **ausgebildet; 2.** Fähigkeiten, Blätter, Organe: form, develop

Ausbilder m; -s, -, **~in** f; -, -nen instructor (auch Mil.)

Ausbildung f **1.** training; akademische: education; **2.** (Entwicklung) development

Ausbildungs|beihilfe f (study od. training) grant, Am. auch tuition aid; **~beruf** m Wirts. (semi-)skilled trade; **~betrieb** m Wirts. company that takes on trainees; **~dauer** f training (od. qualification) period; **~förderung** f (finanzielle Unterstützung) grant(s Pl.); **~kosten** Pl. cost Sg. of studying (od. of a period of training, of a traineeship); **~lager** n training camp; **~leiter** m, **~leiterin** f chief instructor (od. trainer); **~platz** m Wirts. traineeship; bei Handwerk: apprenticeship; **~stätte** f training cen|tre (Am. -er); **~vergütung** f training grant (od. remuneration); **~verhältnis** n **sie steht noch im ~** she is still a trainee, she still has a trainee position; **~versicherung** education(al endowment) insurance; **~vertrag** m articles Pl. of apprenticeship; **~zeit** f → **Ausbildungsdauer**

ausbitten v/t. (unreg., trennb., hat -ge-); geh.: **sich** (Dat.) **etw.** ~ ask for s.th., request s.th.; (verlangen) expect s.th., demand s.th.

ausblasen v/t. (unreg., trennb., ist -ge-) **1.** (Kerze etc.) blow out; **2.** (Ei) blow;

3. (Dampf, Rauch) blow off

ausbleiben v/i.; (unreg., trennb., ist -ge-) **1.** (nicht kommen) Erfolg, Folgen etc.: not come, fail to materialize; Regen: fail to arrive; Ereignis: not take place; Gäste etc.: not come (od. show, turn up); (wegbleiben) stay away; **es konnte nicht ~, dass ...** it was inevitable that ...; **i-e Periode blieb aus** she missed her period; **2.** (aussetzen) Atmung, Puls: stop; **3.** (nicht heimkommen) stay out

Ausbleiben n; -s, kein Pl. absence; e-r Zahlung: non-payment; Jur. default

ausbleichen[1] v/t. (trennb., hat -ge-) bleach

ausbleichen[2] v/i. (unreg., trennb., ist -ge-) (bleich werden) bleach, fade

ausblenden (trennb., hat -ge-) Funk. **I.** v/t. fade out; plötzlich: cut out; **II.** v/refl. go off the air, leave the (od. a) broadcast

Ausblick m (auf + Akk.) **1.** view (of); **2.** fig. forward look (at), preview (of); (Aussichten) outlook (for), prospects Pl. (for); **ausblicken** v/i. (trennb., hat -ge-); lit.: **nach j-m ~** look out for s.o., keep an eye out for s.o.

ausblühen v/i. (trennb., -ge-) **1.** (hat ausgeblüht) **ausgeblüht haben** Blumen: be finished; **2.** (ist) Chem., Min. effloresce

ausbluten v/i. (trennb., -ge-) **1.** (hat ausgeblutet) Wunde: stop bleeding; **2.** (ist) Schlachttier: bleed (dry); (verbluten) bleed to death; **~ lassen** bleed; **3.** (ist) fig. be bled dry (od. white); → **ausgeblutet**

ausbomben v/t. (trennb., hat -ge-) bomb out; → **ausgebombt**

ausbooten v/t. (trennb., hat -ge-) **1.** Naut. take ashore, disembark; **2.** umg. fig. oust, get rid of

ausborgen v/t. (trennb., hat -ge-); umg. → **ausleihen**

ausbrechen (unreg., trennb., -ge-) **I.** v/i. (ist ausgebrochen) **1.** (sich befreien) aus e-m Gefängnis, Käfig: break out (**aus** of), escape (**aus** from); Mil. escape; fig. aus e-r Gemeinschaft, auch Sport: break away (**aus** from); **2.** Haken, Halterung: break off, come away (**aus** from); **3.** Auto, Pferd, seitlich: swerve, veer; (außer Kontrolle geraten) Auto: career (od. veer) out of control; Pferd: bolt; **4.** Feuer, Krieg, Seuche etc.: break out; Vulkan: erupt; Ölquelle: blow out; Beifall, Jubel: erupt, explode; → **Wohlstand; 5.** in Schweiß ~ break out in a sweat; **j-m bricht der Schweiß aus** s.o. breaks into a sweat; **in Beifall ~** break into applause; **in Gelächter/Tränen ~** burst out laughing/crying, burst into laughter/tears; **II.** v/t. (hat) **1.** (losbrechen) break out (od. off); (Steine) quarry (out); **sich** (Dat.) **e-n Zahn ~** break one's tooth; **2.** (Fenster, Tür) put in; **3.** Agr. (unerwünschte Triebe abschneiden) prune, lop (off); **4.** (erbrechen) vomit, bring up

Ausbrecher m; -s, -, **~in** f; -, -nen escaped prisoner (od. convict), escapee; **Ausbrecherkönig** m, **Ausbrecherkönigin** f (habitual) jail-breaker, escape artist

ausbreiten (trennb., hat -ge-) **I.** v/t. **1.** allg. spread (out); (Arme, Flügel) auch stretch out, extend; (Landkarte etc.) auch unfold, spread out; (Waren) lay out; (Werkzeug etc.) display; **mit ausgebreiteten Armen** with arms spread; **sein Leben** etc. **vor j-m ~** fig.

lay one's (whole) life *etc.* out before s.o.; **2.** *fig.* (*Macht*) extend; (*Geschäft etc.*) expand; **II.** *v/refl.* **1.** *Feuer, Gerücht, Krankheit etc.*: spread (**auf** + *Akk.* to); *sich* ~ *auf* (+ *Akk.*) *Kämpfe etc.*: *auch* spill over into; **2.** (*sich erstrecken*) spread, stretch (out), extend (*alle* **auf** + *Akk.* to) (*vor j-m* before [*od.* in front of] s.o.'s eyes / s.o.); **3.** *umg.* (*sich breit machen*) spread o.s. out; **4.** *fig. auch pej.* (*ausführlich werden*) go into detail, go on about; *über ein Thema*: enlarge on; *verweilen*: dwell (*od.* brood) on; **Ausbreitung** *f*; *nur Sg. -s Gerüchts etc.*: spreading; *der Macht*: extension; expansion

ausbremsen *v/t.* (*trennb., hat -ge-*): *j-n* ~ *mit dem Auto*: cut s.o. up, cut in in front of s.o.; *umg. fig.* outwit s.o., trick s.o.

ausbrennen (*unreg., trennb., -ge-*) **I.** *v/i.* (*ist*) **1.** *Feuer, Kerze*: burn (itself) out, go out; **2.** *Haus etc.*: be burnt out, be gutted; **II.** *v/t.* (*hat*) **1.** (*Ungeziefer*) burn out; **2.** *Med.* (*Wunde*) cauterize; **3.** (*Erde etc.*) scorch, parch; → *ausgebrannt* II

ausbringen *v/t.* (*unreg., trennb., hat -ge-*) **1.** *Naut.* (*Boot*) lower, launch; (*Anker*) drop; **2.** *Agr.* (*Saatgut*) sow; (*Dünger*) spread; **3.** *Druck.* (*Zeile*) space out; **4.** *e-n Toast* ~ *auf j-n* / *j-s Gesundheit* propose a toast to s.o. / s.o.'s health, toast s.o. / propose (*od.* drink) s.o.'s health; **5.** *umg.* (*ausbekommen*) (*Schuh etc.*) get off; **6.** *altm. od. schw.* (*Geheimnis*) let out, divulge; **Ausbringung** *f* **1.** *Naut.* (*Boot*) lowering, launch(ing); (*Anker*) dropping; **2.** *Agr.* (*Saatgut*) sowing; (*Dünger*) spreading; **3.** *Druck.* spacing out

Ausbruch *m* **1.** *e-r Krankheit, e-s Kriegs etc.*: outbreak; *e-s Vulkans*: eruption; *e-r Ölquelle*: blow-out; (*Gefühlsausbruch*) outburst; *zum* ~ *kommen* break out; *Gefühle*: *auch* erupt, boil over; *stärker*: explode; *hat er oft solche Ausbrüche?* does he often have these outbursts?; **2.** (*Flucht*) escape; *von mehreren*: breakout; **3.** *Agr.* wine from selected fully ripe grapes

ausbruchsicher *Adj.* escape-proof

Ausbruchsversuch *m* escape attempt; *Mil.* sortie, sally

ausbrüten *v/t.* (*trennb., hat -ge-*) **1.** hatch out; *künstlich*: incubate; **2.** *fig.* (*Pläne etc.*) hatch (*od.* cook) up; *umg.* (*Krankheit*) be getting (*od.* coming down with)

ausbuchten *v/t.* → *ausgebuchtet*; **Ausbuchtung** *f* projection, bulge; *Tech. auch* protrusion; *e-r Küste*: indentation; *zum Parken*: lay-by

ausbuddeln *v/t.* (*trennb., hat -ge-*); *umg.* dig up (*auch fig.*)

ausbügeln *v/t.* (*trennb., hat -ge-*) iron out (*auch umg. fig.*); *und ich soll das wohl* ~? and I'm supposed to sort out your mess, am I?

ausbuhen *v/t.* (*trennb., hat -ge-*): *j-n* ~ boo at s.o.; *bei Bühnenauftritt*: boo s.o. off (the stage)

Ausbund *m*; *-(e)s, kein Pl.* model (*an* + *Dat. od. von* of); *ein* ~ *an Tugend* a paragon of virtue; *ein* ~ *von Bosheit* a real villain, evil personified; *ein* ~ *von Dummheit* an arrant fool

ausbürgern *v/t.* (*trennb., hat -ge-*) denaturalize, expatriate; **Ausbürgerung** *f* expatriation

ausbürsten *v/t.* (*trennb., hat -ge-*); (*Haare*) brush; (*Jacke etc.*) brush down; (*Fleck*) brush out

ausbüxen *v/i.* (*trennb., ist -ge-*); *umg., von zu Hause*: run away (from home); (*sich verdrücken*) do a bunk, *Am.* take a powder; bugger off *Sl.*, *Am.* bug off *Sl.*; *j-m* ~ run away from s.o.

auschecken ['aʊstʃɛkn] *v/t/i.* (*trennb., hat -ge-*) *Flug., Hotel etc.*: check out (*aus* + *Dat.* of); *hast du schon* (*dein Gepäck*) *ausgecheckt?* have you picked up (your luggage *od. Am.* baggage) yet?

Ausdauer *f* staying power; (*Beharrlichkeit*) perseverance; (*Zähigkeit*) tenacity; (*Geduld*) patience; (*körperliche*) stamina; **Ausdauergrenze** *f* (physical) limit; **ausdauernd I.** *Adj.* **1.** persevering; (*geduldig*) enduring; (*zäh*) tenacious, persistent; *Läufer, Schwimmer etc.*: tireless; *präd.* with staying power, with stamina; **2.** *Bot.* perennial.; **II.** *Adv.*: ~ *lernen können* be able to study for long stretches; **Ausdauertraining** *n* stamina training

ausdehnbar *Adj. Tech.* extensible; *Wirts.* expansible

ausdehnen (*trennb., hat -ge-*) **I.** *v/t.* **1.** (*Gummiband, Kleidung*) stretch; *Phys., Tech. in die Länge*: stretch, elongate; *räumlich*: expand, extend, enlarge; *bes. durch Wärme*: dilate; **2.** (*auf* + *Akk.*) (*Gesetz, Macht etc.*) extend (to); (*Geschäft etc.*) expand (into); *die Suche* ~ extend the search (*auf* + *Akk.* to); **3.** *zeitlich*: (*Reise tec.*) extend, prolong; → *ausgedehnt* II; **II.** *v/refl.* **1.** *Phys.* stretch; *räumlich*: expand; *bes. durch Wärme*: dilate; **2.** (*sich verbreiten*) spread; *Stadt*: expand, spread; *sich rasch* ~ *über* (+ *Akk.*) *auch* sweep across; **3.** (*sich erstrecken*) extend, stretch (out); *zeitlich*: last, extend; *pej.* drag on (*über* + *Akk.* for)

Ausdehnung *f* **1.** extension (*auch Phys.*), expansion; (*Spanne*) spread; **2.** (*Ausmaß, Bereich, Umfang*) extent, scope, range

Ausdehnungs|gefäß *n Heizung*: expansion tank; ~**koeffizient** *m Phys.* coefficient of expansion (*od.* dilation)

ausdenken *v/t.* (*unreg., trennb., hat -ge-*): *sich* (*Dat.*) *etw.* ~ think *s.th.* up, come up with; (*Plan etc.*) *auch* work out; (*erfinden*) dream up; *es ist nicht auszudenken* it doesn't bear thinking about, it's too dreadful to think about; (*ist unvorstellbar*) the mind boggles (at the thought); *da musst du dir schon was anderes* ~ you don't think I'm going to buy that(, do you?), you'll have to come up with s.th. better than that; *ich hatte mir das so schön ausgedacht* (*vorgestellt*) I had it all so nicely planned

ausdeuten *v/t.* (*trennb., hat -ge-*) interpret; *falsch* ~ misinterpret; **Ausdeutung** *f* interpretation

ausdienen *v/i.* → *ausgedient*

ausdiskutieren *v/t.* (*trennb., hat*) discuss *s.th.* fully (*od.* thoroughly); thrash *s.th.* out *umg.*

ausdorren *v/i.* (*trennb., ist -ge-*) → *ausdörren* I

ausdörren (*trennb., -ge-*) **I.** *v/i.* (*ist*) dry up; *Felder etc.*: *auch* become parched; *m-e Kehle ist wie ausgedörrt* my throat's absolutely parched; **II.** *v/t.* (*hat*) dry up, become parched; (*Pflanze*) wither (up)

ausdrehen *v/t.* (*trennb., hat -ge-*) turn off, switch off

Ausdruck¹ *m*; *-(e)s, Ausdrücke* **1.** (*Wort*) word, term; (*Redewendung*)

expression, phrase; *idiomatischer* ~ idiomatic expression, idiom; *ordinärer* ~ vulgar expression, vulgarism; *technischer* ~ technical term; *veralteter* ~ obsolete expression, archaism; *Ausdrücke gebrauchen* use swearwords, curse; *sie hat sich im* ~ *vergriffen* her choice of words was most unfortunate; *ärgerlich? - das ist gar kein* ~ annoyed? – that's putting it mildly!; **2.** *nur Sg.* expression; *e-m Gefühl etc.* ~ *geben od. verleihen* put into words, give expression to, express; *zum* ~ *bringen* express, voice; *zum* ~ *kommen* be expressed, find expression, manifest itself (*in* + *Dat.* in); *der Erwartung* ~ *geben, dass ...* express the hope that; *als* ~ *m-r Dankbarkeit* as a sign (*od.* token) of my gratitude; *mit dem* ~ *tiefen Bedauerns/Mitgefühls* with deepest regret/sympathy; **3.** *mst Sg.*; (*Gesichtsausdruck*) expression; *ohne jeden* ~ *in der Stimme*: in a deadpan tone; **4.** *nur Sg.* → *Ausdrucksweise*

Ausdruck² *m*; *-(e)s, -e*; *EDV* printout

ausdrucken *v/t.* (*trennb., hat -ge-*) print; *EDV* print out; (*voll* ~) print in full

ausdrücken (*trennb., hat -ge-*) **I.** *v/t.* **1.** (*Schwamm, Zitrone, Pickel etc.*) squeeze (out); **2.** (*Flüssigkeit*) squeeze out (*aus* of); **3.** (*Zigarette*) stub (*od.* put) out; (*Kerze*) pinch (*od.* put) out; **4.** (*formulieren*) express, put into words; *anders ausgedrückt* in other words, to put it another way; *einfach ausgedrückt* to put it simply (*od.* in simple terms); *in Zahlen etc. ausgedrückt* (given *od.* expressed) in numbers; **5.** (*zeigen*) *Haltung, Verhalten etc.*: express, show; *Gesicht: auch* register; **II.** *v/refl.* **1.** *Person*: express o.s.; *drück dich bitte verständlich od. klarer aus* please explain yourself more clearly; *um mich höflich auszudrücken* to put it politely; **2.** *Einstellung, Gefühle etc.*: be revealed

ausdrücklich I. *Adj.* express, (*explizit*) explicit; *Befehl*: strict; (*absichtlich*) intentional; **II.** *Adv.* expressly; (*besonders*) specially; (*absichtlich*) on purpose

Ausdruckskraft *f*; *nur Sg.* expressiveness, expressive power

ausdruckslos *Adj.* expressionless; *Blick, Miene*: *auch* blank, vacant; *Stimme*: deadpan; ~*es Gesicht* poker face; **Ausdruckslosigkeit** *f*; *nur Sg.* expressionlessness, lack of expressiveness; *e-s Blickes*: vacancy, blankness

ausdrucks|schwach *Adj.* unexpressive, weak; ~**stark** *Adj.* (very) expressive

Ausdrucks|tanz *m*; *nur Sg.* character dance; ~**vermögen** *n* ability to express o.s., powers *Pl.* of expression, articulatory powers *Pl.*

ausdrucksvoll *Adj.* (very) expressive; *Blick etc.*: meaningful, significant

Ausdrucksweise *f* way of expressing o.s., wording; (*Stil*) style, diction; *weitS.* language

ausdünnen *v/t.* (*trennb., hat -ge-*) thin out; **Ausdünnung** thinning out

ausdunsten, ausdünsten (*trennb., hat -ge-*) **I.** *v/t.* give off; **II.** *v/i.* evaporate; *Körper*: transpire (*auch Bot.*), perspire; **Ausdunstung** *f*, **Ausdünstung** *f* emanation; *e-r Flüssigkeit*: evaporation; (*Schweiß*) perspiration

auseinander *Adv.* apart; (*getrennt*) *auch* separated; *weit* ~ *räumlich*: be, li-

ve a long way away from each other; *move* apart (*od.* away) from each other; *zeitlich*: (*be*) years (*od. decades etc.*) apart; *fig.* be light-years away from each other; **~ bekommen** get *s.th.* apart; **~ biegen** bend *s.th.* apart; **~ brechen** (*e-n Gegenstand*) break (up); *in zwei Teile*: break in two; *Freundschaft, Beziehung, Bündnis etc.*: break up; **~ breiten** (*Arme, Flügel*) unfold; (*Landkarte etc.*) *auch* spread out; **~ bringen** (*Menschen*) separate, split up; (*etw.*) get *s.th.* apart; **~ dividieren** (*Rechnung*) break down; (*Meinungen etc.*) draw a clear dividing line between; (*Leute*) drive a wedge between; **~ fahren** *fig.* jump (*Köpfe*: jerk) apart; **~ fallen** fall apart (*od.* to pieces); disintegrate; **~ falten** unfold; (*Landkarte etc.*) *auch* spread out; (*auch Zeitung*) open up; **~ fließen** Farbe *etc.*: run; **~ gehen** (*sich verabschieden*) say goodbye; *Menge*: break up, disperse; (*e-e Beziehung beenden*) split up, break up, go one's separate ways; *Ehe*: break up; *Verlobung*: be broken off; *Linien, Wege*: diverge; *Meinungen*: be divided; *umg. Geklebtes etc.*: come (*od.* fall) apart; *umg.* (*dick werden*) fill out, get fat; **~ halten** *fig.* (*unterscheiden*) distinguish (between); *visuell*: *auch* tell … apart; (*trennen*) keep … apart; **~ klaffen** gape; *fig. Meinungen*: differ enormously; **~ klamüsern** *umg.* sort out *allg.*; *j-m etw.* **~ klamüsern** *umg.* spell *s.th.* out to (*od.* for) s.o., explain the ins and outs of *s.th.* to s.o.; **~ kriegen** *umg. s.th.* apart; **~ laufen** *Personen*: run in different directions; *Linien, Wege*: diverge; *Farbe etc.*: run; **sich ~ leben** drift (*od.* grow) apart; **~ nehmen** take apart, tear to pieces (*auch umg. fig. Gegner, Buch etc.*); **~ reißen** tear apart; **~ schneiden** cut *s.th.* apart; (*zerteilen*) cut *s.th.* in two; *etw.* **~ schreiben** write *s.th.* as two words; **~ sein** (*nicht mehr befreundet sein*) have split up, have had a parting of the ways; **sie sind drei Jahre ~** they're three years apart, there are three years between them; **~ setzen** (*Kinder*) separate, make *the children* sit apart; *j-m etw.* **~ setzen** *fig.* explain (*schriftlich*: set out) *s.th.* to s.o.; **sich mit j-m ~ setzen** argue with s.o. (*über + Akk.* about *od.* over); *gründlich*: have it out with s.o. *umg.*; **sich mit e-m Problem etc.** **~ setzen** go into, tackle; *stärker*: grapple with; **~ spreizen** (*Finger, Zehen*) spread out, splay; *weit* **~ stehen** *Augen*: be wide-set; *Zeilen*: have big gaps (between them); **~ stellen** (*Tische etc.*) place (*od.* put) apart from each other; **~ stieben** scatter; **~ streben** *Linien*: diverge; **~ treiben** *Boote etc.*: drift apart; (*Tiere*) *auch* scatter; (*Demonstranten*) disperse; **~ ziehen** *in Teile*: pull apart; *in die Länge*: stretch; (*e-e gemeinsame Wohnung aufgeben*) move out (into separate accommodation); **sich ~ ziehen** *Autokolonne, Teilnehmerfeld bei e-m Rennen*: string out

Auseinandersetzung *f* **1.** (*Streit*) argument; *bes. Pol.* dispute; (*Zusammenstoß*) clash(es *Pl.*); **kriegerische / blutige ~** armed conflict / violent clash; **2.** (*kritische Beschäftigung*) (critical) analysis, examination (**mit** of); *mit e-m Problem etc.*: *auch* attempt to come to terms (**mit** with); **3.** (*Erörterung*) discussion, debate

auserkoren *Adj. geh.* chosen

auserlesen *Adj.* choice, chosen; *Publikum*: select

ausersehen *v/t.* (*unreg., trennb., hat*) choose, select (**für, zu** for); *für ein Amt*: designate (for)

auserwählen *v/t.* (*trennb., hat*) choose; **auserwählt** *Adj.*: **das ~e Volk** the Chosen People; **die Auserwählten** the elect, the chosen few; **s-e Auserwählte** *umg.* his number one girl; **ihr Auserwählter** *umg.* her number one man

ausfädeln *v/refl.* (*trennb., hat -ge-*) *im Straßenverkehr*: filter out (**aus** of); *auf der Autobahn*: get into the exit lane

ausfahrbar *Adj. Tech.* telescopic; *Fahrwerk etc.*: extendible

ausfahren (*unreg., trennb., -ge-*) **I.** *v/i.* (*ist*) **1.** (*Ausflug machen*) go for a drive; **2.** *Zug*: pull out (**aus** from), leave; *Schiff*: put to sea, set sail; *Bergb.* come up, leave the pit (*od.* mine); **3.** *Fahrwerk etc.*: lower; **4. aus j-m** *Geist etc.*: leave s.o.('s body); **II.** *v/t.* (*hat*) **1.** (*j-n*) take out for a drive; (*Kind im Wagen*) walk; **2.** (*Pakete etc.*) deliver; **3.** *Tech.* (*Fahrgestell*) lower, let down; (*Antenne, Leiter*) pull out, extend; *Landeklappen* extend; (*Periskop*) raise; **4.** *Tech.* (*voll ausnutzen*) (*Auto*) run … up to top speed (*od.* flat out); (*Anlage*) utilize to capacity; **5.** (*Kurve*) round; **6.** (*beschädigen*) (*Weg etc.*) rut, damage; → **ausgefahren** II; **7.** *Naut.* (*Anker*) run out; (*Leine*) lay out; (*Pontonbrücke*) construct

Ausfahrer *m; -s, -,* **~in** *f; -, -nen männlich*: delivery man; *weiblich*: delivery woman

Ausfahrt *f* **1.** *Tor, Weg*: exit; *länger*: driveway; *von Autobahn*: exit; **~ freihalten** Exit: (please) keep clear!; **2.** (*Ausflug*) drive, ride; **eine ~ machen** go (out) for a run (*od.* spin); **3.** (*Abfahrt, auch Naut.*) departure; **4.** *Bergb.* ascent

Ausfahrts|signal *n* *Eisenb.* starting-signal, signal for departure; **~straße** *f* exit (road)

Ausfall *m* **1.** *nur Sg.*; *der Haare etc.*: loss; **2.** *des Unterrichts etc.*: cancel(l)ation; **3.** *Tech.* (*Versagen*) failure, breakdown; (*der Produktion*) stoppage; *e-s Arbeiters, Sportlers*: (*Abwesenheit*) absence; (*Absage*) dropping out, retirement; (*Verdienstausfall*) loss (of earnings), drop (in earnings); **ein glatter ~** *umg. pej.* (*Spieler*) a dead (*Am.* total) loss; **5.** *Sport, Fechten*: lunge, lunging, thrust; *auch Turnen*: splits *Pl.*; *Gewichtheben*: jerk; **6.** *Mil. aus e-r Festung*: sally, sortie; **7.** *fig.* (*Beschimpfung*) invective, (abusive) attack; **8.** (*Ergebnis*) outcome, result

Ausfallbürgschaft *f* *Wirts.* deficiency guarantee

ausfallen *v/i.* (*unreg., trennb., ist -ge-*) **1.** *Zähne, Haare, Federn*: fall out; **ihr sind die Haare ausgefallen** her hair fell out; **2.** (*nicht stattfinden*) be cancel(l)ed, be called off; **~ lassen** cancel; **die Schule fällt heute aus** (there's) no school today; **3.** *Tech.* (*versagen*) break down, fail; **bei uns ist der Strom ausgefallen** we've had a power cut (*od.* blackout); **4.** *Arbeiter wegen Krankheit etc.*: be absent; *Sportler im Wettkampf*: pull out, drop out; *Einnahmen, Verdienst*: be lost; **5.** **gut / schlecht ~** *Ergebnis*: turn out well / badly/satisfactorily; *Prüfung*: go well *etc.*; **wie ist die Prüfung ausgefallen?** *für dich*: how did you do in the ex-

am?; *insgesamt*: what were the exam results like?; **es fiel anders aus, als ich erwartet habe** it turned out (rather) differently to (*Am.* from) what I expected; **6.** *Chem.* be precipitated; **7.** *Mil. altm.* make a sortie, sally out

ausfällen *v/t.* (*trennb., hat -ge-*); *Chem.* precipitate

ausfallend I. *Part. Präs.* → **ausfallen**; **II.** *Adj.* → **ausfällig**; **ausfällig** *Adj.* offensive; **~ werden** get personal (*od.* abusive)

Ausfall|quote *f* *Wirts.* failure rate; *in e-m Beruf etc.*: dropout rate; **~schritt** *m* *Sport* dodge, lunge step; *seitlich*: *auch* side-step

Ausfallerscheinung *f* *Med.* deficiency symptom

Ausfallstor *n* **1.** *hist.* sally gate; **2.** *fig.* gateway

Ausfallstraße *f* arterial road

Ausfallswinkel *m* angle of reflection

Ausfällung *f* *Chem.* precipitation

Ausfallzeit *f* *Wirts.* down time; *Versicherung*: excluded period

ausfaltbar *Adj. Stadtplan etc.*: folding; **ausfalten** *v/t.* (*trennb., hat -ge-*) (*Stadtplan etc.*) fold open, open out

ausfechten *v/t.* (*unreg., trennb., hat -ge-*) fight out; **mit j-m e-n Streit ~** *umg.* have it out with s.o.

ausfegen (*trennb., hat -ge-*); *bes. nordd.* **I.** *v/t.* sweep out; (*Zimmer*) *auch* sweep; **II.** *v/i.* sweep the floor

ausfeilen *v/t.* (*trennb., hat -ge-*) **1.** file, smooth down; **2.** *fig.* (*Rede, Aufsatz etc.*) polish (up), add the finishing touches to

ausfertigen *v/t.* (*trennb., hat -ge-*); (*ausstellen*) issue; *Jur.* (*Urkunde*) execute; (*Rechnungen*) make out; **Ausfertigung** *f* *nur Sg.*; (*Ausstellung*) issuing; *Jur.* execution; **2.** (*Abschrift*) (certified) copy; **in doppelter ~** in duplicate

ausfetten *v/t.* (*trennb., hat -ge-*) (*Backform etc.*) grease

ausfiltern *v/t.* (*trennb., hat -ge-*) filter out

ausfindig *Adv.*: **~ machen** find; (*aufspüren*) trace

ausflaggen *v/t.* (*trennb., hat -ge-*) **1.** (*Absperrung, Strecke etc.*) mark out … with flags, flag out; **2.** *Naut.* (*schmücken*) (flag-)dress, dress ship; **3.** *Naut.* (*nationale Flagge ändern*) sail under a new flag

ausflicken *v/t.* (*trennb., hat -ge-*) patch up

ausfliegen (*unreg., trennb., -ge-*) **I.** *v/i.* (*ist*) **1.** *Insekten, Vögel*: fly away; (*flügge werden*) leave the nest; **2.** *umg. fig.*: **sie sind alle ausgeflogen** they've all gone out (for the day), there's nobody at home, they've fled *hum.*; **II.** *v/t.* (*hat*) (*j-n*) fly out

ausfliesen *v/t.* (*trennb., hat -ge-*) (*Badezimmer etc.*) tile

ausfließen *v/i.* (*unreg., trennb., ist -ge-*) flow out (**aus** of); *Flüssigkeit, Fass*: run out (of), leak (from *od.* out of), flow (from), escape; *Eiter etc.*: seep (out of), be discharged (from); *Lava*: well out

ausflippen *v/i.* (*trennb., ist -ge-*); *Sl.* freak out, crack up; (*durchdrehen*) *auch* flip one's lid (*od.* top), go mad (*bes. Am.* crazy); → **ausgeflippt**

ausflocken (*trennb., hat -ge-*); *Chem.* **I.** *v/t.* (*hat*) flocculate, precipitate; *dicker*: coagulate; **II.** *v/i.* (*ist*) flocculate, precipitate; coagulate; **Ausflockung** *f* deflocculation; *dicker*: coagulation

Ausflucht f; -, *Ausflüchte, mst Pl.*; (*Vorwand*) excuse; **Ausflüchte machen** make excuses, prevaricate

Ausflug m excursion (*auch fig.*), outing, (day) trip; (*Spritzfahrt*) jaunt; **e-n ~ machen** go on a trip; **sie machte e-n kurzen ~ nach Brighton** she took a jaunt to Brighton; **Ausflügler** m; -s, -, **Ausflüglerin** f; -, *-nen* day tripper

Ausflugs|dampfer m excursion (*od.* pleasure) steamer (*od.* boat); **~lokal** n popular country pub (*Am.* inn), tourist café (*od.* bar); *am Meer*: seaside café; **~ort** m popular place for outings; *im Grünen*: *auch* beauty spot

Ausflugs|verkehr m weekend traffic, *Brit. auch* (bank) holiday (*Am.* holiday weekend) traffic; **~ziel** n day-trip destination

Ausfluss m **1.** outflow; *Med.* discharge; *von Urin*: *auch* leakage; **2.** (*Abfluss*) outlet, outflow; *von Gas od. Flüssigkeiten*: efflux *fachspr.*; *von Abwässern*: effluent; **3.** *geh. fig. der Fantasie etc.*: product (+ *Gen.* of); **~rohr** n discharge (*od.* drainage) pipe

ausformen (*trennb., hat -ge-*) **I.** v/t. form, shape; *Schriften etc.*: polish, refine; **II.** v/refl. form, take shape

ausformulieren v/t. (*trennb., hat*) formulate (properly); **ich muss es noch ~** I still have to work out how to put it (properly); **Ausformulierung** f formulation

Ausformung f **1.** *nur Sg.*; *Vorgang*: shaping, mo(u)lding; *Schriften etc.*: polishing, refining; **2.** *Ergebnis*: form, shape

ausforschen v/t. (*trennb., hat -ge-*) **1.** (*Versteck etc.*) seek out, find; (*Pläne etc.*) find out about, investigate; (*dahinter kommen*) get to the bottom of; **2.** *j-n ~* sound s.o. out, question s.o. (*über* + *Akk.* on, about); **3.** *österr.* (*Täter*) apprehend, find; **Ausforschung** f **1.** *von Absicht, Plan*: investigating, finding out; **2.** (*Befragung*) questioning; **3.** *österr.* finding

ausfragen v/t. (*trennb., hat -ge-*) question, quiz; *neugierig*: sound s.o. out; *scharf*: grill *umg.*, interrogate

ausfransen (*trennb., -ge-*) **I.** v/i. (*ist*) fray, become frayed; **II.** v/t. (*hat*) fringe, put a fringe on

ausfressen v/t. (*unreg., trennb., hat -ge-*) **1.** *Tier*: (*Trog etc.*) eat s.th. clean; (*Ei*) suck out; *umg. Mensch*: lick s.th. clean *umg.*; **2.** *umg.* (*anstellen*) be naughty (*od.* up to s.th.), do (s.th.) wrong; **er hat etwas ausgefressen** he's been up to something (*od.* his tricks *od.* no good); **was hast du denn nun schon wieder ausgefressen?** what have you (gone and) done this time(, then)?

ausfugen v/t. (*trennb., hat -ge-*); *Archit.* point, joint

Ausfuhr f; -, *-en*; *Wirts.* (*das Ausführen*) export(ing); (*Ausgeführtes*) exports *Pl.*; **~artikel** m export(ed) article

ausführbar *Adj.* **1.** practicable, feasible, workable; *nicht ~* impracticable, not feasible; *schwer ~* difficult to carry out; **2.** *Wirts.* exportable; **Ausführbarkeit** f; *nur Sg.* practicability, feasibility

Ausfuhr|beschränkung f *Wirts.* export restriction; **~bestimmungen** *Pl.* export regulations; **~bürgschaft** f export guarantee

ausführen v/t. (*trennb., hat -ge-*) **1.** (*j-n*) take out; (*Hund*) take ... for a walk; (*teures Kleidungsstück etc.*) pa-

rade (*od.* show off); **2.** *Wirts.* export; **3.** (*durchführen*) carry out; (*Plan*) *auch* put into effect, execute; (*Auftrag*) execute, *Am. auch* fill; (*Experiment*) *auch* conduct; (*Bau etc.*) erect, construct; (*Reparatur*) *auch* undertake; (*Idee*) realize; (*Verbrechen*) commit; perpetrate *förm.*; (*Operation, Konzert etc.*) perform; (*Kunstwerk, Tanzschritt etc.*) execute; (*Gemälde etc.*) do, paint; (*Strafstoß*) take; *Math.* (*Operation*) perform; **4.** (*darlegen*) explain, point out; (*im Detail erläutern*) *auch* elaborate on, specify; *argumentierend*: argue

ausführend I. *Part. Präs.* → **ausführen**; **II.** *Adj. Gewalt, Organ*: executive; **Ausführende** m, f; *-n, -n* soloist; (*Sänger*) singer; *Pl.* performers

Ausfuhr|genehmigung f *Wirts.* export licen|ce (*Am.* -se); **~güter** *Pl.* exports; **~hafen** m port of exit; **~land** n exporting country

ausführlich I. *Adj.* detailed; in-depth ...; *Brief*: long, lengthy; (*umfassend*) comprehensive, full, thorough; **~e Berichterstattung** in-depth (*od.* extended) coverage; **II.** *Adv.* in detail; in depth; *sehr ~* at great length, in great detail; **~er** in greater detail; **Ausführlichkeit** f; *nur Sg.* detail(ed nature); (*Vollständigkeit*) comprehensiveness; **etw. in aller ~ beschreiben** describe s.th. (right down) to the last detail, describe s.th. at great length

Ausfuhr|sperre f export embargo; **~überschuss** m export surplus

Ausführung f **1.** (*das Ausführen*) carrying out; *e-r Aufgabe, e-s Befehls, e-s Plans*: *auch* execution; *e-r Idee*: realization; *e-s Verbrechens*: perpetration; *e-s Gesetzes etc.*: implementation; *Mus.* performance; *e-s Kunstwerks*: execution; *e-s Baus*: construction; (*Fertigstellung*) completion; **zur ~ gelangen** be carried out (*od.* performed, built, implemented *etc.*); **bei ~ des Plans** in pursuance of the plan; **2.** *e-r Ware*: design; (*Stil*) style; (*Typ*) version; (*Modell*) model; (*Qualität*) workmanship, quality; (*Äußeres*) finish; **3.** (*Darlegung*) exposition; **~en** comments, remarks; *Pol. etc.* statement *Sg.*; (*Rede*) speech *Sg.* (*über* + *Akk. od. zu* on); **4.** *Wirts.* export(ation)

Ausführungsbestimmung f *Wirts.* regulation (*od.* statute) of implementation

Ausfuhrverbot n *Wirts.* ban on exports, export embargo

ausfüllen v/t. (*trennb., hat -ge-*) **1.** (*Grube, Loch*) fill; (*Ritzen etc.*) fill in; **2.** (*Formular*) fill in (*od.* out), complete; (*Scheck*) fill in, *bes. Am.* write out; (*Kreuzworträtsel*) do; *vollständig*: *auch* complete; **3.** *fig.* (*Lücke, Stellung*) fill; *s-n Posten gewissenhaft ~* do (*od.* carry out) one's job very conscientiously; **4.** *fig. Sache*: (*Raum, Zeitraum, Freizeit etc.*) take up; **5.** *fig.*: *j-n ~ zeitlich*: occupy s.o. completely, take up all (of) s.o.'s time; *gedanklich etc.*: completely absorb s.o.; (*befriedigen*) fulfil(l) s.o.; **sein Beruf füllt ihn ganz/nicht aus** his job fulfil(l)s him completely / doesn't fulfil(l) him (*od.* doesn't give him enough satisfaction)

Ausfüllung f; *nur Sg.* **1.** *von Löchern etc.*: filling (in *od.* up); *fig.* fulfil(l)ment; **2.** *e-s Formulars*: filling out, completion

ausfüttern v/t. (*trennb., hat -ge-*) line (*auch Tech.*)

Ausgabe f **1.** handing out; (*Verteilung*)

distribution; *von Essen*: serving; **2.** (*e-s Buchs etc.*) edition; (*Buchexemplar*) copy; *e-r Zeitschrift*: issue, number; *Nachrichten etc.*: release; **3.** *von Aktien, Briefmarken etc.*: issue, emission; *von Befehlen*: issue, issuance, briefing; **4.** (*von Geld*) expense, expenditure; *Pl. auch* spending *Sg.*; (*Unkosten*) cost (*Sg.*); **~n einschränken** curtail (*od.* limit) expenditure; **Einnahmen und ~n** receipt and expenditure; **laufende ~n** current expenses, running costs:; **5.** *EDV* output; **6.** (*Ausgabestelle*) counter, desk, office; **7.** (*das Spendieren*) treat(ing), footing the bill; **~datei** f *Computer*: output file; **~kurs** m *Wirts., Fin.* issue price, rate of issue

Ausgaben|begrenzung f *Wirts.* limit on expenditure; **~buch** n accounts book, (petty) cash book; **~kürzung** f expenditure cut, cut in expenditure; **~rückgang** m reduction in expenditure; **~seite** f expenditure column; **auf der ~** on the expenditure (*od.* outgoings) side; **~steigerung** f increase in expenditure

Ausgabestelle f **1.** *Wirts., Fin.* issuing office; **2.** *Mil.* supply point

Ausgang m **1.** (*Tür*) way out, exit; *am Flughafen*: (departure) gate; (*Ende*) *des Dorfes etc.*: end; *des Waldes*: *auch* edge; *der Höhle*: entrance; *des Darms*: opening, outlet; **2.** (*Ende*) end; *zeitlich*: *auch* close; *e-r Geschichte etc.*: ending; (*Ergebnis*) outcome, upshot, result; **tragischer ~** tragic end(ing) (*od.* outcome); **glücklicher ~** happy end(ing); **Unfall mit tödlichem ~** fatal accident, accident with fatal consequences; **e-n guten ~ nehmen** turn out well (*od.* all right, *Am. umg.* alright) in the end; **am ~ des Mittelalters** at the end (*od.* close) of the Middle Ages; **3.** (*Freizeit*) day (*od.* afternoon, evening) off; **~ haben** *Mil.* have a pass; **heute Abend hat m-e Frau ~** tonight is my wife's night out (*od.* off); **4.** *Wirts.* **Ausgänge** outgoings, *Am.* expenses (*od.* expenditures); (*Post*) outgoing mail *Sg.*; (*Waren*) outgoing stocks; **5.** *nur Sg* (*Anfang*) beginning; **s-n ~ nehmen von** start (*od.* originate) with, take *s.th.* as one's starting point

Ausgangs|basis f starting point; **~lage** f situation (*auch e-r Person*: position) at the outset; initial situation (*od.* conditions *Pl.*); **~leistung** f *Etech.* (power) output; **~position** f starting position; *e-s Gesprächs*: point of departure; **~punkt** m *auch fig.* starting point, point of departure; **~sperre** f curfew; **~ haben** be confined to barracks; **~sprache** f *Ling., Übersetzen*: source language; **~stellung** f starting position; *Mil.* line of departure; **~stoff** m basic material; **~stufe** f *Etech.* output stage; *Verstärker*: power stage; **~tür** f exit; **~widerstand** m *Etech.* output resistance

ausgebaut *P.P.* → **ausbauen**

ausgeben (*trennb., hat -ge-*) **I.** v/t. **1.** (*aushändigen*) hand out; (*austeilen*) distribute; (*Spielkarten*) deal; (*Essen*) serve; **2.** *fig.* (*Aktien, Banknoten, Befehl*) issue; (*Nachrichten*) release; **3.** *EDV* output; *auf dem Bildschirm*: display; (*ausdrucken*) print out; **4.** (*Geld*) spend (*für* on); **so viel wollte ich nicht ~** I wasn't planning on spending that much; **Geld mit vollen Händen ~** spend money like it's going out of style (*od.* like there was no tomorrow) *umg.*; **5.** *umg.*: *e-e Runde für alle* ~ buy everyone a drink, stand (*od.* buy) a round (for everyone); *ich geb dir einen aus* let me buy (*od.* get) you a drink; *ich geb einen aus* this one's on me, it's my treat; **6.** ~ *als* pass *s.o.* (*od. s.th.*) off as; **II.** *v/refl.*: **1.** *sich* ~ *als od. für* pass o.s. off as, pose as; **2.** *sich völlig* ~ *beim Sport etc.*: drive (*od.* push) o.s. to the limit

ausgebeult I. *P.P.* → *ausbeulen*; **II.** *Adj. Hose, Taschen*: baggy; *Auto, Hut*: dented

ausgebildet I. *P.P.* → *ausbilden*; **II.** *Adj.* trained; *mst akademisch*: qualified; *Arbeiter*: skilled

ausgeblutet I. *P.P.* → *ausbluten*; **II.** *Adj.*: ~ *sein* have been bled white (*od.* dry)

ausgebombt I. *P.P.* → *ausbomben*; **II.** *Adj.* bombed-out

ausgebrannt I. *P.P.* → *ausbrennen*; **II.** *Adj.* **1.** burnt-out; *nukleare Brennstäbe*: depleted, spent; *Haus*: *auch* gutted; **2.** *umg. fig.* burnt- (*od.* burned-)out

ausgebucht *Adj. Flug etc.*: full, booked-out ..., *präd.* booked out, fully booked; *Musiker etc.*: booked up, *Am.* sold out; *auf Monate* ~ booked (*Am.* sold) out (*od.* fully booked) for months ahead

ausgebuchtet *Adj.* widened, bulging; *Tech. auch* protruding; *e-r Küste*: indented

ausgebufft *Adj. umg.* (*gerissen*) fly, crafty, shrewd; *ein* ~*er Profi* a real pro

Ausgeburt *f geh. fig. pej.* **1.** monstrosity; (*Auswuchs*) excrescence; *e-e* ~ *i-r Fantasie* a vile product of her imagination; **2.** (*Ausbund*) *er ist e-e* ~ *von Hass* he's hatred incarnate (*od.* personified)

ausgedehnt I. *P.P.* → *ausdehnen*; **II.** *Adj.* **1.** *Fläche*: extensive, spacious; (*lang*) long; *eine* ~*e Fläche* a wide area (*od.* extent);; **2.** *zeitlich*: long, lengthy, extended; **3.** *fig. Suche etc.*: extensive; *weit* ~ far-flung

ausgedient *Adj. Spielsachen, alte Kleidungsstücke etc.*: worn-out; *Soldat*: ex--serviceman, veteran; *die alten* ~*en Sachen habe ich verschenkt* I've given away all the old things that are past use (*od.* using); ~ *haben Soldat etc.*: have retired; *umg. Sache*: have had it's day, have outlived it's usefulness

ausgedorrt, ausgedörrt *P.P.* → *ausdörren*

ausgefahren I. *P.P.* → *ausfahren*; **II.** *Adj. Weg etc.*: rutted; *sich in* ~*en Gleisen bewegen fig.* keep to the beaten track

ausgefallen I. *P.P.* → *ausfallen*; **II.** *Adj.* unusual (*auch Kleidung*), eccentric; off-beat *umg.*; strange *pej.*, weird *pej.*, peculiar *pej.*; ~*e Größe* odd size

ausgefeilt *P.P.* → *ausfeilen*

ausgeflippt I. *P.P.* → *ausflippen*; **II.** *Adj. umg.* freaky, weird; **Ausgeflippte** *m, f; -n, -n; umg.* freak, weirdo

ausgefuchst *Adj.* sly, sneaky

ausgeglichen I. *P.P.* → *ausgleichen*; **II.** *Adj. Mensch*: well-balanced, well--adjusted; *Charakter*: balanced; *Klima*: equable; *Wirts.* balanced, settled; *Spiel*: even, balanced-out; *Spielstand*: equal; **Ausgeglichenheit** *f; nur Sg.* balance, harmony; *des Wesens*: equanimity, balanced nature (*od.* character); *e-s Klimas*: equability

ausgegoren *Adj.* **1.** *Wein etc.*: fully fer-

mented; **2.** *mst verneint; fig. Ideen etc.*: mature, fully worked (*od.* thought) out; *der Plan ist noch nicht* ~ the plan is still in gestation (*od.* the planning stages)

ausgehen *v/i.* (*unreg., trennb., ist -ge-*) **1.** (*weggehen, auch zum Vergnügen*) go out; *zum Essen* ~ eat out; *mein Vater ist ausgegangen* my father's out (*od.* isn't in); **2.** ~ *von* (*kommen*) start from (*od.* at); *Anregung, Vorschlag*: come from; *Gefühl, Wärme*: radiate, emanate; *die Sache ging von ihm aus* it was his idea; *der Plan ging von der Regierung aus* the government initiated the plan; *von ihm geht e-e Ruhe/Begeisterungsfähigkeit aus* he radiates calm/enthusiasm; **3.** *fig.*: ~ *von* (*als Grundlage nehmen*) take *s.th.* as a starting point; *fig. bei e-r Entscheidung etc. von etw.* ~ base a decision etc. on s.th.; *wenn wir davon* ~, *dass* ... on the assumption that ..., assuming that ...; *ich gehe davon aus, dass* ... I'm assuming that ..., I'm working on the assumption that ...; *Sie dürfen davon* ~, *dass* ... you can assume (*od.* take it as read, *Am.* given) that ...; *Sie gehen von falschen Voraussetzungen aus* you're starting from false assumptions; **4.** (*resultieren*) end, turn out; *gut etc.* ~ turn out well *etc.*; *der Film geht gut/tragisch aus* the film has a happy ending / the film has a tragic ending, the film ends tragically (*od.* in tragedy); *wie ist die Sache ausgegangen?* how did it work out (*od.* end up)?; *wie ist das Spiel ausgegangen?* how did the match (*Am.* game) end?; *das Spiel ging 1:3 aus* the match (*Am.* game) ended 1-3; *unentschieden* ~ end in a draw; **5.** *Geld, Vorrat etc.*: run out; *allmählich*: run low; *uns ging das Geld / der Gesprächsstoff etc. aus* we ran out of money / things to say to each other; *ihm ging die Luft* (*umg.* die *Puste*) *aus* he ran out of breath (*fig.* steam); **6.** *Licht, Feuer etc.*: go out; *Dial. Kino, Schule etc.*: finish; **7.** *Haare, Federn etc.*: fall out; **8.** *straffrei* ~ go unprosecuted (*od.* unpunished), get off (*scot-free*) *umg.*; *leer* ~ come away empty-handed, end up with nothing; **9.** *auf etw.* (*Akk.*) ~ (*suchen*) be after, be out for, seek; **10.** ~ *auf* (+ *Akk.*) *Wort etc.*: end in (*od.* with, on); **11.** *Dial. Farbe*: run; *Stoff*: fade; **12.** *österr.*: (*sich*) ~ (*ausreichen*) be enough; (*aufgehen*) (*Rechnung*) work (*od.* go) out

ausgehend I. *Part.Präs.* → *ausgehen*; **II.** *Adj.* **1.** *zeitlich*: late *attr.*; *im* ~*en 20. Jahrhundert* towards the end (*od.* close) of the 20th century, in the late 20th century; **2.** *Post*: outgoing, outbound

ausgehfertig *Adj.* ready to go out *präd.*

ausgehöhlt *Adj.* **I.** *P.P.* → *aushöhlen*; **II.** hollow

ausgehungert I. *P.P.* → *aushungern*; **II.** *Adj.* half-starved; starving to death *umg.*; (*abgezehrt*) emaciated; *nach etw.* ~ *sein fig.* be starved of s.th.

Ausgeh|uniform *f* dress uniform; ~*verbot n Mil.* confinement to barracks; *weitS.* curfew

ausgeklügelt I. *P.P.* → *ausklügeln*; **II.** *Adj.* ingenious, clever; (*detailliert*) elaborate; *weitS.* sophisticated

ausgekocht I. *P.P.* → *auskochen*; **II.** *Adj. umg. pej.*: *ein* ~*er Betrüger* a

dirty cheat to the core (*od.* through and through), a thoroughly rotten apple

ausgelassen I. *P.P.* → *auslassen*; **II.** *Adj. Stimmung*: exuberant; *Person*: lively; chirpy *umg.*; *stärker, auch Kind*: boisterous; *Feier*: wild, crazy; **III.** *Adv. feiern*: exuberantly, wildly; *sich benehmen*: happily; *stärker, auch Kind*: boisterously; **Ausgelassenheit** *f; mst Sg.* exuberance, high spirits *Pl.*

ausgelastet I. *P.P.* → *auslasten*; **II.** *Adj.* **1.** *Maschine etc.*: running to capacity, working at full capacity; **2.** (*nicht*) *voll* ~ *sein Person*: be fully stretched (have too much time on one's hands); *ich fühle mich in der neuen Position nicht* ~ I don't feel fulfil(l)ed in my new position, my new job doesn't challenge me

ausgelatscht *Adj. umg.* worn(-out), out of shape

ausgelaugt I. *P.P.* → *auslaugen*; **II.** *Adj.* **1.** *Land etc.*: eroded; **2.** *fig. Person*: drained, washed-out, shattered

ausgelegt *P.P.* → *auslegen*

ausgeleiert I. *P.P.* → *ausleiern*; **II.** *Adj.* worn; (*ausgedehnt*) worn-out ..., out of shape, *präd.* worn out

ausgelernt I. *P.P.* → *auslernen*; **II.** *Adj.* qualified, fully trained

ausgelesen I. *P.P.* → *auslesen*; **II.** *Adj.* choice, select(ed)

ausgeliefert I. *P.P.* → *ausliefern*; **II.** *Adj.*: *j-m* ~ *sein* be at s.o.'s mercy; *sie war dieser Person völlig* ~ she was in complete subjection to this person; *e-r Sache hilflos* ~ *sein* be helpless in the face of s.th.; **Ausgeliefertsein** *n* helplessness; subjection *geh.*

ausgelitten *P.P.*: *sie hat* ~ her sufferings are over

ausgelutscht I. *P.P.* → *auslutschen*; **II.** *Adj. umg. fig.* (*Thema etc.*) done to death

ausgemacht I. *P.P.* → *ausmachen*; **II.** *Adj.* **1.** settled; ~*e Sache* foregone conclusion, accepted fact; **2.** *Gauner, Schlitzohr etc.*: complete (and utter), downright; *Skandal*: full(y)-blown; *ein* ~*er Unsinn* absolute nonsense; **III.** *Adv.* extremely, decidedly

ausgemergelt *P.P.* → *ausmergeln*

ausgenommen I. *P.P.* → *ausnehmen*; **II.** *Konj.* except (for), apart from, with the exception of; ~, *wenn* ... unless ...; saving that ... *geh.*, except ...; *alle,* ~ *er* all except (for) him, everyone apart from him, all but him; *Anwesende* ~ present company excepted; *ich komme,* ~ *ich werde krank* I'll come unless I'm ill

ausgepowert ['ausgəpo:vɐt] **I.** *P.P.* → *auspowern*; **II.** *Adj. umg.* burnt- (*od.* burned-)out, worn out, done in

ausgeprägt I. *P.P.* → *ausprägen*; **II.** *Adj.* distinct, marked, pronounced; *Gesichtszüge, Kinn*: prominent; *Profil*: very distinct; ~*er Sinn für Humor etc.* strongly developed sense of humo(u)r *etc.*

ausgepumpt I. *P.P.* → *auspumpen*; **II.** *Adj. umg.* done, *Am.* pooped

ausgerechnet I. *P.P.* → *ausrechnen*; **II.** *Adv. fig.* just, exactly; ~ *er* he (*od.* him) of all people; ~ *heute* today of all days; *warum musste es* ~ *mir passieren?* why did it have to happen to me (of all people)?; ~ *jetzt muss sie auftauchen* she would have to turn up (right) now (of all times)

ausgereift I. *P.P.* → *ausreifen*; **II.** *Adj.* **1.** completely ripe; *Käse*: *auch* mature (*auch Wein*); **2.** *fig. Idee etc.*: mature; *Konstruktion*: fully developed; **Ausgereiftheit** *f*; *nur Sg.* ripeness, maturity; *Tech.* (degree of) sophistication

ausgereizt *P.P.* → *ausreizen*

ausgerichtet *P.P.* → *ausrichten*

ausgeruht I. *P.P.* → *ausruhen*; **II.** *Adj.* (well) rested; *du siehst richtig ~ aus* auch you look as if you've had a good rest

ausgeschlafen I. *P.P.* → *ausschlafen*; **II.** *Adj.* **1.** (*auch gut ~*) well rested; **2.** *umg.* a) (*bei der Sache*) *präd.* with it, b) (*clever, gewitzt*) *präd.* on the ball, wide-awake, shrewd

ausgeschlossen I. *P.P.* → *ausschließen*; **II.** *Adj.* impossible, out of the question; *eine Gehaltserhöhung ist völlig ~* a (pay) rise (*Am.* raise) is completely out (of the question)

ausgeschnitten I. *P.P.* → *ausschneiden*; **II.** *Adj. Kleid*: low-cut; *tief ~* very low-cut

ausgesorgt I. *P.P.* → *aussorgen*; **II.** *Adj.*: *~ haben umg.* be sitting pretty; *sie hat für den Rest ihres Lebens ~* she won't have to worry about money for the rest of her days

ausgespielt *P.P.* → *ausspielen*

ausgesprochen I. *P.P.* → *aussprechen*; **II.** *Adj.* distinct, marked, pronounced; (*überzeugt*) decided; *das ist ~es Pech* that really is bad luck; *das ist ~er Unsinn* that's complete and utter nonsense; **III.** *Adv.* (*sehr*) really, extremely; (*typisch*) typically *British etc.*

ausgestalten *v/t.* (*trennb., hat -ge-*); (*Idee, Theorie etc.*) develop, elaborate; (*Fest etc.*) organize, arrange; (*Raum, Wohnung*) decorate

ausgestellt I. *P.P.* → *ausstellen*; **II.** *Adj.*: *~e Hosen* flared trousers, flares *Pl.*; *~er Rock* A-line skirt

ausgestorben I. *P.P.* → *aussterben*; **II.** *Adj.* **1.** *Tierart, Pflanzenart*: extinct; **2.** *Stadt etc.*: deserted; *wie ~ sein* be like a ghost town

Ausgestoßene *m, f*; *-n, -n* outcast

ausgesucht I. *P.P.* → *aussuchen*; **II.** *Adj.* **1.** (*erlesen*) exquisite, choice; *Gesellschaft*: select; **2.** *Höflichkeit*: exceptional, extreme; *Worte*: well-chosen; **III.** *Adv.* (*sehr*) exceptionally, extremely

ausgeträumt I. *P.P.* → *austräumen*; **II.** *Adj.*: *~ haben* have finished dreaming; *fig.* have woken up (*od.* awakened) to reality; *der Traum ist ~* that dream is over, the bubble has burst

ausgetreten I. *P.P.* → *austreten*; **II.** *Adj. Schuhe*: well-worn (*od.* -trodden), trodden-out; *Pfad*: well-trodden; *Stufe*: worn down; *~e Pfade gehen fig.* keep to the beaten track

ausgetrocknet *P.P.* → *austrocknen*

ausgewachsen I. *P.P.* → *auswachsen*; **II.** *Adj.* **1.** fully grown, full-grown; *Geweih etc.*: fully developed; **2.** *umg.* Betrüger etc.*: fully fledged, *Am.* full-fledged, outright; *Skandal etc.*: full-blown, major

ausgewählt I. *P.P.* → *auswählen*; **II.** *Adj.* **1.** *Ausdruck*: well-chosen, nicely chosen; **2.** *Gedichte, Werke*: selected (*von* by)

ausgewaschen I. *P.P.* → *auswaschen*; **II.** *Adj.* washed-out ...; *präd.* washed out; *bes. Jeans*: faded

ausgewechselt *P.P.* → *auswechseln*

Ausgewiesene *m, f*; *-n, -n Pol.* expellee

ausgewogen I. *P.P.* → *auswiegen*;

II. *Adj.* (well-)balanced; **Ausgewogenheit** *f*; *nur Sg.* balance, (well-)balanced nature

ausgezackt *Adj.* serrated, jagged

ausgezehrt I. *P.P.* → *auszehren*; **II.** *Adj.* emaciated; *Gesicht*: haggard; *stärker*: cadaverous

ausgezeichnet I. *P.P.* → *auszeichnen*; **II.** *Adj.* excellent, outstanding; *das Lokal hat e-e ~e Küche* the place (*od.* restaurant) serves excellent food; **III.** *Adv.* very well; *hier kann man ~ essen* the food here is excellent; *danke, mir geht's ~* I'm doing just fine, thanks; *das passt mir ~* that suits me very well

ausgiebig I. *Adj. Essen etc.*: big, substantial; *Spaziergang etc.*: long; *Forschungen etc.*: extensive; (*üppig*) abundant; *~en Gebrauch machen von ...* make full (*od.* good) use of ...; *ein ~er Regen* (continuous) heavy rain; **II.** *Adv.* (*eingehend*) in detail; (*anhaltend*) for a long time; *~ essen* have a big meal (*od.* lunch etc.*), have plenty to eat; *~ frühstücken* eat a good (*od.* substantial) breakfast; *~ spazieren gehen* go for a long walk; *häufig*: go for a lot of walks, be a great walker (*od.* be great walkers); **Ausgiebigkeit** *f*; *nur Sg.* extensiveness; abundance

ausgießen *v/t.* (*unreg., trennb., hat -ge-*) **1.** (*Flüssigkeit*) pour out (*aus* of); (*weggießen*) pour away; (*verschütten*) spill; *sie goss das Wasser über s-n od. s-m Kopf aus* she poured the water over his head; *s-n Spott etc. über j-n od. j-m ~ fig.* pour scorn (*od.* ridicule) over s.o.; **2.** (*Flasche, Glas*) empty; **3.** (*Feuer*) extinguish; **4.** *Tech.* (*füllen*) (*Form*) fill; (*Fugen, Risse*) fill in

Ausgleich *m*; *-(e)s, -e, mst Sg.* **1.** (*Gleichgewicht*) balance; *e-s Fehlers, Mangels, Verlustes*: compensation; *von Abweichungen, Unterschieden*: balancing out, equalization; *von Konflikten*: evening out; (*Schlichtung*) (re)conciliation; *als* (*od.* *zum*) *~ für* to compensate for; *auf ~ bedacht sein* be keen (*Am.* eager, ready) for (a) compromise; **2.** *Wirts. von Konten*: balancing, settlement; *steuerlich*: adjustment; *zum ~ e-s Kontos* to balance an account; **3.** *Sport*: (*Treffer etc.*) equalizer; *Tennis*: deuce; *den ~ erzielen* equalize, score the equalizer

ausgleichen (*unreg., trennb., hat -ge-*) **I.** *v/t.* **1.** (*Unterschiedliches*) balance; (*Gegensätze*) cancel; (*Unebenheiten, Unterschiede*) level out; (*Mangel, Verlust*) compensate (for), make up for, outweigh; (*Fehler*) make good; (*Nachteiliges*) offset; (*Meinungsverschiedenheiten, Konflikte*) reconcile, settle, smooth over; (*Spannungen*) ease; *~de Gerechtigkeit* poetic justice; **2.** *Wirts.* (*Konten*) balance, settle; (*Rechnung, Schulden*) settle, pay; **II.** *v/i.* **1.** *Sport* equalize, *Am.* even the score; **2.** (*vermitteln*) mediate, act as a mediator; **III.** *v/refl.* (*Gegensätze*) cancel (out); (*Unterschiede*) even out

Ausgleichs|abgabe *f Jur.* countervailing duty (*od.* charge); *~fonds m Wirts.* equalization fund; *~getriebe n Mot.* differential (gear); *~sport m* recreational sport; *~tor n, ~treffer m* equalizer; *~zahlung f* compensation (payment)

ausgleiten *v/i.* (*unreg., trennb., ist -ge-*) → *ausrutschen*

ausgliedern *v/t.* (*trennb., hat -ge-*) ex-

clude, sift out; *Wirts.* (*Bereiche*) hive off; **Ausgliederung** *f* exclusion; *Wirts.* hive-off, *Am.* spin-off

ausglühen (*trennb., -ge-*) **I.** *v/t.* (*hat*); *Tech.* anneal; **II.** *v/i.* (*ist*) burn out

ausgraben (*unreg., trennb., hat -ge-*) **I.** *v/t.* **1.** (*Vergrabenes*) dig up; (*Pflanzen*) uproot; (*Kartoffeln*) lift; (*Altertümer*) excavate; (*Leichen*) disinter, exhume; **2.** *fig.* (*Geheimnis etc.*) unearth; (*alte Fotos etc.*) dig out; (*wieder*) (*Vergessenes*) dredge up; **II.** *v/i.* dig; **Ausgräber** *m*; *-s, -*, **Ausgräberin** *f*; *-*, *-nen* excavator

Ausgrabung *f* **1.** excavation; *~en archäologische*: auch a dig; **2.** (*Fund*) arch(a)eological find

Ausgrabungs|fund *m* arch(a)eological find; *~ort m, ~stätte f* excavation site

ausgrenzen *v/t.* (*trennb., hat -ge-*) leave aside, ignore; exclude (*aus* from); *den Aspekt sollten wir nicht aus unseren Überlegungen ~* we should take that aspect into consideration; **Ausgrenzung** *f*; *nur Sg.* exclusion

Ausguck *m*; *-(e)s, -e*; *Naut.* lookout; (*Krähennest*) crow's nest; **ausgucken** *v/refl.* (*trennb., hat -ge-*); *umg.* **1.** *sich* (*Dat.*) *j-n/etw. ~* (*aussuchen*) choose s.th. for o.s.; **2.** *sich* (*Dat.*) *die Augen nach j-m/etw. ~* search everywhere for s.o./s.th.

Ausguss *m* (*Ausgussbecken*) sink; (*Öffnung*) drain; (*Tülle*) spout; *~becken n* sink

aushaben *v/t.* (*unreg., trennb., hat -ge-*); *umg.* **1.** (*Kleidungsstück*) have (taken) off; **2.** (*Wein, Buch etc.*) have finished

aushacken *v/t.* (*trennb., hat -ge-*) **1.** *Agr.* hoe up; **2.** *j-m die Augen ~* gouge s.o.'s eyes out; → *Krähe*

aushaken (*trennb., hat -ge-*) **I.** *v/t.* unhook; **II.** *v/i. und v/refl.* **1.** come unhooked; **2.** *umg. fig.*: *da hakt's bei mir aus* (*das verstehe ich nicht*) I just don't get it; (*habe ich kein Verständnis dafür*) I simply can't understand it; *bei ihm hat's ausgehakt* (*er hat e-n Wutanfall*) he's flipped (out *od.* his lid)

aushalten (*unreg., trennb., hat -ge-*) **I.** *v/t.* **1.** put up with, endure; *bes. bei Verneinung*: stand, take; (*standhalten*) bear up under; (*überstehen*) stand up to; *Tech.* (*Belastung*) tolerate, take; *den Vergleich mit j-m/etw. ~* stand comparison with s.o./s.th.; *es nicht mehr ~ vor* (*lauter*) *Angst, Schmerzen, Hitze etc.* be so scared, hurt, hot etc. that one cannot take (it) any more; *nicht auszuhalten* unbearable; *so lässt es sich ~ hum.* I could get used to this (*od.* come to like this); *ich halt's nicht mehr aus* I can't stand (*od.* take) it any longer, I can't take any more of this; *wie hältst du es nur bei ihm aus?* how (on earth) do you put up with him?; *hält er's bis zur nächsten Raststätte aus?* can he hold out (*od.* will he last out) till the next service station?; *er lässt sich von ihr ~* he's her kept man, he lives off her; **2.** *Mus.* (*Note, Ton*) hold; **II.** *v/i.* (*ausdauern*) hold out; *er hält nirgends lange aus* he never lasts long in any place

aushandeln *v/t.* (*trennb., hat -ge-*); (*Vertrag etc.*) negotiate; (*Preis, Lohn etc.*) bargain for; *endgültig*: come to terms on; *endlich haben wir e-n Preis ausgehandelt* we finally agreed on a price

aushändigen *v/t.* (*trennb., hat -ge-*) hand over, deliver (+ *Dat. od.* **an** + *Akk.* to); (*Dokument*) issue; **Aushändigung** *f; nur Sg.* handing over, delivery (**an** + *Akk.* to); (*Dokument*) issue, issuance

Aushang *m* **1.** (*Notiz*) notice, announcement; **2.** (*Brett*) notice (*od.* bulletin) board

aushängen¹ (*trennb., hat -ge-*) **I.** *v/t.* **1.** (*Anzeige etc.*) put up; (*Plakat*) *auch* post; **2.** (*Tür etc.*) take *s.th.* off its hinges; (*aushaken*) unhook, undo; **II.** *v/refl.* **1.** *Kleidung:* smooth (*od.* drop) out; **2.** (*Tür etc.*) come off its hinges; (*sich aushaken*) become unhooked, come undone

aushängen² *v/i.*; (*unreg., trennb., ist -ge-*) **1.** *zur Information:* be (hung) up (*od.* posted) on the notice board; *die Listen hängen aus* the lists are up (*od.* out); **2.** *Fahnen etc.:* have been hung up (*od.* put up)

Aushängeschild *n* **1.** sign, *Am. auch* shingle *umg.*; **2.** *fig.* advertisement (*für* for)

ausharren *v/i.* (*trennb., hat -ge-*) *bis zum Ende etc.:* hold out, persevere; stick it out *umg.*; *irgendwo: auch* stay, remain; *auf s-m Platz ~* stick to one's place; *auf s-m Posten ~* remain (*od.* wait) at one's post

aushärten (*trennb., -ge-*) *v/t.* (*hat*) *und v/i.* (*ist*); *Tech.* harden, age

aushauchen *v/t.* (*trennb., hat -ge-*) **1.** breathe out, exhale; **2.** *fig. geh.:* *sein Leben ~* breathe one's last

aushauen *v/t.* (*unreg., trennb., hat -ge-*) **1.** *aus Eis, Stein etc.:* cut out, hew out; (*Inschrift*) chisel out, carve out; **2.** *Agr.* (*Wald*) clear; (*unerwünschte Triebe*) prune; (*fällen*) thin out; **3.** *umg.* → *verhauen* I 1

aushäusig *Adj. Dial., umg. Person:* out (and about); *auch Arbeit etc.:* out of the house (*attr. nachgestellt*)

ausheben *v/t.* (*trennb., hat -ge-*) **1.** *Sport, Ringen:* lever; **2.** *fig.* (*Vorhaben, Gesetz etc.*) annul, cancel; *j-n aus e-r leitenden Position:* lever out

ausheben *v/t.* (*unreg., trennb., hat -ge-*) **1.** (*Fundament, Grab, Graben etc.*) dig, excavate; **2.** (*Erde etc.*) dig up; **3.** (*aushängen*) take *s.th.* off its hinges; **4.** (*Nest*) rob; (*Eier etc.*) steal; **5.** *fig.* (*Verbrechernest etc.*) raid; (*Verbrecher*) round (*od.* pick) up; (*Bande*) break up; **6.** *altm.* (*Soldaten, Heer*) levy, recruit; **7.** *Sport, Ringen:* execute a pick-up on *s.o.*, lift *s.o.* off his (*od.* her) feet

ausheicken *v/t.* (*trennb., hat -ge-*); *umg.* (*Komplott, Plan etc.*) cook up, hatch

ausheilen *v/i.* (*trennb., ist -ge-*) *Organ, Wunde:* heal (up) (*Krankheit*): be completely cured

aushelfen *v/i.* (*unreg., trennb., hat -ge-*): ([*bei*] *j-m*) ~ help (s.o.) out (*mit* with)

ausheulen *v/refl.* (*trennb., hat -ge-*); *umg.* → *ausweinen*

Aushilfe *f* temporary help; (*Person*) *auch* stand-in; (*bes. Sekretärin*) temp *umg.*; *als ~ arbeiten* help out (on a temporary basis); *im Büro:* work as a temp, temp *umg.*; *zur ~* to help out; *Koch zur ~ gesucht* cook required for temporary work

Aushilfs|job *m* temporary job; *im Büro:* temping job; **~kellner** *m*, **~kellnerin** *f* stand-in waiter; *weiblich:* stand-in waitress; **~koch** *m*, **~köchin** *f* stand-in

cook; **~kraft** *f* casual worker, temporary worker; temp *umg.*; **~lehrer** *m*, **~lehrerin** *f* supply (*Am.* substitute) teacher; **~personal** *n* temporary staff (*mst V. im Pl.*); **~tätigkeit** *f* temporary job

aushilfsweise *Adv.* temporarily; ~ (*bei j-m*) *arbeiten auch* help (s.o.) out

aushöhlen *v/t.* (*trennb., hat -ge-*) **1.** hollow out; *Geol.* excavate, erode; (*Obst*) scoop out; **2.** *fig.* (*etw.*) undermine, erode; (*j-n*) drain *s.o.* (of all strength); → *ausgehöhlt*

ausholen (*trennb., hat -ge-*) **I.** *v/i.* **1.** *zum Schlag:* raise one's hand (*od.* arm), get ready to hit *s.o.*; *zum Wurf:* swing one's arm back, reach back, get ready to throw *s.th.*; *beim Rudern etc.:* pull (back); *mit weit ~den Schritten* with great strides; **2.** *fig., bei e-r Schilderung etc.:* (*weit*) ~ go a long way back; *etwas ~* go back a bit; **II.** *v/t.* **1.** *Dial.* (*j-n*) sound *s.o.* out, quiz *s.o.*; **2.** *Naut.* (*Segel*) haul out (*od.* taut)

aushorchen *v/t.* (*trennb., hat -ge-*) sound *s.o.* out (*über* + *Akk.* about); *er wollte mich ~* he tried to pump me for information

Aushub *m; -(e)s, kein Pl.* **1.** *Vorgang:* excavation; **2.** (*Erde etc.*) (excavated) earth, excavated materials *Pl.*

aushungern *v/t.* (*trennb., hat -ge-*) starve (*auch fig.*); (*Stadt etc.*) starve out; → *ausgehungert* II

aushusten (*trennb., hat -ge-*) **I.** *v/t.* cough up; **II.** *v/refl.* have a good cough; *hast du dich jetzt ausgehustet?* have you finished coughing?

auskämmen *v/t.* (*trennb., hat -ge-*) **1.** (*Läuse, Schmutz*) comb out; **2.** (*Haar, Wolle*) comb

auskämpfen (*trennb., hat -ge-*) **I.** *v/t.* fight *s.th.* out; **II.** *vt/i.:* *ausgekämpft haben* have given up the struggle; *der Kampf ist ausgekämpft* the battle is over

auskehren *vt/i.* (*trennb., hat -ge-*) *bes. südd.* → *ausfegen*

auskeilen *v/i.* (*trennb., hat -ge-*) *Pferd:* lash out, kick; *Person:* lash out in all directions

auskeimen *v/i.* (*trennb., hat od. ist -ge-*) *Bot.* germinate

auskennen *v/refl.* (*unreg., trennb., hat -ge-*): *sich ~* (*in e-m Ort etc.*) know one's way around (a place *etc.*); *Wissensgebiet etc.:* know all about *s.th.*; *sich mit Hunden/Autos ~* be good with dogs / know a lot about cars; *er kennt sich aus* he knows what's what; *ich kenne mich nicht mehr aus* I'm at a complete loss; *da soll sich noch einer ~!* I can't make head nor tail (*Am.* heads or tails) of it!

auskippen *v/t.* (*trennb., hat -ge-*) **1.** tip out, dump; (*Flüssigkeit*) pour out (*od.* away); **2.** (*leeren*) empty

ausklammern *v/t.* (*trennb., hat -ge-*) **1.** *Math.* factor out, put outside the brackets; **2.** *fig.* leave aside, ignore; *aus der Diskussion ~* exclude from the discussion

ausklamüsern *v/t.* (*trennb., hat*); *umg.* figure (*od.* work *od.* puzzle) out

Ausklang *m Mus. od. fig.* end; *zum ~ des Abends fig.* to end (*od.* finish off) the evening

ausklappbar *Adj.* folding, fold-out; *die Couch ist ~* the sofa folds out (into a bed), it's a sofa-bed; **ausklappen** *v/t.* (*trennb., hat -ge-*) fold out

ausklarieren *v/t.* (*trennb., hat*); *Naut.* clear, give clearance to

ausklauben *v/t.* (*trennb., hat -ge-*); *Dial.* pick out; sort out; (*Erz*) select; *etw. aus etw. ~* pick s.th. out of s.th.

auskleiden (*trennb., hat -ge-*) **I.** *v/t.* **1.** *geh.* (*j-n*) undress; **2.** (*innen verkleiden*) line; *Bergb.* case; **II.** *v/refl. geh.* undress; **Auskleidung** *f* lining; *Vorgang: auch* surfacing

ausklingen *v/i.* (*unreg., trennb., ist -ge-*) **1.** die away; **2.** *fig.* come to an end; end (*mit od. in* + *Dat.* with)

ausklinken (*trennb., hat -ge-*) **I.** *v/t. Tech.* disengage, trip; *auch Flug.* release; **II.** *v/refl.* **1.** *Tech.* release (itself); **2.** *fig. hum.* (*nicht mehr mitmachen*) split, opt out; (*nicht mehr zuhören*) stop listening

ausklopfen *v/t.* (*trennb., hat -ge-*) **1.** (*Teppich etc.*) beat; (*Kleidung*) dust (down); (*Pfeife*) knock out; **2.** (*Asche, Schmutz*) beat (*od.* knock) *s.th.* out (*aus* of)

ausklügeln *v/t.* (*trennb., hat -ge-*) work out; → *ausgeklügelt* II

auskneifen *v/i.* (*unreg., trennb., ist -ge-*); *umg.* cut and run, do a bunk, *Am.* take a powder

ausknipsen *v/t.* (*trennb., hat -ge-*); *Etech. umg.* switch off

ausknobeln *v/t.* (*trennb., hat -ge-*) **1.** *mit Händen:* play paper, scissors, stone (*Am.* scissors, rock and paper) (to decide); *mit Münze:* toss (a coin) for; *mit Würfeln:* throw dice for; **2.** *umg. fig.* figure *s.th.* out

ausknöpfbar *Adj. Futter:* detachable, removable

auskochen *v/t.* (*trennb., hat -ge-*) **1.** (*Fleisch etc.*) boil; (*Wäsche*) boil, boil-wash; *Med.* (*Instrumente*) sterilize; *Chem.* decoct; **2.** *umg. fig.* (*Plan etc.*) hatch, concoct; → *ausgekocht* II

auskoffern *v/t.* (*trennb., hat -ge-*) *fachspr.* (*Straße*) excavate, dig out (a roadbed); (*verseuchten Boden etc.*) remove

auskommen *v/i.* (*unreg., trennb., ist -ge-*) **1.** *mit etw. ~* make do with, manage with; *mit s-m Geld ~* make both ends meet; *~ ohne j-n:* manage without; *ohne etw.:* auch do without; *er kommt ohne sie nicht aus auch* he can't live (*od.* survive) without her; **2.** (*gut*) *mit j-m ~* get on (fine *od.* well) with s.o.; *mit j-m glänzend ~* hit it off (really well) with s.o. *umg.*; **3.** *südd. österr. Person, Tier:* escape, get away (*j-m* from s.o.); *j-m ~ Messer etc.:* slip; *Tasse etc.:* slip out of s.o.'s hand

Auskommen *n; -s, kein Pl.* **1.** livelihood; *ein gutes od. sein ~ haben* make a (decent) living, make (more than) enough to live from; **2.** *es ist kein ~ mit ihm* you just can't get along with him, he's impossible to get along with

auskömmlich I. *Adj. Gehalt, Verhältnisse:* reasonable; **II.** *Adv.:* ~ *leben* live reasonably well

auskoppeln *v/t.* (*trennb., hat -ge-*); (*Schlager etc.*) take (*od.* lift) from an album, release *an album track* as a single; **Auskopp(e)lung** *f* (*Single*) cut, follow-up single

auskosten *v/t.* (*trennb., hat -ge-*) savo(u)r, enjoy to the full; *ich habe es ausgekostet iro.* I've had my fill of it

auskotzen (*trennb., hat -ge-*); *vulg.* **I.** *v/t.* throw up, puke (up), hurl; **II.** *v/refl.* **1.** throw up, puke, hurl; **2.** *fig.* let everything out; *sich bei j-m ~* unload (one's problems) to s.o., have a good moan to s.o.

Auskragung *f* projection, overhang

auskramen *v/t.* (*trennb.*, *hat -ge-*) **1.** (*Dinge*) dig out; **2.** (*Schublade etc.*) pull everything out of; **3.** *fig.* (*alte Geschichten etc.*) dig up

auskratzen (*trennb.*, *-ge-*) **I.** *v/t.* (*hat*) **1.** scratch out; *j-m die Augen ~* scratch s.o.'s eyes out; **2.** (*Gefäß*) scrape out (*auch Med.*); **II.** *v/i.* (*ist*), *umg.* (*ausreißen*) cut and run, do a bunk, bugger off, *Am.* take a powder, bug off

auskristallisieren (*trennb.*) **I.** *v/t.* (*hat*) crystallize out; **II.** *v/i.* (*ist*) *und v/refl.* (*hat*) crystallize (out), form into crystals

auskugeln *v/t.* (*trennb.*, *hat -ge-*); *Med.*: *j-m/sich* (*Dat.*) *den Arm ~* dislocate s.o.'s/one's arm

auskühlen (*trennb.*, *-ge-*) **I.** *v/i.* (*ist*); *Sache*: cool (down); *Person*: chill through; *er ist völlig ausgekühlt* he is suffering from hypothermia; **II.** *v/t.* (*hat*) cool (thoroughly)

auskundschaften *v/t.* (*trennb.*, *hat -ge-*) find out; (*j-n*) track down; (*Geheimnisse*) ferret out; (*Informationen*) spy out; *Mil.* reconnoit|re (*Am.* -er), scout (*od.* scope) out

Auskunft *f*; -, *Auskünfte* **1.** (piece of) information, info *umg.* (*über* + *Akk.* about); *Pl. auch* details; *nähere Auskünfte* (further) details (*od.* particulars), more information *Sg.*; *j-m* (*e-e*) *~ erteilen od. geben* give s.o. (*od.* furnish s.o. *od.* provide s.o. with) information; *j-m e-e falsche ~ geben* give s.o. false (*od.* wrong) information, misinform s.o.; *Auskünfte einholen* obtain information, make (some) enquiries; *j-m die ~ verweigern* refuse to give s.o. information; **2.** *nur Sg.*; *Telef.* directory enquiries *Pl.* (*Am.* assistance, information); **3.** *nur Sg.*; *Büro*: information office; *Schalter*: information (desk); *Person*: information clerk

Auskunfts|beamte *m*, **~beamtin** *f* information clerk; **~büro** *n* enquiry office, information office; **~person** *f* informant; **~pflicht** *f*; *nur Sg.* duty to disclose information; **~schalter** *m* information (desk), inquiries *Pl.*, enquiries *Pl.*; **~stelle** *f* **1.** enquiry office, information office; **2.** → **Auskunftsschalter**

auskungeln *v/t.* (*trennb.*, *hat -ge-*); *umg. pej.* plot, scheme

auskuppeln *v/i.* (*trennb.*, *hat -ge-*); *Mot.* disengage the clutch, declutch

auskurieren (*trennb.*, *hat*) **I.** *v/t.* cure (completely); **II.** *v/refl.*: *du solltest dich richtig ~* you should take a proper break until you're really fit again; *bei Grippe etc.*: you should get it out of your system

auslachen (*trennb.*, *hat -ge-*) **I.** *v/t.* (*j-n*) laugh at (*wegen* for *od.* because of); *stärker*: jeer at, ridicule, deride; *lass dich doch nicht ~!* don't be ridiculous!, don't make a fool of yourself!; **II.** *v/refl.* have a good laugh; **III.** *v/i.* stop laughing

ausladen (*unreg.*, *trennb.*, *hat -ge-*) **I.** *vt/i.* (*Wagen, Waren*) unload; **II.** *v/t.* **1.** *Naut.* (*Passagiere*) disembark, take ashore; (*Fracht*) unload, discharge; **2.**: *j-n* (*wieder*) *~* uninvite s.o., tell s.o. not to come

ausladend I. *Part. Präs.* → *ausladen*; **II.** *Adj.* **1.** *Erker etc.*: jutting out; *Dach*: very wide; *Äste*: sweeping; (*überhängend*) overhanging; **2.** *Geste, Bewegung*: sweeping, expansive; *Kinn*: jutting; *Stirn*: prominent; **3.** *fig. Stil*

etc.: elaborate

Ausladung *f* **1.** *von Fahrzeugen, Waren*: unloading; *Naut. von Passagieren*: disembarkation; *von Fracht*: discharging; **2.** *von Gästen*: cancel(l)ation (of an invitation)

Auslage *f* **1.** *Ware*: window display, goods *Pl.* (*Am.* merchandise) on display; **2.** (*Schaufenster*) shop (*Am.* store) window (display); (*Schaukasten*) display cabinet, showcase; **3.** *mst Pl.* (*Ausgaben*) expenses; *j-m s-e ~n erstatten* refund s.o. his *etc.* expenses

auslagern *v/t.* (*trennb.*, *hat -ge-*); (*Bücher etc.*) retrieve from storage; (*Kunstwerke, im Krieg etc.*) evacuate; *Wirts.* take out of the warehouse (*od.* storage); **Auslagerung** *f* evacuation; *Wirts.* taking out of the warehouse (*od.* storage)

Ausland *n*; *nur Sg.* **1.** foreign countries *Pl.*; *ins ~ od. im ~ abroad*; *aus dem od. vom ~* from abroad; *Waren aus dem ~* foreign goods, goods from abroad; *Kontakte mit dem ~* foreign ties, ties abroad; *fürs ~ bestimmte Waren* goods destined for export, export goods; **2.** *fig.* (*die Ausländer*) foreigners; (*die ausländischen Regierungen*) foreign governments; *die Meinung des ~s* opinion abroad, foreign opinion

Ausländer *m*; -s, - foreigner; *Jur.* alien; **~amt** *n* aliens' registration office; **~anteil** *m* proportion (*od.* percentage) of foreigners (*od.* foreign workers, pupils *etc.*); **~beauftragte** *m*, *f*; -*n*, -*n* official dealing with foreigners (*od.* foreign immigrants); **~behörde** *f etwa* immigration authority

ausländerfeindlich *Adj.* xenophobic, hostile to foreigners *präd.*; *sie sind sehr ~* *auch* they hate foreigners; **Ausländerfeindlichkeit** *f*; *nur Sg.* xenophobia, hostility to foreigners

ausländerfreundlich *Adj.* friendly to (*od.* open towards) foreigners; **Ausländerfreundlichkeit** *f* friendliness to (*od.* openness towards) foreigners

Ausländer|gesetz *n Jur.* law governing aliens; **~hasser** *m*, **~hasserin** *f* xenophobe; **~hetze** *f* xenophobic (hate) campaign

Ausländerin *f*; -, -*nen* foreigner; *Jur.* alien

Ausländer|kind *n* child of immigrants (*od.* from an immigrant family); **~politik** *f* policy on immigrants (*od.* aliens); **~referent** *m*, **~referentin** *f* expert (*od.* adviser) on immigration (policy); **~wahlrecht** *n*: *allgemeines/kommunales ~* aliens' right to vote in general/ local elections

ausländisch *Adj.* **1.** foreign; *Wirts. auch* external; *Jur.* alien; *~e Arbeitnehmer* foreign workers; *~e Besucher* visitors from abroad, international visitors; → *Mitbürger*, **2.** *Pflanzen, Tiere*: exotic

Auslands|abteilung *f Wirts.* export (*od.* foreign sales) department; **~amt** *n an Universitäten etc.*: international students' office; *akademisches ~ etwa* international students' (academic) registry; **~anleihe** *f Wirts.* external (*od.* overseas) loan; **~aufenthalt** *m* visit (*od.* stay) abroad; **~beteiligung** *f Wirts.* foreign investment; **~beziehungen** *Pl.* foreign relations; **~brief** *m* letter going abroad (*Am. auch* overseas), foreign (*od.* international) letter; *Pl. auch* letters abroad (*Am. auch* overseas); **~deutsche** *m*, *f* German national living abroad, German expatri-

ate (*od.* expat *umg.*); **~dienst** *m* foreign service; **~einsatz** *m von Soldaten, Journalisten*: deployment abroad; **~flug** *m* international flight; **~geschäft** *n Wirts.* export (*od.* import) business, export-import business; **~gespräch** *n Telef.* international call; **~hilfe** *f* foreign aid; **~investition** *f Wirts.* foreign investment; **~kapital** *n Wirts.* foreign capital; **~korrespondent** *m*, **~korrespondentin** *f* foreign correspondent; **~krankenschein** *m* health insurance document for abroad; **~niederlassung** *f Wirts.* foreign branch; **~presse** *f* international press; **~reise** *f* trip abroad (*Am. auch* overseas); *Pol.*, *Sport etc.*: foreign tour; **~schulden** *Pl.* foreign (*od.* external) debt *Sg.*; **~schutzbrief** *m Mot.* (certificate of) international travel cover; **~studium** *n* course of studies abroad; *ein ~ kann sehr teuer sein* studying abroad can be very expensive; **~tarif** *m Telef.* international rate; **~tournee** *f* foreign tour; **~vermögen** *n Wirts.* external assets *Pl.*, property abroad; **~verschuldung** *f Wirts.* foreign (*od.* external) debt; **~vertretung** *f Wirts.* agency abroad; *Pol.* diplomatic mission

auslangen *v/i.* (*trennb.*, *hat -ge-*); *umg. Vorräte etc.*: be enough, suffice; *das langt noch für e-e Woche aus* *auch* that'll last for another week

Auslass *m*; -*es*, *Auslässe* outlet

auslassen (*unreg.*, *trennb.*, *hat -ge-*) **I.** *v/t.* **1.** (*Wort etc.*) leave out, omit; (*überspringen*) skip, pass over; (*Gelegenheit etc.*) miss; (*j-n*) miss (*od.* leave) out; **2.** (*Wasser*) let out; (*Badewanne etc.*) empty; **3.** *Gastr.* (*Fett*) melt; (*Speck*) render; **4.** (*Saum*) let down (*od.* out); (*Fell*) let out; **5.** *umg.* (*Licht, Feuer, Ofen etc.*) leave off; **6.** *umg.* (*nicht anziehen*) leave off, not put on; **7.** *s-e Wut etc. an j-m ~* take one's anger *etc.* out on s.o., vent one's anger (*od.* spleen) on s.o.; **8.** *südd.*, *österr.* → *freilassen*; **II.** *v/refl.*: *sich ~ über* (+ *Akk.*) talk about; *langatmig*: hold forth on; *sie ließ sich sehr negativ darüber aus* she was very negative about it; *er ließ sich nicht weiter darüber aus* he didn't say any more about it; **III.** *v/i.* *südd.*, *österr.* (*loslassen*) let go; → *ausgelassen* II, III; **Auslassung** *f* **1.** omission; **2.** *~en* (*Äußerungen*) remarks (*über* + *Akk.* about)

Auslassungs|punkte *Pl.* ellipsis *Sg.*, three dots, omission marks; **~satz** *m Ling.* ellipsis; **~zeichen** *n* apostrophe

auslasten *v/t.* (*trennb.*, *hat -ge-*) **1.** (*Maschine etc.*) use to capacity, utilize to the full; *die Kapazität ist zu 70% ausgelastet* capacity is at 70%, it's at 70% capacity; **2.** *der Haushalt lastet mich voll/nicht aus* I've got plenty on my hands (*od.* plate) with the housework / I need to be doing something else apart from the housework, the housework doesn't fulfil me; → *ausgelastet* II; **Auslastung** *f* (full) utilization

Auslauf *m* **1.** (*Öffnung*) outlet, drain; **2.** *für Kinder, Tiere*: space to run about (in); **3.** *nur Sg.* (*Bewegung*) exercise; *große Hunde brauchen viel ~* large dogs need plenty of exercise; **4.** *Sport, Strecke nach dem Ziel etc.*: run-out; *Fechten*: run-back

auslaufen (*unreg.*, *trennb.*, *-ge-*) **I.** *v/i.* (*ist*) **1.** *Flüssigkeit*: run out; *durch*

Leck: leak out; *Eiter*: drain; **2.** *Wanne etc.*: empty; *durch Leck*: leak; *Auge etc.*: drain; **3.** *Naut.* sail; **4.** *Farbe*: run; **5.** *Läufer, Motor, Propeller etc.*: run out; *(stehen bleiben)* come (*od.* roll) to a stop; **6.** *(aufhören)* end, come to an end; *Vertrag etc.*: expire; run out; *Modell*: be discontinued; *allmählich*: be phased out; **~** *lassen* (*Produkt, Fernsehserie etc.*) phase out; **7.** **~** *in* (+ *Akk.*) *in e-e Ebene etc.*: end in; *(sich zuspitzen)* taper (in)to, narrow (in)to; **8.** *umg.* → *ausgehen* 4; **II.** *v/refl.* (*hat*) **1.** get some exercise; *im Garten kön-nen sich die Kinder richtig* **~** the chil-dren can have a really good run around in the garden (*Am.* yard) (*od.* can run around to their hearts' con-tent); **2.** *nach Rennen, Training*: cool down, have a cool-down run

Ausläufer *m* **1.** *e-s Gebirges*: foothills *Pl.*; **2.** *Met.* fringe(s *Pl.*); **3.** *e-s Erdbe-bens*: coda; **4.** *Bot.* runner

Auslaufmodell *n* discontinued (*od.* phaseout) model *od.* line

auslaugen *v/t.* (*trennb., hat -ge-*) **1.** (*Er-ze, Boden*) exhaust; (*Boden*) *auch* leach (out); **2.** *fig.*: *j-n* **~** drain s.o. (of every ounce of strength), exhaust s.o.; → *ausgelaugt* f; **Auslaugung** f ex-haustion (*des Bodens* of the soil)

Auslaut *m Ling.* final sound; *im* **~** at the end of a (*od.* the) word, in final position; **auslauten** *v/i.* (*trennb., hat -ge-*) end (*auf* + *Akk.* in *od.* with); *auf „t"* **~** have "t" in (the) final position; **Auslautverhärtung** f *Ling.* devoicing (*od.* hardening) of final consonants

ausleben (*trennb., hat -ge-*) **I.** *v/t.* (*Fan-tasie*) live out; (*Gefühle*) let (*od.* act) out; (*Talente*) realize, develop, apply; **II.** *v/refl.* **1.** enjoy life, live life to the full; (*in Saus und Braus leben*) live it up *umg.*; **2.** *Fantasie*: run free; **III.** *v/i.*: *ausgelebt haben* have lived (out) one's life

auslecken *v/t.* (*trennb., hat -ge-*); (*Schüssel etc.*) lick out (*od.* clean); (*Teig etc.*) lick up

ausleeren *v/t.* (*trennb., hat -ge-*) **1.** (*Ei-mer, Tasche etc.*) empty; (*austrinken*) *auch* drain; **2.** (*Inhalt*) empty out; (*ausschütten*) tip (*od.* pour, *Am.* auch dump) out

auslegbar *Adj.* interpretable; *der Text ist so oder so* **~** there are two ways of interpreting the text, the text can be interpreted in two ways; *es ist nur so* **~** that's the only possible interpreta-tion

auslegen *v/t.* (*trennb., hat -ge-*) **1.** (*Ka-bel, Minen*) lay; (*Netze etc.*) put out; (*Gift, Köder*) put down; (*Saatgut*) sow; (*Kartoffeln etc.*) plant, set; **2.** *zur Ansicht*: (put on) display; (*Listen etc.*) put out; (*Broschüren etc.*) make avail-able for use (*od.* reference); *ausgelegt* on display; **3.** (*Boden*) cover; (*Schub-lade*) line; *mit e-m Teppich* **~** carpet; (*Boden*) *auch* put a carpet down on (*Zimmer*: in); **4.** (*verzieren*) inlay; **5.** (*vorstrecken*) advance; *etw. für j-n* **~** lend s.o. s.th., pay s.th. for s.o.; **6.** (*deu-ten*) interpret; *falsch* **~** misinterpret; (*j-m*) *etw. als Eitelkeit etc.* **~** put s.th. down to (s.o.'s) vanity *etc.*; **7.** (*entwer-fen*) design; *ausgelegt für Produktion*: designed to produce; *Geschwindigkeit*: designed to do; *der Saal ist für 2000 (Personen) ausgelegt* is designed to seat 2000

Ausleger *m*; *-s*, *-* **1.** *e-s Krans*: jib, boom; **2.** *Naut.* outrigger; **3.** *am Ru-*

derboot: rowlock; **~boot** *n* outrigger; **~brücke** *f* cantilever bridge; **~kran** *m* jib crane

Auslegeware *f* **1.** floor coverings *Pl.*; **2.** (*Teppichboden*) (wall-to-wall) car-pet(ing)

Auslegung *f* **1.** interpretation; *kirchl.* exegesis; *falsche* **~** misinterpretation; **2.** *nur Sg.*; *Tech.* layout, design (*auf* + *Akk.* for); **Auslegungsfrage** *f*: *das ist e-e* **~** it all depends which way you look at it

ausleiern (*trennb., -ge-*) *v/t.* (*hat*) *und v/i.* (*ist*) wear out; → *ausgeleiert*

Ausleihe *f*; *-*, *-n* **1.** *nur Sg.* (*das Auslei-hen*) lending; **2.** (*Schalter*) issue (*od.* issuing) desk (*od.* counter)

ausleihen *v/t.* (*unreg., trennb., hat -ge-*) **1.** (*verleihen*) lend s.th. (out) (+ *Dat. od. an* + *Akk.* to), lend (*Am. auch* loan) s.o. s.th., *ich habe ihm mein Fahrrad ausgeliehen* I lent (*Am. auch* loaned) him my bicycle, I let him use my bicycle; **2.** *sich* (*Dat.*) *etw.* **~** bor-row s.th. (*bei od. von* from)

Ausleihfrist *f* lending period; *die* **~** *be-trägt drei Wochen* books may be bor-rowed for (a period of) up to three weeks

auslernen *v/i.* (*trennb., hat -ge-*) finish one's training; *Lehrling*: complete one's apprenticeship; *ein ausgelernter Bäcker etc.* a qualified baker *etc.*; *man lernt nie aus* Sprichw. you (*od.* we) live and learn, you learn something new every day

Auslese *f* **1.** (*Auswahl*) choice, selec-tion; *natürliche* **~** *Bio.* natural selec-tion; *e-e strenge* **~** *treffen* make a careful selection; **2.** (*Elite*) elite, *the* crème de la crème, *the* cream of the crop; **3.** *deutscher Wein*: Auslese, su-perior (*od.* choice) white wine; **4.** *aus der Literatur*: anthology

auslesen (*unreg., trennb., hat -ge-*) **I.** *v/t.* **1.** select, choose, pick (*od.* sort) out; **2.** (*verlesen*) (*Erbsen, Linsen etc.*) sort; **3.** (*Buch*) read (to the end), fin-ish; **4.** *EDV* (*Daten*) read out; **II.** *v/i.*: *hast du endlich ausgelesen?* have you finally finished reading?, you're surely not still reading?

Ausleseprozess *m* selection process (*od.* procedure)

ausleuchten *v/t.* (*trennb., hat -ge-*) illu-minate (*auch fig.*); (*Bühne*) *auch* floodlight

auslichten *v/t.* (*trennb., hat -ge-*); (*Bäu-me, Gestrüpp etc.*) prune

ausliefern (*trennb., hat -ge-*) **I.** *v/t.* **1.** *an Person*: hand over (+ *Dat. od. an* + *Akk.* to); *Wirts.* (*Ware etc.*) deliv-er; (*verteilen*) distribute; *Jur.* surren-der; (*politische Gefangene*) hand over; (*ausländische Verbrecher*) extradite; **2.** *fig.* deliver (+ *Dat.* to); *j-n s-m Schicksal* **~** deliver s.o. to his (*od.* her) fate; → *ausgeliefert* II; **II.** *v/refl.*: *sich j-m* **~** surrender (*od.* give o.s. up) to s.o.; *fig.* put o.s. at s.o.'s mercy (*od.* in s.o.'s power), throw o.s. on s.o.'s mercy

Auslieferung *f* **1.** *Wirts.* delivery, dis-tribution; **2.** *Jur.* surrender; *e-s politi-schen Gefangenen*: handing over; *e-s ausländischen Verbrechers*: extradition; **3.** *Wirts.* → *Auslieferungslager*

Auslieferungs|abkommen *n Pol.* ex-tradition treaty; **~antrag** *m Pol.* re-quest for extradition; **~haft** *f Jur.* ex-tradition custody; **~lager** *n Wirts.* sup-ply depot, distribution cent|re (*Am.* -er); **~verfahren** *n Jur.* extradition

proceedings *Pl.*

ausliegen *v/i.* (*unreg., trennb., ist -ge-*) *Waren*: be on display (*od.* displayed); *Zeitungen*: be available; *Listen*: be available for inspection; *Fallen*: set; *... liegen zur Einsichtnahme aus ...* may be viewed by (the public)

Auslinie *f* **1.** *Fußball etc.*: (*Seitenlinie*) touchline; (*Torauslinie*) byline, goal line; **2.** *Tennis etc.*: (*Seitenlinie*) side-line; (*Grundlinie*) base line

ausloben *v/t.* (*trennb., hat -ge-*); *Jur.* (*Summe*) offer (as a reward); (*Preis*) offer (as a prize); **Auslobung** *f* offer-(ing) (of a reward *od.* prize)

auslöffeln *v/t.* (*trennb., hat -ge-*) **1.** (*Schüssel etc.*) scrape s.th. clean; **2.** (*Speise*) spoon up; **3.** *umg. fig.*: *etw. (selber)* **~** *müssen* have to face the music; → *Suppe*

auslöschen *v/t.* (*trennb., hat -ge-*) **1.** (*Licht etc.*) put out; (*Feuer*) *auch* extinguish; (*Kerze*) *auch* snuff (out); (*Zigarette*) stub (*od.* put) out; **2.** (*Schrift*) an der Tafel: rub out; (*ra-dieren*) *auch* erase; (*Steinschrift etc.*) efface; (*Spuren*) wipe out, obliterate; **3.** *fig.* (*vernichten*) wipe out; (*j-n*) de-stroy; (*Erinnerungen etc.*) obliterate, blot out; **Auslöschung** *f fig.* wiping out, destruction

Auslöseknopf *m Tech.* release button; *Fot.* shutter release (button)

auslosen *v/t.* (*trennb., hat -ge-*) draw lots (*Am.* straws) for; *den Gewinner* **~** draw lots (*Am.* straws) to decide the winner (*od.* who wins)

auslösen *v/t.* (*trennb., hat -ge-*) **1.** (*che-mische Reaktion, physikalischen Vor-gang etc.*) set off; (*Streik, Krieg etc.*) trigger off, spark off; (*Krankheit*) bring on; (*Gefühl, Reaktion*) cause, touch off; (*Begeisterung, Wut*) arouse; (*Beifall*) draw; *das auslösende Mo-ment* the decisive moment; *es löste allgemeine Heiterkeit aus* it gave ev-eryone a (good) laugh, it caused great mirth *geh.*; **2.** (*Mechanismus, auch Kameraverschluss*) release; (*Alarm, Schuss*) trigger (off); **3.** (*Knochen*) take out (*aus* of); **4.** (*Gefangene, Gei-seln*) release; (*Pfand*) redeem

Auslöser *m*; *-s*, *-* **1.** *Tech.* release; *Fot.* shutter release; **2.** (*Ursache*) cause; *der* **~** *war ...* what triggered it off was ...; *für Gefühle*: *auch* what set it off was ...; *für Krankheit*: *auch* what brought it on was ...

Auslosung *f* draw(ing of lots)

Auslösung *f* **1.** (*Verursachung*) initia-tion, causing; **2.** (*Betätigung*) trigger-ing, setting off; **3.** *von Geiseln etc.*: re-lease; (*Lösegeld*) ransom (money); **4.** *von Knochen*: taking out (*aus* of)

ausloten *v/t.* (*trennb., hat -ge-*) **1.** *Naut.* sound (the depth of); **2.** *Archit.* plumb; *mit Wasserwaage*: level; **3.** *fig.* (*Seele etc.*) plumb the depths of; (*Ab-sichten*) sound out; (*Sache, Problem*) explore the ins and outs of, try to get to the bottom of

auslüften *v/t.* (*trennb., hat -ge-*); (*Klei-dung, Zimmer*) air

auslutschen *v/t.* (*trennb., hat -ge-*); *umg.* **1.** (*Zitronenscheibe etc.*) suck; **2.** (*Saft*) suck s.th. out (*aus* from *od.* of); **3.** *fig.* → *ausgelutscht*

ausm, aus'm *Präp.* + *Art. gespr.* → *aus* I

ausmachen *v/t.* (*trennb., hat -ge-*) **1.** (*Feuer, Licht etc.*) put out; (*Zigaret-te*) *auch* stub out; (*Gas, Radio etc.*) turn off, switch off; **2.** (*sichten, ermit-*

teln) make out; (*orten*) locate; (*feststellen*) find out, determine; **auf diese Entfernung ist das schwer auszumachen** it's hard to tell from this distance; **3.** (*vereinbaren*) arrange (**mit** with); **e-n Termin ~** arrange (*od.* fix) a time (*od.* date *od.* time and date); (*Arzttermin*) make an appointment (**bei** with); **der Termin ist fest ausgemacht** the date's definite (*od.* firmly fixed); **zur ausgemachten Stunde** at the agreed time; **4.** (*Streit, Sache*) settle; **das müsst ihr unter euch ~** you'll have to sort (*od.* fight) it out between yourselves; **mach das mit dir selbst aus** settle it with your own conscience, let your conscience be your guide; → **ausgemacht** II 1; **5.** (*darstellen*) (*Teil, Wesen*) make up, constitute; **was macht den wahren Künstler aus?** what goes to make a great artist?; **das macht den Reiz an der Sache aus** that's what makes it so attractive; **6.** (*betragen*) come (*od.* add up) to; **was macht das in Euro aus?** what is that in Euros?, what would that come to in Euros?; **der Unterschied macht 2 Stunden** etc. **aus** there's 2 hours' etc. difference; **7.** (*ins Gewicht fallen*): **es macht viel aus** it makes a big difference, it matters a lot (*od.* a great deal); **das macht nichts aus** it doesn't matter, it doesn't make any difference; **8.** (*stören*) matter (+ *Dat.* to); **macht es Ihnen etwas aus, wenn ich Klavier spiele?** do you mind if I play the piano?, would you mind if I played the piano?; **macht es dir was aus, dass ich später komme?** do you mind my (*od.* me) coming late?; **das macht mir nichts aus** I don't mind; (*ist mir gleichgültig*) I don't care; I'm easy *umg.*; **die Kälte macht ihm nichts aus** the cold doesn't bother him; → **ausgemacht** II, III

ausmalen *v/t.* (*trennb., hat -ge-*) **1.** (*Bild, Stich* etc.) colo(u)r; **2.** (*Saal* etc.) paint, decorate (*auch anstreichen*); **3.** *fig.* (*Gefahr, Zukunft*) depict (+ *Dat.* for); **sich** (*Dat.*) **etw. ~** picture s.th. (to o.s.), imagine (*od.* visualize) s.th.; **er kann sich nicht ~, was ...** he can't figure out what ...; **etw. in rosigen Farben ~** paint s.th. in glowing colo(u)rs; **4.** *fig.* (*Erzählung*) (*ausschmücken*) embroider, embellish; amplify *förm.*

ausmanövrieren *v/t.* (*trennb., hat*) **1.** outmanoeuvre, *Am.* outmaneuver; **2.** *pej.* (*austricksen*) outsmart

Ausmaß *n*; *räumlich mst Pl.* size, square footage, dimensions *Pl.*; *fig. auch* extent; *größer.* magnitude; (*Größenordnung*) scale; **ein Haus mit den ~en e-s Palastes** a house the size of a palace; **Konkurse von bisher unbekanntem ~** bankruptcies on an unprecedented scale; **in großem ~** *fig.* to a great (*od.* large) extent; **Reformen in großem ~** large(-)od. wide-)scale reforms; **ein erstaunliches ~ an** (+ *Dat.*) an astounding degree of; **erschreckende ~e annehmen** assume (*od.* take on) alarming proportions; **das ganze ~ der Katastrophe ist noch nicht bekannt** the full extent of the damage caused by the disaster is not yet known

ausmergeln *v/t.* (*trennb., hat -ge-*) **1.** (*entkräften*) drain, emaciate; **völlig ausgemergelt sein** be completely emaciated (*od.* gaunt); **2.** (*Boden*) exhaust, impoverish; leach *fachspr.*

ausmerzen *v/t.* (*trennb., hat -ge-*)

1. (*Unkraut*) weed out; (*Schädlinge*) eradicate; (*ausrotten*) wipe (*od.* stamp) out; **2.** (*Fehler* etc.) weed out, eliminate; (*Erinnerung*) blot out, erase, obliterate; (*Schandfleck*) cut out, eradicate; **3.** (*für die Zucht ungeeignete Tiere*) cull; **Ausmerzung** *f* **1.** (*Unkraut*) weeding (out); (*Schädlinge*) eradication; **2.** (*Fehler* etc.) elimination; (*Erinnerung*) blotting out, obliteration; (*Schandfleck*) eradication; **3.** (*von für die Zucht ungeeigneten Tieren*) cull(ing)

ausmessen *v/t.* (*unreg., trennb., hat -ge-*) measure (out *od.* up); **Ausmessung** *f* **1.** (*das Messen*) measuring (out *od.* up); **2.** **~en** (*Maße*) dimensions *Pl.*

ausmisten (*trennb., hat -ge-*) **I.** *v/t.* **1.** (*Stall*) muck (*od.* clean) out; **2.** *umg. fig.* (*Garage, Zimmer* etc.) tidy (*Am.* clean) up, sort out, do out; (*Gerümpel* etc.) clear out; **Bücher** etc. **~** clear out old books etc.; **II.** *v/i. umg. fig.* have a (good) clear-out

ausmustern *v/t.* (*trennb., hat -ge-*) **1.** discard, reject; (*Fahrzeug* etc.) take out of service; **2.** *Mil.* discharge (as unfit), *Brit.* invalid out; (*befreien*) exempt (from military service); **Ausmusterung** *f* **1.** rejection; **2.** discharge; exemption (from military service)

Ausnahme *f*, -, -*n* exception; **mit ~ von** (*od.* + *Gen.*) except (for), excepting, with the exception of; **e-e ~ bilden** *od.* **darstellen** be an exception; (**bei** etc. **j-m, für j-n**) **e-e ~ machen** make an exception (in s.o.'s case); **~n bestätigen die Regel** *od.* **keine Regel ohne ~** *Sprichw.* the exception proves the rule; **e-e ~ von der Regel** an exception to the rule; **von wenigen ~n abgesehen** disregarding rare exceptions; **eine rühmliche ~** a notable exception

Ausnahme|erlaubnis *f Jur.* exemption permit; **~erscheinung** *f* exception, exceptional phenomenon; **dieser Spieler ist e-e absolute ~** this player is one in a million; **~fall** *m* exceptional (*od.* special) case, exception; **in Ausnahmefällen** in special (*od.* exceptional) circumstances; **~genehmigung** *f* exemption, special authorization; **~regelung** *f* exemption; **~situation** *f* **1.** unusual situation; **2.** (*Sonderfall*) exceptional case; **~stellung** *f* special (*od.* privileged) position; **~zustand** *m* **1.** *Pol.* (state of) emergency; **den ~ verhängen** declare a state of emergency (**über** + *Akk.* in); **den ~ aufheben** lift the state of emergency; **2.** exception; **das ist ein ~** *auch* it's not always like this

ausnahmslos I. *Adv.* without exception; (*einstimmig*) unanimously; **~ alle** all of them, without exception, every single one of them; **II.** *Adj.*; *nur attr.*; *Billigung* etc.: unanimous; **die ~e Anwesenheit aller Beteiligten** the presence of all involved without exception

ausnahmsweise I. *Adv.* exceptionally, by way of exception; (*für diesmal*) for once, just this once; *iro.* gönnerhaft: because it's you; **II.** *Adj.*; *nur attr.*; *Zustimmung* etc.: exceptional

ausnehmen (*unreg., trennb., hat -ge-*) **I.** *v/t.* **1.** (*Fisch, Wild*) gut; (*Geflügel*) draw; (*Eingeweide*) disembowel, eviscerate; **2.** (*Nest*) rob; (*Eier* etc.) steal (**aus** from); **3.** *umg. pej.* (*j-n*) fleece s.o.; **4.** (*ausschließen*) except, exclude (**von** from); **ich nehme keinen aus** I make no exceptions; → **ausgenom-**

men II; **5.** *österr.* (*erkennen*) make out; **6.** *umg. pej.* (*aushorchen*) sound s.o. out; **II.** *v/refl.* look; **das nimmt sich gut/schlecht aus** that looks good/bad

ausnehmend I. *Part.Präs.* → **ausnehmen**; **II.** *Adj.* exceptional; **von ~er Schönheit** exceptionally beautiful; *bes. Frau:* of exceptional beauty; **III.** *Adv.* exceptionally, extremely

ausnüchtern (*trennb., -ge-*) *v/i.* (*ist*) und *v/t.* (*hat*) sober up; **Ausnüchterungszelle** *f* drying-out cell

ausnutzen, ausnützen *v/t.* (*trennb., hat -ge-*) use, make use of; (*voll ~*) make the most of; (*den Vorteil ziehen aus, auch unfair*) take advantage of; (*Arbeiter, auch Energie* etc.) exploit; **die Windenergie ~ für ...** harness the power of wind for ...; **Ausnutzung, Ausnützung** *f*; *nur Sg.* use; exploitation

auspacken (*trennb., hat -ge-*) **I.** *v/t.* unpack; (*Geschenk* etc.) unwrap; **II.** *v/i. umg. fig.* blab, talk; (*Geheimnisse verraten*) tell, squeal, spill the beans; **pack aus!** come on, out with it (*od.* spit it out)

ausparken *v/i.* (*trennb., hat -ge-*) get out of a (*od.* the) parking space

auspeitschen *v/t.* (*trennb., hat -ge-*) whip; *nach Verbrechen:* flog

auspennen *v/i. und v/refl.* (*trennb., hat -ge-*); *umg.* have a good long sleep (*od.* a good lie-in, *Am.* sleep-in)

auspfeifen *v/t.* (*unreg., trennb., hat -ge-*) boo (at); *Theat. auch* boo off the stage

auspflanzen *v/t.* (*trennb., hat -ge-*); *Agr.* plant out

Auspizien *Pl. geh.*: **unter den ~ von** (*od.* + *Gen.*) under the auspices (*od.* aegis) of

ausplaudern (*trennb., hat -ge-*) **I.** *v/t.* let out, blab; (*Geheimnis*) spill the beans; **II.** *v/refl.* have a good old chat (*od. umg.* natter od. chinwag)

ausplündern *v/t.* (*trennb., hat -ge-*) **1.** (*Stadt, Haus* etc.) loot, ransack; (*j-n*) rob; **2.** (*Rohstoffquellen*) exploit; (*Land*) bleed (white); **3.** *umg.* (*Kasse*) clean out; (*Kühlschrank* etc.) raid; **4.** *umg.* (*j-n*) (*ausnehmen*) fleece s.o.

ausposaunen *v/t.* (*trennb., hat*); *umg.* broadcast

auspowern *v/refl.* (*trennb., hat -ge-*); *Sl.* (*sich verausgaben*) exhaust o.s.; → **ausgepowert**

ausprägen (*trennb., hat -ge-*) **I.** *v/refl.* **1.** (*sich formen*) develop, take shape; → **ausgeprägt** II; **2. sich ~ in** (+ *Dat.*) (*sich zeigen*) be reflected in, show (*od.* reveal) itself in; (*Ausdruck finden*) find its expression in, be manifest in; **II.** *v/t.* coin, mint; (*Metall zu Münzen*) stamp; **Ausprägung** *f* **1.** (*Ausdruck*) expression; **2.** *nur Sg.*; (*Ausgeprägtheit*) markedness; **3.** *nur Sg.*; (*Formung*) shaping, mo(u)lding

auspreisen *v/t.* (*trennb., hat -ge-*); *Wirts.* (*Waren*) price, put a price tag on

auspressen *v/t.* (*trennb., hat -ge-*) **1.** (*Saft*) press out; *mit der Hand:* auch squeeze out (*auch Schwamm, Tube* etc.); (*Frucht*) squeeze; **j-n ~** (*wie e-e Zitrone*) *umg. fig.* grill s.o.; **2.** *fig.* (*ausbeuten*) squeeze dry, bleed white (*od.* dry)

ausprobieren *v/t.* (*trennb., hat*) try (out), test (**an** + *Dat.* on)

Auspuff *m*; -(*e*)*s*, -*e*; *Mot.* exhaust; **~anlage** *f* exhaust system; **~gase** *Pl.*

exhaust fumes; **~rohr** *n* exhaust pipe; **~topf** *m* silencer, *Am.* muffler

auspumpen *v/t.* (*trennb.*, *hat -ge-*) **1.** (*Wasser*) pump out (*aus* out); (*Luft*) evacuate; **2.** (*Keller etc.*) pump out, drain; *j-m den Magen ~* pump out s.o.'s stomach; **3.** *umg. fig.* (*j-n*) grill; → *ausgepumpt*

auspunkten *v/t.* (*trennb.*, *hat -ge-*) **1.** *Boxen*: beat on points, outpoint; **2.** *fig.* (*Rivalen*) cut out, outdo

auspusten *v/t.* (*trennb.*, *hat -ge-*) **1.** (*Kerze etc.*) blow out; *j-n ~ umg. fig.* (*erschießen*) blow s.o. away; **2.** (*Ei*) blow

ausputzen (*trennb.*, *hat -ge-*) **I.** *v/t.* **1.** (*reinigen*) clean out; **2.** *Agr.* (*Baum etc.*) prune; **II.** *v/i. Fußball:* sweep up at the back

ausquartieren *v/t.* (*trennb.*, *hat*) move *s.o.* out; *zwangsweise:* turn *s.o.* out; (*Truppen*) billet out

ausquatschen (*trennb.*, *hat -ge-*); *umg.* **I.** *v/t.* blurt out, blab; (*Geheimnis*) spill the beans; **II.** *v/refl.* have a good old natter (*od.* chinwag), have a heart-to--heart (*bei j-m* with s.o.); **III.** *v/i. pej.:* *hast du endlich ausgequatscht?* are you 'still going (*od.* blathering) on?

ausquetschen *v/t.* (*trennb.*, *hat -ge-*) → *auspressen*

ausradieren *v/t.* (*trennb.*, *hat*) **1.** rub out, erase; *aus dem Gedächtnis ~ fig.* erase from one's mind (*od.* memory); **2.** *fig. pej.* (*Volk*) wipe out, eradicate; (*Stadt etc.*) raze (*od.* rase) (*mst Passiv*); *völlig ausradiert* razed to the ground

ausrangieren *v/t.* (*trennb.*, *hat*) **1.** (*aussortieren*) sort out; (*wegwerfen*) throw out, get rid of, discard; (*Maschinen etc.*) scrap; **2.** *Eisenb.* shunt out; **ausrangiert I.** *P.P.* → *ausrangieren*; **II.** *Adj. Auto, Maschinen etc.:* scrap; *Kleidung etc.:* cast-off

ausrasieren *v/t.* (*trennb.*, *hat*); (*Achseln, Nacken, Haare*) shave

ausrasten[1] *v/i.* (*trennb.*, *ist -ge-*) **1.** *Tech.* disengage, be released; **2.** *umg. fig.* (*ausflippen*) flip, freak out; *vor Ärger:* go ballistic (*od.* postal *Am. Sl.*); *sie ist völlig ausgerastet* she went off her rocker (*Am.* trolley).

ausrasten[2] *v/i. und v/refl.* (*trennb.*, *hat -ge-*); *südd., österr.* (have a) rest

ausrauben *v/t.* (*trennb.*, *hat -ge-*) rob; (*plündern*) ransack

ausrauchen *v/t.* (*trennb.*, *hat -ge-*): *s-e Pfeife etc. ~* finish one's pipe *etc.*

ausräuchern *v/t.* (*trennb.*, *hat -ge-*) **1.** (*Raum*) fumigate; **2.** (*Bienen, Fuchsbau, fig. Schlupfwinkel*) smoke out

ausraufen *v/t.* (*trennb.*, *hat -ge-*): *sich* (*Dat.*) *die Haare ~* tear (*od.* pull) one's hair out; *ich könnte mir die Haare ~!* I could kick myself!

ausräumen *v/t.* (*trennb.*, *hat -ge-*) **1.** (*Zimmer, Schrank etc.*) clear out; **2.** (*entfernen*) remove (*aus* from); **3.** *Med.* (*Magen, Darm*) purge; (*Gebärmutter*) curet(te); (*Tumor, Stein*) remove; **4.** *fig.* (*Bedenken, Verdacht, Missverständnis etc.*) clear up; (*Bedenken etc.*) dispel, eliminate; (*Meinungsverschiedenheit*) settle, overcome; **5.** *umg.* (*ausplündern*) clear out

ausrechnen *v/t.* (*trennb.*, *hat -ge-*) work out (*auch fig.*); (*Summe*) *auch* calculate; *sich* (*Dat.*) *etw. ~* (*können*) (be able to) guess s.th., figure s.th. out; *ich rechne mir gute Chancen aus* I reckon (*od.* think) I've got a good

chance; → *ausgerechnet* II

ausrecken (*trennb.*, *hat -ge-*) **I.** *v/t.* stretch; *sich* (*Dat.*) *den Hals ~ nach ...* crane one's neck to see ...; **II.** *v/refl.* stretch out (*nach* to reach)

Ausrede *f* excuse; *faule ~* feeble (*od.* lame) excuse; *nie um e-e ~ verlegen sein* never be short of (*od.* at a loss for) an excuse

ausreden (*trennb.*, *hat -ge-*) **I.** *v/i.* finish speaking; *j-n ~ lassen* let s.o. finish (speaking), hear s.o. out; *j-n nicht ~ lassen* cut s.o. short, interrupt s.o.; **II.** *v/t.:* *j-m etw. ~* talk s.o. out of s.th.; **III.** *v/refl.* **1.** *bes. südd.:* *sich bei j-m ~* unburden o.s. to s.o.; **2.** *altm.* → *herausreden*

ausregnen *v/unpers.* (*trennb.*, *hat -ge-*): *es hat* (*sich*) *ausgeregnet* that's the end of the rain now (*od.* for a while)

ausreiben *v/t.* (*unreg.*, *trennb.*, *hat -ge-*) **1.** (*Glas etc.*) wipe out; (*Topf*) rub clean; **2.** (*Fleck*) rub off, remove; **3.** *sich* (*Dat.*) *die Augen ~* rub one's eyes

ausreichen *v/i.* (*trennb.*, *hat -ge-*) **1.** be enough, suffice; *über e-n Zeitraum:* last; *m-e Kenntnisse reichen nicht aus* I don't know enough; *s-e Ausbildung reicht für die Stelle nicht aus* his training isn't (quite) adequate for the job; **2.** *~ mit* (*auskommen*) get by (*od.* manage) with (*od.* on); **ausreichend I.** *Part.Präs.* → *ausreichen*; **II.** *Adj.* **1.** enough, sufficient; *nicht ~ auch* insufficient, inadequate; **2.** *Note:* *etwa* D, unsatisfactory

ausreifen *v/i.* (*trennb.*, *ist -ge-*) ripen (fully); *Käse: auch* mature (fully), age (*beide auch Wein*); → *ausgereift* II

Ausreise *f* departure (*nach* for); *bei der ~* on leaving the country; *Verkehrsmeldung:* *10 Kilometer Stau bei der ~* (there's a) ten-kilomet|re tailback (*Am.* traffic is backed up 10 kilometers) at the border (crossing); *j-m die ~ verweigern* refuse s.o. permission to leave the country; *~antrag m* application for an exit visa; *~erlaubnis f, ~genehmigung f* exit permit

ausreisen *v/i.* (*trennb.*, *ist -ge-*) leave (the country); *nach Spanien / in die USA ~* leave for (*od.* go to) Spain / the United States

Ausreise|sperre *f* ban on exit visas, ban on leaving the (*od.* a) country, exit embargo; *~verbot n* prohibition from leaving the (*od.* a) country; *~verkehr m* traffic leaving the country; *~visum n* exit visa; *~welle f* wave of departures, emigration wave

ausreisewillig *Adj.* wanting to leave the country, keen to emigrate *präd.*

ausreißen (*unreg.*, *trennb.*, *-ge-*) **I.** *v/t.* (*hat*); (*Haare, Seiten*) tear out (*aus* of); (*Zahn*) pull; (*Bäume, Pflanzen*) pull up (*od.* out); *e-r Fliege ein Bein ~* pull a fly's leg off; *er hat sich dabei kein Bein ausgerissen umg., fig.* he didn't exactly overexert himself, he didn't exactly bust a gut over it *umg.*; *ich könnte Bäume ~ fig.* I feel full of beans *umg.*; **II.** *v/i.* (*ist*) **1.** (*reißen*) *Stoff, Naht etc.:* split; (*Knopfloch*) tear; **2.** (*abreißen*) *Ärmel, Knopf etc.:* come off (*od.* away); **3.** *umg.* (*weglaufen*) do a bunk, *Am.* take a powder; *von zu Hause:* run away; *~ vor* run away from; **4.** *Sport* break away (from the field), put on a spurt

Ausreißer[1] *m; -s, -, ~in f, -, -nen; umg.* **1.** (*Kind etc.*) runaway; **2.** *Sport* break-

away

Ausreißer[2] *m; -s, -; umg.* **1.** *Tech. Messwert etc.:* runaway; **2.** *Schuss:* stray bullet; **3.** (*starke Abweichung*) blip

Ausreißversuch *m* **1.** attempt to escape; **2.** *Sport* attempt to break away

ausreiten (*unreg.*, *trennb.*, *-ge-*) **I.** *v/i.* (*ist*) ride out, go for a ride; *Spazierritt:* go for a hack; **II.** *v/t.* (*hat*); (*Pferd*) exercise; *voll ~* ride *a horse* to its limit

ausreizen *v/t.* (*trennb.*, *hat -ge-*) **1.** *s-e Karten ~* make the most of one's hand, bid up to strength; *j-n ~* outbid s.o.; **2.** (*Thema*) thrash out; *das Thema ist ausgereizt* that subject has been exhausted (*od.* done to death *umg.*)

ausrenken *v/t.* (*trennb.*, *hat -ge-*): *j-m/sich* (*Dat.*) *den Arm etc. ~* dislocate s.o's/one's arm *etc.*; *sich* (*Dat.*) *fast den Hals nach etw. ~ fig.* crane one's neck to see s.th., nearly pull a muscle trying to see s.th. *umg.*

ausrichten (*trennb.*, *hat -ge-*) **I.** *v/t.* **1.** (*Nachricht etc.*) pass on (*j-m* to s.o.); *ich werd's ~* I'll tell him *etc.*, I'll pass it on; *richten Sie ihm Grüße* (*von mir*) *aus* give him my regards, remember me to him; *kann ich etwas ~?* can I take a message?; *sie ließ ihm* (*durch ihren Bruder*) *..., dass ...* she let him know (through her brother) that ...; **2.** (*erreichen*) achieve; *nichts ~* get nowhere; *das wird nicht viel ~* that won't make much (*od.* any) difference; *mit Güte richtest du bei ihr mehr aus als mit Strafen* kindness will get you much further with her than force; *allein konnte er gegen so viele nichts ~* on his own he was no match for so many; **3.** (*gerade richten*) straighten; *in Linie:* align; (*einstellen*) adjust; **4.** *fig.:* *~ auf* (+ *Akk.*) *od. nach* adjust to; *auf Ziel:* aim at, direct at, gear to(wards); *geistig:* orient to(wards); (*angleichen*) bring into line with; *kommunistisch etc. ausgerichtet* communist *etc.* in orientation; *ihr Verhalten war darauf ausgerichtet zu provozieren* her behaviour was designed to provoke; *das Programm auf den od. nach dem Geschmack des Publikums ~* tailor the program(me) to the audience's taste; **5.** (*Veranstaltung*) organize; (*Olympiade etc.*) host; (*Fest, Hochzeit*) make (the) arrangements (*für* for a wedding, *etc.*); **6.** *südd., österr. umg.* (*schlecht machen*) (*j-n*) run s.o. down, bitch about s.o.; **7.** *schw.* (*auszahlen*) pay (out); **II.** *v/refl.* **1.** (*aufstellen*) line up; *Mil.* fall in; **2.** *fig.:* *sich ~ nach* orient(ate) o.s. to (*od.* on) s.th.

Ausrichter *m, ~in f Sport* organizer; *e-r Olympiade etc.:* host

Ausrichtung *f* **1.** (*das Ausrichten 3, 4*) adjustment; alignment; **2.** *Pol.* (*Couleur*) orientation; **3.** *e-r Veranstaltung:* organization; *e-r Olympiade etc.:* hosting; *e-r Hochzeit etc.:* arrangement; **4.** *Bergb.* opening-out (*od.* -up), development

Ausritt *m* ride, (*Spazierritt*) hack, *Am.* nag

ausrollen (*trennb.*, *hat -ge-*) **I.** *v/t.* (*hat*) (*Teppich, Teig*) roll out; (*Kabel*) run (*od.* pay) out; **II.** *v/i.* (*ist*) **1.** *Fahrzeug:* come to a standstill, coast to a stop; *Flug. auch* taxi to a halt; **2.** *Welle:* break

ausrotten *v/t.* (*trennb.*, *hat -ge-*); (*Unkraut*) pull up; (*Tierart, Volk*) wipe out, eradicate, exterminate (*auch fig.*); *fig. auch* root (*od.* stamp) out; *alte Vorurteile ~* uproot old prejudices;

Ausrottung *f* wiping out; *mit Stumpf und Stiel*: extirpation; *e-s Volks*: *auch* genocide

ausrücken (*trennb.*, *-ge-*) **I.** *v/i.* (*ist*) **1.** *Heer, Polizei etc.*: move out; *Feuerwehr*: turn out, go out on call; **2.** *umg.* → *ausreißen* II 3; **II.** *v/t.* (*hat*) **1.** *Tech.* disengage; (*Kupplung*) *auch* shift; **2.** *Druck.* set out (in the margin)

Ausruf *m* cry; *bes. mit Worten*: exclamation; *Ling.* interjection

ausrufen *v/t.* (*unreg., trennb., hat -ge-*) **1.** cry, shout, exclaim; (*Namen etc.*) call out; (*Schlagzeile*) cry out, scream; (*Waren, Zeitung*) cry, hawk (loudly); **2.** *über Lautsprecher etc.*: announce; *Haltestellen* ~ call out (the names of) the stops; *j-n* ~ (*lassen*) page s.o.; **3.** (*Herrscher, Republik etc.*) proclaim *förm.*; (*Streik*) call; *sein Sohn wurde zum König ausgerufen* his son was proclaimed king; *den Notstand* ~ declare a state of emergency; **4.** *zur Versteigerung*: invite bids *for s.th.*

Ausrufer *m*; *-s, -*; *hist.* town crier; *Jahrmarkt*: barker; *Wirts.* hawker

Ausrufezeichen *n Ling.* exclamation mark

Ausrufung *f* proclamation; *e-s Streiks*: call

ausruhen (*trennb., hat -ge-*) **I.** *v/i. und v/refl.* (have a) rest; → *ausgeruht* II, *Lorbeer* 3; **II.** *v/t.*: *die Beine etc.* ~ rest one's legs *etc.*, give one's legs *etc.* a rest

ausrupfen *v/t.* (*trennb., hat -ge-*) pull out; (*Federn*) pluck out; (*Unkraut etc.*) pull up

ausrüsten *v/t.* (*trennb., hat -ge-*) **1.** (*mit* with; *für* for) (*Expedition, Auto, Schiff*) fit out; (*j-n*) equip, supply; *mit Waffen*: *auch* arm; **2.** *fig.* equip (with); **Ausrüstung** *f* **1.** *nur Sg.*; (*das Ausrüsten*) fitting-out, equipping; **2.** *allg.* equipment (*auch Tech. Geräte*); *Sport etc.*: gear; *des Soldaten*: kit

ausrutschen *v/i.* (*trennb., ist -ge-*) **1.** slip (*auf* + *Dat.* on); **2.** *j-m rutscht das Messer / der Pinsel etc. aus* s.o.'s knife/brush *etc.* slips; *manchmal rutscht mir die Hand aus umg.* I sometimes lose my temper and slap him, her, the child *etc.*; **Ausrutscher** *m*; *-s, -*; *umg.* faux pas, gaffe, blunder

Aussaat *f* **1.** sowing; **2.** (*das Gesäte*) seed; **aussäen** *v/t.* (*trennb., hat -ge-*) **1.** sow; **2.** *fig.* sow the seeds of

Aussage *f* **1.** statement (*über* + *Akk.* about); *nach* ~ *von* according to; **2.** *Jur.* testimony (*zu* to); *von Zeugen*: evidence (*auch Pl.*); (*Bericht*) *auch* report; *e-e eidliche/schriftliche* ~ a sworn/written statement; *e-e* ~ *machen* → *aussagen* II; *j-s* ~ *aufnehmen* *Polizei*: take down s.o.'s statement; *die* ~ *verweigern* refuse to make a statement; *vor Gericht*: refuse to give evidence (*od.* testify); *hier steht* ~ *gegen* ~ it's one person's word against another's; *aufgrund der* ~ *von* on the evidence of; **3.** *Ling.* predicate; **4.** *Phil.* proposition; **5.** (*künstlerische* ~) message

Aussagekraft *f* expressiveness; (*Beweiskraft*) validity; **aussagekräftig** *Adj.* expressive; *Statistiken etc.*: sound, convincing

aussagen (*trennb., hat -ge-*) **I.** *v/t.* *Sache*: express, convey; *Person*: state, declare, say; *das Kunstwerk sagt etwas aus* has something to say, has a message; **II.** *v/i. Jur.* make a statement, give evidence; *vor Gericht*: testify, give

evidence (*od.* testimony) in court (*für* in s.o.'s favo[u]r; *gegen* against s.o.; *zu* on); *als Zeuge / vor Gericht* ~ give evidence (*od.* testify) as a witness / in court

aussägen *v/t.* (*trennb., hat -ge-*) saw out

Aussage|satz *m Ling.* declarative sentence, (clause of) statement; ~**verweigerung** *f Jur.* refusal to testify (*od.* give evidence); ~**verweigerungsrecht** *n Jur.* right to refuse to give evidence (*od.* make a statement); *etwa* right to remain silent; ~**weise** *f Ling.* mood

Aussatz *m Med.* leprosy; **aussätzig** *Adj.* leprous; **Aussätzige** *m, f; -n, -n* leper (*auch fig.*)

aussaufen *v/t.* (*unreg., trennb., hat -ge-*) **1.** *Tier*: (*Wasser*) drink up; (*leeren*) empty; **2.** *umg., oft pej. Person*: guzzle; (*Flasche etc.*) finish off, drain

aussaugen *v/t.* (*geh. auch unreg., trennb., hat -ge-*) **1.** (*Saft, Gift etc.*) suck out; (*Frucht, Wunde*) suck; **2.** *fig.* (*Land, Volk*) suck dry; (*bis aufs Blut*) ~ bleed s.o. dry (*od.* white)

ausschaben *v/t.* (*trennb., hat -ge-*) scrape out; *Med. auch* curette; (*Fruchtfleisch, Melone etc.*) scoop out (*aus* of); **Ausschabung** *f Med., der Gebärmutter*: (womb) scrape, curettage

ausschachten *v/t.* (*trennb., hat -ge-*) **1.** (*Keller etc.*) dig out; (*Brunnen, Schacht etc.*) sink; **2.** (*Erde*) dig up, excavate

ausschaffen *v/t.* (*unreg., trennb., hat -ge-*) *schw.* (*aus e-m Land ausweisen*) expel (*aus* from)

Ausschaltautomatik *f* automatic stop (*od.* shutoff)

ausschalten (*trennb., hat -ge-*) **I.** *v/t.* **1.** switch (*od.* turn) off; **2.** *fig.* (*Fehler*) avoid; (*störende Einflüsse, s-e Gefühle*) shut out, exclude; (*Zweifel*) dismiss; **3.** *fig.* (*Konkurrenz, Rivalen*) put out of the running, get rid of; *bes. Sport* eliminate; (*Parlament etc.*) inactivate; (*ermorden*) eliminate; bump off *umg.*; **II.** *v/refl.*: *sich* (*automatisch od. von selbst*) ~ switch (*od.* turn) itself off (automatically)

Ausschalter *m Etech.* circuit breaker

Ausschank *m; -(e)s, Ausschänke* **1.** *nur Sg.* sale of alcoholic drinks; ~ *von Bier etc.* sale of beer *etc.*; **2.** (*Kneipe*) pub, *Am.* bar; **3.** (*Schanktisch*) bar, counter; ~**erlaubnis** *f* licen|ce (*Am.* -se) (to sell alcoholic drinks), *Am. auch* liquor license

Ausschau *f*: ~ *halten* keep a lookout; ~ *halten nach* look out for, be on (*od.* keep) a lookout for; keep one's eyes peeled for *umg.*; *nach e-r Stelle etc.*: look around for; **ausschauen** *v/i.* (*trennb., hat -ge-*) **1.** ~ *nach* look out for; *nach e-r Stelle etc.*: look around for; **2.** *südd., österr.* → *aussehen*

ausschäumen *v/t.* (*trennb., hat -ge-*); *Archit., Tech.* foam

ausscheiden (*unreg., trennb., -ge-*) **I.** *v/t.* (*hat ausgeschieden*) **1.** *Physiol.* excrete; (*Urin*) pass; (*Schweiß etc.*) secrete, exude; (*Gas, Wasser*) expel; **2.** (*aussondern*) sort (*od.* take) out, separate (out); (*beseitigen*) get rid of, remove; **3.** (*aussortieren*) sort out (*aus* from), reject; **II.** *v/i.* (*ist*) **1.** *aus e-m Amt*: retire from; *aus e-r Firma, Regierung etc.*: leave; *aus s-m Amt* ~ *Pol.* withdraw from office; *als Mitarbeiter* ~ leave (the employ of) the company; *als Kabinettsminister* ~ leave one's

post as cabinet minister (*od.* one's cabinet post); **2.** *Sport* be eliminated (*aus* from), drop out (of), retire (from); **3.** (*nicht infrage kommen*) have to be ruled out; *Person*: not be eligible; *sie scheidet von vornherein aus* she can't be considered, she's out of the running already

Ausscheidung *f* **1.** *nur Sg.*; *Physiol.* excretion; *von Urin*: passing; (*Absonderung*) secretion; *von Gas, Wasser etc.*: expulsion; → *ausscheiden* I; **2.** *Physiol.* (*Ausgeschiedenes*) excreted matter; (*Stuhl*) excrement; ~*en* (*Stuhl, Urin*) excreta (*Pl.*); (*Ausfluss*) *auch Pl.* discharge; **3.** *Sport* qualifying contest (*od.* match *od.* round), qualifier; **4.** *Chem.* separation

Ausscheidungs|kampf *m Sport* qualifying contest, qualifier, *Am.* tryout; *bei Leichtathletik*: (qualifying) heat; ~**organ** *n Physiol.* excretory organ; ~**produkt** *n Physiol.* waste product; ~**runde** *f Sport* qualifying round; ~**spiel** *n Sport* qualifying match; ~**wettkampf** *m Sport* qualifying contest, qualifier; *bei Leichtathletik*: (qualifying) heat

ausscheißen *v/i.* (*unreg., trennb., hat -ge-*); *vulg.*: *bei mir hat er ausgeschissen!* I've had it (up to here) with him!, he's really fucked (it) up with me!

ausschenken *v/t.* (*trennb., hat -ge-*) **1.** *als Wirt*: sell, serve (*an* + *Akk.* to); **2.** (*eingießen*) pour out; (*servieren*) serve

ausscheren *v/i.* (*trennb., ist -ge-*) **1.** swerve to the right (*od.* left); *zum Überholen*: pull out; *aus der Kolonne*: leave the convoy; *Soldat*: break rank; *Flugzeug*: break formation; *Schild*: *Achtung, Fahrzeug schert aus!* attention - vehicle swings out when turning (*Am.* vehicle makes wide turns); **2.** *fig.* go one's own way, step out of line; ~ *aus e-m Bündnis etc.*: pull out of; *aus e-r Partei*: leave

ausschicken *v/t.* (*trennb., hat -ge-*) send out

ausschießen *v/t.* (*unreg., trennb., hat -ge-*) **1.** *j-m ein Auge* ~ shoot s.o.'s eye out; **2.** *Sport, Schießen*: (*Preis etc.*) shoot for; (*Meisterschaft*) hold a shooting competition for

ausschiffen (*trennb., hat -ge-*) *Naut.* **I.** *v/t.* put ashore; (*Ladung*) *auch* unload, discharge; (*Passagiere*) *auch* disembark, put ashore; **II.** *v/refl.* disembark, land, go ashore; **Ausschiffung** *f* (*Ladung*) unloading; (*Passagiere*) disembarkation

ausschildern *v/t.* (*trennb., hat -ge-*) signpost, *Am.* sign, mark *s.th.* with signs; *die Umleitung ist ausgeschildert auch* the diversion is marked

ausschimpfen *v/t.* (*trennb., hat -ge-*) give *s.o.* a (good) telling-off (*od.* tongue-lashing *umg.*, bollocking *Brit. umg.*)

ausschirren *vt/i.* (*trennb., hat -ge-*) (*Pferd*) unharness; (*Ochsen*) unyoke

ausschlachten *v/t.* (*trennb., hat -ge-*) **1.** (*Tier*) cut up; **2.** *umg.* (*Auto etc.*) cannibalize, break up for spare parts; **3.** *fig., mst pej.* (*ausnutzen*) exploit, make *political etc.* capital out of; (*Roman, Briefe etc.*) quarry *s.th.* for information *etc.*

ausschlafen (*unreg., trennb., hat -ge-*) **I.** *v/i. und v/refl.* get a good night's sleep; *sonntags etc.*: have a lie-in (*Am.* sleep-in); *hast du jetzt ausgeschla-*

fen? have you had enough sleep?, have you slept for as long as you wanted?; → *ausgeschlafen* II; **II.** *v/t.*: *s-n Rausch etc.* ~ sleep (it) off
Ausschlag *m* **1.** *Med.* rash; *e-n* ~ *bekommen* break (*od.* come) out in a rash (*Pickel: auch* in spots); **2.** *e-s Zeigers:* deflection; *e-s Pendels:* swing; **3.** *fig.:* *den* ~ *geben* decide the issue, clinch matters; *bei knappem Ergebnis:* tip the balance, be the deciding factor; *den* ~ *geben für etw.*: decide; *bei e-r Wahl etc., für j-n:* tip the scales in *s.o.'s* favo(u)r; *er gab den* ~ *für unseren Sieg* without him we would have lost; *das gab den* ~ *für i-e Entscheidung* that was the crucial factor in her decision
ausschlagen (*unreg., trennb., -ge-*) **I.** *v/t.* (*hat*) **1.** (*Zahn etc.*) knock out; → *Fass* 2; **2.** (*ablehnen*) turn down; (*j-n*) *auch* reject; (*etw.*) *auch* refuse; *Jur.* (*Erbschaft etc.*) disclaim, waive; **3.** (*auskleiden*) line; **4.** (*Feuer*) beat out; **5.** (*breit schlagen*) (*Metall*) beat out; **6.** (*Staubtuch*) shake out; **II.** *v/i.* **1.** (*hat*) *Pferd:* kick out; *Person:* hit (*od.* lash) out (in all directions); **2.** (*hat/ist*) *Pendel:* swing; *Zeiger:* deflect; *Geigerzähler, Messgerät:* deviate; *Waage:* turn; *Wünschelrute:* dip; **3.** (*hat/ist*) *Bot.* sprout, bud; *Bäume:* come into leaf, leaf out; **4.** *ihr Herz / die Turmuhr hat ausgeschlagen* her heart beat its last / the clock in the tower finished striking (*od.* chiming), **5.** (*ist*) (*sich entwickeln*) turn out; *zum Guten* ~ turn out fine (*od.* well)
ausschlaggebend *Adj.* decisive; ~ *sein auch* be the deciding factor; ~*e Stimme* casting vote; *von* ~*er Bedeutung* of crucial (*od.* prime) importance; *das war* (*für ihn*) ~ *bei e-r Wahl etc.*: that tipped the scales (in his favo[u]r; *das ist für mich nicht* ~ that doesn't cut any ice with me
ausschließen (*unreg., trennb., hat -ge-*) **I.** *v/t.* **1.** (*j-n, auch Arbeiter*) lock out; **2.** (*nicht zulassen*) bar *s.o.* (*aus* from); *aus e-r Partei, Schule etc.*: expel (from); *Sport* disqualify (from); *vorübergehend:* suspend (from); (*ausnehmen*) exclude (*von* from); *aus Gemeinschaft:* ostracize; *aus der Kirche* ~ excommunicate; *die Öffentlichkeit* ~ exclude the public; *sich ausgeschlossen fühlen* feel left out (in the cold); **3.** (*Irrtum, Möglichkeit, Verbrechen etc.*) rule out, preclude; (*Zweifel*) remove; *vom Umtausch ausgeschlossen* non-exchangeable, non-refundable; *der Rechtsweg ist ausgeschlossen bei Preisausschreiben etc.*: etwa the judges' (*od.* court's) decision is final; *auch* no appeal is permitted; *das eine schließt das andere nicht aus* the one does not exclude the other; *einander od. sich (gegenseitig)* ~ be mutually exclusive; *es ist nicht auszuschließen, dass ...* one cannot rule out the possibility that ...; → *ausgeschlossen* II; **4.** *Druck.* justify, space; **II.** *v/refl.* **1.** exclude o.s. (*von* from); *das gilt für alle, da schließe ich mich nicht aus* that applies to everyone, including myself; **2.** *umg.* (*aussperren*) lock (*od.* shut) o.s. out
ausschließlich I. *Adj.* exclusive, sole; **II.** *Adv.* exclusively, solely; *er interessiert sich* ~ *für ...* all he's interested in is ..., he's only interested in ...; *sie trägt* ~ *Kleider* she only ever wears

dresses; ~ *für Mitglieder* (for) members only; *das ist* ~ *m-e Sache* it is my business (*od.* problem) and mine alone; *das ist* ~ *deine Schuld* it's all your own fault, the blame is entirely your own; **III.** *Präp.* (+ *Gen. od. Dat.*) excluding, exclusive of; *der Preis versteht sich* ~ *Mehrwertsteuer* the price does not include VAT; **Ausschließlichkeit** *f, nur Sg.* exclusiveness
Ausschließung *f* **1.** (*Aussperrung*) lockout; **2.** → *Ausschluss* 1
ausschlüpfen *v/i.* (*trennb., ist -ge-*) *Tier:* hatch out
ausschlürfen *v/t.* (*trennb., hat -ge-*) slurp, sip up
Ausschluss *m* **1.** exclusion; *von Möglichkeiten etc.*: ruling out; *unter* ~ *von* (*od.* + *Gen.*) to the exclusion of; **2.** (*Ausweisung*) expulsion, exclusion; *Sport* disqualification (*auch von e-m Amt*); *zeitweiliger:* suspension; *unter* ~ *der Öffentlichkeit Jur.* in camera, behind closed doors, in private; ~*frist* *f* time limit; ~*verfahren* *n* disqualification system (*od.* procedure)
ausschmieren *v/t.* (*trennb., hat -ge-*) **1.** (*Backform etc.*) grease; **2.** *Tech.* lubricate; *mit Fett:* grease; *mit Öl:* oil; **3.** *umg. fig.* (*betrügen*) put one over on *s.o.*; *ätsch, ausgeschmiert!* ha, tricked you! (*od.* gotcha!)
ausschmücken *v/t.* (*trennb., hat -ge-*) **1.** decorate; **2.** *fig.* (*Erzählung*) embroider, embellish; **Ausschmückung** *f* **1.** decoration; **2.** *fig.* embellishment
ausschnaufen *v/i. und v/refl.* (*trennb., hat -ge-*); *südd., österr. umg.* **1.** (*zu Atem kommen*) get one's breath back; **2.** (*Pause machen*) take a breather
Ausschneidebogen *m* cut-out sheet (*od.* piece of cardboard)
ausschneiden *v/t.* (*unreg., trennb., hat -ge-*) **1.** cut out; *aus der Zeitung: auch* take a clipping (*Am. auch* cutting); **2.** (*angefaultes Obst etc.*) cut away; **3.** (*Bäume*) prune; **4.** → *ausgeschnitten* II
Ausschnitt *m* **1.** *am Kleid:* neck; *weitS.* neckline; *mit tiefem* ~ with a low neckline; **2.** (*Zeitungsausschnitt*) clipping, *Am. auch* cutting; **3.** *Math., e-s Kreises:* sector; **4.** *fig.* (*Teil*) part; *e-s Bildes:* detail; *e-s Buches:* extract; *e-s Films, Konzerts:* excerpt; ~*e* (*Höhepunkte*) highlights (*aus* of, from); *ich habe es nur in* ~*en gesehen* I only saw parts of it
ausschnitt(s)weise I. *Adv.* partially; **II.** *Adj.; nur attr.* in extracts
ausschöpfen *v/t.* (*trennb., hat -ge-*) **1.** scoop out; (*Boot*) bail (*od.* bale) out; **2.** *fig.* (*Möglichkeiten, Thema*) exhaust
ausschrauben *v/t.* (*trennb., hat -ge-*) unscrew, screw off (*od.* out); (*Glühbirne*) *auch* take out, remove
ausschreiben *v/t.* (*unreg., trennb., hat -ge-*) **1.** (*Wort etc.*) write out (in full); **2.** (*Scheck*) make (*od.* write) out (*j-m* to *s.o.*); *j-m ein Rezept etc.*: write out a prescription *etc.*; **3.** (*ankündigen*) announce; (*Stelle etc.*) advertise; (*e-e Belohnung*) offer; (*Steuern*) impose; *Wirts.* put *s.th.* out to tender; *Wahlen* ~ call elections, *in GB: auch* go to the country; **Ausschreibung** *f e-r Stelle:* advertisement; *Wirts.* tender, call for tenders; *Sport* invitation to a competition
ausschreien (*unreg., trennb., hat -ge-*) **I.** *v/refl.* have a good scream, cry one's fill; **II.** *v/refl. und v/i.* (*aufhören zu*

schreien) stop screaming; **III.** *v/t.* shout out
ausschreiten *v/i.* (*unreg., trennb., ist -ge-*) step out, stride (out); **Ausschreitungen** *Pl.* (*Aufruhr*) rioting *Sg.*, riot *Sg.*, riots, violent clashes; *es kam zu* ~ there was rioting, there were violent clashes; ~ *der Polizei gegen die Demonstranten* police violence against the demonstrators
Ausschuss *m* **1.** (*Komitee*) committee; **2.** *nur Sg.*: (*fehlerhafte Ware*) rejects *Pl.*, seconds *Pl.*; (*Abfall*) waste; **3.** (*Wunde am Austrittsstelle e-s Geschosses*) exit wound; ~*mitglied* *n* committee member; ~*quote* *f* waste rate, rate of rejects; ~*sitzung* *f* committee meeting; ~*ware* *f* rejects *Pl.*, seconds *Pl.*
ausschütteln *v/t.* (*trennb., hat -ge-*); (*Staub, Tuch*) shake out
ausschütten (*trennb., hat -ge-*) **I.** *v/t.* **1.** (*Flüssigkeit*) pour out; (*verschütten*) spill; (*Kartoffeln etc.*) empty out; (*Kohle*) *auch* dump; **2.** (*Gefäß, Behälter*) empty; → *Herz*[1] 8, *Kind* 2; **3.** *Lotterie:* pay out; *Wirts.* (*Dividenden etc.*) distribute; **II.** *v/refl.*: *sich* ~ *vor Lachen umg.* kill o.s. laughing, split one's.sides with laughter, crease (*od.* double) up; **Ausschüttung** *f Lotterie:* payout; *Wirts. von Dividenden:* distribution, dividend
ausschwärmen *v/i.* (*trennb., ist -ge-*) **1.** *Bienen:* swarm out; **2.** *fig.* scatter (to the four winds)
ausschweifen *v/i.* (*trennb., ist -ge-*) **1.** go to extremes; *allg.* lead a dissolute life; **2.** *beim Erzählen:* digress, go off on a tangent; *Fantasie:* run riot; **ausschweifend I.** *Part.Präs.* → *ausschweifen* II. **Adj.** (*übertrieben*) excessive; *Fantasie:* wild; *Leben:* dissolute, licentious; **Ausschweifung** *f*; *mst Pl.* excess; *wüste* ~*en* wild excesses; ~*en der Fantasie* products of *s.o.'s* wild (*od.* vivid) imagination
ausschweigen *v/refl.* (*unreg., trennb., hat -ge-*) remain silent (*zu od. über* + *Akk.* on), refuse to speak (about); *Politiker etc.*: refuse to comment (on)
ausschwemmen *v/t.* (*trennb., hat -ge-*) **1.** (*herausschwemmen*) wash out; **2.** (*aushöhlen*) (*Ufer etc.*) hollow out, erode; **3.** (*reinigen*) flush (*od.* wash) out
ausschwenken (*trennb., hat -ge-*) **I.** *v/t.* **1.** (*Behälter*) swill out; (*Wäsche*) rinse (out); **II.** *v/i.* *Kran etc.*: swivel, swing out; *Anhänger etc.*: veer (a)round, veer to the left (*od.* right)
ausschwingen *v/i.* (*unreg., trennb., hat -ge-*) **1.** (*aufhören zu schwingen*) stop swinging; **2.** (*weit*) ~ swing out (wide)
ausschwitzen *v/t.* (*trennb., hat -ge-*); (*Harz, Feuchtigkeit etc.*) sweat (out), exude; (*Krankheit etc.*) sweat out
Aussegnungshalle *f* chapel of rest
aussehen (*unreg., trennb., hat -ge-*) *v/i.* **1.** *äußerlich:* look; *gut/schlecht* ~ be good-looking / ugly; *gesundheitlich:* look well/ill; *du siehst schlecht aus auch* you don't look very well (*od.* too good); ~ *nach od. wie* look like; *wie sieht er aus?* what does he look like?; ~ *wie das blühende Leben* look the very picture of health, *Am. umg.* look like a million dollars (*od.* bucks); *wie siehst du denn aus?* *umg.* what happened to you?; *er sah vielleicht aus!* *umg.* he looked a real sight; you should have seen him; **2.** *umg., fig.* (*e-e Leistung erbringen*): *gut/schlecht*

~ be good/bad (**bei, in** at, in); **im Ma-the-Test habe ich ganz schlecht aus-gesehen** I did really badly in the maths (*Am.* math) test; **im letzten Spiel haben sie schlecht ausgesehen** *umg.* they lost their last game miserably (*od.* big time *umg.*); **3.** (*e-n Eindruck machen*) look; **nach etwas/nichts ~** look impressive/pathetic; **es sieht nach Regen aus** it looks like rain (*od.* as if it's going to rain); **es sieht (ganz) danach aus** it (certainly) looks like it; **er sieht ganz danach aus** *umg.* he looks the sort; **sehe ich etwa so aus?** *umg.* what do you take me for?; **so siehst du aus!** *umg.* that's what 'you think; **4.** *fig. Situation etc.*: look, seem; **schlecht/gefährlich etc. ~** look bad/dangerous *etc.*; **das sieht nach Betrug etc. aus** that looks like fraud *etc.*; **es sieht so aus, als käme er** it looks like he's coming; **mit dem** *od.* **für unseren Ausflug sieht es schlecht aus** things aren't looking good for our trip; **wie sieht's aus?** *umg.* (wie geht's) how are things?; (*wie geht die Sache voran*) how are you *etc.* getting on (*Am.* along)?; (*wie findest du's*) what's the verdict?; **wie sieht's bei od. mit dir aus?** how about you?; **5. ~ nach** (*Ausschau halten*) look out for

Aussehen *n*; *-s, kein Pl.* appearance, looks *Pl.*; **dem ~ nach** judging by appearances; **man sollte nicht nach dem ~ urteilen** one shouldn't judge (*od.* go) by appearances

außen *Adv.* **1.** (on the) outside; **von ~** from (the) outside; **nach ~** (to the) outside; **von innen nach ~** from (the) inside out; **nach ~ dringen** get out; *Flüssigkeit, Geheimnis etc.*: *auch* leak out; *Geräusch*: get through to the outside; **dringt die Musik nach ~?** can you hear the music through the walls?; **die Füße nach ~ drehen** turn one's feet (*od.* toes) out; **~ liegende** *od.* **gelegene Zimmer etc.** rooms *etc.* with windows to the outside (of the building); **~ hui, innen pfui** *umg.* it's all show; **2.** *fig.*: **nach ~** (*hin*) outwardly, on the outside (*od.* surface); **nach ~ (hin) erscheint sie sehr höflich** *auch* she has a veneer of politeness; **nach ~ tragen** make *s.th.* public; **Hilfe etc. von ~** outside help *etc.*; **~ stehende Beobachter etc.** outside observers *etc.*; **davon darf nichts nach ~ gelangen** nothing should leak (*od.* get) out about this; **etw. ~ vor lassen** *nordd.* (*ausschließen*) exclude *s.th.*; (*Tatsache, Aspekt etc.*) disregard *s.th.*, ignore *s.th.*; **~ vor bleiben** *od.* **sein** *nordd.* (*Person*) be excluded, be left out; (*Tatsache, Aspekt etc.*) be disregarded, be ignored

Außen *m*; *-, -*; *Sport*: **~ spielen** play on the wing

Außen\anlagen *Pl. e-s Gebäudekomplexes*: grounds *Pl.*, outside facilities *Pl.*; **~ansicht** *f* exterior view; **~arbeiten** *Pl. beim Bau*: outside work *Sg.*; **~aufnahme** *f Fot.* outdoor shot; *Film*: location shot; **~bahn** *f Sport* outside lane; **~beleuchtung** *f* exterior (*od.* external) lighting; **~bereich** *m* outside; **sind sie für den ~ geeignet?** are they suitable for use outdoors?; **~bezirk** *m* outlying area (*od.* suburb); **~e e-r Stadt**: *auch* outskirts

Außenborder *m*; *-s, -* **1.** outboard (motor); **2.** (*Boot*) outboard motorboat

Außenbordmotor *m* outboard motor

aussenden *v/t.* (*auch unreg., trennb., hat -ge-*) **1.** (*Boten etc.*) send out; **2.** *TV etc.* (*ausstrahlen*) *auch* transmit, broadcast; **3.** (*Paket*) dispatch

Außendienst *m* field service; *Mil.* field duty; **im ~** in the field; **~ haben** *od.* **machen** work outside the office

Außendienstler *m*; *-s, -*, **~in** *f*; *-, -nen* → **Außendienstmitarbeiter**

Außendienstmitarbeiter *m*, **~in** *f* sales (*od.* field) representative (*od.* rep *umg.*); *Pl. auch* sales force, field staff *Sg.* (*mst V. im Pl.*); **~ sein** *auch* work in the field

Außenfeldspieler *m Sport, Baseball*: outfielder

Außenhandel *m Wirts.* foreign (*od.* export) trade

Außenhandels\bilanz *f Wirts.* balance of foreign trade; **~defizit** *n* foreign trade (*od.* export) deficit; **~überschuss** *m* foreign trade (*od.* export) surplus

Außen\kante *f* outside edge; **~linie** *f Sport* boundary line; *engS.* sideline; **~luft** *f* external air, air from outside; **~maße** *Pl.* outside measurements; **~mauer** *f* outer (*od.* exterior) wall

Außen\minister *m*, **~ministerin** *f Pol.* foreign minister (*od.* secretary); *in GB*: Foreign Secretary; *in den USA*: Secretary of State; **~ministerium** *n* foreign ministry; *in GB*: Foreign and Commonwealth Office; *in den USA*: State Department

Außenpolitik *f Pol.* foreign affairs *Pl.*; *bestimmte*: foreign policy; **außenpolitisch** *Adj.* foreign-policy ...; international; **~er Sprecher** spokesperson on foreign affairs; **~e Debatte** debate on foreign policy

Außenposten *m bes. Mil.* outpost; *vorgeschobener*: advance(d) post

Außenseite *f* outside, exterior

Außenseiter *m*; *-s, -*, **~in** *f*; *-, -nen*; *Sport und fig.*: outsider; **gesellschaftlicher ~** social misfit; *Pl. auch* fringes of society; **~chance** *f*: **e-e ~ haben** have an outside chance; **~position** *f* fringe existence; **in e-e ~ geraten** end up on the fringes; **~rolle** *f* role of an (*od.* the) outsider (*od.* [the] outsiders); **in e-e ~ gedrängt werden** be pushed onto the sidelines, be marginalized

Außen\ski *m Sport* outside ski; **~spiegel** *m Mot.* wing mirror; **~stände** *Pl. Wirts.* outstanding accounts, accounts receivable; **~stehende** *m, f; -n, -n* outsider; (*Beobachter*) outside observer, observer on the outside; **~stelle** *f* branch (office), field agency; **~stürmer** *m*, **~stürmerin** *f Sport* winger; **linker ~** outside left; **~tasche** *f* outside pocket; **~temperatur** *f* outdoor temperature; **~toilette** *f* outside toilet; **~übertragung** *f Funk., TV* outside broadcast; **~verteidiger** *m*, **~verteidigerin** *f Sport* full-back; **~viertel** *n* suburb; **in e-m ~ leben** live in a suburb (*od.* the suburbs); **~wand** *f* outer wall; **~welt** *f* outside world; **von der ~ abgeschnitten** *auch* cut off from the world around (*od.* outside world); **~winkel** *m Math.* exterior angle; **~wirtschaft** *f*; *nur Sg.* foreign trade

außer I. *Präp.* (*+ Dat.*) **1.** (*Ggs. in*) out of; **~ Reichweite** out of (*od.* beyond) reach; **~ Frage** out of the question; **~ Haus sein/essen** be/eat out; → **Land** 5; **2.** **~ sich sein** be beside o.s. (*vor* with); **~ sich geraten** lose control over o.s.; *umg.* flip one's lid, go mad;

3. a) (*abgesehen von*) apart from, *bes. Am.* aside from; except (for); **alle ~ mir** all except (*od.* but) me; **~ ihr kenne ich keine Künstler** I don't know any artists other than (*od.* apart from) her; **täglich ~ montags** every day except (for) Mondays; **sie geht nicht gern aus, ~ zum Tanzen / ins Kino** she doesn't like to go out much, apart from dancing / to the cinema, **b)** (*zusätzlich zu*) besides, in addition to; **~ Spanisch spricht sie auch noch Russisch und Polnisch** as well as Spanish she also speaks Russian and Polish; **~ Pamela und Pia kommt auch noch Eva** as well as Pamela and Pia, Eva's coming too; **II.** *Konj.*: **~ (wenn)** unless; **~ dass** except that, apart from the fact that; **s-e Theorie versteht niemand ~ er selbst** no one can understand his theory except him, he is the only one who understands his theory

außer... *im Adj.* extra(-)...

äußer... *Adj.*; *nur attr.* **1.** *Mauer, Schicht etc.*: outer, outside; *Verletzung, Angelegenheit, Umstände, Ursache*: external; *Druck*: outside, external, from outside; *Gefahr*: external, from outside; *Ähnlichkeit, Eindruck*: (on the) surface, outward; **~er Rahmen** setting (*+ Gen.* for); **~e Erscheinung** → **Äußere** 2; **2.** *Wirts., Pol.* foreign

Außerachtlassung *f*; *nur Sg.* disregard, neglect (*+ Gen.* of); **unter ~ der Vorschriften** disregarding (*od.* ignoring) the regulations

außer\beruflich *Adj.* private, outside one's job; **~betrieblich** *Adj.* external, private

außerdem *Adv.* **1.** (*zusätzlich*) as well, in addition; **er besitzt e-e Hotelkette und ~ (noch) e-e Fluggesellschaft** and an airline as well, plus (*od.* as well as) an airline, and an airline on top (of it), and an airline besides; **~ gibt es was zu essen** and there'll be something to eat too (*od.* as well); **~ benötigen wir einen neuen Rechner** furthermore, we need a new PC, we also need a new PC; **2.** *bei Begründung*: and anyway, and apart from that (*betonter*: anything); *betonter*: *auch* and on top of that

außerdienstlich *Adj.* unofficial, private; *Mil.* off-duty ...

Äußere *n*; *-n, kein Pl.* **1.** outside; **2.** (*Erscheinung*) (outward) appearance; externals *Pl.*; **nach dem Äußeren urteilen** go (*od.* judge) by appearances; **von angenehmem ~n** pleasant, personable

außer\ehelich *Adj. Kind*: illegitimate, out-of-wedlock; **~er Verkehr** extramarital intercourse (*od.* sex); **~europäisch** *Adj.* non-European; **~fahrplanmäßig** *Adj. Zug etc.*: special, unscheduled; **~gerichtlich** *Adj.* out-of-court *attr.*, out of court *präd.*, extra-judicial; **~er Vergleich** out-of-court settlement

außergewöhnlich I. *Adj.* unusual; *Begabung, Leistung, Mensch etc.*: exceptional, remarkable; **das ist für ihn ~** that's not typical of him (*od.* like him) at all; **~e Belastungen** *Steuererklärung*: extraordinary expenses, non-recurring expenditure; **II.** *Adv.* (*sehr*) extremely, exceptionally; **~ gut** *auch* exceptional, outstanding

außerhalb I. *Präp.* (*+ Gen. od. von*) outside; (*jenseits*) beyond (*auch fig.*); **~ der Stadt/Arbeitszeit** out of town / working hours; **~ m-r Reichweite** out of (*od.* beyond) my reach; **II.** *Adv.* out

of town; *weit* ~ far away (from town); *von* ~ *kommen* come from out of town; ~ *stehen fig.* be on the outside
Außerhausverkauf *m* takeaway(s *Pl.*), *Am.* take-out, carry-out
außerirdisch *Adj.* extraterrestrial; ~*es Wesen auch* being from outer space, alien (from outer space)
Außerkraftsetzung *f* annulment; *e-s Gesetzes*: repeal; *zeitweilige*: suspension
äußerlich I. *Adj.* **1.** external; *Verletzung, Wunde etc.*: surface ...; *Erscheinung*: outward; *nur zur* ~*en Anwendung Med.* for external use only; **2.** *fig.* on the surface; (*oberflächlich*) superficial; *s-e* ~*e Ruhe verbarg s-e Erregung* his outward calm hid (*od.* disguised) his excitement; **II.** *Adv.* **1.** on the outside; *Oberfläche*: on the surface; **2.** *fig.* outwardly, on the surface; *rein* ~ *betrachtet* on the surface, on the face of it; **Äußerlichkeit** *f; mst Pl.; mst pej.* **1.** *bei Person*: (*Aussehen*) (outward) appearance, externals *Pl.*; (*Umgangsformen*) formalities *Pl.*, manners *Pl.*; **2.** *fig. bei Sache*: (*Formalität*) formality; (*Unwesentliches*) minor detail, triviality
äußern I. *v/t.* **1.** (*sagen*) say; (*Anerkennung, Mitgefühl, Wunsch etc.*) express, show; (*Unzufriedenheit, Verdacht, Vermutung*) voice; (*Worte*) utter; *s-e Meinung* ~ voice one's opinion, put one's point of view; *sie äußerte Kritik an s-m Verhalten* she criticized his behavio(u)r; **II.** *v/refl.* **1.** say something (*über* + *Akk. od.* *zu* about); (*s-e Meinung sagen*) *auch* say what one thinks (about), give one's opinion (on); *sich* ~ *über* (+ *Akk.*) *offiziell*: comment on, make a statement on; *sich kritisch/lobend* ~ *über* (+ *Akk.*) criticize/praise, be critical about / be full of praise for; *sich dahin gehend* ~, *dass ...* make a comment to the effect that ...; *sie wollte sich nicht dazu* ~ she didn't want to comment (on that); **2.** *Sache*: show; *die Krankheit äußert sich in* (+ *Dat.*) the symptoms of the disease are ..., the disease manifests itself in ...
außerordentlich I. *Adj.* **1.** extraordinary; (*hervorragend*) exceptional, outstanding; (*erstaunlich*) remarkable, astonishing, amazing; (*ungewöhnlich*) uncommon, unusual, singular; (*ungeheuer*) immense, enormous, extreme; *Außerordentliches leisten* achieve remarkable things (*od.* a remarkable amount); **2.** *nur attr.*; (*Sonder...*) special, extraordinary; ~*e Ausgaben* extras, extraordinary expenditure *Sg.*; ~*es Gericht* special court; ~*er Professor etwa* reader, senior lecturer, *Am. etwa* associate professor; **II.** *Adv.* (*sehr*) → I 1; ~ *schwierig* extremely difficult; *ich bedaure es* ~ I very much regret it; *es freut mich* ~ I'm very pleased indeed, I'm incredibly pleased; ~ *viel Mühe* an enormous amount of trouble
außerorts *Adv. österr., schw.* out of town
außer|parlamentarisch *Adj.* extraparliamentary; ~*e Opposition* (*abgek.* *APO*) *anti-authoritarian and non-parliamentary reform movement* (*particularly during the German Grand Coalition of 1966-1969*); ~*planmäßig Adj.* additional; *Beamter*: supernumerary; *Gelder*: unbudgeted; *Eisenb. etc.*: special, unscheduled; ~*schulisch Adj.* private, outside school *präd.*; ~*e Erzie-*

hung non-formal education; ~*sinnlich Adj.*: ~*e Wahrnehmung* extrasensory perception, ESP
äußerst *Adv.* extremely, exceedingly; ~ *verwirrend auch* confusing in the extreme
äußerst... I. *Sup.* outermost; → *äußer...*; **II.** *Adj.* **1.** (*entferntest*) furthest (*od.* farthest), ... furthest (*od.* farthest) away; *Ort*: *auch* remotest; *im* ~*en Norden* in the far (*od.* extreme) north; **2.** *zeitlich*: latest possible; *das ist der* ~*e Termin auch* that's the latest possible deadline; **3.** *tiefste/höchste Preis*: extremely high/low, rock--bottom/top; *das ist mein* ~*es Angebot* I can't go any lower/higher than that; *für beide*: that's my final offer; **4.** (*extrem*) extreme; (*völlig*) utter; *im* ~*en Fall* (*höchstens*) at the most; (*schlimmstenfalls*) if worst comes to worst, if it comes to that; *mit* ~*er Konzentration* with the utmost concentration; *mit* ~*er Kraft* by a supreme effort; *fahren etc.*: (at) full speed; *von* ~*er Wichtigkeit* extremely important, of the utmost importance; **5.** *aufs* ~*e* od. *Äußerste erregt etc.* extremely, incredibly *excited etc.*; excited etc. in the extreme
außerstande, außer Stande *Adj.; nur präd.*: ~ *zu* (+ *Inf.*) unable to (+ *Inf.*); (*vollkommen unfähig*) incapable of (+ *Ger.*); *ich fühle od. sehe mich* ~, *es zu tun auch* I can't possibly do it, I am not in a position to do it; *sie zeigte/erklärte sich* ~ *zu helfen* she indicated/explained that she was unable to help
Äußerste *n; -n, kein Pl.* **1.** the limit; the maximum, *the* most; (*das Schlimmste*) the worst; *auf das* ~ *gefasst* prepared for the worst; *das* ~ *wagen* risk everything (*od.* it all); *sein* ~*s tun* do one's utmost; *zum* ~*n entschlossen* prepared to go to any lengths; *wenn es zum* ~*n kommt* if worst comes to worst; *es zum* ~*n kommen lassen* let it (*od.* things etc.) get to this (stage); *bis zum* ~*n gehen od. es bis zum* ~*n treiben* push things to the limit, go on (un)til the bitter end; **2.** → *äußerst...* II 5
äußerstenfalls *Adv.* **1.** (*höchstens*) at (the) most, at best, at the outside; *ich warte* ~ *bis 19 Uhr* I'll wait until 7 o'clock at the latest; **2.** (*schlimmstenfalls*) at worst, if worst comes to worst
außer|tariflich *Adj.* outside the agreed scale; ~*e Leistungen* fringe benefits; ~*tourlich Adj. österr.* (*zusätzlich*) additional, special
Äußerung *f* **1.** (*Bemerkung*) remark, comment; (*Aussage*) statement, comment; *sich jeder* ~ *enthalten* refuse to comment; **2.** (*Ausdruck, Zeichen*) expression, sign
aussetzen (*trennb., hat -ge-*) **I.** *v/t.* **1.** (*Kind, Tier*) abandon; *auf e-r Insel*: maroon; **2.** (*Fische, wilde Tiere*) release (into the wild); *Agr.* (*Pflanzen*) plant out; **3.** *Naut.* (*Boote*) launch, lower; (*Passagiere*) put ashore, disembark; **4.** (*preisgeben*) expose (*Dat.* to); (*Kritik, Spott etc.*) *auch* lay open to; *Wind und Wetter ausgesetzt sein* be exposed to the weather; *j-s Launen hilflos ausgesetzt sein* be at the mercy of s.o.'s moods; **5.** *im Testament*: bequeath, leave; (*Belohnung, Preis*) offer, promise; *e-n Kopfpreis auf j-n* ~ put a price on s.o.'s head; **6.** (*unterbrechen*) interrupt; *Jur.* (*Verfahren, Ur-*

teil) suspend; **7.** *Jur.*: *zur Bewährung* ~ give a suspended sentence; **8.** *etwas* ~ (*od. auszusetzen haben*) *an* (+ *Dat.*) object to, find fault with; *was ist od. gibt es daran auszusetzen?* what's wrong with it?; *er hat immer etwas auszusetzen* (*an* + *Dat.*) he's never satisfied (with), he never stops criticizing; *er hat dauernd was an mir auszusetzen* he's always going on at (*Am.* picking on) me about something (or other); *ich habe nichts daran auszusetzen* I have no objections, I have nothing against it; *an* (*Gerät etc.*: I have no complaints (about it); **II.** *v/i.* **1.** (*unterbrechen*) stop, break off; *Herz, Pulsschlag*: miss a beat; *öfter*: be irregular; *völlig*: stop (beating); *Motor*: stall; **2.** (*e-e Pause machen*) take a rest; *beim Spiel*: (*e-e Runde*) ~ (*müssen*) (have to) miss a turn, (have to) sit (a round) out; *mit etw.* ~ stop (+ *Ger.*); *sie hat mit der Pille ausgesetzt* she's stopped taking the pill; *ohne auszusetzen* without stopping; **III.** *v/refl.* → I 4
Aussetzer *m umg.*: *e-n* ~ *haben* have a blackout, faint
Aussetzung *f* **1.** *e-s Kindes etc.*: abandonment; **2.** *e-s wilden Tieres*: release (into the wild); *von Pflanzen*: planting (out); **3.** *e-s Preises*: offer; **4.** *Jur., e-s Urteils*: suspension; *zur Bewährung*: deferment
Aussicht *f* **1.** view (*auf* + *Akk.* of; *über* + *Akk.* over *od.* upon); *ein Zimmer mit* ~ *aufs Meer* a room overlooking the sea (*od.* with seaview); *hier oben hat man* ~ *ist* ~*e schöne* ~ there's a lovely view from up here; *j-m die* ~ *versperren* obstruct (*od.* block) s.o.'s view; **2.** *fig.* prospect(s *Pl.*), chance (*auf* + *Akk.* of; *zu* + *Inf.* of + *Ger.*); *die weiteren* ~*en Met.* the further outlook; *gute/schlechte* ~*en haben* have good/poor chances; ~*(en) haben auf* (+ *Akk.*) be in the running (*od.* in line) for; *das Projekt hat große* ~ *auf Erfolg* the project stands a good chance (of succeeding); *in* ~ *sein* be coming up, be in the offing; *e-e Gehaltserhöhung ist für dieses Jahr nicht in* ~ there's no prospect of a pay rise (*Am.* raise) this year; *in* ~ *stellen* promise, hold out the prospect of; *in* ~ *haben* have s.th. in prospect; *e-e neue Stelle in* ~ *haben* have the possibility of getting a new job (*od.* a job prospect); *in* ~ *nehmen geh.* take s.th. into consideration, consider s.th.; *das sind ja schöne* ~*en! iro.* that's a fine view
aussichtslos *Adj.* hopeless; ~*! auch* no chance; *es ist ein* ~*es Unterfangen* it's a hopeless venture, it's doomed to fail(ure); *e-e* ~*e Situation* a no-win situation; *es ist* ~, *es* (*auch nur*) *zu versuchen* there's no point in (even) trying; **Aussichtslosigkeit** *f; nur Sg.* hopelessness, futility
Aussichts|plattform *f* viewing (*od.* observation) platform; ~*punkt* *m* lookout (*od.* vantage) point
aussichtsreich *Adj.* promising; *es ist ein* ~*er Posten* the job has good prospects
Aussichtsturm *m* observation (*od.* lookout) tower
aussickern *v/i.* (*trennb., ist -ge-*) seep (*od.* ooze) out (*aus* from); (*tröpfeln*) trickle out (of)
aussieben *v/t.* (*trennb., hat -ge-*) **1.** (*entfernen*) sift (*od.* sieve) out; *Funk.* (*Störungen*) filter (out); **2.** (*befreien von*)

sift; **3.** *fig.* (*Kandidaten*) screen; (*die Guten*) select, pick (out); (*die Schlechten*) sift (*od.* weed) out
aussiedeln *v/t.* (*trennb., hat -ge-*) resettle (*aus* from); (*evakuieren*) evacuate; **Aussiedelung** *f, nur Sg.* resettlement; forced migration; (*Evakuierung*) evacuation
Aussiedler *m*, **~in** *f* emigrant, *auch* refugee, evacuee; *deutscher: auch* ethnic German (emigrant)
Aussiedlung *f →* **Aussiedelung**
aussinnen *v/t.* (*unreg., trennb., hat -ge-*); *geh. →* **ausdenken**
aussitzen *v/t.* (*unreg., trennb., hat -ge-*) **1.** *umg. fig.* (*Probleme etc.*) wait out; **2.** *Reiten*: (*Trab*) sit; **3.** (*Hose, Rock*) wear *s.th.* out of shape, make *s.th.* go baggy; (*Sessel*) make *s.th.* go saggy
aussöhnen *v/t. und v/refl.* (*trennb., hat -ge-*): *j-n/sich ~ mit j-m/etw.* reconcile s.o./o.s. with s.o. / to s.th.; *sich ~ mit auch* make one's peace with; **Aussöhnung** *f* reconciliation
aussondern *v/t.* (*trennb., hat -ge-*) **1.** (*aus* from) sort out, separate; (*Unbrauchbares*) *auch* reject; (*Gutes*) *auch* select, pick (out); *ausgesonderte Ware* reject goods *Pl.*, seconds *Pl.*, imperfects *Pl.*; **2.** *Physiol.* excrete; (*Schweiß etc.*) secrete; **Aussonderung** *f* **1.** *nur Sg.*; (*Auslese*) selection; *von Schlechtem*: rejection; **2.** *Physiol.* excretion; (*Schweiß etc.*) secretion
aussorgen *v/i. →* **ausgesorgt** II
aussortieren *v/t.* (*trennb., hat*) sort out; (*Gutes*) *auch* select; (*Unbrauchbares*) *auch* reject
ausspähen (*trennb., hat -ge-*) **I.** *v/t.* spy out; **II.** *v/i.*: *~ nach* look out for
ausspannen (*trennb., hat -ge-*) **I.** *v/t.* **1.** (*Pferde*) unharness; (*Wagen*) unhitch; **2.** (*lösen*) take out; *Tech.* release, unclamp; **3.** *umg. fig.*: *j-m etw. ~* talk s.o. into giving one s.th.; (*Geld*) *auch* wheedle s.th. out of s.o.; *j-m die Freundin ~* steal s.o.'s girlfriend, take s.o.'s girlfriend away (from s.o.); **II.** *v/i.* **1.** (*ausruhen*) relax, take it easy; **2.** (*abschirren*) (*Pferde*) unharness, unhitch; (*Ochsen*) unyoke; **III.** *v/refl. →* II 1
aussparen *v/t.* (*trennb., hat -ge-*) **1.** (*frei lassen*) leave free; (*Zeile etc.*) leave free (*od.* blank); (*Öffnung*) leave; *Tech.* recess; **2.** *fig.* (*nicht berücksichtigen*) leave out, omit; **Aussparung** *f* **1.** empty space, gap; **2.** *Tech.* recess; *in e-m Tisch etc.*: cut-out section; **3.** (*das Aussparen*) leaving out, omitting
ausspeien *v/t/i.* (*unreg., trennb., hat -ge-*) **1.** spit out; *vor j-m ~* spit at s.o.'s feet; **2.** *fig.* spew (out), belch
aussperren *v/t. und v/refl.* (*trennb., hat -ge-*) lock out (*auch Arbeiter*); **Aussperrung** *f von Arbeitern*: lockout
ausspielen (*trennb., hat -ge-*) **I.** *v/t.* **1.** (*Karte*) play; (*anspielen*) lead; *fig. →* **Trumpf**, **2.** *Sport* (*Pokal etc.*) play for; **3.** *Sport* (*Gegner*) outplay; **4.** (*Gewinne*) offer (*od.* give) as a prize; *es werden Gewinne von drei Millionen etc. ausgespielt* there is a total of three million *etc.* to be won, there's three million *etc.* in the pot; **5.** *fig.*: *j-n gegen j-n ~* play s.o. off against s.o.; **6.** (*Können, Einfluss etc.*) bring to bear; **7.** *Theat.* act out; **II.** *v/i.* **1.** (*fertig spielen*) finish (*od.* stop) playing; *habt ihr bald ausgespielt?* will your game be over soon?; *er hat ausgespielt umg. fig.* he's through (*od.* done for);

der hat bei mir ausgespielt umg. fig. I'm through with him, I've had it up to here with him; **2.** *Kartenspiel*: lead; *wer spielt aus?* whose lead (is it)?, who has the lead?
Ausspielung *f* **1.** *Lotterie etc.*: draw-(ing of lots); **2.** (*Ausschüttung*) distribution, paying (out); **3.** *e-s Pokals*: competition
ausspionieren *v/t.* (*trennb., hat*) spy out; (*Person*) spy on
Aussprache *f* **1.** pronunciation; (*un*)*deutliche: auch* articulation; *die haben aber e-e seltsame ~!* what a funny accent they've got, don't they speak funny?; *sie hat eine undeutliche ~* she doesn't enunciate very well; *e-e feuchte ~ haben umg. hum.* splutter when speaking; **2.** discussion; *auch Parl.* debate; *offene ~* heart-to-heart (talk); *eine offene ~ herbeiführen* bring things out into the open; *~angabe f Ling.* phonetic transcription; *~regel f Ling.* pronunciation rule; *Pl. auch* rules of pronunciation; *~wörterbuch n Ling.* pronouncing dictionary
aussprechbar *Adj.* pronounceable; *schwer ~* hard to pronounce; *nicht ~* unpronounceable; *fig.* unspeakable, unrepeatable
aussprechen (*unreg., trennb., hat -ge-*) **I.** *v/t.* **1.** (*Laut*) pronounce; (*Wort, Satz*) *auch* say; (*un*)*deutlich: auch* articulate, enunciate; *nicht ausgesprochen werden Ling.* (*stummer Laut*) be silent (*od.* mute); *weitS.* remain unspoken; *stimmhaft ausgesprochen werden* be voiced; **2.** (*äußern*) express, utter; (*Meinung, Zweifel*) *auch*: voice; *Jur.* (*Urteil*) pronounce, pass; (*Scheidung*) grant; *j-m s-e Anerkennung / sein Beileid ~* express one's respect for / sympathy to s.o.; *der Regierung das Vertrauen/Misstrauen ~ Parl.* pass a vote of confidence / no confidence in the government; **II.** *v/refl.* **1.** (*sich äußern*) express one's views (*über* + *Akk.* on); *sich anerkennend od.* *lobend ~* speak highly of *s.o.*; *sich ~ für/ gegen* speak out (*od.* come out *od.* declare o.s.) in favo(u)r of / against; *für/gegen Plan etc. auch* support/reject; **2.** (*sein Herz ausschütten*) unbosom o.s.; unload o.s. *umg.*; *sich* (*mit j-m*) *~ zur Klärung e-s Problems*: have it out (with s.o.); *sie haben sich über alles ausgesprochen* they had everything (*od.* it all) out; *sprich dich nur aus!* get it off your chest, speak your mind; spit it out *umg.*; **3.** *sich leicht/ schwer ~* be easy/hard to pronounce; **III.** *v/t/i.* finish (speaking); *lass ihn doch ~!* let him finish; *→* **ausgesprochen** II, III
ausspritzen (*trennb., -ge-*) **I.** *v/t.* (*hat*) **1.** (*Flüssigkeit*) squirt out; (*sprühend*) spray out; (*Samen*) ejaculate; **2.** (*reinigen*) (*Schwimmbecken etc.*) rinse; *Med.* (*Ohr*) syringe; *Med.* (*ausspülen*) irrigate; **II.** *v/i.* (*ist*) squirt out; *sprühend*: spray out
Ausspruch *m* utterance; (*Bemerkung*) remark; (*Spruch*) saying, dictum; *den ~ tun* (+ *Zitat*) say the (following) words
ausspucken (*trennb., hat -ge-*) **I.** *v/t.* **1.** spit out; (*erbrechen*) bring up; throw up *umg.*; **2.** *umg. fig.* (*Geld*) cough up; (*Fakten etc.*) regurgitate *förm.*; *Computer*: spew out; (*größere Mengen*) churn out; **3.** *umg. fig.*: *los, spuck's aus!* (*sag schon!*) come on - spit it out!; **II.** *v/i.* spit; *vor j-m ~* spit

at s.o.'s feet; *fig.* spit on s.o.
ausspülen *v/t.* (*trennb., hat -ge-*) **1.** (*säubern*) rinse; **2.** (*entfernen*) rinse out; **3.** *Med.* (*Wunde etc.*) wash (out); irrigate *fachspr.*; (*Vagina*) douche; (*Hals*) gargle; **4.** *Geol.* (*Ufer, Küste*) erode; (*Sand etc.*) wash away
ausstaffieren *v/t.* (*trennb., hat*) **1.** *→* **ausstatten** 1; **2.** (*schmücken*) trim; **3.** *pej.* (*j-n*) (*herausputzen*) dress up; kit out *umg.*
Ausstand *m* **1.** *mst Pl.*; (*Streik*) strike; *in den ~ treten* go on strike; **2.** *bes. südd., österr.*: *s-n ~ geben* have a farewell (*od.* going-away) party
ausstanzen *v/t.* (*trennb., hat -ge-*) punch (*od.* stamp) out
ausstatten *v/t.* (*trennb., hat -ge-*) **1.** *allg.* fit out, equip; (*j-n*) *mit Kleidung*: provide, fit out; *mit Lebensmitteln*: supply; (*Wohnung*) furnish, get up; (*Auto etc.*) (*Buch*) get up, produce; *ein prächtig ausgestatteter Band* a beautifully produced volume; *mit Personal ~* staff; *e-e Praxis mit Teppichböden ~* have a surgery (*Am.* doctor's office) fitted with carpets, have carpets laid (*od.* put) in a surgery (*Am.* doctor's office); *das Hotel / der Wagen ist sehr gut ausgestattet* the hotel has all mod cons (*od.* everything you could wish for) / the car's got all the trimmings; **2.** *fig.*: *~ mit Fähigkeiten*: endow with; *mit Befugnissen*: vest with
Ausstatter *m*; *-s, -*, **~in** *f*; *-, -nen*; (*Herrenausstatter*) gentleman's outfitter, haberdasher *altm.*; *Firma*: men's clothes shop (*Am.* clothing store); (*Raumausstatter*) interior decorator; *Firma*: firm of interior decorators, interior decorating company
Ausstattung *f* **1.** (*Ausrüstung*) equipment; (*Armaturen*) fittings *Pl.*; *e-r Wohnung*: furnishings *Pl.*; *Theat.* sets and costumes *Pl.*; **2.** (*Gestaltung*) design; (*Buchausstattung*) getup
ausstauben *v/t.* (*trennb., hat -ge-*); (*ausschütteln*) shake out
ausstechen *v/t.* (*unreg., trennb., hat -ge-*) **1.** (*Graben*) dig; (*Rasen, Torf*) cut (out); (*Disteln etc.*) dig up (by the roots); (*Plätzchen*) cut out; (*Apfel*) core; (*Muster etc.*) *mit Nadel*: prick out; (*Augen*) gouge (*od.* put) out; *unabsichtlich*: poke out; **2.** *fig.* (*übertreffen*) outdo; (*Rivalen*) cut out; *sie wollte mich ~, ganz klar* she obviously wanted to put me in the shade; *j-n bei j-m ~* oust s.o. in s.o.'s affections (*od.* esteem)
Ausstecher *m*; *-s, -*; *umg. für Plätzchen*: pastry cutter; *für Äpfel*: (apple-)corer; *für Pfahlwurzeln*: root tool
Ausstechform *f* pastry cutter
ausstecken *v/t.* (*trennb., hat -ge-*) **1.** (*Strecke*) mark out; **2.** *Etech.* pull the plug out
ausstehen (*unreg., trennb., -ge-*) **I.** *v/t.* (*hat*) **1.** (*erleiden*) put up with, suffer, endure; *es ist ausgestanden* it's all over, we've *etc.* made it; **2.** *ich kann ihn/es nicht ~* I can't stand him/it; *ich kann laute Musik nicht ~* I can't bear loud music; **II.** *v/i.* (*hat / südd., österr., schw. ist*) **1.** *Entscheidung*: be pending, be still to be taken (*Am.* made); *Zahlungen*: be outstanding; *Geld*: be owing; *Lösung*: be still to be found; *Sendungen*: be overdue; *s-e Antwort steht noch aus* we're still waiting for his answer, he has yet to give us an answer; *ausstehende Forderungen* outstand-

ing demands; **2.** (*ausgestellt sein*) be on display (*od.* exhibited)

aussteigen *v/i.* (*unreg., trennb., ist -ge-*) **1.** get out (*aus* of), alight (from) *geh.*; *aus Flugzeug*: disembark (from); *Flug.* (*abspringen*) bale (*bes. Am.* bail) out; *aus dem Zug/Bus* ~ get off the train/bus; *alles* ~*!* all change!; **2.** *fig.* drop out (*aus* of), opt out (of) (*auch aus der Gesellschaft*); *aus e-m Geschäft*: back out (of), get out (of); *aus der Kernenergie* ~ back (*od.* opt) out of the nuclear energy program(me); **3.** *Fußball*: *j-n* ~ *lassen* outplay s.o.

Aussteiger *m*, ~**in** *f fig.* dropout

ausstellen (*trennb., hat -ge-*) **I.** *v/t.* **1.** *zur Schau*: show, display; (*Kunstwerk*) exhibit; **2.** (*Urkunde, Pass*) issue (+ *Dat.* for); (*Rechnung, Scheck*) make out (to); (*Quittung, Rezept*) write out; *einen Scheck auf j-n* ~ make out a cheque (*Am.* check) to s.o., make a cheque (*Am.* check) payable to s.o.; *j-m ein Rezept* ~ write (*od.* give) s.o. a prescription; **3.** *umg.* (*ausschalten*) switch off, turn off; **4.** (*aufstellen*) (*Posten*) post; (*Schild*) put up; (*Falle*) set; **5.** (*Fenster*) open out; **6.** → *ausgestellt* II; **II.** *v/i. in Galerie, auf Ausstellung*: exhibit

Aussteller *m; -s, -,* ~**in** *f; -, -nen* **1.** *e-s Passes etc.*: issuer; *Behörde*: issuing authority; **2.** *auf e-r Messe*: exhibitor; **3.** *Fin., e-s Wechsels*: drawer

Ausstellfenster *n Mot.* quarterlight, *Am.* vent window

Ausstellung *f* **1.** (*Kunstausstellung od. Messe*) exhibition, *Am.* exhibit; (*Messe*) *auch* trade fair; (*Schau*) show; **2.** *von Waren*: display; **3.** *mst Sg.*; *e-r Rechnung etc.*: issue, issuing; *e-r Rechnung etc.*: making out, writing (out)

Ausstellungs|datum *n* date of issue; ~**eröffnung** *f* opening of an exhibition; *Zeremonie*: opening ceremony of an exhibition; ~**fläche** *f* exhibition area; ~**gelände** *n* exhibition site (*od.* grounds *Pl.*); ~**halle** *f* exhibition hall; ~**katalog** *m* exhibition catalog(ue); ~**ort** *m e-s Passes etc.*: place of issue; ~**raum** *m* showroom; ~**stand** *m* exhibition stand; ~**stück** *n* exhibit; *im Schaufenster*: display item; ~**tag** *m* date of issue

ausstemmen (*trennb., hat -ge-*) **I.** *v/i.* *Skisport*: stem; **II.** *v/t. Tech.* chisel out

ausstempeln *v/i.* (*trennb., hat -ge-*) clock out

aussterben *v/i.* (*unreg., trennb., ist -ge-*) die out (*auch fig.*); *Tierart*: *auch* become extinct, suffer extinction; *e-e vom Aussterben bedrohte Art* an endangered species; → *ausgestorben* II, *Dumme*; **Aussterben** *n e-r Art*: *auch* disappearance

Aussteuer *f e-r Braut*: trousseau; (*Mitgift*) dowry

aussteuern (*trennb., hat -ge-*) **I.** *vt/i. Etech.* modulate; (*regeln*) control the recording level (of); **II.** *v/t. Versicherung*: disqualify, end *s.o.'s* entitlement to benefits; **Aussteuerung** *f* **1.** *Etech.* modulation; (*Regelung*) level control; **2.** *Versicherung*: disqualification, termination of *s.o.'s* entitlement to benefits

Aussteuerversicherung *f* endowment insurance

Ausstieg *m; -(e)s, -e* **1.** (*Ausgang*) *Bus etc.*: exit, way out; *aus Kanal*: manhole; *aus U-Boot, Panzer etc.*: (escape *od.* opening) hatch; *am Dach*: trapdoor; **2.** *nur Sg.*; (*das Aussteigen*) *aus*

U-Boot etc.: climbing out (*aus* of); **3.** *fig.*: ~ *aus der Kernenergie etc.* withdrawal from (*od.* opting out of) the nuclear energy program(me) *etc.*

Ausstiegs|beschluss *m* decision to opt out; ~**luke** *f Raumf., Landekapsel*: egress (*od.* exit) hatch

ausstopfen *v/t.* (*trennb., hat -ge-*) (*Kissen, Tiere*) stuff; *mit Watte etc.*: pad; (*Löcher, Ritzen*) fill (in)

Ausstoß *m* **1.** *Wirts.* output, production; **2.** *Phys., Tech.* expulsion, ejection; *e-s Vulkans*: belch

ausstoßen *v/t.* **1.** (*Luft, Plazenta*) expel; (*Dampf etc.*) give off; (*Rauchwolken*) send out; *Tech.* (*Kassette etc.*) eject; (*Geschoss*) fire, discharge; *Vulkan*: belch; *der Tintenfisch stößt bei Gefahr Farbwolken aus* the octopus releases clouds of ink when threatened; **2.** (*Fluch*) utter; (*Schrei*) give, let out; (*Seufzer*) heave; **3.** *Wirts.* (*produzieren*) turn out, produce; **4.** (*Zahn*) knock out; (*Auge*) gouge (*od.* put) out; **5.** (*ausschließen*) expel (*aus* from); (*verbannen*) exile (*aus der Gesellschaft*) ~ ostracize, banish; *sich ausgestoßen fühlen* feel like an outcast, feel ostracized; *aus der Armee* ~ discharge (dishono[u]rably) from the army; *aus der Kirche* ~ excommunicate *s.o.*

ausstrahlen (*trennb., hat -ge-*) **I.** *v/t.* **1.** *Funk., TV* broadcast, transmit; *ausgestrahlt werden Sendungen*: *auch* be put on (the) air; **2.** *Phys.* radiate, emit; **3.** *fig.* (*Güte etc.*) radiate; (*Selbstbewusstsein*) exude; *das Bild strahlt Ruhe aus* the picture gives you a great sense of calm; **4.** (*Zimmer*) illuminate; **II.** *v/i.* **1.** radiate, emanate (*auch fig.*) (*von* from); *auf j-n* ~ (*sich übertragen*) influence s.o., communicate itself to s.o., extend to s.o.; **2.** *Schmerz*: spread (*in* + *Akk.* to); *in die Beine* ~ spread down (into) one's legs

Ausstrahlung *f* **1.** *Phys.* radiation, emission; *Funk., TV* transmission, broadcast(ing); **2.** *fig. e-r Person*: personality; *stärker*: personal magnetism, charisma; *von ihm geht e-e starke* ~ *aus* he has tremendous personal magnetism; **3.** *fig. von Ruhe, Zufriedenheit etc.*: radiation; **4.** *von Schmerzen*: transference, spreading; **Ausstrahlungskraft** *f fig.* → *Ausstrahlung* 2

ausstrecken (*trennb., hat -ge-*) **I.** *v/t.* stretch out; (*Fühler*) put out; (*Zunge*) stick out; (*ausdehnen*) stretch; *die Hand* ~ *nach* reach out for; *mit ausgestrecktem Arm* with outstretched arm; **II.** *v/refl.* stretch (o.s.) out; (*sich recken*) stretch (o.s.)

ausstreichen *v/t.* (*unreg., trennb., hat -ge-*) **1.** (*Geschriebenes*) cross out, delete; *j-s Namen auf e-r Liste* ~ cross s.o.'s name off a list; **2.** (*glätten*) smooth out (*od.* down); **3.** (*Fugen, Ritzen*) fill, smooth over; **4.** *mit Farbe*: paint; (*Backform etc.*) grease; **5.** (*verteilen*) (*Farbe*) distribute; (*Teig*) spread out; **6.** (*Pinsel*) get all the paint off *a brush etc.*

ausstreuen *v/t.* (*trennb., hat -ge-*) scatter, distribute; *auch fig.* (*Gerücht*) spread

ausströmen (*trennb., -ge-*) **I.** *v/i.* (*ist*) **1.** *Flüssigkeit*: gush (*od.* pour) out (*aus* of); *Gas, Dampf*: escape (from); *Lava*: well out; ~ *von Licht, Hitze*: emanate from; **2.** *fig.* radiate (*aus* from); **3.** *Menschen etc.*: *ein- und* ~

pour in and out; **II.** *v/t.* (*hat*) **1.** (*Wärme etc.*) radiate, emit; (*Duft*) give off, exhale; **2.** *fig.* radiate, exude

aussuchen *v/t.* (*trennb., hat -ge-*) **1.** pick, choose; *suchen Sie sich was aus* take your pick; → *ausgesucht* II, III; **2.** (*aussortieren*) sort (out); **3.** *umg.*: *der Wühltisch etc. ist schon ganz ausgesucht* all the good stuff is (already) gone

austapezieren *v/t.* (*trennb., hat*); (*Raum*) paper

austarieren *v/t.* (*trennb., hat*) **1.** *Tech.* (*Waage*) balance; **2.** *fig.* balance (*od.* equal) out

Austausch *m* exchange; *von Gedanken*: *auch* interchange; *Wirts. von Gütern*: barter; *Phys.* (*Wärme-, Luftaustausch*) exchange, interchange; *Sport* substitution; *e-s defekten Teils*: replacement; *im* ~ *gegen* in exchange for; ~**aktion** *f* new-for-old campaign

austauschbar *Adj.* (*ersetzbar*) replaceable; *untereinander*: interchangeable; **Austauschbarkeit** *f; nur Sg.* replaceability; interchangeability

austauschen (*trennb., hat -ge-*) **I.** *v/t.* **1.** (*ersetzen*) exchange (*gegen* for); (*Batterie, Glühbirne etc.*) change; (*Motor, Reifen etc.*) replace (*gegen* by) (*auch Math.*); *gegeneinander*: interchange; *auch Chem., Sport* substitute; *Bio.* (*Gene*) cross over; *A gegen B* ~ replace A by B, substitute B for A; **2.** (*Botschafter, Schüler etc.*) exchange (*gegen* for); **3.** *EDV* (*Daten, Informationen*) exchange, interchange; **4.** (*Blicke, Briefe, Gedanken*) exchange (*mit* [*einander*] with [each other]); (*Beleidigungen*) trade; *Blicke* ~ *auch* look at each other; *Erfahrungen* ~ compare notes; *Erinnerungen* ~ reminisce (about the past); **5.** *Wirts. im Tauschhandel*: exchange, barter, swap *umg.*; **II.** *v/refl.*: *sich mit j-m* ~ exchange views, experiences *etc.* (with each other) (*über* + *Akk.* about)

Austausch|motor *m* reconditioned engine; ~**programm** *n* exchange program(me); ~**schüler** *m*, ~**schülerin** *f* exchange pupil (*Am.* student); ~**spieler** *m*, ~**spielerin** *f Sport* substitute; ~**stoff** *m Wirts., Tech.* substitute (material); ~**student** *m*, ~**studentin** *f* exchange student

austausch(s)weise I. *Adv.* as part of an exchange; **II.** *Adj.*; *nur attr.* for a change

austeilen (*trennb., hat -ge-*) **I.** *v/t.* hand out, distribute (+ *Dat. od. an* + *Akk.* to; *unter* + *Dat.* among); *gleichmäßig*: share out (among); (*Befehle*) give, issue; (*Essen*) serve, dish up; *Reli.* (*Kommunion etc.*) administer; *mit vollen Händen* ~ be very lavish with; **II.** *vt/i.* (*Hiebe, Karten*) deal; *wer teilt aus?* who's dealing, whose (turn to) deal is it?; *wer austeilt, muss auch einstecken können* if you dish it out, you have to be able to take it too; **Austeilung** *f* distribution

Auster *f; -, -n*; *Zool.* oyster

Austern|bank *f*; *Pl. Austernbänke* oyster bed; ~**fischer** *m* **1.** *Orn.* oyster catcher; **2.** oyster fisher(man); ~**fischerei** *f* oyster fishing; ~**pilz** *m* oyster mushroom; ~**zucht** *f* oyster culture; *konkret*: oyster farm

austesten *v/t.* (*trennb., hat -ge-*) test; *EDV* (*Programm etc.*) debug

austilgen *v/t.* (*trennb., hat -ge-*); *allg.* get rid of; *völlig*: eradicate; (*Unkraut*)

auch wipe out; (*Ungeziefer*) *auch* ex-terminate; *fig.* (*Erinnerung*) blot out
austoben *v/refl.* (*trennb.*, *hat -ge-*) **1.** *beim Tanzen etc.*: let one's hair down *umg.*; *Kinder, Tiere*: have a good romp *umg.*; **er hat sich auf der Leinwand ausgetobt** he expressed himself passionately on the canvas; **2.** *fig.* (*ungezügelt leben*) have one's fling, indulge o.s.; *Jugendliche*: *auch* sow one's wild oats; **3.** (*Wut etc. entladen*) let one's anger *etc.* out, vent one's anger *etc.*; **4.** *Fieber, Leidenschaft, Sturm etc.*: spend itself
Austrag *m*; *-(e)s, Austräge* **1.** *von Streit etc.*: settlement, resolution; **zum ~ bringen** settle, resolve; **zum ~ kommen** *Amtspr.* be settled *allg.*; **2.** *südd., österr.*: **im ~ leben** *Bauer, Bäuerin*: have retired (*auch fig.*)
austragen (*unreg., trennb., hat -ge-*) **I.** *v/t.* **1.** (*Briefe etc.*) deliver; *Zeitungen ~* deliver (news)papers, do a (news)paper round; **2.** *Med.* (*Kind*) carry to term; **sie will das Kind ~** (*will nicht abtreiben*) she wants to have the child (*od.* baby); **3.** (*Meinungsverschiedenheiten*) argue out; (*zu Ende bringen*) settle, resolve; (*Kampf*) fight out, carry on; **einen Streit mit j-m ~** have it out with s.o. *umg.*; **etw. vor Gericht ~** take s.th. to court; **4.** (*Wettkampf*) hold; (*Spiel*) play; **5.** (*Daten, Zahlen*) delete; *aus Liste*: take (*od.* cross) *s.o.'s name* (*od. s.th.*) off the list; **II.** *v/refl.* take one's name off the list; *vor dem Weggehen*: sign out
Austräger *m*; *~s, ~in f männlich*: delivery man (*od.* boy); *weiblich*: delivery woman (*od.* girl); *von Zeitungen, männlich*: newspaper man (*od.* boy); *weiblich*: newspaper woman (*od.* girl)
Austrag(s)haus *n südd., österr. small house for farmers in retirement*
Austragung *f* **1.** *e-s Streits*: settlement, resolution; **2.** *Sport*: **die ~ des Spiels findet hier statt** the game will be held here
Austragungs|modus *m Sport* procedure; **~ort** *m* venue, *Am. auch* location, arena
austrainiert *Adj. Sport* fighting fit
Australasier *m*; *-s, -, ~in f; -, -nen* Australasian, *weiblich auch* Australasian woman (*od.* girl *etc.*); **australasisch** *Adj.* Australasian
Australien (*n*); *-s; Geog.* Australia; **Australier** *m*; *-s, -*, **Australierin** *f; -, -nen* Australian, *weiblich auch* Australian woman (*od.* girl *etc.*); **australisch** *Adj.* Australian
austräumen *vt/i.* → **ausgeträumt** II
austreiben (*unreg., trennb., hat -ge-*) **I.** *v/t.* **1.** (*Vieh*) drive out; **2.** (*vertreiben*) drive (*od.* turn) out; (*Geister*) exorcize, cast out; (*Winter*) drive out; **3.** *fig.*: **j-m etw. ~** cure s.o. of s.th.; *mit Gewalt*: knock s.th. out of s.o. *umg.*; **4.** *Bot.* (*Blätter, Blüten*) produce, put forth; **II.** *v/i. Bot.* sprout; *Bäume*: (come out in) bud
Austreibung *f* expulsion (*auch Med., e-s Kindes*); *von Geistern*: exorcism; **Austreibungsphase** *f bei Geburt*: expulsive stage (of labo[u]r)
austreten (*unreg., trennb., -ge-*) **I.** *v/t.* (*hat*) **1.** (*Feuer, Glut*) stamp out; **2.** (*Schuhe*) wear out; *neue*: break in; **3.** (*Treppe, Stufen*) wear down; (*Pfad*) tread, *Am. auch* walk (on); → **ausgetreten** II; **II.** *v/i.* (*ist*) **1.** *allg.* come out (*aus* of from); *Dampf, Gas*: escape (from); *Blut*: issue (from); *Harz,*

Schweiß: be secreted (from); *Eiter*: be discharged (from); *Licht*: emanate (from); *Med. Bruch etc.*: protrude; **der Kopf des Kindes ist schon ausgetreten** the head of the baby has already appeared; **2. ~ (aus)** *aus e-m Verein etc.*: leave, *Am. auch* quit; *aus e-r Partei*: *auch* resign from; *aus e-m Bündnis*: *auch* pull out of, withdraw from; **3.** *umg.*: **~ (gehen)** (*zur Toilette gehen*) go and spend a penny, pay a visit, *Am.* go to the bathroom; **ich muss mal ~** *auch* I must disappear for a minute, nature calls; **III.** *v/refl.* (*hat*) *Schuhe*: wear in
Austriazismus *m*; *-, Austriazismen*; *Ling.* Austriacism
austricksen *v/t.* (*trennb., hat -ge-*); *umg.* outsmart, outwit; *Sport* (*Gegenspieler*) trick
austrinken *vt/i.* (*unreg., trennb., hat -ge-*); (*Getränk*) drink up, finish; (*leeren*) empty; (*auch Flasche*) finish
Austritt *m* **1.** *aus e-r Partei*: resignation (*aus* from); *aus e-m Verein*: withdrawal (from); **sein ~ aus der Kirche hat viele schockiert** many people were shocked when he left the church; **s-n ~ erklären** *aus e-r Partei*: hand in one's resignation; *aus der Kirche, e-m Verein*: announce (*od.* say) that one is leaving; **2.** *von Luft, Gas*: escape; *von Blut*: issue; *von Eiter*: discharge; *von Harz etc.*: secretion; *Med., e-s Bruchs*: protrusion; *e-r Kugel bei Schussverletzungen*: exit
Austritts|erklärung *f* (letter of) resignation; *Verein etc.*: notice of withdrawal; **s-e ~ aus der Kirche kam überraschend** his announcement that he is (*od.* was) going to leave the church came as a surprise; **~welle** *f* wave of resignations; **~wunde** *f bei Schussverletzung*: exit wound
Austro... *im Subst.* Austro-; **Austrofaschismus** Austro-fascism
austrocknen (*trennb., hat -ge-*) **I.** *v/t.* dry; (*Boden, Kehle*) dry up, parch; (*Sumpf, Flussbett etc.*) drain; (*Holz*) season; **II.** *v/i.* dry up; *Neubau etc.*: dry out; *Haut*: go (*od.* become) dry; **m-e Kehle ist ausgetrocknet** my throat is parched; **Austrocknung** *f* drying up; *von Sümpfen etc.*: draining; *Med.* dehydration
austüfteln *v/t.* (*trennb., hat -ge-*); *umg.* work out (carefully), think out, *Am.* figure out
ausüben *v/t.* (*trennb., hat -ge-*) **1.** (*Beruf*) carry out *a trade*, have *a profession*; practi|se (*Am. -ce*) *law, medicine etc.*; pursue *a career*; (*Tätigkeit*) carry out, be involved in; (*ein Amt*) hold *an office*; (*Pflicht*) carry out, perform; (*Sportart*) participate in, go in for *umg.*; **welche Tätigkeit üben Sie aus?** what is your occupation?; **den Beruf des Musikers ~** be a professional (*od.* practi|sing [*Am. -cing*]) musician; **2.** (*Herrschaft, Macht, Recht etc.*) exercise; (*Druck, Einfluss*) exert (*auf +* *Akk.* on); (*Wirkung*) have *an effect* (on); (*Zwang*) use (on), apply (to); **e-n Reiz ~ auf** (+ *Akk.*) hold an attraction for; **ausübend I.** *Part. Präs.* → *ausüben*; **II.** *Adj. Pol.*: **~e Gewalt** executive power (*od.* authority)
Ausübung *f* **1.** **die ~ e-s Berufs** the execution of a profession; **in ~ s-s Dienstes** in the line of duty; **2.** *von Macht etc.*: exercise; *von Druck etc.*: exertion, wielding; *von Zwang*: use, application; → *ausüben* 2

ausufern *v/i.* (*trennb., ist -ge-*) **1.** *Stadt*: (begin to) sprawl; *Konflikt etc.*: escalate; *Diskussion etc.*: get out of control (*od.* hand); **2.** *Fluss*: overflow (its banks), break its banks
Ausverkauf *m* **1.** sale; (*Sommer-, Winterschlussverkauf*) end of season sale; (*Räumungsverkauf*) clearance sale; *wegen Geschäftsaufgabe*: closing-down (*od.* liquidation, going-out-of-business) sale; **im ~ kaufen** at (*od.* in) the sales; **2.** *nur Sg.*; *Handlung*: selling off; **3.** *fig. Pol. etc.* sellout (+ *Gen.* of)
Ausverkaufs|preis *m* (special) sale price; **das sind ~e!** these are real bargains!; **~ware** *f* sale goods *Pl.* (*Am.* merchandise *Sg.*)
ausverkauft *Adj.* sold out (*auch Theat. etc.*); *Haus*: packed; **die Größe ist ~** *auch* we've (*od.* they've) sold out of that size, that size is out of stock (at the moment); **~es Konzert** sellout concert; **Ausverkauft!** *Plakat*: Full House!, Sold Out!; **vor ~em Haus spielen** play to a full (*od.* packed) house, play in front of a capacity crowd
auswachsen (*unreg., trennb., -ge-*) **I.** *v/i.* (*ist*) **1.** → **ausgewachsen** II; **2.** *Salat etc.*: go to seed; *gelagerte Kartoffeln, Zwiebeln, Getreide am Halm*: sprout; **3.** *umg.*: **das ist ja zum Auswachsen!** it's enough to drive you up the wall!; **es ist zum Auswachsen mit dir!** you drive me (a)round the bend!; **II.** *v/refl.* (*hat*) **1.** *Gehfehler etc.*: disappear (*od.* sort itself out) in time; **2.** **sich ~ zu** grow into; *fig. auch* develop into
Auswahl *f* **1.** (*das zur ~ Stehende*) choice, selection (+ *Gen. od.* **an** + *Dat. Pl.* of); *Wirts.* range; (*das Ausgewählte*) choice; (*mehreres*) *auch* selection; (*Vielfalt*) variety; *Marktforschung*: sample; *Kleider etc.* **in großer ~** a large range of; **e-e ~** aus a selection from; **die ~ ist nicht besonders gut** (*gering*) there isn't much choice; **e-e ~ treffen** choose (*aus od.* **unter** + *Dat.* from); **e-e sorgfältige ~ treffen** make a careful choice (*mehreres*: selection); **zur ~** to choose from; **2.** *Sport* select(ed) team; **3.** (*Auslese*) selection; (*von Gedichten, Erzählungen*) anthology
auswählen *v/t.* (*trennb., hat -ge-*) choose, pick; select (*aus* from); *mit Sorgfalt*: *auch* pick out; **wähle dir das Beste aus!** take your pick; → *ausgewählt* II
Auswahl|band *m* anthology; **~gremium** *n* selection board; **~kriterium** *n* criterion (*Pl.* criteria) for selection; **~mannschaft** *f Sport* select(ed) (*od.* represenative) team; **~möglichkeit** *f* choice; **es sind** (*od.* **gibt**) **nicht viele ~en** there isn't much choice, there aren't many alternatives; **~prinzip** *n* selection principle (*od.* method); **~spieler** *m*, **~spielerin** *f Sport* selected (*od.* representative) player; **~verfahren** *n* selection procedure
auswalken *österr.*, **auswallen** *südd., schw. v/t.* (*trennb., hat -ge-*); (*Teig*) roll out
auswalzen, auswälzen *v/t.* (*trennb., hat -ge-*) **1.** (*Blech, Teig*) roll out; **2.** *fig. pej.*: (*breit*) ~ make a big thing out of; *begeistert*: go to town on; (*Geschichte, Rede*) drag out (endlessly)
Auswanderer *m* emigrant; **Auswandererschiff** *n* emigrant ship; **Auswanderin** *f* emigrant; **auswandern**

v/i. (*trennb., ist -ge-*) emigrate (*von od. aus* from; *nach* to); *Volksstamm*: migrate; *in die USA* ~ emigrate to the United States; *er musste* ~ he had to leave the country; **Auswanderung** *f* emigration; *e-s Volksstammes*: migration; *fig.* exodus; **Auswandrerin** *f* → *Auswanderin*

auswärtig *Adj.* **1.** outside ..., from outside; (*in/von e-m anderen Ort*) in/from another town; ~*e Studenten* non-local (and foreign) students; **2.** *Pol.* foreign; *das Auswärtige Amt* → *Außenministerium*; ~*e Angelegenheiten* foreign affairs; *im* ~*en Dienst tätig sein* be in the foreign service; **Auswärtige** *m, f; -n, -n* **1.** (*Ggs. Ortsansässige*) non-local (person), person from somewhere else; (*Fremde*) stranger; **2.** (*Ausländer*) foreigner

auswärts *Adv.* **1.** (*nach außen*) outwards; ~ *gehen od. laufen* walk with one's toes turned out; **2.** (*nicht zu Hause*) out, away (from home); (*außerhalb der Stadt*) out of town; (*an e-m anderen Ort*) in another town; ~ *essen/schlafen etc.* eat/sleep *etc.* out; ~ *spielen Sport* play away from home; **3.** *umg. hum.*: ~ *sprechen* speak *a foreign language*

Auswärts|niederlage *f* away defeat; ~*sieg* *m* away victory (*od.* win); ~*spiel* *n* away match (*od.* game)

auswaschen (*unreg., trennb., hat -ge-*) **I.** *v/t.* **1.** (*Fleck, Farbe*) wash out; **2.** (*Kleidung*) rinse (out); **3.** *Med.* wash out, bathe; **4.** *Geol.* erode, scour out, wash out; **II.** *v/refl. Farbe*: wash out; → *ausgewaschen* II

auswechselbar *Adj.* exchangeable (*gegen* for); *untereinander*: interchangeable; (*ersetzbar*) replaceable

auswechseln (*trennb., hat -ge-*) **I.** *v/t.* exchange (*gegen* for); (*ersetzen*) replace (by); *untereinander*: interchange (*alle auch Tech.*); (*Rad, Reifen, Batterie*) change; *Sport* (*Spieler*) substitute; *A gegen B* ~ substitute B for A; *die Batterien etc.* ~ *auch* put new batteries *etc.* in; *wie ausgewechselt fig.* (like) a different person; **II.** *v/i. Sport* make a substitution; **Auswechselspieler** *m*, **Auswechselspielerin** *f* substitute; **Auswechslung** *f* exchange; (*Ersetzen*) replacement; *auch Sport* substitution

Ausweg *m* **1.** way out (*aus* of); *letzter* ~ last resort; *es gibt sonst keinen* ~ *auch* there's no other solution, there's no alternative; *ich weiß (mir) od. sehe keinen* ~ *mehr* I don't know where to turn any more; *sich (Dat.) e-n* ~ *offen lassen* leave o.s. an escape route (*od.* loophole); **2.** (*Öffnung*) outlet

ausweglos *Adj.* hopeless; **Ausweglosigkeit** *f; nur Sg.* hopelessness

ausweichen *v/i.* (*unreg., trennb., ist -ge-*) **1.** (*Platz machen*) make way (+ *Dat.* for); (*auch den Zusammenstoß vermeiden*) swerve to avoid (the way of); *e-m Fußgänger etc.* ~ avoid hitting a pedestrian *etc.*; *e-m Schlag etc.* ~ dodge a blow *etc.*; *nach rechts/links* ~ swerve to the right/left; *ich konnte ihm gerade noch* ~ *Autofahrer*: I just missed him, I just managed to swerve out of the way in time; *Fußgänger*: he just missed me, I just managed to jump out of the way in time; **2.** *fig.* (*ausweichend antworten*) be evasive (*od.* non-committal), hedge; *j-m/etw.* ~ avoid s.o./s.th.; *e-m Thema: auch* talk (a)round; *e-r Entscheidung* ~ avoid

making a decision; *er weicht m-n Fragen aus* he won't answer my questions; **3.** ~ *auf* (+ *Akk.*) switch to; (*Straße etc.*) *auch* take (... instead); (*Termin, Möglichkeit, Nächstbestes*) fall back on; **4.** *Mus.* modulate (*in* + *Akk.* into)

ausweichend I. *Part.Präs.* → *ausweichen*; **II.** *Adj.*: ~*e Antwort* evasive answer; **III.** *Adv.*: ~ *antworten* answer evasively, be non-committal in reply

Ausweich|flughafen *m* alternative airport; ~*manöver* *n* **1.** *Mot.* evasive driving action, swerve to avoid hitting *s.o.* (*od. s.th.*); *das war ein geschicktes* ~ that was a nice bit of dodging (*od.* piece of driving); **2.** *fig.* evasive action; *s-e Antwort war ein reines* ~ with his answer he was just trying to avoid the issue; ~*möglichkeit* *f* way out; ~*quartier* *n* alternative accommodation(s); ~*stelle* *f Verk.* passing point; *Eisenb.* siding; ~*strecke* *f bei Stau*: alternative route, diversion

ausweiden *v/t.* (*trennb., hat -ge-*) **1.** (*Wild*) gut, disembowel; (*Auto*) strip; **2.** *fig.* (*Thema etc.*) exploit

ausweinen (*trennb., hat -ge-*) **I.** *v/refl.* have a good cry; *sich bei j-m* ~ (have a) cry on s.o.'s shoulder; **II.** *v/t.*: *sich (Dat.) die Augen* ~ cry one's eyes out; **III.** *v/i.*: *ausgeweint haben* have (*od.* be) finished crying

Ausweis *m; -es, -e* **1.** (*Personalausweis*) identity card, ID (card); (*Mitglieds-, Zulassungsausweis etc.*) membership (*od.* admission *etc.*) card; *weitS.* pass, permit; *an der Grenze: mst* passport; *den od. j-s* ~ *verlangen* ask for identification; ~ *bitte* your papers please; **2.** (*Nachweis*) proof, evidence; *nach* ~ (+ *Gen.*) *Amtsspr.* according to

ausweisen (*unreg., trennb., hat -ge-*) **I.** *v/t.* **1.** (*aus* from) *aus dem Land*: expel, deport; *aus der Schule*: expel; **2.** *Wirts.* show (on the books); **3.** *j-n* ~ *als* identify s.o. as; *fig.* prove s.o. to be; **II.** *v/refl.* **1.** identify o.s., prove one's identity; **2.** *fig.*: *sich* ~ *als Fachmann etc.* prove o.s. (to be) an expert *etc.*

Ausweis|fälschung *f* forging of IDs; ~*karte* *f* → *Ausweis* 1; ~*kontrolle* *f* ID check; ~*leser* *m Computer*: badge reader; ~*papiere* *Pl.* (identification *od.* ID *od.* identity) papers

Ausweisung *f* expulsion, deportation; *Jur.* eviction; **Ausweisungsbeschluss** *m* deportation decision

ausweiten (*trennb., hat -ge-*) **I.** *v/t.* **1.** extend (*zu* into); (*Handschuhe, Schuhe*) stretch; **2.** *fig.* (*Kredit, Produktion, Zuständigkeit etc.*) extend (to); **II.** *v/refl.* **1.** *Material*: expand; *Pullover etc.*: stretch; **2.** *fig. Organisation etc.*: expand, grow; *Konflikt*: spread; *sich* ~ *zu* grow (*od.* develop) into; *Konflikt: auch* escalate into; **Ausweitung** *f konkret und fig.*: extension, expansion; *e-r Hose etc.*: stretching; *e-s Konfliktes*: spreading, escalation (*zu* into)

auswendig *Adv.* by heart; ~ *lernen auch* learn *s.th.* (off) by heart; ~ *spielen* play from memory; (*in- und*) *kennen od. können oft pej.* (*etw.*) know *s.th.* inside out, know *s.th.* like the back of one's hand; (*j-n*) know *s.o.* better than he, she *etc.* knows himself, herself *etc.*; **Auswendiglernen** *n; -s, kein Pl.* learning by heart, memorization

auswerfen *v/t.* (*unreg., trennb., hat*

-ge-) **1.** throw out; (*Angel, Anker, Netz*) cast; (*Erde*) throw up; **2.** *Med.* (*Schleim, Blut*) cough up; **3.** (*Lava*) spew out; *Tech.* eject; **4.** (*Graben*) dig (out); **5.** (*Fenster*) break, smash; *j-m ein Auge* ~ put s.o.'s eye out; **6.** (*produzieren*) turn out; *Computer*: (*Lösung etc.*) return; **7.** *Wirts.* (*e-e Summe*) allocate, set aside; (*Prämie*) give; (*Dividende*) pay out

auswertbar *Adj.* **1.** *Ergebnisse etc.*: evaluable, analy|sable (*Am.* –zable); *schwer* ~ *sein* be difficult to analy|se (*Am.* –ze) and evaluate; **2.** *kommerziell*: exploitable; (*nutzbar*) utilizable

auswerten *v/t.* (*trennb., hat -ge-*) **1.** evaluate (*auch Math.*), analy|se (*Am.* -ze); (*Statistiken*) *auch* interpret; **2.** (*ausnützen*) utilize, make (full) use of; *auch kommerziell*: exploit; **Auswertung** *f* **1.** (*Bewertung*) evaluation (*auch Math.*), analysis; *von Statistiken: auch* interpretation; **2.** (*Verwertung*) utilization; *auch kommerzielle*: exploitation

auswetzen *v/t.* (*trennb., hat -ge-*) → *Scharte* 1

auswickeln *v/t.* (*trennb., hat -ge-*) **1.** unwrap, undo; **2.** *ein Kind* ~ take a baby's nappie (*Am.* diaper) off; *j-n/sich aus e-r Decke* ~ take a blanket off s.o./o.s., take s.o./o.s. out of a blanket

auswiegen *v/t.* (*unreg., trennb., hat -ge-*) weigh out (*auch Sport*); → *ausgewogen*

auswinden *v/t.* (*unreg., trennb., hat -ge-*); *bes. südd., schw.* wring out

auswirken *v/refl.* (*trennb., hat -ge-*) have an effect (*auf* + *Akk.* on); (*s-e Wirkung zeigen*) have its effect; *bes. negativ: auch* make itself felt; *sich* ~ *auf* (+ *Akk.*) *auch* affect; *sich* ~ *in* (+ *Dat.*) result in; *sich ungünstig* ~ *auf* (+ *Akk.*) have a negative (*stärker*: an adverse) effect on; *sich zu j-s Vorteil* ~ work in s.o.'s favo(u)r (*od.* to s.o.'s advantage)

Auswirkung *f* effect (*auf* + *Akk.* on); (*Folge*) consequence(s *Pl.*) (for); (*Implikation*) implication(s *Pl.*) (for); (*Rückwirkung*) repercussions *Pl.* (on, for); (*Ergebnis*) outcome, result(s *Pl.*); *diplomatische etc.* ~*en auch* diplomatic *etc.* fallout

auswischen (*trennb., -ge-*) **I.** *v/t.* (*hat*) **1.** (*reinigen*) wipe (*od.* clean) out; **2.** (*Schrift, Staub etc.*) wipe out (*od.* off); **3.** *sich* (*Dat.*) *die Augen* ~ rub one's eyes; **4.** *umg. fig.*: *j-m eins* ~ get s.o., get one over on s.o.; (*zurückzahlen*) get one's own back on s.o.; **II.** *v/i.* (*ist*); *Dial.* (*entwischen*) get away, escape (*from*)

auswringen *v/t.* (*unreg., trennb., hat -ge-*) wring out

Auswuchs *m; -es, Auswüchse* **1.** *Med., Bot.* growth; excrescence *förm.*; (*Missbildung*) deformity; (*Buckel*) hump; **2.** *fig.* (*Nebenprodukt*) negative spin-off; *Auswüchse* (*Extreme*) excesses; *das ist ein* ~ *s-r krankhaften Fantasie* it's a product of his sick imagination; **3.** *Agr., von Getreide*: premature sprouting

auswuchten *v/t.* (*trennb., hat -ge-*); *Tech.* (*Räder*) (counter)balance

Auswurf *m* **1.** *Tech.* ejection; **2.** *Med.* sputum; *blutigen* ~ *haben* be coughing up blood; **3.** *nur Sg.*: *fig. pej.* → *Abschaum*

auswürfeln *v/t.* (*trennb., hat -ge-*) throw dice for; *lass uns* ~*, wer fahren muss* let's throw dice to see (*od.* de-

cide) who is going (*od.* has) to drive
auszahlen (*trennb.*, *hat* -*ge*-) **I.** *v/t.*
1. (*etw.*) pay (out) (*j-m* to s.o.); *bar*:
pay in cash; *wie viel bekommst du
ausgezahlt? an Gehalt etc.*: what do
you get cash in hand, *Am.* what's your
take-home pay?; **2.** (*Arbeiter, Gläubiger etc.*) pay off; (*Partner*) buy out;
II. *v/refl. fig.* (*sich lohnen*) pay off; *es
zahlt sich nicht aus* it doesn't pay, it's
not worth it (*od.* the effort *etc.*)
auszählen (*trennb.*, *hat* -*ge*-) **I.** *v/t.*
1. count (out); (*Stimmen*) count;
2. (*Boxer*) count out; **II.** *vt/i. Kinderspiel*: count out
Auszahlung *f* **1.** *von Geld*: payment;
zur ~ gelangen od. kommen geh. be
paid out; **2.** *e-s Erben etc.*: paying off;
e-s Partners: buying out; **3.** (*das Ausgezahlte*) payment; *an Erben, Partner*:
payoff
Auszählung *f* **1.** *von Stimmen etc.*:
counting (up); **2.** *e-s Boxers*: count
(out)
Auszahlungs|anweisung *f Wirts.* payment order; **~beleg** *m* payment slip,
receipt; **~betrag** *m* amount payable,
amount paid out; **~kurs** *m* out-payment rate; **~schalter** *m* cashier's desk
(*od.* counter)
auszehren *v/t.* (*trennb.*, *hat* -*ge*-): *j-n ~*
drain s.o., debilitate s.o., exhaust s.o.;
völlig: drain s.o. of all his (*od.* her)
strength (*od.* of every ounce of
strength); *ein Land ~* drain a country
of (all) its resources, bleed a country
white; → *ausgezehrt*; **Auszehrung** *f*
1. (*Abmagerung*) emaciation; **2.** *altm.*
(*Schwindsucht*) consumption
auszeichnen (*trennb.*, *hat* -*ge*-) **I.** *v/t.*
1. (*markieren*) mark; (*Waren*) label;
mit Preisen: price, put a price tag on;
Druck. mark up; **2.** (*ehren*) hono(u)r;
j-n mit e-m Preis etc. ~ award a prize
etc. to s.o.; *mit Orden ~* decorate; *der
Film wurde in Cannes ausgezeichnet*
the film (*Am. auch* movie) received
an award at Cannes; *X, ein mehrfach
ausgezeichneter Musiker* X, winner of
several music prizes; **3.** (*j-n od. etw.
hervorheben*) distinguish, single out
(for attention); *vor allem ihre Ausdauer zeichnet sie aus* above all she's
known for her stamina; *was dieses
Buch auszeichnet ...* what distinguishes this book ..., what sets this
book apart from others ..., what is so
special about this book ...; → *ausgezeichnet* II, III; **II.** *v/refl.* distinguish
o.s., excel (*als* as; *durch* by; *in* + *Dat.*
at, in)
Auszeichnung *f* **1.** (*Ehrung*) hono(u)ring; *konkret*: (mark of) distinction,
hono(u)r (*für* for); (*Orden*) decoration, medal; (*Preis*) award, prize; *mit ~
bestehen* pass with distinction, get a
distinction; **2.** (*Markierung*) marking;
Wirts. label(l)ing; pricing; *Druck.*
markup, display; **3.** *Wirts.* (*Etikett etc.*)
price label (*od.* tag)
Auszeit *f Sport* time out, timeout
ausziehbar *Adj.* extendible, extending;
Möbel: *auch* pull-out ...; *Antenne etc.*:
telescopic
ausziehen (*unreg.*, *trennb.*, -*ge*-) **I.** *v/t.*
(*hat*) **1.** (*Antenne, Tisch etc.*) pull out,
extend; (*Nagel, Zahn*) pull (out), extract, draw; (*Metall*) draw out (*zu
Draht* [in]to wire); (*Gold*) spin;
2. (*Kleidung*) take off, remove;
(*Handschuhe*) *auch* pull off; (*j-n*) undress; *j-m/sich* (*Dat.*) *die Schuhe etc. ~*
take off s.o.'s/one's shoes *etc.*; *j-n* (*bis*

aufs Hemd) *~ umg. fig.* fleece s.o.; *das
zieht einem ja die Schuhe aus! umg.
pej.* it's enough to make you cringe!;
3. *Math. und Chem.* extract (*aus*
from); **4.** (*ausbleichen*) (*Farbe*) bleach
(out); **II.** *v/i.* (*ist*) **1.** *aus e-r Wohnung*:
move (*aus* out of); **2.** (*losziehen*) set
out (*od.* off) (*zu* + *Inf.* to); *auf Abenteuer/Raub ~* set out in search of adventure / for the hunt; *zum Kampf ~*
set out to battle; **III.** *v/refl.* (*hat*) get
undressed, take one's clothes off
Auszieh|leiter *f* extension ladder;
~platte *f e-s Tisches*: leaf; **~tisch** *m*
extendible table
auszirkeln *v/t.* (*trennb.*, *hat* -*ge*-)
1. mark out with compasses; **2.** *fig.*
figure out, calculate
auszischen *v/t.* (*trennb.*, *hat* -*ge*-);
Theat. hiss (at)
Auszubildende *m*, *f*; -*n* -*n* trainee; *im
Handwerk*: apprentice
Auszug *m* **1.** *aus e-r Wohnung*: move
(*aus* out of); **2.** departure (*aus* from);
(*Marsch*) march (out of); *zeremoniell*:
procession (*out of*); *Mil.*, *Pol.* (*Abzug*)
pullout (from); *e-s Volkes und fig.*: exodus (from); **3.** *Chem.* (*Vorgang*) extraction; (*Produkt*) extract, essence;
4. (*Ausschnitt*) extract, excerpt (*aus*
from); (*Zusammenfassung*) summary,
abstract; (*Kontoauszug*) (bank) statement, statement of account; (*Grundbuchauszug*) extract; *Mus.* arrangement; *etw. nur in Auszügen kennen*
know only parts of s.th.
Auszugsmehl *n* superfine flour
auszugsweise *Adv.* in parts; *etw. ~
vorlesen* read extracts from s.th.
auszupfen *v/t.* (*trennb.*, *hat* -*ge*-) pluck
out; *sich* (*Dat.*) *die Augenbrauen ~*
pluck one's eyebrows
autark *Adj.* self-sufficient, independent; **Autarkie** *f*; -, -*n* (economic) self-sufficiency, autarky, autarchy
authentisch I. *Adj.* authentic; (*echt*)
genuine; *aus ~er Quelle* on good authority; **II.** *Adv.* authentically; **Authentizität** *f*; -, *kein Pl.* authenticity
Autismus *m*; -, *kein Pl.*; *Med.* autism;
Autist *m*; -*en*, -*en*, **Autistin** *f*; -, -*nen*
person with autism, autistic person;
autistisch *Adj.* autistic
Auto *n*; -*s*, -*s* car, *bes. Am.* auto(mobile), *bes. Brit.* motor *umg.*; *~ fahren*
drive (a car); *mit dem* (*od.* im) *~ fahren* go by car, take the car; *ich bin mit
dem ~ da* I've come by car, I've got
my car with me; *j-n im ~ mitnehmen*
give s.o. a lift
auto... *im Adj.*, **Auto...** *im Subst.* **1.** (*eigen*) auto(-)..., self-...; **2.** (*Fahrzeug*)
car ..., *bes. Am.* auto(mobile) ...
Auto|abgase *Pl.* car exhaust fumes;
~apotheke *f* (driver's *od.* car) first-aid kit; **~atlas** *m* road atlas; **~aufbruch** *m* car break-in; **~aufkleber** *m*
bumper sticker
Autobahn *f* motorway, *Am. etwa* highway, freeway; *Am.* gebührenpflichtig:
tollway, turnpike; *in Deutschland etc.*:
autobahn; *innerstädtisch*: *Am.* expressway; **~abfahrt** *f* motorway *etc.* exit;
~anschlussstelle *f* motorway *etc.*
junction; **~auffahrt** *f* motorway *etc.*
access road, slip road, *Am. auch* on-ramp; **~ausfahrt** *f* motorway *etc.* exit;
~brücke *f* motorway *etc.* bridge;
~dreieck *n* motorway *etc.* junction;
~gebühr *f* motorway *etc.* toll, *Am.*
turnpike toll; **~kreuz** *n* motorway *etc.*
intersection; **~meisterei** *f* motorway
etc. maintenance agency; **~netz** *n* mo-

torway *etc.* network; **~polizei** *f* motorway *etc.* police; **~raststätte** *f* motorway *etc.* services (*od.* service area);
~ring *m* motorway *etc.* ring road;
~trasse *f* motorway *etc.* embankment;
~vignette *f* motorway *etc.* toll disc
(*od.* badge), *Am.* tollway smart card;
~zubringer *m* motorway *etc.* approach (*od.* feeder) road
Autobatterie *f* car battery
Autobiografie, **Autobiographie** *f* autobiography; **autobiografisch**, **autobiographisch** *Adj.* autobiographical
Auto|bombe *f* car bomb; **~brille** *f*: (*e-e
~* a pair of) driving glasses *Pl.*; **~bus**
etc. → *Bus etc.*; **autochthon** *Adj. geh.*
autochthonous
Auto|club *m* car (*bes. Am.* automobile) club; **~dach** *n* car-roof
Autodidakt *m*; -*en*, -*en*, **~in** *f*; -, -*nen*
self-taught (*od.* self-educated) person;
autodidaktisch I. *Adj.* autodidactic;
II. *Adv.* autodidactically
Auto|dieb *m*, **~diebin** *f* car thief;
~diebstahl *m* car theft; **~fabrik** *f* car
factory; **~fähre** *f* car ferry; **~fahren** *n*
driving; **~fahrer** *m*, **~fahrerin** *f* motorist, driver; **~fahrt** *f* drive; **~fenster** *n*
car window
Autofokuskamera *f Fot.* autofocus
camera
autofrei *Adj.* car-free
Autofriedhof *m* car dump, breaker's
yard, *Am.* junkyard
autogen *Adj. Psych.*, *Tech.* autogenic;
~es Training autogenic training,
(self-)relaxation exercises
autogerecht *Adj.* car-friendly
Autogramm *n*; -(*e*)*s*, -*e* autograph; **~e
geben** sign autographs; **~jäger** *m*, **~jägerin** *f* autograph hunter; **~karte** *f* autograph card; **~stunde** *f* autograph
session; *e-e ~ geben* have an autograph session, sign autographs
Autograph *n Mus.* (*handschriftliche
Originalpartitur*) autograph
Auto|händler *m*, **~händlerin** *f* car
(*Am. auch* automobile) dealer;
~handschuhe *Pl.* driving gloves;
~haus *n* car (*Am. auch* automobile)
dealer(ship); *Gebäude*: car (*Am. auch*
automobile) showroom; **~hersteller**
m, **~herstellerin** *f* car manufacturer(s
Pl.); (*Am. auch* maker[s]); **~hupe** *f*
(car) horn
Autoimmunerkrankung *f Med.* autoimmune disease
Auto|industrie *f* car (*od.* automobile,
Am. auch automotive) industry; **~karte** *f* road map; **~kennzeichen** *n* car
registration (*Am.* license) number;
wissen Sie noch das ~? auch can you
remember the number of the car?;
~kino *n* drive-in (cinema, *Am.* theater); **~klau** *m*; -*s*, *kein Pl.* car theft;
~knacker *m*; -*s*, -, **~knackerin** *f*; -,
-*nen*; *umg.* car thief
Autokrat *m*; -*en*, -*en* autocrat; **Autokratie** *f*; -, -*n* autocracy; **Autokratin** *f*;
-, -*nen* autocrat; **autokratisch I.** *Adj.*
autocratic; **II.** *Adv.* autocratically
Auto|lawine *f* solid line of cars, large
volume of traffic; **~leder** *n* chamois
(leather), chammy *umg.*; **~marder** *m*
umg. fig. car thief; **~marke** *f* make (of
car), marque
Automat *m*; -*en*, -*en* **1.** (*Maschine*) machine; **2.** (*Verkaufsautomat*) vending
machine; (*Musikbox*) juke box; *für
Glücksspiel*: slot machine; (*Geldautomat*) cash machine (*od.* dispenser),
Am. ATM (*od.* automatic teller machine); *für Zigaretten*: cigarette ma-

chine
automatenhaft *Adj. Bewegungen etc.*: robot(-)like *attr.*, like a robot *präd.*
Automaten|knacker *m*; *-s*, *-*, **~knacke-rin** *f*; *-*, *-nen*; *umg.* slot machine bandit; **~packung** *f* vending pack; **~restaurant** *n* automat
Automatik *f*; *-*, *-en* **1.** automation; **2.** (*Anlage*) automatic system; (*Mechanik*) automatic mechanism; **3.** *Mot.* (*Getriebe*) automatic transmission; **4.** *Radio*: automatic tuning; **~getriebe** *n* automatic transmission; **~gurt** *m* *Mot.* (inertia) reel seatbelt; **~kamera** *f* automatic camera, point and shoot camera *umg.*; **~wagen** *m* automatic (car)
Automation *f*; *-*, *kein Pl.* automation
automatisch I. *Adj.* automatic; *fig. auch* mechanical; (*Druckknopf...*) push-button ...; **II.** *Adv.* automatically
automatisieren *v/t. Tech.* automate
Automatismus *m*; *-*, *Automatismen* automatism
Auto|mechaniker *m*, **~mechanikerin** *f* car (*od.* motor) mechanic; **~minute** *f*: **nur fünf ~n von hier entfernt** only five minutes (away) by car *etc.* (*od.* in the car)
Automobil *n*; *-s*, *-e* → *Auto*; **Automobil...** → *Auto...*; **~club** *m* automobile association; **Allgemeiner Deutscher ~** (*abgek.* **ADAC**) *etwa* Automobile Association (*abgek.* AA), American Automobile Association (*abgek.* AAA)
Automobilist *m*; *-en*, *-en*, **~in** *f*; *-*, *-nen*; *altm. od. schw.* motorist, (car) driver
Automodell *n* **1.** model; **2.** (*Spielzeug*) model car
autonom *Adj.* **1.** autonomous (*auch fig.*), self-governing; *System etc.*: self-contained; **2.** *Pol.*: **~e Gruppen** independent groups; **Autonome** *m*, *f*; *-n*, *-n*; *Pol.* independent; **Autonomie** *f*; *-*, *-n* autonomy; **Autonomiebestrebungen** *Pl.* efforts towards gaining autonomy (*od.* independence)
Auto|nummer *f* registration (*Am.* license) number; **~panne** *f* breakdown, car trouble *umg.*
Autopilot *m* *Flug.* autopilot
Autopsie *f*; *-*, *-n*; *Med.* autopsy, post-mortem (examination) (+ *Gen. od.* **an** + *Dat.* on); **e-e ~ vornehmen** conduct a post-mortem (examination)
Autor *m*; *-s*, *-en* author, writer
Auto|radio *n* car radio; **~reifen** *m* (car) tyre (*Am.* tire); **~reisezug** *m* motorail train
Autoren|exemplar *n* author's copy;

~film *m* film written and directed by the same person; **~honorar** *n* author's fee (*od.* royalty); **~kino** *n* (*cinematography of*) films written and directed by the same person; **~kollektiv** *n* bes. hist., ehem. DDR authors' collective; **~lesung** *f* (author's) reading, reading by the author
Auto|rennen *n* motor (*Am.* car) race; **~rennsport** *m* motor (*Am.* car) racing
Autoreparatur *f* car repair; **~werkstatt** *f* garage, car repair shop
Autorin *f*; *-*, *-nen* author; authoress *altm.*
Autorisation *f*; *-*, *-en*; *geh.* authorization; **autorisieren** *v/t.* authorize (**zu** to)
autoritär *Adj.* authoritarian; *Eltern*: *auch* very strict; **~e Erziehung** authoritarian upbringing
Autorität *f*; *-*, *-en* **1.** *nur Sg.* authority; **2.** (*Experte*) authority (**auf dem Gebiet** + *Gen.* on), expert (on)
autoritativ *Adj.* authoritative
Autoritätsanspruch *m* claim of authority
autoritätsgläubig *Adj.*: **~ sein** have blind faith in authority
Auto|salon *m* motor (*Am.* automobile) show(room); **~schalter** *m* drive-up counter; *Bank*: *auch* drive-in till (*Am.* window); **~schau** *f* motor (*Am.* automobile) show; **~schieber** *m*, **~schieberin** *f* car smuggler; **~schlange** *f* line of cars; **~schlosser** *m*, **~schlosserin** *f* panel beater, *Am.* bodywork man, woman; **~schlüssel** *m* car key; **~skooter** *m* dodgem (*od.* bumper) car; **~ fahren** go on the dodgems (*od.* bumper cars); **~sport** *m* motor sport; **~stellplatz** *m* (car) parking space; **~stopp** *m* hitchhiking; **per ~ fahren** hitchhike; **~straße** *f* *etwa* expressway, freeway; **~strich** *m* *umg.* *etwa* kerb-crawling (*Am.* pick-up) area; *sie arbeitet am ~* she works (on) the streets, she's a streetwalker; **~stunde** *f*: **sechs ~n entfernt** six hours (*od.* a six-hour) drive away (*od.* from here), six hours by (*od.* in the) car
Autosuggestion *f* autosuggestion
Auto|telefon *n* carphone; **~transporter** *m* car transporter; **~tür** *f* car door; **~typ** *m* car make, type of car; **~unfall** *m* car accident, car crash; **~verkehr** *m* road traffic; **~verleih** *m*, **~vermietung** *f* car hire(*Am.* rental); **~versicherung** *f* car insurance; **~waschanlage** *f* car wash; **~werkstatt** *f* garage, car repair shop; **~wrack** *n* wrecked car

Autozoom ['au̯tozuːm] *m* *Fot.* automatic zoom
Autozubehör *n* car accessories *Pl.*; *Wirts.* car components *Pl.*
autsch *Interj.* ouch!
Auwald *m* riverside wood (*od.* forest)
auweh, **auwei(a)** *Interj.* oh no!, *Am. hum. auch* oy veh!
Auxiliar *n*; *-s*, *-e*; *Ling.* auxiliary (verb)
Avancen [a'vãːsən] *Pl.*: **j-m ~ machen** make approaches to s.o.
avancieren [avã'siːrən] *v/i.* be promoted; **~ zu** *auch* rise (*od.* advance) to the position (*od.* post) of
Avantgarde [avã'gard] *f*; *-*, *-n* avant-garde; **Avantgardismus** *m*; *-*, *kein Pl.* avant-gardism; **Avantgardist** *m*; *-en*, *-en*, **Avantgardistin** *f*; *-*, *-nen* avant-gardist; **avantgardistisch** *Adj.* avant-garde
Aversion *f*; *-*, *-en* aversion (**gegen** to); **er hat ~en gegen mich** he doesn't like (*od.* has taken against) me
Avocado, **Avokado** *f*; *-*, *-s*; *Bot.* avocado
AVON *Abk.* (*Amtliches Verzeichnis der Ortsnetzkennzahlen*) *etwa* official dial(l)ing code register
axial *Adj. Tech.* axial
Axel *m*; *-s*, *-* *Eiskunstlauf*: axel
Axiom *n*; *-s*, *-e*; *Math., Philos. etc.* axiom; **axiomatisch I.** *Adj.* axiomatic; **II.** *Adv.* axiomatically
Axt *f*; *-*, *Äxte* axe, *Am.* ax; **mit der ~ erschlagen** ax(e) to death, kill with an ax(e); **sich wie die ~ im Wald benehmen** *fig.* behave like a peasant (*stärker*: savage); **die ~ an die Wurzel(n) legen** *fig.* strike at the root; **die ~ im Haus erspart den Zimmermann** *Sprichw.* (it saves trouble if you) do it yourself; **~hieb** *m* blow of an (*od.* the) ax(e)
Ayatollah *m* → *Ajatollah*
AZ, **Az** *Abk.* → *Aktenzeichen*
Azalee *f*; *-*, *-n*; *Bot.* azalea
Azetat *etc.* → *Acetat*
Azoren *Pl. Geog.* the Azores; **~hoch** *n* *Met.* high over the Azores
Azteke *m*; *-n*, *-n*; *hist.* Aztec; **Aztekin** *f*; *-*, *-nen* Aztec woman (*od.* girl *etc.*); **aztekisch** *Adj.* Aztec, Aztecan
Azubi *m*; *-s*, *-s und f*; *-*, *-s*; *Abk. umg.* (*Auszubildende*) trainee
Azur *m*; *-s*, *kein Pl.* **1.** *Min.* lapis (lazuli); **2.** *poet.* azure, sky blue; **3.** *poet.* (*Himmel*) (azure) sky, heavens; **azurblau** *Adj.* azure, sky-blue
azyklisch I. *Adj.* acyclic; *zeitlich*: irregular; **II.** *Adv.* acyclically, irregularly

B¹, b [be:] *n*; -, - *gespr. auch -s* **1.** B, b; *B wie Berta* Buchstabieren: "b" for (*od.* as in) "Benjamin" (*Am.* "Baker"); **2.** *Mus.* B flat; *Mus.* (*Versetzungszeichen*) flat

B² *f*; -, *kein Pl.*; *Abk.* → *Bundesstraße*

babbeln *v/t/i.* (*auch: dummes Zeug* ~) babble, babble away, prattle; *was babbelt er?* what's he babbling on about?

Babel *n*; -*s*, - **1.** *bibl.* Babel; *der Turm zu* ~ the Tower of Babel; **2.** *fig.* (*Sündenbabel*) Babylon

Baby ['be:bi] *n*; -*s*, -*s* baby; *sie bekommt ein* ~ she's expecting (*od.* going to have) a baby; ~**alter** *n*: *im* ~ at the baby stage, as a baby; *bei mehreren:* as babies; ~**artikel** *Pl.* baby goods (*od.* things); *Kaufhausabteilung:* baby department *Sg.*; ~**ausstattung** *f* (*Wäsche*) layette; ~**boom** *m* baby boom; ~**flasche** *f* (baby's) bottle; ~**gesicht** *n* babyface; ~**jahr** *n* (one year's) maternity leave; *Rentenversicherung:* year credited to a woman's pension scheme for each child she has raised; ~**jogger** *m* (*Kinderwagen, Buggy*) baby jogger, baby stroller; ~**klappe** *f* anonymous baby-flap *for safe, legal surrender of unwanted newborn babies;* ~**korb** *m* bassinet; ~**kost** *f* baby food; ~**lift** *m* *Skifahren:* baby lift

Babylonier [baby'lo:niɐ] *m*; -*s*, -, ~**in** *f*; -, -*nen* Babylonian, *weiblich auch:* Babylonian woman (*od.* girl *etc.*); **babylonisch** *Adj.* Babylonian; ~*es Sprachengewirr* *fig.* babel of languages; ~*e Sprachverwirrung* *bibl.* Confusion of Tongues (at Babel); *fig.* babel, confusion of tongues

Baby|nahrung *f* baby food; ~**pause** *f* *umg.* maternity (*bzw. selten* paternity) leave *allg.*; *e-e* ~ *einlegen* have (*od.* take *od.* go on) maternity (*bzw.* paternity) leave; *sie will e-e einjährige* ~ *einlegen* she wants to take a one-year break to have a baby; ~**phon** *n*; -*s*, -*e* *od.* -*s* babyphone

babysitten *v/i.* babysit; **Babysitter** *m*; -*s*, -, **Babysitterin** *f* -, -*nen* babysitter

Baby|speck *m*; *nur Sg.*; *umg., auch fig.* puppy (*od.* baby) fat; ~**sprache** *f* baby talk; ~**strich** *m* *umg.* **1.** *nur Sg.* child prostitution; **2.** *Gebiet:* child prostitution area; ~**tragetasche** *f* carrycot, *Am.* portable bassinet; *geflochtene:* Moses basket; ~**wäsche** *f* babies' clothes *Pl.*, babywear *Sg.*; ~**zelle** *f* *Etech.* round cell

Bach *m*; -(*e*)*s*, *Bäche* **1.** stream; *kleiner: auch* brook, rivulet, *Am. auch* creek; *den* ~ *runtergehen* *umg. fig.* go up in smoke, go down the pan, go down the drain; **2.** *abfließendes Regenwasser etc., auch fig.* stream; *der Regen lief in Bächen über die Scheiben* the rain was streaming down the windowpanes; *Bäche von Schweiß flossen ihr den Rücken herunter* the sweat was pouring down her back; *e-n* ~ *machen* Kin-

derspr., *auch umg.* do (*Am.* take) a wee(-wee)

Bachbett *n*; -(*e*)*s*, -*en od.* -*e* stream bed

Bachblüten *Pl. Med.* Bach flower extracts; ~**therapie** *f* Bach flower remedy

Bache *f*; -, -*n*; *Zool.* (wild) sow

Bachforelle *f Zool.* brook (*od.* river) trout

Bächlein *n oft poet.* little brook, brooklet; *ein* ~ *machen* Kinderspr. do (*Am.* take) a wee(-wee)

Bachstelze *f*; -, -*n*; *Orn.* wagtail

Back|aroma *n* aromatic essence; ~**blech** *n* baking tray, *Am.* cookie sheet

Backbord *Naut., Flug.* **I.** *n*; -(*e*)*s*, *kein Pl.* port (side); *nach* ~ to port; **II. backbord** *Adv.* to port

Backbuch *n* baking book

Bäckchen *n* (little) cheek

Backe *f*; -, -*n* **1.** (*Wange*) cheek; *mit vollen* ~*n kauen* eat with one's mouth full, munch away (heartily); *e-e dicke od. geschwollene* ~ *haben* have a swollen cheek (*od.* face); ~*n wie ein Hamster haben* have chubby (*od.* hamster) cheeks; *er strahlte über beide* ~*n umg.* he was beaming from ear to ear; *au* ~*! umg.* oh no!; **2.** (*Gesäßhälfte*) cheek; *etw. auf e-r* ~ *absitzen od. abreißen Sl.* sail through s.th.; **3.** *am Gewehr:* cheek piece; **4.** *am Ski:* toe piece; **5.** *Tech.* jaw; (*Bremsbacke*) shoe

backen¹; *bäckt od. backt, backte od. buk, hat gebacken* **I.** *v/t/i.* **1.** (*Brot, Kuchen*) bake; *im Hotel, Restaurant:* *wir* ~ *selbst* we do all our own baking; *e-e frisch gebackene Mutter/Krankenschwester umg. fig.* a young mother / a fledgling (*od.* newly trained) nurse; **2.** *Dial.* (*braten*) (*Eier, Fisch etc.*) fry; (*dörren*) (*Obst*) dry; **II.** *v/i.* Brot *etc.:* bake, stay in the oven

backen²; *backte, hat gebacken* **I.** *v/i.* (*kleben*) Lehm, Schnee: stick (*an* + *Dat.* to); **II.** *v/t.* stick (*an* + *Akk.* to, onto)

Backen|bart *m* sideburns *Pl.*; ~**bremse** *f Mot.* shoe brake; *am Fahrrad:* brake block; ~**hörnchen** *n Zool.* chipmunk; ~**knochen** *m* cheekbone; ~**tasche** *f Anat.* (cheek) pouch; ~**zahn** *m* molar

Bäcker *m*; -*s*, - baker; *Brot vom* ~ baker's bread; *zum* ~ *gehen* go to the baker's

Backerbse *f* small round soup noodle

Bäckerei *f*; -, -*en* **1.** *Laden:* baker's (shop), bakery; **2.** (*Backstube*) bakery, bakehouse; **3.** *nur Sg.*; (*das Backen*) baking; **4.** *nur Sg.*; *Handwerk:* baker's trade; **5.** *mst Pl.*; *bes. österr.* (*Kleingebäck*) (biscuits *od. Am.* cookies and) pastries *Pl.*

Bäckerin *f*; -, -*nen* (female) baker; (*Bäckersfrau*) baker's wife

Bäcker|innung *f* bakers' guild; ~**laden**

m → *Bäckerei* 1; ~**lehrling** *m* apprentice (*od.* trainee) baker, baker's apprentice; ~**meister** *m* master baker

Bäckersfrau *f* baker's wife

backfertig *Adj.* oven-ready

Back|fett *n* cooking fat; *für Kuchen etc.:* shortening; ~**fisch** *m* **1.** fried fish; **2.** *fig. altm.* (young) teenager, teenage girl; ~**form** *f* baking tin, *Am.* cake pan

Backgammon [bɛk'gɛmən] *n*; -*s*, *kein Pl.* backgammon

Background ['bɛkgraʊnt] *m*; -*s*, -*s* **1.** background; **2.** *Mus.* background music; (*Begleitung*) backing

Back|hähnchen *n Gastr.* fried chicken; ~**haus** *n* bakehouse; ~**hendl** *n österr.*, ~**huhn** *n* fried chicken; ~**mischung** *f* baking mixture; ~**obst** *n* dried fruit

Back|ofen *m* oven; ~**ofenhitze** *f umg. fig.* sweltering heat; *das ist e-e* ~*!* it's sweltering; ~**papier** *n* grease(-)proof paper; ~**pfeife** *f umg.* clout (*od.* clip) (a)round the ears; ~**pflaume** *f* (dried) prune; ~**pulver** *n* baking powder; ~**rezept** *n* baking recipe; ~**rohr** *n Dial., österr.*, ~**röhre** *f* oven

Backslash ['bɛkslɛʃ] *m* (*umgekehrter Schrägstrich*) backslash

Backstein *m* brick; ~**bau** *m* brick building

Back|stube *f* bakery, bakehouse; ~**teig** *m* dough; *flüssiger:* batter; ~**trog** *m* kneading trough

Backup ['bɛkʔap] *m*; -*s*, -*s*; *EDV* backup; ~**-Datei** *f EDV* backup file

Back|waren *Pl.* bread, cakes and pastries; ~**werk** *n*; *nur Sg.* pastries *Pl.*; ~**zeit** *f* baking time; ~**zutaten** *Pl.* baking ingredients

Bad *n*; -(*e*)*s*, *Bäder* **1.** *in Wanne:* bath; (*sich* [*Dat.*]) *ein* ~ *einlaufen lassen* run a bath; *ein* ~ *nehmen* have (*od.* take) a bath; → *Kind* 2; **2.** *im Meer, See:* swim; *ein* ~ *nehmen* go for a swim (*od.* dip *umg.*); *ein* ~ *in der Menge fig.* a walkabout, *Am. a public figure's walk among people;* **3.** (*Badezimmer*) bathroom; *Zimmer mit* ~ room with bath; **4.** (*Badeanstalt*) swimming pool, swimming (*od.* public) baths *Pl.*; **5.** (*Kurort*) spa; (*Seebad*) seaside resort; **6.** *Chem., Med.* bath; *medizinische Bäder nehmen*, *verordnen* a course of therapeutic baths

Bade|anstalt *f altm.* swimming pool, swimming baths *Pl.*; ~**anzug** *m* swimsuit; ~**arzt** *m* spa doctor; ~**bekleidung** *f* swimwear; ~**gast** *m* **1.** *im Schwimmbad:* bather; **2.** (*Kurgast*) spa visitor; ~**gelegenheit** *f* place to swim; *mit* ~ with swimming facilities; ~**haube** *f* bathing cap; ~**hose** *f* swimming (*od.* bathing) trunks *Pl.*; *e-e* ~ a pair of swimming (*od.* bathing) trunks; ~**kappe** *f* bathing cap; ~**lustige** *m, f*; -*n*, -*n*, *mst Pl.* keen (*Am.* avid) swimmer; *beim Baden:* bather, swimmer; ~**mantel** *m* bathrobe; (*Morgenmantel*) auch dressing gown; **~matte** f bathmat; **~meister** m pool attendant; **~mode** f swimwear, beachwear; **~mütze** f bathing cap

baden I. v/i. **1.** (*ein Bad nehmen*) have (*od.* take) a bath, *Am. auch* bathe; **warm/kalt ~** have (*od.* take) a hot/cold bath; **wann möchtest du ~?** when do you want your bath?; **2.** (*schwimmen*) swim; **~ gehen** go swimming, go for a swim; *umg. fig.* come a cropper (**bei, mit** over); **II.** v/t. (*Kind etc.*) bath, *Am.* bathe; (*Wunde, Auge etc.*) bathe; → **Schweiß** 1, **schweißgebadet, heiß** II 1; **III.** v/refl. → I 1; *fig.* bask (**in** + *Dat.* in), revel (in)

Badende m, f; *-n, -n* bather, swimmer

Badener m; *-s, -* man from Baden; **~ sein** *mst* come from Baden; **Badenerin** f; *-, -nen* woman from Baden

Badenixe f bathing beauty

Badenser m; *-s, -; umg., neg.!* → **Badener**

Baden-Württemberg (*n*); *-s* Baden-Württemberg; **baden-württembergisch** *Adj.* Baden-Württemberg …, from Baden-Württemberg

Bade|ofen m bathroom boiler; **~öl** n bath oil; **~ort** m **1.** *am Meer*: seaside resort; *am See*: lakeside resort; **2.** (*Kurort*) health spa, spa town (*od.* resort); **~platz** m place for swimming; *förm.* bathing place

Bader m; *-s, -; altm.* **1.** (*Barbier*) barber; **2.** (*Arzt, Kurpfuscher*) quack

Bade|reise f health cure; **e-e ~ machen** go on a health cure; **~sachen** *Pl.* swimming things; **~saison** f swimming season; **~salz** n bath salts *Pl.*; **~schwamm** m (bathroom) sponge; **~schuhe** f beach (*od.* bathing) shoes; **~see** m (bathing) lake; **~strand** m (bathing) beach; **mit eigenem ~** with private (access to the) beach; **~thermometer** n bath thermometer; **~tuch** n bathtowel; **~urlaub** f holiday at the seaside, *Am.* vacation by the sea; **~ machen** go to the seaside for one's holiday (*Am.* vacation); **~wanne** f bath(tub); **~wasser** n bathwater; **~wetter** n weather for the beach (*od.* for swimming); **~zeit** f **1.** *begrenzte Dauer*: maximum swimming period; **2.** (*Öffnungszeiten*) pool opening hours *Pl.*; **~zeug** n *umg.* swimming things *Pl.*; **~zimmer** n bathroom; **~zimmerschrank** m bathroom cabinet; **~zusatz** m bath essence (*od.* product)

badisch *Adj.* Baden …, from Baden

Badminton ['bɛtmɪntən] n; *-s, kein Pl.* badminton

baff *Adj.; nur präd.; umg.:* **~ sein** be flabbergasted, be struck dumb, be gobsmacked *Sl.*; **da war ich aber ~** I was completely floored, I was gobsmacked; **da bist du ~, was?** you weren't expecting that, were you?

BAföG, Bafög n; *-(s), kein Pl.; Abk.* (**Bundesausbildungsförderungsgesetz**) **1.** *Gesetz: federal law governing financial assistance for students*; **2.** *Zuschuss zur Ausbildung:* grant; **~ bekommen** get a (government) grant

Bagage [ba'ga:ʒə] f; *-, -n, Pl. ungebräuchlich; pej.* rabble, shower; **die ganze ~** *umg.* the whole lot of them; rag, tag and bobtail

Bagatell|betrag m petty sum, insignificant (*od.* trifling, trivial) amount; **~delikt** n petty (*od.* minor) offen|ce (*Am.* -se)

Bagatelle f; *-, -n* **1.** trifle; **2.** *Mus.* bag-

atelle

Bagatellfall m *Jur.* petty lawsuit

bagatellisieren vt/i. play down, minimize

Bagatell|sache f **1.** minor affair; **es ist e-e ~** *auch* it's small beer (*Am.* small potatoes); **2.** *Jur.* petty lawsuit; **~schaden** m superficial (*od.* minor *od.* petty) damage

Bagger m; *-s, -* excavator, digger, *Am. auch* backhoe; (*Schwimmbagger*) dredger; **~führer** m driver of the excavator, *Am.* backhoe operator; *e-s Schwimmbaggers:* dredgerman

baggern vt/i. **1.** excavate; *nass:* dredge; **2.** *beim Volleyball:* dig (the ball); **3.** *umg.* (*flirten*) chat up

Baggersee m flooded gravel pit

Baguette f; *-, -n; auch n; -s, -s* baguette, French stick

bah, bäh *Interj.* **1.** *Schaf:* baa!; **2.** *bei Schadenfreude:* ha, ha!; **3.** *bei Ekel:* ugh!, yuck!

Bahamas *Pl.: die ~* the Bahamas

Bahn f; *-, -en* **1.** (*Weg*) way, path; **~ frei!** make way!, stand aside!; **2.** *fig.: die ~ ist frei* the road is clear; **freie ~ haben** have the go-ahead, have the green light *umg.* (**für** for); **du hast freie ~** it's all yours; **sich** (*Dat.*) **~ brechen** (*sich durchsetzen*) win through; *Idee etc.:* gain acceptance; (*vorwärts kommen*) forge ahead; **e-r Sache ~ brechen** pioneer s.th., blaze the trail for s.th.; **auf die schiefe ~ geraten** *od.* **kommen** go astray, stray off the straight and narrow; **in die richtigen ~en lenken** direct into the right channels; **sich in den gewohnten ~en bewegen** move along the same old track, be stuck in the same old rut *pej.*; *bewusst:* keep to the well-trodden paths; **wieder in geregelten ~en verlaufen** be back to normal again; **j-n aus der ~ werfen** *od.* **bringen** throw s.o. off track; *seelisch etc.:* knock s.o. sideways; **3.** a) (*Eisenbahn*) railway, *Am.* railroad; (*Zug*) train; (*Straßenbahn*) tram, *Am.* streetcar, trolley; **in der ~** on the train; **mit der ~** by train; **Waren per ~ schicken** *Wirts.* send goods by rail; (*mit der*) **~ fahren** travel by train; **ich fahre gern** (**mit der**) **~** *auch* I enjoy travel(l)ing on trains, I enjoy rail travel; **j-n zur ~ bringen** take s.o. to the station, see s.o. off (at the station); **j-n von der ~ abholen** (go and) meet s.o. at the station, b) *nur Sg.; Unternehmen:* railway (*Am.* railroad) authorities *Pl.* (*od.* operators *Pl.*); **bei der ~ arbeiten** work for the railway (*Am.* railroad); **4.** (*Fahrbahn*) lane; **5.** (*Flugbahn*) trajectory; **6.** *Astron., von Mond, Sonne:* course; (*Umlaufbahn*) orbit (*auch e-s Elektrons*); *von Komet:* path; **7.** *Sport* a) (*Rennbahn*) track; (*Eis-, Rollschuhbahn*) rink; (*Schlitten-, Bobbahn*) run; (*Kegelbahn*) alley, b) *für einzelne Läufer, Schwimmer etc.:* lane; **8.** *von Tapete:* length; *aus Papier, Kunststoff:* web; *Tuch etc.:* width; *e-s Rocks:* gore; **9.** *Tech., Amboss, Hammer, Hobel:* face; **10.** *Tech.* (*Führung*) guide, track

Bahn|angestellte m, f railway (*Am.* railroad) employee; **~anschluss** m rail connection; **~arbeiter** m, **~arbeiterin** f railway (*Am.* railroad) worker; **~beamte** m, **~beamtin** f *altm.* railway (*Am.* railroad) official

bahnbrechend I. *Adj.* pioneering, *attr. auch* pioneer …; *stärker:* trailblazing; *Erfindung etc.:* revolutionary, epoch-

-making; **II.** *Adv.:* **~ wirken** be pioneering, blaze the trail; **Bahnbrecher** m, **Bahnbrecherin** f pioneer, trailblazer

Bahn|bus m railway (*Am.* rail) bus, bus operated by the railway (*Am.* railroad); **~Card®** f; *-, -s* rail card, rail pass, *rail pass entitling s.o. to reduced fares;* **~damm** m railway (*Am.* railroad) embankment

bahnen v/t.: **e-n Weg ~** clear a path (+ *Dat.* for); **sich** (*Dat.*) **e-n Weg durch etw. ~** fight (*od.* force) one's way through s.th.; **j-m den Weg nach oben ~** *fig.* put s.o. on the road (*od.* path) to the top

Bahn|fahrt f train journey; *kürzere: auch* train ride; *längere:* train (*od.* rail) journey; **~fracht** f rail freight; **♀frei** *Adj. und Adv. Wirts., Sendung etc.:* carriage paid, free on rail (*abgek.* f.o.r.); **~gelände** n railway area (*od.* complex), *Am.* rail yard; **~gleis** n railway (*Am.* railroad) track

Bahnhof m **1.** (*railway od. Am.* train) station; **~ Neustadt** Neustadt Station; **auf dem ~** at the station; **ich verstehe nur ~** *umg. fig.* I don't know what he's *etc.* talking about, it's all Greek to me; **2.** *umg. fig.:* **j-n mit großem ~ empfangen** (*od.* **j-m e-n großen ~ bereiten**) roll out the red carpet for s.o., give s.o. the red carpet (*od.* the real VIP) treatment; **es gab e-n großen ~** they had the red carpets out

Bahnhofs|bereich m station concourse (*od.* premises *Pl.*); **~gaststätte** f station restaurant; **~halle** f (station) concourse, main concourse (of the station); **~mission** f Travel(l)ers' Aid (Office); **~nähe** f: **in ~** near the station; **~platz** m station square; **~restaurant** n station restaurant; **~uhr** f station clock; **~viertel** n (seedy) area around the main station; **~vorplatz** m station forecourt (*od.* square); **~vorsteher** m stationmaster; **~vorsteherin** f (lady) stationmaster

…bahnig *im Adj.* …-lane; **vier-** four-lane; **mehr~** multiple-lane

Bahn|kilometer m kilomet|re (*Am.* -er) (travel(l)ed) by rail, *etwa* passenger mile; **~körper** m permanent way, roadbed

bahnlagernd I. *Adv.:* **etw. ~ senden** send s.th. to be called for at the station; **II.** *Adj.* *Ware etc.:* to be called for at station

Bahn|linie f **1.** (*Strecke*) railway (line), *Am.* railroad (line); **2.** (*Gleiskörper*) (rail) track; **~meisterei** f railway (*Am.* railroad) maintenance division; **~polizei** f station police; **~reise** f train (*od.* rail) journey; **~reisende** m, f rail travel(l)er (*od.* passenger); **~schranke** f level (*od. Am.* grade) crossing barrier (*od.* gate); **~schwelle** f sleeper, *Am.* tie; **~station** f railway (*Am.* train) station (*od.* stop)

Bahnsteig m platform; **~kante** f edge of the platform; **Vorsicht an der ~!** mind the gap!, *Am.* watch your step!; **~karte** f *altm.* platform ticket

Bahn|strecke f (railway) line, *Am.* (railroad) track; **~transport** m rail transport; **~überführung** f railway bridge, *Am.* railroad overpass; **~übergang** m level (*Am.* grade) crossing; → **beschrankt, unbeschrankt**; **~unterführung** f railway (*Am.* railroad) underpass; **~verbindung** f rail connection; **~versand** m rail dispatch; **~wärter** m **1.** level (*Am.* grade) crossing attendant, gatekeeper; **2.** → **Strecken-**

wärter, **~wärterhäuschen** n gate-keeper's cabin

Bahre f; -, -n; (Tragbahre) stretcher; (Totenbahre) bier; → **Wiege** 2; **Bahrtuch** n pall

Bai f; -, -en bay

bairisch Ling. **I.** Adj. Bavarian; **II. Bairisch** n; -en Bavarian; **das Bairische** Bavarian

Baiser [bɛ'zeː] n; -s, -s meringue

Baisse ['bɛːsə] f; -, -n; Fin. slump, bear market, fall (in prices), sharp drop in prices; **auf ~ spekulieren** speculate for a fall, sell short; **Baissier** m; -s, -s; Fin. bear

Bajonett n; -(e)s, -e bayonet; **mit aufgepflanztem ~** with bayonets (at the) ready

Bajuware m; -n, -n, **Bajuwarin** f; -, -nen; altm. noch hum. Bavarian, weiblich auch: Bavarian woman (od. girl etc.); **bajuwarisch** Adj. Bavarian

Bake f; -, -n **1.** an Bahnübergang, Autobahnausfahrt: countdown marker; für Schiffs- und Flugverkehr: beacon; **2.** Landvermessung: marking pole

Bakelit® n; -s, kein Pl. Bakelite

Bakkarat ['bakara] n; -s, kein Pl. baccarat

Bakschisch ['bakʃɪʃ] n; -(e)s, -e baksheesh; **j-m ein ~ geben** give s.o. baksheesh; fig. (bestechen) give s.o. a backhander (Am. bribe)

Bakterie [bak'teːrɪə] f; -, -n, mst Pl. bacterium (Pl. bacteria), germ; **bakteriell** Adj. bacterial; **~e Infektion** bacteria(l) infection

bakterienfrei Adj. germ-free, free of bacteria

Bakterien|kultur f (bacteria[l]) culture; **~stamm** m strain (of bacteria); **~träger** m, **~trägerin** f germ carrier; **~zucht** f growing of bacteria; konkret: bacteria culture

Bakteriologe m; -n, -n, **Bakteriologin** f; -nen bacteriologist; **Bakteriologie** f; -, kein Pl. bacteriology; **bakteriologisch** Adj. bacteriological

Bakterium n; -s, Bakterien; altm. → **Bakterie**

bakterizid Adj. Med. bactericidal; **Bakterizid** n; -s, -e bactericide

Balalaika [bala'laika] f; -, -s od. Balalaiken; Mus. balalaika; **~ spielen** play the balalaika

Balance [ba'lãːsə] f; -, kein Pl. balance; **die ~ halten/verlieren** keep/lose one's balance; **sie halten sich die ~** they balance each other out; → auch **Gleichgewicht**; **~akt** m auch fig. balancing act; **~regler** m Etech. balance control

balancieren I. v/t. (hat balanciert) balance; **etw. auf etw.** (Dat.) **~** balance s.th. on (top of) s.th.; **II.** v/i. (sein) balance; **über etw.** (Akk.) **~** do a balancing act across s.th.; **Balancierstange** f (balancing) pole

bald Adv.; eher, am ehesten **1.** soon; **~ darauf** od. **danach** soon (od. shortly) after(ward[s]); **~ ist dein Geburtstag** it's (od. it'll be) your birthday soon; **möglichst ~** (od. **so ~ wie** od. **als möglich**) as soon as possible; **das wird's so ~ nicht wieder geben** we won't see the likes of that again soon; **wird's ~?** umg. how much longer is it going to take?, come on!; **ich hab's ~** umg. I'm nearly ready, I won't be a minute; **wirst du ~ ruhig sein!** umg. will you be quiet!; **bis** od. **auf ~!** umg. see you soon, be seeing you; **2.** umg. (fast) almost, nearly; **~ hätte ich was gesagt!** I

nearly said something I shouldn't have, I nearly put my foot in it (Am. in my mouth); **das ist ~ nicht mehr lustig** it's getting beyond a joke, Am. it's not funny any more; **3.** geh.: **~ so, ~ so** one moment this, one (od. the next) moment that; **~ hier, ~ da** here, there and everywhere

Baldachin m; -s, -e **1.** über Bett, bei Prozession etc.: canopy; **2.** Archit. baldachin, canopy

Bälde f altm.: **in ~** soon, before long

baldig im Adj.; nur. attr., ohne Steigerung speedy; **auf (ein) ~es Wiedersehen** hope to see you again soon; **wir hoffen auf ~e Antwort** förm. we look forward to an early reply; **baldigst** Adv. as soon as possible

baldmöglichst I. Adj.; nur attr. earliest (od. soonest) possible; **zum ~en Zeitpunkt** as soon as possible; **II.** Adv. as soon as possible

Baldrian m; -s, -e **1.** Bot. valerian; **2.** nur Sg.; Extrakt: valerian; **~tee** m valerian tea; **~tropfen** Pl. valerian Sg. (drops)

Balearen Pl.: **die ~** the Balearics

Balg¹ m; -(e)s, Bälge **1.** (Haut) von Mensch, Tier: skin, hide; **e-m Tier den ~ abziehen** skin an animal; **2.** (Bauch) Sl., auch hum. von Mensch: belly; **3.** von Orgel, auch Fot.: bellows Pl.

Balg² m od. n; -(e)s, Bälge(r); umg. pej. (Kind) brat

balgen v/refl. scuffle, tussle, scrap umg. (**um** over); **Balgerei** f; -, -en scuffle, tussle, scrap umg. (**um** for, over)

Bali (n); -s; Geog. Bali; **Balinese** m; -n, -n, **Balinesin** f; -, -nen Balinese, weiblich auch: Balinese woman (od. girl etc.); **balinesisch** Adj. Balinese

Balkan m; -s; Geog.: **der ~ 1.** Halbinsel: the Balkans Pl; **2.** Gebirge: Balkan Mountains Pl.; **Balkanhalbinsel** f Balkan peninsula; **Balkanstaat** m Balkan state

Balken m; -s, - **1.** Archit. beam; (Dachbalken) rafter; (Decken-, Querbalken) joist; (Träger) girder; **ein tragender ~** a supporting (od. load-bearing) beam etc.; **lügen, dass sich die ~ biegen** umg. fig. lie like a trooper, lie through one's teeth; **Wasser hat keine ~** Sprichw. water's a bad floor to walk on, you must either sink or swim; **2.** Sport, beim Weitsprung: take-off board; → **Schwebebalken**; **3.** Mus. crossbar; **4.** TV bar; **5.** auf Flaggen, Schildern: fess(e); **6.** an Waage: (balance) beam; **~decke** f beamed roof (od. ceiling); **~diagramm** n bar chart; **~überschrift** f banner headline; **~waage** f beam scales Pl.; **~werk** n timbering, timberwork

Balkon [bal'kɔn] m; -s, -s od. -e **1.** balcony; **2.** a) Theat. dress circle, Am. balcony, b) im Kino: (upper) circle; **3.** Sl. hum. (Busen) (big) boobs Pl.; **~blume** f balcony plant; **~kasten** m balcony planter; **~pflanze** f outdoor (potted) plant; **~tür** f balcony door, French window(s Pl.)

Ball¹ m; -(e)s, Bälle **1.** ball; **~ spielen** play ball; **den ~ köpfen** head the ball, Am. butt the ball with one's head; **am ~ sein** have the ball, be in possession of the ball; **er ist am ~** fig. it's his turn, the ball's in his court; (ist aktiv) he's very involved; (weiß Bescheid) he's on the ball; **am ~ bleiben** hold onto the ball; fig. keep at it (stärker: keep one's nose to the grindstone); → **zuspielen**

II.; **2.** fig. aus Wolle, Papier etc.: ball; **der glühende** od. **leuchtende ~ der Sonne** geh., lit. the sun's glowing orb

Ball² m; -(e)s, Bälle ball, dance; **auf e-m ~** at a ball; **auf e-n ~ gehen** go to a ball

balla(balla) Adj.; nur präd.; umg. nuts

Ballabgabe f Sport pass; **bei der ~** when the ball was played, when he (od. she) played the ball

Ballade f; -, -n ballad; **balladenhaft** Adj. ballad(-)like; **Balladensänger** m ballad-singer, balladeer

Ballannahme f Sport stopping and controlling the ball; aus der Luft: bringing down the ball

Ballast m; -(e)s, kein Pl. ballast; fig. (Last, Belastung) auch burden; unnützer: deadwood; (Behinderung) handicap; **~ abwerfen** dump ballast; fig. shed some ballast; **er ist nur ~** fig. he's just deadwood

Ballaststoffe Pl. roughage Sg.; fib|re (Am. -er) Sg.; **ballaststoffreich** Adj. high-fib|re (Am. -er) ..., präd. auch high in fib|re (Am. -er); **~e Nahrung** high-fib|re (Am. -er) food(s Pl.) (od. diet); food(s Pl.) with plenty of roughage

Ball|beherrschung f Sport ball control; **~besitz** m: **im ~ sein** have possession, have (od. be in) possession of the ball

ballen I. v/t. (Faust) clench; **die Hand zur Faust ~** clench one's fist; **II.** v/refl. **1.** form into a ball (od. balls); **der Schnee ballte sich zu Klumpen** the snow became lumpy; **2.** Wolken, Menschen: gather; bedrohlich: move in on; fig. Probleme etc.: mount, build up, pile up; **sich ~ um** um e-e Stadt etc.: build up around, cluster around; → **geballt** II, III

Ballen m; -s, - **1.** Anat. ball of one's (od. the) foot (od. hand); bei Tieren: pad; Med., entzündet: bunion; **2.** (Maßeinheit) Stroh, Stoff: bale; Papier: ten reams Pl.; **3.** (Bündel) Baumwolle, Tabak etc.: bale; **~presse** f baling press

ballenweise Adv. by the bale, in bales

Ballerei f; -, -en; umg. shoot(-)out; ständiges, unsinniges Schießen: constant shooting (od. sniping)

Ballerina¹ f; -, Ballerinen ballerina

Ballerina² m; -s, -s; (Schuh) ballerina shoe

Ballermann m umg. gun, Am. rod, Am. piece Sl.

ballern umg. **I.** v/i. **1.** (schießen) bang (away) (auch Fußball); **durch die Gegend ~** shoot away (at random); **2.** (schlagen) **an** od. **gegen etw. ~** hammer away at s.th.; **II.** v/t. **1.** (werfen) hurl; (Fußball) bang; **etw. irgendwohin ~** fling (od. hurl) s.th. somewhere; **2.** umg. (Schnaps trinken) put away, knock back; **e-n ~** knock one back; **3.** umg. (Schlag versetzen): **j-m e-e ~** sock s.o. one

Ballett n; -(e)s, -e ballet; Truppe: ballet company; **beim ~ sein** be with the ballet; engS. be a ballet dancer; **zum ~ gehen** join a ballet company, become a ballet dancer; **~ tanzen** do ballet-dancing; **~abend** m ballet performance, evening of ballet

Ballett|meister m ballet master; **~meisterin** f ballet mistress; **~musik** f ballet music; **~röckchen** n tutu; **~schuh** m ballet shoe; **~schule** f ballet school; **~tänzer** m, **~tänzerin** f ballet dancer; **~truppe** f ballet company

ballförmig Adj. ball-shaped, spherical

Ball|führung f Sport ball control; **~gefühl** n Sport feel for the ball; **kein ~ haben** have no feel for the ball
Ballistik f ballistics Pl. (als Fach: V. im Sg.); **Ballistiker** m; -s, - ballistics expert; **ballistisch I.** Adj.; nur attr. ballistic; **II.** Adv. ballistically
Balljunge m Sport ball boy
Ballkleid n ball dress
Ball|kontrolle f Sport ball control; **~künstler** m wizard with the ball; Fußball: auch football wizard; **~mädchen** n ball girl
Ballnacht f night at the ball; bestimmte: night of the ball
Ballon m; -s, -s od. -e **1.** (hot-air) balloon; **~ fahren** go up in a balloon; auch regelmäßig: go ballooning; **2.** Flasche: auch Chem. carboy; für Wein: demijohn; **3.** Sl. (Kopf) noddle, Am. noggin; **er hat so e-n ~ gekriegt** he went bright red; **~fahrer** m, **~fahrerin** f balloonist; **~fahrt** f balloon ride (od. trip); **e-e ~ machen** go up in a balloon; **~führer** m, **~führerin** f balloon pilot; **~mütze** f Mao cap; **~reifen** m balloon tyre (Am. tire), doughnut umg.; **~seide** f balloon (od. parachute) silk
Ballsaal m ballroom
Ball|spiel n ball game; **~spielen** n ball games Pl.; **~ verboten!** no ball games
Ballung f agglomeration; fig. concentration, buildup
Ballungs|gebiet n, **~raum** m conurbation; der Industrie: area of concentrated industry; pej. congested area; **~zentrum** n hub of a conurbation, population cent|re (Am. -er); der Industrie: cent|re (Am. -er) of industry
ballverliebt Adj. umg. Fußballspieler: attr. selfish; **~ sein** hold onto (od. refuse to let go of) the ball
Ball|wechsel m Tennis etc.: rally; **~wurfmaschine** f Tennis: ball thrower
Balneologie f; -, kein Pl. balneology; **balneologisch** Adj. balneological
Balsa n; -, kein Pl., **Balsaholz** n balsa (wood)
Balsam m; -s, -e; Pharm. balsam; auch fig. balm; **das ist ~ für m-e Seele** geh. fig., bes. iro. it is a great comfort to my soul; **Balsamessig** m; -s, Sorten: -e balsamic vinegar; **balsamieren** v/t. (Leichen) embalm; **Balsamierung** f embalming; **balsamisch I.** Adj. **1.** (wohlriechend) balmy; (lindernd) soothing, balsamic; **2.** (Balsam enthaltend) Öl: balsamic; **II.** Adv. soothingly, balmily; **~ wirken** have a soothing effect
Balte m; -n, -n Balt, person from the Baltic; **die ~n** the Baltic peoples; **Baltikum** n; -s: **das ~** the Baltic (region), the Baltic States; **Baltin** f; -, -nen Balt, woman from the Baltic; **baltisch** Adj. Baltic; **die ~en Länder** the Baltic countries; **die ~en Staaten** the Baltic States
Balustrade f; -, -n balustrade
Balz f; -, -en; Zool., Orn. (Werbung) courtship; (Paarung) mating; (Balzzeit) mating season; **balzen** v/i. (locken) court, call, display; (sich paaren) mate
Balz|laut m Zool., Orn. mating (od. display) sound; **~ruf** m mating (od. display) call; **~verhalten** n mating (od. courtship) display (od. behavio[u]r); **~zeit** f mating season
Bambus m; - od. -ses, -se **1.** Bot. bamboo; **2.** nur Sg.; Material: bamboo; **~bär** m panda; **~hütte** f bamboo hut;

~rohr n bamboo (cane); **~sprossen** Pl. bamboo sprouts (od. shoots); **~stab** m, **~stock** m (bamboo) cane; **~vorhang** m **1.** bamboo curtain; **2.** Pol. fig. Bamboo Curtain
Bammel m; -s, kein Pl.; umg. dread; **(e-n) ~ haben vor** be scared stiff of
bammeln v/i. umg. Dial. dangle, swing (to and fro)
banal Adj. trite, banal; (alltäglich) run-of-the-mill ...; (simpel) very straightforward; **banalisieren** vt/i. trivialize; **Banalität** f; -, -en **1.** nur Sg.; e-r Situation etc.: banality, triteness, banal nature; **2.** mst Pl. (Bemerkung) trite (od. banal) remark, banalities Pl.
Banane f; -, -n banana
Bananen|buchse f Etech. banana jack; **~dampfer** m auch fig. banana boat; **~flanke** f Fußball: curving cross; **~republik** f pej. banana republic; **~schale** f banana skin (od. peel); **~staude** f banana tree; **~stecker** m Etech. banana plug
Banause m; -n, -n; pej. philistine, low-brow umg.; **banausenhaft** Adj. philistine, low-brow umg.
Band¹ n; -es, Bänder **1.** (Mess-, Zielband) tape; von Schürze etc.: string; am Hut: band; (Farb-, Schmuck-, Ordensband) ribbon; **2.** (Tonband) (magnetic) tape; **auf ~ aufnehmen** tape, record; **hast du's auf ~?** have you got it on tape?; **auf ~ sprechen** speak onto (a) tape, (etw.) record s.th. onto (a) tape, tape s.th.; **3.** Archit. tie, bond; **4.** Tech., von Säge: blade; von Scharnier: hinge; **5.** (Förderband) (conveyor) belt; (Fließband) assembly (od. production) line; **am ~ arbeiten** work on an assembly line; **vom ~ rollen** od. **laufen** roll off the assembly line; **am laufenden ~** umg. fig. one after the other; (pausenlos) nonstop; **wir hatten Schwierigkeiten am laufenden ~** there was no end of problems, it was just one problem (od. thing) after another; **er macht das am laufenden ~** he does it all the time; **6.** Anat. von Sehne, Gelenk: ligament; **7.** Radio: (wave)band
Band² n; -es, -e **1.** fig. (Bindung) bond(s Pl.), ties Pl.; **das ~ der Ehe** the bond of marriage; **familiäre ~e** family ties; **das ~ der Liebe/Freundschaft** the bonds of love/friendship; **zarte ~e knüpfen** lit. od. hum become romantically involved; **2.** lit.: **~e** (Fesseln) bonds, fetters
Band³ m; -es, Bände Buch: volume; **das spricht Bände** that speaks volumes, that's very revealing
Band⁴ f; -, -s; (Musikgruppe) band
Bandage [ban'da:ʒə] f; -, -n bandage; **j-m e-e ~ anlegen** put a bandage on s.o., bandage s.o. up; **mit harten ~n kämpfen** umg. fig. go at it hammer and tongs, go at it with a vengeance; **bandagieren** v/t. bandage (up), put a bandage on
Band|arbeiter m, **~arbeiterin** f assembly-line worker; **~archiv** n tape library (od. archive); **~aufnahme** f, **~aufzeichnung** f tape recording; **~breite** f **1.** Radio: frequency range, bandwidth; **2.** Statistik: spread; **3.** Börse: fluctuation margin; **4.** von Warenangebot: range; **5.** fig. range; bes. von Wissen etc.: spectrum
Bändchen n **1.** (schmales Stoffband etc.) little ribbon; **2.** (kleines Buch) slim volume
Bande¹ f; -, -n **1.** Verbrecher etc.: gang,

ring; **2.** umg. pej. shower, rabble; **e-e ~ von ...** a bunch of ...; **die ganze ~** the whole lot (of them); **e-e saubere ~!** a fine (od. nice) lot (od. bunch)!
Bande² f; -, -n **1.** Billard, Kegeln: cushion; **2.** Eishockey etc.: boards Pl.; Fußball, Sportplatz: touchline, edge; **3.** Reitbahn: rails Pl.
Bandeisen n strip iron
Bändel n od. m; -s, -; (Stoffband) ribbon; (Schnürsenkel) shoelace; **j-n (fest) am ~ haben** umg. fig. keep (od. have) s.o. on a string, have s.o. at one's beck and call
Bandendabschaltung f Etech. automatic shut(-)off
Banden|führer m gang leader (od. boss), ringleader; **~krieg** m gang war(fare); **~kriminalität** f gang crime; **~mitglied** n member of a (od. the) gang, gang member, gangbanger Sl.
Bandenwerbung f touchline (od. perimeter board) advertising
Bandenwesen n gangsterism
Bänderdehnung f Med. stretched (od. pulled) ligament
Banderole f; -, -n **1.** revenue stamp; Zigarre: band; **2.** um Drucksachen, Banknoten: sleeve, wrapper; **3.** Kunst: scroll
Bänderriss m Med. torn ligament
Bänderung f (Musterung) stripes Pl.; von Gestein: banding
Bänderzerrung f Med. stretched (od. pulled) ligament
Band|gerät n reel-to-reel (tape recorder); **~geschwindigkeit** f **1.** tape speed; beim Aufnehmen: auch recording speed; **2.** von Fließband: (assembly-)line speed
...bändig im Adj.: **e-e mehr~e/fünf~e Ausgabe** a multi-volume/five-volume edition
bändigen v/t. (Zirkustiere etc.) tame; (Pferde) break in; fig. restrain, (bring under) control; (Naturkräfte) harness, (bring under) control; (s-e Freude, Hass etc.) restrain, control; (Kinder etc.) get (od. keep under) control; **die Kinder waren nicht zu ~** the children were uncontrollable; **Bändiger** m; -s, -, **Bändigerin** f; -, -nen tamer; **Bändigung** f taming; breaking in; fig. control; harnessing; → **bändigen**
Bandit m; -en, -en **1.** bandit; **2.** umg. fig. crook; **3.** umg.: **einarmiger ~** one-armed bandit
Bandkeramik f Archäol. band ceramics Pl.; Epoche: Danubian I stage
Bandleader ['bɛntliːdɐ] m Mus. bandleader
Band|maß n tape measure, measuring tape; **~montage** f line assembly; **~nudel** f; mst Pl. **~nudeln** tagliatelle, ribbon noodles; **~rauschen** n tape noise (od. hiss); **~riss** m tape break; **~säge** f band saw; **~salat** m umg. chewed-up tape, spaghettied tape
Bandscheibe f Anat. (intervertebral) disc
Bandscheiben|schaden m Med. damaged disc (Am. disk); **~vorfall** m slipped disc (Am. disk)
Band|sortenschalter m Tonband: tape select(or) switch; **~speicher** m EDV magnetic tape storage
Bandwurm m tapeworm; **~satz** m umg. fig. run-on sentence, long, convoluted sentence, sentence that goes on forever
bang Adj. anxious (um about); (besorgt) worried (about); Gefühl: uneasy; Erwartung: anxious; Stunde etc.:

of anxious waiting (*od.* suspense) (*nachgestellt*); **~e Ahnung** foreboding, awful feeling; **e-e ~e Sekunde** (*lang*) for one dreadful (*od.* awful) moment; **mir wird ~ ums Herz** I'm frightened (to death); **ihm wurde ~ und bänger** *hum.* he was getting increasingly anxious; **er wird schon noch kommen, da ist mir gar nicht ~** he'll come, I have no fear of (*od.* no worries about) that

bange *Adj. umg.* → **bang**; **ihm** (*od.* **er**) **ist ~** he's afraid (*od.* scared, frightened) (**vor** + *Dat.* of)

Bange *f*; *, kein Pl.*: (**nur**) **keine ~!** don't (you) worry; **j-m ~ machen** frighten s.o.; **~ machen gilt nicht!** (*sei nicht feige!*) don't be such a coward; (*du machst mir keine Angst*) you can't scare me

bangen *v/i.*, *v/refl.*: (**sich**) **~ um** be worried about; **um sein Leben ~** fear for one's life; (**sich**) **~ nach** *Dial.* long for; *unpers.*: **mir bangt es vor** (+ *Dat.*) I'm frightened (*od.* scared) of (*od.* about), I'm afraid of; **Bangigkeit** *f*; *nur Sg.*; *geh.* (*Angst*) anxiety; (*Beklemmung*) uneasiness

Bangladesch (*n*); *-s* Bangladesh; **Bangladescher** *m*; *-s*, *-*, **Bangladescherin** *f*; *-*, *-nen* Bangladeshi, *weiblich auch:* Bangladeshi woman (*od.* girl *etc.*); **bangladeschisch** *Adj.* Bangladeshi

Banjo *n*; *-s*, *-s* banjo; **~ spielen** play the banjo

Bank¹ *f*; *-*, *Bänke* **1.** (*Sitzbank*) bench, seat; (*Schulbank*) desk; *in Kirche*: pew; *im Parlament*: bench; (*Anklagebank*) dock; *Sport* (*Auswechselbank*) bench; **in der vordersten ~** in the front row; **durch die ~** *umg. fig.* right down the line, every one of them, the whole lot (of them); **etw. auf die lange ~ schieben** *fig.* put s.th. off, shelve s.th. for the time being; **vor leeren Bänken spielen** play before an empty house; **2.** *Tech.* (*Werkbank*) (work)bench; → **Drehbank**, **Hobelbank**, **3.** *Geol.* layer, bed, stratum; (*Sandbank*) sandbank; (*Austernbank*) bed; (*Korallenbank*) reef; (*Wolkenbank*) band

Bank² *f*; *-*, *-en* **1.** *Fin.* bank; **Geld auf der ~** money in the bank; **auf die ~ gehen** go to the bank; **ein Konto bei der ... ~ haben** have an account at (*od.* with) ... (bank); **bei e-r ~ sein** *od.* **arbeiten** work for a bank; **2.** *bei Glücksspielen*: **die ~ halten** hold the bank; **die ~ sprengen** break the bank

Bank|angestellte *m*, *f* bank employee; **~(r) sein** *auch* work for a bank; **~anleihe** *f* bank loan; **~anweisung** *f* banker's order; **~auftrag** *m* banker's order; **~automat** *m* cash dispenser (*od.* machine *umg.*), hole in the wall *umg.*; *förm.* automated teller machine, ATM; **~bürgschaft** *f* bank (*od.* banker's) guarantee; **~darlehen** *n* bank loan; **~direktor** *m*, **~direktorin** *f* bank manager; **~einlage** *f* (bank) deposit; **~einzug** *m* direct debit, *Am.* automatic payment; **mit** (*od.* **per**) **~ zahlen** pay by direct debit (*Am.* by automatic draft); **~einzugsverfahren** *n* automatic payment transfer, direct debiting

Bänkel|lied *n Mus.* (street) ballad; **~sang** *m*; *-(e)s, kein Pl.* ballad-singing; **~sänger** *m hist.* roving minstrel; *moderner*: balladeer

Banken|aufsicht *f* bank supervision; *konkret*: bank supervisory authority; **~konsortium** *n* banking syndicate (*od.* group); **~viertel** *n* financial district, banking area

Banker ['bɛŋkɐ] *m*; *-s, -*, **Bankerin** *f* -, *nen* banker; *umg.* (*Bankangestellte*) bank employee; *weitS.* financier

Bankett¹ *n*; *-(e)s, -e* banquet; **auf e-m ~** at a banquet; **ein ~ geben** hold (*od.* throw) a banquet

Bankett² *n*; *-(e)s, -e*, **Bankette** *f*; *-*, *-n Straßenbau*: shoulder; *unbefestigt*: verge; **~ nicht befahrbar** soft verges (*Am.* shoulder)

Bankfach *n* **1.** *nur Sg.* banking; **2.** (*Schließfach*) safe(-deposit) box; **~frau** *f* (female) banking professional; **~mann** *m* banking professional

Bank|filiale *f* branch bank; **~gebäude** *n* bank; **~geheimnis** *n* banking secrecy; **~geschäft** *n* **1.** banking transaction; **2.** *nur Sg.*: (*Bankwesen*) banking (trade); **~guthaben** *n* bank balance; *in Bar*: money in the bank; **~halter** *m Spielbank*: croupier; **~haus** *n* banking house

Bankier *m*; *-s, -s* **1.** *Inhaber*: banker; *weitS.* financier; *Vorstandsmitglied*: banking executive; **2.** *bei Spielen*: banker

Banking ['bɛŋkɪŋ] *n*; *-(s), kein Pl.*; *Fin.* banking

Bank|kauffrau *f* (female) bank employee; **~kaufmann** *m* bank employee; **~konto** *n* bank account; **~konzern** *m* banking group; **~kredit** *m* bank loan; **~kunde** *m*, **~kundin** *f* bank customer; **~lehre** *f* bank traineeship; **~lehrling** *m* bank apprentice; **~leitzahl** *f* (bank) sort code

Banknachbar *m*, **~in** *f Schule*: **mein ~** the boy I sit next to (in class), the boy who sits next to me (in class)

Banknote *f* (bank)note, *Am. auch* (bank) bill

Bankomat *m*; *-en od. -s, -en* cash dispenser, hole-in-the-wall *umg.*, *Am.* ATM; **~karte** *f* cash card, *Am.* ATM card

Bank|raub *m* bank robbery; **~räuber** *m*, **~räuberin** *f* bank robber

Bankrott I. *m*; *-(e)s, -e*; *auch fig.* bankruptcy; (business) failure; **s-n ~ erklären** (*od.* **~ anmelden**) file for (*od.* declare) bankruptcy; **~ machen** go bankrupt, go bust *umg.*, go to the wall *umg.*; *fig.* (*mit e-r Politik*) be thoroughly discredited; **vor dem ~ stehen** face (*od.* be on the verge of) bankruptcy; **es bedeutet** (**den**) **politischen ~** *fig.* it amounts to political bankruptcy; **II. bankrott** *Adj.* **1.** bankrupt; *umg.* (*abgebrannt*) (stony) broke *Sl.*; **bankrott gehen/sein** go/be bankrupt; **j-n bankrott machen** drive s.o. bankrupt, bankrupt s.o.; **sich** (**für**) **bankrott erklären** declare (*od.* file for) bankruptcy; **j-n** (**für**) **bankrott erklären** declare s.o. bankrupt; **2.** *fig. moralisch, emotional etc.*: bankrupt; **er ist moralisch bankrott** he's morally bankrupt; **innerlich bankrott** crushed, devastated; **Bankrotterklärung** *f auch fig.* declaration of bankruptcy; **Bankrotteur** *m*; *-s, -e* bankrupt; (*Firma*) bankrupt firm

Bank|safe *m* bank safe; **~schalter** *m* (bank) counter (*od.* window); **~scheck** *m* banker's cheque (*Am.* check); **~schließfach** *n* safe(-deposit) box; **~tresor** *m* bank('s) vault; **~überfall** *m* bank raid (*od.* robbery), raid on a bank; **~überweisung** *f* banker's order, bank transfer; **~üblich** *Adj.*: **~e Zinsen** normal bank (interest) rates; **~verbindung** *f* **1.** (*Konto*) bank account; **geben Sie uns bitte Ihre ~ an**

please let us have your bank account details; **2.** *e-r Bank*: correspondent; **~verkehr** *m* banking business, dealings *Pl.* between banks; **~wesen** *n*; *nur Sg.* (world of) banking; **~wirtschaft** *f*; *nur Sg.* banking industry

Bann *m*; *-(e)s, -e* **1.** *hist.* banishment; (*Kirchenbann*) excommunication; **den ~ aussprechen über j-n** (*od.* **j-n in den ~ tun, j-n mit dem ~ belegen**) banish s.o., outlaw s.o.; *kirchlich*: excommunicate s.o.; *gesellschaftlich*: ostracize s.o.; *geschäftlich*: boycott s.o.; **2.** *fig.* (*Zauber*) charm, spell; **unter dem ~ stehen von** (*e-r Person*) be (*od.* have come) under the spell (*od.* sway) of; (*Musik etc.*) be spellbound by, be under the spell of; (*Alkohol etc.*) be in the grip of; **in j-s** (*Akk.*) **~ geraten** come under s.o.'s spell (*od.* sway); **in den ~ der Musik etc. geraten** be enthralled (*od.* spellbound) by the music *etc.*; **j-n in s-n ~ schlagen** *od.* **ziehen** captivate s.o., spellbind s.o.; **j-n in ~ halten** have s.o. spellbound; **den ~ brechen** break the spell (*od.* charm; *bei Verlegenheit*: ice)

bannen *v/t. geh.* **1.** *auch fig.* (*Person*) banish; (*Gefahr*) avert, ward off; (*böse Geister*) exorcize, cast out; *kirchl.* excommunicate; **die Gefahr ist gebannt** the danger has been averted; **2.** *fig.* (*fesseln*) captivate, transfix, spellbind; → **gebannt**; **3.** *etw. auf die Leinwand* **~** capture s.th. on film (*od.* canvas)

Banner *n*; *-s, -* **1.** *auch fig.* banner, standard; **2.** *Internet*: banner ad; **~träger** *m auch fig.* standard-bearer

Bannfluch *m hist.* ban; *kirchl.* excommunication; **j-n mit dem ~ belegen** *kirchl.* excommunicate s.o.

bannig *Adv. nordd. umg.* really, extremely; **das war ~ gut** that was really (*od.* extremely) good

Bann|kreis *m geh. fig.* sphere of influence, spell; **in j-s** (*Akk.*) **~ geraten** come under s.o.'s sway (*od.* spell); **~meile** *f* **1.** *hist.* Precincts *Pl.*; **2.** *e-s Staatsgebäudes*: protected zone; **~wald** *m* protective forest

Bantam|gewicht *n* **1.** *Person*: bantamweight; **2.** *nur Sg.*; *Gewichtsklasse*: bantamweight; **~gewichtler** *m*; *-s, -*; *Sport* bantamweight; **~huhn** *n Orn.* bantam

Bantu *m*; *-(s), -(s)* Bantu; **~frau** *f* Bantu (woman); **~mann** *m* Bantu; **~neger** *m*, **~negerin** *f* Bantu, *weiblich auch:* Bantu woman (*od.* girl *etc.*)

Baptist *m*; *-en, -en*; *kirchl.* Baptist

Baptisterium *n*; *-s, Baptisterien*; *kirchl.* **1.** (*Taufbecken*) (baptismal) font; *bei Baptisten*: baptistry; **2.** (*Taufkirche*) baptistry

Baptistin *f*; *-*, *-nen*; *Reli.* Baptist, *weiblich auch:* Baptist lady (*od.* woman *etc.*); **baptistisch** *Adj.* Baptist

bar *Adj.* **1.** cash; *präd.* in cash; **~es Geld** (ready) cash; **gegen ~** for cash, cash down; **500 Euro in ~** 500 euros (in) cash; (**in**) **~ bezahlen** pay cash; **zahlen Sie ~ oder mit Scheck?** are you paying by cash or cheque (*Am.* check)?; **e-e Summe ~ auf den Tisch legen** put cash on the table; *fig.* offer cash down; **2.** *geh.* (*rein*) pure; *Gold*: pure, sheer; *fig. pej. auch* downright; **~er Unsinn** sheer (*od.* utter) nonsense; → **Münze** 1; **3.** *geh.* (+*Gen.*) devoid of, lacking in; **~ jeglichen Gefühls** totally lacking in feeling; **~ jeder Vernunft** without rhyme or reason, completely pointless; **4.** *geh. altm.*: **~en**

Hauptes bareheaded

Bar¹ *f; -, -s* **1.** (*Lokal*) bar; (*Nachtlokal*) nightclub; *in e-e ~ gehen* go (in)to a bar; **2.** (*Theke*) bar; *an der ~* at the bar; *Möbelstück*: drinks (*Am.* liquor) cabinet, bar

Bar² *n; -s, -s; Phys., Met.* bar

Bär *m; -en, -en* **1.** *Zool.* bear; *schlafen wie ein ~* sleep like a log (*od.* top); *hungrig wie ein ~ umg.* starving, as hungry as a horse (*Am.* a bear); *stark wie ein ~* as strong as an ox; *ein ~ von e-m Mann umg.* a bear (*od.* giant) of a man; → *aufbinden* 3; **2.** *Astron.: der Große/Kleine ~* the Big/Little Bear, Ursa Major/Minor, the Big/Little Dipper *umg.*; *der Große ~ auch* the Plough

Baraber *m; -s, -; österr. pej.* (builder's) labo(u)rer, building worker; **barabern** *v/i. österr.* **1.** *als Hilfsarbeiter*: work as a casual labo(u)rer; **2.** *umg.* (*hart arbeiten*) slave away

Baracke *f; -, -n* hut; *bes. pej.* shack; *elende ~* hovel

Baracken|lager *n* hut camp; *für Flüchtlinge*: refugee camp; **~siedlung** *f* hut camp, temporary accommodation

Bar|ausgaben *Pl.* cash expenditure *Sg.*; **~auslagen** *Pl.* (out-of-pocket) expenses, cash outlays (*od.* outlay *Sg.*); **~ausschüttung** *f* cash dividend, cash distribution; **~auszahlung** *f* cash payment

Barbar *m; -en, -en* **1.** *pej. roh*: savage, ruffian, lout; *ungebildet*: boor, philistine *geh.*; **2.** *hist.* barbarian

Barbarei *f; -, -en* barbarism, savagery; (*barbarische Tat*) barbarous (*od.* savage) act; **Barbarentum** *n* barbarism; **Barbarin** *f; -, -nen* **1.** *pej. roh*: (female) savage; *ungebildet*: boor, philistine *geh.*; **2.** *hist.* barbarian

barbarisch I. *Adj.* **1.** *auch fig. pej.* barbaric, barbarous; *Volk etc.*: barbarian; (*grausam*) barbaric, savage, cruel; (*brutal*) brutal; **2.** *umg.* (*schlimm*) dreadful; *ich habe e-n ~en Hunger/Durst* I'm ravenous, I could eat a horse / I'm parched, I'm dying for a drink; **II.** *Adv.* **1.** *sich ~ benehmen* behave abominably; *~ stinken umg.* smell *etc.* awful (*od.* appalling); **2.** *umg.* → I 2

Barbe *f; -, -en; Zool.* barbel

Barbecue ['baːbikjuː] *n; -(s), -s* **1.** *Fest*: barbecue; **2.** *Gerät*: barbecue; **3.** *Bratgut*: barbecued meat (*od.* food *etc.*)

bärbeißig *Adj. Miene etc.*: surly, bad-tempered; **Bärbeißigkeit** *f; nur Sg.* surliness, bad temper

Bar|bestand *m* cash in hand; *e-r Bank*: cash reserve(s *Pl.*); **Barbestände** cash holdings; **~betrag** *m* cash sum; *größere Barbeträge mit sich führen* carry around large sums in cash (*od.* amounts of cash); **~bezüge** *Pl.* remuneration *Sg.* (*od.* payment[s]) in cash

Barbier *m; -s, -e; altm. od. hum.* barber

Barbiturat *n; -s, -e; Pharm.* barbiturate

barbusig *Adj.* topless, bare-breasted, bare-bosomed

Bärchen *n Jungtier*: (bear) cub; *kleiner Bär*: little bear

Barcode ['baːɛ ɛkoːt] *m; -s, -s* bar code

Bardame *f* barmaid

Barde *m; -n, -n; hist., iro.* bard

Bar|einlage *f* cash deposit; **~einnahmen** *Pl.* takings, cash receipts; **~einzahlung** *f* (cash) deposit, (cash) payment (*auf + Akk.* into)

Bären|dienst *m: j-m e-n ~ erweisen od. leisten* do s.o. a disservice, do s.o. a bad turn; *da hast du mir e-n ~ geleistet! iro.* that was a great help!, I suppose you meant it well!; **~dreck** *m; südd., österr., schw.* liquorice; **~fell** *n* bearskin

bärenhaft *Adj.* (*schwerfällig*) lumbering, ponderous; **~e Gestalt** (great) hulk

Bären|hatz *f* bear-baiting; **~haut** *f* bearskin; **~höhle** *f* bear's den; **~hunger** *m umg.: ich habe e-n ~* I'm ravenous, I could eat a horse; **~jagd** *f* bear-hunt(ing), bear-shoot; **~junge** *n Zool.* (bear) cub; **~klau** *m; -s, -, auch f; -, -; Bot.* **1.** (*Acanthus mollis / A. spinosus*) bear's-breech(es), acanthus; **2.** (*Heracleum*) cow parsnip, hogweed; **~kraft** *f auch Pl.* the strength of a horse; Herculean strength; **Bärenkräfte od. e-e ~ haben** *auch* be as strong as an ox; **~natur** *f umg.: e-e ~ haben* have the constitution of a horse, be as tough as they come *umg.*

bärenstark *Adj.* **1.** (as) strong as an ox; **2.** *umg. fig.* (*toll*) great, *präd. auch* brill; *Werbesprache*: **~e Preise** sensational (*od.* unbelievable) prices, great bargains; *ein ~es Angebot* a great (*od.* unrepeatable) offer, a terrific bargain

Bären|tatze *f* bear's paw; **~zucker** *m österr.* liquorice; **~zwinger** *m* bear pit

Barett *n; -(e)s, -s od. -e* beret, cap; *e-s Richters, Professors*: cap; *e-s Lehrers*: cap, mortarboard, square; *e-s kath. Geistlichen*: biretta, cap

Barfrau *f* barmaid, female bartender

barfuß I. *Adj.* barefoot(ed); **II.** *Adv.* barefoot; *~ herumlaufen auch* run around in one's bare feet; **Barfüßer** *m; -s, - Mönch*: barefooted monk; **barfüßig** *Adj.* barefoot(ed)

barg *Imperf.* → *bergen*

Bargeld *n* cash, ready cash; **bargeldlos** *Adj.* cashless; **~er Zahlungsverkehr** (payment by) money transfer, non-cash payment, cashless payment; **~er Einkauf** cashless shopping

Bar|geschäft *n Wirts.*: cash transaction (*od.* deal); *allg.*: cash dealing (*od.* business); **~guthaben** *n* cash in hand, cash balance, ready money

barhäuptig *Adj.* bareheaded, hatless; *auch Adv.* without a hat (on)

Barhocker *m* bar stool

bärig *Adj.* **1.** *österr., auch Dial. Kerl*: powerful, brawny; **2.** *umg.* (*toll*) great, *präd. auch* brill; *eine ~e Stimmung* a fantastic (*od.* tremendous) atmosphere

Bärin *f; -, -nen* she-bear, female bear

Bariton *m; -s, -e* **1.** *nur Sg.; Stimmlage*: baritone; **2.** *Sänger*: baritone; **3.** *nur Sg.; Partie*: baritone, baritone part (*od.* line); *den ~ singen* sing baritone, be the baritone

Barium *n; -s, kein Pl.; Chem.* barium

Barkarole *f; -, -n; Mus.* barcarol(l)e

Barkasse¹ [bar'kasə] *f; -, -n; Naut.* (*Beiboot*) launch, tender, longboat; (*Motorboot*) (motor) launch

Bar|kasse² ['barkasə] *f; -, -n; Fin.* (*Geld*) petty cash; (*Abteilung*) cash department, cash office; **~kauf** *m* cash purchase

Barke *f; -, -n; Naut.* (rowing) boat, skiff; *poet.* bark, barque

Barkeeper ['baːɛkiːpɐ] *m; -s, -* barman, bartender

Bärlapp *m; -s, -e; Bot.* club moss

Bärlauch *-(e)s, -e; Bot.* bear's garlic

Barmann *m* barman, bartender

barmen I. *v/i. nordd. pej.* (*jammern*) wail, lament *allg.*, keen *Dial.* (*um od. wegen* for); **II.** *v/t. altm.* fill with pity

barmherzig *Adj. Menschen*: compassionate, kind-hearted, caring, merciful *altm.*; (*mildtätig*) charitable; *Gott*: merciful (*gegen* to[ward(s)], unto *altm.*); *~ sein gegen od. mit auch* have pity (*od.* mercy) on; *die Barmherzigen Brüder/Schwestern* (*Krankenpflegeorden*) the Brothers Hospitallers / the Sisters of Mercy (*od.* Charity); → *Samariter* 1; **Barmherzigkeit** *f; nur Sg. der Menschen*: compassion, mercy *altm.*; (*Mildtätigkeit*) charity; *Gottes*: mercy; *~ üben* have pity (*od.* mercy) (*an + Dat.* on, upon *altm.*)

Barmittel *Pl. Fin.* cash *Sg.*, cash resources

Barmixer *m* barman, bartender

Barock I. *m od. n; -s, kein Pl.* **1.** *Epoche*: Baroque (period *od.* era *od.* age); **2.** *Stil*: Baroque (*od.* baroque) (style); **II.** *barock Adj.* **1.** (*aus der Barockzeit*) Baroque, baroque; **2.** *geh.* (*seltsam*) *Fantasie etc.*: baroque, bizarre, eccentric *allg.*

**Barock|... *im Subst.* Baroque (*od.* baroque); *Barockbau* Baroque building; *Barockkirche* Baroque (*od.* baroque) church; *Barockzeit(alter)* Baroque (period *od.* era *od.* age)

barockisieren *v/t.* make Baroque; **barockisierend** *Adj.* in a baroque manner, slightly baroque (style), tending to the Baroque

Barometer *n, österr., schw. auch m; -s, -; auch fig.* barometer (*für* of); *das ~ steht hoch/tief* the barometer (*od.* glass *umg.*) is high/low; *das ~ steigt/fällt* the barometer (*od.* glass *umg.*) is rising/falling; *das ~ steht auf „Regen"* the barometer says "Rain"; *das ~ steht auf Sturm fig.* there's a storm brewing; **~stand** *m* barometer reading, barometric pressure; *den ~ ablesen* read the barometer

Baron *m; -s, -e* baron; *als Anrede*: *Herr ~* My Lord; *fig.* (*auch Industriebaron*) baron, magnate, tycoon *umg.*, captain of industry *umg.*, *mst iro.*; *fig. Rauschgifthandel*: baron; **Baroness(e)** *f; -, Baronessen* baroness, baron's daughter; **Baronin** *f; -, -nen* baroness, baron's wife; *als Anrede*: (*Frau*) *~* Madam

Bar|preis *m* cash price; **~reserven** *Pl.* cash reserves

Barrakuda *m; -s, -s; Zool.* barracuda

Barras *m; -, kein Pl.; umg.: beim ~ sein* be in the army; (*Wehrdienst*) *auch* be doing one's military service; *nach dem Abitur muss er zum ~* after his Abitur he (still) has to do his military service (*od.* his year in the army)

Barrel ['berəl] *n; -, -s* barrel; *5 ~ Öl* 5 barrels of oil

Barren *m; -s, -* **1.** *aus Gold etc.*: bar, ingot; *Pl. auch* bullion *Sg.*; **2.** *Turngerät*: (parallel) bars *Pl.*; **3.** *österr., schw.* (*Futtertrog*) (feeding) trough; **~gold** *n* gold bullion; **~silber** *n* silver bullion; **~turnen** *n Sport* exercise(s *Pl.*) (*od.* work) on the (parallel) bars

Barriere [ba'riɛːrə] *f; -, -n* **1.** *auch fig.* barrier, bar; *e-e ~ abbauen fig.* break down barriers; **2.** *Eisenb., hist.* (*zur Fahrkartenkontrolle*) ticket barrier; (*Schranke*) level- (*Am.* grade-)crossing gate

Barrikade *f; -, -n* barricade; *auf die ~n steigen od. gehen auch fig.* go on the barricades (*für* for)

Barrikaden|kämpfe *Pl.* street battles (*od.* fighting *Sg.*); **~kämpfer** *m,**

~kämpferin f street fighter
Barsch m; -(e)s, -e; Zool. perch
barsch I. Adj. gruff, brusque (**gegen** towards), short (with); **~e Antwort** gruff (od. curt) reply; **II.** Adv. → I; **j-n ~ zurechtweisen/anfahren** give s.o. a sharp reprimand / ticking off, speak roughly to s.o.
Bar|schaft f; Pl. selten ready money, cash umg.; **m-e ganze ~ beläuft sich auf ...** all I have on me is ...; **~scheck** m cash cheque (Am. check)
Barschheit f; nur Sg. Wesensart: gruffness, brusqueness, gruff (od. brusque) manner; von Äußerungen: curtness, sharpness, brusqueness
barst Imperf. → **bersten**
Bart m; -(e)s, Bärte **1.** beard; **mit ~** with a beard; **e-n ~ tragen** have (stolz: sport) a beard; **sich** (Dat.) **e-n ~ stehen** od. **wachsen lassen** grow a beard; **j-m den ~ stutzen/schneiden** trim/ shave s.o.'s beard; **etw. in s-n ~ brummen** od. **murmeln** fig. mutter s.th. under one's breath; **j-m um den ~ gehen** od. **streichen** umg. soft-soap s.o., chat s.o. up, butter s.o. up; **das hat ja so e-n ~!** umg. pej. that's as old as the hills; **der ~ ist ab!** umg. that's done it; → **Kaiser**, **Witz** 1; **2.** von Katze etc.: whiskers Pl.; von Muschel: beard; **3.** von Schlüssel: bit, ward
Bärtchen n little beard; spitz, am Kinn: auch goatee (beard)
Barthaar n einzelnes: hair from s.o.'s beard; **~e** Pl. einzelne: hairs from s.o.'s beard; alle zusammen: beard Sg.
bärtig Adj. bearded; **Bärtige** m; -n, -n bearded man (od. person), man with a beard
bartlos Adj. rasiert: clean-shaven; unreif etc.: beardless
Bart|nelke f Bot. sweet william; **~stoppel** f; mst Pl. stubble Sg.; **~träger** m bearded man (od. person); **~ sein** have a beard; **~wuchs** m beard growth; bei Frauen: (growth of) facial hair; **er hat e-n starken/schwachen/spärlichen ~** he has a strong/slow/sparse growth of beard
Bar|verkauf m cash sale; **~vermögen** n cash assets Pl., cash in hand; **~wert** m cash value
Bar|zahlung f Wirts. cash payment; (Verkauf) **nur gegen ~** cash terms only; **~zahlungsrabatt** m Wirts. cash discount
basal Adj. fachspr., bes. Geol., Med. basal; allg. auch: basic, fundamental
Basalt m; -(e)s, -e; Geol., Min. basalt
Basaltemperatur f Med. basal (body) temperature
basaltisch Adj. basaltic
Basalwert m basal value, base level
Basar [ba'zaːɐ] m; -s, -e **1.** Veranstaltung: bazaar, (charity) sale; **2.** Markt: bazaar, market(place); Ladenstraße: indoor market, arcade
Base¹ f; -, -n **1.** altm. (female) cousin; **2.** österr., schw. (Tante) aunt
Base² f; -, -n; Chem. base
Baseball ['beːsbɔːl] m; -s, kein Pl. baseball; **~mütze** f baseball cap; **~schläger** m baseball bat
Basedow'sche Krankheit f Med. exophthalmic goit|re (Am. –er), Graves' disease
Basel (n); -s Basle
basieren I. v/i.: **~ auf** (+ Dat.) be based on; Theorie etc.: auch be founded on; **II.** v/t. base (**auf** + Dat. on)
Basilika f; -, Basiliken basilica
Basilikum n; -s, -s od. Basiliken **1.** Bot.

(sweet) basil; **2.** (Gewürz) basil
Basilisk m; -en, -en **1.** Myth. basilisk; bibl. cockatrice; **2.** Zool. basilisk
Basis f; -, Basen **1.** (Grundlage) basis, foundation; **die ~ bilden für etw.** be (od. constitute) the basis of (od. for) s.th.; **auf breiter/gesunder ~** on a broad/sound basis; **auf gleicher ~** on equal terms, on an equal footing; **auf solider ~** on a solid (od. firm) footing; **auf der ~ von ... beruhen** be founded on ...; **2.** Pol. grass roots Pl., base; in der Partei: rank and file; **an der ~ arbeiten** work (od. be active) at grass-roots level; **3.** Marxismus: (economic) base (od. structure); **4.** Archit., Math., Mil. base; **~arbeit** f Pol., im Wahlkreis: constituency-level work, work at the grass-roots (level); Vorbereitung e-r Konferenz etc.: groundwork
basisch I. Adj. Chem. basic; **II.** Adv.: **~ reagieren** react as a base
Basisdemokratie f Pol. grass-roots democracy; **basisdemokratisch** Adj. Pol. grass-roots mst attr.
Basis|einkommen n basic income; **~gruppe** f Pol. grass-roots group (od. cell); **~kurs** m Fin. basic rate (od. price); **~lager** n Bergsteigen: base camp; **~wissen** n basics Pl., fundamentals Pl., basic knowledge
Baske m; -n, -n Basque
Basken|land n: **das ~** the Basque country, the Basque Provinces; **~mütze** f beret
Basketball ['baːskətbal] m Sport basketball; **Basketballer** m; -s, -, **Basketballerin** f; -, -nen basketball player
Baskin f; -, -nen Basque, Basque woman (od. girl etc.); **baskisch I.** Adj. Basque; **II. Baskisch** n; -en; Ling.: **das Baskische** Basque
Basrelief ['baːrelief] n bas-relief
bass Adv. altm.: **~ erstaunt sein** be greatly astonished
Bass m; -es, Bässe, Mus. **1.** nur Sg.; Stimme: bass (voice); **2.** Sänger: bass (singer); **3.** Partie: bass (part); **4.** Instrument: double bass; (Bassgitarre) bass (guitar); **5.** mst Pl.; an Radio etc.: bass control
Bass... im Subst. bass ...; **~bariton** bass baritone; **~geige** double bass; **~gitarre** bass guitar; **~saite** bass string
Bassin [ba'sɛ̃:] n; -s, -s **1.** zum Schwimmen: pool; **2.** im Park etc.: pool, basin; **3.** Behälter: tank, container; **4.** Hafenanlage: basin, dock
Bassist m; -en, -en, **~in** f; -, -nen; Mus. **1.** Sänger(in): bass (singer); **2.** Instrumentalist(in): (double) bass player
Bassschlüssel m Mus. bass clef
Bast m; -(e)s, -e **1.** zum Binden: raffia; **2.** Bot. phloem, bast; **3.** am Geweih: velvet
basta Interj. umg. that's enough (of that)!; **und damit ~!** and that's that!
Bastard m; -(e)s, -e **1.** Bot. hybrid; **2.** Zool. crossbreed; Hund: mongrel; **3.** umg. pej. bastard; **4.** hist. (uneheliches Kind) bastard, illegitimate child (od. offspring)
Bastei f; -, -en bastion
Bastel|arbeit f **1.** Gegenstand: piece of hobby-work, handmade article; **e-e ~ verschenken** give (away) something one has made oneself; **2.** nur Sg.; Betätigung: (amateur) handicraft(s Pl.), making things umg.; **~buch** n activities book; **~ecke** f in Zeitschrift: hobbies corner (od. page)
Bastelei f; -, -en **1.** (Gegenstand) piece of hobby-work; **sich viel mit ~en be-**

schäftigen do a lot of handicraft work; **2.** pej. fiddling around, tinkering (around)
Bastelmaterial n hobby (od. model(-l)ing) materials Pl.
basteln I. v/i. **1.** do (amateur od. home) handicrafts; **er bastelt gern** he likes to do things with his hands (od. make things); **mit Papier etc. ~ make** things (od. models) out of paper etc.; **2.** umg. **an etw.** (Dat.) ~ tinker around with s.th.; **II.** v/t. make; (Modelle, elektrische Geräte etc.) build; **III. Basteln** n; -s, kein Pl. (amateur od. home) handicrafts Pl., model(l)ing, making things umg.
Bastel|raum m hobbies room; **~stunde** f in Kindergarten, Schule etc.: handicraft lesson; **~vorlage** f Sticken etc.: pattern; Modellbau etc.: plan(s Pl.), drawing(s Pl.)
Bastion f; -, -en; auch fig. bastion, bulwark
Bastler m; -s, -, **~in** f; -, -nen handicraft (-s) enthusiast (od. worker); umg. DIYer (von DIY = do it yourself); **er ist ein leidenschaftlicher/guter ~** he loves to make things / he's good at making things (od. doing things with his hands)
Bastmatte f Fußboden: bast-fib|re (Am. –er) mat; Tisch: raffia mat
bat Imperf. → **bitten**
Bataillon [batal'joːn] n; -s, -e Mil. battalion
Batik m; -s, -en od. f; -, -en **1.** nur Sg.; Verfahren: batik; **2.** Stoff: batik; **~druck** batik (work)
batiken I. v/i. do batik; **II.** v/t. add batik decoration to; **ein gebatikter Schal** a batik shawl; **ein Halstuch ~** ornament a scarf with batik work
Batist m; -(e)s, -e cambric, batiste
Batterie f; -, -n **1.** Elektr. battery; **mit ~ betreiben** run on batteries (od. a battery); **2.** Mil. battery; **3.** fig. von Flaschen etc.: battery, array, army; **~anzeiger** m battery meter; **~betrieb** m battery operation; **mit ~** battery-operated; **Ωbetrieben** Adj. battery-operated (od. -powered); **~fach** n battery compartment; **~gerät** n battery-operated device (od. set); **es ist ein ~** auch it runs on batteries; **~huhn** n battery hen; **~ladegerät** n battery charger
Batzen m; -s, -; umg. **1.** (Klumpen) clump; **2.** fig. pile, heap; **es hat e-n ~ Geld gekostet** it cost a packet (Am. bundle); **sie verdient e-n ~ Geld** she's making (od. earning) a lot of money; **das ist ein ~ Geld** that's a tidy (od. handy) sum; **3.** hist. (Geldstück) batz
Bau¹ m; -s, -ten **1.** nur Sg.; Vorgang: construction, building; fabrikmäßig: manufacture; von Musikinstrumenten: building; **im** od. **in ~** under construction, being built; **sich im** od. **in ~ befinden** be under (od. in the process of) construction; **mit dem ~ beginnen** start building, begin construction; **2.** (Gebäude) building; **~ten** Film: set(s Pl.); **3.** nur Sg.; Tech. design, (auch Aufbau) structure; **4.** nur Sg.; (Baugewerbe) building; **er ist beim ~** he's in building, he's in the building (od. construction) business; **5.** nur Sg.; (Baustelle) (building od. construction) site; **er arbeitet auf dem ~** he's a building worker; **6.** Mil. Sl. guardhouse; **fünf Tage ~** five days detention (od. confined to barracks); **7.** nur Sg.; (Körperbau) build
Bau² m; -(e)s, -e e-s Tiers: von Dachs:

sett; *von Fuchs*: earth, hole; *von Kaninchen*: burrow, hole; *von Biber*: lodge

Bau|abnahme *f Begutachtung*: inspection of a new building, building inspection; *positiv*: acceptance of work; **~abschnitt** *m* construction (*od.* building) stage; **~amt** *n* Department of Planning and Building Control, planning authority; **~anleitung** *f* construction manual; **~antrag** *m* building proposal; **~arbeiten** *Pl.* **1.** *Hoch- und Tiefbau*: construction work *Sg.*; **2.** *an Straße*: roadworks, *Am.* roadwork *Sg.*; **~arbeiter** *m* building (*od.* construction) worker, labo(u)rer on a building site; **~art** *f* style (of construction); *Tech.* design; (*Typ*) type, model; **~aufsicht** *f* building (standards) control; *wer hat die ~?* who is the (building control) inspector?; **~aufsichtsbehörde** *f* building inspectorate; **~aufzug** *m* builder's hoist; **~beginn** *m* start of construction (work); **~behörde** *f* planning authority (*od.* department)

baubiologisch *Adj.* organic; *nach ~en Gesichtspunkten* using organic materials; *~e Bedenken haben* have reservations relating to proper building practice

Bau|boom [-bu:m] *m* building (*od.* construction) boom; **~branche** [-brã:ʃə] *f*; *nur Sg.* building trade (*od.* construction industry); **~bude** *f* building-site hut; **~büro** *n* (building-)site office

Bauch *m*; *-(e)s, Bäuche* **1.** stomach, tummy *umg.*, *bes. Kinderspr.*; belly *umg.*, *bes. hum. od. pej.*; *Anat.* abdomen; *bibl.* belly; *dicker*: paunch, pot belly, beer belly; *auf dem ~ schlafen* sleep face down (*od.* on one's stomach *od.* in the prone position); *auf dem ~ liegen* lie on one's stomach, lie prone; *mit vollem/leerem ~* on a full / an empty stomach; *nichts im ~ haben* have had nothing to eat; *sich* (*Dat.*) *den ~ voll schlagen umg.* stuff (*od.* gorge *allg.*) o.s.; *ein voller ~ studiert nicht gern Sprichw.* you can't study well on a full stomach; *sich* (*Dat.*) *den ~ halten vor Lachen* split one's sides laughing, fall about *umg.*; (*mit etw.*) *auf den ~ fallen umg.* fall flat on one's face; *vor j-m auf dem ~ kriechen fig.* crawl (*od.* suck up *umg.*) to s.o.; *ich hab e-e Wut im ~* I am blazing mad, I'm ready to explode; *aus dem ~ heraus reagieren umg.* act on instinct, go with a gut feeling *umg.*; *ich hab aus dem ~ heraus reagiert auch umg.* it was a gut reaction; *aus dem hohlen ~ reden umg.* say s.th. off the top of one's head (*od.* off the cuff); *es geht direkt in den ~ umg.* it really hits you; → *Loch* 1; **2.** (*das Innere*) *e-s Schiffs*: belly, bowels; *e-s Gebäudes etc.*: interior; *der Erde*: bowels, interior; **3.** *fig.* (*dicker Teil*) *e-r Flasche etc.*: bulge

Bauch|ansatz *m* beginnings *Pl.* of a paunch, bit of a spare tyre (*Am.* tire) *umg.*; **~atmung** *f* abdominal breathing; **~binde** *f* **1.** *um Zigarre, Buch*: band; **2.** *Med.* abdominal bandage; **~decke** *f Anat.* abdominal wall; **~fell** *n Anat.* peritoneum; **~fellentzündung** *f Med.* peritonitis; **~fleisch** *n Gastr.* (pork) belly; **~flosse** *f Zool.* ventral fin; **~gegend** *f* abdominal region, stomach area; **~gurt** *m beim Pferd*: girth, belly band; **~höhle** *f Anat.* abdominal cavity; **~höhlenschwangerschaft** *f Med.* extra-uterine pregnancy

bauchig *Adj. Vase*: bulbous, pot-bellied

Bauch|klatscher *m umg.* belly flop; **~kneifen** *n umg.* tummy pains *Pl.*; *~ haben* have tummy pains, have a touch of colic, *Am.* have a stomachache; **~laden** *m* vendor's tray; **~lage** *f* prone position; *in ~ schlafen* sleep on one's front (*od.* stomach); **~landung** *f e-s Flugzeugs*: belly landing; *ins Wasser*: *auch* belly flop *umg.*; *e-e ~ machen* land on one's belly, do a belly landing (*ins Wasser*: belly flop *umg.*); *umg. fig.* (*Misserfolg haben*) fall flat on one's face, (only) get egg on one's face

Bäuchlein *n* (*Magen*) tummy; (*Korpulenz*) pot (belly), paunch, corporation *hum.*; **bäuchlings** *Adv.* face down, flat

Bauch|muskel *m*; *mst Pl.* stomach (*od.* tummy) muscle; **~n** *umg.* abs; *umg.*, *durchtrainiert*: six-pack *Sg.*; **~nabel** *m* navel

bauchpinseln *v/t. umg.* → *gebauchpinselt*

Bauchredekunst *f* (art of) ventriloquism; **bauchreden** *v/i.*; *mst Inf.* ventriloquize; **Bauchredner** *m*, **Bauchrednerin** *f* ventriloquist

Bauch|schmerzen *Pl.* stomach(-)ache *Sg.*, stomach pains; *~ haben* have a stomach(-)ache (*od.* stomach pains); **~schuss** *m* stomach wound; **~speck** *m Gastr.* pork belly, belly of pork, streaky pork; *umg.* (*Korpulenz*) spare tire, flab; **~speicheldrüse** *f Anat.* pancreas

Bauchtanz *m* belly dance (*od.* dancing); **bauchtanzen** *v/i.*; *nur Inf.* belly-dance, do some belly dancing; **Bauchtänzerin** *f* belly dancer

Bauch|tasche *f Zool.* pouch; **~umfang** *m* belly girth (*od.* dimensions *Pl.*); **~wand** *f Anat.* abdominal wall; **~weh** *n umg.* tummy(-)ache; **~zwicken** *n umg.* → *Bauchkneifen*

Bau|darlehen *n* building loan; **~denkmal** *n* listed building, historical building, architectural monument; **~dezernat** *n* → *Bauamt*; **~element** *n Bauwesen* component, unit, module; *Archit.* element, component; *Tech.* component; *Etron.* (circuit) component

bauen I. *v/t.* **1.** build; (*errichten*) erect, put up; (*herstellen*) make, build, manufacture, produce; *Tech. auch* construct; **2.** *umg. auch fig.* (*machen*) do; (*Examen*) take; *Betten ~* make (the) beds; *den od. s-n Doktor ~* take a (*od.* one's) doctorate, do a PhD; *e-e Eins/ Sechs ~* get a first-class mark / fail (badly), *Am.* get an A / F; *e-n Unfall ~* have (*od.* be involved in) an accident; → *Mist¹* 3; **3.** *fig.*: *s-e Hoffnungen etc. auf etw.* (*Akk.*) *~* base one's hopes etc. on s.th.; **II.** *v/i.* **1.** build; (*ein Eigenheim*) build a house; *wir werden nächstes Jahr ~* we are going to start building next year; *in unserer Straße wird viel gebaut* there's a lot of building going on in our street; *er hat jetzt gebaut* he has had a house built; *an etw.* (*Dat.*) *~* work on s.th.; *großzügig/ umweltbewusst ~* build on a generous scale / with environmental considerations in mind; **2.** *fig.*: *~ auf* (+ *Akk.*) count (*od.* depend *od.* rely) on

Bauentwurf *m* (architectural) drawing (*od.* plan)

Bauer¹ *m*; *-n, -n* **1.** (*Landwirt*) farmer; *hist.*, *auch pej.* peasant; *die dümmsten ~n haben die dicksten od. größten*

Kartoffeln *Sprichw.* fortune favo(u)rs fools; *was der ~ nicht kennt, frisst er nicht Sprichw.* (it's) caviar to the general; **2.** *in Spielen, Schach*: pawn; *in Karten*: jack

Bauer² *n*; *-s, -*: (*Käfig*) (bird)cage

Bäuerchen *n umg.* burp; *ein ~ machen Baby*: burp, do (*od.* produce) a burp

Bäuerin *f*; *-, -nen* **1.** (*weibl. Landwirt*) (woman) farmer; **2.** (*Frau eines Bauern*) farmer's wife

bäuerlich *Adj. Bauern betreffend*: rural, farming; *Stil etc.*: rustic

Bauern|aufstand *m hist.* peasants' revolt; **~brot** *n* farmhouse bread, coarse brown bread; **~bursche** *m* country (*od.* farm) lad (*Am.* boy); **~dorf** *n* farming village; **~fang** *m*: *auf ~ ausgehen umg.* go out looking for suckers; **~fänger** *m umg. pej.* con man, swindler, fraud; **~fängerei** *f umg. pej.* con (game), swindling, fraud; **~frühstück** *n Gastr.* fried potatoes, diced ham and scrambled eggs; **~haus** *n* farmhouse; **~hochzeit** *f* country (*od.* rustic) wedding; **~hof** *m* farm; *Ferien auf dem ~* farmhouse holiday (*Am.* vacation) *Sg.*; **~junge** *m* country (*od.* farm) lad (*Am.* boy); **~kalender** *m* country lore (*kein Pl.*); **~knecht** *m* farm labo(u)rer, farmhand; **~krieg** *m hist.* Peasants' War; *in England*: Peasants' Revolt; **~lümmel** *m* country bumpkin; *Am.* hick, hayseed; *pej.* ignorant lout; **~mädchen** *n* country girl (*od.* lass); **~magd** *f* farm girl; **~möbel** *Pl.* rustic furniture *Sg.*; **~opfer** *n Schach, auch fig.* sacrifice of a pawn; **~regel** *f* (piece of) country lore

Bauernschaft *f* (farming) community

bauernschlau *Adj.* cunning, shrewd, hard-headed; **Bauernschläue** *f* (native) cunning, shrewdness

Bauern|schrank *m* farmhouse cupboard, cupboard in rustic style; **~schwank** *m Theat.* rustic farce; **~stand** *m*; *mst Sg.* farmers *Pl.*, farming community; *bes. hist.* peasantry; **~stube** *f* **1.** farmer's living room; *zum Wohnen und Kochen*: farmhouse kitchen; **2.** *Stil*: rustic(-style) room; **~theater** *n* rural folk theat|re (*Am. auch* -er); **~tölpel** *m pej.* dolt, yokel, country bumpkin; **~verband** *m* farmers' union; *weitS.* farm(ing) lobby

Bauers|frau *f* → *Bäuerin*; **~leute** *Pl.* farm people; *hist.*, *auch arme*: peasants

Bau|erwartungsland *n* (potential *od.* prospective) development land; **~fach** *n*; *nur Sg.* **1.** architecture; **2.** *Gewerbe*: building trade; **~fachmann** *m* construction expert

baufällig *Adj.* dilapidated, *präd. auch* in bad repair; *Wohnung etc.*: *auch* unfit for habitation; *Dach, Gewölbe*: dilapidated, *präd. auch* in bad repair, falling in; **Baufälligkeit** *f*; *nur Sg.* dilapidated state, (state of) dilapidation (*od.* disrepair)

Bau|finanzierung *f* construction financing, construction (*od.* building) finance; **~firma** *f Häuserbau etc.*: (firm of) builders (and contractors) *Pl.*; *Großprojekte, auch Straßenbau*: construction company, contractors *Pl.*; **~gelände** *n* development area (*od.* site); **~geld** *n* building capital; **~genehmigung** *f* planning permission; **~genossenschaft** *f* cooperative building association; **~gerüst** *n* scaffolding; **~gesellschaft** *f* building (*od.* construction) firm; **~gewerbe** *n* building trade

baugleich *Adj. Modell*: structurally similar (*od. präd.* alike); **~ sein** (*mit*) be similarly constructed (to)

Bau|grube *f* building pit, excavation (pit); **e-e ~ ausheben** excavate (the) foundations; **~grund** *m* **1.** (*Gelände*) building land, development site; **2.** (*Grundstück*) site, (building) plot; **~gruppe** *f Tech.* assembly; **~hand-werk** *n* building trade, *Am.* construction business; **~herr** *m* builder-owner; *größerer*: (property) developer; **~:** *Stadt München* commissioned by the City of Munich; *die Gemeinde ist der ~* it is (being) paid for (*od.* financed) out of public funds, it is a public project; **~herrenmodell** *n* tax-efficient building finance plan; **~herrin** *f →* **Bauherr**, **~hof** *m einer Baufirma*: builder's yard; *der Gemeinde*: plant (*od.* materials) depot; **~holz** *n*; *nur Sg.* (building) timber, *Am.* lumber; **~ingenieur** *m* construction engineer; *bes. bei Tiefbau auch* civil engineer; **~jahr** *n* construction year; *von Auto*: year of manufacture; **~ 2002** 2002 model; *welches ~ ist Ihr Auto?* what year is your car?; *in Anzeigen*: *Rei-henhaus, ~ 1994* terraced house (*Am.* townhouse), built 1994; 1994 terraced house (*Am.* townhouse)

Baukasten *m* (*Spielzeug*) box of bricks; *anspruchsvoller*: construction kit (*od.* set); **~prinzip** *n*; *mst Sg.* modular (assembly) concept (*od.* principle); **~system** *n*; *mst Sg.* modular (assembly) system

Bau|klotz *m* building brick; *da staunst du Bauklötze umg.* it's absolutely amazing (, isn't it?); it (fairly) takes your breath away; **~kolonne** *f* work gang, gang of workmen; **~kosten** *Pl.* building costs; *weitS.* production costs; **~kostenzuschuss** *m* building subsidy; **~kran** *m* (construction *od.* builder's) crane; **~kunst** *f*; *nur Sg.* architecture; **~land** *n*; *nur Sg.* building land, development site; **~leiter** *m*, **~leiterin** *f* site manager (*od.* supervisor); **~leitung** *f*; *mst Sg.* site management (*od.* supervision)

baulich I. *Adj.*; *nur attr.*; *Archit.* architectural; *Tech.* structural; *in gutem/ schlechtem ~en Zustand* in good/bad repair, structurally sound/unsound; **II.** *Adv.*: *etw. ~ verändern* make structural alterations to s.th.; *die Hafenge-gend ~ neu gestalten* redevelop (*od.* re-plan) the harbour (*od.* port) area

Baulichkeiten *Pl. förm.* buildings, architecture *Sg.*

Bau|löwe *m umg., mst pej.* property tycoon, speculative developer; **~lücke** *f* vacant lot, empty site

Baum *m*; *-(e)s, Bäume* **1.** tree; *ein ab-gestorbener ~* a dead tree; *stark wie ein ~ sein* be as strong as an ox; *ein ~ von e-m Mann* a giant of a man; *die Bäume wachsen nicht in den Himmel* there's a limit to everything, you can't have everything, you can't win them all *umg.*; *zwischen ~ und Borke ste-cken od. sitzen* be between the devil and the deep blue sea, be between a rock and a hard place; *es ist, um auf die Bäume zu klettern umg.* it's enough to (*od.* it would) drive you up the wall(s); *der ~ der Erkenntnis fig.* the Tree of Knowledge; *e-n alten ~ soll man nicht verpflanzen Sprichw.* if the roots run deep, leave the tree where it is; *→ ausreißen* I; **2.** *Naut.*

boom

Baumarkt *m* **1.** *Wirts.* building (*od.* construction) market, property development market, new property market; **2.** *Warenhaus*: DIY (building supplies) superstore, *Am.* home improvement warehouse; *kleiner*: builder's yard

baumarm *Adj.* relatively treeless

Bau|maschine *f* piece (*od.* item) of construction equipment, *Pl. auch* construction equipment *Sg.*, heavy (*od.* contractors') plant *Sg.*; **~maßnahmen** *Pl.* building operations; **~material** *n* building material(s *Pl.*)

Baum|bestand *m*; *nur Sg.* stock of trees, tree population; *ein Garten mit altem ~* a garden with mature trees; **~blüte** *f* **1.** (*das Blühen*) blossoming (*od.* flowering) (of a tree); **2.** *Zeit*: blossom time, flowering season

Bäumchen *n* small (*od.* little) tree

Baumchirurgie *f* tree surgery

Baumeister *m* **1.** *auf dem Bau*: master builder; **2.** (*Architekt, auch fig.*) architect

baumeln *v/i. umg.* **1.** dangle, swing (*an + Dat.* from); *mit den Beinen ~* (*od. die Beine ~ lassen*) dangle (*od.* swing) one's legs; *die Seele ~ lassen umg. fig.* let it all hang out; **2.** *am Galgen*: swing

Baum|fäule *f von Holz*: dry rot; *im Baum*: rot in living tree; **~frevel** *m* malicious (*od.* unlawful) damaging of (*od.* damage to) trees; **~ begehen** maliciously damage trees; **~grenze** *f* tree-line, timberline; **~gruppe** *f natürlich*: clump of trees; *angelegt*: group of trees; **~haus** *n* tree(-)house

baumhoch *Adj.* (as) tall as a tree (*od.* trees)

Baum|höhle *f* hollow trunk (of a tree); **~krone** *f* treetop, crown; **~kuchen** *m* cylindrical cake built up from horizontal layers baked successively

baumlang *Adj.* very (*od.* exceptionally) tall

Baumläufer *m Orn.* (tree) creeper

baumlos *Adj.* treeless, bare

Baummarder *m Zool.* pine marten

baumreich *Adj.* densely wooded (*od.* forested)

Baum|riese *m* giant tree; **~rinde** *f* bark (of a tree); **~schere** *f* pruning shears *Pl.*, loppers *Pl.*; *e-e ~* (a pair of) pruning shears *Pl.* (*od.* loppers); **~schule** *f* (tree) nursery; **~schwamm** *m Bot.* agaric; **~stamm** *m* (tree) trunk; *gefällter*: log; **~steppe** *f Geog.* tree savanna; **~sterben** *n Öko.* tree death; *weitS.* forest decline; **~stumpf** *m* (tree) stump; **~wipfel** *m* treetop

Baumwolle *f*; *nur Sg.* cotton; *ein Kleid aus ~* a cotton dress; **baumwollen** *Adj.*; *nur attr.* cotton

Baumwoll|hemd *n* (100%) cotton shirt; **~pflücker** *m*, **~pflückerin** *f* cotton picker; **~plantage** *f* cotton plantation; **~spinnerei** *f* cotton mill

Bau|norm *f* building standard(s *Pl.*); **~objekt** *n* building (*od.* construction) project; **~ordnung** *f* building regulations *Pl.*; **~plan** *m* architect's plan; *Tech.* blueprint; **~planung** *f* project planning; **~platz** *m* site, (building) plot; **~plastik** *f Archit.* (architectural) sculpture

Baupolizei *f* building control authority (*od.* department); **baupolizeilich I.** *Adj.* building control ...; **~e Verord-nungen** *etc.* Building Code; **II.** *Adv.*: **~ genehmigt** covered by a building permit

Baurecht *n Jur.* **1.** *Rechtsgebiet*: building law(s *Pl.*); **2.** *Anspruch*: (owner's conditional) building right

baureif *Adj. Tech.* developed; *Archit.* ready for building; *ein ~es Gelände* a piece of land (*od.* site) suitable for development; *ein ~es Grundstück* a plot (*od.* site) ready for building (on), *Am. auch* a building lot

bäurisch I. *Adj. pej.* coarse, crude; *Be-nehmen auch* boorish, graceless; **II.** *Adv.* coarsely, crudely; *benehmen auch* boorishly; *benimm dich nicht so ~!* don't be so boorish!, don't be such a boor!

Bau|ruine *f* half-finished (*od.* abandoned) building; **~sachverständige** *m, f* construction (*od.* building) expert, surveyor; **~saison** *f* building season; **~satz** *m* construction kit

Bausch *m*; *-(e)s, Bäusche* wad (*auch aus Watte*), ball, roll; *in ~ und Bogen fig.* lock, stock and barrel; *etw. in ~ und Bogen verurteilen* condemn (*od.* denounce) s.th. lock, stock and barrel

bauschen I. *v/i., v/refl.* billow (out), puff out; *Segel*: *auch* fill; *stärker*: belly out; *Kleidungsstück*: puff out, bulge *mst pej.*; **II.** *v/t.* puff out; (*Segel*) swell, fill

bauschig *Adj.* puffed out, full, baggy

Bau|schlosser *m* building fitter; **~schutt** *m* builder's rubble (*od.* rubbish)

Bauspardarlehen *n* building loan

bausparen *v/i.*; *mst Inf.* save with a building society

Bau|sparer *m*, **~sparerin** *f* building society investor; **~sparkasse** *f* building society, *Am.* building and loan association; **~sparvertrag** *m* building society savings agreement

Baustahl *m* structural steel

Baustatik *f* statics *Pl.* (*als Fach V. im Sg.*) for structural engineering, architectural statics; **baustatisch** *Adj.* static(al); **~e Berechnung** stress analysis

Bau|stein *m* **1.** (*Gestein*) stone; (*Zie-gel, auch Spielstein*) brick; **2.** *fig.* element, component; (*Beitrag*) important contribution; **3.** *Chem.* building block; *Tech.* component; *Etron.* building block, module; **~stelle** *f* building site; *auf Straßen*: roadworks *Pl.*, *Am.* roadwork; *Achtung ~!* Danger, Men at Work!; *bei Straßenbauarbeiten*: *auch* Road Up; *Betreten der ~ verboten!* Keep Out, No Admittance, Authorized Personnel Only; **~stil** *m* (architectural) style

Baustoff *m* **1.** *Archit.* building material; **2.** *Bio.* nutrient; **~handel** *m* building materials trade (*Am.* business); **~händler** *m* building materials dealer, *Am.* lumber merchant

Bau|stopp *m* embargo on building, building freeze; *e-n ~ verordnen od. verhängen* halt building (works); **~substanz** *f*; *nur Sg.* structural fabric; *e-r Stadt*: architectural fabric (*od.* core); *ein Viertel mit viel gut erhalte-ner ~* a district which has a lot of well-preserved building stock; **~sum-me** *f* (total) building (*od.* construction) costs *Pl.*; **~sünde** *f* (architectural) eyesore, unsightly development, blot on the landscape *umg.*, carbuncle *umg.*; **~tätigkeit** *f*; *nur Sg.* building (activity); **~technik** *f* (*Sachgebiet*) construction (*od.* structural) engineering; *konkret*: construction method, building technique

bautechnisch *Adj.* constructional

Bauteil n (Element) component (part)
Bauten Pl. → **Bau¹** 2
Bau|träger m Person: building contractor, (property) developer; Firma: (property) developers Pl.; **~unternehmen** n 1. (Firma) (firm of) building contractors Pl., building firm, (property) developers Pl.; 2. (Projekt) building (od. construction) project; **~unternehmer** m, **~unternehmerin** f building contractor, (property) developer; **~verbot** n building ban (od. embargo); **~vorhaben** n building (od. construction) project; **~vorschriften** Pl. building regulations; **~weise** f 1. (Methode) construction (method), building technique; 2. (Stil) style (of architecture), architectural style, design; **~werk** n building; (Brücke etc.) structure; förm. edifice; **~wesen** n; nur Sg. civil and structural engineering; **~wirtschaft** f; nur Sg. building (od. construction) industry; **~wut** f building craze
Bauxit [bau'ksi:t] m; -s, -e; Min. bauxite
Bau|zaun m hoarding; **~zeichner** m, **~zeichnerin** f architectural draughts(wo)man (Am. drafts(wo)man); **~zeichnung** f construction plan, architect's plan (od. drawing); **~zeit** f completion (od. construction) period; die ~ betrug zwei Jahre it took two years to build; nach zweijähriger ~ having taken two years to build, completed after two years' work
Bayer m; -n, -n, **~in** f; -, -nen Bavarian, weiblich auch: Bavarian woman (od. girl etc.); **bayerisch** → **bayrisch**; **Bayern** (n); -s Bavaria; **bayrisch I.** Adj. Bavarian; der Bayrische Wald the Bavarian Forest; **II.** Adv. in the Bavarian manner (od. way od. style)
Bazar m; -s, -e bazaar
Bazi m; -, -; südd., österr.; umg. mst hum. (Schlingel, Lump) rascal, rogue, varmint
Bazille f; -, -n, mst Pl. 1. Med. germ; 2. umg. fig.: er ist e-e linke ~ Pol. he's a pinko bastard; (hinterhältig) he's a slimy customer
Bazillus m; -, Bazillen 1. Bio., Med. germ; fachspr. bacillus (Pl. bacilli); 2. nur Sg.; fig., geh. seed(s Pl.), virus geh.
Bd. m Abk. (Band) vol.
Bde. Pl. Abk. (Bände) vols.
beabsichtigen v/t. intend (zu + Inf. to + Inf.); (planen) plan, aim; das war (so) beabsichtigt it was deliberate (od. intentional), he etc. did it on purpose (od. meant to do it), that was what he etc. meant to do, that was the idea; das war nicht beabsichtigt it wasn't intentional, I etc. didn't mean to (do it), it wasn't (done) on purpose; was hast du damit beabsichtigt? what were you trying to do (od. achieve) (by that)?, what was the idea (of that umg.)?; **beabsichtigt I.** P.P. → **beabsichtigen**; **II.** Adj. 1. (angestrebt) intended; Wirkung: desired; die ~e Wirkung blieb aus bei Medizin etc.: it didn't have the desired effect; bei Schaueffekten etc.: the effect didn't come off; 2. (absichtlich) intentional; Lüge: deliberate
beachten v/t. 1. (befolgen) obey, heed, comply with, observe; (Anweisungen) follow; (Warnung) heed; (Regeln) auch keep to; (Gesetz) obey, comply with, observe; (Verkehrsschilder) obey, heed; (Verbot) observe, respect; nicht

~ (ignorieren) ignore, take no notice of, pay no heed to; (Ratschläge etc.) auch disregard; → **Vorfahrt**; 2. (Aufmerksamkeit schenken) pay attention to; (zur Kenntnis nehmen) note, take note of; j-n nicht ~ (ignorieren) ignore s.o., pay s.o. no attention; (nicht bemerken) not (od. fail to) notice s.o., miss s.o.; bitte ~ Sie please note; die Ereignisse etc. wurden kaum beachtet were scarcely noticed, aroused little attention, passed almost unnoticed; 3. (berücksichtigen) bear in mind, take into account; man muss dabei ~, dass ... you've got to bear in mind (od. remember) that ....
beachtenswert Adj. notable, noteworthy; Buch, Film etc.: significant, präd. auch of note; e-e ~e Leistung auch quite an achievement
beachtlich I. Adj. 1. (beträchtlich) considerable; mengenmäßig: auch siz(e)able; Fortschritt: considerable, respectable; Erfolg: notable, considerable; Verbesserung: considerable, real; das war e-e ~e Leistung that was quite an achievement (od. [quite] some feat umg.); 2. (bemerkenswert) remarkable; (ernst zu nehmen) serious; Gegner, Widerstände: auch formidable, daunting; ~! umg. pretty good!; er hat Beachtliches geleistet he (has) achieved a lot; **II.** Adv. (beträchtlich) considerably; ~ steigen climb sharply (od. steeply)
Beachtung f; nur Sg. 1. (Befolgung) compliance, observance, heed; von Anweisungen: following; von Regeln: obeying, compliance (od. complying) with, adherence (od. adhering) to; von Verbot: compliance (od. complying) with, acceptance; die ~ der Hausordnung etc. fordern ask that the house rules etc. be observed (od. kept to); 2. (Aufmerksamkeit) attention; ~ finden be taken note of; keine/kaum ~ finden be ignored / more or less be ignored; Leistung etc.: pass unnoticed / virtually unnoticed; (keine) ~ schenken pay (no) attention to; ~ verdienen Begebenheit: be worthy of note; Vorschlag etc.: merit serious consideration, be one to be taken seriously; Künstler etc.: command respect; dieses Buch / seine Leistung verdient ~ this is a notable (od. impressive) book / his performance (od. achievement) is (od. was etc.) impressive; j-m wird ~ zuteil s.o. receives (od. s.o.'s views receive) attention; „zur (gefälligen) ~" (please) note; 3. (Berücksichtigung) consideration; unter ~ der besonderen Umstände in view of the circumstances (of this case), taking the (particular) circumstances into account
beackern v/t. 1. umg. fig. (Thema) work through; (auf j-n einreden) work on, keep (on) at, keep working on; wir ~ ihn, bis er Ja sagt we'll just keep (on) at him till he says yes; 2. (Feld etc.) plough, Am. plow
beamen ['bi:mən] **I.** v/refl. beam o.s.; **II.** v/t.; **Beamer** ['bi:mɐ] m; -s,- digital projector, LCD projector
Beamte m; -n, -n official; bei Polizei, Zoll: officer; staatlich: government official, civil servant; umg. (Angestellter) employee; **~r sein** be a civil servant; ein typischer ~r pej. a typical bureaucrat; ein kleiner ~r a minor (od. bes. pej. petty) official (od. bureaucrat); ein hoher ~r a high-ranking civil servant

Beamten|anwärter m civil service applicant; **~apparat** m civil service machinery, bureaucracy; **~beleidigung** f insulting (od. defamation of) a civil servant (Polizist: a police officer) on duty; **~bestechung** f bribery of an official (od. officials); **~deutsch** n pej. officialese
beamtenhaft Adj. bureaucratic
Beamten|karriere, **~laufbahn** f civil service career; **~recht** n; nur Sg. civil service law
Beamtenschaft f; mst Sg. civil service, civil servants Pl., officialdom umg.
Beamten|seele f iro. pej. (typical) petty bureaucrat; **~staat** m bureaucratic state; **~status** m civil service status; ~ haben have civil service status, be a civil servant; **~stelle** f civil service post, position in the civil service; **~verhältnis** n; nur Sg. (contractual) position as civil servant; ins ~ übernommen werden be given civil servant status, become a civil servant; im ~ stehen be a civil servant, have civil service status; aus dem ~ ausscheiden leave / be dismissed from the civil service; **~willkür** f official (od. bureaucratic) whim
beamtet Adj. Amtsspr.: ein ~er Lehrer a teacher with permanent (civil servant) status; auch präd.: ~ sein have permanent (civil servant) status, have tenure as a civil servant
Beamtin f; -, -nen → **Beamte**
beängstigend I. Adj. frightening, alarming; sein Zustand ist ~ his condition is alarming (od. giving rise to (some) alarm); **II.** Adv. alarmingly, frighteningly; sein Zustand verschlechterte sich ~ schnell his condition worsened at an alarming rate
beanspruchen v/t. 1. (fordern) (Recht, Erbteil) claim, lay claim to; er beansprucht für sich, wie ein großer Künstler behandelt zu werden he wants people to treat him as a major artist; 2. (erfordern) (Geschick, Geduld) demand, require, call for; (Platz, Zeit) take up; 3. (Gebrauch machen von) use, make use of; (auch j-s Hilfe etc.) avail o.s. of, accept; (j-s Gastfreundschaft) avail o.s. of, accept; geistig-seelisch: preoccupy; stärker: absorb; ich will Ihre Zeit nicht länger ~ I'll not take up any more of your time; 4. (strapazieren) strain, be (od. put) a strain on, tax; Tech. stress, strain, load; stark ~ (Sache) be (od. put) a heavy strain (od. load) on; (Person) keep s.o. very busy, take up a lot of s.o.'s time (and energy), make heavy demands on s.o. (od. s.o.'s time); innerlich: preoccupy s.o. greatly
beansprucht I. P.P. → **beanspruchen**; **II.** Adj.: stark ~ Person: very (od. extremely) busy; sie ist zur Zeit stark ~ auch she's under (a lot of) pressure at the moment, she's got a lot on her plate at the moment umg.
Beanspruchung f 1. (Forderung) claim (+ Gen. on od. against); 2. von Zeit, der Kräfte etc.: demand (on); starker/geringer ~ ausgesetzt sein be in heavy/little demand; 3. (Gebrauch) use; 4. (Anstrengung) strain; Tech. stress, strain, load; ~ durch die Arbeit etc. demands Pl. of work etc.; 5. Tech.: für starke od. hohe ~ for heavy-duty service, heavy-duty materials etc.; (Abnutzung) auch for hard wear; für normale ~ for normal use; bei normaler ~ under normal (working) conditions, in

normal use, normally

beanstanden *v/t.* (*Einwände erheben gegen, zurückweisen*) object to; (*Zustände etc.*) complain about; (*in Frage stellen*) (*auch Rechnung etc.*) query, dispute; (*kritisieren*) criticize; *die Lieferung/Arbeit wurde beanstandet* the delivery / the job quality (*od.* quality of the work) was queried (*od.* questioned); *was ich an ihm etc. zu ~ habe* what I don't like about him *etc.*, the thing I have against him *etc.*; *ich habe nichts daran zu ~* I can't see anything wrong with it, I have no criticisms; *das Einzige, was ich daran zu ~ habe* the only criticism (*od.* objection) I have, the only problem I have with that; **Beanstandung** *f* (*Beschwerde*) complaint (+ *Gen.* about); (*Infragestellung*) query (about); (*Kritik*) criticism (of, about); (*Einwand*) objection (to); *Anlass zu ~en geben* *förm.* be open to criticism, give cause for complaint

beantragen *v/t.* apply for, put in an application for; *Jur.* (*Strafe*) ask for, demand; *Parl.* (*Gesetzesänderung*) move for; (*vorschlagen*) propose; *Parl.*: *~ zu* + *Inf.* move that *s.th.* be done; (*vorschlagen*) propose that *s.th.* be done; **Beantragung** *f* application; *Parl.* motion; (*Vorschlag*) proposal

beantwortbar *Adj.* answerable; *das ist nicht ohne weiteres ~* there is no easy answer to that (question); **beantworten** *v/t. auch fig.* answer (*mit* with), reply to; (*Gruß, Beleidigung*) respond to, return; *mit Ja ~* answer yes; **Beantwortung** *f* answer, reply; *in ~* (+ *Gen.*) in answer (*od.* reply) to

bearbeiten *v/t.* **1.** (*Sachgebiet etc.*) work on; (*Fall etc.*) *auch* deal with, handle; (*Bestellung*) process, deal with; **2.** (*Werkstoff*) work, (*Leder*) *auch* dress; (*Metall, Holz*) *spanlos*: work, *spanabhebend*: machine; (*behandeln*) treat; **3.** (*Feld, Boden etc.*) work, cultivate, till; **4.** (*Buch*) edit; *neu*: revise; *für die Bühne etc.*: adapt; *Mus.* arrange; **5.** *fig.*: *j-n ~ beeinflussend*: work on s.o., try to persuade s.o.; *umg.* (*verprügeln*) give s.o. a working (*od.* going) over, beat s.o. up; *j-n mit den Fäusten ~* punch s.o. repeatedly, take one's fists to s.o., belabo(u)r s.o.; **Bearbeiter** *m*, **Bearbeiterin** *f* **1.** *e-s Falles etc.*: person in charge (*od.* dealing with) the case *etc.*; **2.** *e-s Buchs*: editor; *e-r Neufassung*: adapter; *Mus.* arranger

Bearbeitung *f* **1.** *e-s Themas etc.*: treatment; *von Akten etc.*: processing; *die ~ dieses Falles übernimmt Kollege Meier* the (*od.* this) case has been assigned to Mr Meier, Mr Meier will be dealing with the (*od.* this) case; **2.** *von Werkstoffen*: working, machining; (*Behandlung*) treatment; **3.** *des Bodens etc.*: working, cultivation; **4.** *e-s Buchs*: (*Überarbeitung*) revision; (*neu bearbeitete Ausgabe*) revised edition; *Theat.* adaptation; *bes. Mus.* arrangement

Bearbeitungs|gebühr *f e-s Antrags*: handling charge; *Bank*: (bank) service (*od.* management) charge; **~zeit** *f* processing time, lag time; *e-e ~ von sechs Monaten* a processing time (*od.* delay) of six months, six months in the pipeline; *e-e sechsmonatige ~* a six-month processing delay (*od.* lag time)

beargwöhnen *v/t.* be suspicious of, feel suspicious about, suspect; *beargwöhnt*

werden be suspected

Beat [biːt] *m*; *-(s)*, *kein Pl.* **1.** (*Musik*) rock, pop; *älter*: beat; *~ hören* listen to rock (*od.* pop); *~ spielen* play rock (*od.* pop) music; **2.** *im Rhthmus*: beat; **~band** [-bɛnt], **~gruppe** *f* rock (*od.* pop) group, rock band

beatmen *v/t.*: *j-n* (*künstlich*) *~* give s.o. (artificial) respiration; *im Operationssaal*: ventilate s.o.; **Beatmung** *f*: (*künstliche*) *~* (artificial) respiration, ventilation; **Beatmungsgerät** *n* respirator, ventilator

Beaufortskala [boˈfoːr-] *f*; *nur Sg.*; *Met.* Beaufort scale

beaufsichtigen *v/t.* supervise; (*Kind*) look after, mind; (*Häftlinge*) supervise, have charge of; (*Prüfung*) invigilate, supervise; *die Kinder bei i-n Hausaufgaben ~* supervise the children's homework; *j-n bei der Arbeit ~* supervise (*od.* keep an eye on *umg.*) s.o.'s work; **Beaufsichtigung** *f* supervision

beauftragen *v/t.* ask; *förm.* instruct, charge; (*Künstler etc.*) commission; (*Anwalt, Firma*) engage, employ; (*Ausschuss*) ask, instruct, give the remit (*Am.* responsibility) (to); *wer hat Sie dazu beauftragt?* on whose instructions are you acting?, who told you to do this? *umg.*; *j-n mit e-m Fall ~* put s.o. in charge of a case; *j-n mit e-r Arbeit ~* entrust s.o. with a job (*od.* task); *bei Entlohnung*: *auch* commission s.o. to do (*od.* carry out) a job; **Beauftragte** *m*, *f*; *-n*, *-n* (authorized) representative; (*Abgeordneter*) delegate; **Beauftragung** *f* (*das Beauftragen*) commissioning, engagement; *förm.* instruction

beäugen *v/t.* have (*od.* take) a good look at; *misstrauisch ~* peer suspiciously at

Beauty|-Case [-keːs] *n od. m*; *-*, *- od. -s* make(-)up bag; *älter*: vanity case; **~farm** *f* health farm

bebaubar *Adj.* developable; **bebauen** *v/t.* **1.** (*Grundstück etc.*) build on; *die Gegend ist jetzt mit Mietshäusern bebaut* they have built the land over with flats (*Am.* apartment buildings); **2.** (*Boden etc.*) cultivate; **bebaut** **I.** *P.P.* → **bebauen**; **II.** *Adj. Gebiet, Gelände*: built-up *attr.*

Bebauung *f* **1.** a) *nur Sg.*; (*das Bebauen*) development, building over, b) (*mit Gebäuden*) development, built-up area; **2.** *Agr.* cultivation

Bebauungs|dichte *f* building density; **~plan** *m* building (*od.* development) plan

beben *v/i.* shake, tremble, quake; *Knie*: shake, wobble; *Stimme*: tremble, quiver; (*vibrieren*) vibrate; *vor Wut/Kälte ~* tremble (*od.* quiver) with rage / shiver with cold; **Beben** *n*; *-s*, *-* trembling; *Geol.* tremor; *stärker*: (earth)quake; *ein leichtes ~ in s-r Stimme* a slight tremor (*od.* tremble) in his voice

bebildern *v/t.* illustrate; **Bebilderung** *f* illustrations *Pl.*

bebrillt *Adj. auch hum.* bespectacled

bebrüten *v/t.* **1.** incubate; (*Eier*) *auch* sit on; **2.** *umg. fig.* brood over; **Bebrütung** *f von Bakterienkulturen, Eiern etc.*: incubation

Béchamel|kartoffeln *Pl. Gastr.* béchamel potatoes; **~soße** *f* béchamel (sauce)

Becher *m*; *-s*, *-* **1.** a) *aus Ton, Porzellan, Metall*: mug; *aus Plastik*: beaker,

tumbler; *aus Glas*: glass, tumbler; *mit Joghurt*: carton, b) *für Eis etc.*: cup; *aus Pappe*: tub, c) *zum Würfeln*: cup, d) (*Kelch*) cup, goblet; **2.** *Bot.* cup, calix

becherförmig *Adj.* cup-shaped; *förm.* cupular

Becherglas *n* **1.** *Chem.* beaker; **2.** *Trinkgefäß*: glass, tumbler

bechern *vt/i. umg. auch hum.* booze; *einen ~* have a few; *wir haben ganz schön gebechert* we had a real booze-up, *Am.* we really tied one on

becircen [bəˈtsɪrtsn] *v/t. umg.* **1.** bewitch; **2.** (*charmant überreden*) sweet-talk

Becken *n*; *-s*, *-* **1.** (*Brunnen-, Hafenbecken*) basin; *Küche*: sink; *Bad*: (wash)basin; *Klosett*: bowl; (*Schwimmbecken*) pool; (*Planschbecken*) paddling pool; **2.** *Geol.* basin; **3.** *Anat.* pelvis; *ein breites/schmales ~ haben* have broad/narrow hips; → *gebärfreudig*; **4.** *mst Pl.*; *Mus.* cymbal

Becken|bruch *m Med.* fractured pelvis; **~endlage** *f Med.* breech position (*od.* presentation); **~gurt** *m im Flugzeug etc.*: lap belt, *Am.* seatbelt; **~knochen** *m* hip bone, pelvic bone; **~rand** *m von Schwimmbecken*: edge of the pool

Beckmesserei *f*; *-*, *-en*; *pej.* carping, faultfinding; **beckmesserisch** *Adj. pej.* carping

Becquerel [bɛkəˈrɛl] *n*; *-s*, *-* becquerel

bedacht¹ *Adj.* (*mit Dach*) roofed; *e-e ~e Brücke* a roofed bridge

bedacht² **I.** *P.P.* → **bedenken**; **II.** *Adj.* (*besonnen*) *Mensch, Handeln*: careful, cautious; *auf etw.* (*Akk.*) *~* intent on (doing) s.th.; *darauf ~ sein zu* (+ *Inf.*) (*sich Mühe geben*) be intent on (+ *Ger.*), be anxious to (+ *Inf.*); *darauf ~ sein, nett zu sein etc.* make a point of being friendly *etc.*; *er ist nur auf s-n eigenen Vorteil ~* he's only out for his own advantage, *Am.* he's only in it for himself

Bedacht *m geh.*: *mit ~* (*überlegt*) with due consideration; (*umsichtig*) circumspectly; (*vorsichtig*) carefully; (*absichtlich*) deliberately; *voll ~* cautiously; *ohne ~* (*unüberlegt*) without thinking; (*übereilt*) rashly, without stopping to think; (*unvorsichtig*) carelessly

bedächtig **I.** *Adj.* (*langsam, gemessen*) *Schritte*: measured, unhurried, slow; (*wohl überlegt*) *Worte, Sprache*: deliberate, well-considered; (*umsichtig*) *Wesen*: cautious, careful; **II.** *Adv.* (*überlegt*) with deliberation; (*langsam*) deliberately, slowly; *langsam und ~ sprechen/kauen* speak slowly and fastidiously / chew with slow deliberation; **Bedächtigkeit** *f*; *nur Sg.* care; (*Umsicht*) circumspection; (*Langsamkeit*) slowness; *e-r Handlung, Bewegung etc.*: deliberation

bedachtsam **I.** *Adj. geh.* (*besonnen, vorsichtig*) circumspect; **II.** *Adv.* circumspectly; *~ handeln od. vorgehen* exercise caution; **Bedachtsamkeit** *f*; *nur Sg.*; *geh.* circumspection

Bedachung *f* roof(ing); **~en** *Tech.* roofing, roofs

bedanken **I.** *v/refl.* say thank you; *förm.* express one's thanks (*bei* to); *sich bei j-m ~ auch* thank s.o. (*für* for); *ich bedanke mich herzlich* thank you very much indeed, *Am.* thank you so much; *dafür bedanke ich mich* *umg. iro.* no thank you very much; *dafür kannst du dich bei deiner*

B

Schwester ~ *umg. iro.* you've got your sister to thank for that; **II.** *v/t. südd., österr.*: *der Redner wurde bedankt* the speaker was thanked; *seien Sie bestens od. herzlich bedankt* please accept our (*od.* my) sincere thanks

Bedarf *m; -(e)s, -e, Pl. nur fachspr.* need (*an + Dat.* for); *Wirts.* (*Nachfrage*) demand (for); (*Erfordernisse*) requirements *Pl.*; (*Bedarfsmenge*) supply (of); ~ *haben an* (+ *Dat.*) need, be in need of; *bei* ~ if required (*od.* necessary); (*je*) *nach* ~ as the need arises; *auch mengenmäßig*: as required; *es besteht* ~ *an neuen Wohnungen* there's a demand for new housing; *für j-s* ~ for s.o.; *für den eigenen* ~ for oneself, for one's personal requirements; *Dinge für den täglichen/häuslichen* ~ everyday/household essentials; *Gegenstände des gehobenen* ~*s* luxury and semi-luxury items; *etw. über* ~ *haben Wirts.* have an oversupply of s.th.; *den* ~ *decken* meet the demand; *s-n* ~ *decken* keep oneself in good supply; *mein* ~ *ist* (*reichlich*) *gedeckt iro.* I've had enough (*an + Dat.* of); *für heute ist mein* ~ *an Abwechslung gedeckt!* I've had enough for one day!; *danke, kein* ~*! umg.* no thank you (very much)

...bedarf *m, im Subst.* **1.** *mit Subst.*: *Wärme~* need for warmth; *Wohnungs~* housing requirement; **2.** *seltener mit V.*: *Mal~* painting materials *Pl.*; *Schreib~* writing materials *Pl.*

Bedarfs|ampel *f* pelican crossing, *Am.* pedestrian crossing; *~analyse f Wirts.* demand analysis; *~artikel m* commodity, requisite; *Pl. auch* consumer goods; *~befriedigung f* satisfaction of demand; *~deckung f* supply of needs; *~ermittlung f* assessment of demand; *~fall m: im* ~ in case of need, if (and when) required; *für den* ~ (*vorsorglich*) for a time of need

bedarfsgerecht I. *Adj. Produktion, Sortiment*: tailored to market requirements; *e-e* ~*e Bildungspolitik* an education policy tailored to (the country's *etc.*) needs; **II.** *Adv.*: *etw.* ~ *gestalten* tailor s.th. according to need

Bedarfs|güter *Pl.* consumer goods; *~haltestelle f* request stop, *Am.* flag stop

bedarfsorientiert *Adj.* demand-oriented

bedauerlich *Adj.* regrettable, unfortunate; *das ist sehr* ~ that's a great pity; **bedauerlicherweise** *Adv.* unfortunately, regrettably, I regret to say (that)

bedauern I. *v/t.* **1.** (*Ereignisse etc.*) regret; (*es*) ~*, etw. tun zu müssen* regret having (*od.* to have) to do s.th.; (*es*) ~*, etw. getan zu haben* regret doing (*od.* having done) s.th.; *das habe ich immer bedauert* I've regretted it ever since; *ich bedauere sehr, dass* I very much regret that; (*es tut mir Leid*) I'm very sorry that; *so sehr ich es* (*auch*) *bedauere* much as I regret it; **2.** *j-n* ~ feel sorry for s.o.; *er ist zu* ~ you can't help feeling (*od.* you have to feel) sorry for him; *er lässt sich gern* ~ he likes people to feel sorry for him, he craves pity; **II.** *v/i.: bedauere!* sorry!

Bedauern *n; -s, kein Pl.* **1.** (*Betrübnis*) regret (*über + Akk.* at); *zu m-m* (*großen*) ~ (much) to my regret; *mit* ~ *habe ich gehört, dass...* I was very sorry to hear that; **2.** (*Mitgefühl*) sympathy; *j-m sein* ~ *ausdrücken* offer one's

sympathy to s.o.; *bei Todesfall*: offer one's condolences to s.o.

bedauernswert, bedauernswürdig *Adj.* **1.** *Mensch*: pitiable; **2.** *Lage etc.*: regrettable; *stärker*: deplorable

bedecken I. *v/t.* cover (*mit* with); (*zudecken*) *auch* cover up; **II.** *v/refl.* cover o.s.; *Himmel*: cloud over; **bedeckt I.** *P.P.* → *bedecken*; **II.** *Adj. Himmel*: overcast; *teils* ~ partly cloudy; *mit Staub* ~ covered in dust; *mit Ruhm* ~ decked in glory; ~*en Hauptes* with one's head covered; *sich* ~ *halten fig.* play one's cards close to one's chest; **Bedeckung** *f* **1.** *nur Sg.*; (*das Bedecken*) covering; **2.** *Gegenstand*: cover, covering; **3.** (*Geleitschutz*) escort

bedenken (*unreg.*) **I.** *v/t.* **1.** (*erwägen*) consider; (*überlegen*) think *s.th.* over; (*beachten*) bear in mind; (*berücksichtigen*) *auch* take into account; *wenn man es recht bedenkt* if you (really) think about it; *j-m etw. zu* ~ *geben* draw s.o.'s attention to s.th (*od.* to the fact that …); *ich gebe dir* (*nur*) *zu* ~*, dass* I'd just like to make the point that (*od.* make you aware [of the fact] that); **2.** *j-n mit etw.* ~ give s.o. s.th.; *förm.* bestow s.th. on s.o.; *j-n reich* ~ shower s.o. with presents (*od.* money); *j-n mit Applaus* ~ applaud s.o.; *die Rede etc. wurde mit heftigem Applaus bedacht* was greeted with loud applause; *j-n in s-m Testament* ~ remember s.o. in one's will; **II.** *v/refl.* think it over; *ohne mich lange zu* ~ without much hesitation, without thinking twice about it

Bedenken *n; -s, -, mst Pl.* **1.** *nur Sg.*; (*Überlegung*) thought, reflection; *nach einigem/kurzem* ~ after some/ a moment's thought (*od.* reflection); **2.** *mst Pl.* (*Zweifel*) doubt; (*Einwand*) objection; (*Skrupel*) *auch moralisch*: scruple, *Pl. auch* qualms; (*Vorbehalt*) reservation, misgiving; ~ *anmelden* raise objections; ~ *äußern gegen* express one's reservations about; *ich habe da m-e* ~ I have my doubts (about it), I'm not so sure (about it); *sie hat* ~*, ob sie ihm das Geld leihen soll* she has (certain) misgivings about lending him the money; *kommen dir da keine* ~*?* don't you have any reservations about it at all?; *j-m die* ~ *nehmen od. j-s* ~ *zerstreuen* allay s.o.'s doubts; *ohne* ~ without hesitation, without giving it a second thought

bedenkenlos I. *Adj.* (*skrupellos*) unscrupulous; (*ohne Zweifel*) unhesitating; **II.** *Adv.* (*ohne nachzudenken*) without thinking; (*ohne lange zu überlegen*) without hesitation, without thinking twice; *förm.* without demur; (*vorbehaltlos*) without reservation; (*skrupellos*) without scruple; *da kannst du* ~ *hingehen* you'll be perfectly all right going there; **Bedenkenlosigkeit** *f, nur Sg.*; (*Skrupellosigkeit*) unscrupulousness; (*Mangel an Überlegung*) unthinkingness; **bedenkenswert** *Adj. Vorschlag.*: worth considering

bedenklich *Adj.* **1.** (*zweifelhaft*) Geschäfte, Mittel: dubious, questionable; (*Verdacht erregend*) suspicious; **2.** (*Besorgnis erregend*) worrying, alarming; (*ernst*) critical, serious; (*gefährlich*) risky; *ich halte das für äußerst* ~ I find that quite worrying (*od.* alarming); *das ist höchst* ~ *auch* that is cause for alarm; *der Himmel sieht* ~ *aus* the sky looks threatening;

3. (*zweifelnd, besorgt*) doubtful; (*skeptisch*) sceptical, *Am.* skeptical; (*besorgt*) worried; *ein* ~*es Gesicht machen* look sceptical (*Am.* skeptical); (*besorgtes*) look worried; *das stimmt mich sehr* ~ *geh.* (*skeptisch*) I find that rather strange, that (really) makes me think; **Bedenklichkeit** *f; nur Sg.* **1.** (*Zweifelhaftigkeit*) questionable nature, dubiousness; **2.** (*Ernsthaftigkeit*) serious (*od.* alarming) nature (+ *Gen.* of), seriousness

Bedenkzeit *f; nur Sg.* time to think it over (*od.* think about it); *sich* (*Dat.*) ~ *erbitten* ask if one can think about it for a while; *ich gebe dir bis morgen* ~ I'll give you till tomorrow (to think about it); *nach kurzer* ~ after briefly thinking about it

bedeppert *Adj. umg., oft pej.* **1.** (*ratlos*) baffled; **2.** (*dümmlich*) gormless, sheepish, *Am.* slow-witted; *blicken, aussehen*: *auch* blank; **3.** (*niedergeschlagen*) crestfallen, downcast

bedeuten *v/t.* **1.** (*heißen, bezeichnen*) mean; *Symbol etc.*: *auch* stand for, signify; *was* ~ *diese Schriftzeichen?* what do these characters mean (*od.* say)?; *was soll das* ~*?* what does it mean?; *was soll das denn* ~*?* (*od.* was *hat das zu* ~*?*) empört: what's the idea?, what's the meaning of this?, what's that supposed to mean?; *das hat was zu* ~ that says something; **2.** (*zur Folge haben*) mean; *das bedeutet nichts Gutes* that's a bad sign, that doesn't augur (*Am.* bode) too well, that's rather ominous; *dieser Wind bedeutet e-n Wetterwechsel* this wind means (*od.* is a sign) that the weather is going to change; *es bedeutet e-e erhöhte Gefahr* it means (*od.* implies) an increased risk; **3.** (*wichtig sein*): *j-m viel/nichts* ~ mean a lot/ nothing to s.o.; *sie bedeutet mir alles* she's (*od.* she means) everything (*od.* the world) to me; *dieser Name bedeutet etwas in Fachkreisen* he (*od.* she) is well known in the field; *es hat nichts zu* ~ it doesn't mean a thing; (*es macht nichts*) it doesn't matter; **4.** *altm.* (*zu verstehen geben*): *j-m etw.* ~ indicate s.th. to s.o.; *j-m* ~*, dass* give s.o. to understand that

bedeutend I. *Part. Präs.* → *bedeuten*; **II.** *Adj.* **1.** (*wichtig*) important, major, significant; *e-e* ~*e Hafenstadt* a major (*od.* an important) seaport; *ein* ~*er Tag im Leben* a significant day in my *etc.* life; **2.** (*von hoher Qualität*) Beitrag, Film: significant; *Wissenschaftler etc.*: leading, distinguished; (*hervorragend*) outstanding; (*bemerkenswert*) remarkable; (*berühmt*) distinguished; *sie hat Bedeutendes auf diesem Gebiet geleistet* she has made a major (*od.* significant) contribution to this field; **3.** (*groß, beträchtlich*) considerable, major, significant; ~*e Fortschritte machen* make significant (*od.* major) progress, forge ahead; **III.** *Adv.* intensivierend (*wesentlich*) considerably, significantly; *sich* ~ *verbessern etc.* improve *etc.* significantly (*od.* markedly); ~ *besser/länger etc.* much (*od.* a great deal) better/longer *etc.*

bedeutsam I. *Adj.* **1.** (*wichtig, bedeutend*) Augenblick, Entschluss etc.: significant, important; **2.** (*viel sagend*) Blick etc.: knowing, meaningful; **II.** *Adv.* knowingly; *j-n* ~ *anblicken/ anlächeln auch* give s.o. a knowing look/smile; **Bedeutsamkeit** *f; nur Sg.*

1. (*Wichtigkeit*) significance, importance; **2.** *geh.* (*Bedeutung*) significance
Bedeutung *f* **1.** *e-s Wortes*: meaning, sense; *dieses Wort hat mehrere ~en* this word has several meanings; **2.** *nur Sg.*; (*Wichtigkeit*) importance, significance; (*Tragweite*) import; *von ~ sein* be important; (*bezeichnend*) be significant; *sachlich*: be relevant (*für* to); *das hat keine ~* (*will nichts heißen*) it doesn't mean anything; *nichts von ~* nothing important (*od.* significant), nothing worth mentioning; **3.** (*Ansehen*) importance; *ein Mann von ~* an important person, a man of some repute
Bedeutungserweiterung *f Ling.* extension of meaning
bedeutungsgleich *Adj.* identical in meaning; *die Wörter sind ~ auch* the words have the same meaning (*od.* mean the same)
bedeutungslos *Adj.* unimportant, insignificant; (*ohne Sinn, nichts sagend*) meaningless; **Bedeutungslosigkeit** *f*; *nur Sg.* insignificance
bedeutungsschwer *Adj. geh.* fraught with meaning; (*folgenschwer*) momentous
Bedeutungs|unterschied *m Ling.* difference in meaning; *~verengung f Ling.* narrowing (down) of meaning
bedeutungsvoll *Adj.* **1.** (*wichtig*) significant; **2.** (*viel sagend*) meaningful; *Blick etc.: auch* knowing; *~es Schweigen* pregnant silence
Bedeutungswandel *m Ling.* semantic change
bedienen I. *v/t.* **1.** (*auch Kunden*) serve; *im Restaurant: auch* wait on; *gut bedient werden im Restaurant etc.*: get good service; *dort wird man immer freundlich bedient* the service is very friendly there; *werden Sie schon bedient?* can I help you?; *im Restaurant auch*: are you being served?; *zu Hause lässt er sich gern ~* he likes to be waited on at home; *j-n von vorn und hinten ~* (*müssen*) *umg.* (have to) wait on s.o. hand and foot; **2.** *fig.*: *ich bin damit gut bedient mit Gegenstand*: it's serving me well, it's doing a good job *umg.*; *mit Rat*: it's a good piece of advice; *damit wärst du besser bedient* you'd be better off with that (one); *ich bin bedient! umg. iro.* I've had enough; **3.** (*Maschine*) work, operate; **4.** a) (*versorgen*) *mit öffentlichen Verkehrsmitteln sind wir hier gut bedient* we have a good bus and train service here, b) (*Flugroute*) serve; *e-e Strecke täglich ~* offer daily flights (*od.* service) on a route; **5.** *umg. Sport* pass (the ball) to; **6.** *Karten: du musst Herz ~* you've got to play a heart, you've got to follow suit in hearts; **7.** (*entsprechen*) cater for (*Vorstellungen*); *ein Bedürfnis ~* cater for a need; **II.** *v/i.* **1.** *bei Tisch*: serve; *wer bedient an diesem Tisch?* who's serving (at) this table?; **2.** *Karten*: follow suit; *falsch ~* revoke; **III.** *v/refl.* **1.** *bei Tisch*: help o.s.; *bedien dich! / bedient euch!* help yourself/yourselves; **2.** (*benutzen*): *sich ~* (*+ Gen.*) use (*od.* make use of), avail o.s. of; *sich e-r List ~* use a strategem
bedienerfreundlich *etc.* → *bedienungsfreundlich etc.*
Bedienerin *f*, *-*, *-nen*; *österr.* cleaning lady
Bedienstete *m, f; -n, -n* **1.** employee; *im öffentlichen Dienst*: public sector

employee, *Am.* government employee; **2.** *altm.* (*Diener*) servant; *Pl. auch* household staff (*V. mst im Pl.*)
Bedienung *f* **1.** *nur Sg.* service; *drei Mann ~ und drei in der Küche* three serving and three in the kitchen; **2.** (*Kellner/Kellnerin*) waiter/waitress; *~! waiter!/waitress!, excuse me!*; **3.** *nur Sg.; Tech.* operation; *die ~ geht ganz einfach* it's very easy to operate; **4.** (*Bedienungsgeld*) service (charge); *~ inbegriffen* service included
Bedienungs|anleitung *f* instructions *Pl.* for use; *für Geräte: auch* operating instructions *Pl.*; (*Buch*) instruction manual; *~fehler m* operating error
bedienungsfreundlich *Adj.* user-friendly; **Bedienungsfreundlichkeit** *f* user-friendliness; (*Zweckmäßigkeit*) serviceability
Bedienungs|geld *n* service charge; *~komfort m* operational ease, ease of operation; *~personal n* operating staff (*V. mst im Pl.*); *~vorschriften Pl.* operating instructions; *~zuschlag m* service charge
bedingen *v/t.* (*verursachen*) cause, give rise to; (*bestimmen*) determine; (*erfordern*) require, call for; (*voraussetzen*) presuppose; *die hohe Arbeitslosigkeit ist durch die Rezession bedingt* the high unemployment rate is a result of (*od.* has been caused by) the recession; *bedingt werden durch* be caused by, go back to; *das bedingt ...* (*bringt mit sich*) it would imply ...; *einander od. sich gegenseitig ~* be mutually dependent (*od.* conditional), go hand in hand *umg.*
bedingt I. *Adj.* **1.** conditional; (*eingeschränkt*) qualified; *~er Reflex* conditioned reflex; *~ durch od. von* conditional (up)on; (*abhängig*) dependent on, contingent (up)on; *es ist psychisch ~* it's psychological; **2.** *Jur.* conditional; *~er Straferlass* (*teilweise*) suspended sentence; **II.** *Adv.* **1.** *das ist nur ~ richtig etc.* this is only partly correct *etc.*; (*in gewissem Sinn*) this is only correct in a sense; (*bis zu e-m gewissen Punkt*) this is only correct/valid up to a point; **2.** (*unter bestimmten Bedingungen*) under certain circumstances; (*mit Vorbehalt*) with some reservations; *~ tauglich* fit for limited service
...bedingt *im Adj.* ...-related, ...-induced
Bedingtheit *f förm.* **1.** (*Bedingtsein*) conditionality, conditional nature (*+ Gen.* of); *e-n Konflikt etc.* *in s-r historischen ~ sehen* see a conflict in its historical context; **2.** (*Begrenztheit*) limitation(s *Pl.*), limited nature (of); (*Ursache*) cause; (*Abhängigkeit*) dependence (*durch* on); **3.** *selten*: (*Bedingungen*) conditions *Pl.*
Bedingung *f* **1.** (*Forderung*) condition, requirement; *~en stellen* make stipulations; *jetzt will er auch noch ~en stellen!* now he's trying to lay down the rules; *e-e ~ erfüllen* fulfil(l) (*od.* satisfy) a condition (*od.* requirement); *es zur ~ machen, dass* make it a condition that; *daran ist die ~ geknüpft, dass er ...* it is conditional on his (*+ Ger.*); *er knüpfte daran die ~, dass wir ...* he made it conditional on our (*+ Ger.*); *nennen Sie mir Ihre ~en* what are the conditions?; **2.** (*Voraussetzung*) *auch* prerequisite; *unter der ~, dass* on condition that, provided (that); (*nur*) *unter einer ~* on one condition

(only); *was ist die ~?* under what condition?; *unter diesen ~en* under these circumstances; *unter keiner ~* on no account, under no circumstances; **3.** *nur Pl.*; (*Verhältnisse, Zustände*) conditions; (*Umstände*) *auch* circumstances; *unter erschwerten ~en arbeiten* work under aggravated conditions; *wenn die äußeren ~en stimmen, dann ...* if the overall conditions are right, then ...; *klimatische ~en* climatic conditions; **4.** *nur Pl.*; *Wirts.* terms; *zu den üblichen ~en* on the usual terms; *zu günstigen ~en* on easy terms; *wie lauten Ihre ~en?* what are your terms?
...bedingungen *Pl.*, *im Subst.* conditions; terms; → *Bedingung* 3, 4
bedingungslos I. *Adj. Liebe, Kapitulation etc.*: unconditional; (*uneingeschränkt*) unreserved; *Gehorsam etc.*: unquestioning; *Vertrauen*: implicit; *Zustimmung*: unqualified; **II.** *Adv.* unconditionally; *j-m ~ vertrauen* have (*od.* place) implicit trust in s.o.; *~ akzeptieren* accept without reservation; **Bedingungslosigkeit** *f*; *nur Sg.* unconditional nature (*+ Gen.* of); *von Hilfe etc.*: wholeheartedness; *von Zustimmung etc.*: complete lack of reservation; *die ~ s-r Treue* his unquestioning loyalty
Bedingungssatz *m Ling.* conditional clause
bedrängen *v/t.* **1.** pressurize, *Am.* pressure, hassle *umg.*; *mit Bitten etc.*: pester, plague *umg.*; *auf aggressive Art*: harass; *j-n ~ auch* put s.o. under pressure, breathe down s.o.'s neck *umg.*; **2.** *Sport* hustle; (*Torwart*) challenge; **3.** (*Feind*) harry; **4.** (*bedrücken*) worry; **Bedrängnis** *f*, *-*, *kein Pl.*; *geh.* predicament, plight; *in ~ sein* be in trouble, be in a very difficult situation; *stärker*: be in distress; *finanziell*: be in financial (*od.* dire) straits; *in ~ geraten* get into (great) difficulty; *j-n in ~ bringen* get s.o. into trouble; **Bedrängung** *f* **1.** pressurization; *durch Bitten etc.*: pestering; *aggressive*: harassment; **2.** *durch den Feind*: harrying
bedrohen *v/t.* threaten; *ihr Leben ist bedroht* her life is in danger (*od.* threatened); *j-n mit dem Tod ~* threaten to kill s.o.; (*vom Aussterben*) *bedrohte Tierarten etc.* endangered (*od.* threatened) species *etc.*; *von Hochwasser bedrohte Gebiete* areas threatended by floods, areas in danger of flooding
bedrohlich I. *Adj.* threatening, menacing; *Lage*: dangerous; *Ausmaß etc.*: alarming; (*unheilvoll*) ominous; *in ~e Nähe rücken* come (*od.* get) dangerously (*od.* threateningly) close; *~e Ausmaße annehmen* take on alarming proportions; **II.** *Adv.* threateningly; *~ nahe* dangerously (*od.* threateningly) close; *... hat sich ~ verschlechtert / ist ~ angestiegen* there's been an alarming deterioration/increase in ...; **Bedrohlichkeit** *f*; *nur Sg. der Lage etc.*: dangerous (*od.* threatening, menacing) nature (*+Gen.* of)
Bedrohung *f* threat (*für* to); *die ~ unserer Umwelt durch ...* the threat to our environment by ...; *tätliche ~ Jur.* threatening behavio(u)r, criminal assault
bedrucken *v/t.* print; *etw. mit etw ~* print s.th. onto s.th.; **bedruckt I.** *P.P.* → *bedrucken*; **II.** *Adj.* printed; *mit Blumen ~* floral-print ...; *die Rückseite war nicht ~* the other side was

blank, there was nothing printed on the back (*od.* on the other side)

bedrücken *v/t.* **1.** *seelisch:* depress, get *s.o.* down; *was bedrückt dich?* what's troubling you?; **2.** (*unterdrücken*) oppress; **bedrückend I.** *Part. Präs.* → *bedrücken;* **II.** *Adj. Situation etc.:* depressing; *Atmosphäre etc.:* oppressive; *~es Elend* grinding poverty (*od.* misery)

bedrückt I. *P.P.* → *bedrücken;* **II.** *Adj.* depressed; *Schweigen:* oppressed; *~ sein* be (*od.* feel) depressed, feel dejected; *warum bist du so ~?* what's making you so depressed?, what's getting you down?; **Bedrücktheit** *f; nur Sg. seelische:* (feeling of) dejection; *e-e gewisse ~ war allgemein spürbar* there was a general mood of dejection

Bedrückung *f* oppression; *seelische:* dejection

Beduine *m; -n, -n* Bedouin

bedürfen *v/i.* (*unreg.*) *geh.* **1.** *unpers.: es bedarf* (+ *Gen.*) … is (*bzw.* are) required; (*in Anspruch nehmen*) it takes …; *es bedurfte all s-r Kraft* it took all his strength; *es bedurfte keiner Beweise* no evidence was necessary; *das bedarf keiner Erklärung* it needs no explanation; *es hätte nur e-s Wortes (von Ihnen) bedurft* you should have said so, it would have taken no more than a word from you; **2.** *~* (+ *Gen.*) need; *der Patient bedarf noch der Schonung* the patient still needs to take things easy

Bedürfnis *n; -ses, -se* **1.** (*Wunsch*) desire, wish (*nach* for; *zu* + *Inf.* to + *Inf.*); *ein ~ nach Ruhe/Unterhaltung haben* need some peace and quiet / want to be entertained; *ein großes ~ nach Schlaf haben* be desperate for some sleep; *es ist ihm ein (dringendes) ~ zu* (+ *Inf.*) he feels the need (an urgent need) to (+ *Inf.*); *ich hatte das ~ zu* (+ *Inf.*) I felt the urge to (+ *Inf.*); *das war mir ein ~!* ernst gemeint: I'm glad I've got that out of the way!; *iro.* I'd do that again any time; **2.** *mst Pl.:* need (*nach* for), requirement; *die ~se des Alltags* (one's) everyday needs; **3.** *Wirts.* (*Nachfrage*) demand; **4.** *altm.: ein od. sein ~ verrichten* relieve o.s.

Bedürfnis|anstalt *f Amtsspr.* public convenience, *Am.* public restroom; *~befriedigung* *f* satisfaction (*od.* fulfil[l]ment) of a need (*od.* needs); *der od. zur ~ dienen* serve (*od.* satisfy) a need

bedürfnislos *Adj. Leben:* frugal; *Mensch: auch* undemanding; *er ist ~ auch* he doesn't need much; (*bescheiden*) he's very modest; **Bedürfnislosigkeit** *f; nur Sg.* frugality

bedürftig *Adj. Familien etc.:* needy, poor; *e-r Sache ~ sein geh.* be in need of s.th.

…bedürftig *im Adj.* in need of …

Bedürftige *m, f; -n, -n* poor (*od.* destitute) person; *die ~n* the poor, the needy; **Bedürftigkeit** *f; nur Sg.* want, need(iness); (*Armut*) poverty; *soziale:* want (*od.* deprivation)

beduselt *Adj. umg.* (*angetrunken*) slightly drunk; (*benommen*) punch-drunk, dazed; (*schwindlig*) dizzy; *ich fühle mich ~ auch* my head's spinning

Beef|burger ['biːfbɚːɡɐ] *m; -s, -* (beef)burger; *~steak* *n* **1.** steak; **2.** *deutsches ~* beefburger

beehren I. *v/t. geh., oft hum., auch iro.* hono(u)r; *j-n mit s-m Besuch / s-r*

Anwesenheit *~* hono(u)r s.o. with a visit / grace s.o. with one's presence; *in Restaurant, Geschäft:* *~ Sie uns bald wieder altm.* hope to see you again soon; **II.** *v/refl. geh., förm. in Anzeigen etc.: i-e Verlobung beehren sich anzuzeigen* … the engagement is announced between …

beeiden *etc.* → *beeidigen etc.*

beeidigen *v/t. geh.* (*Aussage*) swear to; (*Person*) put *s.o.* under oath; **beeidigt I.** *P.P.* → *beeidigen;* **II.** *Adj. Jur. Aussage, Übersetzer:* sworn; *~er Sachverständiger* (accredited) expert; **Beeidigung** *f* affirmation by oath

beeilen *v/refl.* **1.** hurry; *sich mit od. bei etw. ~* hurry up with s.th.; *beeil dich!* hurry up!, get a move on! *umg.; du brauchst dich nicht zu ~* there's no hurry (*od.* rush), take your time; **2.** *sich ~, etw. zu tun* (*nicht zögern*) hasten to do s.th., quickly do s.th.; **Beeilung** *f; nur Sg.; umg.: ~* (*bitte*)*! od. los, ein bisschen ~!* get a move on(, will you)!, step on it!

beeindrucken *v/t.* impress; *er war sehr/tief beeindruckt auch* it etc. made quite an impression / a deep impression on him; *er ließ sich (dadurch) nicht im Geringsten ~* he wasn't at all impressed (by it); **beeindruckend I.** *Part. Präs.* → *beeindrucken;* **II.** *Adj.* impressive

beeinflussbar *Adj.: ein ~er Mensch* a suggestible person; *sie ist sehr od. leicht ~* she's easily influenced (*od.* swayed); *sie ist schwer ~* she isn't easily influenced (*od.* swayed), she's hard to influence (*od.* sway); **Beeinflussbarkeit** *f; nur Sg.* suggestibility

beeinflussen *v/t.* influence; (*sich auswirken auf*) affect, have an effect on; *negativ/positiv ~* have a bad/good influence (*Sache:* effect) on; *er lässt sich nicht ~* he won't be swayed; **Beeinflussung** *f* (*das Beeinflussen*) influencing; (*Einfluss*) influence; *die systematische ~ der Öffentlichkeit durch die Presse* the manipulation of the public by the press; *wegen unzulässiger ~* (+ *Gen.*) because of undue influence on

beeinträchtigen *v/t.* interfere with; (*Rechte*) *auch* encroach on, infringe; (*behindern*) impede; (*negativ beeinflussen*) affect, have a negative effect on; (*verderben*) mar, spoil; (*schmälern*) lessen, diminish, detract from; *j-n in s-r Freiheit ~* restrict *s.o.*'s freedom; *das beeinträchtigt den Wert erheblich* that reduces the value considerably; *Alkohol beeinträchtigt die Reaktionsfähigkeit* alcohol impairs (*od.* slows down) your reactions; *es beeinträchtigte i-e gute Laune keineswegs* it in no way detracted from her (*bzw.* their) good mood; *jetzt regnet es zwar, das soll uns aber nicht ~* it's started to rain, but that needn't put us off; **Beeinträchtigung** *f* interference (+ *Gen.* with); encroachment (on); infringement (of); impeding (of); negative (*od.* adverse) effect (on); reduction (in); diminution (of); → *beeinträchtigen*

Beelzebub [beˈɛltsəbuːp] *m; -s; bibl.* Beelzebub; *den Teufel mit od. durch ~ austreiben* replace one evil by another

beend(ig)en *v/t.* end; (*Streik*) *auch* call off; (*zum Abschluss bringen*) bring to an end (*od.* a close); (*fertig stellen*) finish; (*Arbeit, Studium etc.*) *auch*

complete; (*Vertragsverhältnis*) terminate; (*Sitzung, Rede etc.*) close, wind up, conclude; (*Schulstunde, Gespräch etc.*) finish; *damit ist der Abend / unsere Diskussion beendet* that brings the evening / our discussion to an end; *er beendete sein Leben in Armut* he ended his days in poverty

Beend(ig)ung *f* ending; completion; termination; conclusion, close; → *beend(ig)en; nach ~ des Krieges etc.* after the war *etc.* (had) ended, at the end of the war *etc.; nach ~ s-s Studiums* after he (had) finished studying (*od.* his studies), after (finishing *od.* completing) his degree; *nach der erfolgreichen ~ der Verhandlungen* after the negotiations had been successfully completed (*od.* concluded)

beengen *v/t.* cramp; *Kleidung:* be too tight for; *Kragen: auch umg.* choke; *fig.* cramp, restrict; (*beschränken*) *stärker:* oppress; **beengend I.** *Part. Präs.* → *beengen;* **II.** *Adj.* oppressive; **beengt I.** *P.P.* → *beengen;* **II.** *Adj.* cramped; *in ~en Verhältnissen leben* live in cramped (*od.* confined) conditions; *sich ~ fühlen* feel cramped; *geistig:* feel stifled; **Beengtheit** *f; nur Sg. e-r Wohnung etc.:* cramped conditions *Pl.;* (*Einschränkungen*) restrictiveness; *ein Gefühl der ~ haben* feel stifled, have a feeling of oppression; **Beengung** *f; nur Sg.* restriction

beerben *v/t.: j-n ~* be *s.o.*'s heir; *sobald sie i-n Onkel beerbt hat* … as soon as she has come into her uncle's inheritance (*od.* has inherited her uncle's estate)

beerdigen *v/t.* bury; *j-n kirchlich ~* give *s.o.* a Christian burial; **Beerdigung** *f* burial; *feierliche: auch* funeral; *auf e-e od. zu e-r ~ gehen* go to a funeral; *auf der falschen ~ sein umg. fig.* (*am falschen Ort*) have come to the wrong place; (*fehl am Platz*) *auch* be a square peg in a round hole; (*e-e irrige Meinung haben*) be barking up the wrong tree; → *Stille*

Beerdigungs|feier *f* funeral ceremony; *Gottesdienst:* funeral service; *~institut* *n* undertaker's; *förm.* funeral directors *Pl.; Am.* funeral home (*od.* parlor); *~kosten* *Pl.* funeral expenses

Beere *f; -, -n* berry; *am Weinstock:* grape; *~n sammeln* (*od. in die ~n gehen Dial.*) go berry-picking, go gathering berries; *~n einkochen* make berry preserves, preserve berries

Beeren|auslese *f* beerenauslese, *quality wine made from selected overripe grapes; ~obst n* berries *Pl.,* soft fruits *Pl.; ~wein m* berry wine; *~zeit f* berry-picking (*od. –gathering*) season

Beet *n; -(e)s, -e* (flower) bed; *zur Umrandung:* border; *mit Gemüse:* patch

Beete *f* → *Bete*

befähigen *v/t.* enable; *Ausbildung etc.:* qualify (*zu* for); *j-n (dazu) ~, etw. zu tun* qualify *s.o.* to do s.th.

befähigt I. *P.P.* → *befähigen;* **II.** *Adj.* (*fähig, begabt*) *Arzt, Lehrer etc.:* capable, competent; (*qualifiziert*) qualified (*zu* + *Inf.* to + *Inf.*); *zu e-r Aufgabe etc. ~ sein* be capable of handling a task *etc.,* be able to cope with a task *etc.; zum Richteramt / zur Ausübung e-s Berufs ~ sein* be qualified as a judge / be qualified to carry out a profession (*od.* an occupation); **Befähigung** *f; nur Sg.* ability; (*Begabung*) aptitude, talent; (*Qualifikation*) qualifications *Pl.; s-e ~ nachweisen* provide evidence of one's qualifications; **Befähigungsnachweis** *m Amtsspr.* proof of qualification (*od.* competence), certificate of competency, qualifying certificate

befahl *Imp.* → **befehlen**

befahrbar *Adj. Straße*: passable, fit for traffic; *Fluss*: navigable; **nicht** ~ closed (*od.* not open) to traffic; **der Pass ist im Winter nur mit Schneeketten** ~ in winter the pass is only accessible with snow chains; **wegen Unfall nur einspurig** ~ traffic is down to a single lane due to an accident; → **Bankett²**, **Seitenstreifen**; **Befahrbarkeit** *f; nur Sg.* practicability, suitability for traffic, *Am.* trafficability; (*Straßenzustand*) (road) conditions *Pl.*; *e-s Flusses*: navigability

befahren **I.** *v/t.* **1.** (*Straße*) drive on (*od.* along); (*benutzen*) use; (*Strecke*) cover; *Linienbus etc.*: serve a route; (*Wasserweg*) sail (up *od.* down), navigate; **2.** (*bereisen*) (*Land, Gegend*) drive across (*od.* through); **II.** *Adj.*: **sehr** *od.* **stark** ~ busy; **wenig** *od.* **kaum** ~ (very) quiet; *Straße*: little used (*od.* frequented); **die Strecke ist kaum** ~ *auch* there's very little traffic on that (part of the) road

Befall *m; -s, kein Pl. durch Insekten*: attack (+ *Gen.* on); **dem** ~ **durch Schädlinge vorbeugen** prevent infestation by pests

befallen **I.** *v/t.* (*unreg.*) *auch Med.* attack; *Schädlinge*: *auch* infest; *Missgeschick, Unglück*: strike; ~ **werden von** *Angst etc.*: be seized (*od.* stricken) by (*od.* with); *von Müdigkeit, Schwäche*: be overcome by; *von Krankheit*: be laid low by (*od.* with), *lit.* be struck down by (*od.* with); *von Fieber*: be laid low with; *von Parasiten etc.*: be infested by; *von Zweifeln*: be assailed by; **e-e plötzliche Schwäche befiel ihn** he suddenly felt faint; **II.** *Adj.*: **von Insekten** ~ insect-infested; **von Fieber** ~ fever-stricken

befangen *Adj.* **1.** inhibited, shy, self-conscious; *vorübergehend*: *auch* embarrassed; **2.** (*voreingenommen*) *auch Jur.* bias(s)ed; **j-n/sich für** ~ **erklären** declare s.o./o.s. to be prejudiced; **j-n als** ~ **ablehnen** disqualify s.o. on grounds of bias; **in etw.** ~ **sein** *e-r falschen Vorstellung etc.*: be caught up in s.th.; *stärker*: be blinded by s.th.; **in e-m Irrtum** ~ **sein** labo(u)r under a delusion; **Befangenheit** *f; nur Sg.* **1.** shyness, self-consciousness, inhibition(s *Pl.*); *vorübergehende*: *auch* embarrassment; **2.** (*Voreingenommenheit*) bias, prejudice; **e-n Richter** *etc.* **wegen** ~ **ablehnen** disqualify a judge *etc.* on grounds of bias; **Befangenheitsantrag** *m Jur.* challenge on grounds of bias; **e-n** ~ **gegen j-n einbringen** challenge s.o. on the grounds of bias, object to s.o. on grounds of interest (*od.* partiality)

befassen **I.** *v/refl.* **1.** **sich mit etw.** ~ concern o.s. with s.th.; (*Problem, Angelegenheit*) deal with s.th.; (*Themenbereich*) work on s.th.; (*untersuchen*) look into s.th.; *aus Interesse*: take interest in s.th.; **damit kann ich mich jetzt nicht** ~ I haven't got time for that now; **befass dich nicht mit so e-m Unsinn** don't get involved in that kind of nonsense; **2. sich mit j-m** ~ spend time with s.o.; *mit Problemfall etc.*: deal with s.o.; **mit solchen Leuten befasse ich mich nicht** I won't have anything

to do with that sort; **II.** *v/t.* **1.** *oft im Passiv; Amtsspr.*: **die Rechtsabteilung wurde mit der Sache befasst** the matter was handed over to the legal department; **die mit Ihrem Fall befasste Dienststelle** the department dealing with your case

befehden *v/t.* **1.** *geh.* (*j-n*) (*bekämpfen*) attack; **sich** (*Pl.*) ~ be feuding, be having a feud; **2.** *hist.* (*e-e Stadt etc.*) feud with, have a feud with

Befehl *m; -(e)s, -e* **1.** *allg. und Mil.* order (**zu** to); **j-m e-n** ~ **geben** *od.* **erteilen** give s.o. an order, issue an order to s.o.; **e-n** ~ **ausführen** *od.* **befolgen** obey (*od.* carry out) an order; **e-n** ~ **verweigern** flout (*od.* refuse to obey) an order; **auf** ~ **des Generals** on the orders of (*od.* by order of) the general; **wie auf** ~ (*mechanisch*) like clockwork; (*als ob es so verabredet wäre*) as if on cue; **auf** ~ **handeln** act on orders; **auf höheren** ~ on orders from above; **bis auf weiteren** ~ until further orders; **den** ~ **haben, etw. zu tun** have (*od.* be under) orders to do s.th.; ~ **vom Chef!** boss's orders!; ~ **ist** ~**!** orders are orders; **zu** ~**!** yes, sir!; **dein Wunsch ist** *od.* **sei mir** ~ *umg. hum.* your wish is my command; **2.** *EDV* command, instruction; **3.** *nur Sg.* (*Befehlsgewalt*) command; **den** ~ **haben/übernehmen über** (+ *Akk.*) be in / take (*od.* assume) command of; **j-s** ~ **unterstellt sein** be under s.o.'s command

befehlen; *befiehlt, befahl, hat befohlen* **I.** *v/t.* **1.** order, give the order (*Mil. auch* command) for; **j-m etw.** ~ order s.o. to do s.th.; **von dir lasse ich mir nichts** ~ I won't be ordered about by you; **du hast hier nichts zu** ~ since when have you been giving orders around here?; **in** ~**dem Ton** in an imperious (*od.* a peremptory *od.* commanding) tone (of voice); **2.** *Mil.* → **befehligen**; **3.** (*beordern*) **j-n zu sich** (*Dat.*) ~ send for s.o.; **4.** *geh., altm.* (*anvertrauen*) commit, commend; **s-e Seele in Gottes Hand** ~ commend one's soul to God (*od.* into God's hands *Pl.*); **Gott befohlen!** God bless you!, God be with you!; **II.** *v/i.* give the orders; ~ **über** (+ *Akk.*) be in command of, have *s.o./s.th.* at (*od.* under) one's command; **er befiehlt gern** he likes to order (*od.* boss) people around; **wer** ~ **will, muss erst gehorchen lernen** *Sprichw.* he who will command must first learn to obey; **der Herr** ~**?** *altm.* your order, Sir?; **wie Sie** ~ *altm.* as you wish; **befehligen** *v/t. Mil.* command, be in command of; (*Armee etc.*) *auch* be commander-in-chief of

Befehls|ausgabe *f Mil.* issuing of orders, briefing; ~**bereich** *m* (area of) command; ~**empfänger** *m*, ~**empfängerin** *f* **1.** recipient of an order; **wer war der** ~**?** who received the order?; **2.** *fig.* apparatchik; ~**form** *f Gram.* imperative; ²**gemäß** *Adj.* as instructed; ~**gewalt** *f Mil.* command, authority; ~ **haben** be in command (**über** + *Akk.* of), have command (over); ~**haber** *m; -s, -* commander(-in-chief); ~**notstand** *m Jur.*: **unter** ~ **handeln** act under binding orders; ~**satz** *m Ling.* imperative clause; ~**sprache** *f EDV* command language; ~**ton** *m; nur Sg.* imperious (*od.* peremptory) tone (of voice); **im** ~ in an imperious tone; ~**verweigerung** *f* refusal to obey orders;

befehlswidrig **I.** *Adj.* contrary to orders; **II.** *Adv.* → I

befeinden *v/t. geh.* attack, be hostile towards; **die Parteien** ~ **sich offen** the parties are openly hostile to one another; **befeindet werden** be treated with hostility

befestigen *v/t.* **1.** (*festmachen*) fix (**an** + *Dat.* onto), attach (to); *mit Nadel etc.*: fasten ([on]to); *mit Klebstoff*: stick (onto); (*loses Brett etc.*) secure, make secure; **ein Boot an e-m Pfahl** ~ moor a boat to a post; **2.** (*haltbar machen*) (*Straße etc.*) surface; (*pflastern*) pave; (*Mauer, Deich etc.*) reinforce; (*Ufer*) protect; **3.** *fig.* (*Landesgrenze etc.*) secure; (*Herrschaft*) secure, consolidate; (*festigen*) (*Freundschaft etc.*) cement; **4.** *Mil.* fortify; **Befestigung** *f* **1.** *nur Sg.*; (*das Befestigen*) fixing, attaching, fastening; sticking; surfacing; *fig.* securing, consolidation; cementing; → **befestigen**; **2.** *Mil.* fortification; *von Ufer etc.*: reinforcement; **Befestigungsanlage** *f* fortifications *Pl.*, defen|ces (*Am.* -ses) *Pl.*

befeuchten *v/t.* moisten; (*Briefmarke*) (*lecken*) *auch* lick; (*nass machen*) wet; (*Bügelwäsche*) sprinkle, dampen; **Befeuchtung** *f* moistening; wetting; dampening; → **befeuchten**

befinden (*unreg.*) **I.** *v/refl.* **1.** *konkret*: be; *förm. Gebäude etc.*: *auch* be located; **neben der Kirche befand sich ein Gasthaus** next to the church was a restaurant; **er befindet sich im Ausland / auf Reisen** he's abroad / he's away (travel[l]ing); **das Bild befindet sich im Nationalmuseum** the painting is (to be found) in the National Museum; **2.** *in e-m Zustand*: **sich im Irrtum** ~ be mistaken; **die ganze Familie befand sich in heller Aufregung** the whole family was in a state of great excitement; **die beiden Länder** ~ **sich im Kriegszustand** the two countries are at war with each other; **sich in gutem Zustand** ~ be in good shape (*od.* condition); **3.** *geh., förm.* (*sich fühlen*) be, feel; **wie befindet er sich?** how is he?; **II.** *v/t. geh.* (*beurteilen, erachten*) consider; *förm.* judge; **etw. für gut/ richtig etc.** ~ consider (*od.* judge) s.th. to be good/right etc.; → **schuldig** I 1; **III.** *v/i.* **1.** (*entscheiden*) decide (**über** + *Akk.* on); **ich habe darüber nicht zu** ~ that's not for me to decide; **2.** (*urteilen, äußern*) conclude, judge; **Tod durch Erfrieren, befand der Arzt** death from exposure, was the doctor's verdict

Befinden *n; -s, kein Pl.* **1.** *gesundheitlich*: (state of) health; **wie ist sein** ~**?** how is he (feeling)?; **sie erkundigte sich nach deinem** ~ she was asking how you were (*od.* after your health); **2.** *geh.* (*Meinung, Urteil*): **nach m-m** ~ in my view (*od.* opinion *od.* judgement), as I see it

befindlich *Adj.* **1.** *an einem Ort*: **die im Museum** ~**en Skulpturen** the sculptures (contained) in the museum; **die im Hauptgebäude** ~**en Abteilungen** the departments (located *od.* to be found) in the main building; **2.** *in einem Zustand*: **die an der Macht** ~**e Partei** the party (currently) in power; **ein in Bearbeitung** ~**es Gesetz** a law currently being drafted (*od.* being drawn up); **Befindlichkeit** *f; nur Sg.; altm., geh.* state (of mind)

befingern *v/t. umg.* finger

beflaggen *v/t.* (*Gebäude*) decorate with flags, put flags out on, flag; (*Stra-*

B

ße) line with flags; *das Schiff* ~ dress ship; **beflaggt I.** *P.P.* → **beflaggen**; **II.** *Adj. Gebäude*: flagged; *Straße*: flag-lined; *Schiff*: (*bei festlichem Anlass*) fully dressed; *warum sind heute alle öffentlichen Gebäude beflaggt?* why are there flags flying on all public buildings today?; **Beflaggung** *f* 1. decorating (*od.* lining) with flags; 2. *konkret*: flags *Pl.*

beflecken *v/t.* 1. stain, soil; *mit Blut befleckt* bloodstained; *s-e Hände waren mit Farbe befleckt* he had paint (stains) on his hands; 2. *geh. fig.* (*Ehre, Ruf*) tarnish, sully

befleißigen *v/refl. geh.* take great pains (*zu* + *Inf.* to), endeavo(u)r (to); *sich etw.* (*Gen.*) ~ take care (*od.* pains) to (+ *Inf.*), strive for (*od.* after) s.th.; *sich größter Zurückhaltung* ~ take great pains to exercise as much restraint as possible

befliegen *v/t.* (*unreg.*) (*Strecke*) fly; *e-e stark beflogene Strecke* a busy (*od.* heavily flown) route; *diese Strecke wird nicht mehr beflogen* that route is no longer operated (*od.* served)

beflissen *Adj. geh.* assiduous, very keen; ~ *sein zu* (+ *Inf.*) (*od. sich* ~ *zeigen zu* [+ *Inf.*]) (always) be eager to (+ *Inf.*), take great pains to (+ *Inf.*); **Beflissenheit** *f*; *nur Sg.* assiduousness, assiduity, keenness

beflügeln *v/t.* (*j-n*) spur on, inspire; (*Fantasie*) fire; *lit.* give wing to; *j-s Schritte* ~ quicken s.o.'s pace; *lit.* lend wings to s.o.'s feet; *das Lob beflügelte ihn zu noch besseren Leistungen* the praise spurred him on to do even better

befohlen *P.P.* → **befehlen**

befolgen *v/t.* (*Rat, Befehl*) follow; (*Vorschrift*) *auch* observe, comply with; (*Grundsatz*) keep to, stick to; *förm.*: abide by; *nicht* ~ *auch* ignore; **Befolgung** *f*; *nur Sg.* following, compliance (+ *Gen.* with); observance (of)

befördern *v/t.* 1. transport, carry, take; *förm.* convey; (*verschicken*) send; *Wirts. auch* ship, forward; *die Post® befördert täglich 7 Millionen Sendungen* the postal service handles (*liefert*: delivers) 7 million items a day; *j-d an die frische Luft* ~ *hum.* show s.o. the door; → *Jenseits*, → *auch transportieren* I; 2. *im Rang etc.*: promote (*zu* to, to the position [*Mil.* rank] of); *wann wirst du befördert?* when is your promotion due (*od.* coming through)?; *er wurde zum Abteilungsleiter befördert* he was promoted to head of department

Beförderung *f* 1. *nur Sg.* transport(ation); *förm.*: conveyance; (*Verschickung*) sending; *Wirts. auch* shipping, forwarding; shipment; *die* ~ *der Passagiere zum Flughafen* the transfer of passengers to the airport; 2. *im Rang*: promotion (*zu* to, to the position [*Mil.* rank] of); 3. → *Förderung* 3

Beförderungs|art *f* mode of transport(ation) (*od.* conveyance); ~**aussichten** *Pl.* promotion prospects, chances (*od.* prospects) of promotion; ~**entgelt** *n Amtsspr.* fare; ~**mittel** *n* (means of) transport(ation); *öffentliche* ~ public transport *Sg.*; *förm.* means of public conveyance; ~**stopp** *m Wirts. etc.* promotion moratorium, moratorium on promotion

befrachtet *Adj.* loaded (*mit* with); *der Kurs war mit zu viel Theorie befrachtet* the seminar was overloaded with

theory

befrackt *Adj.* in tails, wearing tails

befragen *v/t.* 1. ask (*über* + *Akk.*, *nach, zu* about); (*ausfragen*) question (about); (*Zeugen*) question (about, on), examine; *auf Befragen* on being asked, when questioned; *j-d nach dem Verbleib e-s Gegenstandes* ~ question s.o. as to the whereabouts of an object; 2. (*konsultieren*) (*Experten, Arzt*) consult (*wegen, in* + *Dat.* about, on); (*Karten, Orakel, Sterne*) consult; *j-n nach s-r Meinung* ~ ask s.o.'s opinion; (*sich wenden an*) turn to; **Befragte** *m*, *f*; *-n, -n* person asked, interviewee; *Statistik*: respondent; *die* ~*n auch* those (*od.* the people) asked (*od.* interviewed); **Befragung** *f* questioning; (*Interview*) interview; *e-s Zeugen*: *auch* examination; *der Öffentlichkeit*: public opinion poll; *Pol.* referendum

befreien I. *v/t.* 1. free, set free (*auch Tier*), release (*aus* from); (*Land etc.*) liberate, free (*von* from); (*retten*) rescue (*aus* from); *j-n aus e-m Auto etc.* ~ get s.o. out of a car *etc.*; *mit großen Schwierigkeiten*: extricate s.o. from a car *etc.*; *etw. von s-r Verpackung* ~ unwrap s.th., unpack s.th., remove the wrapping from s.th.; 2. (*freistellen*) *behördlich*: exempt; *von Verbindlichkeiten, Haftpflicht*: *auch* release; *von e-r Pflicht*: relieve; *vom Unterricht*: excuse (*alle von* from); *vom Wehrdienst befreit sein* be exempt from military service; 3. (*erlösen*) *von Schmerzen, Last, Sorge*: relieve (*von* from); *von etw. Lästigem*: rid (of); *sie wird niemals von diesem Leiden befreit sein* she'll have to live with the illness *etc.* for the rest of her life; 4. *geh.* (*reinigen*) free (*von* of); *etw. vom Rost etc.* ~ take the rust *etc.* off s.th., get rid of the rust *etc.* on s.th.; *etw. von Schmutz*: ~ clean (the dirt *etc.* off) s.th., get rid of the dirt *etc.* on (*od.* in) s.th.; *die Parkwege vom Eis* ~ clear the ice from the paths in the park; *Pflanzen von Ungeziefer* ~ rid plants of pests; **II.** *v/refl.* free o.s. (*von* of); *aus Schwierigkeiten*: extricate o.s. (*aus* from); *von Tradition, Vorurteil*: *auch* get rid of, rid o.s. of

befreiend I. *Part. Präs.* → **befreien**; **II.** *Adj. fig.* liberating; ~*es Gelächter* laughter that breaks the tension

Befreier *m*; *-s, -,* ~**in** *f*; *-, -nen* liberator; (*Retter*) rescuer

befreit I. *P.P.* → **befreien**; **II.** *Adj.* (*erleichtert*) *Lachen*: relieved; ~ *aufatmen* give (*od.* breathe) a sigh of relief

Befreiung *f* 1. freeing, setting free, release; liberation; rescue (*alle*: *von* from); 2. exemption; (*von* from); 3. relief (*von* from); 4. ridding (of); → *befreien*

Befreiungs|aktion *f militärische etc.*: liberation campaign; ~**armee** *f* liberation army; ~**bewegung** *f* liberation movement; ~**front** *f* liberation front; ~**kampf** *m* fight for independence (*od.* liberation); ~**krieg** *m* war of independence (*od.* liberation); ~**schlag** *m* 1. *Sport Eishockey*: icing; *Fußball*: clearance; 2. *umg. fig.* coup; ~**theologe** *m*, ~**theologin** *f* liberation theologian; ~**theologie** *f* liberation theology; ~**versuch** *m* 1. rescue attempt; 2. attempt to escape, attempted flight (*od.* escape)

befremden *v/t.*: *j-n* ~ take s.o. aback; *seltsam*: *auch* strike s.o. as strange; *es hat mich befremdet auch* I found it

quite disconcerting; **Befremden** *n*; *-s, kein Pl.* astonishment (*über* + *Akk.* at); *ich habe mit* ~ *festgestellt, ...* I was (rather) disconcerted to discover ...; *ihr Verhalten erregte allgemeines* ~ everyone was taken aback by her behavio(u)r; **befremdend I.** *Part. Präs.* → **befremden**; **II.** *Adj.* → **befremdlich**; **befremdlich** *Adj. geh.* strange, queer, odd; (*unangenehm*) disconcerting; **Befremdung** *f* → **Befremden**

befreunden *v/refl.* 1. (*Freundschaft schließen*) make friends (*mit* with); *sich* (*miteinander*) ~ become friends; 2. (*gewöhnen*) *sich mit etw.* ~ get used (*od.* accustomed) to the idea of) s.th.; **befreundet I.** *P.P.* → **befreunden**; **II.** *Adj.*: (*miteinander*) ~ *sein* be friends; *wir sind mit ihnen* ~ they're friends of ours; *eng* ~ *sein* be good (*od.* close) friends; *ich bin mit ihr* ~ she's a friend (of mine), we're friends; *sind sie mit irgendwelchen Nachbarn* ~? are they friendly with any of the neighbo(u)rs?; ~*er Staat* friendly nation; *das* ~*e Ausland* friendly nations *Pl.*; *ein* ~*er Lehrer* a teacher friend of mine *etc.*; *zwei* ~*e Familien* two families on close terms

befrieden *v/t. geh.* (*Land*) bring peace to; **Befriedung** *f* establishment of peace (+ *Gen.* in)

befriedigen I. *v/t.* 1. (*Hunger, Ansprüche etc.*) *auch sexuell*: satisfy; (*j-n*) *auch* please; (*Wünsche, Neugierde etc.*) satisfy, gratify; (*Erwartungen*) satisfy, meet, come up to; (*Gläubiger*) pay off; *leicht/schwer zu* ~ *sein* be easily pleased / hard to please; 2. (*innerlich ausfüllen*) *Beruf*: fulfil(l); *die Arbeit befriedigte ihn nicht mehr* he no longer found his job fulfilling; 3. (*zufrieden stellend sein*) be satisfactory; *die Lösung befriedigt mich nicht* I'm not satisfied with the solution; **II.** *v/i. Leistung etc.*: be satisfactory; *Arbeit etc.*: give *s.o.* (enough) satisfaction, be fulfilling; **III.** *v/refl.*: *sich* (*selbst*) ~ *sexuell*: masturbate

befriedigend I. *Part. Präs.* → **befriedigen**; **II.** *Adj.* 1. *Lösung, Ergebnis etc.*: satisfactory; 2. *Schulnote*: C, pass; *in e-m Fach* „~" *haben/bekommen* have/ get a C (*od.* pass) in a subject

befriedigt I. *P.P.* → **befriedigen**; **II.** *Adj.* satisfied, pleased; **III.** *Adv.* with satisfaction; *er blickte* ~ *in den vollen Saal* he cast a satisfied look into the full hall

Befriedigung *f* 1. *auch Jur., Wirts. und sexuelle* satisfaction; *von Wünschen, Neugier etc.*: *auch* gratification; 2. (*Zufriedenheit*) satisfaction; *im Beruf*: *auch* fulfil(l)ment; *mit großer* ~ *sah er, wie...* it gave him great satisfaction to see ...

befristen *v/t.* set (*od.* place, put) a time limit on; *auf eine Woche* ~ limit to one week, set (*od.* place, put) a limit of one week on; **befristet I.** *P.P.* → **befristen**; **II.** *Adj.* 1. limited (in time); *Visum, Genehmigung*: restricted; *Arbeitsvertrag etc.*: fixed-term; *ein auf 3 Jahre* ~*er Mietvertrag* a three-year fixed-term lease (*od.* tenancy agreement); *das Handelsabkommen ist auf drei Jahre* ~ the trade agreement has a time limit of 3 years; 2. *Fin.*: *lang/ kurz* ~ with a long/short time limit on; ~*e Einlagen* time deposits; **III.** *Adv.* for a limited (*od.* fixed) period; **Befristung** *f* (setting of a) time limit

(*auf* + *Akk.* of *10 days etc.*)
befruchten *v/t.* **1.** (*Eizelle*) fertilize; (*weibliches Tier*) impregnate; (*Blüte*) pollinate; **künstlich ~** artificially inseminate; **2.** *fig.* (*anregen*) stimulate, be (very) fruitful for; **befruchtend** **I.** *Part. Präs.* → **befruchten**; **II.** *Adj. fig.* fruitful, stimulating; **III.** *Adv. fig.*: **sich ~ auswirken** (*od.* **~ wirken**) prove very fruitful (*auf* + *Akk.* for), have a stimulating effect (on); **Befruchtung** *f* **1.** fertilization, impregnation; *von Blüten*: pollination; **künstliche ~** artificial insemination; **2.** *fig.* stimulation; **gegenseitige ~** cross-fertilization

Befugnis *f*; -, -*se*; *auch Pl.* authority, power(s *Pl.*); *j-m* (*die*) **~ erteilen/entziehen** authorize s.o. / take away s.o's authority (*zu* + *Inf.* to + *Inf.*); **die ~ zu etw. haben** have the authority to do sth.; *s-e ~se überschreiten* act outside (*od.* go beyond) one's authority (*od.* powers); **befugt** *Adj.* authorized, entitled (*zu* + *Inf.* to + *Inf.*); **zur Unterschrift/Ausführung** etc. **~** authorized to sign / carry s.th. out etc.; *er ist dazu nicht ~* auch he has no authority (*od.* right) to do so

befühlen *v/t.* feel

befummeln *v/t. umg. pej.* **1.** (*Waren etc.*) finger, touch; **2.** *sexuell*: paw, feel up *Sl.*; *bes. unerlaubt*: touch up *Sl.*, *Am.* fondle *Sl.*

Befund *m*; (*e*)*s*, -*e* findings *Pl.*, *auch Med.* results *Pl.*; *e-n negativen/positiven ~ haben* be negative/positive; *ohne ~ Med.* negative

befürchten *v/t.* fear; (*erwarten*) *auch* expect; (*Angst haben vor*) be afraid of; (*den Verdacht haben*) fear, suspect; *wir ~ das Schlimmste* we're prepared for the worst; *es ist od. steht zu ~, dass* it is feared that; *weitere Anschläge sind od. stehen zu ~* there is a danger of further attacks; *... ist od. sind nicht zu ~* there's no danger (*od.* risk) of ...; *das ist nicht zu ~* there's no danger of that; *so etwas hatte ich* (*schon*) *befürchtet* I was afraid of something like this

Befürchtung *f* fear; (*Bedenken*) misgivings *Pl.*, apprehensions *Pl.*; *ich habe die ~, dass* I'm afraid that, I've got a funny feeling that *umg.*; *das übersteigt m-e schlimmsten ~en* it's far worse than I thought; *wir hatten schon die schlimmsten ~en* we've been fearing the worst; *ich habe* (*so*) *m-e ~en* I have certain apprehensions

befürworten *v/t.* (*unterstützen*) support, back; (*billigen*) endorse; **Befürworter** *m*; -*s*, -, **Befürworterin** *f*; -, -*nen* supporter (+ *Gen.* of), backer (of), advocate (of); believer (in); *ein entschiedener ~* a staunch supporter (*od.* advocate) (+ *Gen.* of); **Befürwortung** *f*; *nur Sg.* support, backing, endorsement; → **befürworten**

begabt *Adj.* talented, gifted; **~ sein für** have a gift for; *er ist handwerklich ~* he is good with his hands; *dafür bin ich nicht ~* that's not my strong point; *du bist mit genügend gesundem Menschenverstand ~* you are lucky enough to have plenty of common sense; → **vielseitig** II; **Begabte** *m*, *f*; -*n*, -*n* gifted person; **Begabtenförderung** *f* **1.** *finanziell*: scholarship system, (*provision of*) *scholarships for outstanding pupils or students*; **2.** *pädagogisch*: extra (*od.* specialized) tuition for gifted students (*od.* pupils *etc.*)

Begabung *f* **1.** gift, talent; *e-e hohe ~*

für etw. haben have a real talent for sth.; *es ist e-e ~ auch* he (*od.* she) was born with it; *sie hat e-e ~ zum Organisieren* she's got a talent for organizing things; **2.** *geh.* (*Person*) talent, (very) gifted person; *er ist e-e außergewöhnliche künstlerische ~* he is a person of outstanding artistic talents

begaffen *v/t. umg. pej.* gape (*od.* gawk *od.* gawp) at

begann *Imperf.* → **beginnen**

begatten **I.** *v/t. Zool.* mate (*od.* copulate) with; *geh.*, *hum.* mate with; **II.** *v/refl.* mate, copulate; **Begattung** *f* mating, copulation

begeben (*unreg.*) **I.** *v/refl. geh.* **1.** (*gehen*) make (*od.* wend) one's way; *sich nach Hause / auf den Heimweg ~* make one's way home / set off for home; *sich zu j-m ~* *auch* join s.o.; *sich an die Arbeit od. geh. ans Werk ~* set to work; *sich auf die Reise ~* set out (on one's journey); *sich in ärztliche Behandlung ~* seek medical treatment, see a doctor; *sich unter j-s Schutz od. Obhut ~* place o.s. under s.o.'s protection; *sich auf die Suche ~* set out on a search; *sich auf s-n Platz ~* take one's place; *sich in Lebensgefahr ~* put o.s. in danger; → *Gefahr*, *Ruhe* 4; **2.** *oft altm.* (*sich ereignen*) happen, occur; *es begab sich, dass ... lit.*, *bibl.* it came to pass that ...; **3.** *einer Sache*: forfeit, forgo; *bes. Jur.* (*e-s Anspruchs*, *Privilegs etc.*) waive, relinquish, renounce; **II.** *v/t. Wirts.* (*in Umlauf setzen*) (*Wertpapiere*) float, issue, launch

Begebenheit *f geh.* (*Ereignis*) occurrence, event; (*Vorfall*) incident; *dem Roman liegt e-e wahre ~ zugrunde* the novel is based on a true incident (*od.* on fact)

begegnen *v/i.* (*ist begegnet*) **1.** (*treffen*) meet, come across; *j-m/etw. ~* meet s.o./s.th., come across s.o./s.th.; *sich od. einander ~* meet; *ihre Blicke begegneten sich* their eyes met; **2.** (*stoßen auf*) meet with; (*Schwierigkeiten etc.*) meet with, come up against, have to face up to; *diesem Wort begegnen wir häufig in diesem Werk* this word occurs often (*od.* crops up often *umg.*) in this work; **3.** (*entgegentreten*) confront, face; (*abwehren*) counter; (*bekämpfen*) (*auch Krankheit*) fight; (*aufhalten*) check; *e-r Gefahr etc. mit Mut etc. ~* auch respond to a danger etc. with courage etc.; **4.** *geh.* (*behandeln*) treat, behave very coolly etc. towards; *j-m abweisend / mit Respekt ~* treat s.o.off-handedly / with respect; **5.** (*passieren*): *mir ist das schon einmal begegnet* it's happened to me before; *das Schlimmste, was dir ~ kann* the worst that can happen to you

Begegnung *f* **1.** meeting; *auch feindliche*: encounter; *ein Ort kultureller/internationaler ~* a place where cultures/nations meet; **2.** *Sport* match, meeting; **Begegnungsstätte** *f* meeting place, social cent|re (*Am.* -er)

begehbar *Adj.* **1.** *Weg etc.*: passable; *ist der Weg ~?* can you walk on (*od.* along) the path?; *der Weg ist schwer / nur selten ~* access to the path is difficult / only possible on occasion; *bei Glätte/Schnee nicht ~* impassable in icy/snowy conditions; **2.** *~er Schrank* walk-in cupboard (*Am.* closet)

begehen *v/t.* (*unreg.*) **1.** *geh.* (*feiern*) (*Geburtstag*) celebrate; (*Feiertag*) observe; **2.** (*Fehler*) make; (*Selbstmord*,

Verbrechen etc.) commit; *e-e Dummheit ~* do something stupid; *Verrat ~ an* (+ *Dat.*) betray *s.o./s.th.*; *e-n Mord an j-m ~* murder s.o.; *ein Unrecht ~* do something wrong; *ein häufig begangener Fehler* a common mistake; **3.** (*Weg*, etc.) walk on (*od.* along); *regelmäßig*: *auch* use; *besichtigend*: inspect; *ein viel begangener Fußweg* a well-used (foot)path

Begehr *m auch n*; -*s*, *kein Pl.*; *geh.*, *altm.* wish; *nach j-s ~ fragen* inquire about s.o.'s wish (*od.* wishes)

begehren *v/t.* **1.** *auch sexuell*: desire, want; *heftig*: crave for; *neidvoll*: long for; *du sollst nicht ~ ... bibl.* thou shalt not covet ...; *ein Mädchen zur Frau ~* *altm.* ask for a girl's hand in marriage; **2.** *geh.* (*verlangen*) demand; *er begehrte Einlass* he demanded entry; → *Herz*[1] 8; **Begehren** *n*; -*s*, -, *Pl.* selten; *geh.* desire; *auf mein ~* (*hin*) at my wish; → *Begehr*, **begehrenswert** *Adj.* desirable; **begehrlich** *Adj. Blicke etc.*: covetous; **Begehrlichkeit** *f* **1.** (*Neid*, *Besitzgier*) envy; **2.** (*Verlangen*) desire, longing; **begehrt** **I.** *P.P.* → **begehren**; **II.** *Adj.* (much) sought-after; *auch Lokal etc.*: (very) popular; *präd. auch* very much in demand; *Wagen*, *Theaterrolle*, *Trophäe etc.*: coveted; *Posten*: sought-after

Begehung *f* **1.** *nur Sg. e-s Fests*: celebration; *e-s Feiertags*: observance; **2.** *e-r Strecke*: inspection

begeistern **I.** *v/t.* fill with enthusiasm, inspire, enthuse; (*Publikum*) delight; *stärker*: enthrall (*durch od. mit* with); *j-n ~ für* get s.o. interested in (*stärker*: enthusiastic about); *Mexiko hat mich begeistert* I loved Mexico; *sie ist für nichts zu ~* you can't get her interested in anything; *das kann mich nicht ~* that doesn't interest me; *diese Nachricht begeistert mich nicht gerade euph.* (*entsetzt mich*) I'm not exactly thrilled about the news; **II.** *v/refl.*: *sich für etw. ~* get enthusiastic about s.th., show enthusiasm about s.th.; (*sehr interessiert sein an*) be very much interested in (*od.* very keen on) s.th., *Am.* be hot on s.th.; *ich kann mich dafür nicht ~* I can't work up any enthusiasm for it, it just doesn't appeal to me (*od.* grab me *umg.*)

begeisternd **I.** *Part. Präs.* → **begeistern**; **II.** *Adj. Rede*, *Aufführung*: inspiring; (*mitreißend*) rousing

begeistert **I.** *P.P.* → **begeistern**; **II.** *Adj.* **1.** *attr.* enthusiastic; *Sportler etc.*: keen; (*leidenschaftlich*) passionate; *ein ~er Jazzanhänger* a great jazz fan etc.; **2.** *präd.*: *~ sein* be enthusiastic; *er war ~ von dem Plan/Konzert* he was all for (*od.* very enthusiastic about) the plan / he thought the concert was marvel(l)ous; *sie waren ~* they were quite taken (*von* with); *ich bin total ~!* *umg.* I think it's great (*od.* marvel[l]ous); **III.** *Adv.* enthusiastically, with (great) enthusiasm; *~ aufnehmen Person*: give a warm (*stärker*: rapturous) welcome to; *Sache*: take on board enthusiastically *umg.*; *~ mitmachen* join in wholeheartedly

...begeistert *im Adj.* ...-mad, ...-crazy *umg.*; *präd.* mad about ..., crazy about ... *umg.*; *sie ist total sport~* she's really keen on sports, she's absolutely sports-crazy, *Am.* she's really hot on sports

Begeisterung *f* enthusiasm (*für* for, about); *mit ~* enthusiastically, with

B

(great) enthusiasm; *in* (*große od. helle*) ~ *geraten* get all enthusiastic (*od.* excited) (*über + Akk.* about); *beim Reden*: go into raptures (about); *ohne* (*rechte*) ~ without much enthusiasm, halfheartedly; *e-n Sturm der ~ entfesseln* unleash a storm of enthusiasm

begeisterungsfähig *Adj. Publikum*: easy to carry along; *er ist sehr/nicht ~* he can get very enthusiastic about things / you can't get him excited about anything; **Begeisterungsfähigkeit** *f; nur Sg.* ability to get enthusiastic

Begeisterungs|sturm *m* storm of enthusiasm; **Begeisterungsstürme** (*Applaus*) storms of applause, rapturous applause *Sg.*; **~taumel** *m* frenzy of enthusiasm

Begierde *f; -, -n* desire, appetite (*nach* for); *fleischliche*: desire, lust; *fleischliche ~n* desires of the flesh; **begierig I.** *Adj. Person*: eager (*nach* for); *pej.* greedy (for); *Blicke etc.*: greedy; (*lüstern*) lustful; *ich bin ~ zu erfahren etc.* I am eager (*od.* keen) to find out etc.; *~ auf etw.* (*Akk.*) *sein* be eager for s.th.; **II.** *Adv.* eagerly; *~ lauschen* listen intently (+ *Dat.* to)

begießen *v/t.* (*unreg.*) **1.** pour water etc. over (*od.* on); (*Blumen*) water; (*Braten*) baste; **2.** *umg.* (*mit Alkohol feiern*) drink to, celebrate (with a drink); *das muss begossen werden auch* that calls for a drink

Beginn *m; -(e)s, kein Pl.* beginning, start; *förm.* commencement; *zu ~ auch* at the outset; *seit ~* since the beginning (+ *Gen.* of); *bei od. zu Beginn der Konferenz* at the start of the conference; *gleich zu ~* right at the outset; *mit ~* (+ *Gen.*) at the start of, when ... starts (*od.* begins); *~ der Vorstellung*: *20 Uhr* performance starts at 8 pm; → *auch Anfang*

beginnen; *beginnt, begann, hat begonnen* **I.** *v/i.* begin, start; *förm.* commence; *berufliche Laufbahn*: begin; *mit der Arbeit etc.* ~ start work etc., get down to work etc.; *die Rede begann mit ...* the speech started off with ..., he etc. opened the speech with ...; *die Firma hat ganz bescheiden begonnen* the company started in a small way; *das Auto beginnt zu rosten* the car is starting to rust; *der Prozess begann mit einer persönlichen Erklärung* the trial commenced with a personal statement; **II.** *v/t.* **1.** (*anfangen*) (*Gespräch, Studium etc.*) begin; *förm.* commence; *ein Arbeitsverhältnis ~* commence employment; **2.** *geh.* (*tun*) do; *sie wusste nicht, was sie mit ihrer Zeit ~ sollte* she didn't know what to do with her time; → *auch anfangen I, II*

beginnend I. *Part. Präs.* → *beginnen*; **II.** *Adj. förm.* incipient; *im ~en 20. Jahrhundert* at the beginning of (*od.* in the opening years of) the 20th century; *bei ~er Dunkelheit* as it gets dark; *mit ~em Frühling* at the start of spring; *e-e ~e Grippe* the beginnings of flu; *der ~e Schneefall etc.* the first of the snow *etc.*

beglaubigen *v/t.* **1.** (*bescheinigen*) certify; *etw. notariell ~ lassen* have s.th. notarized; **2.** (*Diplomaten*) accredit (*bei* to); **beglaubigt I.** *P.P.* → *beglaubigen*; **II.** *Adj.* **1.** *Unterschrift etc.*: certified; *~e Abschrift* certified copy; *als Vermerk*: true copy; **2.** *Diplomat*: accredited; **Beglaubigung** *f* **1.** certifica-

tion; **2.** *e-s Gesandten*: accreditation; **Beglaubigungsschreiben** *n* credentials *Pl.*

begleichen *v/t.* (*unreg.*) **1.** (*Rechnung, Zeche etc.*) pay, settle; **2.** *geh. fig.*: *e-e Schuld ~* pay (back) a debt; **Begleichung** *f* **1.** *von Rechnung*: settlement, payment; *zur ~ Ihrer Rechnung* in settlement of your invoice; **2.** *geh. fig. e-r Schuld*: payment *of a debt*

Begleit|brief *m* covering (*Am.* cover) letter, advice-note; **~buch** *n, zu e-r Fernsehsendung*: TV tie-in; *zu e-m Kurs etc.*: book (*od.* accompanying) book; **~dokumente** *Pl.* accompanying documents

begleiten *v/t.* **1.** *allg.*: accompany; *zu Fuß auch*: walk along with; *j-n zur od. an die Bahn ~* see s.o. off at the station; *j-n zu e-m Konzert ~* go to a concert with s.o.; *als derjenige, der einlädt*: take s.o. to a concert; *j-n nach Hause ~* take (*od.* walk) s.o. home; (*schützend geleiten*) *auch Mil., Naut., Mot.* escort; **2.** *Mus.* accompany (*auf + Dat. od. am* on); **3.** *Sache, Umstände*: accompany, attend; *begleitet von* accompanied by; (*Gefahren etc.*) fraught with; *von Erfolg begleitet* very successful; *die Expedition war vom Unglück begleitet* the expedition was attended (*od.* plagued) by bad luck; *m-e besten Wünsche ~ dich* my best wishes go with you

begleitend I. *Part. Präs.* → *begleiten*; **II.** *Adj. Worte etc.*: accompanying; *Umstände*: attendant

Begleiter *m; -s, -,* **~in** *f; -, -nen* **1.** companion; *dienstlicher*: attendant (+ *Gen.* to, of); (*Begleitperson*) *auch zum Schutz*: escort; **2.** *Mus.* accompanist; → *ständig I*

Begleit|erscheinung *f* concomitant; *Med.* side effect; *es ist e-e ~ von* (*od.* + *Gen.*) *auch* it goes with; *das sind so die ~en des Alters umg.* they're all signs of old age, it's all part (and parcel) of growing old; **~fahrzeug** *n* escort vehicle; **~instrument** *n Mus.* accompanying instrument; **~material** *n* backup (*od.* accompanying) material(s *Pl.*); **~musik** *f* incidental (*od.* background) music; *fig.* accompaniment; **~papiere** *Pl.* accompanying documents; **~person** *f* escort; **~schein** *m Wirts.* dispatch note, waybill; **~schreiben** *n* covering (*Am.* cover) letter; **~schutz** *m* escort; **~symptom** *n bes. Med.* accompanying symptom; **~text** *m* accompanying text; **~umstand** *m*; *mst Pl.* surrounding (*od.* attendant) circumstances

Begleitung *f* **1.** *nur Sg.*; (*auch das Begleiten*) company; *Kinder nur in ~ Erwachsener od. von Erwachsenen* children must be accompanied by adults; *in ~ e-r Frau* in female company, with a woman; **2.** (*Begleiter*) escort; *e-s Prominenten etc.*: entourage; *schützende*: escort; *ohne ~* alone, unaccompanied; *in ~ sein* be with someone; *sie geht nur in ~ aus* she never goes out without a companion; *ich komme nur zur od. als ~ mit* I'll just come to keep you company; *sind Sie allein oder in ~?* are you alone or with someone?; **3.** *Mus.* accompaniment; *ohne ~ singen* sing unaccompanied; *Chor*: sing a cappella

Begleitzettel *m* accompanying note; *Wirts.* dispatch note

beglücken *v/t.*: *j-n ~* make s.o. happy; *bes. iro.* delight s.o.; *sie hat uns mit*

ihrer Anwesenheit beglückt iro. she hono(u)red us with her presence; **beglückend I.** *Part. Präs.* → *beglücken*; **II.** *Adj.* heartening; *stärker*: exhilarating; **beglückt I.** *P.P.* → *beglücken*; **II.** *Adj.* (very) happy (*über + Akk.* about), thrilled (with) *umg.*; *~es Lächeln* blissful smile; **Beglückung** *f* **1.** (*das Beglücken*) making s.o. happy; **2.** (*Glück*) (deep) happiness, bliss

beglückwünschen *v/t.* congratulate (*zu* on); *förm.* felicitate (*zu* on)

begnadet *Adj. Künstler etc.*: exceptionally (*od.* highly) gifted; *~ sein mit* be endowed (*od.* favo(u)red) with, have the extraordinary gift of *being able to ...*; *e-e ~e Stimme haben* have an exceptional voice

begnadigen *v/t.* pardon, reprieve; (*amnestieren*) grant an amnesty to, amnesty; *e-n zum Tode Verurteilten zu lebenslänglicher Haft ~* give someone condemned to death a commuted life sentence; **Begnadigung** *f* pardon; *Pol.* amnesty; *~ durch den Präsidenten USA*: executive clemency

Begnadigungs|gesuch *n* petition for pardon; **~recht** *n* right of pardon, prerogative of mercy

begnügen *v/refl.* (*sich mit etw. zufrieden geben*) *sich mit etw. ~* make do with s.th., be satisfied (*od.* content) with s.th., content o.s. with s.th.; *sich damit ~, etw. zu tun* be content with doing s.th.; *ich möchte mich damit ~ zu bemerken, dass ...* I will merely point out that ...

Begonie *f; -, -n; Bot.* begonia

begonnen *P.P.* → *beginnen*

begossen I. *P.P.* → *begießen*; **II.** *Adj.* → *Pudel 1*

begraben *v/t.* (*unreg.*) **1.** (*Tote*) bury; *förm.* (*bestatten*) inter; *da möchte ich nicht ~ sein umg.* I wouldn't live there if you paid me; → *Hund* 8; **2.** *fig.* (*Hoffnungen*) bury; (*Pläne etc.*) give up, abandon; *das Kriegsbeil ~ fig.* bury the hatchet; **3.** (*verschütten*) bury, engulf; *die Lawine begrub ein ganzes Dorf unter sich* the avalanche buried (*od.* engulfed) a whole village

Begräbnis *n; -ses, -se* burial; *feierlich*: *auch* funeral; **~feier** *f*, **~feierlichkeiten** *Pl.* funeral (ceremony) *Sg.*; *förm.* obsequies; **~kosten** *Pl.* funeral expenses; **~stätte** *f* place of burial; *archäologische*: *auch* burial site

begradigen *v/t.* straighten, (*Flusslauf etc.*) regulate; *fig.* (*Missverständnis etc.*) straighten out; **Begradigung** *f* straightening; *von Flusslauf*: regulation; *fig. von Missverständnis*: straightening out

begrapschen *v/t. pej.* → *befummeln*

begreifbar *Adj.* comprehensible; *schwer ~ sein* be difficult to understand

begreifen (*unreg.*) **I.** *v/t.* **1.** understand; *intellektuell*: *auch* grasp; (*Metaphysisches etc.*) *auch* apprehend; *hast du das endlich begriffen?* have you got that into your head?; *begreif doch endlich, was hier gespielt wird!* just try to understand what's going on here!; *ich begann zu ~, dass ...* I began to realize that ...; *es ist kaum zu ~* it's almost incomprehensible; **2.** (*ansehen*) see, view (*als* as); **3.** *geh., altm.* (*einschließen*): *etw. in sich* (*Dat.*) ~ include s.th.; **II.** *v/i.* understand, catch on *umg.*; *schnell/langsam ~* be quick/slow on the uptake; **III.** *v/refl.*: *sich ~ als* see o.s. as

begreiflich *Adj.* understandable; *leicht/schwer* ~ easy/hard to understand; *j-m etw.* ~ *machen* make s.th. clear to s.o.; *es ist mir nicht* ~, *wie ...* I don't understand (*od.* see) how; *es wird mir allmählich* ~, *wie ...* I'm beginning to see how; *so etwas ist mir einfach nicht* ~ (*dafür fehlt mir jedes Verständnis*) I just can't understand that; **begreiflicherweise** *Adv.* understandably (enough), naturally

begrenzbar *Adj.* limitable; *ist es* ~? can it be limited?

begrenzen *v/t.* **1.** *Grundstück etc.*: mark off; (*die Grenze bilden von*) form the boundary of; *der Sportplatz wird von Linien begrenzt* the playing-field is bounded by lines; **2.** *fig. Geschwindigkeit, Risiko, Schaden etc.*: limit, restrict (*auf + Akk.* to); *die Redezeit auf zehn Minuten* ~ restrict speakers to ten minutes

begrenzt I. *P.P.* → *begrenzen*; **II.** *Adj.* restricted; *auch Möglichkeiten, Verstand etc.*: limited; *eng od. genau* ~ *Aufgabe, Bedeutung etc.*: clearly defined; *es ist zeitlich nicht* ~ there's no time limit (on it), it's open-ended; *e-e zeitlich* ~*e Aufenthaltsgenehmigung* a visa with limited validity; *wir sind hier räumlich recht* ~ we haven't got much room here; **III.** *Adv.* to a certain extent; *zeitlich*: for a limited period; ~ *verfügbar sein Waren*: be available in limited supply; *von Person*: only be available at certain times; ~ *haltbar sein* be perishable; **Begrenztheit** *f der Möglichkeiten, des Verstands etc.*: limitations *Pl.* (+ *Gen* of); (*Engstirnigkeit*) narrowness, narrow-mindedness

Begrenzung *f* **1.** (*Grenze*) *e-s Grundstücks etc.*: boundary, perimeter; (*das Begrenzen*) demarcation; **2.** *fig.* (*Einschränkung, auch das Begrenzen*) restriction; *auch zeitlich*: limitation

Begriff *m*; -(e)s, -e **1.** (*Vorstellung, Auffassung*) idea, concept, notion; *sich* (*Dat.*) *e-n* ~ *machen von* form (*od.* get) an idea of; (*sich vorstellen*) imagine; *du machst dir keinen* ~ (*davon*)! you have no idea; *das geht über m-e* ~*e* that's beyond me; *über alle* ~*e schön etc.* beautiful *etc.* beyond words; *für m-e* ~*e* (*wie ich es verstehe*) as I see it, if you ask me; (*für m-e Verhältnisse*) for me, as far as I'm concerned; *nach heutigen* ~*en* in today's thinking; *schwer od. langsam von* ~ *umg.* slow on the uptake, a bit dense *umg.*; **2.** (*Ausdruck*) term; *weitS.* expression; *fester* ~ common expression; *alltäglicher*: household word; **3.** (*bekannte Ware, Person etc.*) household name; *ein* ~ *in der Modewelt etc.* a big name in fashion *etc.*; *ist dir das ein* ~? does that mean anything to you?; *Peter Wolf? Ist mir kein* ~ Peter Wolf? Never heard of him; **4.** *im* ~ *sein od. geh. stehen, etw. zu tun* be about to do s.th., be on the point of doing s.th.

begriffen I. *P.P.* → *begreifen*; **II.** *Adj.*: *in etw.* (*Dat.*) ~ *sein* be in the process of (doing) s.th.; *im Aufbruch* ~ about to leave; *im Entstehen* ~ *sein* be forming; *e-e im Entstehen* ~*e Organisation* an organization that is just forming; *förm.* a nascent organization

begrifflich I. *Adj.* conceptual; (*nicht wirklich*) notional; ~*es Denken* thinking in concepts, abstract thinking; **II.** *Adv.*: ~ *erfassen* conceptualize; *etw.* ~ *verständlich machen* make s.th. conceptually clear

Begriffs|bestimmung *f* definition; *e-e* ~ *vornehmen* define; ~**bildung** *f; nur Sg.* conception, forming of concepts

begriffsstutzig *Adj. pej.* dense, dull, slow-witted, slow (on the uptake); **Begriffsstutzigkeit** *f; nur Sg.; pej.* denseness, obtuseness, slowness

Begriffs|system *n* system of concepts; ~**vermögen** *n* grasp, capacity to understand; *über j-s* ~ *hinausgehen* be beyond s.o.'s grasp

begründen I. *v/t.* **1.** (*Behauptung etc.*) give reasons for, explain; (*rechtfertigen*) justify, back up; (*Handlung*) explain; *wie od. womit begründest du d-n Entschluss?* how do you explain your decision?; *er begründete es damit, dass ...* he explained (*od.* justified) it by the fact that ...; *durch nichts zu* ~ completely unfounded (*od.* unjustified); *etw. näher* ~ explain s.th. in more detail; *ein Urteil* ~ *Jur.* give the reasons for a verdict; **2.** (*gründen*) found, establish; (*Geschäft etc.*) *mst* set up; *fig.* (*j-s Ruf etc.*) establish; (*j-s Glück etc.*) lay the foundations for (*od.* of); (*Haushalt*) set up; **II.** *v/refl.* be explained; *wie begründet sich seine Forderung?* what is the reason for his claim?

Begründer *m*; -s, -, ~**in** *f*; -, -*nen* founder

begründet I. *P.P.* → *begründen*; **II.** *Adj.* (*gerechtfertigt*) valid, justified; (*auch wohl* ~) well-founded; *Verdacht, Zweifel*: reasonable; *nicht* ~ unfounded, unjustified, groundless; ~*er Einwand* reasonable (*od.* valid) objection; *ein sachlich* ~*er Einwand* an objection with a clear factual basis; *es besteht* ~*e Hoffnung, dass ...* there is cause for hope that; *in e-r Sache* ~ *liegen od. sein* go back to, have a (root) cause; *das ist in der Natur der Sache* ~ that arises from (*od.* comes from) the nature of the thing

Begründung *f* **1.** (*Motivierung*) reason(s *Pl.*); (*Erklärung*) explanation; (*Argument*) argument; (*Rechtfertigung*) justification; *mit der* ~, *dass* on the grounds that; *ohne jede* ~ *tun*: without giving any reasons (*od.* explanation); *als od. zur* ~ by way of explanation, as an explanation (*od.* justification) (+ *Gen. od. für od.* for); **2.** (*Gründung*) founding, establishment; *von Geschäft etc.*: setting up; **Begründungssatz** *m Ling.* causal clause

begrünen I. *v/t.* plant with grass (*od.* trees, bushes *etc.*), plant over *s.th.*; **II.** *v/refl. geh.* turn green; **begrünt I.** *P.P.* → *begrünen*; **II.** *Adj.* green; *engS.* planted with grass (*od.* trees, bushes *etc.*); ~*e Flächen* green areas (*od.* spaces); **Begrünung** *f; nur Sg.* **1.** (*das Begrünen*) planting of grass (*od.* trees *etc.*); **2.** (*Pflanzen, Wiese etc.*) greenery

begrüßen *v/t.* **1.** greet; (*Gast*) *förm.* receive; *als Gastgeber, auch freudig*: welcome; *gespreizt*: *ich begrüße Sie* I bid you welcome; *wir wurden herzlich begrüßt* we were given a warm welcome; *in Prospekten*: *wir würden uns freuen, Sie bald in unserem Haus* ~ *zu dürfen* we look forward to receiving (*od.* welcoming) you in our house; *begrüße unsere Gäste!* say hello to our guests; **2.** *fig.* (*positiv aufnehmen*) welcome; *das wäre zu* ~ that would be very welcome, that would be a welcome development (*od.* improvement *etc.*); *es ist*

zu ~, *dass* we (*od.* I) welcome the fact that, we are (*od.* I am) pleased to see that; *ich würde es* ~, *wenn* I'd be very pleased if; **begrüßenswert** *Adj.* welcome; *deine Haltung ist* ~ I'm glad you're taking that attitude

Begrüßung *f* welcoming, greeting; *Veranstaltung*: welcome; *förm.* reception; *zur* ~ *gab es ein Glas Sekt* on arrival we were offered a glass of champagne; *zur* ~ *gab sie mir die Hand* she shook my hand in welcome; → *begrüßen*

Begrüßungs|ansprache *f* welcoming speech; ~**geld** *n hist.* sum of money given to residents of former East Germany who visited former West Germany before the two Germanies reunified in 1990; ~**schluck** *m umg.*, ~**trunk** *m* welcoming drink; ~**worte** *Pl.* words of welcome

begucken *umg.* **I.** *v/t.* have a good look at; **II.** *v/refl. auch* eye o.s. *in the mirror etc.*

begünstigen *v/t.* **1.** (*bevorzugen*) favo(u)r; *vom Schicksal begünstigt* favo(u)red by fate; *e-e vom Klima begünstigte Gegend* a region with a favo(u)rable climate; **2.** (*positiv beeinflussen*) help (along), further; *das begünstigt unsere Pläne* this makes our plans more likely to succeed; **3.** *Jur.*: *ein Verbrechen* ~ be guilty of aiding and abetting a crime; **Begünstigte** *m, f; -n, -n; Jur.* beneficiary; **Begünstigung** *f* **1.** (*Bevorzugung*) preferential treatment, favo(u)ritism; **2.** (*Förderung*) furtherance; **3.** *Jur.* aiding and abetting; *j-n wegen* ~ *verurteilen* sentence s.o. for aiding and abetting

begutachten *v/t.* **1.** give an (expert's) opinion on; (*prüfen, besichtigen*) examine; (*Schaden etc.*) assess; *etw.* ~ *lassen* get an expert's opinion on s.th., get an assessment of s.th., get the experts to have a look at s.th. *umg.*; **2.** *umg., mst hum.* (*anschauen*) have a (close) look at; *genau*: scrutinize; **Begutachtung** *f* **1.** (*das Begutachten*) examination; (*Bewertung*) appraisal; **2.** *selten* → *Gutachten*

begütert *Adj.* **1.** (*vermögend*) wealthy, well-to-do, well-off; **2.** *altm.* (*Land besitzend*) landed; ~ *sein* own land

begütigend I. *Adj. Worte*: calming, soothing; **II.** *Adv.*: ~ *auf j-n einreden/einwirken* speak soothingly to s.o. / calm s.o. down

behaart *Adj.* hairy; *förm.* hirsute; *stark* ~ covered in hair, very hairy; **Behaarung** *f* hair(s) (+ *Gen.* of, on)

behäbig I. *Adj.* **1.** *Wesensart*: sedate; (*phlegmatisch*) phlegmatic; *Gestalt*: portly; **2.** *schw.* well to do; **II.** *Adv.* sedately; phlegmatically; **Behäbigkeit** *f; nur Sg.* sedateness; (*Phlegma*) phlegmatic nature; *von Gestalt*: portliness

behaftet *Adj.*: *mit Fehlern* ~ flawed; *mit Problemen* ~ fraught with problems; *ein mit negativen Assoziationen* ~*er Begriff* a negatively loaded term; *mit e-m negativen Beigeschmack* ~ marred by (*od.* tainted with) negative associations; *mit e-m Makel* ~ *sein* be tainted; *stärker*: bear a stigma; *mit e-r Krankheit* ~ *sein* suffer from an illness, be afflicted with a disease; *mit Schuldgefühlen* ~ guilt-ridden; *mit e-m unangenehmen Geruch etc.* ~ *sein* have an unpleasant smell *etc.* about it

behagen I. *v/i.* (*j-m*) suit; *das behagt mir* I feel comfortable with it; *diese*

Leute **~** *mir nicht* I don't like these people; *das behagt mir ganz und gar nicht* I don't like it one bit; **II. Behagen** *n*; *-s*, *kein Pl.* comfort, ease; (*Vergnügen*) pleasure; *stärker*: relish; (*Zufriedenheit*) contentment; *mit od. voll Behagen essen/zuhören etc.* eat/listen with relish

behaglich I. *Adj.* comfortable; (*heimelig*) cosy (*Am.* cozy), homely, *Am.* homey; (*zufrieden*) contented *smile etc.*; *es j-m/sich* (*Dat.*) **~** *machen* make s.o./o.s. comfortable; **II.** *Adv.* comfortably; (*zufrieden*) contentedly; (*genießerisch*) appreciatively, with enjoyment; **Behaglichkeit** *f*; *nur Sg.*; (*Atmosphäre*) comfort; (*Heimeligkeit*) cosiness (*Am.* coziness), homeliness, *Am.* homeyness

behalten *v/t.* (*unreg.*) **1.** (*festhalten, nicht hergeben*) keep; *darf ich das Buch* **~?** may I keep the book?; **2.** *weiterhin, bes. trotz Schwierigkeiten*: *auch* hold onto; *Recht* **~** be right (in the end); *er hat s-n Humor* **~** he hasn't lost his sense of humo(u)r; *s-e gute Laune* **~** keep up one's good spirits; *die Nerven* **~** keep cool; → *Auge* 2; **3.** *j-n* **~** keep s.o.; (*Angestellte weiterbeschäftigen*) keep s.o. on; *Freunde über Nacht bei sich* **~** have friends stay overnight; **4.** (*am selben Ort lassen*) keep; *den Schirm in der Hand* **~** keep hold of one's umbrella; *die Hände in den Hosentaschen* **~** keep one's hands in one's pockets; *etw. bei sich* (*Dat.*) **~** (*Nahrung*) keep s.th. down; **5.** (*aufrechterhalten*) *auch* maintain; (*Wert*) retain; *s-e Gültigkeit* **~** keep its value; *die Übersicht* **~** keep an overview of; **6.** (*nicht loswerden*) be left with; *die Narbe wird er den Rest s-s Lebens* **~** he'll have the scar for the rest of his life; **7.** *im Gedächtnis*: remember; *Math.* (*e-e Zahl*) carry; *ich kann keine Namen* **~** I'm no good at remembering names; *etw. für sich* **~** (*Geheimnis etc.*) keep s.th. to o.s.; *behalt das für dich!* *auch* keep that under your hat *umg.*; *er kann nichts für sich* **~** *auch* he's a blabbermouth *umg.*; *d-e blöden Kommentare kannst du für dich* **~** *umg.* you may keep your silly remarks to yourself; *in guter Erinnerung* **~** have good memories of

Behälter *m*; *-s*, *-* container; *förm.* receptacle; (*Schachtel, Karton etc.*) box; *für Flüssigkeit*: tank; *hast du dafür e-n* **~?** have you got something to put it in?

Behältnis *n*; *-ses*, *-se* container; *geh.* receptacle

behämmert *Adj. Sl.* nuts, potty, batty, crazy; *Sache*: dumb; *du bist ja total* **~** you are completely crazy

behände *Adj.* (*flink*) nimble; *auch geistig*: agile; (*gewandt*) dext(e)rous; **Behändigkeit** *f*; *nur Sg.* agility; (*Gewandtheit*) dexterity

behandeln *v/t.* **1.** (*Person*) treat; (*schwierige Person etc.*) handle; *j-n von oben herab* **~** treat s.o. condescendingly; **2.** (*handhaben*) (*Maschine etc.*) handle; *e-e Maschine fachmännisch* **~** handle a machine like an expert; **3.** (*bearbeiten*) (*Material etc.*) treat (*mit* with); **4.** (*Thema, Problem, Frage etc.*) treat, deal with; *in der Schule etc.*: go through, do *umg.*; *e-e Sache vertraulich* **~** treat s.th. in confidence, treat s.th. as confidential; *e-n Antrag bevorzugt* **~** give priority to an application; **5.** (*Kranke, Krankheit*)

treat; *sich* (*ärztlich*) **~** *lassen* get (medical) treatment (*gegen, auf* + *Akk.* for); *e-e Wunde mit etw.* **~** treat a wound with s.th., put s.th. on a wound; *j-n homöopathisch/medikamentös* **~** give s.o. hom(o)eopathic/medical treatment; *ambulant/stationär behandelt werden* get out-patient treatment / treatment in (a) hospital; *der* **~***de Arzt* the doctor responsible for the treatment; *wer ist der* **~***de Arzt?* which doctor is treating you (*od.* him *etc.*)?

Behandlung *f allg.* treatment; (*Handhabung*) handling; *bei sachgerechter* **~** ... *auf Garantieschein*: if used as instructed ...; *in* (*ärztlicher*) **~** *sein* be receiving medical treatment, be under medical treatment; *sich in ärztliche* **~** *begeben* seek medical treatment

Behandlungs|kosten *Pl. Med.* treatment (*od.* medical) costs, cost *Sg.* of treatment; **~raum** *m* surgery, consulting room, *Am.* examining room; *im Krankenhaus*: treatment room; **~stuhl** *m* doctor's chair; **~zimmer** *n* surgery, consulting room, *Am.* (doctor's) office

behandschuht *Adj. Hand*: with a glove on

Behang *m*; *-(e)s, Behänge* **1.** (*Wandbehang*) hangings *Pl.*; *schmückender*: decoration(s *Pl.*); **2.** *am Weihnachtsbaum*: tree decorations

behangen *Adj. Baum etc.*: laden (*mit* with); *Christbaum*: *auch* decorated, decked (with); *mit Blumen etc.*: decorated (with); *lit.* bedecked (with); *mit Schmuck*: decorated (with)

behängen *v/t.* hang, drape (*mit* with); (*schmücken*) decorate (*mit* with); *sich mit etw.* **~** *umg. pej.* drape o.s. with (*od.* cover o.s. in) s.th.

beharren *v/i.*: *auf etw.* (*Dat.*) **~** insist on (*od.* stick to) s.th.; *darauf* **~**, *dass* insist that

beharrlich I. *Adj.* (*ausdauernd*) persevering; *Fleiß etc.*: *auch* determined, dogged; (*unerschütterlich*) steadfast, unwavering; (*hartnäckig*) persistent; *mit Fragen etc.*: *auch* importunate; (*uneinsichtig*) stubborn; **II.** *Adv.*: **~** *dabei bleiben od.* **~** *darauf bestehen, dass* insist that; *er bleibt* **~** *dabei, dass* auch he will insist that; *sich* **~** *weigern* doggedly (*od.* stubbornly) refuse; **~** *schweigen* refuse to speak (*od.* say anything), maintain a determined silence; **Beharrlichkeit** *f*; *nur Sg.* perseverance; *von Fleiß etc.*: doggedness, tenacity; (*Sturheit*) stubbornness; → *beharrlich* I

Beharrungsvermögen *n* **1.** (*Ausdauer*) stamina; **2.** *Phys.* (*Trägheit*) inertia

behaucht *Adj. Ling. Laut*: aspirated

behauen *v/t.* (*Holz, Stein*) hew; *roh* **~** roughly hewn

behaupten I. *v/t.* **1.** claim, maintain, say; (*in e-r Diskussion*) argue; *förm.* assert, allege; *er behauptet zu wissen, ...* he claims to know, ..., he maintains (*od.* says) that he knows ...; *j-m gegenüber* **~**, *dass* tell s.o. that; *steif und fest* **~**, *dass* insist (*od.* swear) that; *Sie wollen also tatsächlich* **~**, *dass ...* are you trying to tell me that ...?, do you (actually) mean to say that ...?; *das kann man nicht gerade* **~** you can't exactly say that; *es wird von ihm behauptet, dass ...* he is said to (+ *Inf.*), it is said (*od.* they say) that he ...; *ich will nicht* **~**, *dass ...* I'm not arguing that ...; **2.** (*erfolgreich verteidigen*) defend; (*Meinung*) maintain;

s-n Platz **~** maintain one's position; *das Feld* **~** stand one's ground; **II.** *v/refl.* **1.** assert o.s.; *gegenüber Widerständen*: *auch* hold one's own, stand one's ground; *bes. Mil.* prevail; *sich* **~** *gegen* auch stand up against; *sich in s-r Stellung* **~** maintain one's position; **2.** *Sport* come out on top; **3.** *Wirts., Kurse, Preise*: remain firm

Behauptung *f* **1.** claim, assertion; *förm.* contention; *bes. gegen j-n*: *auch* allegation; *e-e* **~** *aufstellen* make an assertion; *das ist e-e bloße* **~** that's simply an assertion; *die* **~**, *er würde zurücktreten, ist nicht richtig* what people say about him (*od.* his) resigning isn't true; *ich bleibe bei m-r* **~**, *dass ...* I still say (*od.* maintain) that ...; *er bleibt bei s-r* **~**, *dass ...* auch he still insists that ...; *wie kommst du zu dieser* **~?** what makes you say that?; **2.** *Math.* assertion; **3.** *mst Sg.* (*Aufrechterhaltung*) maintenance; *e-r Stellung etc.*: defen|ce (*Am.* -se)

Behausung *f geh.* accommodation; *auch hum.* (*Wohnung*) dwelling, home; *menschliche* **~***en* human habitations; *s-e ärmliche* **~** his humble dwelling

beheben *v/t.* (*unreg.*) **1.** (*Schaden*) repair; (*Panne*) attend to; (*Fehler, Schwierigkeit etc.*) get rid of; (*Missstand*) remedy, redress; (*Elend*) alleviate; (*Zweifel*) remove; (*Störung*) remove; **2.** *österr.* (*abheben*) (*Geld*) withdraw; **Behebung** *f* **1.** *von Schaden*: repair; *von Schwierigkeiten, Zweifeln etc.*: removal; *von Missständen*: redressal; → *beheben* 1; **2.** *österr.* (*das Geldabheben*) withdrawal

beheimatet *Adj.* resident; **~** *sein in* (+ *Dat.*) come from; *Tiere etc.*: *auch* be native to; *er/es ist in X* **~** auch his/its home is (in) X; *der in Wien* **~***e Künstler* the artist whose home is in Vienna

beheizbar *Adj.* heatable, able to be heated; *nicht* **~** unheatable; **~***e Heckscheibe* heated rear window; **beheizen** *v/t.* heat

Behelf *m*; *-(e)s, -e*; (*Notlösung*) makeshift; (*Ersatz*) substitute; *das ist nur ein* **~** that's just a makeshift solution; *als* **~** *dienen* be a makeshift solution; **behelfen** *v/refl.* (*unreg.*) **1.** (*als Notlösung*) make do (*mit* with); **2.** (*zurechtkommen*) manage, get by; *sich ohne etw.* **~** do without s.th.

Behelfs... *im Subst.* (*improvisiert*) makeshift; (*Not...*) emergency; (*vorübergehend*) temporary, stopgap; **~ausfahrt** temporary exit; *ständige*: emergency exit; **~quartier** temporary (*für Notfall auch* emergency) accommodation

behelfsmäßig I. *Adj.* (*improvisiert*) makeshift; (*für Notfälle*) emergency ...; (*vorübergehend*) temporary, stopgap ...; **II.** *Adv.* as a makeshift; (*vorübergehend*) for the time being, as a stopgap; *etw.* **~** *reparieren* repair s.th. temporarily, patch s.th. up

behelfsweise *Adv.*: *der Raum dient* **~** *als Küche* the room serves as a makeshift kitchen (when needed); **~** *können wir auch im Nachbarhaus Gäste unterbringen* in an emergency we can put up guests next door

behelligen *v/t.* bother, trouble, pester; *stärker*: annoy; *behelligt werden von* be pestered by; *darf ich Sie mit e-r Frage* **~?** may I bother you with a question; **Behelligung** *f auch Pl.* pestering

behelmt *Adj.* wearing a helmet

behende → *behände*; **Behendigkeit** → *Behändigkeit*

beherbergen *v/t.* **1.** (*Gäste*) put up, accommodate; (*Flüchtlinge*) take in; **2.** (*Platz bieten für etw.*) provide space for; **Beherbergung** *f*; *nur Sg.*; *von Gästen*: (*das Unterbringen*) putting up; (*Unterkunft*) accommodation

beherrschbar *Adj.* governable; *weitS.* controllable

beherrschen I. *v/t.* **1.** (*regieren über*) rule (over), govern; *fig.* dominate (*auch j-n*); (*e-e Familie, ein Unternehmen*) *auch* rule (over), hold sway over, run *umg.*; **den Luftraum ~** control airspace, have air supremacy; **es beherrscht sein ganzes Denken** *fig.* it governs (*od.* dominates, determines) his whole way of thinking; **2.** *fig.* (*im Griff haben: Lage, Fahrzeug etc.*) control, be in control of, have *s.th.* under control; (*Markt etc.*) control, dominate; (*Technik, Situation etc.*) be in control of; **3.** (*gut können*) (*Sprache*) have a good command of, speak (fluently); (*Musikinstrument*) have complete command of; (*Handwerk*) have mastered; (*sich angeeignet haben: Regeln, Übung etc.*) have internalized; **s-e Schwester beherrscht drei Fremdsprachen** his sister speaks three foreign languages; **4.** (*zügeln*) (*Leidenschaften etc.*) (keep under) control; **5.** (*überragen, bestimmen*) command, dominate, tower (*od.* soar) above; **alte Eichen ~ die Landschaft** the landscape is dominated by ancient oaks; **II.** *v/refl.* control o.s., restrain o.s.; **beherrsch dich!** get yourself under control; **sie kann sich gut/schlecht ~** she keeps herself / cannot keep herself under control; **sie kann sich nicht ~** *auch* she just can't hold back; (*wird schnell wütend*) she has a quick temper; **ich kann mich ~!** *umg. iro. ablehnend*: you'll be lucky!; *stärker*: not likely!

beherrschend I. *Part. Präs.* → *beherrschen*; **II.** *Adj.* (*vorherrschend*) dominating; **~es Thema der Verhandlungen war …** topic number one (*od.* the leading topic) at the talks was …

beherrscht I. *P.P.* → *beherrschen*; **II.** *Adj. Person, Stimme*: restrained, disciplined; *Miene*: controlled; **III.** *Adv.* with restraint; **Beherrschtheit** *f*; *nur Sg.* self-restraint, self-possession

Beherrschung *f*; *nur Sg.* **1.** *Pol. etc.* rule (+ *Gen.* over); **2.** *fig.* control (+ *Gen.* of, over); **3.** (*Können*) mastery (+ *Gen.* of); *e-r Sprache*: command (of); **4.** (*Selbstbeherrschung*) self-control; **die** *od.* **s-e ~ verlieren** lose control, lose one's self-control (*od.* cool *umg.*)

beherzigen *v/t.* take to heart, heed; (*befolgen*) *auch* follow; **beherzigenswert** *Adj.* worth heeding; **Beherzigung** *f*; *nur Sg.* heeding (+ *Gen.* of); **zur ~!** (*Ermahnung*) just remember!, mark well!, take good heed!

beherzt *Adj.* courageous, brave, plucky; (*entschlossen*) determined; **Beherztheit** *f*; *nur Sg.* courage, bravery, pluck; (*Entschlossenheit*) determination

behexen *v/t.* bewitch; (*verzaubern*) put a spell on

behilflich *Adj.*: **j-m ~ sein** help s.o. (**bei** with); *förm.* assist s.o. (with, in + *Ger.*); **darf ich Ihnen ~ sein?** can I help you?; *beim Mantelablegen etc.*: al-

low me

behindern *v/t.* hinder, impede (**bei** in); (*Sicht, Verkehr*) *auch* obstruct; (*stören*) *auch* be (*od.* get) in the way, handicap; **j-n beim Überholen ~** obstruct s.o. while overtaking; **die Brille behindert mich beim Sport** my glasses are (*od.* get) in the way when I'm doing sport (*Am.* sports)

behindert *Adj.* handicapped, disabled; *USA politisch korrekt*: challenged; **ein ~es Kind** a handicapped child; **geistig ~** mentally handicapped; *USA politisch korrekt*: mentally challenged; **körperlich ~** physically handicapped (*od.* disabled); *USA politisch korrekt*: physically challenged; **schwer ~** seriously handicapped; *körperlich auch*: severely disabled; **Behinderte** *m, f*; *-n, -n* handicapped (*od.* disabled) person; **die ~n** the disabled, people with special needs

Behindertenausweis *m* disabled pass

behindertengerecht *Adj.* suitable for disabled users (*od.* for wheelchairs); *Gebäude*: *auch* with wheelchair access

Behinderten|sport *m* disabled sport; **~toilette** *f* disabled (*od.* handicapped) toilet; **~werkstatt** *f* sheltered workshop

Behinderung *f* **1.** hindrance, impediment; *im Verkehr*: obstruction; **mit ~en muss gerechnet werden** *Verkehrsmeldung*: delays can be expected; **~ der Sicht** *wegen Nebel etc.*: obstructed vision; **Falschparken mit ~** illegal parking with obstruction; **2.** *Med.* handicap; **geistige ~** mental handicap; **e-e (geistige) ~ haben** be (mentally) handicapped (*od.* retarded); *USA politisch korrekt*: be (mentally) challenged; **3.** *Sport* obstruction

Behörde *f*; *-, -n* **1.** (public) authority; (*Amt*) *auch* administrative body; *städtisch*: (town) council; **welches ist die zuständige ~?** who is the responsible authority?; **2.** (*Amtsgebäude*) public offices

Behördensprache *f* officialese

behördlich I. *Adj. Anweisung, Verordnung etc.*: official; (*staats~*) government …; **auf ~e Anordnung** on official instructions; **II.** *Adv.* officially; **etw. ~ genehmigen lassen** get official approval for s.th.; **~ genehmigt** officially authorized; **~ anerkannt** officially recognized; **behördlicherseits** *Adv. Amtsspr.* on the part of the authorities

behost *Adj. umg., hum.* trousered, *Am.* wearing pants

Behuf *m*; *-(e)s, -e*; *altm. od. hum.*: **zu diesem ~e** for this purpose

behum(p)sen *v/t. umg. Dial.* swindle, diddle

behüten *v/t.* **1.** (*bewachen*) look after; (*Geheimnis*) keep; (*Schatz*) guard; **2.** (*schützen*) *vor Gefahren etc.*: protect (**vor** + *Dat.* from); (*Gott*) **behüte!** God forbid!, perish the thought!; **Behüter** *m*, **Behüterin** *f geh.* protector; **behütet I.** *P.P.* → *behüten*; **II.** *Adj. Kindheit, Leben* sheltered; **III.** *Adv.*: **~ aufwachsen** grow up in a protected environment

behutsam I. *Adj.* (*vorsichtig*) cautious; (*sachte*) gentle; **II.** *Adv.*: **j-n ~ umgehen mit** be gentle on s.o. / handle s.th. with care; **~ vorgehen** tread carefully; **Behutsamkeit** *f*; *nur Sg.*; (*Vorsicht*) caution; (*Sanftheit*) gentleness

bei *Präp.* **1.** *räumlich, auch fig.*: a) (*in der Nähe von*) near; **~ Berlin** near Ber-

lin; **die Schlacht ~ Waterloo** the Battle of Waterloo; **~m Rathaus** (just) near (*od.* by) the town hall; (*am Rathaus*) at the town hall; **dicht ~ der Schule** just next to the school; **etw. ~ der Hand haben** have s.th. to hand; **der Wert liegt etwa ~ 5000 Euro** its value is around 5000 euros, b) *an e-m bestimmten Ort*: at; **~m Metzger** at the butcher's; **hast du das ~ Woolworth gekauft?** did you buy that at Woolworth's?; **Herr Müller ist gerade ~ Tisch** Mr Müller is just at the table; **~ ihr zu Hause** in her house, at her place; **~ uns in Hessen / auf dem Land** where I come from in Hessen / in the country; **wir sind morgen ~ Kollegen eingeladen** we have been invited to visit colleagues tomorrow; **er wohnt ~ mir nebenan / um die Ecke** he lives next door / on the corner where I live (*od.* of my place); **sie wohnt ~ e-m alten Ehepaar** she lives with an old couple; **~ Schmidt** (*per Adresse*) c/o (= care of) Schmidt; **hier ~ Müller am Telefon**: this is the Müllers', Müller speaking; **~ den Schotten heißt das anders** the Scots call it something else; **Amerika wacht gerade erst auf; ~ uns ist es aber schon 13 Uhr** in America they're just waking up, but here it's already 1 o'clock; **2.** a) *bezeichnet Arbeitsverhältnis etc.*: for; **sie ist ~ Langenscheidt** she is with (*od.* works for) Langenscheidt; **er arbeitet ~ der Bahn** he works for the railway (*Am.* railroad); **sie ist ~m Fernsehen** she works for (the) TV; **~m Militär** in the armed forces, b) **~ j-m Stunden nehmen** have lessons with s.o.; **~ welchem Arzt bist du?** which doctor do you go to?; *Brit. auch* who's your GP?; **3.** *an e-r bestimmten Stelle*: **j-n ~m Kragen packen** grab s.o. by the collar; **j-n ~ der Hand etc. nehmen** take s.o. by the hand *etc.*; **~ Fuß!** (to) heel!; **4.** *dabei, mit*: with; **ich habe kein Geld ~ mir** I have no money on me; **er hatte s-n Hund ~ sich** he had his dog with him; **das ist oft so ~ Kindern** that's fairly common with children; *pej.* children are like that; **~ mir machst du das lieber nicht** you'd be advised not to try that with me; **die Entscheidung liegt ~ dir** it's your decision; **hilfst du mir ~m Umzug?** will you help me with my move?; **j-n ~m Namen nennen** call s.o. by (his *od.* her) name; **5.** *bezeichnet Teilnahme*: **~ e-r Veranstaltung sein** be in on an event; **~ e-r Aufführung mitwirken** take part in a performance; **~ dieser Runde setze ich aus** *bei Spielen*: I'll sit this round out; **6.** *von Werken, Künstlern etc.*: in the work of; **~ Schiller steht** in one of Schiller's works it says, Schiller says; **~ Tizian findet man dieses Motiv** you find this motif in the works of Titian; **7.** *zeitlich, Umstände, Zustände*: a) *zu e-m gewissen Zeitpunkt*: on, at; **~ m-r Ankunft** when I arrived, on my arrival; **~ Tagesanbruch** at dawn; **~ schönem Wetter** when the weather is fine; **der Park schließt ~ anbrechender Dunkelheit** the park closes at dusk; **~ dieser Gelegenheit möchte ich …** I should like to take this opportunity to …; **~ e-m Unfall** in an accident; **Vorsicht ~ Abfahrt des Zuges!** take care when the train leaves, b) (*während*) during, at, by; **~ Nacht** at night; **~ Tag** during the daytime, by day; **~m Unter-**

B

richt during a (*od.* the) lesson; ~ *e-m Glas Wein* over a glass of wine; *~m Lesen der Zeitung fiel mir auf ...* while (*od.* when) I was reading the paper it struck me ...; ~ *der Arbeit einschlafen* fall asleep while working; *~m Essen etc.* while eating *etc.*, c) (*im Falle von*) if there is, in case of; ~ *Gefahr Knopf drücken* press the button in case of danger; ~ *Regen wird das Fest verschoben* if it rains the party will be postponed; ~ *Nebel* if it is foggy; *Vorsicht ~ Nässe!* take care in wet conditions; *~m nächsten Mal* (the) next time; ~ *so etwas wird mir schlecht* that sort of thing makes me feel ill; **8.** (*unter*) among; ~ *den alten Fotos* among the old photos; *heute war nichts für dich ~ der Post* there was nothing for you in the post (*Am.* mail) today; ~ *Strafe von* under penalty of; **9.** (*betreffend*): ~ *Alkohol muss ich aufpassen* I have to be careful with alcohol; ~ *Geldfragen muss ich passen* when it comes to (questions of) money, I have to pass; ~ *Männern hat sie Pech* she's unlucky with men; **10.** (*angesichts*): ~ *m-m Gehalt kann ich mir das nicht leisten* I can't afford that on (*od.* with) my salary; ~ *25 Euro pro Stunde* at 25 euros an hour; ~ *so vielen Schwierigkeiten* considering all the difficulties; ~ *so viel Hilfe sind wir schnell fertig* with all this help we should be ready soon; ~ *diesem Lärm kann man nicht schlafen* with all this noise one can't sleep; **11.** (*trotz*): ~ *aller Liebe, das ist zu viel verlangt* much as I sympathize - that's asking too much; *und das ~ all s-r Mühe!* and that in spite of all his efforts; **12.** *in bestimmtem Zustand*: ~ *Kräften sein* be in good health; ~ *guter Gesundheit sein* be in good health; ~ *Besinnung sein* be conscious; *er ist heute nicht ~ Laune* he's not in a very good mood today; *gut ~ Kasse sein* have plenty of money; **13.** *bei bestimmten Bedingungen*: *~m besten Willen* with the best will in the world; ~ *Wasser und Brot* with just bread and water; ~ *offenem Fenster* with the window open; ~ *Kerzenlicht* by candlelight; ~ *Licht besehen ist es nur halb so schlimm* seen in the light of day it's not so bad; **14.** *Maß*: ~ *weitem* by far; **15.** *Anrufung*: *schwören* ~ swear by; ~ *Gott!* by God!; ~ *meiner Ehre! altm.* on my hono(u)r!

beibehalten *v/t.* (*unreg., trennb., hat*) keep, retain, maintain; (*Gewohnheit etc.*) keep up, stick to; (*Tradition etc.*) keep up, uphold; (*Richtung*) carry on in; (*Tempo*) keep to, stick to; **Beibehaltung** *f; nur Sg. von Gesetz etc.*: upholding; *von Tradition etc.*: *auch* preservation; *unter ~ von* while maintaining

beibiegen (*unreg., trennb., hat -ge-*) **I.** *v/t. umg.*: *j-m etw. ~ schonend*: break s.th. to s.o. (gently); (*erklären*) get s.th. through to s.o.; **II.** *v/i. Naut.* heave to

Bei|blatt *n in e-r Zeitung, im Katalog etc.*: insert; *~boot n Naut.* dinghy, ding(e)y; *mit Segeln*: pinnace, jolly boat

beibringen *v/t.* (*unreg., trennb., hat -ge-*) **1.** *j-m etw.* ~ (*lehren*) teach s.o. s.th.; *j-m das Schwimmen/Lesen etc.* ~ teach s.o. (how) to swim/read *etc.*; *dir werd ich's schon noch ~!* umg. I'll show you what's what!; → *Flötenton!* **2.** *j-m etw.* ~ (*mitteilen*) tell s.o. s.th.;

schonend: *auch* break s.th. to s.o.; (*verständlich machen*) make s.th. clear to s.o., get s.th. across to s.o.; **3.** (*zufügen*) (*Wunde, Verluste etc.*) inflict (+ *Dat.* on); *j-m e-e schwere Niederlage* ~ inflict a heavy defeat on s.o.; **4.** (*be-, herbeischaffen*) produce, come up with; *Beweise/Zeugen* ~ produce (*od.* adduce) evidence / produce (*od.* bring forward) witnesses

Beichte *f; -, -n* **1.** *Reli.* confession; *die* ~ *ablegen* confess; *j-m die* ~ *abnehmen* hear s.o.'s confession; *Priester*: confess s.o.; **2.** *fig.* (*Geständnis*) confession; **beichten** *vt/i.* **1.** *Reli.* confess (*bei j-m* to s.o.); ~ *gehen* go to confession; **2.** *fig.* (*gestehen*) confess; *ich muss dir etwas* ~ I've got something to confess (to you), I've got a confession to make (to you), *auch* I've got to get something off my chest *umg.*

Beicht|geheimnis *n Reli.* seal of confession; *das* ~ *wahren* observe the seal of confession; *~stuhl m* confessional (box); *~vater m* (father) confessor

beid|armig *Adj. Sport* two- (*od.* both-)handed; ~ *rudern* row with two hands; *~beinig Adj.* two-footed; ~ *abspringen* take off from both feet

beide *unbest. Pron. und Zahlw.* **1.** *adj., mst mit Art. od. Pron.*; *betont Gemeinsamkeit*: both; *unbetont*: the two; *m-e ~n Brüder* both my brothers, *unbetont*: my two brothers; ~ *Brüder wohnen in Wien* both brothers live in Vienna; *die ersten/letzten ~n Strophen* the first/last two verses (*od.* strophes); ~ *Male hat er sich geirrt* he was wrong both times; *zu ~n Seiten* on both sides, on either side; *mit euer ~r Hilfe* with the help of you both; **2.** (*das eine oder das andere*) either (*Sg.*); ~ *Tage passen mir* either day would suit me, *beide Tage zusammen*: both days would suit me; *in ~n Fällen* in both cases, in either case; *welcher von ~n?* which one?, which of them?, which of the two?; *ein(e)s od. eine(r) von ~n* one of each; *kein(e)s od. keine(r) von ~n* neither (of them *od.* of the two); **3.** *wir* ~ both of us, the two of us; *wir* ~ *gehen jetzt* we're both off now, the two of us are off now; *ihr* ~ you two; *jeder der ~n hat ein Auto* each of them has (*od.* both of them have) a car; *alle* ~ both of them; *sie gefallen mir alle* ~ *nicht* I don't like either of them; **4.** *subst.*: ~ *sind angekommen* both of them have arrived, they've both arrived; *sie kommen* ~ *nicht* neither of them is coming; *nehmen Sie Milch oder Zucker?-beides* both, please; *~s ist richtig* both are right; *ich mag ~s nicht* I don't like either (of it, of them); **5.** *Sport, Tennis*: *15* ~ 15 all; → *Bein 1*

beiderlei *Gattungsz. undekl.* (of) both kinds; ~ *Geschlechts* of either sex

beiderseitig *Adj.* **1.** (*gegenseitig*) mutual; *sich in ~em Einvernehmen trennen* separate by mutual agreement; *zur ~en Zufriedenheit* to the satisfaction of both sides; *auf ~en Wunsch* by mutual request; **2.** *Pol. etc.* bilateral, two-sided; **3.** → *beidseitig 2*

beiderseits I. *Präp.* on both sides (+ *Gen.* of), on either side (of); **II.** *Adv.* on both sides; (*wechselseitig*) mutually, reciprocally; ~ *wurde behauptet, ...* both sides claimed that ...; *der Plan wurde* ~ *gebilligt* the plan was accepted by both parties

beid|füßig *Adj. Spieler*: two-footed; ~ *abspringen* take off from both feet;

~händig Adj. **1.** *gleichmäßig geschickt*: ambidextrous; ~ *schreiben können* (be able to) write with both hands; **2.** *Sport, Schlag etc.*: two-handed

beidrehen *vt/i.* (*trennb., hat –ge-*); *Naut.* (*verlangsamen*) heave to; *ein Schiff* ~ heave to, bring to; *beigedreht liegen* be hove to; *der Kapitän drehte bei* the captain hove to

beidseitig *Adj.* **1.** (*auf beiden Seiten*) on both sides; *Lungenentzündung*: double; *Lähmung*: bilateral, on both sides *nachgestellt*; **2.** *altm.* → *beiderseitig 1*

beidseits *schw.* → *beiderseits*

beieinander *Adv.* together; ~ *bleiben* stay (*od.* stick *umg.*) together; ~ *haben* have *s.th.* together; (*Summe*) have (ready); *er hat (sie) nicht alle* ~ *umg.* he's not all there, he's got a screw loose; *du hast (sie) wohl nicht mehr alle ~?* umg. have you gone mad (*od.* crazy)?; ~ *halten* keep together; ~ *hocken* sit (*eng*: huddle) together; ~ *liegen* be next to each other; *gut/ schlecht ~ sein umg. gesundheitlich*: be in good/bad shape; *er ist nicht gut* ~ he's not his usual self / he's not (too) well; *sie ist gut ~ umg. euph.* ([zu] *kräftig gebaut*) she's well proportioned; (*dicht*) ~ *stehen etc.* stand (*od.* be) next to each other (stand close together); *nahe ~ wohnen* live near (to) each other

Beieinandersein *n; -s, -: das ~* being together (with *s.o. od.* people); *geselliges ~* cosy (*Am.* cozy) get-together

Beifahrer *m,* *~in f* **1.** *im Pkw*: (front--seat) passenger; *im Lkw*: co-driver, driver's mate *umg.*; (*Soziusfahrer*) pillion rider; **2.** *beim Rennen*: co-driver, *navigierend*: navigator; *~sitz m* front passenger seat; (*Soziussitz*) pillion (seat)

Beifall *m; nur Sg.* applause, clapping; *durch Zurufe*: (loud) cheers *Pl.*; *fig.* (*Billigung*) approval; ~ *klatschen* applaud, clap; ~ *ernten od. finden* draw applause; *fig.* meet with approval; ~ *spenden* applaud (*j-m* s.o.); ~ *heischend* seeking (*od.* looking for) approval; *ein ~ heischender Blick* a look inviting (*od.* begging for) applause; *sich ~ heischend umsehen* look around for applause; *stürmischer ~* thunder of applause

beifällig I. *Adj.* approving; *~es Lächeln* smile of approval; **II.** *Adv.* approvingly; ~ *nicken* nod (in) approval; *etw. ~ aufnehmen* welcome s.th.

Beifall|klatschen *n* applause, clapping; *~ruf m* cheer(s *Pl.*)

Beifalls|bekundung *f,* *~bezeigung f; mst Pl.* show of approval; *~klatschen n* applause, clapping; *~ruf m* cheer(s *Pl.*); *~sturm m* thunderous (*od.* rapturous) applause

beifügen *v/t.* (*trennb., hat -ge-*) **1.** (*noch sagen*) add (+ *Dat.* to); *e-e Klausel ~ im Vertrag etc.*: append a clause (+ *Dat.* to); **2.** (*mitschicken*) enclose, include; *e-m Brief e-e Anlage ~* add an enclosure to a letter; **3.** (*dazutun*) *bes. in Kochrezepten*: add; **Beifügung** *f* **1.** *nur Sg.* addition (+ *Gen.* of); *unter ~ von* (by) adding; *bei Brief etc.*: enclosure; **2.** *Ling.* attribute

Beifuß *m; -es, -: Bot.* mugwort

Bei|futter *n Agr.* supplementary fodder; *~gabe f* **1.** addition; *in Kochrezepten*: *den Saft unter ~ von Zucker erhitzen* heat the juice while adding

sugar; **2.** (*etw. Zusätzliches gratis*) extra; *etw. als* ~ *bekommen* get s.th. for free; **3.** *in Grab*: burial offering
beige [beːʃ] *Adj.* beige; *ein* ~ *od. umg.* ~*r Rock* a beige skirt; **Beige** *n*; -, -, *umg. auch -s* beige
beigeben (*unreg., trennb., hat -ge-*) **I.** *v/t.* **1.** (*hinzufügen*) add (+ *Dat.* to); **2.** (*mitgeben*) *als Berater, zur Aufsicht etc.*: *j-m j-n* ~ assign s.o. to s.o.; **II.** *v/i. umg.*: *klein* ~ climb (*od.* back) down, yield, submit; *j-m klein* ~ give in to s.o., give way to s.o.
beigefarben ['beːʃfarbn̩] *Adj.* beige(--colo(u)red); *ein* ~*er Teppich* a beige(--colo(u)red) carpet
Beigeordnete *m*, *f*; -*n*, -*n* assistant; *Pol.* (town) council(l)or
Beigeschmack *m*; *nur Sg.* (unpleasant) taste; *e-n* ~ *haben von* taste of, *auch fig.* smack of; *bitterer etc.* ~ slightly bitter *etc.* taste; *e-n unangenehmen* ~ *haben auch fig.* have an unpleasant taste (to it); *fig. Wort etc.*: have a negative connotation
beigesellen (*trennb., hat -ge-*) **I.** *v/t.* *zur Gesellschaft, als Gefährten*: *j-n j-m od. j-m j-n* ~ put s.o. together with s.o.; **II.** *v/refl. geh.*: *sich j-m / e-r Gruppe* ~ join s.o./a group, attach o.s. to s.o. / to a group
Beiheft *n* *zu e-m Lehrbuch, e-r Zeitschrift*: supplement; *zu e-r CD etc.*: (sleeve) notes *Pl.*; **beiheften** *v/t.* (*trennb., hat -ge-*): *etw. e-r Sache* ~ attach (*mit Heftklammer*: staple) s.th. to s.th.
Beihilfe *f* **1.** *für Industrie, Ausland*: subsidy, grant; *für Kleider, Miete etc.*: allowance; *für kinderreiche Familien etc.*: *auch* allowance; (*Erziehungs-, Ausbildungsbeihilfe*) grant; ~ *beantragen* apply for a grant *etc.*; *e-e einmalige* ~ *erhalten* receive a one-off (*Am.* one-time) grant *etc.*; **2.** *nur Sg.*; *Jur.* aiding and abetting; ~ *leisten* aid and abet (*j-m s.o.*); *wegen* ~ *zum Mord verurteilt werden* be condemned for aiding and abetting in a murder, be condemned for acting as (*od.* being) an accessory to a murder; **beihilfefähig** *Adj. Kurs etc.*: eligible for a grant
beiholen *v/t.* (*trennb., hat -ge-*); *Naut.* take in (the sail)
Beiklang *m* *auch fig.* overtone(s *Pl.*)
Bei|koch *m*, ~*köchin* *f* assistant cook
beikommen *v/i.* (*unreg., trennb., ist -ge-*) **1.** *j-m* ~ get at s.o., *fig. auch* get the better of s.o.; (*zu fassen bekommen*) get hold of s.o.; *ihm ist nicht beizukommen* there's no getting at him; *mit Argumenten ist ihr nicht beizukommen* she won't listen to any arguments, she's deaf to argument; **2.** *e-r Sache* ~ (*fertig werden mit*) cope with s.th., get to grips with s.th.; (*auf den Grund kommen*) get to the root of s.th.; **3.** *Dial.* (*herbeikommen*) come; **4.** *Dial.* (*etw. erreichen können*) get at *s.th.*
Beikost *f* food supplement(s *Pl.*), supplementary diet
Beil *n*; -(e)*s*, -*e* *zum Holzhacken*: axe, *Am.* ax; *kleiner*: hatchet; *von Metzger*: (meat) cleaver; *des Henkers*: axe, *Am.* ax; (*Fallbeil*) guillotine
Beilage *f* **1.** *in e-r Zeitung*: supplement; *Reklame*: insert; *in Buch*: insertion; **2.** *Gastr.* side dish; *Gemüse*: vegetables *Pl.*; *Salat*: side salad; *Fleisch mit* ~ */ mit verschiedenen* ~*n* meat and vegetables / meat and a selection of vegetables; *was gibt es als* ~? what comes

with it?, what is it served with?; *es gibt Pommes frites als* ~ it comes (*od.* it is served) with French fries; **3.** (*das Beilegen*) enclosing, enclosure; *Antwort gegen* ~ *von Rückporto* (please) enclose return postage for reply; **4.** *österr.* (*Anlage*) *im Brief*: enclosure
beiläufig **I.** *Adj.* casual; ~*e Bemerkung* passing (*od.* throwaway) remark; ~*e Frage* passing query; **II.** *Adv.* **1.** casually; ~ *erwähnen etc.* mention *etc.* in passing; ~ *sei erwähnt* (*od. gesagt*) (be it said) by the way, incidentally, parenthetically; **2.** *österr.* (*ungefähr*) around; **Beiläufigkeit** *f*; *nur Sg.* (*Nebensächlichkeit*) *e-r Bemerkung etc.*: casual nature; (*Ungerührtheit*) *im Erzählen etc.*: offhandedness; *er sprach davon mit erschreckender* ~ he spoke about it in a shockingly offhand way (*od.* with alarming casualness)
beilegen (*trennb., hat -ge-*) **I.** *v/t.* **1.** add (+ *Dat.* to); (*e-m Brief*) enclose, include (with); **2.** (*beimessen*) attach; *e-r Sache Wert od. Bedeutung* ~ attach (great) importance to s.th.; **3.** (*schlichten*) settle; *s-e Meinungsverschiedenheiten* ~ settle the (*od.* one's) differences; **4.** (*Titel*) confer (*j-m* on s.o.), (*Namen*) give; *sich* (*Dat.*) *e-n Titel etc.* ~ assume (*od.* take on) a title *etc.*; **II.** *v/i. Naut.* bring to
Beilegung *f*; *nur Sg.* **1.** *e-s Streits*: settlement, reconciliation; *friedliche/gütliche* ~ peaceful/amicable settlement; **2.** *e-s Titels, Namens*: conferral, bestowal
beileibe *Adv.*: ~ *nicht!* certainly not, not by a long shot *umg.*; *das war* ~ *nicht zu verachten* this was by no means to be scoffed at (*od.* to be sneezed at *umg.*); *es war* ~ *kein Spaß!* it was certainly no picnic (*Am. auch* hayride); *sie ist* ~ *nicht kritisch, aber ...* she's far from (being) critical, but ...
Beileid *n*; *nur Sg.* condolences *Pl.*, sympathy; *j-m sein* ~ *aussprechen* offer s.o. one's condolences; *j-m sein* ~ *bekunden* express one's sympathy (to s.o.); *mein aufrichtiges* ~ may I offer my sincere condolences; → *herzlich* I 1
Beileids|besuch *m* visit of condolence; ~*bezeigung* *f*, ~*bezeugung* *mst Pl.* condolences *Pl.*; *von* ~*en bitten wir abzusehen* no cards or flowers please; ~*brief* *m*, ~*schreiben* *n* letter of condolence
Beilhieb *m* blow of an axe (*Am.* ax)
beiliegen *v/i.* (*unreg., trennb., hat -ge-*) **1.** be enclosed (*e-m Brief etc.* with), be attached (to); *der Reservierung muss ein Scheck* ~ all reservations must be accompanied by a cheque (*Am.* check); **2.** *Naut.* lie to; **beiliegend** **I.** *Part. Präs.* → *beiliegen*; **II.** *Adj. und Adv. Schriftspr.* enclosed; ~ *übersenden wir Ihnen* enclosed please find, we are enclosing, we enclose
beim *Präp. + Art.*; *Kurzf. von bei dem*; a) *bei präziser Zeitangabe*: ~ *nächsten Ton ist es drei Uhr zehn* at the next (*mst.* third) stroke the time will be three ten; ~ *ersten Glockenton standen alle auf* at the first stroke of the bell everyone got up, b) (*während*): ~ *Essen sollst du nicht reden* you shouldn't talk while you're eating; *stör ihn nicht* ~ *Arbeiten* don't disturb him while he's working; *er hat sich* ~ *Sport verletzt* he injured himself while (he

was) playing sports; ~ *Überholen genügend Platz lassen* leave plenty of room when overtaking (*Am.* passing); *ich bin gerade* ~ *Kochen* I'm just (*od.* in the middle of) cooking, c) *in festen Wendungen*: ~ *besten Willen nicht* not with the best will in the world; *j-n* ~ *Kragen / die Gelegenheit* ~ *Schopf packen* grab s.o. by the scruff of his neck / seize (*od.* jump at) the opportunity; *alles bleibt* ~ *Alten* nothing's changed
beimengen *v/t.* (*trennb., hat -ge-*) → *beimischen*
beimessen *v/t.* (*unreg., trennb., hat -ge-*): *j-m / e-r Sache Bedeutung od. Wert etc.* ~ attach (great) importance *etc.* to s.o./s.th.; *ich messe der Sache keinen großen Wert bei* I don't attach any great importance to the matter, I don't regard it as being terribly important
beimischen (*trennb., hat -ge-*) **I.** *v/t.*: *e-r Sache etw.* ~ mix s.th. with s.th.; add s.th. to s.th.; **II.** *v/refl.*: *sich e-r Sache* ~ combine with s.th., be added to s.th.; *der Freude mischte sich etwas Nostalgie bei* the joy was tinged with some nostalgia; **Beimischung** *f* **1.** (*beigemischte Substanz*) admixture; *fig. auch* touch, tinge; **2.** *nur Sg.*; (*das Beimischen*) addition; *unter* ~ *von* while (*od.* by) adding
Bein *n*; -(e)*s*, -*e* **1.** *auch e-s Tisches, e-r Hose etc.*: leg; *krumme/schlanke* ~*e haben* have crooked (*Person auch*: bandy) / slim legs; *die* ~*e übereinander schlagen* cross one's legs; *mit übereinander geschlagenen* ~*en* cross-legged, (with) legs crossed; *von e-m* ~ *aufs andere treten umg.* shift from one foot to the other; *geh du, du hast jüngere* ~*e umg.* you go, your legs are in better shape (*od.* younger) than mine; *ich kann mich nicht mehr auf den* ~*en halten* I could hardly stand on my (own two) feet; *das geht in die* ~*e!* *bei körperlicher Anstrengung*: you really feel it in your legs, it goes for your legs; *bei zu viel Alkohol*: it goes straight to your knees; *von Tanzmusik*: it makes you want to get up and dance; *j-m ein* ~ *stellen auch fig.* trip s.o. up; *beim Fußball*: *das* ~ *stehen lassen* trip up one's opponent, trip *s.o.* up; (*schon*) *auf den* ~*en sein* be up and about (already); *dauernd auf den* ~*en sein* always be on the go; *ich muss mich auf die* ~*e machen* I must (*od.* have to) get moving, I must (*od.* have to) be off (*od.* be making tracks); *j-m* ~*e machen* (*fortjagen*) send s.o. packing; (*antreiben*) get s.o. moving; *die* ~*e in die Hand od. unter den Arm nehmen müssen umg.* have to scoot off, have to stir one's stumps, have to step on it; *j-m auf die* ~*e helfen* help s.o. up, help s.o. onto his (*od.* her) feet, *fig.* set s.o. up, give s.o. a leg up; *e-r Sache auf die* ~*e helfen fig.* get s.th. going; *wieder auf den* ~*en sein* (*gesund sein*) be back on one's feet again; *wir werden dich bald wieder auf die* ~*e bringen!* we'll have you back on your feet (*od.* running around) again in no time; *schwach auf den* ~*en sein* be a bit shaky (*od.* wobbly); *auf schwachen od. wack(e)ligen* ~*en stehen fig.* be shaky, be a shaky affair; *etw. auf die* ~*e stellen* get s.th. up and running, launch (*od.* start) s.th.; *auf eigenen* ~*en stehen* stand on one's own two

B

feet; *mit beiden ~en im Leben stehen* have both feet firmly on the ground; *mit 'einem ~ im Gefängnis stehen* stand a good chance of ending up in prison; *sich (Dat.) (kurz) die ~e vertreten umg.* stretch one's legs; *mein Schlüssel hat (wohl) ~e bekommen od. gekriegt umg.* my key seems to have walked off; *die ganze Stadt war auf den ~en* the whole town had turned out; *alles, was ~e hat* anyone and everyone, the whole population (*od.* town *etc.*); → *ausreißen* I, *Grab, Klotz* 1, *Knüppel* 1, *link...* 1; → *auch Fuß*[1] 3; **2.** *Med., österr., schw., südd., sonst altm.* (*Knochen*) bone; *diese Nachricht etc. ist ihm in die ~e gefahren* the news *etc.* shook him to the core; **3.** *bes. nordd., Dial.* (*Fuß*) foot

beinah(e) *Adv.* almost, nearly, approximately; *betont:* auch very nearly; *er hätte ~ gewonnen auch* he came very close to winning; *man könnte ~ glauben, sie ...* you'd almost think she ...; *es ist ~ Zeit* it is nearly time; *das ist ja ~ dasselbe* it is very much (*od.* pretty much *od.* pretty nearly) the same thing

Beinahzusammenstoß *m* near miss, near collision; *Flug. auch* airmiss

Beiname *m* epithet; (*Spitzname*) nickname

Beinamputation *f* leg amputation; **beinamputiert** *Adj.* with an amputated leg; with both legs amputated; *er ist ~ auch* he's had a leg (*od.* both legs) amputated, he's lost a leg (*od.* both legs); **Beinamputierte** *m, f* person (*od.* man, *f* woman) with an amputated leg (*od.* with both legs amputated), amputee

Bein|arbeit *f* footwork; *Schwimmen:* legwork; **~bruch** *m* fractured (*od.* broken) leg; *ein komplizierter ~* a complex leg fracture; *das ist doch kein ~! umg. fig.* it's not the end of the world; *Hals- und ~! umg.* break a leg!; **~freiheit** *f* in *Auto, Flugzeug etc.:* legroom, room to stretch one's legs

beinern *Adj. aus Knochen:* nur attr. bone ...; made of bone; *aus Elfenbein:* nur attr. ivory ...; made of ivory

beinhalten [bə'?ınhaltn] *v/t.* contain; (*besagen*) say; *stillschweigend:* imply

beinhart *Adj. südd.* **1.** (as) hard as rock (*od.* stone); *der Boden ist ~ gefroren* the ground is frozen solid; **2.** *mst Jugendspr. Person:* hard as nails; *Verhandlungen etc.:* tough

...beinig *im Adj.* **1.** *mit Zahlw.: acht~* eight-legged; *mehr~* multi-legged; **2.** *mit Adj.: krumm~* bandy-legged; *lang~* long-legged

Bein|kleid *n; mst Pl.; altm.* trousers *Pl.;* **~prothese** *f* artificial leg, leg prosthesis; **~schiene** *f* **1.** *Med.* splint; **2.** *Sport* shin pad; **3.** *hist. bei Rüstung:* greave; **~schützer** *m Sport* shin pad; **~stumpf** *m* stump of a leg

beiordnen *v/t. (trennb., hat -ge-)* **1.** *j-m j-n ~* assign s.o. to s.o.; **2.** *Jur.: (als Plichtverteidiger) beigeordnet werden* be assigned as counsel for the defence (*Am.* defense); *j-m e-n Anwalt ~* assign counsel to s.o.; **3.** *Ling.* coordinate; **Beiordnung** *f (das Beigeordnetwerden)* assignment

beipacken *v/t. (trennb., hat -ge-): e-r Ware etw. ~* enclose (*od.* include) s.th. with (*od.* in) s.th.; **Beipackzettel** *m* **1.** *Med.* (patient) package insert; **2.** *bei Warensendungen:* despatch note

beipflichten *v/i. (trennb., hat -ge-):*

j-m/etw. ~ agree with s.o./s.th. (*in* + *Dat.* on); **beipflichtend I.** *Part. Präs.* → *beipflichten;* **II.** *Adj.* approving

Beiprogramm *n* supporting program(me); *im ~ zeigen wir e-n Zeichentrickfilm* the supporting program(me) includes a cartoon film

Beirat *m; -(e)s, Beiräte;* (*Ausschuss*) advisory board

Beiried *n; -(e)s, kein Pl. od. f; -, kein Pl.; österr. Gastr.* piece of beef loin

beirren [bə'?ırən] *v/t.* (*irritieren*) disconcert; (*abbringen*) put *s.o.* off; *er lässt sich von niemandem ~ od. durch nichts ~* he won't be put off; *sich nicht durch Kritik ~ lassen* remain unfazed by criticism

beisammen *Adv.* **1.** together; *gute Nacht ~!* goodnight everyone (*od.* all); **2.** *er ist gut ~* he's in good shape; (*etwas gut ~ kräftig gebaut:* he's quite a big chap (*Am.* fellow, guy); *geistig:* he's got all his wits about him; *er ist schlecht od. nicht so gut ~* he's not (too) well; **~bleiben** *v/i. (unreg., trennb., ist -ge-)* stay (*od.* remain) together; **~haben** *v/t. (unreg., trennb., hat -ge-);* (*Geld*) have, have raised; (*Gruppe*) have together; *s-e Gedanken ~* have one's wits about one; (*noch*) *s-e fünf Sinne ~* have all one's wits about one; *er hat nicht alle ~ umg. pej.* he's not all there, he's got a screw loose

Beisammen|leben *n nur Sg.* living together; **~sein** *n* (*Treffen*) get-together; *geselliges ~* (social) get-together *od.* gathering

Beisatz *m Ling.* apposition

Beischlaf *m geh. Jur.* sexual intercourse; *den ~ vollziehen od. ausüben* have sexual intercourse; **Beischläfer** *m; -s, -,* **Beischläferin** *f; -,-nen* bedfellow

Beisein *n* presence; *im ~ von* (*di. + Gen.*) in the presence of, in front of; *im/ohne ~ s-s Anwalts* in the presence of his solicitor (*Am.* lawyer) / without his solicitor (*Am.* lawyer) being present; *in m-m etc. ~* in my *etc.* presence, in front of me *etc.*; *im ~ anderer od. dritter* with others present, in the company of others

beiseite *Adv.* aside; *Spaß od. Scherz ~!* seriously now; *j-n ~ drängen* push s.o. aside, elbow s.o. out; *~ gehen* step aside; *~ lassen* (*Überlegung etc.*) leave aside, ignore, disregard; *~ legen* put aside, (*Geld sparen*) auch set aside, stash away *umg.*; (*Brille, Buch*) put down (*od.* aside); *j-n ~ nehmen auf ein Wort etc.*: take (*od.* draw) s.o. aside; *~ schaffen* (*aus dem Weg räumen*) remove; (*Geld, Beute*) hide (*od.* stash away.) away; (*loswerden*) *umg.* get rid of *s.o./s.th.; euph.* (*umbringen*) bump *s.o.* off; *~ sprechen Theat.* make an aside, say in an aside; *~ stehen* (*zurückstehen*) stand aside

Beisel, Beisl *n; -s, -(n); südd., österr. umg.* pub, *Am.* bar

beisetzen *v/t.* **1.** (*Leichnam, Urne*) bury; (*Urne in Nische*) instal(l) (in its resting place); *geh.* (*Sarg*) bury *allg.,* inter *förm.,* lay to rest *lit.; mit militärischen Ehren ~* lay to rest with (full) military hono(u)rs; **2.** *Naut.* (*Segel*) set, spread; **Beisetzung** *f von Leichnam, Urne:* burial; *von Sarg:* burial, entombment *förm.,* interment *förm.; feierliche: auch* funeral; **Beisetzungsfeierlichkeiten** *Pl.* funeral ceremony *Sg.; förm.* obsequies

beisitzen *v/i. (unreg., trennb., hat -ge-): e-m Ausschuss ~* sit on a committee; **Beisitzer** *m, -s, -,* **Beisitzerin** *f -, -nen* **1.** *e-s Komitees etc.:* member (of a committee *etc.*); **2.** *bei Gericht:* assessor; **3.** *bei e-r Prüfung:* observer; *aktiver:* co-examiner

Beispiel *n* **1.** example (*für* of); *praktisches/treffendes ~* concrete/apt example; *zum ~* for instance, for example (*Abk.* e.g.); *wie zum ~ ...* (such as) ..., for example; *~e anführen od. geben* give examples; *etw. mit ~en belegen* give examples of (*od.* to support) s.th.; *j-n als ~ zitieren für ...* cite s.o. as an instance of ...; *ohne ~* without a precedent; *das ist ohne ~* (*noch nie vorgekommen*) that's unheard of; **2.** (*Vorbild*) model; *ein warnendes od. abschreckendes ~* a warning; *j-m ein ~ sein od. geben* set an example to s.o.; *sich (Dat.) ein ~ nehmen an* (+ *Dat.*) take *s.o./s.th.* as an example, *an j-m: auch* take a leaf out of *s.o.'s* book; *mit gutem ~ vorangehen* set an (*od.* a good) example; *es soll uns ein ~ sein* let it be a lesson (*od.* an example) to us all; *er ist ein hervorragendes ~ für einen fairen Sportler* he is an excellent exemplar of a fair sportsman

beispiel|gebend *Adj.* exemplary; *für j-n/etw. ~ sein od. wirken* serve as (*od.* be) an example to s.o. / for s.th.; **~haft I.** *Adj.* exemplary; *nur attr.* model ...; **II.** *Adv.: sich ~ benehmen* behave impeccably; *~ vorangehen* set a positive example

beispiellos *Adj.* unequal(l)ed, unparalleled, without parallel; (*unvergleichlich*) matchless, peerless; (*noch nie dagewesen*) unprecedented, unheard of; *das ist eine ~e Frechheit!* he's (*od.* she's, they've *etc.*) got an incredible cheek (*Am.* a lot of nerve); **Beispiellosigkeit** *f; nur Sg.* uniqueness

Beispielsatz *m* example (sentence)

Beispielsfall *m* example, instance

beispiels|halber *Adv.* for example, for instance; **~weise** *Adv.* for example, for instance; *ein ~ oft angewandter Trick* one trick, for example, that is often used

beispringen *v/i. (unreg., trennb., ist -ge-); j-m ~ come* (*schnell:* rush) to s.o.'s aid; (*aushelfen*) help s.o. out

beißen; *biss, hat gebissen* **I.** *v/t. auch Insekt:* bite; *j-n ins Bein / in den Finger ~* s.o.'s leg/finger; *sich (Dat.) auf die Zunge/Lippe ~* bite one's tongue/lip; *ein Loch in etw. ~* bite a hole into s.th., take a bite out of s.th.; *das kann man ja kaum ~!* it's as hard as rock, you can hardly get your teeth into it; *nichts zu ~ haben umg.* not have a bite to eat; *er kann nicht mehr richtig ~* (*kauen*) he can't chew properly any more; *er wird dich schon nicht ~ iro.* he won't bite (*od.* eat) you; **II.** *v/i.* **1.** *auch Insekt und Fisch:* bite; *in etw.* (*Akk.*) ~ bite (into) s.th.; *sie biss fest in den Apfel* she bit hard into the apple; *auf etw.* (*Akk.*) ~ bite on s.th.; *~ nach* snap at; *wild um sich ~ Tier:* snap wildly; → *Apfel* 2, *Granit, Gras* 2; **2.** (*brennen*) in *Wunde:* bite, burn; *in den Augen:* sting; **III.** *v/refl.* **1.** bite o.s.; *sich auf die Zunge/Lippe ~* bite one's tongue/lip; → *Hintern* 2; **2.** *fig. Farben, Töne etc.*: clash; **beißend I.** *Part. Präs.* → *beißen;* **II.** *Adj. Wind, Kälte:* biting; *Geruch:* sharp, acrid; *Schmerz:* sharp; *fig. Bemerkung etc.*: biting, caustic, acrid, acerbic; *Kri-*

tik: *auch* mordant *criticism*

Beißerchen *n umg.*, *Kinderspr.* toothy-peg, *Am.* toofer

Beißerei *f*; -, *-en* **1.** (*das Beißen*) biting; **2.** *zwischen Hunden*: fight

Beiß|korb *m* muzzle; **~ring** *m* (*für Baby*) teething ring; **~wütig** *Adj.* vicious; **~zange** *f* **1.** pliers *Pl.*; *e-e* **~** a pair of pliers; **2.** *umg.* (*zänkische Frau*) shrew, bitch *Sl.*

Beistand *m* **1.** *nur Sg.*; *geh.* help, support, assistance; *fig.* support; *j-m* (*ärztlichen*) **~** *leisten* come to s.o.'s aid; **2.** *Jur.* legal adviser; *im Prozess*: counsel

Beistands|pakt *m*, **~vertrag** *m Pol.* mutual assistance pact

beistehen *v/i.* (*unreg.*, *trennb.*, *hat / südd.*, *schw.*, *österr. auch ist -ge-*): *j-m* **~** help s.o., stand by s.o., give s.o. one's support; *sich gegenseitig* **~** support each other (*od.* one another); *Gott steh mir bei!* God help me; → *Rat*[1]

beistellen *v/t.* (*trennb.*, *hat -ge-*) **1.** *umg.* (*daneben stellen*) put *s.th.* next to (+ *Dat.* s.th.); **2.** *österr.* provide, supply; **Beistelltisch** *m* side table

beisteuern *vt/i.* (*trennb.*, *hat -ge-*) contribute (*zu* to), chip *s.th.* in *umg.*

beistimmen *v/i.* (*trennb.*, *hat -ge-*) agree (+ *Dat.* with); **~d nicken** nod one's approval

Beistrich *m Ling. altm.* comma *allg.*

Beitel *m*; *-s*, -; *Tech.* (*Stemmeisen*) (ripping) chisel; (*Hohlbeitel*) gouge

Beitrag *m*; *-(e)s*, *Beiträge* **1.** *auch fig.* contribution; *e-n* **~** *leisten* contribute (*zu* to), make a contribution (to); **2.** *zu Versicherung*: contribution, premium; (*Mitgliedsbeitrag*) subscription (fee); **3.** (*Zeitungsartikel etc.*) article (*von* by), *bes. Pl. auch* contributions (by, from); (*Funk- und Fernsehsendung*) report (by)

beitragen *vt/i.* (*unreg.*, *trennb.*, *hat -ge-*) contribute (*zu* to); (*förderlich sein*, *dienen*) *auch* help, *mit Inf. auch* serve to + *Inf.*; *er hat* (*wesentlich*) *zum Gelingen des Abends beigetragen* the success of the evening was in (large) part due to him; *das trägt nur dazu bei, s-e Lage zu verschlechtern* it will only serve to worsen the situation; *sein Teil* (*dazu*) **~** contribute one's share, do one's bit (*Am.* part) *umg.*, play one's (*od.* its) part; *viel dazu* (*um*) *die Lage erträglicher zu machen auch* go a long way toward(s) alleviating the situation

Beitrags|bemessungsgrenze *f in Sozialversicherung etc.*: income threshold; **~erhöhung** *f* increase in contributions, increased contributions *Pl.*

beitragsfrei *Adj.* non-contributory; **Beitragsfreiheit** *f*; *nur Sg.* exemption from contributions

Beitragspflicht *f*; *nur Sg.* liability for contributions; **beitragspflichtig** *Adj. Person, Gehalt*: liable to contributions

Beitrags|rückerstattung *f* contribution refund; **~zahler** *m*, **~zahlerin** *f* contributor

beitreiben *v/t.* (*unreg.*, *trennb.*, *hat -ge-*); (*Gelder, Steuern*) collect; (*Schulden*) recover, (*einklagen*) sue for

beitreten *v/i.* (*unreg.*, *trennb.*, *ist -ge-*) **1.** (*e-m Verein, e-r Partei etc.*) join, become a member of; (*e-m Bündnis*) *auch* enter (into), accede to *förm.*; (*e-m Abkommen etc.*) enter into; **2.** *Jur.* intervene in; **Beitritt** *m* joining (*zu* of *a party etc.*); *zu e-m Bündnis*:

auch entry (into), membership (of); *den* **~** *beantragen* *zu e-m Verein*, *Bündnis*, *e-r Partei*: apply for membership; *s-n* **~** *erklären* become a member, join

Beitritts|erklärung *f* application for membership, declaration of membership; *zu Bündnis*: declaration of accession *förm.*; **~verhandlungen** *Pl.* membership talks (*od.* negotiations); **~vertrag** *m* accession treaty

beitrittswillig *Adj.* willing to join

Beiwagen *m* **1.** *Motorrad*: sidecar; **2.** *altm. an Straßenbahn*, *U-Bahn*: extra carriage

Beiwerk *n* trimmings *Pl.*, frills *Pl. umg. pej.*; *Mode*: accessories *Pl.*

beiwilligen *v/i.* (*trennb.*, *hat -ge-*); *schw.* agree (+ *Dat.* to)

beiwohnen *v/i.* (*trennb.*, *hat -ge-*) **1.** *e-r Veranstaltung etc.* **~** attend an event *etc.*, be present at an event *etc.*; *als Zeuge*: witness an event *etc.*; **2.** *geh.*, *lit. und euph.*: *e-r Frau* **~** lie with a woman

Beiwort *n*; *Pl.* *-wörter* **1.** epithet; **2.** *Gram. selten* adjective

Beize[1] *f*; -, *-n* **1.** *Chem.*: *Mittel*: corrosive; *Vorgang*: corrosion etching; **2.** *Agr.* dressing; **3.** *für Holz*: *Mittel*: stain; *Vorgang*: staining; **4.** *Färberei*: mordant; **5.** *Gerberei*: bate; **6.** *Tabak*: sauce; **7.** *Gastr.* marinade, pickle; **8.** *Med.* caustic; **9.** *für Metall*: pickle, pickling solution

Beize[2] *f*; -, *-n*; (*Beizjagd*) hawking, falconry

Beize[3] *f*; -, *-n*; *Dial.* (*Kneipe*) pub, *Am.* bar

beizeiten *Adv.* in good time; *du solltest dich* **~** *darum kümmern* you'd better not leave it too long, you ought to see to it soon

beizen[1] *v/t.* **1.** (*ätzen*) corrode; *Metall.* pickle, dip; **2.** *Agr.* dress; **3.** (*Holz*) stain; **4.** *Färberei*: bate; **5.** (*Häute*) bate; **6.** (*Tabak*) sauce; **7.** *Gastr.* marinade, pickle; **8.** *Med.* cauterize

beizen[2] *vt/i. Jagd*: hawk

beiziehen *v/t.* (*unreg.*, *trennb.*, *hat -ge-*); *bes. südd. und österr.* (*Experten etc.*) call in, (*auch Bücher etc.*) consult; **Beiziehung** *f*; *nur Sg.* consultation, consulting

Beizjagd *f* → *Beize*[2]

Beizmittel *n* → *Beize*[1] 1-6, 8, 9

bejahen I. *v/t.* **1.** (*Frage*) answer (*od.* say) yes to, answer *a question* in the affirmative *förm.*; **2.** (*gutheißen*) see *s.th.* positively (*od.* as positive); *diesen Plan kann ich nur* **~** the plan has my full support; *das Leben* **~** have a positive outlook on life; *die Zukunft* **~** feel positive about the future; **II.** *v/i.* say yes, answer in the affirmative; **bejahend I.** *Part. Präs.* → *bejahen*; **II.** *Adj.* **1.** *Antwort*: affirmative; **2.** (*gutheißend*) positive, affirmative; optimistic

bejahrt *Adj. geh.* old, advanced in years; **Bejahrtheit** *f*; *nur Sg.* advanced age

Bejahung *f* **1.** affirmation; **2.** (*Gutheißung*) affirmation; **~ des Lebens** positive outlook on life

bejammern *v/t.* (*Person, Lage*; *j-s Tod*) lament, bemoan *lit.*

bejubeln *v/t.* (loudly) acclaim, (*j-n*) *auch* cheer; (*Sache*) rejoice at, (loudly) acclaim

bekämpfen *v/t.* fight (against); (*angehen gegen*) *auch* combat; (*Feuer*) fight;

(*Schädlinge*) fight, control; *sich gegenseitig* **~** fight (against) each other; **Bekämpfung** *f*; *mst Sg.* fight, struggle (+ *Gen.* against); *von Schädlingen*: control (of)

bekannt I. *P.P.* → *bekennen*; **II.** *Adj.* **1.** *Person, Lied, Geschichte*: known (+ *Dat.* to); (*berühmt*) well-known (*wegen* for), (*mst berüchtigt*) notorious; (*vertraut*) familiar; *allgemein* **~** well-known, generally known; *mit j-m* **~** *sein* know s.o.; *wir sind bereits* **~** *umg.* (*wir kennen uns bereits*) we have met; *etw. als* **~** *voraussetzen* assume that s.th. is known; *das ist mir* **~** I know that, I'm aware of that; *soviel mir* **~** *ist* as far as I know (*od.* I'm aware); *das Wort ist mir* **~** I've come across the word, I've heard (*od.* seen) the word used; *er kommt mir* **~** *vor* I'm sure (*od.* I know) I've seen him (*od.* his face) before; *es kommt mir* **~** *vor* it looks (*od.* sounds *etc.*) familiar; *die Geschichte kommt mir* **~** *vor iro.* I think I've heard that one before; *mir ist nichts von e-r neuen Regelung* **~** I know nothing about any new regulations; *dafür* **~** *sein, dass* have a reputation for (+*Ger.*), (*berüchtigt*) *auch* be notorious for (+*Ger.*); *er ist* **~** *für s-n Humor* he's known for his (great) sense of humour; *er ist als Lügner* **~** he's a notorious liar, everybody knows he's a liar; **2.** *mit Verb*: **~** *geben* announce; *öffentlich*: *auch* make s.th. public; *sie wollen es nicht* **~** *geben* they don't want to say anything (*od.* give anything away); *etw.* **~** *machen* (*veröffentlichen*) announce s.th., make s.th. known (*od.* public); (*berühmt machen*) make s.th. famous; *j-n* **~** *machen mit* introduce s.o. to; *sich mit etw.* **~** *machen* get to know s.th., familiarize o.s. with s.th.; **~** *werden* become known, become public; (*durchsickern*) get out, leak out; *mit j-m* **~** *werden* (*j-n kennen lernen*) get to know s.o.; *es ist* **~** *geworden, dass …* we've been informed that, news has come in that (*od.* of) …

Bekannte *m*; *f*; *-n -n* friend; *flüchtige(r)*: acquaintance; *euph.* friend; (*Partner*) *auch* boyfriend; (*Partnerin*) *auch* girlfriend; *eine* **~** *von mir* a friend of mine; *flüchtige*: somebody I know; *er ist ein guter* **~r** I know him well; **Bekanntenkreis** *m* circle of friends; *e-n großen* **~** *haben* have a lot (*od.* plenty) of friends, have a wide circle of friends; *zu j-s* **~** *zählen* be a friend of s.o., belong to s.o.'s circle of friends; *niemand aus i-m* **~** none of her friends, nobody she knows

bekanntermaßen *Adv.* → *bekanntlich*

Bekanntgabe *f*; *mst Sg.* announcement

Bekanntheit *f* familiarity; **Bekanntheitsgrad** *m* (degree of) familiarity; (*Berühmtheit*) degree of fame; *e-r Person*: extent of s.o.'s fame; *der* **~** *ist sehr hoch* it's *etc.* very widely known

bekanntlich *Adv.* as everybody knows, as we all know; *das ist* **~** *e-e Fälschung* it's a known forgery (*od.* fake), it's known to be a forgery (*od.* fake)

Bekanntmachung *f* **1.** announcement; *Pol.* (*Verlautbarung*) *auch* communiqué; **2.** (*Anschlag*) announcement, notice

Bekanntschaft *f* **1.** *nur Sg.* acquaintance; *mit e-r Sache*: familiarity; *j-s* **~** *machen* get to know s.o., meet s.o.; *mit etw.* **~** *machen unangenehm*: en-

B

counter s.th., experience s.th.; **~ schließen mit** mit Person: make s.o.'s acquaintance; mit Sache: get to know s.th.; vertraut werden: become familiar with; **bei näherer ~** on closer acquaintance; **in der ersten Zeit unserer ~** when we first got to know each other; **2.** Person: acquaintance; (Bekanntenkreis) acquaintances Pl.

bekehren I. v/t. convert (**zu** to); weitS. (Sünder, Abtrünnigen etc.) reclaim; (überzeugen) von e-r anderen Meinung: bring s.o. round; **er lässt sich nicht ~** he won't be persuaded; **II.** v/refl. become converted; **sich zu etw. ~** auch become a convert to s.th.; **sich zum Katholizismus** etc. **~** auch turn Catholic etc., become a Catholic etc.; **Bekehrte** m, f; -n, -n convert; (Neubekehrte) proselyte förm.; **Bekehrung** f conversion; weitS. von Sündern etc.: reclamation

bekennen I. v/t. (unreg.) **1.** (offen gestehen: Sünden) confess (to); (Wahrheit, Schuld) admit, confess; (Fehler) admit; **~, etw. getan zu haben** confess (od. admit) to having done s.th.; **Farbe ~** fig. nail one's colo(u)rs to the mast, put one's cards on the table, come down on one or other side of the fence; **2. s-n Glauben ~** profess one's faith; **II.** v/refl.: **sich zu etw. ~** zu e-r Tat: confess to s.th.; zu e-m Bombenanschlag etc.: admit (od. claim) responsibility for s.th.; zu e-m Glauben etc.: profess s.th.; **sich zur Demokratie / zum Islam ~** profess one's belief in democracy/Islam; **sich zu s-r Vergangenheit ~** acknowledge one's past; **sich zu j-m ~** stand by s.o.; (eintreten für) stand up for s.o.; **sich schuldig ~** admit one's guilt, admit to being guilty; **bekennend I.** Part. Präs. → **bekennen**; **II.** Adj. mst Reli. confessed; **die Bekennende Kirche** the Confessional Church

Bekenner m supporter (+ Gen. of); **~brief** m, **~schreiben** n (written) responsibility claim, letter claiming (od. admitting) responsibility

Bekenntnis n; -ses, -se **1.** (Geständnis) confession; **ein ~ ablegen** make a confession, confess; **2.** Reli., auch Pol. etc. creed; **3.** (Sichbekennen) auch Pol. (public) avowal (**zu** of), profession of loyalty (to); **~ zum Glauben** profession (od. confession) of faith; **unser ~ zu Europa** our commitment to Europe; **ein ~ zum Buddhismus ablegen** confess to the Buddhist faith; → auch **Glaubensbekenntnis**; **4.** (Konfession) denomination; **5.** österr. auch (Steuererklärung) tax declaration

bekenntnislos Adj. Person, Schule: non-denominational

bekifft Adj. Sl. smashed nur präd umg.

beklagen I. v/t. lament, grieve; **es sind tausende von / keine Menschenleben zu ~** the death toll runs into thousands / there are no casualties; **II.** v/refl.: complain (**bei** to; **über** + Akk., **wegen** about); **er hat sich darüber beklagt, dass** ... he complained about the fact that ...; **sie beklagte sich ständig über die Kosten** she was constantly fretting about (od. at) the costs; **ich kann mich nicht ~** I can't complain, I have no complaints; konzedierend: I mustn't grumble umg.; **beklagenswert** Adj. geh. lamentable, sad; Person: pitiable; **in e-m ~en Zustand** in a sorry state

beklagt Adj. Jur.: **die ~e Partei** the de-

fendant (od. accused); bei Scheidung: respondent; **Beklagte** m, f; -n, -n; Jur. defendant, accused; bei Scheidung: respondent

beklatschen v/t. applaud

beklauen v/t. umg.: **j-n ~** steal s.th. from s.o. allg.; **ich bin beklaut worden** I've been robbed allg.

bekleben v/t. stick s.th. onto; **mit Bildern ~** stick pictures all over, cover with pictures; **die Wand war mit e-r scheußlichen Tapete beklebt** the wall was covered in the most ghastly wallpaper

bekleckern umg. **I.** v/t. mess up; mit etw. Flüssigem: auch spill s.th. on; mit etw. Breiigem: auch drop s.th. on; **ich habe mir die Bluse bekleckert** I've spil|t (Am. -led) something on (od. messed up) my blouse; **ein bekleckertes Lätzchen** a filthy bib; **II.** v/refl. spill (od. drop) s.th. on one's tie (od. blouse etc.), mess up one's tie etc.; **du hast dich mit Tinte bekleckert** auch you've got ink on (od. all over) your shirt etc.; **du hast dich nicht gerade mit Ruhm bekleckert** you didn't exactly cover yourself with glory

bekleiden v/t. **1.** dress; **mit etw. bekleidet sein** auch be dressed (od. clothed) in s.th.; **2.** geh. fig. (Amt, Stelle) hold; **bekleidet I.** P.P. → **bekleiden**; **II.** Adj. dressed, clothed lit. (**mit** in); **~ mit** auch wearing; **leicht ~** lightly dressed; **spärlich ~** scantily dressed (od. clad); **Bekleidung** f **1.** (Kleider) clothing, clothes Pl., dress; **2.** nur Sg.; von Amt, Stellung etc.: tenure

Bekleidungs|artikel m item of clothing; Pl. clothes, garments, clothing Sg.; **~industrie** f clothing (od. textile) industry

beklemmen v/t. make s.o. (feel) uneasy; stärker: oppress s.o.; **beklemmend I.** Part. Präs. → **beklemmen**; **II.** Adj. oppressive, suffocating, stifling (alle auch fig.); Schweigen: embarrassed; **~es Gefühl** uneasy feeling; **Beklemmung** f **1.** durch Enge verursacht: suffocating feeling; **2.** fig. feeling of unease, sense of anxiety; (Angst) feeling of fear; stärker: oppressive feeling; **bei diesem Gedanken bekomme ich ~en** the thought of it makes me feel oppressed (od. full of apprehension od. trepidation); **~en haben** feel very uneasy; bei enger Kleidung: feel restricted

beklommen Adj. Stimme etc.: anxious, uneasy; **~es Gefühl** auch feeling of anxiety; **Beklommenheit** f; nur Sg. uneasiness, anxiety

beklopfen v/t. tap

bekloppt Adj. nordd. umg. **1.** Person: crazy, präd. auch nuts; **Mensch, bist du total ~?** have you gone completely off your head (Am. rocker)?; **so was macht nur ein Bekloppter!** only a nutter (od. fool) would do that; **2.** Vorschlag, Einfall etc: crazy; **so was Beklopptes!** what a crazy thing to do (od. happen etc.)

beknabbern v/t. umg. nibble at

beknackt Adj. umg. **1.** Person: crazy, präd. auch nuts, off one's head (Am. rocker); **ein total ~er Typ** a complete nutter (Am. psycho); **2.** Sache: (ärgerlich) rotten, stupid; **so was Beknacktes!** what a pain!

beknien v/t. umg. beg s.o.. (**zu** + Inf. to + Inf.), go on at s.o. (to + Inf.)

bekochen v/t. umg. cook for s.o.

bekommen I. v/t. (unreg., hat bekom-

men) **1.** (erhalten) weitS. get, auch be given; ohne Zutun: receive; durch Anstrengung: obtain; **hast du m-n Brief ~?** did you get (od. receive) my letter?; **ich bekomme schon seit Tagen keine Post mehr** I haven't had any mail for days now; **ich bekomme noch 20 Euro von dir** you still owe me 20 euros; **er bekam e-e gute Stellung** he got a good position; **hast du noch Karten ~?** did you manage to get tickets?; **das bekommt man überall** you can get that anywhere; **~ Sie schon?** im Geschäft: can I help you?; im Lokal: have you ordered (yet)?; **was ~ Sie?** a) im Geschäft: yes, please?, can I help you?; im Lokal: are you ready to order?, b) (wie viel kostet das) how much is that?; **was haben Sie von uns zu ~?** how much do we owe you?; **~ Sie noch etwas?** anything else?; am Telefon: **ich bekomme keinen Anschluss** I can't get through; **keine Verbindung ~** get a bad line; **e-n Schlag auf die Hand ~** get a slap on the wrist; **e-n Tritt ans Bein ~** get kicked in the leg; **e-n Schneeball an den Kopf ~** get hit on the head by a snowball; **2.** (entwickeln) get; **ein Kind ~** (be going to) have a baby; **Junge ~** have pups etc.; → **Junge**[2]; **e-n Bauch ~** develop a (bit of a) paunch; **e-e Glatze ~** go bald, develop a bald patch; **graue Haare ~** go grey, get grey hair; **Hunger ~** get hungry; **Durst ~** get thirsty, develop a thirst; **Schnupfen ~** get (od. come down with) a cold; **Kinder ~ leicht Fieber** children are quick to run a temperature; **das Baby bekommt Zähne** the baby's teething; **e-n epileptischen Anfall ~** have an epileptic seizure (od. fit umg); **die Bäume ~ Blätter** the trees are coming into leaf; **Knospen ~** begin to bud, get new buds; (seelische Zustände): **Angst ~** get scared (od. frightened); **es mit der Angst zu tun ~** get scared, get the wind up umg.; **e-n Wutanfall ~** lose one's temper; **e-n roten Kopf ~** go red, blush; **Heimweh ~** get (od. start to feel) homesick; **da kann man doch zu viel ~!** umg. it's enough to drive you mad; **3.** umg. (Wetter): **ich glaube, wir ~ bald Regen** I think there's rain on the way; **endlich ~ wir wärmeres Wetter** there's warmer weather on the way at last; **4.** Zustand: **e-n Riss ~** get od. be torn, get a tear; **Flecken ~** get od. be marked (od. stained); **es hat Löcher ~** it's got holes (in it), it's full of holes; **5.** (Zug, Flug etc.) get, catch; **6.** umg. (etw. bewerkstelligen): **ich bekomme den Nagel nicht aus der Wand** I can't get this nail out of the wall; **~ wir das ganze Gepäck in den Kofferraum?** will we get all the luggage into the boot (Am. trunk)?; **7.** mit zu + Inf.: **etw. zu sehen ~** get to see s.th.; **etw. zu spüren ~** get to know s.th., get a taste of s.th.; **wo kann man hier etwas zu essen/ trinken ~?** is there anywhere you can get something to eat/drink around here?; **j-n/etw. zu fassen ~** get hold of s.o./s.th.; **das bekomme ich von allen Leuten zu hören** that's what I've been hearing from everyone; **das wird er noch jahrelang zu hören ~** he won't be allowed to forget about that for years; **er bekommt es nicht über sich, das zu tun** umg. he can't bring himself to do it; **8.** mit Part.: **etw. geschenkt ~** get a present, be given s.th. (as a present); **er bekommt zu Hause *alles gemacht* he has (*od.* gets) everything done for him at home; *er bekommt e-n Dienstwagen gestellt* he gets the use of a company car; → *auch kriegen*; **II.** *v/i.* (*ist*): *j-m* (*gut*) ~ *Essen, Wetter etc.*: agree with s.o., suit s.o.; *Ruhe etc.*: do s.o. good, be good for s.o.; *j-m nicht od. schlecht* ~ *Essen, Wetter*: disagree with s.o.; *das Wetter bekommt ihm nicht auch* he can't cope with the weather; *es bekommt ihm ausgezeichnet* it's doing him the world of (*Am.* a world of) good; *es bekommt ihm überhaupt nicht* it doesn't agree with him at all; *wohl bekomm's!* cheers!, *iro.* the best of luck, *Brit.* the best of British

bekömmlich *Adj. Essen*: easily digestible, easy on the stomach; (*leicht*) light; *Medikament*: innocuous, with (next to) no side effects; *Klima etc.*: (very) agreeable; *ein leicht ~es Essen* a light (*od.* an easily digestible) meal; *schwer* ~ *Essen*: hard to digest, hard on the stomach (*od.* digestion), heavy; **Bekömmlichkeit** *f; nur Sg.* digestibility

beköstigen I. *v/t.* feed, cook for; *dort wo er wohnt, wird er auch beköstigt* they also provide him with meals where he lives; **II.** *v/refl.*: *sich selbst* ~ cook (*od.* cater) for o.s.; **Beköstigung** *f; mst Sg.* **1.** (*Essen*) food; **2.** (*Vorgang*) catering (+ *Gen.* for), feeding (*s.o.*)

bekräftigen *v/t.* **1.** (*bestätigen*) confirm (*durch* with, by + *Ger.*); (*Meinung etc.*) support, *durch Beweise etc.*: *auch* corroborate; *weitS.* (*verstärken*) reinforce; (*unterstützen*) endorse; *s-e Aussage durch od. mit e-m Eid* ~ swear to (*od.* take an oath on) one's statement; *e-e Vereinbarung mit e-m Handschlag* ~ confirm an agreement with a handshake; **2.** *etw. bekräftigt j-n in etw.* (*Dat.*) s.th. confirms s.o. in s.th.; *das bekräftigte ihn in s-m Entschluss* it confirmed him in his decision; **Bekräftigung** *f* support(ing); corroboration; reinforcement; endorsement; confirmation; → *bekräftigen*; *zur* ~ (+ *Gen.*) in support (*od.* corroboration) of; *zur* ~ *gab er ihm die Hand* he shook his hand in affirmation

bekränzen *v/t.* place a wreath on; *j-n mit Lorbeer* ~ crown s.o. with a laurel wreath

bekreuzigen *v/refl. Reli.* cross o.s., make the sign of the cross

bekriegen *v/t.* wage war against; *sich od. geh. einander* ~ go to (*od.* be at) war with one another

bekritteln *v/t. pej.* criticize, find fault with

bekritzeln *v/t.* scribble on; *du hast ja dein ganzes Heft bekritzelt* you've scribbled all over your exercise book (*Am.* notebook)

bekümmern I. *v/t.* worry; (*traurig machen*) grieve; *das bekümmert ihn gar nicht* it doesn't worry (*od.* bother) him in the slightest; *das braucht Sie nicht zu* ~ you needn't worry about that; **II.** *v/refl. geh.* concern o.s. (*um* with); **bekümmert I.** *P.P.* → *bekümmern*; **II.** *Adj.* worried, anxious *look etc.*; *er macht e-n ~en Eindruck* something seems to be worrying him; **III.** *Adv.* anxiously; *j-n* ~ *ansehen* give s.o. a look of concern; **Bekümmerung** *f; nur Sg.* concern; *stärker*: anxiety, grief

bekunden I. *v/t.* **1.** (*zeigen*) show, display; *Interesse* ~ show *od.* display (an) interest; **2.** (*erklären*) state, declare;

Jur. testify; **II.** *v/refl. geh.* reveal itself; **Bekundung** *f* **1.** show, display, manifestation; **2.** (*Erklärung*) declaration, avowal

belächeln *v/t.* smile (condescendingly *od.* pityingly *etc.*) at

belachen *v/t.* laugh at

beladen I. *v/t.* (*unreg.*); (*Fahrzeug, Schiff, Lasttier*) load (up); *j-n mit etw.* ~ *mit Gepäck*: load s.o. (down) with s.th.; *fig. mit Arbeit etc.*: load s.o. down with s.th.; *mit Problemen etc.*: burden s.o. with s.th.; **II.** *Adj.* (fully) loaded; *mit etw.* ~ *sein* be loaded with s.th.; *Tisch etc.*: *auch* be piled high with s.th.; *mit Problemen/Schuld* ~ weighed down (*od.* burdened with) problems/guilt; **Beladung** *f; nur Sg. von Fahrzeug, Schiff*: loading (up)

Belag *m*; *-(e)s, Beläge* **1.** (*Überzug*) coat(ing); (*Schicht*) layer; (*Auskleidung, Brems-, Kupplungsbelag*) lining; *auf Fußboden*: covering; *von Brücken, Straßen*: surface; *von Skiern*: base, (running) surface; **2.** *fig.; Med. auf Zunge*: coating; (*Zahnbelag*) plaque, tartar; **3.** *mst Sg.; auf Brot, Pizza, Kuchen*: topping, (*Aufstrich*) spread, *auf Sandwich*: (sandwich) filling; *belegte Brote mit verschiedenem* ~ open sandwiches with various toppings

Belagerer *m*; *-s, -, mst Pl.* besieger; **belagern** *v/t. auch fig.* besiege, beleaguer; *Mil.* (*völlig einschließen*) invest; *umg. fig. auch* throng, crowd (round); *er wird von s-n Gläubigern belagert fig.* he's being beleaguered by his creditors; *die Fenster* ~ *fig.* crowd the windows; **Belagerung** *f* siege; **Belagerungszustand** *m*; *nur Sg.; Jur.* state of siege; *im* ~ in a state of siege, under siege; *den* ~ *ausrufen* declare a (state of) siege; *den* ~ *über e-e Stadt verhängen* lay siege to a city

belämmert *v/t.* **1.** (*leicht dümmlich*) dop(e)y; **2.** (*betreten, verlegen*) sheepish

Belang *m*; *-(e)s, -e* **1.** *nur Sg.*; (*Wichtigkeit*) importance, significance; *von* ~ of importance (*für* to); *sachlich*: relevant (to); *was schreibt er? - nichts von* ~ what is he writing? – nothing significant (*od.* of importance); *ohne* ~ unimportant (*für* for), of no consequence *od.* importance (to); *sachlich*: irrelevant (to), immaterial (to); **2.** *~e* (*Angelegenheiten*) concerns, issues, affairs; (*Interessen*) interests; *öffentliche ~e* public issues, matters of public concern (*od.* interest); *j-s ~e wahrnehmen/vertreten* look after (*od.* safeguard) / represent s.o.'s interests

belangen *v/t. Jur.* sue (*wegen* for); *auch strafrechtlich*: prosecute *s.o.*

belanglos *Adj.* unimportant, insignificant; *sachlich*: irrelevant (*für* to); **Belanglosigkeit** *f* **1.** *nur Sg.*; (*Unwichtigkeit*) insignificance; irrelevance; **2.** (*Unbedeutendes*) insignificant matter, triviality, irrelevancy; *Pl. auch* trivia; **3.** *~en* (*belangloses Gerede*) trivial talk *Sg.*

Belangsendung *f österr.* party political broadcast

belassen *v/t.* (*unreg.*) **1.** (*nicht verändern*) leave *s.th.* (as it is); *etw. an s-m Platz* ~ leave s.th. where it is; *j-n in dem Glauben* ~, *dass ...* let s.o. go on thinking (*od.* believing) that ...; *wollen wir ihn bei s-m Glauben/Irrtum* ~! let's not spoil his illusion / disabuse him of his mistake; *es dabei* ~ leave it at that; **2.** (*überlassen, nicht abneh-*

men): *j-m etw.* ~ leave s.th. to s.o.; **Belassung** *f; nur Sg. im Amt etc.*: retention

belastbar *Adj.* **1.** *Tech.* loadable; ~ *bis ... bei Fahrzeug*: maximum loading capacity ...; *bei Brücke*: maximum load ...; **2.** *Mensch*: resilient; ~ *sein arbeitsmäßig*: be able to cope with a heavy workload, be able to work under pressure; *nervlich*: be able to take the strain (*od.* pressure); *er ist nicht* ~ he can't cope with any kind of pressure (*nervlich: auch* strain); *im Alter ist der Kreislauf/Magen nicht mehr so* ~ as you get old, your circulation/stomach can't take as much as it used to; *sein Herz ist wieder voll* ~ his heart is back to normal again; *die Umwelt ist nicht unbeschränkt* ~ there's a limit to the amount of pollution the environment can take, we can't go on polluting our environment forever

Belastbarkeit *f; nur Sg.* **1.** *Tech.* loading capacity; *von Seilen etc.*: tensile strength; *e-r Brücke*: load-bearing capacity; *Etech.* power rating; *e-s Lautsprechers*: power handling (capacity); **2.** *e-s Menschen*: ability to cope with pressure (*nervliche: auch* strain); *von Organen*: resilience; *bis zur Grenze der* ~ to the breaking point

belasten I. *v/t.* **1.** (*Fahrzeug*) *auch Tech.* load; (*Brücke, Balken*) put weight on; *Tech.* (*beanspruchen*) stress; (*beschweren*) (*auch Ski*) weight; *beide Beine gleichmäßig* ~ weight both legs evenly; *der Aufzug darf mit max. 300 kg belastet werden* the lift (*Am.* elevator) can take a maximum load of 300 kg; *e-e Brücke mit 3 t* ~ put a 3-ton(ne) load on a bridge; *der Anhänger ist zu sehr belastet* the trailer is overloaded; **2.** (*Person*) physisch, psychisch etc.*: strain, put a strain on; *stark* ~ put a heavy strain on; *arbeitsmäßig*: put *s.o.* under (a lot of) pressure; *durch zusätzliche Arbeit*: give *s.o.* a heavy workload; *mit Verantwortung*: place a heavy burden on; *auch nervlich*: be a (great) strain on *s.o.*; (*Sorgen machen*) be a (big) worry for *s.o.*; *gewissensmäßig*: give *s.o.* a (really) bad conscience; *ich möchte dich nicht mit m-n Problemen* ~ I don't want to burden you with my problems; *es belastet mich* (*allmählich*) *auch* it's getting to me; *sein Gedächtnis mit unnützem Wissen* ~ fill one's head with useless knowledge; *sein Gewissen* ~ *mit* burden one's conscience with; *er ist durch s-e Vergangenheit* (*stark*) *belastet politisch*: he is (seriously) discredited by his past, he has a (very) shady past; *dieses Wissen od. diese Erkenntnis belastet mich* (*beunruhigt mich*) knowing that bothers (*od.* worries) me; *diese Entscheidung scheint dich sehr zu* ~ that decision seems to be causing you some distress; **3.** *Med.* (*Organ, Kreislauf etc.*) strain; *beim EKG etc.*: exert; *Alkohol belastet die Leber* alcohol is a strain on the liver; **4.** (*Umwelt etc.*) pollute, contaminate, add to the pollution of *the environment*; **5.** *Etech.* (*Stromnetz etc.*) load; *wenn das Computernetz plötzlich zu stark belastet wird* when the computer network is suddenly overloaded; **6.** *Fin.*: *j-n/j-s Konto* ~ debit s.o. / s.o.'s account (*mit* with); *j-n finanziell* (*stark*) ~ be a (heavy) burden on s.o., present a (heavy) financial strain on s.o.;

durch Steuern: place a (heavy) tax burden on s.o.; *den Staatshaushalt durch neue Ausgaben ~* burden the national budget with additional spending; **7.** (*Grundstück, Haus*) encumber, mortgage; *ein Haus mit e-r Hypothek ~* encumber a house with a mortgage; **8.** *Jur., durch Indizien etc.*: incriminate; **II.** *v/refl.*: *sich mit etw. ~ mit Arbeit, Verantwortung*: burden (*od.* saddle) o.s. with s.th.; *damit kann ich mich nicht ~* auch I haven't got time to deal with that sort of thing; **III.** *v/i.*: *Besitz belastet* property (*od.* riches) can be a burden; *nur bei Skiern*: *du belastest falsch* you're weighting the wrong ski

belastend I. *Part. Präs.* → *belasten*; **II.** *Adj.* **1.** *Jur.* incriminating; **2.** *~ sein* be a strain; **belastet I.** *P.P.* → *belasten*; **II.** *Adj.* **1.** *Grundstück etc.*: encumbered; *das Haus ist nicht ~* the house is not mortgaged; **2.** *Med. Organ etc.*: under strain, overworked, overtaxed; *ihr Kreislauf ist zu stark belastet* her circulation is under too much strain; → *erblich* II

belästigen *v/t. mit ständigen Fragen*: pester, annoy; *mit Problem etc.*: trouble, bother; (*Mädchen*) molest; *darf ich Sie noch einmal (kurz) ~ geh.* I wonder if I could I trouble you again (very briefly); *ich möchte Sie nicht länger mit m-r Anwesenheit ~ förm. od. gespreizt* I won't take up any more of your precious time; *sich belästigt fühlen durch* find s.o./s.th. irritating (*od.* a nuisance); **Belästigung** *f auch Pl.* pestering; *auf der Straße*: molestation; *als ~ empfinden* find s.o./s.th. irritating (*od.* a nuisance)

Belastung *f* **1.** *Tech.* (*Last*) load, stress; (*das Belasten*) loading; *zulässige ~* maximum permissible load, safe load; *für Aufzug*: maximum load; **2.** *physisch, psychisch etc.*: (*Anstrengung*) strain; (*Last*) burden (*für* on); *e-s Verhältnisses etc.*: strain (on); *e-e starke ~* a great (*od.* real) strain; *wir sind heute anderen ~en ausgesetzt als früher* we're subject to different pressures today than in the past; **3.** *Med.* strain (*für* on); (*das Belasten*) straining; *beim EKG etc.*: exertion; *unter od. bei ~* under exertion; *unnötige ~en vermeiden* avoid unnecessary strain; **4.** *der Umwelt*: pollution, contamination (*für* of); **5.** *Etech. im Versorgungsnetz*: load (+ *Gen.* on); (*das Belasten*) loading (+ *Gen.* of); **6.** *e-s Kontos*: charge, debit; *finanzielle*: (financial) burden (+ *Gen.* on); **7.** *e-s Grundstücks*: encumbrance, (*Hypothek*) mortgage; *die ~ e-s Hauses mit e-r Hypothek* mortgaging a house; **8.** *Jur.* incrimination

Belastungs|-EKG *n Med.* exercise ECG (*Am.* EKG), ECG (*Am.* EKG) stress test; *~grenze f* **1.** maximum load; **2.** *fig.* limit(s *Pl.*) of what s.o. can take; *ich habe m-e ~ erreicht* I can't take any more, I've had just about all I can take *umg.*; *~probe f* **1.** *Tech.* load test; **2.** *fig.* test (of endurance); *~schwankung f Etech.* fluctuation of load; *~spitze f auch Etech.* peak load; *~zeuge m Jur.* witness for the prosecution

belauben *v/refl.* come into leaf; **belaubt I.** *P.P.* → *belauben*; **II.** *Adj.* leafy, *präd. auch* in leaf; *spärlich/dicht ~e Bäume* trees with sparse/thick foliage

belauern *v/t.* lie in wait for; *weitS.*

watch *s.o.* closely; (*beobachten*) spy on; *einander od. sich gegenseitig ~* spy on each other

belaufen *v/refl.* (*unreg., hat*): *sich auf etw.* (*Akk.*) *~ Schulden, Kosten, Schaden, Barschaft*: amount to s.th., run up to s.th., total s.th.

belauschen *v/t.* **1.** (*Gespräch*) eavesdrop on; **2.** (*Wohnung abhören*) bug; **3.** (*beobachten: Tiere*) watch, observe; **Belauschung** *f; nur Sg.* **1.** *e-s Gesprächs*: eavesdropping; **2.** *von Tieren*: observation

Belcanto [bel'kanto] *m; -s, kein Pl.; Mus.* belcanto

beleben I. *v/t.* **1.** (*in Schwung bringen*) liven up, get (*od.* put) some life into; (*Wirtschaft etc.*) stimulate, get s.th. going; (*munter machen*) *Getränk etc.*: revive, freshen; (*auch Kreislauf*) get s.o. *od.* s.th. going (again), buck up *umg.*; (*kräftigen*) invigorate; **2.** (*Zimmer, Bild*) brighten up; (*Unterhaltung*) liven up; *eine bunte Menge belebte den Platz* the square was filled with a motley crowd of people; **3.** (*zum Leben erwecken*) (*alte Sitten*) revive; *frisches Grün belebt die Natur* fresh green gives new life to nature; *neu ~* put/ breathe new life into; → *wieder* 2; **4.** *oft lit.* (*bevölkern*) populate; **II.** *v/refl.* liven up; *Straße, Lokal etc.*: come to life; *Gesicht*: brighten up; *Natur*: come alive; *Wirtschaft, Konjunktur*: pick up, revive; **III.** *v/i.* (*eine aufmunternde Wirkung haben*) be invigorating, get s.o. going; *Kaffee belebt* coffee is a stimulant, coffee gets you going / gives you a kick *umg.*; **belebend I.** *Part. Präs.* → *beleben*; **II.** *Adj.* stimulating, invigorating; *Getränk*: refreshing; **belebt I.** *P.P.* → *beleben*; **II.** *Adj.* **1.** (*lebhaft*) lively, animated; *Szene, Straße etc.*: busy, bustling; **2.** (*lebendig*) living; *die ~e Natur* animate nature; **Belebtheit** *f; nur Sg. e-r Straße etc.*: hustle and bustle (+ *Gen.* of), bustling life (of); **Belebung** *f; nur Sg.* livening up; *des Kreislaufs, der Wirtschaft etc.*: stimulation; *ein Mittel zur ~ des Kreislaufs / der Wirtschaft* something to get the circulation going / to boost the economy

Beleg *m; -(e)s, -e* **1.** record; (*Quittung*) receipt; (*Beweis*) *auch Pl.* proof, evidence; *mehrere ~e für den Gebrauch e-s Wortes* several instances of the use of a word; **2.** (*Beispiel*) example (*für* of); (*Quelle*) reference

Belegarzt *m Med.* private doctor in a hospital

belegbar *Adj.* verifiable, provable

Beleg|bett *n Med.* private bed (*allotted to a specific practitioner*); *~bogen m Univ.* form recording the seminars and lectures for which a student registers

belegen I. *v/t.* **1.** (*bedecken*) cover; (*auskleiden*) (*auch Bremsen etc.*) line; *mit Schutzüberzug etc.*: coat; *mit Teppichboden ~* carpet; *Brot/Tortenboden mit etw. ~* put s.th. on bread / a cake base; **2.** (*Zimmer, Wohnung etc.*) occupy; *im Notfall ~ wir das Doppelzimmer mit 3 Personen* if necessary, we'll put 3 people up in the double room; **3.** (*reservieren*) reserve; (*vorbestellen*): *auch* book; **4.** (*Kurs etc.*) sign up for, register for, enrol(l) for; **5.** *Sport*: *den ersten/letzten Platz ~* take first/ last place, come first/last; **6.** *fig.*: *mit e-r Strafe / Steuern ~* impose a penalty / taxes on s.o./s.th.; **7.** (*nachweisen*) (*Ausgaben etc.*) produce evidence for;

(*beweisen*) give evidence for, substantiate, back up, prove; (*verifizieren*) verify; (*Textstelle, Wort*) give (*od.* quote) a reference for; **8.** *Mil.* (*beschießen*) bombard; **II.** *v/refl.*: get covered (*mit* with); *selber*: form a layer of; *Med. Zunge*: fur; *Stimme*: get husky; → *belegt* II; **III.** *v/i.* (*sich einschreiben*) register

Beleg|exemplar *n* (*Buch*) specimen copy; *für Autor*: *auch* author's copy; *~krankenhaus n Med.* general practitioners' hospital; *~material n* documentary evidence

Belegschaft *f* personnel (*mst V. im Pl.*); *in Fabrik auch*: work force; *die einzelnen Mitarbeiter*: employees *Pl.*; *bes. an Schule, Universität, in Organisationen etc.*: staff (*mst V. im Pl.*); *die ~ der Firma X streikt seit e-r Woche* staff (*od.* employees) at X have been on strike for a week

Belegschaftsaktie *f Wirts.* employee share (*Pl. auch* stock *Sg.*)

Beleg|schein *m* voucher; (*Quittung*) receipt; *~stelle f* reference

belegt I. *P.P.* → *belegen*; **II.** *Adj.* **1.** *Zunge*: coated, furred; *Stimme*: husky; **2.** *Platz, Raum*: taken, occupied; (*voll ~*) full (up); **3.** *Telef.* engaged, *Am.* busy; **4.** *~es Brot* (open) sandwich; *~es Brötchen* filled roll; **5.** (*nachweisbar sein*): *~ sein bei* occur in; *es ist nirgends ~* there's no evidence for it

belehnen *v/t.* **1.** *hist.* enfeoff; **2.** *schw.* (*beleihen*) loan, lend (on security); **Belehnung** *f* **1.** *hist.* enfeoffment; **2.** *schw.* granting of a loan

belehrbar *Adj.* teachable

belehren *v/t.* teach, instruct; (*aufklären*) inform (*über* + *Akk.* of); *Jur. j-n über s-e Rechte ~* advise s.o. of their rights; *sich ~ lassen* (*Rat einholen*) take some advice; (*Vernunft annehmen*) listen to reason; *du musst dich eines anderen ~ geh.* I must put you right there; → *besser* II 2; **belehrend I.** *Part. Präs.* → *belehren*; **II.** *Adj.* **1.** *Film, Vortrag*: instructive; **2.** *pej. Ton etc.*: schoolmasterly; *bei e-r Frau*: schoolmarmish; **Belehrung** *f* **1.** (*Belehrtwerden*) instruction; (*Rat*) advice; *Jur. von Zeugen*: instruction; *er will keine ~(en) annehmen* he won't listen to any advice; **2.** *pej.* (*Zurechtweisung*) lecture; *spar dir deine ständigen ~en* I wish you'd stop lecturing (*od.* preaching)

beleibt *Adj.* stout, portly; **Beleibtheit** *f; nur Sg.* stoutness, portliness

beleidigen *v/t. auch Auge, Gefühl etc. und fig.* offend; (*verletzen*) hurt; *gröblich*: insult; *öffentlich*: affront; (*beschimpfen*) abuse; *Jur.* slander; *schriftlich*: libel; *ich wollte dich nicht ~ auch* I didn't mean any offen|ce (*Am.* -se)

beleidigend I. *Part. Präs.* → *beleidigen*; **II.** *Adj.* offensive; *grob*: insulting; *Jur.* slanderous; *schriftlich*: libel(l)ous; *~ werden* become (*od.* get) abusive, start insulting *s.o.*

beleidigt I. *P.P.* → *beleidigen*; **II.** *Adj.* **1.** offended; *zutiefst ~* deeply offended, *bes. iro.* mortally wounded; *sei nicht gleich ~, aber ...* I don't mean to offend you, but ...; *ach komm, sei nicht gleich wieder ~!* oh come on, don't get all offended again; *sie ist wegen jeder Kleinigkeit ~* she takes offen|ce (*Am.* -se) at the slightest thing; **2.** *nur attr.* offended, in a huff *umg.*; *ein ~es Gesicht machen*

look hurt (*od.* offended); *die ~e Leberwurst spielen* umg. be (*od.* go off) in a huff, sulk (in a corner somewhere); *e-e ~e Antwort geben* answer indignantly, answer in a huff *umg.*
Beleidigung *f* **1.** insult; *Jur.* slander; *schriftliche*: libel; *etw. als ~ empfinden* take offen|ce (*Am.* -se) at s.th., consider s.th. an offen|ce (*Am.* -se); *sich (Pl.) ~en an den Kopf werfen* trade insults; **2.** *nur Sg.*; (*das Beleidigen*) insulting; **Beleidigungsklage** *f Jur.* libel action
beleihbar *Adj.* **1.** eligible as collateral; *etw. ist ~* s.th. can serve as collateral; **2.** *Fin. Sicherheit*: pledgeable; *Haus etc.*: that can be mortgaged
beleihen *v/t.* (*unreg.*); *Wirts.* (*Haus, Grundstück*) mortgage, raise a mortgage on; (*Wertpapiere*) advance money on; (*Schmuck*) raise a loan on; *etw. mit 30.000 Euro ~ lassen* raise a 30,000 euro mortgage (*od.* loan) on s.th.; **Beleihung** *f* raising of a loan (*od.* mortgage) (+ *Gen.* on); **Beleihungswert** *m* loan value
belemmert *Adj.* → *belämmert*
belesen *Adj.* well-read; *er ist auf diesem Gebiet sehr ~* he knows a great deal about the subject; **Belesenheit** *f*; *nur Sg. literarische*: (wide) knowledge of literature; *allg.* knowledge, erudition; *ich staune über s-e ~* I'm amazed at how well-read he is (*od.* at how much he has read)
beleuchten *v/t.* **1.** light (up); *festlich auch*: illuminate; *e-n Saal festlich ~* decorate a hall with festive lighting; **2.** *fig.* examine, take a look at; *kritisch/genauer ~* take a critical/closer look at; *von allen Seiten ~* examine (*od.* look at) s.th. from every angle
Beleuchter *m*; *-s*, *-*, *~in* *f*; *-*, *-nen*; *Theat.* stage-lighter; *Film* lighting technician, lighter
beleuchtet I. *P.P.* → *beleuchten*; **II.** *Adj.* lit (up), illuminated; *gut/schlecht ~* well-lit / badly lit
Beleuchtung *f* **1.** *kollektiv*: lighting, light(s *Pl.*); *die ~ einschalten* switch (*od.* put) on the lights (*od.* lighting); *bei künstlicher ~* in artificial light(ing); **2.** *nur Sg.*; (*das Beleuchten*) lighting, illumination; **3.** *fig.* investigation
Beleuchtungs|anlage *f* lighting (system); *~technik* *f* light(ing) engineering
beleumdet, beleumundet *Adj.*: *gut/schlecht ~* held in good (bad) repute
belfern *v/i.* umg. **1.** (*kläffen*) bark; **2.** *Dial.* (*schimpfen*) rant
Belgien (*n*); *-s* Belgium; **Belgier** *m*; *-s*, *-*, **Belgierin** *f*; *-*, *-nen* Belgian, *weiblich auch*: Belgian woman; **belgisch** *Adj.* Belgian
belichten *vt/i.* **1.** *Fot.* expose; *kurz/lang ~* use a short/long exposure (time); **2.** *Tech.* (*Bühne*) light up, illuminate; **Belichtung** *f Fot.* exposure
Belichtungs|automatik *f Fot.* automatic exposure (*od.* timer); *~dauer* *f* exposure (time); *~messer* *m* light meter, exposure meter; *~zeit* *f* exposure (time)
belieben *geh.*, *auch altm.* **I.** *v/t. bes. iro.*: *~ zu* (+ *Inf.*) deign to (+ *Inf.*); *Sie ~ wohl zu scherzen?* you are joking, of course; *tu, was dir beliebt* do as you like, suit yourself; **II.** *v/i.*: *wie es Ihnen beliebt* as you wish; *wie es hum.* what say?, how'zat?; **III. Belieben** *n*; *-s*, *kein Pl.*; *geh.*

pleasure; (*Gutdünken*) discretion; *nach Belieben* at will, *auch ganz nach Belieben* (just) as you like (*od.* one likes *etc.*); *es steht in Ihrem Belieben* it's (entirely) up to you (*zu* + *Inf.* to + *Inf.*)
beliebig I. *Adj.* any (… you like); (*willkürlich*) *auch* arbitrary; *e-e ~e Menge* any amount, as much (*od.* many) as you like; *zu jeder ~en Zeit* at any time (you please); *jede ~e Arbeit annehmen* take any job (*od.* work) that comes along; *e-e ~e Auswahl treffen* (*irgendeine*) choose anything (*od.* whatever) you like; *die Anordnung ist ~* they can be arranged any way at all (*od.* any way you like); **II.** *Adv.* just as you like (*od.* one likes *etc.*); *~ lang/oft etc.* as long/often *etc.* as you like; *das kann man ~ variieren* it can be varied at will (*od.* any way you like); **Beliebige** *f*, *m*; *-n*, *-n*: *jeder Beliebige / alle Beliebigen* anyone; **Beliebigkeit** *f* arbitrariness, randomness
beliebt I. *P.P.* → *belieben*; **II.** *Adj.* popular (*bei* with); *Ware*: (very much) in demand (among); *sich bei j-m ~ machen* (try and) get into s.o.'s good books, suck up to s.o. *umg. pej.*; **Beliebtheit** *f*; *nur Sg.* popularity (*bei* among); *sich allgemeiner/großer od. e-r großen ~ erfreuen* be very popular, enjoy great popularity *geh.*
Beliebtheitsgrad *m* popularity (rating)
beliefern *v/t.* supply (*mit* with); *e-n Markt ~* supply a market; **Belieferung** *f* supply; *die ~ von j-m mit etw.* supplying s.o. with s.th.
bellen *auch fig.* **I.** *v/i.* **1.** *Hund*: bark; **2.** (*mit heiserer Stimme sprechen*) croak; **3.** *Geschütz*: crack; *Kanone*: boom; **II.** *v/t.* (*Befehle*) bark out; **bellend I.** *Part. Präs.* → *bellen*; **II.** *Adj.* *fig.* **1.** *Husten*: hacking; **2.** *Geschütz*: cracking; *Kanone*: booming
Belletristik *f*; *-*, *kein Pl.* (poetry and) fiction; *engS.* belles lettres (*Sg.*); **belletristisch** *Adj. Literatur*: fictional; *engS.* belletristic; *nur attr.* fiction …; *Zeitschrift*: literary; *~e Werke* works of (poetry and) fiction; *ein ~er Verlag* a fiction publisher
belobigen *v/t. altm.* praise, commend; **Belobigung** *f* praise, commendation
belohnen *v/t.* reward, give *s.o.* a reward; (*Vertrauen, Mühe etc.*) reward; *mit etw. belohnt werden* receive a reward of s.th., *auch fig.* be rewarded with s.th.; **Belohnung** *f* reward; *als od. zur ~* as a reward (*für* for), in return (for); *e-e ~* (*in Höhe von …*) *aussetzen* offer a reward (of …)
belüften *v/t.* ventilate; (*Gewässer*) aerate; **belüftet I.** *P.P.* → *belüften*; **II.** *Adj.*: *gut/schlecht ~* well-ventilated / poorly ventilated; **Belüftung** *f* ventilation; *von Gewässern*: aeration
Belüftungs|anlage *f* ventilation (system); *~rohr* *n* air pipe; *~ventil* *n* ventilation valve
Belugawal *m Zool.* beluga whale
belügen (*unreg.*) **I.** *v/t.* lie to, tell *s.o.* a lie (*od.* lies); **II.** *v/refl.*: *sich selbst ~* delude o.s., deceive o.s.
belustigen I. *v/t.* amuse; (*unterhalten*) entertain; **II.** *v/refl. geh. od. altm.* → *amüsieren*; **belustigt I.** *P.P.* → *belustigen*; **II.** *Adj.* amused; **III.** *Adv.*: *~ schmunzeln* smile in amusement; **Belustigung** *f* **1.** (*Veranstaltung*) amusement; (*Unterhaltung*) entertainment; **2.** (*Erheiterung*) amusement; *zur großen ~* (+ *Gen.*) much to the amuse-

ment of; *zur allgemeinen ~* to everybody's amusement
bemächtigen *v/refl.* (+ *Gen.*) **1.** *e-r Person*: seize; *e-r Sache*: *auch* take possession of; *widerrechtlich, der Macht etc.*: usurp *power*; **2.** *geh. fig.* (*überkommen*) take hold of, seize; *Furcht bemächtigte sich seiner* he was seized with fear, fear took hold of him
bemäkeln *v/t.* umg. criticize, find fault with
bemalen I. *v/t.* **1.** (*anstreichen*) paint; **2.** (*verzieren: Porzellan etc.*) decorate; *etw. mit Blumen ~* paint flowers on s.th.; **3.** (*schminken: Lippen etc.*) paint; **II.** *v/refl.* umg. (*sich schminken*) paint one's face, put one's face on; *du hast dich zu stark/ordinär bemalt* you've got too much makeup on / you look tarty (*od.* cheap) with all that makeup on; *wie du dich wieder bemalt hast!* you've really slapped on the makeup again; **Bemalung** *f* **1.** *nur Sg.*; (*das Anstreichen*) painting; *von Wänden*: *auch* decorating; **2.** a) *nur Sg.*; (*das Verzieren*) decorating, b) (*Verzierung*) decoration, c) *Kunst* (*Gemälde*) painting; (*Fresko*) fresco; **3.** (*Schminke*) makeup, war paint *umg.*
bemängeln *v/t.* criticize, find fault with; *ich habe nichts / verschiedene Dinge zu ~* I have no criticisms (*od.* complaints) / a number of complaints; *an s-m Benehmen war einiges zu ~* there were a number of things you (*od.* one) could criticize about his behavio(u)r
bemannen *v/t. Schiff, Flugzeug, Raumstation*: man; **bemannt I.** *P.P.* → *bemannen*; **II.** *Adj.* **1.** manned (*mit* by); *wir sind nicht ausreichend ~* umg. *von Messestand etc.*: we're understaffed; **2.** umg. hum.: *~ sein* have a man; **Bemannung** *f* **1.** (*das Bemannen*) manning; **2.** (*Besatzung*) crew
bemänteln *v/t.* disguise, cover up; (*beschönigen*) gloss over; **Bemäntelung** *f* disguising, covering up
bemerkbar *Adj.* noticeable; *es ist kaum ~* you can hardly tell (*od.* notice); *sich ~ machen Person*: draw (*od.* attract) attention to o.s.; *Sache*: show, become apparent; (*spürbar werden*) make itself felt; *der macht sich schon ~, wenn ihm etwas nicht passt* umg. he'll soon let you know if something doesn't suit him; *die Anstrengung machte sich bei ihm (allmählich) ~* the strain began to tell on him; *mein Zahn macht sich wieder ~* my tooth is giving me trouble again
bemerken *v/t.* **1.** (*wahrnehmen*) notice, become aware of; *förm.* note; (*sehen*) *auch* see; (*erkennen*) realize; *ich bemerkte sie zu spät* I saw her too late; *ich habe es sehr wohl bemerkt!* it hasn't (*od.* hadn't) escaped my notice; **2.** (*äußern, sagen*) say, remark; *förm.* note, observe; (*erwähnen*) mention; *~, dass auch* make the point that; *haben Sie (dazu) etwas zu ~?* would you like to comment?, do you have any comments to make?; *nebenbei bemerkt* by the way, incidentally
bemerkenswert I. *Adj.* remarkable (*wegen* for); (*beachtenswert*) noteworthy (for); *das Bemerkenswerte an der Sache ist, dass …* the remarkable thing about it is that …; **II.** *Adv.*: *~ echt etc.* remarkably convincing etc.
Bemerkung *f* remark (*über* + *Akk.* on, about); comment (on); *schriftliche*:

auch note; (*Anmerkung*) annotation; **~en machen** *od.* **fallen lassen über** (+ *Akk.*) remark (*od.* comment) on, make remarks about, make comments on; **was soll diese ~?** what's that (remark) supposed to mean?, what's that? *umg.*

bemessen I. *v/t.* (*unreg.*); (*berechnen*) calculate; *zeitlich: auch* time; (*Leistung*) rate; (*Strafe, Preis etc.*) fix; *fig.* (*bewerten*) measure (**nach** by); → **knapp** II; **II.** *v/refl.* (*unreg.*): **etw. bemisst sich nach** s.th. is calculated (*od.* measured) by (*od.* according to); **III.** *Adj.* (*knapp*) limited; **ein großzügig/knapp ~es Trinkgeld** a generous/measly tip; → **knapp** II 3

Bemessung *f* calculation; *e-r Leistung:* rating; *des Preises etc.:* assessment

Bemessungs|grundlage *f von Steuern:* assessment basis; **~zeitraum** *m Steuer:* income year, assessment period, *Am.* tax year

bemitleiden *v/t.* feel sorry for, pity; **sich selbst ~** feel sorry for oneself; **bemitleidenswert** *Adj.* pitiable; *stärker:* wretched; **er ist schon ~** you have to feel sorry for him

bemoost *Adj.* **1.** *Baumstamm etc.:* mossy, moss-covered; **2.** *altm., hum.:* **~es Haupt** *umg.* (*Student*) eternal student; (*alter Mann*) old codger *allg.*

bemühen I. *v/refl.* **1.** (*sich anstrengen*) go to a lot of trouble (*od.* effort) (**zu** + *Inf.* to + *Inf.*), make an effort, try (hard); *beständig:* endeavo(u)r; *angestrengt:* strive; **sich ~ um** *um Eintrittskarten, Wohnung etc.:* try to get; *um Ersatz, Nachfolger etc.:* try to find; *um j-s Vertrauen:* try to gain (*od.* win); **sich um Pünktlichkeit/Ordnung etc. ~** try (*od.* strive) to be punctual/tidy *etc.*; **sie hat sich mit Erfolg um diese Stelle bemüht** she succeeded in getting the job; **er hat sich vergeblich bemüht** his efforts were in vain, he was wasting his time *umg.*; **ich habe mich nach besten Kräften bemüht, ihm zu helfen** I did my (very) best to help him; **~ Sie sich nicht!** don't go to any trouble, don't bother *umg.*; **2.** (*sich kümmern*): **sich um j-n ~** look after s.o.; *schmeichlerisch:* court s.o.('s favo[u]r); *um Verletzten etc.:* (try to) help s.o.; **sich um j-s Wohl ~** look after s.o.'s welfare; **3.** *geh., oft iro.* (*gehen*): **ich bemühte mich zum Finanzamt / nach oben** I proceeded (*iro.* betook myself) to the tax office / upstairs; **sich zu j-m ~** take the trouble to go and see s.o.; **II.** *v/t. geh.* **1.** (*beanspruchen*) trouble (**mit** with; **um** for); (*Arzt, Fachmann etc.*) call in; **dürfte ich Sie zu mir ~** *geh.* may I ask you to come into my office (*od.* surgery etc.)?; **dürfte ich Sie bitte noch einmal kurz ~?** I wonder if I could trouble you again for a moment?; **2.** *als Beweis:* quote from, draw on; **Shakespeare ~** quote from Shakespeare

Bemühen *n; -s, kein Pl.; geh.* (*Bestreben*) endeavo(u)r, effort; **unser ~ muss** *od.* **soll es sein, diese Krise zu überwinden** we must make every effort to overcome this crisis; **trotz eifrigen ~s ist es uns nicht gelungen** despite all our efforts, we failed

bemüht I. *P.P.* → **bemühen**; **II.** *Adj.* **1.** **~ sein zu** (+ *Inf.*) take care to (+ *Inf.*); *stärker:* be at pains to (+ *Inf.*); *eifrig:* be anxious to (+ *Inf.*); **wir sind stets um das Wohl unserer Gäste ~** we make every effort to ensure the

comfort and welfare of our guests; **2.** *Lächeln etc.:* (*angestrengt*) labo(u)red; (*gezwungen*) forced; (*unnatürlich*) unnatural, artificial

Bemühung *f* **1.** effort(s *Pl.*) (**um** towards, *Am. auch* toward); *mst negativer gesehen:* trouble; **alle s-e ~en waren umsonst** he went to all that trouble (*od.* effort) for nothing; **vielen Dank für Ihre ~en** thank you for (all) your help; **2.** *auf Arzt- und Anwaltsrechnungen:* **für m-e ~en erlaube ich mir, Ihnen € 100.- zu berechnen** for my efforts I beg to charge you €100

bemüßigt *Adj. geh.:* **sich ~ fühlen zu** (+ *Inf.*) feel obliged (*od.* duty bound) to (+ *Inf.*)

bemuttern *v/t.* mother; *weitS. auch* nanny; **Bemutterung** *f* mothering; **ihre ständige ~ geht mir auf die Nerven** I hate the way she keeps nannying me (*od.* people)

benachbart *Adj.* neighbo(u)ring; (*angrenzend*) adjoining, adjacent; *fig.* related

benachrichtigen *v/t.* inform, notify (**von** of), let s.o. know (about), send s.o. word (of); *Wirts.* advise

Benachrichtigung *f* **1.** *nur Sg;* (*das Benachrichtigen*) notification; **die ~ der Betroffenen erfolgte unverzüglich** all persons concerned were immediately notified; **2.** (*Nachricht*) notification; *Wirts.* advice; **ich bitte um kurze ~** I would be grateful if you could briefly notify me (*od.* let me know); **ich warte noch auf e-e ~ von der Versicherung** I'm still waiting to hear from the insurance company

benachteiligen *v/t.* put s.o. at a disadvantage; *bes. sozial:* (*Minoritäten etc.*) discriminate against; **j-n in s-m Testament ~** treat s.o. unfairly in one's will, make s.o. come off badly in one's will

benachteiligt I. *P.P.* → **benachteiligen**; **II.** *Adj. Personen, sozial:* disadvantaged, underprivileged; **~ sein** be at a disadvantage; **er fühlt sich von s-m Vater / vom Schicksal ~** he feels he has been unfairly treated by his father / by fate; **e-e klimatisch/wirtschaftlich ~e Region** a climatically disadvantaged / an economically deprived region; **Benachteiligte** *m, f; -n, -n* disadvantaged person; **die ~n** the disadvantaged, the underprivileged

Benachteiligung *f* **1.** (*das Benachteiligen*) discrimination (+ *Gen.* against); **2.** (*Nachteil*) handicap, disadvantage

benagen *v/t.* gnaw at, nibble at

Bendel *m od. n* → **Bändel**

benebeln *v/t.* (*j-n, auch die Sinne*) befuddle; *Narkose etc.:* make s.o. dop(e)y; **benebelt I.** *P.P.* → **benebeln**; **II.** *Adj. umg.* (be)fuddled; (*benommen*) dop(e)y, groggy, woozy; (*angeheitert*) slightly tiddly; **Benebelung** *f durch Alkohol:* befuddlement, (alcoholic) stupor; *durch Narkose:* dopiness, grogginess, wooziness; *durch Müdigkeit:* dopiness

benedeien *v/t.* (*hat* [*ge*]*benedeit*); *bibl. geh.* bless

Benediktiner *m; -s, -, ~in f; -, -nen; Reli.* Benedictine (monk/nun); **~orden** *m; nur Sg.; Reli.* Benedictine order, Order of St. Benedict

Benefiz|konzert *n* charity concert; **~spiel** *n Sport* charity fixture, benefit match; **~vorstellung** *f* charity performance

benehmen (*unreg.*) **I.** *v/refl.* behave (**gegenüber** + *Dat.* towards, *Am. auch*

toward); **sich schlecht ~** behave badly, misbehave; **sich gut ~** behave (oneself), behave well; **sich anständig** etc. **~** behave properly etc.; **er hat sich unmöglich benommen** he was impossible, his behavio(u)r was appalling; **sie weiß sich überall zu ~** you can take her anywhere; **benimm dich!** behave yourself!; **II.** *v/t. geh.* (*wegnehmen*) take away; **es benahm mir den Atem** it took my breath away

Benehmen *n; -s, kein Pl.* **1.** behavio(u)r, conduct; (*Manieren*) good, bad manners *Pl.*; **er hat kein ~** he has no manners, he doesn't know how to behave; **2.** *Amtsspr.:* **im ~ mit** in agreement with; **sich mit j-m ins ~ setzen** (*in Verbindung setzen*) contact s.o.; (*sich besprechen*) confer with s.o.; (*j-n zu Rate ziehen*) consult s.o.

beneiden *v/t.* envy (**um, wegen** s.th.); **sie beneidet mich um mein neues Auto** she envies me my new car, she's envious of my new car; **ich beneide (dich um) d-e Geduld** I envy your patience, I wish I had your patience; **sie ist zu ~** (she's a) lucky woman; **er ist nicht zu ~** I wouldn't like to be in his shoes, he's not to be envied

beneidenswert I. *Adj.* enviable; **du hast e-e ~e Figur!** I wish I had your figure; **sie hat ~es Glück gehabt** she's had enviable luck; **II.** *Adv.* enviably; **~ gut aussehen** be enviably good-looking

Benelux ['be:neluks] (*f*); - the Benelux; **~staaten** *Pl.* the Benelux (countries)

benennen *v/t.* (*unreg.*) **1.** (*Namen geben*) name (**nach** after, *Am. auch* for), call; **sie ist nach ihrer Tante benannt** she's named after (*Am. auch* for) her aunt; **neu ~** rename; **2.** (*bestimmen*) name; (*Termin*) fix; (*Kandidaten*) nominate; **j-n als Zeugen ~** call s.o. as a witness; **Benennung** *f* **1.** *nur Sg.* (*das Benennen*) naming; **2.** *konkret:* name; (*Benennungssystem*) nomenclature; *Wirts., Wertpapier.* title; **falsche ~** misnomer

benetzen *v/t. geh.* moisten, dampen, wet; (*bespritzen*) sprinkle

Bengale *m; -n, -n* Bengali; **Bengali** *n; -s, kein Pl.; Ling.* Bengali; **Bengalin** *f; -, -nen* Bengali (woman); **bengalisch** *Adj.* Bengali; **~es Feuer** Bengal lights

Bengel *m; -s, -, nordd. -s; umg.* (*frecher Kerl*) (little) rascal; (*kleiner Junge*) young lad, *Am.* youngster

Benimm *m; -s, kein Pl.; umg.* manners *Pl.*; **er hat keinen ~** he has no manners, he doesn't know how to behave (himself); **los jetzt, ein bisschen mehr ~!** come on, let's try and behave ourselves!

Benjamin *m; -s, -e; fig., mst hum.* the youngest, the baby

benommen I. *P.P.* → **benehmen**; **II.** *Adj.* dazed, dop(e)y *umg.*; **j-n ~ machen** make s.o. dop(e)y; **Benommenheit** *f; nur Sg.* dazed feeling, dopiness *umg.*; **in e-m Zustand der ~** in a daze(d state)

benoten *v/t.* mark, *Am.* grade; **e-e Arbeit mit einer Eins** etc. **~** give a piece of work a one (*od.* an A); **wie ist d-e Arbeit benotet worden?** what mark (*Am.* grade) did you get for your (home)work?

benötigen *v/t.* need; **dringend ~** badly need, need s.th. urgently, be badly in need of, be in urgent need of; **benötigt I.** *P.P.* → **benötigen**; **II.** *Adj.* required; *das ~e Visum* the necessary visa

Benotung *f* **1.** *nur Sg.*; (*das Benoten*) marking, *Am.* grading; **2.** (*Noten*) marks *Pl.*, *bes. Am.* grades *Pl.*

benutzbar *Adj.* usable; *Straße*: passable; *der Lift ist zurzeit nicht ~* the lift (*Am.* elevator) is out of service at the moment; *dieses Messer ist kaum noch ~* you can hardly use this knife any more; *schwer ~ Werkzeug etc.*: difficult to use

benutzen, *südd.* **benützen** *v/t.* use, (*Gebrauch machen von*) auch make use of; (*Verkehrsmittel*) take, go by; (*Nachschlagewerke*) use, consult *geh.*; *sie benutzte den Feiertag um auszuschlafen* she took the opportunity of the (bank) holiday to have a lie in (*Am.* to sleep in); *etw. gemeinsam ~* share s.th.; *etw. wird (ständig) benutzt* s.th. is in (constant) use

Benutzer, *südd.* **Benützer** *m*; *-s, -,* *~in f*; *-, -nen* **1.** *allg., EDV etc.*: user; **2.** *e-r Bibliothek*: borrower; (*Mitglied*) member; (*Besucher*) visitor

benutzerfreundlich *Adj.* user-friendly; **Benutzerfreundlichkeit** *f*; *nur Sg.* user-friendliness; *Tech. auch* ease of operation (*od.* use)

Benutzer|handbuch *n* user's guide; *~kreis m* users *Pl.*; *~oberfläche f Computer*: user interface

benutzt, *südd.* **benützt I.** *P.P.* → **benutzen**; **II.** *Adj.* used; *es ist ~* it's been used; *~e Bettwäsche/Tassen* dirty (bed) linen / cups

Benutzung, *südd.* **Benützung** *f*; *nur Sg.* use; *mit od. unter ~ von* by using, with the aid of; *etw. in ~ nehmen* start using s.th.; *etw. zur ~ freigeben* open s.th. to use; *„~ auf eigene Gefahr"* "use at your own risk"; *missbräuchliche ~* misuse, improper use

Benutzungs|gebühr *f* fee, charge; *~ordnung f* terms of use; *~recht n* right to use, use

Benzin *n*; *-s, Pl. Arten: -e; Mot.* petrol, *Am.* gas(oline); *für Feuerzeug*: lighter fuel; *Chem., zur Reinigung*: benzine; *~bombe f* petrol (*Am.* gasoline) bomb; *~einspritzung f Mot.* fuel injection

Benziner *m*; *-s, -; Mot., umg.* petrol--driven (*Am.* gasoline-driven) car

Benzin|feuerzeug *n* fuel lighter; *~fresser m Mot. umg.* fuel-guzzler, *bes. Am.* gas-guzzler; *~gutschein m* petrol (*Am.* gas) coupon; *~hahn m bei Motorrädern*: petrol cock, *Am.* gas-(oline) cock; *~kanister m* petrol can, jerry can *umg., Am.* gas(oline) can

Benzinkosten *Pl.* petrol (*Am.* gas od. gasoline) costs, fuel costs; *~beteiligung f in Annonce*: share petrol (*Am.* gas od. gasoline) costs; *Mitfahrgelegenheit nach ... gegen ~* lift (*Am.* ride) to ..., share petrol (*Am.* gas) costs

Benzin|leitung *f* fuel pipe; *~motor m* petrol (*Am.* gasoline) engine; *~preis m auch Pl.* cost of petrol (*Am.* gas od. gasoline), petrol (*Am.* gas od. gasoline) prices *Pl.*; *~pumpe f* fuel pump; *~tank m* petrol (*Am.* gas od. gasoline) tank, fuel tank; *~uhr f* petrol (*od.* fuel) ga(u)ge, *Am.* gas(oline) (*od.* fuel) ga(u)ge; *~verbrauch m* fuel consumption

Benzoe ['bɛntsoe] *f*; *-, kein Pl.* benzoin; *~säure f Chem.* benzoic acid

Benzol *n*; *-s, Pl. nur verschiedenen Arten: -e; Chem.* benzol(e), benzene

beobachtbar *Adj.* observable

beobachten I. *v/t.* **1.** watch; *Med. und Polizei auch*: observe; (*Horizont etc. absuchen*) scan; (*Satelliten etc. verfolgen*) track; *j-n bei etw. ~* watch s.o. doing s.th.; *sich beobachtet fühlen* sense that one is being watched; *j-n ~ lassen* put s.o. under surveillance; **2.** *zufällig*: see; *ich beobachtete, wie sie das Haus verließ* I saw her leave (*od.* leaving) the house; **3.** (*wahrnehmen*) notice; *ich beobachtete, wie sie immer apathischer wurde* I noticed her getting (*od.* how she got) more and more listless; **4.** *geh.* (*Gesetze, Vorschriften*) observe; **II.** *v/i.; nur mit Adv.*: *Kinder ~ ganz genau* children are very observant (*od.* have keen powers of observation)

Beobachter *m*; *-s, -,* *~in f*; *-, -nen* observer (*auch Pol., Mil. etc.*); (*Zuschauer*) onlooker; (*Aufpasser*) watcher; *~status m* observer status; *bei e-r Konferenz etc. ~ haben* take part in a conference etc. as an observer

Beobachtung *f* **1.** (*auch Feststellung*) observation; *unter ~ stehen* be under observation; *aus eigener ~ weiß ich, ...* I know from my own observations ...; **2.** *geh. von Gesetz, Vorschrift*: observation

Beobachtungs|flugzeug *n* observation (*od.* observer) plane; *~gabe f* powers *Pl.* of observation; *e-e gute ~ besitzen* be very observant; *~posten m* lookout (man); *~station f* **1.** *Med.* observation ward; **2.** *Met.* observation station, observatory; **3.** *für Satelliten etc.*: tracking station; *~zeitraum m* period of observation

beordern *v/t.* order (*nach* [to go] to), send (to); (*wegschicken*) send away (to); *j-n zu sich* (*Dat.*) *~* summon s.o., send for s.o.

bepacken *v/t.* load (up); (*mit Einkäufen*) *bepackt wie ein Lastesel* loaded (with shopping) like a packhorse; *schwer bepackt* fully (*od.* heavily) loaded (*od.* laden)

bepflanzen *v/t.* plant; *mit Bäumen/Gemüse etc. ~ auch* plant trees/vegetables etc. on (*od.* along etc.); **Bepflanzung** *f* **1.** (*das Bepflanzen*) planting; **2.** *Koll.* (*Blumen und Sträucher*) plants (and shrubs) *Pl.*; *abwechslungsreiche ~ vor dem Eingang* a variety of plants at the entrance

bepflastern *v/t.* **1.** *umg.* a) (*Wunde*) put a plaster (*Am.* bandage) on, b) (*vollkleben*) plaster; *e-e Wand mit Reklame ~* plaster a wall with advertisements; **2.** (*Straße*) pave; **3.** *Mil. Sl.* (*bombardieren*) clobber, plaster (with shells), carpet-bomb

bepinkeln *umg.* **I.** *v/t.* pee (*od.* tinkle) on; **II.** *v/refl.* wet o.s.

bepinseln *v/t.* **1.** *auch Gastr.* brush (over); *mit Fett ~* grease; **2.** *Med.* (*Wunde etc.*) paint; **3.** *umg.* (*bemalen*) paint (over); *pej.* (*schminken*) paint; (*flüchtig beschreiben*) scribble on; (*bemalen*) slap some paint on

bequatschen *v/t. umg.* **1.** *etw. mit j-m ~* chat about s.th. with s.o.; **2.** *j-n ~ talk s.o.* into doing *s.th.*, get s.o. (a)round to *s.th.*

bequem I. *Adj.* **1.** *Schuhe, Sessel etc.*: comfortable; (*gemütlich*) co|sy (*Am.* -zy); *es sich* (*Dat.*) *~ machen* make o.s. at home; *fig.* (*sich etw. einfach machen*) take the easy way out; *ist Ihnen das so ~?* is that comfortable enough for you?; **2.** (*mühelos, einfach*)

easy; *~e Lösung* easy way out; *e-e ~e Stelle* a cushy job; *es ~ haben* have an easy time of it; **3.** (*praktisch, keine Umstände machend*) *auch Ausrede etc.*: convenient; (*zur Hand*) handy; *fürs Einkaufen ist es sehr ~* it's very convenient for shopping (*od.* the shops); *Person*: comfort-loving; (*träge*) indolent; (*faul*) lazy; *er ist zu ~ zu* (+ *Inf.*) he just can't be bothered to (+ *Inf.*), he's too lazy to (+ *Inf.*); **II.** *Adv.* **1.** comfortably, in comfort; *hier sitzt man sehr ~* this is a very comfortable armchair (*od.* sofa etc.); *sitzen/liegen Sie ~?* are you sitting/lying comfortably?, are you comfortable?; **2.** (*leicht*) easily; *wir haben ~ Zeit umg.* we've got plenty of time; **bequemen** *v/refl.*: *sich in die Küche / zu j-m etc. ~* bring o.s. to go into the kitchen / go and see s.o. etc.; *sich dazu ~, etw. zu tun* take the trouble to do s.th.; (*sich herablassen*) deign to do s.th.; *nach längerem Aufschub*: finally force o.s. to do s.th.; *sich zu e-r Antwort etc. ~* deign to give an answer *etc.*

Bequemlichkeit *f* **1.** *nur Sg.*; (*Behaglichkeit*) comfort, ease; **2.** *nur Sg.*; (*Trägheit*) indolence; (*Faulheit*) laziness; *etw. aus ~ nicht tun* be too lazy to do s.th.; **3.** (*bequeme Einrichtung, Annehmlichkeit*) convenience, *Pl. auch* amenities

beranken *v/t. Bot.* cover with creepers; *e-e berankte Mauer* a creeper-covered wall

berappen *v/t. umg.* cough up, fork out

beraten I. *v/t.* (*unreg.*) **1.** *j-n ~* advise s.o., give s.o. (some) advice (*bei* on); *j-n gut/schlecht ~* advise s.o. well/badly, give s.o. some good/bad advice; *sich* (*von j-m*) *~ lassen* consult s.o.; *ich habe mich von ihm ~ lassen auch* I asked him for his (*od.* some) advice; **2.** *etw. ~* discuss s.th.; **II.** *v/i.* (*unreg.*) deliberate (*über + Akk.* about, on); **III.** *v/refl.* (*unreg.*): *sich mit j-m* (*über etw.* [*Akk.*]) *~* consult (*od.* confer) with s.o. (on s.th.), *auch* discuss s.th. with s.o.; **IV.** *Adj.*: *gut/schlecht ~ sein zu* (+ *Inf.*) be well-advised/ill-advised to (+ *Inf.*); *mit diesem Gerät sind Sie gut ~* you'd be well-advised to get this appliance; *mit diesem Kauf wären Sie schlecht ~* I wouldn't advise you to buy it

beratend I. *Part. Präs.* → **beraten**; **II.** *Adj.* advisory, consultative; *in ~er Funktion* in an advisory capacity; *e-e ~e Tätigkeit ausüben* act (*od.* work) as a consultant, be a consultant; **III.** *Adv.* in an advisory capacity, as an adviser; *j-m ~ beistehen* act as s.o.'s adviser

Berater *m*; *-s, -,* *~in f*; *-, -nen* adviser, consultant; *enger*: aide; *~stab m* team of advisers, think tank *umg.*; *~tätigkeit f* consultancy, consulting; *~vertrag m* consultancy contract

beratschlagen *v/i.* → **beraten** II, III; **Beratschlagung** *f* discussion

Beratung *f* **1.** (*Besprechung*) discussion; *förm.* conferral; *Parl.* deliberation; *sich zur ~ zurückziehen* adjourn for (further) consultation; *bei Gericht*: adjourn (*od.* retire) for deliberation; *e-e ~ haben* be in a session, be in a meeting; **2.** (*Rat*) advice; **3.** (*Beratungsdienst*) advisory service; **4.** (*beratendes Gespräch, Konsultation*) consultation

Beratungs|dienst *m* consultancy; *~gespräch n* consultation; *~kosten Pl.* consultation fee *Sg.* (*od.* fees); *~punkt*

m auf Tagesordnung: item on the agenda; **~stelle** *f* advice cent|re (*Am.* -er); **~unternehmen** *n* consulting firm
berauben *v/t.* **1.** (*ausrauben*) rob *s.o.* (+ *Gen.* of); **2.** *fig.* deprive *s.o.*, rob *s.o.* (+ *Gen.* of); *e-s Rechts etc.*: divest *s.o.* (of); *e-r Hoffnung etc.*: bereave *s.o.* (of); **beraubt I.** *P.P.* → **berauben**; **II.** *Adj.* deprived (+ *Gen.* of); *lit.* bereft (of); *aller Macht etc.* **~ sein** *auch lit.* be shorn of all power *etc.*; **Beraubung** *f* **1.** robbing (+ *Gen.* of); **2.** *fig.* deprivation (of)
berauschen I. *v/t.* **1.** make *s.o.* drunk; *auch fig. Duft etc.*: intoxicate; *Droge:* give *s.o.* a high, make *s.o.* high; **2.** *fig. Macht etc.*: go to *s.o.'s* head; *Musik:* intoxicate; *Gewalt etc.* **kann ~** *violence etc.* can act like a drug; **II.** *v/refl.*: **sich ~ an** (+ *Dat.*) **1.** *konkret, an Alkohol:* get drunk on; *an Drogen:* get high on; **2.** *fig. an Musik, Duft:* become intoxicated by, get high on *umg.*; *an Geschwindigkeit:* become exhilarated by, get high on *umg.*; *an Gewalt etc.*: get seized (*od.* carried away) by; *sich am Klang der eigenen Stimme ~* love the sound of one's own voice; **berauschend I.** *Part. Präs.* → **berauschen**; **II.** *Adj.* **1.** *Getränk:* intoxicating, alcoholic; **2.** *fig. Duft:* heady, intoxicating; *Schönheit, Anblick:* breathtaking; *Klänge:* ravishing; *nicht gerade ~ umg. iro.* nothing to shout (*od.* write home) about; **III.** *Adv.*: **~ wirken** have an intoxicating effect (*auf + Akk.* on); **berauscht I.** *P.P.* → **berauschen**; **II.** *Adj.* drunk (*von* with); *fig. auch* heady (with); *vom Erfolg ~* drunk with success
Berber *m; -s, -* **1.** *Nordafrikaner:* Berber; **2.** *Teppich:* Berber rug (*od.* carpet); **3.** *Sl.* (*Nichtsesshafter*) hobo, *Am.* bum; **~teppich** *m* Berber rug (*od.* carpet)
berechenbar *Adj.* **1.** *Mensch, Verhalten:* predictable; **2.** *Kosten:* calculable; **Berechenbarkeit** *f; nur Sg.* **1.** *des Verhaltens etc.*: predictability; **2.** *von Kosten etc.*: calculability; **3.** *von Ergebnissen:* computability
berechnen *v/t.* **1.** (*ausrechnen*) (*Größe, Entfernung etc.*) *auch fig.* calculate, compute, assess, figure out *umg.*, work out *umg.*; *s-e Reaktion lässt sich genau ~* you can predict exactly how he's going to react; **2.** *fig.* (*berücksichtigen*) take into account; *dabei berechnest du nicht, wie unsicher die Sache ist* you're not taking into account how uncertain the whole thing is; **3.** (*in Rechnung stellen*) charge; (*fakturieren*) invoice; *j-m etw. ~* charge *s.o.* for *s.th.*; *j-m etw. mit € 50.- ~* charge *s.o.* €50 for *s.th.*; *j-m zu viel ~ auch* overcharge *s.o.*; *dein Kaffee ist nicht berechnet worden* they haven't included (*od.* charged you for) your coffee; **4.** (*kalkulieren*) calculate, work out; *den Kredit auf zehn Jahre Laufzeit ~* calculate the credit for a period of ten years; *alle Rezepte sind für vier Personen berechnet* all recipes are based on four servings; *darauf berechnet sein zu* (+ *Inf.*) *fig.* be calculated (*od.* intended *od.* meant) to (+ *Inf.*)
berechnend I. *Part. Präs.* → **berechnen**; **II.** *Adj. fig.* calculating
Berechnung *f* **1.** calculation; *konkret: auch* figure(s *Pl.*); **~en anstellen** calculate; *nach m-r ~* according to my calculation(s); **2.** charge; (*Fakturierung*) invoicing; (*Belastung*) debit; **3.** *nur*

Sg.; *fig.* calculation; *mit ~* with deliberation; *etw. nur aus ~ tun* do *s.th.* purely out of self-interest; *bei ihr ist alles ~* it's all a matter of calculation with her, *Am.* she has everything figured out in advance
Berechnungs|grundlage *f* basis of calculation; *Steuer:* basis of assessment; **~tabelle** *f* calculation (*od.* computation) table
berechtigen I. *vt/i.* entitle; *zu etw. ~* entitle *s.o.* to (do) *s.th.*; (*ermächtigen*) authorize (to + *Inf.*); *das Abitur berechtigt Sie zum Studium* passing the Abitur qualifies you to study (at university); *dieser Ausweis berechtigt zum freien Eintritt* this ID (*od.* pass *od.* document) entitles you to free admission; **II.** *v/i.*: *dieses Wetter berechtigt zu der Annahme/Hoffnung, dass* this weather warrants the assumption/hope that; *zu* (*den schönsten*) *Hoffnungen ~* give cause for hope; (*vielversprechend sein*) be promising
berechtigt I. *P.P.* → **berechtigen**; **II.** *Adj.* **1.** *sein, etw. zu tun* be entitled (*od.* allowed) to do *s.th.*; (*ermächtigt*) be authorized to do *s.th.*; *es ist vollkommen ~, wenn er sich beschwert etc.* he's perfectly justified in complaining *etc.*, he has every reason to complain *etc.*; **2.** *Anspruch, Angst:* legitimate; *Zweifel, Klage etc.*: *auch* justified, justifiable; *dieser Vorwurf / deine Sorge ist ~* it's a justified reproach / you're right to be worried; **Berechtigte** *m, f; -n, -* (rightful) claimant; *Versicherung:* beneficiary
berechtigterweise *Adv.* rightly, (quite) legitimately; *allein stehend:* (and) rightly so
Berechtigung *f* **1.** right; (*Ermächtigung*) authorization; (*Vollmacht*) power, authority; *die ~ haben zu* (+ *Inf.*) have the right to (+ *Inf.*), be authorized to (+ *Inf.*); *die ~ zu etw. erwerben* acquire the right to *s.th.*; **2.** (*Rechtmäßigkeit*) legitimacy, justification; **Berechtigungsschein** *m* permit
bereden I. *v/t.* (*Problem, Sache*) talk *s.th.* over, discuss; *ich muss etw. mit dir ~* there's *s.th.* I've got to talk to you about; **II.** *v/refl.* (*sich beraten*): *sich mit j-m über* (+ *Akk.*) talk to *s.o.* about, *auch* talk *s.th.* over with *s.o.*, discuss *s.th.* with *s.o.*; *wir müssen uns erst mal ~* we'll have to talk it over
beredsam *Adj.* eloquent; (*redefreudig*) talkative; **Beredsamkeit** *f; nur Sg.* eloquence; (*Mitteilsamkeit*) talkativeness; *mit großer ~* with great persuasiveness; *über große ~ verfügen* be very eloquent; *die Kunst der ~* the art of oratory (*od.* rhetoric)
beredt *Adj. auch fig. Schweigen etc.*: eloquent; **Beredtheit** *f; nur Sg.* eloquence; *von großer ~ sein* be very eloquent
beregnen *v/t.* (*Felder*) spray, water; (*Rasen*) sprinkle, water; **Beregnung** *f von Feldern:* spraying, watering; *des Rasens:* sprinkling, watering; **Beregnungsanlage** *f* sprinkler system
Bereich *m* **1.** *konkret:* area; *militärischer ~* military zone (*od.* area); *im ~ der Stadt/Schule* (with)in the town / (with)in the area of the school; *diese Ecke ist mein ~* this corner is my territory; **2.** *Met.* area; *wir befinden uns im ~ e-s Hochdruckgebiets* we are currently under the influence of an

anticyclone; **3.** *fig.* (*Sachgebiet*) field, sphere, area; (*Einflussbereich*) sphere (of influence *od.* action); *förm.* ambit; *im ~ des Möglichen* within the bounds of possibility; *in j-s ~ fallen* fall within *s.o.'s* field of responsibility (*od. s.o.'s* province); *ein Thema aus dem ~ der Politik etc.* a topic from the realm (*od.* field) of politics *etc.*; *ein Ausdruck aus dem medizinischen etc. ~* an expression from the field of medicine *etc.*; (*Gehälter*) *im staatlichen/privaten ~* state (salaries) / private sector (salaries)
bereichern I. *v/t.* (*Leben etc.*) enrich; (*Wissen, Erfahrung, Sammlung*) expand, increase; *e-e Bibliothek um einige wertvolle Bände ~* add some valuable books to a library's collection; *es hat mich sehr bereichert* I gained (*od.* learned) a lot from it; **II.** *v/refl.*: get rich (*an + Dat.* on), *auch* make money (out of); *pej., auch umg.* line one's pockets, feather one's nest; *sich auf Kosten anderer ~* get rich at the expense of others; **III.** *v/i.*: *Reisen/Lesen bereichert ungemein* travel/reading is a great enrichment
Bereicherung *f* **1.** enrichment; *des Wissens etc.*: expansion (+ *Gen.* of), increase (in); *zur ~ e-r Sammlung etc. beitragen* *auch* add to a collection *etc.*; *dieser Nachlass ist e-e große ~ für unsere Sammlung* this bequest is a great addition to our collection; **2.** (*Sichbereichern*) personal enrichment; **3.** (*Gewinn*) gain; *es war e-e große ~ für mich* I gained (*od.* learned) a lot from it
bereifen *v/t. Mot.* put tyres (*Am.* tires) on
bereift[1] **I.** *P.P.* → **bereifen**; **II.** *Adj. Mot.*: *neu ~ sein* have new (*od.* fresh) tyres (*Am.* tires); *gut ~ sein* have good tyres (*Am.* tires); *es ist ein gut ~es Auto* the car has good tyres (*Am.* tires), it's a well-shod car *umg.*
bereift[2] *Adj.* (*reifbedeckt*) covered with (hoar)frost, frost-covered
Bereifung *f Mot.* tyres *Pl.*, *Am.* tires *Pl.*; (*Satz Reifen*) set of tyres (*Am.* tires)
bereinigen I. *v/t.* **1.** (*Streit*) settle; (*Missverständnis*) clear up; (*ausgleichen*) iron out; **2.** (*Konto*) settle; (*Wertpapiere*) validate; (*Statistiken, Zahlen*) adjust, correct; (*Buchausgabe, Text*) expurgate; **II.** *v/refl.* resolve itself; **Bereinigung** *f* **1.** *von Streit:* settlement; *von Missverständnis:* clearing up; **2.** *e-s Kontos:* correction, adjustment; *von Wertpapieren:* validation; *von Statistik, Zahlen:* adjustment, correction; *von Text:* expurgation
bereisen *v/t.* **1.** (*Land*) tour, travel around (*od.* through); *fremde Länder ~* travel around foreign countries; *die Meere ~* sail the seas; **2.** *Wirts.* (*Vertreterbezirk etc.*) cover, do *umg.*; *Handelsmessen ~* tour (*od.* do) tradefairs
bereit *Adj.; nur präd.* **1.** (*fertig*): *~ sein zu etw.* be ready for *s.th.*; *zur Abfahrt ~* ready to leave; *sich ~ halten* (*in Bereitschaft sein*) stand by (at the ready); **2.** (*gewillt*): *~ sein zu etw.* be prepared/willing to do *s.th.*; *zu Konzessionen ~* prepared to make concessions; *wir sind gern ~ zu* (+ *Inf.*) *Geschäftsbrief:* we shall be pleased to (+ *Inf.*); *zu allem ~* game for anything, prepared to try (*od.* risk) anything; *sich ~ erklären. finden zu* (+ *Inf.*) agree to (+ *Inf.*), *freiwillig:* volunteer

to (+ *Inf.*); → **bereithaben, bereithalten, bereitlegen, bereitliegen, bereitmachen, bereitstehen, bereitstellen**
...bereit im *Adj.* **1.** (*fertig für*) mit *Subst. od. V.*: **funktions~** operational, ready to go *umg.*; **reise~** ready for departure; **anzieh~** ready to wear; **2.** (*gewillt zu*) mit *Subst.*: **friedens~** prepared (*od.* willing) to make peace; **widerstands~** ready to fight back, ready to resist

bereiten *v/t.* **1.** prepare, get *s.th.* ready; (*zubereiten*) (*Essen etc.*) make; (*Bad*) run; (*Leder*) dress; **2.** *geh. fig.* (*verursachen*) cause; (*Kopfschmerzen, Freude, Empfang etc.*) give; *j-m schlaflose Nächte ~* give s.o. sleepless nights; *dieser Termin etc. bereitet mir keine Schwierigkeiten* that date *etc.* isn't a problem for me; *na, hat er dir Schwierigkeiten bereitet?* (*war Kind unfolgsam?*) was he being difficult then?; (*hat Chef Vorschlag etc. nicht akzeptiert?*) wouldn't he listen to you then?; → *Empfang* 2, *Ende* 3, *Freude* 1

bereit|gestellt I. *P.P.* → **bereitstellen**; **II.** *Adj.*: **~e Gelder** *etc.* available funds *etc.*, funds *etc.* provided; **~haben** *v/t.* (*unreg., trennb., hat -ge-*) have *s.th.* ready; **~halten** (*unreg., trennb., hat -ge-*) **I.** *v/t.* have *s.th.* (at the) ready; **II.** *v/refl.* **sich ~** be ready; *Truppen etc.*: be on standby; **~legen** *v/t.* (*unreg., trennb., hat -ge-*) (*Kleider, Bücher zur Einsicht*) lay out, get *s.th.* ready; **~liegen** *v/i.* (*unreg., trennb., ist, -ge-*) be ready; *Kleider, Werkzeug: auch* be laid out (ready); **~machen** (*unreg., trennb., hat -ge-*) **I.** *v/t.* get *s.th.* ready, prepare *s.th.*; **II.** *v/refl.* get ready (*zu* for)

bereits *Adv.* **1.** (*schon*) already; *ich habe ~ drei* I've got three already, I've already got three; *er schläft ~ seit zwei Stunden* he's been asleep for two hours (already); *es ist ~ morgen / in zwei Wochen fertig* it'll be ready by tomorrow / within two weeks; *das gab es ~ vor 50 Jahren* that was (already) around fifty years ago; *~ 1810* by 1810, already in 1810, as early as 1810; *~ damals* already at that time; **2.** (*nur*) even; *~ fünf Tropfen können tödlich wirken* even (*od.* just) five drops (*od.* five drops alone) a small amount can be lethal

Bereitschaft *f. nur Sg.* readiness; (*Bereitwilligkeit*) willingness; *in ~ haben od. halten* have *s.th.* (at the) ready; *die innere ~ zu etw. haben* be (inwardly) motivated to do *s.th.*; *solange dir die innere ~ dazu fehlt, wirst du es nie schaffen* unless you really want it, you'll never succeed; **2.** *nur Sg.*; (*Bereitschaftsdienst*) standby duty; *~ haben Arzt*: be on call; *Krankenhauspersonal*: be on duty; *Apotheke*: be on rota (*Am.* revolving) duty (*for dispensing out of hours*); *Polizist*: be on standby (duty); *in ~ sein Arzt*: be on call; *Polizei, Soldaten*: be on standby; **3.** (*Polizeieinheit etc.*) squad; **4.** *nur Sg.*; *Tech.* standby mode

Bereitschafts|arzt *m* duty doctor; **~dienst** *m* **1.** (*Einsatzsystem*) stand-by (system); (*Polizei*) riot squad; **2.** (*Dienstschicht*) standby duty; *~ haben od. machen* be on standby; *Arzt*: *auch* be on call; *Apotheke*: be open all night; **~polizei** *f* riot squad

bereitstehen *v/i.* (*unreg., trennb., ist -ge-*) be ready; (*verfügbar sein*) be available; *Polizei etc.*: stand by, be on

standby
bereitstellen *v/t.* (*trennb., hat -ge-*) place (*od.* get) *s.th.* ready; (*liefern*) provide, supply; (*zur Verfügung stellen*) von *Geld etc.*: make available; (*Geldmittel*) *zweckbestimmt: auch* allocate; (*vorsehen*) earmark; (*Truppen*) marshal; **Bereitstellung** *f; mst Sg.* getting *s.th.* ready; (*Lieferung*) supply, provision; von *Geldmitteln, zweckbestimmt*: allocation; (*Bestimmung, Vorsehung*) earmarking; *Mil.* (final) assembly

Bereitung *f* preparation
bereitwillig I. *Adj.* willing; (*eifrig*) eager; (*dienstfertig*) obliging; **II.** *Adv.* willingly; *er bot uns ~ s-e Hilfe an* he didn't hesitate to offer his help, he obligingly offered his help; **Bereitwilligkeit** *f; nur Sg.* willingness; (*Dienstfertigkeit*) readiness (to oblige); *mit großer ~* with alacrity

bereuen I. *v/t.* regret; (*Sünden*) repent of; *er bereut, dass er nicht mitkommen kann / dass er mitgekommen ist* he regrets not being able to come / having come; *das wirst du noch ~* you'll be sorry (*od.* regret it) (yet); *ich bereue gar nichts* I have no regrets (about anything); **II.** *v/i. Reli. etc.* repent

Berg *m*; *-(e)s, -e* **1.** *einzelner*: mountain; *kleiner*: hill, hillock; *über ~ und Tal* over hill and dale; *~e versetzen* (*können*) *fig.* move mountains; *über den ~ sein umg. fig.* be out of the wood(s), be over the worst; (*längst*) *über alle ~e sein umg.* be over the hills and far away, be miles away; *mit etw. nicht hinterm ~ halten fig.* make no bones about s.th., not beat about (*od.* around) the bush with s.th.; *mit etw. hinterm ~ halten fig.* keep quiet about s.th., not come forward with s.th.; *wenn der ~ nicht zum Propheten kommen will, muss der Prophet zum ~e gehen Sprichw.* if the mountain will not come to Muhammad, then Muhammad must go to the mountain; *da stehen einem die Haare zu ~e* it makes your hair stand on end; **2.** *die ~e* (*Gebirge*) the mountains; *in die ~e fahren* drive (up in)to the mountains; **3.** *mst Pl.*; (*e große Menge*): *~e von Schnee, Akten, Papier etc.* piles of / heaps of / a huge pile of / a mountain of *alle umg.*

...berg *m, im Subst.* **1.** *allzu viele*: huge number of; *Arbeitslosen~* huge number (*od.* mass) of unemployed; **2.** *ein Haufen*: huge pile of; *Bücher~* huge pile of books

berg|ab *Adv. auch fig.* downhill; *e-n Weg ~ gehen* go down a path, follow a path downhill; *mit ihm etc. geht es (immer mehr) ~ umg. fig.* things are going from bad to worse with him *etc.*; → *rapid* II; **~abwärts** *Adv.* downhill; down the mountain
Bergahorn *m Bot.* sycamore
bergan *Adv.* uphill; up the mountain
Bergarbeiter *m*, **~in** *f* miner, mine worker
berg|auf *Adv.* uphill; *e-n Weg ~ gehen* go up a path, follow a path uphill; *es geht wieder ~ mit unserem Land etc. fig.* things are looking up for our country *etc.*; **~aufwärts** *Adv.* uphill
Berg|bahn *f* mountain railway (*Am.* railroad); (*Seilbahn*) cable railway (*Am.* railroad); **~bau** *m; nur Sg.* mining (industry); **~bauer** *m* mountain farmer; **~bäuerin** *f* (female) mountain

farmer; *Gattin*: mountain farmer's wife; **~bauingenieur** *m*, **~bauingenieurin** *f* mining engineer; **~bewohner** *m*, **~bewohnerin** *f* mountain dweller, *Pl. auch* mountain people; **~dorf** *n* mountain village
bergen *v/t.*; *birgt, barg, hat geborgen* **1.** (*retten*) (*Verletzte*) rescue; (*Leichen, Güter*) recover; (*Schiff*) salvage; *j-n tot/lebend ~* recover s.o.'s body/rescue s.o. alive; *drei der fünf Bergsteiger konnten nur noch tot geborgen werden* it was not possible to rescue three of the five mountaineers alive; **2.** (*einholen*) (*Ernte*) gather in; (*Segel*) take in; **3.** *geh.* (*enthalten*) hold, contain; *weitS.* hold; (*Gefahr, Risiko, Vorteile*) *auch* involve; *dieser Versuch birgt erhebliche Probleme* this attempt involves (*od.* holds) serious problems; **4.** *geh.* (*verstecken*) conceal, hide; *das Gesicht in den Händen ~* bury one's face in one's hands
bergeweise *Adv. umg.* masses of; *~ Fanpost etc. bekommen* get masses (*od.* piles) of fan mail *etc.*
Berg|fahrt *f* **1.** *mit Seilbahn*: ascent, uphill (*od.* upward) journey; **2.** (*Bergtour*) trip in(to) the mountains; **~fex** *m*; *-es, -e; südd., österr.* mountaineering freak *umg.*; **~fried** *m hist.* keep; **~führer** *m*, **~führerin** *f* mountain guide; **~geist** *m* mountain troll; **~gipfel** *m* mountain top, summit; **~grat** *m* (mountain) ridge; **~hang** *m* mountain slope
berghoch I. *Adj. Wellen*: mountainous; **II.** *Adv. aufsteigen*: to a mountainous height
Berg|hotel *n* mountain hotel; **~hütte** *f* mountain hut (*od.* refuge)
bergig *Adj.* mountainous; (*hügelig*) hilly
Berg|kamm *m* (mountain) crest; **~kette** *f* mountain range
bergkrank *Adj.*: *~ sein* have (*od.* be suffering from) mountain (*Am.* altitude) sickness; **Bergkrankheit** *f; nur Sg.* mountain (*Am.* altitude) sickness
Berg|kristall *m Geol.* rock crystal, quartz; **~kuppe** *f* round(ed) (*od.* dome-shaped) mountain top; **~land** *n* mountainous country; **~landschaft** *f* mountain(ous) landscape, mountain scenery
Bergler *m*; *-s, -* mountain-dweller
Bergluft *f* mountain air
Bergmann *m*; *-(e)s, Bergleute; Bergb.* miner, mine worker; **bergmännisch** *Adj.* miners' ..., mining ..., in miner's fashion; **Bergmannssprache** *f* mining terminology
Berg|massiv *n* mountain mass, massif; **~not** *f*: *in ~ geraten/sein* get into / be in a dangerous situation up in the mountains; *j-n aus ~ retten* rescue s.o. from danger in the mountains; **~pfad** *m* mountain path; **~predigt** *f; nur Sg. mit best. Art.; bibl. the* Sermon on the Mount; **~rettungsdienst** *m* → *Bergwacht*; **~rutsch** *m* landslide; **~salz** *n* rock salt; **~sattel** *m* saddle; **~schuh** *m; mst Pl.* climbing (*od.* mountaineering) boot(s); **~ski** *m* upper ski; **~spitze** *f* mountain peak(*od.* top); (*Gipfel*) summit; **~sport** *m* mountaineering, mountain climbing; **~station** *f* top (*od.* upper) station
bergsteigen I. *v/i.* (*unreg., untr., hat/ist; nur Inf. und P.P.*) go mountain climbing (*od.* mountaineering); **II. Bergsteigen** *n* mountaineering; **Bergsteiger** *m*; *-s, -*, **Bergsteigerin** *f*;

B

-, *-nen* mountain climber, mountaineer; **bergsteigerisch I.** *Adj. Können, Leistung*: mountaineering; **II.** *Adv.* from a mountaineering point of view

Berg|stiefel *m*; *mst Pl.* mountaineering boot(s); **~stock** *m* **1.** *zum Wandern*: alpenstock; **2.** *Geol.* massif; **~straße** *f* **1.** mountain road; **2.** *nur Sg.*; *Geog.* German winegrowing area along the western escarpment of the Odenwald between Heidelberg and Darmstadt; **Zwingenberg an der ~** Zwingenberg on the Bergstraße; **~tod** *m* death in the mountains; **~tote** *m, f*; *mst Pl.* person killed in the mountains; **die Zahl der ~n nimmt ständig zu** the number of deaths in the mountains is constantly rising; **~tour** *f* mountain hike; *per Auto, Bus etc.*: mountain tour

Berg-und-Tal|-Bahn *f altm.* roller coaster, *Brit. auch* big dipper; **~-Fahrt** *f* **1.** *mit Seilbahn*: ascent and descent; **2.** *fig.* roller coaster ride; **das war die reinste ~** it was just like a ride on a roller coaster

Bergung *f* **1.** *(Rettung)* rescue; *von Toten, Fahrzeugen*: recovery; *Naut.* salvage; **2.** *(Einbringen) von Ernte*: gathering in; *der Segel*: taking in; **3.** *von Verfolgten*: sheltering

Bergungs|aktion *f* rescue operation; *Naut.* salvage operation; **~arbeiten** *Pl.* rescue work *Sg.*; *Naut.* salvage operation *Sg.* (*od.* operations); **~dienst** *m* recovery (*Naut.* salvage) service; **~fahrzeug** *n* rescue (*Flug.* crash) vehicle; *Naut.* salvage vessel; **~flotte** *f* salvage fleet; **~hubschrauber** *m* rescue helicopter; **~kosten** *Pl.* rescue costs; *Naut.* salvage costs; **~mannschaft** *f* rescue team; *Naut.* salvage party; **~schiff** *n* salvage vessel; **~versuch** *m* rescue attempt; *Naut.* salvage attempt (*od.* bid)

Berg|volk *n* mountain tribe (*od.* people [*Sg.*]); **~vorsprung** *m* spur; (*Absatz*) (mountain) ledge; **~wacht** *f* *Institution*: mountain rescue service; *Mannschaft*: mountain rescue team; **~wald** *m* mountain wood; **~wand** *f* rock face; **~wandern** *n* mountain hiking; **~wanderung** *f* mountain hike; **~welt** *f*; *nur Sg.* mountain landscape, mountains; **~werk** *n* mine; **im ~ arbeiten** work in a mine; **~wiese** *f* mountain pasture

Beriberi *f*; -, *kein Pl.*; *Med.* beriberi

Bericht *m*; *-(e)s, -e*; (*auch Reportage*) report (*über* + *Akk.* on); (*Beschreibung*) account (of); (*Kommentar*) commentary (on); (*Verlautbarung*) bulletin; *amtlicher*: return, statement; **~ erstatten** (give a) report (*über* + *Akk.* on; + *Dat.* to); **nach ~en von** (*od.* + *Gen.*) according to reports by; **~ zur Lage** account of the situation; **~ zur Lage der Nation** *Pol.* State of the Nation message; *in USA*: State of the Union message

berichten I. *v/t.* report; (*erzählen*) tell; *förm.* relate; **j-m etw. ~** (*melden*) inform s.o. of s.th., report s.th. to s.o.; (*erzählen*) tell s.o. about s.th.; **wie berichtet** as reported; **II.** *v/i.* report; give a report (on); (*erzählen*) give an account (*über* + *Akk.* of); **ausführlich ~** give a detailed account; **j-m ~** report to s.o. (*od.* give s.o. a report) (*über* + *Akk.*, *von* on); (*erzählen*) tell s.o. (about); **wie uns bereits gestern berichtet wurde, ...** as we already learn|t (*Am.* -ed) from yesterday's reports, ...; **wie uns soeben aus Brüssel be-**

richtet wird, ... according to reports just received from Brussels, ...; **mir ist berichtet worden, dass ...** it has been reported to me that ..., I have been informed that ...; **wir werden fortlaufend über die neuesten Ereignisse ~** we will provide constant updates on the latest developments

Berichterstatter *m*; *-s, -*, **~in** *f*; *-, -nen* **1.** *Presse*: reporter; *auswärtiger*: (foreign) correspondent; *Radio, TV*: commentator; **2.** *Jur.* referee; (*Referent*) *bei Kongressen etc.*: rapporteur; **Berichterstattung** *f*; *nur Sg.* **1.** reporting; *in der Presse*: *auch* coverage; **2.** (*Bericht*) report; *Radio, TV*: *auch* commentary; **j-n zur ~** (*zu sich*) **rufen** summon s.o. to make a report

berichtigen I. *v/t.* **1.** (*Fehler*) correct; *förm.* rectify; (*Text, Jur. Urteil, Parteianträge, Vorschrift*) amend, *Am. auch* revise; *Tech.* correct, adjust; **2.** *Wirts.* (*Buchung, Konto*) adjust; **3.** *Pol.* (*Grenze*) rectify; **II.** *v/refl.* correct o.s.; **Berichtigung** *f* correction; rectification; amendment; adjustment; **e-e ~ vornehmen** make a correction (*od.* an amendment *od.* an adjustment); → **berichtigen**

Berichtigungsanzeige *f* notice of error

Berichts|heft *n von Auszubildenden*: record book; **~zeitraum** *m* period under report (*od.* review)

berieseln *v/t.* **1.** (*Land*) irrigate, water; (*besprengen*) sprinkle; **2.** *fig.*, *pej.* subject (*mit* to); **mit Musik etc. berieselt werden** be subjected to a constant background of music *etc.*; **Berieselung** *f* **1.** irrigation; (*Besprengung*) sprinkling; **2.** *fig.* constant subjection (*mit* to); → *Musikberieselung*; **Berieselungsanlage** *f* sprinkler system

beringen *v/t.* (*Vogel*) ring; **ein beringter Finger** a finger wearing a ring, a ringed finger; **Beringung** *f* (*von Vögeln*) ringing

beritten *Adj.* mounted, *präd. auch* on horseback; **~e Polizei** mounted police

Berliner[1] **I.** *m*; *-s, -*; Berliner; **II.** *Adj.* (of) Berlin; **die ~ Mauer** *hist.* the Berlin Wall; **~ Weiße** (*mit Schuss*) *Gastr.* fizzy, low-alcohol white beer (*with a dash of raspberry juice*)

Berliner[2] *m*; *-s, -*; *Gastr. etwa* doughnut

Berlinerin *f*; *-, -nen* woman (*od.* girl) from Berlin, Berliner; **berlinerisch** *Adj. umg.* Berlin; **berlinern** *v/i.* speak the Berlin dialect

Bermudadreieck *n* Bermuda triangle; **Bermudas** *Pl.* **1.** *Geog.*: **die ~** the Bermudas, Bermuda *Sg.*; **2.** *Hose*: → **Bermudashorts**; **Bermudashorts** *Pl.* Bermuda shorts, Bermudas

Berner *Adj. Geog.*: **das ~ Oberland** the Bernese Oberland

Bernhardiner *m*; *-s, -*; *Zool.* St. Bernard (dog)

Bernstein *m* amber; **bernsteinfarben** *Adj.* amber-colo[u]red

Berserker *m*; *s, -* **1.** madman; **wie ein ~ toben/arbeiten** go berserk / work like crazy; **sich gebärden wie ein ~** carry on like a madman; **2.** *hist.* berserk(er)

bersten *v/i.* *birst, barst, ist geborsten*; *auch fig.* burst; *geh. Eis, Glas etc*: crack; (*explodieren*) explode; **zum Bersten voll** ready to burst, full to bursting (*von* with), jam-packed (with) *umg.*, chock-a-block (with) *umg.*; **~ vor Lachen** split one's sides laughing; **vor Wut/Neugier** *etc.* be bursting with rage/curiosity *etc.*

berüchtigt *Adj.* notorious (*wegen od. für* for), infamous; **er ist als Spieler ~** he is a notorious gambler

berücken *v/t. lit.* enchant, bewitch; **berückend I.** *Part. Präs.* → **berücken**; **II.** *Adj.* enchanting; *Schönheit*: ravishing; **das ist kein ~er Anblick** *iro.* it's not exactly a pleasant sight

berücksichtigen *v/t.* **1.** consider, take into consideration; (*beachten*) bear in mind; *Gesetz, Änderungen etc.*: reflect; (*einberechnen*) allow for; **2.** (*in Betracht ziehen*) (*Wünsche*) take into account; (*Bewerber, Antrag*) consider; (*überhaupt*) **nicht ~** *auch* (completely) disregard (*od.* ignore); **Sonderwünsche ~ wir gerne / können nicht berücksichtigt werden** we will gladly / cannot consider any special requests; **Berücksichtigung** *f* consideration, regard; **unter *od.* bei ~** (+ *Gen.*) considering; **unter ~ aller Vorschriften** subject to all regulations; **ohne ~** (+ *Gen.*) regardless of

Beruf *m*; *-(e)s, -e* job, occupation; *höherer, freier*: profession; (*Berufung*) vocation; (*Gewerbe*) trade; (*Geschäft*) business; (*Fach*) line; (*Laufbahn*) career; *förm.* calling; **e-n ~ ergreifen** take up a career (*od.* profession); **e-n ~ ausüben** *od.* **e-m ~ nachgehen** pursue a career; **den ~ wechseln** change one's occupation; **Erfolg im ~ haben** be successful in one's career; **was ist sie von ~?** what does she do (for a living)?; **sie ist Lehrerin/Hausfrau von ~** she's a teacher (by profession) / housewife (by occupation); **e-n freien ~ haben** be in an independent profession; **ich glaube, ich habe den falschen ~** I think I'm in the wrong (kind of) job; **den ~ verfehlt haben** have missed one's vocation; **~ und Haushalt** work and home; **von ~s wegen** on account of one's job; **wenn man voll im ~ steht, dann ...** when one has a full-time job ...

berufen I. *v/t.* (*unreg.*) **1.** *zu e-r Funktion*: **j-n zum Vorsitzenden / zu e-m Amt ~** appoint s.o. chairman / to an office; **j-n auf *od.* an e-n Lehrstuhl ~** offer s.o. a chair (at university); **an e-n Ort: nach Berlin ~ werden** be called to Berlin; **2.** *umg.* → **beschreien**; **II.** *v/refl.* (*unreg.*): **sich ~ auf** (+ *Akk.*) *als Autorität, Quelle etc.*: cite, quote, refer to; *auf j-n persönlich*: mention s.o.'s name; **sich auf j-n als Zeugen ~** appeal to s.o. as a witness; **sich darauf ~, dass ...** plead that ...; **darf ich mich auf Sie ~?** may I mention your name?; (*zitieren*) may I quote you?; **III.** *v/i.* (*unreg.*) *österr. Jur.* appeal; **IV.** *Adj.* **1.** (*befähigt*) qualified, competent; **aus ~em Munde** from a reliable source, on good authority, straight from the horse's mouth *umg.*; **~ sein / sich ~ fühlen zu** (+ *Inf.*) be/feel competent enough (*od.* qualified) to (+ *Inf.*); *moralisch*: have / feel one has a mission to (+ *Inf.*); **ich fühlte mich (nicht) einzugreifen** I felt called upon / I didn't feel it was for me to intervene; **2.** *zum Priester etc.* **~ sein** have a calling to be a priest (*od.* to the priesthood *etc.*); **zur Malerei etc. ~ sein** have a vocation for painting *etc.*; **sich zu Höherem ~ fühlen** feel one is destined for higher things

beruflich I. *Adj.* professional; *nur attr.* work ...; *Ausbildung etc.*: vocational; **~er Aufstieg** advancement (in one's job *od.* career); **~er Ärger** *etc.* trouble *etc.* at work; ~*e Aussichten* job (*od.* career) prospects; ~*e Eignung* suitability for a (*od.* the) job (*od.* career); ~*er Werdegang* career path; *aus* ~*en Gründen* for job-related (*od.* professional) reasons; *bedingt durch i-e* ~*e Tätigkeit* as a result of her work; → *Fortbildung*; **II.** *Adv.* as far as work (*od.* one's job, career, profession) is concerned; *was machen Sie* ~? what do you do (for a living)?, what's your line of work?; ~ *unterwegs* away on business; ~ *stark beansprucht sein* have a heavy workload; ~ *sehr erfolgreich sein* have a very successful career; *sich* ~ *verändern/verbessern* change one's job / get a better job; ~ *gesehen ist das die richtige Entscheidung* this is the right decision from a career point of view, this is the right career move; *sich* ~ *fort-* *od.* *weiterbilden* do further (vocational) training

Berufs|anfänger *m*, ~*anfängerin* *f* first-time employee; ~*aufbauschule* *f* vocational college providing continuation courses leading to a technical college entrance qualification; ~*ausbildung* *f* vocational (*od.* professional) training *Pl.*; ~*aussichten* *Pl.* career prospects; ~*ausübung* *f; nur Sg.* pursuit of one's career; *j-m die* ~ *untersagen* not allow s.o. to pursue his (*od.* her) career, exclude s.o. from his (*od.* her) profession; *nach langjähriger* ~ after many years of work, after a career lasting many years

berufs|bedingt I. *Adj.* occupational, work-related, job-related; *Ortswechsel*: because of one's job; **II.** *Adv.* for work (*od.* professional) reasons; ~*begleitend* *Adj.* *Kurse, Fortbildung*: in-service

Berufs|berater *m*, ~*beraterin* *f* careers adviser (*od.* officer), job counsel(l)or; ~*beratung* *f* careers guidance, *Am.* career counseling; *zur* ~ *gehen* go to the careers guidance (*Am.* career counseling) session; ~*beratungsstelle* *f* careers guidance (*Am.* career counseling) office; ~*bezeichnung* *f* job title

berufsbezogen *Adj.* job-related; *Unterricht*: vocationally oriented

Berufsbild *n* job profile

berufsbildend *Adj.*: ~*e Schulen* vocational schools

Berufs|chancen *Pl.* job (*od.* career) prospects; ~*erfahrung* *f; nur Sg.* (work) experience; *Redakteur mit langjähriger/vielseitiger* ~ editor with many years experience / varied experience on the job; ~*ethos* *n geh.* professional ethics *Pl.*; ~*fachschule* *f* vocational college; ~*fahrer* *m*, ~*fahrerin* *f* **1.** driver (*who drives for a living*); **2.** *Motorrennen*: professional (racing) driver; *Radrennen*: professional (cyclist); ~*feuerwehr* *f* fire service (*Am.* department *od.* company); ~*fotograf* *m*, ~*fotografin* *f* professional photographer

berufsfremd *Adj.* unconnected with one's work; ~*e Tätigkeiten* activities outside the scope of one's job

Berufs|geheimnis *n* **1.** professional (*od.* trade) secret; **2.** *nur Sg.*; (*Schweigepflicht*) professional secrecy (*od.* discretion); *das* ~ *wahren/verletzen* maintain/violate professional secrecy; ~*genossenschaft* *f* professional (*Gewerbe*: trade) association; ~*grundbildungsjahr* *n* year of basic vocational training; ~*grundschuljahr* *n* basic

one-year vocational college course; ~*gruppe* *f* professional group; ~*heer* *n* professional (*od.* regular) army; ~*kleidung* *f* work(ing) clothes *Pl.*; ~*krankheit* *f* occupational (*od.* industrial *od.* job-related) illness; ~*leben* *n* professional (*od.* working) life; *ins* ~ (*ein*)*treten* start work, start one's first job; *im* ~ *stehen* be at work, have a job; *Frau*: be a working (*od.* career) woman

berufsmäßig I. *Adj.* professional; **II.** *Adv.* professionally, as a profession; → *auch* **beruflich** II

Berufs|politiker *m*, ~*politikerin* *f* professional (*od.* career) politician; ~*praktikum* *n* (practical) work experience; *von Arzt, Lehrer etc.*: practical; ~*revolutionär* *m pej.* professional revolutionary; ~*richter* *m*, ~*richterin* *f* professional judge; ~*risiko* *n* occupational hazard; ~*schule* *f* vocational school (*od.* college); ~*schüler* *m*, ~*schülerin* *f* vocational school (*od.* college) student; ~*soldat* *m*, ~*soldatin* *f* regular (soldier); ~*spieler* *m*, ~*spielerin* *f* **1.** *Sport* professional (player *od.* athlete); **2.** *Glücksspiel*: professional gambler; ~*sportler* *m*, ~*sportlerin* *f* professional (athlete); ~*stand* *m* profession, professional group; *der* ~ *der Juristen/Mediziner etc.* the legal/medical *etc.* profession

berufstätig *Adj.* (*Amtsspr.* gainfully) employed; *Eltern etc.*: *nur attr.* working ...; ~ *sein* (go to) work, have a job; ~*e Mütter* working mothers; *nicht mehr* ~ *sein* be no longer employed; *halbtags* ~ *sein* work part-time; **Berufstätige** *m, f; -n, -n* employed person; **Berufstätigkeit** *f; nur Sg.* employment; *konkret*: *auch* job

berufsunfähig *Adj.* unable to work; **Berufsunfähigkeit** *f; nur Sg. allg.*: inability to work; *occupational disability*; **Berufsunfähigkeitsrente** *f* disability pension (*od.* benefit)

Berufs|unfall *m* workplace accident; ~*verband* *m* professional association; ~*verbot* *n* exclusion from a profession (*Pol.* from public service); *Jur.* (professional) disbarment; *mit* ~ *belegt werden* be excluded from one's profession (*Pol.* from public service); *Jur.* be disbarred; ~ *erhalten aus politischen Gründen*: be barred from pursuing one's career; ~*verbrecher* *m*, ~*verbrecherin* *f* professional criminal; ~*verkehr* *m* **1.** (*Stoßverkehr*) rush-hour traffic; *in den* ~ *kommen* be caught up in rush-hour traffic; **2.** weekday traffic; ~*vorbereitungsjahr* *n* preparatory (training) year; ~*wahl* *f; nur Sg.* **1.** (*das Wählen*) choosing a career; *j-n bei der* ~ *beraten* advise s.o. on a choice of career; **2.** (*gewählter Beruf*) one's choice of career; *wie sieht d-e* ~ *aus?* what career are you considering?; ~*wechsel* *m* change of career (*od.* profession); switching careers (*od.* professions); ~*wunsch* *m* desired career; ~*ziel* *n* **1.** (*geplanter Beruf*) planned career; **2.** *im Beruf*: professional aim; ~*zweig* *m* line of work

Berufung *f* **1.** *Jur.* appeal; *in die* ~ *gehen* (*od.* ~ *einlegen*) (file an) appeal (*gegen* against); **2.** *innere*: calling, vocation (*zu* for, to [be]); *er fühlte die* ~, *Priester zu werden* he felt he had a vocation to be a priest (*od.* for the priesthood); **3.** *mst Sg.*; (*Ernennung*) appointment; *e-e* ~ *an e-e Hochschule*

etc. *erhalten* be offered an appointment (*od.* be appointed) at a university *etc.*; **4.** (*Sichberufen*) reference; *unter* ~ *auf* with reference to

Berufungs|antrag *m Jur.* petition for appeal; ~*gericht* *n*, ~*instanz* *f Jur.* court of appeal, appellate court; ~*klage* *f Jur.* appeal; ~*verfahren* *n Jur.* appeal proceedings *Pl.*

beruhen *v/i.* **1.** ~ *auf* (+ *Dat.*) be based on, be founded on; (*zurückzuführen sein auf*) stem from, go back to; *es beruht auf e-m Missverständnis* it was (all) a misunderstanding; *das beruht auf Gegenseitigkeit umg.* *von Gefühlen*: the feeling is mutual; **2.** *etw. auf sich* ~ *lassen* let s.th. rest; *lassen wir die Sache auf sich* ~ let's let the matter rest; *wir können das nicht auf sich* ~ *lassen* we can't leave it at that (*od.* leave things as they are)

beruhigen I. *v/t.* calm (down); (*versichern*) reassure; (*das Gewissen*) ease; (*die Nerven*) calm, soothe; (*den Magen*) settle; (*entspannen*) relax; *es beruhigt mich zu hören, dass er gut angekommen ist* I'm relieved (*od.* glad) to hear that he arrived safely; *da bin ich aber beruhigt!* that's all right (*Am.* alright) then; *stärker*: that's a relief; *seien Sie beruhigt!* there's no need to worry; *dann kann ich ja beruhigt schlafen / in Urlaub fahren* now I can sleep in peace / go on holiday (*Am.* vacation) with an easy mind; **II.** *v/refl.* calm down; *Lage*: quieten down; *Sturm, Wind*: die down; *See, Wellen*: calm down; *Markt, Börse*: settle down; *Verkehr*: become lighter; *sie konnte sich deswegen gar nicht mehr* ~ she simply couldn't get over it; **III.** *v/i.*: *das beruhigt* that'll calm you down (*od.* relax you); *die Farbe Grün beruhigt* green has a calming effect; **beruhigend I.** *Part. Präs.* → **beruhigen**; **II.** *Adj.* **1.** *Gedanke etc.*: comforting, reassuring; **2.** *Musik, Farbe etc.*: relaxing; *seine Stimme hat (so) etwas Beruhigendes* his voice has a calming (*od.* soothing) quality; **3.** *Med.* sedative; **III.** *Adv.*: *etw. wirkt* ~ *auf* (+ *Akk.*) s.th. has a calming (*Musik etc.*: relaxing) effect on

Beruhigung *f* **1.** (*das Beruhigen*) calming (down); reassurance; easing; soothing; → **beruhigen**; *ich brauche etwas zur* ~ I need something to calm me down; **2.** (*das Ruhigwerden*) *e-r Lage*: calming down; *stärker*: stabilization; *von Spannungen*: easing; *e-e* ~ *des Wetters / der politischen Lage ist nicht zu erwarten* there is no prospect of more settled weather / of an easing of the political situation; *zur* ~ *der Gemüter* to set people's minds at rest; **3.** (*Sicherheit*) reassurance; *zu unserer großen* ~ much to our relief; *s-e Anwesenheit gibt mir ein Gefühl der* ~ I find his presence reassuring; *zu Ihrer* ~ *kann ich Ihnen versichern, dass ...* to put your mind at rest, I can assure you that ...

Beruhigungs|mittel *n Med.* sedative, tranquil(l)izer; ~*pille* *f Med.* sedative (tablet *od.* pill), tranquil(l)izer; ~*spritze* *f Med.* sedative (shot), tranquil(l)izer; ~*tablette* *f Med.* → **Beruhigungspille**

berühmt *Adj.* famous, renowned (*wegen, für* for); (*gefeiert*) celebrated (for); *durch diese Rolle wurde sie* ~ this part (*od.* role) made her famous; *nicht* ~ *umg. fig.* nothing to shout

B

about; **berühmt-berüchtigt** *Adj.* notorious, infamous (**wegen** for); **Berühmtheit** *f* 1. *nur Sg.* fame, renown; **~ erlangen** *Person*: rise to fame; *Film, Gebäude, Melodie etc.*: become famous; **zu trauriger ~ gelangen** gain a doubtful reputation; *durch tragisches Ereignis*: achieve tragic fame; **2.** (*Person*) celebrity, big name
berühren *v/t.* **1.** touch; *Menschen, Hände etc.*: *auch* come into contact, meet; (*streifen*) graze; *weitS.* (*angrenzen an*) touch on; **Berühren verboten!** do not touch; **auf unserer Schiffsreise berührten wir mehrere Länder** on our cruise we paid brief visits to several countries; **2.** *fig.* (*Thema etc.*) touch on; **sich** *od.* **einander ~** meet; *Meinungen, Interessen etc.*: coincide; **3.** *fig. seelisch*: touch (to the quick), move, have an effect on; **das berührt mich (überhaupt) nicht** that doesn't concern me (in the slightest); **es hat mich seltsam/schmerzlich berührt** I found it strangely/painfully moving; **es war angenehm/unangenehm berührt** I was pleased / I didn't like it; → **peinlich** II 1
Berührung *f* 1. (*das Berühren*) touch; (*Kontakt*) contact; **in ~ kommen mit** *auch mit Krankheit, Armut etc.*: come into contact with; (*berühren*) *auch* touch; **bei der leisesten ~** at the slightest touch; **2.** *nur Sg.*; *fig.* contact; **in ~ bleiben** keep in touch; **in ~ kommen mit** *mit e-r Lehre, Kultur etc.*: be introduced to, come across; **3.** *nur Sg.*; *fig. von Thema, Frage*: mention
Berührungs|angst *f* fear of physical contact; *Psych.*: **unter ~ leiden** *Psych.* be afraid of physical contact; **s-e Berührungsängste überwinden** overcome one's fear (*od.* phobia) of physical contact; *fig.* overcome one's initial reservations; **~punkt** *m* 1. *auch fig.* point of contact; **2.** *Math.* tangential point; **3.** **~e** *fig.* (*Gemeinsamkeiten*) common ground *Sg.*
besabbern *umg.* **I.** *v/t.* dribble, *Am.* drool; *stärker*: slobber all over *s.th.*; **II.** *v/refl.* dribble, *Am.* drool; *stärker*: slobber
besagen *v/t.* (*aussagen*) say; (*bedeuten*) mean; **das besagt noch gar nichts** that doesn't mean (*od.* prove) a thing; **das besagt nicht, dass** it doesn't mean (to say) that; **was besagt das schon?** what does that prove?; **besagt I.** *P.P.* → **besagen**; **II.** *Adj.* said; *bes. Jur.* the aforementioned
besaiten *v/t. Mus.* string; **das Cello muss neu besaitet werden** the cello needs restringing; → **zartbesaitet**
besamen *v/t.* **1.** inseminate; **2.** *Bot.* pollinate; **Besamung** *f* 1. insemination; **2.** *Bot.* pollination
besammeln *v/t. schw.* assemble; **Besammlung** *f schw.* assembly
besänftigen I. *v/t.* appease; (*beruhigen*) calm (down); **j-s Zorn ~** pacify s.o.'s anger; **II.** *v/refl.* calm down; *Wellen, Meer*: become calm; *Sturm*: ease, abate; **Besänftigung** *f* appeasement; calming (down); → **besänftigen**
Besan|mast *m Naut.* mizzen mast; **~segel** *n Naut.* mizzen sail
besät *Adj. fig.*: **~ mit** *od.* **von** covered (*od.* strewn) with
Besatz *m*; *-es, Besätze* **1.** *Mode*: trimming(s *Pl.*); **2.** (*Tierbestand*) stock
Besatzer *m*; *-s, -*; *pej. einzelner Soldat*: occupying soldier; *Pl.* occupying forces
Besatzung *f* 1. *Mil.* (*Besatzer*) occupying forces *Pl.*; (*Garnison*) garrison; *Zustand*: occupation; **2.** *Naut., Flug.* crew; **mit fünf Mann ~** with a crew of five
Besatzungs|armee *f* occupying army (*od.* forces *Pl.*); **~macht** *f* occupying power; **~mitglied** *n* crew member; **~soldat** *m* soldier in the occupying army; **~truppen** *Pl.* occupying forces; **~zone** *f* occupied zone
besaufen *v/refl.* (*unreg.*); *umg.* get plastered, get sloshed *Sl.*; **Besäufnis** *n*; *-ses, -se, auch f*; *-, -se*; *umg.* booze-up; **die Party artete in ein allgemeines ~ aus** the party degenerated into a general booze-up (*od.* drinking orgy)
besäuselt *Adj. umg.* slightly sozzled (*Am.* tipsy)
beschädigen *v/t.* damage; **Beschädigung** *f* 1. (*das Beschädigen*) damaging; **2.** (*der Schaden*) *auch Pl.* damage (+ *Gen.* to)
beschaffen¹ *v/t.* get, procure *förm.*; *mit Mühe*: get hold of *umg.*; (*Arbeit, Wohnung etc.*) *auch* find; **j-m/sich e-e Genehmigung etc. ~** obtain a permit *etc.* for s.o./oneself; **das Buch ist nicht / nur schwer zu ~** the book is unobtainable/difficult to get hold of
beschaffen² *Adj.* **1.** (*geartet*) made; **die Sache ist so ~** it's like this, the situation is as follows; **so ~, dass** *Material*: made in such a way that; **ein so ~es Material** a material made like this; **so ist er eben ~** *Mensch*: that's the way he's made; **2.** *Zustand*: **gut/schlecht ~** in a good/bad state; **wie ist die Straße ~?** what state is the road in?; **Beschaffenheit** *f*; *nur Sg.* **1.** (*Eigenschaft*) quality; (*Art*) nature; (*Struktur*) structure; **weiche/raue** *etc.* **~** softness/roughness *etc.*; **von welcher ~ ist dieser Stoff?** what is the nature of this material?; **2.** (*Zustand*) state, condition; **3.** *körperliche*: (physical) constitution; *seelische*: (psychological) makeup
Beschaffung *f*; *nur Sg.* procurement, acquisition; (*Versorgung*) provision; **~ von Lebensmitteln** provision of food supplies
Beschaffungs|kosten *Pl.* cost *Sg.* of acquisition; **~kriminalität** *f* drug-related crime
beschäftigen I. *v/t.* **1.** (*etw. zu tun geben*) keep s.o. busy, occupy s.o.; (*j-m Arbeit geben*) find s.o. something to do; **2.** (*anstellen*) employ, give s.o. a job *umg.*; **wie viele Leute beschäftigt er?** how many people has he got working for him (*od.* does he employ)?, how many employees has he got?; **3.** (*j-n, j-s Geist od. Aufmerksamkeit*) occupy, absorb; *Problem*: preoccupy; *stärker*: engross; **was beschäftigt dich denn so?** what's on your mind?, what's bothering you?; **es beschäftigt mich ständig** I can't get it out of my mind; **II.** *v/refl.*: **sich ~ mit** busy (*od.* occupy) o.s. with; *jetzt gerade*: be busy (*od.* occupied) with; (*sich kümmern um*) look after; (*arbeiten an*) work at (*od.* on); *mit e-m Problem, Thema etc.*: deal with; *mit Kindern etc.*: *auch* spend (a lot of) time with; *mit Kunst, Literatur etc.*: concern o.s. with; **er beschäftigt sich nie mit den Kindern** he never has time for the children; **wie hast du dich heute beschäftigt?** how did you occupy yourself today?, what did you do with yourself today?; **unser Sohn kann sich gut alleine** *od.* **selbst ~** our son is

good at keeping himself occupied; **ich muss mich mal mit was anderem ~** I must concentrate on something else for a change; **wir ~ uns derzeit mit ...** *in Forschung*: we are currently studying ...
beschäftigt I. *P.P.* → **beschäftigen**; **II.** *Adj.* **1.** busy (**mit** with); **damit ~ sein, etw. zu tun** be busy doing s.th. (*od.* with s.th.); **mit Briefeschreiben ~ sein** be busy writing letters; **mit etwas anderem ~ sein** be busy with (*od.* doing) something else (*od.* other things), have something else (*od.* other things) to do; **2.** (*angestellt*) employed; **~ sein bei** work for, have a job with (*od.* at), be employed with (*od.* at)
Beschäftigte *m, f*; *-n, -n* employee; **Zahl der ~n** number of employees
Beschäftigung *f* 1. *allg.*: (*Tätigkeit*) something to do; (*bestimmte*) activity; **keine ~ haben** have nothing to do; **das ist e-e nützliche/Zeit raubende ~** that's a useful thing (to be doing) / a time-consuming activity; **das ist doch keine ~ für dich!** you don't want to be doing that kind of thing; **für ~ ist gesorgt!** *hum.* there's not exactly a shortage of things to do; **das mache ich nur zur ~** (*nicht aus Interesse*) I'm only doing this to keep busy (*od.* for something to do); **2.** (*Anstellung*) employment; (*Stelle*) job; *Arbeitsmarkt*: employment; *Industrie*: activity; **e-r ~ nachgehen** have work; **ohne ~** unemployed; **3.** *nur Sg.*; *mit e-m Thema*: treatment (*mit* of); *mit e-m Problem*: preoccupation (with); *mit Literatur*: study (*mit* of); *mit e-m Projekt*: involvement (*mit* in); **4.** *nur Sg.*; (*das Beschäftigen*) occupying; **die ~ von Kindern erfordert viel Fantasie** keeping children occupied requires plenty of imagination
Beschäftigungs|lage *f* employment situation; **~los** *Adj.* (*arbeitslos*) unemployed, out of work *umg.*; **~nachweis** *m* proof of employment; **~programm** *n* work scheme (*Am.* program), job creation scheme (*Am.* program); **~therapie** *f* occupational therapy; **~verhältnis** *n* employment; *Amtsspr.* employed status; **in was für e-m ~ stehen Sie?** what type of employment are you in?
beschallen *v/t.* **1.** *mit Lautsprecher*: fill with sound; *am Mischpult*: do the sound; **2.** *Med., Tech.* treat with ultrasound; **Beschallung** *f* 1. *hum. mit lauter Musik etc.*: subjection to a barrage of sound; **2.** *Med., Tech.* treatment with ultrasound
beschämen *v/t.* (put to) shame; (*verlegen machen*) embarrass; **ich will mich nicht ~ lassen** I don't want to disgrace myself; **d-e Offenheit beschämt mich** your frankness puts me to shame (*od.* makes me feel ashamed)
beschämend I. *Part. Präs.* → **beschämen**; **II.** *Adj.* **1.** (*schändlich*) shameful; *stärker*: disgraceful; **2.** (*demütigend*) humiliating, shaming; **es ist ~** *auch* it's a disgrace; **es ist ein ~es Gefühl** it makes you feel ashamed; **~ für j-n sein** *auch* put s.o. to shame; **III.** *Adv.* shamefully; (*peinlich*) *auch* embarrassingly; **~ naiv** embarrassingly naive; **es kamen ~ wenige Zuschauer** there were shamefully few visitors; **beschämenderweise** *Adv.* shamefully, to my, his *etc.* shame
beschämt I. *P.P.* → **beschämen**; **II.** *Adj.* ashamed; (*verlegen*) embar-

rassed; **ein ~es Gesicht machen** look ashamed; **III.** *Adv.*: **~ die Augen senken** look down in shame (*verlegen*: with embarrassment)

Beschämung *f; mst Sg.* shame; (*Demütigung*) humiliation; **~ empfinden** feel ashamed (**über** + *Akk.* about); *verlegen sein*: feel embarrassed (about); **zu m-r ~** I'm ashamed to say (that)

beschatten *v/t.* **1.** *geh.* (*Schatten werfen*) shade; *fig.* overshadow, cast a shadow over (*od.* on); **2.** *fig.* (*verfolgen*) shadow, tail; **3.** *Sport* mark (closely); **Beschattung** *f; mst Sg.* **1.** *fig.* shadowing, tailing; **2.** *Sport* (close) marking, shadowing

Beschau *f; -, kein Pl. von Schlachtvieh etc.*: inspection; **beschauen** *v/t.* **1.** (*betrachten*) (have a) look at; *prüfend*: *auch* examine; **2.** *amtlich*: inspect; **Beschauer** *m; -s, -*, **Beschauerin** *f; -, -nen* **1.** (*Betrachter[in]*) viewer; **2.** *amtlich*: inspector

beschaulich **I.** *Adj.* (*voll Muße*) leisurely; (*ruhig*) quiet, peaceful; (*kontemplativ*) contemplative; **ein ~es Dasein führen** lead a quiet (*od.* contemplative) life; **Musik für ~e Stunden** music for tranquil moments; **II.** *Adv.* peacefully, tranquilly; **Beschaulichkeit** *f; nur Sg.* leisureliness; peace and quiet; contemplativeness; contemplation; → **beschaulich**

Bescheid *m; -(e)s, -e* **1.** *nur Sg.*; (*Nachricht*) notification; **~ bekommen** be told, be informed; (**j-m**) **~ geben** *od.* **sagen** let s.o. know (**über** + *Akk.* about); **gib bitte ~!** let me know; **2.** (*Antwort*) answer, reply; *offiziell*: *auch* notification; (*Entscheidung*) decision; **ein günstiger ~** a favourable reply (*Entscheidung*: decision); **ein abschlägiger ~** a rejection, a refusal; **wir warten noch auf e-n ~** we are still waiting for a reply (*Entscheidung*: decision; *Jur.* ruling); **3.** *nur Sg.*: **~ wissen** (*informiert sein*) know, be in the picture *umg.* (**über** + *Akk.* about); (*sich auskennen*) know about things (*od.* how things work *etc.*); **er weiß dort ~ in e-r Stadt etc.**: he knows his way around there; **über j-n ~ wissen** *auch* know all about s.o.; **auf e-m Gebiet ~ wissen** know about a subject; **in e-r Sache genau ~ wissen** know all the ins and outs of s.th.; **ich weiß überhaupt nicht ~** I've no idea (how it works *etc.*); **ich weiß überhaupt nicht mehr ~** I don't know what's going on any more; **Sie brauchen nur m-n Namen zu nennen, dann weiß er schon ~** just mention my name and he'll know what it's about; **ich weiß ~!** *auch iro.* I know all about it; **j-m gehörig ~ sagen** *od.* **stoßen** *umg.* give s.o. a piece of one's mind

bescheiden¹ **I.** *Adj.* **1.** (*genügsam*) modest; *Person*: *auch* unassuming; (*anspruchslos*) undemanding; **2.** (*einfach, schlicht*) *Zimmer*: simple, modest; **~e Mittel** modest means; **mit ~en Mitteln** *etw. aufbauen etc.*: *auch* ... on a shoestring; **aus ~en Anfängen** from humble (*od.* small) beginnings; **aus ~en Verhältnissen kommen** come from a modest background; **e-e ~e Frage**: ... would it be unreasonable to ask ...; **3.** (*gering*) *Lohn etc.*: meag|re (*Am.* -er), very modest; **4.** *euph.* (*beschissen*) awful; **II.** *Adv.*: **sehr ~ leben** get by on very little, live modestly, lead a frugal existence; **sehr ~ woh-**

nen/essen live in very modest surroundings / eat very frugally; **etwas ~er leben müssen** have to get by on less (*od.* tighten one's belt)

bescheiden² (*unreg.*) **I.** *v/refl.* **1.** make do with what one has got; **sich mit etw. ~** be content (*od.* satisfied) with s.th., content o.s. with s.th., make do with s.th.; **II.** *v/t.* **1.** *geh.*: **es war ihm nicht beschieden zu** (+ *Inf.*) it wasn't given to him to (+ *Inf.*), he wasn't destined (*od.* meant) to (+ *Inf.*); **es war ihm nicht beschieden** it wasn't (meant) to be; **ihm / der Sache war kein Erfolg etc. beschieden** he/it wasn't destined to succeed *etc.*; **2.** *förm.* (*entscheiden*) make a decision on; *auch Jur.* (*informieren*) (*j-n*) notify, advise; **ein Gesuch abschlägig** *od.* **negativ ~** reject a petition; **3.** *geh., förm.* (*beordern*) summon (**zu j-m** to appear before s.o.)

Bescheidenheit *f; nur Sg.* modesty; *e-r Person*: *auch* unassuming nature; (*Schlichtheit*) simplicity; (*Kümmerlichkeit*) humility, lowliness; **nur keine falsche ~!** come on, no false modesty!; **bei aller ~** with all due modesty; **aus lauter ~ hat er nicht gefragt** he was too modest to ask

bescheinen *v/t.* (*unreg.*) shine on; *Feuer, Scheinwerfer*: light up; **von der Sonne / vom Mond beschienen** sunlit/moonlit, bathed in sunlight/moonlight

bescheinigen *v/t.* certify; (*Echtheit*) *auch* authenticate; (*bestätigen*) confirm (in writing); *weitS.* (*für etw. bürgen*) confirm, vouch for; **den Empfang ~ e-s Briefes**: acknowledge receipt of; *e-r Summe*: give a receipt for; **hiermit wird bescheinigt, dass** this is to certify that; **sich** (*Dat.*) **die Teilnahme an e-m Kurs ~ lassen** have one's participation in a course certified; **könnten Sie mir ~, dass** could you give me something in writing stating that, could I have written confirmation that; **sich gegenseitig Unfähigkeit etc. ~** accuse each other of incompetence *etc.*; **j-m Ehrlichkeit ~** testify to s.o.'s honesty

Bescheinigung *f* **1.** *allg.*: something in writing; (*Bestätigung*) (written) confirmation, statement; (*Schein*) certificate; (*Quittung*) receipt; **e-e ~ über die Teilnahme an etw.** (*Dat.*) a certificate of participation in s.th.; **e-e ärztliche ~** a medical certificate; **2.** *nur Sg.*; (*das Bescheinigen*) certification, (written) confirmation

bescheißen (*unreg.*) *vulg.* **I.** *v/t.* do (**um** out of), cheat (**um** [out] of); **man hat ihn ziemlich beschissen** he's been properly done (*Am. auch* had); **II.** *v/i.* cheat

beschenken *v/t.*: **j-n ~** give s.o. a present (*od.* presents), give a present (*od.* presents) to s.o.; **j-n mit etw. ~** give s.o. s.th. (as a present); **sich** (**gegenseitig**) **~** give each other presents; **j-n reich / mit Büchern etc. ~** shower s.o. with presents / with books *etc.*; **Beschenkte** *m, f; -n, -n* recipient (of a present)

bescheren **I.** *v/t.* **1.** *fig.* (*zukommen lassen*) bring s.o. s.th.; *Positives, auch iro.*: *auch* bless s.o. with s.th.; **das hat uns viel Ärger beschert** this caused us much hassle; **was uns wohl die Zukunft ~ wird?** what will the future bring?; **2.** **j-n ~** give s.o. presents; **j-n mit etw. ~** give s.o. s.th.; **was hat dir das Christkind beschert?** what did

Santa Claus bring you?; **II.** *v/i.*: **wann wird bei euch beschert?** when do you have (*od.* open) your (Christmas) presents?

Bescherung *f* **1.** *Weihnachten*: opening of (Christmas) presents; **wann ist bei euch ~?** when do you have (*od.* open) your (Christmas) presents?; **2.** *umg. iro.*: **e-e schöne ~!** a fine mess that is, we're in a fine mess now; **da haben wir die ~!** there you are, what did I say?, I told you this would happen!

bescheuert *Adj. umg.* **1.** (*dumm, verrückt*) cracked, *präd. auch* nuts; **er ist ~** *auch* he's gone off his nut (*Am.* rocker); **ich bin doch nicht ~!** I'm not that stupid; **j-n ~ finden** think s.o. is crazy; **2.** (*dumm, ärgerlich*) *Situation, Idee etc.*: stupid, crazy; **so was Bescheuertes!** what a nuisance (*od.* pain)!

beschichten *v/t.* coat; **beschichtet** *Adj. und P.P.* coated; **Beschichtung** *f* **1.** (*Schicht*) coat(ing); **2.** *nur Sg.* (*das Beschichten*) coating

beschicken *v/t.* **1.** *Tech.* (*Reaktor, Hochofen etc.*) load, charge; **2.** (*Ausstellung etc.*) *mit Leuten*: send representatives to; *mit Dingen*: send exhibits *etc.* to; (*Markt, Laden*) supply; **die Messe war gut beschickt** the trade fair had a good display; **3.** *nordd.* (*erledigen*) deal with

beschickert *Adj. umg.* tiddly, slightly sozzled, *Am.* tipsy

Beschickung *f* **1.** *Tech.* (*Füllung*) charge; **2.** *mst Sg.* (*das Beschicken*) charging

beschießen *v/t.* (*unreg.*) **1.** fire at; *Mil.* bombard, shell; **2.** *Phys. mit Neutronen etc.*: bombard; **3.** *fig. mit Fragen etc.*: bombard; **Beschießung** *f Mil.* bombardment, shelling

beschildern *v/t.* **1.** (*mit Schildern versehen*) signpost; (*den Weg*) mark *the route*; **gut beschilderte Wege** clearly signposted paths; **2.** (*Waren etc.*) label; **Beschilderung** *f* **1.** *Verkehr*: signposting; (*Schilder*) signposts *Pl.*; **2.** *von Waren etc.*: label(l)ing

beschimpfen *v/t.* call s.o. names; (*beleidigen*) insult; *mit Kraftausdrücken*: swear at *s.o.*; **j-n als Lügner etc. ~** call s.o. a liar *etc.*; **Beschimpfung** *f* **1.** (*das Beschimpfen*) calling names, abusing; **die ständige ~ der Regierung durch die Opposition** the constant abuse hurled at the government by the opposition; **2.** *auch Pl.*; (*Schimpfworte etc.*) abuse; (*Beleidigung*) insult(s *Pl.*)

beschirmen *v/t.* protect; (*Augen*) shield; **Beschirmung** *f geh.* protection

Beschiss *m; -es, kein Pl.; Sl.* swindle, rip-off *umg.*; **ist doch alles ~!** the whole thing's a rip-off (*od.* con) *umg.*

beschissen *vulg.* **I.** *P.P.* → **bescheißen**; **II.** *Adj.* lousy, rotten, *präd. auch* (bloody) awful *Sl.*; **III.** *Adv.*: **mir geht's ~ physisch, psychisch**: I feel lousy; *finanziell etc.*: things are pretty lousy (at the moment)

Beschlag *m; -(e)s, Beschläge* **1.** *an Möbeln, Koffer*: metal fitting(s *Pl.*); *an Türen, Fenstern*: fittings *Pl.*, furniture; (*Schließe*) clasp; (*Scharnier*) hinge; **2.** *nur Sg.* (*Überzug*) film; (*Feuchtigkeit*) condensation; *Chem.* efflorescence, bloom; **das Silber / der Spiegel hat e-n ~** the silver is tarnished/the mirror is misted up; **3.** *nur Sg., ohne Art.*: **in ~ nehmen** *od.* **mit ~**

belegen (*Plätze etc.*) reserve, bag *umg.*; *fig.* (*j-n, Unterhaltung, Badezimmer etc.*) monopolize; *sein Hobby nimmt ihn ganz in ~* his hobby takes up all his time

beschlagen I. *v/t.* (*unreg.*) **1.** (*Tür etc.*) put metal fittings on; (*Schuhe*) put metal tips on; *mit Nägeln etc.*: stud; *ein Fass mit Reifen ~* put hoops on a barrel; **2.** (*Pferd*) shoe; *das Pferd muss neu ~ werden* the horse must be reshod (*od.* needs new shoes); **3.** (*anlaufen lassen*) (*Fenster, Spiegel*) mist up; (*Wände*) make sweat; (*Silber*) tarnish; (*Metall*) make dull; **II.** *v/i. und v/refl.* (*unreg.*): (*sich*) ~ *Glas, Brillengläser*: mist up; *Wände*: sweat; *Metall*: go dull, tarnish; (*schimmeln*) go mo(u)ldy; *die Wurst ist schon leicht ~* the sausage already has a slight sheen; **III.** *Adj.* **1.** *Glas etc.*: misted up; *Metall*: dull, tarnished; *~e Autofenster* misted up car windows; **2.** (*sich auskennend*) *sehr ~ sein in etw.* (*Dat.*) be very knowledgeable about (*od.* well up on) s.th. / a subject; *wenig ~ sein in* (+ *Dat.*) know very little about, be ignorant about; → I, II; **Beschlagenheit** *f; nur Sg.*; (*Kenntnisse*) (sound) knowledge (*in* + *Dat.* of)

beschlagnahmen *v/t.* (*untr.*) seize; (*konfiszieren*) confiscate; *der Zöllner beschlagnahmte die Ware* the customs officer impounded the goods; **Beschlagnahmung** *f* seizure; (*Konfiszierung*) confiscation; (*Inanspruchnahme*) requisition(ing); (*Zwangsverwaltung*) sequestration

beschleichen *v/t.* (*unreg.*) **1.** *fig. Angst etc.*: steal (*od.* creep) over (*od.* up on); *Schlaf*: creep over; *allmählich beschleicht mich der Verdacht, dass ...* I am gradually coming to suspect that ...; **2.** (*Person*) steal up to; (*Wild*) stalk

beschleunigen I. *v/t. auch Mot., Phys.* accelerate; (*auch Vorgang, Produktion etc.*) speed up; (*Niedergang, Ende*) hasten; *die Schritte ~* quicken one's pace; *das Tempo ~* speed up, pick up the pace; **II.** *v/refl.* speed up, gather speed; *Mot.* accelerate; *Puls*: go faster; **III.** *v/i. Mot.* accelerate

Beschleuniger *m Mot., Phys.* accelerator

Beschleunigung *f* **1.** (*das Schnellerwerden*) *von Wachstum, Arbeit*: speeding up; *von Niedergang, Ende*: hastening; *ein Mittel zur ~ des Wachstums / Wirts. der Wachstumsrate* a means of speeding up growth / increasing the growth rate; *das führt zu e-r ~ des Pulses* it causes a quickening of the pulse; **2.** *umg.* (*Beschleunigungsvermögen*) acceleration; *das Auto hat e-e gute ~* the car has good acceleration; **3.** *Phys.* acceleration, speeding up; **Beschleunigungsvermögen** *n Mot.* acceleration

beschließen (*unreg.*) **I.** *v/t.* **1.** *allg.*: decide (*zu* + *Inf.* to + *Inf.*); *stärker*: make up one's mind (to + *Inf.*); (*Entschluss fassen*) resolve (to + *Inf.*); *Parl.* vote; *e-n Antrag ~* carry a motion; *in Versammlungen*: pass a resolution; *ein Gesetz ~* pass a bill; **2.** (*beenden*) end; *endgültig: auch* settle; (*Rede, Schreiben*) *auch* conclude; *s-e Tage ~ geh.* end one's days; **II.** *v/i.*: ~ *über* (+ *Akk.*) reach a decision on

beschlossen I. *P.P.* → **beschließen**; **II.** *Adj.* agreed, settled; *das ist ~e Sache* that's settled, that's a closed mat-

ter; *es ist ~e Sache, dass er geht* it's definite that he's going, he's definitely going

Beschluss *m*; *-es, Beschlüsse* decision; *stärker und Pol.*: resolution; *e-n ~ fassen geh.* reach a decision; *Parl.* pass a resolution; *laut ~ vom 3. Juni* in accordance with the resolution of 3 June; *auf od. laut ~ des Gerichts* in accordance with the court's ruling

beschlussfähig *Adj.* quorate; *~ sein* constitute (*od.* have) a quorum; *~e Mehrheit* majority competent to pass a resolution; **Beschlussfähigkeit** *f; nur Sg.* (presence of a) quorum; *~ haben* constitute (*od.* have) a quorum

Beschlussfassung *f; nur Sg.* passing of a resolution; *e-n Entwurf zur ~ vorlegen Amtsspr.* submit a draft resolution

beschlussreif *Adj.* ready to be voted on, ready for the vote

beschlussunfähig *Adj.* inquorate; *die Versammlung ist ~* there is no quorum; **Beschlussunfähigkeit** *f; nur Sg.* absence of quorum

beschmieren I. *v/t.* **1.** (*schmutzig machen*) get s.th. dirty; (*mit Farbe usw.*) smear paint etc. on s.th.; **2.** *pej.* (*bekritzeln*) scrawl on; (*Mauer etc.*) smear all over a wall etc., smear s.th. on (*od.* all over), daub a wall etc. with s.th.; *e-e Mauer mit Graffiti ~* cover a wall with graffiti; **3.** (*bestreichen*) spread; *Brot mit Butter ~* put (*od.* spread) butter on bread; **4.** (*einreiben*): *etw mit Fett/Öl ~* smear grease/oil on s.th., grease/oil s.th.; *die Haut mit Salbe ~* spread ointment on the skin; **II.** *v/refl.* get o.s. dirty; *mit Farbe*: smear paint etc. on one's clothes etc.; *mit Tinte*: get ink etc. all over o.s.

beschmutzen I. *v/t.* **1.** dirty, get s.th. dirty, soil; *mit Flecken*: stain; *beschmutz dir nicht das Kleid* don't get your dress dirty; **2.** *fig.* (*Ruf, Ehre*) sully, stain; → *Nest* 1; **II.** *v/refl.* get o.s. dirty; *auch euph.* dirty o.s.; **Beschmutzung** *f* soiling, dirtying; *fig.* sullying, staining

beschneiden *v/t.* (*unreg.*) **1.** (*Hecke*) trim; (*Baum, Strauch etc.*) prune; (*Finger-, Fußnägel*) cut; (*Buch*) cut; **2.** *fig.* (*kürzen*) trim, cut (down); (*Gehalt*) cut; (*Betrieb etc.*) pare down, whittle down; *j-s Rechte ~* restrict (*od.* curtail) s.o.'s rights; *j-n in s-r Freiheit ~* restrict (*od.* curb) s.o.'s freedom; **3.** *Med. und rituell*: circumcise; → *Flügel* 1; **Beschneidung** *f* **1.** trimming; pruning; cutting; → **beschneiden**; **2.** *fig.* curtailment (+ *Gen.* of), cutting down (on); *des Einkommens*: reduction, cut (+ *Gen.* in); *der Ausgaben*: cut (+ *Gen.* in); **3.** *Med. und rituelle*: circumcision

beschneien *v/t.* (*Piste*) cover in artificial snow

beschnüffeln *v/t.* **1.** *Hund*: sniff (at); **2.** *umg. fig.* a) *sich gegenseitig ~* (*abschätzen*) size each other up, have a good look at each other, b) *j-n ~* (*bespitzeln*) spy out s.o., suss s.o. out *Sl.*

beschnuppern *v/t.* → **beschnüffeln** 1, 2 a

beschönigen *v/t.* put s.th. in a favo(u)rable light; (*Fehler etc.*) gloss over; (*bemänteln*) cover up; *ich will nichts ~* I'm not trying to cover anything up, I'm telling it the way it is *umg.*; **beschönigend I.** *Part. Präs.* → **beschönigen**; **II.** *Adj.* Wort etc.: euphemistic; *~er Ausdruck* euphemism;

III. *Adv.* ausdrücken: euphemistically; *... fügte er ~ hinzu* he added in an attempt to gloss over the matter; **Beschönigung** *f* glossing over; (*Darstellung*) euphemistic description; → **beschönigen**; *etw. ohne ~ darstellen* describe s.th. (quite) plainly (*od.* without mincing one's words)

beschränken I. *v/t.* limit, restrict (*auf* + *Akk.* to); (*einengen*) (*Ausgaben etc.*) curb; *die Redezeit ist auf fünf Minuten beschränkt* speakers are restricted to five minutes each; **II.** *v/refl.* restrict o.s., confine o.s. (*auf* + *Akk.* to); *sich darauf ~ zu* (+ *Inf.*) confine o.s. to (+ *Ger.*)

beschrankt *Adj.*: *~er Bahnübergang* guarded (*od.* protected) level crossing (*Am.* grade crossing); *~ sein* be protected with barriers

beschränkt I. *P.P.* → **beschränken**; **II.** *Adj.* **1.** *auch Anzahl, Zeit* limited, restricted (*auf* + *Akk.* to); *~e Mittel* limited means (*od.* resources); *in ~en Verhältnissen leben* live in straitened circumstances; → *Haftung* 2; **2.** *pej.* (*einfältig*) simple-minded; (*begriffsstutzig*) slow-witted; **3.** *pej.* (*engstirnig*) narrow-minded; *~e Ansichten* narrow (--minded) views, blinkered outlook; *e-n ~en Horizont haben* have very narrow horizons; **III.** *Adv.*: *~ lieferbar od. verfügbar* in limited supply

Beschränktheit *f; nur Sg.* **1.** *der Mittel etc.*: limited (*od.* restricted) nature; **2.** (*Einfältigkeit*) simple-mindedness, limited intelligence; *in i-r ~ hat sie das nicht verstanden* she was too simple-minded (*od.* she lacked the intelligence) to understand this; **3.** (*Engstirnigkeit*) narrow-mindedness, narrowness of outlook

Beschränkung *f* **1.** *nur Sg.*; (*das Beschränken*) limitation, restriction (*auf* + *Akk.* to); *bei e-r ~ der Teilnehmerzahl* if the number of the participants is limited; *e-e ~ der Redezeit/Kosten vereinbaren* agree to limit the length of the speeches / keep the costs within limits; **2.** (*Maßnahme*) restrictive measure; restraint (+ *Gen.* on); *Pl.* wirtschaftliche, finanzielle: restrictions; (*Kürzungen*) cuts; *j-m ~en auferlegen* impose restrictions on s.o.

beschreiben *v/t.* (*unreg.*) **1.** (*schildern*) describe; *anschaulich: auch* depict, portray; *es ist nicht zu ~* you can't describe it; *stärker*: it's indescribable, it's beyond description; *ich kann dir (gar) nicht ~, wie ...* I cannot (begin) to tell you how ...; *etw. genau ~* describe s.th. in detail, give a detailed description of s.th.; *könnten Sie es etwas näher ~?* could you describe it in more detail?, could you be a bit more precise?; *ich kann dir den Weg ~* I can tell you how to get there; *~de Grammatik* descriptive grammar; **2.** (*Blatt etc.*) write on; *er hat zwei ganze Seiten mit Zahlen beschrieben* he covered two whole pages with figures; *die Karte war eng beschrieben* the card was filled (*od.* stärker: crammed) with writing; **3.** *Bewegung*: (*Kreis etc.*) describe

Beschreibung *f* **1.** description; (*Darstellung*) depiction, portrayal; (*Bericht*) account; *kurze ~* brief description, outline; *der Ereignisse auch*: rundown; **2.** (*Gebrauchsanweisung*) instructions *Pl.*; → **spotten**

beschreien *v/t.* (*unreg.*); *umg.*: *ich will es nicht ~* touch (*Am.* knock on) wood, I don't want to put the kiss of death on it

beschreiten *v/t.* (*unreg.*); *geh.* walk along, tread; **neue Wege** ~ *fig.* tread (*Am.* walk) new paths; (*e-n neuen Kurs einschlagen*) try a new tack *umg.*; **andere/bessere Wege** ~ adopt different/better methods; → **Rechtsweg**; **Beschreitung** *f*; *nur Sg.*; *bes. fig.* treading

beschriften *v/t.* write on; (*Umschlag*) address; (*Ware etc.*) label; (*Bild etc.*) caption, add a caption to; (*Grabstein etc.*) inscribe, put an inscription on; **Beschriftung** *f* **1.** *nur Sg.*; (*das Beschriften*) writing, lettering; label(l)ing; **2.** (*Aufschrift*) address; (*Warenaufkleber*) label; *e-s Bildes etc.*: caption; (*Inschrift*) inscription; → **beschriften**

beschuldigen *v/t.* accuse (+ *Gen.* of); *Jur. auch* charge (with); **Beschuldigte** *m, f, -n* (-*n* supposed) culprit; *auch Jur.* alleged offender; *Jur. auch* accused, defendant; **Beschuldigung** *f* accusation; *Jur. auch* charge; **gegen j-n** ~**en erheben** bring (*förm. auch* prefer) charges against s.o.

beschummeln *v/t/i. umg. beim Spiel etc.*: cheat; **j-n** ~ diddle s.o. (**um** out of)

Beschuss *m; -es, kein Pl.* **1.** *Mil.* shelling, bombardment; **unter** ~ **geraten** come under fire (*fig. auch* attack) (**wegen** for); **unter** ~ **stehen** *auch fig.* be under fire (*od.* attack); **unter** ~ **nehmen** fire at; *mit Granaten*: shell, bombard *fig.* attack; **2.** *Phys.* bombardment; **durch** ~ **mit Neutronen** by (means of) neutron bombardment, by bombarding it/them with neutrons

beschützen *v/t.* protect; *bes. physisch: auch* shield (**vor** + *Dat.*, **gegen** from); **ich werde dich schon** ~**!** I'll protect (*od.* look after) you, I'll see that you come to no harm; ~**de Werkstätte für Behinderte**: sheltered workshop; **Beschützer** *m; -s, -*, **Beschützerin** *f; -, -nen* **1.** guardian; (*Schirmherr*) patron; *kirchl.* patron (saint); *umg.* (*Begleiter*) friend and protector; ~ **des Glaubens** defender (*od.* guardian) of the faith; **2.** *euph.* (*Zuhälter*) pimp

beschwatzen, *südd. auch* **beschwätzen** *v/t. umg.* **1.** (*überreden*) talk s.o. (a)round (**zu** to); **j-n zu etw.** ~ *auch* talk s.o. into (doing) s.th.; **lass dich nicht** ~ don't let them persuade you, don't let yourself be prevailed upon *förm.*; **2.** (*reden über*) chat about *s.th.*; **wir müssen das mal** ~ we must have a chat about that, *Am.* we need to talk about that

Beschwerde *f; -, -n* **1.** (*Klage*) complaint (**über** + *Akk.* about); *Jur.* appeal; *Grund*: grievance; ~ **führen** *od.* **einlegen** *od. förm.* **erheben gegen** lodge a complaint against (**bei** with); **2.** *nur Pl.*; *körperliche*: aches and pains; problems (**mit** with), trouble *Sg.* (with); (*Schmerzen*) pain *Sg.*; **die** ~**n des Alters** the infirmities (*od.* aches and pains *umg.*) of old age; ~**n beim Atmen / bei der Verdauung haben** have trouble breathing / have problems digesting (*od.* with one's digestion); (*wieder*) **ohne** ~**n sein** have recovered; (*schmerzfrei*) be free from pain; **3.** *auch Pl.* (*Anstrengung*) discomfort; (*Belastung*) burden, inconvenience; *stärker*: strain; **j-m** ~**n machen** cause s.o. great discomfort (*od.* a lot of trouble), be a (great) strain on s.o.; **die** ~**n des Alltags** the difficul-

ties of daily life

Beschwerde|brief *m* (letter of) complaint, written complaint; ~**buch** *n* complaints book

beschwerdefrei *Adj.* (*schmerzfrei*) free of pain; *nach e-r Krankheit*: fully recovered; ~ **sein** (*schmerzfrei*) *auch* have (*od.* feel) no pain; **ich bin seit längerem** ~ I've had no problems (*od.* pain) for a while now

Beschwerdeführer *m* person who lodges a complaint, complainer; *Jur.* complainant

beschweren I. *v/refl.* **1.** complain (**über** + *Akk.* about; **bei** to); **ich möchte mich** ~ I have a complaint (to make), I'd like to make a complaint; **du kannst dich doch** (**überhaupt**) **nicht** ~ you can't (possibly) complain, you have (absolutely) no cause for complaint; **2.** (*sich belasten*) *auch fig.* encumber oneself *geh.*; **II.** *v/t.* weigh (-t) down; *fig.* weigh down

beschwerlich *Adj.* (*mühevoll*) hard, difficult; *stärker*: arduous; (*lästig*) troublesome, *präd.* a nuisance; (*unbequem*) inconvenient; (*ermüdend*) tiring; *Weg, Reise*: arduous, wearisome; **im Alter wird das Leben** ~**er** life becomes more difficult (*od.* burdensome) in old age; **Beschwerlichkeit** *f* **1.** *nur Sg.*; (*das Beschwerlichsein*) difficulty, *stärker*: arduousness; (*Lästigkeit*) troublesomeness; **2.** ~**en** *Pl.* (*Anstrengungen*) strains and stresses; (*Unbequemlichkeit*) inconvenience

beschwichtigen *v/t. auch Pol.* appease; (*aufgebrachte Menge, Zorn*) placate, pacify; (*Kind*) calm down, soothe; (*Gewissen*) ease; (*Zweifel, Befürchtungen etc.*) set at rest, allay; ~**d Worte**: calming, soothing; *Ton etc.*: soothing; *Geste*: pacifying; **Beschwichtigung** *f* appeasement; pacifying; calming down, soothing; easing; → **beschwichtigen**

beschwindeln *v/t.* **1.** (*belügen*) lie to s.o., tell s.o. a lie (*od.* lies), tell s.o. a fib (*od.* fibs) *umg.*; **2.** (*betrügen*) swindle, hoodwink; *umg.* bamboozle

beschwingen *v/t.* get s.o. going; (*aufmuntern*) cheer; *stärker*: elate

beschwingt I. *P.P.* → **beschwingen**; **II.** *Adj.* (*froh gestimmt*) buoyant; *stärker*: elated; *Melodie*: lively, lilting; ~**es Gefühl** (feeling of) elation; ~**en Schrittes** *od.* **Fußes** with a spring (*od.* bounce) in one's step; **III.** *Adv.* buoyantly, in buoyant mood; ~ **tanzen/gehen** dance with great elan/walk with a spring in one's step; **Beschwingtheit** *f; nur Sg.* buoyant mood; elation, elatedness; liveliness; *der Schritte*: springiness; → **beschwingt** I

beschwipst *Adj. umg.* tiddly, tipsy

beschwören *v/t.* (*unreg.*) **1.** (*etw.*) swear to; **ich könnte** ~, **dass** I could swear (that); **e-e Aussage** ~ swear a statement under oath *Jur.*; **2.** (*anflehen*) implore, beseech; **3.** (*Geister, auch fig. Erinnerungen etc.*) conjure up, invoke; (*Schlangen*) charm; **4.** (*bannen*) exorci|se (*auch Am. -ze*)

beschwörend I. *Part. Präs.* → **beschwören**; **II.** *Adj. Geste, Blick, Worte*: imploring, beseeching; **j-m e-n** ~**en Blick zuwerfen** glance imploringly at s.o.; **III.** *Adv.*: **j-n** ~ **ansehen** give s.o. an imploring look; ~ **die Hände heben** raise one's hands in an imploring gesture

Beschwörung *f* **1.** oath; **2.** (*Flehen*) entreaty; **3.** *von Geistern*: invocation;

(*Bannung*) exorcism; **Beschwörungsformel** *f* incantation

beseelt *Adj.* **1.** *Lebewesen*: animate; *Dinge*: full of life; **2.** *fig.* (*Vortrag, Spiel, etc.*) inspired; **3. von Hoffnung beseelt sein** be inspired (*od.* buoyed up) by hope

besehen *v/t.* (*unreg.*) (have a) look at; *prüfend*: examine; **das will ich** (**mir**) **erst mal genau** ~ I want to have a good look at it first; **sie besah sich im Spiegel** she looked at herself in the mirror

beseitigen *v/t.* **1.** (*entfernen*) (*Hindernis*) move out of the way, remove; (*Abfälle etc.*) dispose of, get rid of; (*Flecken, Spuren*) remove, get rid of; (*Missstände*) remedy; (*Problem, Fehler*) eliminate; (*Störungen etc.*) get rid of; (*Schäden*) repair; (*abschaffen*) get rid of; (*Brauch etc.*) *auch* do away with, put an end to; (*Konkurrenz*) dispose of, eliminate; **2.** *euph.* (*ermorden*) get rid of, bump *s.o.* off *umg.*; **Beseitigung** *f* **1.** removal; *von Abfällen*: disposal; *von Missständen*: remedying; *von Störungen, Problemen, Fehlern, Konkurrenz etc.*: elimination; *von Schäden*: repair; **2.** *des Gegners*: elimination

beseligend *Adj.* blissful; **beseligt** *Adj.* blissful

Besen *m; -s, -* **1.** broom; (*Reisigbesen*) besom; (*Handbesen*) (sweeping) brush; **Schaufel und** ~ dustpan and brush; **neue** ~ **kehren gut** *fig. Sprichw.* a new broom sweeps clean; **ich fresse e-n** ~ *umg.* I'll eat my hat; **mit eisernem** ~ **kehren** *fig.* adopt drastic measures (to restore order); **2.** *umg. pej.* (*Frau*) old bag

besenrein *Adj.* well-swept, *präd. auch* swept clean; **e-e Wohnung** ~ **hinterlassen** *beim Auszug*: leave a flat (*Am.* apartment) swept and dusted

Besen|schrank *m* broom cupboard (*Am.* closet); ~**stiel** *m* broomstick; **steif wie ein** ~ *umg.* (as) stiff as a poker (*od.* board)

besessen I. *P.P.* → **besitzen**; **II.** *Adj.* **1.** obsessed (**von** with), possessed (by); (*rasend*) frantic; (*leidenschaftlich*) passionate; **von e-r Idee/Leidenschaft / e-m Wunsch** ~ **sein** be obsessed with an idea / consumed with a passion/possessed by a desire; **ein** ~**er Spieler/Jazzmusiker** an obsessive (*od.* a compulsive) gambler / a fanatical (*od.* mad keen *umg.*) jazz musician; **2.** *von Geistern etc.*: possessed (**von** by); **wie** ~ like a maniac; **wie vom Teufel** ~ as though possessed of the devil; **Besessene** *m, f; -n, -n* maniac; **Besessenheit** *f; nur Sg.* obsession; (*Begeisterung*) fanatical zeal

besetzen *v/t.* **1.** (*Sitzplatz*) take, occupy; (*freihalten*) reserve; **kannst du e-n Platz für mich** ~**?** can you keep a seat for me?; **2.** (*Land*) occupy; *Mil.* (*feindliche Stellung*) take; **3.** (*Gebäude*) occupy; (*Straße, Zufahrt*) *von Polizei*: occupy; *von Demonstranten*: block; **ein Haus** ~ squat (in a house); **4.** (*Amt, Stelle*) fill, **e-e Stelle mit j-m** ~ put s.o. in a position; **die Stelle soll neu besetzt werden** someone new is to take over the job; **5.** (*Stück, Rolle*) cast; **neu** ~ recast; **die Rollen e-s Stückes** ~ cast a play; **die Hauptrollen sind mit bekannten Sängern besetzt** the leading parts are taken by well-known singers; **6.** *Mus.* score (**mit** for); **7.** *fig.* (*Wort, Terminus, Begriff*) reserve; **ein**

Wort mit einer neuen/negativen Bedeutung ~ invest a word with a new meaning / a negative sense; **8.** *mit Juwelen, Perlen, etc.*: set (*mit* with); *mit Spitzen etc.*: trim (with); **9.** *mit Fischen etc.*: stock (*mit* with); *auch mit Wild etc.*: populate (with)

besetzt I. *P.P.* → *besetzen*; **II.** *Adj.* **1.** *auch Mil., Pol., Gebäude etc.*: occupied; *Platz*: *auch* taken; *Bus etc.*: full (up); *Stelle, Amt*: filled; *Telef.* engaged, *bes. Am.* busy; *„~" an Toilettentür*: "occupied"; *ist dieser Platz ~?* is this seat taken?; *diese Woche ist bereits jeder Abend ~* there is already something on (*Am. auch* scheduled) every evening this week; *Herr Meier ist heute ~ umg.* Herr Meier is busy today; ~ *halten* (*Gebäude etc.*) hold, occupy; **2.** *mit Personal etc.*: manned; ~ *mit Gremium etc.*: made up of; *unsere Telefone sind bis 22 Uhr ~* our telephones will be manned (*od.* the lines will be open) until 10 p.m.; *ist der Empfang durchgehend ~?* is there always someone at the reception desk?; **3.** *Mus.*: *das Orchester ist mit fünf Violinen ~* the orchestra has five violins, there are five violins in the orchestra; **4.** *mit Edelsteinen etc.* ~ set with jewels *etc.*; *auffällig*: jewel-studded *etc.*; *mit Pailletten ~* sequined; *mit Spitzen etc.* ~ trimmed with lace *etc.*

Besetztzeichen *n Telef.* engaged tone (*od.* signal), *bes. Am.* busy signal

Besetzung *f* **1.** *e-s Landes*: occupation; **2.** *e-s Gebäudes*: occupation; (*Hausbesetzung*) squatting; **3.** *Amt, Stelle*: filling (+ *Gen.* of); **4.** (*Belegschaft e-r Firma etc.*) staff; *wir arbeiten seit Monaten mit voller ~ umg.* we have been working for months at full strength (*od.* with a full team); **5.** (*Mitglieder e-s Gremiums etc.*) members *Pl.*; **6.** (*Wettkampfteilnehmer*) entry, entrants *Pl.*; **7.** *Theat.* a) cast; *in welcher ~ hast du das Stück gesehen?* who was in the play when you saw it?, b) (*das Besetzen*) casting; **8.** *Mus.* instruments *Pl.*; (*Spieler*) players *Pl.*; *in großer od. voller / kleiner ~ spielen* play with a full complement/a reduced number of players; **Besetzungsliste** *f Theat., Film etc.*: cast (list)

besichtigen *v/t.* **1.** have a look at; *förm.* view; (*Sehenswürdigkeiten*) *auch* visit; (*Stadt etc.*) *auch* do a tour of; (*Schloss, Museum*) *auch* go (a)round; (*auf die Schnelle*) do; (*Truppen*) inspect; *hum.* (*Baby, neue Freundin etc.*) inspect, view; *sie haben London in zwei Tagen besichtigt* they did London in two days; *zu ~ sein* be on view; *Haus etc.*: be open to the public; **2.** *prüfend*: inspect; (*Fabrik etc.*) *auch* tour, go (a)round

Besichtigung *f* **1.** *e-r Sehenswürdigkeit*: visit (+ *Gen.* to); *e-r Stadt*: sightseeing tour; *e-s Museums etc.*: *auch* tour (of); *e-s Kunstwerks etc.*: look (at), viewing (of) *förm.*; *e-e ~ mitmachen* join in a (guided) tour; ~ *des Domes ab 10 Uhr* the cathedral is open to the public from 10 am; *etw. zur ~ freigeben* open s.th. to the public; **2.** *prüfende*: inspection (+ *Gen.* of); *e-r Fabrik etc.*: *auch* tour (of, around)

Besichtigungs|tour sightseeing tour; **~zeiten** *Pl.* hours of opening

besiedeln *v/t.* **1.** (*sich ansiedeln in*) settle in; (*kolonisieren*) colonize; (*bevölkern*) populate; **2.** *Tiere, Pflanzen*: es-

tablish themselves in; **3.** *Regierung etc.*: (*Gebiet*) settle; *e-e Gegend mit Flüchtlingen ~* settle an area with refugees, settle refugees in an area; **besiedelt I.** *P.P.* → *besiedeln*; **II.** *Adj.* settled *area etc.*; populated (*von* by); *dicht/dünn ~* densely/sparsely populated; **Besied(e)lung** *f* **1.** (*das Besiedeln*) settling; **2.** (*das Besiedeltsein*) settlement; colonization; *weitS.* (*Bevölkerung*) population; **Besied(e)lungsdichte** *f* population density

besiegeln *v/t.* **1.** (*Schicksal etc.*) seal; *damit war ihr Schicksal besiegelt* that sealed her fate, her fate was sealed; **2.** (*bekräftigen*) confirm; *stärker*: seal; *mit Blut ~* seal in blood; *mit Handschlag ~* shake hands on; **Besiegelung** *f* (*Bekräftigung*) confirmation; *zur ~ dieses Vertrags* to set the seal on this contract

besiegen *v/t.* **1.** *auch Sport, Pol. etc.* defeat, beat; *Mil.* defeat, conquer; *den Gegner mit 2:1 ~* beat one's opponent (-s) 2-1; **2.** *fig.* overcome; *lit.* conquer; *sich selbst ~ fig.* overcome one's weakness, discipline oneself; **Besiegte** *m, f; -n, -n auch Sport* loser; *die ~n* the losers; *bes. Mil.* the defeated

besingen *v/t.* (*unreg.*) **1.** (*im Lied loben*) celebrate, sing of; **2.** (*verherrlichen*) extol, sing the praises of; **3.** (*Tonband etc.*) record songs on

besinnen *v/refl.* (*unreg.*) **1.** (*nachdenken*) reflect, think; *sich anders ~* change one's mind; *sich e-s Besseren ~* think better of it; *ohne sich lang zu ~* without thinking twice; **2.** *geh.* a) (*sich erinnern*) remember; *sich auf j-n ~* remember s.o.; *ich besinne mich nicht, ihn je getroffen zu haben* I don't recall ever meeting him; *sich auf sich* (*Akk.*) *selbst ~* become self-aware; *wenn ich mich recht besinne* if I remember rightly, b) (*zur Vernunft kommen*) come to one's senses; (*in sich gehen*) think about things, do a bit of thinking *umg.*

besinnlich *Adj. Mensch*: contemplative, pensive; *Wochenende etc.*: *auch* quiet; *Geschichte, Lied etc.*: serious, thought-provoking, *auch* emotional; *ein paar ~e Stunden verbringen* spend a couple of quiet hours; → *heiter-besinnlich*; **Besinnlichkeit** *f*; *nur Sg.* contemplativeness; contemplation, reflection

Besinnung *f*; *nur Sg.* **1.** (*Bewusstsein*) consciousness; *ohne od. nicht bei ~ sein* be unconscious; *die ~ verlieren* lose consciousness; (*wieder*) *zur ~ kommen* regain consciousness, come (a)round; **2.** (*Vernunft*) senses *Pl.*; (*wieder*) *zur ~ kommen* come to one's senses; *j-n zur ~ bringen* bring s.o. back to his (*od.* her, their) senses, make s.o. listen to reason; **3.** (*Nachdenken*) reflection, contemplation; *man kommt überhaupt nicht zur ~* you don't get time to think; **4.** (*das Besinnen*): *e-e ~ auf das Wesentliche* remembering essentials; **Besinnungsaufsatz** *m Päd.* discursive essay

besinnungslos *Adj.* **1.** *Med.* unconscious; ~ *werden* lose consciousness; **2.** *Wut etc.*: blind, uncontrolled, insensate *förm.*; ~ *vor Wut* raging (*od.* blind) with fury (*od.* anger); ~ *vor Angst* out of one's mind with fear; **Besinnungslosigkeit** *f*; *nur Sg.* **1.** *Med.* unconsciousness; **2.** *umg. fig.*: *bis zur ~ sich betrinken* to oblivion; *etw. wiederholen, üben*: ad nauseam

Besitz *m*; *-es, kein Pl.* **1.** *konkret*: (*Habseligkeiten, Habe*) possession(s *Pl.*); (*Eigentum*) property; *privater ~* private(ly owned) property; *staatlicher ~* state(-owned) property; *s-n ganzen ~ verlieren* lose everything one has; **2.** (*das Besitzen*) ownership, possession (*an + Dat., von od. + Gen.* of); *unerlaubter ~ von Waffen* illegal possession of weapons; *im ~ sein von Dokumenten etc.*: be in possession of; *im vollen ~ s-r geistigen Kräfte sein* be in full possession of one's mental faculties; *das befindet sich noch im ~ der Familie* this is still in the family; *sich in privatem/staatlichem ~ befinden* be in private/state ownership; *in j-s ~ übergehen* pass into s.o.'s ownership (*od.* hands); *etw. in ~ nehmen* (*od. von etw. ~ ergreifen*) take possession of s.th.; *von j-m ~ ergreifen fig.* Gefühl: take hold of s.o.; *in den ~ e-r Sache* (*Gen.*) *gelangen* come into possession of s.th.; *j-m den ~* (*e-r Sache Gen.*) *streitig machen* contest s.o.'s ownership (of s.th.); **3.** (*Besitzung*) estate

Besitzanspruch *m* claim to ownership, ownership claim; *Besitzansprüche od. s-n ~ geltend machen* assert one's claim to ownership (*Jur.* title); *auf etw.* (*Akk.*) ~ *erheben* lay claim to s.th.

besitzanzeigend *Adj. Ling.*: ~*es Fürwort* possessive pronoun

besitzen *v/t.* (*unreg.*) **1.** have, own; *förm.* possess; *mit Stolz*: boast; (*Dokumente, Wertpapiere*) have, hold, be in possession of; (*Eigenschaft, Talent etc.*) have; *sie besaß keinen Pfennig* (*mehr*) *umg.* she had lost every penny; *sie besitzt e-e tolle Bibliothek* she boasts an extraordinary library; **2.** (*ausgestattet sein mit*) have, be fitted with; *das Haus besitzt e-e Alarmanlage* the house is fitted with a burglar alarm (*od.* alarm system); **3.** *altm., euph., neg!*: *e-e Frau ~* have sex with a woman, possess a woman; **besitzend I.** *Part. Präs.* → *besitzen*; **II.** *Adj.*: *die ~en Klassen* the propertied classes; **Besitzer** *m*; *-s,* - owner; (*Inhaber*) *auch* proprietor; *Jur.* possessor; *von Land, Haus*: occupant, occupier; *e-s Dokuments*: holder; *er ist stolzer ~ e-r Wohnung* he's the proud owner of a flat (*Am.* an apartment *od.* a condominium); *den ~ wechseln* change hands

Besitzergreifung *f* taking possession (*von* of); *gewaltsame*: seizure; *widerrechtliche*: usurpation

Besitzerin *f*; *-, -nen* → *Besitzer*

Besitzerstolz *m*; *nur Sg.* pride of ownership; *voller ~ führte er uns im Haus herum* very much the proud owner, he showed us (a)round the house

Besitzgier *f*; *nur Sg.* acquisitiveness, (material) greed

besitzlos *Adj.* (*ohne Eigentum*) propertyless; unpropertied; (*entwurzelt*) dispossessed; **Besitzlose** *m, f; -n, -n* unpropertied (*entwurzelt*: dispossessed) person; *die ~n* the unpropertied (*od.* dispossessed), the have-nots *umg.*

Besitz|nahme *f*; *-, kein Pl.* appropriation; ~**stand** *m* **1.** *Eigentum*: amount of property owned; **2.** *Wirts.* (*Aktiva*) assets *Pl.*; **3.** *fig.* vested rights; (*bezüglich des Gehalts*) salary status; *das Weihnachtsgeld ist ein sozialer ~* the Christmas bonus is a vested right

Besitztum n; -s, Besitztümer **1.** nur Sg.; kollektiv: possession; **2.** mst Pl. (Grundbesitz) property nur Sg.
Besitzung f (Grundbesitz) estate
Besitz|urkunde f title deed; **~verhältnisse** Pl. **1.** (Verteilung von Besitz) distribution of property; **2.** Jur. **die ~ sind unklar** the (legal) position regarding ownership is unclear, there is no clear title
besoffen I. P.P. → besaufen; **II.** Adj. umg. plastered, stoned, sloshed Sl.; **da muss ich ~ gewesen sein** I must have been drunk; fig. auch I must have been out of my mind; **Besoffene** m, f; -n, -n; umg. drunk
besohlen v/t. sole; **neu ~** resole
besoldet Adj. salaried; **Besoldung** f **1.** nur Sg.; (das Besolden) payment; **2.** Geldbetrag: salary; Mil. pay; **Besoldungsstufe** f salary bracket
besonder... Adj. **1.** special; (bestimmt) particular, specific; betont: auch special; **dazu brauchst du e-e ~e Ausbildung** you need special training for that; **~e Kennzeichen im Pass:** distinguishing marks; **zur ~en Verwendung** for use in special cases; **in diesem ~en Fall** in this particular case; **gibt es e-n ~en Grund?** is there any particular reason?; **2.** (außergewöhnlich) very special, exceptional; **heute ist ein (ganz) ~er Tag** today is a (very) special day; **ein Ort von ~er Schönheit** a place of exceptional beauty; **es ist mir e-e ~e Freude zu** (+ Inf.) it gives me great pleasure to (+Inf.); **keine ~en Vorkommnisse** no unusual incidents, nothing unusual; **mit ~er Sorgfalt** with particular care, particularly carefully; **3.** (getrennt, extra) separate; **4. etwas Besonderes** something special; (etwas Spezifisches) something particular, a particular one; **nichts Besonderes** nothing unusual; auch pej. nothing special, no great shakes umg.; (nichts Spezifisches) nothing in particular; **im Besonderen** in particular, above all; **im Besonderen möchten wir darauf hinweisen, dass ...** specifically, we would like to point out that ...; **du hältst dich wohl für etwas Besonderes?** I suppose you think you're somebody special?; **das ist doch nichts Besonderes** it's nothing special (od. nothing to write home about umg.)
Besonderheit f **1.** (Eigenheit) specific feature (od. characteristic); auch merkwürdige: peculiarity; merkwürdige: auch quirk; e-s Menschen: auch foible; **die ~ daran war ...** what was so unusual (od. remarkable) about it was ...; **ein solches Talent ist e-e große ~** such talent is really remarkable (od. special); **2.** e-s Autos etc.: special feature
besonders Adv. **1.** (insbesondere) particularly, in particular, (e)specially; (vor allem) auch above all; **dieser gefällt mir ~** I specially (od. particularly) like this one; **~ du hast das nicht nötig** you of all people have no need for that; **~ heute** today of all days; **ich werde mich darum ~ kümmern** I will pay particular attention to it; **2.** (sehr) particularly, (e)specially; (außergewöhnlich) exceptionally; **es waren ~ viele Leute da** there were a lot more people (there) than usual; **es kamen nicht ~ viele Zuschauer** there weren't that many people there; **er kommt nicht ~ häufig** he doesn't come all that often; **das Essen ist heute ~ gut**

gelungen today's meal was particularly successful; **3.** (ausdrücklich) specially, expressly; **~ erwähnen** give special mention to; **4.** gefällt es dir? - **nicht ~** not particularly; wie war es? - **nicht ~** nothing special, nothing to write home about umg.; **es geht ihm nicht ~** umg. he's not (feeling) too well, he's feeling a bit under the weather; **5.** (getrennt) separately; behandeln: auch as a separate item
besonnen I. P.P. → besinnen; **II.** Adj. (vernünftig) sensible, level-headed; (umsichtig) circumspect; (vorsichtig) prudent; (ruhig) calm; Urteil: well-considered; **in einer solchen Situation hilft nur ~es Handeln** the only answer in a situation like this is to keep calm; **III.** Adv. sensibly; circumspectly; prudently; calmly; **~ handeln** act sensibly (od. prudently); **Besonnenheit** f; nur Sg. level-headedness; circumspection; prudence; (Ruhe) composure; **mit ~ reagieren** react in a level-headed way
besorgen v/t. **1.** (beschaffen) get; (Taxi) auch find; j-m etw. ~ get s.o. s.th.; förm. provide s.o. with s.th.; bes. mit Mühe: get hold of s.th. for s.o. umg.; sich (Dat.) etw. ~ get (od. buy) s.th.; umg. (stehlen) organize s.th.; j-m e-e Stelle ~ get (od. find) s.o. a job, fix s.o. up with a job; **ich habe einiges zu ~** I've got a bit of (Am. auch a little) shopping to do; **ihm werd' ich's ~** umg. I'll sort him out; **es j-m ~** vulg. (sexuell befriedigen) have it off with s.o., Am. do it with s.o.; **2.** (erledigen, sich kümmern um) see to; (auch Haushalt, Kranken) look after; **die Auswahl der Stücke besorgte ...** the pieces were chosen (od. compiled) by ...; **was du heute kannst ~, das verschiebe nicht auf morgen** Sprichw. never put off till tomorrow what you can do today
Besorgnis f; -, -se concern; stärker: anxiety (um for; über + Akk. about, at); **~ erregen** cause concern; **es besteht kein Grund zur ~** there's no cause for concern, there's no need to worry; **besorgniserregend, Besorgnis erregend** Adj. worrying; stärker: alarming; **~ sein** auch be causing (great) concern; **der Zustand des Patienten ist ~** the patient's condition gives cause for alarm
besorgt I. P.P. → besorgen; **II.** Adj. **1.** (mit Sorgen) worried, concerned (um, wegen about); **e-e ~e Miene** a troubled face; **2.** (bemüht sein): **~ um** j-s Wohlergehen etc.: concerned for (od. about); **3.** (ängstlich bemüht) concerned, anxious (zu + Inf. to + Inf.); **Besorgtheit** f; nur Sg. **1.** concern, worry, worries Pl. (um, wegen about); **2.** (Fürsorglichkeit) concern, (tender) care, solicitousness (um for)
Besorgung f **1.** (Einkauf) purchase; **~en machen** go shopping; **ich muss noch ein paar ~en machen** I've still got some shopping to do (od. a few things to buy); **2.** nur Sg.; (Beschaffung) (hold of) (+ Gen. s.th.); **3.** nur Sg.; (Erledigung) e-r Arbeit: dealing with (+ Gen. s.th.); von Geschäften: management of affairs; **die ~ von Haus und Garten** looking after (Am. taking care of) the house and garden
bespannen v/t. **1.** (Musikinstrument, Tennisschläger etc.) string; **neu ~** restring; **2.** mit Stoff: cover; **3.** mit Pferden ~ harness horses to; **Bespannung**

f **1.** (das Bespannen) a) von Musikinstrument, Tennisschläger etc.: stringing; b) von Wand, Liegestuhl etc.: covering; **2.** a) (Saiten) strings Pl., b) (Überzug) cover; **3.** (Zugtiere) team (of horses, oxen etc.)
bespielbar Adj. **1.** Tonband, Video: suitable for recording; **Kassetten vom Videoverleih sind nicht ~** you cannot record on rented videos; **2.** Sport: **der Platz ist wieder ~ / nicht ~** the pitch (Am. field) is playable again / unplayable
bespielen v/t. **1.** (Tonband etc.) record (od. make a recording) on; **2.** Theat. perform in a town (od. on a stage etc.); **3.** Sport play on a pitch (Am. field); **bespielt I.** P.P. → bespielen; **II.** Adj. Kassette etc.: (pre)recorded; **dieses Band ist noch nicht ganz ~** part of this tape is still blank
bespitzeln v/t. spy on s.o.; **Bespitzelung** f spying (+ Gen. on)
besprechen (unreg.) **I.** v/t. **1.** discuss, talk s.th. over; **wie besprochen** as arranged; **2.** (Buch, Film etc.) review; **3.** (Tonband etc.) record s.th. on; **e-n Anrufbeantworter ~** record a message on an answering machine; **4.** (beschwören) Warzen etc.: say a magic spell to get rid of; **II.** v/refl. discuss the matter (od. talk things over) (mit with); **Besprechung** f **1.** e-s Problems etc.: discussion; **2.** (Sitzung) meeting; (Konferenz) conference; **in e-r ~ sein** (od. [gerade] eine ~ haben) be in a meeting; **3.** e-s Buches etc.: (book) review, write-up; e-s Theaterstücks: auch criticism; **4.** (Beschwörung) magic spell
besprengen v/t. (Rasen) sprinkle; (Wäsche) dampen; (Straße) spray, Am. water down
bespringen v/t. (unreg.); Zool. cover, mount
bespritzen I. v/t. splash, spatter; mit Schmutz: spatter; mit Wasserstrahl: spray; **II.** v/refl. mit Wasser: splash o.s.; mit Schmutz: spatter o.s.; mit Wasserstrahl: spray o.s.
besprühen v/t. spray
bespucken v/t. spit at (od. on)
besser I. Komp. → gut, wohl[2]; **II.** Adj. **1.** better; **ein ~er Stoff** a better (od. superior) material; **~ werden** improve, get better; **er ist ~ dran als ich** he's better off than me; **es wäre ~, wenn sie das nicht wüsste** it would be better if she did not know this (od. for her not to know this); **es wurde noch ~** iro. that wasn't all, it gets better; **das wäre ja noch ~!** iro. you must be joking!; **umso ~** so much the better, that's even better; **~ als nichts** better than nothing(, I suppose); → Hälfte 1; **2.** subst.: **das Bessere ist des Guten Feind** Sprichw. the search for something better leads to the neglect of what is good; **j-n e-s Besseren belehren** put s.o. right, weitS. open s.o.'s eyes; **sich e-s Besseren besinnen** change one's mind, think better of s.th.; **ich habe Besseres zu tun** I've got better (od. more important) things to do; **e-e Wende zum Besseren** a change for the better; **3.** (sozial) höher gestellt: superior, better-class; Gegend, Adresse: auch respectable; (fein, elegant) Geschäft, Restaurant etc.: upmarket, Am. an upscale; **in ~en Kreisen verkehren** move in higher (od. more elevated) circles; **e-e Wohngegend für ~e Leute** a residential area for a better class of people (od. for

B

the well-to-do); *in e-m ~en Restaurant essen* eat in a better (*od.* upmarket, *Am.* upscale) restaurant; *etwas Besseres* something better; *sie meint, sie sei etwas Besseres* she thinks she's superior; **4.** *pej.* (*kaum besser als*): *e-e ~e Tippse etc.* a glorified typist *etc.*; **III.** *Adv.* **1.** better; *es ~ wissen* know better; *es ~ machen als j-d* do better than s.o., go one up on s.o.; *ich hoffe, du hast es mal ~* I hope things will start looking up for you; *bes. finanziell*: I hope you'll be better off; *es geht ihm heute ~* he's feeling better today; *wenn es dir wieder ~ geht, darfst du nach Hause* when you feel better (*od.* have recovered) you can go home; *es geht* (*wirtschaftlich etc.*) *~* things are looking up; *du kannst es ~ als er* you're better at it than him (*od.* he is); *sich ~ stellen* better o.s., improve one's (financial) position; *durch den Berufswechsel stellt er sich ~* he will be better off with his change of career; *~ gestellt* financiell *etc.*: better--off; *die ~ Gestellten* those who are better off, the well-to-do, the better--off people; *~ verdienen* earn more; *die ~ Verdienenden* those who are earning more (*od.* on higher incomes), the upper-income brackets; *du tätest ~ daran zu gehen* it would be better if you went; *~ gesagt* or rather; **2.** (*lieber*): *gehen wir ~* (*od. wir sollten ~ gehen*) I think we should go, I think (*od.* perhaps) we'd better go; *möchtest du noch ein Glas?- ~ nicht* I'd better not; → *Ruf* 4

bessern I. *v/t.* make *s.th.* better, improve; (*j-n*) reform; (*Bedingungen*) better; **II.** *v/refl.* improve, get better; *Wetter: auch* brighten up; *moralisch*: mend one's ways; *er hat sich nicht gebessert* he hasn't changed, he's still the same (as ever)

Besserstellung *f*; *nur Sg.* (financial, social *etc.*) betterment

Besserung *f*; *nur Sg.* improvement; (*Wende zum Besseren*) change for the better; (*Erholung, auch Med. Genesung*) recovery; *auf dem Arbeitsmarkt zeichnet sich e-e allmähliche ~ ab* there is a gradual improvement (*od.* upswing) in the job market; *auf dem Wege der ~ sein* be recovering, be on the road to recovery; *gute ~!* I hope you feel better soon; *auf Karten*: get well soon!

Besserungsanstalt *f* altm. *Brit.* community home, *Am.* reform school

Besser|wessi *m*; *-s, -s*; *umg. iro. pej.* West German who thinks he (*or* she) is superior to East Germans; *~wisser m*; *-s, -*; *umg. pej.* know-all, *Am.* know-it-all, smart aleck; *~wisserei f*; *-, -en*; *umg. pej.* know-all attitude; *der mit s-r ~* he thinks he knows it all; *~wisserin f*; *-, -nen* know-all, *Am.* know-it-all, smart aleck; ②*wisserisch Adj. umg.* know-all, *Am.* know--it-all...; *sei nicht so ~* stop pretending you know better

best... **I.** *Sup.* → *gut, wohl²*; **1.** best; *im ~en Falle* at best; *im ~en Alter od.* *in den ~en Jahren* in the prime of life; *bei ~er Gesundheit/Laune* in the best of health /spirits *Pl.*; *in ~em Zustand* in perfect (*od.* mint) condition; *aus ~em Hause* from one of the best families; *mit den ~en Wünschen Briefschluss*: with (all) best wishes; *~en Dank!* thank you very much; *mit ~em Dank Briefschluss*: with many thanks;

→ *Familie, Kraft* 1, *Seite* 3, *Stück* 4, *Weg* 2, *Wille, Wissen etc.*; **2.** *am ~en* best; *es ist am ~en, wenn du da bleibst* (*od. am ~en bleibst du da*) the best thing would be for you to stay here, it would be best for you to stay here; *am ~en tun wir gar nichts* it would be best for us to do nothing; **II.** *im Adj.* best-...; *~bekannt* best--known; *~bezahlt* best-paid

bestallen *v/t. Amtsspr.*: *j-n zum Richter etc. ~* appoint s.o. judge *etc.*; **Bestallung** *f Amtsspr.* appointment

Bestand *m* **1.** *nur Sg.* a) (*Weiterbestehen*) (continued) existence; (*Überleben*) *auch* survival, b) (*Dauer*) duration; *von ~ sein* (*od. ~ haben*) be lasting; last; *von kurzem ~ sein* be short-lived; *es ist nicht von ~* it won't last, c) *österr.* (*Bestehen*) existence; *wir feiern den 50-jährigen ~ des Clubs* we are celebrating the club's 50th anniversary; **2.** *auch Pl.* (*Vorrat*) a) stock, supplies *Pl.* (*an + Dat.* of); *~ aufnehmen auch fig.* take stock (*Am. auch* inventory); *Bestände auffüllen* replenish one's stocks (*od.* supply), b) *e-s Museums, e-r Bibliothek etc.*: holdings *Pl.*, c) *an Bäumen, Fischen etc.*: numbers *Pl.* (*an + Dat.* of), d) (*Kassenbestand*) cash in hand; *e-r Bank*: liquid assets *Pl.*, e) *an Wertpapieren*: holdings *Pl.*; **3.** *Forstwesen*: stand *of trees*

bestanden¹ I. *P.P.* → *bestehen*; **II.** *Adj. Examen etc.*: (successfully) passed; *j-m zur ~en Prüfung gratulieren* congratulate s.o. on passing his (*od.* her) exam

bestanden² *Adj.* (*bepflanzt*): *mit Bäumen ~* covered in trees, tree-covered ...; *Straße*: lined with trees, tree-lined *avenue*

beständig I. *Adj.* **1.** (*dauerhaft*) permanent; (*von Dauer, länger anhaltend*) lasting; (*andauernd*) continual, constant, incessant; (*ununterbrochen*) continuous; **2.** *auch Wirts.* (*unveränderlich, stabil*) steady, stable; *Wetter*: settled; **3.** (*beharrlich*) persevering, **4.** (*widerstandsfähig*) resistant (*gegen* to); *Farben*: fast; **II.** *Adv.* (*dauernd, immerzu*) constantly, continually; **Beständigkeit** *f*; *nur Sg.* **1.** (*Dauer*) permanence; (*Dauerhaftigkeit*) lasting nature (*od.* quality); **2.** (*Stabilität*) stability; **3.** (*Beharrlichkeit*) perseverance; **4.** (*Widerstandsfähigkeit*) resistance (*gegen* to)

...beständig *im Adj.*: -resistant

Bestands|aufnahme *f auch fig.* stocktaking, *Am.* inventory; *~ machen* take stock (*Am.* inventory); *~liste f* inventory, stock list

Bestandteil *m* **1.** (*einzelnes Element*) component, part, constituent (part); (*Grundbestandteil*) element; *etw. in s-e ~e zerlegen* take s.th. apart (*od.* to pieces); *sich in s-e ~e auflösen* disintegrate; *umg. weitS.* fall apart; **2.** (*Merkmal*) feature

bestärken *v/t.* (*ermuntern, unterstützen*) encourage; (*bestätigen*) confirm (*in + Dat.* in); (*These etc.*) *auch* reinforce, strengthen; *j-n in s-r Meinung ~* confirm s.o.'s opinion, back s.o. up; *es hat mich in m-m Entschluss bestärkt* it made me all the more determined, it strengthened my resolve *förm.*; **Bestärkung** *f* (*Ermunterung*) encouragement; (*Bestätigung*) confirmation; *e-r Sache*: *auch* reinforcement, strengthening

bestätigen I. *v/t.* **1.** (*Aussage, Mitteilung etc.*) confirm; (*unterstützen*) back up; (*Vermutung, Theorie etc.*) *auch* bear out, corroborate; *ich kann das nur ~* I couldn't agree (with you) more; *sich bestätigt fühlen* feel vindicated (*in + Dat.* in); *er sah od. fand sich in s-r Annahme/ Meinung bestätigt* his assumption was borne out / his opinion was confirmed; *j-m etw. ~* give s.o. confirmation of s.th.; → *Ausnahme*; **2.** (*offiziell bescheinigen*) certify; *hiermit wird bestätigt, dass ...* this is to certify that ...; **3.** *Wirts.* (*Aufträge*) confirm; (*Empfang*) acknowledge receipt; **4.** *Jur.* (*für gültig erklären*) *Urteil*: uphold; **5.** *j-n im Amt ~* confirm s.o. in office; *die Kollegen bestätigten ihn für ein weiteres Jahr* (*in s-r Funktion*) *als Sprecher* his colleagues reappointed him as spokesman for another year; **II.** *v/refl.* be confirmed, be borne out, prove (to be) correct (*od.* true); *mein Verdacht hat sich nicht bestätigt* my suspicion proved (*od.* turned out) to be unfounded; *er muss sich dauernd selbst ~* he constantly has to prove himself

Bestätigung *f* **1.** confirmation; *von Theorie etc.* corroboration; *s-e ~ finden* be confirmed (*od.* borne out, corroborated) (*in + Dat.* by); **2.** (*Bescheinigung*) written confirmation, certificate; **3.** *von Auftrag*: confirmation; *von Post*: acknowledgement; **4.** *Jur. von Urteil*: upholding; **5.** *im Amt*: confirmation of *s.o.'s* appointment

bestatten *v/t. geh.* bury; inter *förm.*; *bestattet werden* be buried; *wo ist er bestattet?* where is he buried?, where is his grave?; **Bestattung** *f geh.* burial; interment *förm.*

Bestattungs|institut *n* (firm of) undertakers; funeral directors *Pl. förm.*; *Am.* funeral home (*od.* parlor); *~kosten Pl.* funeral expenses

bestäuben *v/t.* **1.** dust, sprinkle; *mit Flüssigkeit*: spray; *mit Mehl, Puderzucker*: dust; **2.** *Bot.* (*befruchten*) pollinate; **Bestäubung** *f* **1.** dusting; **2.** *Bot.* pollination

bestaunen *v/t.* look at *s.th.* in amazement; *verblüfft*: gape at; *voller Bewunderung*: marvel at; *vergiss nicht, s-e Fortschritte / sein neues Auto zu ~* don't forget to say something nice about his progress / to admire his new car

beste *Adj.* → *best..., Beste* 4

Beste *m, f, n*; *-n, -n* **1.** (the) best; *das ~* (*od. die ~n*) *auch umg.* the pick of the bunch; *das ~ vom ~n* the very best; *sein ~s tun od. geben* do one's (level) best; *ich werde mein ~s tun auch* I'll do what I can; *ich sage das zu d-m eigenen ~n* I'm telling you this for your own good; *ich will nur dein ~s* I only want what is best for you; *das ~ herausholen od. draus machen* make the best of it (*od.* of a bad job); *ich halte diese Lösung für das ~* I think this is the best answer; *nimm nicht das erste od. nächste ~* don't take the first one you come across; **2.** *Person*: *der/die ~* the best (person); *so geht das nicht, mein ~r / m-e ~!* umg. my dear fellow, that just won't do; **3.** *mit ihr / mit unserer Firma steht es nicht zum ~n* things aren't looking too good for her / things are not going too well for our firm (*od.* our firm is in a bad way); *zum ~n geben* (*Geschichte etc.*) tell; (*Lied*) sing; *er gab e-e Geschich-*

te/*ein Lied zum ~n auch* he recounted a little story /he gave us *etc.* a little song; *j-n zum ~n haben od. halten* pull s.o.'s leg, have s.o. on; *du hältst mich wohl zum ~n? auch* you must be joking! you can't be serious!; **4.** (*sehr gut*): *wir verstehen uns auf das ~* we get on (*Am.* along) perfectly (together); *aufs ~ geregelt* all taken care of

bestechen (*unreg.*) **I.** *v/t.* **1.** bribe; *Jur.* (*Zeugen*) *auch*: suborn; *j-n ~ auch* grease s.o.'s palm *umg.*, square s.o. *umg.*; *sich ~ lassen* take bribes, be open to bribery; **2.** *fig.* (*fesseln*) fascinate, captivate (*durch* with); **II.** *v/i.* be fascinating (*od.* captivating), fascinate (*od.* captivate) people (*durch* with)

bestechend I. *Part. Präs.* → **bestechen**; **II.** *Adj.* fascinating; *Äußeres*: captivating, enchanting; *Lächeln*: winning, charming; *Argument*: persuasive, *stärker*: irresistible; *Angebot*: tempting, *stärker*: irresistible; *~e Leistung* brilliant performance; *von ~er Einfachheit/Logik* delightfully simple/irresistibly logical; *dieser Vorschlag hat etwas Bestechendes* there is something irresistibly attractive about this proposal; **III.** *Adv.*: *~ einfach* delightfully simple

bestechlich *Adj. Beamter*: corruptible; *~ sein* be open to bribery; **Bestechlichkeit** *f*; *nur Sg.* corruptibility

Bestechung *f* bribery; *aktive/passive ~ Jur.* offering/taking of bribes (*od.* a bribe); *wegen versuchter ~* for attempted bribery

Bestechungs|affäre *f* corruption scandal; *~geld* *n* bribe; *~summe* *f* bribe; *~versuch* *m* attempted bribery

Besteck *n*; *-(e)s, -e, umg. auch -s* **1.** (*Essbesteck*) knife, fork and spoon; *Koll.* cutlery, *Am.* flatware; *aus Silber*: (table) silverware; *sechsteiliges ~* six-piece set (of cutlery, *Am.* flatware); *~ putzen* clean the silverware; *hier fehlt noch ein ~* another place setting is needed here; **2.** *Med.* (*chirurgisches ~* surgical) instruments *Pl.*

Besteck|kasten *m* cutlery canteen, *Am.* flatware chest; *~schublade* *f* cutlery (*Am.* flatware *od.* silverware) drawer

bestehen (*unreg.*) **I.** *v/t.* **1.** (*Prüfung*) pass; (*e-e Probe*) stand (*od.* pass) the test; *nicht ~* fail; *e-e Prüfung knapp ~* scrape through an exam; **2.** a) (*durchstehen*) (*e-e Krise etc.*) come (*od.* go) through, survive, b) (*Gefahr*) survive; (*Kampf*) win through in; *wir hatten e-n schweren Kampf zu ~* we had a hard battle to fight; **II.** *v/i.* **1.** exist, *weitS. Bedenken, Grund etc.: auch* be; *weiterhin*: continue, last; *noch*: remain, survive, have survived; *besteht diese Firma noch?* does this firm still exist?; *~ bleiben* (*fortdauern*) continue (to exist); *Gefahr etc.*: remain; (*gültig bleiben*) remain valid, (still) hold good; *~ lassen* retain; *es besteht/bestehen ... auch* there is/are ...; *es besteht die Gefahr, dass sich das Feuer ausbreitet* there's a danger of the fire spreading; *über den Hergang besteht noch keine Klarheit* it is still not clear what happened; **2.** *~ aus* be made (up) of; consist of; *auch weitS.* consist of, comprise; **3.** *~ in* (+ *Dat.*) consist in, be; *das Problem besteht darin, dass* (*od.* *zu* + *Inf.*) the problem is that (*od.* is + *Ger.*); *der Unterschied besteht darin, dass* the difference is (*od.* lies in the fact) that; **4.** *~*

auf (+ *Dat.*) insist (up)on; *darauf ~, etw. zu tun* insist on doing s.th.; *darauf ~, dass etw. getan wird* insist on s.th. being done; *ich bestehe darauf(, dass er kommt)* I insist (that he comes *od.* on his coming *förm.*); *ich bestehe nicht darauf* I'm not insisting, you *etc.* don't have to; *ich bestehe auf m-m Vertrag* I insist that the terms of my contract are hono(u)red; **5.** (*sich behaupten*) hold out, hold (*od.* stand) one's ground, hold one's own (*gegen* against); *in e-r Gefahr etc. ~ auch* prove o.s. in a danger *etc.*; **6.** *in e-r Prüfung ~* pass, get through *umg.*; *mit „gut"/Auszeichnung ~ etwa* pass with a B / a distinction

Bestehen *n*; *-s, kein Pl.* **1.** existence; *seit ~ unserer Firma* ever since our firm was founded; *seit ~ der Regierung* ever since the government came into power; *das 50-jährige ~ feiern* celebrate the fiftieth anniversary *of s.th.*; **2.** (*j-s*) *~ auf* (+ *Dat.*) (s.o.'s) insistence on; **3.** *e-r Prüfung*: passing; *nach ~ der Prüfung* having passed the exam

bestehend I. *Part. Präs.* → **bestehen**; **II.** *Adj.* existing; (*gegenwärtig*) present, current; (*vorherrschend*) prevailing; (*noch ~*) extant

bestehlen *v/t.* (*unreg.*) steal from; *bes. auf der Straße*: rob; *bestohlen werden* be robbed

besteigen *v/t.* (*unreg.*) **1.** (*Berg, Treppe etc.*) climb (up); (*Pferd, Fahrrad*) mount, get onto; (*Thron*) ascend; *e-n Turm ~* climb up to the top of a tower; **2.** (*Bus, Flugzeug, Zug*) get on; (*Auto*) get into; (*Schiff*) get on, board; **3.** *Zool.* (*bespringen*) cover, mount; **Besteigung** *f e-s Bergs*: ascent; *e-s Throns*: accession to the throne

Bestellblock *m* order pad

bestellen I. *v/t.* **1.** order (*bei* from); (*Zimmer, Flugschein etc.*) book, *Am. auch* reserve; (*Zeitung*) subscribe to; *ich bestelle mir noch e-n Kaffee* I'm going to order myself another coffee; *was möchten Sie ~?* can I take your order?; *wie bestellt und nicht abgeholt umg.* like a lost soul, all dressed up and nowhere to go; → *Aufgebot* 1; **2.** (*zu sich* [*Dat.*]) *~* ask *s.o.* to come (and see one); (*kommen lassen*) send for; *beim Arzt bestellt sein* have an appointment with the doctor; *j-n in ein Café ~* arrange to meet s.o. in a café; **3.** (*Nachricht*) give s.o. a message; *kann ich etwas ~?* can I pass on a message?; *j-m etwas ~ lassen* send s.o. a message, pass a message on to s.o.; *bestell ihr bitte ...* would you tell her ...; *bestell ihm e-n schönen Gruß von mir* give him my regards; **4.** *er hat nichts / nicht viel zu ~ umg.* he doesn't have much (of a) say; *die Opposition hatte bei der Wahl nichts zu ~ umg.* the opposition didn't get a look-in (*Am.* didn't show at all) in the election; **5.** *auch Jur.* (*ernennen*) appoint; *j-n zum Vormund etc. ~* appoint s.o. guardian *etc.*; **6.** *es ist gut/schlecht um sie ~* bestellt things are looking good /aren't looking too good for her *etc.*; **7.** *Agr.* (*Feld*) cultivate; *das Feld ~ auch* till the soil; **II.** *v/i. im Lokal*: order; *haben Sie schon bestellt?* have you ordered?; **Besteller** *m*; *-s, -;* (*Kunde*) customer; (*Käufer*) buyer

Bestell|formular *n* order form; *~karte* *f* order card; *~liste* *f* order list; *~nummer* *f* order number; *~praxis* *f* ap-

pointments-only surgery (*Am.* doctor's office), surgery (*Am.* doctor's office) with an appointments system; *~schein* *m* order form

Bestellung *f* **1.** a) (*Auftrag*) order; *auf ~ anfertigen* make to order; *e-e ~ aufgeben* place an order (*bei* with); *im Restaurant*: give one's order; *die ~ läuft* the order is being processed, b) (*bestellte Ware*) order; **2.** (*Reservierung*) booking, *Am. auch* reservation; **3.** (*Übermittlung*) delivery; (*Botschaft*) message; *e-e ~ ausrichten* pass on a message; **4.** (*Ernennung*) appointment; *das Gericht hat die ~ e-s Vormundes angeordnet* the court arranged for the appointment of a guardian; **5.** *Agr.* cultivation

Bestellzettel *m* order form

bestenfalls *Adv.* at best; (*höchstens*) *auch* at (the) most; (*frühestens*) at the earliest

bestens *Adv.* (*ausgezeichnet*) extremely (*od.* very) well; *ich habe mich ~ unterhalten* I had a wonderful time, I enjoyed myself immensely; *ihm geht's ~ umg.* he's fine; *gesundheitlich auch*: he's in the best of health; *wie geht's? - danke, ~* fine thanks, very well thanks; *alles läuft ~ umg. in Beziehung*: we're getting along (*od.* on) really well; *von Maschine*: it's running like clockwork

besteuern *v/t.* tax; *wir werden mit 40% besteuert* we're taxed at 40%, *Brit.* we're taxed at 40 pence in the pound (*Am.* 40 cents on the dollar); *Tabak wird höher besteuert* taxes on tobacco are going up; **Besteuerung** *f*; *mst Sg.* taxation

Bestfall *m*; *nur Sg.*: *im ~* at (the) best

Bestform *f*; *nur Sg.*; *Sport* top form; *sie ist weit von ihrer ~ entfernt* she's nowhere near her best

best|gehasst *Adj. umg.* most hated; *~gekleidet Adj.* best-dressed

bestialisch [bɛs'tɪaːlɪʃ] **I.** *Adj.* **1.** *pej.* (*sehr grausam*) brutal; **2.** *umg.* (*unerträglich*) *Hitze etc.*: unbearable; **II.** *Adv. umg. intensivierend*: dreadfully; *~ kalt auch Sl.* cold as hell; *es tut ~ weh Sl.* it hurts like hell; *es stinkt ~ umg.* it smells (something) awful, it stinks like hell *Sl.*; **Bestialität** *f* **1.** *nur Sg.*; (*Eigenschaft*) brutality; **2.** *Handlung: auch* atrocity, bestial act

besticken *v/t.* embroider; *ein mit Perlen besticktes Kleid* a dress embroidered with pearls

Bestie ['bɛstiə] *f*; *-, -n* beast; *fig. pej. auch* brute

bestimmbar *Adj.* determinable; *sein Alter ist schwer ~* it's hard to tell how old he is

bestimmen I. *v/t.* **1.** (*festsetzen*) determine, decide; (*Preis, Termin etc.*) fix, *Am.* set; **2.** (*befehlen*) give (the) orders; *Gesetz*: require, stipulate; *nichts zu ~ haben* have no say in s.th; *du hast hier nichts zu ~ umg.* who asked you (for your opinion)?; **3.** (*beeinflussen*) (*Pläne etc.*) determine, control; **4.** (*prägen*) characterize; *dunkle Wälder ~ das Bild der Landschaft* the landscape is dominated by dark forests; **5.** (*ausersehen*) choose; *j-n/etw. zu od. für etw. ~* intend s.o. to be s.th. / intend s.th. for s.th.; (*Geld*) *auch* allocate s.th. for s.th., set s.th. aside for s.th.; *er bestimmte sie zu s-r Stellvertreterin* he chose (*od.* designated) her as his successor; *bestimmt sein für* be meant for; *bestimmt sein zu* be destined for (*od.* to be); (*verurteilt*) *auch* be fated to (+ *Inf.*); *dieser Ring ist für dich bestimmt* this ring is (*od.* is meant) for you; *zum sofortigen Verzehr bestimmt* Aufdruck auf Ware: for immediate consumption; *es war ihm vom Schicksal* (*nicht*) *bestimmt zu* (+ *Inf.*) he was fated (not) to (+ *Inf.*); **6.** (*ermitteln*) ascertain; *auch Math., Chem., Phys.* determine; (*festlegen*) (*Begriff, Wort*) define; (*Satz etc.*) determine the meaning of; (*Pflanzen, Tiere*) identify; *neu gefundene*: classify; *s-n Standort ~* determine one's position, take one's bearings; **7.** (*j-n veranlassen*) induce (*zu* + *Inf.* to + *Inf.*); *sich von etw. ~ lassen* (let o.s.) be influenced by s.th.; *weitS.* let s.th. get the better of one; **II.** *v/i.* **1.** (*entscheiden*) decide; (*befehlen*) give the orders (for); *wer hat hier zu ~?* who gives the orders around here?; **2.** (*verfügen*) *über j-n ~* (*Arbeitskräfte etc.*) have s.o. at one's disposal; *über sein Geld / s-e Zeit ~* decide how to spend one's money /what to do with one's time; *über s-e Angelegenheiten selbst ~* decide one's affairs for oneself

bestimmend I. *Part. Präs.* → *bestimmen*; **II.** *Adj.* determining, decisive; *Ling.* determinative; *für den Erfolg etc. ~ sein* be crucial for success

bestimmt I. *P.P.* → *bestimmen*; **II.** *Adj.* **1.** *nur attr.* (*speziell*) Anzahl, Zeit, Dinge etc.: certain; (*Absicht, Plan etc.*: particular, specific; *er sagt das mit e-r ~en Absicht* he's saying that for a (particular) reason; *ein Preis in e-r ~en Höhe* a price set (*od.* fixed) at a particular level, a fixed (*od.* set) price; *~e Vorstellungen von etw. haben* have very definite ideas (*pej.* fixed ideas) about s.th.; *suchst du etwas Bestimmtes?* are you looking for anything in particular?; *wir wissen noch nichts Bestimmtes* we don't have any definite (*od.* firm *od.* hard) information yet; **2.** *Ling.*: *~er Artikel* definite article; **3.** *Math.* Größe, Zahl: determinate; **4.** (*entschlossen*) determined; *im Auftreten etc.*: firm, resolute; *ihr Ton war höflich, aber ~* her tone was polite but firm; **III.** *Adv.* **1.** (*ganz sicher*) definitely; *er kommt ~* he's sure to come; *machst du es auch* (*ganz*) *~?* can I rely on you to do it?, do you promise to do it?; *ich hab's ~ nicht gemacht* I really didn't do it; honestly, it wasn't me; *war er es wirklich? - ganz ~!* no question about it, absolutely; *vergiss deinen Schlüssel nicht! - nein, ~ nicht!* don't forget your key - no, I certainly won't!; *~ wissen, dass* know for sure (*od.* for certain *od.* for a fact) that; **2.** (*aller Wahrscheinlichkeit nach*) probably; *er hat ~ den Bus verpasst* auch he must have missed the bus, I expect he missed the bus; *das hat er doch ~ gewusst* he must have known that; *das ist doch ~ richtig?* that must be right, mustn't it?; **3.** (*mit Entschiedenheit*) firmly, decidedly

Bestimmtheit *f; nur Sg.* **1.** (*Entschlossenheit*) determination; *im Auftreten*: firmness; (*Kraft*) force; *etw. mit* (*aller*) *~ sagen etc.* (*überzeugt*) say s.th. with (complete) certainty (*od.* confidence); (*mit Nachdruck*) say s.th. emphatically (*od.* categorically); **2.** (*Sicherheit*) certainty; *ich kann es nicht mit ~ sagen* I can't say for certain (*od.* with certainty); *mit ~ wissen* know for certain

Bestimmung *f* **1.** (*Vorschrift*) regula-

tion, rule; *gesetzliche ~en* legal requirements; *e-e ~ erlassen* lay down (*od.* introduce) a regulation; *nach den geltenden ~en ...* according to (the) current regulations; **2.** *nur Sg.* (*Festsetzung*) e-s Datums, Termins, Strafmaßes etc.: fixing; *von Preis*: setting; **3.** *mst Sg.* (*Zweck*) (intended) purpose; *die Straße etc. wurde i-r ~ übergeben* the road etc. was officially opened; **4.** *nur Sg.*; (*Berufung*) calling, vocation; (*persönliches Schicksal*) destiny; *das ist göttliche ~* it's a sacred calling; *das war ~* (*musste so kommen*) it was fate; **5.** *nur Sg.*; (*das Ermitteln*) *auch Phys., Math. etc.* determination; *von Pflanze, Tier*: identification, classification; (*Begriffsbestimmung*) definition; *an der ~ der Bestandteile e-r Legierung etc. arbeiten* identify the different constituents of an alloy; **6.** *Ling.* qualification; *adverbiale ~* adverbial modification (*od.* modifier)

Bestimmungs|bahnhof *m* destination (of the train); *~buch* *n* für Pflanzen: field guide, reference guide; *~flughafen* *m* (flight) destination

bestimmungsgemäß *Adj. und Adv.* as directed, as agreed; *bezüglich e-s Vertrags etc.*: according to (*od.* in accordance with) the regulations (*od.* rules)

Bestimmungs|hafen *m* (port of) destination; *~land* *n* (country of) destination; *~ort* *m* destination; *~wort* *n*; *Pl. -wörter*; *Ling.* determinative pronoun, determiner

Best|leistung *f* **1.** best performance; **2.** *mst Sport*: best performance, record; *s-e persönliche ~ übertreffen* beat one's (*od.* set a new) personal best; *i-e persönliche ~ liegt bei 11,12 Sekunden* she has a personal best of 11.12 seconds; *bei dieser Hitze sind keine ~en zu erwarten* we can't expect any records to be broken in this heat; *~marke* *f Sport* record

bestmöglich *Adj.* Lösung, Nutzen: best possible, optimum; *ich werde mein Bestmögliches tun* I will do my level best; *wir haben das Bestmögliche in der Situation getan* we did the best we could in the circumstances

bestrafen *v/t. auch Jur.* punish (*wegen*, *für* for; *mit* with); *Jur.* (*verurteilen*) sentence (*mit* to); *mit e-r Geldstrafe*: fine; *bestraft werden mit Jur. Handlung*: be punishable by; *das wird mit Gefängnis etc. bestraft* offenders are liable to imprisonment etc.; *Zuwiderhandlungen werden bestraft* offenders will be prosecuted; *du wirst für d-n Leichtsinn bestraft fig.* you're being punished for (*od.* you're paying for) your own carelessness; **Bestrafung** *f* **1.** (*das Bestrafen*) punishment; sentencing; **2.** (*Strafe*) punishment; *auch* penalty; (*Urteil*) sentence; (*Geldstrafe*) fine

bestrahlen *v/t.* **1.** shine on; (*beleuchten*) light up, illuminate; *Phys.* irradiate; **2.** *Med.* (*Patient*) give *s.o.* radiation treatment (*od.* radiotherapy); *mit Höhensonne*: give *s.o.* sun-lamp treatment, put *s.o.* under the sun lamp; (*Tumor*) irradiate; **Bestrahlung** *f Phys.* irradiation; *Med.* radiation treatment, radiotherapy; *er hat zehn ~en verordnet bekommen* he was prescribed ten radiation treatments; *etw. mit ~en behandeln* treat s.th. with radiotherapy; **Bestrahlungsdosis** *f* irradiation dose, exposure dose

Bestreben *n*; *-s, kein Pl.* endeavo(u)r, effort; (*Ziel*) aim; *stärker*: desire; *es ist sein ~ zu* (+ *Inf.*) he is endeavo(u)ring to (+ *Inf.*); *in dem ~ zu* (+ *Inf.*) in an attempt (*od.* effort) to (+ *Inf.*), while trying to (+ *Inf.*); **bestrebt** *Adj.*: *~ sein zu* (+ *Inf.*) endeavour to (+ *Inf.*), be anxious to (+ *Inf.*); **Bestrebung** *f*; *mst Pl.* endeavour, attempt, effort(s *Pl.*); *es sind ~en im Gange, die Mehrwertsteuer zu erhöhen* moves are afoot (*od.* efforts are being made) to increase value-added tax

bestreichen *v/t.* (*unreg.*) **1.** *etw. ~ mit* mit Butter: spread s.th. with *butter*; mit Honig etc.: spread *honey* etc. on s.th.; mit Fett, Öl: coat s.th. with; mit Eigelb: brush (*od.* coat) s.th. with; mit Milch: drizzle (*od.* sprinkle) s.th. with; mit Salbe, Klebstoff: apply s.th. to s.th.; *etw. mit Farbe ~* paint s.th., give s.th. a coat of paint; **2.** *fig.*: *~ mit* mit Kugeln, Schüssen etc.: spray with; mit Scheinwerfern etc.: sweep with

bestreiken *v/t.* go out on (*od.* be on) strike against; *vor den Ferien wurden die Flughäfen bestreikt* before the holidays the airports were (*od.* disrupted) by strikes; **bestreikt I.** *P.P.* → *bestreiken*; **II.** *Adj.* disrupted (*od.* affected) by a strike (*od.* strikes), strike-hit (*attr.*); (*ganz außer Betrieb*) strike-bound; **Bestreikung** *f* strike(s *Pl.*), strike action (+ *Gen.* against)

bestreitbar *Adj.* open to question, contestable, disputable

bestreiten *v/t.* (*unreg.*) **1.** (*anfechten*) contest, dispute, challenge; (*abstreiten*) deny; *es lässt sich nicht ~, dass* there's no denying that; → *energisch* II; **2.** (*Kosten etc.*) bear, pay, meet *the costs etc.*; (*finanzieren*) pay for, finance; *sie bestreitet i-n Lebensunterhalt allein* she provides for herself, she is her own provider; **3.** (*gestalten*) (*Programm*) fill; *er bestritt die Unterhaltung allein* he did all the talking, he monopolized the conversation; **4.** (*Wettkampf etc.*) hold, stage; *ein weiteres Spiel ~* play (*od.* have) another match; **Bestreitung** *f*; *nur Sg.* **1.** *der Kosten etc.*: payment, financing; *zur ~ der Unkosten* (in order) to meet the costs; **2.** *e-r These etc.*: challenge, contestation; *geh.* disputation

bestreuen *v/t.* strew (*mit* with); *Gastr.* dredge (with/in); (*Kuchen*) dust; *mit Zucker*: auch sprinkle (with); *e-n Weg mit Kies ~* lay gravel on a path, coat a path with gravel

bestricken *v/t.* **1.** *fig.* charm, bewitch; **2.** *umg.*: *die ganze Familie ~* knit for the whole family; **bestrickend I.** *Part. Präs.* → *bestricken*; **II.** *Adj.* charming; *stärker*: captivating

Bestseller *m*; *-s, -* bestseller; *~autor* *m* bestselling author; *~liste* *f* bestseller list, list of bestsellers; *von Popmusik*: charts *Pl.*, *Am. auch* top 40

bestsellerverdächtig *Adj. umg.*: *das Buch ist ~* the book has the makings of a bestseller, the book looks as if it might become a bestseller

bestücken *v/t. Mil.* arm (with guns); *weitS.* equip (*mit* with); (*Lager*) supply; (*Geschäft*) stock, supply; **bestückt I.** *P.P.* → *bestücken*; **II.** *Adj.* **1.** *~ mit* equipped with; **2.** *gut ~* Geschäft etc.: well-stocked; *mit etw. gut ~ sein* auch have a wide range of s.th.; **3.** *fig. hum.*: *gut ~ sein* Frau: be well-endowed; *Mann*: be well-hung; **Bestü-**

ckung f; mst. Sg. **1.** (das Bestücken) a) mit Waffen: arming, b) e-s Lagers: supply(ing); **2.** (Ausstattung) equipment

bestuhlen v/t. put seats (od. seating) in, provide with seats (od. seating); **der Saal ist nicht ausreichend bestuhlt** there aren't enough seats in the hall, the hall doesn't have enough seats; **Bestuhlung** f **1.** (das Bestuhlen) provision of seating; **2.** Koll. (Sitze) seating; seats Pl.

bestürmen v/t. **1.** fig. (bedrängen) urge; bittend: implore; mit Fragen, Bitten etc.: bombard, assail (mit with); **2.** Mil. (Festung, Stellung etc.) storm, attack; **3.** (Fußballtor) attack, lay siege to

bestürzen v/t. dismay; stärker: shock, stun; **die Nachricht bestürzte uns sehr** the news struck us with consternation, the news really shook us umg.; **bestürzend I.** Part. Präs. → bestürzen; **II.** Adj. Tatsache, Nachricht: alarming, shocking; **bestürzt I.** P.P. → bestürzen; **II.** Adj. dismayed (über + Akk. by, at), completely taken aback; stärker: shocked, stunned; **ein ~es Gesicht machen** look dismayed; stärker: look aghast; **III.** Adv. in dismay

Bestürzung f dismay (über + Akk. at); stärker: shock (at); **zu m-r größten ~** to my utter consternation; **~ empfinden** feel shocked (über + Akk. bei); **ihr Tod löste große ~ aus** everybody was shocked by her death, her death caused great shock (od. shocked everybody); **die Entscheidung wurde mit ~ aufgenommen** the decision came as a shock

Best|wert m optimum (value); Tech. best (od. maximum) performance; Sport: best perfomance; (Rekord) record; **bei e-m Test ~e erzielen** reach optimum performance in a test; **~zeit** f best (od. record) time; **persönliche ~** personal best; **~zustand** m in Anzeigen: Wohnwagen, ~, ... caravan (Am. trailer), (in) perfect condition

Besuch m; -(e)s, -e **1.** visit (bei, in od. + Gen. to); kurzer: call (on); (Aufenthalt) stay (with); (bei j-m) zu od. auf ~ sein be visiting (s.o.); **j-m e-n ~ abstatten** förm pay s.o. a visit; **m-e Schwester kommt zu ~** my sister's coming to see me; **sie kommt für zwei Wochen zu ~** she's coming to stay (with me od. us) for two weeks; **es ist e-n ~ wert** it's worth seeing (Stadt etc.: auch visiting od. a visit); **wir danken für Ihren ~** Geschäft: thank you for your custom (Am. patronage); **2.** nur Sg.; (das Besuchen) von Schule, Gottesdienst etc.: attendance (+ Gen. at); **nach dem ~ der Universität** after going to university; **3.** nur Sg.; (Besucher) visitor(s Pl.); **ich erwarte ~** I'm expecting visitors (od. a visitor); **wir haben ~** we've got a visitor (od. visitors); **wir bekommen (gleich / nächste Woche) ~** our visitor is (od. visitors are) about to arrive / we'll be having a visitor (od. visitors) next week; **hoher ~** a) Sg. an important guest (od. visitor), b) Pl. important guests (od. visitors); **für Samstag haben wir ~ eingeladen** we're having people round (Am. over) on Saturday; geh. auch: we're entertaining on Saturday

...besuch m, im Subst. **1.** Besuch a) bei j-m: Arzt~ visit to the doctor('s), Am. doctor's appointment; **wir machen morgen einen Verwandten~**

we're visiting relatives tomorrow, b) von j-m: Arzt~ visit from the doctor; **wir hatten gestern Familien~** we had some of the family round (Am. over) yesterday; unerwartet: some of the family dropped in (od. besonders Am. by) yesterday; **Vertreter~** visit from a salesman, sales visit; **2.** e-s Ortes: Museums~ visit (od. trip) to a museum; Kino~ visit (od. trip) to the cinema (Am. movies); **Haus~** von Arzt: house call; **Deutschland~** visit (od. trip) to Germany

besuchen v/t. **1.** j-n ~ visit s.o., go and see s.o.; formeller: pay s.o. a visit; bes. offiziell: (Patienten) visit s.o.; kurz, auch Wirts.: (Kunden) call on s.o.; **m-e Tante besucht uns oft** od. umg. viel my aunt often comes to see (od. visit) us; **besuch uns bald wieder!** come and see us again soon!, hope we'll see you again soon!; **2.** (Ort) visit; (Theater, Kino etc.) go to; (Geschäft, Lokal) regelmäßig: patronize; **bisher haben wir nur Cornwall besucht** so far we've only been to Cornwall; **wann haben wir diese Ausstellung / dieses Schloss besucht?** when did we go and see that exhibition / did we visit that castle?; **~ Sie uns bald wieder!** in Geschäften etc.: we look forward to your next visit; weniger formell: (hope to) see you again soon!; **3.** (Vortrag, Schule etc.) go to; attend förm.; (Kurs) auch take; → besucht II

Besucher m; -s, -, ~in f; -, -nen visitor (+ Gen. to); (Gast) guest; formell, e-s Kinos, Lokals etc.: patron; geschäftlich etc.: caller; → auch Kinobesucher etc.; **~rekord** m record number of visitors; Sport record attendance; **die Ausstellung könnte e-n ~ verzeichnen** the exhibition could break all attendance records; **~ritze** f umg., in Doppelbett: **du kommst in die ~** you can get in (od. sleep) between us, you can lie in the middle; **~strom** m stream of visitors; **~tribüne** f in Sporthalle etc.: spectators' gallery; **~zahl** f number of visitors; attendance figures Pl.; **durchschnittliche ~** average attendance

Besuchs|erlaubnis f **1.** für Gefängnis, Krankenhaus etc.: permission to visit; konkret: visitor's permit; **2.** zum Besuchsempfang: permission to receive visitors; **~recht** n bei Scheidung: visiting rights Pl.; **~tag** m visiting day; **~zeit** f auf Schild: visiting hours Pl.; **wochentags ist nur eine Stunde ~** there's only an hour's visiting time on weekdays; **~zimmer** n visitors' room

besucht I. P.P. → besuchen; **II.** Adj.: **gut ~** Veranstaltung: well-attended; Lokal etc.: much-frequented; weitS. popular; **schlecht ~** poorly attended; Lokal etc.: half-empty; **in den ersten Tagen war die Ausstellung gut ~** the exhibition attracted a lot of visitors in the first few days

besudeln I. v/t. pej. (Hände, Tischtuch etc.) dirty, soil; fig. soil, sully; lit. besmirch; (entweihen) defile; **II.** v/refl. get dirty; **sich mit Blut ~** (morden) get blood on one's hands

Beta ['be:ta] n; -(s), -s beta; **~blocker** m Med. beta blocker

betagt Adj. geh. old, advanced in years; lit. aged; von Dingen, oft hum.: antique, elderly; **Betagtheit** f; nur Sg. old age, advancing years

betanken v/t. (Flugzeug) refuel; (Fahrzeug) fill up

betasten v/t. touch; (befühlen) feel;

Med. auch palpate; **Betasten der Ware verboten** Schild: please do not handle the goods (Am. merchandise)

Beta|strahlen Pl. Phys. beta rays; **~strahlung** f beta radiation; **~teilchen** n beta particle

betätigen I. v/t. Tech. **1.** (bedienen) operate, work; (einschalten) switch on, turn on; (Schalter etc.) press, push; (drehen) turn; (in Gang setzen) get s.th. going (od. working); (in Bewegung bringen) auch set s.th. in motion; (Bremse) apply; (Gehirn) get working; **2.** (steuern) control; **3.** geh. (verwirklichen) put into effect, put into practice, implement; **II.** v/refl. be active; im Haushalt etc.: busy o.s., work; ohne bestimmtes Ziel: potter (Am. putter) around umg.; **du könntest dich ruhig auch mal etwas ~** oft iro. (du sollst helfen) perhaps you could stir yourself into action (and help us); **sich ~ als** act as; arbeitend: work as; **sich politisch ~** be active (od. involved) in politics; **sich sportlich ~** do sport(s); **sich schriftstellerisch ~** do some writing; **sich gärtnerisch ~** hum. potter (Am. putter) around in the garden

Betätigung f **1.** (Tätigkeit) activity; (Arbeit) job, work, occupation; allg.: something (od. things) to do; **körperliche ~** physical exercise; **sportliche ~** sporting activity (od. activities); **ich brauche mehr geistige ~** I need more intellectual stimulation; **das ist keine sinnvolle ~!** it's a pointless exercise; **2.** nur Sg.; (das Betätigen) Tech. operation, activation; von Bremse: application

Betätigungs|drang m urge to be doing something; **Kinder haben e-n großen ~** children always want to be doing something; **~feld** n field (of activity), sphere of activity; individuelles: area of activity (od. competence); weitS. outlet

betatschen v/t. umg. paw; sexuell: feel up; **hör auf, den Monitor zu ~!** get your dirty paws (od. mitts) off the monitor!

betäuben v/t. **1.** Med. (Patienten) an(a)esthetize, give an an(a)esthetic to; (Nerven) deaden; (Schmerz) auch kill; fig. (berauschen) intoxicate; **2.** durch Lärm: deafen; durch e-n Schlag etc.: stun; auch fig. daze; **er wurde durch den Schlag betäubt** he was knocked senseless; **3.** (Hunger) numb, deaden, stave off, suppress the hunger pangs; (abstumpfen, Sinne etc.) blunt, dull; (Gewissen) ease, salve; (unterdrücken) stifle; **s-n Kummer mit Alkohol ~** drown one's sorrows (in alcohol); **betäubend I.** Part. Präs. → betäuben; **II.** Adj. Lärm: deafening; Duft: intoxicating; **die Salbe hat eine ~e Wirkung** the ointment has a numbing effect; **betäubt I.** P.P. → betäuben; **II.** Adj. Nerv: dead; (wie) ~ dazed, stunned, in a daze; **sie war wie ~** she seemed to be dazed; (wie) ~ vor Schreck numbed with shock

Betäubung f **1.** Med. an(a)esthetization; (örtliche) ~ (Narkose) (local) an(a)esthetic; **2.** nur Sg.: zur ~ des Hungers/Gewissens to stave off hunger / to ease (od. salve) one's conscience; **3.** (Benommenheit) daze; stärker: stupor; **in e-m Zustand der ~** in a daze

Betäubungsmittel n an(a)esthetic; **~gesetz** n drug law

Betbruder m umg. pej. holy Joe, Am. holy roller; mit Namen: Saint ...

B

Bete f; -, -n; Bot.: **Rote** ~ beetroot, Am. beet

beteiligen I. v/t.: **j-n an etw.** (Dat.) ~ (aktiv mitwirken lassen) give s.o. a share in s.th.; **an Verhandlungen**: bring s.o. into s.th.; **j-n am Gewinn** ~ give s.o. a share in the profits; **j-n an e-m Geschäft** ~ bring (od. let) s.o. in on a deal; **II.** v/refl. **1. sich** ~ **an** (+ Dat.) od. **bei** take part (od. participate) in; Beitrag leistend: contribute to; helfend: cooperate in; **2.** finanziell: **sich** (mit **50 €**) **an den Unkosten** ~ contribute (-€50) toward(s) the expenses

beteiligt I. P.P. → **beteiligen; II.** Adj.: **an etw.** (Dat.) ~ **sein** an Unfall, Verhandlungen: be involved in s.th.; (beitragen zu) auch have a share in s.th.; **an e-r Abmachung, e-m Verbrechen** etc.: be a party to s.th.; Wirts. have a share in s.th., have an interest in s.th.; **am Gewinn**: share in s.th.; **mit wie viel Prozent bist du beteiligt?** what percentage share do you have?; **mit 50 000 Euro / 30% an e-r Firma** ~ **sein** have a 50 000 euro / 30% share (od. stake) in a firm (Am. company od. business); **Beteiligte** m, f; -n, -n person concerned (od. involved); an Spiel, Wettkampf: participant, contestant, competitor; (Teilhaber) partner; an e-r Abmachung etc.: party; Pl. auch those involved; **alle am Gewinn** ~**n** (all) those with a share in the profits

Beteiligung f **1.** (Teilnahme) participation (an + Dat. in), involvement (in); **2.** (Teilnehmerzahl) attendance (an + Dat., bei at); bei Wahlen etc.: turnout; **bei ausreichender** ~ **wird der Kurs angeboten** the course will run (od. be offered) if there are sufficient numbers (od. registrants); **3.** Wirts. (Anteil) share, interest (an + Dat. in); durch Kapitalanlage: investment; durch Aktienbesitz: holdings Pl.; (Teilhaberschaft) partnership

Beteiligungs|gesellschaft f Wirts. holding company; ~**kapital** n investment capital

Betelnuss f Bot. betel nut

beten I. v/i. pray (für, um for; zu to); (Gebet sprechen) say a prayer; say one's prayers; bei Tisch: say grace; **wird in d-r Schule noch gebetet?** do they still have morning prayer(s) in the school?; **II.** v/t. say; **das Vaterunser** ~ say the Lord's Prayer

beteuern v/t. protest, declare (solemnly); **er beteuerte s-e Unschuld** he protested his innocence, he swore innocence; (versichern) (solemnly) swear; **er beteuerte** (mir), **dass er nichts von dem Plan wusste** he swore (to me) that he knew nothing of the plan; **Beteuerung** f protestation; solemn declaration; **die** ~ **s-r Unschuld/ Liebe** his protestation(s) of innocence / his declaration of love

betiteln v/t. **1.** (Buch etc.) give a title to, name; find (od. decide on) a title for; **wie ist die Zeitschrift betitelt?** what's the name (od. title) of the magazine?, what's the magazine called?; **2.** → **titulieren**

Beton [be'tɔŋ] m; -s, Pl. nur Sorten: -s od. -e concrete; **aus** ~ made of concrete, concrete ...; ~**bau** m; Pl. -bauten **1.** nur Sg.; Bauweise: concrete structure; **2.** (Gebäude) auch concrete building; ~**bunker** m **1.** concrete bunker; (Luftschutzbunker) (concrete) air-raid shelter; **2.** pej. → **Betonklotz** 2; ~**decke** f **1.** im Raum: concrete ceil-

ing; **2.** auf Straße: concrete (surface)

betonen v/t. **1.** Ling., Mus. stress; **wie wird das Wort betont?** how is that word stressed?, where does the stress come in that word?; **falsch** ~ wrong(ly) stress, put the wrong stress on; **2.** (unterstreichen) stress, emphasize, underline, underscore; **besonders** ~ place particular emphasis on; **man kann es nicht genug** ~ it can't be emphasized (strongly) enough; **wobei ich „sauber" betone** 'clean' being the operative word; **3.** optisch etc.: (j-s Figur, Augen etc.) emphasize, accentuate, bring out

Betonfußboden m concrete floor

betonieren I. v/t. **1.** concrete (over); Vorsicht, frisch betoniert auf Warnschild: warning, fresh (od. wet) concrete; **2.** fig. firm up; **II.** v/i. Sport, bes. Fußball: pack the defen|ce (Am. -se)

Beton|klotz m **1.** concrete block; **2.** pej. (Hochhaus) concrete monstrosity, tower block, Am. high-rise; ~**kopf** m Pol. umg. pej. hardliner; ~**mauer** f concrete wall; ~**mischer** m, ~**maschine** f cement mixer; ~**pfeiler** m concrete pillar; ~**platte** f concrete slab, slab of concrete

betont I. P.P. → **betonen; II.** Adj. **1.** Silbe: stressed; **diese Silbe ist schwach** ~ **ohne Betonung**: this syllable is unstressed; **mit leichter Betonung** this syllable has a secondary stress; **2.** fig. emphatic, deliberate; Eleganz, Höflichkeit etc.: studied; **mit** ~**er Gleichgültigkeit** with studied indifference; **III.** Adv. emphatically, deliberately; ~ **einfach** strikingly simple; ~ **langsam und deutlich sprechen** speak slowly and clearly, pronoucing each syllable; **sie antwortete** ~ **sachlich** her answer was short and to the point; ~ **gleichgültig** etc.: with studied indifference etc.; **sie gab sich** ~ **lässig** she was behaving with studied nonchalance

...betont im Adj., zeigt, dass etwas besonders hervorgehoben wird: **gefühls**~ emotional; **körper**~ figure-hugging, tight; **leistungs**~ performance-driven, goal-oriented

betontermaßen Adv. deliberately, conspicuously

Betonung f **1.** Ling. a) (Akzent) stress, emphasis; (Intonation) intonation, b) nur Sg. (das Betonen) stressing; **2.** fig. emphasis, stress; **die** ~ **legen auf** (+ Akk.) stress, emphasize, put (od. place) the emphasis on; **mit der** ~ **auf „bald"** "soon" being the operative word, with the emphasis on "soon"; **zur** ~ **der Augen** etc. to highlight the eyes; **3.** Mus. stress, accent; **Betonungszeichen** n **1.** Ling. stress mark; **2.** Mus. accent mark

Beton|wand f concrete wall; ~**wüste** f pej. concrete jungle

betören v/t. geh. **1.** (verliebt machen) beguile, turn s.o.'s head; **2.** altm. (verführen): **j-m die Sinne / das Herz** ~ charm s.o.'s senses / capture s.o.'s heart; (irreführen) lead s.o.'s heart astray; **betörend I.** Part. Präs. → **betören; II.** Adj. bewitching; Worte: auch beguiling; stärker: seductive

betr. Abk. (betreffend, betreffs) re, concerning; **Betr.** Abk. (Betreff) re, concerning

Betracht m: **außer** ~ **lassen** disregard, leave out of consideration; **außer** ~ **bleiben** be disregarded, be left out of consideration, not be taken into ac-

count; **in** ~ **kommen** be a possibility (od. consideration); (Kandidat) be a possible candidate (für for); **nicht in** ~ **kommen** be out of the question; (Kandidat) be unsuitable (für for); **er kommt als nächster Parteivorsitzender nicht in** ~ he can be ruled out as the next party leader; **in** ~ **ziehen** take into consideration (od. account), take account of; **wenn man ... in** ~ **zieht** considering ...

betrachten v/t. look at, observe; fig. auch view; **aufmerksam** ~ pay close attention to; ~ **als** look (up)on (od. regard) s.o./s.th. as, consider s.o./s.th. (as od. to be); **wir können das als erledigt** ~ we can consider it done; **etw. als s-e Pflicht** ~ see s.th. as one's duty, consider s.th. one's duty; **e-e Sache anders** ~ take a different view of things (od. events); **genau(er) betrachtet** (bei näherem Betrachten) on closer examination (od. inspection); (genau genommen) strictly speaking; **so betrachtet** from that point of view; **objektiv betrachtet** objectively speaking; **Betrachter** m; -s, -, **Betrachterin** f; -, -nen e-s Gemäldes etc.: viewer; (Beobachter) auch fig. observer; **links vom Standpunkt des** ~**s** to the left as you're facing (the building etc.)

beträchtlich I. Adj. considerable, substantial, siz(e)able; Verluste: auch heavy; **um ein Beträchtliches** considerably, substantially; **er ist uns um ein Beträchtliches voraus** he's a long way ahead of us; **II.** Adv. considerably, a great deal faster etc.

Betrachtung f **1.** (das Ansehen) viewing, observation (+ Gen. of); besinnliche: contemplation (of); **bei näherer** ~ on closer inspection (od. examination); **2.** (Erwägung) consideration (of); (Nachdenken) reflection; **bei näherer** ~ on reflection; ~**en anstellen über** (+ Akk.) reflect on; **in** ~**en versunken** lost (od. wrapped up) in thought

Betrachtungsweise f approach (+ Gen. to), view (of); (Standpunkt) point of view, perspective; (Lebenseinstellung) outlook

Betrag m; -(e)s, Beträge amount, sum; (Gesamtbetrag) auch total; (Ziffer) figure; **e-e Rechnung über e-n** ~ **von** ... an invoice (od. bill) for the amount of ...; **ein Scheck über e-n** ~ **von 400 €** a cheque (Am. check) for €400; **große Beträge ausgeben/abheben** etc. spend/withdraw large sums; ~ **dankend erhalten** auf Quittung: received with thanks (the sum of ...)

betragen (unreg.) **I.** v/t. (sich belaufen auf) amount to, come to; (sein) (Entfernung etc.) be; **II.** v/refl. (sich benehmen) behave (o.s.) (gegenüber + Dat. od. gegen towards, Am. bes. toward); **sich anständig** ~ behave o.s., behave properly; **sie hat sich stets tadellos** ~ her conduct has always been faultless; **Betragen** n; -s; kein Pl. behavio(u)r, conduct; im Schulzeugnis: conduct; **sie hat in** ~ **eine gute Note** she's got good marks for conduct, her conduct (od. behavio[u]r) has been good

betrauen v/t.: **j-n mit etw.** ~ entrust s.o. with s.th., entrust s.th. to s.o.; **mit e-m Amt**: appoint s.o. to s.th.; **j-n damit** ~ **zu** (+ Inf.) entrust s.o. with (the task of) (+ Ger.)

betrauern v/t. (Tod) mourn (over); (e-n Toten) mourn (for); (Schicksal) lament, bewail

beträufeln *v/t.*: *mit etw.* ~ put a few drops of s.th. on; *mit Wasser* ~ *auch* sprinkle a few drops of water on; *mit Zitrone* ~ squeeze a few drops (*od.* a bit) of lemon (juice) on

Betrauung *f; nur Sg.* entrusting

Betreff *m; -(e)s, -e; Wirts., Amtsspr.* reference; *im Briefkopf*: (*abgek.* **Betr.**) Re

betreffen *v/t.* (*unreg.*) **1.** (*angehen*) concern; *was mich betrifft* as for me, as far as I'm concerned; *was das betrifft* as far as that is concerned (*od.* goes), as for that; → *betroffen* II 2; **2.** *geh.* (*seelisch berühren*) affect (deeply); → *betroffen* II 1; **3.** *Unglück etc.*: hit; *lit.* befall; *betroffen werden von* fall victim to; *Land etc.*: be ravaged by; *der Krieg hat die Kinder am schwersten betroffen* the children were worst hit by the war; → *betroffen* II 2

betreffend I. *Part. Präs.* → *betreffen*; **II.** *Adj.* **1.** + *Gen.* (*zum Thema*) concerning, regarding; **2.** (*fraglich*) ... concerned, in question; **3.** (*jeweilig*) respective; **4.** (*zuständig*) relevant; **Betreffende** *m, f; -n, -n* person concerned, person in question; *der Mann himself, the lady herself umg.*; *die* ~*n auch* those concerned, the people in question

betreffs *Präp.* (+ *Gen.*) *Amtsspr.* regarding, concerning, with regard (*od.* respect *od.* reference) to (*abgek.* re)

betreiben I. *v/t.* (*unreg.*) **1.** (*Tätigkeit, Hobby*) pursue, take part in; (*Sportart*) play, go in for; (*Politik*) go in for, be involved in; **2.** (*Gewerbe*) carry on (*od.* out), ply *a trade*; (*Unternehmen, Fabrik, Hotel etc.*) run; **3.** (*vorantreiben*) (*Aufgabe etc.*) press on with, move forward; *Am. auch* progress; prosecute *förm*; *ein Projekt energisch* ~ work busily on a project; **4.** *Tech.* (*antreiben*) run, operate; *ein mit Kohle betriebenes Kraftwerk* a coal-fired power station; *ein mit Solarzellen betriebener Taschenrechner* a solar-powered calculator; *das U-Boot wird mit Atomkraft betrieben* the submarine is powered by nuclear energy; **II. Betreiben** *n: auf j-s* ~ (*hin*) at s.o.'s instigation

Betreiber *m,* ~**in** *f* operator; *Firma*: operating company

betreten¹ *v/t.* (*unreg.*) step (*od.* walk) on; (*Raum, Haus*) enter, walk (*od.* step, come) into; *zum ersten Mal*: set foot in; (*Gebiet*) set foot on; *die Bühne* ~ come (*od.* walk) on stage, come (*od.* walk) onto the stage; *sie betrat das Haus nie wieder* she never set foot in the house again; **II. Betreten** *n: Betreten verboten! von Rasen etc.*: keep off (the grass); *von Gelände*: no trespassing; *von Gebäude, Raum*: no entry, keep out

betreten² **I.** *Adj.* embarrassed; *Lächeln, Blick*: *auch* sheepish; *Schweigen*: awkward; **II.** *Adv.* sheepishly; ~ *dreinschauen* look rather sheepish; ~ *schweigen* be too embarrassed to say anything, be tongue-tied with embarrassment, maintain an embarrassed silence *förm*.; ~ *schaute er zu Boden* he stared at the ground in embarrassment; **Betretenheit** *f; nur Sg.* embarrassment, (feeling of) awkwardness

betreuen *v/t.* **1.** (*Kinder, Alte, Kranke*) look after, care for; (*Kunden*) see to, attend to; (*Reisegruppe*) be in charge of, lead; (*Sportler*) coach; *gut betreut*

werden be well looked after; **2.** (*Gebiet, Gemeinde etc.*) serve; *leitend*: (*auch Projekt etc.*) be in charge of, be responsible for

Betreuer *m; -s, -,* ~**in** *f; -, -nen allg.*: person in charge; *für Kinder, Alte, Kranke*: carer, attendant; *minder umg.*; *für Jugendgruppe*: (group) leader; *Sport* doctor, physio; *für Kinder*: child-minder, *Am.* daycare worker; *für Jugendliche*: youth leader; *für Reisegruppe*: courier, guide; *für Sozialfälle*: case worker, social worker; *für ehemalige Häftlinge*: probation officer, rehabilitation officer

Betreuung *f* **1.** (*das Betreuen*) looking after, taking care of; *von Patienten, Senioren etc.*: care; *medizinische* ~ medical care; *soziale* ~ (social) welfare; *mit der* ~ *von ... / e-s Projekt(e)s beauftragt sein* be in charge of ... / of a project; *Herr X übernimmt die* ~ *Ihres Kontos* Mr X has taken over responsibility for handling your account; **2.** *Person*: person (*od.* someone) to look after...; *... suchen e-e* ~ *für älteren Menschen in Anzeigen*: ... seek someone to care for (*od.* look after) an elderly person

betreut **I.** *P.P.* → *betreuen*; **II.** *Adj.*: ~*es Wohnen* sheltered (*od.* supportive) housing (for seniors *od.* slightly handicapped), *Am. auch* assisted living accommodation

Betreuungsstelle *f* supporting institution; *soziale*: welfare cent|re (*Am.* -er)

Betrieb *m; -(e)s, -e* **1.** *Wirts.* (*Unternehmen*) business, firm, company; (*Fabrik*) factory, works (*V. im Sg.*); *ein landwirtschaftlicher* ~ an agricultural enterprise (*od.* concern); *ein handwerklicher* ~ a firm of craftsmen; *ein staatlicher/privater* ~ a state enterprise/private company *etc.*; *sie ist im* ~ *auch* she is at work, she is at the office; *in den* ~ *gehen auch* go to work, go to the office; **2.** *nur Sg.* (*Belegschaft*) workforce, staff; **3.** *nur Sg.*; (*Leitung e-s Unternehmens*) running, management; **4.** *nur Sg.*; (*Tätigkeit*) *von Maschine*: operation, running; *von Fähre, Schiff*: operation, running, in operation; *Maschine, Fahrzeug etc.*: *auch* running; *außer* ~ not working; (*defekt*) *auch* out of order; *außer* ~ *setzen* (*ausschalten*) stop, switch off; (*funktionsunfähig machen*) put out of action; *in* ~ *gehen od. den* ~ *aufnehmen Maschine etc.*: begin working; *Kraftwerk*: go on-stream (*od.* on-line); *Unternehmen*: open; *den* ~ *wieder aufnehmen Unternehmen*: resume work; *in* ~ *nehmen Tech.* start running, bring (*od.* put) into operation; (*Verkehrsmittel etc.*) bring (*od.* put) into service; *weitS.* (*eröffnen*) open; *den* ~ *einstellen von Maschine*: switch off; *von Verkehrsmittel*: take out of service; *weitS.* close; *von Bergwerk, Kraftwerk*: take out of commission, shut down; **5.** *nur Sg.* (*Betriebsamkeit*) activity; (*Trubel*) (hustle and) bustle; (*Verkehr*) heavy traffic; *wir hatten heute viel* ~ we were very busy today; *hier ist immer viel* ~ there's always a lot going on around here; *im Lokal etc.*: it's always full (*od.* packed) in here; *den ganzen* ~ *aufhalten umg.* hold everything up; *am Vormittag ist in der Stadt weniger* ~ it's very quiet (*od.* there aren't many people about) in town in the mornings (*Am.* morning); *an den Badestränden*

/ *auf dem Flughafen herrschte reger* ~ the beaches were packed / the airport was very busy; **6.** *umg. pej.* business, caboodle *umg.*; *hast du diesen* ~ *nicht satt?* aren't you just fed up of the whole thing (*od.* business)?

betrieblich **I.** *Adj.* internal; company *attr.*; ~*e Ausbildung* in-house training; ~*e Altersversorgung* company pension plan, *in GB auch* occupational (*od.* company *od.* employee) pension scheme, *Am.* company retirement plan; ~*e Sozialleistungen* company (*od.* employee) benefits; **II.** *Adv.*: ~ *bedingte Entlassungen* redundancies (*Am.* layoffs) due to company restructuring

Betriebsablauf *m* (operational) procedure

betriebsam *Adj.* active, busy; bustling; ~ *hin und her eilen* bustle back and forth; **Betriebsamkeit** *f; nur Sg.* activity; (*Geschäftigkeit*) bustle; *e-e hektische* ~ *an den Tag legen* show an appearance of frenzied activity; *es herrschte emsige* ~ there was a general air of hustle and bustle

Betriebs|angehörige *m, f* (company) employee; *Pl. auch* (company) personnel (*Pl.*); ~**anlage** *f* **1.** (*Gelände*) plant; **2.** ~*n* (*Maschinen etc.*) plant, equipment; ~**anleitung** *f,* ~**anweisung** *f* operating instructions *Pl.*; ~**art** *f von Computer*: (operating) mode; ~**aufgabe** *f* (*Schließung*) closure; ~**aufnahme** *f* startup, putting into operation; ~**ausflug** *m* (annual) works (*Am.* company) outing

betriebs|bedingt *Adj.* required for (*od.* by the) business, work-related, structural; ~*e Ausgaben* running expenses; ~**bereit** *Adj. Gerät, Anlage*: operational, in working order

Betriebsbesichtigung *f* tour of a (*od.* the) factory

betriebsblind *Adj.* blind to the company's failings; **Betriebsblindheit** *f; nur Sg.* blindness to company failings

betriebseigen *Adj.* company-owned, company ...; ~*e Wohnungen* company flats (*Am.* apartments *od.* housing); *e-e* ~*e Kantine* a staff canteen

Betriebserlaubnis *f* operating licen|ce (*Am.* -se)

betriebsfähig *Adj.* in (good) working order (*od.* condition)

Betriebs|ferien *Pl.* company holiday *Sg.*; ~ *von ... bis ... Schild*: closed for holidays (*Am. auch* vacation) from ... till ...; ~ *haben* be (*od.* have) closed down (over the holidays); ~**fest** *n* annual (*od.* company) do *umg.*; *in kleinerem Rahmen*: office party

betriebsfremd *Adj.* outside ..., external; ~*en Person* outsider; ~*en Personen ist der Zutritt verboten* no entry except for company personnel; *auf Toilettentür etc.*: private

Betriebs|frieden *m* industrial peace; *Störung des* ~*s* disruption due to industrial action; ~**geheimnis** *n* trade secret; *das* ~ *verletzen* give away a trade secret; ~**größe** *f* (size of the) workforce; *e-e* ~ *von 2000 Mitarbeitern* a workforce of 2000; ~**inhaber** *m,* ~**inhaberin** *f* owner of the company

betriebsintern I. *Adj. Absprache, Regelung etc.*: internal; in-house ..., (intra-)company ...; **II.** *Adv.*: *etw.* ~ *regeln* settle s.th. within the company

Betriebs|kapital *n; nur Sg.; Fin.* working (*od.* business) capital; (*Anfangskapital*) initial capital, *Am. auch* start-up

B

capital; **~klima** n; nur Sg. Verhältnis mit Mitarbeitern etc.: working atmosphere, company culture; **gutes ~** Büro, Firma: congenial (work) atmosphere; **~kosten** Pl. von Maschine: running costs; von Unternehmen: overheads, Am. overhead; **~krankenkasse** f company health insurance fund (od. Brit. scheme); **~leiter** m, **~leiterin** f (works, factory, plant) manager; **~leitung** f (works, factory, plant) management; **~mittel** Pl. Gebäude, Maschinen etc.: buildings and plant; **~nudel** f umg. **1.** the life and soul of the office, resident comedian; **2.** (überaktiver Mensch) live wire; **~obmann** m works (Am. shop) steward; **~praktikum** n industrial placement; Pl. auch industrial training Sg.; **~prüfer** m auditor; **~prüfung** f (company) audit; **~rat** m **1.** Institution: works committee, works council, Am. employee organization; **2.** Mitglied: member of the works committee (od. council), Am. employee representative; **~rätin** f (woman) member of the works committee (od. council), Am. employee representative **Betriebsrats|mitglied** n member of the works committee (od. council), Am. employee representative; **~sitzung** f works committee (od. council) meeting, Am. employee organization meeting; **~vorsitzende** m, f; -n, -n chair of the works committee (od. council), Am. employee organization head; **~wahl** f works committee (od. council) (Am. employee organization) elections Pl.

Betriebs|rente f company pension; **~ruhe** f shutdown (of the factory); **zwischen den Jahren haben wir ~** we close (down) between Christmas and New Year's; **~schalter** m Etech. operating switch; **~schließung** f shutdown (of the factory); ständig (factory) closure; **bei ~** when the factory etc. is closed; **~schluss** m; nur Sg. closing hours Pl.; **wir haben um 5 Uhr ~** we close at 5 o'clock; **5 Minuten nach ~** 5 minutes after closing time; **nach ~** after hours; in der Freizeit: after work **betriebssicher** Adj. safe (to operate); (zuverlässig) reliable (in service); **Betriebssicherheit** f; nur Sg. **1.** operational safety; **2.** innerbetriebliche: (factory) security

Betriebs|spannung f Etech. operating voltage; **~stätte** f Jur. (buildings and) premises; **~stilllegung** f shutdown, (factory) closure; **~störung** f (work) stoppage, interruption of work; e-r Maschine: breakdown; **~system** n EDV operating system; **~unfall** m **1.** industrial accident, accident at work; **2.** umg. (ungewollte Schwangerschaft) accident, unwanted pregnancy; **~urlaub** m company holiday; **~verfassung** f framework for industrial relations (within the company), industrial relations charter; **~verfassungsgesetz** n; nur Sg.; Jur. etwa industrial relations law; **~verlagerung**, **~verlegung** f (company) relocation; **~versammlung** f employees' meeting, factory meeting, meeting of the working body; **~werk** n der Eisenbahn: rolling-stock division; privates: rolling-stock company; **~wirt** m, **~wirtin** f business administrator, graduate in business administration (od. management); etwa MBA (= Master of Business Administration)

Betriebswirtschaft f → Betriebswirt-

schaftslehre; **Betriebswirtschaftler** m, **Betriebswirtschaftlerin** f umg. business administrator; **betriebswirtschaftlich** Adj. economic; management ...; administrative; **ein ~es Studium absolvieren** graduate (od. obtain a degree) in business studies (od. business administration); **~ gesehen** in economic terms, from an economic point of view; **Betriebswirtschaftslehre** f (abgek. BWL) business administration od. economics (V. im Sg.) **Betriebs|zeit** f e-r Maschine: period of operation; **~zugehörigkeit** f; nur Sg. employment (with a company); zeitlich: period of employment; **nach zehnjähriger ~** after ten years(' employment) with the company, after working for the company for ten years **betrinken** v/refl. (unreg.) get drunk; **sich sinnlos ~** get blind drunk, drink o.s. senseless

betroffen I. P.P. → betreffen; **II.** Adj. **1.** (bestürzt) Schweigen: shocked, stunned; **~ sein** be (completely) taken aback; **die Nachricht machte ihn sehr ~** he was completely taken aback by the news; **ein ~es Gesicht machen** look shocked etc.; **wir sind alle sehr ~** oft als Floskel: we are all deeply shocked; **2.** (berührt) affected (von by); von e-r Katastrophe etc.: auch hit (by); **am schwersten ~** worst affected (od. hit); **von der Hungersnot/ Flutkatastrophe** etc. **~** famine-stricken /flood-stricken etc.; **III.** Adv. **~ schweigen** be too shocked to speak, be dumbfounded, maintain a stunned silence; **Betroffene** m, f; -n, -n person concerned (od. affected); **die ~n** those concerned (od. affected); **Betroffenheit** f; nur Sg. dismay; stärker: shock **betrogen I.** P.P. → betrügen; **II.** Adj. cheated; Ehepartner etc.: deceived; **~er Ehemann** cuckold altm.; **in s-n Hoffnungen ~ sein** have had one's hopes dashed (od. frustrated); **Betrogene** m, f; -n, -n: **der ~ sein** be the dupe **betrüben I.** v/t. sadden; stärker: grieve, distress; **dein Verhalten betrübt mich** I am saddened (od. very disappointed) by your behavio(u)r; **II.** v/refl. altm. grieve; **betrüblich** Adj. Tatsache etc.: sad, saddening; stärker: distressing, grievous; **betrüblicherweise** Adv. unfortunately; stärker: sadly; **Betrübnis** f; -, -se; geh. sadness; stärker: distress, misery; **~se** sorrows; **betrübt I.** P.P. → betrüben; **II.** Adj. sad (über + Akk. about, at); stärker: distressed (about, at); **zu Tode ~ sein** be in the depths of despair; **~ zusehen, wie ...** watch in despair (od. distress) as ...; **Betrübtheit** f; nur Sg. sadness; stärker: grief, distress

Betrug m; -(e)s, kein Pl. swindle, cheating; Jur. auch fraud; (Täuschung) deceit, deception; **e-n ~ begehen** commit an act of deception; **wegen ~(e)s angeklagt** be charged with deception; ernstlicher: be charged with fraud; **ein gemeiner ~** a mean piece of trickery; **ein frommer ~** (Selbstbetrug) a pipe dream; (Notlüge) a white lie; **das ist ja (glatter) ~!** that's plain fraud!, that's a swindle! **betrügen** (unreg.) **I.** v/t. **1.** cheat, swindle; Jur. defraud; **j-n um etw. ~** cheat (od. do umg.) s.o. out of s.th., defraud s.o. of s.th.; **in s-n Hoffnungen betrogen werden** have (od. see) one's hopes dashed; → betrogen II; **ich fühle mich betrogen** I feel cheated (od.

betrayed); **j-n um seine Rechte ~** deprive s.o. of their rights; **2.** (Ehepartner etc.) be unfaithful to, cheat on, two-time umg.; **s-e Frau mit einer Kollegin ~** cheat on one's wife with a colleague from work; **II.** v/i. cheat; be a swindler (od. cheat); **III.** v/refl.: **sich selbst ~** deceive (od. delude) o.s.

Betrüger m; -s, - bei Spiel, Geschäft: swindler, cheat; (Hochstapler) confidence trickster, con man umg.; Jur. fraud; **Betrügerei** f; -, -en; im Spiel: cheating; im Geschäft, auch Jur.: fraud; (Unterschlagung) embezzlement; **kleinere ~en** minor deceptions; **Betrügerin** f; -, -nen swindler; cheat; confidence trickster; fraud; **betrügerisch I.** Adj. deceitful; Jur. fraudulent; **in ~er Absicht** Jur. with intent to defraud; **II.** Adv. fraudulently, by fraud **betrunken I.** P.P. → betrinken; **II.** Adj. präd. drunk; Fahrer, Stimme, Verhalten etc.: auch drunken ...; förm. intoxicated, inebriated; **in ~em Zustand** Jur. under the influence of alcohol; **leicht ~** tipsy; **III.** Adv. drunk, in a drunken state, in a state of drunkenness bes. Brit.; **~ fahren** drink-drive, Am. drink and drive; **Betrunkene** m, f; -n, -n drunk; **Betrunkenheit** f; nur Sg. drunkenness

Betschwester f umg. pej. churchy type (od. woman); mit Namen: umg. Saint ..., the Blessed ...

Bett n; -(e)s, -en **1.** allg. (auch Geol., Tech.) bed; **ein französisches ~** a double bed; **im ~** in bed; **ins** od. **zu ~ gehen** go to bed, turn in umg.; **j-n ins** od. **zu ~ bringen** put s.o. to bed; **ab ins ~!** off to bed (with you)!; **die Kinder ins ~ schicken** send the children to bed; **bei j-m am** od. **an j-s ~ sitzen** sit at s.o.'s bedside, sit by s.o.'s bed; **aus dem ~ springen** leap (od. jump) out of bed; **ich komme od. finde morgens nicht aus dem ~** I can't get out of bed in the mornings; **das ~ hüten (müssen)** be confined to bed, be laid up umg. (wegen with); **ans ~ gefesselt sein** be bedridden; **mit dieser Grippe legst du dich lieber ins ~** you ought to go to bed with that flu; **mit j-m das ~ teilen geh.** share a bed with s.o., share s.o.'s bed; **mit j-m ins ~ gehen** od. **steigen** umg. go to bed with s.o.; **sie hat sich ins gemachte ~ gelegt** fig. she gets everything handed to her on a plate, she's landed (herself) a cushy number umg.; → finden III; **2.** (Federbett) duvet, Am. comforter; **das ~ machen** make the bed; für ankommenden Gast make up the bed; **die ~en lüften** air the bedclothes od. bedding; **das ~ frisch beziehen** change the sheets (od. bed od. bed linen) **Bettag** m → Buß- und Bettag **Bett|anzug** m schw. duvet cover; **~bank** f österr. sofa bed; **~bezug** m duvet cover; **~couch** f sofa bed; **~decke** f wollene: blanket; gesteppte: eiderdown, quilt; (Tagesdecke) bedspread

Bettel m; -s, kein Pl.; pej. umg. rubbish, junk; **j-m den (ganzen) ~ vor die Füße werfen** throw the whole thing back in s.o.'s face, tell s.o. where they can stick it vulg.

bettelarm Adj. desperately poor, poverty-stricken; **Bettelei** f; -, mst Sg. **1.** begging; **2.** umg. pleading; **hör auf mit der ewigen ~!** stop pestering me about it all the time!; **Bettelmönch** m Reli. mendicant (friar); **betteln** v/i.

1. beg (*um* for); **~** *gehen* go begging; **2.** (*bitten*) beg (*um* for); *er bettelte so lange, bis ich ja sagte* he kept pestering me (*od.* went on at me) until I said yes

Bettel|orden *m Reli.* mendicant order; **~stab** *m*: *j-n an den* **~** *bringen* reduce s.o. to poverty (*od.* penury); *an den* **~** *kommen* be reduced to poverty *usw.*

betten I. *v/t.* **1.** bed; (*hinlegen*) lay (down), bed down; *j-n zur letzten Ruhe* **~** lay s.o. to rest; **2.** *fig.*: *j-n in Watte* **~** wrap (*od.* keep) s.o. in cotton wool; *ein Heilbad, in herrliche Landschaft gebettet* a spa town surrounded by (*od.* set in) magnificent countryside; **II.** *v/refl.* make a bed for o.s.; *sich weich* **~** *fig.* make a comfortable life for o.s., land a cushy number *umg.*; *wie man sich bettet, so liegt man* Sprichw. he's made his bed, let him lie in it; you've made your bed, now lie in it

Betten|machen *n* making (the) beds; *beim* **~** *sein* be making the beds; **~zahl** *f im Hotel etc.*: bedspace, number of beds

Betteppich *m* prayer mat (*od.* rug)

Bett|feder *f* **1.** *aus Metall*: bedspring; **2.** *Pl.* (*Daunen*) duvet (*Am.* comforter) feathers; **~genosse** *m*, **~genossin** *f* bedmate; **~geschichte** *f*; *mst Pl.*; *pej.* **1.** amorous escapade; **2.** *in der Zeitung etc.*: kiss and tell story; **~gestell** *n* bedstead; **~häschen** *n umg. Sl.* bit of all right, (bit of a) goer, sex fiend, sex kitten; **~hupferl** *n*; *-s, -*; *Dial.* bedtime treat; *im Hotel: mst* chocolate on one's pillow; **~jäckchen** *n* bed jacket; **~kante** *f* edge of the bed; *ich würde sie/ihn nicht von der* **~** *stoßen* *umg. hum.* I wouldn't kick her/him out of bed; **~kasten** *m* bedding drawer (*od.* box)

bettlägerig *Adj.* laid up *umg.*, confined to bed *förm.*; *längerfristig*: bedridden

Bett|laken *n* sheet; **~lektüre** *f* bedtime reading

Bettler *m*; *-s, -*, **~in** *f*; *-, -nen* beggar

Bett|nässen *n*; *-s, kein Pl.*; *Med.* bed-wetting; **~nässer** *m*; *-s, -*, **~nässerin** *f*; *-, -nen* bed-wetter

Bett|pfanne *f* bedpan; **~pfosten** *m* bedpost; **~rand** *m* edge of the bed; **⚲reif** *Adj. umg.* ready for bed, ready to hit the sack (*Am. auch* hay); **~ruhe** *f* bed rest; *der Arzt hat mir* **~** *verordnet* the doctor told me to stay in bed, the doctor prescribed bed rest; **~schwere** *f umg.*: *die nötige* **~** *haben* be ready to fall into bed; **~szene** *f Film*: bedroom scene; **~tuch** *n* sheet; **~vorleger** *m* bedside rug; **~wäsche** *f* bed linen, sheets (and covers) *Pl.*; **~zeug** *n umg.* bedclothes *Pl.*, bedding

betucht *Adj.*: (*gut*) **~** well-heeled

betulich *Adj.* overattentive, fussy; **Betulichkeit** *f*; *nur Sg.* fussing

betupfen *v/t.* dab; *Med.* swab

betütern *nordd. umg.* **I.** *v/t.* (*umsorgen*) mollycoddle; **II.** *v/refl.* get tipsy; **betütert** *Adj. nordd. umg.* (*beschwipst*) tipsy

Beuge *f*; *-, -n*; *auch Sport und Anat.* bend; **~haft** *f Jur.* coercive detention; **~muskel** *m Physiol.* flexor (muscle)

beugen I. *v/t.* **1.** (*Rücken, Arm etc.*) bend; (*Kopf*) bow; incline; → *gebeugt* II; **2.** *fig.* (*Willen, Starrsinn*) break; **3.** *das Recht od.* *Gesetz* **~** pervert the course of justice; **4.** *Phys.* deflect; *durch enge Öffnung* diffract; **5.** *Ling.* inflect; (*Substantiv, Adjektiv*) decline;

(*Verb*) conjugate; **II.** *v/refl.* **1.** bend (*über* + *Akk.* over); *sich aus dem Fenster* **~** lean out of (*Am. auch* out) the window; *sich nach vorn/hinten* **~** lean forward / (over) backward; **2.** *fig.* (*sich fügen*) bow, yield, submit (+ *Dat.* to); *sich dem Schicksal* **~** bow (*od.* submit) to one's fate

Beugung *f* **1.** bending; **2.** *Jur.* perverting (the course of justice); **3.** *Phys.* diffraction; **4.** *Ling. von Verb*: conjugation; *von Subst.*: declension; *Endung etc.*: inflection

Beule *f*; *-, -n* bump, swelling; *am Körper*: bruise; *im Blech*: dent; *in der Hose*: bulge; *dicke* **~** *am Kopf etc.*: big bump, great big lump *umg.*; *e-e eiternde* **~** a boil

beulen *v/i. Hosen-, Jackentasche*: bulge; *Hose, Pullover*: be baggy

Beulenpest *f* bubonic plague

beunruhigen I. *v/t.* worry, get s.o. worried; *stärker*: alarm; *es beunruhigt mich auch* I feel uneasy (*od.* nervous) about it; **II.** *v/refl.* worry, be worried (*über* + *Akk.* about); **beunruhigend** **I.** *Part. Präs.* → *beunruhigen*; **II.** *Adj.* unsettling, worrying, disconcerting; *Ereignisse etc.*: disturbing; *stärker*: alarming; **Beunruhigung** *f*; *mst Sg.*; (*Unruhe*) uneasiness; *stärker*: anxiety; (*Sorge*) worry

beurkunden I. *v/t.* **1.** (*schriftlich festhalten*) record; (*Geburt etc.*) register; **2.** (*beglaubigen*) certify; *ein Dokument* **~** *lassen* have a document authenticated; **II.** *v/refl. geh.* (*sich zeigen*) manifest itself, be revealed; **Beurkundung** *f* registration; certification; *gerichtliche* **~** legal registration

beurlauben *v/t.* **1.** *für Ferien etc.* give s.o. time off; *Mil.* give (*od.* grant) s.o. leave; *für Forschungszwecke*: grant s.o. a sabbatical; *sich* **~** *lassen Antrag stellen*: ask for time off; *für Forschungszwecke*: apply for a sabbatical; (*freinehmen*) take (some) time off, go on (*od.* take a) sabbatical; *sich eine Woche* **~** *lassen* ask for / take a week's leave (*od.* a week off); **2.** *vom Amt*: suspend s.o. (from office); *beurlaubt werden* be relieved of one's duties; **Beurlaubung** *f* time off; *Mil.* leave; (*Forschungsurlaub*) sabbatical; *vom Amt*: suspension (from office)

beurteilen *v/t.* (*Person*) judge (*nach* by, from); (*Leistung, Wert etc.*) rate, assess, gauge (*Am. auch* gage) (on, according to); *falsch* **~** misjudge; *etw. gut* **~** *können* be a good judge of s.th.; *das ist schwer zu* **~** that is difficult to judge, it's hard to tell; *das kannst du doch nicht* **~** how do you know?, how can you tell?, you're in no position to tell; *nicht dass ich das* **~** *könnte* not that I'm any judge, but who am I to judge?; *wie* **~** *Sie die Lage / unsere Aussichten?* what's your view of the situation / what do you reckon (*od.* think) of our chances?; *man soll Leute nicht danach* **~***, wie sie aussehen* you shouldn't judge (people) by appearances; **Beurteilung** *f* **1.** *nur Sg.*; (*das Beurteilen*) judging, assessing; *bei nüchterner* **~** *der Lage erweist sich ...* a calm assessment of the situation shows ...; **2.**; **3.** (*schriftlicher Bericht*) *von Waren, Personen*: assessment, report, review; *von Situation*: judg(e)ment (+ *Gen.* of, on); (*Einschätzung*) assessment (+ *Gen.*); *in Personalakten*: confidential report (on)

Beuschel *n*; *-s, -*; *österr. Gastr.* traditio-

nal dish of veal or lamb offal, usually served with dumplings

Beute *f*; *-, kein Pl.* **1.** booty; (*Diebesbeute*) *auch* loot, haul; (*Kriegsbeute*) spoils *Pl.* of war; *j-m zur* **~** *fallen* fall into the hands of s.o., *fig.* fall victim to s.o.; *reiche od. fette* **~** *machen* make a big haul; **2.** *von Tieren*: prey, quarry; *auf* **~** *ausgehen* go out hunting, go on a foray; **~** *schlagen* capture (*od.* catch) prey; **3.** *fig.* (*Opfer*) prey (+ *Gen.* to), victim (of); *reiche od. fette* **~** *auch fig.* rich pickings; (*e-e*) *leichte* **~** a sitting duck (*od.* target), easy prey; **4.** *Jagd*: bag

Beutekunst *f*; *nur Sg.* stolen art treasures (*during war*), looted art, booty (*od.* trophy) art

Beutel *m*; *-s, -* **1.** bag; (*Tragetasche*) carrier bag; *für Tabak*: pouch; **2.** *umg.* (*Geldbeutel*) (*einer Frau*) purse; (*eines Mannes*) wallet; **3.** *Zool.* pouch; **4.** *österr. Sl. pej.* idiot, fool

beuteln *v/t.* **1.** *südd., österr.* shake; **2.** *fig.*: *vom Schicksal/Leben gebeutelt werden* be knocked about (*Am.* around) by fate / life's vicissitudes

Beutel|ratte *f Zool.* opossum, possum *umg.*; **~schneider** *m umg. pej.* shark, rip-off artist, swindler, con man; *altm.* (*Taschendieb*) *auch* pickpocket; **~schneiderei** *f umg.* a rip-off, con; **~tier** *n Zool.* marsupial

Beute|stück *n* piece of booty, piece of the loot *umg.*; **~tier** *n* prey, quarry; **~zug** *m* raid, foray; *auf* **~** *ausgehen* *Tier, Jäger*: go out hunting; *fig.* go on a foray

bevölkern I. *v/t.* **1.** populate; (*bewohnen*) inhabit; *fig.* (*Straße etc.*) fill, crowd; **2.** (*besiedeln*) *Regierung etc.*: settle, populate, colonize; *e-n Landstrich* **~** populate an area; **II.** *v/refl.* become inhabited; *fig.* be filling up (with people), become crowded; → *dicht* II 1

Bevölkerung *f* population; *förm.* populace; (*Einwohner*) *auch* inhabitants *Pl.*; (*das Volk*) the people *Pl.*; *die einheimische* **~** the native (*od.* indigenous) people, the natives; *die ganze* **~** *auch* the whole country; *die* **~** *Moskaus* the people of Moscow, Moscow's inhabitants; *statistisch*: the population of Moscow

Bevölkerungs|abnahme *f* population decrease, decrease in population; **~dichte** *f* population density; **~explosion** *f* population explosion; **~gruppe** *f* section (*od.* segment) of the population; **~politik** *f* population (*od.* demographic) policy; **⚲politisch** *Adj.* demographic(ally *Adv.*); **⚲reich** *Adj.* densely populated; **~rückgang** *m* fall (*od.* decline) in population; **~schicht** *f* social stratum (*od.* class); **~struktur** *f* population structure; **~überschuss** *m* overspill; **~wachstum** *n* growth in population; **~zahl** *f statistisch*: population figures *Pl.*; (*Gesamtbevölkerung*) total population; **~zunahme** *f*, **~zuwachs** *m* population growth (*od.* increase)

bevollmächtigen *v/t.* authorize (*zu* + *Dat. od. Inf.* to + *Inf.*); *Jur.* give s.o. power of attorney; **Bevollmächtigte** *m*, *f*; *-n, -n* authorized person (*Jur.* representative); *Pol.* plenipotentiary; **Bevollmächtigung** *f* authorization; (*Vollmacht*) authority, power; *Jur.* power of attorney

bevor *Konj.* **1.** *zeitlich*: before; **~** *du ins Bett gehst, musst du noch die Zähne*

putzen before you go to bed you have to clean (*od.* brush) your teeth; **2.** *drückt Bedingung aus*: **nicht ~** not before, not until; **sag nichts, ~ er kommt** don't say anything until he comes; **wir können nicht gehen, ~ du nicht aufgeschlossen hast** we can't go unless you unlock the door (*od.* before you've unlocked the door)

bevormunden *v/t.* tell *s.o.* what to do (all the time), treat *s.o.* patronizingly (*od.* like a child); **ich lass' mich nicht von dir ~** *auch* I'm not going to let you run my life; **Bevormundung** *f* patronizing attitude; **~ durch den Staat** paternalism, patronage by the state; **ich verbitte mir jede ~** I won't be treated like a child, I won't have my decisions made for me; **ich habe ihre dauernde ~ satt** I'm fed up of (*Am.* with) her telling me what to do all the time, I'm fed up of (*Am.* with) her trying to run my life

bevorrechtigt *Adj.* **1.** *Straße*: having right of way; *auch* major; **2.** privileged; *Anspruch etc.*: preferential; **Bevorrechtigung** *f* privileges *Pl.* (+ *Gen.* granted to); preferential treatment

bevorstehen *v/i.* (*unreg., trennb., hat -ge-*) **1.** *Ereignis*: be approaching; **2.** *Schwierigkeiten etc.*: lie ahead; *Gefahr*: be imminent; (*j-m*) be in store for, await; **ihm steht e-e große Enttäuschung bevor** he's in for a big disappointment; **das Schlimmste steht (mir) noch bevor** the worst is yet (*od.* still) to come; **das steht uns noch bevor** *iro.* we've still got that to look forward to; **s-e Entlassung stand bevor** he was about to be dismissed

bevorstehend I. *Part. Präs.* → **bevorstehen**; **II.** *Adj.* forthcoming, approaching; *bes. Wahlen etc.*: *auch* upcoming; next *week etc.*; *pleasures etc.* to come; *Gefahr etc.*: impending; **ein (unmittelbar) ~es Ereignis** an imminent event

bevorzugen *v/t.* **1.** (*lieber mögen*) prefer (*vor* + *Dat.* to); **2.** (*begünstigen*) favo(u)r (*above*); (*bevorzugt behandeln*) give preferential treatment to; (*Kandidaten, Kind etc.*) give preference to; **hier wird keiner bevorzugt** everyone is treated equally here, there's no favo(u)ritism around here; **3.** (*Fall, Sache, auch j-n vorlassen*) give priority to; *Jur.* privilege; **bevorzugt I.** *P.P.* → **bevorzugen**; **II.** *Adj.* preferred; (*Lieblings...*) favo(u)rite; *Gegend*: popular; *Behandlung*: preferential; *Stellung*: privileged *position*; **~e Lage** prime location; **III.** *Adv.*: **~ behandeln** → **bevorzugen** 2; **Bevorzugung** *f* preference (*j-s* given to s.o.); preferential (*od.* priority) treatment (of s.o.)

bewachen *v/t.* (*Gefangene*) guard; (*behüten*) *auch* watch over; *Sport* mark; **bewacht werden von Sport** mark (*od.* shadowed) by; **Bewacher** *m*; *-s*, *-*, **Bewacherin** *f*; *-*, *-nen* guard; (*Spitzel*) shadow; *hum.* watchdog; *Sport* marker

bewachsen *Adj.* overgrown; **~ mit** covered with (*od.* in), overgrown (with); **mit Moos ~** *auch* moss-covered; **wenn die Mauer erst einmal ~ ist, dann ...** once the wall is overgrown, ...

bewacht I. *P.P.* → **bewachen**; **II.** *Adj.* guarded; *Parkplatz*: supervised **streng ~** closely (*od.* heavily) guarded

Bewachung *f* **1.** *nur Sg.*; (*das Bewachen*) guarding; (*Überwachung*) sur-

veillance; *Sport* marking; **unter ~ stellen/halten** put/keep under guard; **2.** (*Person*) guard(s *Pl.*), escort

bewaffnen I. *v/t.* *auch fig.* arm; **II.** *v/refl.* arm *o.s.*; **bewaffnet I.** *P.P.* → **bewaffnen**; **II.** *Adj.* *auch fig.* armed (*mit* with); **bis an die Zähne ~** armed to the teeth; **Bewaffnung** *f* **1.** *nur Sg.*; (*das Bewaffnen*) arming; **2.** (*Waffen*) arms *Pl.*, weapons *Pl.*

bewahren *v/t.* **1.** (*aufrechterhalten, behalten*) (*Tradition etc.*) keep, preserve; (*Eigenschaft, Aussehen etc.*) *auch* retain; **er hat s-n Humor bewahrt** he's kept (*od.* he hasn't lost) his sense of humo(u)r; **bitte Ruhe ~** please keep calm; → **Fassung** 3; **2.** (*behüten*): **~ vor** (+ *Dat.*) protect (*od.* keep) *s.o.* from; (*retten*) *auch* save *s.o.* from; **j-n vor e-r Dummheit ~** stop *s.o.* (from) doing something stupid; **s-n Ruf ~** maintain one's reputation; **(Gott) bewahre!** God forbid!, heaven forbid!; **(Gott) bewahre, nein!** good heavens, no!

bewähren *v/refl.* Person, Maßnahme *etc.*: prove *o.s.* (*od.* itself), prove one's (*od.* its) worth; *Idee, neues Produkt etc.*: *auch* prove a success, prove successful, prove to be a good investment; *Grundsatz*: hold good; *zeitlich*: stand the test of time; **sich bestens ~** *Person*: give a (very) good account of *o.s.* (*od.* itself), *Am.* show what one (*od.* it) can do; *Sache*: do a good (*od.* an excellent) job; *Methode*: pay off, be worthwhile; **sich ... als Lehrer** *etc.* prove (to be) a good teacher *etc.*; **sich nicht ~** prove a failure, prove not (to be) worthwhile

bewahrheiten *v/refl.* prove (to be) true (*od.* well-founded); *Hoffnungen, Befürchtungen etc.*: be confirmed, prove to be right (*od.* justified); (*sich erfüllen*) come true; **die Gerüchte über e-n Regierungswechsel scheinen sich zu ~** the rumo(u)rs about a change of government seem to be coming true

bewährt I. *P.P.* → **bewähren**; **II.** *Adj.*; *nur attr.*; (*erprobt*) well-tried, tried and tested; *Methode*: proven; *Grundsatz*: established; (*zuverlässig*) reliable; (*wirksam*) effective; (*fähig*) capable, experienced; **~es Mittel** proven (*od.* old, ancient, time-hono(u)red *iro.*) remedy; **unter ihrer ~en Führung** under her excellent guidance, in her capable hands

Bewahrung *f*; *nur Sg.* preservation (*vor* + *Dat.* from), conservation, protection

Bewährung *f* **1.** (*Tauglichkeitsbeweis*) demonstration of one's (*od.* its) worth (*od.* reliability); **bei ~** on qualifying, provided it (*od.* he *etc.*) proves reliable; **die ~ bestehen** pass the test; **2.** *Jur.* (*nach einer Gefängnisstrafe*) parole; (*statt einer Gefängnisstrafe*) probation; **zwei Jahre Gefängnis mit/ohne ~** a suspended / an unconditional sentence of two years; **er hat ein Jahr mit ~ bekommen** he's got (*od.* he was given) a suspended sentence of one year; **e-e Strafe zur ~ aussetzen** suspend a sentence; **er ist auf ~ draußen** he is out on parole

Bewährungs|auflage *f* *Jur.* probation order; **gegen die ~n verstoßen** break one's (terms of) probation; **~helfer** *m* *Jur.* probation officer; **~hilfe** *f* *Jur.* probation service, public protection service; **~probe** *f* (acid) test; **~strafe** *f* *Jur.* suspended sentence, (period of)

probation; **~zeit** *f* (time *od.* period) of probation

bewaldet *Adj.* wooded, forested, tree--covered; **die Gegend ist dicht ~** the area is densely wooded (*od.* forested); **Bewaldung** *f* **1.** (*Waldbestand*) woods *Pl.*, woodland, forests *Pl.*; **2.** (*Aufforstung*) afforestation

bewältigen *v/t.* **1.** (*Arbeit, Essen etc.*) cope with, manage; (*Berg*) conquer; (*Strecke*) cover; **2.** *fig.* (*Problem*) come to grips with, handle; (*Schwierigkeit*) cope with, overcome; (*Vergangenheit, Trauma etc.*) come to terms with; (*Lehrstoff*) master, assimilate, absorb, digest *umg.*; **Bewältigung** *f*; *nur Sg.* (*von Arbeit etc.*): coping with one's work *etc.*; *von Lehrstoff*: assimilation; *von Vergangenheit etc.*: coming to terms with, getting over *the past etc.*

bewandert *Adj.*: **in etw.** (*Dat.*) **(gut** *od.* **sehr) ~ sein** be well up (*od.* well versed) in s.th., be familiar with (*od.* experienced in) s.th.; **da bin ich nicht besonders ~** I'm not very well up in that, I'm not very familiar with that

Bewandtnis *f*: **es hat e-e** *od.* **s-e besondere ~ mit** you have to know the background (to), there is something about; **mit diesem Ring/Zimmer**: there's a very strange thing about *this ring/room*, *this ring/room* has a special story; **damit** (*od.* **mit ihm** *etc.*) **hat es folgende ~** the matter is as follows; **das hat e-e ganz andere ~** it's completely different; **was hat es eigentlich mit ... für e-e ~?** what's the story behind ...?; **das hat s-e eigene ~** *hum.* (and) thereby hangs a tale

bewässern *v/t.* (*Boden, Felder*) irrigate; (*auch Pflanzen*) water; **Bewässerung** *f* **1.** (*das Bewässern*) watering; **2.** (*System*) irrigation

Bewässerungs|anlage *f* irrigation plant; **~graben** *m* irrigation channel (*od.* ditch); **~kanal** *m* irrigation channel (*od.* ditch); **~pumpe** *f* irrigation pump; **~system** *n* irrigation system

bewegen¹ I. *v/t.* **1.** move; (*Schweres*) *auch* shift *umg.*; **ich kann m-n linken Arm nicht ~** *auch* I have no movement in my left arm; **es lässt sich nicht von der Stelle ~** it won't budge; **2.** (*Wasser, Blätter etc.*) stir; **e-e leichte Brise bewegte die Oberfläche des Sees** a gentle breeze ruffled (*od.* rippled) the surface of the lake; **3.** *Tech. und fig.* set *s.th.* in motion; (*antreiben*) drive; **4.** *fig.* (*rühren*) move, touch; (*beschäftigen*) (pre)occupy; *lästiges Problem etc.*: *auch* bother; **5.** (*Pferd*) exercise; **II.** *v/refl.* **1.** move; *leicht*: stir; *Fahne*: flap; **2.** (*sich körperlich betätigen*) get (some) exercise; **du musst dich mehr ~** you need (to get) more exercise; **er bewegt sich zur Zeit kaum** *auch* he hardly gets out of the house these days; **3.** *fig.*: **sich in Politikerkreisen** *etc.* **~** move in political *etc.* circles; **sich in e-e Richtung ~** *Gedanken etc.*: tend in a (certain) direction; **die Kosten ~ sich zwischen ...** the costs range between ...; **in welcher Höhe ~ sich die Kosten?** roughly how high are the costs?

bewegen² ** *v/t*; *bewegt, bewog, hat bewogen*: **j-n zu etw. ~ get (*od.* bring) *s.o.* to do *s.th.*; **j-n dazu ~, etw. zu tun** get (*od.* bring) *s.o.* to do s.th.; **was hat ihn (wohl) dazu bewogen?** (I wonder) what made him do it?; **sich zu etw. ~ lassen** (allow *o.s.* to) be persuaded to do s.th.; *sich nicht ~ lassen* stand firm, remain adamant, refuse to budge *umg.*; *es konnte ihn nichts dazu ~ zu* (+ *Inf.*) wild horses couldn't make him (+ *Inf.*)

bewegend I. *Part. Präs.* → *bewegen*[1], *bewegen*[2]; **II.** *Adj. fig.* (*rührend*) moving, touching; *Rede:* stirring

Beweggrund *m* (*Motiv*) motive; (*Überlegung*) consideration; *aus moralischen etc. Beweggründen* out of moral etc. considerations; *der tiefere ~ war ...* the real motive was ..., what was at the back (*od.* bottom) of it was ...

beweglich *Adj.* **1.** mobile; *Festtage auch* movable; *~e Teile* moving parts; *~e Güter od. Werte Jur.* movables; *mit e-m Auto ist man ~er* you can get around more easily (*od.* you're more mobile) with a car; *ohne Gepäck ist man ~er* you're freer to move (*od.* you can move around better) without luggage; **2.** (*gelenkig*) *Person:* agile; **3.** *Tech.* (*auch elastisch*) flexible; *Mot. etc.* manoeuvrable, *Am.* maneuverable; *schwer ~* hard to move; **4.** *fig.* (*flexibel*) flexible, adaptable; *geistig ~* mentally agile, on the ball, with it *umg.*; **Beweglichkeit** *f; nur Sg.* **1.** mobility; **2.** (*Behändigkeit*) agility; **3.** (*Biegsamkeit*) flexibility; *Mot. etc.* manoeuvrability, *Am.* maneuverability; **4.** *fig.* flexibility; *geistige ~* mental agility

bewegt I. *P.P.* → *bewegen*[1]; **II.** *Adj.* **1.** (*gerührt*) moved, touched; *Stimme:* choked-up; *stärker:* trembling (with emotion), quavering; **2.** *Zeiten, Leben:* exciting; (*ereignisreich*) *auch* eventful; (*aufgewühlt*) turbulent, stirring; (*problembeladen*) troubled; *wir leben in ~en Zeiten* these are exciting (*od.* turbulent) times; **3.** (*lebhaft*) animated (*auch Diskussion*); *mit ~en Worten schildern* give a dramatic account of; **4.** *See:* (*stürmisch*) rough; (*unruhig*) choppy; *stärker:* heavy

Bewegung *f* **1.** movement; *auch Phys.* motion; *mit bestimmter Absicht:* move; (*Handbewegung*) gesture; *Fin. auf Konto:* transfer; *in ~* moving; *Tech. auch* in motion; *fig. astir; Person:* on the move; *ständig in ~ sein* be constantly on the move (*od.* moving); *in ~ bringen* get s.o./s.th. moving; *etw. in ~ setzen auch fig.* start s.th., set s.th. in motion; *in ~ geraten od. sich in ~ setzen* start to move; *Tech. auch* start (working); *fig.* get going; *in ~ halten* keep s.th. moving (*od.* going); *es kam plötzlich ~ in die Menge* there was a sudden stir in the crowd; (*ein bisschen*) *~ bringen in* (+ *Akk.*) *fig.* liven s.th. up, get s.th. going; (*aufstacheln*) stir up; *keine falsche ~!* don't move!, no false moves!, freeze!; → *Hebel* 3; **2.** *nur Sg.;* (*körperliche Betätigung*) exercise; *an der frischen Luft* fresh air and exercise; *ich brauche etwas ~* I need some exercise, I need to stretch my legs; *dir fehlt ~* you need to get some exercise; **3.** *nur Sg. emotional:* emotion; **4.** *Pol. etc.* movement; *künstlerische: auch* trend

Bewegungs|ablauf *m* motions *Pl.;* **~drang** *m; nur Sg.* **1.** *Kind:* urge to move (*od.* be active), motor activity; *Kinder haben e-n grossen ~* children have an incredible amount of energy, children are very restless; **2.** *Med.* hyperkinesia; **~energie** *f Phys.* kinetic energy; **~freiheit** *f; nur Sg.* **1.** room to move, elbowroom; *der enge Rock behinderte ihre ~* the tight skirt hampered (*od.* restricted) her movements; **2.** *fig.* personal freedom, freedom of action; *uneingeschränkte ~ auch Pol.* full liberty of action; **3.** (*Spielraum*) latitude

bewegungslos I. *Adj.* motionless, completely still, immobile; *mit ~er Miene* with a stony stare, poker-faced; **II.** *Adv.:* *~ daliegen* lie there motionless (*od.* without moving); **Bewegungslosigkeit** *f; nur Sg.* immobility

Bewegungs|mangel *m; nur Sg.* lack of (*od.* too little) exercise; *Sie leiden an ~* you don't get enough exercise; **~störung** *f Med.* motor disturbance; **~therapie** *f Med.* therapeutic exercises *Pl.*, kinesitherapy

bewegungsunfähig *Adj.* unable to move (*od.* get about), immobilized; **Bewegungsunfähigkeit** *f* inability to move (*od.* get about), immobility

beweibt *Adj.* **1.** *altm.* married; **2.** *umg. hum.* hitched (up) (with a woman)

beweihräuchern *v/t. fig.* (*j-n*) adulate; (*auch Sache*) praise to the skies (*od.* to high heaven), eulogize; *sich selbst ~* sing one's own praises, blow (*od.* toot) one's own horn *umg.*; **Beweihräucherung** *f* adulation, eulogizing

beweinen *v/t.* mourn, weep (for *od.* over); **Beweinung** *f* mourning; *die ~ Christi Kunst* the Lamentation (of Christ)

Beweis *m; -(e)s, -e* **1.** proof (*für* of), evidence (of); *Jur. auch Pl.* proof; (*Beweismittel*) (piece of) evidence; (*Zeichen*) evidence, sign, indication; *den ~ antreten* offer (*od.* furnish) evidence (*für* for); *den ~ erbringen* furnish proof, provide (*Jur.* produce) evidence (*für* of); *~e erheben Jur.* hear (*od.* take) evidence; *einen ~ führen* prove one's case; *s-e Naivität etc. unter ~ stellen* prove one's naivety etc.; *ein eindeutiger/schlagender ~* incontrovertible/decisive evidence; *als od. zum ~* (*für od.* + *Gen.*) as proof (*od.* evidence) (of), in evidence (of), *auch* to prove s.th.; (*für*) *j-s Zuneigung, Vertrauen etc.*: as a token of; *als ~, dass ich dir glaube* to prove (*od.* show) that I believe you; *das Experiment ist ein klarer ~ dafür, dass ...* the experiment is a clear demonstration (*od.* clearly demonstrates) that ...; *ein ~ von Unfähigkeit* a show of incompetence; *wir danken für die vielen ~e der Anteilnahme* (*bei Todesfällen*) thank you for all the messages of sympathy; *bis zum ~ des Gegenteils* until there is proof to the contrary; *Freispruch aus Mangel an ~en Jur.* acquittal due to lack of evidence; → *mangels;* **2.** *Math.* proof; *e-n ~ führen/antreten* conduct/offer a proof

Beweis|antrag *m Jur.* motion to take (*od.* hear) evidence; **~aufnahme** *f Jur.* hearing of evidence; *die ~ eröffnen/schliessen* open/close the taking (*od.* hearing) of evidence; *zur ~ schreiten* begin with the hearing of the evidence

beweisbar *Adj.* provable, demonstrable; *das ist nicht/leicht ~* that is difficult/easy to prove

beweisen (*unreg.*) **I.** *v/t.* **1.** (*nachweisen*) *auch Math.* prove (*durch* with), back up; (*Ausdruck sein*) be evidence of; *j-m etw. ~* prove s.th. to s.o.; *die Richtigkeit e-r Behauptung ~* prove the accuracy of (*od.* back up) a claim; *dass man Recht hat* prove o.s. right; *das beweist, dass du Recht hast* that proves you right; *man konnte ihm s-e Schuld nicht ~* they couldn't prove that he was guilty, they couldn't prove his guilt; *das beweist zur Genüge, dass ...* it's ample proof (*od.* evidence) that, it proves beyond doubt that ...; *es ist e-e bewiesene Tatsache, dass ...* it's a proven fact that ...; *das beweist noch gar nichts* that doesn't prove a thing; *das musst du mir erst einmal ~!* I'd like to see you prove it; *was zu ~ war bes. Math., Schlussformel bei Beweis:* QED (quod erat demonstrandum); **2.** (*zeigen*) show; (*an den Tag legen*) *auch* display; *sie hat großen Mut bewiesen* she displayed great courage; **II.** *v/refl.* prove o.s./itself

Beweis|führung *f* **1.** argument, line of argument(ation) (*od.* reasoning); **2.** *Jur. engS.* giving of evidence; → *lückenlos;* **3.** *Math.* proof; **~grund** *m* argument; **~kette** *f* chain of evidence; → *lückenlos*

Beweiskraft *f; nur Sg.;* (*Schlüssigkeit*) conclusiveness, cogency, strength; *etw. hat ~* s.th. is cogent; *Jur.* s.th. has evidential value (*od.* conclusive force); **beweiskräftig** *Adj.* **1.** *Argument:* conclusive, cogent; *Resultat:* conclusive, decisive; **2.** *Jur.* evidential, probative

Beweis|lage *f; nur Sg.; Jur.* body of evidence; **~last** *f; nur Sg.; Jur.* burden of proof, onus; *ihm obliegt die ~* the burden of proof lies with him; **~material** *n; mst Sg.; Jur.* (body of) evidence; *~ sammeln* collect evidence; *aufgrund des ~s* on the evidence (available); **~mittel** *n; Jur.* (piece of) evidence; *Pl.* evidence *Sg.* (*für* of); **~not** *f; nur Sg.; Jur.* lack of evidence; *in ~ sein od. sich in ~ befinden* have no evidence (to bring forward)

Beweispflicht *f; nur Sg.; Jur.* → *Beweislast;* **beweispflichtig** *Adj.; Jur.:* *er ist ~* the burden of proof lies with him

Beweis|sicherung *f Jur.* perpetuation of evidence; **~stück** *n* (piece of) evidence; *vom Gericht zugelassenes:* exhibit

bewenden *v/t. nur in: es bei od. mit etw. ~ lassen* be content with s.th.; *es dabei ~ lassen* leave it at that; *sie ließen es bei e-r Verwarnung ~* they decided to let him *etc.* off with a warning; *lassen wir es dabei ~!* let's leave it at that!

Bewerb *m; -(e)s, -e. österr. Sport* competition

bewerben (*unreg.*) **I.** *v/refl.* apply (*um* for); *sich als Koch etc. ~* apply as a chef etc.; *er hat sich bei X beworben* he's applied to X (for a job); *sich um e-e Stelle ~* apply for a post (*Am.* position); *sich ~ um* (*kandidieren*) stand for, *bes. Am.* run for *presidency etc.*; *auch Partei:* contend for; *um e-n Preis:* compete (*od.* contend) for; *um e-n Auftrag:* bid for, tender for; **II.** *v/t. Wirts.* (*Produkt*) advertise, promote; (*Kunden, Zielgruppe*) woo *umg.*

Bewerber *m*, **~in** *f* **1.** applicant; candidate; *Wirts. bei e-r Ausschreibung:* bidder, competitor; *Sport* entrant, competitor; **2.** *nur m altm. od. hum.* (*Freier*) suitor; **Bewerbung** *f* application (*um* for)

Bewerbungs|bogen *m*, **~formular** *n* application form; **~gespräch** *n* (job) interview; **~schreiben** *n* (letter of) application; **~unterlagen** *Pl.* application *Sg.*, application papers; CV (*Am. mst* résumé) and references

bewerfen *v/t.* (*unreg.*) **1. j-n mit etw. ~** throw (*od.* hurl) s.th. at s.o.; pelt s.o. with s.th.; (*Politiker etc.*) *auch* greet s.o. with s.th.; *j-s Ehre / guten Namen mit Schmutz ~ fig.* sling (*od.* throw) mud at s.o. / s.o.'s good name, *Am.* drag s.o.'s name in the dirt; **2.** *Archit.* plaster; **~** *roh:* rough-cast

bewerkstelligen *v/t.* manage, effect; **(es) ~, dass j-d ...** arrange for s.o. to ...; **Bewerkstelligung** *f; nur Sg.;* (*das Bewerkstelligen*) managing

bewerten *v/t.* **1.** (*Leistung, Chancen etc.*) assess (**nach** by, according to); (*j-n*) judge (by); (*Aufsatz*) mark, correct; **~ als** judge *s.o./s.th.* to be, see *s.o./s.th.* as; *e-n Aufsatz mit e-r guten Note ~ etwa* give an essay a good mark (*bes. Am.* grade); *e-e Arbeit gerecht ~* mark (*Am.* grade) a piece of work fairly; *zu hoch/niedrig ~ Eigenschaft:* overrate/underrate; *der Sprung wurde nicht bewertet / mit 7 Punkten bewertet* the jump was disqualified / scored 7 points; **2.** *Wirts.* value (*mit* at); **Bewertung** *f* **1.** *e-r Leistung:* assessment; *Päd.* mark(s *Pl.*), *bes. Am.* grade(s *Pl.*); *Sport* scoring, score(s *Pl.*); **2.** *Wirts.* valuation; **Bewertungsmaßstab** *m* set of criteria, criteria of assessment

bewies *Imperf.* → *beweisen;* **bewiesen** *P.P.* → *beweisen*

bewiesenermaßen *Adv.* demonstrably, as can be proved (*Am. mst* proven); *diese Darstellung ist ~ unwahr* it has been proved that this account is untrue; *das war ~ s-e Absicht* that was his proven intent

bewilligen *v/t.* allow (*j-m etw.* s.o. s.th.); (*Antrag, Mittel*) grant; *Parlament:* sanction; (*genehmigen*) consent to; *die Regierung will die notwendigen Mittel nicht ~* the government doesn't want to provide the finances necessary; *dem Institut sind zwei neue Planstellen bewilligt worden* two new posts (*Am.* positions) have been approved for the institute; **Bewilligung** *f* approval; (*Erlaubnis*) permission; *von Mitteln:* granting *of funds etc.*

bewillkommnen *v/t. geh.* welcome

bewirbt → *bewerben*

bewirken *v/t.* (*zustande bringen*) bring s.th. about; (*verursachen*) cause; (*hervorrufen*) give rise to, result in; (*erreichen*) achieve; **~, dass j-d etw. tut** get s.o. to do s.th.; *nichts / das Gegenteil ~* achieve nothing/ produce (*od.* have) the opposite effect; *was willst du damit ~?* what do you hope to achieve by that?

bewirten *v/t.* feed (*mit* with, on); (*Gesellschaft*) cater for; *mit etw. bewirtet werden* be offered s.th.; *lit.* be regaled with s.th.; *womit wollen wir die Gäste ~?* what shall we offer our guests?

bewirtschaften *v/t.* **1.** (*Acker*) cultivate, work; (*Gut, Betrieb*) run; **2.** *Wirts.* (*Mangelware*) ration; (*Devisen*) control; **bewirtschaftet I.** *P.P.* → *bewirtschaften;* **II.** *Adj.* **1.** *Berghütte etc.:* open (to the public); (*mit Schankerlaubnis*) licensed; **2.** *Wirts.:* *ein ~er Markt* a managed market; *~e Waren* rationed goods; **Bewirtschaftung** *f* **1.** *Agr.* cultivation; *e-s Guts etc.:* running, managing *an estate etc.;* **2.** *Wirts. von Mangelware:* rationing; *von Devisen:* control

Bewirtung *f* (*Versorgung*) catering (+

Gen. for); *im Gasthaus:* food and service; *vielen Dank für die ~!* thank you for looking after (feeding *umg.*) us *etc.* so well, thank you for your hospitality *förm.;* **Bewirtungskosten** *Pl. Fin.* entertainment expenses

bewog *Imperf.* → *bewegen²;* **bewogen** *P.P.* → *bewegen²*

bewohnbar *Adj.* (in)habitable; **Bewohnbarkeit** *f; nur Sg.* habitability

bewohnen *v/t.* live in, occupy; (*Gebiet etc.*) inhabit; (*Stockwerk etc.*) live on; → *auch* **bewohnt** II

Bewohner *m; -s, -,* **~in** *f, -, -nen; von Haus, Zimmer etc.* occupier, *Am.* occupant; (*Mieter*) tenant; *e-s Gebiets etc.:* inhabitant (*auch Tiere*); *...bewohner m, im Subst.* ...dweller, inhabitant *of ...;* *Höhlen~* cave dweller; *Schloss~* inhabitant(s) of a/the castle

Bewohnerschaft *f* inhabitants *Pl.,* residents *Pl.; e-s Hauses:* occupants *Pl.*

bewohnt I. *P.P.* → *bewohnen;* **II.** *Adj. Land, Gegend:* inhabited; *Gebäude, Raum:* occupied; *das Haus ist ~ auch* somebody lives (*od.* people live) in the house, there's somebody (*od.* there are people) living in the house; *das Haus ist nicht ~* the house is empty (*od.* vacant, unoccupied), nobody lives (*od.* there's nobody living) in the house

bewölken *v/refl.* **1.** get cloudy; *völlig:* cloud over, become overcast; **2.** *fig. Gesicht etc.:* darken; **bewölkt I.** *P.P.* → *bewölken;* **II.** *Adj.* **1.** cloudy; *völlig: auch* overcast; *im Wetterbericht: leicht/stark ~* scattered/heavy cloud(s); *~ bis bedeckt* cloudy, overcast; **2.** *fig.* dark, gloomy; **Bewölkung** *f* **1.** cloud, clouds *Pl.; starke ~* heavy cloud cover; *leichte ~* scattered cloud(s); *zunehmende ~* increasing cloudiness (*od.* cloud cover); *vereinzelte ~* scattered cloud(s); *wechselnde ~* variable cloud cover; *auflockernde ~* heavy cloud(s) to begin with, breaking up later; **2.** *nur Sg.;* (*Aufziehen von Wolken*) clouding over (*od.* up)

beworben *P.P.* → *bewerben*

Bewuchs [bə'vu:ks] *m; -es, kein Pl.* vegetation (+ *Gen.* on), plant life

bewundern *v/t.* **1.** admire (*wegen* for); *etw. an j-m ~* admire s.th. about s.o.; *ich bewundere an ihr/ihm, wie ...* I admire his/her ... (+ *Ger.*), I admire the way he/she ...; *ich bewundere ihn wegen s-r Ausdauer auch* I admire his perseverance; *s-e Ausdauer ist zu ~* his perseverance is admirable (*od.* amazing); **2.** (*ansehen*) go and see; *mst iro.* go to admire; **bewundernswert** *Adj.* admirable; *etw. ist ~* s.th. is admirable; **bewundernswerterweise** *Adv.* admirably, incredibly; **bewundernswürdig** *Adj.* admirable, amazing; **Bewunderung** *f* admiration (*von* of; *für* for); *mit ~* with admiration, admiringly

Bewurf *m; -(e)s, Bewürfe; Archit.* facing; (*Rohbewurf*) rough cast

bewusst I. *Adj.* **1.** conscious (+ *Gen.* of); *sich* (*Dat.*) *e-r Sache* (*Gen.*) *~ sein* be aware (*od.* conscious) of s.th.; *sich* (*Dat.*) *e-r Sache* (*Gen.*) *~ werden* realize, become aware of (the fact that), wake up to the fact that; *erst dann wurde mir ~, dass ... auch* only then did it dawn on me that ...; *er war sich der Situation vollkommen ~* he knew exactly what was going on; *er war sich*

dessen nicht mehr ~ he couldn't remember; *j-m etw. ~ machen* make s.o. realize s.th., open s.o.'s eyes to s.th., bring s.th. home to s.o.; *j-m etw. ~er machen* heighten s.o.'s awareness of s.th.; *sich* (*Dat.*) *etw. ~ machen* make s.th. clear to o.s., keep telling o.s. s.th. *umg.;* **2.** *nur attr.; Mensch:* aware; *seiner selbst ~* self-aware; *ein ~er Bürger* an active citizen; *ein ~er Arbeiter ehem. DDR:* a class-conscious worker; **3.** (*absichtlich*) deliberate, conscious; (*berechnet*) calculated, intentional; *das war ein ~er Affront* that was deliberately rude; **4.** (*besagt*) said, *nachgestellt:* in question; *zur ~en Stunde* at the said hour; **II.** *Adv.* **1.** consciously; (*in vollem Bewusstsein*) with full awareness, with all one's wits about one; *~ wahrnehmen* (consciously) register; *er hat es nicht ~ miterlebt* he was too young (*od.* ill, drunk *etc.*) to know what was going on; *das habe ich gar nicht ~ mitbekommen* I (must have) missed that; *~ leben* live life to the full; *~er leben* live more (health-)-consciously; **2.** (*absichtlich*) deliberately, consciously, wittingly, intentionally; *er hat ~ gelogen auch* he knew he was lying, it was a calculated lie

...bewusst *im Adj.* -conscious; *gesundheits~* health-conscious; *umwelt~ planen, leben:* environmentally consciously

bewusstlos *Adj.* unconscious; *~ werden* lose consciousness, faint, black out *umg.,* pass out *umg.; ~ zusammenbrechen* collapse onto the floor (*od.* ground) unconscious, faint; *j-n ~ schlagen* knock s.o. unconscious; *in ~em Zustand sein* be unconscious, be out cold *Sl.;* **Bewusstlose** *m, f; -n, -n* unconscious person (body *umg.*); *da liegt ein ~r* there's somebody lying there unconscious; **Bewusstlosigkeit** *f; nur Sg.* unconsciousness; (*Koma*) coma; *in tiefer ~* in a deep state of unconsciousness, in a coma; *aus s-r ~ erwachen* come (a)round (*Am. auch* to) (again), regain consciousness; *bis zur ~ umg. fig.* ad nauseam; *arbeiten, üben:* to death

Bewusstsein *n; -s, -e, Pl.: nur Med. od. Psych.* **1.** *Med. Psych. Philos. etc.* consciousness; *bei ~* conscious; *der Eingriff erfolgte bei vollem ~* the patient was fully conscious during the operation, the operation was conducted without (any) ana(e)sthetic; *ohne ~ sein* be unconscious; *das ~ verlieren* lose consciousness; (*in Ohnmacht fallen*) faint; *j-n wieder zu(m) ~ bringen* bring s.o. (a)round (*Am. auch* to); *wieder zu ~ kommen* regain consciousness, come (a)round (*Am. auch* to) (again); **2.** awareness, consciousness; realization; *j-m etw. ins ~ bringen* make s.o.fully aware (*od.* conscious) of s.th.; *es kam mir zu(m) ~, dass ...* I realized that ..., I became aware (of the fact) that ..., it occurred to me that ..., it dawned on me that ...; *sich* (*Dat.*) *etw. ins ~ zurückrufen* remind o.s. of s.th.; *sie tat es mit ~* in vollem ~ she was fully aware of (*od.* she knew exactly) what she was doing; *im ~ zu + Inf., im ~, dass ...* conscious of + *Ger.,* aware of the fact that ...; **3.** *nationales, religiöses etc.:* awareness, consciousness; *politisches ~ entwickeln* develop a political awareness; **Bewusstseins|bildung** *f; nur Sg.* raising of (people's) awareness, consciousness raising; *politische* ~ *betreiben* shape political ideas; ~*ebene* f plane of consciousness

bewusstseinserweiternd *Adj. Drogen:* mind-expanding, psychedelic; **Bewusstseinserweiterung** f heightening of (one's *od.* people's) awareness

Bewusstseins|spaltung f *Psych.* schizophrenia; ~*störung* f *Psych.* disturbance of consciousness; ~*trübung* f *Med.* clouded awareness, disorientation; ~*veränderung* f change in awareness (*od.* outlook); ~*zustand* m state of consciousness

Bewusstwerdung f; -, *kein Pl.* (growing) realization (*od.* awareness)

bez. *Abk.* 1. → *bezüglich* I; 2. (*bezahlt*) paid

bezahlbar *Adj.* payable, affordable; *es war nicht* ~ we *etc.* couldn't afford it (*od.* pay for it); *es war gerade noch* ~ we *etc.* just about managed to pay for it; *so e-e Miete ist nicht/kaum* ~ that rent is impossible / barely possible to pay

bezahlen I. *v/t.* 1. *mit Geld etc.:* pay; (*Ware, Leistung*) pay for; (*Schulden*) pay (off), settle; (*entlohnen*) pay; *etw. mit Kreditkarte* ~ pay for s.th by credit card; *das kann ich nicht* ~ I can't afford (*od.* pay for) that, that's beyond my means(, I'm afraid); *das ist einfach nicht mehr zu* ~ who can afford that?, that's daylight (*Am.* highway) robbery *Sl.*; *er hat mir die Reise bezahlt* he paid for my trip (*auch* holiday); *die Getränke bezahle ich* I'll pay for (*od.* get) the drinks, the drinks are on me *umg.*; *das ist nicht mit Geld zu* ~ it's priceless, no amount of money could buy that; 2. (*entlohnen*) pay, reward; *dafür bezahlt werden, dass* get (*od.* be) paid for (+ *Ger.*); *als ob er es bezahlt bekäme umg.* he did it *etc.* like crazy (*od.* mad); *ich bezahle dich nicht fürs Herumstehen* I'm not paying you to stand around; 3. *fig.* (*büßen*) pay for; (*bereuen*) regret; *etw. teuer* ~ pay dearly for s.th.; *das wirst du teuer* ~! you'll pay for that, you'll live to regret that; **II.** *v/i.* 1. pay; *ich möchte gern* ~ *im Restaurant etc.:* can I have the bill (*Am.* check), please?; 2. *fig.:* ~ *für* → I 3

Bezahlfernsehen n *TV, umg.* pay TV

bezahlt I. *P.P.* → *bezahlen*; **II.** *Adj.* 1. *Ware:* paid for; 2. paid; ~*e Kräfte* paid employees; ~*er Urlaub* paid leave; 3. *sich* ~ *machen* pay (off); *es macht sich* ~ *zu* (+ *Inf.*) it pays to (+ *Inf.*); *es hat sich* ~ *gemacht* it paid off, it was worth it

Bezahlung f; *mst Sg.* payment; (*Honorar*) fee; (*Entlohnung*) pay; (*Gehalt*) salary; (*Lohn*) wages *Pl.*; *gegen* ~ for money; (*Honorar*) for a fee (price *umg.*)

bezähmen I. *v/t.* 1. (*Leidenschaft, Neugier, Wut etc.*) curb, restrain, control; *s-e Zunge* ~ curb (*od.* bridle) one's tongue; 2. *lit. altm.* (*Bestie*) tame; **II.** *v/refl.* control o.s., restrain o.s.; **Bezähmung** f 1. restraint, control; 2. *lit. altm.* taming

bezaubern *v/t. fig.* charm, captivate; *stärker:* bewitch (*durch* with); *er war bezaubert von i-r Stimme* her voice captivated him, he was captivated by her voice; **bezaubernd I.** *Part. Präs.* → *bezaubern*; **II.** *Adj.* charming, delightful

bezecht *Adj.* drunk, tiddly, *Am.* tipsy *umg.*, pissed *umg.*

bezeichnen *v/t.* 1. (*benennen*) call;

(*auch wertend beschreiben*) describe; *wie bezeichnet man …?* what do you call …?, what's the name for …?; *wie würdest du das* ~? what would you call that?, how would you describe that?; *es wird verschieden bezeichnet* it has several names (*od.* descriptions), it's referred to in various ways; 2. (*beschreiben*) *Wort:* describe; refer to; (*stehen für*) stand for; (*bedeuten*) mean; 3. (*markieren*) mark; (*angeben*) *auch* indicate; *die Route ist mit roten Pfeilen bezeichnet* the route is marked (*od.* signposted) with red arrows; 4. (*charakterisieren*): *j-n als …* ~ call s.o. a …, refer to s.o. as a …; *er bezeichnet sich selbst als Schriftsteller* he calls himself a writer; *er wird als intolerant bezeichnet* he's said (*od.* meant) to be intolerant, he's described as (being) intolerant; *es wurde als große Blamage bezeichnet* it was described (*od.* put down) as a big disgrace; *solche Preise kann man nur als überteuert* ~ you have to admit these prices are extortionate, these prices can only be called outrageous

bezeichnend I. *Part. Präs.* → *bezeichnen*; **II.** *Adj.* 1. characteristic, typical (*für* of); *es ist* ~ *für s-n Egoismus, dass* it's a reflection of his selfishness that; 2. (*von besonderer Bedeutung*) significant, indicative; (*aufschlussreich*) revealing; *es ist* ~, *dass sie die Sitzung aufgeschoben hat* it says something about (*od.* for) her that she postponed the meeting; **bezeichnenderweise** *Adv.* 1. typically (enough); 2. significantly

Bezeichnung f 1. (*Benennung*) name; (*Begriff*) term, designation *förm.*; *falsche* ~ misnomer, wrong description; *es hat verschiedene* ~*en* it has several names, it's referred to by various names; 2. *nur Sg.* (*das Bezeichnen*) marking, indication, designation

bezeigen *v/t.* (*Liebe, Mitgefühl*) show, express; (*Gunst*) grant; *j-m Achtung* ~ show respect to(ward[s]) s.o., treat s.o. with respect; *j-m sein Beileid* ~ express one's sympathy with s.o., offer s.o. one's condolences; *j-m Ehre* ~ pay hono(u)r to s.o.; **Bezeigung** f show (+ *Gen.* of), display (of)

bezeugen *v/t.* 1. *Jur. und fig.* testify (to); (*bestätigen*) vouch for; (*bescheinigen*) certify; *der Angeklagte bezeugte unter Eid dass, …* the defendant deposed that …; 2. (*historisch nachgewiesen*): *die Siedlung ist für das ausgehende 11. Jahrhundert bezeugt* there is (firm) evidence for (*od.* of) the settlement's existence in the late 11th century, the settlement is known to have existed in the late 11th century; *das Wort ist für das 19. Jahrhundert bezeugt* the word is recorded (*od.* attested) in the 19th century; 3. → *bezeigen*; **Bezeugung** f 1. testimony; 2. → *Bezeigung, Ehrenbezeigung*; 3. *nur Sg.* (*das Bezeugen*) attestation

bezichtigen *v/t.* accuse (+ *Gen.* of); *j-n* ~, *etw. getan zu haben* accuse s.o. of doing (*od.* having done) s.th.; **Bezichtigung** f accusation

beziehbar *Adj.* 1. *Haus:* ready for occupation (*od.* occupancy), ready to move into; 2. *Wirts. Ware:* obtainable (*über* + *Akk.* through); 3. *fig.* referable (*auf* + *Akk.* to)

beziehen (*unreg.*) **I.** *v/t.* 1. (*Sessel, Schirm*) cover; (*Bett*) put clean sheets

on; (*Kopfkissen*) put a new pillowcase on; *mit Saiten:* string; *das Sofa neu* ~ reupholster the sofa; 2. (*Haus, Wohnung*) move into; 3. (*Ware*) get; (*kaufen*) *auch* buy; (*Zeitung*) take, subscribe to; (*Informationen*) get (hold of); *Prügel* ~ get beaten up; 4. (*Gelder, Gehalt etc.*) receive; *sie bezieht e-n Teil i-s Einkommens aus Mieteinkünften* some of her income is from rent (*od.* rental payments); 5. *etw.* ~ *auf* (+ *Akk.*) (*in Zusammenhang bringen*) relate s.th to, (*anwenden auf*) apply s.th. to; *er bezog es auf sich* he took it personally; 6. a) *Mil.* (*Stellung*) take up (a position), b) *e-n klaren Standpunkt* ~ take a (firm) stand; **II.** *v/refl.* 1. *Himmel:* cloud over, become overcast; 2. *sich* ~ *auf* (+ *Akk.*) refer to; (*in Verbindung stehen mit*) relate to; (*betreffen*) concern, apply to; *wir* ~ *uns auf Ihr Schreiben vom …* with reference to your letter of …(, we …); *diese Beschreibung bezieht sich nicht auf dich / nicht auf hiesige Verhältnisse* this description has nothing to do with you / is independent of local conditions

Bezieher m; -s, -, ~*in* f; -, *-nen von Zeitung:* subscriber (+ *Gen.* to); *Wirts.* importer; (*Kunde*) customer; *von Rente etc.:* recipient, drawer *altm.* (*Sozialhilfe*) claimant

Beziehung f 1. (*Zusammenhang*) *von Dingen:* relation (*zu* to), relationship (with, to); connection (with, to); *wechselseitige* ~ interrelationship; *in* ~ *stehen zu* be connected to (*od.* with), be linked to, have a relation to; *etw. mit etw. in* ~ *bringen* (*od. etw. zu etw. in* ~ *setzen*) relate s.th. to s.th, see (*od.* establish) a link between s.th.; 2. (*Hinsicht*): *in dieser* ~ from that point of view, in that respect; (*in diesem Zusammenhang*) in this connection; *in mancher* ~ in some ways (*od.* respects); *in gewisser* ~ in a way; *in jeder* ~ in every way (*od.* respect); *in* ~ *auf* (+ *Akk.*) with regard to, as far as … goes (*od.* is concerned); *in politischer* ~ politically (speaking), in political terms; *in wirtschaftlicher* ~ (seen) in economic terms, seen from an economic point of view; 3. *mit Partner oder Partnerin:* relationship (*zu* with, to); (*Affäre*) affair; *in ihrer* ~ *kriselt es* she is having problems in her relationship (*od.* with her partner); 4. ~*en* *Pl.* (*Verbindungen*) connections (with, to); (*Kontakt*) contact (with), contacts (with, to); *menschliche, diplomatische etc.:* relations; *mit e-m Staat wirtschaftliche/politische* ~*en aufnehmen/abbrechen* establish/ break off economic/political relations (*od.* contact) with a country; *gute* ~*en haben* *zu einzelner Person:* be on good terms *with s.o.*; *zu höheren Stellen etc.:* have good (*od.* the right) connections, know the right people *umg.*; *du brauchst* ~*en* you need connections, you've got to know the right people *umg.*; *er hat es durch* ~*en bekommen* he got it through contacts, he got it through knowing the right people; *s-e* ~*en spielen lassen* pull a few strings; 5. *innere:* relationship (*zu* to); affinity (for, to); feeling (for); understanding (of); *zur Kunst etc.:* *auch* appreciation (for, of); *ich habe keine* ~ *zur Musik* *auch* I can't relate to music, music doesn't mean anything (*od.* means nothing) to me; *ich habe keine*

~ zu ihm I can't relate to him, I feel no affinity for (*od.* towards) him, I can't warm to him

Beziehungskiste *f; nur Sg.; umg.* relationship *allg.*, (romantic) set-up *umg.*

beziehungslos *Adj.* unconnected, without any connection, (completely) unrelated; **~ nebeneinander stehen** *Ideen, Aussagen etc.*: auch bear no relationship to one another; **Beziehungslosigkeit** *f; nur Sg.* unconnectedness, lack of (any) connection (**zu** with, to)

beziehungsweise *Konj.* (*abgek.* **bzw.**) **1.** (*oder auch*) (either …) or (…, as the case may be); **2.** (*oder vielmehr*) or rather, that's to say, i.e.; **3.** (*und im andern Fall*) respectively; **zwei Bücher in englischer ~ deutscher Sprache** two books in English and German respectively

bezifferbar *Adj.* quantifiable; **nicht ~** unquantifiable; **beziffern I.** *v/t.* **1.** (*nummerieren*) number; *Mus.* figure; **2.** (*schätzen*) estimate (**auf** + *Akk.*, **mit** at); **II.** *v/refl.*: **sich auf etw.** (*Akk.*) **~ Schaden etc.**: amount to, come to

Bezirk *m; -(e)s, -e* **1.** *allg.* (*Bereich, Gegend*) area, region, district; *fig.* sphere, realm; **2.** *Verwaltung, in Ländern*: district; *in Stadt*: auch borough, *Am. auch* township; **3.** (*kommunaler Wahlbezirk*) ward; (*Parlamentswahlkreis*) constituency; *Am.* (*Polizei-, Wahlbezirk*) precinct; **4.** *ehem. DDR*: unit of local goverment, *etwa* county

Bezirks|amt *n* district office; **~direktor** *m*, **~direktorin** *f von Bank, Versicherung etc.*: area manager; **~ebene** *f*: **auf ~** at the (*od.* on a) regional level; **~gericht** *n österr. schw.* district court; **~grenze** *f* regional boundary; **~hauptmann** *m Österr.* chief officer of local government; **~krankenhaus** *n Med.* a) *allg.*: regional (*od.* local) hospital, b) *mst. psychiatrische Klinik*: psychiatric clinic, mental hospital; **~liga** *f Sport* regional league; **~regierung** *f Pol., in best. Bundesländern, Österreich, Schweiz*: regional administration; **~tag** *m in der ehem. DDR und best. Bundesländern*: regional parliament elected to govern a *Bezirk*, *etwa* county council, *Am. auch* board of county commissioners

bezirzen *v/t. umg.* bewitch *allg.*

bezog *Imperf.* → *beziehen*; **bezogen** *P.P.* → *beziehen*

...bezogen *im Adj.*: **praxis~er Unterricht** practical (*od.* hands-on) training; **sach~e Argumente** relevant (*od.* pertinent) arguments; **zukunfts~** forward-looking, related to the future

Bezogene *m, f; -n, -n Scheck*: drawee

bezopft *Adj.* pig-tailed

Bezug *m; -(e)s, Bezüge* **1.** (*Überzug*) cover; *von Kissen*: cushion cover; *Kopfkissen*: pillowcase, pillow slip; **2.** *nur Sg.*; (*das Beziehen*) *von Ware*: buying; *e-r Zeitung*: subscription (+ *Gen.* to); *e-r Rente etc.*: drawing (of); **bei ~ von 25 Stück etc.** on orders of; **3.** *Bezüge* (*Einkommen*) income *Sg.*, earnings; **4.** *fig.* reference; **mit od. unter ~ auf** (+ *Akk.*) with reference to; **in ~ auf** (+ *Akk.*) (*hinsichtlich*) as far as … goes (*od.* is concerned); **~ nehmen auf** (+ *Akk.*) refer to; **~ nehmend auf Ihr Schreiben vom ...** *auch* with reference to your letter of …; **5.** *fig.* (*Verknüpfung*) connection (**zu** with, to); **der ~ war mir nicht ganz klar** *auch*

I wasn't quite sure how it *od.* they related (*od.* what the connection was); **den ~ zu etw. herstellen** make the connection (*od.* link) to s.th.; → *auch* **Beziehung** 1; **6.** *fig.* (*innerer ~, Verhältnis*) relationship (**zu** to); → *auch* **Beziehung** 5

Bezüge *Pl.* income *Sg.*, earnings

bezüglich I. *Präp.* (+ *Gen.*) (*abgek.* **bez.**); *Amtsspr.* regarding, concerning *allg.*; **~ Ihres Schreibens** with reference to your letter; **II.** *Adj.* **1.** *Ling.*: **~es Fürwort** relative pronoun; **2.** **~ auf** (+ *Akk.*) relating to, relative to; **der darauf ~e Brief** the letter relating to (*od.* concerning) that

Bezugnahme *f; -, -n; Amtsspr.*: **unter ~ auf Ihr Schreiben** with reference to your letter, further to your letter; **unter ~ auf unser Telefongespräch vom ...** *auch* following our telephone conversation of …

Bezugs|aktie *f Fin.* preemptive share; **~bedingungen** *Pl.* terms (*od.* conditions) of sale; *für Zeitungen etc.*: terms of subscription

bezugsberechtigt *Adj. von Rente etc.* entitled to draw (a pension *etc.*); *von Aktien*: **~ sind alle Aktionäre und Mitarbeiter** all shareholders and employees are beneficiaries; **Bezugsberechtigte** *m, f* beneficiary

Bezugsdauer *f* delivery period; *für Zeitung etc.*: subscription period

bezugsfertig *Adj. Wohnung*: ready for occupancy

Bezugs|größe *f* standard for comparison; **~person** *f* person to whom someone relates; *Psych.* role model; psychological parent; **Kinder brauchen e-e feste ~** children need someone they can relate to; **s-e einzige ~ ist ...** the only person he can relate (*od.* look up) to is …; **~preis** *m* purchase price; *Zeitung etc.*: subscription (price); **~punkt** *m* reference point, point of reference; (*Maßstab*) benchmark; **~quelle** *f* supply source, supplier; **~recht** *n Fin. auf Aktien*: (stock) subscription right; **mit/ohne ~** cum/ex rights

Bezugsschein *m* (ration) coupon; **bezugsscheinpflichtig** *Adj. Lebensmittel*: rationed, available only on coupons; **Benzin war ~** petrol was rationed

Bezugs|stoff *m* covering; **~system** *n* **1.** (*Koordinatensystem*) reference system; **2.** (*Denkschema*) frame of reference

bezuschussen *v/t. Amtsspr.* subsidize; **Bezuschussung** *f Amtsspr.* **1.** (*das Bezuschussen*) subsidizing, subsidization; **2.** (*Zuschusssumme*) subsidy

bezwecken *v/t.* aim at (bringing about); *Person*: auch have s.th. in mind; *Sache*: auch have as its object; **was bezweckt er mit s-m Besuch?** what's the aim (*od.* object) of his visit?; **was bezweckst du damit?** what do you hope (*od.* are you trying to) achieve by that?; **was soll das ~?** what's the point of that (meant to be)?

bezweifeln *v/t.* doubt; *verbal*: question; **ich bezweifle das** *od.* **das möchte ich ~** I doubt it, I have my doubts (about it); **ich bezweifle, dass es sich so verhält** I doubt that it's really like that; **das ist nicht zu ~** there's no doubt about that

bezwingbar *Adj. Berg*: conquerable; *Mannschaft*: beatable, defeatable; **be-**

zwingen (*unreg.*) **I.** *v/t.* **1.** (*Volk, Berg etc.*) conquer; **2.** (*besiegen: Feind, Mannschaft*) defeat; **3.** (*Schwierigkeiten, etc.*) overcome; (*Gefühle*) auch control, get the better of; (*Leidenschaften*) subdue; **II.** *v/refl.* master one's emotions (*od.* wishes); **Bezwinger** *m; -s, -*, **Bezwingerin** *f; -, -nen* conqueror; *Sport* winner; **Bezwingung** *f; mst Sg.* defeat; conquest; *von Gefühlen*: control, mastery

BGB *n; -s, kein Pl.; Abk.* (**Bürgerliches Gesetzbuch**)

BGH *m; -s, kein Pl.; Abk.* (**Bundesgerichtshof**)

BH *m; -s, -s; umg.* bra

Bhf. → **Bahnhof**

bi *Adj. Sl.* AC/DC, bi

Biathlon ['bi:ʔatlɔn] *n; -en, -en, mst Sg.; Sport* biathlon

bibbern *v/i.* tremble (**vor** + *Dat.* with); *vor Kälte*: shiver (with)

Bibel *f; -, -n*; (*Heilige Schrift*) Bible; *fig.* bible; **~auslegung** *f* **1.** biblical exegesis; **2.** *konkret*: interpretation of the Bible; **2fest** *Adj.*: **~ sein** know one's Bible; **~sprache** *f* biblical language; **~spruch** *m* biblical saying; verse from the Bible; **~stelle** *f* passage in (*od.* from) the Bible; verse from the Bible; **~stunde** *f auch Pl.* Bible study; **~text** *m* (*gesamter Text*) text of the Bible; (*Absatz*) text from the Bible; **~übersetzung** *f* translation of the Bible, Bible translation; **~vers** *m* verse from (*od.* of) the Bible; **~wort** *n*; *Pl.*: **~e** biblical saying (*od.* quotation), quotation from the Bible

Biber¹ *m; -s, -* **1.** *Zool.* beaver; **2.** *Fell*: beaver, castor

Biber² *m od. n; -s; kein Pl. Stoff*: flanelet(te); **~betttuch** *n* flannelet(te) sheet

Biber|burg *f* beaver's lodge; **~pelz** *m* beaver (fur), auch castor; **~ratte** *f* (*Pelz*) nutria, *Am. mst* coypu; **~schwanz** *m* **1.** beaver's tail; **2.** *Dachziegel*: flat (*od.* plain *od.* plane) tile

Bibliographie *f; -, -n* **1.** (*Verzeichnis*) bibliography, (**zu** of); *in Artikel*: references *Pl.*; **2.** (*Bücherkunde*) bibliography; **bibliographieren** *v/t.* (*Verzeichnis anlegen*) compile a bibliography; (*Text*) take the bibliographical details (of); **bibliographisch** *Adj.* bibliographical

bibliophil *Adj. Person*: bibliophile …; **~e Ausgabe** fine edition; **Bibliophile** *m, f; -n, -n* book-lover, bookworm *umg.*, bibliophile *förm.*

Bibliothek *f; -, -en* library; **Bibliothekar** *m; -s, -e*, **Bibliothekarin** *f; -, -nen* librarian; **bibliothekarisch** *Adj. Ausbildung*: library, concerning libraries; *Arbeiten*: librarian; **~e Laufbahn** librarian's career

Bibliotheks|gebäude *n* library (building); **~saal** *m* reading room; **~wesen** *n; nur Sg.* librarianship; *Wissenschaft*: library science

biblisch *Adj.* biblical, scriptural; **~e Geschichte** story from the Bible; **das ~e Alter von ... erreichen** *fig.* live to the ripe old age of …

Bickbeere *f nordd., Bot.* (*Heidelbeere*) bilberry, *Am.* blueberry

Bidet [bi'de:] *n; -s, -s* bidet

bieder I. *Adj.* **1.** *pej.* (*spießig*) conventional, conservative, worthy, proper; *Frisur*: proper; *Miene*: goody-goody, *Am.* goody-two-shoes, holier-than-thou *pej.*; **2.** *altm. Handwerker etc.*: honest, upright; (*einfältig*) simple;

II. *Adv. pej.*: **sich sehr ~ anziehen** dress very conservatively; **Biederkeit** *f*; *nur Sg.* **1.** *im Aussehen*: conservativeness; *im Lebensstil*: conventionality; **2.** *von Handwerker*: honesty, uprightness

Biedermann *m*; *altm. od. iro.* honest man (*od.* citizen); *pej.* (*Spießbürger*) petty bourgeois

Biedermeier *n*; *nur Sg.*; *Kunst, Lit.* Biedermeier (period *od.* style); **~sträußchen** *n* posy; **~zeit** *f* Biedermeier period

biegbar *Adj.* flexible, pliable

Biegefestigkeit *f Tech.* bending strength

biegen I. *v/t.*; *biegt, bog, hat gebogen* **1.** bend; (*krümmen*) curve; **etw. nach oben/unten ~** bend s.th. up/down; **wir müssen das Rohr irgendwie gerade ~** we have to get the pipe straight somehow; **2.** *umg. fig.* → **hinbiegen**; **3.** *Ling. österr.* (*beugen*) inflect; **II.** *v/i.*; *ist gebogen*; (*ab-, einbiegen*) turn; **nach links/rechts ~** turn left/right; **um e-e Ecke ~** turn a corner; **der Weg biegt plötzlich scharf nach links** the path suddenly veers off (*od.* turns sharply) to the left; **III.** *v/refl.* bend; *Holzbalken etc.*: warp; **der Tisch bog sich** (*war mit Essen überladen*) the table was heaving (with food); **er bog sich vor Lachen** he was doubling over (*od.* creasing up) with laughter, he was killing himself laughing *umg.*; → **Balken** 1; **Biegen** *n umg.*: **auf ~ oder Brechen** come hell or high water; **es geht auf ~ oder Brechen** it's do or die

biegsam *Adj.* **1.** *Stock*: pliable, flexible; *Körper*: supple, lithe; *Silber*: malleable, ductile; **2.** *fig. Charakter*: malleable, pliable, pliant; **Biegsamkeit** *f*; *nur Sg.* **1.** pliability, flexibility, ductility; (*Geschmeidigkeit*) suppleness, litheness; **2.** *fig.* malleability, pliability

Biegung *f* **1.** bend; (*Kurve, von Weg, Fluss*) curve; *e-r Fläche etc.*: curvature; **e-e ~ machen** curve; **2.** *Ling. österr.* (*Flexion*) inflection

Biene *f*; -, -n **1.** *Zool.* bee; **männliche ~** drone; **fleißig wie e-e ~** (as) busy as a bee; **2.** *umg. altm.* (*Mädchen*) girl, bird, *Am.* chick *Sl.*; **e-e flotte ~** a nice-looking bird, *Am.* a hot chick, a babe

Bienenfleiß *m* industriousness; sedulousness *förm.*; **bienenfleißig** *Adj.* very hard-working (*od.* industrious)

Bienen|gift *n* bee poison; **~haus** *n* apiary; **~honig** *m* honey; **~kasten** *m* (bee)hive; **~königin** *f* queen bee; **~korb** *m* (bee)hive; **~schwarm** *m* swarm of bees; **~staat** *m* colony of bees, bee colony; **~stich** *m* **1.** bee sting; **2.** *Gastr. Kuchen*: almond-covered cake filled with cream or custard; **~stock** *m* beehive; **da geht es zu wie in e-m ~** *fig.* it's swarming with people; **~volk** *n* colony of bees, bee colony; **~wabe** *f* honeycomb; **~wachs** *n* beeswax; **~wachskerze** *f* beeswax candle; **~zucht** *f* beekeeping; apiculture *förm.*; **~züchter** *m* beekeeper, apiarist *förm.*

Biennale [biɛ'naːlə] *f*; -, -n biennial (film or arts festival)

Bier *n*; -(e)s, -e beer; **helles ~** *etwa* lager, light (*od.* pale) ale, *Am. auch* light beer; **dunkles ~** *etwa* brown (*od.* dark) ale, *Am.* dark beer; **~ vom Fass** draught (*Am.* draft) beer; **ein großes/kleines ~** *Brit.* a pint / half-pint (of beer), *beim Bestellen auch*: half a pint

of bitter, lager *etc.*; **zwei ~ bitte!** two beers, please; **gehen wir noch auf ein ~?** do you fancy a beer?, *Am.* do you want to go for a beer (*od.* brew *Sl.*)?; **etw. wie sauer** *od.* **saures ~ anpreisen** *umg.* extol the virtues of s.th.(in order to get rid of it) *allg.*; **das ist nicht mein ~!** *umg. fig.* that's not my affair (*od.* problem); **das ist dein ~!** *umg. fig.* that's your business; **~bauch** *m umg.* beer belly, paunch, beer gut; **~brauer** *m* brewer; **~brauerei** *f* brewery

Bierchen *n umg.* **1.** (*gutes Bier*): **das ist ein ~!** that's quite some beer!; **2.** (*Glas Bier*) (glass of) beer

Bier|deckel *m* beer mat, *bes. Am.* (beer) coaster; **~dose** *f* beer can

bierernst *umg.* **I.** *Adj.* deadly serious; **II. Bierernst** *m* deadly seriousness

Bier|fahne *f umg.* beery breath; **e-e ~ haben** smell of beer; **~fass** *n* beer barrel; **~filz** *m* → **Bierdeckel**; **~flasche** *f* beer bottle; **~garten** *m* beer garden; **~glas** *n* beer glass; **~hahn** *m* beer tap; **~halle** *f etwa* large pub (*Am.* bar); **~hefe** *f* brewer's yeast; **~kasten** *m* beer crate (*Am.* case); **~keller** *m* **1.** *Lokal*: beer cellar; **2.** *zur Aufbewahrung*: beer cellar; **~krug** *m aus Zinn*: tankard; *aus Steingut*: beer mug, (beer) stein; **~krügel** *n österr.* tankard for a half-lit|re (*Am.* -er) of beer; **~kutscher** *m* brewer's drayman *altm.*, beer delivery driver; **fluchen wie ein ~** curse (*Am.* swear) like a sailor; **~laune** *f* jolly mood, high spirits *Pl.*; **in ~ sein** be in an exuberant mood; **~leiche** *f umg. hum.* drunk, drunken heap; **am Schluss gab es e-e Menge ~n** there were quite a few drunks littered about the place at the end; **~ruhe** *f umg.* unflappability; **sich nicht aus s-r ~ bringen lassen** remain unflappable, cool; **er saß da und las s-e Zeitung mit (e-r) ~** he sat there and read his paper, cool as a cucumber; **~schinken** *m Gastr.* (*Wurstsorte*) ham slicing sausage; **~seidel** *n* beer mug, (beer) stein; **~selig** *Adj. umg. hum.* (*Stimmung*) merry, boozed up; **~sieder** *m Beruf.* brewery worker who heats the mash; **~stube** *f Br.* small pub, *Am.* beer bar; **~suppe** *f Gastr.* gruel made of beer, sugar and egg(s); **~teig** *m Gastr.* pastry made with beer; **~wärmer** *m* beer warmer, device inserted into a glass of beer to warm it; **~wurst** *f Gastr.* smoked slicing sausage made of beef, pork and bacon; **~zelt** *n* beer tent

Biese *f*; -, -n **1.** (*Fältchen*) tuck; **2.** *an Uniformen*: *auch Pl.* piping

Biest *n*; -(e)s, -er; *pej.* **1.** (*Tier*) beast, creature; **so ein heimtückisches ~!** what a sneaky (old) devil (*od.* bugger *Sl.*)!; **2.** *umg. Kind*: brat; *Mann*: swine *Sl.*; *Frau*: cow; **freches ~** *Kind*: cheeky brat; *Frau*: cheeky cow; **faules ~** *Kind*: lazy brat; *Mann, Frau*: lazy sod (*od.* bugger *Sl.*), *Am.* lazybones; **3.** *Sache*: beast, bugger *Sl.*; **das ~ klemmt!** *Tür etc.*: the damn thing's jammed; **Biesterei** *f*; -, -en; *umg. pej.* **1.** (*Gemeinheit*) horrible thing; **2.** (*Unanständiges*) obscenity; **3.** *Dial.* (*Schufterei*) beast of a job; **biestig** *Adj. umg. pej.* **1.** (*gemein*) *Mensch* horrible, beastly *altm.*; **2.** (*sehr schlecht*) *Wetter*: foul, terrible

bieten; *bietet, bot, hat geboten* **I.** *v/t.* **1.** (*anbieten*) offer (*j-m etw.* s.o. s.th.); (*Anblick, Schwierigkeiten, Möglichkeit*) present; **was hast du mir zu ~?**

what can you offer me?; **2.** (*geben*) give; (*Schutz*) provide; **j-m Hilfe/Trost ~** help/comfort s.o.; **e-m Flüchtling Asyl ~** grant asylum to a refugee; **3.** (*gewähren*) afford; **das neue Büro bietet uns mehr Platz** the new office is more spacious; **dieser Wagen bietet mehr Komfort** this car is more comfortable; **4.** (*Programm*) show; **im Kino etc. geboten werden** be on at the cinema (*bes. Am.* movies *etc.*); **was hast du uns heute zu ~?** *auch iro.* what have you got to offer us today?, what have you got lined up for us today?; **dieser Ort hat viele Ausflugsmöglichkeiten zu ~** this spot is perfect for a wide variety of day trips; **5.** (*darbieten*) present; **der Garten bot e-n traurigen Anblick** the garden looked a sorry sight; **die Unfallstelle bot ein Bild des Grauens** the scene of the accident was a horrific sight; **6.** *sich* (*Dat.*) **etw. ~ lassen** (*Frechheit*) stand for s.th.; **das lass ich mir (von dir, ihr etc.) nicht ~!** I won't take (*od.* stand for) that (from you, her *etc.*)!; **das solltest du dir nicht ~ lassen** I wouldn't stand for it if I were you; **du hast dir genug von ihr ~ lassen** you've put up with enough from her already; **und das lässt du dir einfach ~?** and you just sit back and take it?; **II.** *v/t.* **1.** *auf Auktion*: bid; **mehr/weniger ~ als** outbid/underbid; **wer bietet mehr?** any more bids?; **bis zu 50 000 Euro ~** go as high as 50,000 euros; **2.** *Kartenspiel*: bid; **III.** *v/refl. Gelegenheit*: come up, present itself; **so e-e Gelegenheit bietet sich dir nie wieder!** it's the chance of a lifetime; **es bot sich ihr e-e traumhafter Anblick** a wonderful scene unfolded before her eyes; **e-e grauenvolle Szene bot sich i-n Augen** she was met with (*od.* confronted by) a scene of horror

Bieter *m*; -s, -, **~in** *f*; -, -nen bidder

bifokal *Adj. Opt.* bifocal; **Bifokalbrille** *f* bifocal glasses (*od.* spectacles); **e-e ~** bifocals *Pl.*, bifocal glasses *Pl.*; **Bifokalglas** *n* bifocal glass

Bigamie *f*; -, -n bigamy; **Bigamist** *m*; -en, -en bigamist

bigott *Adj. pej.* overdevout, churchy *umg.*; (*selbstgerecht*) self-righteous, (over)sanctimonious *förm.*, holier-than-thou *umg.*; (*scheinheilig*) hypocritical; **Bigotterie** *f*; -, -n; *pej* (*religiös*) bigotry; (*over)sanctimoniousness; self-righteousness; hypocrisy; → **bigott**

Bijou [bi'ʒuː] *m od. n*; -s, -s; *schw.* (piece of) jewel(le)ry; **Bijouterie** [biʒutə'riː] *f*; -, -n; *schw.* **1.** (*Laden*) jeweller's (shop); **2.** (*Schmuck*) jewel(le)ry; **Bijoutier** [biʒu'tje:] *m*; -s, -s; *schw.* jewel(l)er

Bikini *m*; -s, -s bikini

bi|konkav *Adj.* biconcave; **~konvex** *Adj.* biconvex

Bilanz *f*; -, -en **1.** *Wirts.* balance; (*Aufstellung*) balance sheet; **e-e ~ aufstellen** draw up (*od.* make out) a balance sheet; **~ machen** *umg.* check one's finances, take stock *auch fig.*; **e-e ausgeglichene ~** a harmonious balance; **die ~ frisieren** *umg.* cook the books; **2.** *fig.* (*Endergebnis*) result, outcome; (*Prüfung*) stocktaking, inventory; (*Überblick*) survey; **(die) ~ ziehen** take stock (*aus s-m Leben* of one's life); **traurige ~** sad outcome; *bei Toten*: tragic toll; **~buchhalter** *m*, **~buchhalterin** *f Wirts.* accountant

B

bilanzieren I. *v/i.* **1.** make out a balance sheet, balance; **2.** show (in the balance sheet); *das Konto bilanziert mit 365 Euro* the account shows a balance of 365 euros; **II.** *v/t.* (*Konten*) balance; **Bilanzierung** *f Wirts.* balancing, preparation of balance sheet
Bilanz|jahr *n* financial (*od.* fiscal) year; **~posten** *m* balance sheet item
bilateral *Adj.* bilateral
Bild *n*; *-(e)s, -er* **1.** a) *auch TV und fig.* picture, b) (*Gemälde*) painting; (*Porträt*) *auch* portrait, c) (*Foto*) photo, picture; (*Schnappschuss*) snap(shot); *ein ~ aufnehmen od. umg. knipsen* take a picture (*od.* photo); *hier sind ~er von unseren Ferien* here are our holiday (*Am.* vacation) snaps, d) in *Büchern:* illustration, picture, e) *Spielkarte:* court card, *Am.* face card; **2.** a) (*Ab-, Ebenbild*) *auch TV* image; *ein ~ von e-m Mädchen* a lovely girl, a peach of a girl *umg.,* b) (*Nachbildung*) effigy; **3.** (*Bühnenbild*) scene; *im Filmvorspann:* camera; *ein Trauerspiel in fünf ~ern* a tragedy in five scenes; *lebende ~er Theater:* tableaux (vivants), living pictures; **4.** (*Anblick*) picture, sight; (*Szene*) scene; *ein ~ der Zerstörung / des Grauens* a scene of destruction/horror; *ein ~ des Jammers* a picture of misery; *die Stadt bot ein verändertes ~* the city's appearance had altered considerably; *ein ~ für (die) Götter! umg. hum.* that's a sight worth seeing!; **5.** (*Vorstellung*) idea, picture; *e-s Landes, e-s Dichters etc.:* image; (*Schilderung*) picture, description, portrait; *ein falsches ~ bekommen* get the wrong idea (*od.* impression, picture); *sich* (*Dat.*) *ein ~ machen* form an impression (in one's mind) (*von* of); *von j-m/etw.:* (*sich vorstellen*) *auch* visualize *s.o./s.th.; von etw.:* (*selber ansehen*) see *s.th.* for *o.s.; sich* (*Dat.*) *ein falsches / zu optimistisches etc. ~ machen von* see *s.o./s.th.* in the wrong light / too optimistically *etc.; sich* (*Dat.*) *ein wahres od. rechtes ~ von etw. machen od. verschaffen* form a true notion of *s.th.; du machst dir kein ~ (davon)* you have no idea (of it); **6.** *rhetorisch:* image, metaphor; (*Gleichnis*) simile; *in ~ern sprechen* use a metaphor, speak metaphorically; **7.** *fig.* picture; *im ~e sein* be in the picture; *jetzt bin ich im ~e* now I get the picture, now I get it, I'm with you now *umg.; j-n ins ~ setzen* put *s.o.* in the picture (*über + Akk.* about); *kann ich dich darüber mal ins ~ setzen? auch* can I fill you in on this one?; → *düster* I 2
Bild|abtastung *f TV* scanning; **~archiv** *n* photo (*od.* picture) library; **~auflösung** *f Tech.* definition, (picture) resolution; **~aufzeichnung** *f TV* recording; **~ausfall** *m TV* picture loss; **~ausschnitt** *n* detail; **~autor** *m,* **~autorin** *f* photographer (*for a book*); **~band** *m* illustrated book; **~beilage** *f* colo(u)r supplement; **~bericht** *m* picture story, photographic report; **~berichterstatter** *m,* **~berichterstatterin** *f* photojournalist; **~beschreibung** *f* decription of a picture; **~breite** *f* picture width; **~dokument** *n* documentary photo (*od.* drawing, film, footage *etc.*); **~dokumentation** *f* picture (*od.* photo, film *etc.*) documentary; **~ebene** *f Math.* focal plane; **~einstellung** *f* (image) focus(s)ing

bilden I. *v/t.* **1.** form; (*gestalten*) *auch* shape, mo(u)ld (*alle auch den Charakter*), make; (*Satz*) make (up); (*Neuwort*) coin; *sich* (*Dat.*) *e-e Meinung ~* form an opinion; *sich* (*Dat.*) *ein Urteil über j-n/etw. ~* form an opinion of *s.o.* / about *s.th.; von e-m Wort den Plural ~* form the plural of a word; **2.** (*schaffen*) create; (*gründen*) establish, set up; (*Regierung*) form; *Vermögen ~* acquire a fortune; **3.** (*hervorbringen*) (*neue Triebe, Kruste etc.*) form, develop; **4.** (*darstellen*) (*Bestandteil etc.*) form, constitute, make up, comprise; (*Attraktion, Grenze, Gefahr etc.*) *auch* be; *e-e Ausnahme / die Regel ~* be an exception / the rule; **5.** (*bestimmte Form annehmen*): *e-n Kreis / e-e Schlange ~* form a circle/queue (*Am.* line); **6.** (*j-n*) *geistig:* educate, (*j-s Geist*) *auch* cultivate; → *gebildet* II; *das Volk politisch ~* politicize the masses, raise the political consciousness of the masses; **II.** *v/i.* broaden the mind; *Reisen bildet auch* there's nothing like travel for broadening the mind; **III.** *v/refl.* **1.** (*entstehen*) *Gruppe, Schicht etc.:* form, *Tumor etc.:* grow, develop; **2.** *geistig:* educate *o.s.,* get some culture *umg.; weitS.* broaden one's horizons; *ich bilde mich durch Lesen* I read to improve my mind; **bildend** I. *Part. Präs.* → *bilden;* **II.** *Adj.* **1.** educational; **2.** *die ~den Künste* the fine arts; *ein ~er Künstler* an artist
Bilder|atlas *m* picture atlas; **~bogen** *m Kunst:* illustrated broadsheet; **~buch** *n* picture book; *ein Wetter wie im ~ umg.* the best weather you can imagine; *Schottland wie aus dem ~* (a) picture-book Scotland
Bilderbuch|... *im Subst. umg. fig.* perfect ...; *Person: auch* model ...; *Leistung, Beispiel, auch Sport* textbook ..., copybook ...; **~ehemann** *m* a model husband, *the* perfect husband; **~hochzeit** *f* fairytale wedding; **~landschaft** *f* storybook landscape; **~landung** *f* textbook landing; **~sommer** *m* perfect summer; **~wetter** *n* perfect (*od.* glorious, unbelievable) weather
Bilder|folge *f* → *Bildfolge;* **~galerie** *f* picture gallery; **~geschichte** *f* picture story; (*Comic*) comic strip, strip cartoon; **~haken** *m* picture hook; **~rahmen** *m* picture frame; **~rätsel** *n* **1.** (*Rebus*) rebus, picture puzzle; **2.** (*Vexierbild*) picture puzzle
bilderreich *Adj.* richly illustrated; *fig. Sprache etc.:* rich in imagery
Bilder|schrift *f* pictographic system; (*Hieroglyphen*) hieroglyphics *Pl.;* **~sprache** *f* imagery (and metaphor); **~streit** *m hist.* iconoclastic controversy
Bilder|sturm *m; nur Sg.; hist.* iconoclasm; iconoclastic movement; **~stürmer** *m auch fig.* iconoclast; **~stürmerei** *f; nur Sg.; hist.* iconoclasm
Bild|fang *m Video:* frame hold; **~fläche** *f TV* image area; *Film:* screen; *von der ~ verschwinden umg. fig.* disappear from the scene, do a vanishing trick *umg.; er ist wie von der ~ verschwunden* he seems to have vanished into thin air; *auf der ~ erscheinen* (suddenly) appear on the scene, suddenly appear from nowhere; **~folge** *f* **1.** picture sequence; **2.** *nur Sg.; TV* picture frequency; **~format** *n* size of picture; *Film* frame size; **~frequenz** *f Film, TV* picture frequency
bildhaft I. *Adj.* **1.** (*visuell*) visual; **2.** *Stil:* rich in imagery; **3.** *Beschreibung etc.:*

vivid, graphic; **II.** *Adv.: etw. ~ beschreiben* give a vivid (*od.* graphic) description of *s.th.; sich* (*Dat.*) *etw. ~ vorstellen* (try and) visualize *s.th.,* conjure *s.th.* up in one's mind; **Bildhaftigkeit** *f; nur Sg.* **1.** *e-r Sprache etc.:* rich imagery (+ *Gen.* of, in); **2.** *e-r Beschreibung:* vividness, graphic nature (*od.* quality) (+ *Gen.* of)
Bildhauer *m; -s, -; Kunst* sculptor; **Bildhauerei** *f; -, kein Pl.* sculpture *ohne best. Art.;* **Bildhauerin** *f; -, -nen* (female) sculptor, sculptress; **Bildhauerkunst** *f* sculpture; **Bildhauerwerkstatt** *f* sculptor's workshop (*od.* studio)
bildhübsch *Adj.* lovely(-looking); *Gegenstand:* beautiful, lovely
Bild|journalist *m,* **~journalistin** *f* photojournalist; **~karte** *f* (*Reliefkarte*) relief map; *mit Bildern:* pictorial map; (*Ansichtskarte*) picture postcard; *Spielkarte:* court card, *Am.* face card; **~komposition** *f* composition of a (*od.* the) picture *od.* painting; **~konserve** *f Film, TV* film picture recording
bildlich I. *Adj.* pictorial, graphic; (*visuell*) visual; **~e Umsetzung** visualization; **~er Ausdruck** figurative expression, metaphor(ical expression); **II.** *Adv.: ~ gesprochen* figuratively speaking; *sich* (*Dat.*) *etw. ~ vorstellen* → *bildhaft* II; **Bildlichkeit** *f; nur Sg.* figurativeness
Bild|material *n in Buch:* illustrations *Pl.;* (*Fotos*) photos *Pl.;* **~nachweis** *m* acknowledg(e)ment; *Pl.* photo credits
bildnerisch *Adj.* **1.** artistic; *weitS.* creative; **~e Darstellung** artistic representation; **2.** (*bildhauerisch*) sculptural
Bildnis *n; -ses, -se* portrait; *auf Münzen:* effigy, head
Bild|platte *f TV* video disc, *Am.* videodisk, DVD; **~plattenspieler** *m* video disc (*Am.* videodisk) player, DVD player; **~qualität** *f* picture quality; **~reportage** *f* picture story; *TV* film documentary; **~reporter** *m,* **~reporterin** *f* photo-journalist; **~röhre** *f TV* tube, picture (*od.* cathode ray) tube; **~säule** *f etwa* statue; *vor Schreck zur ~ erstarren* freeze with terror; **~schärfe** *f* definition, sharpness *nur Sg.*
Bildschirm *m* screen; *Computer: auch* display; (*Gerät*) monitor, VDU *fachspr.* ; *umg.* (*Fernseher*) TV, the box *umg.;* **~anzeige** *f* monitor (*od.* screen) display; **~arbeitsplatz** *m* workstation; **~gerät** *n* visual display unit, VDU *fachspr.;* **~schoner** *m Computer:* screen saver; **~seite** *f* screen page; **~text** *m* **1.** *nur Sg.; System:* viewdata; **2.** *Text, Grafik:* screen text, text on the screen
Bild|schnitzer *m,* **~schnitzerin** *f; -, -nen* (wood) carver; (*auch Herrgottschnitzer*) image-maker; **~schnitzerei** *f* (wood) carving
bildschön *Adj.* beautiful; *e-e ~e Braut* a very attractive bride, a (most) beautiful bride; *es ist ~ auch* it's amazing
Bild|seite *f* **1.** *im Buch etc.:* picture page; **2.** *e-r Münze:* face, obverse; **~signal** *n* picture signal; **~stelle** *f* picture (*od.* film) library; **~stock** *m* **1.** *österr., schw., südd.* wayside shrine; **2.** (*Druckplatte*) block, cut; **~störung** *f* (TV) interference; **~streifen** *m* **1.** *Film:* film; *Fot. auch* film strip; *Bild- und Tonstreifen Film TV* picture and sound tracks; **2.** *Comic etc.:* comic (*od.* picture) strip; **~sucher** *m Fot.* viewfinder; **~suchlauf** *m Video:* picture

search; **~ rückwärts** review; **~ vorwärts** cue; **~symbol** n pictogram; *Computer:* icon

bildsynchron *Adj.* synchronized (with the picture)

Bild|tafel f plate; **~telefon** n videophone; **~übertragung** f picture transmission

Bildung f 1. *nur Sg. geistige:* education; (*Gelehrsamkeit*) learning, erudition; (*Kultur*) culture; **~ haben** be educated, be cultured, be cultivated; **ein Mensch mit ~** an educated (*od.* a cultured) person; **er hat überhaupt keine ~** he's completely uneducated (*od.* uncultured), he's got no education (*od.* culture); 2. a) *nur Sg.;* (*das Bilden*) *von Gruppen, Meinung etc.:* (*Entstehung*) formation; (*Entwicklung*) *auch* development, b) (*das Geschaffene, Entwickelte etc.*) formation, *auch* creation; 3. (*Schaffung*) creation, formation; (*Gründung*) *auch* establishment; *e-s Ausschusses:* setting up; 4. *von Neuwörtern:* coinage; *e-r Satzform etc.:* forming, formation; 5. (*Wort*) form

Bildungsanstalt f *Amtsspr.* educational establishment

bildungsbeflissen *Adj.* eager to learn, eager for knowledge

Bildungs|bürgertum n; *nur Sg.* the educated classes *Pl.;* **~chancen** *Pl.* educational opportunities; **gleiche ~** equal opportunities in education; **~drang** n → *Bildungseifer;* **~dünkel** m intellectual snobbery (*od.* conceit); **~eifer** m desire for education; **~einrichtung** f educational institution; **~fabrik** f *umg.* educational mill, *Am.* diploma mill

bildungsfähig *Adj.* educable, educatable; **Bildungsfähigkeit** f educability, educatability

bildungsfeindlich *Adj.* anti-education; *Politik etc.: auch* (educationally) retrogressive; **Bildungsfeindlichkeit** f opposition to education (*od.* culture), philistinism

Bildungs|gut n established material for general education; **etw. gehört zum allgemeinen ~** s.th. is part of the cultural heritage; **~hunger** m thirst for knowledge (*od.* education); **~ideal** n educational ideal; **~lücke** f gap in one's knowledge; **~minister** m, **~ministerin** f education minister, minister for education; *in GB:* Secretary of State for Education, Education Secretary; *in den USA:* Secretary of Education; **~ministerium** n ministry of education, education ministry; *in GB:* Department of Education and Science; *in den USA:* Department of Education; **~möglichkeit** f educational opportunity; **~monopol** n monopoly on education; **das ~ haben** *auch* control education; **~niveau** n (level of) education, educational standard(s *Pl.*); **~notstand** m education crisis; **~politik** f educational policy

bildungspolitisch *Adj.* educational, education policy ...; politico-educational

Bildungs|reform f educational reform; **~reise** f educational trip; **~roman** m novel describing the spiritual development or education of the main character, Bildungsroman; **~stand** m; *nur Sg.* level of education; **~stätte** f *geh.* educational institution; **~system** n education system; **~urlaub** m educational leave; **~weg** m 1. education; *es gibt* **verschiedene ~e** there are various types of educational paths; 2. *nur Sg.;*

zweiter ~ evening classes *Pl.* (*with a view to obtaining school or university qualifications*), *Am.* continuing education; **auf dem zweiten ~** through evening classes (*Am. auch* continuing education classes); **~wesen** n; *nur Sg.* education; **~zentrum** n educational cent|re (*Am.* -er)

Bild|unterschrift f caption; **~vorlage** f subject for a picture; **~wand** f projection screen; **~wandler** m *Opt.* image converter; **~wörterbuch** n picture *od.* pictorial dictionary; **~zähler** m *Fot.* frame counter; **~zeile** f *TV* (scanning) line; **~zuschrift** f reply with photograph enclosed

Bilge ['bɪlgə] f; -, -n; *Naut.* bilge; **~wasser** n *Naut.* bilge water

Bilharziose [bɪlhar'tsĭoːzə] f; -, -n; *Med.* bilharzia

bilingual *Adj. fachspr.* (*Sprecher*) bilingual

Billard ['bɪljart] n; -s, -e, *österr.* -s 1. (*Spiel*) billiards (*Sg.*); **e-e Partie ~ spielen** play (a game of) billiards; 2. (*Billardtisch*) billiard table; **~kugel** f billiard ball; **~queue** [-køː] n billiard cue; **~saal** m billiard room, *Am.* poolroom; **~stock** m (billiard, *Am.* pool) cue; **~tisch** m billiard (*Am.* pool) table

Billet [bɪl'jɛt] n; -(e)s, -e 1. *schw. od. altm.* (*Fahrkarte*) (train, tram, bus) ticket; (*Eintrittskarte*) (entrance) ticket; 2. *österr.* (*kurzer Brief*) note, greetings card; **Billeteur** [bɪljeˈtøːr] m; -s, -e 1. *österr.* (*Platzanweiser*) usher; 2. *schw.* (*Schaffner*) conductor; **Billeteuse** [bɪljɛˈtøːzə] f; -, -n *österr.* (*Platzanweiserin*) usherette

Billett [bɪl'jɛt] n; -(e)s, -s und -e → *Billet*

Billiarde [bɪ'liardə] f; -, -n (*1015*) quadrillion, *Brit.* thousand billions

billig I. *Adj.* 1. cheap, inexpensive; *Preis:* low, cheap; **~ er Kauf** a bargain; **das Hotel ist nicht ganz ~** *euph.* (*ziemlich teuer*) the hotel is pretty expensive; 2. *fig.* cheap, shabby; *Ausrede:* lame; *auch Rat:* poor; **~er Trost** small consolation, cold comfort; 3. *altm.* (*berechtigt, gerecht*) just; (*angemessen*) fair; → *recht*² I 1; **II.** *Adv. herstellen:* cheaply; *bekommen, verkaufen: auch* get/sell s.th. cheap(ly) (*od.* at a low price); **etw. auf ~ machen** do s.th. on the cheap; **~ wegkommen** get off cheaply (*fig.* lightly); **~ abzugeben** *Überschrift:* cheap sale, bargains; **Schallplatten ~ abzugeben** cheap (*od.* bargain) records

Billigangebot n cut-price offer, sale

billigen *v/t.* approve of; sanction *förm.;* (*beipflichten*) endorse; *amtlich:* approve; **ich kann es nicht ~, dass du so viel rauchst** I don't approve of you (-r) smoking so much; **billigend I.** *Part. Präs.* → *billigen;* **II.** *Adv.* approvingly

Billig|flug m cheap flight; **~fluganbieter** m no-frills airline; **~flugpreise** *Pl.* cut-price (*Am.* bargain) (air) fares; **~importe** *Pl.* cut-price (*od.* cheap) imports

Billigkeit f; *nur Sg.* 1. cheapness, 2. *fig.* cheapness, shabbiness; 3. *altm.* (*Berechtigung*) justness; (*Angemessenheit*) fairness, equity

Billig|kopie f cheap imitation; **~lohnland** n low-wage country; **~preis** m low price; **~preisland** n country with low prices (*od.* costs), low-cost country; **~reise** f cheap holiday (*Am.* vaca-

tion); *Pl. Koll. auch* cut-price (*Am.* bargain) travel *Sg.*

Billigstpreise *Pl.* rock-bottom prices; **etw. zu ~n verschleudern** dump s.th. at a rock-bottom price

Billigtarif m cheap rate, off-peak rate; **zum ~ reisen/telefonieren** travel/make phone calls on the cheap

Billigung f; *nur Sg.* approval, approbation; endorsement; **j-s ~ finden** meet with s.o.'s approval

Billigware f cheap goods *Pl.* (*Am.* merchandise *Sg.*)

Billion [bɪ'lioːn] f; -, -en; (*1012*) trillion; *Brit. altm.* billion, million million; **Billionstel** n; -s, - trillionth; *Brit. altm.* billionth, million millionth

bim *Interj.* ding; **~, bam** ding dong

Bimbam¹ n; -s, *kein Pl.; Kinderspr.* ding-dong

Bimbam² m *umg. hum.:* (**du**) **heiliger ~!** Good Heavens!, good gracious!, (Oh) crikey!, Gordon Bennett!, hell's bells! *Sl.*

Bimbo m; -s, -s *rassistisch:* nigger *neg!,* wog *neg!*

Bimetall n *Tech.* bimetal; (*Streifen*) bimetal(lic) strip

Bimmel f; -, -n; *umg.* 1. (small) bell *allg.;* 2. *umg. Dial.* tram bell; **~bahn** f *umg.* narrow-gauge railway (*with a warning bell*)

Bimmelei f; -, -en; *umg. pej.* (incessant) ringing *allg.;* **bimmeln** *v/i. umg.* ring *allg.;* **es hat gebimmelt** there's someone at the door *allg.*

bimsen *v/t. umg.* 1. (*lernen*) swot up, mug up, *Am.* cram; 2. *Mil.* drill hard, put *recruits etc.* through their paces; 3. (*prügeln*) beat up

Bimsstein m pumice (stone)

bin *Präs.* → *sein*¹

binär *Adj. Math., Phys. etc.* binary

Binär|code m *Computer:* binary code; **~system** n binary system; **~zahl** f binary number; **~zeichen** n binary digit; bit

Binde f; -, -n 1. *Med.* bandage; (*Armschlinge*) sling; (*Augenbinde*) blindfold; **e-e ~ über dem linken Auge tragen** have a patch over one's left eye; 2. (*Damenbinde*) sanitary towel (*Am.* napkin); 3. *am Hals:* necktie; *am Arm:* armband; **sich** (*Dat.*) **e-n hinter die ~ gießen** *od.* **kippen** *umg.* have a tipple, have a drink or two

Bindegewebe n *Anat.* connective tissue

Bindegewebs|entzündung f *Med.* fibrositis; **~schwäche** f; *mst Sg.* weakness of the connective tissue

Bindeglied n (connecting) link, connection; **fehlendes ~** *fig.* missing link

Bindehaut f *Anat.* conjunctiva; **~entzündung** f *Med.* conjunctivitis

Binde|kraft f *von Klebstoff etc.:* binding (*od.* bonding) power; **~mittel** n 1. *Tech.* bonding agent; 2. *Gastr.* thickening

binden *bindet, band, hat gebunden* **I.** *v/t.* 1. (*fesseln*) *auch fig.* tie (*an + Akk.* to); **j-n an sich ~** *fig.* tie s.o. to o.s.; **j-n an Händen und Füßen ~** bind s.o. hand and foot; **mir sind die Hände gebunden** *fig.* my hands are tied; **mich bindet nichts an diesen Ort** *fig.* I have no real ties to this place; 2. (*festmachen*) tie down (*an + Akk.* to); **e-n Strick an e-n Pfahl ~** tie a rope (up) to a post; → *gebunden* II, *Nase*¹ 5; 3. (*zusammenbinden, zubinden*) tie (up); (*Knoten*) tie; (*Schlips*) tie (a knot in); (*Strauß, Kranz*) make;

(*Schleife, Besen*) make; **Rosen zu e-m Strauß ~** tie roses into a bouquet, make a bouquet of roses; **4.** (*verpflichten*) bind, commit; **j-n mit e-m Eid ~** bind s.o. by oath; **5.** (*Buch*) bind; **zum Binden geben** have *a book* bound; **6.** *Chem.* (*Substanz*) bind; *auch Phys.* (*Wärme*) absorb; **7.** *Tech.* bond, cement; **8.** *Gastr.* (*Soße etc.*) thicken, bind; **9.** *Mus.* (*gleiche Noten*) tie; (*legato spielen*) slur; **10.** *Ling.* link; **11.** *Wirts.* (*Geldmittel*) tie up; (*Preise*) fix; **II.** *v/i.* **1.** bind; **2.** *Gastr.* bind, thicken; **3.** *Klebstoff:* stick; *Zement etc.:* harden, set; *Kunststoff:* bond; **4.** *fig.* (*Gemeinsamkeit schaffen*) create a bond; **Verpflichtungen ~** obligations bind; **III.** *v/refl.* **1.** commit o.s., tie o.s. down (**an** + *Akk.* to); *vertraglich:* bind o.s. (to); *ehelich:* tie o.s. down; *pej.* get tied down; **wir möchten uns überhaupt nicht ~** we don't want to get involved at all; **sie will sich noch nicht ~** *auch* she doesn't want to commit herself yet; **2.** *Chem.* bind, combine; **etw. bindet sich an etw.** (*Akk.*) s.th binds with s.th.

bindend I. *Part. Präs.* → **binden;** **II.** *Adj. fig. Zusage etc.:* binding (**für** upon); **wir betrachten den Liefertermin nicht als ~** we don't consider the delivery date binding; **III.** *Adv.* bindingly, for definite, *Am.* for sure; **es ist ~ vorgeschrieben, dass ...** it is stipulated that ...

Binder *m*; *-s*, - **1.** *altm.* (*Krawatte*) tie *allg.*; **2.** *fachspr.* (*Bindemittel*) binder

Binde|strich *m* hyphen; **hat es e-n ~?** has it got a hyphen?, is it hyphenated?; **~wort** *n*; *Pl.:* *-wörter; Ling.* conjunction

Bindfaden *m* string; *starker:* twine; *dicker:* cord; **zum Nähen und Schnüren:** packthread; **ein ~** a piece of (*od.* some) string; **es regnet Bindfäden** *fig.* it's pouring, it's coming down in buckets *umg.*, the rain is coming down in sheets

Bindung *f* **1.** *zu j-m:* (close) relationship (**zu** with, to); (*Verbundenheit*) bond (**an** + *Akk.* with); *auch Pol.* ties *Pl.* (to, with); *an etw.:* attachment (to); **2.** (*Verpflichtung*) commitment, obligation; **e-e ~** (*od.* **~en**) **eingehen** commit o.s., tie o.s. down (**mit** to); **ohne ~(en)** *Person:* without (any) obligation(s); *eheliche etc.:* unattached; **3.** (*Skibindung*) binding; **4.** *Chem., Phys., Tech.* bond(ing); *Weberei:* weave; **5.** (*Atombindung*) linkage (*auch Bio.*); **6.** *Phys.* absorption; (*Verschmelzung*) fusion; **7.** *Mus.* ligature

Bindungsangst *f* fear of getting too involved (with anyone), fear of commitment

bindungsfähig *Adj. Mensch:* capable of commitment; **nicht ~ sein** be incapable of having a (personal) relationship; **Bindungsfähigkeit** *f* ability to form a (personal) relationship

Bingo ['bɪŋgo] *n*; *-(s)*, *kein Pl.* bingo

binnen *Präp.* within; **~ kurzem** before long, within a short space of time; **~ acht Tagen** within a (*od.* the) week

binnendeutsch I. *Adj. Handel etc.:* internal, domestic (German); **II. Binnendeutsch** *n* German (as) spoken in Germany, German German *umg*

Binnen|fischerei *f* freshwater fishing; **~gewässer** *Pl.* inland waters; **~hafen** *m* inland (*od.* river) port; **~handel** *m* domestic (*od.* home) trade

Binnenland *n* interior, inland area; **im ~** inland; **binnenländisch** *Adj.* inland ...

Binnen|markt *m* home (*od.* domestic) market; *EU:* single market; **~meer** *n* inland sea; **~reim** *m Lit.* internal rhyme; **~schiffer** *m* crew member (on inland waterways), (*auf Schleppkahn*) bargeman; **~schifffahrt** *f* inland navigation; **~see** *m* inland lake; **~staat** *m* inland (*od.* landlocked) state *od.* country; **~verkehr** *m* inland traffic; **~wanderung** *f* internal migration; **~wirtschaft** *f* domestic economy; **~zoll** *m* inland duty

Binom *n*; *-s*, *-e Math.* binomial; **binomisch** *Adj. Math.* binomial

Binse *f*; *-*, *-n* **1.** *Bot.* rush; **2.** *umg fig.:* **in die ~n gehen** *Plan etc.:* go up in smoke, go for a burton *Brit.* (*gesprochen*); *Geld:* go down the drain

Binsenweisheit *f* truism, commonplace, platitude

Bio *f*, *-*, *kein Pl.; Abk. umg.* (*Fach*) biology, bio(l) *Jugendspr.*

bio *Adj. umg.:* **das ist alles ~** it's all organic food

Bio|abfall *m* biological waste; **²aktiv** *Adj. Waschmittel:* biological; **~bauer** *m* organic farmer; **Gemüse vom ~** organic vegetables; **~chemie** *f* biochemistry; **~chemiker** *m*, **~chemikerin** *f* biochemist; **²chemisch** *Adj.* biochemical; **²dynamisch** *Adj.* biodynamic; **~gas** *n* biogas, *oft auch* methane

biogen *Adj.* biogenic

Biograph *m*; *-en*, *-en* biographer; **Biographie** *f* biography; **Biographin** *f*; *-*, *-nen* biographer; **biographisch** *Adj.* biographical

Bio|kost *f* organic food; **~laden** *m Brit.* wholefood shop, *Am.* health food store; **~Lebensmittel** *Pl.* organic food, *Am.* health food

Biologe *m*; *-n*, *-n* biologist; **Biologie** *f*; *-*, *nur Sg.* biology; **Biologin** *f*; *-*, *-nen* biologist

biologisch I. *Adj.* biological (*auch aus Naturstoffen hergestellt*); **~er Anbau** organic farming (*od.* gardening); **Gemüse aus ~em Anbau** organically-grown vegetables; **~e Waffen** biological weapons; **~e Abfallbeseitigung** organic waste disposal; **II.** *Adv.:* **~ abbaubar** biodegradable; **biologisch-dynamisch** *Adj. Agr.* organic, biological

Biomasse *m*; *nur Sg.* biomass

Biomedizin *f* biomedicine

Biometrie *f*; *-*, *kein Pl.* biometry, biometrics (*mst V. im Sg.*); **biometrisch** *Adj.* biometric

Bionik [bi'o:nɪk] *f*; *nur Sg.* bionics (*V. im Sg.*); **bionisch** *Adj.* bionic

Bio|physik *f* biophysics (*V. im Sg.*); **~physiker** *m*, **~physikerin** *f* biophysicist

Biopsie *f*; *-*, *-; Med.* biopsy

Bio|rhythmus *m* biorhythm; **~sphäre** *f*; *nur Sg.* biosphere; **~technik** *f*; *nur Sg.* biotechnology, bioengineering; **²technisch** *Adj.* biotechnological; **~tonne** *f* compost bin

Biotop [bio'to:p] *m od. n*; *-s*, *-e* biotope

Biowissenschaft *f* life science, bioscience; **Biowissenschaftler** *m*, **Biowissenschaftlerin** *f* bioscientist

bipolar *Adj.* bipolar; **Bipolarität** *f*; *nur Sg.* bipolarity

Birke *f*; *-*, *-n* **1.** *Baum:* birch (tree); **2.** *nur Sg.; Holz:* birch(wood)

Birken|grün *n* birch branches *od.* greenery; **ein Strauß mit frischem ~** a

bouquet with fresh birch leaves; **~hain** *m* birch grove; **~holz** *n* birch(wood); **~pilz** *Bot.* birch boletus; **~wald** *m* birch(wood) forest, birch wood; **~wasser** *n*; *Pl.:* *-wässer* hair lotion (*made from birch sap*)

Birk|hahn *m Orn.* black cock; **~huhn** *n* black grouse

Birma *n*; *-s Geog.* Burma; **Birmane** *m*; *-n*, *-n*, **Birmanin** *f*; *-*, *-nen* Burmese; **birmanisch** *Adj.* Burmese

Birnbaum *m* **1.** *Baum:* pear tree; **2.** *nur Sg.; Holz:* pear(-)wood

Birne *f*; *-*, *-n* **1.** *Baum:* (*Baum*) pear tree; **2.** *Etech.* (electric) (light) bulb; **3.** *umg. fig.* (*Kopf*) noddle, nut, *Am.* noggin; **e-e weiche ~ haben** be (going) soft in the head

birnenförmig *Adj.* pear-shaped

Birnensaft *m* pear juice

bis I. *Präp.* **1.** *bei Zeitdauer:* till, until; **~ heute** so far, to date; *betont:* to this day; **~ dato** *förm.* to date *allg.*; **~ jetzt** up to now; so far; **~ jetzt noch nicht** not (as) yet; **ich habe ~ jetzt nichts gehört** I haven't heard anything yet (*od.* so far); **~ dahin** until then; (*in der Zwischenzeit*) in the meantime; → *auch* 2; **~ auf weiteres** for the present; **~ in die Nacht** into the night; **~ spät in die Nacht** until the early (*od.* wee) hours; **die Sonne schien ~ zum Sonntag** the sun shone (up) until Sunday; **~ zum späten Nachmittag** till late in the afternoon; **~ vor einigen Jahren** until a few years ago; **~ Ende Mai habe ich zu tun** I'm busy until the end of May, *Am. auch* I'm busy through May; **~ zum Ende** (right) to the end; **~ wann wird es dauern?** how long will it last?; *mit Datum:* **in der Zeit vom ... ~ ...** between ... and ...; **von morgens acht ~ abends sechs** from eight in the morning until six at night; **von Montag ~ Freitag** Monday to (*Am. auch* through) Friday; **~ einschließlich/ausschließlich** up to and including / not including; **~ morgen/Montag!** see you tomorrow/(on) Monday; **~ dann/später!** *umg.* see you then (*od.* later) /later; **2.** (*~ spätestens*) by; *mit Verbkonstruktion:* by the time ...; **~ er zurückkommt, ist es schon dunkel** by the time he gets back, it will be dark; **es muss ~ Freitag eingereicht werden** it has to be handed in by Friday; **~ wann ist es fertig?** when will it be ready by?; **~ wann willst du es wieder haben?** by when do you want it back?; **die Fotos sind ~ frühestens übermorgen fertig** the photos will be ready the day after tomorrow at the earliest; **alle ~ ... eingegangenen Bewerbungen** all applications received by (*od.* before) ...; **~ dahin werden wir fertig sein** *etc.* by then, by that time; **3.** *räumlich:* to, up to, as far as; **~ hierher** up to here; **~ hierher und nicht weiter** *auch fig.* this far and no further; **~ dahin** as far as that (*od.* there); **~ dahin ist es nicht weit** that's not far; **~ wohin?** how far?; **~ ans Knie** up to one's knees; *Kleid:* down to the knee; **von hier ~ New York** from here to New York; **wie weit ist es noch ~ nach Innsbruck?** how far is it to Innsbruck?, how far have we got to go (before we get) to Innsbruck?; **weiterlesen ~ Seite zwölf** continue to read to page twelve; **~ vor das Haus fahren** drive up to the front door of the house, drive (right) up to the house; **er folgte mir ~ ins Hotelfoyer** he followed me (right) into the lobby of the hotel (*nicht weiter*: as far as the lobby of the hotel); *der Blick reicht ~ weit ins Tal* the view stretches right into the valley; *der Ball flog ~ hinter den Zaun* the ball went over the fence; → *hier* 1, *oben* 1; **4.** *Zahlenangabe*: ~ *zu 100 Mann* up to ..., as many as ...; ~ *zu 9 Meter hoch* up to ..., as high as ...; ~ *20 zählen* count (up) to 20; *Kinder ~ zwölf Jahre* children up to the age of twelve *od.* up to twelve years of age; ~ *auf das letzte Stück* down to the last bit (*Kuchen etc.*: piece); **5.** ~ *aufs Äußerste* to the utmost; ~ *auf die Haut nass werden* be soaked to the skin; ~ *auf weiteres* until further notice; ~ *ins Kleinste* down to the last detail; ~ *zur Tollkühnheit* to the point of rashness; ~ *zum Überdruss* ad nauseam; → *Bewusstlosigkeit etc.*; **6.** (*mit Ausnahme von*): ~ *auf* except, with the exception of; *alle ~ auf einen* all except (*od.* but) one; ~ *auf drei sind alle gekommen* all except three have come; → *letzt...* 1; **II.** *Konj.* **1.** till, until; (~ *spätestens*) by the time; *es wird e-e Zeitlang dauern*, ~ *er es merkt* it will take a while for him to find out (*od.* before he finds out); *er kommt nicht*, ~ *ich ihn rufe* he won't come until (*od.* unless) I call him; *du gehst nicht*, ~ *du aufgeräumt hast* you're not going until (*od.* before) you've tidied (*Am.* cleaned) up; ~ *dass der Tod euch scheidet* until death do you part; ~ *ich das gefunden habe! verärgert*: if I don't find it soon!, by the time I find it ...!; **2.** *zwischen Zahladjektiven*: to; *7 ~ 10 Tage* from 7 to 10 days, between 7 and 10 days; *5 ~ 6 Wagen* 5 to 6 cars; **3.** *heiter ~ wolkig / sonnig ~ leicht bedeckt im Wetterbericht*: generally fine, cloudy in places / sunny with light cloud cover; *die Tendenz war lustlos ~ verhalten an der Börse* the tendency was slack to cautious

Bisam *m*; *-s*, *-e und -s* **1.** *Zool.* musk; **2.** *Pelz*: musquash *od.* muskrat (fur); **~ratte** *f Zool.* muskrat

Bischof *m*; *-s*, *Bischöfe*, *Bischöfin* *f*; *-*, *-nen Reli.* bishop; **bischöflich** *Adj.* episcopal

Bischofs|amt *n Reli.* episcopate, bishopric; **~konferenz** *f* bishops' conference; **~mütze** *f* mit|re (*Am.* -er); **~sitz** *m* episcopal see, diocesan town; **~stab** *m* crosier, crozier; **~stuhl** *m* cathedra, bishop's seat; **~synode** *f* episcopal synod, synod of bishops; **~tracht** *f* pontificals

Bisexualität *f*; *nur Sg.*; *Bio. Med.* bisexuality; **bisexuell** *Adj.* bisexual

bisher *Adv.* up to now, so far; ~ (*noch*) *nicht* not (as) yet; *wie* ~ as before, as always; *das ~ beste Ergebnis* the best result so far

bisherig *Adj. Ergebnisse, Leistungen etc.*: so far, up to now, up till (*od.* until) now (*alle nachgestellt*); (*vorhergehend*) previous, former; (*jetzig*) present; *das Amt etc. aufgebend*: outgoing, retiring; *mein ~es Zimmer* the room I had till now; *die ~en Regelungen gelten nicht mehr* the regulations previously (*od.* presently) in force are no longer valid; *nach m-n ~en Erfahrungen* in my experience (to date)

Biskaya [bɪsˈkaːja] *f*; *-*, *kein Pl.*; *Geog.*: *die ~ od. der Golf von ~* the Bay of Biscay

Biskuit [bɪsˈkviːt] *n*, *m*; *-(e)s*, *-s auch*

-e; *Gastr.* (fatless) sponge (cake); **~boden** *m Gastr.* flan base; **~rolle** *f Gastr.* Swiss roll; **~teig** *m Gastr.* sponge mixture

bislang *Adv.* → **bisher**

Bismarckhering *m Gastr.* Bismarck (*od.* marinaded) herring

Bison *m*; *-s*, *-s*; *Zool.* bison

Biss *m*; *-es*, *-e* bite (*auch Bisswunde*, *Med. und fig. Schärfe*); *der ~ ist von e-m Hund* the bite is from a dog, it is a dog bite; *sie spielten mit/ohne ~ fig.* they played with a lot of fight (*od.* guts) / they didn't put up much of a fight

biss *Imperf.* → **beißen**

bisschen I. *Adj.*: *ein ~* a (little) bit of; a little; *bei Flüssigkeiten*: *auch* a drop of; *ein kleines ~* a tiny bit, just a little (bit); *das ~ Geld, das sie hat* what little money she has; *wegen dem ~ Dreck hat sie sich aufgeregt?* she got upset about a bit of dirt?; *kein ~ Geld etc.* no money *etc.* at all; *sie hatte kein ~ Angst* she wasn't scared at all; **II.** *Adv.*: *ein ~* a bit; slightly; *kein ~ müde* not (in) the least bit tired, not tired at all; *ein ~ viel* a bit (*od.* little) (too) much; *das ist ein ~ zu viel verlangt* that's asking a bit much; *wenn du ein ~ wartest* if you wait a while (*od.* hang on a bit *umg.*); *ein ~ schneller!* a bit (*od.* little) faster, (*mach schnell*) get a move on! *umg.*; **III.** *substantiviert*, *aber kleingeschrieben*: a (little) bit; a little; *kein ~* not a bit; *ach du liebes ~! umg.* goodness (me)!, good grief!

Bissen *m*; *-s*, *-* **1.** bite (*von* of); *winziger*: morsel; *schmackhafter*: titbit, *Am.* tidbit; *ich brachte keinen ~ hinunter* I couldn't eat a thing; *er rührte keinen ~ an* he didn't touch (*od.* eat) a thing; *mir blieb der ~ im Hals stecken fig.* I nearly choked, it went down the wrong hole (*od.* tube) *umg.*; *sich* (*Dat.*) *den letzten ~ vom Mund absparen fig.* pinch and scrape, scrimp and save, go short o.s., watch every penny one spends; *das ist ein fetter ~ umg. fig.* (*ein gutes Geschäft*) that's a good deal; **2.** (*Imbiss*) bite, snack; *nur schnell e-n ~ essen od. nehmen* just have a quick bite (*od.* snack)

bissig *Adj.* **1.** *Hund*: vicious; *der Hund ist ~ / nicht ~ auch* the dog bites / doesn't (*od.* won't) bite; *Vorsicht, ~er Hund!* beware of the dog; **2.** *fig. Bemerkung*: cutting, caustic, waspish; *bes. Witz*: *auch* mordant; *Kritik*: scathing; *Person*: snappy; *ein ~er Spieler Sport* an attacking player; **Bissigkeit** *f* **1.** *nur Sg.*; *von Bemerkung*: acerbity; *von Kritik*: sharpness; *von Person*: snappiness; **2.** (*bissige Bemerkung*) *mst Pl.* cutting (*od.* caustic) remark

Bisswunde *f* bite

bist *Präs.* → **sein¹**

Bistro [ˈbɪstro] *n*; *-s*, *-s* bistro; **~stuhl** *m* bistro chair (*made of cast iron*); **~tisch** *m* bistro table (*made of cast iron*)

Bistum *n*; *-s*, *Bistümer*; *kirchl.* bishopric, diocese; *e-e Kirche im ~ Limburg* a church in the diocese of Limburg

bisweilen *Adv. geh.* at times, from time to time, occasionally *allg.*

Bit *n*; *-(s)*, *-(s)*; *EDV* bit; **~dichte** *f* bit density; **~rate** *f* bit rate

Bittbrief *m* petition

Bitte *f*; *-*, *-n* request; (*Anliegen*) *auch kirchl.* petition; *dringende ~* urgent appeal (*od.* plea) (*an* + *Akk.* to); *e-e*

~ an j-n richten request *s.th.* of *s.o.*; *dringende*: appeal to *s.o.*; *auf m-e ~* at my request; *ich habe e-e (große) ~ an Sie* I want to ask you a (big) favo(u)r

bitte *Interj.* **1.** *anfragend*: please; ~, *gib mir die Zeitung* would you pass me the paper, please; **2.** *Antwort auf e-e Bitte*: *darf ich mal? - (aber) ~! od. ~ sehr* of course, certainly, go ahead *umg.*, by all means, please do *förm.*; **3.** *Antwort auf ein Angebot*: *möchtest du noch einen Kaffee? - (ja,) ~* yes please; **4.** *Antwort auf*: *danke od. vielen Dank - (sehr od. schön)* that's all right (*od.* OK), don't mention it, not at all, my pleasure, you're welcome, *Am.* (that's) alright; **5.** *Antwort auf*: *Entschuldigung! - (aber) ~!* it's all right (*Am.* alright), *bes. Am.* that's okay, no problem *umg.*; **6.** *nachfragend*: *wie ~?* sorry(, what did you say)?, pardon?, I beg your pardon? *förm.*, what? *umg.*, *Am.* excuse me?; **7.** *bei höflicher Entschuldigung*: *entschuldigen Sie ~, wo ...* please excuse (*od.* forgive me), but where ...; **8.** *am Telefon, im Büro etc.*: *ja, ~? (Sie wünschen?)* yes?, can I help you?; **9.** *beim Anbieten* (*mst unübersetzt*): ~ (*sehr od. schön*) there you are, there you go *umg.*; **10.** *hinweisend*: *~(!)* there you are; **11.** *triumphierend*: *~!, auch na ~!* what did I say?, didn't I tell you?, told you so!; **12.** *Aufforderung zum Eintreten*: (*ja*) *~!* come in, please, enter; *beim Vorlassen*: ~ after you, go ahead; **13.** *~! bei Filmaufnahmen*: action!

bitten *vt/i.*; *bittet, bat, hat gebeten* **1.** ask (*j-n um etw.* *s.o.* for *s.th.*); (*ersuchen*) request (*s.th.* of *s.o.*); *dringend*: beg; (*anflehen*) implore, beseech, pray; *immer wieder, belästigend*: solicit; *demütig*: supplicate; ~ *um* (*bemühen*) trouble *s.o.* for; ~ *für* (+ *Akk.*) intercede for; *darf ich um Ihren Namen ~?* would you mind telling me your name?; *darf ich Sie um Feuer ~?* may I trouble you for a light?; *dürfte ich Sie ~* could I ask you (*zu* + *Inf.* to + *Inf.*), would you mind (+ *Ger.*); ... *werden gebeten zu* (+ *Inf.*) ... are asked (*od.* requested) to (+ *Inf.*); → *dringend III*; *er lässt sich nicht lange ~* he doesn't have to be asked twice; *wenn ich ~ darf* if you don't mind; *ich bitte darum* if you wouldn't mind; *ich bitte dich! empört*: (well,) really!; *das ist doch selbstverständlich, unmöglich etc.* oh, come on, not at all; *darum möchte ich aber auch gebeten haben! umg.* I should jolly well hope so, *Am.* I would (certainly) hope so; *ich muss doch sehr ~! empört*: I beg your pardon!; ~ *und betteln* beg and plead; *sich aufs Bitten verlegen* resort to pleading; *wir ~ dich, erhöre uns im Gebet*: hear us, we beseech Thee, Lord hear our prayer; **2.** (*einladen*): *j-n zu sich ~* ask *s.o.* to come and see one (*od.* to come into the office *etc.*); *j-n zum Essen ~* invite *s.o.* (round, *Am.* over) to dinner; *j-n zu Tisch ~* ask *s.o.* to come to table; *Herr X lässt ~* Mr. X would like to (*od.* can) see you now; *darf ich ~?* a) *e-n Weg weisend*: would you come this way, please?, b) *beim Tanzen*: may I have (the pleasure of) this dance?, c) *beim Essen*: dinner is served; **bittend I.** *Part. Präs.* → **bitten**; **II.** *Adj.* pleading; *stärker*: beseeching

bitter I. *Adj.* **1.** bitter; ~ *schmecken* taste bitter, have a bitter taste; **2.** *fig.*

B

Kälte etc.: bitter; **~e Not** dire need; **e-n ~en Nachgeschmack hinterlassen** leave a sour aftertaste (od. taste in one's mouth); **~e Tränen weinen** weep bitterly; **j-m ~e Vorwürfe machen** reproach s.o. bitterly; **es ist mein ~er Ernst** I (really) mean it, I'm deadly serious; **bis zum ~en Ende** right to the bitter end; **das ist ~** that's hard (od. tough umg.); **das war eine ~e Lehre** that was a tough lesson (to learn); **er musste die ~e Erfahrung machen, dass ...** he had to find out the hard way that ...; **II.** fig. Adv. bitterly; **etw. ~ nötig haben** need s.th. badly, be in desperate (od. dire) need of s.th.; **sich ~ beklagen** complain bitterly; **es hat sich ~ gerächt** I etc. had to pay dearly for it

bitter|böse Adj. (zornig) furious, livid umg.; (schlimm) wicked; **ein ~s Weib** a villainous woman; **~ernst** Adj. dead serious; **es ist mir ~ (damit)!** I'm serious, I mean it, I'm dead serious (about it); **~kalt** Adj. bitter(ly) cold

Bitterkeit f; nur Sg.; auch fig. bitterness

bitterlich I. Adv.: **~ weinen** weep bitterly; **~ frieren** freeze to the bone; **II.** Adj. (leicht bitter) slightly (od. rather) bitter

Bittermandelöl n Gastr. bitter almond oil; Chem. benzaldehyde

Bitternis f, -, -se **1.** bitterness; **2.** Pl. geh.: **die ~se des Lebens** the trials and tribulations of life

Bitter|salz n Pharm. Epsom salts Pl.; **~schokolade** f plain chocolate; **~stoff** m bitter constituent

bittersüß Adj. auch fig. bittersweet

Bitt|gang m **1.** kirchl. pilgrimage; (Prozession) Rogation procession; **2.** fig., geh. approach (zu to; wegen for); **e-n ~ machen** (go to) request s.th.; **~gesuch** n petition; **~schrift** f petition; **~steller** m, -s, -, **~stellerin** f, -, -nen petitioner

Bitumen n; -s, - auch Bitumina; Chem. bitumen

bitzeln v/i. Dial. **1.** (sprudeln) von Mineralwasser etc.: fizz, tingle; **das Wasser bitzelt zu sehr** the water is too fizzy (Am. auch bubbly); **2.** cut into small pieces

Biwak n; -s, -s auch -e bivouac; **biwakieren** v/i. bivouac

bizarr Adj. Einfälle, Mensch: bizarre, strange, weird, grotesque

Bizeps m; -(es), -e; Anat. biceps

Blabla n; -s, kein Pl.; umg. rubbish, hot air, blah-blah, twaddle altm.

Blackbox, Black Box ['blɛkbɔks] f, -, -es; Tech. black box

Black-out, Blackout ['blɛkˌaʊt] m od. n; -(s), -s **1.** a) (Erinnerungsverlust) (mental) blackout; **ich hatte e-n ~** my mind went completely blank (od. was a complete blank), I had a (mental) blackout; (momentane Unzurechnungsfähigkeit) (temporary od. mental) blackout; temporary lapse, b) Med. durch Kreislaufstörung: blackout; **e-n ~ haben** auch black out, pass out; **2.** Theat. blackout; **3.** a) Mil. (Verdunkelung) blackout, b) (totaler Stromausfall) power cut; **4.** Phys. Raumfahrt: blackout

blaffen, bläffen v/i. umg. Hund: yap, yelp; Person: snap; **Blaffer, Bläffer** m; -s, -; umg. grump

Blag n; -s, -en, **Blage** f; -, -n; umg. pej. brat

Blähbauch m swollen belly

blähen ['blɛːən] **I.** v/i.: Zwiebeln ~

onions give you wind (Am. gas); **II.** v/t. (Bauch, Segel etc.) swell; (Segel, Gardine etc.) auch fill; (Nüstern) dilate; **III.** v/refl. fill out; fig. puff o.s. up; **Blähung** ['blɛːʊŋ] f wind Sg., flatulence Sg. förm.; **~en haben** have wind (Am. gas)

blamabel Adj. disgraceful; Ergebnis etc.: auch shaming; (peinlich) embarrassing; stärker: humiliating; **Blamage** [bla'maːʒə] f, -, -n disgrace; **es war e-e ~** (peinlich) it was (really) embarrassing; **es war e-e (große) ~ für ihn** he made a (real) fool of himself; **blamieren I.** v/t. (Begleiter etc.) show s.o. up; (lächerlich machen) make a fool of s.o.; **II.** v/refl. show o.s. up (vor + Dat. in front of); (sich lächerlich machen) make a fool of o.s.

blanchieren [blã'ʃiːrən] v/t. Gastr. blanch

blank Adj. **1.** (leuchtend) shiny, shining; (~ geputzt) auch polished; Schuhe: shiny; **~ putzen** polish (od. clean) s.th. till it shines (Schuhe, Messing etc.) put a good shine on; **2.** (abgewetzt) shiny (with wear); **3.** (nackt, bloß) Boden, Körper etc.: bare; Schwert, Degen: naked; **4.** fig. Unsinn, Neid etc.: pure, sheer; **das ist doch ~er Unsinn** that's sheer (od. just plain) nonsense!; **5.** im Kartenspiel: **e-e Karte ~ haben** have only one card of a suit, have a singleton heart/spade etc.; **6.** umg. (pleite): **~ sein** be broke

blanko Wirts. **I.** Adj. blank; **II.** Adv. in blank; **j-m e-n Scheck ~ geben** give s.o. a blank cheque (Am. check)

Blanko|scheck m Fin. blank cheque (Am. check); **~unterschrift** f blank signature; **~vollmacht** f Wirts. full discretionary power(s Pl.); fig. carte blanche

Blankvers m Lit. blank verse

Bläschen n; -s, - **1.** Anat., Bot. vesicle; **2.** Med. auf der Haut: (small) blister; eitrig: pustule; **~ausschlag** m blistery rash, blisters Pl.

Blase f, -, -n **1.** (Luft♀) bubble; ~ werfen od. ziehen Tapete: blister; Teig: get frothy; fig. cause a few (od. a lot of) problems; **2.** Med. (auf der Haut) blister (an + Dat. on); sich (Dat.) **~n laufen** get blisters on one's feet from walking; **3.** Anat. bladder; **er hat's mit der ~** umg. he's got bladder trouble, he's having trouble with his waterworks umg.; **4.** Chem. still; **5.** (Sprechblase) balloon, (speech) bubble; **6.** Tech. (Gießblase) blow(n) hole, bubble, hollow, flaw; Glasherstellung: bleb, nodule, bubble; beim Schweißen: blow(-)hole; **7.** umg. pej. (Bande) crowd, lot, shower

Blasebalg m; Pl.: Blasebälge (pair of) bellows Pl.

blasen; bläst, blies, hat geblasen **I.** v/t. **1.** blow; (Suppe etc.) blow on; Mus. (spielen) play; (Blechblasinstrument zum Tönen bringen) blow; **jetzt will ich mal zum Aufbruch ~** umg. now it's really time to get a move on; → **Marsch**[1] 3, **Trübsal**, **2.** vulg.: **j-m e-n ~** suck s.o. off Sl., give s.o. a blow job Sl., (bes. Am.) give s.o. head Sl.; **II.** v/i. auch Wind: blow; **es bläst ganz schön** there's quite a wind (going)

Blasen|bildung f **1.** Med., Tech. blistering; **2.** (Lack) cissing; Etech. (Batterie) formation of bubbles, Am. gassing; **~entzündung** f Med. cystitis, bladder infection; **~katarrh** m Med. cystitus ohne best. Art.; **~leiden** n

Med. bladder complaint; **~spiegelung** f Med. cystoscopy; **~sprung** m Med. rupture of the fe(o)tal membranes, breaking of waters; **~stein** m Med. bladder stone

Bläser m; -s, - **1.** Mus. wind player; **die ~** the wind (section); **2.** Tech. blower; fan

blasiert Adj. pej. smug, pompous, blasé; **Blasiertheit** f **1.** nur Sg. Wesensart: smugness, blasé attitude; **2.** Äußerung: pomposity

blasig Adj. (Flüssigkeit) full of bubbles, aerated; (Teig) frothy; (Haut) blistered

Blas|instrument n Mus. wind instrument; **~kapelle** f Mus. brass band; **~musik** f music for brass band, brass band music; **am Sonntag gibt es ~** a brass band will be playing on Sunday; **~orchester** n Mus. brass band

Blasphemie [blasfe'miː] f; -, -n blasphemy; **blasphemisch** Adj. blasphemous

Blasrohr n **1.** (Waffe) blowpipe; **2.** (Spielzeug) peashooter; **3.** (Glasherstellung) glassblower's pipe, blowing iron

blass Adj. **1.** (fast weiß) pale (vor + Dat. with); krank aussehend: pallid, wan; fig. colo(u)rless; **~ vor Neid** fig. green with envy; **2.** (nicht kräftig) Farbe: pale; **3.** (schwach) Lichtschein: pale, faint; Schimmer: vague; **~e Erinnerung** dim recollection; → **Ahnung** 2, **Schimmer** 2; **4.** (rein) sheer, pure; **blassblau** Adj. pale (od. fading) blue, auch Cambridge blue; **Blässe** f, -, kein Pl. paleness, pallor; **blassgrün** Adj. pale green

Blässhuhn n Orn. coot

blässlich Adj. rather (od. slightly) pale

blassrosa Adj. pale pink

Blatt n; -(e)s, Blätter **1.** Bot. leaf; von Blüte: petal; Kelch: sepal; **kein ~ vor den Mund nehmen** fig. not mince matters (od. one's words); **2.** Buch: leaf; (Seite) page; (Papier) sheet; **hast du ein ~ Papier?** do you have a piece of paper?; **500 ~ Papier** 500 sheets of paper; **ist das Blatt voll geschrieben?** have you used (od. filled) up that page?; **das steht auf e-m anderen ~** fig. a) that's a completely different matter,, b) that's another story umg.; → **unbeschrieben**; **3.** Mus. (Notenblatt) sheet; **vom ~ spielen/singen** sight-read / sight-sing; **etw. vom ~ spielen/singen** auch play/sing s.th. at sight; **4.** (Zeitung) (news)paper; **5.** Kunst: (Druck) print; (Zeichnung) drawing; (Stich) engraving; **6.** a) (Spielkarte) card; (gezogene Karten) hand; **ein gutes/schlechtes ~ haben** have a good/bad hand; **das ~ hat sich gewendet** fig. the tide has turned, b) Spielfarbe im deutschen Kartenspiel: spade; **7.** Tech. plate, lamina, (Folie) foil; Säge, Ruder etc.: blade (auch Flug.); **8.** Mus. für Blasinstrumente: reed; **9.** Jagd: shoulder

Blattader f Bot. leaf vein

Blättchen n **1.** Anat., Bot., Chem. lamella; Tech. membrane; **2.** slip (of paper); **3.** local newspaper (od. rag umg.)

blätterig Adj. leafy; Teig: flaky; **...blätterig** im Adj. → **...blättrig**

blättern I. v/i. **1.** **~ in** (+ Dat.) in e-m Buch: leaf through; in e-m Fotoalbum, e-r Illustrierten: have a look at; **2.** Computer: scroll; **3.** (abblättern) Farbe, Anstrich: flake (off); (ausbrechen) *Töpferware*: chip (off); **der Verputz blättert von der Decke** the plaster is crumbling off the ceiling; **II.** *v/t.* (*hinblättern*): **Geldscheine / Spielkarten auf den Tisch ~** count out notes (*Am.* bills) / deal (playing) cards on the table

Blätter|pilz *m Bot.* agaric; **~teig** *m Gastr.* flaky (*od.* puff) pastry; **~teiggebäck** *n Gastr.* puff pastries *Pl.*; **~teigpastete** *f Gastr.* vol-au-vent; **~wald** *m hum.* the press; **es rauscht im deutschen/englischen ~** the German press is in a flurry / there are goings-on on Fleet Street

blattförmig *Adj.* leaf-shaped

Blatt|gemüse *n* leafy vegetables *Pl.*; **Spinat ist ein ~** spinach is a leafy vegetable; **~gold** *n* gold leaf, beaten (*od.* leaf *od.* laminated) gold; **~grün** *n Bot.* chlorophyll; **~laus** *f Zool.* greenfly, aphid

blattlos *Adj.* leafless; *Baum: auch* bare

Blattpflanze *f* foliage (*od.* leafy) plant

blattreich *Adj.* leafy, foliose *fachspr.*

blättrig *Adj.* → **blätterig**

...blättrig *im Adj.: mit der genannten Art od. Zahl von Blättern*: **groß~** large-leaved; **vier~es Kleeblatt** four-leaved (*od.* -leaf) clover

Blatt|salat *m* green salad; **~schuss** *m Jägerspr.* chest shot; **~werk** *n; nur Sg.; Bot.* foliage

blau *Adj.* **1.** blue; **~es Auge** *umg.* black eye; **~er Fleck** *umg.* bruise; **er hatte überall ~e Flecke** he was black and blue (all over); **du hast ~e Lippen bekommen** your lips have gone (*Am.* turned) blue; **im Gesicht ~ anlaufen** go (*Am.* turn) blue in the face; **der Blaue Planet** (*die Erde*) Planet Earth; **2.** *fig.*: **~es Blut in s-n Adern haben** be blue-blooded; **mit e-m ~en Auge davonkommen** get off lightly; **j-m ~en Dunst vormachen** pull the wool over s.o.'s eyes; **~er Montag** Monday on which one skips work; **~er Brief** a) (letter of) dismissal; *von Vermieter*: notice to quit; *von Betrieb*: one's cards, marching orders *umg.*, *Am.* pink slip *umg.*, b) *Päd.* (letter of) warning (*that a child may have to repeat a school year*); **die ~e Blume** *Kunst.*, *Lit.* the Blue Flower; **der Blaue Reiter** *Kunst* the Blue Rider, the Blaue Reiter; → **Junge**[1], **Wunder** 1; **3.** *umg.* (*betrunken*) plastered, tight *Sl.*; **total ~** *Sl.* pissed, blotto; **er war ~ wie ein Veilchen** he was (as) drunk as a lord; **4.** *Gastr.* au bleu; **Forelle ~** trout au bleu

Blau *n*; **-s**, *kein Pl.* blue (colo[u]r); **in ~ gekleidet** dressed in blue; **das ~ des Himmels** the colo[u]r of the sky, sky-blue

blauäugig *Adj.* blue-eyed; *fig.* starry-eyed, dewy-eyed, naive; **Blauäugigkeit** *f*; *nur Sg.* blue-eyedness *umg.*; *fig.* naive|ty (*Am. auch* –té)

Blaubeere *f Dial. Bot.* bilberry, *Am.* blueberry

blaublütig *Adj. umg.* blue-blooded

Blaue[1] *n*; **-n**, *kein Pl.*: **das ~ vom Himmel herunterlügen** *umg.* lie through one's teeth, lie like a trooper; **ins ~ hinein reden** prattle (on), talk one's head off; **j-m das ~ vom Himmel versprechen** promise s.o. the moon; **Fahrt ins ~** jaunt (through the countryside); *organisiert*: mystery tour; **Schuss ins ~** random shot

Blaue[2] *m*; **-n**, **-n**; *hist.*, *umg.* hundred mark note

Bläue *f*; **-**, *kein Pl.* blue(ness)

Blaufuchs *m Zool.* Arctic fox

blau|grau *Adj.* blue-grey (*Am.* -gray), bluish-grey (*Am.* -gray); **~grün** *Adj.* blue-green, bluish-green

Blauhelm *m*; *mst Pl.*; *Pol.*, *Mil.* UN peace-keeping soldier; **~einsatz** *m* deployment of UN soldiers

Blaukraut *n*; *nur Sg.*; *österr. Gastr.*, *auch Dial.* red cabbage

bläulich *Adj.* bluish

Blaulicht *n*; *nur Sg.* von Polizei etc.: flashing (blue) light(s *Pl.*); *Lampe*: blue light; **mit ~** with (its *od.* their) (-blue) light(s) flashing; **mit ~ ins Krankenhaus gebracht werden** be rushed to hospital (in an ambulance)

blaumachen *v/i.* (*trennb.*); *umg.* skip work, skive off work; *Schule schwänzen*: skip classes; *Brit. auch* skive (off), *Am.* play hooky; **er macht heute blau** he's skiving (off) today, he's skived off today, *Am.* he's playing hooky today

Blau|mann *m*; *Pl.*: -männer; *umg.* boilersuit, *Am.* coveralls *Pl.*; **~meise** *f* blue tit; **~papier** *n* blue carbon paper; **~pause** *f* blueprint

blaurot *Adj.* purple

Blau|säure *f*; *nur Sg.*; *Chem.* prussic (*od.* hydrocyanic) acid; **~schimmel** *m Bot.* blue mo(u)ld

blauschwarz *Adj.* blue-black, bluish-black

Blaustich *m Fot.* blue cast; **blaustichig** *Adj.*: **~ sein** have a blue cast

Blau|strumpf *m altm. fig.* bluestocking; **~tanne** *f Bot.* blue spruce; **~wal** *m Zool.* blue whale

Blazer ['ble:zɐ] *m*; **-s**, **-** blazer

Blech *n*; **-(e)s**, **-** **1.** metal, tin; *Tech.* (*Werkstoff*) sheet metal; (*Erzeugnis*) metal sheet; *am Auto*: bodywork; **ein Eimer** etc. **aus ~** a metal bucket etc.; **das ist doch bloß ~** that's just cheap (*od.* ordinary) metal; **aufs ~ hauen** *umg. fig.* blow (*od.* toot) one's own horn; **2.** (*Backblech*) baking tray, *Am.* cookie sheet; **3.** *Mus.* (*Blechbläser*) brass; **4.** *nur Sg.*; *umg. fig.* (*Unsinn*) rubbish, *Am.* garbage; **red doch nicht so'n ~!** don't talk such rubbish (*od.* rot *umg.*, *Am.* garbage, nonsense)

Blech|bläser *m Mus.* brass player; **die ~** the brass (section); **~blasinstrument** *n Mus.* brass instrument; **~büchse** *f*, **~dose** *f* **1.** *für Lebensmittel*: tin (can), *bes. Am.* can; **2.** tin, (metal) bucket (*od.* container); **~eimer** *m* metal bucket

blechen *umg.* **I.** *v/t.* (*bezahlen*) fork out, cough up, stump up; **II.** *v/i.* (*die Rechnung bezahlen*) foot the bill *allg.*

blechern *Adj.* **1.** (*aus Blech gemacht*) tin ...; **2.** *Klang*: tinny; (*hohl*) hollow

Blech|hütte *f* corrugated iron hut; **~kanister** *m* (metal) canister; **~kiste** *f umg. pej.* (*Auto*) banger, crate, heap; **~lawine** *f umg.* endless stream of traffic, solid line of cars; **~napf** *m* tin bowl; **~schachtel** *f* tin, (metal) box; **~schaden** *m Mot.* bodywork damage; **es gab nur ~** it was just a bump; *weitS.* nobody got hurt; **~schere** *f* metal shears *Pl.*; **e-e ~** a pair of metal shears *Pl.*; **~schüssel** *f* tin (*od.* aluminium, *Am.* aluminum) bowl; **~trommel** *f* tin drum

blecken *v/t.*: **die Zähne ~** show one's teeth; *Tier*: bare its teeth

Blei *n*; **-(e)s**, **-e** **1.** lead; **aus ~** lead ..., made of lead; **~ gießen als Silvesterbrauch**: *custom of pouring molten lead*

into cold water in order to tell one's fortune for the coming year from the resulting shapes; (*schwer*) **wie ~** like lead, like a lead (*od.* dead) weight, leaden; **es liegt mir wie ~ im Magen** it lies heavily on my stomach; *fig.* it is preying on my mind; **~ in den Gliedern haben** *fig.* be weighed down; **2.** → **Senkblei**, **3.** *Jagd*: shot; (*Kugel*) bullet; **4.** *fachspr. Zoll*: (*Plombe*) lead seal

bleiarm *Adj.* low-lead ...

Bleibe *f*; **-**, **-n**, *mst Sg.* place to stay; *bei Bekannten: auch* crash pad *umg.*; **keine ~ haben** have nowhere to stay

bleiben *v/i.*; **blieb**, **ist geblieben** **1.** (*nicht wegbewegen*) stay; (*verweilen*) *in Hotel etc.*: stay, stop *umg.*; *zu lange*: tarry, linger; **zu Hause ~** stay in; *nicht ausgehen: auch* stay in; **im Bett ~** stay in bed; **draußen ~** stay out; **zum Essen ~** stay for dinner; **bleib, wo du bist!** stay where you are!, don't move!; **~ Sie bitte am Apparat** please hold (the line); **bleib auf d-m Platz** stay where you are, don't move; **und wo bleibe ich?** *umg.* what about me?, and where do I come into it?; **wir müssen sehen, wo wir ~** we'll just have to fend for ourselves (do our own thing *umg.*); **sieh zu, wo du bleibst!** *umg.* you're on your own, kid!; **bleib mir damit vom Hals!** don't bother me with such things; **das bleibt unter uns!** that's between you and me, keep that under your hat *umg.*; **im Krieg** etc. **~** (*fallen*) fall, be killed; → **Ball**[1] 1, **Leib** 1; **2.** **~ bei** keep to, stick to; *bei e-r Meinung*, *Entscheidung etc.*: stick to, stand by; *bei Meinung*, *Versprechen*: abide by; **bei der Wahrheit ~** stick to the truth; **wir wollen doch bei der Sache ~** let's stick (*od.* keep) to the point (*od.* subject), let's get back on track *umg.*; **ich bleibe dabei** I'm not going to change my mind; **ich bleibe dabei, dass ...** I still think (*od.* maintain etc.) that ...; **ich bleibe lieber beim Bier** (I think) I'll stick to beer, thanks; → **Sache** 2, **Stange** 3, **Takt**[1] 1, **treu** I; **3.** *in e-m Zustand*: remain, stay, continue (to be), keep; **an/aus ~** stay *od.* be kept on/off; **geschlossen/trocken ~** stay closed/dry; **gesund ~** stay (*od.* keep) healthy; **bleib gesund!** mind how you go, now, take care!, keep well (*od.* fit); **am Leben ~** stay alive; **ruhig/gelassen ~** keep quiet / one's temper; **unbestraft/unentdeckt ~** go unpunished/undiscovered; **ungenannt/anonym ~** remain unnamed/anonymous; **er bleibt immer freundlich** he's always very pleasant; **sie wird sich immer treu ~** she will always be the same; **unsere Bemühungen blieben ohne Erfolg** all our efforts were in vain; **die Sache bleibt ein Geheimnis** the affair remains a mystery; **für sich ~** keep to o.s.; **bleib, wie du bist** stay the way you are; → **ruhig** I 3; **4.** *mit Verb*: remain, stay; **~ Sie (doch) sitzen!** don't get up, please; **bleib doch sitzen!** *ungeduldig*: can't you sit still (for one minute)?; → **hängen**[1] 6, **liegen** 7, **sitzen** 9, **stehen** I 3 - 5; **5.** **etw. ~ lassen** (*nicht tun*) not do *s.th.*, leave (*s.th*) alone; **dann lass es eben bleiben** don't, then; nobody's forcing you; **das wirst du schön ~ lassen!** you'll do nothing of the sort (*od.* kind)!, don't you dare!; **lass es lieber bleiben** (better) leave it; **6.** **etw. ~ lassen** (*aufhören mit*) stop (doing) *s.th.*; **lass das ~!** stop it (*od.* that)!, don't do that!, leave it alone!; *er kann es nicht ~ lassen* he won't stop (doing it); *das Rauchen etc. ~ lassen* stop (*od.* quit *umg.*) smoking *etc.*; **7.** (*übrig ~*) be left (over), remain; *uns bleibt nicht mehr viel Zeit* we haven't got (*od.* there isn't) much time left; *mir bleibt keine* (*andere*) *Wahl* I have no choice (*als zu + Inf.* but to *+ Inf.*); *es bleibt ihr nur die Erinnerung an ihn* all she has left are the memories of him; *jetzt bleibt uns nur noch e-e Chance* we have only one chance left, this is our last chance; → *vorbehalten* III; **8.** (*wegbleiben*): *wo bleibt er denn?* what's taking him (so long)?, where's he got to?; *wo bist du so lange geblieben?* where've you been all this time?, what took you so long?; *wo ist denn der Peter geblieben?* where's Peter got to (*od.* gone)?, what's happened to Peter?; *wo ist nur mein Schlüssel geblieben?* what have I done with my key?; *Kinder, wo ist nur die Zeit geblieben?* Goodness, what's happened to the time?; **9.** *unpers.*: *es bleibt dabei!* that's final (*od.* settled) then, agreed!; *und dabei bleibt es!* and that's that, and that's final; *dabei wird es nicht ~* that won't be the end of it (*od.* the last we'll *etc.* hear of it), matters won't rest (*od.* stop *umg.*) there; *dabei muss es ~* there the matter must rest, we'll have to leave it there *umg.*; *es wird nicht bei nur e-m Fehler ~* that won't be the only mistake (*od.* fault); *bleibt nur noch zu hoffen, dass ...* we can only hope (that) ..., (well,) let's hope (that) ...; → *abwarten* I, *überlassen etc.*

bleibend I. *Part. Präs.* → *bleiben*; **II.** *Adj. Eindruck:* lasting; *auch Schaden,Werte etc.:* permanent

bleiben lassen → *bleiben* 5, 6

Bleiberecht *f* law concerning temporary residence status

bleich *Adj.* pale (*vor + Dat.* with), pallid; (*kränklich aussehend*) wan; *Sache:* (*verblasst*) faded; *ganz ~ Person: auch* (as) white as a sheet; *lit.* pale as death; **Bleiche** *f*, *-*, *-n* **1.** *nur Sg.* paleness, pallor; **2.** (*Bleichmittel*) bleach; **bleichen I.** *v/t.* bleach; **II.** *v/i.* bleach; (*verblassen*) fade

Bleichgesicht *n* paleface

Bleichheit *f; nur Sg.* paleness, pallor

Bleich|mittel *n* bleach(ing agent); *~sellerie m Bot.* celery (stalks *Pl.*)

bleiern *Adj.* **1.** *Rohre etc.:* lead; **2.** *fig. Glieder, Himmel, Farbe etc.:* leaden; *~e Schwere* leaden feeling; *e-e ~e Müdigkeit spüren* feel (absolutely) exhausted

Bleifarbe *f* lead paint

bleifrei I. *Adj. Farbe, Benzin:* unleaded, lead-free; **II.** *Adv.:* ~ *tanken* fill up with unleaded (petrol, *Am.* gas); *kann man dort ~ tanken?* have they got unleaded (petrol, *Am.* gas)?; **III. Bleifrei** *n; -s, kein Pl.* unleaded, lead-free

Blei|fuß *m: mit ~ fahren* put one's foot to the floor (*od.* put one's foot down), *Am. auch* drive with a lead foot; *~gehalt m* lead content; *~gießen n; -s, kein Pl. Silvesterbrauch: custom of pouring molten lead into cold water in order to tell one's fortune for the coming year from the resulting shapes; ~glas n* lead glass

blei|grau *Adj.* lead-colo(u)red; *~haltig Adj.* containing lead; *~ sein* contain lead

Blei|konzentration *f* lead concentra-

tion; *~kristall n; nur Sg.; Min.* lead crystal, galena; *~kugel f* lead bullet; *~platten Pl.* lead plates (*od.* sheets); *~rohr n* lead pipe; *~satz m Druck.* hot metal type; *~schürze f* lead apron

bleischwer *Adj.* like lead, like a lead weight

Bleistift *m* pencil; *~absatz m* stiletto heel; *~mine f* (pencil) lead; *~spitzer m* pencil sharpener; *~stummel m* pencil stub; *~zeichnung f* pencil drawing

Bleivergiftung *f Med.* lead poisoning

bleiverglast *Adj. Fenster:* leaded; *die Scheiben waren ~* the panes were leaded (*od.* made of leaded glass)

bleiverseucht *Adj.* lead-polluted

Blende *f*, *-*, *-n* **1.** *Fot.* a) diaphragm, b) *als Öffnung:* aperture, c) (*Öffnungsweite*) f-stop; (*bei*) *~ 8* (at) F8 (*od.* F/8); **2.** (*Schirm*) screen; *Mil.* shield; *im Auto:* (sun) visor; **3.** *Archit.* (*Fensterblende*) transom; (*Verzierung*) blind arch (*od.* door *etc.*); **4.** *am Kleid:* (*decorative*) facing; **5.** *an Möbeln:* trim

blenden I. *v/t.* **1.** (*j-n, j-s Augen*) blind, dazzle (*mit* by); *du blendest mich! auch* you're blinding me, you're shining it (*od.* the torch *etc.* *Am.* flashlight *etc.*) right into my eyes; *von j-s Schönheit ganz geblendet sein* be dazzled by s.o.'s beauty; **2.** *fig.* (*täuschen*) deceive, delude, blind; (*beeindrucken*) take *s.o.* in; **3.** *Bauwesen:* (*abdecken*) camouflage, mask, disguise; **4.** *hist.:* j-n ~ (*j-s Augen ausstechen*) blind s.o., gouge (*od.* put) s.o.'s eyes out; **II.** *v/i.* dazzle, be dazzling; *das blendet aber!* that light's strong (*od.* too strong for my eyes); **Blenden** *n Mot. etc.* glare

Blendenautomatik *f Fot.* automatic aperture (control)

blendend I. *Part. Präs.* → *blenden*; **II.** *Adj.* **1.** *Licht:* dazzling; **2.** *fig.* (*großartig, genial*) brilliant; (*prächtig*) dazzling; *~es Aussehen* stunning good looks; *~ aussehen* look great; (*sehr gut aussehen*) be extremely good-looking (*od.* attractive *od.* splendid); **III.** *Adv.* **1.** *~ weiß Schnee etc.:* dazzlingly white; **2.** *fig.:* *sich ~ amüsieren* have a great time; *sich ~ verstehen od. ~ miteinander auskommen* get along brilliantly (*od.* just great, like a house on fire *umg.*); *es geht ihr ~* she's getting along great, she's doing fine; *iro. es geht ihm nicht gerade ~* he could be doing worse(, I suppose)

Blenden|einstellung *f Fot.* aperture setting; *~zahl f Fot.* f-stop, f-number

Blender *m; -s, -; fig. pej.* fake, phon(e)y; *er ist ein richtiger ~ auch* he's all show (*od.* talk)

blendfrei *Adj. Bildschirm etc.:* anti-glare ..., anti-dazzle ..., non-dazzling

Blendschutz *m* glare shield; *~zaun m Verk. entlang e-r Straße:* anti-dazzle barrier; *~scheibe f* anti-glare screen

Blendung *f* **1.** blinding; *Mot.* dazzle, glare; **2.** *fig.* (*Täuschung*) deception

Blendwerk *n geh.* (*Täuschung*) deception; (*Illusion*) illusion; (*Tricks*) tricks *Pl.*, trickery; *es ist alles ~ auch* it's all a fake

Blesse *f; -, -n* blaze

Blesshuhn *n Orn.* coot

Blessur *f; -, -en; geh.* wound *allg.*; *leichte ~en* superficial wounds, a few scratches *umg.*

bleu [blø:] **I.** *Adj.* (pale) blue; **II. Bleu**

n; -s, - auch umg. -s (pale) blue

Blick *m; -(e)s, -e* **1.** (*Hinsehen*) look (*auf + Akk.* at); *langer, scharfer:* gaze; *kurzer:* glimpse; (*Blickrichtung*) eye(s *Pl.*); *ein flüchtiger ~* a (quick) glance; *mit einem ~ erkennen etc.:* immediately, straight away; *auf den ersten ~* at first sight (*od.* glance), when you first look at it (*od.* see it); *Liebe auf den ersten ~* love at first sight; *das sieht man doch auf den ersten ~* you can see that straightaway (with half an eye *umg.*); *erst auf den zweiten ~ ...* it's only when you look at it again that ...; *ihre ~e begegneten sich* their eyes met; *sein ~ fiel auf ...* (*+ Akk.*) his eye(s) *od.* gaze fell on ...; *den ~ heben/senken* look up/down, raise one's eyes /cast one's eyes down, lower one's gaze; *s-n* (*od.* den) *~ richten auf* (*+ Akk.*) look at (*od.* towards *od.* in the direction of), cast one's eye(s) on (*od.* in the direction of) *lit.*; *die beiden wechselten verliebte ~e* the two exchanged amorous glances, they made eyes at each other *umg.*; *den ~ wenden von* look away from, turn one's eyes away from; *er wandte den ~ nicht von ...* he wouldn't take his eyes off ...; *e-n* (*kurzen*) *~ werfen auf* (*+ Akk.*) have (*od.* take) a (quick) look at, cast a (quick) glance at (*od.* over); *j-m e-n ~ zuwerfen* give s.o. a look; *j-m e-n fragenden ~ zuwerfen* give s.o. an inquisitive look; *sie warf mir e-n betrübten ~ zu* she cast a troubled glance at me; *e-n ~ hinter die Kulissen werfen auch fig.* take a look behind the scenes; *j-n keines ~es würdigen* not deign to look at s.o.; *wenn ~e töten könnten* if looks could kill; → *durchbohren, starr* II 1; **2.** *nur Sg.* (*Augenausdruck*) look (in one's eyes), eyes *Pl.*; *e-n traurigen/verzweifelten ~ haben* look sad / have a look of despair; *der böse ~* the evil eye; **3.** *nur Sg.;* (*Aussicht*) view; *mit ~ auf* (*+ Akk.*) with a view of, overlooking; *von hier aus haben Sie e-n schönen ~* you have a nice view from here; **4.** *nur Sg.; fig.* (*Empfänglichkeit*) eye(s *Pl.*); (*Horizont*) outlook, horizon(s *Pl.*); *e-n ~ haben für* have an eye for; *dafür hat er keinen od. nicht den richtigen ~* he has no eyes for (*od.* he just doesn't see) that kind of thing; *den ~ für etw. verstellen od. trüben* obscure s.th.; *j-m den Blick für etw. verstellen/trüben* distort/cloud s.o.'s view of s.th. (*od.* outlook on s.th.)

blickdicht *Adj. Strumpfhosen:* opaque

blicken *v/i.* **1.** (*sehen*) look (*auf + Akk.* at; *in + Akk.* into); *durch die Wolken etc. ~ fig. Sonne etc.:* peep through the clouds *etc.*; *das lässt tief ~ fig.* that's very revealing, it makes you think *umg.*; **2.** (*Augenausdruck haben*): *traurig/streng etc. ~* look sad/severe; **3.** *sich ~ lassen umg.* (*auftauchen*) show up, turn up; (*erscheinen*) *auch* put in an appearance; (*vorbeikommen*) drop in (*bei* on), drop by (at); *er lässt sich nicht mehr ~* you never see him (any more) these days; *lass dich ja nicht mehr ~!* don't you ever show your face around here again!

Blick|fang *m; nur Sg.* eyecatcher, eye candy *umg.*; *es soll als ~ dienen* it's meant to catch people's eyes (*od.* be eyecatching); *~feld n auch fig.* field of vision; (*mehr und mehr*) *ins ~ der Öffentlichkeit rücken fig.* (increasingly) become the focus of public attention;

~kontakt *m* eye contact; **~ mit j-m aufnehmen/suchen** catch /try to catch s.o.'s eye

blicklos *Adj. Augen*: blank; **j-n ~ ansehen** look at s.o. blankly

Blick|punkt *m* **1.** *Opt.* visual focus; **2.** *fig. im ~ (der Öffentlichkeit) stehen* be the focus of (public) attention, be in the limelight (be very much in the public eye); **3.** *fig.* → *Blickwinkel* 2; **~richtung** *f* line of vision; *fig. auch* direction; *in ~ links/rechts* looking to the left/right; **~winkel** *m* **1.** angle of view; **2.** *fig.* point of view, perspective; **es kommt auf den ~ an** it depends which angle you look at it from; **aus diesem ~** seen from this angle (*od.* point of view, perspective)

blieb *Imperf.* → *bleiben*

blies *Imperf.* → *blasen*

blind I. *Adj.* **1.** *auch fig.* blind; **auf einem Auge ~** blind in one eye; **bist du (denn) ~?** *umg.* are you blind?, haven't you got eyes in your head?, can't you see?; **~ geboren** blind from birth; **ein ~ geborenes Kind** a child who was born blind *od.* who has been blind from birth; **2.** *fig. Glaube, Vertrauen, Zufall etc.*: blind; *Vertrauen: auch* implicit; **~e Gewalt** uncontrolled violence, brute force; **~ sein (gegen, für** to; **vor** with); **j-n ~ machen** blind s.o. (**gegen** to); **Liebe macht ~** love is blind; **~ Alarm, Eifer, Passagier**, **3.** *Fensterscheiben*: clouded; *Spiegel*: cloudy; *Metall: auch* tarnished; *Wein*: dull; **4.** *Archit., Tech. Boden, Fenster etc.*: invisible, concealed; *Knopfloch*: concealed; **die Bluse wird ~ geknöpft** the blouse has concealed buttons; **5.** *Mil. Patrone*: blank; **II.** *Adv.* **1.** *fliegen, spielen etc.*: blind; **~ (Maschine) schreiben** touch-type; **~ Klavier spielen können** be able to play by heart *od.* blind; **etw. ~ können** be able to do s.th. blindfolded (*od.* with one's eyes closed); **2.** *glauben, vertrauen etc.*: blindly, implicitly; **3.** → *blindlings*

Blinddarm *m Anat.* **1.** appendix; **er lässt sich am ~ operieren** he is having an operation on his appendix; **ich muss mir den ~ herausnehmen lassen** I have to have my appendix (taken) out; **2.** c(a)ecum; **~entzündung** *f Med.* appendicitis; **~operation** *f Med.* appendectomy; **sich e-r ~ unterziehen** *förm. auch* have one's appendix (taken) out

Blinde *m, f; -n -n* blind man / woman, blind person, visually impaired (*Am. auch* challenged) person; **die ~n** the blind (*Pl.*); **das sieht doch ein ~r (mit Krückstock)!** *umg., neg.!* anyone (*od.* any idiot) can see that!; **unter den ~n ist der Einäugige König** *Sprichw.* in the land of the blind, the one-eyed man is king

Blindekuh *f; nur Sg.* blind man's buff (*bes. Am.* bluff); **~ spielen** play blind man's b(l)uff

Blinden|hund *m* guide dog, *Am.* seeing-eye dog; **~schrift** *f* braille; **~schule** *f* school for the blind; **~stock** *m* white stick, (blind person's) cane

Blind|flug *m* blind flight; *Pl. auch* blind flying *Sg.*; **~gänger** *m; -s, -* **1.** *Mil.* dud; **2.** *umg. fig. pej.* (*Versager*) dead loss; **~geborene** *m, f; -n, -n* someone blind from birth, a person who was born blind

blindgläubig I. *Adj.* (utterly) credulous; **II.** *Adv.* unquestioningly; blindly

Blindheit *f; nur Sg.; auch fig.* blindness (**gegenüber** to); **er ist mit ~ geschlagen** *fig.* he must be blind (not to see it)

Blindlandung *f Flug.* instrument (*od.* blind) landing

blindlings *Adv.* blindly; **~ in sein Verderben rennen** rush headlong into disaster

Blind|probe *f Gastr.* blind tasting; **~schleiche** *f Zool.* blindworm; **~schreiben** *n Schreibmaschine*: touch typing; **~versuch** *m Med., Psych.* blind test

blindwütig I. *Adj.* raging, blind with rage; **mit ~em Eifer** with incredible enthusiasm; **in ~em Hass** in blind fury (*od.* rage); **II.** *Adv.* in a blind fury (*od.* rage); **~ um sich schlagen** lash out wildly (in all directions)

blinken *v/i.* **1.** (*funkeln*) sparkle; *Sterne*: twinkle; (*aufleuchten*) flash; (*signalisieren, auch v/t.*) (flash a) signal; **2.** *Mot.* indicate; **Blinker** *m; -s, -* **1.** *Mot.* indicator, *Am.* blinker; **2.** *Angeln*: spoon bait

Blink|licht *n* **1.** *Verkehrszeichen*: flashing light(s *Pl.*); *bei Fußgängerübergang: auch* beacon; **2.** *Mot.* → *Blinker* 1; **~lichtanlage** *f* warning light(s *Pl.*), *Am.* flasher(s *Pl.*); **~signal** *n* flashlight signal; **~zeichen** *n* **1.** flashing signal; **ein ~ geben** flash a signal; **2.** *Mot.* indicator (*beim Überholen*: passing) signal; **der Fahrer gab mir Blinkzeichen** *Pl.* per Lichthupe: the driver flashed me

blinzeln *v/i.* (*auch mit den Augen ~*) blink; *als Zeichen*: wink; **in die Sonne ~** squint against the sun (*od.* in the bright sun)

Blister ['blɪstɐ] *m; -s, - Verpackung*: blister (*od.* bubble) pack

Blitz *m; -es, -e* **1.** lightning; *Strahl*: flash (of lightning); **der ~ schlug in den Turm ein** the tower was struck by lightning; **vom ~ getroffen werden** be struck by lightning; **wie vom ~ getroffen** *fig.* stunned, thunderstruck; **wie der ~** like (a flash of) lightning; **like** (*od.* in) a flash; **wie ein geölter ~** *umg.* like greased lightning, in a flash; **wie ein ~ aus heiterem Himmel** like a bolt from (*od.* out of) the blue; **wie ein ~ einschlagen** *Nachricht etc.*: take everyone by surprise; *stärker*: come like a bomb; **potz ~!** good heavens!; **2.** *Fot. umg.* flash

Blitz|ableiter *m* **1.** lightning conductor (*Am.* rod); **2.** *fig.* easy target (for emotions); **j-n als ~ benutzen** *umg.* take it out on s.o., vent one's spleen on s.o.; **~aktion** *f* lightning operation, blitz *umg.; die Werbung war e-e ~* it was a big publicity blitz; **wir renovierten s-e Wohnung in e-r ~** we had a blitz on his apartment and got it all decorated; **~angriff** *m Mil.* lightning attack

blitzartig I. *Adj. Reaktion etc.*: lightning; **II.** *Adv.* like (a flash of) lightning; like (*od.* in) a flash

Blitz|aufnahme *f Fot.* flash shot; **~besuch** *m* flying (*od.* lightning) visit; **~birne** *f* flashbulb

blitz(e)blank *Adj.* spotless, squeaky clean *umg.*, spick and span

Blitzeinschlag *m* lightning (strike); **man sah den ~ (in den Baum etc.)** you could see the lightning strike (*od.* striking the tree etc.); **beim ~** when the lightning struck

blitzen I. *v/i.* **1.** *unpers.*: **es blitzt** there's

lightning; **es blitzte** there was (a flash of) lightning; **es blitzt und donnert** there's thunder and lightning, it thunders and lightens; **2.** *fig.* flash; (*glänzen*) sparkle; **i-e Augen blitzten vor Wut/Vergnügen** her eyes flashed with anger / her eyes sparkled with pleasure; **die Küche blitzt vor Sauberkeit** the kitchen is gleaming; **3.** *Fot.* flash; **hat es geblitzt?** *auch* did the flash work?; **4.** *umg.* (*früher: sich öffentlich nackt zeigen, um zu provozieren*) streak *allg.*; **II.** *v/t.* **1.** take (*od.* photograph) s.th. with a flash; **2.** *Mot.*: **ich wurde gestern geblitzt** I was caught speeding yesterday; **Achtung, in der Müllerstraße wird geblitzt!** watch out, there's a speed trap in Müllerstraße

Blitzer *m; -s, -; umg.* streaker

Blitzesschnelle *f: in ~* quick as a flash, at lightning speed

Blitzgerät *n Fot.* flashlight, flash(gun)

blitzgescheit *Adj.* very bright; **sie ist ~** *auch* she's a bright spark

Blitz|karriere *f* lightning career, meteoric rise; **~kontakt** *m* flash socket; **~krieg** *m* blitzkrieg; **~lampe** *f* flashbulb

Blitzlicht *n Fot.* flashlight, flash(gun); (*etw.*) **mit ~ fotografieren** use a flash (for s.th.); **~aufnahme** *f* flash shot; **~gewitter** *n umg.* popping of flashlights (*Am.* flashguns)

Blitzreise *f* whirlwind tour (**nach** to; **durch** of), flying visit

blitzsauber *Adj.* spotless, squeaky clean *umg.*

Blitz|schach *n* lightning chess; **~schlag** *m* lightning (strike); **vom ~ getroffen werden** be struck by lightning

blitzschnell I. *Adj.* (as) quick as lightning, *attr. auch* lightning …, split-second …; **II.** *Adv.* quick as a flash, like a flash (*od.* shot); *reagieren etc.*: instantaneously; **es verbreitete sich ~** it spread like wildfire

Blitz|schutz *m Etech.* lightning protection; *Vorrichtung*: (lightning) arrester; **~sieg** *m* lightning victory; **~start** *m* lightning (*od.* jump) start; **~strahl** *m* flash (*od.* streak) of lightning; **~umfrage** *f* lightning poll, instant opinion poll; **~würfel** *m Fot.* flashcube

Blizzard ['blɪzɐt] *m; -s, -s; Met.* (*Schneesturm*) blizzard

Block *m; -(e)s, -s od. Blöcke* **1.** *Pl. Blöcke*; (*Quader*) *Holz etc.*: block *of wood etc.*; (*Felsblock*) *auch* boulder; *Seife, Schokolade etc.*: bar; *Metall.* ingot, pig; **2.** (*Wohnblock*) block of flats, *Am.* apartment building; (*Häuserblock*) block (of houses); **sie wohnen im gleichen ~** (*Gebäude*) they live in the same building (*od.* block of flats); (*Häuserblock*) they live on the same block; **noch einmal um den ~ fahren** go (*od.* drive) (a)round the block again; **3.** *zum Schreiben*: writing pad; *für Notizen*: notepad; *klotzförmig*: scribbling block; **4.** *Pl. Blöcke*; *Karten*: book (of tickets); *von Daten, Themen etc.*: block; **etw. im ~ kaufen/verkaufen = en bloc**; **5.** *Pl. mst Blöcke*; *Parl., Pol., Wirts.* bloc; **e-n ~ bilden od. sich zu e-m ~ zusammenschließen** form a bloc; **6.** *Pl. nur Blocks*; *Eisenb.* (*Streckenblock*) block; **7.** *Pl. Blocks*; *Sport, beim Basketball, Volleyball*: wall, screen, block; **8.** *Pl. mst Blocks*; *Briefmarken*: block; **9.** *beim Kartenspielen*: pack, *Am.* deck; **10.** *Pl. Blöcke*; *Med.* (*Herz-*

block) block, irregular beating, arrhythmia *fachspr.*; **mentaler ~** *Psych.* mental block

Blockade *f*; -, *-n* **1.** blockade; **die ~ brechen** run the blockade; **e-e ~ aufheben** *od.* **beenden** end a blockade; **2.** *Druck.* turned letter(s *Pl.*), black; **3.** *Physiol., Psych.* barrier, block; **e-e ~ (auf)brechen** break down a barrier

Block\bildung *f Pol.* forming of blocs (*od.* a bloc); **~buchstabe** *m* block letter; **~diagramm** *n Geol., EDV* block diagram(me)

blocken *v/t.* **1.** *Sport* block; **2.** *Eisenb.* (*e-e Strecke*) block

Block\floating *n Wirts.* exchange-rate union; **~flöte** *f Mus.* recorder

blockfrei *Adj. Pol.* nonaligned; **~e Staaten** nonaligned countries (*od.* nations); **Blockfreiheit** *f; nur Sg.* nonalignment; *Zustand:* nonaligned status

Block\haus *n* log cabin; **~hütte** *f* log cabin

blockieren I. *v/t.* **1.** (*e-e Blockade errichten*) blockade; **2.** (*den Weg versperren*) block, obstruct; **ein umgestürzter Baum blockiert die Schienen** a fallen tree is blocking the tracks; **3.** (*verstopfen*) clog (up); **4.** *Wirts.* block; **5.** (*zum Stillstand bringen*) (*Räder*) lock; (*Maschine*) jam; **6.** *Druck.* mark with turned letters (*to indicate missing material*); **7.** *Psych.* block; **da bin ich vollkommen blockiert** I have a real problem with that; **II.** *v/i. Räder:* lock; *Maschine:* jam; **Blockierung** *f* blocking; obstruction

Block\parteien *Pl.* **1.** *hist., ehem. DDR:* party bloc *Sg.*; **2.** coalition; **~satz** *m Druck.* justified (*od.* flush) setting, flush (*od.* justified) left and right margins *Pl.*; **~schokolade** *f* cooking (*od.* baking) chocolate; **~schrift** *f; nur Sg.* block letters (*od.* capitals) *Pl.*; **~staat** *m* aligned *od.* bloc country (*od.* state, nation); **~stunde** *f Päd.* double period; **~unterricht** *m Päd.* teaching by topics *ohne Art.*; **~wart** *m*; *hist., Nationalsozialismus:* Nazi party warden (*in charge of a block of houses*)

blöd, blöde I. *Adj.* **1.** *umg.* (*dumm*) stupid *allg.*, daft, thick., *bes. Am.* dumb; (*albern*) silly, foolish *allg.*; **er ~ auch** he's an idiot, he's silly; **ich war so ~, ihm zu glauben** (and) I was stupid (*od.* daft *umg.*) enough to believe him; **ich kam mir ziemlich ~ dabei vor** I felt really foolish doing it; **2.** *umg.* (*ärgerlich*) stupid *allg.*; (*peinlich*) *auch* embarrassing *allg.*; (*heikel*) awkward *allg.*; **blöder Kerl** *od.* **Hund** silly fool; *aggressiver:* stupid bastard *Sl.*; **diese blöde Tür!** this damn door!; **blöde Angelegenheit** stupid situation; **so was Blödes!** how stupid!; (*Ärgerliches*) what a (damn *umg.*) nuisance; **das Blöde daran** the stupid thing about it; **das war ein blödes Gefühl** it wasn't a very pleasant feeling; **das wird mir jetzt zu ~** this (*od.* it) is a waste of (my) time; **3.** *altm. und Med.* (*schwachsinnig*) feeble-minded; **~ sein** *auch* be an imbecile; **II.** *Adv.:* **~ daherreden** talk a lot of nonsense (*od.* rubbish); **~ grinsen** give a stupid grin; **grins nicht so ~!** take that silly grin off your face; **sich ~ anstellen** be hopeless; *bewusst:* act stupid; **stell dich nicht so ~ an!** stop being so dop(e)y *umg.*, snap out of it; *bewusst:* stop acting (*od.* being) the fool, stop acting so stupid

Blödel *m*; -s, -; *umg. pej.* fool, idiot *allg.*

Blödel\gedicht *n* humo(u)rous poem, limerick; **~laune** *f:* **in ~** in a silly mood

Blödelei *f*; -, *-en* **1.** nonsense; (*Witz*) silly joke; **2.** *nur Sg.*; (*Herumalbern*) clowning (*od.* messing) about (*Am. auch* around); **blödeln** *v/i.* talk nonsense; (*Witze machen*) crack (silly) jokes; (*herumalbern*) clown about (*Am.* around)

blöderweise *Adv.* stupidly *umg.*

Blödheit *f*; *nur Sg.* stupidity

Blödian *m*; -s, *-e*; *umg. pej.* idiot, blockhead

Blödmann *m*; *umg. pej.* idiot; *aggressiv:* bastard *Sl.*

Blödsinn *m*; *nur Sg.* rubbish; (*auch Unfug*) nonsense; **ausgemachter ~** complete rubbish; **~ reden** talk nonsense; **mach keinen ~!** don't be silly!; (*stell bloß nichts an*) don't do anything silly; **er hat nur ~ im Kopf** his head is full of nonsense; **blödsinnig** *Adj.* **1.** *umg.* stupid; *stärker:* idiotic; **2.** → **blöd I 3**

blöken *v/i. Schaf:* bleat; *Rind:* low

blond *Adj. Mann:* blond; *Frau:* blonde; *beide:* fair(-haired); **~es Gift** *hum.* blonde bombshell; peroxide blonde *altm.*; **~ gefärbt** *Haar:* dyed blond(e); **~ gelockt** with blond(e) curls; **~ gelocktes Haar** blond(e), curly hair, curly blond(e) hair; **Blonde** *n umg.:* **ein kühles ~s** *etwa* a pint of lager, *auch* a glass of light ale; **blondieren** *v/t.* dye one's hair blond(e), bleach; **Blondine** *f*; -, *-n* blonde *umg.*

Blond\kopf *n*, **~schopf** *m* **1.** (head of) blond(e) (*od.* fair) hair; **2.** fair-haired person

bloß I. *Adj.* **1.** naked; (*unbedeckt*) bare (*auch Erdboden*); **mit ~en Füßen** barefoot, barefooted (*auch Adv.*); **mit ~em Oberkörper** stripped to the waist; **mit ~en Händen** with one's bare hands; **mit dem ~en** *od.* **mit ~em Auge** nicht erkennbar etc. with the naked eye; **2.** *attr.*; (*nichts als*) nothing but, mere, just; *Worte:* empty; *Zufall:* sheer; **im ~en Hemd** in just a shirt; **das ist ~es Gerede** that's just (empty) talk; **der ~e Gedanke (daran)** the mere thought (of it); **auf den ~en Verdacht hin** on the mere suspicion; **II.** *Adv.* (*nur*) **1.** just, only; **er ist ~ ein einfacher Mann** he's just a simple man; **es war ~ ein bisschen kalt** it was just a bit cold(, that's all); **das ist wahr, es glaubt mir ~ keiner** it's true, it's just that nobody believes me; **es ist ~ (so), dass ...** it's just that ...; **2.** *verstärkend in Ausrufen und Fragen:* what, how, who *etc.* on earth; **wie machst du das ~?** how on earth do you do it?; **wer soll das ~ alles bezahlen?** (and) who is meant to pay for all that?; **was hat er ~?** I wonder (*od.* I'd love to know) what's wrong with him; **was ist denn ~ los?** what on earth is wrong?; **hätte ich's ~ nicht gemacht!** I wish (*od.* if only) I hadn't done it; **3.** *drohend, warnend:* **soll ich's ~ nicht sagen? ~ ~ nicht!** (good-ness,) no!; *stärker:* don't you dare!; **lass ihn ~ nicht raus!** don't let him out, whatever you do; *stärker:* don't you dare let him out!; **~ jetzt nicht!** not now, please!; **hör ~ auf damit!** just stop that (will you); **4.** **sag ~, ...!** don't say ..., don't tell me ...; → *auch* **nur**

Blöße *f*; -, *-n* **1.** *geh.* nakedness; **s-e ~ bedecken** cover one's nakedness;

2. *wodurch man sich verrät:* giveaway; *bes. Sport* opening; **sich (Dat.) e-e ~ (empfindliche) ~ geben** leave o.s. wide open; (*sich bloßstellen*) give o.s. away, expose o.s. (**gegenüber** in front of); **j-m e-e ~ bieten** *od.* **zeigen** reveal (*od.* show) s.o. a weakness; **3.** (*Lichtung*) clearing; **4.** *Leder:* smoothed skin

bloß\legen *v/t.* (*trennb., hat -ge-*) uncover, expose, lay bare (*alle auch fig.*); **~liegen** *v/i.* (*unreg., trennb., ist -ge-*) be (*od.* lie) exposed

bloßstellen (*trennb., hat -ge-*) **I.** *v/t.* **j-n** (*öffentlich*) **~** expose (*od.* unmask) s.o. (*publicly*), compromise s.o.in public; **II.** *v/refl.* show o.s. up, give o.s. away; **Bloßstellung** *f* showing up; *stärker:* exposure; **aus Angst vor e-r ~** for fear of losing face

Blouson [blu'zõː] *n*, *m*; -s, *-s Frauen:* blouson; *Männer:* bomber (*od.* flying) jacket

blubbern *umg.* **I.** *v/i Lava, Wasser etc.:* bubble (away); **II.** *vt/i. fig.* (*undeutlich reden*) mumble

Blue Jeans, Bluejeans ['bluː dʒiːns] *n* (pair of) jeans (*od.* denims) *Pl.*; **meine ~ ist** *od.* **sind kaputt** *umg.* my jeans are past it (*od.* falling apart)

Bluff [blœf] *m*; -s, *-s* bluff; **bluffen** ['blœfn] *vt/i.* bluff; **sich nicht ~ lassen** not let o.s. be fooled

blühen *v/i.* **1.** blossom, flower (*auch fig.*); (*in Blüte stehen*) be in bloom (*od.* blossom); **blau** *etc.* **~ have** blue *etc.* flowers (*od.* blossoms); **e-e ~de Wiese** a meadow in full bloom (*od.* full of flowers); **die Rosen blühten den ganzen Sommer** the roses bloomed (*od.* were in bloom) all summer; **2.** *fig.* (*gedeihen*) prosper, thrive; *Geschäft, Handel:* boom; **im Verborgenen ~** blossom in obscurity; **3.** *iro.:* **wer weiß, was uns noch blüht** who knows what's in store for us (*od.* what we're in for); **es kann dir noch ~, dass ...** don't be surprised if ...; **das kann uns auch ~** we're not immune (either); **... dann blüht dir was!** ... you'll be in for it!

blühend I. *Part. Präs.* → **blühen**; **II.** *Adj. fig. Aussehen:* healthy; *Gesundheit:* glowing, radiant; *Fantasie:* vivid; *Unsinn:* complete, utter, arrant; **e-n ~en Handel treiben** do a roaring trade (**mit** in); **wie das ~e Leben aussehen** be the picture of health; **im ~en Alter** in his *od.* her prime; **im ~en Alter von** at the early age of

Blümchen *n* small flower; **~kaffee** *m umg. hum.* weak coffee, dishwater; **~muster** *n* (small) floral pattern

Blume *f*; -, *-n* **1.** (*Blüte*) flower; **~n pflücken** pick flowers; **~n streuen** strew (*od.* scatter) flowers; **die blaue ~** *Lit.* the Blue Flower; **durch die ~** *fig.* in as many words; **j-m durch die ~ sagen / zu verstehen geben, dass ...** *fig. auch* hint to s.o. that / tell s.o. in a roundabout way that ...; **lasst s-n sprechen** say it with flowers; **danke für die ~n!** *iro.* thanks for nothing!; **2.** (*Blütenpflanze*) flowering plant; **~n säen** sow flowers; **3.** (*Topfpflanze*) (flowering) pot plant, *auch* plant; **die ~n gießen** water the plants; **4.** *Wein:* bouquet; *Bier:* froth, head; **5.** *Jägerspr. Schwanz des Hasen etc.:* scut, tail; *Schwanzspitze des Fuchses:* tag

Blumen\ampel *f* hanging basket; **~beet** *n* flowerbed; **~draht** *m* florist's wire; **~erde** *f* potting compost, garden mo(u)ld; **~fenster** *n* window with (*od.*

for) flowers; **~garten** m flower garden; **~geschäft** n florist('s), flower shop
blumengeschmückt Adj. adorned (od. decorated) with flowers
Blumen|gruß m (bouquet of) flowers; **~händler** m, **~händlerin** f florist; **~handlung** f flower shop, florist('s); **~kasten** m window box
Blumenkohl m cauliflower
Blumen|korso m flower carnival, floral procession; **~kranz** m garland (of flowers); (bei Beerdigungen) wreath (of flowers); **~kübel** m flower tub; **~laden** m flower shop, florist('s); **~meer** n sea of flowers; wildes: riot of flowers; **~muster** n floral design (od. pattern); **~pracht** f magnificent display of flowers; **~rabatte** f flower-border, herbaceous border
blumenreich Adj. fig. Stil, Ausdrucksweise: flowery, ornate
Blumen|schmuck m flower arrangement(s Pl.), floral decoration(s Pl.), flowers Pl.; **~spende** f flowers Pl.; **~sprache** f language of flowers; **~stand** m flower stall; **~stängel** m, **~stiel** m (flower) stalk; **~stock** m flowering (pot) plant; **~strauß** m bunch of flowers, bouquet; **j-m e-n ~ schenken** give s.o. (some) flowers
Blumentopf m flowerpot; **damit kannst du keinen ~ gewinnen** umg. fig. that won't get you very far; **~erde** f potting compost
Blumen|vase f (flower) vase; **~zucht** f flower-growing; **~züchter** m, **~züchterin** f flower-grower; **~zwiebel** f (flower) bulb
blümerant Adj. umg.: **mir ist ganz ~** (zumute) I feel queasy (od. queer)
blumig Adj. flowery (auch fig.); Wein: auch with a fine bouquet; Parfum: flowery
Bluse f, -, -n **1.** für Frauen: blouse; **die hat ganz schön was in** (od. unter) **der ~!** Sl. she's got a nice pair (of boobs od. tits vulg.), she's well stacked (od. endowed); **2.** Mil. und altm. tunic, Am. blouse
Blut n; -(e)s, kein Pl. **1.** blood; **~ spenden** give (od. donate) blood; **~ spucken** spit blood; **~ verlieren** lose blood; **j-m ~ abnehmen** take a blood sample from s.o.; **ein ~ bildendes Medikament** h(a)ematinic (od. blood enriching) medicine; **~ bildend wirken** help to form blood; **ein ~ saugendes Insekt** a blood-sucking insect; **sich mit ~ bespritzen** get o.s. bloody; **das Hemd etc. war voll ~** covered in blood; **in s-m ~ liegen** be covered in blood; **stärker**: be lying in a pool of blood; **~ im Urin haben** be passing blood (with one's urine); **ich kann kein ~ sehen** I can't stand the sight of blood; **das ~ schoss ihr ins Gesicht** (vor Scham/Zorn) she blushed with shame / her face was red with anger; **alles ~ wich aus ihrem Gesicht** her face went deathly pale; **das ~ pocht in den Schläfen** one's head is throbbing; **ins ~ gehen** Sekt etc.: go (straight) to one's head; fig. Musik etc.: get into one's bloodstream; **etw. im ~ haben** have s.th. in one's bloodstream (fig. blood); **ihm stockte od. gefror das ~ in den Adern** his blood froze; **~ und Wasser schwitzen** fig. sweat blood; be terrified; **an ihren Händen klebt ~** she's got blood on her hands; **an diesem Geld klebt ~** this money is tainted (with blood); **mit ~ befleckt od. besu-**

delt fig. stained with blood; **es ist viel ~ vergossen worden / geflossen** there was a great deal of bloodshed / much blood (has) flowed; **mit ~ geschrieben** geh. written in blood; **etw. mit s-m ~ besiegeln** poet. (für etw. sterben) lay down one's life for s.th.; **j-n bis aufs ~ ärgern** od. **reizen** etc. get s.o.'s blood up; **j-n bis aufs ~ peinigen** torture s.o. to the utmost; **er hat ~ geleckt** fig. he's tasted blood, he has a taste for blood; **2.** fig.: **heißes** od. **feuriges ~ haben** be hot-blooded; **dickes ~ haben** be lethargic (od. apathetic); **blaues/französisches** etc. **~ in den Adern haben** have blue/French etc. blood in one's veins; **von edlem/königlichem ~(e) sein** geh. be of noble/royal blood; **von reinem ~(e)** geh. pure(-blooded); **kaltes** od. **ruhig ~ bewahren** keep calm; **ruhig ~!** take it easy!, don't get excited!, keep your hair (Am. shirt) on! Sl.; **es liegt ihm im ~** it's in his blood; **das wird böses ~ geben** od. **machen** od. **schaffen** that'll stir up bad feeling; **3.** fig. (Personen): **junges ~** young blood; **e-m Vorhaben frisches** od. **neues ~ zuführen** infuse fresh od. new blood into a project → **Fleisch** 1
Blut|ader f vein; **~ahorn** m Bot. copper maple; **~alge** f, mst Pl.; Bot. red algae mst Pl.
Blutalkohol m, **~gehalt** m, **~spiegel** m Med. blood alcohol level
blutarm Adj. **1.** Med. an(a)emic; **2.** fig. (utterly) destitute, penniless; **Blutarmut** f Med. an(a)emia
Blut|auffrischung f Tierzucht: blood replacement (therapy); **~austausch** m Med. exchange transfusion; **~bad** n bloodbath, massacre; **ein ~ anrichten** carry out a massacre, cause a bloodbath; **~bahn** f **1.** nur Sg. bloodstream; **2.** einzelne: blood vessel; **~bank** f; Pl. -en blood bank
blut|befleckt Adj. bloodstained; **~beschmiert** Adj. bloodstained, bloody; **~bespritzt** Adj. blood-spattered; **~besudelt** Adj. tainted with blood
Blut|bild n Med. blood count (od. picture); **~bildung** f Physiol. formation of blood; **~blase** f Med. blood blister; **~brechen** n Med. vomiting of blood, h(a)ematemesis fachspr.; **~buche** f Bot. copper beech
Blutdruck m; nur Sg.; Physiol. blood pressure; **hoher/niedriger ~** high/low blood pressure, hypertension/hypotension fachspr.; **diastolischer/systolischer ~** diastolic/systolic blood pressure; (bei) **j-m den ~ messen** take s.o.'s blood pressure; **~abfall** m; nur Sg. drop (od. fall) in blood pressure
Blutdruck|messer m, **~messgerät** n blood-pressure meter (od. ga[u]ge); fachspr. sphygmomanometer; **~messung** f (taking of a) blood pressure reading
blutdruck|senkend Adj. hypotensive; **~steigernd** Adj. hypertensive
blutdürstig Adj. bloodthirsty
Blüte f; -, -n **1.** flower, blossom, bloom; **~n tragend** blossoming; fachspr. floriferous; **e-e ~ bestäuben** pollinate a flower; **seltsame ~n treiben** fig. come up with some strange things (od. effects); **üppige ~n treiben** fig. produce extravagant effects, ideas etc.; **2.** nur Sg.; Gesamtheit der Blüten: blossom; **in** (voller) **~ stehen** be in (full) bloom (od. flower od. blossom); **3.** nur Sg. (Blütezeit) flowering time; bes. bei Bäumen: blossom; **e-e Pflanze nach**

der ~ zurückschneiden prune a plant after flowering; **4.** fig. (Höhepunkt) height; der Macht, e-r Mode etc.: auch heyday; (Elite) cream, elite; Wirts. time of prosperity; e-r Kultur, e-r Kunst: flowering, height; **in der ~ s-r Jugend/Jahre** geh. in the prime of youth/life; **zur ~ gelangen** come to fruition; **s-e ~ erleben** flourish, reach its peak, have its heyday; **zu neuer ~ gelangen** experience a revival; weitS. reach new heights; **5.** umg. (falsche Banknote) dud, Am. fake; **6.** → **Stilblüte; 7.** umg. altm. (Pickel) rash, pimple, Brit. spot
Blutegel m Zool. leech
bluten v/i. **1.** bleed (auch Bäume) (aus from; aus dem Mund: auch out of); **~ wie ein Schwein** umg. bleed like a (stuck) pig; **mir blutet das Herz, wenn ich sehe, wie ...** fig. my heart bleeds to see ...; **~den Herzens** fig. with a heavy heart; **2.** umg. fig. (bezahlen) cough up, Brit. stump up; **wir haben dafür schwer ~ müssen** it cost us enough; **j-n ~ lassen** bleed s.o. dry
Blüten|blatt n Bot. petal; **~boden** m Bot. receptacle; **~honig** m honey (made from blossoms and flowers); **~kelch** m Bot. calyx; **~knospe** f Bot. flower bud; **~krone** f Bot. corolla; **~lese** f fig. anthology; iro. collection of howlers (Am. auch bloopers)
blütenlos Adj. flowerless; Bot. non-flowering
Blüten|meer n sea of blossom; **~pflanze** f Bot. flowering plant; **~stand** m Bot. inflorescence; **~staub** m Bot. pollen
Blutentnahme f Med. (taking of a) blood sample
Blütentraube f Bot. cluster of blossoms
blüten|weiß Adj. snow-white; **e-e ~e Weste haben** fig. iro. be whiter than white, be (as) pure as the driven snow; **~zart** Adj. kitten-soft
Blütenzweig m flowering twig, spray
Bluter m; -s, -; Med. h(a)emophiliac
Bluterguss m Med. h(a)ematoma; (blauer Fleck) bruise
Bluterkrankheit f Med. h(a)emophilia
Blutersatz m Med. blood substitute, artificial blood
Blütezeit f → **Blüte** 3, 4
Blut|farbstoff m Physiol. h(a)emoglobin; **~fehde** f blood feud, vendetta
Blutfett n Physiol. blood lipids Pl.; **~werte** Pl. Med. blood lipid concentration Sg.
Blut|fleck m bloodstain; **~fluss** m; nur Sg. flow of blood, h(a)emorrhage; **~gefäß** n Anat. blood vessel; **~geld** n blood money; **~gerinnsel** n Med. blood clot; **~gerinnung** f Physiol. (blood) clotting od. coagulation; **~gerinnungszeit** f Physiol. (blood) coagulation time
blutgetränkt Adj. blood-soaked
Blut|grätsche f Fußball (schweres Foul) scything tackle (od. lunge); **~gruppe** f Physiol. blood group; **j-s ~ bestimmen** determine s.o.'s blood group, type s.o.'s blood; (die) **A haben** be (od. belong to) blood group A, have A-type blood; **welche ~ haben Sie?** which blood group are you (od. do you belong to)?
Blutgruppen|bestimmung f blood-typing; **~zugehörigkeit** f membership of a blood group
Blut|hochdruck m Med. high blood pressure, hypertension; **an ~ leiden**

have high blood pressure; **~hochzeit** f hist.: **die Pariser ~** the Massacre of St. Bartholomew; **~hund** m Zool. bloodhound (auch fig.)

blutig Adj. **1.** Nase etc.: bloody; (blutbefleckt) auch bloodstained; Wunde: bleeding; **j-m die Nase ~ schlagen** give s.o. a bloody nose; **du bist ja ganz ~!** you're covered in blood!; **sich** (Dat.) **die Hände ~ machen** fig. bloody one's hands; **sich** (Dat.) **die Köpfe ~ schlagen** fig. have a real go at each other; **sich** (Dat.) **e-n Kopf holen** fig. get o.s. a bloody nose; **2.** Schlacht, Revolution etc.: bloody; Konflikt, Krieg: auch sanguinary; **e-e ~e Szene** a bloody sight (od. scene); im Film: a bloody scene, a scene full of blood (and violence); a blood and guts scene umg.; **~e Unruhen** violent unrest, violence and bloodshed; **es kam zu ~en Zwischenfällen** od. **Auseinandersetzungen** there were bloody (od. violent) clashes (**zwischen** between); **3.** Steak: rare; **4.** fig.: **~er Anfänger** absolute beginner; im Beruf etc.: raw recruit umg., greenhorn umg.; **~er Laie** complete layman; **es ist mein ~er Ernst** I'm dead(ly) serious, (and) I bloody well mean it umg.; **~e Tränen weinen** shed bitter tears

blutjung Adj. very young; **ich war ~, als ...** umg. auch I was just a kid when ...

Blut|konserve f unit of (stored) blood; **~körperchen** n Physiol. blood corpuscle, blood cell; **weißes ~** leucocyte; **rotes ~** erythrocyte; **~krankheit** f Med. blood disease; **~krebs** m Med. leuk(a)emia; **~kreislauf** m Physiol. (blood) circulation; **großer/kleiner ~** body (od. systematic) / pulmonary circulation; **~kuchen** m Physiol. blood clot; **~lache** f pool of blood

blutleer Adj. bloodless (auch fig.), an(a)emic; **~ aussehen** look ana(e)mic, be ana(e)mic-looking; **Blutleere** f hypox(a)emia; **ich hatte e-e plötzliche ~ im Kopf** the blood suddenly just went (od. drained) from my head

Blutlinie f Tierzucht: blood line

blutlos Adj. bloodless (auch fig.)

Blut|mangel m blood deficiency, an(a)emia fachspr.; **~mehl** n Agr. blood meal; **~opfer** n **1.** blood sacrifice; **2.** (Opfer an Menschenleben) human sacrifice; **dem Land wurden hohe ~ abverlangt** the blood toll for the nation was great, the scale of human sacrifice for the nation was vast; **~orange** f blood orange; **~pfropf** m Physiol. thrombus, blood clot; **~plasma** n Physiol. blood plasma; **~plättchen** n Physiol. platelet; **~probe** f blood test; (entnommene) blood sample; Jur. blood (alcohol) test; **bei j-m e-e ~ machen** od. **entnehmen** take s.o.'s blood, take a blood sample from s.o.; **~rache** f (bloody) vendetta; **~ schwören** swear vengeance; **~rausch** m bloodlust

blutreinigend Adj. blood-cleansing; **Blutreinigung** f cleansing (od. purification) of the bloodstream; **Blutreinigungstee** m blood-cleansing tea

blut|rot Adj. blood-red, (dark) crimson; **~rünstig** Adj. bloodthirsty; weitS. bloody; Film, Geschichte etc.: gory, attr. auch blood and guts ... umg.

Blutsauger m Zool. bloodsucker (auch fig.)

Blutsbruder m blood brother; **Blutsbrüderschaft** f blood brotherhood;

miteinander ~ schließen become blood brothers

Blut|schande f incest; **~schuld** f blood guilt; **~schwamm** m Med. strawberry (birth) mark; **~senkung** f Med. blood sedimentation; **~serum** n Physiol. blood serum; **~spende** f blood donation; **zur ~ gehen** go to give blood; **die Bevölkerung zur ~ aufrufen** appeal for blood (donors); **~spendeaktion** f campaign for (more) blood donors, Am. blood drive; **~spenden** n → **Blutspende**; **~spender** m, **~spenderin** f blood donor; **~spenderausweis** m blood donor card; **~spiegel** m Med. blood level; **~spur** f **1.** trail of blood; **die Hunde folgten der ~** the dogs followed the trail of blood; **e-e ~ hinterlassen** einzelne: leave traces of blood; Armee im Krieg etc.: leave a trail of blood; **2.** nur Pl. traces of blood; auffällig: auch bloodstains; **die ~en beseitigen** get rid of (od. remove) (all) traces of blood; **~stauung** f congestion; **~stein** m Min. h(a)ematite

blutstillend Adj. (auch **~es Mittel**) styptic

Blut|strahl m spurt of blood, spurting blood; **~strom** m flow of blood

Blutstropfen m drop of blood

Blutsturz m Med. h(a)emorrhage

blutsverwandt Adj. related by blood (**mit** to); **Blutsverwandte** m, f blood relation (od. relative); Jur.: **der nächste ~** the next of kin; **Blutsverwandtschaft** f blood relationship, kinship

Blut|tat f bloody deed; **e-e ~ begehen** commit (an act of) murder; **~test** m blood test; **~transfusion** f Med. blood transfusion

blut|triefend Adj. dripping with blood; **~überströmt** Adj. covered in blood; **ein ~es Gesicht** a face covered in blood

Blutübertragung f Med. blood transfusion

Blutung f bleeding; starke ~: h(a)emorrhage; **starke ~(en)** heavy bleeding; bei der Menstruation: heavy flow; **monatliche ~** monthly period; **innere ~en haben** have internal bleeding

blutunterlaufen Adj. Augen: bloodshot

Blut|untersuchung f blood test; **~verdünnung** f Med. h(a)emodilution, thinning of the blood; **~verdünnungsmittel** n Pharm. anticoagulant; **~vergießen** n bloodshed; **~vergiftung** f Med. blood poisoning; **~verlust** m loss of blood, blood loss; **starker ~** heavy loss of blood

blut|verschmiert Adj. bloodied, bloodstained; **~voll** Adj. fig. full-blooded

Blut|wäsche f Med. (blood) dialysis; **e-e ~ vornehmen** carry out dialysis; **~wurst** f Gastr. blutwurst, etwa black-pudding, Am. blood sausage; → **Rache**; **~zirkulation** f Physiol. blood circulation; **~zoll** m; nur Sg. (death) toll, toll of lives; **e-n schweren ~ fordern** take a heavy toll (of lives)

Blutzucker m Physiol. blood sugar; **mein ~ ist zu niedrig** umg. my blood sugar has dropped; **~spiegel** m Med. blood sugar level

Blutzufuhr f blood supply; **die ~ abschneiden** cut off the blood supply

BLZ f; -, kein Pl.; Abk. → **Bankleitzahl**

b-Moll n (abgek. **b**) Mus. B flat minor

BMX-Rad n BMX (bike)

BND m; -, kein Pl.; Abk. → **Bundesnachrichtendienst**

Bö f; -, -en gust; mit Niederschlag:

squall; Flug. turbulence

Boa f; -, -s **1.** Zool. Schlange: boa (constrictor); **2.** (Federboa) boa

Bob m; -s, -s Sport bob(sleigh); **für Kinder:** sledge, Am. sled; **~bahn** f bobsleigh run; **~fahren** n bobsleighing; **~fahrer** m bobber; **~rennen** n bob(sleigh) race (od. racing); **~schlitten** m bob(sleigh)

Bobtail ['bɔpteːl] m; -s, -s; Zool. Old English sheep(-)dog

Bock¹ m; -(e)s, Böcke **1.** bei Ziege: he-goat, billy goat; Schaf: ram; Kaninchen: buck; Reh: ~(bo)ck; Gämse: (chamois) buck; **ein kapitaler ~** Jägerspr. a large buck; fig. (Fehler) a boob; **e-n ~ schießen** umg. fig. boob; (ins Fettnäpfchen treten) drop a clanger; **den ~ zum Gärtner machen** fig. set the fox to keep the geese; **die Böcke von den Schafen trennen** od. **scheiden** fig. separate the wheat from the chaff (od. the men from the boys); **2.** umg. fig.: **sturer ~** pej. stubborn old so-and-so (od. git); (geiler) **alter ~** pej. (randy) old goat; **ein steifer ~ sein** pej. be (as) stiff as a poker (od. board); **3.** bes. Jugendspr. (Lust): **null ~!** can't be bothered!; **ich hab keinen** od. **null ~ (drauf)** it doesn't really grab me; **~ auf etw.** (Akk.) **haben** fancy (Am. feel like) doing s.th.; **4.** (Gestell) stand; (Hebebock) jack; (Sägebock) sawhorse; **5.** Sport buck; **~ springen** vault (over the buck); im Spiel: (play) leapfrog; **6.** (Kutschbock) box (seat); **7.** Zool. Käfer: longhorn

Bock² n, m; -s, - Bier: bock (type of strong beer)

bockbeinig Adj. umg. stubborn allg.

Bockbier n bock (beer) (type of strong beer)

bocken v/i. **1.** Pferd etc.: buck, refuse (a jump); **2.** fig. be stubborn, play up; (schmollen) sulk; **3.** Mot. umg. buck, refuse to start (od. go properly); **4.** Sl.: **das bockt nicht** (macht keinen Spaß) it's no fun

bockig Adj. **1.** stubborn; **2.** (schmollend) sulky; **Bockigkeit** f; nur Sg. **1.** (Sturheit) stubbornness; **2.** (Schmollen) sulking; sulkiness

Bock|leiter f stepladder; **~mist** m umg. crap, bullshit Sl.

Bocksbeutel m **1.** bocksbeutel (od. Franconian) wine; **2.** Flasche: bocksbeutel

Bocksfuß m **1.** goat's foot; **2.** Myth. cloven hoof; **bocksfüßig** Adj. Myth.: **der ~e Gott Pan** the cloven-hooved god Pan

Bockshorn n umg. fig.: **j-n ins ~ jagen** put the wind up s.o., lead s.o. up the garden path; **sich ins ~ jagen lassen** let o.s. be intimidated (od. flurried); **lass dich von ihm nicht ins ~ jagen!** auch don't let him put you off, don't let him get to you

Bock|springen n **1.** leapfrog; **2.** Sport (buck) vaulting; **~sprung** m (buck) vaulting; **Bocksprünge machen** fig. cut capers, jump for joy

Bockwurst f Gastr. (fat) frankfurter, bockwurst

Boden m; -s, -; flache Bucht: etwa shallow bay

Boden m; -s, Böden **1.** (Erdreich) soil; **fruchtbarer/magerer ~** fertile/barren soil; **sandiger/steiniger ~** sandy/stony ground; **leichter/mittelschwerer/schwerer ~** light/loamy/heavy (od. clayey) soil; **den ~ bebauen** od. **bestellen** develop (od. till) land; (**wie Pilze**)

aus dem ~ schießen mushroom (up); *auf fruchtbaren ~ fallen* fig. fall on fertile ground, have an effect; *etw. aus dem ~ stampfen* fig. conjure s.th. up (out of thin air); *wie aus dem ~ gewachsen* as if by magic; *sie wäre am liebsten vor Scham in den ~ versunken* she wished that the earth would open up and swallow her; → *Grund* 1; **2.** *nur Sg.;* (*Erdoberfläche*) ground; (*Fußboden*) floor (*auch im Wagen etc.*); *fester ~* firm ground; *auf den od. zu ~ fallen od. zu ~ stürzen* fall to the ground (*innen:* floor); *zu ~ gehen* (*beim Boxen etc.*) go down; *auf dem od. am ~ liegen* lie on the ground; *fig.* be finished (*od.* bankrupt); *etw. vom ~ aufheben* pick s.th. up (off the ground); *j-n zu ~ schlagen od. strecken* knock s.o. down (to the ground), floor s.o.; *die Augen zu ~ schlagen* cast one's eyes down (to the ground); *j-n zu ~ drücken* konkret: pin (*od.* press *od.* weigh) s.o. down; *fig.* destroy s.o., bear s.o. down; (*festen*) *~ fassen* get a (firm) footing *od.* foothold; *fig.* find one's feet; *Idee etc.:* take hold (*od.* root); *festen ~ unter den Füßen haben* be standing on firm ground, be on terra firma; *den ~ unter den Füßen verlieren* konkret: lose one's footing; (*unsicher werden*) be thrown off balance; *fig.* get out of one's depth; *j-m den ~ unter den Füßen wegziehen* fig. pull the rug out from under s.o.; *sich auf unsicherem etc. ~ bewegen* be treading on slippery ground, be skating on thin ice; *der ~ wurde ihm zu heiß od. der ~ brannte ihm unter den Füßen* fig. things got too hot for him; *den ~ für etw. bereiten* prepare the ground for s.th.; *am ~ zerstört* umg. (*entsetzt*) (completely) devastated; (*erschöpft*) completely drained, washed out; (*an*) *~ gewinnen/ verlieren* gain/lose ground; *~ zurückgewinnen* make up for lost ground; **3.** *e-s Gefäßes:* bottom; *e-e Kiste etc. mit doppeltem ~* with a false bottom; *Moral mit doppeltem ~* fig. double standards *Pl.;* **4.** *nur Sg.;* (*Grund*) *e-s Gewässers:* bottom; *auf dem od. am ~ des Meeres* on the sea(-)bed (*Am. auch* ocean floor); **5.** (*Gebiet*) *auf britischem etc. ~* on British *etc.* soil; *heiliger ~* holy (*od.* consecrated) ground; *heimatlicher ~* home territory; **6.** *fig.* (*Grundlage*) basis; *auf dem ~ des Grundgesetzes stehen* be within the Constitution; *auf dem ~ der Tatsachen bleiben* stick (*od.* keep) to the facts; *den ~ der Tatsachen verlassen* get away from (*od.* forget) the facts; *e-m Argument etc. den ~ entziehen* knock the bottom out of; *Handwerk hat goldenen ~* you can't go wrong if you learn a trade; **7.** (*Tortenboden*) base; **8.** (*Dachboden*) loft, attic; (*Heuboden*) hayloft; (*Trockenboden*) drying room; → *Fass* 2, *Grund* 5

Boden|abstand *m Mot.* (ground) clearance; **~abwehr** *f Mil.* ground defen|ce (*Am.* -se); **~bearbeitung** *f* cultivation of the land, tillage; **~belag** *m* floor covering; **~beschaffenheit** *f* **1.** surface conditions *Pl.;* **2.** *Agr.* properties *Pl.* of the soil; **~-Boden-Rakete** *f Mil.* surface-to-surface missile; **~brüter** *m Orn.* ground nester, ground--nesting bird; **~decker** *m; -s, -; Agr.* ground cover *Sg.;* **~dienst** *m Flug.* ground services *Pl.;* **~erhebung** *f* elevation; **~erosion** *f* soil erosion; **~er-**

~trag *m Agr.* crop yield; **~falte** *f* furrow; **~feuchtigkeit** *f Erde:* soil (*od.* ground *od.* surface) humidity; (*Bodennässe*) soil moisture; *Haus:* rising damp; **~fläche** *f Agr.* acreage; *Archit.* groundspace; *Tech.: Zimmer:* floor space; **~fliese** *f* floor tile; **~freiheit** *f Mot.* (ground) clearance; **~frost** *m* ground frost; **~frostgefahr** *f* likelihood of ground frost; **~fund** *m* arch(a)eological find; **~gefecht** *n* ground battle; *auch Pl.* ground combat (*od.* fighting)

bodengestützt *Adj.:* **~e Rakete** *etc.* ground-launched missile *etc.*

Boden|gymnastik *f* floor exercises *Pl.;* **~haftung** *f Mot.* (road) holding; **~haltung** *f; nur Sg.: Hühner in ~* free--range chickens; *Eier aus ~* free-range eggs; **~höhe** *f* ground level; *in ~* on ground level; **~kampf** *m → Bodengefecht;* **~karte** *f Geol.* soil map; **~kontrolle** *f,* **~kontrollstation** *f Flug.* ground control

Bodenkredit *m* mortgage credit; **~anstalt** *f* land mortgage bank

Boden|krume *f* surface soil, topsoil; **~kunde** *f; nur Sg.* soil science

bodenlang *Adj. Kleid:* full-length, floor-length

Bodenleger *m,* **~in** *f* floor layer

bodenlos I. *Adj.* bottomless; *fig.* incredible; **~er Leichtsinn** *fig.* unbelievable recklessness; *das war e-e ~e Frechheit! fig.* what an incredible cheek (*od.* nerve); *ins Bodenlose fallen* fall into an abyss; *fig.* fall into a black hole; **II.** *Adv. fig.* incredibly

Boden|-Luft-Rakete *f Mil.* ground-to--air missile; **~matte** *f* floor mat; **~nähe** *f:* (*in ~* at) ground level; *Flug.* zero altitude; **~nährstoff** *m* soil nutrient; **~nebel** *m* ground fog; **~nutzung** *f* cultivation (of the soil); **~personal** *n Flug.* ground staff (*mst V. im Pl.*), ground crew (*auch V. im Pl.*); **~pflege** *f* floor care; **~platte** *f Tech.* base plate; **~probe** *f* soil sample (*od.* specimen), bottom-hole sample; **~raum** *m* loft; **~recht** *n; nur Sg.; Jur.* land law; **~reform** *f* land reform; **~rente** *f* ground rent; **~satz** *m* **1.** deposit, sediment, residue; (*Magma*) cumulate; *im Kaffee:* grounds *Pl.,* dregs *Pl.;* **2.** *fig. pej. e-s Volkes: mst sozialer ~* dregs of society *Pl.;* **~schätze** *Pl.* mineral resources; *reich an ~n sein* be rich in (*od.* have rich) mineral resources; **~schutz** *m* soil conservation; **~sediment** *n Geol.* bottomset; bottomset bed; **~see** *m: der ~* Lake Constance; **~senke** *f* depression (of ground), hollow; sink, swale; **~senkung** *f Geol.* ground submergence (*od.* subsidence), sag(ging); **~sicht** *f Flug.* ground contact; **~spalte** *f* crevice, fissure, crack (in the ground); **~spekulant** *m* land jobber (*Am.* speculator); **~spekulation** *f* land speculation

bodenständig *Adj.* native, indigenous, autochthonous *fachspr.; Industrie etc.:* rooted to the soil, long-established; *Mensch:* rooted to one's native soil; **Bodenständigkeit** *f e-s Menschen:* rootedness to one's native soil, autochthony *fachspr.*

Boden|station *f Flug.* ground control; *Satellit etc.:* tracking (*od.* earth) station; **~staubsauger** *m* canister type vacuum cleaner; **~stewardess** *f* ground hostess; **~streitkräfte** *Pl. Mil.* ground forces; **~truppen** *Pl. Mil.* ground forces; **~turnen** *n Sport* floor

exercises *Pl.;* **~übung** *Sport* floor work (*od.* exercises *Pl.*); **~untersuchung** *f Erdreich:* soil test(ing) (*od.* analysis); *auf Baustelle:* site exploration, foundation testing; **~vase** *f* large vase, floor vase; **~verdichtung** *f Agr.* soil compression; **~verhältnisse** *Pl.* ground conditions; **~versalzung** *f; nur Sg.; Agr.* soil alkalization; **~versauerung** *f; nur Sg.; Öko.* soil acidification; **~verseuchung** *f Öko.* contamination of the soil; soil pollution; **~versiegelung** *f; nur Sg. von Parkettböden etc.:* floor (protection) sealing; **~vertiefung** *f* hollow (in the earth); **~welle** *f* **1.** bump; **2.** *Etech.* ground (*od.* earth) wave; **~wind** *m Met.* ground wind; **~ziel** *n Mil.* ground target

Bodmerei *f; -, -en; Naut.* bottomry

Body ['bɔdi] *m, -s, -s* **1.** *umg., bes. hum.* (*Körper*) body; **2.** *Kleidungsstück:* body(suit)

Body|builder ['bɔdibɪldɐ] *m; -s, -,* **~builderin** *f; -, -nen* bodybuilder, weightlifter; **~building** [-bɪldɪŋ] *n; -s, kein Pl.* bodybuilding; *~ machen* do (*od.* go to) bodybuilding; **~check** *m Sport: beim Eishockey:* body-check; **~guard** [-gaːd] *m; -s, -s* bodyguard; **~stocking** [-stɔkɪŋ] *n; -s,* **~suit** [-suːt] *m; -(s), -s; fachspr. → Body* 2

Böe *f; -, -n → Bö*

bog *Imperf. → biegen*

Bogen *m; -s, - od.* Bögen **1.** (*Krümmung*) curve; *e-s Flusses, Weges etc.: auch* bend; *Math., Etech., Astron.* arc; (*Wölbung*) arch; *im Rohr:* bend; *im Holz:* camber; *Skisport:* turn; *Eislauf:* curve, circle; *der Weg macht od. beschreibt e-n ~* the path curves (a)round; *e-n ~ machen um* go (*od.* curve) around, (do a) bend (a)round *umg.;* fig. steer clear of, give *s.o./s.th.* a wide berth; *e-n großen ~ fahren* go the long way (a)round; *mit dem Zirkel e-n ~ schlagen* draw a (arc with (a pair of) compasses (*bes. Am.* with a compass); *in hohem ~ werfen, fliegen etc.:* up high, in a high arc; *in hohem ~ rausfliegen* umg. fig. be turned (*od.* thrown, kicked) out on one's ear; *jetzt hat sie beim Radfahren den ~ raus* umg. fig. now she's got the hang of riding a bike; **2.** *Archit.* arch; *ein spitzer ~* a pointed arch; **3.** (*Waffe*) bow; *mit Pfeil und ~ schießen* shoot with bow and arrow; *den ~ spannen* draw the bow; *den ~ überspannen* fig. overstep the mark, overdo it, go too far, push one's luck (too far); **4.** (*Geigenbogen etc.*) bow; **5.** *Papier:* sheet (of paper), piece of paper; *Geschenkpapier etc.:* sheet; *Druck:* (printed) sheet; *Briefmarken:* sheet (of stamps); **6.** *Mus.: Verbindung zwischen zwei Noten:* (*Bindebogen*) slur (mark); (*Haltebogen*) tie; → *Bausch*

Bogen|brücke *f* arched bridge; **~fenster** *n* arched window

bogenförmig *Adj.* arched, arch--shaped; *Geol.* arcuate

Bogen|führung *f Mus.* bowing (technique); **~gang** *m* arcade; (*Verbindungsgang*) archway; **~gewölbe** *n* arched vault; **~grad** *m Math.* degree of arc; **~lampe** *f* **1.** *Etech.* arc lamp; **2.** *Sport* umg. banana shot, sliced (*od.* hook) shot; **~länge** *f Math.* arc length; **~maß** *n Math.* radian (*od.* circular) measure; **~minute** *f Astron.* arc minute; **~pfeiler** *m Archit.* flying buttress; **~säge** *f* coping saw; **~schießen** *n* archery; **~schütze** *m,* **~schützin** *f* archer; **~sehne** f bowstring; **~sekun-de** f Astron. arc second; **~strich** m Mus. stroke of the bow; weitS. bowing (technique); **~technik** f Mus. bowing technique; **~weite** f span (of an od. the arch)

Boheme [bo'(h)ɛːm] f; -, kein Pl. Bohemian world; **Bohemien** [bo(h)e'miɛ̃ː] m; -s, -s Bohemian

Bohle f; -, -n plank

Bohlen|brücke f plank bridge; **~weg** m corduroy road

Böhme m; -n, -n Bohemian (man od. boy); **Böhmen** (n); -s Bohemia; **~ und Mähren** hist. Bohemia and Moravia; **Böhmin** f; -, -nen Bohemian (woman od. girl); **böhmisch** Adj. Bohemian; **das sind ~e Dörfer für mich** fig. it's all Greek to me; **Böhmerwald** m; nur Sg.: **der ~** (the) Bohemian Forest

Bohne f; -, -n 1. Pflanze, Frucht, Samen: bean; (Saubohne) broad bean; **grüne ~n** French (od. string od. runner) beans; **weiße ~n** haricot beans, Am. navy beans; **gelbe ~n** wax beans; **dicke ~n** broad beans; **fadenlose ~n** stringless (green) beans; **blaue ~n** altm. fig. hum. bullets, slugs; 2. umg. fig.: **nicht die ~ wert** not worth a fig (od. cent); **nicht die ~!** not a bit!; **es kümmert ihn nicht die ~** he doesn't care two hoots about it, he doesn't give a toss about it Sl.; **er versteht nicht die ~ davon** he doesn't know the first thing about it, Am. auch he doesn't know beans about it; **~n in den Ohren haben** umg. fig. be deaf allg.; 3. Kakao: cocoa bean; Kaffee: coffee bean

Bohnen|eintopf m Gastr. bean casserole (od. stew), cassoulet; **~gemüse** n Gastr. green (od. French) beans Pl.; **~kaffee** m 1. (gemahlene) Bohnen: ground coffee, filter coffee; 2. Getränk: filter coffee, real coffee; **~kraut** n; nur Sg. Bot., Gastr. savo(u)ry; **~ranke** f Bot. beanstalk, tendril; **~salat** m Gastr. (French) bean salad; **~sprosse** f bean sprout; **~stange** f beanpole (auch umg. fig.); **~stroh** n: **dumm wie ~** umg. as thick as two short planks (Am. as a board); **~suppe** f Gastr. bean soup

Bohner m; -s, -, **Bohnerbesen** m floor polisher; **Bohnermaschine** f electric floor polisher; **bohnern** vt/i. polish, wax; (the floor[s]); **Vorsicht, frisch gebohnert!** freshly polished (floor, stairs etc.), cleaning in progress; **Bohnerwachs** n floor polish

Bohrarbeiten Pl. drilling (work) Sg., drilling operations

bohren I. vt/i. 1. (ein rundes Loch) ausbohren: bore; Tech., Med., mit Bohrer, Bohrmaschine: drill; (Brunnen) sink; (Tunnel) drive; **mit dem Finger ein Loch in die Tischdecke ~** poke a hole in the tablecloth (with one's finger); 2. e-n Pfahl etc. **in den Boden ~** drive (od. sink) a post etc. into the ground; **j-m ein Messer in die Brust ~** plunge a knife into s.o.'s chest; **ein Schiff in den Grund ~** send a ship to the bottom; 3. etw. **aus etw. ~** pick s.th. out of s.th.; **Rosinen aus dem Kuchen ~** pick raisins out of the cake; **II.** vt/i. Zahnarzt: drill; **er hat mir zwei Zähne gebohrt** umg. I had to have two fillings; **er hat überhaupt nicht gebohrt** I didn't need any fillings (od. any work done); **III.** v/i. 1. Tech. drill (nach for); **nach Öl ~** drill for oil; **wo sollen wir ~?** where should we start drilling?;

2. **mit den Zehen im Sand ~** poke (od. play with) one's toes in the sand; **in der Nase ~** pick one's nose; 3. fig. (eindringen) probe (**in** + Dat. into); **in j-s Vergangenheit ~** delve (od. probe) into s.o.'s past; 4. fig. (aufdringlich sein) persist, go on and on umg.; **er bohrt** auch he's very persistent, he'll go on and on at you; **IV.** v/refl.: **sich in/durch j-n/etw. ~** bore (its way) into/ through s.o./s.th.; **die Rakete bohrte sich in den Boden** the rocket buried itself in the ground; **ein Dorn bohrte sich in ihren Finger** a thorn worked its way into her finger; **seine Blicke bohrten sich in ihren Rücken** fig. his eyes made holes in her back

bohrend I. Part. Präs. → **bohren**; **II.** Adj. Blick: piercing, penetrating; Schmerz: gnawing; Frage: penetrating, probing; Zweifel nagging; Angst: persistent; Hunger: gnawing

Bohrer m; -s, - 1. Tech. drill; (Schlagbohrer) hammer drill; (Nagelbohrer) gimlet; (Bohrstange) bit; (Spiralbohrer) twist drill (od. bit); für Holz: wood drill; 2. Dent. drill; Med., für Schädeloperationen: trepan; 3. Arbeiter: driller

Bohr|futter n drill chuck; **~hammer** m drill hammer, rock drill; **~insel** f drilling rig; für Öl: oilrig; **~kopf** m drilling (od. boring) head, bit; **~loch** n drill(ed) hole; (Sprengloch) blast hole; ausgebohrt: bore hole (auch bei Holz); **~maschine** f Tech., Med. drill; **~plattform** f drilling platform; **~schablone** f drilling template; **~schlüssel** m chuck key; **~schrauber** m drilldriver; **~turm** m (drilling) derrick, boring tower; **~ für Erdölbohrungen** oil-well derrick; **schwimmender ~** floating derrick; **~wurm** m Zool. shipworm

Bohrung f drilling, boring; (Bohrloch) (drilled od. bore) hole; Mot., in Zylinder: bore

Bohrversuch m trial drilling

böig Adj. gusty; Flug. umg. bumpy

Boiler m; -s, -; Tech. boiler; im Haushalt: auch water heater, Brit. auch geyser

Boje f; -, -n; Naut. buoy

Bolero m; -s, -s 1. Mus. bolero; 2. Hut, Jacke: bolero hat, bolero jacket; **~jäckchen** n (little) bolero jacket

Bolid m; -en, -en 1. Astron. fireball, bolide; 2. Mot. racer

Bolide m; -n, -n 1. → **Bolid** 2; 2. fig. high-performance amplifier(, computer etc.)

Bolivianer m; -s, -, **~in** f; -, -nen Bolivian, weiblich auch: Bolivian woman (od. girl etc.); **bolivianisch** Adj. Bolivian

bölken v/i. nordd. 1. → **blöken**; 2. (aufstoßen) belch, burp

Böller m; -s, - saluting gun; **böllern** v/i. fire (a salute); **Böllerschuss** m gun salute; **drei Böllerschüsse** a three-gun salute

Bollerwagen m nordd. (wooden) cart (Am. auch wagon)

Bollette f; -, -n; österr. Amtsspr. customs declaration

Bollwerk n Mil. und fig. bulwark (**gegen** against) mst. fig. bastion, stronghold; **ein ~ des Friedens** fig. a bastion of freedom

Bolschewik m; -en, -i od. pej. -en; hist. Bolshevik; **Bolschewismus** m Bolshevism; **Bolschewist** m; -en, -en, **Bolschewistin** f; -, -nen Bolshevist; **bolschewistisch** Adj. Bolshevist

bolzen umg. **I.** v/i. Fußball: kick around (auch schlecht spielen); **II.** v/t. umg. (Ball) boot

Bolzen m; -s, - 1. Tech. bolt; pin; 2. hist., von Armbrust: bolt

bolzengerade Adj. (as) straight as a poker, bolt upright

Bolzen|gewehr n pop-gun; **~schneider** m Tech. bolt cutters Pl.; **~schussapparat** m bolt apparatus, humane killer

Bolzerei f; -, -en; umg. kick-about; **Bolzplatz** m playing field

Bombardement [bɔmbardə'mãː] n; -s, -s bombardment (auch Phys. und fig.); Mil. bombing; Artillerie: shelling; **bombardieren** v/t. 1. bomb, bombard; mit Granaten: auch shell; 2. fig. (bewerfen) pelt (mit with); 3. fig. mit Bitten, Fragen etc.: bombard, assail (with); **Bombardierung** f → **Bombardement**

Bombast m; -(e)s, kein Pl.; pej. bombast ohne best. Art.; **bombastisch I.** Adj. bombastic; **II.** Adv. bombastically

Bombe f; -, -n 1. bomb; **e-e ~ legen** plant a bomb; **e-e ~ abwerfen** drop a bomb (**auf** + Akk. on); **e-e ~ entschärfen** defuse a bomb; **die Nachricht** etc. **schlug ein wie e-e ~** fig. the news etc. came as a (real) bombshell; **die ~ ist geplatzt** fig. the cat's out of the bag; (etw. Unangenehmes ist passiert) the worst has come to the worst; **mit ~n und Granaten durchfallen** umg. fig. fail miserably (od. spectacularly); 2. nur Sg.: **die ~** (Atombombe) the bomb; **seit wann hat Indien die ~?** how long has India had the bomb (od. had nuclear missiles)?; 3. Fußball: fantastic shot; 4. Geol. bomb

Bomben|... im Subst., umg. oft tremendous ...; **~abwurf** m bombing, bomb release; **gezielter/ungezielter ~** targeted/indiscriminate bombing; **~alarm** m bomb alert; **~angriff** m bomb attack, air raid; **~anschlag** m 1. bomb attack; 2. (Attentat) bomb attempt; **~attentat** n bomb attempt; **~auftrag** m umg. fantastic order (od. job); **~besetzung** f umg. Film etc.: star cast; **~drohung** f bomb threat, bomb scare; **~erfolg** m umg. tremendous (od. huge) success; Theat. box-office hit; (Musik-CD) smash hit

bombenfest I. Adj. 1. (Keller etc.) bombproof; (Material, Gebäude etc.) bomb-resistant; (Panzer etc.) shellproof; 2. Entschluss, Überzeugung: umg. dead certain, unshak(e)able allg.; **II.** Adv. umg. fig.: **~** (davon) überzeugt sein, dass ... be absolutely convinced that ... allg.; **die Naht** etc. **hält ~** is absolutely secure allg.; **das steht ~** that's a dead cert(ainty) (od. a sure thing)

Bomben|form f Sport, umg.: **in ~ sein** be in great shape; **~gehalt** n umg. (Spitzenverdienst) fantastic salary allg.; **~geld** n umg.: **ein ~ verdienen** earn a packet (Am. bundle); **ein ~ machen/ gewinnen** make/win a fortune allg.; **~geschäft** n umg. roaring business; **ein ~ machen** do a roaring trade; **etw. ist ein ~** s.th is a gold mine; **~hitze** f umg. sweltering heat; **~krater** m bomb crater; **~lage** f umg. für Geschäft, Wohnung: prime location, plum site; **~leger** m, **~legerin** f bomber, bomb planter; **der ~** auch the man (od. person) who planted the bomb; **~preis** m umg. 1. niedriger: rockbottom price;

zu e-m ~ *auch* for next to nothing;
2. *hoher*: top price; incredible price;
e-n ~ erzielen obtain the top price;
~räumkommando *n*, **~räumtrupp** *m*
Mil. bomb-disposal (*od.* bomb-clearing) squad; **~räumung** *f* bomb disposal (*od.* bomb clearing); **~rolle** *f* *umg.*
Film etc.: dream part; **~sache** *f umg.*
knockout; **das ist doch e-e ~!** that's
fantastic!; **~schacht** *m* Mil. (*in Flugzeug*) bomb bay; **~schaden** *m* air-raid
damage; **~schuss** *m* Sport umg.
cracking shot; **~schütze** *m* **1.** *Mil.*
bombardier; **2.** *umg.* (*guter Schütze*)
good (*od.* crack) shot
bombensicher *Adj.* **1.** (*Unterstand
etc.*) bombproof; **2.** *umg.* (*ganz sicher*)
surefire, dead certain; **es ist e-e ~e
Sache** it's a dead cert(ainty), it's as
sure as death (*od.* as fate *od.* as a
gun)
Bomben|splitter *m* Mil. bomb splinter; **~stellung** *f umg. beruflich*: plum
job, fantastic job; **~stimmung** *f*; *nur
Sg.*; *umg.* (*gute Stimmung*) terrific
(*od.* tremendous) atmosphere; **er war
in ~** he was (*od.* felt) on top of the
world; **~teppich** *m* Mil. blanket (*od.*
carpet) bombing; **e-n ~ legen** blanket-
(*od.* carpet-)bomb (an area); **~terror**
m terrorist bombing(s) *od.* attacks *Pl.*;
~trichter *m* bomb crater, crater left
by a (*od.* the) bomb
bombenvoll *Adj. umg.* (*gestopft voll*)
full to bursting
Bomber *m*; *-s*, *-* **1.** *Mil. Flug.* bomber;
2. *umg. fig. Fußball*: star striker; **~geschwader** *n* Mil. bomber group (*Am.*
wing); **~jacke** *f* bomber jacket
bombig *umg.* **I.** *Adj. Stimmung, Wetter
etc.*: super, smashing, terrific; **II.** *Adv.*:
~ verdienen earn a packet (*Am.* bundle, wad)
Bommel *m*; *-s*, *-*, *auch f*; *-*, *-n*; *umg.*
bobble, pom-pom
Bon [bɔŋ] *m*; *-s*, *-s* **1.** (*Gutschein*)
voucher; (*Gratisbon*) coupon; **e-n ~
einlösen** redeem a voucher (*od.* coupon); **2.** (*Kassenzettel*) receipt
Bonbon [bɔŋ'bɔŋ] *m*, *n*; *-s*, *-s* **1.** sweet,
sweetie, *Am.* (piece of) candy; *Pl.
Am.* candy; **ein od. e-n ~ lutschen**
suck (on) a sweet (*Am.* piece of candy); **2.** *fig.* treat; **ein echter od. echtes
~ für Kenner** a real treat for the connoisseur; **3.** *umg. hum. rundes Abzeichen etc.*: badge, *Am.* pin *allg.*; **bonbonfarben, bonbonfarbig** *Adj.* sickly
pink (*od.* yellow *etc.*) *Am.* candy-colored
Bonbon(n)iere [bɔŋbɔ'njeːrə] *f*; *-*, *-n*
(*Pralinenschachtel*) box of chocolates
Bonbonpapier *n* sweet-wrapper, sweetie paper, *Am.* candy wrapper
bonbonrosa **I.** *Adj.* candy pink;
II. **Bonbonrosa** *n* candy pink
bongen *v/t. umg.* (*Betrag, Ware an
Kasse*) ring up *allg.*; **ist od. schon gebongt!** sorted!, okey-doke!
Bongo *n*; *-s*, *-s und f*; *-*, *-s*, *mst. Pl.*
bongo (drum), bongos *Pl.*
Bonität *f*; *-*, *-en* **1.** *nur Sg.*; *Wirts., finanzielle*: credit standing, creditworthiness, reliability; **2.** *Wirts.* (*Warengüte*) quality; **3.** *Agr.* quality of the soil
Bonmot [bõ'moː] *n*; *-s*, *-s* witty remark,
witticism; **ein ~ zum Besten geben** entertain with (*od.* make) a witty remark
Bonsai *m*; *-(s)*, *-s* bonsai (tree)
Bonus *m*; *-* od. *-ses*, *-* od. *-se* od. *Boni*
1. *Wirts.* bonus, premium; **j-m e-n ~
gewähren** give s.o. a bonus; **2.** *Wirts.*
special (*od.* extra) dividend; **3.** *Päd.*,

Sport bonus points *Pl.*; **~aktien** *Pl.*
Wirts. dividend shares; **~-Malus-System** *n* bonus-malus system, bonus and
penalty system (in insurance); **~system** *n* bonus system
Bonze *m*; *-n*, *-n* **1.** *umg. pej.* bigwig;
die ~n der Partei the party bigwigs;
die ~n der Wirtschaft the tycoons (*od.*
captains) of industry; **2.** *umg. pej.* (*reicher Angeber*) big shot; **3.** *Reli.* (*buddhistischer Priester od. Mönch*) bonze;
Bonzentum *n*; *-s*, *kein Pl.*; *umg. bes.
Am.* bossism; **Bonzenwirtschaft** *f*;
nur Sg.; *umg.* boss rule
Bookmark ['bʊkmɑːk] *f*; *-*, *-s*; *EDV*
bookmark
Boom [buːm] *m*; *-s*, *-s*; *Wirts.* boom;
boomen *v/i. umg. Geschäft*: boom
Boot *n*; *-(e)s*, *-e*; (*auch umg. für Schiff*)
boat; (*Paddelboot*) canoe; (*Schiffs-,
Ruder-, Vergnügungsboot*) dingh(e)y;
flaches, viereckiges: punt; **ein schnittiges ~** a racy boat; **~ fahren** go boating; **das ~ legt ab/an** the boat is casting off / berthing; **das ~ ist leck** the
boat is leaky; **das ~ kentert** the boat is
capsizing; **das ~ sinkt od. geht unter**
the boat is sinking; **wir sitzen alle im
selben ~** *fig.* we're all in the same
boat
booten [buːtn] *EDV* **I.** *v/t.* (*ein Programm*) boot (up); **II.** *v/i. Computer,
Programm*: boot
Boots|anhänger *m* boat trailer; **~eigner** *m*, **~eignerin** *f* boat-owner; **~fahrt**
f boat trip; *kürzere*: boat ride; **e-e
machen** go for a boat trip; **~führer** *m*,
~führerin *f* Sport coxswain; **~hafen** *m*
marina; **~haken** *m* boat hook; **~haus**
n boathouse; **~länge** *f* (boat's) length;
um zwei ~n gewinnen win by two
lengths; **~leute** *Pl. → Bootsmann*;
~mann *m*; *Pl. -leute*; *Naut.* boatswain;
Mil. petty officer; **~rennen** *n* boat
race; **~schuppen** *m* boatshed; **~steg**
m landing stage; **~verleih** *m* boat hire
(*Am.* rental); *auf Schild*: boats for hire
(*Am.* rent)
Bor *n*; *-s*, *kein Pl.*; *Chem.* boron
Borax *m*; *-(es)*, *kein Pl.*; *Chem.* borax
Bord¹ *m*; *-es*, *-e* **1.** *Naut., Rand des
Schiffes*: side; **2.** *Naut., Flug., in Wendungen*: **an ~** on board, aboard (*e-s
Schiffes / der Titanic etc.* a ship / the
Titanic *etc.*); **an ~ e-s Schiffes/Flugzeugs gehen** board a ship/plane; **an ~
gehen** *Naut.* go aboard, board ship;
Flug. board (the aircraft); **von ~ gehen** *Naut.* disembark; *Flug.* leave the
aircraft; **an ~ nehmen** *Naut.* take
aboard; *Flug.* take onto the plane;
über ~ gehen fall overboard; **über ~
werfen** throw overboard (*auch fig.*);
(*Ladung*) jettison; **alle Mann an/von ~**
all aboard / abandon ship; **Mann über
~!** man overboard!
Bord² *n*; *-es*, *-e für Bücher*: shelf
Bord|buch *n* log book; **~case** [-keːs]
n, *m*; *-*, *-* *od.* *-s* flight case; **~computer**
m Flug. on-board computer; *Mot.
auch* dashboard computer; *Naut.*
ship's computer
Börde *f*; *-*, *-n*; *Geog.* fertile plain
bordeaux [bɔr'doː] **I.** *Adj.* burgundy,
claret; **II.** **Bordeaux** *n*; *-*, *- Farbe*: burgundy, claret; **III.** **Bordeaux** *m*; *-*, *-
Wein*: claret, Bordeaux (wine)
bordeigen *Adj.*; *attr.* on-board ...,
ship's, plane's *etc.* ...
Bordelektronik *f* avionics *Pl.*
Bordell *n*; *-s*, *-e* brothel; **~besucher** *m*
brothel patron; **~viertel** *n* red-light
district; **~wirtin** *f* madam

Bord|funk *m* Naut. ship's radio; *Flug.*
aircraft radio equipment; **~funker** *m*
Naut., *Flug.* radio operator; **~ingenieur** *m* Flug. flight engineer; *Naut.*
ship's engineer; **~instrumente** *Pl.*
Flug. on-board instruments *Pl.*; **~kanone** *f* (air)craft cannon; **~kante** *f*
kerb, *Am.* curb; **~karte** *f* Flug. boarding pass; **~kino** *n* Flug. in-flight movies *Pl.*; *Naut.* ship's cinema; **~küche**
f Naut. galley; **~mittel** *n*; *mst Pl.*: **mit
~n wörtlich**: with our (their, his *etc.*)
on-board equipment; *fig.* with the
means we have (*od.* had) at our disposal (*bzw.* they *etc.* have *od.* had at
their *etc.* disposal); **~personal** *n* Flug.
flight crew; **~programm** *n* Flug. in-
-flight entertainment program(me);
~radar *n* Flug. airborne radar; **~sender** *m* airborne transmitter; **~sprechanlage** *f* (on-board) radio telephone
Bordstein *m* kerb, *Am.* curb; **den ~
mitnehmen** *umg.* scrape the kerb (*od.*
curb); **~kante** *f* kerb, *Am.* curb;
~schwalbe *f umg.* (*Straßenprostituierte*) streetwalker, *bes. Am.* hooker,
working girl *Sl.*
Bord|telefon *n* Naut., *Flug.* interphone; **~unterhaltung** *f Flug.* in-flight
entertainment
Bordüre *f*; *-*, *-n* border, trimming
Bord|verpflegung *f* Flug. in-flight
meals *Pl.* (*od.* catering, fare), meals
Pl. on the plane *umg.*; **~waffen** *Pl.*
Mil. Flug. aircraft weapons; *Panzer*:
tank armament *Sg.*
boreal *Adj. Geog.* boreal
Borg → Pump
borgen *v/t.* **1.** (*sich* [*Dat.*]) *etw.* **~** borrow s.th. (**bei** *od.* **von** from *od.* off
s.o.); *fig.* (*plagiieren*) borrow (*od.* lift)
s.th.; **es ist nur geborgt** I've *etc.* just
borrowed it; **kann ich mir 10 Euro von
dir ~?** can I borrow 10 euros?; **2.** (*verleihen*): **j-m etw. ~** lend s.o. s.th., lend
s.th. (out) to s.o., *bes. Am.* loan s.o.
s.th., loan s.th. to s.o.; **das ist aber nur
geborgt** (*das will ich zurückhaben*)
it's just a loan (though); **kannst du
mir was ~?** can you lend me some
money?; **Borgen bringt Sorgen**
Sprichw. he who goes a-borrowing
goes a-sorrowing
Borke *f*; *-*, *-n*; *nordd.* **1.** *von Bäumen*:
bark; **2.** (*Schorf*) crust; **3.** (*Schmutzkruste*) crust of dirt; **Borkenkäfer** *m*
bark beetle
borniert *Adj. pej.* **1.** (*engstirnig*) narrow-minded; **2.** (*beschränkt*) dense;
Borniertheit *f*; *nur Sg.* **1.** narrow-
-mindedness; **2.** denseness
Borreliose *f*; *-*, *-n*; *Med.* borreliosis
Borretsch *m*; *-(e)s*, *kein Pl.*; *Bot.*,
Gastr. borage
Bor|salbe *f* boric acid ointment; **~säure** *f* bor(ac)ic acid
Borschtsch *m*; *-*, *kein Pl.*; *Gastr.*
borscht
Börse *f*; *-*, *-n* **1.** *Wirts.*: (*Wertpapierbörse*) stock exchange; *Handel*: stock market; *für Waren*: commodities market;
Devisen: foreign exchange market;
(*Frachtbörse*) freight market; (*Termin-, Optionsbörse*) futures (*od.* options) market; (*Gebäude, Ort*) stock
exchange; **die Londoner ~** the London
Stock Exchange; **die Frankfurter/Pariser** *etc.* **~** *auch* the Frankfurt/Paris *etc.*
bourse; **an der ~** on the stock exchange (*od.* market); **an der ~ spekulieren/spielen** speculate/dabble on the
stock market; **an der ~ notierte Aktien**
(officially) quoted shares, listed stock;

an die ~ **gehen** (*Aktien ausgeben*) issue shares, go public, enter the stock exchange; *die ~ haussiert/boomt* the market is bullish/booming; *die ~ eröffnet flau/lustlos/lebhaft etc.* the market opens slack/dull(y)/brisk(ly) *etc.*; *die ~ schließt fest/müde etc.* the market closes strongly/weakly *etc.*; **2.** *altm.* (*Geldbeutel*) purse; *für Männer und Am.*: wallet; **3.** *Sport, Boxen*: purse

...börse *f*, *im Subst.* fair; *Briefmarken~* stamp fair; *Schallplatten~* record fair

Börsen|aufsicht *f Wirts.* stock exchange supervisory board; *~auftrag m* stock market transaction (*od.* deal); **~beginn** *m* opening of the stock market; *bei ~* when the stock market opened (*od.* opens); *~barometer n* (stock) market barometer; **~bericht** *m* stock market report; *~entwicklung f* (stock) market trend *od.* tendency; *~eröffnung* opening of the stock market

börsenfähig *Adj. Wirts.* **1.** listed; *Aktien*: negotiable on the stock exchange; **2.** (*lieferbar*) marketable; **3.** *Person*: qualified to enter (*od.* trade) on an exchange

Börsengang *m Wirts.* introduction to the stock exchange; *ein Unternehmen vor/nach dem ~* a company before/after entering the stock exchange, *auch* a company before/after floatation; **börsengängig** *Adj.* marketable, negotiable

Börsen|geschäft *n Wirts.* stock market transaction; *~handel m* stock exchange trading; *~index m* stock exchange index; *~krach m umg.* (stock market) crash, stock market collapse, collapse of the stock market; *~kurs m* market price (*od.* rate), (stock exchange) quotation; *die ~e notieren heute höher/niedriger* the market prices were quoted higher/lower today; *~makler m*, *~maklerin f* stockbroker; *~nachrichten Pl.* financial news (*od.* report) *Sg.*; *~notierung f* quotation; *~option f* option; *e-e ~ kaufen/verkaufen* buy/sell options *Pl.*, *Am. auch* call/put; *~platz m* financial cent|re (*Am.* –er); *~saal m* trading room; *~schluss m* close of the stock market; *bei ~* when the stock market closed (*od.* closes); *~segment n* sector of the stock market; *~spekulant m* stock exchange speculator; *~spekulation f* speculation on the stock market; *~spiel n Wettbewerb mit fiktiven Börsengeschäften*: stock market simulation game; *~sprache f* stock exchange jargon; *~termingeschäft n*, *~terminhandel m* trading in futures; *~tipp m* market tip; *~umsätze Pl.* market turnover *Sg.*; *~wert m* **1.** market value; **2.** *nur Pl. Wertpapiere*: stocks and shares *Pl.*, *Am.* securities *Pl.*; *die Favoriten unter den ~en* the top stocks (and shares); *~zeiten Pl.* trading hours, market times; *~zettel m* stock list

Börsianer *m*; *-s, -*; *Wirts.* (*Makler*) broker, operator *umg.*; (*Spekulant*) speculator

Borste *f*; *-, -n* **1.** (*Schweinehaar*) bristle *mst. Pl.*; *ein Pinsel mit echten ~n* a brush with real bristles; **2.** *künstlich*: bristle *mst. Pl.*; *e-e Zahnbürste mit abgerundeten ~n* a toothbrush with rounded tufts; *seine ~n aufstellen fig.* put one's defen|ces (*Am.* –ses) up, *Am. auch* bristle up, raise one's bristles

Borsten|besen *m* coarse broom; *~kopf m* spike; *~pinsel m* bristle brush; *~tier n*, *~vieh n* pig; *Pl. Koll.* swine *Sg.*

borstig *Adj.* bristly; *umg. fig.* gruff; **Borstigkeit** *f*; *nur Sg.* gruffness

Borte *f*; *-, -n* border; (*Besatz*) braid, trimming; (*Tresse*) galloon

bös *Adj.* → **böse**

bösartig *Adj.* **1.** (*boshaft, gemein*) malicious, nasty; *Tier.* vicious; *Gerede*: spiteful; *unser Nachbar ist richtig ~* our neigbo(u)r is really malevolent; **2.** *Med.*, *Tumor etc.*: malignant; *Krankheit*: *auch* pernicious, malign *förm.*; *es war etwas Bösartiges* it was a malignancy; **Bösartigkeit** *f*; *nur Sg.* **1.** spitefulness, malignancy *förm.*; *Tier*: vicious nature, visciousness; **2.** *Med. Krankheit*: malignancy, pernicious nature

Böschung *f* embankment; *Geol.* scarp (face); *steile*: escarpment; (*Neigung, Gefälle*) gradient

böse I. *Adj.* **1.** *Menschen, Taten*: bad; (*verrucht*) evil, wicked; (*böswillig*) spiteful; *~ Zeiten* hard times; *e-e ~ Zunge haben* have a wicked (*od.* malicious) tongue; *der ~ Geist* (the) evil spirit; *die ~ Sieben* the unlucky seven; *die ~ Fee* the Wicked Fairy; *in ~r Absicht* with evil intent; → *Blick 2*, *gut I 7*; **2.** (*unartig*) bad, naughty; *pfui, ~r Hund!* bad (*od.* naughty) dog!; **3.** *oft umg.* (*schlimm*) *Ende, Fehler, Husten etc.*: bad; *Ende*: *auch* sticky; (*wund*) *auch* sore; *Krankheit, Sache, Schrecken, Überraschung, Wunde etc.*: nasty; *Erkältung*: *auch* rotten *umg.*; *Folgen*: dire; (*unangenehm*) unpleasant; *sich in e-r ~n Lage befinden* be in dire straights; *e-e ~ Wende nehmen* take a nasty turn, take a turn for the worse; *das gibt ein ~s Erwachen* he (*od.* she etc.) will have a rude awakening (*od.* come down to earth with a bump *umg.*); *es sieht ~ aus* things don't look too good, things look (*umg.* pretty) bad (*od.* grim) (*für* for); **4.** (*wütend, aufgebracht*) angry, cross, *bes. Am.* mad *umg.*; *wegen der Lüge war sie ~ auf ihn od. mit ihm od. war sie ihm ~* she was angry with him about (*od.* because of) the lie, she was angry with him because he lied; *~ werden* get angry *etc.*; *ein ~s Gesicht machen* scowl; → *Blut 2*; **II.** *Adv.* **1.** (*sehr*) *sich schneiden, verbrennen etc.*: badly; *sich ~ erschrecken* get a real fright, get the fright of one's life; *sich (ganz) ~ irren* make a fatal (*od.* very bad) mistake; *sich (ganz) ~ verirren od. verlaufen* get hopelessly lost; *ich war ~ erschrocken* I got a bad shock; *das hat sie ~ mitgenommen* it really took it out of her; **2.** (*schlimm*): *das wird ~ enden od. ausgehen* it will come to a bad end, it will end in tears *umg.*; *~ dran sein umg.* not have an easy time (of it); **3.** (*gemein*) nasty; *ich habe es nicht ~ gemeint* I didn't mean any harm; **4.** (*zornig*): *j-n ~ ansehen* scowl at s.o.; *stärker*: give s.o. a black look, look daggers at s.o.; *schau nicht so ~!* don't look so grumpy!

Böse¹ *m, f*; *-n, -n* bad person; *Kind*: bad boy (*bzw.* girl); *die ~n im Film etc.*: the baddies (*Am.* bad guys) *umg.*; *der ~* (*Teufel*) the Evil One, the Devil; *den ~n spielen* play the villain (*od.* baddy, *Am.* bad guy *umg.*)

Böse² *n*; *-n, nur Sg.* **1.** evil; (*Schaden*) harm; *~s tun* do evil; *j-m* (*etwas*) *~s*

antun do s.o. harm; *~s im Sinn haben od. im Schilde führen* be up to no good; *~s reden über* speak ill of; *j-m ~s nachsagen* spread nasty rumo(u)rs about s.o., bitch about s.o. *umg.*; *das ~ in ihm siegte* the evil in him triumphed; *vom ~n* (*ab*)*lassen geh.* turn away from evil, repent; **2.** (*Schlimmes*) *nichts ~s ahnen* be unsuspecting; *sich* (*Dat.*) *nichts ~s dabei denken* not mean any harm by it; *j-m nichts ~s wünschen* wish only the best for s.o.; *keine Angst, es geschieht dir nichts ~s* don't worry, nothing bad will happen to you; **3.** *nach Streit*: *im ~n auseinander gehen* part on bad terms; → *auch schlimm, Gute²*

Bösewicht *m*; *Pl. –er od. -e*; *altm., hum.* villain, rogue (*beide auch fig., iro.*)

boshaft *Adj. Menschen*: malicious, nasty; *Gelächter, Grinsen*: malicious; *Kritik, Spott*: vicious; **Boshaftigkeit** *f* **1.** *nur Sg.* maliciousness, malicious nature; *lit.* wickedness; **2.** *Äußerung, Handlung*: malicious (*od.* nasty) remark, thing to do *etc.*

Bosheit *f* **1.** *nur Sg.* malice; *aus* (*reiner*) *~* out of (pure) spite; **2.** *Äußerung*: nasty remark; *so e-e ~!* what a nasty thing to do (*od.* say)

Boskop *m*; *-s, -* etwa russet (apple)

Bosnien (*n*); *-s* Bosnia; **Bosnien-Herzegowina** (*n*); *-s* Bosnia-Herzegovina; **Bosnier** *m*; *-s, -*, **Bosnierin** *f*; *-, -nen* Bosnian, *weiblich auch*: Bosnian woman (*od.* girl *etc.*); **bosnisch** *Adj.* Bosnian

Boss *m*; *-es, -e*; *umg.* boss; *von Partei etc.*: leader; *ich werde dir zeigen, wer hier der ~ ist!* I'll show you who's boss

bosseln *v/i. umg.*: *an etw.* (*Dat.*) *~* tinker *od.* fiddle (around *od.* about) with s.th., beaver away at s.th.; *fig. an e-m Problem etc.*: tinker with s.th.; *sie bosselt an der letzten Fassung ihrer Abschlussarbeit* she is putting the finishing touches to her thesis

böswillig I. *Adj.* malicious; *Jur. auch* wil(l)ful; *in ~er Absicht Jur.* with malice aforethought, with malicious intent; *e-e ~e Verleumdung schriftlich*: malicious libel *mst. ohne best. Art.*; *mündlich*: malicious slander *mst. ohne best. Art.*; **II.** *Adv.* out of spite; *Jur.* with malice aforethought, with malicious intent; **Böswilligkeit** *f*; *nur Sg.* malevolence, ill-will; *Jur.* wil(l)fulness

bot *Imperf.* → **bieten**

Botanik *f*; *-, kein Pl.* **1.** botany; **2.** *umg. hum.* great outdoors; **Botaniker** *m*; *-s, -*, **Botanikerin** *f*; *-, -nen* botanist; **botanisch** *Adj.* botanic(al); *ein ~er Garten* botanical gardens *Pl.*

Bote *m*; *-n, -n* **1.** *allg.*: messenger; (*Abgesandter*) emissary; (*Kurier*) courier; *ein reitender ~* a messenger on horseback; *der hinkende ~ kommt nach fig.* the worst (*od.* bad news) is still to come; **2.** *im Büro*: messenger; (*Laufbursche*) männlich: errand boy; *weiblich*: errand girl; *bes. Am.* gofer, *auch* gopher *umg.*; **3.** *fig.* (*Sendbote*) apostle; (*Vorbote*) herald, harbinger; *die ~n des Todes* the harbingers of death; *die ~n des Frühlings* the heralds of spring

Boten|dienst *m* **1.** (*Einrichtung*) courier service; **2.** *~e leisten* run errands; *~gang m* errand; *Botengänge machen* run errands; *~lohn m* delivery fee; *Trinkgeld*: tip for the messenger

Botin *f*; *-, -nen* → **Bote**

Botschaft[1] *f* **1.** message (**an** + *Akk.* to); **2.** (*Nachricht*) news *Sg.*; **e-e freudige/willkommene** ~ good/welcome news (*V. im Sg.*); **die** ~ **hör ich wohl (, allein mir fehlt der Glaube**) I'll believe that when I see it!; **3.** *fig.* message; **ein Lied mit e-r** ~ a song with a message; **4.** *Reli.*: **die Frohe** ~ the Gospel

Botschaft[2] *f Pol.* embassy

Botschafter *m*; *-s*, *-*, ~**in** *f*; *-*, *-nen* ambassador; **unser** ~ **in Spanien / in Madrid** our ambassador to Spain / in Madrid; **e-n** ~ **entsenden/abberufen** post an ambassador / relieve an ambassador of his *od.* her post; ~ **des guten Willens** *fig.* a good will ambassador; ~**ebene** *f*: **auf** ~ at ambassadorial level

Botschafts|angehörige *m*, *f* embassadorial employee; ~**besetzung** *f* occupation of the (*od.* an) embassy; ~**gelände** *n* embassy grounds *Pl.* (*od.* compound); **auf dem** ~ in the embassy grounds

Bott *n*; *-(e)s*, *-e*; *schw.* general meeting

Böttcher *m*; *-s*, *-* cooper

Bottich *m*; *-s*, *-e* tub, vat

Bottleparty ['bɔtlpaːɐ̯ti] *f* (bring-a-)bottle party, *Am.* BYOB (= bring your own booze) party

Botulismus *m*; *-*, *kein Pl.*; *Med.* botulism *kein Pl.*

Bougainvillea [bugɛ̃'vɪlea] *f*; *-*, *Bougainvilleen*; *Bot.* bougainvillea *mst. Sg.*

Bouillon [bʊl'jɔŋ] *f*; *-*, *-s*, *mst Sg. Gastr.* consommé, clear soup, bouillon; ~ **mit Ei/Einlage** consommé with egg/noodles, dumplings *etc.*; ~**würfel** *m* stock cube

Boulevard [bulə'vaːɐ̯] *m*; *-s*, *-s* boulevard; ~**blatt** *n* popular newspaper, rag *umg.*; *kleinformatiges*: tabloid; ~**presse** *f* popular (*pej.* gutter) press; ~**stück** *n* light comedy; ~**theater** *n* **1.** (*Gattung*) light comedy; **2.** comedy theat|re (*Am. auch* -er); ~**zeitung** *f* popular newspaper; *kleinformatige*: tabloid

Bouquet [bu'keː] *n*; *-s*, *-s* → **Bukett**

bourgeois [bʊr'ʒoa] **I.** *Adj.* bourgeois (*auch pej.*), **II. Bourgeois** [bʊr'ʒoa] *m*; *-*, *-* bourgeois; **Bourgeoisie** [bʊrʒoa'ziː] *f*; *-*, *n* bourgeoisie, middle classes *Pl.*

Boutique [bu'tiːk] *f*; *-*, *-n* boutique

Bovist *m*; *-(e)s*, *-e*; *Bot.* puffball, bovista *fachspr.*

Bowle ['boːlə] *f*; *-*, *-n* **1.** (*Getränk*) (cold) punch; **die** ~ **ansetzen** make the punch; **2.** (*Gefäß*) punchbowl

bowlen ['boːlən] *v/i. Sport* bowl; **Bowler** ['boːlɐ] *m*; *-s*, *-*, **Bowlerin** *f*; *-*, *-nen*; *Sport* tenpin bowler, bowls player

Bowling *n*; *-s*, *-s*; *Sport* **1.** bowling; **2.** *auf dem Rasen*: bowls *Pl.* (*V im Sg.*), *Am.* lawn bowling; ~**bahn** *f* bowling alley; ~**kugel** *f* bowling ball; (*auf dem Rasen*) bowl

Box *f*; *-*, *-en* **1.** *für Pferde*: box; **2.** (*Lautsprecher*) speaker; **3.** *zum Parken*: parking space; **4.** *Behälter*: box, tub; **5.** *beim Autorennen*: pit; **an den** ~**en** in the pits; **6.** *beim Tischtennis*: playing area; **7.** *Kamera*: box camera

boxen I. *v/i.* fight; *Sport* box (**gegen** against; **um** for); **II.** *v/t.* (*schlagen*) hit, punch; **j-n in die Seite/Nieren** ~ punch s.o. in the side/kidneys; **III.** *v/refl.* **1.** *sich* (**mit j-m**) ~ have a fight (with s.o.); **2.** *sich durch die Menge / aus dem Getümmel etc.* ~ fight one's way through the crowd / out of the hurly-burly; *sich nach oben* ~ *fig.* fight one's way to the top

Boxen *n*; *-s*, *kein Pl.* boxing

Boxen|gasse *f beim Autorennen*: pit lane; ~**stopp** *m beim Autorennen*: pit stop

Boxer *m*; *-s*, *-* **1.** boxer, fighter; **2.** *Hund*: boxer; **3.** *umg.* (*Boxhieb*) punch; **boxerisch** *Adj.*; *nur attr. Können, Talent*: boxing

Boxer|aufstand *m*; *nur Sg.*; *hist.* Boxer Rebellion; ~**motor** *m Mot.* opposed cylinder (*Am. auch* -piston) engine; ~**nase** *f* boxer's nose; ~**shorts** *Pl.* boxer shorts, boxers

Box|handschuh *m* boxing glove; ~**hieb** *m* punch; ~**kampf** *m* boxing match, fight; ~**ring** *m* boxing ring; ~**sport** *m* boxing

Boy [bɔy] *m*; *-s*, *-s* **1.** (*Hotel-, Liftboy*) pageboy, *bes. Am* bellhop; **2.** *Jugendspr.* (*Junge*) boy, boyfriend; ~**group** *f*; *-*, *-s*; *Mus.* boy band

Boykott *m*; *-(e)s*, *-e* boycott; **e-n** ~ **verhängen über** boycott; **zum** ~ **aufrufen** call a boycott; **etw. mit e-m** ~ **belegen** impose a boycott on s.th.; **e-m Land den** ~ **erklären** declare a boycott on a country; ~**drohung** *f* threat of a boycott

boykottieren *v/t.* boycott; **Boykottierung** *f* boycott

Boykottmaßnahme *f* boycott (action)

Bozen (*n*); *-s* Bolzano; **Bozner I.** *m*; *-s*, *-*, **Boznerin** *f*; *-*, *-nen* person (*od.* man, woman *etc.*) from Bolzano; **II.** *Adj.* Bolzano, from Bolzano

brabbeln I. *vt/i. umg.* **1.** (*murmeln*) mumble, mutter; **was brabbelst du da in deinen Bart?** *hum.* what are you muttering away into your beard about?; **2.** (*Unsinn reden*) witter on, ramble on; **II.** *v/i. Baby*: babble

brach I. *Imperf.* → **brechen**; **II.** *Adj. Agr.* fallow; **Brache** *f*; *-*, *-n*; *Agr.* (piece of) fallow land; **Brach(e)feld** *n Agr.* fallow land (*od.* field); **Brach(e)jahr** *n Agr.* fallow year; *EU Regelung*: set-aside

brachial *Adj.* **1.** *nur attr.*; *geh. Gewalt*: violent, brute; **2.** *Med.* brachial; **Brachialgewalt** *f*: (**mit**) ~ (by) (sheer) brute force

Brachland *n Agr.* fallow (land)

brach|legen *v/t.* (*trennb.*, *hat* -ge-); *Agr.* leave fallow; ~**liegen** *v/i.* (*unreg.*, *trennb.*, *hat od. ist* -ge-); *Agr.* lie fallow; *fig.* go to waste; ~**liegend** *Adj. Agr.* fallow; ~**e Talente** *fig.* wasted talents

brachte *Imperf.* → **bringen**

Brachvogel *m Orn.* curlew

brackig *Adj.* brackish; **Brackwasser** *n* brackish water

Brägen *m* → **Bregen**

Brahmane *m*; *-n*, *-n*, **Brahmanin** *f*; *-*, *-nen* Brahman, *auch* Brahmin; **brahmanisch** *Adj.* Brahmin, Brahminic(al), Brahmanic(al); **Brahmanismus** *m*; *-*, *kein Pl.* Brahmanism, Brahminism

Brailleschrift ['braj-] *f*; *nur Sg.* braille

Brain|storming ['breːnstɔːmɪŋ] *n*; *-s*, *-s* **1.** brainstorming; **2.** *konkret*: brainstorming session; ~**trust** [-trast] *m*; *-(s)*, *-s* (*allg.*) brains trust; *Am.* brain trust, think tank

bramarbasieren *v/i. geh. pej.* brag, boast *allg.*

Bramsegel *n Naut.* topgallant sail

Branche ['brãːʃə] *f*; *-*, *-n*; *Wirts.* **1.** industrial sector, (branch of) industry; **2.** line of business, trade; **s-e** ~ **ist die Chemie** he is in the chemical business

Branchen|buch *n Telef.* classified directory, the yellow pages *Pl. umg.*; ~**erfahrung** *f* experience in the trade

branchen|fremd *Adj.* new to the trade; ~**führend** *Adj. Unternehmen*: market-leading, market-dominating

Branchen|führer *m* market leader; ~**kenner** *m* market expert, person with a good knowledge of the trade (*Am. auch* business); ~**kenntnis** *f* knowledge of the trade (*Am. auch* business)

branchen|kundig *Adj.* experienced in the trade (*Am. auch* business); ~**üblich** *Adj.* customary (in the trade, *Am. auch* business)

Branchenverzeichnis *n Telef.* classified directory, the yellow pages *Pl. umg.*

Brand *m*; *-(e)s*, *Brände* **1.** fire; (*Großbrand*) *auch* blaze; **in** ~ (**stehen**) (be) on fire, (be) in flames, (be) ablaze; **in** ~ **geraten** catch fire; **in** ~ **stecken** set fire to, set on fire, set alight; (*Brennholz etc.*) kindle; (*Pfeife etc.*) light; **e-n** ~ **bekämpfen/legen/löschen** fight / start (*od.* set) / put out a fire; **e-n** ~ **eindämmen** contain a fire, bring a fire under control; **der** ~ **griff um sich** the fire spread; **ein** ~ **wütet** a fire is raging (out of control); **beim** ~ **des Hotels kamen drei Menschen um** three people died in the hotel fire; **2.** *Dial.*, *umg. fig.* (*Durst*) raging thirst; **e-n riesigen** ~ **haben** be parched, be dying of thirst *allg.*; **3.** (*brennendes Holzstück*) firebrand; **4.** *Bot.* blight, mildew; **5.** *nur Sg.*; *Med.* (*Nekrose*) gangrene *ohne Art.*; **feuchter/trockener** ~ moist/dry gangrene; **6.** *von Keramik etc.*: firing; **7.** *nur Sg.* (*Heizmaterial*) fuel, firewood

brandaktuell *Adj. Information*: up-to-the-minute; *Frage*, *Nachricht*: highly topical; *Meldung*: präd. hot off the press; *Buch*: präd. hot from the presses; *Mode etc.*: the very latest ...; *Hit etc.*: the latest ..., präd: the latest thing *umg.*

Brand|anschlag *m* arson attack; **e-n** ~ **verüben auf** (+ *Akk.*) set fire to; ~**bekämpfung** *f* fire fighting; ~**blase** *f* (burn) blister; ~**bombe** *f* fire (*od.* incendiary) bomb; ~**brief** *m umg.* **1.** (*Mahnschreiben*) urgent reminder; **2.** (*Bittbrief*) urgent request; ~**direktor** *m* fire chief

brandeilig *Adj.* extremely urgent; **er hat's** ~ he's in a terrible hurry (**mit** for); **es ist schon wieder** ~ as usual it's all terribly urgent

Brandeisen *n* branding iron

branden *v/i.*: **gegen** *od.* **an etw.** (*Akk.*) ~ **1.** *Meer*, *Wellen*: surge against s.th., break on (*od.* against) s.th.; **2.** *fig. Menschenmenge*, *Verkehr etc.*: surge against s.th.; **brandend I.** *Part. Präs.* → **branden**; **II.** *Adj.*; *nur attr.*; *Applaus*: thunderous, tumultuous

Brandenburger I. *m*; *-s*, *-*, ~**in** *f*; *-*, *-nen* man *bzw.* woman from Brandenburg; ~ **sein** *mst* come (*od.* be) from Brandenburg; **II.** *Adj.* Brandenburg ..., präd. *auch* from Brandenburg; **das** ~ **Tor** the Brandenburg Gate; **brandenburgisch** *Adj.* of Brandenburg; **die Brandenburgischen Konzerte** (**von Bach**) the Brandenburg concert|os (*auch* –i) (by Bach); → **Brandenburger II**

Brand|ente *f Orn.* sheldrake; ~**fackel** *f* firebrand (*auch fig.*); ~**fleck** *m* burn (mark), burnt patch (*od.* spot); ~**gans** *f Orn.* shelduck; ~**gasse** *f* narrow lane

between houses (*to prevent the spreading of fire*); **~gefahr** *f* risk of fire (breaking out), fire risk; *e-e ~ darstellen* be a fire hazard (*od.* risk); **~geruch** *m* smell of burning; *bei Angebranntem:* burnt smell; **~glocke** *f* fire-bell, fire alarm
brandheiß *Adj. Nachrichten:* the very latest *news*, *präd. auch* hot off the press
Brandherd *m* source *od.* focus of (the) fire; *fig.* trouble spot
brandig **I.** *Adj.* **1.** *Geruch, Geschmack:* burnt; **2.** *Med., Wunde, Bein etc.:* gangrenous; **3.** *Bot., Agr.* blight-ridden, suffering from blight; **II.** *Adv.:* ~ *riechen* smell of burning
Brand|kasse *f* fire insurance company; **~katastrophe** *f* fire disaster; **~loch** *n in Kleidung etc.:* burn hole, cigarette burn; **~mal** *n*; *Pl. -e*; *geh.* brand; *fig.* stigma; **~malerei** *f Kunst* pokerwork
brandmarken *v/t.* (*untr., hat ge-*); *fig.* brand; *j-n als Mörder ~* brand s.o. a murderer; **Brandmarkung** *f*; *nur Sg.*; *fig.* branding
Brand|mauer *f* fire(proof) wall; **~meister** *m* chief fire officer, *Am.* fire chief; **~narbe** *f* burn scar, scar from a burn
brandneu *Adj.* brand-new
Brand|opfer *n* **1.** fire victim; **2.** *rituelles:* burnt offering; *ein ~ darbringen* make a burnt offering; **~pfeil** *m* burning arrow, fire arrow; **~rede** *f* inflammatory speech; **~rodung** *f* clearance by fire
brandrot *Adj.* bright red, crimson (*Wangen, Haar etc.*) flaming
Brand|salbe *f Med.* burn ointment; **~satz** *m* incendiary mixture *od.* compound; *e-n ~ werfen* throw a petrol bomb (*Am.* Molotov cocktail); **~schaden** *m* fire damage
brandschatzen *v/t./i.* (*untr., hat ge-*); *hist.* (*mit Plünderung und Feuerlegen drohen*) pillage and threaten to burn; **Brandschatzung** *f hist.* pillaging and threat of burning
Brandschneise *f* fire lane
Brandschutz *m* fire prevention; **~beauftragte** *m, f* fire prevention (*od.* safety) officer
Brand|sohle *f* insole; **~spur** *f* trace of a (*od.* the) fire; **~stätte** *f* scene of the fire; **~stelle** *f* **1.** scene of the fire; **2.** → *Brandfleck*; **~stifter** *m*, **~stifterin** *f* arsonist, fire raiser; **~stiftung** *f* arson
Brandteig *m* chou(x) pastry
Brandung *f*; *nur Sg.* surf; *fig.* surge, wave; *tobende od. tosende ~* surging waves; *bei starker ~* when the surf is high *od.* up; *die ~ donnert gegen die Felsen* the waves crash against the rocks
Brand|ursache *f* cause of the fire; **~verhütung** *f* fire prevention; **~wache** *f* **1.** firewatch; **2.** (*Posten*) fire watcher; **3.** *schw.* (*Berufsfeuerwehr*) fire brigade; **~wirtschaft** *f*; *nur Sg.*; *Agr.* cultivation of land by burn-beating; **~wunde** *f* burn; *durch Verbrühen:* scald; **~zeichen** *n* brand
brannte *Imperf.* → *brennen*
Branntkalk *m* burnt lime
Branntwein *m* brandy; (*Schnaps*) spirits *Pl.*; **~brenner** *m* distiller; **~brennerei** *f* **1.** distillery; **2.** (*Vorgang*) distilling; **~monopol** *n* alcohol (*od.* spirits) monopoly; **~steuer** *f* tax on spirits, *Am.* liquor tax
Brasilianer *m*; *-s, -,* **~in** *f*; *-, -nen* Brazilian, *weiblich auch:* Brazilian woman

(*od.* girl *etc.*); **brasilianisch** *Adj.* Brazilian; **Brasilien** (*n*); *-s* Brazil
Brasse *f*; *-, -n* **1.** *Zool.* bream; **2.** *Naut.* brace
Brät *f*; *-s, kein Pl.*; *südd., schw. Gastr.* (*Bratwurstbrät etc.*) pork sausage meat
Bratapfel *m Gastr.* baked apple
braten **I.** *v/t.* roast; *auf dem Rost:* grill; (*mit Fett*) *in der Pfanne:* fry; *im Ofen, außer Fleisch:* bake; *am Spieß ~* roast on a spit; *in schwimmendem Fett ~* deep-fry; **II.** *v/i.* **1.** → I; **2.** *umg. in der Sonne:* roast (*od.* broil *od.* bake) (in the sun); *in der Hölle ~* burn (*od.* rot) in hell
Braten *m*; *-s, -*; *Gastr.* roast; (*Keule*) joint; *kalter ~* cold meat; *ein fetter ~ fig.* a good (*od.* fine) catch; *den ~ riechen fig.* smell a rat; **~duft** *m* smell of roasting; **~fett** *n* dripp|ing (*Am. -ings Pl.*); **~saft** *m* **1.** juice from the meat; **2.** (*Soße*) gravy; **~soße** *f* gravy
Bräter *m*; *-s, -* roasting pan
bratfertig *Adj.* oven-ready
Brat|fett *n Gastr.* cooking fat *od.* oil; **~fisch** *m* fried fish; **~folie** *f* tin (*Am.* aluminum) foil; **~hähnchen** *n*, **~hendl** *n südd., österr.* → *Brathuhn*; **~hering** *m* grilled (and pickled) herring; **~huhn** *n*, **~hühnchen** *n* roast (*od.* grilled, broiled) chicken; *zum Braten:* broiler; **~kartoffeln** *Pl.* fried (*od.* sauté) potatoes, *Am.* home fries; *rohe/gekochte ~* fried potatoes made from raw/boiled potatoes, *Am.* hash browns *Pl.*, home fries *Pl.*; **~klops** *m ostd.* rissoles of fried potatoes
Bratling *m Gastr.* vegeburger, vegetarian rissole
Brat|ofen *m* oven; **~pfanne** *f* frying pan; **~röhre** *f* oven; **~rost** *m* grill, *Am. auch* broiler
Bratsche *f*; *-, -n*; *Mus.* viola; **Bratschist** *m*; *-en, -en*, **Bratschistin** *f*; *-, -nen* viola player, violist
Brat|spieß *m* **1.** skewer; *Grill:* spit; **2.** *Gastr.* (*Gericht*) kebab; **~wurst** *f*, **~würstchen** *n Gastr.* fried (*od.* grilled) sausage, bratwurst; *zum Braten:* sausage for frying (*od.* grilling); *frische ~* sausage meat; *geräucherte ~* smoked cooking sausage
Brauch *m*; *-(e)s, Bräuche*; (*Sitte*) custom, tradition; (*Usus*) practice; *alter ~* tradition; *allgemeiner ~* general practice; *nach altem ~* according to tradition (*od.* custom), the traditional way; *e-n ~ pflegen* keep up (a) tradition; *e-n ~ wieder aufleben lassen* revive an old custom (*od.* tradition); *es ist hier der ~* (*, dass die Männer ...*) it's the custom (*od.* it's customary) around here (for the men to ...); *es ist bei uns so ~* that's the way we've always done it, that's our custom; *so wie es der ~ will* as custom has it; *es kommt außer ~* it's falling into disuse; *weitS.* people don't do it (so much) any more
brauchbar **I.** *Adj.* **1.** *Gegenstände:* (*nützlich*) useful, handy; (*noch verwendbar*) usable; **2.** *Plan, Vorschlag, Idee etc.:* (*durchführbar*) practicable; (*nicht schlecht*) useful, decent, not bad; **II.** *Adv. umg.* (*nicht schlecht*) quite well; **Brauchbarkeit** *f*; *nur Sg.* usefulness; usability; practicability; → *brauchbar* I
brauchen **I.** *v/t.* **1.** (*nötig haben*) need (*für od. zu* for *od.* (in order) to); *e-e Brille ~* need glasses; *Hilfe ~* (*bei*) need help (with); *alles, was man zum Leben braucht* everything necessary for

life; *eigentlich bräuchte ich ...* I could really do with ...; *Sie ~ den Vierer(-bus)* you need (to take) the number four (bus); *wozu brauchst du es?* what do you need it for?; *was du brauchst ist ein Schirm* what you want is an umbrella; *ich brauche diese Bücher dringend* I am in great want of these books, I really want these books; *wir ~ Kohlen* we lack coal; **2.** (*erfordern*) require; (*in Anspruch nehmen, bes. Zeit, Energie*) take; *ich brauche zwei Stunden, um zu* (+ *Inf.*) it takes me two hours to (+ *Inf.*); *das braucht* (*seine*) *Zeit* it takes time; *diese Arbeit braucht Ausdauer* one needs (*od.* you need *umg.*) stamina for this work; **3.** (*verbrauchen*) use (up); *im Urlaub haben wir viel Geld gebraucht* we used up (*od.* spent) a lot of money on holiday (*Am.* vacation); *das Auto braucht sechs Liter auf hundert Kilometer* the car uses six lit|res (*Am. -ers*) for a hundred kilomet|res (*Am. -ers*), the car does sixteen kilomet|res (*Am. -ers*) a lit|re (*Am. -ers*); **4.** (*anwenden, gebrauchen*) use, make use of; *Gewalt ~* make use of violence; *seinen Verstand ~* use one's brain, think clearly; *er ist heute zu nichts zu ~ umg.* he's no good for anything (*od.* useless) today; **5.** *j-d kann etw. ~* s.o. can use (*od.* do with) s.th.; *das Geld kann ich gut ~* I can really do with the money; *kannst du noch Hilfe ~?* do you still need any help?; *ich kann dich hier nicht ~ umg.* I can do without you here; *ich kann es nicht ~, wenn er ständig anruft umg.* I can do without him ringing up (*Am.* calling) all the time; *ich kann jetzt keine Störung ~* I don't need any interruptions right now; *das kann ich gerade ~! iro.* that's all I needed!; **II.** *Hilfsv.*; + *zu* + *Inf.*, *umg. auch nur* + *Inf.*; (*müssen*) need, have to; *alles, was du zu wissen brauchst* everything (*od.* all) you need to know; *du brauchst* (*es*) *mir nicht zu sagen* you don't have to tell me; *er brauchte nicht zu kommen* he didn't have to come; *er hätte nicht zu kommen ~* he needn't have come; *du brauchst es nur zu sagen* just say the word; *du brauchst keine Angst zu haben* there's no need to be scared; *das braucht keiner zu hören/wissen* no-one (*od. bes. Am.* no one) need hear/know that; *du brauchst nicht gleich in die Luft zu gehen* there's no need to lose your temper; *es braucht wohl nicht gesagt zu werden, dass ...* I suppose there's no need to stress that ..., needless to say, ...; *das brauche ich mir nicht gefallen zu lassen* I don't need to put up with that; *es braucht nicht sofort zu sein* it doesn't have to be straight away (*od.* right now); *das hätte nicht zu sein ~* that needn't have happened, that didn't have to happen; *es braucht nicht immer ... zu sein* it doesn't always have to be ...; **III.** *v/i.*, *unpers. umg.:* *das braucht es nicht* it isn't necessary; *das hätte es doch nicht gebraucht* there was really no need; *das hat es jetzt gebraucht!* that was important right now!; *hat es das gebraucht?* was that really necessary?; **IV.** *v/i.:* *lange ~* take long (*für* for; *zu* to + *Inf.*); *wie lange wird er ~?* how long will it take him?
Brauchtum *n*; *-s, Brauchtümer, mst Sg.*

customs *Pl.*, tradition(s *Pl.*)

Brauchwasser *n*; *nur Sg.*; *fachspr.* **1.** industrial (*od.* service) water; **2.** (*Abwasser*) sewage

Braue *f*, -, -*n* (eye)brow; *buschige ~n* bushy eyebrows; *die ~n hochziehen* raise one's eyebrows (*od.* an eyebrow)

brauen *v/t.* (*Bier*) brew; *bes. hum.* (*Tee, Punsch etc.*) make, concoct; **Brauer** *m*; -*s*, - brewer; **Brauerei** *f*; -, -*en* brewery; **Brauhaus** *n* brewery; **Braumeister** *m*, **Braumeisterin** *f* master brewer

braun *Adj.* **1.** brown; *von der Sonne*: *auch* tanned; *~e Butter* browned (*od.* fried) butter; *~es Pferd* bay (horse); *~ werden Person*: get a tan, go brown; *schnell ~ werden von Natur aus*: tan easily (*od.* quickly), go brown quickly; *du bist aber ~ geworden!* you're very brown, you've got quite a tan; *~ gebrannt* tanned, bronzed; **2.** *Pol. umg.* Nazi; *ein ~er Politiker* a politician with Nazi tendencies; *e-e ~e Vergangenheit haben* have a Nazi past; → *auch blau*; **Braun** *n*; -*s*, - *od. umg.* -*s* brown

Braunalge *f*; *mst Pl.*; *Bot.* brown alga(e)

braunäugig *Adj.* brown-eyed

Braun|bär *m* *Zool.* brown bear; *~bier* *n* brown (malt) beer; *aussehen wie ~ und Spucke umg.* look like death warmed up

Braune¹ *m*; -*n*, -*n* **1.** *Pferd*: bay; **2.** *österr.* *ein großer ~r* a large white coffee (*od.* coffee with milk)

Braune² *n*; -*n*, *nur Sg.* brownness; (*braune Stelle*) blemish; *das ~ wegschneiden* (*von e-m Apfel etc.*) cut away the bad bits (*Am.* parts) *umg.*

Braune³ *m*, *f*; -*n*, -*n*; *hist.*, *umg.* fifty-mark note

Bräune *f*; -, *kein Pl.* brown(ness); (*Sonnenbräune*) (sun)tan

bräunen **I.** *v/i. und v/refl.* get brown; *Haut*, *Person*: *auch* get a tan; **II.** *v/t.* brown; *Sonne*: tan

Braunfäule *f* *Bot.*, *Agr.* blight

braun|haarig *Adj.* brown-haired; *~häutig* *Adj.* brown-skinned

Braun|hemd *n* *hist.* **1.** *Hemd*: brown shirt; **2.** *Person*: Brown Shirt; *~kohle* *f* brown (*Am.* soft) coal, lignite

bräunlich *Adj.* brownish

Braun'sche Röhre *f* *Tech.* cathode-ray tube

Braunschweig (*n*); -*s* Braunschweig, *hist.* Brunswick

Bräunungsstudio *n* solarium, *Am.* tanning salon

Braus → *Saus*

Brause *f*; -, -*n* **1.** (*Dusche*) shower; *sich unter die ~ stellen* have (*od.* take) a shower; **2.** (*Gießbrause*) sprinkler, nozzle, shower head; **3.** → *Brauselimonade*; **4.** → *Brausepulver*; *~bad* *n* shower (bath); *~limonade* *f* fizzy drink, *Brit. auch* lemonade, pop, soda *umg.*; *Am.* (*Flasche*) bottle of pop (*od.* soda)

brausen **I.** *v/i.* **1.** (*hat gebraust*); (*rauschen*) roar; (*dröhnen*) boom; (*toben*) rage; *mir braust es in den Ohren* my ears are buzzing (*od.* ringing); **2.** (*ist*); *umg. fig.* (*stürmen*) zoom; *Auto etc.*: *auch* roar; *um die Ecke ~* come (*od.* go) zooming round the corner; (*hat*) (*duschen*) have (*od.* take) a shower; **II.** *v/t.* (*hat*) spray; *stärker*: shower; **III.** *v/refl.* (*hat*) have (*od.* take) a shower; **brausend** **I.** *Part. Präs.* → *brausen*; **II.** *Adj.*: *~er Beifall* thunderous applause

Brause|pulver *n* sherbet (powder), *Am. powdered fizzy fruit drink mix*; *~stäbchen* *n*, *~stange* *f* sherbet dip; *~tablette* *f* effervescent tablet

Braut *f*, -, *Bräute* **1.** *am Hochzeitstag*: bride; **2.** (*Verlobte*) fiancée, intended *umg.*; **3.** *umg.* (*Freundin*) girl; (*Mädchen*) bird, chick *Sl.*; *~auto* *f* wedding car (*od.* limousine); *~bett* *n* nuptual (*od.* bridal) bed; *~eltern Pl.* parents of the bride, bride's parents; *~examen* *n* *kath.* pre-wedding religious examination; *~führer* *m* man (father, brother, relative, friend) who gives away the bride; *~gemach* *n* *altm.*, *bes. iro.* nuptial chamber

...braut *f*, *im Subst. umg.*: *Räuber~* robber bride; *Rocker~* rocker queen; *Fußball~* footballer's girl (*od.* moll *Sl.*), *Am.* jock chick *Sl.*

Bräutigam *m*; -*s*, -*e*, *umg. auch* –*s* **1.** *am Hochzeitstag*: (bride)groom; **2.** (*Verlobter*) fiancé

Braut|jungfer *f* bridesmaid; *~kleid* *n* wedding dress; *~kranz* *m* bridal wreath; *~leute Pl.* bride and groom; *~mutter* *f* mother of the bride, bride's mother; *~nacht* *f* *altm.* wedding night *allg.*; *~paar* *n* **1.** *am Hochzeitstag*: bride and (bride)groom; **2.** (*Verlobte*) engaged couple; *~schau* *f*: *auf ~ gehen umg. hum.* look for a wife *allg.*; *~schleier* *m* bridal (*od.* bride's) veil; *~schmuck* *m* wedding jewel(le)ry; *~strauß* *m* bridal bouquet; *~suche* *f*: *auf ~ sein* be looking for a wife; *~unterricht* *m* *kath.* religious instruction before marriage; *~vater* *m* father of the bride, bride's father; *~werber* *m* (professional) matchmaker

Brauwesen *n*; *nur Sg.* brewing industry

brav **I.** *Adj.* **1.** (*artig*) good, well-behaved; *sei schön ~!* be good now; *Fabian, sei ~!* Fabian, be a good boy!; *Laura, sei ~ und geh ins Bett!* Laura, go to bed like a good girl; *wenn du ~ bist, dann ...* if you're good, ...; **2.** (*ehrlich*, *rechtschaffen*) good, honest and upright, honest, upright; **3.** *umg. pej.* (*konventionell*) very conventional, ordinary, boring; (*bieder*, *einfach*) plain; *das Kleid ist viel zu ~ für die Party* that dress is much too straightlaced (*od.* plain) for the party; **4.** (*ganz ordentlich*): *e-e ~e Leistung* a good attempt; **5.** *altm. Soldat*: brave; **II.** *Adv.* **1.** (*artig*): *sie hat ~ aufgegessen* she finished her food (*od.* ate up) like a good girl; *~ gemacht!* well done!, good boy *od.* girl!; **2.** (*ganz ordentlich*): *~ gespielt* nicely played; *er hat sich ~ geschlagen* he tried hard, he did his best; **3.** (*tapfer*): *sich ~ halten* be brave; **Bravheit** *f*; *nur Sg.* **1.** (*Artigkeit*) good behavio(u)r; **2.** (*Ehrlichkeit*, *Rechtschaffenheit*) honesty; **3.** *umg. pej.* (*Konventionalität*) conventionality

bravissimo *Interj.* bravissimo

bravo **I.** *Interj.* well done!; *Theat. etc.* bravo!; **II. Bravo** *n*; -*s*, -*s*, **Bravoruf** *m* bravo, *Pl. auch* cheers

Brav(o)ur [bra'vu:r] *f*; -, -*en*, *mst. Sg.* **1.** (*Schwung*) spirit; *mit ~* brilliantly; **2.** *Mus.* bravura; **3.** (*Tapferkeit*) bravery; **brav(o)urös** *Adj.* courageous, bold; *Mus.* brilliant, bravura ...; **Brav(o)urstück** *n* **1.** daring feat; **2.** *Mus.* bravura

BRD *f*; -, *kein Pl.*; *Abk. für* **Bundesrepublik Deutschland**

Break [bre:k] *m*, *n*; -*s*, -*s*; *Sport* **1.** (*un-*

erwarteter Durchbruch) break; **2.** (*Tennis*) break; **3.** *Mus.* break

Breakdance ['bre:kda:ns] *m*; -(*s*), *kein Pl.*; *Mus.* breakdance; **Breakdancer** *m*; -*s*, -; *Jugendspr.* breakdancer

Break-even-Point [bre:k'ʔi:vnpɔynt] *m*; -*s*, -*s*; *Wirts.* break-even point

brechbar *Adj.* breakable

Brech|bohne *f* French bean, *Am.* green bean, wax bean; *~durchfall* *m* *Med.* diarrh(o)ea with vomiting; *~eisen* *n* crowbar

brechen; *bricht*, *brach*, *hat bzw. ist gebrochen* **I.** *v/t.* (*hat*) **1.** (*Stock*, *Stange etc.*) break; *j-m/sich den Arm etc. ~* break s.o.'s/ one's arm *etc.*; *Blumen ~* *poet.* pluck flowers; → *Genick* 1, 2, *Hals* 1, *Knie* 1, *Lanze*, *Stab* 1, *Zaun etc.*; **2.** *fig.* (*überwinden*, *beenden etc.*) (*Bann*, *Rekord*, *Schweigen*, *Stolz*, *Widerstand*, *Willen etc.*) break; *j-m das od. j-s Herz ~* break s.o.'s heart; *j-s Trotz ~* break s.o.'s defiance; *j-n ~* break s.o. (down); → *Bahn* 2, *Blockade* 1, *Eis¹* 1; **3.** *fig.* (*missachten*) (*Eid*, *Gesetz*, *Schwur*, *Streik*, *Vertrag*, *Waffenstillstand*) break, violate; *Ehe ~* commit adultery, be unfaithful; *das Fasten ~* *Reli.* break fast; *j-m die Treue ~* be unfaithful to s.o.; *ein Versprechen ~* break a promise; *sein Wort ~* break one's word; *Bundesrecht bricht Landesrecht* *Jur.*, *Pol. etwa* federal law is superior to (*od.* overrides) regional law; **4.**; **5.** *im Steinbruch*: quarry; **6.** *Opt.*, *Phys.* (*Lichtstrahl*, *Schallwelle*) refract, rebound; (*Farben*) refract; *das Wasser bricht das Licht* the water makes the light refract; **7.** (*erbrechen*) (*Blut*, *Galle*) vomit, be sick, bring up; **8.** *Agr.* (*Flachs*, *Hanf*) break; **II.** *v/i.* **1.** (*ist*) break; *Ast*, *Stock*: snap; *Arm*, *Bein*, *Knochen*: break; *Leder*: crack (at the folds), rub; *Seide*: rub out in the folds, split, wear; *zum Brechen voll umg.* → *brechend* III; **2.** (*ist*); *fig. Stimme*: break; *Widerstand etc.*: break down; *ihre Augen brachen* *lit. beim Sterben*: she passed away; *j-m bricht das Herz (bei etw.)* s.o.'s heart is breaking (at the sight of s.th); *es bricht mir das Herz, aber ...* *iro.* I'm sorry to have to tell you; **3.** (*ist*): *~ aus etw.* (*hervorkommen*) burst out of s.th.; *Tränen*: pour from s.th.; *~ durch durch Eis*, *Mauer etc.*: break (*stärker*: crash) through; *in die Knie ~* *fig.* give up; *die Sonne brach durch die Wolken* the sun broke through the clouds; *der Räuber brach aus dem Gebüsch* the robber (*od.* thief) came out from the bushes; **4.** (*hat*); *umg.* (*sich übergeben*) be sick, vomit, puke *etw.*, vom *umg.*, hurl *umg.*; *ich muss ~* I have to be sick, I'm going to puke *umg.*; **5.** *umg. j-m/etw. ~* break with s.o./s.th.; *mit e-r Gewohnheit ~* break with tradition; *mit s-r Familie völlig ~* break (off) contact with one's family; **III.** *v/refl.* (*hat*) **1.** *Wellen*: *sich ~ an* (+ *Dat.*) break on (*od.* against); *stärker*: crash against; **2.** *Opt.*, *Phys.*, *Licht etc.*: refract; *das Licht bricht sich im Wasser* (the) light refracts in water; *das Echo bricht sich an der Felswand* the echo rebounds from the cliff; → *gebrochen* II, III

brechend **I.** *Part. Präs.* → *brechen*; **II.** *Adj.* *Opt.*, *Phys.* refractive; **III.** *Adv.*: *~ voll umg.* crammed, packed, jampacked, chock-a-block

Brecher *m*; -*s*, - **1.** (*Welle*) breaker; **2.** *Tech.* crusher, breaker

Brechkraft f Opt. refractive power

Brech|mittel n **1.** Med. emetic; **2.** er/ es ist ein echtes (od. das reinste) ~ umg. he's/it's enough to make you want to puke Sl.; **~reiz** m (feeling of) nausea; e-n ~ verursachen auch make one feel sick (od. nauseous, nauseated)

Brechstange f crowbar; es mit der ~ versuchen fig. try it with a sledgehammer

Brechung f Opt., Phys. refraction; Ling. fracture; Mus. arpeggio

Brechungswinkel m Opt., Phys. refracting angle

Bredouille [bre'duljə] f umg. in der ~ sein be in a fix, be in a bit of a mess; in die ~ geraten get (o.s.) into a fix (od. a bit of a mess)

Bregen m; -s, -; nordd. Gastr. brains Pl.

Brei m; -(e)s, -e **1.** für Kinder: pudding, baby food; (Grießbrei) semolina ohne best. Art.; (Haferbrei) porridge, Am. oatmeal; (Kartoffelbrei) mashed potat|o (Am. –oes Pl.), potato puree; Am. (bes. Maisbrei) mush; **~ anrühren** stir porridge (od. semolina etc.); um den heißen ~ herumreden fig. beat about (od. bes. Am. around) the bush; j-m ~ ums Maul schmieren umg. butter s.o. up; **2.** (breiige Masse) pap, auch mush pej.; (Lavabrei) magma; zu ~ kochen cook to a pulp; zu ~ zerstampfen trample s.th. to a pulp; zu ~ schlagen umg. fig. beat s.o. to a pulp; → Koch

breiig Adj. mushy; e-e ~e Masse a thick paste

Brei|gläschen n jar of baby food; **~pulver** n baby food powder

breit I. Adj. **1.** wide, broad; Kinn, Schultern: broad, square; (ausgedehnt) large, wide, broad; Brett, Fluss: wide; Grinsen Lächeln: wide; Hüften: broad; Loch, Lücke: wide; Nase: broad; ~ drücken flatten (out), press s.th. flat; etw. ~er machen, auch ~er werden widen; e-n ~en Buckel od. Rücken haben umg. fig. have broad shoulders; sich ~ machen Person: spread o.s. out; fig. throw one's weight around; fig. Angst etc.: spread; mach dich nicht so ~! move (od. shove) up a bit! umg.; die Beine für j-n ~ machen umg. pej. (sexuell) spread one's legs for s.o.; er wollte sich in m-r Wohnung / m-m Leben ~ machen fig. he wanted to make himself comfortable (od. at home) in my flat (Am. house) /life; Begeisterung macht sich ~! iro. I, we etc. can't wait od. I am, we are etc. on tenterhooks!; **2.** nachgestellt; mit Maßangabe: zwei Finger/Zoll ~ two fingers/ inches wide; 120 Zentimeter ~ 120 centimet|res (Am. -ers) wide (od. across); **3.** fig. Publikum etc.: wide, broad; Echo: wide; Grundlage: broad; Interesse: widespread; ein ~es Angebot a wide (od. broad) range; die ~e Masse the masses (od. populace); die ~e Öffentlichkeit the public at large; **4.** fig. Aussprache, Akzent: broad; **5.** fig. Erzählung etc.: longwinded, rambling; **6.** umg., mst. Jugendspr. (angetrunken) tipsy; (betrunken) plastered, pissed; **II.** Adv. **1.** broadly (auch lächeln etc.); ~ gebaut broadly (od. squarely) built; der Stoff liegt doppelt ~ the material is double width; **2.** fig.: ~ gefächert wide(-ranging); diversified; **3.** fig.: etw. (lang und) ~ erzählen give a longwinded account of s.th.; ~ angelegt

Erzählung, Roman etc.: expansive, epic; **4.** Mus. largo; → lang¹ II 1, weit II 4

Breitband|... im Subst. Telek. broadband, wide-band ...; Pharm. bes. Antibiotika etc.: broad-spectrum ....; **~antibiotikum** n Med. broad-range antibiotics Pl.; **~kabel** n Etech., Telek. high frequency carrier cable, wide band (od. television) cable; **~netz** n Telek. broadband network

breitbeinig Adj. und Adv. with (one's) legs apart; ~ gehen walk with a rolling gait; ~ auf etw. (Dat.) stehen straddle s.th.

Breitbild n TV wide screen television (od. TV)

Breite f; -, -n **1.** seitliche Ausdehnung: width, breadth; e-s Schiffs: beam; es hat e-e ~ von sechs Metern it is six met|res (Am. -ers) wide; der ~ nach hinlegen, nehmen breadthwise, breadthways; **2.** bes. große Ausdehnung: von ungeheurer ~ extremely wide; in die ~ gehen Person: put on weight, grow broad, spread out umg.; in s-r vollen ~ vor j-m stehen stand smack (od. straight) in front of s.o.; **3.** Astron., Geog. latitude; etwa auf der ~ von Rom at about the latitude of Rome; auf dem 25. Grad südlicher/ nördlicher ~ liegen lie at latitude 25 degrees south/north; **4.** nur Pl.; Geog.: in gemäßigten ~n in temperate climes; in diesen ~n in these latitudes; **5.** nur Sg.; fig. breadth, scope, range; (Weitschweifigkeit) longwindedness; die ~ des Angebots the breadth of the range; in epischer ~ in great (od. epic) detail; zu sehr in die ~ gehen Darstellung etc.: be rather long-winded

breiten I. v/t. **1.** ~ über (+Akk.) spread s.th. on (od. over); e-e Decke über j-n ~ put a blanket over s.o.; **2.** lit. (ausbreiten) (Arme, Flügel, Schwingen) spread; **II.** v/refl.: sich ~ über (+ Akk.) spread (out) over (od. across); Nebel breitete sich über das Land fog spread across the land

Breiten|grad m Geog. (degree of) latitude, latitude degree; auf dem od. am 30. ~ on the 30th parallel; in diesen ~en in these latitudes; fig. auch in these spheres, in this part of the world; **~kreis** m Geog. parallel (of latitude), latitude circle; **~sport** m mass sport(s Pl.); **~wirkung** f effectiveness; von großer ~ Film etc.: with wide (od. popular, mass) appeal; Maßnahmen, Neuerungen etc.: with far- (od. wide-)-reaching effects

breit|flächig I. Adj. wide; **II.** Adv. on a wide scale; **~hüftig** Adj. broad-hipped; **~krempig** Adj. wide-brimmed

Breitleinwand f Film: wide-screen

breit|nasig Adj. broad- (od. flat-)-nosed; **~randig** Adj. broad-brimmed; **~räumig** Adj. und Adv. wide(ly)

Breitreifen m Mot. wide tyre (Am. tire) (od. wheel)

breitschlagen v/t. (unreg., trennb., hat -ge-); umg. fig.: j-n ~ talk s.o. (a)round; j-n zu etw. ~ talk s.o. into (doing) s.th.; sich ~ lassen give in, allow o.s. to be swayed (od. persuaded); sich zu etw. ~ lassen be cajoled into (doing) s.th.

breitschult(e)rig Adj. broadshouldered

Breitseite f Naut. und fig. broadside; e-e ~ abfeuern od. abgeben auf (+ Akk.) auch fig. deliver a broadside against

Breitspektrum... im Subst. Pharm.

broad-spectrum ...

breit|spurig Adj. **1.** Eisenb. broad--ga(u)ge; **2.** umg. fig. pej. Person: bumptious, full of o.s.; **~treten** v/t. (unreg., trennb., hat -ge-); umg. fig., mst pej. spin out; das muss man nicht so ~ there is no need to labo(u)r the point; **~walzen** v/t. (trennb., hat -ge-); umg. fig. mst pej. thrash to death

Breitwand f Film: wide screen; **~film** m wide-screen film (Am. auch movie)

Bremer I. m; -s, -, **~in** f; -, -nen person from Bremen; **II.** Adj. Bremen; die ~ Stadtmusikanten (Märchentitel) the musicians of Bremen

Brems|... im Subst. mst brake ...; **~backe** f Tech. brake shoe; **~belag** m brake lining; den ~ erneuern reline the brakes; neue Bremsbeläge brauchen need new brake linings

Bremse¹ f; -, -n; Mot. brake; auf die ~ treten / umg. steigen step on / umg. slam on the brake(s); die ~ betätigen apply (od. put on) the brakes; die ~ (an)ziehen pull on the brakes; umg. fig. slow things down (a bit); die ~ durchtreten slam on the brakes

Bremse² f; -, -n; Zool. **1.** bes. südd. (Stechfliege) biting fly; **2.** (Pferdebremse) horsefly

bremsen I. v/i. **1.** brake, apply (od. put on) the brakes; scharf ~ brake sharply; ich bremse auch für Tiere Autoaufkleber: I slow down for horses (od. animals); **2.** (hemmend wirken) act as a brake, slow things down; der Gegenwind bremst enorm the headwind slows it, me etc. down considerably; **3.** umg. fig. Person: (sich zurückhalten) slow down, ease up; (sich einschränken) cut down on things; mit etw. ~ cut down on s.th.; **II.** v/t. **1.** (Auto, Zug) brake; (Fall) cushion; der Fallschirm bremste s-n Fall the parachute cushioned his fall; **2.** fig. check, curb; (verlangsamen) slow down (Entwicklung, Produktion, Vorgang) restrict, limit; j-s Begeisterung ~ dampen s.o.'s enthusiasm; **3.** umg.: j-n ~ slow s.o. down; (zurückhalten) hold s.o. back; er war nicht zu ~ there was no holding him (back); sie ist nicht zu ~ there's no stopping her; **III.** v/refl. restrain o.s., hold (o.s.) back (in + Dat. from)

Bremser m; -s, - brakeman

Bremsfallschirm m brake parachute

Bremsflüssigkeit f Mot. brake fluid; **Bremsflüssigkeitsanzeiger** m brake fluid indicator

Brems|hebel m brake lever (od. handle); **~klappe** f Flug. brake flap; **~klotz** m brake block; Flug. (wheel) chock

Bremskraft f braking power (od. force); **~verstärker** m brake booster od. servo

Brems|leistung f braking power, brake performance; **~leuchte** f, **~licht** n stop light, brake light; **~pedal** n brake pedal; **~probe** f brake test; **~rakete** f retro(-)rocket; **~schlussleuchte** f stop and tail lamp; **~schuh** m Tech. brake shoe; **~seil** n brake cable; **~spur** f skid mark(s Pl.); **~strecke** f braking distance

Bremsung f braking (effect)

Brems|verzögerung f brake retardation; **~vorrichtung** f brake mechanism; **~weg** m Mot. braking (od. stopping) distance; **~widerstand** m braking resistance; **~wirkung** f braking action

brennbar *Adj.* combustible, burnable; (*entzündlich*) (in)flammable; **leicht ~** highly (in)flammable; **Brennbarkeit** *f*; *nur Sg.* combustibility; (in)flammability

Brenn|dauer *f* **1.** *e-r Glühbirne*: life; **2.** *im Brennofen*: firing time; **~element** *n → Brennstab*

brennen; *brennt, brannte, hat gebrannt* **I.** *v/i.* **1.** burn (*auch fig. Sonne*); *Haus etc.*: auch be on fire; **es brennt!** fire!; **bei den Nachbarn hat es gestern gebrannt** there was a fire at the neighbours' (house) yesterday; **lichterloh ~** blaze fiercely; **das ganze Dorf brannte** the whole village was in a flame; **die Sonne brennt uns auf den Pelz** *umg.* the sun is scorching us *allg.*; **ihm brannte der Boden unter den Füßen** *fig.* the place was getting too hot for him; **wo brennt's (denn)?** *umg. fig.* where's the fire? (*od.* what's the panic?); **vor Ungeduld** etc. **~** *fig.* be burning with impatience *etc.*; **darauf ~ zu** (+ *Inf.*) *umg.* be dying (*od.* itching) to (+ *Inf.*); **er brannte vor Aufregung** etc. *fig.* he was ablaze (*od.* burning) with excitement *etc.*; **2.** *Licht, Herd etc.*: burn, be on; **lass das Licht ~** leave the light on; **bei ihr brennt noch Licht** her light is still on; **die Laterne brannte** the (street) lamp was lit; **3.** (*entflammbar sein*) burn; **schlecht ~** burn poorly; **wie Stroh** *od.* **Zunder ~** burn like straw (*od.* kindling); **4.** *fig. Nessel, Säure etc.*: sting; *Gewürz, Speise etc.*: be hot; **das Shampoo brennt in den Augen** the shampoo stings (in) one's eyes; **das Essen brennt auf der Zunge** the food burns one's tongue; → *Nagel* 2; **5.** *Füße etc.*: be sore, hurt; *Augen*: sting, burn, smart, be sore; *Wunde etc.*: sting, be sore, hurt; **II.** *v/t.* **1.** burn; (*sengen*) singe; **ein Loch in etw.** (*Akk.*) **~** burn a hole in(to) s.th.; **2.** (*Branntwein*) distil(l); **3.** (*Keramik, Porzellan*) fire; (*Ton, Ziegel*) bake; (*Kalk*) burn, calcine; **4.** (*Kaffee, Mehl etc.*) roast; **5.** *Tech.* (*Holz, Kohle*) burn, fire; → *gebrannt* II; **III.** *v/refl. umg.: sich* (**an etw.** [*Dat.*]) **~** burn oneself (on s.th.)

Brennen *n* **1.** burning *etc.*; **2.** *von Schnaps*: distillation; **3.** *im Hals, auf der Haut etc.*: soreness; (*Jucken*) itchiness; **4.** *von Vieh*: branding

brennend I. *Part. Präs.* → *brennen*; **II.** *Adj.* **1.** *fig.* (*Frage, Interesse, Leidenschaft etc.*) burning; **2.** *Med.* (*ätzend*) caustic; **3.** *Hitze*: burning, scorching, searing; **sie lagen in der ~en Sonne** they were lying in the glaring sun; **III.** *Adv.* **1. ~ heiß** scorching hot; **2.** *fig.*: **es interessiert ihn ~** he's desperately interested (to know); **es interessiert mich ~, ob ...** I'm dying to know if ...; **ich würde ~ gern ...** I would love to ...; **ich würde sie ~ gern kennen lernen** I'd really love to meet (*od.* get to know) her

Brenner *m*; *-s, -* **1.** (*Schnapsbrenner*) distiller; **2.** *Tech.* (*Gasbrenner*) burner; **Brennerei** *f*; *-, -en* distillery

Brenn|form *f Porzellanherstellung*: firing mo(u)ld; **~glas** *n* burning glass; **~holz** *n*; *nur Sg.* firewood; **~kammer** *f Flug.* combustion chamber; *Kraftwerk*: burners *Pl.*; **~kolben** *m zum Destillieren*: still; **~material** *n* fuel; **kann man das als ~ verwenden?** can that be used for heating?; **~nessel** *f Bot.* (stinging) nettle; **~ofen** *m* kiln; *Metall.* furnace; **~öl** *n* fuel oil; **~punkt** *m* **1.** *Opt. und fig.* focus, focal point; **in**

den ~ rücken (*v/t.*) bring into focus; *fig. auch* focus attention on; (*v/i.*) pass into focus; *fig.* become the focus of attention; **im ~ des** (**öffentlichen**) **Interesses stehen** *fig.* be the focus of (public) attention; **2.** *Chem.* burning point, fire point; **~schere** *f hist.* curling tongs *Pl.*; **e-e ~** (a pair of) curling tongs (*Am.* irons) *Pl.*; **~schneider** *m* oxyacetylene cutter; **~spiegel** *m Opt.* burning mirror (*od.* reflector); **~spiritus** *m* methylated spirits *Pl.*; **~stab** *m Kerntechnik*: fuel rod (*od.* pin); **~stelle** *f Etech.* lighting point

Brennstoff *m allg.* fuel; *Kerntechnik*: nuclear fuel; **~element** *n* fuel element; **~verbrauch** *m* fuel consumption

Brenn|weite *f Opt.* focal length (*od.* distance); **~wert** *m* calorific value

brenzlig *Adj.* **1.** *umg. fig.* dangerous *allg.*; **es wird mir zu ~** things are getting too hot for me; **2.** *altm. Geruch etc.*: burnt

Bresche *f*; *-, -n* breach; **e-e ~ schlagen** *auch fig.* clear the way; **e-e ~ schlagen in** (+ *Akk.*) *auch fig.* breach, make a breach in; **in die ~ springen** *od.* **sich in die ~ werfen** *fig.* step (*od.* throw o.s.) into the breach (**für** for)

Bretagne [bre'tanjə] *f*; *-*; *Geog.* Brittany; **Bretone** *m*; *-n, -n*, **Bretonin** *f*; *-, -nen* Breton; **bretonisch** *Adj.* Breton

Brett *n*; *-(e)s, -er* **1.** board; (*Bohle*) plank; (*Latte*) slat, lath; **mit ~ern belegen** board; **mit ~ern vernageln** (*od.* **einzäunen**) board up; **hier ist die Welt mit ~ern vernagelt** *umg. fig.* this is the back of beyond (*od.* the middle of nowhere); **j-n auf die ~er schicken** *Sport, beim Boxen*: floor s.o., send s.o. to the floor; **ein ~ vor dem Kopf haben** *umg. fig. pej.* be thick, be as thick as two short planks (*Am.* as a board); **sie ist flach wie ein ~** *fig. neg!* she's as flat as a pancake; → *Stein* 3; **2.** *von Regal*: shelf; *zum Schneiden*: chopping board; (*Holzteller*) (wooden) platter; (*Tablett*) tray; (*Spielbrett*) board; *zum Surfen*: board; (*Sprungbrett*) spring-board; **3.** **schwarzes ~** noticeboard (*bes. Am.* bulletin board); *fig. im Internet*: bulletin board; **4.** *nur Pl., Theat.*: **die ~er(, die die Welt bedeuten**) the stage; **auf den ~ern stehen** be on the stage (*od.* boards); **5.** *nur Pl., Sport umg.* (*Skier*) boards

Brettchen *n* **1.** (*kleines Brett*) small plank; **2.** *zum Essen, Schneiden*: board, wooden platter; **Brettel** *n*; *-s, -(n) südd., österr.* **1.** *Dim.* small board; **2.** *mst Pl.* skis

Bretter|boden *m* wooden floor; **~bude** *f* wooden hut, shack; (*Verkaufsstand*) (market) stall

brettern *v/i. ugs.* (*schnell fahren*) race (along), bomb it (*od.* shoot) down *the road etc.*

Bretter|tür *f* plank door; **~verkleidung** *f* wood panel(l)ing; **~verschlag** *m* **1.** wooden partition; **2.** wooden shed; **~wand** *f* boarding; wooden partition; **~zaun** *m* wooden fence

bretthart I. *Adj. Bett, Matratze etc.*: hard as a board *mst. präd.*; **II.** *Adv.* hard, solidly; **die Wäsche ist ~ gefroren** the washing is frozen solid

Brettl *n*; *-s, -* **1.** *Theat.* (political) satire; **2.** → *Brettel*

Brettspiel *n* board game

Brevier *n*; *-s, -e* **1.** *kath.* breviary; **2.** *altm.* (*Ratgeber*) guide (*Gen.* to)

Breze *f*; *-, -n*; *südd.*, **Brezel** *f*, *österr.*

auch *n*; *-, -n* pretzel; **Brezelbacken**, **Brezenbacken** *n*: **das geht ja wie's ~** *umg.* it's no trouble at all, it's easy as pie

Bridge [brɪtʃ] (*n*); *-, kein Pl.* bridge *kein Pl.*; **e-e Partie ~** a game of bridge

Brie *m*; *-, -s*; *Gastr.* brie

Brief *m*; *-(e)s, -e* letter; *kurzer*: note, a few lines *Pl. umg.*; epistle *bibl. und iro.*; **~e** *auch* correspondence *Sg.*; **eingeschriebener ~** registered letter; **j-m / an j-n e-n ~ schreiben** write s.o., *mst. Am.* / write to s.o.; **darauf gebe ich Ihnen ~ und Siegel** *fig.* I give you my word (on it), you can take my word for it; → *blau* 2, *offen* I 8; **~ablage** *f* letter file; **~anfang** *m* opening (of a *od.* the letter); **~beschwerer** *m*; *-s, -* paperweight; **~block** *m* writing pad; **~bogen** *m* sheet (*od.* piece) of writing paper; **~bombe** *f* letter bomb

Briefchen *n* **1.** (*heimlich zugesteckter Zettel, bes. in der Schule*) note; **2.** (*Heftchen*): **ein ~ Nähnadeln** a packet of needles; **ein ~ Streichhölzer** a book of matches

Brief|drucksache *f auch Pl.* printed matter; **~einwurf** *m* letterbox, *Am.* mailbox; (*Schlitz*) slot; *als Aufschrift*: letters

briefen ['bri:fṇ] *v/t. Wirts.* brief

Brief|fach *n* pigeonhole; **~form** *f*: **in ~** in letter form; (*mittels e-s Briefes*) by letter; **~freund** *m*, **~freundin** *f* pen-friend, pen pal; **~freundschaft** *f* correspondence with a penfriend; **~geheimnis** *n*; *nur Sg.* privacy of correspondence

Briefing ['bri:fɪŋ] *n*; *-s, -s; Wirts.* briefing

Briefkarte *f* letter card

Briefkasten *m* **1.** letterbox, postbox, *Am.* mailbox; **elektronischer ~** *EDV* electronic mailbox; **2.** (*Zeitungsrubrik*) letters page; *als Überschrift: auch* letters from our readers; *für Vorschläge etc.*: suggestion box; **4. toter ~** *Spionage*: dead letter box; **~firma** *f umg.* letterbox company; **~onkel** *m umg.* agony uncle; **~tante** *f umg.* agony aunt, *bes. Am.* sob sister; **~werbung** *f*; *nur Sg.* junk mail, unsolicited (advertising) mail

Brief|klammer *f* (small) paper clip; **~kontakt** *m* written contact; **in ~ stehen mit** correspond with, write to; **wir bleiben in ~** we'll stay in contact by mail; **~kopf** *m* letterhead; *handgeschrieben*: heading; **~kurs** *m Wirts.* selling rate; **~kuvert** *n* envelope; **~laufzeit** *f* postal delivery time

brieflich I. *Adj.* written, in writing; **~e Anfrage** letter of enquiry (*od.* inquiry); **~er Verkehr** correspondence; **II.** *Adv.* in writing; **~ verkehren mit** correspond with; (*miteinander*) **~ verkehren** correspond; **er teilte uns ~ mit, dass ...** *auch* he sent us a letter to the effect that ...

Brief|mappe *f* portfolio; **~marke** *f* (postage) stamp

Briefmarken|album *n* stamp album; **~automat** *m* stamp machine; **~bogen** *m* sheet of stamps; **~heftchen** *n* book of stamps; **~sammler** *m* stamp collector, philatelist; **~sammlung** *f* stamp collection; **~serie** *f* stamp issue

Brief|muster *n* specimen letter; **~öffner** *m* paper knife, letter opener; **~papier** *n* notepaper, writing paper; **~porto** *n* letter rate; **~post** *f* letter post, *Am.* first-class mail; **~roman** *m Lit.* epistolary novel; **~schluss** *m* close (of a letter); *ein geeigneter ~ auch* an appropriate way of signing off; **~schreiber** *m*, **~schreiberin** *f* letter writer, correspondent; **~schulden** *Pl.* unanswered letters; *s-e ~ erledigen* answer (*od.* write) some letters, catch up on one's correspondence; **~sendung** *f → Briefpost*, **~tasche** *f* wallet, *Am. auch* pocketbook, billfold; *e-e dicke ~ haben umg.* be loaded; **~taube** *f* carrier pigeon; **~träger** *m* postman, *Am. auch* mailman, letter carrier; **~trägerin** *f* postwoman, *Am.* letter carrier; **~umschlag** *m* envelope; **~verkehr** *m* correspondence; **~waage** *f* letter scale(s *Pl.*); **~wahl** *f Pol.* postal vote, absentee ballot; *per ~ wählen* vote by post (*Am.* mail), have a postal vote; **~wähler** *m* absentee voter; **~wechsel** *m auch konkret:* correspondence; *mit j-m in ~ stehen* be corresponding with s.o.; *mit j-m in ~ treten* take up correspondence with s.o.; (*miteinander*) *in ~ stehen* correspond

Bries *n; -es, -e* **1.** *Zool.* thymus (gland); **2.** *Gastr.* (throat) sweetbread

briet *Imperf. → braten*

Brigade *f, -, -n* **1.** *Mil.* brigade; **2.** *hist., ehem. DDR* work team (*od.* brigade); **~führer** *m*, **~führerin** *f* **1.** *Mil.* brigadier; **2.** *hist., ehem. DDR* work team (*od.* brigade) leader; **~general** *m Mil.* (*Armee*) brigadier *Brit.*, brigadier general *Am.*; (*Luftwaffe*) air commodore *Brit.*, brigadier general *Am.*

Brigadier[1] [briga'djeː] *m; -s,-s; Mil.* brigadier

Brigadier[2] [briga'djeː] *m; -s, -s,* [briga-'diːɐ] *m; -s, -e,* **~in** *f; -, -nen; hist., ehem. DDR* work team (*od.* brigade) leader

Brigant *m; -en, -en* **1.** (*Freiheitskämpfer*) guerilla; **2.** (*Straßenräuber*) brigand

Brigg *f; -, -s; Naut.* brig

Brikett *n; -s, -s / selten -e* briquette

brillant [brɪl'jant] *Adj.* brilliant; (*sehr gut*) excellent

Brillant [brɪl'jant] *m; -en, -en* (cut) diamond; **~feuerwerk** *n* cascade

Brillantine [brɪljan'tiːnə] *f; -, -n* brilliantine

Brillant|ring *m* diamond ring; **~schliff** *m* brilliant cut; **~schmuck** *m* diamond jewel(le)ry

Brillanz [brɪl'jants] *f; -, kein Pl.; auch Fot. und akustische:* brilliance

Brille *f; -, -n* **1.** (*e-e ~* a pair of) glasses *Pl.*, spectacles *Pl.*, specs *Pl. umg.*; (*Schutzbrille*) goggles *Pl.*; *e-e ~ tragen* wear glasses; *s-e ~ aufsetzen/abnehmen* put one's glasses on / take one's glasses off; *etw. durch e-e rosa(rote)/schwarze ~ betrachten fig.* take a rosy/gloomy view of s.th.; **2.** *von Klosett:* toilet seat

Brillen|bügel *m* ear piece, *Am.* temple; **~etui** *n*, **~futteral** *n* spectacle (*od.* glasses) case; **~fassung** *f*, **~gestell** *n* (spectacle) frame(s *Pl. bes. Am.*); **~glas** *n* glass, lens; **~kette** *f* spectacle chain; **~schlange** *f* **1.** *Zool.* spectacled cobra; **2.** *umg. fig. hum od. pej.* (speccy) four-eyes *Pl.* (*V. im Sg.*); **~träger** *m*, **~trägerin** *f* spectacle (*od.* glasses) wearer; *~ sein* wear glasses (*od.* spectacles)

brillieren [brɪl'jiːrən] *v/i.* be brilliant; *als Redner etc. ~* prove (to be) a brilliant speaker *etc.*; *generell:* be a brilliant speaker *etc.*; *~ mit* mit Kenntnissen *etc.*: impress everybody with; (*angeben*) show off (with), display; *er bril-*

lierte mit e-r Chopin-Etüde he gave a brilliant rendering of a Chopin etude

Brimborium *n; -s, kein Pl.; umg. pej.* fuss, to-do; *ein riesiges ~ machen um* make a great big fuss about (*od.* over)

bringen; *bringt, brachte, hat gebracht; v/t.* **1.** *an diesen Ort* (*auch fig.*): bring; (*holen*) *auch* get, fetch; *bring doch mal das Salz aus der Küche* would you fetch the salt from the kitchen?; *das Essen auf den Tisch ~* serve the food; *die Wolken ~ Regen* these clouds bring (*od.* mean) rain; *was wird uns morgen ~?* what will tomorrow hold in store (for us)?; *etw. ans Licht od. an den Tag ~ fig.* bring s.th. to the light of day (*od.* out into the open); *mit sich ~* involve; (*erfordern*) require; *die Umstände ~ es mit sich* it's inevitable under the circumstances; *das bringt das Leben so mit sich* life is like that, that's life, that's the way the cookie crumbles *umg.*; **2.** *an e-n anderen Ort* (*auch fig.*): take; *ins Gefängnis, in Lage:* put (*in + Akk.* in); (*tragen*) *auch* carry; (*setzen, legen, stellen*) put; (*begleiten*) take, see; *j-n zur Bahn ~* take (*od.* see) s.o. to the station; *bring es ins Haus* take (*od.* put) it inside; *er wurde ins Krankenhaus gebracht* he was taken to (*Am.* to the) hospital; *ich brachte ihm Pralinen* I took him some chocolates; *die Kinder ins od. zu Bett ~* put the children to bed; *j-n vor Gericht ~* take s.o. to court, bring s.o. up before the court; *etw. auf den Markt od. in den Handel ~* bring (*od.* introduce) s.th. onto the market; *etw. in Umlauf ~* introduce s.th. into circulation; **3.** (*verursachen, zur Folge haben*) cause; (*verschaffen*) (*Glück, Unglück etc.*) bring; (*Erleichterung, Linderung*) *auch* give; *Unglück über j-n ~* bring s.o. bad luck; *j-m Trost ~* comfort s.o.; *das bringt nur Ärger* that'll cause nothing but trouble; **4.** (*einbringen*) (*Gewinn etc.*) bring in; (*Zinsen*) bear, yield; *die Bücher haben auf dem Flohmarkt noch 20 Euro gebracht umg.* the books fetched 20 euros at the flea market, I got 20 euros for the books at the flea market; *das bringt nichts umg.* that won't get you *etc.* anywhere, that's no use; *es bringt nicht viel, wenn man ...* one does not get much mileage out of ... (*+Ger.*); *was bringt das? umg.* what's the point?; **5.** (*schaffen*) do; (*erreichen*) manage; *welche Leistung bringt der Motor?* what can the engine do?; *er brachte es auf acht Punkte in Prüfung etc., auch Sport:* he managed eight points; *es auf achtzig Jahre ~* live to be eighty; *es zu etwas/nichts ~* go far / get nowhere; *es (bis) zum Major ~* make it to major *etc.*; *es zu Ruhm und Ehre etc. ~* achieve fame and fortune; *er könnte es noch weit ~* he could go far yet; *es dahin ~, dass* manage to (+ *Inf.*); *j-n dahin ~, dass* bring s.o. to (+ *Inf.*), make s.o. (+ *Inf.*); *→ zuwege* 1; **6.** *mst mit präpositionalen Obj.* (*etw., e-n Zustand, e-e Handlung bewirken*) *j-n aus der Ruhe ~* upset s.o.; *j-n aus dem Gleichgewicht ~* throw s.o. off balance; *j-n außer sich ~* drive s.o. mad; *j-n in Gefahr/Schwierigkeiten etc. ~* get s.o. into danger/difficulties; *etw. in Ordnung od. ins Lot ~* sort s.th. out; *in Einklang/Kontakt/Zusammenhang etc. ~ mit* harmonize/ bring into contact/connection with; *j-n zur Verzweiflung*

~ drive s.o. to despair; j-n zum Lachen/Reden etc. ~ make s.o. laugh/talk *etc.*; *etw. zum Einsturz/Explodieren ~* make s.th. collapse/explode; *sie brachte den Wagen zum Stehen* she stopped the car (*od.* pulled up); *sie brachte Abwechslung etc. in mein Leben* she brought variety *etc.* to my life; *wir müssen endlich System in die Sache ~* we have to give it some kind of system; **7.** (*Programm, Film etc.*) *auch* show; *Theat.* bring, stage; *Mus.* perform, play, (*Lied*) sing; *Zeitung etc.*: bring; *was bringt das 1. Programm heute Abend?* what's on channel one this evening?; *die letzte Ausgabe brachte ...* the last issue had ...; *haben sie schon etwas über das Unglück gebracht?* have they already reported on the accident?; **8.** *umg., mst Jugendspr.* a) (*schaffen*): *das bring ich nicht!* I (just) can't do it; *ich weiß nicht, ob ich das bringe* I'm not sure I can manage it; *es ~ umg.* make it; (*zuwege ~*) pull it off, b) (*tun*): *das kannst du doch nicht ~!* you can't possibly do that!, that's not on!; *du glaubst nicht, was sie heute wieder gebracht hat!* you'll never believe what she did today!, c) (*gut/schlecht sein*): *es* (*nicht*) *~* be great / no good; *das bringt's* (*voll*) *umg.* that's (really) excellent *od.* brilliant; **9.** *umg.* (*kriegen*) get *s.o./s.th.* somewhere; *ich bring das Ding nicht in die Schachtel* I can't get the thing into the box; *ich bring den Schmutz nicht von den Schuhen* I can't get the dirt off these shoes; **10.** (*lenken*): *das Gespräch etc. auf etw.* (*Akk.*) *~* change the subject to s.th.; *j-n auf etw.* (*Akk.*) *~* (*erinnern*) remind s.o. about s.th.; (*anregen*) make s.o. think about, do *etc.* s.th.; *du bringst mich auf etwas* now that you mention it; *j-n auf die schiefe Bahn / den richtigen Weg ~* lead s.o. off/onto the straight and narrow; *etw. auf den Punkt ~* sum s.th. up; **11.** *mit Präp.*: *an sich* (*od. in s-n Besitz*) *~* acquire, take possession of; *hinter sich ~* get it over with; *ich kann es nicht über mich* (*od. übers Herz*) *~* I can't bring myself to do it; *j-n um etw. ~* deprive s.o. of s.th.; (*betrügen*) do s.o. out of s.th. *umg.*

Bringschuld *f allg.:* obligation to fulfil(l)

brisant *Adj.* **1.** highly explosive, shattering; **2.; 3.** *geh. fig. Problem etc.*: highly charged, explosive; *Situation:* volatile; *politisch ~* politically charged; **Brisanz** *f; -, kein Pl.* **1.** explosive effect; **2.** *geh. fig.* explosiveness; *die ~ des Problems* the volatile nature of the issue; *von höchster ~ sein* be highly explosive

Brise *f; -, -n* (light) wind; *steife ~* strong breeze

Britannien [bri'tanjən] (*n*); *-s; hist.* Britannia; **britannisch** *Adj. hist.* Britannic; **Brite** *m; -n, -n* British man, Briton, Brit *umg.*; *die ~n* the British (*Pl.*); *er ist ~* he's British; **Britin** *f; -, -nen* British woman (*od.* girl), Briton, Brit *umg.*; *sie ist ~* she's British; **britisch** *Adj.* British; *die Britischen Inseln* the British Isles; **~es** *Englisch* British (*umg.* English) English; *das Britische Weltreich* the British Empire

Bröckchen *n* bit

bröckelig *Adj.* crumbly; (*zerfallend*) crumbling; (*zerbrechlich*) brittle; **bröckeln I.** *v/i.* crumble; *Farbe:* flake

(**von** off); **II.** v/t. → **brocken**
brocken v/t.: **Brot in die Suppe ~** break (pieces of) bread into the soup
Brocken m; -s, - **1.** piece, bit; (Bissen) morsel; (Klumpen) lump, chunk; **das war ein harter ~** umg. fig. that was tough (going); **j-m die besten ~ vor der Nase wegschnappen** umg. fig. snap up the best bits (od. parts od. bargains etc.) from under s.o.'s nose; **2.** Pl. fig. snatches of conversation etc., scraps of English etc.; **ich spreche nur ein paar ~** Italienisch etc. I have only basic Italian etc.; **3.** umg. whopper; **das ist ein dicker** od. **schwerer** od. **ganz schöner ~!** that's a humdinger; **fetter ~** big haul; (gutes Geschäft) brilliant deal; **brockenweise** Adv. bit by bit, little by little
brodeln v/i. **1.** bubble (auch Lava etc.), simmer; **2.** fig. seethe; **es brodelt im Volk** there's growing unrest among the people; **es brodelte in ihm (vor Zorn)** he was seething with rage
Broiler m; -s, -; ostd. altm. roast chicken
Brokat m; -(e)s, -e brocade
Broker ['broːkɐ] m; -s, -; Wirts. broker
Brokkoli m; -(s),-(s) Bot. broccoli
Brom n; -s, kein Pl.; Chem. bromine
Brombeere f **1.** Frucht: blackberry; wild wachsend: bramble; **2.** Strauch: blackberry (bush); wild wachsend: bramble
Brombeer|gestrüpp n (im ~ among the) blackberry bushes Pl.; wild wachsend: brambles Pl., Am. briar patch; **~marmelade** f blackberry jam (Am. jelly), bramble jelly; **~strauch** m blackberry bush; wild wachsend: bramble
Bronchial|asthma n Med. bronchial asthma; **~katarrh** m bronchial catarrh
Bronchien ['brɔnçiən] Pl. Anat. bronchial tubes, bronchi; **Bronchitis** f; -, Bronchitiden, mst. Sg.; Med. bronchitis
Bronze ['broːsə] f; -, -n **1.** nur Sg.; Metall: bronze; **2.** nur Sg.; Farbe: bronze; **3.** Statue etc.: bronze; **4.** nur Sg.; Sport bronze (medal)
Bronze|farbe f bronze; **~guss** m **1.** nur Sg.; Handlung: bronze casting; **2.** Produkt: (cast) bronze; **~medaille** f Sport bronze medal
bronzen Adj. (of) bronze
Bronze|plastik f bronze figure; größer: auch bronze statue (auch abstrakte); **~zeit** f; nur Sg. Bronze Age
Brosche f; -, -n brooch
broschiert Adj. paperback; antiquarisch: in wrappers, with dust cover
Broschur f; -, -en; Druck. cut flush binding, brochure (od. paperback) edition
Broschüre f; -, -n pamphlet; (Werbung) dünne: leaflet
Brösel m; -s, - crumb; **bröselig** Adj. crumbly; **bröseln** v/t. und v/i. crumble
Brot n; -(e)s, -e **1.** bread; (Laib) loaf (of bread); **zwei ~e** two loaves of bread; **flüssiges ~** hum. liquid nourishment; **e-e Scheibe ~** a slice of bread; **nur trocken ~** only dry bread; **für ein Stück ~** fig. for a crust; **wes ~ ich ess, des Lied ich sing** Sprichw. he who pays the piper calls the tune; **2.** (belegtes ~) sandwich; Brit. umg. sarnie; **~e (zurecht)machen** od. umg. **schmieren** make sandwiches; **3.** fig. (Unterhalt) living, livelihood; **sein ~ verdienen** earn one's daily bread (od. a crust), make (od. earn) a living; **sein ~ hart** od. **schwer verdienen müssen**

have to work hard for a living; **das ist ein hartes** od. **schweres ~** that's a tough way to make a living (od. make a crust); **4.** kirchl. (Hostie) the Host; **~ und Wein** (the) Eucharist, (the) sacrament; **das ~ brechen** administer the sacrament; → **Butter, täglich** I, **Wasser** 1
Brot|aufstrich m something to spread on one's bread, sandwich spread; **er nimmt nur Butter etc. als ~** he only has butter etc. on his bread; **~belag** m sandwich topping; **~beruf** m bread and butter job
Brötchen n roll; **~s-e ~ verdienen** umg. fig. earn one's bread and butter; **s-e ~ sauer verdienen müssen** umg. fig. work one's fingers to the bone; **kleine/kleinere ~ backen müssen** umg. fig. have to make do with what one has / have to cut down on things; **wer verdient denn hier die ~?** who is bringing in the money (od. bringing home the bacon) (round, Am. around) here?; **~geber** m umg. fig. hum. employer allg., boss
Brot|einheit f Med. (abgek. **BE**) bread unit; **~erwerb** m (earning a) living; **zum** (od. **als**) **~** for a living; **~frucht** f Bot. breadfruit; **~getreide** n bread grain; Koll. bread cereals Pl.; **~kasten** m bread bin (od. box); **~korb** m bread basket; **j-m den ~ höher hängen** fig. put s.o. on short rations; durch Lohnkürzung: cut s.o.'s income; **~krume** f, **~krümel** m breadcrumb; **~kruste** f crust (of bread); **~laib** m loaf of bread
brotlos Adj. fig. **1.** ohne Arbeit: jobless; **j-n ~ machen** deprive s.o. of his (od. her) living, put s.o. out of his (od. her) work; **~ werden** lose one's job; **2.** (nicht einträglich) unprofitable; **... ist e-e ~e Kunst** there's no money (to be earned) in ...
Brot|messer n breadknife; **~rinde** f (bread)crust; **~scheibe** f slice (od. piece) of bread; **~schneidemaschine** f bread slicer; **~suppe** f bread gruel; **~teig** m dough; **~würfel** m bread cube; geröstete ~ auch croutons; **~zeit** f Dial. (Pause) break (for a bite to eat); (Essen) snack; **~ machen** have a snack (od. a bite to eat)
Browser ['brauzɐ] m; -s, - Internet: browser
brr Interj. **1.** (halt) whoa!; **2.** (kalt) brr; **3.** (igitt) ugh!, yuck!
Bruch¹ m; -(e)s, Brüche **1.** (das Brechen) breaking; (gebrochene Stelle) break, fracture, rupture; im Eis etc.: crack, split; e-s Damms: breach, rupture; Tech. break, fracture; fig. e-r Verbindung: breaking-off (+ Gen. of), rupture (in); (Stilbruch) inconsistency (of style); **~ mit der Vergangenheit** (clean) break with the past; **zu ~** od. **in die Brüche gehen** break, be broken, go to pieces; umg. fig. Ehe etc.: break up; **zu ~ fahren** umg. (Auto etc.) smash (up); **es kam zum ~ zwischen ihnen / beiden Ländern** they broke up / the two countries broke off relations; **2.** Med. a) (Knochenbruch) fracture, break; **ein glatter/offener ~** a clean break /an open (od. compound) fracture; **e-n ~ einrichten/schienen** set/splint a break (od. a broken arm od. leg etc.), b) (Leistenbruch etc.) rupture, hernia; **eingeklemmter ~** strangulated hernia; **sich** (Dat.) **e-n ~ heben** give o.s. a hernia; **3.** (Zerbrochenes) debris, breakage; (Trümmer) wreckage; (Schrott) scrap; Schokolade etc.:

broken pieces; Steine: rubble; **4.** fig. e-s Versprechens, des Friedens etc.: breach; e-s Gesetzes etc.: violation; infringement; **5.** Math. fraction; **gemeine Brüche** vulgar fractions; **ein echter/unechter ~** a proper/improper (od. top-heavy) fraction; **gleichnamige Brüche** fractions with a common denominator; **e-n ~ kürzen** reduce a fraction to the lowest common denominator, cancel (down) a fraction; **6.** Geol. fault; tektonisch: fracture; **frischer ~** fresh cleavage; **7.** (Steinbruch) quarry; **8.** Flug. umg. (Bruchlandung) crash; **~ machen** crash(-land); **9.** Sl. (Einbruch) break-in allg.; **e-n ~ machen** do a break-in; **10.** (scharfe Falte) fold, crease
Bruch² m und n; -(e)s, Brüche od. Dial. Brücher; (Moor) marsh, marshy ground, bog, mire
Bruch|band n Med. truss; **~bude** f umg. pej. **1.** run-down place, hovel allg.; (Raum) dump; **2.** fig. lousy joint
bruchfest Adj. unbreakable, breakproof
Bruchfläche f fractured surface, fracture
brüchig Adj. **1.** (zerbrechlich) fragile; (spröde) brittle; Leder: auch cracked; (bröckelig) crumbly; (zerfallend) crumbling; (zerbrochen) broken; (geborsten) cracked; **~ werden** (bröckelig) begin to crumble; (Risse bekommen) start to get cracks; **2.** fig. Stimme: cracked; Ehe, Argument etc.: shaky
bruchlanden v/i. crash-land; **Bruchlandung** f crash landing; **e-e ~ machen** fig. fall flat on one's face, do a belly-flop umg. (mit with)
Bruchoperation f Med. hernia operation
bruchrechnen v/i. Math. do fractions nur Inf.; **Bruchrechnen** n, **Bruchrechnung** f Math. fractions Pl., fractional arithmetic
Bruch|schaden m breakage; **~schokolade** f broken chocolate
bruchsicher Adj. breakproof, unbreakable
Bruchstein m quarrystone; beim Mauern: undressed stone; **~mauer** f quarry stone wall, Am. rubble masonry wall
Bruch|stelle f crack, break; Math. point of fracture; **~strich** m Math. (horizontal od. fraction) line (od. bar); **~stück** n fragment (auch fig.); **~e e-r Unterhaltung** etc. snatches of a conversation etc.
bruchstückhaft I. Adj. fragmentary; **II.** Adv. in fragments, fragmentarily; **ich habe es nur ~ mitbekommen** I only caught snatches of it
Bruch|teil m fraction; **im ~ e-r Sekunde** in a fraction of a second; **~wald** m Ökol. fenwood, carr, Am. swamp thicket; **~zahl** f Math. fraction; **~zone** f Geol. fault (od. rift) zone
Brücke f; -, -n **1.** bridge; fig. link (**zu** with); **schwimmende ~** pontoon bridge; **die ~ führt über den Fluss / überspannt den Fluss** the bridge leads over the river / crosses the river; **e-e ~ schlagen über** (+ Akk.) build a bridge across; fig. forge links (**zwischen** between), breach the gap (**zwischen** between); zwischen Völkern etc.: bring together, create a common bond between; **alle ~n hinter sich abbrechen** burn one's bridges (behind one); **j-m goldene ~n bauen** bend over backwards to make it easy for s.o., hold out rosy prospects to

s.o.; **2.** *Naut.* (*Kommandobrücke*) bridge; (*Landungsbrücke*) gangway, gangplank; **3.** *beim Ringen*: bridge, *beim Turnen*: (Boston) crab, back-bend (position), bridge; *e-e ~ machen* bridge; **4.** *Dent.* bridge, bridgework; **5.** *Teppich*: (scatter) rug; **6.** *e-r Brille*: bridge; *e-r Waage*: platform, table

Brücken|bau *m* bridge building (*od.* engineering); **~bogen** *m* arch (of a *od.* the bridge); **~geländer** *n* bridge railing; *bes. aus Stein*: parapet; **~haus** *n* pilothouse, toll house; **~kopf** *m Mil. und fig.* bridgehead; **~pfeiler** *m* bridge pier; **~schlag** *m* building of a bridge; *fig.* breaching of the gap (*zwischen* between); **~steg** *m* footbridge; **~tag** *m* working day between a public holiday and weekend, often taken as holiday; **~träger** *m* bridge girder (*od.* truss); **~waage** *f* platform scale; **~zoll** *m* bridge toll

Bruder *m; -s, Brüder* **1.** brother; *kleiner/großer ~* little/big brother; *leiblicher ~* full brother; *die Brüder Meier/ Grimm* the Meier brothers / the Brothers Grimm; *Brüder im Geiste geh.* spiritual brothers (*od.* brethren); *an j-m handeln wie ein ~* treat s.o. like one's own brother; *das kostet unter Brüdern umg.* between friends; *unter Brüdern ist der Ring 10 Pfund wert* the ring is a bargain at 10 pounds; **2.** *kirchl. Anrede allg.*: brother (*Pl.* brethren); *für Mönche*: Brother; (*Mönch*) monk; (*Klosterbruder*) friar; *Brüder in Christo* brothers in Christ; **3.** a) *umg.* fellow, bloke, *Am.* guy; *ein lustiger ~* a jolly dog (*od.* fellow); *~ Lustig hum.* happy-go-lucky guy, b) *umg. pej.* bird, *Am.* lucky stiff; *ein schlimmer od. böser ~* a bad lot (*od.* egg); *ein warmer ~* a poof, a fairy; *die Brüder kenn ich* I know his, their etc. sort (*od.* kind); **4.** *umg. Anrede*: (*Freund*) mate, old chap

Brüderchen *n* **1.** *Baby*: baby brother; **2.** little brother

Bruder|hand *f: j-m die ~ reichen* extend to s.o. the hand of brotherhood; **~herz** *n; nur Sg.; hum.* dear brother; *als Anrede*: brother dear; **~krieg** *m* fratricidal war(fare); **~kuss** *m* brotherly kiss; **~land** *hist., ehem. DDR* brother nation

Brüderlein *n; Dim.* **1.** *Baby*: baby brother; **2.** little brother

brüderlich I. *Adj.* brotherly; **II.** *Adv.* like brothers; *~ teilen* share and share alike

Bruder|liebe *f* brotherly love; **~mord** *m* fratricide; **~mörder** *m* fratricide

Bruderschaft *f* **1.** *kirchl.* brotherhood, society; **2.** *nur Sg.* brotherhood; *mit j-m ~ schließen* become close friends with s.o.; *~ trinken* agree to use the familiar 'du' form of address over a drink; *Brüderschaft → Bruderschaft 2*

Bruder|volk *n* cousins *Pl.*; **~zwist** *m* fraternal strife

Brügge (*n*); *-s; Geog.* Bruges

Brühe *f; -, -n* **1.** *Gastr.* broth; *klare ~* clear soup; **2.** *Pulver, Würfel*: stock; **3.** *umg. pej. Getränk etc.*: dishwater, slop; *schmutziges Gewässer*: bilge water; **4.** *umg.* (*Schweiß*) sweat; *mir läuft die ~ runter* I'm sweating like a pig, I'm sweating buckets

brühen *v/t.* **1.** (*Kaffee*) make coffee (in the pot); (*Tee*) brew (*od.* make tea); **2.** (*Mandeln, Tomaten etc.*) blanch; **3.** *hist.* (*Wäsche*) boil

brüh|heiß *Adj.* boiling hot, scalding (hot); **~warm** *fig.* **I.** *Adj. Nachricht etc.*: hot off the press; **II.** *Adv.*: *j-m etw. ~ weitererzählen* run off to tell s.o. s.th. straightaway; *er hat's mir ~ weitererzählt auch* he couldn't wait to tell me

Brüh|würfel *m Gastr.* stock cube; **~wurst** *f* sausage for heating in simmering water

Brüllaffe *m* **1.** *Zool.* howling monkey; **2.** *umg. pej.* screaming idiot

brüllen I. *v/i.* **1.** *Löwe, Tiger etc.*: roar; *Rind*: bellow; (*muhen*) low; *Esel*: bray; **2.** (*wortlos schreien*) scream; (*heulen*) scream, howl; *spielende Kinder*: shout and scream; *vor Lachen/Schmerzen ~* roar with laughter / scream with pain; *~ wie am Spieß* scream one's head off; **3.** *fig. Geschütz, Motor etc.*: roar; **~des Gelächter** roars of laughter *Pl.*; **II.** *v/t.* **1.** (*Befehle etc.*) bawl (out), shout, bark; **III.** *v/refl.: sich heiser etc. ~* shout o.s. hoarse

Brüllen *n; -s, kein Pl.* roar; *... ist ja zum ~ umg. ...* is a (real) scream

Brüller *m; -s, -; umg.* **1.** *Mann*: loudmouth; *Baby*: screamer; **2.** (*Schrei*) shout; **3.** (*komisches Ereignis, komische Person*) hoot; **4.** *Jugendspr.: ein ~ sein* (*Witz, Gag, lustiger Film etc.*) be a scream

Brumm|bär *m fig.* grumbler, grouch *umg.*; **~bass** *m Stimme*: growling bass; *Bassgeige*: double bass

brummeln *v/t./i.* mutter *od.* mumble (away *od.* into one's beard)

brummen I. *v/i.* **1.** *Bär etc.*: growl; *Fliege, Käfer etc.*: hum, buzz; *Flugzeug, Motor etc.*: drone; *Lautsprecher etc.*: hum; *mir brummt der Kopf od. Schädel* my head's throbbing; **2.** *umg. im Gefängnis*: *~ müssen* have to do time; **II.** *v/t./i.* (*murren*) growl, grumble (*über + Akk.* about); (*leise sagen*) mutter; *ein Lied ~* hum a tune; **III. Brummen** *n; -s, kein Pl.* **1.** *Handlung*: growling, muttering, humming; **2.** *Geräusch*: growl, mutter, hum

Brummer *m; -s, -; umg.* **1.** (*Fliege*) bluebottle; (*Hummel*) bumblebee; (*Käfer*) bug; **2.** *ein* (*dicker*) *~* (*gefangener Fisch etc.*) a (real) whopper

Brummi *m; -s, -s; umg. hum.* lorry, truck *bes. Am. allg.*; **Brummifahrer** *m*, **Brummifahrerin** *f umg. hum.* lorry-driver, truckdriver *bes. Am. allg.*

brummig *Adj. umg.* grumpy; **Brummigkeit** *f; nur Sg.* grumpiness, bad temper

Brumm|kreisel *m* humming top; **~schädel** *m umg.* throbbing headache; (*Kater*) hangover; **~ton** *m Etech.* low(-pitched) hum, humming noise

Brunch [brantʃ] *m; -(e)s, -(e)s und –e* brunch

brünett *Adj.* dark(-haired), brunette; **Brünette** *f; -n, -n* brunette

Brunft *f; -, Brünfte, mst. Sg.* rut; **brunften** *v/i.* rut; **brunftig, brünftig** *Adj.* (*männlich*) rutting; (*weiblich*) on (*Am.* in) heat; **Brunftschrei** *m* rutting call; **Brunftzeit** *f* rutting season

Brunnen *m; -s, -* **1.** well; (*Quelle*) spring; (*Spring-, Trinkbrunnen*) fountain (*auch fig.*); (*Heilquelle*) mineral spring, (*mineral*) waters *Pl.*; *ein artesischer ~* an artesian well; *e-n ~ bohren od. schlagen* drill (*od.* sink, bore) a well; *da war das Kind schon in den ~ gefallen fig.* the damage had already been done; **2.** (*Wasser*) mineral water; *→ Krug 1*

Brunnen|anlage *f große*: spa house; *dekorative*: fountain; **~kresse** *f Bot.* watercress; **~kur** *f* mineral water cure; *e-e ~ machen auch* take the waters; **~vergiftung** *f* **1.** *hist.* well-poisoning, water-poisoning; **2.** *fig. pej.* calumny; **~wasser** *n* well water

Brunst *f; -, Brünste, mst. Sg.* **1.** *Zool.* rut(ting); *des Weibchens*: heat, (o)estrus; **2.** (*Paarungszeit*) rutting season; **brünstig** *Adj. Zool.* rutting; *von Weibchen: präd.* on (*Am.* in) heat

brüsk I. *Adj.* brusque, curt, abrupt; **II.** *Adv.* brusquely, abruptly; *j-n ~ abfertigen* give s.o. short shrift; **brüskieren** *v/t.* snub; **Brüskierung** *f* snub(bing)

Brüssel (*n*); *-s* Brussels; **Brüss(e)ler I.** *m*, **Brüss(e)lerin** *f; -, -nen* man/woman from Brussels; **II.** *Adj.* Brussels *attr.*, from Brussels; *~ Spitzen* Brussels lace *Sg.*

Brust *f; -, Brüste* **1.** breast; (*Brustkasten*) chest; *Anat.* thorax; *j-n an s-e ~ ziehen/drücken* pull s.o. close; *komm an meine ~* let me give you a hug; *sich* (*Dat.*) (*reuevoll*) *an die ~ schlagen* beat one's breast (in repentance); *~ raus!* chest out! chin up!; **2.** *einzelne weibliche*: breast; (*Busen*) breast(s *Pl.*), boob *umg.*; (*Büste*) bust, bosom; *hängende/straffe Brüste* sagging/firm breasts; *e-m Baby die ~ geben* breastfeed (*od.* nurse) a baby; *lit.* put a baby to one's breast; **3.** *innere Organe*: chest; *es auf der ~ haben* have chest trouble; *schwach auf der ~ sein* have a weak chest; *umg. fig. finanziell*: be hard up; *in e-m Wissensbereich etc.*: not be very well up in; **4.** *fig.* breast, bosom, heart; *aus voller ~* with all one's heart; *sich in die ~ werfen* give o.s. airs, strut around; (*sich* [*Dat.*]) *j-n an die ~ nehmen umg.* have a heart to heart with s.o.; *e-n zur ~ nehmen umg.* have a quick one; **5.** *nur Sg.; Gastr.* breast; **6.** *nur Sg.; Sport* breaststroke; *100 Meter ~* 100 met|res (*Am.* –ers) breaststroke; **7.** *Kleidung*: front; *→ Pistole, schwellen²* 1

Brust-an-Brust-Rennen *n* neck-and-neck race, photo finish

Brust|amputation *f Med.* mastectomy; **~atmung** *f* thoracic breathing; **~bein** *n Anat.* breastbone, sternum; **~beutel** *m* money bag (*worn around the neck*); **~bild** *n* head-and-shoulders portrait; **~drüse** *f Anat.* mammary gland

brüsten *v/refl. pej.* boast (*mit* about)

Brust|entzündung *f Med.* mastitis, infection of the mammary gland; **~fell** *n Anat.* pleura (*Pl.* pleurae); **~flosse** *f* pectoral fin; **~haar** *n* chest hair

brusthoch *Adj.* chest-high; **Brusthöhe** *f nur Sg.* chest height; *in ~* at chest height

Brust|höhle *f Anat.* thoracic cavity; **~kasten** *m umg.* chest; **~kind** *n umg.* breastfed baby; **~korb** *m Anat.* rib cage, thorax; **~krebs** *m Med.* breast cancer; **~lage** *f Sport* prone position; **~leiden** *n* chest complaint (*od.* trouble *nur Sg.*); **~muskel** *m Anat.* chest (*fachspr.*) pectoral) muscle; **~operation** *f Med.* breast operation; *Schönheitschirurgie*: breast enhancement, boob job *umg.*; **~panzer** *m hist., von Rüstung*: breastplate, cuirass; **~plastik** *f Med.* cosmetic breast surgery, mammoplasty; **~schmerz** *m* pain in the chest, *Pl. auch* chest pains (*od.* pain *Sg.*)

brustschwimmen I. *v/i.* do (the) breaststroke; **II. Brustschwimmen** *n* breaststroke

Brust|stimme *f Mus.* chest voice; **~stück** *n* **1.** *Gastr.* brisket; *Lamm, Kalb, Geflügel:* breast; **2.** *Zool.* thorax; **~tasche** *f Außentasche:* breast pocket; *Innentasche:* inside pocket

Brust|ton *m Mus.* chest note; *im ~ der Überzeugung fig.* with deep conviction; **~umfang** *m* chest measurement; *bei Frauen:* bust (measurement)

Brüstung *f* balustrade; *(Fenster2)* breast

Brust|verletzung *f* chest injury; **~warze** *f Anat.* nipple; *fachspr.* papilla; **~wehr** *f Mil., bes. hist.* parapet; **~weite** *f* chest measurement; bust (measurement); **~wickel** *m Med.* chest compress; **~wirbel** *m Anat.* thoracic vertebra (*Pl.* vertebrae)

Brut *f; -, -en, mst. Sg.* **1.** *nur Sg.; (das Brüten)* brooding; *Vögel:* hatching; *in der ~ sein Vögel:* be hatching; **2.** *(Junge)* brood; *(Laich)* spawn; *Bot.* shoot; **3.** *umg.* a) *hum. (Kinder)* brood, b) *pej. (Gesindel)* shower, rabble

brutal I. *Adj.* **1.** brutal; *Film:* auch violent; *(grausam)* cruel; *mit ~er Gewalt* with (sheer) brute force; **2.** *umg. (schwer)* tough, hard; *~e Tatsachen* cold (*od.* hard *od.* brutal) facts; *das war (ziemlich) ~!* that was (rather) tough (*od.* hard), that was a bit stiff (*od.* brutal); **II.** *Adv.* **1.** brutally; *misshandeln:* violently; **2.** *umg. (sehr)* really, brutally; *gut:* incredibly; *kalt:* perishingly; *das tut ~ weh* that hurts like hell

brutalisieren *v/t.* brutalize; **Brutalisierung** *f* brutalization

Brutalität *f; -, -en* **1.** *nur Sg.; Eigenschaft:* brutality; *(Gewalt)* violence; **2.** *Handlung:* act of brutality (*od.* violence); **Brutalo** *m; -s, -s; umg.* **1.** *Mann:* (big) brute, (real) Rambo *umg.*; **2.** *Film:* blood and guts film, *Am.* splatter movie *etc.*; *Video:* video nasty

Brut|apparat *m* incubator; **~ei** *n* **1.** egg for hatching; **2.** addled, rotten egg

brüten *v/i.* **1.** brood, hatch; *Henne:* sit; **2.** *fig. Hitze, Stille, Unheil etc.:* brood (*über + Dat.* over); **3.** *fig. (nachdenken)* brood (*über + Dat.* on, over); **brütend I.** *Part.Präs.* → **brüten**; **II.** *Adj. Hitze:* sweltering; **III.** *Adv.:* **~ heiß** sweltering (hot); **Brüter** *m; -s, -; Phys.* breeder; **schneller ~** fast breeder (reactor)

Brut|henne *f Orn.* sitting hen; **~hitze** *f* sweltering (*od.* stifling) heat; **~kasten** *m Med. und Agr.* incubator; **~platz** *m Orn.* breeding place; *Fische:* spawning ground; **~ofen** *m: wie in e-m ~ umg.* like (in) a furnace; **~pflege** *f Zool.* brood care; **~pflegeinstinkt** *m Zool.* brood care instinct; **~schrank** *m Agr.* incubator; **~stätte** *f* **1.** *fig.* breeding ground (*+ Gen.* for), hotbed (of); **2.** → *Brutplatz*

brutto *Adv. Wirts.* gross; *~ für netto* gross for net; *2000 Euro ~ bekommen* earn (*od.* get) 2000 euros before tax, gross 2000 euros

Brutto|betrag *m Wirts.* gross amount; **~einkommen** *n* gross income (*od.* earnings *Pl.*); **~ertrag** *m* gross return; **~gehalt** *n* gross salary; **~gewicht** *n* gross weight; **~gewinn** *m* gross profit; **~inlandsprodukt** *n (abgek. BIP)* gross domestic product (*abgek.* GDP); **~lohn** *m* gross pay; **~preis** *m* gross

price; **~registertonne** *f Naut. (abgek. BRT)* gross register ton (*abgek.* GRT); **~sozialprodukt** *n Wirts. (abgek. BSP)* gross national product (*abgek.* GNP)

Brutzeit *f* hatching time

brutzeln *umg.* **I.** *v/t.* fry; **II.** *v/i.* sizzle, crackle, sputter

BSE *f; -, kein Pl.; Abk. Med., Agr.* BSE (= bovine spongiform encephalopathy), mad cow disease *umg.*; **BSE-frei** *Adj.* BSE-free, free of BSE; **BSE-Krise** *f* BSE crises; **BSE-Risikomaterial** *n* specified risk material (*Abk. SRM*); **BSE-Seuche** *f* BSE epidemic; **BSE-verseucht** *Adj. Fleisch:* BSE-contaminated, contaminated with BSE

BTX *Abk.* → *Bildschirmtext*

Bub *m;-en, -en; südd., österr., schw.* boy

Bube *m; -n, -n* **1.** *Kartenspiel:* jack, *altm.* knave; **2.** *altm.: böser ~* bad (*od.* naughty) boy

Bubi *m; -s, -s; umg.* **1.** *in der Anrede:* sonny, my lad; **2.** *pej.* little squirt; **~kopf** *m* pageboy cut, bob

bübisch *Adj. Grinsen:* mischievous

Buch *n; -(e)s, Bücher* **1.** book; *(Band)* volume; *(Drehbuch)* script; *ein schlaues ~ umg.* a clever book; *(Nachschlagewerk)* a reference book; *(Lehrbuch)* a textbook; *das ~ der Bücher* the Book of Books; *die fünf Bücher Mose(s)* the Pentateuch; *ein ~ mit sieben Siegeln fig.* a closed book; *er ist für mich ein offenes ~ fig.* I can read him like a book, I know exactly how his mind works; *über s-n Büchern sitzen/schwitzen* sit at / sweat over one's books, swot *Brit umg.*, cram *Am. umg.*; *Bücher wälzen* pore over books; *er redet wie ein ~* he never stops talking, he could talk the hind legs off a donkey *umg.*; *ein/e-e ..., wie es/er/sie im ~e steht* a perfect (*od.* textbook) example of a ..., your archetypal ... *umg.*; **→** *golden* I 2; **2.** *Wirts.* book, *Pl. auch* records; *~ führen* keep accounts *Pl.*, do (the) bookkeeping; *~ führen über (+ Akk.)* keep a record of; *zu ~e schlagen* show favo(u)rably in the books, *fig.* make a difference

Buch|besprechung *f* book review; **~bestände** *Pl.* stocks (*od.* stock *Sg.*) of books, collection *Sg.* of books

Buchbinder *m* bookbinder; **Buchbinderei** *f* **1.** bookbinder's (shop); *Abteilung:* bookbinding department, bookbinder('s); **2.** *Gewerbe:* bookbinding; **Buchbinderin** *f; -, -nen* bookbinder

Buchdeckel *m* (book) cover

Buchdruck *m; nur Sg.* printing; **Buchdrucker** *m* **1.** printer; **2.** *Zool.* typographical (*od.* eight-dentated bark) beetle, *Am.* engraver beetle; **Buchdruckerei** *f* **1.** printer's; (printing) press; **2.** *Gewerbe:* printing; **Buchdruckerin** *f* printer

Buche *f; -, -n; Bot.* **1.** *Baum:* beech (tree); **2.** *nur Sg.; Holz:* beech(wood); **Buchecker** *f; -, -n* beechnut

Bucheinband *m* binding, cover

buchen[1] **I.** *vt/i. (Zimmer, Sitzplatz etc.)* book, reserve; *(Flug)* book; make a reservation; *hast du schon gebucht?* have you booked (yet)?, have you made a reservation (yet)?; *haben Sie gebucht? Hotel, Flughafen etc.:* have you got a reservation?; **II.** *v/t. Wirts.* enter in the books; *fig. als Erfolg etc.:* put down, notch up *umg.*

buchen[2] *Adj.* beech(wood) ..., made of beech(wood)

Buchen|scheit *n* beech log (*od.* piece of wood); **~wald** *m* beech(wood) forest

Bücher|basar *m* book shop *od.* sale; **~bord** *n*, **~brett** *n* bookshelf; **~bus** *m* mobile library, *Am.* bookmobile

Bücherei *f; -, -en* library

Bücher|narr *m*, **~närrin** *f* book fanatic, real bookworm *umg.*; **~regal** *n* bookshelf; **~schrank** *m* bookcase; **~sendung** *f* **1.** book post (*Am.* rate); *Aufschrift:* printed papers at reduced rates; **2.** parcel (*Am.* package) of books; **~ständer** *m* bookstand; **~stütze** *f* bookend; **~verbrennung** *f* burning of books; **~verzeichnis** *n* **1.** book catalog(ue), list of books; **2.** *in e-m Buch:* bibliography; **~wand** *f* **1.** wall of books; **2.** wall-to-wall bookshelves *Pl.*; **~wurm** *m* bookworm (*auch fig. hum.*)

Buchfink *m Orn.* chaffinch

Buch|form *f: in ~* in book form, as a book; **~format** *n* book format (*od.* size); **~führung** *f Wirts.* bookkeeping, accounting, accountancy; **einfache/doppelte ~** single-entry/double-entry bookkeeping; *die ~ machen* keep the accounts (*od.* books); **~gemeinschaft** *f* book club

Buchhalter *m*, **~in** *f Wirts.* accountant; **buchhalterisch** *Adj.* accounting ..., accounts ..., bookkeeping ...; **Buchhaltung** *f* **1.** → *Buchführung*; **2.** *Abteilung:* accounts department

Buchhandel *m* book (*od.* publishing) trade; *im ~ erhältlich* available in bookshops; **Buchhändler** *m*, **Buchhändlerin** *f* bookseller; *Pl. Koll. auch* bookshops, *bes. Am.* bookstores; **Buchhandlung** *f* bookshop, *bes. Am.* bookstore

Buch|hülle *f (Umschlag)* dustjacket; *(Schutzhülle)* book wrapper; **~klub** *m* book club; **~kredit** *m Jur., Wirts.* book (*od.* open account) credit; **~kritik** *f* book review; **~kritiker** *m*, **~kritikerin** *f* book critic; **~laufkarte** *f* stock-control card in book shop

Büchlein *n; -s, -* little book

Buch|macher *m Sport* bookmaker, bookie *umg.*; **~malerei** *f* **1.** *Kunst:* book illumination; **2.** *Koll.* illuminated manuscripts *Pl.*; **~messe** *f* book fair; *die Frankfurter/Leipziger ~* the Frankfurt/Leipzig Book Fair; **~preisbindung** *f* net book agreement, *Am.* agreement under which booksellers will not offer discounts; **~prüfer** *m Wirts.* auditor; **~prüfung** *f Wirts.* audit; **~reihe** *f* series (of books); **~rücken** *m* spine

Buchs *m; -(es), -e Bot.* **1.** *Baum:* box (tree); **2.** *Holz:* boxwood; **~baum** *m* box (tree)

Buchse *f; -, -n; Etech.* jack; *Tech.* bush(ing); *(Muffe)* sleeve; *(Zylinderbuchse)* liner, lining

Büchse *f; -, -n* **1.** tin, *bes. Am.* can; *größere: auch* box; *(Sammelbüchse)* (collecting) box; *e-e ~ Erbsen etc.* a can of peas *etc.*; *die ~ der Pandora* Pandora's box; **2.** *(Gewehr)* gun, rifle

Büchsenfleisch *n* tinned (*bes. Am.* canned) meat

Büchsenmacher *m* gunsmith

Büchsen|milch *f* tinned (*Am.* canned) *od.* evaporated milk; **~öffner** *m* canopener, *Brit. auch* tin-opener

Buchstabe *m; -n, -n* letter; *(Schriftzeichen)* character (*auch Anschlag*); *großer ~* capital (letter); *Druck.* uppercase letter; *kleiner ~* small (*Druck.*

lowercase) letter; **~ für ~** letter by letter; **auf den ~n genau** to the letter; **nach dem ~n des Gesetzes** according to the letter of the law; **am ~n kleben** take *s.th.* (*od.* things) very literally; **die vier ~n** *umg. hum.* the bottom, the behind; **setz dich auf deine vier ~n** *umg. hum.* plonk yourself down, take a pew

buchstabengetreu I. *Adj.* literal; **II.** *Adv. wiedergeben etc.*: word for word, verbatim

buchstabieren I. *vt/i.* spell (out); (*mühsam lesen*) spell out; *falsch ~* misspell; **ich buchstabiere: A wie Anton, B wie Berta** *etc.* I'll spell it out (for you): A for Alpha, B for Bravo; **II. Buchstabieren** *n*; *-s*, *kein Pl.* spelling

buchstäblich I. *Adj.* literal (*auch fig.*); **II.** *Adv.* literally (*auch fig.*); **~ nichts** *auch* absolutely nothing

Buchstütze *f* bookend, book support

Bucht *f*; *-*, *-en* bay; *kleine*: *auch* inlet; *kleine schmale*: creek; *im Meer*: *auch* cove; *fjordähnliche*: fiord

Buch|titel *m* (book) title; **~umschlag** *m* dustjacket

Buchung *f* **1.** booking, reservation; **2.** *Wirts.* booking; (*Posten*) entry; *laufende ~* current (*od.* running) booking

Buchungs|beleg *m Wirts.* accounting record, voucher; **~bestätigung** *f* confirmation (of booking); **~fehler** *m* false (*od.* incorrect) entry, bookkeeping error; **~gebühr** *f* booking (*od.* transaction) fee; **die ~ beträgt ...** the fee amounts to...

Buch|verlag *m* book publisher(s *Pl.*) *od.* publisher's; **~versand** *m* **1.** book distribution; **2.** a) mail-order bookselling, b) mail-order bookseller

Buchweizen *m* buckwheat

Buch|wert *m Wirts.* book value; **~wissen** *n* knowledge from books, book knowledge; *pej.* bookish knowledge

Buckel *m*; *-s*, *-* **1.** *am Rücken*: hump; (*buckliger Rücken*) hunchback; (*schlechte Haltung*) stoop, round shoulders *Pl.*; **e-n ~ machen** stoop; (*sich schlecht halten*) hunch one's shoulders; *Katze*: arch its back; **2.** *umg.* (*Rücken*) back; **e-n breiten ~ haben** *fig.* have a thick skin; **e-e Menge auf dem** *od.* **am ~ haben** *fig.* have a lot on one's plate; **... Jahre auf dem ~ haben** *fig.* have notched up ... years; **er hat schon etliche Jahre auf dem ~** *fig.* he's been around for a while (*od.* a bit); **den ~ hinhalten** *fig.* carry the can (**für** for); **du kannst mir den ~ runterrutschen** *od.* **raufsteigen!** you know what you can do; **den ~ voll kriegen** get a good hiding; **j-m den ~ voll lügen** *fig.* tell s.o. a pack of lies; **3.** (*Hügel*) hillock; (*Unebenheit*) bump; *Skifahren*: mogul; (*Ausbuchtung*) bulge; (*Verzierung*) boss; (*Beschlag*) knob

buckelig, Buckelige → **bucklig, Bucklige**

buckeln I. *v/i.* **1.** *fig. pej.* (*kriechen*) bow and scrape, kowtow (**vor** + *Dat.* to); **2.** *Katze etc.*: arch one's back; **II.** *v/t.* (*schultern*) shoulder

Buckel|piste *f Skisport*: mogul field (*od.* piste); **~rind** *n Zool.* zebu; **~wal** *m Zool.* humpback whale

bücken *v/refl.* bend over; bend down *od.* stoop (**nach** to pick *s.th.* up)

bucklig *Adj.* **1.** hunchbacked; **2.** *Gegend*: hilly; *umg. Weg etc.*: bumpy; **Bucklige** *m*, *f*; *-n*, *-n* hunchback,

humpback

Bückling *m*; *-s*, *-e* **1.** *Gastr.* bloater, buckling; **2.** *umg. hum.* (*Verbeugung*) bow

Buddel *f*; *-*, *-n*; *nordd. umg.* bottle *allg.*; **~schiff** *n* ship in a bottle

buddeln *vt/i. umg. bes. Kinder*: dig (*od.* play) in the sand *allg.*

Buddhismus *m*; *-*, *kein Pl.*; *Reli.* Buddhism; **Buddhist** *m*; *-en*, *-en*, **Buddhistin** *f*; *-*, *-nen* Buddhist; **buddhistisch** *Adj.* Buddhist

Bude *f*; *-*, *-n* **1.** (*Verkaufsstand*) kiosk; *auf dem Jahrmarkt*: stall; **2.** *umg.*, *oft pej.* (*Haus*) place; (*auch Lokal*) joint *Sl.*; *Wohnung*: digs *Pl.*; (*Zimmer*) pad, place *allg.*; **er wohnt in e-r elenden ~** he lives in an awful hole; **die ~ zumachen** shut up shop; **j-m die ~ einrennen** badger (*od.* keep pestering) s.o. (**mit** with); **j-m auf die ~ rücken** crash in on s.o.; → **Kopf** 1, **Leben** 4, **sturmfrei**; **Budenzauber** *m umg.* party *allg.*; *Brit. hum.* knees-up, *Am.* hoedown

Budget [by'dʒe:] *n*; *-s*, *-s*; *Pol.*, *Wirts.* budget; **budgetär** *Adj.* budgetary

Budget|ausgleich *m Pol.*, *Wirts.* balancing of the budget; **~ausschuss** *m* budget committee; **~beratung** *f* budget(ary) debate, debate on the budget; **~entwurf** *m* budget proposals *Pl.*

budgetieren *v/t. Pol.*, *Wirts.* budget; **Budgetierung** *f* budgeting

Budike *f*; *-*, *-n*; *Dial.* **1.** *Laden*: small shop; **2.** *Kneipe*: (small) pub *bes. Brit.*, bar

Büfett *n*; *-(e)s*, *-s od. -e* **1.** (*Geschirrschrank*) sideboard; **2.** (*Schanktisch*) counter; **3.** *Gastr.* buffet; *kaltes ~* cold buffet; *kaltes und warmes ~* hot and cold buffet (*od.* dishes); **Büfettdame** *f*, **Büfettfrau** *f* woman behind the counter, counter-assistant, server; **Büfettier** [byfɛ'tje:] *m*; *-s*, *-s* barman

Büffel *m*; *-s*, *-* **1.** *Zool.* buffalo; **2.** *umg. fig.* lout, oaf

Büffelei *f*; *-*, *kein Pl.*; *umg.* swotting, *Am.* cramming

Büffel|fell *n* buffalo hide; **~gras** *n Bot.* buffalo grass; **~herde** *f* herd of buffalo (*od.* buffalo[e]s); **~leder** *n* buffalo hide (*od.* leather)

büffeln *vt/i. umg.* swot (up on), cram; **~ für** *auch* swot up (*Am.* cram) for

Buffet [by'fe:] *n*; *-s*, *-s etc.* → **Büfett** *etc.*

Buffo *m*; *-s*, *-s und Buffi*; *Theat.* buffo

Bug¹ *m*; *-(e)s*, *-e od. Büge*, *mst.Sg.* **1.** *Naut.* bow; *Flug.* nose; **j-m e-e od. eins vor den ~ knallen** *umg.* sock s.o. in the mouth (*od.* in the jaw), sock s.o.one; *verbal*: sock it to s.o.; → **Schuss** 1; **2.** *von Pferd*, *Rind*: shoulder; **3.** *Gastr.* shoulder; **4.** *Archit.* brace, strut

Bug² [bak] *m*; *-s*, *-s*; *EDV* bug

Bügel *m*; *-s*, *-* **1.** (*für Kleider*) (coat) hanger; **auf den ~ hängen** hang up, put on a (coat) hanger; **2.** (*Steigbügel*) stirrup; **3.** *Brille*: ear piece, *Am.* temple; **4.** (*Handgriff*) handle; *an der Säge*: bow, frame; **5.** (*Verschluss*) clamp; **6.** *Gewehr*: trigger guard, cross; **7.** *Kopfhörer*: harness; **8.** *Skilift*: T-bar; **9.** *Etech.* (*Stromabnehmer*) (collector) bow; **~brett** *n* ironing board; **~eisen** *n* iron; **~falte** *f* crease

bügelfrei *Adj.* drip-dry, no(n)-iron ...; *Etikett*: wash-and-wear, no(n)-iron

Bügelmaschine *f* (electric) ironing machine

bügeln I. *v/t.* iron; (*Hose*) press; **II.** *v/i.* iron, do the (*od.* some) ironing

Bügelsäge *f* hacksaw

Bügeltisch *m* ironing table

Bügelverschluss *m an Bierflasche etc.*: swing top

Bügelwäsche *f* ironing

Buggy ['bagi] *m*; *-s*, *-s* **1.** (*Kinderwagen*) buggy; **2.** (*Auto*) beach buggy; **3.** (*Pferdewagen*) buggy

buglastig *Adj.* nose-heavy

Bugrad *n Flug.* nose wheel

Bugsierboot *n Naut.* tug(boat); **bugsieren** *v/t.* **1.** *Naut.* tow, tug; **2.** *umg. fig.* steer, manipulate, man|oeuvre (*Am.* -euver); (*Unhandliches*) man|oeuvre (*Am.* -euver)

Bug|spriet *n und m*; *Naut.* bowsprit; **~welle** *f* bow wave

buh I. *Interj.* boo!; **II. Buh** *n*; *-s*, *-s* boo; *Buhs* booing *Sg.*; **buhen** *v/i.* boo

buhlen *v/i.*: **~ um** *altm.* court *s.o.*, woo *s.o.*; **um j-s Gunst ~** *oft pej.* curry favo(u)r with s.o., court s.o.'s favo(u)r

Buhmann *m*; *Pl. -männer* scapegoat; *Schreckgestalt*: *umg.* bogeyman (*auch fig.*); **j-n zum ~ machen** *auch* paint s.o. as the bogeyman, make s.o. the fall guy

Buhne *f*; *-*, *-n* breakwater, groyne, *Am.* groin

Bühne *f*; *-*, *-n* **1.** *Theat.* stage; **auf der ~** on stage; **hinter der ~** backstage (*auch fig.*); **auf die ~ bringen** stage, produce; **auf der ~ stehen** *auch fig.* be on stage; **die ~ betreten** walk on stage; **von der ~ abtreten** take one's last curtain call, leave the stage; *fig.* (*sterben*) pass away; **von der politischen** *etc.* **~ abtreten** *od.* **verschwinden** *fig.* bow out of politics *etc.*, quit the political *etc.* scene; **über die ~ gehen** *Stück*: be put on stage, be staged; *fig.* go off (*glatt* smoothly); **über die ~ bringen** *umg. fig.* (*erledigen*) get *s.th.* out of the way; **wir haben es gut über die ~ gebracht** we managed (it) quite well; **2.** (*Theater*) theat|re (*Am. auch* -er); **3.** (*Podium und Tech.*) platform

Bühnen|anweisung *f Theat.* stage direction; **~arbeiter** *m*, **~arbeiterin** *f* stage hand; **~aussprache** *f* standard diction; **~ausstattung** *f* set(s *Pl.*); **~autor** *m*, **~autorin** *f* playwright, dramatist; **~bearbeitung** *f* stage adaptation; *e-s Romans etc.*: dramatization; **~beleuchtung** *f* stage lighting

Bühnenbild *n Theat.* (stage) set, stage setting; **Bühnenbildner** *m*; *-s*, *-*, **Bühnenbildnerin** *f*; *-*, *-nen* stage (*od.* set) designer

Bühnen|eingang *m* stage entrance; **~erfahrung** *f* experience of the stage, theatrical experience; **~erfolg** *m* box-office success; **~fassung** *f* stage version

bühnengerecht *Adj. Theat.* stageworthy, suitable (*od.* adapted) for the stage; **~ machen** adapt (*od.* arrange) for the stage

Bühnen|haus *n Theat.* fly tower; **~held** *m* (stage) hero; **~heldin** *f* heroine; **~himmel** *m* cyclorama; **~künstler** *m* stage artist, actor; (*Sänger*, *Tänzer*, *Alleinunterhalter*) artiste; **~künstlerin** *f* stage artist, actress; (*Sängerin*, *Tänzerin*, *Alleinunterhalterin*) artiste; **~maler** *m* scene painter; **~malerei** *f* scene painting; **~malerin** *f* scene painter; **~meister** *m*, **~meisterin** *f Theat.* stage manager; **~musik** *f* incidental music; **~name** *m* stage name; **~raum** *m* stage area; **~rechte** *Pl.* stage rights

bühnenreif *Adj.* ready for the stage;

s-e Nachahmung des Chefs ist ~ he could go on stage with his impersonation of the boss

Bühnen|schaffende *m und f Theat.* dramatic artist; **~schriftsteller** *m*, **~schriftstellerin** *f* playwright; **~stück** *n* play; **~technik** *f Theat.* stage technique; **~werk** *n* drama, play

bühnenwirksam *Adj. Theat.* stageworthy; (theatrically) effective; **Bühnenwirksamkeit** *f; nur Sg.* stageworthiness; (theatrical) effectiveness; **Bühnenwirkung** *f* dramatic (*od.* theatrical) effect, effect on stage

Buhrufe *Pl.* booing *Sg.*, boos

buk *Imperf.* → **backen**¹

Bukarest (*n*); *-s Geog.* Bucharest

Bukett *n*; *-s, -e od.* –s **1.** bouquet; **2.** *Wein:* bouquet, nose, aroma; **bukettreich** *Adj.:* ~ *sein Wein:* have a full bouquet (*od.* nose)

bukolisch *Adj. geh.* bucolic

Bulette *f; -, -n; nordd.* meatball; *ran an die ~n! umg. hum.* let's go (for it)!

Bulgare *m; -n, -n* Bulgarian; **Bulgarien** (*n*); *-s Geog.* Bulgaria; **Bulgarin** *f; -, -nen* Bulgarian woman (*od.* girl); **bulgarisch** *Adj.* Bulgarian

Bulimie *f; -, kein Pl.; Med.* bulimia; **bulimisch** *Adj.* bulimic

Bullauge *n Naut.* porthole

Bulldog® *m; -(s), -s; südd.* (*Traktor*) tractor

Bulldogge *f Zool.* bulldog

Bulldozer ['buldo:zɐ] *m; -s, -* bulldozer

Bulle¹ *m; -n, -n* **1.** *Zool.* bull (*auch Elefant etc.*); **2.** *umg. fig.* (*bulliger Mann*) gorilla, heavyweight; **3.** *umg.* (*Polizist*) screw *Sl.; die ~n* the law *Sg.,* the cops *auch Sl.;* **4.** *Wirts. umg.* bull; **5.** *Mil. umg.* big shot, brass

Bulle² *f; -, -n* **1.** (*Siegel*) seal; **2.** (*Urkunde*) (*päpstliche* ~ papal) bull

Bullenhitze *f umg.* scorching (*od.* sweltering) heat; *heute ist aber e-e* ~ it's absolutely sweltering today

bullenstark *Adj.* (as) strong as an ox *präd.*

bullern *v/i. umg.* **1.** *kochendes Wasser, Suppe etc.:* bubble (away); *Feuer im Kamin:* roar; **2.** (*klopfen, trommeln*) bang (*an* on; *gegen* against, on)

Bulletin [byl'tɛ̃:] *n; -s, -s; geh.* bulletin (*über* + *Akk.* about)

bullig I. *Adj.* **1.** *oft pej. Person:* beefy, hefty; **2.** *umg. Hitze:* scorching, sweltering; **II.** *Adv.:* ~ *warm* boiling (*od.* swelteringly) hot

Bullterrier *m Zool.* bull terrier

bum *Interj.* bang!: *dumpfer:* boom!

Bumerang *m; -s, -e od.* –s boomerang (*auch fig.*); *sich als* ~ *erweisen fig.* have a boomerang effect, backfire; *für j-n:* auch come back *at s.o.*; **~effekt** *m* boomerang effect

Bummel *m; -s, -; umg.* **1.** (*Spaziergang*) stroll, walk *allg.; e-n* ~ *machen* go for (*od.* take) a walk; **2.** (*Kneipenbummel*) pub crawl, *Am.* bar hop; *e-n* ~ *machen* go on a pub crawl, *Am.* go bar-hopping

Bummelant *m; -en, -en; umg. pej.* → **Bummler** 2, 3; **Bummelei** *f; -, kein Pl. umg.* dawdling; (*Faulenzen*) idling (around); **bummelig** *Adj. umg.* (*langsam*) slow *allg.;* (*trödelig*) dawdling *allg.;* **bummeln** *v/i. umg.* **1.** (*ist*) (*schlendern*) stroll; go for a stroll *allg.;* **2.** (*hat*) (*faulenzen*) mess around; (*trödeln*) dawdle; **3.** ~ *gehen* (*Lokale besuchen*) have a night out (on the tiles)

Bummel|streik *m* go-slow, *Am.* slow-

-down; *im öffentlichen Dienst:* work-to-rule; **~zug** *m umg.* slow train *allg.*

Bummler *m; -s, -, ~in* *f; -, -nen; umg.* **1.** stroller *allg.;* **2.** (*Trödler*) dawdler; (*langsamer Mensch*) dawdler *allg.,* slowcoach, *Am.* slowpoke; **3.** (*Nichtstuer*) idler *allg.*

bums *umg.* **I.** *Interj.* bang!; **II. Bums** *m; -es, -e; umg.* bang, *dumpfer:* thud *allg.*

bumsen I. *v/i.* **1.** (*ist*) *umg.* (*sich stoßen*) bang, bump (*gegen od. an* + *Akk.* against *od.* on); *sie ist mit dem Kopf an den Schrank gebumst* she bumped her head on (*od.* against) the cupboard; **2.** (*hat*); *umg.* (*krachen*) bang, crash; *plötzlich bumste es* suddenly there was a loud crash(ing sound); *es hat gebumst* there's been a crash (*od.* an accident); **3.** (*hat*); *umg.* (*koitieren*) have it off, bonk, shag *Brit. vulg.;* screw *vulg.; mit j-m* ~ have it off (*Am.* do it) with s.o., shag s.o. *Brit. vulg.;* **II.** *v/t.* (*hat*); *umg.* bonk, bang, shag *vulg.;* **Bumslokal** *n umg.* dive

bumsvoll *Adj. umg.* full to bursting *präd.*

Bund¹ *m; -(e)s, Bünde* **1.** *Pol.* (*Bündnis*) alliance (+ *Gen. Pl.* between); *von Staaten, Städten auch:* federation, league; (*Staatenverbund*) union; *e-n* ~ *schließen mit* enter into an alliance with; *im* ~ *stehen mit* be allied to (*od.* with), be in league with *s.o.;* **2.** *Pol.:* ~ *und Länder* the Federal Government and the Länder (*od.* Lands); **3.** *Mil., umg.* (*die Bundeswehr*): *der* ~ the army; *beim* ~ in the army; *er muss zum* ~ he's got to do his national service; **4.** *zwischen Personen:* *den* ~ *fürs Leben schließen geh.* enter into the bond of marriage, take marriage vows; *der Dritte im* ~*e* the third in the trio; *im* ~*e mit* together with, in association with; **5.** *bibl.* covenant; **6.** *an Hosen etc.:* waistband; (*Bundweite*) waist; **7.** *an der Gitarre etc.:* fret

Bund² *n; -(e)s, -(e);* (*Bündel*) bundle; *Schlüssel, Radieschen etc.:* bunch; *Heu, Stroh:* truss ; *Baumwolle, Flachs* hank

BUND *m; -, kein Pl.; Abk.* (**Bund für Umwelt und Naturschutz Deutschland**) German union for environmental and nature concerns

Bündchen *n am Hals:* neck(-)band; *am Ärmel:* arm(-)band; *an der Hüfte:* waistband; *am Knöchel:* ankle-band

Bündel *n; -s, -* **1.** bundle; *längliches:* sheaf, wad (*auch Banknoten*); *Radieschen etc.:* bunch; *Heu, Stroh:* sheaf; *ein* ~ *Briefe/Zeitungen* a packet (*Am.* bundle) of letters/newpapers; *ein schreiendes etc.* ~ *fig.* a screaming little bundle; *sein* ~ *schnüren fig.* pack one's bags, pack up; *jeder hat sein* ~ *zu tragen* everyone has his, her etc. cross to bear; **2.** *Opt.* (*Strahlen*) bundle, pencil, beam; **3.** *Anat. von Muskeln etc.:* fascicle; **4.** *Wirts.* package, parcel; **bündeln** *v/t.* bundle up; *Etech.* bunch; *Phys., Opt.* focus; **Bündelung** *f* **1.** *nur Sg.* bunching; **2.** *Opt.* focus(s)ing, concentration; **3.** *Wirts.* bundling; **bündelweise** *Adv.* in bundles

Bundes|... *im Subst. Pol.* (*bezieht sich für gewöhnlich auf Institutionen der BRD*): *oft* federal, Federal ...; **~adler** *m* Federal Eagle; **~agentur** *f:* ~ *für Arbeit hist.* Federal Labo(u)r Agency; **~amt** *n* Federal Agency *od.* Office (*für ...* for ...); **~angestelltentarif** *m;*

nur Sg. (*abgek.* **BAT**) official pay scale for federal employees; **~anleihe** *f* government bond; **~anstalt** *f:* ~ *für Arbeit hist.* Federal Labo(u)r Office; **~anwaltschaft** *f; nur Sg.* Federal German Bar; **~anzeiger** *m* Federal Gazette; **~ausbildungsförderungsgesetz** *n* (*abgek.* **BAföG** *od.* **Bafög**) Federal Education and Training Assistance Act; **~autobahn** *f* autobahn; **~bahn** *f österr., schw., in Deutschland bis 1994:* Federal Railway(s *Pl.*); **~bank** *f; nur Sg.* (*auch* **Deutsche** ~) German Central Bank; **~beauftragte** *m, f:* ~ *für Datenschutz* Federal official responsible for data protection; **~behörde** *f* federal authority; **~bürger** *m* German citizen, citizen of the Federal Republic

bundesdeutsch *Adj. Pol.* (German) Federal ...; **Bundesdeutsche** *m, f* → **Bundesbürger**

Bundesebene *f Pol.:* *auf* ~ on a national (*od.* federal) level; *auf Bundes- und Länderebene* on a federal and state (*od.* länder) level

bundeseigen *Adj. Pol.* national, federal

Bundes|feier *f schw., Pol.* Swiss national commemoration holiday on August 1st; **~finanzhof** *m* Federal Fiscal Court; **~gartenschau** *f* national garden show; **~gebiet** *n:* *im gesamten* ~ throughout (*od.* across the whole of) Germany/Austria *etc.*

Bundes|genosse *m,* **~genossin** *f altm.* ally, confederate

Bundes|gericht *n Pol.* federal court; **~gerichtshof** *m* (*abgek.* **BGH**) Federal High Court; **~gesetzblatt** *n* (*abgek.* **BGBl.**) Federal Law Gazette; **~grenzschutz** *m; nur Sg.;* (*abgek.* **BGS**) Federal Border Guard; **~hauptstadt** *f* federal capital; **~haushalt** *m* federal budget; **~heer** *n; nur Sg.* (Austrian) armed forces *Pl.;* **~kabinett** *n* (German) federal cabinet; **~kanzler** *m* **1.** German/Austrian (*od.* Federal) Chancellor; **2.** *Schweiz:* Chancellor of the Confederation; **~kanzleramt** *n* Federal Chancellery; **~kriminalamt** *n* (*abgek.* **BKA**) Federal Bureau of Criminal Investigation

Bundeslade *f bibl.* Ark of the Covenant

Bundesland *n Pol.* (federal) state, land, Land; *die neuen* (*die alten*) *Bundesländer* the newly-formed German (the old West German) states (*od.* Länder)

Bundesliga *f Sport:* (*erste, zweite* ~ First, Second) Division; **Bundesligist** *m; -en, -en* national league team

Bundes|minister *m,* **~ministerin** *f Pol.* minister, Secretary of State *Brit.,* Secretary *Am.* (*für* of, for); ~ *für Justiz* Minister of Justice; ~ *für Verkehr* Minister for Transport; ~ *für Verteidigung* Defen|ce (*Am.* –se) Minister; ~ *für Wirtschaft* Minister for Trade and Industry; **~ministerium** *n* ministry (*für* of); **~mittel** *Pl.* federal funds; **~nachrichtendienst** *m* (*abgek.* **BND**) Federal Intelligence Service; **~post** *f; nur Sg.; hist.: die* (**Deutsche**) ~ the Federal Post Office; **~präsident** *m,* **~präsidentin** *f* **1.** German/Austrian (*od.* Federal) President; **2.** *Schweiz:* President of the Confederation; **~rat** *m* **1.** *BRD und Österreich:* Bundesrat, Upper House (of the German/Austrian Parliament); **2.** *Schweiz:* Bundesrat, Executive Federal Council; **3.** *Ös-*

terreich, *Schweiz*: (*Person*) member of the Bundesrat; **~rechnungshof** *m* Federal Audit Office; **~recht** *n* Federal Law; **~ bricht Landesrecht** Federal Law invalidates (*od.* abrogates) the Law of a Land; **ℒrechtlich** *Adj. und Adv.* under federal law; **~regierung** *f* Federal Government; **~republik** *f*: **~ Deutschland/Österreich** Federal Republic of Germany/Austria; **~richter** *m*, **~richterin** *f* Federal High Court judge; **~schatzbrief** *m* Wirts. Federal Saving Bond
Bundesstaat *m Pol.* **1.** federal state; **2.** *Gesamtheit der einzelnen*: (con)federation; **bundesstaatlich** *Adj.* federal
Bundes|straße *f* (*abgek. B*) *Verk.* major road; **~tag** *m* **1.** *Pol.* Bundestag, Lower House (of the German Parliament); **2.** *hist.* (*1815-1866*) Diet of the German Confederation
Bundestags|abgeordnete *m*, *f Pol.* member of the Bundestag; **~debatte** *f* debate of the Bundestag; **~mitglied** *n* (*abgek. MdB*) member of the Bundestag; **~präsident** *m*, **~präsidentin** *f* Speaker of the Bundestag, parliamentary speaker; **~wahl** *f* parliamentary elections *Pl.*
Bundes|trainer *m*, **~trainerin** *f* Sport national team manager (*od.* coach); **~verdienstkreuz** *n* Pol. Order of Merit (of the Federal Republic of Germany); **~verfassungsgericht** *n*; *nur Sg.* (*abgek. BVG*) Federal Constitutional Court; **~versammlung** *f* **1.** *Deutschland*: Federal Assembly *od.* Convention; **2.** *Schweiz*: Federal Assembly; **~versicherungsanstalt** *f*: **~ für Angestellte** (*abgek. BfA*) Federal Insurance Institution for Employees
Bundeswehr *f*; *nur Sg. Mil.* (German) armed forces *Pl.*; **~soldat** *m* soldier
bundesweit *Adj. und Adv.* nationwide
Bundfalte *f* tuck; **Bundfaltenhose** *f*: (*e-e* ~ a pair of) pleated trousers (*Am.* auch slacks, pants) *Pl.*
bündig *Adj.* **1.** *Tech.* flush; (*auf gleicher Höhe*) level, even; **~ abschließen** finish flush; **2.** (*kurz und*) **~** (*überzeugend*) conclusive; *Stil etc.*: concise, terse; (*genau*) precise
Bündnis *n*; *-ses*, *-se Pol.* **1.** alliance; **ein ~ eingehen** enter into an alliance; → **Bund¹** 1; **2.** (*Vertrag*) agreement; **3.** ~ **90/Die Grünen** *Partei*: Alliance 90/The Green Party; **ℒfrei** *Adj. Pol.* nonaligned; **~grüne** *m*, *f* member of the Alliance 90/Green Party; **die ~n** *etwa* the Green Party; **~partner** *m* ally; **~politik** *f* policy of alliances
Bundweite *f* waist (measurement)
Bungalow ['bʊŋgalo] *m*; *-s*, *-s* bungalow
Bungeejumping ['bandʒidʒampɪŋ] *n*; *-s*, *kein Pl.*, **Bungeespringen** *n* bungee jumping
Bunker *m*; *-s*, - **1.** *gegen Luftangriffe*: air-raid shelter; **2.** *Mil.* dugout; **3.** *für Kohlen*: bunker; **4.** *für Getreide*: silo, bin; **5.** *Golf*: bunker; **6.** *Sl.* (*Gefängnis*) clink, *Am.* slammer; **bunkern** *v/t.* **1.** (*Treibstoff etc.*) bunker; **2.** *umg.* (*verstecken*) stash away
Bunsenbrenner *m Chem.* Bunsen (*od.* bunsen) burner
bunt I. *Adj.* **1.** (*gefärbt*) colo(u)red; (*mehrfarbig*) colo(u)rful, multicolo(u)red; (*farbenfroh*) bright, colo(u)rful; (*schreiend, grell*) gaudy; *Glas*: stained; (*gefleckt*) spotted; → **Hund** 8; **2.** *fig.* colo(u)rful; (*ab-*

wechslungsreich) *Programm, Reihenfolge etc.*: varied; **~er Abend** evening of entertainment; **~e Platte** (dish of) varied kinds of sliced meat and sausages; **~er Teller** plate of nuts, cakes and sweets (*Am.* candy); **3.** a) (*gemischt*) mixed, motley, b) (*ungeordnet, wirr*) confused, higgledy-piggledy; **~es Durcheinander** complete muddle, confusion, chaos; **~es Treiben** lively goings-on; **das wird mir doch zu ~!** umg. I've had enough!, I'm fed up with this!; **II.** *Adv.* **1.** in different colo(u)rs; *gemustert, gestreift etc.*: brightly; **~ bemalt** brightly colo(u)red, multi-colo(u)red, painted in (all sorts of) different colo(u)rs; **~ geblümt** with a colo(u)rful floral pattern *präd.*; **~ gefiedert** with brightly-colo(u)red feathers *präd.*; **~ gestreift** brightly striped; **~ kariert** with colo(u)red checks; **~ schillernd** iridescent; **2.** *fig.*: **~ durcheinander** in a complete jumble (*od.* muddle), chaotic; **das geht ~ durcheinander** there's no system in it, it goes all over the place; **~ gemischt** motley ..., mixed, assorted; **er treibt es zu ~** umg. he takes things too far, he overdoes it
Buntheit *f*; *nur Sg.* colo(u)rfulness; *fig.* vividness
Bunt|metall *n Chem.* non-ferrous metal; **~papier** *n* colo(u)red paper; **~sandstein** *m Min.* new red sandstone
buntscheckig *Adj.* spotted; *Pferd* (*mit Schwarz*): piebald; *Pferd* (*ohne Schwarz*): skewbald
Bunt|specht *m Orn.* spotted woodpecker; **~stift** *m* crayon, colo(u)red pencil; **~wäsche** *f*; *nur Sg.* colo(u)reds *Pl.*
Bürde *f*, -, *-n*; *geh.* burden (*auch fig.*), (heavy) load; **j-m e-e ~ auferlegen** *fig.* place a (heavy) burden on s.o.; **e-e ~ auf sich** (*Akk.*) **nehmen** *fig.* take on a (heavy) burden
Bure *m*; *-n*, *-n*, **Burin** *f*; *-*, *-nen* Boer; **Burenkrieg** *m hist.* Boer War
Bürette *f*; *-*, *-n*; *Chem.* burette
Burg *f*; *-*, *-en* **1.** *hist.* castle; (*Festung*) *auch* fortress, citadel (*beide auch fig.*); **2.** (*aus Sand*) (sand) castle; *am Strand*: (protective) wall of sand; **3.** *e-s Bibers*: (beaver's) lodge; **~anlage** *f hist.* castle buildings *Pl.*
Bürge *m*; *-n*, *-n*; *Jur.* guarantor (*auch fig.*), surety; (*Referenz*) reference; **e-n ~n stellen** offer (*od.* provide) bail; **für j-n als ~ eintreten** stand (*od.* act) as guarantor for s.o.; **bürgen** *v/i.* **1.** **~ für** *für etw.*: (*garantieren*) vouch for, guarantee; (*geradestehen für*) answer for; **der Name bürgt für Qualität** the name guarantees quality; *stärker.* it's (*od.* the make etc.) is a byword for quality; **2.** *Jur.*: **~ für** *für j-n*: go bail for, stand surety for
...burger [-bøːɐgɐ] *m*, *im Subst.*; *-s*, *-*; *Gastr.* ...burger; **Cheese~** cheeseburger; **Fisch~** fishburger; **Soja~** soy(a)-burger
Bürger *m*; *-s*, *-*, **~in** *f*; *-*, *-nen* **1.** citizen; *weitS. auch* member of society; (*Stadtbewohner*) resident, inhabitant; **braver ~** upright citizen (*od.* member of society); **~ in Uniform** soldier; **2.** *soziologisch*: middle-class citizen, member of the middle classes; bourgeois; **3.** *hist.* burgher, freeman
Bürger|begehren *n Pol.* public petition; **~beratungsstelle** *f etwa* citizens' advice bureau; **~entscheid** *m* local

referendum; **~forum** *n* public (*od.* open) debate; **~haus** *n* **1.** *historisches Wohnhaus*: town house (*od.* residence); *öffentliches Gebäude*: village (*od.* community) hall; **2.** *altm.* (*Bürgerfamilie*) family of the mercantile class, bourgeois family; **~initiative** *f* **1.** citizens' (action) group, civic action group; **2.** civic action
Bürgerkrieg *m* civil war; **bürgerkriegsähnlich** *Adj.*: **in dem Land herrschen ~e Zustände** the country is virtually in a state of civil war
bürgerlich *Adj.* **1.** *auch Jur.* Pflichten *etc.*: civil, civic; (*Zivil...*) civilian; **~es Recht** civil law; **~e Rechte** civic rights; **im ~en Leben** in civil (*od.* civilian) life; **Bürgerliches Gesetzbuch** (*abgek. BGB*) (German) Civil Code; **2.** (*Mittelstands...*) middle-class, *pej.* bourgeois; **die ~en Parteien** *Pol.* the non-socialist parties; **er führt ein sehr ~es Leben** he has (*od.* leads) a very bourgeois lifestyle; **~es Trauerspiel** Lit. domestic tragedy; **3.** (*nicht adelig*) untitled; **4.** (*einfach*) plain, simple; **~e Küche** home cooking, good plain cooking (*od.* food); **5.** *pej.* (*spießig*) conventional, plebeian, philistine; **Bürgerliche** *m*, *f*; *-n*, *-n* commoner; **bürgerlich-rechtlich** *Adj.* civil law ...; under civil law
Bürgermeister *m* mayor; *in Schottland*: provost; **~amt** *n 1. Würde*: mayor's office; *förm.* mayoralty; **2.** *Dienststelle*: mayor's office; *weitS.* town hall, *Am. auch* city hall
Bürgermeisterei *f* town hall, mayor's office
Bürgermeisterin *f* mayoress (*bes. Brit.*)
bürgernah *Adj.* grass-roots *attr.*; *Politik*: populist; **Bürgernähe** *f* populism; **er versteht sich auf ~** he has people skills
Bürgerpflicht *f* civil (*od.* civic) duty; **Ruhe ist die erste ~** law and order is the primary civic duty
Bürgerrecht *n* civil rights *Pl.*; **Bürgerrechtler** *m*; *-s*, *-*, **Bürgerrechtlerin** *f*; *-*, *-nen* civil rights campaigner (*od.* activist); **Bürgerrechtsbewegung** *f* civil rights movement
Bürger|schaft *f*; *-*, *-en*, *mst. Sg.* **1.** *alle Bürger*: citizens; **2.** *Pol.* Bremen, Hamburg: city parliament (*od.* assembly); (*Stadtrat*) town (*od.* city) council; **~schreck** *m* -, *-(e)s* -e anti(-)establishment figure, iconoclast *förm.*; **~sinn** *m*; *nur Sg.* public spirit
Bürgersmann *m*; *Pl.* *–leute*; *altm.* **1.** member of the middle-class; *Pl.* middle-class people,; **2.** *Ggs. Adliger*: commoner
Bürger|stand *m*; *nur Sg.*; *the* middle classes *Pl.*; bourgeoisie; **~steig** *m* pavement, *Am.* sidewalk
Bürgertum *n*; *-s*, *kein Pl.* → **Bürgerstand**
Bürger|versammlung *f* town meeting; **~wehr** *f*; *-*, *-en* vigilante group; *bes. hist.* militia
Burg|fräulein *n hist.* daughter of the lord of the castle; **~friede(n)** *m* **1.** *hist.* (area of) jurisdiction; **2.** *fig.* truce (*auch Pol.*); **~n schließen** make a truce; **~graben** *m hist.* moat; **~graf** *m* burgrave; **~gräfin** *f* burgrave's wife; **~herr** *m* lord (*od.* knight *od.* governor) of the castle, castellan; **~herrin** *f* lady of the castle, chatelaine; **~hof** *m* bailey, castle yard; **~ruine** *f* ruined castle, castle ruins *Pl.*

Bürgschaft *f*; -, -en; *Jur.*, *Wirts.* (*Sicherheit*) surety; *auch fig.* guarantee; *im Strafrecht*: bail; **~ leisten**, **e-e** *od.* **die ~ für j-n übernehmen** stand surety for s.o.; *im Strafrecht, als Bürge*: go bail for s.o.; **für e-n Kredit/Wechsel** *etc.* **~ leisten** guarantee a loan/bill of exchange *etc.*; **gegen ~ freilassen** release on bail

Bürgschafts|erklärung *f Jur.*, *Wirts.* declaration of surety; **~leistung** *f* surety

Burgund (*n*); –*s Geog.* Burgundy; **Burgunde** *m*; -*n*, -*n*; *hist.* Burgundian, inhabitant of the Kingdom of Burgundy

Burgunder[1] *m*; -*s*, -, **~in** *f*; -, -*nen*; *hist.* Burgundian, *weiblich auch*: Burgundian woman (*od.* girl)

Burgunder[2] *m*; -*s*, - *Wein*: burgundy; **~wein** *m* Burgundy (wine)

burgundisch *Adj.* Burgundian

Burg|verlies *n hist.* dungeon; **~vogt** *m hist.* castellan; **~wall** *m* (castle) mound

burisch *Adj.* Boer

burlesk *Adj.* burlesque, farcical; **Burleske** *f*; -, -*n* burlesque, farce

Burma (*n*) → **Birma**

Burn-out-Syndrom ['bœrn? aut-] *n*; *nur Sg.*; *Med.*, *Psych.* burnout syndrome

Burnus *m*; -*ses*, -*se* burnous(e)

Büro *n*; -*s*, -*s* office; **~angestellte** *m*, *f* office employee; *weitS.* white-collar worker; **~arbeit** *f* **1.** *in Firma*: office work; **2.** *Schreibarbeit zu Hause*: desk work; **~bedarf** *m* office supplies *Pl.*; **~gebäude** *n* office building (*od.* block); **~gehilfe** *m*, **~gehilfin** *f* office junior, clerical assistant; **~haus** *n* office block (*od.* building); **~hengst** *m umg. pej.* pencil pusher; **~hochhaus** *n* high-rise office block (*od.* building), commercial tower; **~kauffrau** *f*, **~kaufmann** *m* trained clerical worker, office administrator; **~klammer** *f* paper clip; **~kram** *m umg.* odd jobs *Pl.*, odd bits *Pl.* of paperwork

Bürokrat *m*; -*en*, -*en*; *pej.* bureaucrat; **Bürokratie** *f*; -, -*n*; *pej.* **1.** bureaucracy; (*Beamte*) officialdom; **2.** (*Amtsschimmel*) red tape; **bürokratisch** *Adj.*; *pej.* bureaucratic(ally *Adv.*); **bürokratisieren** *v/t. pej.* bureaucratize; **Bürokratisierung** *f pej.* bureaucratization; **Bürokratismus** *m*; -, *kein Pl.*; *pej.* bureaucracy, bureaucratism

Büro|maschinen *Pl.* (electronic) office equipment *Sg.*; **~material** *n* office supplies *Pl.*, stationery; **~mensch** *m umg.* pencil pusher; **~möbel** *Pl.* office furniture *Sg.*; **~personal** *n* office staff (*mst V. im Pl.*), office workers (*od.* employees) *Pl.*; **~schluss** *m* (office) closing time; **nach ~** after office hours; **um 17 Uhr haben wir ~** we leave the office (*od.* stop work) at five o'clock; **~stunden** *Pl.* office hours; **~tätigkeit** *f* office work; **~vorsteher** *m hist.* senior (*od.* chief) clerk

Bürschchen *n umg. in der Anrede*: my lad (*Am.* boy), sonny; **freches ~** cheeky (little) so-and-so (*od.* bugger *umg.*); **ein sauberes ~** *iro.* a fine figure of a man, a bad lot; **du verwöhntes ~** you spoiled (*od.* spoilt) little brat

Bursche *m*; -*n*, -*n* **1.** (*Knabe*) lad (*Am.* boy); **2.** (*junger Mann*): **ein fescher** *toller* **~** some (*od.* a great) guy, quite a lad; **3.** *pej.* (*Kerl*) character, guy; **das ist ein übler ~** he's a nasty sort (*od.* piece of work) *umg.*; **4.** *hist. Mil.* e-s *Offiziers*: orderly., *Brit.* batman;

5. *umg.* (*großes Exemplar*) **prächtiger ~** whopper, big fellow

Burschenschaft *f* (student) society (*od. Am.* fraternity), student league; **Burschenschaft(l)er** *m*; -*s*, - member of a student society (*od.* fraternity)

burschikos *Adj.* **1.** *Frauen*: (tom)boyish; (*lässig*) sporty, jaunty; **2.** *Kleidung*: (*salopp*) casual; *pej.* careless

Bürste *f*; -, -*n* **1.** brush (*auch Tech.*, *Etech.*); **2.** *umg.* (*Frisur*) crew cut; (*Schnurrbart*) clipped (*od.* toothbrush) moustache

bürsten *v/t.* **1.** brush; **Fusseln vom Anzug ~** brush the fluff (*od.* fuzz) from one's suit; **sich** (*Dat.*) **die Haare ~** brush one's hair; **sich** (*Dat.*) **die Zähne ~** brush (*od.* clean) one's teeth; **2.** *vulg.* (*koitieren*) screw, shag *Brit.*

Bürstenschnitt *m* crew cut

Bürzel *m*; -*s*, -; *Orn.* rump; *Gastr.* parson's (*Am.* pope's) nose; (*Schwanz*) tail; **~drüse** *f* preen (*od.* coccygeal) gland

Bus *m*; -*ses*, -*se* **1.** bus; (*Überland-, Reisebus*) *auch* coach; **mit dem ~ fahren** go by bus, take the bus; **2.** *EDV* bus(bar); **~bahnhof** *m* (bus) terminal, bus station; *für Überlandbus in GB*: *auch* coach station

Busch *m*; -(*e*)*s*, *Büsche* **1.** bush; (*Strauch*) shrub; (*kleines Gehölz*) copse, thicket, *Am.* bush; **da ist etwas im ~** *umg. fig.* (I'm sure) they're up to something, there's something brewing; **auf den ~ klopfen** *umg.* put out one's feelers, fish for information; **bei j-m auf den ~ klopfen** sound s.o. out (about *s.th.*); **sich** (**seitwärts**) **in die Büsche schlagen** *umg.* sneak (*od.* slip) away, go behind a tree; **2.** (*Strauß*) bunch; **3.** *in Afrika, Australien etc.*: bush; *umg.* (*Urwald*) jungle; **~bohne** *f Bot.* dwarf (*Am. auch* bush) bean

Büschel *n*; -*s*, - bunch; (*Bündel*) bundle; *Haare etc.*: tuft, *Federn*: *auch* crest; *Phys.*, *Math.* pencil; **büschelweise** *Adv. Haare ausreißen, verlieren etc.*: in handfuls

Busch|feuer *n* bushfire; **~hemd** *n* bush jacket

buschig *Adj.* bushy (*auch Haar*)

Busch|krieg *m Mil.* bush fighting; **~mann** *m*; *Pl.* -männer bushman; **~land** *n* bushland, shrub; **~messer** *n* machete; **~rose** *f Bot.* polyantha (rose), bushrose; **~trommeln** *Pl. umg. fig.* bush telegraphy *Sg.*, grapevine *Sg.*; **etw. über die ~ erfahren** hear s.th. on the bush telegraph (*Am.* on *od.* through the grapevine); **~werk** *n*; *nur Sg.* bushes *Pl.*; **~windröschen** *n Bot.* (wood) anemone

Busen *m*; -*s*, - **1.** (*Brust*) breasts *Pl.*; *verhüllt.*: *mst.* bust, chest; *lit.* bosom; *fig.* bosom, breast, heart; *umg.* boobs *Pl.*, knockers *Pl.*; **voller ~** big breasts (*od.* bust *od.* chest); **schlaffer/straffer ~** sagging/firm breasts; **am ~ der Natur** *fig.* in nature's bosom; **2.** (*Oberteil e-s Kleids*) bodice; **~freund** *m*, **~freundin** *f* close friend, bosom buddy *umg.*

Bus|fahrer *m*, **~fahrerin** *f* bus driver; **~fahrplan** *m* bus timetable (*Am.* schedule); **~fahrt** *f* bus ride; *mit Reisebus*: coach (*Am.* bus) trip, (*Rundfahrt*) coach tour (**durch** of, through); **~geld** *n* bus fare; **~haltestelle** *f* bus stop; **~ladung** *f* busload of *tourists etc.*; **~linie** *f* bus route; **die ~ 8** bus number 8, the number 8 (bus)

Bussard *m*; -*s*, -*e Orn.* buzzard

Buße *f*; -, -*n* **1.** penance; (*Reue*) repentance; (*Sühnung*) atonement, expiation; **~ tun** do penance; **für etw. ~ tun** atone (*weitS.* make amends) for s.th.; **2.** (*Strafe*) penalty; (*Geldstrafe*) *auch* fine

büßen I. *v/t.* **1.** (*Verbrechen etc.*) pay for; *fig. auch* suffer for; **er büßte es mit s-m Leben** *fig.* he paid for it with his life, he sacrificed his life for it; **das sollst** *od.* **wirst du mir ~!** you'll pay for that, I'll make you pay for that; **2.** *kirchl.* atone for; (*bereuen*) repent of; **II.** *v/i.* **1.** **~ für** pay for; *fig. auch* suffer for; **dafür habe ich schwer ~ müssen** *fig.* I had to pay dearly for it; **2.** *kirchl.* do penance; (*bereuen*) repent

Büßer *m*; -*s*, - penitent; **~gewand** *n* penitential robe; **~hemd** *n* hair shirt

Büßerin *f*; -, -*nen* penitent

Busserl *n bes. südd. österr.* kiss, peck *allg.*

bußfertig *Adj.* repentant, contrite

Bußgang *m* penitential pilgrimage

Bußgeld *n* fine; **zu e-m ~ in Höhe von ... verurteilt werden** be sentenced to a fine of ..., be fined ...; **~bescheid** *m* penalty notice; **~katalog** *m* list of (traffic offen|ce, *Am.* -se) penalties; **~verfahren** *n* fining system

Bußgottesdienst *m kath.* penitential service

Bussi *n*; -*s*, -*s*; *bes. südd.*, *österr. umg.* kiss; **~~Gesellschaft** *f umg.* (*Schickeria*) in-crowd, smart set

Busspur *f* bus lane

Buß- und Bettag *m day of prayer and repentance*

Büste *f*; -, -*n* bust

Büstenhalter *m* bra; *formell*: brassiere

Bustier [bys'tie:] *n*; -*s*, -*s* bustier, halter top

Bus|unternehmen *n* bus company; **~verbindung** *f* bus connection (*od.* service)

Butan *n*; -*s*, *kein Pl.*; *Chem.* butane; **~gas** *n*; *nur Sg.* butane (gas)

Butler ['batlɐ] *m*; -*s*, - butler

Butt *m*; -(*e*)*s*, -*e*; *nordd. Zool.* flounder

Bütt *f*; -, -*en* speaker's platform; *umg.* soap(-)box

Bütte *f*; -, -*n* vat, tub

Büttel *m*; -*s*, - **1.** *altm.* (*Polizist*) cop(-per); (*Häscher*) bailiff; **2.** *pej.* lackey, minion, slave; **das lässt er s-e ~ machen** he'll get his lackeys (*od.* minions) (in) to do that

Büttenpapier *n* deckle-edge(d) (*od.* hand-made) paper

Bütten|rede *f* carnival speech; **~redner** *m*, **~rednerin** *f* carnival orator

Butter *f*; -, *kein Pl.* butter; **braune ~** melted butter; **mit ~ bestreichen** butter, spread butter on; **er gönnt ihr nicht die ~ auf dem/das Brot** *fig.* he begrudges her every little thing; **sie lässt sich die ~ nicht vom Brot nehmen** she can stick up for (*od.* look after) herself; **alles in ~** *umg.* everything's just fine (*od. umg.* hunky-dory), couldn't be better *allg.*; **~berg** *m umg.* butter mountain; **~birne** *f Bot.* butter pear; **~blume** *f Bot.* buttercup

Butterbrot *n* (piece *od.* slice of) bread and butter, *Brit. auch umg.* butty; **für** *od.* **um ein ~** *umg. fig.* (billig) for a song, *arbeiten*: for peanuts; → *auch* **Brot** 2; **~papier** *n* greaseproof paper

Buttercreme *f* buttercream; **~schnitte** *f* buttercream slice; **~torte** *f* buttercream cake

Butter|dose f butter box; *am Tisch*: butter dish; **~fahrt** f *umg.* duty-free cruise; **~fass** n (butter) churn; **~flöckchen** n; *mst. Pl.* knob (*od.* pat) of butter; **~keks** m *etwa* rich tea biscuit, butter biscuit; **~kugel** f pat of butter; **~messer** n butter knife; **~milch** f buttermilk

buttern I. v/t. **1.** (*bestreichen*) butter; (*Backblech etc.*) grease (with butter); **2.** *umg. fig.*: **Geld in etw. ~** pour (*umg.* sink) money into s.th.; **3.** *Sport umg.* (*den Ball*) slam; **II.** v/i. make butter, churn; *Rahm*: thicken

Butter|säure f *Chem.* butyric acid;

~schmalz n *Gastr.* clarified butter

butterweich *Adj.* **1.** *Gemüse etc.*: lovely and soft (*Fleisch*: tender); **die Karotten sind ~** *auch* the carrots just melt on your tongue; **2.** *fig.* (*nachgiebig*) soft; **3.** *fig. Sport, Zuspiel*: delicate

Button ['batn] m; *-s*, *-s* badge, *bes. Am.* button

Butzemann m *umg. bes. Kinderspr.* bogeyman

Butzenscheibe f bull's eye (pane)

Büx f; *-*, *-en*, **Buxe** f; *-*, *-n*; *nordd.* (pair of) trousers (*Am. auch* pants, slacks) *Pl.*

b.w. *Abk.* (*bitte wenden*) PTO, pto (= please turn over)

BWL (f) *Abk.* → *Betriebswirtschaftslehre*

BWV (n) *Abk.* (*Bach-Werke-Verzeichnis*) list of J. S. Bach's works

Bypass ['baipas] m; *-es*, *Bypässe* (heart) bypass; **j-m e-n ~ legen** perform a bypass (operation) on s.o.

Byte [bait] n; *-s*, *-s*; *EDV* byte

byzantinisch *Adj.* Byzantine; **~e Zeitrechnung** Byzantine calendar; **Byzantinistik** f; *-*, *kein Pl.* Byzantine studies *Pl.*

bzgl. *Abk.* → *bezüglich* I

bzw. *Abk.* → *beziehungsweise*

C¹, c *n*; -, - *od. umg.* -s **1.** C, c; **C wie Cäsar** *Buchstabieren:* "c" for (*od.* as in) "Charlie"; **2.** *Mus.* C; **das hohe C** top C

C² *Abk.* → **Celsius**

C³, c *Abk.* → **Cent**

ca. *Abk.* → **circa, zirka**

Cabaret [kaba're:] *n* → **Kabarett**

Cabrio(let) [ka:brio('le:)] *n* → **Kabrio**

Cache-Speicher ['kaʃ-] *m Computer:* cache memory

Cadmium *n* → **Kadmium**

Café [ka'fe:] *n*; -s, -s café; **ins ~ gehen** go to a (*od.* the) café

Cafeteria *f*; -, -s *od. Cafeterien* snack bar, cafeteria

cal *Abk.* → **Kalorie**

Call|box ['kɔ:lbɔks] *f für Handys:* voice-mail (*od.* message) box; **~boy** *m* call boy; **~center** *n* call cent|re (*Am.* -er); **~girl** *n* call girl

Calvinismus *m*; -, *kein Pl.*; *Rel.* Calvinism

Camcorder *m*; -s, -; *Etech.* camcorder

Camembert ['kaməmbe:ɐ] *m*; -s, -s; *Gastr.* Camembert

Camp [kɛmp] *n*; -s, -s **1.** (*Ferienlager*) (holiday) camp; **2.** *Mil.* compound, camp

campen ['kɛmpn̩] *v/i.* camp, go camping

Camper¹ ['kɛmpɐ] *m*; -s, - *Fahrzeug:* camper, *Brit. auch* camper van

Camper² *m*; -s, -, **~in** *f*; -, -nen camper

Camping ['kɛmpɪŋ] *n*; -s, *kein Pl.* camping; **~anhänger** *m* caravan, *Am.* travel trailer, motor home; **~ausrüstung** *f* camping equipment; **~bedarf** *m* camping supplies; **~bus** *m* camper, *Brit. auch* camper van; **~platz** *m* camping site, campsite; **~stuhl** *m* folding chair; **~tisch** *m* folding table; **~urlaub** *m* camping holiday (*Am.* vacation); **~machen** go on a camping holiday (*Am.* vacation), go camping; **~wagen** *m* camper, *Brit. auch* camper van

Campus *m*; -, -; *Univ.* campus; **auf dem ~** on (the) campus

Cannabis *m*; -, *kein Pl.* **1.** *Bot.* hemp; **2.** (*Haschisch*) cannabis; → **Haschisch, Marihuana** *etc.*

Canossa (*n*) → **Kanossa**

Canyoning ['kɛnjənɪŋ] *n*; -, *kein Pl.*; *Sport* canyoning

Cape [ke:p] *n*; -s, -s cape

Cappuccino [kapu'tʃi:no] *m*; -(s), -(s) cappuccino

Caravan ['karavan] *m*; -s, -s **1.** (*Kombi*) estate (car), *Am.* station wagon; **2.** (*Wohnwagen*) caravan, *Am.* travel trailer

Cardio... *im Subst. siehe* **Kardio...**

Carepaket ['kɛɐ-] *n* CARE package

Car|port [ka:ɐpɔːt] *m*; -s, -s; (*überdachter Autoabstellplatz*) carport; **~sharing** [-'ʃɛːrɪŋ] *n*; -s, -s; *Verk.* car-sharing (scheme)

Cartoon [kar'tu:n] *m*, *n*; -(s), -s **1.** (*Zeichnung*) cartoon; **2.** (*Geschichte*)

comic (*od.* cartoon) strip; **Cartoonist** [kartu'nɪst] *m*; -en, -en, **Cartoonistin** *f*; -, -nen cartoonist

Casanova *m*; -(s), -s; *umg. fig.* Casanova, Don Juan

Cash [kɛʃ] *n*; -, *kein Pl.*; *Sl.* cash

cash *Adv. Sl.:* **~ bezahlen** pay (in) cash; **ich will das aber ~** I'd like that in cash (please)

Cashflow ['kɛʃflo:] *m*; -s, *kein Pl.*; *Wirts.* cash flow

Cäsium *n*; -s, *kein Pl.*; *Chem.* ca(e)-sium

Cassette *etc.* → **Kassette**

Casting ['ka:stɪŋ] *n*; -s, -s; *Theat., Film:* casting session

Castor® *m*; -s, -en; *Abk.* (**Cask for Storage and Transport of Radioactive Material**) Castor; **Castortransport** *m* Castor transport (*transport of spent nuclear fuel rods*)

catchen ['kɛtʃn̩] *v/i.* do all-in (*od.* catch) wrestling (**gegen** *od.* **mit** against); **Catcher** ['kɛtʃɐ] *m*; -s, -, **Catcherin** *f*; -, -nen all-in wrestler

CB-Funk *m* CB radio, citizens' band radio; **CB-Funker** *m*, **CB-Funkerin** *f* CB radio enthusiast (*od.* hacker *umg.*)

CD *f*; -, -s; *Etech.* CD, compact disc (*Am. auch* disk); **~-Box** *f* CD case, jewel box; **~-Brenner** *m Computer:* CD-writer; **~-Laufwerk** *n Computer:* CD(-ROM) drive; **~-Rekorder** *m Etech.* CD recorder; **~-Rohling** *m*; -s, -e; *Etech.* blank CD; **~-ROM** *f*; -, -s; *EDV* CD-ROM; **~-Spieler** *m Etech.* CD player; **~-Ständer** *m* CD rack; *Turm: auch* CD tower

CDU *f*; -, *kein Pl.*; *Abk.* (**Christlich-Demokratische Union**) Christian Democratic Party

C-Dur *n*; -, *kein Pl.*; *Mus.* C major; **~-Tonleiter** *f* C major scale

CD-Wechsler *m Etech.* CD changer

Cellist [tʃɛ'lɪst] *m*; -en, -en, **~in** *f*; -, -nen; *Mus.* cellist, cello player; **Cello** ['tʃɛlo] *n*; -s, -s *od. Celli* cello

Cellophan® *n*; -s, *kein Pl.* cellophane®; **Cellophanbeutel** *m*, **Cellophantüte** *f* cellophane bag

Celsius (*abgek.* **C**) centigrade, Celsius; **... Grad ~** ... degrees centigrade (*od.* Celsius); **~skala** *f* Celsius (*od.* centigrade) scale; **~thermometer** *n* centigrade (*od.* Celsius) thermometer

Cembalo ['tʃɛmbalo] *n*; -s, -s *od Cembali* harpsichord

Cent [tsɛnt, sɛnt] *m*; -(s), -(s); (*abgek.* **C** *od.* **c** *od.* **Ct.** *od.* **ct.**) cent

...center *n*; -s, -; *im Subst. allg.* ... cent|re (*Am* -er); **Einkaufs~** shopping cent|re (*Am* -er); **Garten~** garden cent|re (*Am* -er); **Schuh~** (large) shoe shop, *Am.* shoe superstore (*od.* outlet)

Cerealien *Pl. Gastr.* cereals *Pl.*

Cervelat *m*; -s, -s; *schw.*, **~wurst** *f Gastr.* cervelat (sausage)

ces, Ces *n*; -, -; *Mus.* C flat; **Ces-Dur** *n* C flat

Cevapcici [tʃe'vaptʃitʃi] *n*; -(s), -; *Gastr.* spicy minced meat sausages

Cevennen *Pl. Geog.* Cévennes

Ceylonese *m*; -n, -n, **Ceylonesin** *f*; -, -nen Ceylonese, *weiblich auch:* Ceylonese woman (*od.* girl *etc.*); **ceylonesisch** *Adj.* Ceylonese; Ceylon ...

Ceylontee *m* Ceylon tea

CH *Abk.* (**Confoederatio Helvetica**) CH

Cha-Cha-Cha ['tʃatʃa'tʃa] *m*; -(s), -s cha-cha(-cha)

Chaise ['ʃɛːzə] *f*; -, -n; *umg.* banger, *Am.* beater

Chaiselongue [ʃɛzə'lɔŋ] *f*; -, -n *od.* -s chaise longue, divan

Chalet [ʃa'le:] *n*; -s, -s; *schw.* chalet; *aus Holz:* Swiss cottage

Chamäleon [ka'mɛːleɔn] *n*; -s, -s; *Zool.* chameleon (*auch fig.*); **chamäleonartig** *Adj.* chameleon(-)like; (*wankelmütig*) fickle

Champagner [ʃam'panjɐ] *m*; -s, - champagne; **2farben** *Adj.* champagne(-colo[u]red); **~glas** *n* champagne glass

Champignon ['ʃampɪnjɔŋ] *m*; -s, -s; *Bot.* button mushroom; **~cremesuppe** *f Gastr.* cream of mushroom soup

Champion ['tʃɛmpiən] *m*; -s, -s; *Sport* champion(s *Pl.*); **der ~ im Speerwerfen** the javelin champion, the champion javelin-thrower; **Championat** *n*; -(e)s, -e championship

Chance ['ʃãːsə] *f*; -, -n chance (**zu** + *Inf. od.* **auf** + *Akk.* to + *Inf. od.* of + *Ger.*); (*Gelegenheit*) *auch* opportunity (to + *Inf.*); *Pl.* (*Aussichten*) prospects; **e-e** *od.* **die ~ haben zu** (+ *Inf.*) have the chance to (+ *Inf.*); **geringe ~n** a slim chance, fat chance *hum.*; **dieser Beruf hat gute ~n** good prospects; **nicht die geringste ~** not a chance; **das ist die ~ m-s Lebens!** it's the chance of a lifetime!, it's a once in a lifetime opportunity!; **bei j-m ~n haben** *umg.* stand a chance with s.o.; **sich** (*Dat.*) **~n ausrechnen** fancy (*Am.* reckon) one's chances; **wie sind** *od.* **stehen die ~n?** what are the odds?; **die ~n stehen gut** the odds are in our *etc.* favo(u)r; *weitS.* the prospects are good, things look (quite) hopeful; **die ~n stehen gleich** it's fifty-fifty, the odds are even; **s-e ~ nutzen** jump at (*od.* grab) the chance; **s-e ~ wahrnehmen** seize the opportunity (with both hands); **s-e ~ verpassen** miss one's chance, miss the boat; **keine ~!** *umg.* no way, not a chance, not a hope in hell *hum.*

Chancengleichheit *f* equal opportunities *Pl.*

chancen|los *Adj.:* **die Mannschaft ist ~** the team's got no chance; **~reich** *Adj.:* **~e Aussichten** good prospects (for the future); **~er Beruf** *etc.* job *etc.* with good prospects

changieren [ʃã'ʒiːrən] *v/i.* (*schillern*) iridesce, shimmer

C

Chanson [ʃã'sõ:] *n*; *-s*, *-s*; *Mus.* chanson; *politisches*: political song

Chaos *n*; -, *kein Pl.* chaos; **hier herrscht ja das reinste ~** it's absolute chaos (*od.* sheer bedlam) in this place; **~forschung** *f Math., Phys.* research into chaos theory; **~tage** *Pl. Sl.* **1.** *Pol.* meeting of the lunatic fringe; **2.** *umg., fig.* chaos days, chaotic period

Chaot *m*; *-en, -en*, **~in** *f*; -, *-nen* **1.** *Pol.* (young) radical, anarchist; *Pl. auch* lunatic fringe (*od.* element) *Sg.*; **2.** *umg. pej.* completely disorganized person, scatterbrain *hum.*; **er ist ein absoluter ~** he just can't get his act together, he's a complete scatterbrain; **chaotisch I.** *Adj.* chaotic; **~e Zustände** chaos, chaotic situation; **II.** *Adv.*: **es ging ziemlich ~ zu** *umg.* it was pretty chaotic

Charakter *m*; *-s*, *-e* **1.** *e-r Person*: character; (*sittliche Stärke*) (strength of) character, (moral) backbone; (*Persönlichkeit*) personality; **das formt den ~** it's character-forming (*od.* -building); **ein Mann von ~** a man of character; **ein Mensch mit ~ hätte ...** anyone with a bit of character (*od.* backbone) would have ...; **sie hat ~** she's got (real) character (*od.* spunk *umg.*); **sie hat keinen ~** she's got no character (*od.* backbone), she's spineless *umg.*; **~ beweisen** show some character (*od.* backbone); **vom ~ her** as far as his *etc.* character goes, *weitS.* personalitywise; **2.** *e-r Sache, bes. mit den Sinnen wahrnehmbar*: character; (*Natur*) nature; *Gespräche vertraulichen* **~s** of a confidential nature; **das Gespräch nahm allmählich den ~ e-s Verhörs an** the conversation gradually turned into a cross-examination; **3.** (*Mensch*) personality; *komischer etc.*: character; *in der Literatur etc.*: character

Charakter|anlage *f* disposition; **~bild** *n* **1.** (*Schilderung*) character sketch (*od.* study); **2.** *Merkmale*: character, personality

charakterbildend *Adj.* character-forming (*od.* -mo[u]lding); **Charakterbildung** *f*; *nur Sg.* **1.** character (*od.* personality) development; **2.** *von außen*: character-mo(u)lding

Charakter|darsteller *m*, **~darstellerin** *f Theat.* character actor, *weiblich auch*: character actress; **~eigenschaft** *f* (personality *od.* personal) trait; **~fehler** *m* (character) weakness, flaw in one's character, character (*od.* personality) flaw

charakterfest *Adj.* of strong character, stable; **Charakterfestigkeit** *f*; *nur Sg.* strength of character

charakterisieren *v/t.* **1.** (*schildern*) describe; (*Sache*) *auch* depict, portray; (*zusammenfassen*) sum up; **2.** (*kennzeichnen*) mark; (*j-n*) be typical of; **charakterisiert sein durch** be marked by; **es wird durch Folgendes charakterisiert** *auch* it has the following characteristics; **Charakterisierung** *f* characterization; (*Schilderung*) description; (*Zusammenfassung*) summary; **Charakteristik** *f*; -, *-en* **1.** characterization; **2.** *Math., Tech.* characteristic; **Charakteristikum** *n*; *-s*, *Charakteristika* characteristic feature; **charakteristisch** *Adj.* characteristic, typical (*für* of); **~e Eigenschaft** characteristic (feature); **charakteristischerweise** *Adv.* characteristically

Charakter|komödie *f Theat.* comedy of character; **~kopf** *m* striking (*od.* interesting) face; **e-n ~ haben** *auch* have striking features

charakterlich I. *Adj.*; *nur attr.* character ..., in (one's) character; personal; **~e Schwäche** weakness in character, character flaw; **II.** *Adv.* in character; *sich ~ verändern* change in character; *völlig*: change one's personality; **er hat sich ~ völlig geändert** *auch* he's a completely different person (*od.* character; personality); **j-n ~ einschätzen** assess s.o.'s character

charakterlos *Adj.* **1.** *Person*: unprincipled; *Handlung(sweise)*: *auch* condemnable; **2.** (*nichts sagend*) colo(u)rless, bland; *Person*: colo(u)rless, (totally) lacking in personality; **Charakterlosigkeit** *f* **1.** *nur Sg.* lack of character; **2.** blandness

Charakter|rolle *f Theat.* character part; **~schilderung** *f* characterization

charakterschwach *Adj.* weak(-charactered); (*willensschwach*) weak-willed; **Charakterschwäche** *f* weakness (of character); *einzelne*: *auch* character flaw

Charakterschwein *n umg., fig.* low character; rat *Sl.*, pig *Sl.*, *bes. Am. auch* low-life(r)

charakterstark *Adj.* of strong character, stable; **Charakterstärke** *f* strength of character; *einzelne*: strength, strong point

Charakter|stück *n* **1.** *Theat.* character play; **2.** *Mus.* piece; **~studie** *f* character study

charaktervoll *Adj.* full of character; *Gesicht etc.*: interesting, striking; *Person*: ... of character

Charakterzug *m* (personality *od.* personal) trait

Charge ['ʃarʒə] *f*; -, *-n* **1.** *Theat.* supporting part; **2.** *Metall.* charge, heat; **3.** *Mil.* rank; **die ~n** the non-commissioned ranks, the NCOs; **die oberen/unteren ~n** *fig.* the lower ranks / the upper echelons; **4.** *Pharm.* batch, lot; **Chargennummer** *f Pharm.* batch number

Charisma ['ça:rɪsma] *n*; *-s*, *Charismen* charisma; **charismatisch** *Adj.* charismatic

charmant I. *Adj.* charming; **II.** *Adv.*: **~ lächeln** give a charming smile; **Charme** [ʃarm] *m*; *-s*, *kein Pl.* charm; (*Ausstrahlung*) personality; **s-n (ganzen) ~ spielen lassen** *umg.* turn on the old charm; **Charmeur** [ʃar'møɐ] *m*; *-s*, *-s od. -e* charmer

Charta ['karta] *f*; -, *-s*; *Pol.* charter; **die ~ der Vereinten Nationen** the United Nations Charter

Charter ['tʃartɐ] *m*; *-s*, *-s*; *Wirts.* charter; **~flieger** *m Flug., umg.* charter plane; **~flug** *m Flug.* charter flight; **~gesellschaft** *f Flug.* charter company; **~maschine** *f Flug.* charter plane

chartern ['tʃartɐn] *v/t.* charter, hire

Charterverkehr *m Flug.* charter flights *Pl.*

Charts [tʃarts] *Pl. umg.* charts; **in die ~ kommen** get into the charts

Chassis [ʃa'si:] *n*; -, -; *Mot., Radio etc.*: chassis

Chatroom ['tʃɛtru:m] *m*; *-s*, *-s*; *EDV im Internet*: chatroom; **chatten** ['tʃɛtn] *v/i.* chat

Chauffeur [ʃɔ'fø:ɐ] *m*; *-s*, *-e*, **~in** *f*; -, *-nen* driver, chauffeur; **chauffieren I.** *v/t.* chauffeur (*od.* drive) around; **II.** *v/i.* drive

Chaussee [ʃɔ'se:] *f*; -, *-n*; *altm.* country road; *in der Stadt*: avenue; **~baum** *m*

roadside tree; **~graben** *m* (roadside) ditch

Chauvi ['ʃo:vi] *m*; *-s*, *-s*; *umg. pej.* male chauvinist (pig *umg.*), MCP *umg.*; **Chauvinismus** *m*; -, *kein Pl.*; *pej.* **1.** chauvinism, jingoism; **2.** (*männlicher ~*) male chauvinism; **Chauvinist** *m*; *-en, -en*; *pej.* **1.** chauvinist; **2.** male chauvinist; **chauvinistisch** *Adj. pej.* chauvinist(ic)

Cheat [tʃi:t] *m*; *-s*, *-s*; (*Code in Computerspiel*) cheat (code)

Check [tʃɛk] *m*; *-s*, *-s* **1.** *Eishockey*: check; **2.** *umg.* (*kurze Überprüfung*) check

checken ['tʃɛkn̩] **I.** *v/t.* **1.** (*überprüfen*) check; **2.** *umg.* (*verstehen*) get, *Brit. auch* twig, cotton on (to); **hast du's endlich gecheckt?** have you got that into your thick skull yet?; **der checkt aber auch gar nichts!** he just doesn't get it (*od.* the message)!; **II.** *vt/i. Sport* barge

Check-in ['tʃɛkʔɪn] *m, n*; *-(s)*, *-s*; *Flug.* check-in; **Checkliste** *f* check list; **Check-up** ['tʃɛkʔap] *m, n*; *-(s)*, *-s*; *Med.* check(-)up

Chef *m*; *-s*, *-s* **1.** head of the company *etc.*; (*Vorgesetzter*) boss, supervisor *geh., s.o.'s* superior; (*Abteilungsleiter*) *auch* head of department; *umg. in der Anrede auch*: chief, *Brit. auch* guv; **wer ist hier der ~?** who's in charge around here?; **ich möchte mit dem ~ sprechen** oft: I'd like to speak to the manager; **den ~ markieren** *umg.* act as if one owns the place; **2.** (*Küchenchef, Chefkoch*) (head) chef

Chefin *f*; -, *-nen* **1.** → **Chef**; **2.** *umg.* the boss's wife

Chef|koch *m*, **~köchin** *f* chef; **~pilot** *m*, **~pilotin** *f* (flight) captain; **~redakteur** *m*, **~redakteurin** *f* editor (in chief); **~redaktion** *f* (*Büro*) main editorial office; (*Aufgabe*) (chief) editorship; **~sache** *f*: **etw. zur ~ machen** *od.* **erklären** decide that s.th. is (a matter *od.* problem *etc.*) for the bosses to deal with (*od.* to decide); (*vorrangig behandeln*) give top priority to s.th.; **~sekretär** *m*, **~sekretärin** *f* personal assistant, PA; **~sessel** *m umg. fig.*: **es auf den ~ abgesehen haben** have one's eye on the boss's job; **~visite** *f Med.* consultant's (*Am.* specialist's) round

Chef|... *im Subst.* **1.** *leitend*: head ..., senior ..., chief ...; **2.** *maßgebend*: leading ...; **~arzt** *m*, **~ärztin** *f* senior consultant, *Am.* chief of staff; **~dirigent** *m*, **~dirigentin** *f* principal conductor; **~etage** *f* executive floor; **~ideologe** *m*, **~ideologin** *f* chief ideologist

Chemie *f*; -, *kein Pl.* **1.** chemistry; (*an)organische ~* (in)organic chemistry; **2.** (*chemische Industrie*) chemicals industry; **3.** (*chemische Vorgänge*) chemistry; **die ~ zwischen ihnen stimmt** *fig.* they have great chemistry; **zwischen uns stimmt die ~** our chemistry is right; **4.** *umg.* (*Chemikalien*) chemicals *Pl.*; **das schmeckt nach ~** it tastes of chemicals (*od.* artificial); **das esse ich nicht, da ist mir zu viel ~ drin** that's too processed, that's full of chemicals

Chemie|arbeiter *m*, **~arbeiterin** *f* chemical worker; **~fabrik** *f* chemical plant (*od.* factory); **~faser** *f* man-made (*od.* synthetic) fib|re (*Am.* -er); **~industrie** *f* chemicals industry; **~konzern** *m* chemicals group; **~labor**

n chemical laboratory; **~laborant** *m*, **~laborantin** *f* (chemical) laboratory (*od.* lab *umg.*) assistant (*od.* technician); **~unfall** *m* chemical accident

Chemikalien *Pl.* chemicals; *giftige ~* toxic chemicals

Chemiker *m*; *-s*, *-*, **~in** *f*; *-*, *-nen* chemist

chemisch I. *Adj.* chemical; **~e** *Elemente* chemical elements; **~e** *Erzeugnisse* chemicals; **~e** *Reinigung Vorgang*: dry cleaning; *Unternehmen*: dry cleaner('s); **~e** *Wirkung* chemical action; **~e** *Zusätze* chemical additives; → *Keule* 3; **II.** *Adv.*: *etw. ~ reinigen lassen* have s.th. dry-cleaned, take s.th. to the dry cleaner('s)

Chemo|technik *f* chemical engineering; **~techniker** *m*, **~technikerin** *f* laboratory (*od.* lab *umg.*) technician; **~therapie** *f Med.* chemotherapy

...chen *n*; *-s*, *-*; *im Subst.* little, small; *Äpfel~* little apple; *Auto~* little car; *Bär~* little (*od.* baby) bear

Cheque *m* → *Scheck*

Cherub ['çe:rʊp] *m*; *-s*, *-im od. -inen*; *bibl.* cherub (*Pl.* cherubim)

chic [ʃɪk] *Adj.*, **Chic** *m* → *schick*, *Schick*

Chicorée ['ʃɪkore] *m*; *-s od. f*; *-*, *kein Pl.*; *Bot.* chicory, *Am. mst.* endive

Chiemsee *m Geog.* (Lake) Chiemsee

Chiffon ['ʃɪfõ] *m*; *-s*, *-s / österr. -e* chiffon

Chiffre ['ʃɪfrə] *f*; *-*, *-n* cipher, code; *Anzeige*: box number; *Zuschriften unter ~ 360* replies to box no. 360; **~anzeige** *f* box number advertisement, blind ad; **~nummer** *f* box number

chiffrieren [ʃɪ'fri:rən] *v/t.* (en)code

Chile (*n*); *-s*; *Geog.* Chile

Chilene *m*; *-n*, *-n*, **Chilenin** *f*; *-*, *-nen* Chilean, *weiblich auch*: Chilean woman (*od.* girl); **chilenisch** *Adj.* Chilean

Chili ['tʃi:li] *m*; *-s*, *kein Pl.* chil(l)i; **~pulver** *n* chil(l)i powder; **~schote** *f* chil(l)i (pepper); **~soße** *f* chil(l)i sauce

Chimäre [çi'mɛ:rə] *f*; *-*, *-n*; *Myth., fig., Bot.* chimera

China (*n*); *-s*; *Geog.* China; *die Volksrepublik ~* the People's Republic of China

China|kohl *m* Chinese cabbage (*od.* leaves *Pl.*); **~restaurant** *n* Chinese restaurant; **~rinde** *f Pharm.* chinchona bark

Chinchilla [tʃɪn'tʃɪla] **I.** *f*; *-*, *-s*; *Zool.* chinchilla; **II.** *m*; *-s*, *-s* **1.** (*Pelz, Mantel*) chinchilla; **2.** (*Kaninchen*) chinchilla (rabbit)

Chinese *m*; *-n*, *-n* **1.** Chinese; **2.** *umg.* Chinese restaurant; *zum ~n gehen* go to a Chinese (restaurant); *in der Nähe ist ein ~* there's a Chinese place near here; **Chinesenviertel** *n* (*auch das ~*) Chinatown; **Chinesin** *f*; *-*, *-nen* Chinese (woman *od.* girl *etc.*)

chinesisch *Adj.* Chinese; *die Chinesische Mauer* the Great Wall (of China); **Chinesisch** *n*; *-en*; *Ling.* Chinese; *das ~e* Chinese, the Chinese language; *das ist ~ für mich fig.* that's all Greek (*od.* double Dutch) to me; *ja, red ich denn ~? umg.* am I talking to a brick wall?

Chinin [çi'ni:n] *n*; *-s*, *kein Pl.*; *Pharm.* quinine

Chintz [tʃɪnts] *m*; *-(es)*, *-e* chintz

Chip [tʃɪp] *m*; *-s*, *-s* **1.** (*Spielmarke*) chip; *Pl. Gastr.* (potato) crisps, *Am.* potato chips; **3.** *Etron.* chip; **~karte** *f* smart card

Chiro|praktik [çiro'praktɪk] *f*; *nur Sg.*; *Med.* chiropractic; **~praktiker** *m*, **~praktikerin** *f* chiropractor

Chirurg *m*; *-en*, *-en* surgeon; **Chirurgie** *f*; *-*, *kein Pl.* **1.** surgery; **2.** (*Krankenhausabteilung*) surgical ward; *in der ~ liegen auch* be in surgery; **Chirurgin** *f*; *-*, *-nen* surgeon; **chirurgisch** *Adj.* surgical; *ein ~er Eingriff* surgery (*auch Pl.*), an operation; *e-n ~en Eingriff vornehmen* operate (*bei* on), carry out surgery (on)

Chitin *n*; *-s*, *kein Pl.*; *Zool.* chitin; **~panzer** *m* exoskeleton

Clochard [klo:'ʃaːɐ] *m* tramp, down-and-out

Chlor *n*; *-s*, *kein Pl.*; *Chem.* chlorine; **chloren** *v/t.* chlorinate; **Chlorgas** *n* chloric gas; **chlorhaltig** *Adj.* chlorinated; **Chlorid** *n*; *-(e)s*, *-e* chloride; **chlorieren** *v/t.* chlorinate

Chloroform *n*; *-s*, *kein Pl.*; *Chem., Med.* chloroform; **chloroformieren** *v/t. Med.* chloroform

Chlorophyll *n*; *-s*, *kein Pl.*; *Bot.* chlorophyll

Choke [tʃo:k] *m*; *-s*, *-s*; *Mot.* choke

Cholera *f*; *-*, *kein Pl.*; *Med.* cholera; **~epidemie** *f* cholera epidemic

Choleriker *m*; *-s*, *-*, **~in** *f*; *-*, *-nen*; *Psych.* choleric type; **cholerisch** *Adj.* choleric

Cholesterin *n*; *-s*, *kein Pl.*; *Zool., Med.* cholesterol; **Qarm** *Adj. attr.* low-cholesterol ..., *präd.* low in cholesterol; **~gehalt** *m* cholesterol content; **Qreich** *Adj. attr.* high-cholesterol ..., *präd.* high in cholesterol; **~spiegel** *m* cholesterol level

Chor *m*; *-(e)s*, *Chöre* **1.** (*Gruppe*) choir; **2.** (*Chorsatz, -gesang*) chorus; *im ~ rufen etc.*: in chorus, all together; **3.** (*Instrumentengruppe*) section; **4.** *im Drama*: chorus; **5.** *Archit.* choir, chancel

Choral *m*; *-s*, *Choräle* chorale, hymn; *gregorianischer*: Gregorian chant; (*Psalmodie*) plainsong

Choramt *n* choir office

Choreograf *etc.* → *Choreograph etc.*

Choreograph *m*; *-en*, *-en* choreographer; **Choreographie** *f*; *-*, *-n* choreography; **choreographieren** *vt/i.* choreograph; **Choreographin** *f*; *-*, *-nen* choreographer; **choreographisch I.** *Adj.* choreographic; **II.** *Adv.* choreographically

Chor|gang *m Archit.* choir aisle; **~gebet** *n* canonical hour(s *Pl.*); **~gesang** *m* **1.** *Koll.* choral music; **2.** singing of a (*od.* the) choir; **~gestühl** *n* (choir) stalls *Pl.*; **~hemd** *n* surplice; *auch des Bischofs*: rochet; **~herr** *m kath.* canon

Chor|knabe *m* choirboy, **~konzert** *n* choral concert; **~leiter** *m*, **~leiterin** *f* choirmaster, choir director; **~musik** *f* choral music; **~probe** *f* choir practice; **~sänger** *m*, **~sängerin** *f* member of a (*od.* the) choir, chorister; **~stuhl** *m* (choir) stall

Chose ['ʃo:zə] *f*; *-*, *-n*; *umg.* **1.** (*Sache*) business; *die ganze ~ hinschmeißen* chuck the whole thing; **2.** (*Dinge*) stuff

Chow-Chow [tʃau'tʃau] *m*; *-s*, *-s*; *Zool.* chow (chow)

Christ *m*; *-en*, *-en*, **~in** *f*; *-*, *-nen* Christian

Christbaum *m* Christmas tree; **~schmuck** *m* Christmas tree decorations *Pl.*

Christdemokrat *m*, **~in** *f Pol.* Christian Democrat; **christdemokratisch** *Adj. attr.* Christian Democrat

Christen|gemeinde *f* **1.** (*Christenheit*) Christian community; **2.** *~ der Frühzeit* early Christian church; **~glaube(n)** *m* the Christian faith

Christenheit *f*: *die ~* Christendom, the Christian world; *die gesamte ~* the whole of Christendom, the entire Christian world

Christen|mensch *m* Christian (person); **~pflicht** *f*; *nur Sg.*: *s-e ~* one's duty as a Christian

Christentum *n*; *-s*, *nur Sg.*: *das ~* Christianity

Christenverfolgung *f* persecution of (the) Christians

Christfest *n altm.* Christmas

christianisieren *v/t.* convert to Christianity; **Christianisierung** *f* christianization, conversion *of a country etc.* to Christianity

Christkind *n*; *nur Sg.*, **Christkindl** *n*; *nur Sg.*, *südd., österr.* **1.** *das ~ in der Krippe*: the infant Jesus, the Christ child, the Holy child; *Kindersprache*: (the) baby Jesus; *das Geschenke bringt*: *etwa* Father Christmas, Santa Claus; **2.** *südd., österr.* (*Weihnachtsgeschenk*) Christmas present; **Christkindl(es)markt** *m* Christmas market

christlich I. *Adj.* Christian; **~e** *Nächstenliebe* Christian charity, love for one's fellow man; → *Seefahrt* 1; **II.** *Adv.* like a Christian; *~ teilen umg.* share (*s.th.*) out evenly; **~-demokratisch** *Adj. Pol.* Christian Democrat; *Christlich-Demokratische Union* (*abgek.* CDU) Christian Democratic Party; **~sozial** *Adj. Pol.*: *Christlich-Soziale Union* (*abgek.* **CSU**) Christian Social Union

Christ|messe *f Reli.* midnight mass; **~mette** *f kath.* midnight mass; *ev.* midnight service; **~rose** *f Bot.* Christmas rose; **~stollen** *m Gastr.* stollen (cake)

Christus (*m*); *Christi*, *kein Pl.* Christ; *vor Christi Geburt od. vor ~* (*abgek. v. Chr.*) before Christ (*Abk.* BC); *nach Christi Geburt od. nach ~* (*abgek. n. Chr.*) Anno Domini (*Abk.* AD); **~bild** *n* image of Christ; *am Kreuz*: crucifix; **~figur** *f* figure (*od.* statue) of Christ

Chrom *n*; *-s*, *kein Pl.*; *Chem., Legierung*: chrome; *Element*: chromium

Chromatik *f*; *-*, *kein Pl.*; *Mus., Opt.* chromatics *Pl.* (*Verb mst im Sg.*); **chromatisch I.** *Adj.* chromatic; **II.** *Adv.* chromatically; **~e** *Tonleiter* chromatic scale

chromblitzend *Adj.* gleaming (with metal)

Chromdioxidkassette *f* chromium dioxide cassette

chrom|gelb *Adj.* chrome yellow; **~grün** *Adj.* viridian (*od.* chrome) green

Chromosom *n*; *-s*, *-en*; *Bio.* chromosome

Chromosomen|anomalie *f* chromosome abnormality; **~paar** *n* pair of chromosomes; **~satz** *m* set of chromosomes, genome *fachspr.*; **~zahl** *f* chromosome number

Chrom|silber *n Min.* silver chromate; **~stahl** *m* chrome (*od.* chromium) steel

Chronik *f*; *-*, *-en* chronicle, annal *altm.*; *in e-r ~ aufzeichnen* chronicle

chronisch I. *Adj. Med. und fig.* chronic; **II.** *Adv.* chronically

Chronist *m*; *-en*, *-en*, **~in** *f*; *-*, *-nen* chronicler

Chronologie *f*; *-*, *-n* chronology; *die ~ der Ereignisse auch* the sequence of

C

events; **chronologisch** *Adj.* chronological; *in ~er Folge* in chronological order, chronologically

Chronometer *n*; *-s*, - chronometer

Chrysantheme *f*; *-*, *-n*; *Bot.* chrysanthemum

Chuzpe ['xʊtsspə] *f*; *-*, *kein Pl.*; *umg. pej.* chutzpah

ciao [tʃau] *Interj.* bye!, see you!

Cidre ['siːdrə] *m*; *-s*, *kein Pl. etwa* cider, *Am.* hard cider

Cinch|buchse ['sɪntʃ-] *f Etech.* coaxial socket; **~stecker** *m* coaxial plug

Cineast *m*; *-en*, *-en*, **~in** *f*; *-*, *-nen* **1.** filmmaker, cinematographer; **2.** movie buff, cineaste; **cineastisch** *Adj. Ereignis, Genuss:* cinematographic

circa *Adv.* → *zirka*

cis, Cis *n*; *-*, *-*; *Mus.* C sharp

City ['sɪti] *f*; *-*, *-s* town (*od.* city) centre, *Am.* downtown, city center; *wann willst du in die ~?* when are you going (in)to town?; **~lage** *f* central location; *in ~* central, (situated) in the town (*od.* city) cent|re (*Am.* -er), *Am. auch* downtown

citynah *Adj.* close to the town (*od.* city) cent|re (*Am.* -er), central; **Citynähe** *f*; *in ~* central(ly)

cl *Abk.* → *Zentiliter*

Clan *m*; *-s*, *-e*; *auch iro. pej.* clan

Claqueur [kla'køːɐ] *m*; *-s*, *-e*; *Theat., TV* claqueur

clean [kliːn] *Adj. umg.* (*nicht mehr drogenabhängig*) clean, straight

Clearing ['kliːrɪŋ] *n*; *-s*, *-s*; *Wirts.* clearing; **~stelle** *f* clearinghouse, clearing house; **~verkehr** *m* clearing (transactions *Pl.*)

Clementine *f Obst:* → *Klementine*

clever *Adj. oft pej.* clever; *schlau:* shrewd, smart; *gerissen:* crafty, sly; **Cleverness** *f*; *-*, *kein Pl.* cleverness; *Schlauheit:* shrewdness; *Gerissenheit:* craftiness, slyness

Cliché [kli'ʃeː] → *Klischee*

Clinch [klɪntʃ] *m*; *-(e)s*, *kein Pl. Boxen:* clinch; *mit j-m im ~ liegen od. sein umg. fig.* be at loggerheads with s.o; *mit j-m in den ~ gehen umg. fig.* get stuck into s.o., take s.o. on; *j-n in den ~ nehmen* put s.o. under pressure

Clip *m*; *-s*, *-s* **1.** → *Klipp*; **2.** (*Filmclip*) clip, excerpt; (*Videoclip*) video

Clipart *f*; *-*, *kein Pl. Computergrafik:* clip art

Clique ['klɪkə] *f*; *-*, *-n*; (*Freundeskreis*) crowd *umg.*; *pej.* clique, coterie; *Pol. auch* faction; *wir gehen mit der ganzen ~ zum Tanzen* we're off to the disco with the whole gang; **Cliquenwirtschaft** *f pej.* cliquism

Clou [kluː] *m*; *-s*, *-s* main attraction, high spot; (*Höhepunkt*) climax; (*Witz*) point; *jetzt kommt der ~!* wait for this, now here's the good part; *das ist doch gerade der ~!* but that's the whole point!, that's just it!

Clown [klaun] *m*; *-s*, *-s* clown; *den ~ spielen* clown around, play the fool; *sich zum ~ machen* make o.s. look foolish; **Clownerie** *f*; *-*, *-n* clowning around

Club → *Klub*

cm *Abk.* → *Zentimeter;* **cm²** *Abk.* → *Quadratzentimeter;* **cm³** *Abk.* → *Kubikzentimeter*

c-Moll *n* C minor; **~-Tonleiter** *f* C minor scale

Co *Abk.* (*Compagnie*) Co.

c/o *Abk.* (*care of*) c/o

Co... *im Subst. siehe auch Ko...*

Coach [koːtʃ] *m*; *-(s)*, *-s*; *Sport* coach, trainer; *bei Fußball:* manager; **coachen** *v/t.* coach, train

Coca *f*, *n* → *Cola*

Cockerspaniel *m Zool.* cocker spaniel

Cockpit *n*; *-s*, *-s* cockpit; *Flug. auch* flight deck

Cocktail ['kɔkteːl] *m*; *-s*, *-s* **1.** cocktail; **2.** cocktail party; **~kleid** *n* cocktail dress; **~party** *f* cocktail party; **~tomate** *f* cherry tomato

Code *m* → *Kode*

codieren *etc.* → *kodieren etc.*

Cognac® ['kɔnjak] *m*; *-s*, *-s französischer:* cognac; *umg.* (*Weinbrand*) brandy

cognacfarben *Adj.* cognac(-colo[u]red)

Cognacschwenker *m* brandy glass

Coiffeur [koa'føːɐ] *m*; *-s*, *-e*, **Coiffeuse** *f*; *-*, *-n* hairdresser, hair stylist

Cola *f*; *-*, *-s od. n*; *-s*, *-s* coke®; *zwei ~* two cokes; **~dose** *f* coke can; **~nuss** *f* cola nut

Collage [kɔ'laːʒə] *f*; *-*, *-n* collage

College ['kɔlɪtʃ] *n*; *-(s)*, *-s* college

Collie *m*; *-s*, *-s*; *Zool.* collie

Colorfilm *m* colo(u)r film

Colt® *m*; *-s*, *-s* Colt ® revolver; *umg.* revolver, gun

Combo *f*; *-*, *-s* combo

Come-back, Comeback [kam'bɛk] *n*; *-(s)*, *-s* comeback; *ein ~ erleben od. sein ~ feiern* make (*od.* stage) a comeback

Comedy-Serie *f* (television) comedy series, sitcom

Comic *m*; *-s*, *-s* **1.** (*Geschichte*) comic (*od.* cartoon) strip; **2.** (*Heft*) comic, *Am. auch* comic book; **~figur** *f* cartoon character; **~heft** *n* comic, *Am. auch* comic book; **~strip, ~ Strip** *m* → *Comic* 1, 2; **~zeichner** *m*, **~zeichnerin** *f* cartoonist

Coming-out [kamɪŋ'ʔaut] *n*; *-(s)*, *-s* coming out

Compactdisc, Compact Disc *f*; *-*, *-s*; *Etech.* compact disc (*Am. auch* disk)

Computer [kɔm'pjuːtɐ] *m*; *-s*, *-*; *EDV* computer; *am ~ arbeiten/spielen* work/play on a computer; *am ~ sitzen* sit at (*od.* in front of) a computer; *es läuft über ~* it's all computerized (*od.* done by computer)

Computeranimation *f EDV* computer animation; **computeranimiert** *Adj.* computer-animated

Computer|arbeitsplatz *m EDV* computer workplace; **~ausdruck** *m EDV* computer printout; **~befehl** *m* computer command; **~bildschirm** *m* computer screen, monitor; **~brief** *m* personalized computer letter; **~chip** *m* computer chip; **~diagnostik** *f* computer diagnostics *Pl.* (*als Fach:* V. *im Sg.*), computer-aided diagnosis; **~erfahrung** *f* computer experience, experience with computers; **~fachmann** *m* computer consultant (*od.* expert); **~fahndung** *f* computer-aided search(es *Pl.*); **~fehler** *m* computer-generated error; **~firma** *f* computer firm (*od.* company); **~freak** *m umg.* (computer) geek, computer freak; **~generation** *f* generation of computers, computer generation

computer|gerecht *Adj. EDV* computer-compatible; **~gesteuert** *Adj.* computer-controlled (*od.* -operated); **~gestützt** *Adj.* computer-aided, computerized

Computer|grafik *f EDV* computer graphics *Pl.* (*als Fach:* V. *im Sg.*); **~hersteller** *m* computer manufac-

turer(s *Pl.*)

computerisieren *v/t. EDV* computerize

Computer|kriminalität *f EDV* computer crime; **~kurs** *m* computer course

computerlesbar *Adj. EDV* machine-readable

Computermesse *f* computer fair

computern *v/i. umg.* be (*od.* work, play *etc.*) on the computer

Computer|netzwerk *n EDV* computer network; **~programm** *n* computer program; **~satz** *m Druck.* computer(ized) typesetting; **~simulation** *f* computer simulation; **~spezialist** *m*, **~spezialistin** *f* computer specialist (*od.* expert); **~spiel** *n* computer game; **~sprache** *f* computer language

Computer|tomogramm *m Med.* (*abgek.* CT) computer tomogram, CT (*od.* CAT) scan; **~tomograph** *m*; *-en*, *-en*; (*abgek.* CT) computer tomograph, CAT (*od.* CT) scanner; **~tomographie** *f* computer tomography, CAT

computerunterstützt *Adj. EDV* computer-aided

Computervirus *m*, *n EDV* computer virus

Conférencier [kõferã'sjeː] *m*; *-s*, *-s* compere, Master of Ceremonies, emcee, MC

Connaisseur [kɔnɛ'søːɐ] *m*; *-s*, *-e* connoisseur

Container [kɔn'teːnɐ] *m*; *-s*, - container; *für Müll:* waste container; *für Bauschutt:* (rubbish) skip, *Am.* Dumpster®; *für Altglas:* bottle bank, *Am.* glass recycling bin; **~bahnhof** *m* container depot (*od.* terminal); **~dorf** *n temporary camp consisting of prefabricated huts;* **~hafen** *m* container port (*od.* terminal); **~schiff** *n* container ship; **~zug** *m* container train

Contenance [kõtə'nãːsə] *f*; *-*, *kein Pl.*; *geh.* composure; *die ~ verlieren/wahren* lose/maintain one's composure

Contergankind *n Med.* thalidomide baby (*od.* child, victim)

contra → *kontra*

Controller [kɔn'troːlɐ] *m*; *-s*, *-*, **~in** *f*; *-*, *-nen*; *Wirts.* (cost) controller; **Controlling** *n*; *-s*, *kein Pl.* cost control, controlling

cool [kuːl] *Adj. umg.* **1.** (*gelassen*) cool, laid-back; *~ bleiben* keep one's cool; **2.** (*gut, toll*) cool, fantastic; **3.** (*fair*) reasonable, fair

Copilot *m* → *Kopilot*

Copyright ['kɔpirait] *n*; *-s*, *-s* copyright; *das ~ haben auf* (+ *Akk.*) *od.* *für etw.* hold (*od.* have) the copyright on (*od.* for) s.th.

Cord *m* → *Kord*

Corner ['kɔːnɐ] *m*; *-s*, *-*; *österr., schw., mst Sport* corner

Cornflakes ['kɔːnfleːks] *Pl. Gastr.* cornflakes

Cornichon [kɔrni'ʃõː] *n*; *-s*, *-s*; *Gastr.* cocktail gherkin, *Am. auch* cornichon

Corpus *n* **1.** → *Korpus¹, Korpus²;* **2.** *~ Delicti* corpus delicti

Costa Rica *n*; *-s*; *Geog.* Costa Rica

Costa-Ricaner *m*; *-s*, *-*, **~in** *f*; *-*, *-nen* Costa Rican, *weiblich auch:* Costa Rican woman (*od.* girl *etc.*); **costa-ricanisch** *Adj.* Costa Rican

Couch *f*; *-*, *-s od. -en* sofa, couch; **~garnitur** *f* three-piece suite; **~tisch** *m* coffee table

Couleur [ku'løːɐ] *f*; *-*, *-s*; *Pol. etc.* complexion; *jeder ~ auch* of every shade and colo(u)r

Count-down, Countdown ['kaunt-

'daun] *m, n; -(s), -s* countdown; *der ~ läuft* we're into the final countdown

Coup [kuː] *m; -s, -s* coup; *e-n ~ landen* pull off (*od.* land) a coup

Coupé *n; -s, -s* **1.** *Mot.* coupé, *Am. mst* coupe; **2.** *altm. od. österr.* (*Zugabteil*) compartment

Coupon [kuˈpõː] *m; -s, -s* **1.** coupon, voucher; (*Zinsschein*) (interest) coupon, dividend warrant; *im Scheckbuch*: counterfoil; **2.** *Textilien*: length (of material)

Courage [kuˈraːʒə] *f; -, kein Pl.; umg.* courage, pluck; *~ zeigen* show some courage (*od.* pluck *od.* bottle); *Angst vor der eigenen ~ kriegen* get the wind up; **couragiert** *Adj.* bold, plucky *umg.*

Courtage [kʊrˈtaːʒə] *f; -, -n; Wirts.* brokerage

Cousin [kuˈzɛ̃ː] *m; -s, -s* (male) cousin; **Cousine** *f; -, -n* (female) cousin

Couturier [kutyˈrjeː] *m; -s, -s* couturier, fashion designer

Cover ['kavɐ] *n; -s, -(s)* **1.** (*Titelseite*) (front) cover, front page; **2.** (*Schallplattenhülle*) cover, sleeve, jacket; *~girl n* cover girl; *~version f Mus.* cover (version)

Cowboy ['kaubɔy] *m; -s, -s* cowboy; *~film m* western; *~hut m* cowboy hat, Stetson®; *~stiefel m* cowboy boot

Coyote *m → Kojote*

Crack¹ [krɛk] *m; -s, -s;* (*Sportler*) tennis *etc.* ace, crack tennis player *etc.; umg.* (*Könner*) (real) buff, dab hand, whiz

Crack² *n; -(s), kein Pl.;* (*Droge*) crack

Cracker ['krɛkɐ] *m; -s, -(s)* **1.** *Gastr.* cracker; **2.** (*Knallbonbon*) banger, firecracker

Crash|kid [krɛʃ-] *n* joyrider; *~kurs m* *Päd.* crash course; *~test m Mot.* crash test

Credo *n → Kredo*

Creme *f; -, -s od. österr. schw. -n* cream; (*Dessert*) crème; *die ~ der Gesellschaft fig.* the crème de la crème

creme *Adj.; nur präd., ~farben Adj.* cream(-colo[u]red)

cremen *v/i.* put cream on

Creme|schnitte *f* cream slice; *~speise f* crème; *~torte f* cream cake (*od.* gateau)

cremig *Adj.* creamy

Crêpe [krɛp] *f; -, -s; Gastr.* crêpe, pancake

Crescendo [krɛˈʃɛndo] *n; -s, -s od. Crescendi; Mus.* crescendo

Creutzfeldt-Jakob-Krankheit *f; nur Sg.; Med.* Creutzfeldt-Jakob disease (*od.* syndrome), CJD, CJS

Crew [kruː] *f; -, -s* crew (*Verb auch im Pl.*)

Croissant [krʊaˈsãː] *n; -(s), -s; Gastr.* croissant

Cromagnonmensch [kromaˈɲõ-] *m* Cro-Magnon man

Cromargan® *n; -s, kein Pl.* stainless steel

Cross-over ['krɔsoːvɐ] *Mus.* crossover

Croupier [kruˈpieː] *m; -s, -s* croupier

Crux *f; -, kein Pl.* **1.** (*Last*) trouble, nuisance; *man hat schon s-e ~ mit ihm* he certainly doesn't make life easy, it's a real trial with him; *man muss s-e ~ tragen* we all have our crosses to bear; **2.** (*Schwierigkeit*) crux; *die ~ dabei ist …* the crux of the matter is …; *das ist eben die ~* that's the problem, that's just it

C-Schlüssel *m Mus.* C clef

CSU *f; -, kein Pl.; Abk.* (*Christlich-Soziale Union*) Christian Social Union

Ct., Ct, ct., ct *Abk. → Cent*

c.t. *Abk.* (*cum tempore*): *14 Uhr ~* 2.15 pm; *~ oder s.t.?* quarter past or sharp?

CT *Abk. → Computertomogramm, Computertomograph*

Cup *m; -s, -s; Sport* cup; *~finale n* cup final; *~sieger m, ~siegerin f* cup winner

Curriculum *n; -s, Curricula; Päd.* curriculum

Curry ['kœri] *m, n; -s, kein Pl.* **1.** (*Gewürz*) curry powder; **2.** *nur n;* (*Gericht*) curry; *~pulver n* curry powder; *~soße f* curry sauce; *~wurst f* curried, grilled sausage

Cursor ['kɔːɐsɐ] *m; -s, -(s); EDV* cursor

Cutter ['katɐ] *m; -s, -, ~in f; -, -nen Film etc.*: cutter

CVJM *m; -, kein Pl.; Abk.* (*Christlicher Verein Junger Männer*) *etwa* YMCA

Cyber|sex ['saibɐ-] *m* cybersex; *~space m; -, -s, ~welt f* cyberspace

Cyclamat *n; -(e)s, -e; Chem.* cyclamate

D

D, d *n*; -, - *od. umg.* -s **1.** D, d; *D wie Dora* Buchstabieren: "d" for (*od.* as in) "Delta"; **2.** *Mus.* D

da I. *Adv.* **1.** (*dort*) there; *hier und ~* here and there; *~, wo* where; *~ vorn(e)/hinten* there at the front/back; *~ oben/unten* up/down there; *~ drinnen od. hinein* in there; *~ drüben od. hinüber* over there, *Am.* yonder *umg.*; *wer ~?* who goes there?; *ist ~ jemand?* is there anybody there?; *he du ~!* *umg.* hey you (over there)!; *den od. das ~ umg.* that one; *der/die ~ umg.* that man/woman over there; *der/die ~ war's umg.* it was him/her; **2.** (*hier*) here; *~ und dort* here and there; *dieser od. diese od. dies(es) ~* this one; *~ bin ich* here I am; *~, nimm schon! umg.* here (you go), take it!; *~ (hast du's)! umg.* there you are (*auch fig.*); *~ haben wir's umg.* (ich hab's gefunden) there it is, got it; (das ist geschafft) done it; (jetzt ist es passiert) that had to (go and) happen, didn't it?; *ich bin gleich wieder ~* I'll be back in a minute; *ist noch Brot ~?* is there any bread left?; *es ist keine Milch mehr ~* we've run (*od.* we're) out of milk; *jetzt ist er wieder ~ fig.* (bei Bewusstsein) he's come (a)round again; (wieder voll) *~ sein umg. fig.* be (back) in top form; **3.** *~ sein* (existieren) be there; (noch leben) still be alive; *~ sein für od. zu* Zweck: be there for; *noch nie ~ gewesen* unheard-of, unprecedented; *er ist nur für sie ~* he's only got time for her; *weitS.* he lives for her; *ich bin immer für dich ~* I'll always be around when you need me; **4.** *umg.*; *in* Ausrufen: *sieh ~!* well just look at that!; *iro.* lo and behold!; *... und siehe ~, auf einmal klappt es!* surprise surprise, all of a sudden it works!; *nichts ~!* forget it!; → *heda*; **5.** *als* Füllwort: *als ~ sind od. wären* for instance, such as; *was ~ kommen mag* whatever happens; **6.** *zeitlich*: (dann, damals) then, at that time; *~ erst* only then; *von ~ an* from then on, since then; *hier und ~* now and then; *~ gab es noch keinen Strom* there was no electricity in those days; **7.** (in diesem Fall) there, in that case, under the circumstances; *was lässt sich ~ machen?* what can be done about it?; *~ wäre ich (doch) dumm* I would be stupid to do so; *~ fragst du noch?* do you really need to ask?; *~ kann man nichts machen* what can you do about it?, there's not much you can do about it; **8.** *umg.*; (aus diesem Grund) therefore, so; *er ist sehr reich, ~ kann er sich das leisten* he's very (*od.* really) rich, so he can afford it; **9.** *umg.*; *einleitend*: *~ fällt mir etwas ein* it's just occurred to me, the thought strikes me; *~ soll es jetzt ein neues Mittel geben, das ...* supposedly there's a new medicine which ...; *wo*

ist das? - ~ gehst du erst geradeaus, dann ... go straight ahead first (*od.* to begin with), then ...; **10.** *~ ... bei, für, nach etc. nordd.* → *dabei, dafür, danach etc.*; **II.** *Konj.* **1.** (weil) (seeing) as, since, because; *~ aber od. jedoch* but since; since ..., however *~ sie ja od. doch od. nun schon einmal hier ist, ...* seeing as she's here, ...; *~ ich keine Nachricht erhalten hatte, ging ich weg* not having received any news, I left; **2.** *zeitlich* a) (nachdem, wo) after; *jetzt, ~ es entschieden war* now that it has been decided, b) *geh.* (als) as, when, while; *in dem Augenblick, ~ er ...* the moment he ...

d.Ä. *Abk.* (der Ältere) sen., *Am.* mst Sr.

DAAD *m*; -(s), kein Pl.; *Abk.* (**Deutscher Akademischer Austauschdienst**) German Academic Exchange Service

dabehalten *v/t.* (unreg., trennb., hat); (Unterlagen etc.) hold onto; (Häftling) detain; (Schüler) keep behind; *sie behielten ihn gleich (zur Beobachtung) da im Krankenhaus*: they kept him in (for observation)

dabei *Adv.* **1.** with it; (nahe) nearby, close by; *ein Haus mit Garten ~* a house with a garden; *~ sein* (anwesend sein) be there; (teilnehmen) take part (in it); (mit ansehen) see it; *darf ich ~ sein?* can I come too?; (teilnehmen) can I join in?; *ich bin ~!* (you can) count me in!, I'm game!; *er muss immer ~ sein* he's got to be in on everything; *ist ein Brief für mich ~?* is there a letter for me there?; *es war ziemlich viel Glück ~* I was *etc.* pretty lucky there; **2.** (im Begriff): *~, etw. zu tun* just doing s.th., in the middle of doing s.th.; (kurz davor) about (*od.* going) to do s.th., on the point of doing s.th.; *tu das endlich! - ja, ja, ich bin ja schon ~! umg.* alright, alright, I'm doing it!; **3.** (gleichzeitig) at the same time, while doing so; *sie strickt und liest ~* she knits and reads at the same time; *er aß und sah mich ~ fragend an* while he ate, he gave me a questioning look; **4.** (überdies) besides, what is more; *sie ist hübsch und ~ auch noch klug* auch she's attractive and intelligent into the bargain (*Am.* intelligent to boot); **5.** (dennoch) nevertheless, yet, for all that, at the same time; *und ~ ist er doch schon alt* and he's an old man, after all; **6.** (obwohl) although, even though; *jetzt schreibt sie immer noch, ~ könnte sie schon längst fertig sein* she's still writing, even though she could have been finished ages ago; *~ hätten wir gewinnen können* to think we could have won; *sie suchte danach, ~ hatte er ihn in der Hand* she was looking for it and he had it in his hand all the time; **7.** (bei dieser Gelegenheit) on the occasion, then; (während) while, in the

process; (dadurch) as a result; *j-n ~ ertappen od. erwischen, wie er ...* catch s.o. red-handed as he ...; *~ kam es zu e-r heftigen Auseinandersetzung* this gave rise to (*od.* resulted in) a heated argument; *man könnte verrückt werden ~* it's enough to drive you mad; **8.** (bei dieser Handlung, Angelegenheit) about it; *das Schwierige ~ ist, ...* the difficult thing about it is ...; *es kommt nichts ~ heraus umg.* it's no use, it's not worth it; *~ dürfen wir nicht vergessen* here we must not forget; *ich dachte mir nichts Böses ~* I meant no harm; *ich dachte mir nichts ~ (zu + Inf.)* I thought nothing of it (of + Ger.); (bei einer Bemerkung) I didn't mean anything by it; *was hast du dir eigentlich ~ gedacht?* what on earth made you do (*od.* say etc.) that?; *weitS.* whatever possessed you?; *was ist schon ~? umg.* so what?; *was ist schon ~, wenn ...?* what difference does it make if ...?, what harm does it do if ...?; *da ist doch nichts ~ umg.* (ist nicht schwer) that's child's play, there's nothing to it; (ist nicht bedenklich) it's nothing to worry about; (schadet nichts) it can't do any harm; (ist nicht gefährlich) it's perfectly safe; **9.** abschließend: *ich bleibe ~* I'm not changing my mind; *und ich bleibe ~, in X ist es am schönsten* I'm still convinced X is the most beautiful place in the world; *du kommst mit, und ~ bleibt's umg.* you're coming with us, and that's that; *lassen wir es ~* let's leave it at that

dabei|bleiben *v/i.* (unreg., trennb., ist -ge-); (bei Tätigkeit etc.) keep (*od.* stick) to it; (bei Stelle, Firma) stay on, remain; → *dabei* 9; *~haben* *v/t.* (unreg., trennb., hat -ge-); *umg.*: *er hat keinen Schirm dabei* he didn't bring his umbrella; *ich hab kein Geld dabei* I haven't got any money on me; *niemand wollte ihn ~* nobody wanted him to come (*od.* to be in on it)

Dabeisein *n*: *~ ist alles* it's taking part that counts

dabeistehen *v/i.* (unreg., trennb., hat / südd., österr., schw. ist -ge-) stand by watching; *zufällig*: happen to be there

dableiben *v/i.* (unreg., trennb., ist -ge-) stay (there *od.* here); *bleib doch noch ein bisschen da* can't you stay a bit longer?; *länger od. noch ~ müssen in der Schule*: be kept in, have to stay behind; *halt, dageblieben!* stop right there!, stay right where you are!

da capo [da'ka:po] **I.** *Adv. Mus.*: *~ (al fine)* da capo (al fine); **II.** *Interj. Theat., Konzert*: encore!; → *Dakapo*

Dach *n*; -(e)s, Dächer **1.** (Hausdach) roof; *ein/kein ~ über dem Kopf haben* have a/no roof over one's head; *sie wohnen alle unter einem ~* they all live under the same roof; *unterm ~ (juchhe umg. hum.) wohnen* live (right up) under the roof; *das ~ der Welt Geog. fig.* the roof of the world; **2.** *Mot.* roof, top; *mit offenem ~ fahren* drive with the top down; **3.** *fig.*: *unter ~ und Fach (in Sicherheit)* under cover, safely sheltered; *Vertrag etc.*: all settled (*od.* signed and sealed), in the bag *umg.*; *eins aufs ~ bekommen od. kriegen umg. fig.* get a clip (a)round the ears; (*getadelt werden*) get a real ticking-off (*Am.* dressing-down) (*od.* bollocking *Sl.*), get it in the neck; *j-m eins aufs ~ geben umg.* (*schlagen*) give s.o. a clip (a)round the ears; *fig.* (*kritisieren etc.*) show s.o. what's what; (*auch j-m aufs ~ steigen*) (*tadeln*) come down on s.o. like a ton of bricks, give s.o. hell, haul (*od.* rake) s.o. over the coals

Dach|antenne *f* roof aerial (*od.* antenna); **~ausbau** *m Archit.* loft (*Am. auch* attic) conversion; **~balken** *m Archit.* roof beam (*od.* joist); *schräger*: rafter

Dach|boden *m* loft, attic; **~decker** *m; -s, -*, **~deckerin** *f; -, -nen* roofer; *mit Ziegeln*: tiler; *mit Schiefer*: slater; *mit Stroh*: thatcher

Dach|fenster *n* **1.** dormer (window); **2.** (*Dachluke*) skylight; **~first** *m Archit.* (roof) ridge

dachförmig *Adj.* roof-shaped

Dach|garten *m* roof(-top) garden; **~gaube** *f*, **~gaupe** *f Archit.* dormer (window); **~gepäckträger** *m Mot.* roofrack

Dachgeschoss *n, österr.* **Dachgeschoß** *m* top floor; *im ~* in the attic, on the top floor; **~ausbau** *m* loft conversion; **~wohnung** *f* attic flat, *Am.* (converted) loft

Dach|gesellschaft *f Wirts.* parent (*od.* holding) company; **~giebel** *m Archit.* gable; **~isolierung** *f Archit.* roof insulation; **~kammer** *f* attic (room), garret *poet.*; **~koffer** *m Auto:* roof (*od.* top) box; **~lawine** *f* roof snowslide

Dach|luke *f* skylight; **~organisation** *f Wirts. etc.* umbrella (*od.* parent) organization; **~pappe** *f* roofing felt, *Am.* tarpaper; **~pfanne** *f* roof tile, pantile; **~rinne** *f* gutter

Dachs *m; -es, -e; Zool.* badger; *frecher ~ umg. fig.* cheeky (little) rascal (*od.* pup); *junger ~ umg. fig.* young upstart (*od.* squirt), whipper-snapper

Dachsattel *m Archit.* (roof) ridge

Dachsbau *m; Pl. Dachsbaue* badger's earth (*od.* set)

Dach|schaden *m* roof damage; *e-n ~ haben umg. fig.* have a screw loose (*od.* lost one's marbles); **~schindel** *f* (roof) shingle

Dachshund *m Zool.* dachshund

Dächsin *f; -, -nen; Zool.* female badger, badger sow

Dach|sparren *m Archit.* rafter; **~stuhl** *m Archit.* roof truss (*od.* timbering)

dachte *Imperf.* → **denken**

Dach|terrasse *f* roof terrace; **~traufe** *f* gutter; **~verband** *m Wirts. etc.* umbrella (*od.* parent) organization; **~wohnung** *f* attic flat, *Am.* (converted) loft; **~ziegel** *m* (roofing) tile; **~zimmer** *n* attic (room), garret *poet.*

Dackel *m; -s, -; Zool.* dachshund, sausage dog *hum.*; **~beine** *Pl. umg.* (short) bandy legs

Dada *m; -(s), kein Pl.; Kunst* Dada; **Dadaismus** *m; -, kein Pl.* Dadaism; **Dadaist** *m; -en, -en*, **Dadaistin** *f; -, -nen* Dadaist; **dadaistisch I.** *Adj.* Dadaist(ic); **II.** *Adv.* Dadaistically

dadran *umg.*, **dadrauf** *umg.*, **dadraus** *umg. etc.* → **daran, darauf, daraus** *etc.*

dadurch *Adv.* **1.** *räumlich*: through (it, there *etc.*); that way; *muss ich wirklich ~?* do I really have to go through there?; **2.** (*auf solche Weise*) by it, in this way, that's how; *~, dass* by (+ *Ger.*); *die ~ gewonnene Zeit* the time saved by doing *etc.* that; *was willst du ~ gewinnen?* what do you hope to gain by that?; **3.** (*aus diesem Grund*) because of that, as a result, that's why; *~, dass* because, due to the fact that; *er kaufte e-e Zeitung und verpasste ~ den Zug* he bought (himself) a newspaper and missed his train as a result

dafür *Adv.* **1.** *allg.* for it, for them, for that, for this; *ein anderes Wort ~* another word for it; *ein Beispiel ~ ist ...* an example of this is (*od.* would be) ...; *er kann nichts ~* (*für den Unfall etc.*) it's not his fault; (*für s-e Art etc.*) he can't help it; *er wurde ~ bestraft, dass er gelogen hatte* he was punished for telling lies; *~ sorgen, dass* see to it that; **2.** (*als Ersatz*) instead, in *s.th.'s* place; (*als Gegenleistung*) in return; *was willst du ~?* (*Geldbetrag*) what do you want for it?; (*Tauschobjekt etc.*) what do you want in exchange (*od.* return)?; *was kriege ich ~?* wenn ich dir diesen Gefallen tue: what's in it for me?; *ich möchte mich ~ bedanken, dass ...* I would like to express my thanks for ...; **3.** (*als Ausgleich*) but; *er ist blind, hat aber ~ ein sehr gutes Gehör* but has extremely good ears (to make up for it); **4.** (*zugunsten*) for it, in favo(u)r of it; *~ sein od. stimmen* be in favo(u)r; *~ sein, etw. zu tun* be for doing *s.th.*; *~ bin ich immer zu haben* I'm always up for that, I never say no to that; *es lässt sich vieles ~ und dagegen sagen* it has its pros and cons; *alles spricht ~, dass ...* all the evidence seems to indicate that, it looks very much as if ...; **5.** *Zweck:* (*dazu*) for it; *nimm doch den Hammer ~* why not use the hammer (for that)?; *~ ist er ja da* that's what he's there for (after all), that's his job, isn't it?; **6.** *umg.* (*schließlich*) *er müsste es wissen, ~ ist er ja Lehrer* after all, he's a teacher(, isn't he?); **7.** (*im Hinblick darauf*) considering (that), given (that); *~, dass du so klein bist, bist du ganz schön stark* you're pretty strong considering (that) you're so small (*od.* for someone so small)

Dafürhalten *n: nach m-m ~* as I see it, in my opinion

dafürstehen *v/i.* (*unreg., trennb., ist -ge-*) *bes. österr.*: *es steht nicht dafür* it's not worth it

DAG *f; -, kein Pl.; Abk.* (*Deutsche Angestelltengewerkschaft*) *etwa* Trade Union of German White-collar Workers

dagegen *Adv.* **1.** *drücken, halten, lehnen etc.*: against it (*od.* them); *klopfen*: on it; *~ stoßen Auto etc.*: crash into it (*od.* them); *Person*: bump; **2.** *fig. Kampf, Protest, Widerstand etc.*: against it (*od.* them); *ich bin allergisch ~* I'm allergic to it; *man kann nichts ~ machen od. tun* there's nothing you can do about it; *s-e Gründe ~* his objections to it; *~ sein* be against (*od.* opposed to) it; *bei Abstimmungen*: be against; *er sprach sich entschieden ~ aus* he opposed it strong-

ly; *was spricht ~, dass wir ...?* why shouldn't we ...?; *es spricht nichts ~ od. es ist nichts ~ einzuwenden od. zu sagen* there is no reason why not; *ich habe od. hätte nichts ~ umg.* that's fine by me, I'm up (*od.* on) for that; *alles spricht ~* (*, dass es geschehen wird*) the odds are (stacked) against it; *etw. ~ haben* object to *s.th.*, have *s.th.* against it; *haben Sie etwas ~, wenn ich rauche?* do you mind if I smoke?; *wenn Sie nichts ~ haben* if you don't mind, if it's alright by you (*auch iro.*); *ich habe Husten, können Sie mir was ~ geben?* could you give me *s.th.* for it?; **3.** (*im Austausch dafür*) in return (*od.* exchange (for it)); **4.** (*im Vergleich dazu*) in comparison, by contrast; *unsere Qualität ist nichts ~* can't compare; **5.** (*jedoch, hingegen*) whereas, while, *Brit. auch* whilst; (*andererseits*) on the other hand, however

dagegen|halten *v/t.* (*unreg., trennb., hat -ge-*); (*entgegnen*) argue, counter; (*einwenden*) object; **~setzen** *v/t.* (*trennb., hat -ge-*) put forward (in opposition), object; *ich habe nichts dagegenzusetzen* (*nichts einzuwenden*) I have no objection; (*kann es nicht leugnen*) I don't deny it (*od.* that); **~stellen** *v/refl.* (*trennb., hat -ge-*) oppose it; **~stemmen** *v/refl.* (*trennb., hat -ge-*) fight (*od.* oppose) *s.th.* (bitterly)

Dagewesene *n: das übertrifft alles ~* that beats everything (*od.* it all *od.* them all), that puts everything else in the shade

Daguerreotypie [dageroty'pi:] *f; -, -n; Fot. hist., Verfahren, Bild:* daguerreotype

dahaben *v/t.* (*unreg., trennb., hat -ge-*); *umg.*: *haben wir noch Brot da?* do we have (*od.* is there) any bread left?; *hast du mal 'nen Euro/Hammer etc. da?* have you got a euro/hammer handy?; *sie kann nicht kommen, wir wollten euch zum Essen ~* we wanted to have you round (*od.* in) to (*Am.* over for) dinner

daheim I. *Adv. bes. südd., österr., schw.* (*zu Hause*) at home, in; (*in der Heimat*) back home; *~ ist ~* there's no place like home; *bei mir ~* at my place; *wenn er anruft, bin ich nicht ~* if he calls, tell him I'm not in; *wo sind Sie ~?* where do you come from?, where's home for you?; *~ anrufen* ring (*od.* phone) home; **II. Daheim** *n; -s, kein Pl.* home; **Daheimgebliebene** *m, f; -n, -n* person left at home; *die ~n* those left at home

daher *Adv.* **1.** *räumlich:* (*von da*) from there; (*hierher*) here; *das Wasser ging mir bis ~* the water was up to here; **2.** (*deshalb*) that's why, that's the reason for; (*folglich*) and so, as a result; *~* (*stammt*) *die ganze Verwirrung* hence the confusion; *~ kam es, dass ...* that's why (*od.* how) ...; *das kam ~, dass/weil ...* it was (*od.* happened) (like that) because ...

daher|geflogen *P.P.:* *~ kommen* come flying along (*od.* up); **~gelaufen I.** *P.P.:* *~ kommen* come running along (*od.* up); **II.** *Adj. umg.:* *~er Kerl* bum, nobody; *jeder ~e Kerl* any Tom, Dick or Harry, anybody who comes along

daher|kommen *v/i.* (*unreg., trennb., ist -ge-*) come along; (*auftreten*) turn up; *wie kommst 'du denn daher? umg.* what do you 'look like?, look at the state of you; **~reden** *vt/i.* (*trennb., hat -ge-*) *umg.* talk away, prattle; *dummes*

Zeug od. **Unsinn** *od.* **dumm** ~ talk nonsense, blather on

dahier *Adv. österr., schw., sonst altm.* here

dahin *Adv.* 1. *räumlich:* there; *das gehört nicht* ~ that doesn't belong there; ~ *fahren, wo es am schönsten ist* drive to where it is nicest; 2. *fig.:* *es* ~ *bringen, dass j-d etw. tut* bring s.o. to the point where s.o. will do s.th.; *es wird noch* ~ *kommen, dass ...* it will reach the stage when ...; 3. *zeitlich:* *bis* ~ until then, till then; *hoffentlich bist du bis* ~ *fertig* I hope you'll be finished by then (*od.* by that time); 4. *Ziel, Zweck:* *m-e Meinung geht* ~, *dass ...* I tend to think (*od.* hold the opinion) that ...; ~ *gehend* *Antrag, Äußerung etc.:* to the effect; *man hat sich* ~ *gehend geeinigt, dass ...* it was agreed that...; 5. ~ *sein* (*vorbei sein*) be past; *gerade:* be over; (*verloren sein*) lost; (*tot sein*) have passed away, be dead; (*kaputt sein*) be broken (*od.* ruined), have had it *umg.*; *Hoffnungen:* be dashed

dahinauf *Adv.* up there (*od.* that way)

dahinaus *Adv.* out there (*od.* that way)

dahin|bewegen *v/refl.* (*trennb., hat*) move along, move on one's way; ~**dämmern** *v/i.* (*trennb., ist od. hat -ge-*) be semi-conscious, be in a stupor; ~**eilen** *v/i.* (*trennb., ist -ge-*) 1. hurry along; 2. *fig. Zeit:* fly

dahinein *Adv.* in there

dahin|fahren *v/i.* (*unreg., trennb., ist -ge-*) 1. drive (*od.* ride) along; 2. *lit.* (*wegfahren*) depart; (*sterben*) pass away; *alle Hoffnung etc.* ~ *lassen* *fig.* lose all hope *etc.*; ~**fliegen** *v/i.* (*unreg., trennb., ist -ge-*) 1. fly along; 2. *fig. Zeit:* fly; ~**fließen** *v/i.* (*unreg., trennb., ist -ge-*) 1. flow along; 2. *fig. Jahre etc.:* pass by

Dahingegangene *m, f; -n, -n; geh. euph.* departed

dahingegen *Adv. geh.* on the other hand

dahingehen *v/i.* (*unreg., trennb., ist -ge-*) 1. go along; 2. *fig. Zeit:* pass; (*sterben*) pass away

dahin|gestellt *Adj.:* *es* ~ *sein lassen, ob ...* leave it open as to whether ...; *das sei* ~ who knows?; *es bleibt* ~ it remains to be seen; ~**kriechen** *v/i.* (*unreg., trennb., ist -ge-*) 1. creep (*od.* crawl) along; 2. *fig. Zeit:* drag (on); *Jahre:* drag by (slowly); ~**leben** *v/i.* (*trennb., hat -ge-*) live (from day to day); ~**plätschern** *v/i.* (*trennb., ist -ge-*) *Bach:* trickle along; *Gespräch:* meander along; *Musik:* tinkle away (in the background); ~**raffen** *v/t.* (*trennb., hat -ge-*) *geh. euph.* carry off; ~**sagen** *v/t.* (*trennb., hat -ge-*): *das habe ich od. das war nur so dahingesagt* I just said that without thinking, that was just a casual remark; ~**scheiden** *v/i.* (*unreg., trennb., ist -ge-*) *geh. euph.* pass away; ~**schleichen** *v/i.* (*unreg., trennb., ist -ge-*) 1. creep (*od.* slink) along; 2. → *dahinkriechen*; ~**schmelzen** *v/i.* (*unreg., trennb., ist -ge-*) 1. *Eis etc.:* melt away; 2. *fig. Vorräte etc.:* dwindle (away); 3. *fig. Person, vor Rührung, Liebe:* melt (away); ~**schwinden** *v/i.* (*unreg., trennb., ist -ge-*) 1. *Vorräte etc.:* dwindle (away); 2. *Person:* waste away; *aus Kummer:* pine away; 3. *fig. Schönheit:* fade; *Mut, Interesse:* dwindle; ~**siechen** *v/i.* (*trennb., ist -ge-*); *geh.* languish, waste

away; ~**siechend** I. *Part.Präs.* → *dahinsiechen*; II. *Adj. fig. Wirtschaft, Gebiet etc.:* ailing

dahinten *Adv.* back there

dahinter *Adv.* 1. *räumlich:* behind it (*od.* them); *liegen, sein:* at the back; *bringen, schaffen:* to the back; 2. *fig.:* ~ *sein od.* **stehen** be behind it; *unterstützend: auch* (fully) support it; *es ist od.* **steckt was** ~ Positives: there's something in it; *heimliche Absicht:* there's more to it than that, there's something funny (*od.* fishy) about it *umg.*; *weiß man schon, ob die Mafia* ~ *steckt?* *umg.* is it known (yet) whether the mafia is involved?; *sich* ~ *klemmen od.* **knien** *od.* **setzen** *umg.* (*anstrengen*) buckle down to s.th., pull one's finger out; ~ *kommen* *umg.* (*herausfinden*) get to the bottom of it, find out (about it), *Brit. auch* suss it out; (*es kapieren*) get it, cotton on, *Brit. auch* twig

dahinterher *Adv. umg.:* wenn du Erfolg haben willst, *musst du schon* ~ *bleiben od.* **sein** you have to make a real effort; *i-e Mutter ist sehr* ~, *dass sie ihr Zimmer in Ordnung hält* her mother is always going on to her about keeping her room tidy

dahintreiben *v/i.* (*unreg., trennb., ist -ge-*) *Boot etc.:* drift along; *er lässt sich einfach so* ~ *fig.* he just goes with the flow

dahinüber *Adv.* over (*od.* across) there, *Am. auch* yonder *umg.*

dahinunter *Adv.* down there

dahin|vegetieren *v/i.* (*trennb., hat*) vegetate (away); ~**ziehen** (*unreg., trennb., -ge-*) I. *v/i.* (*ist*) move along; *Wolken:* drift past; II. *v/refl.* (*hat*) 1. *zeitlich:* go on and on; 2. *räumlich:* stretch (out) for miles

Dahlie *f; -, -n; Bot.* dahlia; **Dahlienknolle** *f* dahlia bulb

dahocken *v/i.* (*trennb., hat / südd., österr., schw. ist*) 1. *in hockender Stellung:* squat (*od.* crouch) there; 2. *Dial.* (*dasitzen*) sit there

Dakapo *n; -s, -s; Mus., Theat.* encore

Daktylus *m; -, Daktylen; Lit.* dactyl

dalassen *v/t.* (*unreg., trennb., hat -ge-*) *dort:* leave there; *hier:* leave here; *zurück:* leave behind

daliegen *v/i.* (*unreg., trennb., hat / südd., österr., schw. ist -ge-*) *dort:* lie there; *hier:* lie here; *untätig:* lie there motionless

dalli *Adv. umg.:* ~, ~*!* get a move on!, hurry up!; *aber ein bisschen* ~*!* and make it snappy!

Dalmatien (*n*); *-s; Geog.* Dalmatia

Dalmatiner[1] *m; -s, -;* (*Hund*) Dalmatian

Dalmatiner[2] *m; -s, -,* ~**in** *f; -, -nen* Dalmatian, *weiblich auch:* Dalmatian woman (*od.* girl etc.)

dalmat(in)isch *Adj.* Dalmatian

damalig... *Adj.; nur attr.* then, of (*od.* at) that time; *der* ~*e Besitzer* the then owner; *sein* ~*es Versprechen* the promise he made then

damals *Adv.* (*back*) then, at that time, in those days; *schon* ~ even then, even at that time; *Ereignisse von* ~ events of the time

Damaskus (*n*); *-; Geog.* Damascus

Damast *m; -(e)s, -e* damask

Damast|serviette *f* damask napkin (*Brit. auch* serviette); ~**tuch** *n* damask cloth

Damaszener *m; -s, -,* ~**in** *f; -, -nen* Damascene

Dame *f; -, -n* 1. lady; *beim Tanz:* partner; ~*n* Toilette: Ladies; *e-e* ~ *von Welt* a woman of the world; *die große alte* ~ (+ *Gen.*) the grand old lady (of); *j-s alte* ~ *umg. hum.* (*Mutter*) s.o.'s old woman; *ganz* ~ *sein* be every inch a lady; *die große od. feine* ~ *spielen* play the lady; ~ *des Hauses* the lady of the house; (*Gastgeberin*) hostess; *m-e* ~*n und Herren!* ladies and gentlemen; 2. (~*spiel*) draughts *Pl., Am.* checkers *Pl.* (*beide Verb im Sg.*); 3. (*Doppelstein*) king; *Schach und Kartenspiel:* queen; ~**brett** *n* draughtboard, *Am.* checkerboard

Damen|bart *m* facial hair; ~**begleitung** *f: in* ~ in female company, with a woman; ~**bekanntschaft** *f* lady friend; *e-e* ~ *machen* get acquainted with a lady; ~**besuch** *m* lady visitor(s *Pl.*); ~**binde** *f* sanitary towel (*Am.* napkin); ~**doppel** *n* Tennis etc.: women's doubles *Pl.* (*Match: Verb im Sg.*); ~**fahrrad** *n* ladies' bicycle; ~**friseur** *m* 1., *auch* ~**friseurin** *f* ladies' hairdresser, *Am. auch* beautician; 2. (*Geschäft*) → *Damensalon*; ~**fußball** *m* women's football (*od.* soccer); ~**gesellschaft** *f* 1. ladies-only party, *Am.* shower; *vor einer Hochzeit:* wedding shower, hen party *umg.*; 2. *in* ~ in female company, with a woman; ~**größe** *f* ladies' size

damenhaft I. *Adj.* ladylike; II. *Adv.:* *sich* ~ *benehmen* behave like a lady (*od.* in a ladylike way)

Damen|hose *f* women's trousers (*Am.* pants) *Pl.; e-e* ~ (a pair of) women's trousers (*Am.* pants); ~**hut** *m* woman's hat; ~**kleidung** *f* ladies' wear, *Am.* womenswear; ~**kränzchen** *n* ladies' circle (*od.* afternoon); *weitS.* coffee klatsch; *sie gehört zu unserem* ~ she's one of the ladies' afternoon crowd, *Am.* she belongs to our coffee klatsch; ~**mannschaft** *f* women's team; ~**mode** *f* women's fashions *Pl.*; ~**oberbekleidung** *f* ladies' wear, *Am.* womenswear; ~**rad** *n* ladies' bicycle (bike *umg.*); ~**salon** *m* ladies' hairdresser's, *Am.* beauty salon; ~**sattel** *m hist.* side-saddle; *im* ~ *reiten* ride side-saddle; ~**schneider** *m,* ~**schneiderin** *f* ladies' (*Am.* women's) tailor; ~**sitz** *m: im* ~ *reiten* ride side-saddle; ~**toilette** *f* ladies' toilet, *the ladies Pl.* (*Verb im Sg.*), *Am.* women's room; ~**wahl** *f* ladies' choice; ~**wäsche** *f* ladies' (*Am.* women's) underwear; *elegante:* lingerie; ~**welt** *f* the ladies *Pl.*

Dame|spiel *n* draughts *Pl., Am.* checkers *Pl.* (*beide Verb im Sg.*); ~**stein** *m* draughtsman, *Am.* checker

Damhirsch *m Zool.* fallow buck

damit I. *Adv.* 1. with it (*od.* them); *betont:* with that (*od.* those); (*mittels*) by (*od.* with) it (*betont:* that), *Pl.* with them (*betont:* those); *her* ~*!* *umg.* give it to me, hand it over; *weg* ~*!* *umg.* take (*od.* put) it away; *heraus* ~*!* *umg.* (*sag schon*) spit it out!; (*gib her*) hand it over!; *was will er* ~ *sagen?* what's he trying to say?; *was soll ich* ~*?* what am I supposed (*od.* meant) to do with it?; *wie steht's od. wär's* ~*?* how about it?; *wir sind* ~ *einverstanden* we have no objections; ~ *wirst du nichts erreichen* that won't get you anywhere; *er fing* ~ *an, dass er ...* he began by (+ *Ger.*); ~ *soll nicht gesagt sein, dass ...* that doesn't mean (to say) that ...; 2. (*folglich, somit*) as a result, (and) so; (*mit diesen Worten*) with that, with these words; *und* ~ *Schluss!* and let that be the end of it!; **~ steht der Sieger fest** that decides (who is) the winner; **~ war alles wieder beim Alten** things were back to where we started; **II.** *Konj.* so that, in order to (+ *Inf.*), so as to (+ *Inf.*); **~ nicht** so as not to (+ *Inf.*); *stärker*: for fear that *s.o. od. s.th.* might ...; **~ er nicht kommt** so that he doesn't come

dämlich *umg. pej.* **I.** *Adj.* stupid, idiotic; **II.** *Adv.* idiotically; **Dämlichkeit** *f umg. pej.* **1.** *nur Sg.* silliness; **2.** *konkret*: silly prank, *Pl. auch* nonsense *Sg.*

Damm *m*; *-(e)s, Dämme* **1.** (*Staudamm*) dam; (*Deich*) sea wall, dike (*od.* dyke); **2.** (*Bahndamm*) embankment; (*Hafendamm*) embankment, (harbour) wall; (*Dammweg*) causeway; (*Schutzwall*) embankment, *bes. Am.* levee; (*Fahrdamm*) street, road(way); (*Fahrbahn*) carriageway; **3.** *fig.* (*Hindernis*) barrier; **4.** *umg. fig.*: **wieder auf dem ~ sein** be fighting fit again, be back on one's feet; **nicht ganz auf dem ~ sein** be (feeling) a bit under the weather; **nicht recht auf dem ~ sein** be not up to the mark; **5.** *Anat.* perineum; **~bruch** *m Vorgang*: bursting of a dam; *Stelle*: breach in a dam

dämmen *v/t.* **1.** *geh.* (*Fluss, Fluten*) dam (up), obstruct; **2.** *Tech.* (*Wärme, Schall*) insulate; **3.** *fig.* check, curb, restrain

dämmerig *Adj.* → **dämmrig**

Dämmerlicht *n* twilight; *weitS.* dim light

dämmern *v/i.* **1. es dämmert** *morgens*: it's getting light; *abends*: it's getting dark; **der Morgen** *od.* **Tag dämmert** day is breaking; **der Abend dämmert** night is falling; **2.** *fig.*: **langsam dämmert's (bei) ihm** it's beginning to get through to him; *iro. auch* he's getting there; **vor sich hin ~** doze; *Kranker*: be very dop(e)y

Dämmer|schlaf *m* light sleep, doze, snooze; *Med.* twilight sleep; **~schoppen** *m* sundowner; **~stunde** *f* twilight hour

Dämmerung *f* **1.** *morgens*: dawn; **bei ~** at dawn, at daybreak; **2.** *abends*: twilight, dusk; **in der** *od.* **bei Einbruch der ~** at dusk, at nightfall

Dämmerzustand *m Med.* semiconscious state; *weitS.* daze

Dämmmaterial *n Tech.* insulating (*od.* insulation) material

dämmrig *Adj. Licht*: dim (*auch fig.*), crepuscular *lit.*; *Tag*: dull; *Raum*: dimly lit, twilit

Dammriss *m Med.* perineal tear

Dämmschicht *f Tech.* insulating (*od.* insulation) layer

Dammschutz *m Med.* episiotomy

Dämmung *f* (*Wärmeisolierung etc.*) insulation

Damoklesschwert *n fig.* sword of Damocles; **wie ein ~ über j-m hängen** *od.* **schweben** hang over s.o. like a sword of Damocles

Dämon *m*; *-s, -en* demon, evil spirit; **Dämonenglaube** *m* demonism; **dämonisch** *Adj.* demonic, demoniac(al); *weitS. auch* diabolical; **dämonisieren** *v/t.* demonize; **sie wurde von der Presse dämonisiert** she was portrayed as a demon (*od.* villified) by the press

Dampf *m*; *-(e)s, Dämpfe* steam; *Phys.* vapo(u)r; (*Rauch*) smoke; (*Dunst*) vapo(u)r, haze; (*Ausdünstung*) exhalation; (*chemische*) **Dämpfe** fumes; **~ablassen** *Tech.* blow off steam; *umg. fig.* let off steam; **aus dem Projekt** *etc.*

ist der ~ raus *umg. fig.* the project *etc.* has run out of steam; **~ dahinter machen** *od.* **setzen** *umg. fig.* speed things up a bit, get things moving; **j-m ~ machen** *umg. fig.* give s.o. a kick in the pants, hurry s.o. up (*od.* along); **~bad** *n* steam bath

dampfbetrieben *Adj.* steampowered, steam-driven

Dampf|bügeleisen *n* steam iron; **~druck** *m*; *Pl. -drücke*; *Tech.* steam pressure

dampfen *v/i.* **1.** (*hat gedampft*) steam; (*rauchen*) smoke (*auch umg. Person*); fume; *Zug*: puff; **die Suppe dampft** the soup is steaming (*od.* piping) hot; **2.** (*ist*) *Zug, Dampfer*: **~ aus dem Bahnhof, Hafen**: chug out

dämpfen *v/t.* **1.** (*mit Dampf behandeln*) steam; (*Wäsche*) *mit Dampfbügeleisen*: steam-iron; *mit Tuch*: press with a damp cloth; **2.** *Gastr.* steam, stew; **3.** (*Geräusche, Schall*) muffle, deaden; **4.** *Mus.* (*Trompete, Geige etc.*) mute; (*Schlaginstrumente*) muffle; (*Klavier*) (use the) soft-pedal, soften; **5.** (*Stimme*) lower; **6.** (*Farbe*) subdue, soften, tone down; **7.** (*Licht*) dim, turn down; **8.** (*Stoß, Schlag*) cushion, absorb (*auch Tech.*); *Etech.* (*Schwingungen*) attenuate; **9.** *Med.* (*Schmerzen*) alleviate, assuage; (*Fieber*) supress, lessen, reduce; **10.** *fig.* (*Stimmung*) put a damper on, dampen; (*Leidenschaft*) subdue, check; (*Wut*) assuage; (*Freude*) temper, diminish; (*unterdrücken*) suppress; → **gedämpft** II; **11.** *Wirts.* (*Kosten, Konjunktur*) curb; (*auch Kostenanstieg etc.*) slow down

Dampfer *m*; *-s, -* steamer, steamship; **er befindet sich** *od.* **ist** *od.* **sitzt auf dem falschen ~** *umg. fig.* he is on the wrong track, he is barking up the wrong tree, he has got the wrong end of the stick

Dämpfer *m*; *-s, -* **1.** → **Schalldämpfer, Stoßdämpfer**, **2.** *Mus. am Klavier*: damper; *Streich- und Blasinstrumente*: mute; **3.** *Tech., Etech.* damper; *Lautsprecher*: baffle; **4.** *umg. fig.* damper; **j-m / e-r Sache e-n ~ aufsetzen** put a damper on s.o./s.th.; **e-n ~ bekommen** *Begeisterung etc.*: be dampened; (*gerügt werden*): get a rap over (*od.* across) the knuckles

Dampferfahrt *f* steamboat trip

dampfig *Adj.* steamy

Dampf|kessel *m* boiler; **~kochtopf** *m* pressure cooker; **~kraftwerk** *n* steam (--generating) power station; **~lok(omotive)** *f* steam engine; **~maschine** *f* steam engine; **~nudel** *f südd. Gastr.* sweet yeast dumpling; **aufgehen wie e-e ~** *umg. hum.* blow up (*od.* fill out) like a balloon; **~radio** *n umg. hum.* wireless; **~ramme** *f* steam(-operated) pile-driving engine (*od.* pile driver); **~reiniger** *m für Teppiche*: steam cleaner

Dampfschiff *n* steamship, steamer; *vor dem Schiffsnamen*: SS; **~fahrt** *f* steam(-ship) navigation; **~fahrtsgesellschaft** *f* steamship company (*od.* line)

Dampf|strahl *m* steam jet; **~turbine** *f Tech.* steam turbine

Dämpfung *f* steaming *etc.*; → **dämpfen**; *Phys., von Energien*: loss; *Etech.* attenuation

Dampf|walze *f* steamroller; **~wolke** *f* cloud of steam

Damwild *n Zool.* fallow deer *Pl.*

danach *Adv.* **1.** *zeitlich od. räumlich*: after that (*od.* it), *Pl.* after them; (*an-*

schließend) then, afterwards; (*später*) afterwards, later on; **bald ~** soon after(wards); **zwei Wochen ~** two weeks later (on); **zuerst kamen sie, ~ (folgten** *od.* **kamen) wir** they came first, then we followed along (*od.* we came later); **2.** *Richtung*: toward(s) it, *Pl.* toward(s) them; **er drehte sich ~ um** he turned (a)round toward(s) it; **sie griff ~** she reached for it; (*schnell*) she grabbed (*od.* made a grab) for it; **3.** *Ziel*: **ich sehnte mich ~ zu** (+ *Inf.*) I longed to (+ *Inf.*); **ich fragte ihn ~** I asked him about it; **sie sucht ~** she's looking for it (*od.* that); **4.** (*so*): **er sieht ganz/nicht ~ aus** he looks the sort / he's not that sort of person (*od.* the type); **es sieht (ganz) ~ aus, als ob ...** it looks as though ...; **5.** (*gemäß*) according to it (*od.* that); (*entsprechend*) accordingly; **das sind die Vorschriften - richte dich ~!** those are the rules - stick to them!; **es war billig, aber es ist auch ~** *umg.* it was cheap, and it looks it; **mir ist nicht ~ zumute** *od.* **nicht ~** *umg.* I don't feel like it, I'm not in the mood; **wenn es ~ ginge, was ...** if it was (*od.* were) a matter *od.* case of what ...

Dandy ['dɛndi] *m*; *-s, -s*; *pej.* dandy; **dandyhaft** *Adj. pej.* dandyish

Däne *m*; *-n, -n* Dane, Danish man (*od.* boy); **er ist ~** he's Danish

daneben *Adv.* **1.** *räumlich*: beside it (*od.* them), next to it (*od.* them); (*am Ziel vorbei*) off the mark; **das Zimmer ~** the room next door, the next room; **rechts/links ~** *Sache*: to the right/left (of it); *Person*: on his *etc.* right/left; **~!** missed!; **total ~!** *umg.*, *auch fig.* way out!; **weit ~** *fig.* way off (way off *umg.*) the mark; **völlig ~ sein** *Antwort*: be completely wrong (*od.* way off the mark); *Vorschlag*: be completely out of order (*od.* unacceptable); (*sich unwohl fühlen*) be off form (*od.* under the weather), feel really awful; **2.** (*außerdem*) in addition; (*gleichzeitig*) at the same time; **3.** (*im Vergleich*) beside it (*od.* him *etc.*), in comparison

daneben|benehmen *v/refl.* (*unreg., trennb., hat*); *umg.* show o.s. up, step out of line, be out of order; **du hast dich natürlich mal wieder danebenbenommen** can't take you anywhere, can we?, you made an exhibition of yourself again; **~gehen** *v/i.* (*unreg., trennb., ist -ge-*) **1.** *Schuss etc.*: miss, be off target; *Fußball etc.*: *auch* go wide; **2.** *fig.* (*Schätzung*) be wide of the mark; *Pläne etc.*: misfire, fail, (be a) flop *umg.*; **das geht bestimmt daneben** *umg.* it's bound to be a disaster; **~greifen** *v/i.* (*unreg., trennb., hat -ge-*) **1.** miss; *Mus.* play a (few) wrong note(s); **2.** *fig.* (*sich verschätzen etc.*) be way out, be wide of the mark; **im Ton ~** put one's foot in it (*Am.* in one's mouth), be tactless; **~hauen** *v/i.* (*unreg., trennb., hat -ge-*) **1.** miss; **2.** *umg. fig.* be way out (*od.* wide of the mark); **~liegen** *v/i.* (*unreg., trennb., ist -ge-*); *umg.*: **weit ~** be way off the mark (*mit* with); **da liegst du völlig daneben** you're completely wrong about that; **~schießen** *v/i.* (*unreg., trennb., hat -ge-*) miss; **~schlagen** *v/i.* (*unreg., trennb., hat -ge-*) miss; **~tippen** *v/i.* (*trennb., hat -ge-*); *umg.* guess wrong(ly), make a wrong guess; **~treffen** *v/i.* (*unreg., trennb., hat -ge-*) miss

Dänemark (*n*); *-s*; *Geog.* Denmark

D

dang *Imperf.* → *dingen*

daniederliegen *v/i.* (*unreg., trennb., hat / südd., österr., schw. ist -ge-*) **1.** *Handel etc.*: be stagnating (*od.* depressed); **2.** (*krank sein*) be laid low (*od.* up) (*an* + *Dat.* with)

Daniel *m; -s, -s; bibl.* Daniel; ~ *in der Löwengrube* Daniel in the lion's den

Dänin *f; -, -nen* Dane, Danish woman (*od.* girl); **dänisch I.** *Adj.* Danish; **II. Dänisch** *n; -en; Ling.* Danish; *das Dänische* Danish, the Danish language

dank *Präp.* (+ *Gen. od. Dat.*) thanks to (*auch iro.*); ~ *einem Zufall od. eines Zufalls* by chance (*od.* coincidence)

Dank *m; -(e)s, kein Pl.*; (*für* for) thanks *Pl.*; (*Dankbarkeit*) gratitude; (*Lohn*) reward; *wenig/keinen ~ ernten für etw.* get meag|re (*Am.* -er) / no thanks for s.th.; (*hab od. haben Sie*) *besten od. herzlichen od. schönen od. tausend od. vielen ~!* many thanks, thank you very much, thanks a million *umg.*; *mit ~ zurück* returned with thanks, thanks for the loan *umg.*; *vielen ~ für die Blumen! iro.* thanks a lot (*od.* for nothing)!; *j-m ~ sagen od. abstatten geh.* thank s.o.; *kirchl.* give thanks; *j-m ~ schulden od. j-m zu ~ verpflichtet sein* be deeply indebted to s.o., owe s.o. a debt of gratitude; *ist das der ~ für m-e Mühe?* is that all (the thanks) I get for the trouble I went to?; *das ist nun der ~ dafür! iro.* that's gratitude for you; *zum ~ für s-e Dienste* in (grateful) recognition of his services; *zum od. als ~ dafür, dass Sie ihm geholfen haben* in appreciation of your help, as a way of saying thanks to you for helping him *umg.*; ~ *sei Gott im Himmel od. dem Herrn!* thanks be to God (in Heaven)

dankbar I. *Adj.* **1.** grateful (*für* for), appreciative (of); *Publikum:* appreciative; *ich wäre Ihnen ~, wenn ...* I'd be much obliged if ... (*auch iro.*), I'd appreciate it if ...; *man muss für alles ~ sein* you have to be thankful for small mercies (*od.* for every little thing); **2.** (*lohnend*) worthwhile; *Aufgabe: auch* rewarding; *er ist ein ~es Opfer für ihre Sticheleien* he's an easy target (*od.* a sitting duck) for her gibes; **3.** *umg.* (*strapazierfähig*) *Stoff:* hard-wearing, durable; (*anspruchslos*) *Pflanze:* easy(-care), hardy; **II.** *Adv.* gratefully; *etw. ~ annehmen* accept s.th. gratefully (*od.* with thanks); **Dankbarkeit** *f* **1.** gratitude; *aus ~ für* out of gratitude for; **2.** *e-r Aufgabe:* profitableness; **3.** *umg. e-s Stoffes etc.:* durability, durableness; *e-r Pflanze:* hardiness

Dankbrief *m* letter of thanks, thank-you letter *umg.*

danke *Interj.*: ~ (*schön od. sehr*)! (many) thanks, thank you (very much); ~ *od. Danke sagen* say thanks; *~(, ja)!* thank you; *~(, nein)!* no, thank you; no, thanks; ~ *der Nachfrage* nice of you to ask, thanks for asking; *iro. auch* so kind of you to ask; *mir geht's ~ umg.* can't complain; *sonst geht's dir aber ~? umg.* have you taken leave of your senses?, are you feeling alright?

danken I. *v/i.* thank (*j-m für etw.* s.o. for); *kurz ~* say a brief thanks; *er lässt ~* he says thank you; *nichts zu ~!* you're welcome, not at all, don't mention it; *na, ich danke! iro.* no thanks, I can do without (it); *du kannst od.*

solltest Gott/mir *etc.* **auf** (**den**) **Knien ~ für/dass ...** you should thank God/me *etc.* on your knees for/that ...; **II.** *v/t.* **1.** *j-m etw. ~* (*verdanken*) owe s.th. to s.o.; *ihm ~ wir, dass ...* we owe it to him that ..., it's due (*od.* thanks) to him that ...; **2.** *j-m etw. ~* (*dankbar sein*) thank s.o. for s.th.; (*belohnen*) reward (*od.* repay) s.o. for s.th. (*mit* with); *iro.* repay s.o. for.s.th.; *wie kann ich dir das jemals ~?* how can I ever thank (*od.* repay) you?; **dankend I.** *Part.Präs.* → *danken*; **II.** *Adv.* with thanks; *Betrag ~ erhalten* amount gratefully received

dankenswert *Adj.* **1.** commendable; *in ~er Weise* (most) commendably; (*Hilfe*) kind; **2.** *Aufgabe etc.*: rewarding; **dankenswerterweise** *Adv.* kindly (enough), generously

Dankes|bezeigung *f* (expression of) thanks *Pl.*; *konkret:* token of one's gratitude; *~brief m* → *Dankbrief*; *~rede f* speech of thanks

Dankeschön *n; -s, kein Pl.* thank-you; (*Dankeswort*) word of thanks; *als* (*kleines*) ~ as a (small) token (*od.* gesture) of my *etc.* thanks (*od.* gratitude)

Dankeswort *n Pl. -worte* word of thanks

Dank|gebet *n* thanksgiving (prayer); *~opfer n* thanks offering; *~sagung f* **1.** *allg.* expression of thanks; **2.** *für Beileidsbrief:* acknowledg(e)ment, note of thanks; **3.** *kirchl.* thanksgiving; *~schreiben n* letter of thanks

dann *Adv.* **1.** (*danach, später*) then, after that, afterwards; *was geschah ~?* what happened then (*od.* next)?; *anfangs war es noch schwer, aber ~ ging es auf einmal* but then it got easier all of a sudden; **2.** (*zu der Zeit*) then; ~ *und ~ umg.* at such and such a time, round about then; ~ *und wann* now and then; *bis ~* until then; *als Abschied:* see you (then); *erst ~* only then; *von ~ bis ~ umg.* from then till then, from such and such a date (*od.* time) until such and such a date (*od.* time); **3.** *Reihenfolge:* (*dahinter*) then, after(wards); *zuerst kommt die Dampflok, ~ die Güterwaggons* the engine comes first, followed by the goods wagons (*Am.* freight cars); **4.** (*in dem Fall*) in that case, then; ~ *eben nicht! umg.* all right, forget it!; *wenn du mich brauchst, ~ sag mir Bescheid* if you need me, just let me know; *ich mache nur ~ mit, wenn ...* I'll only join in if (*od.* on the condition that) ...; *selbst ~, wenn ...* even if ...; *also od. na ~! umg.* (*wenn das so ist*) well in that case; *um Gespräch zu beenden:* right then, okeydoke; **5.** *umg.* (*also*) so; ~ *stimmt das* (*also od. etwa*) *gar nicht?* so that isn't true then?; **6.** *in Fragen:* (*sonst*) *wer/wo/wie etc. ~?* who/where/how *etc.* else then?; *wenn er es nicht weiß, wer ~?* if he doesn't know, who does?

dannen *Adv. altm. od. hum.: von ~* away, off, thence; *von ~ gehen* go hence

daran *Adv.* **1.** *räumlich: stellen, lehnen etc.*: against that *od.* it; *sich setzen etc.*: at that *od.* it; *hängen etc.*: on that *od.* it; *befestigen etc.*: to that *od.* it; ~ *fassen/riechen/schlagen* touch/smell/hit it; *halt dich ~ fest* hold on to it tight(ly); ~ *herumfummeln umg.* fiddle about with s.th.; **2.** *fig.*: ~ *glauben* believe in it; *das ändert nichts ~* that doesn't change anything (about it); *im*

Anschluss ~ following that, after that; *erinnere mich bitte ~, dass ...* please remind me that ...; *was ist schon ~?* what harm is there in that (*od.* it)?; ~ *kann man sehen, wie etc.* that goes to show how *etc.*; *du tätest gut ~ zu* (+ *Inf.*) you would do well (*od.* be well-advised) to (+ *Inf.*); *das Beste/Schlimmste etc.* ~ the best/worst thing about it *etc.*; → *die mit daran verbundenen Adjektive, Substantive und Verben*; **3.** (*daneben*) next to it; *nahe od. dicht ~* nearby; *zu nahe ~* too close (to it); ~ *vorbei* past it; *nahe ~ sein zu* (+ *Inf.*) *fig.* be on the point of (+ *Ger.*), come close to (+ *Ger.*), be just about to (+ *Inf.*); *ich war nahe ~, ihn zu schlagen* I nearly hit him, I was on the verge of hitting him; **4.** *Ursache:* ~ *leiden* suffer from it; ~ *sterben* die of it; ~ *ersticken* choke on it; ~ *scheitern, dass ...* fail because of ...; *das liegt ~, dass ...* that's because (of) ..., that's due to the fact that ...; **5.** *umg.* → *dran*

daran|geben *v/t.* (*unreg., trennb., hat -ge-*); *geh.: alles / sein Leben ~* (, *dass/zu ...*) sacrifice everything / one's life (to ...); (*tun*) do everything in one's power (to ...); *~gehen v/i.* (*unreg., trennb., ist -ge-*) get down to it, set about it; ~ *zu* (+ *Inf.*) get down to (+ *Ger.*); *~halten v/refl.* (*unreg., trennb., hat -ge-*) → *dranhalten*; *~machen v/refl.* (*trennb., hat -ge-*); *umg.* → *darangehen*; *~setzen* (*trennb., hat -ge-*) **I.** *v/t.* (*aufs Spiel setzen*) risk, stake; *alles ..., um zu* (+ *Inf.*) do everything in one's power to (+ *Inf.*); **II.** *v/refl.* get cracking *umg.*

darauf *Adv.* **1.** *räumlich:* (*auf*) on it (*od.* them); (*oben darauf*) on top of it (*od.* them); *e-e Straße/Wiese mit vielen Kindern ~* a street/meadow with lots of children in it; **2.** *Reihenfolge: der ~ folgende Läufer* the runner following on behind, the next runner; **3.** *zeitlich, Reihenfolge:* after that, then, thereupon *lit.*; (*als Nächstes*) next; *bald ~* soon after (that), soon thereafter; *gleich ~* immediately afterwards; *am Tag od. tags ~* the day after, the next (*od.* following) day; *zwei Jahre ~* two years later (*od.* on); **4.** *Richtung, Ziel:* ~ *aus sein zu* (+ *Inf.*) be aiming to (+ *Inf.*); ~ *hinarbeiten, dass od. zu* (+ *Inf.*) work towards *od.* on (+ *Ger.*); ~ *schießen* shoot at it; *sich ~ vorbereiten* prepare o.s. for it; **5.** *fig.*: ~ *beruhen* be based on it; ~ *bestehen* insist on it; *sich ~ freuen* look forward to it; ~ *hoffen* hope for it; ~ *kommen* think (of) that; *stolz ~ sein* be proud of it; ~ *warten, dass etw. geschieht / j-d etw. tut* wait for s.th. to happen / for s.b. to do s.th.; *mein Wort ~* my word on it; → *die mit darauf verbundenen Adjektive, Verben und Substantive*; **6.** → *daraufhin*

daraufhin *Adv.* **1.** after that, then; *im Nebensatz:* whereupon; **2.** (*aufgrund dessen*) as a result; **3.** (*als Antwort*) in reply; **4.** (*im Hinblick darauf*): *etw. ~ prüfen od. untersuchen, ob ...* examine s.th. to see if ...

daraus *Adv.* **1.** *räumlich:* from *od.* out of it (*od.* them); **2.** *Veränderung:* ~ *schnitzen/formen/machen etc.* carve/form/make *etc.* from (*od.* out of) it; ~ *bauen etc.* build *etc.* of it; ~ *wird nichts werden* (*wird keinen Erfolg haben*) nothing will come of it; (*das ist unmöglich*) we (*od.* you) can forget about that; ~ *wird nichts!* *umg.* nothing doing!; **3.** *Herkunft, Quelle:* ~ *lernen, zitieren etc.* learn/quote *etc.* from it; ~ *geht hervor, dass ...* from this it follows that ...; ~ *kann man schließen, dass ...* one may conclude from that, that ...; *er hat mir nie einen Vorwurf ~ gemacht* he never made an issue out of it; **4.** *fig.:* **ich mache mir nichts ~** (*es stört mich nicht*) it doesn't bother me; (*ich mag es nicht besonders*) I'm not that keen on it; (*es macht mir keine Sorgen*) it doesn't worry me; *mach dir nichts ~!* don't worry about it!, don't let it get you down!

darben *v/i.* *geh.* **1.** live in want; (*Entbehrungen ertragen*) suffer privations, go short; **2.** (*hungern*) go hungry; *stärker:* starve

darbieten (*unreg., trennb., hat -ge-*) **I.** *v/t.* **1.** *Mus., Theat.* perform, play; (*zeigen*) present, show; (*singen*) sing; **2.** (*darstellen*) (*Thema etc.*) present; **3.** *geh.* (*anbieten*) offer (+ *Dat.* to); **II.** *v/refl.* **1.** *Sache, Gelegenheit:* (*sich bieten*) present itself; (*entstehen*) arise; **2.** *Person:* offer o.s., volunteer; *als Opfer:* sacrifice o.s.; **Darbietung** *f* presentation; *Theat. etc.* performance (*auch Veranstaltung*); (*Nummer*) number, act

darbringen *v/t.* (*unreg., trennb., hat -ge-*) present (+ *Dat.* to), give (to); (*Opfer*) offer, make (to); (*Ovation*) give

Dardanellen *Pl. Geog.:* **die** ~ the Dardanelles

darein *Adv.* **1.** *räumlich:* in(to) it (*od.* them); **2.** *fig.:* *sich* ~ *ergeben od. fügen* → **dareinfinden**; **~finden** *v/refl.* (*unreg., trennb., hat -ge-*) come to terms with it, resign o.s. to the fact, put up with it; *sich* ~ *zu* (+ *Inf.*) come to terms with (+ *Ger.*), resign o.s. to (+ *Ger.*), put up with (+ *Ger.*); **~reden** *v/i.* (*trennb., hat -ge-*) → **dreinreden**; **~schicken** *v/refl.* (*trennb., hat -ge-*); *geh.* → **dareinfinden**

darf *Präs.* → **dürfen**

darin *Adv.* **1.** *räumlich:* in it (*od.* them); (*da drinnen*) in there; *was ist ~?* what's inside?; *da ist ... ~* there's ... in it, it contains ...; **2.** *fig.:* *die Schwierigkeit / der Unterschied / der Fehler liegt ~, dass ...* the difficulty/difference/mistake is that ...; *wievielmal ist diese Zahl ~ enthalten?* how many times can one find this number in it?; *die Autorin berichtet ~ von ...* the author reports on ... in this, the author uses this to report on ...; **3.** (*in dieser Hinsicht*) in this respect; ~ *irren Sie sich* there you are mistaken; *es unterscheidet sich von anderen ~, dass ...* it distinguishes itself from others in that ...; **4.** (*auf diesem Gebiet*) at it (*od.* that); ~ *ist er gut* he's good at it (*od.* that); *er kennt sich ~ gut aus* he knows a lot about it

darinnen *Adv. geh.* → **darin** 1

darlegen *v/t.* (*trennb., hat -ge-*); (*Meinung etc.*) present; (*erklären*) explain; (*aufführen*) state; *s-e Position ~* set out one's position; **Darlegung** *f* (*Darstellung*) presentation; (*Erklärung*) explanation, exposition

Darlehen *n; -s, -; Wirts.* loan; *ein ~ aufnehmen* take out (*od.* raise) a loan; *j-m ein ~ geben od. gewähren* give (*od.* grant) s.o. a loan

Darlehens|geber *m,* **~geberin** *f* lender; **~nehmer** *m,* **~nehmerin** *f* borrower; **~summe** *f* amount of a (*od.* the)

---

loan, sum borrowed; *eine ~ von ...* a loan amounting to ...; **~zinsen** *Pl.* interest *Sg.* on loans

Darlehn *etc.* → **Darlehen** *etc.*

Darm *m; -(e)s, Därme* **1.** *Anat.* intestine, bowels *Pl.*; *von Tieren:* gut(s); *den ~ entleeren* empty (*od.* evacuate) one's bowels; **2.** (*Wursthülle*) skin

Darm|ausgang *m Anat.* anus; **~bakterie** *f; mst Pl.; Physiol.* intestinal flora *Pl.*; **~bewegung** *f Med.* peristalsis; **~entleerung** *f Physiol.* evacuation of the bowels; **~entzündung** *f Med.* (gastro)enteritis; **~flora** *f Physiol.* intestinal flora *Pl.*; **~grippe** *f Med.* gastroenteritis, gastric flu *umg.*; **~infektion** *f Med.* intestinal infection; **~inhalt** *m* contents of the intestine, intestinal contents; **~kolik** *f Med.* abdominal (*od.* intestinal) colic; **~krebs** *m Med.* cancer of the intestine; *des Dickdarms:* colon (*od.* colorectal) cancer; **~saite** *f Mus.* catgut (string); **~spiegelung** *f Med.* enteroscopy; **~tätigkeit** *f Physiol.* bowel movement; **~trägheit** *f; nur Sg.; Med.* underactivity of the bowels; (*Verstopfung*) constipation; **~trakt** *m Anat.* intestinal tract; **~verschlingung** *f Med.* volvulus *fachspr.*, twisting of the bowels; **~verschluss** *m Med.* intestinal occlusion (*od.* obstruction); **~wand** *f Anat.* wall of the intestine, intestinal wall; **~wind** *m geh.* (intestinal) wind

darniederliegen → **daniederliegen**

Darre *f; -, -n* **1.** *Vorrichtung:* (drying) kiln (*od.* oven); *für Getreide:* oast; **2.** *Vorgang:* drying; *von Getreiden:* oasting

darreichen *v/t.* (*trennb., hat -ge-*); *geh.:* *j-m etw.* ~ hand s.o. s.th.; (*anbieten*) offer s.o. s.th.; *Med. und kirchl.* administer s.th. to s.o.; *j-m ein Geschenk* ~ present s.o. with a gift; **Darreichungsform** *f* presentation; *von Medikamenten:* (form of) administration

darren *v/t.* kiln-dry; (*Getreide*) oast; **Darrofen** *m* kiln

darstellbar *Adj.* **1.** *es ist in Worten /numerisch/ auf der Leinwand nicht* ~ it can't be described in words / expressed in numbers / portrayed on the screen; *ist das grafisch ~?* can that be shown graphically?; **2.** *Theat.* actable, playable

darstellen (*trennb., hat -ge-*) **I.** *v/t.* **1.** (*schildern*) describe; (*Tatsachen etc.*) present; *falsch* ~ misrepresent; *negativ* ~ portray in a negative light; **2.** *grafisch etc.:* represent; *Math.* describe; *in Umrissen:* outline, sketch; *in e-m Diagramm* ~ draw a graph of; **3.** *künstlerisch:* show, depict, portray; *was soll dieses Bild ~?* what is this picture supposed to represent?; **4.** *Theat.* act (*od.* play) (the part of); **5.** (*bedeuten*) be, represent, constitute; *was stellt das eigentlich dar?* what is it supposed to be?; *er stellt etwas dar umg. fig.* he's somebody, *Brit. auch* he looks the part; **6.** *Chem.* prepare, synthesize; *industriell:* produce; **II.** *v/refl. Sache:* present itself, appear; *Person:* present (*od.* portray) o.s.; *sich ~ als* (*sich erweisen als*) show o.s. to be

darstellend I. *Part. Präs.* → **darstellen**; **II.** *Adj.:* **~e Geometrie** descriptive geometry; **~e Künste** (*Schauspielerei etc.*) performing (*od.* interpretative) arts; (*Malerei etc.*) plastic arts

Darsteller *m; -s, -,* **~in** *f; -, -nen* **1.** *Theat., Film, TV, männlich:* actor; *weiblich auch:* actress; *der ~ des Faust*

---

the actor playing (the part of) Faust; *die Darsteller* the cast (*V. im Sg. od. Pl.*); **2.** *Sänger, Tänzer etc.:* performer

darstellerisch I. *Adj.* acting, theatrical, dramatic; *s-e ~e Leistung* his performance; **II.** *Adv.* in terms of acting

Darstellung *f* **1.** (*Schilderung*) description, portrayal; (*Bericht*) account; (*Diagramm*) representation; *von Tatsachen etc.:* presentation; *falsche* ~ misrepresentation; *i-e ~ des Vorfalls* her account of the incident; **2.** *künstlerische:* representation; (*Interpretation*) interpretation; **3.** *Theat., e-r Rolle:* interpretation, acting; *e-s Stückes:* production; **4.** *Chem.* preparation

Darstellungs|kraft *f; nur Sg.* powers *Pl.* of interpretation; *e-s Schriftstellers:* descriptive powers *Pl.*; **~kunst** *f; nur Sg.* art of interpretation; *Theat.* acting ability (*od.* technique); **~weise** *f* style

Darts *n; -, kein Pl.; Sport* darts *Sing.*; *möchtest du ~ spielen?* do you want (*Brit. auch* do you fancy) a game of darts?, do you want to play darts?

dartun *v/t.* (*unreg., trennb., hat -ge-*) show, demonstrate; (*aufzeigen*) set out; (*erklären*) explain

darüber *Adv.* **1.** *räumlich:* ~ *legen/liegen/breiten* lay/lie/spread *etc.* over it (*od.* them) (*betont:* over that [*od.* those]; *quer darüber:* across it *etc.*); ~ *schweben etc.* hover *etc.* above it; *das Zimmer* ~ the room above; *mit e-m Dach etc. ~* with a roof *etc.* on top; *mit der Hand ~ fahren od. streichen* run one's hand over it; ~ *schreiben* write over it; (*Namen etc.*) write at the top; *es geht nichts ~ fig.* there's nothing like it; *da steht er ~ fig.* he is above that (*od.* such things); **2.** *fig.* (*mehr*) more; (*höher*) higher; *sechs Jahre und ~ Alter:* six years (of age) and above (*od.* over), from six years of age upwards; *Zeitraum:* six years and over; **3.** *zeitlich:* in the meantime; *ich bin ~ eingeschlafen* I fell asleep over it; ~ *werden Jahre vergehen* that will take years; **4.** *fig.* (*über e-e Sache*) about that (*od.* it); (*über dieses Thema*) on that (*od.* it); *ich freue mich ~, dass ...* I'm glad (that) ...; ~ *vergaß er s-e Probleme* it took his mind off his problems; ~ *wird morgen verhandelt* we'll *etc.* be discussing that tomorrow; ~ *lässt sich streiten* that's a matter of opinion, that's a debatable point; *er beklagt sich ~, dass er unfair behandelt worden sei* he complains of having been treated unfairly; **5.** ~ *hinaus* beyond it, past it; *fig.* in addition, on top of it; (*was das Übrige angeht*) beyond that; ~ *hinaus möchte ich noch sagen ...* furthermore (*od.* moreover) I would like to say ...; *wir sind ~ hinweg fig.* we've got(ten) over it

darum *Adv.* **1.** *räumlich:* around it (*od.* them); *betont:* around there; **2.** *fig.:* *j-n ~ bitten zu* (+ *Inf.*) ask s.o. to (+ *Inf.*); *es geht ~, dass ...* the thing is that ...; ~ *geht es gar nicht* that's not the point; *er kümmert sich nicht ~* he doesn't care (about it); *ich gäbe was/ viel ~ zu wissen umg.* I wouldn't mind knowing / I'd love to know; *du wirst nicht ~ herumkommen* you won't be able to avoid it; *es ist mir nicht ~ zu tun, dass ...* it is not my intention (*od.* aim) to ...; **3.** (*deshalb*) that's why; *ich habe es ~ getan, weil ...* the reason I did it was because ...; *warum? - ~! umg.* (just) because!, that's why!; *sie ist zwar jung, aber ~ nicht*

dumm she may be young but that doesn't necessarily make her stupid

darum|binden v/t. (unreg., trennb., hat -ge-) tie (a)round it (od. them); **~kommen** v/i. (unreg., trennb., ist -ge-); (verlieren) lose it (od. them); (versäumen) miss, lose; **~, etw. zu tun** miss the opportunity of doing s.th. (od. chance to do s.th.); miss out on (doing) s.th.; **~legen** v/t. (trennb., hat -ge-) put around it (od. them); **~stehen** v/i. (unreg., trennb., hat / südd., österr., schw. ist -ge-) stand around

darunter Adv. **1.** räumlich: under it (od. them); betont: under there; (direkt **~**) underneath; (weiter unten) further down; s-n Namen **~** schreiben od. setzen write at the bottom; **s-e Unterschrift ~ setzen** sign (it), sign at the bottom; **~ (an)ziehen** (Pullover etc.) put on as well; (Unterhemd etc.) put on underneath; **2.** (in e-r Menge) among them; (einschließlich) including; **mitten ~** right in the middle (of it od. them); **etw. ~ mischen** add, mix s.th. into it; **sich ~ mischen** mix with them (od. the crowd etc.); **den Eischnee vorsichtig ~ heben** fold (od. mix) in the beaten egg-white carefully; **~ fallen** be included; be covered by it; **3.** (weniger) less; (niedriger) lower; **zehn Jahre und ~** Alter: ten years (of age) and below; Zeitraum: ten years and less; **~ bleiben** od. **liegen** Angebot, Preis: be lower; Ergebnisse, Leistungen: not reach (od. not come up to) this level; **4.** fig.: **~ leiden, dass ...** suffer from (+ Ger.); **er leidet sehr ~** unter dem Verlust etc.: he's taking it hard; **was verstehst du ~?** what do you understand by it?; **~ kann ich mir nichts vorstellen** it doesn't mean a thing to me

das I. best. Art. the; **~ Gute** the good; **~ Laufen** running; **eine ist falsch, ~ andere richtig** one is wrong, the other (one) is right; **das Tier** (alle Tiere) the animal kingdom; **ich wusch mir ~ Gesicht** I washed my face; **zwei Euro ~ Kilo** two euros a kilo; **II.** Dem. Pron. that, this, those Pl.; **~ ist der neue Chef** that's the new boss; **~ sind m-e Bücher** those are my books; **~ da** that one (there); **~, was er sagt** what he says; **~ ist es ja!** that's just it (od. the point)!; sie wurde gelobt, **auch ~ noch!** that's all I need, that tops the lot!; **und ~ mit Recht** and quite right too, Am. auch and how! umg.; **nur ~ nicht!** anything but that!; **III.** Rel. Pron. bei Personen: who (Nom.); whom (Akk.); bei Sachen: which; **~ Kind, ~ ich meine** the child I'm referring to; **~ Haus, ~ abgerissen wird** the house which (Am. mst that) is being demolished; → **der**

Dasein n **1.** existence; life; **ein jämmerliches ~ fristen** eke out a wretched existence, scrape by; **ins ~ rufen** bring s.th. into existence, call s.th. into being; (gründen) found s.th.; → **Kampf**, **2.** (Anwesenheit) presence

Daseins|berechtigung f; nur Sg. **1.** (Legitimation) right to exist; **hat unser Verein noch eine ~?** can our club justify its continuing existence?; **2.** (Grund) raison d'être; **~form** f way of life; **~kampf** m; nur Sg. struggle for existence (od. survival); **~recht** n; nur Sg. right to exist(ence)

dasitzen v/i. (unreg., trennb., hat / südd., österr., schw. ist -ge-) **1.** hier: sit here; dort: sit there; **(nun) sitz nicht**

untätig od. **einfach so da - tu etwas!** umg. don't just sit there - do something!; **2.** umg. fig.: **ohne Geld ~** be left without a penny (to one's name)

dasjenige Dem. Pron.; desjenigen, diejenigen **1.** subst.: Sg.: the one; Pl.: those (ones); **~, das** od. **welches** the one which (Am. mst that); **diejenigen, die** od. **welche** those which (Am. mst that); **2.** adj.: **~ Amt** etc., **das** od. **welches** the (betont: that) office etc. which (Am. mst that); **diejenigen ..., die** od. **welche** the (betont: those) ... which (Personen: who, Am. mst that); → **derjenige**

dass Konj. **1.** im Subjekt: that; **es ist nett, ~ du anrufst** it's nice of you to ring; **es sind zwei Jahre, ~ ich ihn nicht gesehen habe** it's two years now since I've seen him; **~ es schneien wird, ist unwahrscheinlich** it's unlikely to snow; **2.** im Objekt: **er weiß, ~ es wahr ist** he knows (that) it's true; **entschuldigen Sie, ~ ich Sie störe** sorry to disturb you; **3.** im Attribut: **angenommen, ~ ...** assuming (od. given) that ...; **vorausgesetzt, ~ ...** provided that ...; **für den Fall, ~ du kommst, lege ich den Schlüssel raus** I'll leave the key out in case you come; **ihr Wunsch, ~ es gelingen möge, erfüllte sich nicht** her hopes of success were dashed; **4.** anstelle e-s präpositionalen Objekts: → **dadurch, dafür, daher** etc.; **sie löste das Problem dadurch** od. **damit, ~ ...** she solved the problem by (+ Ger.); **ich ärgere mich darüber, ~ es regnet** I'm annoyed that it is raining; **sie leidet darunter, ~ er lügt** she suffers from his deception; **5.** Folge: **es war so kalt, ~ der Fluss zufror** it was so cold that the river froze; **der nasse Hund schüttelte sich, ~ es nur so spritzte** the wet dog shook himself so the spray went everywhere; **sie lachte (so), ~ ihr die Tränen kamen** she laughed until she cried; → **auch sodass**; **6.** umg. (weil, da) because, since; **bist du taub, ~ du mir nicht antwortest?** why aren't you answering me - are you deaf?; **er entschuldigte sich, ~ er zu spät kam** he apologized for being late; **7.** Ziel: (damit) so that; **sie bemühen sich sehr, ~ sie mich zufrieden stellen** they are doing their best (in order) to please me; **zeig her, ~ ich es selbst sehen kann** show me, so that I can see for myself; **8.** in Wendungen: **es ist zu kalt, als ~ man baden könnte** it is too cold to swim; **er läuft lieber, als** od. **(an)statt ~ er sein Fahrrad repariert** he'd rather walk than repair his bicycle; **auf ~ es gelingen möge!** here's to success!; **wir fahren, außer** od. **es sei denn ~ es schneit** unless it's snowing, we'll drive; **nicht, ~ ich wüsste** not that I know of; **nicht, ~ es etwas ausmachte** not that it mattered; → **auch als** 2, **anstatt** II; **9.** umg.; Wunsch, Drohung etc.: **~ du mir ja nichts anrührst!** don't go and touch anything, now; **~ du ja kommst!** you had better be there!; **~ ich es bloß nicht vergesse!** I hope I don't forget it, I'd better not forget it; **~ er so was sagen konnte!** how could he say such a thing?

dasselbe Dem. Pron.; desselben, dieselben **1.** the same; **das ist ein und ~** that is (od. amounts to) one and the same (thing); **wenn zwei das Gleiche tun, ist es noch lange nicht ~** Sprichw. what counts for one doesn't

necessarily count for the other; **2.** umg. (das Gleiche) the same; **~ noch einmal, bitte** the same again please; **3.** altm., statt Pron.: **die Bombe traf das Haus und zerstörte ~** and destroyed it; → **derselbe**

dasselbige Dem. Pron. m; des-, dem-, das-, dieselbigen; altm. → **dasselbe**

Dasselfliege f Zool. warble fly

dass-Satz, Dasssatz m Ling. that-clause

dastehen v/i. (unreg., trennb., hat / südd., österr., schw. ist -ge-) **1.** hier: stand here; dort: stand there; **nicht liegen** etc.: stand; **untätig:** just stand there (doing nothing); **2.** fig.: **ganz allein ~** be left all on one's own; **dumm ~** umg. be left looking the fool; **gut ~** be doing all right; weitS. be in a good position; **mit leeren Händen ~** be left without a penny (to one's name); **wie stehe ich nun da!** and where does that leave me?, I look a right idiot (now) umg., Am. auch I look like a dope umg.

Dat. Abk. → **Dativ**

Datei f; -, -en; bes. EDV (data) file; **e-e ~ abspeichern/benennen/löschen/öffnen/schließen** save/name/delete/open/close a file; **~manager** m file manager; **~name** m filename; **~verwaltung** f file-management; **~verzeichnis** n (file) directory

Daten Pl. **1.** → **Datum**; **2.** EDV data Pl. (V. auch im Sg.); **~ austauschen/auswerten/erfassen/löschen/speichern** exchange/evaluate/capture (od. collect) /delete/save data; **3.** allg. Tatsachen, Resultate etc.: data, facts; **technische ~** specifications; **4.** (Personalangaben) particulars, personal data

Daten|abfrage f EDV (data) query; **~aufbereitung** f data preparation (od. editing); **~austausch** m data exchange; **~auswertung** f data evaluation; **~autobahn** f information superhighway

Datenbank f; Pl. -banken; EDV database, data bank; **~aufbau** m database construction (od. design)

datenbankgestützt Adj. EDV database-supported

Datenbank|pflege f EDV database management (od. maintenance); **~verwaltung** f database management

Daten|bestand m EDV data bank; **~eingabe** f data input; **~erfassung** f data capture (od. acquisition); **~erhebung** f survey; **~fehler** m data-sensitive fault; **~fernübertragung** f data remote transfer

Datenfluss m EDV data flow; **~plan** m data flowchart

Daten|highway ['daːtn̩'haɪve] m; -s, -s; EDV information superhighway; **~material** n data; **~netz** n data network; **~satz** m record

Datenschutz m Jur. data protection; **~beauftragte** m, f data protection registrar (Am. agency)

Datenschutzgesetz n Jur. data protection law

Daten|sicherheit f EDV data security; **~sichtgerät** n visual display unit, VDU; **~sicherung** f data storage (od. backup); **~speicher** m data memory (od. storage); **~technik** f data systems technology; **~träger** m data medium (od. carrier); **~typist** m; -en, -en, **~typistin** f; -, -nen data typist (od. entry clerk), keyboarder; **~übertragung** f data transfer; **~verarbeitung** f data processing; **elektronische ~** (abgek.

D

EDV) electronic data processing; *als Fach*: computer science; **~verarbeitungsanlage** *f* data processor; **~verbund** *m* data network; **~verlust** *m* data loss; **~verwaltung** *f* data management; **~zugriff** *m* data access

datierbar *Adj.*: *die Funde sind nicht genau ~* cannot be dated exactly; **datieren I.** *v/t.* (*Brief, Funde*) date; **II.** *v/i.*: *~ aus, seit od.* **von** date from (*od.* back to); *der Brief datiert vom 2. Mai* the letter is dated May 2nd; **Datierung** *f* dating

Dativ *m*; *-s*, *-e*; *Ling.* (*abgek.* **Dat.**) dative (case); **dativisch** *Adj.* dative; **Dativobjekt** *n* indirect object

dato *Adv.*: *bis ~* up to now, to date

DAT-Kassette *f* DAT cassette; **~-Rekorder** *m* DAT recorder, digital audio tape (recorder)

Datscha *f*; *-*, *-s od. Datschen*, **Datsche** *f*; *-*, *-n*; *ostd.* da(t)cha

Dattel *f*; *-*, *-n*; *Bot.* date; **~baum** *m*, **~palme** *f* date palm; **~pflaume** *f* persimmon

Datum *n*; *-s*, *Daten* date; *heutigen ~s* of today; *ohne ~* undated; *welches ~ haben wir heute?* what's the date today?; *der Brief trägt das ~ vom 2. Mai* the letter is dated May 2nd; *älteren/ früheren/neueren ~s* older/earlier/ more recent; → *Daten*

Datums|angabe *f* date; *ohne ~* undated; **~grenze** *f* (international) date line

Datum(s)stempel *m* date stamp; (*Gerät*) dater, date stamper

Daube *f*; *-*, *-n* **1.** *von Fass*: stave; **2.** *beim Eisstockschießen*: tee

Dauer *f*; *-*, *kein Pl.* **1.** duration; (*Zeitspanne*) period (of time); *bes. Wirts., Jur.* term; *für die / während der ~ unseres Aufenthalts* for the course (*od.* duration) / during (the course) of our stay; **2.** (*Länge*) length; *Mus.* duration; *Ling., e-s Vokals*: quantity, duration; **3.** (*Dauerhaftigkeit*) durability; **4.** *auf ~ angestellt, geregelt*: permanently; *auf ~ angelegt/gearbeitet* designed/made to last; *das ist keine Lösung auf ~* that's no long-term solution; *auf die ~* in the long run (*od.* term); *auf die ~ wird es unerträglich* it becomes unbearable after a time; *sie können auf die ~ nicht so weitermachen* they can't go on like this for ever; **5.** *Lösung etc.* *von ~* long-term solution *etc.*; *von ~ sein* last; *von kurzer od. begrenzter od. nicht von (langer) ~ sein* be short-lived

Dauer|arbeitslose *m, f* long-term unemployed person; *Pl.* the long-term unemployed; **~auftrag** *m Wirts.* standing order; *etw. per ~ überweisen* pay s.th. by standing order (*Am.* by automatic draft); **~ausstellung** *f* permanent exhibition; **~beanspruchung** *f Tech.* endurance stress; *e-s Menschen*: constant stress; **~behandlung** *f* prolonged treatment; **~behinderung** *f* permanent disability; **~belastung** *f* **1.** *Tech.* constant load; **2.** *e-s Menschen*: constant strain (*od.* stress); **~beschäftigung** *f Wirts.* permanent employment; **~beschuss** *m*: *unter ~ stehen Mil.* experience sustained bombardment; *fig.* be under constant attack (*od.* fire); **~betrieb** *m*; *nur Sg.* continuous operation; **~beziehung** *f* long-term (*od.* permanent) relationship, LTR *umg.*; **~brenner** *m* **1.** *Tech.* slow-combustion stove; **2.** (*Erfolgsstück etc.*) long-running success; **3.** (*Diskussionsthema*) long-running issue;

4. *umg.* (*Kuss*) long (passionate) kiss; **~einrichtung** *f auch fig.* permanent institution; **~erfolg** *m* long-running (*od.* -lasting) success; **~frost** *m* permafrost; **~frostgrenze** *f* permafrost line; **~funktion** *f Tastatur*: locking function; **~gast** *m Hotel*: permanent resident; *er ist bei uns ~ umg.* he's a permanent fixture here; **~geschwindigkeit** *f* cruising speed

dauerhaft I. *Adj. Beziehung, Friede, Lösung etc.*: lasting; (*belastbar*) durable; (*lang anhaltend*) long-term ...; *Einrichtung, Zustand*: permanent; *Farbe*: fast; *Stoff*: hard-wearing; *Gebäude*: solid; **~e Konsumgüter** (consumer) durables; **II.** *Adv.* lastingly, with long-lasting effect; *~ gearbeitet* made to last; *~ geregelt* settled once and for all; **Dauerhaftigkeit** *f* durability

Dauer|institution *f* → *Dauereinrichtung*; **~kalender** *m* perpetual calendar; **~karte** *f* season ticket; **~kunde** *m*, **~kundin** *f* regular customer; **~lauf** *m* long-distance run(ning); *im ~* at a jog; **~leistung** *f* **1.** *Tech.* continuous output; **2.** *e-s Menschen*: long-term performance; **~lösung** *f* long-term solution; **~lutscher** *m* lollipop; **~mieter** *m*, **~mieterin** *f* permanent tenant; *im Parkhaus*: holder of a reserved space

dauern¹ *v/i.* **1.** last, go on; *wie lange dauert die Sitzung denn noch?* how much longer will the meeting last (*od.* take)?; *die Saison dauert von Mai bis September* the season lasts (*od.* runs) from May until (*Am. auch* through) September; **2.** (*Zeit beanspruchen*) take; *es wird lange ~, bis er kommt* it'll be a long time before he comes; *es wird nicht lange ~, dann ...* it won't be long before ...; *das dauert mir zu lange* that's too long for me; *mit Argwohn*: it's taking too long for my liking; *das dauert aber! umg.* it doesn't half take a long time, *Am.* it seems to take forever

dauern² *v/t. geh. altm.*: *er dauert mich* I feel sorry for him; *es dauert mich, dass od. zu* (+*Inf.*) ... I regret to ..., I am sorry that ...

dauernd I. *Part.Präs* → *dauern¹*; **II.** *Adj.* **1.** (*ständig*) constant, perpetual; (*unaufhörlich*) incessant; **2.** *Wohnsitz*: permanent; **3.** → *dauerhaft* I; **III.** *Adv.*: *er lachte ~* he kept laughing; *unterbrich mich nicht ~!* stop interrupting me (all the time)!; *~ ist was los umg.* there's always something going on

Dauer|parker *m*, **~parkerin** *f* long-term parker; (*Anlieger*) resident with a parking permit; *im Parkhaus*: holder of a reserved space; **~problem** *n* constant problem; **~regelung** *f* permanent arrangement; **~regen** *m* continuous rain; **~schaden** *m Med.* permanent damage; **~stellung** *f* permanent post; **~test** *m* endurance test; **~ton** *m* continuous tone; **~visum** *n* permanent visa; **~welle** *f* perm; *sich e-e ~ machen lassen* get one's hair permed, get a perm; **~wirkung** *f* lasting effect; **~wurst** *f* hard smoked sausage; **~zustand** *m* permanent condition (*od.* state of affairs); *zu e-m ~ werden* become permanent (*od.* a permanent state of affairs)

Däumchen *n*: *~ drehen umg.* twiddle one's thumbs (*auch fig.*)

Daumen *m*; *-s*, *-* thumb; *am ~ lutschen* suck one's thumb; *j-m den od. die ~ halten od. drücken fig.* keep one's fin-

gers crossed (for s.o.); *~ drehen umg.* twiddle one's thumbs (*auch fig.*); *den ~ auf etw.* (*Akk.*) *haben od. halten umg. fig.* keep tabs on s.th., watch over s.th.; *etw. über den ~ peilen umg.* make a rough guess at s.th.

Daumenabdruck *m* thumbprint

Daumenbreite *f*: *um ~* by about an inch

daumendick I. *Adj.* as thick as a (*od.* one's) thumb, about an inch thick; **II.** *Adv.*: *du hast das Brot wieder ~ geschnitten* you cut the loaf into doorsteps again *umg.*

Daumen|kino *n* flip-book; **~lutschen** *n*; *-s*, *kein Pl.* thumb-sucking; **~nagel** *m* thumbnail; **~register** *n in Wörterbüchern etc.*: thumb index; **~schraube** *f hist.* thumbscrew; *j-m ~n anlegen fig.* put the screws on s.o.

Däumling *m*; *-s*, *-e* **1.** *Schutzkappe*: thumbstall; *am Handschuh*: thumb; **2.** *Märchenfigur*: Tom Thumb

Daune *f*; *-*, *-n* downy feather; **~n** down *Sg.*

Daunen|anorak *m* down anorak (*Am.* parka); **~bett** *n*, **~decke** *f* eiderdown, (down-filled) duvet (*Am.* comforter); **~feder** *f* down feather; **~kissen** *n* down-filled cushion; (*Kopfkissen*) down(-filled) pillow

daunenweich *Adj.* downy, *präd. auch* soft as down

David(s)stern *m* Star of David

Daviscup [ˈdeːvɪskap] *m*; *nur Sg. Tennis*: Davis Cup

davon *Adv.* **1.** *räumlich, Herkunft*: from it (*od.* them), from there (*weg*) away; *nicht weit ~* (*entfernt*) *sein* be not far (away) from; *fig.* be not a million miles away from; *ich bin weit ~ entfernt, das zu glauben fig.* the last thing I'm going to do is believe that; → *auf* II 5; **2.** *Teil*: of it (*od.* them); *trink nicht ~* don't drink from that; *etwas ~ wegnehmen* take s.th. away from it; *ich habe zehn Mark ~ ausgegeben* I've spent ten marks of it; *sie hatten vier Kinder, zwei ~ sind schon tot* they had four children, two of whom are already dead; **3.** *Ursache etc.*, *mit Passiv*: by it; *~ sterben die* from (*od.* of) it; *~ krank/gesund werden* become ill/well through it; *~ wurde er wach* he was awakened by it; *~ wird man müde* it makes you tired; *~ kannst du etwas lernen* you can learn (something) from that; *das kommt ~, dass du so faul bist od.* *wenn man so faul ist* that's what comes of being so lazy; *das kommt ~!* what did you expect?; *was habe 'ich ~?* what do I get out of it?; *was 'habe ich ~?* why should I?; *das hast du nun ~! umg.* that's what comes of it!; *mit Schadenfreude*: serves you right; **4.** *Thema*: (*darüber*) about it, of it; *genug ~!* enough of that!, *Am. auch* enough already!; *weiß sie schon ~?* does she know (about it) already?; *ich will nichts ~ hören!* I don't want to hear a word about it (*od.* on the subject)!; **5.** *Material*: out of, from; *sie hat sich ~ Schuhe gemacht* she made shoes from it; **6.** *Grundlage*: *~ leben* live off it; *er lebt ~, Hunde zu züchten* he makes his living (from) breeding dogs; **7.** *fig.*: *es hängt ~ ab, ob* it depends (on) whether; *abgesehen ~* leaving that aside, ignoring that; → *die mit davon verbundenen Adjektive, Substantive und Verben*

davon|brausen *v/i.* (*trennb.*, *ist -ge-*);

D

umg. speed off (*od.* away); **~fahren** *v/i.* (*unreg., trennb., ist -ge-*) drive (*od.* ride) off *od.* away; *mir ist der Bus davongefahren* I just missed the bus; **~gehen** *v/i.* (*unreg., trennb., ist -ge-*) walk away (*od.* off); **~jagen** *v/t.* (*trennb., hat -ge-*) chase away

davonkommen *v/i.* (*unreg., trennb., ist -ge-*) get away, escape; (*mit dem Leben*) **~** escape, survive; **~ mit leichten** *Verletzungen etc.:* escape (*od.* get away) with; *e-r Geldstrafe etc.:* get away (*od.* off) with; *wir sind noch einmal davongekommen* it was a close shave, we had a narrow escape, we escaped by the skin of our teeth; → *blau* 2, *Schrecken* 1

davonlassen *v/t.* (*unreg., trennb., hat -ge-*) → *Finger* 1

davonlaufen *v/i.* (*unreg., trennb., ist -ge-*) **1.** run away (*j-m* from s.o.); *fig.* (*s-r Frau etc.*) *auch* desert *s.o.; von zu Hause* **~** run away from home; *ihm ist die Freundin davongelaufen fig. auch* his girlfriend (got up and) left him (*od.* walked out on him); *es ist zum Davonlaufen! umg. fig.* it's enough to drive you (a)round the bend (*od.* make you weep); **2.** *fig. Preise etc.:* get out of control (*od.* hand), spiral; *die Preise laufen den Löhnen davon* prices have outstripped wages

davon|machen *v/refl.* (*trennb., hat -ge-*); *umg.* make off; (*heimlich*) sneak away; **~schleichen** (*unreg., trennb., -ge-*); *v/i.* (*ist*) *und v/refl.* (*hat*) sneak off (*od.* away); **~stehlen** *v/refl.* (*unreg., trennb., hat -ge-*) sneak off (*od.* away); **~tragen** *v/t.* (*unreg., trennb., hat -ge-*) **1.** carry away (*od.* off); **2.** *fig.* (*Verletzung*) come away with, receive, sustain *geh.*; (*Krankheit*) get, catch, end up with *umg.*; *den Sieg* **~** win, be victorious; **~ziehen** *v/i.* (*unreg., trennb., ist -ge-*) **1.** *Soldaten etc.:* move (*od.* march) off; *Vögel:* move away, migrate; *Wild etc.:* migrate; **2.** *Sport umg.* pull away (*j-m* from s.o.)

davor *Adv.* **1.** *räumlich:* before *od.* in front of it (*od.* them); *den Riegel* **~** *schieben* slip the bolt across; **2.** *zeitlich:* beforehand; *vor e-m bestimmten Zeitpunkt:* before that; *e-e Stunde* **~** an hour earlier; **3.** *fig.:* *keine Achtung* **~** *haben* have no respect for s.th.; *sich* **~** *ekeln* be disgusted by s.th.; *er fürchtet sich* **~** he's afraid of it, it scares him; *ich habe dich* **~** *gewarnt* I warned you about that

DAX® *m; -, kein Pl.; Abk.* (*Deutscher Aktienindex*) DAX Index

dazu *Adv.* **1.** *räumlich:* there; *soll ich es 'hierzu legen? - nein,* **~** no, (over) there; **2.** (*dabei, damit*) (together) with it; (*außerdem*) besides, in addition, into the bargain; *noch* **~** on top of it (*od.* that); *etwas* **~** *hinzugeben* add s.th. to s.th.; *möchtest du ein Glas Bier* **~**? would you like a (glass of) beer with that?; **3.** *Zweck, Aufgabe etc.:* (*dafür*) for it (*od.* that); **~** *gehört Zeit* it takes time; *es gehört viel Mut* **/** *schon einiges* **~** *zu* (+ *Inf.*) it takes a lot of courage / quite a lot (*od.* a fair bit) to (+ *Inf.*); **~** *ist er ja da* that's what he's there for, that's his job; **~** *hast du's doch* that's what you've got it for (*od.* it's there for), isn't it?; **4.** *Thema:* (*darüber*) about it (*od.* that); *sich* **~** *äußern* give one's view (*od.* voice one's opinion) on it, comment (on it); *hast du etwas* **~** *zu sagen?* do you have anything to say

about that?; *sie schwieg* **~** (*zu diesen Vorwürfen*) she made no comment (*od.* remained silent); *es ist alles* **~** *gesagt* it's all been said already; **5.** *Veränderung, Ziel:* *das führt* **~**, *dass ...* that leads to ...; *ich war früher nicht so misstrauisch, m-e Erfahrungen haben mich* **~** *gemacht* my experiences have made me it (*od.* this way); *wie ist es* **~** *gekommen?* how did it happen?; *wie konnte es nur* **~** *kommen?* how could it turn out this way?; *es wird/darf niemals* **~** *kommen!* it won't/mustn't ever come to that!; *doch es kam nie* **~** but it never came to that; **6.** *Anlass:* *darf ich* **~** *gratulieren?* may I congratulate you (on your birthday etc.)?; **7.** *Zugehörigkeit:* *der Deckel/Schlüssel* **~** its lid/key, the lid/key belonging to (*od.* going with) it; **8.** *fig.:* *Liebe/Neigung* **~** love/affection for it; *Erlaubnis/Recht* **~** permission/right to it; *wie bist du* **~** *gekommen?* (*zu diesem Buch etc.*) how did you get hold of (*od.* come by) it?; (*Stelle*) how did you get into (*od.* come to be doing) this?; **9.** *anstelle od. vor zu + Inf.:* *ich habe keine Lust* **~** (*aufzuräumen*) I don't want to (tidy up), I can't be bothered (tidying up *od.* to tidy up); *er tut das Seine* **~**(, *das Problem zu lösen*) he's doing his share (*od.* bit) (to solve the problem); *die Gelegenheit* **~** *haben*(, *ins Ausland zu gehen*) have the opportunity (*od.* chance) (to go abroad *od. Am. auch* overseas); *wie kamst du* **~**, *für sie zu arbeiten?* how did you come to work (*od.* be working) for them?; *ich kam nie* **~**(, *es zu lesen*) I never got (a)round to (reading) it; *wie komme ich* **~**? *empört:* why should I?; *wie kommst du* **~**? *empört:* how could you?; → *die mit dazu verbundenen Adjektive, Substantive und Verben*

dazu|geben *v/t.* (*unreg., trennb., hat -ge-*) add; *j-m etw.* **~** give s.o. s.th. toward(s) it; → *Senf;* **~gehören** *v/i.* (*trennb., hat*) belong to it (*od.* that); (*Teil davon sein*) be part of it; *zu e-m Kreis etc.: auch* belong; *sie gibt einem das Gefühl dazuzugehören* she makes you feel like you belong; *das gehört mit/unbedingt dazu* that's part (and parcel) of it / that's a must; → *auch dazu* 3; **~gehörig** *Adj.* belonging to it (*od.* them); (*passend*) appropriate; it; **~gewinnen** *vt/i.* (*unreg., trennb., hat*): *es hat dadurch viel dazugewonnen* it gained a lot through that; *es kann nur* **~** it (*od.* things) can only get better; **~kommen** *v/i.* (*unreg., trennb., ist -ge-*) **1.** *Person:* come along; (*sich anschließen*) join them (*od.* us etc.); *er kam gerade/zufällig dazu, als ...* he arrived/ happened to arrive just as ...; **2.** *Sache:* be added; *kommt noch was dazu?* is there anything else?; *im Geschäft:* will that be all?, *Brit. auch* is that the lot?, *Am. auch* is that everything? *umg.;* → *auch dazu* 5, 8, 9; **~können** *v/t.* (*unreg., trennb., hat -ge-*) *bes. nordd.:* *er kann nichts* **~** (*dass es passiert ist*) it's not his fault; (*dass er so ist*) he can't help it; **~legen** (*trennb., hat -ge-*) **I.** *v/t.* lay (*od.* put) beside it; (*hinzufügen*) add to s.th.; **II.** *v/refl.* lie down with s.o. (*od.* s.th.); **~lernen** *vt/i.* (*trennb., hat -ge-*) learn (something new); *schon wieder etwas dazugelernt!* you live and learn!

dazumal *Adv.* → *anno*

dazu|rechnen *v/t.* (*trennb., hat -ge-*)

add on; **~sagen** *v/t.* (*trennb., hat -ge-*) (*hinzufügen*) add; *das hättest du* **~** *sollen* you should have said that; **~setzen** (*trennb., hat -ge-*) **I.** *v/t.* *schriftlich:* add; *dürfen wir Ihnen j-n* **~**? would you mind sharing the table etc. with s.o.?; **II.** *v/refl.:* *darf ich mich* **~**? may I join you (*od.* sit here)?; **~stellen** (*trennb., hat -ge-*) **I.** *v/t.* put (*od.* place) beside it; (*hinzufügen*) add to it; **II.** *v/refl.* stand next to s.o.; *bei Warteschlange:* join the queue (*Am.* line)

dazutun *v/t.* (*unreg., trennb., hat -ge-*) add; → *auch dazu* 9

Dazutun *n:* *ohne sein* **~** without any help from him, without his assistance

dazuverdienen *vt/i.* (*trennb., hat*) earn *s.th.* extra

dazwischen *Adv.* **1.** *räumlich:* between (them), in between; → *dazwischen liegen;* **2.** (*darunter*) among(st) them, in with them; **3.** *zeitlich:* in between; **~** *lagen zwei Monate* there were two months in between them; → *dazwischen liegen;* **4.** *fig.:* *ich kann mich nicht* **~** *entscheiden* I can't decide between them; → *die mit dazwischen verbundenen Substantive und Verben*

dazwischen|fahren *v/i.* (*unreg., trennb., ist -ge-*) step in; *im Gespräch:* butt in; **~fragen** *v/i.* (*trennb., hat -ge-*): *darf ich mal kurz* **~**? could I ask a quick question before you (*od.* we) go on?; **~funken** *v/i.* (*trennb., hat -ge-*) *umg.* **1.** interfere (*j-m* with s.o. 's plans etc.), put one's oar in; (*Pläne etc. vereiteln*) put a spoke in the wheel (*od.* a spanner *od. Am.* wrench in the works); **2.** *im Gespräch:* butt in; **~geraten** *v/i.* (*unreg., trennb., ist*) **1.** *mit den Fingern etc.* **~** get one's fingers etc. caught; **2.** (*in etw. verwickelt werden*) get involved; **~kommen** *v/i.* (*unreg., trennb., ist -ge-*): *wenn nichts dazwischenkommt* if all goes well, as long as there are no hitches; *es od. mir etc. ist etw. dazwischengekommen* s.th.'s cropped up

dazwischen| liegen *v/i.* (*unreg., trennb., hat* **/** *südd., österr., schw. ist*) **1.** *räumlich:* lie (*od.* be) in between; **2.** *zeitlich:* lie between; **3.** *zwischen zwei Extremen:* be in the middle (*od.* between); **~ liegend I.** *Part. Präs.* → *dazwischen liegen;* **II.** *Adj.* intervening; *die* **~en** *Ereignisse* the events that occurred in the meantime; **~reden** *v/i.* (*trennb., hat -ge-*) **1.** interrupt (*j-m* s.o.), butt in; **2.** (*sich einmischen*) meddle, interfere; **~rufen** (*unreg., trennb., hat -ge-*) **I.** *v/t.* shout *s.th.* (in between); **II.** *v/i.* interrupt a speech *etc.* with shouts, shout

dazwischen|schalten *v/t.* (*trennb., hat -ge-*) **1.** *Tel.:* fig. call (*od.* bring) *s.o., s.th. etc.* in; **2.** *Etech.:* insert; **~schieben** (*unreg., trennb., hat -ge-*) **I.** *v/t.* **1.** *räumlich:* put (*od.* insert) in between; *knapper:* squeeze in between; **2.** *zeitlich:* fit (*od.* squeeze) in; **II.** *v/refl.:* *anstatt sich hinten anzustellen, hat er sich einfach irgendwo dazwischengeschoben* instead of joining the queue (*Am.* line) at the back, he just pushed in somewhere; **~schlagen** *v/i.* (*unreg., trennb., hat -ge-*) *umg.* (*od.* wade) in, use force to break up a fight *etc.;* **~stehen** *v/i.* (*unreg., trennb., hat* **/** *südd., österr., schw. ist*) **1.** *räumlich:* stand among(st) them; **2.** *zwischen zwei Extremen:* be (*od.* stand) in the middle (*od.* between);

D

3. *fig. störend*: stand in the way, be obstructive; **~treten** *v/i. (unreg., trennb., ist -ge-); fig.* interfere; *(sich einschalten)* step in, intervene; **~werfen** *(unreg., trennb., hat -ge-)* **I.** *v/t. fig. (Frage etc.)* throw in; **II.** *v/refl.* jump in, try and break up the fight

DB *f; -, kein Pl.; Abk. (bis 1993 Deutsche Bundesbahn)* German Federal Railways; *(ab 1994 Deutsche Bahn AG)* German Rail; *(Deutsche Bundesbank)* the (German *od.* Deutsche) Bundesbank

DDR *f; -; Abk., hist. (Deutsche Demokratische Republik)* GDR (= German Democratic Republic), East Germany *umg.*; **~Bürger** *m,* **~Bürgerin** *f* citizen of the GDR, East German (citizen) *umg.*; **~Regierung** *f* GDR *(od.* East German *umg.)* government

D-Dur *n; -, kein Pl.; Mus.* D major; **~Tonleiter** *f* D major scale

dealen [ˈdiːlən] *v/i. umg.* push drugs; **Dealer** *m; -s, -,* **Dealerin** *f; -, -nen* drug dealer, pusher *umg.*

Debakel *n; -s, - débâcle,* debacle

Debatte *f; -, -n* debate *(auch Parl.),* discussion *(über + Akk.* on); **zur ~ stehen** be up for discussion; **zur ~ stellen** put *s.th.* forward for discussion, open *s.th.* up to debate; **das steht hier nicht zur ~** that's not the issue here

debattieren I. *v/t.* debate, discuss; **II.** *v/i.* debate; **über etw.** *(Akk.)* **~** debate *(od.* discuss) s.th.

Debet *n; -s, -s; Wirts.* debit; **~saldo** *m* balance due

debil *Adj. Med.* mentally subnormal, feeble-minded; **Debilität** *f; -, kein Pl.* debility, feeble-mindedness

debitieren *v/t. Wirts.* charge, debit; **j-m e-n Betrag ~** charge a sum to s.o. 's account, debit s.o. with a sum

Debitoren *Pl. Wirts., Bilanz:* accounts receivable

Debüt *n; -s, -s* debut, début; **sein → geben → debütieren; Debüt... im Subst.** debut ..., first ...

Debütant *m; -en, -en* débutant, debutant; **Debütantin** *f; -, -nen* débutante, debutante; **Debütant(inn)enball** *m* debutantes' *(od.* débutantes') ball; **debütieren** *v/i.* make one's debut *od.* début *(als* as)

Dechant [dɛˈçant] *m; -en, -en; kirchl.* dean

dechiffrierbar [deʃɪˈfriːɐ̯baːɐ̯] *Adj.* decipherable; **dechiffrieren** *v/t.* decipher, decode

Deck *n; -(e)s, -s* **1.** *Naut.* deck; **an** *od.* **auf ~** on deck; **alle Mann an ~!** all hands on deck!; **unter** *od.* **von ~ gehen** go below (deck); **2.** *e-s Busses:* **oberes ~** top *(od.* upper) deck; **3.** *(Parkdeck)* level; **4.** *(Kassettendeck)* deck

Deckadresse *f* cover address

Deckanstrich *m* top coat

Deck|bett *n* duvet, eiderdown, *Am.* comforter, *Brit. auch* (continental) quilt; **~blatt** *n* **1.** *e-r Zigarre:* wrapper; **2.** *Bot.* bract; **3.** *für Schriftstücke:* correction sheet; *durchsichtig:* overlay

Deckchen *n* small tablecloth; *(Zierdeckchen)* doily, small cloth *(od.* mat)

Decke *f; -, -n* **1.** *(Wolldecke)* blanket; *(Pferde-, Reisedecke)* rug, *Am.* blanket; *(Babydecke)* cot *(Am.* baby) blanket; *(Krabbeldecke)* activity mat; **2.** *auf Bett:* (bed)cover, bedspread; *(Federbett)* duvet, eiderdown, *Am.* comforter, *Brit. auch* (continental) quilt; *(Steppdecke)* quilt, *Am. auch* comforter; *(Tagesdecke)* bedspread,

coverlet; **unter die ~ kriechen** *od.* **schlüpfen** crawl under the cover(s), pull the cover(s) up over one's head; **unter einer ~ stecken mit j-m** *umg. fig.* be hand in glove *(od.* be in league *od.* in cahoots) with s.o.; **sich nach der ~ strecken** *umg. fig.* cut one's coat according to one's cloth, make the best of it; **3.** *(Tischdecke)* tablecloth; **4.** *(Zimmerdecke)* ceiling; **ein Raum mit hoher/niedriger ~** a room with a high/low ceiling, a high-/low-ceilinged room; **(vor Freude) (bis) an die ~ springen** *umg. fig.* jump for joy, be over the moon; **an die ~ gehen** *umg. fig.* hit the roof, blow one's top; **5.** *(Abdeckung)* cover(ing); *(Plane)* awning, tarpaulin; *(Hülle)* envelope; *(Überzug)* lining; **6.** *(Bedeckendes)* cover(ing); *(Schicht)* layer, coat; *aus Eis:* sheet; *aus Schnee:* blanket; *(Oberfläche, Straßenbelag etc.)* surface; **7.** *Jägerspr.* skin; **e-m Reh die ~ abziehen** skin a deer; **8.** *Mus., e-r Geige, Gitarre etc.:* soundboard, belly

Deckel *m; -s, -* **1.** lid, cover; *von Gefäß:* lid, top; *(Kronenkorken)* (crown) cap *(od.* cork), stopper; *(Schraubdeckel)* screw top (lid); *zum Schieben:* sliding lid; *zum Aufklappen:* cap, flap; **2.** *e-s Buchs:* cover; *e-r Uhr:* (watch) cover; *Klavier:* lid, top; *Orgelpfeife:* stopper, tampion; *Blasinstrumente:* cup; **3.** *umg. fig. pej. od. hum.* (Hut) lid; **eins auf den ~ kriegen** get a clip (a)round the ears *(od.* a clout); *fig.* get a real ticking-off *(Am.* dressing-down); **4.** *(Bierdeckel)* beer-mat, *Am.* coaster; **5.** *Bot., Zool.* operculum

Deckel... *im Subst.* with a lid *(nachgestellt)*

deckeln *v/t.* **1.** *(Dosen)* put a *(od.* the) lid on; *(Waben)* cover *(od.* seal) with wax; **2.** *umg. fig.: j-n ~ (scharf kritisieren)* take s.o. to task, tear a strip off s.o.; **3.** *Wirts., umg. (Kostenobergrenzen setzen)* cap, limit, impose an upper limit on

decken I. *v/t.* **1.** *(Dach)* cover; *(Haus)* roof; *mit Ziegeln:* tile; *mit Schiefer:* slate; *mit Schindeln:* shingle; *mit Stroh:* thatch; **2.** *(Tuch etc.)* put, spread *(über + Akk.* over); **3.** *(schützen)* cover, protect *(auch Mil., Schach etc.); durch Schutzschild etc.:* shield *(alle auch sich* o.s.); **4.** *fig. (j-n, j-s Flucht, Fehler etc.)* cover (up) for; → **Rücken** 1; **5.** *Wirts. (Bedarf, Kosten etc.)* cover, meet; *(Bedarf) auch* satisfy; **der Scheck ist nicht gedeckt** the cheque *(Am.* check) isn't covered; **wird der Schaden von der Versicherung gedeckt?** will the insurance cover the damage?; *fig.* → **Bedarf.** **6.** *Zool.* cover, *Am.* service; **eine Stute ~ lassen** have a mare served *(od.* covered, *Am.* serviced); **7.** *Kartenspiel, bes. Bridge:* cover (with a higher card); **8.** *geh.* → **bedecken; II.** *v/i.* **1.** **den Tisch ~** lay *(od.* set) the table; **es ist gedeckt** dinner *etc.* is served; **2.** *Sport* mark, *bes. Am.* cover; *Boxen:* cover (up); *(etw.)* guard; *Fußball etc.:* cover; **III.** *v/i. Farbe etc.:* cover; **IV.** *v/refl.* **1.** *(sich schützen)* cover o.s., protect o.s. *(auch Mil., Schach etc.); durch Schutzschild etc.:* shield o.s.; *Boxen:* guard o.s.; **2.** *Math.* coincide, be congruent *(mit* with); **3.** *fig.: Ansichten, Aussagen etc.:* correspond, tally; *exakt:* be identical *(alle: mit* with); → **gedeckt**

Decken|balken *m* ceiling beam *(od.* joist); **~beleuchtung** *f* ceiling lamp(s

Pl.); **~gemälde** *n* ceiling fresco; **~strahler** *m* uplighter

Deck|farbe *f* body *(od.* opaque) colo(u)r, topcoat (paint); **~feder** *f Zool.* deck feather, cover; **~flügel** *m Zool., Käfer:* wing case *(od.* cover); **~haar** *n* top hair

Deckhengst *m* stallion, stud

Deck|mantel *m,* **~mäntelchen** *n* cover; **unter dem ~ der Freundschaft** in the guise of friendship; **~name** *m* alias, assumed name; *e-s Schriftstellers:* pseudonym, pen name, nom de plume; *e-s Spions etc.:* code name

Deck|offizier *m Naut. etwa* warrant officer; **~passagier** *m,* **~passagierin** *f* deck passenger

Deck|platte *f* cover plate; *aus Stein:* covering slab

Deckschicht *f* top *(od.* surface) layer; *von Straße:* surface

Deckstation *f Agr.* stud (farm)

Deckung *f* **1.** *(Schutz, auch Mil.)* cover, shelter; *(Tarnung)* camouflage; *(Feuerschutz)* covering fire; **j-m ~ geben** cover s.o., give s.o. cover; **in ~ gehen** take cover **(vor + Dat.** from); **2.** *Sport* marking, *Am.* covering; **3.** *Sport (Verteidiger)* defen|ce *(Am.* -se); *Boxen:* guard; *Schach etc.:* cover, guard; **4.** *Sport (Hintermannschaft)* defen|ce *(Am.* -se); **5.** *fig. (Vertuschung)* hushing *(od.* covering) up, cover-up; **6.** *Wirts., der Kosten etc.:* cover; *(Zahlung)* payment; *(Sicherheit)* security; *der Währung:* backing; *(Mittel)* funds *Pl.;* **zur ~ der Nachfrage/Unkosten** to meet the demand / to cover the costs; **~ e-s Verlustes** making up a loss; **7.** *Math.* coincidence, congruence; **8.** *fig. (Übereinstimmung)* correspondence

Deckungsbeitrag *m Wirts. e-s Buches etc.:* contribution margin, profit contribution, variable gross margin

Deckungsfehler *m Sport* case of bad marking *(bes. Am.* covering); **er hat einen ~ begangen** he failed to mark *s.o. (od.* pick *s.o.* up)

deckungsgleich *Adj.* **1.** *(übereinstimmend)* identical; **2.** *Math.* congruent

Deckungs|grenze *f Wirts.* cover limit; **~kapital** *n* covering funds *Pl.*

deckungslos *Adj.* uncovered; **~es Gelände** open ground

Deckungs|loch *n umg.,* **~lücke** *f* **1.** *Mil.* foxhole; *bei Fußball:* gap in the marking; **2.** *Wirts.* deficit, shortfall, hole in the budget; **~spieler** *m,* **~spielerin** *f Sport* defender; **~summe** *f Wirts.* sum insured; **~zusage** *f Wirts.* cover(ing) note, *Am.* binder

Deckweiß *n* whitener

decodieren *etc.* → **dekodieren** *etc.*

Deduktion *f; -, -en* deduction; **deduktiv** *Adj.* deductive

Deeskalation *f; -, -en* de-escalation; **deeskalieren** *v/i.* de-escalate

de facto *Adv.* de facto; **De-facto-...** *im Subst.* de facto ...

Defäkation *f; -, -en; Med.* defecation

Defätismus *m; -, kein Pl.; geh.* defeatism; **Defätist** *m; -en, -en,* **Defätistin** *f; -, -nen* defeatist; **defätistisch** *Adj.* defeatist

defekt *Adj.* faulty; *(beschädigt)* damaged; **„~“ Schild:** "out of order"; **Defekt** *m; -(e)s, -e* fault; *Psych., Med.* defect, deficiency; **e-n ~ haben** *Tech.* be faulty

defensiv I. *Adj.* defensive, non-aggressive; **II.** *Adv.:* **sich ~ verhalten** be on the defensive; **Defensive** *f; -, -n; Mil.*

defensive; *Sport* defensive (play); *in der* ~ on the defensive; *j-n in die* ~ *drängen* force s.o. onto the defensive
Defensiv|krieg *m Mil.* defensive war(-fare); ~**spiel** *n Sport* defensive play; ~**taktik** *f* defensive tactic; ~**waffe** *f* defensive weapon
defilieren *v/i.* march past; **Defiliermarsch** *m Mus.* parade march
definieren I. *v/t.* define; *neu* ~ redefine; *etw. genau(er)* ~ define s.th. (more) precisely; **II.** *v/refl.*: *sich durch* od. *über j-n/etw.* ~ define (*od.* describe) o.s. through s.o. / in terms of s.th.; *es lässt sich nicht* (*gut*) ~ it defies (*od.* eludes) (easy) definition; **Definition** *f*; -, *-en* definition
definitiv I. *Adj.* **1.** (*bestimmt*) definite, positive; **2.** (*endgültig*) definitive, final; **II.** *Adv.* **1.** (*bestimmt*) definitely, positively, for certain; ~ *zusagen* give one's word, make a firm acceptance; **2.** (*endgültig*) definitively, finally; *etw.* ~ *entscheiden* make a final decision on s.th.; ~ *feststehen* be absolutely final
Defizit *n*; -(e)s, -e *Wirts.* deficit; **defizitär** *Adj.* in deficit; ~*er Haushalt etc.* deficit budget *etc.*; **Defizitfinanzierung** *f* deficit spending
Deflation *f*; -, *-en*; *Wirts.* deflation; **deflationär** *Adj.*, **deflationistisch** *Adj.* deflationary; **Deflationspolitik** *f* deflationary policy
Defloration *f*; -, *-en*; *Med.* defloration; **deflorieren** *v/t.* deflower
Deformation *f* **1.** deformation (*auch Med.*); (*Verzerrung*) distortion; **2.** *Med.* (*Missbildung*) deformity; *des Gesichts*: disfigurement; (*Verstümmelung*) mutilation; **deformieren** *v/t.* deform; *Med. auch* disfigure; (*verstümmeln*) mutilate; *Phys., Tech. auch* distort
deftig *Adj. umg.* **1.** *Essen*: solid, substantial; *ein* ~*es Essen auch* a good square meal; **2.** *Witz etc.*: coarse, crude, near the knuckle; **3.** *Kritik, Ohrfeige*: sharp, hefty; *Abfuhr, Niederlage*: sound, thorough; **4.** *Preis*: steep
Degen *m*; -s, - sword; *Fechten*: épée
Degeneration *f*; *nur Sg.* degeneration; **Degenerationserscheinung** *f* sign of degeneration; **degenerieren** *v/i.* degenerate (*zu* into); **degeneriert I.** *P.P.* → *degenerieren*; **II.** *Adj.* degenerate; *Adlige, Macht etc.*: *auch* effete
Degen|fechten *n* épée fencing; ~**fechter** *m*, ~**fechterin** *f* épéeist; ~**klinge** *f* sword (*od.* rapier) blade
degradieren *v/t. Mil.* demote (*zu* to the rank of); *fig.* degrade (*zu* to)
Degression *f*; -, *-en*; *Wirts.* degression, progressive reduction (in costs); **degressiv** *Adj.* degressive; ~*e Abschreibung* declining-balance depreciation
dehnbar *Adj.* **1.** flexible, elastic; *Stoff*: stretch(y); *Phys.* expansible; *Metall*: malleable; **2.** *fig.*: ~*er Begriff etc.* elastic term *etc.*; **3.** *der Vokal ist* ~ can be lengthened; **Dehnbarkeit** *f* elasticity; expansibility; malleability; → *dehnbar*
dehnen I. *v/t.* **1.** (*Glieder, Gummiband, Pullover etc.*) stretch; (*in die Länge ziehen*) *auch* extend, lengthen; (*ausweiten*) *auch* widen; *Phys.* (*Volumen vergrößern*) expand; *Med.* dilate; *übermäßig*: distend; **2.** (*Vokale*) lengthen; (*Wörter*) drawl; (*Ton*) hold; → *gedehnt*; **3.** *fig.* (*Begriff, Recht etc.*) stretch, extend, make s.th. flexible (*od.* elastic); *Gespräch etc. in die Länge* ~ spin out, drag out; **II.** *v/refl.* **1.** *Mate-*

rial: stretch; *in die Länge*: *auch* extend, lengthen; *in die Breite*: *auch* widen; *Phys., Volumen*: expand; **2.** *Person*: stretch (o.s.); **3.** *fig. Landschaft etc.*: extend, stretch out; *Zeit, Gespräch etc.*: drag on; *die Straße dehnte sich endlos* the street went (*od.* seemed to go) on forever
Dehnübung *f Sport* stretching exercise
Dehnung *f* **1.** stretch(ing); *der Länge nach*: lengthening; (*Weitung*) widening; *Phys.* expansion; **2.** *Ling.* lengthening; **3.** *fig. e-s Begriffs etc.*: elasticity, flexibility
Dehnungs|fuge *f Tech.* expansion joint; ~**zeichen** *n Ling.* length mark
dehydrieren *v/t. Chem.* dehydrate
Deibel *m*; -s, -; *nordd. umg.* → *Teufel*
Deich *m*; -(e)s, -e dike, dyke; *e-s Flusses*: embankment, *Am. auch* levee; ~**bruch** *m Vorgang*: bursting of a dike; *Stelle*: breach (*Am. auch* break) in a dike; ~**krone** *f* dike top (*od.* summit)
Deichsel *f*; -, *-n* pole, shaft; (*Gabeldeichsel*) thills *Pl.*; *für Schlepperzug*: drawbar, towbar; **deichseln** *v/t. umg.* manage; *ich werde das schon* ~ I'll see to it all right, I'll wangle it somehow
Deichverband *m* association of owners of diked land
dein I. *Poss. Pron.* **1.** *adjektivisch*: your; *e-r* ~ *Freunde* a friend of yours, one of your friends; *im Brief*: *viele Grüße*, ~ *Martin* with best wishes, yours Martin; ~ *blöder Hund umg.* that stupid dog of yours; **2.** *substantivisch*: yours; ~*er*, ~*e*, ~*(e)s*, *der* (*die, das*) ~*e* yours; *der/die Deine* od. ~*e* (*dein Mann/d-e Frau*) your husband/wife, your spouse; *du und die Deinen* od. ~*en* (*d-e Familie*) you and yours; *du musst das Deine* od. ~*e* (*dazu*) *beitragen* od. *tun*(, *damit ...*) you'll have to do your bit (*od.* share, *Am. auch* part) (for it ...); **II.** *pers. Pron. altm.* od. *poet.* → *deiner*
deiner *pers. Pron.* (*Gen. von du*) of you; *ich werde* ~ *gedenken* I shall remember you
deinerseits *Adv.* for (*od.* on) your part
deines|gleichen *Pron.* people like yourself, (the) likes of you, your sort, you and your ilk
deinet|wegen *Adv.* **1.** (*wegen dir*) because of you, on your account; (*dir zuliebe*) because of you, for your sake; **2.** (*in d-r Sache*) on your behalf; ~**willen** *Adv.*: (*um*) ~ for your sake; (*in d-r Sache*) on your behalf
deinige → *dein* I 2
Deinstallation *f*; -, *-en*; *EDV* de-installation; **deinstallieren** *vt/i.* de-install
Déjà-vu-Erlebnis [deʒaˈvyː-] *n Psych.* feeling (*od.* sense) of déjà vu, déjà vu experience
de jure *Adv.* de jure; **De-jure-...** *im Subst.* de jure ...
Deka *n*; -(s), -; *österr.*: *zehn* ~ *Käse* 100 gram(me)s of cheese
Dekade *f*; -, *-n* **1.** (*10 Jahre*) decade; **2.** (period of) ten days (*od.* ten weeks, ten months) *Pl.*
dekadent *Adj.* decadent; **Dekadenz** *f*; -, *kein Pl.* decadence; **Dekadenzerscheinung** *f* sign of decadence
Dekalog *m*; -(e)s, *kein Pl.*; *Reli.* Decalogue
Dekan *m*; -s, -e; *kath. und Univ.* dean; *ev.* superintendent; **Dekanat** *n*; -s, -e **1.** *Univ.* dean's office, office of the dean; **2.** *kath.* deanery; *ev.* superintendent's district

dekantieren *v/t.* (*Wein etc.*) decant
Deklamation *f*; -, *-en*; *geh.* declamation, recitation; *fig. auch* harangue; **deklamatorisch** *Adj.* declamatory; *pej.* empty, rhetorical; **deklamieren** *vt/i.* declaim, spout *umg.*
Deklaration *f*; -, *-en* declaration; **deklarieren** *v/t.* declare
deklassieren *v/t.* downgrade (*zu* to); *Sport* outclass
Deklination *f*; -, *-en* **1.** *Ling.* declension; *schwache/starke* ~ strong/weak declension; **2.** *Astron., Phys.* declination; **deklinierbar** *Adj.* declinable; **deklinieren** *v/t.* decline
dekodieren *v/t.* decode; **Dekodierung** *f* decoding
Dekolleté, Dekolletee [dekɔlˈteː] *n*; -s, -s low neckline, décolletage, décolleté; *tiefes* ~ plunging neckline; **dekolletiert** *Adj.* low-cut, décolleté; *tief* ~ very low-cut; rather revealing *umg. hum.*
Dekompression *f*; -, *-en*; *fachspr.* decompression
dekontaminieren *v/t.* decontaminate
Dekor *m*, *n*; -s, -s *und* -e decoration; *Theat.* décor, scenery, set; **Dekorateur** [dekoraˈtøːɐ] *m*; -s, -e, **Dekorateurin** *f*; -, *-nen* (painter and) decorator; *von Schaufenstern*: window dresser; *Theat.* scene painter; (*Bühnenbildner*) set designer; **Dekoration** *f*; -, *-en* decoration (*auch Orden*); *Schaufenster*: window display; *Theat.* set(s *Pl.*); **dekorativ** *Adj.* decorative; **dekorieren** *v/t.* decorate (*auch mit e-m Orden*); (*Schaufenster*) *auch* dress
Dekret *n*; -(e)s, -e decree; **dekretieren** *v/t.* decree, pass a decree
Delegation *f*; -, *-en* delegation
Delegationsmitglied *n* member of the (*od.* a) delegation
delegieren *vt/i.* (*j-n, Aufgaben*) delegate (*an + Akk.* to); **Delegierte** *m*, *f*; -n, -n delegate
delektieren *v/refl. geh.*: *sich an etw.* (*Dat.*) ~ (take) delight in s.th.; *fig. pej.* gloat about s.th.
Delfin → *Delphin*[1], *Delphin*[2]; **Delfinarium** → *Delphinarium*
delikat *Adj.* **1.** (*köstlich, lecker*) delicious, exquisite; **2.** (*heikel*) delicate, ticklish; **3.** (*taktvoll*) tactful, discreet; **Delikatesse** *f*; -, *-n* **1.** (*Leckerbissen*) delicacy; **2.** *nur Sg.*; *geh.* (*Feingefühl*) tact(fulness), discretion; **Delikatessengeschäft** *n* delicatessen, deli *umg.*
Delikt *n*; -(e)s, -e offen|ce (*Am.* -se)
Delinquent *m*; -en, -en, ~**in** *f*; -, *-nen*; *geh.* offender
Delirium *n*; -s, *Delirien* delirium; *im* ~ *liegen* od. *sein* be delirious
Delle *f*; -, *-n*; *umg.* dent
Delphin[1] *m*; -s, -e; *Zool.* dolphin, porpoise
Delphin[2] (*n*); -s, *kein Pl.*; *Sport* butterfly (stroke)
Delphinarium *n*; -s, *Delphinarien* dolphinarium
Delphin|schwimmen *n*, ~**stil** *m* butterfly (stroke)
Delta *n*; -(s), -s delta; ~**flieger** *m* hang-glider; ~**flügel** *m* delta wing
dem (*Dat. Sg. von der, das*) **I.** *Art.* → *der* I; **II.** *Dem. Pron.* **1.** → *der* II; **2.** *in Wendungen*: *an* ~ *und* ~ *Ort umg.* at such and such a place; *nach* ~, *was ich gehört habe* from (*od.* according to) what I've heard; *wie* ~ *auch sei* be that as it may; **III.** *Rel. Pron.* to whom, to which, who (*od.* which) ...

D

to; *das Spielzeug, mit ~ sie gespielt hatte* the toy (which *od. Am. mst* that) she had played with (*od.* with which she had played); → *der* III
Demagoge *m; -n, -n; pej.* demagogue; **Demagogie** *f; -, -n; pej.* demagogy; **Demagogin** *f; -, -nen; pej.* demagogue; **demagogisch** *pej.* **I.** *Adj.* demagogic; **II.** *Adv.* demagogically
Demarkationslinie *f Pol.* demarcation line
demaskieren I. *v/t.* unmask; *fig. auch* expose (*als* as); **II.** *v/refl.* unmask (*od.* reveal) o.s.; *fig. auch* drop one's mask, reveal one's true identity (*od.* colo[u]rs)
Dementi *n; -s, -s* (official) denial, disclaimer; **dementieren** *v/t.* deny, disclaim
dementsprechend I. *Adj.* corresponding, *präd.* as expected; *sie machte e-e ~e Bemerkung* she made an appropriate remark; **II.** *Adv.* accordingly, correspondingly
Demenz *f; -, -en; Med.* dementia
demgegenüber *Adv.* **1.** (*im Vergleich dazu*) compared with this; **2.** (*andererseits*) on the other hand
Demission *f; -, -en; Pol.* resignation
demnach *Adv.* **1.** thus, so; **2.** (*demgemäß*) according to that
demnächst *Adv.* soon, before long; *~ stattfindend etc.* forthcoming; *~ im Kino etc.* coming soon
Demo I. *f; -, -s; umg.* (*Demonstration*) demo; **II.** *n; -s, -s; bes. EDV umg.*; (*Demonstrationsbeispiel, -version*) demo (version); **Demo|...** *im Subst. umg.* demo ...; *~band n umg.* demo tape
demobilisieren *v/t/i. Mil.* demobilize
Demodulation *f Etech.* demodulation; **demodulieren** *v/t.* demodulate
Demograph *m; -en, -en* demographer; **Demographie** *f; -, -n* demography; **Demographin** *f; -, -nen* demographer; **demographisch I.** *Adj.* demographic, population ...; **II.** *Adv.* demographically
Demokassette *f umg.* demo tape
Demokrat *m; -en, -en; Pol.* democrat
Demokratie *f; -, -n; Pol.* democracy; *~auffassung f, ~begriff m* concept of democracy; *~verständnis n: was ist das für ein ~?* what sort of understanding of (the meaning of) democracy is that?
Demokratin *f; -, -nen; Pol.* democrat; **demokratisch I.** *Adj.* democratic; **II.** *Adv.* democratically; **demokratisieren** *v/t.* democratize
Demokratisierungsprozess *m Pol.* process of democratization, democratic process
demolieren *v/t.* (*beschädigen*) damage; (*zerstören*) wreck (*auch umg. Auto etc.*); *mutwillig:* vandalize, smash up
Demonstrant *m; -en, -en, ~in f; -, -nen* demonstrator
Demonstration *f; -, -en* **1.** (*Kundgebung*) demonstration, demo *umg.* (*für/gegen* for *od.* in favo[u]r of / against); **2.** *geh.* (*Bekundung*) demonstration (+ *Gen. od.* **von** of); *von Macht, gutem Willen etc.: auch* show (of); **3.** *geh.* (*Veranschaulichung*) demonstration; *zur ~* (+ *Gen. od.* **von**) to demonstrate (*od.* illustrate) *s.th.*
Demonstrations|aufruf *m* call to protest (*od.* demonstrate), appeal for demonstration; *~flug m* demonstration flight; *~freiheit f; nur Sg.* freedom to demonstrate (*od.* hold demonstra-

tions); *~material n* demonstration (*od.* teaching) material; *~objekt n* demonstration exhibit (*od.* object), teaching aid; *~recht n; nur Sg.* right to demonstrate; *~teilnehmer m, ~teilnehmerin f* demonstrator; *~verbot n* ban on demonstrations; *~zug m* **1.** *Aktion:* demo(nstration), protest march; **2.** *Personen:* demonstrators *Pl.*; *~zweck m:* (**nur**) *zu ~en* for demonstration purposes (only)
demonstrativ I. *Adj.* **1.** (*auffallend*) ostentatious; *Schweigen etc.:* pointed; **2.** (*anschaulich*) graphic, clear; **3.** *Ling.* demonstrative; **II.** *Adv.* ostentatiously; (*aus Protest*) in protest, to make a point; *~ den Saal verlassen* walk out (in protest)
Demonstrativpronomen *n Ling.* demonstrative pronoun
demonstrieren *v/t/i.* demonstrate (*für/gegen* for *od.* in favo[u]r of / against)
Demontage [demɔnˈtaːʒə] *f; -, -n* **1.** dismantling, disassembly; **2.** *fig.* dismantling (process); **demontieren** *v/t.* **1.** dismantle; (*zerlegen*) *auch* take apart; (*entfernen*) *auch* take off; **2.** *fig.* (*Vorurteile*) break down; (*Ruf*) chip away at, damage
demoralisieren *v/t.* demoralize; (*Moral untergraben*) corrupt
Demoskop *m; -en, -en* (public) opinion pollster (*od.* researcher); **Demoskopie** *f; -, -n* **1.** *nur Sg.* public opinion research; **2.** (*Umfrage*) opinion poll; **Demoskopin** *f; -, -nen* (public) opinion pollster (*od.* researcher); **demoskopisch** *Adj.: ~es Institut* public opinion research institute
demotivieren *v/t/i.* put *s.o.* off, demotivate
Demoversion *f bes. EDV* demo version
demselben → *derselbe*
Demut *f; -, kein Pl.* humility; *in ~* with humility; **demütig** *Adj.* humble; (*unterwürfig*) submissive; **demütigen I.** *v/t.* humiliate; **II.** *v/refl.* humble o.s.; (*sich herabwürdigen*) grovel; **Demütigung** *f* humiliation
Demutsgebärde *f* submissive gesture
demzufolge *Adv.* **1.** accordingly; **2.** (*daher*) consequently
den I. *best. Art.* **1.** (*Akk. Sg. von der*) the; **2.** (*Dat. Pl. von der, die, das*) the; **II.** *Dem. Pron.* (*Akk. Sg. von der*) that; *betont: ja - ~ meinte ich!* yes, that's the one I meant!; **III.** *Rel. Pron.* (*Akk. Sg. von der*) *bei Personen:* who(m *förm.*), that; *bei Sachen:* that, which
denaturieren I. *v/t.* (*hat denaturiert*); *Chem., auch geh.* denature; **II.** *v/i.* (*ist*); *geh. Person:* degenerate (*zu* into)
denen (*Dat. Pl. von der, die, das*) **I.** *Dem. Pron.* them; *trau ~ nicht!* don't trust them!; **II.** *Rel. Pron.*; *bei Personen:* who(m), who ... to, to whom *förml.*; *bei Sachen:* that, which; *die Leute, ~ er misstraute* the people (whom) he didn't trust; *die Spielsachen, mit ~ sie gespielt hatte* the toys (which *od. Am. mst* that) she had played with (*od.* with which she had played)
Den Haag (*n*); *-s; Geog.* The Hague
Denitrifikation *f; -, -en; Bot., Chem.* denitrification
Denk|ansatz *m* (intellectual) approach; *~anstoß m: ein ~* cause (*od.* food) for thought; *das war für mich der ~* that was what gave me the idea; *~arbeit f* mental effort; *~art f* way of thinking;

(*Gesinnung*) mentality, mindset
denkbar I. *Adj.* conceivable, possible; **II.** *Adv.: in der ~ kürzesten Zeit* in the shortest possible time; *das ist ~ einfach* it's the easiest thing in the world
Denkblockade *f: e-e ~ haben* have a block, be blocked
denken; *denkt, dachte, hat gedacht* **I.** *v/t/i.* **1.** think; (*nachsinnen*) reflect; *logisch:* reason; *bei od. für sich ~* think to o.s.; *ich habe od. das war nur laut gedacht* I was just thinking aloud (*od.* out loud); *es gibt einem zu ~* it makes you think; *ich denke, also bin ich* I think, therefore I am; *der Mensch denkt, (und) Gott lenkt Sprichw.* man proposes, God disposes; **2.** (*vermuten*) think, imagine; *ich denke schon* I (should) think so; *wer hätte das gedacht!* who would have thought it; *das hättest du dir ~ können* you should have known (that); *dachte ich's mir doch!* I knew it!, I thought so (*od.* as much)!; **3.** *e-e Meinung haben:* think (*über* + *Akk.* about; *von* of); *sich* (*Dat.*) *sein Teil ~* have thoughts (*od.* opinions) of one's own, think for o.s.; *ich kann mir auch mein Teil ~* I can put two and two together; *nichts Gutes od. schlecht über j-n od. von j-m ~* think ill (*od.* badly) of s.o., have a low opinion of s.o.; **4.** *sich* (*Dat.*) *etw. ~* (*vorstellen*) imagine; *~ Sie nur!* just imagine!; *das kann ich mir ~* I can well (*od.* just) imagine; *das habe ich mir schon od. beinahe gedacht* I thought (*od.* suspected) as much; *das habe ich mir gleich gedacht* I almost thought as much from the start; *das hätte ich mir doch ~ können* I should have realized; *ich habe mir das so gedacht: ...* this is what I had in mind, I imagined it like this; *ich habe mir nichts Böses dabei gedacht* I didn't mean anything (*od.* any harm) by it; *das hast du dir so gedacht! umg.* → *denkste*; → *dabei* 8; **II.** *v/i.* **1.** *e-e Gesinnung haben:* *fortschrittlich/konservativ ~* think progressively/conservatively; *großzügig/kleinlich ~* be generous of spirit / pettyminded; *anders Denkende Pl.* people of differing viewpoints (*od.* opinions); **2.** *~ an* (+ *Akk.*) think of; (*sich erinnern an, nicht vergessen*) remember; *so lange ich ~ kann* as long (*od.* as far back) as I can remember; *denk daran!* don't forget!; *ich darf gar nicht daran ~* I it doesn't bear thinking about!; *der wird noch an mich ~!* *drohend:* I'll give him something to remember me by!, he'll have me to reckon with!; **3.** (*im Sinn haben*) have in mind, think of; *es war für dich gedacht* it was meant (*od.* intended) for you; *ans Heiraten ~* think of marrying (*od.* getting married); *er denkt daran zu* (+ *Inf.*) he's thinking of (+ *Ger.*); *er denkt gar nicht daran zu* (+ *Inf.*) he has no intention of (+ *Ger.*); *ich denke nicht daran!* I wouldn't dream of it, no way! *umg.*, not on your life *umg.*, not in a million years *umg.*; *ich muss an meine Karriere ~* I have to consider (*od.* think of) my career; *daran ist (zur Zeit) gar nicht zu ~* that's completely out of the question (at the moment)
Denken *n; -s, kein Pl.* thinking, thought; (*logisches ~*) reasoning; (*Denkart*) way of thinking
...denken *n, im Subst. oft pej.* **1.** *Wert legend auf:* attitude, way of thinking; *Erfolgs~* success-oriented attitude; *pej.*

worship of success; **Nützlichkeits~** utilitarian thinking; **2.** *in Kategorien*: way of looking at things; **Freund-Feind--Denken** "friend or foe" way of dealing with people, us-and-them attitude; **Schwarz-Weiß-Denken** black and white view of the world; **3.** *typisch für*: mentality, mind set; **Beamten~** bureaucratic mentality (*od.* logic)

denkend I. *Part.Präs.* → **denken**; **II.** *Adj.* (*vernunftbegabt*) thinking, sentient; (*vernünftig*) rational, reasonable

Denker *m*; *-s, -*, **~in** *f*; *-, -nen* thinker; **großer Denker** great thinker (*od.* mind); **Denkerstirn** *f* lofty brow

denkfähig *Adj.* intelligent, rational, capable of (logical *od.* rational) thinking; **ich bin heute nicht** (*mehr*) **~** *umg.* I can't think straight (any more) today; **Denkfähigkeit** *f* intelligence, mental capabilities *Pl.*

denkfaul *Adj.* mentally lazy; **~ sein** have a lazy mind; **sei doch nicht so ~!** *umg.* come on, get your brain working!

Denk|fehler *m* logical error, mistake in one's reasoning; **~gewohnheit** *f* (habitual) way of thinking; **~hilfe** *f* clue

Denkmal *n*; *-(e)s, Denkmäler* monument (+ *Gen.* to); (*Ehrenmal*) memorial (to); (*Standbild*) statue (of); **j-m ein ~ setzen** erect (*fig.* create) a monument to s.o.; *fig. auch* hono(u)r s.o.'s memory; **denkmalgeschützt** *Adj.* (*Gebäude*) listed (on a historic register); *Monument*: scheduled; *Baum etc.*: protected

Denkmal(s)|pflege *f* preservation of historic buildings and monuments; **~pfleger** *m*, **~pflegerin** *f* curator of historic buildings and monuments; **~schutz** *m* protection of historic buildings and monuments; **unter ~ stehen** *Gebäude*: be listed (*od.* a listed building), *Am.* be (listed) on a historic register; *Monument*: be scheduled; *Baum etc.*: be protected; **unter ~ stellen** put a preservation order on; (*Gebäude*) *auch* list; (*Monument*) *auch* schedule; **~schützer** *m*, **~schützerin** *f* preservationist

Denk|modell *n* working model, (working) hypothesis; **~pause** *f* pause for reflection (*od.* thought); **eine ~ einlegen** take a break to think things over; **~prozess** *m* thought process; **~richtung** *f* line of thought (*od.* thinking); (*Schule*) school of thought; **~schema** *n*: **in kein ~ passen** not fit into any scheme of thought; **~schrift** *f* memorandum; **~sport** *m* mental exercise; **~sportaufgabe** *f* brainteaser

denkste *Interj. umg.* (*da täuscht du dich*) that's what you think; (*da wird nichts draus*) no way!; (*das hat nicht geklappt*) no such luck

Denkungsart *f* → **Denkart**

Denk|vermögen *n* intellectual capacity; **~weise** *f* → **Denkart**

denkwürdig *Adj.* memorable (*wegen* for); **ein ~er Tag** *auch* a day to be remembered; **Denkwürdigkeit** *f* memorability, notability

Denk|zentrum *n im Gehirn*: thought cent|re (*Am.* -re); **~zettel** *m fig.* lesson; **j-m e-n ~ geben** *od.* **verpassen** *umg.* teach s.o. a lesson, give s.o. what for

denn I. *Konj.* **1.** *begründend*: because, since, for; **2.** *nach Komp.*: (*als*) than; **mehr etc. ~ je** more etc. than ever; **II.** *Adv.* **1. es sei ~**(, *dass*) unless;

2. *in Fragen, unbetont*: *mst* unübersetzt: **wie heißt du ~?** what's your name then?; **wieso ~?** why?, how come?; **was machen wir ~ jetzt?** what shall we do now?; **was ist ~?** *umg.* what's up?; *verärgert*: what (is it)?; **3.** *in Fragen, betont*: (*sonst, dann*) then; *unbetont*: **~ dann** *od.* **sonst** then; **was sollen wir ~ machen** *od.* **'dann etc. machen?** what are we supposed to do then?; **4.** *überrascht, zweifelnd etc.*: **ist er ~ so arm?** is he really that poor?; **ist das ~ zu fassen!** *umg.* that's really incredible (*od.* unbelievable)!; **5.** *umg.*; *folgernd etc.*: (*dann, nun*) then; **das war ~ doch zu viel** that was just too much, that was the limit; **6.** *nordd. zeitlich*: then; **~ man los!** off you/we go!; **na, ~ prost!** *umg.* well cheers, then!; *iro.* that's brilliant!, that's just great (*od. Am.* swell)!

dennoch *Adv.* (yet ...) still, nevertheless, nonetheless, all the same; **er wollte es ~ machen** (yet) he still wanted to do it, he wanted to do it all the same

dennschon → **wennschon** II

denselben → **derselbe**

dental *Adj.* dental; **Dentallabor** *n* dental laboratory; **Dentallaut** *m Ling.* dental

Denunziant *m*; *-en, -en*, **~in** *f*; *-, -nen*; *pej.* informer

Denunziation *f*; *-, -en*; *pej.* denunciation; **denunzieren** *v/t. pej.* inform on; **j-n bei der Polizei ~** *auch* report s.o. to the police, grass *s.o.* up *umg., Am.* fink on *s.o. umg.*

Deo *n*; *-s, -s*; *umg.*, **Deodorant** [de?odo'rant] *n*; *-s, -s und -e* deodorant; **deodori(si)erend** *Adj.* deodorant

Deo|roller *m* roll-on (deodorant); **~spray** *m, n* deodorant spray

Departement [departə'mãː] *n*; *-s, -s od. schw. -e* [departə'mɛnt] **1.** *in Frankreich*: depart(e)ment; **2.** *schw.* (*Ministerium*) ministry; (*Abteilung*) department

Dependance [depã'dãːs] *f*; *-, -n* **1.** *Wirts.* branch; **2.** *fachspr.* (*Nebengebäude*) annex(e)

depilieren *v/t.* depilate

deplaciert [depla'siːʀt] *altm.*, **deplatziert** *Adj.* out of place; *Bemerkung etc.*: *auch* misplaced

Deponie *f*; *-, -n* **1.** (refuse) tip, waste disposal site, landfill, dump; **2. wilde ~** uncontrolled (*od.* indiscriminate) dumping; **3.** *fig.* dumping ground; **~gas** *n* gas produced by decomposing waste

deponieren *v/t.* deposit, leave

Deportation *f*; *-, -en* deportation; **deportieren** *v/t.* deport; **Deportierte** *m, f*; *-n, -n* deported person, deportee

Depositen *Pl. Wirts.* deposits; **~bank** *f* deposit bank; **~geschäft** *n* deposit banking

Depot [de'poː] *n*; *-s, -s* **1.** (*Lager*) depot (*auch Mil.*); *für Waren*: warehouse; (*Aufbewahrtes*) deposits *Pl.*; *Ort: auch* depository; *in Bank*: strongroom; (*Schließfach*) safe(ty) deposit box; **2.** *Wirts. Konto*: deposit; *für Wertpapiere*: securities account; **3.** *Pharm.* depot; **4.** *Verk.* (*Bus-, Straßenbahndepot*) depot, garage; **5.** *schw.* (*Pfand*) deposit; **~auszug** *m Wirts.* statement of deposited securities; **~effekt** *m Pharm.* controlled sustained release; **~fett** *n Physiol.* adipose tissue; **~gebühr** *f Wirts.* safe custody charges; **~wirkung** *f* → **Depoteffekt**

Depp *m*; *-en und -s, -en*; *umg. pej.* idiot, twit; **deppert** *Adj. südd., österr.* (*dumm, blöd*) stupid, daft

Depression *f*; *-, -en*; *Psych., Wirts. etc.* depression; **an** *od.* **unter ~en leiden** *Psych.* suffer from depression(s); **depressiv** *Adj. Psych.* depressive; **in e-r ~en Stimmung sein** be depressed; **~ sein** *Psych.* suffer from depression, be depressive; *fig.* (*in schlechter Stimmung*) be depressed (*od.* down *umg.*)

deprimieren *v/t.* get *s.o.* down; *stärker*: depress; **deprimiert** I. *P.P.* → **deprimieren**; **II.** *Adj.* down in the dumps *umg.*, fed up *umg.*, *stärker*: depressed

Deputat *n*; *-(e)s, -e* **1.** *Wirts.* payment in kind; **2.** *Päd.* teaching load; **volles/ halbes ~ haben** *od.* **unterrichten** teach full-time/half-time

Deputation *f*; *-, -en* delegation; **deputieren** *v/t.* delegate

der I. *best. Art.* **1.** *m*; (*Nom. Sg.*) the; **~ eine ist fleißig, ~ andere faul** (the) one is hard-working, the other one is lazy; **~ Tod** death; **~ Mensch** (*alle Menschen*) man(kind), humankind; **~ arme Peter** poor Peter; **~ Peter, den ich kenne** the Peter (who *od.* that) I know; **2.** (*Gen. Sg. von die*) of the; **die Mauern ~ Stadt** *auch* the city walls; **3.** (*Dat. Sg. von die*) to the; **den Schlüssel habe ich ~ Nachbarin gegeben** I gave the key to the neighbo(u)r; **4.** (*Gen. Pl. von der, die, das*) of the; **die Ankunft ~ Kinder** *auch* the children's arrival; **II.** *Dem. Pron.* **1.** *m*; (*Nom. Sg.*) that (one), this (one); (*er*) he, it; **~ Mann hier** this man; **~ mit dem Bart** the one with the beard; **nur ~ kann das verstehen, ~ ...** only he (*od.* that man) who ... can understand it; **~ und baden gehen?** you won't catch him going swimming; **2.** (*Dat. Sg. von die*) **zu ~ und ~ Zeit** *umg.* at such and such a time; **III.** *Rel. Pron.* **1.** *m*; (*Nom. Sg.*) *bei Personen*: who, that; *bei Sachen*: which, that; **~ Bezirk, ~ e-n Teil von X bildet** the district forming part of X; **er war ~ Erste, ~ es erfuhr** he was the first to know; **jeder, ~ ...** anyone who ...; **2.** (*Dat. Sg. von die*) *bei Personen*: who(m), who ... to, to whom *förm.*; *bei Sachen*: that, which; **die Freundin, ~ ich m-e Sorgen erzählte** the friend (whom) I told about my problems (*od.* to whom I told my problems)

derart *Adv.* so; *nachgestellt*: like that; (*so sehr*) so much; (*in solchem Ausmaß*) to such an extent; **er hat ~ geschrien, dass ...** he screamed so much (*od.* loud) that ...; **ein ~ hübsches Kind** such a pretty child

derartig I. *Adj.* such; **ein ~er Fehler** a mistake like that; **es war e-e ~e Kälte** it was so cold (*od.* such a bitter cold); **ich habe nie etwas Derartiges gesagt** I have never said anything of the sort (*od.* anything like that); **II.** *Adv.* → **derart**

derb I. *Adj.* **1.** *Material*: (*rau, grob*) rough, coarse; *Leder*: tough; (*strapazierfähig*) strong, sturdy; *Schuhe*: sturdy, stout; **2.** *fig.* (*urwüchsig*) earthy; (*unfein*) crude; *Sprache*: coarse; *Leute*: uncouth; **3.** *fig.* (*unfreundlich, grob*) gruff, brusque; **4.** *Kost etc.*: solid, substantial; **5.** *Geol.* massive; **II.** *Adv.* **1.** *kritisieren etc.*: strongly; **2.** *zupacken*: roughly; **Derbheit** *f* **1.** *nur Sg.*; *Benehmen*: coarse behavio(u)r; **2. ~en Witze**: crude jokes; *Äußerungen*: crude remarks

Derby ['dɛrbi] n; -(s), -s;(Pferderennen) Derby; bei Fußball etc.: derby; → **Lokalderby**

dereinst Adv. geh. some (od. one) day

deren I. Rel. Pron. **1.** (Gen. Sg. von die) whose; bei Dingen: auch of which; **Frau Meier und ~ Sohn** Mrs(.) Meier and her son; **2.** (Gen. Pl. von der, die, das) whose; **die Anwesenden, ~ Namen ich nicht kenne** those present whose names I don't know; **die Eltern und ~ Kinder** the parents and their children; **II.** Dem. Pron. **1.** (Gen. Sg. von die) **~ erinnere ich mich nicht geh.** I don't remember her; **2.** (Gen. Pl. von der, die, das) of those (od. them); **ich habe ~ viele** altm. I have lots of those

derent|wegen Adv. for her (od. their) sake; **die Frau, ~ er s-e Frau verließ** the woman for whom he left his wife, the woman he left his wife for; **~willen** Adv.: **(um) ~ →** derentwegen

derer Dem. Pron. (Gen. Pl. von der, die, das) of those; **die Namen ~, die da waren** the names of those present

dergestalt Adv. geh. Weise: in such a way; Ausmaß: to such an extent; **~ bewaffnet etc.** thus armed etc.; → **auch derart**

dergleichen Dem. Pron. (abgek. **dgl.**) such, like that, of that kind; substantivisch: the like, such a thing, something like that; **nichts ~** no such thing, nothing of the kind; **und ~ (mehr)** and the like, and so forth

Derivat n; -(e)s, -e; Chem., Ling. derivative; **Derivativ** n; -s, -e; Ling. derivative

derjenige Dem. Pron m; des-, dem-, den-, diejenigen; Sg.: the one; Sache: auch that one; Pl.: those (ones), the ones; **~, der od. welcher** the one who; **diejenigen, die od. welche** those who, the ones who

derlei Dem. Pron. → **dergleichen**

dermaßen Adv. → **derart**

Dermatologe m; -n, -n; Med. dermatologist, skin specialist; **Dermatologie** f; -, kein Pl. dermatology; **Dermatologin** f; -, -nen dermatologist, skin specialist; **dermatologisch** Adj. dermatological

derselbe Dem. Pron. m; des-, dem-, den-, dieselben **1.** the same; Person: the same person; **er ist immer ~ geblieben** he always stayed (true to) himself; **2.** umg. (der Gleiche) the same one (od. man); **sie trugen denselben Hut** they were wearing the same hat; **3.** altm., statt pers. Pron.: **als er den Pfarrer traf, grüßte er denselben freundlich** when he met the priest he greeted him pleasantly

derselbige Dem. Pron. m; des-, dem-, den-, dieselbigen; altm. → **derselbe**

derweil(en) I. Konj. while, Brit. auch whilst; **II.** Adv. meanwhile

Derwisch m; -(e)s, -e; Reli.: (tanzender) **~** (whirling) dervish

derzeit Adv. **1.** at present, at the moment; **2.** altm. (früher) at that time, then; **derzeitige** Adj. **1.** (jetzige) present, current; **2.** (damalige) then; nachgestellt: at the time

des[1] (Gen. Sg. von der, das) **I.** best. Art. of the; **~ Langen und Breiten** geh. (ausführlichst) at great length; **~ Weiteren** (außerdem) in addition, furthermore; **II.** Dem. und Rel. Pron.; altm. → **dessen** II.; **~ ungeachtet** geh. nevertheless, notwithstanding (that etc.)

des[2], **Des** n; -, -; Mus. D flat

Desaster n; -s, -; geh. disaster; **mit e-m ~ enden** end disastrously (od. in disaster); **desaströs** Adj. geh. disastrous

Des-Dur n D flat

desensibilisieren v/t. Med., Fot. desensitize (**gegenüber** to); (j-n) harden (to)

Deserteur [dezɛr'tøːɐ] m; -s, -e; Mil. deserter; **desertieren** v/i. desert (**von** from); **zum Feind ~** run over to the enemy; **Desertion** f; -, -en desertion

desgleichen Adv. likewise, the same; (ebenso) auch similarly; **ich stand auf und mein Freund tat ~** and so did my friend

deshalb Adv. that's why, so; therefore förm.; **~ musst du nicht gleich weinen** there's no need to cry (about it); **die Lage ist ~ nicht besser** that doesn't mean to say (that) things have improved; **~, weil** because; **er tat es gerade ~** that's precisely why he did it

Design [di'zain] n; -s, -s design; **Designer** m; -s, - designer

Designer|... im Subst. designer ...; **~brille** f designer glasses; **~droge** f designer drug

Designerin f; -, -nen designer

Designermöbel Pl. designer furniture Sg.

designiert Adj. nachgestellt: designate, elect; **der ~e Präsident** the President elect

desillusionieren v/t. disillusion

Desinfektion f Med. disinfection; **Desinfektionsmittel** n disinfectant; zur Wundbehandlung: antiseptic; **desinfizieren** v/t. disinfect; **desinfizierend I.** Part. Präs. → **desinfizieren**; **II.** Adj. disinfectant; **Desinfizierung** f disinfection; von Gefässen etc. sterilization

Desinformation f Pol. disinformation

Desintegration f fachspr. disintegration

Desinteresse n; nur Sg. indifference (**an + Dat.** towards); stärker: apathy (toward[s]); **desinteressiert** Adj. uninterested (**an + Dat.** in), indifferent (to, toward[s])

Desktoppublishing, Desktop-Publishing ['dɛsktɔp'pablıʃıŋ] n; -(s), kein Pl.; EDV (abgek. **DTP**) desktop publishing (= DTP)

Desodorant etc. → **Deo** etc.

desolat Adj. geh. Zustand: wretched, desperate; Anblick: pitiable

Desorganisation f geh. **1.** breakdown of order; **2.** lack of organization; state of disarray; (Chaos) chaos

desorientiert Adj. disorient(at)ed; (verwirrt) confused; **Desorientierung** f disorientation

Desoxyribonukleinsäure f Bio., Chem. (abgek. **DNS**) deoxyribonucleic acid (= DNA)

despektierlich Adj. geh. disrespectful; stärker: contemptuous; (abfällig) disparaging

Despot m; -en, -en despot; **Despotin** f; -, -nen despot; **despotisch I.** Adj. despotic; **II.** Adv. despotically; **Despotismus** m; -, kein Pl. despotism

desselben → **dasselbe, derselbe**

dessen (Gen. Sg. von der, das) **I.** Rel. Pron. whose; Sache: auch of which; **ein Fass, ~ Boden ein Loch hat** a barrel which (Am. bes. that) has a leak in its base; **mein Bekannter und ~ Frau** my friend and his wife; **ein Raum, an ~ Ende ein Tisch steht** a room with a table at one end; **II.** Dem. Pron.: **bin ich sicher** I'm absolutely certain about that; **ist er sich ~ bewusst?** is

he aware of it?; **~ ungeachtet** notwithstanding (that), nevertheless, all the same

dessent|wegen Adv. for his sake; **das Mädchen, ~ er s-e Frau verließ** the girl for whom he left his wife; **der Stuhl, ~ er gekommen war** the chair for which he had come; **~willen** Adv.: **(um) ~ →** dessentwegen

Dessert [dɛ'seːɐ] n; -s, -s; Gastr. dessert; **als (od. zum) ~** for dessert; **~löffel** m dessertspoon; **~teller** m dessert plate; **~wein** m dessert wine

Dessin [dɛ'sɛ̃ː] n; -s, -s design, pattern

Dessous [dɛ'suː] n; - [dɛ'suːs], - [dɛ'suːs], mst Pl. (ladies) underwear Sg.; Pl. elegante: lingerie Sg.

destabilisieren v/t. Pol. destabilize

Destillat n; -(e)s, -e; Chem. distillate; **Destillation** f; -, -en distillation; **destillieren** v/t. distil(l); **Destillierkolben** m distillation (od. distilling) flask

desto Konj. (all) the; **je älter er wird, ~ besser spielt er** etc. the better he plays etc.; **je mehr ..., ~ besser** the more ... the better

destruktiv Adj. Med. und geh. destructive; **Destruktivität** f; -, kein Pl.; geh. destructiveness

deswegen Adv. → **deshalb**

Deszendent m; -en, -en; Astron., Astrol. descendant

Detail [de'tai] n; -s, -s; geh. detail; **die kleinen ~s** the finer points, the fine details; **bis ins kleinste ~** (down) to the last detail; → **Teufel** 3; **~frage** f **1.** (treffende Frage) penetrating question; **2.** (Sache) matter (od. question) of detail

detailgenau Adj. accurate in every detail; **detailgetreu** Adj. präd. od. nachgestellt: accurate in every detail; **Detailkenntnis** f; mst Pl. detailed knowledge

detaillieren [deta'jiːrən] v/t. geh. specify; **detailliert I.** P.P. → **detaillieren**; **II.** Adj. detailed

Detailschilderung f detailed account

Detektei f; -, -en detective agency, private investigators Pl.

Detektiv m; -s, -e (private) detective; **(den) ~ spielen** fig. play the sleuth (od. detective); **~büro** n → **Detektei**

Detektivin f; -, -nen (private) detective; **detektivisch** Adj. detective; **mit ~em Scharfsinn** with the keen perception of a detective

Detektivroman m detective story (od. novel); Koll. auch detective fiction

Detektor m; -s, -en; Tech., Funk. detector

determinieren v/t. geh., fachspr. determine; **Determiniertheit** f geh., fachspr. determined nature, determinacy

Detonation f; -, -en detonation

Detonationsdruck m force of the blast

detonieren v/i. detonate

Deubel m; -s, -; Dial. → **Teufel**

deucht, deuchte → **dünken**

Deut m: **keinen od. nicht einen ~ wert** not worth a penny; **(um) keinen ~ besser** not the slightest bit better

deutbar Adj. (auslegbar) interpretable; (erklärbar) explainable; **es ist nicht anders ~** it can't be explained (od. interpreted) any other way

deuteln v/i. pej.: **daran gibt es nichts zu ~** there are no two ways about it, there are no ifs and buts about it umg.

deuten I. v/i. **1.** point (**auf j-n/etw.** at s.o./s.th.; **nach Norden, unten** etc. to);

D

2. *fig.*: **~ auf** (+ *Akk.*) point to, indicate, suggest; (*ankündigen*) point to(-ward[s]); **alles deutet darauf, dass es ein Unfall war** all the signs indicate (*od.* evidence indicates) that it was an accident; **II.** *v/t.* (*auslegen*) interpret; (*erklären*) explain; (*Traum, Zukunft*) *auch* read; **falsch ~** misinterpret

deutlich I. *Adj.* **1.** *Ahnung, Erinnerung, Gefühl etc.*: clear, distinct; *Fortschritt, Unterschied*: *auch* marked; (*merklich*) noticeable; **2.** *Aussprache*: clear, intelligible; *Schrift*: legible; **3.** (*eindeutig*) clear, plain; *Antwort, Worte*: plain; (*unverblümt*) blunt, plainspoken; **~er Wink** broad hint; **etw. ~ machen** make s.th. clear (*od.* plain) (+ *Dat.* to); **j-m etw. ~ machen** *auch* explain s.th. to s.o.; *weitS.*: drive s.th. home to s.o.; **sehr ~ werden** not pull any punches, talk straight with *s.o. umg.*; **muss ich noch ~er werden?** am I making myself understood?, have I not made myself clear enough?; **e-e ~e Sprache sprechen** *Person*: not to mince matters (*od.* one's words); *Sache*: speak volumes; **II.** *Adv.* → I; **~ besser** *etc.* much better *etc.*; **um es ganz ~ zu sagen** to put it quite bluntly, not to put too fine a point on it; **habe ich mich ~ genug ausgedrückt?** have I made myself understood (*od.* clear)?

Deutlichkeit *f* **1.** *nur Sg.* clearness, distinctness *etc.*; → **deutlich** I; **etw. in** *od.* **mit aller ~ sagen** put s.th. quite bluntly; **an ~ nichts zu wünschen übrig lassen** leave no room for doubt; **2. j-m ein paar ~en sagen** tell s.o. a few home truths, not mince one's words

deutsch I. *Adj.* **1.** German; **~ reden** talk (in) German; *umg. fig.* not mince matters (*od.* one's words), tell it like it is; **der ~e Michel** the simple honest German; **~e Schrift** German (*od.* Sütterlin) script; **die ~e Schweiz** German-speaking Switzerland; **2.** *in Bezeichnungen großgeschrieben*: **Deutsche Bahn** (*abgek.* **DB**) German Rail; **die Deutsche Bucht** *Geog.* the German Bight; **Deutsche Demokratische Republik** (*abgek.* **DDR**) *hist.* German Democratic Republic; **Deutsche Lebens-Rettungs-Gesellschaft** (*abgek.* **DLRG**) German Life Saving Society; **Deutsche Mark** (*abgek.* **DM**) *hist.* the (German) Mark, the Deutschmark; **Deutsches Reich** *hist.* the German Reich (*od.* Empire); **II.** *Adv.*: **~ gesinnt sein** think of o.s. as (a) German, feel a kinship with Germans

Deutsch *n*; *-en*; *Ling.* German; **das ~e** the German language; **~ sprechend** (*der Sprache mächtig*) German-speaking; **sprechen Sie ~?** do you speak German?; **sie kann** *od.* **spricht/versteht kein ~** she can't speak German / she doesn't understand German (at all); **das heißt auf** *od.* **zu ~ ...** that is called ... in German; *fig.* that is to say: ...; **auf** (**gut**) **~** (**gesagt**) *fig.* in plain English, to put it plainly

Deutschamerikaner *m*, **~in** *f* German--American; **deutschamerikanisch** *Adj.* German-American

Deutscharbeit *f schriftliche Prüfung*: German test

deutsch-deutsch *Adj. hist.* German--German, East-West German

Deutsche *m, f; -n, -n* German, *weiblich auch*: German woman (*od.* girl *etc.*); **er/sie ist ~r/~** he/she's (a) German

Deutschen|feind *m*, **~feindin** *f* German-

manophobe, anti-German; **~freund** *m*, **~freundin** *f* Germanophile; **~hasser** *m*, **~hasserin** *f* Germanophobe

deutschfeindlich *Adj.* anti-German, Germanophobic

deutsch-französisch *Adj.* Franco--German; **der Deutsch-Französische Krieg** *hist.* (*1870/71*) the Franco-Prussian War

deutsch-freundlich *Adj.* Germanophilic, pro-German

Deutsch|kenntnisse *Pl.* knowledge of German *Sg.*; **~kurs** *m* German course, German lessons *Pl.*

Deutschland (*n*); *-s, h ist. -s; Geog.* Germany; **~bild** *n* image of the Germans; **~frage** *f hist.* German question; **~lied** *n*; *nur Sg.* German national anthem

Deutschlandpolitik *f* **1.** *hist.* intra-German policy; **2.** *Innenpolitik*: domestic (*od.* home) policy; **3.** *des Auslands*: policy towards Germany; **deutschlandpolitisch** *Adj.*: **der ~e Sprecher der Partei** the party's speaker for intra-German affairs

Deutschlandreise *f nach Deutschland*: trip to Germany; *Rundreise*: tour of Germany

Deutsch|lehrer *m*, **~lehrerin** *f* German teacher; **~national** *Adj. hist.* German National; **~note** *f Päd.* German mark; **~schweiz** *f schw.* German-speaking Switzerland; **~schweizer** *m*, **~schweizerin** *f schw.* German-speaking Swiss (person)

deutsch|sprachig *Adj. attr.* **1.** *Zeitschrift etc.*: German-language ...; **die ~e Literatur** German literature; **2.** (*Person*) German-speaking

deutschstämmig *Adj.* ethnic German, of German origin

Deutschstunde *f Päd.* German class (*od.* lesson)

Deutschtum *n*; *-s, kein Pl.*; (*Wesensart*) Germanness; (*Volkszugehörigkeit*) German nationality; (*die Deutschen*) Germans *Pl.*; **Deutschtümelei** *f*; *-, -en; pej.* jingoistic hyper-Germanness

Deutschunterricht *m* German lesson(s *Pl.*) *od.* class(es *Pl.*); *das Lehren*: teaching of German

Deutung *f* (*Auslegung*) interpretation; (*Erklärung*) explanation; **falsche ~** misinterpretation; **Deutungsversuch** *m* attempt at (*od.* to make an) interpretation

Devise *f*; *-, -n* motto; **als oberste ~ gilt: Ruhe bewahren** the most important thing is to keep calm

Devisen *Pl.* **1.** → **Devise**; **2.** *Wirts.* foreign exchange (*od.* currency) *Sg.*; **~abkommen** *n* foreign exchange agreement; **~beschränkungen** *Pl.* foreign exchange restrictions; **~bestimmungen** *Pl.* currency regulations; **~bringer** *m*; *-s, -; umg.* currency (*od.* foreign exchange) earner; **~einnahmen** *Pl.* currency receipts; **~knappheit** *f* exchange stringency, shortage of foreign exchange; **~kurs** *m* rate of exchange; **~makler** *m*, **~maklerin** *f* (foreign) exchange broker; **~notierung** *f* quotation of foreign exchange rates; **~reserven** *Pl.* foreign exchange reserves; **~schmuggel** *m* currency smuggling; **~vergehen** *n* currency offen|ce (*Am.* -se), breach of exchange control regulations; **~verkehr** *m* foreign exchange transactions *Pl.*

Devon *n*; *-(s), kein Pl.*; *Geol.*: **das ~** the Devonian (period)

devot *Adj. geh.* **1.** *pej.* obsequious, ser-

vile; **2.** *altm.* humble, deferential; **Devotionalien** *Pl. Reli.* devotional objects

Dextrose *f*; *-, kein Pl.*; *Chem.* dextrose

Dezember *m*; *-s, -, mst Sg.*; (*abgek.* **Dez.**) December; → **April**

dezent *Adj.* **1.** *Lächeln, Verhalten etc.*: discreet, unobtrusive; **2.** *Farbe, Licht*: soft, subdued; *Musik*: gentle, quiet; **3.** *Kleidung*: tasteful; *Geschmack*: refined; *Parfüm*: subtle

dezentral *Adj. geh.* decentralized; **dezentralisieren** *v/t.* decentralize; **Dezentralisierung** *f* decentralization

Dezernat *n*; *-(e)s, -e* department; → **Morddezernat**, **Rauschgiftdezernat** *etc.*; **Dezernent** *m*; *-en, -en*, **Dezernentin** *f*; *-, -nen; Amtsspr.* department head

Dezibel *n*; *-s, -; Phys.* (*abgek.* **dB**) decibel

dezidiert *geh.* **I.** *Adj. Forderungen etc.*: firm; **II.** *Adv.* decidedly

Deziliter *m, n* (*abgek.* **dl**) decilit|re (*Am.* -er)

dezimal *Adj.* decimal; **Dezimalbruch** *m* decimal

Dezimal|komma *n* *Math.* decimal point; **~rechnung** *f* decimals *Pl.*; **~stelle** *f* decimal (place); **auf zwei ~n genau** to two decimal places; **~system** *n* decimal system; *Maße und Gewichte*: *auch* metric system; **auf das ~ umstellen** (*Währung*) decimalize; *ohne Objekt*: go decimal; **~währung** *f* decimal currency; **~zahl** *f* decimal

Dezimeter *m, n* (*abgek.* **dm**) decimet|re (*Am.* -er)

dezimieren *v/t.* decimate; **Dezimierung** *f* decimation

DFB *m*; *-, kein Pl.*; *Abk.* (**Deutscher Fußball-Bund**) German Football Association

DGB *m*; *-, kein Pl.*; *Abk.* (**Deutscher Gewerkschafts-Bund**) German Trade Union Federation

d.Gr. *Abk.* (**der Große**) the Great

d.h. *Abk.* (**das heißt**) i.e.

d.i. *Abk.* (**das ist**) i.e.

Dia *n*; *-s, -s; Fot.* slide; **~s machen** take slides

Diabetes *m*; *-, kein Pl.*; *Med.* diabetes; **Diabetiker** *m*; *-s, -*, **Diabetikerin** *f*; *-nen* diabetic; **er ist ~** he's (a) diabetic; **Diabetikerkost** *f* diabetic food; **Diabetikerzucker** *m* sugar substitute for diabetics, artificial sweetener; **diabetisch** *Adj.* diabetic

Diabetrachter *m* slide viewer

diabolisch *Adj. geh.* devilish; **diachronisch** *Adj.* diachronic

Diadem *n*; *-s, -e* diadem

Diadochenkämpfe *Pl. geh. fig.* battle *Sg.* for the succession

Diafilm *m* slide film

Diagnose *f*; *-, -n; Med.* diagnosis; **e-e ~ stellen** make a diagnosis; **die ~ lautet ...** the diagnosis is ...; **~verfahren** *n* diagnostic method; **~zentrum** *n* diagnostic clinic (*od.* centre *od. Am.* center)

Diagnostik *f*; *-, kein Pl.*; *Med.* diagnosis; **diagnostisch I.** *Adj.* diagnostic; **II.** *Adv.* diagnostically; **diagnostizieren** *vt/i.*: **e-e** *od.* **auf Lungenentzündung ~** diagnose pneumonia

diagonal I. *Adj. Math.* diagonal; **II.** *Adv.* diagonally; **ein Buch ~ lesen** *fig.* skim(-read) a book; **Diagonale** *f*; *-, -n* diagonal

Diagonal|pass *m Sport* diagonal ball; **~reifen** *m Mot.* cross-ply (tyre, *Am.* tire), *Am. auch* bias-ply (tire)

D

Diagramm n; -s, -e; fachspr. graph; ~papier n graph paper

Diakon m; -s und -en, -e und -en; Reli. deacon; **Diakonie** f; -, kein Pl.; ev. social (welfare) work; **Diakonin** f; -, -nen deaconess; **diakonisch** Adj. ev.: ~es Werk welfare and social work; **Diakonisse** f; -, -n, **Diakonissin** f; -, -nen; ev. deaconess

diakritisch Adj. Ling.: ~es Zeichen diacritic(al mark)

Dialekt m; -(e)s, -e; Ling. dialect; ~ sprechen speak (a) dialect

Dialekt|ausdruck m Ling. dialect word (od. expression); ~dichter m, ~dichterin f dialect poet; ~forschung f dialectology

dialektfrei Adv. Ling.: ~ sprechen speak standard English etc.

Dialektik f; -, kein Pl.; bes. Philos. dialectics Pl. (V. im Sg.); **Dialektiker** m; -s, -, **Dialektikerin** f; -, -nen dialectician; **dialektisch** Adj. dialectical

Dialog m; -(e)s, -e 1. dialogue, Am. auch dialog (auch EDV); 2. fig. (Kommunikation) auch discourse; 3. TV, Film: Koll. script

dialogbereit Adj. Pol.: ~ sein be willing to negotiate (od. have talks); **Dialogbereitschaft** f willingness to negotiate (od. have talks), openness for talks

dialogfähig Adj. 1. open to communication; 2. → dialogbereit; 3. EDV, Computer: interactive

Dialog|feld n EDV dialog(ue) field; ~fenster n EDV dialog(ue) window; ~form f: in ~ in dialogue (form); ~partner m, ~partnerin f conversational partner, interlocutor geh.; ~regie f TV, Film: script supervision

Dialyse f; -, -n; Chem., Med. dialysis; an der ~ hängen umg. be on dialysis; fig. (~-Patient sein) need dialysis; ~-Patient m, ~-Patientin f dialysis patient; ~zentrum n Med. (kidney) dialysis clinic

Diamagazin n slide tray

Diamant m; -en, -en 1. diamond; 2. Plattenspieler: stylus

diamanten Adj. diamond ...; ~e Hochzeit diamond wedding (anniversary)

diamantenbesetzt Adj. diamond-studded

Diamantenschmuck m diamond jewel(le)ry, diamonds Pl., ice umg.

Diamant|kollier n diamond necklace; ~ring m diamond ring; ~schleifer m, ~schleiferin f diamond cutter; ~schmuck m → Diamantenschmuck; ~schrift f Druck. diamond type

diametral I. Adj. 1. Math. diametric(al); 2. geh. fig. diametrically opposed; in ~em Gegensatz stehen be diametrically opposed (zu to); II. Adv. geh. fig.: ~ entgegengesetzt diametrically opposed (+ Dat. to)

Diaphragma n; -s, Diaphragmen 1. Anat. diaphragm; 2. Med. diaphragm; das ~ einführen od. einlegen insert the diaphragm

Dia|projektor m slide projector; ~rähmchen n, ~rahmen m slide frame

Diarrhö(e) [dia'rø:] f; -, Diarrhöen; Med. diarrh(o)ea

Diashow f slide talk (od. show)

Diaspora f; -, kein Pl. diaspora

Diastole f; -, -n; Physiol. diastole; **diastolisch** Adj.: ~er Blutdruck diastolic blood pressure

Diät f; -, -en (special) diet; ~ halten be on (od. keep to) a diet; j-m e-e ~ ver-

ordnen od. j-n auf ~ setzen umg. put s.o. on a diet; ~ kochen cook according to a diet; streng ~ leben keep to (od. follow) a strict diet; ~assistent m, ~assistentin f dietician

Diäten Pl. 1. → Diät; 2. Parl. emoluments, parliamentary (Am. etwa congressional) pay Sg.; ~erhöhung f increase in parliamentary (Am. etwa congressional) allowances

diätetisch Adj. Med. diet(etic); Lebensmittel: dieting

Diät|kost f dietary food; ~kur f diet cure

Diatonik f; -, kein Pl.; Mus. diatonicism; **diatonisch** I. Adj. diatonic; II. Adv. diatonically

Diavortrag m slide talk (od. show)

dich (Akk. von du) I. pers. Pron. you; II. refl. Pron. yourself; nach Präp.: you; oft unübersetzt: beruhige ~! calm down!

dicht I. Adj. 1. dense, thick; Verkehr: auch heavy; Hecke: auch close-set; Gewebe: dense, closely-woven; (gedrängt) tightly packed; 2. (undurchlässig) für Wasser: watertight, waterproof; für Luft: airtight; Vorhang: thick, heavy; nicht mehr ~ sein Gefäß etc.: leak, be leaky; ~ machen Gefäß: seal, stop the leak(s), make watertight; Dach: seal (the cracks); Fenster: seal; er ist nicht ganz ~ umg. fig. he's got a screw loose; 3. fig. Stil: compact, dense; Atmosphäre: dense; Programm: tightly-packed, full; 4. umg. (geschlossen, zu) closed, shut; Grenze: blocked; Eugen war gestern wieder total ~ umg. (betrunken) Eugene was pissed (Am. plastered) again last night; II. Adv. 1. densely, thickly; ~ behaart (very) hairy, hirsute geh.; ein ~ bepflanztes Beet a closely planted (flower)bed; ~ besiedelt od. bevölkert densely populated; ~ gedrängt tightly packed; 2. (nahe) closely; ~ an od. bei close to; ~ an-, bei- od. nebeneinander close together; ~ daneben stehen: close by, right next to; schießen: right by; ~ hinter j-m her sein be hot on s.o.'s heels; → auffahren I 2; 3. fig.: ~ bevorstehen be imminent; ich war ~ daran od. davor aufzugeben I was just about to give up (od. on the verge of giving up); 4. ~ schließen shut tight(ly); Tür: shut tight (od. properly); nicht mehr ~ halten not close (od. shut) properly any more

dichtauf Adv. closely

Dichte f; -, -n, mst Sg. 1. density, thickness; 2. Phys. (spezifisches Gewicht) specific gravity; 3. fig. fullness

dichten¹ vt/i. write poetry (od. plays, novels etc.); (verfassen) write

dichten² vt/i. (abdichten) seal; (Dach) repair; (Leck) fix; (Fuge) flush; mit Kitt: caulk, lute; Naut. caulk; etw. dichtet (nicht) gut s.th. does not seal well

Dichter m; -s, - poet; (Schriftsteller) author, writer; **Dichterfürst** m geh. prince among poets; **Dichterin** f; -, -nen poet, poetess altm.; (Schriftstellerin) author(ess), writer; **dichterisch** I. Adj. Sprache, Werk: literary; (poetisch) poetic; ~e Freiheit poetic licen|ce (Am. -se); II. Adv. poetically; **Dichterlesung** f (author's) reading; e-e ~ halten read from one's own works

dichthalten v/i. (unreg., trennb., hat -ge-); umg. keep mum, keep one's mouth (od. trap) shut

Dichtheit, **Dichtigkeit** f 1. density, thickness; 2. tightness; → dicht I

Dichtkunst f poetry

dichtmachen (trennb., hat -ge-); umg. I. v/t. 1. (Laden etc.) am Abend: close (od. shut up) (for the night); für immer: close down, shutter; 2. die Luken od. Schotten ~ auf Schiff: batten down the hatches; II. v/i. 1. Laden etc., am Abend: close, shut; für immer: close down, put up the shutters; 2. Sport: (hinten) ~ put up a defensive barrier; bes. Fußball: close up in front of goal; 3. Person: (nicht mehr zuhören) switch off, stop listening; (keine Gefühle an sich heranlassen) shut (od. close) o.s. off

Dichtung¹ f 1. nur Sg.; Koll. literature; (Lyrik) poetry; 2. (Gesamtwerk e-s Dichters) work(s Pl.), writing(s Pl.); (Lyrik) poetry, poetic works Pl.; 3. (Gedicht) poem; (Prosawerk) work (of literature); sinfonische ~ symphonic poem; 4. fig.: ~ und Wahrheit fact and fiction, truth and fantasy

Dichtung² f 1. nur Sg.; Handlung: sealing; 2. seal; (Packung) packing; (Manschette) gasket; (Unterlegscheibe) washer; (Fuge) joint; mit Kitt: luting, caulking; Naut. caulking

Dichtungs|masse f, ~material n sealing compound, sealant; ~ring m, ~scheibe f sealing ring; am Wasserhahn etc.: washer, gasket

dick I. Adj. 1. allg.: thick; Ast, Baum etc.: big; Buch: fat, long; Seil: strong; 2. Maßangabe: drei Meter ~ three met|res (Am. -ers) thick; 3. Lippen: thick; Backen: chubby; (geschwollen) swollen; e-n ~en Bauch haben umg. (hochschwanger sein) have a bun in the oven; 4. (beleibt) Person: fat, corpulent; Bauch: large, fat; Beine etc.: chubby, heavy; ~ werden get fat, put on weight; ~ und fett pej. big and fat; mach dich nicht so ~! umg. do you have to spread (yourself) out like that?, budge (Am. scrunch) up a bit!; 5. Brei, Soße etc.: thick; ~ werden Blut, Eiweiß: coagulate; → Blut 2; 6. Nebel, Rauch etc.: thick, dense, heavy; hier ist od. herrscht ~e Luft umg. there's something in the air, feelings are running high; 7. umg. attr. (groß) (great) big ..., whopping great ... Sl.; ein ~es Gehalt einschieben earn a fat (od. hefty) salary; ein ~es Lob ernten be praised to the skies; → Brocken 3, Ei 2, Hund 8; 8. umg. fig.: mit j-m durch ~ und dünn gehen stick by s.o. through thick and thin; das ~e Ende kommt noch the worst is yet to come; sie sind ~e Freunde they're (as) thick as thieves, they're very thick; e-n ~en Kopf haben (Kopfweh haben) have a thick head; bei Kater: have a hangover; II. Adv. 1. Schicht: ~ mit Staub bedeckt thick with dust; die Salbe ~ auftragen apply the cream generously; sich ~ anziehen wrap up well; 2. ~ geschwollen very swollen; 3.; 4. umg. fig.: ~ auftragen (übertreiben) lay it on thick; ~(e) haben/kriegen be/get sick and tired of, have one's fill of; es ~(e) haben be well off; wenn es ~ kommt when push comes to shove

dick|bauchig Adj. Vase: bulbous; ~bäuchig Adj. fat-bellied, pot-bellied

Dickdarm m Anat. colon

dicke Adv. umg. (reichlich) easily; das reicht ~ od. damit kommen wir ~ aus that will be plenty (od. easily enough);

D

→ *dick* II 3

Dicke[1] *f; -, -n, mst Sg.* **1.** thickness; (*Durchmesser*) diameter; *e-e Mauer von 40 cm ~* a 40-cm thick wall; **2.** (*Beleibtheit*) fatness

Dicke[2] *m, f; -n, -n,* **Dickerchen** *n umg. hum.* fatty, chubby (cheeks), *Brit. auch* podge, *Am. auch* pudge

dickfellig *Adj. umg. pej.* thick-skinned

dickflüssig *Adj.* syrupy; viscous *fachspr. und Tech.*

Dickhäuter *m; -s, -; Zool.* pachyderm; *umg. fig.* (*Mensch*) thick-skinned person; **dickhäutig** *Adj.* **1.** *Zool.* pachydermatous; **2.** *fig.* thick-skinned

Dickicht *n; -s, -e* **1.** thicket; **2.** *fig.* labyrinth, jungle

Dickkopf *m umg.:* *ein ~ sein od. e-n haben* be pigheaded (*od.* stubborn); *so ein ~!* he's so pigheaded, how stubborn can you get; **dickköpfig** *Adj. umg.* pigheaded, stubborn

dickleibig *Adj.* **1.** *Person:* corpulent, obese; portly *euph.,* stout *euph.;* **2.** *Buch:* fat, thick

dicklich *Adj.* **1.** slightly plump, a bit on the plump side, chubby; **2.** *Flüssigkeit:* thick

Dick|macher *m umg.* fattener; *Pl. auch* fattening food *Sg.* (*od.* foods); *das ist ein ~ auch* that's very fattening; *~milch* f sour(ed) milk

Dickschädel *m umg.* → **Dickkopf**

dickschalig *Adj.* thick-skinned, *nachgestellt:* with a thick skin

dicktun (*unreg., trennb., hat -ge-*); *umg. pej.* **I.** *v/refl.* act big; **II.** *v/i.:* ~ *mit* show off with

dickwandig *Adj.* thick-walled, *nachgestellt:* with thick walls

Dickwanst *m umg. pej.* tub of lard, fat slob, fatso

Didaktik *f; -, -en* didactics *Pl.* (*V. im Sg.*); *~ und Methodik des Englischunterrichts etc.* theory and methodology of English teaching; **Didaktiker** *m; -s, -,* **Didaktikerin** *f; -, -nen* educationalist, expert in teaching methods; **didaktisch I.** *Adj.* didactic; *~e Analyse* analysis of teaching method; **II.** *Adv.* didactically; *~ geschickt/falsch vorgehen* use skilful/wrong teaching methods

die I. *best. Art.* **1.** (*Nom. Sg.*) the; *~ eine ist fleißig, ~ andere faul* the one is hard-working, the other (one) is lazy; *~ Frau* (*alle Frauen*) woman(kind); *~ Erde* earth; *~ Chemie* chemistry; *~ kleine Maria* little Mary; *~ Maria, ~ ich meine* the Mary (who) I mean; **2.** (*Akk. Sg.*) the; *~ Regel kennen* know the rule; **3.** (*Nom. Pl. von der, die, das*) the; *~ Menschen sind sterblich* man(kind) is (but) mortal; **4.** (*Akk. Pl. von der, die, das*) the; **II.** *Dem. Pron.* **1.** (*Nom. Sg.*) that (one), this (one); she; *~ Frau hier* this woman; *~ mit dem Hut* the one with the hat; *nur ~ kann das verstehen, ~ ...* only she (*od.* that woman) who ... can understand; *~ und ehrlich? Dass ich nicht lache!* her - honest? Pull the other one! (*Am.* Give me a break!); *~ Frage ist ~:* ... the question is (this): ...; **2.** (*Akk. Sg.*) that (one), this (one); *er hat ~ und ~ Lösung probiert umg.* he tried this and that solution; **3.** (*Nom. Pl. von der, die, das*) these, those, they, them; *das entscheiden ~ da oben* that is decided by them up top; **4.** (*Akk. Pl. von der, die, das*) these, those, they, them; **III.** *Rel. Pron.* **1.** (*Nom. Sg.*) *bei Personen:*

who; *bei Sachen:* which, that; *sie war ~ Erste, ~ es erfuhr* she was the first to know; *jede, ~ ...* anyone who ...; **2.** (*Akk. Sg.*) *bei Personen:* who(m förm.), that; *bei Sachen:* which, that; **3.** (*Nom. Pl. von der, die, das*) *bei Personen:* who, that; *bei Sachen:* which, that; *~ Blumen, ~ blühen* the flowers that are blooming (*od.* in bloom); **4.** (*Akk. Pl. von der, die, das*) *bei Personen:* who, that, whom *förm.*; *bei Sachen:* which, that; *~ Blumen, ~ ich gepflückt habe* the flowers (that) I picked

Dieb *m; -(e)s, -e* thief (*Einbrecher*) burglar; *haltet den ~!* stop, thief!; *die kleinen ~e hängt man, die großen lässt man laufen Sprichw.* there's one law for the rich and another (one) for the poor; → **Ladendieb** *etc.*

Diebes|bande *f pej.* gang of thieves; *~beute f, ~gut n; nur Sg.* stolen goods *Pl.*

diebessicher I. *Adj.* theftproof; (*einbruchsicher*) burglarproof; **II.** *Adv.:* *etw. ~ aufbewahren* keep s.th. in a safe place (*od.* under lock and key)

Diebestour *f:* *auf ~ gehen* go (out) thieving (*od.* on the rob *umg.*), go on a robbery (*od.* burglary) spree

Diebin *f; -, -nen* thief (*Einbrecherin*) burglar; → **Ladendieb** *etc.*; **diebisch I.** *Adj.; nur attr.* **1.** thieving; → **Elster**, **2.** *fig. Vergnügen, Freude:* malicious, fiendish; **II.** *Adv.:* *sich ~ freuen* secretly rejoice (*über* + *Akk.* at)

Diebstahl *m; -(e)s, Diebstähle* theft; *Jur. mst* larceny; *einfacher/schwerer ~* theft (*Am.* petty larceny) / aggravated theft (and burglary) (*Am.* grand larceny); *geistiger ~* plagiarism; → **Ladendiebstahl** *etc.*

diebstahlsicher *Adj.* → **diebessicher**, **Diebstahlsicherung** *f Mot.* anti-theft device

diejenige *Dem. Pron*; *derjenigen, diejenigen*; *Sg.*: the one; *Sache: auch* that one; *Pl.*: those (ones), the ones; *~, die od. welche* the one who *od.* that

Diele *f; -, -n* **1.** *Brett:* (floor)board; *stärkere:* plank; **2.** (*Vorraum*) hall

dienen *v/i.* **1.** *Sache:* serve (*j-m* s.o.; *als* as); *dazu ~ zu* (+ *Inf.*) serve to (+ *Inf.*); *es dient dazu zu* (+ *Inf.*) it's for (+ *Ger.*); *wozu soll das ~?* what's that (meant) for?; *Handlung etc.:* what's that supposed to achieve?; *lass es dir als Warnung ~* let that serve as a warning to you; **2.** *e-r Sache ~* (*nützlich sein*) help (*od.* contribute to) s.th.; *es dient e-m guten Zweck* it's all for a good purpose; *damit ist mir nicht gedient* that doesn't help me at all, that's no use to me; **3.** *Mil.* serve one's time; *15 Monate ~* do 15 months' service; *bei der Marine ~* serve in the Navy; *haben Sie gedient?* have you been in the services?; **4.** *als Diener:* help; *geh. e-r Firma, guten Sache etc.:* be of help (*od.* service); *womit kann ich (Ihnen) ~?* what can I do for you?, how can I help?; *damit kann ich leider nicht ~* I'm afraid I can't help you there

Diener *m; -s, -* **1.** servant (*auch fig.*); *persönlicher:* valet, manservant; *livrierter:* footman; (*Gefolgsmann*) attendant; **2.** (*Verbeugung*) bow; *vor j-m e-n ~ machen* bow to (*od.* before) s.o.; **3.** *stummer ~* (*Kleiderständer*) valet; (*Serviertisch*) dumb waiter; **Dienerin** *f; -, -nen* maid; *fig.* handmaid(en); **dienern** *v/i. fig., pej.* bow and scrape (*vor*

+ *Dat.* to); **Dienerschaft** *f* servants *Pl.*, domestics *Pl.*, domestic help

dienlich *Adj.* useful, helpful (+ *Dat.* to); (*zweckdienlich*) expedient; *e-r Sache ~ sein* further s.th.

Dienst *m; -(e)s, -e* **1.** *allg.* service (*an* + *Dat.* to); *j-m gute ~e leisten* serve s.o. well; (*j-m zugute kommen*) stand s.o. in good stead; *Person:* be a great help (to s.o.); *j-m e-n schlechten ~ erweisen* do s.o. a disservice (*od.* bad turn); *j-m zu ~en sein od. stehen* be at s.o.'s disposal (*od.* command); *~ am Kunden* customer service; (*das ist*) *~ am Kunden umg.* (that's) all part of the service, madam (*od.* sir); *sich in den ~ e-r Sache stellen* offer one's services *to,* devote o.s. *to;* *in/außer ~ nehmen od. stellen* (*Verkehrsmittel etc.*) put in (out of) service (*od.* commission); *die Beine versagten ihm den ~* his legs gave way; **2.** *nur Sg.;* (*Ggs. Freizeit*) duty; *den od. zum ~ antreten* go on duty, start work; *sich zum ~ melden* report for duty; *im/außer ~* on/off duty; *wann hast du ~?* when are you working, when are you on?; *der ~ habende od. tuende Arzt/Offizier od. der Arzt/Offizier vom ~* the doctor on call (*od.* duty) / the duty officer; *Unteroffizier vom ~* the duty NCO; *Chef vom ~ Druckw.* duty editor; *Torschütze vom ~ umg. fig.* goal machine; *~ nach Vorschrift* work-to-rule; *~ ist ~, und Schnaps ist Schnaps umg.* never mix business with pleasure; **3.** (*Stellung*) *beim Militär, König etc.:* service; *beim Staat:* civil service; *als Dienstbote:* service, employ; *bei e-r Firma:* work; *in j-s ~(e) treten* enter s.o.'s employ; *bei e-r Firma in ~ treten* start work with; *bei j-m im ~ od. in j-s ~ sein od. stehen bei Firma etc.:* work for; *bes. pej. heimlich etc.:* be in the pay of; *bei König etc.:* serve; *den ~ quittieren* resign; *außer ~* (*abgek. a.D.*) (*im Ruhestand*) retired, in retirement, emeritus; **4.** *mit Adj.: aktiver ~ Mil.* active service; *gehobener od. höherer / mittlerer ~* executive/clerical (grade of the) civil service; *öffentlicher ~* civil service; **5.** *Kunst* respond

...dienst *m, im Subst.* **1.** *Einrichtung:* service; *Ansage~* telephone information service; *Apothekennot~* emergency chemist's (*od. bes. Am.* pharmacy); **2.** *Aufgabe:* *Abhol~* collecting (*od.* picking-up) duty; *Abspül~* washing-up (*Am.* dishwashing) duty; *Vertretungs~Ärzte:* locum (*Am.* substitute doctor) service; *Sekretariatsarbeit:* temp(ing) agency; *Lehrer:* supply (*Am.* substitute) teacher agency

Dienstabteil *n Eisenb.* guard's (*Am.* conductor's) compartment

Dienstag *m; -(e)s, -e;* (*am*) *~* on Tuesday; *~, der 1.Mai* Tuesday, the first of May, *Am.* Tuesday, May 1; *sie kommt ~* she's coming on Tuesday; *letzten/diesen/nächsten ~* last/this/next Tuesday; *in der Nacht von Montag auf od. zu ~* in the night from Monday to Tuesday (*od.* between Monday and Tuesday), on Monday night; *~ früh* on Tuesday morning (early); *den ganzen ~ (lang od. über)* all day (on) Tuesday; *e-s ~s* one Tuesday; *~ in/vor acht Tagen* Tuesday week (*Am.* next Tuesday) /a week ago Tuesday

Dienstagabend *m* Tuesday evening; (*am*) *~ um 7 Uhr* (on) Tuesday at 7 o'clock

dienstagabends *Adv.* on Tuesday evenings

dienstägig *Adj.* Tuesday; *unsere ~e Sendung* our Tuesday('s) program(me); **dienstäglich** *Adj.* (regular) Tuesday

Dienstagmittag *m* Tuesday noon (*od.* lunchtime); *(am) ~* at Tuesday lunchtime, Tuesday noon; **dienstagmittags** *Adv.* on Tuesday lunchtimes

Dienstagmorgen *m* Tuesday morning; *(am) ~* on Tuesday morning; **dienstagmorgens** *Adv.* on Tuesday mornings

Dienstagnachmittag *m* Tuesday afternoon; *(am) ~ um 4 Uhr* (on) Tuesday afternoon at four o'clock; **dienstagnachmittags** *Adv.* on Tuesday afternoons

Dienstagnacht *f* Tuesday night; *(in der) ~* (on) Tuesday night; **dienstagnachts** *Adv.* on Tuesday nights

dienstags *Adv.* on Tuesday(s); *~ abends/mittags etc.* on Tuesday evenings/lunchtimes *etc.*

Dienstagvormittag *m* Tuesday morning; *(am)~ um 10 Uhr* (on) Tuesday morning at ten o'clock; **dienstagvormittags** *Adv.* (on) Tuesday mornings

Dienstalter *n* length of service; *nach ~* according to seniority

dienstältest... *Adj.* most senior; **Dienstälteste** *m, f* senior member of staff

Dienst|antritt *m: bei ~* on taking up one's/her/his *etc.* post; *~anweisung f* instruction; *laut ~* according to regulations *Pl.*; *~auffassung f* work ethic, conception of duty; *~aufsicht f* supervision; *~ausweis m* identity (*od.* ID) card, pass

dienstbar *Adj.* (*ergeben*) subservient (+ *Dat.* to); *~er Geist umg. hum.* helpful soul; *sich* (*Dat.*) *j-n/etw. ~ machen* make use of s.o./s.th.

dienstbeflissen *Adj.* zealous, eager; (*übereifrig*) officious; **Dienstbeflissenheit** *f* zeal, eagerness

Dienst|beginn *m: ~ ist 8 Uhr* work starts at 8 o'clock; *bei ~* when starting work; *~bereich m* area of responsibility, competence

dienstbereit *Adj.* **1.** (*gefällig*) obliging; **2.** *Arzt etc.*: on call; *Apotheke*: open; *~er Arzt* auch duty doctor; **Dienstbereitschaft** *f* **1.** obligingness; **2.** standby duty

Dienst|besprechung *f* (official) meeting; *~bezeichnung f* title; *~bezüge Pl.* salary *Sg.*

Dienstbote *m altm.* (domestic) servant; **Dienstbotin** *f altm.* (domestic) servant

Diensteifer *m* zeal, eagerness; *übertriebener*: officiousness

dienstfähig *Adj.* → *diensttauglich*

Dienst|fahrt *f* business trip; *e-s Beamten*: auch official trip; *~fahrzeug n* official (works) vehicle

dienstfrei *Adj.: ~ haben* be off (duty); *~er Tag* day off

Dienst|gang *m* business errand; *e-s Beamten*: official errand; *e-n ~ machen* do (*od.* run) a business (*Beamter*: official) errand; *~gebrauch m: nur für den ~* for official use only; *~geheimnis n* **1.** trade secret; *im Staatsdienst*: official secret; **2.** *nur Sg.*; (*Geheimhaltung*) trade secrecy; *staatlich*: official secrecy; *~geschäfte Pl.* business *Sg.*; *e-s Beamten*: official business *Sg.*; *~gespräch n* **1.** business call; **2.** *e-s Beamten*: official call;

~grad *m* rank; *Am. Unteroffiziere und Mannschaften*: grade; *Naut.* rating; *~herr m* employer; *~hund m* dog used for police or security work, *Am.* police (*od.* guard) dog; *~jahre Pl.* years of service; *~jubiläum n* anniversary; *~kleidung f* work(ing) clothes *Pl.*; uniform

Dienst|leister *m; -s, -;* (*Person, Firma*) contractor (*od.* person, company *etc.*) working in the service sector (*od.* industry); *die Datenerfassung haben wir an ~ vergeben* we have outsourced the data collection; *~leistung f* service (rendered); *der Anteil der ~en am Bruttosozialprodukt* the share of services in the gross national product

Dienstleistungs|abend *m etwa* late--night shopping; *Bank, Behörde*: late--night opening, late opening hours; *~beruf m* job in the service sector; *~betrieb m* business (*od.* company) in the service sector; *~gesellschaft f* service-orient(at)ed society; *~gewerbe n* service industries *Pl.*

Dienstleute *Pl.* → *Dienstmann*

dienstlich I. *Adj.* official, formal; *~ werden* take on an official tone; **II.** *Adv.: ~ unterwegs sein* be away on (*Beamter*: official) business; *er ist ~ verhindert* he's tied up with business (matters) (*Beamter*: official business)

Dienst|mädchen *n altm.* maid, home help; *~mann m; Pl. -männer od. -leute; südd., österr. altm.* (*Gepäckträger*) porter; *~marke f* (*Ausweis*) identity disc, *Am.* identification (*od.* dog *umg.*) tag; *~ordnung f* regulations *Pl.*; *~personal n e-s Hotels etc.*: staff (*V. im Sg. od. Pl.*); *im Haushalt*: domestic staff (*V. mst im Pl.*)

Dienstpflicht *f* (official) duty, compulsory service; **dienstpflichtig** *Adj.* liable for compulsory service

Dienst|pistole *f* service pistol; *~plan m* duty roster; *~programm n EDV* utility program; *~rang m* → *Dienstgrad*; *~räume Pl.* offices; *~reise f* business trip; *e-s Beamten*: auch official trip; *~schluss m: nach ~* after (office) hours; *~stelle f* (*Behörde*) department; (*Arbeitsstelle, Büro*) office; *~stunden Pl.* (office) hours

dienst|tauglich *Adj. bes. Mil.* fit for service (*od.* duty); *~unfähig Adj.* unfit for work (*Mil.* duty); *ständig*: disabled

Dienst|vergehen *n* disciplinary offen|ce (*Am.* -se); *~verhältnis n* contractual relationship

dienstverpflichten *v/t.* (*nur Inf. und P.P., hat*) *zu Militärdienst*: conscript, call up, *Am. auch* draft; *zu Arbeit*: force *s.o.* to work, rope *s.o.* in *hum.*

Dienst|vorschrift *f* regulation(s *Pl.*); *~wagen m* **1.** (*Firmenwagen*) company car; **2.** *für Minister etc.*: official car; **3.** *Mil.* staff car; *~weg m: auf dem ~* through (the) official channels; *den ~ einhalten* go through the proper (*od.* official) channels

dienstwidrig I. *Adj.: ~es Verhalten* breaking of the regulations; **II.** *Adv.: sich ~ verhalten* go against the regulations; **Dienstwidrigkeit** *f* **1.** *nur Sg.* insubordination; **2.** disciplinary offen|ce (*Am.* -se)

Dienst|wohnung *f e-s Betriebes, der Armee etc.*: company/army *etc.* flat (*Am.* apartment), company/army *etc.* house; flat (*Am.* apartment) (*od.* house) provided by the company/army *etc.*; *~zeit f* **1.** working (*od.* office)

hours *Pl.*; **2.** *Mil.* term of service

dies *Dem. Pron. n* → *dieser*

diesbezüglich I. *Adj. nur attr.*; *nachgestellt*: concerning this, in this connection; **II.** *Adv.* concerning this, in this connection

diese *Dem. Pron. f* → *dieser*

Diesel *m; -(s), -; Mot., umg.* **1.** (*Fahrzeug, Motor*) diesel; **2.** *nur Sg.*; (*Kraftstoff*) diesel, *Brit. auch* derv; *~antrieb m* diesel drive; *mit ~* diesel-driven

dieselbe *Dem. Pron.*; *derselben, dieselben* **1.** the same; *Person*: the same person; *ein und ~ Frau* one and the same woman; *sie ist immer ~ geblieben* she always stayed (true to) herself; **2.** *umg.* (*die Gleiche*) the same one (*od.* woman); *sie trugen ~ Jacke* they were wearing the same jacket; **3.** *altm., statt pers. Pron.*: *als er die Lehrerin traf, grüßte er ~ freundlich* when he met the teacher, he greeted her pleasantly; *statt Poss. Pron.*: *er erwähnte Frau X und sagte, er sei der Bruder derselben* and said he was her brother (*od.* the brother of the same *förm.*)

dieselbige *Dem. Pron.*; *derselbigen, dieselbigen; altm.* → *dieselbe*

dieselelektrisch I. *Adj.* diesel-electric; **II.** *Adv.* diesel-electrically

Diesel|kraftstoff *m* diesel fuel; *~motor m* diesel engine

dieser *Dem. Pron. m*, **diese** *f*, **dies(es)** *n*, **diese** *Pl.* **1.** *attr.* this; (*jener etc.*) that; *Pl.* these; (*jene*) those; *dieser Tage* the other day; *zukünftig*: soon; *diese Nacht vergangene*: last night; *kommende*: tonight; *am 1. dieses Monats* on the first of this month; *diese Ihre Bemerkung förm.* this remark of yours; *diese Kinder!* those children (*od.* kids *umg.*)!; *dieser Idiot! umg.* what an idiot!; *diese Frechheit!* what a cheek!, *Am.* what nerve!, the cheek of it!; **2.** *subst.*: *diese(r) hier/da* this one (here) / that one (there); *Pl.* these, those; (*Letztere[r] etc.*) the latter; *diese ~ sind es* this is the one; *diese sind es* these are the ones; *dieser und jener* (*einige*) some (*od.* a few) people; *dieser oder jener* (*der eine oder andere*) someone or other; (*mancher*) some people *Pl.*; *ich muss noch dies und das od. dieses und jenes einkaufen/ erledigen* I still have a few bits and pieces to buy / a few things to do (*od.* to sort out); **3.** *rückbezüglich*: he, she, it; *Pl.* they; *sie fragte den Nachbarn, doch dieser wusste von nichts* she asked the neighbo(u)r but he didn't know anything about it

dieses *Dem. Pron. n* → *dieser*

diesig *Adj. Wetter*: hazy

diesjährig... *Adj.: der etc. ~e ...* this year's ...

diesmal *Adv.* this time; (*dieses e-e Mal*) for once

diesmalig... *Adj.: sein ~er Auftritt war ein voller Erfolg* his performance this time was a complete success

diesseitig *Adj.* **1.** *das ~e Ufer* this side of the river (*od.* lake); **2.** *fig.* worldly; **diesseits I.** *Präp.* (on) this side of; **II. Diesseits** *n; -, kein Pl.: das ~* this life, life on earth; *im ~* in this life

Dietrich *m; -s, -e* skeleton key, picklock; *ein Schloss mit e-m ~ öffnen* pick a lock

dieweil(en) *altm.* **I.** *Konj.* (*während*) while; (*weil*) because, since; **II.** *Adv.* meanwhile

diffamieren *v/t.* slander; **diffamierend I.** *Part.Präs.* → *diffamieren*; **II.** *Adj.*

defamatory; **Diffamierung** f defamation, slander(ing)

Differential etc. → **Differenzial** etc.

Differenz f; -, -en **1.** Math., Wirts., geh. difference; (Rest) balance; (Überschuss) surplus, the rest umg.; **2.** mst ~en (Unstimmigkeiten) difference(s) of opinion; ~**betrag** m difference; (Rest) balance

Differenzial n; -s, -e **1.** Math. differential; **2.** Mot. differential (gear); ~**getriebe** n Mot. differential (gear); ~**rechnung** f Math. differential calculus

differenzieren geh. **I.** v/t. **1.** (voneinander ~) distinguish (od. make a distinction) between; **2.** Math. differentiate; **II.** v/i. make distinctions, differentiate; **III.** v/refl. (sich verfeinern) become more and more sophisticated; (sich auseinander entwickeln) diversify; **differenziert I.** P.P. → **differenzieren**; **II.** Adj. sophisticated; Geschmack etc.: auch discriminating, refined; **Differenzierung** f distinction; (Sprache etc.) complexity; (Abänderung) modification

differieren v/i. geh. differ, vary (um by)

diffizil Adj. geh. **1.** Sache: difficult, tricky; (heikel) delicate; **2.** Person: difficult; (schwer zufrieden zu stellen) hard to please, fastidious

diffus Adj. **1.** Phys., Licht: diffuse, diffused, scattered; **2.** geh. fig.; Ideen etc.: vague, foggy, hazy; Lage etc.: confused, unclear; **Diffusion** f; -, -en **1.** Chem., Phys. diffusion; **2.** Phys., von Licht: refraction

Digicam ['dɪdʒɪkɛm] f; -, -s; Etron. digicam

digital Adj. Tech., EDV digital

Digital|-**Analog-Umsetzer** m, ~**Analog-Wandler** m Tech., EDV digital-analog converter; ~**anzeige** f digital display; ~**aufnahme** f, ~**aufzeichnung** f digital recording; ~**fernsehen** n digital television (od. TV)

digitalisieren v/t. Tech., EDV (Daten) digitize

Digital|**kamera** f Tech. digital camera; ~**rechner** m EDV digital computer; ~**uhr** f digital clock (od. watch)

Diktafon, Diktaphon n; -s, -e Dictaphone®

Diktat n; -(e)s, -e **1.** dictation; **ein ~ aufnehmen** take (a) dictation; **etw. nach ~ schreiben** write (od. type) s.th. (up) from dictation; **ein ~ schreiben / schreiben lassen** Schule: do/give a dictation; **2.** geh. (Befehl, Zwang) dictates Pl.; Pol. auch diktat

Diktator m; -s, -en, **Diktatorin** f; -, -nen; pej. dictator; **diktatorisch** Adj. mst pej. dictatorial; **Diktatur** f; -, -en; mst pej. **1.** nur Sg.; System: dictatorship; **2.** Land: dictatorship; **in e-r ~ leben** live under a dictatorship

diktieren vt/i. dictate (auch geh. fig.); **j-m e-n Brief ~** dictate a letter to s.o.; **Diktiergerät** n dictating machine

Dilemma n; -s, -s od. -ta dilemma, fix umg.; **sich in e-m ~ befinden** be in (od. on the horns of) a dilemma

Dilettant m; -en, -en, **Dilettantin** f; -, -nen; geh. pej. dilettante, amateur; **dilettantisch** Adj. geh. pej. amateurish, attr. auch dilettante ...; **Dilettantismus** m; -, kein Pl.; geh. pej. dilettantism, amateurism

Dill m; -(e)s, -e; Bot., **Dille** f; -, -n; bes. österr. dill

Dimension f; -, -en **1.** Phys., Math. dimension; Pl. (Maße) auch size Sg.;

2. fig. Pl. dimensions; (Ausmaß) proportions, extent Sg.; **gigantische ~en annehmen** assume vast proportions; **dimensional** Adj. dimensional; **dimensionieren** v/t. dimension

diminutiv Ling. **I.** Adj. diminutive; **II. Diminutiv** n; -s, -e diminutive

Dimmer m; -s, -; Elektr. dimmer (switch)

DIN® Abk. **1.** (**Deutsches Institut für Normung**) German Institute for Standardization; **2.** (**Deutsche Industrie Norm**) German Industrial Standard; **DIN A4** A4; **DIN A5** A5

DIN-A4-|... im Subst. A4-...; ~**Blatt** n A4(-sized) paper

Diner [di'ne:] n; -s, -s dinner (party); (Bankett) banquet

Ding n; -(e)s, -e od. umg. -er **1.** Pl. -e; (Sache) thing; (Gegenstand) auch object; **gut ~ will Weile haben** Sprichw. Rome wasn't built in a day; **aller guten ~e sind drei** Sprichw. good things come in threes; **nach zwei missglückten Versuchen:** third time lucky, Am. third time's the charm; → **Name** 1; **2.** ~**e** (Angelegenheiten) things, matters; **der Stand der ~e** the state of affairs (od. play); (**so,**) **wie die ~e liegen** od. **stehen** as matters stand; **das geht nicht mit rechten ~en zu** umg. there's something fishy about it; **über den ~en stehen** be above it all; **das ist ein ~ der Unmöglichkeit** that's absolutely impossible, that's completely out of the question; **unverrichteter ~e** without having achieved anything; → **Lage** 3; **3.** fig.: **guter ~e sein** (fröhlich) cheerful; (voll Hoffnung) (be) in good spirits; **vor allen ~en** above all; **4.** Pl. -er; umg., oft pej. (Gegenstand, Exemplar) thing; euph. Geschlechtsteil: thingy, knob, Am. johnson; **5.** Pl. -er; umg. (Kind, Mädchen, Tier) thing; **6.** Pl. -er; umg.: **ein krummes ~** something dodgy; **ein (krummes) ~ drehen** pull a job Sl., get up to something (dodgy od. fishy); **j-m ein ~ verpassen** get one over on s.o., get one's own back on s.o.; **das ist aber ein ~** now there's something, you don't say; **das war (vielleicht) ein (tolles) ~!** that was really (od. quite) something!; **7.** Pl. -e; Philos. thing, substance, entity; **die letzten ~e** death and the life to come; **die Lehre von den letzten ~en** eschatology

dingen v/t.; dingte od. selten dang, hat gedungen od. selten gedingt **1.** geh. pej. (Mörder etc.) hire; → **gedungen**; **2.** altm. (anheuern) hire, take on

dingfest Adj.: **j-n ~ machen** (festnehmen) arrest s.o.; (einsperren) put s.o. behind bars

dinglich Adj. real (auch Jur.)

Dings m, f, n; -, -, **Dingsbums** m, f, n; -, -(e), **Dingsda** m, f, n; -s, -s; umg. Sache: thing, what-d'you-call-it; auch Ort: what's-its-name; Person: what's-his/her-name, thingumajig, whosie

Dingwort n; Pl. Dingwörter; Ling. noun, naming word

dinieren v/i. geh. dine (**bei** at)

Dinkel m; -s, kein Pl.; Bot. spelt

DIN-Norm f German Industrial Standard

Dino m; -s, -s; Zool., umg., ~**saurier** m dinosaur

Diode f; -, -n; Etech. diode

Dioptrie f; -, -n; Opt. diopter

Dioxid n Chem. dioxide

Dioxin n; -s, -e; Chem. dioxin

dioxin|**belastet** Adj. Öko., Chem.

präd. polluted with dioxin; attr. dioxin-polluted; ~**verseucht** Adj. präd. contaminated with dioxin; attr. dioxin-contaminated

Diözesanbischof m kirchl. diocesan bishop, bishop of the diocese; **Diözese** f; -, -n diocese

Diphtherie f; -, -n; Med. diphtheria

Diphthong m; -s, -e; Ling. diphthong; **diphthongieren** v/t. diphthongize

Dipl.-|... im Subst. Abk. (**Diplom...**) qualified ..., certified ...; ~**Chem.** etwa BSc Chem, Am. B.S. in Chemistry; ~**Ing.** etwa BSc Eng, Am. B.S. in Engineering

diploid Adj. Bio. diploid(ic)

Diplom n; -s, -e diploma, degree; **ein ~ machen** do (od. take) a diploma (od. degree)

Diplom|... im Subst. (abgek. **Dipl.-**) qualified ..., certified ...; ~**arbeit** f dissertation (submitted for a diploma)

Diplomat m; -en, -en; Pol. diplomat (auch fig.)

Diplomaten|**gepäck** n diplomatic pouch (od. bags Pl.); ~**koffer** m executive briefcase, attaché case, VIP briefcase; ~**laufbahn** f diplomatic career; ~**pass** m diplomatic passport

Diplomatie f; -, kein Pl.; Pol. diplomacy (auch fig.); **Diplomatin** f; -, -nen diplomat; **diplomatisch I.** Adj. diplomatic (auch fig.); ~**es Korps** diplomatic corps; ~**e Vertretung** diplomatic mission; **II.** Adv. diplomatically

Diplom|**bibliothekar** m, ~**bibliothekarin** f qualified librarian; ~**dolmetscher** m, ~**dolmetscherin** f qualified (od. trained) interpreter

diplomiert Adj. qualified

Diplom|**ingenieur** m, ~**ingenieurin** f etwa qualified engineer; Univ. engineering graduate; ~**kauffrau** f, ~**kaufmann** m etwa business graduate; MBA (= Master of Business Administration); ~**landwirt** m, ~**landwirtin** f graduate in agriculture (od. from agricultural college); ~**pädagoge** m, ~**pädagogin** f graduate in teaching (od. from teacher training college); ~**studiengang** m degree (od. diploma) course, course of study leading to a degree (od. diploma)

Dipol m Etech. dipole; ~**antenne** f dipole (aerial od. antenna)

dippen v/t. **1.** (eintauchen) dip (**in** + Akk. in); **2.** Naut. dip

dir I. pers. Pron. (Dat. von du) (to) you; **ich werde es ~ erklären** I'll explain it to you; **ein Freund von ~** a friend of yours; **II.** refl. Pron. (auch ~ **selbst**) yourself; **wasch ~ die Hände** (go and) wash your hands

direkt I. Adj. **1.** (gerade) direct; ~**e Verbindung** od. ~**er Zug nach ...** Eisenb. ohne Umsteigen: through train to ...; **2.** (unmittelbar) direct, immediate; Informationen: firsthand; **3.** (unumwunden) Antwort, Frage: straight, frank; Art: direct; **4.** mst verneint; umg. (richtig, wirklich) real, actual; **es war kein ~er Fehler** it wasn't really a mistake; **5.** Ling.: ~**e Rede** direct speech; ~**es Objekt** direct object; **II.** Adv. **1.** (geradewegs) direct(ly), straight; **sie kam ~ auf uns zu** she came straight up to us; **Eier ~ beim Bauern kaufen** buy eggs direct from the farmer; **2.** (gleich) räumlich und zeitlich: directly, immediately; (sofort) auch at once; ~ **am Bahnhof** right at the station; ~ **gegenüber** directly opposite; **es liegt ~ vor d-r Nase** umg. it is right in front of

D

you (*od.* your nose); **~ nach dem Essen** right (*od.* straight) after dinner; **3.** (*ohne Umschweife*) point-blank, straight to s.o.'s face; **4.** *umg.* (*wirklich*) really; **nicht ~ falsch** not exactly (*od.* really) wrong; **man müsste es ~ mal versuchen** one (*od.* you) really ought to try it out; **5.** *umg. erstaunt*: really, actually; **du bist ja ~ einmal pünktlich!** you are actually on time for once!; **das hat jetzt ~ Spaß gemacht!** that was really (good) fun!; **6.** *TV, Radio*: live; **Direktbank** *f* direct banking service

Direktheit *f* directness

Direktion *f*; -, -en **1.** *nur Sg.*; *Wirts.* (*Leitung*) management; (*Vorstand*) board of directors, (board of) management; (*Räume*) manager's office; (*Hauptgeschäftsstelle*) head office; **2.** *schw., Pol.* (*Ministerium*) ministry, *Am.* department, administration, agency

Direktions|assistent *m*, **~assistentin** *f Wirts.* assistant manager; **~sekretär** *m*, **~sekretärin** *f* personal assistant, PA, administrative assistant, AA

Direktive *f*; -, -n; *geh.* instruction(s *Pl.*), directive

Direkt|kandidat *m*, **~kandidatin** *f Pol., Parl.* candidate with a direct mandate; **~marketing** *n Wirts.* direct marketing

Direktor *m*; -s, -en; *Wirts.* director, manager; *Bank*: bank manager; *Gefängnis*: governor, *Am.* warden; *Polizei*: chief inspector; *Schule*: headmaster, *bes. Am.* principal; *Zoo*: director; **leitender ~** managing director, chief executive officer, CEO

Direktorat *n*; -(e)s, -e **1.** *Amt*: directorship; **2.** (*Raum des Schuldirektors*) headmaster's (*Am.* principal's) office

Direktorin *f*; -, -nen manageress; director; (*Schulleiterin*) headmistress, *bes. Am.* principal

Direktorium *n*; -s, *Direktorien* board of directors; (*Vorstand*) management committee; (*Aufsichtsrat*) board of supervisors

Direktpass *m Sport* first-time pass

Direktrice [dɪrɛkˈtriːsə] *f*; -, -n; *Wirts., e-s Geschäfts*: manager(ess); *Modebranche*: head designer

Direkt|schuss *m Sport* volley (shot); **~übertragung** *f Radio, TV*: live broadcast; **~verbindung** *f Zug, Flug*: direct connection; *bei Flug*: direct flight; *bei Zug*: through train; **~verkauf** *m Wirts.* direct sale(s *Pl.*); **~vermarktung** *f Wirts.* direct marketing; **~wahl** *f* **1.** *Pol.* direct elections *Pl.*; **2.** *Telef.* direct dial(l)ing; **~werbung** *f Wirts.* direct advertising

Dirigent *m*; -en, -en; *Mus.* conductor, *Am. auch* director; *das waren die Wiener Philharmoniker unter dem ~en ...* conducted by, directed by, under the direction of ...

Dirigenten|podium *n Mus.* (conductor's) rostrum; **~pult** *n* (conductor's) desk

Dirigentin *f*; -, -nen; *Mus.* conductor, *Am. auch* director

dirigieren I. *v/t.* direct; *j-n in e-e Parklücke ~* help s.o. get into a parking space; **II.** *vt/i. Mus.* conduct

dirigistisch *Adj. Pol., Wirts.* dirigiste

Dirndl *n*; -s, -(n) **1.** *Dial.* (*Mädchen*) girl, lass; **2.** (*Kleid*) dirndl; **~kleid** *n* dirndl

Dirne *f*; -, -n prostitute; **Dirnenmilieu** *n* red light district

dis, Dis *n*; -, -; *Mus.* D sharp

dis... *im Adj. und V.*, **Dis...** *im Subst.* dis...

Disagio [dɪsˈʔaː dʒo] *n Wirts.* discount

Discount... [dɪsˈkaʊnt] *im Subst. Wirts.* discount ...; *Laden, Artikel*: *auch* cut-price ...

Discounter [dɪsˈkaʊntɐ] *m*; -s, - **1.** *Wirts.* discount (*od.* cut-price) retailer, *Am.* discounter; **2.** (*Billigfluganbieter*) no-frills airline

Dis-Dur *n Mus.* D sharp major

Disharmonie *f* **1.** *Mus.* dissonance, discord; **2.** *Farben*: clash; **3.** *geh. fig.* dissonance, disharmony (+ *Gen. od.* **von** between); **~n innerhalb der Koalition** disagreements within the coalition; **disharmonieren** *v/i.* **1.** *Mus.* be discordant (*od.* dissonant); **2.** *Farben*: clash; **3.** *fig.*: **die beiden ~ grundsätzlich** those two just don't get on (together); **disharmonisch** *Adj.* **1.** *Mus.* discordant, dissonant; **2.** *attr. Farben*: clashing ...; **3.** *fig.* dissonant, disharmonious

Diskant *m*; -s, -e; *Mus.* treble

Diskette *f*; -, -n; *EDV* diskette, floppy (disk); **Diskettenlaufwerk** *n* (floppy) disk drive

Disk|jockey *m* [ˈdɪskdʒɔke] disc jockey, DJ *umg.*, deejay *umg.*; **~man®** [-mɛn] *m*; -, *Diskmen* Discman ®

Disko *f*; -, -s; *umg.* disco; **~musik** *f* disco music

Diskont *m*; -s, -e; *Wirts.* discount; (*Satz*) discount rate; **~erhöhung** *f* increase in (*od.* raising of) the discount rate

diskontieren *v/t. Wirts.* discount

diskontinuierlich *Adj. geh.* intermittent, discontinuous

Diskont|politik *f Wirts.* discount policy; **~satz** *m* discount rate

Diskothek *f*; -, -en discotheque

diskreditieren *v/t. geh.* (bring into) discredit

Diskrepanz *f*; -, -en; *geh.* discrepancy

diskret *Adj.* **1.** *geh.* discreet; *j-m ein ~es Zeichen geben* give s.o. a subtle hint; **2.** *geh.; Farbe etc.*: unobtrusive; **3.** *Math., Phys., Tech.* discrete; **Diskretion** *f*; -, *kein Pl.*; *geh.* discretion; (*Verschwiegenheit*) *auch* secrecy; *~ Ehrensache!* discretion guaranteed

diskriminieren *v/t. geh.* discriminate against (**wegen** on account of); **diskriminierend I.** *Part. Präs.* → *diskriminieren*; **II.** *Adj. geh.* discriminating, discriminatory; **Diskriminierung** *f geh.* discrimination (+ *Gen. od.* **von** against); *~ am Arbeitsplatz* discrimination in the workplace; **Diskriminierungsverbot** *n* ban on discrimination

Diskurs *m*; -es, -e; *geh.* **1.** (*Gespräch*) discourse; **2.** (*Abhandlung*) discourse, treatise

Diskus *m*; -(ses), -se *od. Disken*; *Sport, Gerät*: discus; *Sportart*: discus

Diskussion *f*; -, -en discussion (**über** + *Akk.*, **um** on, about), debate (on); *sich zur ~ melden* request (*od.* put one's hand up) to speak; *sich auf keine ~en einlassen mit ...* not enter (*od.* get drawn) into any discussion with ...; *zur ~ stehen/stellen* be/put on the agenda; *das steht nicht zur ~* that's not what we're here to discuss, that is not under discussion; *ich will keine ~en!* and I don't want any arguments, and that's an end to it!

Diskussions|bedarf *m*: *es besteht ~* we *etc.* need to talk about this; **~beitrag** *m* contribution to the discussion

diskussions|bereit *Adj.* open to discussion; **~fähig** *Adj. Person*: präd. willing (*od.* prepared) to discuss *s.th.*; *Thema, Vorschlag etc.*: able to be discussed

Diskussions|grundlage *f* basis for discussion; **~leiter** *m*, **~leiterin** *f* (panel) chairman; **~partner** *m*, **~partnerin** *f* discussion partner, partner in discussion; *Pol.* negotiating partner; **~runde** *f* **1.** *Personen*: discussion group; **2.** round of discussions; **~stoff** *m*: *~ liefern* provide matters (*od.* topics) for discussion; **~teilnehmer** *m*, **~teilnehmerin** *f* participant; *TV etc.*: panel(-l)ist, member of the panel, *oft* guest; **~thema** *n* subject for discussion; **~veranstaltung** *f* forum

Diskus|werfen *n* discus (throwing); **~werfer** *m*, **~werferin** *f* discus thrower

diskutabel *Adj. geh.* worth discussing; **diskutieren I.** *v/i.* have a discussion; **über etw.** (*Akk.*) *~* discuss s.th., have a discussion about s.th.; *darüber lässt sich (durchaus) ~* we can talk about it; (*das ist fragwürdig*) that's debatable; *ich hab keine Lust, mit dir zu ~* I don't want to argue with you

dis-Moll *n Mus.* D sharp minor

disparat *Adj. geh.* disparate

Dispens *m*; -es, -e, *österr. und kath. f*; -, -en dispensation; **dispensieren** *v/t.* **1.** *geh.* (*j-n*) exempt (**von** from); **2.** *Pharm.* dispense

Dispokredit *m Fin. umg.* overdraft

Disponent *m*; -en, -en; *Wirts.* managing clerk; **disponibel** *Adj. geh.* available; **Disponibilität** *f*; -, *kein Pl.*; *geh.* availability

disponieren I. *v/i.* **1.** *geh.* make arrangements, plan (ahead); **2.** *geh.*: *~ über* (+ *Akk.*) (*verfügen können*) have at one's disposal; (*entscheiden*) do what one likes with; **3.** *Wirts.* place orders; **II.** *v/t. geh.* allot (**für** to)

disponiert I. *P.P.* → *disponieren*; **II.** *Adj.* **1.** *geh.*: *gut/schlecht ~ sein* be in good/bad form; **2.** *Med.*: *~ sein für od. zu* be prone to

Disposition *f*; -, -en **1.** *Med.* proneness, susceptibility (**für, zu** to); *e-e ~ haben für od. zu* be prone (*od.* susceptible) to; **2.** *mst ~en* (*Vorkehrungen*) arrangements; (*Planung*) plans; (*Anweisungen*) instructions; **3.** (*Anlage, Entwurf*) outline, plan; **4.** (*Verfügung*) disposal; *hier haben Sie ... zur freien ~* here you have ... at your disposal; (*j-m*) *zur ~ stehen* be at s.o.'s disposal; **Dispositionskredit** *m Wirts.* drawing credit, overdraft (facility)

Disput *m*; -(e)s, -e; *geh.* dispute, argument (**über** + *Akk.* about); **disputieren** *geh.* **I.** *v/i.* **1.** dispute (**über etw.** [*Akk.*] [on *od.* about] s.th.), debate ([on] s.th.), argue (about s.th.); **2.** (*streiten*) argue, quarrel; **II.** *v/t.* discuss

Disqualifikation *f Sport od. geh.* disqualification; **disqualifizieren I.** *v/t. Sport* disqualify (**wegen** for); **II.** *v/refl. geh.* lose one's (*od.* all) credibility (**als** as)

dissen *v/t. umg. Popkultur*: dis(s)

Dissens *m*; -es, -e; *geh.* dissent, disagreement

Dissertation *f*; -, -en; *Päd.* (doctoral) thesis (*od.* dissertation)

Dissident *m*; -en, -en; *geh.* dissident

Dissidenten|bewegung *f geh.* dissident movement; **~gruppe** *f geh.* group of dissidents

dissonant *Adj. Mus.* dissonant; **Disso-**

nanz f; -, -en dissonance; fig. auch Pl. (note of) discord

Distanz f; -, -en **1.** distance; *aus e-r ~ von 10 Metern* from 10 met|res (*Am.* -ers) away, from a distance of 10 met|res (*Am.* -ers); **2.** geh. fig. distance (*zu* from); (*Objektivität*) auch detachment; (*Zurückhaltung*) auch reserve; *~ halten od. wahren od. auf ~ bleiben* keep one's distance (*zu j-m od. j-m gegenüber* from s.o.); *j-n auf ~ halten* fig. keep s.o. at arm's length; *auf ~ gehen* back off, start cooling the relationship, become distant (*zu j-m* towards s.o.); *etw. mit ~ betrachten* take a detached view of s.th.; *~ gewinnen zu ...* get a bit of distance from ...; **3.** *Sport* distance; *das Rennen geht über e-e ~ von 100 km* the race covers a distance of 100 km; *der Kampf ging über die volle ~ Boxen:* the fight went the (whole) distance

distanzieren I. v/refl. geh. dissociate o.s. (*von* from); **II.** v/t. *Sport* leave *s.o.* trailing (*um* by), outdistance; (*schlagen*) auch beat, outclass

distanziert I. P.P. → *distanzieren*; **II.** Adj. geh. reserved, aloof pej.

Distanzschuss m long-range shot; *Fußball:* long(-range) ball

Distel f; -, -n; *Bot.* thistle; *~fink* m *Orn.* goldfinch

distinguiert [dɪstɪŋ'giːɐt] Adj. geh. distinguished; **Distinguiertheit** f geh. distinguished manner, appearance *etc.*, distinction

Distribution f; -, -en; *Wirts., Ling. etc.* distribution; **distributiv** Adj. distributive

Distrikt m; -(e)s, -e district, area

Disziplin f; -, -en **1.** nur Sg. discipline; *~ halten od. wahren* be disciplined, maintain discipline; *hier herrscht ~* things are very disciplined around here; **2.** (*Fachgebiet, Sportart*) discipline; *olympische, leichtathletische etc.:* event

Disziplinar|gericht n disciplinary court; *~gewalt* f; nur Sg. disciplinary power(s Pl.)

disziplinarisch I. Adj. disciplinary; **II.** Adv.: *~ vorgehen* take disciplinary action (*gegen* against)

Disziplinar|recht n disciplinary law; *~strafe* f **1.** *Sport* disciplinary penalty; **2.** *Eishockey:* misconduct penalty; *~verfahren* n disciplinary proceedings Pl.

disziplinieren I. v/t. discipline; **II.** v/refl. discipline o.s.; **diszipliniert I.** P.P. → *disziplinieren*; **II.** Adj. disciplined; **III.** Adv.: *sich ~ verhalten* be (very) disciplined; **Disziplinierung** f disciplining

disziplinlos Adj. undisciplined; **Disziplinlosigkeit** f **1.** nur Sg. lack of discipline; **2.** *Handlung:* disobediant act

dito Adv. umg. ditto

diuretisch Adj. diuretic

Diva f; -, -s od. Diven; (*Sängerin*) diva; (*auch Schauspielerin*) star

divergent Adj. *Math., Phys.,* geh. divergent; **Divergenz** f; -, -en divergence (*auch geh. fig.*); **divergieren** v/i. diverge (*von* from)

divers... Adj.; nur attr.; geh. various, divers; *Diverses* various things Pl.; bes. *Wirts.* sundries Pl.; *als Überschrift:* Miscellaneous

Diversifikation f; -, -en; *Wirts.* diversification; **diversifizieren** v/t. diversify

Dividend m; -en, -en; *Math.* dividend

Dividende f; -, -n; *Wirts.* dividend;

(*Satz*) dividend rate

Dividendenausschüttung f *Wirts.* dividend distribution, distribution of dividends

dividieren v/t. *Math.* divide (*durch* by); *zwölf dividiert durch drei ist* (*gleich*) *vier* twelve divided by three is (*od.* equals) four

Division f; -, -en; *Math., Mil.* division; **Divisionszeichen** n *Math.* division sign; **Divisor** m; -s, -en; *Math.* divisor

Diwan m; -s, -e **1.** (*Sofa*) divan, ottoman; **2.** hist. divan, diwan; **3.** *Lit.* divan, diwan

d.J. Abk. **1.** (*dieses od. diesen Jahres*) of this year; **2.** (*der Jüngere*) jun., *Am.* Jr.

DJH m; -, kein Pl.; Abk. (*Deutscher Jugendherbergsverband*) German Youth Hostel Association

DKP f; -, kein Pl.; Abk. hist. (*Deutsche Kommunistische Partei*) Communist Party of Germany

DLG f; -, kein Pl.; Abk. (*Deutsche Landwirtschafts-Gesellschaft*) German Agricultural Society; *~-Siegel* n seal (of approval) of the German Agricultural Society

DLRG f; -, kein Pl.; Abk. (*Deutsche Lebens-Rettungs-Gesellschaft*) → *deutsch* I 2

DM Abk. (*Deutsche Mark*) DM

D-Mark f; Abk. hist. (*Deutsche Mark*) Deutschmark, D-Mark, D-mark

d-Moll n *Mus.* D minor; *~-Tonleiter* f D minor scale

D-Netz n; nur Sg.; *Funk.* digital mobile (*Am.* cellular) phone network

DNS f; -, kein Pl.; Abk. *Bio.* (*Desoxyribonukleinsäure*) DNA; *~-Strang* m DNA strand

doch I. Konj. (*aber*) but, however; **II.** Adv. **1.** (*dennoch*) however, yet, still; all the same, nevertheless; (*wider Erwarten*) after all; *der Film war traurig und ~ schön* the film was sad and yet beautiful; *er kam also ~?* then he did come after all?; *ich hab's dann ~ nicht getan* I didn't do it after all; *wo er ~ genau wusste, ...* knowing very well ...; **2.** (*Ggs. nein*) yes it is, I was *etc.*; *das ist nicht wahr! - ~!* yes it is!; *willst du denn nicht? - ~!* yes, I do; **3.** (*schließlich*) after all; *das war denn ~ zu viel für sie* it was too much for her after all; *du kennst das ~, kannst du mir helfen?* you know it, can't you help me then?; *er ist ~ ganz nett, warum magst du ihn nicht?* he's really nice, so why don't you like him?; **4.** (*gewiss*) surely; *du weißt ~, dass ... um Zustimmung bittend:* you know (that) ..., don't you?, surely you know (that) ...; *du kommst ~?* you will come, won't you?; *sie ist ~ nicht* (*etwa*) *krank?* she isn't it, is she?; *das ist ~ Peter da drüben* überrascht: look, there's Peter over there; *unsicher:* isn't that Peter over there?; *das wäre ~ schön!* that would be lovely!; **5.** *auffordernd:* do (+ Inf.); *setzen Sie sich ~* do sit down; *sei ~ mal still!* ärgerlich: be quiet, will you!; *lass ihn ~!* leave him alone, can't you?; **6.** *verstärkend:* *ja/nicht ~!* of course! / of course not!, certainly not!; *ich hab's ~ gewusst!* I knew it!; *mir ~ egal!* umg. verärgert: I don't care (*od.* give a damn); *wie schön das ~ ist!* oh isn't that lovely; *das gibt's ~ nicht!* umg. I don't believe it!; *du musst ~ immer Recht haben!* verärgert: you just have to be right, don't you?; **7.** *zurückweisend:*

mach die Heizung an - das hab ich ~ schon! umg. I already did; *das konnte ich ~ nicht wissen!* how was I supposed (*od.* meant) to know that?; *lass nur, du kannst mir ja ~ nicht helfen* just leave it, you can't help me anyway (*od.* there's nothing you can do to help me); **8.** (*bloß, nur*) if only ...; *hättest du das ~ gleich gesagt!* why didn't you say that (from the start)?, why didn't you tell me straightaway?; **9.** (*noch, gleich*) again; *wer war das ~* (*gleich*)? who was that again?

Docht m; -(e)s, -e wick

Dock n; -s, -s; *Naut.* dock(s Pl.), dockyard; *auf ~ legen* (put into) dock

Docke f; -, -n **1.** *Garn:* skein, hank; **2.** *Agr., Getreide:* stook, *Am.* shock; **3.** *Dial.* (*Puppe*) doll

docken[1] v/t. **1.** (*Garn*) wind into skeins; **2.** *Agr.* (*Getreide*) stook, *Am.* shock; (*Tabak*) bundle

docken[2] v/t/i. **1.** *Naut.* dock; **2.** *Raumfahrt:* *~ an* (+ Akk.) dock onto

Doge ['doːʒə] m; -n, -n; hist. doge

Dogge f; -, -n; *Zool.:* *Dänische od. Deutsche ~* Great Dane; (*Englische*) *~* mastiff

Dogma n; -s, Dogmen; kath. od. geh. pej. dogma; *etw. zum ~ erheben* make s.th. into a dogma; **Dogmatik** f; -, -en **1.** *Reli.* dogmatics Pl. (*V. im Sg.*); **2.** nur Sg.; geh. pej. dogmatism; **Dogmatiker** m; -s, -, **Dogmatikerin** f; -, -nen; geh. pej. dogmatist; **dogmatisch** kath. od. geh. pej. **I.** Adj. dogmatic; **II.** Adv. dogmatically; **Dogmatismus** m; -, kein Pl.; geh. pej. dogmatism

Dohle f; -, -n; *Orn.* jackdaw

Doktor m; -s, -en **1.** (*abgek. Dr.*) *Univ.* doctor; *den od. s-n ~ machen od. bauen* umg. do (*od.* get) one's doctorate (*od.* Ph.D.); *den ~* (*der Chemie etc.*) *haben* have a docorate (*od.* Ph.D.) in chemistry; *Herr od. Frau Dr. Schubert* Dr. Schubert; *Anrede e-s Arztes:* doctor Schubert; **2.** umg. (*Arzt*) doctor; *~ spielen* play doctors and nurses, *Am.* play doctor; → *Onkel* 2

doktern v/i. umg.: *an j-m/etw. ~* have a go at treating s.o., mess about with s.th., *Am.* doctor s.o./s.th.

Doktorand m; -en, -en doctoral candidate, Ph.D. student

Doktor|arbeit f thesis, doctoral (*od.* Ph.D.) thesis; *das wäre ein Thema für e-e ~* somebody ought to write a thesis on that; *~frage* f umg. fig. (really) tricky question; *~grad* m doctor's degree; *den ~ erwerben* do (*od.* get) one's doctorate; *~hut* m doctor's cap; umg. fig. → *Doktorgrad*; *~prüfung* f viva (voce), *Am.* defense; *~titel* m (*Grad*) doctorate; *im Namen:* doctor's title; *~vater* m (Ph.D. *od.* dissertation) supervisor; *~würde* f doctorate; *die ~ erlangen* get (*od.* obtain) one's doctorate

Doktrin f; -, -en; *Pol. und* geh. doctrine

Dokument n; -(e)s, -e **1.** document; *amtlich:* record (*beide auch* fig.); **2.** fig.: *ein ~* (*Beweis, Zeugnis*) proof (+ *Gen.* of), evidence (of)

Dokumentar|bericht m documentary report; *~film* m documentary (film); *~filmer* m, *~filmerin* f documentary filmmaker

dokumentarisch geh. **I.** Adj. documentary; **II.** Adv.: *etw. ~ belegen* provide documentary evidence of s.th.; *~ belegt* documented

Dokumentarspiel n documentary drama, docudrama

Dokumentation f; -, -en documentation (*über* + *Akk. od.* **zu** about *od.* on); *fig. auch* demonstration
dokumentenecht *Adj. Tinte*: indelible, waterproof
dokumentieren I. v/t. **1.** document; **2.** *fig.* (*beweisen*) show, demonstrate; **II.** v/refl. be shown, be revealed
Dokumentvorlage f *EDV* template
Dolch m; -(e)s, -e dagger
Dolchstoß m dagger thrust; *fig.* stab in the back; *j-m einen ~ versetzen fig.* wound s.o. deeply (*od.* to the core); **~legende** f *hist.* stab-in-the-back legend
Dolde f; -, -n; *Bot.* umbel
Dolden|blüte f *Bot.* umbellate flower; ℓ**förmig** *Adj.* umbellate
Dole f; -, -n; *schw.* (*Gully*) drain
Doline f; -, -n; *Geol.* doline, dolina, sink(hole)
doll *Adj. bes. nordd. umg.* → **toll**
Dollar m; -(s), -(s) dollar; **~imperialismus** m *Wirts. pej.* imperialism of the dollar; **~kurs** m value of the dollar; *der ~ ist gestiegen auch* the dollar has gone up (in value); **~zeichen** n ($) dollar sign
Dolmetsch m; (e)s, -e **1.** *österr.* interpreter; **2.** *fig.* spokesman; **dolmetschen** vt/i. interpret, act as interpreter (*j-m* for s.o.)
Dolmetscher m; -s, -, **~in** f; -, -nen interpreter; **~institut** n, **~schule** f school for interpreters
Dolomiten *Pl. Geog.* the Dolomites
Dom m; -(e)s, -e **1.** cathedral; *der Kölner ~* Cologne Cathedral; **2.** *Tech., Geol. etc.* dome, cupola
Domain [dɔ'meːn-] f; -, -s; *EDV* domain; *e-e ~ (auf s-n Namen) registrieren lassen* get a domain registered (in one's name); **~adresse** f *EDV* domain address
Domäne f; -, -n **1.** (*Besitz*) domain, estate; **2.** *fig.* sphere; *~ s.o.'s* province (*od.* domain); **3.** *EDV* → **Domain**
Domestikation f; -, -en; *Bio.* domestication; **domestizieren** v/t. domesticate
Dom|freiheit f *hist.* cathedral close (*od.* precincts *Pl.*); **~herr** m *kath.* canon
Domina f; -, -s; *euph.* dominatrix
dominant *Adj. Bio. und geh.* dominant; **Dominantakkord** m *Mus.* dominant chord; **Dominante** f; -, -n; *Mus.* dominant; *fig.* dominant feature; **Dominanz** f; -, -en; *Bio. und geh.* dominance; **dominieren** *geh.* **I.** v/i. *Person*: dominate; have the upper hand; *Sache*: predominate, be predominant; **II.** v/t. dominate; **dominierend I.** *Part. Präs.* → **dominieren**; **II.** *Adj.* dominant; *Person*: dominating
Dominikaner m; -s, -, **~in** f; -, -nen **1.** *kath.* Dominican (*männlich*: friar; *weiblich*: nun); **2.** *Geog.* Dominican (man, woman *etc.*); person, woman *etc.* from the Dominican Republic; **~orden** m Dominican Order, Order of St(.) Dominic
dominikanisch *Adj.* **1.** *kath.* Dominican; **2.** *Geog.* Dominican; *die Dominikanische Republik* the Dominican Republic
Domino¹ m; -s, -s domino
Domino² n; -s, -s dominoes *Pl.* (*V. im Sg.*); **~maske** f domino; **~stein** m domino
Domizil n; -s, -e domicile (*auch Wirts.*); *sein ~ aufschlagen* take up residence; **~wechsel** m *Wirts.* domiciled bill (of exchange)
Domkapitel n *kath.* (cathedral) chapter
Dompfaff m; -s *od.* -en, -en; *Orn.* bullfinch
Dompteur [dɔmp'tøːɐ] m; -s, -e, **Dompteuse** [dɔmp'tøːzə] f; -, -n (animal) trainer
Donau f; -; *Geog.* Danube; **~monarchie** f; *nur Sg.*; *hist.* Austro-Hungarian Empire
Donner m; -s, - thunder (*auch fig.*); *wie vom ~ gerührt* thunderstruck; **~getöse** n thunderous din (*od.* racket); **~grollen** n rolling thunder
donnern I. v/i. **1.** (*hat gedonnert*); *unpers.*: thunder; *es blitzt und donnert* there's thunder and lightning; **2.** (*hat*); *fig. Stimme, Wasserfall etc.*: thunder, roar; *Stimme*: *auch* boom; **3.** (*ist*); *umg.* (*fahren, fallen etc.*) thunder; *zu Boden ~* crash (on)to the floor (*od.* ground); **4.** (*hat*); *umg.* (*schlagen*): *an die Tür ~* hammer *od.* pound (away) at the door; *mit der Faust auf den Tisch ~* bang one's fist on the table; **II.** v/t. (*hat*) **1.** *umg.* (*schleudern*) fling; (*Ball*) slam; **2.** *umg.*: *e-e gedonnert kriegen* get a clip (a)round the ears; (*angebrüllt werden*) get shouted at (good and proper)
donnernd I. *Part. Präs.* → **donnern**; **II.** *Adj.* thundering, roaring; *Applaus*: thunderous; **~es Gelächter** roars of laughter
Donner|rollen n roll(ing) of thunder; **~schlag I.** m clap (*od.* peal) of thunder, thunderclap; **II.** *Interj. umg.*; *staunend*: wow; *verärgert*: damn (it), *Brit. auch* bugger *Sl.*
Donnerstag m Thursday; → **Dienstag**; **~abend** etc. → **Dienstagabend** etc.
donnerstags *Adv.* on Thursday(s); → **dienstags**
Donner|stimme f thundering voice; **~wetter** *umg.* **I.** n: *ein ~ ging auf ihn nieder* he got a real roasting, all hell was let loose (for him); **II.** *Interj.* **1.** *staunend*: wow!, *Brit. auch* (well) blow me!, blimey!; **2.** *als Fluch*: *zum ~!* damn (it)!
Donquichotterie [dɔnkiʃɔtə'riː] f; -, -n; *geh.* quixotism
doof *umg.* **I.** *Adj.* **1.** (*dumm*) stupid, silly, *Am. auch* dumb; *~ bleibt ~* once a fool, always a fool; **2.** (*langweilig*) boring; **3.** (*lästig, ärgerlich*) silly, stupid; **II.** *Adv.* stupidly; *guck nicht so ~!* take that silly look off your face!; **Doofheit** f **1.** *nur Sg.* stupidity; **2.** *Handlung*: stupid remark (*od.* idea *etc.*); **Doofi** m; -(s), -s; *umg.* dumbo, twit; *Klein ~ mit Plüschohren hum.* a right (*Am.* complete) idiot, *Brit. auch* a proper charlie; **Doofkopp** m; -s, *Doofköppe*, **Doofmann** m; *Pl. Doofmänner*; *umg. pej.* dummy, blockhead
dopen I. v/t. (*Sportler etc.*) administer drugs (*or* steroids) to; (*Rennpferd etc.*) dope; **II.** v/refl. take drugs; → **gedopt**
Doping n; -s, -s; *Sport, Med.* drug use (by athletes); *auch bei Tieren*: doping; **~kontrolle** f drug(s) (*od.* doping) test; *weitS.* doping (*od.* drug) control; **~mittel** n doping substance; **~sünder** m, **~sünderin** f drug-taker; **~vergehen** n drug-taking (*od.* doping) offen|ce (*Am.* -se)
Doppel n; -s, - **1.** duplicate; **2.** *Tennis etc., Match*: doubles *Pl.* (*V. im Sg.*); *Spieler*: doubles team; *gemischtes ~* mixed doubles *Pl.*; **~adler** m double eagle; **~agent** m, **~agentin** f double agent; **~b** n *Mus.* double flat (sign);

~band m double(-sized) volume; **~bedeutung** f double meaning; **~belastung** f double load; **~belegung** f *e-s Zimmers*: double occupancy; **~belichtung** f *Fot.* double exposure; **~bereifung** f twin tyres (*Am.* tires) *Pl.*; **~beschluss** m *Pol., hist.* twin-track decision; **~besteuerung** f double taxation; **~bett** n double bed; **~bild** n *TV* double-image; *ich habe ein ~* I have ghosting (on my screen); **~bindung** f *Chem.* (chemical) double bond
Doppelblindversuch m *Pharm.* double-blind trial (*od.* test)
Doppel|chor m **1.** *Archit.* double choir; **2.** *Mus.* double choir (*od.* chorus); **~decker** m; -s, - **1.** *Flug.* biplane; **2.** *umg.* (*Bus, Brot etc.*) double-decker
doppeldeutig *Adj.* ambiguous, (*anzüglich*) suggestive; **Doppeldeutigkeit** f **1.** *nur Sg.* ambiguity; (*Anzüglichkeit*) suggestiveness; **2.** *Bemerkung*: ambiguous (*od.* suggestive) remark
Doppel|ehe f bigamy; *e-e ~ führen* have (*od.* live with) two wives *od.* husbands, live bigamously; **~erfolg** m double victory (*od.* success); **~fehler** m *Tennis*: double fault; **~fenster** n double(-glazed) window; *Pl. Koll. auch* double glazing *Sg.*; **~flinte** f double-barrel(l)ed gun; **~gänger** m; -s, -, **~gängerin** f; -, -nen double, lookalike; **~garage** f double garage
doppel|geschlechtig *Adj.* hermaphroditic, hermaphrodite; **~gesichtig** *Adj. fig.* two-faced, deceitful; **~gleisig** *Adj.* → **zweigleisig**
Doppelgriff m *Mus.* double stop
Doppelhaus n pair of semi-detached houses (*od.* semis *umg.*), *Am.* duplex; **~hälfte** f semi-detached house, semi *umg.*, *Am.* (half of a) duplex
Doppel|heft n *Schulheft*: extra-thick exercise book; *e-r Zeitschrift etc.*: double issue; **~hochzeit** f double wedding; **~kassettendeck** n dual cassette deck; **~kinn** n double chin; **~klick** m; -s, -s; *EDV* double-click; *einen ~ machen* (*auf etw.*) double-click (on s.th.); **~klinge** f: *Rasierer mit ~* twin-blade (-d) razor; **~konsonant** m *Ling.* double (*od.* geminate *fachspr.*) consonant; **~konzert** n double concerto
doppelköpfig *Adj. Monster etc.*: two-headed
Doppel|korn m (strong) corn schnapps; **~kurve** f S-bend, double curve
Doppellauf m double barrel; **doppelläufig** *Adj. Gewehr*: double-barrel(l)ed
Doppel|laut m *Ling.* (*Diphthong*) diphthong; (*Konsonant*) double (*od.* geminate *fachspr.*) consonant; (*Vokal*) double vowel; **~leben** n double life; **~mitgliedschaft** f *in zwei Parteien, Vereinen etc.*: dual membership; **~moral** f double standards *Pl.*
doppeln v/t. *südd., österr.* resole
Doppel|naht f double-stitched seam; **~name** m double-barrel(l)ed (*od.* hyphenated) name; (*Vorname*) double name; **~pack** m: *im ~* in a double-pack; *fig.* as a pair; **~pass** m *Fußball*: one-two; **~passspiel** n; *nur Sg. Fußball*: one-two (move); **~punkt** m colon; **~rahmkäse** m full-fat cheese; **~reifen** m twin tyre (*Am.* tire);
doppelreihig *Adj. Jacke*: double-breasted
Doppel|rolle f *Theat. und fig.* double role; **~salto** m double somersault; **~schicht** f *Arbeit*: double shift; *eine ~*

fahren work a double shift; **~schräg-strich** m double slash (forward); **um-gekehrter ~** double backslash

doppelseitig I. *Adj.* **1.** **~e** *Anzeige* double-page spread; **2.** *Gewebe:* reversible; *Klebeband:* double-sided; **3.** *Med.* double; **~e** *Lungenentzündung* double pneumonia; **II.** *Adv.* on both sides; → *gelähmt* II

Doppel|spalte f *in Zeitung etc.:* double column; **~spiel** n **1.** *fig.* double dealing; **ein ~ mit j-m treiben** *umg.* double-cross s.o.; *(in e-r Beziehung)* two-time s.o.; **2.** *Sport, im Tennis etc.:* (game of) doubles *Sg.;* **~spülbecken** n double(-bowl) kitchen sink; **~steck-dose** f *Etech.* two-socket outlet, double socket; **~stecker** m *Etech.* double plug; *(Verteiler)* two-way adapter; **~stern** m *Astron.* binary star

doppelstöckig *Adj. attr. Gebäude:* two-stor(e)y ..., *präd.* two-storeyed, *Am.* two-storied; *Autobahn etc.:* two-tiered, *attr. auch* two-tier ...; **~er** *Bus etc.* double-decker bus *etc.;* **~es** *Bett* bunk bed; **~er** *Whisky etc. umg.* double whisk(e)y *etc.*

Doppel|strategie f dual strategy; **~strich** m *Mus.* double bar; **~stunde** f *Päd.* double period

doppelt I. *Adj.* double *(auch Whisky etc.);* *(Fahrbahn, Funktion, Staatsbürgerschaft etc.)* dual; **die ~e** *Breite/Menge etc.* twice *(od.* double) the width/amount; **in ~er** *Ausfertigung* in duplicate; **~e** *Buchführung* double-entry bookkeeping; **~es** *Übel* twin evils; → *Boden* 3, *Moral* 1, *Spiel* 7; **II.** *Adv.* **1.** double; *(zweimal)* twice; **etw. ~ ha-ben** have two (copies) of s.th.; **~ so alt wie ich** twice my age; **~ so lang** twice as long; **~ so groß** twice the size; **~ so viel** twice as much, double the amount *(od.* price *etc.);* **das ist ~ gemoppelt** *umg. hum.* that's saying the same thing twice over; **~ genäht hält besser** *Sprichw.* it's better to be on the safe side, better safe than sorry; **2.** *(sehr, noch mehr) vor Adj.:* doubly, twice as; **aus d-m Munde kränkt mich das ~** I find that even more *(od.* doubly) hurtful coming from you; **3.** *umg.:* **~ und dreifach** *bereuen:* deeply; *sich entschuldigen:* profusely; *erklären, machen, überprüfen:* thoroughly

Doppelte[1] n; -n, *kein Pl.* double; *(doppelt so viel)* twice as much *(od.* many); **das ~ des Betrags** double the amount

Doppelte[2] m; -n, -n; *umg. Getränk:* double (whisk[e]y *etc.*)

doppeltkohlensauer *Adj. Chem.:* **dop-peltkohlensaures** *Natron* bicarbonate of soda

Doppeltür f double door(s *Pl.*)

Doppelung f doubling

Doppel|verdiener m **1.** *Person:* double wage-earner; **~ sein** have (an) income from two jobs; **2.** *Pl.; Paar:* dual-income couple *Sg.;* **~verdienst** m dual income; **~vergaser** m dual carburet(t)or; **~verglasung** f double glazing

doppel|wandig *Adj.* double-walled; **~zeilig** *Adv.:* **~ getippt** double-spaced

Doppelzimmer n double room; **mit zwei Einzelbetten:** twin-bedded room

doppelzüngig *Adj. pej. Person:* two-faced; *Bemerkung etc.:* ambiguous; **Doppelzüngigkeit** f **1.** *nur Sg.; e-r Person:* two-facedness, deceitfulness; *e-r Bemerkung:* ambiguity; **2.** *(Bemerkung)* ambiguous remark

Dopplereffekt m *Phys.* Doppler effect

Dorf n; -(e)s, *Dörfer* village; **auf dem ~**

wohnen live in a village; **er stammt vom ~** he's from the country; **die Welt ist ein ~** it's a small world; **das ist ja hier ein richtiges ~** *pej.* this place is so provincial; **der ist auch nie aus s-m ~ herausgekommen** *umg. fig. pej.* he's a real country bumpkin *(od.* hick, yokel); **potemkinsche Dörfer** *fig.* façade *Sg.,* sham *Sg.,* Potemkin village(s *Pl.*); **leider sind das nur potemkinsche Dörfer** sadly that is all just window-dressing; **das sind böhmische Dörfer für mich** it's all Greek *(od.* double Dutch) to me

Dorf|älteste m, f; -n, -n village elder; **~bewohner** m, **~bewohnerin** f villager

Dörfchen n little village; *(Weiler)* hamlet

Dorf|eingang m: **am ~** at the entrance to *(od.* start of) the village; **~erneue-rung** f village regeneration (scheme); **~jugend** f young people *(od.* youngsters) *Pl.* in the village, village youth *Pl.*

dörflich *Adj. Leben etc.:* village ...; *(bäuerlich)* rustic

Dorf|pfarrer m country vicar; **~platz** m village green; **~schänke** f, **~schenke** f *altm.* village inn *(od. Brit. auch* pub); **~schönheit** f *iro.* village beauty; **~schule** f village school; **~trottel** m village idiot

dorisch *Adj.* **1.** *Archit.* Doric; **2.** *Mus.* Dorian

Dorn[1] m; -(e)s, -en **1.** thorn *(auch fig.);* **voll(er) ~en** thorny *(auch fig.);* **ihr Le-bensweg war voller ~en** life was no bed of roses for her, she had a hard life; **er ist ihr ein ~ im Auge** *fig.* he's a thorn in her side *(od.* flesh); **2.** *Bot.* thorn, spine; **3.** *Zool.* spine

Dorn[2] m; -(e)s, -e **1.** *am Sportschuh:* spike, *Am. auch* cleat; *an e-r Schnalle:* tongue; **2.** *(Bolzen, Stift)* pin, bolt; **3.** *Tech., Werkzeug:* awl

Dornbusch m thorn-bush, briar; **der brennende ~** *bibl.* the burning bush

Dornen|gestrüpp n thorn-bushes *Pl.,* brambles *Pl.;* **~hecke** f prickly hedge, hedge of thorns; **~kranz** m, **~krone** f *bibl.* crown of thorns

dornen|reich, ~voll *Adj. fig.* hard, difficult; *(Problem) auch* thorny

dornig *Adj.* thorny *(auch fig.),* prickly

Dornröschen n Sleeping Beauty; **~schlaf** m: **im ~ liegen** be in (a state of) hibernation

dörren I. *v/t. (hat gedörrt)* dry, desiccate; *im Darrofen:* kiln-dry; **II.** *v/i. (ist)* dry (up)

Dörr|fisch m *Gastr.* dried fish; **~obst** n dried fruit; **~pflaume** f prune

Dorsch m; -(e)s, -e; *Zool.* cod, *Am. auch* codfish

dort *Adv.* there; **~ drüben** over there; **von ~ (aus)** from there; **~, wo ich her-komme** (the place) where I'm from; **wer spricht ~ bitte?** *am Telefon:* who's speaking please?; **sie haben ihn gleich ~ behalten** *(im Krankenhaus etc.)* they've kept him in; → *auch* da

dort|her *Adv.:* **(von) ~** from there; **~hin** *Adv. Ziel:* there; *Richtung:* that way; **bis ~** as far as there; **~hinab** *Adv.* down there; *Richtung:* down that way; **~hinauf** *Adv.* up there; *Richtung:* up that way; **bis ~** up to there; **~hinaus** *Adv.* out there; *Richtung:* out that way; **bis ~** *umg. fig.* incredibly ...; **das ärgert mich bis ~** *umg.* that really gets on my nerves; **~hinein** *Adv.* in there; **~hinüber** *Adv.* over there, *Am. auch*

yonder *umg.;* **~hinunter** *Adv.* down there

dortig *Adj.:* **die ~en** *Verhältnisse* the conditions there

dortzulande, dort zu Lande *Adv.* there, in those parts

Dose f; -, -n **1.** *aus Blech:* tin; *aus Holz:* box; *aus Glas od. Porzellan:* jar; *für Zucker:* bowl; *für Butter:* dish; *für Puder:* compact; **2.** *(Konserve, Bier etc.)* can, *Brit. auch* tin; **3.** *Etech. (Abzweigdose)* box; **Dosen... im Subst.** canned ..., *Brit. auch* tinned ...

dösen *v/i. umg. Adv.:* **(vor sich hin) ~** daydream; **ein bisschen ~** have a little doze

Dosen|bier n beer in a can; **~milch** f condensed milk; **~öffner** m can *(Brit. auch* tin) opener; **~pfand** n deposit on beverage tins *(od. bes. Am.* cans)

dosierbar *Adj.:* **gut/schlecht ~** easy/hard to measure into exact doses; **do-sieren** *v/t.* **1.** measure out; **richtig ~** *(Medizin)* give *(od.* take) the right dose of; **2.** *fig.* mete out, dispense; **Dosierung** f dosage, dose

Dosis f; -, *Dosen* dose *(auch fig.),* dosage; *fig. Ironie etc.:* touch, dash

Dossier [dɔ'sie:] n; -s, -s file, dossier

dotiert *Adj.:* **gut** *od.* **hoch ~ sein** *Stellung etc.:* be well paid; *Rennen etc..* be endowed with a good purse *(od.* good prize money); *Preis etc.:* have *(od.* offer) good prize money; **die Stellung ist mit 5000 Euro ~** the monthly salary for the post *(od.* position) is 5,000 euros; **die Auszeichnung ist mit 25000 Euro ~** the award includes prize money of 25,000 euros; **Dotierung** f *(Entgelt)* remuneration, salary; *(Preis)* prize

Dotter m; -s, - (egg) yolk; **~blume** f *Bot.* marsh marigold; **²gelb** *Adj.* deep yellow; **~sack** m *Zool.* yolk-sac

doubeln ['du:bḷn] *v/t.:* **j-n ~** *Film:* be *(od.* act as) s.o.'s stand-in; *(bei Stunts)* be *(od.* act as) s.o.'s stuntman *od.* stuntwoman *(od.* double); **er musste in dieser Szene gedoubelt werden** they had to bring in a stuntman *(od.* double) for that scene; **Double** ['du:bḷ] n; -s, -s **1.** *Film:* stand-in; *(bei Stunts)* stuntman, stuntwoman, double; **2.** *Mus.* double; **3.** *(Doppelgänger)* double, lookalike; **4.** *Sport* double

Dow Jones ['dau'dʒo:nz] m, **Dow-Jo-nes-Index** m; -, *kein Pl.; Wirts.* Dow(-Jones Industrial Index)

down [daun] *Adj. umg.:* **~ sein** be (feeling) down

Down-Syndrom n; *nur Sg.; Med.* Down's syndrome

Dozent m; -en, -en **1.** *allg.* (university) lecturer; **2.** *(Ggs. Professor)* lecturer, *Am.* assistant professor; **dozieren** *v/i.* lecture **(über + Akk.** on) *(auch fig.);* **er doziert an e-r Universität** he's a university lecturer

dpa f; -, *kein Pl.; Abk. (Deutsche Pres-se-Agentur)* German Press Agency

Dr.(.) *Abk.* → *Doktor*

Drache m; -n, -n; *Myth.* dragon

Drachen m; -s, - **1.** *aus Papier etc.:* kite; **e-n ~ steigen lassen** fly a kite; **2.** *fig. pej. (böses Weib)* shrew, battle-ax(e) *umg.;* **3.** *Fluggerät:* hang-glider; **4.** *Segelboot:* dragon; **~fliegen** n hang-gliding

Drachenflieger[1] m *Fluggerät:* hang glider

Drachenflieger[2] m, **~in** f hang(-)glider (pilot)

Drachme f; -, -n drachma

Dragee, Dragée [dra'ʒeː] *n*; *-s*, *-s* (sugar)coated tablet, dragee

Dragoner *m*; *-s*, - **1.** *hist.* dragoon; **2.** *umg. fig. pej.* dragon, (old) battle-ax(e)

Draht *m*; *-(e)s*, *Drähte* **1.** wire; *Drähte spannen od. ziehen* stretch wires, pull wires tight; **2.** *fig.* (*Verbindung*) line; *heißer ~ Pol.* hotline; *direkter ~ zum Chef etc.*: direct line (*zu* to); **3.** *umg. fig.*: *auf ~ sein* be on the ball; **4.** *nur Sg.*; *altm. umg.* (*Geld*) lolly, dosh, *Am.* dough; *~auslöser m Fot.* cable release; *~bürste f* wire brush

Draht|esel *m umg. hum.* pushbike; *klappriger*: boneshaker; *~geflecht n* wire mesh; *~gitter n* wire netting; *~glas n* wire (reinforced) glass

Drahthaar|dackel *m Zool.* wirehair(ed dachshund)

drahtig *Adj.* wiry (*auch Person*)

drahtlos *Adj.* wireless, radio ...

Draht|saite *f* wire string; *~schere f* wire cutter(s *Pl.*)

Drahtseil *n* wire rope, (wire) cable; *im Zirkus etc.*: tightrope; → *Nerv*, *~akt m* **1.** tightrope (*od.* high-wire) act; **2.** *fig.* razor-edge affair; *~bahn f* cable railway; *~künstler m* tightrope artist; **Drahtseilkünstlerin** *f* tightrope artist(e)

Draht|sieb *n* wire sieve; *~spule f* wire coil; *~wurm m Zool.* wireworm; *~zange f* wire cutter; *~zieher m*; *-s*, -, *~zieherin f*; *-*, *-nen*; *fig.* puppet master, string puller; *Pol.* powerbroker; *er war schon immer der ~* he was always the brains of the operation

Drainage [drɛ'naːʒə] *f bes. Med.* drainage; **drainieren** [drɛ'niːrən] *v/t.* drain

drakonisch *Adj.* draconian

drall *Adj. Frau*: buxom, strapping; *Brüste*: full; *Wangen*: round

Drall *m*; *-(e)s*, *-e*, *mst Sg.* **1.** *Phys.* (*Rotation*) spin (*auch von Ball, Kugel etc.*); (*Impuls*) angular momentum; (*Verdrehung*) torsion; **2.** *Faden etc.*: twist

Drama *n*; *-s*, *Dramen*; *Lit., Theat.* (*Gattung*) drama (*auch fig.*); (*Stück*) *auch* play; *das elisabethanische ~* Elizabethan drama; *mach kein ~ draus fig.* don't make a big thing out of it

Dramatik *f*, *-*, *kein Pl.* **1.** *Lit., Theat.* drama; **2.** *fig.* (high) drama, excitement

Dramatiker *m*; *-s*, -, *~in f*; *-*, *-nen Lit., Theat.* dramatist, playwright

dramatisch I. *Adj. Lit., Theat.* dramatic (*auch fig.*); **II.** *Adv.* dramatically; **dramatisieren** *v/t.* **1.** *Lit., Theat.* adapt for the stage; **2.** *fig.* dramatize

Dramaturg *m*; *-en*, *-en*, *~in f*; *-*, *-nen Lit., Theat.* script editor, dramaturg(e); **dramaturgisch** *Adj.* dramaturgical

dran *Adv. umg.* **1.** → *daran*; **2.** *an ihm / dem Hühnchen ist nichts ~* he's / the chicken's all skin and bones; *es ist etwas/nichts ~* (*ist wahr / nicht wahr*) there's something in it / nothing to it; (*ist etwas/nichts Besonderes*) there's something/nothing special about it; **3.** *früh/spät ~ sein* be early/late; *er ist gut ~* he's got it good, he's doing all right; *er ist schlecht od. arm ~* (*ist bedauernswert*) he's in a bad way; *finanziell*: he's scraping the barrel; *ich weiß nie, wie ich* (*bei od. mit ihr*) *~ bin* I never know where I stand (with her); **4.** *ich bin ~* it's my turn; *jetzt ist er aber ~! fig.* he's really in for it now; → *drauf* 3, *Drum*, *glauben* II 2

Dränage *f*; *-*, *-n*; *bes. Tech.* drainage

dranbleiben *v/i.* (*unreg., trennb., ist -ge-*); *umg.* **1.** stay on (*an etw.* [*Dat.*] s.th.); (*kleben*) stick; **2.** *fig.*: *an etw.* (*Dat.*) *~* keep at it; *an j-m ~* keep on at s.o.; *bleib dran! am Telefon*: hang on

drang *Imperf.* → *dringen*

Drang *m*; *-(e)s*, *Dränge*, *mst Sg.* **1.** (*Trieb*) urge; (*Wunsch*) wish, desire; (*Bedürfnis*) need (*nach, zu* for; *zu + Inf.* to + *Inf.*); *~ nach Freiheit* urge for freedom; *~ zum Lügen* urge (*od.* compulsion) to tell lies; *e-n ~ nach Höherem haben* aspire to higher things; *ich habe e-n ~ umg.* I'm really dying to go (to the loo, *Am.* bathroom); **2.** (*Druck, Bedrängnis*) pressure

Drängelei *f*; *-*, *-en*; *umg. pej.* **1.** pushing and shoving, jostling; **2.** *fig.* pestering; **drängeln** *umg.* **I.** *vt/i.* **1.** push, jostle, shove; **2.** *fig.* pester *s.o.*, bother *s.o.*; *mit Gerede*: go on at *s.o.*; **II.** *v/refl.*: *sich nach vorn ~* push (*od.* elbow) one's way to the front; *beim Anstehen*: jump the queue (*Am.* line); → *auch drängen* II 1

dran|geben *umg.* → *darangeben*; *~gehen umg.* → *darangehen*

drängen I. *v/t.* **1.** (*schieben*) push, shove; *j-n zur Seite ~* push s.o. aside (*od.* out of the way); → *Defensive, Ecke* 1, *Hintergrund*; **2.** (*dringend bitten, auffordern*) press (*zu + Inf.* into + *Ger.*); *stärker*: urge (*to + Inf.*); (*unter Druck setzen*) pressurize, *bes. Am.* pressure (into + *Ger.*); (*zur Eile antreiben*) rush; *ich lasse mich nicht ~* I'm not going to let anyone (*od.* them etc.) rush me; **3.** *es drängte mich zu* (+ *Inf.*) *unwiderstehlich*: I felt (*od.* had) the urge to (+ *Inf.*); *zu danken etc.*: I felt I ought to (*od.* had to) (+ *Inf.*); *Notwendigkeit*: I felt compelled to (+ *Inf.*); *Verpflichtung*: I felt obliged to (+ *Inf.*); **II.** *v/i.* **1.** push (and shove); *nach vorn ~* push one's way forward (*od.* to the front); *zum Eingang ~ Menge*: push its *od.* their way (*od.* crowd) toward(s) the entrance; *~ in* (+ *Akk.*) (*e-n Beruf etc.*) flood into; **2.** (*eilig sein*) be urgent; *die Zeit drängt* time's running out (*od.* pressing); **3.** *~ auf* (+ *Akk.*) press for; *darauf ~, dass etw. tut* press (for) s.o. to do s.th.; *darauf ~, dass etw. getan wird* press for s.th. to be done; **4.** *zum Aufbruch / zur Eile ~* insist that we, they etc. should leave/hurry, urge *s.o.* to leave/hurry; **III.** *v/refl.* **1.** push (and shove); → *auch* II 1; *Menge*: *sich um j-n ~* crowd (a)round s.o.; *die Leute ~ sich auf den Straßen* people are crowding the streets, the streets are teeming with people; → *gedrängt* II, III; **2.** *fig.*: *sich ~ nach ...* be keen on ...

Drängen *n*; *-s*, *kein Pl.* **1.** pushing and shoving; **2.** *fig.* urging; *stärker*: insistence; *auf ~ der Regierung* on the government's urging (*od.* insistence); *ich habe es auf sein ~ hin getan* he persuaded (*stärker*: forced) me to do it

drängend I. *Part. Präs.* → *drängen*; **II.** *Adj.* urgent; *~e Probleme* pressing problems

drangsalieren *v/t. pej.* pester, plague; (*schikanieren*) pick on

drangvoll *Adj.*: *~e Enge* oppressive restriction

dranhalten (*unreg., trennb., hat -ge-*); *umg.* **I.** *v/t.*: *etw. (an etw.) ~* hold s.th. up (to s.th.); **II.** *v/refl.* (*sich beeilen*) hurry up, get a move on; (*sich anstrengen*) put one's back into it (*od.* the

job); *beharrlich*: keep (plugging away) at it, stick at it

dranhängen¹ (*trennb., hat -ge-*); *umg.* **I.** *v/t.* tag on; *wir beschlossen spontan, noch eine Woche Urlaub dranzuhängen* we decided on the spur of the moment to add on another week('s holiday, *Am.* vacation); **II.** *v/refl.* tag along; *an e-e Bewegung etc.*: jump on the bandwagon

dranhängen² *v/i.* (*unreg., trennb., hat -ge-*); *umg.* **1.** *Schild, Gegenstand etc.*: be attached (*od.* tied on) (*an + Dat.* to); **2.** *fig.* involve; *an dem Bild hängt viel Mühe dran* that picture is a lot of work

dränieren *v/t.* drain; **Dränierung** *f* draining

dran|kommen *v/i.* (*unreg., trennb., ist -ge-*); *umg.* **1.** (*erreichen*) get at it, reach it; **2.** *Schüler*: be called; *ich komme jetzt dran* it's my turn, I'm next; *das kommt nächste Woche dran* we'll be doing that next week; *das ist in der Prüfung nicht drangekommen* that wasn't asked (*od.* tested) in the exam; *~kriegen v/t.* (*trennb., hat -ge-*); *umg.* **1.** *zu e-r Arbeit*: get s.o. to do it; **2.** (*reinlegen*) fool s.o., catch s.o. out, *Am. auch* trip s.o. up; *~lassen v/t.* (*unreg., trennb., hat -ge-*); *umg.* **1.** (*nicht abmachen*) leave s.th. (*an + Dat.* on); **2.** (*benutzen, nehmen lassen*) let s.o. *od.* s.th. have a go (*Am.* try) (*an + Akk.* at); (*gelangen lassen*) let s.o. *od.* s.th. near (*od.* touch) s.th.; *an die Reihe*: let s.o. go (first); *~machen* (*trennb., hat -ge-*); *umg.* **I.** *v/t.*: *~* (*an + Akk.*) attach (to), put on (to); **II.** *v/refl.* get down to it; *sich ~ zu* (+ *Inf.*) set about (+ *Ger.*); *~nehmen v/t.* (*unreg., trennb., hat -ge-*); *umg.* (*Patienten*) take; (*Kunden*) see to, serve; (*Schüler*) ask; *~setzen* (*trennb., hat -ge-*); *umg.* **I.** *v/t.* alles ~ make every effort; **II.** *v/refl.* get down to it

drapieren *v/t.* drape (*mit* with)

drastisch I. *Adj.* drastic; **II.** *Adv.* drastically; *~ kürzen* (*Gelder etc.*) slash

drauf *Adv. umg.* **1.** → *darauf*; **2.** *gut/ schlecht ~ sein* be on the ball / not on (*Am.* in) good form; *seelisch*: feel good/bad, be in a good/bad mood; *wie ist 'der denn ~?* verwundert *od.* verärgert: what's up (*od.* the matter) with him then?; **3.** *~ und dran sein zu* (+ *Inf.*) be on the point of (+ *Ger.*), be about to (+ *Inf.*); **4.** *Ausruf*: (*immer feste*) *~!* get stuck in there!, let them have it!; *~bekommen v/i.* (*unreg., trennb., hat -ge-*); *umg.* → *draufkriegen*; *~fahren v/i.* (*unreg., trennb., ist -ge-*); *umg.*: *j-m* (*hinten*) *~* drive into (the back of) s.o.('s car)

Draufgänger *m*; *-s*, -, (*Teufelskerl*) daredevil; (*Frauenheld*) womanizer, lady-killer; **Draufgängerin** *f*; *-*, *-nen* daredevil; **draufgängerisch** *Adj. attr.* daredevil ..., *auch präd.* daring; **Draufgängertum** *n*; *-s*, *kein Pl.* derring-do, daredevil(t)ry

drauf|geben *v/t.* (*unreg., trennb., hat -ge-*); *umg.* **1.** (*dazugeben*) add some more (on); *gut - ich gebe noch eine Woche drauf* all right, I can give you another week; **2.** *j-m eins ~* belt s.o. one, give s.o. a belt round the ears (*Am.* a good smacking); *~gehen v/i.* (*unreg., trennb., ist -ge-*); *umg.* **1.** (*verbraucht werden*) be used (up); (*verloren gehen*) be lost; *Geld*: go down the drain; *dabei sind zwei Stunden draufgegangen* two hours were wasted on

D

that; **2.** (*kaputtgehen*) go to pot; **3.** (*sterben*) be killed, snuff (*Am.* buy) it; **~haben** *v/t.* (*unreg., trennb., hat -ge-*); *umg.* **1.** (*Sprüche, Masche, Technik*) have *s.th.* at one's fingertips, have *s.th.* off (*Am.* down) pat; **technisch hat er nichts drauf** he hasn't got a clue about technical things; **sie hat was drauf** she's really good, she's got what it takes; *fachlich:* she knows her stuff; (*ist gut in Form*) she's in top form; **2.** *Geschwindigkeit:* **100 Sachen / e-n ordentlichen Zahn ~** be doing a ton / a fair speed; **~halten** (*unreg., trennb., hat -ge-*); *umg.* **I.** *v/t.* hold *s.th.* on (*auf + Akk.* s.th.); **II.** *v/i.:* **auf j-n/etw. ~** (*zielen*) aim for s.o./s.th.; **~hauen** *v/i.* (*unreg., trennb., hat -ge-*); *umg.:* **auf j-n/etw. ~** hit s.o./s.th. (hard)
draufkommen *v/i.* (*unreg., trennb., ist -ge-*); *umg.* **1.** *das kommt da* (*oben*) *drauf* (*wird gelegt etc.*) that goes up there; **was kommt vorne / auf das Schild drauf?** (*geschrieben*) what's going on the front/sign?; **2.** *auf Lösung etc.:* **ich bin einfach nicht draufgekommen** it just didn't occur to me; **3.** (*j-m*) **~** find s.o. out
drauf|kriegen *v/t.* (*trennb., hat -ge-*); *umg.:* **eins ~** get a belt round the ears (*Am.* a good smacking; (*zurechtgewiesen werden*) get a (real) roasting; **~legen** (*trennb., hat -ge-*); *umg.* **I.** *v/t.* lay (*auf + Akk.* on); **da musst du schon noch ein paar Euro ~** *fig.* you'll have to fork out a few more euros for that; **II.** *v/refl.* lie down on s.th.
drauflos *Adv. umg.:* **immer** *od.* **munter ~!** get stuck in!, keep it up!; **~arbeiten** *v/i.* (*trennb., hat -ge-*); *umg. ohne Zögern:* get cracking, set to work (straight away); *ohne Plan:* work away without a clue; **~gehen** *v/i.* (*unreg., trennb., ist -ge-*); *umg.* (*anfangen*) go at it, set to work; *auf ein Ziel:* make straight for it; *ohne Ziel:* set off, get going; **~fahren** *v/i.* (*unreg., trennb., ist -ge-*); *umg.* drive (straight) towards *s.th.*; **~reden** *v/i.* (*trennb., hat -ge-*); *umg.* start talking (*od.* rattling) away; **~schießen** *v/i.* (*unreg., trennb., hat -ge-*); *umg.* start shooting wildly
drauf|machen *v/t.* (*trennb., hat -ge-*); *umg.:* **einen ~** have (*od.* go on) a binge; **~satteln** *v/t.* (*trennb., hat -ge-*); *umg.* slap on top; **10% ~** throw in another 10%; **~schlagen** (*unreg., trennb., hat -ge-*); *umg.* **I.** *v/i.* hit (*auf + Akk.* s.th.); **II.** *v/t.:* **auf den Preis noch etw. ~** add s.th. to the price
Draufsicht *f* top view
drauf|stehen *v/i.* (*unreg., trennb., hat / südd., österr., schw. ist -ge-*); *umg.* **1.** *Mensch, Sache:* be (*od.* stand) on it; *Schrift:* be (written) on it; **2.** *magst du Pizza? - da steh ich drauf* I love it, I'm wild about it; **~stoßen** *v/t.* (*unreg., trennb., hat -ge-*); *umg.:* **j-n ~** rub s.o.'s nose in it, spell it out (to s.o.) *iro.*; **~zahlen** (*trennb., hat -ge-*); *umg.* **I.** *v/t.:* **20 Euro** *etc.* **~** pay an extra 20 euros *etc.*; **II.** *v/i.* **1.** make a bad deal (on it); **2.** *fig.* lose out
draus *Adv. umg.* → *daraus*; **~bringen** *v/t.* (*unreg., trennb., hat -ge-*); *südd., österr. umg.* distract, confuse; **~kommen** *v/i.* (*unreg., trennb., ist -ge-*); *südd., österr. umg.* lose track
draußen *Adv.* **1.** outside; (*im Freien*) *auch* in the open; **da ~** out there; *nach* **~** outside; **im Garten** out in the garden; **~ bleiben!** stay outside!; **2.** *in der*

Welt: in the world outside; *im Ausland:* abroad; *auf See:* (out) at sea; *an der Front:* (out) at the front; *weit ~ auf dem Meer:* far out at sea; **~ auf dem Lande** out in the country
drechseln I. *v/t.* **1.** (*etw.*) turn *s.th.* on the lathe; **2.** *fig.* turn *s.th.* out; (*Phrasen*) over-elaborate, over-do; **II.** *v/i.* work the lathe; **Drechsler** *m, -s, -* wood turner; **Drechslerbank** *f* (wood-turning) lathe; **Drechslerei** *f, -, -en* **1.** *Werkstatt:* wood-turner's workshop, turnery; **2.** *nur Sg.; Handwerk:* wood turning; **Drechslerin** *f, -, -nen* wood turner
Dreck *m; -(e)s, kein Pl.; umg.* **1.** dirt; *stärker:* muck, filth; (*Schlamm*) mud; **vor ~ starren** be filthy (*od.* covered in muck); **~ machen** make a mess; **j-n wie den letzten ~ behandeln** treat s.o. like dirt (*od.* shit *Sl.*); **2.** *fig.:* **mit ~ bewerfen** sling mud at; **durch** *od.* **in den ~ ziehen** drag through the mud (*od.* mire); **ganz schön im ~ sitzen** *od.* **stecken** be in a fine (*od.* real) mess (*od.* jam), be up shit creek *Sl.*; **j-n aus dem ~ ziehen** get s.o. out of trouble, help s.o. out; **~ am Stecken haben** have a skeleton in the cupboard (*Am.* closet), have blotted one's copybook; **3.** *fig. pej.* (*Sache*): **mach doch d-n ~ alleine!** (*Brit.* bloody well) do it yourself then!; **kümmere dich um deinen eignen ~** mind your own business!; **4.** *fig. pej.* (*Schund*) rubbish, *bes. Am.* garbage; **das ist doch ein / der reinste ~ dagegen** it's nothing compared (with that), there's no comparison; **er ist der letze ~** he's scum (*od.* the lowest of the low); **5.** *pej., als Verneinung:* **e-n ~** (**hat er das gesagt**) like hell!, the hell he said that!; **er kümmert sich e-n ~ darum** he doesn't give (*od.* care) a damn; **das geht dich e-n ~ an!** that's none of your (bloody) business
Dreck|... *im Subst. umg. pej.* **1.** *schmutzig:* dirty ...; **2.** *fig. verabscheuungswürdig etc.:* lousy ..., filthy ...; *verdammt:* damn ...; **~arbeit** *f umg. pej.* dirty work (*auch fig.*); *pej.* (*niedrige Tätigkeit*) drudgery; **~finger** *m; mst Pl.; umg. pej.* dirty finger; **~fleck** *m umg.* dirty mark (*od.* speck); **~haufen** *m umg.* pile of dirt
dreckig I. *Adj. umg.* **1.** dirty; *stärker:* filthy (*beide auch Witz etc.*); **2.** *fig. pej.* (*gemein*) nasty; **II.** *Adv.* **1.** *es geht ihm ~ finanziell:* he's going through a bad patch, he's pretty badly off; *gesundheitlich:* he's not in the best of health; *stärker:* he's in a pretty bad state, he's in a bad way; **2.** *sie grinste/lachte ~* she gave a dirty grin/laugh
Dreck|loch *n umg. pej.* pigsty, hole; **~nest** *n umg. pej.* dump, hole, hovel
Drecks... *im Subst.* → *Dreck...*
Dreck|sack *m vulg. pej.* (dirty) bastard *Sl.*; **~sau** *f vulg. pej.* (dirty) pig; *moralisch:* swine *Sl.*; **~schleuder** *f umg. pej.* **1.** *Fabrik, Auto etc.:* environmental hazard; **2.** *Person:* foul-mouth; *nasty piece* (*od.* bit) of work; **e-e ~ sein** *auch* have a wicked tongue (*od.* dirty mouth)
Dreckskerl *m umg. pej.* swine, louse, pig
Dreckspatz *m umg. pej.* mucky pup; *pej.* filthy bugger (*Am.* jerk)
Dreckszeug *n umg. pej.* rubbish, *bes. Am.* garbage
Dreckwetter *n umg. pej.* filthy (*Am.* lousy) weather
Dreh *m; -(e)s, -s* *od.* *-e; umg.* **1.** (*Trick*)

trick, knack; **jetzt hab ich den ~ heraus** now I've got the hang of it; **2.** (*so*) **um den ~** *zeitlich:* (a)round about then; *Summe, Menge:* or so, or thereabouts; **3.** (*Drehung*) turn; **4.** *umg.* (*Dreharbeiten*) shooting; **beim ~** at (*od.* during) the shooting; **~achse** *f* axis of rotation; **~arbeiten** *Pl. Film:* shooting *Sg.*, filming *Sg.*; **bei den ~ sein** be on set; **~bank** *f; Pl. -bänke; Tech.* lathe
drehbar *Adj. Tür, Bühne:* revolving; *Trommel, Antenne:* rotating; (*schwenkbar*) *attr.* swivel ... (*auch Stuhl*); **Drehbarkeit** *f* turnability
Dreh|beginn *m Film:* start of shooting; **~bewegung** *f* turn; *Tech.* rotation, rotary motion, revolution; **e-e schnelle ~ machen** turn (*od.* spin) (a)round quickly; **~bolzen** *m Tech.* pivot pin; **~brücke** *f* swing bridge
Drehbuch *n* (film) script, screenplay; **~autor** *m,* **~autorin** *f* screenwriter, scriptwriter
Drehbühne *f* revolving stage
drehen I. *v/t.* **1.** *allg.* turn; (*winden, verdrehen*) twist; *um e-e Achse:* rotate; (*schwenken*) swivel; (*zwirbeln*) twirl; **s-e Runden ~** *umg. zu Fuß:* go for a stroll; *im Auto:* go for a spin; **das Gas kleiner** *od.* **auf klein ~** turn down the heat; **das Radio lauter/leiser ~** turn the radio up/down; **j-m den Arm auf den Rücken ~** twist s.o.'s arm (behind their back); **man kann es ~ und wenden(, wie man will)** *od.* **wie man es auch dreht und wendet** *fig.* whichever way you look at it; → *Däumchen*; **2.** (*herstellen*) (*Pille etc.*) roll; (*Faden, Seil etc.*) twist; *Tech.* (*Schrauben etc.*) screw (in), turn; **sich e-e Zigarette ~** roll a cigarette; **sich** (*Dat.*) *Locken ~* curl one's hair, put one's hair in curlers; → *Strick* 1; **3.** *durch den Fleischwolf ~* (*Fleisch etc.*) mince, *bes. Am.* grind, put through the mincer (*bes. Am.* grinder); *umg., fig.* put *s.o.* through the mill; **4.** *umg. fig.* (*deichseln*) wangle, fix; **es so ~, dass ...** *umg.* wangle it so that ...; → *Ding* 6; **II.** *vt/i.* (*Film, Szene*) shoot; *Schauspieler:* make (a film); **III.** *v/i.* **1.** turn; *Wind:* → IV 2; **am Schalter/Radio ~** flick a switch / turn the radio dial (*od.* knob); **3.** *umg. fig. pej.:* **~ an** (+ *Dat.*) fiddle with; **IV.** *v/refl.* **1.** turn; *im Kreis:* go (a)round; *schnell:* spin ([a]round); *die Erde dreht sich um ihre Achse / die Sonne* rotates on its axis / revolves around the sun; *sich auf den Bauch/Rücken ~* turn (over) onto one's stomach (tummy *umg.*) /back; *sich im Kreis ~* turn in a circle; *schneller:* spin (a)round; *fig.* go (a)round in circles; *mir dreht sich alles umg.* my head's spinning; *sich ~ und winden fig.* hedge; **2.** *Wind:* shift, veer ([a]round); **3.** *fig.:* *sich ~ um e-n Mittelpunkt:* revolve (a)round (*auch Gedanken etc.*); *alles drehte sich um ihn* he was the cent|re (*Am.* -er) of attention; **4.** *umg. fig.:* *sich ~ um* (*betreffen*) be about, concern; *es dreht sich darum, ob ...* it's a question (*od.* matter) of whether ...; *worum dreht es sich?* what's it all about?
Dreher *m; -s, -;* **~in** *f; -, -nen; Tech.* turner, lathe operator
Dreh|erlaubnis *f* filming permission; **~feld** *n Etech.* rotating field; **~geschwindigkeit** *f* speed (of rotation), rotating speed; **~knopf** *m* knob; **~kraft** *f Phys.* torque; **~kran** *m* swing

crane; **~kreuz** n turnstile; **~leiter** f turntable (od. revolving) ladder; **~maschine** f Tech. lathe; **~moment** n Phys. torque; **~orgel** f barrel organ, hurdy-gurdy; **~orgelspieler** m, **~orgelspielerin** f organ grinder; **~ort** m Film: location; **~pause** f Film: break in shooting; **~punkt** m 1. Tech. fulcrum; 2. fig.: **Dreh- und Angelpunkt** pivot; **~richtung** f direction (od. sense) of rotation; **~schalter** m Etech. rotary switch; **~scheibe** f 1. turntable; Töpferei: potter's wheel; Telef. etc. dial; 2. fig. hub, nerve cent|re (Am. -er); **~strom** m Etech. three-phase (od. rotary) current; **~stuhl** m swivel chair; **~tag** m Film: shooting day; **~tür** f revolving door

Drehung f turn; um e-e Achse: rotation (**um** on); um e-n Körper: revolution ([a]round); schnelle: spin (auch e-s Balls); (Verwindung) twist; **e-e halbe/ganze ~** a half/complete turn; **e-e ~ um 180° (machen)** (do) a 180° turn (od. a complete about-face)

Drehwurm m 1. Zool. coenurus, dog tapeworm; 2. umg. fig.: **den ~ kriegen/haben** get/feel dizzy (od. giddy)

Drehzahl f Tech., Mot. speed, revolutions Pl. per minute (rpm), revs umg.; **~bereich** m speed range; **im niederen/hohen** od. **unteren/oberen ~** at lower/higher revs umg.; **~messer** m revolution counter; Mot. rev counter, Am. tachometer

Drehzeit f Film: shooting time

drei Zahlw. 1. three; **einer von uns/euch ~(en)** one of the three of us / you three; **kennst du die ~ da drüben?** do you know those three over there?; **sie kamen zu ~en** there were three of them; **ehe man bis ~ zählen konnte** before you could say Jack Robinson (od. knew it); **er sieht aus, als ob er nicht bis ~ zählen könnte** umg. (harmlos) he looks as if butter wouldn't melt in his mouth; (dumm) he looks a right (Am. complete) idiot (od. as thick as two short planks [Am. as a board hum.]); → auch **acht**[1], **Ding** 1; 2. das Glas ist ~ viertel voll three-quarters full; **~ Viertel der Bevölkerung** three quarters of the population; **~ viertel acht** Uhrzeit: quarter to eight

Drei f, -, -en 1. Zahl: (number) three; → auch **Acht**[1] 1, 2, 4; 2. Päd. (Note): etwa e-e ~ schreiben get a C

Dreiachser m; -s, -; Mot. six-wheeler

Dreiachteltakt m Mus.: **(im) ~** (in) three-eight time

Dreiakter m; -s, -; Theat. three-act play

drei|armig Adj. Leuchter: three-armed; **~bändig I.** Adj. attr. three-volume ..., nachgestellt, auch präd. in three volumes; **II.** Adv. in three volumes

dreibeinig Adj. three-legged

Dreibettzimmer n three-bed room

dreiblätt(e)rig Adj. Klee: three-leaved

Drei-D-|... im Subst. 3-D ...; **~Brille** f 3-D glasses

dreidimensional Adj. three-dimensional; **~es Sehen** stereoscopy, three-dimensional vision

Dreieck n; -s, -e triangle; Sport top corner (of the goal); **Dreieckgeschäft** n Wirts. three-way deal; **dreieckig** Adj. triangular; **Dreiecksgeschichte** f: **e-e ~** a case of the eternal triangle; **Dreiecksverhältnis** n love triangle, ménage à trois; **ein ~ haben** take part in a ménage à trois

dreieinhalb Zahlw. three and a half

dreieinig Adj. kirchl.: **der ~e Gott** the

---

triune God(head); **Dreieinigkeit** f Trinity

Dreier m; -s, - 1. umg. → **Drei**; 2. **e-n ~ haben** Lotto: have (got) three right, have matched three numbers; 3. umg.: flotter ~ threesome, three-way deal; **~gruppe** f group of three

dreierlei Adj. indekl. three (different) kinds of; subst. three things; **aus ~ Gründen** for three reasons

Dreier|pack m three-pack; **~reihe** f row of three; **in ~** three abreast; **~takt** m triple (Am. auch three-four) time

dreifach I. Adj. triple; **in ~er Ausfertigung** in triplicate; **etw. in ~er Ausfertigung schicken** send three copies of s.th.; **II.** Adv. three times; → **achtfach**; **Dreifache** n; -n, kein Pl.: **um ein ~s steigen** triple, rise (od. go up) threefold; → **Achtfache**

Dreifach|... im Subst. triple ...; **~steckdose** f Etech. triple socket

Dreifaltigkeit f kirchl. Trinity; **Dreifaltigkeitsfest** n Trinity Sunday

Dreifarbendruck m; -(e)s, -e 1. nur Sg. three-colo(u)r printing; 2. (Bild etc.) three-colo(u)r print; **dreifarbig** Adj. three-colo(u)red

Drei|felderwirtschaft f; nur Sg.; Agr. three-field system

dreiflächig Adj. three-faced; Math. trihedral

dreifüßig Adj. three-legged

Dreigang|rad n three-speed bicycle (od. bike umg.); **~schaltung** f Fahrrad: three-speed gears Pl.

drei|geschossig, österr. **~geschoßig** Adj. attr. three-stor(e)y ...

Drei|gespann n 1. three-horse carriage, troika; 2. fig. trio, threesome; **~gestirn** n poet. fig. triumvirate

drei|gestrichen Adj. Mus.: **das ~e C** the C two octaves above middle C; **~geteilt** Adj. divided into three parts; Artikel etc.: auch three-part ...; **~gliedrig** Adj. 1. Anat. three-membered; 2. Math. Ausdruck: trinomial, three-term(ed); Operation: triadic

Dreigroschen|heft n, **~roman** m bes. Brit. penny dreadful, Am. dime novel, (work of) pulp fiction

Dreiheit f trinity

dreihundert Zahlw. three hundred; **Dreihundertjahrfeier** f tercentenary, Am. tercentennial

dreijährig Adj. 1. attr. three-year-old ...; 2. attr. (drei Jahre dauernd) three year ...; **Dreijährige** m, f, n; -n, -n three-year-old

dreijährlich I. Adj. three-yearly, triennial; **II.** Adv. every three years, triennially; **Dreikampf** m Sport triathlon

dreikantig Adj. Feile etc.: attr. three-square ..., auch präd. triangular; Frucht etc.: trigonal; Math. trihedral, three-cornered

dreikarätig Adj. attr. three-carat ...

Dreikäsehoch m; -s, -(s); umg. titch, little nipper, Am. squirt

Drei|klang m Mus. triad

Dreikönige Pl., **Dreikönigsfest** n, **Dreikönigstag** m Reli. Epiphany, Twelfth Day

drei|köpfig Adj. 1. **~e Familie** etc. family etc. of three; 2. Monster etc.: three-headed; **~lagig** Adj. three-ply

Drei|ländereck n; nur Sg.; Geog. triangle (where three countries meet); **~mächteabkommen** n Pol. three-power (od. tripartite) agreement

dreimal Adv. three times; **dreimalig** Adj.: **~e Wiederholung** etc. three repeats etc.; **nach ~er Warnung** etc. after

---

three warnings etc., after being warned etc. three times; → **achtmalig**

Dreimaster m; -s, -; Naut. three-master

Dreimeilenzone f three-mile limit

Dreimeterbrett n Sport three-met|re (Am. -er) board

dreimonatig Adj. 1. attr. Baby etc.: three-month-old; 2. attr. Zeitraum: three-month ...; **nach e-m ~en Englandaufenthalt** after three months (od. a three-month stay) in England; **dreimonatlich I.** Adj. attr. three-monthly ..., quarterly; **II.** Adv. every three months

drein Adv. umg. → **darein**; **~blicken** v/i. (trennb., hat -ge-); umg.: fröhlich/traurig etc. ~ look happy, sad etc.; **~finden** v/refl. (unreg., trennb., hat -ge-); umg. get used to s.th., become resigned to s.th.

Dreingabe f Dial. (added) extra, bonus

drein|reden v/i. (trennb., hat -ge-); umg. 1. interrupt, butt in; **j-m ~** butt into s.o.'s conversation; 2. (sich einmischen) interfere (**bei** with; **in** + Akk. in); **er lässt sich in s-e Arbeit nicht** od. **von niemandem ~** he won't let anyone tell him what to do; **~schauen** v/i. (trennb., hat -ge-); umg. → **dreinblicken**; **~schlagen** v/i. (unreg., trennb., hat -ge-); umg. 1. → **dazwischenschlagen**; 2. **mit den Fäusten ~** use one's fists

Dreiparteiensystem n Pol. three-party system

Dreipfünder m; -s, - Brot: three-pound loaf (of bread); Fisch etc.: three-pounder

drei|phasig Adj. Etech. attr. three-phase ...; **~polig** Adj. Etech. attr. three-pole ...; Kabel: three-core ...; Stecker: three-pin ...; **~prozentig** Adj. attr. three percent ...

Dreipunktgurt m Mot. three-point (od. lap and diagonal) (seat)belt

Dreirad n tricycle; **dreiräd(e)rig** Adj. attr. three-wheeled ...; with three wheels

dreisaitig Adj. Mus. three-stringed

Dreisatz m Math. rule of three (od. proportion); **~rechnung** f calcuation (od. sum umg.) using the rule of three

drei|schichtig Adj. attr. Torte: three-layered; Anstrich: three-coat(ed); Leimholzplatte: three-ply; **~schiffig** Adj. Archit. attr. with three naves; **diese Kirche ist ~** this church has a nave and two aisles

dreiseitig Adj. 1. Körper: three-sided; Math. auch trilateral; 2. attr. Aufsatz etc.: three-page ...

dreisilbig Adj. Ling. attr. three-syllable ..., trisyllabic

dreisitzig Adj. nachgestellt: with three seats

dreispaltig Adj. Druck. nachgestellt: with three columns

Dreispitz m tricorn(e), three-cornered hat, tricorn

dreisprachig Adj. trilingual; **~ sein** auch speak three languages fluently, be fluent in three languages, be trilingual

Dreisprung m triple jump

dreispurig Adj. attr. three-lane ...

dreißig Zahlw. thirty; **Anfang/Mitte/Ende ~ (sein)** be in one's early/mid/late thirties; → auch **achtzig**

Dreißig f; -, -en, mst Sg. Zahl: (number) thirty; → auch **Achtzig**

dreißiger Adj.: **in den ~ Jahren** in the thirties; **er ist in den Dreißigern** he's in his thirties

D

Dreißiger *m*; *-s*, *-*, *~in f*; *-*, *-nen* man/woman in his/her thirties; thirtysomething *umg.*

Dreißigerjahre *Pl.*: *in den ~n* in the thirties

dreißigjährig *Adj. attr.* (*Dauer*) thirty years' ...; *nachgestellt*: lasting thirty years; (*Alter*) *attr.* thirty-year-old ...; *präd.* thirty years old; *der Dreißigjährige Krieg* the Thirty Years' War; **Dreißigjährige** *m*, *f*; *-n*, *-n* thirty-year-old man *od.* woman, thirty-year-old

dreißigst... *Zahlw.* thirtieth; → *achtzigst...*

dreist *Adj. Person*: bold as brass; (*frech*) cheeky, impudent; *Bemerkung*: impudent; *Lüge*: brazen, barefaced

dreistellig *Adj. attr. Zahl*: three-digit ...

Dreisternehotel *n* three-star hotel

Dreistheit *f*, **Dreistigkeit** *f* 1. *nur Sg.* boldness, audacity; (*Frechheit*) impudence, brazenness; 2. *Äußerung*: impudent remark

drei|stimmig *Mus.* I. *Adj. attr.* three-part ...; II. *Adv.*: *~ singen* sing in three-part harmony; *~stöckig Adj. attr.* three-stor(e)y ...

Dreistufenplan *m* three-stage plan

drei|stufig *Adj. attr.* three-stage ...; *~stündig Adj. attr.* three-hour(-long); *der Zug kam mit ~er Verspätung an* the train arrived three hours late; *~stündlich* I. *Adj.* three-hourly; II. *Adv.* every three hours

Dreitagebart *m umg.* designer stubble

dreitägig *Adj.* 1. *attr.* three-day(-long); 2. (*drei Tage alt*) *attr.* three-day-old

dreitausend *Zahlw.* three thousand

Dreitausender *m Berg*: 3000 met|re (*Am.* -er) peak

dreiteilig *Adj.* 1. *Aufsatz, Plan*: *attr.* three-part, tripartite, *nachgestellt*: in three parts; 2. *Anzug, Couchgarnitur etc.*: *attr.* three-piece ...

Dreitonner *m*; *-s*, *-*; *Mot.* three-tonner, three-ton lorry (*Am.* truck)

Dreiuhr|nachrichten *Pl.* three o'clock news; *~zug m* three o'clock train

Dreiviertel|literflasche *f* 75 cl bottle; *~mehrheit f* three-quarter majority; *~stunde f* three quarters of an hour, 45 minutes *Pl.*; *~takt m Mus.*: (*im*) *~* (in) three-four (*od.* triple) time

Dreiwege|... *im Subst.* three-way ...; *~katalysator m Mot.* three-way catalyst (*od.* catalytic converter)

drei|wertig *Adj. Chem.* trivalent; *~wöchig Adj.* 1. *Zeitraum etc.*: *attr.* three-week ...; 2. *Baby etc.*: *attr.* three-week-old

Dreizack *m*; *-s*, *-e* trident

dreizehn *Zahlw.* thirteen; *jetzt schlägt's ~!* *umg.* that's going too far, that's a bit much; → *acht¹*; **dreizehnt...** *Zahlw.* thirteenth; **Dreizehntel** *n* thirteenth (part)

Dreizimmerwohnung *f* two-bedroom(ed) flat (*Am.* apartment)

dreizinkig *Adj. attr.* three-pronged

Dreschboden *m Agr.* threshing floor

Dresche *f umg.*: *~ bekommen* get a good hiding (*od.* thumping)

dreschen; *drischt*, *drosch*, *hat gedroschen* I. *vt/i.* 1. (*Getreide etc.*) thresh; → *Phrase* 1, *Stroh*; 2. *umg. mit Wucht*: bang; *mit der Faust auf den Tisch ~* thump one's fist on the table; II. *vt. umg.* (*prügeln*) thrash, thump, wallop

Dresch|flegel *m Agr.* flail; *~maschine f Agr.* threshing machine

Dress *m*; *-es*, *-e*; *österr.* *f*; *-*, *-en*; *Sport* kit; *Fußball auch*: strip

Dresseur [drɛ'søːʀ] *m*; *-s*, *-e*, *~in f*; *-*, *-nen* (*animal*) trainer; **dressierbar** *Adj.* trainable; *nicht/gut ~* untrainable / easy to train

dressieren *vt.* 1. train (*zu + Inf.* to + *Inf.*); (*zureiten*) *auch* break in; 2. *fig. pej.* drill; 3. *Gastr.* (*Torte etc.*) decorate; *Spritzguss*: pipe; 4. *Gastr.* (*Geflügel*) truss (up), dress; **dressiert** I. *P.P.* → *dressieren*; II. *Adj.* trained; *~er Seehund etc.* performing seal *etc.*; *der Hund ist auf den Mann ~* he's *od.* she's been trained as an attack dog

Dressing *n*; *-s*, *-s*; *Gastr.* 1. *für Salate*: dressing; 2. *für Geflügel*: stuffing, *Am. auch* dressing

Dressman ['drɛsmən] *m*; *-s*, *Dressmen* male model (*auch euph.*)

Dressur *f*; *-*, *-en* 1. *mst Sg.* training; 2. *Kunststück*: trick; 3. *mst Sg.*; *Sport*, *Reiten*: dressage; *~reiten n Sport* dressage

Dr.h.c. *Abk.* (*doctor honoris causa*) honorary doctorate (*od.* PhD)

dribbeln *vi. Sport* dribble (the ball); **Dribbling** *n*; *-s*, *-s* dribble

Drift *f*; *-*, *-en*; *Naut.* 1. *Strömung*: drift current; 2. *Treiben*: drift(ing); **driften** *vi.* drift

Drill *m*; (*e*)*s*, *kein Pl.*; *Mil.* drill (*auch fig.*)

Drillbohrer *m* drill; **drillen** *vt.* 1. *Mil.* drill (*auch fig.*); (*schulen*) coach; *auf etw.* (*Akk.*) *gedrillt sein umg.* be trained to do s.th.; 2. *Tech.* (*bohren*) drill; 3. *Agr.* drill

Drillich *m*; *-s*, *-e* drill; *~anzug m* overalls *Pl.*; *~hose f* dungarees *Pl.*

Drilling *m*; *-s*, *-e* 1. triplet; 2. (*Gewehr*) triple-barrel(l)ed shotgun

drin *Adv. umg.* 1. → *darin*, *drinnen*; 2. *fig.*: *das ist nicht ~!* that's not on, *Am.* no way!; *das ist bei mir nicht ~* that's out of the question for me; (*da mach ich nicht mit*) you can count me out on that

dringen *vi/i.*; *dringt*, *drang*, *gedrungen* 1. (*ist*); *Person*, *gewaltsam*: force one's way (*od.* break) (*aus* out of *od.* from; *durch* through; *in* + *Akk.* into); *Messer*, *Licht*, *Kugel etc.*: penetrate, pierce; *Wasser etc.*: leak (*od.* seep) (*aus* out from; *durch* through; *in* + *Akk.* into); *~ bis zu* reach, get as far as; *aus der Küche drang lautes Gelächter* you could hear loud laughter coming from the kitchen, loud laughter emanated from the kitchen; *an die Öffentlichkeit ~* *fig.* leak (*od.* get) out, become public; 2. (*hat*) *auf etw.* (*Akk.*) *~* press for s.th., urge s.th.; *darauf ~*, *dass etw. getan wird* press for s.th. to be done; 3. (*ist*): *in j-n ~* press s.o.; *mit Bitten*: plead with s.o.; *mit Fragen*: ply (*od.* press) s.o. with questions

dringend I. *Part. Präs.* → *dringen*; II. *Adj.* 1. urgent; (*vordringlich*) *attr.* priority ...; *~er Fall* emergency; 2. *Verdacht*, *Rat*: strong; *Bedürfnis*: urgent, extreme; *Gründe*: compelling; III. *Adv.* urgently; *~ notwendig* absolutely essential; *~ brauchen* desperately need, need *s.th.* very badly (*schnell*: urgently); *j-m ~ raten zu* (+ *Inf.*) urge (*od.* strongly advise) s.o. to (+ *Inf.*); *ich rate Ihnen ~ davon ab* I would urge (*od.* strongly advise) you not to (do it), I would strongly advise you against it; *... werden ~ gebeten zu* (+ *Inf.*) ... are urged (*od.* urgently requested) to (+ *Inf.*); *der Tat ~ ver-*

dächtig strongly suspected of the crime

dringlich *Adj.* urgent; *~es Problem* pressing issue (*od.* problem); **Dringlichkeit** *f* urgency; (*Vordringlichkeit*) priority; *von größter ~* of the utmost urgency

Dringlichkeits|antrag *m* emergency motion; *~liste f* priority list; *~sitzung f* emergency (*od.* crisis) meeting; *im Parlament*: emergency sitting (*Am.* session); *~stufe f* priority (class); *höchste ~* top priority

drinnen *Adv.* inside; (*im Haus*) *auch* indoors; *nach ~ gehen* go inside (*od.* indoors)

drin|stecken *vi/i.* (*trennb.*, *hat* / *südd.*, *österr.*, *schw. ist -ge-*); *umg.*: *da steckt viel Arbeit/Geld drin* there's a lot of work/money in that; *~stehen vi/i.* (*trennb.*, *hat* / *südd.*, *österr.*, *schw. ist -ge-*); *umg.* be (written) in

drischt *Präs.* → *dreschen*

dritt *Adv.*: *zu ~* three of; → *acht²*

dritt... *Zahlw.* third; *in der ~en Person Ling.* in the third person; *~en Ranges* third-rate *attr.*; *die ~en Zähne* dentures, (one's) false teeth *umg.*; *ein Drittes erwähnen etc.* a third point (*od.* thing); *das Dritte Reich hist.* the Third Reich; *die Dritte Welt Pol.* the Third World; → *acht...*

dritt|ältest... *Adj.* third eldest ...; *~best... Adj.* third best ...

Dritte *m*, *f*; *-n*, *-n* 1. (the) third; *der ~ im Bunde* the third member of the trio (*od.* league *umg.*), number three (in the trio) *umg.*; *der lachende ~* the lucky bystander (*od.* third party); *wenn zwei sich streiten, freut sich der ~ Sprichw.* when two people are busy quarrelling, a third person can take advantage; → *Achte.*; 2. *weitS.* another person; *Jur.* third party; *im Beisein ~r* in front of others (*od.* other people)

drittel *Adj.*: *e-e ~ Sekunde* a third of a second

Drittel *n*; *-s*, *-* third; *zwei ~* two thirds

drittens *Adv.* third(ly)

Dritte-Welt-|Laden *m* charity shop with products from the Third World; *Brit. etwa* Oxfam

dritt|größt... *Adj.* third-largest ..., third-biggest ...; *~klassig Adj. attr.* third-class ...; *fig.* third-rate ...

Drittklässler *m*, *-s*, *-*, *~in f*; *-*, *-nen* third-year pupil (*Am.* student), third-former (*Am.* -grader)

Drittland *n Pol.* third country; *EU etc.*: non-member country

drittletzt... *Adj.* third last; *das ~e Haus* the third house from the end, the third(-to-the)-last house *umg.*

Drittmittel *Pl. Univ.* external funds

drittrangig *Adj. attr.* third-rate ...

Drive [draif] *m*; *-s*, *kein Pl.*; *umg.* (*Schwung*) drive, swing; (*Antrieb*) drive, enterprise, ambition

droben *Adv. geh. od. südd.*, *österr.* up there; *im Haus*: upstairs

Droge *f*; *-*, *-n* drug; *harte/weiche ~n* hard/soft drugs; *j-n unter ~n setzen* put s.o. on medication; *unter ~n stehen* be on medication

dröge *Adj. nordd. pej.* dry

drogenabhängig *Adj.* addicted to (*od.* dependent on) drugs; *~ sein auch* be a drug addict

Drogen|abhängige *m*, *f* drug addict, junkie *Sl.*; *~abhängigkeit f* drug addiction; *~beratungsstelle f* drugs advice cent|re (*Am.* -er); *~boss m umg.*

drug(s) boss; **~fahnder** *m*, **~fahnderin** *f* drug squad (*Am.* narcotics) officer (*od.* agent), narco *Sl.*

drogengefährdet *Adj.*: **~e Gruppe** *etc.* drug-risk group *etc.*

Drogen|handel *m* drug trafficking; **~händler** *m*, **~händlerin** *f* drug trafficker (*od.* dealer); **~karriere** *f* escalating drug habit, graduation to harder drugs; **~konsum** *m* drug consumption; **~kurier** *m* drug courier, mule *Sl.*; **~mafia** *f* drug mafia; **~missbrauch** *m* drug abuse; **~problem** *n* drug (--dependency) problem; **er hat ~e** he has a drug problem

Drogensucht *f*; *nur Sg.* drug addiction; **drogensüchtig** *Adj.* → **drogenabhängig**

Drogen|szene *f* drug scene; **~tote** *m*, *f* drug victim; **die Zahl der ~n** the number of deaths caused by drugs (*od.* drug overdose); **~umschlagplatz** *m* drug-dealing area

Drogerie *f*; -, -*n* chemist's (shop), *Am.* drugstore, pharmacy; **Drogist** *m*; -*en*, -*en*, **Drogistin** *f*; -, -*nen* chemist, *Am.* pharmacist

Drohbrief *m* threatening letter; *Pl. auch* hate mail *Sg.*

drohen *v/i.* **1.** *Person*: threaten (*j-m* s.o.; *zu* + *Inf.* to + *Inf.*); **er drohte** (*ihm etc.*) **mit der Polizei** he threatened to call the police; **sie drohte** (**ihm**), **ihn anzuzeigen** *od.* **sie drohte ihm mit e-r Anzeige** she threatened to report him to the police; **j-m mit der Faust / dem Finger ~** shake one's fist/ finger at s.o.; *Gefahr, Gewitter etc.*: threaten, approach; **er weiß noch nicht, was ihm droht** he doesn't know what's in store for him (*od.* what he's in for) yet; **ihm droht e-e Gefängnisstrafe** if he's unlucky he could get (*od.* he runs the risk of) a prison sentence; **der Wirtschaft droht der Kollaps** the economy is threatened with (*od.* is on the brink of) collapse; **3.** (*im Begriff sein*): **~ zu** (+ *Inf.*) threaten to (+ *Inf.*); *auch Person*: be in danger of (+ *Ger.*); **es drohte zu regnen** it looked like rain

drohend I. *Part. Präs.* → **drohen**; **II.** *Adj.* threatening, menacing; (*bevorstehend*) *auch* imminent, impending; **Drohgebärde** *f Mensch*: threatening gesture; *Tier*: threatening attitude

Drohne *f*; -, -*n* **1.** *Zool.* drone; **2.** *fig. pej.* drone, parasite; **3.** *Mil., Flug.* drone

dröhnen *v/i.* **1.** *laut*: boom, roar; *eintönig*: drone; *grollend*: rumble; *Donner. auch* roll; **2.** *Raum*: ring, echo (**von** with); **mir dröhnt der Kopf** my head's pounding (*od.* throbbing) (**von** with); **mir ~ die Ohren** my ears are ringing; **3.** *bes. nordd. pej.* (*reden*) drone (*od.* go) on; **4.** *Sl. Droge, Alkohol*: **das Zeug dröhnt tierisch** this stuff gives you a real high; → **voll gedröhnt**; **dröhnend I.** *Part. Präs.* → **dröhnen**; **II.** *Adj.*: **~es Gelächter** roars *Pl.* of laughter; **III.** *Adv.*: **~ lachen** roar with laughter

Drohnendasein *n*: **ein ~ führen** *pej.* lead the life of a parasite

Dröhnung *f Sl.* **1.** *nur Sg.*; (*Zustand unter Rauschmittel*) high; **2.** (*Dosis, Menge Alkohol etc.*) fix; **s-e tägliche ~ Bier** his daily fix of beer

Drohung *f* threat; **leere ~** empty threat; **~en ausstoßen** make threatening remarks, utter threats; **unter ~en** amid threats

drollig *Adj.* funny, comical; (*niedlich*) cute; (*seltsam*) odd, strange

Dromedar *n*; -*s*, -*e*; *Zool.* dromedary

Drops *Pl.*: **saure ~** acid drops

drosch *Imperf.* → **dreschen**

Droschke *f*; -, -*n* **1.** *hist.* cab, hackney carriage; **2.** *Mot. altm.* taxi, cab

Drossel¹ *f*; -, -*n*; *Orn.* thrush

Drossel² *f*; -, -*n* **1.** *Tech.* throttle; **2.** *Etech.* choke, choking coil; **Drosselklappe** *f Tech.* throttle valve; **drosseln** *v/t.* **1.** *Tech.* throttle, choke; *Etech.* choke; **2.** (*Geschwindigkeit*) slow down; **3.** *fig.* curb, cut (down); **4.** *altm.* (*j-n*) throttle, strangle; **Drosselung** *f* (*Heizung etc.*) turning down, reducing; (*Tempo*) cutting down

drüben *Adv.* **1.** over there; (*auf der anderen Seite*) on the other side (of the lake etc.); (*auf der anderen Straßenseite*) across the road; *wohnen*: *auch* across the way; *im anderen Gebäude*: over in the other building; **2.** *umg. hist.* (*in der DDR/BRD*) in East/West Germany; **sie kamen von ~** they came from East Germany; **3.** (*in Amerika*) over in America (*od.* the States), *bes. Am.* stateside; **4.** *fig.* (*im Jenseits*) in the next world

drüber *Adv. umg.* → **darüber**; **~stehen** *v/i.* (*unreg., trennb., hat / südd., österr., schw. ist* -*ge*-); *umg.* **1.** *Überschrift*: be (written) above it; **2.** *fig. Person*: be above such things

Druck¹ *m*; -(*e*)*s*, *Drücke* **1.** *Phys.* pressure; **unter ~ stehen/setzen** be under pressure / pressurize; **2.** *nur Sg.* touch, press; **ein ~ auf den Knopf genügt** just press the button; **3.** *nur Sg.*: *Gefühl*, *im Kopf*: tension; *im Magen*: tight feeling; **4.** *nur Sg.*, *fig.* (*Zwang*) pressure; (*Bedrängnis*) *auch* stress; (*Belastung*) burden; *nervlich*: stress; **~ auf j-n ausüben** *od.* **j-n unter ~ setzen** put s.o. under pressure, put the screws on s.o. *umg.*; **unter ~ stehen** be under pressure; (*j-m*) **~ machen** *umg.* put (the) pressure on (s.o.); **~ hinter etw.** (*Dat.*) **machen** *umg.* speed s.th. up; **in ~ kommen/sein** *umg.* (*Zeitnot haben*) get/be pushed for time

Druck² *m*; -(*e*)*s*, -*e*; *Druck.* **1.** *nur Sg.* printing; **in ~ geben/gehen** send/go to press; **im ~ sein** be in (the) press; **2.** (*Buch*) edition; (*Bild, Stoff*) print; **3.** *nur Sg.*; (**~art**) print, type

Druck|abfall *m* drop (*od.* fall) in pressure; **~anstieg** *m* increase (*od.* rise) in pressure; **~anzug** *m Flug.* pressure suit; **~ausgleich** *m* pressure equalization; **ich kann keinen ~ machen** *beim Tauchen*: I can't equalize (the pressure); **~bleistift** *m* drop-action pencil

Druck|bogen *m Druck.* printed sheet; **~buchstabe** *m* block letter; **in ~n schreiben** print

Drückeberger *m*; -*s*, -; *umg. pej.* shirker, *Brit. auch* skiver, *Am. auch* goldbrick(er); **drückebergerisch** *Adj. umg. pej.* idle, *Brit. auch* skiving, *Am. auch* goldbricking

druckempfindlich *Adj. Med.* tender, sore to the touch; *Obst*: easily bruised; *Samt*: easily crushed; **diese Stelle ist ~** *Med.* this part hurts when you touch (*od.* press on) it

drucken *v/t./i. Druck.* print (**auf** + *Akk.* on[to]); **~ lassen** have s.th. printed, publish; → **gedruckt** II

drücken I. *v/t./i.* **1.** **~** (**auf** + *Akk.*) *Hupe, Klingel, Taste etc.*: press (on); *Knopf, Taste*: *auch* push; → **Tränendrüse, Tube** 1; **2.** (*j-n*) *Rucksack etc.*: hurt, rub;

Schuhe etc.: pinch, be too tight, rub; **der Kuchen drückt mich schwer im Magen** the cake is lying heavily on (*od.* like a lead weight in) my stomach; → **Schuh**; **3.** *fig.*: **auf die Stimmung ~** put a damper on things; **aufs Gemüt ~** depress (one's spirits), get one down; **4.** *Sl.*: (**sich** [*Dat.*] **etw.**) **~** shoot (*od.* fix) up; **II.** *v/t.* **1.** press (**nach unten** down; **an** *od.* **gegen die Wand** up against the wall); (*schieben*) push; (*quetschen*) squeeze; **breit** *od.* **flach ~** flatten; **den Senf aus der Tube ~** squeeze the mustard out of the tube; **j-n in e-n Stuhl ~** push s.o. into a chair; **e-n Stempel ~ auf** (+ *Akk.*) stamp; **sich** (*Dat.*) **den Hut in die Stirn ~** pull one's hat down over one's brow; **j-m die Hand ~** shake hands with s.o., shake s.o.'s hand; *stärker*: squeeze s.o.'s hand; **j-m etw. in die Hand ~** give (*od.* hand) s.o. s.th.; *bes. heimlich*: slip s.th. into s.o.'s hand; **j-m e-n Kuss auf die Stirn ~** kiss s.o. on the forehead; **j-n** (**an sich** *od.* **ans Herz**) **~** give s.o. a hug; *länger*: hold s.o. tight; → **Daumen, Schulbank, Wand**; **2.** (*zerdrücken*) (*Obst etc.*) squash; (*Blumen, Kleid*) crush; **3.** *geh. fig.* (*bedrücken*) worry; *stärker*: depress; *Verantwortung etc.*: weigh (heavily) on; **was drückt dich denn?** what's up *umg.* (*od.* on your mind)?; **4.** (*Preise etc.*) bring (*od.* force) down; (*Leistung, Niveau etc.*) lower; (*Rekord*) better (**um** by); **er drückte den Rekord um zwei Sekunden** *auch* he took two seconds off the record; **5.** *umg. fig.* (*j-n*) (*unterdrücken*) keep down, repress; **6.** *Flug.* nose (*od.* point) down; **7.** *Gewichtheben*: press; **8.** *Kartenspiel*: discard; **III.** *v/refl.* **1.** **sich in e-e Ecke ~** huddle into a corner; **sich an j-n ~** cuddle up to s.o.; **2.** *umg.*: **sich** (**heimlich**) **aus dem Saal ~** sneak out of the hall; **3.** *umg. fig.*: **sich ~ um** *od.* **vor** (+ *Dat.*) (*Einladung*) um: avoid / *vor*: get out of; (*Verantwortung, Arbeit*) shirk, *Brit. auch* skive; *ängstlich*: chicken out of; **er drückt sich mal wieder** he's shirking (*Am. auch* goldbricking) again, *Brit. auch* he's on the skive again; **er drückt sich dauernd** he somehow always manages to get out of it (*od.* things); **IV.** *v/i.* **1.** *um Darm zu entleeren*: strain, push; **2.** *Hitze*: be oppressive; **3.** *Sl. Haustürwerbung*: hawk, flog, sell door-to-door

drückend I. *Part. Präs.* → **drücken**; **II.** *Adj.* **1.** *Verantwortung*: onerous, burdensome; *Last*: heavy; *Armut*: dire, wretched; *Sorgen*: serious; *Steuern*: crippling; **2.** *Wetter*: close, sultry, muggy; *Hitze*: oppressive; **III.** *Adv.*: **~ heiß** oppressively hot

Drucker¹ *m*; -*s*, -, **~in** *f*; -, -*nen*; *Druck.* (*Beruf*) printer

Drucker² *m*; -*s*, -; *EDV* printer

Drücker¹ *m*; -*s*, - **1.** (*Druckknopf*) (push)button; *Türschloss*: latch; *Tech.*, *Gewehr*: trigger; **2.** *umg. fig.*: **am ~ sein** be at the controls (*od.* in charge); **auf den letzten ~** at the last minute; **die Hand am ~ haben** be ready to act

Drücker² *m*; -*s*, -, **~in** *f*; -, -*nen*; *umg. pej.* (*bes. Zeitschriftenwerber*) hawker

Druckerei *f*; -, -*en Druck.* printers *Pl.*

Drückerkolonne *f umg. pej.* door-to-door sales force

Druckerlaubnis *f Druck.* permission to print, imprimatur

Drucker|presse *f Druck.* (printing) press; **~schwärze** *f* newsprint, print-

D

ing (*od.* printer's) ink

Druckerzeugnis *n* publication, printed matter

druckfähig *Adj.* printable; *s-e Antwort war nicht ~ fig.* his answer wasn't printable (*od.* fit to be printed)

Druck|fahne *f Druck.* (galley) proof; **~farbe** *f* printing (*od.* printer's) ink; **~fassung** *f* final version for printing

Druckfeder *f* compression spring

Druckfehler *m Druck.* misprint, printing (*od.* typographical) error; **~teufel** *m hum.*: *der ~ hat zugeschlagen* the gremlin strikes again

druckfertig *Adj. Druck.* ready for press; **~es Manuskript** fair copy

druckfrisch *Adj. Druck.* hot off the press

Druck|grafik, **~graphik** *f* graphic reproduction, print

Druck|kabine *f* pressurized (*od.* pressure) cabin; **~knopf** *m Tech.* (push)button; *am Kleid etc.*: press stud, *bes. Brit. umg.* popper, *Am.* snap (fastener)

Druckkosten *Pl. Druck.* printing costs; **~beteiligung** *f* (*durch Autor e-s Buches*) author's contribution to printing costs; *etwa* vanity payment

Drucklegung *f Druck.* printing; *mit der ~ beginnen* go to press

Druckluft *f; nur Sg.* compressed air

Druckluft|... *im Subst. mst* pneumatic ...; **~bremse** *f* air brake

Druck|maschine *f Druck.* printing press; **~messer** *m; -s, -; Tech.* pressure ga(u)ge; **~mittel** *n fig.* lever; *~ anwenden* apply pressure, put the screws on *umg.*

Druckplatte *f* plate

Druckregler *m* pressure controller (*od.* regulator)

druckreif *Adj.* **1.** → **druckfertig; 2.** *fig.*: *s-e Reden sind ~* he ought to have his speeches published

Druck|sache *f; auch Pl.*: printed matter, *Am. auch* fourth-class (matter); **~schrift** *f* **1.** *nur Sg.* block letters *Pl.*; *in ~ schreiben* print; *bitte in ~ ausfüllen* please write in capital letters; **2.** *Art*: print, type(face); **3.** (*Veröffentlichung*) publication; *kleine*: pamphlet; **~seite** *f* printed page

drucksen *v/i. umg.* hum (*Am.* hem) and haw, beat about the bush

Druckstelle *f Med.* tender spot; *stärker*: bruise (*auch auf Obst*)

Druck|stock *m Druck.* printing (*od.* relief) plate; **~stoff** *m* printed cloth (*od.* material)

Druck|taste *f* (push)button; **~unterschied** *m* difference in pressure; **~verband** *m Med.* compression (*od.* pressure) bandage

Druck|verfahren *n Druck.* printing process; **~vorlage** *f* printer's (*od.* setting) copy; **~walze** *f* (printing) platen

Druck|wasserreaktor *m Tech.* pressurized water reactor; **~welle** *f* blast, shock wave

Druide *m; -n, -n; hist.* Druid

drum *Adv. umg.* **1.** → **darum; 2.** *~ rumkommen/rumreden* → **herumkommen, herumreden; 3.** *sei's drum!* never mind, too bad, what the hell!

Drum *n*: *das ganze ~ und Dran* all the little things (that go with it), all the trappings; *mit allem ~ und Dran* with all the trimmings (*od.* frills)

Drumherum *n; -s, kein Pl.; umg.*: *das ganze ~* the whole shooting-match, the whole nine yards, the works

drunten *Adv. bes. südd., österr. umg.*

down there; *im Haus*: downstairs

drunter *Adv. umg.* **1.** → **darunter. 2.** *fig.*: *es ging alles ~ und drüber* it was absolutely chaotic; **~fallen** *v/i.* (*unreg., trennb., ist -ge-*); *umg.* **1.** be included (*unter + Akk.* in); **2.** *fig. unter Regelung, Kategorie etc.*: come (*od.* fall) under

Drüse *f; -, -n* gland

Drüsen|fieber *n Med.* glandular fever, *Am.* (infectious) mononucleosis, mono *umg.*; **~schwellung** *f* swelling of the glands, swollen glands *Pl.*

Dschibuti (*n*); *-s; Geog.* Djibouti

Dschungel *m; -s, -* jungle (*auch fig.*)

Dschunke *f; -, -n; Naut.* junk

DTP *n; -(s), kein Pl.; Abk. EDV* (**Desktop-Publishing**) DTP

du *pers. Pron.* **1.** you; *bist ~ es?* is that you?; *oft unübersetzt, z. B.*: *~, komm mal her* come here a minute, will you?; *~, ~! tadelnd zu Kind*: naughty, naughty; *wie ~ mir, so ich dir Sprichw.* an eye for an eye, a tooth for a tooth; tit for tat *umg.*; *per ~ sein* say 'du' to each other; *etwa* be on familiar terms (*mit j-m* with s.o.); → *deiner, dich, dir, duzen*; **2.** *umg.* (*man*) you; **3.** *bibl.* thou *altm. od. lit.*; **Du** *n*: *er hat mir das ~ angeboten* he suggested we drop the polite form of address (*od.* use the familiar form of address, use the familiar 'du'); *auf ~ und ~ sein od. stehen mit j-m*: be good friends (with); *fig. mit Sache*: be familiar with

dual *Adj.* **1.** *Math., EDV* binary; **2.** *Wirts., Öko.*: *das Duale System* waste disposal and recycling system

Dualismus *m; -, kein Pl.; geh.* dualism; **dualistisch** *geh.* **I.** *Adj.* dualistic; **II.** *Adv.* dualistically

Dual|system *n Math., EDV* binary system; **~zahl** *f Math., EDV* binary number

Dübel *m; -s, -* rawlplug; *aus Holz*: dowel (pin); **dübeln** *v/t.i.* (rawl)plug (*an + Akk.* to); *mit Holzdübeln*: dowel; *ein Regal an die Wand ~* fix a shelf to the wall (with rawlplugs)

dubios *Adj. geh.* dubious

Dublee *n; -s, -s* rolled gold; *... aus ~* gold-plated ...

Dublette *f; -, -n* **1.** *zum Tauschen*: double, duplicate, swap *umg.*; **2.** *Boxen*: double blow, one-two; **3.** *Schmuck*: doublet

ducken I. *v/t.* **1.** (*den Kopf*) duck; **2.** *fig. pej.* (*j-n*) put *s.o.* down, humiliate; **II.** *v/refl.* **1.** duck; *vor Angst*: cower, cringe; *sich zum Sprung ~* crouch ready to spring; *sich vor e-m Schlag ~* dodge a blow, duck to avoid a blow; **2.** *fig.* knuckle under (*vor + Dat.* to)

Duckmäuser *m; -s, -; pej.* (moral) coward, spineless jellyfish *umg.*; (*Jasager*) yes-man; **Duckmäuserei** *f; -, kein Pl.* moral cowardice, servility; **duckmäuserisch** *Adj.* submissive; *stärker*: servile, cringing

Dudelei *f; -, -en, mst. Sg.; umg. pej.* tooting; *e-s Radios etc.*: droning; **dudeln** *v/i. umg. pej. Radio etc.*: drone (on); *~ auf* (*+ Dat.*) (*Flöte etc.*) tootle away on

Dudelsack *m* bagpipes *Pl.*; **~pfeifer** *m* (bag)piper

Due Diligence [ˌdjuːˈdɪlɪdʒəns] *f; -, -es, mst Sg.; Wirts.* due diligence (analysis, report, process *etc.*)

Duell *n; -s, -e* **1.** *hist.* duel; *j-n zum ~ fordern* challenge s.o. to a duel; **2.** *Sport od. geh. fig.* contest, battle; *sich* (*Dat.*) *ein ~ mit j-m liefern* fight

(*od.* have) it out with s.o.; **Duellant** *m; -en, -en* duellist; **duellieren** *v/refl.* fight a duel (*mit* with)

Duett *n; -(e)s, -e; Mus.* duet; *im ~ singen* sing a duet

Duft *m; -(e)s, Düfte* **1.** (pleasant) smell; *von Blumen, Parfüm*: *auch* scent, fragrance; *von Essen, Kaffee*: *auch* aroma; *der ~ der großen, weiten Welt fig.* the taste of the big, wide world; **2.** *Zool.* scent; **Duftdrüse** *f Zool.* scent (*od.* olfactory) gland

duften *v/i.* smell (*nach* of); (*gut riechen*) smell good; *hier duftet es aber!* what a nice smell!, *iro. umg.* what a pong (*Am.* stench)!; *hier duftet es nach ...* I can smell ...; **duftend I.** *Part. Präs.* ~ **duften; II.** *Adj.* nice-(*od.* sweet-)smelling; *Blumen, Parfüm*: *auch* fragrant

Dufthauch *m* breath, waft

duftig *Adj.* **1.** fragrant; *Wein*: *auch* scented; **2.** *Kleid etc.*: airy, light

Duft|kissen *n* sachet; (*Kopfkissen*) scented pillow; **~marke** *f Zool.* scent mark; **~note** *f* scent, fragrance; **~öl** *n* perfumed (*od.* aromatherapy) oil; **~probe** *f* perfume sample; **~stoff** *m* scent; **~wolke** *f umg.* cloud of perfume

Dukaten *m; -s, -; hist.* ducat; **~esel** *m umg.*, **~scheißer** *m vulg.*: *ich habe doch keinen ~* I'm not made of money(, you know)

dulden I. *v/t.* **1.** *Person*: (*zulassen*) tolerate; *stillschweigend*: condone, shut one's eyes to; (*hinnehmen*) put up with, stand for; *keinen Widerspruch ~* stand for (*od.* brook) no contradiction; *er ist hier nur geduldet* he's only here on sufferance; *ich dulde es nicht* I won't have it; **2.** *geh.*: *keinen Aufschub ~* admit no delay; **II.** *v/t.i. geh.*: (*etw.*) *~* (*ertragen*) endure (s.th.), suffer (s.th.)

Dulder *m; -s, -*, **~in** *f; -, -nen* patient sufferer, martyr; **~miene** *f iro.* martyred expression; *mit ~* with an air of patient suffering

duldsam *Adj.* tolerant (*gegen* of); (*nachsichtig*) indulgent (to), forbearing; **Duldsamkeit** *f* tolerance (*gegen* of), forbearance

Duldung *f* toleration; *stillschweigende ~* (tacit) connivance

dumm; *dümmer, am dümmsten* **I.** *Adj.* **1.** stupid, thick *umg.*; *sich ~ stellen umg.* act the fool; *er ist nicht* (*so*) *~* he's no fool; *er ist dümmer, als die Polizei erlaubt umg.* he's as thick as two short planks (*Am.* as a board); *sich nicht für ~ verkaufen lassen* not be taken in (*od.* fooled); *willst du mich für ~ verkaufen?* you must think I'm stupid; *~es Zeug! umg.* rubbish!; *~es Zeug reden umg.* talk nonsense; *das ist gar nicht so ~* that's not a bad idea; *das war ~ von mir* how stupid of me; *schön ~ wärst du umg.* you'd be a fool; *j-n wie e-n ~en Jungen behandeln* treat s.o. like a child; **2.** (*albern*) silly; (*töricht, unklug*) foolish; *~e Gans pej.* silly goose; **3.** *Sache*: (*unangenehm*) awkward, nasty; (*lästig*) annoying, tiresome; (*ärgerlich*) annoying, irritating; *Angewohnheit*: unpleasant; *Zufall*: terrible, awful; *ich hatte ein ~es Gefühl dabei* I had an awful feeling about it; *zu od. wie ~!* what a nuisance; *schließlich wurde es mir zu ~* in the end I got tired of the whole business; *mir ist was Dummes passiert* (*habe Unangenehmes erlebt*)

something awful happened to me;
4. *umg. fig.*: *mir ist ganz ~ im Kopf*
(*schwindelig*) I feel really weird; (*verwirrt*) my head is swimming; *dein Gerede macht mich ganz ~* your wittering (*Am.* blathering) (on) is confusing
me; **II.** *Adv.* **1.** stupidly; *sich ~ anstellen* be stupid, do s.th. stupid; (*ungeschickt*) be clumsy; *~ daherreden* (*um.* witter (*Am.* blather) on; *~ aus der Wäsche schauen umg.* look stupid; *jetzt steh ich ganz schön ~ da umg. fig.* now I'm the one left looking stupid; **2.** *umg.*: *das hätte ~ ausgehen können* that could have ended badly; *es ist ~ gelaufen* (*für ihn*) he's had (a run of) bad luck; *j-m ~ kommen* (*unverschämt sein*) be cheeky to s.o.; *ich hab mich ~ und dämlich geredet, um ihn zu überzeugen umg.* I talked until I was blue in the face trying to persuade him; *sich ~ und dämlich verdienen umg.* be raking it in
Dummchen *n umg.* silly (billy)
dummdreist *Adj. pej.* insolent, impertinent
Dumme *m, f; -n, -n* fool, mug *umg.*; *der ~ sein* be left holding the baby (*od.* carrying the can); *e-n ~n findet man immer* there are plenty of mugs (*Am.* fools) around; *die ~n sterben nicht aus od. werden nicht weniger* there's another one born every minute; *da musst du dir schon e-n Dümmeren suchen umg.* you'll have to find (yourself) another mug (*Am.* sucker)
Dummejungenstreich *m* silly prank
dümmer *Komp.* → **dumm**
Dummerchen *n; -s, -e; umg.* silly (billy)
dummerweise *Adv. umg.* **1.** stupidly; *ich habe ~ zugesagt* I was stupid enough to say yes; **2.** (*leider*) unfortunately
Dummheit *f* **1.** *nur Sg.* stupidity; (*Unwissenheit*) ignorance; *vor ~ brüllen etc. umg.* be as thick as two short planks (*Am.* as a board); *gegen ~ ist kein Kraut gewachsen* some people are born that way; *wenn ~ wehtäte, müsste er den ganzen Tag schreien umg.* he's so thick that it hurts,; **2.** (*Handlung*) stupid thing to do; (*Fehler*) silly mistake; *e-e ~ begehen* do s.th. stupid, get up to mischief; *mach keine ~en!* don't do anything stupid; (*drohend*: no funny business!; *er hat nur ~en im Kopf* he's always up to something, his head's always full of silly ideas; **Dummkopf** *m pej.* idiot; *er ist kein ~* he's no fool; **dümmlich** *pej.* **I.** *Adj.* **1.** (*beschränkt*) simple-minded, foolish; **2.** *Grinsen etc.*: silly, foolish; **II.** *Adv.*: *~ grinsen* grin stupidly
dümmst... *Sup.* → **dumm**
dümpeln *v/i. Naut.* roll gently, bob up and down; *der Kurs dümpelt bei ... Dollar fig.* the rate is hovering in the doldrums at ... Dollars
dumpf I. *Adj.* **1.** *Geräusch*: dull, muffled; *~er Aufprall, Schlag etc.* thud; **2.** (*schwül*) sultry, close; *Wetter: auch* muggy; **3.** (*muffig*) stuffy; (*modrig*) mo(u)ldy, musty; **4.** *Schmerz*: dull; **5.** *Schweigen, Stimmung etc.*: gloomy; **6.** *Gefühl, Ahnung*: vague, hazy; **7.** *Erinnerung*: dim, hazy; **II.** *Adv.*: *~ aufprallen* hit (*od.* collide) with a (dull) thud; *~ grollen* rumble dully; *~ riechen* smell damp (*od.* mo[u]ldy); *~ vor sich hin brüten/starren pej.* brood/stare apathetically into space; **Dumpfbacke** *f umg. pej.* dimwit, bonehead; **Dumpf-**

heit *f* apathy, torpor; **dumpfig** *Adj.* musty; (*feucht*) dank
Dumping ['dampıŋ] *n; -s, kein Pl.; Wirts.* dumping; *~preis m* dumping price
Düne *f; -, -n* dune
Dung *m; -(e)s, kein Pl.* manure, dung
Düngemittel *n* → **Dünger**, **düngen** *v/t/i.* manure, dung; *mit Kunstdünger*: fertilize; *Kompost düngt gut* compost is a good fertilizer; **Dünger** *m; -s, -* fertilizer; *natürlicher*: manure, dung
Düngung *f* manuring; *mit Kunstdünger*: fertilizing
dunkel I. *Adj.* **1.** *mit wenig Licht*: dark; *draußen wird es schon ~* it's already getting dark; *im Sommer wird es erst spät ~* it doesn't get dark until late in the summer; *~ machen* darken; *im Dunkeln* in the dark; *im Dunkeln ist gut munkeln umg. hum.* darkness is the friend of lovers; **2.**; **3.** *farblich*: dark (*auch Bier, Haar*); *dunkles Brot* brown bread; *ein dunkler Typ sein* (*Ggs. blass sein*) be dark; *ein Dunkles, bitte!* in GB etwa: a (pint of) brown ale please; **4.** *Stimme, Ton*: dark, deep; *Vokal*: dark; **5.** *fig.* (*unklar, geheimnisvoll*) dark, mysterious; *in dunkler Vorzeit* in the dim and distant past; *j-n im Dunkeln lassen* keep (*od.* leave) s.o. in the dark; *das liegt noch im Dunkeln* (*ist unklar*) that's still a mystery; (*ist ungewiss*) that remains to be seen; *im Dunkeln tappen* grope (about) in the dark; **6.** *fig.* Ahnung, Erinnerung: vague, dim; **7.** *fig.* (*unerfreulich*) dark, gloomy; *ein dunkles Kapitel der Geschichte* a dark chapter in history; **8.** *fig.* (*zweifelhaft*) Existenz, Geschäft, Vergangenheit: shady, dubious; *ein dunkler Punkt in j-s Vergangenheit* a black spot in s.o.'s past, a skeleton in s.o.'s cupboard (*Am.* closet); *dunkle Machenschaften* sinister machinations; **II.** *Adv.* **1.** *~ gekleidet* dressed in dark colo(u)rs (*od.* clothes); *e-e ~ getönte Brille* dark (*od.* tinted) glasses *Pl.*; **2.** *fig.*: *ich kann mich ~ daran erinnern* I can remember that vaguely (*od.* dimly)
Dunkel *n; -s, kein Pl.* **1.** *geh.* the dark, darkness; **2.** *fig.* darkness, mystery; *das ~ um etw. aufhellen* shed light on s.th.
Dünkel *m; -s, kein Pl.; pej.* arrogance; *er hat e-n akademischen ~* he thinks he's something special because he's got a degree
dunkel|äugig *Adj.* dark-eyed; *~blau Adj.* dark blue; *~blond Adj. Haar*: light brown; *~ sein* have light brown hair; *~braun Adj.* dark brown; *~grau Adj.* dark grey (*Am.* gray); *~grün Adj.* dark green; *~haarig Adj. attr.* dark-haired; *~ sein* have dark hair
dünkelhaft *Adj. pej.* arrogant, conceited
dunkelhäutig *Adj.* dark(-skinned); *Mann: auch* swarthy
Dunkelheit *f* darkness; *bei/nach Einbruch der ~* at/after nightfall; *im Schutze der ~* under cover of darkness; *etw. in ~ hüllen fig.* conceal s.th. in darkness
Dunkel|kammer *f Fot.* darkroom; *~mann m; Pl. -männer; umg. pej.* shady character
dunkeln I. *v/i.* **1.** *auch unpers.* (*hat gedunkelt*); *lit.*: *es od. der Abend dunkelt* it is getting (*od.* growing) dark; **2.** (*ist*); *Haar, Holz etc.*: go darker, darken; **II.** *v/t.* (*hat*) make darker,

darken
dunkel|rot *Adj.* dark red; *~weiß Adj.* off-white
Dunkelziffer *f* number of unreported cases (*od.* crimes, victims)
dünken *lit.* **I.** (*altm. deucht, deuchte, hat gedeucht*); *v/unpers.*: *es dünkt* (*altm. deucht*) *mich od. mir od. mir od. mich dünkt* (*altm. deucht*) it seems to me, methinks *altm. od. iro.*, I ween *altm. od. iro.*; **II.** *v/refl.*: *sich sehr schlau etc. ~* think one is very clever etc.
Dünkirchen (*n*); *-s; Geog.* Dunkirk
dünn I. *Adj.* **1.** *allg.* thin; *Faden, Haar etc.*: fine; *Briefpapier*: lightweight; **2.** *Person etc.*: thin, skinny *umg.*; *~er werden* lose weight; *er ist sehr ~ geworden* he's gone (*od.* got, *Am.* gotten) really thin; *sich ~ machen fig.* make room, squeeze up, breathe in *umg.*; **3.** *Flüssigkeit, Luft*: thin; *Nebel, Regen*: fine; *Luft: auch* rarefied; *Teig*: runny; **4.** (*wenig gehaltvoll*) *Suppe*: thin; *Kaffee, Tee*: weak, watery; *Bier*: watery; **5.** *Stimme*: thin, weak; **6.** *Besiedlung, Bewuchs, Haarwuchs*: thin, sparse; **7.** *umg. fig.* (*dürftig*) weak, poor; *Argument: auch* flimsy; **II.** *Adv.* thinly; *Farbe ~ auftragen* apply paint thinly; *~ besiedelt od. ~ bevölkert* sparsely populated; *~ gesät fig.* scarce, few and far between
Dünn|brettbohrer *m umg. pej.* slacker, *Brit. auch* skiver; *er ist ein ~* he always takes the easy way out; *~darm m* small intestine
Dünndruckausgabe *f* thin (*od.* India) paper edition
Dünne *m, f; -n, -n; umg.* thin (*od.* skinny) man (*f* woman *etc.*)
dünn|flüssig *Adj.* watery; *Öl*: light, thin(-bodied); *Honig*: runny; *Stuhlgang*: loose, sloppy; *~häutig Adj. geh. fig.* very sensitive (*od.* delicate)
Dünnheit *f* thinness
dünnmachen *v/refl.* (*trennb., hat -ge-*); *umg.* (*verschwinden*) make o.s. scarce
Dünnpfiff *m; nur Sg.; umg.* the runs *Pl.*
Dünnsäure *f Chem.* dilute acid; *Umweltverschmutzung: auch etwa* sewage sludge; *~verklappung f Öko.* dumping of dilute acid (*od.* sewage sludge)
Dünnschiss *m vulg.* the shits *Pl.*
Dunst *m; -(e)s, Dünste* **1.** *nur Sg.*; (*Dampf*) vapo(u)r, steam; (*Rauch*) smoke; (*Schwaden*) fumes *Pl.*; (*Nebel*) haze, mist; (*Smog*) smog; **2.** (*Geruch*) smell; (*Ausdünstung*) vapo(u)r, fumes *Pl.*; (*stickige Luft*) fug; **3.** *umg. fig.*: *j-m e-n blauen ~ vormachen* throw dust in s.o.'s eyes; *er hat keinen blassen ~ davon* he hasn't the foggiest (idea) about it; *von etw. ~ bekommen* get wind of s.th.; *~abzugshaube f* extractor hood
dünsten *vt/i.* steam
Dunstglocke *f* blanket of smog
dunstig *Adj.* hazy, misty
Dunst|kreis *m fig.* sphere of influence; *~schleier m* haze
Dünung *f Naut.* swell
Duo *n; -s, -s; Mus.* duo (*auch fig.*)
Duodezimalsystem *n Math.* duodecimal system
Duplex... *im Subst.* Etech., Tech., EDV duplex ...
Duplikat *n; -(e)s, -e* duplicate (copy); (*Kopie*) copy; *Kunst*: replica; **duplizieren** *v/t. geh.* duplicate; **Duplizität** *f; -, -en; geh.*: *die ~ der Ereignisse* the duplication of events
Dur *n; -, kein Pl.; Mus.* major (key);

D

A-~ A major; **~akkord** *m* major chord

durch I. *Präp.* (+ *Akk.*) **1.** *räumlich, auch fig.:* **~** (*hindurch*) through; (*quer*) **~** across; (*kreuz und quer*) all over; **über/unter/zwischen** *etw.*(*Dat.*) over/under/between s.th.; **~** *die Luft fliegen* fly through the air; **~** *die Fußgängerzone bummeln* stroll through the pedestrian precinct; → *Bank*[1] 1, *dick* I 8, *mitten*; **2.** (*von*) *Passiv*: by; **3.** (*mittels*) through, by, by means of; **~** *Zuhören* through listening; *ich habe sie ~ m-n Freund kennen gelernt* I met her through my boyfriend (*od.* a friend of mine); *etw.* **~** *die Zeitung* / **~** *Lautsprecher bekannt geben* announce s.th. in the paper / over loudspeakers; **4.** (*infolge von*) because of; **~** *Nachlässigkeit* due to negligence; **~** *den Regen wird das Gras nass* the grass gets wet from the rain, the rain makes the grass wet; *Tod* **~** *Ertrinken/ Erfrieren* death by drowning / from exposure; **5.** *Math.:* (*geteilt*) **~** divided by; **6.** *zeitlich:* through(out), during; *das ganze Jahr* **~** throughout (*od.* over) the whole year, all year (long); *den ganzen Tag* **~** all day (long); **II.** *Adv. umg.* **1.** **~** *sein* (*durchgekommen sein*) be gone; *ist der ICE schon* **~?** has the express train already left?; **2.** **~** *sein Hose, Schuhe etc.:* be worn through, have had it; **3.** **~** *sein Antrag etc.:* be (*od.* have got, *Am.* gotten) through; **4.** **~** *sein Person, durch Schwierigkeiten etc.:* be out of the wood(s); *bei Krankheit: auch* be over the worst; *durch Prüfung:* have made it, be through; **~** *sein mit e-r Arbeit / e-m Buch* be finished (*Am. auch* through) with one's work / have finished with (*od.* reading) a book, *Am. auch* be through with a book; *ich bin* **~** *mit ihm od. er ist bei mir unten* **~** I'm through with him; **5.** *Gastr.* (*gar*) done; *ich esse mein Steak am liebsten* **~** I prefer (my) steak well-done; **6.** **~** *und* **~** completely, ... through and through; *Person: auch* to the core; *ein Politiker* **~** *und* **~** a dyed-in-the-wool politician; *ein Gentleman* **~** *und* **~** a gentleman born and bred; **~** *und* **~** *nass* soaked to the skin, drenched; *das geht einem* **~** *und* **~** it goes right through you; *Kälte: auch* it chills you to the bone; **7.** *es ist acht Uhr* **~** it's past (*od.* gone) eight o'clock

durch|ackern *v/t. und v/refl.* (*trennb., hat -ge-*); *umg. fig.* plough (*Am.* plow) through *s.th.;* **~arbeiten** (*trennb., hat -ge-*) **I.** *v/t.* **1.** *Buch etc.:* work through *s.th.,* go through *s.th.* thoroughly; (*ausarbeiten*) work out (in detail); **2.** → *durchkneten;* **II.** *v/refl.: sich* **~** *durch den Dschungel etc.:* fight one's way through; *durch Arbeit, Schnee etc.:* plough (*Am.* plow) through; **III.** *v/i.* work through without a break, work nonstop; *die ganze Nacht* **~** work through the night (without a break)

durcharbeitet *Adj.: nach e-r* **~***en Nacht* after working through the night, *bes. Am. auch* after an all-nighter *umg.*

durchatmen *v/i.* (*trennb., hat -ge-*) breathe deeply; *tief* **~** *auch* take deep breaths

durchaus *Adv.* **1.** (*unbedingt*) absolutely; *wenn du es* **~** *willst* if you absolutely must, if you insist; *ist das wirklich nötig? -* **~***!* absolutely!; **2.** *bekräftigend:* quite, perfectly; *das ist* **~** *richtig* that is entirely correct; *es hat mir* **~** *gefallen unerwarteterweise:* I re-

ally liked it, actually; *ich hätte* **~** *Lust dazu, aber ich kann nicht* I'd really love to, actually; **3.** *verneint:* **~** *nicht* not at all, not in the least, by no means; **~** *nicht arm* far from poor, not in the least bit poor; *sie ist* **~** *nicht zufrieden* she's by no means satisfied; *das ist* **~** *kein Versehen* that's certainly no mere oversight; **4.** (*ganz und gar*) thoroughly, completely

'durchbeißen[1] (*unreg., trennb., hat -ge-*) **I.** *v/t.* bite through *s.th.,* bite *s.th.* in two; **II.** *v/refl. umg. fig.* struggle through

durch'beißen[2] *v/t.* (*unreg., untr., hat*) bite through *s.th.*

durch|bekommen *v/t.* (*unreg., trennb., hat*) → *durchbringen* I 1, 2, 5; **~betteln** *v/refl.* (*trennb., hat -ge-*) beg one's way (through); **~biegen** (*unreg., trennb., hat -ge-*) **I.** *v/t.* bend back (as far as possible); **II.** *v/refl.: sich* (*unter e-r Last*) **~** sag, bend (under a weight); **~blasen** (*unreg., trennb., hat -ge-*) **I.** *v/i.: der Wind bläst durch die Ritzen durch* the wind blows through the cracks; **II.** *v/t.* **1.** (*Ohren, Rohr etc.*) *reinigend:* clear (by blowing through it); **2.** *etw.* (*durch etw.*) **~** (*bewegen*) blow through; **3.** *Wind:* (*j-n*) blow (right) through; **~blättern** *v/t.* (*trennb., hat -ge-*) leaf (*od.* thumb, flick *umg.*) through *s.th.*

Durchblick *m* **1.** view (*auf od. in* + *Akk.* of); **2.** *umg. fig.: sich* (*Dat.*) *den nötigen* **~** *verschaffen* find out what's what; (*den nötigen*) **~** *haben* know what's going on; *er hat überhaupt keinen* **~** he has no idea (about) what's going on, he hasn't got a clue; *den* **~** *verlieren* lose track of what's going on

durchblicken *v/i.* (*trennb., hat -ge-*) **1.** (*auch* **~** *durch*) look through; *etw.* **~** *lassen fig.* hint at; **~** *lassen, dass ...* hint (at the fact) that ..., intimate that ...; **2.** *umg. fig.: ich blick da nicht durch* I don't get it, I can't make head (-s) or tail(s) of it; *da blick ich nicht mehr durch* I'm lost; *blickst du bei dem Film durch?* d'you know what the film (*Am. auch* movie) is on about?

durch'bluten[1] *v/t.* (*untr., hat*); *Physiol.* supply with blood

'durchbluten[2] *v/i.* (*trennb., -ge-*) **1.** (*hat*); (*Wunde*) bleed through; *die Wunde blutete durch* blood from the wound soaked through the bandage; **2.** (*ist*); (*Verband*) become soaked (through) with blood

durchblutet *I. P.P.* → *durchbluten*[1]; **II.** *Adj.:* **~***e Haut* live skin; *das Gehirn ist gut/schlecht* **~** the blood flow (*od.* circulation) in the brain is good/bad

Durchblutung *f* blood flow, circulation (+ *Gen. od. in* + *Dat.* in); **Durchblutungsstörung** *f* circulatory problem (*od.* disturbance)

durchbohren *v/t.* (*untr., hat*) *Nagel, Pfeil etc.:* pierce; *mit Bohrer:* drill through; (*durchlöchern*) perforate; (*j-n*) *mit Hörnern:* gore (through); (*aufspießen*) skewer (s.o.); *mit dem Dolch:* stab; *mit dem Schwert:* run through; *j-n mit Blicken* **~** *fig.* look daggers at s.o.

durch|boxen (*trennb., hat -ge-*); *umg.* **I.** *v/t. fig.* push *s.th.* through; **II.** *v/refl.* **1.** battle (*od.* fight) one's way through; **2.** *fig.* struggle through; **~braten** *v/t.* (*unreg., trennb., hat -ge-*) cook well; → *durchgebraten*

'durchbrechen[1] (*unreg., trennb., -ge-*)

I. *v/t.* (*hat*) **1.** break *s.th.* (in two); (*Zweig etc.*) snap; **2.** (*Mauer*) break through; **3.** *ein Fenster etc.* **~** put a window *etc.* in a (*od.* the) wall; **II.** *v/i.* (*ist*) **1.** break (in two); *unter e-r Last:* collapse; **2.** *durchs Eis etc.:* fall through; **3.** *mit Gewalt:* break through; *Zähne, Sonne:* come through, appear; **4.** *fig.* (*zum Vorschein kommen*) come out; **5.** *Med., Geschwür etc.:* burst, perforate; *Blinddarm: auch* rupture

durch'brechen[2] *v/t.* (*unreg., untr., hat*) **1.** break through *s.th.;* (*Schallmauer*) break; (*Blockade*) run; **2.** *fig.* (*Regel etc.*) break; **Durch'brechung** *f* breaking (through)

durch|brennen *v/i.* (*unreg., trennb., -ge-*) **1.** (*hat*); (*nicht ausgehen*) stay alight (*od.* lit); **2.** (*ist*); *Birne:* burn out, go *umg.; Sicherung:* blow; *fig.* → *Sicherung* 1; **3.** (*ist*); *umg. fig.:* (*[mit] j-m*) **~** run away (with/from s.o.); *Verliebte:* elope (with s.o.); *mit dem Geld etc.* **~** make off with the money *etc.,* take the money and run; **~bringen** (*unreg., trennb., hat -ge-*) **I.** *v/t.* **1.** (*durch etw.*) **~** get *s.th. od. s.o.* through; **2.** (*Kranken*) save *s.o.;* **3.** (*Kinder etc.*) support, feed, provide for; **4.** *pej.* (*Geld*) squander, get (*od.* go) through (quickly), blow *umg.;* **5.** *umg.* (*zerteilen können*) get through; **II.** *v/refl.* support o.s., make (both) ends meet; *mühsam:* scrape by (*od.* through)

Durchbruch *m* **1.** *Sportler, Soldaten:* breakthrough; *Zähne:* cutting; *Fluss:* rise, resurgence; *Damm, Geschwür:* bursting, rupture; *Geschwür: auch* perforation; **3.** (*Loch*) gap, opening, breach; **4.** *fig.* breakthrough; *ihm ist der* **~** *gelungen* he finally made the breakthrough (*od.* made it); *zum* **~** *kommen* show, become apparent, reveal *o.s.; Idee:* gain acceptance; *e-r Idee zum* **~** *verhelfen* help to get an idea accepted

durchchecken *v/t.* (*trennb., hat -ge-*) check thoroughly; *das Auto* **~** *lassen* have the car thoroughly checked over; *sich* **~** *lassen umg.* have a thorough checkup

durchdacht *I. P.P.* → *durchdenken*[2]; **II.** *Adj.: gut/schlecht* **~** well (*od.* carefully) / badly thought-out

'durchdenken[1] *v/t.* (*unreg., trennb., hat -ge-*) think *s.th.* through; (*überlegen*) think *s.th.* over, give *s.th.* some thought

durch'denken[2] *v/t.* (*unreg., untr., hat*) think *s.th.* through

durch|drängen *v/refl.* (*trennb., hat -ge-*): *sich* **~** (*durch*) push one's way through; **~drehen** (*trennb.,-ge-*) **I.** *v/t.* (*hat*) **1.** (*Fleisch*) mince, *Am.* grind, put through the grinder (*od.* mincer); **II.** *v/i.* **1.** (*hat*); *Räder:* spin; *Motor:* rev (up), roar; **2.** (*ist*); *umg. fig. nervlich:* crack up, go to pieces; *vor Wut:* go spare, do one's nut, *Am.* go ballistic, *vor Angst:* panic, go into a flat panic, *Am. auch* have kittens

'durchdringen[1] *v/i.* (*unreg., trennb., ist -ge-*) **1.** (*auch* **~** *durch*) get through; *Flüssigkeit: auch* seep through; *Nachricht:* get out, leak (out); **~** *zu Nachricht:* reach, get to; **2.** *fig. Person:* succeed (*mit* with); *mit etw.* **~** *auch* get s.th. accepted

durch'dringen[2] *v/t.* (*unreg., untr., hat*) **1.** penetrate; *er durchdrang mich mit s-m Blick* his look went right through me; **2.** *fig. mit dem Verstand:* fathom, grasp; **3.** (*erfüllen*) pervade, permeate; → *durchdrungen* II

durchdringend I. *Part. Präs.* → *durchdringen*[1], *durchdringen*[2]; **II.** *Adj.* **1.** penetrating, piercing (*auch Blick*); **2.** *Kälte, Wind*: biting; *Stimme*: piercing, shrill; **3.** *Verstand*: keen, penetrating; **III.** *Adv.*: *j-n ~ ansehen* give s.o. a penetrating (*od.* piercing) look, **~ riechen** smell pungent

durchdrücken (*trennb., hat -ge-*) **I.** *v/t.* **1. ~** (*durch*) *durch Sieb etc.*: force (*od.* pass) through; **2.** (*Knie etc.*) straighten; *drück die Knie nie ganz durch* don't lock your knees; (*Rücken*) stretch; **3.** *Kupplung, Gaspedal*: press down; **4.** (*durchbiegen*) sag; **5.** *fig.* → *durchsetzen*[1] I; **II.** *v/refl.* **1.** *umg. Person*: squeeze (*od.* push) one's way (through); **2.** *Schrift*: show (*od.* come) through; **Durchdrückpackung** *f* bubble pack; **~en** *Kollekt.* bubble packaging (*od.* plastic, wrap) *Sg.*

durch'drungen I. *P.P.* → *durchdringen*[2]; **II.** *Adj.* **1.** *Person*: filled; *positiv*: *auch* inspired, suffused (*von* with) *lit*, **2.** *Sache*: **~ von** steeped in

durchdürfen *v/i.* (*unreg., trennb., hat -ge-*); *umg.*: (*auch ~ durch*) be allowed through; *darf ich mal durch?* excuse me, can I get through?

durch'eilen[1] *v/t.* (*untr., hat*); *geh.* rush through (*auch fig.*); (*ein Land*) rush across

'durcheilen[2] *v/i.* (*trennb., ist -ge-*) rush through

durcheinander *Adv.* **1.** (*in Unordnung*) in a mess, mixed up; *alles ~ essen* eat everything as it comes; *aufgeregt ~ laufen* run around excitedly all over the place; *~ reden* all talk at the same time; *der Wind wirbelt die Blätter ~* the wind blew the leaves all over the place; *mein ganzer Zeitplan ist* (*mir*) *~ geraten* my schedule is all over the place now; *in s-r Wohnung fliegt alles ~ umg.* his flat (*Am.* apartment) is a complete mess (*od.* tip, *Am.* dump); *sie hat mir alles ~ gebracht* she got me all in a muddle; **2.** (*verwirrt*) confused; *emotional*: mixed up; *sie ist noch ganz ~* she's still all over the place; *~ bringen* (*verwirren*) get s.o. all flustered; (*verwechseln*) mix up, mistake *s.o.* for *s.o.* else

Durcheinander *n*; *-s, kein Pl.* mess, muddle; (*Wirrwarr*) confusion; *stärker*: chaos; *laut*: pandemonium

durchexerzieren *v/t.* (*trennb., hat*); *umg.* go through *s.th.* (*auch erproben*); (*üben*) *auch* practi|se (*Am.* -ce)

'durchfahren[1] *v/i.* (*unreg., trennb., ist -ge-*) **1. ~** (*durch*) pass (*od.* go) through; *Mot. auch* drive through; *Naut.* sail through; **2.** *die Nacht ~* drive (*od.* travel) all (*od.* through the) night; *bis X ~* drive *etc.* nonstop to X; *der Zug fährt in X durch* the train doesn't stop in X; *bei Rot ~* run a (red) light

durch'fahren[2] *v/t.* (*unreg., untr., hat*) **1.** go (*od.* pass) through; *Mot. auch* drive through; *Naut.* sail through; *go etc.* across; (*Strecke*) drive; **2.** *fig.*: *mich durchfuhr der Gedanke, dass ...* it suddenly struck (*od.* hit) me that ...; *ein Schreck etc. durchfuhr ihn* he was suddenly hit by a shock *etc.*; *stärker*: fear *etc.* suddenly gripped him

Durchfahrt *f* **1.** *Handlung*: passage; *~ verboten!* no through road, no thoroughfare, access only; *freie ~ haben* have right of way; *die ~ freigeben* al-

low (*od.* signal) vehicles through; **2.** *Weg*: way, access road; *die ~ zur Kirche* the road leading up to the church; *~ freihalten!* please keep (access) clear (*od.* do not obstruct); **3.** → *Durchreise*; **Durchfahrtsstraße** *f* through road

Durchfall *m* **1.** *Med.* diarrh(o)ea *ohne Art.*; **2.** (*Misserfolg*) failure; *Theat. etc.* flop *umg.*

'durchfallen (*unreg., trennb., ist -ge-*) *v/i.* **1.** (*auch ~ durch*) fall through (*auch Licht*); **2.** *umg.* in e-r *Prüfung*: fail, flunk; *bei e-r Wahl*: be defeated, be beaten, not get in; *beim Publikum*: be a flop; *Vorschlag*: be turned down; (*j-n*) *~ lassen* fail (s.o.); *im Examen ~* fail (flunk *umg.*) the *od.* one's exam; **Durchfallquote** *f* failure rate

durchfeiern *v/i.* (*trennb., hat -ge-*); *umg.*: (*die Nacht*) *~* celebrate all night, make a night of it; *wir haben durchgefeiert auch* the party went on all night

durchfeiert *Adj. nach ~er Nacht etc.* after celebrating (*od.* partying) all night *etc.*, after a night *etc.* (spent) celebrating

durch|ficken *v/t.* (*trennb., hat -ge-*); *vulg.* fuck, screw; *die gehört mal ordentlich durchgefickt pej.* what she needs is a good shafting; **~finden** *v/refl.* (*unreg., trennb., hat -ge-*): *sich ~* (*durch*) find one's way (around *od.* through); *sich nicht mehr ~* be lost; *sich nicht mehr ~ in Durcheinander etc.*: be unable to make head(s) or tail (-s) of *s.th.*

durch'fliegen[1] *v/t.* (*unreg., untr., hat*) **1.** (*Gebiet, Wolken*) fly through; (*Luftkorridor*) fly along; (*e-e Strecke*) fly, cover; **2.** *fig.* (*Buch etc.*) skim through *s.th.*

'durchfliegen[2] *v/i.* (*unreg., trennb., ist -ge-*) **1. ~** (*durch*) fly through; *unter e-r Brücke ~* fly under a bridge; *zwischen Bergen ~* fly between mountains; **2.** *ohne Zwischenlandung*: fly non-stop (*bis* [*zu*] to); **3.** *umg.* in e-r *Prüfung*: flunk (the *od.* one's exam)

'durchfließen[1] *v/i.* (*unreg., trennb., ist -ge-*) flow (*od.* run) through

durch'fließen[2] *v/t.* (*unreg., untr., hat*) flow (*od.* run) through

Durchflug *m* flight (*durch* through); *Luftrecht*: (air) transit; *Passagiere auf dem ~* transit passengers

Durchfluss *m* **1.** *nur Sg.* flow; **2.** *Tech. Öffnung*: opening, outlet

durchfluten *v/t.* (*untr., hat*) **1.** flow through; **2.** *fig. Licht, Gefühl*: flood, infuse; *Licht durchflutete das Zimmer* the room was flooded with light

durchforschen *v/t.* (*untr., hat*) **1.** (*Land*) explore; (*Gelände*) search; (*Bibliothek etc.*) search, comb (*od.* sift) through; **2.** *Sachgebiet*: investigate (thoroughly); (*genau betrachten, untersuchen*) scrutinize; **Durchforschung** *f* exploration; search(ing); investigation; scrutiny

durchforsten *v/t.* (*untr., hat*) **1.** (*Wald*) thin (out); **2.** *fig.* comb (*od.* sift) through *s.th.*

durch|fragen *v/refl.* (*trennb., hat -ge-*) ask one's way (*nach, zu* to); **~fressen** (*unreg., trennb., hat -ge-*) **I.** *v/t. auch Chem.* eat through; **II.** *v/refl.* **1.** *Wurm etc.*: eat its way through; **2.** *umg. pej.*: *sich bei j-m ~* sponge off s.o., take advantage of *s.o.*'s hospitality

durchfroren *Adj.* (*ganz od. völlig*) *~* frozen stiff, chilled to the bone; *Flüs-*

sigkeit: frozen solid

durchführbar *Adj.* practicable, feasible; **Durchführbarkeit** *f* practicability, feasibility

durchführen (*trennb., hat -ge-*) **I.** *v/t.* **1.** (*auch ~ durch*) lead (*od.* take) through *od.* across; *durch Museum etc.*: take through (*od.* [a]round); *durch Wohnung etc.*: show (a)round; **2. ~** (*durch*) (*Draht etc.*) pass through; **3.** *fig.* carry out; (*in Angriff nehmen*) go ahead with; (*zu Ende führen*) carry *s.th.* through; (*Untersuchung*) carry out; (*Expedition*) undertake; (*Kurs, Prüfung, Wahl*) hold; (*Konzept*) realize; (*Gesetz*) enforce, implement; (*Messung*) take; **II.** *v/i. Straße etc.*: *~ durch/unter/zwischen* (+ *Dat.*) go (*od.* lead) through/under/between

Durchführung *f e-s Projekts etc.*: realization; *e-s Gesetzes*: enforcement

Durchführungsbestimmung *f Jur.* implementing regulation

Durchfuhr|verbot *n Wirts.* transit embargo; **~zoll** *m* transit duty

durchfurcht *Adj. Gesicht*: lined, wrinkled; **~e Stirn** lined forehead, furrowed brow *lit*.

durchfüttern *v/t.* (*trennb., hat -ge-*) feed; (*j-n*) *auch* support; *sich von j-m ~ lassen* live off s.o.

Durchgang *m* **1.** *nur Sg.* passage; *~ verboten!* no through road, no thoroughfare, private (road); *j-m den ~ versperren* block s.o.'s way (*od.* passage); **2.** *Weg, Tor etc.*: passageway; *zwischen Stuhlreihen*: aisle; **3.** *Phase, bei Wahl*: stage; *Sport* round; *Rennen*: heat; **4.** *Wirts., Astron.* transit

durchgängig I. *Adj.* **1.** *Meinung etc.*: general, universal; *Preise*: uniform; **2.** *Einlass etc.*: continual, nonstop; **3.** *Med., Ader, Eileiter*: open, free; **II.** *Adv.* generally; (*überall, immer*) throughout

Durchgangs|bahnhof *m Eisenb.* through station; **~lager** *n* transit camp; **~stadium** *n* transitional stage (*od.* phase); **~station** *f auf e-r Reise*: stopover, stopping-off place (*auch fig.*); **~straße** *f* through road; **~verkehr** *m* through traffic; *Wirts.* transit trade

durch|gebacken *Adj.*: *nicht richtig od. ganz ~* not properly cooked (through); **~geben** *v/t.* (*unreg., trennb., hat -ge-*) **1.** *Radio*: announce; (*Hinweis, Meldung etc.*) give; *j-m etw. telefonisch ~* (tele)phone *s.th.* through to s.o., let s.o. know *s.th.* by telephone; **2.** → *durchreichen*; **~gebraten I.** *P.P.* → *durchbraten*; **II.** *Adj.* well-done; *es ist noch nicht ~* it isn't done (properly) yet; **~gedreht I.** *P.P.* → *durchdrehen*; **II.** *Adj.* crazy, mad; **~gefroren** *Adj.* **1.** *See*: frozen over; **2.** → *durchfroren*

durchgehen (*unreg., trennb., ist -ge-*) **I.** *v/i.* **1. ~** (*durch*) *Person*: go (*od.* walk) through, pass (through); *im Bus etc.*: *bitte nach hinten ~* please pass (*od.* move) right down (to the back); **2.** *umg.* (*durchpassen, durchgelangen*) go through; *unter e-r Brücke ~* pass under a bridge; **3.** *Zug etc.*: go (*right*) through, go direct; *geht der Zug durch, oder muss ich umsteigen?* is this a through-train or will I have to change?; **4.** *Party, Sitzung*: carry (*od.* go) on, last; **5.** *unpers.*: *geht es da durch?* is that the way (through)?; *hier geht's nicht durch* this isn't the way (through); **6.** *Pferd*: bolt (*j-m* with s.o.); **7.** *umg. fig.* → *durchbrennen* 3;

s-e Fantasie etc. **geht manchmal mit ihm durch** *fig.* sometimes his imagination *etc.* gets the better of him; **sein Temperament ging mit ihm durch** he got carried away; **8.** *umg. Antrag*: be accepted; *Gesetz*: be passed, go through; **9.** *(geduldet werden)* pass, be tolerated; **etw. ~ lassen** let s.th. pass, turn a blind eye to s.th.; **j-m etw. ~ lassen** let s.o. get away with s.th.; **10.** *umg.*: **~ für** *(gehalten werden)* be taken for; **II.** *v/t. (Unterlagen etc.)* go through *(od. over)*; **ich ging es nochmal auf Tippfehler hin durch** I checked it over *(od.* went through it) again for typos

durchgehend I. *Part. Präs.* → **durchgehen**; **II.** *Adj. attr.* **1.** *Flug, Zug*: through, direct; *(ohne Halt etc.)* non--stop; **2.** *Betrieb etc.*: continuous, non--stop; **3.** *Linie etc.*: continuous; *Bank, Tischplatte*: one-piece ...; **III.** *Adv.* **1.** *(allgemein)* generally; **2.** *(ständig)* continuously; **~ geöffnet** open all day; **~ von 9 - 18.30 geöffnet** open 9 a.m. - 6.30 p.m.; **~ arbeiten** work through; *Einlass* **~** non-stop admission; **3.** *(durchweg)* throughout; **~ gefüttert sein** be fully lined

durchgeistigt *Adj.* (very) cerebral

durchgeknallt I. *P.P.* → **durchknallen**; **II.** *Adj. umg.* crazy, whacky

durch|gelegen I. *P.P.* → **durchliegen**; **II.** *Adj.* **1.** *Bett, Matratze*: saggy, worn (down); **2.** *Rücken etc.*: bedsore, *präd.* suffering from bedsores; **~geschwitzt I.** *P.P.* → **durchschwitzen**; **II.** *Adj.* sweaty; *völlig*: soaked with sweat; **~gesessen** *Adj. Sofa etc.*: saggy, worn out; *Hose etc.*: worn through; **~gestaltet** *Adj.* worked out to the last detail; **~gestylt** ['-gəstailt] *Adj. umg.* carefully styled; **ein ~er Yuppie** a yuppie from head to toe; **~gewetzt I.** *P.P.* → **durchwetzen**; **II.** *Adj.* worn through, worn-out

durch|graben *(unreg., trennb., hat -ge-)* **I.** *v/t.*: **~** *(durch etw.)* dig through (s.th.); **II.** *v/refl.*: **sich ~** *(durch)* dig *(od.* burrow) one's way through

durch|greifen *v/i. (unreg., trennb., hat -ge-)* **1.** **~** *(durch)* reach through; **2.** *fig.*: *(hart od. energisch)* **~** take (tough) action, do something (drastic) *umg.*; **rücksichtslos ~** take ruthless steps *(od.* measures); **~greifend I.** *Part. Präs.* → **durchgreifen**; **II.** *Adj.* drastic; radical, sweeping

durchhaben *v/t. (unreg., trennb., hat -ge-); umg. allg.* have got through; *Buch etc.*: have finished

durchhalten *(unreg., trennb., hat -ge-)* **I.** *v/i.* hold out, stick it out, persevere *umg.*; *Patient*: hold on, make it; **du musst ~** *auch* you mustn't give up, *bes. Am.* hang in there *umg.*; **II.** *v/t.* **1.** *(durchstehen)* *(Belastung, Tempo etc.)* stand; *(Zeit, Kampf etc.)* survive; *(Streik)* see through; *(Diät)* stick *(od.* keep) to, stay on; *(Rennen)* stay (the course); **2.** *(beibehalten)* *(Lebensweise, Tempo etc.)* keep s.th. up

Durchhaltevermögen *n* staying power

durchhängen *v/i. (unreg., trennb., hat / südd., schw., österr. ist -ge-)* **1.** *(nach unten)* **~** sag; **2.** *umg. fig.* have *(od.* be going through) a low *(od.* downer); **lass dich nicht so ~** come on, get a grip of yourself; **Durchhänger** *m umg.* low; **e-n ~ haben** have *(od.* be going through) a low, be on a downer

durch|hauen *v/t. (hieb / umg. haute durch, hat -ge-)* **1.** chop in two; *(spal-*

---

ten) split; **2.** *umg. (prügeln)* give s.o. a thrashing; **~hecheln** *v/t. (trennb., hat -ge-); umg.* **1.** *pej. (mst Abwesende)* gossip about; **2.** *(Lernstoff, Buch etc.)* run through; **~heizen** *(trennb., hat -ge-)* **I.** *v/t.* heat properly; **II.** *v/i.* keep the heating on night and day; **~helfen** *v/i. (unreg., trennb., hat -ge-):* **~** *(durch)* help *s.o.* through; **sich** *(Dat.)* **~** get by, manage; **~hören** *v/t. (trennb., hat -ge-)* **1.** hear (through the wall *etc.*); **2.** *fig.* sense, detect; **~, dass ...** be able to tell that ...; **~hungern** *v/refl. (trennb., hat -ge-):* **sich ~** *(durch e-n Krieg etc.)* have to survive (a war *etc.*) on very little; **wir haben uns durch den Krieg durchgehungert** *auch* we had very little *(od.* virtually nothing) to eat during the war; **~jagen** *(trennb., -ge-)* **I.** *v/i. (ist):* **~** *(durch)* race *(od.* tear) through; **II.** *v/t. (hat)* rush through *(auch fig.)*

'durchkämmen¹ *v/t. (trennb., hat -ge-)* **1.** *(Haar)* comb out; **2.** *fig. (Gebiet etc.)* comb *(nach* for)

durch'kämmen² *v/t. (untr., hat); fig.* comb *(nach* for)

durch|kämpfen *(trennb., hat -ge-)* **I.** *v/t. (Antrag, Vorschlag etc.)* fight *s.th.* through; **II.** *v/refl.* **1. sich ~** *(durch)* fight one's way through *(auch fig.)*; **2.** *fig.*: **sich ~ zu** → **durchringen**; **~kauen** *v/t. (trennb., hat -ge-)* **1.** chew well; **2.** *umg. fig.* go over *s.th.* again and again; **~klingen** *v/i. (unreg., trennb., -ge-)* **1.** *(hat)* sound through; **2.** *(hat od. ist); fig.*: **es klang etwas Neid durch** you could detect a tinge of envy; **~knallen** *v/i. (trennb., ist -ge-); umg. Sicherung*: blow; → **durchgeknallt**; **~kneten** *v/t. (trennb., hat -ge-)* knead (thoroughly); *(Muskeln)* knead

durch|kommen *v/i. (unreg., trennb., ist -ge-)* **1.** **~** *(durch)* come through *(auch Sonne, Wasser, Zahn)*; **mit Mühe**: (manage to) get through *(auch Telef.)*; **bei m-n Haaren kommt immer mehr Grau durch** I keep getting more grey *(Am.* gray) hairs; **kommst du mit der Hand durch das Gitter durch?** can you reach through the grille with your hand?; **es gab kein Durchkommen** there was no way through; **2.** **~** *(durch) auf Weiterfahrt etc.*: come *(od.* pass) through; **3.** *fig. (zum Vorschein kommen) Charakterzug etc.*: become apparent; **wenn sie aufgeregt ist, kommt ihr französischer Akzent durch** her French accent comes through; **manchmal kommt bei ihm der Geizhals durch** sometimes the miser in him comes out *(od.* to the fore); **4.** *umg. fig. (sein Ziel erreichen)* make it; *in e-r Prüfung*: pass; *Kranker*: pull through; **~ mit** *(Erfolg haben)* get somewhere with *s.th.*; *mit e-r Frechheit etc.*: get away with; **damit kommst du** *(bei ihm)* **nicht durch** that won't work *(od.* that won't cut any ice) (with him); **5.** *umg.*: **~ mit wenig Geld**: get by with; *viel Arbeit*: cope with

durchkönnen *v/i. (unreg., trennb., hat -ge-); umg.*: **~** *(durch)* be able to get through

durch'kreuzen¹ *v/t. (untr., hat)* **1.** *geh. (Länder, Meere)* cross; **2.** *fig. (Pläne etc.)* thwart, frustrate, foil

'durchkreuzen² *v/t. (trennb., hat -ge-)* cross out

Durchkreuzung *f fig.* foiling, thwarting

'durchkriechen¹ *v/i. (unreg., trennb., ist -ge-):* **~** *(durch)* crawl through

---

durch'kriechen² *v/t. (unreg., untr., hat)* crawl through

durch|kriegen *v/t. (trennb., hat -ge-); umg.* → **durchbringen** I 1, 2, 3, 5; **~laden** *v/t./i. (unreg., trennb., hat -ge-)* *(Gewehr etc.)* reload

Durchlass *m; -es, Durchlässe* passage-(way); *(Öffnung)* opening, gap; **j-m ~ gewähren** *geh.* let s.o. pass *(od.* through); **durchlassen** *v/t. (unreg., trennb., hat -ge-)* **1.** *Person*: **~** *(durch)* let *s.o. od. s.th.* pass *(od.* through); **den Ball ~** *Torwart*: let a goal in; **2.** *(Licht, Wasser etc.)* let *s.th.* through; *nach innen/außen*: let *s.th.* in/out; *Wasser* **~** *Boot, Gefäß*: *auch* leak; **3.** *umg. fig. (Antrag, Prüfling)* pass; *(Frechheit etc.)* let *s.th.* pass; **j-m etw. ~** let s.o. get away with s.th.; **durchlässig** *Adj.* **1.** *für Wasser, Licht, Luft*: permeable, pervious *(für* to); *für Licht*: translucent; **2.** *(porös)* porous; **3.** *(undicht) Gefäß, Schuhe etc.*: leaky; **4.** *fig. Grenze, Schulsystem etc.*: open; **Durchlässigkeit** *f* perviousness; translucence; porosity; leakiness; → **durchlässig**

Durchlaucht *f; -, -en: Euer/Seine/Ihre* **~** Your/His/Her (Serene) Highness *(Herzog*: Grace)

Durchlauf *m* → **Durchgang** 3

durch'laufen¹ *v/t. (unreg., untr., hat)* **1.** run through; *(e-e Strecke)* cover; *Astr., Phys. (Bahn)* travel through; **2.** *fig. (Phase, Schule etc.)* pass through; **3.** *geh. fig.*: **mich durchlief es heiß/eiskalt** I had a hot flush / my blood ran cold; **ein Schauder durchlief ihn** he shuddered, a shiver ran down his spine

'durchlaufen² *(unreg., trennb., -ge-)* **I.** *v/i. (ist)* **1.** *Person*: **~** *(durch)* run through; *(durcheilen)* rush through; *(vorbeikommen)* pass through; **~ unter** *(+ Dat.)* run under; **zwischen den Pfählen ~** run between the posts; **2.** **~** *(durch) Sache*: pass through; *Flüssigkeit etc.*: flow through; *Sanduhr*: trickle through; **der Kaffee ist durchgelaufen** the coffee is finished filtering *(od.* is ready); **3.** *umg. ohne Pause, Person*: run without stopping *(bis* to *od.* until); *Fernseher, Heizung etc.*: run non-stop; **II.** *v/t. (hat)*: *Schuhe*: **~** go through a pair of shoes

durchlaufend I. *Part. Präs.* → **durchlaufen¹, durchlaufen²**; **II.** *Adj.* continuous *(auch Tech.)*; *Wirts.* transitory

Durchlauferhitzer *m* instant *(od.* continuous-flow) water heater

durchlavieren *v/refl. (trennb., hat); umg.*: **sich ~** *(durch)* wangle one's way through

durchleben *v/t. (untr., hat)* go *(od.* live) through, experience; *(im Geiste)* **noch einmal ~** relive

durch|leiten *v/t. (trennb., hat -ge-):* **~** *(durch)* lead through; *Verkehr*: direct; *Kabel*: run; **~lesen** *v/t. (unreg., trennb., hat -ge-):* *(sich [Dat.])* **etw. ~** read s.th. through; **wenn du den Bericht durchgelesen hast, ...** when you've finished (reading) the report, ...

'durchleuchten¹ *v/i. (trennb., hat -ge-):* **~** *(durch)* shine through; *fig. auch* show

durch'leuchten² *v/t. (untr., hat)* **1.** *Med.* x-ray, screen; *am Flughafen etc.*: x-ray, put through the scanner; *(Eier)* test; **2.** *fig. (untersuchen)* investigate *(auf + Akk. [hin]* for); *(Bewerber etc.)* screen, *Brit. auch* vet; *(Vergan-*

genheit) probe into

Durchleuchtung *f Med.* x-ray (examination); **Durchleuchtungsgerät** *n am Flughafen etc.*: (x-ray) scanner

durchliegen (*unreg., trennb., hat -ge-*) **I.** *v/t.* **1.** *Matratze*: wear out (in the middle); **2.** *Med.*: **sich** (*Dat.*) **den Rücken** ~ develop bedsores; **II.** *v/refl. Med.* get bedsores; → **durchgelegen** II

durch|löchern *v/t.* (*untr., hat*) **1.** make holes in; *durch Tragen*: wear holes in; (*durchbohren*) pierce; *mit Kugeln*: riddle with bullets; **2.** *fig.* shoot holes in, undermine; **~löchert I.** *P.P.* → **durchlöchern**; **II.** *Adj.* full of holes, *attr. auch* holy … *umg.*; *von Kugeln*: riddled with bullets; **völlig** ~ *auch* riddled with holes

durchlotsen *v/t.* (*trennb., hat -ge-*): ~ (**durch**) pilot (*Auto*: guide) through

'durchlüften[1] *v/t.* (*trennb., hat -ge-*) air, give *s.th.* a good airing

durch'lüften[2] *v/t.* (*untr., hat*); (*Getreide, Holzstoß etc.*) ventilate; (*Aquarium, Boden*) aerate

durch|machen (*trennb., hat -ge-*) **I.** *v/t.* (*durchlaufen, erleiden*) go through; (*Entwicklung, Wandlung etc.*) undergo; (*Krankheit*) suffer from, have; *Operation*: have, undergo; **er hat einiges durchgemacht** he's been through a lot, he hasn't had an easy time of it; **II.** *v/i. umg.* (*durcharbeiten*) work through, not take a break; (*weitermachen*) carry on (**bis** until); (**die ganze Nacht**) ~ *umg.* (*durchfeiern*) make a night of it, do an all-nighter

Durchmarsch *m* **1.** march through; **2.** *nur Sg.; umg.* (*Durchfall*) the runs *Pl.*; **3.** *umg., bes. Skat*: **e-n** ~ **haben/machen** have a grand slam / take all the tricks; **durchmarschieren** *v/i.* (*trennb., ist*): ~ (**durch**) march through

durchmessen *v/t.* (*unreg., untr., hat*); *geh.*: **er durchmaß das Zimmer** he paced the floor; **Durchmesser** *m; -s, -* diameter; **e-n** ~ **von drei Metern haben** be three met|res (*Am.* -ers) in diameter

durch|mogeln *v/refl.* (*trennb., hat -ge-*); *umg. pej.* wangle one's way through; *in e-r Prüfung*: cheat; **~müssen** *v/i.* (*unreg., trennb., hat -ge-*); *umg.* (*auch* ~ **durch**) have to get (*od.* go) through; **da muss ich** (**einfach**) **durch** *fig.* I've (just) got to get through it somehow, I've got to ride this one out

durchnässt *Adj.*: **völlig** ~ soaking wet; *Person*: *auch* soaked to the skin, drenched

durch|nehmen *v/t.* (*unreg., trennb., hat -ge-*); (*Lehrstoff*) go through, do; **~nummerieren** *v/t.* (*trennb., hat*) number (consecutively) all the way through; **~organisiert** *Adj.* (**gut**) well-organized; **alles war** ~ it was all organized down to the last detail; **~pauken** *v/t.* (*trennb., hat -ge-*); *umg. pej.* (*Gesetz etc.*) force (*od.* push) through; **~pausen** *v/t.* (*trennb., hat -ge-*) trace; **~peitschen** *v/t.* (*trennb., hat -ge-*) **1.** give *s.o.* a whipping, flog *s.o.*; **2.** *fig.* (*Gesetz etc.*) rush *s.th.* through

durchprobieren *v/t.* (*trennb., hat*) try in turn; **sie hat alle Kleider durchprobiert** she tried on every dress one after another

durchqueren *v/t.* (*untr., hat*) cross; *Zug*: travel across; (*Land*) pass through; **Durchquerung** *f* crossing

durchquetschen (*trennb., hat -ge-*) *v/refl.*: **sich** ~ (**durch**) squeeze through

'durchrasen *v/i.* (*trennb., ist -ge-*): ~ (**durch**) race (*od.* tear, shoot) through

durch|rasseln *v/i.* (*trennb., ist -ge-*); *umg.*: (**in der Prüfung**) ~ flunk (the exam *od.* test); **~rauschen** *v/i.* (*trennb., ist -ge-*); *umg.* **1.** → **'durchrasen**; **2.** → **durchrasseln**; **~rechnen** *v/t.* (*trennb., hat -ge-*) make an estimate of; (*nochmals rechnen*) go over, check; **~regnen** *v/i.* (*trennb., hat -ge-*); *unpers.* **1. hier regnet es durch** the rain's coming in here; **2. es hat die ganze Nacht durchgeregnet** it rained all (through the) night

Durchreiche *f, -, -n* (serving) hatch, pass-through; **durchreichen** *v/t.* (*trennb., hat -ge-*) pass (*od.* hand) *s.th.* through

Durchreise *f*: **auf der** ~ (**durch**) on one's way through; **wir sind nur auf der** ~ we're just passing through

durch'reisen[1] *v/t.* (*untr., hat*) travel through; (*auch die Welt*) travel around

'durchreisen[2] *v/i.* (*unreg., trennb., ist -ge-*): ~ (**durch**) pass through; **Durchreisende** *m, f* travel(l)er, *Am. auch* transient; *Flug.* transit (*Eisenb.* through) passenger; **Durchreisevisum** *n* transit visa

durchreißen (*unreg., trennb., -ge-*) **I.** *v/t.* (*hat*) tear (in two *od.* half); **II.** *v/i.* (*ist*) tear, get torn; *Faden*: snap, break (in two)

'durchreiten[1] (*unreg., trennb., -ge-*) **I.** *v/i.* (*ist*) **1.** ~ (**durch**) ride through; ~ **unter/zwischen** (+ *Dat.*) (through) under/between; **2.** *Zeitraum*: **die ganze Nacht etc.** ~ ride all night *etc.*; **II.** *v/t.* (*hat*): **sich** (*Dat.*) **die Hosen** ~ wear out the trousers (through riding)

durch'reiten[2] *v/t.* (*unreg., untr., hat*) ride through

durchrennen *v/i.* (*unreg., trennb., ist -ge-*): ~ (**durch**) run through

durchrieseln *v/t.* (*untr., hat*); *unpers.*: **es durchrieselte ihn kalt** a cold shiver ran down his spine; *fig.* a ghost walked over his grave

durch|ringen *v/refl.* (*unreg., trennb., hat -ge-*): **sich** (**dazu**) ~ **zu** (+ *Inf.*) finally make up one's mind to (+ *Inf.*); **sich zu e-m Entschluss** ~ force o.s. to make a decision; **~rosten** *v/i.* (*trennb., ist -ge-*) rust through; **~rühren** *v/t.* (*trennb., hat -ge-*) stir (*od.* mix) thoroughly; **~rutschen** *v/i.* (*trennb., ist -ge-*): ~ (**durch**) slip through (*auch fig.*); **sie ist bei der Prüfung gerade noch durchgerutscht** *umg. fig.* she (just about) scraped through the exam, she passed on (*Am.* by) the skin of her teeth; **~rütteln** *v/t.* (*trennb., hat -ge-*) shake around (*Am.* around)

durchs *Präp. + Art.* **1.** → **durch**; **2.** *in Wendungen*: **für j-n** ~ **Feuer gehen** go through fire for s.o.; **mit j-m** ~ **Leben gehen** go through life with s.o.

durchsacken *v/i.* (*trennb., ist -ge-*); *Flug.* stall; *bei Landung*: pancake

Durchsage *f* announcement; *Radio*: (news) flash; ~ **der Polizei** police message (*od.* announcement); **Achtung, Achtung, e-e** ~**!** your attention please (for the following announcement); **durchsagen** *v/t.* (*trennb., hat -ge-*) **1.** *Lautsprecher, Radio*: announce; **2.** (*weitergeben*) pass *s.th.* on; **j-m etw. telefonisch** ~ tell s.o. s.th. on the (tele)phone

durchsägen *v/t.* (*trennb., hat -ge-*) saw

through (*od.* in two)

Durchsatz *m fachspr.* throughput

durchschaubar *Adj. Motiv etc.*: obvious, transparent; **schwer** ~ inscrutable; *Person: auch* enigmatic; **er ist leicht** ~ you can read him like a book

'durchschauen[1] *v/i.* (*trennb., hat -ge-*): ~ (**durch**) look through; **man kann durch die Fenster kaum** ~ you can hardly see through the windows

durch'schauen[2] *v/t.* (*untr., hat*); (*j-n, Lüge, Motive etc.*) see through; (*begreifen*) understand; **du bist durchschaut** you've been caught (out)

durchscheinen *v/i.* (*unreg., trennb., hat -ge-*): ~ (**durch**) shine through (*auch fig.*); *Schrift etc.*: show through; **durchscheinend I.** *Part. Präs.* → **durchscheinen**; **II.** *Adj.* translucent

durch|scheuern (*trennb., hat -ge-*) **I.** *v/t.* **1.** (*Stoff*) wear through; **2. sich** (*Dat.*) **die Haut** ~ rub one's skin off, chafe one's skin; **II.** *v/refl.* wear through; **~schieben** *v/t.* (*unreg., trennb., hat -ge-*): ~ (**durch**) push (through); **etw. unter der Tür** ~ push *s.th.* under a door

'durchschießen[1] *v/i.* (*unreg., trennb., -ge-*): ~ (**durch**) **1.** (*hat*) shoot through; **2.** (*ist*); *umg.* shoot (*od.* flash) through

durch'schießen[2] *v/t.* (*unreg., untr., hat*) **1.** shoot through *s.th.*; **ein Gedanke durchschießt j-n** *fig.* a thought occurs to s.o.; **2.** *Druck.* space (out); **3.** *mit Papier*: interleave; **4.** *mit Fäden*: interweave

durchschimmern *v/i.* (*trennb., hat -ge-*): ~ (**durch**) shimmer through; *Schrift etc.*: come (*od.* show) through

'durchschlafen[1] *v/i.* (*unreg., trennb., hat -ge-*) sleep (right) through

durch'schlafen[2] *Adj.*: **nach e-r ~en Nacht** after sleeping all night, after a good night's sleep

Durchschlag *m* **1.** (*Kopie*) (carbon) copy; **2.** (*Sieb*) sieve, strainer; *für Gemüse*: colander; **3.** *Werkzeug*: punch; **4.** *Mot.* puncture; **5.** *Etech.* disruptive discharge, *Am.* puncture; *von Sicherungen*: blowout; **6.** *Bergb.* crosscut, breakoff

durch'schlagen[1] *v/t.* (*unreg., untr., hat*) *Kugel etc.*: go through

'durchschlagen[2] (*unreg., trennb., -ge-*) **I.** *v/t.* (*hat*) **1.** (*zerschlagen*) break *s.th.* in two; **2.** ~ (**durch**) (*Nagel etc.*) drive (*od.* knock) (through); (*Wand etc.*) make a hole in; *Bergb.*: (break) open, cut across; **3.** *Gastr.* pass *s.th.* through a strainer; **II.** *v/i.* **1.** (*ist*); *Nässe, Erbanlage etc.*: ~ (**durch**) come through; *Farbe: auch* show through; **bei ihm schlägt die Mutter durch** *fig.* he takes after his mother; **2.** (*ist*); *fig.* (*wirken*) have an effect (**auf** + *Akk.* on); **3.** (*hat*); (*abführend wirken*) go straight through (**bei j-m** s.o.); **4.** (*ist*); *Etech. Sicherung*: blow; **III.** *v/refl.* (*hat*) **1. sich** ~ (**durch**) fight one's way through; **2.** *fig.* get by (**mit** on); **sich mühsam** ~ have a hard time of it

durchschlagend I. *Part. Präs.* → **durchschlagen**[1], **durchschlagen**[2]; **II.** *Adj.* **1.** *Beweis*: conclusive, irrefutable; **2.** *Erfolg*: resounding, sweeping; **e-e ~e Wirkung haben** *umg. fig. Essen etc.*: give you the runs; **3.** *Effekt, Maßnahme*: decisive, effective

Durchschlagpapier *n* carbon paper

Durchschlagskraft *f; nur Sg.* **1.** striking force; **2.** *fig. e-s Arguments etc.*: force

durch|schlängeln *v/refl.* (*trennb., hat -ge-*): **sich** ~ (**durch**) **1.** *Fluss etc.*: wind

durchschleppen – durchtasten

(its way) through, meander; *Person*: weave one's way through; **2.** *fig.* muddle through, (manage to) get (a)round; **~schleppen** *v/t.* (*trennb., hat -ge-*); *umg., oft pej.*: **j-n (mit) ~** (*ernähren*) keep s.o.; (*j-n mit schlechter Leistung*) carry s.o.; **~schleusen** *v/t.* (*trennb., hat -ge-*) **1.** (*Schiff etc.*) pass *s.th.* through a lock; **2.** *fig.*: **~ (durch)** guide *s.o. od. s.th.* through; *durch den Zoll etc.*: hustle *s.o.* through; *heimlich*: smuggle *s.o. od. s.th.* through; **~schlüpfen** *v/i.* (*trennb., ist -ge-*): **~ (durch)** slip through (*auch fig.*); **unter dem Zaun ~** squeeze under the fence **durch|schmecken** (*trennb., hat -ge-*) **I.** *v/t.* (be able to) taste; **II.** *v/i.*: **der Senf schmeckte durch** you could taste the mustard (quite strongly); **~schmoren** *v/i.* (*trennb., ist -ge-*); *umg. Kabel etc.*: burn through

'durchschneiden[1] *v/t.* (*unreg., trennb., hat -ge-*); (*Papier, Band*) cut (in two); (*Faden etc.*) cut through; (*Nabelschnur*) cut; **j-m die Kehle ~** slit s.o.'s throat

durch'schneiden[2] *v/t.* (*unreg., untr., hat*) **1.** cut (in two); **2.** *geh.; optisch*: (*Land etc.*) cut through; (*Linie*) intersect; (*kreuzen*) cross; (*die Wellen*) plough (*Am.* plow) through

Durchschnitt *m* **1.** average; **im ~** on (an) average; **über/unter dem ~ liegen** be above/below average; **im ~ betragen, erzielen, verdienen** etc. average; **2.** *fig.*: **sie ist guter ~** she's not a bad player etc.; **er ist schlechter/nur ~** he's very/only average; **der ~ unserer Kunden** (*die Mehrheit*) our average customer, most (*od.* the majority) of our customers; **3.** *Math.* mean; **4.** *fachspr. Darstellung*: (cross-)section **durchschnittlich I.** *Adj.* **1.** *nur attr.* average; **die ~e Jahrestemperatur beträgt ...** the average annual temperature is ...; **2.** (*normal*) *Begabung, Qualität etc.*: average; *Leben, Mensch etc.*: ordinary; **3.** (*mittelmäßig*) *Begabung, Leistung*: modest, mediocre *pej.*, fair to middling *umg.*; *Aussehen pej.*: nondescript, average; **II.** *Adv.* on (an) average; **~ begabt/groß** of average talent/height; **~ betragen, leisten, verdienen** etc. average; **sie arbeitet ~ zehn Stunden am Tag** she works an average of ten hours a day, she works ten hours a day, on average

Durchschnitts|... *im Subst. mst* average ...; **~alter** *n* average age; **~bürger** *m*, **~bürgerin** *f* average citizen; **der ~** the (your *umg.*) average citizen, the man in the street, Mr(.) Average *umg.*; **~einkommen** *n* average income; **~geschwindigkeit** *f* average speed; **~gesicht** *n* nondescript face; **~leistung** *f* average performance; **~mensch** *m* ordinary person, *the* man in the street; **~note** *f* average mark (*bes. Am.* grade); **~temperatur** *f* average (*od.* mean) temperature; **~typ** *m* umg. ordinary sort of person; **~wert** *m* average (value), mean; **~zeit** *f* average time (it takes)

durchschnüffeln *v/t.* (*untr., hat*); *umg. pej.* snoop around in; (*auch Briefe etc.*) nose around in

durchschreiben *v/t.* (*unreg., trennb., hat -ge-*) make a (carbon) copy of

durchschreiten *v/t.* (*unreg., untr., hat*) **1.** *geh.* walk through (*od.* across); *mit großen Schritten*: stride through; **2.** *Truppen*: (*Grenze*) pass, traverse; (*Fluss*) ford

Durchschrift *f* (carbon) copy
Durchschuss *m* **1.** (*Wunde*) penetration wound; **das war ein glatter ~ durch den Arm**: the shot went right through his (*od.* her) arm; **2.** *Druck.* space; **3.** *Weberei*: woof

'durchschwimmen[1] *v/i.* (*unreg., trennb., ist -ge-*): **~ (durch)** swim (*Sachen*: float) through (*od.* across); **~ unter** (+ *Dat.*) **/zwischen** (+ *Dat.*) swim under/between (*od.* through)

durch'schwimmen[2] *v/t.* (*unreg., untr., hat*) swim through (*od.* across), cross; (*e-e Strecke*) swim

durchschwitzen *v/t.* (*trennb., hat -ge-*): **ich habe mein Hemd durchgeschwitzt od. mein Hemd ist durchgeschwitzt** my shirt's soaked (*od.* soaking, drenched) with sweat

durchsegeln *v/i.* (*trennb., ist -ge-*) **1.** sail through; **~ unter** (+ *Dat.*) **/zwischen** (+ *Dat.*) sail under/between (*od.* through); **2.** *umg. fig.* flunk (it); **er ist in der od. durch die Prüfung durchgesegelt** he flunked the exam

durch|sehen (*unreg., trennb., hat -ge-*) **I.** *v/i.* **~ (durch)** see (*od.* look) through; **II.** *v/t.* **1.** look (*od.* go) through, go over, check; **etw. auf Fehler ~** look (*od.* check) s.th. through for mistakes; **2.** (*durchblättern*) glance (*od.* flick) through *s.th.*; **3.** *umg. fig.* → **durchblicken** 2; **~seihen** *v/t.* (*trennb., hat -ge-*) strain

durchsetzbar *Adj.*: **schwer ~ präd.** hard to enforce, barely enforceable; **nicht ~ präd.** not enforceable

'durchsetzen[1] (*trennb., hat -ge-*) **I.** *v/t.* (*Plan etc.*) get s.th. through (*od.* accepted); **mit Nachdruck**: push s.th. through; **~, dass etw. getan wird** succeed in getting s.th. done; **s-e Meinung ~** get (the) others to agree; **s-n Kopf od. Willen ~** have one's way; **II.** *v/refl.* **1.** *Person*: get one's way; *im Leben*: assert o.s.; *im Konflikt*: prevail; **sie kann sich bei den Kindern nicht ~** the children always get their own way with her, she has no control over the children; **du musst lernen, dich durchzusetzen** you've got to (learn to) assert yourself more, you've got to be more self-assertive (*od.* forceful); **2. sich ~ gegen** (*j-n*) come out on top against (*auch Sport*), prevail over; (*etw.*) overcome; **3.** *Idee etc.*: catch on, gain acceptance (**bei** with); *Ware*: catch on, sell

durch'setzen[2] *v/t.* (*untr., hat*) intersperse, permeate; (*bes. Schriftliches*) *auch* interlard (**mit** with); *mit Spionen etc.*: infiltrate (with); **durchsetzt I.** *P.P.* → **durchsetzen**[2]; **II.** *Adj.*: **ein mit Unkraut ~er Rasen** a weed-ridden lawn

Durchsetzung *f* putting (*od.* getting) s.th. through; (*von Zielen*) achievement, accomplishment; **zur ~ unserer Ziele/Forderungen** to achieve our aims / enforce our goals

Durchsetzungs|kraft *f*, **~vermögen** *n* (powers *Pl.* of) self-assertion, self-assertiveness; **er hat nicht genügend ~** he isn't forceful enough

Durchseuchung *f* contamination; **geringe/hohe ~** low/high amount (*od.* degree) of contamination

Durchsicht *f* (*Überprüfung*) checking; **bei ~** (+ *Gen.*) on (*od.* while) looking through (*prüfend*: checking) *s.th.*

durchsichtig *Adj.* **1.** transparent; *attr. Bluse etc.: auch* see-through ...; *Haut*: translucent; **2.** *fig.* obvious, transparent; *Lüge*: patent; **Durchsichtigkeit** *f* transparency (*auch fig.*); *der Haut*: translucence, translucent quality

durchsickern *v/i.* (*trennb., ist -ge-*) **1. ~ (durch)** seep through; *tröpfelnd*: trickle through; **2.** *fig. Informationen*: filter through; *ungewollt*: leak out; **~ bis** *auch* filter (*od.* trickle) down to

durchsiebt *Adj.* *mit Kugeln*: riddled with bullets

durchsoffen *Adj.* *umg. pej. Nacht*: drunken

durch|spielen (*trennb., hat -ge-*) **I.** *v/t.* **1.** *ohne Pause*: play s.th. right (*Am.* all the way) through; **2.** *in Gedanken*: go through; **II.** *v/i.* **1. die ganze Nacht ~** play all night (long); **2.** *Sport* (*nicht ausgewechselt werden*) last the whole match (*Am. auch* game); **III.** *v/refl. Sport*: weave one's way (*od.* get) through; **~sprechen** (*unreg., trennb., hat -ge-*) *v/t.* talk s.th. over (**mit** with), discuss (thoroughly)

durch|spülen *v/t.* (*trennb., hat -ge-*): (**gut**) **~ 1.** (*Wäsche etc.*) rinse thoroughly; **2.** (*Nieren*) flush; **~starten** *v/i.* (*trennb., hat -ge-*) **1.** *Flug.* reaccelerate (*od.* climb) for a new landing approach; *Mot.* rev up; **2.** *fig.* get going (again) properly, make a good start

durchstechen *v/t.* (*unreg., untr., hat*) **1.** pierce; *leicht, mit e-r Nadel*: prick; **2.** *Tech.* (*Damm*) cut

durch|stecken *v/t.* (*trennb., hat -ge-*): **~ (durch)** pass (*od.* put) through; **etw. unter der Tür ~** slip (*od.* push) s.th. under a door; **~stehen** *v/t.* (*unreg., trennb., hat -ge-*); *umg.* get through, stick s.th. out *umg.*; → *auch* **durchhalten** II; **~stellen** *v/t.* (*trennb., hat -ge-*) *Telef.*: **j-n / ein Gespräch (zu j-m) ~** put s.o. / a call through (to s.o.)

durchstöbern *v/t.* (*untr., hat*) rummage through *s.th.* (**nach** for)

'durchstoßen[1] (*unreg., trennb., -ge-*) **I.** *v/i.* (*ist*); *auch Mil. und Sport* break through ([**bis**] **zu** to); *Mil.: auch* penetrate; **II.** *v/t.* (*hat*). **~ (durch)** push *s.th.* through

durch'stoßen[2] *v/t.* (*unreg., untr., hat*) pierce; *Mil., Flug.* (*Wolken*) break through, clear

durch|strecken *v/t.* (*trennb., hat -ge-*); (*völlig strecken*) stretch out (fully); **~streichen** *v/t.* (*unreg., trennb., hat -ge-*) cross out

durchstreifen *v/t.* (*untr., hat*) *Mensch*: roam, wander (through); *Raubtier*: prowl; *suchend*: scour *s.th.*; *kontrollierend*: patrol

durchströmen *v/t.* (*untr., hat*) **1.** flow (*od.* run) through; **2.** *fig.*: **ein Gefühl der Zufriedenheit durchströmte sie** she was filled with a great sense of satisfaction

durchsuchen *v/t.* (*untr., hat*) search (**nach** for); **Durchsuchung** *f* search; **Durchsuchungsbefehl** *m* search warrant

durchtanzen *v/i.* (*trennb., hat -ge-*) dance nonstop; **~ bis** dance (away) until (*od.* till); **die ganze Nacht ~** dance the night away; **durchtanzt** *Adj.* **1. ~e Nacht** night spent dancing; **wir hatten gerade eine ~e Nacht hinter uns** we had just spent the whole night dancing; **2.** *Schuhe*: *nachgestellt*: worn out (by dancing)

durch|tasten *v/refl.* (*trennb., hat -ge-*): **sich ~ (durch)** grope one's way through; **~testen** *v/t.* (*trennb.*, *hat -ge-*) test out (thoroughly)

durchtrainiert *Adj.* well-trained, very fit; *Körper*: athletic; **ein gut ~er Körper** a body in peak condition

durchtränkt *Adj.*: **~ von** soaked (*od.* steeped) in; *lit. fig.* suffused with

durchtreiben *v/t.* (*unreg.*, *trennb.*, *hat -ge-*): **~** (**durch**) (*Vieh*) drive through; (*Nagel*) drive (*od.* force) through

'durchtrennen¹ *v/t.* (*trennb.*, *hat -ge-*) → **durch'trennen²**

durch'trennen² *v/t.* (*untr.*, *hat durchtrennt*) tear (in two), divide; (*schneiden*) cut (in two); (*Nerv etc.*) sever; **Durchtrennung** *f* division, severance

durchtreten (*unreg.*, *trennb.*, *-ge-*) **I.** *v/t.* (*hat*); *Mot.* (*Pedal*) floor; (*Starter*) kick; **II.** *v/i.* (*ist*); *im Bus etc.*: **nach hinten ~, bitte** move through to the back please

durchtrieben *Adj. pej.* sly, crafty; **das ist ein ~er Kerl** he's a sly one; **Durchtriebenheit** *f* slyness

durch'wachen¹ *v/t.* (*untr.*, *hat durchwacht*): **die Nacht ~** be (*od.* lie, stay) awake all night; **bei j-m**: stay by s.o.'s bedside (*od.* stay up with s.o.) all night; **ich habe die Nacht durchwacht** *auch* I didn't sleep a wink (*od.* get a wink of sleep) all night; → **durchwacht**

'durchwachen² *v/t.* (*untr.*, *hat -ge-*): **die Nacht ~** be (*od.* lie, stay) awake all night; **bei j-m**: stay by s.o.'s bedside (*od.* stay up with s.o.) all night; **ich habe die Nacht durchgewacht** *auch* I didn't sleep a wink (*od.* get a wink of sleep) all night

'durchwachsen¹ *v/i.* (*unreg.*, *trennb.*, *ist -ge-*): **~** (**durch**) grow through

durch'wachsen² *Adj.* **1.** *Fleisch*: marbled; *mit Knorpel etc.*: gristly; *Speck*: streaky; **2.** *umg. fig. Befinden*: so-so, fair to middling; *Wetter*: up and down, mixed

durchwacht I. *P.P.* → **durchwachen¹**; **II.** *Adj.*: **nach e-r ~en Nacht** after not getting any sleep all night

Durchwahl *f Telef.* **1.** *Vorgang*: direct dial(l)ing; **2.** (*Nummer, Anschluss*) extension (number), direct line (number); **durchwählen** *v/i.* (*trennb.*, *hat -ge-*) dial through (*od.* direct); *Am.* direct dial; **Durchwahlnummer** *f* extension (number), direct line (number)

'durchwandern¹ *v/i.* (*unreg.*, *trennb.*, *ist -ge-*) walk (*od.* hike) through, cross (by foot)

durch'wandern² *v/t.* (*untr.*, *hat*) walk (*od.* hike) through *s.th.*; do (*od.* go on) a walking *od.* hiking tour through

durchwärmen *v/t.* (*trennb.*, *hat -ge-*) warm *s.o. od. s.th.* up

durchwaschen *v/t.* (*unreg.*, *trennb.*, *hat -ge-*); *umg.* wash through

'durchwaten *v/i.* (*trennb.*, *ist -ge-*): **~** (**durch**) wade through

durchweg *Adv.* entirely, without exception; **sie waren ~ defekt** they were all faulty, every (last) one of them was faulty; **durchwegs** *Adv. bes. südd., österr., schw.* → **durchweg**

'durchweichen¹ *v/i.* (*trennb.*, *ist -ge-*) become (*od.* go) soft (*od.* soggy)

durch'weichen² *v/t.* (*untr.*, *hat*) soften; *durch Nässe*: soak; **durchweicht I.** *P.P.* → **durchweichen²**; **II.** *Adj.* soaked; *Erde, Brot etc.*: soggy

durch|werfen *v/t.* (*unreg.*, *trennb.*, *hat -ge-*): **~** (**durch/zwischen** + *Dat.*) throw through (*s.th.*); **~wetzen** *v/t.* (*trennb.*, *hat -ge-*); (*Ärmel*) wear

through; (*Hose*) wear out; **~winken** *v/t.* (*trennb.*, *hat -ge-*) wave *s.o.* through

durchwirkt *Adj. Stoff, mit Goldfäden etc.*: interwoven (**mit** with)

'durchwühlen¹ (*trennb.*, *hat -ge-*) **I.** *v/t.* → **durchwühlen²**; **II.** *v/refl.*: **sich ~ durch** burrow (one's *od.* its way) through; *fig.* plough (*Am.* plow) through

durch'wühlen² *v/t.* (*untr.*, *hat*) **1.** (*Erde*) dig (*od.* churn) up; *Schweine*: root up; **2.** (*Koffer etc.*) rummage through; (*Papiere etc.*) rif(f)le through; (*Haus etc.*) turn upside down

durchwurs(ch)teln *v/refl.* (*trennb.*, *hat -ge-*); *umg.* muddle through; **sich durch etw. ~** muddle one's way through s.th.

durch|zählen (*trennb.*, *hat -ge-*) **I.** *v/t.* count (up); **II.** *v/i.*: **sich in e-r Reihe aufstellen und ~** line up and count (*od.* number) off

durchzecht *Adj.*: **nach ~er Nacht** after a night spent (*od.* of) drinking

'durchziehen¹ (*unreg.*, *trennb.*, *-ge-*) **I.** *v/t.* (*hat*) **1.** **~** (**durch**) pull *s.th.* through; **2.** *umg.* (*Plan etc.*) carry *s.th.* through (to the end); **II.** *v/i.* (*ist*): **~** (**durch**) pass through; **III.** *v/refl.* (*hat*): **sich ~** (**durch**) go right through; *Motiv etc.*: run all the way through

durch'ziehen² *v/t.* (*unreg.*, *untr.*, *hat*) pass (*od.* go) through; *Flüsse etc.*: run through (*auch Motiv etc.*); *Geruch etc.*: pervade, fill

durchzucken *v/t.* (*untr.*, *hat*) *Schmerz, Empfindung*: shoot through; **der Gedanke durchzuckte sie, dass ...** it flashed into her mind that ...

Durchzug *m 1. nur Sg.*: (*Luft*) draught, *Am.* draft; **~ machen** air the room *etc.* through; **auf ~ schalten** *od.* **die Ohren auf ~ stellen** *umg. fig.* switch off, let it go in one ear and out the other; **2.** *von Vögeln*: passage; *von Truppen*: march through

durch|zwängen (*trennb.*, *hat -ge-*) **I.** *v/t.*: **~** (**durch**) force (*od.* squeeze) through; **II.** *v/refl.*: **sich ~** (**durch**) squeeze (o.s. *od.* one's way) through

dürfen *v/i.*; *darf, durfte, hat* (+ *Inf.*) *dürfen* / *hat gedurft* **I.** *Modalv.* (*hat* (+ *Inf.*) *dürfen*) **1.** *Erlaubnis bzw. Verbot*: be allowed to (+ *Inf.*); **darf ich rausgehen?** can (*höflich*: may) I go out?; **ich darf keinen Alkohol trinken** I'm not allowed (to drink) any alcohol; **man wird doch wohl noch fragen ~** you're allowed to ask, aren't you?; **2.** *Ratschlag, Aufforderung, Warnung etc.*: **du darfst den Hund nicht anfassen** you mustn't touch the dog, don't touch the dog; **wir ~ den Bus nicht verpassen** we mustn't (*bes. Am.* can't) miss the bus; **so etwas darf einfach nicht vorkommen** something like that simply cannot be allowed to happen; **so etwas darfst du nicht sagen** you mustn't (*od.* shouldn't) say things like that; **das hättest du nicht sagen ~** you shouldn't have said that; **das darf keiner erfahren** nobody's to know, nobody must find out; **3.** (*können*) *mit gutem Grund*: **wenn man es so nennen darf** if one can call it that; **du darfst stolz auf ihn sein** you can be proud of him; **du darfst es mir glauben** you can take my word for it; **das darf man wohl sagen** *iro.* you can say that again; **ich darf Ihnen mitteilen, dass ...** I am able to inform you that ...; **das darf wohl nicht wahr sein!**

that's incredible, I don't believe it!; **4.** *Vermutung*: **das dürfte der Neue sein** that must be the new guy (*od.* teacher etc.); **es dürfte bald zu Ende sein** it should be finished soon; **das dürfte die beste Lösung sein** that's probably (*od.* that seems to be, I think that's) the best solution; **es dürfte Regen geben** it might rain, there could be rain; **das dürfte reichen** that should be enough (*od.* suffice); **5.** *als Höflichkeitsform*: **was darf's sein?** what can I do for you?; *als Gastgeber*: what would you like (to drink)?, what's your poison? *umg. hum.*; **ich darf mich jetzt verabschieden** I'm afraid I've got to go now; **dürfte ich mir die Frage erlauben?** may I ask a question?; **wenn ich mich kurz entschuldigen dürfte** if you would excuse me for a moment; **dürfte ich um das Salz bitten?** would you pass (me) the salt please?; → **bitten** 1, 2; **II.** *vt/i.* (*hat gedurft*); *umg.* **1.** *Erlaubnis, Verbot*: **darf ich od. man?** may I?; **nein, du darfst nicht** no you can't; *bestimmter*: no you may not; **das darf man nicht** you're *etc.* not allowed, it isn't permitted; **er darf nicht nach draußen** he's not allowed out; **ich darf heute ins Kino** I'm allowed (out) to go to the cinema (*Am.* movies) tonight; **das hätte er eigentlich nicht gedurft** he wasn't really allowed (to do it); **2.** *Ratschlag etc.*: **ich geb's auf!** - **nein, das darfst du nicht!** no you shouldn't (do that)

durfte *Imperf.* → **dürfen**

dürftig *Adj.* **1.** *pej.* (*unzulänglich*) poor; *Einkommen, Mahlzeit*: meag|re (*Am. -er*), paltry; *Beleuchtung, Ausstattung etc.*: scanty, sparse; *Kleidung*: scanty, skimpy; *Argument*: weak, flimsy, feeble; *Ausrede, Erklärung*: feeble, lame; *Chance, Mehrheit*: measly; *Aussehen*: puny, scrawny, feeble; **2.** (*ärmlich*) *Verhältnisse*: humble; *stärker*: wretched

dürr *Adj.* **1.** *Äste, Gras etc.*: dry, withered; **2.** *Boden*: dry, arid, parched; (*unfruchtbar*) barren; **3.** (*hager*) thin, skinny, scraggy (*auch Arme*); *Hals*: scrawny; *Beine*: spindly; **4.** *fig. Jahre*: lean; **in ~en Worten** in sober terms

Dürre *f*, *-*, *-n* **1.** *Zeit*: drought; **von e-r ~ heimgesucht werden** be drought-ridden; **2.** *nur Sg.*; *Zustand*: dryness; *des Bodens*: aridity; (*Unfruchtbarkeit*) barrenness; **~periode** *f* period of drought; *fig.* barren period

Durst *m*; *-(e)s, kein Pl.* **1.** thirst (**auf** + *Akk. od.* **nach** for); **großer, heftiger** *etc.* **~** great thirst; **~ bekommen/haben** get/be thirsty; **ich habe großen ~** I'm really thirsty (*od.* parched); **hab ich e-n ~!** I'm dying of thirst; **ich habe ~ auf ein Bier** *umg.* I could just drink (*od.* do with) a beer; **das macht ~** it makes you thirsty; **Gartenarbeit macht ~** gardening is thirsty work; **s-n ~ löschen** *od.* **stillen** quench one's thirst; **e-n über den ~ getrunken haben** *umg.* have had one too many (one over the eight); **2.** *lit. fig.* thirst (**nach** for); **~ nach Ruhm/Wissen** a thirst for fame/ knowledge

dursten *v/i. geh.* **1.** be thirsty; **~ müssen** go thirsty; **2.** *fig.* → **dürsten** 2; **dürsten** *v/i.*, *unpers. poet.* **1.** *j-n dürstet* (*es*) s.o. is thirsty; **2.** *fig.*: **ihn dürstete** (*es*) **nach Freiheit** he was thirsty (*od.* desperate) for freedom; **durstig** *Adj.* thirsty; **Gartenarbeit macht ~** gardening is thirsty work; **er ist e-e ~e**

D

Seele fig. hum. he's fond of the bottle

durst|löschend, ~stillend *Adj.* thirst-quenching

Durststrecke *f fig.* long hard haul, lean period

Dur|tonart *f Mus.* major key; **~tonleiter** *f Mus.* major scale

Duschbad *n* shower (bath); (*Raum*) shower room; (*Duschgel*) shower gel

Dusche *f; -, -n* shower; *e-e ~ nehmen* have (*od.* take) a shower; *unter der ~* in the shower; *das war e-e kalte ~ für ihn fig.* that brought him down to earth with a bump; **duschen I.** *v/i. und v/refl.* have (*od.* take) a shower; **II.** *v/t.* give *s.o.* a shower; *j-m/sich die Beine ~* spray (down) s.o.'s/one's legs

Dusch|gel *n* shower gel; **~gelegenheit** *f* shower facilities *Pl.*; **~haube** *f* shower cap; **~kabine** *f* shower (cubicle); **~kopf** *m* shower head; **~raum** *m* shower room, showers *Pl.*; **~vorhang** *m* shower curtain; **~wanne** *f* shower tray

Düse *f; -, -n; Tech.* nozzle; *Flug.* jet; *zum Spritzen:* jet

Dusel *m; -s, kein Pl.; umg.* (*Glück*) luck; → *Glück* 1; **duselig** *Adj. umg.* dop(e)y; *mir ist ganz ~* (*im Kopf*) I feel really dop(e)y, I'm in a fuddle

düsen *v/i. umg.* dash, whiz(z), zoom; *durch die Welt ~* jet around the world

Düsen|antrieb *m Flug.* jet propulsion; *mit ~* jet-propelled ...; **~clipper** *m; -s, -, ~flieger** *m umg.* jet (plane); **~flugzeug** *n* jet aircraft, jet (plane); **♀getrieben** *Adj.* jet-propelled; **~jäger** *m*

Mil. jet fighter; **~triebwerk** *n* jet engine

Dussel *m; -s, -; umg.* dope, twit, dumbo; **duss(e)lig** *Adj. umg.* stupid, dopey, *Brit. auch* gormless

duster *Adj. Dial.* → *düster* I 1

düster I. *Adj.* **1.** (*dunkel*) dark, gloomy; *Licht:* dim; *Farben:* dark, somb|re (*Am.* -er); **2.** (*bedrückend*) *Aussichten:* dismal, grim, depressing; *Atmosphäre, Prognose, Wetter:* gloomy, somb|re (*Am.* -er); *Musik:* somb|re (*Am.* -er); *ein ~es Bild von etw. zeichnen etc. fig.* paint a black picture of s.th.; *die Zukunft in ~en Farben ausmalen fig.* paint the future in dark colo(u)rs; *es sieht ~ aus (für uns)* things are looking grim (for us); **3.** (*bedrückt*) *Blick:* ominous, forbidding; *Gedanken:* black; *Schweigen:* gloomy; *Stimmung:* grim; *ein ~es Gesicht machen* have a gloomy expression (on one's face); **4.** *Gestalt:* sinister; (*verdächtig*) shady; **II.** *Adv.:* **~ dreinblicken** look gloomy; **Düsterkeit** *f* gloom(iness)

Dutyfreeshop, Duty-free-Shop ['djuːtɪ'friːʃɔp] *m* duty-free (shop)

Dutzend *n; -s, -e, mit Mengenangabe: -* **1.** (*12 Stück*) dozen; *zwei ~ Eier* two dozen eggs; *10 Euro das ~* 10 euros (for) a dozen; *im ~ billiger* cheaper by the dozen; the more you buy, the more you save; **2.** *umg., verstärkend:* **~e od. dutzende von Leuten** dozens of people; *sie kamen in od. zu ~en od. dutzenden* dozens (of them) came, they came in their dozens (*Am.* by the

dozen); *einige od. ein paar ~ od. dutzend* some dozens; *das habe ich dir schon (ein) ~ Mal gesagt* I've told you that dozens of times already

dutzendfach I. *Adj.; nur attr.* dozens of; **II.** *Adv.* in dozens of ways; (*oft*) dozens of times

Dutzend|gesicht *n pej.* nondescript face; **~mensch** *m pej.* nonentity; **~ware** *f pej.* cheap stuff

dutzendweise *Adv.* by the dozen, *Brit. auch* in (their) dozens

duzen *v/t.* say 'du' to *s.o.*, *etwa* be on first-name terms with; **Duzfreund** *m,* **Duzfreundin** *f etwa* good friend, bosom buddy; *sie sind ~e auch* they're good mates *umg.* (*od.* pals *umg.*)

DVD *f; -, -s; Abk.* (*Digital Video Disc*) DVD

Dynamik *f; -, -en* **1.** *Phys., Mus., auch e-s Romans etc.:* dynamics *Pl.* (*Lehre:* V. im Sg.); **2.** *fig.* (*Kraft*) dynamic force; *e-r Person:* dynamism, (tremendous) drive; **dynamisch I.** *Adj.* **1.** dynamic (*auch fig.*); **2.** *fig. Rente, Versicherung:* index-linked; **II.** *Adv.* dynamically

Dynamit *n; -s, kein Pl.* dynamite; **~stange** *f* stick of dynamite

Dynamo *m; -s, -s* dynamo, *Am.* generator

Dynastie *f; -, -n; geh.* dynasty

D-Zug *m* express, fast train; *ein alter Mann ist doch kein ~! umg.* I'm going as fast as I can!

E, e *n*; -, - *od. umg.* -s **1.** E, e; *E wie Emil* Buchstabieren: 'e' for (*od.* as in) 'Echo'; **2.** *Mus.* E

Eau| de Cologne ['oː də koˈlɔnjə] *n*; - - -, *Eaux* - - [oː] eau de Cologne; **~ de Toilette** ['oː də toaˈlɛt] *n*; - - - -, *Eaux* - - [oː] eau de toilette, toilet water

Ebbe *f*; -, -*n* (*Niedrigwasser*) low tide; (*Bewegung*) ebb tide; **~ und Flut** high and low tide, ebb and flow; *es ist ~* the tide's out, it's low tide; *mit der ~ auslaufen* set sail with the tide; *in m-m Geldbeutel / im Staatssäckel ist od. herrscht ~ umg. fig.* I'm a bit hard up (*od.* strapped for cash) at the moment / the state coffers are empty

ebd. *Abk.* (**ebenda**) ibid

eben¹ I. *Adj.* **1.** (*flach*) even, level, flat; *zu ~er Erde* at ground level; *auf ~er Strecke* on the flat, on level roads *etc.*; **2.** (*glatt*) smooth; **II.** *Adv.*: *der Weg verläuft ~* the path runs (on the) level

eben² *Adv.* **1.** (*jetzt*) just (now); *ich wollte ~ gehen* I was just about (*od.* going) to leave; **2.** (*vor kurzer Zeit*) *gerade ~ od. ~ erst* only just, *Am.* just now; *sie war ~ noch hier* she was here just a moment (*od.* minute) ago; **3.** (*genau, gerade*) just, exactly; *~ das wollte ich sagen* that's just what I was going (*od.* about) to say; *~! exactly, that's right; *das ist es ja*) *~!* that's it, that's what I've been trying to say all along; *~ nicht!* no - that's the whole point; **4.** *Dial.*: *hast du ~ mal Zeit?* have you got (*od.* can you spare) a minute?; *zieh mal ~ die Jacke an* just put the jacket on for a minute; **5.** *~ noch od. so* (*gerade noch*) only just, just about; *ich habe den Zug ~ noch geschafft* I only just (*Am.* I just barely) caught my train; **6.** (*nun einmal, halt*) just; *ich weiß es ~ nicht* I just don't know; *dann komme ich ~ nicht!* well, I'll just not (*Am.* I just won't) come, then; *er will ~ nicht* he doesn't want to - it's as simple as that; *er ist ~ müde* he's tired, that's all; *es taugt ~ nichts* I told you it was no good; *dann ~ nicht!* all right, nobody's forcing you; *da kann man ~ nichts machen* well, it can't be helped, that's the way it is; *er ist ~ der Bessere* he's better (*od.* the better man) - there's no denying it; *das ist ~ so* well, that's how it is; **7.** *mit Verneinung*: *nicht ~ klug etc.* not exactly clever *etc.*; **8.** *verstärkend*: *so schnell etc. es ~ geht* just as fast *etc.* as possible

Ebenbild *n geh.* image; *sie ist das ~ i-r Mutter* she is the spitting image (*od.* spit and image) of her mother

ebenbürtig *Adj.* equal, of equal rank (*od.* quality); *j-m ~ sein* be on a level (*od.* par) with s.o.; *sie ist ihm an Intelligenz ~* she's every bit as intelligent as he is; *ein ~er Gegner/Nachfolger* a well-matched opponent / worthy suc-

cessor; **Ebenbürtigkeit** *f* equality

ebenda *Adv.* (*abgek.* **ebd.**) just there; *bei Quellenangaben*: ibidem (*Abk.* ib-id.)

eben|der(selbe), **~die(selbe)**, **~das(selbe)** *Dem. Pron.* that very one; *auch Person*: the very same; *attr.* that very ...; **~deswegen** *Adv.* that's precisely why; *allein stehend*: that's exactly (the reason) why I did it *etc.*

Ebene *f*; -, -*n* **1.** *Geog.* plain; (*Hochebene*) plateau, *Am.*, *in SW USA auch* mesa; **2.** *Math.* plane; *Tech.* plane surface; *schiefe ~* inclined plane; **3.** (*Stockwerk*) level, floor; **4.** *fig.* (*Stufe*) level; *auf politischer/staatlicher ~* on a political / at government level; *auf höchster ~ entschieden werden etc.*: at the highest level, (right) at the top; *Gespräche auf höchster ~* top-level talks; *auf gleicher ~ liegen mit* be on a level (*od.* par) with

ebenerdig *Adj. attr.* ground-level ..., *auch präd.* at ground level

ebenfalls *Adv.* likewise, also; *nachgestellt*: too, as well; *~ nicht/kein* not ... either; *sie hat ~ kein Auto* she doesn't have a car either; *danke, ~!* you too; → *auch* **auch** 1

Ebenheit *f* (*Flachheit*) evenness; (*Glätte*) smoothness

Ebenholz *n* ebony; *Haar etc.* schwarz *wie ~* ebony hair

eben|jener, **~jene**, **~jenes** *Dem. Pron.* he, she, it; *sprichst du von Laura? - ebenjene meine ich* that's exactly who I mean

Ebenmaß *n*; *nur Sg.* harmony, symmetry, regularity; *e-r Person*: shapeliness; **ebenmäßig** *Adj.* regular; (*wohlproportioniert*) well-proportioned; *Person*: shapely

ebenso *Adv.* **1.** *Intensität, Ausmaß etc.*: just as; *ich habe ihn ~ gern wie du/dich* I like him (*od.* every bit) as much as you (do) / as (I do) you; *es ist ~ voll wie gestern* it's (just) as full as it was yesterday; *er ist ~ fleißig wie hilfreich* he's as hard-working as he is helpful; **2.** *Art*: (in) the same way; *ich reagierte ~ auch* my reaction was the same; *mir geht es ~* that's exactly how I feel, it's exactly the same for me; *in Europa ~ wie in Amerika* in Europe and America alike

eben|solch, **~solche**, **~solche**, **~solches** *Dem. Pron.* (just) the same; *ich hatte ~e Angst wie du* I was every bit (*od.* just) as scared as you were

Eber *m*; -*s*, -; *Zool.* boar

Eberesche *f Bot.* mountain ash, rowan (tree)

ebnen *v/t.* level (off *od.* out); *fig.* → **Weg** 2

echauffieren [eʃoˈfiːrən] *v/refl.* get all excited (*od.* worked up, hot and bothered) (*über* + *Akk.* about)

Echo *n*; -*s*, -*s* **1.** echo; *ein ~ geben od. zurückwerfen* echo; **2.** *fig.* response

(*auf* + *Akk.* to), echo; *ein begeistertes ~ finden* go down well; *stärker*: meet with an overwhelming response; *Vorschlag etc.*: be welcomed with open arms; *es fand kein ~* there was no response (*Zustimmung*: support) (*bei* from); *ein weltweites ~ hervorrufen Entdeckung etc.*: be hailed throughout the world; *politische Handlung etc.*: have worldwide impact (*od.* repercussions)

Echolot *n Tech.* sonic depth finder, echo sounder

Echse *f*; -, -*n Zool.* saurian; (*Eidechse*) lizard

echt I. *Adj.* **1.** (*nicht nachgemacht*) genuine; *Unterschrift, Urkunde etc.*: *auch* authentic; *Gold, Leder etc.*: *auch* real; *Haarfarbe*: natural; *das Gemälde etc. ist nicht ~ auch* is a forgery (*od.* fake); *für ~ erklären* authenticate; **2.** (*wahr*) real; *Liebe, Freundschaft*: *auch* true; *Gefühle*: *auch* sincere; (*nicht vorgetäuscht*) genuine; (*unverfälscht*) real, genuine; *ein ~er Verlust* a real (*od.* great) loss; *ich möchte das ~e Wien erleben* I want to see (*od.* experience) the real Vienna; **3.** *nur attr.*; (*typisch*) typical, true; *ein ~er Engländer* a real (*od.* true) Englishman, an Englishman born and bred; **4.** *nur attr.*; (*reinrassig*) *Pferd*: thoroughbred; *Hund, Katze, Rind*: pedigreed; **5.** *Math., Bruch*: proper; **6.** *Chem. etc., Farbe*: fast; **7.** *umg.* (*geistig normal*) with it; *bist du noch ~?* are you feeling all right?; *der ist doch nicht ganz ~!* that one's off his head (*od.* not all there)!; **II.** *Adv.* **1.** really; *die Uhr ist ~ Gold* the watch is (made of) real (*od.* genuine) gold, the watch is really gold; **2.** *umg.* (*wirklich*) really; *das war ~ gut!* it was really good; *das hat sie gesagt - ~ wahr od.* (*in*) *~?* did she really (*od.* honestly)?; **3.** *umg.* (*typisch*) typically; *das ist mal wieder ~ Martin* that's Martin all over, that's just typical of Martin; *das war mal wieder ~ Mann!* that was just so typically male! **...echt** *im Adj. allg.* ...proof; *bügel~* ironable; *motten~* mothproof; *säure~* acid-proof; *schweiß~* sweat-proof

Echtheit *f* genuineness; *e-r Urkunde etc.*: authenticity; *die ~ überprüfen von* (*od.* + *Gen.*) check whether *s.th.* is genuine (*od.* authentic); *die ~* (+ *Gen.*) *od. von etw. bescheinigen* authenticate *s.th.*

Echtzeit *f*; *nur Sg.*; *EDV* real time

Eck *n*; -(*e*)*s*, -*e* *od.* *österr.* -en **1.** *südd.*, *österr.* → **Ecke**; **2.** *über* (*od.* *südd.*, *österr. übers*) *~* diagonally (across *od.* opposite), *Am. umg. auch* kitty-corner from; **3.** *Sport*: *das lange/kurze ~* the far/near corner (of the goal) **...eck** *n*; -*s*, -*e*; *im Subst.* *Math.* ...angle

Eck|ball *m Sport* corner; *e-n ~ verwandeln* score from a corner; **~bank** *f*; *Pl.* -*bänke* corner seat(ing unit)

E

Eckchen *n* little corner
Eckdaten *Pl.* key features
Ecke *f*; -, *-n* **1.** *in e-m Raum*: corner; *sich in e-e ~ verkriechen* crawl into a corner; *in die ~ drängen* corner; *fig.*, *in den Hintergrund*: push *s.o.* into the background; **2.** *von zwei Straßen*: corner; *um die ~ kommen* come (a)round the corner; *an der ~* at (*Haus*: on) the corner; *~ Weinstraße* at (*od.* on) the corner of Weinstraße; *gleich um die ~* just (a)round the corner; **3.** *von Gegenstand*: edge; *die ~n* (*und Kanten*) *abschleifen* smooth away the rough edges; **4.** *Fußball*: corner; *die kurze/ lange ~* the near/far corner; *e-e ~ ausführen od. treten* take a corner; **5.** *umg.* (*Gegend*) corner; *aus welcher ~ Deutschlands kommen Sie?* which area of (*od.* whereabouts in) Germany are you from?; **6.** *umg. fig.* (*Strecke*) stretch; *das ist noch e-e ganze ~* that's still a fair way to go; *e-e ganze ~ besser/schlechter etc.* quite a bit (*od.* lot) better/worse; **7.** *fig. in Wendungen*: *es fehlt an allen ~n und Enden* we're *etc.* short on everything; *er ist ein Mann mit ~n und Kanten fig.* he rubs people (up) the wrong way; *ich bin um fünf etc. ~n mit ihm verwandt fig.* I'm a distant relation (*od.* relative) of his; *j-n um die ~ bringen umg. fig.* bump *s.o.* off, do away with *s.o.*
Eckensteher *m umg. altm.* loafer, idler, good-for-nothing
Eck‖fahne *f Fußball etc.*: corner flag; **~fenster** *n* corner window
eckig *Adj.* **1.** *Tisch etc.*: rectangular; *Gestalt*: angular, *Gesicht, Kinn, Klammer etc.*: square; **2.** *fig.* (*ungeschickt*) awkward, stiff; (*ungeschliffen*) rough; → *Klammer* 2
...eckig *im Adj.* ...-cornered; *Math.* ...angular
Eck‖lohn *m Wirts.* minimum (*od.* basic) wage; **~pfeiler** *m* corner pillar; *fig.* cornerstone; **~preis** *m Wirts.* price which is one cent, euro *etc.* below a round figure; **~schrank** *m* corner cupboard; **~stein** *m* cornerstone (*auch fig.*); **~stoß** *m Fußball*: corner kick; **~wert** *m Wirts.* benchmark figure, (piece of) key data; **~zahn** *m* eyetooth, canine (tooth), dogtooth; **~zimmer** *n* corner room; **~zins** *m Wirts.* basic interest rate, base rate, *Am.* prime rate
Economy-Klasse [i'kɔnəmi-] *f Flug.* coach (class), *Brit. auch* economy class; **~ fliegen** fly coach
Ecstasy ['ɛkstəzi] *n*; -, -(*s*) ecstasy
Ecuador (*n*); *-s*; *Geog.* Ecuador; **Ecuadorianer** *m*; *-s*, -, **Ecuadorianerin** *f*; -, *-nen* Ecuador(i)an, *weiblich auch*: Ecuador(i)an woman (*od.* girl *etc.*); **ecuadorianisch** *Adj.* Ecuadorian
Edamer *m*; *-s*, -; *Gastr.* Edam (cheese)
edel *Adj.* **1.** *Gesinnung, Tat etc.*: noble, hono(u)rable; *Person: auch* noble-minded, generous, magnanimous; → *Spender* 1; **2.** *Qualität, Schmuck, Wein etc.*: fine; *Metall*: precious; *Pferd*: thoroughbred; *Rose etc.*: species ...; *Holz*: fine, precious; → *Tropfen*; **3.** *geh.* (*wohlgeformt*) noble, finely-shaped; *von edler Gestalt* of noble stature; **4.** *altm.* (*adelig*) noble, aristocratic; *aus edlem Geschlecht* of noble birth
Edel‖fäule *f Wein*: noble rot; *Käse*: mo(u)ld; **~frau** *f hist.* noblewoman; **~fräulein** *n hist.* (unmarried) noble-

woman
Edelgas *n Chem.* noble (*od.* inert) gas
Edel‖holz *n* fine (*od.* precious) wood; **~kastanie** *f Bot.* sweet chestnut; **~kitsch** *m pej.* glorified (*od.* elevated) kitsch; **~knabe** *m hist.* page, squire; **~leute** *Pl.* nobles, nobility *Sg.*; **~mann** *m hist.* nobleman; **~metall** *n* precious metal
Edelmut *m geh.* noble-mindedness, magnanimity; **edelmütig** *Adj. geh.* noble-minded, magnanimous
Edel‖nutte *f umg. pej.* high-class callgirl (*od.* tart); **~pilzkäse** *m* blue (--veined) cheese; **~stahl** *m* high--grade steel; **~stein** *m* precious stone; *geschnitten etc.*: jewel, gem(stone); **~tanne** *f Bot.* silver fir; **~weiß** *n Bot.* edelweiss; **~western** *m etwa* classic western (film), 'message' western
Eden *n*; *-s*, *kein Pl.* **1.** *bibl.*: (*der Garten*) ~ (the Garden of) Eden; **2.** *fig.* Eden
edieren *v/t.* **1.** edit; be the editor of; → *editieren*; **2.** (*veröffentlichen*) publish
Edikt *n*; *-(e)s*, -*e* edict
Edinburg (*n*); *-s*; *Geog.* Edinburgh
editieren *v/t. EDV* edit; **Editierfunktion** *f* editing function
Edition *f*; -, *-en* edition; (*Veröffentlichung*) publication
Edle *m, f*; *-n*, -*n* noble(wo)man; *Klara, ~ von Drachenstein* Lady Klara von (*od.* of) Drachenstein
E-Dur *n Mus.* E major; **~-Tonleiter** *f* E major scale
EDV *f*; -, *kein Pl.*; *Abk.* (**Elektronische Datenverarbeitung**) (electronic) data processing, computing; **~-Kenntnisse** *Pl.* computing expertise *Sg.* (*od.* know-how *Sg. umg.*)
EEG *n*; *-(s)*, *-s*; *Abk. Med.* (**Elektroenzephalogramm**) EEG
Efeu *m*; *-s*, *kein Pl.*; *Bot.* ivy
Effeff *n umg.*: *etw. aus dem ~ können* be able to do *s.th.* blindfold(ed) (*od.* standing on one's head); *etw. aus dem ~ kennen* know *s.th.* inside out (*od.* like the back of one's hand)
Effekt *m*; *-(e)s*, -*e* **1.** effect; (*Ergebnis*) *auch* result; *Tech.* (*Wirkungsgrad*) *auch* efficiency; *~ haben* have an effect; **2.** *Theat. etc.* (*special*) effect
Effekten *Pl. Wirts.* stocks and bonds, securities; **~bank** *f*, *Pl.* *-en* investment bank; **~börse** *f* stock exchange; *auf dem europäischen Festland*: *auch* bourse; **~handel** *m* trading in stock; **~händler** *m*, **~händlerin** *f* stock dealer; **~makler** *m*, **~maklerin** *f* stockbroker; **~markt** *m* stock market
Effekthascherei *f*; -, *-en* showing-off; *stärker*: sensationalism; *in Wort und Schrift*: claptrap; *billige ~* cheap showmanship; *bei ihm ist es bloß ~ auch* he's just out for show, it's all show for him
effektiv **I.** *Adj.* **1.** (*tatsächlich*) actual; *Wirts. auch* effective; *~e Verzinsung* net yield; *der ~e Jahreszins für ein Darlehen*: the net annual interest rate; **2.** (*wirksam*) effective; **II.** *Adv.* **1.** effectively; **2.** (*wirklich*) really, literally; (*ganz sicher*) definitely
Effektivität *f*; -, *kein Pl.* effectiveness
Effektiv‖kosten *Pl.* actual cost *Sg.*; **~leistung** *f Tech.* effective output; **~lohn** *m* actual earnings *Pl.*
effektvoll *Adj.* effective
effizient *Adj. geh., fachspr.* (*wirtschaftlich*) efficient; (*wirksam*) effective; **Effizienz** *f*; -, *-en*; *geh., fachspr.* efficiency; effectiveness

EG *f*; -, *kein Pl.*; *Abk. Pol., hist.* (**Europäische Gemeinschaft**) EC, European Community; *fälschlich oft*: EEC
EG... *Pol., hist.* → *EU*
egal **I.** *Adj.* **1.** *nur präd.*; *umg.*: *das ist ~* it doesn't matter, it doesn't make any difference; *das ist mir ~* (*stört mich nicht*) I don't mind, it doesn't matter (*od.* make any difference) to me; *verärgert*: I couldn't care less, why should I care, I don't give (*od.* couldn't give) a damn; *ist ~!* never mind, forget it; *er/sie ist mir ~* he/she means nothing to me; *ihr ist alles ~* she doesn't care about anything; *das kann dir doch ~ sein* that's none of your business (*od.* nothing to do with you); *~ wo/warum/wer etc.* no matter where/why/who *etc.*; *stärker*: I don't care where/why/who *etc.*; **2.** *präd.*, *umg. auch attr.*; (*gleich*) the same; (*gleich lang*) the same length (*od.* size); (*gleichmäßig*) even; **II.** *Adv. Dial.* (*ständig*) non-stop, constantly
egalitär *geh.* **I.** *Adj.* egalitarian; **II.** *Adv.* in an egalitarian way
Egel *m*; *-s*, -; *Zool.* leech
Egerling *m*; *-s*, -*e*; *Bot.*: *brauner ~* chestnut (*od.* brown cap) mushroom
Egge *f*; -, *-n* harrow; **eggen** *vt/i.* harrow
Ego *n*; -, *-s*; *Psych.* ego
Egoismus *m*; -, *Egoismen* selfishness, ego(t)ism; **Egoist** *m*; *-en*, *-en*, **Egoistin** *f*; -, *-nen* selfish person, ego(t)ist; **egoistisch** *Adj.* selfish, ego(t)istical
Egotrip *m umg.*: *auf dem ~ sein* be on an ego trip
Egozentriker *m*; *-s*, -, **~in** *f*; -, *-nen* self-centred (*Am.* -centered) person, egocentric (person); **egozentrisch** *Adj.* self-centred (*Am.* -centered), egocentric
eh *umg.* **I.** *Adv.* **1.** *bes. südd., österr.* (*sowieso*) anyway, anyhow; *er weiß es ~ schon auch* he already knows (anyway); **2.** *das ist seit ~ und je so* it's always been like that, it's been like that ever since I can remember, *Brit. auch* it's been like that for donkey's years; *es ist wie ~ und je* it's the same as ever, it's the same old story; *er ist optimistisch wie ~ und je* he's as optimistic as ever; **II.** *Interj.* **1.** *~?* eh?, huh?; **2.** *~! empört*: hey!; **III.** *Konj.* → *ehe*
eh., e.h. *Abk.* → *ehrenhalber*
ehe *Konj.* before; *nicht ~* not until, not before; *~ er mir das Zimmer versaut, renoviere ich es selber* rather than let him ruin the room, I'll do it up myself
Ehe *f*; -, *-n* marriage (*auch fig.*); (*Eheleben*) married life; *aus erster ~* by one's first marriage, by one's first husband (*od.* wife); *e-e glückliche ~ führen* be happily married; *sie hat zwei Kinder mit in die ~ gebracht* she's got two children from a previous marriage; *er ist in zweiter ~ verheiratet mit ...* his second wife is ...; *j-m die ~ versprechen* promise to marry *s.o.*; *e-e ~ schließen als Paar*: get married (*mit* to); *als Priester etc.* (*trauen*) marry a couple; *in den* (*heiligen*) *Stand der ~ treten* enter into (holy) matrimony; *in wilder ~ leben altm.* live in sin; *die ~ vollziehen förm.* consummate a marriage; *eine ~ auflösen* dissolve a marriage; → *Hafen¹* 2
eheähnlich *Adj.*: *sie leben in e-m ~en Verhältnis* they live together as man and wife
Eheberater *m*, **~in** *f* marriage guidance

counsel(l)or; **Eheberatung** f **1.** marriage guidance (counsel[l]ing); **2.** (*Stelle*) marriage guidance bureau; **Eheberatungsstelle** f marriage guidance bureau

Ehebett n **1.** (*Doppelbett*) double bed; **2.** fig. marriage (od. marital) bed; **ehebrechen** v/i. nur Inf. und Part. Präs.; geh. altm. commit adultery; *du sollst nicht ~ bibl.* thou shalt not commit adultery; **Ehebrecher** m; -s, -, **Ehebrecherin** f; -, -nen männlich: adulterer; weiblich: adulteress; **ehebrecherisch** Adj. adulterous; **Ehebruch** m adultery; **~ begehen** commit adultery

ehedem Adv. geh. formerly; **wie/von** like/from former times: **seit ~** since time immemorial, Am. auch since day one umg.

Ehefähigkeitszeugnis n certificate (od. proof) of marriageability

Ehefrau f **1.** wife (Pl. wives); **2.** (*verheiratete Frau*) married woman; Pl. auch wives

Ehegatte m, **Ehegattin** f Jur. spouse; *beide Ehegatten* (both) husband and wife; → **Ehefrau, Ehemann**

Ehegattensplitting n taxation of the total income of a married couple on the basis of equal halves

Ehe|gelübde n geh. marriage vows Pl.; **~glück** n marital (od. wedded) bliss; **~hindernis** n impediment to marriage; **~joch** n hum. yoke of marriage; **~krach** m umg. marital row(s Pl.) (Am. spat[s] Pl.); **~krieg** m marital feud; **~krise** f marital crisis; **~krüppel** m umg. hum. od. pej. casualty of marriage (od. married life); **~leben** n married life; **~leute** Pl. married couple Sg.; (die) ~ Miller Mr(.) and Mrs(.) Miller

ehelich I. Adj. **1.** marital, conjugal; *die ~e Gemeinschaft* marriage, married life, matrimony förm.; **~e Rechte** conjugal rights; **2.** Kind: legitimate; **II.** Adv.: *das Kind ist ~ geboren* he's (she's) a legitimate child, the child was born in wedlock förm.; **ehelichen** v/t. altm. od. hum. marry, wed; **Ehelichkeit** f e-s Kindes: legitimacy

ehelos Adj. unmarried; kirchl. celibate; **Ehelosigkeit** f unmarried state; für Männer: bachelorhood; für Frauen: spinsterhood; kirchl. celibacy; *die ~ auch* not being married

ehemalig Adj. nur attr. former, ex-...; bes. Am. auch one-time ...; (alt) old; (verstorben) late; *die ~e Sowjetunion etc. auch* what used to be the Soviet Union etc.; *die ~e Fleet Street etc. auch* Fleet Street etc. as it was; **ehemals** Adv. formerly, once; *es war ~ ... auch* it used to be ...

Ehemann m; Pl. Ehemänner **1.** (*Partner*) husband; **2.** (*verheirateter Mann*) married man, Pl. auch husbands

ehe|müde Adj. tired of married life; **~mündig** Adj. Jur. of marriageable age

Ehe|name m Amtsspr. married name; **~paar** n married couple; **(das) ~ Peters** Mr(.) and Mrs(.) Peters; **~partner** m husband; wife; förm. spouse; *der ~ auch* the husband or wife; *beide ~* both partners in marriage, (both) the husband and the wife

eher Adv. **1.** (*früher*) earlier, sooner; *~ als auch* before; *je ~, desto lieber* od. *besser* the sooner the better; *ich konnte leider nicht ~ kommen* I'm afraid I couldn't make it any earlier;

---

2. (*lieber*) rather; *~ würde ich ...* I'd rather (od. sooner) ...; **3.** (*mehr*) more; (*wahrscheinlicher*) more likely; *das lässt sich schon ~ hören* that sounds more like it; *das wäre schon ~ was für mich umg.* that's more to my taste, that's more my cup of tea; *es ist ~ grün als blau* it's more green than blue, it's more on the green side; *man sollte ~ annehmen* you'd think (od. expect), you would have thought; **4.** (*relativ, vielmehr*) rather; *er ist ~ klein* he's rather (od. somewhat) small, he's on the small side

Ehe|recht n; nur Sg. matrimonial law; **~ring** m wedding ring

ehern Adj.; nur attr. **1.** lit. brass; **2.** geh. fig. firm, unshak(e)able; Gesetz, Wille: iron; (kühn) bold, brazen

Ehe|sakrament n; nur Sg.; kath. the (holy) sacrament of mariage; **~scheidung** f divorce; **~scheu** Adj. not keen on marriage (od. getting married), Am. auch wedding-shy umg.; **~schließung** f **1.** marriage; **2.** → **Trauung**

ehest... **I.** Adj. earliest, first; **II.** Adv. **1.** am **~en** (zuerst) (the) soonest, (the) earliest, first; **2.** (noch am besten) best, most easily; (noch am liebsten) most of all; (am wahrscheinlichsten) most likely; *am ~en würde ich noch nach England ziehen* if I had to choose, I'd probably go to England; *am ~en würde ich wohl die braunen Stiefel nehmen* (for lack of anything better) I suppose I would take the brown boots; *am ~en finden wir ihn in der Bibliothek* he's most likely to be in the library, the library is the likeliest place to find him; *er kann uns am ~en helfen* if anyone can help us, it's him; *so geht es wohl am ~en* that's probably the best way

Ehestand m; nur Sg.; Amtsspr. matrimony, married state, marriage; *in den ~ treten* enter into matrimony; **Ehestandsdarlehen** n low-interest bank loan given to newlyweds

ehestens Adv.: **~** ([am] Montag etc.) (Monday etc.) at the earliest

Ehestifter m, **~in** f matchmaker

Ehe|versprechen n: *j-m das ~ geben* promise to marry s.o.; *Bruch des ~s* breach of promise (to marry s.o.); **~vertrag** m marriage contract

Ehrabschneider m pej. slanderer, calumniator

ehrbar Adj. geh. Beruf, Person etc.: respectable, reputable; Person: auch upright, upstanding; Absichten: hono(u)rable; **Ehrbarkeit** f respectability, worthiness

Ehrbegriff m code of hono(u)r

Ehre f; -, -n **1.** (*Zeichen der Wertschätzung*) hono(u)r; *es ist mir e-e (große) ~* it is an (a great) hono(u)r for me; *mit wem habe ich die ~? oft iro.* to whom have I the pleasure of speaking?; *habe die ~! bes. österr.* good day; (beim Treffen) pleased to meet you; *was verschafft mir die ~?* to what do I owe this hono(u)r (od. the pleasure)?; *geben sich (Dat.) die ~, zu ... einzuladen ...* request the hono(u)r of your company at ...; *um der Wahrheit die ~ zu geben* to be quite honest (od. frank); *j-m die letzte ~ erweisen* pay one's last respects to s.o.; *~ wem ~ gebührt Sprichw.* credit where credit is due; *j-n mit* od. *in ~n entlassen* give s.o. an hono(u)rable discharge; *wieder zu ~n kommen* come back into favo(u)r; *ihm zu ~n* in his hono(u)r; *zu*

---

s-r ~ muss gesagt werden, dass ... in his defen|ce (Am. -se) it ought to be said that ...; *zur (grösseren) ~ Gottes* to the (greater) glory of God; **2.** (Ansehen) hono(u)r, reputation; (Ruhm) glory; *bei m-r ~!* upon my oath!; *j-m/etw. alle/keine ~ machen* be a/no credit to s.o./s.th.; *es gereicht ihm zur ~ geh.* it is to his credit; *es zu hohen ~n bringen* achieve (great) eminence; *in ~n halten* (hold in) hono(u)r; *in ~n gehalten* revered; *dein Eifer etc. in (allen) ~n, aber ...* with all due respect, ...; *~ sei Gott in der Höhe!* glory (be) to God in the highest!; **3.** nur Sg.; (Ehrgefühl) sense of hono(u)r; (Selbstachtung) self-respect, pride; *auf ~ und Gewissen* in all conscience; *j-n bei der* od. *s-r ~ packen* appeal to s.o.'s sense of hono(u)r; *er fühlte sich dadurch in s-r ~ gekränkt* it hurt (od. wounded) his pride, he felt rather piqued by it; *s-e ~ dareinsetzen, etw. zu tun* make it a point of hono(u)r to do s.th.; *etw. in allen ~n tun* do s.th. in good faith; **4.** nur Sg.; altm. (Jungfräulichkeit) (virgin) hon(u)r; *e-r Frau ihre ~ rauben* rob a woman of her hono(u)r

ehren v/t. **1.** (*Ehre erweisen*) hono(u)r; *Ihr Vertrauen ehrt mich sehr* your confidence flatters me greatly; *mit e-r Medaille geehrt werden* be presented with a medal; *sich geehrt fühlen* be (od. feel) hono(u)red; **2.** (zur Ehre gereichen) do s.o. credit; **3.** altm. (achten) respect; *du sollst Vater und Mutter ~ bibl.* hono(u)r thy father and thy mother; → **ehrend, geehrt, Pfennig**

Ehrenamt n honorary post; **ehrenamtlich I.** Adj. Mitarbeiter etc.: honorary; Mitarbeit etc.: voluntary; **~er Helfer** voluntary worker, volunteer; **II.** Adv. in an honorary capacity; **~ arbeiten bei** do voluntary work for

Ehren|bezeigung f, **~bezeugung** f mark of respect, tribute; Mil. salute; **~bürger** m, **~bürgerin** f honorary citizen; männlich auch: freeman; *er wurde zum ~ der Stadt ernannt* he was given the freedom (od. he was made freeman) of the city

ehrend I. Part. Präs. → **ehren**; **II.** Adj.: *j-m ein ~es Andenken bewahren* hono(u)r s.o.'s memory

Ehrendoktor m **1.** (*Person*) honorary doctor; **2.** (Titel) honorary doctorate; **~würde** f honorary doctorate; *ihm wurde die ~ der Universität München verliehen* he was given an honorary doctorate by the University of Munich

Ehren|erklärung f public (od. formal) apology; **~gast** m guest of hono(u)r; (berühmte Person) auch guest celebrity; **~geleit** n escort, guard of hono(u)r; *j-m das ~ geben* escort s.o.

Ehrengericht n disciplinary court, tribunal; **ehrengerichtlich** Adj. disciplinary

ehrenhaft Adj. Person: respectable, upright; Absichten: hono(u)rable; **Ehrenhaftigkeit** f respectability, uprightness

ehrenhalber Adv. Univ.: Doktor ~ honorary doctor, förm. doctor honoris causa

Ehren|kodex m code of hono(u)r; **~legion** f Legion of Hono(u)r; **~loge** f VIP (od. royal) box; im Stadion: directors' box, Am. skybox; **~mal** n; -(e)s, -e od. -mäler monument (für to); Mil. memorial (to); **~mann** m; Pl. -männer man of hono(u)r; *er ist nicht gerade ein ~* he's a dubious (od. shady) character; **~medaille** f medal (of hono[u]r); **~nadel** f badge of hono(u)r; **~name** m complimentary nickname; **den ~n ... erhalten/tragen** be hono(u)red by being given the name / by being called ...; **~pflicht** f: **es für s-e ~ halten zu** (+ Inf.) be duty-bound to (+ Inf.); **~platz** m place (od. seat) of hono(u)r; **e-m Bild etc. den ~ geben** give a picture etc. pride of place; **~präsident** m, **~präsidentin** f honorary president; **~preis** m **1.** prize; **2.** (Trostpreis) consolation prize; **~rechte** Pl.: **bürgerliche ~** civil rights; **~rettung** f vindication (of s.o.'s hono[u]r); **zu s-r ~ muss gesagt werden, dass ...** in his defen|ce (Am. -se) it ought to be said that ...

ehrenrührig Adj. Arbeit, Behauptung etc.: defamatory; Geste etc.: insulting

Ehren|runde f Sport lap of hono(u)r; **e-e ~ drehen** do a lap of hono(u)r; Jugendspr. fig. have to repeat a year; **in der 11. Klasse habe ich eine ~ gedreht** I had to repeat year 11 (Am. junior year); **~sache** f matter of hono(u)r; **das ist doch ~!** that goes without saying; **~!** umg. you can count on me; **~schuld** f debt of hono(u)r; **~tag** m geh. great (od. big) day; **~titel** m honorary title; **~tor** n consolation goal; **~tribüne** f VIP stand; **~urkunde** f certificate

ehrenvoll Adj. hono(u)rable; (ruhmvoll) glorious

Ehrenwache f **1.** (Person[en]) guard of hono(u)r; **2.** (Dienst) sentry duty; **~ halten** be on sentry duty

ehrenwert Adj. respectable

Ehrenwort n; Pl. -e word of hono(u)r; (großes) **~!** umg. I promise (you); stärker: cross my heart, I swear, honest to God, auch scout's (od. Brit. auch guide's) hono(u)r umg. iro.; **sein ~ geben/brechen** give/break one's word

ehrerbietig Adj. respectful, deferential (gegen towards); **Ehrerbietung** f deference; stärker: reverence; **aus ~ gegen** in (od. out of) deference to(-wards)

Ehrfurcht f respect (vor + Dat. for); stärker: awe (of); **~ gebietend** awe-inspiring; **in ~ erstarren** od. **vor ~ erschauern** iro. be awestruck, nearly die of awe umg.; **ehrfürchtig I.** Adj. respectful; stärker: reverential; Schweigen: awed; **II.** Adv.: **~ lauschen** listen in awe; **Ehrfurchtsbezeigung** f mark of respect; **ehrfurchtslos** Adj. disrespectful, irreverent; **ehrfurchtsvoll** Adj. geh. reverential

Ehrgefühl n sense of hono(u)r; (Selbstachtung) self-respect, self-esteem; (Stolz) pride; → auch Ehre 3

Ehrgeiz m ambition; krankhafter/großer **~** fanatical/great (od. enormous) ambition; **vor lauter ~** driven (od. fired) by ambition; **sie macht es aus ~** she does it out of ambition (od. because she's ambitious); **er hat den ~, Weltmeister zu werden** his ambition is (od. he wants) to become world champion; **s-n ~ an etw. setzen** set one's heart on doing s.th., make it a point of hono(u)r to do s.th.; **ehrgeizig** Adj. ambitious; Pläne: auch high--flown; **Ehrgeizling** m; -s, -e; umg. pej. pushy person, Am. auch bulldozer

ehrlich I. Adj. **1.** Antwort, Gesicht, Person etc.: honest; Bedauern, Wunsch etc.: genuine; (aufrichtig) sincere; (wahrheitsgetreu) truthful; (offen) open, frank; **~ mit** od. **zu j-m sein** be

honest with s.o.; **sei doch mal ~, stimmt das?** umg. be honest with me, is it true?; **seien wir ~** let's face it, let's be honest (with ourselves); **wenn ich ~ bin, (muss ich zugeben,) ich mag es gar nicht** to be quite honest, (I must admit) I don't like it at all; **~ währt am längsten** Sprichw. honesty is the best policy; **2.** Spiel, Handel etc.: fair; präd. auch above board; **~e Absichten** hono(u)rable intentions; → Finder; **3.** altm. Name: good; Handwerk: honest; **~er Leute Kind** (child) of a good family; **II.** Adv. **1.** → I; **mal ganz ~ - hat er das gesagt?** umg. seriously now, did he say that?; **~ spielen** play fair; **~ gesagt** to tell you the truth, to be absolutely honest; **er meint es ~** he means well; **ich mein's ~ mit dir** I'm only thinking of your own good; **2.** (wirklich) really, honestly; **den Urlaub etc. hat sie sich ~ verdient** she's really earned this holiday etc.; **davon bin ich ~ überzeugt** I am absolutely convinced of that

ehrlicherweise Adv.: **er hat es ~ zugegeben** he was honest enough to admit it; **ich muss ~ sagen** in all honesty (od. to be quite honest) I have to say (od. admit)

Ehrlichkeit f honesty; openness etc.; → ehrlich I

ehrlos Adj. disreputable; stärker: disgraceful; **Ehrlosigkeit** f Benehmen: disreputable (od. disgraceful) behavio(u)r; **die ~ e-r Tat** etc. the disreputable (od. disgraceful) nature of a deed etc.

Ehrung f hono(u)r (+ Gen. conferred on s.o.); (Anerkennung) tribute (to); (Handlung) hono(u)ring (of); paying tribute (to); (Zeremonie) presentation ceremony (for)

ehrverletzend Adj. insulting

Ehrwürden m; -(s), kein Pl. als Anrede: Reverend; **Seine ~ ...** the Reverend (Abk. Rev.) ...; **ehrwürdig** Adj. venerable; kirchl. reverend; **Ehrwürdigkeit** f venerableness, claim to veneration

Ei n; -(e)s, -er **1.** egg; **ein ~ legen** lay an egg; **~er legend** Zool. egg-laying, oviparous; **aus dem ~ schlüpfen** hatch (out); **ein ~ aufschlagen/trennen** crack/separate an egg; **ein weiches/hartes** od. **weich/hart gekochtes ~** a soft-/hard-boiled egg; **wie auf (rohen) ~ern gehen** tread carefully; **sich gleichen wie ein ~ dem andern** be alike as two peas (in a pod); **wie ein rohes ~ behandeln** handle with kid gloves; **aussehen wie aus dem ~ gepellt** look very smart, look as if one has just stepped out of a fashion magazine; **2.** fig.: **das ist das ~ des Kolumbus!** that's it(, why didn't I od. we think of that before?), that's the answer (od. solution) we've all been looking for; **das sind noch ungelegte ~er** we'll cross that bridge when we come to it; **kümmere dich nicht um ungelegte ~er** you can worry about that when the time comes, we'll cross that bridge when we get to it; **ach du dickes ~!** umg. well I never, my goodness!; **ein ~ legen** umg. (etw. austüfteln) think up something; (e-n Plan ausbrüten) work out a plan; (Darm entleeren) have a dump (od. shit Sl.); **das ~ will klüger sein als die Henne** you etc. are trying to teach your grandmother to suck eggs; **das ist wie die Frage mit der Henne und dem ~** that's a chicken-an-

d-egg question; → Apfel 2; **3.** Physiol. ovum; **4. ~er** umg. (Geld) euros, hist. marks; Brit. quid; Am. bucks; **3000 ~er** auch three grand; **5. ~er** vulg. (Hoden) balls, bes. Am. nuts; **j-m in die ~er treten** kick s.o. in the balls; **6.** Sport umg. (Ball) ball

ei Interj. **1.** oh!; **~, ~!** iro. (well,) what do you know!, Brit. auch well fancy that!; **~, wer kommt denn da?** look who's here!; **2.** Kindersprache: **~ ~ machen** (bes. die Wange streicheln) pet; **~ ~!** beim Streicheln: nice doggy etc.; tröstend etc. zu Kind: there there

Eibe f; -, -n; Bot. **1.** (Baum) yew (tree); **2.** nur Sg.; (Holz) yew

Eichamt n in GB: Office of Weights and Measures; in den USA: Bureau of Standards

Eiche f; -, -n; Bot. **1.** (Baum) oak (tree); **2.** nur Sg. (Holz) oak

Eichel f; -, -n **1.** Bot. acorn; **2.** Anat. glans (penis); **3.** nur Sg.; Kartenspiel: German card suit equivalent to clubs; **~häher** m Zool. jay

eichen[1] v/t. (Maße, Gewichte) adjust; (Messgeräte, Skalen, Gefäße) calibrate; → geeicht

eichen[2] Adj. nur attr. oak, lit. oaken

Eichen|blatt n oak leaf; **~holz** n oak

Eichgewicht n standard weight

Eich|hörnchen n Zool. squirrel; **~kätzchen** n squirrel

Eich|maß n standard (measure od. weight); **~stab** m ga(u)ging rod; **~stempel** m verification stamp; **~strich** m official calibration; (an Trinkglas) line measure; **bis zum ~ einschenken** fill up to the line

Eichung f adjustment; calibration

Eid m; -(e)s, -e oath; **an ~es statt** in lieu of (an) oath; **e-n ~ ablegen** od. **leisten** take an oath; **e-n ~ auf die Bibel ablegen** swear by the (Holy) Bible; **j-m e-n ~ abnehmen** administer an oath to s.o.; **e-n ~ auf die Verfassung leisten** solemnly swear to preserve, protect and defend the constitution; **unter ~ aussagen** testify (od. give evidence) on oath; **unter ~ stehen** be under oath; **etw. auf s-n ~ nehmen** swear to s.th.; **der ~ des Hippokrates** the Hippocratic oath; **tausend ~e schwören, dass ...** umg. swear by all that is holy (od. sacred)

Eidbruch m breach (od. breaking) of an oath; **e-n ~ begehen** break one's oath; **eidbrüchig** Adj.: **~ werden** break one's oath

Eidechse f; -, -n; Zool. lizard

Eider|daune f, **~daunen** Pl. eiderdown Sg.; **~ente** f, **~gans** f umg. eider (duck)

Eidesformel f (wording of an) oath

eidesstattlich Adj. in lieu of an oath; **e-e ~e Erklärung abgeben** make a declaration in lieu of an oath

Eidgenosse m **1.** confederate; **2.** Swiss (citizen); **Eidgenossenschaft** f **1.** confederation; **2. die Schweizer ~** the Swiss Confederation, Switzerland; **Eidgenossin** f **1.** (female) confederate; **2.** (female) Swiss (citizen); **eidgenössisch** Adj. **1.** confederate; **2.** Swiss

eidlich I. Adj. sworn; **~e Aussage** sworn statement; schriftlich: affidavit; **e-e ~e Erklärung abgeben** make a declaration on oath, make a sworn declaration (Am. affidavit); (schriftlich) swear an affidavit; **II.** Adv. on (od. under) oath

Eidotter m, n (egg) yolk, yolk of an

egg
Eierbecher *m* egg cup
Eierchen *Pl.* **1.** little eggs; **2.** *umg.*
(*Geld*) cash, dosh, *Am.* dough (*alle
Sg.*)
Eier|frau *f* egg-woman; **~frucht** *f Bot.*
aubergine, *Am.* eggplant; **~kocher** *m*
egg boiler; **~kohle** *f* egg(-shaped)
coal; **~kopf** *m umg. hum. od. pej.*
1. egg-shaped head; **2.** (*Intellektueller*)
egghead, boffin; **~kuchen** *m Gastr.*
pancake; **~laufen** *n* egg-and-spoon
race; **~likör** *m* advocaat, *Am. etwa*
eggnog; **~löffel** *m* egg spoon
eiern *v/i. umg.* be wonky
Eier|nudeln *Pl. Gastr.* (egg) noodles;
~pfannkuchen *m* pancake; **~punsch**
m eggnog
Eierschale *f* eggshell; **eierschalenfar-
ben** *Adj.* eggshell(-colo[u]red)
Eier|schneider *m* egg slicer;
~schwammerl *m österr. Bot.* chanterelle; **~speise** *f Gastr.* **1.** egg dish;
2. *österr.* scrambled egg(s *Pl.*); **~stich**
m Gastr. cooked-egg garnish
Eierstock *m Anat.* ovary; **~entzün-
dung** *f Med.* inflammation of the
ovaries
Eier|tanz *m fig.*: **e-n ~ aufführen** per-
form a skil(l)ful balancing act; *der ~
der Regierung um die Steuerreform*
the government's shilly-shallying
about the tax reform; **~tomate** *f* plum
tomato; **~uhr** *f* egg timer; **~wärmer** *m*
egg cosy
Eifer *m*; *-s, kein Pl.* keenness, eagerness; *stärker*: zeal, fervo(u)r; (*Begeisterung*) enthusiasm; *voller ~* full of enthusiasm, with great fervo(u)r; *blinder
~* blind zeal; *blinder ~ schadet nur
Sprichw.* haste makes waste; *sich mit
~ ans Werk machen* set to work with
a will (*stärker*: vengeance); *im ~ des
Gefechts* in the heat of the moment;
→ **missionarisch** I
Eiferer *m*; *-s, -, pej.* fanatic; **eifern** *v/i.*
1. *nach etw. ~* strive for; **2.** *pej.*: *für
etw. od. j-n ~* campaign for; *gegen etw.
od. j-n ~* campaign against; (*schmähen*)
rail against
Eifersucht *f; nur Sg.* jealousy (*auf +
Akk.* of); **Eifersüchtelei** *f*; *-, -en* petty
jealousy; **eifersüchtig I.** *Adj.* jealous
(*auf + Akk.* of); **II.** *Adv.*: *~ über
j-n/etw. wachen* guard s.o./s.th. jealously
Eifersuchts|szene *f* jealous scene;
(*dramatic*) display of jealousy; *er
machte ihr e-e ~* in a fit of jealousy he
made a scene; **~tat** *f* act of jealousy
eiförmig *Adj.* egg-shaped, oval
eifrig I. *Adj.* keen, eager; (*begeistert*)
auch enthusiastic; (*fleißig*) hard-working, diligent; (*emsig*) busy, assiduous;
(*übereifrig*) officious, fussy; **II.** *Adv.*:
enthusiastically, eagerly; *~ lernen/ar-
beiten* study/work hard; *~ die Kirche
besuchen etc.* go to church *etc.* regularly (*od.* as often as one can); *~ bemüht sein zu* (+ *Inf.*) be anxious to (+
Inf.)
Eigelb *n*; *-(e)s, -e, bei Mengen*: *-* (egg)
yolk, yolk of an egg; *vier ~* four egg
yolks, the yolks of four eggs
eigen *Adj.* **1.** *nur attr.*; one's own, of
one's own; *~e Ansichten* personal
views; *darüber habe ich m-e ~en Ansichten* I have my own (personal)
opinion about that; *ein ~es Zimmer* a
room of one's own; *er braucht ein ~es
Zimmer auch* he needs a room to himself (*od.* his own room); *Zimmer mit
~em Bad* room with a private bath

(*od.* an en suite bathroom); *mit ~em
Eingang* with a separate entrance; *für
den ~en Bedarf* for personal (*od.* private) use; *auf ~e Gefahr* at one's own
risk; → **Antrieb** 1, **Faust**, **Fleisch** 1,
Herr 3; **2.** *nur attr.*; (*unabhängig*) *Gemeinde, Staat*: independent; **3.** *nur
attr.*; (*besonder...*) special (+ *Dat.* to),
typical (+ *Dat.* of); (*charakteristisch*)
auch particular (to), characteristic
(of), specific (to); (*innewohnend*) inherent (in); *mit dem ihm ~en Sarkasmus* with his characteristic sarcasm;
mit e-m ganz ~en Reiz with a charm
of (*od.* all) its own; **4.** (*genau, wählerisch*) particular (*in* + *Dat.* about);
stärker: fussy (about); **5.** (*seltsam*)
strange, odd, peculiar; *mir ist so ~ zumute* I have the strangest feeling, I
feel really peculiar
Eigen *n*; *-s, kein Pl.*; *geh.*: *etw. sein ~
nennen* call s.th. one's own; *sich
(Dat.) etw. zu ~ machen* make s.th.
one's own; (*Ansicht*) adopt; (*Gewohnheit*) make a habit of s.th.; *als Widmung*: *m-r lieben Frau zu ~* (dedicated) to my dear (*od.* beloved) wife
...eigen *im Adj.* *...*-owned; *betriebs~*
company-owned; *gewerkschafts~* uni-
on-owned, owned by a (trade) union
präd.
Eigenanteil *m* excess
Eigenart *f* **1.** characteristic feature, peculiarity, peculiar characteristic; *e-r
Person*: foible, idiosyncrasy; **2.** *nur
Sg.*; (*Gesamtheit der Merkmale*) dis-
tinctiveness, specific *od.* special character (*od.* nature); *die ~ s-r Musik besteht in ... auch* his music is characterized by ..., the special quality of his
music lies in ...; **eigenartig** *Adj.*
strange, peculiar, odd; **eigenartiger-
weise** *Adv.* strangely (*od.* oddly)
enough; **Eigenartigkeit** *f* **1.** *nur Sg.*
strangeness; **2.** *Verhaltensweise*: odd
behavio(u)r
Eigen|bau *m*; *nur Sg.*: *es ist ~* it's
homemade (*Gemüse etc.*: home-
grown); *Marke ~ umg.* à la Jones *etc.*;
~bedarf *m* one's personal needs *Pl.*;
e-s Landes: domestic requirements *Pl.*;
~ geltend machen als Vermieter: notify
a tenant *etc.* that one needs a flat *etc.*
for personal use; **~bericht** *m* correspondent's report, report from one's
own correspondent; **~beteiligung** *f
im Schadensfall*: excess
Eigenblut *n Med.*: *~ bekommen bei
Transfusion*: be given a transfusion of
one's own blood; **~behandlung** *f*
autoh(a)emotherapy
Eigenbrötelei *f*; *-, -en* **1.** (*Sichabson-
dern*) solitary ways *Pl.*; **2.** (*exzentri-
sches Verhalten*) eccentricity; **Eigenbrötler** *m*; *-s, -*, **Eigenbrötlerin** *f*; *-,
-nen*; *oft pej.* loner; *er ist ein ziemlicher Eigenbrötler* he's a bit of a loner,
he keeps very much to himself; **2.** (*Ex-
zentriker[in]*) eccentric; **eigenbrötle-
risch** *Adj.* **1.** solitary; **2.** eccentric
Eigen|dynamik *f fig.* momentum (of
its own); *e-e (gewisse) ~ entwickeln*
develop a life (*od.* momentum) of its
own; **~finanzierung** *f* self-financing;
~frequenz *f* natural frequency, eigen-
tone *Tech.*
eigengenutzt *Adj. Wohnung etc.*: owner-occupied
eigengesetzlich *Adj.* autonomous;
Dynamik etc.: self-contained; **Eigen-
gesetzlichkeit** *f* autonomy; (*innewoh-
nende Ordnung*) inherent order; order
of its (*od.* one's) own; *e-e gewisse ~*

entwickeln create an order of its (*od.*
one's) own
Eigengewicht *n Tech.* dead weight;
Wirts. net weight; *Phys.* specific
weight
eigenhändig I. *Adj. Delikt etc.*: personal; **~es Testament** holographic will;
es muss Ihre ~e Unterschrift sein it
has to be signed by you personally, it
needs your signature; **II.** *Adv.* personally; (*ohne Hilfe*) oneself, on one's
own, without any (outside) help; *bau-
en etc.*: with one's own two hands; *~
übergeben* deliver personally (*od.* in
person)
Eigenheim *n* house *od.* home (of one's
own), one's own house (*od.* home);
~zulage *f state subsidy available to
people who buy a home*
Eigenheit *f →* **Eigenart**
Eigen|initiative *f* **1.** (*Antrieb*) initiative
(of one's own); *ohne jede ~ sein auch*
be completely unresourceful; **2.** *es ist
e-e ~ von ihm* it was his own idea, he
came up with it (*od.* the idea) himself;
~interesse *n* vested interest, self-interest *pej.*; *aus ~* out of self-interest,
to serve one's own interests; **~kapital**
n Wirts. capital resources *Pl.*, equity
capital; **~leben** *n; nur Sg.* one's own
way of life, *a* life of one's own; *ein ~
führen auch* live one's own life, be independent, be an individual (in one's
own right); *etw. entwickelt/hat ein ~*
s.th. is developing/has a life of its
own; **~leistung** *f* personal contribution; *... wurde in ~ erstellt* they *etc.*
built ... themselves; **~liebe** *f nur Sg.*
love of self; *Psych.* narcissism; (*Egoismus*) self-centredness, (*Am.* -centered-
ness); **~lob** *n* self-adulation; *~ stinkt!*
umg. don't blow your own trumpet!
eigenmächtig I. *Adj.* (*anmaßend*)
high-handed; (*unbefugt*) unauthorized;
II. *Adv.* high-handedly, without anyone's permission, without instructions
from anyone, just like that *umg.*; *etw.
~ entscheiden* decide s.th. for oneself;
~ handeln act on one's own authority,
take the law into one's own hands; **Eigenmächtigkeit** *f* **1.** *nur Sg.* high-
-handedness; **2.** (*Handlung*) unauthorized act
Eigen|mittel *Pl.* one's own resources
(*od.* funds, capital *Sg.*); *aus ~n finanzieren* finance with one's own resources *etc.*; **~name** *m* proper name;
Ling. proper noun
Eigennutz *m*; *-es, kein Pl.*; *pej.*: *aus ~*
out of self-interest; **eigennützig** *Adj.
pej.* selfish
Eigen|nutzung *f e-r Wohnung*: owner-
-occupation; **~produktion** *f* (*Schallplatte, CD etc.*) own-label production
(*od.* record); (*Fernsehsendung*): *~ des
ORF etc.* ORF *etc.* production; **~regie**
f: *in ~ bauen etc.* build *etc.* s.th. oneself
eigens *Adv.* specially; (*ausdrücklich*)
auch specifically, expressly; *~ für dich
auch* just for you; *ich bin ~ wegen dir
gekommen auch* I came for your sake
(*od.* on your account)
Eigenschaft *f* quality; (*Merkmal*) (distinctive) feature, characteristic; *Phys.,
Chem.* property; (*Wesen*) nature; (*Eigentümlichkeit*) peculiarity; *gute/
schlechte ~en e-r Person*: good/bad
points (*od.* habits), positive/negative
traits; *e-r Sache*: good/bad points, ad-
vantages/disadvantages (*od.* draw-
backs); *in s-r ~ als* in his capacity of
(*od.* as), acting as; **Eigenschaftswort**
n; *Pl.* **Eigenschaftswörter**; *Ling.* adjec-

E

tive

Eigensinn *m*; *nur Sg.* stubbornness, obstinacy; **eigensinnig** *Adj.* stubborn, headstrong; ~ *sein auch* have a will of one's own; **Eigensinnigkeit** *f* **1.** *nur Sg.* stubbornness, obstinacy; **2.** *Handlung*: stubborn (*od.* obstinate) behavio(u)r

eigenständig *Adj.* independent; **Eigenständigkeit** *f* independence

Eigensucht *f*; *nur Sg.* selfishness; (*Egoismus*) self-centredness (*Am.* -centeredness); **eigensüchtig** *Adj.* selfish; (*egoistisch*) self-centred (*Am.* -centered)

eigentlich I. *Adj. nur attr.* **1.** (*wirklich*) actual, real; *Beweggründe*: *auch* true; (*genau*) specific; **~e Ursache e-s Übels**: root cause; **im ~en Sinne** (**des Wortes**) in the true sense (of the word); **2.** (*ursprünglich*) *Absicht, Grund, Plan etc.*: original; **II.** *Adv.* **1.** (*in Wirklichkeit*) actually, really; **~ heißt er Manfred** his real name's Manfred; **~ ist er ganz vernünftig** he's actually quite sensible, I suppose he's quite sensible, really; **kann ich ihn nicht ausstehen** to be honest (*od.* to tell you the truth), I can't stand him; **2.** (*genau genommen*) strictly speaking; (*von Rechts wegen*) by rights; **~ nicht/schon, aber ...** (well) not/yes really, but ...; **~ bin ich froh darüber** actually I'm quite pleased about it; **~ sollte sie schon längst hier sein** they really ought to (*od.* should) be here by now; **3.** *vorwurfsvoll*: anyway; **was wollen Sie ~?** what do you want anyway?, what do you actually want?; **das hättest du mir ~ sagen müssen** you really ought to have told me; **was hast du dir ~ dabei gedacht?** what on earth were you thinking of?; **4.** (*übrigens*) by the way; **wie spät ist es ~?** what time is it(, by the way)?; **hast du das ~ gewusst?** did you know (about) that?; **was ist ~ passiert?** what actually (*od.* exactly) happened?; **5.** (*vermutlich*) probably; **das müsste jetzt ~ reichen** that will probably be enough, that should do it; **6.** (*ursprünglich*) originally; **~ wollte ich früher hier sein** I was (actually) hoping to be here earlier

Eigentor *n Sport*: an own goal (*auch fig.*); **ein ~ schießen** *auch fig.* score an own goal

Eigentum *n*; *-s, kein Pl. auch öffentliches*: property; *e-r Firma*: *auch* assets *Pl.*; *Jur.* (*Eigentumsrecht*) ownership (**an** + *Dat.* of), title; **es ist mein ~** *auch* it belongs to me; **sich an fremdem ~ vergreifen** steal; ~ **verpflichtet** (*Verfassungsgrundsatz*) property entails responsibility; ~ **erwerben** acquire title; → **geistig** I

Eigentümer *m*; *-s, -,* **~in** *f*; *-, -nen* owner; (*Inhaber*) proprietor; (*von Effekten*) holder

eigentümlich I. *Adj.* **1.** (*seltsam*) peculiar, strange, odd; **2.** (*typisch*) peculiar (+ *Dat.* to), characteristic (of), typical (of); **II.** *Adv.*: *j-n* ~ **berühren** have a curious effect on; **eigentümlicherweise** *Adv.* strangely (*od.* oddly) enough; **Eigentümlichkeit** *f* **1.** *nur Sg.*; (*Eigenartigkeit*) peculiarity; **2.** (*Merkmal*) peculiarity, characteristic; (*merkwürdige Gewohnheit*) peculiar habit

Eigentums|delikt *n* property offence, *Am.* crime against property; **~nachweis** *m* proof of ownership; **sie konnte keinen ~ erbringen** she was not able to provide any proof of ownership;

~recht *n* **1.** ownership (**an** + *Dat.* of); **2.** *Jur.* ownership law(s *Pl.*); **~urkunde** *f* title deed; **~verhältnisse** *Pl.* distribution of property *Sg.*; **~wohnung** *f* flat, *Am.* apartment; *bei Eigennutzung*: *auch* owner-occupied flat, *Am.* condominium, condo *umg.*; **sie haben e-e ~** *auch* they own a flat (*Am.* a condo), they've got a flat (*Am.* a condo) of their own

Eigenurin *m Med.* one's own urine; **~behandlung** *f* urine therapy

eigenverantwortlich I. *Adj.* independent, autonomous; **II.** *Adv.* on one's own authority; **er muss ~ handeln** he must act as he sees fit; **Eigenverantwortung** *f*: **in ~ entscheiden etc.**: on one's own responsibility

Eigen|verbrauch *m* private consumption; **~wärme** *f* **1.** *Physiol.* body temperature; **2.** *Phys.* specific heat; **~werbung** *f* self-advertising (*od.* -publicity); ~ **treiben** promote o.s.; **~wert** *m* **1.** intrinsic value; **2.** *Math.* eigenvalue; **~widerstand** *m Etech.* inherent resistance

eigenwillig *Adj.* **1.** *Stil etc.*: very individual, unusual, unconventional, original; **2.** *Person*: wayward, wil(l)ful; (*eigensinnig*) headstrong, obstinate *pej.*

eignen *v/refl. Sache*: be suitable (**für** for); *Person*: be suited (**für** for; **als** as; **zu** as, for); **sich schlecht ~** be unsuitable; **sich hervorragend ~ für** be ideal for (*od.* as); **es eignet sich gut als Geschenk** it makes (*od.* would make) a good present; **die Äpfel ~ sich gut zum Kochen** they're good cooking apples, these apples are ideal for cooking; **er würde sich als Lehrer** (**nicht**) ~ he'd make (*od.* be) a good teacher (he's not cut out for teaching); **er / das Holz etc. eignet sich überhaupt nicht** *auch* he just isn't the right kind of person / it's the wrong kind of wood etc.

Eigner *m*; *-s, -,* **~in** *f*; *-, -nen* owner

Eignung *f* suitability (**für** for; **zu** as, for), aptitude (**für** for); **keine ~ haben für** show no aptitude for, have no talent for; **fachliche ~** professional qualification; ~ **von Waren** fitness of goods

Eignungs|prüfung *f*, **~test** *m* aptitude test

Eiland *n*; *-(e)s, -e; altm. od. lit.* island, isle *lit.*

Eil|antrag *m* urgent appeal (*od.* motion); **~auftrag** *m* rush order; **~bote** *m Post.*: **per ~n** express, *Am.* (by) special delivery; **~brief** *m Post.* express letter, *Am.* special delivery (letter); **ein Schreiben als ~ schicken** send a letter express

Eile *f*, *-, kein Pl.* hurry, rush; **ich habe keine/große ~** (**zu** + *Inf.*) I'm in no hurry / in a great hurry (to + *Inf.*); **damit hat es keine ~** there's no hurry (for it), there's no (great) rush; **j-n zur ~ antreiben** hurry s.o. up; **in ~ sein** be in a hurry; **in der ~ habe ich es übersehen etc.**: in the (general) rush (*od.* hectic); **in aller ~** hurriedly, in a rush; **ein paar Zeilen in aller ~** just a quick note, a few hurried lines

Eileiter *m Anat.* Fallopian tube; **~schwangerschaft** *f Med.* ectopic pregnancy

eilen I. *v/i.* **1.** (*ist geeilt*); *Person*: hurry, hasten; *stärker*: rush; *j-m zu Hilfe ~* rush to s.o.'s aid (*od.* assistance); **zu den Waffen ~** hasten to (take up) arms; *kannst du mir mal helfen? etc.* - *ich eile! hum.* coming!; **eile mit Weile!**

Sprichw. more haste, less speed; **2.** (*hat*); *Sache*: be urgent; **es eilt nicht** *od.* **damit eilt es** (**mir**) **nicht** there's no hurry (for it), there's no (great) rush; **eilt!** *Aufschrift*: urgent; **II.** *v/refl.* (*hat*) *umg.* → **beeilen**; **eilends** *Adv.* hastily, in haste

eilfertig *Adj. geh. pej.* **1.** (*übereilt*) rash, (over)hasty; **2.** (*dienstbeflissen*) zealous

Eil|fracht *f* express (*Am.* fast) freight; **~gebühr** *f Post.* express delivery charge; **~gut** *n* express (*Am.* fast) freight; **als ~ schicken** send s.th. express (freight) (*Am.* fast freight)

eilig I. *Adj.* **1.** (*schnell*) hurried, quick; **mit ~en Schritten** hurriedly; **wohin so ~?** what's the hurry (*od.* rush)?, where are you off to in such a hurry?; **2.** (*dringend*) urgent; **nichts Eiligeres zu tun haben als ...** *iro.* have nothing better to do than ...; **3. es ~ haben** be in a hurry (*od.* rush); **ich hab's mit dem Brief nicht sehr ~** I'm in no hurry for the letter to be done; **II.** *Adv.* hurriedly; **eiligst** *Adv.* in a great hurry; (*so schnell wie möglich*) as quickly (*od.* soon) as possible

Eil|marsch *m* speed (*od.* forced) march; **~schritt** *m*: **im ~** at a fast pace; **im ~ vorbeirauschen** breeze past; **~sendung** *f Post.* express post (*od.* mail); **~tempo** *n umg.*: **im ~** in double-quick time; **~verfahren** *n Jur.* summary proceeding(s *Pl.*); **im ~ durchnehmen** *fig.* rush through *s.th.*; **im ~ herstellen etc.** rush *s.th.* off; **~zug** *m hist.* fast stopping train, *Am.* limited

Eimer *m*; *-s, -* **1.** bucket, *bes. Am.* pail; **ein ~** (**voll**) **Wasser** a bucket(ful) of water; **es gießt wie aus ~n** *umg.* it's bucketing down, it's raining cats and dogs; **2.** *umg. fig.*: **im ~ sein** *Auto, Uhr etc.*: have had it, be up the spout; *Gesundheit, Kuchen, Ruf etc.*: be ruined (*od.* buggered *Sl.*); *Ehe etc.*: be in tatters; **damit sind unsere Pläne im ~** bang go our plans; **3.** *umg. fig. pej.* (*Schiff*) tub

eimerweise *Adv.* in bucketfuls; *umg.* (*in großen Mengen*) by the bucket(ful)

ein¹ I. *unbest. Art.* **1.** a, an; **~ anderer/jeder** somebody else / each and every one; **welch ~ Glück!** what luck!; **war das ~ Spaß!** that was fun!; **das konnte nur ~ Nero behaupten** only somebody like Nero could say that; **~** (**gewisser**) **Herr Braun** a (certain) Mr(.) Braun; **~ Kind** (*jedes Kind*) **macht viel Freude** children bring such joy; **2.** *Zeitangabe*: one; **~es Tages** one day; *zukünftig*: *auch* some day; **II.** *Adj.* **1.** *Zahl*: one, a, an; **um ~ Uhr** at one o'clock; **~ halbes Pfund** half a pound; **~ für alle Mal** once and for all; **nur ~** (**einziges**) **Mal** once (and once only), one time (only); **nicht ~ Fehler** not one (*od.* a single) mistake; **nicht ~e Sekunde lang** not even for a second; **an ~em** (**einzigen**) **Tag** in a single day; **in ~em fort geh.** continuously, all the time; **er ist ihr Ein und Alles** he means the world to her, he's her one and only; **~es sage ich dir!** I'll tell you something (for nothing); → **acht¹**; **2.** (*gleich*) same; **wir sind ~er Meinung** we are of the same opinion, we agree; **~ und dieselbe Frau** one and the same woman; **an ~ und demselben Tag** on the very same day; **III.** *unbest. Pron.*: **das ~e, das ich meine** the one I mean; **der ~e oder andere** the one or (the) other;

E

die ~en sagen so, die anderen so some say this, the others say that; *du bist mir ~er! umg.* you're a (fine) one; → *einer*

ein² *Adv.* **1.** *am Schalter:* on; *~ - aus* on - off; **2.** *~ und aus gehen* come and go; *bei j-m:* be a frequent visitor of s.o. (*od.* at s.o.'s place), always be (a)round at s.o.'s place; *ich weiß weder ~ noch aus* I'm at my wit's end

Einakter *m; -s, -; Theat.* one-act play

einander *Adv.* each other, one another; *sie sind ~ im Weg* in each other's way; *~ ausschließende Vorstellungen* mutually exclusive ideas

einarbeiten (*trennb., hat -ge-*) **I.** *v/t.* **1.** (*j-n*) show *s.o.* the ropes, train *s.o.;* **2.** (*einfügen*) work in; (*hinzufügen*) add; **3.** (*Zeitverlust*) make up for; *auch im Voraus:* work in; **II.** *v/refl.* familiarize o.s. with the work (*od.* subject *etc.*), get to know the ropes; *sich ~ in* (+ *Akk.*) *auch* get into; *sich schnell in e-e neue Stelle ~* settle into a new job very quickly; **Einarbeitungszeit** *f* settling-in (*od.* training) period

einarmig I. *Adj. Person, Hebel etc.:* one-armed; *er ist ~ mst* he's only got one arm; *ein ~er Mann auch* a man with (just) one arm; **II.** *Adv.* with one arm

einäschern *v/t.* (*trennb., hat -ge-*) **1.** burn to ashes; **2.** (*j-n*) cremate; **Einäscherung** *f e-r Leiche:* cremation; **Einäscherungshalle** *f* crematorium

einatmen (*trennb., hat -ge-*) **I.** *v/t.* breathe in, inhale; **II.** *v/i.* breathe in; *tief ~* take a deep breath (*od.* deep breaths)

einäugig *Adj.* **1.** one-eyed; *er ist ~ auch* he's only got one eye; *unter den Blinden ist der Einäugige König Sprichw.* in the country of the blind, the one-eyed man is king; **2.** *fig.* short-sighted

Einbahn|straße *f* **1.** one-way street; **2.** *fig.* dead end, cul-de-sac; *~verkehr m* one-way traffic

einbalsamieren *v/t.* (*trennb., hat*) embalm; **Einbalsamierung** *f* embalming, embalmment

Einband *m* binding; *konkret:* cover

einbändig *Adj. attr.* one-volume ..., single-volume ..., *nachgestellt und präd.* in one volume

Einbau *m; Pl. Einbauten* **1.** *nur Sg.;* (*das Einbauen*) installation, fitting; **2.** (*Eingebautes*) fixture, fitting; (*Regale etc.*) fitted (*Am. auch* built-in) shelves *etc.;* **3.** *fig.* (*Einfügung*) insertion, incorporation; **einbauen** *v/t.* (*trennb., hat -ge-*): *~ (in)* (+ *Akk.*) **1.** (*Möbel*) fit (*od.* build) in; *~* in(to); **2.** *Tech.* install (into); (*Motor*) fit; **3.** *fig.* (*einfügen*) (*Satz etc.*) work in(to), insert, incorporate; → *eingebaut*; **Einbauküche** *f* fitted kitchen

Einbaum *m* dugout (canoe)

Einbau|möbel *Pl.* fitted furniture *Sg.;* *~schrank m* built-in *od.* fitted cupboard(s *Pl.*) (*für Kleider:* wardrobe, *Am.* closet)

einbegriffen *Adj.:* (*mit*) *~* included (*in + Dat.* in)

einbehalten *v/t.* (*unreg., trennb., hat*) withhold, keep, hold onto *umg.;* (*abziehen*) deduct

einbeinig *Adj.* one-legged; *er ist ~ mst* he's only got one leg; *ein ~er Mann auch* a man with (just) one leg

einberechnen *v/t.* (*trennb., hat*): (*mit*) *~* take into account (*bei* in)

einberufen *v/t.* (*unreg., trennb., hat*) **1.** (*Versammlung*) call; *Parl.* summon, convene; **2.** *Mil.* call up (*zu* for), conscript, *Am.* draft (into); **Einberufene** *m; -n, -n; Mil.* conscript, *Am.* draftee; **Einberufung** *f* **1.** *e-r Versammlung:* calling; *Parl.* summoning, convening; **2.** *Mil.* conscription, call-up, *Am.* draft

Einberufungsbefehl *m Mil.* call-up orders *Pl., Am.* draft papers *Pl.*

einbetonieren *v/t.* (*trennb., hat*) embed in concrete; *Pfosten in den Boden ~* set posts in concrete

Einbett|kabine *f* single-berth cabin, stateroom; *~zimmer n* single room

einbeziehen *v/t.* (*unreg., trennb., hat*) include (*in + Akk.* in), cover; (*integrieren*) incorporate (into), integrate (into); *j-n in ein Gespräch* (*mit*) *~* involve (*od.* include) s.o. in a conversation; **Einbeziehung** *f* inclusion (*in + Akk.* in), incorporation (into); *unter ~ von ...* taking ... into account

einbiegen (*unreg., trennb.*) **I.** *v/t.* (*hat eingebogen*) bend in(wards); **II.** *v/i.* (*ist*): *in e-e Straße ~* turn into; (*nach*) *links ~* turn left

einbilden *v/t.* (*trennb., hat -ge-*) **1.** *sich* (*Dat.*) *etw. ~* (*sich vorstellen*) imagine s.th.; (*glauben*) think s.th.; *er bildet sich ein, beliebt zu sein* he thinks (*od.* likes to think) he's popular; *sich steif und fest ~, dass ...* be (firmly) convinced that ...; *bilde dir ja nicht ein, dass ...* you needn't (for one minute) think that ..., don't go running away with the idea that ...; *was bildest du dir eigentlich ein?* what on earth has got (*Am. auch* gotten) into you?, who do you think you are?; *bei Handlung: auch* what on earth do you think you're doing?; *bilde dir doch nichts ein!* don't fool (*od.* kid *umg.*) yourself; *ich bilde mir nicht ein, ein Genie zu sein* I don't pretend (*od.* claim) to be a genius; **2.** *umg., mst pej.: sich* (*Dat.*) *etw. ~* (*stolz sein*) be proud (*od.* conceited) (*auf + Akk.* about); *darauf brauchst du dir nichts einzubilden* that's nothing to be proud of (*od.* to write home about); *er bildet sich auf s-n Erfolg was ein* his success has gone to his head, he's gone (*Am.* gotten) all stuck-up since his success; *bilde dir ja nicht zu viel ein!* don't let it go to your head(, now); → *eingebildet* II.; **3.** *Dial.: sich* (*Dat.*) *etw. ~* (*unbedingt haben wollen*) set one's mind on s.th.

Einbildung *f* **1.** (*Fantasie*) imagination; (*falsche Vorstellung*) fantasy; *~en* illusions; *das ist reine ~* you're (*od.* he's *etc.*) imagining things, it's all in your *etc.* mind; *nur in j-s ~ existieren* be a figment of s.o.'s imagination; **2.** *nur Sg.;* (*Dünkel*) conceitedness

Einbildungs|gabe *f*, *~kraft f*, *~vermögen n* (powers *Pl.* of) imagination

einbinden *v/t.* (*unreg., trennb., hat -ge-*) **1.** (*Buch*) bind; **2.** *in Taschentuch etc.:* tie up (*in + Akk.* in); **3.** *Med.* bandage; **4.** (*integrieren*) integrate (*in + Akk.* into); *ein Dorf ins Verkehrsnetz ~* link a village to the transport (*Am.* transportation) system

einbläuen *v/t.* (*trennb., hat -ge-*): *j-m etw. ~* drum s.th. into s.o.('s head), get s.th. into s.o.'s head

einblenden (*trennb., hat -ge-*) **I.** *v/t.: ~ (in + Akk.*) (*Musik etc.*) fade in; *nachträglich:* dub in(to); (*Zweitbild, Schrift*) superimpose (on); (*Werbespot etc.*) slot in; **II.** *v/refl.: wir blenden uns* (*jetzt*) *ein* we're joining (*od.* going

over to) the other studio (*od.* our crew at Wembley Stadium *etc.*); **Einblendung** *f* fade-in; (*Zweitbild etc.*) insert

Einblick *m* **1.** (*Blick*) view (*in + Akk.* of); *~ in j-s Garten haben* be able to see into s.o.'s garden; **2.** (*das Einsehen*) look (*in + Akk.* at); (*Zugang*) access to; *j-m ~ gewähren in Dokumente etc.:* allow s.o. access (*in + Akk.* to); *~ nehmen in* (+ *Akk.*) (*Akten etc.*) take a look at (*od.* examine) s.th.; **3.** (*Kenntnis*) insight (into); *e-n gewissen ~ haben* have some idea (*in + Akk.* of, about); *~ gewinnen od. sich* (*e-n*) *~ verschaffen in* (+ *Akk.*) get some sort of idea, get a general idea of, get (*od.* gain) an insight into

einbrechen (*unreg., trennb.*) **I.** *v/i.* **1.** (*hat/ist eingebrochen*): *~ (in + Akk.*) *Dieb:* break in(to); *~ in* (+ *Akk.*) (*Wohnung etc.*) *auch* burgle; *bei ihm wurde eingebrochen* his house (*od.* flat, *Am.* apartment) was burgled (*Am. auch* burglarized), he had burglars, he was burgled, he got broken into; **2.** (*ist*) *Höhle, Dach etc.:* collapse, cave in; **3.** (*ist*) *im Eis:* fall (*od.* go) through the ice; **4.** (*ist*) *fig.* suffer a severe defeat (*od.* setback); **5.** (*ist*) *geh. Kälte, Winter etc.:* set in; *bei ~der Dunkelheit* at nightfall; **II.** *v/t.* (*hat*); (*niederreißen*) break down, demolish

Einbrecher *m* burglar; *~bande f* gang of burglars

Einbrecherin *f; -, -nen* burglar

Einbrenne *f; -, -n; südd., österr. Gastr.* roux

einbrennen (*unreg., trennb., hat -ge-*) **I.** *v/t.* **1.** *~ (in + Akk.*) burn in(to); *e-m Tier ein Zeichen ~* brand; **2.** *südd., österr. Gastr.* (*Mehl*) brown; (*Soße, Suppe*) thicken with roux; **II.** *v/refl. geh.: sich in j-s Gedächtnis ~* become engraved (*od.* etched) on s.o.'s memory

einbringen (*unreg., trennb., hat -ge-*) **I.** *v/t.* **1.** (*Geld*) bring in; (*Gewinn, Zinsen etc.*) *auch* yield; *netto:* net; (*Preis*) fetch; *j-m etw. ~* (*Ruf, Ruhm etc.*) earn s.o. s.th.; *es bringt mir ... ein* it gets me ...; *es hat mir nur Ärger eingebracht* it caused me nothing but trouble; *das bringt nichts ein* it doesn't pay, it isn't worth it (*od.* the candle); *wieder ~ Kosten etc.:* recover; **2.** (*mitbringen*) (*Kapital, Ideen etc.*) contribute (*in + Akk.* to); *etw. in die Ehe ~* bring s.th. into (*od.* contribute s.th. to) a marriage; **3.** (*Antrag etc.*) introduce; *e-e Klage ~ Jur.* file an action; **4.** (*Ernte, Heu etc.*) bring in, harvest; (*Schiff*) bring in (*in den Hafen* to port); **5.** (*Verlust, Zeit*) make up (for); **6.** *Druck.* (*Zeile*) get (*od.* take) in; **7.** *Amtsspr.* (*Entflohene*) capture, catch; **II.** *v/refl.: sich in e-e od. e-r Beziehung, Diskussion etc. ~* make a contribution (to); *sich voll ~* put a lot of time (and energy) into it

einbrocken *v/t.* (*trennb., hat -ge-*) **1.** *etw. ~ (in + Akk.*) crumble s.th. in(to); **2.** *umg. fig.: j-m/sich etwas* (*Schönes*) *~* get s.o./o.s. into a real fix, land o.s. in it; *das hast du dir selbst eingebrockt* it's your own fault, you've shot yourself in the foot

Einbruch *m* **1.** *in ein Haus:* burglary (*in + Akk.* in); *e-n ~ verüben* commit burglary; *e-n ~ verüben in* (+ *Akk.*) break into; **2.** *Mil.* invasion (*in + Akk.* of); **3.** (*Einsturz*) collapse; **4.** (*Anfang*) onset; *bei ~ der Dunkelheit* at nightfall, when night closes in; *bei ~ der Kälte* when the cold (weather) sets in;

5. (*schwere Niederlage*) severe defeat (*od.* setback); (*Leistungsabfall*) drop in performance (*od.* form); **in der 2. Halbzeit erlitt die Mannschaft einen ~** the team slumped in the second half; **6.** *Wirts.* slump; **e-n ~ erleiden** (*Aktienkurse etc.*) (suffer a) crash

Einbruch(s)|diebstahl *m* burglary; **~gefahr** *f* **1. es besteht ~ beim Dach** *etc.*: the roof *etc.* is in danger of collapsing; *bei Eis*: the ice is dangerously thin (in places); **2.** (*Diebstahlgefahr*) likelihood of a burglary (*od.* of being burgled); **~melder** *m* burglar (*od.* security) alarm; **~serie** *f* series of break-ins (*od.* burglaries); **⌂sicher** *Adj.* burglar-proof; **~werkzeug** *n* housebreaking tool; **sie haben die ~e gefunden** they found the instruments he *etc.* used to (try and) break in

einbuchen *v/refl.* (*trennb.*, hat -ge-) *Handy in Netz*: register

einbuchten *v/t.* (*trennb.*, hat -ge-); *umg.* (*j-n*) → **einlochen** I 2

Einbuchtung *f* **1.** (*Delle*) indentation, dent; **2.** *Geol.* bay, inlet

einbuddeln (*trennb.*, hat -ge-); *umg.* **I.** *v/t.* bury (*in* + *Akk.* in); **II.** *v/refl.*: **sich ~** (*in* + *Akk.*) dig o.s. in(to)

einbürgern (*trennb.*, hat -ge-) **I.** *v/t.* **1.** (*Person*) naturalize; **sich ~ lassen** become naturalized; **2.** (*Pflanze, Tier, Brauch etc.*) introduce; **II.** *v/refl. Sache*: take root, establish itself; *Brauch etc.*: come into use, gain currency; **sich in e-r Sprache ~** *auch* find its (*od.* their) way into a language; **es hat sich so eingebürgert** it's become a habit (*bei* with); (*wird erwartet*) it's become the done thing (,*dass man ...* to + *Inf.*); **es hat sich bei uns so eingebürgert, dass wir uns die Hausarbeit teilen** we got in(to) the habit of sharing the housework

Einbürgerung *f* **1.** naturalization; **2.** *fig. e-s Brauchs etc.*: establishment

Einbürgerungsantrag *m* application (*od.* petition) for naturalization; **e-n ~ stellen** apply for naturalization

Einbuße *f* loss (*an* + *Dat.* of), setback; **unter ~ von** (*od.* + *Gen.*) at the cost of; **schwere ~n hinnehmen müssen** *od.* **erleiden** suffer (*od.* sustain) heavy losses, be badly out of pocket *umg.*; **einbüßen** (*trennb.*, hat -ge-) **I.** *v/t.* (*verlieren*) lose; (*opfern müssen*) forfeit; **II.** *v/i.*: **an etw.** (*Dat.*) **~** lose (some of) s.th.

Eincentstück *n* one-(euro)cent piece

einchecken *v/i.* (*trennb.*, hat -ge-) check in

Einchecken *n*; -s, *kein Pl.* checking in, check-in; **beim ~** as I was *etc.* checking in; **das ~ dauert immer furchtbar lange** it always takes ages to check in

eincremen (*trennb.*, hat -ge-) **I.** *v/t.*: **j-m den Rücken / j-n ~** rub cream into s.o.'s back / onto s.o.; **sich** (*Dat.*) **die Hände ~** put some handcream on; **die Schuhe ~** put polish on the shoes; **II.** *v/refl.* put some cream on

eindämmen *v/t.* (*trennb.*, hat -ge-) **1.** (*Wasserlauf*) dam up; (*Land*) dyke, dike, embank; **2.** (*Fluten, Inflation etc.*) stem, curb; (*Feuer etc.*) check, get under control; (*Kriminalität etc.*) curb, control; *bes. Pol.* contain

eindecken (*trennb.*, hat -ge-) **I.** *v/refl.* stock up (*mit* on); **sich mit Vorräten ~** lay in provisions; **II.** *v/t.* **1.** (*bedecken*) cover (up); (*Dach*) cover; (*Haus*) roof; (*Tisch*) → **decken** II 1; **2.** *umg. fig.* inundate; **j-n mit Aufträgen/Fragen** *etc.* **~** swamp s.o. with work / bombard s.o. with questions; *mit Geschenken etc.*: shower; → **eingedeckt** II; **III.** *v/i. im Restaurant*: (*decken*) lay (*od.* set) the table(s)

Eindecker *m*; -s, - *Flugzeug*: monoplane; *Schiff*: single-deck(ed) ship; *Bus*: single decker

eindeichen *v/t.* (*trennb.*, hat -ge-) dyke, dike

eindellen *v/t.* (*trennb.*, hat -ge-); *umg.* dent

eindeutig I. *Adj.* clear, obvious, straightforward, explicit; (*nicht zweideutig*) unambiguous, unequivocal; *Geste etc.*: unmistakable; *Beweis*: indisputable, definite; *Sieger*: clear, undisputed; **II.** *Adv.* clearly; definitely; unambiguously; obviously; **es ist ~ s-e Schuld** it was clearly his fault, there's no doubt that it was his fault; **j-m ~ zu verstehen geben, dass ...** make it quite clear to s.o. that ..., make no bones about the fact that ...; **~ Stellung beziehen** take an unequivocal stand (*zu* on); **Eindeutigkeit** *f* clarity, unambiguity, explicitness

eindeutschen *v/t.* (*trennb.*, hat -ge-) Germanize; **muss ich dir das erst ~?** *umg.* do I have to spell it out for you?; **Eindeutschung** *f* Germanization

eindicken *v/t.* (*trennb.*, hat eingedickt) *und v/i.* (*ist*) thicken

eindimensional *Adj.* one-dimensional (*auch fig.*)

eindösen *v/i.* (*trennb.*, ist -ge-); *umg.* doze off, nod off

eindrängen (*trennb.*, hat -ge-) *v/i.*: **auf j-n ~** *Erinnerungen etc.*: crowd in on s.o.

eindrehen (*trennb.*, hat -ge-) **I.** *v/t.* **1.** (*Glühbirne, Schraube*) screw in; **2. sich** (*Dat.*) **die Haare ~** put curlers (*od.* rollers) in one's hair, put one's hair in curlers; **3. die Füße etc. ~** turn one's feet in, be pigeon-toed; **II.** *v/i.* (*einschwenken*) turn (*od.* swing) onto a new course, take a different tack

eindreschen *v/i.* (*unreg.*, *trennb.*, hat -ge-); *umg.*: **~ auf** (+ *Akk.*) beat; **das Eindreschen auf die Gewerkschaften** *etc. fig.* union-bashing *etc.*

eindringen *v/i.* (*unreg.*, *trennb.*, ist -ge-) **1. ~** (*in* + *Akk.*) *Person*: get in(to); *gewaltsam*: force one's way in(to); *Einbrecher*: break in; *Truppen*: invade; **er drang in sie ein** he penetrated her; **2. ~** (*in* + *Akk.*) *Sache*: get in(to); *Wasser, Sand etc.*: *auch* seep in(to); *Pfeil etc.*: penetrate, pierce; **der Stachel drang tief in den Finger ein** the thorn went deep into his *etc.* finger; **3.** *fig. in e-n Markt*: penetrate, make inroads into (*od.* on); *Idee etc.*: penetrate, find its way in; *Sprache*: become established in; **Fremdwörter dringen in die Sprache ein** foreign words come into common usage in the language; **ihre Worte sind in ihn eingedrungen** her words registered with him, her words really hit home (with him); **4.** *fig.*: **~ in** (+ *Akk.*) (*ergründen*) go into; (*erfassen*) comprehend, fathom; **5. ~ auf j-n** *Feinde etc.*: close in on s.o.; *fig. mit Fragen etc.*: press s.o.; *Gefühle*: crowd in on s.o.

eindringlich I. *Adj.* **1.** *Warnung, Bitte etc.*: urgent; **2.** *Rede, Stimme etc.*: forceful, powerful; **II.** *Adv.*: **aufs ~ste** *od.* **Eindringlichste** (most) urgently; **ich rate Ihnen aufs ~ste** *od.* **Eindringlichste ab** I strongly advise you

against it, I urge you not to do it; **Eindringlichkeit** *f* urgency

Eindringling *m*; -s, -e intruder; (*Angreifer*) invader

Eindruck *m* **1.** impression; **es hat keinen ~ auf mich gemacht** it didn't impress me at all, it didn't make the slightest impression on me; **sie macht e-n intelligenten ~** *od.* **den ~ e-r intelligenten Frau** she seems to be quite intelligent, she gives the impression of being quite intelligent; **e-n schlechten ~ machen** make a bad impression (*auf* + *Akk.* on); **den ~ erwecken, dass ...** give s.o. (*od.* create) the impression that ...; **ich habe den ~, dass ...** I have (*od.* get) the impression (that) ...; (*das Gefühl*) I have a feeling (that) ...; **ich werde den ~ nicht los, dass ...** I can't help thinking (that) ..., I have the distinct feeling (that) ...; **welchen ~ haben Sie von ihm?** what's your impression of him?, what do you think (*od.* make) of him?; **sie stand noch unter dem ~ dieses Erlebnisses** she was still captivated by (*od.* under the spell of) that experience; *im neg. Sinn*: she was still haunted by that experience; → **erwehren** 2, **schinden** I 3; **2.** (*Spur*) imprint, impression

eindrücken (*trennb.*, hat -ge-) **I.** *v/t.* **1.** (*zerbrechen*) break; (*zerschlagen*) smash (in) (*auch Nase*); (*Tür*) force, break down; (*platt drücken*) flatten; (*zerdrücken*) crush (*auch Rippen*); (*verbeulen*) dent; **2. etw. ~** (*in* + *Akk.*) press s.th. in(to); **II.** *v/refl. auch fig.* make (*od.* leave) an impression (*in* + *Akk.* in); **eindrücklich** *Adj. bes. schw.* impressive

eindrucksvoll *Adj.* impressive

eine → **ein¹**, **einer**

einebnen *v/t.* (*trennb.*, hat -ge-) **1.** (*Beet, Unebenheiten etc.*) level (off); **2.** *fig.* (*Unterschiede*) level out

Einehe *f* monogamy

eineiig *Adj.*: **~e Zwillinge** identical (monozygotic *fachspr.*) twins

eineinhalb *Adj.* one and a half; **~ Stunden** one and a half hours; **~fach** *Adj.*: **die ~e Menge** one and a half times the amount, half as much again; **~mal** *Adv.* one and a half times

einen *v/t. geh.* unite

einengen *v/t.* (*trennb.*, hat -ge-) **1.** (*Bewegungsfreiheit, Spielraum etc.*) restrict, limit, curb; (*Person*) hem in, restrict, constrict; **j-n in s-n Rechten ~** restrict s.o.'s rights; → **eingeengt**, **2.** (*Begriff*) narrow down (*auf* + *Akk.* to), limit (to); **Einengung** *f* limitation; restriction

einer, **eine**, **ein(e)s** *unbest. Pron.* **1.** *Person*: one; *Sache*: one (thing); **einer m-r Freunde** a friend of mine; **einer von beiden** *od.* **ihnen** one (or other) of them; **gib mir ein(e)s davon** give me one of them; **alles in einem** all in one go; **ein(e)s ist sicher** one thing is certain; **einer** *od.* **ein(e)s nach dem andern** one after the other; (*nicht gleichzeitig*) one at a time; **es kam ein(e)s zum andern** one thing led to another; **schlau** *etc.* **wie kaum/nur einer** clever *etc.* with few equals / like nobody else; **du bist ja einer!** *umg.* you're a fine one!; **lass dir ein(e)s gesagt sein** take it from me; **noch ein(e)s (, bevor ich es vergesse)** and another thing (before it slips my mind); **einer für alle und alle für einen** one for all and all for one; **2.** (*jemand*) one; (*man*) you; **das soll einer verstehen!** and we *etc.*

are meant to understand that?; *kennst du eine, die das macht?* do you know anyone who does that?; *das tut einem gut* that does you good; *sieh mal einer an!* well I never, well what do you know!; **3.** (*der, die, das gleiche*) the same; *es kommt alles auf ein(e)s heraus* it all boils (*od.* comes) down to the same thing; **4.** *umg., in Wendungen: j-m eine kleben* thump (*od.* belt) s.o.; *einen in der Krone haben* have had a drop too much (to drink); *eine od. eins draufkriegen* get thrashed; → *ein*[1] III

Einer *m; -s, -* **1.** *mst Pl.*; *Math.* unit, digit; **2.** (*Boot*) single (sculler); *~kajak m Sport* single-seater kayak

einerlei I. *Adj. indekl.* **1.** *präd.*: *das ist mir ~* it's all the same to me; *~, ob/ wer etc.* no matter whether/who; *~, wir tun es einfach!* it doesn't matter, we'll do it anyway!; **2.** (*gleichartig*) the same; the same sort (*od.* kind) of; **II. Einerlei** *n; -s, kein Pl.* monotony; *das ~ des Alltags* the daily grind (*od.* rut)

einerseits *Adv.* on the one hand
Einerstelle *f Math.* unit (place)
eines I. *unbest. Pron.* → *einer*, **II.** *unbest. Art.* (*Gen. von* → *ein*[1] I)
einesteils *Adv.* on the one hand
Eineuro|centstück *n* one-(euro)cent piece; *~stück n* one-euro piece
einexerzieren *v/t.* (*trennb., hat*) **1.** (*einüben*) drill, train; **2.** *j-m etw. ~* drill (*od.* train) s.o. in s.th.
einfach I. *Adj.* **1.** (*leicht*) *Aufgabe, Rechnung etc.*: easy, simple; *Lösung, Problem etc.*: straightforward; (*einleuchtend*) *Erklärung, Grund*: obvious, simple; *es ist ~ zu verstehen, warum* you can (easily) understand (*od.* see) why; *nichts ~er (als das)!* no problem at all!; *du machst es dir reichlich ~ mit der Entscheidung* you're making it really easy for yourself to make the decision; *warum ~, wenn's umständlich auch geht?* *umg. iro.* the option would be too simple, I suppose!; **2.** (*Ggs. mehrfach*) *Ausführung, Knoten etc.*: single; *Bruch, Mehrheit*: simple; *Buchführung*: single-entry; **3.** *~e Fahrkarte* single (ticket), *Am.* one-way ticket; *X ~, bitte* a single (*Am.* one--way) to X, please; **4.** (*schlicht*) simple; *auch Essen*: plain; (*bescheiden*) modest; *Mensch*: ordinary; *er ist nur ein ~er Soldat* (*kein Offizier*) he is just an ordinary soldier; **II.** *Adv.* **1.** easily, simply; *zu ~ darstellen/dargestellt* oversimplify/oversimplified; **2.** *~ gefaltet etc.* folded etc. once; **3.** *~ leben* live simply (*od.* a simple life); **4.** *umg. verstärkend*: simply, just; *das ist ~ unglaublich/toll!* that's just incredible / really great; *das ist ~ e-e Unverschämtheit* it's a downright cheek; **5.** *umg.* (*ohne Zögern, Nachdenken etc.*): *warum tust du's nicht ~?* why don't you just do it?; *er ist ~ gegangen* he just got up and left (*without so much as a by-your-leave*); **6.** *umg.* (*nun mal*): *ich hab ~ nicht genug Geld dafür* I quite simply (*Am.* I just) don't have enough (*od.* the) money for that; *die Sache ist ~ die, dass ...* it's like this ...; *ich weiß nicht warum, ich hab ~ ein komisches Gefühl dabei* I just feel really funny (*od.* have a funny feeling) about it; **Einfachheit** *f* simplicity; (*Schlichtheit*) plainness; *der ~ halber* to simplify matters, for the sake of simplicity

einfädeln (*trennb., hat -ge-*) **I.** *v/t.* **1.** (*Nadel, Faden, Film etc.*) thread (*in + Akk.* into); **2.** *fig. geschickt*: arrange, fix up, engineer; (*tun*) go about s.th. *od.* (*+ Ger.*); *alles geschickt ~* set things up well; **II.** *v/refl. Mot.* merge, filter in; *sich links ~* filter (*Am.* merge) left; **III.** *v/i. Skislalom*: straddle a gate

einfahren (*unreg., trennb.*) **I.** *v/i.* (*ist eingefahren*): *~* (*in + Akk.*) *mit Auto*: drive in(to); (*ankommen*) arrive (in, at); *Zug*: *auch* come in(to), pull in(to); **II.** *v/t.* (*hat*) **1.** (*Auto*) run in; **2.** *Tech.* (*Antenne, Fahrgestell etc.*) retract; **3.** (*Zaun etc.*) drive into; (*umfahren*) *auch* knock down; **4.** (*Ernte*) bring in, harvest; **5.** *Wirts.* (*Gewinne etc.*) make, bring in; (*Verluste*) make, suffer; **III.** *v/refl.* (*hat*) **1.** (*sich an ein Auto etc. gewöhnen*) get used to a car etc., break a car etc. in; **2.** (*sich einspielen*) start to run smoothly; (*zur Gewohnheit werden*) become a habit (*bei* with); *es hat sich bei uns so eingefahren, dass ...* *auch* we just got into the habit of (*+ Ger.*); → *eingefahren* II

Einfahrt *f* **1.** *zu Grundstück, Hafen, Tunnel etc.*: entrance; (*Auffahrt*) drive; *~ freihalten!* keep clear; *keine ~!* no entry; **2.** *nur Sg.*; (*das Hineinfahren*) entry; *Vorsicht bei der ~* (*des Zuges*) please stand back (from the platform, *Am.* track); **3.**; **4.** *zur Autobahn*: access road

Einfall *m* **1.** (*Gedanke*) idea (*zu + Inf.* of *+ Ger.*); *er hatte den plötzlichen ~ zu* (*+ Inf.*) he had (*od.* took) a sudden notion to (*+ Inf.*); *auf den ~ kommen, etw. zu tun* hit upon the idea of doing something; *das war nur so ein ~ (von mir*) it was just an idea (I had *od.* of mine); **2.** *Mil.* invasion (*in + Akk.* of); (*Überfall*) raid (on); **3.** *nur Sg.*; *Phys., Licht*: incidence; **4.** *geh.* (*plötzliches Einsetzen*) onset

einfallen *v/i.* (*unreg., trennb., ist -ge-*) **1.** *Idee*: *mir fällt gerade ein* it has just occurred to me; *mir fällt nichts Besseres ein* I can't think of anything better; *da musst du dir schon was Besseres ~ lassen* you'll have to do (*od.* come up with something) better than that; *ihm fällt immer was ein* he always comes up with (*od.* thinks of) something, he's never at a loss for ideas (*od.* an excuse etc.); *zu dem Thema fällt mir nichts mehr ein* I can't think of anything else to say on the subject; *dazu fällt mir gar nichts ein* my mind's a blank (on that); *ich werde mir schon was ~ lassen* I'll think of (*od.* come up with) something; *was fällt dir ein?* *vorwurfsvoll*: what do you think you're doing?; *abwehrend*: you must be joking!; *lass dir ja nicht ~, mich anzulügen!* don't you even think about lying to me!; *wie's ihm gerade einfällt* just as the mood takes him; *wo's mir gerade einfällt* while I think of it; *fällt mir gar nicht ein!* *umg.* who do you think I am?, you must be joking!; *so etwas würde mir nie od. im Traum nicht ~* I wouldn't dream of it; **2.** *Erinnerung*: *es fällt mir im Moment nicht ein* I can't think of it right now; *mir fällt gerade ein* I've just remembered; *es wird mir schon wieder ~* it'll come back to me (eventually); **3.** *in ein Land ~ Mil.* invade a country; **4.** *~* (*in + Akk.*) *Licht*: enter, come in(to); **5.** *~* (*in + Akk.*) (*einstim-*

men) join in; *in ein Lied*: come in; *in ein Gespräch*: butt (*od.* break) in (on); **6.** (*einstürzen*) collapse, cave in; → *eingefallen* II; *einfallend* **I.** *Part. Präs.* → *einfallen*; **II.** *Adj. Licht*: incident

einfallslos *Adj.* unimaginative; (*langweilig*) boring; **Einfallslosigkeit** *f* lack of imagination, unimaginativeness

einfallsreich I. *Adj.* full of ideas, original; (*findig*) resourceful; **II.** *Adv.* imaginatively, with plenty of imagination; **Einfallsreichtum** *m; nur Sg.* wealth of ideas (*od.* imagination), imaginativeness; (*Findigkeit*) resourcefulness; *dieser ~! auch* where does he etc. get all these ideas from?

Einfallswinkel *m* angle of incidence
Einfalt *f; -, kein Pl.*; *geh.* **1.** naivety, *bes. Am.* naiveté; (*Beschränktheit*) simple-mindedness; *heilige ~!* how naive can you be!; **2.** (*Reinheit*) innocence, simplicity; **einfältig** *Adj.* naive; (*beschränkt*) simple-minded; *Lächeln etc.*: stupid, dumb *umg.*; **Einfaltspinsel** *m umg. pej.* nincompoop, numskull, simpleton

Einfamilienhaus *n* detached house, *Am.* single family house (*od.* home)

einfangen *v/t.* (*unreg., trennb., hat -ge-*) **1.** (*Flüchtige, Tiere*) catch, capture; **2.** *fig.* (*Stimmung etc.*) capture; **3.** *umg.*: *sich* (*Dat.*) *e-n Schnupfen ~* catch a cold; *du fängst dir gleich eine Ohrfeige ein* you're heading for a slap!

einfärben *v/t.* (*trennb., hat -ge-*) dye
einfarbig I. *Adj. Stoff*: plain, single-colo(u)r; *Fot., Druck.* monochrome, monochromatic; **II.** *Adv.*: *~ blau etc.* solid blue etc.; *~ streichen* paint s.th. one colo(u)r, paint s.th. all the same colo(u)r; *~ gestalten* design s.th. in one (basic) colo(u)r

einfassen *v/t.* (*trennb., hat -ge-*) enclose; *mit e-m Zaun*: fence in; (*Beet, Rasen*) border, edge; (*Quelle*) build a wall around, wall in; (*umsäumen*) line; (*Kleidung*) trim; (*Bild, Brillengläser*) frame; (*Edelstein*) set; **Einfassung** *f* enclosure; (*Umsäumung*) lining; (*Rand*) edge, border; (*Saum*) trim(ming); (*Rahmen*) frame; *e-s Edelsteins*: setting

einfetten *v/t.* (*trennb., hat -ge-*) grease; *mit Öl*: oil; *Tech. auch* lubricate; (*Haut*) rub (some) cream into; (*Schuhe etc.*) soften s.th. up with dubbin

einfinden *v/refl.* (*unreg., trennb., hat -ge-*) arrive, turn up *umg.*; (*sich versammeln*) assemble, gather; *sich bei j-m ~* present o.s. (*od.* report) to s.o.

einflechten *v/t.* (*unreg., trennb., hat -ge-*) **1.** *~* (*in + Akk.*) weave in(to); *sich* (*Dat.*) *Bänder ins Haar ~* braid (*od.* plait) ribbons into one's hair; **2.** (*Haare*) plait, *Am.* braid; **3.** *fig.*: *~* (*in + Akk.*) work in(to); (*beiläufig erwähnen*) mention in passing; *~, dass ... auch* throw in that ...

einfliegen (*unreg., trennb., -ge-*); *Flug.* **I.** *v/i.* (*ist eingeflogen*) **1.** *~* (*in + Akk.*) fly in(to), enter; **2.** (*sich dem Flughafen nähern*) approach; **II.** *v/t.* (*hat*) **1.** (*Truppen, Vorräte etc.*) fly in (*nach* to); **2.** (*Flugzeug*) test-fly

einfließen *v/i.* (*unreg., trennb., ist -ge-*) **1.** *~* (*in + Akk.*) *Wasser etc.*: flow into; *kalte Luft*: enter; **2.** *fig.*: *etw. ~ lassen* slip s.th. in; (*andeuten*) let s.th. be known, drop a hint; *~ lassen, dass ...* let it be known that ...; *er hat es gesprächs-*

weise ~ lassen he slipped it into the conversation

einflößen v/t. (trennb., hat -ge-): **j-m etw. ~** (Medizin etc.) give s.o. s.th.; (Alkohol) make s.o. drink s.th.; Med. auch administer s.th. to s.o. förm.; (Suppe) auch feed s.o. s.th.; fig. fill s.o. with s.th.; (Mut) give s.o. s.th.; **j-m Respekt ~** instil(l) respect in s.o., teach s.o. a bit of respect; **j-m Vertrauen ~** inspire confidence in s.o.; **j-m Furcht/ Respekt ~d aussehen** look forbidding / have an air of authority

Einflug m Flug. flight (**in + Akk.** into); **beim ~ in den russischen Luftraum beobachtet werden** be observed flying into (od. entering) Russian airspace

einflüg(e)lig Adj. Tür: attr. single-wing …

Einflugschneise f Flug. approach corridor

Einfluss m influence (**auf etw./j-n** on s.th. / on od. over od. over s.th.); clout umg.; (Macht) power (over); (Wirkung) effect (on); **~ haben auf** (+ Akk.) influence; (einwirken auf) auch affect; **~ ausüben** od. **nehmen auf** (+ Akk.) have (od. exert) an influence on; **e-n schlechten ~ haben auf** (+ Akk.) Mensch: be a bad influence on; Sache: have a bad effect on; **unter j-s ~ ste- hen/geraten** be/come under s.o.'s influence; **unter dem ~ von Drogen** etc. under the influence of drugs etc.; **s-n** (**ganzen**) **~ geltend machen** bring (all) one's influence to bear (**bei** od. **auf +** Akk. on); **es entzieht sich m-m ~** it's beyond my control, I have no influence in the matter; **ein Mann von** (**großem**) **~** a (highly) influential man, a man with (considerable) clout umg.; **~bereich** m sphere of influence; **Deutschland liegt im ~ e-s Azorenhochs** Germany's weather is being affected by a ridge of high pressure over the Azores

einflusslos Adj. lacking influence; (machtlos) powerless; **Einflusslosigkeit** f lack of influence; (Machtlosigkeit) powerlessness

Einflussnahme f; -, kein Pl. exerting influence (**auf +** Akk. on); **wegen versuchter ~ auf die Zeugin** for attempting to influence the witness

einflussreich Adj. influential; (mächtig) powerful

Einflusssphäre f sphere of influence

einflüstern v/t. (trennb., hat -ge-): **j-m etw. ~** whisper s.th. to s.o.; fig. pej. (heimlich einreden) put s.th. into (od. plant s.th. in) s.o.'s mind; **Einflüsterung** f insinuation

einfordern v/t. (trennb., hat -ge-) demand (payment of); (Buch etc.) recall, demand the return of

einförmig Adj. uniform; (eintönig) monotonous; **Einförmigkeit** f uniformity; monotony

Einfriedung f enclosure

einfrieren (unreg., trennb.) **I.** v/i. (ist eingefroren) **1.** Wasser: freeze; Rohre etc.: freeze (up); Bach, Teich: freeze (over); Schiff, Hafen: become icebound; **2.** fig. Verhandlungen: reach (a) deadlock; **3.** fig. Lächeln: freeze; **II.** v/t. (hat) **1.** (Lebensmittel) (deep-)- freeze; **2.** fig. (Löhne, Kapital, Preise) freeze; (Beziehungen, Verhandlungen) suspend, put on hold; (Projekt, Plan) shelve, put into cold storage

einfügen (trennb., hat -ge-) **I.** v/t.: **~** (**in + Akk.**) (einpassen) fit in(to); bes. in e-n Text: insert (in); als Zusatz: add

(to),; **II.** v/refl. fit in (well); Person: adapt (**in + Akk.** to); **Einfügetaste** f Computer: insert key; **Einfügung** f insertion; (Zusatz) addition

einfühlen v/refl. (trennb., hat -ge-): **sich in j-n ~** empathize with s.o., put o.s. in s.o.'s shoes; **sich in etw.** (Akk.) **~** get the feel of s.th.; **einfühlsam** Adj. sensitive; (verständnisvoll) understanding

Einfühlungsvermögen n; nur Sg. (powers Pl. of) empathy; (Verständnis) intuitive understanding; bei Interpretation etc.: sensitivity

Einfuhr f; -, -en; Wirts. importing, importation; konkret: (Waren) imports Pl.; **~beschränkungen** Pl. import restrictions; **~bestimmungen** Pl. import regulations

einführen (trennb., hat -ge-) **I.** v/t. **1.** als Neuerung: introduce (**in + Akk.** into); (Einrichtungen) establish, set up; **das wollen wir gar nicht erst ~** umg. we're not going to start that sort of thing, we're not having any of that; **2.** Wirts. (Waren) import; **3.** (j-n) in Familie, Gesellschaft: introduce (**in + Akk.** into; **bei j-m** to s.o.); **j-n bei Hofe ~** present s.o. at court; **in die Gesellschaft eingeführt werden** junge Dame: be initiated into society; **4.** (j-n) in Arbeit etc.: introduce (**in + Akk.** to); (einweisen, vorstellen) initiate (into); (vertraut machen) familiarize (with); feierlich, in ein Amt: instal(l) (in); **5.** (etw.) in e-e Öffnung etc.: insert (**in + Akk.** into); (zuführen) (Draht, Leitung) feed in(to); **II.** v/refl.: **sich gut ~** Person: make a good first impression; Ware: be successfully launched; → **eingeführt** II; **einführend I.** Part. Präs. → **einführen**; **II.** Adj.: **~e Worte** introductory words; **~e Worte sprechen** give a spoken introduction

Einfuhr|erklärung f Wirts. import declaration; **~genehmigung** f import licen|ce (Am. -se); **~hafen** m port of entry; **~quote** f import quota; **~stopp** m import ban

Einführung f **1.** allg. introduction; von Einrichtungen: establishment; in Arbeit etc.: initiation; in Amt: installation; in Öffnung etc.: insertion; **2.** Wirts. importation; **3.** (Text) introduction (**in + Akk.** to)

Einführungs|angebot n Wirts. introductory offer; **~kurs** m **1.** Päd., Univ. introductory (od. beginner's) course; **2.** Wirts., von Aktien: issue price; **~preis** m Wirts. introductory price

Einfuhr|verbot n Wirts. import ban; **~zoll** m import duty

einfüllen v/t. (trennb., hat -ge-): **~** (**in + Akk.**) (Flüssiges, Getreide etc.) pour in(to); in Flaschen: bottle; (Kartoffeln etc.) fill (od. put) in(to); Kartoffeln etc. **in Säcke ~** auch fill (the) sacks with potatoes etc.

Einfüllstutzen m Mot. filler neck (od. pipe)

Eingabe f **1.** (Bitte) application; (Gesuch) petition (**an + Akk.** to; **um** for); (Beschwerde) complaint; **e-e ~ machen** file a petition, apply (**um** for); **2.** nur Sg.; (das Einreichen) submission (**bei** to); **3.** EDV input; **nach ~ der Daten** after inputting the data; **4.** nur Sg.; Med. administering (+ Gen. of); **~fehler** m EDV input error; **~maske** f EDV input mask; **~taste** f Computer: enter (od. return) key

Eingang m **1.** entrance (+ Gen. of od. to), way in; **kein ~!** no entry; **2.** des

Darms, Magens etc.: inlet; e-r Höhle, e-s Tunnels: entrance, mouth; **am ~ des Dorfes** where you enter the village; **3.** nur Sg.; (Eintritt) entry (**in + Akk.** into); (Zugang) access (**zu** to); **~ finden in** (+ Akk.) fig. Sache: become established in; (in e-e Gruppe) Person: be accepted into; **sich ~ verschaffen in** (+ Akk.) gain admission to; **4.** Wirts., Amtspr. von Waren: arrival; von Schreiben, Summe: receipt; **Eingänge von Waren/Zahlungen** goods/ payments received; (Einnahmen) receipts; **„Eingänge"** Aufschrift: "In"; **bei** od. **nach ~** on receipt; **5.** nur Sg.; geh. (Anfang) beginning; **zu ~** at the beginning; **6.** Etech., Etron. source, input

eingängig I. Adj. **1.** Melodie: catchy; **2.** geh. (verständlich) comprehensible, easy to grasp (od. understand); **II.** Adv. geh.: **~ erläutern** explain in simple terms

eingangs I. Adv. at the beginning (od. start, outset); (einleitend) by way of introduction; **~ erwähnt** mentioned at the start; (oben erwähnt) mentioned above; **II.** Präp. + Gen.; geh. at the beginning of

Eingangs|bereich m e-s Gebäudes: entrance area, lobby; bes. Theater etc.: foyer; **~bestätigung** f acknowledg(e)- ment of receipt; **~datum** n date of receipt; von Schecks: value date; **~halle** f entrance hall, lobby; bes. Theater etc.: foyer; **~leistung** f Etech. input (power); **~spannung** f Etech. input voltage; **~stempel** m date stamp; **~strom** m Etech. input current; **~tor** n (entrance) gate; **~tür** f entrance; **~vermerk** m file mark

eingebaut I. P.P. → **einbauen**; **II.** Adj. built-in

eingeben v/t. (unreg., trennb., hat -ge-) **1.** in e-n Computer: feed, enter, input (**in + Akk.** into); **2.** (Arznei) give, administer (+ Dat. to); **3.** j-m e-n Gedanken **~** give s.o. an idea

eingebettet Adj. embedded (**in + Akk.** in); **~ zwischen Bergen/Wäldern** etc. tucked away (od. nestling) between mountains / among woods and trees etc.

eingebildet I. P.P. → **einbilden**; **II.** Adj. **1.** conceited (**auf + Akk.** about), arrogant; **er ist auf s-e neue Stelle furchtbar ~** his new job has gone to his head completely; **2.** Krankheit etc.: imaginary; Schwangerschaft: phantom; **ein ~er Kranker** a hypochondriac

eingeboren Adj. **1.** attr.; (einheimisch) native; **2.** geh. (angeboren) innate; **3.** Reli.: **Gottes ~er Sohn** the only begotten Son of God; **Eingeborene** m, f; -n, -n; neg! native; bes. Australiens: aborigine

Eingeborenen|sprache f native language; **~stamm** m native tribe

Eingebung f: (**e-e göttliche** divine) inspiration; (Regung) impulse; (Einfall) brainwave; **e-r ~ folgend** acting on impulse

eingedeckt I. P.P. → **eindecken**; **II.** Adj.: **gut ~ sein** be well stocked; **mit etw.**: auch have plenty of s.th.; **mit Arbeit**: have plenty of work to do (od. to be getting on with)

eingedenk Adj. präd. geh. mindful (+ Gen. of); **e-r Sache ~ bleiben** keep s.th. in mind, remember s.th.; **~ der Tatsache, dass …** bearing in mind that …

eingeengt I. *P.P.* → *einengen*; **II.** *Adj.* restricted; *sich ~ fühlen* feel cramped

eingefahren I. *P.P.* → *einfahren*; **II.** *Adj.* **1.** *Auto etc.*: run in, *Am.* broken in; **2.** *fig. Verhaltensweise etc.*: ingrained; *das ist bei ihr vollkommen ~* it's become second nature to her, it's second nature with (*od.* for) her; *sich in ~en Bahnen od. Gleisen bewegen* keep to well-trodden paths, stay on the beaten path

eingefallen I. *P.P.* → *einfallen*; **II.** *Adj.* **1.** *Haus*: dilapidated; **2.** *Gesicht, Aussehen*: haggard; *Wangen, Augen*: hollow, sunken

eingefleischt *Adj.*; *mst attr.* **1.** *Gegner, Raucher etc.*: inveterate, ingrained, hardened; *Junggeselle*: confirmed; **2.** *Gewohnheit, Vorurteil etc.*: deep-rooted

eingeführt I. *P.P.* → *einführen*; **II.** *Adj.* **1.** *ein (gut) ~es Geschäft* a well-established business; **2.** *~e Waren* imported goods, imports

eingehen (*unreg., trennb., ist -ge-*) **I.** *v/i.* **1.** *Kleidung*: shrink; **2.** *Tier, Pflanze*: die (*an + Dat.* of); *dabei geht man ja ein!* *umg., bei großer Anstrengung etc.*: it's enough to finish you off; *bei dieser Hitze geht man ja ein* this heat kills you; *ich gehe noch od. fast ein vor Durst/Hitze etc. umg.* I'm dying of thirst/heat *etc.*; **3.** *umg. fig. Firma, Zeitung*: fold, go under; **4.** *umg. fig.* (*e-n Misserfolg erleiden*) come to grief; *auch* come a cropper (*bei* with); **5.** *~ auf* (+ *Akk.*) (*Interesse zeigen für*) show an interest in; (*sich befassen mit*) deal with; *auf e-e Frage etc.*: go into; *auf e-n Scherz etc.*: go along with; *auf e-n Plan etc.*: accept; *auf j-n* respond to; *zuhörend*: listen to; *nachsichtig*: humo(u)r; *auf die Frage* (+ *Gen.*) *~ auch* address the issue of; *näher ~ auf* elaborate on, expand on, amplify; (*überhaupt*) *nicht ~ auf auch* ignore (completely); *darauf will ich jetzt nicht ~* I don't want to go into that now; **6.** *Wirts., Amtsspr.* (*eintreffen*) *Geld, Post, Waren*: come in, arrive; *ist mein Schreiben bei Ihnen eingegangen?* have you received my letter?; **7.** *~ in* (+ *Akk.*) (*Eingang finden*) enter; *in die Annalen od. Geschichte ~* go down in history; *in das Reich Gottes ~* enter the Kingdom of God; *sind diese Überlegungen in Ihren Artikel / in die Planung eingegangen?* have these considerations found a place in your article / been taken up in the plans?; **8.** *umg.*: *das will mir nicht ~!* (*ich verstehe es nicht*) I can't grasp it; (*ich will es nicht wahrhaben*) I can't accept it, I can't come to terms with it; **II.** *v/t.* **1.** (*Vertrag*) enter into; (*Verpflichtung etc.*) take on; (*Risiko*) take; (*Wette*) make; (*Kompromiss*) accept; *e-n Vergleich ~* come to an arrangement; *mit Gläubigern*: reach a settlement(*od.* compound *fachspr.*); *die Ehe ~ mit geh.* enter into marriage with; *darauf gehe ich jede Wette ein* I bet you anything that'll happen; **2.** *Chem.* (*Verbindung*) form; (*Reaktion*) undergo

eingehend I. *Part. Präs.* → *eingehen*; **II.** *Adj. nur attr.* **1.** *Post etc.*: incoming; **2.** (*ausführlich*) detailed; *Bericht: auch* full ...; (*gründlich*) thorough; *Artikel etc.*: in-depth ...; (*sorgfältig*) careful; **III.** *Adv.* in detail; in depth; (*sorgfältig*) carefully; *sich ~ mit etw. befassen etc. auch*

look at s.th. from every angle

eingehüllt I. *P.P.* → *einhüllen*; **II.** *Adj. fig.*: *in Nebel etc. ~* enveloped (*od.* shrouded) in mist *etc.*

eingekeilt *Adj.* wedged in (*zwischen + Dat.* between); *in Stau, Parklücke etc.*: hemmed in

eingekerbt I. *P.P.* → *einkerben*; **II.** *Adj.* scalloped, notched

eingeklammert I. *P.P.* → *einklammern*; **II.** *Adj.* in brackets, *bes. Am.* in parentheses; bracketed off

eingeklemmt I. *P.P.* → *einklemmen*; **II.** *Adj.* stuck; *Nerv*: trapped; *Bruch*: strangulated

eingeknickt I. → *einknicken*; **II.** *Adj.*: *ein Hund mit eingeknicktem Ohr/ Schwanz* a dog with a bent ear / with a kink in his tail

eingekniffen I. *P.P.* → *einkneifen*; **II.** *Adj.*: *mit ~em Schwanz abziehen* slink off with its (*auch fig.* one's) tail between its (*fig.* one's) legs

eingelagert I. *P.P.* → *einlagern*; **II.** *Adj. Möbel etc.*: *präd. od. nachgestellt.*: in storage

eingelegt I. *P.P.* → *einlegen*; **II.** *Adj.* **1.** *~e Gurke* gherkin, pickled cucumber, *Am.* pickle; **2.** *~er Schrank* inlaid cupboard; **3.** *Mot.*: *mit ~em Gang parken* park with the car *etc.* in gear, leave the car *etc.* in gear when parking

Eingemachte *n*; *-n, kein Pl.* preserves *Pl.*; *Obst*: preserved fruit; *in Essig*: pickles *Pl.*; *jetzt geht's ans ~ umg. fig.* we're really scraping the barrel now

eingemeinden *v/t.* (*trennb., hat*) incorporate; **Eingemeindung** *f* incorporation

eingenommen I. *P.P.* → *einnehmen*; **II.** *Adj.* **1.** *~ sein von* be taken with; *von sich selbst ~ sein* be full of o.s.; **2.** *~ sein für/gegen* be bias(s)ed *od.* prejudiced in favo(u)r of / against; **Eingenommenheit** *f* **1.** partiality; *für/gegen* bias *od.* prejudice) in favo(u)r of / against; **2.** (*~ von sich selbst*) conceitedness

eingerechnet I. *P.P.* → *einrechnen*; **II.** *Adj.*: *... (nicht) ~* (not) including ..., *weitS.* (not) taking into account ...; *alles ~* including everything, *weitS.* all in all

eingerostet I. *P.P.* → *einrosten*; **II.** *Adj.*: (*völlig*) *~* (completely) rusted up, rusted solid

eingeschenkt I. *P.P.* → *einschenken*; **II.** *Adj.*: *ein gut ~es Glas* a generously filled glass

eingeschlechtig *Adj. Bot.* unisexual

eingeschlechtlich *Adj.* **1.** *umg.* (*Bot.*) unisexual; **2.** *Ling. attr.* single-gender; **3.** *Gruppe, Klasse: attr.* single-sex

eingeschlossen I. *P.P.* → *einschließen*; **II.** *Adj.* **1.** *Geld etc.*: locked up; *Person*: locked in; (*umgeben*) enclosed; (*umzingelt*) surrounded, encircled; **2.** *im Preis ~* included in the price; *es ist alles (im Preis) ~* the price is all-inclusive

eingeschnappt I. *P.P.* → *einschnappen*; **II.** *Adj. präd.* in a huff (*Am. auch* snit), *Brit. auch* miffed; *er ist schnell ~* he's quick to take offen|ce (*Am.* -se)

eingeschneit *Adj. Dorf, Haus*: snowbound; *wir waren e-e Woche ~* we were snowed in (*od.* snowbound) for a week

eingeschnitten I. *P.P.* → *einschneiden*; **II.** *Adj.*: *ein tief ~es Tal* a deep(ly carved) valley

eingeschossig *Adj. attr.* one-stor(e)y

...

eingeschränkt I. *P.P.* → *einschränken*; **II.** *Adj.* limited, restricted; *~es Halteverbot* ban on parking except for certain purposes; *sich ~ fühlen* feel restricted

eingeschrieben I. *P.P.* → *einschreiben*; **II.** *Adj.* **1.** *Brief*: registered; **2.** *Univ.*: *~ sein* be registered (*Am.* enrolled) (*an + Dat.* at); **3.** *Math.* inscribed; *~er Kreis* inscribed circle, incircle

eingeschüchtert I. *P.P.* → *einschüchtern*; **II.** *Adj.* frightened; *er war völlig ~* he was too intimidated (*od.* scared) to say or do anything

eingeschworen I. *P.P.* → *einschwören*; **II.** *Adj.* confirmed; (*treu*) *auch* committed; *~e Gemeinschaft* closely-knit community; *~ sein auf* swear by; *Politik*: be committed to

eingespannt I. *P.P.* → *einspannen*; **II.** *Adj.*: *stark ~ sein* be heavily committed, have a heavy workload

eingespielt I. *P.P.* → *einspielen*; **II.** *Adj.*: *sie sind gut aufeinander ~* they make a good team, they work (*Sport, Mus.* play) well together; *sie sind ein ~es Team auch* they're a well-coordinated team, they've been working (*Sport, Mus.* playing) together for years

eingesprengt I. *P.P.* → *einsprengen*; **II.** *Adj.*: *mit ~en ...* interspersed with ..., scattered with ...

eingestandenermaßen *Adv.* admittedly; **Eingeständnis** *n* admission; *e-r größeren Schuld*: confession

eingestaubt I. *P.P.* → *einstauben*; **II.** *Adj.* very dusty, covered in dust

eingestehen *v/t.* (*unreg., trennb., hat*) admit; *Verbrechen*: confess to; *sie hat die Tat eingestanden* she admitted that she had done it; *er wollte (es) sich nicht ~, dass er Angst hatte* he didn't want to admit to himself that he was afraid

eingestellt I. *P.P.* → *einstellen*; **II.** *Adj.* **1.** *gegen j-n/etw. ~ sein* be opposed to s.o./s.th.; **2.** *~ auf* (+ *Akk.*) (*vorbereitet auf*) prepared for; (*ausgerichtet, abgestimmt auf*) geared to; *ich bin schon ganz auf Urlaub ~* I'm in a really holiday mood, *Am.* I'm really ready for (a) vacation; **3.** *mit Adj. od. Adv.*: *sozial ~* socially-minded; *materialistisch ~* materialistic (in one's attitudes); *sehr fortschrittlich ~ sein* be very progressive (in one's views), have very progressive views; *wie ist er politisch ~?* what are his political leanings?

eingestimmt I. *P.P.* → *einstimmen*; **II.** *Adj. fig.*: *aufeinander ~ sein* be attuned to (*od.* in harmony with) one another

eingestrichen I. *P.P.* → *einstreichen*; **II.** *Adj. Mus.*: *das ~e C/A* middle C / A above middle C

eingesunken I. *P.P.* → *einsinken*; **II.** *Adj.*: *~e Wangen* sunken cheeks

eingetragen I. *P.P.* → *eintragen*; **II.** *Adj.*: *~er Verein* (*abgek. e.V.*) registered association; *~es Warenzeichen* registered trademark

eingewachsen I. *P.P.* → *einwachsen*[1]; **II.** *Adj.* **1.** *Zehennagel etc.*: ingrown; **2.** *Garten*: mature

eingewandert I. *P.P.* → *einwandern*; **II.** *Adj.*: *~e Familie etc.* immigrant family *etc.*

Eingeweide *Pl. Anat.* inside *Sg.*, innards *umg.*; *fachspr.* viscera; (*Gedär-*

E

me) intestines, guts

eingeweiht I. *P.P.* → *einweihen*; **II.** *Adj.*: ~ *sein* (*Mitwisser sein*) be in the know, be in on it *umg.*; **Eingeweihte** *m, f*; *-n, -n* insider; *die* ~*n auch* those in the know

eingewöhnen (*trennb., hat*) **I.** *v/refl.* get used to one's new surroundings, settle in; *sich* ~ *in* (+ *Dat.*) get used to; **II.** *v/t.*: *j-n/ ein Tier* ~ (*in* + *Dat.*) settle (in); **Eingewöhnungszeit** *f* settling-in period

eingezwängt I. *P.P.* → *einzwängen*; **II.** *Adj.* **1.** ~ *in* (+ *Dat.*) packed (*od.* jammed) into; **2.** *fig.* straitjacketed; *sich* ~ *fühlen auch* feel severely restricted

eingießen *v/t.* (*unreg., trennb., hat -ge-*): ~ (*in* + *Akk.*) pour in(to); (*einschenken*) pour (out); *Tech.* (*Metall*) cast (into)

eingipsen *v/t.* (*trennb., hat -ge-*) **1.** *Med.* put in plaster, put a (plaster) cast on; **2.** (*Haken etc.*) plaster in

eingleisig I. *Adj. attr.* single-track ..., *präd.* single-tracked; **II.** *Adv.*: ~ *denken* take a very narrow view of things; **Eingleisigkeit** *f fig.* narrow-mindedness

eingliedern (*trennb., hat -ge-*) **I.** *v/t.* **1.** integrate (*in* + *Akk.* into); *in etw. Größeres*: incorporate (into) (*auch Gebiet, Dorf*); (*Land*) annex (to); **2.** (*zuweisen*) assign (*in* + *Akk.* to); **II.** *v/refl.*: *sich* ~ (*in* + *Akk.*) fit in(to), integrate (with); **Eingliederung** *f* integration (*in* + *Akk.* into); *in etw. Größeres*: incorporation (into); *e-s Landes*: annexation (to); (*Zuweisung*) assignment (to); **Eingliederungshilfe** *f für Behinderte, Spätaussiedler etc.*: assistance with social integration

eingraben (*unreg., trennb., hat -ge-*) **I.** *v/t.* (*vergraben*) bury; (*Pflanze*) plant; (*Pfahl*) dig in; **II.** *v/refl.* **1.** *Soldaten*: dig in; *sich* ~ (*in* + *Akk.*) dig o.s. (*Tier*: itself) in(to); **2.** *Geschoss etc.*: embed itself (*in* + *Akk.* in); *die Räder graben sich in den Sand ein* the wheels dig into the sand; *der Fluss hat sich tief ins Hügelland eingegraben* the river has carved a deep channel in the hills; **3.** *geh.* (*einmeißeln*) carve; *sich in j-s Gedächtnis* ~ engrave itself in s.o.'s memory

eingravieren *v/t.* (*trennb., hat*) engrave (*in* + *Akk.* on)

eingreifen (*unreg., trennb., hat -ge-*) *v/i.* **1.** step in, intervene (*in* + *Akk.* in); *unerlaubt, störend*: interfere (in); *bes. Jur.* encroach (on); *in j-s Privatsphäre* ~ intrude on s.o.'s privacy; **2.** *Tech., Zahnrad*: engage, mesh (*in* + *Akk.* with)

Eingreifen *n*; *-s, kein Pl.* intervention; *durch beherztes* ~ *e-s Passanten wurde Schlimmeres verhindert* due to the courageous action of a passerby more serious consequences were averted; **eingreifend I.** *Part. Präs.* → *eingreifen*; **II.** *Adj.* (*entscheidend*) crucial; (*einschneidend*) far-reaching; **Eingreiftruppe** *f Mil.* task force; *schnelle* ~ rapid deployment (*od.* reaction) force

eingrenzen *v/t.* (*trennb., hat -ge-*) **1.** enclose; **2.** (*beschränken*) limit (*auf* + *Akk.* to); *stärker*: narrow down (to)

Eingriff *m* **1.** *auch Pl.* intervention (*in* + *Akk.* in); *unerlaubter, störender*: *auch Pl.* interference (in); *bes. Jur.* encroachment (on); **2.** *Med.* operation; *e-n* ~ *vornehmen* operate (*bei od. an* + *Dat.* on), perform an operation

---

(*on*); **3.** *Unterhose mit* ~ underpants *Pl.* with a fly

eingruppieren *v/t.* (*trennb., hat*) assign (*in* + *Akk.* to)

einhacken *v/i.* (*trennb., hat -ge-*): ~ *auf* (+ *Akk.*) *mit Beil etc.*: hack (away) at; *Vogel*: peck at; *fig.* have a go at *s.o., Am.* hit on *s.o.*

einhageln *v/i. unpers.* (*trennb., hat -ge-*); *fig.*: ~ *auf* (+ *Akk.*) rain down on

einhaken (*trennb., hat -ge-*) **I.** *v/t.* hook (*in* + *Akk.* into), fasten; (*Fensterläden*) fasten back; **II.** *v/refl.*: *sich bei j-m* ~ take s.o.'s arm; *eingehakt gehen* walk arm in arm; **III.** *v/i. fig. im Gespräch*: come (*od.* break) in (*bei* on); *hier möchte ich mal* ~ if I could just take up that point

...einhalb *im Adj.* ... and a half

Einhalt *m*: ~ *gebieten e-r Sache*: call a halt to, put a stop to; *e-r Seuche, dem Vormarsch*: halt; *j-m*: stop

einhalten (*unreg., trennb., hat -ge-*) **I.** *v/t.* (*Vereinbarung etc.*) keep to, comply with; (*Diät, Regeln*) *auch* stick to; (*Versprechen*) keep, stick to; (*Verpflichtung*) meet; (*Verabredung*) keep; *die Gesetze* ~ observe (*od.* comply with) the law, be law-abiding; *den Termin / die Zeit* ~ keep to (*od.* meet) the deadline / time limit; *den Kurs od. die Richtung* ~ keep going in the same direction; **II.** *v/i. lit.*: *halte ein!* stop!; *mit od. im Lesen etc.* ~ stop reading *etc.*; **Einhaltung** *f* adherence (+ *Gen.* to), keeping (of); *von Vereinbarung, Vorschriften etc.*: compliance (with), observance (of); *unter* ~ *der Regeln* (while) complying with the rules

einhämmern *v/t.* (*trennb., hat -ge-*) **1.** (*in* + *Akk.*) hammer in(to); **2.** ~ *auf* (+ *Akk.*) *Boxer etc.*: rain blows on, pummel; *er hämmerte auf das Klavier ein* he pounded away at the piano; **3.** *fig.*: *j-m die Regeln etc.* ~ drum the rules *etc.* into s.o.

einhandeln *v/t.* (*trennb., hat -ge-*) **1.** trade; *etw. gegen od. für etw.* ~ trade (*od.* swap) s.th. for s.th.; **2.** *fig.*: *sich* (*Dat.*) *etw.* ~ land o.s. (with) s.th.; *damit handelst du dir garantiert Ärger ein* that's asking for trouble

einhändig I. *Adj.* one-handed; **II.** *Adv. auch* with (only) one hand

einhängen (*trennb., hat -ge-*) **I.** *v/t.* (*Tür etc.*) put on its hinges, hang; **II.** *vt/i. Telef.*: (*den Hörer*) ~ hang up, *Brit. auch* ring off; **III.** *v/refl.*: *sich bei j-m* ~ take s.o.'s arm; *eingehängt gehen* walk arm in arm

einhauchen *v/t.* (*trennb., hat -ge-*), *geh. fig.*: *j-m / e-r Sache neues Leben* ~ give s.o. new vigo(u)r / breathe new life into s.th.

einhauen (*unreg., trennb., hat -ge-*) **I.** *v/t.* **1.** → *einschlagen* I 1, 2; **2.** (*Inschrift etc.*) carve (*in* + *Akk.* into); **II.** *v/i.*: *auf j-n / ein Tier* ~ lay into s.o. / thrash away at an animal

einheften *v/t.* (*trennb., hat -ge-*); (*Akten etc.*) file; (*Ärmel, Futter*) tack in

einheimisch *Adj.* local, native; *auch Bot., Zool.* indigenous; *Wirts.* domestic; ~*e Agrarprodukte* home-grown produce *Sg.*; ~*e Mannschaft* home team; **Einheimische** *m, f*; *-n, -n*: *ein* ~*r* one of the locals; *die* ~*n* the people (who live) here (*od.* there), the natives; *e-r Stadt*: *auch* the locals

einheimsen *v/t.* (*trennb., hat -ge-*), *umg.* (*Gewinn, Preis etc.*) pocket; (*größere Mengen*) rake in; (*Ruhm etc.*)

---

take

Einheirat *f*: ~ *in* (+ *Akk.*) marriage into; **einheiraten** *v/i.* (*trennb., hat -ge-*): ~ *in* (+ *Akk.*) marry into

Einheit *f* **1.** *nur Sg.* unity; *die drei* ~*en Theat.* the three unities; *e-e* ~ *bilden* form a (unified) whole; *Tag der deutschen* ~ German Unity Day; **2.** *nur Sg.*; (*Einheitlichkeit*) uniformity; **3.** (*Maßeinheit*) unit (*auch Telef.*); *zehn* ~*en vertelefonieren* use ten telephone units; **4.** *Mil.* unit

einheitlich I. *Adj.* **1.** *Kleidung etc.*: uniform; (*genormt*) standardized; *Methode etc.*: consistent; *ein* ~*es Vorgehen* concerted action; **2.** (*in sich geschlossen*) homogenous; ~*e Front* united front; **II.** *Adv.* uniformly; ~ *gekleidet* wearing (*od.* dressed in) the same clothes; (*uniformiert*) (dressed in) uniform; ~ *vorgehen* take concerted action, act consistently; *die Öffnungszeiten sind in allen Schwimmbädern der Stadt* ~ *geregelt* the opening times have been made consistent (*od.* the same) for all the town's swimming pools; **Einheitlichkeit** *f* **1.** uniformity; *des Vorgehens, der Methode etc.*: consistency; **2.** (*Geschlossenheit*) homogeneity; *e-s Werks*: unity

Einheits|bestrebungen *Pl.* unitary tendencies; *Pol. auch* efforts toward(s) (*od.* striving for) political union; ~**brei** *m fig.*: *das ist alles ein* ~ it's all one mish-mash; ~**fraß** *m umg. pej.*: *wir bekommen e-n* ~ we all get the same disgusting food; ~**gebühr** *f* flat (*od.* standard) rate; ~**gewerkschaft** *f* unified trade (*Am.* labor) union; ~**gewicht** *n* standard weight; ~**größe** *f* standard size; ~**kleidung** *f* uniform(s *Pl.*); ~**kurs** *m Wirts.* standard quotation; ~**look** [-luk] *m umg. pej.* standard look; ~**partei** *f* united party; *es gibt nur eine* ~ there's only one (central) party; ~**preis** *m Wirts.* standard price; (*Pauschale*) flat rate; ~**steuer** *f* flat-rate tax; ~**tarif** *m* flat rate

einheizen *v/t.* (*trennb., hat -ge-*) **I.** *v/i.* **1.** (*Kaminfeuer anzünden*) light the fire; (*Heizung einschalten*) turn the heat(ing) on; **2.** *umg. fig.*: *j-m* ~ give s.o. a piece of one's mind; **II.** *v/t.* (*Zimmer*) warm up; (*Ofen*) put on

einhellig *Adj.* unanimous; **Einhelligkeit** *f* unanimity

einher|... *im V.* ... along; ~**gehen** *v/i.* (*unreg., trennb., ist -ge-*) **1.** *geh.* walk along; *auf j-n zu*: come walking along; **2.** ~ *mit* accompany; *Arbeitslosigkeit geht mit Konjunkturrückgang einher* unemployment goes hand in hand with (*od.* is a concomitant of *förm.*) economic decline; ~**schreiten** *v/i.* (*unreg., trennb., ist -ge-*) *geh.* stride along; *auf j-n zu*: come striding along; ~**stolzieren** *v/i.* (*trennb., ist*) strut along; *auf j-n zu*: come strutting along

einhöck(e)rig *Adj. Zool. attr.* one-humped

einholen (*trennb., hat -ge-*) **I.** *v/t.* **1.** (*j-n, Auto etc.*) catch up with; **2.** *verlorene Zeit / Versäumtes* ~ make up for lost time / what one has missed; *e-n Rückstand* ~ catch up with one's (arrears of) work; **3.** (*Segel*) strike; (*Flagge*) lower; (*Anker, Netz, Tau*) haul in; **4.** (*Auskunft, Genehmigung*) get, obtain; *Rat* ~ take advice (*bei* from); *bei j-m*: *auch* consult s.o.; *Informationen* ~ seek information, make enquiries; **5.** *umg.* (*einkaufen*) pick up; **II.** *v/i.*: *umg.*: ~ *gehen* go shopping

Einhorn n; Pl. Einhörner; Myth. unicorn

einhüllen (trennb., hat -ge-) **I.** v/t. **1.** wrap (up) (**in** + Akk. in), cover (with); Tech. encase (in); **Nebel hüllt die Gipfel ein** fig. mist is shrouding the peaks; → **eingehüllt**; **II.** v/refl. wrap o.s. up (**in** + Akk. in); in e-e Decke: auch snuggle into umg.

einhundert Zahlw. a hundred, betont: one hundred; → auch **hundert**

einig Adj. **1.** ~ **sein mit** be in agreement with; (**sich**) ~ **werden** come to an agreement (**über** + Akk. about); **mit j-m** ~ **gehen** agree with s.o. (**in** + Dat. about, on); **sich nicht** ~ **sein** disagree, differ (**über** + Akk. on); **die Fachleute ist sich** ~ **darüber, dass ...** the experts are agreed that ...; **man ist sich noch nicht** ~ **darüber, was/ wie** etc. there's still some disagreement as to what/how etc.; **er ist sich selbst nicht** ~, **was er tun soll** he can't make up his mind what to do; **2.** Volk etc.: united

einige unbest. Pron. **1.** Sg.: (etwas) some; **~s Aufsehen erregen** cause something of a stir; **aus** ~**r Entfernung** from a certain distance; **mit** ~**m guten od. gutem Willen** with a bit of effort; **es wird noch** ~ **Zeit dauern** it'll be some time (od. take a while) yet; **es hat ihn schon** ~ **Selbstüberwindung gekostet** it cost him an effort of will; → **einiges**; **2.** Pl.: (ein paar) some, a few; (mehrere) several; ~ **von uns** some of us; ~ **wenige** a few; ~ **tausend Frauen** several thousand women; ~ **Mal(e)** several times; **schon** ~ **Male** (quite) a number of times

einigeln v/refl. (trennb., hat -ge-) **1.** curl up (into a ball); **2.** fig. (sich zurückziehen) hide o.s. away, shut o.s. off from the (rest of the) world

einigen I. v/refl. agree (**über** od. **auf** + Akk. on); bes. Pol. reach (an) agreement od. a settlement (on); **sich** ~ **auf** (+ Akk.) auch settle on; **sich auf e-n Kompromiss** ~ agree on (od. come to) a compromise; **wir müssen uns irgendwie** ~ we'll have to come to some sort of agreement; **II.** v/t. unite; (versöhnen) reconcile

einigermaßen Adv. (relativ, ziemlich) vor Adj.: fairly, reasonably; mit Verb: reasonably well, fairly well; (in gewissem Grad) to some extent, up to a point; umg. als Antwort: (leidlich) not too bad; **es geht ihm** ~ he's not doing too badly; gesundheitlich: he's reasonably (od. fairly) well; ~ **Bescheid wissen** have a fairly good idea (**über** + Akk. of)

einiges unbest. Pron. **1.** adjektivisch → **einige** 1; **2.** substantivisch: (manches) something, a few things; (schon) ~ quite a bit, a fair amount (bit umg.); Pl. quite a few things; ~ **an ...** (+ Dat.) quite a bit of ..., quite a few ...; **es gäbe noch** ~ **zu tun** there are (still) a number of things to do; **dazu möchte ich noch** ~ **sagen** I'd just like to make a few comments on that; **ich könnte dir** ~ **erzählen** I could tell you a thing or two; **dazu gehört schon** ~ that takes a fair bit of courage (od. nerve)

Einigkeit f unity; (Übereinstimmung) agreement (**über** + Akk. on, about); **es herrschte** ~ **darüber, dass ...** it was (od. everybody) agreed that ...; **es herrscht noch keine** ~ **darüber, was/ wo** etc. there's still no agreement (consensus förm.) as to what/how etc.; ~

macht stark Sprichw. (there is) strength in unity

Einigung f **1.** agreement, settlement; ~ **erzielen** reach (an) agreement, reach a settlement (**über** + Akk. on); **2.** e-s Volkes etc.: unification

Einigungs|versuch m attempt to reach agreement; ~**vertrag** m hist. unification treaty

einimpfen v/t. (trennb., hat -ge-) umg. fig.: **j-m etw.** ~ (Hass etc.) instil(l) s.th. into s.o.; (Glauben etc.) auch indoctrinate s.o. with s.th.; (einbläuen) drum s.th. into s.o.

einjagen v/t. (trennb., hat -ge-) umg.: **j-m Angst** ~ give s.o. a fright, frighten s.o.; **hast du mir e-n Schrecken eingejagt!** you scared me out of my wits, I nearly jumped out of my skin

einjährig Adj. attr. **1.** Kind etc.: one--year-old ...; **2.** (ein Jahr dauernd) year-long ..., one-year ...; Frist, Pause, Abwesenheit etc.: ... of a year; **3.** Pflanze: annual

Einjährige m, f, n; -n, -n one-year-old (child)

einkalkulieren v/t. (trennb., hat) take into account, allow for; im Preis: include; **die Möglichkeit** etc. **hatten wir nicht einkalkuliert** we hadn't reckoned with that possibility etc.

einkarätig Adj. attr. one-carat ...

einkassieren v/t. (trennb., hat) **1.** (Beiträge etc.) collect; **2.** umg. fig. (einstecken) pocket, swipe; **3.** Sl. fig. (festnehmen) collar umg.

Einkauf m **1.** (das Einkaufen) shopping; Wirts. purchasing; **beim** ~ **von ...** when buying ...; **Einkäufe machen** go shopping; **ich muss noch einige Einkäufe machen** I've still got some shopping to do; **2.** (eingekaufte Ware) purchase; **die Einkäufe auf den Tisch legen** put the shopping on the table; **3.** Wirts. (Abteilung) purchasing (department); **4.** Sport, von Spielern, auch (Spieler) purchase, signing; **er ist der bisher teuerste** ~ **der Bayern** he's the most expensive player Bayern have (Am. has) acquired (od. Bayern's most expensive signing) so far

einkaufen (trennb., hat -ge-) **I.** v/t. buy, purchase förm.; Sport (Spieler) auch sign; **II.** v/i. shop; ~ (**gehen**) go shopping; **wo kaufst du ein?** where do you shop (od. do your shopping)?; **da hast du aber gut/teuer eingekauft** you got some good bargains / paid some high prices there; **III.** v/refl.: **sich** ~ **in** (+ Akk.) in Altenheim, Firma etc.: buy into

Einkaufs|abteilung f purchasing department; ~**beutel** m shopping bag; ~**bummel** m: **e-n** ~ **machen** go on a shopping spree, have a look around the shops (Am. stores); ~**korb** m shopping basket; ~**leiter** m, ~**leiterin** f Wirts. head buyer; ~**liste** f shopping list; ~**meile** f long (pedestrianized) shopping street; ~**passage** f shopping arcade; ~**preis** m purchase price; **zum** ~ at cost price; ~**roller** m wheelie shopping bag; ~**tasche** f shopping bag; ~**wagen** m (supermarket) trolley, Am. shopping cart; ~**zentrum** n shopping cent|re (Am. -er), Am. auch mall; (Großmarkt) hypermarket; ~**zettel** m shopping list

Einkehr f; -, kein Pl. **1.** geh.: **innere** ~ (self-)contemplation, reflection; prüfende: soul-searching; ~ **halten** search one's soul; **2.** altm. in Gaststätte: stop for refreshment; **einkehren** v/i.

(trennb., ist -ge-) **1.** altm. stop for refreshment; **in e-m Gasthof** ~ auch stop (off) at an inn; **2.** fig. Freude etc.: come (**bei** to); **endlich kehrt wieder Ruhe ein** at last peace returns

einkellern v/t. (trennb., hat -ge-) store in a (od. the) cellar, cellar

einkerben v/t. (trennb., hat -ge-) **1.** (Holz etc.) put a notch (od. notches) in; **2.** (Zeichen etc.) notch (**in** + Akk. into); (Bild, Namen) auch carve (in); → **eingekerbt**; **Einkerbung** f notch

einkerkern v/t. (trennb., hat -ge-); hist. od. geh. throw into prison, incarcerate

einkesseln v/t. (trennb., hat -ge-); Mil. encircle, surround; in e-r Falle: trap

einklagbar Adj. Jur. legally recoverable; (Recht) legally enforceable; **einklagen** v/t. (trennb., hat -ge-); **etw. bei j-m** ~ sue s.o. for s.th.; **e-e Schuld / ein Recht** ~ take legal action for the recovery of a debt / the enforcement of a right

einklammern v/t. (trennb., hat -ge-) bracket, put in brackets (bes. Am. parentheses); → **eingeklammert**; **Einklammerung** f bracketing; konkret: brackets Pl., bes. Am. parentheses Pl. (+ Gen. around)

Einklang m; nur Sg. **1.** Mus. unison; **2.** fig. harmony; **in** ~ **bringen** bring into line, harmonize; (versöhnen) reconcile; **in** ~ **mit** in line with; **in** ~ **sein od. stehen** be compatible, be in accord (**mit** with); **miteinander in** ~ **sein od. stehen** Tatsachen etc.: tally; Personen: be in accord (od. of one mind); **nicht im** ~ **sein od. stehen** be incompatible; auch Personen: be at odds; be at variance förm.

einkleben v/t. (trennb., hat -ge-): ~ (**in** + Akk.) stick in(to)

einkleiden v/t. (trennb., hat -ge-) **1.** clothe, fit out; (Soldaten) auch kit out, Am. outfit; (Mönch, Nonne) provide with a habit, accept as a novice; **neu** ~ buy new clothes for; **ich musste ihn ganz neu** ~ I had to buy him a whole new set of clothes; **2.** fig. (Gedanken etc.) couch (**in** + Akk. in)

einkleistern v/t. (trennb., hat -ge-) paste

einklemmen (trennb., hat -ge-) **I.** v/t. **1.** wedge in; Tech. clamp; **2.** (j-n) jam; **sich den Finger** etc. ~ get one's finger etc. jammed (od. caught); **er wurde bei dem Unfall in s-m Fahrzeug eingeklemmt** he was trapped in his car as a result of the accident; **II.** v/refl. get jammed (od. caught); → **eingeklemmt**

einklinken (trennb.) **I.** (hat eingeklinkt); (Tür) shut (properly), latch; (Seil etc.) hitch up (**an** +Dat. to); **II.** v/i. (ist) click shut, click to

einkneifen v/t. (unreg., trennb., hat -ge-); (Bauch) pull in; **den Schwanz** ~ Hund: put its tail between its legs; → **eingekniffen**

einknicken (trennb.) **I.** v/t. (hat eingeknickt) **1.** (Papier, Serviette) fold; (Ecke e-r Buchseite) fold over; (Kissen) put a fold in; **2.** (Ast, Stiel etc.) (biegen) bend; (brechen) break, snap; **3.** (Arm) bend; **II.** v/i. (ist); (sich biegen) bend; (brechen) break, snap; Knie, Regalbrett, Pfeiler etc.: give out; **mit dem Fuß** ~ go over on one's ankle; **ich bin mit dem Knie eingeknickt** my knee (just) gave out; → **eingeknickt**

einknüppeln v/i. (trennb., hat -ge-): **auf j-n** ~ beat s.o. up with a cudgel (Polizei: a baton, Am. blackjack)

einkochen (*trennb., hat -ge-*) *vt/i.* **1.** (*einmachen*) preserve; *Marmelade*: make; **2.** (*eindicken*) boil down; (*Soße*) thicken (*auch dickflüssig werden*)

einkommen *v/i.* (*unreg., trennb., ist -ge-*); *geh.*: ~ **um** apply for (*bei* to)

Einkommen *n; -s, -* income (*aus* from), earnings *Pl.*; *des Staates*: revenue

Einkommens|einbuße *f* loss of income; ~**buße** *f* loss of income *Sg.* of income; ~**gefälle** *n* income differential; ~**grenze** *f* income limit; ~**gruppe** *f* income bracket

einkommens|schwach *Adj. attr.* low-income …; ~**stark** *Adj. attr.* high-income …

Einkommen(s)steuer *f* income tax; ~**bescheid** *m* income tax assessment; ~**erklärung** *f* income tax return; *s-e* ~ **abgeben** send in (*Am.* file) one's income tax return

einkommen(s)steuerpflichtig *Adj.* liable for income tax

Einkommens|verhältnisse *Pl.* income level *Sg.*; ~**zuwachs** *m* increase in income

einköpfen *vt/i.* (*trennb., hat -ge-*) *Fußball*: head (the ball) in

einkratzen *v/refl.* (*trennb., hat -ge-*) *umg. fig.*: **sich bei j-m** ~ (*wollen*) (try to) get in with s.o. (*od.* rub s.o. up the right way)

einkreisen *v/t.* (*trennb., hat -ge-*) **1.** (*Feind, Wild*) surround; *Mil. auch* encircle; *Pol.* (*Land*) isolate; **2.** (*Zahl etc.*) put a ring (a)round; **3.** *fig.* (*Problem etc.*) narrow down

einkremen → *eincremen*

einkriegen *v/refl.* (*trennb., hat -ge-*); *umg.*: **wir konnten uns vor Lachen nicht mehr** ~ we were rolling about (*Am.* rolling on the floor) (with uncontrollable laughter); **jetzt krieg dich mal wieder ein** come on, get a hold on yourself

Einkünfte *Pl.* income *Sg.*, earnings; *des Staates*: revenue *Sg.* (*alle aus* from)

einkuscheln *v/refl.* (*trennb., hat -ge-*); *umg.* snuggle up (*in* + *Akk.* into; *bei* next to)

einladen (*unreg., trennb., hat -ge-*) **I.** *v/t.* **1.** (*j-n*) invite, ask round (*Am.* over) (**zum Abendessen etc.** to *od.* for dinner *etc.*); **j-n ins Konzert etc.** ~ ask s.o. (out) to a concert *etc.*; **j-n auf ein** *od.* **zu e-m Bier etc.** ~ buy (*od.* stand) s.o. a beer *etc.*; **ich bin heute Abend eingeladen** I've been invited out tonight; **wir haben Freunde eingeladen** we've invited (*od.* we're having) some friends round (*Am.* over); **ich lad dich ein zum Bier etc.**: let me treat you; *beim Zahlen od. Bestellen*: it's on me; **2.** (*Waren*) load; *in den Kofferraum*: *auch* stow; **II.** *v/i.*: **zu Missbrauch etc.** ~ invite abuse *etc.*; **zum Verweilen etc.** ~ be (*od.* look) very inviting; **das schöne Wetter lud zum Baden ein** the fine weather made you want to go swimming

einladend I. *Part. Präs.* → *einladen*; **II.** *Adj.* inviting; (*verlockend*) tempting; (*lecker*) delicious(-looking)

Einladung *f* **1.** invitation; **auf** ~ **von X** at …X's invitation; ~**en verschicken** send out invitations; **2.** (*Fest etc.*) party

Einladungs|karte *f* invitation card; ~**schreiben** *n* letter of invitation

Einlage *f* **1.** *im Brief*: enclosure; *in Zeitungen etc.*: insert; **2.** *im Schuh*: (arch) support; (*Einlegesohle*) insole; **3.** *in Kleidung*: padding; *im Kragen*: stiffen-

er; **4.** *im Zahn*: temporary filling; **5.** *Gastr. in der Suppe*: meat balls, vegetables *etc.* inserted in a clear soup; **6.** *Fin. von Kapital*: contribution; (*Investition*) investment; *in e-r Bank*: deposit; **7.** *Theat. etc.* interlude; **er bringt gern humoristische** ~**n** he likes to do comic cameos; **8.** *Tech.* insert; **9.** (*Intarsie*) inlay

einlagern (*trennb., hat -ge-*) **I.** *v/t.* **1.** store; (*Möbel etc.*) *auch* put into storage; → *eingelagert*; **2.** *Med., im Gewebe, Knochen*; *Geol., in Gesteinsschicht*: deposit; **II.** *v/refl. Med., Geol.* settle (*in* + *Akk.* od. *Dat.* in[to]), be (-come) deposited (in); **Einlagerung** *f* **1.** storage; **2.** *Geol., Med.* deposit

einlagig *Adj. attr.* one-ply

Einlass *m; -es, Einlässe* admission, admittance (*zu* to); ~ **ab 17 Uhr** doors open at 5 p.m.; ~ **begehren** *geh.* request admission (*od.* admittance); **j-m** ~ **gewähren** *geh.* grant s.o. admission, admit s.o.; **sich** (*Dat.*) ~ **verschaffen** gain admission (*od.* admittance, entry)

einlassen (*unreg., trennb., hat -ge-*) **I.** *v/t.* **1.** ~ (*in* + *Akk.*) (*Person, Licht etc.*) let in(to); **2.** (*Wasser*) run (*in* + *Akk.* into), let in(to); (*Wanne*) fill; **sich** (*Dat.*) **ein Bad** ~ run (o.s.) a bath; **3.** (*Edelstein etc.*) set (*in* + *Akk.* in); **4.** *Tech.*: ~ (*in* + *Akk.*) insert (in); fit (in); **5.** *südd., österr. mit Wachs etc.*: wax; *mit Farbe*: paint; *mit Firnis*: varnish; **II.** *v/refl.* **1.** **sich** ~ **auf** (+ *Akk.*) let o.s. in for; *auf ein Gespräch, e-n Streit etc.*: get involved in; *auf e-e Frage*: go into; *auf e-n Vorschlag*: agree to; **lass dich nicht darauf ein!** don't get involved, keep out of it, *engS.* don't let them talk you into it; **da hab ich mich auf was Schönes eingelassen!** I've really let myself in for something there; **2.** **sich mit j-m** ~ get involved (*od.* mixed up) with s.o.; *sexuell*: *auch* have an affair with s.o.; *Mädchen*: *auch* go with s.o.; (*streiten mit*) get into an argument (*od.* a fight) with s.o.; **3.** *Jur.* testify

Einlasskontrolle *f* ticket inspection

Einlass|ventil *n Tech.* inlet valve; ~**zeit** *f* opening time

Einlauf *m* **1.** *Sport, ins Ziel*: finish; *Reihenfolge*: order (at the finish), placings *Pl.*; **beim** ~ **in die Zielgerade** on entering the finishing straight; **2.** *Med.* enema; **j-m e-n** ~ **machen** give s.o. an enema; **3.** *Gastr.* thickening; **4.** *Wirts.* → *Eingang* 4

einlaufen (*unreg., trennb.*) **I.** *v/i.* (*ist eingelaufen*) **1.** ~ (*in* + *Akk.*) *Zug*: come in, arrive; *Naut.* put in(to); *Sportler, ins Ziel*: finish; *ins Stadion etc.*: make his (*od.* her) entrance; **2.** *Wasser*: ~ (*in* + *Akk.*) run in(to); *Wanne*: be filling; **3.** *Kleidung*: shrink; **läuft nicht ein** *Etikett*: non-shrink; **4.** *Wirts.* → *eingehen* I 6; **5.** *Tech.*: ~ **lassen** (*Maschine, Motor*) run in (*Am.* break in); **II.** *v/t.* (*hat*) **1.** (*Schuhe*) wear in; **2.** *umg.* → *einrennen*; **III.** *v/refl.* (*hat*) **1.** *Sport* warm up; **2.** *Tech., Motor, Maschine*: run in, *Am.* be broken in; **3.** *fig. Sache*: get going

einläuten *v/t.* (*trennb., hat -ge-*) (*Sonntag etc.*) ring in; **die letzte Runde wird eingeläutet** *bei Mittel- und Langstreckenläufen*: there goes the bell (for the last lap)

einleben *v/refl.* (*trennb., hat -ge-*) **1.** settle in; **sich in e-m Haus / an e-m Ort** ~ settle into a house / settle down in a

place; **2.** *fig.*: **sich in ein Bild** etc. ~ project o.s. into a picture *etc.*

Einlegearbeit *f* inlaid work, intarsia

einlegen *v/t.* (*trennb., hat -ge-*) **1.** **etw.** (**in etw.** [*Akk.*]) ~ put s.th. in (s.th.), insert s.th. (in s.th.); *in e-n Brief*: enclose s.th. (with s.th.); **2.** *Mot.*: **den zweiten** etc. **Gang** ~ engage (*od.* go into) second *etc.* gear; **3.** *fig.* (*Ruhetag, Sonderschicht*) put in; (*Pause, Rast*) have, take; **e-e Gedenkminute** ~ observe a minute's silence; **e-n Spurt** ~ put on a spurt; **4.** *Gastr. in Essig*: pickle; *in Salz*: salt, brine; *in Rum*: preserve; (*marinieren*) marinate; **5.** **mit Elfenbein** etc. ~ inlay with ivory *etc.*; **6.** **j-m/sich die Haare** ~ set s.o.'s/one's hair; **7.** (*Berufung, Beschwerde, Revision etc.*) lodge (**gegen** against); (*Rechtsmittel*) file; **der Trainer legte Protest gegen die Wertung des Spiels ein** the coach entered a protest against the scoring of the match; → *Veto, Wort* 2; **8.** *Wirts. in Bank*: deposit; *in Firma*: invest; **9.** *schw.* (*abgeben*) hand in; → *eingelegt*

Einleger *m; -s, -*, ~**in** *f; -, -nen*; *Wirts. bei Bank*: depositor, account holder

Einlegesohle *f* insole

einleiten *v/t.* (*trennb., hat -ge-*) **1.** start, begin; (*Kampagne, Untersuchung, Verhandlungen*) open; (*veranlassen*) (*Verfahren*) initiate; (*Maßnahmen etc.*) implement, introduce; (*Buch*) write a preface (*od.* an introduction) to; (*Nebensatz*) introduce; **e-n Prozess / rechtliche Schritte** ~ (**gegen**) go to court (with) / take legal action (*od.* institute proceedings) (against); **2.** *Med.* (*Geburt etc.*) induce; **3.** *Sache*: mark the beginning of; (*Zeitalter etc.*) *auch* usher in; **4.** (*Schadstoffe in Fluss etc.*) discharge (*in* + *Akk.* into)

einleitend I. *Part. Präs.* → *einleiten*; **II.** *Adj.* introductory, opening, preliminary; **III.** *Adv.* by way of introduction

Einleitung *f* **1.** *zu Buch, Musikstück etc.*: introduction (*zu* to); (*Vorwort*) preface (+ *Gen.* to); *zu e-m Gesetz etc.*: preamble (+ *Gen. od. zu* to); **2.** *Vorgang*: starting; *von Kampagne, Untersuchung, Verhandlungen*: opening; *von Verfahren*: initiation; *von Maßnahmen*: implementation, introduction; *Med., e-r Geburt*: induction; → *einleiten*; **3.** *von Schadstoffen*: discharge

Einleitungskapitel *n* introductory chapter

einlenken *v/i.* (*trennb., hat -ge-*); *fig.* relent; soften one's tone; **wenn er nicht einlenkt, übergebe ich die Sache m-m Anwalt** if he doesn't back down I'll place the matter in the hands of my solicitor (*Am.* attorney)

einlesen (*unreg., trennb., hat -ge-*) **I.** *v/refl.*: **sich** ~ **in** (+ *Akk.*) get into, read one's way into; **II.** *v/t. EDV*: **Daten** etc. ~ (*in* + *Akk.*) read in (*od.* input) data *etc.* (into)

einleuchten *v/i.* (*trennb., hat -ge-*) make sense (*j-m* to s.o.); **es leuchtet ein** *auch* it stands to reason, it's obvious why; **es leuchtet mir nicht ein, dass …** I don't see why (*od.* how) …;

einleuchtend I. *Part. Präs.* → *einleuchten*; **II.** *Adj.* (*klar*) (quite) clear, quite plain; (*offensichtlich*) obvious; (*überzeugend*) convincing; *Argument*: *auch* cogent; ~ **sein** *auch* make sense, stand to reason

einliefern *v/t.* (*trennb., hat -ge-*) **1.** (*j-n*) take (*in* + *Akk.* to); *ins Krankenhaus*:

admit (to); *ins Gefängnis*: put (into); *er wurde ins Gefängnis eingeliefert auch* he was imprisoned (*od.* placed in prison); **2.** (*Waren*) deliver; *etw. bei der Post* etc. ~ take s.th. to the post office *etc.*; **Einlieferung** f **1.** *ins Krankenhaus*: admission (*in + Akk.* to); *ins Gefängnis, in e-e Anstalt*: committal (to) *förm.*; **2.** *von Waren*: delivery; **Einlieferungsschein** m receipt; *Post.* certificate of posting (*Am. auch* mailing)

Einliegerwohnung f granny annexe (*od.* flat), *Am.* in-law apartment

einlochen (*trennb., hat -ge-*) **I.** *v/t.* **1.** (*Golfball*) hole; (*Billardkugel*) pot; **2.** *umg.*: *j-n* ~ clap s.o. in jail, put s.o. in the slammer; **II.** *v/i. Golf*: hole out; *Billard*: pot the ball

einloggen *v/refl.* (*trennb., hat -ge-*); *EDV in e-n Rechner etc.*: log on (*od.* in); *sich ins Internet* ~ log onto the Internet

einlösen *v/t.* (*trennb., hat -ge-*) **1.** (*einreichen*) (*Pfand, Gutschein*) redeem; **2.** *Wirts., Fin.* (*Schuldschein, Wechsel*) call in; (*Scheck*) cash; *durch die Bank*: hono(u)r; **3.** *fig.* (*Wort*) keep; (*Versprechen*) *auch* hono(u)r; **Einlösung** f **1.** *von Pfand, Gutschein*: redemption; **2.** *Wirts., Fin. von Scheck*: cashing; *von Schuldschein, Wechsel*: calling in; *durch die Bank*: hono(u)ring; **3.** *fig. e-s gegebenen Wortes*: keeping; *e-s Versprechens*: *auch* hono(u)ring

einlullen *v/t.* (*trennb., hat -ge-*) **1.** lull to sleep; **2.** *fig.* lull into a false sense of security

einmachen *v/t.* (*trennb., hat -ge-*) preserve, *Am. auch* put up (*od.* by), can; *in Gläsern*: bottle, *Am.* can; *in Dosen*: can; *in Flaschen*: bottle; *in Essig*: pickle

Einmach|glas n preserving (*Am.* canning *od.* Mason) jar; **~gummi** m *umg.*, **~ring** m rubber ring (*for a preserving* [*Am. canning*] *jar*)

einmal *Adv.* **1.** once; ~ *eins ist eins* one times one is one; ~ *im Jahr* once a year; *ein- bis od. oder zweimal* once or twice; *noch* ~ once more, (once) again; *betont*: one more time; *versuch's noch* ~ *auch* have another go (*Am.* try); *noch* ~ *so viel* twice as much; *noch* ~ *so alt wie er* etc. twice his *etc.* age; ~ *mehr / wieder* ~ once again; ~ *hell,* ~ *dunkel* sometimes light, sometimes dark; ~ *sagst du ja, dann sagst du nein* one moment (*od.* first) it's yes, then it's no; *Ferien* ~ *anders* quite a different sort of holiday (*Am.* vacation); ~ *ist keinmal Sprichw.* once (*od.* one time) doesn't count; ~ *und nie wieder* never again; *das gibt's nur* ~ *Sache*: that's unique; *Ereignis*: that won't happen again; **2.** (*früher*) once; (*zuvor*) before; *ich war (schon)* ~ *da* I've been there before, I was there once; *das war* ~ that's all in the past; *es war* ~ *ein(e)* ... once upon a time there was a ...; *haben Sie schon* ~ *...?* have you ever ...?; **3.** (*in der Zukunft*) one day, some day (or other); (*später* ~) later on (some time); *wenn du* ~ *groß bist* when you grow up, when you're a big boy (*od.* girl); *das wird er noch* ~ *bereuen* he'll live to regret it; **4.** *auf* ~ (*plötzlich*) suddenly; (*gleichzeitig*) at the same time; (*auf einen Sitz*) in one go; *alle(s) auf* ~ all at once; *zwei etc. auf* ~ two at the same time (*od.* at once); **5.** *erst* ~ first; **6.** *nicht* ~ not even, not so much as; *er*

hat mich nicht ~ *angesehen* he didn't even (deign to) look at me; **7.** *nun* ~ (*eben*) just, simply; *ich habe nun* ~ *keine Lust dazu* I just don't feel like it at the moment; *ich bin nun* ~ *so* that's the way I am, I can't help it; *er ist nun* ~ *so auch* he's like that; *es ist nun* ~ *so* that's the way it is, that's life; **8.** *freundlich*: *hör* ~! listen; *stell dir* ~ *vor* just imagine, can you imagine; *kommst du bitte* ~ *her?* can you come here for a moment?; **9.** *ärgerlich*: *sei endlich* ~ *ruhig!* be quiet, will you!, how many times do I have to tell you to be quiet!; ~ *muss Schluss sein* all good things (must) come to an end; **10.** (*zum einen, erstens*) firstly, for one thing; ~ *weil ..., zum anderen weil ...* for one thing because ..., for another because ...

Einmal... *im Subst.* (*Wegwerf...*) disposable

Einmaleins n; -, *kein Pl.* **1.** (multiplication) tables *Pl.*; *das kleine/große* ~ the (*od.* one's) tables up to ten / over ten; *das* ~ *aufsagen* say one's tables; **2.** *fig.* *das* ~ (+ *Gen.*) the basics *Pl.*, the fundamentals *Pl.* of

Einmalhandtuch n paper towel

einmalig I. *Adj.* **1.** *nur attr.*; *Zahlung etc.*: single ...; *auch Ausgabe etc.*: single ..., *Am.* one-time ...; *das ist e-e ~e Anschaffung* it's a once-in-a-lifetime purchase, you only buy that sort of thing once in your life; *nach* ~*em Durchlesen* after reading it once; **2.** (*unwiederholbar*) unique; *sie ist* ~ she's one of a kind; *e-e* ~*e Gelegenheit auch* a once-in-a-lifetime chance; **3.** (*hervorragend*) brilliant, fantastic *umg.*; **II.** *Adv.*: ~ *schön* absolutely beautiful; ~ *gut* brilliant, fantastic; **Einmaligkeit** f uniqueness

Einmann|... *im Subst.* one-man ...; **~betrieb** m **1.** (*Geschäft etc.*) one-man business (show *umg.*); **2.** (*das Betreiben*) one-man operation

Einmarkstück n *hist.* one-mark piece

Einmarsch m marching in; (*Einfall*) *auch* invasion; **einmarschieren** *v/i.* (*trennb., ist*): ~ *in* (+ *Akk.*) march in(-to), enter; (*einfallen in*) invade

einmassieren *v/t.* (*trennb., hat*) rub in (gently); ~ *in* (+ *Akk.*) rub (gently) into

Einmaster m; -s, -: *Naut.* single-master

einmauern *v/t.* (*trennb., hat -ge-*) wall in, immure; (*einbauen*) fix (*od.* embed) in a wall

einmeißeln *v/t.* (*trennb., hat -ge-*) chisel (*in + Akk.* into)

Einmeterbrett n *Sport* one-met|re (*Am.* -er) board

einmieten (*trennb., hat -ge-*) **I.** *v/refl.* rent a room (*bei* at); **II.** *v/t. Agr.* (store in a) clamp

einmischen (*trennb., hat -ge-*) **I.** *v/refl.* interfere (*in + Akk.* in *od.* with), meddle (in *od.* with); *neugierig*: poke one's nose in(to) *umg.*; *sich in ein Gespräch* ~ join in (*störend*: butt in on) a conversation; *misch dich lieber nicht ein* better not get involved; *misch dich da nicht ein!* *drohend*: (you) just keep out of it; **II.** *v/t.*: ~ *in* (+ *Akk.*) mix in(to), add (to); **Einmischung** f interference; *bes. Pol.* intervention

einmonatig *Adj.* **1.** *Baby etc.*: one-month-old; **2.** *Zeitraum etc.*: one-month ..., *nach e-m* ~*en Englandaufenthalt* after a month's stay (*od.* staying a month) in England

einmontieren *v/t.* (*trennb., hat*): ~ (*in + Akk.*) instal(l) (in)

einmotorig *Adj.* single-engined

einmotten *v/t.* (*trennb., hat -ge-*) **1.** (*Kleidung*) put in mothballs; **2.** *fig.* (*Schiff, Auto etc.*) mothball

einmumme(l)n (*trennb., hat -ge-*); *umg.* **I.** *v/t.* wrap up, muffle up; **II.** *v/refl.* wrap (o.s.) up, get wrapped up, muffle up

einmünden *v/i.* (*trennb., ist -ge-*): ~ *in* (+ *Akk.*) *in e-n Fluss*: flow into; *Nebenfluss*: *auch* join; *Straße*: join, lead into; *fig.* lead to; **Einmündung** f *von Fluss*: mouth, estuary; *von Straße*: junction

einmütig I. *Adj.* unanimous; **II.** *Adv.* unanimously; *etw.* ~ *tun* be unanimous in doing s.th.; ~ *der Meinung sein, dass ...* be unanimous that ...; **Einmütigkeit** f unanimity (*über + Akk.* about)

einnähen *v/t.* (*trennb., hat -ge-*) **1.** ~ (*in + Akk.*) sew in(to); **2.** (*enger machen*) take in

Einnahme f; -, -n **1.** *Wirts.* receipt; **~n** (*Erlös*) proceeds *Pl.*; (*Verdienst*) earnings *Pl.*; (*Einkommen*) income; *des Staates*: revenue; **~n und Ausgaben** income and expenditure; **2.** *nur Sg.*; *e-r Arznei*: taking; *e-r Mahlzeit*: eating; **3.** *nur Sg.*; *Mil.* capture; *e-s Landes*: occupation; **~ausfall** m *Wirts.* drop in takings (*Am.* revenue); *des Staates*: revenue shortfall; **~quelle** f source of income; *des Staates*: source of revenue

einnässen *vt/i.* (*trennb., hat -ge-*): (*das Bett*) ~ wet one's bed

einnebeln (*trennb., hat -ge-*) **I.** *v/t.* **1.** (*mit Rauch einhüllen*) envelope in smoke; *Mil.* put a smokescreen around; **2.** *umg. fig.* (*Zimmer etc., mit Rauch*) fill with smoke; (*Menschen*) smoke out; **II.** *v/refl.* **1.** *Schiff etc.*: put up a smokescreen; **2.** *unpers.*: *es nebelt sich ein* it's getting foggy, the fog seems to be settling

einnehmen *v/t.* (*unreg., trennb., hat -ge-*) **1.** (*Geld*) take; (*verdienen*) earn; **2.** (*Arznei*) take; *geh.* (*Mahlzeit*) have; **3.** *Mil.* capture; (*Land*) occupy; **4.** (*ausfüllen*) (*Platz, Raum*) take up; **5.** (*Platz, Position, Standort*) take (up) (*auch fig.*); (*innehaben*) hold; *s-n Platz* ~ take one's seat; *e-e kritische Haltung* ~ adopt a critical attitude; **6.** *fig.*: *j-n* (*für sich*) ~ win s.o. over; *stärker*: charm s.o.; *j-n gegen sich* ~ turn s.o. against one; *das kann die Leute gegen ihn ein* it didn't do much for his popularity; → *eingenommen*

einnehmend I. *Part. Präs.* → *einnehmen*; **II.** *Adj.* winning, engaging; *Äußeres, Lächeln*: *auch* fetching; *er hat ein* ~*es Wesen* he has a very engaging personality; *umg. iro.* (*ist raffgierig*) he just can't get enough

einnicken *v/i.* (*trennb., ist -ge-*); *umg.* nod off, drop off

einnisten *v/refl.* (*trennb., hat -ge-*) **1.** (build one's) nest (*in + Dat.* in); **2.** (*sich festsetzen*) lodge itself, get lodged, settle (*in + Dat.* in); **3.** *fig.*: *sich bei j-m* ~ *Idee etc.*: take hold of s.o.; *umg. Person*: park o.s. on s.o.

Einöde f; -, -n; (*unfruchtbares Land*) barren waste; (*Wildnis*) wilderness; **Einödhof** m *südd., österr.* isolated farm

einölen *v/t.* (*trennb., hat -ge-*) **1.** (*ölen*) oil; **2.** (*Arme etc.*) rub (some) oil into; *j-n/sich* ~ rub oil into s.o.'s/one's skin, massage s.o. with oil

einordnen (*trennb., hat -ge-*) **I.** *v/t.*
1. (*einsortieren*) sort out (and put in their proper place); *in Akten*: file (away); ~ *in* (+ *Akk.*) sort into; ~ *nach* arrange according to; **alphabetisch** ~ arrange alphabetically (*od.* in alphabetical order); **2.** *fig.* (*klassifizieren*) classify (**unter** + *Akk.* as); (*kategorisieren*) categorize (**in** + *Akk.* among); (*Kunstwerk etc.*) place; *zeitlich*: *auch* date; **j-n** ~ put s.o. down as a certain type; → *auch* **einreihen** II; **II.** *v/refl.*
1. *Verk.* get in lane; **sich rechts/links** ~ get into the right/left lane; **2.** *fig. Person*: fit in (**in** + *Akk.* with), fall into line (with); *Sache*: fit in(to)
Einordnung *f* **1.** (*Ordnung*) *Vorgang*: sorting, arrangement (**in** + *Akk.* into, **nach** according to); *in Akten*: filing; *Ergebnis*: arrangement; **2.** (*Klassifizierung*) classification (**unter** + *Akk.* as); categorization (**in** + *Akk.* among); *von Kunstwerk*: placing; *zeitlich*: *auch* dating
einpacken (*trennb., hat -ge-*) **I.** *v/t.*
1. (*Sache*) pack (up) (**in** + *Akk.* into); (*einwickeln*) wrap up; (*Paket etc.*) *auch* do up; **2.** *umg.* (*j-n*) wrap up; **II.** *v/i.* pack; **da können wir** ~ *umg. fig.* we might as well pack up and go home; **III.** *v/refl.*: **sich** (**warm**) ~ wrap (o.s.) up (warmly)
einparken *v/i.* (*trennb., hat -ge-*) park; **rückwärts** ~ back into a parking space
Einparteien... *im Subst.* one-party ...
einpassen (*trennb., hat -ge-*) **I.** *v/t.*: ~ (**in** + *Akk.*) fit in(to); **II.** *v/refl.* **sich** ~ (**in** + *Akk.*) fit in(to)
einpauken (*trennb., hat -ge-*) *umg.*: **etw.** ~ bone (*Brit. auch* swot, mug) up on s.th.; **j-m etw.** ~ drum (*od.* hammer) s.th. into s.o.
Einpeitscher *m; -s, -, ~in f; -, -nen*; *Parl.* (party) whip
einpendeln *v/refl.* (*trennb., hat -ge-*) level out (**auf** + *Akk. od. Dat.* at)
einpennen *v/i.* (*trennb., ist -ge-*); *umg.* nod off
Einpersonen|haushalt *m* one-person (*od.* single-person) household; **~stück** *n Theat.* monodrama, one-man show
einpferchen *v/t.* (*trennb., hat -ge-*)
1. (*Tiere*) pen in; **2.** *fig.* (*Menschen*) coop up; ~ **in** (+ *Akk.*) *auch* cram (*od.* crowd) into; (*treiben*) herd into
einpflanzen *v/t.* (*trennb., hat -ge-*)
1. plant; **2.** *Med.* (*Organ etc.*) implant; **j-m e-e fremde Niere** ~ give s.o. a kidney transplant
Einphasen... *im Subst.* single-phase ...; **einphasig** *Adj. Etech. attr.* single-phase
einpinseln *v/t.* (*trennb., hat -ge-*); *Med.* paint (**mit** with); **mit Jod** *etc.* ~ put (*od.* dab) iodine *etc.* on
einplanen *v/t.* (*trennb., hat -ge-*) include (in the plan), plan; (*berücksichtigen*) allow for; **das war nicht eingeplant** *umg.* that wasn't part of the plan, that wasn't supposed to happen
einpökeln *v/t.* (*trennb., hat -ge-*) salt, pickle
einpolig *Adj. attr. Etech.* single-pole ...; *Stecker*: one-pin ...
einprägen (*trennb., hat -ge-*) **I.** *v/t.*
1. *Siegel etc.*: imprint, stamp (**in** + *Akk.* on); **2.** *fig.*: **j-m etw.** ~ impress s.th. (up)on s.o.; **sich** (*Dat.*) **etw.** ~ remember s.th.; *lernend*: memorize s.th.; **II.** *v/refl.*: **sich j-m** ~ stick in s.o.'s mind; (*j-n beeindrucken*) make an (*od.* a lasting) impression on s.o.; **sich leicht** ~ be easy to remember; *durch*

Reim, Rhythmus *etc.*: *auch* be catchy;
einprägsam *Adj.* easy to remember, memorable; *Spruch, Melodie etc. auch* catchy; **Einprägsamkeit** *f* memorableness; *von Spruch, Melodie etc.*: *auch* catchiness
einprogrammieren *v/t.* (*trennb., hat*); *EDV* input (as a program)
einprügeln *v/i.* (*trennb., hat -ge-*): ~ **auf** (+ *Akk.*) beat, bash *umg.*
einpudern *v/t.* (*trennb., hat -ge-*) powder
einquartieren (*trennb., hat*) **I.** *v/t. Mil.* billet (**bei** on); *zivil*: put up (**bei j-m** at s.o.'s place); **II.** *v/refl.*: **sich** ~ **bei** move in with; **ich habe mich bei m-m Bruder einquartiert** *auch* I'm staying with my brother; **Einquartierung** *f Mil.* billeting
einquetschen *v/t.* (*trennb., hat -ge-*) jam; **sich** (*Dat.*) **den Finger** ~ get one's finger stuck (*od.* jammed)
Einrad *n* unicycle
einräd(e)rig *Adj.* one-wheeled
einrahmen *v/t.* (*trennb., hat -ge-*) (*Bild, Dia*) frame; **sie wurde von ihren Söhnen eingerahmt** *fig.* she had her sons sitting (*od.* standing) on either side of her
einrammen *v/t.* (*trennb., hat -ge-*) **1.** ~ **in** (+ *Akk.*) ram in(to); (*Pfahl*) drive in(to); **2.** (*zertrümmern*) (*Tür, Tor*) batter down
einrangieren *v/t.* (*trennb., hat*) **1.** ~ **in** (+ *Akk.*) (*Auto etc.*) manoeuvre (*Am.* maneuver) into; **2.** *rangmäßig*: rank, put, place
einrasten *v/i.* (*trennb., ist -ge-*) click into place; *Tech.* engage
einräuchern *v/t.* (*trennb., hat -ge-*) envelope in smoke; (*Zimmer*) fill with smoke
einräumen *v/t.* (*trennb., hat -ge-*)
1. (*Zimmer etc.*) put the furniture in; (*Schrank etc.*) put (the) things in; **2.** (*Bücher, Wäsche etc.*) put (*od.* clear) away; **3.** (*gewähren*) (*Recht*) grant (+ *Dat.* to); *Wirts.* (*Kredit etc.*) grant, allow; **e-r Sache den Vorrang** ~ give s.th. precedence; **4.** (*zugeben*) concede, admit, acknowledge (**dass** that); **j-m etw.** ~ admit s.th. to s.o.; **einräumend I.** *Part. Präs.* → **einräumen**; **II.** *Adj. Ling.* concessive; **Einräumung** *f* (*Zugeständnis*) admission, concession; (*das Gewähren*) granting; **Einräumungssatz** *m Ling.* concessive clause
einrechnen *v/t.* (*trennb., hat -ge-*) include; (*einkalkulieren*) allow for, take into account; → **eingerechnet**
Einrede *f Jur.* objection, plea
einreden (*trennb., hat -ge-*) **I.** *v/t. umg.*
1. **j-m etw.** ~ talk s.o. into (believing) s.th.; **j-m** ~, **dass** ... persuade s.o. that ...; **wer hat dir das eingeredet?** who put that (idea) into your head?; **du willst mir doch wohl nicht** ~, **dass** ... you're not trying to tell me that ...;
2. **sich** (*Dat.*) **etw.** ~ persuade o.s. of s.th.; **das redest du dir (doch) nur ein!** you're imagining it; **II.** *v/i.*: **auf j-n** ~ talk away at s.o.; (*nicht lockerlassen*) keep (*od.* go) on at s.o.
einregnen (*trennb., hat -ge-*); *v/refl., unpers.*: **es regnet sich ein** the rain is settling in
Einreibemittel *n Pharm., für die Muskeln und Gelenke*: liniment; *für die Haut*: ointment; **einreiben** (*unreg., trennb., hat -ge-*) **I.** *v/t.*: ~ (**in** + *Akk.*) rub in(to); *vorsichtig*: put on (in); **die Haut etc. mit etw.** ~ rub s.th. on (*fest*:

into) the skin; **II.** *v/refl.*: **sich mit etw.** ~ put s.th. on; *fest*: rub s.th. in
einreichen *v/t.* (*trennb., hat -ge-*); (*einsenden*) send in; *persönlich*: hand in; (*Bewerbung, Bittschrift etc.*) *auch* submit; (*Beschwerde*) lodge; **e-e Klage** ~ *Jur.* file (*od.* bring) an action; **die Scheidung** ~ file a petition for divorce
einreihen (*trennb., hat -ge-*) **I.** *v/refl.* take one's place (**in** + *Akk.* among); *Sache*: take its place; *in e-e Schlange*: get in line; **sich** ~ **in** (+ *Akk.*) *auch* join; **II.** *v/i.* **1.** → **einordnen** I; **2.** *fig.*: **j-n** ~ **unter** (+ *Akk.*) rank s.o. with (*od.* among); **eingereiht werden unter** *auch* be counted among
Einreiher *m; -s, -* single-breasted suit; **einreihig** *Adj. Anzug etc.*: single-breasted
Einreise *f* entry (**in** + *Akk. od.* **nach** into); **bei der** ~ (**in** + *Akk.*) on arrival (in), when entering; **j-m die** ~ **verweigern** refuse s.o. entry; **~erlaubnis** *f* entry permit
einreisen *v/i.* (*trennb., ist -ge-*) enter the country; ~ **in** (+ *Akk.*) *od.* **nach** enter
Einreise|verbot *n*: ~ **haben** have been refused entry (to the country), not be allowed to enter the country; **~visum** *n* entry visa
einreißen (*unreg., trennb.*) **I.** *v/t.* (*hat eingerissen*) **1.** (*Riss machen*) tear; **sich** (*Dat.*) **e-n Fingernagel** ~ tear a fingernail; **2.** (*Haus etc.*) pull down; **3. sich** (*Dat.*) **e-n Splitter** *etc.* ~ get a splinter in one's skin; **II.** *v/i.* (*ist*)
1. tear; **2.** *umg. fig. Unsitte*: (start to) spread, take hold; **das dürfen wir gar nicht erst** ~ **lassen** we'd better put a stop to that before it takes hold, we'd better nip that in the bud
einreiten (*unreg., trennb.*) **I.** *v/t.* (*hat eingeritten*); (*Pferd*) break in; **II.** *v/i.* (*ist*): ~ (**in** + *Akk.*) ride in(to), enter on horseback; **III.** *v/refl.* have a warming-up ride
einrenken (*trennb., hat -ge-*) **I.** *v/t.*
1. *Med.* set; **2.** *fig.* put right, straighten out; **II.** *v/refl. fig.* sort (*od.* straighten) itself out
einrennen *v/t.* (*unreg., trennb., hat -ge-*) (*Tür etc.*) break (*od.* batter) down; **offene Türen** ~ *fig.* preach to the converted; → **Bude** 2
einrichten (*trennb., hat -ge-*) **I.** *v/t.*
1. (*Zimmer etc.*) furnish; (*Küche, Geschäft etc.*) fit out; (*Labor, Praxis etc.*) equip; **sie sind nett eingerichtet** their place is nicely furnished (*allg.* fixed up); **2.** (*justieren*) adjust; (*Druckmaschine etc.*) set up; *Med.* (*Knochen*) set; **3.** (*schaffen*) establish; (*Organisation*) *auch* set up; (*Filiale*) open; (*gründen*) found; (*Buslinie*) start; (*Konto*) open; **4.** (*ermöglichen, organisieren*) arrange (for); **es** ~, **dass** ... see to it that ...; **wenn du es** ~ **kannst** if you can manage it; **kannst du es irgendwie** ~ **dass** ...? can you possibly arrange things so that ...?; **5.** (*bearbeiten*) (*Musik*) arrange; (*Roman, Stück*) adapt; **6.** *Druck.* (*Seiten*) lay out, set up; **II.** *v/refl.* **1.** furnish one's home (*place umg.*); *weitS.* (*sich einleben*) settle in; **sich neu** ~ refurnish one's home (*place umg.*), get new furnishings; **du hast dich nett eingerichtet** you've made the place really nice, you've set yourself up nicely; → **häuslich** II; **2.** (*auskommen*) make ends meet; (*sich anpassen*) adapt to circumstances; **3. sich** ~ **auf** (+ *Akk.*) prepare

for, get ready for; *organisatorisch*: *auch* make arrangements for; (*rechnen mit*) be prepared for; **auf so etwas sind/waren wir nicht eingerichtet** we're not geared to that sort of thing / we weren't prepared for anything like that

Einrichtung *f* **1.** (*Mobiliar*) furnishings *Pl.*; *e-s Geschäfts*.: fittings *Pl.*; (*Ausrüstung*) equipment; **2.** (*Anlage*) installation, facility; **sanitäre ~en** sanitary facilities; **3.** (*das Einrichten*) *e-r Wohnung etc.*: furnishing; *e-r Küche, e-s Geschäfts*: fitting out; *e-s Labors etc.*: equipping; (*Einbau*) installation; **4.** (*Justierung*) adjustment; *Med.* setting, reduction *fachspr.*; **5.** (*Eröffnung*) setting up, establishment; *e-r Filiale*: opening; **6.** (*Institution*) institution; **öffentliche ~en** public institutions (*od.* services); **7. ständige ~** (*Gepflogenheit*) permanent institution, fixture
Einrichtungs|gegenstände *Pl.* furnishings; *e-r Küche, e-s Geschäfts*: fittings, fixtures; **~haus** *n* furniture store (*od.* showrooms *Pl.*)
Einriss *m* tear; *Med.* laceration
einritzen *v/t.* (*trennb.*, hat -ge-) **1.** scratch (**in** + *Akk.* into the surface of); **2.** (*Haut*) scratch
einrollen (*trennb.*) **I.** *v/t.* (*hat eingerollt*) roll up; **sich** (*Dat.*) **die Haare ~** put one's hair in curlers; **II.** *v/i.* (*ist*); *Zug*: come in; **III.** *v/refl.* (*hat*) curl up; *Tier*: *auch* curl itself up, curl up into a ball
einrosten *v/i.* (*trennb.*, ist -ge-) **1.** get rusty; (*unbeweglich werden*) *auch* get rusted up; → **eingerostet**; **2.** *umg. fig. Kenntnisse*: get rusty; *Glieder*: get stiff (from lack of use); *Person*: stagnate, vegetate
einrücken (*trennb.*) **I.** *v/i.* (*ist eingerückt*) **1.** *bes. Mil.* (*Ggs. ausrücken*): ~ (**in** + *Akk.*) move (*od.* march) in(to), enter; **2.** *Mil.* (*eingezogen werden*) enlist (**zum Militär** in the army); (*sich melden*) report for duty; **II.** *v/t.* (*hat*) **1.** (*Zeile*) indent; **2.** *Tech.* (*Kupplung etc.*) engage; **3.** *fachspr.* (*Anzeige etc.*) (*veröffentlichen*) insert, put in (a newspaper); **Einrückung** *f e-r Zeile*: indentation
einrühren *v/t.* (*trennb.*, hat -ge-): ~ (**in** + *Akk.*) stir in(to)
einrüsten *v/t.* (*trennb.*, hat -ge-); *Archit.* put up scaffolding around, cover in scaffolding
eins I. *Zahlw.* one; *Uhrzeit*: one (o'clock); **~ zu ~** *Sport* one all; **~ zu null für dich** *umg.* that's one up to you; **~ a** (*od.* **I a**) *Wirts.* prime quality ...; *umg.* (*hervorragend*) A1, *Brit. auch* ace *Sl.*; → *auch* **acht¹**; **II.** *Adj.* **1.** (*einig*): **~ sein** *od.* **werden mit j-m** agree with s.o.; **2.** *in Wendungen*: **ihn sehen und weglaufen war ~** the very moment I, he *etc.* saw him I, he *etc.* ran for it, the sight of him resulted in instantaneous flight; **~ werden mit** (*verschmelzen*) become as one with; **III.** *unbest. Pron.* **1.** one thing; **~ gefällt mir nicht** there's one thing I don't like about it; **noch ~** another one; **~ wollte ich dir noch sagen** there's something else (*od.* another thing) (I wanted to say); **es kam ~ zum andern** one thing led to another; **~ nach dem andern!** one thing at a time; **2.** *umg.* (*Schlag*): **j-m ~ auf die Nase** *etc.* **versetzen** land s.o. one on the nose *etc.*; → **einer**
Eins *f*, -, -en **1.** (*Zahl*) (number) one; → *auch* **Acht¹** 1, 2; **2.** *Päd.* (*Note*)

etwa A; **e-e ~ schreiben** get an A
einsacken¹ *v/t.* (*trennb.*, hat -ge-) **1.** sack, put in sacks; **2.** *umg. fig.* (*Geld*) pocket; (*scheffeln*) rake in
einsacken² *v/i.* (*trennb.*, ist -ge-) *umg.* sink; *Dach etc.*: sag; *Boden, Straßendecke*: subside; **~ im Schnee etc.**: sink into
einsagen *vt/i.* (*trennb.*, hat -ge-); *bes. südd., österr.*: **j-m etw. ~** (*Antwort, Lösung etc.*) whisper s.th. to s.o.; **j-m ~** prompt s.o.; → *auch* **vorsagen** I
einsalben *v/t.* (*trennb.*, hat -ge-) put some ointment (*od.* cream) on
einsalzen *v/t.* (*unreg.*, *trennb.*, hat -ge-) salt
einsam *Adj.* **1.** *Person*: lonely; (*zurückgezogen*) *auch Leben*: solitary; **sich ~ fühlen** *auch* feel (very) isolated; **2.** (*abgelegen*) *Haus, Gegend etc.*: lonely, isolated, secluded; *Straße, Strand etc.*: lonely; (*menschenleer*) empty, deserted; **~e Insel** lonely (*unbewohnt*: uninhabited) island; *tropische*: *auch* desert island; **3.** (*einzeln*) *Baum etc.*: solitary, lone; **4.** *umg.*: **~e Spitze sein** be absolutely brilliant (*stärker*: sensational); **Einsamkeit** *f* loneliness (*Abgelegenheit*) *auch* seclusion; isolation; (*Alleinsein*) *auch* solitude
einsammeln *v/t.* (*trennb.*, hat -ge-) **1.** (*Obst etc.*) gather; *vom Boden*: pick up; **2.** (*Geld, Hefte etc.*) collect; **3.** *umg.* (*Personen*) pick up
einsargen *v/t.* (*trennb.*, hat -ge-) put in a coffin (*od.* coffins)
Einsatz *m* **1.** (*eingesetztes Stück*) insert; *Tisch*: (extension) leaf; *am Kleid, im Topf etc.*: inset; *im Filter*: element; *im Koffer etc.*: compartment; **2.** *beim Spiel*: stake (*auch fig.*); (*Flaschenpfand etc.*) deposit; **den ~ erhöhen** raise the stakes *Pl.*; **s-n ~ machen** *beim Roulette*: put down one's stake; **3.** *Mus.* entry; **4.** (*Anstrengung*) effort, hard work; (*Hingabe*) dedication; (*Engagement*) commitment; **~ zeigen** show commitment (*od.* dedication); **beide Seiten haben mit vollem ~ gekämpft** both sides fought with total commitment, it was an all-out battle; **5.** (*das Einsetzen*) employment, use; *von Truppen*: deployment; **unter ~ s-s Lebens** at the risk of one's life; **unter ~ aller Kräfte** by a supreme effort; **zum ~ kommen** *od.* **gelangen** be used; *Truppen etc.*: be sent in; *Spieler*: come on; **im ~ sein** *Sache*: be in use (*od.* operation); **6.** (*Aktion*) *der Armee, Feuerwehr, Polizei etc.*: operation; (*Auftrag*) mission; *Mil. auch* sortie; **im ~ sein** be on duty; *Mil.* be in action; **e-n ~ fliegen** fly a sortie; **7.** *schw. kirchl.* (*Amtseinführung*) induction; **~befehl** *m Mil.* combat order; *Polizei*: operational order
einsatzbereit *Adj.* **1.** *Person*: ready for duty (*Mil.* action), operational; *Sport* match-ready, *Am.* ready to play; **sich ~ halten** stand by; **2.** (*bereitwillig*) willing, keen, *Am. auch* eager; (*opferwillig*) dedicated; **3.** (*kühn*) daring; **4.** *Tech.* operational, ready for use; **Einsatzbereitschaft** *f* **1.** readiness for duty (*Mil.* action); **2.** (*Bereitwilligkeit*) willingness; (*Opferwille*) dedication; **3.** (*Kühnheit*) daring; **4.** *Tech.* readiness for use
Einsatzbesprechung *f* briefing; *nach dem Einsatz*: debriefing
einsatzfähig *Adj.* operational; (*verfügbar*) available; *Sportler*: fit (to play), *Brit. auch* match-fit; **voll ~** fully opera-

tional; *Sportler*: a hundred percent fit; **Einsatzfähigkeit** *f* operational state; (*Verfügbarkeit*) availability; *Logistik etc.*: utilizability; *e-s Sportlers*: fitness (to play), *Brit. auch* match-fitness
Einsatzfahrzeug *n Sanitäter, Notarzt*: emergency vehicle; *Polizei*: police vehicle; *Feuerwehr*: operations vehicle
Einsatzfreude *f*; *nur Sg.* keenness, *Am.* eagerness, alacrity *geh.*; **einsatzfreudig** *Adj.* keen, *Am.* eager; **~ sein** *Sport* put a lot into the game
Einsatz|gebiet *n Mil.* operational area; *weitS.* field of operations; **~kommando** *n* task force; **~leiter** *m*, **~leiterin** *f allg.* head of operations; *e-s Kommandos*: task force commander; **~plan** *m* plan of operations; **~truppe** *f* task force; **~wille** *m* willingness to make a commitment
einsaugen *v/t.* (*mst. unreg.*, *trennb.*, hat -ge-) suck in; (*Luft*) *auch* draw in; → **Muttermilch**
einsäumen *v/t.* (*trennb.*, hat -ge-) **1.** (*Kleid etc.*) hem; **2.** *mit Bäumen etc.*: border
einscannen *v/t.* (*trennb.*, hat -ge-); *EDV, Etron.* scan (**in** + *Akk.* into)
einschalen *v/t.* (*trennb.*, hat -ge-); *Archit.* board, shutter
einschalten (*trennb.*, hat -ge-) **I.** *v/t.* **1.** (*Licht, Gerät etc.*) switch (*od.* turn) on; (*Motor*) start; (*Sender*) tune into; (*auch Fernsehkanal*) put on, switch on; **das 1. Programm eingeschaltet haben** *im Fernsehen*: *auch* be switched onto channel 1, have got channel 1 on *umg.*; **2.** (*einfügen*) add, insert, interpolate *förm.*; **3.** (*j-n*) call in, bring in; **die Presse ~** involve the press; **II.** *v/refl.* **1.** step in, intervene; **2.** *Gerät*: switch itself on
Einschalt|hebel *m* starting lever; **~knopf** *m* on/off button, power button; **~quote** *f TV, Radio*: ratings *Pl.*; *TV auch* viewing figures *Pl.*; **die höchste ~** the top ratings; **~taste** *f* on/off button (*od.* switch), power button
Einschaltung *f* **1.** *e-r Person*: involvement (+ *Gen.* of); **2.** *Ling.* interpolation
Einschaltzeit *f bei Timer*: preset time
einschärfen *v/t.* (*trennb.*, hat -ge-): **j-m ~, etw. zu tun** impress on s.o. the importance of doing s.th.; *bes. e-m Kind*: (*ermahnen*) admonish (*od.* warn) s.o. to do s.th.; **j-m ~, dass ...** impress (up)on s.o. that ...
einscharren (*trennb.*, hat -ge-) **I.** *v/t.* bury; (*j-n*) put in a shallow grave; **II.** *v/refl. Tier*: burrow (its way) (**in** + *Akk.* into)
einschätzbar *Adj.* assessable
einschätzen *v/t.* (*trennb.*, hat -ge-) **1.** (*Einkommen, Kosten, Wert etc.*) assess; (*schätzen*) estimate (**auf** + *Akk.* at); **2.** *fig.* (*beurteilen*) judge; (*einstufen*) rate, assess; **~ als** rate (*od.* see) as; **hoch/niedrig ~** rate highly / not rate highly, think highly / not think highly of; **zu hoch/niedrig ~** overalue/undervalue; **j-n/ die Lage völlig falsch ~** misjudge s.o. / the situation entirely; **etw. richtig ~** judge s.th. right, be right about s.th.; **das ist schwer einzuschätzen** it's hard to say
Einschätzung *f* **1.** assessment; (*Beurteilung*) judg(e)ment; **nach m-r ~** the way I see it; **2.** *e-r Summe etc.*: estimate; *bes. Steuer*: assessment
einschäumen *v/t.* (*trennb.*, hat -ge-) **1.** *mit Schaum*: lather; **2.** *Tech.*, *mit Schaumstoff*: wrap in plastic foam

E

einschenken *v/t.* (*trennb., hat -ge-*) **1.** pour (out); *j-m Wein* ~ pour s.o. some wine; → *Wein* 1; **2.** (*Glas, Tasse*) fill; *j-m e-e Tasse Tee* ~ pour s.o. a cup of tea; → *eingeschenkt*

einscheren *v/i.* (*trennb., ist -ge-*); *Mot.* cut in (*vor* + *Dat.* on *od.* in front of); *nach rechts/links* ~ move across (*od.* change lanes) to the right/left

einschicken *v/t.* (*trennb., hat -ge-*) send (in) (*an* + *Akk.* to)

einschieben *v/t.* (*unreg., trennb., hat -ge-*): ~ (*in* + *Akk.*) push (*od.* slide) in(to); (*Worte etc.*) add (to), insert (in); (*j-n, etw.*) *in e-n Zeitplan etc.*: fit in(to), slot in(to); **Einschiebung** *f* addition, insertion; (*Textstelle*) *auch* interpolation *förm.*

Einschienenbahn *f* monorail

einschießen (*unreg., trennb.*) **I.** *v/t.* (*hat eingeschossen*) **1.** (*Gebäude, Mauer*) demolish with gunfire; (*Fenster etc.*) shoot in; *mit e-m Ball etc.*: smash in; **2.** (*neues Gewehr*) break in; **3.** *Fußball*: (*Ball*) drive into the net; **4.** *fig.* (*Geld*) contribute (*in* + *Akk.* to), invest (in); (*Kapital*) inject (into); **5.** *Tech.* (*Dübel, Nieten etc.*) drive in; **6.** *Druck.* (*Blatt*) interleave; **II.** *v/refl.* (*hat*) *Artillerie*: get the range (*auf* + *Akk.* of); *sich* ~ *auf* (+ *Akk.*) *auch fig.* zero (*od.* home) in on; **III.** *v/i.* **1.** (*hat*); *Sport* score; *zum 2:0* ~ score to make it 2-0 (= two-nil, *Am.* two-nothing); **2.** (*ist*); *Flüssigkeit*: rush in; *Muttermilch*: come in

einschiffen (*trennb., hat -ge-*) **I.** *v/t.* (*Waren*) *auch* ship; **II.** *v/refl.* embark (*nach* for), board (the) ship

einschiffig *Adj. Archit., Kirche*: consisting only of a nave, with no side-aisles

Einschiffung *f* embarkation

einschl. *Abk.* (*einschließlich*) incl.

einschlafen *v/i.* (*unreg., trennb., ist -ge-*) **1.** fall asleep, go to sleep; *ich konnte letzte Nacht nicht* ~ I couldn't get to sleep last night; *wieder* ~ go (*od.* get) back to sleep; *beim Fernsehen / am Steuer* ~ go to sleep (*od.* drop off) in front of the television / at the wheel; *komm, schlaf nicht ein!* get a move on, don't go to sleep!; **2.** *Glieder*: go to sleep; *mir ist der rechte Arm eingeschlafen auch* I've got pins and needles in my right arm; **3.** *euph.* (*sterben*) pass away; **4.** *Briefwechsel, Unterhaltung etc.*: peter out, fizzle out *umg.*; *Freundschaft*: cool off; *Brauch*: die out

einschläfern *v/t.* (*trennb., hat -ge-*) **1.** send to sleep; (*schläfrig machen*) make (feel) sleepy, be soporific; **2.** *Med.* (*betäuben*) put to sleep, an(a)esthetize; **3.** (*Tier*) put down, put to sleep; **4.** (*Gewissen*) salve; (*Gegner etc.*) lull into a false sense of security; **einschläfernd I.** *Part. Präs.* → *einschläfern;* **II.** *Adj. auch fig.* (*langweilig*) soporific; *Med.* an(a)esthetic; **III.** *Adv.: die Musik etc. wirkt* ~ the music *etc.* has a soporific effect (*od.* sends you to sleep)

Einschlafstörungen *Pl.* difficulties in getting to sleep

Einschlag *m* **1.** *e-s Geschosses etc.*: impact; (*Einschlagstelle*) point of impact; *die Einschläge der Bomben hören/sehen* hear the bomb explosions / see where the bombs struck (*in den Boden*: landed); *beim* ~ *des Blitzes* when the lightning struck; **2.** *fig.* (*Beimischung*) element; *sie hat türkisches* ~ she's got some Turkish (blood) in her; **3.** *Mot., der Räder*: lock; *des Lenkrades*: turning; **4.** *am Kleid, Ärmel*: tuck, fold; **5.** *Weberei*: weft, woof; **6.** *Agr. von Bäumen*: felling; *konkret*: amount (of timber) felled

einschlagen (*unreg., trennb., hat -ge-*) **I.** *v/t.* **1.** ~ (*in* + *Akk.*) (*Nagel etc.*) hammer in(to); **2.** (*zerbrechen*) smash in; *j-m den Schädel / die Zähne / die Nase* ~ smash s.o.'s head in / knock s.o.'s teeth out / flatten s.o.'s nose; **3.** (*Kurs, Richtung etc.*) take; *e-e Laufbahn* ~ take up (*od.* pursue) a career; *e-e andere Richtung* ~ change course (*auch fig.*); **4.** *Mot.* (*Räder, Steuer*) turn; *das Steuer nach rechts* ~ turn the steering wheel to the right, lock over to the right; **5.** (*einwickeln*) wrap up (*in* + *Akk.* in); (*Buch*) put a dust jacket on; **6.** (*Betttuch etc.*) tuck in; **7.** *Agr.* (*Bäume, Holz*) fell; **II.** *v/i.* **1.** *Geschoss*: hit; *Blitz*: strike; *unpers.*: *es schlug in der Kirche ein* the church was struck by lightning; **2.** *fig.* (*Erfolg haben*) be a big hit (*bei j-m* with s.o.), go down a bomb *Brit. umg., Am.* hit the big time; → *Blitz* 1, *Bombe* 1; **3.** *beim Handel*: shake hands (on the deal); *schlag ein!* shake on it!; **4.** *auf j-n* ~ rain blows on s.o., hit out at s.o.; **5.** *Mot.*: (*nach*) *links/rechts* ~ turn the steering wheel (*od.* lock over) to the left/right; *Anweisung*: left/right hand down

einschlägig I. *Adj.* relevant (*auch Literatur*), appropriate; *in allen* ~*en Geschäften zu finden* available at all stockists (*Am.* specialty stores); **II.** *Adv.: er ist* ~ *vorbestraft* he's been previously convicted for the same (*od.* for a similar) offen|ce (*Am.* -se)

einschleichen *v/refl.* (*unreg., trennb., hat -ge-*): *sich* ~ (*in* + *Akk.*) creep in(-to) (*auch fig. Fehler*); *sich in j-s Vertrauen* ~ *fig.* worm one's way into s.o.'s confidence

einschleifen (*unreg., trennb., hat -ge-*) **I.** *v/t.* **1.** (*Brillengläser etc.*) grind; **2.** (*eingravieren*) engrave, cut (*in* + *Akk.* into); **II.** *v/refl. Verhalten etc.*: become a habit, become ingrained; *Gewohnheit*: take root

einschleppen *v/t.* (*trennb., hat -ge-*) **1.** ~ (*in* + *Akk. od. nach*) (*Krankheit*) bring in(to), introduce (to, into); **2.** ~ (*in* + *Akk.*) (*Schiff*) tow in(to)

einschleusen *v/t.* (*trennb., hat -ge-*) ~ (*in* + *Akk.*) (*Rauschgift, Flüchtlinge etc.*) smuggle in(to); *fig.* (*Agenten*) infiltrate (into)

einschließen (*unreg., trennb., hat -ge-*) **I.** *v/t.* **1.** (*einsperren*) lock up; ~ *in* (+ *Akk.*) lock (up) in; *bes. Tier, Kind*: shut in; **2.** (*umgeben*) enclose; *Berge etc. auch* shut in; (*umzingeln*) surround, encircle; **3.** *fig.* include; **II.** *v/refl.: sich* ~ (*in* + *Akk. od. Dat.*) lock (*od.* shut) o.s. in; → *eingeschlossen*

einschließlich I. *Präp.* (+ *Gen. od. Dat.*) including; *bes. Wirts.* inclusive of; **II.** *Adv.: bis* ~ *Seite 7* up to and including page 7, *Am. auch* through page 7; *vom 1. bis* ~ *4. Mai* from the 1st to the 4th of May inclusive(ly), *Am.* (from) May 1st through May 4th; *von Montag bis* ~ *Mittwoch* Monday to Wednesday inclusive(ly), *Am.* Monday through Wednesday; *bis* ~ *Freitag* up to and including Friday, *Am. auch* through Friday

einschlummern *v/i.* (*trennb., ist -ge-*) **1.** *geh.* doze off; **2.** *umg. Freundschaft etc.*: peter out

Einschluss *m* **1.** *Geol.* inclusion; **2.** *unter* ~ (+ *Gen. od. von*) including, with the inclusion of

einschmeicheln *v/refl.* (*trennb., hat -ge-*): *sich bei j-m* ~ play up to s.o., ingratiate o.s. with s.o., butter s.o. up *umg.*; **einschmeichelnd I.** *Part. Präs.* → *einschmeicheln;* **II.** *Adj.* beguiling; *Art*: ingratiating; *Stimme*: *auch* silky; **Einschmeich(e)lung** *f* attempt to ingratiate o.s.

einschmeißen *v/t.* (*unreg., trennb., hat -ge-*); *umg.* → *einwerfen* I 1, 2, 3

einschmelzen (*unreg., trennb.*) *v/t.* (*hat eingeschmolzen*) *und v/i.* (*ist*) melt (down)

einschmieren (*trennb., hat -ge-*) *umg.* **I.** *v/t.* **1.** ~ *in* (+ *Akk.*) (*Öl*) rub into (*od.* on); (*Creme*) *auch* put on; *sich* (*Dat.*) *die Hände etc.* ~ put (some) cream (*od.* lotion) on one's hands *etc.*, rub (some) cream (*od.* lotion) into one's hands *etc.*; **2.** (*Kuchenform etc.*) grease; *Tech.* lubricate; *mit Fett*: grease,; **II.** *v/refl. mit Creme*: rub (*od.* put) some cream (*od.* lotion) on; *mit Öl*: rub some oil in

einschmuggeln (*trennb., hat -ge-*) **I.** *v/t.:* ~ (*in* + *Akk.*) smuggle in(to); **II.** *v/refl.: sich* ~ (*in* + *Akk.*) sneak in(to)

einschnappen *v/i.* (*trennb., ist -ge-*) **1.** *Schloss etc.*: snap shut; *Tür*: click shut; *Verschluss*: click into place; **2.** *umg. pej.* (*beleidigt sein*) go into a huff

einschneiden (*unreg., trennb., hat -ge-*) **I.** *v/t.* **1.** cut into; **2.** (*einritzen*) carve (*in* + *Akk.* into); **3.** *Tech.* (*Nut, Gewinde*) cut; **4.** *fig.* → III; **II.** *v/i. Kragen etc.*: cut, pinch; *die Träger schneiden an den Schultern ein* the straps cut into your shoulders; **III.** *v/refl.: der Fluss hat sich tief ins Tal eingeschnitten* the river has cut a deep bed in the valley; → *eingeschnitten;* **einschneidend I.** *Part. Präs.* → *einschneiden;* **II.** *Adj. fig. Maßnahmen*: decisive; (*radikal*) drastic; *Reformen*: radical, drastic, major; (*weitreichend*) far-reaching; *von* ~*er Bedeutung* of far-reaching significance

einschneidig *Adj.* one-edged, single--edged

Einschnitt *m* **1.** cut; *bes. Med.* incision; **2.** (*Kerbe*) notch; **3.** *im Gelände*: cleft; **4.** *fig.* crucial (*od.* decisive) event; (*Wendepunkt*) turning point; (*Zäsur*) break

einschnitzen *v/t.* (*trennb., hat -ge-*) carve (*in* + *Akk.* into)

einschnüren *v/t.* (*trennb., hat -ge-*); (*Paket*) tie up; *j-n/sich* ~ *in Korsett*: lace s.o./o.s. up; *j-m den Hals* ~ *Kragen*: (nearly) strangle s.o.

einschränken (*trennb., hat -ge-*) **I.** *v/t.* **1.** (*verringern*) (*Ausgaben, Verbrauch, Produktion etc.*) reduce, cut (down) (*auf* + *Akk.* to); (*Forderungen*) moderate; *das Rauchen/Trinken etc.* ~ cut down on smoking/drinking *etc.*; **2.** (*begrenzen*) (*Macht, Freiheit etc.*) limit, restrict (*auf* + *Akk.* to); *j-n in s-n Rechten/Möglichkeiten* ~ limit s.o.'s rights / what s.o. can do (*formeller*: s.o.'s sphere of action); **3.** (*relativieren*) (*Behauptung etc.*) qualify; → *eingeschränkt;* **II.** *v/refl.* cut down (on things), economize; *sich* ~ *müssen auch* have to tighten one's belt *umg.*

einschränkend I. *Part. Präs.* → *einschränken*; **II.** *Adj.* qualifying; *Ling.* restrictive; **III.** *Adv.*: **dazu muss ich ~ hinzufügen** I should qualify that by saying

Einschränkung *f* **1.** reduction, cut (+ *Gen.* in); (*Begrenzung*) restriction (+ *Gen.* of); **~en vornehmen** make cuts; *finanziell*: *auch* make economies; **~en vornehmen in** (+ *Dat.*) *auch* cut down on; **e-e ~ der Ausgaben** a cutback in expenditure; **j-m/sich ~en auferlegen** impose restrictions (*finanzielle*: economies) on s.o. / practi|se (*Am.* -ce) self-denial; *finanziell*: make economies; **2.** (*Vorbehalt*) qualification (+ *Gen* of); **ohne ~ sagen etc.**: without reservation; **mit der ~, dass ...** with the (one) reservation that ...

einschrauben *v/t.* (*trennb.*, *hat -ge-*): **~** (*in* + *Akk.*) screw in(to)

Einschreibe|brief *m* registered letter; **~gebühr** *f Post.*, *Univ.* registration fee

einschreiben I. *v/t.* (*unreg.*, *trennb.*, *hat -ge-*); (*eintragen*) *in Liste etc.*: enter; *als Mitglied*, *Teilnehmer*: enrol(l); **sich ~ lassen** → II; **II.** *v/refl.* sign up; *Univ.* register, *Am.* enrol(l); **sich in e-e Liste ~** enter one's name on a list; → *eingeschrieben*

Einschreiben *n*: **per** *od.* **als ~ schicken** send *s.th.* registered (*od.* by registered mail); (**per**) **~!** registered, certified

Einschreibung *f* signing up; *Univ.* registration, *Am. auch* enrollment

einschreien *v/i.* (*unreg.*, *trennb.*, *hat -ge-*): **auf j-n ~** shout at s.o.

einschreiten *v/i.* (*unreg.*, *trennb.*, *ist -ge-*) intervene, step in; **~ gegen** take action against; **energisch ~ gegen** take firm measures against, clamp down on

einschrumpeln *umg.*, **einschrumpfen** *v/i.* (*trennb.*, *ist -ge-*) shrivel (up); *umg. Mensch*: shrink

Einschub *m* **1.** (*Text*) insertion; **2.** *Tech.* plug-in unit

einschüchtern *v/t.* (*trennb.*, *hat -ge-*) intimidate; (*erschrecken*) scare; *durch Drohungen*: *auch* browbeat; **lass dich von ihm nicht ~** don't be intimidated by him; → *eingeschüchtert*; **Einschüchterung** *f* intimidation; *durch Drohung*: browbeating

Einschüchterungsversuch *m* attempt to intimidate s.o.; *Pol.* scare tactic

einschulen *v/t.* (*trennb.*, *hat -ge-*) send to school; **eingeschult werden** start school; **Einschulung** *f* **1.** enrol(l)ment; **ein Kind von der ~ zurückstellen** postpone the date a child starts school; **2.** (*Tag*) first day at school

Einschulungs|alter *n* age for starting school, school age; **~test** *m* pre-school test

Einschuss *m* **1.** (*Treffer*) hit, shot; (*Loch*) bullet hole; (*Stelle*) entry; *Med.* entry wound; **2.** *Sport* shot into goal, scoring shot; **3.** *Wirts.* (*Einlage*) capital invested; *im Differenzgeschäft*: margin; **4.** *Weberei*: woof, weft; **5.** → *Einschlag* 2

einschussbereit *Adj. Sport* in a good scoring position

Einschuss|loch *n* bullet hole; **~stelle** *f* point of entry; **~winkel** *m* **1.** *beim Fußball*, *Hockey etc.*: shooting (*od.* scoring) angle; **2.** *von Geschoss*: angle of entry

einschwärzen *v/t.* (*trennb.*, *hat -ge-*) blacken; *Druck.* ink

einschweben *v/i.* (*trennb.*, *ist -ge-*) *Flugzeug*, *Spaceshuttle etc.*: glide in (to land)

einschweißen *v/t.* (*trennb.*, *hat -ge-*) **1.** **etw. in etw.** (*Akk.*) **~** weld s.th. into s.th.; **2.** *in Plastikfolie*: shrink-wrap

einschwenken (*trennb.*) **I.** *v/i.* (*ist eingeschwenkt*) **1.** turn in (*in* + *Akk.* -to); **nach links ~** turn (to the) left; **2.** *fig.*: **~ auf** (+ *Akk.*) switch to; (*sich anpassen*) fall in line with; **auf e-n neuen Kurs ~** change course; **II.** *v/t.* (*hat*) swivel *s.th.* into position; **~ in** (+ *Akk.*) swivel into

einschwören *v/t.* (*unreg.*, *trennb.*, *hat -ge-*) (*vereidigen*) swear in; *fig.* (*verpflichten*) commit; → *eingeschworen*

einsegnen *v/t.* (*trennb.*, *hat -ge-*) **1.** *kath.* (*Kirche etc.*) consecrate; (*Haus*, *Gläubige*) bless; **2.** *ev.* (*konfirmieren*) confirm; **Einsegnung** *f* consecration; *von Gläubigen*: blessing; (*Konfirmation*) confirmation

einsehbar *Adj.* **1.** visible; **der Garten ist von der Straße her nicht ~** you can't see into the garden from the road; **2.** (*zugänglich*) (*Akten etc.*) open (to view); **3.** (*verständlich*) understandable; **es ist nur schwer ~, warum ...** it is difficult to see why ...

einsehen *v/t.* (*unreg.*, *trennb.*, *hat -ge-*) **1.** (*Garten*, *Fenster etc.*) see into; **etw. ~ können** be able to see into s.th.; (*Garten etc.*) overlook s.th.; **2.** (*Unterlagen etc.*) have a look at; **die Dokumente dürfen eingesehen werden** the documents may be viewed (*od.* consulted); **3.** *fig.* (*verstehen*) see; (*erkennen*) realize; (*richtig einschätzen*) appreciate; (*akzeptieren*) accept; **e-n Fehler ~** recognize one's mistake; **das sehe ich nicht ein** I don't see why; **er will es einfach nicht ~** he just refuses to accept it (*od.* see it)

Einsehen *n*; *-s*, *kein Pl.*: **ein ~ haben** show some consideration (*od.* understanding); (*vernünftig sein*) be reasonable; (*nachsichtig sein*) be lenient, show some leniency; **das Wetter hatte ein ~ mit uns** *hum.* the weather was kind to us

einseifen *v/t.* (*trennb.*, *hat -ge-*) **1.** soap; (*Bart*) lather; **j-n ~ beim Baden**, *Duschen*: lather (*od.* soap) s.o.; *beim Rasieren*: lather s.o.'s face; **j-n mit Schnee ~** *umg.* rub snow in s.o.'s face; **2.** *umg. fig.* (*betrügen*) con, take for a ride

einseitig I. *Adj.* **1.** *oft pej.* (*Ausbildung*, *Begabung*, *Bericht*, *Sichtweise etc.*) one-sided; (*parteiisch*) partial, bias(s)ed; **2.** *Pol.*, *Jur.* unilateral; (*Liebe*, *Zuneigung*) one-sided; (*unerwidert*) unrequited; **3.** *Med.* on one side; **e-e ~e Lungenentzündung** single pneumonia; **~e Lähmung** paralysis on one side, hemiplegia *fachspr.*; **4.** (*unausgeglichen*) unbalanced, one-sided; **~e Ernährung** unbalanced diet; **5.** (*Druck etc.*) one-sided; **II.** *Adv.* **1.** *pej.*: **etw. ~ darstellen** give a (very) one-sided view of s.th.; **~ begabt sein** be one-sided; **2.** *Pol.*, *Jur.* unilaterally; **3.** **~ bedruckt/beschrieben** printed/written on one side; **4.** *Med.*: **~ gelähmt** paralysed on one side, hemiplegic *fachspr.*; **Einseitigkeit** *f* one-sidedness; (*Parteilichkeit*) partiality, bias

einsenden *v/t.* (*mst unreg.*, *trennb.*, *hat -ge-*) send in; **etw. an e-e Zeitung ~** send (in) s.th to a newspaper; **Einsender** *m*, **Einsenderin** *f* sender; *Wettbewerb*: entrant; *an e-e Zeitung*: contributor; **Einsendeschluss** *m* closing date (for entries); **Einsendung** *f* **1.** (*Einsenden*) sending in; **2.** (*Beitrag*)

contribution; *für Wettbewerb*: entry; (*Zuschrift*) letter, reply

einsenken *v/t.* (*trennb.*, *hat -ge-*) sink (*in* + *Akk.* into); **Einsenkung** *f* **1.** (*Einsenken*) sinking; **2.** (*Vertiefung*) depression

Einser *m*; *-s*, *-*; *umg.* → *Eins*

einsetzen (*trennb.*, *hat -ge-*) **I.** *v/t.* **1.** **~** (*in* + *Akk.*) put in(to); (*einpassen*) fit in(to); (*einfügen*) *auch* insert (in); *in ein Formular etc.*: enter (*in* + *Akk.* in); (*Pflanzen*) plant (in); **Fische** (*in e-n Teich*) **~** put fish in a breeding pool; **2.** (*Sonderzug etc.*) put on; **3.** (*anwenden*) use, employ; (*Gewalt*, *Kraft etc.*) *auch* apply, exert; *fig.* (*Einfluss*, *Können*) bring to bear; **4.** (*Personen*) (*beschäftigen*) employ, put to work; (*Polizei etc.*) call in; *Mil.* put into action; *Sport* (*aufstellen*) play; **5.** (*Ausschuss etc.*) set up; (*Person*) *in ein Amt*: appoint (*in* + *Akk.* to); *als Präsident*, *Bischof etc.*: install; *als Bevollmächtigten*, *Erben etc.*: appoint, name; **6.** (*Geld*) bet; **sein Leben ~** risk one's life (**für** for), put one's life at risk (for); **II.** *v/refl.* **1.** (*sich anstrengen*) do what one can, make an effort; **du musst dich mehr ~** you must make more of an effort; **sich voll ~** do one's utmost, give one's all; **2.** **sich ~ für** (*unterstützen*) support; (*plädieren für*) speak up for; (*verfechten*) champion; *weitS.* do what one can for, do one's best to help; **ich werde mich dafür ~, dass ...** I will do what I can to see that ...; **sich für etw. voll ~** do all one can (*od.* make every effort) to support s.th.; **sich** (*bei j-m*) **für j-n ~** put in a good word for s.o. (with s.o.), intercede (with s.o.) on s.o.'s behalf *förm.*; **III.** *v/i.* **1.** *Mus.* come in; **2.** (*beginnen*) start; *Fieber*, *Schlechtwetter etc.*: set in; *Unwetter*: break; **einsetzend I.** *Part. Präs.* → *einsetzen*; **II.** *Adj.*: **die ~e Dämmerung** the gathering twilight; **plötzlich ~er Regen** a sudden burst of rain

Einsetzung *f* **1.** *e-r Person*: appointment (*in* + *Akk.* to); *e-s Ausschusses*: setting up; **2.** (*Einfügung*) insertion; → *auch* **Einsatz** 5, 7

Einsicht *f* **1.** (*Einblick*) **~** (*in* + *Akk.*) view in(to); **2.** *nur Sg.*; (*Prüfung*) examination (**in Akten** of records); **~ nehmen in** (+ *Akk.*) examine, take a look at; **j-m ~ gewähren in** (+ *Akk.*) allow s.o. to look at; **3.** *fig.* (*Erkenntnis*) insight (**in** + *Akk.* into); **zur ~ kommen, dass ...** come to realize that ...; **4.** *nur Sg.*; *fig.* (*Vernunft*) sense; (*Verständnis*) understanding; **~ haben** show understanding (**mit** for); **zur ~ kommen** come to one's senses; **hab doch ~!** do be reasonable!; **gegen s-e bessere ~** against one's better judg(e)ment

einsichtig I. *Adj.* **1.** (*vernünftig*) reasonable; (*verständnisvoll*) understanding; (*reumütig*) contrite; **2.** (*verständlich*) understandable; *Argumente*: cogent; **mir ist nicht ~, warum ...** I cannot see why ...; **II.** *Adv.* understandingly; (*reumütig*) contritely

Einsichtnahme *f Amtsspr.* inspection; **zur ~** for attention; **nach ~ in** (+ *Akk.*) after inspecting ...

einsichtslos *Adj.* (*unvernünftig*) unreasonable; (*verständnislos*) lacking in understanding; (*reuelos*) unrepentant; **einsichtsvoll** *Adj.* understanding; (*verständig*) reasonable

einsickern *v/i.* (*trennb.*, *ist -ge-*): **~** (*in*

+ *Akk.*) seep *od.* trickle in(to); *fig. Gäste, Meldungen etc.*: trickle in(to); *Spione etc.*: infiltrate (into)

Einsiedelei *f*, -, *-en* **1.** hermitage; **2.** *nur Sg.*; (*Lebensweise*) (life of) solitude; **Einsiedler** *m*, **Einsiedlerin** *f auch fig.* hermit, recluse; **einsiedlerisch** *Adj.* hermit(-)like, *weitS.* solitary

Einsiedler|krebs *m Zool.* hermit crab; **~leben** *n* hermit's life, life of a hermit; **ein ~ führen** lead the life of a hermit, live like a hermit

einsilbig *Adj.* **1.** monosyllabic; **~es Wort** monosyllable; **2.** *fig.* (*wortkarg*) taciturn; (*kurz angebunden*) curt, short; **~e Antworten geben** answer in monosyllables; **Einsilbigkeit** *f fig.* taciturnity; (*kurz angebundene Art*) curtness

einsinken *v/i.* (*unreg., trennb., ist -ge-*) **1.** ~ (*in + Akk.*) sink in(to); **bis zu den Knien ~** sink in up to one's knees; **2.** *Boden, Dach etc.*: subside, cave in; **in den Knien ~** sink to one's knees

einsitzen *v/i.* (*unreg., trennb., hat* / *südd., österr., schw. ist -ge-*); *Jur.* serve a sentence

Einsitzer *m*; *-s*, *-*; (*Fahrzeug, Flugzeug*) single-seater; **einsitzig** *Adj.* (*Fahrzeug, Flugzeug*) *attr.* single-seater ...

einsortieren *v/t.* (*trennb., hat*) sort (**in** *+ Akk.* into); (*Karteikarten etc.*) (sort and) file

einspaltig I. *Adj. Zeitungsmeldung, Satz etc.*: *attr.* single-column; **II.** *Adv.*: **~ gedruckt/gesetzt** printed/set in one column

einspannen *v/t.* (*trennb., hat -ge-*) **1.** *Tech.* clamp; (*Schreibpapier*) put in(to the typewriter *etc.*); (*Film*) load, put in; **2.** (*Pferd*) harness; **3.** *umg. fig.*: *j-n ~* rope s.o. in (**zu etw.** for s.th. *od.* to do s.th.); *j-n zur Arbeit ~* make s.o. work hard; → **eingespannt**

Einspänner¹ *m*; *-s*, *-* (*Kutsche*) one-horse carriage

Einspänner² *m*; *-s*, *-*; *österr.* (*Kaffee*) *glass of black coffee with whipped cream topping*

einsparen *v/t.* (*trennb., hat -ge-*) save; (*Kosten, Stellen*) cut; **Einsparung** *f* saving (**an** *+ Dat. od.* **von** in); *bes. Pl.* economies (in); **~ von Arbeitsplätzen** job cuts; **Einsparungsmaßnahme** *f* economic measure

einspeichern *v/t.* (*trennb., hat -ge-*) *EDV* input, enter (**in** *+ Akk.* into)

einspeisen *v/t.* (*trennb., hat -ge-*) **1.** *Tech.* feed (**in** *+ Akk.* into; *+ Dat.* to); **2.** *EDV* (*Daten*) input, enter (**in** *+ Akk.* into)

einsperren (*trennb., hat -ge-*) **I.** *v/t.* lock up (**in** *+ Akk. od. Dat.* in); *im Gefängnis: auch* put behind bars; *in e-n Käfig:* put in a cage, cage; **II.** *v/refl.*: **sich ~** (**in etw.** *Akk. od. Dat.*) lock o.s. in (s.th.)

einspielen (*trennb., hat -ge-*) **I.** *v/refl.* **1.** *auch Sport* warm up; **sich auf e-m Instrument ~** get the feel of (*od.* get used to) an instrument; **2.** *Sache*: get going (properly); **das neue System hat sich noch nicht eingespielt** the new system has yet to settle down; **3. sich aufeinander ~** learn to work (*Sport*) play) together, get used to one another → **eingespielt**; **II.** *v/t.* **1.** (*Instrument*) break in; **2.** (*aufnehmen*) record; **3.** *TV* (*in Sendung einfügen*) insert, play in; **4.** (*Geld*) bring in, gross; **der Film hat die Produktionskosten bereits im ersten Monat eingespielt**

the film covered its production costs in its first month

Einspielergebnisse *Pl.* box-office (returns *od.* takings)

Einspielung *f* (*Aufnahme*) recording (**von** by)

einspinnen (*unreg., trennb., hat -ge-*) **I.** *v/refl.* **1.** *Zool.* cocoon itself; **2.** *fig.* cocoon o.s.; *in Gedanken*: be wrapped up; **II.** *v/t. Spinne*: spin a web around

Einsprache *f österr., schw.* → **Einspruch**

einsprachig I. *Adj.* monolingual; *Fremdsprachenunterricht*: in the foreign language; **II.** *Adv.*: **~ aufwachsen** have a monolingual upbringing; **s-e Kinder ~ erziehen** bring up one's children monolingually

einsprengen *v/t.* (*trennb., hat -ge-*); (*Wäsche, Rasen*) sprinkle; → **eingesprengt**; **Einsprengsel** *n*; *-s*, - embedded particle

einspringen (*unreg., trennb.*) **I.** *v/i.* (*ist eingesprungen*) **1.** *fig.* (*aushelfen*) step in(to the breach), help out; *finanziell*: help out, chip in *umg.*; **für j-n ~** stand in for s.o.; **2.** *Tech.* (*einschnappen*) click (into place); **3.** *Archit.* recede; **II.** *v/refl.* (*hat*); *Sport* do practice jumps

Einspritzdüse *f Mot., Diesel*: injection (*od.* injector) nozzle

einspritzen *v/t.* (*trennb., hat -ge-*) inject (**in** *+ Akk.* into); *j-m etw. ~* give s.o. an injection of s.th., inject s.o. with s.th.

Einspritz|motor *m Mot.* fuel injection engine; **~pumpe** *f Mot.* (fuel) injection pump

Einspruch *m auch Jur.* objection (**gegen** to); *Jur.* (*Berufung*) appeal (against); *Patentrecht*: opposition (to); **~ erheben** *od.* **einlegen** raise an objection (**gegen** to), object (to); *Jur.* (file an) appeal (against); **ich erhebe ~!** I object!; *Jur.* objection!

Einspruchsrecht *n* right to appeal; *Pol.* (power of) veto

einsprühen *v/t.* (*trennb., hat -ge-*) spray; (*Haar*) put hairspray on; *Wäsche auch* sprinkle

einspurig I. *Adj. Eisenb. attr.* single-track ..., *präd.* single-tracked; *Straße*: *attr.* single-lane ...; **II.** *Adv.*: **nur ~ befahrbar** with only one lane open

Einssein *n geh.* oneness, unity (**mit** with)

einst *Adv. geh.* **1.** (*vormals*) once; ... **~ und jetzt** ... past and present, ... then and now; **das England von ~** the England of days past (*od.* of yore), England as it once was; **2.** (*künftig*) one day, some day; **~ kommt der Tag, da ...** the day will come when ...; **Einst** *n*; *-*, *kein Pl.* (distant) past

einstampfen *v/t.* (*trennb., hat -ge-*) **1.** (*Kohl etc.*) press; (*Erde*) tamp, stamp down; **2.** (*Papier, Bücher*) pulp

Einstand *m* **1.** *nur Sg.*; *Tennis*: deuce; **2.** *bes. südd., österr.* first day (in a new job *etc.*); *s-n ~ feiern* celebrate the start of one's new job; **s-n ~ geben** *auch Sport* make one's debut (*od.* début)

Einstandspreis *m Wirts.* cost price

einstanzen *v/t.* (*trennb., hat -ge-*); *Tech.*: ~ (**in** *+ Akk.*) stamp in(to)

einstauben (*trennb., -ge-*) **I.** *v/i.* (*ist*) get covered in dust; **II.** *v/t.* (*hat*) **1. sich** (*Akk., Dat.*) **die Kleidung** *etc.* ~ get one's clothes *etc.* covered in dust; → **eingestaubt**; **2.** *österr.* (*pudern*) (*Gesicht*) powder, dust one's face with

powder

einstechen (*unreg., trennb., hat -ge-*) **I.** *v/t.* **1.** (*Teig etc.*) prick; (*Folie etc.*) *auch* pierce; **2.** (*Loch*) pierce (**in** *+ Akk.* in); (*Nadel*) stick in(to); (*Spritze*) insert (in), stick in(to) *umg.*; *Tech., Werkzeugmaschine*: cut (in); (*eingravieren*) engrave (in); **II.** *v/i.* **1. mit e-r Nadel** *etc.* **in etw.** (*Akk.*) ~ stick a needle *etc.* into s.th.; **2. auf j-n ~** stab s.o. repeatedly

einstecken *v/t.* (*trennb., hat -ge-*) **1.** (*Stecker etc.*) put in; (*Bügeleisen, Radio etc.*) plug in; **etw. in etw.** (*Akk.*) ~ put s.th. into s.th.; **2.** *in die Tasche*: put in one's pocket (*Handtasche* bag); (*Pistole, Messer*) put away; (*einpacken*) take; **stecks schnell ein!** put it away quick!; **hast du genug Geld eingesteckt?** have you got enough money on you?; **3.** *umg.* (*Brief*) stick in (*od.* pop into) the letterbox (*Am.* mailbox); **4.** *umg. pej.* (*stehlen, einkassieren*) pocket; **5.** *fig.* (*Vorwurf etc.*) swallow; (*Schlag*) take; **er kann viel ~** he can take a lot (of punishment); **viel ~ müssen** have to take a lot of stick; **e-e Niederlage ~** (*müssen*) take a beating; **6.** *umg. fig.*: *j-n ~* (*überlegen sein*) put s.o. in the shade; **den steckst du leicht ein** you're miles better than him

Einstecktuch *n* breast-pocket handkerchief

einstehen *v/i.* (*unreg., trennb., ist -ge-*) **~ für** answer for, take responsibility for; (*garantieren*) vouch for; (*Behauptung etc.*) stand by, stick by; **für s-e Überzeugung ~** have the courage of one's convictions; **ich stehe dafür ein, dass ...** I guarantee (you) that ...

einsteigen *v/i.* (*unreg., trennb., ist -ge-*) **1.** ~ (**in** *+ Akk.*) get in(to); *in Bus, Zug, Flugzeug*: get on; (*einklettern*) climb in(to); **alle(s) ~!** all aboard!; **steigt ein!** jump in!; **2.** *fig. umg.*: **in ein Unternehmen ~** join a firm; **in die Politik** etc. ~ go into politics etc.; **in ein Thema ~** get to grips with a subject; **3.** *Sport umg.*: **hart ~** go in hard; **Einsteiger** *m*, **Einsteigerin** *f* newcomer (**in** *+ Dat.* to)

einstellbar *Adj.* adjustable

einstellen (*trennb., hat -ge-*) **I.** *v/t.* **1.** put in; (*wegräumen*) put away; (*Möbel*) store; (*Wagen*) put in(to) the garage, put away; **2.** (*Arbeitskräfte etc.*) take on, hire; **3.** (*beenden*) stop; (*Produktion*) *auch* cease, discontinue; (*Feindseligkeiten, Kampfhandlungen*) end, cease; (*Buslinie, Zugverkehr*) discontinue, close down; (*Streik, Suche*), call off; **etw. vorübergehend ~** suspend s.th. temporarily; **die Arbeit ~** *Person*: stop work; (*streiken*) down tools; *Fabrik*: cease production; **das Feuer ~** *Mil.* cease fire, stop shooting (*od.* firing); **das Verfahren ~** *Jur.* suspend proceedings, drop the case; **bitte stellen Sie jetzt das Rauchen ein** please stop smoking now; **die Zeitung hat ihr Erscheinen eingestellt** the newspaper has ceased publication; **4.** *Sport* (*Rekord*) equal; **5.** *Tech.* (*regulieren*) adjust (**auf** *+ Akk.* to); (*Uhr, Messgerät*) set (to); (*Entfernung, Zeit etc.*) adjust (to), set (at); (*Radio*) tune (to); *TV* switch (to); *Opt., Fot.* focus (on); **den Hauptwaschgang ~** select main wash; **6.** *fig.* (*anpassen*) adjust, adapt (**auf** *+ Akk.* to); (*Gedanken etc.*) focus (on); **e-e Mannschaft** (*taktisch*) **auf den Gegner ~** adjust a team's tactics to suit the opponent; **7.** *Med.*, *auf Medikament*: stabilize (*auf* + *Akk.* on); **den Zucker e-s Diabetikers ~** *Med.* adjust a diabetic's blood sugar; **II.** *v/refl.* **1.** (*kommen*) appear, turn up; *Sommer etc.*: arrive; *Fieber, Schmerzen, Regen etc.*: start; *Sorgen, Schwierigkeiten*: arise; *Folgen etc.*: ensue, appear; **sich wieder ~** come back (again); **Zweifel stellten sich bei mir ein** I began to have doubts; **2. sich ~ auf** (+ *Akk.*) (*sich anpassen an*) adapt (*od.* adjust) (o.s. *od.* itself) to; (*sich vorbereiten auf*) prepare (o.s.) for, get ready for, gear (o.s.) up for *umg.*; (*rechnen mit*) be prepared for; (*Aufmerksamkeit darauf richten*) focus one's attention on; (*Lebenstil*) adjust one's lifestyle (*od.* way of thinking) to; **sich auf e-n Gegner ~** prepare to face an opponent; **du musst dich darauf ~** (*daran gewöhnen*) you'll have to get used to it (*od.* learn to accept it); → **eingestellt** II, **einrichten** II 3

einstellig *Adj. attr.* (*Zahl*) single-figure; (*Dezimalzahl*) one-place

Einstell|knopf *m* control (knob); *Radio*: tuning knob; **~platz** *m in Großgarage*: parking space; *unter Schutzdach*: carport; **~ring** *m* adjusting ring; *Fot., am Objektiv*: focus(s)ing ring; **~schraube** *f* adjusting screw

Einstellung *f* **1.** *von Arbeitskräften*: employment; **2.** *Tech.* (*Regulierung*) adjustment, setting; *von Ventil, Zündmoment*: timing; *Opt., Fot.* focus, focus(s)ing; **3.** (*Beendigung*) stopping; *von Zahlungen*: *auch* suspension; *des Betriebs*: shutdown; *von Buslinie, Zugverkehr*: closing down; *e-s Streiks etc.*: ending; **~ des Verfahrens** *Jur.* stay (*od.* discontinuance) of proceedings; *bei Klage*: dismissal; **~ der Feindseligkeiten** cessation of hostilities; **4.** (*Haltung*) attitude (*zu od.* **gegenüber** to[wards]), approach (to); *zum Leben*: outlook (on); **politische ~** political views *Pl.*; **das ist e-e Frage der ~** it depends on how (*od.* the way) you look at it; **5.** *Film*: shot; **6.** *Sport, e-s Rekords*: equal(l)ing; **7.** *Med., e-s Patienten auf ein Medikament*: stabilization

Einstellungs|gespräch *n* (job) interview; **~stopp** *m* job freeze, freeze on (further) recruitment; **~termin** *m* starting date; **~test** *m* test for job applicants, recruitment (*od.* employment) test; **~untersuchung** *f* medical examination for a new employee; **~voraussetzung** *f* job requirement

Einstich *m e-r Spritze*: prick

Einstieg *m*; -(e)s, -e **1.** (*Eingang*) entrance; **2.** *nur Sg.*; (*Einsteigen*) entry, getting in; **~ nur vorn** im Bus etc.: enter only at the front; **3.** *fig.* start; *Päd., e-r Stunde*: *etwa* introduction (*technique or approach to introduce class to the subject matter of a lesson*); **der ~ war schwierig** it was hard at the beginning; **der ~ ins Berufsleben** starting (*od.* embarking on) a career; **der ~ in ein solches Thema ist nicht einfach** it's not easy to get to grips with that kind of subject; **~luke** *f* (access) hatch

Einstiegs|... *im Subst.* starting, starter; **~droge** *f* starter (*od.* gateway) drug

einstig *Adj.* former, erstwhile *förm.*; *Person*: *auch* one-time

einstimmen (*trennb., hat -ge-*) **I.** *v/i.* **1.** *in Gesang*: join in; **in den Beifall / die Klagen** *etc.* **~** join in the applause /

the complaints *etc.*; **2.** *altm.* (*zustimmen*) agree (*in* + *Akk.* to); **II.** *v/t.* **1.** *Mus.* (*Instrument*) tune; **2.** *fig.* (*j-n*) get into the right mood (*auf* + *Akk.* for); **III.** *v/refl. fig.* get into the right mood (*auf* + *Akk.* for); → **eingestimmt**

einstimmig **I.** *Adj.* **1.** (*einmütig*) unanimous; **2.** *Mus.* for one voice; **II.** *Adv.* **1.** unanimously, to a man; **2.** *Mus.*: **~ singen** *etc.* sing *etc.* in unison; **Einstimmigkeit** *f* unanimity, consensus; **~ erzielen** come to an agreement, reach a consensus (*über* + *Akk.* on)

Einstimmung *f*: *als od.* **zur ~** in order to get into the right mood (*auf* + *Akk.* for)

einstmalig *Adj.* → **einstig**, **einstmals** *Adv. geh. altm.* → **einst**

einstöckig **I.** *Adj. attr.* single-stor(e)y ...; **II.** *Adv.*: **~ bauen** put up single-stor(e)y buildings

einstöpseln *v/t.* (*trennb., hat -ge-*); (*Korken etc.*) put in; (*Stecker, Telefon etc.*) plug in

einstoßen *v/t.* (*unreg., trennb., hat -ge-*) **1. ~** (*in* + *Akk.*) push in(to); **2.** (*Fensterscheibe etc.*) smash (in); (*Tür*) break down; *j-m/sich* (*Dat.*) **die Zähne ~** knock in s.o.'s/one's teeth

einstrahlen (*trennb.*) **I.** *v/i.* (*ist eingestrahlt*); *Licht, Sonne*: shine in (*in* + *Akk.* -to; *auf* + *Akk.* on); **II.** *v/t.* (*hat*); (*Wärme, Licht*) radiate (*auf* + *Akk.* onto); **Einstrahlung** *f* radiation

einstreichen *v/t.* (*unreg., trennb., hat -ge-*) **1. mit Kleister ~** (*Tapete*) spread paste on, paste; **mit Butter/Fett ~** butter/grease; **2.** *umg., auch pej.* (*Geld*) pocket; → **eingestrichen**

Einstreu *f Agr.* litter; **einstreuen** *v/t.* (*trennb., hat -ge-*) **1. ~** (*in* + *Akk.*) (*Körner, Salz etc.*) sprinkle in(to); (*Stroh etc.*) strew, scatter; **2.** *fig.*: **~** (*in* + *Akk.*) put in(to), slip in(to); *Zitate etc. in etw.* (*Akk.*) **~** scatter (*od.* intersperse) s.th. with quotations *etc.*

einströmen *v/i.* (*trennb., ist -ge-*): **~** (*in* + *Akk.*) *Wasser, fig. Menschen*: pour in(to), stream in(to); *Luft*: come in(-to); *stärker*: stream in(to)

einstrophig *Adj. attr.* (*Gedicht, Lied*) one-verse ..., ... consisting of one verse

einstudieren *v/t.* (*trennb., hat*); (*Rolle*) learn; (*Gedicht etc.*) learn (by heart); (*üben*) rehearse; *neu ~* *Theat.* (*Inszenierung, Stück*) revive; **einstudiert** **I.** *P.P.* → **einstudieren**; **II.** *Adj. pej.* studied; **Einstudierung** *f Theat.* production

einstufen *v/t.* (*trennb., hat -ge-*) class, classify (*als* as); *nach Leistung, Qualität etc.*: assess; **~ in** (+ *Akk.*) (*e-e Steuerklasse, Kategorie etc.*) put in(to); **hoch/niedrig ~** rate high/low

einstufig *Adj. Tech. attr.* single-stage ...

Einstufung *f* classification; rating

einstündig *Adj. attr.* one-hour(-long) ...

einstürmen *v/i.* (*trennb., ist -ge-*) **1. ~ auf** (+ *Akk.*) rush at, charge (*auch Mil.*); **2.** *fig.*: **auf j-n ~** assail s.o. (*auch Gedanken etc.*); (*mit Fragen, Bitten*) besiege

Einsturz *m* collapse; **vom ~ bedroht** in danger of collapsing; **etw. zum ~ bringen** cause s.th. to collapse (*od.* cave in); **einstürzen** *v/i.* (*trennb., ist -ge-*) **1.** *Wand, Zaun, Gebäude etc.*: collapse; *Dach, Stollen etc.*: cave in; **2.** *fig.* **~ auf** (+ *Akk.*) assail; *Ereignis-*

se: overwhelm; *Sorgen*: crowd in on; **Einsturzgefahr** *f*; *nur Sg.*: **„Achtung, ~!"** danger - building unsafe; **einsturzgefährdet** *Adj.* in danger of collapsing

einstweilen *Adv.* meanwhile, in the meantime; (*vorläufig*) for the time being; **einstweilig** *Adj. Amtsspr.* temporary, provisional; *bes. Jur. attr.* interim ...; **~e Verfügung** *Jur.* interim order; (*Unterlassungsbefehl*) interim injunction; **in den ~en Ruhestand versetzen** be suspended from duty

eintägig *Adj.* **1.** one-day ...; **2.** *Zool., Bot., Med.* ephemeral

Eintagsfliege *f* **1.** *Zool.* mayfly, dayfly; **2.** *fig. Person, Sache*: nine days' wonder; *Leidenschaft, Affäre*: flash in the pan

eintasten *v/t.* (*trennb., hat -ge-*) *EDV* key in

eintätowieren *v/t.* (*trennb., hat*) tattoo

eintauchen (*trennb. -ge-*) **I.** *v/t.* (*hat eingetaucht*) dip (*in* + *Akk.* in, into); (*Brötchen in Suppe etc.*) dunk (in); **II.** *v/i.* (*ist*) *ins Wasser*: dive in

Eintausch *m* exchange; **im ~ für od. gegen** in exchange for; **eintauschen** *v/t.* (*trennb., hat -ge-*) exchange (**gegen** for)

eintausend *Zahlw.* a thousand; *betont*: one thousand; → *auch* **tausend, Tausend**

einteilen *v/t.* (*trennb., hat -ge-*) **1.** divide (up) (*in* + *Akk.* into); (*anordnen*) arrange (*in* + *Akk.* in; *nach* according to); *in Gruppen*: *auch* group; *Bio.* (*klassifizieren*) classify; *hierarchisch*: grade, rate (*nach* according to); *Phys., Tech.* (*Thermometer in Grade etc.*) calibrate; **2.** (*Arbeit, Zeit etc.*) organize, plan; (*Geld*) budget; (*Vorräte*) conserve, plan to make s.th. last; (*sparsam verwenden*) consume carefully; **du musst dir dein Geld besser ~** you must plan your expenditure (*od.* finances) more carefully; **3.** (*j-n*) assign, *Mil.* detail (**für** *od.* **zu** to); **zur Wache ~** put on guard duty

einteilig *Adj. attr.* one-piece ...

Einteilung *f* **1.** division; *Bio.* classification; *von Thermometer etc.*: calibration; **2.** (*Anordnung*) organization, arrangement; *zeitliche*: planning, schedule; *der Finanzen*: budgeting; **3.** (*Delegieren*) assignment; *Mil.* detailing

Eintel *n*, *schw. mst m*; -s, -; *Math.* whole

eintönig **I.** *Adj.* monotonous; *Leben*: *auch* humdrum, dull; **II.** *Adv.*: **~ vorlesen** read out in a monotonous tone (of voice) (*od.* in a monotone); **Eintönigkeit** *f* monotony

Eintopf *m Gastr.* stew, casserole; **eintopfen** *v/t.* (*trennb., hat -ge-*); (*Pflanzen*) pot; **Eintopfgericht** *n Gastr.* stew, casserole

Eintracht *f*; -, *kein Pl.* harmony, concord; (*Einheit*) unity; **völlige ~** perfect harmony; **einträchtig** *Adj.* harmonious; (*friedlich*) peaceful

Eintrag *m*; -(e)s, *Einträge* **1.** (*Notiz, in Tage- od. Wörterbuch etc.*) entry; (*Buchungsposten*) *auch* item; **e-n ~ ins Klassenbuch bekommen** have one's bad behavio(u)r noted in the class register; **2.** *fachspr., von Schadstoffen*: input

eintragen (*unreg., trennb., hat -ge-*) **I.** *v/t.* **1.** *in e-e Liste*: enter (*in* + *Akk.* on), put down (on); (*buchen*) enter (in); *in Schulheft etc.*: write in(to); *in Karte etc.*: enter (on), include (on); *j-n*

E

ins Klassenbuch ~ note s.o.'s bad behavio(u)r in the class register; **2.** *amtlich*: register (*bei* with); *sich ~ lassen* be registered; *etw. auf s-n Namen ~ lassen* have s.th. registered in one's name; **3.** *als Mitglied*: enrol(l) (in); **4.** (*Gewinn etc.*) bring in; *netto*: net; **5.** *fig.*: *j-m etw. ~* (*Lob, Neid, Ehre etc.*) earn s.o. s.th.; **II.** *v/refl.* put one's name down (on the list); *für etw.*: *auch* sign up; *im Hotel*: register, check in; *als Mitglied, Teilnehmer*: register

einträglich *Adj.* profitable, lucrative

Eintragung *f* entry; *amtliche*: registration; (*Posten*) item

einträufeln *v/t.* (*trennb., hat -ge-*): *sich* (*Dat.*) *Tropfen in das Ohr etc.* ~ put some drops in one's ear *etc.*

eintreffen *v/i.* (*unreg., trennb., ist -ge-*) **1.** (*ankommen*) arrive (*an* + *Dat.* at; *in* + *Dat.* in); come, get here (*od.* there); *Schild*: *„frisch eingetroffen"* just in; *bei m-m Eintreffen* when I arrived; → *auch* **eingehen** I 6; **2.** (*geschehen*) happen; (*sich erfüllen*) prove true

eintreiben *v/t.* (*unreg., trennb., hat -ge-*) **1.** (*Schulden etc.*) collect; **2.** (*Vieh*) drive home; **3.** ~ (*in* + *Akk.*) (*Nagel, Pfahl etc.*) drive in(to); **Eintreiber** *m*, **Eintreiberin** *f* (debt) collector

eintreten (*unreg., trennb.*) **I.** *v/i.* **1.** (*ist eingetreten*): ~ (*in* + *Akk.*) go in(to), come in(to), enter; *treten Sie doch ein!* do come in!; *durch das Loch ist Wasser eingetreten* water came in through the hole; **2.** (*ist*); *fig.*: ~ *in* (+ *Akk.*) (*e-n Beruf, ein Amt*) take up; *in den Krieg, ein Kloster, e-e Phase*: enter; *in die Armee, e-e Firma, e-n Klub etc.*: join; *in Verhandlungen*: enter into; *in die Politik, ein Kloster*: go into; **3.** (*ist*); *fig.* (*kommen*) *Regen*: start; *Kälte etc.*: set in; *Dunkelheit, Nacht, Stille*: descend; *Winter etc.*: come; (*sich ereignen*) happen, take place, occur; *Fall, Notwendigkeit, Umstände*: arise; *Tod*: occur; *der Tod trat auf der Stelle ein* death was instantaneous; *es ist noch keine Besserung eingetreten* there has been no improvement as yet; *wenn der Fall eintritt, dass ...* if it happens that ..., in case ...; **4.** (*ist*); *fig.*: *für j-n ~* (*verteidigen*) stand (*od.* speak) up for s.o.; (*intervenieren*) intervene on s.o.'s behalf; *für etw. ~* speak out in favo(u)r of s.th., support s.th.; *voll*: give s.th. one's full backing; (*plädieren für*) argue for s.th.; → *auch* **einsetzen** II 2; **5.** (*hat*): ~ *auf* (+ *Akk.*) *mit den Füßen*: kick; **6.** (*ist*); *schw. fig.* ~ *auf* (+ *Akk.*) → **eingehen** I 5; **II.** *v/t.* (*hat*) **1.** (*Tür*) kick down; **2.** *in den Boden*: stamp in(to the ground); *in den Teppich*: (*Krümel etc.*) tread (*od.* grind) in(to the carpet); **3.** *sich* (*Dat.*) *etw.* ~ get s.th. in one's foot; **4.** (*Schuhe*) wear in

Eintreten *n*; *-s, kein Pl.* **1.** → **Eintritt** 1 - 4; **2.** (*Einsatz*) intervention (*für* on behalf of); (*Unterstützung*) support, backing (for)

eintrichtern *v/t.* (*trennb., hat -ge-*) **1.** → **einflößen**; **2.** *umg., fig.*: *j-m etw. ~* drum s.th. into s.o.

Eintritt *m* **1.** entry (*in* + *Akk.* into) (*auch fig.*); *theatralischer etc.*: entrance (into); *„~ verboten!"* no admittance; *beim ~ in die Erdatmosphäre* on entering the earth's atmosphere; **2.** (*Beitritt*) entry (*in* + *Akk.* into); ~ *in e-e Firma/Partei* joining a company/party; **3.** (*Anfang*) beginning, start; *von Wet-*

ter, Winter, Med. etc.: onset; *bei/nach ~ der Dunkelheit* when darkness falls / after dark; **4.** *e-s Umstandes etc.*: occurrence; *bei ~ des Todes* when death occurs; **5.** (*Einlass*) admission; ~ *frei* admission free; *was verlangen sie für den ~?* what do they charge for admission?; **6.** *Gebühr*: admission fee; *Sport* gate money

Eintritts|geld *n* → **Eintritt** 6; **~karte** *f* (admission) ticket; **~preis** *m* admission (*od.* entrance) charge

eintrocknen *v/i.* (*trennb., ist -ge-*) **1.** dry up; **2.** (*einschrumpfen*) shrivel up

eintrommeln *v/i.* (*trennb., hat -ge-*) pound (bash *umg.*) away (*auf* +*Akk.* at)

eintrüben *v/refl.* (*trennb., hat -ge-*) *Himmel*: become overcast; *unpers.*: *es trübt sich ein* it's clouding over; **Eintrübung** *f* cloudy spell

eintrudeln *v/i.* (*trennb., ist -ge-*); *umg. Personen*: drift in; *Briefe etc.*: turn up eventually

eintürig *Adj.* with one door

eintüten *v/t.* (*trennb., hat -ge-*) put into paper bags

einüben *v/t.* (*trennb., hat -ge-*) practi|se (*Am.* -ce); (*Theaterstück*) rehearse; (*aneignen*) (*soziale Fertigkeiten etc.*) acquire by constant practice

Einuhr... *im Subst.* one o'clock ...

einverleiben *v/t.* (*trennb., hat*) **1.** add (+ *Dat. od.* in + *Akk.* to); (*Land*) annex (to); **2.** *hum.*: *sich* (*Dat.*) *etw.* ~ (*Essen etc.*) stow (*od.* put) away s.th.; (*Kenntnisse*) assimilate s.th.; **Einverleibung** *f e-s Landes etc.*: annexation

Einvernahme *f*; *-, -n*; *Jur., bes. österr., schw.* examination; **einvernehmen** *v/t.* (*unreg., trennb., hat*); *Jur., bes. österr., schw.* examine

Einvernehmen *n*; *-s, kein Pl.* agreement, understanding; *in gutem ~* on good (*od.* friendly) terms; *zusammenarbeiten, -leben*: amicably; *im ~ mit* in agreement with; *nach Rücksprache mit*: after consultation with; *im gegenseitigen ~* by mutual agreement; *sich mit j-m ins ~ setzen* come to an understanding (*od.* agreement) with s.o.; **einvernehmlich I.** *Adj. Abkommen etc.*: amicable; **II.** *Adv.* amicably, by mutual agreement

einverstanden *Adj.*: ~ *sein* (*mit*) *od.* *sich ~ erklären* (*mit*) *zustimmend*: agree (to), consent (to); *billigend*: approve (of); *damit ~ sein, dass j-d etw. tut* agree (*od.* consent) to (*billigend*: approve of) s.o.('s) doing s.th.; *damit ~ sein zu* (+ *Inf.*) agree to (+ *Inf.*); *damit bin ich ganz und gar nicht ~* (*bin anderer Meinung*) I disagree totally with that; (*lehne ich ab*) I find that completely unacceptable; *sie ist mit allem ~* she has no objections; (*ihr ist es gleich*) she doesn't mind one way or another; *ich bin damit ~* it's all right with me; ~*!* okay, all right, it's a deal *umg.*; **einverständlich** → *einvernehmlich*

Einverständnis *n* **1.** (*Zustimmung*) consent (*zu* to); (*Billigung*) approval (of); *sein ~ geben* (give one's) consent (*zu* to); *dein ~ vorausgesetzt* assuming that you agree (*od.* approve); **2.** (*Übereinkommen*) agreement, understanding; *stillschweigendes ~* tacit understanding; → *auch* **Einvernehmen**

Einwaage *f Wirts.* contents *Pl.*

einwachsen[1] *v/i.* (*unreg., trennb., ist eingewachsen*) *Nagel*: grow in; → *ein-*

gewachsen II 1

einwachsen[2] *v/t.* (*trennb., hat eingewachst*); (*Boden, Skier*) wax

einwählen *v/refl.* (*trennb., hat -ge-*); *Telek.* dial in; *sich ins Internet ~* log onto the Internet

Einwähl|knoten *m*, **~punkt** *m Telek., EDV* point of presence

Einwand *m* objection (*gegen* to); *e-n ~ vorbringen* raise an objection

Einwanderer *m*, **Einwanderin** *f* immigrant; *im gleichen Land*: incomer; **einwandern** *v/i.* (*trennb., ist -ge-*) immigrate (*in* + *Akk.* to); *auch Tiere, Pflanzen*: migrate; → *eingewandert*; **Einwanderung** *f* immigration

Einwanderungs|behörde *f* immigration authorities *Pl.*; **~quote** *f* immigration quota; **~verbot** *n* ban on immigration; **~welle** *f* wave of immigrants

einwandfrei I. *Adj.* **1.** (*fehlerfrei*) perfect, flawless; (*tadellos*) impeccable; *Ware*: flawless; *Lebensmittel etc.*: perfectly fresh; *es ist alles ~* everything's perfect (*od.* in perfect condition); *er spricht ein ~es Englisch* his English is perfect, he speaks perfect (*od.* flawless) English; **2.** (*Beweis*) definite; (*unanfechtbar*) indisputable, incontestable; **II.** *Adv.*: ~ *falsch / der Beste* undoubtedly wrong / the best; ~ *funktionieren Gerät*: work perfectly, be in perfect working order; *Sache*: work out perfectly; *es ist ~ erwiesen* it's proved (*Am. auch* proven) beyond doubt; *es steht ~ fest, dass ...* it's indisputable that..., there's no question that ...

Einwandrerin *f* (female) immigrant

einwärts *Adv.* inward(s); ~ *gebogen od. gewölbt* concave

einweben *v/t.* (*unreg., trennb., hat -ge-*) *auch fig.*: ~ (*in* + *Akk.*) work in(to)

einwechseln (*trennb. -ge-*) **I.** *v/t.* (*hat eingewechselt*) **1.** (*Geld*) change; (*einlösen*) cash; **2.** *Sport* (*Spieler*) bring on (as a substitute), substitute (*für od. gegen* for); **II.** *v/i.* (*ist*) *Wild*: change location (*in* + *Akk.* to)

einwecken *v/t.* (*trennb., hat -ge-*) preserve, *Am. auch* put up, can; *in Gläsern*: bottle, *Am.* can; *in Dosen*: can; *in Flaschen*: bottle; *in Essig*: pickle; **Einweckglas** *etc.* → **Einmachglas** *etc.*

Einweg|... *im Subst.* (*Wegwerf...*) disposable ...; **~flasche** *f* non-returnable bottle; **~geschirr** *n* single-use crockery, *Am.* disposable dishes *Pl.*; **~kondom** *n* non-returnable (*od.* throwaway) condom; **~spiegel** *m* one-way mirror; **~verpackung** *f* throwaway pack

einweichen *v/t.* (*trennb., hat -ge-*) soak

einweihen *v/t.* (*trennb., hat -ge-*) **1.** *feierlich*: (*Gebäude, Straße etc.*) open (officially), dedicate; *kirchl.* consecrate; **2.** *umg.* (*erstmals benutzen*) christen; *s-e Wohnung / sein Haus ~* have a housewarming (*Brit. auch* flatwarming) party / housewarming party; **3.** *j-n ~ in* (+ *Akk.*) let s.o. in on; *sie weihte ihn ein* she let him in on the secret; *j-n ~ in die Kunst/Geheimnisse* (+ *Gen.*) *fig. hum.* initiate s.o. into the art/mysteries of (+ *Ger.*); → *eingeweiht*, **Eingeweihte**; **Einweihung** *f* (formal) opening, dedication; *kirchl.* consecration

Einweihungs|feier *f* opening ceremony; *für Haus etc.*: housewarming party; **~rede** *f* inaugural address

einweisen *v/t.* (*unreg., trennb., hat*

-ge-) **1. ~ in** (+ *Akk.*) *ein Heim, Krankenhaus etc.*: admit to; **in e-e Anstalt ~** institutionalize; **2. j-n in e-e Aufgabe ~** show s.o. what to do; **3.** *in ein Amt*: instal(l) (**in** + *Akk.* in), inaugurate (into); **4.** (*Fahrzeug*) direct (**in** + *Akk.* into); **Einweiser** *m*; **-s, -, Einweiserin** *f*; -, -*nen*; *Flug.* marshal(l)er; **Einweisung** *f* **1.** *in ein Heim, Krankenhaus*: admission (**in** + *Akk.* to); **2.** *in e-e Aufgabe, Stelle etc.*: introduction (**in** + *Akk.* to); (*Kurs*) induction course; **3.** *in ein Amt etc.*: induction, inauguration

einwenden *v/t.* (*mst unreg., trennb., hat* -ge-): **~, dass** ... object (*od.* argue) that ...; **er wandte** *od.* **wendete** (**dagegen**) **ein, dass** ... *auch* he raised (*od.* made) the objection that ...; **dagegen lässt sich ~, dass** ... it could be objected that ...; **ich habe nichts dagegen einzuwenden** I have no objections; **es lässt sich nichts dagegen ~** there's nothing to be said against it; **sie hat immer irgendetwas einzuwenden** she always has some objection or other, she always finds something to object to; **Einwendung** *f* objection (**gegen** to); **~en erheben gegen** raise objections to

einwerfen (*unreg., trennb., hat* -ge-) **I.** *v/t.* **1.** (*Brief*) post, *Am.* mail; (*Geld*) insert, put in; *Sport* (*Ball*) throw in; **2.** (*Fenster*) smash in, break; **3.** *umg.*: **Tabletten ~** pop pills; **4.** *fig.* (*Bemerkung etc.*) throw in; **~, dass** ... object (*od.* argue) that ...; **II.** *v/i. Sport* take the throw-in

einwertig *Adj.* **1.** *Chem.* monovalent; **2.** *Ling.* (*Verb*) one-place; **Einwertigkeit** *f* monovalence

einwickeln *v/t.* (*trennb., hat* -ge-) **1.** wrap up (**in** + *Akk.* in); **2.** *umg. fig.* take in, fool; *durch Schmeicheleien*: soft-soap; **lass dich nicht von ihm ~** don't be taken in by him, don't fall for his line; **Einwickelpapier** *n* wrapping paper

einwilligen *v/i.* (*trennb., hat* -ge-); (*zustimmen*) agree (**in** + *Akk.* to); (*s-e Erlaubnis geben*) consent (to); **Einwilligung** *f* approval (**in** + *Akk.* of), consent (to); *in ein Angebot*: acceptance (of); **s-e ~ zu etw. geben** consent to s.th.

einwinken *v/t.* (*trennb., hat* -ge-) **~** (**in** + *Akk.*) *Mot.* wave in(to), guide in(-to); *Flug.* marshal (into)

einwirken *v/i.* (*trennb., hat* -ge-) **1. ~ auf** (+ *Akk.*) have an effect on; (*angreifen*) affect; (*beeinflussen*) influence; **etw. ~ lassen** let s.th. take effect (**auf** + *Akk.* on); (*Fett etc.*) let s.th. work itself in(to); *Creme etc.* **fünf Minuten ~ lassen** leave on for five minutes (to take effect); **2.** *fig. überredend*: (*j-n*) work on; **etw. auf sich ~ lassen** let s.th. sink in; **Einwirkung** *f* effect (**auf** + *Akk.* on); *e-s Medikaments etc.*: *mst* effects *Pl.* (on); (*Einfluss*) *auch Pl.* influence (on)

einwöchig *Adj. attr.* **1.** week-long ..., one-week ...; **2.** (*eine Woche alt*) week-old ...

Einwohner *m*; -s, -, **~in** *f*; -, -*nen* inhabitant; *e-r Stadt*: *auch* resident; **Einwohnermeldeamt** *n* local residents' registration office; **Einwohnerschaft** *f* inhabitants *Pl.*, population; **Einwohnerzahl** *f* (total) population, number of inhabitants

Einwurf *m* **1.** *Fußball*: throw-in; **2.** *e-s Briefes*: posting, *bes. Am.* mailing; *e-r*

Münze etc.: insertion; **~ 1 Euro** insert 1 euro:; **3.** *am Automaten*: slot; *am Briefkasten*: opening, slit; **4.** (*Bemerkung*) interjection; *kritisch*: objection

einwurzeln (*trennb.*) *v/refl.* (*hat eingewurzelt*) *und v/i.* (*ist*) take root; *fig.* put down (one's) roots, settle down

Einzahl *f*; *mst Sg.*; *Ling.* singular

einzahlen *v/t.* (*trennb., hat* -ge-) pay in; *in e-e Bank*: deposit (**in** + *Akk.* at); **etw. auf ein Konto ~** pay s.th. into (*Am.* deposit s.th. in) an account; **Einzahlung** *f* payment; *in e-e Bank*: deposit; (*Teilzahlung*) instal(l)ment

Einzahlungs|beleg *m* paying-in counterfoil, *Am.* deposit stub; **~formular** *n* paying-in form; **~schein** *m* paying-in slip, *Am.* deposit slip

einzäunen *v/t.* (*trennb., hat* -ge-) fence in; **Einzäunung** *f* enclosure; (*Zaun*) fence

einzeichnen *v/t.* (*trennb., hat* -ge-) draw in, sketch in; (*markieren*) mark (in) (**in** *od.* **auf** + *Akk.* on)

einzeilig *Adj. Nachricht*: *attr.* one-line ...

Einzel *n*; -s, - *Tennis etc.*: singles *Pl.* (*Match*: *V. im Sg.*)

Einzel|abteil *n* separate compartment; **~aktion** *f* independent action, solo effort; **~anfertigung** *f* one-off, *Am.* one-time; **es ist e-e ~** *auch* it's (been) specially made (*od.* custom-built); **~antrieb** *m Tech.* separate drive; **~beispiel** *n* isolated example; **~behandlung** *f* individual treatment; **~bett** *n* single bed

Einzelbild *n Video*: (single) frame

Einzel|darstellung *f* individual study; (*Abhandlung*) monograph; **~disziplin** *f Sport* individual event; **~ergebnis** *n* individual result; **~erscheinung** *f* isolated instance; **~exemplar** *n* unique specimen (*Buch*: copy); **~fall** *m* individual case; (*Ausnahmefall*) isolated case; **kein ~** no exception; **~frage** *f* individual question; (*Detailfrage*) detail question

Einzelgänger *m*; -s, -, **~in** *f*; -, -*nen* loner, lone wolf; *Tier*: rogue elephant *etc.*; **einzelgängerisch** *Adj.* solitary, lone ...

Einzel|gespräch *n* one-to-one conversation; **~haft** *f* solitary confinement

Einzelhandel *m* retail trade; **es kostet im ~...** it costs ... retail

Einzelhandels|geschäft *n* retail store, *Brit. auch* retail shop; **~kette** *f* chain of retail stores, retail chain; **~kauffrau** *f*, **~kaufmann** *m* (qualified) retail business person; **~preis** *m* retail price

Einzelhändler *m*; -s, -, **~in** *f* retailer

Einzel|haus *n* detached (*Am. auch* freestanding) house; **~heft** *n* individual (*od.* single) issue

Einzelheit *f* detail; **nähere ~en** further details; **bis in alle ~en** down to the last detail; **auf ~en eingehen** go into detail (*od.* particulars); **ich will nicht auf alle ~en eingehen** I won't bore you with (all) the details

Einzel|interessen *Pl.* individual (*od.* personal) interests; **~kabine** *f Naut.* single cabin; **~kampf** *m* **1.** *Mil.* single combat, hand-to-hand fighting; **2.** *Sport* individual competition; **~kämpfer** *m*, **~kämpferin** *f* **1.** *Mil.* solo combatant; **2.** *fig.* lone wolf, loner; **~kind** *n*: **~ sein** be an only child; **~kosten** *Pl.* itemized costs; **Aufschlüsselung der ~** cost breakdown

Einzeller *m*; -s, -; *Bio.* protozoon, protozoan, monad; **einzellig** *Adj. attr.*

---

single-cell ..., *auch präd.* single-celled; *fachspr.* monocellular

einzeln I. *Adj.* **1.** (*allein*) individual, single; (*getrennt*) separate; (*abgeschieden*) isolated; (*besonder...*) particular; *Baum, Wolke*: single, solitary, lone *geh.*; *Schuh etc.*: odd, single; **jedes ~e Stück** (*für sich*) each individual piece; (*alle*) every single piece (*od.* one); **jede(r) Einzelne** every (single) one (of them); *Mensch*: *auch* every (single) person *etc.*; **vom Einzelnen zum Ganzen** from the particular to the general; **Einzelnes** (*manches*) some *Pl.*, a few *Pl.* (things, points, details *etc.*); **2. ~e** *Pl.* (*vereinzelt*) a few, some, one or two; *Regen-, Schneeschauer*: scattered, occasional; *lokal begrenzt*: isolated; **3. im Einzelnen geht es um folgende Fragen** the points at issue (*od.* specific questions) are (as follows); **ins Einzelne gehen** go into detail(s); **II.** *Adv.* individually, singly; (*getrennt*) separately; (*nicht gleichzeitig*) *auch* one by one, one at a time; **~ angeben** specify, list, itemize; **~ stehend** *Baum, Haus*: solitary, isolated; **~ stehende Gehöfte** *auch* scattered farms

Einzel|paar *n Schuhe etc.*: odd pair; **~packung** *f* single pack; **~person** *f* single person; *ohne Begleitung*: unaccompanied person; **für e-e ~** for one person (only); **~posten** *m* item; **~preis** *m* unit price; *e-r Zeitung, Illustrierten*: price per copy; **~radaufhängung** *f Mot.* independent suspension; **~reisende** *m, f* solo (*od.* individual) travel(l)er; **~richter** *m*, **~richterin** *f Jur.* judge sitting singly, sole presiding judge; **~schicksal** *n* individual destiny; **~spiel** *n Tennis etc.*: singles *Pl.* (*V. im Sg.*), singles match; **~stück** *n* **1.** (*aus e-m Satz*) odd piece; **2.** (*einziges Exemplar*) unique specimen, one-off *umg.*, *Am.* one-of-a-kind specimen *etc.*; **~täter** *m*, **~täterin** *f* lone (*od.* solo) operator, s.o. working alone (*od.* on his *od.* her own); **~teil** *n* (component) part; **etw. in s-e ~e zerlegen** take s.th. apart (*od.* to pieces), reduce s.th. to its component parts; **~unterricht** *m* private (*od.* individual) lessons *Pl.*, private tuition (*od.* coaching, *Am. auch* tutoring); **~wertung** *f Sport* individual scoring; **~wesen** *n* individual (being); **~zelle** *f im Gefängnis*: single cell; **~zimmer** *n* single room

einzementieren *v/t.* (*trennb., hat*) cement in (**in** + *Akk. od. Dat.* into)

einziehbar *Adj.* **1.** *Tech.* retractable; **2.** *Geld*: collectible; *Güter*: seizable

einziehen (*unreg., trennb.*) **I.** *v/t.* (*hat eingezogen*) **1. ~** (**in** + *Akk.*) *in Bezug*: put in(to); (*Faden, Gummi*) thread in(to); (*Kabel*) feed (*od.* pay) in(to); *Gerät*: (*Papier*) feed in(to); *sich* (*Dat.*) **e-n Dorn/Splitter ~** get a thorn/splinter in one's hand *etc.*; **2.** (*einbauen*) put in; (*Wand*) *auch* put up; **3.** (*Fahne*) lower, haul down; (*Segel*) take in; (*Netz*) haul in, pull in; *Tech.* retract; **das Fahrgestell ~** *Flug.* retract the landing gear; **4.** (*Bauch*) pull in; (*Fühler, Krallen*) draw in; (*Krallen*) *auch* sheathe; **den Kopf ~** duck (one's head); **den Bauch ~** *auch* breathe in *umg.*; **den Schwanz ~** *Hund*: put its *etc.* tail between its legs; *umg. fig. pej.* cave in; **5.** (*Luft, Rauch*) draw in; *Person*: *auch* breathe in, inhale; **6.** *Mil.* call up, conscript, *Am.* draft; **7.** (*Steuer, Gelder etc.*) collect; (*Schulden*) recover; **8.** (*beschlagnahmen*) seize, confiscate; (*Führerschein etc.*) take away, confiscate, withdraw; **9.** (*Banknoten etc.*) withdraw (from circulation); **10.** *Amtsspr.* (*Auskünfte etc.*) gather, collect; **Erkundigungen** ~ enquire, make enquiries (*über + Akk.* about, into); **11.** *Druck.* (*Absatz, Zeile*) indent; **II.** *v/i.* (*ist*) **1.** (*in + Akk. e-e Wohnung etc.*) ~ move in(to); **bei j-m** ~ move in with s.o.; (*als Mieter*) *auch* move to s.o.'s (place); **2.** ~ (*in + Akk.*) *Truppen*: march in(to), enter; *in ein Stadion etc.*: enter; *Zirkus etc.*: arrive in town; **in den Bundestag** ~ *Partei*: win seats in the Bundestag, enter the Bundestag; *Abgeordnete(r)*: take up one's seat in the Bundestag; **3.** ~ (*in + Akk.*) *Flüssigkeit, Creme*: soak in(to), be absorbed (in, into), be soaked up; **4.** *fig. Frühling etc.*: come, arrive; *Resignation etc.*: follow, take over; **wenn wieder Ruhe im Haus einzieht** when things settle down

Einziehung *f* **1.** *Mil.* conscription, *Am.* drafting (*od. the* draft); **2.** (*Beschlagnahme*) confiscation, seizure; *des Führerscheins*: confiscation, withdrawal; **3.** *von Steuern etc.*: collection; **4.** *von Münzen etc.*: withdrawal; **5.** *Amtsspr.*: **die** ~ **von Erkundigungen** pursuance of enquiries

einzig I. *Adj.* **1.** only; **mein** ~**er Freund** my (one and) only friend, my one friend; **der** ~**e Einzige** the only one, the only person, the one person; *Sache*: the only thing, the one thing; **sie ist die Einzige, die ...** she's the only woman who ...; *ein Einziger etc.*: just one (person etc.), one single (*od.* solitary) person; **kein Einziger etc.** not (a single) one; **wir waren die Einzigen am Strand** we were the only people on the beach, we had the beach to ourselves; **Lisa ist unsere Einzige** Lisa is our only child, we've only got Lisa; **mein** ~**er Gedanke** my one thought; **ein** ~**es Buch** (just) one book; **kein** ~**es Auto** not a single car, not one car; **kein** ~**es Wort** not a word; **sein** ~**er Halt** his sole support, the one thing etc. he could count on; **ein** ~**es Mal** (just) once; **nicht ein** ~**es Mal** not once, not a single time; **sie hat keinen** ~**en Fehler gemacht** she didn't make a single mistake; **2.** (*ausgesprochen*) pure, sheer, nothing but; **sein Leben war e-e** ~**e Flucht** he spent his life running away from things; **3.** *unvergleichlich:* ~ **in s-r** etc. **Art sein** be unique (of its kind), be unequal(l)ed, stand alone; → **einzigartig** I; **II.** *Adv.* only; ~ (**und allein**) solely; **das** ~ **Richtige od. Wahre** the only answer (*od.* solution, thing to do etc.); **das** ~ **Vernünftige wäre ...** the only sensible thing to do is (*od.* would be) ...; **es hängt** ~ **und allein davon ab, ob** ... it depends entirely (*od.* solely) on whether ...

einzigartig I. *Adj.* unique; *Leistung*: unequal(l)ed, unrival(l)ed; *Schönheit*: peerless, matchless, supreme; (*großartig*) *auch* tremendous; **II.** *Adv.* uniquely; ~ **gut** amazingly good; *Waren etc.*: *auch* of unmatched quality; ~ **schön** *auch weitS.* wonderful, exquisite; **Einzigartigkeit** *f* uniqueness

Einzimmer|appartement *n*, ~**wohnung** *f* one-room (*Am. auch* efficiency *od.* studio) apartment; *Brit. auch* bedsit(ter), one-room flat

Einzug *m* **1.** *in ein Haus etc.*: moving in; *Amtsspr.* entry; **2.** (*auch Ein-*

marsch) entry (**in** + *Akk.* into); *Mil.* march(ing) in; **3.** *fig. e-r Jahreszeit etc.*: arrival, coming, onset, advent *lit.*; (**s-n**) ~ **halten** make its arrival; arrive (on the scene *umg.*); **4.** *Druck.* indent(ation); **5.** *e-r Fahne*: lowering; *e-s Netzes*: hauling in; *e-s Segels*: reefing, taking in; **6.** → **Einziehung** 2 - 4

Einzugs|bereich *m* → **Einzugsgebiet**; ~**ermächtigung** *f Wirts.* direct-debit mandate, *Am. auch* automatic draft order; ~**gebiet** *n Geogr., Wirts.* catchment area (*auch e-r Schule*); *Am. Geog.* drainage basin; *auch e-r Schule: Am.* school district; *e-r Stadt etc.*: hinterland; *engS.* commuter belt; ~**verfahren** *n Wirts.* direct debit; **im** ~ by direct debit

einzwängen (*trennb., hat -ge-*) **I.** *v/t.* **1.** squeeze (*od.* force) in, jam in *umg.*; **2.** *fig.* constrain, straitjacket; → **eingezwängt**; **II.** *v/refl.*: **sich** ~ **in** (+ *Akk.*) squeeze (o.s.) into

Einzylinder *m*, ~**motor** *m Mot.* single--cylinder (engine)

Ei|pulver *n* dried egg; ~**reifung** *f Physiol.* maturation of the ovum

Eis¹ *n*; *-es, -* **1.** *nur Sg.*; ice; ~ **laufen** (ice-)skate; **im** ~ **eingeschlossen** icebound, frozen in; **das** ~ **trägt** the ice is thick enough; **das ewige** ~ perpetual ice and snow; **Whisky** etc. **mit** ~ Scotch etc. on the rocks, with ice; **auf** ~ **legen** *auch fig.* put on ice; **das** ~ **brechen** *fig.* break the ice; → **Glatteis**; **2.** *Gastr.* (*Speiseeis*) ice cream; ~ **am Stiel** ice lolly, *Am.* Popsicle®

eis, Eis² ['eːʔ ɪs] *n*; *-, -*; *Mus.* E sharp

Eis|bahn *f* ice rink; ~**bär** *m Zool.* polar bear; ~**becher** *m Gastr.* sundae; ♀**bedeckt** *Adj.* Gipfel: ice-capped; *See etc.*: frozen, ice-covered; ~**bein** *n Gastr.* pickled knuckle of pork; ~**berg** *m* iceberg; → **Spitze¹** 1; ~**beutel** *m Med.* ice bag; ♀**blau** *Adj.* glacial blue, icy blue; ~**block** *m*; *Pl. -blöcke* block of ice; ~**blume** *f* frost flower; ~**n** frostwork *Sg.*; ~**bombe** *f Gastr.* bombe glacée; ~**brecher** *m Naut.* icebreaker; ~**café** *n* ice-cream parlo(u)r

Ei|schale *f* eggshell; ~**schnee** *m* beaten egg white

Eis|creme *f* ice cream; ~**decke** *f* sheet of ice, ice sheet; ~**diele** *f* ice-cream parlo(u)r

Eisen *n*; *-s, -* **1.** *nur Sg.*; iron (*auch Pharm.*); **die** ~ **schaffende/verarbeitende Industrie** iron production / iron--processing (industry); **2.** (*Werkzeug, Golfschläger, Bügeleisen etc.*) iron; (*Hufeisen*) horseshoe; (*Fangeisen*) (gin) trap; **altes** ~ scrap iron; **j-n in** ~ **legen** clap s.o. in irons; **3.** *fig.*: **zum alten** ~ **werfen** throw on the scrapheap, scrap; **zum alten** ~ **gehören** be past it, have had one's day; **ein heißes** ~ a tricky (*od.* dicey *umg.*) affair (*od.* business); **ein heißes** ~ **anfassen** risk**ant**: tread on thin ice; *mutig*: grasp the nettle; **mehrere od. noch ein** ~ **im Feuer haben** have more than one string to one's bow (*od.* iron in the fire); (**man muss**) **das** ~ **schmieden, solange es heiß ist** (you have to) strike while the iron is hot, make hay while the sun shines

Eisenbahn *f Eisenb.* railway, *Am.* railroad; (*Zug*) train; *Spielzeug*: model railway (*Am.* railroad), train set; **mit der** ~ by rail, by train; → **Bahn** 3; **es ist (aller)höchste** ~ *umg. fig.* it's high time we got going etc.; ~**... im Subst.** → *auch* **Bahn**, **Zug**, ~**brücke** *f* railway

(*Am.* railroad) bridge

Eisenbahner *m*; *-s, -,* ~**in** *f*; *-, -nen*; *Eisenb., männlich*: railwayman, *Am.* railroader; *weiblich*: (woman) railway (*Am.* railroad) employee; ~**streik** *m* rail strike

Eisenbahn|knotenpunkt *m Eisenb.* (railway, *Am.* railroad) junction; ~**netz** *n* railway (*Am.* rail) network (*od.* system); ~**schaffner** *m*, ~**schaffnerin** *f* guard, *Am. auch* conductor; ~**strecke** *f* railway (*Am.* railroad) line; ~**wagen** *m* railway carriage, coach, *Am.* railroad car

Eisen|beschlag *m* iron mounting(s *Pl.*) (*od.* fittings *Pl.*); ~**draht** *m* steel wire; ~**erz** *n* iron ore; ~**gehalt** *m* iron content; ~**gießerei** *f Tech.* iron foundry; ~**gitter** *n* iron grille, (iron) bars *Pl.*

eisen|haltig *Adj.* **1.** ~ **sein** contain iron; ~**e Diät** diet with plenty of iron, iron-rich diet; **2.** *Min.* ferruginous; ~**hart** *Adj.* hard as iron, rock-hard

Eisenhut *m Bot.* monk's-hood, wolfsbane, aconite

Eisen|hütte *f*, ~**hüttenwerk** *n Tech.* ironworks *Pl.* (*V. mst im Sg.*); ~**industrie** *f Tech.* iron industry; ~**kern** *m Etech., e-r Spule*: core

Eisen|mangel *m Physiol.* iron deficiency; ~**oxid** *n*, ~**oxyd** *n Chem.* ferric oxide; ~**präparat** *n Pharm.* iron preparation; *oft auch* iron tablets *Pl.*; ~**rost** *m* (*Gitter*) iron grating (*od.* grid); ~**stange** *f* iron (*od.* steel) rod; ~**verhüttung** *f Tech.* iron production, iron--smelting

Eisenwaren *Pl.* ironware *Sg.*, ironmongery *Sg., auch Am.* hardware *Sg.*; ~**händler** *m*, ~**händlerin** *f* ironmonger, *auch Am.* hardware dealer; ~**handlung** *f* ironmonger's, hardware shop (*Am.* store)

Eisenzeit *f*; *nur Sg.*; *Archäol.* Iron Age

eisern I. *Adj.* **1.** (*aus Eisen*) iron, *fachspr.* ferrous; *Ferric*; *präd.* of iron; ~**e Lunge** *Med.* iron lung; ~**er Vorhang** *Theat.* safety curtain; **der Eiserne Vorhang** *hist.* the Iron Curtain; → **Jungfrau** 1; **2.** *fig.* (*unerschütterlich*) iron, steely; *präd.* of iron (*od.* steel); (*unnachgiebig*) adamant, hard; (*fest, unerschrocken*) firm; *Energie*: tireless, inexhaustible; *Sparsamkeit etc.*: rigorous; ~**e Regel** hard and fast rule, absolute rule; **mit** ~**em Besen auskehren** take a radical new broom to; **mit** ~**er Faust niederschlagen** (*Revolte etc.*) crush (ruthlessly); **mit** ~**em Griff** with a grip of iron (*od.* steel); **mit** ~**er Hand herrschen** rule with a rod of iron; ~**e Hochzeit** seventieth (*od.* seventy-fifth) wedding anniversary; ~**e Ration/Reserve** iron rations *Pl.* / emergency reserves *Pl.*; **mit** ~**er Ruhe** with imperturbable calm; **sie hat e-e** ~**e Gesundheit** she's got a cast-iron constitution; **II.** *Adv.* (*fest*) firmly; (*unnachgiebig*) unyieldingly, rigidly, implacably; (*unbeirrbar*) resolutely, unswervingly, with iron (*od.* steely) determination; ~ **lernen/üben** etc. study/practi|se (*Am.* -ce) etc. hard; **in etw.** (*Dat.*) ~ **sein** stick rigidly to s.th., take a hard line on s.th.; ~ **festhalten an** hold on rigidly to; ~ **durchhalten** keep going to the (bitter) end

Eiseskälte *f geh.* bitter (*od.* icy) cold

Eis|fach *n* freezing compartment; ~**fischerei** *f* ice fishing; ~**fläche** *f* expanse (*od.* sheet) of ice; *e-s Sees*: frozen surface, ice cover; ♀**frei** *Adj.* free of ice, ice-free; *Wasser: auch*

open

eisgekühlt *Adj.* cold, chilled

eisglatt *Adj. Straße*: icy, treacherous; **Eisglätte** *f* icy roads *Pl.*, black ice

eisgrau *Adj.* grey (*Am.* gray), silver--grey (*Am.* -gray)

Eis|grenze *f* glacial boundary; **~heilige** *Pl.*: **die ~n** the Ice Saints

Eishockey *n Sport* ice hockey, *Am. auch* hockey; **~schläger** *m* ice-hockey (*Am. auch* hockey) stick; **~spieler** *m*, **~spielerin** *f* ice-hockey (*Am. auch* hockey) player

eisig I. *Adj.* **1.** icy; **2.** *fig.*: **~er Blick** icy (*od.* frosty) stare; **~es Schweigen** an icy (*od.* frosty) silence; **II.** *Adv.* **1.** **~ kalt** ice-cold, icy cold; **2.** *fig.*: **j-n ~ anblicken/empfangen** give s.o. an icy (*od.* frosty) stare/welcome (*od.* reception)

Eiskaffee *m Gastr.* iced coffee

eiskalt I. *Adj.* **1.** *Temperatur*: icy cold, ice-cold, freezing; **~e Getränke** ice--cold drinks; **2.** *fig. Blick etc.*: icy, frosty; *Vernunft*: cold; *Mensch*: cold (as ice); **II.** *Adv.* **1.** *als Gefühl*: **dabei überlief es mich ~** it sent shivers down my spine; **2.** *umg.*, (*berechnened, rücksichtlos*): **j-n ~ umbringen** kill s.o. in cold blood; **~ kalkulieren** calculate cold-bloodedly; **sie haben ~ 800 Mitarbeiter entlassen** they dismissed (*Am.* laid off) 800 workers just like that (*od.* without a qualm)

Eis|kappe *f* ice cap; **an den Polen**: *auch* polar ice (cap); **~keller** *m fig.* icebox; **~krem** *f →* **Eiscreme**; **~kristall** *m* ice crystal; **~kübel** *m* ice bucket

Eiskunstlaufen *m*, **Eiskunstlaufen** *n Sport* figure skating; **Eiskunstläufer** *m*, **Eiskunstläuferin** *f* figure skater

Eislauf *m; nur Sg.*, **Eislaufen** *n* (ice-)skating; **Eisläufer** *m*, **Eisläuferin** *f* (ice-)skater

Eis|mann *m* ice-cream man; **~maschine** *f* ice(-cream) maker; **~meer** *n Geog.* polar sea; **Nördliches/Südliches ~** Arctic/Antarctic Ocean; **~pickel** *m* ice axe (*Am.* ax); **~platte** *f* ice sheet, sheet of ice; **~prinz** *m* star skater, prince on ice; **~prinzessin** *f* star skater, princess on ice

Eisprung *m Physiol.* ovulation; **e-n ~ haben** ovulate, be ovulating

Eis|pulver *n* ice-cream powder; **~regen** *m mit Glatteisbildung*: freezing rain; *Hagel*: hail; *Schneeregen*: sleet; **~revue** *f* ice show; **~salat** *m Gastr.* iceberg lettuce; **~schicht** *f* layer of ice; **~schießen** *n etwa* curling

Eisschnell|lauf *m Sport* speed skating; **~läufer** *m*, **~läuferin** *f* speed skater

Eis|schokolade *f* iced chocolate; **~scholle** *f* ice floe; **~schrank** *m altm. Brit. mst* fridge, *Am. od. Brit. förm.* refrigerator; **~sport** *m* ice sports *Pl.*; **~sporthalle** *f* ice rink; **~stadion** *n* ice stadium; **~stand** *m* ice-cream kiosk

Eisstock *m etwa* curling stone; **~schießen** *n etwa* curling

Eis|tanz *m*, **~tanzen** *n Sport* ice-dancing; **~tee** *m* iced tea; **~torte** *f Gastr.* ice-cream gateau; **~tüte** *f* ice-cream cone; **~umschlag** *m Med.* ice pack; **~verkäufer** *m*, **~verkäuferin** *f* ice--cream seller (*od.* vendor); **~vogel** *m* **1.** *Orn.* kingfisher; **2.** (*Schmetterling*) white admiral (butterfly); **~waffel** *f* **1.** *zum Eis gegessen*: wafer; **2.** (*Tüte*): ice-cream cone; **~wasser** *n* ice(d) water; **~wein** *m* eiswein; *very sweet wine from grapes harvested in hard frost*

Eiswürfel *m* ice cube; **~schale** *f* ice-

-cube tray

Eis|wüste *f* frozen waste(s *Pl.*) (*od.* wilderness); **~zapfen** *m* icicle

Eiszeit *f* ice age; **es herrscht ~ zwischen ...** *fig.* relations have cooled off dramatically between ...; **eiszeitlich** *Adj. attr.* ice-age ..., glacial

Eiteilung *f Bio.* segmentation of the ovum

eitel *Adj.* **1.** *pej.* vain; (*eingebildet*) conceited, stuck-up *umg.*; **~ wie ein Pfau** just a peacock, as stuck-up as they come *umg.*; **2.** *geh. altm.* (*nichtig*) vain; (*fruchtlos*) futile, in vain; **eitles Gerede** idle (*od.* empty) talk; **eitle Hoffnung** vain hope; **3.** *undekl.; altm. od. hum.* (*rein*) sheer, pure, nothing but; **es herrschte ~ Freude** there was general rejoicing; **Eitelkeit** *f* **1.** *pej.* vanity, conceit; **verletzte ~** wounded vanity; **2.** *geh. altm.* vanity, futility

Eiter *m; -s, kein Pl.; Med.* pus; **~ absondern** suppurate; **~beule** *f* abscess, boil; **~bläschen** *n* pustule; **~herd** *m* suppurative focus

eitern *v/i. Med.* fester, suppurate

Eiter|pfropf *m Med.* core (of a boil *etc.*); *e-s Pickels*: head (of a spot *od.* pimple); **~pickel** *m* spot, *bes. Am.* pimple

Eiterung *f Med.* suppuration

eitrig *Adj. Med., Wunde*: suppurating; *Entzündung*: septic

Eiweiß *n; -es, - od. -e* **1.** *Pl. Eiweiß* white of an egg, egg white; *Zool.* albumen; **2.** *Pl. Eiweiße; Bio., Chem.* protein, albumin, albumen; **pflanzliches/tierisches ~** vegetable/animal protein; **eiweißarm** *Adj. präd.* low in protein; *attr.* low-protein; **Eiweißbedarf** *m* protein requirement

Eiweißgehalt *m* protein content; **eiweißhaltig** *Adj.* albuminous *fachspr.*, containing protein; **~ sein** contain protein

Eiweiß|körper *m Chem., Bio.* protein; **~mangel** *m* protein deficiency

eiweißreich *Adj. präd.* rich in protein; *attr.* high-protein ...

Eizelle *f Bio.* egg cell, ovum

Ejakulat *n; -(e)s, -e; Physiol.* ejaculate, ejaculated semen; **Ejakulation** *f; -, -en* ejaculation; **ejakulieren** *vt/i.* ejaculate

Ekel[1] *m; -s, kein Pl.* revulsion (**vor +** *Dat. od.* **gegenüber** at), disgust (at); **~ wie an Pfau**: → **empfinden** *od.* **e-n ~ haben vor →** **ekeln** I; **~ erregend** disgusting, sickening, revolting, repulsive; **es ist mir ein ~** I loathe it, I can't stomach (*od.* stand) it *umg.*; **Spinnen sind mir ein ~** I loathe spiders, spiders give me the creeps *umg.*; **sich vor ~ abwenden** look (*od.* turn) away in disgust

Ekel[2] *n; -s, -; umg. pej.* (*widerliche Person*) obnoxious (*od.* repulsive) person; **du ~!** you beast, you rotten old so--and-so; **er ist ein altes ~** he's a real creep

ekelerregend *Adj.*: **äußerst** *od.* **sehr ~** absolutely (*od.* utterly) disgusting, sickening, revolting, nauseating, repulsive

ekelhaft I. *Adj.* **1.** revolting, disgusting; **2.** (*gemein*) horrible, disgraceful, beastly *umg.*; **3.** *umg. Wetter etc.*: nasty, awful, dreadful; **II.** *Adv.* **1.** *riechen, schmecken*: revolting, disgusting; **2.** *umg.*: **~ kalt** *etc.* beastly (*od.* horribly) cold *etc.*; **~ wehtun** hurt horribly

ekelig *Adj. →* **ekelhaft**

ekeln I. *v/refl. und v/t. unpers.*: **es ekelt mich** *od.* **mich ekelt, ich ekle mich davor** it turns me (right) off, it revolts

me, it gives me the shivers (creeps *umg.*); **ich ekle mich** *etc.* **vor ihm** *etc.* he *etc.* gives me the creeps *umg.*; **II.** *v/t. umg.*: **j-n aus dem Haus ~** make life in the same house intolerable for s.o.

EKG *n; -, -s; Abk. Med.* (**Elektrokardiogramm**) ECG, *Am.* EKG

Eklat [e'klaː] *m; -s, -s;* (*Skandal*) scandal, sensation; (*Krach*) confrontation, row, *Am. auch* blow-up *umg.*; **es wird zu e-m ~ kommen** there'll be (a) scandal (*od.* a row), there's going to be (big) trouble; **eklatant I.** *Adj.* **1.** (*offenkundig*) *Beispiel*: striking, conspicuous; *Unterschied: auch* glaring; *Fehler, Verstoß, Widerspruch*: startling, flagrant; *Ungerechtigkeit, Lüge*: blatant; **2.** (*Aufsehen erregend*) spectacular, sensational; **~er Vorfall** sensation; **II.** *Adv.*: **sich ~ unterscheiden/widersprechen** differ/conflict strikingly

eklig *Adj. →* **ekelhaft**

Eklipse *f; -, -n; Astron.* eclipse; **ekliptisch** *Adj.* ecliptic(al)

Ekstase *f; -, -n* ecstasy, rapture; **in ~ geraten** go into ecstasies (*od.* raptures) (**über +** *Akk.* over), get carried away (by); **j-n in ~ versetzen** send s.o. into ecstasies (*od.* raptures); **ekstatisch I.** *Adj.* ecstatic, rapturous; **II.** *Adv.* ecstatically, rapturously

Ekto|parasit *m Med., Zool.* ectoparasite; **~plasma** *n Bio.* ectoplasm

Ekuador *etc. →* **Ecuador** *etc.*

Ekzem *n; -s, -e; Med.* eczema

Elaborat *n; -(e)s, -e; geh.* **1.** (*Abhandlung*) discourse, treatise; **2.** *pej.* piece of hack writing

Elan *m; -s, kein Pl.; geh.* vigo(u)r, brio; **sich mit ~ an die Arbeit machen** set to (work) with a will; **sie haben ohne ~ gespielt** they played without real spirit

Elaste *Pl. Chem., bes. ehem. DDR*: elastomers

Elastik *n; -s, -s od. f; -, -en* elastic; **~binde** *f* elastic (*od.* stretch) bandage

elastisch I. *Adj.* **1.** elastic; (*federnd*) springy; (*biegsam*) flexible; **~er Gang** springy walk (*od.* gait *geh.*); **er kam mit ~en Schritten daher** he came bouncing along; **2.** *fig. Regeln etc.*: flexible; **II.** *Adv.* elastically; **Elastizität** *f; -, -en, mst. Sg.* elasticity; springiness; flexibility

Elativ *m; -s, -e; Ling.* absolute superlative

Elba (*n*); *-s; Geog.* (Isle of) Elba

Elbe *f; -; Geog.*: **die ~** the (river) Elbe; **Elbkähne** *Pl. umg. hum.* size twelves, size twelve shoes

Elch *m; -(e)s, -e; Zool.* elk; *in Nordamerika*: moose; **ich glaub, mich knutscht ein ~** *umg. fig.* I don't believe it!; **~bulle** *m* bull elk; *in Nordamerika*: bull moose; **~kalb** *n* elk calf; *in Nordamerika*: moose calf; **~kuh** *f* cow elk; *in Nordamerika*: cow moose; **~test** *m hum.* elk test, *Am.* moose test; *fig.* litmus test

Eldorado *n; -s, -s; fig.* Eldorado, paradise, happy hunting-ground (**für** for)

Elefant *m; -en, -en; Zool.* elephant; **sich wie ein ~ im Porzellanladen benehmen** *umg. fig.* behave like a bull in a china shop, *Am. auch* be a klutz; → **Mücke** 1

Elefanten|baby *n* baby elephant; *umg. pej.* (*dicke[r] Jugendliche[r]*) young fatso; **~bulle** *m* bull (*od.* male) elephant; **~haut** *f fig.* thick skin; **~hochzeit** *f Wirts. umg.* jumbo merger;

~kalb n elephant calf; **~kuh** f cow (od. female) elephant; **~rennen** n umg. hum. duel between two huge trucks (one trying to overtake the other); **~robbe** f Zool. elephant seal; **~rüssel** m elephant's trunk

elegant I. Adj. **1.** (vornehm, geschmackvoll) elegant, smart; modisch: auch fashionable, chic; **2.** (geschickt) elegant; Bewegung: auch graceful; Lösung: elegant, neat; **auf ~e Weise** elegantly, skil(l)fully, neatly; **3.** (kultiviert, erlesen) elegant, sophisticated; **II.** Adv.: **sich ~ aus der Affäre ziehen** umg. get (o.s.) out of it nicely, extricate o.s. neatly (from …); **Eleganz** f; -, kein Pl. elegance, smartness, chic

Elegie f; -, -n; Lit. elegy; **elegisch** Adj. elegiac; fig. auch melancholy, mournful

elektrifizieren v/t. Etech. electrify; **Elektrifizierung** f electrification

Elektrik f; -, -en; Etech. **1.** (Anlage) electrical system (od. equipment), electrics umg.; **2.** nur Sg.; umg., Fachgebiet: electricity, electrics Pl. umg.

Elektriker m; -s, -, **~in** f; -, -nen electrician

elektrisch I. Adj. Heizofen, Klavier, Stuhl etc.: electric; Defekt, Energie, Kontakt etc.: electrical; **~er Schlag/Strom** electric shock/current; **II.** Adv.: **~ geladen/gesteuert** etc. electrically charged/control[l]ed etc.; **~ heizen** etc. heat etc. with od. by electricity; **~ betrieben sein** be run on electricity

Elektrische f; -n -n; umg. altm. tram

elektrisieren Elektr. **I.** v/t. electrify (auch fig.); **II.** v/refl. get (od. give o.s.) an electric shock; **elektrisiert I.** P.P. → **elektrisieren; II.** Adj. electrified; **er sprang (wie) ~ auf** fig. he jumped up as if he'd been shocked; **Elektrisierung** f electrification

Elektrizität f; -, kein Pl.; Elektr. electricity; (Strom) (electric) current

Elektrizitäts... im Subst. siehe auch **Strom...**

Elektrizitäts|versorgungsunternehmen n electricity supplier (od. supply company); **~werk** n power (od. electricity generating) station

Elektroakustik f Phys., Tech. electroacoustics Pl. (V. im Sg.); **elektroakustisch** Adj. electroacoustic(al)

Elektro|antrieb m Etech. electric drive (od. propulsion); **~artikel** m electrical item (Pl. auch goods, Am. household electronics Pl.); **~auto** n electric car, electric; **~bohrer** m electric (od. power) drill

Elektrode f; -, -n; Phys. electrode; **negative ~** negative electrode, cathode; **positive ~** positive electrode, anode

Elektro|enzephalogramm n Med. (abgek. EEG) electroencephalogram, EEG; **~fahrzeug** n Etech. electric vehicle, electric; **~gerät** n electrical appliance; Pl. auch electrical equipment Sg.; im Kaufhaus, Katalog etc.: electrical goods; **~geschäft** n electrical shop (Am. store), electrical supplier's; **~gitarre** f Mus. electric guitar; **~grill** m electric grill; **~herd** m electric cooker (Am. range); **~industrie** f electrical industry; **~ingenieur** m, **~ingenieurin** f electrical engineer; **~installateur** m, **~installateurin** f electrician; **~kardiogramm** n Med. (abgek. EKG) electrocardiogram, ECG, Am. EKG; **~lok(omotive)** f electric locomotive

Elektrolyse f; -, -n; Chem., Phys. electrolysis; **Elektrolyt** m; -en, -e od. -s,

-en electrolyte; **elektrolytisch** Adj. electrolytic

Elektromagnet m Phys. electromagnet; **elektromagnetisch I.** Adj. electromagnetic; **II.** Adv. electromagnetically

elektromechanisch Adj. Etech. electromechanical

Elektromotor m (electric) motor

Elektron n; -s, -en; Chem., Phys. electron

Elektronen|blitz m, **~blitzgerät** n Fot. electronic flash(gun); **~gehirn** n EDV umg. electronic brain, computer; **~hülle** f Chem. electron shell; **~mikroskop** n electron microscope; **~rechner** m EDV computer; **~röhre** f Phys., Tech. electronic valve (Am. tube); **~schleuder** f Phys. betatron, electronic accelerator

Elektronik f; -, -en **1.** nur Sg.; electronics Pl. (V. im Sg.); **2.** electronic system; **~industrie** f electronics industry; **~schrott** m electronic junk, discarded electronic gadgets

elektronisch I. Adj. electronic; **~e Datenverarbeitung** electronic data processing, EDP; **II.** Adv. electronically

Elektro|ofen m Tech. (Schmelzofen) electric (smelting) furnace; (Heizofen) electric heater; (Kochherd) electric cooker; **~rasierer** m electric shaver (od. razor); **~rasur** f electric shaving (konkret: shave); **~schock** m Med. electroshock; **~schweißen** n electronic welding; **~smog** m electronic smog umg.

elektrostatisch Phys. **I.** Adj. electrostatic; **II.** Adv. electrostatically

Elektrotechnik f Etech. electrical engineering; **Elektrotechniker** m, **Elektrotechnikerin** f electrical engineer; **elektrotechnisch** Adj. electrotechnical; Bauteil, Industrie etc.: electrical

Elektro|therapie f Med. electrotherapy; **~zaun** m electric fence

Element n; -(e)s, -e **1.** (Naturgewalt) element; **die (vier) ~e** the (four) elements; **das feuchte** od. **nasse ~** geh. the watery element; **die entfesselten ~e** the unleashed power of the elements; **2.** Lebensraum: (natural) element; **in s-m ~ sein** od. **sich in s-m ~ fühlen** fig. be in one's element; **3.** (Bestandteil) element, component (part); (Faktor) (contributory) factor; **das gemeinsame/treibende ~** the common/motivating factor; **ein besinnliches ~ in den Abend bringen** introduce a reflective note into the evening('s proceedings etc.); **4.** ~e (Grundbegriffe) elements, rudiments, basics; **5.** mst Pl.; fig. pej.: **unliebsame/kriminelle** etc. **~e** undesirable/criminal etc. elements; **6.** Chem. element; **einwertiges/zweiwertiges ~** monovalent (od. univalent) / divalent (od. bivalent) element; **radioaktives ~** radioactive element; **7.** Etech. element, cell, battery; **galvanisches ~** galvanic cell; **8.** (Bauteil) element; **9.** Math., Mengenlehre: element (aus od. von out of, from)

elementar Adj. **1.** (grundlegend) elementary, basic; **~er Fehler** fundamental (od. basic) mistake (od. flaw); **2.** Gewalt, Kraft etc.: elemental; **3.** (primär) elementary, primary; **4.** Chem. (ungebunden) elemental

Elementar|begriff m fundamental idea; **~gewalt** f elemental power (od. force), power of the elements; **~kenntnisse** Pl. rudiments, basics; **~ladung** f Phys. elementary charge; **~stufe** f elementary grade

Elementarteilchen n Phys. elementary particle; **~physik** f particle physics Pl. (V. im Sg.)

Elementarunterricht m elementary instruction

Elen n, auch m; -s, -; Zool. → **Elch**

elend I. Adj. **1.** (unglücklich, beklagenswert) miserable, wretched, pitiable; **ein ~es Leben führen** live a life of misery; **2.** (ärmlich) poverty-stricken; **in ~en Verhältnissen leben** live in wretched conditions (od. dire poverty); **3.** (krank) (very) unwell; **~ aussehen** look dreadful; **sich ~ fühlen** feel terrible (od. wretched); **4.** pej. (gemein) despicable; **5.** nur attr.; umg. Durst, Hunger etc. (stark): terrible; **II.** Adv. **1.** miserably; **~ zugrunde gehen** come to a wretched end; **~ verhungern** die of slow (and painful) starvation; **2.** umg. (sehr) dreadfully; **es tut ~ weh** it's terribly sore, it hurts dreadfully (od. like hell Sl.); **es ist ~ kalt** it's absolutely freezing

Elend n; -s, kein Pl. **1.** (Leid) misery; **wie das leibhaftige ~ aussehen** umg. look like death warmed up (Am. over), look (utterly) wretched; **es ist ein ~ mit ihm** umg. he's a hopeless case, he'd break your heart; **er bekam das heulende ~** umg. he got the miseries, he just went to pieces; **da könnte man das heulende ~ kriegen** umg. it's enough to make you weep; **2.** (Armut) (dire od. abject) poverty, destitution; **soziales ~** social hardship; **ins ~ geraten** be reduced to poverty; **ins ~ stürzen** plunge into poverty (and distress); **3.** umg. fig.: **langes ~** beanpole, long (thin) streak of misery pej.; → **Häufchen** 3

elendig Adj. und Adv. Dial. → **elend**; **elendiglich** Adv. geh. → **elend** II

Elends|quartier n hovel, slum (dwelling); **~viertel** n slum(s Pl.)

Eleve m; -n, -n, **Elevin** f; -, -nen; Theat. etc. student

elf Zahlw. eleven; → **acht**[1]

Elf[1] f; -, -en **1.** Zahl: (number) eleven; → **Acht**[1] 1, 2; **2.** Fußball: team, eleven

Elf[2] m; -en, -en, **Elfe** f; -, -n elf

elf... im Adj. od. Adv. → **acht...**

Elfenbein n ivory; **elfenbeinern** Adj. ivory; **elfenbeinfarben, elfenbeinfarbig** Adj. ivory (-colo[u]red)

Elfenbein|küste f Geog. Ivory Coast, Côte d'Ivoire; **~schnitzerei** f ivory carving; konkret: auch ivory; **~turm** m fig. ivory tower

elfenhaft Adj. elfin, elfish, elf(-)like

Elfenreigen m poet. dance of the elves

Elfer m; -s, -; umg. **1.** eleven; → **Acht**[1] 1, 2; **2.** Fußball: penalty (kick); **~rat** m im Karneval: Committee of Eleven; **~wette** f Sport kind of football pool betting involving 11 matches

Elfmeter m Fußball: penalty (kick); **~marke** f, **~punkt** m penalty spot; **~schießen** n penalty shootout; **~schütze** m penalty kicker; **~tor** n penalty (goal)

elft Adv.: **zu ~** eleven of; **wir/sie waren zu ~** there were eleven of us/them; → **acht**[2]

elft... Adj. eleventh; → **acht...**

elftel I. Adj.: **e-e ~ Sekunde** an (od. one) eleventh of a second; **II. Elftel** n; -s, - eleventh (part); **elftens** Adv. (point) eleven, eleventhly mst hum.

eliminieren v/t. geh. eliminate; **Eliminierung** f geh. elimination

elisabethanisch Adj. hist. Elizabethan; **das ~e Drama** Elizabethan drama

elitär I. *Adj.* **1.** *pej.* elitist; **2.** *nur attr.*; (*zur Elite gehörig*) elite ...; **II.** *Adv. pej.*: ~ **denken** have elitist attitudes

Elite *f; -, -n* elite; ~**denken** *n* elitism, elitist mindset; ~**schule** *f* elite school; ~**truppe** *f* crack regiment (*Pl. auch* troops); ~**universität** *f* top (*od.* first--class) university, *Am.* ivy league school

Elixier *n; -s, -e* elixir, (magic) potion

Ellbogen *m* elbow; **sich mit den ~ e-n Weg bahnen durch** elbow one's way through; **s-e ~ gebrauchen** *fig.* use one's elbows; ~**freiheit** *f auch fig.* el-bowroom, room to move; ~**gelenk** *n* elbow joint; ~**gesellschaft** *f; nur Sg.*; *pej.* dog-eat-dog society; (*permanenter Konkurrenzkampf*) rat race; ~**mensch** *m pej.* pushy type, ruthless go-getter *umg.*

Elle *f; -, -n* **1.** *Anat.* ulna; **2.** *hist.* ell; *bibl.* cubit; **3.** *altm.* (*Maßstock*) yard--stick; **alles mit der gleichen ~ messen** *fig.* measure everything by the same yardstick

Ellenbogen → **Ellbogen**

ellenlang *Adj. umg.* **1.** *Geschichte etc.*: endless, never-ending; **2.** *Person*: ex-tremely (*od.* exceptionally) tall

Ellipse *f; -, -n* **1.** *Math.* ellipse; **2.** *Ling.* ellipsis; **elliptisch** *Adj.* elliptical

Elmsfeuer *n Astron.* St(.) Elmo's fire

Eloge [e'lo:ʒə] *f; -, -n; geh.* eulogy (**auf** + *Akk.* to)

E-Lok *f* electric loco(motive)

eloquent *Adj. geh.* eloquent; **Elo-quenz** *f; -, kein Pl.; geh.* eloquence, rhetoric

eloxieren *v/t. fachspr.* coat with eloxal

Elritze *f; -, -n; Zool.* minnow

Elsass *n; -(es); Geog.*: **das ~** Alsace; **Elsässer** *m; -s, -*, **Elsässerin** *f; -, -nen* Alsatian, *weiblich auch* Alsatian woman (*od.* girl *etc.*); **~ sein** *auch* be (*od.* come) from Alsace; **elsässisch** *Adj.* Alsatian, *attr. auch* Alsace ...; ~**e Weine** wines from the Alsace, Alsa-tian wines

Elster *f; -, -n; Orn.* magpie; **er ist e-e diebische ~** *fig.* he'd steal the shirt off your back *umg.*

elterlich *Adj.*; *nur attr.* parental; *Woh-nung etc.*: *auch* parents' ...; **die ~en Pflichten** one's duties as a parent, one's parental duties; ~**e Gewalt** *Jur. altm.* parental authority

Eltern *Pl.* parents; **nicht von schlech-ten ~** *umg.* not bad at all, classy; *Ohr-feige etc.*: *attr.* resounding, *präd.* one to remember; ~**abend** *m in der Schu-le*: parent-teacher meeting, parents' evening; ~**beirat** *m* parents' council; ~**generation** *f Bio.* parental genera-tion; ~**haus** *n* **1.** *konkret*: one's par-ents' house, house one grew up in; **2.** *weitS.* home, background; **aus gu-tem ~ stammen** come from a good (*od.* respectable) family (*od.* home), have a good family background; ~**lie-be** *f* parental love

elternlos *Adj. attr.* orphan ..., *auch präd.* orphaned

Eltern|pflicht *f* parental duty; **die ~en** *auch* one's duties as a parent; ~**recht** *n* parental right(s *Pl.*)

Elternschaft *f* **1.** *nur Sg.*; parenthood; **2.** *konkret*: parents *Pl.*

Eltern|schlafzimmer *n* parents' bed-room; *auf Bauplänen*: master bed-room; ~**sprechtag** *m* open day; ~**teil** *m* parent; ~**tier** *n Zool.* parent animal; ~**vertretung** *f* parents' council

EM *Abk.* (*Europameisterschaft*[*en*])

Sport European Championship(s); *Fußball*: *auch* European Cup

E-Mail ['i:me:l] *f; -, -s; EDV* e(-)mail; **e-e ~ schicken** send an email

Email [e'mai] *n; -s, -s* enamel

Emailarbeit *f* enamel work

Emaille [e'maljə] *f; -, -n* → **Email**

Emaillack *m* high-gloss coating

emaillieren [ema'ji:rən] *v/t.* enamel

Emanze *f; -, -n*; *umg., oft pej.* women's libber; **Emanzipation** *f; -, -en* emanci-pation; **die ~ der Frau** women's libera-tion (lib *umg.*); **emanzipatorisch** *Adj.* emancipatory; **emanzipieren I.** *v/t.* emancipate; **II.** *v/refl.* become emancipated (**von** from)

Embargo *n; -s, -s; Pol.* embargo; **ein ~ verhängen über** (+ *Akk.*) embargo, place (*od.* impose) an embargo on

Emblem *n; -s, -e* emblem; (*Symbol*) symbol

Embolie *f; -, -n*; *Med.* embolism

Embryo *m; -s, -s od. -nen*; *Med.* em-bryo; **Embryologie** *f; -, kein Pl.* em-bryology; **embryonal** *Adj. attr.* embry-onic, embryo ...

emeritieren *v/t. Univ.* retire, give *s.o.* emeritus status; **emeritiert I.** *P.P.* → *emeritieren*; **II.** *Adj.* retired; ~**er Pro-fessor** retired (*od.* emeritus) profes-sor, professor emeritus

emeritus *Adj.*: **Professor ~** emeritus professor; **Emeritus** *m; -, Emeriti* emeritus professor

Emigrant *m; -en, -en* emigrant; (*Flücht-ling*) refugee; *hist. politischer*: émigré; **Emigrantenliteratur** *f* literature of exile; *hist.* émigré literature; **Emigran-tenschicksal** *n* one's fate as an exile (*od.* refugee *od.* émigré); **Emigran-tentum** *n; -s, kein Pl.* life in exile, life as an exile (*od.* refugee *od.* émigré); **Emigrantin** *f; -, -nen* (female) emi-grant; (*Flüchtling*) refugee; *hist.* émi-grée; **Emigration** *f; -, -en* **1.** *Handlung*: emigration; *innere ~ geh. fig.* inner emigration; **2.** *nur Sg.*; (*die Fremde*) exile; **in die ~ gehen** go into exile; **emigrieren** *v/i.* emigrate (*nach od. in* + *Akk.* to)

eminent I. *Adj. österr. od. geh.*: ~**e Be-gabung** outstanding talent; **von ~er Wichtigkeit** of the utmost importance; **II.** *Adv.* (*sehr*) exceptionally, extreme-ly; *förm.* most; ~ **gefährlich** extremely (*od.* exceptionally) dangerous

Eminenz *f; -, -en* **1.** *kath. Titel*: Emi-nence; **Seine/Eure ~** His/Your Emi-nence; *Träger des Titels Eminenz*: car-dinal; **2.** *fig.*: **graue ~** éminence grise, grey (*Am.* gray) eminence, power be-hind the throne

Emir *m; -s, -e* emir; **Emirat** *n; -(e)s, -e* emirate

Emissär *m; -s, -e* emissary; (*Agent*) agent; (*Bote*) envoy

Emission *f; -, -en* **1.** *Phys., Öko.* emis-sion; **2.** *Wirts. etc.* (*Ausgabe*) issue; (*Wertpapier*) issue; **3.**; **4.** *Schw.* (radio) broadcast

Emissions|bank *f Wirts.* bank of issue; ~**grenzwerte** *Pl. Öko.* emission standards; ~**schutz** *m Öko.* emission control

emittieren *v/t.* **1.** *Wirts.* issue; **2.** *Phys., Etron.* emit

Emmentaler I. *m; -s, -*; Emmental (cheese), Emmental-type cheese, *Am. mst* Swiss (cheese); **II.** *Adj.*: **~ Käse** → **I**

e-Moll *n Mus.* E minor; **~-Tonleiter** *f* E minor scale

Emotion *f; -, -en* emotion; **von ~en er-**

füllt highly emotional, emotionally charged, full of emotion; **emotional** *Adj.* emotional; **emotionalisieren** *v/t. geh., fachspr.* emotionalize; **Emotio-nalität** *f; -, kein Pl.; geh., fachspr.* emotionality, emotionalism; **emotio-nell → emotional**; **emotionsfrei** *Adj.* free of emotion, dispassionate; **emoti-onsgeladen** *Adj. attr. Atmosphäre etc.*: highly-charged, emotionally char-ged, very emotional; *Thema etc.*: emo-tive; **emotionslos** *Adj.* unemotional, emotionless

empfahl *Imperf.* → **empfehlen**

empfand *Imperf.* → **empfinden**

Empfang *m; -(e)s, Empfänge* **1.** *nur Sg.*; (*Erhalt*) receipt; **nach od. bei ~** on receipt; *von Waren*: on delivery (+ *Gen. od.* **von** of); **in ~ nehmen** (*Waren etc.*) receive, take delivery of; **2.** *nur Sg.*; *geh.* (*Begrüßung, Aufnahme*) re-ception, welcome; **j-m e-n begeister-ten/kühlen ~ bereiten** give s.o. an en-thusiastic / a cool reception; **3.** (*Veran-staltung*) reception; **e-n ~ geben** hold a reception; **4.** *nur Sg.*; *Funk., TV* re-ception; **auf ~ gehen/bleiben** switch to / stay on 'Receive'; **5.** *im Hotel etc.*: reception (desk), (front) desk

empfangen *v/t.*; **empfängt, empfing, hat empfangen 1.** *geh.* (*erhalten*) re-ceive; (*annehmen*) accept; (*Strafe, Schl ä ge*) receive, suffer; (*Eindrücke*) form, get, receive; **2.** *Funk., TV* re-ceive, get (**auf** *Kurzwelle etc.*: on); **3.** (*begrüßen*) welcome; *formell*: re-ceive; *am Bahnhof etc.*: welcome, meet; *Besucher ~* see (*od.* receive) visitors; **j-n mit Jubel ~** *etc.* ~ greet s.o. with cheers *etc.*; **4.** *geh., Med.* (*ein Kind*) conceive

Empfänger[1] *m; -s, -*, ~**in** *f; -, -nen* **1.** re-cipient, receiver; *Wirts.*, *von Waren*: consignee; **2.** *e-s Briefes*: addressee; **~ unbekannt** addressee (*od.* address) unknown; **~ unbekannt verzogen** gone away, not known at this address; **3.** *ei-ner Zahlung*: payee; *einer Erbschaft*: beneficiary

Empfänger[2] *m; -s, -*; (*Radio*) receiver; *ohne Verstärker*: tuner

empfänglich *Adj.* receptive, responsive (**für** to); *für Eindrücke*: impressiona-ble; *für Krankheiten, Schmeicheleien etc.*: susceptible (to); *Med. auch* prone to; **~ für neue Ideen** open to new ideas; **Empfänglichkeit** *f* **1.** (*Zugäng-lichkeit*) receptiveness (**für** to); *für Suggestion*: *auch* susceptibility (**für** to), impressionableness; **2.** *Med.* sus-ceptibility (**für** to), proneness (to)

Empfängnis *f; -, kein Pl.* conception; **die Unbefleckte ~** *kath.* the Immacu-late Conception

empfängnisverhütend *Adj. Med.* (*auch* ~**es Mittel**) contraceptive; **Emp-fängnisverhütung** *f* contraception; **Empfängnisverhütungsmittel** *n* con-traceptive

Empfangs|antenne *f Radio etc.*: re-ceiving aerial (*od.* antenna); ~**berech-tigt** *Adj.* authorized to receive goods *etc.*; ~**bereich** *m Funk.* **1.** *in dem man e-n Sender empfangen kann*: reception area; **2.** (*Frequenzbereich*) frequency range; ~**bescheinigung** *f* receipt; ~**bestätigung** *f* acknowledg(e)ment of receipt; ~**chef** *m*, ~**chefin** *f* recep-tion (*od.* front desk) manager, recep-tion (*Am.* room) clerk; ~**dame** *f* re-ceptionist; ~**halle** *f* reception (area), lobby, foyer; ~**komitee** *n* reception committee; ~**saal** *m* reception room;

~störung f Funk. auch Pl. interference; atmosphärische: static
empfängt → *empfangen*
empfehlen; *empfiehlt, empfahl, hat empfohlen* **I.** *v/t.* **1.** recommend (**als** as; **für** od. **zu** for); **j-m etw.** (**wärmstens**) **~** (warmly) recommend s.th. to s.o.; **nicht zu ~** not to be recommended, not advisable; **wir ~ den Filter regelmäßig zu wechseln** the filter should be changed regularly, we advise (od. recommend) changing the filter regularly; **2.** förm.: **~ Sie mich Ihrer Frau** etc. give my regards to your wife etc.; **II.** *v/refl.* **1.** Sache: recommend itself; Verfahren etc.: suggest itself; **der Tee empfiehlt sich bei ...** the tea is recommended for ...; unpers.: **es empfiehlt sich zu** (+ Inf.) it is advisable to (+ Inf.); **2.** (s-e Dienste anbieten) offer one's services (**als** as); **3.** (weggehen) take one's leave geh.; beim Schlafengehen: retire, say goodnight; **ich empfehle mich!** Abschiedsgruß: (I'll say) goodbye!
empfehlenswert Adj. (lohnend etc.) recommendable, worth doing (od. seeing etc.); (ratsam) advisable; Warentest: **sehr/besonders ~** highly/particularly recommended; **weniger ~** less recommendable
Empfehlung f **1.** recommendation; **auf ~** (**von j-m**) on (s.o.'s) recommendation; **2.** beruflich: **gute ~en haben** have good references; **3.** förm.: **m-e ~ an** (+ Akk.) give my regards to, remember me to; Briefschluss: **mit den besten ~en** (**von**) Yours (very) truly, with best regards; **Empfehlungsschreiben** n letter of recommendation (od. introduction)
empfiehlt → *empfehlen*
empfinden; *empfindet, empfand, empfunden; vt/i.* **1.** (Freude, Schmerzen etc.) feel; **Mitleid ~ für** auch have sympathy for; **ich empfinde mit Ihnen** I feel for you; **was empfindest du dabei?** what kind of feeling does it (od. that) give you?, what (od. how) do you feel when you do (od. see etc.) it (od. that)?; **2. ~ als** (auffassen) find, see as; **etw. als lästig** etc. **~** find s.th. (od. regard s.th. as) a nuisance; **3.** (lieben): **etwas/nichts für j-n ~** feel s.th./nothing for s.o., have (no) feelings for s.o.; **viel/wenig für j-n ~** have a deep attachment to (od. be emotionally involved with) s.o. / have no special (od. particular) feeling(s) for s.o.
Empfinden n (Gefühl) feeling; (Meinung) opinion; (Sinn) sense, instinct; **nach m-m ~** (Ansicht) the way I see it, to my mind; (Gefühl) for me, as far as I'm concerned
empfindlich I. Adj. **1.** (fein reagierend, anzeigend) Messgerät etc.: sensitive (**gegen** to), delicate; Film: fast; **2.** (verletzbar, leicht beschädigt, schmerzempfindlich) Haut, Zahn etc.: sensitive (**gegen** to); Haut: auch delicate; Gesundheit, Stoff, Teppich etc.: delicate; Pflanze: tender, delicate; Person: (leicht gekränkt) touchy (**gegen** about), (very) sensitive (about); pej. over-sensitive (about), easily offended, präd. auch quick to take offen|ce (Am. -se); (anfällig) susceptible (**gegen** to); **~e Stelle** sore spot (auch fig.), tender spot (od. area); **3.** (stark, schwer, streng, auffallend) Kälte: severe, biting, bitter; Schmerz: sharp, severe; Mangel, Verlust(e) etc.: serious,

disturbing, major; Verluste: auch heavy; Strafe etc.: severe, heavy, sharp; **II.** Adv. **1.** (fein) sensitively; **~ reagieren** (**auf** + Akk.) react sensitively (to); auf Einflüsse: respond readily (od. easily) (to); (beleidigt) → 2; **2.** (verletzbar, reizbar) sensitively; pej. over-sensitively, badly; (beleidigt) touchily; pej. huffily; **3.** (stark, scharf) severely, badly; **~ kalt** bitter(ly) (od. bitingly) cold; **j-n ~ treffen** Bemerkung etc.: hit (od. strike) home, hit s.o. hard, cut s.o. to the quick
...empfindlich im Adj. ...-sensitive; **frost~** susceptible to frost, not frost-resistant (od. hardy); **korrosions~** attr. easily corroding, präd. prone to corrosion, of low corrosion resistance
Empfindlichkeit f **1.** von Messger ät etc.: sensitivity, delicacy, sensiveness; **2.** (Reizbarkeit) touchiness, sensitiveness; pej. (over-)sensitivity, quickness (od. readiness) to take offen|ce (Am. -se); e-r Körperstelle: tenderness, soreness
empfindsam Adj. (zartfühlend) sensitive; (gefühlvoll) sentimental; **Empfindsamkeit** f (Feinfühligkeit) sensitivity; (Sentimentalit ät) sentimentality; Lit. Sentimentalism
Empfindung f **1.** (körperliches Gefühl) feeling, sensation; (sinnliche Wahrnehmung) (sensory) perception; weitS. feeling, sense; **2.** (Emotion) emotion, feeling; **empfindungslos** Adj. **1.** körperlich: numb, präd. auch without feeling; **2.** (seelisch gefühllos) insensitive (**für** to); pej. unfeeling
Empfindungs|nerv m sensory nerve; **~vermögen** n sensitivity; für Seelisches: auch sensibility
empfing Imperf. → *empfangen*
empfohlen I. P.P. → *empfehlen*; **II.** Adj. recommended
empfunden P.P. → *empfinden*
Emphase f **-, -n**; geh. emphasis (Pl. emphases); **emphatisch I.** Adj. geh. emphatic; **II.** Adv. emphatically
Emphysem n; **-s, -e**; Med. emphysema
Empire¹ [ˈɛmpaɪɐ] n; **-(s)**, kein Pl.; hist.: **das ~** the (British) Empire
Empire² [ãˈpiːɐ] n; **-(s)**, kein Pl.; Kunst Empire (period); **~stil** m; nur Sg. Empire (style)
Empirik f **-, -en**; geh. empiricism; **Empiriker** m; **-s, -**, **Empirikerin** f; **-, -nen**; geh. empiricist; **empirisch** Adj. geh. empirical
empor Adv. geh. up, upward(s); **empor...** im V.; geh. → auch **hoch...**, **hinauf...**; **~arbeiten** v/refl. (trennb., hat -ge-); geh. work one's way up; **~blicken** v/i. (trennb., hat -ge-); geh. look up (**zu** at; fig. to)
Empore f **-, -n**; Archit. gallery
empören I. v/t. (aufbringen) anger; stärker: infuriate, outrage; (beleidigen) insult, affront geh.; (schockieren) shock; stärker: scandalize, appal; **II.** v/refl. **1.** be outraged (**über** + Akk. at, by), be furious (od. angry) (about), express (one's) outrage (at); **2.** Volk etc.: rebel, rise up (in arms) (**gegen** against); **empörend I.** Part. Präs. → *empören*; **II.** Adj. outrageous, infuriating; shocking, scandalous; **empörerisch** Adj. **1.** Ideen: rebellious; Rede: inflammatory; **2.** Personen: rebellious, insurgent
emporheben v/t. (unreg., trennb., hat -ge-); geh. lift, raise
emporkommen v/i. (unreg., trennb., ist -ge-); geh. **1.** come up, rise to the sur-

face; **2.** fig. get on in life, prosper; **Emporkömmling** m; **-s, -e**; pej. upstart, parvenu
empor|ragen v/i. (trennb., hat -ge-); geh.: **~ aus** rise (od. tower up) from (od. out of); **~schießen** v/i. (unreg., trennb., ist -ge-); geh. **1.** (häufig werden) shoot (od. spring) up; Neubauten etc.: auch mushroom; **2.** (aufspringen) Person etc.: jump (od. spring, leap) up (od. to one's feet); Wasserstrahl: gush up; **~schwingen** v/refl. (unreg., trennb., hat -ge-); geh. Mensch, Tier: swing o.s. up; Vogel: rise (**zu** to); fig. **sich zu großen künstlerischen Leistungen ~** achieve artistic mastery; **~steigen** (unreg., trennb., ist -ge-); geh. **I.** v/i. rise (up), climb (up); **II.** v/t. climb (auch fig.); **~streben** v/i. (trennb., ist -ge-); geh. Bergsteiger etc.: climb higher; mühsam: plod (od. toil) upwards; Pfeiler, Vogel etc.: soar (up, upwards); fig. Person: aspire (**zu** to)
empört I. P.P. → *empören*; **II.** Adj. (schockiert) shocked; stärker: appalled (**über** + Akk. at); (entrüstet) indignant (at), angry (about); (beleidigt) insulted; **III.** Adv. indignantly, angrily, resentfully; **Empörung** f **1.** nur Sg.; indignation (**über** + Akk. at, over); outrage (at, over), shock and resentment; **s-r ~ Ausdruck verleihen** express (stärker: give vent to) one's anger etc.; **2.** (Aufstand) revolt, (up)rising, rebellion (**gegen** against)
emsig Adj. (geschäftig) busy; (fleißig) industrious, hardworking, diligent; (eifrig) eager, keen; **~es Treiben** concentrated activity, hive of activity (od. industry), hustle and bustle umg.; **Emsigkeit** f (Geschäftigkeit) bustle, busyness umg.; (Fleiß) industry, diligence; (Eifer) zeal, enthusiasm
Emu m; **-s, -s**; Zool. emu
Emulgator m; **-s, -en**; Chem. emulsifier, emulsifying agent; **Emulsion** f; **-, -en** emulsion
E-Musik f; nur Sg. serious (od. classical) music
EN Abk. (**europäische Norm**) European standard
en bloc [ãˈblɔk] Adv. en bloc, wholesale
End|abrechnung f final account; fig. final reckoning; **~abschaltung** f Tech.: **automatische ~** automatic (tape) shut-off; **~achtziger** m, **~achtzigerin** f man/woman in his/her late eighties; **~ sein** auch be in one's late eighties; **~anwender** m, **~anwenderin** f EDV end user; **~ausscheidung** f Sport final elimination (round); **~betrag** m (sum) total, final total; **~buchstabe** m last (od. final) letter; **~darm** m Anat. rectum; **~dreißiger** m, **~dreißigerin** f man/woman in his/her late thirties; **~ sein** auch be in one's late thirties
Ende n; **-s, -n 1.** räumlich: end; **am ~ des Zuges einsteigen** get in at the back of the train; **das vordere/hintere ~** the front (end) (od. forward end) / the back, the rear (end); **das obere/ untere ~** the top (end) / bottom (end); **etw. am verkehrten ~ anpacken** fig. tackle s.th. the wrong way (a)round, put the cart before the horse; **2.** nur Sg.; e-s Zeitraums: end, close; **~ Januar** at the end of January; **am** od. **gegen ~ des Monats** at/toward(s) the end of the month; **noch vor ~ dieser Woche** by the end of this week, before the week is out geh.; **bis ans ~ al-**

ler Tage until the end of time; **~ *der Dreißigerjahre** od. **dreißiger Jahre** in the late thirties, at the end of the thirties; **sie ist ~ zwanzig** she's in her late twenties; **3.** (*Schluss*) end, close; *e-s Films etc.*: ending; *Auslaufen e-s Vertrags*: expiry; *e-r Frist*: end, expiry; (*Ergebnis*) result, outcome; **~!** *Funk.* over!; **ohne ~** endless, unending; **er findet kein ~** he can't stop, he doesn't know where (*od.* when) to stop; **letzten ~s** after all, ultimately, in the end, at the end of the day, when all is said and done; **die Arbeit geht ihrem ~ entgegen** is nearing completion; **... und kein ~ in Sicht** with no end in sight; **e-r Sache ein ~ machen** od. **bereiten** put a stop (*od.* an end) to s.th.; **s-m Leben ein ~ machen** od. **setzen** die by one's own hand *geh.*, end it all *umg.*; **alles hat einmal ein ~** all (good) things come to an end; **das muss ein ~ haben** it's got to stop; **es nimmt kein ~** it just goes on and on; **ein schlimmes** od. **böses ~ nehmen** come to a bad end; **das dicke ~ kommt noch** *umg.* the worst is yet to come, there's worse to come, it gets worse; **das ~ vom Lied war** *fig.* the end of the story was, what happened in the end was, the upshot of it (all) was *umg.*; **~ gut, alles gut** *Sprichw.* all's well that ends well; **4. am ~** (*schließlich*) in the end, eventually; (*auf die Dauer*) in the long run, eventually; **am ~ mussten wir hinlaufen** we ended (*od.* wound *umg.*) up having to walk (there); **5. am ~** (*fertig, erledigt, kaputt*) finished, done, on one's last legs; **ich bin am ~** (*kann nicht mehr*) I'm finished, I've had it *umg.*, *Brit. auch* I'm all in *umg.*; **ich bin mit m-r Geduld / m-n Nerven am ~** I've been patient (for) long enough / I can't stand the strain any longer; **6. am ~** (*vielleicht, womöglich, etwa*) maybe, could be, perhaps; **am ~ stimmt das sogar!** it could even be true!; **meinst du das am ~ ernst?** are you actually serious about this?, I'm beginning to think you mean it; **7. zu ~ bringen** od. **führen** finish, complete, see *s.th.* through; **zu ~ gehen** (*enden*) (come to an) end, finish; *allmählich*: draw to a close; (*knapp werden*) run short (*od.* low); **etw. zu ~ denken** think s.th. out fully, think s.th. through; **zu ~ lesen** *etc.* finish reading *etc.*; **zu ~ sein** *Schule, Krieg, Wartezeit etc.*: be over; *Film, Spiel etc.*: have finished; *Geduld, Vorräte*: be at an end, be exhausted, have run out; *Vorräte*: *auch* be finished; **8.** *nur Sg.*; *lit.* (*Zweck*) end, purpose; **9.** *nur Sg.*; *lit. euph.* (*Tod*) end; **sein ~ nahen fühlen** sense that one's end is near (*od.* that one has not long to live); **es geht zu ~ mit ihm** he's going (*od.* slipping) fast, it won't be long now; **10.** *nur Sg.*; *umg.*: **es ist noch ein ganzes ~** it's a long way (off) yet, there's quite a distance still; **11.** *Jägerspr., des Geweihs*: point; **12.** *Naut.* line, rope

Endeffekt *m* end (*od.* net) result, outcome; **im ~** ultimately, in the long run; **im ~ bleibt sich das gleich** it comes to the same thing in the end

endemisch I. *Adj. Bio., Med.* endemic; **II.** *Adv.* endemically

enden I. *v/i.* **1.** (*räumlich aufhören*) (come to an) end, stop; **der Zug endet hier** the train terminates (*od.* stops *umg.*) here, this is the end of the line (for this train); **2.** (*zeitlich aufhören,*

ausgehen) end, finish; *Frist*: *auch* run out, be up, expire; *Vertrag etc.*: expire, lapse; **~ mit** *Sache*: end (up) with, end in; *Person*: finish (up) with (*od.* by + *Ger.*); **schlimm** od. **böse ~** come to a bad (*od.* sorry) end; **wo soll das nur** (*alles*) **~?** whatever are things coming to?; **der Film endet tragisch/gut** the film (*Am. auch* movie) ends tragically/happily, the film (*Am. auch* movie) has a sad ending / happy end; **nicht ~ wollend** unending, never-ending; *Beifall*: prolonged; **3.** *Rede etc., Redner(in)*: finish, end, conclude *geh.*; **sie endete mit den Worten ...** she finished by saying..., finally, she said...; **4.** *euph.* (*sterben, sein Leben beschließen*) end one's days, finish (up); **du wirst noch im Knast ~!** you'll finish (*od.* end) up in jail!; **5.** *Ling.*: **~ auf** (+ *Dat.*) end in (*od.* with); **II.** *v/t. geh.* (*beenden*) end, (bring to a) close, terminate

...ender *m*; *-s, -*; *im Subst.*; *Jägerspr.* *...pointer*

End|ergebnis *n* final result (*auch Sport und Math.*), end result; **~erzeugnis** *n* end product; **~fassung** *f* final version; *Aufsatz etc.*: *auch* fair copy; **~fünfziger** *m*, **~fünfzigerin** *f* man/woman in his/her late fifties; **~ sein** *auch* be in one's late fifties

endgültig I. *Adj.* final; *Beweis*: *auch* conclusive, definitive; *Antwort*: final, definitive; **ich kann noch nichts Endgültiges sagen** I can't say anything (*od.* be *umg.*) definite at the moment, I am not yet in a position to resolve the matter *förm.* (*od.* make a definitive statement); **II.** *Adv.* finally; (*für immer*) for good; (*ein für alle Mal*) once and for all; **das steht ~ fest** that's definite (*od.* fixed); **damit ist es ~ aus** (**und vorbei**) that's over for good, that's finished and done with *umg.*; **jetzt ist aber ~ Schluss!** it really is time to stop now!; *Brit. auch energischer*: right - that's your lot! *umg.*;

Endgültigkeit *f* finality, irrevocability

End|haltestelle *f* terminus; **~haus** *n* end-of-terrace (*Am.* -row) house

endigen *v/i. altm.* → **enden**

Endivie *f*; *-, -n*; *Bot.* endive; **Endiviensalat** *m*; *Gastr.* endive salad

End|kampf *m* **1.** *Sport* final; **2.** *Mil.* final phase of fighting, final stage (of the war), final struggle; **~konsonant** *m Ling.* final consonant

Endlager *n Öko.* final disposal site; **endlagern** *v/t.* (*hat -ge-*) *nur Inf. und P.P.* dispose of *s.th.* permanently; **Endlagerstätte** *f* final disposal site; **Endlagerung** *f* final disposal

Endlauf *m Sport* final

endlich I. *Adv.* (*nach langer Zeit*) finally, at (long) last; (*schließlich*) in the end, eventually; *bei Aufzählungen*: (and) last(ly), (and) finally; **hör ~ auf!** stop it, will you!; *for goodness' etc.* sake stop it (*od.* that)!; (*na*) **~!** *umg.* at last!, about time too!; **bist du ~ fertig?** have you quite finished?; *iro.* are you sure you've finished?; **II.** *Adj.* **1.** (*begrenzt*) limited, finite; **2.** *Philos. und Math.* finite; **Endlichkeit** *f* finiteness, finite nature (+ *Gen.* of)

endlos I. *Adj.* **1.** (*Ggs. kurz*) endless, never-ending, unending; *Rede etc.*: interminable; (*unaufhörlich*) incessant; **2.** *fig.* (*grenzenlos*) infinite, boundless; **3.** (*ohne Ende*) infinite; *Tech.* continuous; **II.** *Adv.* endlessly, interminably; **es zog sich ~ hin** it went on forever

(*od.* for ages); **Endlosigkeit** *f* endlessness

Endlospapier *n* continuous (*od.* fan-fold) paper

End|lösung *f hist., in der NS-Propaganda*: Final Solution; **~montage** *f Tech.* final assembly; **~moräne** *f Geog.* terminal moraine; **~neunziger** *m*, **~neunzigerin** *f* man/woman in his/her late nineties; **~ sein** *auch* be in one's late nineties; **~nummer** *f* final (*od.* last) digit

endogen *Adj. fachspr.* endogenous

Endoskop *n*; *-s, -e*; *Med.* endoscope; **Endoskopie** *f*; *-, -n* endoscopy

End|phase *f* final (*od.* last) stage(s *Pl.*), final phase; **~preis** *m* retail (*od.* shop, *Am.* store) price; **~produkt** *n* end (*od.* final, finished) product; **~punkt** *m e-r Reise etc.*: end, (final) destination; *bei Linienverkehr*: terminus, end; **~reim** *m Lit.* end rhyme; **~resultat** *n* final result

Endrunde *f Sport, e-s Turniers*: final(s *Pl.*); *Boxen*: final round (*auch fig.*); *bei Rennen*: last lap (*auch fig.*), final lap

End|sechziger *m*, **~sechzigerin** *f* man/woman in his/her late sixties; **~ sein** *auch* be in one's late sixties; **~siebziger** *m*, **~siebzigerin** *f* man/woman in his/her late seventies; **~ sein** *auch* be in one's late seventies; **~sieg** *m hist., in der NS-Propaganda*: final victory; **~silbe** *f Ling.* final syllable; **~spiel** *n Sport* final(s *Pl.*); **das ~ erreichen** make it to (*od.* get into) the final(s); **~spurt** *m* final spurt (*auch fig.*), (strong) finish; *fig. auch* final burst; **~stadium** *n* final stage(s *Pl.*); **im ~** in the final (*od.* last) stages; *Krebs im ~* terminal cancer; **~stand** *m Sport, Fußball etc.*: final result (*od.* score); *Rennen etc.*: final positions *Pl.*, final ranking(s *Pl.*); **~station** *f* terminus, end of the line; *fig.* end of the road; **~! Alles aussteigen, bitte!** all change please!; **~stück** *n allg.* end (piece), last piece (*od.* bit); *e-s Brotes*: heel, end (of the loaf); **~stufe** *f Rakete*: final stage; **~summe** *f* (sum) total, final total

Endung *f Ling.* ending; **endungslos** *Adj. nachgestellt*: with no ending

End|ursache *f* final (*od.* ultimate) cause; **~verbrauch** *m* final consumption; **~verbraucher** *m*, **~verbraucherin** *f* end user, (ultimate) consumer, retail customer; **~verstärker** *m Etron.* final amplifier; *Etech.* power amplifier; **~vierziger** *m*, **~vierzigerin** *f* man/woman in his/her late forties; **~ sein** *auch* be in one's late forties; **~vokal** *m Ling.* final vowel

Endzeit *f bibl.* last days *Pl.*; *weitS.*: end of the world; **endzeitlich** *Adj.* eschatological; **Endzeitstimmung** *f* doomsday atmosphere

End|ziel *n* final objective, ultimate goal; **~ziffer** *f* last (*od.* final) digit; **~zustand** *m* final state; **~zwanziger** *m*, **~zwanzigerin** *f* young man/woman in his/her late twenties; **~ sein** *auch* be in one's late twenties; **~zweck** *m* final (*od.* ultimate) purpose, ultimate aim

Energetik *f*; *-, kein Pl.*; *Phys.* energetics *Pl.* (*V. im Sg.*); **energetisch** *Adj.* **1.** *Phys.* energetical; *Ling.* energetic; **2.** *umg.* (*voller Energie*) *Handlung*: energetic, vigorous, forceful; *Person*: energetic, dynamic

Energie *f*; *-, -n*; *Phys.* energy; *Etech. auch* power; *fig.* energy, drive; **~ spa-**

rend energy-saving, energy-efficient, *attr. auch* low-energy ...; *fig. Körperbewegungen etc.:* economical, efficient

Energie... *im Subst. siehe auch* **Kraft..., Strom...**

energiearm *Adj.* **1.** *attr.* low-energy, *präd.* low in energy; **2.** *Land etc.:* low in energy resources, energy-poor

Energie|aufwand *m* expenditure of energy, (amount of) energy involved; **~bedarf** *m* energy requirement(s *Pl.*) (*od.* demand); **~bilanz** *f* energy budget (*od.* balance); **~bündel** *n fig.* bundle of energy, live wire; **~einsparung** *f auch Pl.* energy saving, economy in the use of energy; **~erhaltungssatz** *m* → **Energiesatz**; **~erzeugung** *f* energy production, generation of energy; **~form** *f* form of energy, energy form

energiegeladen *Adj. fig.* energetic, bursting with energy

Energie|gewinnung *f* energy production; **~haushalt** *m* **1.** *des Körpers:* energy balance; **2.** *Wirts.* energy budget (*od.* requirements *Pl.*); **~krise** *f* energy (*od.* power) crisis; **~lieferant** *m* energy supplier

energielos *Adj.* lacking in energy, listless, lethargic; **Energielosigkeit** *f* lack of energy, listlessness, lethargy

Energie|mangel *m* energy shortage; **~mix** *m* energy mix; **~prinzip** *n* → **Energiesatz**; **~quelle** *f* **1.** *allg.* energy source, source of energy; **2.** *Etech. etc.* power source

energiereich *Adj.* **1.** *Nahrung etc.:* attr. high-energy ..., *präd. und nachgestellt:* high in energy; **2.** *Land etc.:* energy-rich, rich in energy resources

Energie|reserven *Pl.* energy reserves; *e-r Person: auch* spare energy *Sg.*, physical reserves; **~satz** *m*; *nur Sg. Phys.* principle of the conservation of energy

energiesparend *Adj.:* **äußerst** *od.* **sehr ~** absolutely (*od.* utterly) energy-saving (*od.* -efficient)

Energiespar|haus *n* energy-saving house (*od.* home), low-energy house; **~lampe** *f* low-energy bulb; **~programm** *n* energy-saving program(me)

Energie|spender *m* (*Nahrung*) energy booster; **~träger** *m* energy source, source of energy; **~umwandlung** *f Phys.* conversion of energy; **~verbrauch** *m* energy consumption; **~verlust** *m* energy loss, waste of energy; **~verschwendung** *f* waste of energy; **~versorgung** *f* energy supply; **~wirtschaft** *f* energy (*od.* power-supply) industry; **~zufuhr** *f* energy supply

energisch I. *Adj.* energetic; *Geste etc., auch Persönlichkeit:* forceful; *Art, Auftreten etc.:* brisk, dynamic; *Maßnahmen etc.:* firm, vigorous, decisive; *Protest, Widerstand etc.:* spirited, vehement; *Kinn etc.:* firm, decisive, craggy; **~ werden** put one's foot down, get tough, stop messing about *umg.;* **II.** *Adv.* → I; **~ bestreiten** (*nachdrücklich*) firmly (*od.* stoutly) deny; (*leidenschaftlich*) vehemently deny; **~ vorgehen** take firm measures (*od.* action) (*gegen* against); **~ vorantreiben** push (*od.* drive) forward (hard *od.* energetically)

enervierend *Adj. geh. Angewohnheit, Geräusch etc.:* nerve-fraying, maddening

Enfant terrible [ãfãtɛ'ribl] *n*; - -, -s -s; *geh.* enfant terrible

eng I. *Adj.* **1.** *Straße, Tal etc.:* narrow; *Wohnung, Raum etc.:* cramped, *pr äd.* *auch* short of space; (*klein*) small; (*zu klein*) cramped, poky, dinky *pej.;* (*voller Menschen*) crowded; **~e Kurve** tight (*od.* hairpin) bend; **auf ~stem Raum** crowded together (in a small space); **es ist bei uns etwas ~** we don't have a lot of room here, we're a bit cramped for space; **2.** *Kleidung etc.:* tight; **~er machen** (*Gürtel, Halsband etc.*) tighten; (*abnähen*) take in; **die Hose ist mir zu ~ geworden** these trousers don't fit (me) any more (*od.* are too tight for me now); **3.** *Umarmung, Schrift:* close; **~ an** (+ *Dat.*) close to; **4.** *fig. Freund, Freundschaft, Kontakt, Zusammenhang etc.:* close; **im ~sten Kreis** with (the family and) a few close friends; **im ~sten Kreis der Familie** with the close family members (*od.* immediate family); → **Sinn** 4, **Wahl** 1; **5.** *fig.* (*beschränkt*) *Auslegung, Sichtweise etc.:* narrow; → **Horizont** 2; **6.** *umg.:* **das kann ~ werden** *umg.;* *finanziell:* it will be touch-and-go (financially), it will be tight; *zeitlich:* it could (*od.* will) be very tight (timewise); **das war ~** *umg.* (*hätte fast e-n Unfall gegeben*) that was close (*od.* a close call, a near thing); **II.** *Adv.* **1.** narrowly; tightly; closely; → I; **~ anliegen** fit tightly, be a tight fit; **~ anliegend** tight(-fitting); **~ bedruckt/beschrieben** closely printed/written; **~ nebeneinander** close together; **~ umschlungen** in close embrace, locked in embrace; **2.** *fig.* (*nahe*) *verbunden, verwandt, zusammenarbeiten etc.:* closely; **~ befreundet sein** be close friends; **3.** *fig.:* **etw. ~ auslegen** interpret s.th. narrowly; **~ begrenzt** narrow, restricted; **das darfst du nicht so ~ sehen** *umg.* you mustn't take it so seriously (*od.* too literally)

Engadin *n*; -s; *Geog.* the Engadine

Engagement [ãgaʒə'mã] *n*; -s, -s **1.** *nur Sg.; geh.* commitment, involvement (**für** to, on behalf of; **in** + *Dat.* in); **2.** *Theat. etc.* engagement; **engagieren** [ãga'ʒiːrən] I. *v/t.* employ, take on; (*Künstler*) engage; **II.** *v/refl.* get (*od.* be) involved (**in** + *Dat.* in); **sich ~ für** be very involved (*od.* active) in, do a lot (*od.* a great deal) for; **engagiert I.** *P.P.* → **engagieren**; **II.** *Adj.* committed; **politisch ~** politically involved (*od.* active), (very) into politics *umg.;* **Engagiertheit** *f geh.* commitment

engbrüstig *Adj.* narrow-chested

Enge *f*; -, -n **1.** *nur Sg.; e-r Straße etc.:* narrowness; *e-r überfüllten Wohnung etc.:* cramped (*bedrückend:* claustrophobic) conditions *Pl.*, crampedness, pokiness *pej.;* *von Kleidung:* tightness; **2.** (*enge Stelle*) narrow passage, bottleneck, constriction; **3.** *Geog.* (*Meerenge*) strait (*auch Pl.*) narrows *Pl.*, channel; **4.** *nur Sg.; fig.* (*Beschränktheit*) narrow(minded)ness, blinkered outlook; (*Engpass*) bottleneck; **in die ~ treiben** drive into a corner, get *s.o.* cornered *umg.;* **in die ~ getrieben** with one's back to the wall, up against it

Engel *m*; -s, - **1.** angel; *guter* an angel; **die ~** (*im Himmel*) **singen hören** *umg. hum.* be in agony, think one is sent for *Dial.;* **2.** *fig.:* **du bist ein ~!** you're an angel (*od.* a real dear)!; **er ist auch nicht gerade ein ~** he's not exactly an angel himself; **j-s rettender ~ sein** be s.o.'s salvation; **die gelben ~** *Mot.* angels in yellow (*in Germany, road breakdown patrol*)

engelhaft I. *Adj.* angelic, angel-like;

II. *Adv.* angelically, like an angel

Engel|macher *m*, **~macherin** *f umg.* backstreet abortionist

Engels|chor *m* choir of angels; **~geduld** *f* endless (*od.* infinite) patience, *the* patience of Job; **~gesicht** *n* angelic face (*od.* looks *Pl.*); **♀gleich** *Adj.* angelic, angel-like, saintly; **~haar** *n* (*Baumschmuck*) angel('s) hair; **~miene** *f* innocent (*od.* demure) look; **~zunge** *f:* **mit ~n auf j-n einreden** do everything in one's power to persuade s.o., cajole (*od.* coax) s.o. with honeyed words

Engelwurz *f*; -, -en; *Bot.* angelica

Engerling *m*; -s, -e; *Zool.* white (*od.* cockchafer) grub

engherzig *Adj.* small- (*od.* mean-)-minded; **Engherzigkeit** *f* small- (*od.* mean-)mindedness, pettiness

England *n*; -s; *Geog.* **1.** *weitS.* Britain, the UK; **2.** *engS.* England

Engländer¹ *m*; -s, - **1.** *weitS.* Briton, British man, Brit *umg.;* **2.; 3.** *engS.* English, Englishman; **die ~** the British (*Pl.*), (the) Brits *umg.;* *engS.* the English (*Pl.*); **er ist ~** he's British (*od.* a Brit *umg.*); *engS.* he's English

Engländer² *m*; -s, -; *Tech.* adjustable spanner (*Am.* wrench), monkey wrench

Engländerin *f*; -, -nen British woman (*od.* girl); *engS.* Englishwoman (*od.* English girl etc.); *e-e junge ~ auch* a British (*engS.* English) girl; **sie ist ~** she's British; *engS.* she's English

englisch I. *Adj.* **1.** *weitS.* British; *engS., auch Sprache:* English; **die Englischen Fräulein** *kath.* an order of teaching nuns; **ein ~er Garten** a landscape garden; **~er Trab** riding trot; **II.** *Adv. Gastr.:* **~** (*gebraten*) rare, underdone

Englisch¹ *n*; -en; *Ling.* English; **das ~e** the English language, English; **auf ~** in English; **aus dem ~en** from (the) English; **~ sprechend** (*der Sprache mächtig*) English-speaking; **als Muttersprache:** *auch* anglophone *fachspr.*

Englisch² *Adj.:* **der ~e Gruß** *kirchl. altm., Kunst* the Angelic Salutation

Englisch|horn *n Mus.* cor anglais, *bes. Am.* English horn; **~kenntnisse** *Pl.* (knowledge *Sg.* of) English, English language skills; **perfekte ~ erforderlich** perfect English required (*od.* essential); **~lehrer** *m*, **~lehrerin** *f* English teacher; *Privatunterricht: auch* English tutor; **~note** *f* mark (*Am.* grade) in (*od.* for) English, English mark (*Am.* grade)

englischsprachig *Adj.* **1.** *Zeitschrift etc.:* English-language ...; **~e Literatur** English literature; **2.** *Personen:* English-speaking; *als Muttersprache: auch* anglophone *fachspr.*

Englisch|traben *n* rising trot; **~unterricht** *m* **1.** *Tätigkeit:* teaching of English, English language tuition (*Am.* teaching), tuition in (*Am.* teaching) English; **2.** (*Stunde[n]*) English lesson(s *Pl.*), English class(es *Pl.*)

engmaschig *Adj. Stoff etc.:* fine(ly)-meshed; *fig.* close-knit; *Fußball etc.:* close

Engpass *m* **1.** defile, (narrow) pass; *e-r Straße:* width restriction, narrow part (*od.* bit *umg.*); **2.** *fig.* (supply) bottleneck (**in** + *Dat.* in), supply problem (with); (*Mangel*) shortage (of); **Engpässe in der Produktion** production bottlenecks

en gros [ã'gro] *Adv. Wirts.* wholesale; **Engroshandel** *m* wholesale trade

(*od.* business)

Engstelle *f* narrow place, constriction

engstirnig *Adj.* narrow-minded; **Engstirnigkeit** *f* narrow-mindedness, tunnel vision

Enkel[1] *m*; *-s*, *-*, **~in** *f*; *-*, *-nen neutral*: grandchild; *männlich*: grandson; *weiblich*: granddaughter; *weitS.* (*Nachkomme*) descendant

Enkel[2] *m*; *-s*, *-*; *Dial.* ankle

Enkel|kind *n* grandchild; **~sohn** *m* grandson; **~tochter** *f* granddaughter

Enklave *f*; *-*, *-n*; *Pol.* enclave

enkodieren *v/t. fachspr.* (en)code, encrypt

en masse [ã'mas] *Adv. umg.* en masse

enorm I. *Adj. Summe*: enormous, huge, vast; *Wissen*: vast, encyclop(a)edic; *Belastung*: enormous, immense; *positiv*: tremendous, (absolutely) great; *negativ*: dreadful, appalling; **II.** *Adv.*: **~** **hoch** *etc.* enormously (*od.* immensely) tall *etc.*; **die Preise sind ~ gestiegen** prices have risen dramatically (*od.* shot up); **~ viel Geld** vast (*od.* huge) amounts of money

en passant [ãpa'sã] *Adv. geh.* in passing; *Schach*: en passant

Enquete [ã'keːt] *f*; *-*, *-n* **1.** *Pol.* (*Untersuchung*) (comprehensive) inquiry, review; **2.** *österr.* (*Arbeitstagung*) working meeting, conference; **~kommission** *f Pol. etwa* (parliamentary) select (*Am. auch* special) committee

Ensemble [ã'sãːbl̩] *n*; *-s*, *-s* **1.** *Mus.* ensemble; *Theat. auch* company; (*Besetzung*) cast; **2.** *Kleidung*: ensemble; **3.** *geh.*, *von Kunstwerken, Möbeln etc.*: ensemble, grouping, overall layout (*od.* design)

entarten *v/i.* degenerate, become degenerate; **entartet I.** *P.P.* → **entarten**; **II.** *Adj.* degenerate; *fig. auch* decadent; **~e Kunst** *hist.*, *in der NS-Propaganda*: degenerate art; **Entartung** *f* degeneration

entbehren I. *v/t.* **1.** (*auskommen ohne*) do (*stärker*: live) without; (*zur Verfügung stellen*) spare; **könntest du den Computer ein paar Stunden ~?** could you do (*od.* manage) without the computer for a few hours?; **2.** *geh.* (*vermissen*) miss; **II.** *v/i. geh.*: *e-r Sache* **~** be without, lack; **die Beschuldigung entbehrt jeder Grundlage** the charge is totally (*od.* completely) unfounded; **das entbehrt nicht e-r gewissen Ironie** it's not without a degree of irony; **entbehrlich** *Adj.* dispensable; (*nicht unbedingt erforderlich*) non-essential; **Entbehrlichkeit** *f* dispensability; (*Überflüssigkeit*) superfluousness

Entbehrung *f* privation, want, deprivation; **unter großen ~en** in circumstances of great hardship; **entbehrungsreich** *Adj.* disadvantaged, full of privation

entbeinen *v/t. Gastr.* bone

entbieten *v/t.* (*unreg.*); *geh.*: *j-m e-n Gruß* **~** bid s.o. good day

entbinden (*unreg.*) **I.** *v/t.* **1.** (*befreien*) release, excuse (**von** *od. geh.* + *Gen.* from); **2.** (*Frau*) deliver (**von** of); **entbunden werden von** give birth to; **3.** *Chem.* set free, liberate, release; **II.** *v/i. Frau*: be confined, give birth; **Entbindung** *f* **1.** release (**von** from); **2.** *e-r Frau*: delivery

Entbindungs|pfleger *m* male midwife; **~station** *f* maternity ward

entblättern I. *v/t.* (*Pflanze*) strip of leaves; **II.** *v/refl.* **1.** *Pflanze*: shed its leaves; **2.** *umg. fig.* strip, peel (*od.*

---

pull) one's clothes off

entblöden *v/refl. altm. pej.*: **sich nicht ~ zu** (+ *Inf.*) have the cheek (*od.* gall, nerve, audacity) to (+ *Inf.*)

entblößen I. *v/t.* **1.** (*Brust, Zähne*) bare, expose; (*Haupt*) uncover, bare; (*Schwert*) draw; **2.** *fig.* (*offenbaren*) lay bare; **j-n e-r Sache ~** strip (*od.* deprive) s.o. of s.th.; **II.** *v/refl.* take one's clothes off; *exhibitionistisch*: expose o.s.; **entblößt I.** *P.P.* → **entblößen**; **II.** *Adj.* **1.** bare; **2.** *fig.* destitute, stripped (+ *Gen.* of); **Entblößung** *f* **1.** baring, exposing; uncovering; → **entblößen** I; **2.** *fig. einer Person*: exposure; *von Gefühlen etc.*: laying bare, revealing, uncovering

entbrennen *v/i.* (*unreg.*); *geh. fig.* **1.** *Kampf*: break out; *Zorn etc.*: flare up; **2.** *Person*: **in Hass entbrannt** burning (*od.* consumed) with hatred; **in Liebe für j-n ~** fall passionately in love with s.o.

entbürokratisieren *v/t.* deregulate; **Entbürokratisierung** *f* deregulation, cutting (the) red tape *umg.*

entdecken *v/t.* **1.** (*etw. bislang Unbekanntes finden*) discover; **2.** (*etw. Verborgenes, Gesuchtes finden*) find, discover, spot, see; (*Fehler etc.*) *auch* detect; (*herausfinden*) find out, discover, ascertain, establish; (*feine Unterschiede etc.*) discern *geh.*; **3.** (*auf etwas stoßen*) discover, spot; **zufällig ~** stumble (*od.* happen) (up)on, come across, happen to find; **sie entdeckte ihr Herz für die Bretagne** Brittany came to occupy a special place in her affections

Entdecker *m*; *-s*, *-* discoverer; (*Forscher*) explorer; **Entdeckerin** *f*; *-*, *-nen* discoverer; **~ e-r Sache** *auch* woman (*od.* girl) who discovered/discovers …;

Entdeckerstolz *m* pride of discovery; **Entdeckung** *f* (*auch Gegenstand, Sachverhalt, Person*) discovery; (*Gegenstand*) *auch* find

Entdeckungs|reise *f* **1.** voyage of discovery, expedition; **2.** *umg. hum.*: *auf* **~ gehen** (go out and) explore; **~reisende** *m*, *f* explorer

entdramatisieren *v/t.* cool (down), defuse, take the heat out of

Ente *f*; *-*, *-n* **1.** *Orn.* duck; **junge ~** duckling; **schwimmen wie e-e bleierne ~** *umg.* swim like a brick (*od.* stone); → **lahm** 3; **2.** *umg.*, *in Zeitung*: canard, hoax; **3.** *umg.* (*Citroën*) 2CV, deux chevaux; **4.** *umg. Med.* bottle, (bed) urinal *förm.*; **5.** *Gastr.*: **kalte ~** kind of white wine cup with fruit

entehren *v/t.* **1.** dishono(u)r, disgrace; (*entwürdigen*) degrade; **2.** *altm.* (*Frau*) compromise *euph.*, dishono(u)r; **entehrend I.** *Part. Präs.* → **entehren**; **II.** *Adj.* disgraceful, discreditable; (*entwürdigend*) degrading; **Entehrung** *f* dishono(u)r(ing); (*Entwürdigung*) degradation

enteignen *v/t.* (*Besitz*) expropriate, sequestrate; (*Besitzer*) dispossess; **Enteignung** *f von Besitz*: expropriation, sequestration; *eines Besitzers*: dispossession, expropriation

enteilen *v/i. geh.* **1.** *Person*: hasten off (*od.* away); **2.** *Zeit*: fly past (*od.* by), speed by

enteisen *v/t.* clear of ice; (*Kühlschrank, Autoscheibe*) defrost; *Flug.* de-ice

enteisent *Adj. Mineralwasser*: iron-reduced

Enteisung *f* de-icing; *Kühlschrank*: defrosting; **Enteisungsanlage** *f Mot.*

---

de-icing installation; *Flug.* de-icing system

entemotionalisieren *v/t.* defuse, cool (down), get (*od.* take) the emotional heat out of; **Entemotionalisierung** *f* (emotional) defusing, cooling, chilling *umg.*

Enten|braten *m Gastr.* roast duck; **~ei** *n* duck('s) egg; **~grütze** *f Bot.* duckweed; **~jagd** *f allg.*: duck shooting; *Partie*: duck shoot; **~klein** *n Gastr.* duck giblets (and trimmings); **~küken** *n* duckling; **~schnabel** *m* duck's bill

Entente [ã'tãːtə] *f*; *-*, *-n*; *Pol.* entente; **~ cordiale** [ãtãkɔr'djal] *hist.* entente (cordiale); **Große/Kleine ~** *hist.* Great/Little Entente

Ententeich *m* duck pond

enterben *v/t.* disinherit; **Enterbung** *f* disinheriting

Enterhaken *m hist.* grappling iron, grapnel

Enterich *m*; *-s*, *-e*; *Orn.* drake

entern I. *v/t.* (*hat geentert*); *hist.* board; **II.** *v/i.* (*ist*); *Naut.*: **~ in** (+ *Akk.*) climb (up) (*s.th.*), scramble up (*s.th.*)

entfachen *v/t.* **1.** (*Feuer*) kindle, start, light; **2.** *fig.* (*Leidenschaft*) kindle, arouse, ignite *geh.*; (*Gefühle*) rouse, incite; (*Begeisterung etc.*) stimulate; *stärker*: whip up; (*Diskussion, Streit etc.*) provoke, spark off, start (off), trigger (off)

entfahren *v/i.* (*unreg.*, *untr.*, *ist*): **ihr entfuhr ein Fluch/Seufzer** *etc.* she let slip an imprecation / heaved a sudden sigh *etc.*

entfallen *v/i.* (*unreg.*, *untr.*, *ist*) **1.** **der Name ist mir ~** the name escapes me, I forget the name, I can't remember (*od.* think of) the name; **2.** (*wegfallen*) be cancel(l)ed, be dropped; *Wort etc.*: be omitted, be left out; (*nicht infrage kommen*) be inapplicable; **entfällt in Formularen**: not applicable (*Abk.* N/A); **3.** **~ auf** (+ *Akk.*) *statistisch*: occur in (*bzw.* at *etc.*); *Anteil etc.*: fall to s.o.; **auf jeden ~ 10 Euro** it comes to 10 euros per person, each person pays (*zahlt*) / gets (*bekommt*) 10 euros; **4.** *geh.*: **j-s Händen** *od.* **j-m ~** slip from s.o.'s hands (*od.* grasp)

entfalten I. *v/t.* **1.** (*Tuch, Zeitung etc.*) unfold; (*Zeitung*) *auch* open; (*ausbreiten*) spread (*od.* open) out; *rollend*: unroll, roll out; **2.** *Pflanze*: (*Blätter etc.*) unfurl, open out; (*Flügel*) *Vogel*: spread; *Schmetterling*: open (out) (*od.* unfold, spread); **3.** *fig.* (*Fähigkeiten etc.*) develop (**zu** into); (*zeigen*) display, reveal; **II.** *v/refl.* **1.** *Blüte etc.*: open up; *Gefieder*: open out, fan out, spread out; *Fallschirm*: open (up), mushroom (out); *Fahne*: unfurl; **2.** *fig.* develop (**zu** into); **hier kann man sich frei ~** this is a good place for discovering your (own) potential, there's plenty of scope for personal development here; **3.** *fig.* (*sich zeigen*) display itself, blossom *lit.*; **Entfaltung** *f* **1.** (*Entwicklung*) development; **zur ~ kommen** (be able to) develop, blossom; *Begabung, Potential etc.*: *auch* be realized, find its full expression; **zur ~ bringen** draw out, bring out, help realize; **2.** (*Zurschaustellung*) display; **Entfaltungsmöglichkeiten** *Pl.* scope *Sg.* for self-realization, opportunities for (personal) development

entfärben I. *v/t.* take the colo(u)r (*od.* dye) out of; (*bleichen*) bleach; **II.** *v/refl. Sache*: fade, lose its colo(u)r, become colo(u)rless; *Person, Gesicht*:

blanch, (go) pale (suddenly); **Entfärber** *m*; *-s*, *-* dye remover; (*Bleichmittel*) bleach(ing agent); **Entfärbung** *f* removal of the dye (+ *Gen.* from); **Entfärbungsmittel** *n* → **Entfärber**

entfernen I. *v/t.* **1.** (*beseitigen*) remove (*von od. aus* from); (*wegnehmen*) take away; (*herausnehmen*) take out, extract; *mit Messer*: excise; (*abnehmen*) take off; (*wegräumen*) clear (away); *EDV* delete, wipe *umg.*; **2.** *j-n ~ aus Haus, Zimmer*: turn s.o. out (**aus** of); *aus Amt*: remove s.o. (from); *aus Schule*: exclude s.o. (from), expel s.o. (from), kick s.o. out *umg.*; **3.** *euph.* (*töten*) eliminate, dispose of; **4.** (*Ggs. näher bringen*) put at a distance (*auch fig.*), distance *fig.*, estrange *fig.*; **II.** *v/refl.* **1.** leave; *Person: auch* go away, take o.s. off *umg.*; (*sich zurückziehen*) withdraw; **2.** *Schritte*: recede, move away, get fainter; **3.** (*verschwinden*) (gradually) disappear; **4.** *fig. von e-m Thema*: deviate (**von** from), digress, stray (from); *von e-r Meinung*: distance o.s. (from); **5.** *fig.*: *sich* (*voneinander*) *~* drift (*od.* grow) apart; *stärker*: become estranged

entfernt I. *P.P.* → **entfernen**; **II.** *Adj.* **1.** (*entlegen*) remote, distant; *Entfernungsangabe: e-e Meile/Stunde von X ~* a mile / an hour (away) from X; *zwei Meilen voneinander ~* two miles apart; **3.** *fig. Ähnlichkeit etc.*: remote, faint, vague; *~e Verwandte* distant relations (*od.* relatives); *ich bin weit davon ~ zu* (+ *Inf.*) I haven't the slightest intention of (+ *Ger.*); **III.** *Adv.* **1.** (*entlegen*) far away, a long way away; **2.** *fig.*: *~ verwandt* distantly related; *nicht im Entferntesten* not in the least (*od.* slightest); *ich habe nicht im Entferntesten daran gedacht zu* (+ *Inf.*) I never even dreamed (*od.* dreamt) of (+ *Ger.*), it never occurred to me to (+ *Inf.*)

Entfernung *f* **1.** (*Abstand*) distance; (*Schussweite*) range; *aus e-r / in e-r ~ von* from/at a distance (*od.* range) of; *aus der ~* from (*od.* at) a distance; *aus einiger ~* from a distance, from some distance away; *aus nächster/ großer ~* at short (*od.* close) / long range, from close to / from a long way away; **2.** (*Beseitigung*) removal, clearing (out); **3.** (*Entlassung*) dismissal (*aus* from), removal (from); *aus Schule*: exclusion, expulsion; **4.** *euph.* elimination, removal; **5.** (*Weggehen*) *Mil.* *unerlaubte ~ von der Truppe* absence (*Am.* away) without leave, AWOL

Entfernungs|messer *m* *Fot.* rangefinder; *~***ring** *m* *Fot.* focus(s)ing ring; *~***skala** *f* *Fot.* focus(s)ing scale

entfesseln *v/t.* (*Krieg, Streit*) provoke, trigger, start; (*Streit*) *auch* touch off, spark; (*Leidenschaft*) arouse, kindle, stimulate; *stärker*: unleash; (*Begeisterungsstürme*) draw, bring (forth), earn; **entfesselt I.** *P.P.* → **entfesseln**; **II.** *Adj. Elemente etc.*: raging, untamed; *Leidenschaft*: wild, tempestuous, unbridled; **Entfesselungskünstler** *m* escape artist, Houdini

entfetten *v/t.* remove the grease (*od.* fat) from; (*Wolle*) degrease, scour; (*Haut*) dry (out), make dry; *Chem.*, *Tech.* degrease

entflammbar *Adj. auch Tech.* flammable, inflammable; *leicht/schwer ~* flammable/flame-resistant (*od.* -retardant), non-flam(mable); **entflammen** *geh.* **I.** *v/t.* (*hat entflammt*) → **entfa-**

chen; **II.** *v/i.* (*ist*) **1.** burst into flames; *Tech.* ignite; (*aufblitzen*) flash; **2.** *fig.* → **entbrennen**; **entflammt I.** *P.P.* → **entflammen**; **II.** *Adj. fig.*: *~ von Gefühl*: consumed (*od.* inflamed) with; (*in Liebe*) *für j-n ~ sein* be passionately in love with s.o.

entflechten *v/t.* (*unreg.*) **1.** *Wirts.* (*aufteilen*) break (*od.* split) up, demerge; (*Kartelle*) decartelize; **2.** (*entwirren, auflösen*) *auch fig.* disentangle, unravel, straighten out; (*Zöpfe etc.*) unplait, unbraid, undo; **Entflechtung** *f* **1.** *Wirts.* break-up, demerger; **2.** (*Entwirrung*) *auch fig.* unravelling, disentangling

entfleuchen *v/i. hum.* → **entfliehen**

entfliegen *v/i.* (*unreg.*) fly away (+ *Dat.* from); *„grüner Papagei entflogen"* lost (*od.* escaped): green parrot

entfliehen *v/i.* (*unreg.*) **1.** escape (*aus od.* + *Dat.* from), flee (from *s.th.*, *s.o.*); **2.** *geh. fig.*: *dem Schicksal ~* escape a grim fate, be snatched from the jaws of Destiny; *dem Alltag ~* escape from (*od.* flee) everyday reality, escape from the daily grind *umg.*; **3.** *geh. fig. Jugend etc.*: slip away, be fleeting; *schnell*: fly past (*od.* by)

entfremden I. *v/t.* **1.** (*Person*) alienate (+ *Dat.* from); **2.** *etw. s-m Zweck ~* put s.th. to an unintended use, use s.th. in a way not intended; **II.** *v/refl.*: *sich* (*einander*) *~* become estranged; **Entfremdung** *f* estrangement (*von* from; *zwischen* between), alienation

entfrosten *v/t.* defrost, de-ice; **Entfroster** *m*; *-s*, *-*; *Mot.* de-icer (spray)

entführen *v/t.* **1.** (*Person*) kidnap, abduct; (*Flugzeug*) hijack, *bes. Am. auch* skyjack; **2.** *umg. hum.* (*j-s Kugelschreiber etc.*) liberate, appropriate, nick, run away with; *dürfte ich Ihnen kurz einmal Ihren Mann ~?* may I borrow your husband for a moment?; **Entführer** *rer m*, **Entführerin** *f* kidnapper; *Flug.* hijacker, *bes. Am. auch* skyjacker; **Entführung** *f* kidnapping, abduction; *Flug.* hijacking, *bes. Am. auch* skyjacking

entgegen I. *Präp.* (+ *Dat.*) *Gegensatz*: contrary to, against; *~ s-n Anweisungen* in defiance of (*od.* contrary to) his instructions; **II.** *Adv. Richtung*: towards; *dem Wind etc.*: against; *~***arbeiten** *v/i.* (*trennb., hat -ge-*) *bes. Mensch*: work against; *~***blicken** *v/i.* (*trennb., hat -ge-*) → **entgegensehen**; *~***bringen** *v/t.* (*unreg., trennb., hat -ge-*) *fig.* (*Gefühle*) show (*j-m* for s.o.); *e-r Sache Interesse etc. ~* show (an) (*od.* some) interest *etc.* in s.th., be actively interested in s.th.; *~***eilen** *v/i.* (*trennb., ist -ge-*) rush toward(s); (*j-m*) *auch* rush to meet; *~***fahren** *v/i.* (*unreg., trennb., ist -ge-*): *j-m ~* drive (out) to meet s.o.; *~***fiebern** *v/i.* (*trennb., hat -ge-*): *e-r Sache ~* feverishly await s.th.; *ängstlich*: wait for (*od.* await) s.th. with fear and trembling (*od.* with bated breath); *~***gehen** *v/i.* (*unreg., trennb., ist -ge-*) **1.** (*j-m*) walk toward(s), go to meet; **2.** *fig.* approach; (*e-r Gefahr, der Zukunft*) face (up to), confront; *dem Untergang etc.*) be heading for; *dem Ende ~* be drawing to(ward[s]) a close, be nearing the end

entgegengesetzt I. *Adj.* **1.** *Ende, Ufer, Richtung*: opposite; *Ufer: auch* far; **2.** (*gegensätzlich*) (mutually) contradictory, opposing; (*widersprüchlich*) conflicting; *s-e Meinung ist Ihrer völlig ~* his opinion completely contra-

dicts yours (*od.* is completely opposed to yours), he takes exactly the opposite view to you; **II.** *Adv.*: *genau ~ handeln* do the exact opposite, do exactly the opposite

entgegen|halten *v/t.* (*unreg., trennb., hat*) **1.** (*reichen*): *j-m etw. ~* hold s.th. out to s.o.; **2.** *fig.* (*entgegnen*) say (*od.* argue) *s.th.* in reply (+ *Dat.* to); *j-m etw. ~* point s.th. out to s.o., remind s.o. of s.th.; *~***handeln** *v/i.* (*trennb., hat -ge-*) act (*od.* work) against (+ *Dat. s.th.*)

entgegenkommen (*unreg., trennb., ist -ge-*) *v/i.* **1.** *wörtlich*: (*j-m*) come toward(s), come to meet; *j-m auf halbem Wege ~* *auch fig.* meet s.o. halfway; **2.** *fig. Person*: make concessions to (s.o.) (*od.* toward[s] s.o.'s wishes *etc.*); (*gefällig sein*) oblige *s.o.*; (*j-s Wünschen*) comply with; *können Sie mir mit dem Preis noch etwas ~?* can you do anything for me on the price?; → *auch* 1; **3.** *fig. Sache*: *j-m od. j-s Vorstellungen sehr ~* be very convenient for s.o., suit s.o. fine (*od.* very well), fit in well with s.o.'s plans (*od.* ideas)

Entgegenkommen *n* **1.** (*Gefälligkeit*) obligingness, helpfulness, co(-)operativeness; *sie zeigte wenig ~* she was unco(-)operative (*od.* not very helpful); **2.** (*Zugeständnis*) concession(s *Pl.*)

entgegenkommend I. *Part. Präs.* → **entgegenkommen**; **II.** *Adj.* **1.** *fig.* obliging, helpful, accommodating; **2.** *Fahrzeug, Verkehr*: oncoming, *nachgestellt*: coming the other way

entgegenlaufen *v/i.* (*unreg., trennb., ist -ge-*) **1.** (*j-m*) run toward(s), run to meet; **2.** *fig. Sache*: (*j-s Plänen etc.*) go against, run counter to, be unhelpful to, militate against

Entgegennahme *f* acceptance; *bei ~* (+ *Gen.*) on receipt (of); **entgegennehmen** *v/t.* (*unreg., trennb., hat -ge-*); (*Brief, Dank, Geschenk*) accept; (*Bestellung, Gespräch*) take, accept; (*Befehl*) take; (*Glückwünsche*) receive

entgegen|schallen *v/i.* (*auch unreg., trennb., hat*) ring out toward(s); *~***schauen** *v/i.* (*trennb., hat -ge-*) → **entgegensehen**; *~***schlagen** *v/i.* (*unreg., trennb., -ge-*); *fig.* **1.** (*ist entgegengeschlagen*); *Flammen*: lick up, leap up; *Rauchschwaden etc.*: billow, swirl toward(s); *Gestank*: assail, meet, hit; *Lärm*: assail, hit; **2.** *Hass, Verachtung*: come across (to), be palpable (to); **3.** (*hat*): *j-m ~ Herzen*: go out to s.o.; *~***sehen** *v/i.* (*unreg., trennb., hat -ge-*) **1.** *fig.* await; *mit Freude*: look forward to; *e-r Gefahr*: face; *e-r baldigen Antwort ~d förm.* in anticipation of your early reply, I look forward to hearing from you shortly; **2.** (*in Richtung auf j-n, etw.* [*Herankommendes*] *sehen*) look (*od.* gaze) toward(s), watch; (*noch Unsichtbares*) watch for; *~***setzen** (*trennb., hat -ge-*) *v/t.*: *e-m Argument etc. etw. ~* counter (*od.* meet) an argument *etc.* with s.th.; *Widerstand etc. ~* put up a resistance, offer (some) resistance (+ *Dat.* to); *dem habe ich nichts entgegenzusetzen* I can't think of any objection, I don't see (*od.* have) any problem(s) with that, it sounds fine to me *umg.*

entgegenstehen *v/i.* (*unreg., trennb., hat* |*südd., österr., schw. ist -ge-*) **1.** (*e-m Plan etc.*) stand in the way of; **2.** (*widersprechen*) conflict with; *dem*

steht nichts entgegen there's nothing to be said against that

entgegen|stellen (*trennb., hat -ge-*) **I.** *v/t.* **1.** *j-m etw.* ~ set s.th. against s.o., oppose (*od.* obstruct) s.o. with s.th., put s.th. in s.o.'s way, stymie s.o. (with s.th.) *umg.*; **2.** → **entgegensetzen**; **II.** *v/refl. fig.*: **sich** *j-m od. e-r Sache* ~ oppose, resist; (*e-r Sache*) *auch* combat; **~strecken** *v/t.* (*trennb., hat -ge-*): *j-m etw.* ~ hold s.th. out to(ward[s]) s.o.; **~treten** *v/i.* (*unreg., trennb., ist -ge-*) **1.** (*j-m*) walk (*od.* go) toward(s) (*od.* over to *od.* up to); **2.** *fig.* (*bekämpfen, hindern*) oppose, resist; *Missständen etc.*: take steps (*od.* measures *od.* action) against; *e-r Gefahr etc.*: confront, face up to; *Vorwürfen, Drohungen etc.*: counter, stand up to; *Gerüchten etc.*: contradict, speak out against, counter; **3.** *fig. Sache*: *j-m* ~ present itself to s.o.; **~wirken** *v/i.* (*trennb., hat -ge-*) counteract, combat; *stärker*: fight

entgegnen *vt/i.* reply; *schlagfertig, kurz*: retort; **Entgegnung** *f* reply (*auf* + *Akk.* to); *kurze*: retort

entgehen *v/i.* (*unreg.*) **1.** (*verschont bleiben*) escape; *durch List etc.*: evade *geh.*, dodge *umg.*; *peinlicher Situation etc.*: avoid, get out of *umg.*; *knapp e-m Attentat etc.* ~ narrowly escape assassination *etc.*; *e-r Strafe* ~ evade punishment / the law; **2.** *fig.*: *sich* (*Dat.*) *etw.* ~ *lassen* miss s.th., let s.th. slip; *er ließ sich die Gelegenheit nicht* ~ he took (*od.* his) chance; *stärker*: he seized (*od.* grabbed *umg.*) the opportunity; *das darfst du dir nicht* ~ *lassen* don't miss it, don't let this chance go, don't pass up this chance; **3.** *fig.*: (*unbemerkt bleiben*): *j-m od. j-s Aufmerksamkeit* ~ escape s.o., escape s.o.'s notice (*od.* attention), be missed (*od.* overlooked) by s.o.; *ihr entgeht nichts* she doesn't miss a thing, she overlooks nothing

entgeistert *Adj. und Adv.* (*verstört*) dumbfounded, flabbergasted, speechless; (*entsetzt*) *auch* horrified, aghast; *was siehst du mich so* ~ *an?* what are you looking so startled (*od.* surprised *od.* shocked) about?

Entgelt *n*; *-(e)s, -e*; (*Vergütung*) remuneration; (*Gebühr, Honorar*) fee; (*Belohnung*) reward; *gegen/ohne* ~ subject to payment / free of charge, gratis; *als* ~ *für* in return for; **entgelten** *v/t.* (*unreg., untr., hat*): *j-m etw.* ~ *mit Geld*: pay s.o. for s.th.; (*Gefälligkeit*) repay s.o. for s.th.; *j-n etw.* ~ (*büßen*) *lassen* make s.o. pay for s.th.; **entgeltlich** *Adj. und Adv. Amtsspr.* against payment

entgiften *v/t. Chem., Med.* detoxify; *von Gasen etc.*: decontaminate; (*Abgase*) filter, clean up *umg.*

entgleisen *v/i.* **1.** *Schienenfahrzeug*: be derailed, *bes. Am.* jump the track; **2.** *fig.* (*sich taktlos benehmen*) commit a faux pas (*od.* gaffe) (*zu weit gehen*) overstep the mark; **3.** *fig. Diskussion etc.*: get off the track, get sidetracked, lose direction; *Redner etc.*: stray from the point, wander; **Entgleisung** *f* **1.** derailment; **2.** *fig.* faux pas, gaffe; **3.** descent into irrelevance

entgleiten *v/i.* (*unreg.*) **1.** *wörtlich*: *j-m* ~ slip out of s.o.'s hand(s); **2.** *fig.*: *j-m* (*j-s Kontrolle*) ~ slip out of s.o.'s control, slip away from s.o.; *Kind etc.*: drift away from s.o.

entgräten *v/t.* bone, fillet

enthaaren *v/t.* remove (the) hair from, depilate; **Enthaarungscreme** *f* hair removal cream, depilatory (cream)

enthalten (*unreg.*) **I.** *v/t. allg.* contain; (*fassen*) *auch* hold, take; (*umfassen*) comprise, include, embrace *geh.*; *Werbesprache*: feature; *mit* ~ *sein in* (+ *Dat.*) be included in; *3 ist in 12 viermal* ~ three goes into twelve four times, three into twelve makes four; **II.** *v/refl.* **1.** *Pol.*: *sich* (*der Stimme*) ~ abstain (from voting); **2.** *geh.*: *sich* ~ (+ *Gen.*) (*des Alkohols etc.*) abstain from; *e-r Handlung*: refrain from (+ *Ger.*); *ich konnte mich nicht* ~ *zu* (+ *Inf.*) I couldn't restrain myself from (+ *Ger.*)

enthaltsam *Adj.* (*abstinent*) abstemious; *im Trinken*: teetotal; (*mäßig*) moderate, frugal; *im Trinken*: moderate, temperate; *sexuell*: continent, restrained; **Enthaltsamkeit** *f* abstinence; moderation; continence; → **enthaltsam**; *vollkommene* ~ total abstinence; *im Trinken*: *auch* teetotalism

Enthaltung *f* **1.** *bei Abstimmungen*: abstention; **2.** *nur Sg.* → **Enthaltsamkeit**

enthärten *v/t.*; (*Wasser*) soften; **Enthärter** *m*; *-s, -*, **Enthärtungsmittel** *n* (water) softener, (water) softening agent

enthaupten *v/t.* behead, decapitate *geh.*, execute by beheading; **Enthauptung** *f engS.*: beheading, decapitation *geh.*; (*Hinrichtung*) execution

enthäuten *v/t.* **1.** (*j-n, Tier*) skin, flay; **2.** (*Obst etc.*) skin, peel

entheben *v/t.* (*unreg., untr., hat*) *e-r Verantwortung etc.*: relieve of; *e-r Pflicht etc.*: *auch* release (*od.* exempt) from; *des Amtes*: remove from; *j-n vorläufig s-s Amtes* ~ suspend s.o. (from office *od.* his/her post); **Enthebung** *f von Pflicht etc.*: release, exemption (*von* from); ~ *vom Amt* dismissal (*od.* removal) from office

enthemmen I. *v/t.* disinhibit, help *s.o.* lose his (*od.* her) inhibitions; **II.** *v/i.* have a disinhibiting (*od.* liberating) effect; **enthemmend I.** *Part. Präs.* → **enthemmen**; **II.** *Adj.* disinhibitory *fachspr.*; **III.** *Adv.*: ~ *wirken* have a disinhibiting effect (*auf* + *Akk.* on); **enthemmt I.** *P.P.* → **enthemmen**; **II.** *Adj.* free of inhibitions, uninhibited; **Enthemmung** *f* breaking down of (*s.o.'s*) inhibitions

enthüllen I. *v/t.* **1.** (*Statue etc.*) unveil; (*Gesicht*) unveil, lift the veil from, reveal; (*zeigen*) show, reveal; **2.** *fig.* (*Geheimnis, Zukunft*) reveal; (*aufdecken*) *auch* bring to light; (*entlarven*) unmask, expose; **II.** *v/refl. fig. Person*: reveal o.s., be revealed; *Sache*: be revealed *od.* disclosed (+ *Dat.* to)

Enthüllung *f e-r Statue, e-s Gesichts*: unveiling; *fig., e-s Geheimnisses etc.*: disclosure (+ *Gen.* of), revelation (of); (*e-s Betrügers etc.*) unmasking (of); ~*en Pl. auch in der Presse*: revelations (*über* + *Akk.* about), disclosures (about)

Enthüllungsjournalismus *m* investigative journalism

Enthusiasmus *m*; *-, kein Pl.* enthusiasm; **Enthusiast** *m*; *-en, -en*, **Enthusiastin** *f*; *-, -nen* enthusiast, fan *umg.*; **enthusiastisch I.** *Adj.* enthusiastic, keen, eager; **II.** *Adv.* enthusiastically

entjungfern *v/t.* deflower; **Entjungferung** *f* deflowering

entkalken *v/t.* **1.** (*Kaffeemaschine etc.*) descale, delime; **2.** *Med.* (*Knochen*) demineralize; **Entkalker** *m*; *-s, -* descaler

entkernen *v/t.* **1.** (*Pfirsiche, Pflaumen etc.*) stone; (*Äpfel*) core; (*Trauben etc.*) (de)seed; (*Zitrusfrüchte*) remove the pips from; **2.** (*Wohngebiet*) reduce the density of, disperse; **3.** (*Gebäude*) gut

entkleiden; *geh.* **I.** *v/t.* **1.** undress, take *s.o.'s* clothes off; *rücksichtslos*: strip; (*bes. Bewußtlose[n]*) remove *s.o.'s* clothing; **2.** *fig.* (*e-s Amtes etc.*) divest of, strip of; **II.** *v/refl.* undress, get undressed, take one's clothes off, remove (all) one's clothes *f örm.*; *vollständig, schnell*: *auch* strip (off *umg.*)

entkoffeiniert *Adj.* decaffeinated; ~*er Kaffee auch* decaf *umg.*

entkolonialisieren *v/t.* decolonize; **Entkolonialisierung** *f* decolonization

entkommen *v/i.* (*unreg.*) escape (+ *Dat. od. aus* from), get away (from); *s-n Verfolgern etc.* ~ *auch* escape one's pursuers *etc.*; → *knapp* I 5

entkoppeln *v/t.* (*Fahrzeuge etc.*) uncouple; (*Radio*) decouple

entkorken *v/t.* uncork

entkräften *v/t.* **1.** (*Person*) (*schwächen*) weaken, enfeeble *geh.*, debilitate *fachspr.*; (*entnerven*) enervate; (*erschöpfen*) exhaust; **2.** *Jur.* (*ungültig machen*) invalidate; (*widerlegen*) refute; **Entkräftung** *f* **1.** *Vorgang*: weakening, debilitation; *Zustand*: (state of) exhaustion (*od.* collapse), weakened condition, debilitation; *vor* ~ *sterben* die of exhaustion; **2.** *Jur.* (*Ungültigmachen*) invalidation; (*Widerlegung*) refutation

entkrampfen I. *v/t.* **1.** (*Muskeln etc.*) relax; **2.** *fig.* (*Stimmung*) lighten, help, relieve; (*Verhältnis etc.*) take the tension out of, ease, smoothe, defuse; **II.** *v/refl.* **1.** *körperlich*: relax; **2.** *fig. Stimmung*: lighten, get (*od.* become) more relaxed; *Verhältnis etc.*: become easier (*od.* less strained); **Entkrampfung** *f* **1.** relaxation; **2.** *fig.* easing

entkriminalisieren *v/t.* decriminalize; **Entkriminalisierung** *f* decriminalization

entladen I. *v/t.* (*unreg.*) **1.** (*Fahrzeug, Ladung, Schusswaffe*) unload; *Naut. auch* discharge; (*Schüttgut*) dump; **2.** *Etech.* discharge; **3.** *fig.* (*Zorn*) vent, give vent to; **II.** *v/refl.* **1.** *Etech.* discharge; **2.** *Gewitter*: break; **3.** *Schusswaffe*: go off, fire; **4.** *fig. Spannung*: be released; *Zorn etc.*: break out, erupt; *sein Zorn entlud sich über uns* he took his anger out on us, we took the full force (*od.* the brunt) of his anger; **Entladung** *f* **1.** unloading; dumping; discharge; **2.** *fig.* release; eruption; → **entladen**

entlang **I.** *Präp.*: *den Fluss etc.* ~ *od.* ~ *dem Fluss etc.* along the coast/river *etc.*; *den Wald* ~ *etc.* along the edge of (*od.* along by) the woods, skirting the woods; *die Straße* ~ along the street (*od.* road); *laufen etc.*: *auch* up (*od.* down) the street (*od.* road); *die ganze Straße* ~ all the way up (*od.* down) the street (*od.* road), all along the street (*od.* road); **II.** *Adv.*: *an etw.* (*Dat.*) ~ along s.th.; *hier/da* ~ ... this/that way

entlang|fahren *v/i.* (*unreg., trennb., ist -ge-*) **1.** *Zug etc.*: run (*od.* go) along; *mit Auto*: drive along; *mit Fahrrad*: ride along; **2.** (*parallel zu etw.*) *Zug etc.*: run along (*od.* beside *od.* by); *an Kanal, Fluss etc.*: *auch* alongside; *mit*

Auto: drive along (*od.* beside); *mit Fahrrad*: ride along (*od.* beside); **3.** *fig.*: **mit dem Finger ~** trace (*od.* follow) (with one's finger), trace out; **~führen** (*trennb., hat -ge-*) **I.** *v/i.* *Weg etc.*: **am Ufer** *etc.* **~** (*Fluss*) lead (*od.* run) along the (river) bank, follow the river; (*See*) run by the lake(side); (*großer See, Küste*) lead along (*od.* follow *od.* skirt) the shore; **II.** *v/t.* (*j-n*) lead *s.o.* along; (*Behinderte etc.*) *auch* guide (*od.* help) *s.o.* along; **~gehen** *v/i.* (*unreg., trennb., ist -ge-*) **1.** *Person*: go (*od.* walk *etc.*) along, follow; **2.** → **entlangführen** I

entlarven I. *v/t.* unmask, expose; **II.** *v/refl.*: **sich ~ als** turn out (*od.* prove) to be; **Entlarvung** *f* unmasking, exposure

entlassen *v/t.* (*unreg.*) **1.** (*Patienten*) discharge (**aus** from); (*Gefangene*) release, let go; *geh.* (*Besucher*) dismiss; **aus der Schule ~ werden** *nach Abschluss etc.*: leave school; **j-n aus e-r Verpflichtung ~** release (*od.* free) *s.o.* from an obligation; **2.** (*Arbeitnehmer*) dismiss, fire *umg., Brit. auch* give *s.o.* the sack *umg.*, make redundant *euph., Am. auch* lay *s.o.* off *euph.*; (*Arbeitsteam etc.*) disband; **als Strafe, aus der Schule**: expel (*od.* exclude) (from school); *Mil.* discharge (**aus** from); → **fristlos; Entlassung** *f* **1.** (*von Patienten*) discharge; (*von Gefangenen*) release; *aus der Armee*: discharge; *geh.* (*von Besuchern*) dismissal; **um s-e ~ ersuchen** *bei Arbeitgeber*: hand in one's notice (*od.* resignation), tender one's resignation *förm.*; **2.** (*Kündigung etc.*) dismissal; sacking *umg.*, firing *umg.*, making redundant *umg., Am. auch* laying off *euph.*; *von e-m Arbeitsteam etc.* disbanding; **3.** *als Strafe, aus der Schule*: expulsion, exclusion; *Mil.* discharge; **unehrenhafte ~** discharge with ignominy, *Am.* dishonorable discharge

Entlassungs|feier *f* *Schule*: (school-)leaving (*Am.* graduation) ceremony, *Brit. auch* final prize day (at school); **~gesuch** *n* (letter of) resignation; **~papiere** *Pl. Mil.* discharge papers, marching orders *umg., Am.* walking papers *umg.*, pink slip *Sg. umg.*; **~welle** *f* wave of redundancies (*Am.* job losses); **~zeugnis** *n* *Schule*: leaving report, final (school) report

entlasten *v/t.* **1.** (*Person, Kreislauf, Leitungen etc.*) reduce (*od.* relieve) the strain on; (*Person*) *auch* make life easier for; *psychisch*: ease the burden on; *arbeitsmäßig*: reduce (*od.* lighten) the workload of, relieve; **~** (**von**) relieve (of); **den Verkehr ~** reduce the traffic load; **2.** *Jur.* (*Angeklagte*) *teilweise*: be a mitigating (*od.* extenuating) factor (*od.* circumstance) *in s.o.'s case*, be a point in *s.o.'s* favo(u)r; (*Verdächtige*) speak for (*s.o., s.o.'s* innocence); *völlig*: clear *s.o.* of a charge, exonerate; *Beweis etc.*: exculpate; **3.** *Wirts.* (*Konto*) credit; (*Schuldner*) discharge; **4.** *Wirts.* (*Vorstand etc.*) formally approve past actions of the board; (*Vereinsvorstand etc.*) approve action(s) taken by the committee; **5.** *Skisport*: (*Ski*) unweight; **entlastend I.** *Part. Präs.* → **entlasten; II.** *Adj. Jur. teilweise*: mitigating, extenuating; *völlig*: exculpating, exonerating; **Entlastung** *f* **1.** *Vorgang*: reduction (*od.* relief) of the strain (*od.* pressure) (+ *Gen.* on), easing the burden

etc. (of, on); → **entlasten; 2.** *Person*: help; *Sache*: relief; **3.** *Jur. teilweise*: mitigation, extenuation; *völlige*: exoneration

Entlastungs|material *n Jur.* evidence for the defen|ce (*Am.* -se); **~straße** *f* relief road; **~zeuge** *m*, **~zeugin** *f* witness for the defen|ce (*Am.* -se), defen|ce (*Am.* -se) witness; **~zug** *m* relief train

entlauben I. *v/t.* strip of its leaves; *mit chemischen Mitteln*: defoliate; **II.** *v/refl.* shed its leaves, abscise *fachspr.*; **entlaubt I.** *P.P.* → **entlauben; II.** *Adj.* bare, leafless; **Entlaubung** *f* defoliation; **Entlaubungsmittel** *n* defoliant

entlaufen¹ *v/i.* (*unreg.*) run away (+ *Dat.* from); „*Siamkatze ~*" lost (*od.* missing): Siamese cat

entlaufen² **I.** *P.P.* → **entlaufen¹; II.** *Adj.* Sklave etc.: runaway; *Sträfling*: escaped; *Hund, Katze*: lost, missing

entlausen *v/t.* delouse

entledigen *v/refl.; geh.*: **sich** *j-s / e-r Sache* **~** get rid of *s.o./s.th.*; (*Sache*) *auch* relieve o.s. of, dispose of; *e-s Kleidungsstücks*: take off, remove; *e-r Aufgabe*: carry out; *e-r Verpflichtung*: fulfil(l), meet

entleeren I. *v/t.* empty; (*Tank, Teich etc.*) *auch* drain; (*Briefkasten*) clear; *Phys. und Physiol.* evacuate; **II.** *v/refl.* *Tank*: empty, run dry; *Physiol.* empty; (*s-e Notdurft verrichten*) empty one's bowels; **Entleerung** *f* emptying, draining, clearing; *Phys. und Physiol.* evacuation

entlegen *Adj.* **1.** remote, out-of-the--way *umg.*; **2.** *fig.* *Gedanke etc.*: strange, offbeat *umg.*, way-out *umg.*

entlehnen *v/t.*; (*Wort, Idee etc.*) borrow (**aus** *od.* + *Dat.* from); **Entlehnung** *f* (*auch Ausdruck etc.*) borrowing (**aus** from)

entleihen *v/t.* (*unreg.*) borrow; *aus Bibliothek etc.*: *auch* take (*od.* check) out *umg.*; **Entleiher** *m*; *-s, -*, **Entleiherin** *f*; *-nen* borrower

Entlein *n* duckling; **hässliches ~** *umg.* *fig. hum.* ugly duckling

entlocken *v/t.*: **j-m etw. ~** *durch Schmeichelei, mit Geduld etc.*: coax (*od.* wheedle) s.th. out of *s.o.*; **j-m ein Geheimnis ~** persuade *s.o.* to reveal a secret, worm a secret out of *s.o.*, get *s.o.* to squeal *umg.*; **e-r Sache etw. ~** *fig.* draw s.th. out of s.th.

entlohnen, *schw.* **entlöhnen** *v/t.* pay; **Entlohnung** *f*, *schw.* **Entlöhnung** pay, payment; → *auch* **Entgelt**

entlüften *v/t.* **1.** (*Bremse, Heizung*) bleed; **2.** (*lüften*) air, ventilate; **Entlüfter** *m*; *-s, -* - **1.** *von Bremse, Heizung*: bleed(er) valve; **2.** (*Stutzen*) air vent; **3.** (*Gerät*) ventilator; **Entlüftung** *f* ventilation

Entlüftungs|anlage *f* ventilation system; **~ventil** *n* ventilation valve; *Mot., Heizung etc.*: bleed(er) valve

entmachten *v/t.* strip *s.o.* of (political) power (*od.* of all power[s]), topple (*s.o.* from power), take all power(s) away from *s.o.*; (*Monarchen*) dethrone; **Entmachtung** *f* loss of power; *Vorgang*: toppling (+ *Gen.* of); *e-s Monarchen*: *auch* dethronement

entmagnetisieren *v/t.* demagnetize

entmannen *v/t.* (*kastrieren*) castrate, emasculate *euph.*; **Entmannung** *f* (*Kastration*) castration, emasculation

euph.

entmaterialisieren *v/t.* dematerialize

entmensch(lich)en *v/t.* dehumanize; **entmensch(lich)t I.** *P.P.* → **entmensch(lich)en; II.** *Adj.* inhuman; **Entmensch(lich)ung** *f* dehumanization

entmilitarisieren *v/t.* demilitarize; **Entmilitarisierung** *f* demilitarization

entminen *v/t.*; *Mil.* clear of mines

entmündigen *v/t.* (legally) incapacitate; **Entmündigung** *f* (legal) incapacitation; *wegen Unzurechnungsfähigkeit*: interdiction

entmutigen *v/t.* discourage, dishearten; **lass dich nicht ~!** don't be put off, don't let them get you down, don't lose heart; **entmutigt I.** *P.P.* → **entmutigen; II.** *Adj.* disheartened, dispirited, downhearted; **Entmutigung** *f* disheartenment, discouragement

entmystifizieren *v/t.* take the mystique out of, demystify, debunk *umg.*; **Entmystifizierung** *f* demystification, debunking *umg.*

Entnahme *f* *von Geld*: withdrawal; **~ von Blut / e-r Probe** *etc.* taking of blood / of a sample *etc.*

entnazifizieren *v/t. hist.* denazify; **Entnazifizierung** *f* denazification

entnehmen *v/t.* (*unreg.*) **1.** (*Geld, Blutprobe etc.*) take (+ *Dat.* from, out of); (*Organe*) remove; *e-m Buch etc.*: *auch* borrow (from); (*zitieren*) quote (from); **2.** *fig.* (*erfahren*) learn (+ *Dat.* from); (*folgern*) take it (from); gather (from), infer (from); **ich entnehme Ihrem Schreiben, dass ...** I infer (*od.* it appears) from your letter that ...; **(aus) s-n Worten war zu ~, dass ...** from what he said it seemed (*od.* appeared) that ...; **ich entnehme Ihren Worten, dass Sie ...** I take it (from what you say) that you ..., I think you're telling me (that) you ...

entnerven *v/t.* get on *s.o.'s* nerves; *stärker*: fray *s.o.'s* nerves; **entnervend I.** *Part. Präs.* → **entnerven; II.** *Adj.* enervating; *stärker*: harrowing, nerve--fraying; **entnervt I.** *P.P.* → **entnerven; II.** *Adj. und Adv.* enervated; **ich bin völlig ~** my nerves are shot to pieces

Entomologe *m*; *-n -n; fachspr.* entomologist; **Entomologie** *f*; *-, kein Pl.* entomology; **Entomologin** *f*; *-, -nen* (woman) entomologist; **entomologisch** *Adj.* entomological

entpacken *v/t.* (*Datei*) unzip

entpersönlichen *v/t.* depersonalize, take the human element out of, make impersonal

entpolitisieren *v/t.* depoliticize; **Entpolitisierung** *f* depoliticization

entprivatisieren *v/t.* deprivatize, (re-)nationalize; **Entprivatisierung** *f* deprivatization, (re-)nationalization

entpuppen *v/refl.*: **sich ~ als** turn out (*od.* prove) to be, reveal o.s. to be

entrahmen *v/t.*; (*Milch*) skim; **Milch ~ in e-r Zentrifuge**: separate the cream from the milk; **entrahmt I.** *P.P.* → **entrahmen; II.** *Adj.*: **~e Milch** skimmed milk

enträtseln *v/t.* solve, puzzle (*od.* work) out; (*Schrift etc.*) decipher; **ein Geheimnis ~** *auch* unravel (*od.* get to the bottom of *umg.*) a mystery

entrechten *v/t.* deprive *s.o.* of his (*od.* her) rights; **Entrechtete** *m, f*; *-n, -n* person (*Pl. auch* those) deprived of his (*od.* her; *Pl.* their) rights; **Entrechtung** *f* deprivation of rights

Entrecote [ãtrə'ko:t] *n*; *-s, -s; Gastr.*

entrecote, (sirloin) steak

Entree [ã'tre:] *n*; *-s*, *-s* **1.** *Gastr.* first course, appetizer, *bes. Brit. auch* starter; *Mus.* opening music; **2.** *bes. österr.* (*Eintritt*) admission, entry; **3.** *altm.* (*Eingangshalle*) entrance hall, foyer

entreißen *v/t.* (*unreg.*): *j-m etw. ~ auch fig.* snatch (*stärker*: wrest) s.th. from s.o., tear s.th. from s.o.'s grasp; *j-n dem Tod ~ fig.* snatch s.o. from the jaws of death

entrichten *v/t.* **1.** *Amtsspr.* (*Summe etc.*) pay; **2.** *fig.*: *j-m s-n Tribut ~* pay (one's) tribute to s.o.; **Entrichtung** *f* payment (+ *Gen.* of)

entriegeln *v/t.* unbolt, unlock, release; **Entriegelung** *f* unbolting, unlocking, release

entrinden *v/t.* debark, remove (*od.* strip) the bark from

entringen (*unreg.*); *geh.* **I.** *v/t.: j-m etw. ~* wrest s.th. from s.o *auch fig.*, wrench s.th. away from s.o., wrestle s.th. off s.o.; **II.** *v/refl.* **1.** *sich j-m etc. ~* break away from, free o.s. from; (*e-r Umarmung*) *auch* disentangle o.s. from *hum.*; **2.** *fig.*: *ein Seufzer etc. entrang sich i-r Brust* a sigh told of her (inner) feelings

entrinnen *v/i.* (*unreg.*) **1.** *geh.* (*entkommen*) escape, get away (+ *Dat.* from); **2.** *poet.* (*aus etw. herausrinnen*) trickle (*od.* flow) from; **3.** *poet.* (*verrinnen*) flee (*od.* fly) away

Entrinnen *n*; *-s*, *kein Pl.* escape; *es gibt kein ~* there's no escaping (*vor* + *Dat. s.th.*), there's no escape (from *s.th.*)

entrollen I. *v/t.* unroll; (*Fahne, Segel*) unfurl; **II.** *v/refl. fig.* unfold

entromantisieren *v/t.* deromanticize, take the romance (*od.* glamo[u]r) out of, debunk *umg.*; **Entromantisierung** *f* deromanticization

entrosten *v/t.* remove (the)rust from; **Entrostung** *f* removal of (the) rust, rust removal

entrücken *v/t.* ; *geh.* (*entziehen*) carry away, transport (+ *Dat.* from); (*verzücken*) enrapture, entrance, enthral(l); **entrückt I.** *P.P. →* **entrücken**; **II.** *Adj. geh.* (*in Gedanken*) rapt, (utterly) engrossed; (*verzückt*) rapt, transported; *oberflächlicher*: captivated; **Entrücktheit** *f*; *mst Sg.*; *geh.* state of rapture (*od.* ecstasy *od.* entrancement); **Entrückung** *f geh. Zustand*: (state of) rapture (*od.* ecstasy *od.* entrancement); (*das Entrücken*) entrancement

entrümpeln *v/t.* **1.** (*Wohnung etc.*) clear out, rid of its clutter; **2.** *fig.* (*Ideologie etc.*) clean up, modernize; **Entrümp(e)lung** *f* **1.** clearing out; **2.** *fig.* clean-up

entrußen *v/t.* (*Ofen, Schornstein etc.*) free from soot (deposits)

entrüsten I. *v/t.* (*erzürnen*) fill *s.o.* with indignation, anger, incense; *stärker*: infuriate; (*schockieren*) shock; **II.** *v/refl.* become (*od.* be) very indignant (*über* + *Akk.* at, about *s.th.*), get (*od.* be) angry (at, about *s.th.*, with *s.o.*); be up in arms (over, about); (*schockiert sein*) be shocked (at); **entrüstet I.** *P.P. → entrüsten*; **II.** *Adj.* indignant, aggrieved, angry, up in arms *präd.*; *stärker*: furious; (*schockiert*) shocked; **Entrüstung** *f* (shock and) indignation (*über* + *Akk.* at); anger (at, over); **Entrüstungssturm** *m* storm of indignation

entsaften *v/t.* juice, extract the juice from; (*Zitrone etc.*) *auch* squeeze; **Entsafter** *m*; *-s*, *-* juice extractor, *Am.*

juicer

entsagen *v/i.* ; *geh.*, *der Welt*, *e-m Genuss etc.*: renounce, forswear *förm.*; *der Welt ~ auch* turn one's back on the world, renounce all worldly things; *dem Alkohol etc. ~* give up (*od.* stop) drinking, give up alcohol, get on the wagon *umg.*; **Entsagung** *f geh.* renunciation (+ *Gen.* of); (*Selbstentsagung*) self-denial; *ein Leben voller ~en* a life of (sacrifice and) self-denial; **entsagungsreich** *Adj. Leben etc.*: full of hardship (*od.* privation); **entsagungsvoll** *Adj. Leben etc.*: full of hardship (*od.* privation); *Person*: self-denying; *Blick etc.*: resigned

entsalzen *v/t.* desalinate; **Entsalzung** *f* desalination; **Entsalzungsanlage** *f* desalination plant

Entsatz *m*; *nur Sg.*; *Mil.* relief (troops *od.* forces *Pl.*)

entsäuern *v/t.* de-acidify, reduce the acidity of; **Entsäuerung** *f* de-acidification, acid neutralization

entschädigen *v/t.: Person*: compensate (*od.* recompense) (*für* for); *als Entschuldigung*: make amends to; *fig. Sache*: compensate, reward, make up *for s.th. umg.*; **Entschädigung** *f* compensation (*auch fig.*); (*Entgelt*) *auch* remuneration

Entschädigungs|anspruch *m* claim for compensation (*od.* damages); **~summe** *f* amount of compensation, damages *Pl.*, indemnity; **~zahlung** *f* (*Zahlen*) payment of damages (*od.* compensation); (*Betrag*) damages *Pl.*, damages sum, compensation

entschärfen I. *v/t.* **1.** (*Sprengkörper*) defuse, disarm, make (*od.* render) safe; (*Munition*) deactivate; **2.** *fig.* (*Lage etc.*) defuse, ease, take (some of) the tension out of; (*Kritik etc.*) tone down, soften, make more conciliatory; (*Buch etc.*) tone (*od.* water) down; (*Obszönes etc. herausnehmen*) remove offensive material from, bowdlerize; **II.** *v/refl. Lage etc.*: ease, lose its tension; **Entschärfung** *f* **1.** *von Sprengkörpern, Waffen etc.*: defusing, disarming; **2.** *fig. der Lage etc.*: defusing, easing; *e-r Kritik etc.*: toning (*od.* watering) down; *e-s Buches etc.*: removal of offensive material (+ *Gen.* from), bowdlerization

Entscheid *m*; *-(e)s*, *-e*; *Amtsspr.* decision, ruling, decree; *→ Entscheidung*

entscheiden (*unreg.*) **I.** *v/t.* **1.** (*Streitfall etc.*) decide, determine; *endgültig*: settle, resolve; *Gericht*: *auch* rule (*od.* pronounce *geh.*) on, reach a verdict (*od.* finding) on; *das musst du ~* that's (*od.* it's) up to you, that's for you to say; *der Fall ist noch nicht entschieden Jur.* the case is not settled yet, the case is continuing; **2.** (*den Ausschlag geben*) decide, settle, be decisive for; *e-n Kampf etc. für sich ~* win (*od.* emerge the winner in) a fight; **II.** *v/i.* **1.** (*Urteil fällen, bestimmen*) decide, rule, make the (*od.* a) decision, determine *Jur.*; *Gericht*: *auch* rule; *~ über* (+ *Akk.*) decide (on) *s.th.*, determine *s.th.*; *in e-m Fall ~ Jur.* rule (*od.* find) on a case; *zu j-s Gunsten/Ungunsten ~ Jur.* rule (*od.* find) for (*od.* in favour of) / against s.o.; **2.** (*den Ausschlag geben*) be decisive, decide (*od.* settle) the issue; **III.** *v/refl.* **1.** *Person*: decide, make up one's mind; *er konnte sich nur schwer ~* he found it hard to make up his mind (*od.* reach a decision); *sich anders ~* change

one's mind, have a change of heart; *sich für/gegen j-n/etw. ~* decide in favo(u)r of / against s.o./s.th.; *sich für einen Bewerber etc. ~* choose (*od.* select, decide on, decide in favo(u)r of, go for *umg.*) an applicant; *sich ~, etw. zu tun* decide (*od.* choose, opt, make up one's mind) to do s.th.; **2.** (*sich herausstellen*) be decided (*od.* resolved, settled), be(come) clear, prove

entscheidend I. *Part. Präs. → entscheiden*; **II.** *Adj.* (*ausschlaggebend*) decisive (*für* for, in); *Frage, Problem*: crucial, vital, *attr. auch* key ...; *Augenblick, Phase*: *auch* critical; *Fehler etc.*: crucial; (*verhängnisvoll*) *auch* fatal; *Änderungen*: fundamental; *von ~er Bedeutung* crucial, vital, crucially (*od.* vitally) important, of critical importance; *der ~e Faktor* the deciding factor; *die ~e Stimme* the casting vote; *im ~en Augenblick hat sie der Mut verlassen* she lost her nerve at the critical moment, when the (critical) moment came she funked (*Am.* blew) it *umg.*; **III.** *Adv.* decisively; *etw. ~ ändern* bring about fundamental changes in s.th.; *~ zu etw. beitragen* be instrumental in bringing s.th. about

Entscheidung *f* decision (*über* + *Akk.* on); *Jur. auch* ruling (on); *der Geschworenen*: verdict (on); *e-e ~ treffen* make (*od.* come to) a decision, decide; *e-e ~ fällen* announce a decision; *Jur.* announce (*od.* pronounce *förm.*) a verdict; *zur ~ kommen* (*zur ~ vorliegen*) come up for decision; (*entschieden werden*) be decided; *um die ~ spielen Sport* play (*od.* be) in the final; *die ~ ist noch nicht gefallen* there is still no decision, there has been no decision (*od.* declaration) (as) yet, it could go either way; *Sport, bei Gleichstand*: they (*od.* the teams *etc.*) are still level, it's still a draw (*od.* tie); *die ~ fiel in der 80. Spielminute* the decisive goal etc. (*od.* the decider) came in the 80th minute; *die ~ fällt mir schwer* I can't decide, I'm finding it hard to decide, I'm having difficulty making my mind up

Entscheidungs|befugnis *f* competence, authority; **~frage** *f Ling.* yes--or-no question; **~freiheit** *f* freedom of choice, discretion

entscheidungsfreudig *Adj.* decisive, unafraid (*od.* not afraid) of making (*od.* to make) decisions

Entscheidungs|gewalt *f*: *die ~ liegt bei j-m* s.o. has the authority (to take decisions); **~grund** *m* decisive factor, (principal) reason; **~hilfe** *f* help in reaching a decision; *j-m e-e ~ geben* help s.o. (to) reach a decision; **~kampf** *m* decisive (*od.* deciding) battle; *fig.* showdown; *Sport* decisive (*od.* deciding) match; **~möglichkeit** *f* possibility, possible decision, option; **~prozess** *m* decision-making process; **~reif** *Adj. präd.* due for (*od.* requiring) decision; **~schlacht** *f* decisive (*od.* deciding) battle; **~spiel** *n Sport allg.*: deciding match, decider, play-off; (*Endspiel*) final; **~spielraum** *m* scope, range of possibilities (*od.* options) (to choose from); **~stunde** *f* moment of truth, hour of decision; **~träger** *m*, **~trägerin** *f* decision-maker; (*Gremium*) decision-making body; *politischer ~* politician responsible; *auf Regierungsebene*: *auch* (responsible) minister

entschieden I. *P.P. → entscheiden*;

II. *Adj.* **1.** (*entschlossen*) determined, resolute; *Verfechter, Gegner etc.: auch* strong, uncompromising; **2.** (*nachdrücklich*) emphatic, decided, uncompromising, categorical; (*brüsk*) peremptory; (*Respekt einflößend*) authoritative; **3.** (*ausgesprochen*) *attr.* decided, out-and-out; (*unbestreitbar*) unquestionable; **ein ~er Gegner von** a declared opponent (*od.* enemy) of; **III.** *Adv.* **1.** (*fest*) firmly, resolutely; (*nachdrücklich*) emphatically; (*brüsk*) peremptorily; **etw. ganz ~ bestreiten/zurückweisen** strongly (*od.* vigorously) dispute s.th. / categorically (*od.* flatly) reject s.th., reject s.th. outright; **sich ~ aussprechen für/gegen** come out strongly in favo(u)r of/against; **2.** (*zweifellos*) definitely, without (a) doubt, decidedly, distinctly *mst iro.*; **~ zu wenig** *etc. auch* far too little *etc.*; **Entschiedenheit** *f; nur Sg.* determination, resoluteness, resolution, steadfastness; **mit (aller) ~** categorically

entschlacken *v/t.* **1.** *Tech.* remove (*od.* clear) the cinders (*od.* slag) from; **2.** *Med.* (*Blut etc.*) purify; (*Darm*) purge; **den Körper ~** *auch* detox (*od.* cleanse) one's system, flush one's system through, get rid of all the toxins in one's system (*od.* bloodstream); **Entschlackung** *f Med.* detox(ification), purification; *des Darms:* purging, purge

entschlafen *v/i.* (*unreg.*); *geh. euph.:* (*sanft*) **~** pass away (peacefully); **Entschlafene** *m, f; -n, -n; geh. euph.* the deceased *mst Sg.*, the departed *mst Pl.*

entschleiern ; *geh.* **I.** *v/t.* **1.** unveil, remove *s.o.'s* veil; **2.** *fig.* reveal, disclose, unveil; (*Geheimnis*) *auch* unravel, penetrate; **II.** *v/refl.* **1.** (*den Schleier entfernen*) take off (*od.* remove) one's veil, unveil (o.s.); **2.** *fig. Berg etc.:* shed its veil, emerge, be revealed; *Geschichte etc.:* be exposed (*als* as), revealed (as, to be); **Entschleierung** *f auch fig.* unveiling; *fig. auch* revelation, exposure

entschließen *v/refl.* (*unreg.*) decide (*zu, für* on; *zu* + *Inf.* to + *Inf.*); make up one's mind (to + *Inf.*); **sich anders ~** change one's mind, have a change of mind (*od.* heart); **er kann sich zu nichts ~** he (just) can't make up his mind; **Entschließung** *f e-r Einzelperson:* decision; *bes. Pol.* resolution; **Entschließungsantrag** *m Pol.* proposal for a resolution

entschlossen I. *P.P.* → **entschließen**; **II.** *Adj.* determined, resolute; **zu allem ~** utterly determined, prepared to go to any length(s); **e-n ~en Eindruck machen** seem very determined, have an air of determination (about one), seem to be s.o. who knows his (*od.* her) own mind; **III.** *Adv.* resolutely, steadfastly, with determination; **kurz ~** *als Reaktion:* without a moment's hesitation, without further ado; (*plötzlich*) suddenly, out of the blue, on the spur of the moment; **Entschlossenheit** *f; nur Sg.* determination, resolution, resoluteness

entschlummern *v/t.* (*untr., ist*); *geh.* **1.** fall asleep; **2.** *euph.* (*sterben*): (*sanft*) **~** pass away (peacefully)

entschlüpfen *v/i.* **1.** **dem Ei ~** hatch, emerge from the egg; **2.** (*entkommen*) slip (*od.* get) away (+ *Dat.* from), escape (+ *Dat.* from *od. s.th.*); **j-m ~** *auch* give s.o. the slip; **3.** *fig. Wort etc.:* slip out; **ihm ist ein unbedachtes**

Wort entschlüpft he let slip a thoughtless remark

Entschluss *m* decision, resolution, resolve *geh.*; **e-n ~ fassen** *od.* **zu e-m ~ kommen** make (*od.* take, reach, come to) a decision, make up one's mind, form a resolve *geh.*; **zu dem ~ kommen zu** (+ *Inf.*) make up one's mind (*od.* decide) to (+ *Inf.*); **es ist sein fester ~ zu** (+ *Inf.*) he firmly intends to (+ *Inf.*), it is his firm intention to, he is resolved *geh.* to; **aus eigenem ~** on one's own (initiative), *Brit. auch* off one's own bat *umg.*

entschlüsseln *v/t.* decipher (*auch Rätsel*); (*dekodieren*) *auch* decode; **Entschlüsselung** *f* decipherment, deciphering; (*Dekodierung*) *auch* decoding

entschlussfähig *Adj.* capable of deciding, able to decide, competent

entschlussfreudig *Adj.* decisive, not afraid of taking (*od.* to take) decisions; (*unternehmend*) enterprising

Entschlusskraft *f; nur Sg.* determination, decisiveness, resolution

entschuldbar *Adj.* excusable, forgivable, pardonable, venial *geh.*

entschulden *v/t.* free of debts

entschuldigen I. *v/t.* **1.** (*Versäumnis, Fernbleiben etc.*) excuse (*mit* on grounds of, because of); **sein Kind in der Schule ~** have (*od.* get) one's child excused (from) school, send an excuse for one's child missing school; **sich** (*Akk.*) **~ lassen** make one's excuses (*od.* apologize) (for not coming *etc.*); *schriftlich: auch* send an apology (*od.* excuse); **Herr X lässt sich** (*Akk.*) **~** Mr(.) X sends his apologies, Mr(.) X regrets he is unable to attend (*od.* be present) *förm.*; **2.** (*verzeihen*) excuse, forgive; **~ Sie, dass ich nicht gekommen bin** (I'm) sorry I didn't come, please forgive me for not coming, I apologize for not coming *förm.*; **~ Sie die Störung!** (I'm) sorry to bother (*od.* disturb) you; **3.** *Sache:* (*verständlich erscheinen lassen*) excuse, explain; **das ist durch nichts zu ~** nothing can justify that, that is inexcusable (*od.* indefensible); **II.** *v/i.:* **~ Sie (bitte)!** *od.* **entschuldige (bitte)!** *beim Ansprechen:* excuse me; (*Verzeihung!*) sorry!, *Am. auch* excuse me; **III.** *v/refl.* apologize, say (one is) sorry; *bei Abwesenheit, beim Weggehen:* make one's excuses, excuse o.s.; **sich bei j-m ~** apologize *od.* say sorry (to s.o.) (*wegen* for, about); **ich habe mich bei ihm entschuldigt** *auch* I told him I was sorry; **ich entschuldigte mich, dass ich es vergessen hatte** I apologized for having forgotten (it)

entschuldigend I. *Part. Präs.* → **entschuldigen**; **II.** *Adj.* apologetic, *nachgestellt:* of apology; **III.** *Adv.* apologetically; **... fügte er ~ hinzu ...** *auch* he added by way of apology ...

Entschuldigung *f* **1.** *Äußerung:* apology; **~!** (*Verzeihung!*) sorry!, I'm sorry, *Am. auch* excuse me; **~, darf ich mal vorbei?** excuse me, ...; **als ~ für** by way of (*od.* as an) apology for; **2.** (*Grund, Vorwand etc.*) excuse; **als ~ für** as an excuse (*od.* explanation) for, to excuse; **dafür gibt es keine ~** there's no excuse for it; **es muss zu i-r ~ gesagt werden** it has to be said in her defen|ce (*Am.* -se); **3.** (*Nachsicht*) forgiveness, tolerance; **ich bitte Sie vielmals um ~** I do apologize (**wegen** for, about), I am extremely sorry (about);

4. *Schule, schriftliche:* (excuse) note; **ohne ~ fehlen** be absent (*od.* miss school) without explanation

Entschuldigungs|grund *m* excuse; **~schreiben** *n* (letter of) apology, written apology

Entschuldung *f Wirts.* disencumberment, reduction of debt burden

entschwefeln *v/t.* *Chem.* desulphurize, *Am.* desulfurize; **Entschwefelung** *f* desulphurization, *Am.* desulfurization; **Entschwefelungsanlage** *f Tech.* desulphurization (*Am.* desulfurization) plant

entschwinden *v/i.* (*unreg.*); *geh.* disappear, vanish (**in** + *Dat.* into, in); *Zeit:* fly by (*od.* past); **j-s Blicken ~** vanish from (s.o.'s) sight, be lost to sight; **j-s Gedächtnis ~** slip s.o.'s memory

entseelt *Adj. geh., auch fig.* dead, lifeless

entsenden *v/t.* (*unreg.*); *geh.* send, dispatch; **Entsendung** *f geh.* dispatch, sending

entsetzen I. *v/t.* **1.** (*in Schrecken versetzen*) horrify, appal(l); (*Angst einjagen*) terrify; (*bestürzen*) shock, dismay; **2.** *Mil.* (*Festung, Truppen*) relieve; **II.** *v/refl. vor Grauen etc.:* be horrified (*od.* appalled) (**über** + *Akk.* at, by), react with horror (to); *bei Gefahr:* be terrified (by); (*bestürzt sein*) be shocked (at, by), be dismayed (by); *moralisch:* be shocked (at, by)

Entsetzen *n; -s, kein Pl.*; (*Schrecken*) horror; (*Erschrecken*) terror; (*Bestürzung*) (utter) dismay, shock; **starr vor ~** rigid with horror (*od.* terror), horror- (*od.* terror-)struck; **mit ~ vernahmen wir** we were horrified (*od.* shocked) to hear (*od.* learn); **zu unser aller ~** *geh.* to (our) universal horror; **Entsetzensschrei** *m* cry of horror (*od.* terror), scream of terror

entsetzlich I. *Adj.* **1.** (*furchtbar*) horrifying, dreadful, terrible, appalling; (*Schrecken erregend*) terrifying; (*ekelhaft*) horrible; (*bestürzend*) shocking, awful; **2.** *umg. Angst, Hunger, Kälte etc.:* dreadful, terrible, awful; **II.** *Adv.* dreadfully, terribly, awfully (*alle auch umg. sehr*); **~ langweilig** *umg. auch* deadly boring; **~ dumm** *umg. auch* incredibly thick; **Entsetzlichkeit** *f* **1.** *nur Sg.; Zustand:* dreadfulness, awfulness; **2.** (*Ereignis, Handlung*) horror; (*Handlung*) *auch* atrocity

entsetzt I. *P.P.* → **entsetzen**; **II.** *Adj.* horrified, appalled (*beide über* + *Akk.* at, by), aghast (at); terrified (at, by); shocked (at, by); **~er Blick** look of (absolute) horror; **ein ~es Gesicht machen** look shocked (*od.* horrified)

entseuchen *v/t.* decontaminate; *Med.* disinfect, sterilize; **Entseuchung** *f* decontamination; disinfection

entsichern *v/t.* ; (*Waffe*) release the safety catch of, cock; **entsichert I.** *P.P.* → **entsichern**; **II.** *Adj.:* **~ sein** have the safety catch off, be cocked

entsiegeln *v/t.* (*Tür, Brief*) unseal, break the seal on

entsinnen *v/refl.* (*unreg.*) recall, recollect, remember (+ *Gen. od.* **an** + *Akk.* s.o., s.th.); **wenn ich mich recht entsinne** if I remember rightly, if my memory serves me right, if I'm not mistaken

entsorgen *v/t.* **1.** (*Abfall, auch Atommüll etc.*) dispose of; **2.** (*Haushalte etc.*) provide refuse disposal (services) for; (*Anlage etc.*) clean (up); *bei Radioaktivität: auch* decontaminate; **Ent-**

sorgung *f* **1.** *von Abfall*: (waste) disposal; *radioaktivem*: nuclear waste disposal; **2.** *e-r Anlage etc.*: cleaning (up); *bei Radioaktivität*: decontamination
Entsorgungs|anlage *f* waste disposal plant; **~firma** *f* waste disposal company (*od.* contractor); *engS.* nuclear waste disposal contractor; **~park** *m* euph. (temporary nuclear) waste disposal site
entspannen I. *v/refl.* **1.** *Person*: relax, unwind, chill *umg.*; *Gesicht*: relax, lose the (*od.* its) tension; *Muskeln*: relax, slacken, loosen up; *seine Züge entspannten sich* his face cleared; **2.** *Lage, Beziehungen*: ease, become less fraught (*od.* tense *od.* more relaxed), settle down; **3.** (*Erholungspause machen*) relax, unwind, wind down; *sich beim Lesen ~* read for relaxation, relax over a book (*od.* magazine *etc.*); *man kann sich dabei gut ~* it helps you (*to*) relax (*od.* unwind), it's good (*od.* great) for relaxing (to); **II.** *v/t.* **1.** (*Muskeln etc.*) relax, loosen (up), slacken; *das entspannt die Nerven* that will soothe (*od.* help) your nerves; **2.** (*Lage, Beziehungen*) ease, take the tension (*od.* heat) out of, normalize; **3.** (*j-m e-e Erholungspause verschaffen*) relax, have a relaxing effect on, help unwind, soothe; **4.** (*von e-r Spannung befreien*) (*Feder, Seil etc.*) slacken, take the tension off; (*Bogen*) release; (*Wasser*) reduce the surface tension of; **III.** *v/i.* **1.** *Sache*: be relaxing (*od.* soothing), have a relaxing (*od.* soothing) effect; **2.** *Person*: → I 3
entspannt I. *P.P.* → *entspannen*; **II.** *Adj.* **1.** *Person*: *völlig ~ sein* be completely relaxed (*od.* totally chilled out *umg.*); *psychisch*: *auch* be completely at ease; **2.** *fig. Verhältnis*: relaxed, easy(going), laid back *umg.*
Entspannung *f* **1.** *Person*: relaxation, rest, time off, time to unwind *umg.*; **2.** *Wirts.* easing; *Pol.* easing of tension, détente; **3.** *des Bogens*: release, discharge; *der Feder*: release, uncoiling; *des Wassers*: reduction of surface tension
Entspannungs|bemühungen *Pl. Pol.* efforts to achieve détente, conciliation attempts; **~politik** *f* policy of détente; **~prozess** *m* process of détente
Entspannungsübung *f* relaxation exercise
entspiegelt *Adj.*: *~es Glas* coated (*od.* anti-reflection) glass; **Entspieg(e)lung** *f* (anti-reflection) coating
entspinnen *v/refl.* (*unreg.*) (*sich entwickeln*) arise, develop (*aus* from); (*folgen*) ensue (from), follow
entsprechen *v/i.* (*unreg.*) **1.** (*übereinstimmen*) correspond to, tie up with; (*e-r Beschreibung*) *auch* fit, agree with, match, conform to; (*gleichwertig sein*) be equivalent to; (*sich decken mit*) tally (*od.* tie up) with, match; **2.** (*erfüllen*) fulfil(l); (*j-s Anforderungen, Erwartungen*) meet, come (*od.* live *od.* match) up to; (*e-r Bitte*) comply with, fulfil(l), meet; *Erwartungen etc. nicht ~* fall short of, fail to meet (*od.* come up to)
entsprechend I. *Part. Präs.* → *entsprechen*; **II.** *Adj.* **1.** (*übereinstimmend*) corresponding (+ *Dat.* to); *sinngemäß*: analogous (to); *im Verhältnis*: proportionate (to), commensurate (with), due (to); (*gleichwertig*) equivalent (to); *der ~e französische Aus-*

druck the French equivalent; **2.** (*angemessen*) appropriate (+ *Dat.* to), adequate, right (for); (*erforderlich*) necessary (for, to); *hart arbeiten und ein ~es Gehalt bekommen* receive a commensurate salary (*od.* a salary in keeping); **3.** (*jeweilig*) respective; (*betreffend*) relevant, *nachgestellt: auch* concerned, affected; (*zuständig*) appropriate, competent; **III.** *Adv.* correspondingly *etc.*; → II; *er verhielt sich ~* he acted accordingly (*od.* responded appropriately); *~ hat er geantwortet* he gave a fitting reply; **IV.** *Präp.* (+ *Dat.*); (*gemäß*) according to, in line with *umg.*; (*befolgend*) in compliance with; *sich s-m Alter ~ benehmen* act one's age, act in a manner befitting one's age *förm.*; *wie geht es ihr? - den Umständen ~* as well as can be expected (in the circumstances); *wie ist die Stimmung? - den Umständen ~* (much) as one might expect in the circumstances, much as you'd expect *umg.*
Entsprechung *f* **1.** (*Übereinstimmung*) correspondence (*mit* with, to), match (with, for); (*Gleichwertigkeit*) equivalence (to); (*Analogie*) analogy (with, to), parallelism (with); **2.** *konkret*: equivalent (*auch Ling.*); (*Gegenstück*) counterpart; (*Analogie*) analogy, analogue *geh.*; (*Parallele*) parallel
entsprießen *v/i.* (*unreg.*); *geh.* **1.** *dem Boden etc.*: spring from, grow in; *bes. Unkraut: auch* sprout from (*od.* in); **2.** *altm. od. hum. fig. e-r Familie*: be a scion (*od.* son *od.* daughter) of; *e-m bestimmten Milieu*: come from, have grown up in, be a child of, have ... origins (*od.* a ... background); *e-m Gebiet*: hail (*od.* come) from
entspringen *v/i.* (*unreg.*) **1.** *Fluss*: rise, have its source (+ *Dat. od.* **in** + *Dat.* in, at); *Quelle*: spring (from); **2.** *fig.*: (*s-n Ursprung haben in*) *~ aus* (*od.* + *Dat.*) spring (*od.* arise, come) from, originate from (*od.* in), have one's origins in; **3.** (*entfliehen*) escape; → *entsprungen*; **4.** *etc.* → *entstammen* 1; **entsprungen I.** *P.P.* → *entspringen*; **II.** *Adj.*: *ein ~er Häftling* an escaped convict (*od.* prisoner)
entstaatlichen *v/t.* denationalize, privatize; **Entstaatlichung** *f* denationalization, privatization
entstalinisieren *v/t.*; *Pol., hist.* destalinize; **Entstalinisierung** *f* destalinization
entstammen *v/i.* (*untr., ist*) **1.** (*abstammen von*) be descended from, come (*od.* descend) from; **2.** *e-m bestimmten Milieu, Gebiet etc.*: come from, have grown up in, be of ... stock; *e-m Milieu: auch* have a ... background; **3.** (*herrühren von*) come from, originate from (*od.* in), derive from, stem from, go back to
entstauben *v/t.* (*Möbel etc.*) dust; *nach längerer Zeit*: dust off; *flüchtig*: dust (a)round; (*Gerät etc.*) remove (the) dust from; *fig.* (*modernisieren*) take a new broom to
entstehen *v/i.* (*unreg.*) **1.** (*zu bestehen beginnen*) come into being, form, take shape, begin; *allmählich*: emerge (*aus* from), form (from); (*sich entwickeln*) develop (from), evolve (from); *Nation*: be born (*od.* formed); (*s-n Ursprung haben*) originate (in); *dadurch könnte bei ihm der Eindruck ~, dass ...* he might get the impression that ..., it might make him think that ...; *e-e*

peinliche Pause entstand there was an embarrassed silence; **2.** (*geschaffen werden*) be made (*aus* from), be created (from); (*gebaut, geschrieben etc. werden*) be built/written *etc.*; *hier ~ 20 Eigentumswohnungen* Schild: Coming soon: 20 homes (*Am. auch* condominiums); *hier entsteht das Gewerbegebiet X* Schild: (Location) Under Development for X Business (*od.* Office *od.* Industrial) Park; **3.** *Kosten, Schwierigkeiten etc.*: arise (*aus* from, as a result of); *Kosten: auch* be incurred (through, over, as a result of); *Wirts.* accrue (from); *~ durch* result from, be caused by, be a result of; **4.** *Chem., Phys. allg.* result, be caused; *Reibung*: be caused (*od.* produced), occur; *Verbindung*: form, be formed (*od.* created); *Wärme etc.*: be generated (*od.* produced) (*alle aus* from; *bei in od.* under conditions of); **5.** *im Enstehen begriffen* developing, *nachgestellt und präd.* in the making; incipient *förm.* (*auch Med.*), inchoate *förm.*; *Staat*: emergent; *Chem.* nascent
Entstehung *f* **1.** (*Ursprung*) beginning(s *Pl.*), origin(s *Pl.*), formation, emergence; *e-s Staates etc.*: birth; (*Entwicklung*) development, evolution; **2.** (*Schaffung*) creation, formation; *e-s Staates etc.*: *auch* foundation; **3.** *von Kosten*: accrual, build-up, generation; *Chem., Phys.*: *von Wärme, Reibung etc.*: generation, production
Entstehungs|geschichte *f* history of the origin(s) (+ *Gen.* of), earliest history (of); *e-s Kunstwerks etc.*: genesis; *bibl.* Genesis; *die ~ der Menschheit* the evolution (*od.* earliest history) of man (*od.* the human race); **~ort** *m* place of origin, home, source; **~ursache** *f* root cause; **~zeit** *f* period (*genau*: date) (of origin)
entsteigen *v/i.* (*unreg.*); *geh.* **1.** *e-r Raumkapsel etc.*: emerge (*od.* climb) from, step (*od.* climb) out of; *e-r Badewanne etc.*: emerge from, step (*od.* get) out of; *e-m Wagen etc.*: get (*od.* climb) out of; *e-r Luxuslimousine*: step (*od.* alight) from; **2.** *fig. Dämpfe etc.*: rise (up) from
entsteinen *v/t.* (*Kirschen etc.*) stone, *bes. Am.* pit
entstellen *v/t.* **1.** (*Gesicht etc.*) (*hässlich machen*) disfigure; (*verzerren*) distort; (*Schönheit, Landschaft etc.*) mar, spoil, disfigure; *stärker*: blight, ruin; **2.** *fig.* (*Tatsachen, Wahrheit etc.*), distort, misrepresent, falsify, twist *umg.*; (*Text*) garble; **entstellt I.** *P.P.* → *entstellen*; **II.** *Adj.* **1.** *Gesicht etc.*: disfigured; *stärker*: deformed, ravaged; *Schönheit, Landschaft etc.*: marred, spoil|t (*Am.* -ed), defaced; *stärker*: ruined, ravaged; *vor Wut/Schmerz ~ Gesicht*: distorted with rage / twisted (*od.* contorted) with pain; **2.** *fig. Wahrheit etc.*: distorted; *Text*: garbled; **Entstellung** *f* disfigurement; marring; distortion, misrepresentation; garbled account (*od.* version); → *entstellen*
entstöpseln *v/t.* (*Abfluss*) unplug, take the plug out of; (*Gefäß*) unstopper, uncork, take the cap off
entstören *v/t.*; *Tech.* (*Radio*) radio-shield, screen; (*Motor etc.*) fit with a suppressor; *Telef.* clear; **Entstörer** *m*; *-s, -* (interference) suppressor; **entstört I.** *P.P.* → *entstören*; **II.** *Adj. Mot.* noise-suppressed; *Radio etc.*: interference-free; **Entstörung** *f* interference suppression; *bei absichtlicher Störung*:

anti-jamming; *Mot.* shielding

Entstörungsstelle *f Telef.* fault-clearing service; *die ~ anrufen* report a (*od.* the) fault, call the engineers

entströmen *v/i. geh.* **1.** *Flüssigkeit:* flow (*od.* pour *od.* surge) out (+ *Dat.* of); *Gas etc.:* escape (from), come out (of); *Aroma etc.:* be given off (by), emanate (from); **2.** *Menschen etc.:* pour (*od.* stream) out (+ *Dat.* of *od.* from), flood out (of *od.* from)

enttabuisieren *v/t.* remove the taboo (*od.* stigma) from, destigmatize, treat as acceptable; (*Ausdruck*) *auch* remove the taboo value from, destigmatize

enttarnen *v/t.* unmask, expose; *e-n Spion ~ auch* blow a spy's cover *umg.*; **Enttarnung** *f* unmasking, exposure

enttäuschen I. *v/t.* disappoint; (*im Stich lassen*) let *s.o.* down; *enttäuscht werden in der Liebe:* suffer a disappointment; *j-s Hoffnung:* be dashed, be disappointed, come to nothing; *angenehm enttäuscht werden* be pleasantly surprised; *der Film hat mich zutiefst enttäuscht* the film was a big disappointment (for me), I was really (*od.* very) disappointed with the film; **II.** *v/i.* be disappointing, be a disappointment (*od.* letdown), not live (*od.* come) up to expectations

enttäuscht I. *P.P.* → *enttäuschen*; **II.** *Adj.* **1.** *Person:* aus spezifischem *Anlass:* disappointed; *Zustand:* (*desillusioniert*) disenchanted, disillusioned; *zutiefst ~* bitterly (*od.* terribly) disappointed (*über + Akk.* at, about; *von* with); *er ist ~ von dir auch* he feels let down by you; **2.** *Erwartungen:* disappointed, *nachgestellt:* not realized; *Hoffnung:* frustrated, vain; *Liebe:* disappointed, unwanted, unreciprocated; *stärker:* frustrated; **III.** *Adv.* disappointedly, in disappointment

Enttäuschung *f* disappointment, letdown; *es war e-e einzige ~* it was one big disappointment (*od.* letdown), it was a huge (*od.* terrible) letdown, it was a fiasco

entthronen *v/t. geh.* dethrone (*auch fig.*), depose, oust from the throne; **Entthronung** *f* dethronement, deposing, ousting

entvölkert *Adj.* **1.** (*nicht mehr bevölkert*) depopulated; **2.** (*leer*) deserted, unpopulated

entwachsen *v/i.* (*unreg.*) **1.** *der elterlichen Gewalt etc.:* outgrow, grow out of; → *Kinderschuhe*; **2.** *geh. dem Boden etc.:* grow out of, come up out of, sprout from (*od.* in)

entwaffnen *v/t.* disarm (*auch fig.*); **entwaffnend I.** *Part. Präs.* → *entwaffnen*; **II.** *Adj. fig.* disarming, *mst attr.* winning; *von ~er Ehrlichkeit etc.* disarmingly honest *etc.*; **Entwaffnung** *f* disarming

Entwaldung *f; nur Sg.* deforestation; clearing

entwarnen *v/i.* give the all clear; **Entwarnung** *f* all clear (signal)

entwässern *v/t.* **1.** (*Wiese etc.*) drain; **2.** *Chem.* dehydrate; *Med.* (*Körper, Ödem etc.*) diurese; **Entwässerung** *f* **1.** *Vorgang:* draining; *Koll.* drainage; **2.** *Chem.* dehydration

Entwässerungs|graben *m* drainage ditch (*od.* channel); *~kanal m* drainage canal

entweder *Konj.:* ~ ... *oder* either … or; ~ *oder!* take it or leave it; ~ *alles oder gar nichts* it's all or nothing; **Entwe-**

der-oder *n*; -, - two-way choice; *da gibts kein ~* there's no choice (about this), there is no alternative

entweichen *v/i.* (*unreg.*) **1.** *Person:* escape (+ *Dat. od. aus* from); *unauffällig:* auch disappear (from), vanish (from); **2.** *Gase etc.:* escape (+ *Dat. od. aus* from); *bei Undichtigkeit:* auch leak (from); *Blut aus dem Gesicht etc.:* drain (from *od.* out of)

entweihen *v/t.* desecrate; (*Feiertag etc.*) profane; **Entweihung** *f* desecration; profanation

entwenden *v/t.* steal, pilfer, appropriate *geh.*, purloin *geh. od. iro.*; (*unterschlagen*) embezzle; **Entwendung** *f* theft, pilfering, purloining *geh. od. iro.*; (*Unterschlagung*) embezzlement

entwerfen *v/t.* (*unreg.*) **1.** (*skizzieren*) *auch schriftlich:* sketch, outline, (*Kleidung, Gerät etc.*) design; (*Garten, Haus etc.*) design; *weitS.* auch plan (the layout of); *ein Bild ~* (+ *Gen. od. von*) *fig.* draw a picture of, depict, portray; **2.** (*in s-n wesentlichen Punkten festlegen*) (*Plan, Vertrag etc.*) draw up, draft, set out

entwerten *v/t.* **1.** *Wirts.* (*Währung*) völlig: make (*od.* render) worthless; (*abwerten*) devalue; *entwertet werden Währung etc.:* auch fall in value; *stärker:* lose its value; **2.** *fig.* devalue, reduce the value of; (*erniedrigen*) debase, degrade; **3.** (*Wertzeichen, Fahrkarte etc.*) cancel; (*Wertzeichen*) auch postmark; (*Fahrschein etc.*) auch punch; **Entwerter** *m; -s, -* ticket-cancel(l)ing machine; **Entwertung** *f* **1.** *von Währung:* devaluation, devaluing; *von Wertzeichen etc.:* cancel(l)ation; **2.** *fig.* devaluing, devaluation; (*Erniedrigung*) debasement

entwickeln I. *v/t.* **1.** (*fördern, vorwärtsbringen*) develop (*aus* from; *zu* into); (*j-n*) auch bring on; (*Appetit*) build up, develop; **2.** (*hervorbringen, entfalten, zeigen*) (*Wärme etc.*) generate, produce; (*Dampf, Geruch*) give off, emit, produce; (*Initiative, Tatkraft, Talent, Phantasie etc.*) display, show; (*Geschmack*) auch acquire (*für* for); **3.** (*erfinden, konstruieren*) develop; (*Theorie, Verfahren etc.*) auch evolve; **4.** (*darlegen*) explain (in detail), give a detailed account of; **5.** *Fot.* develop; **II.** *v/refl.* **1.** (*allmählich entstehen, sich herausbilden*) develop, evolve, grow (*aus* from; *zu* into); *Gase etc.:* form, be given off, be generated; (*Gestalt annehmen*) form, take shape; *aus der Raupe entwickelt sich der Schmetterling* the caterpillar develops into a butterfly; *daraus entwickelte sich e-e Krise* it became (*od.* turned into) a crisis, a crisis ensued, it gave rise to a crisis; **2.** (*Reife erlangen*) develop, mature, reach (*od.* come to) maturity; **3.** (*vorankommen*) (make) progress, advance, come on *umg.*; *sich gut ~* be shaping up (well), be coming on (well) *umg.*, be making good (*od.* steady) progress

Entwickler *m; -s, -; Fot.* developer; *~bad n* developing bath

Entwicklung *f* **1.** development; *von Ideen, Tierarten, Verfahren etc.:* auch evolution; *neuer Produkte:* auch research (+ *Gen.* od. on; *od.* into); *von Kenntnissen:* advancement, furthering; *in der ~ sein* be developing; *Kind:* auch be growing, be at the (*od.* a) formative stage; *Verfahren etc.:* be at the development stage, be under (*od.*

in the course of) development; *zur ~ bringen* develop; (*Anlagen etc.*) auch bring out (*od.* on); *in der ~ zurückgeblieben sein* körperlich: be physically underdeveloped, be a late developer (physically); *in der ~ zurückgebliebene Kinder* retarded (*od.* special needs) children; *geistig:* mentally retarded children; *lernbehindert:* children with a learning disability; **2.** *konkret:* (*Geschehen*) development; (*Tendenz*) trend; **3.** (*Erzeugung*) generation, production; **4.** *Fot.* developing, development; *von Dias:* processing

Entwicklungs|ablauf *m* development, evolution; *~abteilung f* (research and) development department, R and D *umg.*; *~alter n* **1.** (*entwicklungsmäßiges Alter*) developmental age; *geistiges:* mental age; *körperliches:* physical (*od.* biological) age; **2.** (*Pubertät*) adolescence, puberty; *~dienst m* overseas development (*od.* aid) service; *Brit. etwa* Voluntary Service Overseas, VSO; *Am. etwa* the Peace Corps

entwicklungsfähig *Adj. präd. od. nachgestellt:* capable of development, *nachgestellt:* auch with potential; *Posten etc.:* progressive; (*viel versprechend*) promising; *Bio.* (*lebensfähig*) viable; **Entwicklungsfähigkeit** *f; nur Sg.* capacity for development, potential (for development); *Bio.* viability

Entwicklungsgeschichte *f* history; *Bio.* (history of) evolution, evolutionary history, biogenesis *fachspr.*; (*Stammesgeschichte*) phylogeny; *des Einzelwesens:* ontogeny; *die ~ der Menschheit Bio.* the history of evolution, the evolution of man, human evolutionary history; (*Zivilisationsprozess*) the history of mankind (*od.* civilization); **entwicklungsgeschichtlich I.** *Adj.* historical; *Bio.* biogenetic; **II.** *Adv.* historically; *Bio.* biogenetically; *~ gesehen* (seen) from a historical (*od.* an evolutionary) point of view (*od.* perspective)

Entwicklungshelfer *m, ~in f* development aid worker (*od.* volunteer) (*Pl auch* personnel); *Brit. etwa* VSO worker, *Am. etwa* Peace Corps volunteer

entwicklungshemmend *Adj. Hormon etc.:* growth-inhibiting

Entwicklungs|hilfe *f Pol.* aid to developing countries, foreign aid; *~jahre Pl.* adolescence, puberty; *in den ~n* (*od.* during) adolescence, at (*od.* during) puberty; *~kosten Pl. e-s neuen Automodells etc.:* development costs; *~land n* developing nation (*od.* country); *die Entwicklungsländer* (the) developing countries, the developing world, the Third World; *~lehre f; nur Sg.* theory of evolution, evolutionary theory; *~möglichkeit f* possibility (of [*od.* for] development), (development) potential; *~phase f* stage (of development), development stage (*od.* phase); *~politik f* Third World aid policy, development aid policy; *~programm n* development program(me) *od.* plan; *~prozess m* (process of) development, development process; *~psychologie f* developmental psychology; *~roman m Lit.* novel of personal development; *~stadium n, ~stand m* stage (of development); *~störung f* developmental disturbance (*od.* disorder); *~stufe f* stage (of development); *~zeit f* **1.** period of (*od.* time for) development; **2.** (*Pubertät*) adolescence, puberty; **3.** *Med.* incubation period; **4.** *Fot.* developing time

entwinden (*unreg.*) *geh.* **I.** *v/t.*: *j-m etw.* ~ wrest s.th. from s.o.; **II.** *v/refl.* extricate o.s. (*aus* from), wriggle free (from)

entwirrbar *Adj. Knäuel etc.*: *präd. od. nachgestellt*: not beyond disentangling; *Problem*: soluble; *Konflikt etc.*: resolvable; **schwer** ~ *präd.* hard to untangle (*od.* disentangle), *attr.* knotty; **entwirren** *v/t.* disentangle, sort out (*beide auch fig.*); *Wolle*: *auch* unravel; **Entwirrung** *f* disentanglement, unravel(l)ing (*beide auch fig.*)

entwischen *v/i. umg.* slip (*od.* get) away (+ *Dat.* from), escape (from *od. s.th.*), do a runner *umg.*; *j-m* ~ *auch* give s.o. the slip

entwöhnen *v/t.* **1.** (*Säugling, Jungtier*) wean; **2.** *geh. j-n* cure (+ *Gen.* of); **Entwöhnung** *f* **1.** *e-s Säuglings*: weaning; **2.** *von Drogen etc.*: withdrawal; **Entwöhnungskur** *f* withdrawal treatment (*od.* therapy)

entwürdigen I. *v/t.* (*erniedrigen*) degrade, debase; (*Schande bringen über*) disgrace, bring shame (up)on; **II.** *v/refl.* degrade o.s., debase o.s.; (*Schande bringen über sich*) disgrace o.s., engage in shameful conduct *geh.*; **entwürdigend I.** *Part. Präs.* → **entwürdigen**; **II.** *Adj.* degrading; (*entehrend*) disgraceful, dishono(u)rable; **Entwürdigung** *f* degradation, debasement

Entwurf *m* **1.** (*Skizze*) sketch; *für ein Gemälde*: *auch* study; (*Modell*) model, mock-up; *Tech. etc.* design, blueprint (*für od.* + *Gen.* of); *e-s Gebäudes etc.*: plan, blueprint; **2.** (*schriftliche Festlegung in wesentlichen Punkten*) outline, draft; *e-s Gesetzes*: bill; *im* ~ *sein Vorhaben etc.*: be at the planning stage; *Bauwerk, Automodell etc.*: *auch* be at the design stage, be on the drawing board

entwurmen *v/t. Med.* worm; **Entwurmung** *f* worming, worm (*od.* anthelmint[h]ic *fachspr.*) treatment

entwurzeln *v/t.* uproot (*auch fig.*); **Entwurzelung** *f* uprooting (*auch fig.*)

entzaubern *v/t.* **1.** break the spell on, release (*od.* free) *s.o. od. s.th.* from a (*od.* the) (magic) spell; **2.** *fig.* break the spell of, take the magic away from, rob *s.th.* of its magic, cast the cold light of day (*od.* of reason *etc.*) on; *entzaubert werden* lose its magic (*od.* spell); **Entzauberung** *f* breaking of *s. th.'s* spell, restoration of *s.th.* to reality, debunking *umg. pej.*

entzerren *v/t.* **1.** (*Signal etc.*) correct; *Fot.* rectify; **2.** *zeitlich*: distribute (more evenly), space more evenly, space out, stagger; **3.** *fig.* (*falsche Vorstellung etc.*) rectify, set straight, straighten out; **Entzerrung** *f* **1.** *Radio*: distortion correction; *Fot.* rectification; **2.** *fig. falscher Vorstellungen etc.*: rectification, straightening out, setting straight

entziehen (*unreg.*) **I.** *v/t.* **1.** (*von j-m wegziehen*) withdraw, pull away (*von* from); *sie entzog mir ihre Hand auch* she took her hand out of mine, she detached herself from my hand; **2.** (*wegnehmen, nicht länger überlassen*) withdraw, take away; (*Rechte etc.*) deprive *s.o.* of *s.th.*; *j-m die Erlaubnis etc.* / *Unterstützung* ~ withdraw s.o.'s permission *etc.* / (one's) support from s.o.; *j-m das Vertrauen* ~ cease to trust

s.o., stop trusting s.o., no longer trust s.o., no longer have confidence in s.o. *förm.*; *j-m das Wort* ~ impose silence on s.o.; *e-m Redner*: cut s.o. short, stop s.o.; *j-m den Führerschein* ~ take s.o. 's driving licence (*Am.* driver's license) away, disqualify (*od.* ban) s.o. from driving; **3.** (*von etw. fernhalten*) keep away (+ *Dat.* from), separate (from), keep apart (from); *j-s Blicken* ~ hide from s.o., keep out of s.o.'s sight; *j-s Einfluss/Zugriff* ~ remove from (*od.* put out of) s.o.'s reach/influence; **4.** (*aus etw. ziehen*) take (up) from; *Chem.* (*Sauerstoff etc.*) remove (from), extract (from); *dem Körper Wärme* ~ take heat (away) from s.o. 's body; *der Wind entzieht dem Boden Feuchtigkeit* the wind dries (*od.* draws) moisture out of the ground, the wind dries the soil out; (*aus etw. ziehen und in sich aufnehmen*) *Wurzeln etc.*: absorb, suck, draw (*alle* + *Dat.* from *od.* out of); **5.** *umg.* (*Trinker, Süchtige*) detox; **II.** *v/refl.* **1.** (*sich von j-m losmachen*): *sich j-m* ~ *körperlich*: detach o.s. (from s.o.); *mit Gewalt*: break free (from s.o.); *fig. e-m Freund etc.*: stop seeing s.o., part ways with s.o.; *sich j-s Griff/Umarmung* ~ free o.s. from (*gewandt*: slip out of) s.o.'s grip (*od.* grasp) /embrace; *er konnte sich ihrem Charme nicht* ~ he was not immune to her charm(s); **2.** *geh.* (*sich von j-m, etw. zurückziehen, fernhalten*) *sich j-s Blicken* ~ *Person*: (*vermeiden*) hide from s.o., keep out of s.o.'s sight, avoid encountering s.o.; *Sache*: (*versteckt sein*) remain hidden (*od.* invisible *od.* unnoticed); *Person, Sache*: (*verschwinden*) disappear (from s.o.'s view, from sight); **3.** (*e-e Aufgabe etc. nicht erfüllen, vermeiden*) fail to fulfil, evade *geh.*, shirk, dodge *umg.*; *sich der Verantwortung* ~ evade (*od.* shirk) (one's) responsibility, be unwilling to accept (one's) responsibility; **4.** (*entgehen, entkommen*) *Verfolgern etc., Verhaftung*: escape, elude, evade; (*sich befreien von*) free o.s. from; *sich der Gerechtigkeit* ~ flee from justice; **5.** (*nicht Gegenstand von etw. sein*) be beyond (*od.* not within) (*j-s Kontrolle etc.* one's control *etc.*); *Sache*: escape; (*der Definition etc.*) elude, defy; *es entzieht sich m-r Kenntnis/Kontrolle auch* I have no knowledge of (*od.* information about) that / I have no control over that, there's nothing I can do about that; **III.** *v/i. umg. Alkoholiker*: be dried out; *Drogenabhängiger*: be detoxed, be in detox

Entziehung *f* **1.** *von Unterstützung, Vertrauen etc.*: withdrawal; confiscation (+ *Gen. od.*); (*Verweigerung*) denial; (*Verbot*) prohibition; **2.** → **Entzug** 2

Entziehungs|anstalt *f* (drug) detoxification cent|re (*Am.* -er) (*od.* facility); *für Alkoholiker*: drying-out cent|re (*Am.* -er); ~**kur** *f* withdrawal treatment

entzifferbar *Adj.* decipherable, intelligible; **schwer** ~ barely decipherable (*od.* intelligible), *präd. auch* hard to read; **entziffern** *v/t.* (*Handschrift etc.*) decipher, make out, read; (*dechiffrieren*) decode, decipher; *bei unbekanntem Schlüssel*: break the key of; (*enträtseln*) puzzle (*od.* work) out

entzücken *v/t.* charm, delight; **Entzücken** *n*; *-s, kein Pl.*; *geh.* → **Entzückung**; **entzückend I.** *Part. Präs.* →

entzücken; **II.** *Adj.* charming, delightful, lovely; **entzückt I.** *P.P.* → **entzücken**; **II.** *Adj.* delighted, thrilled (*über* + *Akk.* at; *von* with); *wenig* ~ *sein iro.* be less than pleased, *Brit. auch* be not too chuffed *umg.*; **Entzückung** *f geh.* delight; *stärker*: ecstasy; *in* ~ *geraten* go into raptures (*über* + *Akk.* over), be ecstatic (about); *in* ~ *versetzen* send into raptures, absolutely delight

Entzug *m* **1.** *von Rauschgift etc.*: withdrawal; *j-n auf* ~ *setzen* detox s.o., give s.o. withdrawal treatment; *auf* ~ *sein* be in detox (*od.* in withdrawal); **2.** *Chem. von Sauerstoff etc.*: removing; **3.** ~ *des Führerscheins* taking away s.o.'s licen|ce (*Am.* -se); → **Entziehung**

Entzugs|blutung *f Med.* withdrawal bleeding; ~**erscheinung** withdrawal symptom

entzündbar *Adj.* **1.** (*leicht brennbar*) flammable, *nachgestellt*: easily set on fire, *Brit. auch* inflammable; **2.** *fig.* excitable, easily excited; **entzünden I.** *v/refl.* **1.** *geh.* catch fire; *Brennstoffe*: ignite; **2.** *Med.* become inflamed; **3.** *geh. fig. Leidenschaften*: (*geweckt werden*) be (a)roused (*an* + *Dat.* by); (*sich erregen*) run high (over), become heated (over); *Streit*: be sparked off (by); **II.** *v/t.* **1.** *geh.* (*Feuer, Kerze etc.*) light; **2.** *geh. fig.* (*Gefühle etc.*) arouse, incite, provoke, give rise to; **entzündet I.** *P.P.* → **entzünden**; **II.** *Adj.* inflamed; *Augen*: *auch* red; **entzündlich** *Adj.* **1.** (*leicht brennbar*) flammable, *nachgestellt*: easily set on fire, *Brit. auch* inflammable; **2.** *fig.* excitable, easily excited; **3.** *Med.* inflammatory; **Entzündung** *f Med.* inflammation; **entzündungshemmend** *Adj.* anti-inflammatory; **Entzündungsherd** *m Med.* focus of inflammation

entzwei *Adv. nur präd.* (*zerbrochen*) broken (in two), in pieces; (*zerrissen*) torn (apart *od.* in two); (*defekt*) broken, kaput(t) *umg.*; ~**brechen** (*unreg., trennb.*) **I.** *v/t.* (*hat entzweigebrochen*) break in two (*od.* into two pieces); **II.** *v/i.* (*ist*) break in two, come apart

entzweien I. *v/t.* divide, separate; *er versuchte sie zu* ~ he tried to turn them against each other; **II.** *v/refl.* fall out (*mit* with)

entzwei|gehen *v/i.* (*unreg., trennb., ist -ge-*) **1.** *Fenster, Tasse etc.*: break (in two); *Buch etc.*: come apart; *Maschine etc.*: break down; *Radio etc.*: stop working, go phut *umg.*; **2.** *fig. Ehe etc.*: break up (*od.* down), go to pieces; ~**reißen** (*unreg., trennb. -ge-*) **I.** *v/t.* (*hat entzweigerissen*) tear in two (*od.* into two pieces); (*zerreißen*) tear up; **II.** *v/i.* (*ist*) tear; ~**schlagen** *v/t.* (*unreg., trennb., hat -ge-*) smash to pieces; ~**schneiden** *v/t.* (*unreg., trennb., hat -ge-*) cut in two; (*zerschneiden*) cut into pieces, cut up

Entzweiung *f* division, split, rupture, rift

Enzian *m*; *-s, -e* **1.** *Bot.* gentian; **2.** (*Enzianbranntwein*) enzian (schnapps), spirit distilled from the roots of yellow gentian

Enzyklika *f*; *-, Enzykliken*; *kath.* encyclical

Enzyklopädie *f*; *-, -n* encyclop(a)edia; **enzyklopädisch** *Adj. auch Wissen*: encyclop(a)edic

Enzym *n*; *-s, -e*; *Bio.* enzyme

Epauletten [epoˈlɛtn] *Pl. Mil.* epaulettes, *Am.* epaulets

Epheser *m*; *-s*, *-*; *hist.* Ephesian; **~brief** *m bibl.*: **der ~** the (*od.* St Paul's) Epistle (*od.* Letter) to the Ephesians, Ephesians *Pl.* (*V. im Sg.*)

Epidemie *f*; *-*, *-n*; *Med.* epidemic; **Epidemiologie** *f*; *-*, *kein Pl.* epidemiology; **epidemisch** *Adj.* epidemic; **~e Ausmaße** *od.* **Formen annehmen** take on (*od.* reach) epidemic proportions

Epigone *m*; *-n*, *-n*; *geh.*, *mst pej.* Epigone, epigonus; (*Nachahmer*) imitator; **epigonenhaft** *Adj.* epigonic, derivative

Epigramm *n*; *-(e)s*, *-e*; *Lit.* (*Sinngedicht*) epigram

Epik *f*; *-*, *kein Pl.*; *Lit.* **1.** *weitS.* Gattung: narrative (*od.* epic) literature, the epic (genre); **2.** *engS.* (*epische Dichtung in Versen*) epic poetry; **Epiker** *m*; *-s*, *-*, **Epikerin** *f*; *-*, *-nen* **1.** *weitS.* narrative author (*od.* writer); **2.** *engS.* epic poet

Epikureer *m*; *-s*, *-*, **~in** *f*; *-*, *-nen* **1.** *hist.* Epicurean; **2.** *fig.* (*Genussmensch*) bon viveur, epicurean, gourmand *pej.*; (*Feinschmecker*) epicure, gourmet; **epikureisch** *Adj.* **1.** *hist.* Epicurean; **2.** *fig.* epicurean, pleasure-loving

Epilepsie *f*; *-*, *-n*; *Med.* epilepsy; **Epileptiker** *m*; *-s*, *-*, **Epileptikerin** *f*; *-*, *-nen* epileptic; **epileptisch** *Adj.* epileptic; **~er Anfall** epileptic seizure (*od.* fit *umg.*)

Epilierer *m*; *-s*, *-* hair remover, epilator; (*Damenrasierer*) lady's shaver

Epilog *m*; *-s*, *-e*; *Lit.* epilog(ue)

episch *Adj.* epic; **~e Dichtung** *Koll.* epic (*od.* narrative) literature; *einzelnes Werk*: epic (narrative); *in Versen*: epic (*od.* narrative) poem; **~e Breite** epic scope (*od.* scale *od.* dimensions *Pl.*); **etw. in ~er Breite erzählen** *umg. fig.* give *s.o.* the whole saga, tell *s.o.* (about) s.th. at great (*od.* enormous) length

episkopal *Adj.* *Reli.* (*bischöflich*) episcopal; *Anhänger etc.*: Episcopalian (*England*: *auch* Anglican); **Episkopat** *n*, *m*; *-(e)s*, *-e* (*Amt*) office of bishop, bishopric; (*Bischöfe*) episcopate

Episode *f*; *-*, *-n* episode (*auch Mus.*); **Episodenfilm** *m* film in instal(l)-ments, serial film; **episodenhaft**, **episodisch I.** *Adj.* episodic; **II.** *Adv.* episodically

Epistel *f*; *-*, *-n.* **1.** *bibl.* (*Apostelbrief*) Epistle, Letter; **2.** *im Gottesdienst*: (*Lesung*) (New Testament) reading; **3.** *mst pej. od. iro.* (*Brief*) epistle, screed

Epizentrum *n* *Geol.* epicent|re (*Am.* -er)

epochal *Adj.* **1.** (*bedeutsam*) epoch--making, momentous; *Erfindung etc.*: revolutionary; *Entscheidung etc.*: attr. landmark, momentous; (*Aufsehen erregend*) sensational; **2.** *Päd.* end-on, sequential; **Epoche** *f*; *-*, *-n* era, age, epoch; **~ machen** have a profound (*stärker*: revolutionary) impact; usher in a new age; **~ machend** nur attr. epoch-making, momentous; *Idee*, *Erfindung etc.*: revolutionary; *Idee*: *auch* seminal, transforming; (*Aufsehen erregend*) sensational

Epos *n*; *-*, *Epen*; *Lit.* epic; *in Versen*: *auch* epic poem

Equalizer ['i:kvəlaizɐ] *m*; *-s*, *-*; *Etech.* equalizer

Equipe [e'kip] *f*; *-*, *-n*; *Sport* team

er *pers. Pron.* **1.** he; *von Dingen*: it; *von Mond*, *Dampfer*, *Wagen*: *auch* she; *von Hund etc.*: he, it; **~ ist es** it's him

umg.; **~ ist es gewesen, der …** it was he who (*od.* that) …, he was the one who (*od.* that) …; **2.** *altm.*, *Anrede*: **Er** *etwa*: Verwendung des Passivs *od.* you; **Er** *m*; *-*, *-s*; *umg.* **1. es ist ein ~** *auch bei Tieren*: it's a he; **2.** *auf Handtüchern etc.*: His

erachten *v/t. geh.* consider, think, judge, deem; **etw. für unnötig ~** consider s.th. (to be) unnecessary, regard s.th. as unnecessary; **es als s-e Pflicht ~ zu** (+ *Inf.*) consider it (*od.* see it as) one's duty to (+ *Inf.*)

Erachten *n*; *-s*, *kein Pl.*; *geh.* opinion, judg(e)ment; **m-s ~s** (*abgek. m. E.*) *od.* **nach m-m ~** in my opinion (*od.* judgment *od.* view), as I see it; **m-s ~s war es ein Fehler** *auch* I regard it as (*od.* consider it) a mistake, I think (*od.* feel) it was a mistake; **nach s-m ~** *auch* he takes the view that

erahnen *v/t.* → **ahnen** I

erarbeiten *v/t.* **1.** (*durch Arbeit erwerben*) (**sich** *Dat.*) **etw. ~** work (hard) for *s.th.*, get (*od.* gain) *s.th.* through one's own efforts; **2.** (*sich geistig zu eigen machen*) (*Wissen*, *Kenntnisse etc.*) acquire, master, gather; (*Unterrichtsstoff etc.*) cover, master, (thoroughly) prepare; (*Begriff etc.*) explore, research; **3.** (*erstellen*, *entwickeln*) (*Programm etc.*) work out, put together, compile; (*Modell etc.*) design, develop, create; **Erarbeitung** *f* **1.** achievement, attainment; **2.** (*von Lernstoff etc*) mastering, preparation; (*von Wissen etc.*) acquisition; **3.** (*Erstellung*) development, creation, compilation

Erb|adel *m* hereditary nobility, aristocracy; **~anlage** *f Bio.* genes *Pl.*, genetic make-up (*od.* endowment); *Med.* hereditary disposition; **~anspruch** *m* (hereditary) title (**auf** + *Akk.* to), claim to an inheritance

erbarmen I. *v/refl.* **1.** *geh.*: **sich j-s ~** take (*od.* have) pity on s.o.; *Reli.* have mercy on s.o.; **Herr, erbarme Dich unser** *kirchl.* Lord, have mercy upon us; **2.** *umg. hum.*: **sich des Kuchens etc. ~** take pity on *the cake etc.*; **II.** *v/t.* move *s.o.* to pity

Erbarmen *n*; *-s*, *kein Pl.* pity, compassion; **er kennt kein ~** he's merciless; **zum ~** (*Mitleid erregend*) pitiful, pathetic; (*entsetzlich*) appalling; (*schlecht*) wretched, pathetic, awful; **erbarmenswert** *Adj. Person*: pitiable, wretched; *Anblick etc.*: pitiful, wretched, heartrending

erbärmlich I. *Adj.* **1.** (*elend*) wretched, pitiful, miserable; **in e-m ~en Zustand** in a wretched state; **2.** *pej.* (*schlecht*, *unzulänglich*) *Leistung*, *Qualität etc.*: appalling, dreadful, pathetic, deplorable; *Summe*, *Menge etc.*: (*gering*) paltry *geh.*, pathetic; *stärker*: insulting; *präd.* an insult; **3.** *pej.* (*gemein*) mean, contemptible; **4.** *nur attr.*; *Durst*, *Hunger etc.*: appalling, dreadful, tormenting; **sie hatte ~e Angst** she was dreadfully (*od.* horribly) frightened; **II.** *Adv.* (*äußerst*) terribly, dreadfully, excruciatingly; **~ wenig** precious little; **Erbärmlichkeit** *f*; *nur Sg.* **1.** (*Elend*) misery; wretchedness; **2.** (*Unzulänglichkeit*) (total) inadequacy; *e-r Summe*, *Menge etc.*: *auch* paltriness; **3.** (*Gemeinheit*) *e-r Tat etc.*: deplorable nature *geh.*, meanness

erbarmungslos I. *Adj.* merciless, pitiless; **II.** *Adv* mercilessly, pitilessly; *oberflächlicher*: *necken etc.*: unmercifully; **Erbarmungslosigkeit** *f*; *nur Sg*

mercilessness, pitilessness

erbauen I. *v/t.* **1.** (*Haus etc.*) build, construct; **2.** *geh. fig.* (*erfreuen*, *Gemüt erheben*) edify; **er war nicht besonders erbaut davon** he wasn't exactly over the moon about it *umg.*, he was not too pleased (*od.* thrilled); **II.** *v/refl. geh.*: **sich ~ an** (+ *Dat.*) find great pleasure in, derive great pleasure from; *stärker*: be uplifted by; **Erbauer** *m*; *-s*, *-*, **Erbauerin** *f*; *-*, *-nen* architect, builder; (*Gründer*) founder; **erbaulich** *Adj.* edifying (*auch iro.*), elevating; *Schrift*: devotional

Erbauung *f* **1.** (*Errichtung*) construction, erection, building; **2.** *fig. des Gemüts*: edification

Erbauungs|literatur *f Lit.* devotional literature; **~schrift** *f* religious (*od.* devotional) tract; *Pl.* *auch* devotional writings (*od.* literature *Sg.*)

Erbbaurecht *n* inheritable (*od.* hereditary) building rights *Pl.*

erbberechtigt *Adj. präd.* entitled to inherit; **Erbberechtigte** *m*, *f* (legitimate) heir

erbbiologisch *Adj.*: **~es Gutachten** *Jur. bei Vaterschaftsklage*: genetic evidence

Erbe[1] *m*; *-n*, *-n* heir (*auch fig.*); (*Nachfolger*) successor (*beide*: **e-s Vermögens** to an estate); (*Begünstigter*) beneficiary; (*Vermächtnisnehmer*) legatee; *e-s noch Lebenden*: heir apparent; **alleiniger ~** sole heir; **gesetzlicher ~** legal heir, heir-at-law *fachspr.*; **mutmaßlicher ~** heir presumptive; **j-n zum ~n einsetzen** make s.o. (*od.* designate s.o. as) one's heir; → **lachend** II

Erbe[2] *n*; *-s*, *kein Pl.* **1.** inheritance; **ein ~ antreten/ausschlagen** succeed to (*od.* come into) / refuse (*od.* disclaim) an inheritance; **2.** *fig. Koll.*: heritage; *spezifisches mst*: legacy

erbeben *v/i. auch Person und fig.*: shake, tremble (*Person*: *auch* quake) (**alle vor** + *Dat.* with; **bei** at); **etw. ~ lassen** make s.th. shake (*od.* tremble), shake s.th.

erben I. *v/t.* **1.** inherit (*auch fig.*); (*Geld*) *auch* come into; **du hast wohl geerbt?** *hum.* (have you) won the pools (*Am.* the lottery) or something?; **das hat er von der Mutter geerbt** *fig.* he's got (*od.* he has) that from his mother; **2.** *umg. fig.* (*kriegen*) get; **bei mir / hier ist nichts zu ~** *umg.* you'll get no joy from me / there's nothing doing here; **II.** *v/i.* inherit, come into an inheritance

Erbengemeinschaft *f* community of heirs

erbetteln *v/t.*: (**sich** *[Dat.]*) **etw. ~** beg s.th., get s.th. by begging; *pej.* scrounge, cadge s.th. (**von** off *od.* from); *schmeichelnd*: wheedle s.th. (out of)

erbeuten *v/t.* **1.** *Dieb etc.*: get away with, take, grab *umg.*; **2.** *bes. Mil.* seize, capture, take (*od.* gain) possession of; **3.** *umg. fig.* (*Preis etc.*) carry off, manage to get; **Erbeutung** *f*; *nur Sg.* capture

Erb|faktor *m Bio.* gene; **~fall** *m Jur.*: **im ~** on succession (to the estate); **~fehler** *m Med.* hereditary defect; **~feind** *m* **1.** *Volk*: traditional (*od.* age-old) enemy (*od.* foe); **2.** *Einzelmensch* (*auch* **~feindin** *f*) sworn (*od.* lifelong) enemy; **3.** *euph.* (*Teufel*) the adversary; **~feindschaft** *f* traditional (*od.* longstanding) enmity

Erbfolge *f* succession; **~krieg** *m hist.*

war of succession

Erbgut n **1.** nur Sg.; Bio. genetic make-up; **2.** Jur. (Nachlass) estate; weitS. inheritance, patrimony

erbgut|schädigend, **~verändernd** Adj. Bio., Med. mutagenic

erbieten v/refl. (unreg.); geh.: **sich ~ zu** (+ Inf.) offer (od. volunteer) to (+ Inf.)

Erbin f; -, -nen reiche: heiress; → **Erbe¹**

Erbinformation f Bio. genetic information

erbitten v/t. (unreg.); geh.: (**sich** [Dat.]) etw. **~** ask for, request, solicit förm.

erbittern I. v/t. (erzürnen) anger; stärker: enrage, infuriate; (verbittern) make s.o. (feel) very bitter (od. resentful), embitter; **II.** v/refl. (sich entrüsten) get angry (über + Akk. about), get upset (about, over), deeply resent; (verbittern) become embittered (about), become bitter (about); **erbittert I.** P.P. → **erbittern**; **II.** Adj. **1.** präd. (grollend) embittered (über + Akk. at, by), bitter (about); (deeply) resentful (about od. of); **2.** attr. (leidenschaftlich) Gegner etc.: bitter; (heftig) fierce; (verbissen) stubborn, unyielding, intransigent; **~en Widerstand leisten** fight back fiercely, put up a fierce resistance; **III.** Adv.: etw. **~ bekämpfen** fight s.th. tooth and nail; **Erbitterung** f; nur Sg. bitterness, embitterment

Erbkrankheit f hereditary disease

erblassen v/i. geh. go (od. turn od. grow) pale, go (od. turn) white

Erblasser m; -s, -, **~in** f; -, -nen; the deceased; testamentarisch, männlich: testator; weiblich: testatrix

Erblast f burden of the past; Technik, Wirtschaft etc.: inherited problem(s Pl.); **die ~ der Nazizeit** the burden (od. stigma) of the (od. their, our, your) Nazi past

Erblehre f; nur Sg.; Bio. genetics

erblich I. Adj. hereditary, (in)heritable; **II.** Adv.: **er ist ~ belastet** Med. he has a hereditary disease; bei Eigenschaft: it runs in the family, it's hereditary; **Erblichkeit** f; nur Sg. hereditary character (od. nature)

erblicken v/t. geh. **1.** (sehen) behold, see; plötzlich: auch catch sight of; **sie erblickte das Licht der Welt in** (+ Dat.) / **am** (+ Datum) she first saw the light of day (od. entered this world) in … on …; **2.** (erkennen, zu erkennen glauben) see; **in j-m s-n Feind** etc. **~** fig. see s.o. as one's enemy etc.

erblinden v/i. **1.** (blind werden) go blind, lose one's sight; **auf einem Auge ~** go blind in one eye, lose the sight of one eye; **2.** (glanzlos werden) Glas etc.: (grow) dull, fog, lose its brilliance; **Erblindung** f loss of (one's) sight; (Blindheit) blindness

erblühen v/i. geh. **1.** Blume: blossom, open (out); **2.** fig.: **~** (**zu**) blossom (into)

Erb|masse f **1.** Jur. (Nachlass) estate; **2.** Bio. genetic make-up, biological inheritance; **~merkmal** n Bio. hereditary (od. inherited) characteristic; **~onkel** m umg. hum. rich uncle

erbost Adj. angry (über + Akk. etw.: about, j-n: with)

Erbpacht f Jur. hereditary leasehold; **ein Grundstück in ~ erwerben** lease a piece of land in perpetuity

erbrechen (unreg.) **I.** v/t. **1.** Med. vomit, bring (od. throw) up; **2.** geh. (gewaltsam öffnen) break open; (Tür) auch force (open); **3.** altm. (Brief) open; (Siegel) break; **II.** v/i. und v/refl. vomit, throw up, be sick, hurl umg.; **er musste sich ~** he vomited, he threw up, bes. Brit. auch he was sick; **Erbrechen** n; -s, kein Pl.; Med. vomiting; **bis zum ~** umg. fig. ad nauseam

Erbrecht n Jur. **1.** nur Sg.; Gesetze: law of succession, law(s Pl.) of (od. governing) inheritance; **2.** (Anspruch) right of succession, hereditary title

erbringen v/t. (unreg.) **1.** (ergeben) produce, yield, bring, return; (liefern, stellen) provide, deliver, supply; (Beweise) auch furnish geh.; **Leistungen ~** produce results; **2.** (aufbringen) (Geldbetrag etc.) raise, find

Erbrochene n; -n, kein Pl. vomit, sick (od. puke) umg., vomitus fachspr.

Erbschaden m Bio., Med. genetic defect

Erbschaft f inheritance; **e-e ~ machen** receive (od. get umg.) a legacy, come into an inheritance; → **Erbe²**

Erbschaftssteuer f inheritance (od. death od. estate) tax

Erbschein m Jur. certificate of inheritance

Erbschleicher m; -s, -; pej. legacy hunter; **Erbschleicherei** f; -, -en; pej. legacy hunting; **Erbschleicherin** f; -, -nen legacy hunter

Erbse f; -, -n **1.** Bot. pea; **gelbe** od. **getrocknete ~** dried peas; **wie die Prinzessin auf der ~** like the princess and the pea; **2.** Sl. (Kopf) nut, head; **hast du was an der ~?** umg. fig. pej. are you off your head?

Erbsen|brei m Gastr. pureed peas Pl., Brit. auch pease pudding; **~eintopf** m Gastr. thick pea broth (od. soup); **2groß** Adj. pea-sized, präd. od. nachgestellt: the size of a pea; **~schote** f Bot. pea pod; **~suppe** f Gastr. pea soup

Erbsenzähler m pej. bean-counter umg., pedant; **Erbsenzählerei** f; -, -en; pej. nit-picking umg., pedantry; **Erbsenzählerin** f; -, -nen bean-counter umg., schoolmarm umg.

Erb|sprung m Bio. saltation; **~streitigkeit** f inheritance dispute, quarrel over a will (od. legacy); **~stück** n heirloom; **~substanz** f Bio. genetic make-up, genome; **~sünde** f original sin

Erb|tante f umg. hum. rich aunt; **~teil** n **1.** Jur. share (od. portion) of the inheritance (od. estate); **2.** Bio. inherited characteristic (od. trait); **~vertrag** m Jur. testamentary contract; **~verzicht** m Jur. renunciation of inheritance rights

Erdachse f earth's axis

erdacht I. P.P. → **erdenken**; **II.** Adj. (erfunden) imaginary, invented, fictitious, concocted pej.; (Geschichte) auch: attr. made-up, präd. made up; **ein schlau ~er Plan** an ingenious (od. a clever) scheme (od. plan), a cleverly thought-out scheme (od. plan)

Erd|altertum n; nur Sg.; Geol. the Palaeozoic (era); **~anziehung** f Phys. (earth's) gravity, earth's pull; **~apfel** m südd., österr. potato; **~arbeiten** Pl. earth-moving operations, excavation work Sg., excavations; **~atmosphäre** f; nur Sg. (earth's) atmosphere; **~bahn** f earth's orbit (od. [a]round the sun); **~ball** m (the) earth, our planet, the globe

Erdbeben n earthquake; **kleines ~** (earth) tremor(s Pl.); **schweres ~** major (od. strong, bad umg.) earthquake; **das ~ von San Francisco** etc. the San

Francisco etc. earthquake, the earthquake in San Francisco etc.; **bei e-m ~ umkommen** die (od. perish geh.) in an earthquake; **~gebiet** n **1.** gefährdet: earthquake (od. seismic) zone; **2.** betroffen: area hit by the (bzw. an) earthquake; **2gefährdet** Adj. earthquake-prone, präd. at risk of an earthquake; **~herd** m focus of the (bzw. an) earthquake, seismic focus; **~opfer** n earthquake victim (od. casualty); **~schutz** m earthquake protection; **2sicher** Adj. earthquake-proof; **~warte** f seismographical station; **~welle** f seismic wave

Erdbeerbecher m Gastr. strawberry coupe (od. sundae)

Erdbeere f Bot. strawberry

Erdbeereis n Gastr. strawberry ice cream

erdbeerfarben Adj. strawberry(-colo[u]red)

Erdbeer|kuchen m Gastr. strawberry cake; **~marmelade** f strawberry jam; **~sekt** m sparkling strawberry wine, strawberry sekt, strawberry champagne; **~torte** f strawberry flan (od. tart)

Erd|bestattung f burial, interment förm.; **~bewegung** f **1.** Geol. movement(s Pl.) in the earth's crust; **2.** Tech. earth-moving; **~bewohner** m inhabitant of the earth, earth-dweller geh., earthling umg. hum.; **~biene** f Zool. mining bee; **~boden** m ground, earth; **dem ~ gleichmachen** raze (to the ground); **vom ~ verschwinden** disappear from (od. off) the face of the earth; **es war wie vom ~ verschluckt** it was as if the earth had swallowed it up, it had (just) vanished (into thin air); **ich wäre (vor Scham) am liebsten im ~ versunken** (I was so ashamed [od. mortified,]) I just wished the earth would swallow me up; **~brocken** m clod (od. clod of earth)

Erde f; -, -n **1.** (Erdreich) earth, soil; (Bodenart) (type of) soil; **in fremder/geweihter ~ ruhen** rest in foreign/consecrated soil; **zu ~ werden** geh. euph. (re)turn to dust; **~ zu ~, Staub zu Staub** kirchl. ashes to ashes, dust to dust; **2.** Chem. earth; **seltene ~n** rare earths, lanthanides; **3.** (Boden) ground; (Fußboden) floor; **die ~ bebt** the earth shakes (od. trembles); **über der ~** above ground; **unter der ~** underground, below the surface; **auf die** od. **zur ~ fallen** fall to the ground (Fußboden: auch to [od. on] the floor); **auf der bloßen** od. **nackten ~** on the bare ground; **j-n unter die ~ bringen** umg. (beerdigen) bury; fig. (Tod verschulden) cause s.o.'s death, be the death of s.o. umg.; **unter der ~ liegen** geh. euph. be no longer with us, have gone to one's long home; → **Boden** 1, 2, **Erdboden**; **4.** nur Sg.; (Welt) the world, the earth; **auf der ganzen ~** all over the world, the world over, everywhere on earth; **niemand auf der ganzen ~** nobody in the whole (wide) world, nobody on earth; **auf ~n** bibl., geh. on earth, here below; **5.** nur Sg.; (Planet) Earth (ohne Art.), the earth; **Mutter ~** poet. Mother Earth; **6.** Etech. earth, Am. ground

erden v/t. Etech. earth, Am. ground

Erden|bürger m mortal; **ein neuer ~** another little human being; **~glück** n earthly (od. human) happiness

erdenken v/t. (unreg.) think up, devise, invent; → **erdacht**; **erdenklich** Adj.

imaginable, conceivable, possible; **auf jede ~e Weise** (in) every possible (*od.* imaginable, conceivable) way, every way imaginable; **sich alle ~e Mühe geben** *od.* **alles Erdenkliche tun** do one's utmost (**um zu** + *Inf.* to + *Inf.*), make every possible effort (to + *Inf.*), go to all possible lengths (to + *Inf.*)

Erden|leben *n* earthly life, life on earth; **~rund** *n poet.*: **auf dem ~** (all) over the world, at the round earth's imagined corners *poet.*; **~wurm** *m geh.* puny (*od.* mere) mortal

Erd|erschütterung *f* earth tremor; **~erwärmung** *f* global warming

erdfarben *Adj.* earth-colo[u]red, brownish, dull brown

Erdferkel *n Zool.* aardvark

erdfern *Adj. Mond*: far (*od.* furthest) from the earth; *Planet etc.*: distant, remote; **Erdferne** *f Astron.* apogee

Erdgas *n* natural gas; **~leitung** *f* (natural) gas pipeline

Erd|geist *m* **1.** *allg., Lit.* earth spirit; **2.** (*Kobold*) gnome; **~geruch** *m* earthy smell

Erdgeschichte *f; nur Sg.; weitS.* history of the earth; *engS.* geological record; (*Wissenschaft*) geology; **erdgeschichtlich** *Adj.* geological

Erd|geschoss *n,* **Erd|geschoß** *n österr.*: (**im** on the) ground (*Am. auch* first) floor; **~halbkugel** *f* hemisphere; **~haufen** *m* heap (*od.* pile *od.* mound *geh.*) of earth; **~höhle** *f* (*Tierbehausung*) burrow, earth; *natürlich entstandene*: cave; **~hörnchen** *n Zool.* ground squirrel; **~hügel** *m* mound (of earth [*od.* soil])

erdichten *v/t.* make up, think up, dream up *umg.*, invent; *pej. auch* fabricate, concoct; **erdichtet** *Adj. attr.* made-up, *präd.* made up; **es ist ~ auch** it's a fabrication (*od.* a fiction); **Erdichtung** *f* invention; fabrication

erdig *Adj.* **1.** *Geruch, Geschmack etc.*: earthy; **2.** *geh.* (*mit Erde beschmutzt*) soiled, earth-stained; **3.** (*aus Erde bestehend*) *Boden*: *attr.* earth, earthen *altm., präd.* of earth

Erd|innere *n Geol.* interior of the earth; **~kabel** *n Etech.* underground cable; **~kern** *m* earth's core; **~klumpen** *m* clod (of earth); **~kröte** *f Zool.* common toad; **~krume** *f Agr.* topsoil, tilth; **~kruste** *f Geol.* earth's crust; **~kugel** *f* **1.** **die ~** (*Erde*) the earth, our planet, the globe; **2.** (*Globus*) globe

Erdkunde *f; nur Sg.* geography; **erdkundlich** *Adj.* geographic(al)

Erd|leiter *m Etech.* earth (*Am.* ground) wire (*od.* lead); **~leitung** *f* **1.** *Etech.* earth (*Am.* ground) wire (*od.* lead); **2.** *Tech.* underground pipe(line); **~loch** *n* hole (in the ground); *Mil.* foxhole

erdmagnetisch *Adj. Phys.*: **~es Feld** earth's magnetic field; **Erdmagnetismus** *m* geomagnetism

Erd|männchen *n* **1.** *Zool.* meerkat; **2.** *Bot.* mandrake (root); **3.** *Myth.* goblin, gnome, dwarf; **~mantel** *m Geol.* earth's mantle; **~massen** *Pl.* masses of earth, earth masses; **~messung** *f* geodesy; **~mittelalter** *n Geol.* the Mesozoic (era)

erdnah *Adj. Astron., Mond*: close (*od.* closest) to earth; *Planet etc.*: near; **Erdnähe** *f Astron.* perigee, point nearest to earth; **in ~** at perigee

Erdneuzeit *f Geol.* the Cenozoic (*od.* Cainozoic) (era)

Erdnuss *f Bot.* peanut; **~butter** *f* peanut butter

Erdoberfläche *f; nur Sg.* earth's surface, surface of the earth

Erdöl *n* (crude) oil, petroleum; **~ exportierende/fördernde Länder** *od.* **Staaten** oil- (and petroleum-)exporting/oil- (and petroleum-)producing countries (*od.* nations)

Erdöl... *im Subst. siehe auch* **Mineralöl..., Öl...**

erdolchen *v/t.* stab to death

Erdöl|feld *n* oilfield; **~förderung** *f* oil (and petroleum) production; **~gesellschaft** *f* oil company; **~lager** *n Geol.* oil deposit(s *Pl.*); **~leitung** *f* (oil) pipeline; **~produkt** *n* petroleum product; **~raffinerie** *f* oil refinery; **~vorkommen** *n Geol.* oil deposit(s *Pl.*) oilfield(s *Pl.*)

Erd|pol *m* pole (of the earth); **~probe** *f* soil sample; **~reich** *n* earth, soil

erdreisten *v/refl. geh.*: **sich ~ zu** (+ *Inf.*) dare to (+ *Inf.*); have the cheek (*od.* nerve *od.* audacity) to (+ *Inf.*)

Erdrinde *f; nur Sg.; Geol.* earth's crust

erdröhnen *v/i. Raum, Luft etc.*: resound (**von** with), reverberate (with), re-echo (to, with); *Saal etc. vom Gelächter*: re-echo (to, with), erupt (in); *Motor*: roar; *Glocken*: boom out

erdrosseln *v/t.* (*erwürgen*) strangle, throttle; *fig.* (*unterbinden*) smother, suppress; **Erdrosselung** *f* strangulation

Erdrotation *f* → **Erdumdrehung**

erdrücken *v/t.* **1.** (*zu Tode drücken*) crush (to death); **2.** *fig.* (*überbelasten*) overwhelm; (*niederdrücken*) weigh down; **von Arbeit fast erdrückt** snowed under (*od.* swamped) with work, hopelessly overworked; **3.** *fig.* (*Raum*) *Möbelstück etc.*: be too overpowering for; (*Kunstwerk etc.*) *auch* kill *umg.*; **erdrückend I.** *Part. Präs.* → **erdrücken; II.** *Adj. Hitze*: intolerable, unbearable; *Sorgen etc.*: oppressive; *stärker*: crippling; *Beweislast, Übermacht*: overwhelming

Erdrutsch *m* landslide (*auch fig., Pol.*); **erdrutschartig** *Adj. Pol.*: **~e Verluste** devastating losses

Erd|schatten *m Astron.* earth's shadow; **~schicht** *f* **1.** (*Schicht Erde*) layer of earth; *untere*: subsoil; **2.** *Geol.* stratum; **~scholle** *f* clod (of earth); *fig.* soil; **~schluss** *m Etech.* earth (*Am.* ground) leakage, accidental earth (*Am.* ground); **~spalte** *f* fissure, cleft; **~stoß** *m* tremor; seismic shock, earthshock; **~strahlung** *f* ground radiation; **~teil** *m Geog.* continent; **~trabant** *m; nur Sg.; Astron., geh.* earth satellite

erdulden *v/t.* bear, endure, put up with, suffer *geh.*; **Erduldung** *f; nur Sg.* endurance, enduring

Erd|umdrehung *f* earth's rotation; *auch einzelne*: rotation of the earth; **~umfang** *m* earth's circumference, circumference of the earth; **~umkreisung** *f Astron.* orbit (a)round the earth; **~umlaufbahn** *f Astron., e-s Satelliten*: (earth) orbit; **in die ~ schießen** send into orbit; **~umrundung** *f* (a)round-the-world voyage (*od.* flight etc.), circumnavigation of the earth, circling the globe; **~umsegelung** *f* circumnavigation of the earth, voyage (*od.* sailing) (a)round the world

Erdung *f Etech.* **1.** (*Erden*) earthing, *Am.* grounding; **2.** (*Draht*) earth (*Am.* ground) (wire)

erdverbunden *Adj. engS.* close to the soil; *weitS.* close to (*od.* in harmony with) nature (*od.* Nature)

Erd|wall *m* earthwork(s *Pl.*), earth bank; **~wärme** *f Geol.* geothermal heat, internal heat of the earth; **~zeitalter** *n Geol.* geological era

ereifern *v/refl.* get worked up (**über** + *Akk. od.* **wegen** about), get hot under the collar *umg.* (about)

ereignen *v/refl.* happen, occur, take place *geh.*; **es hat sich nichts Ungewöhnliches ereignet** nothing much happened; **Ereignis** *n; -ses, -se* event; (*Vorfall*) incident; (*Sensation*) sensation; *freudiges ~ euph.* (*Geburt*) happy event; **ereignislos** *Adj.* uneventful; **Ereignislosigkeit** *f; nur Sg.* uneventfulness; **ereignisreich** *Adj.* (very) eventful; (*aufregend*) exciting

ereilen *v/t.* catch up with, overtake *lit.*; *Schicksalsschlag etc.*: befall *lit.*; *Nachricht*: reach; **der Tod hat ihn ereilt** death caught up with (*od.* overtook) him; **der Tod hat ihn in ... ereilt** he met his death in ...

Erektion *f; -, -en* erection

Eremit *m; -en, -en* hermit

ererbt *Adj.* **1.** *Besitz*: inherited; **2.** *Bio., Veranlagung etc.*: inherited, hereditary

erfahrbar *Adj.*: **~ sein** be real (*od.* tangible *od.* palpable)

erfahren¹ (*unreg.*) **I.** *v/t.* **1.** (*Kenntnis erhalten*) learn (of); (*gesagt bekommen*) hear (about), be told (about, of); (*entdecken*) find out (about); discover; **ich habe nichts davon ~ auch** nobody told me anything (*od.* about it); **sie hat es durch die Zeitung ~** she read about it in the newspaper(s); **2.** *geh. Person*: (*erleben*) experience; (*erleiden*) suffer, undergo; (*empfangen*) get; **etw. am eigenen Leibe ~** experience s.th. personally, go through s.th. o.s.; **3.** *Sache*: (*Entwicklung, Veränderung etc.*) undergo; (*Negatives*) *auch* suffer; **II.** *v/i.*: **~ von** get to know about, hear about (*od.* that ...)

erfahren² **I.** *P.P.* → **erfahren¹; II.** *Adj.* experienced (**in** + *Dat.* in), practi[s]ed (*Am.* -ced) (in); **~ in** (+ *Dat.*) (*bewandert*) *auch* well versed in; **er ist sehr ~ auch** he's got a lot of experience, he really knows the score *umg.* (*od.* what he's doing); **er ist in diesen Dingen sehr ~ auch** he's an old hand at that sort of thing; **Erfahrenheit** *f; nur Sg.* (long) experience

Erfahrung *f* **1.** (*Erlebnis*) experience; (*Kenntnis, Praxis*) experience (*nur Sg.*); *technische*: know-how; **aus (eigener) ~ kennen, sprechen**: from (one's personal *od.* one's own) experience; **~en sammeln** *od.* **machen** gain (*od.* pick up) experience; **durch ~ wird man klug** *Sprichw.* you live and learn; **durch ~ klug werden** learn the hard way; **die ~ machen, dass ...** find that ...; **ich musste die traurige ~ machen, dass ...** sadly, I found that ...; **schlechte ~en machen** have problems *od.* trouble (**mit** with), fare *geh.* badly (with); **die ~ hat gezeigt, dass ...** (past) experience has shown that ...; **da bin ich wieder um e-e ~ reicher** *allg.* you learn something new every day, you live and learn; *bei Enttäuschung*: I'll just have to put it down to experience; (*das ist mir e-e Lehre*) I suppose I have learn[t (*Am.* -ed) s.th.; *nachdrücklicher*: that's another lesson (for me); **2. in ~ bringen** learn; (*herausfinden*) find out

Erfahrungs|austausch *m* exchange of views; **sich zu e-m ~ treffen** get together (*od.* meet) to compare notes; **~bereich** *m* field (of competence *od.* special interest), (professional) experience; **~bericht** *m* *Wirts.* progress report

erfahrungsgemäß *Adv.*: **~ dauert es eine Stunde** experience has shown (*od.* shows) that (*od.* we know from experience) that it takes an hour

Erfahrungs|sache *f*: **das ist ~** it's (just) a question of experience; **~schatz** *m* store (*großer*: wealth) of experience; (*gesamter*) sum total of one's experience; **~tatsache** *f* well--known (*od.* well-established) fact; **~wert** *m* typical figure (*od.* value *od.* quantity), figure *etc.* based on experience

erfassbar *Adj.* *Daten*: recordable; *Statistik*: ascertainable; *Begriff etc.*: comprehensible, graspable, *präd. od. nachgestellt*: *auch* accessible to the understanding

erfassen *v/t.* **1.** (*packen*) seize (*auch fig.*), grasp; **von Furcht** *etc.* **erfasst werden** *fig.* be seized with (*od.* gripped by) fear *etc.*; **2.** (*mit sich reißen*) *Auto*: hit, strike, collide with; *Wirbel, Strömung etc.*: sweep (*od.* carry) away; **von den Rädern erfasst werden** be caught under the wheels; **von e-m Auto erfasst werden** be hit (*od.* knocked down, run over) by a car; **3.** *fig.* (*verstehen*) grasp, understand, appreciate, get *umg.*; (*erkennen*) realize, see; **du hast's erfasst!** *umg.* you've got it!, you've cracked it!, you've got there! *iro.*; **4.** (*mit einbeziehen*) include, cover; (*abdecken*) cover; *statistisch*: register, record, list; *zahlenmäßig*: count; (*Daten*) collect, record, file; **steuerlich ~** tax; **wir sind vermutlich erfasst** vom *Verfassungsschutz etc.*: they've probably got us down on their files *umg.*, they'll probably have a file on (each of) us; **5.** (*Text am PC*) put on disk (*od.* on the computer); *mit Scanner*: scan in; **Erfassung** *f* **1.** (*Verstehen*) understanding, comprehension; **2.** (*Registrierung*) registration, recording; **3.** *e-s Textes am PC*: putting *s.th.* on disk (*od.* on the computer), capture, input

erfechten *v/t.* (*unreg.*); (*Sieg, Anerkennung etc.*) gain, win, achieve; (*Medaille etc.*) win, carry off

erfinden *v/t.* (*unreg.*) (*etw. Neues*) invent; (*Unwahres*) invent, make up, concoct *pej.*; **er hat die Arbeit / das Pulver auch nicht erfunden** *umg.* he's not (exactly) one of the world's workers / he's not going to set the Thames (*Am.* the world) on fire; → **erfunden**; **Erfinder** *m*; *-s, -*, **~in** *f*; *-, -nen* inventor; **der ~** (+ *Gen.*) *auch* the man (*od.* woman) who invented ...;

Erfindergeist *m*; *nur Sg.* inventiveness, inventive genius, resourcefulness; **erfinderisch** *Adj.* (*findig*) inventive, resourceful; (*fantasievoll*) imaginative; (*schöpferisch*) creative; → **Not** 1

Erfindung *f* **1.** *von etwas Neuem*: invention; (*Idee*) idea, notion, concept; **e-e ~ machen** invent something; **2.** (*Erdichtetes*) invention, fabrication; **das ist reine ~** *auch* he's *etc.* made it all up, it's fiction (*od.* a fabrication) from start to finish; **Erfindungsgabe** *f*; *nur Sg.* inventive talent (*od.* genius), inventiveness; (*Fantasie*) imagination; **erfindungsreich** *Adj.* inventive, resourceful, imaginative; **Erfindungsreichtum** *m*; *nur Sg.* inventiveness, re-

sourcefulness, imaginative resources *Pl.*

erflehen *v/t.* *geh.* implore, beseech, plead for; *von Gott*: pray (to God) for

Erfolg *m*; *-(e)s, -e* **1.** (*positives Ergebnis*) success; (*Leistung*) achievement; *Wirts.* *bilanzmäßig*: profit or loss; **~ haben** succeed, be successful; **hattest du ~?** *auch* did you get what you wanted?; **keinen ~ haben** be unsuccessful, fail; **er hatte keinerlei ~ bei ihr** he didn't get anywhere with her; **er hat bei den Frauen keinen ~** he's not very successful with women, he's not much of a hit with women, he doesn't get (*Am.* hit it) off with women a lot *umg.*; **von ~ gekrönt** crowned with success; **mit/ohne ~** successfully/unsuccessfully; **mit ~ teilgenommen** passed; **~ versprechend** promising; **der ~ blieb aus** it didn't come off, things didn't work out; **ich wünsche Ihnen viel ~** I wish you every success; **viel ~!** good luck!, all the best!; **2.** (*Ausgang*) result, outcome; (*Folge*) consequence(s *Pl.*), upshot *nur Sg.*; (*Wirkung*) effect; **durchschlagender ~** decisive (*od.* emphatic) result

erfolgen *v/i.* (*sich ereignen*) happen, take place, occur; **~ auf** (+ *Akk.*) *od.* **nach** follow, come after; **es ist noch keine Antwort erfolgt** there has been no (*od.* is) no reply so far, we haven't had a (*od.* any) reply yet; **die Zahlung muss sofort ~** payment must be made immediately

erfolglos *Adj.* unsuccessful; (*fruchtlos*) fruitless; (*wirkungslos*) ineffective, ineffectual; **die Bemühungen etc. blieben ~** *auch* were to no avail; **Erfolglosigkeit** *f*; *nur Sg.* *j-s*: lack of success, run of failures; *e-r Sache*: failure; *e-s Plans*: *auch* miscarriage; (*Wirkungslosigkeit*) ineffectiveness, lack of effect

erfolgreich I. *Adj.* successful; **II.** *Adv.*: **e-e Prüfung ~ bestehen** pass (*od.* get through) an exam

Erfolgs|aussicht *f*; *mst Pl.* chance (*od.* prospect) of success; **~autor** *m*, **~autorin** *f* best-selling author; **~bilanz** *f* (*Erfolge*) list (*od.* string) of successes; (*bisherige Leistungen*) track record; *Wirts.* operating statement; **~erlebnis** *n* sense of achievement, elation *geh.* of winning; **jeder braucht mal ein ~** everyone needs a lift now and again, you have to win some of them some of the time; **~film** *m* box-office hit (*od.* success), successful film (*Am.* *auch* movie), film success; **~garantie** *f*: **es gibt keine ~** there's no guarantee of success, we're *etc.* making no promises; **~geheimnis** *n* secret behind (*od.* of) s.o.'s success

erfolgsgewohnt *Adj.* *präd. od. nachgestellt*: used (*od.* accustomed) to success (*od.* winning)

Erfolgs|honorar *n* contingent fee, payment by results; **~kontrolle** *f* performance (*od.* efficiency) review; **~kurs** *m* *umg.*: **auf ~ sein** be on one's way to the top; **~kurve** *f* *rückblickend*: rise (and fall); *aktuell*: record, performance curve; *e-r Person*: career, achievement record; **~leiter** *f* ladder of success; **~meldung** *f* *allg.* (piece of) good news; *e-e Person betreffend*: *auch* news of s.o.'s success; **~mensch** *m* high-flier, achiever, go-getter *umg.*, whizz-kid *umg. iro.*

erfolgsorientiert *Adj.* *Einzelmensch*: achievement-oriented; *Firma*: profit--oriented

Erfolgs|prämie *f* efficiency bonus, incentive payment; **~quote** *f* success rate; **~rezept** *n* recipe for success; **~schlager** *m* (top) hit, hit success; **~story** *f* *umg.* success story; **~zwang** *m*: **unter ~ stehen** be under pressure to succeed (*od.* do well)

erforderlich *Adj.* necessary; required; **unbedingt ~** essential; **~ machen** require, necessitate; **die ~en Maßnahmen ergreifen** take the necessary steps; **erforderlichenfalls** *Adv.* *Amtsspr.* if required; **erfordern** *v/t.* (*untr., hat*) require, demand, call for, necessitate *geh.*; (*Zeit*) take, require *geh.*; (*Geduld, Mut etc.*) take, require, demand; **Erfordernis** *n*; *-ses, -se*; *geh.* requirement, prerequisite, demand *mst Pl.*

erforschen *v/t.* **1.** (*untersuchen*) inquire into, investigate, study, research (into), do research on; (*Land, Weltraum*) explore; **2.** *sein Gewissen ~* examine (*od.* search) one's conscience, do a bit of soul-searching *umg.*; **Erforscher** *m*, **Erforscherin** *f* explorer; **Erforschung** *f* investigation (+ *Gen.* of, into); *wissenschaftliche*: research (into, on); *e-s Gebiets*: exploration (of)

erfragen *v/t.* ask (for), inquire (about); **zu ~ bei** apply to, inquiries should be directed to

erfreuen I. *v/t.* please, give *s.o.* pleasure; *j-s Herz* ~ gladden s.o.'s heart *lit.*, delight s.o.; **II.** *v/refl.* **1.** (*Freude empfinden*) **sich ~ an** (+ *Dat.*) enjoy, take delight in; **2.** *geh.* (*genießen*) **sich e-r Sache ~** enjoy s.th.; **sich großer Beliebtheit ~** be very popular, enjoy great popularity; **sich keines guten Rufes ~** have a dubious (*stärker*: bad) reputation; → **erfreut**

erfreulich I. *Adj.* pleasing; *Nachrichten*: good, welcome; (*ermutigend*) encouraging, heartening; **II.** *Adv.*: **es waren ~ wenig Leute da** we were *etc.* pleased to find so few people there; **es sind ~ wenig Unfälle passiert** *bei Meldung*: and it's nice to report that there were not many accidents; **ich habe ~ viel geschafft** I'm pleased at how much I got done; **Erfreuliche** *n*; *-n*, *kein Pl.*: **das ~ daran** the nice thing about it; **es gibt wenig ~s zu berichten** the news isn't very good, I'm afraid; **erfreulicherweise** *Adv.* fortunately, happily; **~ hat es geklappt** *auch* I'm glad to say it worked

erfreut I. *P.P.* → **erfreuen**; **II.** *Adj.* pleased (*über* + *Akk.* at, about), delighted (with, about, at); **sehr ~** *altm.* pleased to meet you, how do you do?; **III.** *Adv.*: **..., sagte sie ~ ...**, she said delightedly

erfrieren (*unreg.*) **I.** *v/i.* (*ist erfroren*) **1.** (*Erfrierungstod sterben, eingehen*) freeze to death; *Pflanzen*: be killed by frost; **2.** (*verderben, absterben*) *Äpfel, Ernte*: suffer frost damage; **ihm sind zwei Finger erfroren** he lost two fingers through frostbite; **mir sind die Finger erfroren** *übertreibend*: my fingers were frozen solid (*od.* to the bone); **II.** *v/t.* (*hat*): **er hat sich zwei Finger erfroren** he got frostbite on two fingers; **Erfrierung** *f* *auch Pl.* frostbite (*an* + *Dat.* on); **sich** (*Dat.*) **~en zuziehen** get frostbite, get frostbitten

erfrischen I. *v/t.* **1.** (*neu beleben*) refresh; *stärker*: revive; **2.** (*geistig anregen*) (mentally) refresh, stimulate, help *s.o.* refocus; **II.** *v/refl.* refresh o.s., take some refreshment; *durch Waschen*: freshen up; (*sich abkühlen*) cool (o.s.) down; **erfrischend I.** *Part. Präs.* → *erfrischen*; **II.** *Adj.* refreshing (*auch fig.*); *von ~er Offenheit fig.* refreshingly frank; **Erfrischung** *f* refreshment; *e-e ~ od. ~en zu sich nehmen* have (*od.* take) some refreshment

Erfrischungs|getränk *n* **1.** *alkoholfreies*: soft drink; **2.** *kühlendes*: cool (*od.* cold) drink; *~raum m* refreshment room, cafeteria; *~tuch n* wipe, moist (*od.* moistened) tissue (*od.* towelette)

erfroren I. *P.P.* → *erfrieren*; **II.** *Adj.* **1.** *Finger, Zehen etc.*: frostbitten; **2.** *umg.*: *völlig ~* (*durchgefroren*) frozen stiff

erfüllbar *Adj. Traum, Wunsch*: realizable, not impossible; *Bedingungen*: fulfillable, not unreasonable

erfüllen I. *v/t.* **1.** *auch fig.* fill (*mit* with); *i-e Worte erfüllten ihn mit Sorge/Stolz auch* what she said left him very worried / made him (*od.* his heart) swell with pride; *die Kinder ~ das Haus mit Leben* the children keep the house full of life (*od.* buzzing); *der Raum war von e-m köstlichen Duft erfüllt* the room was pervaded by an exquisite aroma; **2.** (*j-n*) (*befriedigen*) satisfy, fulfil(l); *m-e Arbeit erfüllt mich sehr* I find my work very fulfilling (*od.* satisfying); **3.** (*Aufgabe etc.*) (*entsprechen*) fulfil(l); (*Bedingung*) *auch* meet, fulfil(l), satisfy, comply with; (*Wunsch*) grant, fulfil(l); (*Erwartungen*) meet, come (*od.* live) up to; (*Pflicht, Vertrag etc.*) carry out; (*Versprechen*) keep, fulfil(l); (*Zweck*) serve, fulfil(l); *das Auto erfüllt noch s-n Zweck* the car still serves its purpose (*od.* does its job); *den Tatbestand der Nötigung etc. ~ Jur.* constitute (*od.* meet the definition of) coercion; **II.** *v/refl.* come true, be realized

erfüllt I. *P.P.* → *erfüllen*; **II.** *Adj.*: *~ von* filled with, full of; *von Begeisterung etc.*: *auch* bubbling over with; *~ von dem Wunsch zu* (+ *Inf.*) filled with (*od.* possessed by) the desire to (+ *Inf.*); *ein ~es Leben* a full (and active) life, a fulfilled life; *ein ~er Traum* a dream come true, a dream fulfilled, the fulfil(l)ment of a dream; *nicht ~e Forderungen etc.* unmet (*od.* unsatisfied) demands *etc.*

Erfüllung *f* fulfil(l)ment (*auch Befriedigung*); *in ~ gehen* come true, be fulfilled (*od.* realized); **Erfüllungsgehilfe** *m* **1.** *Jur. allg.* agent, proxy; *bei e-m Auftrag*: subcontractor; *bei e-m Verbrechen etc.*: accomplice, accessory; **2.** *fig. pej.* accomplice, creature *umg.*, (willing) tool; *j-s ~ auch* one who does the dirty work for s.o.; **Erfüllungsort** *m Wirts., Vertrag*: place of fulfil(l)ment; *Zahlung*: place of settlement

erfunden I. *P.P.* → *erfinden*; **II.** *Adj.* imaginary, fictitious, invented; *frei ~* pure invention, a complete fabrication; *das ist alles ~ auch* he's *etc.* made it all up, it's pure fabrication (*od.* wholly imaginary *od.* completely fictitious)

Erg *n*; *-s, -*; *Phys.* erg

ergänzen *v/t.* **1.** (*vervollständigen*) complete; (*weiter ausbauen*) add to, supplement; (*ersetzen*) replace; (*Lager, Vorräte*) replenish, restock; (*Summe*) make up; (*wiederherstellen*) restore; (*abrunden*) complement; *bei e-m Gespräch*: (*hinzufügen*) add; **2.** *sich od.*

einander ~ complement one another, be complementary; *sie ~ sich hervorragend* they are a perfect foil for each other; *Personen: auch* they make the perfect (man-and-wife) team

ergänzend I. *Part. Präs.* → *ergänzen*; **II.** *Adj.* (*komplementär*) complementary; (*nachträglich*) supplementary; (*zusätzlich*) additional; (*zum Ganzen gehörig*) integral; **III.** *Adv.*: *~ möchte ich noch hinzufügen, dass ...* (as a rider to that) I would just like to add that ..., I would amplify that by saying ...

Ergänzung *f* **1.** (*Vervollständigung*) completion; (*Hinzufügung*) supplementation, amplification; (*Einsetzung*) addition; (*Ersetzung*) replacement, correction; *zur ~* (+ *Gen.*) to add to, to supplement, in addition to; **2.** (*das Ergänzende*) complement (*auch Math.*); supplement; addition; *zu e-m Gesetz*: amendment; **3.** *Ling.* (*Objekt*) object; *weitS.* complement

Ergänzungs|band *m* supplement(ary volume); *~bindestrich m Ling.* (omission) hyphen; *~frage f* **1.** *Ling.* wh-question; **2.** (*Zusatzfrage*) follow-up (*od.* supplementary) question; *Parl.* supplementary; *~haushalt m* supplementary budget; *~material n* supplementary material

ergattern *v/t.* (*untr., hat*); *umg.* (manage to) get hold of, wangle, organize

ergaunern *v/t. umg.*: (*sich* [*Dat.*]) *etw. ~* get s.th. in some racket or other (*od.* through a fiddle *od.* by devious means); (*j-m etw. abluchsen*) swindle (*od.* diddle) *s.o.* out of s.th.

ergeben¹ (*unreg.*) **I.** *v/t.* **1.** (*hervorbringen*) result in; (*betragen*) come to, make; (*abwerfen*) yield, produce; (*Sinn*) make; *ergibt 4 Portionen Packungsaufschrift*: serves 4, contains approx(imately) 4 servings; *Kochrezept*: sufficient (*od.* makes enough) for 4; **2.** *Untersuchung etc.*: show, establish, prove; *es hat nichts ~ auch* nothing came of it, the results were inconclusive; **II.** *v/refl.* **1.** (*aus etw. entstehen od. folgen*) arise; *Schwierigkeiten etc.*: *auch* crop up; *es ergab sich e-e Diskussion* a discussion ensued, this (*od.* that) led to a discussion; *sich ~ aus* result (*od.* arise) from; *daraus ergibt sich, dass ...* it follows that ...; *es ergab sich, dass ...* it turned out that ...; *es hat sich so ~* it happened to work out like that; *es hat sich so ~, dass ...* it so happened that ..., as it turned out, ...; **2.** (*sich j-m, e-r Sache hingeben*) devote (*od.* dedicate) o.s. (+ *Dat.* to); (*e-m Laster*) take to (doing) *s.th.*; *stärker*: give in to *s.th.*, surrender to *s.th.*, abandon o.s. to *s.th.*; **3.** (*sich fügen*) accept *s.th.*, resign o.s. (to [doing] *s.th.*); *sich in sein Schicksal ~* resign o.s. to one's fate; **4.** *Mil. etc.*: surrender (+ *Dat.* to), give o.s. up (to); *Sport etc.*: give in; *ich ergebe mich!* I give up

ergeben² **I.** *P.P.* → *ergeben¹*; **II.** *Adj.* **1.** *e-m Schicksal*: resigned (to); *dem Laster ~ altm.* a slave to vice; **2.** (*hingebungsvoll*) devoted (+ *Dat.* to); **3.** (*treu*) loyal (+ *Dat.* to), faithful (to); *Diener*: trusty *lit.*, obedient; *Ihr sehr ~er X od. Ihr ~ster Diener X altm. Briefschluss*: (I am, Sir *etc.*,) Your obedient servant; **Ergebenheit** *f; nur Sg.* (*Hingabebereitschaft*) devotion; (*Treue*) loyalty; (*Fügsamkeit*) resignation, submissiveness, humility

Ergebnis *n*; *-ses, -se* result (*auch Sport etc.*), outcome; (*Folgen*) result, consequence(s *Pl.*); (*Punktzahl*) (final) score; *e-r Untersuchung*: findings *Pl.*, results *Pl.*, outcome; (*Lösung, Antwort*) solution, answer; (*Folgerung, Schluss*) conclusion; *zu keinem ~ führen Verhandlungen etc.*: come to nothing, be inconclusive, be (*od.* prove) unsuccessful; *das ~ war, dass sie nicht kam* as a result (*od.* the result was that) she did not come; *ich will ~se sehen* I want (to see) results; **ergebnislos** *Adj.* without result; (*erfolglos*) unsuccessful, fruitless; *~ bleiben* be (*od.* remain) unsuccessful, lead nowhere; *Gespräche, Versuch etc.*: *auch* fail

ergehen (*unreg.*) **I.** *v/i.* (*ist ergangen*) **1.** *Befehl etc.*: be issued (*an* + *Akk.* to), go out (to); *Gesetz*: come out, be promulgated *geh.*; (*geschickt werden*) be sent (to); *Jur., Urteil, Beschluss*: be passed (*od.* pronounced); *~ lassen* issue; (*Einladung*) send (*an* + *Akk.* to), extend (to *förm.*); *als Rundschreiben*: send out (to); *Jur.* (*Beschluss*) pass, pronounce, deliver; *es erging die Aufforderung an die Mitglieder zu* (+ *Inf.*) the members were called on to (+ *Inf.*); → *Gnade* 1; **2.** *etw. über sich* (*Akk.*) *~ lassen* (patiently) endure, submit to; **3.** *unpers.*: *es ist ihm schlecht ergangen* things did not go well for him, he had a bad (*od.* rough) time of it; *wie ist es dir ergangen?* how did you get on?, *Am.* how was it?, how did it go?; *mir ist's genauso ergangen* it was (exactly) the same with me, I had (just) the same experience; **II.** *v/refl.* (*hat*) **1.** *sich über* (+*Akk.*) (*ein Thema*) ~ hold forth on, expatiate on; *sich ~ in* (+ *Dat.*) indulge (at some length) in; (*Verwünschungen etc.*) utter a stream of; **2.** *lit.* take a walk (*od.* stroll)

ergiebig *Adj.* **1.** *Farbe, Waschpulver etc.*: *attr.* high-quality, high-yield, concentrated; *der Tee ist sehr ~* this tea goes a long way (*od.* is a good strong one); **2.** *Quelle, Vorkommen*: (highly) productive, rich; *Boden*: *auch* fertile; *Geschäft*: profitable, lucrative; **3.** *fig. Gespräch*: useful, productive, fruitful; *Thema*: productive, rewarding, rich, worthwhile; **Ergiebigkeit** *f*; *nur Sg.* **1.** *von Farbe etc.*: yield; **2.** *von Quelle etc.*: productiveness; *e-s Bodens*: fertility; *hohe*: richness; **3.** *e-s Geschäfts*: lucrativeness, returns *Pl.* (+ *Gen.* from); **4.** *fig. e-s Gesprächs*: usefulness; *e-s Themas*: richness, interest, stimulus value

ergießen (*unreg.*) **I.** *v/refl.*: *sich ~ in/ auf/über* (+ *Akk.*) flow (*od.* pour) into/onto/over; *sich ~ in* (+ *Akk.*) *Fluss*: flow (*od.* empty) into; *e-e Flut von Verwünschungen ergoss sich über sie fig.* she was subjected to a torrent of abuse (*od.* flood of imprecations); **II.** *v/t. lit.* pour (*in/auf/über* + *Akk.* into/onto/over)

erglühen *v/i. geh.* **1.** *Berge, Himmel etc.*: (begin to) glow, take on a (fiery) glow, catch (*od.* be on) fire *lit.*; **2.** *fig. Gesicht*: glow, blush, flush, go red (*alle*: *vor* + *Dat.* with)

Ergonomie *f*, *-*, *kein Pl.* ergonomics *Pl.* (*V. im Sg.*), human-factor engineering; **ergonomisch I.** *Adj.* ergonomic; **II.** *Adv.* ergonomically

Ergotherapie *f Med., Soziol.* ergotherapy

ergötzen *geh.* **I.** *v/t.* amuse, entertain; *(auch das Auge od. Ohr)* delight; **II.** *v/refl.:* **sich ~ an** (+ *Dat.*) enjoy; *stärker:* delight (*od.* revel) in, love; *(sich amüsieren über)* be amused by; *(e-m schönen Anblick)* feast one's eyes on; *schadenfroh:* gloat at (*od.* over); **III. Ergötzen** *n: **zu j-s Ergötzen** to s.o.'s delight

ergrauen *v/i.* turn (*od.* go) grey (*Am.* gray); **im Dienst / in Ehren ergraut sein** *fig.* have served for many years / have had a long and hono(u)rable career

ergreifen *v/t.* (*unreg.*) **1.** (*nach etw., e-r Person greifen und es/sie festhalten*) grasp; *energischer:* seize, grab; *bei Gefahr:* catch (*od.* grab *umg.*) hold of; (*Macht, Gelegenheit*) take, seize; **ein Kind bei der Hand ~** grasp (*od.* grab *umg.*) a child by the hand; → *auch* 6; **2.** (*festnehmen*) (*Dieb etc.*) seize, catch, get hold of; **3.** (*erfassen*) *Gefühle etc.:* seize, take hold of; *Flammen:* (*Haus etc.*) envelop, engulf, take hold in; *Wellen etc.:* engulf, carry *s.o.* away; **4.** (*erschüttern*) move (*od.* stir) deeply; **5.** (*überkommen*) overcome, overwhelm, carry *s.o.* away; **von Angst ergriffen werden** be seized (*od.* gripped) by fear; **6.** *fig.* (*wählen, anfangen*) (*Initiative, Maßnahme*) take; (*Beruf*) take up, begin; **von etw. Besitz ~** take possession of s.th., take s.th. over; **die Flucht ~** (turn tail and) flee *geh.*, opt for flight *lit.*; *zu Fuß:* auch run away, take to one's heels; *j-s od.* **für j-n Partei ~** come in on s.o.'s side, take up the cudgels for s.o. *umg., Am. auch* go to bat for s.o. *umg.;* **das Wort ~** (begin to) speak; **ergreifend I.** *Part. Präs.* → **ergreifen;** **II.** *Adj.* (deeply) moving, stirring; (*herzzerreißend*) heartbreaking, heart-rending; **Ergreifung** *f; mst Sg.* **e-s Verbrechers etc.:** capture; (*Verhaftung*) arrest, detention *förm.*

ergriffen I. *P.P.* → **ergreifen; II.** *Adj. und Adv.* (*bewegt*) deeply moved (**von** by); (*erschüttert*) shaken (by); **sie schwiegen ~** they were moved to silence, (for a moment) (their) feelings ran too deep for words; *iro.* there was a respectful silence; **von Panik ~** panic-stricken, in (a state of) panic; **von Trauer ~** grief-stricken, overcome with grief; **Ergriffenheit** *f; nur Sg.* (deep) emotion; **in tiefer ~** deeply moved (*od.* touched)

ergründen *v/t.* (*untr., hat*) get to the bottom of; (*Verhalten*) *auch* fathom (out); (*Ursache etc.*) find out, determine; **Ergründung** *f; mst Sg.;* (*Erklärung*) explanation (+ *Gen.* for); *e-s Rätsels:* solving

Erguss *m* **1.** discharge (*auch Physiol.*); **2.** *Geol. von Lava:* (lava) flow; **3.** (*Samenerguss*) emission, ejaculation; **4.** (*Bluterguss*) contusion, bruise; **5.** *fig. pej.* effusion, outburst, *Pl. auch* outpourings; *von Worten:* flood (*od.* torrent) (of words), tirade; *schriftlich:* screed; **~gestein** *n Geol.* volcanic (*od.* igneous) rock

erh. *Abk.* (**erhalten**) rec. (= received)

erhaben *Adj.* **1.** *bei Relief etc.:* raised, *nachgestellt:* in relief; **~e Arbeit** embossed (*od.* raised) work; **2.** (*großartig*) grand, magnificent; *stärker:* sublime; *Gedanken etc.:* lofty, noble, sublime; *Philos.* sublime; **3.** *fig.:* **~ über** (+ *Akk.*) above (doing) *s.th.*, superior to; *über Lob, Tadel:* beyond; **über jeden Verdacht ~** above suspicion; **Erhaben-**

heit *f; nur Sg.; fig.* **1.** (*Großartigkeit*) grandeur, loftiness, sublimity; **2.** (*kleine Anhöhe*) rise, area of high(er) ground; → **erhaben**

Erhalt *m; -(e)s, kein Pl.; Amtsspr.* **1.** receipt; **nach ~ Ihres Schreibens** on receiving (*od.* receipt of *förm.*) your letter; → *auch* **Empfang** 1; **2.** → **Erhaltung**

erhalten I. *v/t.* (*unreg.*) **1.** (*bekommen*) get, receive; (*erlangen, gewinnen*) get, obtain; (*Geschenk, Befehl, Name, Preis*) be given; (*Preis*) *auch* be awarded; (*Eindruck*) get, form; **e-e Geldstrafe ~** be (*od.* get *umg.*) fined, get a fine; **5 Jahre / lebenslänglich ~** be sentenced to 5 years / life imprisonment, get *umg.* (*od.* be given) 5 years / life (*od.* a life sentence); **2.** (*bewahren*) keep; (*Kunstwerke etc.*) preserve, conserve; (*Brauch*) maintain, keep up; (*Frieden*) maintain, preserve; (*retten*) save; **am Leben ~** keep *s.o.* alive; **j-n bei guter Laune ~** keep s.o. in a good mood; **sich s-n Optimismus ~** keep thinking positive(ly), stay optimistic, accentuate the positive; **3.** (*ernähren*) keep, support, maintain; **II.** *v/refl.* survive, support o.s.; **sich am Leben ~** stay alive, survive; **sich gesund ~** stay (*od.* keep) healthy (*od.* fit and well); **III.** *P.P.* → I, II; **IV.** *Adj.:* **gut/schlecht ~** in good/poor condition, well / not well preserved; **~ bleiben** survive; **noch ~ sein** remain, be left; **er bleibt uns noch ~** he'll be around for a while (*od.* some time) yet; *euph.* (*ist nicht gestorben*) he has pulled through, he's been spared

erhaltenswert *Adj. präd. od. nachgestellt:* worth preserving

erhältlich *Adj.* obtainable, available; **schwer ~** *präd. od. nachgestellt:* hard to get (hold of), hard to come by, difficult to obtain

Erhaltung *f; nur Sg.* preservation; *von Kunstwerken etc.:* auch conservation; *e-r Familie, von Häusern etc.:* upkeep, maintenance

Erhaltungs|kosten *Pl.* maintenance costs, cost *Sg.* of upkeep; **~zustand** *m* condition; **wie ist der ~?** what kind of condition is it in?; *bei alten Dingen:* auch what's its state of preservation?

erhängen *v/t. und v/refl.* hang (**sich** o.s.); **erhängt werden** be hanged; **zum Tod durch Erhängen verurteilen** sentence *s.o.* to be hanged

erhärten I. *v/t.* (*hat erhärtet*) **1.** *fig.* (*bekräftigen*) bear out, confirm, corroborate, substantiate, support; *Tatsache etc.:* auch bear out; **2.** *geh.* (*Zement etc.*) harden, set; **II.** *v/refl.* (*hat*); *Darstellung etc.:* be corroborated, be substantiated, be supported; *durch etw.:* auch be borne out by; **III.** *v/i.* (*ist*); *geh. Zement etc.:* harden, set; *Lava:* solidify; **Erhärtung** *f* **1.** *fig.* corroboration, substantiation; **2.** *von Zement etc.:* hardening, setting

erhaschen *v/t.* **1.** (*fangen*) catch, pounce on; **2.** *fig.* (*Worte*) (just) catch, pick up; **e-n flüchtigen Blick von etw. ~** catch a (fleeting) glimpse of s.th.

erheben (*unreg.*) **I.** *v/t.* **1.** (*in die Höhe heben*) (*Arm, Glas, Augen*) raise, lift (up); **s-e Hand gegen j-n ~** lift a hand against s.o.; **erhobenen Hauptes** *geh.* with head held high; **s-e Stimme ~** (*zu sprechen anfangen*) (begin to) speak, make one's voice heard; (*sich einsetzen*) speak (out) **für/gegen** in support of / against), declare o.s. (for/

against); (*s-e Meinung sagen*) express one's view(s); (*lauter sprechen*) raise one's voice, talk louder; → **erhoben;** **ein großes Geschrei ~** *umg.* make (*od.* kick up) a great fuss (**wegen** about *s.th.*), make a great song and dance about nothing; (*protestieren*) be up in arms (at once), protest furiously; *Interessengruppe etc.:* respond with a storm of protest; **2.** *lit. fig.* (*erbauen*) (*Geist, Gemüt*) elevate, edify, improve, focus on higher things; **3.** (*in e-n höheren Rang einsetzen*) elevate, promote, raise in status; *in Redewendungen häufig:* make; **ein Dorf zur Stadt ~** make a village a town, give a village town status; **etw. zum Prinzip ~** make s.th. a principle *etc.*; **zum König etc. erhoben werden** be made king *etc.*; **4.** *Math.* raise; **ins Quadrat ~** square; **zur dritten/vierten Potenz ~** cube / raise to the fourth power; **5.** (*einfordern, einziehen*) (*Steuern, Zoll etc.*) impose; (*Gebühr*) charge; (*Beiträge*) require; **6.** *bes. südd., österr.* (*amtlich feststellen*) assess, register, record; **7.** (*Daten etc.*) (*sammeln*) collect, compile, assemble; **Beweise ~** *Jur.* assemble evidence; **8.** (*vorbringen, geltend machen*) (*Bedenken*) express (*od.* voice) (**gegen** about); (*Einwand*) raise (*od.* put forward) (**gegen** to); **Beschuldigungen/Vorwürfe gegen j-n ~** criticize/reproach s.o. (**wegen** for); **Protest ~ gegen** (make a) protest against; → *auch* 1; → **Anspruch** 1, **Einspruch, Klage** 3; **II.** *v/refl.* **1.** (*aus dem Liegen od. Sitzen hochkommen*) stand up, get up, rise *förm.*, get (*od.* rise *förm.*) to one's feet; *geh.* (*Bett verlassen*) rise; **2.** (*in die Höhe steigen*) *Flugzeug, Vogel etc.:* rise, climb; *schnell, mühelos:* soar (up); **3.** (*emporragen*) *Berg, Turm etc.:* rise; *stärker:* tower (up); **sich ~ über** (+ *Akk.*) rise (*od.* tower) above; *fig.* (*hinauskommen*) rise above; (*überlegen sein*) be superior to; **4.** (*rebellieren*) *Volk:* rise (up) (**gegen** against), rebel (against), revolt (against); **5.** *fig. geh.* (*aufkommen, ausbrechen*) *Sturm:* arise, come up, break; *Wind:* rise, get up, begin to blow; *Frage:* arise, be raised; *Schwierigkeit:* arise, crop up, occur; *Zweifel etc.:* arise, begin to form; *Geschrei, Wehklagen etc.:* break out, fill the air; **es erhob sich lauter Protest** there were (*od.* this brought) loud protests

erhebend I. *Part. Präs.* → **erheben; II.** *Adj. fig. Anblick, Augenblick:* impressive, memorable, inspiring; *stärker:* exalting; *Gefühl:* inspiring, uplifting, solemn; **ein ~es Gefühl** *auch* a feeling of exaltation

erheblich I. *Adj.* **1.** (*beträchtlich*) considerable; *Schaden, Verlust:* serious, major; *Verluste: auch* heavy; *Summe:* considerable, large, significant; **2.** (*wichtig*) important; (*relevant*) relevant (**für, in** + *Dat.* to); **II.** *Adv.* considerably; **~ besser** much (*od.* significantly *geh.*) better; **~ größer/teurer etc.** much (*od.* a great deal) bigger / more expensive *etc.*; **Erheblichkeit** *f* importance; (*Relevanz*) relevance (**für, in** + *Dat.* to)

Erhebung *f* **1.** *im Boden:* (*ansteigendes Gelände*) rise, rising ground; (*kleiner Hügel*) hill(ock); (*Berg*) hill, mountain; (*Gipfel*) top, summit; **2.** (*Einziehen*) *von Steuern, Zoll:* levying, imposition; *von Gebühren:* charging; **3.** *amtliche:* (*Ermittlung*) inquiry, assessment;

E

(*Zählung*) census; *statistische*: survey; ~en statistics; **wie statistische ~en zeigen, ...** (the) statistics show that ...; **4.** *in e-n höheren Stand*: elevation, promotion (**in** + *Akk.* to); *e-r Sache*: making (**zu** to *od. ohne Präp.*); **5.** *Math.* involution; ~ **ins Quadrat** squaring; ~ **in die dritte Potenz** cubing; **6.** (*Aufstand*) uprising, popular revolt; **7.** *fig.* (*Glücksgefühl*) exaltation, heightened mood; **Erhebungszeitraum** *m Statistik*: survey period
erheischen *v/t. geh.* demand, call for; (*Respekt*) command
erheitern I. *v/t.* **1.** (*lustig stimmen*) amuse; **ich finde das wenig ~d** *iro.* I don't find that very amusing; **2.** (*aufheitern*) cheer (up); **II.** *v/refl.* **1.** *geh. Gesicht*: brighten; *stärker*: light up; *Himmel*: brighten up, clear; **2. sich ~ über** (+ *Akk.*) be amused by; **Erheiterung** *f*; *mst Sg.* amusement; **zur allgemeinen ~** to everyone's amusement
erhellen I. *v/t.* **1.** (*hell machen*) light up, illuminate; **2.** (*Farbe*) lighten; **3.** *fig.* shed (*od.* throw) light (up)on, help (to) explain; **II.** *v/refl.* **1.** brighten; *Gesicht*: *auch* light up; **2.** *fig. Problem etc.*: become clearer; **III.** *v/i. geh.*: **daraus erhellt, dass/wie** *etc.* ... from this it is evident (*od.* can be seen) that/ how *etc.* ...; **erhellend I.** *Part. Präs.* → **erhellen**; **II.** *Adj.* illuminating; **wenig ~e Äußerungen** unilluminating remarks; **Erhellung** *f e-s Raums etc.*: illumination, lighting; *des Himmels*: brightening
erhitzen I. *v/t.* **1.** heat (up); (*j-n*) make s.o. hot; **2.** *fig.* (*Leidenschaften*) arouse, turn s.o. on *umg.*; (*Fantasie*) fire; **II.** *v/refl.* **1.** get hot; **2.** *fig. Gespräch*: become heated; *Gefühle*: be (a)roused; *Person*: get worked up (*od.* excited *od.* steamed up *umg. od.* steamed up *umg.*) (**über** + *Akk.* about); **die Gemüter erhitzten sich** feelings ran (*od.* were running) high; **erhitzt I.** *P.P.* → **erhitzen**; **II.** *Adj.* **1.** hot; *Person*: *auch* flushed; **2.** *fig. Debatte*: heated; *Person*: worked up, hot under the collar *umg.*, steamed up *umg.*; **~e Gemüter** raised tempers; **Erhitzung** *f*; *mst Sg.* **1.** heating (up); **2.** *fig.* agitation, excitement
erhoben I. *P.P.* → **erheben**; **II.** *Adj.*: **mit ~er Stimme** raising his (*od.* her) voice, at the top of his (*od.* her) lungs
erhoffen *v/t.*: (**sich** [*Dat.*]) ~ hope for; (*erwarten*) expect (**von** from, of); **erhofft I.** *P.P.* → **erhoffen**; **II.** *Adj.* hoped-for, looked-for *umg.*
erhöhen I. *v/t.* **1.** (*Mauer, Damm, Zaun etc.*) raise, make higher; **2.** (*steigern*) raise, increase (**auf** + *Akk.* to; **um** by); (*verstärken*) intensify; (*verbessern*) improve (by); (*Preis*) raise, put up (**auf** + *Akk.* to; **um** by); (*Wirkung, Eindruck etc.*) enhance, heighten, strengthen, reinforce; (*Appetit*) sharpen, whet; (*Kredit*) increase; **etw. um das Doppelte/ Dreifache** *etc.* ~ double/triple (*od.* treble) s.th.; **3.** *im Rang*: promote; **4.** *Mus.* (*Ton*) sharpen (**um e-n Halbton** by a semitone, *Am. auch* half tone); **II.** *v/refl.* increase (**auf** + *Akk.* to; **um** by); *Preis etc.*: *auch* rise, go up; *Temperatur, Zahl etc.*: rise, go up; *Spannung*: grow, increase; *Wirkung etc.*: be heightened (*od.* enhanced); *Ansehen, Ruf etc.*: grow
erhöht I. *P.P.* → **erhöhen**; **II.** *Adj.* **1.** *Plattform etc.*: raised, elevated; **2.** *Preise etc.*: increased, higher; *Span-*

nung, Bewusstsein etc.: *auch* heightened; **~e Temperatur / ~en Blutdruck haben** have (*od.* be running) a temperature / have high blood pressure; **mit ~er Aufmerksamkeit fahren** drive extra carefully; **in ~em Maße** more, to a greater extent; **3.** *Mus.*: **~es C** C sharp
Erhöhung *f* **1.** *e-r Mauer etc.*: raising; **2.** (*Anhöhe*) hill, (area of) high ground; (*Hügel*) hill(ock); **3.** (*Steigerung*) increase (+ *Gen.* in); *der Qualität*: improvement (in); *e-r Wirkung etc.*: enhancement, heightening (of); *der Löhne*: rise (in), *Am.* raise; *der Preise*: increase, rise (in); → **erhöhen**; **4.** *Mus.* sharpening (+ *Gen.* of; **um** by)
erholen *v/refl.* **1.** recover (*auch fig.*) (**von** from); *von Krankheit*: *auch* recuperate (from, after); *nach der Arbeit*: (take a) rest, have a rest; (*sich entspannen*) relax, unwind; *im Urlaub*: have a (good) rest, unwind properly; **sich vom Schreck** *etc.* ~ *fig.* get over (*od.* recover from) the shock *etc.*; **2.** *Wirts., Kurse etc.*: recover, rally, stage a recovery; *Börse*: *auch* pick up; *Wirtschaft*: pick up, be on the rebound
erholsam *Adj.* restful, relaxing; **ich wünsche Ihnen e-n ~en Urlaub** *auch* I hope you come back from your holiday refreshed
erholt I. *P.P.* → **erholen**; **II.** *Adj.* rested; **du siehst gut ~ aus** *auch* you look your old self again
Erholung *f*; *nur Sg.* **1.** (*Wiedererlangen der Kraft*) recovery; (*Genesung*) recuperation, convalescence; **er ist zur ~ nach X** he's gone to X to convalesce; **2.** (*Entspannung*) rest, relaxation; (*Freizeitgestaltung*) recreation; (*Ferien*) holiday, *Am.* vacation; **wir fahren zur ~ hin** we're going there for a holiday (*Am.* vacation) (*od.* to relax); **gute ~!** have a good rest (*od.* break); **für ~ suchende Städter** for city-dwellers (*od.* urbanites) in search of a break; **~ Suchende** → **Erholungsuchende**; **3.** *Wirts.* recovery, rally
Erholungsaufenthalt *m* holiday, *Am.* vacation
erholungsbedürftig *Adj.* in need of (*od.* needing) a rest (*od.* holiday, *Am.* vacation)
Erholungs|gebiet *n* recreational area; (*Urlaubsgebiet*) popular holiday area; *bes. schönes*: *auch* beauty spot; **~heim** *n* (*für Rekonvaleszente*) rest (*od.* convalescent) home; (*Ferienheim*) holiday centre, *Am.* vacation center (*od.* home); **~pause** *f* rest, breather, break; **~raum** *m* recreational and leisure zone; **~reise** *f* holiday (*Am.* vacation) trip, pleasure trip
Erholungsuchende *m, f*; *-n, -n* holidaymaker, *Am.* vacationer; *Wirts.* holiday (*Am.* vacation) customer; *Pl. auch* holiday market *Sg., Am.* tourist trade *Sg.*
Erholungs|urlaub *m* holiday, *Am.* vacation; *Med.* convalescent leave; **~wert** *m*; *nur Sg.* recreational value
erhören *v/t.* **1.** *geh.* (*Bitte*) grant; (*Flehen*) respond to; (*Gebet*) hear, answer; **2.** *geh.*: *j-n* ~ *Gott*: hear (*od.* answer) s.o.'s prayers; *altm. Verehrer*: give in to s.o., accept s.o.'s suit; **Erhörung** *f*; *mst Sg.*: **die ~ e-s Gebets** the answering of a prayer
erigieren *v/i. Physiol.* become erect; **erigiert I.** *P.P.* → **erigieren**; **II.** *Adj.* erect

Erika *f*; *-, -s*; *Bot.* heather, erica
erinnern I. *v/t.*: *j-n* ~ **an** (+ *Akk.*) remind s.o. of; *Sache*: *auch* put s.o. in mind of; **j-n daran ~, etw. zu tun** remind s.o. to do s.th.; **könntest du mich daran ~?** could you remind me (*od.* give me a reminder) (about that)?; **II.** *v/refl.* remember; **sich ~ an** (+ *Akk.*) (*od.* **sich ~** + *Gen. geh.*) remember (*od.* recall, recollect) *s.o./s.th.*; (*zurückdenken an*) think back to, call to mind; **wenn ich mich recht erinnere** if I remember rightly; **jetzt erinnere ich mich vage** it's slowly coming back to me now; **III.** *v/i.* ~ **an** (+ *Akk.*) *Sache*: be reminiscent of, remind one of, recall; **er erinnert an s-n Onkel** he has a strong resemblance to his uncle, he reminds me (*od.* one) of his uncle, he has a lot of his uncle in him *umg.*; **ich erinnere (nur) an ...** (*Tatsachen etc.*) I would remind you *etc.* ..., we should not forget ..., suffice it to recall ...
Erinnerung *f* **1.** *Eindruck*: memory (**an** + *Akk.* of), recollection (of); **e-e ~ wird wach / verblasst** a memory comes back (*od.* stirs *od.* awakens) / fades; **in guter ~ haben** have pleasant (*stärker*: fond) memories of; **ich habe keine ~ daran** I can't (*od.* don't) remember it at all; **s-n ~en nachhängen** bei e-m *Gespräch*: be lost (for a moment) in one's memories; *gewohnheitsmäßig*: dwell on one's memories, live in the past; *stärker*: have nothing left but one's memories; **2.** *nur Sg.*; (*Gedächtnis*) memory, powers *Pl.* of recall (*od.* recollection); **in ~ behalten** remember, keep in mind; **sich** (*Dat.*) **etw. in ~ rufen** call s.th. to mind, (try to) remember s.th.; **sich** (**bei j-m**) **in ~ bringen wollen** want to be kept in mind by s.o. (*od.* want to remind s.o. of one's existence); **3.** *nur Sg.*; (*Gedenken*) memory; *feierlich*: remembrance; **zur ~ an** (+ *Akk.*) in memory (*od.* remembrance) of; **4.** (*Erinnerungsstück*) keepsake, memento; *mst Wirts.*: souvenir; **als ~ an** (+ *Akk.*) as a memento of; **5.** ~**en** (*Memoiren*) reminiscences; *bes. Buch*: memoirs; **6.** *euph.* (*Mahnschreiben*) reminder; → *auch* **Gedächtnis**
Erinnerungs|foto *n von Urlaub etc.*: souvenir photo (*od.* snapshot); *von Verstorbenen etc.*: cherished photo(graph); **~lücke** *f* gap in one's memory; **~vermögen** *n* memory, powers *Pl.* of recall (*od.* recollection), ability to remember; **~wert** *m*; *nur Sg.* sentimental value
Erinnyen *Pl. Myth.* Furies, Erinyes
Eritrea (*n*); *-s*; *Geog.* Eritrea; **Eritreer** *m*; *-s, -*, **Eritreerin** *f*; *-, -nen* Eritrean; **eritreisch** *Adj.* Eritrean
erkalten *v/i.* **1.** *Lava etc.*: cool (down); *Speise etc.*: *auch* get cold; *Leiche*: grow cold; *messbar*: cool; **2.** *fig. Person*: grow (*od.* turn) cool; *Gefühle*: cool off; *Herz*: turn to stone *lit.*, become cold; *Liebe*: wither
erkälten I. *v/refl.* catch (a) cold, get a cold *umg.* (**beim Skifahren** *etc.* [while] skiing *etc.*); **II.** *v/t.*: **sich** (*Dat.*) **die Blase** *etc.* ~ catch a chill in one's bladder *etc.*; **erkältet I.** *P.P.* → **erkälten**; **II.** *Adj.*: ~ **sein** have a cold; **er ist ~** *auch* he's got a cold *umg.*; **stark ~ sein** have a bad (*od.* heavy) cold; **ich bin furchtbar ~** I've got a rotten (*od.* filthy) cold (*od.* a stinker of a cold *umg.*)

E

Erkältung f cold; Med. common cold; **leichte/starke** ~ slight/bad (od. heavy) cold; **e-e ~ bekommen** od. **sich** (Dat.) **e-e ~ holen** catch (a) cold, get a cold umg.; **Erkältungsgefahr** f; nur Sg. risk of catching (a) cold, exposure to cold-type infections; **Erkältungskrankheiten** Pl. coughs and colds, colds and flu

erkämpfen v/t. (kämpfen um) fight for; (gewinnen) achieve, win (through to); Sport win; **etw. hart ~ müssen** have to really fight (od. fight all the way) for s.th., have a real battle on one's hands to attain s.th., have to fight tooth and nail for s.th.

erkaufen v/t.: (**sich** [Dat.]) **etw. ~ mit Geld**: buy euph., obtain (od. secure) through a bribe (od. through bribery), bribe one's way (in)to; fig. **mit Opfern**: buy, secure (**mit** at the cost [od. price] of); **etw. teuer ~ müssen** pay dearly for s.th., (have to) pay a high price for s.th.; **der Sieg war teuer erkauft** it was an expensive (od. costly) victory (Sport: auch win; **die Freiheit mit s-r Ehre ~** pay for one's freedom with one's hono(u)r, buy (one's) freedom at the cost of (one's) hono(u)r, barter (one's) hono(u)r for (one's) freedom

erkennbar Adj. **1.** (wahrnehmbar) perceptible; (sichtbar) visible; gerade noch: discernible; **in der Ferne war die Stadt deutlich ~** you could clearly make out the town; **2.** (zum Wiedererkennen) recognizable; **ohne ~en Grund** for no apparent reason; **3.** Philos. cognizable

erkennen (unreg.) **I.** v/t. **1.** (ausmachen) optisch: make out, see; (Schrift) make out, read; (entdecken) detect, spot; **2.** (wieder) ~ recognize (**an** + Dat. by, from umg.), know (by); (identifizieren) identify; Med. diagnose; ~ **lassen** show, reveal; indirekt: suggest; **zu ~ geben** indicate, give one to understand; **sich zu ~ geben** identify o.s.; nachträglich etc.: disclose (od. reveal) one's identity, say who one is umg.; fig. come out into the open; **man erkennt ihn an s-m Akzent** auch his accent gives him away; **aus ihrem Verhalten war deutlich zu ~, dass ...** her behavio(u)r left no one in any doubt that ..., from the way she behaved (od. acted), it was evident (od. clear) that ...; **3.** (einsehen, verstehen) realize, see, appreciate, understand, recognize; (durchschauen) see through; **etw. als s-e Pflicht ~** acknowledge (od. accept) s.th. as one's duty, accept that s.th. is one's duty; **den Ernst der Lage nicht ~** fail to see how serious the situation is, underrate the seriousness of the situation; **erkenne dich selbst!** know thyself (od. yourself)!; **4.** Jur.: **j-n für schuldig/unschuldig ~** find s.o. guilty / not guilty, return verdict of guilty / a not guilty verdict on s.o.; **etw. für Recht ~** pronounce (od. make a ruling) on s.th.; **II.** v/i. Jur.: **in e-r Sache ~** decide in a matter; **auf e-e Geldstrafe ~** impose a fine; **auf 5 Jahre Haft ~** impose a sentence of [od. sentence s.o. to) 5 years (imprisonment); **auf Freispruch ~** acquit (s.o.), find s.o. not guilty, return a not guilty verdict (on s.o.)

erkenntlich Adj. **1.** geh.: **j-m ~ sein** od. **sich** (j-m) ~ **zeigen** show one's appreciation (**für** for, of) (od. gratitude) (for); **2.** → **erkennbar, Erkenntlich-**

keit f geh. **1.** nur Sg.; appreciation, gratitude; **2.** konkret: mark (od. token) of one's (od. s.o.'s) appreciation

Erkenntnis[1] f; -, -se **1.** (Wissen) auch Pl. knowledge; (Entdeckung) discovery, finding; Pl. (Informationen) findings; **neueste ~se** the latest findings, latest (od. most recent) research Sg.; **2.** (Einsicht) realization, insight, appreciation; (Verständnis) understanding; (Gedanke) idea, notion; **zu der ~ gelangen, dass ...** (come to) realize (od. recognize) that ...; **3.** Philos. cognition; → **Baum** 1

Erkenntnis[2] n; -ses, -se; österr. od. altm. (Gerichtsbescheid) verdict, judg(e)ment, finding, ruling; (Urteil) e-s Richters: judg(e)ment; der Geschworenen: verdict, finding

Erkenntnis|fähigkeit f cognitive powers Pl.; ♀**reich** Adj. informative, instructive; stärker: eye-opening; ~**stand** m state of (our etc.) knowledge, level of knowledge; ~**theorie** f epistemology

Erkennung f; nur Sg. recognition; identification

Erkennungsdienst m (police) records department, etwa criminal records Pl.; (Spurensicherung) crime (od. forensic) lab; (Mitarbeiterstab) (team of) forensic experts (od. people); **erkennungsdienstlich** Adj. und Adv.: **j-n ~ behandeln** get s.o. checked out in Criminal Records, Am. book s.o.; ~ **erfasst** on file in (od. known to) Criminal Records, Am. known to the police

Erkennungs|marke f identity disc (Am. disk); ~**melodie** f signature tune; ~**wort** n password; ~**zeichen** n **1. als ~ werde ich e-e rote Fliege tragen** you'll recognize me by my red bow tie, I'll be wearing a red bow tie (to identify myself); **2.** Med. symptom; **3.** (Abzeichen) badge; **4.** Flug. markings Pl., insignia Pl. (V. im Sg. od. Pl.); **5.** Radio: station identification signal, call-sign

Erker m; -s, - oriel; ~**fenster** n oriel (od. bay) window

erkiesen v/t.; erkiest, erkor, erkoren; Präsens selten; altm. geh. choose (**als** od. **zu** as)

erklärbar Adj. explainable (**durch** by); **es ist ~ durch** auch it can be explained by; **das ist rational nicht mehr ~** there is no rational explanation for it

erklären I. v/t. **1.** Person: explain (j-m to s.o.); (begründen) explain (**mit** by); **sie erklärte i-e Abwesenheit mit Krankheit** she explained her absence by saying that she had been ill, she gave illness as the reason for her absence; **der Absturz lässt sich durch Materialermüdung ~** the crash can be put down to metal fatigue; ~ **Sie mir bitte, warum ...** could you tell me why ...; **ich kann es mir nicht ~** I don't understand it, it's a mystery to me, I can't make anything of it; **ich erkläre mir das so: ...** this is how I explain (od. understand) it:, this is how it seems to me:, the way I see it is: ...; **2.** Sache: account for, explain; Beispiel: illustrate; **3.** (verkünden) declare; (Unabhängigkeit) auch proclaim; (Rücktritt etc.) announce; (Einverständnis) give; **j-m s-e Liebe ~** declare one's love for s.o.; **e-m Land den Krieg ~** declare war on a country; **hiermit erkläre ich die Sitzung für eröffnet** I hereby declare this meeting open; →

Austritt 1, **Beitritt** etc.; **4.** (bezeichnen, nennen) declare (**für** [to be] s.th.), pronounce; **j-n für tot ~** (Patienten, Vermissten) pronounce s.o. dead; **5.** in Interview etc.: say; Jur. (aussagen) declare, state; **II.** v/refl. **1.** Sache: be explained (**aus** od. **durch** by), explain itself (by); **das erklärt sich daraus, dass ...** that can be explained by the fact that ..., the reason for that is that ...; **das erklärt sich von selbst** that is self-explanatory; **2.** Person: explain o.s., give an explanation; **3.** altm., lit.: **sich** (j-m) ~ **Liebeserklärung**: declare o.s. (to s.o.); **4. sich ~ für/gegen** declare o.s. for/against; **5. sich für etw. ~** (bezeichnen) declare oneself (to be) s.th.; **sich einverstanden ~** signify one's agreement; **sich mit etw. zufrieden ~** express one's satisfaction with s.th.; **III.** v/i.: **sie kann gut ~** she's good at explaining things

erklärend I. Part. Präs. → **erklären**; **II.** Adj. explanatory; **III.** Adv.: ~ **hinzufügen** add by way of explanation

erklärlich Adj. **1.** → **erklärbar**; **2.** (verständlich) understandable; (offensichtlich) evident, obvious; **aus ~en Gründen** understandably, for obvious reasons; **erklärlicherweise** Adv. understandably, for obvious reasons

erklärt I. P.P. → **erklären**; **II.** Adj. Gegner etc.: declared, professed, avowed; **der ~e Liebling des Publikums** in Konzert etc.: the obvious favo(u)rite with the audience (od. weitS. the public); **sein ~es Ziel ist es zu** (+ Inf.) it is his stated objective (od. declared aim) to (+ Inf.); **erklärtermaßen** Adv. avowedly, openly

Erklärung f **1.** explanation (**für** of, for); (Gründe) auch reasons Pl.; **das ist die ~ für** that explains, that is the explanation for; **zur ~** (+ Gen.) by way of explanation (for); **2.** (Aussage, Feststellung) declaration, statement (auch Pol.); **e-e ~ abgeben** auch Pol. make a statement (**zu** on)

Erklärungsbedarf m: **es besteht ~** there is need for explanation, there's a need to explain; **erklärungsbedürftig** Adj. in need of (an) explanation

Erklärungs|notstand m: **im ~ sein** have a lot of explaining to do; (nicht wissen, wie man etw. erklären soll) be at a loss to know how to explain s.th.; ~**versuch** m attempt at explanation (od. to explain s.th.)

erklecklich Adj. altm. considerable, hefty; **ein ~es Sümmchen** auch a tidy sum

erklettern v/t. climb (up)

erklimmen v/t. (unreg.); geh. **1.** climb; (Gipfel) auch climb up to; **2.** fig. reach

erklingen v/i. (unreg.) sound; laut: ring out; **Gelächter erklang** you could hear the sound of laughter; lauter: laughter rang out; **ein Lied ~ lassen** strike up a tune

erkor Imperf. → **erkiesen**; **erkoren I.** P.P. → **erkiesen**; **II.** Adj. chosen (**als** od. **zu** for, as), select

erkranken v/i. **1.** Person: fall ill od. sick (**an** + Dat. with); ~ **an** (+ Dat.) auch get; bes. an Infektionskrankheiten: come down with; **erkrankt sein an** (+ Dat.) have, be laid up with umg.; **2.** Organ, Pflanze, Tier etc.: become diseased (**an** + Dat. with); **Erkrankung** f illness, sickness; e-s Organs: disease

erkunden v/t. **1.** (Gelände) explore;

E

Mil. reconnoit|re (*Am.* -er); **2.** (*Versteck, Geheimnis etc.*) discover, find out; (*Möglichkeiten etc.*) investigate, scout out

erkundigen *v/refl.* inquire (*bes. Brit.* enquire) (**über** + *Akk.*, **nach** about), ask (about); (*Erkundigungen einholen*) make inquiries (*bes. Brit.* enquiries); **sich nach etw. ~** *in der Bücherei etc.*: ask for s.th.; **sich nach dem Weg** *etc.* **~** ask the way *etc.*; **sich nach j-m** *etc.* **~** inquire (*od.* enquire) after s.o.('s health) *etc.*; **ich werde mich ~** *auch* I'll try and find out; **Erkundigung** *f* inquiry (*bes. Brit.* enquiry); **~en einziehen** *od.* **einholen** make inquiries (*od.* enquiries) (**über** + *Akk.* about)

Erkundung *f* **1.** *von Gelände*: exploration; *Mil.* reconnaissance; **auf ~ gehen** *Mil.* go on reconnaissance; *fig. in e-m Ort, der einem noch fremd ist*: go exploring, scout around; **2.** *von Tatsachen etc.*: finding out

Erkundungs|fahrt *f in noch fremder Umgebung*: exploratory trip; *e-r Untersuchungskommission etc.*: fact-finding mission; *Mil.* reconnaissance mission; **~flug** *m Mil.* reconnaissance flight; **~tour** *f*: **auf ~ gehen** (go and) have a look around

Erlagschein *m österr.* paying-in (*Am.* deposit) slip

erlahmen *v/i.* **1.** tire, grow weary; **2.** *geh. fig. Geschäft, Sturm*: slacken; *Eifer, Interesse etc.*: flag, wane

erlangen *v/t.* **1.** (*bekommen, gewinnen*) gain; **2.** (*erreichen*) attain; (*Alter, Höhe, Ziel etc.*) reach; **Geltung ~** become valid; → **wiedererlangen**; **Erlangung** *f, nur Sg.* attainment; **nach ~** (+ *Gen.*) on reaching (*od.* attaining) s.th.

Erlass *m*; -es, -e *od. österr.* **Erlässe** **1.** (*Verordnung*) decree, edict; (*Gesetz*) law; **2.** (*Befreiung*) dispensation, exemption (+ *Gen.* from); *von Schulden, e-r Strafe etc.*: remission; **3.** *nur Sg.*; (*das Erlassen*) issuing; *e-s Gesetzes*: enactment

erlassen *v/t.* (*unreg.*) **1.** (*Gebühren, Schulden*) waive; (*Strafe etc.*) remit; **j-m etw. ~** (*Schulden, Strafe, Verpflichtung*) release s.o. from s.th.; (*Verpflichtung*) *auch* let s.o. off from s.th.; (*Prüfung*) exempt s.o. from s.th.; **die Antwort auf die letzte Frage wurde uns ~** we were excused from answering (*od.* we didn't have to answer) the last question; **2.** (*Haftbefehl, Verordnung etc.*) issue; (*Gesetz*) enact; (*Amnestie*) proclaim; (*Aufruf*) issue

erlauben *v/t.* **1.** allow; *formell*: permit (*j-m etw.* s.o. to do s.th.); **j-m ~, etw. zu tun** *auch* give s.o. permission to do s.th.; **ich erlaube nicht, dass sie mit dem Motorrad fahren** I won't allow them to go (*od.* I won't let them go) by motorbike; *stärker*: I refuse to let them go by motorbike; **~ Sie?** may I?; **wenn Sie ~** if you don't mind; **~ Sie mal!** *od.* **was ~ Sie sich?** what do you think you're doing?, who do you think you are?; **ist es erlaubt zu ...** (+ *Inf.*)? can one ...?, is it all right to (+ *Inf.*)?; **es ist alles erlaubt** you can do what you want (*od.* whatever you like), anything goes (around here); **innerhalb der Grenzen des Erlaubten** within the accepted limits; **2.** *fig. Sache*: permit; **wenn es das Wetter erlaubt** weather permitting; **m-e Zeit erlaubt es (mir) nicht** I haven't got (*od.* don't have) (the) time for it; **3.** *sich* (*Dat.*) *etw.* **~** (*gönnen*) treat o.s. to

s.th.; *sich* (*Dat.*) **~ zu** (+ *Inf.*) take the liberty of (+ *Ger.*); (*sich erdreisten*) *auch* dare (to) (+ *Inf.*); *sich* (*Dat.*) **Frechheiten** *od.* **Vertraulichkeiten ~** take liberties; **für ... erlaube ich mir zu berechnen:** ... *förm., etwa*: we calculated our costs for ... as follows: ...; **wenn ich mir die Bemerkung ~ darf** if you don't mind my saying, if I may be permitted to say so *förm.*; **er kann sich** (*Dat.*) **das ~** *weitS.* he can get away with it; **er glaubt, er kann sich** (*Dat.*) **alles ~** he thinks he can get away with anything; **ich kann mir nicht ~ zu** (+ *Inf.*) I can't afford to (+ *Inf.*); *sich* (*Dat.*) **e-n Scherz mit j-m ~** pull s.o.'s leg, have a little fun with s.o.

Erlaubnis *f*; -, -se; *mst Sg.* **1.** permission; (*Ermächtigung*) authority; **j-n um ~ bitten** ask s.o.'s (*od.* s.o. for) permission (**etw. tun zu dürfen** to do s.th.); **mit Ihrer freundlichen ~ würde ich gern ...** if you would be kind enough to permit me (*od.* with your kind permission), I should like ...; **2.** **behördliche ~** (*Schein*) licen|ce (*Am.* -se), permit

erlaucht *Adj. geh. altm. od. iro.* illustrious

Erlaucht *f*; -, -en; *altm.*: **Seine/Ihre ~** His Lordship / Her Ladyship; **Eure ~** Your Lordship/Ladyship

erläutern *v/t.* explain (*j-m* to s.o.); **durch Beispiele ~** illustrate; **erläuternd I.** *Part. Präs.* → **erläutern**; **II.** *Adj.* explanatory; *Beispiele ec.*: illustrative; **III.** *Adv.*: **~ hinzufügen** add by way of explanation; **Erläuterung** *f* explanation; (*Anmerkung*) (explanatory) note, annotation; **mit ~en versehen(e Ausgabe etc.)** annotated (edition *etc.*)

Erle *f*, -, -n; *Bot.* alder

erleben *v/t.* **1.** experience; (*bes. Schlimmes*) *auch* go through; (*mit ansehen*) see, witness; (*Abenteuer, schöne Tage etc.*) have; **er hat viel erlebt** (*gesehen*) he's seen a lot of the world, he's been about (*od.* around) a bit *umg.*; (*ausprobiert*) he's done all sorts of things; (*gelitten*) he's been through a lot; **ich habe etwas Seltsames erlebt** I've had a strange (*od.* weird) experience; **ich habe es oft erlebt(, dass ...)** I've often seen it happen (that ...); **so aggressiv etc. habe ich sie noch nie erlebt** I've never known her to be so aggressive *etc.*; **ich möchte etwas ~!** I want to have a good time (*od.* a bit of fun); **wir werden es ja ~!** we'll see!; **das möchte ich ~!** *skeptisch*: I'd like to see that, I'll believe that when I see it; **das muss man einfach erlebt haben!** (*es ist bzw. war fantastisch*) you had to be there; *als Tipp*: you really mustn't miss it, *Am.* you've got to be there; *um es nachvollziehen zu können*: you've got to have been through it yourself; **2.** *umg., in Drohungen*: **na, du kannst was ~!** you just wait!; **die kann was ~!** she's in for it; *stärker*: she won't know what's hit her; **sonst kannst du was ~!** or else!; **3.** (*noch miterleben*) live to see; **dass ich das noch ~ darf!** I never thought I'd (live to) see the day; **du wirst es nie ~, mich rauchen zu sehen** you won't ever catch me smoking; **4.** *auf e-e Sache bezogen*: have, see; **die Wirtschaft erlebt gerade e-n Aufschwung** the economy is currently experiencing an upturn; **das Land erlebte e-e Zeit des**

Friedens the country enjoyed a time of peace; **das Buch erlebte sechs Auflagen** the book went through six editions; **II.** *v/refl. geh.*: **sich ~ als** feel oneself to be

Erlebensfall *m bei Lebensversicherung*: **im ~** in case of survival

Erlebnis *n*; -ses, -se experience; (*Ereignis*) event; (*Abenteuer*) adventure; **ein großes ~** a tremendous experience; **das war ein ~!** that was quite an experience (*od.* quite something); **das schönste ~ war ...** the nicest (*od.* best) part (*od.* thing about it) was ...

Erlebnis|... *im Subst.* experience ..., adventure ...; **~bad** *n* adventure pool; **~erzählung** *f Päd.* essay (*od.* composition) based on personal experience

Erlebnishunger *m* thirst for adventure; **erlebnishungrig** *Adj.* thirsty for adventure

Erlebnispark *m* adventure (*Am.* amusement) park, theme park

erlebnisreich *Adj.* eventful, exciting

Erlebniswelt *f Psych.*: **die ~ des Kindes** the experiential world of the child

erlebt I. *P.P.* → **erleben**; **II.** *Adj.* *Geschichte etc.*: real-life ..., true; **~e Rede** *Lit.* interior (*od.* inner) monolog(ue)

erledigen I. *v/t.* **1.** (*beenden*) finish (off); **das ist für mich erledigt** that's all over and done with as far as I'm concerned; **damit war der Fall für sie erledigt** that was all there was to it as far as she was concerned; **du bist für mich erledigt** *umg.* I'm through with you; **2.** (*sich kümmern um*) do, deal with, take care of, see to; **würden Sie das für mich ~?** would you do that for me?; **wird gleich erledigt!** *umg.* right away, will do, *Am.* you got it; **das wäre erledigt** that's that; *wann holst du die Post?* - **schon erledigt!** (I've) done it, it's done, *Brit. auch* sorted! *umg.*; **3.** (*hinter sich bringen*) get through with, get s.th. out of the way; **Einkäufe ~** go shopping, do the (*od.* some) shopping; **ich habe in der Stadt einiges zu ~** I have a few things to do (*od.* see to) in town; **4.** (*Frage, Geschäft etc.*) settle; (*Auftrag*) carry out; (*abtun*) (*Thema etc.*) dispense with; **5.** *umg.*: **j-n ~** *allg.* finish s.o. off; (*erschöpfen*) *auch* wear s.o. out; (*ruinieren*) *auch* ruin s.o.; (*umbringen*) *auch* do s.o. in; **II.** *v/refl.*: **sich von selbst ~** take care of itself; **die Sache hat sich inzwischen erledigt** that's been taken care of now; **damit ~ sich die übrigen Punkte** that takes care of the remaining points

erledigt I. *P.P.* → **erledigen**; **II.** *Adj.* **1.** finished, done, settled; **~! Stempel:** closed, actioned; **~e Fälle** *Jur.* closed cases; **2.** *umg.* (*erschöpft*) whacked, bushed; (*ruiniert*) done for, finished; **ich bin ~** *allg. auch* I've had it

Erledigung *f* **1.** *nur Sg.*; *von Aufgaben etc.*: handling, dealing with; *e-s Geschäfts etc.*: settlement; **für die sofortige ~ e-r Sache sorgen** see to it that s.th. is done immediately; **zur umgehenden ~** for immediate attention; **in ~ Ihres Auftrags** *etc. förm.* in fulfil(l)ment of your order; **2.** **einige ~en in der Stadt haben** have a few things to do (*od.* see to) in town

erlegen *v/t.* **1.** *Jägerspr.* shoot; **2.** *österr.* (*Gebühren*) pay

...erlei *Adj.* of ... different kinds; **zwanzigerlei** of twenty different kinds

erleichtern I. *v/t.* **1.** (*Gewicht, Last*) lighten (**um** by); **2.** *fig.* (*Bürde, Gewis-*

sen, Not, Schmerz) ease; *(Not, Schmerz)* auch relieve; *(j-n)* relieve; **sich** *(Dat.)* **das Herz ~** unburden one's heart; **es erleichtert mich zu hören, dass ...** I am relieved to hear that ...; **3.** *fig. (Arbeit, Verständnis etc.)* make easier; *(vereinfachen)* facilitate; **das erleichtert vieles** that makes things a lot easier; **4.** *umg. hum.:* **j-n um** *s-e Brieftasche etc.* **~** relieve s.o. of; **II.** *v/refl.* **1.** unburden o.s.; **2.** *umg. (Kleidungsstücke ausziehen)* make o.s. comfortable (by taking off outer clothing); **3.** *euph. (s-e Notdurft verrichten)* relieve o.s.; **III.** *v/i.:* **weine nur, das erleichtert** have a good cry, it'll make you feel better

erleichtert I. *P.P.* → **erleichtern**; **II.** *Adj.* relieved *(über + Akk.* about); **III.** *Adv.:* **~ aufatmen** breathe *(od.* heave) a sigh of relief

Erleichterung *f* **1.** *nur Sg.; (Beruhigung, Linderung)* relief *(über + Akk.* about); **voller ~** with relief; **j-m ~ verschaffen** give s.o. relief; **zu m-r großen ~** much to my relief; **zur ~ der Schmerzen** to relieve *(od.* ease) the pain; **2.** *(Vereinfachung)* simplification; *(Verbesserung)* alleviation; *(Hilfe)* help; **es stellt e-e große ~ dar** it makes things much easier

erleiden *v/t. (unreg.)* suffer; *(Verlust, Verletzung) auch* sustain; *(Rückfall etc.)* have, suffer; *(durchleben)* go through; **den Tod ~** die, meet one's death *lit.;* → **Schiffbruch**

Erlenmeyerkolben *m Chem.* Erlenmeyer flask

erlernbar *Adj.* learnable; **es ist ~** it can be learnt *(Am.* learned), you can learn it; **leicht ~** easy to learn *(od.* pick up); **erlernen** *v/t. (untr., hat); (Beruf, Handwerk, Sprache etc.)* learn

erlesen *Adj.* select, choice; *(vorzüglich)* exquisite; **ein ~er Kreis** a select circle; **Erlesenheit** *f; nur Sg.* selectness, choiceness; exquisiteness

erleuchten *v/t.* **1.** light up, illuminate; **2.** *fig.* enlighten; **Erleuchtung** *f* **1.** *nur Sg.* illumination; **2.** *fig.* enlightenment; *(Einfall)* inspiration, brainwave *umg.*

erliegen I. *v/i. (unreg., ist)* **1.** *e-r Versuchung:* give in to, succumb to; *e-m Gegner:* be defeated by; *e-m Irrtum ~* be the victim of an error, be misled; **2.** *(sterben an)* die of *(od.* from); *(zum Opfer fallen)* fall victim to; **II. Erliegen** *n:* **zum Erliegen kommen** grind to a halt; **zum Erliegen bringen** bring to a standstill, paraly|se *(Am.* -ze)

erlischt *Präsens* → **erlöschen**

Erlkönig *m* **1.** *Lit.* erlking; **2.** *Mot. umg.* mystery model

erlogen *Adj. präd.* not true; *(erfunden) attr.* made-up ...; *präd.* made up; **das ist von Anfang bis Ende ~** there's not a word of truth in it, it's a pack of lies *umg.;* → **erstunken**

Erlös *m; -es, -e* proceeds *Pl.; (Reingewinn)* net profit(s *Pl.);* **vom ~ des Basars wollen wir ... kaufen** with the money we made at the bazaar, we're going to buy ...

erlosch *Imperf.* → **erlöschen**; **erloschen I.** *P.P.* → **erlöschen**; **II.** *Adj.* **1.** extinct; **2.** *Vertrag etc.:* expired; *Gesetz, Plan:* defunct; **3.** *Blick, Gefühl etc.:* dead; **4.** *Geschlecht etc.:* extinct, defunct

erlöschen *v/i.: erlischt, erlosch, ist erloschen* **1.** *Feuer, Licht etc.:* go out; *Vulkan:* become extinct; **2.** *Anspruch:* ex-

pire, lapse; *Firma:* cease to exist; *Konto:* be closed ; *Mitgliedschaft:* lapse; *Patent:* expire, lapse; *Vertrag etc.:* expire; **3.** *Geschlecht, Name etc.:* die out; **4.** *fig. Augen:* grow dim; *Lächeln, Leidenschaft:* die; *(Leben:* be extinguished

Erlöschen *n; -s, kein Pl.* **1.** *e-s Vulkans:* extinction; **zum ~ bringen** extinguish; **2.** *(Ablauf)* expiry, *Am.* expiration

erlösen *v/t.* **1.** *(retten)* rescue, save *(aus* from); *aus Gefangenschaft etc.:* release, free; **2.** *euph.:* **ein Tier von s-n Qualen ~** put an animal out of its misery; **von s-n Leiden erlöst werden** be released from one's sufferings; **sie ist erlöst** her sufferings are over; **3.** *Wirtsch. altm., als Reingewinn:* net; **4.** *Reli.* save, redeem; **und erlöse uns von dem Bösen** and deliver us from evil; **erlösend I.** *Part. Präs.* → **erlösen**; **II.** *Adj. fig.:* **er sprach endlich das ~e Wort** he finally put us *etc.* out of our *etc.* misery; **Erlöser** *m; -s, -* **1.** *Reli.* Savio(u)r, Redeemer; **2.** *(Befreier)* liberator; *(Retter)* rescuer; **erlöst I.** *P.P.* → **erlösen**; **II.** *Adj. (erleichtert)* relieved; **wie ~ sein** *od.* **sich ~ fühlen** experience a great feeling of release *(od.* relief); **Erlösung** *f; mst Sg.* **1.** *Reli.* redemption, salvation; **2.** *(Rettung)* rescue; *(Befreiung)* release *(aus od. von* from); *(Erleichterung)* relief; **der Tod war e-e ~ für sie** death was a merciful release for her

ermächtigen *v/t.* authorize *(zu* to + *Inf.),* give (official) permission (to + *Inf.);* **Ermächtigung** *f* **1.** *Vorgang:* authorization *(zu* to); *(Befugnis)* authority (to); **2.** *(Urkunde)* warrant; **Ermächtigungsgesetz** *n hist.* Enabling Act (of 1933)

ermahnen *v/t.* admonish, exhort *(j-n zur Vorsicht etc.* s.o. to be careful *etc.); (drängen)* urge; *(warnen)* caution, warn; *Sport* give s.o. a warning; **Ermahnung** *f* admonition, exhortation; *(Warnung)* warning *(auch Sport); (Rüge)* rebuke

Ermangelung *f geh.:* **in ~** *(+ Gen.)* for want *(od.* lack) of, in the absence of; **in ~ e-s Besseren** for want *(od.* lack) of anything better

ermäßigen I. *v/t.* reduce, lower, cut; **II.** *v/refl.* come down (in price); *Preis:* be reduced, be cut *(auf + Akk.* to; *um* by); **ermäßigt I.** *P.P.* → **ermäßigen**; **II.** *Adj.* reduced; **zu ~en Preisen** at reduced prices; *Fahrkarten etc.: auch* at reduced rates; **Ermäßigung** *f* reduction, cut *(von* of); **mit e-r ~ von 15%** *od.* **mit 15% ~** at a reduction *(od.* discount) of 15 per cent *(bes. Am.* percent)

ermatten I. *v/t. (hat ermattet); geh.* tire (out); *(erschöpfen)* wear out; **II.** *v/i. (ist)* **1.** *Person, Tier:* tire; **2.** *fig. (nachlassen)* slacken; *Interesse etc.:* flag; **ermattet I.** *P.P.* → **ermatten**; **II.** *Adj.* tired; *(erschöpft) attr.* worn-out ..., *präd.* worn out; *geistig:* weary, jaded; **Ermattung** *f; nur Sg.* fatigue, weariness

ermessen *v/t. (unreg.); (abschätzen)* assess, ga(u)ge; *(beurteilen)* judge; *(erwägen)* consider; *(begreifen)* realize, understand, appreciate, conceive; *(sich vorstellen)* imagine; *(folgern)* infer, conclude *(aus* from)

Ermessen *n; -s, kein Pl.* judg(e)ment; *(freies)* **~** discretion; **nach m-m ~** as I see it, in my opinion *(od.* estimation); **nach eigenem ~ handeln** act as one sees fit; **das steht nicht in s-m ~** that's

not within his discretion, that's not for him to decide; **das liegt ganz in Ihrem ~ auch** it's entirely up to you; **nach bestem ~** to the best of one's judg(e)ment; **nach menschlichem ~** as far as is humanly possible to tell, in all probability

Ermessens|frage *f* matter of opinion; **~spielraum** *m* latitude

ermitteln I. *v/t.* **1.** *(feststellen)* find out, ascertain, establish; *(bestimmen)* determine; *(j-s Adresse, Schuldigen)* discover; *(Aufenthaltsort etc.)* locate; *(Anrufer)* trace; *(Herkunft)* establish; **j-s Identität ~** identify s.o.; **2.** *(Sieger etc.) durch Wettkampf:* decide; **3.** *(errechnen)* calculate; **II.** *v/i. polizeilich:* investigate, carry out investigations *(gegen j-n:* concerning), hold an inquiry; **in e-m Fall ~** investigate a case; **Ermittler** *m; -s, -,* **Ermittlerin** *f; -, -nen* investigator; **Ermittlung** *f* **1.** *(Feststellung)* establishment; *(Bestimmung)* determination; **~en** *(Feststellungen)* findings; **2.** *(Untersuchung)* investigation, inquiry *(+ Gen. od. in + Dat.* into; *über + Akk.* about); **~en anstellen über** *(+ Akk.)* make inquiries *(bes. Brit.* enquiries) about, investigate; **Ermittlungs|arbeit** *f* investigatory work, investigations; **die ~ behindern** hamper the investigations; **~ausschuss** *m Pol.* fact-finding committee; **~beamte** *m,* **~beamtin** *f* investigator; **~stand** *m* state of the investigations *(od.* the inquiry); **~verfahren** *n Jur.* preliminary proceedings *Pl.,* judicial inquiry; **das ~ einstellen** drop the charge

ermöglichen *v/t.* make s.th. possible, enable s.th. (to be done *etc.); (gestatten)* allow; **den Bau e-s Flughafens ~** make it possible to build an airport, enable an airport to be built; **wenn es sich ~ lässt** if it can be arranged, if it is at all possible

ermorden *v/t.* murder; *durch Attentat:* assassinate; **Ermordete** *m, f; -n, -n* (murder) victim; **Ermordung** *f* murder; *(Attentat)* assassination

ermüden I. *v/t. (hat ermüdet)* tire, wear s.o. out; **II.** *v/i. (ist)* **1.** *Person:* tire, get tired; **2.** **langes Stillsitzen ermüdet** sitting still for a long time makes you feel tired; **3.** *Tech. Material:* fatigue; **ermüdend I.** *Part. Präs.* → **ermüden**; **II.** *Adj.* tiring; *(Arbeit etc.) auch* tedious, wearisome; **Ermüdung** *f; mst Sg.* tiredness; *auch Tech.* fatigue; **vor ~ einschlafen** fall asleep from exhaustion

Ermüdungserscheinung *f* sign of tiredness *(auch Tech.* fatigue)

ermuntern *v/t.* **1.** encourage *(zu + Inf.* to + *Inf.); (anregen)* stimulate (to + *Inf.);* **2.** *(beleben)* get s.o. going (again); **ermunternd I.** *Part. Präs.* → **ermuntern**; **II.** *Adj.* encouraging; **~e Worte** *auch* words of encouragement; **Ermunterung** *f* encouragement

ermutigen *v/t.* encourage *(zu + Inf.* to + *Inf.);* give s.o. courage; **j-n ~ zu** (+ *Inf.)* give s.o. the courage to (+ *Inf.);* **ermutigend I.** *Part. Präs.* → **ermutigen**; **II.** *Adj.* encouraging, reassuring; **~e Worte** *auch* words of encouragement; **Ermutigung** *f* encouragement; **zu s-r ~** to encourage him

ernähren I. *v/t.* **1.** feed, nourish; **künstlich ernährt werden** be fed artificially *(od.* intravenously); → **ernährt**; **2.** *(erhalten)* support, keep; **von m-m Gehalt kann ich keine Familie ~** I can't feed a family on my salary; **dieser Beruf ernährt s-n Mann** there's a good living to be made from this job; **II.** *v/refl.*: **sich ~ von 1.** live on; *Tier: auch* feed on; **2.** *fig.* make a living by (+ *Ger.*); **davon kann ich mich kaum ~** I can hardly survive (*od.* get by) on that; **Ernährer** *m*; *-s*, *-*, **Ernährerin** *f*; *-*, *-nen* e-r *Familie*: earner, breadwinner; **ernährt I.** *P.P.* → **ernähren**; **II.** *Adj.*: **gut ~** well fed; **schlecht ~** malnourished; **Ernährung** *f*; *nur Sg.* **1.** (*Nahrung*) food; *bes. Med.* nutrition; *spezielle*: diet; **schlechte ~** poor diet; **2.** (*das Ernähren*) feeding; **schlechte ~** (*Unterernährung*) malnutrition; **3.** (*Unterhalt*) maintenance

Ernährungs|berater *m*, **~beraterin** *f* nutrition consultant; **~beratung** *f* dietary advice; **⊆bewusst** *Adj.* nutrition-conscious; **~fehler** *m* bad (*od.* unhealthy) eating habit; *Pl. auch* bad (*od.* unhealthy) diet *Sg.*; **~gewohnheiten** *Pl.* eating habits; **~lage** *f* food situation; **~störung** *f* nutritional disorder; *Med.* dystrophy; **~weise** *f* **1.** eating habits *Pl.*; **2.** (*Ernährung*) nutrition; *spezielle*: diet; **~wissenschaft** *f*, *nur Sg.* dietetics *Pl.* (*V. im Sg.*), nutritional science; **~zustand** *m*: **in e-m guten/schlechten ~ sein** be well/poorly nourished (*od.* fed)

ernennen *v/t.* (*unreg.*) appoint; **er wurde zum Vorsitzenden ernannt** he was appointed (*od.* made, elected) chairman; **Ernennung** *f* appointment; **s-e ~ zum Konsul** his appointment as (*od.* to the post of) consul; **Ernennungsurkunde** *f* letter of appointment

erneuerbar *Adj.* **1.** *Teile*: renewable, replaceable; **2.** *Ökol., Energien*: renewable; **Erneuerer** *m*; *-s*, *-*, **Erneuerin** *f*; *-*, *-nen* reviver; **der ~ dieser Bewegung** *auch* the man who revitalized this movement; **erneuern I.** *v/t.* **1.** (*Batterie, Reifen, Verband etc.*) renew, replace; (*wechseln*) change; **2.** (*reparieren*) repair, mend; (*Dach, Haus*) renovate, *Am. auch* rehabilitate, rehab *umg.*; (*Gemälde*) restore; **3.** (*Versprechen, Vertrag*) renew; (*wiederholen*) repeat; (*Ausweis, Lizenz, Patent etc.*) renew; (*System*) reform; **4.** *fig.* (*Bekanntschaft, Freundschaft*) revive; **II.** *v/refl.* be renewed; (*sich regenerieren*) regenerate; **Erneuerung** *f* renewal; replacement; repair; renovation; rehabilitation; restoration; revival; → **erneuern**

erneut I. *Adj.* renewed, new; (*wiederholt*) renewed, repeated; *Versuch: auch* fresh; **II.** *Adv.* once more (*od.* again); **~ Ärger bekommen** run into fresh trouble

erniedrigen I. *v/t.* **1.** (*entwürdigen*) degrade; (*demütigen*) humiliate; **2.** (*reduzieren*) lower; **3.** *Mus.* flatten; **II.** *v/refl.* demean o.s. (**vor j-m** in front of s.o.); **sich** (*dazu*) **~, etw. zu tun** lower o.s. (*od.* stoop) to do s.th.; **erniedrigend I.** *Part. Präs.* → **erniedrigen**; **II.** *Adj.* humiliating, degrading, demeaning; **Erniedrigung** *f* **1.** degradation; (*Demütigung*) humiliation; **2.** *Mus.* flattening; **3.** *von Preisen*: lowering

ernst I. *Adj.* **1.** *Musik, Person, Worte etc.*: serious; (*feierlich*) solemn, grave; (*streng*) severe; (*wichtig*) grave; **~es Gesicht** serious expression (*od.* face), straight face; **~ bleiben** keep a straight face; **j-m ist** (*es*) **~** (**mit etw.**) s.o. is serious (about s.th.); **~e**

Absichten haben have hono(u)rable intentions; **2.** (*wichtig, bedrohlich*) serious, grave; **sich ~e Gedanken machen über** (+ *Akk.*) be really worried about; **es ist doch hoffentlich nichts Ernstes?** I hope it's nothing serious?; **jetzt wird's ~!** this is where it gets serious, this is where we get down to the nitty gritty; **II.** *Adv.* seriously *etc.*; → I; **~ nehmen** take seriously; **ein ~ zu nehmendes Problem** *etc.* a serious problem; **ein ~ zu nehmender Gegner** an opponent to be reckoned with; **ich meine es ~** I'm serious (**mit** about), I mean it, I'm not joking; **das war nicht ~ gemeint** he *etc.* was *etc.* only joking, it was *etc.* (said) tongue-in-cheek; **~ gemeint** *Ratschlag etc.*: serious, genuine, seriously (*od.* sincerely) meant; **es steht ~ um** things aren't looking too good for; → **tierisch** II, → *auch* **ernsthaft**

Ernst *m*; *-es, kein Pl.* **1.** seriousness, earnest; *Einstellung*: seriousness, earnestness; (*Würdigkeit*) gravity, solemnity; **allen ~es** in all seriousness; **es ist mein voller/blutiger ~** I'm being really/deadly serious; **wollen Sie im ~ od. allen ~es behaupten ...?** do you really mean to say ...?; **im ~?** seriously?, you're kidding *umg.*; **ganz im ~!** (*Spaß beiseite*) seriously, though; no, seriously (now); **das kann doch nicht dein ~ sein!** you cannot (*od.* can't) be serious!, you're joking, of course; you don't really mean that, do you?; **~ machen mit** *e-r Absicht, e-m Plan etc.*: go through with; *mit e-r Drohung*: carry out; **jetzt wird es endlich ~ mit dem Bau der Straße** now at last they're actually going to get down to building the road; **2.** (*Wichtigkeit, Bedrohlichkeit*) seriousness, gravity; **der ~ des Lebens** the serious side of life; **jetzt beginnt für dich der ~ des Lebens** life is going to get serious for you from now on; **jetzt beginnt wieder der ~ des Lebens** life begins in earnest again, it's back to the grindstone (again) *umg.*; → **tierisch** I 3

Ernstfall *m* emergency; **im ~** in case of emergency; (*wenn es schlimm wird*) if (the) worst comes to (the) worst; *Mil.* in the event of a war; **auf den ~ vorbereitet** prepared for an (*od.* any) emergency

ernsthaft I. *Adj.* **1.** serious; **ich mache mir ~e Sorgen um ihn** I'm seriously worried about him; **2.** *Absicht, Wunsch etc.*: serious, genuine; **II.** *Adv. krank*: seriously; **~ besorgt** genuinely (*od.* seriously) worried; **Ernsthaftigkeit** *f*; *nur Sg.* e-r *Person, Sache*: seriousness; *e-r Sache: auch* serious nature (+ *Gen.* of)

ernstlich I. *Adj.* **1.** *Risiko, Versuch, Zweifel etc.*: serious; **2.** *Wunsch*: sincere; **II.** *Adv.* seriously; (*aufrichtig*) genuinely; **sonst bin ich dir ~ böse!** or else I'll be really angry with you; **~ in Gefahr sein** be in real danger; → *auch* **ernsthaft** II

Ernte *f*; *-*, *-n*; *Agr.* **1.** harvest (*auch fig.*); **während der ~** during (the) harvest, at harvest time; **der Tod hielt reiche/schreckliche** *etc.* **~ geh.** *fig.* the death toll was enormous/terrible *etc.*; **2.** (*Ertrag*) crop; **die ~ an Äpfeln/Getreide** *etc.* the apple/grain *etc.* harvest (*od.* crop); **die ~ einbringen** bring in (*od.* gather) the harvest; **j-m ist die ~ verhagelt** *umg. fig.* s.o.'s hopes have come to nothing

Ernte|arbeit *f* harvest(ing); **~arbeiter** *m*, **~arbeiterin** *f* harvester; (*Wanderarbeiter[in]*) migrant worker; **~ausfall** *m* crop failure; **~dankfest** *n Brit.* harvest festival, *Am.* Thanksgiving (Day)

erntefrisch *Adj.* farm-fresh, garden-fresh

ernten I. *v/t.* **1.** harvest, reap; (*Obst*) pick; *umg. vom Baum herab*: pick (the apples *etc.* from); **2.** *fig.* (*Ruhm, Applaus etc.*) earn, win; **Undank ~** get nothing but ingratitude; **Spott ~** be laughed at, be(come) a laughing stock; **Lohn ~** reap a reward (*od.* rewards); **die Früchte s-r Arbeit ~** reap the rewards of one's labo(u)r; **gegen diesen Gegner gab es nichts zu ~** there was nothing to be gained by taking on this opponent, this opponent simply didn't give him/her/them *etc.* a look-in (*Am.* a chance) *umg.*; **II.** *v/i.* harvest; **wer ~ will, muss auch säen** *Sprichw.* to reap, one must first have sown

erntereif *Adj.* ready for harvesting/picking

Ernte|schäden *Pl.* crop damage *Sg.*; **~zeit** *f* harvest (time)

ernüchtern *v/t.* **1.** sober up; **2.** *fig.* bring *s.o.* down to earth again; **ernüchternd I.** *Part. Präs.* → **ernüchtern**; **II.** *Adj.* sobering; **III.** *Adv.*: **~ auf j-n wirken** have a sobering effect on s.o.; **Ernüchterung** *f* **1.** sobering-up; **2.** *fig.* disillusionment; (*Enttäuschung*) disappointment

Eroberer *m*; *-s*, *-*, **Eroberin** *f*; *-*, *-nen* conqueror; **erobern** *v/t.* **1.** (*Land*) conquer; (*Festung, Stadt*) seize, capture, take; **im Sturm ~** take by storm; **2.** *fig.* (*Frau, Herz*) win, conquer; (*Macht*) gain; (*mit Gewalt*) seize; **j-n / die Herzen im Sturm ~** sweep s.o. off his (*od.* her) feet / capture everybody's heart; **3.** *fig.*: **sich** (*Dat.*) *etw.* **~** *Sport* gain, win; (*Sympathien*) win; *umg. hum.* (*Eintrittskarten, Sitzplatz etc.*) manage to get hold of; **Eroberung** *f* conquest (*auch hum. Person*); *e-r Stadt etc.*: capture; **e-e ~ machen** *fig.* make a conquest; **auf ~en aus sein** *od.* **ausgehen** *umg. hum.* be aiming (*od.* set out) to make a few conquests

Eroberungs|feldzug *m* campaign of conquest; **~krieg** *m* war of conquest

eröffnen I. *v/t.* **1.** (*Autobahn, Fluglinie, Geschäft etc.*) open; *feierlich: auch* inaugurate; (*Geschäft, Praxis*) open up, start, set up; **wieder ~** reopen; **2.** (*Ausstellung, Fluglinie, Konto, Saison etc.*) open; (*Diskussion, Saison etc.*) *auch* start off; **das Feuer** (**wieder**) **~** (re)open fire, start firing (again); **3.** *Jur.* (*Testament*) open, read; (*Verfahren*) open; **das** *od.* **ein Konkursverfahren ~** institute bankruptcy proceedings; **4.** *Med.* (*Bauchhöhle etc.*) open (up); (*Geschwür*) lance; **5.** **j-m etw. ~** (*mitteilen*) disclose s.th. to s.o., inform s.o. of s.th.; **6.** **j-m neue Möglichkeiten/Perspektiven** *etc.* **~** open (up) new possibilities/perspectives *etc.* for s.o.; **II.** *v/i. Börse, Geschäft etc.*: open; **III.** *vt/i. Schach*: open (the game); **IV.** *v/refl.* **1.** *Möglichkeit etc.*: present itself; **2.** *geh.*: **sich j-m ~** take s.o. into one's confidence

Eröffnung *f* **1.** opening (*auch Schach*); *feierliche*: inauguration; **2.** (*Mitteilung*) disclosure; **j-m e-e ~ machen** reveal (*od.* disclose) s.th. to s.o.

Eröffnungs|angebot *n* introductory offer; **~ansprache** *f* inaugural ad-

E

dress; **~beschluss** *m Jur.* order to proceed; *Konkursverfahren:* bankruptcy order; **~bilanz** *f Wirts.* opening balance sheet; **~feier** *f* opening ceremony; **~feierlichkeiten** *Pl.* opening ceremonies; **~kurs** *m Wirts.* opening quotation; **~phase** *f Med., bei Geburt:* dilation (phase), first stage of labo(u)r; **~sitzung** *f* introductory meeting; *Parl.* opening session; **~spiel** *n* **1.** *Schach:* opening; **2.** *Sport* opening game (*od.* match); **~tag** *m* opening day; **~variante** *f Schach:* variant opening; **~veranstaltung** *f* first event; **~wehen** *Pl. Med.* first-stage contractions

erogen *Adj.:* **~e Zone** erogenous zone

erörtern *v/t. geh.* discuss; *ausführlich* **~** discuss in detail; **Erörterung** *f* **1.** discussion; **2.** *Päd.* (*Aufsatz*) (discursive) essay

Eros *m; -, kein Pl.; Myth. und fig.* Eros; **~center** *n* licensed brothel

Erosion *f; -, -en; Geol.* erosion; **Erosionsschäden** *Pl.* damage *Sg.* caused by erosion; **Erosionsschutz** *m Ökol.* measures to protect against erosion

Erotik *f; -, kein Pl.* **1.** (*Sinnlichkeit*) sensuality; *stärker:* eroticism; **2.** *euph.* (*Sexualität*) sexuality; **3.** (*Eros*) Eros; **Erotika** *Pl.* erotica; (*Literatur*) *auch* erotic (*od. euph.* adult) literature *Sg.*; **erotisch** *Adj.* **1.** (*sinnlich*) sensual; *stärker:* erotic; **2.** *euph.* (*sexuell*) sexual

Erpel *m; -s, -; Orn.* drake

erpicht *Adj.:* **~ auf** (+ *Akk.*) very keen on (*Am.* eager about); *darauf* **~ sein zu** (+ *Inf.*) be bent on (+ *Ger.*), be desperate to (+ *Inf.*) *umg.*

erpressbar *Adj.:* **~ sein** be open (*od.* susceptible) to blackmail; *j-n* **~ machen** lay s.o. open (*od.* make s.o. susceptible) to blackmail

erpressen *v/t.* **1.** (*j-n*) blackmail (*mit* over; *zu* + *Inf.* into + *Ger.*); **2.** (*etw.*) extort (*von* from); *von j-m e-e Unterschrift / ein Zugeständnis etc.* **~** blackmail s.o. into signing *s.th.* / making a concession *etc.*

Erpresser *m; -s, -* blackmailer; **~bande** *f* gang of blackmailers; **~brief** *m* blackmail letter

Erpresserin *f; -, -nen* blackmailer

erpresserisch *Adj. attr.* blackmailing ...; *Preis, Methode:* extortionate; *in* **~er Absicht** with a view to blackmail(-ing s.o.)

Erpressermethoden *Pl.* blackmail *Sg.*

Erpressung *f e-r Person:* blackmail; (*das Erpressen*) blackmailing; *von Geld etc.:* extortion; *räuberische* **~** *Jur.* extortion by means of force (*od.* under threat of force)

Erpressungsversuch *m* blackmail attempt

erproben *v/t.* try (out), test, put to the test; **erprobt I.** *P.P.* → *erproben;* **II.** *Adj.* **1.** *Sache:* well-tried, tried and tested; *klinisch* **~** clinically tested; *in* **~er Manier** in the tried and tested fashion (*od.* manner); **2.** (*erfahren*) experienced; (*zuverlässig*) reliable; **Erprobung** *f* trial, test; **Erprobungsphase** *f* test phase; *befindet sich noch in der* **~** is still undergoing tests (*Maschine, Fahrzeug etc.:* trial runs)

erquicken *v/t. und v/refl. geh.* refresh (*sich* o.s.); revive; **erquicklich** *Adj. geh.* pleasant; *Anblick etc.:* uplifting; *Rede etc.: auch* edifying; *wenig* **~** *iro.* not exactly edifying

Errata *Pl. Druck.* errata

erraten *v/t.* (*unreg.*) guess; *du hast's* **~***!*

you've guessed (it)

erratisch I. *Adj. Geol.* erratic; **~er Block** erratic (block); **II.** *Adv.* erratically

errechenbar *Adj.* calculable

errechnen I. *v/t.* work out, calculate; *sich* (*Dat.*) *s-e Chancen etc.* **~** work out one's chances *etc.* (for oneself); **II.** *v/refl. Amtsspr.:* *daraus errechnet sich ...* as a result we arrive at ...

erregbar *Adj.* excitable (*auch Etech.*); (*reizbar*) irritable; (*empfindlich*) (over)sensitive, touchy; *er ist leicht* **~** *auch* he gets upset (*od.* angry) easily, he is irascible; **Erregbarkeit** *f; nur Sg.* excitability; irritability; oversensitiveness; → *erregbar*

erregen I. *v/t.* **1.** (*j-n*) excite, get *s.o.* excited; *sexuell: auch* arouse; *freudig:* thrill; **2.** (*aufregen*) excite, upset; (*reizen*) irritate; (*wütend machen*) infuriate; *die Gemüter* **~** cause quite a stir; *stärker:* get people's blood (*od.* tempers) up; **3.** (*verursachen*) (*Aufsehen, Heiterkeit, Krebs etc.*) cause; (*Unruhe*) create; (*Neugier, Zorn etc.*) provoke; (*Argwohn, Interesse, Leidenschaft, Mitleid, Neugier, Verdacht etc.*) arouse; (*Aufmerksamkeit, Interesse*) attract; (*Bewunderung, Eifersucht, Interesse, Verdacht*) excite; (*j-s Abscheu, Ekel, Zweifel etc.*) fill s.o. with; *Anstoß od. Ärgernis* **~** cause (*od.* give) offen|ce (*Am.* -se) (*bei* to); *j-s Gefallen/Missfallen* **~** please/displease s.o., arouse s.o.'s pleasure/displeasure; **4.** *Etech.* excite, energize; **II.** *v/refl.* get excited; *stärker:* get all worked up (*über* + *Akk.* about); *zürnend: auch* get angry; → *erregt;* **erregend I.** *Part. Präs.* → *erregen;* **II.** *Adj.* exciting; *sexuell: auch* on-turning *umg.*; **~es Mittel** *Med.* stimulant

Erreger *m; -s, -* **1.** *Med.* pathogen, agent, virus; (*Keim*) germ; **2.** (*Ursache*) cause; **3.** *Etech.* exciter; **~stamm** *m* strain of virus, virus strain

erregt I. *P.P.* → *erregen;* **II.** *Adj.* **1.** excited, agitated; *sexuell:* excited, aroused; *freudig* **~** thrilled; *in* **~em Zustand** excited, in a state of excitement; *sexuell:* sexually aroused; **2.** *Debatte, Gemüter etc.:* heated; *Zeiten:* turbulent; **3.** *Etech.* excited, energized; **III.** *Adv.:* *es ging* **~** *zu* *Debatte etc.:* feelings ran high; *Ereignis etc.:* there was quite a stir (*od.* commotion); **Erregtheit** *f; nur Sg.* excitement; → *Erregung*

Erregung *f* **1.** *Zustand:* (state of) excitement, agitation; (*Zorn*) anger; **2.** *e-s Nervs etc.:* stimulation; *sexuelle:* arousal; **3.** (*Verursachung*) causing; creation; provocation; arousing; → *erregen; wegen* **~** *öffentlichen Ärgernisses Jur.* for creating a public disturbance; **4.** *Etech.* excitation; **Erregungszustand** *m* state of excitement (*bes. sexuell:* arousal); *emotional:* emotional state

erreichbar *Adj.* **1.** (*auch in* **~er Nähe**) within reach; (*zugänglich*) accessible; *leicht* **~ sein** be within easy reach, be easy to get to; *zu Fuß / mit dem Wagen leicht* **~** within easy walking/driving distance; **2.** *fig. Ziel etc.:* attainable, within (one's) reach; **3.** *Person:* available, there, contactable; *er ist nie* **~** you just can't get hold of him; *ich bin telefonisch* **~** (*habe Telefon*) I'm on the phone, *Am.* I have a phone; *ich bin von ... bis ... telefonisch* **~** you can reach me (*od.* get in touch

with me) by phone between ... and ...; **Erreichbarkeit** *f; nur Sg.* **1.** accessibility; reachability; **2.** attainability; **3.** availability

erreichen *v/t.* **1.** *mit der Hand:* reach; **2.** (*Ort*) reach, arrive at; (*auch Ufer*) get to; (*es schaffen bis*) make (it to *od.* as far as); *vom Bahnhof* (*aus*) *leicht zu* **~** within easy reach of the station; → *auch erreichbar* 1; **3.** (*Zug etc.*) catch; (*auch Anschluss*) make; (*einholen*) catch up with; *der Brief erreichte ihn nicht mehr* the letter didn't get to him in time; **4.** *j-n* (*telefonisch*) **~** get hold of s.o. (on the phone); *zu* **~** → *erreichbar* 3; **5.** *fig.* (*hingelangen*) reach; (*schaffen*) achieve; *stärker:* attain; (*erlangen*) obtain, get; (*gleichkommen*) equal, match; (*ein gewisses Maß*) come up to; *ein hohes Alter* **~** live to a ripe old age; *etwas* **~** (*Erfolg haben*) get somewhere, get results, be successful; *hast du* (*bei ihm*) *etwas erreicht?* did you get anywhere (with him)?; *ich erreichte zumindest, dass er mich anhörte* I managed at least to get him to listen to me; *damit erreichst du nur, dass ich wütend werde* the only thing you'll achieve (by that) is to make me lose my temper; → *Höhepunkt* 2, *Klassenziel etc.*

Erreichung *f; nur Sg.* **1.** *bei/nach* **~** *von* on/after reaching *od.* arriving at (*od.* in); **2.** *fig.* attainment; *mit od. nach* **~** *des 50. Lebensjahres* on reaching the age of 50

erretten *v/t.; geh.* save, rescue (*von, aus* from); **Erretter** *m,* **Erretterin** *f geh.* rescuer; *Reli.* Savio(u)r, Redeemer; **Errettung** *f geh.* rescue; *Reli.* → *Erlösung* 1

errichten *v/t.* **1.** (*Statue, Bühne, Barrikaden etc.*) put up, erect; (*Gerüst*) put up; (*Gebäude*) erect, build; (*Zelt*) put up; **2.** *fig.* (*Barrieren etc.*) put up, set up, erect; **3.** *fig.* (*gründen*) found; *bes. Wirts.* set up; **4.** *Jur.* (*Testament*) draw up; **Errichtung** *f* **1.** building; erection; **2.** *fig.* founding; establishment; → *errichten*

erringen *v/t.* (*unreg.*); (*Ansehen, Mehrheit, j-s Vertrauen*) gain, win; *den Sieg* **~** gain victory, win; *e-n Erfolg* **~** be successful; *den ersten Platz* **~** take (*od.* win) first place; **Erringung** *f; nur Sg.* *e-r Leistung etc.:* achievement; → *Errungenschaft*

erröten *v/i. geh., vor Verlegenheit etc.:* blush, go red; *vor Aufregung, Stolz etc.:* flush (*vor* + *Dat. od.* **aus** with; *über* + *Akk.* at)

errungen I. *P.P.* → *erringen;* **II.** *Adj.:* *hart* **~** (*Sieg, Erfolg etc.*) hard-won, hard-earned; **Errungenschaft** *f* **1.** achievement; (*Großtat*) feat; **~en der Technik** technological achievements (*od.* advances); *technische* **~en** (*Geräte*) technical gadgets; *die neuesten technischen* **~en** the latest technology; **2.** *umg. hum.* (*Anschaffung*) acquisition; *ihre neueste* **~** *heißt Peter fig.* her latest conquest is named Peter

Ersatz *m; nur Sg.* **1.** *auch Person:* substitute; *permanenter:* replacement; *Stoff: auch* surrogate, ersatz *pej.*; *Teil:* replacement part; *mitgeliefertes:* spare (part); *Mil.* replacements *Pl.*; **~ schaffen** find a replacement (*od.* replacement) (*für* for); **2.** (*Vergütung*) compensation; (*Entschädigung*) indemnification; (*Schadenersatz*) damages *Pl.*; (*Wiedergutmachung*) reparation;

E

(*Rückerstattung*) restitution; **als ~ für** by way of compensation for; (*im Tausch*) in exchange (*od.* return) for; **~ leisten für** compensate (*od.* make amends) for; **3.** → *Ersetzung;* **~anspruch** *m* claim for compensation; *Ersatzansprüche stellen* claim compensation; **~bank** *f; Pl. -bänke; Sport* substitutes' bench; **~befriedigung** *f Psych.* vicarious satisfaction, compensation *umg.;* **~brille** *f* spare pair of glasses (*od.* spectacles)

Ersatzdienst *m* alternative (*od.* community) service (for conscientious objectors); **~ leisten** do alternative (*od.* community) service (**als** as); **⚲pflichtig** *Adj.* liable for alternative (*od.* community) service

Ersatz|droge *f* substitute drug; **~handlung** *f Psych.* (act of) compensation; **~kaffee** *m* coffee substitute, ersatz coffee; **~(kranken)kasse** *f* health insurance; **~leistung** *f* compensation; (*Schadenersatz*) damages *Pl.;* **~leute** *Pl.* → *Ersatzmann*

ersatzlos I. *Adj. nachgestellt:* without replacement; *die ~e Streichung des Weihnachtsgeldes* the abolition (*od.* discontinuation) of the Christmas bonus; **II.** *Adv.: 12 Arbeitsplätze werden ~ gestrichen* 12 jobs are being axed without replacement

Ersatz|mann *m; Pl. -männer od. -leute* substitute (*auch Sport*), replacement; **~mine** *f* refill; **~mittel** *n* substitute, surrogate, ersatz *oft pej.*

Ersatzpflicht *f* liability (for damages); **ersatzpflichtig** *Adj.* liable for damages

Ersatz|rad *n Mot.* spare wheel; **~reifen** *m* spare tyre (*Am.* tire); **~spieler** *m,* **~spielerin** *f Sport* substitute

Ersatzteil *n Tech.* replacement part; *mitgeliefertes:* spare (part); **~lager** *n* spare parts store

Ersatzwagen *m* replacement car; *von Werkstatt etc. vorübergehend gestellter:* courtesy car

ersatzweise *Adv.* as a substitute; as an alternative

Ersatzzeit *f:* **~ (für Rentenanspruch)** *period during which contributions were not paid into the state pension scheme but which nevertheless counts towards pension entitlement*

ersäufen *v/t. umg.* **1.** (*töten*) drown; **2.** *fig.: s-e Sorgen im Alkohol ~* drown one's sorrows (in drink)

erschaffen *v/t.* (*unreg.*); *geh.* create, make; **Erschaffer** *m; -s, -,* **Erschafferin** *f; -, -nen; geh.* creator; **Erschaffung** *f; nur Sg.; geh.* creation

erschallen *v/i.; erscholl od. erschallte, ist erschollen od. erschallt; geh.* → *ertönen*

erschaudern *v/i. geh.* shudder (with horror); *bei dem Gedanken ~, dass ...* shudder at the thought that ... (*od.* of *s.o. + Ger.*)

erschauern *v/i. geh. vor Angst, Kälte etc.:* tremble, shiver; *vor Glück etc.:* thrill (*alle* **vor** + *Dat.* with; **über** + *Akk.* at)

erscheinen *v/i.* (*unreg.*) **1.** (*sichtbar werden*) appear, become visible; *Sonne:* come out; **2.** (*kommen*) come (**zu** to), turn up (at); (*sich sehen lassen*) *auch* put in an appearance; *vor Gericht ~* appear in court; *nicht erschienen sein* be absent; *er ist heute nicht zum Frühstück / zur Arbeit erschienen* he wasn't at (*od.* didn't come for) breakfast this morning / he didn't turn

up for work today; **3.** *in Dokumenten etc.:* appear, be mentioned; **4.** *Zeitung:* come out; *Buch: auch* be published, appear; *Briefmarken etc.:* be issued; *soeben erschienen* just published, just out; **5.** *j-m ~ Geist:* appear to s.o.; **6.** (*den Anschein haben*) seem, appear, look (*j-m* to s.o.); (*sich darstellen*) present oneself/itself (*in e-m anderen Licht* in a different light); *es erscheint mir merkwürdig* it strikes me as (rather) strange; *es erscheint (mir) ratsam* it would seem (*od.* appear) advisable (to me)

Erscheinen *n; -s, kein Pl.* **1.** appearance; (*Anwesenheit*) attendance; *um pünktliches ~ wird gebeten* you are kindly requested to attend punctually; *wir danken für Ihr zahlreiches ~* we are grateful that so many of you have (been able to) come; **2.** *e-s Buchs:* publication; *im ~ begriffen Buch:* forthcoming; *die Zeitung hat ihr ~ eingestellt* the newspaper has ceased publication

Erscheinung *f* **1.** (*Vorkommnis, auch Phys. und Naturerscheinung*) phenomenon; *zeitlich gesehen: auch* occurrence; (*Anzeichen*) indication (+ *Gen.* of), sign (of); *Med. auch* symptom (of); *das ist e-e ganz normale ~ auch* that's perfectly normal, that's nothing out of the ordinary; **2.** (*Auftreten*) appearance; *in ~ treten* appear; *fig. Sache: auch* emerge, make itself felt; *stark/kaum in ~ treten* be very much in evidence / be hardly noticeable; *er tritt kaum in ~* he keeps very much in the background; **3.** *e-s Geistes:* apparition; (*Vision*) vision; (*Geist*) spect|re (*Am.* -er), phantom; *e-e ~ haben* (*Vision*) have a vision; *e-s Geistes:* see a ghost (*od.* an apparition); **4.** *kirchl.* manifestation; *Fest der ~ des Herrn* Epiphany; **5.** (*Gestalt*) figure; *e-e imposante ~ sein* cut a fine figure; *sie ist e-e sympathische ~* she comes across as very friendly (*od.* likeable); **6.** *äußere:* outward appearance; *von der ~ her* outwardly; *ihrer (äußeren) ~ nach* to look at her, *förmlicher:* judging by her (outward) appearance

Erscheinungs|bild *n* **1.** appearance, look; **2.** *Med.* manifestation; **3.** *Bio.* phenotype; **~form** *f* **1.** (outward) form; **2.** *Med.* manifestation; **3.** *Bio.* phenotype; **4.** *Chem., Geol.* form; **~jahr** *n* year of publication; **~ort** *m* place of publication; **~tag** *m* day (*od.* date) of publication; **~weise** *f* publication dates *Pl.;* **~:** *wöchentlich* published (*od.* appearing) weekly

erschießen (*unreg.*) **I.** *v/t.* shoot (dead), shoot and kill; **~ lassen** have *s.o.* shot; *zum Tod durch Erschießen verurteilen* sentence *s.o.* to be executed by firing squad (*od.* to be shot); **II.** *v/refl.* shoot o.s.; *dann kann ich mich ~!* umg. then I might as well go and shoot myself (*od.* might as well end it all); **Erschießung** *f* shooting; *standrechtliche:* execution (by firing squad); **Erschießungskommando** *n* firing squad

erschlaffen *v/i.* **1.** *Glieder, Penis etc.:* go limp; *Muskel:* grow tired, slacken; *Haut:* (begin to) sag, become (*od.* get, go) flabby; **2.** *Person:* tire, get (*od.* grow) tired; **3.** *fig. Kraft, Interesse etc.:* (begin to) flag

Erschlaffung *f; nur Sg.* **1.** *der Glieder, allmähliche:* tiring; *völlige:* (sudden) limpness; *der Muskeln: auch* slacken-

ing; *der Haut:* flabbiness; **2.** *e-r Person:* (sudden) tiredness; **3.** *fig. des Interesses etc.:* flagging (+ *Gen.* of), drop (in)

erschlagen I. *v/t.* (*unreg.*) kill; *er wurde vom Blitz ~* he was struck (dead) by lightning; *j-n mit Argumenten etc. förmlich ~ umg. fig.* overwhelm s.o. by the force of one's arguments *etc.;* **II.** *P.P.* → I; **III.** *Adj. umg.:* (*vollkommen od. wie*) **~** (*verblüfft*) flabbergasted; (*erschöpft*) whacked, bushed, out for the count

erschleichen *v/t.* (*unreg.*); *pej.* obtain by devious means; *sich* (*Dat.*) *j-s Gunst/Vertrauen ~* worm o.s. into s.o.'s favo(u)r/confidence

erschließbar *Adj.* **1.** *Markt, Gebiet:* capable of being opened up, developable; **2.** *fig.* infer|able (*od.* -ible) (*aus* from); (*ableitbar*) derivable (*aus* from); **erschließen** (*unreg.*) **I.** *v/t.* **1.** open (up), make accessible; (*Märkte*) open up; (*nutzbar machen*) (*auch Baugebiet*) develop; (*Rohstoffquellen etc.*) tap, exploit; **2.** (*folgern*) infer (*aus* from); (*Wort*) reconstruct (from), derive (from); **3.** (*offenbaren*) disclose; **II.** *v/refl.: sich j-m ~ Geheimnis, Bedeutung etc.:* be revealed to s.o.; *Möglichkeiten:* open up before s.o.; **Erschließung** *f* opening (up), development; tapping, exploitation; *Ling.* reconstruction, derivation; → *erschließen;* **Erschließungskosten** *Pl.* development (*od.* start-up) costs

erschollen *P.P.* → *erschallen*

erschöpfen I. *v/t.* **1.** (*ermüden*) wear out, exhaust; **2.** (*Vorräte, Bodenschätze, Kräfte*) deplete, exhaust; **3.** (*Möglichkeiten*) exhaust; (*Thema*) *auch* flog to death *umg.;* **II.** *v/refl.* **1.** *Person:* wear o.s. out; **2.** *sich ~ in e-r Tätigkeit, Begabung etc.:* be limited to, not go (*od.* get) beyond; *die Diskussion erschöpfte sich in leerem Geschwätz* the discussion never got beyond superficial chitchat; **3.** (*zu Ende gehen*) *Vorräte etc.:* run out; *Möglichkeiten:* be exhausted; *Quelle:* run dry; *Boden: auch* be worked to death; *Thema: auch* be flogged to death *umg.;* **erschöpfend I.** *Part. Präs.* → *erschöpfen;* **II.** *Adj.* **1.** exhausting; **2.** (*gründlich*) exhaustive; **III.** *Adv.: ein Thema ~ behandeln* treat a topic exhaustively, look at a topic from every (possible) angle; **erschöpft I.** *P.P.* → *erschöpfen;* **II.** *Adj.* exhausted (*von* by); *Batterie:* run-down; *m-e Geduld ist endgültig ~* my patience is finally exhausted (*od.* at an end); **Erschöpfung** *f; mst Sg.* exhaustion; *bis zur ~* to the point of exhaustion; *vor ~ umfallen* collapse with (*od.* from) exhaustion; **Erschöpfungszustand** *m* (state of) exhaustion

erschossen I. *P.P.* → *erschießen;* **II.** *Adj. umg.* (*erschöpft*) whacked, bushed; *ich bin total ~ auch* I've had it

erschrecken¹ *v/t.* frighten, scare; *plötzlich:* startle, give *s.o.* a shock; *j-n zu Tode ~* frighten s.o. out of his (*od.* her) wits, frighten s.o. to death; *du hast mich zu Tode erschreckt auch* you gave me the fright of my life, I nearly jumped out of my skin

erschrecken² *v/i.; erschrak, ist erschrocken* get a fright (*od.* shock); (*zusammenfahren*) jump, start; *~ über* (+ *Akk.*) be startled (*stärker:* shocked) by; *bin ich erschrocken! umg.* what a fright I got (*od.* you gave me); **erschrick nicht!** *ich bin's nur* don't be frightened!; *gleich wird's kalt* it's nothing to worry about; *er sieht sehr krank aus* I think I'd better warn you, you'd better prepare yourself; it may be a shock

erschrecken[3] *v/refl.*; *erschreckte sich, hat sich erschreckt od. erschrocken* get a fright; (*zusammenfahren*) jump, start; **sich zu Tode ~** get the fright of one's life, be frightened out of one's wits; **er hat sich ganz schön erschrocken** he got quite a fright, it gave him quite a fright (*od.* scare)

Erschrecken *n*; *-s, kein Pl.* fright, scare

erschreckend I. *Part. Präs.* → **erschrecken**[1]; **II.** *Adj.* alarming, frightening; (*furchtbar*) dreadful, terrible; (*entsetzlich*) appalling; *stärker:* horrific; **III.** *Adv.:* **~ wenige** etc. alarmingly few etc.; **~ viel(e)** an alarming amount (number) of; **sie haben ~ wenig gewusst** it was quite frightening how little they knew, they were alarmingly ill-informed (*od.* ignorant)

erschrocken I. *P.P.* → **erschrecken**[2], **erschrecken**[3]; **II.** *Adj.* startled; (*perplex*) *auch* taken aback; **ich war ganz ~** I got (*od.* it gave me) quite a fright *od.* scare; **er war zu Tode ~** he was frightened to death, he got (*od.* it gave him) the fright of his life; **III.** *Adv.* in (*od.* with) fright; **~ zusammenfahren od. auffahren** jump, start; **~ aus dem Schlaf hochfahren** wake up with a start

erschüttern *v/t.* **1.** (*Boden, Gebäude* etc.) shake; **2.** *fig.* (*Entschluss, Gesundheit, Vertrauen, Wirtschaft* etc.) shake; **j-n in s-m Glauben ~** shake s.o.'s faith; **3.** *fig.* (*bestürzen*) shock (deeply), shake (up); (*rühren*) move deeply; **das kann mich nicht ~** that leaves me cold; **ich lasse mich durch nichts ~** I am completely unflappable, nothing ever worries me; **ihn kann nichts mehr ~** he's seen (*od.* been through) it all; **4.** *Med.* (*Gehirn*) concuss; **erschütternd I.** *Part. Präs.* → **erschüttern**; **II.** *Adj.* shocking, devastating; (*ergreifend*) deeply moving; **erschüttert I.** *P.P.* → **erschüttern**; **II.** *Adj. und Adv.:* (*zutiefst*) **~** (deeply) shocked, (absolutely *od.* completely) devastated, (completely) shaken up, (absolutely *od.* completely) shattered (*alle von* by); **Erschütterung** *f* **1.** *der Erde* etc.: vibration; *stärker:* tremor, shock (wave); *Tech.* vibration; *Med.* concussion; **2.** *fig.* shock (+ *Gen.* to), blow (to); (*der Wirtschaft* to the economy); **zur ~ des Systems** etc. **führen** shake the system etc. to its foundations; **3.** *fig.* (*Bestürzung*) shock; *in der Öffentlichkeit* etc.: *auch* shock wave; **~ auslösen bei** be a shock for, shock; *weitläufig:* send shock waves through; **sie konnte vor ~ nichts sagen** she was too shocked to speak

erschweren *v/t.* make (more) difficult, complicate; (*verschlimmern*) aggravate; (*Problem*) *auch* compound; (*hemmen*) impede, hamper; (*stören*) seriously interfere with; **erschwerend I.** *Adj. Jur. Umstände:* aggravating; **II.** *Adv.:* **~ kommt hinzu, dass ...** to aggravate the situation ..., to make the situation worse ...

Erschwernis *f*; *-, -se; geh.* (added) difficulty *od.* burden; (*Hindernis*) impediment, obstacle; **~zulage** *f* hardship al-

lowance

erschwert I. *P.P.* → **erschweren**; **II.** *Adj.* more difficult, harder; **unter ~en Bedingungen** under less favo(u)rable conditions

Erschwerung *f* complication; **e-e ~** (+ *Gen.*) **bedeuten** make *s.th.* more difficult; → **Erschwernis**

erschwindeln *v/t. umg. pej.* obtain by fraud (*od.* dishonest means); (**sich** [*Dat.*]) **etw. von j-m ~** swindle *s.th.* out of *s.o.*

erschwinglich *Adj.* within *s.o.'s* means, affordable; **zu ~en Preisen** at reasonable prices; **das ist für uns nicht ~** we can't afford it

ersehen *v/t.* (*unreg.*): **etw. ~ aus** (*entnehmen*) see (*od.* understand) from; (*schließen*) gather from; **daraus lässt sich ~, dass ...** this shows (*od.* indicates) that ...; **daraus ist nicht zu ~, ob ...** it doesn't indicate (*od.* tell you) whether ...

ersehnen *v/t. geh.* long for, yearn for; **ersehnt I.** *P.P.* → **ersehnen**; **II.** *Adj.* longed-for; **heiß/lang ~** ardently/long wished-for

ersetzbar *Adj.* replaceable (*auch Tech.*); *Schaden:* reparable; *Verlust:* recoverable; **ersetzen** *v/t.* **1.** replace (**durch** by, with); (*j-n*) *auch* take the place of; (*Batterie, Glühbirne*) change; **A durch B ~** replace A by (*od.* with) B, substitute B for A; **diese Maschine ersetzt 5 Arbeitskräfte** this machine does the work of five people; **2.** (*Verlust, Mangel*) compensate for; **j-m s-e Auslagen ~** reimburse *s.o.'s* expenses; **den Schaden ersetzt bekommen** get paid (receive compensation *förm.*) for the damage; **3.** **j-m j-n/etw ~** take the place of *s.o./s.th.* as far as *s.o.* is concerned; **sie ersetzte ihnen die Eltern** she was a father and mother to them; **das ersetzt mir das Abendessen** it takes the place of dinner, as far as I'm concerned, it does me instead of dinner *umg.*; **Ersetzung** *f* replacement; *e-s Verlusts* etc.: compensation; *von Kosten:* reimbursement

ersichtlich *Adj.* apparent, evident (**aus** from); (*klar*) clear; **klar ~** obvious, clearly evident (*od.* apparent); **ohne ~en Grund** for no apparent reason; **daraus wird ~, dass ...** this shows (*od.* indicates) that ..., thus it appears that ...; **aus Ihrem Schreiben ist ~ od. wird ~, dass ...** from your letter it would appear that ...; **wie aus ... ~ ist** as can be seen from ...

ersinnen *v/t.* (*unreg.*) *geh.* think up, dream up; (*erfinden*) invent

erspähen *v/t. geh.* catch sight of, spot; *lit.* espy

ersparen *v/t.* **1.** (**sich** [*Dat.*]) **etw. ~** (*Geld*) save; **erspare dir d-e Bemerkungen** *fig.* just keep your remarks to yourself; **2.** **j-m Arbeit/Kosten** etc. **~** save *s.o.* work/money etc.; **j-m e-e Demütigung** etc. **~** spare *s.o.* a humiliation etc.; **das wird uns nicht erspart bleiben** there's no way we're going to avoid (*od.* get out of *umg.*) it; **mir bleibt aber auch nichts erspart** everything seems to happen to me, I seem to be fated; **Ersparnis** *f*; *-, -se* **1.** *nur Sg.*; saving(s *Pl.*) (**an** + *Dat.* in); **2.** **~se** (*Geld*) savings *Pl.*; **erspart I.** *P.P.* → **ersparen**; **II.** *Adj.:* **~es Geld** *od.* **Erspartes** savings; **vom Ersparten leben** live off one's savings

ersprießlich *Adj. geh.* fruitful; (*förderlich*) beneficial (+ *Dat.* to)

erst *Adv.* **1.** (*als Erstes*) first; (*anfangs, dann nicht mehr*) at first; **~ einmal** first; **wir müssen ~ einmal aufräumen** *auch* we've got to tidy (*Am.* clean) up before we do anything else; **~ mal stimmt das gar nicht, und dann ...** first(ly) (*od.* for a start) it's not true, and then ...; **2.** (*nicht früher als*) only, not until (*od.* till); *zukunftsbezogen:* **auch** not before; **~ als** *od.* **wenn** only when; **~ jetzt wissen wir ...** only now do we know ..., not until (*od.* till) now did we know ...; **~ in zehn Minuten** not for ten minutes, in ten minutes' time; **~ als er anrief, wurde mir klar ...** it was only when he rang up (*Am.* called) that I realized ...; **3.** (*nicht länger zurückliegend als*) only, just; (*eben od. gerade*) **~** just; **~ vor kurzem** only a short while ago; **ich habe sie ~ letzte Woche gesehen** I saw her only last week, it was only last week (that) I saw her; **4.** (*bloß*) only, just; **sie ist ~ zwanzig** she is only twenty; **es ist ~ zwei Tage her** it's only two days ago; **mit e-r Arbeit ~ am Anfang sein** have (only) just begun a job, be still only at the beginning of a job; **5.** *zukünftig:* (*noch*) still, yet; **das muss sich ~ noch zeigen** that remains to be seen; **der muss ~ noch geboren werden, der ...** no one has yet been born who ..., the man has yet to be born who ...; **wenn du ~ so alt bist wie ich** when you get to my age; **wenn wir ~ reich sind, werden wir ...** when (*od.* once) we're rich (*od.* wait till we're rich), then we'll ...; **6.** *hervorhebend, steigernd:* **ich bin so müde - und ich ~!** how about me then!; **was glaubst du, wie mir ~ zumute ist?** how do you think 'I feel?; **du solltest ihn ~ mal sehen!** (just) wait till you see him; **das versuche ich ~ gar nicht** I shan't (*Am.* won't) even bother to try (it); **was wird sie ~ sagen, wenn sie das erfährt?** whatever is she going to say when she hears about that then?; **7. ~ recht** all the more; **jetzt ~ recht nicht!** absolutely definitely not!; that settles it, no!, *Am.* no way!; **dann kann er es ja ~ recht tun** all the more reason (for him) to do it; **jetzt zeig ich's ihr ~ recht!** now I'm really going to show her; **das macht es ~ recht schlimm** that makes it even worse

erst... *Zahlw.* **1.** first; **als Erstes** first of all, to start with; **~es Kapitel** chapter one; **~e Hilfe** first aid; **am ~en Mai** on the first of May, on May the first; **1. Mai** 1st May, *bes. Am.* May 1(st); **heute ist der Erste** it's the first (of the month) today; **am Ersten** (**des Monats**) on the first (of the month); (**am**) **nächsten/letzten Ersten** on the first of next/last month; **j-m zum nächsten Ersten kündigen** give *s.o.* notice for the first of the following month; **er war Erster** he was (*od.* came) first; **er war der Erste, der ...** he was the first to (+*Inf.*); **Karl I.** Charles I (= Charles the First); **zum Ersten, zum Zweiten, (und) zum Dritten!** *Auktion:* going, going, gone!; **100 zum Ersten, zum Zweiten, (und) zum Dritten** 100 for the first time (*od.* once), for the second time (*od.* twice), gone!; **zum Ersten möchte ich festhalten, dass ...** in the first place, first of all; **2.** (*best...*) *Klasse, Wahl:* first; *Qualität:* prime; **~er Rang** *Theat., Kino:* dress circle; **das ~e Haus am Platze** the best hotel in town (*od.* in the place); **sie ging als Erste**

*durchs Ziel od. **sie wurde Erste** she finished first; **Erste(r) von hinten** umg. hum. last; bottom; **die Ersten werden die Letzten sein** bibl. the first shall be last; **3.** (vorläufig) (Entwurf) first; **fürs Erste** for the moment, for the time being; **4. ~e Beste** → erstbest...; → Ehe, Hand[1] 2, Linie 1, Mal[1]*

erstarken v/i. geh. **1.** grow strong(er), gain strength; **wieder ~** regain one's etc. strength; **2.** fig. Glaube, Liebe etc.: strengthen, grow stronger

erstarren v/i. **1.** Gelatine, Sülze, Gips, Zement etc.: set; Öl, Fett: congeal; Lava, Stahl etc.: solidify (auch Chem.); **zu Eis ~** freeze; **2.** Finger, Glieder: grow stiff, stiffen; vor Kälte: go numb; **3.** fig. Person, Lächeln: freeze; Gesicht: turn to stone; **vor Angst ~** freeze (with fear od. terror), be paralysed with fear; **j-s Blut ~ lassen** make s.o.'s blood run cold; **vor Ehrfurcht ~** be completely overawed (od. dumbfounded); → Salzsäule; **4.** fig. Formen, Verhaltensweisen etc.: become rigid; Brauch, Tradition etc.: ossify; **erstarrt I.** P.P. → erstarren; **II.** Adj. **1.** stiff; vor Kälte: auch numb; **2.** fig. Person: paralysed; Formen etc.: rigid; Brauch, Tradition etc.: ossified; **vor Ehrfurcht ~** awestruck; **Erstarrung** f; nur Sg. **1.** stiffness; durch Kälte: numbness; Chem. solidification; von Fett, Öl: auch congealing; von Gelatine, Gips, Zement etc.: setting; **2.** fig. paralysis; von Formen, e-r Haltung etc.: rigidity

erstatten v/t. **1.** (Auslagen etc.) reimburse, refund; **j-m s-e Auslagen etc. ~** reimburse (od. refund) s.o. for expenses etc.; **2.** Anzeige ~ (gegen j-n) report (s.o.) to the police; **j-m Bericht od. Meldung ~** report to s.o. (über + Akk. on); **Erstattung** f **1.** (Rückzahlung) reimbursement, refund(ing); **2.** e-r Anzeige: making; e-s Berichts: auch delivery; **erstattungsfähig** Adj. Kosten: refundable, repayable

erstaufführen v/t. (hat erstaufgeführt); nur Inf. und P.P. perform (in public) for the first time, give the first public performance of, première; **Erstaufführung** f Theat., Film: première; Film: (erste Laufzeit) first run; **Erstaufführungskino** n first-run cinema (Am. theater)

Erstauflage f Druck. first impression

erstaunen I. v/t. (hat erstaunt) astonish; stärker: astound, amaze; **II.** v/i. **1.** (ist) Person: be astonished; stärker: be astounded, be amazed; **2.** (hat) Sache: cause astonishment (od. amazement), astonish (od. amaze) everyone

Erstaunen n; -s, kein Pl. astonishment; stärker: amazement; **in ~ geraten** → erstaunen II; **in ~ (ver)setzen** → erstaunen I; **zu m-m (großen) ~** (much) to my astonishment

erstaunlich I. Adj. astonishing; stärker: astounding, amazing; (beachtlich) remarkable; (unglaublich) unbelievable, incredible; **das Erstaunlich(st)e daran ist, dass ...** the (most) astonishing (od. amazing) thing about it is ...; **II.** Adv. astonishingly; stärker: astoundingly, amazingly; (beachtlich) remarkably; (unglaublich) unbelievably, incredibly; **erstaunlicherweise** Adv. astonishingly, to my etc. surprise; stärker: amazingly, to my etc. amazement; **erstaunt I.** P.P. → erstaunen; **II.** Adj. astonished; stärker: astounded, amazed (über + Akk. at)

Erst|ausfertigung f original (copy);

~ausgabe f **1.** Druck. first edition; **2.** Wirts. von Aktien: first issue; **~ausstattung** f **1.** basic equipment (od. kit); **2.** für Baby: layette; **~ausstrahlung** f TV etc. first (od. virgin) broadcast; **~besitz** m: aus ~ with only one previous owner

erstbest... Adj. first; any old; **er fragte das ~e Kind** he asked the first child he saw (od. he happened to see, that came along); **kauf doch nicht einfach das ~e Auto** don't go and buy just any old car; **der/die Erstbeste** just anyone; am Ort: the first person (od. man, woman) to come along; **das Erstbeste kaufen, tun** etc. any old thing

Erst|besteigung f first (od. maiden od. virgin) ascent; **~bezug** m e-r Wohnung etc.: first occupation

erstechen v/t. (unreg.) stab (to death)

erstehen (unreg.) **I.** v/t. (hat erstanden); (kaufen) buy (o.s.); (bekommen) get; **II.** v/i. (ist) geh. arise, result (aus from), rise up (from); **daraus können uns Unannehmlichkeiten ~** it could cause us trouble

Erste-Hilfe|-Ausrüstung f first-aid kit; **~-Koffer** m fürs Auto: first-aid kit; **~-Kurs** m first-aid course; **~-Leistung** f providing first aid

ersteigen v/t. (unreg.) **1.** climb, ascend; (Gipfel) climb (up to); **2.** fig. (Position) rise to; (gesellschaftliche Stufenleiter) climb, move up

ersteigern v/t. buy at an auction

Erste-Klasse|-Abteil n Eisenb. first-class compartment; **~-Fahrkarte** f Eisenb. first-class ticket; **~-Ticket** n Flug. first-class ticket; **~-Wagen** m Eisenb. first-class carriage (od. car)

erstellen v/t. **1.** (bauen) build, construct; **2.** (Plan etc.) draw up; **Erstellung** f **1.** (Bau) building, construction; **2.** (Anfertigung) drawing-up

erstens Adv. first(ly), first of all; betont: to start with; emotional: auch for a start

erster... Adj. the former; **der, die, das Erstere** the former ...

ersterben v/i. (unreg.); geh. Ton etc.: die (od. fade) away; Lächeln: fade; **das Lächeln erstarb auf s-n Lippen** the smile died on (od. faded from) his lips

Erster-Klasse-... im Subst. first-class-...

erstgeboren Adj. firstborn; **Erstgeborene** m, f, n; -n, -n firstborn

Erstgeburt f **1.** firstborn (child); **2.** nur Sg.; Jur. birthright, (right of) primogeniture; **Erstgeburtsrecht** n; nur Sg.; Jur. birthright, (right of) primogeniture

erstgenannt Adj. first-mentioned; Person: auch first-named; (erstere[r]) former

ersticken I. v/t. (hat erstickt) **1.** suffocate; durch Erdrosselung etc.: choke; **2.** (Feuer) smother, put out; **3.** fig. (Gefühl etc.) suppress; (Geräusch, Lachen) smother, stifle; (Aufstand) suppress, quell; → Keim 4; **II.** v/i. (ist) **1.** suffocate (an + Dat. from), be suffocated (by); **an e-r Gräte etc. ~** choke (to death) on a bone etc.; **2.** fig.: vor Lachen etc. ~ choke with laughter etc.; **in Arbeit ~** be snowed under with work, be drowning in work; **mit erstickter Stimme** in a choked voice

Ersticken n; -s, kein Pl. suffocation; fachspr. asphyxiation; **zum ~** Luft etc.: stifling, suffocating; **zum ~ heiß** stifling(ly) hot; **erstickend I.** Part. Präs.

→ **ersticken**; **II.** Adj. stifling, suffocating

Erstickungs|anfall m choking fit; **~gefahr** f danger of suffocation; **~tod** m: **den ~ sterben** die of suffocation (od. asphyxiation fachspr.)

erstklassig I. Adj. first-class, first-rate; Sportler: auch top-class, crack ... umg., ace ...; Waren: top-quality; **Erstklassiges leisten** do brilliantly (od. outstandingly); **II.** Adv. superbly; **das schmeckt ~** that tastes absolutely wonderful

Erstklässler m; -s, -, **~in** f; -, -nen first-year (primary) pupil, Am. first grader

Erstkommunion f kath. first Communion

Erstkontakt m: **beim ~ mit e-m Allergen** etc. on first contact with

Erstligist m; -en, -en; Sport first-league (od. first-division) team, team in the top division

Erstling m; -s, -e **1.** Buch etc.: first work; **2.** Kind: firstborn child

Erstlings|ausstattung f layette; **~film** m debut film; **~roman** m first novel; **~werk** n first work

erstmalig I. Adj. first; **II.** Adv. → erstmals; **erstmals** Adv. for the first time, first

erstrahlen v/i. shine; Weihnachtsbaum: sparkle, glitter

erstrangig Adj. **1.** (erstklassig) first-rate; **2.** Problem: top-priority; Hypothek: first

erstreben v/t. geh. aim for; (Glück, Macht etc.) strive after; (begehren) desire, covet; **erstrebenswert** Adj. desirable, worthwhile

erstrecken I. v/refl. **1.** extend, stretch (bis zu to, as far as; über + Akk. across, over); **2.** sich ~ über (+ Akk.) zeitlich: cover od. span (a period of); **3.** sich ~ auf (+ Akk.) (betreffen) concern, apply to; (einschließen) include; **II.** v/t. österr. (Frist) extend; (Termin) postpone, put back

erstreiten v/t. (unreg.) geh.: (sich [Dat.]) etw. ~ win (od. secure) s.th.

Erstschlag m Mil. first strike; **~waffe** f first-strike weapon

Erst|semester n new student; etwa freshman, fresher umg.; **~sendung** f; nur Sg.; TV, Radio: **~ am ... vorher**: first broadcast (TV auch shown) on; künftig: to be broadcast (TV auch shown) for the first time on ...; **~stimme** f Pol. first vote

Ersttags|brief m Post. first-day cover; **~stempel** m first-day stamp

Ersttäter m, **~in** f Jur. first-time offender

erstunken Adj. umg.: **das ist ~ und erlogen** that's a dirty lie (od. a pack of lies)

erstürmen v/t. (take by) storm; **Erstürmung** f storming

Erst|versorgung f (giving) first aid; **~wagen** m first car; **~wähler** m, **~wählerin** f first-time voter; **~zulassung** f Mot. first registration

ersuchen I. vt/i.: **j-n ... zu** (+ Inf.) ask (dringend: beseech) s.o. to (+ Inf.); **(j-n) um etw.** request s.th. (from s.o.); **II. Ersuchen** n; -s, - request; **auf sein Ersuchen hin** at his request

ertappen I. v/t. catch (bei at); **j-n beim Stehlen ~** catch s.o. stealing; → Tat 2; **II.** v/refl.: **sich dabei ~, etw. zu tun** catch o.s. doing s.th.

ertasten v/t. feel (the shape of)

erteilen v/t.; (Auftrag, Auskunft, Befehl, Erlaubnis, Rat, Strafe, Unterricht *etc.*) give (*j-m* [to] s.o.); (*ein Recht etc.*) confer (+ *Dat.* on); (*Patent*) grant (to); (*Lizenz*) issue; → **Abfuhr** 2, **Vollmacht**, **Wort** 2; **Erteilung** *f* giving; granting; conferral; issuing

ertönen *v/i.* **1.** *Lachen, Schuss, Stimme etc.*: ring out; *Instrument, Musik, Schritte*: sound; **plötzlich ertönte Musik** suddenly there was the sound of music; *lauter* suddenly music rang out; **e-n Gong** *etc.* **~ lassen** sound a gong *etc.*; **2.** *geh.*: **~ von** (*widerhallen*) resound (*od.* echo) with

Ertrag *m; -(e)s, Erträge* **1.** yield; *Bergb. etc.* output; **2.** *Wirts., finanzieller*: proceeds *Pl.*, returns *Pl.*, profit(s *Pl.*) (**aus** from); **3.** *fig.* fruits *Pl.*, results *Pl.*

ertragen *v/t.* (*unreg.*) **1.** (*aushalten*) bear, stand, endure; **nicht zu ~** intolerable, unbearable, insufferable; **etw. mit Fassung/Geduld ~** bear s.th. with equanimity/patience; **2.** (*dulden*) tolerate, put up with

erträglich I. *Adj.* bearable; (*auch leidlich*) tolerable; **II.** *Adv.* (*leidlich*) tolerably well

ertragreich *Adj.* productive; *Wirts.* profitable

ertragsarm *Adj. attr.* low-yield

Ertragseinbruch *m Wirts.* sudden fall (*od.* downturn) in profits

ertragsfähig *Adj.* productive; *Wirts.* profit-bearing; **Ertragsfähigkeit** *f; nur Sg.* productivity; *Wirts.* earning potential (*od.* capacity)

Ertrags|lage *f* profit situation; **~minderung** *f* decrease (*od.* downturn) in profits; **~schwankung** *f* fluctuating profits (*od.* returns); **2sicher** *Adj.* producing reliable returns; **~steigerung** *f* increase (*od.* upturn *od.* upswing) in profits; **~steuer** *f* profits tax; **~wert** *m* earning power

ertränken I. *v/t.* drown; **s-n Kummer** *etc.* **in** *od.* **im Alkohol ~** drown one's sorrows (in alcohol); **II.** *v/refl.* drown o.s.

erträumen *v/t.*: (**sich** [*Dat.*]) **~** dream of; imagine; **erträumt I.** *P.P.* → **erträumen**; **II.** *Adj.* dreamed-of; imaginary; **nie ~** undreamt-of

ertrinken I. *v/i.* (*unreg.*) drown, be drowned; **in e-r Flut von Beschwerden** *etc.* **~** *fig.* be inundated (*od.* swamped) with complaints *etc.*; **II. Ertrinken** *n*: (**Tod durch**) **Ertrinken** (death by) drowning; **Ertrinkende** *m, f; -n, -n* drowning man/woman

ertrotzen *v/t.; geh.*: (**sich** [*Dat.*]) **etw. ~** get s.th. through sheer stubbornness, stubbornly insist until one gets s.th.

ertüchtigen *v/t. und v/refl.* get (s.o.) in shape; (*stählen*) toughen (s.o.) up; **Ertüchtigung** *f* physical training (*od.* fitness)

erübrigen I. *v/t.* (*Geld*) save, put aside; (*Zeit*) spare; **können Sie zehn Euro / fünf Minuten (für mich) ~?** can you spare (me) ten euros / five minutes?; **II.** *v/refl.* be unnecessary, be superfluous; **es hat sich erübrigt** it's been solved, forget it *umg.*; **es dürfte sich ~** it will hardly be necessary; **jedes weitere Wort erübrigt sich** there's nothing more to be said

eruieren *v/t.* **1.** *geh.* find out, determine; **2.** *österr., schw.* (*Täter etc.*) trace

Eruption *f, -, -en*; *Geol. und Med.* eruption; **eruptiv** *Adj.* eruptive

erwachen I. *v/i. geh.* **1.** wake up, awake *förm.*, awaken *förm.*; (*alle* **aus** from); *aus Narkose, Ohnmacht*: come

(*a*)round, come to; **aus s-n Träumen ~** *fig.*: wake up to reality; **2.** *fig. Tag*: dawn; *Erinnerungen, Interesse*: be awakened; *Argwohn, Ehrgeiz etc.*: be aroused; **zu neuem Leben ~** revive, come to life again; **II. Erwachen** *n* awakening; **böses** *od.* **unsanftes Erwachen** *fig.* rude awakening

erwachsen¹ *v/i.* (*unreg.*); *geh.* arise (**aus** from); **~ aus** *Vorteil, Unkosten etc.*: accrue (*od.* result) from; **daraus können Ihnen Unannehmlichkeiten ~** it may cause you trouble

erwachsen² **I.** *P.P.* → **erwachsen¹**; **II.** *Adj.* grown-up, adult; (*ausgewachsen*) fully-grown; (*mündig*) of age; **er ist ein ~er Mensch** (*er weiß, was er tut*) *auch* he's old enough to know what's what; **sehr ~ sein** be very grown-up for one's age; **Erwachsene** *m, f; -n, -n* grown-up, adult; **nur für ~** (for) adults only

Erwachsenen|bildung *f* adult (*od.* further) education; **~taufe** *f* adult baptism

Erwachsensein *n* adulthood, being an adult (*od.* adults); (*Reife*) maturity

erwägen *v/t.* (*unreg.*) consider, think s.th. over; **~, etw. zu tun** consider doing s.th.; **die Vor- und Nachteile ~** weigh up the pros and cons (*od.* advantages and disadvantages); **es wird ernsthaft erwogen** it's under serious consideration; **erwägenswert** *Adj.* worth considering; **Erwägung** *f* consideration; **aus finanziellen ~en** on financial grounds, for financial reasons; **in ~ ziehen** take into consideration, consider; (*zu tun gedenken*) contemplate, consider (+ *Ger.*); **~en anstellen, ob ...** consider whether ...

erwählen *v/t. geh.* choose; *durch Abstimmung*: elect; **j-n zum Parlamentssprecher** *etc.* **~** elect s.o. (as) parliamentary speaker *etc.*

erwähnen *v/t.* mention; **am Rande** *od.* **nebenbei ~** mention in passing; **j-n namentlich ~** mention s.o. by name, mention s.o.'s name; **ich wurde überhaupt nicht erwähnt** I didn't even get a mention; **erwähnenswert** *Adj.* worth mentioning; *Kunstwerk etc.*: worthy of note; **Erwähnung** *f* mention (+ *Gen.* of), reference (to); **~ finden** be mentioned

erwandern *v/t.*: (**sich** [*Dat.*]) **ein Gebiet ~** discover (*od.* get to know) an area on foot

erwärmen I. *v/t.* **1.** warm *od.* heat (up); **2.** *fig.*: **j-n für etw. ~** get s.o. interested in s.th.; **II.** *v/refl.* **1.** warm up, heat up (**auf** + *Akk.* to), get warm; *Person*: warm o.s. (up); **2.** *fig.*: **sich ~ für** warm to, get to like; **Erwärmung** *f* warming up, heating up; **globale ~** global warming

erwarten *v/t.* **1.** (*Anruf, Besuch, Post etc.*) expect; (*warten auf*) wait for; **ein Kind ~** be expecting a baby; **sehnsüchtig ~** wait longingly for; **j-n am Flughafen ~** wait for s.o. at the airport; **sie kann es kaum ~(, dass i-e Eltern zurückkommen)** she can hardly wait (for her parents to get back); **wenn sie wüsste, was sie erwartet** if she knew what was in store for her; **2.** (*rechnen mit*) expect; **zu ~de Probleme, Beförderung**: likely; **es ist** *od.* **geh steht zu ~** it's to be expected; **das hatte ich erwartet** I thought (*bes. Am.* figured) as much; **von ihm kann man noch allerhand ~** he's somebody to watch; **wenn er heimkommt, hat er**

was zu ~! *umg.* (*Strafe, Vorwürfe etc.*) when he gets home, he'll get what for (*Am.* get what's coming to him)!; **3.** (*fordern, verlangen*) expect (**von** from); (*erhoffen*) hope for (**von** from); (**von s-n Mitarbeitern**) **Pünktlichkeit ~** expect punctuality (from one's employees); **ich erwarte von dir, dass du ...** I expect you to (+ *Inf.*); **sie erwartet sich nicht mehr viel vom Leben** she doesn't expect much from life any more; **4. über/wider Erwarten** beyond/ contrary to all expectation(s)

Erwartung *f* (*Annahme, Anspruch*) expectation (+ *Gen.* of); (*Hoffnung*) hope(s *Pl.*) (for); (*Spannung*) anticipation (of), expectancy (of); **voller ~ →** **erwartungsvoll**; **in der ~, dass ...** in the expectation that ...; **in ~ Ihrer Antwort** *Briefschluss*: looking forward to (*od.* in anticipation of *od.* awaiting) your reply; **große ~en setzen in** (+ *Akk.*) *od.* **knüpfen an** (+ *Akk.*) place great hopes in, expect a great deal of; **die ~en herabsetzen** lower one's expectations (*od.* sights); **entgegen allen ~en** against all expectations, against the odds; **du hast m-e ~en enttäuscht** you disappoint me, I expected you to do better than that; **die in das Projekt gesetzten ~en erfüllten sich nicht** the project did not live up to expectations

Erwartungsdruck *m* stress resulting from other people's expectations

erwartungsgemäß *Adv.* as expected

Erwartungshaltung *f* (level of) expectations *Pl.*

erwartungsvoll *Adj. und Adv.* full of expectation, expectant(ly); **in ~er Haltung** in a state of expectancy

erwecken *v/t.* **1.** *geh.* → **wecken**; **2.** *j-n od. etw.* **wieder zum Leben ~** revive; **von den Toten ~** raise from the dead; **3.** *fig.* (*Interesse, Mitleid, Neugier etc.*) arouse; (*Gefühle*) *auch* awaken, stir up; (*Erinnerung*) bring back, stir up; (*Hoffnung*) raise; (*Vertrauen*) inspire; **bei j-m den Glauben ~, dass ...** make s.o. believe that ...; **den Anschein** *od.* **Eindruck ~, dass ...** give the impression of (+ *Ger.*); **4.** *kirchl.* (*bekehren*) convert

erwehren *v/refl. geh.* **1. sich j-s ~ e-s Angreifers, Verehrers**: ward s.o. off; (*widerstehen*) resist; **2. sich etw.** (*Gen.*) **nicht ~ können** be helpless against s.th., be unable to resist (+ *Ger.*); **ich konnte mich des Eindrucks nicht ~, dass ...** I couldn't help feeling (that) ...

erweichen (*untr.*) **I.** *v/t.* (*hat erweicht*) **1.** soften (up); **2.** *fig.* (*j-n*) soften, mollify; (*rühren*) move, touch; **sich ~ lassen** relent, yield, give in; **II.** *v/i.* (*ist*) soften, go soft

erweisen I. *v/t.* (*unreg.*) **1.** (*beweisen*) prove, show, demonstrate, establish; **es ist erwiesen, dass ...** it has been proved *etc.* that ...; **2.** (*Gefallen, Dienst*) do; (*Gunst*) grant; (*Achtung, Gastfreundschaft*) show; **würden Sie mir die Ehre ~ zu** (+ *Inf.*)? would you do me the hono(u)r of (+ *Ger.*)?; **II.** *v/refl.* **1. sich ~ als** turn out (to be), prove (to be); *Person*: *auch* prove o.s. (to be); **2. sich j-m gegenüber dankbar ~** show one's gratitude to (*od.* towards) s.o.

erweitern I. *v/t.* **1.** (*Straße etc.*) widen; (*Blutgefäße, Pupillen*) dilate; (*Betrieb, Gebäude*) extend; (*Produktion*) expand; (*Buch, Programm etc.*) enlarge; (*Rock etc.*) let out; **2.** (*Einfluss, Be-**

E

fugnisse etc.) extend; (*Kenntnisse*) broaden; **s-e Spanischkenntnisse ~** improve one's Spanish; → **Horizont** 2; **3.** *Math.* (*Bruch*) reduce to higher terms; **II.** *v/refl.* **1.** *Straße etc.*: widen; *Pupille, Blutgefäß*: dilate; *Herz*: become enlarged; **2.** *Kenntnisse*: increase, expand; *Begriff*: take on a wider meaning; **erweitert I.** *P.P.* → **erweitern**; **II.** *Adj.* **1.** enlarged *etc.*; → **erweitern**; **2.** *Ling.*: **~er Satz** compound sentence; **~er Infinitiv** extended infinitive; **Erweiterung** *f* widening; extension; enlargement; broadening; *Med.* dilation; → **erweitern**; **erweiterungsfähig** *Adj.* capable of being enlarged, extendable, expandable; **es ist ~ auch** it can be enlarged (*od.* extended, expanded)

Erwerb *m*; -*(e)s*, -*e* **1.** acquisition; (*Kauf*) *auch* purchase; **2.** (*Verdienst*) earnings *Pl.*; (*Unterhalt*) living; **erwerben** *v/t.* (*unreg.*) **1.** acquire; *käuflich*: *auch* purchase; **2.** (*verdienen*) earn; **sich ein Vermögen ~** make a fortune; **3.** *fig.* (*Kenntnisse, Rechte etc.*) acquire; (*j-s Achtung, Vertrauen etc., Ruhm etc.*) win; **sich um die Organisation etc. große Verdienste ~** serve the organization *etc.* well, do the organization *etc.* great service

erwerbsfähig *Adj.* able to work; fit for work; **~es Alter** employable (*od.* working) age; **Erwerbsfähigkeit** *f*; *nur Sg.* ability to work

Erwerbsleben *n* working life; **im ~ stehen** be working

erwerbslos *Adj.* unemployed; **Erwerbslose** *m, f*; -*n*, -*n* unemployed person; **die ~n** the unemployed *Pl.*; **Erwerbslosenquote** *f* level of unemployment; **Erwerbslosigkeit** *f*; *nur Sg.* unemployment

Erwerbs|minderung *f* reduction in earning capacity; **~quelle** *f* source of income

erwerbstätig *Adj.* (gainfully) employed; **~e Bevölkerung** *auch* working population; **Erwerbstätige** *m, f*; -*n*, -*n* employed person; **die ~n** the working population *Sg.*; **die Zahl der ~n** the number of employed people; **Erwerbstätigkeit** *f* (gainful) employment

erwerbsunfähig *Adj.* unable to work; unfit for work; **Erwerbsunfähigkeit** *f*; *nur Sg.* inability to work

Erwerbs|urkunde *f Jur.* title deed; **~zweig** *m* source of income (*od.* employment), occupation; branch of industry

Erwerbung *f* acquisition

erwidern I. *vt/i.* (*antworten*) reply, answer (*auf + Akk.* to); *treffend, scharf*: retort; **auf m-e Frage erwiderte er …** in reply to my question he said …; **er wusste nicht, was er darauf ~ sollte** he didn't know what to say to that; **II.** *v/t.* **1.** (*Besuch, Blick, Gefälligkeit, Gruß etc.*) return; (*Gefühl*) reciprocate; **2.** *Mil.* (*das Feuer*) return; **Erwiderung** *f* **1.** (*Antwort*) reply, answer; *treffende, scharfe*: retort; **2.** *e-s Gefühls*: reciprocation; **in ~** (+ *Gen.*) in reply to; **keine ~ finden** *Liebe*: be unrequited, not be returned; **3.** *Mil.*: **flexible ~** flexible response

erwiesen I. *P.P.* → **erweisen**; **II.** *Adj.* proved (*bes. Am.* proven), established; **wegen ~er Unschuld** on grounds of proven innocence; **erwiesenermaßen** *Adv.* as has been proved (*bes. Am.* proven *od.* shown, demonstrated, es-

tablished); (*nachweislich*) demonstrably; **sie war ~ dabei** she has been prov|ed (*bes. Am.* -en) to have been present, her presence (*od.* that she was there) is a proven fact

erwirken *v/t. geh.* achieve, bring about; (*erlangen*) secure, succeed in getting; (*Genehmigung etc.*) obtain, secure

erwirtschaften *v/t.* gain (by good management); *Gewinne* ~ make profits

erwischen *v/t. umg.* **1.** (*greifen, fangen*) catch, get; (*treffen*) catch, hit; **nicht ~** *Geschoss etc.*: miss; **ich erwischte ihn gerade noch am Ärmel** I just managed to catch (hold of) (*od.* grab) him by the sleeve; **ihn hat's erwischt** *umg. fig. Krankheit*: he's got it; *Verletzung, Unangenehmes*: he's taken a knock; *Strafe*: he got it in the neck; *Liebe*: he's got it bad, he's smitten; *Tod*: he's had it; **2.** (*ertappen*) catch; **j-n beim Rauchen/Lügen ~** catch s.o. smoking (*od.* lying; **ich hab ihn dabei erwischt** I caught him at it; **sich ~ lassen** get caught; **lass dich ja nicht dabei ~, dass du …!** I don't you dare to …!; **jetzt haben Sie mich erwischt** *bei Wissenslücke*: you've got me there *umg.*; **es hat ihn kalt erwischt** he was caught with his trousers down; **3.** (*erreichen*) catch (*auch j-n*); (*Zug etc.*) *auch* make; **nicht ~** miss; **4.** (*Krankheit*) catch, get; **5.** → **ergattern**

erworben I. *P.P.* → **erwerben**; **II.** *Adj. Med., Bio.* (*Ggs. angeboren*) acquired

erwünscht *Adj.* desired; (*willkommen*) welcome; (*wünschenswert*) desirable; **Rauchen nicht ~** thank you for not smoking; **du bist hier nicht ~** you're not wanted around here; **Computerkenntnisse ~, aber nicht Bedingung** *Zeitungsannonce*: computer skills an advantage (*od.* desirable), but not essential

erwürgen I. *v/t.* strangle; **II. Erwürgen** *n* strangling, strangulation

Erythrozyt *m*; -*en*, -*en*; *Physiol.* erythrocyte, red (blood) cell

Erz *n*; -*es*, -*e* ore

erz… *im Adj. umg. pej.* extremely, really, ultra-; **~dumm** extremely stupid

Erz… *im Subst. umg. pej.* out-and-out, arch-; **~lump, ~schurke** out-and-out scoundrel

Erz|abbau *m Bergb.* ore extraction; **~ader** *f* vein of ore, lode

erzählen *vt/i.* tell a story (*od.* stories); (*etw., auch Geschichte, Witz etc.*) tell; (*Erlebnis, Traum etc.*) recount; *kunstvoll*: narrate; **er kann gut ~** he's a good storyteller → **erzählt**; **~ von** tell s.o. about; tell of *lit.*; **man hat mir erzählt …** I've been told …; **was hat er erzählt?** what did he (have to) say?; **man erzählt sich …** they say …; **er erzählt nur Unsinn** *umg.* he talks a lot of nonsense; **erzähl doch keinen Unsinn!** *umg.* who are you trying to kid?; *zum Kind: auch* don't talk such nonsense; **erzähl keine Märchen!** *umg.* don't tell fibs (*zum Kind: auch* stories); **das kannst du mir nicht ~!** *od.* **das kannst du d-r Großmutter ~!** *umg.* pull the other one; **wem ~ Sie das!** *umg.* you're telling me; **dem werd ich was ~!** *umg.* I'll tell him a thing or two, I'll give him a piece of my mind

Erzählen *n*; -*s*, *kein Pl.* storytelling; *kunstvolles*: narration; **die Kunst des ~s** the art of storytelling (*od.* narrative); **erzählend I.** *Part. Präs.* → **erzählen**; **II.** *Adj. Stil*: narrative; **erzählenswert** *Adj.* worth telling; **e-e ~e**

Geschichte auch a good story; **Erzähler** *m*; -*s*, -, **Erzählerin** *f*; -, -*nen* narrator; *von Geschichten: auch* storyteller; *begabter*: raconteur; (*Schriftsteller*) narrative writer; **erzählerisch** *Adj.* narrative; **~es Talent besitzen** be a good storyteller; **erzählfreudig** *Adj.* communicative

Erzähl|kunst *f* narrative (art), art of narrative; **ein Meister der ~** a master of narrative (*od.* of the narrative art); **~perspektive** *f* narrative perspective

erzählt I. *P.P.* → **erzählen**; **II.** *Adj.*: **~e Zeit** *Lit.* narrative time

Erzähltechnik *f* narrative technique

Erzählung *f* **1.** (*das Erzählen*) telling; *in der Literatur*: narration; **2.** (*Geschichte*) story, tale (*beide auch Lit.*); (*Bericht*) account; *bes. fantasievolle, märchenhafte etc.: auch* tale; **ich kenne das/ihn nur aus ~en** I only know about that/him from stories; **3.** *Koll.* (*Erzählliteratur*) fiction

Erzählweise *f* narrative style

Erzbergwerk *n* ore mine

Erzbischof *m kath.* archbishop; **erzbischöflich** *Adj.* archiepiscopal; **Erzbistum** *n*, **Erzdiözese** *f* archbishopric, archdiocese

Erzengel *m Reli.* archangel

erzeugen *v/t.* **1.** produce; *Agr. auch* grow; *industriell*: manufacture, produce, make; **2.** *Phys., Chem.* generate (*auch Strom*); **3.** *fig.* (*verursachen*) cause, bring about, give rise to; (*Gefühl, Zustand etc.*) create, generate, engender, breed; (*Hass*) incite

Erzeuger¹ *m*; -*s*, -; (*Vater*) (biological) father; begetter; progenitor *geh., iro.*

Erzeuger² *m*; -*s*, -, **~in** *f*; -, -*nen*; *Wirts.* producer, manufacturer; *Agr.* producer, grower

Erzeuger|gemeinschaft *f* group of producers; **~land** *n* country of origin; **~preis** *m* manufacturer's price; *Agr.* producer price, price paid to the farmer

Erzeugnis *n* product; *landwirtschaftliches: mst Pl.* produce *Sg.*; *des Geistes, der Kunst*: creation; *der Fantasie*: product; **eigenes ~** my *etc.* own product (*od.* produce)

Erzeugung *f* production; *Wirts. auch* manufacture; *Phys., Chem.* generation; *fig.* creation; **Erzeugungskosten** *Pl.* production costs

Erzfeind *m*, **~in** *f* arch-enemy; **der ~** (*Satan*) Satan; **Erzfeindschaft** *f* archrivalry

Erzgauner *m*, **~in** *f umg. pej.* (real) crook

Erzgebirge *n*; *nur Sg.*; *Geogr.* Erzgebirge, Erz Mountains

Erz|gehalt *m Bergb.* ore content; **~gewinnung** *f* ore production; **~gießerei** *f* (metal) foundry

erzhaltig *Adj. Bergb.* ore-bearing

Erzherzog *m* archduke; **Erzherzogin** *f* archduchess; **Erzherzogtum** *n* archduchy

erziehbar *Adj.* educable; **schwer ~es Kind** problem child

erziehen *v/t.* (*unreg.*); (*aufziehen*) bring up (*zu* to be); raise; *geistig*: educate; (*Gehör, Körper, Tier*) train (*zu* to be); **j-n zur Sparsamkeit ~** bring s.o. up (*od.* teach s.o.) to be thrifty; **j-n im christlichen etc. Glauben ~** bring s.o. up as a Christian *etc.*; **er wurde streng erzogen** he had a strict upbringing; → **erzogen**

Erzieher *m*; -*s*, - educator; (*Lehrer*) teacher; (*Hauslehrer, Internatslehrer*)

tutor; *Kindergarten*: (qualified) kindergarten teacher; **Erzieherin** *f*; -, *-nen Kindergarten*: (qualified) kindergarten teacher; (*Hauslehrerin*) governess
erzieherisch I. *Adj.* educational; ～**e Probleme/Fragen** *innerhalb der Familie*: problems/questions of upbringing; **II.** *Adv.*: **das ist ～ ganz falsch** you're never going to teach them *etc.* that way *umg.*
Erziehung *f*; *nur Sg.* upbringing; *geistige, politische etc.*: education; (*Ausbildung*) training; (*Lebensart*) breeding; (*Manieren*) *auch* manners *Pl.*; **er hat e-e gute ～ genossen** he had a good upbringing; **ihr fehlt jede ～** she's got no upbringing (*od.* manners)
Erziehungs|anstalt *f altm. Brit. hist.* approved school, *Am.* reformatory, reform school; → **Erziehungsheim**; ～**arbeit** *f* educational activity; ～**beihilfe** *f* educational grant; ～**berater** *m*, ～**beraterin** *f* child guidance counsel(l)or; ～**beratung** *f* child guidance (service); ～**beratungsstelle** *f* child guidance office
erziehungsberechtigt *Adj.* having parental authority; **Erziehungsberechtigte** *m*, *f* **1.** parent; **2.** legal guardian
Erziehungs|fehler *Pl.* wrong upbringing *Sg.* (+ *Gen.* on the part of); ～**geld** *n state benefit paid to unemployed or partially employed parent who is caring for a newborn*; ～**heim** *n* community home, *Am.* supervised home; ～**maßnahme** *f* educational measure; ～**methode** *f* teaching method; method of education; ～**mittel** *n* teaching (*od.* educational) aid; ～**schwierigkeiten** *Pl.* difficulties in upbringing (*od.* education); ～**urlaub** *m* maternity leave; *für Väter*: paternity leave; ～**wesen** *n* **1.** education; **2.** educational system; ～**wissenschaft** *f* educational science
erzielen *v/t.* (*Ergebnis, Effekt*) achieve, attain, get; (*Resultate*) *auch* produce, come up with; (*Erfolg*) achieve, score; (*Gewinn etc.*) make; (*Preis*) *Person*: get; *Ware*: fetch; (*Punkt, Treffer*) score; (*Einigung, Kompromiss, Verständigung*) reach, come to; (*Wirkung*) have; **als Reingewinn ～** clear, net; **Einigung ～** reach (an) agreement (**über** + *Akk.* on)
erzittern *v/i.* tremble, shake (**vor** + *Dat.* with); *etw.* **～ lassen** make s.th. shake
erzkatholisch *Adj.* ultra-Catholic
erzkonservativ *Adj.* ultra- (*od.* arch-)conservative; *in GB*: *auch attr.* true-blue ...; **～ sein** *in GB*: *auch* be true blue, *in USA*: be an old-line (*od.* Old Guard) Republican
Erzlagerstätte *f Bergb.* mineral (*od.* ore) deposit
erzogen I. *P.P.* → **erziehen**; **II.** *Adj.*: **er ist gut/schlecht ～** he's very well-mannered / he's got no manners at all; **gut ～e Kinder** well-behaved children
erzreaktionär *Adj.* ultra-reactionary
Erzrivale *m*, **Erzrivalin** *f* archrival
erzürnen; *geh.* **I.** *v/t.* anger; *stärker*: enrage; **II.** *v/refl.* get angry (**über** + *Akk.* at, about); **erzürnt I.** *P.P.* → **erzürnen**; **II.** *Adj.* angry; *stärker* furious, enraged (**über** + *Akk.* about)
Erzvorkommen *n* ore deposit(s *Pl.*)
erzwingen *v/t.* (*unreg.*) force, get *s.th.* by force; *gesetzlich*: enforce (*auch Gehorsam etc.*); *etw.* **von j-m ～** (*Geständnis etc.*) force s.th. out of s.o.; (*Zugeständnis*) wring s.th. out of s.o.; **e-e Entscheidung ～** force an issue; **Liebe**

---

lässt sich nicht ～ you can't force love; **Erzwingungshaft** *f Jur.* coercive detention; **erzwungen I.** *P.P.* → **erzwingen**; **II.** *Adj.* forced; *Lächeln etc.*: *auch* put-on; **erzwungenermaßen** *Adv.* under pressure
es[1] *pers. Pron.* **1.** (*Nom.*); *Sache*: it; *Kind, Haustier*: it; *bei bekanntem Geschlecht*: he, she; **2.** (*Akk.*) it; **ich nahm ～** I took it; **ich bin ～ leid** I'm (sick and) tired of it; **ich weiß ～** I know; **da hast du's!** what did I say?; **3.** *mit unpers. Verb*: **～ schneit** it's snowing; **～ ist kalt** it's cold; **～ hat geklopft** someone's (knocking) at the door; **mich juckt's** I've got an itch; **mir geht ～ gut** I'm well (*od.* fine); **4.** *als Hilfssubjekt*: **wer ist der Junge? - ～ ist mein Bruder** he's my brother; **wer sind diese Mädchen? - ～ sind m-e Schwestern** they're my sisters; **wer hat angerufen? - ～ war mein Chef** it was my boss; **ich bin's** it's me; **sie sind ～** it's them; **～ war keiner da** there was nobody there, nobody was there; **～ kam der Tag, da...** the day came (*od.* there came the day) when ...; **～ war einmal ein König** once upon a time there was a king; **～ gibt zu viele Probleme** there are too many problems; **～ wird erzählt ...** they say ...; **～ wurde getanzt** they *etc.* danced, there was dancing; **5.** *als Hilfsobjekt*: **er ist reich, ich bin ～ auch** so am I; **ich hoffe ～** I hope so; **er hat ～ mir gesagt** he told me so; *er sagte,* **ich sollte gehen, und ich tat ～** and I did, so I did; *bist du bereit?* - **ja, ich bin ～** yes, I am; **ich kann ～** I can (do it); **ich halte es für leichtsinnig zu** (+ *Inf.*) I think it would be irresponsible to (+ *Inf.*); **～ gefällt mir nicht, dass er so faul ist** I don't like the fact that he's so lazy; **6.** *mit refl. Verben*: **mit diesem Auto fährt es sich gut** this is a nice car to drive; **hier lässt sich's aushalten** *umg.* it's not too bad (*od.* quite bearable) here, there are worse places than this
es[2], **Es** *n*; -, -; *Mus.* E flat
Es *n*; -, *kein Pl.*; *Psych. the* id
Escapetaste [ɛs'keːp-] *f Computer*: escape key
Eschatologie [ɛsçatolo'giː] *f*; -, *-n*; *Reli.* eschatology; **eschatologisch** *Adj.* eschatological
Esche *f*; -, *-n*; *Bot.* **1.** (*Baum*) ash (tree); **2.** *nur Sg.*, (*Holz*) ash (wood); **eschen** *Adj.* ash; **Eschenholz** *n* ash (wood)
Es-Dur *n Mus.* E flat major
Esel *m*; -s, -. **1.** *Zool.* donkey; *seltener*: ass; **männlicher/weiblicher ～** male/female donkey; *seltener*: he-ass (*od.* jackass) / she-ass; **störrisch wie ein ～** (as) stubborn as a mule; **wenn es dem ～ zu wohl wird, geht er aufs Eis** *Sprichw.* etwa you'll *etc.* get a rude awakening one of these fine days, overconfidence makes people reckless; **2.** *umg.* (*Dummkopf*) twit; **alter ～** old fool; **ich ～!** what an idiot!, how stupid can you get!; **Eselin** *f*; -, *-nen* female donkey; *seltener* she-ass
Esels|brücke *f* mnemonic (aid); **ich muss mir e-e ～ bauen** I've got to have something that will help me remember; ～**ohr** *n fig.* dog-ear, turned-down corner; **Buch mit ～en** dog-eared book
Eseltreiber *m*, ～**in** *f* donkey driver
...esk *im Adj. geh.* -esque, (-)like; **ballad～** ballad-like; **donjuan～** Don-Juanesque

---

Eskalation *f*; -, *-en*; *Pol.*, *Mil.* escalation; **eskalieren I.** *v/i.* (*ist eskaliert*); *Konflikt etc.*: escalate; **II.** *v/t.* (*hat*); (*Maßnahmen etc.*) step up, escalate
Eskapade *f*; -, *-n*; *geh.* escapade
Eskapismus *m*; -, *kein Pl.*; *Psych. od. geh.* escapism; **eskapistisch** *Adj.* escapist
Eskimo[1] *m*; -(s), -(s) Inuit, Eskimo *neg!*
Eskimo[2] *n*; -; *Ling.* Inuit, Eskimo *neg!*
Eskimorolle *f Sport* Eskimo roll
Eskorte *f*; -, *-n* escort; *mit Wagen*: *auch* motorcade; **eskortieren** *v/t.* escort
Es-Moll *n Mus.* E flat minor
Esoterik *f*; -, *kein Pl.*; *geh.* **1.** esoteric arts *Pl.*; **2.** esotericism; **3.** *weitS.* New Age (movement); **esoterisch** *Adj.* esoteric
Espe *f*; -, *-n*; *Bot.* aspen; **Espenlaub** *n*: **wie ～ zittern** tremble like a leaf (*od.* an aspen leaf)
Esperanto *n*; -(s), *kein Pl.* Esperanto
Espresso *m*; -(s), -s *od. Espressi* espresso (*Pl.* espressos); ～**automat** *m* espresso machine; ～**bar** *f* espresso bar; ～**maschine** *f* espresso machine
Esprit [ɛs'priː] *m*; -s, *kein Pl.*; *geh.* wit; **e-e Frau mit ～** a (woman of) wit
Essapfel *m* eating apple, eater
Essay [ɛ'seː] *m*, *n*; -s, -s essay; **Essayist** *m*; -en, -en essayist; **Essayistik** *f*; -, *kein Pl.* **1.** (the art of) essay writing; **2.** (*Gesamtheit der Essays*) essayistic writings *Pl.*; **Essayistin** *f*; -, *-nen* essayist; **essayistisch** *Adj.* essayistic
essbar *Adj.* (*Ggs. verdorben*) eatable; (*Ggs. giftig*) edible; ～**er Pilz** (edible) mushroom; **Essbarkeit** *f*; *nur Sg.* edibility
Ess|besteck *n* cutlery (set), *Am.* silverware, flatware; ～**-Brechsucht** *f* bulimia
Esse *f*; -, *-n* **1.** (*Schornstein, Rauchfang*) chimney; **2.** (*Schmiede*) forge
Essecke *f* dining area; → *auch* **Essnische**
essen; *isst, aß, hat gegessen* **I.** *v/i.* eat; **zu Mittag/Abend ～** have lunch/dinner; **viel ～** eat a lot; *generell*: be a big eater; **gut/warm/kalt ～** have a good/hot/cold meal; *das Kind* **isst gut/schlecht** has a good/poor appetite; **wenn du gesund werden willst, musst du tüchtig ～** you must (*Am.* have to) eat well; **man isst dort ganz gut** the food is quite good there; **was gibt es zu ～?** what's for dinner (*od.* lunch)?, what are we having for dinner (*od.* lunch)?; **wir können gleich ～** dinner (*od.* lunch) will be ready in a minute; **～ gehen** *od.* **auswärts, im Restaurant ～** eat out, eat at a restaurant; **ich geh zu m-r Schwester ～** I'm eating (*od.* having a meal) at my sister's; **II.** *v/t.* eat; *etw.* **gern ～** like; **s-n Teller leer ～** clear one's plate; **ich esse kein Fleisch** I don't eat meat; **sie hat noch keinen Bissen gegessen** she hasn't even touched her food, she hasn't eaten a single morsel yet; **du isst mich noch arm!** *umg.* you're going to eat me out of house and home; **nichts wird so heiß gegessen, wie es gekocht wird** *Sprichw.* things are seldom as bad as they seem; **das ist längst gegessen!** *umg. fig.* that's ancient history, that's dead and buried; **III.** *v/refl.*: **sich satt ～** eat one's fill (**an** + *Dat.* of)
Essen *n*; -s, -. **1.** *nur Sg.*; *Handlung*: eating; **wir sind gerade beim ～** we're just having dinner (*od.* lunch), we're in the middle of eating; **lass dich**

E

nicht beim ~ stören don't let me disturb your meal; *das ist nichts zum ~* you can't eat that, that's not for eating; **2.** (*Speise, Kost, Verpflegung*) food; (*Gericht*) dish; **~ und Trinken** food and drink; *gesundes/vegetarisches etc.* ~ healthy/vegetarian food; *~ fassen! Mil.* come and get it!, grub up!, *Am.* chow down!; **3.** (*Mahlzeit*) meal; (*Festmahl*) dinner; **~ auf Rädern** meals on wheels; *das ~ machen od. kochen* make (*od.* cook) the dinner (*od.* lunch); *zum ~ gehen* (*Mittagspause machen*) go for lunch; (*ausgehen*) eat out; *j-n zum ~ einladen* invite s.o. for a meal (*od.* to dinner, lunch); *zum ~ bleiben* stay for dinner (*od.* lunch), stay and eat; *etw. vor/nach dem ~ einnehmen* take s.th. before/after meals; *nach dem ~ sollst du ruhn oder tausend Schritte tun Sprichw.* after dinner sit awhile, after supper walk a mile; **4.** (*Portion*) meal; *20 ~ ausgeben* serve 20 meals

Essen|ausgabe *f*: *~ von 12 - 14 Uhr* meals served from 12 p.m - 2 p.m.; **~marke** meal ticket, *Brit. auch* lunch (-eon) voucher

Essens|ausgabe *f* → *Essenausgabe*; **~geruch** *m* smell of food (*od.* cooking); **~marke** *f* → *Essenmarke*; **~zeit** *f mittags*: lunchtime, lunch hour; *abends*: dinnertime; *er ruft immer zur ~ an* he always phones at mealtimes; **~zuschuss** *m* lunch allowance

essentiell *Adj.* → *essenziell*

Essenz *f*: *-, -en* essence (*auch fig.*); **essenziell** *Adj.* essential (*auch Chem., Bio.*); *von ~er Bedeutung* of paramount importance

Esser *m*; *-s, -,* **~in** *f*; *-, -nen*: *guter/schlechter ~* big/poor (*od.* bad) eater; *zusätzlicher ~* extra mouth to feed

Ess|geschirr *n* crockery, *Am.* dinnerware, dishes *umg.*; (*Service*) dinner service; *Mil.* mess kit; **~gewohnheiten** *Pl.* eating habits; **~gier** *f* greed, gluttony; **~gruppe** *f* dining set, dining table and chairs *Pl.*

Essig *m*; *-s, Sorten*: *-e* vinegar; *damit ist es (jetzt) ~ umg. fig.* it's all off; **~baum** *m Bot.* tanner's sumac(h); **~essenz** *f* vinegar essence; **~flasche** *f* vinegar bottle; **~gurke** *f Gastr.* pickled cucumber; *kleine*: (pickled) gherkin, *Am.* pickle

essigsauer *Adj.* acetic; → *Tonerde*

Essig|säure *f* acetic acid; **~und-Öl-Ständer** *m* cruet stand

Ess|kastanie *f* (sweet) chestnut; **~korb** *m* hamper; **~kultur** *f* gastronomy; (*keine*) **~ haben** have (no) gastronomic finesse, take (no) care over the preparation and eating of food

Esslöffel *m* tablespoon; *zwei (gestrichene/gehäufte) ~* two (level/heaped) tablespoon(ful)s

Ess|lust *f* appetite; **~nische** *f* dining alcove, dinette; **~papier** *n* edible paper; **~stäbchen** *Pl.* chopsticks; **~störung** *f Med.* eating disorder; **~sucht** *f* craving for food; **~tisch** *m* dining table; **~unlust** *f* lack of appetite; **~waren** *Pl.* food *Sg.*; *Wirts.* foodstuffs; **~zimmer** *n* dining room

Establishment [is'tɛblɪʃmənt] *n*; *-s, -s*; *the* establishment, *the* Establishment

Este *m*; *-n, -n* Estonian

Ester *m*; *-s, -*; *Chem.* ester

Estin *f*; *-, -nen* Estonian woman (*od.* girl); **Estland** (*n*) *Geog.* Estonia; **Estländer** *m*; *-s, -,* **Estländerin** *f*; *-, -nen* Estonian, *weiblich auch* Estonian

woman (*od.* girl); **estländisch, estnisch** *Adj.* Estonian

Estragon *m*; *-s, kein Pl.*; *Bot., Gastr.* tarragon

Estrich *m*; *-s, -e* **1.** stone floor; **2.** *schw.* (*Dachboden*) loft, attic

Eszett *n*; *-, - the letter ß as used in German*

etablieren I. *v/refl.* establish o.s. (*od.* itself), become established; *geschäftlich*: set o.s. up, start a business; *häuslich*: settle in; *sich ~ als* set o.s. up as; **II.** *v/t.* (*Geschäft*) set up, establish, found; (*Ordnung*) establish; **etabliert I.** *P.P.* → *etablieren*; **II.** *Adj. Person*: established; *Partei, Verlag etc.*: well-known, well-established; *Machtposition, Ordnung*: entrenched; **Etablierung** *f* establishment

Etablissement [etablısə'mãː] *n*; *-s, -s od. schw. -e* **1.** *Wirts.* (business) establishment; **2.** *geh. euph.* (*Bordell*) establishment; **3.** *geh.* (*Vergnügungsstätte*) place, establishment; *ein gepflegtes ~* (*Lokal*) a well-kept (*od.* well-appointed *förm.*) place

Etage [e'taːʒə] *f*; *-, -n* **1.** floor, stor(e)y; *auf od. in der ersten ~* on the first (*Am.* second) floor; *auf welcher ~ wohnst du?* which floor do you live on (*od.* are you on)?; **2.** *e-s Stockbetts*: bunk; *e-s Gestells*: shelf, tier; **3.** *fig. e-r Hierarchie*: ranking, level

Etagen|bad *n im Hotel*: shared bath; **~bett** *n* bunk bed(s *Pl.*)

etagenförmig *Adj.* terraced, tiered, (arranged) in tiers

Etagen|heizung *f* single-stor(e)y heating (system); **~kellner** *m* floor waiter; **~wohnung** *f* flat (*Am.* apartment) that takes up a whole floor of a building

Etappe *f*; *-, -n* **1.** stage; *Sport auch* leg; *~ des Lebens* stage in life, phase of life; **2.** *Mil.* communication zone; (*Stützpunkt*) base

Etappen|sieg *m* stage win (*od.* victory); **~sieger** *m*, **~siegerin** *f* stage winner

etappenweise I. *Adv.* in stages, step by step, bit by bit *umg.*; **II.** *Adj. attr.* step-by-step ...

Etappenziel *n* end of a (the) stage

Etat [e'taː] *m*; *-s, -s* **1.** *Wirts., Pol.* budget; *veranschlagter: auch* estimates *Pl.*; *das ist nicht im ~ vorgesehen* that hasn't been budgeted for; *das übersteigt m-n ~ für Süßigkeiten umg. hum.* I can't afford that many sweets; **2.** *Mil.* establishment; **~entwurf** *m* budget proposals *Pl.*; **~jahr** *n* fiscal (*od.* financial) year; **~kürzung** *f* cut in the budget, budget cut

etatmäßig *Adj.* budgetary; *Beamter etc.*: permanent; *Torwart etc.*: regular

Etat|posten *m* budget(ary) item; **~überschreitung** *f* spending in excess of the budget

etc. *Abk.* (*et cetera*) etc, etc.; **et cetera** (*abgek. etc.*) etcetera; **~ p.p.** *umg. hum.* and so on and so forth

etepetete *Adj. umg.* **1.** (*geziert*) la-di--da; **2.** (*penibel*) fussy; **3.** (*zimperlich*) squeamish

Eternit® *n, m*; *-s, kein Pl.* asbestos cement; **~platte** *f* asbestos cement slab

Ethanol, Ethyl *etc.* → *Äthanol, Äthyl etc.*

Ethik *f*; *-, -en* ethics *Pl.* (*als Fach V. im Sg.*); **~kommission** *f* ethical (*Am.* ethics) committee; **~konferenz** *f* ethics conference, conference on ethics; **~unterricht** *m* ethics

ethisch *Adj.* ethical; *~e Frage* ethical question, question of ethics; *aus ~en Gründen ablehnen* reject on ethical grounds

Ethnie *f*; *-, -n* ethnic group; **ethnisch I.** *Adj.* ethnic; *~e Säuberung Pol.* ethnic cleansing; **II.** *Adv.* ethnically

Ethno... *im Subst.* ethno-; *Stil*: ethnic; **Ethnorock** ethnic rock

ethnographisch I. *Adj.* ethnographic; **II.** *Adv.* ethnographically

Ethnologe *m*; *-n, -n* ethnologist; **Ethnologie** *f*; *-, kein Pl.* ethnology; **Ethnologin** *f*; *-, -nen* ethnologist

Ethologe *m*; *-n, -n* ethologist; **Ethologie** *f*; *-, kein Pl.* ethology; **Ethologin** *f*; *-, -nen* ethologist

Ethos *n*; *-, kein Pl.* ethos; *weitS.* ethics *Pl.*

Etikett *n*; *-(e)s, -e(n) od. -s* label (*auch fig.*); (*Preisschild*) price tag; *auf dem ~ steht* it says on the label, the label says; *mit e-m ~ versehen fig.* label, pin a label on

Etikette *f*; *-, -n* **1.** etiquette, convention(s *Pl.*); *Verstoß gegen die ~* breach of etiquette; *es ist gegen die ~ zu* (+ *Inf.*) it's bad form to (+ *Inf.*); **2.** *österr., schw.* → *Etikett*; **Etikettenschwindel** *m* **1.** bogus claim(s *Pl.*), fraudulent label(l)ing; **2.** *fig.* (a) fraud; *das ist ja der reinste ~* they ought to be done under the Trades Descriptions Act, *Am.* they should get them for false advertising

etikettieren *v/t.* **1.** put a label on; price-tag; **2.** *fig.* label; *j-n als Betrüger ~* label s.o. a cheat

etlich... I. *unbest. Pron.* **1.** *~e* (*Pl.*) a number of, quite a few; *~e Mal(e)* quite a few times, a number of times; *~e tausend Dollar* several thousand dollars; *~e Millionen* several millions; *Dollar etc.*: several million *dollars etc.*; **2.** *~es* (*Sg.*) a number of things *Pl.*, a thing or two; **II.** *Adj. altm. geh.* (*ziemlich groß, viel*) considerable; *mit ~em Glück* not without a measure of good fortune

Etrusker *m*; *-s, -,* **~in** *f*; *-, -nen hist.* Etruscan; **etruskisch** *Adj.* Etruscan; **Etruskisch** *n*; *-en*; *Ling.* Etruscan; *das ~e* Etruscan

Etüde *f*; *-, -n*; *Mus.* étude

Etui *n*; *-s, -s* case

ETW *Abk.* (*Eigentumswohnung*) owner-occupied flat, *Am.* condo(minium)

etwa *Adv.* **1.** (*in ~*) (*ungefähr*) about, approximately, around *umg.*; *nachgestellt*: or so, or thereabouts; *in ~ fertig etc.*: more or less; *wann ~?* approximately when?; (*um wie viel Uhr?*) *auch* around what time? *umg.*; *wie viel ~?* about how much?; *wie macht man das? - so od. so* something like this; **2.** (*zum Beispiel*) for instance, for example, (let's) say; *viele Vögel, wie od. so ~ die Amsel, ...* many birds, like (*od.* such as) the blackbird for instance; **3.** (*vielleicht*) by any chance, possibly; *war sie ~ da?* was she there by any chance?; *glaubst du das ~?* do you really believe that?, you don't believe that, do you?; *ist das ~ besser?* *zweifelnd*: is that any better?; *ist das ~ nichts?* *herausfordernd*: isn't that something?, what do you think of that then?; *das stimmt doch, oder ~ nicht?* surely that's right - or is it? (*od.* - or do you think not?); **4.** *nicht ~ verstärkend*: surely; not that; *du warst doch nicht ~ da?* you weren't there, were you?, don't tell me you were there;

nicht **~**, *dass es etwas ausmachen würde, aber* ... not that it matters, but ...; **5.** *gegenüberstellend*: *sie ist nicht ~ faul,* (**sondern**) *nur langsam* she's not lazy, just slow; *es war nicht ~ gestern, sondern vorgestern* it wasn't yesterday but the day before

etwaig I. *Adj. attr.* any; (*möglich*) possible; **~e Schwierigkeiten** any difficulties (that might arise); **II.** *Adv.*: *~ auftretende Fehler* any mistakes that may occur

etwas *unbest. Pron.* **1.** *Unbestimmtes, nachfolgend Bestimmtes*: something; *verneinend, fragend od. bedingend*: anything; *~ Merkwürdiges* something strange, a strange thing; *~ anderes* something (*fragend*: anything) else; *ohne ~ zu sagen* without (saying) a word; *~, das od. was ich nicht verstehe, ist ...* something (*od.* one thing) that I don't understand is ...; *da ist noch ~*(*, das ich sagen möchte*): ... there is something else (that I should [*Am.* would] like to say): ...; *so ~ habe ich noch nie gehört* I've never heard anything like it; *so ~ kommt schon vor* that kind of thing does happen; *das hat ~ für sich* there's something to be said for it; *sie haben ~ miteinander* umg. euph. there's something going on between them; *nein, so ~!* umg. *überrascht*: well, there's a thing!; *verärgert*: would you believe it!; **2.** (*ein bisschen*) some; any; a little; a bit of; *~ Englisch* a little English; *~ Petersilie* a touch of parsley; *~ anders* slightly different; *ich muss mich ~ ausruhen* I need to rest for a while (*od.* to have a little rest); *hab ~ Geduld* be patient; *das ist immerhin od. wenigstens ~* that's something, at least; **3.** (*ziemlich*) quite, somewhat; a little, a bit; *ich bin noch nicht fertig, es ist eben ~ schwierig* it is quite (*Am.* fairly) (*od.* a little) difficult, you know; **4.** (*ein Teil von*) some; *nimm dir ~ davon* take some; *er versteht ~ davon* he knows a thing or two about it; *sie hat ~ von e-r Katze* (*an sich*) she's got something catlike (*od.* something of a cat) about her; **5.** (*viel, Wichtiges etc.*) something; *es zu ~ bringen* get somewhere umg., make something of o.s.; *aus ihm wird noch mal ~* he'll go a long way; *das will schon ~ heißen!* umg. now that really is something!; *ihr Wort gilt ~ beim Vorstand* what she says carries weight (*od.* counts for a lot) with the management

Etwas *n*; -, - *od. hum.* -se **1.** *Sache*: thing; *was ist das glitzernde ~ da hinten?* what's that glittering thing back there?; **2.** (*kleines Tier, Baby*) little thing; **3.** *das gewisse ~* that certain something; → *auch* **was** IV

Etymologie *f*; -, -*n* etymology; **etymologisch** *Adj.* etymological

Et-Zeichen *n* (*Zeichen* &) ampersand

EU *f*; -, *kein Pl.*; *Abk. Pol.* (**Europäische Union**) EU, European Union; **~-Beihilfe** *f* EU subsidy; **~-Bestimmung** *f* EU regulation

Euböa -*s*; *Geog.* Euboea

euch (*Dat. und Akk. Pl. von* **du**) **I.** *pers. Pron.* (to) you; *ich hab's ~ gesagt/gegeben* I told you /I gave it to you (*od.* I gave you it); **II.** *refl. Pron.* yourselves; *nach Präp.*: you; *oft unübersetzt*: *setzt ~!* sit down

Eucharistie *f kirchl.*: *die ~* the Eucha-

rist; **~feier** *f* Eucharistic mass

euer I. *Poss. Pron.* (*Nom. Pl. m und n*) **1.** *adjektivisch*: your; *~ Robert am Briefende*: Yours, Robert; *Euer Ehren/Gnaden* Your Hono(u)r/Grace; *e-r eu(e)rer Freunde* a friend of yours; **2.** *substantivisch*: yours; *der/die/das eu(e)re* (*auch großgeschrieben*) yours; → *auch* **dein** I 2; **II.** *pers. Pron.* (*Gen. Pl. von* **du**) of you; *ich gedenke ~* I am thinking of you

Eugenik *f*; -, *kein Pl.*; *Med.* eugenics *Pl.* (*V. im Sg.*); **eugenisch I.** *Adj.* eugenic; **II.** *Adv.* eugenically

EU-Gipfel *m* EU summit

Eukalyptus *m*; -, - *und* Eukalypten; *Bot., Pharm.* eucalyptus (*Pl.* eucalyptuses *od.* eucalypti); **~baum** *m* eucalyptus tree, eucalypt; **~bonbon** *n, m* eucalyptus sweet (*Am.* candy); **~öl** *n* eucalyptus oil

euklidisch *Adj. Math.* Euclidean

EU-konform *Adj. und Adv. Pol.* in line with EU provisions

Eule *f*; -, -*n* **1.** owl; **2.** *geh. fig.*: **~n nach Athen tragen** carry coals to Newcastle; **3.** *Zool.* (*Nachtfalter*) noctuid; **4.** *umg. fig. pej.* old bag

Eulen|ruf *m*, **~schrei** *m* owl's cry, hoot; **~spiegelei** *f*; -, -*en* prank

EU|-Ministerrat *m Pol.* Council of Ministers; **~-Mitglied(sland)** *n* member of the EU, EU member (state *od.* nation); **~-Norm** *f* EU standard

Eunuch *m*; -*en*, -*en* eunuch; **eunuchenhaft** *Adj.* eunuch(-)like; **Eunuchenstimme** *f* high-pitched (*od.* squeaky umg.) voice

Euphemismus *m*; -, *Euphemismen*; *geh.* euphemism; **euphemistisch I.** *Adj. geh.* euphemistic; **II.** *Adv.* euphemistically

Euphorie *f*; -, -*n*; *Med. und geh.* euphoria; **euphorisierend I.** *Adj. Mittel*: euphoriant; **II.** *Adv.*: *~ wirken* have a euphoriant effect; **euphorisch I.** *Adj.* euphoric; **II.** *Adv.* euphorically

Euphrat *m*; -(*s*) *Geog.* Euphrates

Eurasien (*n*); -*s*; *Geog.* Eurasia; **Eurasier** *m*; -*s*, -, **Eurasierin** *f*; -, -*nen* Eurasian; **eurasisch** *Adj.* Eurasian

eure, eurer → **euer**

euerseits *Adv.* for (*od.* on) your part

eures → **euer**

euresgleichen *Pron.* people like yourselves; *pej.* the likes of you umg., your sort umg.

eurethalben *Adv. altm. od. poet.* → **euretwegen**; **euretwegen** *Adv.* **1.** (*wegen euch*) because of you, on your account; (*euch zuliebe*) because of you, for your sake(s); **2.** (*in eurer Sache*) on your behalf; **euretwillen** *Adv.*: (*um*) *~* for your sake(s); (*in eurer Sache*) on your behalf

Eurhythmie *f*; -, *kein Pl.* **1.** *von Bewegungen*: eur(h)ythmics *Pl.* (*V. im Sg.*); **2.** *Med.* eurhythmia

eurige *Poss. Pron.*; *substantivisch*: *der/die/das ~ od. Eurige* yours; → *auch* **dein** I 2

Euro *m*; -*s*, -*s*; *Fin., Wirts.* euro, Euro; **~-Banknote** *f* euro note

Eurocard *f*; -, -*s*; *Wirts.* Eurocard

Eurocentmünze *f* euro cent coin

Eurocheque ['ɔyroʃɛk] → **Euroscheck**

Euro|dollar *m Wirts.* Eurodollar; **~kommunismus** *m Pol., hist.* Eurocommunism

Eurokrat *m*; -*en*, -*en*, **~in** *f*; -, -*nen*; *Pol.* Eurocrat

Euro|land *n* **1.** EMU country (*country that has introduced the euro*); **2.** *Koll.*;

kein Pl. (*alle Staaten der Europäischen Währungsunion*) Euroland; **~münze** *f* euro coin; **~norm** *f* European standard

Europa I. (*n*); -*s*; *Geog., Pol.* Europe; **II.** *f*; -*s*, *kein Pl.*; *Myth.* Europa

Europa|abgeordnete *m*, *f Pol.* Member of the European Parliament, MEP; **~bus** *m Verk.* international tourist bus run by the European rail networks

Europäer *m*; -*s*, -, **~in** *f*; -, -*nen* European

Europaflagge *f* flag of the European Union

europäisch *Adj.* European; *Europäischer Binnenmarkt* European Common Market; *Europäische Freihandelszone* European Free Trade Area; *Europäische Gemeinschaft* hist. (*abgek.* EG) European Community (*abgek.* EC); *Europäisches Parlament* European Parliament; *Europäische Union* (*abgek.* **EU**) European Union (*abgek.* EU); *Europäisches Währungssystem* (*abgek.* **EWS**) European Monetary System (*abgek.* EMS); *Europäische Währungsunion* (*abgek.* **EWU**) European Monetary Union (*abgek.* EMU); *Europäische Wirtschaftsgemeinschaft* (*abgek.* **EWG**) hist. European Economic Community (*abgek.* EEC); *Europäische Zentralbank* (*abgek.* EZB) European Central Bank (*abgek.* ECB); → *Menschenrechtskommission etc.*

europäisieren *v/t.* Europeanize; **Europäisierung** *f* Europeanization

Europa|meister *m*, **~meisterin** *f Sport* European champion (*Mannschaft*: champions *Pl.*); **~meisterschaft** *f* European championships *Pl.*

europamüde *Adj. Pol.* Euro-fatigued (*disillusioned with European politics and taking a more nationalistic stance*); **Europamüdigkeit** *f* Euro fatigue

Europa|parlament *n* European Parliament; **~parlamentarier** *m*, **~parlamentarierin** *f* Euro-MP; **~pokal** *m Sport* European Cup; *~* (*der Landesmeister*) European Cup; *~ der Pokalsieger* früher: European Cup Winners' Cup; **~politik** *f Pol.* Europolitics *Pl.*; **~rat** *m*; *nur Sg.*; *Pol.* Council of Europe; **~rekord** *m Sport* European record; **~straße** *f Verk.* European route; **~wahlen** *Pl. Pol.* Euro-elections

europaweit I. *Adj.* cross-Europe ..., Europe-wide; **II.** *Adv.* Europe-wide, all over (*od.* throughout) Europe

Euroscheck *m* Eurocheque; **~karte** *f* Eurocheque card

Eurotunnel *m*; *nur Sg.* Channel Tunnel

Eurovision *f*; *nur Sg.*; *TV* Eurovision; **Eurovisionssendung** *f* Eurovision broadcast

Eurozeichen *n* (€) euro symbol

eurozentrisch *Adj. Geogr., Pol. etc.* eurocentric; **Eurozentrismus** *m*; -, *kein Pl.* eurocentrism

Eurozone *f* euro zone

Eurythmie → **Eurhythmie** 1

EU-Staat *m* EU state (*od.* country)

eustachisch *Adj. Anat.*: *~e Röhre* Eustachian tube

Euter *n*; -*s*, - udder

Euthanasie *f*; -, *kein Pl.*; *Med.* euthanasia, mercy killing

Eutrophierung *f* eutrophication

EU-weit *Adj. und Adv.* EU-wide

ev. *Abk.* (**evangelisch**) Protestant; (*evangelisch-lutherisch*) Lutheran

e.V. *Abk.* (**eingetragener Verein**) regis-

tered society
Eva *f; -, -s; umg. hum.* Eve
evakuieren *v/t.* evacuate (*auch Med. und Phys.*); **Evakuierung** *f* evacuation
Evangele *m; -n, -n,* **Evangelin** *f; -, -nen; umg., oft pej.* Protestant; **Evangeliar** *n; -s, -e kirchl.* Gospel; **evangelisch** *Adj.* Protestant; **~-lutherisch** Lutheran; **~-reformiert** Reformed; **evangelisieren** *v/t.* evangelize; **Evangelist** *m; -en, -en* evangelist; **Evangelium** *n; -s, Evangelien* **1.** *bibl.* Gospel; **2.** *fig.* gospel; **was s-e Schwester sagt, ist für ihn das ~** what his sister says is gospel as far as he's concerned; → **Matthäusevangelium** *etc.*
Evas|kostüm *n umg.: im ~* in the nude, in one's birthday suit; **~tochter** *f hum.* daughter of Eve, woman
Eventualfall *m: für den ~* for eventualities, just in case
Eventualität *f; -, -en* eventuality; **eventuell I.** *Adj.* possible; (*irgendwelche*) any; **~e Beschwerden** any complaints (that might arise); **II.** *Adv.* possibly; (*vielleicht*) perhaps, maybe; (*notfalls*) if necessary; (*gegebenenfalls*) should the occasion arise; **kommst du mit? - ~** I might; **ich würde es ~ nehmen** I might (well) take it, I might consider taking it
evident *Adj.* obvious, clear; (*einleuchtend*) self-evident; **Evidenz** *f; -, kein Pl.* evident nature, obviousness (+ *Gen.* of)
Evolution *f; -, -en* evolution (*auch weitS. Entwicklung*); **evolutionär** *Adj.* evolutionary
Evolutions|lehre *f,* **~theorie** *f* Theory of Evolution
evozieren *v/t. geh.* evoke
evtl. *Abk.* (*eventuell*) poss. (= possibly)
E-Werk *n* power station
EWG *f; -, kein Pl.; Abk.* (**Europäische Wirtschaftsgemeinschaft**) *hist.* EEC
ewig I. *Adj.* **1.** *Jugend, Liebe, Schnee, Treue etc.*: eternal; (*unaufhörlich*) *auch* everlasting; *Frieden, Glück, Schnee etc.*: *auch* perpetual; *Liebe, Treue etc.*: *auch* undying; (*endlos*) endless; **der Ewige Jude** the Wandering Jew; **das ~e Leben** eternal life, immortality; **die Ewige Stadt** (*Rom*) the Eternal City; **seit ~en Zeiten** from (*od.* since) time immemorial; **das ~e Licht** *kath.* the sanctuary lamp; → **Jagdgründe**; **2.** (*ständig*) eternal, constant, incessant; (*endlos*) endless; **~er Student** eternal student; **der ~e Verlierer** the perennial loser; **~er Zweifler** *etc.* arch-sceptic (*Am.* - skeptic *etc.*); **seit ~en Zeiten** (*schon lange*) for ages; **du mit d-r ~en Meckerei** *etc.* you never stop, do you?; **II.** *Adv.* **1.** forever, eternally; **auf immer und ~** for ever and ever; **2.** *umg.:* **~** (*lange*) for ever, for ages; **~ und drei Tage** for ever and a day; **es dauert ~** it's taking ages (*od.* for ever); **er jammert ~** he never stops moaning; **der ~ gleiche Trott** the same old routine day after day; **3.** *umg.* (*sehr*) very; **es ist ~ schade** it's just too bad
Ewiggestrige *m; f; -n, -n* diehard
Ewigkeit *f* **1.** eternity; **bis in alle ~ to** the end of time; **in ~, Amen** for ever and ever, amen; **in die ~ eingehen** *geh. euph.* pass into eternity; **2.** *umg.* ages; **es ist schon e-e ~ her, seit ...** it's (*od.* it's been) ages since ...; **ich warte schon seit ~en** I've been waiting for ages
EWS *Abk.* (**Europäisches Währungssystem**) EMS (= European Monetary

System)
EWU *Abk.* (**Europäische Währungsunion**) EMU (= European Monetary Union)
ex *Adv. umg.* **1.** **~ trinken** empty one's glass (in one go); **~!** bottoms up!; **2.** (*vorbei*) all over; **3.** **~ sein** (*tot*) have had it
Ex¹ *f; -, -en; Jugendspr.* → **Extemporale**
Ex² *m, f; -, -; mst Sg.; umg.* (*ehemalige[r] Partner[in] etc.*) ex
Ex... *im Subst.* (*ehemalig*) ex-..., former; **~diktator** former dictator; **~weltmeister** former world champion
exakt *Adj.* precise, accurate; *Übersetzung, Wissenschaft:* exact; *Person:* scrupulous, pernickety *pej.*; **Exaktheit** *f; nur Sg.* precision, accuracy, exactitude; scrupulousness; → **exakt**
exaltiert *Adj. geh.* **1.** (over-)excited; **2.** (*überschwänglich*) effusive
Examen *n; -s, - od. Examina* examination, exam; **~ machen** take one's exams (*od.* finals)
Examens|... *im Subst. siehe auch Prüfungs...*; **~arbeit** *f* extended essay; → *auch* **Diplomarbeit, Magisterarbeit** *etc.*
Exegese *f; -, -n; fachspr., geh.* exegesis (*Pl.* exegeses); **exegetisch** *Adj.* exegetic
exekutieren *v/t.* **1.** execute; **2.** *österr. Amtsspr.* → **pfänden**; **Exekution** *f; -, -en* **1.** execution; **2.** *österr. Amtsspr.* → **Pfändung**; **Exekutionskommando** *n* firing squad
exekutiv *Adj. bes. Pol., Jur.* executive; **Exekutivausschuss** *m Pol.* executive committee; *Wirts.* executive board; **Exekutive** *f; -, -n; Jur., Pol.* executive; **Exekutivgewalt** *f Pol.* executive power(s *Pl.*); **Exekutivorgan** *n Pol.* executive organ (*od.* body)
Exempel *n; -s, -; geh. altm.* (*Beispiel*) example; **die Probe aufs ~ machen** put it to the test; → **statuieren**
Exemplar *n; -s, -e;* (*Einzelstück*) piece; *Pflanze, Tier etc.*: specimen; (*Probe, Muster*) specimen, sample; *e-s Buches, e-r Zeitschrift:* copy; **er ist schon ein seltenes ~** (*von Mann*) *umg. hum.* he's a peculiar (*od.* odd) specimen (*od.* an oddball), *Brit. auch* he's a queer fish
exemplarisch: I. *Adj.* (*musterhaft*) exemplary; **~ sein für** be typical of; **II.** *Adv. erklären etc.*: by means of an example (*od.* of examples); **j-n ~ bestrafen** make an example of s.o.
exemplifizieren *v/t. geh.* exemplify (*mit od. an* + *Dat.* by [means of])
exerzieren I. *v/i. Mil.* drill; **II.** *v/t.* **1.** *Mil.* (*Soldaten*) drill; **2.** (*praktizieren*) practi|se (*Am.* -ce); (*Methode*) *auch* use; **3.** *umg.* (*etw. einüben*) practi|se (*Am.* -ce); **Exerzierplatz** *m* parade (ground)
Exerzitien *Pl.* **1.** *kath.* spiritual exercises; **2.** *altm.* exercises
Exhibitionismus *m; -, kein Pl.* exhibitionism (*auch geh. fig.*); *Jur.* indecent exposure; **Exhibitionist** *m; -en, -en,* **Exhibitionistin** *f; -, -nen* exhibitionist (*auch fig.*), flasher *umg.*; **exhibitionistisch I.** *Adj.* exhibitionist(ic); **II.** *Adv.:* **s-e Gefühle ~ zur Schau stellen** make a parade of one's feelings, wear one's heart on one's (shirt)sleeve *umg.*
exhumieren *v/t. Jur., Med.* exhume; **Exhumierung** *f* exhumation
Exil *n; -s, -e* exile (*Land*) *auch* place of exile; **im ~** in exile; **im ~ lebende Person** exile, émigré; **im südamerikanischen ~ leben** live in exile (*od.* as an exile) in South America; **ins ~ gehen**

go into exile; **ins ~ schicken** exile
Exil... *im Subst., mit Nationalität:* ... exile (*od.* émigré), exiled ...; **~deutsche** German exile (*od.* émigré), exiled German
Exilierte *m, f; -n, -n* exile
Exil|land *n* country (*od.* place) of exile; **~literatur** *f* exilic (*od.* émigré) literature; **~regierung** *f* government in exile; **~schriftsteller** *m,* **~schriftstellerin** *f* exiled (*od.* émigré) writer, writer in exile
existent *Adj.* existent; **~ sein** exist; **für ihn war das Problem einfach nicht ~** as far as he was concerned the problem did not exist (*od.* was non-existent)
Existenz *f; -, -en* **1.** *nur Sg.;* existence; (*Leben*) *auch* life; **2.** (*Lebensgrundlage*) livelihood; **gesicherte ~** secure livelihood; **sich in s-r ~ bedroht fühlen** feel that one's livelihood is threatened; **sich** (*Dat.*) **e-e ~ aufbauen** build a new life; **dieses Gesetz bedroht zahllose ~en** this law is threatening the livelihoods of countless people; **3.** *pej.* (*Person*) character; → **verkracht II 2,** **~angst** *f* **1.** *finanziell:* fear for one's livelihood; **2.** *Psych.* existential fear, angst; **~bedrohung** *f für Leben:* threat to one's existence; *für berufliche Existenz:* threat to one's livelihood
Existenzialismus *m; -, kein Pl.* existentialism; **Existenzialist** *m; -en, -en,* **Existenzialistin** *f; -, -nen* existentialist; **existenzialistisch** *Adj.* existentialist
existenzberechtigt *Adj.:* **~ sein** have the right to exist; **Existenzberechtigung** *f* right to exist; (*Grund*) raison d'être
existenziell *Adj.* **1.** *Philos. od. geh.* existential; **2.** *geh.:* **von ~er Bedeutung** vitally important; **~e Bedrohung** *für Leben:* threat to one's existence; *für Lebensgrundlage:* threat to one's livelihood
existenzfähig *Adj.* able to exist; *Wirts. etc.* viable
Existenz|gründer *m,* **~gründerin** *f* person who is setting up a (*od.* in) business (on his/her own); **~grundlage** *f* basis for one's existence (*od.* livelihood); **~gründung** *f* setting up a (*od.* in) business (on one's own); **~gründungsdarlehen** *n* start-up loan; **~kampf** *m* struggle for survival; **~minimum** *n* subsistence level; **am Rande des ~s leben** live on the poverty line (*od.* breadline); **der Lohn liegt unter dem ~** the wages are below the poverty line; **~sicherung** *f* securing one's livelihood
existieren *v/i.* exist, be; (*noch vorhanden sein*) be extant; **davon ~ nur zwei** there are only two of them (in existence *od.* to be found); **nur wenige ~ noch** only a few have survived, there are only a few left; **2.** (*leben*) exist, live (**von** on)
Exitus *m; -, kein Pl.; Med.* exitus, death; **„~", sagte der Arzt** "he's/she's dead", said the doctor
Exkanzler *m,* **~in** *f* former chancellor (*od.* prime minister); → *auch* **Expräsident**
exkl. *Abk.* (*exklusive*) excl. (= exclusive)
Exklave *f; -, -n; Pol.* exclave
exklusiv I. *Adj.* exclusive; **~er Kreis** select circle (*od.* group); **II.** *Adv.:* **aus dem Weißen Haus / über den Skandal**

berichtet ~ ... ... has an exclusive (report) from the White House / on the scandal

Exklusivbericht *m* exclusive (story), scoop

exklusive *Präp.* (+ *Gen.*) *und Adv.* exclusive of, excluding, not counting, not including

Exklusivinterview *n* exclusive interview

Exklusivität *f*; -, *kein Pl.*; *geh.* exclusiveness

Exklusiv|meldung *f* scoop; **~rechte** *Pl.* sole (*od.* exclusive) rights; **~vertrag** *m* exclusive contract (*od.* agreement)

Exkommunikation *f* excommunication; **exkommunizieren** *v/t.* excommunicate

Exkremente *Pl.* excrement *Sg.*

Exkurs *m*; -es, -e; *geh.* **1.** (*Abschweifung*) digression (**in** + *Akk.* into); **2.** (*Behandlung e-s Sonderproblems*) excursus (*Pl.* excursus *od.* excursuses)

Exkursion *f*; -, -en excursion; *auch längere*: field trip

Exlibris *n*; -, - ex libris, bookplate

Exmatrikulation *f*; -, -en; *Univ.* removal of a student's name from the university register at the end of his/her studies; **exmatrikulieren I.** *v/refl.* take one's name off the (university) register; **II.** *v/t.* take *s.o.*'s name off the (university) register

Exminister *m*, **~in** *f* former (government) minister; → *auch* **Expräsident**

Exodus *m*; -, -se **1.** *bibl.* Exodus; **2.** *fig.* (mass) exodus

exogen *Adj. fachspr.* exogenous

exorbitant *Adj. geh.* excessive; *Preise*: *auch* exorbitant

Exorzismus *m*; -, *Exorzismen* exorcism; **Exorzist** *m*; -en, -en, **Exorzistin** *f*; -, -nen exorcist

Exot *m*; -en, -en, **Exote** *m*; -n, -n **1.** *Tier*: exotic animal; *Pflanze*: exotic (*od.* tropical) plant; **2.** *Person*: exotic, stranger from a faraway place; *umg. fig. beruflich etc.*: rare bird, strange creature; *auffällig*: flamboyant character; **3.** *umg. fig. Sache*: exotic, exotic ...; *Exoten Börse*: unlisted securities; *neben den etablierten Parteien stellen sich auch wieder zahlreiche Exoten zur Wahl* in addition to the established parties, a large number of fringe organizations have again offered themselves for election

Exotik *f*; -, *kein Pl.* exoticism; **Exotin** *f*; -, -nen exotic, woman from a faraway place; **exotisch** *Adj.* exotic; *Früchte*: *mst* tropical

Expander *m*; -s, - (chest) expander

expandieren *vt/i.* expand; **Expansion** *f*; -, -en expansion; **expansionistisch** *Adj. Pol.* expansionist

Expansions|bestrebungen *Pl.* expansionist tendencies *Pl.*; **~kurs** *m*: **auf ~ sein** be expanding (*od.* growing)

Expedition *f*; -, -en **1.** (*Forschungsreise, -gruppe*) expedition; **2.** *Wirts.* (*Versandabteilung*) forwarding department; **3.** *Wirts.* (*das Expedieren*) dispatch, forwarding; **4.** *Mil. altm.* (military) expedition

Expeditions|leiter *m*, **~leiterin** *f* expedition leader; **~teilnehmer** *m*, **~teilnehmerin** *f* member of an (*od.* the) expedition

Experiment *n*; -(e)s, -e experiment; *ein ~ machen* (**mit** *od.* **an** + *Dat.*) carry out an experiment (on); *nur keine ~e! umg.* no fancy business!, let's not take

any risks; *mach keine ~e! umg.* if you feel like trying something new, don't!, *Am. etwa* if it's not broke, don't fix it; **experimental** *Adj.* experimental

Experimental|film *m* experimental film; **~filmer** *m*, **~filmerin** *f* experimental film(-)maker; **~physik** *f* experimental physics *Pl.* (*V. im Sg.*); **~theater** *n* experimental theat|re (*Am. auch* -er)

experimentell *Adj.* experimental

experimentieren *v/i.* experiment (**an** + *Dat.* on)

Experimentierfreude *f*; *nur Sg.* eagerness to experiment, readiness to try out something new; **experimentierfreudig** *Adj.*: *er ist sehr ~* he likes to experiment (*od.* try new things out)

Experimentierstadium *n*: (*im ~* in the) experimental stage

Experte *m*; -n, -n expert (**für** *od.* **in** + *Dat.* in), pundit *umg.*; *die ~n mst* the experts (*od.* pundits)

Experten|anhörung *f* specialist evidence; **~gremium** *n* panel of experts, brains (*Am.* brain) trust; **~kreis** *m*: **in ~en heißt es, ...** according to the experts ...; **~meinung** *f* expert opinion; **~system** *n* EDV expert system; **~team** *n* team of experts; **~wissen** *n* expert knowledge

Expertin *f*; -, -nen expert

Expertise *f*; -, -n expert('s) opinion, expertise *fachspr.*

explizit *fachspr.*, *geh.* **I.** *Adj.* explicit; **II.** *Adv.* explicitly; *sie hat es nicht ~ gesagt auch* she didn't say it in so many words

explodieren *v/i.* **1.** explode; **2.** *fig. Person*: explode, hit the roof; **3.** *fig. Preise*: explode, go through the roof

Explosion *f*; -, -en **1.** explosion; *zur ~ bringen* explode, detonate; **2.** *fig. von Zorn, Gewalt etc.*: explosion, flare-up; **3.** *fig. der Kosten etc.*: explosion

explosionsartig *Adj.* like an explosion, explosive; *Wachstum etc.*: explosive, phenomenal, astronomical; **~er Preisanstieg** price explosion; **~es Bevölkerungswachstum** population explosion

Explosions|druck *m* (pressure of the) blast; **~gefahr** *f* danger of explosion; **~kraft** *f* explosive force; **~krater** *m* e-r *Bombe*: bomb crater; *e-s Vulkans*: crater; **~motor** *m* Tech. internal combustion engine; **²sicher** *Adj.* explosion-proof; **~welle** *f* blast (wave)

explosiv *Adj.* **1.** explosive; **2.** *fig. Person, Situation*: volatile; *Preisanstieg etc.*: explosive, *nachgestellt*: ... explosion; **3.** *Ling.*: **~er Laut** plosive, explosive; **Explosivität** *f*; *nur Sg.* explosivity

Explosivstoff *m* explosive(s *Pl.*)

Exponat *n*; -(e)s, -e; *fachspr.* exhibit

Exponent *m*; -en, -en; *Math.* exponent (*auch fig.*)

Exponential|funktion *f* Math. exponential function; **~gleichung** *f* exponential equation; **~größe** *f* exponential; **~kurve** *f* exponential curve

exponentiell *Adj. Math.* exponential

exponieren I. *v/t.* expose (+ *Dat.* to); **II.** *v/refl.* expose o.s. (+ *Dat.* to); **exponiert I.** *P.P.* → *exponieren*; **II.** *Adj. Position etc.*: exposed

Export¹ *m*; -(e)s, -e; *Wirts.* **1.** *Handlung*: exportation, export(ing); *Bereich*: export trade (*od.* business); **2.** (*Waren*) exports *Pl.*

Export² *n*; -, -; *Gastr.* (*Bier*) lager

Export|... *im Subst.* export ...; **~abteilung** *f* export department; **~artikel** *m*

export article (*od.* item), *Pl. auch* exports; **~ausführung** *f Tech.* export model; **~beschränkungen** *Pl.* export restraints; **~bier** *n Brauart*: lager

Exporteur [ɛkspɔr'tøːɐ] *m*; -s, -e, **~in** *f*; -, -nen exporter

Export|firma *f* export(ing) firm (*od.* company, business); **~geschäft** *n* **1.** → *Exportfirma*; **2.** export transaction; **3.** → *Exporthandel*; **~güter** *Pl.* exports, export(ed) goods; **~handel** *m* export trade

exportieren *vt/i.* export (*nach* to)

Export|industrie *f* export industry; **~kauffrau** *f*, **~kaufmann** *m* export merchant; **~land** *n* exporting country; (*Bestimmungsland*) country of destination; **~leiter** *m*, **~leiterin** *f* export manager; **²orientiert** *Adj.* export-oriented; **~quote** *f* export ratio (*value of exports as proportion of gross national product*); **~schlager** *m* highly successful export, export leader; **~überschuss** *m* export surplus; **~ware** *f* export(ed) articles *Pl.*

Exposé, Exposee [ɛkspo'zeː] *n*; -s, -s; (*Erläuterung*) exposé; (*Übersicht*) plan; (*Handlungsskizze*) outline of the plot

Exposition *f*; -, -en **1.** *Lit.* exposition; **2.** *Mus.* exposition; **3.** *Fot.* exposure

Expräsident *m*, **~in** *f* former president; **~ Reagan** former president Reagan

Expremierminister *m*, **~in** *f* former prime minister; → *auch* **Expräsident**

express *altm. Adv.* **1.** **~ schicken** send express (*od.* by special delivery); **2.** *auch Dial.* → **extra** II 3, 4; **Express** *m*; -es, *kein Pl.* **1.** *Zug*: express (train); **2.** *per ~ schicken* → I

Express|brief *m* → *Eilbrief*; **~fahrstuhl** *m* high-speed lift (*Am.* elevator); **~gut** *n*; *nur Sg.* express goods *Pl.*

Expressionismus *m*; -, *kein Pl.* Expressionism; **Expressionist** *m*; -en, -en, **Expressionistin** *f*; -, -nen Expressionist; **expressionistisch** *Adj.* expressionist(ic); *Kunstrichtung*: Expressionist

expressiv *Adj. geh.* expressive

Express|lift *m* high-speed lift (*Am.* elevator); **~reinigung** *f* express dry-cleaning (service); **~zug** *m schw.*, *sonst altm.* express train

exquisit *Adj. geh.* exquisite, choice

Exquisitgeschäft *n hist., ehem. DDR*: *shop in the former GDR selling foreign (luxury) goods that could be paid for in East German marks*

Extemporale *n*; -s, *Extemporalien*; *Päd. altm.* unprepared (written) test

extensiv *Adj.* extensive (*auch Agr.*)

Exterieur [ɛkste'rjøːɐ] *n*; -s, -s *od.* -e exterior

extern I. *Adj.* external; (*auswärtig*) *auch* outside; **~er Schüler** day pupil (*Am.* student); **II.** *Adv.*: *e-e Prüfung ~ ablegen* take an external examination

Externe *m*, *f*; -n, -n; *Päd.* day boy (*weiblich*: girl)

exterritorial *Adj. Pol.* extraterritorial

extra I. *Adj. attr.*; *umg.* extra; (*besondere*) special; **II.** *Adv.* **1.** (*besonders*) extra, (e)specially; **~ sorgfältig** *etc.* extra careful *etc.*; **2.** (*getrennt*) separately; (*zusätzlich*) extra; *Getränke gehen ~* drinks are (*od.* cost) extra, drinks aren't included (in the price); **3.** (*eigens*) specially; **~ deswegen** *auch* for that very reason (*od.* purpose); **~ für dich** just (*od.* specially) for you; *ich habe es ~ mitgebracht* I brought it specially; **4.** *umg.* (*absichtlich*) on purpose

Extra *n; -s, -s*; (*Zubehör etc.*) (optional) extra, option; *ein Wagen mit vielen ~s* a car with a lot of (optional) extras

extra... *im Adj.* (*besonders*) extra, super-; *~dick Küchenpapier etc.*: extra thick; *~fein* extra-fine, superfine; *~zart* extra soft

Extra... *im Subst.* extra, additional; *~aufgabe* additional task; *~platz* extra seat; *~portion* extra helping

Extra|ausgabe *f e-r Zeitung*: special edition; *~ausstattung f Mot.* optional extras *Pl.*, options *Pl.*; *~blatt n* supplement; *e-r Zeitung*: extra

extrahieren *v/t. Med., Chem., Pharm.* extract

Extraklasse *f umg.*: *ein Film/Wagen der ~* a first-rate film (*Am. auch* movie) / a top-line model; *das ist ~* that's great (*od.* fantastic)

Extrakt *m; -(e)s, -e* extract

Extraktion *f; -, -en; Med., Chem., Pharm.* extraction

Extratour *f umg. pej.* something special (*od.* extra)

extravagant *Adj.* (*modisch*) stylish, trendy; (*leicht exzentrisch*) outré; *Kleidung, Lebensstil etc.*: *auch* flamboyant; **Extravaganz** *f; -, -en* stylishness; flamboyance, flamboyant nature (+ *Gen.* of)

Extrawurst *f* 1. *umg. pej.* (*Sonderbehandlung*) special treatment; *ich kann dir nicht immer e-e ~ braten* I can't always give you just what you want, I

can't make an exception for you every time; *sie will immer e-e ~ gebraten haben* she expects special treatment all the time; 2. *österr.* → **Lyoner**

extrem I. *Adj.* extreme; *Pol. auch* radical; *er ist ein bisschen ~ auch* he tends to go to extremes, he takes things a bit too far; **II.** *Adv.* extremely, incredibly *umg.*; *~ kalt auch* freezing cold

Extrem *n; -s, -e* extreme; *bis zum od.* *ins ~* to the extreme; *von einem ~ ins andere fallen* go from one extreme to the other

Extremfall *m*: (*im*) *~* (in an) extreme case

Extremismus *m; -, Extremismen* extremism; **Extremist** *m; -en, -en* extremist; **Extremistengruppe** *f* extremist group, group of extremists; **Extremistin** *f; -, -nen* extremist; **extremistisch** *Adj.* extremist

Extremitäten *Pl.* extremities

Extrem|punkt *m Math.* bend point; *in Polarkoordinaten*: apse (of a curve); *~situation f* extreme situation; *~sport m*, *~sportart f* extreme sport; *~thermometer n* thermometer that records daily high and low temperatures; *~wert m bes. Math.* extreme (value)

extrovertiert *Adj.* (*auch ~e Person*) extrovert; **Extrovertiertheit** *f; nur Sg.* extroversion, extrovert nature (+ *Gen.* of)

Ex-und-hopp-|... *im Subst. umg. pej.* throwaway, disposable; *~Gesellschaft*

f umg. pej. throwaway society; *~Mentalität f; nur Sg.* throwaway mentality

exzellent *Adj. geh.* excellent; *Wein etc.*: *auch* exquisite; *er ist ein ~er Kenner* (+ *Gen.*) he's an expert in, he has an excellent knowledge of

Exzellenz *f; -, -en*: *Eure/Ihre/Seine ~* your/her/his Excellency

Exzentriker *m; -s, -, ~in f; -, -nen* eccentric; **exzentrisch** *Adj.* 1. eccentric; 2. *Math., Tech.* eccentric, off-cent|re (*Am.* -er); **Exzentrizität** *f; -, -en* 1. eccentricity; *~en auch* eccentric behavio(u)r; 2. *Math., Astron.* eccentricity; *Tech. auch* off-cent|re (*Am.* -er) position

exzerpieren *v/t. geh.* (*Stellen*) extract; (*Buch etc.*) excerpt, make extracts from; **Exzerpt** *n; -(e)s, -e* excerpt, extract

Exzess *m; -es, -e* excess; *von Gewalt*: *auch* outrage; *etw. bis zum ~ treiben* go to extremes with s.th., take s.th. to excess; *bis zum ~* to excess; (*bis zum Überdruss*) ad nauseam; *es kam zu wilden ~en sexuell etc.*: it was an absolute orgy; *von Gewalt*: the violence got totally out of hand, there was an orgy of violence; **exzessiv** *geh.* **I.** *Adj.* excessive; (*übertrieben*) exaggerated; **II.** *Adv.* excessively, to excess; *etw. ~ betreiben* go to extremes with s.th.

Eyeliner ['aɪlaɪnɐ] *m; -s, -* eyeliner

EZ *Abk.* (*Einzelzimmer*) single room

F, f n; -, - od. umg. -s **1.** F, f; **F wie Friedrich** *Buchstabieren*: 'f' for (*od. as in*) 'Foxtrot'; **2.** *Mus.* F; → **Schema**

f. *Abk.* (**und folgende**): **S. 38f.** p.38-9, p. 38f

Fa. *Abk.* (**Firma**): **Fa. Schmidt** Messrs. Schmidt

Fabel f; -, -n **1.** *Lit, Gattung*: fable; **2.** *Lit.* (*Handlung e-s Stücks*): plot; **3.** *fig.* (*erdichtete Geschichte*) fable, story; (*Lüge*) tall story; **das gehört ins Reich der ~** that's pure fabrication (*od.* fiction)

fabelhaft I. *Adj.* **1.** (*großartig*) fantastic, fabulous; *Gedächtnis*: auch wonderful; **er ist ein ~er Kerl** he's a marvel(l)ous (*od.* wonderful) person; **2.** *umg., Vermögen etc.*: fabulous, prodigious; **II.** *Adv.* **1.** fantastically, wonderfully; **es hat ~ geklappt** it worked out fantastically well (*od.* marvel[l]ously); **du hast ~ gekocht** your cooking was fantastic; **2.** *umg.* (*sehr*) incredibly; **~ reich** fabulously rich, prodigiously wealthy

Fabel|tier n fabulous (*od.* mythical) beast; **~welt** f **1.** world of fable; **2.** (*Welt der Fantasie*) fantasy (*od.* fairytale) world; **~wesen** n **1.** mythical figure; **2.** → **Fabeltier**

Fabrik f; -, -en factory; *zur Herstellung von Papier, Stahl, Stoffen*: mill; (*Werk*) works *Pl.* (*V. auch im Sg.*); **in die ~ gehen** umg. work in a factory; **Preis ab ~** price ex works, *Am.* factory price, price f.o.b. *Detroit etc.*

...fabrik f, *im Subst.*; *oft pej.* factory; **Agrar~** factory farm; **Bildungs~** education factory; **Hit~** recording studio churning out hit songs; **Ideen~** think tank

Fabrikanlage f (manufacturing) plant; (*Gebäudekomplex*) factory complex

Fabrikant m; -en, -en, **~in** f; -, -nen (*Besitzer*) factory owner; (*Hersteller*) manufacturer

Fabrik|arbeit f **1.** factory work; **2.** → **Fabrikware**; **~arbeiter** m, **~arbeiterin** f factory worker

Fabrikat n; -(e)s, -e **1.** (*Typ*) make; *Nahrungsmittel, Putzmittel etc.*: brand; **2.** (*Erzeugnis*) product

Fabrikation f; -, -en production; **in ~ geben** put into production

Fabrikations|fehler m manufacturing flaw *od.* defect; **~nummer** f serial number; **~verfahren** n production process; **~zweig** m branch of production

Fabrik|besitzer m, **~besitzerin** f factory owner; **~direktor** m, **~direktorin** f works (*Am.* production) manager; **~fahrer** m, **~fahrerin** f *Sport* works driver; *Radrennen*: works rider

fabrik|fertig *Adj.* prefabricated; **~frisch** *Adj. nachgestellt*: straight from the factory; **~ sein** auch have come straight from the factory

Fabrik|gebäude n factory building,

~gelände n factory site; **~halle** f factory building; **~marke** f trade mark of ..., factory mark

fabrik|mäßig *Adj.* using production line (*od.* factory) methods; **~neu** *Adj.* brand-new

Fabrik|nummer f serial number; **~preis** m factory price, *Brit.* price ex works; **~schiff** n factory ship; **~schornstein** m factory chimney, (industrial) smoke stack; **~stadt** f manufacturing town; **~tor** n factory gate; **~verkauf** m (*Laden*) factory shop (*Am. mst* outlet); **~ware** f manufactured article (*Koll.* goods *Pl.*)

fabrizieren v/t. **1.** umg. (*zurechtbasteln*) cobble together; (*Gedicht etc.*) concoct; (*Eigentor*) succeed in scoring; (*Unfall*) succeed in causing; **was hast du denn da wieder fabriziert?** what have you been up to this time?; **2.** *altm. industriell*: manufacture

fabulieren I. v/i. tell wonderful stories (**von** about); **II.** v/t. (*Geschichte*) tell; **Fabulierkunst** f; *nur Sg.* ability as a storyteller

Facette [fa'sɛtə] f; -, -n facet (*auch fig.*); **facettenartig** *Adj.* facet(t)ed; **Facettenauge** n *Zool.* compound eye; **facettenreich** *Adj.* many-facet(t)ed; **Facettenschliff** m facet(t)ing, facets *Pl.*; **Rubin mit ~** facet(t)ed ruby

Fach n; -(e)s, **Fächer** **1.** *in Schublade etc.*: compartment; *in Tasche etc.*: partition; *in Setzkasten*: box; *für Briefe*: pigeonhole; *im Regal etc.*: shelf; **2.** *Schule, Studium*: subject; (*Arbeitsfeld*) field; (*Beruf*) job; (*Branche*) line (of business); **er ist vom ~** he's an expert; **Musiker vom ~** professional musician; **sind Sie vom ~?** is this your line (of business)?; **sein ~ verstehen** know one's job (*od.* stuff umg.)

...fach im *Adj. und Adv.* ...fold; (*...mal*) ... times; → *auch* **achtfach**

Fach... im *Subst.* **1.** (*spezialisiert*) specialist ...; (*technisch*) technical ...; **2.** (*beruflich*) professional ...; *Päd. auch* vocational ...

Fach|abitur n *Päd.* examination entitling the successful candidate to study at a *Fachhochschule* or certain subjects at a university; **~akademie** f etwa vocational college; **~arbeit** f **1.** *Wirts.* skilled work; **2.** *Päd., schriftliche*: paper

Facharbeiter m skilled worker; *Pl. auch* skilled labo(u)r (*od.* manpower) *Sg.*; **Facharbeiterbrief** m skilled worker's certificate; **Facharbeiterin** f skilled (female) worker; **Facharbeitermangel** m shortage of skilled workers

Facharzt m, **Fachärztin** f specialist (**für** in); **fachärztlich I.** *Adj.* specialist; *Attest etc.*: from a specialist; *Untersuchung, Behandlung*: by a specialist; **II.** *Adv.* by a specialist

Fach|ausbildung f special(ized) *od.*

professional training; **~ausdruck** m technical (*od.* specialist) term; **medizinischer** etc. **~** medical etc. term; **~ausschuss** m committee of experts; **~begriff** m → **Fachausdruck**; **~berater** m, **~beraterin** f technical adviser, (specialist) consultant; *im Geschäft*: sales advis|er (*od.* -or); *Schule*: etwa (teaching) adviser; **~bereich** m **1.** *Univ.* faculty, school, *Am.* department, school; **2.** → **Fachgebiet**; **~besucher** m, **~besucherin** f *e-r Messe*: professional visitor

fachbezogen *Adj.* subject-orientated, specialized

Fach|blatt n specialist journal; *gewerbliches*: trade journal (*od.* publication); **~buch** n specialist book (*Pl. auch* literature *Sg.*); (*Lehrbuch*) textbook; **medizinisches** etc. **~** medical etc. book; **~buchhandlung** f specialist book|shop (*Am.* -store); **~ für Medizin** etc. medical etc. book|shop (*Am.* -store); **~chinesisch** n umg. pej. technical jargon (*od.* gobbledygook)

fächeln I. v/t. **1.** fan; **2.** *geh. Wind*: blow gently on; **II.** v/i. geh. **1.** *Blätter etc.*: wave; **2.** *Brise*: blow gently; waft (**über** + *Akk.* through)

Fächer m; -s, - **1.** fan; **2.** *fig.* array; **~besen** m lawn rake

fächerförmig I. *Adj.* fan-shaped, fan-like; **II.** *Adv.*: **sich ~ ausbreiten** od. **verteilen** etc. fan out

Fächerkombination f *Schule, Studium*: combination of subjects

fächern I. v/t. diversify (**in** + *Akk.* into); **II.** v/refl. fan out; → **gefächert**; **fächerübergreifend** *Adj.* → **fachübergreifend**

Fächerung f diversity, variety

Fach|frage f technical question; *für Fachleute*: question for the experts; **~frau** f expert (**in** + *Dat.* in, at; **für** on), specialist (in); *anerkannt auch*: authority (on)

fachfremd I. *Adj.* **1.** unrelated (**to** the subject); **2.** *Person*: unqualified, with no relevant experience; *Unterricht*: given by a non-specialist teacher; **II.** *Adv.*: **~ unterrichten** teach a subject other than one's own

Fach|gebiet n (special) field; **~gelehrte** m, f expert, specialist

fach|gemäß, **~gerecht** *Adj.* skilled, professional

Fach|geschäft n specialist shop, *Am.* specialty store; **~ für Herrenmode** etc. men's clothing store; **~gespräch** n: **ein ~** some shop talk (*auch Pl.*); **~handel** m specialized trade (*od.* dealers *Pl.*); **~händler** m, **~händlerin** f specialist dealer; **erhältlich bei ihrem ~** available from your local specialist

Fachhochschule f *Univ.* specialist college (*with university level courses*); **Fachhochschulreife** f entitlement to study at a *Fachhochschule*

Fach|idiot m, **~idiotin** f pej. person obsessed with his (*od.* her) subject, narrow-minded specialist; **~jargon** *m pej.* technical jargon; **~kenntnis** *f:* **~(se)** knowledge (of the *od.* a subject); *auf Spezialgebiet:* specialist knowledge; (*Sachverstand*) expertise; **~se erwerben** *auch* make a special study of the subject; *mir fehlen die* **~se** I haven't got the expertise; *sie hat sehr gute* **~se** she knows a lot about the subject; **~kompetenz** *f* professional competence; (*Sachverstand*) expertise; **~kraft** *f* skilled worker; **Fachkräfte** *Pl.* skilled (*od.* qualified) personnel *Sg.(V. mst im Pl.)*; **~kräftemangel** *m* lack of skilled (*od.* qualified) personnel; **~kreise** *Pl.:* **in ~n** among experts; **in ~n heißt es** the experts (*od.* specialists) say that ...; *in medizinischen* **~n** in medical circles

fachkundig *Adj.* informed, knowledgeable; (*fähig*) competent, skilled; (*fachmännisch*) expert

Fach|lehrer *m,* **~lehrerin** *f Päd.* specialist (subject) teacher; (*er ist*) **~ für Englisch** (he's an) English specialist; **~leute** *Pl.* experts

fachlich I. *Adj. Arbeit, Wissen:* specialist, specialized; *Ausbildung: auch* in the subject; *Problem etc.:* technical; **~es Können** competence *od.* ability (in a *od.* the field); **II.** *Adv.:* **~ qualifiziert** qualified in one's subject (*od.* field); **~ ausgebildet** ... with specialist training, trained (in one's field); *sich* **~ weiterbilden** do further (specialist) training, extend one's qualifications (in a *od.* the field)

Fachliteratur *f* specialist (*od.* specialized) literature

Fachmann *m; Pl. Fachmänner od. Fachleute* expert (*in + Dat.* in, at; *für* on), specialist (in); *anerkannt auch:* authority (on); **fachmännisch I.** *Adj.* expert ..., specialist ...; *Arbeit:* professional; **~es Auge** expert's eye; **~es Urteil** expert opinion; *unter der* **~en Leitung von** under the expert guidance of; **II.** *Adv.* expertly; **e-e Reparatur ~ ausführen** make an expert (*od.* professional) job of a repair

Fach|markt *m → Fachgeschäft,* **~messe** *f* trade fair; **~oberschule** *f Päd. specialist college preparing students for the Fachhochschule;* **~personal** *n* qualified personnel (*V. mst im Pl.*); **~presse** *f* trade press; **~richtung** *f* field (of study); **~schaft** *f* **1.** *Berufsgruppe:* professional association; **2.** *Univ., Koll.* student body of a faculty (*Am.* department); *Vertretung:* student representatives *Pl.;* **~schule** *f Päd. etwa* technical college, *Am.* vocational high school

Fachsimpelei *f; -, -en; umg., oft pej.* shop talk; **fachsimpeln** *v/i.* (*untr., hat gefachsimpelt*); *umg.* talk shop

fachspezifisch *Adj.* specialist ...

Fachsprache *f* technical language; (*Fachausdrücke*) specialist terminology; *juristische* **~** legal terminology; *in der juristischen* **~ heißt es** ... the legal term is ...; **fachsprachlich** *Adj.* specialized, technical; **~er Ausdruck** technical term

Fach|studium *n* study of (*Lehrgang:* course in) one's specialist subject; **~text** *m* specialist text (*wissenschaftlich:* paper, *Beitrag:* article *etc.*); *medizinischer* **~** medical text (*od.* paper *etc.*)

fachübergreifend I. *Adj.* interdisciplinary; **II.** *Adv. unterrichten:* on inter-

disciplinary lines, across (the) disciplines; *man muss* **~ denken** you must not restrict your ideas to one subject area, you must take a broad view

Fach|übersetzer *m,* **~übersetzerin** *f* specialist (*od.* technical) translator; *er ist* **~ für Medizin** he specializes in medical translation(s); **~übersetzung** *f* specialist (*od.* technical) translation; **~verband** *m* professional association; *Wirts.* trade association; **~verkäufer** *m,* **~verkäuferin** *f* specialist salesperson (*männlich auch:* salesman, *weiblich auch:* saleswoman); **~welt** *f:* (*in der*) **~** (among the) experts *Pl.*

Fachwerk *n Archit.* half-timbering; **~bau** *m* **1.** (*Haus*) half-timbered building; **2.** (*Bauweise*) half-timbering; **~haus** *n* half-timbered house

Fach|wirt *m,* **~wirtin** *f Wirts. qualified professional in a commercial or financial occupation;* **~wissen** *n → Fachkenntnis;* **~wort** *n* technical term; **~wörterbuch** *n* specialist dictionary; *Tech.* technical dictionary; **~wortschatz** *m* technical (*od.* specialized) vocabulary; **~zeitschrift** *f* specialist (*e-s Berufszweiges:* professional) journal; *gewerbliche:* trade journal

Fackel *f; -, -n* torch; **brennen wie e-e ~** blaze fiercely; *wie lebende* **~n** like human torches; *die* **~ des Fortschritts hochhalten** *fig.* hold up the beacon of progress

fackeln *v/i. umg. fig.* dither, shilly-shally; *nicht lange* **~ mit** make short work of; *los, nicht lange gefackelt!* don't mess about (*Am.* around), stop dithering; come on, get on with it; *er fackelte nicht lange* he didn't waste any time

Fackel|schein *m* torchlight; *im* **~** by the light of the torches; **~träger** *m,* **~trägerin** *f* torchbearer; **~zug** *m* torchlight procession

fad *Adj. bes. südd., österr. → fade*

Fädchen *n* narrow thread; *kurz:* short thread

fade *Adj. pej.* **1.** tasteless, insipid; (*schal*) stale; *Bier:* flat; **~ schmecken** have a bland taste; *ohne Geschmack:* be tasteless; **2.** *umg. fig.* (*langweilig*) dull, boring; *Farbe:* dull; **~r Kerl** bore; **e-e ~ Sache** a (real) drag

fädeln *v/t.* thread (*auf + Akk.* onto; *in + Akk.* into; *durch* through)

Faden[1] *m; -s, Fäden* **1.** *allg.* thread; *Marionette etc.:* string; *ein* **~** a piece of thread; *er hatte keinen trockenen* **~ am Leib** *umg.* he was soaked to the skin; **2.** *von Bohnen, Flüssigem etc.:* string; *ein dünner* **~ Blut** a trickle of blood; *Fäden ziehen Suppe, Käse etc.:* go stringy; **3.** *fig.* thread, string; *der rote* **~** the central thread; *sich wie ein roter* **~ durch etw. ziehen** run though s.th. like a thread; *den* **~ verlieren** lose the thread; *den* **~ wieder aufnehmen** pick up the thread; *es hing an e-m* (*dünnen od. seidenen*) **~** it was hanging by a thread; *sie ließ keinen guten* **~ an ihm** she tore him to shreds, she didn't have a good word to say about him; *s-e Fäden spinnen* spin a web of intrigue; *die Fäden laufen in s-r Hand zusammen* he's in control of everything, he's at the controls; **4.** *Med.* suture, stitch; *die Fäden ziehen* take out the stitches; **5.** *Etech., Tech.* filament

Faden[2] *m; -s, -; Naut.* fathom

fadengerade I. *Adj. nachgestellt:* cut on the straight (*Am.* with the weave); **II.** *Adv.: etw.* **~ schneiden** cut s.th. on

the straight (*Am.* with the weave)

Faden|heftung *f Druck.* (thread-)stitching; **~kreuz** *n Opt.* reticule; *auch Computer:* crosshairs *Pl.;* **im ~ haben** *fig.* have *s.o./s.th.* in one's sights

fadenlos *Adj. Bohnen:* stringless

Fadennudeln *Pl.* vermicelli *Pl.*

fadenscheinig *Adj.* threadbare (*auch fig. pej.*); *Ausrede, Argument etc.: auch* flimsy

Faden|spiel *n* cat's cradle; **~stärke** *f* thickness (of wool, thread); **~wurm** *m Zool.* threadworm, nematode *fachspr.*

Fadheit *f; nur Sg.; pej.* **1.** *von Essen:* blandness; *ohne Geschmack:* tastelessness; (*Schalheit*) staleness; **2.** *fig.* (*Langweiligkeit*) dullness

fadisieren *v/refl. österr.* be bored

Fagott *n; -(e)s, -e; Mus.* bassoon; **Fagottist** *m; -en, -en,* **Fagottistin** *f; -, -nen* bassoonist

Fähe *f; -, -n; Jägerspr.* (*Dachs*) sow; (*Fuchs*) vixen; (*Marder*) female marten

fähig *Adj.* **1.** capable (*zu etw.* of s.th.; *zu + Inf.* of + *Ger.*), able (to + *Inf.*); *er ist zu allem* **~** he's capable of anything, he'll stop at nothing; *Verbrecher etc.: auch* he's desperate; *keines klaren Gedankens* **~ sein** *geh.* be incapable of thinking clearly; **2.** (*tüchtig*) able, capable; (*begabt*) talented; *er ist ein* **~er Kopf** he has an astute mind; **Fähigkeit** *f* ability (*zu* to); (*Tüchtigkeit*) capability; (*Begabung*) talent; *geistige/praktische* **~en** intellectual capacity *Sg.* / practical skills; *bei d-n* **~en** with your ability; *sie hat die* **~,** *sich über einen langen Zeitraum zu konzentrieren* she has the ability (*od.* she's able) to concentrate for long periods

fahl *Adj.* pale (and wan), pallid; *Lächeln:* wan; **fahlgelb** *Adj.* pale yellow; **Fahlheit** *f; nur Sg.* paleness, pallor; *e-s Lächelns:* wanness

Fähnchen *n* **1.** (little) flag; (*Wimpel*) pennant; *Sport* marker; *sein* **~ nach dem Wind drehen** *od.* **hängen** *fig. pej.* swim with the tide, go with the flow; **2.** *umg. pej.* (*Kleid*) cheap(, scanty) dress, rag

fahnden *v/i.:* **~ nach** hunt (*od.* search) for; **Fahnder** *m; -s, -,* **Fahnderin** *f; -, -nen* hunter, searcher; (*Ermittler*) investigator; **Fahndung** *f* hunt, search

Fahndungs|aktion *f* (police) hunt, search operation; **~apparat** *m* (police) personnel engaged in a (*od.* the) hunt; **~buch** *n* wanted persons register; **~erfolg** *m* successful result of a (*od.* the) hunt; **~foto** *n* police photo (mugshot *umg.*) of a wanted person; **~liste** *f* wanted persons (*Am.* most wanted) list; *auf der* **~ stehen** be wanted by the police; **~stelle** *f* tracing and search department

Fahne *f; -, -n* **1.** flag; *bes. fig.* banner; *Mil., Naut. auch* colo(u)rs *Pl.; die* **~** (*der Freiheit etc.*) **hochhalten** *fig.* keep the flag (of freedom *etc.*) flying; *etw. auf s-e* **~(n) schreiben** *fig.* champion the cause of s.th.; *→ auch Fähnchen* 1, *fliegend* II 2; **2.** *umg.:* **e-e ~ haben** smell of drink; *stärker:* reek of alcohol; **3.** *Druck.* (galley) proof

Fahnen|appell *m Mil.* rollcall to salute the colo(u)rs; **~eid** *m Mil.* oath of allegiance

Fahnenflucht *f; nur Sg.; Mil.* desertion; **fahnenflüchtig** *Adj.:* **~ sein** be a deserter; **~ werden** desert; **Fahnenflüchtige** *m* deserter

Fahnen|korrektur *f Druck.* proofreading of galleys; **~mast** *m* flagpole; **~stange** *f* flagpole; *das Ende der ~ ist erreicht / in Sicht fig.* we've got / we'll soon be as far as one can get; **~träger** *m*, **~trägerin** *f* standard-bearer (*auch fig.*); **~tuch** *n* bunting; **~weihe** *f* dedication of the flag (*Mil.* colo(u)rs)

Fähnrich *m*; *-s, -e*; *Mil.* officer cadet; *~ zur See Naut.* midshipman

Fahr|anfänger *m*, **~anfängerin** *f auf Rad*: novice rider; *Mot.* learner driver; **~ausweis** *m Amtsspr.* ticket

Fahrbahn *f* carriageway, *Am.* roadway; (*Straße*) road; (*Spur*) lane; **~markierung** *f* lane markings *Pl.*; **~rand** *m* edge of the road; *Autobahn*: hard shoulder, *Am.* shoulder; *fahren Sie am äußersten rechten ~* keep to the edge of the inside lane (*Am.* to the extreme right); **~wechsel** *m* change of lane; *beim ~* when changing lanes

fahrbar *Adj. Bibliothek etc.*: mobile; *Bett etc.*: ... on castors; *Bühne*: movable; → *Untersatz*

fahrbereit *Adj.* **1.** *Auto etc.*: in running order; **2.** (*fertig zur Abfahrt*) ready to leave; **Fahrbereitschaft** *f Einrichtung*: car pool

Fähr|betrieb *m Naut.* ferry service; **~boot** *n* ferryboat

Fähre *f*; *-, -n*; *Naut.* ferry

Fahreigenschaften *Pl. Mot.* handling characteristics, handling *Sg.*

fahren; *fährt, fuhr, gefahren* **I.** *v/i.* (*ist*); **1.** *Person*: (*auch reisen*) go (*mit* by); *selbst lenkend*: drive; *auf Fahrrad, Motorrad*: ride; *längere Strecke*: travel (by); *auf Schiff*: sail; *mit dem Aufzug/Bus etc. ~ auch* take the lift (*Am.* elevator) *a* (*od.* the) bus *etc.*; *öffentlich* (*mit öffentlichen Verkehrsmitteln*) I use (*od.* go by) public transport (*Am.* transportation); *fahr rechts* (*bleib rechts*) keep to the right; (*bieg rechts ab*) turn right; *an den Straßenrand ~* pull over to the side of the road; *nach Köln fährt man sieben Stunden mit dem Auto*: it's a seven-hour drive to Cologne; *mit dem Zug*: it's a seven-hour train journey to Cologne, it's seven hours on the train to Cologne; *langsamer/schneller ~* slow down / accelerate; *über e-n Fluss etc. ~* cross a river *etc.*; *ich will noch mal ~ auf Karussell etc.*: I want another ride; **2.** (*abfahren*) leave, go; *wir ~ in fünf Minuten* we're leaving in five minutes; **3.** (*in Fahrt sein*) be moving; → *fahrend* II 1; **4.** *Fähigkeit*: *sie fährt gut/schlecht* she's a good/bad driver; **5.** (*verkehren*) run; *das Boot/der Zug fährt zweimal am Tag* the boat/train goes twice a day, there are two sailings / two trains a day; **6.** *Mot. etc.* (*funktionieren*) go, run; *das Auto fährt nicht* (*ist kaputt*) the car isn't going (*od.* won't go); *das Auto fährt ruhig* the car is quiet(-running); *mit Benzin/Diesel ~ Fahrzeug*: run on petrol (*Am.* gas) /diesel; *Person*: have a petrol- (*Am.* gas) /diesel-engine car; *mit Strom ~* be driven by electric power; *mit Dampf ~* be steam-driven; **7.** *mit der Hand etc. durch/über etw.* (*Akk.*) *~* run one's hand *etc.* through/over s.th.; **8.** *in etw.* (*Akk.*) *~ Kugel, Messer etc.*: go into s.th.; *Blitz*: hit (*od.* strike) s.th.; *in die Kleider ~* slip into (*od.* slip on) one's clothes; *aus dem Bett ~* jump (*od.* leap) out of bed; *der Hund fuhr ihm an die Kehle* the dog leapt at his throat; → *Himmel* 2, *Hölle* 1;

9. *etw. ~ lassen* (*loslassen*) let go of s.th.; *alle Hoffnung etc. ~ lassen fig.* give up (*od.* abandon) all hope; *einen ~ lassen umg.* let one go, fart *vulg.*; **10.** *fig.*: *sie ist sehr gut/schlecht damit gefahren* she did very well/badly out of it; *was ist nur in ihn gefahren?* what's got into him?; *der Schreck fuhr ihm in die Glieder* he froze with terror; → *Haut* 4, *Mund etc.*; **II.** *v/t.* **1.** (*hat*); (*lenken, besitzen*) drive; (*Fahrrad, Motorrad*) ride; *er hat das Auto gegen den Zaun gefahren* he drove the car into the fence; *ein Auto zu Schrott ~* drive a car into the ground; *bei e-m Unfall*: write a car off, *Am.* total a car; *ein Schiff auf Grund ~* run a ship aground; *j-n über den Haufen ~ umg.* knock s.o. down, run s.o. over; **2.** (*hat*); (*befördern*) take, drive; (*Güter*) *auch* transport; → *spazieren*; **3.** (*ist*) (*Aufzug, Skilift*) ride in; (*Karussell, U-Bahn etc.*) ride on; (*Segelboot*) sail; (*Ruderboot*) row; *Boot ~* go boating; *Rad ~* cycle; *Roller ~* scooter; (*Motorroller*) ride a scooter; *Schlittschuh ~* skate; *Schlitten ~* (*rodeln*) toboggan; (*Pferdeschlitten*) ride in a sledge (*Am.* sleigh); *Ski ~* ski; **4.** (*hat od. ist*) (*Strecke*) cover, travel; (*Kurve, anderen Weg etc.*) take; (*Umleitung*) follow; (*Rennen*) take part in; (*Umweg*) make; *sie fuhren e-e andere Strecke* they took a different route; *Kurven ~* weave about (*Am.* back and forth); *Slalom ~* do a slalom; **5.** (*hat od. ist*); (*Zeit*) record, clock; (*Rekord*) set; *wir fuhren gerade 100 km/h, als ...* we were doing 62 mph when ...; *das Auto fährt 200 km/h* (*leistet*) the car will do (*od.* can reach) 124 mph; **6.** (*hat*); (*Normal, Super*) use, run on; **7.** *Tech.* (*Hochofen*) operate; *EDV* (*Programm*) run; **8.** (*Sonderschicht*) work; **III.** *v/refl.* (*hat*): *dieser Wagen fährt sich gut* this car is pleasant to drive (*od.* handles well); *unpers.*: *auf dieser Straße fährt es sich gut* this is a good road to drive on

fahrend I. *Part. Präs.* → *fahren*; **II.** *Adj.* **1.** *Fahrzeug*: moving; *auf den ~en Zug aufspringen* jump on the moving train (*fig.* on the bandwagon); **2.** (*wandernd*) travel(l)ing, itinerant; *~er Ritter hist.* knight errant; *~er Sänger hist.* wandering minstrel; *~es Volk* travel(l)ers, *Am.* gypsies, migrants

Fahrenheit *undekl.* Fahrenheit; *30 Grad ~* 30 degrees Fahrenheit; **~skala** *f*; *nur Sg.* Fahrenheit scale

Fahrer *m*; *-s, -* **1.** driver; *Rad, Motorrad*: rider; **2.** *beruflich*: driver; (*Chauffeur*) *auch* chauffeur; **~airbag** *m* driver airbag

Fahrerei *f*; *-, selten -en*; *oft pej.* **1.** (*constant*) travel(l)ing (*Mot.* driving); *diese ~!* all this travel[l]ing (*Mot.* driving)!; **2.** (*Fahrstil*) way of driving; *deine ~ macht mich nervös* the way you drive gets on my nerves

Fahrerflucht *f*; *nur Sg.* hit-and-run offen|ce (*Am.* -se); *~ begehen* drive off after causing an accident, commit a hit-and-run offen|ce (*Am.* -se) *Jur.*; *wegen ~* for failing to stop after causing an accident

Fahrerin *f*; *-, -nen* (*woman*) driver; *Rad, Motorrad*: (female) rider

fahrerisch I. *Adj. nur attr.*: *~es Können* driving skill(s); **II.** *Adv.* as a driver; *~ überlegen* be a better driver

Fahrerkabine *f* driver's cab

Fahrerlaubnis *f Amtsspr.* driving li-

cence, *Am.* driver's license; *j-m die ~ entziehen* take away (*od.* suspend) s.o.'s licen|ce (*Am.* -se), disqualify s.o. from driving

Fahrer|sitz *m* driver's seat; **~tür** *f* driver's door

Fahrfehler *m* driver error

Fahrgast *m* passenger; **~aufkommen** *n* number of passengers; **~raum** *m* passenger compartment; *Mot. auch* interior

Fahr|gefühl *n* driving experience; *das ist ein ~!* that's what I call driving; **~geld** *n* fare; **~gelegenheit** *f* means of transport; **~gemeinschaft** *f* car pool; *Pl.* (*Tätigkeit*) car sharing *Sg.*, *Am.* ride sharing *Sg.*; **~geschwindigkeit** *f* speed

Fahrgestell *n* **1.** *Mot.* chassis; **2.** *Flug.* undercarriage; **3.** *umg. fig.* (*Beine*) legs, *Brit. auch* pins *Pl.*; **~nummer** *f Mot.* chassis number

Fährhafen *m Naut.* ferry terminal

fahrig *Adj.* (*nervös*) nerv|y (*Am.* -ous), agitated; (*unaufmerksam*) dithering; *Bewegungen*: fidgety; *er ist furchtbar ~* (*unkonzentriert*) he can't concentrate on anything, he's all of a dither; **Fahrigkeit** *f*; *nur Sg.* agitation; (*Unaufmerksamkeit*) dithering state; *von Bewegungen*: fidgetiness

Fahrkarte *f* ticket; *e-e ~ lösen* buy a ticket (*nach* to)

Fahrkarten|ausgabe *f* ticket office; **~automat** *m* ticket machine; **~entwerter** *m* ticket-cancel(l)ing machine; **~kontrolle** *f* ticket inspection; **~kontrolleur** *m*, **~kontrolleurin** *f* ticket inspector; **~schalter** *m* ticket office

Fahrkomfort *m Mot.* ride comfort

Fahrkosten *Pl.* travel(l)ing (*od.* travel) costs; **~zuschuss** *m* travel(l)ing allowance

Fahrkunst *f* driving skill

fahrlässig *Adj.* careless; *stärker*: reckless; *auch Jur.* negligent; *grob ~* grossly negligent; *~e Tötung Jur.* (involuntary) manslaughter, *Am.* negligent homicide; *~e Körperverletzung Jur.* injury caused by culpable negligence; **Fahrlässigkeit** *f* carelessness, *stärker*: recklessness; *auch Jur.* negligence; *grobe ~* gross negligence

Fahr|lehrer *m*, **~lehrerin** *f* driving instructor; **~leistung** *f* road performance

Fähr|leute *Pl. Naut.* ferrymen; **~mann** *m*; *Pl. -leute od. -männer* ferryman

Fährnis *f*; *-, -se*; *lit.* peril

Fahrplan *m* timetable (*auch fig.*), *bes. Am.* schedule; *den ~ einhalten* run to schedule; *den ~ durcheinander bringen* turn the timetable (*bes. Am.* schedule) upside down; *j-s ~ durcheinander bringen umg.* mess up s.o.'s plans; **~änderung** *f* change in the timetable (*bes. Am.* schedule); **~auskunft** *f* timetable (*bes. Am.* schedule) information

fahrplanmäßig I. *Adj.* scheduled; *der verspätete Intercity, ~e Ankunft 2 Uhr 15, ...* the delayed Intercity train, scheduled (*od.* due) to arrive at 2.15 am ...; **II.** *Adv.* (*rechtzeitig*) on time, according to schedule

Fahrpraxis *f* driving experience, experience behind the wheel

Fahrpreis *m* fare; **~erhöhung** *f* fare increase; *allg. auch* increase in fares; **~ermäßigung** *f* fare reduction; *allg. auch* reduction in fares

Fahrprüfung *f* driving test

Fahrrad *n* bicycle, bike *umg.*; (*mit*

dem) ~ *fahren* cycle; *mit Ziel auch*: go by bicycle; ~**anhänger** *m* bicycle trailer; ~**fahrer** *m*, ~**fahrerin** *f* cyclist
fahrradfreundlich *Adj. Stadt etc.*: bicycle-friendly
Fahrrad|helm *m* cycle helmet; ~**kette** *f* bicycle chain; ~**kurier** *m* cycle courier; ~**pumpe** *f* (bi)cycle pump; ~**reifen** *m* bicycle tyre (*Am.* tire); ~**schlauch** *m* bicycle inner tube; ~**ständer** *m* **1.** am *Rad*: bicycle stand; **2.** (*Abstellplatz*) bicycle rack; ~**taxi** *n* pedicab, cycle cab; ~**tour** *f* bicycle (*od.* cycling) tour; ~**unfall** *m* cycling accident; ~**verleih** *m* (bi)cycle hire (service); ~**weg** *m* cycle path
Fahrrinne *f Naut.* shipping lane
Fahrschein *m Amtsspr.* ticket; ~**entwerter** *m* ticket-cancel(l)ing machine; ~**heft** *n* book of tickets
Fährschiff *n Naut.* ferry
Fahr|schule *f* **1.** driving school; **2.** *umg.* (*Stunden*) driving lessons *Pl.*; ~**schüler** *m*, ~**schülerin** *f* **1.** e-r *Fahrschule*: learner (driver); **2.** (*auswärtiger Schüler*) non-local pupil; ~**sicherheit** *f* road safety; *e-s Fahrers*: (safe) driving; *die ~ erhöhen* improve road safety; ~**spaß** *m* driving pleasure; ~**spur** *f* lane; ~**stil** *m Mot.* (style of) driving; *Motorrad*: (style of) riding; *Skifahren*: (style of) skiing; ~**strecke** *f* **1.** (*Route*) route; **2.** (*Entfernung*) distance ([to be] covered); ~**streifen** *m* lane
Fahrstuhl *m* **1.** lift, *Am.* elevator; *mit dem ~ fahren* take the lift (*Am.* elevator); **2.** → *Rollstuhl*; ~**führer** *m*, ~**führerin** *f* lift attendant, *Am.* elevator operator; ~**schacht** *m* lift (*Am.* elevator) shaft
Fahrstunde *f* driving lesson
Fahrt *f*, -, *-en* **1.** (*Reise*) journey, trip; (*Ausflug*) outing; *im Wagen*: drive, ride; *auf Skiern*: run; *im Schiff, Boot*: trip; *im Karussell etc.*: ride; *gute ~!* have a good trip; *e-e ~ nach Rom machen* make (*od.* go on) a trip to Rome; *während der ~ nicht aus dem Fenster lehnen etc.* while the train (*od.* bus etc.) is in motion (*od.* moving); *auf der ~ nach X* on the way to X; *in ~ kommen* get under way; *einfache ~* (*Fahrkarte, Preis*) single, *Am.* one-way; *jetzt habe ich freie ~* the road's clear now; *fig.* there's nothing to stop me now; → *Blaue[1]*; **2.** *nur Sg.*; (*Tempo*) speed; *die ~ verlangsamen/beschleunigen* slow down / speed up *od.* accelerate; *~ aufnehmen* pick up (*od.* gather) speed; *in voller ~* (at) full speed; **3.** *umg. fig.*: *in ~ kommen* get going; *j-n/etw. in ~ bringen* get s.o./s.th. going; (*j-n wütend machen*) get s.o. steamed up *umg.*; *in ~ sein* be in full swing; *Person*: be going strong; (*wütend*) be all steamed up *umg.*
fährt *Präs.* → *fahren*
fahrtauglich *etc.* → *fahrtüchtig etc.*
Fahrt|antritt *m*: *bei/vor ~* when/before setting out; ~**dauer** *f* travel(l)ing time; *die ~ beträgt etwa drei Stunden auch* it will take about three hours (to get there)
Fährte *f*, -, *-n* **1.** trail, track; (*Witterung*) scent; *die ~ aufnehmen/verlieren* pick up/lose the scent; **2.** *fig.* track; *j-n von der ~ abbringen* throw s.o. off the scent; *j-n auf die falsche ~ locken* put s.o. on the wrong track; *auf der richtigen/falschen ~ sein* be on the right/wrong track
Fahrtechnik *f* driving technique
Fahrten|buch *n Mot.* logbook; ~**mes-**

ser *n* hunting knife; ~**schreiber** *m Mot.* tachograph; ~**schwimmer** *m Sport*: *den ~ machen* take one's advanced swimming test; ~**schwimmerabzeichen** *n Sport* advanced swimmer's badge
Fahrt|kosten *Pl.* **1.** travel(l)ing (*od.* travel) costs; **2.** (*Fahrpreise*) fares; ~**richtung** *f* direction of travel; *in ~ sitzen Eisenb.* sit facing the engine (*od.* the direction of travel); *entgegen der ~ sitzen* sit with one's back to the engine; *die Autobahn ist in südlicher ~ / in ~ Stuttgart gesperrt* the motorway (*Am.* expressway) is closed southbound / in the direction of Stuttgart; ~**richtungsanzeiger** *m Amtsspr.* (*Blinker*) direction indicator, *Am.* turn signal
fahrttüchtig *Adj. Fahrzeug*: roadworthy; *Person*: fit to drive; **Fahrttüchtigkeit** *f*; *nur Sg. e-s Fahrzeugs*: roadworthiness; *e-r Person*: fitness to drive; (*Können*) driving ability
Fahrt|unterbrechung *f* stop, break in the journey, *bes. Am. auch* stopover; ~**wind** *m* airstream
Fährunglück *n Naut.* ferry disaster
fahruntauglich, fahruntüchtig *Adj. Fahrzeug*: not roadworthy; *Person*: unfit to drive
Fährverbindung *f Naut.* ferry service
Fahr|verbot *n* **1.** *als Strafe*: disqualification from driving; *ein ~ erhalten* be banned from driving, lose one's driving licence (*Am.* driver's license); *ein ~ gegen j-n aussprechen od. über j-n verhängen* ban s.o. from driving; **2.** *Verk.* ban on vehicles; *Schild*: (*allgemeines*) ~ all vehicles prohibited, no vehicular traffic; *hier ist ~* you are not allowed to drive along here; → *auch Nachtfahrverbot*; ~**verhalten** *n* **1.** e-r *Person*: behavio(u)r behind the wheel; **2.** e-s *Wagens*: behavio(u)r on the road, road manners
Fährverkehr *m Naut.* ferry traffic
Fahr|wasser *n* **1.** *Naut.* shipping channel, fairway; **2.** *fig.* element; *in s-m ~ sein* be in one's element; *in ein politisches ~ geraten* take a political turn; *in j-s ~ geraten* come under s.o.'s influence; ~**weg** *m* road (suitable for vehicles); ~**weise** *f* (way of) driving; *bei d-r ~* the way you drive; ~**werk** *n* **1.** *Flug.* landing gear, undercarriage; **2.** *Mot.* (*Fahrgestell*) chassis; ~**zeit** *f* running time; → *Fahrtdauer*
Fahrzeug *n*; -(e)s, *-e* vehicle; *Naut.* vessel; *gesperrt für ~e aller Art* closed to all traffic; ~**aufkommen** *n* traffic volume; *hohes ~* heavy traffic; ~**bau** *m*; *nur Sg.* motor manufacturing; *Branche*: motor industry; ~**brief** *m* vehicle title (document); ~**führer** *m*, ~**führerin** *f* driver of a (*od.* the) vehicle; ~**halter** *m*, ~**halterin** *f* vehicle keeper; ~**insasse** *m*, ~**insassin** *f* occupant of a (*od.* the) vehicle; ~**kolonne** *f* line of vehicles; *offizielle*: motorcade; ~**nummer** *f* (vehicle) registration number; ~**papiere** *Pl.* vehicle documents; ~**park** *m Mot.* fleet (of vehicles); *Eisenb.* rolling stock; ~**schein** *m* car licen|ce (*Am.* -se); ~**verkehr** *m*: *für den ~ gesperrt* closed to all traffic
Faible ['fɛːbḻ] *n*; -s, -s weakness; *für j-n*: soft spot; (*Hang*) penchant
fair [fɛːɐ] **I.** *Adj.* fair; **II.** *Adv.* fairly; ~ *spielen* play fair; **fairerweise** *Adv.* fairly; ~ *müsste man ...* to be fair, one would have to ...; **Fairness** *f*, -, *kein Pl.* fairness

fäkal *Adj. bes. Med.* f(a)ecal; **Fäkalien** *Pl.* f(a)eces; **Fäkalsprache** *f*; *nur Sg.*; *pej.* lavatorial (*förm.* scatological) language
Fakir *m*; -s, -e fakir
Faksimile *n*; -s, -s; *fachspr.* facsimile; ~**ausgabe** *f* facsimile edition
Fakt *n*, *m*; -(e)s, -en *od.* -e fact; ~**en** facts; (*Angaben etc.*) data
Fakten|material *n*; *nur Sg.* facts *Pl.*; ~**wissen** *n* factual knowledge
faktisch I. *Adj.* actual, effective; *Jur.* de facto; **II.** *Adv.* **1.** in fact, in reality; ~ *unmöglich* actually impossible; **2.** *bes. österr. umg.* (*praktisch*) virtually
Faktor *m*; -s, -en factor (*auch Math., Bio.*); **Faktorenanalyse** *f* factor analysis
Faktotum *n*; -s, -s *od. Faktoten* factotum
Faktum *n*; -s, *Fakten*; *geh.* → *Fakt*
fakturieren *v/t.* invoice
Fakultät *f*, -, *-en* **1.** *Univ.* faculty, school, *Am.* department, school; *die juristische etc.* ~ the faculty (*od.* school, *Am. auch* department) of law *etc.*; **2.** *Math.* (*Zeichen:!*) factorial; *6 ~ od. 6!* 6 factorial
fakultativ *Adj. geh.* optional
Falangist *m*; -en, -en, ~**in** *f*; -, -nen Falangist
falb *Adj. geh.* dun(-colo[u]red)
Falke *m*; -n, -n; *Orn.* falcon; *Jägerspr. und fig. Pol. auch* hawk; *Augen wie ein ~ haben* have eyes like a hawk
Falken|auge *n fig.* eagle-eye; ~**jagd** *f* falconry
Falkland|inseln *Pl. Geog.* Falkland Islands, Falklands; ~**krieg** *m hist.* Falklands War
Falkner *m*; -s, - falconer; **Falknerei** *f*; -, *-en* **1.** falconry; **2.** (*Anlage*) hawk house; **Falknerin** *f*; -, *-nen* (female) falconer
Fall[1] *m*; -(e)s, *kein Pl.* **1.** fall; *im Fallschirm*: descent; *freier ~ Phys.* free fall; *zu ~ bringen* cause s.o. to fall; *im Kampf*: bring down; *durch Beinstellen*: trip up, *zu ~ kommen* fall; **2.** *der Temperatur, der Kurse, der Preise etc.*: fall, drop; *stärker*: slump; **3.** *fig.* downfall; *e-r Regierung etc.*: *auch* fall, collapse; *e-r Festung etc.*: fall; *zu ~ bringen* (*Regierung etc.*) bring down; (*Pläne etc.*) thwart; (*Gesetzentwurf etc.*) defeat; *zu ~ kommen Person*: come to grief; *Regierung auch*: be brought down; *Plan*: be wrecked (*od.* thwarted); *Gesetzentwurf etc.*: be defeated; → *Hochmut*; **4.** *Art zu hängen*: fall; *von Stoff*: drape
Fall[2] *m*; -(e)s, *Fälle* **1.** case (*auch Med., Jur.*); (*Angelegenheit*) *auch* matter, affair; (*Einzelbeispiel*) instance; (*Vorkommnis*) occurrence; *der ~ Graf* the Graf case; *ein ~ von Typhus* a typhoid case, a case of typhoid; *in vielen Fällen* in many cases, often; *im besten od. günstigsten ~* at best; *im schlimmsten ~* at worst; *in diesem / im anderen ~(e)* in that (*od.* this) case / otherwise; *im ~e es-s ~es umg.* if (the) worst comes to (the) worst; *für alle Fälle* just in case, to be on the safe side; *auf alle Fälle od. auf jeden ~* anyway; (*ganz bestimmt*) definitely; *lass den Schlüssel auf alle Fälle od. in jedem ~ da* whatever you do, leave the key behind; *auf keinen ~* on no account, under no circumstances; (*ganz bestimmt nicht*) definitely not; *sag es ihm auf keinen ~* don't tell him what-

ever you do; **ist das der ~?** is that the case (here)?; **das ist auch bei ihm der ~** it's the same with him; **der ~ liegt so** the situation is as follows; **für den** od. **im ~, dass er kommen sollte** in case he should come; **gesetzt den ~** suppose, supposing, let's assume; **das ist von ~ zu ~ verschieden** that varies from case to case; **das muss man von ~ zu ~ entscheiden** auch you have to decide each case on its merits; **klarer ~, dass er das nicht kann** umg. it's obvious he can't do it; **klarer ~!** umg. (oh,) sure!; **das ist ganz / nicht ganz mein ~** umg. that's right up my street / not exactly my cup of tea; **er ist genau / nicht ganz mein ~** umg. exactly my type; → **hoffnungslos**; **2.** Ling. case; **erster/zweiter/dritter/vierter ~** nominative/genitive/dative/accusative case; **der fünfte ~** the instrumental case; **im Lateinischen**: the ablative case; **der sechste ~** the prepositional case; (Vokativ) the vocative case; **im dritten ~ stehen** be in the dative; **nach „durch" steht der vierte ~** "durch" is followed by the accusative

Fall³ n; -(e)s, -en; Naut. halyard
Fall|apfel m windfall; **~beil** n hist. guillotine; **~beispiel** n case study; **~beschleunigung** f Phys. gravitational acceleration; **~beschreibung** f Med. case description; **~birne** f Tech. demolition (od. wrecking) ball; **~bö** f down gust; **~brücke** f hist. drawbridge
Falle f; -, -n **1.** trap (auch fig.); (Schlinge) snare; (Grube) pit; **mit e-r ~ fangen** auch trap; **e-e ~ stellen** set a trap (j-m for s.o.); **j-n in e-e ~ locken** fig. lure s.o. into a trap, ensnare s.o.; **j-m in die ~ gehen** fig. walk right into s.o.'s trap; **er ist in die ~ gegangen** auch he took the bait; **in der ~ sitzen** be caught in a trap; **2.** umg. fig. (Bett) bed; **in die ~ gehen** hit the sack (od. hay); **3.** schw. (Türklinke) latch
fallen v/i.; fällt, fiel, ist gefallen **1.** fall, drop; (stürzen) fall (down); Regen, Schnee: fall; Klappe, Vorhang: come down; **~ lassen** drop (auch fig.); **zu** od. **auf den Boden ~** fall to the ground, fall over; **aus dem Bett ~** fall out of bed; **j-m aus der Hand ~** fall (od. drop) from s.o.'s hand; **über e-n Stuhl ~** (stolpern) trip over a chair; **in der Nacht sind 30 Zentimeter Schnee gefallen** there was (od. we got) 30 centimet|res (Am. -ers) of snow last night; → **Apfel** 2, **Fuß¹** 1, **gefallen²**, **Nase¹** 1; **2.** (sinken) fall, drop, go down; Barometer: fall, be falling; Melodie, Stimme: descend, fall; **das Gold ist im Wert gefallen** the value of gold has gone down; **im Kurs ~** Aktien, Währung: fall, go down; **3.** Festung etc.: fall, be taken; euph. Soldat: fall, be killed (in action); fig. Barriere, Tabu etc.: be removed; Regierung: fall; Gesetz: be defeated; **4.** heftig: **vor j-m auf die Knie ~** go down on one's knees to s.o.; **j-m ins Lenkrad / in die Zügel ~** try to grab the steering wheel/reins from s.o.; **sich aufs Bett / ins Gras etc. ~ lassen** (heftiger): throw o.s.) onto the bed / into the grass etc.; **die Tür fiel ins Schloss** the door slammed; → **Arm** 1, **Hals** 1, **Rücken** 1; **5.** Blick, Licht, Schatten etc.: fall (auf + Akk. on); Licht: auch come (durch through); **6.** (hängen) Gardine, Haare, Kleid: fall; Stoff: auch be draped; **die Haare fielen ihm ständig ins Gesicht** his hair kept falling in his face; **7.** Ab-

hang, Klippen etc.: drop; Kurve, Linie: fall, descend; **8.** (zustande kommen) Entscheidung: be made; Urteil: be passed; Tor: be scored; **die Entscheidung fiel / zwei Tore fielen in der zweiten Halbzeit** the match was decided / there were two goals in the second half; **es fielen drei Schüsse** there were three shots, three shots were fired; **9.** Bemerkung: fall, be made; **e-e Bemerkung ~ lassen** let fall a remark, make a casual remark; **darüber hat er kein Wort ~ (ge)lassen** he didn't say a word about it; **auch sein Name fiel** his name was also mentioned; **es fielen harte Worte** there were harsh words; **10.** ~ **in** (+ Akk.) (geraten) in Dialekt, Muttersprache: lapse into; in Trance, Schlaf: fall into; **in Schwermut ~** be overcome by melancholy; **in e-n tiefen Schlaf ~** fall into a deep sleep; → **Ohnmacht** 1, **Ungnade**; **11.** j-m leicht/schwer ~ be easy/difficult for s.o.; **12.** fig.: **an j-n ~** fall (od. go) to s.o.; **auf e-n Feiertag** etc. ~ fall (od. be) on a holiday etc.; **auf j-n ~** Verdacht, Wahl: fall on; **das Los fiel auf mich** it fell to me to do it; **in e-e Kategorie / unter e-e Regelung** etc. ~ come under a category/regulation etc.; **13.** umg.: **durch ein Examen ~** fail an exam; → **Extrem**, **Hand¹** 3, **Last** 2, **Nerv** etc.
Fallen n; -s, kein Pl. fall(ing); **im ~ mit sich reißen** take s.o./s.th. with one (od. pull s.o./s.th. to the ground) as one falls
fällen v/t. **1.** (Baum) cut (od. chop) down, fell; **2.** (Entscheidung) make, come to; **ein Urteil ~** Richter: pass sentence (über + Akk. on); Jury: return a verdict; fig. pass judg(e)ment (on); **e-n Schiedsspruch ~** make a ruling; **3.** Chem. precipitate; **4.** Math.: **das Lot ~** drop a perpendicular; **5.** Mil. (Bajonett) lower
Fallensteller m; -s, -, **~in** f; -, -nen trapper
Fall|gatter n portcullis; **~geschichte** f case history; **~geschwindigkeit** f Phys. rate of fall; **~gitter** n portcullis; **~grube** f pit; auch fig. trap; **~höhe** f **1.** Phys. height of fall; **2.** Tech. height of drop; **~holz** n fallen dead wood
fällig Adj. **1.** due; **längst ~** long overdue; **der Haarschnitt war aber längst ~** auch it was high time (od. about time) you etc. had that hair cut; **jetzt wäre eigentlich e-e Entschuldigung ~** an apology would not come amiss now; **2.** (zahlbar) due, payable; **~ werden** become due (od. payable); (verfallen) expire; **~ zum 31. Mai** payable by May 31; **3.** umg. drohend: **jetzt ist er ~!** he's asked for it now; **morgen ist er ~!** I'll be after him tomorrow; **Fälligkeit** f maturity; **Fälligkeitstag** m maturity date, due date
Fall|linie f Skifahren: fall line; **~obst** n windfalls Pl.
Fall-out, Fallout [fɔːl'ʔaut] n, m; -s, -s; Phys. auch Pl.: fallout
Fall|reep n Naut. Jacob's (od. jack) ladder; **~rohr** n drainpipe; **~rückzieher** m Fußball: overhead kick
falls Konj. if; (für den Fall, dass) in case; **~ sie kommt** if she comes, if she should come; **~ er nicht erscheinen sollte** auch should he not turn up, in the event he does not appear förm.
Fallschirm m parachute; **mit dem ~ abspringen** make a parachute jump; **~absprung** m parachute jump; **~ab-**

~wurf m airdrop; **~gurt** m parachute harness; **~jäger** m Mil. paratrooper; **~seide** f parachute silk; **~springen** n parachuting, parachute jumping; Sport, mit längerem freiem Fall und Akrobatik: skydiving; **~springer** m, **~springerin** f parachutist; Sport skydiver
Fallstrick m fig. trap, snare; **j-m ~e legen** set a trap for s.o.
Fallstudie f case study
fällt Präs. → **fallen**
Fall|treppe f foldaway stairs Pl.; **~tür** f trapdoor
Fällung f Chem. precipitation; **Fällungsmittel** n precipitant
fallweise Adv. bes. österr. from case to case
Fall|wind m katabatic (od. down) wind; **~wurf** m Handball: falling throw
falsch I. Adj. **1.** (verkehrt) wrong; (nicht wahr) untrue; Annahme, Ton: false; Antwort, Bezeichnung: auch incorrect; Darstellung, Information, Interpretation etc.: auch mis...; **da bist du an den Falschen geraten** you've come to the wrong place (od. person) for that; → **Hals** 1; **2.** Bart, Zähne etc.: false; (künstlich) auch artificial; Perlen etc.: imitation, fake; (gefälscht) false, forged; Geld: auch counterfeit; Spielkarte: marked; Würfel: loaded; **~er Name** false (od. assumed) name; **unter ~em Namen** under a false name; **~e Schildkrötensuppe** mock turtle soup; **~er Hase** Gastr. meat loaf; **3.** pej. (gelogen) untrue; (unehrlich) auch two--faced; (unaufrichtig) false, insincere; Eid: false; ~ **gegen j-n** od. **gegenüber j-m sein** play false with s.o.; **er ist ein ganz ~er Typ** he's so false; **~er Prophet** false prophet; → **Schlange** 1, **Vorspiegelung** etc.; **4.** (unangebracht) Scham, Bescheidenheit etc.: false; Rücksichtnahme etc.: misplaced; **ein ~es Wort** a word out of place; **5.** Anat.: **~e Rippe** floating rib; **II.** Adv. wrong(ly); ~ **abbiegen** take the wrong turning (Am. turn); **etw. ~ anpacken** go about s.th. the wrong way; ~ **antworten** give the wrong answer, get the answer wrong; **etw. ~ auffassen** misunderstand s.th., get s.th. wrong; ~ **aussagen** make a false statement; ~ **gehen** Uhr: be wrong; ~ **herum** the wrong way (a)round; ~ **liegen im Bett**: lie the wrong way; fig. be mistaken (mit in), be on the wrong track; **da liegst du ~** you're mistaken (od. wrong) about that; **er macht alles ~** he can't do a thing right; ~ **schreiben** misspell, spell wrong(ly); ~ **singen** sing out of tune; ~ **spielen** Mus. play a (od. the) wrong note; pej. (betrügen) cheat; ~ **verbunden** am Telefon: sorry, wrong number; ~ **verstehen** misunderstand; ~ **verstandene Ehre** wrong idea of hono(u)r, misconceived sense of hono(u)r; ~ **wiedergeben** misquote
Falsch m: **ohne ~** guileless; **an ihm ist kein ~** he is guileless, he is completely without guile; **~aussage** f Jur. false statement
fälschen v/t. fake; (Urkunden, Unterschrift etc.) auch forge; (Geld) counterfeit, forge; (Rechnung, Bücher etc.) tamper with, doctor umg.; (Spielkarten) mark; (Würfel) load; weitS. (Geschichte etc.) falsify, doctor umg.; **die Bücher ~** auch cook the books umg.
Fälscher m; -s, - forger, counterfeiter; **~bande** f gang of forgers

Fälscherin *f; -, -nen* → *Fälscher*

Falschfahrer *m* driver going in the wrong direction (*on a motorway or similar*), *Am.* wrong-way driver; → *auch* **Geisterfahrer**

Falschgeld *n* counterfeit money; *Scheine auch* forged money; **~ring** *m* ring of money counterfeiters (*od.* forgers)

Falschheit *f* **1.** *nur Sg.*; (*Ggs. Richtigkeit*) wrongness; (*Unechtheit*) falsehood, falseness; **2.** *nur Sg.*; *pej. e-r Person*: falseness, duplicity; **3.** (*Betrügerei*) deception

Falschinformation *f* piece of false information; (*Ente*) hoax

fälschlich I. *Adj.*; *nur attr.*; (*Beschuldigung etc.*) wrongful, false; (*Annahme*) mistaken; **II.** *Adv.* wrongly; *beschuldigen*: wrongfully; (*aus Versehen*) by mistake, erroneously; **fälschlicherweise** *Adv.* by mistake, erroneously

Falschmeldung *f* false report; (*Ente*) hoax

Falschmünzer *m; -s, -* forger; **Falschmünzerei** *f; -, kein Pl.* forgery, counterfeiting; **Falschmünzerin** *f; -, -nen* forger

Falsch|parken *n* illegal parking; **~parker** *m; -s, -* **1.** parking offender (*Am. auch* scofflaw); *diese!* these people who park their cars all over the place; **2.** *Auto*: wrongly-parked car; **~parkerin** *f; -, -nen* → *Falschparker* **1.**; **~schreibung** *f* misspelling; *mis|spelt* (*Am.* -spelled) word; **~spieler** *m*, **~spielerin** *f* cheat

Fälschung *f* **1.** (*das Fälschen*) forging; *von Geld: auch* counterfeiting; **2.** (*Gefälschtes*) fake, forgery; **fälschungssicher** *Adj.* forgery-proof, *präd. od. nachgestellt*: impossible to counterfeit

Falsett *n; -(e)s, -e; Mus.* falsetto; (*im*) **~ singen** sing falsetto

faltbar *Adj.* folding ...; collapsible; *ist es ~?* can it be folded up?

Falt|blatt *n* leaflet; **~boot** *n* folding canoe

Fältchen *n* crease; *in der Haut: auch* (tiny) wrinkle

Faltdach *n Auto*: soft top, *Am.* convertible

Falte *f; -, -n* **1.** *Papier, Stoff, beabsichtigte*: fold; *am Rock*: pleat; *geknitterte, gebügelte*: crease; **~n werfen** *schöne*: fall in folds; *unschöne*: pucker; **2.** *Haut*: crease; *stärker*: wrinkle; *die Stirn in ~n legen* knit one's brow, frown

fälteln *v/t.* pleat; (*Papier*) fold

falten I. *v/t.* **1.** fold; (*Taschentuch etc.*) *auch* fold up; **2.** *die Hände ~* fold one's hands; → *gefaltet*; **3.** *die Stirn ~* knit one's brow, frown; **4.** *Geol.* fold; **II.** *v/refl.* **1.** *Haut*: wrinkle, crease; **2.** *Geol.* fold

Faltenbildung *f* **1.** wrinkling; **2.** *Geol.* folding, plication *fachspr.*

faltenfrei *Adj.* **1.** *Sitz von Kleidung*: creaseless; **2.** *Haut*: smooth, unlined; **3.** *Textilien: attr.* non-crumple, non-crease

Faltengebirge *n Geol.* folded mountains *Pl.*

faltenlos *Adj. Gesicht etc.*: smooth, unlined; *Kleidungsstück*: uncreased

Falten|rock *m* pleated skirt; **~wurf** *m* drapery

Falter *m; -s, -*; (*Schmetterling*) butterfly; (*Nachtfalter*) moth

faltig *Adj.* **1.** (*zerknittert*) creased; **2.** *Haut*: wrinkled

Falt|karte *f* folding map; **~karton** *m* collapsible cardboard box; **~prospekt**

---

m leaflet; **~tür** *f* folding door

Falz *m; -es, -e* **1.** (*Falte, Knick*) fold; **2.** *Buchbinderei*: fold; *zwischen Buchrücken und -deckel*: shoulder; *zum Einkleben*: guard, stub; **3.** *Tech.* (*Kante*) welt, edge; (*Fuge, Saum*) seam; (*Auskehlung*) groove, notch; *Holz*: rabbet; **4.** *für Briefmarken*: mount, hinge; **~bein** *n Buchbinderei*: folding stick

falzen *v/t.* **1.** fold; **2.** *Tech.* groove; *Blech*: welt; *Holz*: rabbet

Fama *f; -, kein Pl.; geh.* rumo(u)r; *es geht die ~, dass ...* rumo(u)r has it that ...

familiär *Adj.* **1.** (*die Familie betreffend*) family; *aus ~en Gründen* for family (*od.* personal) reasons; **2.** (*ungezwungen*) informal; *Atmosphäre*: easy-going; **3.** *pej.*: (*allzu*) ~ (over)familiar; **4.** *Ling.* familiar, colloquial; **~er Ausdruck** colloquialism

Familie *f; -, -n* family (*auch Ling., Zool., Bot.*); **~ Miller** the Miller family, the Millers; *e-e ~ gründen* start a family; *~ haben* have a family, have children; *sechsköpfige ~* family of six; *das bleibt in der ~* it will go no further; *es liegt in der ~* it runs in the family; *das kommt in den besten ~n vor umg.* it happens to the best of us

Familien|ähnlichkeit *f* family likeness; **~angehörige** *m, f* member of the family; (*direkte[r] Verwandte[r]*) close relative; *Abhängige(r)*: dependant *Amtsspr.*; **~angelegenheit** *f* family affair; *in dringenden ~en* on urgent family business; **~anschluss** *m* contact with a family; *Dalmatinerwelpen suchen ~* Dalmatian pups looking for a good family home; *für Student(in) etc.*: *möbliertes Zimmer mit ~* furnished room for student *etc.* who will be one of the family; **~anzeigen** *Pl. Zeitungsrubrik*: births, marriages and deaths; **~arbeit** *f* work involved in looking after the family, *etwa* family duties *Pl.*; **~ausflug** *m* family outing; **~bande** *Pl. geh.* family ties; **~besitz** *m* family property; *in od. im ~ sein* be family-owned, be in family ownership; **~betrieb** *m* family business; **~buch** *n* (registry office's) record of family details; **~chronik** *f* family chronicle (*od.* history); **~drama** *n* family drama; **~ehre** *f* family hono(u)r; **~feier** *f* family celebration

familienfeindlich *Adj. Politik, Gesetz*: anti-family, unfavo(u)rable to families

Familien|fest *n* family party; **~forschung** *f* genealogy; **~foto** *n* family (group) photo

familienfreundlich *Adj. Politik etc.*: pro-family, favo(u)rable to families; *Hotel etc.*: family ..., *nachgestellt*: ... that welcomes families; *die Partei fordert eine ~e Steuerreform* this party is backing tax reform that favo(u)rs the family

Familiengeheimnis *n* family secret

familiengerecht *Adj. Hotel, Campingplatz etc.*: well arranged for families

Familien|glück *n* domestic bliss; **~grab** *n* family grave; **~karte** *f* family ticket; **~kreis** *m* family circle; *der engste ~* the immediate family, the next of kin; *das Begräbnis findet im engsten ~ statt* only the closest members of the family will be attending the funeral; *in Todesanzeige*: private funeral; **~kutsche** *f hum.* family car; **~leben** *n* family life; **~mitglied** *n* member of the family, family member; *Abhängi-*

---

ge(r): dependant *Amtsspr.*; **~name** *m* surname, family (*Am. auch* last) name; **~oberhaupt** *n* head of the family; **~packung** *f* family pack; **~pass** *m* book of family vouchers; **~pause** *f* time off work for raising a family; **~planung** *f* family planning; **~rat** *m* family council (*od.* tribunal); **~recht** *n Jur.* family law; **~roman** *m Lit.* roman-fleuve, saga; **~sauna** *f* mixed sauna (for couples); **~sinn** *m; nur Sg.* sense of family; **~sitz** *m* family home (*od.* residence); **~stand** *m; nur Sg.* marital status; **~streit** *m* family argument (*od.* row); **~stück** *n* (family) heirloom; **~therapie** *f Psych.* family group therapy; **~tradition** *f* family tradition; **~treffen** *n* family get-together (*umg. iro.* affair); (*Wiedersehen*) family reunion; **~unterhalt** *m* upkeep of the family; **~vater** *m* **1.** (*Familienoberhaupt*) head of the family; **2.** (*Mann mit Familiensinn*) family man; **~verhältnisse** *Pl.* family set-up (*od.* background) *Sg.*; **~wagen** *m* family car; **~zulage** *f* family allowance; **~zusammenführung** *f* family reunification; **~zuwachs** *m* new arrival, addition to the family

famos *Adj. umg. altm.* capital

Fan [fɛn] *m; -s, -s; umg.* fan; *Fußball: auch* supporter

Fanal *n; -s, -e* **1.** *geh.* beacon; **2.** *fig.* signal

Fanatiker *m; -s, -*, **~in** *f; -, -nen* fanatic; **fanatisieren** *v/t.* instil(l) fanaticism in; **fanatisch** *Adj.* fanatic(al); **Fanatismus** *m; -, kein Pl.* fanaticism

Fan|block *m im Stadion*: area occupied by supporters; **~club** *m* fan club; *Fußball*: supporters' club

fand *Imperf.* → *finden*

Fanfare *f; -, -n* **1.** (*Instrument*) trumpet; **2.** (*Stück, ~nstoß*) fanfare; (*Signal*) *auch* flourish (of trumpets); **3.** *Mot.* musical horn, *mst* Colonel Bogey horn *umg.*

Fang *m; -(e)s, Fänge* **1.** *nur Sg.; Handlung*: catching; *mit Fallen*: trapping; (*Jagen*) hunting; *auf ~ ausgehen/ausfahren* go hunting /(*Fischfang*) fishing /(*Walfang*) whaling; **2.** *nur Sg.*; (*Beute*) bag; *von Fischen*: catch, haul (*beide auch fig.*); *e-n guten ~ machen* Fischfang: take a good catch; *Jagd*: take home a good (*od.* rich) haul; *fig.* make a big haul; *das war ein guter ~ fig.* that was a real bargain; *mit ihm haben wir e-n guten ~ gemacht fig.* he was a good catch; **3.** *mst Pl.*; (*Vogelkralle*) claw; (*Reißzahn*) fang; *des Ebers*: tusk; *in den Fängen* (+ *Gen.*) *fig.* in the clutches of; *wenn ich ihn erst in den Fängen habe* once I get hold of him (*od.* lay my fingers on him); **4.** *Jägerspr.* (*Todesstoß*) coup de grâce; **~arm** *m Zool.* tentacle; **~ball** *m, n Spiel*: catch; *mit j-m ~ spielen fig.* treat s.o. as one's plaything; **~eisen** *n Wildfalle*: trap

Fangemeinde ['fɛn-] *f* fan base

fangen; *fängt, fing, hat gefangen* **I.** *v/t.* **1.** catch; (*Menschen*) *auch* capture; *mit Falle*: trap; *mit Netz: auch* net; *mit Schlinge*: snare; *sich ~ lassen* get caught; → *gefangen*; **2.** *fig.* (*fesseln*) captivate; **3.** *Feuer ~* catch fire; *fig.* be bitten (*für etw.* by, with); (*sich verlieben*) be smitten; *für die Fitness-Idee Feuer ~ fig.* be bitten by the fitness bug *umg.*; **4.** *fig.* (*Kunden, Stimmen*) gain; (*Lügner etc.*) trap; **5.** *südd., österr. umg.*: *eine ~* (*e-e Ohrfeige krie-*

gen) cop one, cop it, *Am.* get it; **II.** *vt/i.* (*Ball*) catch; **gut/nicht ~ können** be good / no good at catching; **III.** *v/refl.* **1.** be (*od.* get) caught (*in + Dat.* in); *der Schmutz fängt sich im Sieb* the dirt is caught (*od.* collected) in the filter; **2.** *beim Stolpern etc.*: catch (*od.* steady) o.s.; *Auto, beim Schleudern*: straighten out; *Flugzeug*: level out; **3.** *fig.*: *sich* (*wieder*) *~* get a grip on o.s. (again), recover one's equilibrium; *ich fang mich schon wieder* I'll be all right (in a minute)

Fangen *n*; *-s*, *kein Pl.*; (*Spiel*) catch, *Am.* tag

Fänger *m*; *-s*, *-*, **~in** *f*; *-*, *-nen* catcher

Fang|flotte *f* fishing fleet; **~frage** *f* catch (*od.* trick) question

fangfrisch *Adj.* freshly caught, fresh

Fang|gebiete *Pl.* fishing grounds; **~gründe** *Pl.* fishing grounds; **~leine** *f* **1.** *Naut.* painter; **2.** *Fallschirm*: shroud (line); **~netz** *n* **1.** net; **2.** *Flug.* arrester net; **3.** *Zirkus etc.*: safety net; **4.** *fig.* snare

Fango *m*; *-s*, *kein Pl.* fango; *zehnmal ~ bekommen* receive ten fango treatments; **~packung** *f* mudpack, fango pack

Fang|plätze *Pl.* fishing grounds; **~prämie** *f* bounty; **~quote** *f* fishing quota; **~schaltung** *f* *Telef.* interception; **~schuss** *m* coup de grâce

fängt *Präs.* → **fangen**

Fang|verbot *n* **1.** fishing ban; *Walfang*: whaling ban; **2.** (*Jagdverbot*) hunting ban; **~zahn** *m* *Zool.* (*Reißzahn*) fang; **~zaun** *m* *für Schnee*: snow fence (*od.* guard); **~zeit** *f* fishing season

Fan|klub [ˈfɛnklʊb] *m* fan club; **~post** *f* fan mail; (*einzelner Brief*) *auch* a fan letter

Fantasie *f*; *-*, *-n* **1.** *nur Sg.*; (*Vorstellungskraft*) imagination; *e-e blühende ~* a vivid imagination; *e-e schmutzige ~* a dirty mind; *die ~ anregen* stimulate the imagination; *nichts der ~ überlassen* leave nothing to the imagination; *das ist reine ~ od. das existiert nur in d-r etc. ~* it's all in the mind, you're *etc.* imagining things; → *durchgehen* I 7, *Lauf* 4, *Reich*; **2.** (*Vorstellung*) fantasy (*auch sexuell*); *e-s Kranken*: hallucination(s); *sich in ~n flüchten* escape into a fantasy world (*od.* world of fantasy); **3.** *Mus.* fantasia

fantasiearm *Adj.* unimaginative, lacking in imagination

Fantasie|gebilde *n* figment of the imagination; **~gestalt** *f* imaginary character; **~kostüm** *n* fantastic get-up; **~landschaft** *f* imaginary (*od.* fantastic) landscape

fantasielos *Adj.* unimaginative; (*langweilig*) boring; (*einfallslos*) unresourceful; *sei doch nicht so ~!* be more imaginative!, use your imagination!; **Fantasielosigkeit** *f*; *nur Sg.* lack of imagination; (*Einfallslosigkeit*) unresourcefulness

Fantasie|name *m* invented (*od.* made-up) name; **~preis** *m pej.* exorbitant (*od.* astronomical) price

fantasieren I. *v/i.* **1.** (day)dream, fantasize (*von* about); *umg.* (*Unsinn reden*) talk wildly (*von* about); *er fantasiert nur* he's just talking moonshine; (*erfindet alles*) he's making it up as he goes along; *sie fantasiert davon, Astronautin zu werden* she has this dream of becoming an astronaut; **2.** *Mus.* improvise, extemporize;

3. *Med.* hallucinate, be delirious; **II.** *v/t.* (*Geschichte*) dream up; *was fantasierst du da? umg.* what are you going on about?

fantasievoll *Adj.* imaginative; (*kreativ*) creative

Fantasie|vorstellung *f* fantasy; **~welt** *f* world of fantasy, fantasy world

Fantast *m*; *-en*, *-en*; *pej.* (starry-eyed) dreamer; **Fantasterei** *f*; *-*, *-en*; *pej.* (pure) fantasy; *das ist ~ auch* it's his *etc.* imagination running wild; **~en** (*Unsinn*) crazy ideas

fantastisch *Adj.* **1.** (*unwirklich*) fantastic; (*bizarr*) bizarre; (*überspannt*) wild, extravagant; **2.** *umg.* (*großartig*) fantastic, terrific; (*unglaublich*) incredible

Faradaykäfig [ˈfɛrədi-] *m* *Phys.* Faraday cage

Farb|abstimmung *f* **1.** colo(u)r scheme; **2.** *Fot.*, *TV* colo(u)r balance; **~abweichung** *f* colo(u)r variation; **~aufnahme** *f* colo(u)r photo; **~band** *n* typewriter ribbon; **~beilage** *f* colo(u)r supplement; **~beutel** *m* paint bomb; **~bild** *n* colo(u)r photo; **~bildschirm** *m* colo(u)r screen; **~dia** *n Fot.* colo(u)r transparency; **~druck** *m* **1.** *Verfahren*: colo(u)r printing; **2.** *konkret*: colo(u)r print; **~drucker** *m* colo(u)r printer

Farbe *f*; *-*, *-n* **1.** colour, *Am.* color; (*Farbton*) *auch* shade; *des Gesichts*: *auch* complexion; *in ~* (*nicht schwarzweiß*) in colo(u)r; *von grauer etc. ~ sein* be grey (*Am.* gray) in colo(u)r; *welche ~ hat das Kleid?* what colo(u)r is the dress?; *in allen ~n schillern* be iridescent, be all the colo(u)rs of the rainbow; *ihr Gesicht wechselte die ~* her face went pale; *etw. in den schwärzesten/herrlichsten/rosigsten ~n ausmalen* *fig.* paint s.th. in the blackest/most glowing/rosiest colo(u)rs, paint the gloomiest possible/ most glowing/rosiest picture of s.th.; *e-r Sache ~ verleihen* *fig.* add (*od.* lend) colo(u)r to s.th.; **2.** *zum Anstreichen*: paint; *für Haar, Stoffe*: dye; *zum Drucken*: (printer's) ink; *~n mischen* mix paint; *die ~n laufen ineinander* the colo(u)rs are running into one another; **3.** *nur Sg.*; (*Ggs. Blässe*) colo(u)r; *~ bekommen* get some colo(u)r into one's cheeks; (*braun werden*) get a tan; *du hast richtig ~ bekommen von der Bewegung, frischen Luft etc.*: you've put on a really healthy colo(u)r; *von der Sonne*: you've got yourself a nice tan; *~ verlieren* go pale; **4.** *Spielkarten*: suit; *~ bekennen* follow suit; *fig.* declare o.s., come clean; **5.** *mst Pl.*; *fig. als Symbol für Zugehörigkeit*: colo(u)r; *die ~n s-s Vereins tragen/vertreten* wear the colo(u)rs of one's club / represent one's club; *die ~(n) wechseln* change sides

Färbebad *n* dye bath

farbecht *Adj.* **1.** *Stoff etc.*: colo(u)rfast; **2.** *Fot.* orthochromatic

Farb|effekt *m* colo(u)r effect; **~eimer** *m* paint bucket; *kleiner*: paint kettle

Färbemittel *n* dye

farbempfindlich *Adj.* **1.** *Fot.* colo(u)r-sensitive; **2.** *Stoff, Gewebe*: not colo(u)rfast, subject to fading

färben I. *v/t.* **1.** (*Stoff, Haar*) dye; (*Glas, Papier*) stain; (*tönen*) tint; *sich* (*Dat.*) *die Haare* (*schwarz*) *~* dye one's hair (black); **2.** *Sache*: colo(u)r; *der Herbst färbt die Wälder bunt* autumn decks out the woodlands in bright colo(u)rs; **3.** *fig.* colo(u)r; *s-n Beitrag hu-*

moristisch ~ give one's article a humorous touch; → *gefärbt*; **II.** *v/refl.* colo(u)r; *Laub*: change colo(u)r; *sich blau etc. ~* turn blue *etc.*; *ihr Gesicht färbte sich vor Verlegenheit/Wut rot* she went red in the face from embarrassment/anger, she reddened (*od.* blushed) with embarrassment / flushed with anger; **III.** *v/i.* **1.** *umg.* (*abfärben*) run; **2.** *Farbstoff*: dye

...farben *im Adj.* ...-colo(u)red; *rosen~* rose-colo(u)red

Farben... *siehe auch Farb...*

farbenblind *Adj.* colo(u)r-blind; **Farbenblindheit** *f* colo(u)r-blindness

farben|freudig, **~froh** *Adj.* colo(u)rful

Farbenlehre *f*; *nur Sg.* **1.** *Phys.* theory of colo(u)rs, chromatics *Pl.* (*V. im Sg.*); **2.** *Psych.* colo(u)r psychology

Farbenpracht *f* blaze of colo(u)r; *die Bäume in i-r ganzen ~* the trees in all their colo(u)rful splendo(u)r (*od.* glorious colo(u)rs *Pl.*); **farbenprächtig** *Adj.* gloriously colo(u)rful (*od.* colo(u)red)

Farbenspiel *n* play of colo(u)r

Färber *m*; *-s*, *-* dyer; **Färberei** *f*; *-*, *-en* **1.** dyeworks *Pl.*; **2.** (*Gewerbe*) dyer's trade; **Färberin** *f*; *-*, *-nen* (female) dyer

Färbetablette *f* dental plaque indicator tablet

Farbfernsehen *n* colo(u)r television (*od.* TV); **Farbfernseher** *m*, **Farbfernsehgerät** *n* colo(u)r television (*od.* TV)

Farb|film *m* colo(u)r film; **~filter** *m*, *n* *Fot.* colo(u)r filter; **~fleck** *m* paint spot; **~foto** *n* colo(u)r photo; **~fotografie** *f* **1.** colo(u)r photography; **2.** (*Bild*) colo(u)r photograph; **~gebung** *f* colo(u)ring; (*Kombination*) colo(u)r scheme

farbig I. *Adj.* **1.** colo(u)red, *präd. od. nachgestellt*: in colo(u)r; *(bunt)* colo(u)rful; *Glas in Kirchenfenstern etc.*: stained; *Druck, Kopie etc.*: *attr.* colo(u)r ...; **2.** *Haut, Person*: colo(u)red *neg!*; → *Farbige*, *Schwarze*[1]; **3.** *fig.* colo(u)rful; **II.** *Adv.* **1.** *(bunt)* colo(u)rfully; **2.** *fig.* *etw. ~ schildern* give a colo(u)rful description of s.th.

...farbig *im Adj. und Adv.* → *...farben*

Farbige *m*, *f*; *-n*, *-n* non-white, *Am.* person of color; (*Schwarze[r]*) black; *in USA*: *auch* African American; *in Südafrika*: (Cape) Colo(u)red

Farbigkeit *f*; *nur Sg.* colo(u)r, colo(u)rfulness

Farb|kasten *m* paintbox; **~klecks** *m* **1.** blob (*od.* spot) of paint; **2.** *fig.* spot (*od.* dash) of colo(u)r; *es ist ein netter ~* it adds a nice bit of colo(u)r; **~komposition** *f* colo(u)r composition (*od.* scheme); **~kopie** *f* colo(u)r copy; **~kopierer** *m* colo(u)r copier; **~kreis** *m* colo(u)r wheel; **~lehre** *f*; *nur Sg.* → *Farbenlehre*

farblich I. *Adj. attr.* colo(u)r ..., *nachgestellt*: in colo(u)r; **II.** *Adv.* in colo(u)r; (*~ gesehen*) colo(u)rwise, as far as the colo(u)rs go; *~* (*aufeinander*) *abstimmen* match the colo(u)rs; *die Möbel passen ~ nicht zusammen* the colo(u)rs of the furniture do not match (*od.* don't go together)

farblos *Adj.* **1.** colo(u)rless; *Lack, Glas etc.*: *auch* clear; *Licht*: white; *Schuhcreme*: neutral; **2.** (*blass*) pale; **3.** *fig. Erzählung, Person etc.*: colo(u)rless; *er ist völlig ~ auch* he has no personality; **Farblosigkeit** *f*; *nur Sg.* colo(u)rlessness (*auch fig.*); *fig. e-r Person*: *auch* lack of personality

Farb|monitor m EDV colo(u)r monitor; **~nuance** f shade (of colo[u]r); **~orgie** f riot of colo(u)r; **~palette** f **1.** Brett: (painter's) palette; **2.** Auswahl: palette (od. range) of colo(u)rs; **~pulver** n dry colo(u)r, ground pigment; **~sättigung** f colo(u)r saturation; **~schattierung** f shade (of colo[u]r), hue; **~schicht** f layer of paint; beim Anstrich: coat of paint; **~skala** f colo(u)r range; **~stich** m colo(u)r cast; **~stift** m colo(u)red pencil, crayon; (Filzstift etc.) colo(u)red pen; grüner etc. **~** green etc. pencil (od. crayon, pen); **~stoff** m **1.** dye; für Lebensmittel etc.: auch Pl. colo(u)ring; ohne **~e** Aufschrift: contains no (artificial) colo(u)ring; **2.** Chem., Bio. pigment; **~symbolik** f colo(u)r symbolism; **~tafel** f **1.** im Buch: colo(u)r plate; **2.** (Tabelle) colo(u)r chart; **~temperatur** f colo(u)r temperature; **~ton** m shade, tone; im **~** zusammenpassen match colo(u)rwise, be matching shades; **~tupfer** m dab (od. spot) of paint; fig. spot of colo(u)r

Färbung f **1.** nur Sg.; Handlung: colo(u)ring; von Textilien etc. dyeing; **2.** (Farbe) colo(u)ring; (Tönung) tinge; leichte **~** (slight) tint; **3.** fig. politisch etc.: slant, bias; Politiker aller **~en** politicians of every hue

Farb|walze f ink(ing) roller; **~wiedergabe** f colo(u)r reproduction; **~zusammenstellung** f colo(u)r combination (absichtlich: scheme)

Farce ['farsə] f; -, -n **1.** Theat. farce (auch fig. pej.); **2.** Gastr. stuffing; **farcenhaft** Adj. pej. farcical

Färinger m; -s, -, **~in** f; -, -nen Faroese

Farinzucker m brown sugar

Farm f; -, -en; Agr. farm; **Farmer** m; -s, -, **Farmerin** f; -, -nen farmer

Farn m; -(e)s, -e; Bot. fern; **~kraut** n Bot. fern; **~wedel** m Bot. fern frond

Färöer[1] Pl. Geog. Faroes, Faroe Islands

Färöer[2] m; -s, -, **~in** f; -, -nen Faroese, weiblich auch: Faroese woman (od. girl etc.); **färöisch I.** Adj. Faroese; **II. Färöisch** n; -en; Ling. Faroese; das Färöische the Faroese language

Färse f; -, -n; Zool. young cow, heifer

Fasan m; -s, -e; Orn. pheasant

Fasanenjagd f **1.** pheasant shooting; **2.** konkret: pheasant shoot (od. hunt)

Fasanerie f; -, -n pheasantry

Faschierte n; -n, kein Pl.; österr. mince(d meat), Am. ground meat

Fasching m; -s, -e und -s, mst Sg.; südd., österr. carnival; im **~** at carnival time

Faschings|... im Subst. südd., österr. carnival ...; **~dienstag** m Shrove Tuesday, Am. Mardi Gras; **~kostüm** n carnival costume, fancy dress; **~prinz** m carnival prince; **~prinzessin** f carnival princess

Faschismus m; -, kein Pl.; Pol. fascism; **Faschist** m; -en, -en, **Faschistin** f; -, -nen; oft pej. fascist; **faschistisch** Adj. fascist; **faschistoid** Adj. protofascist; **Fascho** m; -s, -s; Sl. pej. fascist pig

Faselei f; -, -en; umg. pej. drivel; **faseln** umg. pej. **I.** v/i. blather; stärker: drivel on (über + Akk. od. von about); **II.** v/t.: blödes Zeug etc. **~** talk nonsense; was faselt er da? what is he blathering about?

Fasenacht f südd., schw. → Fastnacht

Faser f; -, -n; Anat., Bot. fib|re (Am. -er); (Faden) thread; von Gemüse: string; von Holz: grain; mit jeder **~** m-s Herzens fig. with every fib|re (Am. -er) of my being; **Faserglas** n; nur Sg.; Tech. fibreglass, Am. fiberglass; **faserig** Adj. **1.** fibrous; Fleisch etc.: stringy; **2.** (zerfasert) frayed; **fasern** v/i. fray; **fasernackt** Adj. umg. stark (Am. auch buck) naked, präd. starkers

Faser|optik f fib|re (Am. -er) optics Pl. (V. im Sg.); **~pflanze** f fib|re (Am. -er) plant; **~platte** f fibreboard, Am. fiberboard

Fasler m; -s, -, **~in** f; -, -nen; umg. pej. blatherer; stärker: drivel(l)er, **er ist ein richtiger ~** auch he just blathers on and on

Fasnacht f südd., schw. → Fastnacht

Fass n; -es, Fässer **1.** barrel; für Portwein, Sherry: cask; kleines: keg; (Bottich) vat, tub; zum Buttern: churn; für Öl, Chemikalien etc.: drum; **ein ~ Bier** a barrel (kleines: keg) of beer; **Bier/Wein vom ~** draught (Am. draft) beer / wine from the wood; **2.** fig.: **dick wie ein ~** as fat as a barrel; **~ ohne Boden** bottomless pit; **das ist ein ~ ohne Boden** auch it's never-ending, it just goes on and on; Thema: you could go on talking about that all night; **das schlägt dem ~ den Boden aus** od. **das bringt das ~ zum Überlaufen!** that's the last straw, that takes the biscuit (Am. cake) umg.; **ein ~ aufmachen** umg. have a fling (od. binge)

Fassade f; -, -n façade, front (beide auch fig.)

Fassaden|beleuchtung f **1.** floodlighting; **2.** floodlit building(s Pl.); **~kletterer** m, **~kletterin** f cat burglar; **~malerei** f façade painting

fassbar Adj. **1.** (konkret) tangible; **2.** geistig: comprehensible; **schwer ~** hard to comprehend

Fass|bier n draught (Am. draft) beer; **~daube** f stave

fassen I. v/t. **1.** (ergreifen) take hold of, grasp; (halten) hold; (packen) seize, grab; **j-n an** od. **bei der Hand ~** take s.o. by the hand, take s.o.'s hand; **j-n am Arm ~** take s.o.'s arm; **zu ~ kriegen** get hold of; **2.** (Verbrecher etc.) catch; (festnehmen) arrest; **zu ~ kriegen** apprehend förm.; **3.** → einfassen; **4.** (aufnehmen können) hold; auf Sitzplätzen: auch seat; **5.** (enthalten) contain; **in sich** (Dat.) **~** fig. include; **6.** (formulieren) put, formulate; **in Worte ~** put into words; **das lässt sich nicht in Worte ~** auch it can't be described; **7.** fig. geistig: grasp, understand; **8.** (glauben) believe; **nicht zu ~** unbelievable, incredible; **das ist kaum zu ~** auch it's hard to believe; **9.** (aufnehmen) (Ladung, Treibstoff etc.) hold; **10.** Mil. (Proviant, Munition etc.) draw; → Essen 2; **11.** fig. (Beschluss, Entschluss) make, take, come to; (Abneigung, Mut) take; **e-n Gedanken ~** form an idea; **ich konnte keinen klaren Gedanken ~** I couldn't think straight; → Auge 2, Fuß[1] 1, Vorsatz 1; **II.** v/i. **1. ~ an** (+ Akk.) touch; **~ in/auf** (+ Akk.) put one's hand in/on; **~ nach** reach (od. grasp) for s.th.; **ins Leere ~** grasp thin air; **sich** (Dat.) **an die Stirn** etc. **~** put one's hand to one's forehead etc.; **da kann man sich nur noch an den Kopf ~** it really makes you wonder; **2. fass!** zum Hund: get (Am. sic) him/her/it!; **3.** Tech., Werk-

zeug, Schraube etc.: grip; **III.** v/refl. **1.** regain one's composure; (sich zusammenreißen) pull o.s. together; **er konnte sich vor Glück kaum ~** he was beside himself with joy; → gefasst; **2. sich kurz ~** be brief; **fasse dich kurz!** keep it short, make it brief; **3. sich in Geduld ~** have patience

fässerweise Adv. **1.** by the barrel; **2.** umg. (in großen Mengen) in huge quantities

Fassette f → Facette

fasslich Adj.: **leicht/schwer ~** easy/hard to understand; **Fasslichkeit** f; nur Sg. comprehensibility

Fasson [fa'sõ:] f; -, -s od. südd., österr., schw. mst. -en **1.** (Form) shape; (Schnitt) cut; (Frisur) trim; (Machart) style; **2.** fig.: **aus der ~ geraten** umg. (zunehmen) lose one's figure, put on weight; **nach s-r ~** after one's own fashion; **jeder muss nach s-r ~ glücklich** od. **selig werden** everyone has to work out his own salvation

Fassreifen m (barrel) hoop

Fassung f **1.** e-r Brille: frame; e-r Glühbirne: socket; e-s Edelsteins: setting; e-r Quelle etc.: rim; **2.** (sprachliche Form) form; (Formulierung) wording; (Version) version; **in der vorliegenden ~** in its present form; **3.** kein Pl. (Beherrschung) composure; (inneres Gleichgewicht) auch equanimity; **aus der ~ bringen** upset, faze umg.; **sie ist durch nichts aus der ~ zu bringen** she's unflappable; **die ~ bewahren** maintain one's composure, keep one's cool umg.; **um ~ ringen** nach Ausbruch: try to regain one's composure; vor Ausbruch: struggle to retain one's composure, try not to lose one's temper; **die ~ verlieren** lose one's composure; vor Wut: lose one's temper (cool umg.); **er war ganz außer ~** he was completely beside himself; **etw. mit ~ tragen** bear s.th. with fortitude, grin and bear it; **trag's mit ~!** keep a stiff upper lip; → Abfassung, Einfassung

Fassungskraft f powers Pl. of comprehension, (mental) capacity

fassungslos I. Adj. stunned; (sprachlos) speechless; (verwirrt) perplexed, bewildered; **II.** Adv.: **er sah mich ~ an** he looked at me in amazement (od. disbelief), he just gaped at me; **Fassungslosigkeit** f; nur Sg. stunned state, state of shock; (Verwirrung) bewilderment

Fassungsvermögen n **1.** capacity; **2.** fig. (mental) capacity; **das übersteigt mein ~** that's beyond my (powers of) comprehension, that's above my head

Fasswein m im Ausschank: wine from the barrel; fässerweise: wine in barrels

fast Adv. vor Subst. und Adj.: mst almost; vor Zahlen, Maß- und Zeitangaben: auch nearly; **in ~ allen Fällen** in almost every case; **~ keine** hardly any; **~ nichts** next to nothing; **~ nie** hardly ever; **ich hätte ~ geglaubt, dass ...** I could almost have sworn (that) ...; **~ hätte ich ihn rausgeschmissen** I very nearly kicked him out, I was on the point of kicking him out; **wir haben's ~** umg. we're almost there, we've almost (od. nearly) finished; → auch beinah(e)

fasten v/i. fast; go on a fast

Fasten[1] n fast(ing); **das ~ brechen** break one's fast

Fasten[2] Pl. kirchl **1.** Zeit: Lent Sg.;

F

2. (*Bußübungen*) Lenten acts of penance
Fasten|gebot n obligation to fast; **~kur** f starvation (*od.* fasting) cure; **~speise** f food permitted during fasting (*kirchl.* Lent); **~tag** m **1.** fast (day), day of fasting; **2.** *Med.* fasting day; **~zeit** f **1.** *kirchl.*: **die ~** Lent; **2.** fasting period
Fastnacht f **1.** *Dienstag*: Shrove Tuesday, *Am.* Mardi Gras; **2.** *Zeitraum*: carnival; **Fastnachts...** → **Faschings...**
Faszination f; -, *kein Pl.* fascination; *e-e* **~** *ausüben auf* (+ *Akk.*) hold a great fascination for; **faszinieren** v/t. fascinate; **Faszinosum** n; -s, *Faszinosa*; *geh.* fascinating (*od.* amazing) phenomenon
fatal *Adj.* **1.** (*schicksalhaft*) fateful; (*verhängnisvoll*) disastrous, fatal; **2.** (*unangenehm*) awkward, embarrassing; *Folgen*: (most) unfortunate; (*ärgerlich*) annoying; **fatalerweise** *Adv.* (most) unfortunately; **Fatalismus** m; -, *kein Pl.*; *geh.* fatalism; **Fatalist** m; -en, -en, **Fatalistin** f; -, -nen; *geh.* fatalist; **fatalistisch** *Adj. geh.* fatalist(ic)
Fata Morgana f; - -, - -s *od.* - *Morganen* mirage, fata morgana (*beide auch fig.*)
Fatzke m; -n *od.* -s, -n *od.* -s; *umg. pej.* stupid poser, arrogant twit; *so ein eitler ~!* what a conceited ass!
fauchen v/i. **1.** *Katze*: hiss; *Tiger etc.*: snarl; **2.** *fig. Dampflok etc.*: let off steam; *Wind*: whoosh; **3.** *fig. Person, gereizt*: snarl
faul I. *Adj.* **1.** *Obst, Gemüse, Ei, Zähne etc.*: rotten, bad; *Fisch, Fleisch*: bad, *präd. Brit.* off, *Am.* bad; (*stinkend*) putrid; *Holz*: rotten; *Wasser*: foul, brackish; *Luft*: foul, **2.** (*träge*) lazy, idle; **~es Aas** *umg. pej. Mann*: lazy sod (*Am.* bum) *Sl.*; *Frau*: lazy bitch; *umg. hum.* lazybones (*Sg.*); *auf der* **~en** *Haut liegen od. sich auf die* **~e** *Haut legen* take one's ease; *er, nicht* **~,** *handelte sofort* he was on the ball and took immediate action; *am Wochenende war ich mal so richtig schön* **~** I had a really lazy time at the weekend; **3.** *fig. pej. Ausrede*: lame; *Kompromiss etc.*: shabby; *Friede*: phon(e)y *umg.*; *Witz*: bad; *Scheck, Wechsel*: dud; (*verdächtig*) *Person*: shady; *Sache*: fishy; **~er Zauber** humbug; *da ist doch etwas* **~** there's something fishy about it; *etwas ist* **~** *im Staate Dänemark* something is rotten in the state of Denmark; **4.** (*säumig*) *Zahler*: late; **II.** *Adv.*: **~** *herumliegen* laze around (*od.* about); *häng hier nicht* **~** *rum, hilf mir lieber umg.* instead of hanging around doing nothing you could help me
Faulbaum m *Bot.* black alder, alder buckthorn; **~rinde** f *Pharm.* buckthorn bark
Fäule f; -, *kein Pl.* **1.** *Krankheit*: rot; **2.** *geh.* → *Fäulnis*
faulen v/i. (*ist, auch hat gefault*) go bad, rot; *Zahn, Gewebe etc.*: *auch* decay; *Wasser*: become foul (*od.* brackish); *Aas etc.*: putrefy
faulenzen v/i. laze (*od.* idle) around, be lazy (*od.* idle); **Faulenzer** m; -s, -, **Faulenzerin** f; -, -nen; *hum.* lazybones *Sg.*; *pej.* loafer, *Brit. auch* layabout *umg.*; **Faulenzerleben** n life of idleness
Faulgas n sewer gas
Faulheit f; *nur Sg.* laziness, idleness;

vor **~** *stinken umg. pej.* be bone idle
faulig I. *Adj.* rotten; (*modrig*) mo(u)ldy; (*faulend*) rotting; *Geruch*: foul, putrid; *Wasser*: foul, brackish; **II.** *Adv. riechen, schmecken*: foul
Fäulnis f; -, *kein Pl.* rottenness; *stinkend*: putrefaction; *Med. auch* decomposition, decay; *e-s Zahns*: decay, caries; *fig.* (moral) decay; *in* **~** *übergehen* (begin to) rot; **~** *erregend* putrefactive; **~erreger** m putrefactive agent; **~prozess** m process of decay (*od.* decomposition)
Faulpelz m *umg.* lazybones *Sg.*
Faulschlamm m sludge
Faultier n **1.** *Zool.* sloth; **2.** *umg. fig.* lazybones *Sg.*
Faun m; -(e)s, -e; *Myth.* faun
Fauna f; -, *Faunen* fauna
Faust f; -, *Fäuste* fist; *mit der* **~** *schlagen* punch; *die* **~** *ballen* clench one's fist; *j-m die* **~** *zeigen od. j-m mit der* **~** *drohen* raise one's fist to s.o.; *mit den Fäusten auf j-n losgehen* go for s.o. with fists flying; *es gab Brote auf die* **~** *umg.* there were sandwiches to hold in your hand, *Am.* there was finger food; *etw. aus der* **~** *essen* eat s.th. with one's hands (*od.* fingers); *mit der* **~** *auf den Tisch hauen* bang one's fist on the table; *fig.* put one's foot down; *auf eigene* **~** *fig.* on one's own initiative, off one's own bat *umg.*; *die* **~** *im Nacken spüren fig.* really feel the pressure; *die* **~** *in der Tasche ballen fig.* be seething inwardly (with rage), bottle up one's anger; *das passt wie die* **~** *aufs Auge umg. fig.* (*passt nicht*) they go together like chalk and cheese; (*passt genau*) it's a perfect fit (*od.* match); → *eisern* I 2
Faustball m, n; *nur Sg.; Sport* faustball (*form of volleyball*)
Fäustchen n *fig.*: *sich* (*Dat.*) (*eins*) *ins* **~** *lachen* have a good chuckle, laugh up one's sleeve
faustdick I. *Adj.* **1.** as big as your fist; **2.** *umg. fig.*: *e-e* **~e** *Lüge* a whopping great lie, a whopper; *er hat es* **~** *hinter den Ohren* he's as sly as they come; **II.** *Adv. umg. fig.*: **~** *auftragen* lay it on thick (*od.* with a trowel)
Fäustel m; -s, -; *Bergb.* miner's hammer; *des Steinmetzes*: stonemason's hammer; **2.** *Dial.* (*Fausthandschuh*) mitten
fausten v/t./i. *Sport* punch (the ball)
Faustfeuerwaffe f handgun
faustgroß *Adj.* as big as your fist
Faust|handschuh m mitten; **~hieb** m punch
faustisch *Adj. geh.* Faustian
Faust|kampf m *geh.* **1.** *nur Sg.* (*Boxen*) pugilism, boxing:; **2.** (*Wettkampf*) boxing contest; **~keil** m *Archäol.* hand ax(e)
Fäustling m; -s, -e mitten
Faust|pfand n **1.** pledge, security *altm.*; **2.** *fig.* lever; **~recht** n; *nur Sg.; fig.* jungle law; *dort gilt das* **~** it's dog eat dog there; **~regel** f rule of thumb (*od.* general rule); **~schlag** m punch; **~skizze** f rough sketch
Fauxpas [fo'pa] m; - [fo'pa], - [fo'pas] (*social*) blunder, faux pas, gaffe; *e-n* **~** *begehen* make a blunder, commit a faux pas (*od.* gaffe)
favorisieren v/t. **1.** *Sport* fancy; **2.** *geh.* favo(u)r; (*Kind*) favouritize, *Am.* favor, play favorites with; **favorisiert I.** *P.P.* → *favorisieren*; **II.** *Adj. Sport* strongly fancied; **~** *sein allg.* be (a *od.* the) favo(u)rite, be (the) favo(u)rites;

Favorit m; -en, -en; *auch Sport, Internet*: favo(u)rite (*auf e-n Titel* for); *Pol.* front runner; *hoher/todsicherer* **~** hot/odds-on favo(u)rite; **Favoritenrolle** f role as favo(u)rite; **Favoritin** f; -, -nen favo(u)rite
Fax n; -(es), -(e); *Telek.* **1.** (*Nachricht*) fax; **2.** (*Gerät*) fax (machine); **~abruf** m fax polling; **~empfang** m receipt of a fax; *allg.* fax reception
faxen v/t./i. *Telek.* fax; *j-m etw.* **~** fax s.th. (through) to s.o.
Faxen *Pl. umg.* **1.** *e-s Clowns etc.*: antics, silly pranks; (*Grimassen*) funny faces; **~** *machen od. schneiden* pull (funny) faces; **2.** *fig.* (*Unsinn*) nonsense, silliness *Sg.*; *lass die* **~!** stop acting the goat (*od.* playing the fool); *mach keine* **~!** stop making silly excuses (*od.* difficulties); *ich hab die* **~** *dick* I'm sick of all this nonsense; **~macher** m, **~macherin** f clown
Fax|gerät n *Telek.* fax machine; **~karte** f *für Computer*: fax card; **~nummer** f fax number; **~rolle** f roll of fax paper; **~weiche** f fax selector, reception select
Fayence [fa'jã:s] f; -, -n faïence
Fazit n; -s, -s (net) result, upshot, bottom line *umg.*; *das* **~** *ziehen* sum up (*aus s.th.*), consider the results (*aus* of); **~:** ... to sum up ..., what it boils down to is (that) ...; *sein* **~:** ... his conclusion is (that) ...
FC m; -(s), *kein Pl.; Abk.* (*Fußballclub*) FC
FCKW n, m; -, - CFC, chlorofluorocarbon; **~frei** *Adj.* CFC-free
FDGB m; -, *kein Pl.; Abk. hist., ehem. DDR* (*Freier Deutscher Gewerkschaftsbund*) Free German Federation of Trade Unions (*East German Trade Union organization*)
FDJ f; -, *kein Pl.; Abk. hist., ehem. DDR* (*Freie Deutsche Jugend*) Free German Youth (*East German youth organization*)
FDP f; -, *kein Pl.; Abk.* (*Freie Demokratische Partei*) Free Democratic Party
F-Dur n *Mus.* F major
Feber m; -s, -; *österr.* February
Febr. *Abk.* (*Februar*) Feb(.)
Februar m; -(s), -e, *mst Sg.* February; *im* **~** in February
Fecht|bahn f *Sport* (fencing) piste; **~boden** m fencing hall
fechten; *ficht, focht, hat gefochten* **I.** v/i. **1.** fence (*mit* with; *gegen* against); (*kämpfen, auch fig.*) fight; **2.** *umg.* (*betteln*) scrounge; **II.** v/t. *Sport* (*Degen, Florett etc.*) fence with; (*j-n*) fence against; *e-n Gang* **~** fence a bout
Fechten n; -s, *kein Pl.; Sport* fencing; **Fechter** m; -s, -, **Fechterin** f; -, -nen fencer
Fecht|handschuh m *Sport* fencing glove; **~hieb** m cut; **~kampf** m *Sport* fencing bout; **~kunst** f (art of) fencing; **~maske** f fencing mask
Fedajin m; -s, -; *Pol.* fedayee(n *Pl.*)
Feder f; -, -n **1.** feather; *feste, an Schwanz, Flügel*: quill (feather); *große weiche, als Zierde*: plume; **~n** *Pl.* (*Gefieder*) plumage *Sg.*; *flaumige, für Kissen*: down *Sg.*; *mit weißen/schwarzen* **~n** with white/black feathers, white-/black-feathered; *sich mit fremden* **~n** *schmücken fig.* take the credit (for what s.o. else has done); *sie musste* **~n** *lassen fig.* she did not escape unscathed; **2.** *Pl. umg. fig.*: *noch in den*

F

~n liegen still be in bed; *raus aus den ~n!* time to get up!, rise and shine!; **3.** *zum Schreiben*: (~*kiel*) quill; *aus Metall*: nib; (*Stift*) pen; *zur ~ greifen* put pen to paper; *ein Roman etc. aus s-r ~* written (*od.* penned) by him; *mit spitzer ~ geschrieben* fig. written with a barbed pen; *der Neid führte ihr die ~* fig. her words were inspired by envy; *ein Mann der ~* geh. altm. a man of letters; **4.** Tech. (*Sprung-, Zugfeder*) spring; **5.** Tech., *für Nut*: tongue; ~**antrieb** m Tech. spring drive

Federball I. m shuttlecock; **II.** n; nur Sg.; *Spiel*: badminton; ~**schläger** m badminton racket (*od.* racquet)

Feder|bett n duvet, continental quilt, Am. comforter; ~**blatt** n Tech. spring leaf; ~**boa** f (ostrich-)feather boa; ~**busch** m **1.** Zool. crest; **2.** (*Hutschmuck*) plume; ~**decke** f duvet, continental quilt, Am. comforter; ~**fuchser** m; -s, -, ~**fuchserin** f; -, -nen; pej. **1.** pedant; **2.** (*Schreiberling*) pen-pusher

federführend Adj. chief …; (*verantwortlich*) … in charge, … responsible; **Federführung** f: *unter* (*der*) ~ *von …* with … responsible (*od.* in charge), under the overall control of …

Feder|gewicht n, ~**gewichtler** m; -s, - featherweight; ~**halter** m fountain pen; ~**hut** m feathered hat; *mit großer Feder*: plumed hat

Federkernmatratze f spring interior (Am. innerspring) mattress

Feder|kiel m quill; ~**kissen** n feather pillow; ~**kleid** n lit. plumage

federleicht Adj. (as) light as a feather

Feder|lesen n fig.: *nicht viel ~s machen* mit make short work of, waste no time on; *ohne viel ~(s)* unceremoniously, without much ado; ~**mäppchen** n pencil case; ~**messer** n penknife

federn I. v/i. **1.** (*elastisch sein*) be springy; (*nachgeben*) give; (*springen*) bounce; *gut ~* Mot. give a good ride; **2.** Gymnastik: flex; *in den Knien ~* bend at the knees; **II.** v/t. **1.** (*Sessel etc.*) fit with springs; Tech. spring-load; → *gefedert*; **2.** → *teeren*; **federnd I.** Part. Präs. → *federn*; **II.** Adj. springy; ~*er Gang* springy walk (*od.* step)

Feder|nelke f Bot. feathered pink; ~**pennal** n; -(e)s, -e; österr. pencil case; ~**schaft** m shaft of a feather; ~**schloss** n spring lock; ~**schmuck** m **1.** e-s Indianers: feather headdress; *in Nordamerika*: auch war bonnet; **2.** geh. (*Gefieder*) plumage; ~**strich** m stroke of the pen (*auch fig.*)

Federung f Sessel etc.: springs Pl.; Auto: suspension; *e-e gute ~ haben* be well sprung

Feder|vieh n poultry; ~**waage** f spring scale; ~**weiße** m (fermenting) new wine; ~**wild** n Jägerspr. game birds Pl.; ~**wisch** m altm. feather duster; ~**wölkchen** n fluffy (*od.* fleecy) cloud; ~**wolke** f Met. cirrus (cloud); ~**zeichnung** f pen-and-ink drawing

Fee f; -, -n fairy; *gute ~* good fairy, fairy godmother; *böse ~* wicked fairy

Feed-back, **Feedback** ['fiːtbɛk] n; -s, -s feedback

Feeling ['fiːlɪŋ] n; -s, -s; umg. **1.** (*Empfindung*) feeling; *es ist ein tolles ~* auch it feels great; **2.** (*Einfühlungsvermögen*) feeling (*für* for)

feenhaft Adj. **1.** fairylike; **2.** fig. (*märchenhaft*) ethereal; (*zauberhaft*) magical

Feen|königin f fairy queen; ~**reich** n fairy kingdom; *das ~* auch Fairyland

Fegefeuer n; nur Sg.: *das ~* purgatory

fegen I. v/t. (*hat gefegt*) **1.** bes. norrd. (*kehren*) sweep; *den Schnee von den Stufen ~* sweep the snow from the steps, clear the steps of snow; **2.** schnelle Bewegung: sweep (*von* away *od.* off); → *Tisch* 4; **3.** bes. österr., schw. (*scheuern*) scour; **4.** Jägerspr.: *das Geweih ~* Hirsch: fray its antlers; **II.** v/i. **1.** (*hat*) sweep (*the floor etc.*); **2.** (*hat*) *mit dem Arm über den Tisch ~* sweep the table with one's arm; **3.** (*ist*) umg. fig. (*sausen*) sweep, dash; *Wind*: sweep, rush

Fehde f; -, -n feud (*auch fig.*); *in ~ liegen mit* be feuding (*od.* at war) with; ~**handschuh** m fig.: *j-m den ~ hinwerfen* throw down the gauntlet to s.o.; *den ~ aufheben* take up the challenge

fehl Adv.: *~ am Platz(e)* out of place

Fehl (n) geh.: *ohne ~ (und Tadel)* without blemish

Fehlanzeige f **1.** Amtsspr. negative answer; *„~"* auf Vordruck etc.: negative; *zu Einzelpositionen*: not applicable; (*… ist od. war*) ~ umg. nothing doing, no such luck; **2.** Tech. (*Fehler*) instrument error; **3.** Mil. beim Schießen: nil return

fehlbar Adj. fallible; **Fehlbarkeit** f; nur Sg. fallibility

Fehl|bedienung f operating error; ~**belegung** f Amtsspr. Sozialwohnung: unjustified occupation of low-cost housing (*by someone with adequate means*); ~**besetzung** f Theat. miscasting; *konkret*: miscast actor (*od.* actress); Sport etc.: the wrong man (*od.* woman) for the job; *als Abteilungsleiter ist er e-e glatte ~* he is simply in the wrong job as head of department; ~**betrag** m deficit, shortfall; ~**bildung** f Bio. etc. malformation; (*Missbildung*) deformity; ~**diagnose** f Med. misdiagnosis; diagnostic error; *e-e ~ stellen* misdiagnose, make a wrong diagnosis (*od.* diagnostic error); ~**druck** m; Pl. -e Briefmarke: misprint; ~**einschätzung** f wrong assessment, miscalculation; *auch e-r Person*: misjudg(e)ment

fehlen v/i. **1.** (*nicht vorhanden sein, abhanden gekommen sein*) be missing; (*j-m ermangeln*) be lacking; *bei dir fehlt ein Knopf* you've lost a button, you've got a button missing; *in der Kasse fehlt Geld* money is missing from the till; *ihm ~ zwei Zähne* he has two teeth missing; *mir fehlt …* I have no …, I haven't got (any) …; (*ich habe nicht genug, brauche*) I haven't got enough …, I need …; *ihr fehlten noch 50 Euro* she was short of 50 euros, needed another 50 euros; *mir ~ die Worte* words fail me; *das fehlte gerade noch!* iro. that's the last straw, that's all I/we etc. need(ed); *du hast mir gerade noch (zu m-m Glück) gefehlt!* iro. you're all I need(ed); **2.** (*abwesend sein*) be absent (*in der Schule, bei e-r Sitzung etc.* from); *er hat gefehlt* auch he wasn't there; *du darfst bei der Hochzeit nicht ~* you mustn't miss the wedding, the wedding won't be the same without you; *bei dem Rezept darf ein Schuss Kognak nicht ~* the recipe is not complete without a dash of brandy; **3.** *j-m ~* (*vermisst werden*) be missed by s.o.; *du hast uns*

sehr gefehlt we really missed you; **4.** unpers.: *es fehlt an* (+ Dat.) there's a lack of; (*es gibt kein[e]*) there's (*od.* there are) no; there isn't (*od.* there aren't) enough; *es an nichts ~ lassen* make sure nothing is lacking; (*keine Mühe/Kosten scheuen*) spare no pains/expense; *es fehlt ihm an nichts* he's got everything he wants; *es fehlte an jeder Zusammenarbeit* there was no cooperation whatsoever; *wo fehlt's denn?* what's wrong?, what's the trouble?; *es fehlte nicht viel, und er wäre daran gestorben* he very nearly died of it; *an mir soll's nicht ~* (well,) I'll do what I can; *daran soll's nicht ~* that's no problem; *dazu fehlt's noch weit* that's still a long way off, he's etc. still got a long way to go before he etc. can do that; *bei dir fehlt's wohl da oben od. hier* umg. *mit Stirntippen*: you must be off your head (*od.* out of your mind); → *Ecke* 7; **5.** gesundheitlich etc.: *was fehlt ihr denn?* what's wrong with her?; *fehlt Ihnen etwas?* are you all right?; *dem fehlt schon nichts* beruhigend: there's nothing wrong with him, he's perfectly OK; **6.** (*vorbeischießen*) miss; *weit gefehlt!* fig. (*falsch geraten*) try again; (*nichts dergleichen*) you/he etc. couldn't be more wrong; **7.** geh. (*sündigen*) sin, transgress

Fehlen n; -s, kein Pl. **1.** (*Mangel*) lack, absence; **2.** (*Nichterscheinen*) absence (*bei, in* + Dat. from); *häufiges, bes. von Arbeitnehmern und Schülern*: absenteeism; **fehlend I.** Part. Präs. → *fehlen*; **II.** Adj. missing; (*ausstehend*) outstanding; (*restlich*) remaining; (*abwesend*) absent; **Fehlende I.** n; -n, kein Pl. *das ~* what is missing, the missing item(s); (*Rest, Übrige*) the remainder; **II.** m, f; -n, -n; Person: missing person, absentee

Fehl|entscheidung f wrong decision; *e-e ~ treffen* make the wrong decision; ~**entwicklung** f **1.** Wirts. undesirable trend; **2.** Med. malformation

Fehler m; -s, - **1.** beim Rechnen, Schreiben etc.: mistake, error; EDV: error; *e-n ~ machen* make a mistake; *mir ist ein ~ unterlaufen* I've slipped up; *hier hat sich ein ~ eingeschlichen* an error has crept in here; *häufige ~* common errors; *etw. als ~ anstreichen* mark s.th. wrong; **2.** (*Versehen, Irrtum*) mistake, error; (*Lapsus*) blunder; (*Fehltritt*) slip, lapse; (*Schuld*) fault; *e-n ~ machen* make a mistake; (*taktlos sein etc.*) make a wrong move; *stärker*: put one's foot in it; *in den ~ verfallen zu* (+ Inf.) *od. den ~ begehen zu* (+ Inf.) make the mistake of (+ Ger.); *ich halte es für e-n ~, länger zu warten* I think it would be wrong (*od.* a mistake) to wait any longer; *es ist allein dein ~, dass …* it's all your fault that …, you are entirely to blame for …; **3.** charakterlich: fault, weakness, shortcoming; körperlich: (physical) defect; *jeder hat s-e ~* nobody's perfect, we all have our little failings (*od.* foibles); **4.** am Material etc.: fault, flaw, defect; (*Makel*) flaw, blemish; (*Nachteil, schlechte Seite*) drawback; (*Haken*) snag; Computerprogramm: bug; *mit kleinen ~n* Wirts. with slight flaws; fig. with minor flaws; *das hat den ~, dass …* the drawback (*od.* the trouble with this) is that …; *das hat nur den ~, dass …* the only snag (*od.* problem) is that …; **5.** Springreiten, Tennis etc.:

fault; *auf ~ erkennen od. entscheiden Schiedsrichter:* call a fault
fehleranfällig *Adj.* error-prone
Fehler|anzeige *f EDV* error display; **~berichtigung** *f* error correction; *EDV* debugging; **~beseitigung** *f EDV* debugging
fehlerfrei I. *Adj.* **1.** faultless; *(vollkommen)* flawless, perfect; *(richtig)* correct; **2.** *Springreiten:* **~er Durchgang** *od. Ritt* clear round; **3.** *Person, Charakter:* without blemish; *(makellos)* flawless; **II.** *Adv.* flawlessly; *aufsagen, rechnen etc.:* faultlessly, without a mistake
Fehlergrenze *f* margin of error; *Tech.* tolerance
fehlerhaft *Adj.* **1.** faulty, defective; *Ware:* auch imperfect; **~e Stelle im Stoff** *etc.:* flaw, defect; **2.** *(unrichtig)* incorrect; *schriftliche Arbeit:* containing mistakes; **Fehlerhaftigkeit** *f; nur Sg.* **1.** faultiness, defectiveness; **2.** *(Unrichtigkeit)* incorrectness
Fehlerkorrektur *f* **1.** *EDV* error correction; *CD-Spieler:* auch error concealment; **2.** *Schule etc.: auch Pl.* correction of mistakes; *einzelne:* correction
fehlerlos *Adj. und Adv.* → **fehlerfrei**
Fehlermeldung *f EDV* error message; *Fax:* failure notice
Fehlernährung *f* wrong nutrition; bad eating habits *Pl.*
Fehler|punkt *m Sport* fault; **~quelle** *f* source of error; *Tech.* cause of the fault *(od.* trouble); **~quote** *f* error rate; **~suche** *f Tech.* fault detection; *(Kontrolle)* checking for faults; *allg.* troubleshooting; **~verzeichnis** *n* in *e-m Buch:* errata *Pl.*, corrigenda *Pl.*
Fehl|farbe *f* **1.** *beim Kartenspiel: Spielfarbe, die nicht Trumpf ist:* plain suit; *Karte:* non-trump; *Farbe, die man nicht hat:* void suit; **2.** *(Zigarre)* second choice cigar, discolo(u)red *(od.* off-shade) cigar, cigar with a discolo(u)red wrapper; **~funktion** *f Med. etc.* malfunctioning; **~geburt** *f* miscarriage
fehl|gehen *v/i. (unreg., trennb., ist -ge-); (sich verlaufen, irren)* go wrong; *Schuss:* miss (the target); *gehe ich fehl in der Annahme, dass ...?* fig. am I mistaken in assuming (that) ...?; **~geleitet I.** *P.P.* → *fehlleiten;* **II.** *Adj. fig.* misguided
Fehl|griff *m (Irrtum)* mistake; *(falsche Wahl)* auch wrong *(od.* bad) choice; *e-n ~ tun* make a mistake, make the wrong *(od.* a bad) choice; **~information** *f* wrong *(irreführend:* misleading) information; **~interpretation** *f* misinterpretation; *e-s Texts etc.: auch* wrong interpretation; **~investition** *f* bad investment; *umg. Sache: auch* waste of money; **~kalkulation** *f* miscalculation; **~kauf** *m* bad buy; **~konstruktion** *f* **1.** faulty design, failure; *diese Überführung ist e-e ~* this overpass is badly designed; **2.** *umg.* piece of junk, *Am.* lemon; **~leistung** *f: (Freudsche) ~* (Freudian) slip
fehlleiten *v/t. (trennb., hat -ge-); geh.* **1.** misdirect; **2.** *fig. (j-n)* lead astray; → *fehlgeleitet*
Fehl|pass *m Sport* bad pass; **~planung** *f* (piece of) bad planning
Fehlschlag *m* **1.** *konkret:* miss; **2.** *fig.* failure; *von Hoffnungen:* disappointment; *(Rückschlag)* setback; **fehlschlagen** *v/i. (unreg., trennb., ist) fig.* fail, go wrong; *Hoffnungen:* come to nothing

Fehl|schluss *m* fallacy; **~schuss** *m* miss
fehlsichtig *Adj. Med.* with defective eyesight
Fehl|spekulation *f* **1.** *(falsche Einschätzung)* wrong assessment; *(falsche Annahme)* wrong assumption; *allg.* wrong thinking; **2.** *Wirts.* (e-e) ~ *(auch* a piece of) bad speculation; *e-e Reihe von ~en trieb die Firma in den Ruin* a run of disastrous speculation ruined the firm; **~start** *m* **1.** *Sport* false start; *e-n ~ verursachen auch* jump the gun *umg.;* **2.** *Flug.* unsuccessful takeoff (attempt); *Raumf.* unsuccessful *(od.* aborted) launch
fehltreten *v/i. (unreg., trennb., ist -ge-); geh.* **1.** lose one's footing; **2.** *fig.* commit a faux pas; **Fehltritt** *m* **1.** *konkret:* slip; *ein ~, und ... auch* you put one foot wrong and ... *(auch fig.);* **2.** *fig. (Lapsus)* faux pas; *(Vergehen)* lapse, aberration; *sexueller:* indiscretion
Fehl|urteil *n* misjudg(e)ment; *Jur.* wrong verdict, miscarriage of justice; *e-s Richters:* auch misjudg(e)ment; **~verhalten** *n unangemessenes:* inappropriate behavio(u)r; *konkret:* lapse; *Psych.* abnormal behavio(u)r; **~versuch** *m Sport* unsuccessful attempt, failure; **~zeit** *f gleitende Arbeitszeit:* time debit; *~en durch Krankheit:* working time lost; *Schule:* days *(od.* periods) missed
fehlzünden *v/i. (trennb., hat -ge-); Mot.* backfire; **Fehlzündung** *f* **1.** *Mot.* backfire; *das war e-e ~* it backfired; **2.** *umg. fig.* wrong reaction; *das war bei ihm bestimmt e-e ~* he must have got(ten) hold of the wrong end of the stick
Feier *f; -, -n* celebration; *(Party)* party; *(Festakt)* ceremony; *e-e ~ abhalten* have *(od.* hold) a celebration; *zur ~ des Tages* to mark the occasion; *keine ~ ohne Meier umg. hum.* I've/he's *etc.* never been known to miss a party; *weitS.* he's got a finger in every pie
Feierabend *m* **1.** *(Dienstschluss)* finishing time; *~ machen* finish (work), knock off (work) *umg.; Geschäft:* close; *machen wir ~* let's call it a day; *nach ~* after work; **2.** *(Zeit nach Dienstschluss)* mst evening; *schönen ~!* have a nice evening; **3.** *umg. fig.: jetzt ist aber ~!* that's enough now!; *wenn ..., dann ist (damit) ~* if ..., that's the end of that; *für mich ist ~* I've had enough, I'm chucking *(Am. auch* packing) it in; **~verkehr** *m* evening rush hour (traffic)
feierlich I. *Adj. (ernst, würdevoll)* solemn; *(nach e-m Zeremoniell)* ceremonial; *(förmlich, steif)* ceremonious; *(festlich)* festive; *das ist schon nicht mehr ~ umg.* it's beyond a joke, *Am.* it's not funny anymore; **II.** *Adv.:* ~ *begehen* celebrate; *... wird Mittwoch ~ eröffnet ...* will have a formal *(od.* ceremonial) opening on Wednesday; ~ *versprechen* solemnly promise; **Feierlichkeit** *f* **1.** *nur Sg. (Ernst, Würde)* solemnity; *(steife Förmlichkeit)* ceremoniousness; *(Aufwand)* pomp; **2.** *(Feier) auch Pl.* ceremony; *die ~en* the festivities
feiern I. *v/t.* **1.** celebrate; *(einhalten)* keep, observe; *das muss gefeiert werden* that calls for a celebration; → *Fest* 1; **2.** *(gedenken)* commemorate; *(ehren, rühmen)* celebrate; *(umjubeln)* acclaim; → *gefeiert;* **3.** *fig. (Erfolge, Triumphe)* experience; *(Comeback)* have; *etw. feiert (fröhliche) Auferste-*

hung s.th. is having a (real) comeback; **II.** *v/i.* **1.** celebrate; *(e-e Party halten)* have a party; **2.** *umg. (nichts tun)* take it easy; → *auch krankfeiern*
Feier|schicht *f* cancelled shift; *e-e ~ einlegen* drop a shift; **~stunde** *f* ceremony; *festlich:* celebration
Feiertag *m: (gesetzlicher) ~* (public *od.* bank, *Am. auch* legal) holiday; *kirchlicher ~* religious festival; *halber ~* half-holiday; *schöne ~e!* happy holidays; **feiertags** *Adv.: sonn- und ~* on Sundays and public holidays
feig(e) *pej.* **I.** *Adj.* **1.** cowardly; *sei doch nicht so ~!* don't be such a coward; *er ist viel zu ~, (um) zu (+ Inf.)* he's too much of a coward to (+ *Inf.*); **2.** *(heimtückisch, gemein)* base; *(Mord)* dastardly; **II.** *Adv.* in a cowardly manner
Feige *f; -, -n* fig
Feigen|baum *m Bot.* fig tree; **~blatt** *n* fig leaf *(auch fig.); etw. als ~ benutzen fig.* use s.th. as a cover; **~kaktus** *m* prickly pear
Feigheit *f; nur Sg.; pej.* cowardice, cowardliness; *~ vor dem Feind* cowardice in the face of the enemy
Feigling *m; -s, -e; pej.* coward
feilbieten *v/t. (unreg., trennb., hat -ge-) geh.* offer for sale; *sich ~ pej.* prostitute o.s.
Feile *f; -, -n* file; **feilen I.** *v/t.* file; **II.** *v/i. fig.:* ~ *an (+ Dat.)* hone, polish (up)
feilhalten *v/t. (unreg., trennb., hat -ge-); altm.* → *feilbieten, Maulaffen*
feilschen *v/i. oft pej.* haggle (*um* over)
fein I. *Adj.* **1.** *Linie, Faden etc.:* fine, thin; **~er Regen** (light) drizzle; **2.** *(zart)* fine, delicate; *(zierlich)* graceful; **~e Züge haben** have delicate *(od.* finely etched) features; **~es Stimmchen** finely tuned voice; **3.** *Kamm, Sieb, Sand, Zucker etc.:* fine; **~es Mehl** finely ground *(od.* fine-ground) flour; **4.** *(gering)* fine, subtle; *(kaum wahrnehmbar)* faint, slight; *(winzig)* minute; **~er Unterschied** *der besteht:* subtle difference; **5.** *(genau)* accurate, precise; *(Beobachter)* keen, shrewd; **~er Unterschied** *den man macht:* fine *(od.* subtle) distinction; **6.** *Sinne:* keen, acute; *Gespür:* fine, sensitive; *ein ~es Gehör* a keen ear; *sie hat ein ~es Auge/Ohr für* she has a keen *(od.* good) eye/ear for; **~e Nase** sensitive nose, keen *(od.* good) sense of smell; *fig.* good nose; → *Gaumen;* **7.** *Qualität:* fine; *(erlesen)* choice; *(tadellos)* excellent; *Gebäck:* fancy; *Porzellan:* fine; *Geruch, Geschmack etc.:* exquisite, refined; *die ~e Küche* haute cuisine; *das Feinste vom Feinsten* the very best, the best that money can buy; *das ist Käse vom Feinsten* this cheese is of the finest quality; **8.** *umg. (gut):* ~! *(o.k.)* good!; *(das ist toll)* great!; ~, *dass du da bist* it's great that you're here; *das ist schon e-e ~e Sache* it's really clever *(od.* brilliant); **9.** *Humor:* subtle; *Geschmack:* refined, cultivated; **10.** *(vornehm)* distinguished, refined; *(elegant)* elegant, smart; *Restaurant etc.:* fancy, posh; *der ~e Ton* good form; *die ~en Leute* the upper classes, the top people, *Brit. auch* the nobs *umg. altm.; ein ~er Herr iro.* a (real) gent *umg.; sich (Dat.) für etw. zu ~ sein* think s.th. is beneath one; *ich bin dir wohl nicht ~ genug* I'm not good enough for you, then, am I?; *das ist aber nicht gerade die ~e englische*

F

Art that's not the proper way of doing things; *sich ~ machen* get dressed up, dress up; put on one's best clothes; *du hast dich aber ~ gemacht!* you look very smart (*Am.* really sharp); **11.** *umg.* (*anständig, nett*) nice; *er/sie ist ein ~er Kerl* he's a great fellow (*Am.* guy) / she's really great; *du bist mir ein ~er Freund!* *iro.* a fine friend you are; **II.** *Adv.* **1.** finely; *~ geschnitten* finely cut (*od.* sliced); *~ gemahlenes Mehl* finely ground (*od.* fine-ground) flour; **2.** (*gut*) well, nicely; *~ schmecken* taste good (*stärker*: delicious); *das hast du ~ gemacht!* zum Kind: good boy (*od.* girl); *er ist ~ (he)raus umg.* he's sitting pretty; **3.** (*sehr*) really; *~ säuberlich* nice and neat; **4.** (*elegant*) smartly; **5.** (*genau*) precisely; *Details ~ herausarbeiten* work out details meticulously, pay meticulous attention to detail; **6.** (*brav, schön*) Kindern gegenüber: *jetzt sitz mal ~ still* now sit nice and still; *iss ~ auf* eat it all up, there's a good boy/girl

Fein|abstimmung *f* fine tuning (*auch fig.*); *TV auch* fine adjustment; *~arbeit f* **1.** precision work; **2.** *fig.* fine tuning; *die ~ machen auch* add the finishing touches; *~bäckerei f* patisserie; *~blech n* sheet metal

Feind *m; -(e)s, -e* **1.** enemy (*auch Koll.*); *lit.* foe; *Freund und ~* friend and foe; *keine natürlichen ~e haben* have no natural enemies; *sich ~e machen* make enemies; *sich (Dat.) j-n zum ~ machen* make an enemy of s.o., antagonize s.o.; *ran an den ~! umg. hum.* OK, let's get stuck in (*Am.* let's get going)!; *viel ~, viel Ehr Sprichw.* an hono(u)rable man has many enemies; **2.** *fig.:* *ein ~ der Automatisierung sein* be opposed to automation, be anti-automation; *stärker*: be an enemy of automation; (*hassen*) hate (*od.* loathe) automation

...feind *m, im Subst.* -hater; *mit Wörtern griechischen Ursprungs*: -phobe; *Ausländer~* hater of foreigners, xenophobe; *Katzen~* hater of cats, cat-hater; *ein Krawatten~ sein* hate ties, be anti-ties; *Umwelt~* despoiler of the environment, polluter

Feind|berührung *f Mil.* contact with the enemy; *~bild n: ein ~ aufbauen von* make a bogeyman out of; *~einwirkung f Mil.: durch ~* as a result of enemy action; *er verletzte sich ohne ~* his injury was self-inflicted

Feindeshand *f geh. altm.: in ~ geraten* fall into enemy hands; *von ~ sterben* die at the hands of the enemy

Feindin *f; -, -nen* enemy; *...feindin f, im Subst. → ...feind*

feindlich I. *Adj.* **1.** hostile; *Feuer, Linien etc.*: enemy ...; *~e Truppen* enemy forces; **2.** *Haltung*: hostile (*gegen* to[wards]), antagonistic; *schwächer*: unfriendly; *~e Übernahme* hostile takeover; **II.** *Adv.: ~ gesinnt* hostile (+ *Dat.* to[wards]); *~ eingestellt gegen* opposed to

...feindlich *im Adj.* **1.** (*nachteilig für*) anti-; *verbraucher~* anti-consumer, consumer-unfriendly; **2.** (*ablehnend gegenüber*) hostile (*od.* opposed) to ..., anti-...; *system~* opposed to the system, anti-system

Feindlichkeit *f* animosity, hostility

...feindlichkeit *f; nur Sg., im Subst.* **1.** *von Nachteil für*: unfriendliness (*od.* unhelpfulness) toward(s) ...; *Verbrau-*

cher~ consumer-unfriendliness; **2.** (*ablehnende Haltung gegenüber*) hostility (*od.* opposition, antagonism) to ...; *System~* opposition (*od.* antagonism) to the system

Feindschaft *f* **1.** enmity; *stärker*: hostility; (*Gegnerschaft*) antagonism; (*Groll*) ranco(u)r; (*Hass*) hatred; (*Böswilligkeit*) ill will; *persönliche ~* personal animosity (*od.* enmity); *in ~ mit j-m leben* be at daggers drawn with s.o.; *sich (Dat.) j-s ~ zuziehen* make an enemy of s.o.; **2.** (*Fehde*) feud; (*Streit*) quarrel

feindselig I. *Adj.* hostile (*gegen* to[wards]); (*böswillig*) malevolent; **II.** *Adv.* in a hostile manner; *j-n ~ ansehen* give s.o. a hostile look; **Feindseligkeit** *f* **1.** *nur Sg.*; hostility, animosity; (*Böswilligkeit*) malevolence; **2.** *~en Pl.; Mil.* (*Kampfhandlungen*) hostilities

Feindsender *m Mil.* enemy transmitter

Feineinstellung *f* fine adjustment

feinfühlig *Adj.* sensitive; (*mit Taktgefühl*) tactful; **Feinfühligkeit** *f; nur Sg.* sensitivity; (*Taktgefühl*) tactfulness

Fein|gebäck *n* fancy cakes and pastries, patisserie; *~gefühl n; nur Sg.* **1.** sensitivity, sensibility; **2.** (*Takt*) delicacy, tact; *Mangel an ~* lack of delicacy, tactlessness

Feingehalt *m* fineness; *e-r Münze*: standard; **Feingehaltsstempel** *m* hallmark

Feingewicht *n Münzen etc.*: fineness

feingliedrig *Adj.* slender, gracefully built

Feingold *n* fine (*od.* refined) gold

Feinheit I. *f; nur Sg.* **1.** fineness; (*Zartheit*) delicacy; (*Zierlichkeit, Grazie*) grace(fulness); **2.** (*Stärke*) *von Garn*: size, grist; **3.** *e-s Geräuschs etc.*: faintness, slightness; *e-s Unterschieds*: subtlety; **4.** *des Fühlens*: delicacy, tact; (*Raffinesse*) subtlety, finesse; **5.** (*Qualität*) quality; *e-r Arbeit*: workmanship; **6.** (*Vornehmheit*) distinction, gentility; (*Eleganz*) smartness, elegance; *des Benehmens, Stils etc.*: refinement, elegance; **II. Feinheiten** *Pl.: die ~en* the finer points, the niceties, the subtleties; *die letzten ~en* the final touches

feinhörig *Adj.: ~ sein* have a keen ear

feinkörnig *Adj.* fine-grained; *Fot.* fine-grain

Feinkost *f* delicatessen *Pl.*; *~laden m* delicatessen, deli *umg.*

feinmaschig *Adj.* fine-meshed

Feinmechanik *f* precision mechanics *Pl.* (*V. im Sg.*); **feinmechanisch** *Adj. attr.* precision mechanics; *Gerät*: precision

Feinschliff *m* **1.** *Tech.* (*Vorgang*) finishing; *konkret*: finish; **2.** *fig.* (*in persönlicher Entwicklung*) finish; (*Perfektionierung*) final touch (*od.* polish); (*Raffiniertheit*) sophistication

Feinschmecker *m, ~in f* gourmet; *~lokal n* gourmet restaurant

Fein|schnitt *m Tabak*: fine cut; *~seife f* fine-quality soap; *~silber n* fine (*od.* refined) silver

feinsinnig *Adj. Person*: sensitive; *Humor, Unterscheidung etc.*: subtle; **Feinsinnigkeit** *f; nur Sg. e-r Person*: sensitivity; *von Humor, Unterscheidung etc.*: subtlety

Fein|struktur *f Phys.* microstructure; *~strumpfhose f* sheer tights *Pl.*; *~unze f* troy ounce; *~waage f* precision balance; *~wäsche f* delicate fabrics *Pl.*; *~waschmittel n* gentle washing

powder; *~zucker m* refined sugar

feist *Adj. mst pej.* fat, stout

feixen *v/i. umg.* smirk

Feld *n; -(e)s, -er* **1.** (*Acker*) field; *von Öl, Schnee etc.*: field; *das ~ bestellen* till the fields *Pl.*; **2.** *nur Sg.; geh.* (*freies Land*) (open) country, countryside; *auf freiem ~* in the open countryside; **3.** *Sport* (*Spielfeld*) field, pitch; *des ~es verwiesen werden* be sent off; **4.** *in Formularen etc.*: box, space; (*Kästchen*) *auf Spielbrett*: square; *Archit.* panel; *in der Decke*: coffer; **5.** *nur Sg.; Mil.* field (of battle); *ins ~ ziehen altm.* go into battle (*gegen* against); *auf dem ~ der Ehre fallen euph.* fall on the field of hono(u)r; **6.** *mst Sg.; fig.* (*Gebiet*) field, area; *beruflich*: domain, province; *ein weites ~* a vast area; *es steht ein weites ~ offen für* (*od.* + *Dat.*) *Bereich*: there's considerable scope for; *Möglichkeiten*: there are plenty of (*stärker*: endless) possibilities for; **7.** *Sport* (*Gruppe*) field; *das ~ anführen* lead the field; **8.** *Phys., Psych., EDV, Ling. etc.*: field; **9.** *fig.: das ~ behaupten* stand one's ground; *das ~ räumen* beat a retreat; *aus dem ~ schlagen* defeat, eliminate; *j-m das ~ überlassen* leave the field to s.o., leave the way clear for s.o.; *ins ~ führen* put forward, advance; *zu ~e ziehen gegen* campaign (*od.* crusade) against; *er hat freies ~* he has free rein

Feld|arbeit *f* **1.** work(ing) in the fields; **2.** (*Forschung, auch Außendienst*) fieldwork; *~arbeiter m, ~arbeiterin f* agricultural labo(u)rer, *bes. Am.* farm worker; *~bett n* campbed; *~blume f Bot.* field (*od.* meadow) flower

feldein(wärts) *Adv.* across the fields, (a)cross country

Feld|elektron *n Phys.* field electron; *~flasche f* water bottle, canteen; *~forschung f bes. Soz.* field research, fieldwork; *~frucht f* field crop; *~gottesdienst m Mil.* camp service; *~hase m Zool.* common (European) hare; *~heer n Mil.* field forces *Pl.*; *~herr m Mil. altm.* general; (*Stratege*) strategist; *~hockey n Sport* field hockey; *~jäger m Mil.* military policeman; *Pl.* military police (*Pl.*), MPs; *~konstante f Phys.* space constant; *~küche f Mil.* field kitchen; *~lager n Mil.* bivouac, (military) camp; *~lazarett n Mil.* field hospital, casualty clearing station, *Am.* evacuation hospital; *~lerche f Orn.* skylark; *~linien Pl. Phys.* lines of force, field lines; *~marschall m Mil.* field marshal; *in der NATO*: five-star general; *~maus f Zool.* field mouse; *genauer*: (European) common vole; *~messer m, ~messerin f altm.* surveyor

Feldpost *f Mil.* forces' mail (service), *Am.* APO; *auf See*: FPO; *~brief m* letter from (*od.* to) the front

Feld|rain *m* edge strip, field margin; *~rübe f* turnip; *~salat m* lamb's lettuce, corn salad; *~spat m Min.* feldspar; *~spieler m, ~spielerin f Sport* (*Ggs. Torwart*) player running with the ball; *~stärke f Phys.* field strength; *~stecher m:* (*ein*) *~* (a pair of) binoculars *Pl. od.* field glasses *Pl.*; *~stein m* fieldstone; (*Findling*) erratic block; (*Grenzstein*) boundary stone; *~studie f bes. Soz.* field study; *~stuhl m* camp stool

feldüberlegen *Adj. Sport: ~ sein* dominate play, have more of the ball; **Feldüberlegenheit** *f Sport* territorial superiority

Feldversuch *m* field test

Feld-Wald-und-Wiesen-... *im Subst.* *umg.* common-or-garden ..., run-of--the-mill ..., *Am. auch* garden-variety ...

Feldwebel *m*; *-s*, - **1.** *Mil.* sergeant; **2.** *umg. fig. pej.* sergeant major; **~ton** *m pej.*: **im ~** in a sergeant major's bark

Feld|weg *m* track (*between fields*), *Am.* dirt road; **~zug** *m Mil.* campaign (*auch fig.*), expedition; **e-n ~ führen gegen** conduct a (military) campaign against; *fig.* wage a campaign against, campaign (*od.* crusade) against

Felge *f*; -, *-n* **1.** *Tech., Mot.* rim; **2.** *Turnen:* circle; **Felgenbremse** *f Fahrrad:* rim brake

Fell *n*; *-(e)s*, *-e* **1.** *Zool.* coat; *abgezogenes, von größeren Tieren:* hide; *von kleineren Tieren:* skin; *von Schafen:* fleece; *unbearbeitetes:* pelt; (*Pelz*) fur; **e-m Tier das ~ abziehen** skin an animal; **2.** *Pauke etc.:* skin; **3.** *umg. fig.:* **ein dickes ~** a thick skin; **j-m das ~ gerben** tan s.o.'s hide, give s.o. a hiding; **j-m das ~ über die Ohren ziehen** pull the wool over s.o.'s eyes; **s-e ~e davonschwimmen sehen** see one's hopes dashed, (have to) wave goodbye to one's plans *etc.*; → **jucken** I 2

Fell... *im Subst., Kleidung:* fur ...; *aus Schaffell:* sheepskin ...; *aus Lammfell:* lambskin ...

Fellache *m*; *-n*, *-n*, **Fellachin** *f*; -, *-nen* fellah

Fels¹ *m*; -, *kein Pl.*; (*Gestein*) rock; **auf ~ gebaut** *fig.* built on a firm foundation

Fels² *m*; *-en(s)*, *-en*; *geh.* rock; **wie ein ~ in der Brandung** (as) steady (*od.* firm) as a rock, like the Rock of Gibraltar; **~block** *m*, **~brocken** *m* boulder, (piece of) rock

Felsen *m*; *-s*, - rock; (*Felszacke*) crag; (*Klippe*) cliff; **~burg** *f* mountain fastness

felsenfest I. *Adj.* (as) steady as a rock; *Glaube etc.:* steadfast, unshak(e)able, unwavering; **II.** *Adv.:* **ich bin ~ davon überzeugt** I'm utterly (*od.* unshakably) convinced of it; **sich ~ auf j-n verlassen** rely on s.o. totally (*od.* absolutely)

Felsen|gebirge *n* **1.** rocky (*od.* craggy) mountains; **2.** *Geog.:* **das ~** the Rocky Mountains; **~grab** *n* rock tomb; **~küste** *f* rocky coast(line); **~schlucht** *f* (rocky) ravine, gorge; **~tor** *n* arch of rock

Fels|formation *f* rock formation; **~grat** *m* rocky ridge

felsig *Adj.* rocky

Fels|massiv *n* **1.** mass of rock; **2.** rocky massif; **~nadel** *f* rock pinnacle; **~nase** *f* rock ledge; **~spalte** *f* crevice; **~vorsprung** *m* rock ledge; **~wand** *f* rockface; *hohe:* wall of rock; **~zeichnung** *f* rock drawing, *Archäol.* petroglyph

Feme *f*; -, *-n* **1.** *hist.* vehmgericht; **2.** kangaroo court; **~gericht** *n* → *Feme*; **~mord** *m* (kangaroo court) lynching; *durch Terroristen:* terrorist killing

feminin *Adj.* **1.** feminine (*auch Ling.*); **2.** *pej. Mann:* effeminate; **Femininum** *n*; *-s*, *Feminina*; *Ling.* **1.** *Genus:* feminine; **2.** *Subst.:* feminine noun; **Feminismus** *m*; -, *kein Pl.* feminism; **Feminist** *m*; *-en*, *-en*, **Feministin** *f*; -, *-nen* feminist; **feministisch** *Adj.* feminist

Fenchel *m*; *-s*, *kein Pl.* fennel; **~tee** *m* fennel tea

Fender *m*; *-s*, -; *Naut.* fender

Fenster *n*; *-s*, - **1.** window (*auch im Briefumschlag*); (*Schaufenster*) *auch* shop window; **zum ~ hinausschauen** look out of (*Am. auch* out) the window; **sein Geld zum ~ hinauswerfen** *fig.* throw one's money away; **sich zu weit aus dem ~ lehnen** *fig.* lay o.s. open to attack; **er ist weg vom ~** *umg. fig.* he's right out of it, he's a has--been; **2.** *EDV* window; **ein ~ anklicken** click on a window; **3.** *Pol. fig.* gateway (**nach** to); **ein ~ zur Welt öffnen** open up avenues (*od.* give access) to the outside world; **~bank** *f*; *Pl.* -bänke **1.** *zum Sitzen:* window seat; **2.** (*Sims*) windowsill; **~brett** *n* windowsill; **~briefumschlag** *m* window envelope; **~flügel** *m* casement; **~front** *f* fenestrated facade; **~gitter** *n* (window) grille; **~glas** *n* window glass; *in Brille:* plain glass; **~heber** *m Mot.:* **elektrische ~** electric windows; **~kitt** *m* putty; **~kreuz** *n* mullion and transom; **~laden** *m* shutter; **~leder** *n* wash leather, *mst* chamois (leather)

fensterln *v/i.* *südd., österr.* sneak into one's girlfriend's room through the window at night with the help of a ladder

fensterlos *Adj.* windowless

Fenster|nische *f* window recess; **~platz** *m* window seat; **~putzer** *m*, **~putzerin** *f* window cleaner; **~rahmen** *m* window frame; **~reiniger** *m* *Reinigungsmittel:* glass cleaner; *Beruf:* window cleaner; **~rose** *f Archit.* rose window; **~scheibe** *f* windowpane; **~sims** *m*, *n* windowsill, window ledge; **~stock** *m* *bes. österr.* (outer) window frame; **~sturz** *m* **1.** *Archit.* lintel; **2.** *hist.:* **der Prager ~** the Defenestration of Prague; **~technik** *f EDV* windowing technique; **~tür** *f* French window; **~umschlag** *m* *Kuvert:* window envelope

Ferien *Pl.* holidays; *bes. Jur., Univ. od. Am.* vacation *Sg.*, *Brit. Univ. auch umg.* vac; *Parl.* recess *Sg.*; **die großen ~** the summer holidays (*bes. Am.* vacation *Sg.*); **~ haben** be on holiday (*Am.* vacation); **wann habt ihr ~?** when are (*od.* when do you have) your holidays?, *Am.* when is (*od.* when do you have) your vacation?; **in die ~ fahren** go (away) on holiday (*Am.* vacation); **~ machen** take a holiday (*Am.* vacation), go on holiday (*Am.* vacation); **~ vom Ich machen** *fig.* get away from it all

Ferien|... *im Subst.* → *auch Urlaubs-...*; **~austausch** *m* holiday (*Am.* vacation) exchange; **~beginn** *m* beginning of the holidays (*Am.* vacation); **~dorf** *n* holiday (*Am.* vacation) village; **~ende** *n* end of the holidays (*Am.* vacation); **~gast** *m* holidaymaker, *Am.* vacationer; (*Besucher*) holiday (*Am.* vacation) visitor; **~haus** *n* holiday (*Am.* vacation) home; **~job** *m* holiday (*Am.* vacation) job; *im Sommer: auch* summer job; **~kolonie** *f* → *Ferienlager*; **~kurs** *m* vacation course; *im Sommer: auch* summer course; **~lager** *n* holiday camp; *für Kinder, im Sommer:* summer camp; **ins ~ fahren** go to a holiday (*Am.* vacation) camp; *im Sommer:* go to summer camp; **~ordnung** *f* roster of (school) holidays (*in the different Länder*); **~ort** *m* holiday (*Am.* vacation) resort; **~paradies** *n* holidaymaker's (*Am.* vacationer's) paradise; **~pass** *m* (school pupil's) holiday

(*Am.* vacation) pass (*giving reduced fares etc.*); **~programm** *n in der Gemeinde: program(me)* of activities for children at home during the holidays (*Am.* vacation); **~reise** *f* holiday (*Am.* vacation) trip; **~tag** *m* day on holiday (*Am.* vacation); **am ersten ~** on the first day of the holiday (*Am.* vacation); **~wohnung** *f* holiday (*Am.* vacation) apartment; **~zeit** *f* holiday (*Am.* vacation) period; **~ziel** *n* place for a holiday, *Am.* vacation spot; (*auch Land*) tourist destination

Ferkel *n*; *-s*, - **1.** young pig, piglet; **2.** *umg. fig. pej. schmutzige Person:* pig; *Kind:* mucky pup *umg.*; *unanständiger Mann:* dirty old man; **Ferkelei** *f*; -, *-en*; *umg. fig. pej.* obscenity; *Bemerkung: auch* dirty remark

Ferment *n*; *-(e)s*, *-e*; *altm.* enzyme; **fermentieren** *vt/i.* ferment

fern I. *Adj.* **1.** far; (*entfernt*) far off, distant; **~e Gegenden** *od.* **Länder** faraway places; **der Ferne Osten** the Far East; **~ halten** keep away (**von** from); **j-n von sich** (*Dat.*) **~ halten** keep s.o. at a distance (*od.* at arm's length); **etw. von j-m ~ halten** *fig.* keep s.th. from s.o., protect s.o. from s.th.; **es liegt mir ~ zu** (+ *Inf.*) *fig.* I have no intention of (+ *Ger.*), far be it from me to (+ *Inf.*); **das sei ~ von mir!** *fig.* I wouldn't dream of it; **j-m ~ stehen** *fig.* have no (real) contact with s.o., have no (real) relationship with s.o.; **e-r Sache ~ stehen** *fig.* have nothing to do with s.th.; → *nah* II 1; **2.** *zeitlich:* distant; *vergangen:* long past; *zukünftig:* distant future; **in ~er Vergangenheit** in the distant past; long, long ago; **II.** *Adv.:* **von ~** from (*od.* at) a distance (*auch fig.*), from afar *lit.*; **ich sah ihn von ~ kommen** I could see him coming a long way off (*od.* in the distance); **III.** *Präp.* (+ *Dat.*); *geh.* far (away) from

fernab *Adv. und Präp.*; *geh.* far away (+ *Dat. od.* **von** from)

Fern|abfrage *f Telef.* remote pickup (*od.* interrogation); **~amt** *n Telef. hist.* long-distance (*Brit. auch* trunk) exchange; **~aufklärung** *f Mil.* long-range reconnaissance; **~aufnahme** *f Fot.* long-distance shot; **~auslöser** *m Fot.* (remote) cable release; **~bedienung** *f* remote control

fernbleiben *v/i.* (*unreg., trennb., ist -ge-*) not come *od.* go (+ *Dat.* to); *der Schule etc.:* be absent (from), stay away (from); *e-r Sitzung etc.: auch* not attend

Fern|blick *m* vista, distant view; **~brille** *f*: (**e-e**) **~** (a pair of) distance glasses *Pl.*; **~diagnose** *f Med.* absentee (*od.* remote) diagnosis

Ferne *f*; -, *-n*; *mst Sg.* **1.** distance; **aus der ~** from far away, from a distance (*auch fig.*); **Grüße aus der ~** greetings from far away (*od.* distant parts); **in der ~ verschwinden** disappear in(to) the distance (*od.* out of view), fade out of sight; **es zieht ihn wieder in die ~** he's off to distant parts again; (*er will reisen*) he's got wanderlust again; **ihre Gedanken schweiften in die ~** she was far away with her thoughts; **2.** *zeitlich:* distant past/future; *fig.* far distance; **in weiter ~** a long way off; **in weite ~ gerückt sein** have receded into the far distance; *in der Erinnerung:* have become a distant memory

Fernempfang *m Radio:* long-range reception

F

ferner I. *Adj.* (*Komp.* → **fern**) further; *nichts lag mir* ~ *fig.* nothing was further from my mind, I wouldn't have dreamt of it; **II.** *Adv. geh.* **1.** further(more); (*außerdem*) besides, moreover; (*noch dazu*) on top of that, and then; ~ *liefen Sport* also ran; *er rangierte unter* ~ *liefen umg. fig.* he was among the also-rans; **2.** (*zukünftig*) in future, *Am.* in the future; *daran wird sich auch* ~ *nichts ändern* it's not going to change in any way, it'll go on in the same old way

fernerhin *Adv.* for the (*od.* in, *Am.* in the) future, henceforth

Fern|fahrer *m*, **~fahrerin** *f* long-distance lorry driver, *Am.* long-haul truck driver (*od.* trucker); **~fahrt** *f* long trip; *Lastwagen: auch* long haul; **~flug** *m* long-distance (*od.* long-haul) flight

ferngelenkt I. *P.P.* → **fernlenken**; **II.** *Adj.* → **ferngesteuert** II

Ferngespräch *n Telef.* long-distance call

ferngesteuert I. *P.P.* → **fernsteuern**; **II.** *Adj.* remote-controlled, remote control …; *Flugzeug:* pilotless; **~es Geschoss** guided missile

Fern|glas *n*: (**ein**) ~ (a pair of) binoculars *Pl.*; **~heizung** *f* district heating (system); **~kopierer** *m* facsimile (*od.* fax) machine; **~kurs** *m* correspondence course; **~laster** *m umg.*, **~lastwagen** *m* long-distance lorry, *Am.* long-haul truck, semi *umg.*; **~lastzug** *m* long-distance (*Am.* long-haul) articulated truck, *Am.* tractor-trailer, semi *umg.*; *mit mehreren Anhängern:* road train; **~leihe** *f*; -, -n inter-library loan (system); **~leitung** *f* **1.** *Telef.* long-distance line; **2.** *Etech.* transmission line; **3.** (*Röhrenleitung*) pipeline

fernlenken *v/t.* (*trennb., hat -ge-*) operate (*od.* guide) by remote control; → **ferngelenkt**; **Fernlenkung** *f* remote control; **Fernlenkwaffe** *f* guided weapon (*od.* missile)

Fernlicht *n Mot.* full (*od.* high) beam (position); *mit* ~ *fahren* drive on full beam (*od.* with undipped headlights), *Am.* drive with your brights on

Fernmelde|amt *n* telephone exchange; **~gebühren** *Pl. Amtsspr.* telephone charges; **~geheimnis** *n Jur.* confidentiality of telecommunication; **~satellit** *m* communications satellite; **~technik** *f* telecommunications *Pl.* (*V. im Sg.*); **~wesen** *n* telecommunications *Pl.* (*V. im Sg.*)

fernmündlich *Amtsspr.* **I.** *Adj.* telephone …; **II.** *Adv.* by telephone

Fernost *ohne Artikel:* **in/aus/nach** ~ in/from/to the Far East; **Fernost…** *im Subst.* Far Eastern; **fernöstlich** *Adj.* Far Eastern

Fern|reise *f* **1.** (*Ferienreise*) long-distance (*od.* -haul) holiday (*Am.* vacation); **2.** *hist.* long journey; **~reisende** *m, f*; -n, -n long-haul travel(l)er; **~rohr** *n* telescope; **~ruf** *m Amtsspr.* telephone call; *auf Briefköpfen etc.:* Telephone (*Abk.* Tel.); **~schach** *n* correspondence chess; **~schreiben** *n* telex; **~schreiber** *m* telex machine; **~schuss** *m Fußball:* long-range shot

Fernseh|… *im Subst.* television …, TV …; **~ansager** *m*, **~ansagerin** *f* television *od.* TV presenter (*od.* announcer, *Am. auch* personality); **~ansprache** *f* television (*od.* televised) address; **~anstalt** *f* television company (*Am.* station); **~antenne** *f* television (*od.* TV

aerial (*od.* antenna); **~apparat** *m* television (set), TV (set); **~auftritt** *m* television (*od.* TV) appearance; **~bild** *n* television image (*od.* picture); **~diskussion** *f* (TV) panel discussion; **~empfang** *m* TV reception

Fernsehen *n*; -s, *kein Pl.* **1.** television, TV; *im* ~ on television; *im* ~ *übertragen werden* be televised, be shown on television; **2.** *Anstalt:* television company (*Am.* station); *das Erste Deutsche* ~ the First German Television Channel; *beim* ~ *arbeiten* work in television; *das* ~ *brachte die Meldung in den Abendnachrichten* the report was in the television evening news; **3.** *Programme, Sendungen:* television (programming); *kritisches etc.* ~ *machen* make investigative *etc.* program(me)s; **4.** *umg. Gerät:* television, TV

fernsehen *v/i.* (*unreg., trennb., hat -ge-*) watch television (*od.* TV)

Fernseher¹ *m*; -s, -; *umg.* television, TV

Fernseher² *m*; -s, -, **~in** *f*; -, -nen; *umg.* viewer

Fernseh|fassung *f* television (*od.* TV) adaptation (*od.* version); **~film** *m* TV film (*Am.* movie, *abgek.* TVM), film made for television; **~gebühren** *Pl.* television licen|ce (*Am.* -se) fee *Sg.*; **~gerät** *n* television (set), TV (set); **~gesellschaft** *f* television (*od.* TV) company; **~interview** *n* television interview; **~journalist** *m*, **~journalistin** *f* television (*od.* TV) journalist; **~kamera** *f* television camera; **~kanal** *m* television channel; **~kommentator** *m*, **~kommentatorin** *f* television (*od.* TV) commentator; **~lotterie** *f* televised lottery drawing; **~programm** *n* **1.** (*Sendungen*) television (*od.* TV) schedule (*od.* program(me)s *Pl.*); **2.** (*Heft*) TV program(me) guide; **3.** (*Kanal*) television channel; **~publikum** *n* television audience, viewing public; **~redakteur** *m*, **~redakteurin** *f* program(me) editor; **~reporter** *m*, **~reporterin** *f* television (*od.* TV) reporter; **~röhre** *f* television tube; **~satellit** *m* television satellite; **~schirm** *m* (television) screen; **~sender** *m* **1.** television transmitter; **2.** (*Sendeanstalt*) television (broadcasting) station; **3.** (*Kanal*) television channel; **~sendung** *f* television (*od.* TV) program(me); **~serie** *f* television (*od.* TV) series; **~sessel** *m* television chair; **~show** *f* television (*od.* TV) show; **~spiel** *n* television (*od.* TV) play; **~spot** *m* television commercial; **~star** *m* TV star; **~studio** *n* television (*od.* TV) studio(s *Pl.*); **~techniker** *m*, **~technikerin** *f* television engineer; **~teilnehmer** *m*, **~teilnehmerin** *f Amtsspr.* television viewer; **~truhe** *f* TV cabinet; **~turm** *m* television (*od.* TV) tower; **~übertragung** *f* television (*od.* TV) broadcast; **~unterhaltung** *f* television (*od.* TV) entertainment; **~werbung** *f* **1.** television (*od.* TV) advertising (*od.* commercials *Pl.*); **2.** (*Werbespot*) television (*od.* TV) commercial (*od.* ad); **~zeitschrift** *f* TV program(me) guide; **~zimmer** *n* TV room; **~zuschauer** *m*, **~zuschauerin** *f* television viewer; *Pl. auch* television audience *Sg.*

Fernsicht *f* **1.** (*Aussicht*) view; **2.** *Met.* visibility

Fernsprech|… *im Subst. Amtsspr.* telephone …; *siehe auch* **Telefon…**; **~amt** *n hist.* telephone exchange; **~anlage** *f*

telephone installation; **~automat** *m* pay phone

Fernsprecher *m Amtsspr.* telephone; *öffentlicher* ~ public telephone

Fernsprech|gebühren *Pl.* telephone charges; **~netz** *m* telephone network; **~teilnehmer** *m*, **~teilnehmerin** *f Amtsspr.* telephone subscriber; **~verkehr** *m* telecommunications *Pl.*

fernsteuern *v/t.* (*trennb., hat -ge-*) operate by remote control; → **ferngesteuert**; **Fernsteuerung** *f* remote control

Fern|straße *f* trunk road, *Am.* major highway; *in den USA:* interstate (highway); (*Autobahn*) motorway, *Am.* freeway; **~studium** *n* **1.** *Univ.* correspondence degree course; **2.** *Unterricht:* distance learning; **3.** *hist., ehem. DDR:* part-time university level course; **~tourismus** *m* long-haul tourism; **~transport** *m* long-distance (*od.* long-haul) transport(ation); **~universität** *f* distance learning university, *in GB: the* Open University; **~unterricht** *m* correspondence course(s *Pl.*); **~verkehr** *m* long-distance (*od.* long-haul) traffic; **~waffe** *f Mil.* long-range weapon; **~wahl** *f Telef.* direct (long-distance) dial(l)ing; **~wärme** *f* district heating; *mit* ~ *heizen* use district heating; **~weh** *n* yen to see distant places; *allg.* wanderlust; **~wirkung** *f* **1.** *Phys.* long-distance effect; **2.** *Tech.* remote action; **3.** *Psych.* telepathy; **4.** *fig.* long-range (*od.* long-term) effect; **~ziel** *n* long-term objective; **~zug** *m* long-distance train; **~zündung** *f* remote-control(l)ed ignition

ferromagnetisch *Adj. Phys.* ferromagnetic

Ferse *f*; -, -n **1.** heel (*auch am Strumpf etc.*); **2.** *fig.*: (*dicht*) *auf den* ~*n folgen* follow (hot *od.* hard) on the heels of; *j-m auf den* ~ *sein od.* bleiben be hard on s.o.'s heels; *sich an j-s* ~*n heften* stick to s.o.'s tail

Fersen|bein *n Anat.* heel bone; **~geld** *n umg. fig. hum.*: ~ *geben* take to one's heels; **~sitz** *m* squat

fertig I. *Adj.* **1.** (*beendet, erledigt*) finished, done; *Wirts.* finished; (*fertig gestellt*) finished, completed; (*fertig ausgebildet*) *Krankenschwester, Lehrer etc.:* fully trained (*od.* qualified); ~ *sein mit* have finished with; *mit Buch, Brief, Ausbildung etc.:* have finished; *bist du mit dem Putzen* ~? have you finished (with the) cleaning?; *ich bin* ~ *mit Packen auch* I'm all packed; *seid ihr* ~? have (*umg. auch* are) you finished?; ~ *werden mit* (*Arbeit etc.*) finish, get through *s.th.*; → *auch* 6; *man wird* (*damit*) *nie* ~ there's no end to it, it's never-ending; *etw.* ~ *haben* have s.th. ready, have finished s.th.; *etw.* ~ *machen od.* stellen finish (*od.* complete) s.th.; *etw. nicht rechtzeitig* ~ *bekommen od.* kriegen *umg.* not finish s.th. in time; (*das*) *Essen ist* ~! the meal's ready, grub's up *umg., Am. auch* come and get it! *hum.*; *und damit* ~! *fig.* and that's that!; *mit ihm bin ich* ~! *fig.* I'm through (*od.* I've finished) with him; → *fix I* 3; **2.** (*vorgefertigt*) *Tech.* prefabricated; *Kleidung:* off-the-peg, *Am.* off-the-rack; *Essen:* pre-cooked; (*tischfertig*) ready-to-serve …; *etw.* ~ *kaufen* buy s.th. ready made (*Essen:* precooked); **3.** (*bereit*) ready; ~ *zum Ausgehen/Start* ready to go out / take off; *ich bin gleich* ~ I'll be ready (*od.* with you) in a minute; *Ach-*

tung, ~, los! *Sport* ready, steady (*Am.* on your marks, get set), go!; **sich ~ machen** get ready (**für** for); **j-n/etw. ~ machen** get s.o./s.th. ready; **4.** (*reif*) *Charakter, Person:* mature; **5.** *umg. fig.:* (**fix und**) **~** (*erschöpft*) shattered, bushed; (*ruiniert*) done for; (*sprachlos*) speechless, *präd. auch* floored; **da war ich aber ~!** that really floored me; **der ist ~!** he's had it; **j-n** (**fix und**) **~ machen** *körperlich:* take it out of s.o.; *auch nervlich:* finish s.o. (off); *seelisch:* get s.o. down; (*Konkurrenz etc.*) ruin s.o.; *stärker:* wipe s.o. out; ([*Diskussions-*]*Gegner etc.*) tear s.o. to pieces (*od.* shreds); (*abkanzeln*) tear a strip off s.o.; *durch Kritik:* slam s.o.; (*verprügeln, Sport: besiegen*) give s.o. a (real) clobbering *umg.; Sport auch* clobber s.o. *umg.;* (*umbringen*) finish s.o. off, do s.o. in; **die Sache macht mich langsam ~** it's gradually wearing me out; *seelisch:* it's really starting to get to me; **er macht mich ~** he's getting me down; *nervlich: auch* he's driving me spare (*Am.* crazy); → **Nerv, 6.** *umg. fig.: etw.* **~ bringen** etc. *umg.* (*zustande bringen*) manage s.th., bring s.th. off; *weitS.* (*tun*) do s.th.; **~ bringen** etc. **zu** (+ *Inf.*) manage to (+ *Inf.*); **ich brachte es nicht ~** I couldn't do it; (*brachte es nicht übers Herz*) *auch* I couldn't bring myself to do it; **er brachte es ~, sie rauszuschmeißen** he actually threw her out; **er bringt es** (**glatt**) **~** *iro.* I wouldn't put it past him; **das bringst nur du ~** *iro.* that's just like you, only you could have done that; **7.** *umg. fig.:* **~ werden mit** cope with; *mit Kummer, Enttäuschung: auch* get over; *mit j-m, Stress, Hitze etc.:* cope with, be able to handle (*od.* take); **~ werden ohne** get along (*od.* manage) quite well without; **soll 'er damit ~ werden** that's his problem; **damit musst du allein ~ werden** nobody can help you there, you're on your own there; **er wurde nie damit ~, dass sie ihn verlassen hatte / dass ihm gekündigt wurde** he never got over her leaving him / being fired; **II.** *Adv.* **1.** (*völlig*) ausgebildet, angezogen etc.: fully; **~ lesen/essen** etc.; **2.** (*schon im Voraus*) ready, pre-; **~ geschnitten** pre-cut, ready cut; **~ verpackt** prepacked

...fertig *im Adj.* ready to ..., ...-ready; **küchen~** ready to cook; **ofen~** oven-ready; **pfannen~** ready to fry, pan-ready; **transport~** *verpackt* ready to ship

Fertig|bau *m; Pl.* -ten **1.** (*Haus*) prefabricated building, prefab *umg.;* **2.** *nur Sg.* prefabricated construction; **~bauweise** *f* prefabricated construction; *Haus in* **~** prefabricated; **~beton** *m* ready-mixed concrete

fertigen *v/t.* make, produce, manufacture; → **gefertigt**

Fertig|gericht *n* ready-to-serve dish, hassle-free dish *umg.;* **~haus** *n* prefabricated house, prefab *umg.*

Fertigkeit *f* (*Geschick, Fähigkeit*) skill (**in** + *Dat.* in); (*Können*) proficiency; *im Sprechen:* fluency

Fertig|menü *n* ready-to-serve meal, hassle-free meal *umg.;* **~montage** *f* final assembly; **~nahrung** *f* convenience food(s *Pl.*), hassle-free food(s *Pl.*); **~produkt** *n* finished product; **~stellung** *f; nur Sg.* completion; **~teil** *n* prefabricated part; *fertig bearbeitet:* finished part

Fertigung *f; nur Sg.* manufacture, production

Fertigungs|bereich *m Wirts.* manufacturing sector; **~halle** *f* assembly shop; **~kosten** *Pl.* production costs; **~stätte** *f* production plant (*Am.* facility); **~straße** *f* production (*od.* assembly) line

Fertigware *f* finished product

fes, Fes¹ *n; -, -; Mus.* F flat

Fes² *m; -(es), -(e);* (*Kopfbedeckung*) fez

fesch *Adj. umg.* **1.** smart; (*schneidig*) dashing; **~er Kerl** dashing young man, smart lad, *Am.* cute guy; **2.** *österr.:* **sei ~!** (*mach mit*) be a sport; (*sei brav, lieb*) be good

Fessel¹ *f; -, -n* **1.** (*Strick*) rope; (*Kette*) chain; **j-m ~n anlegen** put s.o. in chains; (*Handschellen*) handcuff s.o.; **2.** *fig.* fetters *Pl.*, shackles *Pl.;* **die ~n abschütteln/sprengen** shake off / break out of one's chains; *etw. als* **~ empfinden** feel tied down by s.th.

Fessel² *f; -, -n; Anat.* ankle; *Zool.* pastern, fetlock

Fesselballon *m* captive balloon

Fesselgelenk *n Zool.* pastern, fetlock, hock

fesseln *v/t.* **1.** tie up, bind; *mit Ketten:* put in chains; *mit Handschellen:* handcuff, manacle; **j-n an Händen und Füßen ~** tie s.o.'s hands and feet, bind s.o. hand and foot; **2.** *fig.:* **j-n an sich ~** tie s.o. to one; **3.** *fig.* (*faszinieren*) captivate; *stärker:* enthral(l); (*Aufmerksamkeit, Auge etc.*) catch; **das Buch hat mich gefesselt** I found the book quite gripping (*od.* enthralling);

fesselnd I. *Part. Präs.* → **fesseln;** **II.** *Adj.* captivating, fascinating, arresting; *Buch etc.:* absorbing; *stärker:* riveting; (*spannend*) gripping, enthralling; **III.** *Adv.:* **~ schreiben/erzählen** (**können**) be a captivating writer/storyteller

fest I. *Adj.* **1.** *Nahrung, Substanz:* solid; **~ werden** harden, solidify; *Pudding, Zement, Gelee etc.:* set; **~er Körper** *Phys.* solid (body); **2.** *Fleisch, Boden etc.:* firm; *Bucheinband:* hard; *Straße:* surfaced, *Am.* paved; **~es Land** terra firma, dry land; **3.** (*stabil*) solid; *Material:* strong; *Schuhe:* sturdy, good; **4.** *Knoten, Verband etc.:* (*gut befestigt*) firm; (*straff*) tight; **~er machen** *od.* **ziehen** tighten; **5.** (*Ggs. beweglich*) fixed, rigid; *Tech.* (*auch ortsfest*) stationary; **~er Punkt** fixed point; **6.** *Händedruck:* firm; *Schlag etc.:* heavy; **~en Halt finden** find something firm to hold onto; *fig.* find security; → **Fuß¹** 1, **Hand¹** 2; **7.** *Blick, Charakter:* steady; *Stimme: auch* firm; *Entschluss, Glaube:* firm, unshak(e)able; *Wirts., Börse, Kurse, Markt:* steady, firm; *Währung:* hard, stable; **ich hatte die ~e Absicht zu gehen** I firmly intended to go, I had every intention of going; **ich war der ~en Meinung, dass ...** I was firmly of the opinion (*od.* convinced) that ...; **in Geschichte ist er** (**nicht sehr**) **~** *fig.* he's (not very) well up in history; **8.** *Schlaf:* sound, deep; **9.** *Einkommen, Kosten, Preis, Termin, Zeitpunkt, Regel etc.:* fixed; *Abmachung:* firm, binding; *Plan:* definite, fixed; *Redewendung:* set; **~er Bestandteil** integral (*od.* permanent) part; **~e Form(en)** *od.* **Gestalt annehmen** take on a definite shape, take shape; **10.** (*dauerhaft*) *Stellung:* permanent; *Freund(in), Job:* steady; *Freundschaft:* close; *Kunde:*

regular; **e-n ~en Freund / e-e ~e Freundin haben** have a steady boyfriend/girlfriend; **ohne ~en Wohnsitz** of no fixed abode; **II.** *Adv.* **1.** binden, packen etc.: tightly; **die Tür ~ schließen** shut the door firmly; **Schrauben ~ anziehen** tighten screws; **j-n ~ anfassen** take s.o. firmly by the hand; *fig.* handle s.o. firmly (with firmness); **etw. ~ in der Hand haben** have a firm hold on s.th.; *fig.* have s.th. under control; **2.** **~ kochende Kartoffeln** salad potatoes; **3.** *glauben etc.:* firmly; *versprechen:* faithfully; **ich bin ~ entschlossen zu** (+ *Inf.*) I'm determined to (+ *Inf.*); **~ gefügt** *fig. Ordnung etc.:* firmly established; **ich bin ~ davon überzeugt, dass ...** I'm absolutely convinced (*od.* positive) that ...; **du kannst dich ~ auf sie verlassen** you can rely on her totally (*od.* absolutely); **ich hab's ihm ~ versprochen** I gave him my word (*od.* I swore to him) (that I would); → **steif** II 3; **4.** (*unlösbar*) anbringen, verbinden etc.: securely; **~ verankert** securely (*od.* firmly) anchored; *fig.* firmly (*od.* deeply) rooted; **~ verwurzelt** *Pflanze:* deeply rooted; *fig. auch* deep-rooted, ingrained; **5.** (*dauerhaft*) permanently; **~ angelegt** *Geld:* tied-up, *präd.* tied up; **Geld ~ anlegen** invest money long-term, make a long-term investment; **~ angestellt sein** be permanently employed, have a permanent post (*od.* job); **~ besoldet** on a regular (full-time) salary; **sie sind ~ befreundet** they're firm (*od.* very good) friends; *Paar:* they're going steady; **6.** (*endgültig*) definitely; **es ist ~ abgemacht** *od.* **vereinbart** there's a firm agreement, it's definite; **~ umrissen** clear-cut, clearly defined; **7. ~ schlafen** *od.* **eingeschlafen sein** be fast asleep; **8.** *umg.* arbeiten, helfen: with a will; *essen:* heartily; *lernen, üben:* hard; **~ zuschlagen** hit out hard; (*immer*) **~e!** *umg.* (*schlag zu*) let him (*od.* her) have it!; (*streng dich an*) go at it!

Fest *n; -(e)s, -e* **1.** celebration; (*Festlichkeiten*) festivities *Pl.;* (*Party*) party; (*Empfang*) reception; (*Festmahl*) banquet; **ein ~ geben** have (*od.* throw) a party; *offiziell:* have (*od.* hold) a reception; **ein ~ feiern** have (*od.* throw) a party; *allg.* celebrate, have a celebration; **man muss die ~e feiern, wie sie fallen** it's not every day you get a chance to celebrate, any excuse for a celebration *umg.; fig.* you've got to take your chances; **2.** *kirchl.* (*Feiertag*) feast, festival; **frohes ~!** Merry Christmas, *bes. Am.* Happy Holidays; *zu Ostern:* Happy Easter; **ein ~ feiern** celebrate a feast; **3.** *umg.* (*Vergnügen*) treat; **ein ~ für die Ohren** a feast for the ears; **es war mir ein ~!** it was a pleasure

...fest *im Adj.* -proof; **bügel~** *Aufdruck, Farbe:* ironable, that can take ironing *präd.;* **krisen~** crisis-proof; **stör~** interference-proof

Festakt *m* ceremony

Festangestellte *m, f* permanent employee

Festansprache *f* (ceremonial) address

Festanstellung *f* permanent appointment

festbeißen *v/refl.* (*unreg., trennb., hat -ge-*) **1. der Hund biss sich an ihrem Bein fest / hatte sich an ihrem Bein festgebissen** the dog sank its teeth into her leg / wouldn't let go of her leg;

F

2. *fig.*: *sich an e-m Problem etc.* ~ become totally absorbed with (get bogged down with *umg.*) a problem *etc.*; *er hat sich an der Idee festgebissen* he's obsessed with (*od.* by) the idea

Festbeleuchtung *f* (festive) illuminations *Pl.*; *weihnachtliche etc.*: (Christmas, party *etc.*) lights *Pl.*; *innen*: *auch* festive lighting

fest|binden *v/t.* (*unreg., trennb., hat -ge-*) tie up; *Tier*: *auch* tether; ~ *an* (+ *Dat.*) tie (firmly) to; *das Kopftuch unter dem Kinn* ~ tie one's headscarf under one's chin; **~bleiben** *v/i.* (*unreg., trennb., ist -ge-*) remain (*od.* stand) firm; (*zu Entscheidung, Versprechen stehen*) stick to one's decision (*Versprechen*: promise)

Festbrennstoff *m* solid fuel

feste *Adv. umg.* → *fest* II 8

Festessen *n* dinner; *üppiges*: banquet; *das ist ja ein richtiges* ~*!* this is a real feast!

fest|fahren (*unreg., trennb., -ge-*) **I.** *v/i.* (*ist*) *und v/refl.* (*hat*) **1.** *Auto etc.*: get stuck (*auch fig.*); *Schiff*: run aground; **2.** *fig. Verhandlungen*: come to a standstill, reach (a) deadlock; **II.** *v/t.* (*hat festgefahren*) *ein Schiff / ein Auto etc.* ~ run a ship aground / get a car etc. stuck; **III.** → *festgefahren*; **~fressen** *v/refl.* (*unreg., trennb., hat -ge-*) **1.** jam; *Maschinenteil*: seize; *Säge*: stick; **2.** *sich* ~ *in* (+ *Dat.*) *Rost*: eat into; → *auch festbeißen* 2; **~frieren** *v/i.* (*unreg., trennb., ist -ge-*) freeze; ~ *an* (+ *Dat.*) freeze to; **~gefahren** **I.** *P.P.* → *festfahren*; **II.** *Adj.* **1.** *Gewohnheiten etc.*: rigid, inflexible; *Meinungen*: fixed; **2.** *Boden*: compacted; **3.** *Fahrzeug*: stuck; *Schiff*: run aground

Fest|gehalt *n* fixed salary; **~gelage** *n bes. pej.* orgy of eating and drinking, feast; **~geld** *n Wirts.* fixed term deposits *Pl., Am. etwa* certificate of deposit, *abgek.* CD; **~gottesdienst** *m* special service, festival (*od.* celebratory) service; **~halle** *f* assembly hall (*for large functions*); *als Name*: festival hall

festhalten (*unreg., trennb., hat -ge-*) **I.** *v/t.* **1.** hold onto; (*stützen*) hold; (*packen*) hold tight, grasp firmly; *j-n am Arm* ~ hold on to (*od.* grasp) s.o.'s arm, grasp s.o. by the arm; *etw. mit den Zähnen* ~ hold (*od.* grip) s.th. with one's teeth; **2.** (*Verdächtigen*) hold, detain; **3.** (*j-n*) (*zurückhalten*) stop; (*aufhalten*) detain, hold up; (*einreden auf*) buttonhole; **4.** (*Brief etc.*) withhold, hold back; **5.** *fig.* (*j-s Blick*) catch; **6.** *fig. in Wort, Ton*: record; *bes. Szene, Stimmung*: capture; *etw. mit der Kamera* ~ capture s.th. on film; *etw. schriftlich* ~ put s.th. down in writing; *das wollen wir mal* ~ let's get that straight (*od.* make that clear), let there be no doubt about that; *nur um das mal festzuhalten* ... just for the record ...; **II.** *v/i. fig.*: ~ *an* (+ *Dat.*) stick to, cling to; *das Festhalten an Traditionen* continued adherence (*stärker*: clinging) to traditions; **III.** *v/refl.*: *sich* ~ (*an* + *Dat.*) hold on(to); *sich* (*krampfhaft*) ~ *an* (+ *Dat.*) clutch (at); *auch fig.* cling to; *halt dich fest!* hold on, hold tight; *umg. fig.* brace yourself (while I tell you this)

festhängen *v/i.* (*unreg., trennb., hat -ge-*) be stuck (*auch fig.*); ~ *an/in* (+ *Dat.*) *an Draht etc.*: be caught on/in, have got (o.s.) caught on/in

festigen I. *v/t.* strengthen; (*Macht etc.*) *auch* consolidate; (*Währung etc.*) *auch* stabilize; (*sichern*) secure; **II.** *v/refl. Freundschaft etc.*: grow stronger; *Währung etc.*: stabilize, become firmer

Festigkeit *f*; *nur Sg.* **1.** *Phys., Tech.* strength, resistance; *e-s Gewebes*: strength; *e-s Knotens*: tightness; *von Eis, Zement etc.*: firmness; **2.** *Wirts.* firmness, stability; *Pol.* stability; **3.** *fig.* (*Entschlossenheit*) firmness, resolution; (*Standhaftigkeit*) steadfastness

Festigung *f* strengthening; consolidation; stabilization; → *festigen*

Festival ['festival] *n*; *-s, -s* festival

Festivität *f*, -, -en; *hum.* festivities *Pl.*

fest|klammern (*trennb., hat -ge-*) **I.** *v/t.* (*Blätter etc.*) clip on; (*Wäsche*) peg (*Am.* pin) on; *Tech.* clamp on; **II.** *v/refl.*: *sich* ~ *an* (+ *Dat.*) clutch (at); *auch fig.* cling to; **~kleben** (*trennb.*) **I.** *v/i.* (*ist festgeklebt*) stick (*an* + *Dat.* to); **II.** *v/t.* (*hat*) stick (*an* + *Dat.* to), glue (to); **~klemmen** (*trennb.*) **I.** *v/t.* (*hat festgeklemmt*) clamp; **II.** *v/i.* (*ist*) *und v/refl.* (*hat*) jam, get jammed, get stuck; **~knoten** *v/t.* (*trennb., hat -ge-*) knot (firmly) (*an* + *Dat.* to)

Festkomma *n EDV* fixed decimal point

Festkonzert *n Mus.* gala concert

Fest|körper *m Phys.* solid; **~kosten** *Pl.* fixed costs

festkrallen *v/refl.* (*trennb., hat -ge-*): *sich* ~ *an* (+ *Dat.*) *Tier*: dig its claws into; *Mensch*: cling to

Festkurs *m Wirts., Börse*: fixed quotation; *Währung*: fixed exchange rate

Festland *n*; *-(e)s, kein Pl.* **1.** *Geog.* continent; *das griechische etc.* ~ im *Gegensatz zu den Inseln*: the Greek mainland; *das europäische* ~ the continent of Europe, the Continent; **2.** (*Ggs. Meer*) (dry) land; **festländisch** *Adj.* **1.** (*Ggs. insular*) mainland; **2.** *Klima etc.*: continental; **Festland(s)sockel** *m Geog.* continental shelf

festlegen (*trennb., hat -ge-*) **I.** *v/t.* **1.** (*Gehalt, Ort, Preis, Strafe, Zeit*) settle (on), fix (*auf* + *Akk.* at); (*Termin*) *auch* set; (*Bedingungen, Regel etc.*) lay down, set; (*Programm*) arrange; *durch Übereinkunft*: agree on; (*vorschreiben*) prescribe; *etw. schriftlich* ~ put s.th. down in black and white; **2.** *Naut.* (*Kurs*) plot; **3.** *Wirts.* (*Kapital*) lock (*od.* tie) up; **4.** *fig.* (*j-n*) pin s.o. down (*auf* + *Akk.* on); (*Schauspieler etc.*) *auf ein Fach*: typecast s.o. (as); **II.** *v/refl.* commit o.s. (*auf* + *Akk.* to); *ich möchte mich noch nicht* ~ *auch* I'd like to leave that open for the time being; **Festlegung** *f* **1.** fixing; *von Termin, Bedingungen etc.*: setting; *von Programm*: arrangement; **2.** (*Bindung*) commitment (*auf* + *Akk.* to)

festlesen *v/refl.* (*unreg., trennb., hat -ge-*); *umg.* become completely absorbed (*in* + *Dat.* while reading ...)

festlich I. *Adj.* festive; (*feierlich*) solemn; (*prächtig*) splendid; *Kleidung etc.*: dressy; **II.** *Adv.*: ~ *geschmückt* decked out with festive decoration; ~ *begehen* celebrate; ~ *bewirten* entertain lavishly; **Festlichkeit** *f* **1.** festivity, celebration; **2.** *nur Sg.* festiveness; *Stimmung*: festive atmosphere; (*Feierlichkeit*) solemnity

festliegen *v/i.* (*unreg., trennb., hat / südd., österr., schw. ist -ge-*) **1.** *Termin etc.*: be fixed, be settled; **2.** *Kapital*: be

tied up; **3.** *Auto etc.*: be stuck; **4.** *Naut.* be moored

Festlohn *m* fixed wage

festmachen (*trennb., hat -ge-*) **I.** *v/t.* **1.** (*befestigen*) fix, *bes. Am.* attach (*an* + *Dat.* to); **2.** *Naut.* moor; **3.** *umg.* (*vereinbaren*) fix, set, settle; **4.** (*zeigen, feststellen*) demonstrate (*an* + *Dat.* with reference to); *er machte seine Argumentation an folgenden Punkten fest* he based his arguments on the following points; **II.** *v/i. Naut.* moor

Festmahl *n geh.* banquet

Festmeter *m, n*: *zwei* ~ *Holz* two cubic met|res (*Am.* -ers) of timber

festnageln *v/t.* (*trennb., hat -ge-*) **1.** nail down; ~ *an* (+ *Dat.*) nail to; *wie festgenagelt dasitzen* be rooted to the spot; **2.** *umg. fig.*: *j-n* ~ tie (*od.* pin) s.o. down (*auf* + *Akk.* to)

Festnahme *f*; -, -n arrest; *bei s-r/i-r* ~ when he was / they were arrested; *sich der* ~ *durch Flucht entziehen* evade arrest by escaping; **festnehmen** *v/t.* (*unreg., trennb., hat -ge-*) (*put under*) arrest; *vorläufig* ~ take into custody; *Sie sind vorläufig festgenommen* I am taking you into custody

Festnetz *n Telek.* fixed-line (*od.* landline) network; **~anschluss** *m Telek.* fixed line (*od.* permanent) connection

Festordner *m*, **~in** *f* steward

Festplatte *f Computer*: hard disk

Festplatz *m* fairground

Festpreis *m Wirts.* fixed price

Fest|programm *n* program(me) of events; **~rede** *f* (ceremonial) address; **~redner** *m*, **~rednerin** *f* speaker; *unser* ~ our speaker on this occasion; **~saal** *m* banquet(ing) hall (*Ballsaal*) ballroom; **~schmaus** *m* banquet

fest|schrauben *v/t.* (*trennb., hat -ge-*) screw on (*od.* down) tightly; (*Mutter*) tighten; **~schreiben** *v/t.* (*unreg., trennb., hat -ge-*) give written form to; (*Regeln*) *auch* codify; (*sanktionieren*) sanction

Festschrift *f* commemorative volume; *für e-n Gelehrten*: festschrift

festsetzen (*trennb., hat -ge-*) **I.** *v/t.* **1.** → *festlegen* I 1; **2.** (*Schaden, Steuer*) assess; (*Zinssatz etc.*) set; **3.** (*verhaften*) arrest; (*inhaftieren*) imprison; *vorläufig*: take into custody; **II.** *v/refl.* **1.** *Schmutz etc.*: settle; *dick*: collect; *der Husten/Schleim hat sich in der Lunge festgesetzt* the cough/mucus has settled in the lungs; **2.** *fig. Idee etc.*: take root; *sich bei j-m* ~ become implanted (*od.* firmly fixed) in s.o.'s mind; **3.** *umg. Person*: settle; **Festsetzung** *f* **1.** → *Festlegung* 1; **2.** (*Verhaftung*) arrest; (*Inhaftieren*) imprisonment; *vorläufig*: taking into custody

festsitzen *v/i.* (*unreg., trennb., hat / südd., österr., schw. ist -ge-*) **1.** be stuck (*auch e-e Panne haben und fig.*); *Schiff*: be stranded (*auch umg. Person*); *im Eis/Schnee* ~ be icebound/snowbound; **2.** *der Schmutz etc. sitzt fest* won't come off

Festspeicher *m Computer*: read-only memory, ROM

Festspiel *n* **1.** (*Stück*) festival play; **2.** **~e** festival *Sg.*; *in deutschsprachigen Ländern*: *auch* festspiele; **~haus** *n* festival theat|re (*Am. auch* -er); **~woche** *f* week of a (*od.* the) festival, festival week

fest|stampfen *v/t.* (*trennb., hat -ge-*) tread down; *mit Gerät*: tamp down; **~stecken** (*trennb., -ge-*) **I.** *v/t.* (*hat festgesteckt*) pin (*an* + *Dat.* [on]to);

(*Haare, Saum*) pin up; **II.** *v/i.* (*hat / südd., österr., schw. ist*) be (*od.* have got, *Am.* gotten) stuck

feststehen *v/i.* (*unreg., trennb., hat / südd., österr., schw. ist -ge-*) (*festgelegt sein*) be fixed; (*bekannt sein*) be known; (*sicher sein*) be certain; **eins steht fest** *od.* **fest steht, dass ...** one thing's (for) certain; **steht schon fest, wer der Mörder ist?** do we know for certain (*Am. auch* sure) who the murderer was?; **feststehend I.** *Part. Präs.* → *feststehen*; **II.** *Adj. Tech.* fixed, stationary; *Bild:* still; *Brauch, Tatsache:* established; **~e Redensart** set phrase

feststellbar *Adj.* **1.** (*ermittelbar*) ascertainable; (*identifizierbar*) identifiable; **schwer ~** difficult to establish (*od.* ascertain); **2.** (*wahrnehmbar*) observable; (*merklich*) noticeable; **3.** *Tech.* lockable; **es ist ~** it can be locked in position

Feststellbremse *f Mot.* parking (*od.* emergency) brake

feststellen *v/t.* (*trennb., hat -ge-*) **1.** (*ermitteln*) find out, discover, ascertain; (*Tatbestand etc.*) establish; *Med.* diagnose; (*bestimmen*) determine; (*Schaden*) assess; (*Ort, Lage, Fehler*) locate; **j-s Personalien ~** establish s.o.'s identity; **2.** (*wahrnehmen*) see; (*bemerken*) notice; (*beobachten*) observe; (*erkennen, einsehen*) realize, see; (*zur Kenntnis nehmen*) note; **an i-r Stimme konnte ich ~, dass sie wütend war** I could tell from her voice that she was furious; **3.** (*aussprechen*) state; (*erklären*) say; **er stellte mit aller Deutlichkeit fest, dass ...** he made it absolutely clear that ...; **j-s Tod ~** *Arzt:* confirm that s.o. is dead; **4.** *Tech.* lock (in position)

Feststell|schraube *f* set screw; **~taste** *f* shift lock

Feststellung *f* **1.** (*Ermittlung*) discovery, establishment; *Med.* diagnosis; *von Schaden:* assessment; *von Lage, Fehler:* location; *Jur. etc.* finding(s *Pl.*); **2.** (*Erkenntnis*) realization; (*Wahrnehmung*) observation; **sie machte die ~, dass ...** she discovered (*od.* realized) that ...; **3.** *Äußerung:* statement; (*Bemerkung*) observation, remark; **e-e ~ machen** *od.* **treffen** make an observation

Feststellungs|bescheid *m Jur.* notice of assessment; **~klage** *f* action for declaratory judg(e)ment

Feststimmung *f* celebratory mood; *zu Weihnachten etc.:* festive mood (*od.* atmosphere)

Feststoff *m* solid matter; **~rakete** *f* solid fuel rocket

Festtafel *f geh.* festive board, banquet table

Festtag *m* **1.** holiday; *kirchl.* feast day, religious festival; *im Kalender (auch Glückstag)*: special day; **2.** *Pl.* (*Festspiele*) festival *Sg.*; **Festtagsstimmung** *f* celebratory *od.* festive mood (*od.* atmosphere)

festtreten (*unreg., trennb., hat -ge-*) **I.** *v/t.* tread down; **II.** *v/refl. umg. hum.:* **das tritt sich fest!** it's good for the carpet

Festung *f* **1.** fortress; (*Burg*) castle; *e-r Stadt:* citadel; (*Fort*) fort; **2.** *fig.* stronghold, fortress; **3.** *hist. Haft:* imprisonment (in a fortress), incarceration

Festungs|anlagen *Pl.* fortifications; **~graben** *m* moat; **~stadt** *f* fortress town; **~wall** *m* rampart

fest|verzinslich *Adj. Wirts.* fixed-interest; **~e Anlagepapiere** investment bonds; **~wachsen** *v/i.* (*unreg., trennb., ist -ge-*) **1.** **~ an** (+ *Dat.*) grow onto; **2.** *Med.* (*Transplantat*) take; **~ an** (+ *Dat.*) adhere to

Festwert *m* **1.** standard value; **2.** *Phys., Math.* constant, coefficient

Fest|wiese *f* festival site; *e-s Volksfests:* fairground; **~woche** *f auch Pl.* festival; **~zelt** *n* marquee, *Am.* function tent

festziehen *v/t.* (*unreg., trennb., hat -ge-*) tighten

Festzug *m* festive procession

festzurren *v/t.* (*trennb., hat -ge-*); *bes. Naut.* lash down; (*Leine*) lash (tightly)

fetal *Adj. Med., Bio.* f(o)etal

Fete *f; -, -n; umg.* party, do; **e-e ~ machen** *etc.* have a party (*od.* do); **da steigt e-e ~** there's (going to be) a party there

Fetisch *m; -s, -e* fetish; **etw. zum ~ machen** make a fetish (out) of s.th.; **Fetischismus** *m; -, kein Pl.* fetishism; **Fetischist** *m; -en, -en*, **Fetischistin** *f; -, -nen* fetishist

fett I. *Adj.* **1.** *pej.* (*dick*) fat; **~ machen** fatten; **2.** *Speisen:* greasy, fatty; *Milch etc.:* creamy; **3.** *Agr., Boden, Weide:* rich; *Gras, Klee:* luxuriant; **4.** *Haare, Salbe:* greasy; (*ölig*) oily; **5.** *Chem., Tech., Erz, Gemisch etc.:* rich; *Kohle:* fat; *Öl:* fatty; **6.** *Druck.* bold; **~ gedruckt** bold(face) ..., in bold type (*od.* print); **7.** *umg. fig. Jahre:* fat; *Beute, Erträge, etc.:* rich; *Posten etc.:* lucrative; **~e Zeiten** times of plenty; **~er Bissen** juicy morsel; **~er Brocken** lucrative deal; **8.** *Dial.* (*betrunken*) sloshed; *Sl.* (*auf Drogen*) stoned; **9.** *Jugendspr.* (*toll*) fab, *Am.* awesome; **II.** *Adv.* **1.** **~ essen** eat a lot of fatty food(s); **~ kochen** use a lot of fat (in one's cooking); **2.** *Druckw.* in bold type (*od.* print)

Fett *n; -(e)s, -e* **1.** fat; (*Schmalz*) lard; *vom Braten:* dripping; *zum Backen:* shortening; **gehärtete ~e** hardened fats; **~ ansetzen** put on weight; *Tier:* get fat, fatten up; **von s-m ~ zehren** live off one's reserves; **~ schwimmt oben** *umg. hum.* fat people don't drown; **das ~ abschöpfen** *fig.* cream off the best; **~ lösend** *Adj.* grease-cutting; **im ~ schwimmen** *umg. fig.* be rolling in it; **er hat sein ~ abgekriegt** *od.* **weg** *umg. fig.* he got what was coming to him; **2.** *zum Schmieren:* grease (*auch unerwünschtes als Film, Fleck etc.*); **~abbau** *m* breakdown of (body) fats; **~ablagerung** *f* deposit of fats, adiposis; *konkret:* fatty deposit; **~absaugung** *f Med.* liposuction; **~ansatz** *m* **1.** (*erste Anzeichen e-s Bauchs*) first signs *Pl.* of a spare tyre (*Am.* tire) *hum.*; *beim Mann:* auch first beginnings *Pl.* of a paunch; **2.** (*Korpulenz*) corpulence; **zu ~ neigen** put on weight easily

fettarm I. *Adj.* low-fat, *präd.* low in fat; **~ sein** *auch* have a low fat content; **II.** *Adv.* **~ essen** eat low-fat food; **~ kochen** use little fat in cooking, cook low-fat

Fettauge *n* blob (*od.* globule) of fat

fettbäuchig *Adj. umg.* fat-bellied, pot-bellied

Fett|bedarf *m* fat requirement; **~creme** *f* rich oil-based cream; **~druck** *m Druck.* bold(faced) *od.* heavy type; **~drüse** *f* sebaceous gland

fetten I. *v/t.* (*Backblech, Stiefel etc.*) grease; *Tech.* grease, lubricate; *mit Öl:*

oil; **II.** *v/i.* be greasy; *Haare:* get greasy

Fett|film *m* greasy film; **~fleck** *m* grease mark (*od.* spot)

fettfrei I. *Adj.* fat-free; *Kost:* auch non-fat; **II.** *Adv.:* **~ kochen** cook without fats

Fett|gebackene *n; -n, kein Pl.* cakes *Pl.* fried in fat; **~gehalt** *m* fat content; **~geruch** *m* smell of hot fat; **~gewebe** *n* fatty tissue

fett|glänzend *Adj.* greasy, shiny; **~haltig** *Adj.* containing fat, fatty; *Creme:* oil-based, oily

Fettheit *f; nur Sg.* fatness

Fett|henne *f Bot.* Stonecrop, sedum; **~herz** *n Med.* fatty heart

fettig *Adj.* **1.** (*schmierig*) greasy; *Creme:* oily; **2.** (*fetthaltig*) fatty; **Fettigkeit** *f; nur Sg.* **1.** greasiness; **2.** (*Fetthaltigkeit*) fattiness

Fett|kloß *m umg. pej.* fatso, *Am. auch* tub (of lard); **~leber** *f Med.* fatty liver

fettleibig *Adj. geh.* obese; **Fettleibigkeit** *f; nur Sg.; geh.* obesity

fettlöslich *Adj.* fat-soluble

Fett|massen *Pl. umg.* mass *Sg.* of fat; **~näpfchen** *n fig.:* **ins ~ treten** put one's foot in it (*Am.* in one's mouth); **~polster** *n* **1.** fatty tissue; *auch Pl.* flab *umg.*; **2.** *fig.* (*Geldreserven*) capital reserves *Pl.*

fettreich *Adj.* high-fat, *präd.* high in fat; fatty; **~ sein** *auch* have a high fat content, be really fat *umg.*

Fett|sack *m vulg. pej.* fatso, *Am. auch* tub (of lard); **~salbe** *f* greasy ointment; **~sau** *f vulg. pej.* fat slob; **~säure** *f* fatty acid; **~schicht** *f* layer of fat; **~stift** *m* **1.** *Farbstift:* wax crayon; *Tech.* grease pencil; **2.** *für die Lippen:* lip salve (*od.* balm)

Fettsucht *f; nur Sg.; Med.* chronic obesity; **fettsüchtig** *Adj.:* **~ sein** suffer from chronic obesity

fetttriefend *Adj.* dripping with fat (*od.* grease)

Fett|wanst *m umg. pej.* **1.** *Person:* fatso, *Am. auch* tub (of lard); **2.** *Bauch:* paunch; **~wulst** *m od.* f roll (*od.* fold) of fat; **~zelle** *f Physiol.* fat (*od.* adipose) cell

Fetus *m; -(ses), Feten od. -se; Bio., Med.* f(o)etus

Fetzen *m; -s, -* **1.** *Papier:* scrap; *Stoff:* shred, rag; (*Lumpen*) rag; **in ~** in shreds, in tatters; **in ~ reißen** tear to shreds; **die Kleidung hing ihr in ~ vom Leib** her clothes hung about her in tatters; **dass die ~ fliegen** *umg. fig.* like crazy; **2.** *Wolke:* shred; *Rauch:* wisp; **3.** *umg.* (*Kleid*) rag; **4.** *Pl.; umg. von Gespräch, Lied etc.:* snatches; **5.** *österr.* (*Lappen*) rag

fetzen *umg.* **I.** *v/i.* **1.** (*ist gefetzt*); (*rasen*) tear; **2.** (*hat*); *unpers.:* **dass es nur so fetzt** like crazy; **das fetzt!** *Jugendspr.* it's really awesome, it blows your mind; **II.** *v/t.* (*hat*) **1.** tear (**von** off); **in Stücke ~** tear to shreds; **2.** *umg.:* **sich** (*Pl.*) **~** (*streiten*) go at one another hammer and tongs

fetzig *Adj. Sl.* awesome, mind-blowing; *Musik:* with a really good beat

feucht *Adj. Gras, Keller, Kleidung, Tuch, Wetter etc.:* damp; *Augen, Lippen, Haut etc.:* moist; *Luft, Klima:* damp, humid; *Hitze:* auch muggy; (*nass*) *auch Schnauze:* wet; (*klebrig, kalt*) clammy; (*nasskalt*) dank; **ein ~es Grab** a watery grave; **das ~e Element** (the) water; **~e Hände** sweaty palms; **er bekam ~e Augen** his eyes became

F

moist with tears; **e-e ~e Aussprache haben** *hum.* spit when speaking
Feuchtbiotop *m, n Ökol.* wet biotope, wetland
Feuchte *f; -, kein Pl.* dampness, humidity
feuchtfröhlich *Adj. umg. hum.* (very) merry; **wir hatten e-n ~en Abend** we had a boozy evening (*od.* a booze-up, *Am.* a bender)
Feuchtgebiet *n Ökol., Geog.* wetland
feuchtheiß *Adj. Klima:* hot and humid
Feuchtigkeit *f; nur Sg.* damp(ness); *bes. der Luft:* humidity; (*leichte Nässe*) moisture; **vor ~ schützen!** keep in a dry place
feuchtigkeits|anziehend *Adj.* hygroscopic; **~beständig** *Adj.* moisture--proof; *Bauteile:* damp-proof
Feuchtigkeits|creme *f* moisturizing cream; **~gehalt** *m* moisture content; **~grad** *m* degree of moisture; *der Luft:* humidity; **~isolierung** *f* damp-proofing; **~messer** *m* hygrometer
feucht|kalt *Adj.* clammy, dank; *Wetter:* cold and damp; **~warm** *Adj.* warm and humid, muggy
feudal I. *Adj.* **1.** *Pol. hist.* feudal; (*aristokratisch*) aristocratic; **2.** *umg.* (*luxuriös*) plush, classy; *Haus:* grand; *Essen:* slap-up, *Am.* first-rate; **II.** *Adv. umg.:* **~ essen** have a slap-up (*Am.* first--rate) meal; **~ leben** live in grand style
Feudal|herr *m hist.* feudal lord; **~herrschaft** *f hist.* feudalism, feudal rule
Feudalismus *m; -, kein Pl.; hist.* feudalism, feudal system; **feudalistisch** *Adj.* feudalistic
Feudalstaat *m hist.* feudal state
Feudel *m; -s, -; nordd.* (floor)cloth; **feudeln** *vt/i. nordd.* wipe with a (floor)cloth
Feuer *n; -s, -* **1.** fire (*auch Brand*); *das olympische ~* the Olympic flame; *am ~ sitzen* sit by the fire; *~ fangen* catch fire; *~ legen* start a fire; *~ legen an* (+ *Akk.*) (*od. in* [+ *Dat.*]) set fire to; *~ speien* spit fire; *Vulkan: auch* erupt; *~ speiender Berg* volcano spewing (*od.* belching) flames; *auf offenem ~ kochen* cook over a fire; *ein Gegensatz wie ~ und Wasser sein* be as different as chalk and cheese; **2.** *für Zigarette:* light; *j-m ~ geben* give s.o. a light; *haben Sie ~?* have you got a light?; **3.** *im/auf Kochherd:* flame; *auf kleinem/großem ~ kochen* cook on a low heat (*od.* flame) / on a high flame; *das Essen vom ~ nehmen* take the food off (the heat); **4.** *Naut.* (*Leuchtfeuer*) beacon; **5.** *fig.* (*Glanz*) fire, sparkle; *i-e Augen* her eyes were blazing; **6.** (*Eifer, Begeisterung*) fire, fervo(u)r; (*Leidenschaft*) *auch* passion; (*Temperament*) fire, spirit; *~ haben Wein:* be fiery, pack a punch; *~ und Flamme sein* be full of enthusiasm (*für* for); *~ fangen* (*sich begeistern*) be fired with enthusiasm; (*sich verlieben*) be smitten; *→ auch fangen* I 3; **7.** *Mil.* fire (*auf + Akk.* at); *das einstellen/eröffnen* cease/open fire; *unter ~ nehmen* fire at; (*gebt*) *~!* fire!; *~ frei!* open fire!; **8.** *fig.: das brennt wie ~* (*ist scharf*) it's like fire on the tongue; (*tut weh*) it causes a burning pain; *durchs ~ gehen für* go through fire and water for; *mit dem ~ spielen* play with fire; *~ hinter etw. machen* get s.th. going, kickstart s.th.; *j-m ~ unter dem Hintern machen umg.* (*antreiben*) give s.o. a kick up the backside, *Am.* set a fire under s.o.; → **Ei-**

sen 3, **Hand**[1] 3, **Kastanie**
Feueralarm *m* fire alarm; **~übung** *f* fire drill
Feuer|anzünder *m* firelighter; **~ball** *m Phys.* fireball; *lit.* ball of fire; **~befehl** *m Mil.* order to (open) fire; **~bekämpfung** *f* fire fighting
feuerbeständig *Adj.* fire-resistant, fireproof
Feuer|bestattung *f* cremation; **~bock** *m am offenen Kamin:* firedog; **~bohne** *f Bot.* scarlet runner; **~brand** *m Bot.* fireblight; **~dorn** *m Bot.* pyracantha, firethorn; **~eifer** *m* great zeal, fervent enthusiasm; **~voll** *od.* **mit ~** with great zeal (*od.* fervo[u]r); **~einstellung** *f Mil.* **1.** cessation of fire; *Befehl zur ~* order to stop firing; **2.** (*Waffenruhe*) ceasefire; **~eröffnung** *f Mil.* opening fire
feuerfest *Adj.* fireproof, fire-resistant; *Geschirr:* heat-resistant; (*unbrennbar*) incombustible
Feuergefahr *f* fire risk; danger of fire (breaking out); **feuergefährlich** *Adj.* (highly) inflammable
Feuer|gefecht *n Mil.* gun battle; **~geist** *m* **1.** fire spirit; **2.** *fig.* (*Person*) fiery spirit; **~haken** *m* poker
feuerhemmend *Adj.* flame-retardant
Feuerholz *n; nur Sg.* firewood
Feuerland (*n*) *Geog.* Tierra del Fuego; **Feuerländer** *m; -s, -,* **Feuerländerin** *f; -,* -nen Fuegian
Feuer|leiter *f* fire ladder; (*Nottreppe*) fire escape; **~linie** *f Mil.* firing line; **~löschboot** *n* fire boat; **~löscher** *m* fire extinguisher
Feuerlösch|fahrzeug *n* fire engine; **~gerät** *n* fire extinguisher; *Pl.* fire--fighting equipment; **~teich** *m* (fire--fighting) water storage pool; **~zug** *m* fleet of fire-fighting vehicles
Feuer|mal *n; Pl. -e; Med.* port wine stain; **~melder** *m* fire alarm
feuern I. *v/t.* **1.** *umg.* (*entlassen*) fire, give *s.o.* the sack; **2.** *umg.* (*schleudern*) fling, hurl; (*Ball*) slam; **3.** *umg.: j-m eine ~* whack s.o. one; **4.** (*Holz, Kohlen*) burn; **5.** (*Ofen*) fire; *den Ofen mit Holz ~* burn wood in the stove; **6.** *Mil.* (*Salut*) fire; **II.** *v/i. Mil.* fire (*auf + Akk.* at)
Feuer|patsche *f* fire beater; **~pause** *f Mil.* pause in (the) fighting
Feuerpolizei *f* fire prevention authorities *Pl., Am.* fire marshal(s *Pl.*); **feuerpolizeilich** *Adj.: nach den ~en Vorschriften ...* in accordance with the fire regulations
Feuer|probe *f* **1.** *hist.* ordeal by fire; **2.** *fig.* acid test; **~qualle** *f Zool.* stinging jellyfish; **~rad** *n* **1.** *Feuerwerk:* Catherine wheel; **2.** (*brennendes Wagenrad*) fire wheel
feuerrot *Adj.* blazing red; **~ werden** *im Gesicht:* turn crimson, go bright red
Feuer|salamander *m* spotted salamander; **~säule** *f* pillar of fire
Feuersbrunst *f geh.* blaze, conflagration
Feuer|schaden *m* fire damage; **~schein** *m* **1.** glow of the fire; **2.** sky glow; **~schirm** *m* fire screen; (*Kamingitter*) fireguard; **~schlucker** *m,* **~schluckerin** *f* fire-eater; **~schutz** *m* **1.** fire prevention; **2.** *Mil.* covering fire; *j-m ~ geben* provide s.o. with covering fire
feuersicher *Adj.* fireproof
Feuer|spritze *f* fire extinguisher; **~stätte** *f* fireplace; **~stein** *m* flint

(*auch im Feuerzeug etc.*); **~stelle** *f* **1.** (*ehemalige:* site of an) open hearth; **2.** (*Brandstelle*) scene of a (*od.* the) fire; **~stoß** *m* burst of fire; **~strahl** *m* jet of fire; *rückwärtiger:* backblast; **~taufe** *f* baptism of (*od.* by) fire; **~teufel** *m umg.* firebug; **~tod** *m geh.: den ~ sterben* be burnt to death; *hingerichtet werden:* be burnt at the stake; **~treppe** *f* fire escape; **~tür** *f* fire door
Feuerung *f* **1.** (*Heizung*) heating; **2.** (*Befeuerung*) firing; **3.** (*Brennstoff*) fuel
Feuerversicherung *f* fire insurance
feuerverzinkt *Adj.* hot-galvanized
Feuer|wache *f* fire station; **~waffe** *f* firearm, gun; **~wasser** *n umg.* firewater
Feuerwehr *f* fire brigade, *Am.* fire department. *konkret:* fire fighters *Pl.*; *wie die ~ umg.* like a flash; *das geht wie die ~ umg.* it's done in a flash; **~auto** *n* fire engine, *Am. auch* fire truck; **~frau** *f* firewoman, woman fire fighter; **~gerätehaus** *n* appliance room; **~hauptmann** *m* fire brigade captain, *Am.* fire chief; **~helm** *m* fireman's helmet; **~leute** *Pl.* firemen, fire fighters; **~mann** *m; Pl. -männer und -leute* fireman, fire fighter; **~übung** *f* fire drill (*od.* practice)
Feuerwerk *n* **1.** fireworks *Pl.*; *als Schauspiel:* firework display; **2.** *fig.: ein ~ von Witz etc.* a sparkling display of wit *etc.*; **Feuerwerkskörper** *m* firework (*mst Pl.*), firecracker
Feuerzange *f* tongs *Pl.*; **Feuerzangenbowle** *f* burnt punch
Feuerzeichen *n* fire signal; *Naut.* beacon
Feuerzeug *n* (cigarette) lighter; **~benzin** *n* lighter fuel
Feuilleton [fœjəˈtõː] *n; -s, -s* **1.** *Zeitungsteil:* feature (*od.* arts) pages *Pl.*; **2.** (*Artikel*) feature (article); **Feuilletonist** *m; -en, -en,* **Feuilletonistin** *f; -, -nen* feature writer, feuilletonist(e); **feuilletonistisch** *Adj.* **1.** *Stil etc.:* journalistic; *pej.* facile; **2.** *~er Beitrag* article for the feature pages
Feuilleton|redakteur *m,* **~redakteurin** *f* features editor; **~redaktion** *f* features department; **~stil** *m* journalistic style; **~teil** *m* feature (*od.* arts) section
feurig *Adj.* **1.** *Blick, Pferd, Temperament:* fiery; *Augen:* flashing, burning; *Rede:* impassioned; *~er Liebhaber* passionate (*od.* fiery) lover; **2.** *geh.* (*funkelnd*) sparkling; **3.** *Wein:* fiery; **4.** *altm. Kohlen:* glowing
Fez[1] [feːts] *m → Fes*[2]
Fez[2] *m; -es, kein Pl.; umg.: ~ machen* fool around; *aus ~* for kicks
ff. *Abk.* (*und folgende Seiten*) ff
FH *f; -, -s; Abk. → Fachhochschule*
Fiaker *m; -s, -; österr. od. hist.* **1.** cab; **2.** (*Kutscher*) coachman
Fiasko *n; -s, -s* fiasco; (*Misserfolg*) *auch* flop; *in e-m ~ enden* end in fiasco
Fibel[1] *f; -, -n* **1.** *Päd.* primer; **2.** (*Handbuch*) manual
Fibel[2] *f; -, -n; hist.* (*Spange*) fibula, brooch
Fiber *f; -, -n; Bio., Med., Tech.* fib|re (*Am.* -er); → *auch Faser*, **~glas** *n* fibreglass, *Am.* fiberglass
ficht → fechten
Fichte *f; -, -n; Bot.* **1.** *Baum.* spruce, *auch allg.* pine (tree); **2.** *nur Sg., Holz:* spruce (wood)
Fichten|holz *n* spruce (wood); **~kreuzschnabel** *m Orn.* crossbill

Fichtennadel f pine needle; **~bad** n pine needle bath; **~extrakt** m pine essence

Fichten|schonung f (protected) pine (od. spruce) plantation; **~wald** m pinewood; größer: pine forest; **~zapfen** m pine (genauer: spruce) cone

Fick m; -s, -s; vulg. fuck; **ficken** vt/i. vulg. **1.** fuck; **fick dich selbst** od. **ins Knie!** fuck off!; **2.** Sl., auch Mil. (schikanieren) bully; **fick(e)rig** Adj. **1.** Dial. fidgety; **2.** vulg. (sexuell erregt) randy Sl., horny Sl.

fidel Adj. cheerful; **er ist ganz ~** auch he's quite chirpy (Am. chipper) umg.

Fidschi (n); -s; Geog. Fiji; **Fidschianer** m; -s, -, **Fidschianerin** f; -, -nen Fijian; **fidschianisch** Adj. Fijian; **Fidschiinseln** Pl.; Geog.: **die ~** the Fiji Islands

Fieber n; -s, -, mst Sg.; Med. fever (auch fig.); (erhöhte Temperatur) (high) temperature; **~ haben** have (od. be running) a temperature; **leichtes/ hohes ~** a slight/high temperature; **([bei] j-m) ~ messen** take s.o.'s temperature; **das ~ fällt/steigt** s.o.'s temperature is falling/rising; **~anfall** m attack of fever; **e-n ~ bekommen** come down with a temperature; **~bläschen** n fever blister; **~fantasie** f (feverish) ravings Pl.; **~n haben** be delirious (with fever), be raving; **~flecken** Pl. fever spots

fieber|frei Adj.; Med.: **sie ist jetzt ~** her temperature's back to normal; **~glänzend** Adj. Augen: ... with a feverish gleam; **~glühend** Adj. Gesicht, Wangen: flushed with fever

fieberhaft I. Adj. feverish (auch fig.); Tätigkeit auch frantic; **~e Suche** mad (od. frantic) search; **II.** Adv. feverishly; suchen, überlegen: frantically; **Fieberhaftigkeit** f; nur Sg. feverishness; fig. auch feverish (od. frantic) activity

Fieberkrampf m infantile (feverish) convulsion

fieberkrank Adj. ill with fever

Fieber|kurve f Med. temperature curve; **~mittel** n antipyretic

fiebern v/i. **1.** Med. have (od. be running) a temperature; **2.** Med. (fantasieren) be delirious, be raving; **3.** fig. be feverish (vor + Dat. with), be in a fever (of); **~ nach** crave (for); **fiebernd I.** Part. Präs. → **fiebern**; **II.** Adj. Med. feverish (fig.: vor + Dat. with)

fiebersenkend Med. **I.** Adj. antipyretic; **II.** Adv.: **das wirkt ~** this brings the temperature down

Fieber|tabelle f Med. temperature chart; **~thermometer** n (clinical) thermometer; **~traum** m feverish dream; **~wahn** m delirium; **im ~ sein** be delirious (with fever); **~zäpfchen** n antipyretic suppository

fiebrig Adj. feverish; → auch **fieberhaft**

Fiedel f; -, -n; Mus., altm., hum. od. pej. fiddle; **fiedeln** vt/i. fiddle

fiederig Adj. feathered

Fiedler m; -s, -, **~in** f; -, -nen; Mus., altm., hum. od. pej. fiddler

fiedrig Adj. feathered

fiel Imperf. → **fallen**

fiepen v/i. Hund: whimper; Vogel: cheep; Jägerspr. Reh: call

Fierant [fiə'rant] m; -en, -en, **~in** f; -, -nen; südd., österr. market trader

fieren v/t. Naut. **1.** (Tau) pay out; **2.** (Boot, Segel) lower

fies umg. **I.** Adj. nasty, horrible; **so ein ~er Typ** what a nasty piece of work, what a (real) bastard; **das war echt ~**

---

von dir that was really mean (od. beastly) of you; **II.** Adv.: **das schmeckt ja ~!** it tastes horrible (od. horrid, revolting); **Fiesling** m; -s, -e; umg. pej. nasty piece of work, bastard

fifty-fifty ['fɪftɪ'fɪftɪ] umg.: **machen wir ~** let's go halves (on it), let's go fifty-fifty, let's split it down the middle; **es steht ~** it's fifty-fifty, there's a fifty-fifty chance

Fight [faɪt] m; -s, -s; umg. fight, battle; **fighten** ['faɪtn] v/i. umg. fight, put up a fight

Figur f; -, -en **1.** mst Sg.; e-r Frau: figure; e-s Mannes: physique; (Körperbau) build; **auf s-e ~ achten** watch one's weight; **2.** Kunst: figure; größere: statue; kleinere: figurine; **3.** Math., geometrische: figure; (Diagramm) diagram; **4.** (Spielfigur) piece; Schach: auch chessman; **5.** im Buch, Film etc.: figure, character; in Politik etc.: figure, person; **6.** Eislauf, Tanz: figure; **~en laufen** skate figures; **7.** Mus. figure; **8.** umg. fig.: **e-e gute/schlechte ~ machen** cut a fine/poor figure; **er gibt e-e lächerliche/traurige ~ ab** he looks ridiculous / cuts a sorry figure

figurativ Adj. **1.** Ling. figurative; **2.** geh. Darstellung etc.: figured

figurbetont Adj. Kleidung: tight-fitting, bodyhugging

Figuren|laufen n figure skating; **~tanz** m figure dance

figurieren v/i. geh. figure (**als** as)

Figurine f; -, -n; Kunst figurine

figürlich I. Adj. **1.** Kunst: (Ggs. abstrakt) figurative; **2.** Ling. figurative; **II.** Adv. **1.** etw. **~ darstellen** show s.th. as a figure, give s.th. human form; → **gegenständlich; 2. sie hat sich ~ verändert** her figure has changed

Figurproblem n problem with one's figure, weight problem

Fiktion f; -, -en; geh. (Einbildung) myth; (Erfindung, auch literarische) fiction; **fiktional** Adj. geh. fictional; **fiktiv** Adj. geh. fictitious

Filet [fi'le:] n; -s, -s **1.** fillet, Am. auch filet; Geflügel: breast; **2.** Gastr. (Steak) fillet steak; **3.** Stoff: fil(l)et, netting

filetieren v/t. Gastr. fillet, Am. auch filet

Filet|steak n Gastr. fillet steak; **~stück** n **1.** Gastr. piece of sirloin; **2.** fig. choicest part

Filiale f; -, -n; Wirts. branch; (Niederlassung) branch (office); → **Filialgeschäft**

Filialist m; -en, -en, **~in** f; -, -nen; Wirts. owner of a chain

Filial|geschäft n Wirts. branch (store od. shop), outlet; **~leiter** m, **~leiterin** f Wirts. branch manager; **~netz** n branch network

filigran Adj. geh. filigree; (zart) auch delicate, gossamer; (durchbrochen) reticulated

Filipina f; -, -s Filipina; **Filipino** m; -s, -s Filipino

Filius m; -, -se; umg. son, boy; **mein** etc. **~** my etc. boy (od. young fellow)

Film m; -(e)s, -e **1.** Fot. (roll of) film; **genug ~e mitnehmen** take enough film Sg.; **2.** (Kinofilm) film, bes. Am. auch movie; **bester ~** Oscar etc.: best picture; **e-n ~ drehen** shoot (od. make) a film (Am. auch movie); **e-n ~ von j-m/etw. drehen** film s.o./s.th.; **in e-n ~ gehen** go to see a film (Am. movie); **warst du schon in dem ~?** have you seen (od. been to) that film (Am. auch movie) yet?; **3.** nur

---

Sg.; Branche: the cinema, bes. Am. the movies Pl.; Industrie: the film (Am. motion picture) industry, Am. auch Hollywood; **beim ~ sein** be in films (bes. Am. auch movies), be in the film (bes. Am. auch movie) business; als Schauspieler: auch be a film (bes. Am. auch movie) actor (weiblich: actress); **zum ~ gehen/wollen** go / want to go into films (bes. Am. auch movies); **4.** (Häutchen, Überzug) film; **~amateur** m, **~amateurin** f home film (bes. Am. movie) maker; **~archiv** n film library (od. archive); **~atelier** n film (Am. auch movie, motion picture) studio; **~aufnahme** f **1.** (Einzelszene) shot, take; **2.** Pl. (Vorgang) shooting (of a film); **~ausschnitt** m film clip; **~autor** m, **~autorin** f screenwriter; **~bauten** Pl. film (Am. auch movie) sets; **~bearbeitung** f film (od. screen) adaptation; **~bericht** m film (Am. auch movie) report; **~bewertungsstelle** f film assessment board; **~debüt** n screen debut; **~diva** f altm. screen goddess

Filmemacher m, **~in** f film maker, bes. Am. auch moviemaker

Filmempfindlichkeit f Fot. film speed

filmen I. v/t. **1.** film, shoot; **2.** umg. (hereinlegen) take s.o. for a ride; **II.** v/i. film, make a film; bei Außenaufnahmen: auch be on location

Film|entwicklung f (film) processing; Negativfilm: developing; **~fassung** f film (od. screen, Am. auch movie) version; **~festival** n, **~festspiele** Pl. film festival Sg.; **~förderung** f financial help for the film (Am. auch movie, motion picture) industry; **~freund** m film (od. movie) buff (od. fan); **~gelände** n studio lot; draußen: location; **~gesellschaft** f film company (Am. studio); **~größe** f film (bes. Am. auch movie) star; **~industrie** f film (Am. motion picture) industry

filmisch I. Adj. cinematic; **II.** Adv. cinematically

Film|kamera f movie camera; für Schmalfilme: auch cine camera; **~karriere** f film (od. screen, bes. Am. auch movie) career; **~komiker** m, **~komikerin** f screen comedian (f auch comedienne altm.); **~komödie** f comedy (film); **~komponist** m, **~komponistin** f film music composer; **~kritik** f film (Am. auch movie) review; **~kritiker** m, **~kritikerin** f film (Am. auch movie) critic; **~kulisse** f gebaut: film set; natürliche: setting for a film; **~kunst** f cinematography; **~kunsttheater** n repertory cinema; **~leinwand** f screen; **~leute** Pl. film (bes. Am. auch movie) people; **~musik** f **1.** Genre: film music; **2.** einzelne: film score; **~partner** m, **~partnerin** f screen partner; **~preis** m film (od. screen, Am. auch movie) award; **~produktion** f film production; **~produzent** m, **~produzentin** f (film) producer; **~projektor** m film (bes. Am. auch movie) projector; **~prüfstelle** f film censorship board; **~publikum** n **1.** **das ~** the cinemagoing (Am. moviegoing) public, cinemagoers (Pl., Am. moviegoers Pl.; **2.** cinema (Am. movie) audience; **~rechte** Pl. film (od. screen, bes. Am. auch movie) rights; **~regisseur** m, **~regisseurin** f film (bes. Am. auch movie) director; **~reklame** f screen advertising; **~reportage** f screen documentary; **~riss** m film tear; **ich hatte e-n ~** umg. fig I had a mental blackout (od. blank), my

F

mind (just) went blank; **~rolle** f 1. (Part) film part (od. role); 2. (Spule) reel of film; leer: film reel; 3. Fot. roll of film; **~schaffende** m, f; -n, -n film maker; **~schauspieler** m, **~schauspielerin** f film (od. screen, bes. Am. auch movie) actor (f actress); **~spule** f film reel; **~stadt** f 1. Kulisse: cardboard town; 2. Zentrum: film (bes. Am. movie) capital; **~star** m film (bes. Am. auch movie) star; **~sternchen** n starlet; **~studio** n film studio(s Pl.); **~theater** n cinema, Am. movie theat|er (od. -re); **~titel** m film (bes. Am. auch movie) title; **~transporthebel** m film advance lever; **~verleih** m 1. Handlung: film distribution; 2. Gesellschaft: film distributors Pl.; **~version** f film (od. screen, Am. auch movie) version; **~vorführer** m, **~vorführerin** f projectionist; **~vorführraum** m projection room; **~vorführung** f 1. (Vorstellung) film; 2. (das Vorführren) showing (of a film); **~vorschau** f für Kritiker: preview; (Ausschnitte, als Reklame) trailer; in Zeitung: forthcoming films Pl. (Am. auch movies Pl.); **~welt** f: die ~ the film world, filmland, Am. umg. auch movieland; **~werbung** f screen advertising; **~wirtschaft** f film (Am. motion picture) industry; **~zeitschrift** f film (Am. auch movie) magazine

Filou [fi'lu:] m; -s, -s; umg. rogue

Filter m, fachspr. n; -s, - filter; Zigarette mit ~ filter(-tipped) cigarette; Zigarette ohne ~ untipped (od. filterless) cigarette; **~anlage** f filtration plant; **~kaffee** m filter coffee; **~kohle** f filtering charcoal; **~mundstück** n filter tip

filtern v/t. filter; (Kaffee) auch percolate

Filter|papier n filter paper; **~rückstand** m Tech. filtration residue; **~staub** m filtration dust; **~tuch** n straining cloth; **~tüte** f (paper) filter, paper cone; **~n** auch filter paper Sg.

Filterung f filtering; Tech. filtration

Filterzigarette f filter(-tipped) cigarette

Filtrat n; -(e)s, -e; fachspr. filtrate; **filtrieren** v/t. filter

Filz m; -es, -e 1. felt; grüner, für Billardtisch etc.: baize; 2. umg. (Hut) felt hat; 3. umg. (Durcheinander) tangle; 4. Pol. fig. cronyism; (Korruption) sleaze; **~deckel** m (Bierdeckel) beer mat, Am. (beer) coaster

filzen I. v/t. 1. (Stoff) felt; 2. umg. (durchsuchen) frisk; II. v/i. Pullover, Wolle: felt

Filzhut m felt hat; weicher: trilby, Am. fedora

filzig Adj. Haar: matted; Bot. downy

Filzlaus f 1. Zool. crab louse; 2. umg. pej. arsehole, Am. asshole

Filzokratie f; -, -n; Pol., umg. cronyism

Filz|pantoffel m felt slipper; **~schreiber** m → Filzstift; **~sohle** f felt sole; **~stift** m felt(-tip) pen, felt tip; **~unterlage** f felt pad

Fimmel m; -s, -; umg. craze; **e-n ~ haben** be crazy (od. mad) (für about); **das ist so ein ~ von ihm** it's a crazy idea (od. fixation) of his; **...fimmel** im Subst. umg. craze about ..., mania for ...; Putz**~** mania for (od. fixation about) cleaning

Final m; -s, -s; schw. → Finale 3

Finale n; -s, -(s) 1. Mus. finale; geh. fig. (grand) finale; 2. Sport final; im ~ stehen be in the final; 3. (Endspurt) final

burst (od. spurt)

Finalgegner m, **~in** f Sport opponent in the final

Finalist m; -en, -en, **~in** f; -, -nen; Sport finalist

Final|satz m Ling. final clause; **~spiel** n final

Finanz f; -, kein Pl.; Wirts., Fin. 1. Bereich: finance; 2. Personen: financial world; **~abteilung** f finance department; **~adel** m plutocracy; **~amt** n 1. tax office; in GB: inland revenue (office); in USA: Internal Revenue Service, abgek. IRS; das ~ auch the taxman umg.; 2. Gebäude: tax office; **~ausgleich** m financial adjustment (between the government and the Länder); **~beamte** m, **~beamtin** f tax officer, taxman; **~behörde** f fiscal (od. tax) authority; **~buchhaltung** f financial accounting; **~chef** m, **~chefin** f umg. head of finance; der langjährige Finanzchef des Konzerns the person who has been responsible for the firm's finances for many years, Am. the company's long-time chief financial officer; **~direktor** m, **~direktorin** f financial director

Finanzen Pl. 1. Fin. (Staatseinkünfte) finances; (Geldwesen) finance; 2. umg. (Geldverhältnisse) money situation Sg.; wie steht es mit d-n ~? how are you off (Am. doing) for money?, how's your money situation?; mit m-n ~ steht es nicht gut my finances are in a bad way, I'm hard up umg.

Finanz|gebaren n e-r Behörde etc. handling of public finances, fiscal policy; e-r Bank etc.: (style of) financial management; **~genie** n financial genius (od. wizard); **~hoheit** f fiscal prerogative

finanziell I. Adj. financial; **~e Krise** auch cash(-flow) crisis; in **~er Hinsicht** financially; II. Adv. financially; **~ schlecht gestellt sein** be badly off (financially); **j-n ~ unterstützen** give s.o. financial support

Finanzier [finan'tsi̯e:] m; -s, -s; Fin. financier

finanzierbar Adj. **es ist ~** it can be financed (od. funded), the money can be found; **finanzieren** I. v/t. finance, fund, bankroll umg.; (bezahlen) pay for; **j-m das Studium ~** pay for s.o. to go to university; II. vt/i. (mit Kredit kaufen) buy on credit; **Finanzierung** f financing, funding; mit Kredit: credit (finance); **steht die ~ eures Hauses?** have you got the finance (od. money) together for your house?

Finanzierungs|bedarf m funding (od. borrowing) requirement; **~gesellschaft** f finance company; **~kosten** Pl. financing (od. funding) cost; **~ für etw.** cost of financing s.th.; **~lücke** f funding shortfall; **~plan** m finance scheme (od. model); **~zusage** f grant of finance (bes. Pol. funding)

Finanz|kauf m credit purchase; **~kraft** f; nur Sg. financial strength (od. clout)

finanzkräftig Adj. financially strong

Finanz|krise f financial crisis; **~lage** f financial situation; die ~ ist schlecht auch funds are low; **~minister** m, **~ministerin** f Pol. minister of finance, finance minister; in GB: Chancellor of the Exchequer; in den USA: etwa Federal Reserve chairman; **~ministerium** n ministry of finance, finance ministry; in GB: Treasury; in den USA: etwa Federal Reserve Bank; **~plan** m financial plan; **~planung** f financial

(od. budgetary) planning; **~politik** f financial (bes. Am. fiscal) policy

finanzschwach Adj. financially weak

Finanzspritze f umg. cash injection, (financial) shot in the arm

finanzstark Adj. financially strong

Finanz|wesen n: das ~ (the world of) finance, public finance; **~wirtschaft** f management of public finances

Findelkind n foundling

finden; findet, fand, hat gefunden I. v/t. 1. find; (entdecken) auch discover; zufällig: auch come across; (Freunde) find, make; schwer zu ~ hard to find (od. come by); Trost ~ in (+ Dat.) find comfort in; keine Worte ~ be lost for words; Zeit ~ find (the) time for; ich finde die Schlüssel nicht I can't find the keys; es wird sich schon e-e Lösung ~ lassen a solution will be found in the end; da haben sich zwei (gesucht und) gefunden! iro. those two were meant for each other; 2. (vorfinden) find; wir fanden ihn schlafend / bei der Arbeit we found him asleep / at work; 3. Meinung: think, believe, find; ich fände es klüger zu (+ Inf.) I think it would be wiser to ...; ich finde es kalt hier I find it cold here; ich finde es gut (Sache) I like it; (Vorschlag) I think it's a good idea; ich finde das zum Lachen/Weinen I find that funny/tragic; ~ Sie nicht (auch)? don't you think so, too?, don't you agree?; wie ~ Sie das Buch? how do you like (od. what do you think of) the book?; wie finde ich denn das? umg. what am I to make of that?; 4. Gefallen ~ an (+ Dat.) take pleasure in; ich weiß nicht, was sie an ihm findet I don't know what she sees in him; ich kann nichts dabei ~ I don't see any harm in it; sie findet nichts dabei, wenn ihre Tochter spät heimkommt she thinks nothing of it (od. doesn't mind) when her daughter comes home late; 5. fig.: reißenden Absatz ~ sell like hotcakes; großen Anklang ~ be very well received; Beachtung ~ receive attention; j-s Beifall ~ meet with s.o.'s approval; → Ende 3, Gehör 2, Glaube 1; II. v/refl. 1. (gefunden werden, anzutreffen sein) be found; Verschwundenes: turn up (again) umg.; es fand sich keinerlei Hinweis etc. there were no clues etc. (at all od. to be found); 2. Person: sich umzingelt / in e-r Notlage etc. ~ find o.s. surrounded/ in dire straits etc.; 3. (in Ordnung kommen) work out; es wird sich schon e-e Lösung ~ an answer will be found; das wird sich schon alles ~ it'll all work out (od. sort itself out) (in the end); 4. geh. Person: find o.s.; 5. Person: sich ~ in (+ Akk.) (sich fügen in) resign (od. reconcile) o.s. to; (sich gewöhnen an) get used to; III. v/i.: nach Hause ~ find one's way home; zur Musik/Kunst etc. ~ discover (od. develop an appreciation for) music/art etc.; zu sich selbst ~ come to terms with o.s., sort o.s. out; er findet nicht aus dem Bett he just can't get (od. drag himself) out of bed; endlich fand die Mannschaft zu ihrem Spiel at last the team got into its (od. their) stride; sie hat noch nicht wieder zu ihrer alten Form gefunden she hasn't yet recovered her old form

Finder m; -s, -, **~in** f; -, -nen finder; der ehrliche ~ potenziell: anyone finding (and returning) the missing item; tat-

sächlich: the person who found the missing item; **~lohn** *m* finder's reward

findig *Adj.* resourceful; (*klug*) clever; **Findigkeit** *f*; *nur Sg.* resourcefulness; (*Klugheit*) cleverness

Findling *m*; *-s*, *-e* **1.** *Geol.* erratic block (*od.* boulder); **2.** (*Findelkind*) foundling

Finesse *f*; *-*, *-n*; *geh.* finesse; *Pl.* tricks; **mit sämtlichen ~n arbeiten** use all the tricks of the trade; *Auto etc.* **mit allen ~n** with every refinement, with all the trimmings (of)

fing *Imperf.* → **fangen**

Finger *m*; *-s*, - **1.** finger (*auch des Handschuhs*); **der kleine ~** the little finger; **e-n ~ breit/dick/lang** the width/thickness/length of a finger, as wide/thick/long as a finger; **e-n Ring am ~ tragen** wear a ring on one's finger; **mit dem ~ drohen** wag one's finger; **mit den ~n schnippen** snap one's fingers; **etw. an den ~n abzählen können** be able to count s.th. on the fingers of one hand; **das kannst du dir an den** *od.* **fünf ~n abzählen** *umg. fig.* that's clear as daylight; **eins auf die ~ kriegen** *umg.* get a rap across the knuckles (*auch fig.*); **sich in den ~ schneiden** cut one's finger; *umg. fig.* make a big mistake; **sich die ~ verbrennen** burn one's fingers (*auch umg. fig.*); **~ weg!** *od.* **lass die ~ davon!** *umg.* hands off!, don't touch!; *fig.* don't you get involved; **mit dem ~ zeigen auf** (+ *Akk.*) point at (*od.* to); *fig.* point one's finger at; **2.** *fig.*: **das sagt mir mein kleiner ~** a little bird told me; **etw. im kleinen ~ haben** *umg.* have s.th. at one's fingertips; **das macht sie mit dem ~ weg** *umg.* she can do that with her eyes shut; **j-n um den (kleinen) ~ wickeln** *umg.* twist s.o. (a)round one's little finger; **gibt man ihm den kleinen ~, nimmt er gleich die ganze Hand** give him an inch, and he'll take (you) a mile; **krumme** *od.* **lange ~ machen** *umg.* get itchy fingers; **mit spitzen ~n anfassen** hold at arm's length; **j-m auf die ~ klopfen** rap s.o.'s knuckles; **j-m auf die ~ sehen** *umg.* keep a close eye on s.o.; **j-m durch die ~ schlüpfen** *od.* **gehen** slip through s.o.'s fingers (*Verbrecher etc.*: *auch* clutches); *Verbrecher etc.*: *auch* give s.o. the slip; **das lasse ich mir nicht durch die ~ gehen** *umg.* I'm not going to let the opportunity slip; **j-m in die ~ geraten** *od.* **fallen** *umg.* fall into s.o.'s hands; **in** *od.* **zwischen die ~ bekommen** *umg.* get hold of, get one's hands on; **der soll mir nur unter die ~ kommen!** *umg. drohend*: just wait till I lay my hands on him!; **wenn ich die in** *od.* **zwischen die ~ kriege!** *umg. drohend*: if I lay my hands on her!; (*überall*) **s-e ~ im Spiel** *od.* **drin haben** have a hand in it (have got a finger in every pie); **keinen ~ rühren** *od.* **krümmen** *od.* **krumm machen** *umg.* not lift a finger (*für j-n* to help s.o.); **er macht sich die ~ nicht gern schmutzig** *umg.* he doesn't like getting his hands dirty; **es juckt** *od.* **kribbelt mich in den ~n, ihn zu schlagen** *umg.* I'm longing (*od.* dying) to hit him; **ich würde mir die** *od.* **alle zehn ~ danach lecken** *umg.* I'd give my right arm for it; **sich** (*Dat.*) **etw. aus den ~n saugen** make s.th. up; **den ~ auf die Wunde legen** touch on a sore point; **sie hat an jedem ~ einen** *od.* **zehn** *umg.* she has one for every day of the week

Fingerabdruck *m* fingerprint; **Fingerabdrücke (ab)nehmen** take fingerprints

fingerbreit I. *Adj.* etwa inch-wide …, *präd.* an inch wide; **II.** *Adv.* an inch wide; **Fingerbreit** *m*; *-*, *- etwa* inch; **keinen ~ nachgeben** not budge (*od.* give) an inch

fingerdick I. *Adj.* as thick as your finger; **II.** *Adv.*: **etw. ~ auftragen** spread s.th. thickly

Finger|druck *m*: **ein ~ genügt, und die Maschine läuft** you just press the button and the machine starts

Fingerfarbe *f* finger paint

fingerfertig *Adj.* dext(e)rous, adroit, nimble-fingered; **Fingerfertigkeit** *f*; *nur Sg.* dexterity; *weitS.* (*Geschicklichkeit*) skill

fingerförmig *Adj.* finger-shaped

Finger|gelenk *n*, **~glied** *n* finger joint; **~hakeln** *n*; *-s*, *kein Pl.* finger-wrestling; **~handschuh** *m* glove; **~hut** *m* **1.** thimble; **ein ~ voll** a thimbleful (of); **2.** *Bot.* foxglove, digitalis; **~knöchel** *m* knuckle; **~kuppe** *f* fingertip

fingerlang *Adj.* finger-length, … the length of one's finger

Fingerling *m*; *-s*, *-e* fingerstall

fingern *v/i.*: **~ an** (+ *Dat.*) finger, fiddle with; *suchend*: fumble (*od.* feel) around on; **~ nach** fumble (*od.* feel) for; **~ aus** pull out of, extract from

Finger|nagel *m* fingernail; **an den Fingernägeln kauen** bite one's nails; **j-m das Schwarze unterm ~ nicht gönnen** *umg. fig.* begrudge s.o. every little thing; **~satz** *m Mus.* fingering; **~schale** *f* finger bowl

Fingerspitze *f* fingertip; **bis in die ~n** *fig.* down to one's fingertips; **etw. in den ~n haben** *fig.* have a feeling (*od.* the right feel) for s.th.; **Fingerspitzengefühl** *n* instinct, flair; (*Takt*) tact; **dazu braucht man ~** you've got to have a feeling (*od.* the right feel) for it

Finger|übung *f Mus.* finger exercise; **~zeig** *m*; *-s*, *-e* pointer, hint; *für die Polizei*: tip-off; **ein ~ Gottes** a sign (from above)

fingieren *v/t. geh.* fake; (*erfinden*) fabricate; **fingiert I.** *P.P.* → **fingieren**; **II.** *Adj.* fake, bogus, faked (*erfunden*) made-up, fictitious, invented

Finish ['fɪnɪʃ] *n*; *-s*, *-s* **1.** *fachspr.* finishing touch; **2.** *Sport*: **im ~** at the finish

finit *Adj. Ling.* finite

Fink *m*; *-en*, *-en* **1.** *Orn.* finch; **2.** *schw.* (*Taugenichts*) rogue, good-for-nothing; **3.** *schw. schmutzig*: mucky pup

Finne[1] *f*; *-*, *-n* **1.** (*Flosse*) fin; **2.** (*Bandwurmlarve*) bladder worm

Finne[2] *m*; *-n*, *-n*, **Finnin** *f*; *-*, *-nen* Finn, *weiblich auch*: Finnish woman (*od.* girl etc.); **finnisch I.** *Adj.* Finnish; **Finnischer Meerbusen** *Geog.* Gulf of Finland; **II. Finnisch** *n*; *-en*; *Ling.* Finnish; **das Finnische** Finnish; **finnisch-ugrisch** *Adj. Ling.* Finno-Ugric

Finn|land (*n*) *Geog.* Finland; **~mark** *f*; *-*, *-*; *hist.* Finnish mark (*ehemalige finnische Währung*); **~wal** *m* fin whale, finback

finster I. *Adj.* **1.** dark; *Gasse, Wald etc.*: *auch* gloomy; **im Finstern** in the dark; **im Finstern tappen** *fig.* grope in the dark; **2.** *fig.* (*düster*) gloomy, dark; (*drohend*) ominous; (*streng*) stern; (*grimmig*) grim; (*böse, unheilvoll*) sinister, evil; *Blick*: black; *Gedanken*: dark, evil; **es sieht ~ aus** the outlook is gloomy (*stärker*: grim); **es geht zu**

wie im ~sten Mittelalter *umg.* we might as well be back in the Dark Ages; **3.** *fig.* (*dubios*) shady; *Gestalt*: sinister; **II.** *Adv.*: **j-n ~ ansehen** give s.o. a black look, glower at s.o.; **Finsterling** *m*; *-s*, *-e*; *pej.* shady customer *umg.*; **Finsternis** *f*; *-*, *-se* darkness; *fig. auch* obscurity; *Astron.* eclipse; (*e-e*) **ägyptische ~** *umg. fig.* pitch darkness; **die Mächte der ~** the powers of darkness

Finte *f*; *-*, *-n* **1.** *geh.* (*Täuschung*) trick; *Pl. auch* trickery; **2.** *Sport* feint; **fintenreich** *Adj. geh.* crafty

Firlefanz *m*; *-es*, *-e*; *umg. pej.* **1.** (*unnützer Kram*) frippery; (*Flitter*) baubles *Pl.*; *auf Kleidung*: fancy trimmings, frills *Pl.*; **2.** (*Unsinn*) nonsense; (*Blödelei*) clowning; **~ treiben** fool around

firm *Adj.*: **~ sein in** (+ *Dat.*) *Fachgebiet*: be well up in, *Am.* be clued up about; *Tätigkeit*: be good at

Firma *f*; *-*, *Firmen* firm, company; (*Firmenbezeichnung*) company name; **die ~ Wellington** Wellingtons; (*An*) **~ X im Brief*: Messrs(.) X; The X Company; **die ~ dankt** *umg. hum.* thanks (but no thanks)

Firmament *n*; *-(e)s*, *kein Pl.*; *lit.* firmament, heavens *Pl.*

firmen *v/t. kath.* confirm

Firmen|angehörige *m*, *f* (company) member of staff; **~aufdruck** *m Brief*: company letterhead; **~bezeichnung** *f* company name; **~chef** *m*, **~chefin** *f* head of the company (*od.* firm), company boss *umg.*

firmeneigen *Adj.* company-owned

Firmen|gelände *n* company site; **~geschichte** *f* company (*od.* corporate) history; **~gründer** *m*, **~gründerin** *f* founder of a *bzw.* the business, company founder; **~gründung** *f Vorgang*: establishment of a *bzw.* the business; (*neu gegründete Firma*) start-up; **~gruppe** *f* group of companies, conglomerate; **~inhaber** *m*, **~inhaberin** *f* owner (of a *od.* the company)

firmenintern I. *Adj. Angelegenheit etc.*: internal (company); *Ausbildung, Abmachung etc.*: *auch* in-house; **II.** *Adv.* in-house, internally

Firmen|jubiläum *n*: **sie hat im 25. ~** she is celebrating 25 years with the firm (*od.* company); **~leitung** *f* company management; **~name** *m* company name; **~schild** *n* company sign (*od.* name); **an e-r Maschine**: company nameplate; **an e-r Baustelle**: contractor's nameplate; **~sitz** *m* (company) headquarters *Pl.* (*V. auch im Sg.*); **~sprecher** *m*, **~sprecherin** *f* company spokesman (*od.* spokesperson); **~verzeichnis** *n* trade directory; **~wagen** *m* company car; **~wert** *m* goodwill; **~zeichen** *n* company logo; (*Markenzeichen*) trademark

firmieren *v/i.*: **~ als** *od.* **unter dem Namen** trade (*Am.* do business) under the name of

Firmling *m*; *-s*, *-e*; *kath.* confirmand; **Firmung** *f* confirmation

Firn *m*; *-(e)s*, *-e(n)* firn, névé; **~eis** *n* firn ice

Firnis *m*; *-ses*, *-se* varnish; *fig.* veneer; **firnissen** *v/t.* varnish

Firnschnee *m* firn snow, névé

First *m*; *-(e)s*, *-e* **1.** (*Dachfirst*) ridge; **2.** *Bergb.* roof; **~balken** *m* ridge beam; **~feier** *f österr.* topping-out ceremony

fis, Fis *n*; *-*, *-*; *Mus.* F sharp

Fisch *m*; *-(e)s*, *-e* **1.** *Zool.* fish; *Pl. mst*

F

fish *Pl.*; *viele ~e zappeln im Netz* a large number of fish are wriggling in the net; *munter wie ein ~ im Wasser* (as) fit as a fiddle; *stumm wie ein ~* tight-lipped, silent as a post; *weder ~ noch Fleisch fig.* neither fish nor fowl; *der ~ stinkt vom Kopf her fig.* the trouble is at the top; **2.** *umg. fig.: großer od. dicker ~* umg. fig. big fish, *Am. auch* big cheese; *kleine ~e (Kleinigkeit)* peanuts; *Leute:* small fry; *das sind kleine ~e ist problemlos:* that's no big deal; **3.** (*Sternzeichen*) Pisces *auch Sg.*; *ein ~ sein* be (a) Pisces, be a Piscean

Fischadler *m Orn.* osprey

fischarm *Adj. Gewässer:* ... containing few fish

Fisch|auge *n Fot.* fisheye lens; **~bein** *n* whalebone; **~bestand** *m* fish stocks *Pl.* (*od.* population); **~besteck** *n* **1.** fish knife and fork; **2.** *Koll.* fish knives and forks *Pl.*; **~blase** *f Zool.* swim (*od.* air) bladder; **~blut** *n fig.:* **~** *in den Adern haben* be (as) cold as a fish; **~braterei** *f* fried fish restaurant, *Brit. etwa* fish and chip shop; **~brötchen** *n Gastr.* fish roll (*Am.* sandwich); **~brut** *f Zool.* fry *Pl.*; **~bude** *f* fish stall in a market; **~bulette** *f* fishcake; **~dampfer** *m* trawler; **~ei** *n* fish egg

fischeln *v/i. bes. österr.* smell of fish, have a fishy smell; *es fischelt* there's a smell of fish

fischen I. *v/i.* fish; *nach etw. ~* fish for s.th. (*auch umg. fig.*); *im Trüben ~ fig.* fish in troubled waters; **II.** *v/t.* fish for (*auch Austern, Perlen*); **2.** *umg. fig.: etw. aus der Tasche etc. ~* fish s.th. out of one's pocket *etc.*; **3.** *umg. fig.: sich (Dat.) j-n ~* hook (o.s.) s.o.; **III. Fischen** *n; -s, kein Pl.* fishing

Fischer *m; -s, -* fisherman; (*Angler*) angler; **~boot** *n* fishing boat; **~dorf** *n* fishing village

Fischerei *f; -, kein Pl.*; (*Fischen*) fishing; (*Gewerbe*) fishing industry; **~abkommen** *n* fisheries agreement; **~flotte** *f* fishing fleet; **~gewässer** *n* fishing grounds *Pl.*; **~grenze** *f* fishing limit; **~hafen** *m* fishing port; **~recht** *n* **1.** fishing rights *Pl.*; **2.** *nur Sg.* (*Gesetze*) fishing laws *Pl.*; **~wesen** *n; nur Sg.* fishing, fisheries *Pl.*

Fischerin *f; -, -nen* **1.** fisherwoman; **2.** (*Anglerin*) (woman) angler

Fischer|hütte *f* fisherman's hut; **~netz** *n* fishing net

Fischers|frau *f* fisherman's wife; **~leute** *Pl.* fisherfolk; **~mann** *m; Pl. -männer od. -leute* fisherman

Fischfang *m* fishing; **~flotte** *f* fishing fleet; **~gebiet** *n* fishing grounds *Pl.*

Fisch|farm *f* fish farm; **~filet** *n Gastr.* fish fillet; **~flosse** *f* fin; **~frikadelle** *f* fishcake; **~gericht** *n* fish (dish); **~geruch** *m* fishy smell, smell of fish; **~geschäft** *n* fishmonger('s), *Am.* fish dealer (*od.* vendor); **~gräte** *f* fishbone; **~grätenmuster** *n* herringbone (pattern); **~gründe** *Pl.* fishing grounds; **~händler** *m*, **~händlerin** *f* fishmonger, *Am.* fish dealer (*od.* vendor); *im Großhandel:* fish merchant

fischig *Adj.* fishy

Fisch|köder *m* bait; **~konserve** *f* canned (*Brit. auch* tinned) fish; **~kunde** *f; nur Sg.* ichthyology; **~kutter** *m* (fishing) trawler; **~laich** *m* (fish) spawn; **~leim** *m* fish glue; **~leiter** *f Ökol.* fish ladder; **~markt** *m* fish market; **~mehl** *n* fish meal; **~messer** *n*

fish knife; **~milch** *f Zool.* milt; **~otter** *m Zool.* otter

fischreich *Adj. Gewässer:* ... rich in fish

Fisch|reiher *m Orn.* heron; **~schuppe** *f* scale; **~schwarm** *m* shoal (of fish); **~stäbchen** *n Gastr.* fish finger, *Am.* fish stick; **~sterben** *n* fish kill; **~suppe** *f Gastr.* fish soup; **~teich** *m* fishpond; **~vergiftung** *f* fish poisoning; **~weib** *n pej.* fishwife; **~wilderei** *f* fish poaching; **~wirtschaft** *f* fishing industry; **~zaun** *m* fish weir; **~zucht** *f* fish farming; **~zug** *m* **1.** *Fischfang:* trawl; **2.** (*Unternehmen mit reicher Beute*) killing; *ein guter ~* a big killing (*od.* haul)

Fis-Dur *n Mus.* F sharp major

Fisimatenten *Pl. umg.* (*Umstände*) fuss *Sg.*; (*Ärger*) trouble *Sg.*; (*Ausflüchte*) excuses; (*Unsinn*) nonsense *Sg.*; *mach keine ~!* stop messing about (*Am.* around) (*od.* making such a fuss)

fiskalisch *Adj. geh.* fiscal; **Fiskus** *m; -, Fisken od. -se, mst Sg.* **1.** Treasury; **2.** (*Staat*) government, State; *in GB: auch* the Crown; *umg.* → **Finanzamt**

fis-Moll *n Mus.* F sharp minor

Fisole *f; -, -n; österr.* green bean

Fissur *f; -, -en; Med., des Knochens:* fissure; *der Haut:* crack

Fistel *f; -, -n; Med.* fistula; **~stimme** *f* **1.** *Mus.* falsetto (voice); **2.** *pej.* high-pitched (*od.* falsetto) voice

fit *Adj.* **1.** fit; *sich ~ machen/halten* get/ keep fit, get into / keep in shape (*auch fig.*); **2.** *~ in* (+ *Dat.*) *e-m Fach etc.:* well up in, *Am.* clued up about; *nicht sehr ~ in* (+ *Dat.*) not too hot on *umg.*; *geistig ~* on the ball

Fitness *f; -, kein Pl.* physical fitness; **~center** *n* health club, fitness cent|re (*Am.* -er); **~programm** *n* fitness programme, *Am.* training regime; **~raum** *m* exercise room; **~studio** *n* → **Fitnesscenter**; **~training** *n* fitness training; **~ machen** *auch* work out

Fittich *m; -(e)s, -e* **1.** *lit.* wing, pinion; **2.** *fig.: j-n unter s-e ~e nehmen* take s.o. under one's wing

Fitzelchen *n; -s, -; Dial.* (tiny) scrap; *nicht ein ~* not a scrap

fix I. *Adj.* **1.** *Gehalt, Preise:* fixed; → **Fixkosten**; *~e Idee* obsession, idée fixe; *das ist so e-e ~e Idee von ihm* he's got a fixation (*umg.* thing) about it; **2.** (*schnell*) quick (*in* + *Dat.* at); (*wendig*) agile; *Person: auch* quick-witted; (*gewandt*) adroit, *bes.Am.* smart; **3.** *umg.: ~ und fertig* completely finished, all ready; *~ und fertig od. alle od. foxi* *Sl. fig.* → **fertig** I 5; **II.** *Adv.* **1.** *umg.* quickly, in a flash; *mach ~ od. jetzt aber ~!* get a move on, make it snappy; **2.** *österr.: ~ angestellt* permanently employed

Fix *m; -(es), -e; Sl.* fix

Fixa *Pl.* → **Fixum**

Fixangestellte *m, f; -n, -n; österr.* permanent employee

fixen *v/i.* **1.** *Sl.* (*Rauschgift spritzen*) have a fix, shoot; *gewohnheitsmäßig:* mainline; **2.** *Wirts.* sell a bear, sell short

Fixer *m; -s, -,* **~in** *f; -, -nen* **1.** *Sl.* (*Drogensüchtiger*) mainliner, junkie; **2.** *Wirts.* (*Baissier*) bear; **~besteck** *n* drug addict's gear, *Am.* works *Sl.*; (*Nadel*) needle; **~stube** *f* cent|re (*Am.* -er) for drug addicts (*where drugs can legally be taken*)

Fixgeschäft *n Fin.* time bargain; *Wirts.* fixed-date transaction

Fixierbad *n Fot.* fixer, fixing bath

fixieren I. *v/t.* **1.** *geh.* (*formulieren*) record; *schriftlich ~* put down in writing; **2.** *Fot.* fix; **3.** (*e-n Punkt etc.*) focus on; (*anstarren*) stare at, fix one's gaze on; **4.** *Med.* (*Bruch etc.*) set; **II.** *v/refl. Psych.: sich ~ auf* (+ *Akk.*) fixate on; → **fixiert**

Fixier|mittel *n* fixative; *Fot.* fixer; **~salz** *n* hypo, fixing salt

fixiert I. *P.P.* → **fixieren**; **II.** *Adj.: ~ auf* (+ *Akk.*) fixated on; *auf s-e Mutter ~ sein Psych.* have a mother fixation; **Fixierung** *f* **1.** fixing (*auch Fot.*); **2.** *Psych.* fixation (*auf* + *Akk.* on); *fig. auch* obsession (with)

Fix|kosten *Pl.* fixed costs; **~punkt** *m* **1.** point of reference; *Opt.* point of focus; **2.** *fig.* focal point; **~stern** *m* fixed star

Fixum *n; -s, Fixa* basic salary

Fixzeit *f* core time

Fjord *m; -(e)s, -e* fiord, fjord

FKK (*n*); -, *kein Pl.*; *Abk.* naturism, nudism; **~-Gelände** *n* nudist camp

FKKler *m; -s, -,* **~in** *f; -, -nen; umg.* nudist, naturist

FKK-Strand *m* nudist beach

flach I. *Adj.* **1.** *Dach, Gelände etc.:* flat; (*eben*) *auch* level, even; *Math.* plane; *~e Brust Frau:* flat chest; *Mann:* hollow chest; *~ gedrückt* flat(tened down); *mit der ~en Hand* with the flat of one's hand; *auf dem ~en Land* in the depths of the countryside; *~ klopfen* beat out; *~ machen* level (off); *~ werden* flatten (out), level (off); **2.** *Atmung, Gewässer, Wasser:* shallow; *~er Teller* dinner plate; **3.** (*niedrig*) *Absätze etc.:* low; *Schuhe:* low-heeled; *Boot:* flat-bottomed; *Math., Kurve:* flat; **4.** *fig. pej.* (*oberflächlich*) shallow, superficial; **II.** *Adv.: ~ liegen* lie flat; *sich ~ hinlegen* lie down flat; *den Ball ~ spielen* keep the ball on the ground; *~ über etw. fliegen/hinwegstreichen etc.* fly/skim *etc.* low over s.th.; *~ atmen* breathe shallow(ly); *bewusst:* take shallow breaths; *ihr Atem geht ~* her breathing is shallow

Flach|bau *m; Pl. -ten* low building; **~bettscanner** *m EDV* flat-bed scanner; **~bildschirm** *m Computer:* flat screen

flachbrüstig *Adj. Frau:* flat-chested; *Mann:* hollow-chested

Flach|dach *n* flat roof; **~druck** *m Druck.* flatbed printing

Fläche *f; -, -n* **1.** (*Gebiet*) area; (*Grundfläche*) area, space; *in Gebäude:* floorspace; *weite ~* wide expanse; *das Dreieck hat e-e ~ von 5 cm²* the triangle has an area of 0.775 sq. in.; **2.** (*Oberfläche*) surface; *Math.* (*Ebene*) plane; *e-s Körpers:* face; *e-s geschliffenen Steins:* facet

Flacheisen *n* flat iron

Flächen|ausdehnung *f* (surface) area; **~berechnung** *f Math.* planimetry; **~blitz** *m* sheet lightning; **~bombardement** *n* saturation (*od.* carpet) bombing; **~brand** *m* extensive fire; *sich zu e-m ~ ausweiten fig.* spread like wildfire

flächen|deckend I. *Adj.* ... giving comprehensive (*od.* overall) coverage; *Gebrauch etc.:* widespread, extensive; *~er Polizeieinsatz etc.* saturation policing *etc.*; *~es Bombardement* saturation (*od.* carpet) bombing; **II.** *Adv.* giving comprehensive (*od.* overall) coverage; *einsetzen etc.:* extensively; **~gleich** *Adj. Math.* ... of equal area,

... equal in area; **~haft I.** *Adj.* extensive; **II.** *Adv. sich ausbreiten*: over a wide area

Flächen|inhalt *m Math.* (surface) area; **~maß** *n* **1.** surface measurement; **2.** (*Einheit*) unit of square measure; **~ton** *m* harmonic; **~messung** *f* planimetry; **~nutzung** *f* land use; **~nutzungsplan** *m* zoning (*od.* land development) plan; **~sanierung** *f* area rehabilitation; **~staat** *m* (*Ggs. Stadtstaat*) territorial state; **~stilllegung** *f EU-Agrarpolitik*: set--aside scheme (*od.* program[me])

flachfallen *v/i.* (*unreg., trennb., ist -ge-*); *umg.* fall through; *Veranstaltung*: be cancel(l)ed; *Fernsehen fällt heute für dich flach* there's no TV for you today

Flach|glas *n* flat (*od.* sheet) glass; **~hang** *m* gentle slope

Flachheit *f* **1.** *nur Sg.*; flatness; **2.** *nur Sg.*; *fig.* shallowness, superficiality; **3.** *pej. Äußerung*: platitude

flächig *Adj.* **1.** flat; (*zweidimensional*) two-dimensional; **2.** (*ausgedehnt*) extensive

...flächig *im Adj. Math.* ...hedral; *zwanzig~* icosahedral; *zwölf~* dodecahedral

Flach|kabel *n Etech.* flat cable; **~kopf** *m umg. pej.* blockhead; **~kopfschraube** *f* countersunk screw; **~küste** *f* flat coast (*od.* shore)

Flachland *n; nur Sg.* lowland, flat country; **Flachländer** *m; -s, -*, **Flachländerin** *f; -, -nen* lowlander, flatlander; **Flachlandtiroler** *m*, **Flachlandtirolerin** *f umg. hum. od. pej.* mountainman wannabe

flach|legen (*trennb., hat -ge-*) **I.** *v/refl. umg.: sich eine Weile ~* lie down for a bit; **II.** *v/t.* **1.** *umg.* (*j-n*) bring *s.o.* down; **2.** *vulg.: er hat sie flachgelegt* he laid her; **~liegen** *v/i.* (*unreg., trennb., ist -ge-*); *umg.* be laid up (in bed)

Flachmann *m; Pl. Flachmänner; umg.* hip flask

...flächner *m; -s, -; im Subst. Math.* ...hedron; *Zwanzig~* icosahedron; *Zwölf~* dodecahedron

Flach|pass *m Fußball*: low pass; **~relief** *n* bas-relief

Flachs *m; -es, kein Pl.* **1.** *Bot.* flax; **~brechen** break flax; **2.** *umg. fig.* kidding; (*Witz*) joke; *kein ~?* no kidding?; *mal ganz ohne ~* seriously though

flachsblond *Adj.* flaxen

Flachschuss *m Fußball*: low shot (*od.* ball)

Flachse *f; -, -n; österr.* sinew; *Pl. im Fleisch*: gristle

flachsen *v/i. umg.* be kidding; (*herumalbern*) kid around

Flach|stahl *m* flat steel; **~stecker** *m Etech.* tab connector; **~wasser** *n; nur Sg.* shallow water, shallows *Pl.*; **~zange** *f*: (*e-e*)*~* (a pair of) flat-nose pliers *Pl.*

flacken *v/i. südd.: auf dem Bett / am Boden ~* lounge on the bed / sprawl on the ground

flackerig *Adj.* flickering

flackern **I.** *v/i. Augen, Feuer, Licht*: flicker; *Kerze im Luftzug*: *auch* gutter; **II. Flackern** *n; -s, kein Pl.* flicker(ing)

flackrig *Adj.* flickering

Flacon [fla'kõː] → **Flakon**

Fladen *m; -s, -* **1.** flat round cake; *süß*: pancake; **2.** *breiige Masse*: dollop; → *Kuhfladen*; **~brot** *n* flat unleavened bread; *griechisches etc.*: pita (bread)

fladern *vt/i. österr.* steal

Flädlisuppe *f schw.* pancake soup

Flagellant *m; -en, -en*, **~in** *f; -, -nen* *kirchl., hist., auch Psych.* flagellant

Flageolett [flaʒo'lɛt] *n; -s, -e od. -s; Mus.* **1.** *Instrument*: flageolet; **2.** *Ton*: harmonic; **~ton** *m* harmonic

Flagge *f; -, -n* flag; *Mil. auch* colo(u)rs *Pl.*; → *auch Fahne* 1; *die ~ hissen od. aufziehen* hoist the flag (*od.* colo[u]rs *Pl.*); *die ~ einholen* lower the flag (*od.* colo[u]rs *Pl.*); *die ~ streichen auch fig.* strike the flag (*od.* colo[u]rs *Pl.*) (*auch fig. kapitulieren*); *die britische ~* the British flag, the Union Jack; *die amerikanische ~* the American flag, the Stars and Stripes, Old Glory; *unter fremder ~* under a foreign flag; *unter falscher ~ fig.* under false colo(u)rs; *~ zeigen fig.* make a stand

flaggen **I.** *v/i.* fly a flag (*od.* flags); *Person*: hoist the flag (*od.* flags); *geflaggt haben* be flying a flag (*od.* flags); **II.** *v/t.* flag; (*signalisieren*) signal (with flags)

Flaggen|alphabet *n Naut.* code of flag signals, semaphore; **~mast** *m* flagpole; **~parade** *f* ceremony of raising/lowering the colo(u)rs; **~signal** *n Mil., Naut.* flag signal

Flaggschiff *n Naut., auch fig.* flagship

flagrant *Adj. geh.* flagrant

Flair [flɛːɐ̯] *n, m; -s, kein Pl.* aura; (*Atmosphäre*) *auch* atmosphere; (*Reiz*) charm

Flak *f; -, -(s); Mil.* **1.** *Waffe*: anti-aircraft gun; **2.** *Koll.* anti-aircraft artillery; **~feuer** *n* flak, anti-aircraft fire; **~helfer** *m*, **~helferin** *f hist.* anti-aircraft auxiliary

Flakon [fla'kõː] *m, n; -s, -s* small bottle

flambieren *v/t.* flambé; *flambiert werden* be flambéed; *flambiert* **I.** *P.P.* → *flambieren*; **II.** *Adj.* flambé(e), *bei Pl.*: flambé(e)s

Flame *m; -n, -n* Fleming; *der ~ Koll.* the Flemish *Pl.*; **Flämin** *f; -, -nen* Flemish woman (*od.* girl *etc.*), Fleming

Flamingo *m; -s, -s* flamingo

flämisch *Adj.* Flemish; **Flämisch** *n; -en; Ling.* Flemish; *das ~e* Flemish

Flamme *f; -, -n* **1.** flame (*auch fig.*); *in ~n* in flames, blazing; *in ~n aufgehen/stehen* go up /be in flames; *in ~n ausbrechen* burst into flames; *auf kleiner ~ kochen* cook on a low flame (*od.* heat); *fig.* get by on (*od.* make do with) very little; → *Feuer* 1; **2.** *am Gasherd*: burner; **3.** *altm. fig.* (*Freundin*) flame

flammen *v/i. geh.* **1.** *altm.* blaze; **2.** *fig. Gesicht etc.*: burn (*vor + Dat.* with); *Zorn flammte in i-n Augen* her eyes were ablaze with anger; **flämmen** *v/t.* (*Rasen*) scorch; *Tech.* (*Metallstück*) deseam; **flammend I.** *Part. Präs.* → *flammen*; **II.** *Adj. fig.* fiery; *Appell*: stirring; **III.** *Adv.: ~ rot* fiery (*od.* flaming) red

Flammen|meer *n* sea of flames; **~schwert** *n* flaming sword; **~tod** *m geh.: den ~ erleiden* be burnt (*bes. Am.* burned) to death; **~werfer** *m Mil.* flame-thrower

Flammpunkt *m Chem.* flashpoint

Flandern (*n*); *-s; Geog.* Flanders

Flanell *m; -s, -e* flannel; **~hemd** *n* flannel shirt

flanieren *v/i.* stroll, saunter; **Flaniermeile** *f hum.* smart (*Am.* upscale) shopping street

Flanke *f; -, -n* **1.** *von Tier, Berg, Truppe*: flank; (*Seite*) side; *j-m in die ~ fal-*

len Mil. attack s.o.'s flank; **2.** *Sport, Sprung beim Turnen*: flank vault; **3.** *Sport, Pass beim Fußball*: cross, cent|re (*Am.* -er); *e-e ~ schlagen* cross (*od.* cent|re, *Am.* -er) the ball; **4.** *Sport* (*Angriffsseite*) wing; *Angriff über die linke ~* attack down the left wing; **flanken I.** *vt/i.* (*hat geflankt*) *Fußball*: (*den Ball*) *~* cross (*od.* cent|re, *Am.* -er) the ball; **II.** *v/i.* (*ist*): *über den Bock / vom Barren ~* flank vault over the horse / from the parallel bars

Flanken|angriff *m* **1.** *Mil.* flank attack; **2.** *Sport, Fußball, Hockey*: attack down the wing; **~ball** *m Sport* cross, cent|re (*Am.* -er); **~deckung** *f Mil.* cover of the flanks; **~schutz** *m Mil.* protection of the flanks

flankieren *v/t.* flank; *das Tor ~* stand on either side of the gate; **flankierend I.** *Part. Präs.* → *flankieren*; **II.** *Adj.: ~e Maßnahmen Wirts., Pol. fig.* supporting measures

Flansch *m; -(e)s, -e; Tech.* flange; **flanschen** *v/t.* flange

Flappe *f; -, -n; bes. nordd. umg.: e-e ~ ziehen* sulk, make a face; *halt die ~!* shut your trap!

Flaps *m; -es, -e; umg.* whippersnapper; (*Flegel*) lout; **flapsig** *Adj.* boorish, uncouth

Fläschchen *n* small bottle; *Pharm.* phial, *bes. Am.* vial; *für Babys*: bottle

Flasche *f; -, -n* **1.** bottle (*auch für Baby*); *bei e-r ~ Wein besprechen etc.*: over a bottle of wine; *Wein in ~n (ab)füllen od. auf ~n ziehen* bottle wine; *e-m Kind die ~ geben* give a baby its bottle; *gewohnheitsmäßig*: bottle-feed a baby; *es kriegt noch die ~ Kind*: he's/she's still on the bottle; *ein Tier mit der ~ aufziehen* rear an animal by bottle-feeding; *e-r ~ den Hals brechen od. e-e ~ köpfen umg. hum.* crack (open) a bottle; *zur ~ greifen* take to (*umg.* hit) the bottle; *an der ~ hängen umg.* be on the bottle; **2.** *für Gas etc.*: cylinder; **3.** *umg. pej.* (*Dummkopf*) dummy; (*Versager*) loser, useless type; (*Weichling*) wimp, weakling

Flaschen|batterie *f umg.* mass (*od.* rows on rows) of bottles; **~bier** *n* bottled beer; **~bürste** *f* bottle brush; **~gärung** *f* fermentation in the bottle; **~gas** *n* bottled gas; **~gestell** *n* bottle rack

flaschengrün *Adj.* bottle green

Flaschen|hals *m* **1.** neck of a bottle; **2.** *fig.* bottleneck; **~kind** *n* bottle(-fed) baby; **~kürbis** *m* bottle gourd; **~milch** *f* bottled milk; **~öffner** *m* bottle opener; **~pfand** *n* deposit (on a *od.* the bottle); **~post** *f* bottle post (*Am.* mail); (*Nachricht*) message in a bottle; **~regal** *n* bottle rack; **~reiniger** *m* bottle brush; **~verschluss** *m* bottle top; **~wärmer** *m* bottle warmer; **~wein** *m* bottled wine; *auf Weinkarte*: *~e* wine by the bottle

flaschenweise *Adv.* by the bottleful

Flaschenzug *m Tech.* block and tackle

Flaschner *m; -s, -; südd., schw.* plumber

Flatrate ['flɛtreːt] *f; -, -s; Telek.* flat rate; *Internet*: flat-rate internet access

Flatter *f umg.: die ~ machen* hop it, *Am.* scram

flatterhaft *Adj. pej.* flighty; (*unstet*) fickle

flatterig *Adj.* **1.** *Puls*: irregular, fluttering; **2.** → *flatterhaft*

Flattermann *m*; *Pl.* *-männer*; *umg.* **1.** (*Hähnchen*) chicken; **2.** *nur Sg.*: **e-n ~ haben** (*Lampenfieber*) have butterflies in the stomach; *allg.* have the jitters

flattern *v/i.* (*hat* / *mit Richtung*: *ist geflattert*) **1.** flutter; (*mit den Flügeln schlagen*) flap its wings; **2.** *Wäsche, Segel etc.*: flap (in the wind); *Blatt, Papier etc.*: flutter; *Haar*: stream; *mir flatterte heute e-e Einladung auf den Tisch fig.* an invitation landed on my desk today; **3.** *Augenlider, Herz, Puls*: flutter; *Hände*: tremble; **4.** *Tech.* flutter; *Räder*: wobble; *Ski*: chatter

Flattersatz *m Druck.* unjustified (*od.* ragged) setting

flattrig *Adj.* → *flatterig*

flau *Adj.* **1.** (*unwohl*) queasy; *mir ist od. wird ganz ~* (*im Magen*) I feel queasy; *ihm wurde ~ vor Angst* he was sick with fear; **2.** *Geschmack, Stimmung*: flat, dull; **3.** *Fot., Negativ*: flat, lacking contrast; **4.** *Wirts. Börse, Geschäft*: slack; **Flauheit** *f*; *nur Sg.* **1.** (*Übelsein*) queasiness; **2.** *Wirts.* slackness; **3.** v *on Geschmack, Stimmung*: dullness

Flaum *m*; *-(e)s, kein Pl. bei Vogel*: down; *bei Baby*: baby (*od.* downy) hair; (*erster Bartwuchs*) down, (peach) fuzz *umg., Brit. auch* bumfluff *umg.*; *auf Früchten*: down, fur; **~bart** *m* downy moustache, *Brit. auch* (bit of) bumfluff *umg.*; **~feder** *f* down(y) feather

flaumig *Adj.* **1.** *Gefieder, Haut*: downy; **2.** *österr.* (*weich*) fluffy

flaumweich *Adj.* soft as down

Flausch *m*; *-(e)s, -e* brushed wool; *synthetisch*: fleece; **flauschig** *Adj.* fleecy

Flausen *Pl. umg.* nonsense *Sg.*, silly ideas; *j-m ~ in den Kopf setzen* put silly ideas into s.o.'s head; *dem werd ich die ~ austreiben* I'll knock all that nonsense out of him, I'll knock some sense into him

Flaute *f*; *-, -n* **1.** *Naut.* calm; *in e-e ~ geraten* be becalmed; **2.** *Wirts. fig.* slack period, bad patch (*auch Sport*); *in der Bauindustrie herrscht ~* the building industry is going through a slack period

fläzen *v/refl. umg. pej.*: *sich aufs od. auf dem Sofa ~* lounge (*od.* sprawl) on the sofa

Flechse *f*; *-, -n* sinew; *Pl. im Fleisch*: gristle; **flechsig** *Adj.* sinewy; *der Braten war total ~* the joint (*Am.* roast) was full of gristle

Flechte *f*; *-, -n* **1.** *Bot.* lichen; **2.** *Med.* eczema; → *auch* **Schuppenflechte**; **3.** *geh.* (*Zopf*) braid

flechten *v/t.*; *flicht, flocht, hat geflochten* **1.** (*Haar*) plait, *Am.* braid; (*Kranz*) bind; (*Korb, Matte*) weave; (*Seil*) twist; *j-m/sich Zöpfe ~* make plaits (*Am.* braids) for s.o. / make o.s. plaits (*Am.* braids); **2.** *hist.*: *j-n aufs Rad ~* break s.o. on the wheel; **3.** *fig.* → *einflechten* 3; **Flechtwerk** *n* **1.** wickerwork; **2.** *Archit., Wand*: wattle and daub

Fleck *m*; *-(e)s, -e* **1.** *von Schmutz*: stain, mark; (*Klecks*) blob; *Tinte*: blot; *kleiner*: spot; *das macht ~e* it stains (*od.* leaves stains); **2.** *auf Haut, Fell*: spot, patch; (*Verletzung, Geburtsmal*) mark; *blauer ~* bruise; **3.** (*Stelle*) spot, place; (*Stück Land*) patch; *blinder/gelber ~ Med., im Auge*: blind/yellow spot; *am falschen ~* in the wrong place; *am falschen ~ sparen fig.* make false econo-

mies; *er hat das Herz auf dem rechten ~ fig.* his heart's in the right place; *ein schöner ~ auf der Landkarte* empty patch on the map, uncharted area; *sich nicht vom ~ rühren* not budge; *rühr dich nicht vom ~!* don't (you) move; *ich krieg den Schrank nicht vom ~* I can't shift (*Am.* budge) this cupboard; *ich komm nicht vom ~* I can't move; (*komme nicht herum*) I can't get about; *fig.* (*komme nicht vorwärts*) I'm not getting anywhere, I'm getting nowhere; *vom ~ weg* (*sofort*) there and then, on the spot; **4.** *fig.* (*Schandfleck*) blemish, blot; *e-n ~ auf der weißen Weste haben* have blotted one's copybook, *Am. etwa* have put another nail in one's coffin; **5.** *Dial.* (*Flicken*) patch

Fleckchen *n* (*Ort*) spot; *ein schönes ~ Erde* a beautiful spot (*größer*: part of the world)

flecken *v/i.* **1.** (*Flecke machen*) stain, make stains; **2.** (*fleckenempfindlich sein*) stain easily

Flecken *m*; *-s, -* **1.** → *Fleck* 1, 2, 4, 5; **2.** (*Dorf*) village; *kleiner*: hamlet; **~entferner** *m* stain remover

flecken|frei *Adj.*, **~los** *Adj.* spotless; *fig. auch* unimpeachable

Fleckenwasser *n* stain remover

Fleckerlteppich *m Dial.* patchwork rug

Fleckfieber *n Med.* (epidemic) typhus

fleckig *Adj.* **1.** *Fell etc.*: spotted; *Gefieder*: speckled; **2.** *Haut*: blotchy; *~ sein Obst*: have spots; **3.** (*befleckt*) stained; *~ machen* stain; *~ werden* stain

Fleck|typhus *m Med.* (epidemic) typhus; **~vieh** *n* spotted cattle

fleddern *v/t.* **1.** *Sl.* (*Wehrlose*) plunder, rob; *Leichen*: rob dead bodies (*od.* corpses); **2.** *umg. hum.* (*Sachen*) help o.s. to

Fleder|maus *f Zool.* bat; **~wisch** *m* feather duster

Fleeceshirt ['fliːsʃøːɐ̯t] *n* fleece shirt

Flegel *m*; *-s, -* **1.** *pej.* (*Lümmel*) lout; **2.** *zum Dreschen*: flail; **~alter** *n pej.* → **Flegeljahre**

Flegelei *f*; *-, -en*; *pej.* loutish behavio(u)r

flegelhaft *Adj. pej.* loutish

Flegeljahre *Pl. pej.*: *in den ~n sein* be at an awkward age

flegeln *v/refl. umg. pej.*: *sich irgendwohin ~* sprawl (about), loll about

flehen *geh. v/i.* beg, plead (*um* for); *zu Gott*: pray; *bei j-m um Hilfe ~* implore (*od.* beg) s.o. to help (one); **Flehen** *n*; *-s, kein Pl.* supplication, entreaty; **flehentlich I.** *Adj. Blick etc.*: imploring, pleading; *~e Bitte* urgent plea; *~es Gebet* fervent prayer; **II.** *Adv.* imploringly, pleadingly; *j-n ~ bitten* implore s.o. (*um* for)

Fleisch *n*; *-(e)s, kein Pl.* **1.** *am Körper*: flesh; *wildes ~ Med.* proud flesh, granulation tissue; *vom ~ fallen umg.* go thin; *stärker*: waste away; *~ werden bibl.* be made flesh; *~ geworden* incarnate; *Menschen von ~ und Blut* flesh and blood, real people; *mein etc. eigen ~ und Blut fig.* my *etc.* own flesh and blood; *in ~ und Blut* (*persönlich*) in the flesh; (*j-m*) *in ~ und Blut übergehen fig.* become second nature (to s.o.); *sich ins eigene ~ schneiden fig.* dig one's own grave; (*sich selbst in etw. reinreiten*) cut off one's nose to spite one's face; → *Fisch* 1, *Pfahl*, *Weg* 2; **2.** *zum Verzehr*: meat; *~ fressend Pflanze, Tier*: carnivorous; *~*

fressende Pflanze *od.* ~ fressendes Tier *auch* carnivore; **3.** *von Früchten*: flesh; **4.** *fig.*: *frisches ~* (*neue Leute*) new blood; *das sündige ~* the flesh; **5.** *Druck.* shoulder; **~abteilung** *f* meat department

fleischarm I. *Adj.* containing little meat; **II.** *Adv.* ~ *essen* eat little meat

Fleisch|beschau *f* **1.** meat inspection; **2.** *umg. hum.* bodywatching; **~beschauer** *m*, **~beschauerin** *f* meat inspector; **~brocken** *m* chunk of meat; **~brühe** *f* **1.** *Gastr., Suppe*: consommé; **2.** *Würfel, Pulver*: (*mst* beef) stock; **~einlage** *f* meat added to soup; **~einwaage** *f* meat content

Fleischer *m*; *-s, -* **1.** butcher; **2.** → *Fleischerei*; **beim ~** at the butcher's

Fleischerbeil *n* meat cleaver

Fleischerei *f*; *-, -en* butcher's shop, *Am. auch* meat market; **~fachverkäufer** *m*, **~fachverkäuferin** *f* specialist meat salesperson

Fleischerhaken *m* meat hook

Fleischerin *f*; *-, -nen* butcher

Fleischer|meister *m*, **~meisterin** *f* master butcher; **~messer** *n* butcher's knife

Fleischeslust *f geh. altm.* carnal lust

Fleischesser *m* meat eater, carnivore *hum.*

fleischfarben, fleischfarbig *Adj.* flesh-colo(u)red

Fleisch|fliege *f Zool.* meat fly; **~fondue** *n Gastr.* meat fondue(e); **~fresser** *m*; *-s, -* carnivore; **~gericht** *n* meat dish; **~hauer** *m*, **~hauerin** *f*; *-, -nen*; *österr.* butcher

fleischig *Adj.* fleshy

Fleisch|käse *m Gastr. etwa* meat loaf; **~klopfer** *m* mallet; **~kloß** *m*, **~klößchen** *n Gastr.* meatball (*for soup*); **~konserven** *Pl.* canned (*bes. Brit. auch* tinned) meat *Sg.*; **~la(i)berl** *n* österr., *Gastr. etwa* meatball

fleischlich *Adj. geh. altm.* **1.** *aus Fleisch*: nachgestellt: comprising meat; **~e Kost/Ernährung** food in the form of meat / meat diet; **2.** *fig.* (*sinnlich*) carnal; **~e Lüste** carnal desires

fleischlos I. *Adj.* **1.** *Kost*: vegetarian; *Tag*: meatless; **2.** (*abgemagert*) emaciated, skinny; **II.** *Adv.*: *sich ~ ernähren* eat no meat

Fleisch|messer *n* carving knife; **~pastete** *f Gastr.* pâté; *größer, mit Teighülle*: meat pie; **~pflanzerl** *n südd., Gastr. etwa* meatball; **~saft** *m* meat juices *Pl.*; **~salat** *m Gastr.* meat salad; **~schaf** *n* mutton sheep; **~spieß** *m* (meat) skewer; **~tomate** *f* beef(steak) tomato; **~ton** *m Kunst*: flesh tint; **~vergiftung** *f* meat poisoning; **~waren** *Pl.* **1.** meat products; **2.** *Supermarktabteilung*: meat department *Sg.*

Fleischwerdung *f bibl.* incarnation

Fleisch|wolf *m* mincer, *Am.* meat grinder; *j-n durch den ~ drehen fig.* (*ausquetschen*) grill s.o., give s.o. the third degree; **~wunde** *f* flesh wound; **~wurst** *f Gastr.* pork sausage; **~zartmacher** *m* (meat) tenderizer

Fleiß *m*; *-es, kein Pl.* **1.** (*Mühe*) hard work, industry; (*Eifer*) application, diligence; *viel ~ verwenden auf* (+ *Akk.*) put a lot of effort (*od.* hard work) into, take great pains over; *mit großem ~ arbeiten* work very diligently; *ohne ~ kein Preis Sprichw.* no pain, no gain, *Brit. auch* you don't get nowt for nowt *umg.*; **2.** *mit od. zum ~ altm. od. Dial.* (*absichtlich*) on purpose, purposely; *ich hab's nicht mit od. zum ~ getan auch* I did-

n't mean to (do it); **~arbeit** f **1.** job requiring hard work; *das war e-e reine ~* he/she *etc.* managed to do it by sheer hard work; (*routinemäßige Arbeit*) it was just a matter of hard work (*od.* application); **2.** *Päd.* (*freiwillige Extraarbeit*) voluntary extra task; **~aufgabe** f *Päd.* voluntary extra task
fleißig I. *Adj.* **1.** *Person*: hard-working, diligent; (*emsig*) busy; *Hände: auch* willing: *ich war gestern sehr ~* I got a lot done yesterday; *Fleißiges Lieschen Bot.* busy Lizzie, *Am.* impatiens; **2.** *Arbeit etc.*: ... showing great application; **3.** *umg.* (*häufig*) *Besucher, Benutzer etc.*: frequent, regular; *Sammler, Spaziergänger*: keen; **II.** *Adv.* **1.** diligently, industriously; *lernen etc.*: hard; **2.** *umg.* (*viel*) *essen etc.*: a lot; (*häufig*) frequently; *etw. ~ benutzen* use s.th. regularly (*od.* all the time); *~ spazieren gehen* do a lot of walking
flektierbar *Adj. Ling.* inflectional; **flektieren I.** *v/t.* inflect; **II.** *v/i.* be inflected; *stark/schwach ~ Verb*: be conjugated as a strong/weak verb
flennen *v/i. umg. pej.* howl; **Flennerei** f; -, -en (constant) howling
fletschen *v/t.*: *die Zähne ~ Tier*: bare its teeth, snarl; *Mensch*: show (*od.* flash) one's teeth, snarl
fleucht *hum.* → *kreucht*
Fleurop® f; -, *kein Pl. etwa* Interflora®
flexibel *Adj. geh.* flexible; *flexible Arbeitszeit* flex(i)time, flexible working hours; *flexibler Wechselkurs* floating exchange rate; **Flexibilität** f; -, *kein Pl.; geh.* flexibility
Flexion f; -, -en; *Ling.* inflection; **Flexionsendung** f *Ling.* inflectional ending; **flexionslos** *Adj. Ling.* uninflected; **Flexionssystem** n *Ling.* inflectional system
flicht *Präs.* → *flechten*
Flickarbeit f *auch pej.* patchwork
flicken *v/t.* **1.** mend; **2.** *umg. fig.* patch up; → *Zeug* 4
Flicken m; -s, - patch; **~decke** f patchwork quilt; **~teppich** m patchwork rug
Flickflack m; -s, -s *Turnen*: backflip
Flick|korb m mending basket, workbasket; **~schuster** m, **~schusterin** f **1.** *altm.* shoe repairer, cobbler; **2.** *fig. pej.* (*Stümper*) bungler; **~schusterei** f *fig. pej.* bungling; *Arbeit(en)*: patch-up job(s *Pl.*); **~werk** n; *nur Sg.; fig. pej.* patch-up job; *stärker*: botch(-up) *umg.*; **~zeug** n sewing kit; *zum Reifenflicken etc.*: repair kit
Flieder m; -s, - **1.** lilac; **2.** *Dial.* (*Holunder*) elder; **~beere** f *Dial.* elderberry
fliederfarben *Adj.* lilac
Flieder|strauch m lilac (bush); **~strauß** m bunch of lilac (blossom)
Fliege f; -, -n **1.** fly; *wie die ~n sterben od. umfallen* go down like flies; *er tut keiner ~ was zuleide fig.* he wouldn't hurt a fly; *zwei ~n mit einer Klappe schlagen fig.* kill two birds with one stone; *die ~ e-e ~ machen umg.* clear off, *Brit. auch* hop it, *Am. auch* vamoose; *mach 'ne ~! umg.* scram!, beat it!; → *Not* 1; **2.** (*Schlips*) bow tie; **3.** (*Bärtchen*) shadow; **4.** *Angeln*: fly; *mit ~n angeln* fly-fish, go fly-fishing
fliegen; *fliegt, flog, geflogen* **I.** *v/i.* (*ist*) **1.** *Vogel, Geschoss, Funken, Blätter etc.*: fly (*durch die Luft* through the air); *in die Höhe od. Luft ~* fly up (into the air); *in die Luft ~* (*explodieren*) blow up; *e-n Drachen etc. ~ lassen* fly a kite *etc.*; *ich kann doch nicht ~ umg.*

I haven't got wings; → *Fetzen* 1, *Funke* 1; **2.** *mit Flugzeug etc.*: fly, go by air (*od.* plane); *wie lange fliegt man nach New York?* how long is the flight to New York?; **3.** *Fahne etc.*: fly, be blowing (*im Wind* in the wind); *Haare*: stream; **4.** *geh. fig.* (*eilen*) fly, rush; *Puls etc.*: race; *ihr Atem flog* her breath came in short gasps, she was panting; *j-m an od. um den Hals ~* hurl o.s. (a)round s.o.'s neck; *ich eile, ich fliege!* hum. I'm coming with the speed of light!; *ein Lächeln flog über ihr Gesicht* a smile flitted across her face; **5.** *umg. fig.* (*fallen*) fall (*von* off, from); (*geworfen werden*) be thrown; (*landen*) land; *auf die Nase ~* fall on one's nose; *aus der Kurve ~* fly off the road on a (*od.* the) curve; *in den Mülleimer ~* land (*od.* end up) in the dustbin (*Am.* garbage can); *in die Ecke ~ Schultasche etc.*: get hurled (*od.* slung) into the corner; **6.** *umg. fig. aus e-r Stellung*: be fired, get the sack; *auch aus der Schule, e-r Wohnung etc.*: be kicked out (*aus od.* von) of; **7.** *umg. fig.*: *durch e-e/die Prüfung ~* fail (*od.* flunk) a/the exam; **8.** *umg. fig.*: *~ auf* (+ *Akk.*) (*begeistert sein von*) really go for, be a sucker for; **II.** *v/t.* (*hat*); (*Flugzeug, Personen etc.*) fly (*nach od. in* + *Akk.* to); **2.** (*hat od. ist*); (*e-e Strecke*) fly, cover; *e-e Kurve ~* fly in a curve; *e-n Angriff/Einsatz ~* make an airborne attack/sortie; **III.** *v/refl.* (*hat*) **1.** *die Maschine fliegt sich gut* the aircraft is good to fly, the machine is airworthy; **2.** *unpers.*: *bei diesem Wetter fliegt es sich schlecht* it's not good to fly in this weather, it's not good flying weather
Fliegen n; -s, *kein Pl.* flying; (*Luftfahrt*) aviation
fliegend I. *Part. Präs.* → *fliegen*; **II.** *Adj.* **1.** flying; *~er Fisch/Hund Zool.* flying fish/fox; *~er Teppich* magic carpet; *~e Untertasse* flying saucer; *~es Personal* flight crew; **2.** *fig.*: *~er Händler* hawker; *~e Blätter Buch*: loose leaves; *~e Achse Tech.* floating axle; *in ~er Eile* in a tearing hurry; *~e Hitze Med.* hot flushes *Pl.* (*Am.* flushes *Pl.*); *mit ~en Fahnen überlaufen* transfer one's allegiance very publicly (*zu* to); *mit ~en Fahnen untergehen* go down with all flags flying
Fliegen|dreck m flies' droppings *Pl.*, *Am.* flyspeck *Sg.*; **~fänger** m flypaper; **~fenster** n fly screen; **~gewicht** n *Boxen*: flyweight; **~gitter** n **1.** *Material*: wire mesh; **2.** *Gestell*: fly screen; **~klatsche** f fly swatter; **~netz** n fly net; **~pilz** m *Bot.* fly agaric; *allg.* (*Giftpilz*) toadstool; **~schwarm** m swarm of flies; **~spray** m, n fly spray
Flieger m; -s, - **1.** (*Pilot*) pilot; *bes. hist.* flyer, aviator; *Mil. auch* airman; *Rang*: *Brit.* aircraftman 2nd class, *Am.* airman basic; *bei den ~n sein umg.* be in the air force; **2.** *Tier*: *guter/schlechter etc. ~* good/poor *etc.* flyer; **3.** *umg.* (*Flugzeug*) plane; *aus Papier*: paper (air)plane; **4.** *Radsport, Pferderennen*: sprinter; **~abzeichen** n *Mil.* (pilot's) wings *Pl.*; **~alarm** m air-raid warning; **~angriff** m air raid, air attack; **~bombe** f airborne bomb
Fliegerei f; -, *kein Pl.* flying
Fliegerhorst m *Mil.* (military) airfield, air base
Fliegerin f; -, -nen (woman) pilot (*bes. hist.* flyer, aviator)
fliegerisch *Adj.* flying, aeronautical; *~e*

Glanzleistung brilliant piece of flying
Flieger|jacke f bomber jacket; **~schule** f flying school; **~sprache** f airman's (*od.* pilot's) slang
fliehen; *flieht, floh, geflohen* **I.** *v/i.* (*ist*) **1.** flee, run away (*vor* + *Dat.*, *aus* from); (*entkommen*) escape; *ins Ausland ~* escape abroad, leave the country; *zu j-m ~* flee to s.o., take refuge with s.o.; **2.** *fig. Zeit*: fly; **II.** *v/t.* (*hat*); *geh.* flee (*od.* escape) from; (*meiden*) shun; **fliehend I.** *Part. Präs.* → *fliehen*; **II.** *Adj.* **1.** *Person*: fleeing, fugitive; **2.** *Kinn, Stirn etc.*: receding
Fliehkraft f *Phys.* centrifugal force
Fliese f; -, -n (wall *od.* floor) tile; *mit ~n auslegen* tile; **fliesen** *v/t.* tile
Fliesen|boden m tiled floor; **~kleber** m tile cement; **~leger** m; -s, -, **~legerin** f; -, -nen tiler
Fließband n assembly (*od.* production) line; (*Förderband*) conveyor belt; *am ~ arbeiten od. stehen umg.* work on the assembly line; *sie produziert die Aufsätze (wie) am ~ fig.* she churns out the essays as if on a conveyor belt; **~arbeit** f assembly-line work; **~arbeiter** m, **~arbeiterin** f assembly-line worker
fließen *v/i.*; *fließt, floss, ist geflossen* **1.** *Blut, Sekt, Tränen, Wasser*: flow; *Fluss, Wasser etc.*: *auch* run (*in* + *Akk.* into; *aus* out of); *in Strömen*: pour, stream; *es ist viel Blut geflossen* there was a lot of bloodshed; **2.** *Verkehr*: flow, run; *durch etw.*: pass; *Gewand, Haar*: flow; **3.** *fig. Rede, Unterhaltung etc.*: flow (easily); *in* (+ *Akk.*) *Gelder etc.*: flow (*od.* pass) into; *reichlich/spärlich ~ Gelder etc.*: pour in / come in a slow trickle; *die Nachrichten flossen spärlich* little news got through; *alles fließt* everything is in (a state of) flux; **fließend I.** *Part. Präs.* → *fließen*; **II.** *Adj.* **1.** flowing; *Wasser*: running; *~es Gewässer* stream of flowing water; *~ Kalt- und Warmwasser* hot and cold running water; **2.** *~er / zäh ~er Verkehr* free-flowing/ /slow-moving traffic; **3.** *fig.* (*unbestimmt*) fluid; *die Grenzen od. Übergänge sind ~* there's no clear(-cut) dividing line (*od.* difference) (*zwischen* + *Dat.* between); **4.** *Stil*: fluent; *in ~em Englisch* in fluent English; **III.** *Adv.* *lesen, sprechen etc.*: fluently; *sie spricht ~ Deutsch* she speaks fluent German
Fließ|heck n *Mot.* fastback; **~komma** n *EDV* floating point; **~papier** n blotting paper; **~text** m *EDV* continuous text
Flimmer m; -s, *kein Pl.; lit.* **1.** shimmer; *von Stern*: twinkle; *von Leuchtschrift etc.*: flicker; **2.** *fig.* glitter; **flimmerfrei** *Adj.* flicker-free
Flimmerhärchen n *Bio.* cilium (*Pl.* cilia)
flimmerig *Adj.* flickering
Flimmerkiste f *umg.* (goggle) box, *Am.* tube
flimmern *v/i.* **1.** (*hat geflimmert*); *Luft, Wasser*: shimmer; *Sterne*: twinkle; *Bildschirm, Bild, Schrift*: flicker; *mir flimmert's vor den Augen* everything's flickering (*od.* dancing) in front of my eyes; **2.** (*hat*); *Herz*: fibrillate; **3.** (*ist*); *umg. fig.*: *über den Bildschirm ~* be shown on our screens
Flimmern n; -s, *kein Pl.* **1.** *Luft, Wasser*: shimmering; *Bildschirm, Bild, Schrift*: flickering; *Sterne*: twinkling; **2.** *Med., Herz*: fibrillation; *ein ~ vor*

F

den Augen (a) flickering in front of one's eyes

flink *Adj.* **1.** quick, agile; *Finger*: nimble; **er ist ~ wie ein Wiesel** he's a real speedy Gonzalez *umg.*; **2.** (*aufgeweckt*) bright, alert; **3.** *Zunge etc.*: rapid; **ein ~es Mundwerk haben** talk nineteen to the dozen; **Flinkheit** *f*; *nur Sg.* **1.** quickness, agility; *von Fingern*: nimbleness; **2.** (*Aufgewecktheit*) brightness, alertness; **3.** *von Zunge*: rapidity

Flinte *f*; -, -n shotgun; *weitS.* gun; **er schießt (auf) alles, was ihm vor die ~ kommt** he shoots everything that comes in his sights; **die ~ ins Korn werfen** *fig.* give up, throw in the towel

Flipchart ['flɪptʃaːɐt] *n*; -s, -s flipchart

flippen *v/i. Sl.* → *ausflippen*

Flipper *m*; -s, -, **~automat** *m* pinball machine; **flippern** *v/i. umg.* play pinball

flippig *Adj. umg.* **1.** *Kleidung etc.*: way-out; **2.** (*unstet*) flighty

flirren *v/i. geh.* **1.** whirr, *Am.* whir; (*surren*) buzz, hum; **2.** *Licht*: shimmer

Flirt [flœɐt] *m*; -s, -s **1.** *Handlung*: flirtation; **2.** *Person*: flirt; **flirten** ['flœɐtn] *v/i.* flirt (around)

Flittchen *n*; -s, -; *umg. pej.* floozie *altm.*, (bit of a) tart

Flitter *m*; -s, - **1.** *Koll.* sequins *Pl.*; **2.** *fig. pej.* glänzend: glitter; *billig*: tinsel; **~kram** *m pej.* frippery

flittern *v/i. umg. hum.* honeymoon; **Flitterwochen** *Pl.* (*mst* one's) honeymoon *Sg.*

Flitz(e)bogen *m umg.* bow (and arrow); **ich bin gespannt wie ein ~** *fig.* I can't wait to find out *etc.*

flitzen *v/i. umg.* **1.** flit, scoot; *Auto*: shoot; **2.** (*abhauen*) flit, beat it; **3.** *nackt*: streak

Flitzer[1] *m*; -s, -; *Mot. umg.* nippy little car, *Am.* sportster

Flitzer[2] *m*; -s, -, **~in** *f*; -, -nen; *umg. nackt*: streaker

floaten ['floːtn] *v/i. Wirts.* float; **Floating** ['floːtɪŋ] *n*; -s, -s floating

flocht *Imperf.* → *flechten*

Flöckchen *n* little flake; *von Staub, Flaum*: little bit of fluff

Flocke *f*; -, -n *Schnee, Hafer, Butter, Seife*: flake; *Wolle*: flock; *Staub, Feder, Flaum*: ball of fluff; **flocken** *v/i. geh.* flake; *Chem.* flocculate; **flockig** *Adj.* fluffy

flog *Imperf.* → *fliegen*

floh *Imperf.* → *fliehen*

Floh *m*; -s, Flöhe **1.** *Zool.* flea; **j-m e-n ~ ins Ohr setzen** *fig.* put an idea into s.o.'s head; **(e-n Sack) Flöhe hüten ist leichter** *umg.* climbing Everest would be simple in comparison; **er hört die Flöhe husten** *umg. fig.* he's forever imagining things; **2.** *Pl. umg.* (*Geld*) dough *Sg.*, *Brit. auch* readies; **~biss** *m* fleabite

flöhen I. *v/t.* deflea, remove fleas from; **II.** *v/refl.* deflea o.s. (*od.* itself), get rid of one's (*od.* its) fleas

Floh|halsband *n* flea collar; **~markt** *m* flea market; **~pulver** *n* flea powder; **~zirkus** *m* flea circus

Flokati *m*; -s, -s flokati (rug)

Flom(en) *m*; -s, *kein Pl.*; *nordd.* lard

Flop *m*; -s, -s **1.** *umg.* flop; **sich als ~ erweisen** *od.* **zum ~ werden** turn out (to be) a flop; **2.** *Hochsprung*: Fosbury flop; **floppen** *v/i.* **1.** (*ist gefloppt*) *umg.* (*scheitern*) flop, be a flop; **2.** (*ist od. hat*) *Hochsprung*: perform the Fosbury flop

Floppydisk *f*; -, -s, **Floppy Disk** *f*; -, -

-s; *EDV* floppy (disk)

Flor[1] *m*; -s, -e, *mst Sg.*; *geh.* **1.** (*Blüte*) bloom; (*Blumenfülle*) mass of flowers (*od.* blossoms); **2.** *fig. von Damen*: bevy

Flor[2] *m*; -s, -e **1.** *auf Samt, Teppich*: pile; **2.** (*dünnes Gewebe*) gauze; **3.** (*Trauerflor*) black crepe (band)

Flora *f*; -, Floren flora (*Pl.* -s *od.* florae); **~ und Fauna** flora and fauna

Florentiner[1] *m*; -s, - **1.** *Hut*: picture hat; **2.** *Gastr.* florentine; **II.** *Adj.* Florentine

Florentiner[2] *m*; -s, -, **~in** *f*; -, -nen Florentine

Florenz (*n*); *Florenz'*; *Geog.* Florence

Florett *n*; -(e)s, -e foil; **~fechten** *n* foil fencing

Florfliege *f Zool.* green lacewing

florieren *v/i.* flourish, prosper, thrive

Florist *m*; -en, -en, **~in** *f*; -, -nen **1.** *Beruf*: florist; **2.** (*Kenner e-r Flora*) expert on the flora (of a region)

Floskel *f*; -, -n; *pej.* meaningless phrase, cliché; *Pl. auch* (empty) words; **floskelhaft** *Adj. pej.* meaningless; (*stereotyp*) stereotyped; **ein ~er Ausdruck** *auch* a cliché

floss *Imperf.* → *fließen*

Floß *n*; -es, Flöße **1.** raft; **2.** *Angeln*: float

Flosse *f*; -, -n **1.** fin; *Wal, Seelöwe etc.*: flipper (*auch Sportgerät*); **2.** *Flug.* stabilizer fin; **3.** *umg. pej.* (*Hand*) paw; **4.** *umg. pej.* (*Fuß*) **~n weg!** hands off!; **zieh d-e ~n ein!** keep your feet to yourself

flößen *v/t.* float

Flossenfüß(l)er *m*; -s, -; *Zool.* pinniped

Flößer *m*; -s, - raftsman; **Flößerin** *f*; -, -nen raftswoman

Floßfahrt *f* trip by raft

Flöte *f*; -, -n **1.** (*Querflöte etc.*) flute; (*Blockflöte*) recorder; (*Pfeife*) whistle; (*Rohrflöte*) pipe; (*Panflöte*) pan pipes *Pl.*; **~ spielen** play the flute *etc.*; **2.** *Glas*: champagne flute; **3.** *Kartenspiel*: flush

flöten I. *v/t./i.* **1.** play the flute (*od.* recorder); (*pfeifen*) whistle; **2.** *Vogel*: sing, warble; **3.** *umg. fig.* say in a honeyed voice (*od.* in honeyed tones); **II.** *v/i. umg. fig.*: **~ gehen** *Pläne etc.*: go by the board; *Geld*: go down the drain; (*kaputtgehen*) go for a burton, *Am.* go kaput; **m-e Hoffnungen sind ~ gegangen** that's put paid to my hopes

Flöten|spieler *m*, **~spielerin** *f* flute-player, flautist, *Am. auch* flutist; **~ton** *m* note of a flute; **Flötentöne** the sound of a flute (*od.* flutes); **j-m (die) Flötentöne beibringen** *umg. fig.* show s.o. what's what

Flötist *m*; -en, -en, **~in** *f*; -, -nen; *Mus.* flute-player, flautist, *Am. auch* flutist

flott *umg.* **I.** *Adj.* **1.** (*schnell*) fast; (*schwungvoll*) lively; (*reibungslos*) smooth; **jetzt aber ~!** get a move on!; **~er Absatz** *Wirts.* brisk trading; **ein ~es Leben führen** live a life in the fast lane; **in ~em Tempo** at a fast (*od.* smart, sprightly) pace; **den ~en Otto haben** *hum.* have the runs; **2.** (*schick*) smart; (*nett, hübsch*) *Mädchen etc.*: captivating; (*unbekümmert*) bubbly, breezy; *Tänzer*: stylish; **3.** (*wieder*) ~ **machen** *od.* **bekommen/sein** (*Schiff*) refloat/be afloat; (*Auto etc.*) get/be going (again); *fig.* (*Geschäft*) put/be back on its feet (again); **II.** *Adv.* **1.** fast; (*glatt, reibungslos*) smoothly, without a hitch; **~ spielen** *Mus.* play very lively

music; **~ leben** lead a fast life; **es geht ihm ~ von der Hand** he's very quick (at it); **es geht ~ voran** things are going very well; **das Geschäft geht ~** business is brisk; **~ geschrieben** (*od.* **gemacht** *etc.*) punchy; **das ging ja ~!** that was quick work, you made short work of that; **2.** (*schick*) smartly

Flotte *f*; -, -n; *Naut.* fleet

Flotten|parade *f* naval review; **~stützpunkt** *m* naval base; **~verband** *m* naval formation

Flottille [flɔ'tɪljə] *f*; -, -n; *Naut., Mil.* flotilla; **Flottillenadmiral** *m* rear admiral

flottweg *Adv. umg.* quickly; (*ohne Unterbrechung*) nonstop

Flöz *m*; -es, -e; *Geol. und Bergb.* seam

Fluch *m*; -(e)s, Flüche **1.** curse (**über** + *Akk.* about); (*Kraftausdruck*) swearword; **heftige Flüche ausstoßen** utter fierce oaths, swear furiously; **2.** (*Verwünschung, Plage*) curse; **mit e-m ~ belegen** *od.* **e-n ~ aussprechen gegen** put a curse on; **ein ~ liegt** *od.* **lastet auf ihm** there's a curse on him; **unter e-m ~ stehen** be under a curse; **der ~ der bösen Tat** the wages of evil; **zum ~ für die Menschheit werden** become the bane of humanity; **fluchbeladen** *Adj. geh.* ill-omened; **fluchen** *vt./i.* curse, swear; **~ auf** *od.* **über** (+ *Akk.*) curse; **~ wie ein Bierkutscher** *etc.* swear like a trooper

Flucht[1] *f*; -, -en, *mst Sg.* **1.** flight (**aus** *od.* **vor** + *Dat.* from); **erfolgreiche**: escape; **auf der ~** while fleeing; *Gefangener*: while attempting to escape, on the run; **die ~ ergreifen** flee (**vor** + *Dat.* from), run away (from); **in die ~ schlagen** put s.o. to flight; **in wilder ~** fleeing headlong; **j-m zur ~ verhelfen** help s.o. to escape; **2.** *fig.* escape; **das ist die ~ vor der Verantwortung** that's trying to evade responsibility; **er versuchte es mit der ~ in den Alkohol** he tried to take refuge in alcohol, he turned to drink (as a refuge); **die ~ in die Öffentlichkeit antreten** go public, make a statement *etc.*; **die ~ nach vorn antreten** take the bull by the horns; **wir müssen die ~ nach vorn antreten** *auch* attack is the best means of defen|ce (*Am.* -se)

Flucht[2] *f*; -, -en **1.** *geh. von Zimmern*: suite; *von Häusern, Fenstern*: row; *von Treppen*: flight; **2.** *Archit., Tech.* straight line

fluchtartig I. *Adj.* hasty, hurried; **II.** *Adv.* in a hurry; **e-n Ort ~ verlassen** *auch* make a quick getaway (*od.* beat a hasty retreat) from a place

Flucht|auto *n* getaway car; **~bewegung** *f* tide of refugees; **~burg** *f hist.* refuge

flüchten *v/i.* (*ist geflüchtet*) *und v/refl.* (*hat*) flee (**vor** + *Dat.* from); (*weglaufen*) run away; *mit Erfolg*: escape (*auch fig.*); **über die Grenze / ins Ausland ~** flee across the border / flee the country; (*sich*) **zu j-m ~** take refuge with s.o.; (*sich*) **~ in** (+ *Akk.*) take refuge in; *fig. auch* resort to, turn to ... (as a refuge)

Flucht|fahrzeug *n* getaway vehicle; **~gefahr** *f* danger of an escape attempt (*Jur.* of absconding); **es besteht ~ bei j-m** s.o. is likely to make an escape attempt; **~geschwindigkeit** *f Phys.* speed required to overcome gravitational pull, escape velocity; **~helfer** *m*, **~helferin** *f Pol.* helper in escape; (*Schlepper*) people smuggler *umg.*;

~hilfe f escape aid; **j-m ~ bieten** offer to help s.o. to escape

flüchtig I. Adj. **1.** (entflohen) escaped, fugitive; **~ sein** Verbrecher: be on the run, be at large; **~ werden** Jur. abscond; **~er Schuldner** runaway (Jur. absconding) debtor; **2.** (eilig) quick, hurried; Augenblick, Eindruck: fleeting; Bekanntschaft, Bemerkung: passing; Besuch: brief, flying; Blick: cursory; Gruß, Kuss: perfunctory; Vorstellung: vague, hazy; **j-m e-n ~en Besuch machen** pay s.o. a brief visit, drop in on s.o.; **~er Einblick** glimpse (**in** + Akk. of); **3.** (oberflächlich) superficial; (schlampig) Arbeit etc.: hurried; stärker: slapdash; **4.** Chem., EDV volatile; **II.** Adv. quickly, hurriedly; sehen: fleetingly; besuchen: briefly; erwähnen etc.: in passing; **~ durchlesen** read cursorily, skim over, scan; **~ mit j-m bekannt sein** know s.o. slightly; **~ arbeiten** work in a slapdash manner; **Flüchtige** m, f; -n, -n fugitive, runaway; **Flüchtigkeit** f **1.** nur Sg.; (Vergänglichkeit) fleeting nature; von Bekanntschaft: passing nature; von Besuch: briefness; von Blick: cursoriness; von Gruß, Kuss: perfunctoriness; von Vorstellung: vagueness; **2.** nur Sg.; (Oberflächlichkeit) superficiality; e-r Arbeit: slapdash nature; **3.** Fehler: careless mistake, slip; **4.** nur Sg.; Chem. volatility

Flüchtigkeitsfehler m careless mistake, slip

Flüchtling m; -s, -e refugee

Flüchtlings|ausweis m refugee's identity card; **~elend** n refugees' hardship; **~lager** n refugee camp; **~schiff** n refugee ship; **~strom** m stream of refugees; Welle: tide of refugees; **~treck** m refugees' long march; **~welle** f tide of refugees

Flucht|linie f Archit. alignment; Opt. vanishing line; **~punkt** m Opt. vanishing point; **~verdacht** m suspicion of an escape attempt; **es besteht ~** it is suspected that there will be an escape attempt; **~verhalten** n Zool. flight response; **~versuch** m escape (aus dem Gefängnis: auch breakout) attempt, attempted escape; **e-n ~ unternehmen** attempt to escape; **~weg** m escape route

Flug m; -(e)s, Flüge **1.** flight; allg. (das Fliegen) auch flying; **im ~** Vogel: in flight; **den Ball im ~ auffangen** catch the ball in the air; **2.** fig.: die Woche verging wie im ~(e) went by very quickly (od. in a flash, in no time), just flew by; **3.** Skispringen: jump; **e-n ~ sicher stehen** land a jump safely; **4.** Jägerspr. (Gruppe von Vögeln) flock; **~abfertigung** f clearing of flights for take-off; **~abkommen** n air traffic agreement; **~abwehr** f Mil. air defen|ce (Am. -se)

Flugabwehr|... im Subst. Mil. anti-aircraft ...; **~kanone** f (abgek. **Flak**) anti-aircraft gun

Flug|angst f fear of flying; **~apparat** m hist. flying machine; **~asche** f flue ash; **~bahn** f trajectory; Flugzeug: flight path; **~ball** m Sport volley; **~begleiter** m, **~begleiterin** f flight attendant; **~benzin** n Flug. aviation fuel (Am. auch gasoline)

flugbereit Adj. ready for take-off

Flug|betrieb m Flug. air traffic; **~bild** n Orn. flight silhouette

Flugblatt n leaflet; **~aktion** f leafleting campaign

Flug|boot n Flug. flying boat; **~datenschreiber** m flight recorder, black box; **~dauer** f flying time; **~dichte** f air traffic density, volume of air traffic; **~drachen** m Sportgerät: hang glider; **~echse** f pterosaurian; **~eigenschaften** Pl. flying characteristics

Flügel m; -s, - **1.** Tier: wing; **mit den ~n schlagen** flap (größerer Vogel: beat) its wings; **e-m Vogel** / fig.: **j-m die ~ stutzen** od. **beschneiden** clip a bird's / s.o.'s wings; **die ~ hängen lassen** fig. lose heart, be down in the mouth; **auf den ~n der Fantasie** fig. on the wings of fantasy; **die Angst verlieh ihr ~** geh. fig. fear lent her wings; **2.** Flugzeug: wing; Propeller, Schiffsschraube, Ventilator: blade; Windmühle: sail; Bot. wing, side petal; **3.** fig. Gebäude: wing; Fenster: casement; Flügeltür: door, panel; Altar: wing, panel; Nase: nostril; **der linke/rechte ~ der Lunge** left/right lung; **4.** Mil. flank; Sport und Pol.: wing; **über die ~ angreifen/spielen** attack/play down the wings; **5.** Musikinstrument: grand piano; **am ~: Elisabeth Platzer** with Elisabeth Platzer at the piano; **zur Begleitung:** auch accompanied by Elisabeth Platzer

Flügel|altar m winged altarpiece; **dreiteiliger ~** triptych; **~decke** f Zool. wing case, elytron; **~fenster** n casement window; **~frau** f → **Flügelmann**; **~horn** n Mus. flugelhorn; **~kampf** m Pol. factional dispute (auch Pl. infighting); **~klappe** f Flug. wing flap

flügel|lahm Adj. **1.** Vogel: broken-winged; Ente: auch lame; **~er Vogel** auch bird with a broken wing; **2.** fig. (mutlos) dejected; (ohne Schwung) limp, weary; Unternehmen: ailing; **er ist ~** auch the fizz has gone out of him; **~los** Adj. wingless

Flügel|mann m **1.** Sport winger; **2.** Pol. member of one wing of a party; **linker/rechter ~** left-/right-winger; **~schlag** m flapping (od. beating) of wings; **~schraube** f Tech. wing bolt; **~spanne** f, **~spannweite** f wingspan; **~spitze** f wing tip; **~stürmer** m, **~stürmerin** f Sport winger; **~tür** f double door(s Pl.)

Flug|ente f Gastr. wild duck; **~erfahrung** f flying experience

flugfähig Adj. **1.** Vogel: able to fly; **2.** Flug. (einsatzbereit) airworthy

Flugfeld n Flug. airfield

Fluggast m Flug. (air) passenger; **~abfertigung** f passenger clearance; (Schalter) check-in desk

flügge Adj. Vogel: (fully) fledged; fig. Person: independent; **~ werden** fledge; fig. begin to stand on one's own two feet

Flug|gepäck n Flug. (air) passenger luggage (Am. auch baggage); **~gerät** n **1.** Mil. Koll. (military) aircraft; **2.** Sportgerät: flying machine; **~geschwindigkeit** f flying speed; Vogel: speed of flight; **~gesellschaft** f airline (company), carrier

Flughafen m Flug. airport; **~bereich** m airport area; **im ~** in the airport and the immediate neighbo(u)rhood; in Flughafennähe: in the vicinity of the airport; **~bus** m airport (shuttle) bus; **~gebühr** f auch Pl. airport tax; **~gelände** n airport (area); **das alte ~** the old airport site; **~nähe** f: **in ~** near (od. in the vicinity of) the (od. an) airport; **~polizei** f airport security Sg. (V. mst im Pl.); **~restaurant** n airport restaurant; **~steuer** f airport tax; **~verwaltung** f airport authority

Flug|halle f Flug. hangar; **~haut** f Zool. flying membrane, patagium fachspr.; **~höhe** f Flug. (flying) altitude; **in e-r ~ von** ... (flying) at an altitude of ...; **~hörnchen** n Zool. flying squirrel; **~hund** m Zool. flying fox; **~ingenieur** m, **~ingenieurin** f Flug. flight engineer; **~kapitän** m (flight) captain; **~kilometer** Pl. e-s Flugzeugs: mileage (covered); e-s Flugkapitäns etwa flying hours; e-s Passagiers: air miles; **er hat mehr als eine Million ~ hinter sich** Pilot, Passagier: he has flown more than 600,000 miles

flugklar Adj. ready (od. clear) for take-off

Flug|komfort m in-flight amenities Pl. (od. service); **~körper** m (Raumfahrzeug) space vehicle; (Geschoss) projectile; **~lärm** m Flug. noise of aircraft taking off and landing; allg. aircraft noise; **~lehrer** m, **~lehrerin** f flying instructor; **~leiter** m, **~leiterin** f air traffic control(l)er; **~leitung** f air traffic control; **~linie** f **1.** Gesellschaft: airline (company), carrier; **2.** Strecke: (air) route; **3.** (Flugbahn) flight path; **~loch** n für Bienen, Tauben etc.: entrance hole; **~lotse** m, **~lotsin** f Flug. air traffic control(l)er; **~nummer** f flight number; **~objekt** n: **unbekanntes ~** unidentified flying object, UFO; **~passagier** m, **~passagierin** f (air) passenger; **~personal** n crew; **~plan** m (flight) schedule, timetable; **~platz** m airfield; großer: airport; **~praxis** f flying experience; **~preis** m (air) fare; **~reise** f journey by air; **~reisende** m, f air travel(l)er; (Passagier) (air) passenger; **~reservierung** f flight reservation; **~route** f air route

flugs Adv. altm. swiftly; (sofort) at once, instantly

Flug|sand m drifting (od. windborne) sand; **~saurier** m Zool. pterosaurian; **~schalter** m Flug. flight desk; **~schanze** f Sport (ski) jump, jumping hill (for ski-flying); **~schau** f Flug. air show (od. display); **~schein** m **1.** (air od. flight) ticket; **2.** (Pilotenschein) pilot's licen|ce (Am. -se); **~schneise** f (airport) flight path; für den Anflug: approach corridor; **~schreiber** m flight recorder, black box; **~schrift** f leaflet, pamphlet; **~schüler** m, **~schülerin** f trainee pilot; **~sicherheit** f air safety; **~sicherung** f air traffic control; **~simulator** m flight simulator; **~sport** m pleasure flying; als Wettbewerb: competitive flying; **~steig** m (airport) gate; (Gang zum Flugzeug) air bridge, Jetway®; **~strecke** f (air) route; zurückgelegte: distance flown (od. covered); (Etappe) leg (of a [od. the] flight); **~stunde** f **1.** Strecke, Zeit: hour's flying; **fünf ~n entfernt sein** be five hours away by air, be a five-hour flight (away); **nach zwei ~n waren wir da** we arrived after a two-hour flight; **2.; 3.** (Unterricht) flying lesson; **~tag** m flying day

flugtauglich Adj. Pilot: fit to fly; Flugzeug: airworthy

Flug|technik f Flug. **1.** Tech., Theorie: aeronautics Pl. (V. im Sg.); Praxis: aeronautical (od. aircraft) engineering; **2.** des Piloten: flying technique; **~ticket** n (air od. flight) ticket

flugtüchtig Adj. Pilot: fit to fly; Flugzeug: airworthy

Flug|überwachung f air traffic con-

F

trol; **~unterbrechung** f stopover

flugunfähig Adj. Pilot: unable to fly; Flugzeug: not airworthy; Vogel: flightless

Flug|verbindung f air connection, air service; **gibt es e-e (direkte) ~?** can you fly there (direct od. nonstop)?; **~verbot** n ban on flying; für Flugzeug: grounding order; **~ erhalten** be grounded; **~verkehr** m air traffic; planmäßiger: air services Pl.; **der ~ nimmt ab/nimmt zu** the volume of air traffic is decreasing/increasing; **~versuch** m 1. e-s Jungvogels etc.: attempt to fly; 2. Flug. test flight; **~wesen** n aeronautics Pl. (V. im Sg.); mit Flugzeugen: aviation; **~zeit** f flying time; **wie ist die ~ nach X?** how long is the flight to X?; **~zettel** m österr. leaflet

Flugzeug n Flug. (aero)plane, Am. (air)plane; auch Pl. Koll. aircraft; **~absturz** m air (od. plane) crash; **~abwehr** f Mil. anti-aircraft defen|ce (Am. -se); **~bau** m aircraft construction; **~besatzung** f aircrew; **~entführer** m, **~entführerin** f hijacker, bes. Am. auch skyjacker; **~entführung** f hijacking, bes. Am. auch skyjacking; **~führer** m, **~führerin** f Flug; zweiter **~** co-pilot; **~halle** f (aircraft) hangar; **~katastrophe** f air disaster; **~modell** n model aeroplane (Am. airplane); **~träger** m Naut., Mil. aircraft carrier; **~typ** m type of aircraft; **~unglück** n air crash, air accident; **~wrack** n wreckage of an (od. the) aeroplane (Am. airplane), wrecked aircraft

Flugziel n (flight) destination

Fluidum n; -s, Fluida; geh. aura; e-s Orts, Gebäudes etc.: auch atmosphere

Fluktuation f; -, -en; geh. fluctuation; im Personal: turnover; **fluktuieren** v/i. geh. fluctuate

Flummi m; -es, -s bouncing rubber ball, springball

Flunder f; -, -n; Zool. flounder

Flunkerei f; -, -en; umg. 1. (tall) story, Koll. (tall) stories Pl.; 2. nur Sg; Handlung: storytelling; (Prahlerei) bragging; **flunkern** v/i. umg. tell (tall) stories; (prahlen) brag

Flunsch m; -es, -e; umg. pout; **e-n ~ machen od. ziehen** pull a face, pout

Fluor n; -s, kein Pl.; Chem. fluorine; als Trinkwasserzusatz etc.: fluoride; **~chlorkohlenwasserstoff** m Chem. (abgek. FCKW) chlorofluorocarbon, CFC

Fluoreszenz f; -, kein Pl.; Chem. fluorescence; **fluoreszieren** v/i. fluoresce, be fluorescent

Fluorid n; -s, -e; Chem. fluoride

Fluortablette f Pharm. fluoride tablet

Flur¹ m; -(e)s, -e; (Eingangsraum) hall(way); (Gang) corridor; **auf dem ~** in the hall

Flur² f; -, -en 1. geh. open fields Pl.; (Wiesen) meadows Pl., meadowland; **durch Wald und ~** through woods and meadows; **allein auf weiter ~ sein** fig. be on one's own, be all alone (with no one to turn to); 2. Agr. (Land) village land(s Pl.) (divided into small parcels); **die ~ bereinigen** reallocate parcels of land to form larger, more economic holdings; **~bereinigung** f 1. land reallocation and consolidation; 2. fig. settling of disputes, smoothing over of difficulties

Flurgarderobe f hall stand

Flur|grenze f boundary of village lands; **~name** m field name; **~schaden** m auch Pl. crop damage

Flurtür f front door, flat (Am. apartment) door

Fluse f; -, -n; nordd. bit of fluff; Pl. fluff

Fluss m; -es, Flüsse 1. river; **am ~ Haus** etc.: by (od. on) the river; Stadt: on the river; 2. nur Sg.; (das Fließen) flow(ing); fig. der Rede, des Verkehrs etc.: flow; **im ~** in (a state of) flux; **etw. in ~ bringen** get s.th. going (od. under way); **in ~ kommen** get going, get under way, get into its stride

flussab(wärts) Adv. downstream, downriver

Fluss|arm m branch of a (od. the) river; **~auen** Pl. river meadows

flussauf(wärts) Adv. upstream, upriver

Fluss|bett n riverbed; **~biegung** f bend in the river

Flüsschen n little river, Am.auch creek

Fluss|dampfer m riverboat; **~delta** n river delta; **~diagramm** n flowchart; **~ebene** f flood plain, fluvial plain; **~fahrt** f river trip; **~fisch** m river (od. freshwater) fish

flüssig I. Adj. 1. liquid; (geschmolzen) molten, melted; **~ machen/werden** liquefy; (schmelzen) melt; **~es Brot** hum. liquid (od. beery) sustenance; 2. Wirts., Kapital etc.: liquid, available; **~ machen** mobilize; (Vermögen) realize; **ich bin im Moment nicht ~** umg. I'm broke at the moment; **wenn er wieder ~ ist** umg. when he's in funds (od. he's liquid) again; 3. fig. Stil etc.: fluent, flowing; Mus., Spiel: smooth; **~er Verkehr** free-flowing traffic; **II.** Adv. 1. in liquid form; **er muss ~ ernährt werden** he can only take fluids; 2. fig. lesen, sprechen etc.: fluently; **~ laufen** Verkehr etc.: flow freely; **das Buch liest sich ~** the book reads well

Flüssig|ei n liquid egg; **~gas** n liquid gas

Flüssigkeit f 1. liquid, fluid; **viel ~ zu sich nehmen** drink plenty of liquids (od. fluids); 2. nur Sg.; Zustand: liquidity; 3. nur Sg.; fig. des Stils: fluency, flow; Mus., des Spiels: smoothness; des Verkehrs: free flow

Flüssigkeits|bedarf m fluids requirement; **~grad** m liquidity; Chem. viscosity; **~haushalt** m des Körpers: fluids balance

Flüssig|kristallanzeige f liquid crystal display, LCD; **~seife** f liquid soap

Fluss|insel f river island, Brit. auch eyot; **~krebs** m Zool. (freshwater) crayfish, Am. auch crawfish, crawdad; **~landschaft** f 1. Geog., Landschaftsform: fluvial topography; 2. konkret: countryside through which a (od. the) river flows; 3. Kunst: riverscape; **~lauf** m course of a (od. the) river; **~mündung** f mouth (of a od. the river), estuary; **~niederung** f flood plain; **~pferd** n Zool. hippopotamus; **~regulierung** f river regulation; **~säure** f Chem. hydrofluoric acid; **~schiff** n Naut. riverboat; **~schifffahrt** f Naut. river navigation; Boote: river traffic; **~spat** m Geol. fluorite, fluorspar; **~tal** n river valley; **~ufer** n river bank, riverside

Flüsterer m; -s, -, **Flüsterin** f; -, -nen (male/female) whisperer

flüstern vt/i. (speak in a) whisper; **wir verständigten uns ~d** we communicated in whispers; **j-m etw. ins Ohr ~** whisper s.th. into s.o.'s ear; **dem werd ich was ~** umg. fig. I'll give him something to think about; **das kann ich dir ~!** umg. fig. you can take that from me

Flüstern n; -s, kein Pl. whisper(ing); **ein ~** a whisper, (some) whispering

Flüster|parole f rumo(u)r; **~propaganda** f whispering campaign; **~ton** m: **im ~** in a whisper; **~tüte** f umg. hum. megaphone; **~witz** m secretly circulating (anti-government) joke

Flut f; -, -en 1. (Ggs. Ebbe) (high) tide; **die ~ kommt/geht** the tide is coming in / going out; **es ist ~** it is high tide; **mit der ~ einlaufen** come in on the tide; → Ebbe; 2. (Wogen) waves Pl.; (Wassermassen) waters Pl.; (Überschwemmung) flood; **in den ~en versinken** disappear beneath the waves; **sich in die ~en stürzen** hum. plunge into the water; 3. fig. von Tränen: flood; von Leuten: (great) crowd, horde; von Flüchtlingen: flood, stream; von Worten: torrent, stream; von Protesten: flood, avalanche; **mit e-r ~ von Zuschriften überschüttet werden** be inundated with letters; **e-e ~ von Schimpfwörtern ergoss sich über ihn** a torrent of abuse rained down on him

fluten I. v/i. (ist geflutet) 1. flood, surge; Licht: stream, pour; 2. fig. Menschen: pour; Verkehr: auch stream; **II.** v/t. (hat) flood

Flut|grenze f high-water mark; **~katastrophe** f flood disaster

Flutlicht n floodlights Pl.; **bei ~** floodlit, under floodlight; **~anlage** f floodlights Pl., floodlighting

Flut|linie f, **~marke** f high-water mark

flutschen v/i. umg. 1. (ist geflutscht) slip; **es ist mir aus der Hand geflutscht** it just slipped out of my hand; 2. (hat); fig. Arbeit: go very well; **es flutscht nur so** it's (od. things are) going like clockwork; **es flutscht nicht recht** things won't go right, it's hard going

Flut|warnung f flood warning; **~welle** f tidal wave

f-Moll n Mus. F minor

focht Imperf. → fechten

Fock f; -, -en; Naut. foremast; **~mast** m foremast; **~segel** n foresail

Föderalismus m; -, kein Pl.; Pol. federalism; **föderalistisch** Adj. federalist; Staatsaufbau etc.: federal; **Föderation** f; -, -en federation; **föderativ** Adj. federal

Fohlen n; -s, -; Zool. foal; männliches: auch colt; weibliches: auch filly; **fohlen** v/i. foal

Föhn m; -(e)s, -e 1. Gerät: (hand) hair dryer; 2. nur Sg.; Wind: foehn, föhn; **bei ~** when the foehn (od. föhn) is blowing; **heute haben wir ~** we've got the foehn (od. föhn) today; **föhnen** v/t. (Haar) blow-dry; **j-n/sich ~** blow-dry s.o.'s/one's hair; **Föhnfrisur** f blow-dry hairstyle; **föhnig** Adj. foehn ..., föhn ...; **Föhnwetter** n foehn (od. föhn) weather

Föhre f; -, -n; Bot. Scots pine (tree)

Fokus m; -, -se; Opt. focus; **fokussieren I.** v/t. Opt. focus; **II.** v/i. Med.: **schlecht ~ können** have difficulty in focus(s)ing

Folge f; -, -n 1. (Ergebnis) consequence; direkt: result; (Wirkung) auch effect; ernste, e-s Krieges etc.: aftermath; Med. aftereffect; **logische ~** natural consequence, logical outcome; auch Philos. corollary; **üble ~n haben od. nach sich ziehen** have (unpleasant) consequences; **die ~n tragen**

od. **auf sich nehmen** bear the consequences; **ohne ~n bleiben** have no consequences; **die ~n blieben nicht aus** it wasn't without (its) consequences; **zur ~ haben** result in, lead to; **als ~ davon** as a result; **die ~ war, dass ...** the result(*od.* outcome, upshot) was that ...; **sie starb an den ~n des Unfalls** she died as a result of the accident; **2.** (*Abfolge*) succession; *Zusammengehöriges*: sequence (*auch* Math.); *von Spielkarten*: *auch* run; (*Reihenfolge*) order; (*Reihe, Serie*) series; **in ~** (*nacheinander*) in succession, in a row; **sechs Siege in ~** *auch* a sequence of six victories; **in rascher ~** in rapid succession; → **zwanglos** 1; **3.** (*Fortsetzung*) *e-s Romans etc.*: instal(l)ment; *e-r Fernsehreihe*: part; *e-s Dramas*: episode; (*bes. zweiter Teil*) sequel; (*Heft, Ausgabe*) number, issue; **in mehreren ~n** in instal(l)ments; **4.** *Amtsspr.*: **~ leisten** *e-m Gesuch*: grant; → **folgen¹** 6

Folge|erscheinung *f* consequence; *Med.* aftereffect; **~jahr** *n* following year; **~konferenz** *f Pol.* follow-up conference; **~kosten** *Pl.* resulting costs; **~modell** *n* replacement model, successor

folgen¹ *v/i.* (*ist gefolgt*) **1.** (*nachgehen*) follow; (*entlanggehen*) *auch* go along; (*begleiten*) *auch* come with, accompany; (*beschatten*) tail; (*verfolgen*) pursue; **e-m Weg ~** follow (*od.* take, go along) a path; **j-s Spur ~** track (*od.* trail) s.o.; **j-m auf Schritt und Tritt ~** dog s.o.'s footsteps; **2.** *mit Blicken etc.*: follow; *mit dem Finger*: trace; **die Straße folgt hier dem Lauf des Flusses** here the road follows the course of the river; **j-m in den Tod ~** *geh.* follow s.o. to the grave; **3.** *geistig*: follow; (*zuhören*) listen to; (*beobachten*) watch; **können Sie mir (noch) ~?** can you follow me?; **ich kann Ihnen da nicht ~** (*zustimmen*) I can't agree with you there; **4.** *Reihenfolge, Rang*: follow, come after; *als Nachfolger*: succeed, follow; **auf Platz 3 folgt ...** in third place we have ..., third is (*od.* are) ...; **der** *od.* **auf die Rede folgte ein Empfang** the speech was followed by a reception; **ein Unglück folgte dem andern** it was one disaster after the other; **Brief folgt** letter to follow; **weitere Einzelheiten ~** further details to come; **es folgt ...** we now have ..., and now ...; **... lautet wie folgt** ... reads as follows; → **Fortsetzung** 1, **Strafe** 5. (*sich richten nach*) follow; *j-s Rat*: *auch* take; **s-m Gefühl ~** do what one's heart tells one, follow one's instinct; (*nach bestem Wissen und Gewissen handeln*) do what one feels is best; **6.** (*Folge leisten*) (*e-m Befehl etc.*) obey; (*e-r Aufforderung etc.*) comply with, carry out; (*e-r Einladung*) accept; **7.** (*sich ergeben*) follow, ensue (*aus* from); **daraus folgt, dass ...** it follows (from this) that ...

folgen² *v/i.* (*hat gefolgt*); *umg.* (*gehorchen*) obey; **nicht ~** disobey; **er folgt nicht** he (just) won't listen; (*j-m*) **aufs Wort ~** *sofort*: obey (s.o.) instantly; *genau*: obey (s.o.) to the letter; **Laura, folge jetzt endlich!** Laura, will you please do as you're told

folgend I. *Part. Präs.* → **folgen¹**, **folgen²**; **II.** *Adj.* following; (*darauf erfolgend*) *auch* ensuing; (*später*) subsequent; (*nächst*) next; **am ~en Tag** the

next (*od.* following) day, the day after; **im Folgenden** in the following passage (*Äußerung*: statement *etc.*), in what follows; **es handelt sich um Folgendes** the matter is as follows, what it's (all) about is this *umg.*; **dazu möchte ich Folgendes sagen** may I just make the following point (*od.* make one thing clear), the way I see it is; **folgendermaßen, folgenderweise** *Adv.* as follows

folgenlos *Adj.* without consequences; **es blieb ~** there were no consequences

folgenreich *Adj.* momentous; (*weitreichend*) far-reaching

folgenschwer *Adj.* (*sehr ernst*) with serious (*od.* grave) consequences; (*schwerwiegend*) momentous, fateful; (*weitreichend*) far-reaching

folgerichtig I. *Adj.* logical; (*konsequent*) consistent; **II.** *Adv.* denken: logically, along logical lines; handeln: consistently

folgern I. *v/t.* deduce (**aus** from); (*daraus*) **~, dass ...** conclude (from this) that ...; **II.** *v/i.*: **richtig ~** come to the right conclusion; **vorschnell ~** jump to conclusions; **Folgerung** *f* conclusion; **e-e ~ ziehen** draw a conclusion (**aus** from); **daraus ergibt sich die ~, dass ...** from this it follows (*od.* one may conclude) that ...

Folge|satz *m* **1.** *Ling.* consecutive clause; **2.** *Math., Philos.* corollary; **~schaden** *m Jur.* consequential damage

folgewidrig *Adj.* illogical; (*inkonsequent*) inconsistent

Folge|wirkung *f* consequence, effect; *Pl. auch* impact *Sg.*; **e-e ~ war ...** one effect (*od.* result) (it had) was ...; **~zeit** *f* period following

folglich *Adv.* (*daher*) consequently, therefore; (*also*) so

folgsam *Adj.* obedient; (*brav*) well-behaved; **Folgsamkeit** *f*; *nur Sg.* obedience

Foliant *m*; *-en, -en* **1.** *Druck.* folio; **2.** *fig.* (*großes, dickes Buch*) hefty tome

Folie *f*; *-, -n* **1.** *Metall*: foil; *aus Plastik*: film, *mst* cling film, *Am.* plastic wrap; *für Overheadprojektor, in Buch*: transparency; **2.** *geh.* (*Hintergrund*) background

Folien|kartoffel *f Gastr.* jacket (*Am.* baked) potato (*baked in alumin[i]um foil*); **~schreiber** *m* erasable marker pen (*for OHP transparencies*)

folienverpackt *Adj. Alufolie*: wrapped in foil, alumin(i)um-wrapped; *Plastikfolie*: wrapped in cling film, *Am.* plastic-wrapped

Folio *n*; *-s, -s od. Folien*; *Druck., Wirts.* folio; **~blatt** *n Wirts.* folio; **~format** *n Druck.* folio

Folk [fo:k] *m*; *-s, kein Pl.* ; *Mus.* folk (music)

Folklore *f*; *-, kein Pl.*; (*Brauchtum, auch Dichtung*) folklore; (*Musik*) traditional music, folk (music); (*Kultur*) folk culture; **folkloristisch** *Adj. Musik*: traditional, folk; *Kleidung*: traditional, ethnic; **~e Abend** *auch* folk elements; **~er Abend** evening of traditional music and dance

Follikel *m*; *-s, -*; *Physiol.* follicle

Folsäure *f*; *nur Sg.*; *Chem., Med.* folic acid

Folter *f*; *-, -n* **1.** torture (*auch fig.*); **es war e-e ~** *fig.* it was torture (*od.* sheer agony); **2.** (*~bank*) rack; **j-n auf die ~ spannen** *fig.* keep s.o. in suspense

(*od.* on tenterhooks); **~bank** *f*; *Pl. -bänke* rack; **~instrument** *n* instrument of torture; **~kammer** *f* torture chamber; **~knecht** *m* torturer; **der General mit s-n ~en** the general and his henchmen torturers

foltern I. *v/t.* torture; *fig. auch* torment; **II.** *v/i.* use (*od.* carry out) torture

Folter|opfer *n* tortured person; **~qualen** *Pl.* **1.** agonies of torture; **2.** *fig.* agony, torment *Sg.*; **~ erleiden** suffer torment, go through absolute agony

Fon → **Phon**

Fön® → **Föhn**

Fond [fõ:] *m*; *-s, -s* **1.** *Mot.* back (of the car); **im ~** *auch* on the back seat, in back; **2.** *Gastr.* (*Grundsoße*) stock

Fonds [fõ:] *m; - [fõ:], - [fõ:s]* **1.** *Wirts.* (*zweckgebundene Geldsumme*) fund; (*Gelder*) funds *Pl.*, capital; **2.** *Wirts.* (*Staatspapiere*) government stocks (*Am.* securities) *Pl.*; **3.** *fig.* fund

Fondue [fõ'dy:] *n*; *-s, -s od. f*; *-, -s*; *Gastr.* fondu(e)

fönen → **föhnen**

fono..., Fono... *siehe* **phono..., Phono...**

Font *m*; *-s, -s*; *EDV, Druck.* font

Fontäne *f*; *-, -n* fountain; (*Strahl*) jet of water

Fontanelle *f*; *-, -n*; *Anat.* fontanel(le)

foppen *v/t.*: **j-n ~** (*necken*) pull s.o.'s leg, kid s.o. *umg.*; (*täuschen*) fool s.o.

forcieren [fɔr'si:rən] *v/t.* **1.** *geh.* (*vorantreiben*) push (on with); (*beschleunigen*) speed up; (*steigern*) step up; (*Anstrengungen*) *auch* intensify; **das Tempo ~** force the pace; **2.** *Mil.* take by force; **3.** *fig.* (*erzwingen*) force; (*Dankbarkeit etc.*) compel

Förde *f*; *-, -n*; *Geog.* long narrow inlet; *bes. in Schottland*: firth

Förder|anlage *f* conveyor (system); **~antrag** *m* application for a grant; **~band** *n* conveyor belt; **~betrag** *m* grant

Förderer *m*; *-s, -*, **Förderin** *f*; *-, -nen* sponsor; *e-r Sache*: supporter, promoter; (*Mäzen*) patron (*weiblich auch* patroness), *bes. Am.* sponsor

Förder|gut *n* material to be transported; **~korb** *m* (pit) cage; **~kreis** *m*: **~ für ...** society for the promotion of ...; **~kurs** *m Päd.* special class; *Pl. auch* special tuition *Sg.*; **~leistung** *f* output, yield

förderlich *Adj.* conducive (+ *Dat.* to); (*günstig*) beneficial (to); (*nützlich*) useful (for, to); (*wirksam*) effective; **e-r Sache ~ sein** *auch* help (*od.* promote, contribute to) s.th.

Förder|maßnahme *f* contributory (*od.* helpful) measure; **~mittel** *Pl.* grants, funding *Sg.*

fordern *v/t.* **1.** (*verlangen*) demand (*von j-m* of s.o.); *rechtlich*: claim; (*Preis*) ask (for); **zu viel ~** be too demanding; **du forderst zu viel** you're asking too much (of me); **zahlreiche Menschenleben** *od.* **Todesopfer ~** *fig.* claim many lives; **2.** (*erfordern*) demand, call for; **3.** (*j-n*) (*anstrengen*) stretch; *stärker*: take it out of; (*e-n Sportler*) push (*od.* stretch); **gefordert werden** be faced with a challenge; **er fühlt sich in s-m Beruf nicht gefordert** he needs a more challenging job; **in dieser Angelegenheit sind wir alle gefordert** this business is putting us all on our mettle (*od.* to the test); **4.** **zum Duell ~** challenge to a duel

fördern *v/t.* **1.** *Person, Sache*: (*Beziehungen, Handel, Künste etc.*) promote, foster; (*Talent, Wachstum etc.*) foster, encourage, nurse; (*Ideal, Karriere, Wahrheitsfindung etc.*) further; (*Absatz, Verbrauch etc.*) boost, increase; *Person*: (*unterstützen*) support; *als Gönner*: patronize, *bes. Firma*: sponsor; *Sache*: (*förderlich sein*) help, be good for; (*verbessern*) improve; (*Appetit etc.*) stimulate; (*Schlaf, Verdauung*) aid; → **fördernd**; **2.** *Bergb.* produce; (*Erz, Kohle*) *auch* mine; (*Öl*) *auch* extract; **3.** *Tech.* (*befördern*) convey, transport; (*zuführen*) feed; → **zutage** 1; **fördernd** I. *Part. Präs.* → **fördern**; II. *Adj.*: **~es Mitglied** supporting member; **~ wirken auf** (+ *Akk.*) have a beneficial effect on

fordernd I. *Part. Präs.* → **fordern**; II. *Adj. Blick etc.*: expectant; (*gebieterisch*) imperious; *Aufgabe*: challenging

Förder|preis m award of sponsorship; **~quote** f output level; **~richtlinie** f guideline for sponsorship (*Finanzierung*: funding); **~schacht** m *Bergb.* mine shaft; **~schule** f special school; **~turm** m *Bergb.* winding tower, pit-head frame

Forderung f **1.** demand, request (**nach** for; **an** + *Akk.* on); *in Aufrufen*: call (for); (*Anspruch*) claim (for); **~en stellen** make demands; **die ~ der Stunde ist ...** the pressing need of the moment is ...; **das ist e-e ~ der Vernunft** common sense demands this; **2.** *nur Sg. Wirts., von Preis, Spesen*: charging; *von Gebühren etc.*: exaction; **3.** *Wirts.* (*geforderter Preis*) asking price, charge; (*Anspruch auf Bezahlung*) claim; **e-e ~ haben an** (+ *Akk.*) have a claim against (*od.* on); **e-e ~ einklagen/eintreiben** sue for payment of / collect a debt; **ausstehende ~en** outstanding debts, accounts receivable; **4.** **~ zum Duell** challenge to a duel

Förderung f **1.** promotion; (*Unterstützung*) support; (*Anregung*) stimulation; *der Künste etc.*: patronage, sponsorship; **2.** *Bergb.* production; *von Öl etc.*: extraction; *von Erz, Kohle*: mining; (*Menge*) output; **3.** *Tech.* (*Beförderung*) conveyance; (*Zuführung*) supply

Förderungsmaßnahme f supportive measure

förderungswürdig *Adj.* worthy of support (*od.* sponsorship); **~ sein** *auch* deserve support (*od.* sponsorship)

Förder|unterricht m *Päd.* extra (*Am.* remedial) lessons *Pl.* (*for weak pupils or beginners*); **~verein** m: **~ für ...** society for the promotion of ...

Forelle f, -, -n; *Zool.* trout; **~ blau** *Gastr.* trout au bleu, poached trout; **~ Müllerin** (*Art*) *Gastr.* trout meunière

Forellen|teich m trout pond; **~zucht** f **1.** trout farming; **2.** (*Anlage*) trout hatchery

forensisch I. *Adj.* forensic; II. *Adv.* forensically

Forke f, -, -n; *nordd.* pitchfork

Form f, -, -en **1.** (*Gestalt*) form, shape; (*Umriss*) outline; *e-r Sache* **~ geben** lend shape to; *aus der* **~ geraten** get out of shape; *aus der* **~ gehen** *umg. hum.* (*dick werden*) lose one's figure; (*feste*) **~(en)** annehmen (*begin to*) take shape; *in* **~ von** (*od.* + *Gen.*) in the form of (*auch fig.*); *die* **~ e-s Halbmonds** *etc.* **haben** be in the shape of a crescent *etc.*, be shaped like a crescent *etc.*; *weibliche* **~en** female curves *umg.*; **2.** *fig. der Erscheinung, Darstel-*

lung etc.: form; (*Gestaltung*) design, style, styling; (*Art und Weise*) form, way; *in angemessener* **~** appropriately; *in höflicher* **~** politely; *der Antrag bedarf schriftlicher* **~** the application must be in writing (*od.* in written form *geh.*); **3.** *fig.* (*guter Ton*) good form; (*Konvention*) convention(s *Pl.*), etiquette; **~en** (*Manieren*) manners; *die* **~ wahren** observe the conventions (*od.* proprieties), stick to the rules (of etiquette); *der* **~ halber** as a matter of form; (*zur Wahrung des Scheins*) to keep up appearances; *in aller* **~** formally; (*feierlich*) solemnly; *sich in aller* **~ entschuldigen** make a formal apology; **4.** *für Kuchen*: tin, *Am.* pan; *zum Ausstechen*: pastry cutter; *für Abguss etc.*: mo(u)ld; *Tech. für Spritzguss*: die; *für Hut*: block; *für Schuh*: last; **5.** *Sport* (*Kondition*) condition, shape, *auch weitS.* form; *in* (*guter*) **~** in good form (*Sport auch* shape, condition); *in bester* **~** in top form; *nicht in* **~** off form, not in form; *in* **~ bleiben** *od.* **sich in** **~ halten** keep in form (*Sport auch* shape); *j-n in* **~ bringen** get s.o. into shape

formal I. *Adj.* formal; *Einwand, Fehler etc.*: technical; *Jur.* procedural; *in* **~er Hinsicht** formally; (*genau genommen*) technically; *Jur.* from a procedural point of view; II. *Adv.* formally; (*genau genommen*) technically; *Jur.* from a procedural point of view; **~ und inhaltlich** in form and content; **~ästhetisch** I. *Adj. Kunst* purely (a)esthetic; II. *Adv.* from a purely (a)esthetic point of view

Formaldehyd n, m; -s, kein Pl.; *Chem.* formaldehyde

Formalie f, -, -n *od. geh. Formalia, mst Pl.* formality

Formalin® n; -s, kein Pl.; *Chem.* formalin

formalisieren v/t. formalize; **Formalismus** m; -, *Formalismen* formalism; **Formalist** m; -en, -en, **Formalistin** f; -, -nen formalist; **formalistisch** *Adj.* formalist(ic); **Formalität** f; -, -en formality

formaljuristisch *Adj.* following the letter of the law, legalistic

Format n; -(e)s, -e **1.** *allg.* size; *von Buch, Bild, Papier*: format; *EDV* format; *welches* **~ hat die Datei?** what format is the file in?; **2.** *fig.* (*Rang, Niveau*) stature, class; *kein* **~ haben** lack stature (*od.* distinction, class), be undistinguished; *ein Musiker von internationalem* **~** a musician of international standing (*od.* stature); **3.** *TV* format

formatieren v/t. *EDV* format; **Formatierung** f formatting

Formatvorlage f *EDV* style sheet

formbar *Adj. Metall. und fig.* malleable

formbeständig *Adj.* shape-retaining, of consistent shape; *Synthetik*: dimensionally stable; **~ sein** retain (*od.* keep) its (*od.* their) shape

Form|blatt n form; **~brief** m form letter

Formel f; -, -n **1.** formula; (*Redensart*) *auch* (set) phrase; *e-s Eides*: wording; *auf e-e* (*einfache*) **~ bringen** reduce to

a simple formula; *auf e-e kurze* **~ gebracht** in a nutshell; **2.** *Mot.*: **~ 1** *etc.* Formula 1 (*od.* One *etc.*)

Formel-1|-Fahrer m, **~-Pilot** m Formula 1 (*od.* One) driver; **~-Rennen** n Formula 1 (*od.* One) racing (*konkret*: race); **~-Wagen** m Formula 1 (*od.* One) car

formelhaft I. *Adj.* stereotyped, formulaic *förm.*; II. *Adv.* reden, schreiben *etc.*: in clichés, in set phrases

formell I. *Adj.* formal; *sehr* **~ sein** *Person*: *auch* stand on ceremony; II. *Adv.* formally; (*der Form halber*) as a matter of form; **~ leitet sie das Projekt** officially she's in charge of the project

Formelsammlung f formulary, collection of formulas (*mst fachspr.* formulae)

formen I. v/t. form, shape (**aus** out of, from; **zu** into); *aus weichem Stoff*: mo(u)ld; shape; (*Gedanken, Laute, Satz*) form; (*j-n, Charakter*) form, mo(u)ld (**zu** into); II. v/refl. form, take shape

Formen|lehre f *Bio., Ling. etc.* morphology; *Grammatik*: *auch* accidence; *Mus.* theory of (musical) forms; **~reichtum** m great (*od.* rich) variety of forms, multitude of forms

Form|fehler m **1.** irregularity; *bei Verfahren auch*: procedural error; **2.** *gesellschaftlicher*: faux pas; **~frage** f question of etiquette; **~gebung** f *Tech.* styling, design

formgerecht *Adj.* correct; *Jur.* in proper form

Formgestaltung f styling, design

formieren v/t. und v/refl. form; *Mil.* line (*od.* draw) up; *sie* **~ sich zu e-r Mannschaft** they are forming themselves into a team

...förmig im *Adj.* -shaped; *apfel~* apple-shaped; *rüssel~* trunk-shaped; *treppen~* in the form of stairs

Formkrise f *Sport* patch of bad form; *in e-r* **~ sein** have lost one's form; *die* **~ des Euro hält an** *Wirts.* the euro continues to perform badly

förmlich I. *Adj.* **1.** formal; (*feierlich*) ceremonious; (*sehr genau*) punctilious; **2.** *umg.* (*regelrecht*) positive; (*Schreck*) real; II. *Adv.* **1.** formally; **2.** (*regelrecht*) positively; (*buchstäblich*) literally; (*wirklich*) really; **Förmlichkeit** f formality; *in aller* **~** in due form, formally; *keine* **~en!** don't stand on ceremony

formlos *Adj.* **1.** (*gestaltlos*) shapeless, amorphous; **2.** (*nicht formell, zwanglos*) informal (*auch Antrag, Schreiben etc.*); **Formlosigkeit** f; nur Sg. **1.** (*Gestaltlosigkeit*) shapelessness; **2.** (*Zwanglosigkeit*) informality

Formsache f matter of form; (*e-e reine*) **~** (a mere) formality

formschön *Adj.* beautifully shaped (*od.* designed); (*Auto etc.*) with beautiful lines

Form|strenge f *Kunst* strict adherence to a form, formal strictness; **~tief** n *Sport* (patch of) bad form; *ein* **~ haben** be badly off form

Formular n; -s, -e form; *ein* **~ ausfüllen** fill in (*bes. Am.* fill out) a form

formulieren I. v/t. formulate; (*Gedanken etc.*) *auch* express, put into words; (*Brief etc.*) formulate, word; *neu* **~** rephrase, reword; *etw. knapp* **~** sum s.th. up, put s.th. in a few words (*od.* briefly); *ich weiß nicht, wie ich es* **~ soll** I don't know how to put it; *das hast du treffend formuliert* you've expressed (*od.* put) it perfectly, I couldn't have put it better myself; **wenn ich es mal so ~ darf** if I may put it like that; **II.** *v/i* express o.s.; **Formulierung** *f* (*das Formulieren, Formuliertes*) formulation; (*Wortlaut*) wording, phrasing

Formulierungs|hilfe *f* help with wording; *schriftliche Anleitung*: guide to self-expression, style guide; *Pl.* (*Mustertexte*) sample texts; *bes.* (*Musterbriefe*) sample letters; **~vorschlag** *m* suggested wording, sample text

Formung *f* **1.** (*das Formen*) forming, shaping; (*Formgebung*) design; *von weichem Stoff*: *auch* mo(u)lding; **2.** *fig.*, *e-r Persönlichkeit*: formation, mo(u)lding

formvollendet *Adj.* perfectly shaped (*od.* designed); *Benehmen etc.*: perfect, immaculate; *Verbeugung, Übung oder Figur im Sport etc.*: flawlessly executed

formwidrig *Adj.* **1.** (*unkorrekt*) Entscheidungsweg: irregular; *Dokument*: incorrectly drafted; **2.** (*Benehmen*) improper; **Formwidrigkeit** *f* **1.** irregularity; *e-s Dokuments*: incorrect drafting; **2.** *des Benehmens*: impropriety

forsch I. *Adj.* (*energisch, tatkräftig*) forceful; (*selbstbewusst*) self-assertive; **II.** *Adv.*: **~ auftreten** have a very self-assertive (*stärker*: brash) manner

forschen *v/i.* **1. ~ nach** search for; **nach den Ursachen braucht man nicht lange zu ~** you don't have to look far to find the reasons; **2.** *wissenschaftlich*: do research; **~ in** (+ *Dat.*) do research in, research; **forschend I.** *Part. Präs.* → **forschen**; **II.** *Adj. Blick*: searching; (*fragend*) questioning, inquiring

Forscher *m*; *-s*, - researcher; (*Naturwissenschaftler*) scientist; (*Entdecker*) explorer; **~drang** *m* intellectual curiosity; *als Entdecker*: urge to explore; **~geist** *m* **1.** intellectual curiosity, inquiring mind; **2.** *Person*: **sie ist ein ~** she has an inquiring mind, she likes to get to the bottom of things

Forschheit *f*; *nur Sg.* forcefulness; (*Selbstbewusstsein*) self-assertiveness, *stärker*: brashness

Forscherin *f*; *-*, *-nen* (female) researcher

Forschung *f* **1.** **~(en)** research (work); **in der ~ tätig sein** work (*od.* be engaged) in research, do research work; **~ und Entwicklung** research and development, R&D; **2.** *nur Sg.*; *Koll.* (*Forscher*) researchers *Pl.*, *naturwissenschaftliche*: scientists *Pl.*

Forschungs|abteilung *f Wirts.* research department; **~arbeit** *f allg.* research (work); *einzelne*: piece of research; **~auftrag** *m* research assignment; **~beitrag** *m* contribution to research; **~ergebnis** *n* result(s *Pl.*) of the research; **~freijahr** *n Univ.* sabbatical (for research); **ein ~ haben** be doing research on sabbatical; **~gebiet** *n* field of research; **~gegenstand** *m* object of research; **~gemeinschaft** *f*: **Deutsche ~** (*abgek.* **DFG**) German Research Council; **~institut** *n* research institute; **~labor** *n* research lab(oratory); **~minister** *m*, **~ministerin** *f* minister for research; **~ministerium** *n* ministry of research; **~mittel** *Pl.* research funding *Sg.*; **~programm** *n* research program(me); **~projekt** *n* research project; **~reaktor** *m Phys.* research reactor; **~reise** *f* **1.** (*Entdeckungsreise*) expedition; **2.** *mit e-m wissenschaftli-*

chen Zweck: field trip; **~reisende** *m, f* explorer; **~satellit** *m Astron.* research satellite; **~schiff** *n* research vessel; **~schwerpunkt** *m* main research aim; **~semester** *n Univ.* half-year (*od.* term's) sabbatical (for research); **ein ~ haben** have the term off for research; **~station** *f* research station; **~stipendium** *n Univ.* research grant (*od.* fellowship); **~tätigkeit** *f* research activity (*od.* work); **~urlaub** *m* sabbatical (for research); **im ~ sein** be (doing research) on sabbatical; **~vorhaben** *n* research project; **~zentrum** *n* research cent|re (*Am.* -er); **~zweck** *m*: **für ~e** *od.* **zu ~en** for research purposes; **~en dienen** be for research purposes

Forst *m*; *-(e)s*, *-e(n)* forest; **~amt** *n* forestry commission office; **~beamte** *m*, **~beamtin** *f* forestry commission officer

Förster *m*; *-s*, - forest warden, forester, *Am.* forest ranger; **Försterei** *f*; *-*, *-en* forest warden's (*Am.* forest ranger's) office; **Försterin** *f*; *-*, *-nen* (female) forest warden (*Am.* ranger); *altm.* forester's wife

Forst|frevel *m* infringement of forest laws; **~haus** *n* forest warden's (*Am.* forest ranger's) lodge; **~meister** *m*, **~meisterin** *f* senior forestry commission (*Am.* forest service) officer; **~verwaltung** *f* forestry commission, *Am.* forest service; **~wesen** *n* forestry

Forstwirt *m*, **~in** *f* forestry engineer; **Forstwirtschaft** *f* forestry (management); **forstwirtschaftlich** *Adj. nur attr.* forestry...; **nach ~en Gesichtspunkten** from the point of view of good forestry management

Forstwissenschaft *f* forestry (science)

Forsythie [fɔr'zy:tsiə] *f*; *-*, *-n*; *Bot.* forsythia; **~n in die Vase stellen** put (sprigs of) forsythia blossom in the vase

Fort [fo:ɐ̯] *n*; *-s*, *-s*; *Mil.* fort

fort *Adv.* **1.** (*abwesend*) away; (*verloren, verschwunden*) gone; **sie sind schon ~** they've already left (*od.* gone); **der Wagen ist ~** the car has gone (*od.* vanished); **~ mit euch!** off with you!; **~ damit!** take it away!; **~ mit Schaden!** good riddance!; → *auch* **weg**, **2. und so ~** and so on (*od.* forth); **in einem ~** continuously, without interruption (*od.* stopping); **er redete in einem ~** *auch* he wouldn't stop talking, he just went on and on *umg.*

fort... *im V. etc. siehe auch* **weg...**

fortan *Adv. geh.* henceforth, from now on

Fortbestand *m* continued existence, continuance; *e-r Einrichtung etc.*: survival; **fortbestehen** *v/i.* (*unreg., trennb., hat*) continue (to exist), survive; *Kunstwerk etc.*: live on

fortbewegen (*trennb., hat*) **I.** *v/refl.* move; *Fahrzeug*: move (along); (*gehen*) walk; **sich nur mit Mühe ~ können** *Person*: have great difficulty walking; **II.** *v/t.* move (away); **Fortbewegung** *f* movement, *Physiol., Tech.* locomotion

Fortbewegungs|art *f* form of locomotion *förm.*; **~mittel** *n* means of transport (*od.* transportation)

fortbilden (*trennb., hat -ge-*) **I.** *v/t.*: (*j-n*) continue *s.o.*'s education; *beruflich*: give *s.o.* further (vocational) training; **II.** *v/refl.* continue one's education; *in Abendkursen*: go to evening classes; **sich** (*beruflich*) **~** do further (vocational) training; **Fortbildung** *f*

continuing education, *Brit. auch*: further education; (*berufliche*) **~** further (vocational) training

Fortbildungs|kurs *m*, **~lehrgang** *m* further training course; **~maßnahme** *f* continuing (*Brit. auch* further) education provision

fortbleiben I. *v/i.* (*unreg., trennb., ist -ge-*) stay away; **II. Fortbleiben** *n*; *-s*, *kein Pl.* absence

fortbringen *v/t.* (*unreg., trennb., hat -ge-*) take away; *von der Stelle*: move

Fortdauer *f* continuation; **fortdauern** *v/i.* (*trennb., hat -ge-*) continue, last; **fortdauernd I.** *Part. Präs.* → **fortdauern**; **II.** *Adj.* lasting; (*ständig*) ongoing, continuous; *Zahlungen etc.*: continuing, recurrent; **III.** *Adv.* continuously

forte *Adv. Mus.* forte; **Forte** *n*; *-s*, *-s od. Forti* forte

fort|entwickeln *v/t.* (*trennb., hat*) → **weiterentwickeln I**; **~fahren** (*unreg., trennb. -ge-*) **I.** *v/i.* **1.** (*ist fortgefahren*) leave, go away; *mit dem Auto*: *auch* drive off (*od.* away); (*e-n Ausflug machen*) go off (on a jaunt); (*e-e Reise machen*) go off on a trip (*od.* on holiday, *Am.* on vacation); **2.** (*hat/ist*) (*etw. fortsetzen*) continue, carry on; **~ zu** (+ *Inf.*) continue (+ *Ger. od.* to + *Inf.*), carry (*od.* go, keep) on (+ *Ger.*); **mit s-r Erzählung ~** continue (with) (*od.* resume) one's story; **fahren Sie fort!** go on; **II.** *v/t.* (*hat*) **1.** **j-n/ ein Auto ~** drive (*od.* take) s.o./ a car away, drive away with s.o. / in a car; **2.** (*abtransportieren*) take (*od.* drive) away; **~fallen** *v/i.* → **wegfallen**; **~fliegen** *v/i.* (*unreg., trennb., ist -ge-*) fly away (*od.* off)

fortführen *v/t.* (*trennb., hat -ge-*) **1.** lead away; **2.** (*fortsetzen*) go on with, continue; (*Geschäft, Krieg*) carry on; (*wieder aufnehmen*) resume; **Fortführung** *f* continuation; (*Wiederaufnahme*) resumption

Fortgang *m*; *nur Sg.* **1.** (*Weggehen*) departure; **seit i-m ~** since her/their departure, since she/they went away; **2.** (*Fortschreiten*) progress; (*Weiterentwicklung*) *auch* further development; (*Fortsetzung*) continuation; **s-n ~ nehmen** progress; **fortgehen** *v/i.* (*unreg., trennb., ist -ge-*) **1.** go away, leave; **2.** *umg.* (*ausgehen*) go out; **3.** *fig.* (*weitergehen*) go on, continue

fortgeschritten I. *P.P.* → **fortschreiten**; **II.** *Adj. Stadium etc.*: advanced; **Kurs für Fortgeschrittene** course for advanced students, advanced course; **Krebs im ~en Stadium** unheilbar: terminal cancer; **in e-m ~en Alter sein** be advanced in years; **zu ~er Stunde** at a (very) late hour; (*nach Mitternacht*) in the small hours

fortgesetzt I. *P.P.* → **fortsetzen**; **II.** *Adj.* continual, constant; (*wiederholt*) *auch* repeated; **III.** *Adv.* continually, constantly; (*wiederholt*) *auch* repeatedly

fortissimo *Adv. Mus.* fortissimo; **Fortissimo** *n*; *-s*, *-s od. Fortissimi* fortissimo

fortjagen *v/t.* → **wegjagen**

fortkommen I. *v/i.* (*unreg., trennb., ist -ge-*) **1.** get away; **mach, dass du fortkommst!** make yourself scarce!; **2.** (*weggebracht werden*) be removed; **3.** (*Erfolg haben*) get on (*auch beruflich*); **II. Fortkommen** *n* progress; *gesellschaftliches, berufliches*: advancement; **j-s Fortkommen hinderlich/förderlich sein** hinder/help to advance s.o.'s career

fort|können *v/i. (unreg., trennb., hat -ge-)* be able to get away; **~lassen** *v/t. (unreg., trennb., hat -ge-)* **1.** *j-n* ~ let s.o. go; **2.** *(auslassen)* leave out, omit

fortlaufen *v/i. (unreg., trennb., ist -ge-)* **1.** run away ([*vor*] *j-m* from s.o.); **2.** *(weitergehen)* continue; **fortlaufend I.** *Part. Präs.* → **fortlaufen**; **II.** *Adj.* continuous, running; *Hefte, Folgen etc.:* consecutive; *mit **~er Nummer*** numbered consecutively; **III.** *Adv.* continuously; ~ *nummeriert* numbered consecutively

fortleben I. *v/i. (trennb., hat -ge-)* live on; **II. Fortleben** *n* survival

fort|legen *v/t. (trennb., hat -ge-)* put aside; *(niedersetzen)* put down; *(wegräumen)* put away; **~locken** *v/t. (trennb., hat -ge-)* lure away; **~machen** *v/refl. (trennb., hat -ge-); umg.* clear off; **~müssen** *v/i. (unreg., trennb., hat -ge-)* have to go; *das muss fort* it's got to go, I've/we've etc. got to get rid of it; **~nehmen** *v/t. (trennb., hat -ge-)* take away

fortpflanzen *(trennb., hat -ge-)* **I.** *v/refl.* **1.** *Bio.* reproduce; *Pflanzen: auch* propagate; **2.** *Phys., Licht, Schall etc.:* be transmitted, travel; **3.** *fig. Idee, Gerücht etc.:* spread, be passed on; **II.** *v/t.* **1.** *Bio.* propagate, reproduce; **2.** *Phys.* transmit; **3.** *fig.* spread; **Fortpflanzung** *f* **1.** *Bio.* reproduction; *von Pflanzen: auch* propagation; **2.** *Phys., von Licht, Schall etc.:* transmission; **3.** *fig. von Idee, Gerücht etc.:* spread(ing), propagation

fortpflanzungsfähig *Adj.* capable of reproduction, procreative; *im **~en** Alter* at the age of reproduction; *von Frau:* at the child(-)bearing age

Fortpflanzungs|medizin *f* reproductive medicine; **~organ** *n* reproductive organ; **~trieb** *m* reproductive (*od.* procreative) instinct

fort|reißen *v/t. (unreg., trennb., hat -ge-):* *(mit sich)* ~ sweep away; **~reiten** *v/i. (unreg., trennb., ist -ge-)* ride off; **~rennen** *v/i.* → **wegrennen**

Fortsatz *m Anat.* process; *(Anhang)* appendix; *e-s Knochens:* eminence

fort|schaffen *v/t.* → **wegschaffen**; **~scheren** *v/refl. (trennb., hat -ge-); umg.: scher dich fort!* get lost!, clear off!; **~schicken** *v/t. (trennb., hat -ge-)* send away; *(verjagen)* send packing; *(Brief etc.)* send off; **~schieben** *v/t. (unreg., trennb., hat -ge-)* push away; **~schleichen** *v/i.* → **wegschleichen**; **~schleppen** *(trennb., hat -ge-)* **I.** *v/t.* drag away; **II.** *v/refl.* **1.** drag o.s. along; **2.** *fig. (sich hinziehen)* drag (on); *Fehler:* be perpetuated

fortschreiben *v/t. (unreg., trennb., hat -ge-)* **1.** *(Statistik)* update; **2.** *fig. (aufrechterhalten)* perpetuate

fortschreiten *fig. v/i. (unreg., trennb., ist -ge-)* progress; *Zeit:* march on; *Epidemie, Missstand etc.:* spread; *die Vernichtung scheint unaufhaltsam fortzuschreiten* the destruction seems unstoppable; *das Jahr ist schon weit fortgeschritten* the year is getting on, it's getting late in the year; → *fortgeschritten;* **Fortschreiten** *n* progress; **fortschreitend I.** *Part. Präs.* → **fortschreiten**; **II.** *Adj.* progressive; *mit **~em Alter*** with advancing years (*od.* age)

Fortschritt *m* progress (*auch Pl.*); *ein* ~ an advance, a step forward; *(Verbesserung)* an improvement; **~e machen**

make progress (*od.* headway), get on (*od.* ahead); *große **~e machen*** make great strides, forge ahead; **fortschrittlich I.** *Adj.* progressive; *Anlage etc.:* (very) modern, up-to-date; **II.** *Adv.* progressively; ~ *denken* be progressive (*od.* forward-looking) in one's thinking; **Fortschrittlichkeit** *f; nur Sg.* progressiveness; *Haltung:* progressive attitude

Fortschrittsfanatiker *m,* **~in** *f* fanatical believer in progress

fortschritts|feindlich *Adj.* reactionary; **~gläubig** *Adj.:* ~ *sein* believe implicitly in progress

fort|schwimmen *v/i. (unreg., trennb., ist -ge-)* swim away; **~sehnen** *v/refl. (trennb., hat -ge-)* long to be somewhere else (*od.* to escape)

fortsetzen *(trennb., hat -ge-)* **I.** *v/t.* continue; *etw. wieder ~ auch* resume s.th., take s.th. up again; **II.** *v/refl.* continue; **Fortsetzung** *f* **1.** *nur Sg.* continuation; *e-r Geschichte etc.: auch* sequel; *(Wiederaufnahme)* resumption; ~ *folgt* to be continued; ~ *auf/von Seite 2* continued on/from page two; **2.** *(Folge)* part, instal(l)ment; *TV, Radio: auch* episode; *in **~en** (erscheinend) auch* serialized

Fortsetzungs|geschichte *f* serialized story, serial; **~roman** *m* serialized novel

fort|stehlen *v/refl. (unreg., trennb., hat -ge-)* steal (*od.* sneak) away (*od.* off); **~stürzen** *v/i. (trennb., ist -ge-)* dash off; **~tragen** *v/t. (unreg., trennb., hat -ge-)* carry away; **~treiben** *(unreg., trennb., -ge-)* **I.** *v/t. (hat)* **1.** drive away; **2.** *Strömung etc.:* sweep away; **3.** *fig. (weiterhin tun)* carry on (with), go on with; **II.** *v/i. (ist); im Wasser:* drift away

Fortuna *(f); -s, kein Pl.; geh.* fortune, luck; *personifiziert:* Dame Fortune, Lady Luck *umg.;* *Göttin:* Fortuna; ~ *war ihr hold* fortune smiled on her

fortwagen *v/refl. (trennb., hat -ge-)* dare to go away (*od.* leave)

fortwährend I. *Adj.* continual, constant; *(ununterbrochen)* continuous, incessant; **II.** *Adv.* continually, constantly; *(ununterbrochen)* continuously, incessantly, all the time; *er ruft* ~ *an* he is constantly (*od.* keeps on) ringing up (*Am.* calling)

fort|werfen *v/t. (unreg., trennb., hat -ge-)* throw away; **~wirken** *v/i. (trennb., hat -ge-)* continue to have an effect (*in* + *Dat.* on; *bei Pl.:* among), continue to make itself felt (in, among); *dieses Erlebnis wirkte lange in mir fort* this experience continued to affect me for a long time

Fortzahlung *f* continued payment

fortziehen *(unreg., trennb. -ge-)* **I.** *v/i. (ist)* **1.** *(umziehen)* move (away) (*aus* from); *aus e-r Wohnung:* move out (*aus* of); **2.** *Soldaten etc.:* leave; *Zugvögel:* migrate; **II.** *v/t. (hat)* pull (*mit Wucht:* drag) away (*von* from)

Forum *n; -s, Foren* **1.** *Pl. auch Fora;* *hist.* forum (*Pl.* forums *od.* fora *geh.*); ~ *Romanum* the Roman Forum; **2.** *fig. von Experten etc.:* forum; *für Diskussionen etc.: auch* platform (*für* for); *Internet:* forum; *(Podiumsgespräch)* panel discussion; *vor e-m ~ sprechen* address a forum

Forumsdiskussion *f n* discussion forum

fossil I. *Adj.* fossil ..., fossilized; **~e** *Brennstoffe* fossil fuels; **II. Fossil** *n*;

-s, -ien fossil

fötal *Adj.* f(o)etal

Foto[1] *n; -s, -s od. schw. auch f; -, -s* photo(graph); *(Schnappschuss) auch* snap *umg.; auf dem ~ ist sie nicht* she isn't in this photo; **~s machen** *od. schießen umg.* take photos

Foto[2] *m; -s, -s; umg. (Kamera)* camera

foto..., Foto... *im Subst., V. und Adj. bes. bei Fachterminologie auch* **photo..., Photo...**

Foto|album *n* photo(graph) album; **~amateur** *m,* **~amateurin** *f* amateur photographer; **~apparat** *m* camera; **~archiv** *n* photographic library (*od.* archive); **~atelier** *n* photographic studio; **~ausrüstung** *f* photographic equipment, camera(s) and lenses *Pl.*; **~ausstellung** *f* photographic exhibition; **~automat** *m* photo booth; **~-CD** *f Computer.* photo CD, photodisk; **~ecke** *f (adhesive)* corner

fotogen *Adj.* photogenic

Fotograf *m; -en, -en* photographer

Fotografie *f; -, -n* **1.** *nur Sg.; Kunst, Technik:* photography; **2.** *(Bild)* photograph, picture

fotografieren I. *v/t.* photograph, take a photograph (*od.* picture) (*mehrere:* photographs *od.* pictures) of; *sich ~ lassen* have one's photograph (*od.* picture) taken; *er lässt sich gut ~* he photographs well, he's photogenic; **II.** *v/i.* take photographs (*od.* pictures); *er fotografiert gern* he likes taking photographs, he's a keen (*Am.* an avid) photographer; *ich fotografiere nicht mehr* I've stopped taking photographs, I've given up photography; **III.** *v/refl.: sich gut/schlecht ~* photograph well/badly, come out well/badly in photographs; **IV. Fotografieren** *n; -s, kein Pl. (Fotografie)* photography; *Handlung:* taking of photographs; *Fotografieren verboten* no photographs

Fotografin *f; -, -nen* photographer

fotografisch I. *Adj.* photographic; **~es** *Gedächtnis* photographic memory; **II.** *Adv.* photographically

Foto|journalist *m,* **~journalistin** *f* photojournalist

Fotokopie *f* photocopy; **fotokopieren** *(untr., hat) vt/i.* photocopy; *er fotokopiert gerade* he's just doing some photocopying; **Fotokopierer** *m,* **Fotokopiergerät** *n* photocopier

Foto|labor *n* photo(graphic) laboratory; **~modell** *n* photographic model; **~montage** *f* photomontage; **~papier** *n* photographic paper; **~reportage** *f* photo reportage; **~reporter** *m,* **~reporterin** *f* photojournalist; **~sachen** *Pl. umg.* cameras and lenses, photographic gear *Sg.;* **~safari** *f* photographic (*od.* picture) safari; **~studio** *n* photographic studio; **~tasche** *f* camera holdall; **~termin** *m* photocall; **~wettbewerb** *m* photographic competition

Fötus *m; -(ses), -se od. Föten* f(o)etus

Fotze *f; -, -n* **1.** *vulg.* cunt; **2.** *mst Fotzen südd., österr. umg. (Ohrfeige)* cuff, slap; **3.** *südd., österr. umg. pej. (Mund)* trap, *Brit. auch* gob; **fotzen** *v/t. südd., österr. umg.* cuff, slap

foul [faul] *Sport* **I.** *Adv.:* ~ *spielen allg.* play dirty; *einmal:* commit a foul; **II. Foul** *n; -s, -s* foul; **Foulelfmeter** *m* penalty (kick); **foulen** ['faulən] **I.** *v/t.* foul; **II.** *v/i.* commit a foul; **Foulspiel** *n* foul

Fox|terrier *m* fox terrier; **~trott** *m; -s, -s od. -e; Mus.* foxtrot; ~ *tanzen* (do the) foxtrot

Foyer [foaˈjeː] *n*; *-s*, *-s* foyer (*auch Theat. etc.*), entrance hall, *bes. Am.* lobby (*auch Theat. etc.*)

FPÖ *f*; *-*, *kein Pl.*; *Abk.* (**Freiheitliche Partei Österreichs**) Austrian Freedom Party

Fr. *Abk.* **1.** *vor Namen:* → **Frau** I 4; **2.** (**Freitag**) Fri(.); **3.** *Wirts.* (**Franken1**) SFr

Fracht *f*; *-*, *-en* **1.** (*Ladung*) load, freight; *Schiff, Flugzeug:* cargo; *allg.* (*Güter*) freight; **die ~ löschen** unload; **2.** (*Beförderung, Preis*) carriage, *Am. auch* freight(age), haulage; *Naut., Flug.* freightage; **~brief** *m* consignment note, *Am.* waybill; **~dampfer** *m* cargo ship, freighter

Frachten|bahnhof *m*, **~station** *f österr.* goods (*Am.* freight) station

Frachter *m*; *-s*, *-* **1.** (*Schiff*) freighter; **2.** → **Frachtflugzeug**

Fracht|flugzeug *n* cargo (*od.* freight) plane, (air) freighter; **~führer** *m*, **~führerin** *f* carrier; **~gebühr** *f*, **~geld** *n* carriage, *Am.* freight (charge); **~gut** *n* freight; *Naut.* cargo; **als ~** *Eisenb.* by goods (*bes. Am.* freight) train; **~kahn** *m* (freight) barge; **~kosten** *Pl.* freight charges; **~maschine** *f* → **Frachtflugzeug**, **~raum** *m* **1.** cargo hold; **2.** (*Kapazität*) freight capacity; **~schiff** *n* cargo ship, freighter; **~sendung** *f* consignment; **~stück** *n* package; **~versicherung** *f* freight (*od.* cargo) insurance

Frack *m*; *-(e)s*, *Fräcke*, *umg. auch -s* tails *Pl.*; *Jacke:* tailcoat; **im ~** in evening dress, in tails; **den ~ voll bekommen** *umg. fig.* be badly beaten up; **~hemd** *n* dress shirt; **~sausen** *n umg.:* **~ haben** have got the wind up, *Am.* have caught a fright; **~schoß** *m*; *mst Pl.* coattail; **~zwang** *m auf Einladungen:* evening dress; **es herrscht ~** tails are compulsory

Frage *f*; *-*, *-n* **1.** question (**über** + *Akk. od.* **zu** about, on); *bes. anzweifelnde od. Auskunft suchende:* query (**nach** *Erkundigung*) inquiry, enquiry (**nach** about); **e-e ~ bejahen/verneinen** answer a question in the affirmative/negative, say yes/no to a question; (**j-m**) **e-e ~ stellen** ask (s.o.) a question, put a question (to s.o.); **ich habe mal e-e ~ (an dich)** can I ask you something?; **es war nur e-e ~** I was only asking; **was soll diese ~?** what kind of question is that?, what are you getting at?; **so e-e ~!** what a question, what a thing to ask; **2.** *fig.* question (*Angelegenheit*) matter, issue; (*Problem*) problem; (*Zweifel*) doubt; **soziale ~n** social issues; **die deutsche ~** *hist.* the German question; **die ~ ist, ob/wie etc.** ... the question (*od.* point) is whether/how *etc.* ...; **das ist eben die ~** that is the question, that's just the point; **das ist noch sehr die ~** that's very much the question, that's very questionable; **das ist die große ~** that's the 64,000 dollar question; **das ist od. steht außer ~**, *kurz:* **keine ~** there's no question about that; (*steht fest*) *auch* that's been decided (*od.* settled); **gar keine ~!** (*natürlich*) of course; *Erlaubnis:* you don't have to ask; **ohne ~** undoubtedly; **es ist nur e-e ~ von Sekunden** *etc.*, **bis/bevor** ... it will only be a matter of seconds until/before ...; **3.** *in* **kommen/stellen** *→* **infrage** **...frage** *f*; *-*, *-n*; *im Subst., bes. Pol.* question; (*Problem*) problem; *Entsor-*

gungs~ question (*od.* problem) of waste disposal; *Frauen~* question (*od.* issue) of women's rights

Fragebogen *m* questionnaire; *Formular:* form; **~aktion** *f* poll

Frage|form *f Ling.* interrogative form; **~fürwort** *n* interrogative (pronoun)

fragen (*Dial. Präs. auch frägst, frägt, Imperf. auch frug*) **I.** *v/t./i.* **1.** ask; (*ausfragen*) question, query; (**j-n**) **etwas ~** ask (s.o.) a question; **viel ~** ask a lot of questions; **ich wollte ~, ob** ... I was wondering if (*od.* whether) ..., I wanted to ask if (*od.* whether) ...; **wenn ich ~ darf** if you don't mind my asking; **da fragst du mich zu viel** (I'm afraid) I can't help you there, I don't know about that; **frag lieber nicht!** don't ask!; (*sonst hörst du etw. Unangenehmes*) you don't want to know!; **man wird ja wohl noch ~ dürfen** sorry I asked; **frag nicht so dumm!** don't ask such silly (*od.* stupid) questions; **da fragst du noch?** (*das ist doch selbstverständlich*) how can you even ask (such a thing)?; (*du wagst es zu ~?*) you've got a nerve; **Fragen kostet nichts** there's no harm in asking; **2.** (*sich erkundigen*) inquire (**nach** *od.* **wegen** about); **nach j-m ~** ask about s.o.; *nach Befinden: auch* ask after s.o.; (*j-n sprechen wollen*) ask for s.o.; **ich fragte ihn nach s-r Frau** I asked him how his wife was; **j-n nach s-m Namen / dem Weg** *etc.* **~** ask s.o. his (*od.* her) name / the way *etc.*; **3.** (*bitten*): (**j-n**) **~ nach** ask (s.o.) for; **j-n um Erlaubnis/Rat ~** ask s.o.'s permission/advice; **fragst du ihn wegen dem Auto?** *umg.* (*ob wir es haben können*) will you ask him about the car (*od.* whether we can have the car)?; → **gefragt**; **II.** *v/i.:* **nicht ~ nach** (*sich nicht kümmern um*) not care about; **wer fragt schon danach?** who cares?; **er fragt e-n Dreck danach, wie das Wetter ist** *umg.* he couldn't care less (*od.* he doesn't give a damn) about the weather; **III.** *v/refl.* **1.** wonder; **ich frage mich, wie er es schafft** *auch* I'd like to know how he does it; **ich frage mich, warum** I (just) wonder why, I can't help wondering why; **2.** *unpers.*: **es fragt sich, ob/wann** *etc.* it's a question of whether/when *etc.*, the question is whether/when *etc.*

fragend I. *Part. Präs.* → **fragen**; **II.** *Adj.* **1.** questioning, inquiring; **2.** *Ling.* interrogative; **III.** *Adv.:* **j-n ansehen** look at s.o. inquiringly; (*auch zweifelnd*) give s.o. a questioning look

Fragen|katalog *m* package (*Am. umg.* slew) of questions; **ein ganzer ~** *auch* a long list of questions; **~komplex** *m* problem area; (*Thema*) topic; **der ganze ~ um** ... the whole set of problems concerning ...

Fragerei *f*; *-*, *en*; *pej.* questions *Pl.*; **hör auf mit d-r ~** I wish you'd stop asking all these questions

Frage|satz *m Ling.* interrogative sentence; *Nebensatz:* interrogative clause; (**in**)**direkter ~** (in)direct question; **~steller** *m*; *-s*, *-*, **~stellerin** *f*; *-*, *-nen* questioner; **~stellung** *f* **1.** way of putting the question; **das ist e-e falsche ~** the question has to be put differently; **2.** (*Problemkreis*) question, problem; **~stunde** *f Parl.* question time; **~und--Antwort-Spiel** *n* quiz; *auch fig.* question-and-answer game; **~wort** *n Ling.* interrogative; **~zeichen** *n* question mark; **etw. mit e-m (großen) ~ verse-**

hen fig. put a (big) question mark against (*Am.* next to) s.th.; **es bleiben noch einige ~** *fig.* there are still a few unanswered questions (*od.* some uncertainties); **wie ein ~ dasitzen, dastehen etc.** all hunched up

fragil *Adj. geh.* fragile

fraglich *Adj.* **1.** (*zweifelhaft*) doubtful, uncertain; **2.** (*betreffend*) ... in question; **an dem ~en Tag** on that particular day, on the day in question

fraglos *Adv.* unquestionably, undoubtedly

Fragment *n*; *-(e)s*, *-e* fragment; **fragmentarisch I.** *Adj.* fragmentary; **II.** *Adv.* in fragmentary form; **fragmentieren** *v/t. geh.* fragment, break up (into fragments); *EDV* fragment; **Fragmentierung** *f EDV* fragmentation

fragwürdig *Adj.* questionable; (*verdächtig*) dubious; **~es Subjekt** shady character; **Fragwürdigkeit** *f* dubious nature, dubiousness; *e-r Person:* dubiousness, shadiness

Fraktion *f*; *-*, *-en* **1.** *Parl.* parliamentary party; (*Untergruppe*) faction; **2.** *Chem.* fraction

Fraktions|beschluss *m Parl.* parliamentary party resolution; **~disziplin** *f* party discipline; **~führer** *m*, **~führerin** *f* parliamentary party leader, *Am.* floor leader

fraktionslos *Adj.* independent

Fraktions|mitglied *n* parliamentary party member; **~sitzung** *f* parliamentary party meeting; **~stärke** *f* **1.** *zahlenmäßige:* size of the (*od.* a) parliamentary party; **2.** *ausreichende:* required strength for recognition as a parliamentary party; **~ haben** be large enough to be recognized as a parliamentary party; **~status** *m* status of a parliamentary party; **~vorsitzende** *m*, *f* parliamentary party leader, *Am.* floor leader; **~zwang** *m* party discipline; **unter ~ stehen** be under the party whip; **den ~ aufheben** remove the whip, allow a free vote

Fraktur *f*; *-*, *-en* **1.** *nur Sg.*; *Druck.* Gothic (type); *Handschrift:* old German-style handwriting; **mit j-m ~ reden** *umg. fig.* tell s.o. what's what, *bes. Am.* talk turkey to s.o.; **2.** *Med.* fracture

Franc [frãː] *m*; *-s*, *-s*; *hist.* franc (*ehemalige fränzösische, belgische etc. Währung*)

Franchise ['frentʃaiz] *m*; *-*, *kein Pl.* franchise; **~geber** *m* franchis|er (*auch* -or); **~nehmer** *m*; *-s*, *-* franchisee

frank *Adv.:* **~ und frei** quite frankly, openly

Franke *m*; *-*, *-n* **1.** *hist.* Frank; **2.** *Geog.* Franconian

Franken1 *m*; *-s*, *-* *Geld:* (Swiss) franc

Franken2 (*n*); *-s*; *Geog.* Franconia; **~reich** *n hist.* the Frankish Empire (*od.* Kingdom), the Kingdom of the Franks; **~wein** *m* Franconian wine

Frankfurt (*n*); *-s*; *Geog.:* **~ am Main / an der Oder** Frankfurt (on the Main) / on the Oder

Frankfurter1 *f*; *-*, *-* Würstchen: frankfurter; **ein Paar ~** two frankfurters

Frankfurter2 *Adj.* **1.** Frankfurt; **2.** **~ Würstchen** → **Frankfurter1**

Frankfurter3 *m*; *-s*, *-*, **~in** *f*; *-*, *-nen* Frankfurter

frankieren *v/t.* stamp; *mit e-r Maschine:* frank; **Frankiermaschine** *f* franking machine, *Am.* postage meter; **frankiert I.** *P.P.* → **frankieren**; **II.** *Adj.* **~**

F

sein mit Marke(n): have a stamp (*od.* stamps) on it; *mit Freistempel*: be post paid (*od.* prepaid); *der Brief ist nicht ausreichend ~* there are not enough stamps on the letter

Fränkin *f*; -, -nen Frank, Frankish woman (*od.* girl)

fränkisch *Adj.* **1.** *hist.* Frankish; *das ~e Reich → Frankenreich*; **2.** *Geog.* Franconian; *Fränkische Alb/Schweiz* Franconian Jura/Switzerland

franko *Adv. Post.* post-free, post paid

Frankokanadier *m*, *~in f* French Canadian; **frankokanadisch** *Adj.* French Canadian

franko|phil *Adj.* Francophile; *~phob Adj.* Francophobe; *~phon Adj. geh.* francophone

Frankreich (*n*); -s; *Geog.* France

Franse *f*; -, -n **1.** *Verzierung*: strand (of a fringe); *die ~n e-s Schals etc.* the fringe *Sg.*; **2.** (*loser Faden*) (loose) thread; *in ~n gehen* be becoming frayed; *in ~n sein* be in shreds (*od.* tatters); **3.** *~n* (*Pony*) fringe, *Am.* bangs; *pej.* (*Strähnen*) strands of hair; **fransen** *v/i.* fray; **fransig** *Adj.* **1.** *verziert*: fringed; **2.** (*ausgefranst*) frayed; *sich* (*Dat.*) *den Mund ~ reden umg. fig.* talk till one is blue in the face

Franzbranntwein *m* rubbing alcohol

Franziskaner *m*; -s, -, *~in f*; -, -nen; *kath.* Franciscan (*männlich*: friar / *weiblich*: nun); *~orden m* Franciscan Order, Order of St(.) Francis

Franzmann *m*; *Pl. Franzmänner*; *umg. altm., oft pej.* Frenchie, Frog *neg!*

Franzose *m*; -n, -n **1.** Frenchman; *die ~n* the French; *er ist ~* he's French; **2.** *Tech.* monkey wrench; **Französin** *f*; -, -nen Frenchwoman; *sie ist ~* she's French

französisch I. *Adj.* French; *~es Bett* double bed; *~e Krankheit altm.* syphilis; *die ~e Küche* French cuisine; *die ~e Schweiz* French-speaking Switzerland; *~e Spielkarten* ordinary (playing) cards; *~er Verkehr* oral sex; **II.** *Adv.* **1.** *geschrieben etc.*: in French; *aussprechen etc.*: in a French way; *sich ~ empfehlen umg. fig.* take French leave; **2.** *es ~ machen* (*oralen Verkehr haben*) have oral sex; **Französisch** *n*; -en; *Ling.* French; *das ~e* French; *sich auf ~ verabschieden umg. fig.* take French leave; → *auch Deutsch*; **französischsprachig** *Adj.* French-speaking, francophone; **französisieren** *v/t.* Gallicize; *bes. pej.* Frenchify

frappieren *v/t.* astonish, amaze; **frappierend** I. *Part. Präs. → frappieren*; **II.** *Adj.* amazing, astonishing, remarkable; *~e Ähnlichkeit* striking resemblance

Fräse *f*; -, -n **1.** *für Metall*: milling machine; *für Holz*: shaper; **2.** *Agr.* rotary hoe; **fräsen** *vt/i.* mill; (*Holz*) shape

Fräser[1] *m*; -s, - *Werkzeug*: cutter

Fräser[2] *m*; -s, -, *~in f*; -, -nen milling machine operator

Fräs|kopf *m* milling head; *~maschine f* milling machine

fraß *Imperf. → fressen*

Fraß *m*; -es, -e, *mst Sg.* **1.** *umg. pej.* (*Essen*) muck, swill; **2.** *für Tiere*: feed, food; *ein ~ der Geier sein* be food for the vultures; *etw. e-m Tier zum ~ werfen* throw s.th. to an animal (to eat), feed s.th. to an animal; **3.** *nur Sg.*; *fig.* (*Opfer*) food (+ *Gen.* for); *j-n der Presse zum ~ vorwerfen* feed s.o. to the press hounds, let the press pick over s.o.'s story; **4.** *nur Sg.*; *durch*

Schädlinge: damage; *durch Säure, Rost*: corrosion; *am Zahn*: caries

Frater *m*; -s, *Fratres*; *kath.* Brother

fraternisieren *v/i. geh.* fraternize; **Fraternisierung** *f geh.* fraternization

Fratz *m*; -es, -e, *bes. österr.* -en, -en **1.** little monkey; *niedlicher od. süßer ~* cute little thing; **2.** *bes. südd., österr. pej.* brat; *eitler ~* vain little so-and-so

Fratze *f*; -, -n **1.** *umg.* (*Grimasse*) grimace; *~n schneiden* pull (*Am.* make) faces; **2.** (*hässliches Gesicht*) grotesque face; **3.** *Sl.* (*Gesicht*) mug; *so e-e ~!* what a face!; *widerliche ~* ugly mug *umg.*; **fratzenhaft** *Adj.* grotesque

Frau I. *f*; -, -en **1.** woman; *in Statistik*: female; *die ~(en) Koll.* women; *typisch ~!* how typical of a woman!; **2.** (*Gattin*) wife; *zur ~ nehmen altm.* marry; *j-m s-e Tochter zur ~ geben altm.* give s.o.'s daughter's hand in marriage; *sie ist ihm e-e gute ~* she is a good wife to him; *willst du m-e ~ werden?* will you be my wife?; *wie geht es Ihrer ~?* how's your wife (the wife *umg.*, the missus *umg.*)?; **3.** (*Hausherrin, Dame*) lady; *die ~ des Hauses* the lady of the house; *gnädige ~ Anrede*: madam; *ist die gnädige ~ da?* is madam (*Adlige*: her ladyship) at home?; **4.** *vor Namen, bei verheirateter Frau*: Mrs, *Am.* Mrs.; *schriftlich*: auch Ms(.); *bei unverheirateter Frau, bes. schriftlich*: Ms(.), Miss *altm.*; *~ Doktor/Ministerin etc.* Doctor/Minister etc.; *~ Holle Myth.* Holda; *~ Holle schüttelt die Betten aus umg. fig.* it's snowing; **5.** *geh.*: *Ihre ~ Mutter* your mother; **II.** *frau unpers. Pron. Sl.* (*Ggs. man*) one; *Petra erklärte mir, wie frau es macht* Petra explained to me how it's done

Frauchen *n* **1.** (*Ggs. Herrchen*) mistress; *komm zu ~!* *zum Hund*: come to mistress!; **2.** *hum.*: *mein ~* (*m-e Frau*) my dear wife

Frauen|anteil *m* percentage of women; *~arbeit f* **1.** *für die Frau geeignet*: woman's job; *allg.* women's work; *das ist keine ~!* that's no job for a woman; **2.** *für die Belange der Frau*: work for the cause of women; *~arzt m*, *~ärztin f* gyn(a)ecologist; *~beauftragte m, f* women's representative; *~beruf m* female profession; *~bewegung f*: *die ~* the women's (*od.* the feminist) movement; *zur Frauenemanzipation*: women's lib *umg.*; *~buchladen m* women- -only bookshop; *~chor m* women's choir; *auch Komposition*: women's chorus

Frauenfeind *m* woman-hater, misogynist; **frauenfeindlich** *Adj.* anti-women; *Person*: *auch* woman-hating ..., misogynous *förm.*; *das Konzept ist ~ auch* the whole concept is hostile to women; **Frauenfeindlichkeit** *f* hostility towards women, misogyny *förm.*

frauenfreundlich *Adj.* favo(u)rable to women, pro-women

Frauen|fußball *m* women's football (*Am.* soccer); *~gefängnis n* women's prison; *~geschichte f umg.* **1.** *Krankheit*: women's trouble; **2.** (*Affäre*) affair (with a woman); *Pl.* affairs (with women), womanizing *Sg.*; *~gestalt f in Dichtung etc.*: female figure (*od.* form); *~gruppe f* **1.** group of women; **2.** *in der Frauenbewegung*: women's group (*od.* association)

frauenhaft *Adj.* feminine

Frauen|hand *f*: *von* (*zarter*) *~ geh.* by a woman's (fair) hand; *~hasser m*

woman-hater, misogynist *förm.*; *~haus n* women's refuge (*Am.* shelter); *~heilkunde f* gyn(a)ecology; *~held m* lady-killer *umg.*; *~kleid n* women's dress; *er trug ~er* he was wearing women's clothes, he was in drag; *~klinik f* gyn(a)ecological hospital (*od.* clinic); *~kloster n* convent; *~krankheit f*, *~leiden n* gyn(a)ecological disorder (*od.* problem); *~liebling m* favo(u)rite with the ladies; *~literatur f* women's literature; *emanzipatorische*: feminist writing(s *Pl.*) *od.* literature; *~mantel m Bot.* lady's mantle; *~mörder m* murderer of a woman (*Serienmörder*: of women); *~parkplatz m* parking space reserved for women; *~quote f* fixed proportion of women

Frauen|rechte *Pl.* women's rights; *~rechtler m* advocate (*od.* supporter) of women's rights; *~rechtlerin f* feminist, women's libber *umg.*; **frauenrechtlerisch** I. *Adj.* concerning women's rights, feminist; **II.** *Adv. kämpfen etc.*: for women's rights; *sich ~ betätigen* get involved with feminist issues

Frauen|referat *n* department for women's affairs; *~referent m*, *~referentin f* consultant on women's affairs

Frauen|rolle *f Theat.* female part; *~sache f* **1.** *Angelegenheit*: women's matter; *das ist ~* that's women's business; **2.** *euph., Krankheit*: women's trouble; *~schänder m* rapist; *~schuh m Bot.* lady's slipper; *~sport m* women's sport(s *Pl.*); *~station f* women's ward; *~stimme f* **1.** woman's (*bes. Mus.* female) voice; **2.** *mst Pl. bei e-r Wahl*: women's votes; *~stimmrecht n* votes *Pl.* for women, women's suffrage; *~treff m umg.* women's meeting place (*od.* haunt, hangout); *~überschuss m* surplus of women; *~wahlrecht n* votes *Pl.* for women, women's suffrage; *~zeitschrift f* women's magazine; *~zimmer n umg. pej., Dial. od. altm.* female, woman; *unverschämtes ~* brazen hussy *umg. altm.*

Fräulein *n*; -s, - *od. umg.* -s **1.** *junges*: (young) lady; *unverheiratetes*: spinster; → *englisch* I 1; **2.** *altm. Anrede, Titel*: Miss; *gnädiges ~ altm.* madam; *an junges Mädchen*: miss; *Ihr ~ Tochter altm. geh.* your daughter; **3.** *altm. neg!* (*Angestellte*) girl; (*Kindermädchen*) governess; (*Erzieherin, Lehrerin*) teacher; (*Verkäuferin*) sales girl, assistant; (*Kellnerin*) waitress; *alle in der Anrede*: Miss; *~!* excuse me; *~ vom Amt Telef. altm.* operator

fraulich *Adj.* feminine; (*reif*) womanly; **Fraulichkeit** *f*; *nur Sg.* femininity; womanliness, womanly quality (*od.* qualities *Pl.*)

Freak [fri:k] *m*; -s, -s; *Sl.* freak; *...freak m*, *im Subst.* freak; *Klassik~* classical music freak; *Motorrad~* motorbike freak (*od.* maniac)

frech I. *Adj.* **1.** (*Person*) cheeky, *bes. Am.* fresh, smart; (*Person, Antwort etc.*) impudent; (*betont unhöflich*) impertinent; (*dreist*) brazen; (*Lüge*) barefaced; *zuletzt wurde sie noch ~* then she started getting impertinent; *der ist ~ wie Oskar umg.* he's a cheeky devil (*Kind*: little brat); **2.** (*kess*) *Hütchen, Lied*: saucy; **II.** *Adv.*: *j-m ~ kommen umg.* get cheeky (*bes. Am.* smart) with s.o.; *~ grinsen* give a cheeky (*od.* impudent) grin; *er hat es ~ geleugnet* he had the cheek (*bes. Am.* nerve) to deny it

Frechdachs *m*; -es, -e; *umg. hum.*

cheeky (little) monkey

Frechheit f **1.** nur Sg. cheek, impudence, impertinence; von Kind: cheekiness, impudence; **die ~ haben zu** (+ Inf.) have the cheek (od. impudence, impertinence, nerve, temerity förm.) to (+ Inf.); **2.** Handlung, Äußerung: bit of cheek (bes. Am. nerve od. impertinence); Äußerung: auch cheeky (od. impudent) remark; **so e-e ~!** what a cheek (od. nerve), of all the cheek (od. nerve); **sich** (Dat.) (**j-m gegenüber**) **~en erlauben** start getting cheeky (od. impertinent, bes. Am. smart) (with s.o.)

Freemail ['fri:me:l] f; -, -s Computer: freemail, free web-based email

Freesie f; -, -n; Bot. freesia

Fregatte f; -, -n **1.** Mil. frigate; **2.** fig. pej. Frau: **e-e aufgetakelte ~** an excessively dolled up woman, a woman dressed up to the nines (od. dressed to kill)

Fregattvogel m Orn. frigate bird

frei I. Adj. **1.** free; **~er Bürger** hist. freeborn citizen, freeman; **ein ~er Mensch** (der tun kann, was er will) a free agent; **sie ist ~ zu gehen, wenn sie will** she is free to go if she wishes; **ich bin so ~** altm. od. hum. sich bedienen etc.: if I may; **ich war so ~, Ihr Auto zu nehmen** od. **und nahm Ihr Auto** I took the liberty of using your car, I helped myself to your car; **2.** Wahl, Wille etc.: free; Zugang: unrestricted, unlimited; (unbehindert) unrestrained; **„~ ab 16"** Film: 16 (= no admission to persons under 16 years), Am. etwa R(-rated); **jetzt haben wir ~e Fahrt mit** Zug: the signal's green now, the train can go now; mit Auto: the road's clear now; fig. there's nothing to stop us now; **auf ~em Fuß sein** be free; Verbrecher: be at large; **j-n auf ~en Fuß setzen** set s.o. free, let s.o. go; **das Recht auf ~e Meinungsäußerung** the right of free speech (od. of self-expression); **aus ~en Stücken** od. **~em Willen** of one's own free will; **die ~e Wahl haben zwischen ... und ...** be free to choose between ... and ...; **3.**; **4.** (unabhängig, selbstständig) Stadt etc.: free; Beruf, Tankstelle etc.: independent; (nicht gebunden) unattached; Journalist, Künstler etc.: freelance; Künste: liberal; **~er Mitarbeiter** freelance(r); → **Freie²**; **5.** im Namen von Organisationen etc.: **Freie Demokratische Partei** (abgek. **FDP**) Free Democratic Party; **Freie Deutsche Jugend** (abgek. **FDJ**) hist., ehem. DDR Free German Youth; **Freier Deutscher Gewerkschaftsbund** (abgek. **FDGB**) hist., ehem. DDR Free German Trade Union Organization; **die Freie Hansestadt Bremen** the Free Hanseatic City of Bremen; **6.** Wirts.: **im ~en Handel** available in the shops (Am. in stores); **~er Markt** open market; Börse: unofficial market; **~e Marktwirtschaft** free market economy; **~er Wechselkurs** floating exchange rate; **~e Wirtschaft** free enterprise; **die Rechte an diesem Buchtitel werden bald ~** the rights in this title will soon be free (od. available); **7.** (unbesetzt) Stuhl, Raum etc.: free, available; Leitung: vacant; Stelle: vacant, open; Straße etc.: clear, empty; (unbeschrieben) Seite, Zeile etc.: blank; **~ am WC**: vacant; am Taxi: for hire; **~e Stelle** vacancy; **ist der Platz noch ~?** is this seat taken?, is anyone sitting here?; **Platz ~ lassen/machen**

für leave/make space for; **j-m den Weg ~ machen** clear the way for s.o.; **zwei Zeilen ~ lassen** leave two blank lines; → **Bahn** 2, **Ring**, **Zimmer**. **8.** (unbedeckt) bare; **der Rock lässt die Knie ~** the skirt is above the knee; **den Oberkörper ~ machen** strip to the waist; **9.** Feld, Himmel, Meer, Sicht: open; **auf ~er Strecke** on an open stretch (Eisenb.: of line / Straße: of road); **in ~er Wildbahn** in the wild; **unter ~em Himmel** in the open (air), outside; **10.** Tag, Zeit etc.: free; nachgestellt: off; Person: free, not busy; **~e Zeit** (od. leisure) time; **nächsten Dienstag ist ~** next Tuesday is a holiday; **hast du morgen ~?** do you have tomorrow off?; **seitdem habe ich keine ~e Minute mehr** since then I haven't had a free moment (od. a moment to myself); **sind Sie ~?** Taxi: are you taken?; Verkäufer: are you serving someone?; **11.** (kostenlos) free (of charge); **~er Eintritt** admission free (für to); **Kinder unter sechs sind ~** umg. von Eintritt, Fahrgeld: children under six are free, no charge for children under six; **20 kg Gepäck sind ~** there is a baggage (bes. Am. luggage) allowance of 20 kg; **~ Haus** carriage paid; **Lieferung ~ Haus** free delivery, no delivery charge; **dazu bekommt sie auch noch e-n Job ~ Haus** fig. what's more, she gets a job handed to her on a plate; **du hast noch zwei Versuche ~** fig. you have two tries left; **12. ~ von** (ohne) von Schmerzen, Schulden etc.: free from (od. of), without; von Eis, Schneeschicht etc.: clear of; von Steuern etc. befreit: exempt from; **niemand ist ~ von Fehlern** nobody is perfect; **13.** sich **~ machen von** (herauskommen aus) get out of; (loswerden) get rid of; **14.** fig. (ungezwungen) free and easy; (offen) open; (moralisch großzügig) liberal; **~e Liebe** free love; **sie ist schon viel ~er geworden** she has loosened up a great deal; **15.** fig. Übersetzung: free; **~e Hand haben** have a free hand (bei with); **j-m ~e Hand lassen** give s.o. a free hand (bei with); **aus** od. **mit der ~en Hand zeichnen** (ohne Hilfsmittel) draw s.th. freehand; **16.** Sport (ungedeckt) unmarked; **der ~e Mann** (vor der Abwehr) the sweeper; **17.** Post. (frankiert) prepaid, post paid; **18.** Phys.; Elektron, Fall, Radikal etc.: free; Chem. uncombined; **im ~en Fall** in free fall; **~ werden** Energie etc.: be released; **II.** Adv. **1.** atmen, herumlaufen etc.: freely; **~ geboren** freeborn; **~ laufende Hühner** free-range hens; **Eier von ~ laufenden Hühnern** free-range eggs; **~ lebende Tiere** wildlife Sg., animals living in the wild (od. out of captivity); **~ praktizierender Arzt** doctor in private practice; **2.** herumliegen etc.: openly; **~ zugänglich von allen Seiten** freely accessible; **für alle**: open to all; **~ stehen** Baum, Haus etc.: stand by itself; Sport, Spieler: be unmarked; **~ stehend** Baum: solitary; Haus, nicht angebaut: detached; einzeln: isolated; Sport, Spieler: unmarked; **3.** Wirts. erhältlich, konvertierbar: freely; **~ finanziert** privately financed; **~ verkäuflich** on general sale, freely available (to buy); **4.** Tech.: **~ beweglich** freely moving, mobile; **~ hängend** od. schwebend unsupported; **5. ~** (und offen) openly, frankly, freely; → **frank**, **freiheraus**; **6. ~ sprechen** Redner:

speak without notes; mit Handy im Auto: phone (od. talk) hands-free, use the speaker phone; **e-n Kreis ~ zeichnen** draw a circle freehand; **das Kind kann schon ~ laufen** etc. the child can walk etc. unaided; **7. ~ erfunden** (entirely) fictitious; **das hat er ~ erfunden** he made that up; **~ nach** (e-m Stück von) **X** freely adapted from (a play by) X; **8.** (liberal) liberally; **~ erzogen sein** have had a liberal upbringing

...frei im Adj. **1.** (ohne ...) Inhalt: ...-free; Krankheit: free from ...; **stickstoff~** nitrogen-free, non-nitrogenous; **tuberkulose~** free from tuberculosis; **2.** nicht geschehend: non-...; **blend~** Beleuchtung: non-dazzle; **repressions~** Erziehung: non-repressive; **3.** nicht verlangt: exempt from ..., ...-exempt; **visum~** not requiring a visa, visa-exempt; **4.** nicht bedeckt: Person: with bare ...; Kleid: leaving ... bare; **nabel~** with a bare midriff; **schulter~** off-the-shoulder; **5.** unabhängig: independent of ...; **bündnis~** independent of any alliance, unallied; **trust~** non-trust

Frei|anlage f oft Pl. **1.** in Wohngebiet: open space; **2.** Sport open-air facility; (Sportplatz) playing field; **~bad** n open-air (od. outdoor) swimming pool; **~ballon** m free balloon; **~bank** f cheap meat counter

freibekommen (unreg., trennb., hat) **I.** vt/i. get off; **bekommst du morgen frei?** do you get tomorrow off?; **ich habe nicht ~** I wasn't able to get off, I didn't get any time off; **II.** v/t. **1.** (Hände etc.) get free; **2.** (j-n) get s.o. free; durch Verhandlungen etc.: obtain s.o.'s release, get s.o. out umg.

Freiberufler m; -s, -, **~in** f; -, -nen freelance(r), self-employed person; **~ sein** be a freelance(r), be freelance (od. self-employed); **freiberuflich I.** Adj. freelance, self-employed; Anwalt, Arzt: in private practice; **II.** Adv.: **~ arbeiten** od. **tätig sein** work (as a) freelance; Arzt etc.: have a private practice, practi|se (Am. -ce) privately

Freibetrag m Steuern: tax allowance

Freibeuter m; -s, -, **~in** f; -, -nen **1.** hist. buccaneer; **2.** fig. pej. shark

Freibier n free beer

freibleibend Adj. und Adv. Wirts., Preis, Angebot: provisional, subject to alteration

Freibord m Naut. freeboard; **~marke** f Naut. Plimsoll line (od. mark)

freiboxen v/t. (trennb., hat -ge-); fig. bail out

Freibrief m **1.** hist. charter; **2.** fig.: **kein ~ für etw. sein** be no excuse for s.th; **j-m e-n ~ ausstellen** give s.o. carte blanche (für to + Inf.); **er glaubt, e-n ~ zu haben für ...** he thinks he has carte blanche for (od. to + Inf.) ...; **er sieht das als ~ an zu ...** he regards this as an open invitation to ...

Freidemokrat m, **~in** f Free Democrat; **freidemokratisch** Adj. nur attr. Free Democrat

Freidenker m, **~in** f freethinker; **Freidenkertum** n; -s, kein Pl. freethinking

Freie¹ n; -n, kein Pl.: **das ~** the open air; **ins ~ gehen** go outdoors; **im ~n** in the open (air), outdoors, outside; **im ~n übernachten** camp out; **Spiele im ~n** outdoor games

Freie² m, f; -n, -n **1.** hist. freeborn citizen; **2.** (freier Mitarbeiter) freelance(r)

Freier m; -s, - **1.** euph. (Prostituiertenkunde) client; **2.** altm. suitor; **Freiers-**

F

füße *Pl. umg. hum.*: **auf ~n gehen** *od.* **wandeln** be looking for a wife; (*um e-e bestimmte Frau werben*) be courting

Frei|exemplar *n* free (*od.* complimentary) copy; **~fahrschein** *m* free ticket; **~fahrt** *f* free ride; **~fläche** *f* open space; *Verkaufsfläche*: outdoor sales area; **~flug** *m Flug.* free flight; **~frau** *f*, **~fräulein** *n* baroness; **~gabe** *f* **1.** *von Gefangenen, Leiche, Meldung etc.*: release; **2.** *e-r Straße etc.*: opening (**für den Verkehr** to traffic); *Flug.* clearance (**zum Start** for take-off); **die ~ e-s Films für e-e Altersgruppe** the passing of a film for an age group; **3.** *Wirts. des Wechselkurses*: floating; **~gang** *m*: **~ haben** be on day release; **er kam vom ~ nicht zurück** he failed to return from day release; **~gänger** *m; -s, -*, **~gängerin** *f; -, -nen*; (*Häftling*) day release prisoner; **~ sein** auch be on day release

freigeben (*unreg., trennb., hat -ge-*) **I.** *v/t.* **1.** (*Gefangene*) release; (*Partner, Angestellte*) release from his (*od.* her) contract; **2.** (*Flugzeug*) **zum Start ~** clear for take-off; **zum Abschuss ~** (*Wild*) declare open season for; *umg.fig.* (*j-n*) throw *s.o.* to the wolves; **für den Verkehr ~** open to traffic; **zur Veröffentlichung ~** release for publication; **j-m den Weg ~** geh. clear the way for *s.o.*, let *s.o.* pass; **freigegeben ab 6** (**Jahren**) *Film*: passed for children over 6; **3. den Blick ~ auf** (+ *Akk.*) open up the view of; **4.** *Wirts.* (*Wechselkurse*) float, remove controls on; (*Mieten, Preise*) decontrol; (*gesperrtes Konto etc.*) release; **II.** *vt/i.*: **j-m ~** let *s.o.* off, give *s.o.* time off; **sie hat sich eine Woche ~ lassen** she has arranged to have a week off

freigebig *Adj.* generous (**gegen** to); **Freigebigkeit** *f; nur Sg.* generosity (**gegen** to), largess(e) *förm.*

Frei|gehege *n* open-air enclosure; **~geist** *m* freethinker; **~gelände** *n* (piece of) open ground, open space; **~gelassene** *m, f; -n, -n* freedman; *Frau*: freedwoman; **~gepäck** *n Flug.* baggage (*bes. Am.* luggage) allowance

freigestellt I. *P.P.* → **freistellen**; **II.** *Adj.* **1.** (*wahlweise*) optional; **2. ~ sein von** be exempt from

freigiebig *etc.* → **freigebig** *etc.*

Freigrenze *f Steuern*: tax exemption limit

freihaben *v/i.* (*unreg., trennb., hat -ge-*); *umg.* have time off; **freitags habe ich frei** I have Friday('s) off, Friday's my day off; **sie hat heute frei** *einmalig*: she's got today (*od.* the day) off; *regelmäßig*: it's her day off today

Freihafen *m Naut.* free port

freihalten (*unreg., trennb., hat -ge-*) **I.** *v/t.* **1.** (*e-n Platz*) keep, save; (*Straße, Einfahrt*) keep clear; (*Angebot, Stelle etc.*) keep open; **„Eingang ~!“** keep clear; **2. j-n ~** treat (*od.* pay for) *s.o.*; **sich von j-m ~ lassen** be treated by *s.o.*, let *s.o.* pay for everything; **3. ~ von** keep free of; (*Eingang, Straße etc.*) keep clear of; **II.** *v/refl.* **1.** keep o.s. free (**für** for); **2. sich ~ von** ward off, avoid

Freihandbücherei *f* open access (*Am.* open stack) library

Freihandel *m Wirts.* free trade

Freihandels|abkommen *n Wirts.* free trade agreement; **~gemeinschaft** *f*: **die Europäische ~** the European Free Trade Association; **~zone** *f* free trade area

freihändig *Adj. und Adv.* **1.** *Radfahren etc.*: with no hands; *Schießen*: without support, offhand *fachspr.*; *Zeichnen etc.*: freehand; **2.** *Jur.* private(ly); *Wirts. Verkauf etc.*: direct; **~er Verkauf von Wertpapieren**: over-the-counter trade

Freihandzeichnen *n* freehand drawing

Freiheit *f; -, -en* **1.** *nur Sg.* freedom, liberty; **in ~** *Tier*: in the wild; (*Ggs. in Haft*) free, at liberty; **in ~ sein** be free; **j-m / e-m Tier die ~ schenken** set *s.o.* / an animal free, give *s.o.* his (*od.* her) freedom / an animal its freedom; **2.** (*Vorrecht*) freedom (**zu** + *Inf.* of + *Ger. od.* to + *Inf.*); (*Freiraum*) scope; (*Unabhängigkeit*) independence; **dichterische ~** poetic licen|ce (*Am.* -se); **die ~ haben zu** (+ *Inf.*) be free to (+ *Inf.*); **sich die ~ nehmen zu** (+ *Inf.*) take the liberty of (+ *Ger.*) (*od.* to [+ *Inf.*]); **sich ~en herausnehmen** take liberties (**gegenüber** with); **j-m völlige ~ lassen** give *s.o.* carte blanche; **in m-r Position genießt man gewisse ~en** you have certain privileges in my position; → **Pressefreiheit**, **Redefreiheit** *etc.*; **3.** *nur Sg.*: **~ von** (*Abwesenheit*) **von** *Mängeln etc.*: freedom from; *von Lasten, Steuern*: exemption from; **4.** *Tech.* (*Spielraum*) free play, clearance

...freiheit *f; nur Sg.; im Subst.* **1.** *Abwesenheit*: freedom from ...; *Fieber~* freedom from fever, feverless condition; *Schaden~* freedom from damage, undamaged condition; **2.** *Recht, Möglichkeit*: freedom of ...; *Auswanderungs~* freedom to emigrate; *Informations~* freedom of information

freiheitlich *Adj.* free; *Gesinnung etc.*: liberal; **die Freiheitliche Partei Österreichs** the Austrian Freedom Party; **Freiheitliche** *m, f; -n, -n*; *Pol.* member of the (Austrian) Freedom Party; **die ~n** the (Austrian) Freedom Party

Freiheits|begriff *m* concept of freedom (*od.* liberty); **~beraubung** *f Jur.* unlawful detention (*od.* imprisonment); **~beschränkung** *f* restriction of personal liberty; **~bewegung** *f* freedom movement; **~drang** *m* desire for independence (*od.* freedom); **~entzug** *m Jur.* imprisonment; **~kampf** *m* struggle for freedom (*od.* [political] independence); (*Aufstand*) revolt; **~kämpfer** *m*, **~kämpferin** *f* freedom fighter; **~krieg** *m* war of liberation (*od.* independence)

Freiheitsliebe *f* love of liberty; **freiheitsliebend** *Adj.* freedom-loving

Freiheits|statue *f; nur Sg.* Statue of Liberty; **~strafe** *f Jur.* prison sentence; **zu e-r ~ von fünf Jahren verurteilt werden** be sentenced to five years' imprisonment

freiheraus *Adv.* openly, straight out, frankly; (*unverblümt*) point-blank; **immer ~!** don't be afraid to speak your mind

Freiherr *m* baron; **Freiherrin** *f* baroness

freikämpfen (*trennb., hat -ge-*) **I.** *v/t.* (fight to) free, liberate; **II.** *v/refl.* fight o.s. free; *aus e-r Menge etc.*: fight (*od.* battle) one's way out (**aus** of)

Freikarte *f* free ticket; *Theat. etc. auch* complimentary ticket

Freikauf *m e-r Geisel*: ransom; **freikaufen** (*trennb., hat -ge-*) **I.** *v/t.* (*j-n*) pay for *s.o.'s* release, ransom; **II.** *v/refl.* **1.** pay for one's release (*od.* freedom);

2. *fig.* buy a clear conscience

Freikirche *f* free church

freikommen *v/i.* (*unreg., trennb., ist -ge-*) get free; (*wegkommen*) get away; *Jur.* be released; (*freigesprochen werden*) be acquitted

Freikörperkultur *f; nur Sg.* naturism, nudism; **~verein** *m* naturist (*od.* nudist) association

Freikorps *n hist.* volunteer corps

frei|kratzen *v/t.* (*trennb., hat -ge-*); (*Autofenster*) scrape clear; **~kriegen** *v/t.* (*trennb., hat -ge-*); *umg.* → **freibekommen**

Freiland *n; nur Sg.* open ground; **ins ~ pflanzen** plant out in open ground, plant outdoors

Freiland... *im Subst.* outdoor ...; *aus Freilandhaltung*: free-range ...; **~anbau** *m* outdoor cultivation; **aus ~ grown outdoors**; **~gemüse** *n* outdoor vegetables *Pl.*; **~haltung** *f* free-range husbandry; **Eier/Hühner aus ~** free-range eggs/chickens; **~versuch** *m* outdoor test planting

freilassen *v/t.* (*unreg., trennb., hat -ge-*) release, set free; **gegen Kaution/ ein Lösegeld ~** release on bail / for a ransom; **Freilassung** *f* release

Freilauf *m Tech.* freewheel; **im ~ fahren** freewheel, coast

frei|laufen *v/refl.* (*unreg., trennb., hat -ge-*); *Sport* get into space; **~legen** *v/t.* (*trennb., hat -ge-*) lay open, expose; (*Verschüttetes*) uncover

Freileitung *f Etech.* overhead (power) line

freilich *Adv.* **1.** *einschränkend*: though, however; **die Entscheidung ist ~ noch nicht endgültig** however the decision is not final; **2.** (*zugegebenermaßen*) of course, admittedly; **3.** *bes. südd.* of course

Freilicht|bühne *f* open-air theat|re (*Am. auch* -er); *für Konzerte*: open-air (concert) platform; **~kino** *n* open-air cinema; (*Autokino*) drive-in (cinema, *Am.* movie theater); **~konzert** *n* open-air concert; **~malerei** *f* plein-air painting; **~museum** *n* open-air museum

freiliegen *v/i.* (*unreg., trennb., hat / südd., österr., schw. ist -ge-*) *Goldader, Leitung etc.*: lie exposed (*od.* uncovered)

Freilos *n* **1.** free (lottery) ticket; **2.** *Sport* bye

Freiluft... *im Subst.* open-air ..., outdoor ...

freimachen (*trennb., hat -ge-*) **I.** *v/t.* (*Brief etc.*) put a stamp (*od.* stamps) on; *mit Freistempel*: frank; **mit 3 Euro ~** put a 3 euro stamp on; *mit mehreren Marken*: put 3 euros worth of stamps (*od.* postage) on; **II.** *v/i.* (*nicht arbeiten*) take time off; **e-n Tag ~** take a day off; → *auch* **frei** I 7; **III.** *v/refl.* **1.** *umg.*; *vom Dienst etc.*: take time off; **sich für ein paar Stunden ~, um einkaufen zu gehen** take a few hours off to go shopping; **2.** (*sich ausziehen*) undress, get undressed; → *auch* **frei** I 7

Freimaurer *m* Freemason, *Am. auch* Mason; **~loge** *f* freemasons' (*od.* Masonic) lodge

freimütig *Adj.* candid, open; **Freimütigkeit** *f* **1.** *nur Sg.* cando(u)r, openness; **2.** *Äußerung*: candid remark

freinehmen *v/i.* (*unreg., trennb., hat -ge-*); *umg.*: (*sich* [*Dat.*]) **~ / e-n Tag ~** take time / a day off

Freiplatz *m* **1.** *im Internat etc.*: free

F

place; **2.** *im Kino etc.*: free seat; **3.** *Sport* outdoor court

freipressen *v/t.* (*trennb., hat -ge-*) obtain *s.o.'s* release

Freiraum *m auch Pl.* (*Spielraum*) (personal) freedom; *zur Selbstentfaltung*: space to be o.s.; **sich Freiräume schaffen** create space for o.s.

frei|räumen *v/t.* (*trennb., hat -ge-*) clear; **~religiös** *Adj. Reli.* non-denominational

Freisasse *m; -n, -n; hist.* yeoman

freischaffend I. *Adj.* freelance; **II.** *Adv.*: **~ tätig sein** work (as a) freelance, be a freelance(r)

freischalten *v/t.* (*trennb., hat -ge-*); *Telef.* (*Leitung*) clear; (*Handy*) connect, enable; **Freischaltung** *f Telef.* clearing; *e-s Handys*: connection (*Brit. auch* connexion), enablement

Freischärler *m; -s, -* **1.** guer(r)illa; **2.** *hist.* irregular

frei|schaufeln *v/t.* (*trennb., hat -ge-*) shovel clear; (*Wagen etc.*) *auch* dig out; **~schießen** *v/t.* (*unreg., trennb., hat -ge-*): *j-m/sich den Weg* ~ shoot s.o.'s/one's way out (*od.* through.)

Freischicht *f* **1.** *Zeit*: free shift; **~ haben** have a free shift; **2.** *Koll., Personen*: workers *Pl.* on a free shift

freischwimmen *v/refl.* (*unreg., trennb., hat -ge-*); *umg. fig.* learn to stand on one's own two feet, make the break *umg.*

Freischwimmer[1] *m, ~in f person who has passed the 15-minute swimming test*

Freischwimmer[2] *m, n umg.* → *Freischwimmerabzeichen*; **~abzeichen** *n*: *das* ~ *haben/machen* hold the Freischwimmer badge / take the Freischwimmer test

freisetzen *v/t.* (*trennb., hat -ge-*) **1.** *Chem., Phys.* (*Energie, Gas*) release; (*Gas*) *auch* give off; (*Elektronen, Strahlung etc.*) emit; **2.** *euph.* (*Arbeitskräfte*) release, make redundant, *Am.* lay off; **Freisetzung** *f* **1.** *Chem., Phys. von Energie, Gas*: release; *von Elektronen, Strahlung etc.*: emission; **2.** *euph. von Arbeitskräften*: release, redundancy

freisinnig *Adj.* liberal(-minded)

Freispiel *n am Automaten etc.*: free game; **freispielen** (*trennb., hat -ge-*) **I.** *v/refl.* **1.** *Sport* get into space; **2.** *Thea., Film*: get over one's stage fright; **II.** *v/t.* (*Spieler*) play *s.o.* clear, create space for

Freisprechanlage *f Telef.* speaker phone, hands-free device (*od.* function)

freisprechen *v/t.* (*unreg., trennb., hat -ge-*) **1.** *vor Gericht*: acquit (*von* of); *von Schuld*: exonerate (from); *von Verdacht*: clear (of); *kirchl.* absolve (from); **2.** *Wirts.* (*Lehrling*) release from his (*od.* her) articles

Freisprechen *n; -s, kein Pl.; Telef.* making calls with a speaker phone

Frei|spruch *m* acquittal; *Urteil*: verdict of not guilty; **~staat** *m* free state; *der* **~ Bayern/Sachsen** the Free State of Bavaria/Saxony; **~statt** *f; -, Freistätten*; *geh.* sanctuary

freistehen *v/i.* (*unreg., trennb., hat / südd., österr., schw. ist -ge-*) **1.** (*leerstehen*) be unoccupied, be empty; **2.** *j-m* ~ be up to s.o.; *es steht Ihnen frei zu* (+ *Inf.*) you are free to ...; *bei Alternativen*: it's up to you whether you want to ...

freistellen *v/t.* (*trennb., hat -ge-*) **1.** *auch*

Mil. exempt, release (**von** from; **für** for); *vom Unterricht*: excuse; **2.** *Wirts., euph.* (*entlassen*) make redundant; **3.** *j-m etw.* ~ leave s.th. (up) to s.o.; *es ist ihm freigestellt zu* (+ *Inf.*) he's free to (+ *Inf.*); → **freigestellt**; **Freistellung** *f* **1.** exemption; (*Befreiung*) release; **2.** *euph.* (*Entlassung*) redundancy; **Freistellungsauftrag** *m Fin., an Bank*: application for exemption from taxation of income from capital

Freistempel *m Post.* franking stamp (*od.* mark)

Freistil *m Sport* freestyle; **~ringen** *n* freestyle wrestling; **~schwimmen** *n* freestyle swimming

Frei|stoß *m Sport, Fußball*: free kick; *e-n* ~ *ausführen* (*od.* *treten umg.*) take a free kick; **~stunde** *f Schule*: free period

Freitag *m* Friday; *der Schwarze* ~ *Fin. hist.* Black Friday; *ein schwarzer* ~ a disastrous Friday; → **Dienstag**, **~abend** *etc.* → *Dienstagabend etc.*

freitags *Adv.* on Friday(s); → *dienstags*

Freitod *m euph.* suicide; *in den* ~ *gehen od. den* ~ *wählen* commit suicide, take one's own life

freitragend *Adj. Archit., Tech.* cantilever ..., self-supporting; *Achse*: floating

Frei|treppe *f Archit.* (flight of) steps *Pl.* (+ *Gen.* of, in front of, leading up to); **~umschlag** *m Post.* stamped addressed envelope, *Brit. auch* sae, *Am. auch* SASE; *vorgedruckt*: prepaid envelope; **~verkehr** *m Wirts.*: *geregelter/ungeregelter* ~ over-the-counter/ /unlisted trading; **~vermerk** *m Wirts.* prepaid notice

freiweg *Adv. umg.* straight out; ~ *reden können* be able to talk openly

Freiwild *n fig.* fair game

freiwillig I. *Adj.* voluntary; (*aus sich heraus*) spontaneous; **~e Feuerwehr** volunteer fire brigade; **~e Leistung** *finanzielle*: ex gratia payment; **~es soziales Jahr** year of voluntary community service; **II.** *Adv. auch* of one's own free will; *sich* ~ *melden* volunteer (*zu* for); **Freiwillige** *m, f; -n, -n* volunteer

Frei|wurf *m Sport* free throw; **~zeichen** *n Telef.* ringing tone; (*Amtszeichen*) dialling (*Am.* dial) tone

Freizeit *f* **1.** *nur Sg.*; free (*od.* spare) time, leisure (time); **2.** *Veranstaltung*: holiday (*Am.* vacation) activity program(me) (*for a common interest group*); **~angebot** *n* (program[me] of) leisure activities *Pl.*; (*Einrichtungen*) recreational facilities *Pl.*; *ein großes* ~ *haben auch* offer a lot of leisure activities; **~beschäftigung** *f* leisure pursuit (*od.* activity); *Koll.* leisure pursuits (*od.* activities) *Pl.*; *recreation*; **~einrichtung** *f* recreational facility; **~gesellschaft** *f Soziol.* leisure-oriented society; **~gestaltung** *f* leisure activities *Pl.*; *die richtige* ~ *ist sehr wichtig* it's very important to organize one's spare time (*od.* leisure) properly; **~hemd** *n* casual shirt; **~hose** *f* casual trousers (*Am. pants od.* slacks) *Pl.*; **~industrie** *f* leisure industry; **~kleidung** *f* leisurewear; **~park** *m* amusement park; **~problem** *n* problem of how to spend one's spare time; **~sektor** *m* leisure sector; **~verhalten** *n* recreational behavio(u)r; **~wert** *m* recreational value; *mit hohem* ~ with a wide range of leisure facilities; **~zentrum** *n* leisure cent|re (*Am.* -er)

---

freizügig I. *Adj.* **1.** (*großzügig*) generous, liberal; (*Auslegung*) loose; **2.** *moralisch*: permissive; (*Beziehungen*) free; (*Film etc.*) explicit; (*gewagt*) risqué; **3.** *Wirts.* unrestricted; **4.** (*nicht ortsgebunden*) free to move, mobile; (*Leben*) nomadic; **II.** *Adv.* **1.** (*großzügig*) *Geld ausgeben*: liberally; *auslegen*: loosely; **2.** ~ *leben* lead a nomadic life, move from place to place; **Freizügigkeit** *f* **1.** (*Großzügigkeit*) generosity; *der Auslegung*: looseness; **2.** *moralische, sexuelle*: permissiveness; *der Beziehungen*: freedom; *e-s Films etc.*: explicitness; (*Gewagtheit*) risqué nature; **3.** (*Ortsungebundenheit*) freedom of movement, mobility

fremd *Adj.* **1.** (*unbekannt, ungewohnt*) strange; **~e Leute** strangers; *in ~er Umgebung* in unfamiliar surroundings; *ich bin hier selbst* ~ I'm a stranger here myself; *sich* ~ *fühlen* feel like a stranger, feel very strange; *er ist mir* ~ he's a stranger to me, I don't know him (at all); *das ist mir nicht* ~ that's nothing new to me; *Eifersucht ist ihm* ~ jealousy is unknown (*od.* alien) to him; *sie tat so* ~ she was very distant (*scheu*: shy); *sich od. einander* ~ *werden* grow apart, become strangers; *im Lauf der Jahre wurde er mir immer* ~*er* over the years we drifted further and further apart (*od.* we had less and less in common); *m-e Heimatstadt ist mir* ~ *geworden* I no longer know (*od.* recognize) my home town; **2.** (*ausländisch*) *Länder, Sprachen etc.*: foreign; *bes. Pflanzen, Tiere*: exotic; **3.** (*Ggs. eigen*) *Eigentum etc.*: other people's; **~es Organ** foreign organ; (*Transplantat*) transplanted organ; **~e Welten** other worlds; *in ~en Händen* in strange hands; *unter ~em Namen* under an assumed name, incognito; *das ist nicht für ~e Ohren bestimmt* this is for your ears only, not a word of this to anyone else; *misch dich nicht in ~e Angelegenheiten* don't go poking your nose into other people's business; *sich mit ~en Federn schmücken fig.* steal someone else's thunder; **4.** (*nicht dazugehörig*) extraneous; (*von außen*) outside ...; **~e Hilfe** outside help; *es ohne ~e Hilfe schaffen* manage without help, do it unaided

...fremd *im Adj.* **1.** (*Ggs. ...nah*) foreign (*od.* alien) to ...; *kultur~* foreign to one's culture; *realitäts~* out of touch with reality; **2.** (*nicht dazugehörig*) unrelated to ...; *berufs~* unrelated to one's profession; *branchen~* from another sector (of industry), new to the industry; *vereins~* not belonging to the club; (*Person*) *auch* who is a non-member

Fremdarbeiter *m, ~in f altm. neg!* foreign worker

fremdartig *Adj.* strange; (*Pflanze, Gericht etc.*) exotic; (*Aussehen, Kleidung*) *auch* outlandish

Fremd|befruchtung *f Bot.* cross-fertilization; **~bestäubung** *f* cross-pollination

fremdbestimmt *Adj. Soziol., Pol. etc.* heteronomous

Fremde[1] *f; -, kein Pl.*: *die* ~ foreign parts *Pl.*; *in die/der* ~ away from home; (*ins od. im Ausland*) abroad; *aus der* ~ *heimkehren* return from abroad (*od.* foreign parts)

Fremde[2] *m, f; -n, -n* **1.** stranger; *er ist mir kein ~r* he is known to me; **2.** (*Ausländer*) foreigner, alien *bes.*

Amtsspr.; **3.** (*Urlauber*) visitor

Fremdeinwirkung *f*; *nur Sg.*; *Jur.*: **ohne ~** without anyone else (*bei Verkehrsunfall*: any other vehicle) being involved

fremden, *schw.* **fremden** *v/i.* be shy (with strangers); **er/sie fremdelt sehr** *auch* he/she doesn't take to strangers at all

Fremden|bett *n* (guest) bed; **~buch** *n* visitors' book

fremdenfeindlich *Adj.* xenophobic, hostile to foreigners; **die Leute hier sind sehr ~** *auch* they don't like foreigners around here; **Fremdenfeindlichkeit** *f*; *nur Sg.* xenophobia, hostility towards foreigners

Fremden|führer *m*, **~führerin** *f* (tourist) guide; **~hass** *m* xenophobia, hatred of foreigners; **~hasser** *m*, **~hasserin** *f* hater of foreigners; **~heim** *n* guest house; **~legion** *f* Mil. Foreign Legion; **~legionär** *m* Mil. (Foreign) Legionnaire; **~polizei** *f* aliens' (police) department; **~verkehr** *m* tourism

Fremdenverkehrs|amt *n*, **~büro** *m* tourist office (*od.* bureau); **~ort** *m* tourist resort; **~verein** *m* tourist association (*od.* board)

Fremdenzimmer *n* im *Gasthaus etc.*: room (to let, *Am.* to rent)

Fremdfinanzierung *f* Wirts. outside financing

fremdgehen *v/i.* (*unreg.*, *trennb.*, *ist -ge-*); *umg.* two-time, be unfaithful, go out with another man *od.* woman

Fremdheit *f*; *nur Sg.* strangeness; (*Unvertrautheit*) unfamiliarity

Fremd|herrschaft *f* foreign rule; **~kapital** *n* Wirts. borrowed capital; **~körper** *m* **1.** Bio., Med. foreign body; **2.** *fig. Sache*: alien element; *Person*: odd man out; **wie ein ~ wirken** be (completely) out of place

fremdländisch *Adj.* foreign; *weitS.* exotic

Fremdling *m*; *-s*, *-e*; *altm.*, *bes. lit.* stranger, alien *förm.*

Fremdsprache *f* foreign language

Fremdsprachen|erwerb *m* Ling. foreign (*od.* second) language acquisition; **~kenntnisse** *Pl.* knowledge *Sg.* of foreign languages; *als Überschrift im Lebenslauf etc.*: foreign languages; **~korrespondent** *m*, **~korrespondentin** *f* foreign language correspondent; **~sekretär** *m*, **~sekretärin** *f* bilingual (*mehrsprachig*: multilingual) secretary

fremdsprachig *Adj.* **1.** *Bevölkerungsteil etc.*: foreign-speaking ...; **2.** *Buch etc.*: foreign-language ...; **~er Unterricht** teaching (*od.* tuition) in a foreign (*od.* second) language

fremdsprachlich *Adj.* foreign-language ...

Fremd|stoff *m* Med. foreign substance; **~verschulden** *n* Jur. involvement of another person; **es liegt eindeutig ~ vor** it is obvious that someone else was involved; **~währung** *f* foreign currency

Fremdwort *n*; *Pl. Fremdwörter* foreign word; (*Latinismus*) hard word; **das ist für ihn ein ~** *fig.* he doesn't know what it means; **Kontoüberziehung ist für uns ein ~** we would never think of becoming overdrawn; **Fremdwörterbuch** *n* dictionary of foreign loan words

frenetisch *Adj. geh.* frenzied; *Applaus*: *auch* wild

frequentieren *v/t. geh.* frequent; **das Lokal wird stark frequentiert** a lot of

people go to this restaurant, this restaurant is very popular

Frequenz *f*; *-*, *-en* **1.** Phys., Funk. frequency; **auf der ~ von 50 Kilohertz senden** broadcast on 50 kilohertz; **2.** Med., des Pulses etc.: (pulse) rate; **3.** *geh.* (*Häufigkeit*) frequency; (*Besucherzahl*) number of visitors; des Verkehrs: density, volume

Frequenz|bereich *m* Phys., Funk. frequency range; **~skala** *f* tuning dial

Fresko *n*; *-s*, *Fresken*; *Kunst* fresco (*Pl.* frescos *od.* frescoes)

Fresken|maler *m* fresco painter; **~malerei** *f* fresco (painting); **~malerin** *f* fresco painter

Fressalien *Pl. umg. hum.* grub *Sg.*, eats, *Brit. auch* nosh *Sg.*

Fresse *f*; *-*, *-n*; *vulg.* **1.** (*Mund*) trap *umg.*, *Brit. auch* gob; **halt die ~!** shut your trap!; **er hat 'ne große ~** he has a big mouth; → *auch* Maul; **2.** (*Gesicht*) mug *umg.*; **j-m die ~ polieren** smash s.o.'s face in; **eins auf die ~ kriegen** get a bash (*od.* punch) in the face; **ich hau dir gleich eins in die ~!** I'll bash your ugly mug if you don't watch it; **3.** *fig.*: (**ach du**) **m-e ~!** *erstaunt*: well I'll be blowed (*Am.* darned)!; *bewundernd*: out of this world!

fressen; *frisst*, *fraß*, *hat gefressen* **I.** *v/t.* **1.** *Tier*: eat; *Raubtier*:(*verschlingen*) devour; (*sich ernähren von*) eat, feed on; **was gibst du ihnen zu ~?** what do you give them to eat?, what do you feed them on?; **2.** *e-n Trog etc.* **leer ~** empty a trough *etc.*; *e-n Baum kahl ~* strip a tree (bare); *Löcher ~ in* (+ *Akk.*) Motten, *fig.* Rost etc.: eat holes in; **3.** *umg. pej. Mensch*: eat; *gierig und viel*: stuff o.s. with, guzzle; *schnell*: gobble; *j-n arm ~* eat s.o. out of house and home; **4.** *umg. fig.* (*Bücher*) devour; (*Geld etc.*) gobble up; (*Kraft, Strom etc.*) consume; (*Benzin*) drink, guzzle; (*zerstören*) eat away; *Kilometer ~* drive endlessly on and on (without stopping); **5.** *umg. fig.*: **er wird dich schon nicht ~!** he won't eat you (*od.* bite); **das habe ich gefressen** (*habe ich dick*) I can't stand it; **er hat's gefressen** (*kapiert*) the penny's dropped; (*geglaubt*) he fell for it; **er hat's immer noch nicht gefressen** (*kapiert*) he still hasn't got it into his thick skull; **die Großen ~ die Kleinen** the big boys swallow up the little fellows, the big fish eat the little fish; **da heißt's ~ oder gefressen werden** it's (a case of) dog eat dog; **j-n zum Fressen gern haben** love s.o. so much one could eat him/her; → *auch* Besen 1, Narr 1; **II.** *v/i.* **1.** *Tier*: eat; **j-m aus der Hand ~** eat out of s.o.'s hand (*auch fig.*); **friss, Vogel, oder stirb!** *umg. fig.* you've got no choice; **2.** *~ an* (+ *Dat.*) Maus etc.: gnaw at; *fig.* Bohrer, Rost, Säure etc.: eat away at; *Feuer, Flammen*: begin to eat up; *Hass, Neid etc.*: gnaw at s.o.; **3.** *umg. pej. Mensch*: eat; *gierig und viel*: stuff o.s.; *schnell*: gobble; **er isst nicht, er frisst** he eats like a pig; **III.** *v/refl.* **1.** *sich ~ durch/in* (+ *Akk.*) *auch* Säure etc.: eat through/into; **2.** *sich satt ~* Tier: eat its fill; *sich dick und rund ~* get rotund by gobbling too much (*auch umg. Mensch*)

Fressen *n*; *-s*, *kein Pl.* für Tier: food, feed; *vulg.* → Fraß 1; **das ist ein gefundenes ~ für ihn** *umg. fig.* that's just what he was waiting for; **erst kommt das ~, dann die Moral** *umg. Sprichw.* morals take second place when you're

hungry

Fresser *m*; *-s*, *-* **1.** Zool.: **ein langsamer etc. ~** a slow etc. eater (*od.* feeder); **2.** *umg. pej.* (*Vielfraß*) glutton; **...fresser** *m*; *im Subst.*; Zool. ...-eater, ...-vore *fachspr.*; **Insekten~** insect-eater, insectivore *fachspr.*; **Plankton~** plankton-eater; **Fresserei** *f*; *-*, *-en*; *umg. pej.* **1.** guzzling; **2.** → Fressgelage

Fressgelage *n umg.* blowout, *Am.* major feed, *Brit. auch* great nosh-up

Fressgier *f* **1.** voracity; *pej.* gluttony, greed(iness); **2.** Med. b(o)ulimia; **fressgierig** *Adj.* voracious; *pej.* greedy, gluttonous

Fress|korb *m umg.* hamper; (*Geschenkkorb*) (food) hamper; **~napf** *m* (feeding) bowl; *für Vögel*: seed dish; **~paket** *n umg.* food parcel; **~sack** *m umg. pej.* glutton; **~sucht** *f* → Fressgier; **~tempel** *m umg.* mecca for gourmets; **~welle** *f* period of overeating; **~werkzeuge** *Pl.* Zool. trophi; **~zelle** *f* Bio. phagocyte

Frettchen *n*; *-s*, *-*; Zool. ferret

Freud *f*; *-*, *nur Sg.*; *geh.* → Freude 3

Freude *f*; *-*, *-n* **1.** *nur Sg.*; joy (*über* + *Akk.* at); (*Vergnügen*) pleasure (**an** + *Dat.* in); (*Entzücken*) delight (in); **~ haben** *od.* **finden an** (+ *Dat.*) enjoy, take pleasure in; **er hat s-e helle ~ daran** it gives him great delight; **j-m ~ machen** *od.* **bereiten** give s.o. pleasure; *stärker*: make s.o. happy; **es macht mir ~ zu** (+ *Inf.*) I take pleasure in (+ *Ger.*), I enjoy (+ *Ger.*); **ich wollte ihr e-e kleine ~ machen** I wanted to give her a nice little surprise; **ich wollte ihr damit e-e ~ machen** I wanted to please her (by doing this); **würden Sie mir die ~ machen, mit mir auszugehen?** would you give me the pleasure of coming out with me?; **aus ~ an der Sache** for the love of it; **vor ~ weinen** weep for (*od.* with) joy; **vor ~ an die Decke springen** *umg.* jump for joy; **außer sich vor ~** overjoyed; **es war e-e ~ zu** (+ *Inf.*) it was a pleasure to (+ *Inf.*); **zu m-r großen ~** to my great delight, much to my delight; **es war keine reine ~** *umg.* it wasn't all beer and skittles (*od.* fun and games), it wasn't exactly fun, *Am. auch* it was no hayride (*od.* picnic); → geteilt II; **2.** *Pl.*: **die kleinen ~n des Alltags** the little everyday pleasures; *iro.* the little things that are sent to try us; **mit ~n!** with the greatest of pleasure; **3.** *geh.*: **Freud und Leid** joy and sorrow; **in Freud und Leid** through thick and thin, in good times and bad

Freuden|... im *Subst. mst* ... of joy; **~botschaft** *f* good news, glad tidings *Pl. lit. und hum.*; **~fest** *n* (joyful) celebration(s *Pl.*); **~feuer** *n* bonfire; **~geheul** *n*, **~geschrei** *n* shouts *Pl.* of joy; cheers *Pl.*, cheering; **~haus** *n* brothel, house of ill repute *altm. od. hum.*; **~mädchen** *n* prostitute

freudenreich *Adj.* joyful; **~er Tag** *auch* day of rejoicing

Freuden|schrei *m* cry of joy; **e-n ~ ausstoßen** shout for joy; **~sprung** *m*: **Freudensprünge machen** jump for joy; **~tag** *m* day of rejoicing; day to be remembered; **~tanz** *m*: **e-n ~ (wahren, wilden etc.) ~ aufführen** dance a jig, dance for joy; **~taumel** *m*: **in e-n ~ geraten** go into ecstasies; **~tränen** *Pl.* tears of joy

freude|strahlend *Adj. und Adv.* beaming (with joy *od.* happiness); **~trunken**

Adj. lit. delirious with joy, deliriously happy, ecstatic

Freudianer *m*; *-s*, *-*, **~in** *f*; *-*, *-nen* Freudian, follower of Freud

freudig I. *Adj.* (*froh*) happy; (*heiter*) cheerful; (*begeistert*) enthusiastic, keen; (*freudvoll*) *Erwartung*: joyful; *Nachricht*: good; *Überraschung*: delightful, wonderful; **sie sieht e-m ~en Ereignis entgegen** *euph.* she has a happy event coming up, she's in the family way; **II.** *Adv.* (*froh*) happily; (*heiter*) cheerfully; (*begeistert*) enthusiastically; (*freudvoll*) joyfully; **j-n ~ begrüßen** greet s.o. joyfully (*od.* warmly), give s.o. a cheerful hello; **~ erregt** happy and excited, overjoyed; **ich war ~ überrascht** it was a pleasant (*stärker*: delightful) surprise (for me)

...freudig *im Adj.* eager to ..., fond of ...ing; **ausgabe~** free with one's money; **diskussions~** eager to discuss, fond of discussing; **gebe~** keen (*Am.* eager) to give, open-handed

freudlos *Adj.* joyless, bleak, cheerless; **ein ~es Dasein fristen** lead a joyless (*od.* cheerless) existence

freudsch *Adj.* Freudian; **~er Fehler** *od.* **Versprecher** Freudian slip

freudvoll *Adj.* joyful, full of joy

freuen I. *v/refl.* be glad, be pleased (*über* + *Akk.* about); **sich über ein Geschenk** *etc.* ~ be pleased with a present *etc.*; **sie hat sich über d-n Besuch gefreut** she was glad (*od.* pleased) that you visited her; **sich mächtig** *od.* **riesig** *etc.* ~ *umg.* be over the moon; **sich an etw.** (*Dat.*) ~ get a lot of pleasure out of s.th.; **sich s-s Lebens ~** enjoy life (to the full); **sich ~ auf** (+ *Akk.*) look forward to; **sich darauf ~ zu** (+ *Inf.*) look forward to (+ *Ger.*); **sich zu früh ~** rejoice too soon; **freu dich nicht zu früh!** *auch* don't start celebrating too soon; **ich freue mich für dich, dass ...** I'm pleased for you that ...; **er freute sich mit ihr über i-n Erfolg** he shared her pleasure in her success; **II.** *v/t.* please; **das freut mich sehr** I'm glad to hear that; *unpers.*: **es würde mich ~, wenn ...** I'd be very pleased if ...; **es freut mich, Sie zu sehen** nice to see you; **freut mich!** *bei Vorstellung*: pleased to meet you; **es hat mich sehr gefreut** *beim Abschied nach Kennenlernen*: I was pleased to meet you; *weniger formell*: (It was) lovely to meet you, it was nice talking to you

Freund *m*; *-(e)s*, *-e* **1.** friend; **~ und Feind** friend and foe; **ein ~ von mir** a friend of mine; **j-m ein guter ~ sein** be a good friend to s.o.; **sich j-n zum ~ machen** make a friend of s.o.; **j-n zum ~ haben** have a friend in s.o.; **e-n guten ~ an j-m haben** have a good friend in s.o.; **du bist mir ein schöner ~!** *iro.* a fine friend you are!; **dadurch hat sie sich viele ~e gemacht** it won (*od.* made) her a lot of friends; **gut ~ sein mit** be good friends with; **unter ~en sein** be among friends; **was kostet das unter ~en?** how much do I get off (as a friend)?; **~ Hein** *lit. euph.* the Grim Reaper; **ein ~ in der Not** a friend in need; → **dick** I 8; **2.** (*Partner*) boyfriend; *älterer*: gentleman friend; **fester ~** steady boyfriend; **3.** *fig.* friend; **ein ~ der Musik** *etc.* a music lover *etc.*; *in Vereinsnamen*: **~e der Universität** *etc.* friends of the university *etc.*; **ein ~ sein von** be fond of; **kein ~ sein von** not be keen on, be no fan of; **er ist**

kein ~ von vielen Worten he's not a man of many words, he's not one for talking much; **sie ist kein ~ von Traurigkeit** she doesn't believe in wasting time on regrets; **4.** *als Anrede*: **alter ~** old chap, old mate; **guter** *od.* **mein ~** *altm. od. leicht herablassend*: my dear fellow; **mein lieber ~!** *drohend*: now look here!

Freundchen *n* (*scherzhaft*) *drohend*: **hör mal, ~** now listen, my friend (*Brit. auch* mate)

Freundeskreis *m* (circle of) friends *Pl.*; **e-n großen ~ haben** have a lot of friends; **im engsten ~ feiern** celebrate with a few good friends (*od.* with one's close[st] friends)

Freund-Feind-Denken *n* us and them attitude

Freundin *f*, *-*, *-nen* **1.** (female) friend; → *auch* **Freund** 1; **2.** (*Partnerin*) girlfriend; *ältere*: lady friend; **feste ~** steady girlfriend

freundlich I. *Adj.* **1.** (*gegen od. zu* to[-ward(s)]) friendly, amiable; (*liebenswürdig*) kind; (*zuvorkommend*) obliging; (*leutselig*) affable; **bitte recht ~!** *beim Fotografieren*: smile please!, say cheese!; **sehr ~ (von Ihnen)!** very kind of you; **~er Empfang** warm welcome; **mit ~er Genehmigung** *des Verlags etc.*: by kind permission of, by courtesy of; **mit freundlichen Grüßen** *Briefschluss*: yours sincerely; **j-n ~ stimmen** put s.o. in a good (*od.* affable) mood; **wären Sie bitte so ~ zu** (+ *Inf.*) would you be so kind as (*od.* good enough) to (+ *Inf.*)?; **sei bitte so ~ und hilf mir** please (be so kind as to) help me; **2.** *Atmosphäre, Umgebung, Wetter*: pleasant; *Klima*: *auch* mild; *auch* fair; *Farben, Zimmer*: welcoming, cheerful; *Farben*: *auch* bright; **das macht das Zimmer ~er** *auch* it brightens up the room; **3.** *Wirts-, Stimmung, Tendenz an der Börse*: favo(u)rable; **II.** *Adv.* in a friendly manner; *begrüßen*: *auch* amiably; **j-n ~ empfangen** give s.o. a warm welcome; **~ gesinnt sein** (+ *Dat.*) be well-disposed toward(s); **~ gesinnt** *Pol.* friendly; **...freundlich** *im Adj.* **1.** (*geeignet für, entgegenkommend*) adapted to the needs of ...; **radfahrer~** adapted to the needs of cyclists, bicycle-friendly; **urlauber~** adapted to the needs of holidaymakers (*Am.* vacationers), welcoming to holidaymakers (*Am.* vacationers); **2.** *Gesinnung*: pro-...; **amerika~** pro-American; **franzosen~** pro-French, francophile

freundlicherweise *Adv.* (very) kindly; **er hat mich ~ hingebracht** he was kind enough to take me there; **würden Sie ~ ...?** please could you ...?, could you possibly ...?, would you be kind enough to ...? *förm.*

Freundlichkeit *f* **1.** *nur Sg.*; friendliness; (*Liebenswürdigkeit*) kindness, obligingness; (*Leutseligkeit*) affability; → **freundlich** I; **würden Sie die ~ haben zu** (+ *Inf.*)? would you be so kind as (*od.* kind enough) to ...?; **2.** (*Handlung*: kind deed; *Äußerung*: kind remark; **j-m e-e ~ erweisen** do s.o. a favo(u)r; **j-m ein paar ~en sagen** say a few nice words to s.o.; *iro.* tell s.o. what's what; **3.** *nur Sg.*; *des Wetters etc.*: pleasantness; *e-s Zimmers*: cheerfulness, brightness

Freundschaft *f*, *-*, *-en* **1.** friendship; **aus ~** from feelings of friendship, because we're *etc.* friends; **aus alter ~** for

old friendship's sake; **in aller ~** in all friendliness, as a friend; **~ schließen mit** make friends with; **in ~ leben mit** be on good terms with s.o.; **da hört die ~ auf** my friendship doesn't extend that far, that's presuming too much of our friendship; **2.** *nur Sg.*; *Dial.* → **Freundeskreis**; **freundschaftlich I.** *Adj.* friendly, amicable; **II.** *Adv.*: **~ gesinnt gegen** well-disposed towards

Freundschafts|band *n*; *Pl.* *-bänder* friendship band; **~bande** *Pl.* ties of friendship; **~besuch** *m Pol.* goodwill visit; **~beweis** *m* token (*od.* proof) of friendship; **~bezeigung** *f* token (*od.* gesture) of friendship; **~dienst** *m* good turn, favo(u)r; **j-m e-n ~ erweisen** do s.o. a good turn (as a friend); **~preis** *m* special price (for a friend), *Brit. auch* mate's rate *umg.*; **~ring** *m* ring given as a token of friendship; **~spiel** *n Sport* friendly (game)

Frevel *m*; *-s*, *-*; *geh.* **1.** (*Untat, auch fig.*) crime, outrage (*an* + *Dat.*, *gegen* against); (*Bosheit*) wickedness, iniquity; **2.** *kirchl.* sacrilege; (*Lästerung*) blasphemy; **frevelhaft** *Adj.* **1.** *geh.* outrageous; *Leichtsinn etc.*: wanton; (*böse*) wicked; **2.** *kirchl.* sacrilegious; **freveln** *v/i.* **1.** *geh.* commit an outrage (*Verbrechen*: a crime); **~ an** (+ *Dat.*) (*od.* **gegen**) trespass against; **2.** *kirchl.* commit sacrilege (*mit Worten*: blasphemy) against; **Freveltat** *f* outrage; (*Verbrechen*) heinous crime; **Frevler** *m*; *-s*, *-*, **Frevlerin** *f*; *-*, *-nen* **1.** *geh.* evil-doer, evil transgressor; **2.** *kirchl.* sacrilegious person; (*Gotteslästerer*) blasphemer; **frevlerisch** *Adj.* → **frevelhaft**

Friede *m*; *-ns*, *Pl. sehr selten*: *-n* → **Frieden**; **~ auf Erden** *kirchl. od. geh.* peace on earth; **~ s-r Asche** *bei Begräbnis*: may his soul rest in peace; **„~ sei mit euch" - „und mit d-m Geiste"** *kirchl.* peace be with you - and with thy spirit; **~, Freude, Eierkuchen** *umg. hum. od. iro.* on the surface everything in the garden's lovely

Frieden *m*; *-s*, *Pl. selten*: *-* **1.** (*Ggs. Krieg*) peace; *Zeit*: (time of) peace, peacetime; **~ schließen** make peace; **den ~ bewahren** keep the peace; **2.** (*Friedensvertrag*) peace treaty; **den ~ diktieren** dictate peace terms (+ *Dat.* to); **3.** (*Ggs. Streit, Ärger*) peace; (*Einklang*) harmony; **häuslicher ~** domestic harmony; **innerer ~** *Pol.* internal peace, peace at home; **~ stiften zwischen** make peace between; **in ~ mit j-m leben** live at peace with s.o.; **s-n ~ machen mit** make one's peace with; **um des lieben ~s willen** for the sake of peace (and quiet); **lass uns ~ schließen** let's make peace, let's let bygones be bygones; **4.** (*Ruhe*) peace, tranquil(l)ity; *in der Natur etc.*: peacefulness; **innerer ~** *e-r Person*: peace of mind; **ich will nur m-n ~ haben** I just want my peace and quiet; **lass mich in ~!** leave me alone; **lass mich mit dem Unsinn in ~!** stop pestering me with that nonsense (of yours); **er gibt keinen ~** *od.* **er kann nie ~ geben** he gives me no peace, he won't leave me in peace; **dem ~ traue ich nicht** things are a bit too peaceful for my liking, things are suspiciously quiet; **(er) ruhe in ~** (may he) rest in peace

Friedens|... *im Subst.* ... of peace, peace ...; **~angebot** *n* peace offer; **~bedingungen** *Pl.* peace terms; **~bemühungen** *Pl.* peace effort *Sg.*, at-

F

tempt *Sg.* to bring about a peace settlement; **~bereitschaft** *f* desire for peace; **~bewegung** *f* peace movement; **~brecher** *m*, **~brecherin** *f*; -, *-nen* violator of the peace; **~bruch** *m Jur.* breach (*Pol.* violation) of the peace; **~demonstration** *f* peace demonstration; **~diktat** *n* dictated peace terms *Pl.*; **~fahne** *f* flag of peace; **~gespräche** *Pl.* peace talks; **~gottesdienst** *m* peace thanksgiving service; **~initiative** *f* peace initiative (*od.* move); **~konferenz** *f* peace conference; **~marsch** *m* peace march; **~mission** *f* peace mission; **~nobelpreis** *m* Nobel Peace Prize; **~pfeife** *f* peace pipe; **die ~ rauchen** *umg. hum.* smoke the pipe of peace, bury the hatchet; **~politik** *f* peace politics *Pl.*; *konkret:* policy of peace; **~preis** *m* peace prize (*od.* award); **~prozess** *m* peace process; **~richter** *m*, **~richterin** *f* lay magistrate; *in GB und den USA:* justice of the peace; **~schluss** *m* conclusion of a (*od.* the) peace treaty; **~sicherung** *f* securing (*od.* preservation) of peace; peacekeeping (measures *Pl.*); **~ im Nahen Osten** *etc. auch* bringing about peace (*od.* a peace settlement) in the Middle East *etc.*
friedensstiftend *Adj.* peacemaking ...; **Friedensstifter** *m*, **Friedensstifterin** *f* peacemaker
Friedens|störer *m*, **~störerin** *f* disturber of the peace; **~symbol** *n* symbol of peace; **~taube** *f* dove of peace; **~truppen** *Pl.* peacekeeping forces; **~verhandlungen** *Pl.* peace negotiations (*od.* talks); **~vertrag** *m* peace treaty; **~wille** *m* desire for peace; **~zeiten** *Pl.* times of peace, peacetime *Sg.*
friedfertig *Adj.* peaceable; *Tier:* gentle, docile; *selig sind die Friedfertigen bibl.* blessed are the peacemakers
Friedhof *m* cemetery; *an e-r Kirche: auch* graveyard; *auf welchem ~ liegt er?* which cemetery is he buried in?
Friedhofs|atmosphäre *f fig. pej.* graveyard atmosphere; **~ruhe** *f* 1. peace of the graveyard; 2. *fig. pej.* deathly stillness
friedlich *Adj.* 1. (*Ggs. kriegerisch*) peaceful; *etw. auf ~em Wege lösen* find a peaceful solution to (*od.* for) s.th.; 2. (*friedfertig*) peaceable; *Tier:* gentle, docile; *j-n ~ stimmen* pacify s.o.; *sei ~ umg.* be quiet; (*beruhige dich*) take it easy, cool it *umg.*; 3. *Atmosphäre etc.:* peaceful; **Friedlichkeit** *f; nur Sg.* peacefulness; (*Friedfertigkeit*) peaceable nature; *e-s Tieres:* gentleness, docility
friedliebend *Adj.* peaceloving
frieren *v/i.; friert, fror, gefroren* 1. (*hat*); *Person:* **ich friere** (*od.* **mich friert, es friert mich**) *umg.* I'm freezing (*od.* frozen); **ich friere** (*od.* **mich friert**) **an den Füßen** (*od.* **mir ~ die Füße**) I've got cold feet, my feet are cold (*stärker:* freezing); 2. (*hat*) *unpers.:* **es friert** it's freezing; *heute Nacht wird es ~* temperatures will be below freezing tonight, there will be a frost tonight; 3. (*ist*); *Boden, Wasser:* freeze; → **gefroren**
Fries *m*; *-es, -e; Archit. und Tuch:* frieze
Friese *m*; *-n, -n*, **Friesin** *f*; -, *-nen* Frisian, *weiblich auch:* Frisian woman (*od.* girl *etc.*); **friesisch I.** *Adj.* Frisian; **II. Friesisch** *n*; *-en; Ling.* Frisian; *das Friesische* Frisian; **Friesennerz** *m umg. fig.* oilskin jacket

frigid(e) *Adj. Psych.* frigid; **Frigidität** *f*; -, *kein Pl.* frigidity
Frikadelle *f*; -, *-n; Gastr.* meatball, *Am. etwa* (ham)burger
Frikassee *n*; *-s, -s; Gastr.* fricassee
Friktion *f*; -, *-en; Phys.* friction
Frisbee® ['frɪsbɪ] *n, m*; *-(s), -s* Frisbee®; **~ spielen** play with a Frisbee
frisch I. *Adj.* 1. *Blumen, Milch, Obst etc.:* fresh; *Ei: auch* new-laid; **~ bleiben** *od.* **sich ~ halten** stay fresh; **~ halten** keep fresh; **~ vom Fass** straight from the barrel; 2. (*neu*) *Schnee etc.:* fresh, new; (*sauber*) clean (*auch Blatt Papier*); *Spur:* fresh; 3. (*ausgeruht*) *Pferde, Truppen:* fresh; *sich wieder ~ fühlen* feel refreshed; **~ und munter** wide awake; *mit ~er Kraft* refreshed, with renewed strength; *sich ~ machen* freshen up; 4. (*Ggs. verblasst*) *Erinnerung, Farben etc.:* fresh; *Farbe: auch* bright; *noch in ~er Erinnerung* fresh in my *etc.* mind; 5. (*erfrischend*) *Luft, Wasser, Wind:* fresh; *an die ~e Luft gehen* go out into the fresh air; *~e Luft schnappen umg.* get a breath of fresh air; *fig.* → **Luft** 1, **Wind** 2; 6. (*kühl*) cool; *stärker:* chilly; *es ist ziemlich ~ geworden* it's gone quite chilly; 7. (*kräftig*) *Brise, Wind:* fresh; *~er werden* freshen; 8. *fig.* (*lebensfroh*) full of life; (*aufgeweckt*) bright; (*lebhaft*) lively; **II.** *Adv.* 1. freshly, newly, recently; *das Bett ~ beziehen* put clean sheets on the bed, change the sheets; **~ gebacken** *Brot etc.:* fresh from the oven; *fig. Ehemann, Ehepaar etc.:* newly-wed; *fig. Lehrer etc.:* fledg(e)ling, newly-qualified; **~ gelegt** *Ei:* new-laid; **~ gekocht** freshly cooked; **~ geputzt** just cleaned; **~ geschnitten** *Blumen etc.:* freshly cut, fresh-cut; **~ gestrichen** newly painted; **~ gestrichen!** *Schild:* wet paint; **~ gewaschen** clean, just washed; *Person:* (nice and) clean; **~ rasiert** clean-shaven; **~ verheiratet** newly-wed; 2. (*erneut*) again; *noch einmal ~ anfangen* start again from scratch; 3. (*direkt*) straight (*von der Universität etc.* from university *etc.*); *sie sind ~ aus dem Urlaub zurück* they've just got back from holiday (*Am.* vacation); 4. (*Ggs. zögerlich*) **~ ans Werk!** let's get straight down to it; *immer ~ drauflos!* come on, look lively!; **~ gewagt ist halb gewonnen** *Sprichw.* nothing ventured, nothing gained
Frische *f*; -, *kein Pl.* 1. (*auch Sauberkeit*) freshness; **~ für den ganzen Tag** all-day freshness; 2. *körperliche:* fitness, vigo(u)r; (*Ggs. Müdigkeit*) freshness, *geistige ~* mental alertness, alert (*od.* lively) mind; *in körperlicher und geistiger ~* fit in mind and body; *in alter ~* as full of life as ever; *arbeiten etc.:* with renewed vigo(u)r; 3. (*Munterkeit*) briskness, liveliness; 4. *im Gesicht:* fresh colo(u)r; 5. (*Kühle*) coolness; *unangenehme:* chill(iness); 6. *von Farben:* liveliness; (*Leuchtkraft*) brightness
Frischei *n* fresh (*od.* new-laid) egg
frischen *v/t. Metall.* refine
Frisch|fisch *m* fresh fish; **~fleisch** *n* fresh meat; **~gemüse** *n* fresh vegetables *Pl.*; **~gewicht** *n* fresh weight
Frischhalte|beutel *m* (airtight) polythene (*Am.* polyethylene) bag; **~dose** *f* cooler box; **~folie** *f* cling film, *Am.* plastic wrap; **~packung** *f* airtight pack
Frischhaltung *f*; *nur Sg. von Lebensmitteln:* preservation; (*Kühlung*) cold

storage; *die ~ von ...* keeping ... fresh
Frischkäse *m* curd (*Am. auch* farmer) cheese
Frischling *m*; *-s, -e* 1. *Zool.* young wild boar; 2. *fig.* greenhorn
Frischluft *f; nur Sg.* fresh air; **~fanatiker** *m*, **~fanatikerin** *f* fresh air fiend (*od.* fanatic); **~zufuhr** *f* fresh air supply
Frisch|milch *f* fresh milk; **~obst** *n* fresh fruit; **~waren** *Pl.* fresh produce *Sg.*; perishables; **~warenabteilung** *f* (fresh) produce section
Frischwasser *n; nur Sg.* (*auch Süßwasser*) fresh water; **~versorgung** *f* supply of fresh water, fresh water supplies *Pl.*
Frischwurst *f; nur Sg.; Gastr.* fresh sausage (*without preservative*)
Frischzelle *f Med.* living cell; **Frischzellenkur** *f* living cell therapy
Frisée [fri'zeː] *m*; *-s, kein Pl.*, **~salat** *m* curly endive, frisée
Friseur [fri'zøːɐ] *m*; *-s, -e*, **~in** *f*; -, *-nen* hairdresser; *für Herren: auch* barber
Friseur|salon *m* hairdresser's (*Am.* beauty) shop, styling salon; *für Herren: auch* barbershop; **~termin** *m* hair appointment
Friseuse [fri'zøːzə] *f*; -, *-n* (female) hairdresser
frisieren *v/t.* 1. *j-n/sich ~ od. j-s/s-e Haare ~* do s.o.'s/one's hair; 2. *umg. fig.* (*Auto, Motor etc.*) hot (*od.* soup) up; *die Bilanz ~* cook the books; *die Zahlen ~* doctor the figures
Frisier|haube *f* hairdrier; **~kommode** *f altm.* dressing table, *Am.* vanity (table); **~salon** *m* → **Friseursalon**
frisiert I. *P.P.* → **frisieren**; **II.** *Adj.* 1. *Person:* **sorgfältig ~** well-groomed; 2. *umg. Auto etc.:* hot, hotted (*od.* souped) up; *Bilanz, Statistik, Zahlen:* doctored
Frisör *etc.* → **Friseur**, **Frisöse** → **Friseuse**
frisst *Präs.* → **fressen**
Frist *f*; -, *-en* 1. (*Zeitraum*) (fixed) period (of time); *äußerste ~* final date (*od.* deadline); *innerhalb e-r ~ von zehn Tagen* within a ten-day period; *in kürzester ~* at (very) short notice; *die ~ verlängern für* extend the period for, postpone the deadline for; *sie haben mir die ~ für Ansprüche verlängert* they have given me more time to make a claim; *die ~ ist abgelaufen* the time (*od.* period) has expired, the deadline has passed; *fig.* your *etc.* time is up, time's up *umg.*; 2. (*Zeitpunkt*) deadline, date; *bis zu dieser ~* by this date; *e-e ~ einhalten* meet a deadline; *e-e ~ setzen* fix a deadline (*od.* date); 3. (*Aufschub*) extension; *für Zahlung:* respite; *für Strafe:* reprieve; *j-m drei Tage etc. ~ gewähren* give s.o. three days' *etc.* grace
fristen *v/t.* 1. *ein kümmerliches etc. Dasein ~* eke out a miserable existence; *sein Leben in Armut ~* lead a life of poverty; *sein Leben mit Gelegenheitsarbeiten ~* scrape a living with occasional work; 2. → **befristen**
Fristenregelung *f für Abtreibung:* abortion limit
fristgemäß, **fristgerecht** *Adj. und Adv.* in time, within the agreed time limit; *bei Anmeldung:* before the closing date
fristlos *Adj. und Adv.* without notice; **~ entlassen werden** be dismissed without notice, be fired on the spot
Frist|überschreitung *f* failure to meet

the deadline; **~verlängerung** f extension (of the deadline), deadline extension

Frisur f; -, -en hairstyle; (*Haarschnitt*) haircut; *i-e ~ sitzt nicht mehr* her hair has come undone

Friteuse etc. → **Fritteuse** etc.

Frittaten Pl. österr. Gastr. strips of pancake

Fritten Pl. umg. chips, Am. (french) fries; **~bude** f umg. chips (Am. fries) stall, Brit. auch chippie stall

Fritteuse [fri'tø:zə] f; -, -n deep (fat) fryer; **frittieren** vt/i. deep-fry

...fritze m; -n, -n; im Subst. umg. pej. **1.** beruflich: man, Brit. auch chap, Am. auch guy; **Heizungs~** heating man (od. chap, Am. guy); **Reparatur~** repairman; **2.** gewohnheitsmäßig: type; **Jodel~** yodeller type; **Nörgel~** grumbling type

frivol Adj. **1.** (*leichtfertig, schnippisch*) frivolous, flippant; **2.** (*unanständig*) Lied, Bemerkung, Witz etc.: risqué, suggestive; **Frivolität** f; -, -en **1.** nur Sg.; frivolity, flippancy, levity; **2.** (*Unanständigkeit*) risqué nature, suggestiveness; **3.** Bemerkung: suggestive remark

Frl. Abk. altm. (**Fräulein**) Miss

froh Adj. **1.** (*erfreut, erleichtert*) glad (*über* + Akk., südd., schw. auch um about); **~ gelaunt** od. **gestimmt** cheerful; **sei ~ ein Mutes** cheerfully; **sei ~, dass du nicht dabei warst** be thankful (od. glad) you weren't there; **bin ich ~, dass das vorbei ist!** auch what a relief that that's over; **er ist s-s Lebens nicht mehr ~ geworden** (*es hat nie aufgehört*) he led a life of unending misery; (*er hat es nie überwunden*) he never got over it; → **Fest** 2, **Ostern** etc.; **2.** (*erfreulich*) Ereignis: happy; Kunde, Nachricht: good; **die ~e Botschaft** kirchl. the Gospel

frohgemut Adj. geh. cheerful

fröhlich I. Adj. **1.** cheerful, happy; (*ausgelassen*) merry; **j-n ~ stimmen** put s.o. in a good mood; → **Weihnachten**; **2.** Spiele, Tänze: merry; **II.** Adv. **1.** → I; **2.** umg. (*unbekümmert*) blithely, merrily; **er schwindelte ~ drauflos** he went on merrily telling lies; **Fröhlichkeit** f; nur Sg. cheerfulness; (*Lustigkeit*) high spirits Pl.

frohlocken geh. v/i. (*untr., hat*) **1.** geh. rejoice (*über* + Akk. at), be jubilant (at); schadenfroh: gloat (over); **2.** kirchl. altm. Engel etc.: sing joyfully; **Frohlocken** n; -s, kein Pl. jubilation; schadenfroh: gloating

Froh|natur f: **e-e ~ haben/sein** have a happy disposition / be a cheerful person; **~sinn** m; nur Sg. cheerfulness

fromm Adj.; frommer od. frömmer, am frommsten od. frömmsten **1.** pious, devout; **~es Getue** pej. sanctimoniousness; **2.** (*scheinheilig*) innocent; **mit ~em Augenaufschlag** with a look of wide-eyed innocence; **3.** (*sanft*) gentle; Tier: docile, quiet; **~ wie ein Lamm** meek as a lamb; **4.** fig.: **~e Lüge** white lie; **ein ~er Wunsch** a pious hope; **5.** altm. (*rechtschaffen*) worthy, upright

Frömmelei f; -, -en; pej. **1.** nur Sg. sanctimoniousness; **2.** Handlung/Äußerung: sanctimonious act/remark; **frömmeln** v/i. pej. be sanctimonious, put on a pious act umg.

frommen v/i. altm. od. lit.: **wem frommt das?** what use is that to anyone?

Frömmigkeit f; nur Sg. piety

Fron f; -, -en, mst Sg. **1.** hist. corvée, statute labo(u)r; **2.** geh. fig. drudgery; **~arbeit** f → **Fron**; **~dienst** m: **~e leisten** hist. perform statute labo(u)r (+ Dat. od. **für** for); fig. slave away (for); schw. do voluntary work (for)

frönen v/i. e-m Laster: indulge in; Gelüsten: gratify; e-m Hobby: pursue, devote o.s. to; **s-n Leidenschaften ~** indulge one's passions; **dem Alkohol ~ ständig:** be a heavy drinker, hit the bottle umg.; bei e-r Feier etc.: imbibe, knock it back umg.

Fronleichnam (m); nur Sg.; kath. Corpus Christi

Front f; -, -en **1.** e-s Gebäudes: front, facade; **die rückwärtige ~** the rear facade; **2.** e-s Autos etc.: front; **3.** e-r angetretenen Truppe: front rank; **die ~ abschreiten** pass along the ranks, inspect the troops; **4.** Mil. (*Kampfgebiet*) front; (*Kampflinie*) front line; **an der ~** at the front; **hinter der ~** behind the lines; **die feindliche ~** the enemy front line, the enemy lines Pl.; **an vorderster ~ stehen** be right in the front line; **die ~en abstecken** fig. mark out one's positions; **klare ~en schaffen** fig. make a clear stand, make one's position clear; **die ~en haben sich verhärtet** fig. their attitudes have hardened; **5.** Pol. Gruppe: front; **e-e geschlossene ~ bilden** fig. form a united front, close ranks (**gegen** against); **~ machen gegen** fig. make a stand against, resist; **6.** Met. front; **die ~ e-s Islandtiefs** the leading edge of a depression over Iceland; **7.** Sport: **in ~ gehen** take the lead; **in ~ liegen** be in the lead

...front f; im Subst. front; Branche, Sektor: sector; **was gibt's Neues von der ....?** what's the latest on the ~ front?; **Heirats~** wedding front; **Urlaubs~** holiday (Am. vacation) front

frontal I. Adj. frontal; Zusammenstoß: head-on; **II.** Adv. zusammenstoßen: head on

Frontal|angriff m frontal attack; **~unterricht** m class teaching, chalk and talk umg.; **~zusammenstoß** m head-on collision

Front|ansicht f front(al) view; **~antrieb** m Mot. front-wheel drive; **~bericht** m Mil. front-line report; **~breite** f Archit. frontage; **~einsatz** m Mil. front-line service (od. action)

Fronten|system n Met. frontal system; **~verhärtung** f hardening of attitudes (od. positions); **~wechsel** m fig. U-turn, volte-face; **e-n ~ vornehmen** do a U-turn, perform a volte-face geh.

Frontfrau f auf Konzertbühne: frontwoman

Frontispiz n; -es, -e; Archit., Druck. frontispiece

Front|kämpfer m, **~kämpferin** f Mil. front-line soldier; **~lader** m **1.** Waschmaschine etc.: front loader; **2.** Fahrzeug: front-end loader; **~linie** f Mil. front line; **~mann** m; Pl. -männer auf Konzertbühne: frontman; **~motor** m front(-mounted) engine; **~scheibe** f Mot. windscreen, Am. windshield; **~soldat** m, **~soldatin** f Mil. front-line soldier; **~stadt** f Mil. front-line city; **~urlaub** m Mil. leave from the front; **~verlauf** m Mil. line of the front; **~zulage** f Mil. front-line supplement, combat pay

fror Imperf. → **frieren**

Frosch m; -(e)s, Frösche **1.** Zool. frog; **2.** fig.: **sei kein ~!** don't be a spoilsport; **e-n ~ im Hals haben** fig. have a

frog in one's throat; **sich aufblasen wie ein ~** fig. puff o.s. up (self-importantly); **kleiner ~** hum. (*nacktes Kind*) little tadpole; **3.** Mus., am Geigenbogen etc.: frog, heel; **~augen** Pl. umg. bulging eyes; **~konzert** n frogs' chorus; **~laich** m frogspawn; **~mann** m; Pl. -männer frogman; **~perspektive** f worm's eye view; Film: auch tilt shot; **etw. aus der ~ sehen** have a worm's eye view of s.th.; fig. take a narrow view of s.th.; **~schenkel** Pl. Gastr. frog's legs; **~teich** m frog pond

Frost m; -(e)s, Fröste **1.** frost; **bei ~** when there's (a) frost, in frosty weather; **bei strengem ~** when there's a hard (od. severe) frost; **~ abbekommen** catch the frost; **2.** bei Fieber: the shivers Pl.; **frostbeständig** Adj. frost-resistant, hardy

Frost|beule f chilblain; **~einbruch** m sudden frost

frösteln I. v/i. shiver (with cold); vor Ekel etc.: auch shudder; **II.** v/t. unpers.: **mich fröstelt** I feel shivery; **da fröstelt's einen ja** (*bei dem Gedanken*) it makes you shudder (to think of it); **Frösteln** n; -s, kein Pl. shivering

frostempfindlich Adj. sensitive to frost, delicate, not hardy

frosten v/t. fachspr. (deep-)freeze; **Froster** m; -s, - freezing compartment

frostfrei Adj. free of frost, frost-free; **wir werden ~e Nächte** we don't get any frost at night (od. any night frosts)

Frostgefahr f; nur Sg. danger of frost

frostgeschützt Adj. protected from frost

Frostgrenze f Met. frost line

frostig I. Adj. **1.** Wetter: frosty; **2.** fig. frosty; stärker: icy; **II.** Adv. fig. frostily; **er wurde ~ empfangen** he got a frosty reception; **Frostigkeit** f; nur Sg.; fig. frostiness; stärker: iciness

frost|klar Adj.: **~e Nacht** clear, frosty night; **~klirrend** Adj. Tag, Nacht: with a sharp frost; **~e Kälte** sharp, tingling cold

Frost|periode f spell of frost; **~schaden** m frost damage; **„Frostschäden"** Schild: frost damage; **~schutz** m frost protection; **~schutzmittel** n Mot. etc.: antifreeze

frostsicher Adj. frostproof; Ort: free of frost

Frottee, österr. **Frotté** [frɔ'te:] n, m; -(s), -s (terry) towel(l)ing, terry(cloth); **~bademantel** m terry bathrobe; **~betttuch** n terry sheet; **~handtuch** n (fleecy) towel; **~socken** Pl. terry socks

Frottier... im Subst. siehe **Frottee...**; **frottieren** v/t. rub down; (*Haare etc.*) rub (with a towel)

Frotzelei f; -, -en; umg. auch Pl. teasing; **hör auf mit der ~!** stop teasing; **frotzeln** umg. vt/i.: **~** (*über* + Akk.) make fun of; (*Person*) auch tease, Brit. auch take the mickey out of

Frucht f; -, Früchte **1.** (*Obst*) und Bot. auch Pl. fruit; **die Früchte des Feldes** geh. the fruits of the field; **Früchte ansetzen** start to fruit; **Früchte tragen** bear fruit (*auch fig.*); **2.** (*Getreide*) crop, Brit. auch corn; **3.** fig. fruit; **Früchte** fruit Sg., fruits, result Sg., results; **die Früchte s-r Arbeit genießen** enjoy the fruits (od. reap the rewards) of one's labo(u)r; **~ der Liebe** altm. euph. love child; → **gebenedeit**, → auch **verboten** II 1; **4.** Med. (*Leibesfrucht*) f(o)etus

fruchtbar Adj. **1.** Bio. fertile; **nicht ~**

F

infertile; **~e Tage** *der Frau*: fertile period; **seid ~ und mehret euch** *bibl.* be fruitful and multiply; **2.** *fig.* fruitful, productive; *Schriftsteller*: prolific; **nicht ~** unfruitful; **auf ~en Boden fallen** fall on fertile ground; **Fruchtbarkeit** *f*, *nur Sg.* **1.** fertility; **2.** *fig.* fruitfulness
Fruchtbarkeits|gott *m*, **~göttin** *f* fertility god/goddess; **~zauber** *m* fertility rite
Frucht|blase *f Anat.* amniotic sac; **~bonbon** *m, n* fruit drop
fruchtbringend *Adj.* fruitful
Früchtchen *n*; *-s, -*; *umg. iro.*: **sauberes ~** really useless character; *Kind*: little devil
Früchte|becher *m* (*Eisbecher*) fruit sundae; **~brot** *n* fruit loaf
Fruchteis *n* fruit-flavo(u)red ice cream
fruchten *v/i. fig.* be of use; (*wirken*) have an effect; **es hat nichts gefruchtet** it was of no avail (*od.* no use)
Früchtetee *m* fruit tea
Frucht|fleisch *n* flesh (of fruit); **~fliege** *f Zool.* fruit fly; **~folge** *f Agr.* crop rotation; **~geschmack** *m* fruity taste; **~gummi** *m, n* fruit gum
fruchtig *Adj.* fruity
Frucht|joghurt *m* fruit yoghurt; **~knoten** *m Bot.* ovary
fruchtlos *Adj. fig.* fruitless, futile
Frucht|mark *n* fruit pulp; **~saft** *m* fruit juice; **~saftgetränk** *n* fruit drink; **~säure** *f* fruit acid; **~stand** *m Bot.* multiple (*Am.* collective) fruit
Fruchtwasser *n Physiol.* amniotic fluid, *the* waters *Pl. umg.*; **das ~ geht ab** *umg.* the waters break; **~punktion** *f* amniocentesis (*Pl.* amniocenteses)
Frucht|wechsel *m Agr.* rotation of crops; **~wein** *m* fruit wine; **~zucker** *m* fruit sugar, fructose
Fructose *f*; *-, kein Pl.*; *Chem.* fructose
frugal *Adj. geh.* frugal
früh I. *Adj.* **1.** early; **ein ~er van Gogh** an early van Gogh (*od.* work of van Gogh's); **am ~en Abend** early in the evening, in the early evening, early evening; **es ist noch zu ~, um das feststellen zu können** it is too soon to establish that; **2.** (*vorzeitig*) premature, untimely; **II.** *Adv.* **1.** early; (*in jungem Alter*) at an early age; (*in frühem Stadium*) early on, at an early stage; **schon ~** early on; **~ genug** soon enough; **zu ~** too soon; **~ am Tag** early in the day; **~ aufstehen** get up early; *gewohnheitsmäßig*: **auch** be an early riser; **~ sterben** die prematurely (*od.* young, before one's time); **zu ~ kommen** be early; **2.** (*am Morgen*) **heute/ morgen ~** this/tomorrow morning; **~ um fünf** (*od.* **um fünf Uhr**) at five (o'clock) in the morning; **von ~ bis spät** from morning till night; → **früher, frühest...**
Früh *f südd., österr.*: **in der ~** in the morning; **heute/morgen in der ~** this/ tomorrow morning
Frühapfel *m* early apple
frühauf *Adv.*: **von ~** from an early age
Früh|aufsteher *m*; *-s, -*, **~aufsteherin** *f*; *-, -nen* early riser (*umg.* bird); **~beet** *n* cold frame; **~blüher** *m*; *-s, -*; *Bot.* early-flowering plant
Frühbucher *m*; *-s, -* *Reise*: early booker; *Pl.* those who book early; **~rabatt** *m* discount for early booking
Frühchen *n umg.* (*Frühgeburt*) premature baby, *Am. auch* preemie
frühchristlich *Adj.* early Christian
Früh|diagnose *f* early diagnosis; **~dienst** *m* early duty (*Schicht*: shift);

~ haben be on early duty/shift
Frühe *f*; *-, kein Pl.*; *geh.* (early) morning; **in aller ~** early (*od.* first thing) in the morning
Frühehe *f* young marriage
früher I. *Komp.* → **früh**; **II.** *Adj.* **1.** earlier; (*älter*) older; **~e Fassung** earlier version; **2.** (*ehemalig*) former; (*vorherig*) *auch* previous; **der ~e Besitzer** the previous owner; **die ~e DDR** former East Germany; **3.** (*vergangen*) past; **in ~en Zeiten** in the past; **III.** *Adv.* **1.** earlier; (*eher*) *auch* sooner; **~ oder später** sooner or later; **2.** (*einst*) in the past; **~, als ...** in the (old) days, when ...; **an ~ denken** think back, think of earlier times; **~ habe ich geraucht / nicht geraucht** I used to / didn't use to smoke; **~ habe ich nie geraucht** I never used to smoke; **warst du ~ wirklich Rennfahrer?** did you really use to be a racing (*Am.* racecar) driver?; **ich hab noch m-e ganzen Bücher von ~** I've still got all my old books (from university *etc.*); **ich kenne ihn von ~** I know him from the old days; **genau wie ~** just as it *etc.* used to be; **es ist alles noch wie ~** nothing has changed
Früh|erkennung *f Med.* early detection (*od.* diagnosis); **~erziehung** *f*: **musikalische ~** first musical training (*in the form of games*)
frühest... I. *Sup.* → **früh**; **II.** *Adj.* earliest; **in ~er Kindheit** at a very early age; **frühestens** *Adv.* at the earliest, not before; **~ am Sonntag** (on) Sunday at the earliest, not before Sunday; **das Haus ist ~ in e-m Jahr fertig** it will take at least a year to finish the house
frühestmöglich I. *Adj.* earliest possible; **der ~e Tag** the earliest possible date; **zum ~en Zeitpunkt** → II; **II.** *Adv.* as soon as possible, as soon as I/you *etc.* can
Frühgeburt *f* **1.** *Vorgang*: premature birth; **2.** *Baby*: premature baby
Frühgeschichte *f*: **die ~** early (*od.* ancient) history; **die ~ der Menschheit** the early history of man(kind); **in der ~ der Bewegung** *auch* in the early days of the movement; **frühgeschichtlich** *Adj. Funde etc.*: early, ancient; *Forschung, Studien*: in ancient history; **aus ~er Zeit** from (the period of) ancient history, dating back to ancient history
Früh|gottesdienst *m* early service; **~herbst** *m* early autumn (*Am. auch* fall); **~jahr** *n*; *-s, -e* spring; **im ~** in (the) spring
Frühjahrs|kollektion *f* spring collection; **~messe** *f Wirts.* spring fair; **~mode** *f* spring fashions *Pl.*; **~müdigkeit** *f* springtime lethargy (*od.* tiredness); **~putz** *m* spring cleaning
Früh|kapitalismus *m* early (days *Pl.* of) capitalism; **~kartoffeln** *Pl.* early potatoes
frühkindlich *Adj. Med., Psych.* infant ...; *Erlebnisse*: early childhood; **die ~e Entwicklung** the child's early development
Frühkultur *f* **1.** *geschichtlich*: early civilization; **die chinesische ~** early Chinese society (*od.* civilization); **2.** *Garten*: forcing; **in ~** (*gezogen*) forced
Frühling *m*; *-s, -e* spring; *Zeit*: *auch* springtime (*auch fig.*); **im ~** in (the) spring, in springtime; **im ~ 2003 / nächsten Jahres** in the spring of 2003 / next spring; **es riecht nach ~** you can smell the spring, spring is in the air; **e-n zweiten ~ erleben** *fig.* experience

a second youth
Frühlings|anfang *m*, **~beginn** *m* Jahreszeit: beginning of spring; *Tag*: first day of spring; **~blume** *f* spring flower; **~bote** *m poet.* harbinger of spring; **~gefühle** *Pl.*: **~ haben** (*auch sexuell*) be feeling frisky
frühlingshaft *Adj.* springlike
Frühlings|luft *f* spring air; **~rolle** *f Gastr.* spring roll; **~sonne** *f* spring sunshine; **~suppe** *f Gastr.* spring vegetable soup (with noodles); **~tag** *m* spring day; **an e-m schönen ~** one fine day in spring; **~Tagundnachtgleiche** *f* spring (*od.* vernal) equinox; **~wetter** *n* spring weather; **~zeit** *f* springtime; **~zwiebel** *m* spring (*Am.* green) onion
Früh|mensch *m hist.*: **der ~** early man; **~messe** *f kath.* early morning mass; **~mette** *f kath., ev.* early morning service
frühmorgens *Adv.* early in the morning
Früh|nachrichten *Pl.* early morning news (bulletin) *Sg.*; **~nebel** *m* early morning mist (*dichter.* fog)
frühneuhochdeutsch *Ling.* **I.** *Adj.* Early New High German; **II. Frühneuhochdeutsch** *n* Early New High German; **das Frühneuhochdeutsche** Early New High German
Früh|obst *n* early fruit, primeurs *Pl.*; **~pensionierung** *f* early retirement; **~phase** *f* early phase
frühreif *Adj.* **1.** *Kind etc.*: precocious; **2.** *Bot.* early-maturing; **Frühreife** *f* **1.** *e-s Kindes etc.*: precociousness; **2.** *Bot.* early maturity
Früh|rente *f* early retirement; **in ~ gehen** take (*od.* go into) early retirement; **~rentner** *m*, **~rentnerin** *f* early retirer; **er ist ~** he took (*od.* went into) early retirement, he retired early; **~schicht** *f* early shift; **~ haben** be on early shift; **~schoppen** *m* pre-lunch drink(s *Pl.*); *Treffen*: *auch* (Sunday) morning get-together for a drink; **~sommer** *m* early summer; **~sport** *m* early morning exercises *Pl.*, daily dozen *Pl. umg. altm.*; **~stadium** *n*: (**im**) **~** (at an) early stage; **~start** *m Sport* false start; **e-n ~ machen** jump the gun
Frühstück *n* **1.** breakfast; **erstes ~** (early) breakfast; **zweites ~** second breakfast, mid-morning snack, *Brit. auch etwa* elevenses *Pl.*; **Zimmer mit ~** bed and breakfast; **2.** *umg. Pause*: morning break; **~ machen** stop for one's second breakfast; **frühstücken** (*untr., hat gefrühstückt*) **I.** *v/i.* have (one's) breakfast, breakfast; **II.** *v/t.* have for breakfast, breakfast on
Frühstücks|brett(chen) *n* wooden breakfast board; **~büffet** *n* breakfast buffet; **~ei** *n* breakfast egg; **~fernsehen** *n* breakfast television; **~fleisch** *n* luncheon meat; **~geschirr** *n* breakfast dishes *Pl.*; **~pause** *f* morning break; **~speck** *m* bacon; *in Scheiben*: bacon rashers (*Am.* slices) *Pl.*; **~tisch** *m* breakfast table; **~zimmer** *n* breakfast room
Früh|warnsystem *n* early warning system; **~werk** *n* early work(s *Pl.*); **e-s** *Schriftstellers*: *auch Koll.* early writings *Pl.*; **~zeit** *f* **1.** early period; **2.** (*Vorzeit*) prehistoric times *Pl.*
frühzeitig I. *Adj.* **1.** (*früh*) early; **2.** (*vorzeitig*) premature; *Tod*: untimely; **II.** *Adv.* **1.** (*früh*) early, in good time; **2.** (*vorzeitig*) prematurely

Früh|zug *m* early train; **~zündung** *f* *Mot.* pre-ignition

Fruktose → *Fructose*

Frust *m*; *-(e)s, kein Pl.*; *umg.* sense of frustration; **hab ich e-n ~!** am I cheesed off (*od.* pissed off); **so ein ~!** what a drag (*od.* pain); **das war der absolute ~!** it was just banging your head against a brick wall; **frusten** *vt/i.* *umg.*: **j-n ~** frustrate s.o.; **das frustet!** it's really frustrating (*od.* a real drag); **gefrustet sein** have come up against a brick wall (**von** with); **Frustessen** *n* comfort eating; **frustig** *Adj. umg.* frustrating; (*nervend*) maddening; **Frustration** *f*; *-, -en*; *Psych.* frustration; **e-e ~ erleben** be frustrated, have a frustrating time (of it); **Frustrationstoleranz** *f Psych.*: **geringe/hohe ~** low/high frustration tolerance; **frustrieren** *v/t. Psych.* frustrate; **j-n ~** (*nerven*) get on s.o.'s nerves; *stärker*: drive s.o. mad *umg.*; (*enttäuschen*) get s.o. down

F-Schlüssel *m Mus.* F clef, bass clef

Fuchs *m*; *-es, Füchse* **1.** *Zool.* fox; *alter od. schlauer ~ fig.* cunning old devil; **wo sich ~ und Hase gute Nacht sagen** *umg. hum.* at the back of beyond, out in the sticks (*Am. auch* boondocks); **2.** → *Fuchspelz*, **3.** *Zool., Pferd*: chestnut; *heller*: sorrel; **4.** *Zool., Schmetterling*: **Großer ~** large tortoiseshell; **Kleiner ~** painted lady; **5.** *umg.* (*Rothaarige[r]*) redhead; **6.** *Univ.* new fraternity member, *Am.* pledge; **~bandwurm** *m Zool.* fox tapeworm; **~bau** *m*; *Pl. -e* fox's earth (*bes. Am.* lair)

fuchsen *umg.* **I.** *v/t.* rile, get to; **II.** *v/refl.* be riled (**über** + *Akk.* about)

Fuchsie *f*; *-, -n*; *Bot.* fuchsia

fuchsig *Adj.* **1.** *Haar*: ginger; **2.** *umg.* (*wütend*) fuming, (hopping) mad

Füchsin *f*; *-, -nen*; *Zool.* vixen

Fuchs|jagd *f* foxhunt; *das Jagen*: foxhunting; **~pelz** *m* fox (fur)

fuchsrot *Adj. Haar*: ginger

Fuchsschwanz *m* **1.** fox's brush, foxtail; **2.** *Bot.* amaranth, love-lies-bleeding; *Süßgras*: foxtail grass; **3.** (*Säge*) handsaw

fuchsteufelswild *Adj. umg.* hopping mad

Fuchtel *f*; *-, -n*; *umg.*: **unter j-s ~ sein od. stehen** be under s.o.'s thumb; **j-n unter s-r ~ haben** have s.o. under one's thumb; **fuchteln** *v/i.*: **~ mit** wave around; *drohend*: brandish; **mit den Händen ~** gesticulate wildly; **fuchtig** *Adj. umg.* fuming, (hopping) mad; **werden** get mad

Fuder *n*; *-s, -* cartload; **ein ~ Heu** a cartload of hay

Fudschijama *m*; *-s*; *Geog.* Fujiyama

Fuffi *m*; *-s, -s*; *umg. hist.* fifty-mark note; **fuffzehn** *Adj. Dial.* → *fünfzehn*; **fuffzig** *Adj. Dial.* → *fünfzig*; **Fuffziger** *m*; *-s, -*; *Dial.* → *Fünfziger²*; **ein falscher ~** *umg. fig.* a shifty type

Fug *m*: **mit ~ und Recht** rightly, with good reason; **sie behauptet mit ~ und Recht** she justifiably claims, she is justified in claiming (*od.* saying); **er tat es mit ~ und Recht** he had every reason to do so

Fuge¹ *f*; *-, -n*; *Mus.* fugue

Fuge² *f*; *-, -n* **1.** *Tech.* joint; (*Zwischenraum*) gap, interstice *förm.*; **aus den ~n gehen** *od.* **geraten** come (*od.* fall) apart; *fig.* be going to pieces; **s-e Welt ist aus den ~n** his world is in ruins; **in allen ~n krachen** *auch fig.* be creaking

at the joints; **2.** *Ling.* juncture; **fugen** *v/t.* **1.** (*zusammenfügen*) joint; **2.** (*verstreichen*) point

fügen I. *v/t.* **1. ~ an** (+ *Akk.*) *od.* **zu** add to; (*befestigen*) join to; *Tech.* fit to; **~ in** (+ *Akk.*) add to, fit into; **2.** *geh.* (*errichten*) build, put together (**aus** from); **Steine zu e-r Mauer ~** build up stones into a wall; **zu e-m Ganzen ~** *fig.* join together to form a whole; **3.** *geh.* (*bewirken*) ordain; **II.** *v/refl.* **1. sich ~ an** (+ *Akk.*) follow (upon); **eines fügte sich ans andere** one thing followed (*od.* led to) another; **2. sich ~ in** (+ *Akk.*) (*passen zu*) fit in well with; **3. sich ~** (+ *Dat. od. in* + *Akk.*) (*nachgeben*) submit to; (*gehorchen*) comply (with); (*sich abfinden mit*) resign o.s. (to); **wir müssen uns ~** we have no choice but to obey (*od.* comply); **sich in sein Schicksal ~** resign o.s. to (*od.* accept) one's fate; **4.** *geh.* (*eintreten, sich treffen*) happen, turn out; *unpers.*: **es fügt sich, dass** it so happens that; **das fügt sich gut** things have turned out well, this is a fortunate turn of events

fugenlos I. *Adj.* smooth; *Mauer etc.*: with no gaps; **II.** *Adv.* *schließen*: perfectly, leaving no gaps

Fugen-s *n Ling.* linking s

fügsam *Adj.* (*gehorsam*) obedient; (*nachgiebig*) compliant; (*leicht lenkbar*) docile

Fügung *f* **1.** *göttliche, des Schicksals*: (act of) providence; (*Zusammentreffen*) coincidence; (*Schicksal*) fate; **durch e-e glückliche ~** by a lucky coincidence; **e-e merkwürdige ~ des Schicksals** a (strange) twist of fate; **2.** *Ling.* construction

fühlbar *Adj.* **1.** (*merklich*) noticeable; (*deutlich*) distinct, marked; (*beträchtlich*) considerable, appreciable; (*wahrnehmbar*) perceptible; **~er Verlust** serious loss; **sich ~ machen** make itself felt; **2.** *mit Tastsinn*: tangible, palpable

fühlen I. *vt/i.* **1.** *körperlich, seelisch*: feel; (*gewahr werden*) *auch* sense; (*Mitleid*) **mit j-m ~** feel (sympathy) for s.o.; **j-n s-e Verachtung ~ lassen** show s.o. one's contempt, show one's contempt for s.o.; **2.** (*ahnen*) feel; (*spüren*) sense; **sie hat ihr Ende kommen ~** she felt her end was near; **ein Unglück nahen ~** have a premonition of disaster; **II.** *v/refl.* **1. sich glücklich etc. ~** feel happy etc.; **sich von j-m verstanden ~** feel s.o. understands one, feel in harmony with s.o.; **sich e-r Situation gewachsen ~** feel equal to a situation; **wie fühlst du dich?** how are you (feeling)?, how do you feel?; **~ Sie sich wie zu Hause!** make yourself at home; **er fühlte sich mehr und mehr bedroht** he felt increasingly threatened, he had a growing sense of menace; **2. sich ~ als** see o.s. as, consider o.s.; **ein geborener Türke, fühlt er sich jetzt eher als Deutscher** although Turkish by birth, he feels more like (*od.* feels himself to be) a German now; **der fühlt sich aber!** *umg.* (*ist eingebildet*) he thinks he's God's gift, *Brit. auch* he doesn't half fancy himself; **jetzt kannst du dich aber ~!** *umg.* now you can be really pleased with yourself; **III.** *v/t.*: **(j-m) den Puls ~** feel (*Med.* take) s.o.'s pulse; **IV.** *v/i.*: **~ nach** (*tasten*) feel (*od.* grope) for; → *Zahn* 3

fühlend I. *Part. Präs.* → *fühlen*; **II.** *Adj. Herz etc.*: feeling; (*mitfühlend*) *auch* sympathetic

Fühler *m*; *-s, -* **1.** *Zool.* feeler, antenna; *bei Weichtieren*: *auch* tentacle; *Schnecke*: horn, feeler; **die ~ ausstrecken** *Schnecke*: put out its horns; *fig.* put out feelers (**nach** for); **2.** *Tech.* sensor; *zum Messen*: probe

Fühl|haar *n* tactile hair; **~horn** *n* horn, feeler

Fühlung *f* contact; **~ haben/verlieren mit** be in /lose touch with; **~ (auf)nehmen mit** contact, get in touch with; **Fühlungnahme** *f*; *-, -n* initial (*od.* first) contact

fuhr *Imperf.* → *fahren*

Fuhre *f*; *-, -n* **1.** (*Ladung*) *Laster*: (truck)load, *Brit. auch* (lorry)load; *Wagen*: cart(load); **e-e ~ Sand** a (truck)load (*Brit. auch* [lorry]load) of sand; **2.** (*Fahrt*) trip; *e-s Taxis*: fare

führen I. *v/t.* **1.** lead (**nach, zu** to); (*geleiten*) *auch* take, escort; *zu e-m Platz*: *auch* usher; (*j-m den Weg zeigen*) lead, guide; (*zwangsweise*) escort; **an** *od.* **bei der Hand ~** take s.o. by the hand; **an der Leine / am Zügel ~** walk on the lead / lead by the reins; *Besucher in ein Zimmer ~* show (*od.* lead, usher) into a room; **j-n durch die Firma ~** show s.o. (a)round the firm (*Am.* company); **die Polizei auf j-s Spur ~** *fig.* put the police on s.o.'s track; **was führt dich zu mir?** *fig.* what brings you here?; **m-e Reise führte mich nach Spanien** *fig.* my trip took me to Spain; → *Versuchung*, **2.** (*irgendwohin gelangen lassen*): **j-m die Hand ~** guide s.o.'s hand (*auch fig.*); **zum Mund ~** raise to one's lips; **ein Kabel durch ein Rohr ~** pass a cable through a pipe; **e-e Straße um e-n Ort ~** take a road (a)round a place, bypass a place; **3.** (*handhaben*) handle, wield; **sie führt den Ball sicher** she's got good ball control; **4.** *Amtsspr.* (*Auto, Zug etc.*) drive; (*Flugzeug etc.*) pilot, fly; (*Schiff*) navigate; **5. bei** *od.* **mit sich ~** have on one, carry; (*Fracht, Ladung etc.*) carry; **Erz ~** bear (*od.* contain) ore; **Strom ~** *Etech.* be live; (*leiten*) conduct current; **der Fluss führt Sand (mit sich)** the river carries sand with it; → *Hochwasser*, **6.** (*anführen*) lead, head; (*Leitung haben*) be in charge of; *Mil. auch* command; (*Geschäft, Haushalt etc.*) manage, run; (*lenkend beeinflussen*) guide; **e-e Armee zum Sieg ~** lead an army to victory; **etw. in den Ruin ~** lead s.th. to ruin; **e-e Klasse zum Abitur ~** take a class through to the Abitur exam; **er führt s-e Mitarbeiter mit fester Hand** he manages his colleagues with a firm hand; → *Aufsicht* 1, *geführt* II, *Kommando* 2, *Vorsitz etc.*; **7.** (*Gespräch, Verhandlung etc.*) carry on, have; (*Telefongespräch*) make; (*Prozess*) conduct; (*Buch, Liste, Protokoll etc.*) keep; (*Konto*) manage; **ein geruhsames etc. Leben ~** lead (*od.* live) a peaceful etc. life; **sie ~ e-e gute Ehe** they're happily married, they have a good (husband-and-wife) relationship; **etw. zu Ende ~** finish s.th.; → *Beweis* 1, *Krieg, Regie etc.*; **8.** (*Namen*) bear, go by (*od.* under) the name of; (*Nummer, Wappen*) have; (*Flagge*) carry, fly; (*Titel*) *Person*: hold; *Buch etc.*: have; **den Titel ... ~** *Buch*: *auch* be entitled ...; **9.** (*Ware*) *auf Lager*: stock; *zum Verkauf*: *auch* sell, have; **~ Sie Campingartikel?** do you have (*od. auch od.* stock) camping gear?; **auf** *od.* **in e-r Liste ~** list, make a list of; (**auf** *od.*

F

in e-r Liste) **geführt werden** appear on a list, be listed; **als vermisst geführt werden** be posted as missing; **10.** (*Reden, Sprache*) use; **ständig im Munde ~** be constantly talking about; (*Wendung*) be constantly using; **11.** *fig.* → **Feld** 9, **Schild**² 1; **II.** *v/i.* **1.** lead (*nach, zu* to); *Tal, Tür etc.*: *auch* open (into); *unser Weg führte durch e-n Wald* our route led (*od.* passed) through a wood; **2.** *beim Tanzen*: lead, steer; **3.** *Sport*: **~ über** (+ *Akk.*) (*dauern*) last; *der Kampf führt über zehn Runden* the fight is over ten rounds; **4.** (*führend sein*) lead; *Sport auch* be in the lead; **mit zwei Toren ~** be two goals ahead, have a two-goal lead; **mit 3:1 ~** be 3-1 up; **mit 3:1 gegen X ~** lead X by 3-1; **5.** *fig.*: *durch das Programm führt X* your guide (*od.* presenter) for the program (-me) is X; **~ zu** lead to, end in; (*zur Folge haben*) result in; *das führt zu nichts* that won't get you/us *etc.* anywhere; *das führt zu keinem Ergebnis* that won't produce a result; *das führt zu weit* that's (*od.* that would be) going too far; *das führt dazu, dass noch mehr Stellen abgebaut werden* it'll lead to (*od.* end in) further staff reductions; as a consequence, there'll be even more downsizing (*od.* job cuts); *wohin soll das noch ~?* where will all this lead (*od.* end up)?; **III.** *v/refl.* conduct o.s.; *bes. Schüler*: behave (o.s.); *sich gut ~* behave (well)

führend I. *Part. Präs.* → **führen; II.** *Adj.* leading; *Politiker etc.*: *auch* senior, top-ranking ...; *auch Künstler etc.*: prominent; **~er Unternehmer** *auch* business leader; **~e Position** senior position; **~ sein** lead, rank in first place; **e-e ~e Rolle spielen** play a leading (*od.* key) role, hold a leading (*od.* key) position

Führer *m; -s, -* **1.** *e-r Partei, Organisation*: leader; *Mil. auch* commander; (*Leiter*) head, chief; *Sport* captain; *der ~ hist.* the Führer (*od.* Fuehrer); **2.** (*Fremdenführer etc.*) guide; **3.** *Buch*: guide (*für, durch, von* to), guidebook (on); **4.** *bes. Amtsspr. und schw.* (*Fahrer*) driver; (*Pilot*) pilot; *e-s Schiffs*: helmsman; **5.** *e-s Fahrstuhls, Krans etc.*: operator; **~ausweis** *m schw.* → **Führerschein; ~haus** *n* driver's cab

Führerin *f; -, -nen* (female) leader; *Mil.* commander; (*Leiter*) head, chief; *Sport* captain

führerlos *Adj.* **1.** without a leader (*od.* guide *etc.*); *Partei etc.*: *auch* leaderless; **2.** *Wagen*: driverless; *Flugzeug*: unpiloted, pilotless

Führer|natur *f* born (*od.* natural) leader; **~rolle** *f* role of (a) leader, leadership role

Führerschaft *f; mst Sg.* leadership; *Koll.* the leaders *Pl.*

Führerschein *m Mot.* driving licence, *Am.* driver's license; **s-n ~ machen** take (*od.* do) one's driving test; (*fahren lernen*) learn to drive; *sie haben ihm den ~ entzogen* they've taken away his licen|ce (*Am.* -se), he's lost his licen|ce (*Am.* -se); **~anwärter** *m*, **~anwärterin** *f* driving test candidate; **~entzug** *m* loss of one's driving licence (*Am.* driver's license), disqualification from driving; **zu e-m Jahr ~ verurteilt werden** be disqualified (*od.* banned) from driving for a year; **~kontrolle** *f* check of one's driving licence (*Am.* driver's license); **~neuling**

m person who has just passed the driving test, newly-qualified driver; **~prüfung** *f*: *praktische/theoretische ~* practical/theoretical part of the driving test

Führer|stand *m* driver's cab; **~stellung** *f* (position of) leadership

Fuhr|mann *m*; *Pl. mst* **Fuhrleute 1.** *altm.* carter; (*Kutscher*) coachman; **2.** *nur Sg.; Astron.* Auriga, the Charioteer; **~park** *m* fleet (of vehicles)

Führung *f* **1.** *nur Sg.; e-r Partei etc.*: leadership; *Mil.* command; *e-s Unternehmens*: management; (*Führungsgewalt*) control; (*Menschenführung*) guidance, direction; *unter der ~ von* headed by, under the direction *etc.* of; *die ~ übernehmen* take charge, take over; *die ~ an sich reißen* seize control; **2.** *nur Sg.; Koll. e-r Partei etc.*: leadership, the leaders *Pl.; e-s Unternehmens*: management; *Mil.* command; **3.** *in e-m Museum etc.*: (guided) tour; *an e-r ~ teilnehmen* take (*od.* go on) a guided tour; **4.** *nur Sg.*; (*Benehmen*) conduct, behavio(u)r; *gute ~* good conduct; **5.** *nur Sg.; Sport und fig.*: lead; *in ~ gehen* (*od.* *die ~ übernehmen*) take the lead; *in ~ sein* be leading (*od.* in the lead); *in ~ bleiben* keep the lead, stay in front; *die ~ ausbauen* increase (*od.* extend) the lead; **6.** *nur Sg.; e-r Kamera etc.*: guiding; (*Handhabung*) handling; **7.** *nur Sg.; von Verhandlungen etc.*: conduct; *von Listen etc.*: keeping; *von Konto*: management; **8.** *nur Sg.; e-s Namens, Titels etc.*: use; **9.** *Amtsspr.*: *zur ~ e-s Kraftfahrzeugs/Flugzeugs/Wasserfahrzeugs berechtigt sein* be licensed to drive a motor vehicle / pilot an aircraft / navigate a watercraft; **10.** *Tech.* guide(way); *Schiene*: guide (rail)

Führungs|anspruch *m* claim to (the) leadership; *e-n ~ anmelden* make a bid for (the) leadership; **~aufgabe** *f* executive function; **~eigenschaften** *Pl.* leadership qualities; **~gremium** *n* management committee; *e-r Partei*: executive committee; **~kraft** *f Wirts.* executive, manager; *Führungskräfte* management personnel (*Pl.*); *Pol.* leaders; **~krise** *f* leadership (*Wirts.* management) crisis

führungslos *Adj. Partei etc.*: without a leader, leaderless; *Firma*: without any management, managerless

Führungs|nachwuchs *m Pol.* future leaders *Pl.; Wirts.* future managers (*od.* executives) *Pl.*; **~position** *f* **1.** *Pol.* (position of) leadership; **2.** *Posten, Sport in der Tabelle etc.*: top (*od.* leading) position; **~qualitäten** *Pl.* leadership qualities; **~ haben** have leadership qualities; **~rolle** *f* **1.** leading role; **2.** *innerhalb e-r Gruppe etc.*: leadership role; **~schiene** *f Tech.* guide rail; **~schwäche** *f* weak leadership; **~spitze** *f* top echelons *Pl.; Wirts.* top management, top executives *Pl.*; **~stab** *m Mil.* command; *Wirts.* top executive team; **~stärke** *f* strong leadership, distinctive leadership qualities *Pl.*; **~ zeigen** be a strong leader; **~stil** *m* style of leadership; *Wirts.* managerial style; **~treffer** *m Sport*: *den ~ erzielen Ballspiele*: (score the goal to) put one's team into the lead; *Fechten*: score a hit to take the lead; **~wechsel** *m* change in leadership, *Pol. auch* regime change; **~zeugnis** *n*: (*polizeiliches ~*) certificate of good conduct (*confirming that the holder has no cri-*

minal record)

Fuhr|unternehmen *n* haulage company, *Am.* (common) carrier; **~unternehmer** *m*, **~unternehmerin** *f* haulage contractor, *Am.* (common) carrier

Fuhrwerk *n* horsedrawn vehicle; *für Personen*: carriage; (*Karren*) cart; **fuhrwerken** *v/i. umg.* bustle around; *laut*: bang around; *mit etw. ~* wave s.th. around; *drohend*: brandish s.th.

Füllanzeige *f Tech.* level indicator, gauge

Fülle *f; -, kein Pl.* **1.** (*Menge, Überfluss*) wealth, abundance; (*große Zahl*) *auch* host; *des Glücks etc.*: profusion; → **Hülle** 5; **2.** *Haar*: fullness; *Körper*: stoutness; *zur ~ neigen* be a bit on the stout side; **3.** *fig. der Stimme, des Klangs*: richness, sonority

füllen I. *v/t.* **1.** (*Behälter, Torte, Zahn*) fill; (*Loch*) *auch* stop; (*Braten, Kissen etc.*) stuff; *den Eimer mit Wasser ~* fill (up) the bucket with water; *bis zum Rand ~* fill to the brim, fill (right) up; → **gefüllt; 2. ~ in** (+ *Akk.*) fill into; (*gießen*) pour into; *in Säcke, Kisten etc.*: put into; *in Flaschen ~* bottle; *Sand in Säcke ~* put sand into sacks, fill sacks with sand; **3.** *Sache*: (*einnehmen*) take up; *der Bericht füllte 15 Seiten* the report took up (*od.* filled) 15 pages; **II.** *v/refl.* fill; *Badewanne, Saal*: fill up; *der Saal füllte sich schnell* (*mit Gästen*) the hall filled up very quickly

Füllen *n; -s, -; Zool., geh.* → **Fohlen**

Füller *m; -s, -* **1.** (fountain) pen; **2.** *in Zeitung*: filler

Füll|federhalter *m* fountain pen; **~gewicht** *n* net weight; **~halter** *m* fountain pen; **~höhe** *f* filling level; **~ technisch bedingt** pack only partially filled for technical reasons; **~horn** *n* horn of plenty, cornucopia

füllig *Adj. Gesicht, Haar*: full; *Figur, Busen*: ample; *Person*: stout, portly

Füll|masse *f* **1.** *Tech.* (*auch Zahnfüllung*) filling compound, amalgam; *für Mauerrisse etc.*: filler; **2.** *Gastr., Braten*: stuffing; *Torte*: filling; **~material** *n* filler

Füllsel *n; -s, -* **1.** *für Lücken*: filler; *im Paket, auch fig. schriftlich*: padding; **2.** *Gastr.* filling; *in Fleisch*: stuffing

Fulltimejob, Full-Time-Job ['fʊltaimdʒɔb] *m* full-time job

Füllung *f* **1.** *Tank, Torte, Zahn*: filling; *Braten, Kissen etc.*: stuffing; *Praline*: cent|re (*Am.* -er); **2.** (*Polsterung*) padding; **3.** *Tür*: panel; **4.** *nur Sg.; Handlung*: filling; *Gastr.* stuffing; *in Flaschen*: bottling

Füllwort *n Ling., Lit.* filler (word)

fulminant *Adj. geh.* brilliant

Fummel *m; -s, -; umg., oft pej.* rag

Fummelei *f; -, -en; umg. pej.* stümperhaft etc.: fumbling; *knifflig*: fiddling; *was für e-e ~!* what a fiddly job!; **Fummelkram** *m umg. pej.* fiddly job, fiddle; **fummeln I.** *v/i. umg.* **1.** *mühsam*: fumble around; **2.** *pej.* fiddle around (*an* + *Dat.* with); **3.** *sexuell*: grope; *mit j-m ~* feel s.o. up *Sl.*; **II.** *v/t.*: *~ aus* drag out; *~ in* (+ *Akk.*) fiddle into

Fund *m; -(e)s, -e* **1.** (*das Finden*) finding; *e-s Schatzes etc.*: discovery; *e-n ~ machen* make a find (*od.* discovery); **2.** (*Gefundenes*) find

Fundament *n; -(e)s, -e* **1.** *Archit.* foundations *Pl.; bis auf die ~e zerstört werden* be razed (to the ground); **2.** *fig.* foundation, basis; *das ~ legen*

für od. **zu** lay the foundation(s) for (od. of); **ein gutes** od. **solides ~** a solid foundation (bes. Wissen: grounding); **auf e-m festen ~ stehen** be on a firm footing; **in s-n ~en erschüttern** destroy the (very) foundations (od. roots) of

fundamental geh. **I.** Adj. fundamental, basic; **~er Irrtum** fundamental error, basic mistake; **II.** Adv.: **~ voneinander abweichen** be fundamentally different (Meinungen: opposed); **Fundamentalismus** m; -, kein Pl. fundamentalism; **Fundamentalist** m; -en, -en, **Fundamentalistin** f; -, -nen fundamentalist; **fundamentalistisch** Adj. fundamentalist

fundamentieren v/t. lay the foundations of

Fund|amt n bes. österr., **~büro** n lost property office; Schild: auch lost and found; **~gegenstand** m → **Fundsache**; **~grube** f fig. goldmine; für etw. Bestimmtes: treasure chest; im Kaufhaus etc.: bargain offers Pl.

Fundi m; -s, -s; Pol. umg. radical Green, Am. auch tree-hugger

fundieren v/t. **1.** (Behauptung, These etc.) substantiate; **2.** Wirts. (Anleihe, Schuld) fund, consolidate; **fundiert I.** P.P. → **fundieren**; **II.** Adj. **1.** Wissen etc.: sound; Tatsachen: well-founded, well-grounded; **wissenschaftlich ~** well-founded, backed up by research; **2.** Wirts. Schuld: funded; Geschäft: solid, sound

fündig Adj.: **~ werden** strike gold (od. oil etc.), auch weitS. make a strike, strike (it) lucky; **bist du ~ geworden?** did you find anything?, did you have any luck?

Fund|ort m place where s.th. was found; archäologischer etc.: site of the discovery etc.; **hier ist der ~ der Statue** this is where the statue was found; **~sache** f lost article, piece of lost property; Pl. lost property Sg.; **~stätte** f Archäol. etc. (Fundort) site of the discovery etc.; **archäologische ~** (Grabungsstätte) arch(a)eological site; **~stelle** f → **Fundort**; **~stück** n find

Fundus m; -, -. **1.** fig. an Wissen etc.: store, fund (an + Dat. of); **2.** Theat. general equipment store

fünf Zahlw. five; **die ~ Weisen** Wirts., Pol. the Five Wise Men (who assess the performance of the German economy); **~ vor zwölf** fig. the eleventh hour; **es ist ~ vor zwölf** fig. time is running out fast, it's almost zero hour; **~(e) gerade sein lassen** fig. stretch a point; **du musst auch mal ~(e) gerade sein lassen** fig. you mustn't be so critical, you must take a more relaxed view of things; → auch **acht¹**, **Finger** 1, **Sinn** 1

Fünf f; -, -en **1.** Zahl: (number) five; → **Acht¹** 1, 2, 4; **2.** Päd. (Note): etwa E, Am. F; **e-e ~ schreiben** get an E (Am. F)

Fünfakter m Theat. five-act play

fünfarmig Adj. Leuchter: five-armed; **fünfbändig** Adj. five-volume ..., präd. und nachgestellt: in five volumes

Fünf-Cent-Münze f Euro: five-(euro)-cent piece

Fünfeck n; -s, -e pentagon; **fünfeckig** Adj. pentagonal

fünfeinhalb Zahlw. five and a half

Fünfer m; -s, - **1.** umg. → **Fünf**; **2.** Geldschein: five-euro etc. note; hist. Münze: five-pfennig/mark etc. piece; Schein: five-mark note; **3.** **e-n ~ haben**

Lotto: have a (prize-winning) sequence of five numbers; **~einmaleins** n five-times table; **~gruppe** f group of five

fünferlei Adj. indekl. five (different) kinds of; subst. five (different) things

Fünfeuro|centstück n five-eurocent piece; **~schein** m five-euro note

fünffach I. Adj. fivefold; **in ~er Ausfertigung** in quintuplicate; **die ~e Menge** five times the amount; **~er Sieger** five-time winner; **II.** Adv. five times; → **achtfach**

Fünf|frankenstück n five-franc piece; **~gangschaltung** f five-speed gears Pl.; **~groschenstück** n hist. five-groschen piece

fünfhundert Zahlw. five hundred

Fünfhundert... im Subst. five-hundred ...; **~euroschein** five-hundred euro note

Fünfjahresplan m five-year plan

fünfjährig Adj. **1.** Kind etc.: five-year-old ...; **2.** Zeitraum: five-year ...; **ein ~es ...** auch five years of ...; **Fünfjährige** m, f; -n, -n five-year-old

Fünfkampf m Sport pentathlon; **moderner ~** modern pentathlon

fünf|karätig Adj. five-carat ...; **~köpfig** Adj. Familie etc.: ... of five; **~e Delegation** etc. auch five-member (od. five-man) delegation etc.

Fünfling m; -s, -e quintuplet, quin, Am. quint umg.

fünfmal Adv. five times; **fünfmalig** Adj.: **nach ~er Wiederholung** etc. after five repetitions etc., after being repeated etc. five times; → **achtmalig**

Fünfmark|schein m hist. five-mark note; **~stück** n hist. five-mark piece

Fünfmeter|brett n five-met|re (Am. -er) board; **~raum** m Fußball: six-yard box

fünf|minütig Adj. Gespräch etc.: five-minute ...; **~monatig** Adj. **1.** Baby etc.: five-month-old ...; **2.** Zeitraum: five-month ...; **~monatlich I.** Adj. five monthly ...; **II.** Adv. every five months

Fünf|pfennigstück n hist. five-pfennig piece; **~prozenthürde** f Parl. five per cent hurdle (od. threshold)

fünfprozentig Adj. five percent ...

Fünf|prozentklausel f Parl. five per cent clause (restricting representation in parliament to parties obtaining more than five per cent of the vote); **~rappenstück** n schw. (Swiss) five-centime piece

fünfsaitig Adj. Mus. five-stringed

Fünfschillingstück n hist. five-schilling piece

fünf|seitig Adj. **1.** Math. pentagonal; **2.** Artikel, Aufsatz: five-page ...; **~silbig** Adj. Ling. five-syllable ...; **~stellig** Adj. Zahl: five-digit ...

Fünfsternehotel n five-star hotel

fünf|stöckig Adj. five-stor(e)y ...; **~stündig** Adj. five-hour(-long) ...

fünft Adv.: **zu ~** five of; **sie waren zu ~** there were five of them; → **acht²**

fünft... Zahlw. mit Endung: fifth; **~e Kolonne** Pol. Fifth Column; **das ~e Rad am Wagen sein** fig. be the odd man out; (stören) be in the way; bei Paaren: play gooseberry, Am. be a third wheel → **acht...**

Fünftagewoche f five-day week

fünftägig Adj. **1.** Frist etc.: five-day (--long) ...; **~ sein** last five days; **2.** Baby etc.: five-day-old ...

fünftausend Zahlw. five thousand; **Fünftausender** m **1.** Berg: five thou-

sand met|re (Am. -er) (etwa sixteen thousand foot) peak; **2.** Geldschein in einigen Währungen: five thousand lira etc. note; **Fünftausendmeterlauf** m, **5000-m-Lauf** m Sport five thousand met|res (Am. -ers) Sg. (race)

Fünfte m, f; -n, -n (the) fifth; → **Achte**

fünfteilig Adj. **1.** Aufsatz, Plan etc.: five-part ..., ... in five parts; **~ sein** be in five parts; **2.** Couchgarnitur etc.: five-piece ...

fünftel I. Adj.: **e-e ~ Sekunde** a fifth of a second; **II. Fünftel** n; -s, - fifth

fünftens Adv. fifth(ly), five

Fünftklässler m, **~in** f fifth-year pupil (in primary school), Am. fifth-grader

Fünfuhr|nachrichten Pl. five o'clock news Sg.; **~tee** m five-o'clock tea; **~zug** m five o'clock train

Fünfunddreißigstundenwoche f, **35-Stunden-Woche** f thirty-five (od. 35) hour (work) week

Fünfvierteltakt m Mus. five-four time

fünf|wertig Adj. Chem. pentavalent; **~wöchig** Adj. **1.** Zeitraum etc.: five-week ...; **~ sein** last five weeks; **2.** Baby etc.: five-week-old ...

fünfzehn Zahlw. fifteen

fünfzehnt Adv.: **zu ~** fifteen of; **wir waren zu ~** there were fifteen of us; → **acht²**

fünfzehnt... Zahlw. fifteenth

fünfzehntel I. Adj.: **e-e ~ Sekunde** a fifteenth of a second; **II. Fünfzehntel** n; -s, - fifteenth (part)

fünfzeilig Adj. five-line ...

fünfzig Zahlw. fifty; **Anfang/Mitte/Ende ~ sein** be in one's early/mid-/late fifties; → auch **achtzig**

Fünfzig f; -, -en, mst Sg. Zahl: (number) fifty; → auch **Achtzig**

fünfziger indekl. Adj.: **in den ~ Jahren** in the fifties

Fünfziger¹ Pl. **sie ist in den Fünfzigern** she's in her fifties

Fünfziger² m; -s, - **1.** Münze: fifty-cent etc. coin; **2.** Schein: fifty-euro etc. note; → **Fuffziger**

Fünfziger³ m; -s, -, **~in** f; -, -nen man/woman in his/her fifties, fiftysomething umg.

Fünfzigerjahre Pl.: **in den ~n** in the fifties

Fünfzig|eurocentstück n fifty-euro-cent piece; **~euroschein** m fifty-euro note; **~frankenschein** m fifty-(Swiss-)franc note; **~groschenstück** n hist. fifty-groschen piece

fünfzigjährig Adj. attr. Person: fifty-year-old ...; Zeitraum: fifty-year ...; **sein ~es Bestehen feiern** celebrate its fiftieth anniversary (od. its half-century); **Fünfzigjährige** m, f; -n, -n fifty-year-old

Fünfzig|markschein m hist. fifty-mark note (Am. bill); **~pfennigstück** n hist. fifty-pfennig piece; **~schillingschein** m hist. fifty-schilling note

fünfzigst... Zahlw. fiftieth; → **achtzigst...**

Fünfzimmerwohnung f five-room apartment (Brit. auch flat)

fungieren v/i.: **~ als** act as; Sache: serve as, function as

Fungizid n; -(e)s, -e fungicide

Funk m; -s, kein Pl. radio; **per** od. **über ~** by radio; → auch **Radio**, **Rundfunk**; **~amateur** m, **~amateurin** f radio ham; **~aufklärung** f radio intelligence; **~ausstellung** f radio (and television) exhibition; **~bild** n radio picture

Fünkchen n **1.** small spark; **2.** fig. scrap; Wahrheit: auch grain; Hoffnung:

flicker

Funke m; -ns, -n **1.** spark; **~n aus e-m Stein schlagen** strike sparks from a stone; **~n sprühten (aus)** sparks were flying (from *od.* out of); **~n sprühend** *Räder etc.*: sending out (showers of) sparks; *fig. Augen*: flashing; *Diskussion*: heated; *Geist*: scintillating; **der zündende ~** *fig.* the trigger; **der ~ ist übergesprungen** *fig.* we (*od.* they) clicked; **sie arbeiteten, dass die ~n flogen** *fig.* they worked so fast you could see the sparks fly; **2.** *fig.* (*bisschen*) scrap (of); *Wahrheit*: *auch* grain (of); *Hoffnung*: flicker (of); **keinen ~n Ehrgeiz etc. haben** not have the slightest trace of ambition

funkeln v/i. **1.** sparkle; *Sterne*: *auch* twinkle; (*glitzern*) glisten, glitter; **2.** *Augen, vor Wut etc.*: flash (**vor** + *Dat.* with); *vor Freude*: sparkle (**vor** + *Dat.* with)

funkelnagelneu *Adj. umg.* brand--spanking new

Funkempfänger m radio receiver

funken I. vt/i. radio; (*Nachricht, Signal etc.*) *auch* send out; **II.** v/i. **1.** (*Funken sprühen*) give off sparks, spark; **2.** *unpers.*; *umg. fig.*: **gleich funkt's!** (*gibt es Schläge*) you'll get it in a moment!; **hat es bei ihm endlich gefunkt?** has the penny finally dropped (with him)?, has he got it (*od.* the message) at last?; **bei od. zwischen ihnen hat es (gleich) gefunkt** they hit it off (from the word go), they clicked (immediately)

Funken m; -s, - → **Funke**; **~bildung** f sparking; **~flug** m flying sparks *Pl.*; **~mariechen** n; -s, - girl Carnival dancer in the 18th century uniform of the *Cologne Town Guard*; **~regen** m shower of sparks

funkentstört *Adj.* suppressed; **Funkentstörung** f; nur Sg. noise suppression; (*Vorrichtung*) static screen

Funker m; -s, -, **~in** f; -, -nen radio operator

Funk|gerät n (two-way) radio, radio transceiver; *tragbar*: walkie-talkie; **~haus** n broadcasting studios *Pl.*

Funk|kontakt m radio contact; **~ haben** be in radio contact (**mit** with); **~meldung** f radio message; **~offizier** m *Naut.* radio officer; **~ortung** f radiolocation; **~peilgerät** n radio direction finder (*Abk.* RDF); **~peilung** f radio direction finding; **~richtstrahl** m directional radio beam; **~rufempfänger** m bleeper; **~schatten** m (reception) blind spot; **~signal** n radio signal

Funksprech|gerät n walkie-talkie; **~verkehr** m radio telephony

Funk|spruch m radio message; **~stille** f **1.** radio silence, blackout; (*Sendepause*) break in transmission; **2.** *fig.* silence; **bei od. zwischen ihnen herrscht ~** they're not on speaking terms; **~störung** f interference; *durch Störsender*: jamming

Funkstreife f **1.** radio patrol; **2.** *Wagen*: squad car; **Funkstreifenwagen** m squad car

Funk|taxi n radio taxi (*bes. Am.* cab); **~technik** f radio engineering; **~techniker** m, **~technikerin** f radio engineer; **~telefon** n cellular phone, cellphone

Funktion f; -, -en **1.** function; (*Zweck*) *auch* purpose; **dies hat die ~ zu** (+ *Inf.*) this is supposed to (+ *Inf.*), this is for (+ *Ger.*); **2.** (*Amt*) office; (*Stellung*) position; **e-e hohe ~ ausüben**

hold a high office (*od.* an important position); **in m-r ~ als ...** in my position as ..., acting as ...; **3.** (*Funktionieren*) functioning; (*Arbeit, Tätigkeit*) working, operation; **außer ~** not working, not in operation; (*im Stillstand*) at a standstill; **außer ~ setzen** put out of action; (*zum Stillstand bringen*) bring to a standstill; **in ~ sein** be in operation, be working; **in ~ treten** *Sache*: come into operation; *Person*: take up one's duties; *Krisenstab etc.*: go into action; **4.** *Math.* function; **5.** *Logik.* function; *Philos., des Denkens etc.*: corollary

funktional *Adj.* functional; **Funktionalismus** m; -, *kein Pl.* functionalism; **funktionalistisch** *Adj.* functionalist

Funktionär m; -s, -e, **~in** f; -, -nen official; **hoher ~** high-ranking (*od.* top) official; **hohe ~e** *auch* (the) top brass *umg.*

funktionell *Adj.* functional

funktionieren v/i. work; *Tech. auch* function, be functioning; **es funktioniert nicht** *allg.* it doesn't work; *momentan*: it's not working, it's out of order; **gut ~** work well; (*ablaufen*) *auch* go well; *Organisation*: be efficient

Funktionsablauf m operational sequence

funktions|fähig *Adj.* functional, working, in working order; *System etc.*: workable; **~gerecht** *Adj.* functional, practical; **~los** *Adj.* without a function; **~ sein** *Person*: have no work to do; *Bauteil etc.*: have no function, serve no purpose

Funktionsprüfung f *Med.* function test

funktionssicher *Adj.* reliable, sound

Funktions|störung f *Med.* malfunction; **~taste** f *Computer*: function key; **~träger** m, **~trägerin** f office-holder

funktionstüchtig *Adj. Ausrüstung*: working efficiently; *Organ*: functioning soundly, sound

Funktions|verb n *Ling.* empty verb; **~weise** f manner of operation

Funk|turm m radio tower; **~uhr** f radio-controlled clock; **~verbindung** f radio contact; **~verkehr** m radio communication; **~wagen** m **1.** (*Ü-Wagen*) radio van; **2.** *Polizei*: radio (patrol) car; **~wecker** m radio-controlled alarm clock; **~zentrale** f (radio) call cent|re (*Am.* -er)

Funsportart ['fan-] f fun sport

Funzel f; -, -n; *umg. pej.* (too) dim light

für I. *Präp.* (+ *Akk.*) **1.** *Zweck, Ziel*: for; **~ mich** for me; (*um meinetwillen*) for my sake; **hier, ~ dich!** this is for you; **~ was ist das?** *umg.* what's that in aid of?, what's that for?; **~ nichts und wieder nichts** *umg.* (*vergebens*) all for nothing; **2.** (*zugunsten von*) for, in favo(u)r of; **alles spricht ~ ihn als** *Kandidat*: he has everything going for him; **als** *Täter*: everything points to him; **das hat viel ~ sich** there's a lot to be said for it; **und du, ~ wen bist du?** who are you rooting for?; **3.** (*wegen*) for; **j-n ~ etw. belohnen/bestrafen** reward/punish s.o. for s.th.; **4.** (*anstelle von*) for; (*im Namen von*) *auch* on behalf of; **~ zwei arbeiten/essen** do as much work as two people / eat enough for two; **gehst du ~ mich hin?** will you go there for me?; **dieses Beispiel steht ~ viele** this example stands for (*od.* is one of) many; **5.** *Preis, Gegenleistung*: for; (*als Ersatz*) *auch* in exchange (*od.* return) for; **~ zwei Euro**

Eis kaufen get two euros' worth of ice cream; **Aktien ~ tausend Euro** a thousand euros of shares; **~ 20 Euro die** *od.* **pro Stunde** for 20 euros an hour; **6.** *mit Zeitangaben*: for; **~ gewöhnlich** usually; **~ immer** for ever; **~ zwei Wochen** for two weeks; **das Treffen ist ~ Montag geplant** the meeting is planned for Monday; **genug ~ heute!** that's enough for today; **7.** *Bezug herstellend*: *Lehrer, Professor, Minister etc.* **~** of; **sie ist Lektorin für Sachbücher** she's a non-fiction editor; **zu alt etc. ~** too old etc. for; **das gilt auch ~ dich!** that applies to (*od.* goes for) you too; **~ ihn heißt es jetzt Geduld haben** now he's just got to be patient; **ist das von Interesse ~ dich?** is that of any interest to you?; **~ mich ist sie die Größte!** for me (*od.* as far as I'm concerned) she's the greatest!; **8.** *Verhältnis, Vergleich*: for; **nicht schlecht ~ den ersten Versuch!** not bad for a first attempt; **9.** *Aufeinanderfolge*: **Schritt ~ Schritt** step by step; **Tag ~ Tag** day after day; **Wort ~ Wort** word for word; **10.** *Eigenschaft zuweisend*: **halten/erklären ~** consider/declare (to be); **ich halte es ~ unklug** I don't think it's (*od.* it would be) a good idea; **ich hätte ihn ~ jünger gehalten** I would have thought he was younger; **die Sitzung ~ eröffnet erklären** declare the meeting open; **j-n ~ tot erklären** pronounce s.o. dead; **11.** *umg.* (*gegen*) for; **ein Mittel ~ Grippe** something for flu; **gut ~ den Durst** good for thirst, good if you're thirsty; **12. ~ sich bleiben** stay on one's own, be alone; **~ sich leben** live by o.s.; **er ist gern ~ sich (allein)** he likes to be on his own; **das ist e-e Sache ~ sich** that's another matter entirely, that's a different story; **13.** *fig.*: **an und ~ sich** actually; **ich ~ m-e Person** *od.* **ich ~ mein Teil** I for my part; **sie singt ~ ihr Leben gern** she just loves singing; **er kann nichts ~ s-e Dummheit** he can't help being stupid; **14.** *umg.*: **was ~ (ein) ...** (*welche Art*) what kind of ...; (*welche[r,s]*) what ...; *als Ausruf*: what (a) ...; **was ~ ein Auto hast du?** what sort (*bes. Am.* kind) of car have you got?; **was ~ ein Unsinn!** what nonsense!; **II.** *Adv.* **1.** *nordd. umg.*: **da/hier/wo ... ~ →** **dafür, hierfür, wofür**; **2.** *altm.*: **~ und ~** for ever and ever

Für n: **das ~ und Wider** the pros and cons *Pl.*

Fürbitte f intercession; **~ einlegen** intercede (**für** for, on behalf of; **bei** with)

Furche f; -, -n *Acker, Gehirn, Haut etc.*: furrow; (*Rille*) groove; (*Wagenspur*) rut; **~n ziehen** make (*mit Pflug*: plough) furrows (**in** + *Akk.* in); **furchen** geh. **I.** v/t. **1.** (*Boden*) make (*mit Pflug*: plough) furrows in; (*Weg*) make ruts in; **2.** **die Stirn ~** furrow (*od.* knit) one's brow; **II.** v/refl. **1.** **i-e Stirn furchte sich** furrows creased her brow; **2.** *Bio., Eizelle*: divide

Furcht f; *kein Pl.* **1.** fear (**vor** + *Dat.* of); *stärker*: dread (of); **~ haben vor** (+ *Dat.*) be afraid (*od.* scared, frightened) of; **aus ~ vor** (+ *Dat.*) because he's etc. afraid (*od.* scared, frightened) of, for fear of (+ *Ger.*); **vor ~ erstarren** be paralysed with fear; **ohne ~ sein** (*od.* **keine ~ kennen**) be fearless, know no fear; **ohne ~ und Tadel** without fear or reproach; **j-m ~ einflößen** *od.* **einjagen** frighten (*od.* scare) s.o.; *stär-*

ker: terrify s.o.; **~ einflößend** *od.* **erregend** frightening; **unter der Bevölkerung ~ und Schrecken verbreiten** spread terror among the people, terrorize the people; **zwischen ~ und Hoffnung schweben** be in a state of trepidation, be on tenterhooks; *längerfristig*: live in fear and trepidation; **2.** *altm.* (*Ehrfurcht*) awe (**vor** + *Dat.*, *oder nur* + *Gen.* of)

furchtbar I. *Adj.* **1.** terrible; *stärker*: fearful; *Gegner etc.*: formidable; **er ist ein ~er Mensch** *umg.* he is an awful person; **es war ~ für mich, nicht helfen zu können** it was terrible for me not to be able to help; **2.** *umg.* (*sehr groß od. schlecht*) terrible, dreadful, awful; **ein ~es Deutsch sprechen** speak terrible (*od.* dreadful, awful, frightful) German; **das ist ja ~!** that's terrible (*od.* frightful)!; **II.** *Adv.* **1.** terribly; **2.** *umg.* (*sehr*) terribly; *negativ*: *auch* dreadfully; **~ heiß** terribly (*od.* dreadfully) hot; **es ist ~ einfach** it's terribly easy; **ich bin ~ erschrocken** I got a terrible (*od.* a dreadful) fright; **wir haben ~ gelacht** we just laughed and laughed

furchteinflößend *Adj.*: **äußerst/sehr ~** extremely/very frightening

fürchten I. *v/t.* **1.** be afraid of; *stärker*: dread; **er fürchtete zu sterben** he was afraid of dying; **ich fürchte wir schaffen es nicht** I don't think we're (*od.* I have a feeling we're not) going to make it; → **gefürchtet**; **2.** *altm.*: **Gott ~** fear God; **II.** *v/i.*: **~ für** (*od. um*) **um** fear for; **ich fürchte um sein Leben** I fear for his life; **III.** *v/refl.* be frightened, be scared, be afraid (**vor** + *Dat.* of); **sich ~ vor** (+ *Dat.*) *auch* dread; **sich** (**davor**) **~ zu** (+ *Inf.*) be afraid of (+ *Ger.*), be scared to (+ *Inf.*); **sich im Dunkeln ~** be afraid (*od.* scared) of the dark; **fürchtet euch nicht!** *bibl.* be not afraid, fear not; **IV.** **Fürchten** *n*: **j-n das Fürchten lehren** put the fear of God (*od.* death) into s.o.; **da kann man das Fürchten lernen** it soon teaches you what fear is all about; **das ist ja zum Fürchten** it's enough to frighten the life (*od.* wits) out of you; **er sieht zum Fürchten aus** he looks a (real) fright *umg.*

fürchterlich *Adj. und Adv.* → **furchtbar**

furchterregend, **Furcht erregend** *Adj.*: **äußerst/sehr furchterregend** extremely/very frightening; *stärker*: really horrific

furchtlos *Adj.* fearless, intrepid; **Furchtlosigkeit** *f; nur Sg.* fearlessness

furchtsam *Adj.* timorous

füreinander I. *Adv.* for each other, for one another; **sie sind immer ~ da** they're always there for one another, they look out for one another; **II. Füreinander** *n; -s, kein Pl.* concern for one another, mutual (care and) concern

Furie *f; -, -n* **1.** *Myth.* Fury; **wie von ~n gejagt** as though the devil were after him, her etc.; **2.** *fig. pej.* virago, hellcat; **wie e-e ~** like a madwoman

furios *Adj. geh. altm.* (*leidenschaftlich*) passionate; (*rasend*) furious; (*mitreißend*) rousing; (*glänzend*) brilliant

Furnier *n; -s, -e* veneer; **furnieren** *v/t.* veneer

Furore *f; -, kein Pl. od. n; -s, kein Pl.*: **~ machen** cause a sensation, cause (*od.* create) quite a stir; (*groß in Mode sein*) be all the rage; **er hat mit s-m**

Buch ~ gemacht his book caused quite a sensation (*od.* stir)

fürs *Präp.* + *Art.* **1.** → **für**, **2.** **~ Erste** for the moment

Fürsorge *f* **1.** care (**für** for); **ärztliche ~** medical care; **2. öffentliche ~** public welfare; **3.** *umg. altm.* (*Sozialamt*) social security (*Am.* welfare) office.; (*Sozialhilfe*) → **Fürsorgeunterstützung**; **~einrichtung** *f* welfare institution; **~empfänger** *m*, **~empfängerin** *f* social security beneficiary, *Am.* welfare recipient; **~ sein** be on social security (*Am.* welfare)

fürsorgend *Adj.* caring

Fürsorge|pflicht *f; nur Sg.*; *Jur.* employer's duty of care (*towards employees*); **~unterstützung** *f* social security, *Am.* welfare, public assistance; **von der ~ leben** be (*od.* live) on social security (*Am.* welfare); **~zögling** *m altm.* juvenile in care

fürsorglich *Adj.* thoughtful, considerate; *stärker*: solicitous

Fürsprache *f* plea, intercession *förm.* (**für** for, on behalf of; **bei** with); (*Empfehlung*) recommendation; (*Unterstützung*) support; (*Vermittlung*) mediation; **für j-n ~ einlegen** intercede on s.o.'s behalf *förm.*, put in a good word for s.o.; **Fürsprech** *m; -s, -e; schw.* → **Rechtsanwalt**; **Fürsprecher** *m*, **Fürsprecherin** *f* **1.** intercessor *förm.*, supporter; (*Vermittler*) mediator; **2.** (*Verfechter*) advocate; **3.** *schw.* → **Rechtsanwalt**

Fürst *m; -en, -en* prince (*auch Titel und fig.*); (*Herrscher*) ruler; **leben wie ein ~** *umg.* live like a lord (*od.* king); **der ~ der Finsternis** *bibl.* the Prince of Darkness

Fürsten|geschlecht *n*, **~haus** *n* royal house, dynasty; **~hof** *m* royal court; **~stand** *m; nur Sg.* princely rank; **in den ~ erheben** raise to the rank of prince; **~tum** *n; -s, Fürstentümer* principality; **das ~ Monaco** the Principality of Monaco

Fürstin *f; -, -nen* princess

fürstlich I. *Adj.* **1.** princely; prince's …; **2.** *fig.* splendid; (*üppig*) lavish; *Mahl*: sumptuous; *Trinkgeld*: generous, lavish; *Gehalt, Summe*: princely; **II.** *Adv.* *leben*: in grand style; *belohnen*: royally; **j-n ~ bewirten** entertain s.o. lavishly, kill the fatted calf, *Brit. auch* push the boat out for s.o. *umg.*; **wir haben ~ gespeist** we dined right royally

Furt *f; -, -en* ford; **e-e ~ durchqueren** ford a river

Furunkel *m, n; -s, -; Med.* boil

fürwahr *Adv. geh. altm. od. hum.* truly, in truth *lit.*

Fürwort *n; Pl. Fürwörter; Ling.* pronoun

Furz *m; -es, Fürze; vulg.* fart; **e-n ~ lassen** fart; **sich über jeden ~ aufregen** *fig.* get worked up about the slightest thing; **er ist doch nur ein kleiner ~!** *fig.* he's a mere nobody; **furzen** *v/i. vulg.* fart

Fusel *m; -s, -, mst Sg.; umg. pej.* rotgut

Fusion *f; -, -en* **1.** *bes. Phys.* fusion; **2.** *Wirts.* merger; *neue Firma*: amalgamation; (*Übernahme*) takeover; **fusionieren** *v/i. Wirts.* merge; amalgamate

Fusions|energie *f Phys.* fusion energy; **~reaktor** *m Phys.* fusion reactor; **~verhandlungen** *Pl. Wirts.* negotiations toward(s) a merger

Fuß¹ *m; -es, Füße* **1.** foot (*Pl.* feet); **zu**

~ on (*Am. auch* by) foot; **zu ~ gehen** walk; **zu ~ (bequem) erreichbar** within (easy) walking distance; **gut/schlecht zu ~ sein** be / not be a good walker; **bei ~!** *zum Hund*: heel!; **so schnell die Füße ihn trugen** as fast as his legs would carry him; **keinen ~ vor die Tür setzen** not set foot outside the door; **ich setze keinen ~ mehr über s-e Schwelle!** I will never again darken his door; **von e-m ~ auf den anderen treten** shift from one foot to the other; **wir werden uns auf die Füße treten** (*wegen der Enge*) we'll be tripping over each other; **j-m auf den ~ od. die Füße treten** *umg.* tread on s.o.'s toes (*auch fig.*); **sich** (*Dat.*) **die Füße vertreten** stretch one's legs; **über die eigenen Füße fallen** *od.* **stolpern** trip over one's own feet (*auch umg. fig. ungeschickt sein*); **trockenen ~es** without getting one's feet wet; **leichten/ schnellen ~es** *geh.* with light/quick steps; **stehenden ~es** *fig.* (*sofort*) immediately, instantly; (**festen**) **~ fassen** get (*fig. auch* gain) a foothold; *fig. Sache*: *auch* catch on; **auf dem ~e folgen** *e-r Person*: follow closely, trail; *fig. e-m Geschehnis*: follow (hard) on the heels of; **auf die Füße fallen** fall on one's feet (*auch fig.*); **sich j-m zu Füßen werfen** *geh.*, *auch fig.* throw o.s. at s.o.'s feet; *fig.* worship s.o.; **j-m etw. zu Füßen legen** *geh.* *fig.* lay s.th. at s.o.'s feet; **j-m etw. vor die Füße werfen** hurl s.th. at s.o.'s feet; *fig.* hurl s.th. back in s.o.'s face; **j-m den ~ in den Nacken setzen** *geh. fig.* keep s.o. under one's thumb, put the screws on s.o.; **auf eigenen Füßen stehen** *fig.* stand on one's own two feet; **auf großem ~ leben** *fig.* live in grand style (*od.* on a grand scale); *hum.* (*große Füße haben*) have huge feet; **auf gutem etc. ~ stehen mit** *fig.* be on good etc. terms with; **mit beiden Füßen im Leben stehen** *fig.* have both feet firmly on the ground; **mit Füßen treten** *fig.* trample on; **sein Glück mit Füßen treten** *fig.* cast away one's fortune; **kalte Füße bekommen** *umg. fig.* get cold feet; **e-n ~ in der Tür haben** *umg. fig.* have a foot in the door; → **Boden** 2, **frei** I 2, **Gewehr**, **Hand¹** 4, **link…** 1; **2.** *e-s Berges, Schranks, e-r Liste, Seite etc.*: foot, bottom; *e-r Säule*: base, pedestal; *e-s Glases*: stem; *e-r Lampe*: stand; *e-s Tisches, e-s Stuhls*: leg; **auf tönernen etc. Füßen stehen** *fig.* be built on sand; **3.** *südd., österr., schw.* (*Bein*) leg; **4.** *am Strumpf*: foot; **5.** *Lit. e-s Verses*: foot

Fuß² *m, n; -es, - Längenmaß*: foot (= 30,48 cm)

Fuß|abdruck *m* footprint; **~abstreifer** *m Matte*: doormat; *Gestell*: shoe scraper; **~angel** *f* **1.** mantrap; **2.** *fig.* trap, pitfall; **j-m ~n legen** set traps for s.o.; **~bad** *n* **1.** footbath; **2.** *hum. in Untertasse*: spilt coffee, tea etc. in a saucer

Fußball *m* **1.** *nur Sg.*; *Spiel*: football, *bes. Am.* soccer; **amerikanischer ~** American football, *Am.* football; **2.** *Ball*: football, *Am.* soccer ball; **~braut** *f umg. hum.* football widow; **~bund** *m*: **Deutscher ~** (*abgek.* **DFB**) German Football Association; **~bundesliga** *f* Bundesliga, (*German*) premier football league; **~bundesligist** *m* Bundesliga club; **~bundestrainer** *m* (*German*) national football manager (*od.* coach); **~elf** *f* football (*Am.* soccer) team

Fußballen *m Anat.* ball of the (*od.* one's) foot

Fußballer *m*; *-s*, *-*, **~in** *f*; *-*, *-nen*; *umg.* footballer, *Am.* soccer player

Fußball|europapokal *m* (Football) European Cup; **~europameisterschaft** *f* European football (*Am.* soccer) championship; **~fan** *m* football (*Am.* soccer) fan; **~feld** *n Anlage*: football ground, *Am.* soccer field; *Spielfeld*: football pitch, *Am.* soccer field; **~klub** *m* football (*Am.* soccer) club; **~länderspiel** *n* international (football, *Am.* soccer) match; **~mannschaft** *f* football (*Am.* soccer) team; **~nationalmannschaft** *f* national football (*Am.* soccer) team (*od.* side); **~platz** *m* football pitch, *Am.* soccer field; **~profi** *m* professional football (*Am.* soccer) player; **~rowdy** *m* football (*Am.* soccer) hooligan; **~schuh** *m* football boot, *Am.* soccer shoe; **~spiel** *n* football match, *Am.* soccer game; **~spielen** *n* playing football (*Am.* soccer); **~spieler** *m*, **~spielerin** *f* football (*Am.* soccer) player; **~stadion** *n* football (*Am.* soccer) stadium; **~star** *m* football (*Am.* soccer) star; **~stiefel** *m* football boot, *Am.* soccer shoe; **~tor** *n* goal; **~toto** *m*, *n* football pools *Pl.*, the pools *Pl. umg.*; **~trainer** *m*, **~trainerin** *f* football (*Am.* soccer) manager (*od.* coach); **~turnier** *n* football (*Am.* soccer) tournament; **~verband** *m* football (*Am.* soccer) association; **~verein** *m* football (*Am.* soccer) club; **~weltmeister** *m* World Cup holders *Pl.*; **~weltmeisterschaft** *f* World Cup

Fuß|bank *f*; *Pl. Fußbänke* footstool; **~bekleidung** *f* shoes (and socks) *Pl.*; (*Schuhe*) footwear; **~bett** *n im Schuh*: footbed

Fußboden *m* 1. floor; 2. (*Belag*) floor covering; **~belag** *m* floor covering; **~heizung** *f* underfloor heating

fußbreit I. *Adj.* as wide as a foot, the width of a foot; **II. Fußbreit** *m*: *er wollte keinen Fußbreit weichen* he refused to budge (*od.* give) an inch

Fußbremse *f* footbrake

Fussel *f*; *-*, *-n od. m*; *-s*, *-(n)* piece of fluff (*Am.* lint); **~n** fluff *Sg.*, *Am.* lint *Sg.*; **fusselig** *Adj.* covered in fluff, *Am.* linty; *sich den Mund ~ reden umg. fig.* talk till one is blue in the face; **fusseln** *v/i.* shed (a lot of) fluff, *Am.* shed, *Brit. auch* mo(u)lt *umg.*

fußeln, füßeln *v/i. umg.* play footsie

fußen *v/i.*: *~ auf* be based (up)on, rest on

Fußende *n* foot of the bed, bottom (of the bed)

Fußfall *m* prostration; *e-n ~ vor j-m tun früher*: throw o.s. at s.o.'s feet; *heute nur fig.* kowtow to s.o.; **fußfällig** *Adv. fig.* on bended knee

Fuß|fehler *m Sport* foot fault; **~fesseln** *Pl.* (foot) shackles

Fuß|gänger *m*, **~in** *f* pedestrian; **~ampel** *f* pedestrian lights *Pl.*; **~brücke** *f* footbridge; **~insel** *f* traffic island; **~überführung** *f* footbridge; **~übergang** *m*, **~überweg** *m* pedestrian crossing; **~unterführung** *f* (pedestrian) underpass, *Brit. auch* subway; **~zone** *f* pedestrian precinct (*Am.* mall)

Fuß|geher *m*, **~geherin** *f österr.* pedestrian; **~gelenk** *n* ankle

fußkalt *Adj.*: *dieses Zimmer ist ~* my feet are always cold in this room

...füßig *im Adj.* 1. *Mensch, Tier*: *...-footed*; *bloß*: barefoot(ed); *platt~* flatfooted; 2. *Stuhl, Tisch etc.*: *...-legged*; *drei~* three-legged; 3. *Lit. ...-foot*; *fünf~* five-foot..., pentameter ...

Fuß|kettchen *n Schmuck*: anklet; **~knöchel** *m* ankle

fuß|krank *Adj.* 1. *vom Marschieren*: footsore; 2. *~ sein* have a foot complaint; **~lahm** *Adj. umg.* footsore and weary

Fußleiste *f* skirting board, *Am.* baseboard

Füßling *m*; *-s*, *-e am Strumpf*: foot

Fuß|marsch *m* (long) walk; *Mil.* march; *wir haben noch e-n langen ~ vor uns* we've still got a long trek ahead; *es ist ein ~ von drei Stunden* it's a three-hour walk, it's three hours on foot; **~matte** *f Haus*: doormat; *Auto*: car mat; **~nagel** *m* toenail; **~note** *f* footnote; **~pfad** *m* footpath; **~pflege** *f kosmetische*: pedicure; *medizinische*: chiropody, podiatry; *häusliche*: care of the feet; **~pfleger** *m*, **~pflegerin** *f* chiropodist, podiatrist; **~pilz** *m Med.* athlete's foot; **~puder** *m* foot powder; **~punkt** *m* 1. *Math.* foot; 2. *Astron.* nadir; **~raste** *f Mot.* footrest; **~reflexzonenmassage** *f Med.* 1. reflexology; 2. *konkret*: zone massage; **~ring** *m* ring (on a bird's leg); **~schalter** *m* pedal switch; **~schemel** *m* footstool; **~schweiß** *m mst* sweaty feet *Pl.*; **~sohle** *f* sole (of the *od.* one's foot); **~sohlenreflex** *m Med.* sole (*od.* Babinski) reflex; **~soldat** *m*, **~soldatin** *f Mil.* foot soldier, infantryman (*weiblich*: infantrywoman); **~spann** *m* instep; **~spitze** *f* tip of one's toes; → *Zehenspitze*; **~spray** *m*, *n* foot spray; **~spur** *f* footprint; (*Fährte*) track; **~stapfe** *f* footstep; *in j-s ~n treten fig.* follow in s.o.'s footsteps; **~stütze** *f* 1. footrest; 2. *Med.* arch support

fußtief *Adj.*, *Adv. Schnee etc.*: ankle-deep

Fuß|tritt *m* 1. *Stoß*: kick; *j-m e-n ~ geben od. versetzen* give s.o. a kick, kick s.o.; *e-n ~ bekommen umg. fig.* (*entlassen werden*) get the boot; (*weggeschickt werden*) be kicked (*Brit. umg.* turfed) out; 2. *Geräusch*: footstep, footfall; **~truppe** *f* infantry; **~volk** *n* 1. *Mil. altm.* infantry; 2. *fig. pej. od. hum.* rank and file (*e-r Partei, Gewerkschaft etc.*); *das übersteigt m-e Kompetenz – ich gehöre nur zum ~* that would be exceeding my authority - I'm a mere underling (*Brit. auch* dogsbody); **~wanderung** *f* hike, walking tour; **~waschung** *f Reli.* foot washing; **~weg** *m* 1. (*Pfad etc.*) footpath; 2. *Strecke*: *ein ~ von einer Stunde* an hour's walk, an hour on foot

fußwund *Adj.* footsore

Fußwurzel *f Anat.* tarsus; **~knochen** *m* tarsal bone

Fußzeile *f Druck.*, *EDV* footer

Futon *m*; *-s*, *-s* futon

futsch *Adj. umg.* (*weg*, *verloren*) gone; (*kaputt*) broken; (*zerschlagen*) smashed (up), bust *Sl.*; kaput *Sl.*; (*verdorben*) ruined; *alles ~! Pläne etc.*: it's all down the tubes, you can forget it

Futter¹ *n*; *-s*, *kein Pl.* 1. *für Tiere*: feed; *für Vieh*: fodder, forage; *für Haustiere, vom Tier gesuchtes*: food; *gut im ~ stehen* be well-fed (*auch umg. hum. Person*); 2. *umg.* (*Essen*) grub, *bes. Am.* chow

Futter² *n*; *-s*, *-* 1. *aus Stoff*: lining; 2. *Archit.* casing; 3. *Tech.* (*Spannvorrichtung*) chuck

Futteral *n*; *-s*, *-e* case; (*Hülle*) cover

Futter|automat *m* automatic feeder; **~beutel** *m* nosebag; **~häuschen** *n* (covered) bird table; **~kammer** *f Agr.* feed store; **~krippe** *f* 1. manger; 2. *fig.* gravy train; *an der ~ sitzen* be doing nicely for o.s.; **~mangel** *m* lack of food; **~mittel** *n auch Pl.* feedstuff; *für Vieh*: fodder; **~mittelindustrie** *f* (animal) feed industry; **~mittelzusatz(-stoff)** *m* feed additive

futtern *umg.* **I.** *v/t.* dig into, scoff; **II.** *v/i.*: *tüchtig ~* stuff o.s., feed one's face

füttern¹ *v/t.* 1. (*Tier, Baby, Kranke*) feed; *j-n mit etw. ~ umg. hum., einmalig*: feed s.o. s.th.; *ständig*: feed s.o. on s.th.; (*vollstopfen*) stuff s.o. with s.th.; *Füttern verboten!* do not feed (the animals)!; 2. *fig.* (*Automaten, Computer etc.*) feed (*mit* with)

füttern² *v/t.* (*Rock etc.*) line; (*auspolstern*) pad

Futter|napf *m* (feeding) bowl; **~neid** *m* 1. jealousy (*od.* possessiveness) (of animals) as regards food; 2. *fig.* (*professional od.* social) jealousy, envy of the better-off; **~pflanze** *f* forage plant (*od.* crop); **~rübe** *f Bot.* mangold, mangel-wurzel; **~stelle** *f* feeding ground

Futterstoff *m* lining (material)

Futter|suche *f* search for food; **~trog** *m* feeding trough

Fütterung *f* feeding; *im Zoo*: feeding time

Futterverwerter *m*, **~in** *f umg.*: *ein guter ~ sein* (*wenig brauchen*) get by on very little (food); (*schnell dick werden*) put it on (*od.* put on the pounds) very quickly *umg.*; *ein schlechter ~ sein* (*viel Essen brauchen*) put away huge amounts (of food) *umg.*; (*nicht dick werden*) never put on weight

Futur *n*; *-s*, *-e*; *Ling.* future (tense); *zweites ~* future perfect

Futurismus *m*; *-*, *kein Pl.* futurism; **futuristisch** *Adj.* futurist

Futurologie *f*; *-*, *kein Pl.* futurology; **futurologisch** *Adj.* futurological

Fuzel *m*; *-s*, *-*; *bes. österr.* (*winziges Stück*) tiny scrap; **fuzelig** *Adj. bes. österr.* 1. *Stück*: (*winzig*) tiny; 2. *Arbeit*: fiddly; **fuzeln** *v/i. bes. österr.* 1. *beim Schreiben*: write very small; 2. *in kleine Stücke*: cut off tiny pieces

G, g n; -, - od. umg. -s **1.** G, g; *G wie Gustav Buchstabieren*: 'g' for (*od*. as in) 'Golf'; **2.** *Mus.* G

g *Abk*. (*Gramm*) g, gr (= gram)

gab *Imperf*. → *geben*

Gabardine ['gabardi:nə] m; -s, -, *od*. f; -, - gaberdine

Gabe f; -, -n **1.** (*Spende*) contribution (*an + Akk*. to); (*Schenkung*) donation; (*Opfer*) offering; (*Geschenk*) gift, present; *um e-e milde ~ bitten* ask for alms; **2.** *fig*. (*Begabung*) gift, talent; (*Geschick*) knack; *die ~ haben zu* (+ *Inf*.) have a gift for (+ *Ger*.); *iro. auch* have a (great) knack of (+ *Ger*.), be (very) good at (+ *Ger*.); **3.** *Med*. (*Verabreichung, Dosis*) dose; **4.** *schw*. (*Gewinn*) prize; winnings

gäbe *Adj*. → *gang*

Gabel f; -, -n **1.** fork; *für Heu, Mist etc*.: pitchfork; **2.** *am Ast, Rad, Weg*: fork; *Telef*. cradle; *Deichsel*: shafts *Pl*.; **3.** *Zool., Geweih*: spire; *~bissen* m *Gastr*. **1.** *small rolled piece of pickled herring*; **2.** canapé

Gabeldeichsel f shafts *Pl*.

gabelförmig *Adj*. forked

Gabelfrühstück n *altm*. mid-morning buffet; fork lunch

gabeln I. *v/t*. **1.** fork *s.th*. up; **2.** *umg. fig*.: *sich* (*Dat*.) j-n *od. etw. ~* pick up; **II.** *v/refl. Ast, Straße etc*.: fork (off *od*. out); → *gegabelt*

Gabelstapler m forklift truck

Gabelung f fork (in the road *etc*.)

Gabel|weihe f *Zool. altm*. red kite; *~zinke* f prong, tine

Gabentisch m table with (the) presents; *ein reich gedeckter ~* a table piled high with presents

Gabun (n); -s; *Geog*. Gabon

G-8-Staat m *Pol*. G8 member (state)

gackern *v/i*. **1.** *Huhn*: cluck; **2.** *fig. Mädchen*: cackle

Gaffel f; -, -n; *Naut*. gaff; *~schoner* m for-and-aft schooner

gaffen *v/i. umg. pej*. gawk, gawp; **Gaffer** m; -s, -, **Gafferin** f; -, -nen; *umg. pej*. gawker, gawper, starer, *Am. auch* rubberneck

Gag [gɛk] m; -s, -s gag; *Werbung: auch* gimmick; (*Clou*) highlight; *~s Film: auch* special effects; *der ~ war ... umg*. the great thing was ...

gaga *Adj*.; *indekl*.; *umg*. gaga

Gage ['ga:ʒə] f; -, -n; *Theat. etc*. fee; *als regelmäßiges Einkommen*: salary

gähnen *v/i*. yawn; **Gähnen** n; -s, kein *Pl*. yawn(ing); *da kommt einem ja das große ~! umg*. it's just one big yawn!; **gähnend I.** *Part. Präs*. → *gähnen*; **II.** *Adj. fig*.: *~er Abgrund* yawning abyss; *~e Leere* gaping void

GAL f; -, *kein Pl*.; *Abk. Pol*. (**Grün-Al-ternative Liste**) list of electoral candidates from an alliance of the Green Party and other alternative parties

Gala f; -, -s **1.** *Veranstaltung*: gala; **2.** *Kleidung*: gala dress; *sich in ~ wer-*

---

fen umg. put on one's glad rags, dress to the nines; *~abend* m gala night; *~diner* n gala dinner, (gala) banquet; *~empfang* m formal reception; *~konzert* n gala concert

galaktisch *Adj*. galactic

Galan m; -s, -e; *altm*. **1.** (*Liebhaber*) beau; **2.** *iro*. (*galanter Mann*) gallant

galant *Adj*. **1.** *altm. Benehmen, Mann*: gallant; **2.** *~es Abenteuer* amorous escapade; **3.** *Lit. Dichtung*: galant

Galanterie f; -, -n *altm*. **1.** *nur Sg*.; *Benehmen*: gallantry; **2.** (*Kompliment*) gallantry; *~waren Pl. altm*. fancy goods, fashion accessories

Galater *Pl. hist*. Galatians; *Brief an die ~ bibl*. the (*od*. St Paul's) Epistle to the Galatians, Galatians *Pl*. (*V. im Sg*.)

Gala|uniform f full dress (uniform); *~vorstellung* f gala performance

Galaxie f; -, -n; *Astron*. galaxy

Galaxis f; -, Galaxien; *Astron*. **1.** *nur Sg*.; (*Milchstraße*) Galaxy, Milky Way; **2.** galaxy

Galeere f; -, -n; *Naut., hist*. galley

Galeeren|sklave m, *~sträfling* m galley slave

Galeone f; -, -n; *Naut., hist*. galleon

Galerie f; -, -n **1.** *Archit., Theat. etc*.: gallery; **2.** (*Kunstgalerie*) art gallery; *e-e ganze ~* (+ *Gen. od. von*) *umg. hum*. a whole battery of; **3.** *Verk., bes. südd., österr*. tunnel (*through a mountainside with openings along one wall*); **Galerist** m; -en, -en, **Galeristin** f; -, -nen (art) gallery owner, art dealer, gallerist; *er ist ~ auch* he owns (*od*. runs) an art gallery

Galgen m; -s, - gallows *Pl*.; *an den ~ bringen/kommen* send to / end up on the gallows; **2.** *für Mikrofon*: (microphone) boom; *~frist* f reprieve; *ich gebe dir eine Woche ~* I'll give you a week's grace; *~humor* m gallows humo(u)r; *~strick* m, *~vogel* m *umg. pej*. good-for-nothing; (*Gauner*) crook, jailbird

Galiläa (n); -s; *Geog., hist*. Galilee

Galionsfigur f figurehead

gälisch *Ling. Adj*. Gaelic; **Gälisch** n; -en Gaelic; *das ~* Gaelic

Gallapfel m *Bot*. oak apple, *Am*. oak gall

Galle f; -, -n **1.** *Anat*. gall bladder; **2.** *Physiol., Sekret*: bile; **3.** *Zool., Bot*. gall; **4.** *fig*. bile, venom; (*s-e*) *~ verspritzen* spit (one's) venom, vent one's spleen *lit*.; *ihm kam die ~ hoch od. lief die ~ über* his blood was up, he was seething; → *Gift* 2

gallebitter *Adj*. **1.** acrid; **2.** *fig*. acrid, caustic

Galleiche f *Bot*. gall oak

Gallen|blase f *Anat*. gall bladder; *~kolik* f *Med*. bilious colic; *~stein* m *Med*. gallstone; *~wege Pl. Anat*. biliary tract *Sg*.

Gallert n; -(e)s, -e jelly; **gallertartig**

Adj. gelatinous, jelly(-)like; *~e Masse* gelatinous (*od*. jelly[-]like) substance *od*. mass

Gallien (n); -s; *hist*. Gaul; **Gallier** m; -s, -, **Gallierin** f; -, -nen Gaul, *weiblich auch*: Gallic woman (*od*. girl *etc*.)

gallig *Adj*. **1.** *Geschmack etc*.: acrid; **2.** *fig. Temperament, Laune etc*.: bilious; *Bemerkung, Humor etc*.: caustic; *Satire etc*.: biting

gallisch *Adj*. Gallic, Gaulic, Gaulish

Gallizismus m; -, Gallizismen; *Ling*. Gallicism

Gallone f; -, -n; (*in GB auch* imperial) gallon (= 4,54 l), (*in den USA auch* US) gallon (= 3,78 l)

Gallwespe f *Zool*. gall wasp

Galopp m; -s, -s *od*. -e **1.** gallop; *leichter ~* canter; *im ~* at a gallop; *in gestrecktem ~* at full gallop; *in ~ fallen* break into a gallop; **2.** *fig*.: *im ~ ankommen* come galloping along; *etw. im ~ erledigen* race (*od*. gallop) through s.th.; **galoppieren** *v/i*. gallop; *leicht, in Dressur etc*: canter; *sein Pferd ~ lassen* gallop one's horse; **galoppierend I.** *Part. Präs*. → *galoppieren*; **II.** *Adj. Med*. galloping; *Wirts. auch* runaway ...

Galopp|rennbahn f racetrack, racecourse; *~rennen* n (horse)race; **Galoschen** *Pl. altm*. (*Überschuhe*) galoshes, overshoes, *Am. auch* rubbers; **2.** *umg. pej*. worn-out old slippers

galt *Imperf*. → *gelten*

galvanisch *Tech*. **I.** *Adj*. galvanic; *~es Element* galvanic cell; **II.** *Adv*. galvanically; **galvanisieren** *v/t*. galvanize (*auch Med*.), *Tech. auch* electroplate; **Galvanometer** n; -s, -; *Phys., Tech*. galvanometer

Gamasche f; -, -n gaiter, legging; *über dem Fuß*: spat; *er hat ~n vor ihr umg. fig*. she puts the wind up him, *Am*. she gives him the willies

Gambe f; -, -n; *Mus*. (viola da) gamba

Gameshow ['ge:mʃoː] f *TV* game show

Gamet m; -en, -en; *Bio*. gamete

Gamma|globulin n *Med*. gamma globulin; *~strahlen Pl. Phys*. gamma rays; *~strahlung* f *Phys*. gamma radiation

gammelig *Adj. umg*. **1.** *Lebensmittel*: mo(u)ldy; *Obst*: rotten; **2.** *pej*. (*ungepflegt*) scruffy; **gammeln** *v/i. umg*. **1.** *pej*. (*faulenzen*) loaf (*od*. bum) around, *Am*. goof off (*od*. around); **2.** *Lebensmittel*: mo(u)ld, go mo(u)ldy; **Gammler** m; -s, -, **Gammlerin** f; -, -nen; *umg. oft pej*. layabout; **gammlig** → *gammelig*

Gamsbart, Gämsbart m tuft of chamois hair worn as a decoration on a hat

Gämse f; -, -n; *Zool*. chamois

Gang[1] m; -(e)s, Gänge **1.** *nur Sg*.; *Art und Weise*: walk, way *s.o*. walks, gait; (*Tempo*) pace; *gemächlicher/schlep-*

G

pender ~ amble/shuffle; **s-n ~ be-schleunigen/verlangsamen** quicken/slow one's pace (*od.* step); **er hatte e-n unsicheren ~** he wasn't very steady on his feet, he walked with an unsteady step; **2.** (*Spaziergang*) walk; (*Besorgung*) errand; (*Weg*) way; **letzter ~ geh.** *fig.* last journey; **~ nach Kanossa** *hist.* journey to Canossa; *geh.* *fig.* (act of) eating humble pie, act of self-abasement; **auf dem ~ zu** on the (*od.* one's) way to; **e-n ~ machen** go (*od.* be) on an errand; **e-n ~ machen zu** go to; **Gänge besorgen** run errands; **das war ein schwerer ~** that wasn't easy, that was no easy business (*od.* matter); **ihr erster ~ war ...** the first thing she did was (to) (+ *Inf.*); **3.** *nur Sg.*; *Tech. und fig.* (*Ggs. Stillstand*) operation; *e-r Maschine etc.*: running, working; (*Wirkungsweise*) action; *fig.* (*Fortschritt*) progress; (*Verlauf*) course (+ *Gen.* of); **e-n leisen ~ haben** *Tech.* run quietly; **in ~ bringen** *od.* **setzen** *Tech.* start, put into operation; *fig.* get *s.th.* going; (*Entwicklung etc.*) set *s.th.* in train; **in ~ sein** *Tech.* be running; *fig.* be under way; **außer ~ setzen** *Tech.* put out of operation; **in ~ halten/kommen** keep/get going; **in vollem ~** *fig.* in full swing; **es ist etwas im ~(e)** *fig.* there's s.th. up (*od.* afoot), there's (fishy) going on; **es ist etwas im ~(e) gegen** *fig.* there's a plot being hatched against; **s-n ~ gehen** *fig.* *Vorgang*: take its course; **s-n gewohnten ~ gehen** *fig.* go (*od.* carry) on as usual; **4.** (*Flur*) corridor; *hinter Haustür*: hallway; *Treppenhaus, oberer Stock*: landing; **auf dem ~** in the corridor (*od.* hallway); *oben*: on the landing; **5.** *unterirdisch od. in Tierbau*: tunnel; *Bergwerk*: *auch* gallery; *im Freien, mit Bogen*: arcade; *mit Säulen*: colonnade; *mit Bäumen etc.*: walk, alley; (*Durchgang*) passage(way); *zwischen Sitzreihen*: aisle; *in Bus, Flugzeug*: *auch* gangway; **6.** *Tech.* speed; *Fahrrad*: speed, gear; *Mot.* gear; **erster ~** first (*od.* bottom) gear; **den ~ wechseln** change (*bes. Am.* shift) gears; **den ~ herausnehmen** change (*bes. Am.* shift) into neutral; **den zweiten ~ einlegen** *od.* **in den zweiten ~ gehen** *od.* **schalten** change (*bes. Am.* shift) into second (gear); **durch die Gänge jagen** run through the gears; **leg mal e-n ~ zu!** *umg.* *fig.* step it up a gear!, *Am.* pick up the pace!; **ich muss e-n ~ zurückschalten** *umg.* *fig.* (*kürzer treten*) I need to ease up a bit; **etw. kommt in die Gänge** *umg.* *fig.* (*in Schwung, geht los*) s.th. is starting to get going (*od.* is really getting under way); **morgens habe ich immer Probleme, in die Gänge zu kommen** I always have problems getting going in the morning; **7.** *Gastr.* course; **Essen mit drei Gängen** three-course meal; **8.** (*Durchgang*) *Arbeit*: operation; *Fechten etc.*: bout; *Rennen*: heat; *Sauna*: session; **9.** *Anat.* duct, canal, passage; **10.** *Geol.* vein; **11.** *Tech. Gewinde*: thread; (*Röhre*) duct

Gang² [gɛŋ] *f*; -, -s gang

gang *Adj.*: **~ und gäbe sein** be quite usual, be the usual thing; **das ist hier ~ und gäbe** *auch* that's nothing unusual around here

Gangart *f* **1.** gait, walk; *Pferd*: pace; *Zool.* locomotory pattern; **2.** *fig.* (*Vorgehensweise*) approach; **e-e andere ~ anschlagen** change the (*od.* one's) pace; **e-e härtere ~ anschlagen** force the pace, take a tougher line (**gegenüber** with)

gangbar *Adj.* **1.** *Weg*: passable; **2.** *fig.* practicable, feasible; *Lösung, Plan*: *auch* workable

Gängelband *n fig.*: **am ~ führen** *od.* **haben, halten** → **gängeln**; **Gängelei** *f*, -, -*en*; *pej.* nursemaiding, nannying; **gängeln** *v/t.* *pej.* nursemaid, nanny, lead *s.o.* by the nose; *Frau, Mutter*: *auch* keep *s.o.* tied to one's apron strings

Ganghebel *m* gearstick, gear lever, *Am.* gearshift, stick

gängig *Adj.* **1.** *Ausdruck*: current; *Methode etc.*: (very) common; **die ~e Meinung** the conventional wisdom; **2.** *Wirts.* sal(e)able, marketable; (*gut gehend*) fast-selling; **gängigst...** best-selling; **3.** *Fin.* (*im Umlauf*) current; **4.** *Tech.* (*beweglich*) *Maschine*: working; *Riegel etc.*: movable; *Schraube etc.*: turnable; **wieder ~ machen** get *s.th.* working again; (*Riegel, Schraube etc.*) loosen; **Gängigkeit** *f*; *nur Sg.* **1.** currency; *e-r Methode etc.*: commonness; **2.** *Wirts.* sal(e)ability, marketability; **3.** *Tech.* operability, being in working order; movability

Ganglion *n*; -s, Ganglien, *mst Pl.*; *Anat.* ganglion (*Pl.* ganglia)

Gangschaltung *f Mot.* gearshift(ing)

Gangster ['gɛnstɐ] *m*; -s, -; *pej.* gangster; **~bande** *f* gang (of criminals); **~boss** *m* gang boss, gangland leader; **~braut** *f umg.* (gangster's) moll

Gangsterin *f*; -, -*nen* gangster

Gangstermethoden *Pl. fig.*: **das sind ja ~!** that's (almost) criminal

Gangstertum *n* gangsterism; *Gangster*: gangland, the underworld

Gangway ['gɛŋweɪ] *f*; -, -s; *Flug.* steps *Pl.*; *Naut.* gangway

Ganove *m*; -n, -n; *umg.* *pej.* crook, hoodlum; **kleiner ~** small-time crook

Ganoven|ehre *f*; *nur Sg.* hono(u)r among thieves; **~sprache** *f* underworld slang, thieves' cant

Ganovin *f*, -, -*nen* crook

Gans *f*; -, Gänse **1.** *Orn.* goose (*Pl.* geese); *Küken*: gosling; **2.** *fig.*: **alberne/dumme ~** silly fool; *milder*: silly thing, silly goose

Gänschen *n* **1.** gosling; **2.** *fig.* stupid thing (*od.* girl)

Gänse|blümchen *n Bot.* daisy; **~braten** *m Gastr.* roast goose

Gänse|distel *f Bot.* sow thistle; **~feder** *f* goose feather; *zum Schreiben*: (goose) quill; **~füßchen** *Pl.* quotation marks, *Brit. auch* inverted commas; **~haut** *f fig.* goose pimples *Pl.*; **ich bekam e-e ~** it sent shivers down my spine, it gave me the creeps *umg.*; **das verursacht mir keine ~** it leaves me cold; **~kiel** *m* (goose) quill; **~klein** *n*; -s, kein *Pl.*; *Gastr.* goose giblets *Pl.*

Gänseleber *f Gastr.* goose liver; **~pastete** *f* pâté de foie gras

Gänsemarsch *m*: **im ~** in single (*bes. Am.* Indian) file

Gänserich *m*; -s, -e gander

Gänse|schmalz *n Gastr.* goose dripping (*Am. auch* grease); **~wein** *m umg. hum.* Adam's ale, water

Gant *f*; -, -*en*; *schw.* public auction; **ganten** *v/t. schw.* auction

Ganter *m*; -s, -; *bes. nordd.* gander

ganz I. *Adj.* **1.** (*gesamt*) whole, entire; (*vollständig*) complete; **~ Deutschland** the whole (*od.* all) of Germany; **die ~e Stadt** the whole town; **in od. durch ~ Amerika** all over America; **in der ~en Welt** all over the world; **~e Länge** total (*od.* overall) length; **~e Note** *Mus.* semibreve, *Am.* whole note; **~e Pause** *Mus.* semibreve (*Am.* whole note) rest; **~e Zahl** *Math.* whole number; **den ~en Morgen/Tag** all morning/day; **die ~e Nacht** (**hindurch**) all night long; **die ~e Zeit** all the time, the whole time; **zwei ~e Stunden** (*nicht weniger*) (for) two solid hours; **den ~en Goethe lesen etc.**: the whole (*od.* all) of Goethe; **von ~em Herzen** with all my *etc.* heart; **2.** *mst präd.*; (*unbeschädigt*) in one piece, intact; **wieder ~ machen** mend; **3.** *mit Pl., attr.; umg.* (*alle*) all (of); **m-e ~en Schuhe** all (of) my shoes; **schau mal, die ~en Leute!** look at all the people!; **4.** *attr.; umg.* (*ziemlich*) quite (a); **e-e ~e Weile** *od.* **Zeit brauchen/dauern** take/last quite a while (*od.* time); **ein ~er Haufen** *od.* **e-e ~e Stange Geld** *umg.* quite a lot of money; **5.** *umg.* (*echt, wahr*) real; **ein ~er Kerl** a real (*od.* proper) man; **die Aufgabe erfordert e-n ~en Mann** this is a job for a real man; **6.** *attr.; umg.* (*nur, bloß*) just, only; **es hat ~e fünf Minuten gedauert** it didn't take more than five minutes, it was all over in five minutes; **er hat mir ~e zehn Euro gegeben** all he gave me was ten euros; **sie ist ~e zehn Jahre alt** she's only ten years old; **II.** *Adv.* **1.** **~** (**und gar**) completely, totally; **~ und gar nicht** not at all; **~ aufessen** eat *s.th.* all up; **etw. ~ bezahlen** pay *s.th.* in full; **~ durcheinander** in total confusion (*od.* disorder); **~ durchnässt** wet (all the way) through; **~ nass** sopping (*od.* dripping) wet, drenched, all wet; **~ zu schweigen von** not to mention; **das ist was ~ anderes** that's a completely different matter, that's something else entirely; **das ist ~ unmöglich** that is quite impossible; **das hab ich ~ allein gemacht** I did it entirely on my own; (**ich bin**) **~ Ihrer Meinung** I quite agree; **nicht ~ zehn** just under ten, coming up for ten *umg.*; **2.** (*sehr*) very, really; **ein ~ kleines Stück** a tiny piece (*od.* bit); **ein ~ kleines bisschen** *od.* **ein ~ klein wenig** a tiny bit; **~ besonders, weil** (e)specially since; **~ gewiss** certainly; (*ohne Zweifel*) (oh,) definitely; **~ in der Nähe** very close by; **3.** (*genau*) just, exactly; quite; **nicht ~ dasselbe** not quite the same thing; **es sieht ~ danach aus, als ob ...** it looks very much as if ...; **4.** (*ziemlich, leidlich*) quite, pretty *umg.*; **~ gut** quite good, not bad *umg.*; **es hat mir ~ gut gefallen** I quite liked (*od.* enjoyed) it; **~ schön viel** quite a lot, a fair bit *umg.*; **~ schön dreckig etc.** *umg.* pretty dirty *etc.*; **ich würde es ~ gern machen, aber ...** I'd like to, but ...; **5.** *umg., verstärkend*: **ich bin ~ Ohr** I'm all ears; **sie ist ~ der** *od.* **ihr Vater** she's just like her father, she's a chip off the old block *umg.*; **~ Kavalier, ließ er ihr den Vortritt** being the perfect gentleman, he let her go first; **er, ~ verfolgte Unschuld, protestierte heftig** all (*od.* the picture of) injured innocence, he protested loudly

Ganzaufnahme *f* full-length portrait (*od.* photograph)

Ganze *n*; -n, -(n), *mst Sg.*; *the* whole; **ein einheitliches etc. ~s** an integrated *etc.* whole; **das ~** the whole thing; (*Gesamtbetrag*) the total (amount); (*Gesamtheit*) the entirety; **das ~ halt!** *Mil.* parade (*od.* company, platoon, *etc.*),

G

halt!; **aufs** (**große**) ~ **gesehen** seen (*od.* viewed) as a whole, all in all; **aufs** ~ **gehen** go all out, go the whole hog *umg.*; **im** ~**n** (*zusammengerechnet*) in all, altogether; *Wirts.* (*als Einheit*) as a unit; **im** (**Großen und**) ~**n** *od.* **im großen** ~**n** on the whole, all in all; **die Summe beträgt im** ~**n 50 Mark** the sum amounts to 50 marks in total; **jetzt geht's ums** ~**!** *umg.* it's all or nothing now; **vier Halbe sind zwei** ~ *Math.* four halves make two wholes; → **halb** I 3

Gänze *f*: **zur** ~ completely, in full; **in s-r** ~ **geh.** in its entirety

Ganzheit *f*; *mst Sg.* wholeness, completeness, entirety; **in s-r** ~ as a whole, in its entirety; **ganzheitlich I.** *Adj.* (*umfassend*) comprehensive, all-embracing; *Päd.* integrated; *Philos., Psych., Med. etc.* holistic; **II.** *Adv.* comprehensively; *Philos., Med. etc.* holistically; ~ **betrachtet** seen as a whole (*od.* in its entirety)

Ganzheits|medizin *f* holistic medicine; ~**methode** *f* **1.** holistic method; **2.** *Päd.* integrated curriculum

Ganzjahresreifen *m Mot.* all-season tyre (*Am.* tire)

ganzjährig I. *Adj.* all-year ...; *Mot., Öl:* all-season ...; **II.** *Adv.* all year round

Ganzkörpermassage *f* whole-body massage

Ganz|leder *n* (full) leather; **in** ~ leatherbound; ~**leinen** *n* full cloth (binding); **in** ~ clothbound

gänzlich I. *Adj.* complete, total; (*absolut*) absolute; **II.** *Adv.* completely, totally, absolutely; **ich habe diesen Plan** ~ **aufgegeben** I've totally given up this plan

ganz|seitig *Adj.* full-page ...; ~**tägig I.** *Adj.* all-day ...; *Beschäftigung:* full-time ...; **II.** *Adv.* all day, (for) the whole day; ~ **geöffnet** open all day; ~ **beschäftigt sein** have a full-time job; ~**tags** *Adv.* → **ganztägig** II

Ganztags|beschäftigung *f* full-time job; ~**betreuung** *f von Kindern etc.:* all-day care; ~**kraft** *f* full-time employee; ~**schule** *f* all-day school(ing)

Ganzton *m Mus.* whole tone; ~**schritt** *m* whole(-tone) step

Ganzwortmethode *f Päd.* whole word method

ganzzahlig *Adj. Math.* integral

gar¹ I. *Adj.* **1.** *Gastr.* done, cooked; **der Braten ist nach zwei Stunden** ~ the roast will be done in two hours; **nicht** ~ underdone; **2.** *südd., österr. umg.* (*aufgebraucht*) used up, finished; **3.** *Agr. Boden:* ready for cultivation; *Kompost:* ready for use, fully composted; **II.** *Adv.: etw.* ~ **kochen** cook s.th. until it's done; ~ **gekocht** done, cooked

gar² *Adv.* **1.** *mit Verneinung:* ~ **nicht** not at all; ~ **nichts** not a thing, nothing at all, absolutely nothing; ~ **keiner** nobody at all; **es hat** ~ **keinen Sinn** there is absolutely no point, it's completely pointless (*od.* senseless, *od.* useless); **es besteht** ~ **kein Zweifel** there's no doubt whatsoever; ~ **nicht schlecht** not bad at all; **das ist** ~ **nichts gegen m-e Geschichte** that's got nothing on my story; **das ist noch** ~ **nichts!** (*ich habe od.* weiß etwas noch Tolleres.*) that's nothing!; (*es kommt noch besser*) *auch* you haven't heard anything (*od.* ain't heard nothing *umg.*) yet; **2.** (*sogar*) even; **viele,**

wenn nicht ~ **alle** many if not all; **ich glaube** ~**, du hast Recht** I do believe you're right; **3.** (*etwa, vielleicht*) perhaps; **sollte sie** *od.* **sie wird doch nicht** ~ **gelogen haben?** could she have been lying? *od.* she couldn't have been lying, could she?; **4.** *verstärkend:* **und** ~ (*erst recht*) even more so, not to mention; **oder** ~ (*erst recht nicht*) let alone; ~ **so** so very; **sie ist** ~ **so heikel beim Essen** she's so very fussy about her food; ~ **zu** (*wirklich zu*) just too, just so; **meine Schwester ist** ~ **zu blöd** *umg.* my sister is just so stupid (*od.* just too stupid for words); **5.** *südd., österr., schw. altm.* (*sehr*) very, passing *altm.*; ~ **mancher** *od.* **viele** many a one

Garage [ga'ra:ʒə] *f*; -, -*n*; *Mot.* garage

Garagen|einfahrt *f Mot.* garage entrance; ~**tor** *n* garage door; ~**wagen** *m* car kept in a garage (*as opposed to one kept in the open or on the street*)

Garant *m*; -*en*, -*en* guarantor; → *auch* **Bürge**

Garantie *f*, -, -*n* **1.** (*Gewähr*) guarantee (**für** of); *Jur., Pol.* undertaking; **dafür kann ich keine** ~ **übernehmen** I can't make any guarantees; **er fällt unter** ~ **durch** *umg.* he's bound (*od.* guaranteed) to fail, there's no way he's going to pass; **sie hat's unter** ~ **vergessen** *umg.* she's bound (*od.* guaranteed) to have forgotten, I bet (you any money) she's forgotten; **2.** *Wirts., auf Ware:* guarantee (**für** *od.* **auf** + *Akk.* on), warranty; **es hat ein Jahr** ~ it's got a year's (*od.* a one-year) guarantee; **die** ~ **ist abgelaufen** the guarantee has run out; **j-m ein Jahr** ~ **auf etw.** (*Akk.*) **geben** give s.o. a year's guarantee on s.th.; **geht die Reparatur noch auf** ~ *od.* **fällt die Reparatur noch unter die** ~**?** is the repair still covered by the guarantee (*Am. auch* warranty)?; **3.** *Bürg., Fin.* (*Sicherheit*) security; (*Bürgschaft*) surety; ~**anspruch** *m Jur.* warranty claim; ~**bedingungen** *Pl.* terms of a (*od.* the) guarantee; ~**erklärung** *f* (statement of) guarantee

garantieren *vt/i.:* ~ (**für**) guarantee (*auch fig.*); **garantiert I.** *P.P.* → **garantieren**; **II.** *Adv.:* ~ **echt** *etc.* guaranteed genuine *etc.*; **sie kommt** ~ **nicht** *umg.* I bet (you) she won't come

Garantie|schein *m* guarantee; ~**zeit** *f* guarantee (period)

Garantin *f*; -, -*nen* guarantor

Garaus *m umg., mst hum.:* **j-m den** ~ **machen** finish (*od.* bump) s.o. off; **e-r Sache den** ~ **machen** put paid to s.th.

Garbe *f*; -, -*n* **1.** *Agr.* sheaf; **in** ~ **binden** bundle, tie up into sheaves; **2.** *Schießen:* burst

Garde *f*; -, -*n* **1.** *Mil.* the guards *Pl.*; **das ist e-r von der alten** ~ *fig.* he's still one of the old school; **2.** *Karneval:* group of members of a carnival society wearing brightly colo(u)red uniforms during carnival

Gardenie [gar'de:niə] *f*; -, -*n*; *Bot.* gardenia

Garde|offizier *m Mil.* guards officer; ~**regiment** *n* guards regiment

Garderobe *f* **1.** (*Kleidung*) clothes *Pl.*, wardrobe; (*Mäntel etc.*) hats and coats *Pl.*; **e-e große** ~ **haben** have a lot of clothes (*od.* a large wardrobe); „**für** ~ **wird nicht gehaftet**" *Schild:* we regret that the management cannot accept responsibility for losses due to theft; **2.** *Gestell:* coatrack; *frei stehend:* hall stand; *Schrank:* wardrobe; **3.** *Raum, zu Hause:* wardrobe, clothes cupboard

(*Am.* closet); *im Museum etc.:* cloakroom, *Am. auch* checkroom; **etw. an der** ~ **abgeben** leave s.th. in the cloakroom (*Am.* checkroom); **4.** *Theat. etc.* (*Umkleideraum*) dressing room

Garderoben|frau *f* cloakroom (*Am.* checkroom) attendant, *Am. auch* hatcheck girl/boy; ~**haken** *m* coat hook; ~**marke** *f*, ~**nummer** *f* cloakroom ticket, *Am.* check; ~**schrank** *m* wardrobe; ~**spiegel** *m* hall mirror; ~**ständer** *m* coatrack; *frei stehend:* hall stand

Garderobier [gardəro'bje:] *m*; -*s*, -*s*, **Garderobiere** [gardəro'bjɛ:rə] *f*; -, -*n* cloakroom (*Am.* checkroom) attendant, *Am. auch* hatcheck girl/boy

Gardine *f*; -, -*n* (net) curtain; **hinter schwedischen** ~**n** *fig.* behind bars

Gardinen|predigt *f umg. hum.* lecture, dressing down; ~**röllchen** *n* curtain runner; ~**stange** *f* **1.** *zum Aufhängen:* curtain rod; **2.** *zum Zuziehen:* curtain pole

garen *vt/i. Gastr.:* ~ (*lassen*) cook slowly, simmer

gären *v/i.:* **gärte** *od.* **gor, hat** *od.* **ist gegoren, seltener gegärt 1.** ~ (*lassen*) ferment; **2.** *fig.* be seething, fester; **es gärte in ihm** he was seething with hatred (*od.* rage *etc.*); **es gärt im Volk** there's growing unrest among the people

Garküche *f altm.* cookshop, eating house

Garn *n*; -(*e*)*s*, -*e* **1.** thread, yarn; *Baumwolle: auch* cotton; **2.** *fig.: (j-m)* **ins** ~ **gehen** walk into the (into s.o.'s) trap; **ein** ~ **spinnen** spin a yarn

Garnele *f*; -, -*n* shrimp (*Am. auch Pl.*); *größere:* prawn

garni *Adj.* → **Hotel**

garnieren *v/t.* decorate; (*Hut etc.*) *auch* trim; *Gastr.* garnish; **Garnierspritze** *f Gastr.* piping bag; **Garnierung** *f* decoration; *am Hut etc.: auch* trimmings *Pl.*; *Gastr.* garnish(ing)

Garnison *f*; -, -*en*; *Mil.* garrison; **Garnisonsstadt** *f* garrison town

Garnitur *f*; -, -*en* **1.** (*Satz*) set; *Unterwäsche:* matching underwear; *Mil.* full uniform; **zwei** ~**en Unterwäsche** two sets of underwear; → *auch* **Sitzgarnitur** *etc.*; **2.** (*Besatz*) trimming(s *Pl.*); *Gastr.* garnish, trimmings *Pl.*; **3.** *umg. fig.: erste* ~ top rank(s *Pl.*); *Person[en]:* top notcher(s *Pl.*); **zweite/dritte** ~ second-/third-rater(s *Pl.*); **Solisten der ersten** ~ top-class (*umg.* top-notch) soloists

Garn|knäuel *m, n* ball of thread; ~**rolle** *f* reel (of thread *od.* cotton); ~**spule** *f* spool, bobbin

Gärprozess *m* fermentation process, (process of) fermentation

garstig *Adj.* **1.** *Benehmen, Geruch etc.:* nasty; *Wetter: auch* filthy; **2.** (*hässlich*) *Hexe, Zwerg:* horrible, horrid

Gärstoff *m* ferment

gärteln *v/i. südd.* → **gärtnern**

Garten *m*; -*s*, **Gärten** garden; **englischer/hängender** ~ English (landscape) / hanging garden; **botanischer/zoologischer** ~ botanical/zoological gardens *Pl.*; **der** ~ **Eden** *bibl.* the Garden of Eden; → *auch* **Gemüsegarten** *etc.*; ~**abfälle** *Pl.* garden waste *Sg.*; ~**anlage** *f* (public) gardens *Pl.*; ~**arbeit** *f* gardening; **sie hat sich bei der** ~ **verletzt** she injured herself while gardening (*od.* working in the garden); ~**architekt** *m*, ~**architektin** *f* landscape gardener; ~**bank** *f*; *Pl.* -*bänke* garden bench

G

Gartenbau m horticulture; ~amt n parks department; ~ausstellung f → *Gartenschau*; ~betrieb m market garden, *Am.* truck farm
Garten|beet n flower (*od.* vegetable) bed; ~blume f garden flower; ~erd-beere f cultivated strawberry; ~fest n garden party; ~freund m keen (*Am.* avid) gardener; ~geräte *Pl.* gardening tools; ~häuschen n *bewohnbar*: summer house; *für Geräte*: garden shed; ~kräuter *Pl.* pot herbs, greens; ~kresse f garden cress; ~laube f *Sitzplatz*: arbo(u)r, bower; *Häuschen*: summer house; ~lokal n → *Gartenwirtschaft*; ~möbel *Pl.* garden (*Am.* outdoor) furniture *Sg.*; ~schau f horticultural show; *größere*: garden festival; ~schaukel f swing(ing) seat; ~schere f: (e-e) ~ (a pair of) pruning shears *Pl.*; ~schlauch m garden hose; ~stadt f garden city; ~stuhl m garden chair; ~tisch m garden table; ~tor n, ~tür f garden gate; ~weg m garden path; ~wirtschaft f outdoor café (*od.* restaurant); (*Biergarten*) beer garden; ~zaun m garden fence; ~zwerg m 1. (garden) gnome; 2. *umg. fig. pej. hässlich*: ugly little thing; *unangenehm*: little squirt; *lächerlich*: short-arse, midget
Gärtner m; -s, - gardener
Gärtnerei f; -, -en 1. *nur Sg.*; *Tätigkeit*: gardening; 2. *Betrieb*: market garden, *Am.* truck farm
Gärtnergurke f garden cucumber
Gärtnerin f; -, -nen gardener; ~art f *Gastr.*: (*auf od. nach*) ~ à la jardinière
gärtnern v/i. do gardening, work in the garden
Gärung f 1. fermentation; *in ~ überge-hen* begin to ferment; 2. *fig.* (state of) unrest
Gärungs|mittel n ferment; ~prozess m fermentation process, (process of) fermentation
Garzeit f cooking time
Gas n; -es, -e 1. *allg.* gas; 2. *Mot.*: ~ ge-ben step on the accelerator (*umg. und Am.* gas); *gib ~!* step on it! *umg.*; ~ wegnehmen *od.* vom ~ gehen *umg.* take one's foot off the accelerator, decelerate, *Am. auch* throttle back; 3. (*Brenner, Herd*) gas; *das Wasser vom ~ nehmen* take the water off the gas (*od.* flame); 4. *Mil.* (*Giftgas*) gas; 5. (*Gaskammer*) gas chamber
Gas|ableser m, ~ableserin f (gas)meter reader; *männlich auch* gas-man; ~anschluss m gas connection; ~anzünder m gas lighter; ~aus-tausch m *Bio., Med.* gaseous interchange; ~behälter m gas tank
gasbeheizt *Adj.* gas-fired, gas-heated; ~e Wohnung flat (*od.* flat, *Am.* apartment) with gas heating
Gas|beleuchtung f gas light(ing); ~be-ton m aerated concrete; ♀betrieben *Adj. Tech.* gas-driven; ~brenner m gas burner; ♀dicht *Adj.* gasproof; ~druck m gas pressure; ~entwicklung f, ~erzeugung f gas production; ~ex-plosion f gas explosion; ~fernleitung f long-distance gas pipe; ~feuerung f gas firing; ~feuerzeug n gas lighter; ~flamme f gas flame; *am Kocher*: burner; ~flasche f gas cylinder
gas|förmig *Adj.* gaseous; ~gefüllt *Adj.* gas-filled, filled with gas; ~gekühlt *Adj.* gas-cooled
Gas|gemisch n gas(eous) mixture; ~geruch m smell of gas; ~hahn m gas tap; *den ~ aufdrehen/abdrehen* turn

the gas on/off; *j-m den ~ abdrehen umg. fig.* put s.o. out of business; ♀haltig *Adj.* gaseous; ~hebel m *Mot. für Hand*: throttle control; ~heizofen m gas fire; ~heizung f gas heating; ~herd m gas cooker (*od.* stove, *Am. auch* range); ~kammer f gas chamber; ~kocher m camping stove; ~lampe f, ~laterne f gas lamp, gaslight; ~leitung f gas pipe; ~licht n gaslight; ~-Luft--Gemisch n *Mot.* fuel-and-air mixture; ~mann m gasman; ~maske f gas mask; ~ofen m gas stove (*od.* oven)
Gasometer m gasometer
Gas|patrone f 1. *für Sodaflasche etc.*: gas (*od.* soda) cartridge; 2. *für Waffe*: gas canister; ~pedal n *Mot.* accelera-tor (pedal), *Am. auch* gas pedal; ~pis-tole f tear-gas pistol; ~rechnung f gas bill; ~rohr n gas pipe
Gässchen n (little) alleyway, narrow lane
Gasse f; -, -n 1. narrow street, (nar-row) lane; *auf der ~* in (*od.* on) the street; *auf allen ~n zu hören sein fig. pej.* be the talk of the town; → *Hans-dampf*; 2. *fig.*: e-e ~ bilden make (*od.* clear) a path; *sich e-e ~ bahnen durch* force one's way through; 3. *österr.* → *Straße*; 4. *Fußball*: opening; *Rugby*: lineout; *ein Pass in die ~* a through pass; *linke/rechte ~ Kegeln*: left-/right--hand alley between the lines of skittles (*Am.* pins)
Gassen|hauer m *altm. umg.* popular song (*od.* tune); ~junge m *pej.* urchin
Gassi *ohne Art., umg.*: (*mit dem Hund*) ~ gehen take the dog out (for a walk), go walkies (with the dog); *komm, wir gehen jetzt ~!* time for walkies!; *der Hund muss ~* the dog needs a walk
Gast m; -(e)s, Gäste guest; (*Besucher*) visitor; *im Wirtshaus etc.*: customer; *Theat.* guest (performer *od.* artist); *Gäste Sport* away (*od.* visiting) team *Sg.*, visitors *Pl. umg.*; *nur für Gäste* for patrons (*od.* customers) only; *Vor-stellung etc.* für geladene Gäste for an invited audience; *er ist ein seltener ~* he's a stranger in these parts; *bei j-m zu ~ sein* be staying with s.o.; *Gäste haben* have visitors (*od.* company); *oft Gäste haben über Nacht*: often have people to stay; (*Einladungen*) do a lot of entertaining; *wir haben heute Abend Gäste* we're having guests (*od.* visitors) tonight, we're having some people round (*Am.* over) tonight; *heu-te Abend haben wir X zu ~* TV etc. our guest tonight is X; *heute bist du mein ~* it's all on me (today); ~arbei-ter m, ~arbeiterin f foreign (*od.* immi-grant) worker
Gäste|bett n 1. *zu Hause*: guest (*od.* spare) bed; 2. *im Hotel etc.*: bed; ~buch n visitors' book; ~handtuch n guest towel; ~haus n guest house; ~liste f guest list; ~-WC n guest toilet; ~zimmer n 1. *zu Hause*: guestroom, spare (bed)room; 2. *im Hotel etc.*: room; (*Aufenthaltsraum*) lounge
Gastfamilie f *für Austauschschüler etc.*: host family
gastfrei *Adj.* hospitable
gastfreundlich I. *Adj.* hospitable; *Land etc.*: *auch* very friendly towards visitors (*od.* tourists); II. *Adv.*: ~ emp-fangen give s.o. a warm welcome; *wir wurden sehr ~ behandelt* we were made to feel at home, we were treated very kindly; **Gastfreundlichkeit**, **Gastfreundschaft** f; *nur Sg.* hospitali-ty

Gastgeber m 1. host; 2. *Pl. Sport* home team *Sg.*; **Gastgeberin** f host-ess
Gast|geschenk n present (for the host[ess]), *Am. auch* hospitality gift; ~haus n → *Gasthof*
Gastherme f gas water heater, *Brit. auch* gas geyser
Gast|hof m restaurant; *mit Unterkunft*: guesthouse; ~hörer m, ~hörerin f *Univ.* auditor
gastieren v/i. (*als Gast auftreten*) give a guest performance, *bes. Am.* guest (*in + Dat.* in; *an + Dat.* at); *weitS.* (*auftreten*) perform, give a perform-ance; *in Japan ~* (*auf Tournee sein*) tour Japan
Gast|konzert n guest concert (*od.* per-formance); ~land n host country
gastlich *Adj.* 1. hospitable; 2. (*einla-dend*) inviting; (*gemütlich*) cosy, *Am.* homey; **Gastlichkeit** f; *nur Sg.* 1. hos-pitality; 2. (*Gemütlichkeit*) cosiness, *Am.* homeyness
Gast|mahl n *geh.* banquet; ~mann-schaft f visiting team; ~professor m, ~professorin f *Univ.* visiting profes-sor; ~recht n (right of) hospitality; *das ~ missbrauchen* abuse s.o.'s hos-pitality; ~redner m, ~rednerin f guest speaker
gastrisch *Adj. Med.* gastric; **Gastritis** f; -, *Gastritiden* gastritis; **Gastroente-ritis** f gastroenteritis
Gastrolle f 1. *Theat.* guest role (*od.* part); 2. *fig.*: e-e ~ geben pay a flying visit (*in + Dat.* to), put in a brief ap-pearance (at, in)
Gastronom m; -en, -en restaurateur; **Gastronomie** f; -, *kein Pl.* 1. *Gewerbe*: catering trade; 2. (*Kochkunst*) gas-tronomy; **Gastronomin** f; -, -nen res-taurateur; **gastronomisch** *Adj.* 1. *Ge-werbe, Betrieb*: catering; 2. gastronomi-c(al)
Gastspiel n 1. *Theat., Konzert*: guest performance; 2. *Sport* away game; 3. *fig.* → *Gastrolle*; ~reise f tour (*in + Dat.* of)
Gaststar m *in Fernsehserie etc.*: guest star
Gaststätte f restaurant; **Gaststätten-gewerbe** n catering trade
Gaststube f restaurant; *bes. wenn nur für Getränke*: bar
Gasturbine f gas turbine
Gast|vorlesung f *Univ.* guest lecture; ~vorstellung f 1. *Theat.* guest per-formance; 2. *fig.* → *Gastrolle*; ~vor-trag m guest lecture
Gastwirt m landlord; (*Inhaber*) propri-etor; **Gastwirtin** f landlady; (*auch In-haberin*) proprietor, proprietress; **Gastwirtschaft** f → *Gasthof*
Gas|uhr f gas meter; ~vergiftung f gas poisoning; ~werk n gasworks *Pl.* (*V. auch im Sg.*); ~wolke f cloud of gas; ~zähler m gas meter
Gatt n; -(e)s, -en *od.* -s; *Naut.* 1. (*Heck*) stern; 2. (*Loch*) hole; (*Speigatt*) scup-per (hole)
GATT n; -s, *kein Pl.; Wirts., Pol.* GATT (= General Agreement on Tariffs and Trade); ~Abkommen n GATT agree-ment
Gatte m; -n, -n; *geh.* husband; *Jur.* spouse; *beide ~n altm.* both spouses; *Ihr ~* your husband, Mr(.) X *förm.*
Gattenwahl f *Zool.* choosing (*od.* choice of) a mate
Gatter n; -s, - 1. *Tor*: gate; 2. *Zaun*: fence; 3. (*Gehege*) preserve; 4. *Reit-sport*: fence; 5. *Etron.* gate; ~tor n,

~tür f gate

Gattin f; -, -nen; geh. wife; Jur. spouse; **Ihre ~** your wife, Mrs(.) X förm.

Gattung f **1.** (Sorte) kind, type; (Tierart) species; **2.** Zool., Bot. genus; **3.** Kunst: form; Literatur: genre

Gattungs|begriff m generic term; **~name** m generic name; Ling. collective (od. common) noun

Gau m; -(e)s, -e **1.** bes. hist. district; **2.** im Nationalsozialismus: administrative district

GAU m; -(s), -s od. -e; Abk. (größter anzunehmender Unfall) maximum credible accident, MCA, Am. worst--case scenario

Gaube f; -, -n; Archit. bes. südd. dormer window

Gaudi f; -, kein Pl., auch n; -s, kein Pl.; umg.: **das war e-e ~!** it was a (real) scream (Am. auch gas); **nur zur ~** just for fun (umg. kicks), just for the fun of it

Gaukelbild n geh. illusion, mirage; (Blendwerk) delusion

Gaukelei f; -, -en; geh. delusion; e-s Clowns: tricks Pl.; **gaukeln** v/i. **1.** (ist gegaukelt); lit. (flattern) flutter (around); **2.** (hat); altm. conjure

Gaukelwerk n geh. altm. delusion

Gaukler m; -s, -, **~in** f; -, -nen; altm. tumbler; (Spaßmacher) clown; (Scharlatan) charlatan

Gaul m; -(e)s, Gäule **1.** pej. nag; **alter ~** (old) jade; **2.** Dial. od. altm. horse; **e-m geschenkten ~ sieht man nicht ins Maul** Sprichw. never look a gift horse in the mouth; **ihm ging der ~ durch** umg. fig. he flew off the handle; → auch **Pferd**

Gauleiter m hist., im Nationalsozialismus: gauleiter

Gaumen m; -s, -; auch fig. palate; **e-n feinen ~ haben** fig. have a fine palate (od. tongue, sense of taste); **für den verwöhnten ~** fig. for the discriminating palate; → **gespalten**; **~bein** n Anat. palatine (bone); **~freuden** Pl. culinary delights; **~kitzel** m: **jetzt gibt es e-n kleinen ~** now for something to tickle your tastebuds; **~mandel** f Anat. (palatine) tonsil; **~platte** f Med. upper plate; **~segel** n Anat. soft palate, velum fachspr.; **~spalte** f Med. cleft palate; **~zäpfchen** n Anat. uvula

Gauner m; -s, -; pej. crook, swindler; (Halunke) rascal; **diese ~!** what a bunch of crooks!; **die kleinen ~ hängt man, die großen lässt man laufen** Sprichw. there's one law for the rich and another for the poor; **~bande** f gang of crooks, band of thieves; **Gaunerei** f; -, -en; pej. swindling, swindle, con game umg.; **gaunerhaft** Adj. crooked umg.; **Gaunerin** f; -, -nen; pej. crook, swindler; (Halunke) minx; **gaunern** v/i. swindle

Gauner|sprache f underworld jargon, thieves' cant; **~streich** m, **~stück** n swindle, con umg.

Gazastreifen ['gɑːza-] m Geog. Gaza Strip

Gaze ['gɑːzə] f; -, -n gauze (auch Med.); Wirts., feine: gossamer; grobe: cheesecloth; Draht: wire gauze

Gazelle f; -, -n gazelle

Gazeschleier m gauze veil

Gazette f; -, -n; altm. newspaper; pej. rag

GB Abk. **1.** GB (= Great Britain); **2.** Gb (= gigabyte)

G-Dur n; -, kein Pl.; Mus. G major

geachtet I. P.P. → **achten**; **II.** Adj. re-

---

spected; **bei allen ~ sein** have everyone's respect

Geächtete m, f; -n, -n outlaw

Geäder n; -s, - **1.** (Blutgefäße) blood vessels Pl.; **2.** (Maserung) veins Pl., veined structure; im Holz: grain; **geädert** Adj. veined; (marmoriert) marbled; Holz: grained; Käse: veiny

geartet I. P.P. → **arten**; **II.** Adj. disposed; **anders ~ sein** be different; **besonders ~er Fall** special case; **so ~, dass ...** the kind of person etc. that would, will etc. ...; **er lässt keine wie auch immer ~e Kritik gelten** he won't accept any criticism whatsoever (od. won't accept criticism of any kind)

Geäst n; -(e)s, kein Pl. branches Pl.

Gebäck n; -(e)s, kein Pl. feines: (fancy) cakes Pl.; (Kekse) biscuits Pl., Am. cookies Pl.; **~schale** f cake dish; **~stück** n, **~teilchen** n pastry; **~zange** f: (e-e) ~ cake tongs Pl.

gebadet I. P.P. → **baden**; **II.** Adj. → **Schweiß**

Gebälk n; -(e)s, -e, mst Sg. beams Pl.; von Säulen: entablature; **es knistert od. kracht im ~** fig. there's trouble brewing (od. in the air)

Geballer(e) n; -s, kein Pl.; umg. pej. banging

geballt I. P.P. → **ballen**; **II.** Adj. **1.** Faust: clenched; **2.** fig. concentrated; Stil: auch compact; Angriff: concerted; **~e Ladung** Mil. concentrated charge; umg. fig. load, pile; **III.** Adv.: **~ auftreten** Probleme etc.: come all at once; nacheinander: come thick and fast

gebannt I. P.P. → **bannen**; **II.** Adj. und Adv. (auch **wie ~**) fascinated, spellbound; **~ zusehen** auch be riveted; **~ vor dem Fernseher sitzen** be glued to the TV; **wie ~ stehen bleiben** stop dead in one's tracks

gebar Imperf. → **gebären**

Gebärde f; -, -n **1.** (Geste) gesture; **2.** geh. fig. air

gebärden v/refl. behave, act (**wie** like); **sich wie toll ~** behave (od. act) like a madman

Gebärden|spiel n gestures Pl.; stummes: pantomime (auch fig.); **~sprache** f **1.** sign language; **2.** Theat. mimicry

Gebaren n; -s, kein Pl. behavio(u)r, demeano(u)r; geschäftlich: conduct

gebären v/t./i.; gebärt od. altm. gebiert, gebar, geboren **1.** (ein Kind) ~ give birth (to a child); **geboren werden** be born; **ich bin am ... geboren** od. **wurde geboren am ...** I was born on ...; **sie gebar ihm e-n Sohn** she bore him a son; **der Mann muss noch geboren werden** fig. that man hasn't been born yet; → **geboren**; **2.** fig. breed s.th., beget s.th.

gebär|fähig Adj. capable of childbearing (Zool. of giving birth); **im ~en Alter** of childbearing age; **~freudig** Adj. fertile; **sie hat ein ~es Becken** umg. hum. she's broad in the beam, Am. she's a wide ride

Gebärmutter f; Pl. Gebärmütter; Anat. womb, uterus; **~hals** m Anat. neck of the uterus (od. womb), cervix (uteri) fachspr.; **~krebs** m Med. cervical cancer, cancer of the womb; **~senkung** f Med. uterine descent; **~vorfall** m Med. (uterine) prolapse

Gebärstuhl m birthing chair

Gebarung f österr. (Buchführung) book-keeping; (finanzielle Geschäftsführung) financial management

---

Gebarungs|bericht m österr. company report; **~jahr** n österr. financial year

gebauchpinselt Adj. umg. hum.: **sich ~ fühlen** be od. feel (quite) tickled

Gebäude n; -s, - **1.** building; (Gefüge) structure; bes. großes, bemerkenswertes: edifice; **2.** fig. (Zusammengefügtes) structure; von Gedanken: edifice; **~flügel** m wing (of a od. the building); **~komplex** m complex (of buildings), group of buildings; **~reinigung** f (commercial) cleaning; Betrieb: contract cleaners; **~schäden** m damage Sg. to a (od. the) building; **~trakt** m part of a (od. the) building; (Flügel) wing; **~versicherung** f buildings insurance

gebaut I. P.P. → **bauen**; **II.** Adj. fig.: **gut ~** Person: well-built (auch iro.); **so wie er ~ ist, schafft er es leicht** umg. hum. a man of his size won't have any problems

gebefreudig Adj. open-handed, (very) generous

Gebein n; -(e)s, -e **1.** geh.: **~e von Toten**: (mortal) remains; kirchl. relics; **2.** altm. bones Pl.; (Knochengerüst) skeleton

Gebell n; -(e)s, kein Pl. barking; (Kläffen) yapping

geben; gibt, gab, hat gegeben **I.** v/t. **1.** give (**j-m etw.** s.o. s.th., s.th. to s.o.); (reichen) auch hand; (schenken) auch present (with); (verleihen) auch lend; (Ball etc.) (weitergeben) pass; **etw. nicht aus der Hand geben** (nicht hergeben) not let go of s.th., not part with s.th.; fig. (Leitung, Verantwortung) refuse to give up s.th. (od. relinquish s.th); **j-m zu trinken/essen ~** give s.o. s.th. to drink/eat; **sich** (Dat.) **etw. ~ lassen** (bitten um, verlangen) ask for s.th.; **j-m etw. zur Aufbewahrung ~** give s.o. s.th. for safekeeping; **~ Sie mir bitte ein Bier / zwei Kilo Äpfel** give me (od. I'd like) a beer / two kilos of apples, please; **~ Sie mir bitte Herrn Müller am Telefon** I'd like to speak to Mr(.) Müller, please, put me through to Mr(.) Müller, please; **ich gäbe was drum zu wissen ...** umg. I'd give anything to know ...; → **Druck²**, **Hand¹ 1, 3, 4, Kommission, Pflege** etc.; **2.** (Anlass, Auskunft, Befehl, Chance, Erlaubnis, Hinweis etc.) give; (gewähren) auch grant; (bieten) give, offer; (Hoffnung, Mut etc.) give, fill s.o. with; **er hat mir nichts zu ~** (bieten) he has nothing to offer me; **der Arzt gibt ihm noch zwei Monate** (**zu leben**) fig. the doctor gives him two more (od. another two) months (to live); → **Antwort, Bescheid 1, Blöße 2, gegeben, Recht, Ruhe 1, Wort 4**; **3.** (Konzert etc.) give; (Theaterstück etc.) perform, do umg.; (Film) show; (Essen, Party) have, give; (Unterricht, Fach) teach; **was wird heute Abend gegeben?** what's on tonight?; **4.** Sport (Ecke, Elfmeter, Freistoß) give; **5.** (Ertrag etc.) give, yield; **Milch ~** give (od. provide) milk; **6.** (ergeben) make; (Flecken) make, leave; **das gibt e-e gute Suppe** it makes a good soup; **das gibt keinen Sinn** it doesn't make (any) sense; **fünf mal sechs gibt dreißig** five sixes are thirty, five times six is thirty; **7.** (tun, legen, stecken etc.) put; (hinzufügen) add; **Salz in die Suppe ~** put salt into (od. add salt to) the soup; **8. von sich ~** (Geräusch, Geruch) give off; Chem. emit; (Äußerung) make; (Schrei etc.) give; (auch

G

Flüche) let out; *Essen* **wieder von sich ~** *umg.* bring up; **nichts als Unsinn von sich ~** talk nothing but nonsense; → *Ton*[1] 1; **9.** *etwas od.* **viel ~** *auf gutes Benehmen etc.*: set great store by; *bes. auf j-n*: think highly *(od.* a lot) of; **wenig/nichts ~** *auf Konventionen etc.*: set little/no store by, not bother much / at all about *umg.*; *auf j-n*: not think much of; **ich gebe nichts auf i-e Worte** I don't believe a word she says, I don't take anything she says seriously; **10.** *umg.*: **es j-m ~** let s.o. have it, give it to s.o.; **gib ihm Saures!** give him hell!; **gut gegeben!** that's telling him *etc.*!; **II.** *v/i.* **1.** give (*mit vollen Händen* freely); **gern ~** give willingly *(od.* gladly); **2.** *Kartenspiel*: deal; **wer gibt?** whose deal is it?; **3.** *Tennis*: serve; **4.** *unpers.*: **es gibt** (*existiert, wird angeboten etc.*) there is, there are; **es gibt Leute, die ...** some people ...; **der beste Spieler, den es je gab** the best player there ever was; **was gibt es da noch zu überlegen?** what is there still to think about?; **was gibt es da zu lachen?** *ärgerlich*: what's funny about that?; **was gibt's?** what's up?; (*was hast du*) what's the matter?; **was gibt's Neues?** what's new?; **was es nicht alles gibt!** *umg.* you don't say!; **das gibt's nicht!** (*existiert nicht*) there's no such thing; (*das darf nicht wahr sein*) you're joking, that can't be true; *verbietend*: that's out; **das gibt's nicht - sie ist tatsächlich noch aufgetaucht!** *umg.* I don't *(od.* can't) believe she actually turned up; **Sachen gibt's, die gibt's nicht** *umg* truth is often stranger than fiction, there are more things in heaven and earth (than are dreamed of in your philosophy); *ungläubig*: would you believe it!; **gibt's den denn noch?** *umg.* is he still around?; **da gibt's nichts!** *umg.* (*ohne Zweifel*) there's no doubt about that, and no mistake about it; (*unter allen Umständen*) even if it kills me *etc.*; **5.** *unpers.*; *zukünftig*: **das gibt Ärger** *umg.* there'll be trouble; **morgen gibt es Schnee** it's going to snow *(od.* there's going to be snow) tomorrow; **heute wird's noch was ~** *(ein Gewitter)* I think we're in for some bad weather *(od.* a storm); (*e-n Krach*) *auch* there's trouble brewing *(od.* in the air); **sei ruhig, sonst gibt's was!** *umg.* be quiet, or else!; **III.** *v/refl.* **1.** (*sich benehmen*) act, behave; (*vorgeben*) play, pretend; **sich natürlich ~** act naturally; **sich als Experte etc. ~** play the expert *etc.*, pose as an expert *etc.*; **2.** (*nachlassen*) ease up; (*vorübergehen*) pass, blow over; *Leidenschaft etc.*: *auch* cool (down); *Schmerzen*: let up; *völlig*: go away; *Fieber*: go down; (*wieder gut werden*) come right; **das gibt sich wieder** *auch* it'll sort itself out; **3.** *sich in sein Schicksal etc. ~* give o.s. up to *(od.* resign o.s. to) one's fate *etc.*; → *gefangen* II 1, *geschlagen* II 1, *verloren* II

Geben *n*; *-s, kein Pl.* **1.** giving; **es ist alles ein ~ und Nehmen** it's all a matter of give and take; **~ ist seliger denn Nehmen** *bibl.* it is more blessed to give than to receive; **2.** *Kartenspiel*: **am ~ sein** be dealing, be the dealer; **er ist am ~** it's his deal

gebenedeit *Adj. kirchl.* blessed; **~ sei die Frucht d-s Leibes** blessed be the fruit of thy womb

Geber *m*; *-s, -,* **~in** *f*; *-, -nen* **1.** giver;

2. *Kartenspiel*: dealer; **3.** *Wirts.*: **~ und Nehmer** *Pl.* sellers and buyers; **~land** *n Pol.*, *Wirts.* donor country; **~laune** *f*: **in ~** in a generous mood

Gebet *n*; *-(e)s, -e* prayer (**an** + *Akk. od.* **zu** to); **beim ~** at (*Am.* in) prayer; **sein ~ verrichten** say one's prayers; **j-n ins ~ nehmen** *umg. fig.* give s.o. a good talking-to; **~buch** *n* prayer book

gebeten *P.P.* → *bitten*

Gebetsläuten *n südd.*, *österr.* angelus

gebetsmühlenhaft *Adj. pej. Wiederholungen*: constant

gebeugt I. *P.P.* → *beugen*; **II.** *Adj.* **1. vom Alter ~** bowed (down) *od.* bent with age; **vom Kummer ~** bowed down with grief; **2.** *Ling.* inflected

gebiert → *gebären*

Gebiet *n*; *-(e)s, -e* **1.** (*Fläche*) area; (*Gegend*) *auch* region; (*Bezirk*) district, zone; (*Territorium*) territory; **benachbarte ~e** neighbo(u)ring territories; (*Länder*) neighbo(u)ring countries; **2.** (*Fachgebiet*) field; (*Bereich*) *auch* area, sphere; (*Thema*) subject; **er ist Fachmann auf dem ~ der Kernspaltung** he's an authority on *(od.* in the field of) nuclear fission; **ich kenne mich in dem ~ überhaupt nicht aus** I don't know anything *(od.* the first thing) about the subject; **das ist nicht mein ~** that's not my field *(od.* line, *umg.* territory)

gebieten; *gebietet, gebot, hat geboten*; *geh.* **I.** *v/t.* **1.** (*erfordern*) require, call for; (*Achtung, Ehrfurcht*) command; **die Vernunft gebietet (uns) zu** (+ *Inf.*) reason demands (of us) that we ...; **2.** (*befehlen*) order; (*anweisen*) instruct (*beide*: **zu** + *Inf.* to + *Inf.*); **er gebot ihnen Einhalt/Schweigen** he ordered them to stop / to be quiet; **II.** *v/i.*: **~ über** (+ *Akk.*) (*etw.*) control; (*auch j-n*) hold sway over; (*herrschen über*) rule (over), govern; (*verfügen über*) have at one's disposal *(od.* command); → *geboten*; **gebietend I.** *Part. Präs.* → *gebieten*; **II.** *Adj.*: **e-e Achtung** *od.* **Ehrfurcht ~e Erscheinung** a figure who commands respect; **Gebieter** *m*; *-s, -* master, lord; (*Herrscher*) ruler; → *Herr* 3; **Gebieterin** *f*; *-, -* mistress; (*Herrscherin*) ruler; **gebieterisch** *Adj. geh.* imperious; *Ton etc.*: *auch* peremptory; **~es Wesen** *auch* imperiousness

Gebiets|abtretung *f* cession of territory; **~en verlangen von** make territorial claims on; **~anspruch** *m* territorial claim; **~erweiterung** *f* territorial expansion; **~hoheit** *f* territorial sovereignty *(od.* jurisdiction); **~körperschaft** *f Jur.* territorial authority; **~krankenkasse** *f österr.* provincial statutory health insurance (scheme, *Am.* plan) (*operating in an Austrian Bundesland*); **~reform** *f* regional reorganization

gebietsweise *Adv.* regionally, locally; by *(od.* according to) regions; **~ Regen** local showers, rain in places

Gebilde *n*; *-s, -*; (*Ding*) thing; (*Form*) form, shape; (*Bau, Gefüge*) structure; (*Werk*) work, creation; (*Erzeugnis*) product; *hum.* (*Vorrichtung etc.*) contraption; *Wirts.*, *Jur.* entity; (*Bildung*) *auch Geol.* formation

gebildet I. *P.P.* → *bilden*; **II.** *Adj.* educated; (*kultiviert*) cultured; (*wissensreich*) well-informed; (*belesen*) well-read; **Gebildete** *m, f*; *-n, -n* educated person; **die ~n** the educated world *(od.* classes), *weitS.* the intellectuals

Gebimmel *n*; *-s, kein Pl.*; *umg. pej.* ringing

Gebinde *n*; *-s, -* **1.** bundle; *von Blumen*: spray; **2.** *von Garn*: skein; **3.** *Archit.* truss; **4.** (*Fass*) barrel, cask; (*Behälter*) container

Gebirge *n*; *-s, -* **1.** mountains *Pl.*; (*Gebirgskette*) mountain range; **2.** *Bergb.* rock; **3.** *fig.* mountain; **gebirgig** *Adj.* mountainous

Gebirgs|... *im Subst. siehe auch* **Berg...**; **~ausläufer** *m* spur; **~bach** *m* mountain stream; *reißender*: (mountain) torrent; **~bewohner** *m*, **~bewohnerin** *f* mountain-dweller; **~blume** *f* mountain *(od.* alpine) flower; **~dorf** *n* mountain village; **~jäger** *m Mil.* mountain infantryman; *Pl.* mountain infantry *Sg.* (*V. auch im Pl.*); **~kamm** *m* mountain ridge; **~kette** *f* mountain range; **~landschaft** *f* **1.** *Geog.* mountainous region *(od.* area); **2.** *Anblick*: mountain scenery; **3.** *Kunst* mountain landscape; **~massiv** *n* massif; **~pass** *m* mountain pass; **~stock** *m* massif; **~straße** *f* mountain road *(od.* route); **~tal** *n* mountain valley; **~zug** *m* mountain range

Gebiss *n*; *-es, -e* **1.** (set of) teeth *Pl.*; **ein scharfes ~** sharp teeth; **2.** *künstliches*: dentures *Pl.*, (set of) false teeth *Pl.*; **ein ~ tragen** wear dentures, have false teeth; **3.** *am Zaum*: bit; **~abdruck** *m* (dental) impression

gebissen *P.P.* → *beißen*

Gebiss|fehlstellung *f* malocclusion; **~regulierung** *f* corrective dentistry, orthodontics *Pl.* (*V. im Sg.*); **~träger** *m*, **~trägerin** *f*: **~ sein** wear dentures

Gebläse *n*; *-s, -* **1.** *Tech.* fan, blower; **2.** *Mot. am Vergaser*: supercharger; *beim Hochofen*: airpipe; **3.** (*Blasebalg*) bellows *Pl.*

geblasen *P.P.* → *blasen*

geblieben *P.P.* → *bleiben*

geblümt, *österr.* **geblumt** *Muster*: floral; *Kleid, Stoff*: flowered, with a floral *(od.* flower) pattern; **blau** *etc.* **~** with blue *etc.* flowers on it

Geblüt *n*; *-(e)s, kein Pl.*; *geh. fig.* blood; (*Geschlecht*) *auch* lineage; **von edlem ~** of noble blood *(od.* birth); *Pferd*: thoroughbred

gebogen I. *P.P.* → *biegen*; **II.** *Adj.* bent; (*geschwungen, rund*) curved; *Nase*: hooked

gebongt *P.P.* → *bongen*

geboren I. *P.P.* → *gebären*; **II.** *Adj.* born; **blind/tot ~** born blind/dead; **er ist ein ~er Deutscher/Berliner** he's German by birth /he was born in Berlin; **~e Schmidt** née Schmidt; **sie ist e-e ~e Schmidt** her maiden name is Schmidt; **~ sein zu** be born to (be/do) s.th.; **zu e-m Beruf**: *auch* be cut out for; **er ist der ~e Geschäftsmann** he is a born *(od.* natural) businessman; **aus der Not ~** *fig.* born of necessity

geborgen I. *P.P.* → *bergen*; **II.** *Adj.* safe, secure, safe and secure; **sich ~ fühlen** feel safe; **sie fühlt sich bei ihm ~** she feels very secure with him, he gives her a sense of security; **Geborgenheit** *f*; *nur Sg.* security; **die ~ des Elternhauses** the warmth and security of the home; **Geborgenheitsgefühl** *n* sense of security

geborsten *P.P.* → *bersten*

Gebot *n*; *-(e)s, -e* **1.** *Reli.* commandment, law; **die Zehn ~e** the Ten Commandments; **2.** *fig.* (*Erfordernis*) requirement, necessity; **es ist ein ~ der Höflichkeit** *etc.* it's a matter of courtesy *etc.*; ... **ist das ~ der Stunde** *od.* ... **ist oberstes ~** ... is top (*od.* the number one) priority, ... is urgently called for, ... is of paramount importance; *es ist ein ~ der Vernunft, dass ...* reason demands that ...; *dem ~ der Vernunft folgen* follow the dictates of reason; **3.** *altm.* (*Befehl*) order, command; (*Vorschrift*) rule; **4.** *lit.*: *j-m zu ~e stehen* be at s.o.'s disposal; *zu ~e stehend* available; *mit allen zu ~e stehenden Mitteln* by fair means or foul; *sie versuchte mit allen ihr zu ~e stehenden Mitteln zu* (+ *Inf.*) she tried every possible means to (+ *Inf.*), she did her utmost to (+ *Inf.*); **5.** *Bridge, Skat, Versteigerung*: bid; *ein ~ abgeben* make a bid; *verkaufe Motorrad gegen ~ in Annonce*: offers invited for motorbike, motorbike for sale: make an offer

geboten I. *P.P.* → **bieten, gebieten**; **II.** *Adj.* **1.** (*notwendig*) necessary; *präd.* called for; (*gehörig*) due; *Jur.* mandatory; *dringend ~* (absolutely) imperative; *es ist Vorsicht ~* caution is called for, it would be as well to be cautious; **2.** *Preis etc.*: bid, offered; *da ist was ~* *umg. fig.* there's something doing (*Am.* going on) there

Gebotsschild *n* traffic sign (*giving an instruction*)

Gebrabbel *n*; *-s*, *kein Pl.*; *umg. pej.* mumbling, muttering

gebracht *P.P.* → **bringen**

gebrandmarkt *P.P.* → **brandmarken**

gebrannt I. *P.P.* → **brennen**; **II.** *Adj.* **1.** burnt; *~es Kind scheut das Feuer Sprichw.* once bitten, twice shy; *ein ~es Kind sein fig.* be cautious (*od.* wary) (due to bad experience); *in dieser Hinsicht bin ich ein ~es Kind* I'm wary of making the same mistake twice, I'm not falling for that again *umg.*; **2.** *Tech., Keramik*: fired; *Ziegel*: baked; *~er Kalk* quicklime; **3.** *Kaffee, Mandeln etc.*: roasted; **4.** *Person*: *braun ~* tanned, bronzed

gebraten *P.P.* → **braten**; *Gebratenes* fried foods (*umg.* stuff)

Gebräu *n*; *-(e)s*, *-e*; *mst pej.* brew; *fig. auch* concoction

Gebrauch *m*; *-(e)s*, *Gebräuche* **1.** *nurSg.* use; (*Anwendung*) application (*auch Pharm., Med.*); *Ling.* usage; *von etw. ~ machen* make use of s.th., use s.th.; *guten/schlechten ~ von etw. machen* put s.th. to good/bad use; *in ~ kommen* come into use; *in ~ sein* be in use, be used; *außer ~ kommen* pass out of use; *allgemein in ~* in common use; *nur zum äußerlichen ~* for external application *od.* use only; *zum persönlichen ~* for personal use; *vor ~ schütteln!* shake before use; **2.** *mst Pl.*; (*Sitte*) custom; (*Gepflogenheit*) practice; *heilige Gebräuche* sacred rites; → *Sitte 1*

gebrauchen *v/t.* (*benutzen*) use; (*anwenden*) apply; *zu nichts zu ~* absolutely useless; *es ist noch gut / nicht mehr zu ~* it's still / no longer usable; *~ können* (*verwenden können*) make use of; *ich könnte jetzt e-n Whisky ~* (*hätte jetzt gern einen*) I could do with a Scotch now; *dich kann ich hier/jetzt nicht ~ umg.* I don't want you here (*od.* around) now; *Geld kann man immer ~* money always comes in useful (*Am.* handy); → *gebraucht*

gebräuchlich *Adj.* (*gewöhnlich*) common; (*üblich*) normal; *Wörter etc.*:

common; *nicht mehr ~* no longer used; (*überholt*) outdated; *das ist hier nicht ~* it's not done (*od.* they don't do that) around here; *~ werden* come into use; **Gebräuchlichkeit** *f; nur Sg. e-s Wortes etc.*: currency

Gebrauchs|anleitung *f*, *~anweisung* *f* directions *Pl.* for use, instructions *Pl.* (for use); *~artikel* *m* (basic) commodity; *Pl. auch* consumer goods

gebrauchsfähig *Adj.* usable; (*betriebsfähig*) in working order

Gebrauchsfahrzeug *n* utility vehicle

gebrauchsfertig *Adj.* ready for use

Gebrauchs|gegenstand *m* → *Gebrauchsartikel*; *~grafik* *f* commercial art; *~güter* *Pl.* (consumer) durables, *Am. auch* durable goods; *~literatur* *f* functional writing; *~möbel* *Pl.* utility furniture *Sg.*

Gebrauchs|muster *n Jur.* utility model; *~wert* *m* practical value; *~zweck* *m* purpose, intended use

gebraucht I. *P.P.* → **brauchen, gebrauchen**; **II.** *Adj.* used; *Wirts. auch* second-hand; *Kleidung: auch* old; *etw. ~ kaufen* buy s.th. second-hand

Gebraucht| ... *im Subst.*; *Wirts.* second-hand, used; *~möbel* *Pl.* used (*od.* second-hand) furniture *Sg.*

Gebrauchtwagen *m* used (*od.* second-hand) car; *~handel* *m* used (*od.* second-hand) car trade; *~händler* *m*, *~händlerin* *f* used (*od.* second-hand) car dealer; *~markt* *m* used (*od.* second-hand) car market

Gebrauchtwaren *Pl.* second-hand goods (*Am. auch* merchandise *Sg.*); *~laden* *m* second-hand shop, *Am. auch* thriftshop

gebräunt I. *P.P.* → **bräunen**; **II.** *Adj.*: *tief ~* bronzed

Gebrechen *n*; *-s*, *-*; *geh.* **1.** affliction; (*Krankheit*) complaint, ailment; *die ~ des Alters* the infirmities of old age; **2.** *fig.* shortcoming

gebrechlich *Adj.* frail; **Gebrechlichkeit** *f; nur Sg.* frailty; (*Altersschwäche*) *auch* infirmity

gebrochen I. *P.P.* → **brechen**; **II.** *Adj.* (*Bein, Herz, Farbe, Stimme, Akkord etc.*) broken; *Med. auch* fractured; *~es Englisch* broken English; *mit ~er Stimme* in a broken voice; *mit ~em Herzen* (*od.* *~en Herzens*) broken-hearted, heartbroken; *sie ist ein ~er Mensch* she's a broken woman; *~es Verhältnis* flawed (*od.* disturbed) relationship; *sie haben ein ~es Verhältnis* (*zueinander*) there are serious problems (*od.* flaws) in their relationship; **III.** *Adv.*: *~ Englisch etc. sprechen* speak (in) broken English etc.

Gebrüder *Pl.* brothers; *~* (*abgek.* *Gebr.*) *Wolfram Wirts.* Wolfram Brothers (*Abk.* Bros.)

Gebrüll *n*; *-(e)s*, *kein Pl. Löwe etc.*: roaring; *Rind*: bellowing; *Esel*: braying; (*Geschrei*) screaming; (*lautes Rufen*) bellowing; (*lautes Weinen*) bawling; *auf sie mit ~! umg. hum.* let them have it!

Gebrumm *n*; *-(e)s*, *kein Pl.* (loud) hum(ming), (loud) humming sound; *Biene, Flugzeug*: drone, droning; *Bär*: growling; *Käfer*: buzz(ing); *Person, beim Singen*: drone, droning; *missmutig*: grumbling

gebückt I. *P.P.* → **bücken**; **II.** *Adj.* bent, bowed (*über* + *Akk.* over); *~ sein auch* stoop; *~e Haltung* stoop; *in ~er Haltung* bent (forward), stooping; **III.** *Adv.*: *~ gehen* walk with a stoop

Gebühr *f*, *-*, *-en* **1.** charge, fee; (*Beitrag*) subscription; (*Satz, Tarif*) rate; (*Porto*) postage; (*Maut*) toll; *~en Radio, TV*: licen|ce (*Am.* -se) fee; *Jur. für Verfahren*: cost; *ermäßigte ~* reduced rate; *~ bezahlt* postage paid; *~ bezahlt Empfänger* postage to be paid by addressee; *e-e ~ erheben* charge a fee, charge postage (*od.* toll etc.); *e-e ~ von hundert Euro erheben auch* charge a hundred euros; *e-e ~ entrichten* pay a fee, pay postage (*od.* toll etc.); **2.** *geh.*: *nach ~* duly, as s.o. deserves; *über ~* excessively, unduly

gebühren *geh.* **I.** *v/i.*: *j-m ~* be due to s.o.; *es gebührt ihm* he deserves it, it's his due; (*gehört sich für ihn*) it befits him; *gib ihm, was ihm gebührt* give him his due; *i-n Bemühungen gebührt Anerkennung* her (*od.* their) efforts deserve recognition; **II.** *v/refl. unpers. altm.*: *sich ~* → *gehören II*

Gebührenanzeiger *m Telef.* call-fee indicator

gebührend I. *Part. Präs.* → **gebühren**; **II.** *Adj.* (*gehörig*) due; (*geziemend, passend*) due, proper, fitting; *j-m die ~e Achtung entgegenbringen* treat s.o. with due respect; *in ~em Abstand iro.* at a respectful distance; **III.** *Adv.* duly, properly, as is fitting; *dem Anlass*: as befits the occasion

gebührendermaßen,   **gebührenderweise** *Adv.* → **gebührend** II

Gebühren|einheit *f Telef.* unit; *~einnahmen* *Pl. bes. TV, Radio*: revenue from licen|ce (*Am.* -se) fees; *~erhöhung* *f* increase in charges *etc.*; → *Gebühr*, rate increase; *~ermäßigung* *f* reduction in fees

gebührenfrei *Adj. und Adv.* free of charge; **Gebührenfreiheit** *f; nur Sg.* exemption from charges

Gebühren|marke *f* revenue stamp; *~ordnung* *f* scale of fees (*od.* charges)

gebührenpflichtig I. *Adj.* subject to charges; *~e Straße* toll road; *~e Verwarnung* ticket, fine; **II.** *Adv.*: *~ verwarnt werden* get ticketed

Gebühren|satz *m* rate; *~zahler* *m*, *~zahlerin* *f bes. TV, Radio*: licen|ce(*Am.* -se) -fee payer; *~zähler* *m* Telef. call-fee indicator

gebunden I. *P.P.* → **binden**; **II.** *Adj.* **1.** *Buch*: bound; (*Ggs. als Taschenbuch*) hardcover; **2.** *fig.* tied (*an* + *Akk.* to); *an Vertrag, Versprechen*: bound (by); (*verlobt etc.*) attached; *anderweitig ~ sein* have already committed o.s.; *förm.* be otherwise engaged; *an e-n Ort etc. ~ sein* be tied to a (particular) place *etc.*; *sich an etw.* (*Akk.*) *~ fühlen* feel committed to s.th.; *mir sind die Hände ~* my hands are tied; **3.** *Wirts., Kapital*: tied (up); (*gesperrt*) blocked; (*zweckgebunden*) earmarked; (*gelenkt*) controlled; *Preise*: fixed; **4.** *Chem.* fixed (*od.* bound) (*an* + *Akk.* to), combined (with); *Phys., Wärme*: latent; **5.** *Mus.* tied; (*auch Adv.*) legato; **6.** *Lit.*: *in ~er Rede* in verse; **7.** *Soße etc.*: thickened

...gebunden *im Adj.* (*...abhängig*) ...dependent, ...bound; *ideologie~* bound by ideology; *saison~* seasonal

Gebundenheit *f; nur Sg.*; (*Verpflichtung*) commitment (*an* + *Akk.* to); (*Beschränkung*) restriction; (*Abhängigkeit*) dependence (on)

Geburt *f*, *-*, *-en* **1.** birth; *Med.* (child)birth; (*Entbindung*) delivery; (*Niederkunft*) confinement; *Vorgang*: parturition; *sanfte ~* natural childbirth; *vor/*

G

nach der ~ (*stattfindend*) antenatal (*bes. Am.* prenatal) /postnatal; *während der* ~ *aus Sicht der Frau:* during labo(u)r; *aus Sicht des Babys:* during the birth; *bei der* ~ *sterben Frau:* die in childbirth; *Baby:* die at birth, be stillborn; *von* ~ *an* from birth; **2.** (*Abstammung*) birth, descent; *von hoher/ niedriger* ~ high-born/low-born; *er ist Deutscher von* ~ he's (a) German by birth; **3.** *fig.* (*Entstehung*) birth, origin, rise; *es war e-e schwere* ~ *umg.* it was a tough job, it was tough going

Geburten|abstand *m* birth spacing; ~**beschränkung** *f* birth (*od.* population) control; ~**buch** *n* register of births; ~**kontrolle** *f* birth control; ~**rate** *f* birthrate; ~**regelung** *f* birth control; ~**rückgang** *m* decline (*od.* drop) in the birthrate

geburten|schwach *Adj. Jahr etc.:* low-birthrate ...; *die* ~*en Jahrgänge auch* the baby-bust generation *umg.;* ~**stark** *Adj. Jahr etc.:* high-birthrate ...; *die* ~*en Jahrgänge auch* the baby-boom-(er) generation *umg.*

Geburten|überschuss *m* excess of births over deaths; ~**ziffer** *f* birthrate, *Am. auch* natality

gebürtig *Adj.: er ist* ~*er Engländer* he's English (*od.* British) by birth; *aus Wales etc.* ~ *sein* be Welsh *etc.* by birth, have been born in Wales *etc.*, be a native of Wales *etc.*

Geburts|adel *m* hereditary nobility; ~**anzeige** *f* birth announcement; (*Meldung*) registration of a (*od.* the) birth; ~**beihilfe** *f* maternity benefit; ~**datum** *n* date of birth; ~**einleitung** *f Med.* induction of labo(u)r; ~**fehler** *m Med.* congenital defect; ~**gewicht** *n Med.* weight at birth; ~**haus** *n: mein etc.* ~ the house where I *etc.* was born; *Shakespeares etc.* ~ Shakespeare's *etc.* birthplace; ~**helfer** *m* **1.** *Arzt:* obstetrician; **2.** (*männliche Hebamme*) male midwife; ~**helferin** *f* **1.** (*Hebamme*) midwife; **2.** *Ärztin:* obstetrician; ~**hilfe** *f durch Hebamme:* midwifery; *Fachgebiet:* obstetrics *Pl.* (*V. im Sg.*); ~ *leisten* assist at a (*od.* the) birth; ~**jahr** *n* year of birth; ~**jahrgang** *m* cohort; ~**lage** *f Med., des Babys:* presentation; ~**land** *n* native country; ~**mal** *n; Pl. -male; Med.* birthmark; ~**name** *m* name at birth; *e-r Frau auch:* maiden name; ~**ort** *m* birthplace; ~ *und -tag* place and date of birth; ~**schein** *m* birth certificate; ~**stadt** *f* native town; ~**stätte** *f* birthplace; ~**stunde** *f* **1.** hour of birth; **2.** *fig.* birth; *am ... schlug die* ~ (+ *Gen.*) on ... *s.th.* was born

Geburtstag *m* **1.** birthday; *wann hast du* ~*?* when's your birthday?; *er hat heute* ~ it's his birthday today; *ich gratuliere od. herzlichen Glückwunsch zum* ~ many happy returns of the day; *alles Gute zum* ~ *auch* happy birthday; *was wünscht du dir zum* ~*?* what would you like for your birthday?; **2.** *Amtsspr.* date of birth

Geburtstags|feier *f,* ~**fest** *n* birthday party; ~**gast** *m* guest (at birthday party); ~**geschenk** *n* birthday present; ~**gruß** *m* birthday greeting; ~**karte** *f* birthday card; ~**kind** *n* birthday boy (*od.* girl) (*auch Erwachsener*); ~**kuchen** *m* birthday cake; ~**tisch** *m* table laden with birthday presents; ~**wunsch** *m: was hast du für Geburtstagswünsche?* what would you like for your birthday?

Geburts|trauma *n Med.* birth trauma;

~**urkunde** *f* birth certificate; ~**vorbereitung** *f* preparation for a (*od.* the) birth; *Kurs zur* ~ antenatal (*Am.* prenatal) classes *Pl.;* ~**wege** *Pl. Anat.* birth canal *Sg.;* ~**wehen** *Pl.* **1.** *Med.* labo(u)r pains, labo(u)r *Sg.; in* ~ *liegen* be in labo(u)r; **2.** *fig.* birth pangs; ~**zange** *f* forceps

Gebüsch *n; -(e)s, -e* bushes *Pl.;* (*Dickicht*) thicket; (*Gehölz*) underbrush, brushwood; *sich ins* ~ *schlagen* take to the bush (*od.* brush, wilds)

Geck *m; -en, -en; pej.* fop; **geckenhaft** *Adj. pej.* foppish

Gecko *m; -s, -s; Zool.* gecko

gedacht I. *P.P.* → *denken;* **II.** *Adj.* **1.** (*vorgestellt*) imagined, imaginary; (*angenommen*) assumed; **2.** (*vorgesehen, geplant*) intended, meant (*als* as *od.* to be; *für* for); *so war das nicht* ~*!* that wasn't what I *etc.* meant (*od.* intended)

Gedächtnis *n; -ses, -se* **1.** *Fähigkeit:* memory; *kurzes/schlechtes* ~ short/ bad memory; *ein* ~ *wie ein Sieb* a memory like a sieve; *ich habe kein gutes* ~ *für Gesichter etc.* I'm no good at remembering faces *etc.; das* ~ *verlieren* lose one's memory; *wenn mich mein* ~ *nicht trügt* if my memory serves me right; **2.** (*Erinnerung*) memory, recollection, remembrance; *aus dem* ~ from memory; (*auswendig*) by heart; *im* ~ *behalten* remember, keep in mind; *sich* (*Dat.*) *etw. ins* ~ *rufen* recall s.th., call s.th. to mind; *das ist m-m* ~ *entfallen* it has slipped my memory; *j-s* ~ *nachhelfen* jog s.o.'s memory; *wir haben unsere Methoden, Ihrem* ~ *nachzuhelfen* we have ways of making you remember; **3.** (*Andenken*) commemoration; *zum* ~ *an* (+ *Akk.*) in memory of

Gedächtnis|... *siehe auch Gedenk...;* ~**hilfe** *f* mnemonic (aid); ~**kirche** *f* memorial church; ~**künstler** *m,* ~**künstlerin** *f* memory artist; ~**lücke** *f* lapse of memory; ~**protokoll** *n* minutes from memory; ~**schwäche** *f* weak memory; *an* ~ *leiden* have a weak (*od.* poor) memory; ~**schwund** *m* loss of memory; ~**störung** *f auch Pl.* partial amnesia; ~**en haben** suffer from partial amnesia *Sg.,* be liable to memory lapses; ~**stütze** *f* mnemonic (aid); ~**test** *m* recall test; ~**training** *n* memory training; ~**übung** *f* memory training exercise; ~**verlust** *m* amnesia, loss of memory

gedämpft I. *P.P.* → *dämpfen;* **II.** *Adj. auch Stimmung, Person etc.:* subdued; *Musik, Licht: auch* soft; *Farben: auch* muted; *Schall:* muffled; *mit* ~*er Stimme* in a low voice, in an undertone; ~*er Optimismus* guarded (*od.* cautious) optimism

Gedanke *m; -ns, -n* **1.** thought (*an* + *Akk.* of); (*Gefühl, Ahnung*) notion; (*Gedankengang, Betrachtung*) thought(*s Pl.*); (*Mutmaßung*) conjecture; *der* ~, *dass* ... the thought that (*od.* of *s.o. od. s.th.* [+ *Ger.*]); *in* ~*n* (*zerstreut*) absent-minded; (*im Geiste*) in spirit; (*in der Fantasie*) in one's mind's eye; *s-n* ~*n nachhängen* lose oneself in thought (*od.* in one's own thoughts); *in* ~*n verloren* (*od.* versunken, vertieft*) lost in thought, miles away *umg.; etw. ganz in* ~*n tun* do s.th. absent-mindedly; *sie ist mit ihren* ~*n nie bei der Sache* she's always got her mind on other things; *wo warst du nur mit d-n* ~*n?* what were you

thinking of?; *j-n auf andere* ~*n bringen* get s.o.'s mind onto other things; (*von Kummer etc. ablenken*) take s.o.'s mind off things; *j-s* ~*n lesen* read s.o.'s mind; *ich kann doch keine* ~*n lesen!* I'm not a mind-reader!; *schon bei dem* ~*n od. allein der* ~ just to think of it, the very thought of it; *kein* ~ (*daran*)*! umg.* no way!; *ich kann keinen klaren* ~*n fassen* I can't think straight; *sich* ~*n machen über* (+ *Akk.*) (*nachdenken*) think about; (*sich fragen*) wonder about; (*sich sorgen*) worry about, be worried about; *mach dir keine* ~*n darüber* don't worry about it, don't let it worry you; *die* ~*n sind frei* thought is free; **2.** (*Idee, Vorstellung, Einfall, Plan*) idea; *guter* ~ good idea; *j-n auf den* ~*n bringen zu* (+ *Inf.*) give s.o. the idea of (+ *Ger.*); *j-n auf dumme* ~*n bringen* put ideas into s.o.'s head; *er kam auf den* ~ *zu* (+ *Inf.*) he had the idea of (+ *Ger.*), it occurred to him to (+ *Inf.*); *auf dumme* ~*n kommen* get ideas; *da kam ihr der rettende* ~ then she hit upon the solution; *mit dem* ~*n spielen zu* (+ *Inf.*) toy with the idea of (+ *Ger.*); *sich mit dem* ~*n tragen zu* (+ *Inf.*) have in mind to (+ *Inf.*), be minded to (+ *Inf.*); **3.** ~*n* (*Ansichten*) thoughts, views (*über* + *Akk.* on); *s-e* ~*n austauschen* exchange ideas (*od.* views); **4.** (*Begriff*) idea, concept; *der* ~ *der Demokratie* the idea (*od.* concept) of democracy

Gedanken|armut *f* lack of ideas; ~**austausch** *m* exchange of ideas; *sich zu e-m* ~ *treffen Pol.* get together for informal talks; ~**blitz** *m umg. hum.* sudden inspiration, brainwave; ~**freiheit** *f; nur Sg.* freedom of thought; ~**gang** *m* line of thought; ~**gebäude** *n* system of thought; (*Philosophie*) philosophy; ~**gut** *n; nur Sg.: christliches/faschistisches etc.* ~ Christian/ Fascist *etc.* thought; ~**lesen** *n* mind-reading; ~**leser** *m,* ~**leserin** *f* mind-reader

gedankenlos I. *Adj.* (*unüberlegt*) thoughtless; (*rücksichtslos*) *auch* inconsiderate; (*mechanisch*) mechanical; (*zerstreut*) absent-minded; **II.** *Adv.* → I; without thinking; **Gedankenlosigkeit** *f* **1.** *nur Sg.* thoughtlessness; **2.** *Handlung, Äußerung:* thoughtless act/remark; *so e-e* ~*!* what a thoughtless thing to do/say, how thoughtless (of her *etc.*)

Gedanken|reichtum *m; nur Sg.* wealth of ideas; ~**schnelle** *f: in* ~ (as) quick as a flash; ~**schritt** *m* step in a thought process

gedankenschwer *Adj. geistiges Erzeugnis:* deep, heavy; *Person:* weighed down with thoughts

Gedanken|sprung *m* mental leap; *das ist jetzt ein* ~ *von mir* to change the subject briefly, this has got nothing to do with what we're talking about, but ...; ~**stimme** *f Film, TV:* voice-over; ~**strich** *m* dash; ~**tiefe** *f; nur Sg.* profundity of thought; ~**übertragung** *f* telepathy

gedanken|verloren *Adj.* lost in thought; ~**voll** *Adj.* pensive

gedanklich I. *Adj. attr.* intellectual; ~*er Fehler* an error in (one's *od. s.o.'s*) reasoning, logical error; ~*e Tiefe* intellectual profundity, profundity of thought; **II.** *Adv.* intellectually; ~ *verarbeiten* (mentally) digest

Gedärm *n; -(e)s, -e, mst Pl.* intestines

Pl.; *Zool.* entrails *Pl.*

Gedeck *n*; *-(e)s*, *-e* **1.** cover; *ein ~ auflegen* set a place; *zwei ~e auflegen* set the table for two; **2.** (*Menü*) set meal, fixed menu; **3.** *Preis*: cover charge

gedeckt I. *P.P.* → *decken*; **II.** *Adj.* covered (*auch Scheck, durch Versicherung etc.*); *Tisch*: laid, set; *Sport, Spieler*: marked, *bes. Am.* covered; *Farben*: subdued; *~er Apfelkuchen* apple pie

gedehnt I. *P.P.* → *dehnen*; **II.** *Adj.*: *~e Sprechweise* drawl; **III.** *Adv.*: *~ sprechen* speak with a drawl, drawl (one's words)

Gedeih *m*: *auf ~ und Verderb* come what may; *j-m auf ~ und Verderb ausgeliefert sein* be completely at s.o.'s mercy

gedeihen *v/i.*: *gedeiht, gedieh, ist gediehen* **1.** *Pflanzen, Kinder etc.*: thrive; (*wachsen*) grow; (*blühen*) flourish; (*überleben*) survive; **2.** *fig. Geschäft, Kunst etc.*: flourish, prosper, thrive; (*vorankommen*) progress (well), get on (well); *die Sache ist nun so weit gediehen, dass ...* the matter has now reached a point where ...; *wie weit bist du gediehen?* *umg.* how far have you got?; **3.** *lit.* turn out; *es gedieh ihr zum Vorteil* it turned out well (*od.* advantageously) for her

Gedeihen *n*; *-s, kein Pl.* prosperity; (*Erfolg*) success

gedeihlich *Adj. geh. Zusammenarbeit*: (*angenehm*) rewarding; (*vorteilhaft*) advantageous, beneficial; (*erfolgreich*) successful

Gedenkausgabe *f* commemorative issue

gedenken; *gedenkt, gedachte, hat gedacht* **I.** *v/i.*: ~ (+ *Gen.*) think of; (*sich erinnern*) remember, recollect; (*bedenken*) bear in mind; (*erwähnen*) mention; (*feiern*) commemorate; *e-r Sache nicht ~* pass s.th. over in silence; **II.** *v/t.*: ~ *zu tun* think of doing, intend (*od.* propose) to do; *was gedenkst du zu tun?* *bes. iro.* what do you propose to do (about it)?

Gedenken *n*; *-s, kein Pl.* memory; *zum ~ an* (+ *Akk.*) in memory (*od.* remembrance) of

Gedenk\|feier *f* commemoration (ceremony); *~gottesdienst* *m* memorial service; *~minute* *f* a minute's silence (*für* in memory of); → *einlegen* 3; *~münze* *f* commemorative coin; *~rede* *f* commemorative address; *~säule* *f* commemorative column; *~stätte* *f* memorial (site); *~stein* *m* memorial (stone); *~stunde* *f* hour of remembrance; *~tafel* *f* commemorative plaque; *~tag* *m* day of remembrance; *~veranstaltung* *f* commemoration (ceremony)

gedeucht *P.P.* → *dünken*

Gedicht *n*; *-(e)s*, *-e* poem; *~e auch* poetry *Sg.*; *das Kleid etc. ist ein ~* *umg. fig.* the dress etc. is pure poetry; *noch ein ~!* *umg. hum.* here's another!; *~band* *m* book of poems (*od.* poetry); *~form* *f* poetic form; *in ~* in verse; *~sammlung* *f* collection of poems; *in Auswahl*: anthology; *~zyklus* *m* cycle of poems

gediegen *Adj.* **1.** *Gold etc.*: pure; (*massiv*) solid; **2.** *Ware*: good-quality ...; (*geschmackvoll*) tasteful; *e-e ~e Arbeit* a solid piece of work (*auch fig.*); *ihre Einrichtung ist ~* her place has got class; **3.** *fig.* solid; *Wissen*: sound; *Mensch*: worthy, upright; **4.** *umg.* (*komisch*) funny; (*seltsam*) *auch* strange;

Gediegenheit *f*; *nur Sg.* **1.** *von Gold etc.*: purity; (*Massivität*) solidity; **2.** *von Waren*: quality; **3.** *fig.* solidity; *j-s Wissens*: soundness; *e-s Menschens*: worthiness, uprightness

gedieh *Imperf.*, **gediehen** *P.P.* → *gedeihen*

Gedöns *n*; *-es*, *kein Pl.*; *umg. pej.* fuss; *mach doch nicht so'n ~!* don't make such a fuss (*od.* hue and cry) about it

gedopt *Sport* **I.** *P.P.* → *dopen*; **II.** *Adj.* *die ~en Schwimmer wurden disqualifiziert* the swimmers who had taken drugs were disqualified

Gedränge *n*; *-s, kein Pl.* **1.** *Vorgang*: pushing (and shoving); **2.** (*Menge*) crowd, crush *umg.*; (*Ansturm*) rush (*nach, um* for); **3.** *fig.*: *ins ~ kommen* get into a (mad) rush; *damit wir nicht ins ~ kommen* so that we don't have to rush things (*od.* don't get pushed for time); **4.** *Rugby*: scrummage

Gedrängel *n*; *-s, kein Pl.*; *umg.* pushing (and shoving); *lass doch das ~!* stop pushing, will you?

gedrängt I. *P.P.* → *drängen*; **II.** *Adj.* **1.** (*dicht*) ~ crowded, packed; **2.** *Stil etc.*: concise, compact, terse; *~e Übersicht* condensed summary, quick rundown *umg.*; **III.** *Adv.* *schreiben etc.*: concisely, tersely, in a concise (*od.* terse) style; *~ voll* (*umg.* jam) packed

Gedröhn(e) *n*; *-s, kein Pl.*; *umg.* droning; *lauter*: roaring

gedroschen *P.P.* → *dreschen*

gedruckt I. *P.P.* → *drucken*; **II.** *Adj.*: *fett/klein ~* in bold / in lower case; *~e Schaltung* *Etron.* printed circuit; *lügen wie ~* *umg.* lie through one's teeth

gedrückt I. *P.P.* → *drücken*; **II.** *Adj.* depressed (*auch Wirts. Kurse, Preise*); *in ~er Stimmung sein* feel depressed, be down in the dumps *umg.*

gedrungen I. *P.P.* → *dringen*; **II.** *Adj.* *Gestalt*: stocky, thickset

geduckt I. *P.P.* → *ducken*; **II.** *Adj.* **1.** *Haltung*: crouched; *Kopf*: bowed, lowered; *ängstlich ~* cowering anxiously; *zum Sprung ~* crouched ready to spring; *in ~er Haltung* crouching; **2.** *fig. Person*: squat; *Häuschen, Hütte etc.*: low; **III.** *Adv.*: *~ sitzen od. hocken* crouch

Gedudel *n*; *-s, kein Pl.*; *umg. pej.* tootling; *im Radio etc.*: racket

Geduld *f*; *-, kein Pl.* patience; (*Ausdauer*) perseverance; (*nur*) *~!* patience, be patient, don't get impatient; *~ haben mit* be patient with; *die ~ verlieren* lose (one's) patience; *sich in ~ fassen* have patience; *j-s ~ auf die Probe stellen* try s.o.'s patience; *er war mit s-r ~ am Ende* his patience was exhausted (*od.* at an end), he couldn't stand it any longer; *mit ~ und Spucke* *umg. fig.* if you wait long enough

gedulden *v/refl.* be patient; *wenn Sie sich noch ein wenig ~ würden* if you wouldn't mind waiting a moment; *geduldig* *Adj.* patient; *~ wie ein Lamm* (*nachgiebig*) meek as a lamb

Gedulds\|arbeit *f*: *das ist reine ~* it takes a lot of patience, you need a lot of patience to do that; *~faden* *m umg.*: *mir riss der ~* I lost my patience; *~probe* *f* test of one's patience; *j-n auf e-e harte ~ stellen* (really) put s.o.'s patience to the test, try s.o.'s patience hard; *~spiel* *n* puzzle; *fig. auch* test of (one's *od.* s.o.'s) patience

gedungen I. *P.P.* → *dingen*; **II.** *Adj.* *Mörder etc.*: hired

gedunsen *Adj.* bloated

gedurft *P.P.* → *dürfen*

geehrt I. *P.P.* → *ehren*; **II.** *Adj.* hono(u)red; *hoch ~* highly esteemed; *in Briefen*: *Sehr ~er Herr N.* Dear Mr(.) N; *Sehr ~e Herren* Dear Sirs; *Sehr ~e Damen und Herren* Dear Sir or Madam, Dear Sir/Madam

geeicht I. *P.P.* → *eichen¹*; **II.** *Adj. fig.*: *darauf ist er ~* he's an expert on that kind of thing, it's right up his street *umg.*

geeignet I. *P.P.* → *eignen*; **II.** *Adj.* **1.** suitable (*für, zu* for); (*passend*) right (for); (*befähigt*) qualified; *körperlich etc.*: fit; *~e Schritte* appropriate action *Sg.*; *gut ~* just right; *er ist nicht dafür ~* he's not the right man (for it); *im ~en Augenblick* at the right moment; *sie ist als od. zur Lehrerin nicht ~* she wasn't cut out to be a teacher; **2.** *das ist* (*eher*) *~, die Kunden abzuschrecken* that's (more) likely to drive customers away

geeist *Adj. Melone, Tee etc.*: iced

Geest *f*, *-, kein Pl.*; *Geog.* geest (North German coastal heathland)

gefächert I. *P.P.* → *fächern*; **II.** *Adj.*: *breit ~ Angebot etc.*: wide-ranging

Gefahr *f*, *-, -en* danger (*für* for, to); hazard; (*Bedrohung*) *auch* threat; (*Risiko*) risk, hazard; *~ für die Gesundheit* health hazard; *es ist ~ im Verzug* *Jur.* there is imminent danger; *weitS.* there is danger ahead; *die gelbe/rote ~ hist. Pol.* the yellow/red peril; *auf eigene ~* at one's own risk, on one's own responsibility; *auf die ~ hin, dass* (*od.* *zu* (+ *Inf.*) at the risk of (+ *Ger.*); *außer ~* out of danger, out of the wood(s) *umg.*; *bei ~* in *od.* (in case of) emergency; *~ bringend* dangerous; *in ~ bringen* → *gefährden*; *sich in ~ begeben* take a risk; *in ~ sein od.* *schweben zu* (+ *Inf.*) be in danger of (+ *Ger.*); *~ laufen zu* (+ *Inf.*) *auch* run the risk of (+ *Ger.*), be liable to (+ *Inf.*); *der ~ aussetzen* expose to danger; *ohne ~* safely; *es besteht keine ~* there's no danger, it's perfectly safe; *mit ~ verbunden sein* involve a certain risk; *unter ~ für Leib und Leben* risking life and limb

gefährden *v/t.* endanger; *Sache*: *auch* threaten; (*in Frage stellen*) jeopardize; (*aufs Spiel setzen*) risk, put at risk; (*Ruf, Stellung*) compromise; *j-s Leben ~* put s.o.'s life at risk; *gefährdet I.* *P.P.* → *gefährden*; **II.** *Adj.* endangered; *stärker*: imperil(l)ed; *präd. und nachgestellt*: *auch* at risk; *Jugend etc.*: *nachgestellt*: at risk, in danger; *am meisten ~ sein Personen*: run the greatest risk; *auch Bäume etc.*: be in greatest danger, be particularly at risk; *Versetzung od. Vorrücken ~ Schule*: in danger of being kept down (*Am.* held back); *Gefährdung* *f Vorgang*: endangering *etc.*; → *gefährden*; (*Gefahr*) danger, threat, menace (+ *Gen.* to)

gefahren *P.P.* → *fahren*

Gefahren\|abwehr *f* protective measures *Pl.*; *~bereich* *m* danger zone; *~moment* *n* hazard; *~potenzial* *n* potential danger; *~punkt* *m* **1.** → *Gefahrenquelle* 2; **2.** *fig.* critical point; *~quelle* *f* **1.** *Ursache*: safety hazard; **2.** *Ort, Stelle*: danger spot, (accident) black spot; *~zone* *f* danger zone; *~zulage* *f* danger money, *Am.* hardship allowance, combat pay *umg.*

gefährlich *Adj.* dangerous; (*gewagt*) risky; (*ernst*) critical, grave, serious;

(*unsicher*) unsafe; **sie kommt in ein ~es Alter** she's getting to a tricky age; **der könnte mir ~ werden** *umg.* I'll have to watch myself with him; **Gefährlichkeit** f; *nur Sg.* danger; (*Ernst*) seriousness, gravity

gefahrlos *Adj.* not dangerous; (*sicher*) safe; (*harmlos*) harmless; **es ist ~ auch** there's no danger

Gefahrstoff m *Jur.* hazardous substance

Gefährt n; -(e)s, -e; *geh.* vehicle; → *auch* **Fuhrwerk**

Gefährte m; -n, -n, **Gefährtin** f; -, -nen companion; → *auch* **Lebensgefährte, Kamerad**

gefahrvoll *Adj.* dangerous

Gefälle n; -s, - 1. *von Land:* slope, incline; *von Fluss etc.:* drop, fall; (*Neigungswinkel*) gradient, *bes. Am.* grade; **zehnprozentiges ~** one-in-ten (*od.* ten-per-cent) gradient, gradient of one in ten, *Am.* ten percent grade; **ein starkes ~ haben** slope (down) steeply, drop sharply; 2. *Math., Etech.* gradient; 3. *fig.* (*Unterschied*) differential(s *Pl.*) (**zwischen** between); **das wirtschaftliche ~ zwischen Norden und Süden** the economic divide between north and south

Gefallen[1] m; -s, - favour, *Am.* favor; **j-n um e-n ~ bitten** ask a favo(u)r of s.o.; **tu mir den ~ und ... do me a favo(u)r and ...(, will you?)**

Gefallen[2] n; -s, *kein Pl.* pleasure; **~ finden an e-r Sache:** enjoy; *an j-m:* like; **~ daran finden zu** (+ *Inf.*) enjoy (+ *Ger.*), take pleasure in (+ *Ger.*) *förm.*; **ich finde kein ~ daran** I don't enjoy it, I don't get anything out of it; **mir zu ~** for my sake, for me, to please me

gefallen[1] v/i.; *gefällt, gefiel, hat gefallen* 1. **j-m ~** please s.o.; **es gefällt mir** I like it; **es gefällt mir sehr gut** I really like it, I like it a lot; **er gefiel mir auf den ersten Blick** I took to him straightaway; **was mir daran gefällt** what I like about it; **solche Filme ~ der Masse** films like that appeal to the masses; **er gefällt mir nicht** (*sieht krank aus*) I don't like the look of him; **das will mir gar nicht ~** I don't like (the look of) that at all; **hat dir das Konzert ~?** did you enjoy the concert?; **wie gefällt es Ihnen in X?** how do you like (it in) X?; **tu, was dir gefällt** please yourself; **erlaubt ist, was gefällt** anything goes; 2. **sich** (*Dat.*) **etw. ~ lassen** (*hinnehmen*) put up with s.th.; (*erlauben*) approve s.th.; (*mögen*) like (*od.* enjoy) s.th.; **das brauche ich mir nicht ~ zu lassen!** I don't have to put up with that!; **er lässt sich alles/nichts ~** he lets people walk all over him / he won't let you get away with anything; **du lässt dir zu viel ~** you're too easy-going; **sie ließ es sich gerne ~, dass er sie streichelte** she was quite happy to let him fondle her; **das lasse ich mir ~!** that's what I like!; **das lasse ich mir schon eher ~!** now you're talking! *umg.*; 3. **sich ~ in** (+ *Dat.*) enjoy (+ *Ger.*); *stärker:* take great pleasure in (+ *Ger.*); **er gefällt sich in der Rolle des Märtyrers** etc. he likes to play *od.* act the martyr *etc.*; **er gefällt sich in der Rolle des Frauenhelden** etc. *auch* he fancies himself as a ladies' man *etc.*

gefallen[2] I. *P.P.* → **fallen**, **gefallen**[1]; II. *Adj.* 1. **frisch ~er Schnee** fresh snowfall; 2. *Mil., Soldat:* killed in action, fallen; *Festung, Stadt:* fallen;

3. *fig. Engel, Mädchen:* fallen; **e-e ~e Größe** *od.* **ein ~er Gott** *etc.* a has-been; **Gefallene** m; -n, -n; *Mil.* soldier killed in the war; **die ~n** the (war) dead *Pl.*, the fallen *Pl.*

Gefallenen|denkmal n war memorial; **~friedhof** m war cemetery

gefällig *Adj.* 1. (*ansprechend*) pleasant, pleasing, agreeable; *Wein:* palatable, pleasing; 2. (*verbindlich*) obliging, complaisant; (*zuvorkommend*) kind; **j-m ~ sein** oblige s.o., help s.o.; **sich j-m ~ zeigen** help s.o. (out), do s.o. a favo(u)r; 3. *präd.;* (*erwünscht*): **etwas zu trinken ~?** would you like something to drink?; **sonst noch was ~?** *iro.* anything else (while I'm at it)?; **wenn's ~ ist** *iro.* if you don't mind, of course; 4. *Wirts.* kind; **zur ~en Beachtung** for your kind attention; → **gefälligst, Gefälligkeit** f obligingness; *konkret:* favo(u)r; → **Gefallen**[1]

Gefälligkeits|... *Fin., Wirts.* accommodation; **~gutachten** n favo(u)rably slanted report

gefälligst *Adv.* 1. *iro.:* if you don't mind; **sei ~ still!** be quiet, will you!; **hör ~ zu!** will you listen to me?; 2. (*freundlicherweise*) kindly

gefaltet I. *P.P.* → **falten**; II. *Adj.:* **mit ~en Händen** (with) hands folded

gefangen I. *P.P.* → **fangen**; II. *Adj.* 1. caught; *Mil.* captive; (*eingekerkert*) imprisoned, in prison; **sich ~ geben** (*od.* **nehmen lassen**) surrender; **~ halten** keep (*od.* hold) s.o. prisoner, keep s.o. imprisoned; **ein Tier ~ halten** keep an animal locked up; *im Zoo etc.:* hold an animal captive; **~ nehmen** arrest; *Mil.* capture, take s.o. prisoner; **~ setzen** put s.o. in prison, imprison; 2. *fig.* captivated (**von** by); **~ halten** hold s.o. under one's spell; *Sache:* have s.o. spellbound; **~ nehmen** captivate, enthral(l); **Gefangene** m, f; -n, -n prisoner; (*Sträfling*) convict

Gefangenen|austausch m exchange of prisoners (of war); **~hilfsorganisation** f prisoners' aid society (*od.* organization); **~lager** n prison camp; *Mil.* prisoner-of-war (*Abk.* POW) camp; **~revolte** f prison riot

Gefangennahme f; -, *kein Pl.* arrest; *Mil.* capture

Gefangenschaft f imprisonment; *Mil. und Tiere:* captivity; **in ~ geraten** be taken prisoner, be captured; **in ~ sein** im Krieg: be a prisoner-of-war

Gefängnis n; -ses, -se 1. prison, jail, *Brit. auch* gaol, *Am.* penitentiary *fachspr.;* **ins ~ kommen** be sent (*of.* go) to prison; **ins ~ stecken** *umg.* put s.o. in prison, lock s.o. up; 2. *Jur.* (*Strafe*) (term of) imprisonment; **fünf Jahre ~ bekommen** get five years in prison, get five years' imprisonment; **mit ~ bestraft werden** *Vergehen:* be punishable by imprisonment; *Person:* be sentenced to prison; → **Bein** 1; **~aufenthalt** m prison term; **~aufseher** m, **~aufseherin** f prison officer, *Am.* warden, guard; **~direktor** m, **~direktorin** f prison governor, *Am.* prison warden; **~geistliche** m prison chaplain; **~hof** m prison yard; **~insasse** m, **~insassin** f (prison) inmate; **~leitung** f prison management (team); **~mauer** f prison wall; **er verbrachte 30 Jahre seines Lebens hinter ~n** he spent 30 years of his life behind bars; **~strafe** f *Jur.* prison (*od.* custodial) sentence, term of imprisonment; **sie verbüßt gerade e-e 3-jährige ~** she is currently

serving a 3-year prison sentence; **~tor** n prison gate; **~verwaltung** f prison administration; **~wärter** m, **~wärterin** f prison officer, *Am.* warden, guard; **~zelle** f prison cell

gefärbt *Adj.* 1. *Haare:* dyed; *Glas etc.:* colo(u)red; *Lebensmittel:* artificially colo(u)red; **~e Lebensmittel** *auch* foods with artificial colo(u)ring; *blond* **~es Haar** hair dyed blond(e), bleach-blond hair; 2. *fig. Aussprache:* tinged (**mit** with); *Bericht etc.:* bias(s)ed; **s-e Aussprache ist** (*italienisch*) **~** he has an (Italian) accent; **das Parteiprogramm ist kommunistisch ~** the party manifesto has a communist bias

Gefasel n; -s, *kein Pl.;* *umg. pej.* drivel

Gefäß n; -es, -e 1. receptacle, container; (*Schale, Schüssel*) bowl; (*Topf*) jar; 2. *Anat., Bot. und bibl. fig.* vessel; **~chirurgie** f *Med.* vascular surgery

gefäßerweiternd *Adj. Med.* vasodilatory; **Gefäßerweiterung** f *Med.* vasodilation

gefasst I. *P.P.* → **fassen**; II. *Adj.* 1. (*ruhig, beherrscht*) calm, composed; 2. **~ sein auf** (+ *Akk.*) be prepared for; **sich ~ machen auf** (+ *Akk.*) prepare for, brace o.s. for; **er kann sich auf etwas ~ machen** *umg.* he's in for it now; **darauf kannst du dich ~ machen!** *umg.* you can bet your bottom dollar on that; 3. *Edelstein:* set (*od.* mounted) (**in** + *Dat.* in); 4. *Brief etc.:* **kurz/verständlich ~** brief/intelligible; III. *Adv.* calmly, with composure; **Gefasstheit** f; *nur Sg.* composure

gefäßverengend *Adj. Med.* vasoconstrictive; **Gefäßverengung** f *Med.* vasoconstriction

Gefäß|verkalkung f vascular calcification; **~verschluss** m *Med.* vascular obstruction, embolism; **~wand** f *Anat.* vascular wall

Gefecht n; -(e)s, -e 1. fight; (*Scharmützel*) skirmish; (*Schlacht*) battle; (*Einsatz*) action; **außer ~ setzen** put out of action (*auch fig.*); (*Kanonen*) *auch* silence; **letztes ~** last-ditch stand; **klar zum ~!** *Naut.* clear for action!; 2. *fig.* conflict; *Argumente etc.* **ins ~ führen** advance; → **Hitze**

gefechts|bereit *Adj. Mil.* ready for combat (*od.* action); **~klar** *Adj. Naut.* cleared for action; **ein Schiff ~ machen** clear a ship for action

Gefechts|kopf m *Mil.:* **nuklearer ~** nuclear warhead; **~stand** m *Mil.* command post

gefedert I. *P.P.* → **federn**; II. *Adj.:* **gut/schlecht ~** *Sessel, Auto:* well/badly sprung; *Auto: auch* having a good/bad suspension

gefehlt I. *P.P.* → **fehlen**; II. *Adj. schw.* (*misslungen*) unsuccessful

gefeiert I. *P.P.* → **feiern**; II. *Adj. Künstler etc.:* (highly) acclaimed, renowned, celebrated

Gefeilsche n; -s, *kein Pl.;* *pej.* haggling

gefeit *Adj.:* **~ gegen** immune to, safe from

gefertigt I. *P.P.* → **fertigen**; II. *Adj.:* **von Hand / industriell ~** hand-made / manufactured

gefesselt I. *P.P.* → **fesseln**; II. *Adj. fig.:* **~ und geknebelt** bound and gagged; **ans Bett ~** *fig.* confined to one's bed, bedridden; **ans Haus ~** house-bound; **an den Rollstuhl ~** wheelchair-bound

gefestigt I. *P.P.* → **festigen**; II. *Adj. Charakter, Position etc.:* stable, firm; **in sich** (*Dat.*) **~ sein** be sure of oneself

Gefieder *n*; *-s*, *-* plumage, feathers *Pl.*; **gefiedert** *Adj.* feathered, feathery; **unsere** *~***en Freunde** our feathered friends

gefiel *Imperf.* → **gefallen**[1]

Gefilde *n*; *-s*, *-*; *geh.* **1.** fields *Pl.*; *hei-matliche* ~ home ground *Sg.*; *die* ~ *der Seligen* the Elysian Fields; **2.** *fig.* realm; *in höheren* ~*n schweben iro.* be up in the clouds

Geflecht *n*; *-(e)s*, *-e* **1.** *aus Weiden*: wickerwork; *aus Garn etc.*: netting; *aus Draht etc.*: auch mesh; *(Gewebe)* weave; **2.** *Anat., von Nerven*: plexus; **3.** *fig. von Lügen etc.*: mesh

gefleckt I. *P.P.* → **flecken**; **II.** *Adj.* spotted; *(gesprenkelt)* speckled; *(marmoriert)* mottled

geflissentlich I. *Adj.* intentional, deliberate; **II.** *Adv.* intentionally, deliberately, studiously; *sie übersah ihn* ~ she deliberately overlooked him

geflochten *P.P.* → **flechten**

geflogen *P.P.* → **fliegen**

geflohen *P.P.* → **fliehen**

geflossen *P.P.* → **fließen**

Geflügel *n*; *-s*, *kein Pl.* poultry *Sg.*; *als Gang*: fowl; *~***cremesuppe** *f* cream of chicken *(od.* turkey *etc.)* soup; *~***farm** *f* poultry farm, chicken *(od.* turkey *etc.)* farm; *~***leber** *f* chicken *(od.* turkey *etc.)* liver *(als Pl.)*; *~***salat** *m* chicken *(od.* turkey *etc.)* salad; *~***schere** *f*: *(e-e)* ~ (a pair of) poultry shears *Pl.*

geflügelt *Adj.* winged; *Ameisen auch* flying; *~***es Wort** *fig.* saying

Geflügelzucht *f* poultry farming, chicken *(od.* turkey *etc.)* farming

Geflüster *n*; *-s*, *kein Pl.* whispering

gefochten *P.P.* → **fechten**

Gefolge *n*; *-s*, *-* **1.** entourage; *(Bediens-tete)* attendants *Pl.*; *(Begleiter)* escort; *(Trauerzug)* cortège, mourners *Pl.*; **2.** *fig.*: *im* ~ *von (od. + Gen.)* in the wake of; *etw. im* ~ *haben* bring s.th. in its wake

Gefolgschaft *f* **1.** *Personen*: *bes. Pol.* followers *Pl.*, following, adherents *Pl.*; *hist.* vassals *Pl.*; **2.** *j-m* ~ *leisten* show one's allegiance to s.o.; *j-m die* ~ *ver-weigern* refuse to be led by s.o., reject s.o. as a leader; *j-m die* ~ *aufkündigen* dissociate o.s. from s.o.

Gefolgsmann *m*; *Pl.* **-männer und -leu-te 1.** *hist.* vassal; **2.** *Pol. etc.* follower, supporter; *pej.* acolyte, henchman, lackey

gefragt I. *P.P.* → **fragen**; **II.** *Adj.* in demand; *nicht mehr* ~ *sein auch* have fallen out of favo(u)r; *ein* ~*er Mann auch* a popular man; *Mut ist nicht* ~ courage is not much in demand *(od.* appreciated)

gefräßig *Adj.* greedy; *bes. Tier*: voracious; **Gefräßigkeit** *f*; *nur Sg.* greediness; *bes. von Tier*: voracity

Gefreite *m*; *-n*, *-n*; *Mil. Heer*: lance corporal, *Am.* private 1st class (Pfc.); *Luftwaffe*: aircraftman 1st class, *Am.* airman 3rd class; *Marine*: able seaman, *Am.* seaman

gefressen *P.P.* → **fressen**

Gefrett *n*; *-s*, *kein Pl.*; *südd., österr.* trouble

gefreut I. *P.P.* → **freuen**; **II.** *Adj. schw.* **1.** *Sache*: pleasant, good; **2.** *Person*: lik(e)able, nice

Gefrier|beutel *m* freezer bag; *~***brand** *m*; *nur Sg.* freezer burn; *~***dose** *f* freezer box

gefrieren *v/i.* gefriert, gefror, ist gefro-ren: ~ *(lassen)* freeze; *j-m gefriert das Blut in den Adern / das Lächeln auf*

den Lippen fig. the blood freezes in s.o.'s veins / the smile freezes on s.o.'s lips

Gefrier|fach *n* freezer, freezing compartment; *~***fleisch** *n* frozen meat

gefriergetrocknet *Adj.* freeze-dried

Gefrier|gut *n*, *~***kost** *f* frozen food(s *Pl.*); *~***punkt** *m*: *(auf dem)* ~ (at) freezing point; *unter dem* ~ below zero, *bes. Am.* below freezing (point); *auf den* ~ *sinken* drop to zero *(Am.* freezing); *~***raum** *m* cold room; *~***schrank** *m* (upright) freezer; *~***schutzmittel** *n* anti(-)freeze; *~***truhe** *f* deep-freeze, (chest) freezer

gefroren I. *P.P.* → **frieren**, **gefrieren**; **II.** *Adj.*: *hart/steif* ~ frozen hard/stiff; **Gefrorene** *n*; *-n*, *kein Pl.*; *österr.* ice cream

Gefüge *n*; *-s*, *-*. **1.** *(Gebautes)* structure; **2.** *(Aufbau)* structure, make-up; *fig. wirtschaftlich, gesellschaftlich*: fabric, system; *syntaktisches* ~ *Ling.* syntactic structure

gefügig *Adj. pej.* compliant, docile; *stärker*: submissive; *(sich [Dat]) j-n* ~ *machen* bring s.o. to heel, make sure s.o. toes the line; **Gefügigkeit** *f*; *nur Sg.* compliance, docility; *stärker*: submissiveness

Gefühl *n*; *-s*, *-e* **1.** *nur Sg.*; *körperlich*: feeling; *(Wahrnehmung)* sensation; *(Tastsinn)* touch; *weitS.* feel; ~ *der* ~ *von Kälte* cold sensation; *ich hab kein* ~ *im Arm* I can't feel anything in my arm, my arm's gone numb *(od.* dead); *dem* ~ *nach ist es Plastik* judging by the feel it's plastic; **2.** *psychisch*: feeling, sense; *bes. kurze Wahrnehmung*: sensation; *emotional*: sentiment, emotion; *ein beängstigendes* ~ a worrying feeling; *widerstreitende* ~*e* conflicting feelings; *ich habe dabei ein ungutes* ~ I've got a funny feeling about it; *e-r Sache mit gemischten* ~*en gegen-überstehen* have mixed feelings about s.th.; *mit viel* ~ *singen* sing with great feeling *(od.* emotion); *für mein* ~ *od. m-m* ~ *nach* my feeling is that; *I wish (that)*; *von s-n* ~*en überwältigt* overcome with emotion; *s-e* ~*e zur Schau tragen* wear one's heart on one's sleeve; *das ist das höchste der* ~*e umg. (ist das Äußerste)* that's the (absolute) limit; **3.** *e-r Person gegenüber*: feeling; *freundliche* ~*e für j-n hegen* feel friendly toward(s) s.o.; *j-s* ~*e erwi-dern* return s.o.'s feelings *(od.* affection); *sich über s-e* ~*e klar werden* be(come) clear about how one feels; **4.** *(Ahnung)* feeling; *(Vorahnung)* presentiment; *das (dumpfe)* ~ *haben, dass od. als ob ...* have a (vague) feeling that ...; **5.** *(Gespür)* sense *(für* of); *(Instinkt)* instinct, intuition, feel(ing); *(besondere Begabung)* flair; ~ *für An-stand* sense of propriety; *nach* ~ *Zuta-ten dosieren* by guess and by God, by rule of thumb; *das muss man mit* ~ *machen* you've got to have the right touch; *etw. im* ~ *haben* have a feeling *(od.* instinct) for s.th.; *(ahnen, wissen)* feel it in one's bones

gefühllos *Adj.* **1.** *Gliedmaßen etc.*: numb; *gegen Schmerzen*: insensitive, insensible *(gegen* to); **2.** *fig. (harther-zig)* unfeeling, callous, heartless; **Ge-fühllosigkeit** *f* **1.** *nur Sg.* numbness; **2.** *nur Sg.*; *fig.* heartlessness; **3.** *fig. Handlung*: cruelty

Gefühlsanwandlung *f* fit of emotion; *in e-r* ~ *auch* suddenly overcome with emotion

gefühlsarm *Adj.* unemotional, cold; *er ist* ~ he's got no feelings; **Gefühlsar-mut** *f* lack of feeling, coldness

Gefühls|ausbruch *m* (emotional) outburst; *~***äußerung** *f* expression of one's feelings

gefühls|bedingt *Adj.* emotional; *~***be-tont** *Adj.* emotional

Gefühlsduselei *f*; *-*, *-en*; *umg. pej.* (sloppy) sentimentality; **gefühlsduse-lig** *Adj. umg. pej.* sentimental, mawk-ish, sloppy

gefühls|echt *Adj. Kondom etc.*: ultra-sensitive; *~***geladen** *Adj.* (very) emo-tional, emotionally charged; *Wort etc.*: *auch* emotive

gefühlskalt *Adj.* (emotionally) cold; **Gefühlskälte** *f* frigidity

Gefühlsleben *n* emotional life

gefühlsmäßig I. *Adj.* emotional; *weitS.* intuitive, instinctive; **II.** *Adv.* emotion-ally *etc.*; *(instinktiv)* by instinct

Gefühls|mensch *m* emotional person; *~***nerv** *m* sensory nerve; *~***regung** *f* emotion; *keine* ~ *zeigen* show no trace of emotion, show no emotion at all; *~***rohheit** *f*; *nur Sg.* hard-heartedness; *~***sache** *f*: *das ist* ~ it's a matter of feeling; *~***stark** *Adj.* very emotional; *~***stau** *m* emotional block; *~***tiefe** *f* emotional depth; *~***überschwang** *m* flood of emotion; *~***umschwung** *m* emotional about-turn; *~***wallung** *f* wave of emotion; *~***welt** *f* emotional world, world of feeling(s); *~***wert** *m* emotional value; *e-s Gegenstands*: sen-timental value

gefühlvoll I. *Adj.* full of feeling; *(emp-findsam)* sensitive; *(zärtlich)* tender; *(gefühlsbetont)* emotional; *(rührselig)* sentimental; **II.** *Adv.* feelingly *etc.*; *sin-gen etc.*: with feeling; *umg. (vorsichtig)* gently

gefuhrig *Adj. südd., österr. Schnee*: good for skiing

geführt I. *P.P.* → **führen**; **II.** *Adj.*: *ein gut* ~*es Hotel* a well-run hotel; *~e Tour* guided tour *(Wanderung: auch* walk)

gefüllt I. *P.P.* → **füllen**; **II.** *Adj.* **1.** filled *(mit* with); *(voll)* full; *~e Tomaten etc.* stuffed tomatoes *etc.*; *~e Bonbons/ Pralinen* sweets/chocolates with soft centres, *Am.* candies/chocolates with soft centers; *gut* ~*e Geldbörse* bulging purse; **2.** *Bot. (Ggs. einfach) Blüten, Dahlien etc.*: double

gefunden I. *P.P.* → **finden**; **II.** *Adj.* → **Fressen**

gefürchtet I. *P.P.* → **fürchten**; **II.** *Adj.* feared, dreaded

gegabelt I. *P.P.* → **gabeln**; **II.** *Adj.*: *ein* ~*er Ast* a forked branch

Gegacker *n*; *-s*, *kein Pl.* **1.** *von Hüh-nern*: clucking; **2.** *umg. fig. von Mäd-chen*: cackling

gegangen *P.P.* → **gehen**

gegeben I. *P.P.* → **geben**; **II.** *Adj.* **1.** *(bekannt, vorhanden)* given; *~e Grö-ße Math.* given quantity; *wenn wir es als* ~ *voraussetzen, dass ...* taking (it) for granted that ...; *aus* ~*em An-lass weisen wir darauf hin, dass ...* for certain reasons (not specified here) we would point out that ..., there are certain reasons why we must point out that ...; *unter den* ~*en Um-ständen/Voraussetzungen* under the circumstances / under these condi-tions; **2.** *(passend)* appropriate, prop-er; *die* ~*e Methode* the correct meth-od; *im* ~*en Fall potenziell*: should the situation arise; *zu* ~*er Zeit (gegebenen-falls)* when the occasion arises; *(ir-*

G

gendwann) at some future time; *das ist das Gegebene* it's the obvious thing; **3.** *Fähigkeit:* **es ist mir nicht ~, mich zu verstellen** I am incapable of hiding my true feelings; **gegebenenfalls** *Adv.* should the occasion arise; (*notfalls*) if necessary; *auf Formularen:* if applicable; **Gegebenheit** *f* given fact; **~en** (*Zustände*) circumstances; (*Tatsachen*) reality *Sg.*

gegen I. *Präp.* (+ *Akk.*) **1.** *räumlich:* (*an*) against; **~ die Wand lehnen/stoßen** lean against / bump into the wall; **~ die Tür klopfen** knock at the door; **etw. ~ das Licht halten** hold s.th. up to the light; **2.** *in Richtung nach:* towards, *bes. Am.* toward; **~ Osten** eastward; **sich ~ die Wand drehen** turn to face the wall; **3.** *in entgegengesetzte Richtung:* against; **~ die Strömung rudern** row against the current; **~ den Strom schwimmen** *fig.* swim against the tide; **4.** *zeitlich:* **~ zehn (Uhr)** around (*od.* about) ten (o'clock); **~ Abend** (*zu od. hin*) toward(s) evening; **es ist ~ Ende nächster Woche fertig** it'll be ready toward(s) the end of next week; **5.** (*Ggs. für*) against; **etw. ~ Kopfschmerzen** something for a headache; **willst du nichts ~ s-e Frechheit tun?** aren't you going to do anything about his cheekiness?; **hast du was ~ mich?** have you got something against me?; **ich bin ~ den Vorschlag** I don't agree with the proposal; **6.** *Kampf, Spiel:* against; *Jur., Sport* versus (*Abk.* v.); **England spielt ~ Deutschland** England are (*bes. Am.* is) playing (against) Germany; **7.** (*entgegen, wider*) contrary to; **~ die Vernunft** *etc.* contrary to reason *etc.*; **~ j-s Befehl/Willen** *auch* against s.o.'s orders/will; **8.** (*gegenüber, zu*) freundlich, grausam *etc.*: to(ward[s]); *allergisch:* to; *streng:* with; **e-n Verdacht ~ j-n haben** be suspicious of s.o.; **9.** (*verglichen mit*) compared with; **das ist nichts ~ das, was ich gesehen habe** that's nothing to what I saw; **gestern fühle ich mich heute ganz gut** I feel quite well today compared to yesterday; **10.** (*im Austausch für*) in return for; **~ bar** for cash; **~ Bezahlung** for money (*od.* payment); **~ Quittung** against (*od.* in return for a) receipt; **A ~ B eintauschen** *od.* **auswechseln** exchange A for B, replace B by A; **ich wette zehn ~ eins** I('ll) bet you ten to one; **II.** *Adv.* (*ungefähr*) about, around; (*fast*) nearly

Gegen... *im Subst., als Reaktion:* counter...; **~angebot** counteroffer; **~anspruch** counterclaim; **~demonstration** counterdemonstration

Gegen|angebot *n* counteroffer; **~angriff** *m auch fig.* counterattack; **e-n ~ führen gegen** counterattack *s.o.*; **zum ~ übergehen** counterattack; **~ansicht** *f* opposing view; **~anzeige** *f Med.* contraindication; **~argument** *n* counterargument; **~behauptung** *f* counterclaim; **~beispiel** *n* example to prove (*od.* show) the opposite; **~besuch** *m* return visit; **j-m e-n ~ machen** return s.o.'s visit; **~beweis** *m* proof to the contrary; *Jur. auch* counterevidence; **den ~ antreten** provide evidence to the contrary; **den ~ antreten für** *od.* **zu etw.** provide evidence against s.th. (*od.* to counter s.th.); **~bitte** *f:* **ich habe e-e ~** could you do me a favo(u)r in return?; **~buchung** *f Wirts.* cross entry

Gegend *f; -, -en* **1.** (*Landschaft*) country(side); (*Gebiet*) area, region, part of the country; **in der ~ von München** (*nahebei*) near Munich; (*um ... herum*) around Munich, in the Munich area; **2.** *in e-r Stadt:* area, part of town; (*Nachbarschaft*) neighbo(u)rhood, vicinity; (*Umgebung*) surroundings *Pl.*, environs *Pl.*; **in unserer ~** in our area (*od.* neighbo[u]rhood), where we live; **üble ~** tough area (*od.* neighbo[u]rhood); **hier in der ~** around here, in this area, in these parts; **wenn Sie mal wieder in der ~ sind** if ever you happen to be in the area (*od.* neighbo[u]rhood) again; **außerhalb der Stadt:** if you ever happen to be in these parts (*od.* in this part of the country *etc.*) again; **die ~ unsicher machen** *umg.* terrorize the neighbo(u)rhood; **3.** (*Körpergegend*) region, area; **die ~ um den Blinddarm** (the area) around the appendix; **4.** *umg.:* **in der ~ herumwerfen** throw things everywhere (*od.* anywhere); **muss dein Zeug denn überall in der ~ herumliegen?** do you have to leave your things (lying) all over the place?; **wie läufst du denn wieder durch die ~?** what do you look like?; **5.** *umg. fig.:* **die ganze ~ kam** everyone (from miles around) came, the whole village *etc.* came; **es kostet 100 Euro oder so, ungefähr in dieser ~** it costs 100 euros or thereabouts (*od.* or something like that)

Gegen|darstellung *f* correction; (*Widerlegung*) refutation; *in der Zeitung:* reply; **s-e ~** his reply; **~dienst** *m* favo(u)r in return, return favo(u)r; **als ~ in return**; **j-m e-n ~ erweisen** return s.o.'s favo(u)r, do s.o. a favo(u)r in return, do s.th. for s.o. in return; **~druck** *m* **1.** counterpressure, back pressure; **2.** *fig.* resistance

gegeneinander I. *Adv.* **1.** *kämpfen, lehnen etc.:* against one another (*od.* each other); **~ halten** *od.* **stellen** put (*od.* place) side by side; (*vergleichen*) *auch* compare; **~ prallen** *od.* **stoßen** run (*od.* bump) into each other; *Dinge:* hit each other, collide; **2.** (*gegenseitig*) mutually; **3.** (*zueinander*) towards one another (*od.* each other); **freundlich ~ sein** be friendly toward(s) each other; **4.** *Gefangene/Reifen ~ austauschen* exchange prisoners / change tyres (*Am.* tires) over; **die Vor- und Nachteile ~ abwägen** weigh up the pros and cons (*od.* advantages and disadvantages); **II. Gegeneinander** *n; -s, kein Pl.* antagonism

Gegen|entwurf *m* alternative concept, counterconcept (*zu* to); **~fahrbahn** *f* opposite (*od.* oncoming) carriageway (*Am.* lane [*s Pl.*]); **~farbe** *f* complementary colo(u)r; **~feuer** *n:* **ein ~ legen** start a backfire; **~forderung** *f* counterdemand; *Jur. etc.* counterclaim; **~frage** *f:* **erlauben Sie mir e-e ~** if I may answer your question with another question, let me ask 'you something; **~fuge** *f Mus.* counterfugue; **~gerade** *f Sport* back straight, *bes. Am.* backstretch; **~geschenk** *n* present (given) in return; **j-m ein ~ machen** give s.o. a present in return; **~gewicht** *n auch fig.* counterweight; **ein ~ bilden** *od.* **darstellen zu** *fig.* act as a counterbalance to, counterbalance *s.th./s.o.*; **als ~ zu etw.** to balance s.th., to set s.th. off; **~gift** *n auch fig.* antidote (*gegen* to, against; *für* for); **~gutachten** *n* opposing opinion;

~kandidat *m,* **~kandidatin** *f* opponent, rival, rival (*od.* opposition) candidate; **ohne ~** unopposed, uncontested; **~klage** *f Jur.* cross action, *Am.* countersuit; **~ erheben** file a cross action (*gegen* against), *Am.* countersue (*s.o.*); **~kraft** *f* counteracting force (*auch fig.*); **~kurs** *m* opposite course (*auch fig.*); **auf ~ gehen** take the opposite course

gegenläufig *Adj.* **1.** *Tech.* moving in opposite direction(s); *rotierend:* counter-rotating; **2.** *fig.* opposite; **~e Tendenz** reversal; **~er Zyklus** anticyclic(al) pattern

Gegenleistung *f* return favo(u)r, quid pro quo; **als ~** in return (*für* for)

gegen|lenken *v/i.* (*trennb., hat -ge-*) → **gegensteuern**; **~lesen** *v/t.* (*unreg., trennb., hat -ge-*) check; **könntest du das bitte ~?** could you check this to see that I haven't missed anything?

Gegenlicht *n; nur Sg.* back light(ing); contre jour; **bei ~** against the light; **~aufnahme** *f* contre-jour shot

Gegen|liebe *f:* **er fand keine ~** his love remained unrequited; **sein Vorschlag stieß auf wenig ~** *fig.* his suggestion didn't go down particularly well; **~maßnahme** *f* countermeasure; *vorbeugende:* preventive measure; (*Vergeltung*) reprisal; **~n ergreifen** *od.* **treffen gegen** take steps against; **~mittel** *n auch fig.* remedy (*gegen* for); (*Gegengift*) antidote (*against*); **~papst** *m hist. kath.* antipope; **~partei** *f Jur.* opposing party, other side; *Pol.* opposition; *Sport* opponents *Pl.*; **die ~ ergreifen** take the other side; **~pol** *m* **1.** *Phys., Etech. etc.* opposite pole; **2.** *fig.* counterpart; (*Ausgleich*) counterbalance; **~probe** *f* cross-check; *Parl.* counter-verification; **die ~ machen** cross-check (*auf etw.* [*Akk.*] s.th.); **~propaganda** *f* counterpropaganda; **~rechnung** *f* **1.** (*Gegenprobe*) cross-checking; **ich muss erst die ~ machen** *fig.* I'll have to see what there is to lose; **j-m die ~ aufmachen** *fig.* counter s.o.'s arguments; **2.** *Wirts.* (*Gegenforderung*) counterclaim; *Buchhaltung:* set-off; **~reaktion** *f* counter-reaction; *heftige:* backlash; **~rede** *f* reply; (*Widerspruch*) contradiction; (*Einwand*) objection; *Rede und ~* dialogue; **~reformation** *f hist.* Counter-Reformation; **~revolution** *f* counter-revolution; **~richtung** *f* opposite direction; *Verkehr aus der ~* oncoming traffic

Gegensatz *m* **1.** *Verhältnis:* contrast (*zu* to, with); *mst Pl. der Meinungen etc.:* differences; **im ~ zu** in contrast to (*od.* with), unlike; **im ~ dazu** by contrast; **e-n krassen** *od.* **scharfen ~ bilden zu** *od.* **im scharfen ~ stehen zu** stand in (*od.* form a) sharp contrast to; *Meinung etc.:* be in sharp opposition to; → *auch* Widerspruch 2; **2.** (*Gegenteil*) the opposite, the contrary (*von* of); *Gegensätze ziehen sich an* opposites (*od.* opposite poles) attract; **3.** *Mus., e-r Fuge:* countersubject; **gegensätzlich** *Adj.* opposite; *Meinungen:* contrary; (*völlig anders*) completely different; (*entgegenwirkend*) opposing, antagonistic; *Befehle, Vorschriften etc.:* conflicting; **Gegensätzlichkeit** *f* oppositeness, opposing (*od.* antithetical) nature (+ *Gen.* of), polarity; antagonism

Gegen|schlag *m* counterblow; *fig. auch* retaliation; **e-n ~ tun** counter; *fig. auch* retaliate; **zum ~ ausholen**

auch fig. start to hit back; **~seite** *f* **1.** opposite (*od.* other) side; **2.** → **Gegenpartei**

gegenseitig I. *Adj. Interesse, Verständnis, Respekt etc.*: mutual; *Hilfe, Rechte, Pflichten*: reciprocal; **~e Abhängigkeit** interdependence; **~e Beziehung** interrelation; correlation; **II.** *Adv.*: **sich ~ helfen** *etc.* help *etc.* one another (*od.* each other); **Gegenseitigkeit** *f; nur Sg.* reciprocity, mutuality; **Abkommen auf ~** mutual agreement; **auf ~ beruhen** be mutual; **das beruht ganz auf ~** *iro.* (I can assure you) the feeling is mutual

Gegen|sinn *m*: **im ~** in the opposite direction; **~spieler** *m*, **~spielerin** *f* antagonist; *auch Sport etc.*: opponent; **~spionage** *f* counterespionage, counterintelligence

Gegensprech|anlage *f* intercom system; **~verkehr** *m* duplex communication

Gegenstand *m; -(e)s, Gegenstände* **1.** object, thing; *bes. Wirts.* article; *einzelner, von Liste etc.*: item; **ein runder ~** a round object, s.th. round; **sie wurde mit e-m stumpfen ~ erschlagen** she was killed with a blunt instrument; **2.** *fig. des Denkens, der Bewunderung*: object; *e-s Gesprächs, Gemäldes etc.*: subject, topic; (*Motiv*) motif, theme; *e-s Vertrags etc.*: subject matter; *e-s Unternehmens*: objects *Pl.*; *e-s Streits*: issue; *der Tagesordnung etc.*: item; **zum ~ haben** deal (*od.* be concerned) with; **er war ~ i-s Mitleids** he was an object of her (*od.* their) pity; **ein ~ des Gespötts** a figure of fun; **3.** *österr. Päd.* subject

gegenständig *Adj. Bot.* opposite

gegenständlich I. *Adj.* concrete (*auch Ling.*); (*anschaulich*) graphic; *Kunst*: (*Ggs. abstrakt*) representational; **II.** *Adv.* graphically; *malen etc.*: representationally

gegenstandslos *Adj.* **1.** (*unbegründet*) *Verdacht, Vorwurf*: groundless; **2.** (*hinfällig*) invalid; (*überflüssig*) superfluous, unnecessary; **der Vertrag etc. ist ~ geworden** the contract etc. is no longer valid; **damit ist Ihre Frage ~ geworden** that makes your question superfluous (*od.* redundant), that takes care of your question; **3.** *Kunst*: abstract, nonrepresentational

gegensteuern *v/i.* (*trennb., hat -ge-*) **1. beim Schleudern ~** steer into a skid; **bei dem starken Wind musste sie ~** as the wind was strong she had to steer slightly into it, she had to correct her steering to allow for the strong wind; **2.** *fig.* take countermeasures

Gegen|stimme *f* **1.** *Parl.* dissenting vote, vote against; **es gab fünf ~n** *auch* there were five votes against (*od.* noes *od.* nays); **ohne ~** unanimously, nem. con.; **2.** (*gegenteilige Meinung*) objection; *mst iro.* dissenting voice; **3.** *Mus.* counterpart; **~strategie** *f* counterstrategy; **~strömung** *f* **1.** countercurrent; **2.** *fig.* countermovement; **~stück** *n* **1.** counterpart; *Kunst* pendant, companion piece; *Figur etc.*: matching piece; *Teil e-s Paars*: fellow, *Am.* mate; **2.** → **Gegenteil**

Gegenteil *n* opposite (**von** of), reverse; **im ~** on the contrary, oh no(, not at all); **ganz im ~** quite the reverse; **genau das** *od.* **das genaue ~** the exact opposite, exactly the opposite; **das ~ behaupten** put (*od.* take) the opposite

point of view, argue the opposite; **das ~ bewirken** have the opposite effect, be counterproductive; **etw. ins ~ verkehren** twist s.th. round (completely); **dann schlug alles ins ~ um** then there was a complete reversal (of events);

gegenteilig *Adj.* contrary, opposite; **~e Behauptung** contradictory claim; **~er Meinung sein** disagree; **e-e ~e Wirkung haben** have the opposite (*od.* a paradoxical) effect

Gegen|tor *n*, **~treffer** *m Sport* goal against; **der Torwart blieb in den letzten vier Spielen ohne ~** has kept a clean sheet in the last four matches

gegenüber I. *Präp.* (+ *Dat.*) **1.** *räumlich*: opposite, facing, vis-à-vis, across from; **2.** *Bezug herstellend*: *freundlich, feindlich etc.*: to(ward[s]); *kritisch, misstrauisch*: of; *streng*: with; **er war mir ~ sehr nachsichtig** he was very forbearing as far as I was concerned; **uns ~ hat sie nie etwas davon erwähnt** she never mentioned anything about it to us; **Männern ~ verhält sie sich komisch** she's funny with men; **3.** (*im Vergleich zu*) compared with, as against; (*im Gegensatz zu*) in contrast to; **~ j-m im Vorteil/Nachteil sein** be at an advantage / a disadvantage compared to s.o.; **II.** *Adv.* opposite; *Personen*: *auch* face to face; *bei Straße etc.*: across the way (*od.* street); **direkt** *od.* **genau ~** right opposite; **schräg ~** diagonally opposite, *Am.* kitty- (*od.* catty-)corner; **sie wohnt im Haus ~** she lives in the house opposite

Gegenüber *n; -s, -* **1.** *räumlich*: person/ house etc. opposite, vis-à-vis; **2.** *fig. Sport* opponent; *Pol. etc.* counterpart, opposite number

gegenüber|liegen *v/i.* (*unreg., trennb., hat / südd., österr., schw. ist -ge-*) be opposite, face (+ *Dat.* s.th.); **~liegend I.** *Part. Präs.* → **gegenüberliegen**; **II.** *Adj.*: **auf der ~en Seite der Straße**: on the opposite side; **im Buch**: on the opposite page; **der ~e Park** the park across the road; **~sehen** *v/refl.* (*unreg., trennb., hat -ge-*): **sich e-r Aufgabe, e-m Gegner etc. ~** be up against; **~sitzen** *v/i.* (*unreg., trennb., hat / südd., österr., schw. ist -ge-*): **j-m ~** sit opposite (*od.* facing) s.o.; **sie saßen sich** *od.* **einander gegenüber** they sat facing one another; **~stehen** *v/i.* (*unreg., trennb., hat / südd., öster., schw. ist -ge-*): **e-r Person**: face s.o. (*auch fig.*), stand in front of (*od.* opposite) s.o., stand face to face with s.o.; **sich** *od.* **einander ~** be facing each other; *fig. als Gegner*: be opponents; *als Feinde*: be enemies; **2.** *e-r Sache, e-m Problem etc.*: be faced (*od.* confronted) with, face, be up against; (*betrachten als*) view, regard, look upon; **e-r Sache kritisch ~** take a critical view of s.th., view s.th. with criticism

gegenüberstellen *v/t.* (*trennb., hat -ge-*) **1.** *j-n j-m ~* *auch fig.* confront s.o. with s.o., bring s.o. face to face with s.o.; **2.** *etw. e-r Sache ~* put s.th. opposite s.th.; *fig.* compare s.th. with s.th.; **Gegenüberstellung** *f* **1.** *auch Jur.* confrontation; **2.** *zur Identifizierung*: identification parade, *Am.* (police) lineup; **3.** (*Vergleich*) comparison

gegenübertreten *v/i.* (*unreg., trennb., ist -ge-*); *auch fig.* face; (*bekämpfen*) oppose (+ *Dat.* s.o., s.th.)

Gegen|verkehr *m* oncoming traffic; *in Autobahnbaustellen*: contraflow traffic; *Verkehrsschild*: two-way traffic; **~ver-**

such *m* control test; **~vorschlag** *m* alternative (suggestion); **darf ich e-n ~ machen?** *auch* may I suggest an alternative?

Gegenwart *f; -, kein Pl.* **1.** (*jetzige Zeit*) the present (time); *Künstler etc.* **der ~** present-day…, … of today; **2.** (*Anwesenheit*) presence; **in der ~ von** in the presence of, with … present (*od.* around); **in s-r ~** when he's *od.* he was *etc.* around (*od.* there); **3.** *Ling.* present (tense); → **vollendet** II 3

gegenwärtig I. *Adj.* **1.** (*jetzig*) present; (*vorherrschend*) prevailing; **zum ~en Zeitpunkt** at the moment, at present; **2.** (*unserer Zeit, heutig*) *attr.* *Probleme, Sprache etc.*: present-day…, … of our time, today's …; *bes. Kunst, Literatur etc.*: contemporary; **3.** *präd.*; (*anwesend*) present (**bei** at); **4.** *geh.*: **etw. ~ haben** (*sich erinnern können*) recall s.th.; **es ist mir im Moment nicht ~** it escapes my memory; **II.** *Adv.* **1.** at the moment, at present, *bes. Am.* at this point in time; **2.** (*heutzutage*) nowadays, these days, today

Gegenwarts… → **gegenwärtig** I 2

gegenwarts|bezogen *Adj.* topical; *Denken etc.*: modern; **~fern** *Adj.* remote, unrealistic; *Mensch*: out of touch

Gegenwartsform *f Ling.* present (tense)

gegenwartsfremd *Adj.* → **gegenwartsfern**

gegenwartsnah *Adj.* topical; **Gegenwartsnähe** *f* relevance to the present; (*Aktualität*) topicality

Gegen|wehr *f* defen|ce (*Am.* -se); resistance; **~ leisten** resist, put up a fight; **keine ~ leisten** offer no resistance; **~welt** *f*; **~en entwerfen** imagine alternative worlds; **~wert** *m* equivalent (value); **im ~ von** to the equivalent value of; **~wind** *m* headwind; **wir haben ~** there's a headwind (blowing); **~winkel** *m Math.* opposite angle; **~wirkung** *f* reaction (**auf** + *Akk.* to), countereffect; *Med.* adverse reaction

gegenzeichnen *vt/i.* (*trennb., hat -ge-*): (*Brief, Vertrag*) countersign; (*Scheck, Wechsel*) endorse; **Gegenzeichnung** *f* countersignature

Gegen|zeuge *m* counterwitness; **~zug** *m* **1.** *Schach und fig.*: countermove; **im ~** (*zu*) as a countermove (to), in reaction (to); **2.** *Eisenb.* oncoming train, train coming from the other direction

gegessen *P.P.* → **essen**

geglichen *P.P.* → **gleichen**

gegliedert I. *P.P.* → **gliedern**; **II.** *Adj.* **1.** (*in* + *Akk*) organized (in), planned; *Aufsatz etc.*: structured (into); **hierarchisch ~ Organisation**: hierarchic(al); **2.** *Tech., Archit.*: **~e Bauweise** sectionalized design; **3.** *Bio. Körper, Gliedmaßen etc.*: jointed; **4.** *Geog., Landschaft etc.*: varied, differentiated; *Küste*: indented

geglitten *P.P.* → **gleiten**

geglommen *P.P.* → **glimmen**

geglückt I. *P.P.* → **glücken**; **II.** *Adj.* *Versuch*: successful; **e-e wenig ~e Kombination** an unsuccessful combination

Gegner *m; -s, -*, **~in** *f; -, -nen* **1.** opponent (*auch Sport*); antagonist; (*Feind[in]*) enemy, foe *lit.*; (*Angreifer[in]*) assailant; (*Rivale, Rivalin*) rival, competitor; *Jur.* opposing party, other side; **sich j-n zum Gegner machen** make an enemy of s.o., antagonize s.o.; **j-n zum Gegner haben** have s.o.

G

as a rival *etc.*, have to compete against s.o.; **2.** (*Ggs. Verfechter[in]*, *Anhänger[in]*) opponent; **ein Gegner** *der Todesstrafe / von Gewalt* **sein** be against, strongly oppose; **gegnerisch** *Adj.* opposing; *stärker*: antagonistic; enemy ...; **die ~e Mannschaft** the opposing side (*od.* team), the other side; **Gegnerschaft** *f* **1.** (*Widerstand*) opposition; *stärker*: antagonism; (*Rivalität*) rivalry; **2.** *nur Sg.*; *Koll.* opponents *Pl.*, opposition

gegolten *P.P.* → **gelten**

gegoren I. *P.P.* → **gären**; **II.** *Adj. Saft*: fermented

gegossen *P.P.* → **gießen**

gegrätscht I. *P.P.* → **grätschen**; **II.** *Adj.*: **mit ~en Beinen** with splayed legs

gegriffen *P.P.* → **greifen**

Gegröle *n; -s, kein Pl.; umg. pej.* bawling, caterwauling

geh. *Abk.* (**gehoben**) *Stil*: form. (= formal)

Gehabe *n; -s, kein Pl.; pej.* silly behavio(u)r, affectation; (*Getue*) fuss

gehaben *v/refl.: altm. od. hum.*: **gehab dich** *od.* **gehabt euch wohl!** farewell

gehabt I. *P.P.* → **haben**; **II.** *Adj.*: (**alles**) **wie ~** same as ever; **es ist alles wie ~** auch nothing's changed; **wie ~** *am Satzende*: mst as always, as usual; **das bleibt wie ~** that stays as it is

Gehackte *n; -n, kein Pl.*, minced (*Am.* ground) meat, *Brit. auch* mincemeat; *vom Rind*: *Brit. auch* mince, *Am. auch* hamburger

Gehalt¹ *m; -(e)s, -e* **1.** *geh.* (*Inhalt*) content; (*Substanz*) substance; **geistiger ~** intellectual content; **2.** (*Anteil*) content; *prozentualer*: percentage; *Chem. auch* concentration (*alle an + Dat.* of); **~ an Öl** oil content; **3.** *von Essen*: nourishment, substance; *von Wein*: body; **4.** (*Fassungsvermögen*) capacity

Gehalt² *n, österr. m; -(e)s, Gehälter* salary, pay; **ein ~ beziehen** *od.* **bekommen / haben** be paid (*od.* draw) / earn a salary; **bei** *od.* **mit vollem ~** on full pay

gehalten I. *P.P.* → **halten**; **II.** *Adj. geh.* **1. ~ sein zu** (+ *Inf.*) be expected to (+ *Inf.*); **ich bin ~ zu** (+ *Inf.*) I am obliged (*od.* required) to (+ *Inf.*); **2.** *altm.* (*zurückhaltend*) restrained, subdued; **3.** (*gestaltet*): **ein freundlich ~er Brief** a friendly letter; **ein ganz in Blau ~es Zimmer** a room decorated entirely in blue

gehaltlos *Adj.* **1.** *Nahrung*: insubstantial; *Wein*: lacking body; **2.** *fig.* empty, lacking in substance; (*bedeutungslos*) meaningless

Gehalts|abrechnung *f* pay slip; **~abzug** *m* deduction from salary; **~anspruch** *m* **1.** entitlement to salary; **mit ~** salaried; **2.** *Pl.* salary expectations; **~aufbesserung** *f* salary increase; **~empfänger** *m*, **~empfängerin** *f* salaried employee; **~erhöhung** *f* (pay) rise, salary increase; **~forderung** *f* salary claim; **~fortzahlung** *f* continued payment of salary; **~gruppe** *f* salary bracket; **~konto** *n* salary account; **~kürzung** *f* salary cut; **~liste** *f* payroll; **~nachzahlung** *f* back payment (of salary); **~pfändung** *f* deduction from salary at source, *Am.* payroll deduction; **~streifen** *m* pay slip; **~stufe** *f* salary bracket; **~vorschuss** *m* advance; **~vorstellung** *f*, **~wunsch** *m* salary expectations *Pl.*; **~zahlung** *f* payment of salary; **~zulage** *f* bonus

gehaltvoll *Adj.* **1.** *Nahrung*: substantial, nourishing; *Wein*: full-bodied; **2.** *fig.* ... of substance; (*tief*) profound

gehandikapt [gə'hɛndikɛpt] *Adj.* handicapped

Gehänge *n; -s, -* **1.** *aus Blumen*: festoon(s *Pl.*); **2.** *Schmuck*: pendants *Pl.*; *für Ohren*: ear drops *Pl.*; **3.** *Sl.* (*männliche Geschlechtsteile*) balls; **4.** (*Koppel*) belt; *für Schwert*: sword-belt

gehangen *P.P.* → **hängen¹**

geharnischt *Adj.* **1.** *Antwort etc.*: withering; **ein ~er Brief** a strongly-worded reply, a nasty letter *umg.*; **2.** *hist.* (*gepanzert*) (clad) in armo(u)r, armo(u)r-clad

gehässig *Adj. pej.* spiteful; **Gehässigkeit** *f* **1.** *nur Sg.* spitefulness; **aus reiner ~** out of sheer spite; **2.** *Bemerkung*: spiteful remark

gehauen I. *P.P.* → **hauen**; **II.** *Adj.*: **e-e in Stein ~e Inschrift / aus Stein ~e Figur** an inscription carved in stone / a figure carved out of stone

gehäuft I. *P.P.* → **häufen**; **II.** *Adj.* **1.** *Löffel*: heaped; **ein ~er Teelöffel** one heaped (*Am.* heaping) teaspoonful; **2.** *Auftreten, Vorkommen*: frequent; **III.** *Adv. zeitlich*: frequently, at frequent intervals, repeatedly; **in letzter Zeit sind ~ Anschläge vorgekommen** there's been a spate of attacks recently

Gehäuse *n; -s, -* **1.** *Tech., von Uhr, Kamera etc.*: casing, case; *von großem Radio*: cabinet; *Fot.* body; *Lager*: housing; **2.** *Zool., Schnecke etc.*: shell; **3.** (*Kerngehäuse*) core

gehbehindert *Adj.*: **sie ist ~** she can't walk properly; **Gehbehinderte** *m, f* person who has problems with walking (*od.* mobility), lame person, *Am. auch* physically-challenged person

Gehege *n; -s, -* **1.** enclosure; *für Tiere*: *auch* pen; *für Pferde*: paddock, *Am.* corral; *von Schutz*: preserve; **2.** *umg. fig.*: **j-m ins ~ kommen** get under s.o.'s feet; **komm mir ja nicht ins ~!** just keep out of my way

geheiligt I. *P.P.* → **heiligen**; **II.** *Adj.* **1.** *Recht, Sonntag etc.*: sacred, sacrosanct; **2.** *umg. hum.*: **j-s ~en Feierabend etc. stören** intrude on s.o.'s precious time of rest *etc.*; **j-s ~e Hallen betreten** enter s.o.'s inner sanctum

geheim I. *Adj.* secret; (*vertraulich*) confidential, private; (*verborgen*) hidden; (*heimlich, unerlaubt*) clandestine, surreptitious; *Lehre etc.*: occult; **~! auf Dokumenten**: Restricted!; **streng ~** top secret; **j-s ~ste Gedanken** *etc.* s.o.'s most secret thoughts; **~ halten** keep s.th. secret (*umg.* under wraps); (*vertuschen*) hush s.th. up; **etw. vor j-m ~ halten** keep s.th. a secret from s.o.; **wir müssen es vor ihm ~ halten** auch he mustn't find out (about it); **das soll noch ~ bleiben** this should be kept secret, don't tell anyone yet *umg.*; **~ tun** *umg. pej.* be secretive; **im Geheimen** secretly (*auch im Innersten*), in secret; **II.** *Adv.*: **~ abstimmen** hold a secret ballot

Geheim|agent *m*, **~agentin** *f* secret agent; **~akte** *f* secret (*od.* classified) document; **~n** secret files; **~auftrag** *m* secret mission; **~bund** *m* secret society; **~dienst** *m* secret service; **~fach** *n* secret drawer; (*Safe*) hidden safe

Geheimhaltung *f; nur Sg.* (observance of) secrecy; (*Verschweigen*) concealment; **zur ~ verpflichtet sein** be sworn to secrecy

Geheimhaltungs|... *im Subst. Mil., Pol.* security ...; **~pflicht** *f* (imposed) secrecy; **~stufe** *f* security classification (*od.* grade, *Am. auch* level); **die ~ e-s Dokuments** *etc.* **aufheben** declassify a document

Geheim|kode *m* secret code; **~konto** *n* **1.** secret account; **2.** *anonym*: numbered account; **~lehre** *f* esoteric doctrine, occult doctrine; **~mittel** *n* secret remedy

Geheimnis *n; -ses, -se* secret; (*Rätselhaftes, Verborgenes*) auch mystery; **ein offenes ~** an open secret; **ein süßes ~ haben** euph. be awaiting a happy (*od.* blessed) event; **ich habe vor dir keine ~se** I have no secrets from you; **ein ~ aus etw. machen** make a secret out of s.th.; **j-n in die ~se der Physik einweihen** initiate s.o. into the mysteries of physics; **das ist das ganze ~** that's all there is to it; **~krämer** *m*, **~krämerin** *f* umg. mysterymonger; **er ist ein richtiger ~** he's terribly secretive, he likes to make a mystery out of everything; **~krämerei** *f; -, -en*: **hör doch auf mit dieser ~** stop making such a big secret of it; **~träger** *m*, **~trägerin** *f* bearer of official secrets

geheimnis|umwittert, **~umwoben** *Adj. geh.* shrouded in mystery, mysterious; (*rätselhaft*) enigmatic; **~voll** *Adj.* mysterious; (*rätselhaft*) auch enigmatic; (*obskur*) arcane; **ein ~es Gesicht machen** put on a mysterious face; **tu nicht so ~!** don't be so secretive, don't make such a big secret out of it

Geheim|nummer *f* **1.** *Telef.* ex-directory (*Am.* unlisted) number; **2.** → **Geheimzahl**; **~polizei** *f* secret police

Geheimrat *m hist.* privy councillor; **Geheimratsecken** *Pl.*: **er hat ~** his hair is receding at the temples, he's got a widow's peak *umg.*

Geheim|rezept *n* secret recipe; **~sache** *f* secret matter; *Pol., Mil.* security matter; **~schrift** *f* secret code; **~sprache** *f* **1.** secret language; **2.** *iro., pej.* jargon; **~tipp** *m umg.* hot tip; *beim Wetten etc.*: insiders' tip; **dieser Ort ist mein ~** this is a place I don't like to tell everyone about; **das Lokal ist ein ~ für Feinschmecker** the restaurant is a mecca for gourmets (*od.* foodies *umg.*) in the know; **~tür** *f* secret door; **~versteck** *n* secret hiding place; **~waffe** *f* secret weapon; **~zahl** *f von Zahlenschloss etc.*: secret number; *für Geldautomat etc.*: PIN (= personal identification number); **~zeichen** *n* secret sign; (*Chiffre*) code, cipher

Geheiß *n geh.*: **auf j-s ~** (*hin*) at s.o.'s behest

geheißen *P.P.* → **heißen¹**

gehemmt I. *P.P.* → **hemmen**; **II.** *Adj.* inhibited; (*befangen*) auch self-conscious; (*scheu*) auch shy; **~ sein** feel inhibited, be (*od.* feel) self-conscious *od.* shy; **Gehemmtheit** *f; nur Sg.* inhibition; (*Befangenheit*) self-consciousness, shyness

gehen I. *v/i.; geht, ging, ist gegangen* **1.** (*zu Fuß*) **~** walk, go (on foot, *Am. auch* by foot); **spazieren ~** go for a walk; **aufrecht/gebückt ~** walk upright / with a stoop; **am Stock ~** walk with a stick (*Am.* cane); **im Schritt/Trab ~** *Pferd*: walk/trot; **wo ich gehe und stehe sehe ich ...** wherever I go ...; **2.** *mit Richtung*: **~ in** (+ *Akk.*) go into, enter; **auf/über die Straße ~** go out into /cross the street; **mit j-m zum Bahn-**

hof *etc.* ~ see s.o. (*od.* go with s.o.) to the station *etc.*; **er geht nie aus dem Haus** he never leaves (*od.* goes out of) the house; → **Licht** 1, **Seite** 1, **Weg** 1, 2; **3.** (*sich irgendwohin begeben*) go; **schwimmen** *etc.* ~ go swimming *etc.*; **j-n suchen** ~ (go and) look for s.o.; **ins** *od.* **zu Bett** ~ go to bed; **in Deckung** ~ take cover; **auf Reisen** ~ go travel(l)ing; **unter Menschen** ~ mix with people; **an/von Bord** ~ go on board / leave the ship, plane *etc.*, embark/disembark; **zu j-m** ~ (*sich hinzugesellen*) join s.o.; **mit e-r Frage** *etc.*: go up to s.o.; (*besuchen*) go and see s.o.; **seit wann bist du unter die Sportler gegangen?** *umg. hum.* since when have you been a sports enthusiast?; **4.** *beruflich etc.*: **als Putzfrau** *etc.* ~ work as a cleaner; **in die Fabrik** *etc.* ~ (*dort anfangen*) start at the factory *etc.*; (*dort arbeiten*) go (in)to the factory; **zur Schule / aufs Gymnasium** *etc.* ~ go to school / grammar (*Am.* high) school; **in die Politik / zum Film** *etc.* ~ go into politics / films (*Am.* motion pictures); **ins Kloster** ~ become a nun; **in** *od.* **auf Urlaub** ~ go on holiday (*Am.* vacation); **in Rente** ~ retire; **5.** *umg.* (*sich kleiden*): **als Clown** *etc.* ~ **im Karneval**: go as a clown *etc.*; **in Zivil** ~ **Soldat**: wear civilian clothes; *Polizist*: wear plainclothes; **ganz in Weiß** *etc.* ~ wear white *etc.*, be all in white *etc.*; **so kannst du nicht** ~**!** you can't go (looking) like that!; **6.** (*beginnen*): **an die Arbeit** *etc.* ~ get down to work *etc.*; *auch unpers.*: **wenn's ans Aufräumen geht** when it comes to clearing up; **7.** *fig.*: **an etw.** (*Akk.*) ~ *umg. ohne Erlaubnis*: touch; *Geldbeutel, Handtasche* go into; (*nehmen*) take; **geh mir ja nicht an m-e Sachen** *umg.* don't you (dare) touch (*od.* interfere with) my things; **sie sind auseinander gegangen** (*haben sich getrennt*) they've split up; **in sich** ~ do a bit of soul-searching; **mit j-m** ~ *umg.* (*fest befreundet sein*) go steady with; **8.** (*weggehen, auch aus Stellung etc.*) go, leave; **gehst du schon?** are you going already?; **jetzt geh schon!** *ermunternd*: go on then; *antreibend*: get going then; **j-n lieber** ~ **als kommen sehen** be glad to see the back of s.o.; **er ist von uns gegangen** *euph.* (*ist tot*) he has passed away; **j-n** ~ **lassen** let s.o. go; *ungestraft*: let s.o. off; ~ **lassen** *umg. fig.* (*Seil etc.*) (*loslassen*) let go; (*j-n, etw.*) (*in Ruhe lassen*) leave alone; **sich** ~ **lassen** *unmanierlich*: let o.s. go; (*die Beherrschung verlieren*) lose one's temper; **er ist gegangen worden** *umg. hum.* he was sacked (*bes. Am.* fired); **geh!** *bes. südd., österr., erstaunt*: really?; **ach, geh** *od.* **geh, geh!** *umg.* come on!, go on!; **geh mir doch mit d-n faulen Ausreden!** *umg. fig.* I don't want to hear any of your excuses; **9.** *Zug etc.*: (*abfahren*) go (**nach** to), leave (*od.* depart) (for); (*verkehren*) go, run; **wann geht der nächste Zug nach Rom?** when does the next train for Rome leave (*od.* depart)?; **der nächste Bus geht erst in zwei Stunden** there isn't another bus for two hours; **hier geht alle zehn Minuten ein Bus** there's a bus every ten minutes here; → *auch* 13; **10.** *allg. Bewegung*: **ging da nicht gerade e-e Tür?** wasn't that a door I heard (going)?; **die Schublade geht so schwer** the drawer is so difficult to open (*od.* shut), the drawer

sticks; **draußen geht ein kalter Wind** there's a cold wind blowing outside; **11.** *mit Ziel*: **der Ball ging ins Tor** the ball went in; **sie ging als Erste durchs Ziel** she was the first to cross the finishing line; **12.** *fig.*: **es geht das Gerücht, dass ...** there's a rumo(u)r going around that ...; **das Erbe ging an ihn** the inheritance went to him; **das geht auf mich** (*zahle ich*) that's on me; **das geht auf die Leber** *etc.* it's bad for your liver *etc.*, it takes its toll on your liver *etc.*; **es geht auf** *od.* **gegen Mitternacht** it's nearly midnight; **sie geht auf die 60** she's nearly 60; **s-e Kritik ging dahin, dass ...** his criticism was to the effect that ..., what his criticism boiled down to was that ...; **der Skandal ging durch die Presse** the scandal was in all the papers; *was ich jetzt sage,* **geht nicht gegen dich** is not aimed at you; ~ **nach** (*sich richten nach*) go by; **wenn es nach mir ginge** if I had my way; **es kann nicht immer alles nach d-m Kopf** ~ you can't get your own way all of the time; **was geht hier vor sich?** what's going on here?; **wie ist das vor sich gegangen?** what happened?; **13.** *Mauer, Weg etc.*: go, lead to; *Treppe*: lead (down/up) to; *Leitung etc.*: lead; *Fenster*: face, look out on; *Tür*: open; ~ **durch** go (*od.* pass) through; **wohin geht die Reise?** where are you *etc.* off to?; **das Fenster geht auf die Straße / nach Norden** looks out onto the street / faces (*od.* looks) north; *die Brücke* **geht über e-e Schlucht** spans (*od.* goes over) a ravine; **zum Zoo geht es die nächste Straße rechts** for the zoo, take the next (street on the) right; **an der Ampel geht es** (**nach**) **links** go left at the lights; **14.** *zur Angabe von Mengen, Grenzen*: **das Wasser geht mir bis ans** *od.* **zum Kinn** the water comes up to my chin; **der Rock geht über die Knie** the skirt comes to below the knee; **tief** ~**d** *Schmerz etc.*: deep; **es** ~ **200 Personen in den Saal** the hall holds (*od.* seats) two hundred people; **wie oft geht fünf in neunzig?** how many times does five go into ninety?; **der Schrank geht nicht durch die Tür** the cupboard won't go through the door; **auf e-n Zentner** ~ **50 Kilogramm** 50 kilogram(me)s make a (metric) hundredweight; **15.** (*erreichen*) *der Schaden* **geht in die Millionen** runs into millions; **die Kämpfe** ~ **in den vierten Tag** fighting has entered its fourth day; **das Spiel geht in die Verlängerung** the game is going into extra time (*Am.* overtime); **16.** (*dauern*) last; **wie lange geht die Sitzung schon/noch?** how long has the meeting been going on (*od.* been under way) / how much longer is the meeting going to take?; **die Ferien** ~ **vom 10. bis 24. Mai** the holidays are (*od.* run) from the 10th to the 24th of May (*Am.* May 10th to 24th); **17.** (*übertreffen, übersteigen*): **das geht über m-n Verstand / m-e Kräfte** it's beyond my understanding / strength, it's more than I can grasp/ manage; **es geht doch nichts über ...** there's nothing like ...; **sie geht ihm über alles** she means everything to him; **18.** *fig.*: **wie hoch kannst/willst du** ~**?** *beim Kaufen*: how much can you afford? / do you want to spend?; *beim Wetten, Pokern etc.*: how high can you / do you want to go?; **das geht zu weit!** that's going too far!; **er**

ging so weit zu sagen ... he went so far as to say ...; **19.** a) (*in Betrieb sein*) *Staubsauger, Radio etc.*: be on, b) (*klingeln*) *Klingel, Telefon*: ring, go; **um 6 Uhr ging mein Wecker** my alarm went off at 6 o'clock; **das Telefon geht schon den ganzen Tag** the phone has been ringing all day, c) *Puls*: beat; **ihr Puls geht zu schnell** her pulse is too rapid; **20.** (*funktionieren*) go, work; **die Uhr geht nicht** has stopped; (*ist kaputt*) is broken; **m-e Uhr geht falsch/richtig** my watch is wrong/right; **keine Angst, das geht ganz leicht** don't worry, it's quite easy; **das Gedicht, Lied geht so** goes like this; **wie soll denn das** ~**?** (*verstehe ich nicht*) how do you do it?; (*glaube ich nicht*) how do you say you do it?; **21.** (*möglich sein*) be possible; (*gut sein*) be all right; **geht** (**es**) **Mittwoch?** is Wednesday OK (*od.* all right)?; **Mittwoch geht gut** Wednesday is fine; **22.** *unpers.*; (*erlaubt sein*) be allowed; *ich hätte morgen gern das Auto,* **geht das?** is that OK?; **geht das** (**aber**) **nicht!** that won't do at all!; **23.** *umg.* (*ausreichen, akzeptabel sein*) do; **der Mantel muss den Winter noch** ~ the coat will have to do for (*od.* last) this winter; **geht das jetzt so?** will it do?, is it all right like that?; **der Hunger ging ja noch, aber der Durst** (*war nicht auszuhalten*)**!** the hunger we could take, but the thirst (was unbearable)!; **24.** *Entwicklung, Verlauf*: **gut** ~ go well, turn out all right; *Geschäfte*: do well, go well; **schief** ~ go wrong; **wie** ~ **die Geschäfte?** how's business?; **gut/schlecht** ~**d** *Geschäft etc.*: flourishing (*od.* thriving) / ailing; **das konnte nicht gut** ~ it was bound to go wrong; **das kann ja nicht gut** ~**!** *umg.* there's no way it's going to work; **wenn das nur gut geht!** well, let's just hope for the best; **das ist noch einmal gut gegangen** that was close (*od.* a close thing, *Am.* a close call), talk about lucky *umg.*; **so geht es, wenn man** *nicht aufpasst etc.*: that's what comes of (+ *Ger.*); → **abwärts** 3, **aufwärts** 3, **vorwärts** 2; **25.** *Ware*: sell (**gut** well), go (well); **26.** *unpers.*; *Befinden*: **wie geht es Ihnen** *od.* **dir?** how are you?; *zu e-m Kranken*: how are you feeling?; **wie geht's(, wie steht's)?** *umg.* how are things?, how's life (with you)?, how's life treating you?; **mir geht's gut/schlecht** I'm fine / not well; *geschäftlich etc.*: I'm doing fine/ badly; **es geht** (**so**) *umg.* not too bad-(ly), (it) could be worse; **es sich** (*Dat.*) **gut** ~ **lassen** have a good time, enjoy o.s.; **ihm ist es** (**auch**) **nicht besser gegangen** he didn't do (*od.* fare) any better; **mir ist es genauso gegangen** it was the same for me, same here *umg.*; **wie geht es dir mit diesem Film?** what do you think (*od.* how do you feel) about this film (*Am. auch* movie)?; **mir geht es genauso** I feel exactly the same way, same here *umg.*; **jetzt geht es ihm ans Leben** *od.* **an den Kragen** *etc. umg.* he's really in for it now; **27.** *unpers.*; (*möglich sein*): **es geht nicht** it can't be done, it's impossible, nothing doing *umg.*, no way *umg.*; **es wird schon** ~ it'll be all right; **es geht auch so/allein** (*ohne das/dich*) we *etc.* can manage without *it/you*; **es geht** (**eben**) **nicht anders** it can't be helped(, I'm afraid); **28.** *unpers.*; *fig.*: **es geht um** *Thema*: it's about; **worum**

G

geht es in dem Film? what's the film (*Am. auch* movie) about?; *es geht um den Frieden etc.*: peace *etc.* is at stake; *es geht darum zu* (+ *Inf.*) it's a question (*od.* matter) of (+ *Ger.*); *darum geht es hier nicht* that's not the point; *persönliches Interesse*: *worum geht es dir eigentlich?* what are you really after?; *es geht ihm nur ums Geld* he's just interested in the money; **29.** *Teig*: rise; *den Teig ~ lassen* let the dough rise; **30.** *als Funktionsverb*: *zu Bruch od. in die Brüche ~* break, get broken; *in Druck ~* go to press; *in Erfüllung ~* be fulfilled (*od.* realized); *in Produktion ~* go into production; → *offline*, *online, verlieren* I 1 - 3, *vonstatten etc.*; **II.** *v/t.*: *e-n Umweg ~* make a detour; *wir gingen die Strecke Altdorf - Neustadt in drei Stunden* we walked from Altdorf to Neustadt in three hours; → *Gang¹* 3, *Weg* 1 - 3; **III.** *v/refl. unpers.*: *in diesen Schuhen geht es sich gut* these shoes are good for walking, these are good walking shoes; *auf dem steinigen Boden ging es sich etwas mühsam* the going was fairly laborious over the stony ground

Gehen *n*; *-s, kein Pl.* **1.** walking; *das ~ fällt ihm schwer* he finds it hard to walk; **2.** *Sport, Disziplin*: walking; *Wettkampf*: walk; **3.** *zum ~ bringen* (*Gerät etc.*) get *s.th.* going; **4.** *fig.* (*Abschied*) leaving

Geher *m*; *-s, -*, *~in f*; *-, -nen*; *Sport* walker

gehetzt I. *P.P.* → *hetzen*; **II.** *Adj.* hunted (*auch Blick etc.*); *fig. Person*: harassed; *er wirkt irgendwie ~* he's got this hunted look

geheuer *Adj.*: *nicht* (*ganz od. recht*) *~* (*unheimlich*) eerie; (*verdächtig*) fishy, strange; (*dubios*) dubious; *es ist dort nicht ganz ~* it's a funny place; *mir ist dieser Ort nicht ~* this place gives me the creeps; *er etc. ist mir nicht ~* I've got a funny feeling about him *etc.*; *ihm war nicht ganz ~ zumute* he felt very uneasy

Geheul *n*; *-s, kein Pl.* howling, howls *Pl.*; **Geheule** *n*; *-s, kein Pl.*; *umg., mst pej.* howling, bawling

gehfähig *Adj.* able to walk

Geh|fehler *m* limp; *~gips m* walking cast; *~hilfe f* walking aid

gehießen *P.P. Dial.* → *heißen¹*

Gehilfe *m*; *-n, -n*, **Gehilfin** *f*; *-, -nen* **1.** assistant; (*Aushilfe*) someone to help out; *im Laden*: shop assistant; *im Büro*: clerk; *im Handwerk*: journeyman; **2.** *Jur.* (*Komplize*) accessory (before the fact); *pej.* henchman

Gehirn *n*; *-s, -e* **1.** *Anat.* brain; **2.** *umg. fig.* brain(s *Pl.*), mind; **Gehirn...** *im Subst.* brain ..., cerebral ..., *nachgestellt*: of the brain; → *auch Hirn*; *~akrobatik f umg.* mental acrobatics (*od.* gyrations) *Pl.*

gehirnamputiert *Adj. umg. fig. pej.* braindead

Gehirn|blutung *f Med.* brain (*od.* cerebral) h(a)emorrhage; *~chirurgie f* brain surgery; *~durchblutung f* blood flow (*od.* circulation) in the brain; *es fördert die ~ auch* it gets your brain cells working *umg.*; *~entzündung f* inflammation of the brain, encephalitis *fachspr.*; *~erschütterung f* concussion; *e-e ~ haben* have (*od.* be suffering from) concussion; → *schwer* I 4; *~erweichung f Med., auch fig.* softening of the brain

Gehirnhaut *f Anat.* cerebral membrane; *~entzündung f Med.* meningitis

Gehirn|kasten *m umg. hum.* skull; *streng d-n ~ an! fig.* use your brains (*umg.* noddle, *Am.* noodle)!; *~lappen m Anat.* lobe of the brain; *~nerv m Anat.* cranial nerve; *~quetschung f Med.* cerebral contusion; *~rinde f Anat.* cerebral cortex; *~schlag m Med.* stroke; *~schmalz n umg. hum.* (little) grey (*Am.* gray) cells *Pl.*; *~stamm m Anat.* brainstem; *~tätigkeit f* cerebral activity; *die ~ hat ausgesetzt* the brain has stopped functioning; *~tod m Med.* brain death; *~tumor m Med.* brain tumo(u)r; *~wäsche f Pol.* brainwashing; *j-n e-r ~ unterziehen* brainwash s.o.; *~zelle f Med.* brain cell

Gehminute *f*: *es ist nur ein paar ~n von hier* it's only a few minutes' walk away (*od.* from here)

gehoben I. *P.P.* → *heben*; **II.** *Adj.* **1.** *Stellung*: high, senior; *der ~e Dienst* the higher levels *Pl.* (*Am.* grades *Pl.*) of the Civil Service; **2.** *Stil*: elevated; *~e Ansprüche* expensive tastes; *Güter des ~en Bedarfs Wirts.* luxuries and semi-luxuries; **3.** *~e Stimmung* high spirits *Pl.*

Gehöft *n*; *-(e)s, -e* farm(stead)

geholfen *P.P.* → *helfen*

Gehölz *n*; *-es, -e* wood, copse; (*Dickicht*) thicket

Gehör *n*; *-(e)s, kein Pl.* **1.** (sense of) hearing; ears *Pl.*; (*Empfinden*) ear; *feines/scharfes ~* sensitive/keen ear; *nach dem ~* by ear; *zu ~ bringen* (*Lied*) sing; (*Gedicht*) recite; (*Musikstück*) play; *mir ist zu ~ gekommen, dass ...* I have heard that ..., it has come to my attention that ... *geh.*; → *absolut* I; **2.** (*Beachtung*) hearing (*auch Jur.*); *j-m ~ schenken* listen to what s.o. has to say; *kein ~ schenken e-r Sache*: turn a deaf ear to; *e-r Person*: refuse to listen to; (*j-n*) *um ~ bitten* request a hearing (from s.o.); *~ finden* get a hearing; *sich* (*Dat.*) *~ verschaffen* make o.s. heard

gehorchen *v/i.* **1.** *j-m* (*nicht*) *~* (dis)obey s.o.; *du musst d-r Mutter ~* you must do as your mother tells you; → *Wort* 3; **2.** *fig.*: *s-e Beine etc. gehorchten ihm nicht mehr* he lost control over his feet *etc.*; *das Schiff gehorcht dem Steuer nicht* the ship isn't responding to the helm

gehören I. *v/i.* **1.** (+ *Dat.*) belong to; *wem gehört das Buch?* whose book is this?, who does this book belong to?; *gehört der Handschuh dir?* is this your glove?; *der Solarenergie gehört die Zukunft fig.* the future belongs to solar energy; *am Wochenende gehöre ich der Familie* my weekends are given over to the family; *ihre ganze Liebe gehört ihren Katzen* she gives all her love to her cats; **2.** *~ zu* belong to; (*zählen zu*) *auch* rank (*od.* be) among; *als Mitglied*: *auch* be a member of; *als Teil*: *auch* be part of; *als Voraussetzung*: be necessary for, be called for; *als Ergänzung*: go with; *unter e-e Rubrik etc. ~* come (*od.* fall) under; *er gehört zu den besten Spielern* he's one of the best players; *das gehört nicht zur Sache* that's irrelevant; *er gehört nicht zu dieser Sorte* he's not like that, he's not that sort of person; *dazu gehört Mut etc.* that takes (*od.* for that you need) courage *etc.*; *es gehört nicht viel dazu* it doesn't take much;

3. (*s-n Platz haben*) belong (*in/auf* + *Akk.*; *in/on*); *die Sachen ~ in den Schrank* (*tu sie hinein*) these things go (*od.* belong) in the cupboard; *das Fahrrad gehört nicht in die Wohnung!* the flat (*Am.* apartment) is no place for a bike; **4.** *bes. südd. und umg.*: *du gehörst ins Bett* you should be in bed; *so etwas gehört doch verboten!* that sort of thing should be forbidden; *dir gehört e-e Ohrfeige!* you deserve a clip round the ear, *Am.* you need your ears boxed; **II.** *v/refl.* (*schicklich sein*) be right (*od.* fitting *od.* right and proper); *das gehört sich nicht* it's not done; *wie es sich gehört* properly; *so gehört es sich auch* that's the way it should be; *er weiß, was sich gehört* he knows how to behave

Gehör|fehler *m* hearing defect, impaired hearing; *~gang m* auditory canal

gehörgeschädigt *Adj.* hearing-impaired

gehörig I. *Adj.* **1.** (*gebührend*) right, due, proper; (*notwendig*) necessary; *mit dem ~en Respekt* with due respect; **2.** *umg. Schrecken*: good; *Achtung, Respekt*: healthy; (*tüchtig*) decent; *sie hatten ~e Angst davor* it really put the wind up them; *ein ~er Schluck* a good gulp (*od.* swig); *e-e ~e Portion Kartoffelbrei* a decent serving (*od.* a good dollop) of mashed potatoes; *dazu gehört e-e ~e Portion Frechheit* that takes a fair bit of cheek (*Am.* nerve); *e-e ~e Tracht Prügel* a good hiding; **3.** (+ *Dat.*) (*gehörend*) belonging to; (*nicht*) *zur Sache ~* (ir)relevant, (not) pertinent; *die ins Haus ~en Dinge* the things that belong in(side) the house; **II.** *Adv.* duly, properly; *ich habe es ihm ~ gegeben umg.* I really let him have it

Gehörknöchelchen *n Anat.* ossicle

gehörlos *Adj.* deaf; **Gehörlose** *m, f*; *-n, -n* deaf person; **Gehörlosenschule** *f* school for the deaf; **Gehörlosigkeit** *f*; *nur Sg.* deafness

Gehörnerv *m Anat.* auditory nerve

gehörnt *Adj.* horned; *~er Ehemann umg. fig.* cuckold

gehorsam I. *Adj.* obedient (*gegen* to); *Bürger*: law-abiding; (*folgsam*) submissive; *die Kinder sind sehr ~* always do as they're told; *Ihr ~(st)er Diener altm. Briefschluss*: your most obedient servant; **II.** *Adv.* obediently; *melde ~st*: ... *Mil. altm.* wish to report, sir; *ich bitte ~st ... altm.* I humbly request

Gehorsam *m*; *-s, kein Pl.* obedience (*gegen[über]* to); *blinder ~* blind (*od.* unquestioning) obedience; *j-m ~ leisten* obey s.o.; *j-m den ~ verweigern* disobey s.o., refuse to carry out s.o.'s orders; *sich bei j-m ~ verschaffen* force s.o. to obey

Gehorsamkeit *f*; *nur Sg.* obedience

Gehorsamsverweigerung *f* disobedience; *Mil.* insubordination

Gehör|schaden *m* hearing defect, impaired hearing; *~sinn m*; *nur Sg.* sense of hearing; *~verlust m* loss of hearing

Gehrock *m altm.* frock coat

Gehrung *f Tech., 450-Winkel*: mit|re (*Am.* -er); *anderer Winkel*: bevel

Gehsteig *m* pavement, *Am.* sidewalk

Gehtnichtmehr *n umg. pej.*: *bis zum ~* till you're sick of it; *tanzen, trinken*: till you drop

gehupft *P.P.* → *hupfen*

Geh|versuch *m* attempt to walk; *erste*

literarische etc. *~e* *fig.* first attempt to write *etc.*, first literary *etc.* effort; **~weg** *m* footpath; (*Bürgersteig*) pavement, *Am.* sidewalk

Geier *m*; *-s, -*; *Orn.* vulture (*auch fig.*); **hol's / hol dich der ~!** *umg.* to hell with it/you!; **weiß der ~!** *umg.* God knows

Geifer *m*; *-s, kein Pl.* **1.** (*Speichel*) dribble, slaver; (*Schaum*) foam, froth; **2.** *geh. fig. pej.* venom, spite; **Geiferer** *m*; *-s, -*; *geh. pej.* vituperator; **geifern** *v/i.* **1.** dribble, slaver; **vor Wut ~** froth at the mouth; **2.** *geh. fig. pej.*: **~ gegen** rail at

Geige *f*; *-, -n*; *Mus.* violin; **~ spielen** play the violin; **die erste/zweite ~ spielen** play first/second violin; *fig.* play first/second fiddle; **geigen I.** *v/i.* **1.** play the violin, fiddle *umg.*; **2.** *poet.* *Grille*: chirp; **II.** *v/t.* **1.** play s.th. on the violin, fiddle *umg.*; **2.** *umg. pej.*: **j-m die Meinung** *od.* **es j-m ~** tell s.o. what's what

Geigen|bau *m* *Mus.* violin-making; **~bauer** *m*, **~bauerin** *f*; *-, -nen* violin--maker; **~bogen** *m* violin bow; **~hals** *m* neck of a violin; **~kasten** *m* violin case; **~spiel** *n* violin playing; **~spieler** *m*, **~spielerin** *f* violinist; **~strich** *m* stroke (of the bow); **~virtuose** *m*, **~virtuosin** *f* virtuoso violinist

Geiger *m*; *-s, -*, **~in** *f*; *-, -nen*; *Mus.* violinist

Geigerzähler *m* *Phys.* Geiger counter

geil *Adj.* **1.** *vulg.* (*sexuell erregt*) randy, horny; (*wollüstig*) lecherous; **~ auf j-n** lusting after; **~er alter Bock** *pej.* randy (*od.* dirty) old man, lech *Sl.*; **j-n ~ machen** turn s.o. on; **2.** *umg. fig.*: **~ auf** (+ *Akk.*) (*verrückt nach*) crazy about; **auf e-n Job** *etc.*: burning to get, leching after *Sl.*; **das macht mich ~ auf/nach** it makes my tongue hang out for; **3.** *umg.* (*toll*) brill *Sl.*, ace *Sl.*, wicked *Sl.*; **4.** *Agr. Pflanzen*: rank; **~e Triebe** suckers

...geil *im Adj. umg. fig.* -mad, -crazy, obsessed with; **katastrophen~ sein** get off on (*od.* have a thing about) disasters *Sl.*; **noten~** obsessed with getting good marks (*Am.* grades); **profit~** profit-mad; **sonnen~** sun-crazy

Geilheit *f*; *nur Sg.* **1.** *vulg.* randiness, horniness; (*Wollüstigkeit*) lecherousness; **2.** *Agr.* rankness

...geilheit *f, im Subst.; nur Sg.; umg. fig.* obsession, thing (about), mania; **Katastrophen~** thing about disasters; **Noten~** obsession with good marks (*Am.* grades); **Profit~** lust for profit, fixation on profits; **Sonnen~** sun lust

Geisel *f*; *-, -n* hostage; **j-n als ~ nehmen/festhalten** take/hold s.o. hostage; **~drama** *n* hostage drama (*od.* crisis), kidnapping drama; **~haft** *f* captivity, being held hostage; **nach drei Jahren ~** *auch* after three years of being held hostage; **~nahme** *f*; *-, -n* taking of hostages (*od.* a hostage), hostage-taking; **~nehmer** *m*, **~nehmerin** *f* hostage-taker, kidnapper, captor

Geiser → *Geysir*

Geisha ['geːʃa] *f*; *-, -s* geisha (girl)

Geiß *f*; *-, -en*; *bes. südd., österr., schw.* (nanny) goat; (*Ricke*) doe; **~bock** *m* billy goat

Geißel *f*; *-, -n* **1.** *hist.* scourge; (*Peitsche*) whip; **2.** (+ *Gen.*) *fig.* scourge (of), plague (of); **3.** *Bio.* flagellum; **geißeln** *v/t. und v/refl.* **1.** whip *s.o.*; *kirchl.* flagellate (**sich** o.s.); **2.** *fig.* castigate, chastise; **etw. als verwerflich ~**

---

condemn s.th. as reprehensible; **Geißeltierchen** *n* *Zool.* flagellate; **Geißelung** *f* **1.** flagellation; **2.** *fig.* castigation; (*Kritik*) severe condemnation

Geißlein *n* *bes. südd., österr., schw.* kid; **der Wolf und die sieben ~** The Wolf and the Seven Kids

Geist *m*; *-(e)s, -er* **1.** *nur Sg.*; (*Verstand*) mind; (*Intellekt*) intellect; (*Sinn, Gemüt*) (*Witz*) wit; (*Seele*) spirit; **~ und Körper** mind and body, body and spirit; **Mann von ~** man of wit; **vor ~ sprühen** *od.* **s-n ~ sprühen lassen** scintillate; **den** *od.* **s-n ~ aushauchen** *geh. euph.* (*sterben*) give up the ghost; **den ~ aufgeben** *umg.* (*kaputtgehen*) give up the ghost, conk out; **j-m auf den ~ gehen** *umg.* get on s.o.'s nerves, drive s.o. crazy; **im ~e** in one's mind's eye; **im ~e sah sie sich schon als Siegerin** she already imagined (*od.* saw) herself as the winner; **wir werden im ~e bei euch sein** we will be with you in spirit; **der ~ ist willig, aber das Fleisch ist schwach** the spirit is willing but the flesh is weak; **2.** *nur Sg.*; (*Einstellung*) spirit; (*Verfassung*) morale; (*Atmosphäre*) atmosphere, vibes *Pl. umg.*; **der olympische ~** the Olympic spirit; **es herrschte ein kameradschaftlicher ~** there was a comradely spirit; **in j-s ~e handeln** act in the spirit of s.o.; **daran sieht man, wes ~es Kind er ist** it says a lot about him; **3.** *überirdischer*: spirit; (*Gespenst*) ghost; (*Erscheinung*) apparition; **böser ~** evil spirit, demon; **hier geht ein ~ um** this place is haunted; **bist du denn von allen guten ~ern verlassen?** are you out of your mind?, have you taken leave of your senses?; **4.** *fig. Person*: **großer ~** great mind (*od.* thinker); **kleiner ~** small-minded person; **dienstbarer ~** *umg. hum.* (*Dienstbote*) servant, domestic treasure; **j-s guter ~** s.o.'s guiding light; **sie ist der gute ~ der Abteilung** she is the moving spirit in the department; **sie ist ein unruhiger ~** she's a restless person (*od.* spirit), she can't sit still for one moment, she's up and down like a yoyo *umg.*; → *scheiden* III

...geist *m, im Subst.; Chem., Gastr.* spirit(s *Pl. Am.*); **Himbeer~** (white) raspberry brandy; **Mirabellen~** plum brandy

Geister|bahn *f* ghost train; **~beschwörer** *m*, **~beschwörerin** *f* (*der Geister ruft*) necromancer; (*der sie austreibt*) exorcist; **~beschwörung** *f* necromancy; (*Austreibung*) exorcism; **~bild** *n* TV ghosting, shadow(s *Pl.*) *umg.*; **~erscheinung** *f* apparition; **~fahrer** *m*, **~fahrerin** *f* driver driving on the wrong side of the road or in the wrong direction down a one-way street; *Am.* wrong-way driver, **plötzlich kam uns ein ~ entgegen** suddenly a car was driving towards us in the wrong direction (*auf der falschen Straßenseite*: on the wrong side of the road); **~geschichte** *f* ghost story; **~glaube** *m* belief in ghosts; (*Aberglaube*) superstition

geisterhaft *Adj.* ghostly, spooky *umg.*

Geister|hand *f*: **wie von** *od.* **durch ~** as if by magic; **~haus** *n* **1.** haunted house; **2.** *Buddhismus etc.*: spirit house

geistern *v/i. fig.* (*mit Richtung: ist gegeistert / ohne Richtung: hat*) **1.** haunt a place; (*um*) *od.* about); (*huschen*) flit

---

around; **was geisterst du nachts durchs Haus?** what are you doing wandering around the house at night?; *Licht etc.*: **~ über** (+ *Akk.*) flit across; **die Idee geistert immer noch durch ihre Köpfe** they still haven't managed to get that idea out of their heads; **dieser Irrtum geistert durch die gesamte Literatur** this error is endemic in the entire (*od.* all the) literature

Geister|reich *n* realm of spirits, spirit world; **~schiff** *n* ghost ship; **~schloss** *n* haunted castle; **~stadt** *f* ghost town; **~stimme** *f* **1.** spooky voice; **2.** *TV* voice-over; **~stunde** *f* witching hour; **~welt** *f* realm (*od.* world) of the supernatural (*od.* spirits)

geistesabwesend I. *Adj.* absent, distracted; **II.** *Adv.* absent-mindedly; (*nachdenklich*) absently; **Geistesabwesenheit** *f*; *nur Sg.* distractedness; (*Zerstreutheit*) absent-mindedness

Geistes|anstrengung *f* mental effort; **~arbeit** *f* brainwork; **~blitz** *m* *umg.* flash of inspiration; (*konkrete Idee*) brainwave, *Am.* brainstorm; **~frische** *f* mental vigo(u)r (*od.* alertness), acumen; **~gaben** *Pl.* intellectual gifts

Geistesgegenwart *f* presence of mind; **geistesgegenwärtig I.** *Adj. Person*: alert, on the ball *umg.*; *auch Antwort, Reaktion etc.*: quick; **II.** *Adv.*: **~ riss er das Kind weg** he had the presence of mind to pull the child away

Geistesgeschichte *f*; *nur Sg.* history of ideas, intellectual history; **die deutsche** *etc.* **~** the history of German *etc.* thought, German *etc.* intellectual history

geistesgestört *Adj.* mentally disturbed; **Geistesgestörte** *m, f; -n, -n* mentally disturbed person; **Geistesgestörtheit** *f*; *nur Sg.* mental imbalance (*stärker*: derangement)

Geistes|größe *f* **1.** *nur Sg.*: **ihr fehlte / sie hatte die ~, sich zu entschuldigen** she lacked/had the grace to apologize; **2.** *Person*: great thinker; **~haltung** *f* attitude, mentality, mindset; **~kraft** *f* mental power; **Geisteskräfte** mental faculties

geisteskrank *Adj.* mentally ill (*od.* disordered); **Geisteskranke** *m, f* mental patient; *Pl. the* mentally ill (*Pl.*); **Geisteskrankheit** *f* mental disease

Geistes|riese *m*, **~riesin** *f* *umg.* genius; **~schaffende** *m, f; -n, -n* brainworker; **~schärfe** *f* acuity of mind, acumen

geistesschwach *Adj.* feebleminded; **Geistesschwäche** *f*; *nur Sg.* feeblemindedness

Geistes|störung *f* mental disorder; **~verfassung** *f* frame of mind, (mental) state

geistesverwandt *Adj.* congenial (*mit* to), *nur attr.* kindred; **~e Menschen** kindred spirits; **Geistesverwandtschaft** *f* (spiritual) affinity

Geistesverwirrung *f* confused state of mind

Geisteswissenschaft *f* arts subject; **die ~en** the arts, the humanities; **Geisteswissenschaftler** *m*, **Geisteswissenschaftlerin** *f* arts (*od.* humanities) scholar (*od.* person, man/woman *umg.*); *Student*: arts student; **geisteswissenschaftlich** *Adj.* arts ...; *Forschung etc., nachgestellt*: in the arts, in the (field of) humanities

Geisteszustand *m* mental state; **j-n auf s-n ~ (hin) untersuchen** examine s.o.'s state of mind; (*förmlich untersu-*

G

chen) subject s.o. to psychiatric tests; *du solltest dich mal auf d-n ~ untersuchen lassen! umg.* you need your head examined

geistfeindlich *Adj.* anti-intellectual

geistig I. *Adj.* **1.** (*seelisch, nicht körperlich*) spiritual; (*die Denkkraft betreffend*) intellectual, mental; *Mensch:* intellectual; *vor j-s ~em Auge* in s.o.'s mind's eye; *~er Austausch* exchange of ideas; *~er Diebstahl* plagiarism; *~es Eigentum* intellectual property; *~er Vater* spiritual father; **2.** *~e Getränke* spirits, alcohol; **II.** *Adv.* mentally *etc.;* → I; *~ anspruchsvoll* highbrow; *~ behindert* mentally handicapped; *~ gesund/zurückgeblieben* sane/backward (*od.* retarded); *~ aktiv sein* (*rege*) have an active mind; (*sich mit geistig Anspruchsvollem befassen*) exercise one's mind; (*viele geistige Interessen haben*) have a lot of intellectual pursuits; *~ arbeiten* work with one's brain; *ich kann ~ nicht mehr folgen* I'm lost, you've *etc.* lost me; **Geistigkeit** *f; nur Sg.* intellectuality; *auf die Seele bezogen:* spirituality

geistig-seelisch *Adj.* mental and spiritual

geistlich *Adj.* religious; *Musik etc.: auch* sacred; (*Priester betreffend*) clerical; (*kirchlich*) ecclesiastical; (*nicht weltlich*) spiritual; *~es Amt* ministry; *~en Beistand brauchen od. wünschen* require someone to tend to one's spiritual needs; → *Stand* 5; **Geistliche** *m, f; -n, -n* member of the clergy, *männlich auch* clergyman, *weiblich auch* clergywoman; (*Pfarrer[in]*) minister; (*Priester*) priest; *in Gefängnis, Armee:* chaplain, padre; *die ~n* the clergy *Pl.;* **Geistlichkeit** *f; nur Sg.; Koll.* the clergy *Pl.*

geistlos *Adj.* (*langweilig*) dull; *Person:* insipid; (*dumm*) stupid, witless; *Unterhaltung:* shallow; **Geistlosigkeit** *f* **1.** *nur Sg.; Eigenschaft:* insipidity; **2.** *Äußerung:* banality, platitude

geistreich *Adj.* witty, clever; *e-e nicht gerade ~e Bemerkung* not the most profound remark

geist|sprühend *Adj.* sparkling, scintillating; *~tötend* *Adj.* deadly boring; *Beschäftigung: auch* mind-dulling, mind-numbing, brainless *umg.; es war ~ auch* it was a crushing bore *umg.; ~voll Adj.* **1.** → *geistreich;* **2.** (*tief*) profound

Geiz *m; -es, kein Pl.* stinginess, miserliness; *aus lauter ~ macht er die Heizung nicht an* he's too stingy to turn the heating on; **geizen** *v/i.: ~ mit* be mean with; *nicht ~ mit* be very generous with, not to stint (on); *mit Worten ~* be very sparing with words; *mit s-r Zeit ~* plan one's time very carefully; *er geizt mit jeder Mark* he counts every mark before he spends it; **Geizhals** *m pej.* skinflint, (*old*) miser; **geizig** *Adj.* stingy, tight-fisted, miserly; **Geizkragen** *m umg. pej.* skinflint, (*old*) miser

Gejammer *n; -s, kein Pl.; umg. pej.* moaning, whining

Gejohle *n; -s, kein Pl.; umg. pej.* shouting

gekannt I. *P.P.* → *kennen;* **II.** *Adj.: ein nie ~es Gefühl* a feeling never felt before; *von nie ~em Ausmaß* of unprecedented size

Gekicher *n; -s, kein Pl.; umg., oft pej.* giggling

Gekläff(e) *n; -s, kein Pl.; umg. pej.* yapping, barking

Geklapper *n; -s, kein Pl.; umg., oft pej.* rattling, clatter

gekleidet I. *P.P.* → *kleiden;* **II.** *Adj.* **1.** *gut/schlecht etc. ~* well/badly *etc.* dressed; *schwarz etc. ~* dressed in black *etc.; in Lumpen ~* dressed in rags; **2.** *fig.: e-e in freundliche Worte ~e Kränkung* an insult cloaked in friendly words, *Am.* a backhanded compliment

Geklingel *n; -s, kein Pl.; umg., oft pej.* ringing; *von Glöckchen etc.:* tinkling, jingling

geklommen *P.P.* → *klimmen*

geklungen *P.P.* → *klingen*

geknickt I. *P.P.* → *knicken;* **II.** *Adj. umg. fig.* crestfallen, crushed

gekniffen *P.P.* → *kneifen*

geknüppelt I. *P.P.* → *knüppeln;* **II.** *Adv. umg.: ~ voll* jampacked, chock-a-block

gekocht I. *P.P.* → *kochen;* **II.** *Adj.* (*Ggs. roh*) cooked; *~es Gemüse* boiled (*od.* cooked) vegetables; *~es Obst* stewed fruit; *gar ~* done; *weich ~* cooked till soft; *Fleisch:* cooked till tender; *hart/weich ~e Eier* hard-/soft-boiled eggs

gekommen *P.P.* → *kommen*

gekonnt I. *P.P.* → *können;* **II.** *Adj.* skil(l)ful; (*meisterhaft*) masterly; *das war ~! auch* it was brilliant; **III.** *Adv.: das hat sie ~ gemacht auch* she made an excellent job of it

gekörnt I. *P.P.* → *körnen;* **II.** *Adj.: ~e Brühe Gastr.* stock granules

gekränkt I. *P.P.* → *kränken;* **II.** *Adj.* hurt, offended (*über + Akk.* at, by); *Stolz:* injured

gekräuselt I. *P.P.* → *kräuseln;* **II.** *Adj. Haar etc.:* curly; *Wasser:* rippled; *Stoff:* gathered

Gekreisch(e) *n; -s, kein Pl.; umg., oft pej.* screeching, screaming; *von Bremsen, Reifen:* screeching

Gekreuzigte *m; -n, kein Pl.; kirchl.: der ~* Christ on the cross, Christ crucified

Gekritzel *n; -s, kein Pl.; pej.* **1.** *Schreiben:* scrawling, scribbling; *Malen:* daubing; **2.** *Schrift:* scrawl, scribble; *Männchen, Muster:* doodle

gekrochen *P.P.* → *kriechen*

gekrönt I. *P.P.* → *krönen;* **II.** *Adj.* **1.** *~e Häupter* crowned heads; **2.** *fig.: von Erfolg ~* crowned with success

Gekröse *n; -s.* **1.** *Gastr. vom Kalb:* tripe; *vom Schwein:* chitterlings, *Am. auch* chitlins; *von Geflügel:* giblets; **2.** *Anat.* mesentery

gekrümmt I. *P.P.* → *krümmen;* **II.** *Adj.* curved; *hakenartig:* hooked; (*gebogen, gebeugt*) bent; (*verzogen, verworfen*) warped; *in ~er Haltung* bent, doubled-over; **III.** *Adv.: sie geht ganz ~* she's almost bent double

gekünstelt *Adj. pej.* artificial, affected; *Stil: auch* stilted, contrived; *Lachen:* forced

Gel *n; -s, -e od. umg. -s* gel

Gelaber *n; -s, kein Pl.; umg. pej.* drivel

Gelächter *n; -s, -, mst Sg.* laughing, laughter; *wieherndes ~* guffaw; *in schallendes ~ ausbrechen* roar with laughter; *j-n/etw. dem ~ preisgeben* expose s.o./s.th. to ridicule; (*j-n*) *auch* make s.o. a laughing stock; (+ *Gen.*) make s.o. the laughing stock of

gelackmeiert *umg.* **I.** *P.P.* → *lackmeiern;* **II.** *Adj.: sich ~ fühlen* feel one has been had (*od.* conned, *od.* taken for a ride); *und ich bin der Gelack-*

meierte! I've been had (*od.* taken for a ride), I'm the sucker (*od.* mug), I'm the one who's left holding the baby

gelackt I. *P.P.* → *lacken;* **II.** *Adj. umg. pej. Person:* slick

geladen I. *P.P.* → *laden¹, laden²;* **II.** *Adj.* **1.** *Waffe:* loaded; **2.** *fig.: ~ mit Energie, Spannung* brimming with; **3.** *Etech., Phys., Batterie etc.:* charged; *Draht:* live; *positiv/negativ ~* positively/negatively charged; **4.** *umg. fig.* (*wütend*) fuming, mad; *auf j-n ~ sein* have it in for s.o.; **5.** *Gast:* invited; *Zeuge:* subpoenaed; *nur für ~e Gäste* by invitation only

Gelage *n; -s, -* feast; *wildes ~* wild carousal

gelagert I. *P.P.* → *lagern;* **II.** *Adj. fig.: anders ~* different; *das hängt davon ab, wie der Fall ~ ist* that depends on the particular case (*od.* on the nature of the case)

gelähmt I. *P.P.* → *lähmen;* **II.** *Adj.* paralysed (*fig. vor + Dat.* with); *rechtsseitig/linksseitig ~* paralysed on the right/left (*od.* down one's right/left side); *einseitig/doppelseitig od. beidseitig ~* paralysed on (*od.* down) one side / both sides of one's body, hemiplegic/paraplegic *fachspr.; wie ~ dastehen* stand rooted to the spot, stand transfixed; *sie war vor Angst wie ~* she was petrified (*od.* paralysed with fear); **Gelähmte** *m, f; -n, -n* person affected by paralysis, disabled person, paralytic

Gelände *n; -s, -* area; (*Boden*) ground, terrain; *zum Bauen:* site; (*Areal*) grounds *Pl.*, complex; (*ein*) *hügeliges ~* hilly ground; (*ein*) *offenes ~* open country (*od.* terrain); (*ein*) *schwieriges ~* difficult terrain; *das ~ erkunden Mil.* to reconnoit|re (*Am.* -er) (the terrain); *~aufnahme f* topographical survey; (*Luftbild*) aerial photograph; *~ausbildung f Mil.* field training; *~erkundung f Mil.* terrain reconnaissance; *~fahrt f* cross-country drive; *~fahrzeug n* all-terrain (*od.* off-road) vehicle; all- (*od.* four-)wheel drive (vehicle)

geländegängig *Adj. attr.* all-terrain, off-road, *präd.* suitable for all types of terrain

Gelände|kunde *f; nur Sg.* topography; *~lauf m Sport* cross-country run (*Wettlauf:* race); *Sportart:* cross-country (running); *~marsch m Mil.* cross-country march

Geländer *n; -s, - auch am Balkon:* railing(s *Pl.*); *an Treppe:* ban(n)ister(s *Pl.*); *~pfosten m* newel (post); *~stange f* handrail

Gelände|reifen *m Mot.* cross-country tyre (*Am.* tire); *~ritt m* cross-country ride; *Reitsport:* cross-country (ride *od.* riding); *~sport m* field sports *Pl.;* *~wagen m* → *Geländefahrzeug*

gelang *Imperf.* → *gelingen*

gelangen *v/i.* **1.** *räumlich: ~ an* (+ *Akk.*) (*od. nach, zu*) reach, get to; *ans od. zum Ziel ~* reach (*od.* arrive at) one's destination; *fig.* reach one's goal; **2.** (*kommen*) reach, come to; *an die Öffentlichkeit ~* become public, reach the public; *in j-s Besitz/Hände ~* come into s.o.'s possession / get (*od.* come) into s.o.'s hands; *an die Macht ~* come to power; *zu der Ansicht od. Überzeugung etc. ~, dass ...* come to the conclusion that ..., decide that ...; → *Erkenntnis¹* 2, *Schluss* 1, 5; **3.** (*erlangen*): *zu Geld ~ durch Arbeit:* make money; *durch Erbe etc.*: come into money; *zu e-m Vermögen, Reichtum etc.*: acquire; **zu Macht/Ruhm** *etc.* ~ gain power/fame *etc.*; **zu Ehren** ~ make a name for o.s.; **4.** *statt Passiv*: **zur Aufführung** ~ be staged, be put on; **zum Einsatz** ~ be used; *Spieler* play, take the field

gelangweilt I. *P.P.* → **langweilen**; **II.** *Adj.* bored; *Gesichter: auch* bored-looking; **zu Tode** ~ *fig.* bored to death (*od.* tears); **III.** *Adv.*: **sie hörten** ~ **zu** they listened, completely bored

gelassen I. *P.P.* → **lassen** I, III; **II.** *Adj.* calm; *(gefasst)* composed; *(besonnen)* cool; *(Ggs. erschüttert)* unperturbed, unruffled; ~ **bleiben** keep calm, keep one's cool *umg.*; **III.** *Adv.*: **etw.** ~ **hinnehmen** take s.th. calmly; *(ungerührt)* take s.th. in one's stride; **Gelassenheit** *f; nur Sg. (Ruhe)* calm(ness); *(Gefasstheit)* composure; *(Besonnenheit)* coolness; *(Unerschütterlichkeit)* imperturbability; → **gelassen**

Geläster *n; -s, kein Pl.; pej.* backbiting, making malicious (*od.* snide) remarks

Gelatine [ʒela'ti:nə] *f; -, kein Pl.* gelatin(e); **kapsel** *f* gelatin(e) capsule, gelcap, *Am.* softgel

gelaufen *P.P.* → **laufen**

geläufig *Adj.* **1.** *(allgemein bekannt)* familiar, common; **das Wort ist mir** *(nicht)* ~ *(bekannt)* I've (never) heard (of) the word; *(vertraut)* it's not a word I know (*od.* I'm familiar with); **2.** *(fließend)* fluent; **Geläufigkeit** *f; nur Sg.* **1.** *e-s Wortes*: widespread use, currency; **2.** *(Gewandtheit)* ease (*beim Spielen* with which one plays)

gelaunt *Adj.*: **gut/schlecht** ~ in a good/bad mood; **froh** ~ happy, cheerful, in a cheerful mood; **wie ist sie heute** ~**?** what kind of mood is she in today?; **wie bist du wieder** ~**!** *iro.* I see you got out of bed the wrong side this morning; *ärgerlich* what's got into you?

Geläut *n; -s, -e* **1.** *nur Sg.* ringing (of bells); **2.** *(die Glocken)* bells *Pl.*, peal, chime(s *Pl.*)

geläutert I. *P.P.* → **läutern**; **II.** *Adj.* **1.** *Tech.* refined; **2.** *fig.* purified, chastened

gelb *Adj.* **1.** yellow; *Verkehrsampel*: amber; *Teint*: sallow; ~ **vor Neid** green with envy; **der Gelbe Fluss** *Geog.* the Yellow River; **die** ~**e Gefahr** *altm. pej.* the yellow peril; **die** ~**e Karte** *Sport* the yellow card; **Gelbe Rübe** carrot; **die Gelben Seiten** the yellow pages; **das** ~**e Trikot** *Sport* the yellow jersey; **2.** *(für Verpackungen)* Container, Sack, Tonne: yellow *used for collecting packaging materials for recycling*

Gelb *n; -s, - od. umg. -s* yellow; **bei** ~ **über die Kreuzung fahren** cross when the lights are at (*od.* on) amber (*Am.* yellow); **er hat bereits** ~ **gesehen** *Sport* he's already been shown the yellow card (*od.* already on a yellow [card]); ~**braun** *Adj.* yellowish- (*od.* yellowy-)brown

Gelbe *n; -s, -n, kein Pl.; vom Ei*: yolk; **das ist auch nicht gerade das** ~ **vom Ei** *umg. fig.* that's not exactly brilliant either, is it?; **II.** *m, f; -n, -n; pej.*: **die** ~**n** Orientals, slants *neg!*, slant-eyes *neg!*

Gelb|fieber *n; nur Sg.; Med.* yellow fever; ~**filter** *m, n Fot.* yellow filter; ~**körper** *m Physiol.* corpus luteum

gelblich *Adj.* yellowish, yellowy; ~ **weiß** yellowish-white

Gelbstich *m; nur Sg.; Fot.* yellow cast; **gelbstichig** *Adj.*: ~ **sein** have a yellow cast

Gelbsucht *f; nur Sg.; Med.* (yellow) jaundice; **gelbsüchtig** *Adj.* jaundiced; ~ **sein** have (yellow) jaundice

Gelb|wurz *f; -, -en*, ~**wurzel** *f Bot.* turmeric

Geld *n; -es, -er* **1.** money, cash *umg.*; **bares** ~ cash; **großes** ~ notes, *Am. auch* bills; **kleines** ~ (small) change; **schmutziges/heißes** ~ *fig.* dirty/hot money; **schnelles** *od.* **leicht verdientes** ~ easy money; **für billiges** *od.* **wenig / teures** *od.* **viel** ~ cheaply / for a lot of money; **das kostet ein irrsinniges** ~ it costs a fortune, it costs an arm and a leg *umg.*; ~ **und Gut** money and property; ~ **oder Leben!** your money or your life!; **etw. für sein** ~ **bekommen** get one's money's worth; **sein** ~ **unter die Leute bringen** go on a spending spree, spend freely; **ohne** ~ **dastehen** *(momentan kein Bargeld bei sich haben)* have no money on one; *(arm sein)* have no money, be penniless; **das geht ins** ~ *umg.* it'll cost you *etc.*, that's going to cost you *etc.* a pretty penny; **zu** ~ **kommen** get hold of some money; *(reich werden)* strike (it) rich *umg.*, hit the jackpot *umg.*; *(Geld erben)* come into money; ~ **machen** *umg.* make money (aus *od.* of); **zu** ~ **machen** turn into cash; **was machst du mit dem vielen** ~**?** what do you do with all that money of yours?; **auf s-m** ~ **sitzen** *umg. fig. pej.* sit on one's money; **um** ~ **spielen** play for money; ~ **waschen** *umg.* launder money; **mit s-m** ~ **um sich werfen** *od.* **schmeißen** *umg.* throw one's money around; **sein** ~ **wert sein** be worth the money; **die wollen nur dein** ~ all they're after is your money; ~ **spielt keine Rolle** money's no object; **2.** *fig. in Wendungen*: **sie hat** ~ **wie Heu** *od.* **schwimmt im** ~, **stinkt vor** ~ *umg.* she's rolling in money (*od.* it); **es/er ist für** ~ **nicht zu haben** it's not for sale (*od.* you can't buy him; **sie ist nicht mit** ~ **zu bezahlen** she's worth her weight in gold; **das** ~ **liegt auf der Straße** the money's there to be had (*od.* for the taking); **das liebe** ~**!** money, money, money!; **nicht für** ~ **und gute Worte** not for love or money; ~ **stinkt nicht** *Sprichw.* money's money, money talks; ~ **regiert die Welt** *Sprichw.* money makes the world go round; → **Fenster** 1, **rinnen**; **3.** *Wirts.* (Anlagekapital) *mst* ~**er** money, funds; *(Einlagen)* deposits; **es geht um die Veruntreuung von** ~**ern in Millionenhöhe** the amounts that have been embezzled run into millions; **sein** ~ **arbeiten lassen** *fig.* make one's money work (for one); **4.** *Fin.* (Geldkurs) bid price

Geld|abwertung *f* (currency) devaluation; ~**adel** *m* the rich (and powerful); ~**angelegenheit** *f* money matter; *j-s* ~**en** s.o.'s financial affairs; → **Gelddinge**, ~**anlage** *f* investment; ~**anleger** *m*, ~**anlegerin** *f* investor; ~**anweisung** *f* money order; ~**aufwand** *m* expenditure(s *Pl.*); ~**automat** *m* cash dispenser (*umg.* machine), hole in the wall *Brit. umg.*, automated teller machine (abgek. ATM), *Am. auch* MAC (= money access center); ~**bedarf** *m* cash requirements *Pl.*; *Geldmarkt*: currency demands *Pl.*; ~**beschaffung** *f* raising funds; ~**bestand** *m* monetary holdings

Pl. (*od.* stock); ~**betrag** *m* amount, sum; ~**beutel** *m* **1.** purse; **2.** *fig.*: **e-n dicken/dünnen** ~ **haben** be well-off/-hard-up; *(nicht)* **für jeden** ~ (not) within everybody's means *od.* reach; *(für etw.)* **tief in den** ~ **greifen** *(müssen)* (have to) dig deep into one's pocket (for s.th); ~**bombe** *f* night safe container; ~**börse** *f geh.* → **Geldbeutel**, ~**bote** *m*, ~**botin** *f* security guard; ~**briefträger** *m hist. postman who delivers money orders*; ~**buße** *f* fine; **zu e-r** ~ **verurteilt werden** be fined; ~**dinge** *Pl.*: **in** ~**n** in money (*od.* financial) matters, when it's a question of money; ~**einnahmen** *Pl.* receipts; ~**empfänger** *m*, ~**empfängerin** *f* payee; ~**entwertung** *f* inflation; ~**erwerb** *m* moneymaking; **zum** ~ to make money

Geld|forderung *f* money due; *Schuld*: outstanding debt; *Anspruch*: monetary claim; ~**frage** *f* financial matter; **e-e** *(reine)* ~ (just) a question of money; ~**geber** *m*, ~**geberin** *f* financial backer; *engS.* sponsor; ~**geschäft** *n* **1.** money transaction; **2.** banking (business); ~**geschenk** *n* (gift of) money; *größeres*: donation

Geldgier *f* greed for money, avarice; **geldgierig** *Adj.* greedy for money, obsessed with money

Geld|hahn *m fig.*: **j-m den** ~ **zudrehen** cut off s.o.'s money supply; **e-m Institut** *etc.* **den** ~ **zudrehen** axe funding for an institute's activities *etc.*; ~**heirat** *f* marriage for money; ~**institut** *n Wirts.* financial institution; ~**karte** *f umg aufladbare*: charge card; ~**kassette** *f* cash box; ~**knappheit** *f* shortage of money; ~**koffer** *m* money chest; *mit Inhalt*: chest (full) of money; *in Geldtransportwagen*: safe, strongbox; *fig.* coffers

Geld|kreislauf *m Wirts.* money circuit; ~**kurs** *m (Kaufkurs)* buying rate; *der Börse*: bid price; ~**leistung** *f* payment

geldlich *Adj.* financial, monetary; **um die** ~**en Dinge kümmert sich seine Frau** his wife takes care of the financial side of things; **hast du** ~**e Probleme?** have you got (*Am. auch* do you have) money problems?

Geldmacherei *f; -, kein Pl.; umg.* moneymaking, money-spinning

Geld|mangel *m* lack of money; ~**markt** *m* money market; ~**menge** *f Wirts.* money supply; ~**mittel** *Pl.* means, funds, (financial) resources; ~**münze** *f* coin; ~**not** *f des Staates*: shortage of money; *e-r Person*: financial difficulties (*od.* straits); ~**politik** *f* financial policy; ~**prämie** *f* bonus; ~**preis** *m Sport* cash prize; ~**quelle** *f* source of money; ~**reserve** *f* money reserve; ~**rolle** *f* roll of coins

Geldrückgabe *f* **1.** *Handlung*: giving money back; *Aufschrift auf Automat*: coin return; **keine** ~ *Aufschrift*: no change given; **2.** *das Geld*: money back; ~**taste** *f* coin-return button

Geld|sack *m* **1.** moneybag; *mit Inhalt*: bag of money; **2.** *umg. pej. (reicher Mann)* moneybags *Sg.*; ~**sammlung** *f* collection, *Brit. umg. auch* whip-round; ~**schein** *m* (bank)note, *Am. auch* bill

Geldschrank *m* safe; ~**knacker** *m*, ~**knackerin** *f; -, -nen; umg.* safecracker

Geld|schuld *f* (money) debt; ~**schwierigkeiten** *Pl.* financial difficulties (*od.* straits); **in** ~ **sein** be in financial difficulties; ~**segen** *m* bonanza, financial

G

godsend; **~sendung** f cash remittance; **~sorgen** Pl. money worries; → auch **Geldschwierigkeiten**; **~sorten** Pl. Fin. currencies; **~spende** f donation; **~spielautomat** m slot machine; **~strafe** f Jur. fine; **zu e-r ~ verurteilen** fine; **~strom** m flow (stärker flood) of money; **~stück** n coin; **~summe** f sum (of money); **~tasche** f money bag; **~töpfe** Pl. coffers; **~transport** m transport(ing) of money; **~transporter** m security van

Geld|umlauf m circulation of money; **~umsatz** m turnover; **~umstellung** f (currency) conversion; **~umtausch** m currency exchange

Geld|verdienen n; -s, kein Pl. money-making; (s-n Unterhalt verdienen) earning a living; **sich ans ~ machen** start earning some money (od. a living); **~verdiener** m, **~verdienerin** f verdient viel Geld: moneymaker; im Hause bread-winner

Geld|verlegenheit f: **in ~ sein** be pushed for money, be hard up (for cash), be in a tight spot (financially); **~verleiher** m, **~verleiherin** f money-lender; **~verlust** m financial loss; **~vermögen** n Wirts., Jur. financial assets Pl.; **~verschwendung** f 1. Sache: waste of money; 2. Handlung: wasting of money; (Luxus) extravagance; **~vorrat** m Wirts. funds Pl.; (Bargeld) cash reserve; (Kassenbestand) cash in hand; **am Geldmarkt**: supply of money; → auch **Geldbestand**

Geldwaschanlage f umg. iro. money-laundering outfit (od. scheme, Am. operation); **Geldwäsche** f umg. iro. money laundering

Geld|wechsel m Wirts. currency exchange; Schild: Bureau de Change, Am. Foreign Exchange; **~wechsler** m 1. Person: moneychanger; 2. Automat: money-changing machine, money-changer; **~wert** m cash value; Wirts. value of (the) currency; **~wesen** n Fin. monetary system, finance

Geldwirtschaft f Fin. money economy; **geldwirtschaftlich** Adj. monetary

Geldzuwendung f 1. dauernde: allowance; 2. einmalige: appropriation of funds; 3. → **Geldgeschenk**

geleckt I. P.P. → **lecken**[1], **lecken**[2]; II. Adj. umg. hum.: **wie ~ aussehen** Wohnung etc.: be spick and span, be squeaky clean umg.; Person: be all spruced up

Gelee [ʒeˈleː] n, m; -s, -s; Gastr. jelly; **Hering in ~** herring in aspic

Gelege n; -s, -; Zool., von Vögeln: clutch (of eggs), eggs; von Reptilien, Insekten: eggs; von Fischen, Fröschen: spawn

gelegen I. P.P. → **liegen**; II. Adj. 1. einsam, schön etc. ~ lying, situated, located; **an e-m See ~** (situated) beside (od. on) a lake; **die nach Norden ~en Fenster** the north-facing windows; **am höchsten ~** highest; 2. (passend) convenient, suitable; (günstig) opportune; **es ist ihr sehr daran ~** it's very important to her, it matters a lot to her; **allgemein**: auch she sets great store by it; **mir ist sehr daran ~, dass er es tut** I'm very anxious od. keen for him to do it (od. that he should do it); **mir ist nichts daran ~** I don't care one way or the other; III. Adv: **es kommt mir ganz / nicht sehr ~** Termin etc.: that suits me just fine / that's not very convenient for me; Sache: that's just what I need / not quite right for me

Gelegenheit f 1. opportunity, chance; (Anlass) occasion; **bei ~** (irgendwann) some time; (wenn möglich) when I etc. get a chance; **bei dieser ~ lernte ich ihn kennen** that's when I got to know him; **bei dieser ~ möchte ich bemerken ...** I'd like to take this opportunity to say (od. of saying) ...; **bei der ersten ~** as soon as I etc. can, the first chance I etc. get umg., at the earliest opportunity geh.; **bei jeder sich bietenden / passenden und unpassenden ~** at any and every opportunity, at the drop of a hat; **~ haben zu** (+ Inf.) have the opportunity (od. chance) to (+ Inf.); **die ~ ergreifen** od. **wahrnehmen, nutzen zu** (+ Inf.) take the opportunity to (+ Inf.) (od. of [+ Ger.]); **die ~ ungenutzt verstreichen lassen** pass up the opportunity; **sie hat die ~ beim Schopf gepackt** she seized the opportunity; **j-m ~ geben zu** (+ Inf.) give s.o. the opportunity to (+ Inf.) (od. of + Ger.), give s.o. a (od. the) chance to (+ Inf.); **es bot sich eine ~** an opportunity came up (od. presented itself); **ein Kleid für besondere ~en** a dress for special occasions; **~ macht Diebe** Sprichw. opportunity makes the thief; 2. Wirts. (günstiges Angebot) bargain

Gelegenheits|arbeit f casual labo(u)r, odd jobs Pl. umg.; **~dieb** m, **~diebin** f sneak thief; **~gedicht** n occasional poem; **~kauf** m bargain; **~käufer** m, **~käuferin** f chance buyer; **~raucher** m, **~raucherin** f occasional smoker

gelegentlich I. Adj. 1. occasional; (zeitweilig) temporary; **~e Anrufe** etc. the occasional (od. odd) phone call etc.; 2. (zufällig) chance ...; (unverbindlich) casual; II. Adv. 1. (manchmal) occasionally, now and then, from time to time; **~ e-e Tasse Kaffee trinken** have the occasional cup of coffee; 2. (bei Gelegenheit) when you get (she gets etc.) a chance; (irgendwann) some time; III. Präp. (+ Gen.) Amtsspr. (anlässlich) on the occasion of

gelehrig Adj. (lernwillig) receptive; auch Tier: eager to learn, teachable; (mit schneller Auffassungsgabe) quick (on the uptake); **Gelehrigkeit** f; nur Sg. receptiveness; auch Tier eagerness to learn; (schnelle Auffassungsgabe) quickness

gelehrsam Adj. 1. → **gelehrig**; 2. altm. → **gelehrt** II; **Gelehrsamkeit** f; nur Sg.; geh. 1. → **Gelehrigkeit**; 2. (hoher Bildungsstand) erudition, learning, scholarship

gelehrt I. P.P. → **lehren**; II. Adj. learned, erudite; (wissenschaftlich) scholarly; pej. highbrow; **die ~e Welt** academia, scholars Pl.; III. Adv. umg., mst pej.: **sich ~ ausdrücken** speak in tongues; **Gelehrte** m, f; -n, -n scholar; **die ~n** scholars

Gelehrten|kreis m scholarly circle, circle of scholars; **in ~en** among scholars, in scholarly circles; **~streit** m academic (od. scholarly) dispute od. debate

Gelehrtheit f; nur Sg. → **Gelehrsamkeit** 2

Geleier n; -s, kein Pl.; pej. (endless) droning

Geleise n; -s, -; österr. od. geh. → **Gleis**

geleistet I. P.P. → **leisten**; II. Adj.: **~e Arbeitsstunden** hours worked (od. put in); **~e Zahlungen** payments made

Geleit n; -(e)s, -e 1. **j-m das ~ geben** geh. escort s.o.; **j-m freies** od. **sicheres ~ geben** od. **gewähren** Jur. give s.o. safe conduct; **j-m das letzte ~ geben** geh. euph. pay s.o. one's last respects; **zum ~** in Büchern: Foreword; 2. escort; Mil. convoy; → auch **Gefolge** 1; **~boot** n Naut. escort vessel; **~brief** m letter of safe conduct

geleiten v/t. geh. accompany; Mil. und schützend: escort; **an die Tür ~** see s.o. to the door

Geleit|fahrzeug n escorting vehicle; Naut. escort vessel; **~schutz** m Mil. escort; **unter ~** under escort, escorted; **~ geben** escort; **~zug** m Mil., Naut. convoy

Gelenk n; -(e)s, -e 1. Anat. joint (auch Tech.); der Hand: wrist; des Fußes: ankle; 2. Bot. articulation, joint; **~bus** m articulated bus; **~entzündung** f Med. arthritis

gelenkig Adj. supple; (flink, gewandt) agile; (geschmeidig) lithe, lissom

Gelenk|kapsel f Anat. articular capsule; **~kopf** m 1. Tech. swivel head; 2. Anat. condyle; **~pfanne** f Anat. socket; **~rheumatismus** m Med. rheumatoid arthritis; **~schmerzen** Pl. Med. pains in one's joints; **~stange** f Tech. toggle link

gelenkt I. P.P. → **lenken**; II. Adj. Presse, Gespräch: controlled; Rakete etc.: guided; **~e Wirtschaft** planned economy

Gelenk|verbindung f Tech. link joint; **~welle** f Tech. cardan shaft

gelernt I. P.P. → **lernen**; II. Adj. (ausgebildet) qualified; Arbeiter: skilled; Handwerker etc.: trained

gelesen I. P.P. → **lesen**[1], **lesen**[2]; II. Adj.: **e-e viel ~e Zeitung** etc. a newspaper etc. with a large circulation (od. readership), a widely-read newspaper etc.

geliebt I. P.P. → **lieben**; II. Adj. beloved lit. od. hum.; **heiß ~** dearly (be)loved; **Geliebte** m, f; -n, -n 1. lover; Frau mst: mistress umg.; 2. altm. Anrede: love, sweetheart

geliefert I. P.P. → **liefern**; II. Adj. umg.: **~ sein** have had it, have had one's chips

geliehen I. P.P. → **leihen**; II. Adj.: **von ~em Geld leben** live on borrowed money

gelieren [ʒeˈliːrən] v/i. gel

Gelier|mittel n gelling (Am. auch jelling) agent; **~zucker** m preserving (Am. canning) sugar

gelind(e) I. Adj. Regen, Wind, Worte: mild; Schmerz, Kälte etc.: slight; Strafe: light; (mäßig) moderate, slight; **gelinde Zweifel** umg. some doubt; **mich packte e-e gelinde Wut** I got really angry; II. Adv.: **gelinde gesagt** to put it mildly

gelingen v/i.: gelingt, gelang, ist gelungen Plan, Versuch: succeed, be successful; (gut) Feier, Kuchen etc.: be a success, turn out well; unpers.: **es gelang ihm zu** (+ Inf.) he managed to (+ Inf.), he succeeded in (+ Ger.); **es gelingt mir einfach nicht zu** (+ Inf.) I just don't seem to be able to (+ Inf.); **m-e Fotos / Aufsätze / Pläne ~ nie** my photos never come out right / my essays never turn out well / my plans never work out; **das Badezimmer** etc. **ist dir gut gelungen** you've made a good job of (od. done a good job on) the bathroom etc.; **die Überraschung ist dir gelungen** auch iro. well that really was a surprise!; → **gelungen**

Gelingen n; -s, kein Pl. success; Ergeb-

nis: successful outcome; *zum ~ e-r Sache beitragen* help (*od.* do one's bit, *Am.* part) to make s.th. a success; (*auf ein*) *gutes ~!* (the) best of luck

gelitten I. *P.P.* → *leiden*; II. *Adj.*: *gut/ schlecht ~* popular/unpopular

gell¹ *Adj. geh.* shrill, piercing

gell² *Adv. südd.*, **gelle** *Adv. Dial.* → *gelt*

gellen *v/i.* 1. *Pfiff, Schrei*: ring out; *ein Schrei gellte durch die Nacht* a shriek shattered the silence of the night; 2. (*widerhallen*) ring (*von* with); *mir ~ die Ohren von d-m Geschrei* my ears are still ringing from all the shouting; **gellend** I. *Part. Präs.* → *gellen*; II. *Adj.* shrill, piercing; *~es Geschrei* screaming, high-pitched screams; III. *Adv.*: *~ lachen* laugh shrilly, give a high-pitched laugh

geloben *v/t. geh.* solemnly promise (*j-m etw.* s.o. s.th.); *eidlich*: vow, pledge; *j-m ewige Treue ~* vow eternal fidelity to s.o.; *ich gelobe hiermit Besserung* I hereby solemnly promise to reform (*oft iro.*); **Gelöbnis** *n; -ses, -se; geh.* (solemn) promise; *eidlich*: pledge, vow; **Gelöbnisfeier** *f Mil.* oath-taking ceremony

gelobt I. *P.P.* → *loben*; II. *Adj.*: *das Gelobte* (*fig.*: *~e*) *Land bibl.* the Promised Land

gelockt I. *P.P.* → *locken¹, locken²*; II. *Adj.*: *~es Haar* curly hair, curls *Pl.*

gelogen *P.P.* → *lügen*

gelöscht I. *P.P.* → *löschen*; II. *Adj. Chem., Kalk*: slaked

gelöst I. *P.P.* → *lösen*; II. *Adj.* 1. *fig. Person*: relaxed; 2. *Substanz*: dissolved (*in + Dat.* in); **Gelöstheit** *f; nur Sg.* relaxed manner (*od.* mood *etc.*)

Gelse *f; -, -n; österr., Zool.* mosquito, gnat

gelt *Adv. südd., österr. umg.*: *sie ist ziemlich reich, ~?* she's quite rich, isn't she?; *das hat dich überrascht, ~?* I bet that surprised you

gelten; *gilt, galt, hat gegolten* I. *v/i.* 1. (*gültig sein*) be valid; (*zählen*) *Fehler, Treffer etc.*: count; *Gesetz etc.*: be effective; *Regel etc.*: apply; *~ für* (*sich anwenden lassen auf*) apply to, go for; *~ lassen* (*akzeptieren*) accept, allow; (*nicht beanstanden*) let s.th. pass; *lassen als* let s.th. pass for; *das lass ich ~!* *od.* *das will ich ~ lassen!* I'll grant you that; *sie lässt nur ihre eigene Meinung ~* she won't accept anybody's opinion but her own; *der Pass gilt nicht mehr* the passport is invalid (*od.* has expired); *gilt das Geld noch?* is this (money) still legal tender?; *in Zweifelsfällen gilt die englische Fassung Jur.* the English version shall prevail; *es gilt die Wette gilt!* you're on!, it's a bet!; → *Bange*; 2. (*wert sein*) be worth s.th.; *etwas ~ Person*: carry weight; *nicht viel ~* not count for much (*bei* with); *was gilt die Wette? - 2 Flaschen Sekt!* what do you bet (me)?; → *Prophet*; 3. *j-m ~ Schuss, Vorwurf etc.*: be for s.o.; *Sympathie etc.*: be for s.o.; *diese spitze Bemerkung galt dir* the remark was aimed at you; 4. *das gilt als unschicklich* that's considered inappropriate (*od.* unseemly); *er gilt als reicher Mann* he is reputed to be a wealthy man, he's said to be rich; *es gilt als sicher od. abgemacht, dass sie kommt* it's taken for granted that she will come; II. *v/i. unpers.* 1. *es gilt, rasch zu handeln* we've got to act

quickly, immediate action is called for; *jetzt gilt's!* this is it; 2. *unpers.; geh.*: *es gilt etw.* (*etw. steht auf dem Spiel*) s.th. is at stake; *es galt unser Leben* it was a matter of life and death

geltend I. *Part. Präs.* → *gelten*; II. *Adj.* 1. valid; *Gesetz etc.*: auch in effect; *Preise, Rechtschreibung etc.*: current; (*allgemein anerkannt*) accepted; (*vorherrschend*) prevailing; *nach ~em Recht* according to the law of the land; 2. *~ machen* (*Ansprüche, Rechte*) assert; (*Gründe*) put forward; (*Einfluss*) bring s.th. to bear, make s.th. felt; (*Einwand*) raise; *~ machen, dass ...* argue that ...; *wieder ~ machen* reassert; 3. *Sache*: *sich ~ machen* make itself felt, be felt

Geltung *f; nur Sg.* 1. (*Gültigkeit*) validity; *~ haben Gesetz etc.*: be valid; (*anwendbar sein*) be applicable (*für* to); (*akzeptiert sein*) be accepted *od.* recognized (*bei* by); *e-m Gesetz / e-r Maßnahme etc. ~ verschaffen* enforce a law/measure *etc.* (*bei* [up]on); *e-r Ansicht etc. ~ verschaffen* get a view *etc.* (generally) accepted (*bei* by); 2. (*Wichtigkeit*) importance; *e-r Person*: auch prestige; (*Achtung*) respect, recognition; (*Wert*) value; *~ erlangen* gain acceptance (*Ansehen*: recognition); *~ haben* carry (a great deal of) weight (*bei* with); *zur ~ bringen* (*Einfluss etc.*) bring to bear; (*hervorheben*) accentuate, bring out; *zur ~ kommen* (begin to) tell, be (*od.* make itself) felt; *Einfluss etc.*: come into play; (*herausragen*) stand out; (*wirkungsvoll erscheinen*) be (very) effective, show to advantage; *sich ~ verschaffen* assert o.s.; (*Ansehen gewinnen*) gain prestige; (*Bedeutung erlangen*) gain importance

Geltungs|bedürfnis *n* → *Geltungsdrang*; *~bereich m* scope; *Gebiet*: area of applicability; *Jur.* (area of) jurisdiction; *e-s Gesetzes*: scope, purview *förm.*; *in den ~ e-s Gesetzes fallen* come within the scope (*förm.* purview) of a law; *~dauer f* (period of) validity; *e-s Patents etc.*: life; *e-s Vertrags*: term; *e-e ~ von ... haben* be valid for ...; *~drang m* need for recognition

Geltungssucht *f; nur Sg.* craving for recognition; **geltungssüchtig** *Adj.*: *~ sein* crave recognition

Gelübde *n; -s, -; geh.* vow; *ein ~ ablegen/brechen* take (*od.* make) /break a vow

gelungen I. *P.P.* → *gelingen*; II. *Adj.* 1. very good, successful, *präd. auch* a success; (*wirkungsvoll*) effective; *das Bild ist gut ~* the picture has turned out well; *das nenne ich e-e ~e Überraschung* that's what I call a surprise!; 2. *Dial.* (*drollig*) funny

Gelüst *n; -(e)s, -e*, **Gelüste** *n; -s, -; geh.* craving (*nach od. auf + Akk.* for); *Pl.* cravings; *sinnliches*: desire, appetite; **gelüsten** *v/t. unpers. mst hum.*: *es gelüstet mich od. mich gelüstet nach* I'm craving for; *es gelüstet mich sehr zu* (+ *Inf.*) I'd love to (+ *Inf.*)

GEMA *f; -, kein Pl.; Abk.* (*Gesellschaft für musikalische Aufführungs- und mechanische Vervielfältigungsrechte*) PRS (*Performing Rights Society*), *Am.* etwa ASCAP, BMI; *~Gebühren Pl.* royalties (payable to the GEMA)

gemach *Adv. hum.*: *~, ~!* gently does it, take it easy

Gemach *n; -(e)s, Gemächer; geh. altm. od. hum.* room, chamber

gemächlich I. *Adj.* leisurely (*auch Leben*); (*langsam*) slow; *~es Tempo* leisurely (*od.* relaxed) pace; *~en Schrittes* at a leisurely pace; II. *Adv.* without any hurry, in one's own time

gemacht I. *P.P.* → *machen*; II. *Adj.* 1. *Bett*: made; *sich ins ~e Bett legen fig.* have it made; 2. *umg.*: *~e Leute* well-to-do people; 3. (*nicht*) *für* (*od. zu*) *etw. ~ sein* (*geeignet sein*) (not) made for (*od.* to)

Gemahl *m; -s, -e, mst Sg.; geh.* husband; *grüßen Sie Ihren Herrn ~ von mir* give my regards to your husband

gemahlen I. *P.P.* → *mahlen*; II. *Adj. Kaffee etc.*: *fein ~* finely ground

Gemahlin *f; -, -nen; geh.* wife, spouse

gemahnen *geh.* I. *v/t.*: *j-n ~ an* (+ *Akk.*) remind s.o. of; II. *v/i.*: *~ an* (+ *Akk.*) recall, remind us (*od.* them) of

Gemäkel *n; -s, kein Pl.; umg. pej.* carping, faultfinding

Gemälde *n; -s, -; Kunst* 1. painting; 2. *fig.* portrait; *~ausstellung f* exhibition of paintings, art exhibition; *~fälscher m, ~fälscherin f* art forger; *~galerie f* art (*od.* picture) gallery

Gemarkung *f* 1. (*Grenze*) boundary; 2. (*Bezirk*) district

gemasert I. *P.P.* → *masern*; II. *Adj.* veined; *Holz*: grained; *Marmor*: marbled

gemäß I. *Präp.* (+ *Dat.*); (*entsprechend*) according to, in accordance with; (*in Übereinstimmung mit*) in compliance (*od.* conformity) with; *~ § 30 BGB* under Article 30 of the Civil Code; II. *Adj.* (*angemessen*) appropriate (+ *Dat.* to), in keeping (with); (*passend*) suited (to); (*entsprechend*) commensurate (with)

...gemäß *im Adj. und Adv.* 1. (*...gerecht*) appropriate to, suitable for; *art~ Tierhaltung*: appropriate for the species; *witterungs~ Kleidung*: suitable for the weather; 2. (*entsprechend*) in accordance with; *anteils~ abrechnen* proportionally; *vereinbarungs~* in accordance with the agreement, as agreed

gemäßigt I. *P.P.* → *mäßigen*; II. *Adj.* 1. moderate; *die ~e Linke/Rechte* the cent|re (*Am.* -er) left/right; *~er Optimismus* guarded optimism; 2. *Zone*: temperate; *Klima*: auch moderate; **Gemäßigte** *m, f; -n, -n* moderate; (*Konservativer*) in *GB*: auch wet *umg.*

Gemäuer *n; -s, -; geh.* walls *Pl.*; *altes od. verfallenes ~* ruins

Gemauschel *n; -s, kein Pl.; umg. pej.* 1. wheeling and dealing; 2. (*undeutliches Reden*) mumbling

Gemecker *n; -s, kein Pl.* 1. *von Ziegen*: bleating; 2. *umg. pej.* (*Nörgeln*) bleating

gemein I. *Adj.* 1. (*boshaft*) mean, nasty; *bes. von Frauen*: auch bitchy *umg.*; *Bemerkung etc.*: mean; (*abfällig*) snide; *~e Lüge* rotten (*od.* dirty, filthy) lie *umg.*; *~er Streich* dirty trick; *das ist ~!* that's not fair, that's mean; *wie kann man nur so ~ sein?* how anyone be so mean (*od.* nasty, cruel)?; 2. *umg.* (*unerfreulich*) awful, terrible; *es regnet schon wieder, wie ~!* how depressing!, what a pain!; *das Gemeine daran* the awful thing about it, what really gets me about it; 3. *umg.* (*schwer*) *Verletzung etc.*: nasty; *die Prüfung, das Interview etc. war ~* was really tough, was a real stinker; 4. (*abstoßend*) *Witz etc.*: vulgar; *Aussehen, Lachen*: coarse; 5. (*gewöhnlich*) common (*auch Bot., Zool.*); **der ~e Mann** the man in the street; **~er Soldat** *Mil.* common soldier; **~er Bruch** *Math.* vulgar fraction; **6. etw. ~ haben mit** have s.th. in common with; **sie haben nichts miteinander ~** they have nothing in common; **sich ~ machen mit** *fig.* rub shoulders with, get chummy with *umg.*; **7.** *attr.; altm. der Allgemeinheit*: common; (*öffentlich*) public; **das ~e Wohl** the common good (*lit.* weal); **8.** *Druck.* (*Ggs. kursiv*) lowercase; **II.** *Adv.* **1.** *umg.*: **~ kalt** awfully cold; **es tut ~ weh** it hurts like hell; **2. ~ an j-m handeln** treat s.o. badly (*od.* shabbily)

Gemeinbesitz *m* public property

Gemeinde *f; -, -n* **1.** *Verwaltungsbezirk*: municipality; *ländlich*: rural commune; *der Kirche*: parish; **2.** *Verwaltung*: local authority; **auf die ~ gehen** *umg.* oft go to the town hall, *Am.* go to city hall; **3.** *Koll.,* (*Bewohner*) residents; *kirchl.* (*Mitglieder*) parish, parishioners *Pl., Am. auch* congregation; *beim Gottesdienst*: congregation; **4.** *fig. Koll.* (*Gemeinschaft*) community; (*Zuhörer*) audience; (*Anhängerschaft*) entourage; **~abgaben** *Pl.* rates, *Am.* local taxes (*od.* assessments); **~ammann** *m schw.* mayor; **~amt** *n* local authority; **~beamte** *m,* **~beamtin** *f* local government officer; **~behörde** *f* local authority; **~betrieb** *m* communal enterprise; **~bezirk** *m* (municipal) district

gemeindeeigen *Adj.* municipal, communal(ly-owned)

Gemeinde|haus *n* **1.** *kirchl.* parish hall; **2.** (*Bürgerhaus*) community cent|re (*Am* -er); **~haushalt** *m* municipal (*od.* local government) budget; **~helfer** *m,* **~helferin** *f kirchl.* parish worker; **~mitglied** *n kirchl.* parishioner, member of the parish; **~ordnung** *f* municipal code; *Brit. auch* byelaws *Pl.;* **~pflege** *f ev.* parish welfare work

Gemeinderat[1] *m Pol., Gremium*: local council

Gemeinde|rat[2] *m,* **~rätin** *f Pol., Person*: municipal council(l)or

Gemeinderats|beschluss *m Pol.* decision taken by the local council; **~mitglied** *n* council(l)or; **~wahl** *f* local election, elections for the local council *Pl.*

Gemeinde|saal *m* church (*od.* parish) hall; **~schwester** *f* district nurse; **~steuer** *f* local tax, *Brit.* council tax

gemeindeutsch *Adj. Ling.* standard German; **das Gemeindeutsche** standard German

Gemeinde|vertreter *m,* **~vertreterin** *f Pol.* local council(l)or; **~vertretung** *f* local council; **~verwaltung** *f* local government

Gemeinde|vorstand *m kirchl.* **1.** *Koll.* parish council; **2.** *Person*: chairman (*od.* chair, *od.* chairwoman) of a (*od.* the) parish council; **~vorsteher** *m,* **~vorsteherin** *f* chair of a (*od.* the) parish council; (*Bürgermeister[in]*) mayor

Gemeinde|wahl *f Pol.* local election(s *Pl.*); **~zentrum** *n* community cent|re (*Am.* -er); *kirchl.* parish rooms *Pl.*

Gemeine *m, f; -n, -n; Mil.* common soldier; **die ~n** the ranks

Gemeineigentum *n* common property; *e-r Gemeinde*: communal property

gemeinerweise *Adv.* meanly; **er hat ~ alles verraten / den Weinkeller abgeschlossen** he meanly went and let it

all out / went and locked the wine cellar, it was mean (*od.* beastly) of him to tell it all / to lock the wine cellar

gemeingefährlich I. *Adj.* dangerous to the public, *präd. auch* a public danger, a danger to the public; **~er Verbrecher** dangerous criminal, *Am. auch* public enemy; **II.** *Adv.*: **~ handeln** endanger public safety

Gemein|geist *m* public spirit; **~gültig** *Adj.* (generally) accepted, recognized; **~gut** *n* common property (*auch fig.*); **zum ~ (der Deutschen) gehören** *fig.* be part of our *etc.* common heritage (be part of Germany's heritage)

Gemeinheit *f* **1.** *nur Sg.* meanness, nastiness; **aus ~** out of (sheer) spite, just to be nasty; **es war e-e ~ zu** (+ *Inf.*) it was really mean of him *etc.* to (+ *Inf.*); **2.** *Handlung*: mean (*od.* dirty) trick, nasty thing to do; *Äußerung*: nasty remark, nasty thing to say; *Umstand, Ereignis*: nuisance, nasty thing to happen; **so e-e ~!** what a nasty thing to do (*od.* say, happen)!

gemeinhin *Adv.* commonly, generally

Gemeinkosten *Pl. Wirts.* overheads *Pl., Am.* overhead *Sg.*

Gemeinnutz *m; -es, kein Pl.; the* common good, *the* public interest; **~ geht vor Eigennutz** public need before private greed; **gemeinnützig** *Adj.* **1.** for the public welfare, *Organisation*: non-profit(-making), (*wohltätig*) charitable, welfare ...; **er wurde zu 40 Stunden ~er Arbeit verurteilt** he was sentenced to forty hours community service; **2.** (*genossenschaftlich*) cooperative; **Gemeinnützigkeit** *f; nur Sg. e-r Organisation*: charitable (*od.* non-profit) status

Gemeinplatz *m pej.* commonplace, platitude; **sich in Gemeinplätzen ergehen** spout platitudes

gemeinsam I. *Adj.* **1.** *Eigenschaft, Interesse, Nenner, Ziel etc.*: common (+ *Dat.* to); *Freund*: mutual; *Aktion, Reise etc.*: joint, combined; *Wirts., Jur.* joint; *Konto: auch* shared; *Besitz: auch* common; **allen ~** common to all; **vieles ~ haben** have a lot in common; **~e Anstrengung** concerted effort; **der Gemeinsame Markt** *Pol., Wirts.* the Common Market; **~e Überzeugung** shared belief; **unsere ~e Zeit** our time together; **auf ~e Rechnung** to a joint account; *im Restaurant etc.*: shared (*od.* split) between us *etc.*; **~e Schritte unternehmen** take joint action; **~e Kasse machen** *umg.* pool resources (**mit** with); **~e Sache machen** *umg.* make common cause (**mit** with); **sie haben ein ~es Zimmer** *etc.* they share a room *etc.*; → **Nenner, II.** *Adv.* together; (*vereint*) jointly; **~ vorgehen** take joint action; **Gemeinsamkeit** *f* **1.** common ground; *der Interessen*: common interest; **sie haben viele ~en** they have a lot (of things) in common; **zwischen ihnen gibt es keinerlei ~** they have absolutely nothing in common; **2.** *nur Sg.*; (*Harmonie*) togetherness, closeness to each other; **in trauter ~** in sweet communion

Gemeinschaft *f* **1.** community (*auch Pol.*); (*Gruppe*) team; *Soziol.* society; **in ~ mit** together (*od.* jointly, in conjunction) with; **in enger ~ arbeiten** work in close association (with); **in enger ~ leben** live in close companionship (**mit** with); **in ehelicher ~ leben** live as man and wife (**mit** with); → **ehelich** I 1; **2.** (*Vereinigung*) associa-

tion; *religiöse*: community; → **europäisch**; **gemeinschaftlich** *Adj. und Adv.* → **gemeinsam**

Gemeinschafts|anschluss *m Telef.* party line; **~antenne** *f* communal aerial (*od.* antenna); **~arbeit** *f* teamwork; *auch Ergebnis*: joint effort; **es ist in ~ entstanden** it's the result of a joint effort; **~aufgabe** *f* joint task; **die ~n von Bund und Ländern** *Pol.* projects jointly involving the Federal Government and the Länder; **~besitz** *m* joint ownership; *konkret*: joint property; **in ~** jointly owned; **~feindlich** *Adj. Verhalten*: antisocial; **~finanzierung** *f* group financing; **~gefühl** *n* sense of community; (*Solidarität*) (sense of) solidarity; **~geist** *m* community spirit; **~haushalt** *m EU*: Community budget; **~hilfe** *f* community welfare services *Pl.; EU*: Community aid; **~kasse** *f* kitty *umg.*; **~küche** *f* **1.** communal (*od.* kleiner shared) kitchen; **2.** (*Kantine*) canteen; **~kunde** *f; nur Sg.; Päd.* social studies *Pl.;* **~leben** *n* communal living; **~praxis** *f* joint (*od.* group) practice; **~produktion** *f* coproduction; **~raum** *m* common room; **~schule** *f* interdenominational school; **~sendung** *f TV, Radio*: joint program(me); **~sinn** *m; nur Sg.* community spirit; **~unterkunft** *f* communal residence, shared accommodation(s); *für Asylbewerber*: hostel; **~verpflegung** *f* canteen meals *Pl.* (*od.* food); **~werbung** *f* joint advertising; *konkret*: joint advertisement; **~werk** *n* collaboration, collaborative work; **~zelle** *f* communal cell

Gemein|schuldner *m,* **~schuldnerin** *f Jur.* bankrupt; **~sinn** *m; nur Sg.* public spirit

Gemeinsprache *f Ling.* standard language; **gemeinsprachlich** *Adj. Ling.* standard

gemeinverständlich I. *Adj.* generally intelligible; **II.** *Adv.*: **sich ~ ausdrücken** express o.s. in a way that everyone can (*od.* will) understand, express o.s. in plain English *etc.*

Gemein|werk *n schw.* voluntary work; **~wesen** *n* community; (*Staat*) polity

Gemeinwirtschaft *f* social economy

Gemeinwohl *n* public welfare (*od.* interest), public (*od.* common) weal *lit.*; **das dient dem ~** it's for the common good

gemeint I. *P.P.* → **meinen**; **II.** *Adj.*: **ernst ~** *Angebot, Vorschlag*: serious

Gemenge *n; -s, -* **1.** mixture (*aus, von* of); **2.** *altm.*: **mit j-m ins ~ kommen** come to blows with s.o.; **3.** *Agr.* mixed crop

gemessen I. *P.P.* → **messen**; **II.** *Adj.* **1.** *Schritte, Worte*: measured (*auch Mus.*); (*feierlich*) grave, solemn; (*würdevoll*) dignified; **~en Schrittes** at a measured pace *lit.*; **mit ~en Worten** with well-considered words; **2. ~ an** (+ *Dat.*) compared with; **3.** *attr.;* (*angemessen*) *Abstand*: appropriate; **Gemessenheit** *f; nur Sg.* measuredness; (*Feierlichkeit*) gravity, solemnity; (*Würde*) dignity

Gemetzel *n; -s, -; pej.* bloodbath, carnage, slaughter; massacre

gemieden *P.P.* → **meiden**

Gemisch *n; -(e)s, -e* **1.** mixture (*auch Chem., Mot.*) (+ *Gen. od.* **aus, von** of); **2.** *fig.* (*Durcheinander*) jumble; *Gastr. umg.* concoction

gemischt I. *P.P.* → **mischen**; **II.** *Adj.* **1.** mixed (*auch Sauna, Tennis etc.*); *Kekse etc.*: assorted; **~er Teller** mixed plate; **bunt ~** very varied; **~e Klasse** mixed class; **2.** *umg. fig.* (*zweifelhaft*) dubious; (*nicht besonders gut*) patchy; → **Gefühl** 2; **III.** *Adv. umg.*: **es ging sehr ~ zu** all sorts of things were going on; **mir geht's ziemlich ~** I'm not doing too well

Gemischtbauweise *f* composite construction

gemischtrassig *Adj. Person*: mixed--race; *Gesellschaft*: multiracial; *Ehe*: mixed; **gemischtsprachig** *Adj.* muiltilingual

Gemischtwaren|händler *m*, **~händlerin** *f* grocer; **~handlung** *f*, **~laden** *m* grocery (store), general store

gemischtwirtschaftlich *Adj.* mixed(-enterprise …)

gemittelt *Adj. Werte*: averaged

Gemme *f*; -, -n **1.** *erhaben*: cameo; *vertieft*: intaglio; **2.** *mst Pl.; Bio.* gemma

gemocht *P.P.* → **mögen** II

gemolken *P.P.* → **melken**

gemoppelt *Adj. umg.* → **doppelt** II 1

Gemotze *n*; -s, *kein Pl.; umg. pej.* moaning

Gemsbart, **Gemse** *etc.* → **Gamsbart**, **Gämse** *etc.*

Gemunkel *n*; -s, *kein Pl.; umg.* whisperings *Pl.*; (*Gerücht*) rumo(u)r(s *Pl.*), gossip, talk

gemünzt → **münzen**

Gemurmel *n*; -s, *kein Pl.* murmuring; *vor sich hin*: muttering; unverständlich: mumbling

Gemurre *n*; -s, *kein Pl.; pej.* grumbling, complaining

Gemüse *n*; -s, - vegetable; *Koll.* vegetables *Pl.*, greens *Pl.*, veggies *Pl. umg.*; **junges ~** *umg. fig.* youngsters *Pl.*; **~(an)bau** *m*; *nur Sg.* vegetable (*Wirts.* market) gardening, *Am.* truck farming; **~beet** *n* vegetable bed; **~brühe** *f Gastr.* **1.** *Suppe*: vegetable soup; **2.** *Pulver, Würfel*: vegetable stock; **~garten** *m* vegetable garden; **~gärtnerei** *f* market garden, *Am.* truck farm; **~händler** *m*, **~händlerin** *f* greengrocer; **~konserven** *Pl.* canned (*bes. Brit.* tinned) vegetables; **~laden** *m* greengrocer's; **~pflanze** *f* vegetable; **~platte** *f* **1.** *Geschirr*: vegetable dish; **2.** *Gastr. als Beilage*: assorted vegetables; **~saft** *m* vegetable juice; **~sorte** *f* type of vegetable; **~suppe** *f Gastr.* vegetable soup

gemusst *P.P.* → **müssen** II

gemustert I. *P.P.* → **mustern*; **II.** *Adj.* patterned; **bunt/klein ~** with (*od. in*) a multicolo(u)red/small-check pattern

Gemüt *n*; -(e)s, -er **1.** *nur Sg.* mind; (*Gefühl*) feeling; (*Seele*) soul; (*Herz*) heart; (*Gemütsart*) nature, disposition; **sonniges ~** sunny disposition (*od.* nature); **das deutsche ~** the German mentality (*od.* soul *od.* mindset); **in s-m kindlichen ~** in his innocence, naively; **von sanftem ~ sein** be soft--hearted; **etwas fürs ~** something for the soul; **sich** (*Dat.*) *etw.* **zu ~e führen** *fig. hum.* (*Essen etc.*) treat o.s. to, indulge in; (*lesen etc.*) take s.th. to heart; **es schlägt ihm aufs ~** it's getting him down; **2.** *fig. Person*: soul; **sie gehört eher zu den schlichten ~ern** she's a simple soul; **die ~er bewegen** *od.* **erregen** cause quite a stir, cause feelings to run high; **wenn sich die ~er wieder beruhigt haben** when things have calmed down (again); → **erhitzen** II 2, **erhitzt** II 2

gemütlich I. *Adj.* **1.** (*behaglich*) comfortable, comfy *umg.*; (*angenehm*) pleasant; *Lokal*: with a friendly at-

mosphere; **es sich ~ machen** make o.s. at home, relax; **der macht sich's aber ~** *iro.* you'd think he owned the place; **2.** (*zwanglos*) cosy, *Am.* cozy; **~es Beisammensein** cosy (*Am.* cozy) get-together; **jetzt beginnt der ~e Teil des Abends** this is where the fun starts; **3.** (*gemächlich*) *Tempo etc.*: leisurely; *Fahrt, Reise etc.*: restful; (*ungestört*) quiet; (*entspannt*) relaxed; **e-e ~e Tasse Tee trinken** have a nice (quiet) cup of tea; **ein ~es kleines Städtchen** a sleepy little town; **4.** *Mensch*: good-natured; (*gelassen*) easygoing; (*leutselig*) affable, genial; **II.** *Adv.* cosily *etc.*; → I; (*ungestört*) in peace and quiet; *etw.* (*ganz*) **~ tun** take one's time doing (*od.* over) s.th.; **jetzt können wir (ganz) ~ e-n Kaffee trinken** now we can sit down and have a nice cup of coffee; **~ dasitzen** sit and relax;

Gemütlichkeit *f*; *nur Sg.* **1.** (*Behaglichkeit*) cosiness, *Am.* coziness; **2.** *Stimmung*: cosy (*Am.* cozy) atmosphere, gemütlichkeit; **3.** (*Gemächlichkeit*) leisureliness; **in aller ~ frühstücken** have breakfast in peace, take one's time over breakfast; **da hört (sich) doch die ~ auf!** *umg.* that's the limit!; **4.** *e-r Person*: good nature; (*Gelassenheit*) easygoing nature; (*Leutseligkeit*) affability, geniality

gemütsarm *Adj.* lacking in feeling; (*kalt*) cold

Gemüts|art *f* disposition, temperament, nature; **~bewegung** *f* emotion; **~erregung** *f* agitation, excitement; *Psych.* affect

gemütskrank *Adj.* emotionally disturbed; (*schwermütig*) depressed, depressive; **Gemütskrankheit** *f* emotional disorder; (*Schwermut*) depression

Gemüts|lage *f* mood, frame of mind; **~leiden** *n* → **Gemütskrankheit*; **~mensch** *m* good-natured person; **nicht aus der Ruhe zu bringen**: imperturbable person; **du bist ein ~!** *iro.* you've got (a) nerve; (*du verlangst zu viel*) is that all?; **~ruhe** *f* composure, calmness; **in aller ~** quite unconcernedly, calmly and collectedly; (*gemütlich*) unhurriedly, as if he *etc.* had all the time in the world; (*eiskalt*) calmly, as cool as you like; **~verfassung** *f*, **~zustand** *m* frame of mind

gemütvoll *Adj.* warmhearted; (*gefühlsbetont*) emotional

gen *Präp.* (+ *Akk.*); *altm. od. poet.* to, toward(s); **~ Osten** eastward; **~ Himmel** heavenward

Gen *n*; -s, -e; *Bio., Gnt.* gene; **~änderung** *f* gene mutation

genagelt I. *P.P.* → **nageln*; **II.** *Adj.* **1.** *Schuhe*: hobnailed; **2.** *umg.*: **~ voll** chock-full

genannt I. *P.P.* → **nennen*; **II.** *Adj.*: (**oben**) **~** (the) said; *schriftlich*: *auch* (the) above-mentioned

genarbt I. *P.P.* → **narben*; **II.** *Adj. Leder*: grained; *Haut etc.*: *auch Bot.* pitted

genas *Imperf.* → **genesen**

genau I. *Adj.* **1.** exact, accurate; *Tech. auch* true; (*exakt*) exact, precise; **die ~e Zeit** the exact time; **2.** detailed; **~er Bericht** detailed account, full report; *etw.* **Genaues** s.th. definite; **Genaueres** further details *Pl.*; **3.** (*sorgfältig, gründlich*) careful, thorough; *stärker*: meticulous; *Person*: (*streng*) strict; (*eigen*) particular; *peinlich* **~** scrupulously exact, absolutely meticulous;

bei ~erer Betrachtung on closer inspection; **in Gelddingen ist sie sehr ~** she's very particular (*od.* scrupulous) in money matters; **II.** *Adv.* exactly *etc.*; → I; **~!** exactly, that's it; **~ dasselbe** (exactly) the same thing; **~ das wollte ich auch sagen** that's exactly (*od.* just) what I was going to say; **~ der Mann, den wir brauchen** just the man we want; **~ in der Mitte** right in the middle; **~ nördlich** *etc.* **von hier/ uns** due north *etc.* of here/us; **~ in diesem Augenblick** at that very moment; **~ um 4 Uhr** at exactly 4 o'clock, at 4 o'clock on the dot; **aufs ~este** *od.* **Genaueste** to a T; **~ aufpassen** pay close attention; (*zusehen*) *auch* watch closely (*od.* carefully); *Vorschriften* **~ befolgen** follow closely; **~ beschreiben** describe exactly; (*ins Einzelne gehend*) describe in detail; **~ gehen** *Uhr*: keep good time; **~ genommen** strictly speaking; (*eigentlich*) actually; **~ kennen** know inside out; **sich** (*Dat.*) *etw.* **~ merken** (*einprägen*) note s.th. precisely, make a careful note of s.th.; (*nachtragend sein*) not forget s.th.; *etw.* **~ nehmen** (*wörtlich*) take s.th. literally; **es ~ nehmen** be very particular *od.* strict (*mit* about); **es mit der Etikette ~ nehmen** stand on etiquette; **du darfst es nicht so ~ nehmen** (*ist nicht so schlimm*) you mustn't take it so seriously; (*du bist zu pedantisch*) you've got to stretch a point here and there; **~ passen** be a perfect fit; **j-m ~ passen** fit s.o. perfectly; **nicht ~ stimmen** *Angabe, Ergebnis, Zeit etc.* not be spot on; *auch Uhr, Waage etc.*: not be quite right, be a bit out; **stimmt ~!** (you're) absolutely right; **ich weiß es noch nicht ~** I'm not sure yet; **ich weiß es ~** I know (for sure); **so ~ wollte ich es gar nicht wissen** *iro.* I didn't really want (*od.* you *etc.* could have spared me) all the gory details; → **Minute**

genauestens *Adv.*: **~ beachten** pay very careful heed to; **~ befolgen** obey to the letter; **sich** (*Dat.*) *etw.* **~ überlegen** think s.th. over very carefully

Genauigkeit *f*; *nur Sg.* accuracy; precision; strictness; care, meticulousness; → **genau** I; (*Wiedergabetreue*) fidelity; **mit ~** accurately

genauso *Adv.* **1.** exactly (*od.* just) the same (way); **~ wie** just like; **ich sehe es ~** I see it exactly the same way; **ich denke darüber ~** I feel exactly the same (way) about it; **2.** *vor Adj.*: **~ gut/lang/oft** *etc.* just as good/long/often *etc.*; **er mag Äpfel ~ gern** he likes apples just as much; **es waren ~ wenig** (*Leute*) **da** *wie am Montag* there were just as few (people) there, the turnout was just as low

Genbank *f*; *Pl.* Genbanken; *Gnt.* gene bank

Gendarm [ʒanˈdarm] *m*; -en, -en; österr. und hist. policeman; **Gendarmerie** *f*; -, -n; österr., schw. police station

Genealoge *m*; -n, -n genealogist; **Genealogie** *f*; -, -n genealogy; **Genealogin** *f*; -, -nen genealogist; **genealogisch** *Adj.* genealogical

genehm *Adj. geh.* convenient, agreeable (+ *Dat.* to); **wann es ihm ~ ist** when it suits him

genehmigen *v/t.* **1.** (*Antrag, Plan etc.*) approve; (*bewilligen*) grant, give; (*erlauben*) sanction; (*einwilligen in*) agree (*od.* consent) to; (*Aufenthalt, Demonstration, Durchreise*) authorize, permit; (*Projekt etc.*) give the go-

G

ahead to, *Am. auch* green-light *umg.*; (*Tagesordnung*) adopt; (*Vorschlag etc.*) accept; (*Vertrag etc.*) ratify; **genehmigt! als** *Antwort*: permission granted; **amtlich genehmigt** (officially) approved; **2.** *umg. hum.*: **sich** (*Dat.*) *etw.* ~ treat o.s. to; **sich einen** ~ have a wee drop

Genehmigung *f* (*Billigung*) approval (+ *Gen.* of); (*Bewilligung*) granting (of); *e-s Vertrags etc.*: ratification; (*Erlaubnis*) permission; (*Ermächtigung*) authorization (**für** for); *behördliche*: permit; (*Zulassung*) licen|ce (*Am.* -se); **mit freundlicher** ~ **von** (*od.* + *Gen.*) by kind permission of; **j-m die** ~ **erteilen zu** (+ *Inf.*) give s.o. permission to (+ *Inf.*), authorize s.o. to (+ *Inf.*); **j-m die** ~ **verweigern** refuse s.o. permission (**zu** + *Inf.* to + *Inf.*)

Genehmigungspflicht *f* licen|ce (*Am.* -se) requirement; **es besteht** ~ **für** a licen|ce (*Am.* -se) is required for (*od.* to + *Inf.*); **genehmigungspflichtig** *Adj.* subject to authorization

Genehmigungsverfahren *n* licensing procedure

geneigt I. *P.P.* → **neigen**; **II.** *Adj.* **1.** ~ **sein zu** (+ *Inf.*) feel inclined to (+ *Inf.*), feel like (+ *Ger.*); **du scheinst dazu nicht sehr** ~ **zu sein** you don't seem to be very keen (on it); **ich bin dazu überhaupt nicht** ~ it's the last thing I feel like doing; **2.** *geh.*: **j-m** ~ **sein** *förm.* be well-disposed towards s.o.; **j-m ein** ~**es Ohr schenken** lend a willing ear to s.o.; ~**er Leser** gentle reader; **3.** (*abschüssig*) sloping; **Geneigtheit** *f*; *nur Sg.* **1.** (*Bereitschaft*) readiness, inclination; **2.** *geh.* (*Wohlwollen*) good will

Genera *Pl.* → **Genus**

General *m*; *-s, -e od. Generäle*; *Mil.* general; **Herr** ~ General

General|amnestie *f* *Jur.* general amnesty; ~**angriff** *m* all-out attack; ~**anwalt** *m*, ~**anwältin** *f* *Jur.*, *des Europäischen Gerichtshofes*: advocate general; ~**bass** *m* *Mus.* (basso) continuo; ~**bevollmächtigte** *m*, *f* *Pol.* plenipotentiary; *Wirts.* universal agent; *im Betrieb*: general manager; ~**bundesanwalt** *m*, ~**bundesanwältin** *f* *Jur.* Chief Federal Prosecutor; ~**debatte** *f* *Pol.* policy (review) debate

General|direktion *f* *Wirts.* executive board; ~**direktor** *m*, ~**direktorin** *f* general manager, chairman, *Am.* CEO (= chief executive officer), president; **stellvertretender** ~ *Am.* executive vice president

Generalfeldmarschall *m* *hist.* field marshal

Generalin *f*; *-, -nen*; *Mil.* general; *altm.* general's wife

General|inspekteur *m* *Mil.*: ~ (**der Bundeswehr**) Chief of Staff (of the German Armed Forces); ~**inspektion** *f* general inspection; ~**intendant** *m*, ~**intendantin** *f* *Theat. etc.* director

generalisieren *v/t./i. geh.* generalize

Generalität *f*; *-, -en* **1.** *Mil.* the generals *Pl.*, *Am. auch* the top brass *Sg. umg.*; **2.** *nur Sg.*; *altm.* (*Gesamtheit*) generality

General|kommando *n* *Mil.* **1.** supreme command; **2.** (*Hauptquartier*) command headquarters *Pl.*(*V. auch im Sg.*); ~**konsul** *m* *Pol.* consul general; ~**konsulat** *n* *Pol.* consulate general; ~**leutnant** *m* *Mil.* lieutenant general; *Flug. Brit.* air marshal; ~**linie** *f* general policy; *e-r Partei*: party line; ~**major**

m *Mil.* major general; *Flug. Brit.* air vice marshal; ~**nenner** *m* *Math. und fig.* common denominator; ~**oberst** *m* *Mil. hist.* colonel general; ~**pause** *f* *Mus.* tacit; ~**probe** *f* **1.** *Theat.* (final *od.* full) dress rehearsal; **2.** *fig.* dress rehearsal; ~**sekretär** *m* *Pol.* secretary general

Generalsrang *m* *Mil.* rank of general; **in den** ~ **erheben** raise to the rank of general, promote to general

General|staatsanwalt *m*, ~**staatsanwältin** *f* *Jur.* chief public prosecutor

Generalstab *m* *Mil.* general staff (*V. auch im Pl.*)

Generalstabs|chef *m* *Mil.* chief of staff; ~**karte** *f* ordnance survey map

generalstabsmäßig I. *Adj.* Planung, Vorbereitung: carried out with military precision; **II.** *Adv.*: ~ **vorbereitet** prepared down to the last detail; **die Werbekampagne wurde** ~ **geplant** the advertising campaign was planned with military precision

Generalstabsoffizier *m* *Mil.* general staff officer

General|streik *m* general strike; ~**superintendent** *m*, ~**superintendentin** *f* *ev.* superintendent general

generalüberholen *v/t.* (*nur Inf. und P.P.*); *Tech.* (give *s.th.* a complete) overhaul; **Generalüberholung** *f* major overhaul

General|versammlung *f* *Wirts.* shareholders' meeting; *Pol.* general assembly; ~**vertreter** *m*, ~**vertreterin** *f* *Wirts.* general agent; ~**vertretung** *f* *Wirts.* general agency; ~**vikar** *m* *kath.* vicar general; ~**vollmacht** *f* *Wirts.*, *Pol.*, *Jur.* full power of attorney; **j-n mit e-r** ~ **ausstatten** give s.o. power of attorney

Generation *f*; *-, -en* generation (*auch fig.*); **die** ~ **unserer Eltern** our parents' generation; *Computer etc.* **der dritten** ~ third-generation ...; **seit** ~**en** for generations

generationsbedingt *Adj.* ... due to the difference in generation(s)

Generations|konflikt *m* generation gap; ~**problem** *n* **1.** *zwischen Generationen*: generation gap, problems *Pl.* between the generations; **2.** *e-r Generation*: problem of (*od.* specifically connected with) the younger *etc.* generation; ~**unterschied** *m* difference in generation; ~**wechsel** *m* **1.** *Bio.* alternation in generations; **2.** **es hat ein** ~ **stattgefunden** a new generation has taken over

Generator *m*; *-s, -en* **1.** *Etech.* generator; *Gleichstrom, für Licht*: dynamo; *Wechselstrom*: alternator; **2.** *Tech., für Gas*: producer

generell I. *Adj.* general; **II.** *Adv.* generally

generieren *v/t. geh. od. Ling.* generate

generös *Adj. geh.* generous, liberal; (*edelmütig*) magnanimous

genervt *umg.* **I.** *P.P.* → **nerven**; **II.** *Adj.*: ~ **sein** be set (*od.* worked) up (**von** about); (*die Geduld verlieren*) go off at the deep end; **sei doch nicht immer gleich** ~**!** keep your hair on!; **III.** *Adv.*: ~ **antworten/reagieren** answer/react irritably

Genese *f*; *-, -n*; *fachspr., geh.* genesis (+ *Gen.* of)

genesen *v/i.*; *genest, genas, ist genesen*; *geh.* **1.** *Med.* recover (**von** from), get well; (*allmählicher*) convalesce; **2.** *fig.* recover; **Genesende** *m, f*; *-n, -n* convalescent

Genesis *f*; *-, kein Pl.* genesis; **die** ~ *bibl.* Genesis

Genesung *f*; *mst Sg.*; *geh.* recovery; *allmähliche*: convalescence (**von** from)

Genesungs|prozess *m* (process of) recovery; *allmähliche*: convalescence; ~**urlaub** *m* *Mil.* sick leave

Genetik *f*; *-, kein Pl.*; *Bio., Gnt.* genetics *Pl.* (*als Fach V. im Sg.*); **Genetiker** *m*; *-s, -*, **Genetikerin** *f*; *-, -nen* geneticist; **genetisch I.** *Adj.* genetic; ~**er Fingerabdruck** *fig.* genetic (*od.* DNA) fingerprint; **II.** *Adv.* genetically; ~ **veränderte Tomaten/Lebensmittel** *etc.* genetically modified tomatoes/food *etc. Sg.*

Genezareth *m*: **der See** ~ *Geog.* the Sea of Galilee

Genf (*n*); *-s*; *Geog.* **1.** *Stadt*: Geneva; **2.** *Kanton*: Geneva

Genfer[1] *m*; *-s, -*, ~**in** *f*; *-, -nen* Genevan

Genfer[2] *Adj.* Geneva *attr.*; ~ **Konvention** *Pol.* Geneva Convention; ~ **See** *Geog.* Lake Geneva

Gen|forscher *m*, ~**forscherin** *f* *Gnt.* genetic researcher, geneticist; ~**forschung** *f* genetic research, genetics *Pl.* (*als Fach V. im Sg.*)

genial *Adj.* ingenious, brilliant; *Künstler etc.*: ... of genius; **e-e** ~**e Leistung** the work of a genius; **ein** ~**er Einfall** a stroke of genius; **er hat etwas Geniales** he has a touch of genius about him; **genialisch I.** *Adj.* brilliant; **II.** *Adv.* with a touch of genius; **Genialität** *f*; *-, kein Pl.* genius; *von Idee, Lösung etc.*: brilliance

Genick *n*; *-(e)s, -e* **1.** (back of the) neck, nape (of the neck); **steifes** ~ stiff neck; **ein Schlag ins** ~ a rabbit punch; **sich** (*Dat.*) **das** ~ **brechen** break one's neck; **2.** *fig.*: **das brach ihm das** ~ that was his ruin (*od.* undoing); **j-m im** ~ **sitzen** be breathing down s.o.'s neck; ~**bruch** *m* *Med.* neck fracture, broken neck; ~**schuss** *m* shot in the back of the neck; ~**starre** *f* stiffness of the neck

Genie [ʒe'niː] *n*; *-s, -s* genius; **sie hat** ~ she's a genius; **er ist ein** ~ **im Kreuzworträtsellösen** he's a genius at (*od.* when it comes to) solving crossword puzzles; **er ist nicht gerade ein** ~ *iro.* he's not exactly an Einstein; → **verkannt** II

genieren [ʒe'niːrən] **I.** *v/refl.*: **sich** ~ feel embarrassed (*od.* awkward) (**vor** in front of, with ... there); (*scheu sein*) be shy (with, in front of); ~ **Sie sich nicht!** make yourself at home; *beim Essen*: help yourself; **du brauchst dich nicht zu** ~ *beim Ausziehen etc.*: no need to be shy (*stärker*: prudish); **er genierte sich nicht zu** (+ *Inf.*) he had the nerve to (+ *Inf.*); **II.** *v/t.* **1.** (*verlegen machen*) embarrass; **2.** *altm.* (*stören*) bother; **das geniert ihn nicht** he doesn't mind, that doesn't bother him; **genierlich** *Adj. umg.* **1.** (*peinlich*) awkward, embarrassing; **2.** (*schüchtern*) shy, bashful; **3.** *umg.* (*lästig*): ~ **sein** be a nuisance

genießbar *Adj.* **1.** *Essen*: eatable; (*unschädlich*) edible; *Getränk*: drinkable; potable *fachspr.*; **das Essen ist ja fast nicht** ~ *umg.* how are you supposed to eat this food?; *umg.* → **ungenießbar**, **2.** *umg. fig.* enjoyable; *Buch: auch* readable; *Person*: bearable; **kaum/nicht** ~ not much / no fun; *Buch*: (almost) unreadable; *Person*: (almost) unbearable; **genießen** *v/t.*; *genießt, genoss, hat genossen* **1.** *mit Freude*: enjoy; **richtig** ~ relish, savo(u)r (auch fig.); (schwelgen in) revel in; **2.** (zu sich nehmen) take; (essen) eat; (trinken) drink; **kaum/nicht zu** ~ **Essen:** (virtually) inedible; Trinken: (virtually) undrinkable; fig. Person: (almost) unbearable; → **Vorsicht; 3.** fig. (Achtung, Ruf, Vorteil etc.) enjoy; **j-s Vertrauen** ~ be in s.o.'s confidence; **e-e gute Ausbildung** od. **Erziehung** ~ receive a good education; **Genießer** m; -s, -, **Genießerin** f; -, -nen epicure; des Lebens: bon vivant; im Essen: gourmet; **er ist ein stiller** ~ he knows how to enjoy life in his own quiet way; **genießerisch I.** Adj. appreciative; Gefühl: ... of pleasure; **II.** Adv. with (great) relish; **sich** ~ **in der Sonne aalen** bask in the sunshine

Genie|streich m **1.** stroke of genius; **2.** iro. auch bright idea; stärker: inspired blunder; **~truppe** f schw. Mil. corps of engineers

genital Adj. bes. Med. genital; **Genitalbereich** m genitals Pl., genitalia Pl. fachspr.; **im** ~ around (od. on) the genitals, in the genital area; **Genitalien** Pl. genitals, genitalia fachspr.

Genitiv m; -s, -e; Ling. genitive; **im** ~ **stehen** be in the genitive; **~attribut** n attributive genitive; **~objekt** n genitive object

Genius m; -, Genien; Myth. od. geh. fig. genius; **guter** ~ guardian angel

Genlabor n Gnt. genetics laboratory

Genmanipulation f Gnt. genetic engineering; **genmanipuliert** Adj. Pflanze, Tier: genetically engineered

Gen|material n genetic material; **~mutation** f gene mutation

Genom n; -s, -e; Bio., Gnt. genome

genommen I. P.P. → **nehmen; II.** Adv: **genau** ~ strictly speaking; (eigentlich) actually

genoppt Adj. aus Plastik: dimpled; Textilien: (k)nubbly

Genörgel n; -s, kein Pl.; umg. pej. niggling, moaning

genoss Imperf. → **genießen**

Genosse m; -n, -n **1.** Pol. comrade; **liebe Genossinnen und** ~n comrades; **2.** umg. (Kumpel) mate; **3.** altm. (Kamerad) companion; **4.** Wirts. altm.: **Braun und** ~n Braun and associates

genossen P.P. → **genießen**

Genossenschaft f association; Wirts. cooperative (society); **landwirtschaftliche** ~ farmers' cooperative; **Genossenschaft(l)er** m; -s, -, **Genossenschaft(l)erin** f; -, -nen member of a cooperative; **genossenschaftlich** Adj. cooperative

Genossenschafts|bank f cooperative bank; **~bauer** m, **~bäuerin** f member of a farming cooperative; **~betrieb** m cooperative

Genossin f; -, -nen → **Genosse**

genötigt I. P.P. → **nötigen; II.** Adj.: **sie sah sich** ~ **zu** (+ Inf.) she felt obliged (od. compelled) to (+ Inf.)

Genotyp m Bio. genotype

Genozid m, n; -(e)s, -e od. -ien; geh. genocide (**an** + Dat. against)

Genre ['ʒãːrə] n; -s, -s genre; **das ist nicht mein** ~ that is not my sort of thing; **~bild** n genre painting; **~maler** m, **~malerin** f genre painter

Gent (n); -s; Geog. Ghent

Gentechnik f Gnt. genetic engineering; **gentechnikfrei** Adj. Lebensmittel: not genetically modified; **Gentechniker** m, **Gentechnikerin** f genetic engineer; **gentechnisch I.** Adj. nachgestellt: re-

lating to genetic engineering; **II.** Adv. genetically; herstellen through genetic engineering; ~ **veränderte Pflanzen/ Lebensmittel** genetically modified plants/food; → **genmanipuliert; Gentechnologie** f **1.** gene technology; **2.** → **Gentechnik**

Gentest m DNA test, genetic test

Gentherapie f Med. gene therapy

Gentleman ['dʒɛntlmən] m; -s, Gentlemen gentleman

Genua (n); -s; Geog. Genoa; **Genuese** m; -n, -n Genoese; **Genueser** Adj. Genoese; **Genuesin** f; -, -nen Genoese (woman od. girl); **genuesisch** Adj. Genoese

genug Adv. enough; **das ist** ~ **für mich** that's enough (od. that'll do) for me; (nicht) **gut** etc. ~ (not) good etc. enough; ~ (**davon**)! od. **jetzt ist es** (**aber**) ~! enough (of that)!, that'll do!; **ich hab** ~ **davon** (mir reicht's) I've had enough, I'm fed up; **ich hab** ~ (kann nicht mehr) I've had enough, I've had it umg.; **hast du denn noch nicht** ~? (sei nicht so gierig) haven't you had enough already?; (gib doch auf) haven't you had as much as you can take?; **es ist auch so schon schwierig** ~ it's difficult enough as it is; **er kann nie** ~ **bekommen** od. **kriegen** he just can't get enough (**von** of); **sag, wenn es** ~ **ist!** beim Einschenken etc.: say when; **sich** (Dat.) **selbst** ~ **sein** be sufficient unto oneself; (gern allein sein) be content with one's own company; → **betonen 2, Mann 5**

Genüge f **1. zur** ~ (often/long) enough; **zur** ~ **kennen** know only too well; **das habe ich zur** ~ **genossen** I've had quite enough of that; **2.** geh.: ~ **tun** od. **leisten** (j-m) give s.o. satisfaction; (e-r Anordnung, Pflicht) fulfil(l); **der Gerechtigkeit ist** (hiermit) ~ **getan** justice has been done

genügen v/i. **1.** be enough (+ Dat. for); **genügt das?** is that enough?; **das genügt** (mir) (reicht aus) that's enough; (ist akzeptabel) that'll do for me; (ist zufrieden stellend) that's satisfactory; **Anruf genügt!** just give me (od. us) a call; **sich** (Dat.) **selbst** ~ be sufficient unto oneself; (gern allein sein) be content with one's own company; **2.** j-s Anforderungen etc.: come up to, meet; e-r Pflicht: fulfil(l); **genügend I.** Part. Präs. → **genügen; II.** Adj. **1.** enough, sufficient; (befriedigend) satisfactory; iro. (mehr als genug) plenty of; **2.** altm. Schulnote: fair; **nicht** ~ fail; **III.** Adv. enough, sufficiently; ~ **viel(e)** enough

genügsam Adj. easily satisfied, easy to please; auch Pflanze, Tier etc.: undemanding; (mäßig) moderate; im Essen: frugal; (bescheiden) modest; **Genügsamkeit** f; nur Sg. modesty; im Essen: frugality

genugtun v/i. (unreg., trennb., hat -ge-); (e-r Sache) satisfy; (j-m) auch please; **Genugtuung** f; mst Sg. **1.** (Befriedigung) satisfaction (**über** + Akk. at); ~ **empfinden über** (+ Akk.) feel (a sense of) satisfaction on account of; **ich habe mit großer** ~ **vernommen, dass ...** od. **es war mir e-e** ~ **zu hören, dass ...** I was gratified to hear that ...; auch bei Schadenfreude: it gave me great satisfaction to hear that ...; **2.** geh. (Wiedergutmachung) satisfaction (**für** for); ~ **leisten** make amends (**für** for); ~ **fordern** od. **verlangen** demand satisfaction

Genus n; -, Genera **1.** Bio. genus (Pl.

genera); **2.** Ling. gender

Genuschel n; -s, kein Pl.; umg. pej. muttering, mumbling

Genuss m; -es, Genüsse **1.** nur Sg.; (Zusichnehmen) consumption; (Essen) auch eating; (Trinken) auch drinking; von Drogen, Medikamenten: auch taking, use; von Zigaretten: auch smoking; **übermäßiger** ~ **von** Alkohol etc.: too much; von Süßigkeiten etc.: too many; (Völlerei) overindulgence in; **2.** (Freude) pleasure, delight; (das Genießen) enjoyment; **mit** ~ with relish; etw. **mit** ~ **essen/trinken/sehen/hören** etc. enjoy eating/drinking/seeing/hearing; **in den** ~ **kommen von** (od. + Gen.) fig. get (the benefit of); weitS. e-s Konzerts etc.: be treated to

genussfreudig Adj. pleasure-loving

Genussgift n Amtsspr. social (od. recreational) drug

genüsslich I. Adj. voluptuous; (schadenfroh) gleeful; **II.** Adv. with (great) relish; (schadenfroh) gleefully

Genuss|mensch m pleasure-seeker, epicure; **~mittel** n semi-luxury; anregendes: stimulant; **Ɂreich** Adj. enjoyable

Genusssucht f hedonism; **genusssüchtig** Adj. hedonistic, pleasure-seeking

genussvoll Adj. und Adv. → **genüsslich**

genverändert Adj. Gnt. genetically modified; → **genmanipuliert**

Geochemie f geochemistry

Geodäsie f; -, kein Pl. geodesy; **Geodät** m; -en, -en, **Geodätin** f; -, -nen geodesist; **geodätisch** Adj. geodetic(al), geodesic(al)

Geodreieck n Math. set square, Am. triangle

geöffnet I. P.P. → **öffnen; II.** Adj. open; **nur vormittags** ~ open mornings only; **von 9 – 18 h** ~ open 9 am – 6 pm; **das Geschäft ist ab 9 h** ~ opens at 9

Geograf, Geograph m; -en, -en geographer; **Geografie, Geographie** f; -, kein Pl. geography; **Geografin, Geographin** f; -, -nen geographer; **geografisch, geographisch** Adj. geographic(al)

Geologe m; -n, -n geologist; **Geologie** f; -, kein Pl. geology; **Geologin** f; -, -nen geologist; **geologisch** Adj. geologic(al)

geölt P.P. → **ölen**

Geometrie f; -, kein Pl.; Math. geometry; **geometrisch** Adj. geometric(al)

Geophysik f geophysics Pl. (V. im Sg.); **Geophysiker** m, **Geophysikerin** f geophysicist

Geopolitik f geopolitics Pl. (als Fach V. im Sg.); **geopolitisch** Adj. geopolitical

geordnet I. P.P. → **ordnen; II.** Adj. tidy, orderly; (systematisch) systematic; **er Rückzug** Mil. orderly retreat; **in ~en Verhältnissen leben** live in well-ordered circumstances; finanziell: have a steady income

Georgien (n); -s; Geog. Georgian; **Georgier** m; -s, -, **Georgierin** f; -, -nen Georgian, weiblich auch Georgian woman (od. girl etc.); **georgisch** Adj. Georgian

Geosphäre f; nur Sg. geosphere

Geowissenschaften Pl. earth sciences

geozentrisch Astron. **I.** Adj. Weltbild etc.: geocentric; **II.** Adv. geocentrically

gepaart I. P.P. → **paaren; II.** Adj. fig.: **Bosheit** ~ **mit Dummheit** maliciousness

coupled (*od.* combined) with stupidy
Gepäck *n*; *-(e)s, kein Pl.* **1.** luggage; *bes. Flug. und Am.* baggage; **großes/ kleines ~** (piece of) large/small luggage; **mit leichtem ~ reisen** travel light; **mit e-m Angebot im ~ anreisen** *fig.* arrive with an offer in one's luggage; **2.** *Mil.* kit; **~abfertigung** *f* **1.** *Schalter*: luggage (*od.* baggage) counter; *Flug.* baggage check-in; **2.** *nur Sg.*; *Handlung*: **bei der ~** when checking in the baggage; **~anhänger** *m* luggage label (*Am.* tag); **~annahme** *f* → *Gepäckabfertigung*; **~aufbewahrung** *f* **1.** *Raum*: left-luggage (office), *Am.* checkroom; **2.** *nur Sg.*; *Handlung*: **bei der ~** when depositing luggage in left-luggage office (*Am.* in the checkroom); **~aufgabe** *f* **1.** *Schalter*: luggage (*od.* baggage) counter; *Flug.* baggage check-in; **2.** *nur Sg.*; *Handlung*: **bei der ~** when checking in the baggage; **~aufkleber** *m* stick-on luggage label (*Am.* tag); **~ausgabe** *f* **1.** *Flug.* baggage claim; **2.** *nur Sg.*; *Handlung*: **bei der ~** when collecting one's luggage (*od.* baggage); **~band** *n Flughafen*: baggage conveyor; **~ermittlung** *f* baggage tracing; **~karren** *m* baggage trolley, *Am.* luggage cart; **~kontrolle** *f* luggage (*od.* baggage) check; **~marsch** *m Mil.* march with full kit; **~netz** *n* luggage (*od.* baggage) rack; **~raum** *m* luggage (*bes. Flug.* baggage) hold; *Mot.* boot, *Am.* trunk; **~schalter** *m* → *Gepäckannahme*; **~schein** *m* luggage ticket, *Am.* baggage check; **~stück** *n* piece *od.* item of luggage (*od.* baggage); **~träger** *m* **1.** *am Fahrrad*: carrier; *auf Autodach*: roofrack; **2.** *Person*: porter; **~wagen** *m Eisenb.* luggage van, *Am.* baggage car

gepanscht, gepantscht *I. P.P.* → *panschen, pantschen*; *II. Adj. Wein etc.*: adulterated

gepanzert *I. P.P.* → *panzern*; *II. Adj.* **1.** *Mot.* armo(u)red; **2.** *Zool.* mailed; *mit Hornhaut*: sclerodermic

Gepard *m*; *-s, -e*; *Zool.* cheetah

gepfeffert *I. P.P.* → *pfeffern*; *II. Adj. umg.* **1.** *Preis etc.*: steep; *Rechnung*: *auch* hefty; **2.** *Brief, Strafe etc.*: stiff; *Kritik etc.*: biting; *Prüfung, Frage*: tough; **3.** *Witz etc.*: spicy

Gepfeife *n*; *-s, kein Pl.*; *umg. pej.* (awful) whistling

gepfiffen *P.P.* → *pfeifen*

gepflegt *I. P.P.* → *pflegen*; *II.*: *Adj.* **1.** very neat; *Sache*: well-looked-after, *Am.* well taken care of; *Garten etc.*: well-kept; *Rasen*: *auch* manicured; **er hat sehr ~e Hände** *etc.* he takes good care of his hands *etc.*; **in ~em Zustand** *in Annoncen, Auto*: immaculate; *Haus*: in first-class decorative order; **2.** *Sprache, Stil etc.*: cultivated, refined; *Atmosphäre*: cultivated; *Restaurant*: high-class; *Speisen*: choice; *Wein*: select; *III. Adv.*: **sich ~ ausdrücken** be well-spoken; **dort kann man sehr ~ essen** it's a very nice place to eat; **~ wohnen** live in style; **Gepflegtheit** *f*; *nur Sg.* **1.** *äußerlich*: (a) neat appearance; **2.** refinement (*der Ausdrucksweise etc.* of speech *etc.*)

geflogen *P.P. altm.* → *pflegen* I 3
Gepflogenheit *f* habit; (*Brauch*) custom; *bes. Wirts.* practi|ce (*Am. auch* -se); **ganz entgegen i-n sonstigen ~en** quite contrary to their normal practice

gepfropft *I. P.P.* → *pfropfen*; *II. Adv.*

umg.: **~ voll** jampacked, chock-a-block
Gepiep(s)e *n*; *-s, kein Pl.*; *umg. pej. von Vögeln*: cheeping; *von Mäusen*: squeaking

geplagt *I. P.P.* → *plagen*; *II. Adj.*: **~ von Problemen etc.**: dogged by; *auch von Schmerzen etc.*: plagued by; *von Mücken etc.*: plagued by; **von der Hitze ~** wilting under the heat; **nicht von Skrupeln ~** not bothered by scruples; **von Sorgen ~** beset with worries; **von Zweifeln ~** racked with doubts; **er ist ein ~er Mann** *umg.* he's got a lot on his plate

Geplänkel *n*; *-s, -* **1.** *Mil. altm.* skirmish; **2.** *fig.* tit for tat; *humorvolles*: banter

Geplapper *n*; *-s, kein Pl.*; *umg., oft pej.* babbling

Geplärr(e) *n*; *-s, kein Pl.*; *umg. pej.* (terrible) bawling

Geplätscher *n*; *-s, kein Pl.* **1.** *e-s Bachs etc.*: babbling; **2.** *fig. pej.* (shallow) chit-chat

geplättet *I. P.P.* → *plätten*; *II. Adj. umg.* floored; **er war ziemlich ~** *auch* that floored him

Geplauder *n*; *-s, kein Pl.* chat(ting), chit-chat *umg.*

gepolstert *I. P.P.* → *polstern*; *II. Adj. Möbel etc.*: upholstered; *Kleidung etc.*: padded; **gut ~** *umg. fig.* well-padded

Gepolter *n*; *-s, kein Pl.* **1.** *Lärm*: din, clatter, banging; **2.** *Schimpfen*: ranting and raving

Gepräge *n*; *-s, -* **1.** *auf Münzen*: impression, stamp; **2.** *nur Sg.*; *geh.* character; (*Aussehen*) *auch* look; **der Seehandel hat der Stadt ihr ~ gegeben** *od.* **verliehen** maritime trade gave the town its distinctive character

Geprahle *n*; *-s, kein Pl.*; *pej.* boasting, big talk *umg.*

Gepränge *n*; *-s, kein Pl.*; *geh.* pomp, splendo(u)r

gepresst *I. P.P.* → *pressen*; *II. Adj.* **1.** *frisch ~er Zitronensaft etc.* fresh(ly squeezed) lemon juice *etc.*; **2.** *fig.*: **mit ~er Stimme** in a choked voice

gepriesen *I. P.P.* → *preisen*; *II. Adj.*: **viel ~** highly praised

gepunktet *I. P.P.* → *punkten*; *II. Adj. Linie*: dotted; *Kleid etc.*: with dots, polka-dot …

Gequake *n*; *-s, kein Pl.*; *umg. pej.* **1.** *von Fröschen*: croaking; *von Enten*: quacking; *vom Kind*: grizzling; *vom Radio etc.*: burbling (*Am.* squawking) away; **2.** *fig.* (*Gequatsche*) blather(ing), yak-yakking (*Gejammer*) whing(e)ing, *Am.* whining, kvetching

gequält *I. P.P.* → *quälen*; *II. Adj. Gesichtsausdruck*: pained; *stärker*: anguished; *Lächeln*: forced; *III. Adv.*: **~ lächeln** give a forced smile

Gequassel, Gequatsche *n*; *-s, kein Pl.*; *umg. pej.* blather(ing), yak-yakking

Gequieke *n*; *-s, kein Pl.*; *umg. pej.* squeaking

Gequietsche *n*; *-s, kein Pl.*; *umg. pej.* squeaking; *von Autoreifen etc.*: squealing; *auch von Metall*: screeching

gequollen *P.P.* → *quellen*
gerade *I. Adj.* **1.** *Math., Zahl*: even; **2.** (*Ggs. krumm*) straight; **e-n ~n Kurs nehmen** go straight (ahead), follow a straight course; **~ biegen** *od.* **legen, machen, richten** *etc.* straighten (out), put *s.th.* straight; → *auch* **geradebiegen, geradestehen**; **3.** (*aufrecht*) *Haltung*: straight, erect; **4.** (*Ggs. schief*) straight; **5.** *fig.* (*aufrichtig*) honest, up-

right; (*unumwunden*) outspoken; **das ~ Gegenteil** the exact (*od.* direct) opposite (*von* of); **in ~r Linie abstammen von** be a direct descendant of, be descended directly from; *II. Adv.* **1.** straight; **~ gegenüber** directly opposite; **~ gewachsen** *Mensch*: erect; *Baum*: straight-stemmed; **das Brett liegt ~** the board is straight; **~ sitzen/ stehen** *od.* **sich ~ halten** sit (up) / stand up straight; **ich konnte (vor Müdigkeit) kaum noch ~ stehen** (I was so tired) I could hardly stand up *od.* stand on my feet; **2.** (*genau*) just, exactly; **~ als wenn** (*od.* **ob**) just as if; **das ist es ja ~!** that's just it, that's the point; **~ entgegengesetzt** diametrically opposed; **sie ist nicht ~ e-e Schönheit** she's not exactly what you might (*od.* would) call beautiful; **das ist (nicht) ~ das Richtige** that's just (not quite) what we need; **~ zur rechten Zeit** just in time (**um zu** + *Inf.* to + *Inf.*); *Hilfe etc.*: *auch* not a moment too soon, in the nick of time *umg.*; **das hat mir ~ noch gefehlt** that's all I needed (*auch iro.*); → **recht²** II 1; **3.** (*nur, knapp*) just; **~ um die Ecke** just (a)round the corner; **sie ist ~ mal** *od.* **eben fünf Jahre alt** she's just turned five; **ich hab's ~ noch geschafft** *auch zeitlich*: I only just made it, *Am.* I just made it (in time); **das ging ~ noch gut** that was close (*od.* a close shave); **wir haben ~ noch genug** we've got just about enough; **4.** *zeitlich*: **ich bin ~ gekommen** I've just arrived; **sie wollte ~ gehen** she was just about (*od.* going) to leave; **ich war ~ beim Lesen** I was just reading, I was in the middle of reading; **könntest du ~ mal runterkommen?** could you come down(stairs) for a minute?; **ich war ~** (*zufällig*) **dort** I happened to be there (at the time); **da wir ~ von Kindern sprechen** speaking of children; **5.** (*besonders*) especially; (*erst recht*) more than ever; **~ im Winter ist es am schlimmsten** *etc.*: winter is the very time when …; **jetzt ~ nicht!** I won't, just try and make me!; **~, weil …** just because; **~ du solltest das doch verstehen!** you of all people ought to understand that; **6.** *umg.* (*ausgerechnet*) of all people/ days *etc.*; **~ heute!** today of all days; **dass ich ~ dich treffe!** fancy (*Am.* imagine) bumping into you of all people!

Gerade *f*; *-, -n* **1.** *Math.* straight line; **2.** *Renn-, Laufsport*: straight; → **Zielgerade**; **3.** *Boxen*: **linke/rechte ~** straight left/right

geradeaus *I. Adv.* straight on (*od.* ahead); **immer ~!** just keep going straight on (*od.* ahead); *II. Adj.*; *präd; fig.* (*direkt*) very outspoken

geradebiegen *v/t.* (*unreg., trennb., hat -ge-*); *umg. fig.*: (*wieder*) **~** straighten *s.th.* out, put *s.th.* right; → *auch* **gerade** I 2

geradeheraus *umg.* *I. Adv.* straight out; (*unumwunden*) bluntly, point-blank; *II. Adj.*; *nur präd.* open, outspoken

gerädert *I. P.P.* → *rädern*; *II. Adj. umg.*: **völlig** *od.* **wie ~** absolutely shattered, *umg.* whacked, *Am. auch* beat

geradeso *Adv.* → **genauso, ebenso** 1

geradestehen *v/i.* (*unreg., trennb., hat / südd., österr., schw. ist -ge-*); *fig.*: **~ für** answer for; (*verantwortlich sein für*) take the responsibility for; *für s-e Überzeugung etc.*: stand up for; → *auch* **gerade** II 1

geradewegs *Adv.* **1.** straight, directly; ~ **auf** *etw.* (*Akk.*) **losgehen** head straight for, make a beeline for; *fig. auf Problem etc.*: get straight down to; **2.** (*sofort*) straightaway

geradezu *Adv.* **1.** (*praktisch*) virtually; (*fast*) almost; (*nichts anderes als*) absolute(ly); (*wirklich*) really; *es machte* ~ *Spaß* we actually (*od.* even) enjoyed it; *es wäre* ~ *ein Wunder* it would be nothing short of a miracle; **2.** → *geradeheraus*

Geradheit *f*; *nur Sg.* **1.** *e-r Linie etc.*: straightness; **2.** *fig.* honesty, uprightness; (*Unumwundenheit*) outspokenness

geradlinig I. *Adj.* **1.** straight; *Math. auch* rectilinear; *Abstammung*: direct; **2.** *fig. Person*: straight; **II.** *Adv.* in a straight line; **Geradlinigkeit** *f*; *nur Sg.* **1.** straightness; *Math. auch* linearity; **2.** *fig.* straightness

gerammelt I. *P.P.* → *rammeln*; **II.** *Adv. umg.*: ~ *voll* jampacked, chock-a-block

gerändert *Adj.*: *rot* ~*e Augen* red (--rimmed) eyes; *schwarz* ~*er Brief* black-bordered letter

Gerangel *n*; *-s*, *kein Pl.*; *umg., mst pej.* wrangling, dispute; *internes*: *auch* infighting (*um* over), free-for-all (for); (*Gedrängel*) scramble (for)

Geranie *f*; *-*, *-n*; *Bot.* geranium

gerann *Imperf.* → *gerinnen*

gerannt *P.P.* → *rennen*

Geraschel *n*; *-s*, *kein Pl.*; *umg.* rustling, rustle

Gerassel *n*; *-s*, *kein Pl.*; *umg.* rattling, rattle; *beim Atmen*: rattle

gerät *Präs.* → *geraten*[1]

Gerät *n*; *-(e)s*, *-e* **1.** (*Vorrichtung*) device, gadget; (*Apparat*) *auch Pl. Koll.* apparatus; *feinmechanisches*: instrument; (*Werkzeug*) tool, implement; *maschinelles*: uni; (*Radio, Fernseher*) set; (*Haushaltsgerät*) appliance; (*Küchengerät*) utensil; *zum Turnen*: piece of apparatus; *Koll. und Pl.* apparatus (*Sg.*); **2.** *nur Sg.*; *Koll.* (*Ausrüstung*) equipment; *kleineres*: *auch* outfit; **3.** *umg.*: *das war 'so ein* ~*!* (*Riesenexemplar*) it was absolutely enormous!

Geräte|haus *n* tool shed; ~**medizin** *f* high-tech(nology) medicine

geraten[1] *v/i.*: *gerät, geriet, ist geraten* **1.** (*ausfallen*) turn out; *gut/schlecht* ~ turn out well/badly; *groß/klein* ~ *sein* be big/small; *relativ*: turn out to be on the big/small side; *die Suppe ist ein bisschen salzig* ~ the soup's a bit on the salty side; *j-m zum Vorteil* ~ turn out to s.o.'s advantage; *ihm gerät alles* (*gut*) everything turns out right with him; **2.** *nach j-m* ~ *Kind*: take after s.o.; *er gerät ganz nach s-m Vater* he really takes after his father; *negativ*: he's getting to be just like his father; **3.** ~ *an* (+ *Akk.*) *an etw.*: (*erlangen*) come by, get hold of; (*stoßen auf*) come across; *an j-n*: meet, come across; *feindlich*: fall foul of; *da sind Sie (bei mir) an den Falschen* ~ you've come to the wrong person, I'm afraid; *wie bist du denn an den* ~*?* *umg.* where did you find him (*od.* pick him up)?; **4.** (*gelangen, kommen*) get; *in Gefahr, Schwierigkeiten, e-n Stau etc.*: get into; *in e-n Sturm etc.*: get caught in; *auf die Gegenfahrbahn* ~ end up on the wrong side of the road; *mit der Hand in die Säge* ~ get one's hand caught in the saw; *in e-e unangenehme Lage* ~ get into a difficult situation; *in j-s Hände* ~ fall into s.o.'s

hands; *in Verdacht / unter j-s Einfluss* ~ come under suspicion / s.o.'s influence (*od.* sway); *aus der Fassung/ Form* ~ lose one's composure/shape; *außer Atem/Kontrolle* ~ get out of breath/control; *außer sich* ~ be beside oneself (*vor* with); *in Panik* ~ panic, get into a panic; *in Verlegenheit/Versuchung* ~ be embarrassed/tempted; *in Bewegung* ~ get under way, start moving; *in Brand* ~ catch fire; *ins Stocken/Stottern* ~ grind to a halt / start to stutter; *in Gefangenschaft* ~ end up in prison; → *Abweg, Adresse* 1, *Haar* 3

geraten[2] **I.** *P.P.* → *raten*[1], *raten*[2], *geraten*[1]; **II.** *Adj.* (*ratsam*) advisable; (*vorteilhaft*) advantageous; *es scheint mir* ~ *zu* (+ *Inf.*) I think it would be advisable to (+ *Inf.*), the best policy would seem to be to (+ *Inf.*)

Geräte|raum *m Sport* equipment room (*Brit. auch* store); *für Werkzeuge* tool room, tool shed; ~**schuppen** *m* (tool)shed; ~**treiber** *m EDV* (device) driver

Geräte|turnen *n Sport* apparatus gymnastics *Pl.*; ~**turner** *m*, ~**turnerin** *f* (apparatus) gymnast; ~**übung** *f* exercise on the apparatus; ~**wart** *m* attendant (in charge of sports equipment)

Geratewohl *n*: *aufs* ~ at random, haphazardly; *es aufs* ~ *tun* take a chance (on it), do it on the off-chance

Gerätschaften *Pl.* equipment *Sg.*; (*Werkzeuge*) tools; (*Instrumente*) instruments

Geratter *n*; *-s*, *kein Pl.*; *umg. pej.* clatter(ing); *von einem Maschinengewehr*: rattle

Geräucherte *n*; *-n*, *kein Pl.*; *Gastr.* smoked meat

geraum *Adj. geh.*: (*e-e*) ~*e Zeit od.* *e-e* ~*e Weile* a fairly long time; *seit* ~*er Zeit* for quite a long time, for a while now

geräumig *Adj.* spacious, roomy, large; **Geräumigkeit** *f*; *nur Sg.* spaciousness

Geraune *n*; *-s*, *kein Pl.* whispering, murmuring

Geräusch *n*; *-(e)s*, *-e* sound; *bes. unangenehm*: noise; ~ *Theat., Film*: sound effects; *beim Atmen*: *auch* rattle; *im Bauch*: rumble

geräuscharm *Adj.* quiet; (*schallgedämpft*) *auch* soundproof; *Kassette*: low-noise …

geräusch|dämmend, ~**dämpfend** *Adj.* noise-reducing

Geräuschdämpfer *m* noise suppressor

Gerausche *n*; *-s*, *kein Pl.*; *umg. pej.* roar(ing); *sanft* rustling

geräuschempfindlich *Adj.* sensitive to noise

Geräuschkulisse *f* background noise; *Theat., Film*: sound effects *Pl.*

geräuschlos I. *Adj.* silent, quiet (*auch Tech.*); **II.** *Adv.* **1.** silently, quietly; **2.** *umg. fig.* (*ohne Aufsehen*) without a fuss; **Geräuschlosigkeit** *f*; *nur Sg.* silence, quietness

Geräusch|minderung *f* noise reduction; ~**pegel** *m* noise level

geräuschvoll *Adj.* noisy, loud; (*lärmend*) boisterous

Geräusper *n*; *-s*, *kein Pl.*; *pej.* throat-clearing

gerben *v/t.* tan; *s-e Haut war von Wind und Wetter gegerbt fig.* his skin was tanned by wind and weather, his skin had a weatherbeaten look; *j-m (tüchtig) das Fell* ~ *fig.* give s.o. a good hid-

ing; **Gerber** *m*; *-s*, *-* tanner

Gerberei *f*; *-*, *-en* **1.** *nur Sg.*; *Beruf*: tanner's trade; **2.** *Betrieb*: tannery

Gerberin *f*; *-*, *-nen* tanner

Gerberlohe *f* tanbark

Gerb|säure *f* tannic acid, tannin; ~**stoff** *m* tanning agent

Gerbung *f* tanning

gerechnet *P.P.* → *rechnen*

gerecht I. *Adj.* **1.** *Person, Urteil*: just, fair (*gegen[über]* toward[s]); (*unparteiisch*) impartial; ~ *werden* (+ *Dat.*) do justice to (*auch fig.*); **2.** *Strafe*: just; (*berechtigt*) justified; (*verdient*) (well-)deserved; ~*er Lohn iro.* one's just deserts *Pl.*; ~*e Sache* good cause; ~*er Zorn* righteous anger; **3.** (*angemessen*) up (+ *Dat.* to); ~ *werden* (+ *Dat.*) *j-s Anforderungen, Bedingungen, Wunsch etc.*: meet; *j-s Erwartungen*: *auch* come up to; *s-m Ruf, Namen*: live up to; *e-r Aufgabe* ~ *werden* (be able to) cope with a task; *allen Seiten e-s Problems etc.* ~ *werden* deal with all aspects; *allen* (*Leuten*) ~ *werden* please everybody; **4.** *bibl.* (*rechtschaffen*) good, righteous; **II.** *Adv.*: ~ *teilen* share *s.th.* (out) fairly; (*aufteilen*) divide *s.th.* (up) fairly

...gerecht *im Adj.* **1.** (*geeignet für*) suitable (*od.* appropriate) for; *behinderten*~ adapted to the needs of disabled people; **2.** (*entsprechend*) in accordance with; *konjunktur*~ cyclically correct; *termin*~ on schedule

Gerechte *m*; *-n*, *-n*; *bibl.* righteous man; *die* ~*n* the righteous (*Pl.*); *den Schlaf des* ~*n schlafen* sleep the sleep of the just

gerechterweise *Adv.* justly; *einräumend*: in fairness

gerechtfertigt I. *P.P.* → *rechtfertigen*; **II.** *Adj.* justified, justifiable; (*legitim*) legitimate

Gerechtigkeit *f*; *nur Sg.* **1.** justice; *der* ~ *Genüge tun* act justly; *j-m/etw.* (*Dat.*) ~ *widerfahren lassen geh.* treat s.o./s.th. justly; do justice to s.o./s.th.; → *ausgleichen* I 1; **2.** (*Billigkeit*) fairness, justness; (*Rechtmäßigkeit*) legitimacy; **3.** (*Rechtschaffenheit*) righteousness

Gerechtigkeits|fanatiker *m*, ~**fanatikerin** *f* stickler for justice, s.o. who is fanatical in the pursuit of justice; ~**gefühl** *n*; *nur Sg.* sense of justice

Gerechtigkeitsliebe *f* love of justice, fair-mindedness; **gerechtigkeitsliebend** *Adj.* fair-minded

Gerechtigkeitssinn *m*; *nur Sg.* sense of justice

Gerede *n*; *-s*, *kein Pl.* **1.** *umg. unnötiges etc.*: talk; *hör dir das* ~ *der Leute nicht an* don't listen to what people say (*od.* are saying); → *leer* I 1; **2.** (*Klatsch*) *auch* gossip; (*Gerücht[e]*) rumo(u)r(s *Pl.*); *sie ist ins* ~ *gekommen* people have started (*od.* are) talking about her; *j-n ins* ~ *bringen* start people talking about s.o.; **3.** *schw.* → *Gespräch*

geregelt I. *P.P.* → *regeln*; **II.** *Adj.* **1.** *Einkommen, Tätigkeit*: regular; *Leben*: orderly; **2.** *Tech.* control(l)ed

gereichen *v/i. geh.*: *es gereicht ihm zur Ehre* it's a credit to him, it does him credit; *es gereicht ihm zum Vorteil/Nachteil od. Schaden* it's to her advantage/disadvantage

gereift I. *P.P.* → *reifen*; **II.** *Adj. fig.* mature

gereizt I. *P.P.* → *reizen*; **II.** *Adj.* (*aufgebracht*) irritated; (*reizbar*) irritable,

G

edgy; *Atmosphäre*: tense, strained; *in ~em Ton antworten* answer irritably (*od.* testily); **Gereiztheit** *f*; *nur Sg.* irritability

Gerenne *n*; *-s, kein Pl.*; *umg., mst pej.* running (around); *~ nach* (*Ansturm*) rush for; *ich hatte ein ziemliches ~, die Papiere zu bekommen* I had to go from pillar to post to get the papers
gereuen *v/t. geh. altm.* → *reuen*
Geriatrie *f*; *-, kein Pl.*; (*auch Abteilung*) geriatrics *Pl.* (*V. im Sg.*); *in der ~ arbeiten* work in geriatrics; **geriatrisch** *Adj.* geriatric
Gericht[1] *n*; *-(e)s, -e* **1.** *Jur., Institution*: (law) court(s *Pl.*); *mst lit. und fig.* tribunal; (*Rechtsprechung*) jurisdiction; **ordentliches** *~* ordinary court (of law); *vor ~ aussagen/laden* testify/summon before a (*od.* the) court; *vor ~ bringen* take s.o. to court; *vor ~ gehen od. das ~ anrufen* go to court; *vor ~ kommen Sache*: come before the court(s); *Person*: go on trial; *vor ~ stehen* be up for trial, be on trial; *sich vor ~ verantworten* stand trial; **2.** *Jur.* (*die Richter*) the bench; *Hohes ~!* Your Lordship (*Am.* Your Honor); *bei Schwurgerichtsverfahren: auch* Members of the Jury; *das ~ zieht sich zur Beratung zurück* the court will adjourn; **3.** *Jur.* (*Verhandlung*) hearing; *im Strafverfahren*: trial; (*Urteil, das Urteilen*) judg(e)ment; *~* (*ab*)*halten* hold court, sit; **4.** *Gebäude*: court, *bes. Am.* courthouse; **5.** *kirchl.*: *das Jüngste od. Letzte ~ kirchl.* the Last Judg(e)ment; *Tag des Jüngsten ~s kirchl.* Day of Judg(e)ment, Judg(e)ment Day; **6.** *fig.*: *mit j-m hart od. scharf ins ~ gehen fig.* take s.o. to task, haul s.o. over the coals
Gericht[2] *n*; *-(e)s, -e* dish (*aus* of); (*Mahlzeit*) meal; (*Gang*) course
...gericht *n*, *im Subst.* dish; *Reis~* rice dish
gerichtlich *Jur.* **I.** *Adj. Untersuchung etc.*: judicial; *Verfahren etc.*: legal; *Entscheidung etc.*: court ..., of the court; *~e Medizin* forensic medicine; *~e Verfügung* court order; *~e Verfolgung* prosecution; *das wird ein ~es Nachspiel haben* the matter is likely to end up in court; **II.** *Adv.* judicially, legally; (*~ angeordnet*) by order of the court; *j-n ~ belangen od. gegen j-n ~ vorgehen* take legal action against s.o.; *etw. ~ austragen* fight s.th. through the courts; *~ vereidigt Übersetzer etc.*: sworn
Gerichtsakten *Pl. Jur.* court records
Gerichtsarzt *m*, **Gerichtsärztin** *f Jur., Med.* forensic pathologist, specialist in forensic medicine; **gerichtsärztlich** *Adj.* medico-legal ...
Gerichts|assessor *m*, *~assessorin* *f Brit. Jur.* junior barrister, *Am. etwa* assistant counsel
Gerichtsbarkeit *f Jur.* jurisdiction
Gerichts|beamte *m*, *~beamtin* *f Jur.* court official; *~befehl* *m* writ, court order; *~beschluss* *m* court order, decree of the court; *~bezirk* *m* (court) circuit, juridical district; *~dolmetscher* *m*, *~dolmetscherin* *f* sworn interpreter; *~entscheid* *m*, *~entscheidung* *f* court decision, judicial ruling; *~hof* *m* court of justice, law court; *mst lit. od. fig.* tribunal; *Oberster ~* supreme court; *~kasse* *f* court cashier's office; *~kosten* *Pl.* legal costs
Gerichtsmedizin *f Jur., Med.* forensic medicine; **Gerichtsmediziner** *m*, *~in*

f forensic pathologist, specialist in forensic medicine; **gerichtsmedizinisch** *Adj.* forensic; *~e Untersuchung* forensic tests
gerichtsnotorisch *Adj.* known to the court(s)
Gerichts|ordnung *f Jur.* rules *Pl.* of the court; *~präsident* *m*, *~präsidentin* *f* presiding judge; *~referendar* *m*, *~referendarin* *f* junior lawyer; *~reporter* *m*, *~reporterin* *f* court reporter; *~saal* *m* courtroom; *~schreiber* *m*, *~schreiberin* *f* clerk; *~sitzung* *f* session, hearing; *~stand* *m* (legal) domicile; *~*: *Berlin auch* any disputes arising hereunder will be settled before a competent Berlin court of law; *~tag* *m* day of hearing; *~ halten* be in session; *~termin* *m* trial date, date fixed (*Am. auch* assigned) for (a) trial; (*bei Zivilverfahren*) date fixed (*Am. auch* assigned) for the hearing; *~urteil* *n* verdict; (*Richterspruch*) judg(e)ment; (*Strafe*) sentence; *~verfahren* *n* formal: court procedure; *konkret*: legal proceedings *Pl.*, lawsuit; (*Strafverfahren*) trial; *ein ~ einleiten gegen* institute legal proceedings against; *~verfassung* *f* **1.** constitution of the courts; **2.** *Zuständigkeit*: judiciary; *~verhandlung* *f* (judicial) hearing; (*Strafverhandlung*) trial; *~vollzieher* *m*, *~vollzieherin* *f* bailiff, *Am. auch* marshal; *~vorsitzende* *m, f* presiding judge; *~weg* *m*: *auf dem ~* by legal action, through the courts; *den ~ einschlagen* take legal action; *~wesen* *n*; *nur Sg.* judicial system, judiciary
gerieben **I.** *P.P.* → *reiben*; **II.** *Adj. umg.* sly, artful; *das ist ein ~er Kerl* he's a sly one; **Geriebenheit** *f*; *nur Sg.*; *umg.* slyness, artfulness
Geriesel *n*; *-s, kein Pl.* trickling; *von Schnee*: soft fall
geriet *Imperf.* → *geraten*[1]
geriffelt *Adj.* grooved, fluted; (*gerippt*) ribbed; (*eng gewellt*) corrugated; (*gezahnt*) serrated
gering **I.** *Adj.* **1.** *bes. bei Mengen*: small; (*wenig*) little; *Gehalt, Preis, Leistung, Produktion, Temperatur, Druck etc.*: low; *Entfernung*: small, short; *Interesse* little interest; *mit ~en Ausnahmen* with few exceptions; *~e Chancen* slim prospects; *~e Kenntnisse* scant knowledge; *in ~er Höhe* fairly low (down); *in ~er Tiefe* not too deep (down); **2.** (*unbedeutend*) insignificant, negligible, minor; (*wenig, schwach*) slight, little; (*bescheiden*) *Einkommen, Preis etc.*: modest; (*beschränkt*) limited; *nichts Geringes* no small matter; *es spielt keine ~e Rolle* it plays no small part; **3.** (*schlecht*) *Qualität*: inferior, poor, low; *Kenntnisse*: poor; *Herkunft etc., auch Ansehen, Meinung*: low; *in ~em Ansehen stehen* be held in low esteem (*bei* by); → *geringer, geringst...*; **II.** *Adv.* **1.** (*geringfügig*) a little; **2.** (*niedrig*) *~ geschätzt* at least, at a conservative estimate; *zu ~* (*ein*)*schätzen konkret*: underestimate; *ideell*: underrate; **3.** (*wenig, schlecht*): *~ achten od. schätzen* (*nicht wichtig nehmen*) place little value on, not care (much) about; (*nicht gut finden*) have a low opinion of, not think much (*od.* very highly) of; (*etw.*) *auch* hold cheap, set little store by; (*verachten*) despise; (*Gefahr*) disregard
Geringachtung *f* **1.** → *Geringschätzung*; **2.** disregard (+ *Gen.* of, for)
geringelt I. *P.P.* → *ringeln*; **II.** *Adj.* So-

cken: hooped; *Pullover etc.*: striped, with (horizontal) stripes, strip(e)y *umg.*
geringer *Komp.* → *gering* I; *Summe etc.*: smaller; (*weniger*) less; (*niedriger*) lower; *Qualität etc.*: inferior; *~ werden Zahl, Menge*: decrease, lessen, diminish, drop; *Kräfte etc.*: *auch* wane; *in ~em Maße* to a lesser extent; *das ~e von zwei Übeln* the lesser of two evils; *nichts Geringeres als* nothing (*od.* no) less than; *kein Geringerer als* no less a person than, none other than; *..., no less*
geringfügig I. *Adj. Abweichung, Unterschied etc.*: slight, small; *Betrag etc.*: paltry; (*unbedeutend*) negligible, insignificant; *Änderung etc.*: minor, marginal; *~es Vergehen* petty crime; → *auch gering* I 1, 2; **II.** *Adv.* very slightly, marginally; **Geringfügigkeit** *f* **1.** *nur Sg.*; (*Unwichtigkeit*) insignificance, trivial nature; *ein Verfahren wegen ~ einstellen Jur.* dismiss a case because of the trivial nature of the offence; **2.** (*Banalität*) triviality; (*Kleinigkeit*) trifle, little thing
geringschätzig I. *Adj.* disdainful, contemptuous; (*herabsetzend*) deprecatory, disparaging; (*herablassend*) condescending; *~e Geste* dismissive gesture; **II.** *Adv.* disdainfully *etc.*; *j-n ~ behandeln* treat s.o. with contempt; *etw. ~ abtun* dismiss s.th.; **Geringschätzigkeit** *f*; *nur Sg.* disdain, contempt; *Art*: deprecatory (*od.* disparaging) manner; **Geringschätzung** *f*; *nur Sg.* **1.** (*Verachtung*) contempt (+ *Gen.* of, for), disdain (of, for); **2.** (*Geringachtung*) scant regard (for)
geringst|... *Sup.* → *gering* I; least, slightest; (*minimal*) minimum; (*kleinste*) smallest; *nicht im Geringsten* not in the least (*od.* slightest); *nicht das Geringste* not a thing; *die ~e Kleinigkeit* the least little thing; *bei der ~en Kleinigkeit* at the drop of a hat; *er hat nicht die ~e Ahnung* he has no idea, he hasn't got the faintest (*umg.* foggiest) idea, he hasn't got a clue *umg.*, *oft pej.*; *nicht den ~en Zweifel* not the slightest doubt, not the shadow of a doubt; *das ist m-e ~e Sorge* that's the least of my worries; **geringstmöglich** *Adj.* least possible
geringwertig *Adj.* inferior, of inferior quality
gerinnen *v/i.*; *gerinnt, gerann, ist geronnen* **1.** *Chem.* coagulate, clot; *durch Kälte*: congeal; *Blut*: clot; *Milch*: curdle; **2.** *fig.*: *ihm gerann das Blut in den Adern* his blood ran cold; *j-m das Blut in den Adern ~ lassen* make s.o.'s blood curdle (*od.* run cold)
Gerinnsel *n*; *-s, -*; *Med.* (blood)clot
Gerinnung *f*; *mst Sg.* coagulation; *Blut*: *auch* clotting
gerinnungs|fähig *Adj. Med.* coagulable; *~hemmend* *Adj.* anticoagulant
Gerinnungsmittel *n* clotting agent, coagulant
Gerippe *n*; *-s, -* **1.** skeleton; *ein wandelndes ~ sein* be a walking skeleton, be nothing but skin and bones; **2.** *umg. fig.* (*dürrer Mensch*) bag of bones; *zum ~ abgemagert* reduced to a skeleton; **3.** *von Flugzeug, Regenschirm etc.*: frame; *von Schiff*: shell; **4.** *fig.* (*Gliederung*) skeleton, outline; *von Aufsatz etc.*: framework
gerippt *Adj.* **1.** ribbed (*auch Tech.*); *Gewebe*: corded; *Säule*: fluted; *Papier*: laid; *Heizkörper*: finned; **2.** *Bot., Blatt*:

ribbed

gerissen I. *P.P.* → *reißen*; **II.** *Adj. umg. (schlau)* sly, crafty; *(alle Schliche kennend)* shrewd, wily; *ein ~er Geschäftsmann etc.* a shrewd businessman *etc.*; **Gerissenheit** *f; nur Sg. (Schlauheit)* slyness, craftiness; shrewdness

geritten *P.P.* → *reiten*

geritzt I. *f;* → *ritzen*; **II.** *Adj. umg.:* *(die Sache* [*od. das*]) *ist ~!* (*ist abgemacht*) that's settled, then; *(wird erledigt)* right you are!

Germ *m; -(e)s, kein Pl., auch f; -, kein Pl.; österr.* yeast

Germane *m; -n, -n* Teuton, ancient German; *die alten ~n auch* the ancient Germanic peoples *(od.* tribes); **Germanien** *n; -s, kein Pl.; hist.* Germania; **Germanin** *f; -, -nen* Teuton (woman), ancient German (woman); **germanisch** *Adj.* **1.** *hist.* Germanic, Teutonic; **2.** *Ling. Sprache:* Germanic; *Wörter im Englischen:* Saxon; **Germanismus** *m; -, Germanismen; Ling.* Germanism; **Germanist** *m; -en, -en* **1.** *Wissenschaftler:* Germanist; **2.** *Student:* student of German (language and literature), German student; **Germanistik** *f; -, kein Pl.* German(ic) philology, German (studies *Pl.*), German language and literature; **Germanistin** *f; -, -nen* **1.** *Wissenschaftlerin:* Germanist; **2.** *Studentin:* student of German (language and literature), German student; **germanistisch** *Adj. Studien:* German; *Arbeit, Zeitschrift:* on (*od.* relating to) German studies

gern(e) *Adv.; lieber, am liebsten* **1.** gladly; *(bereitwillig)* willingly; *~!* of course; *stärker:* I'd love to; *ich helfe ~* I'll be glad to help; *ich bin ~ hier* I like it here; *(bei spezifischer Veranstaltung)* I'm glad to be here; *~ haben od. mögen (j-n)* like, be fond of; *(etw.)* like, enjoy; *(Tätigkeit)* like (+ *Ger.*), enjoy (+ *Ger.*), *Brit. auch* be keen on (+ *Ger.*); *etw. ~ essen/trinken* like eating/drinking s.th.; *du weißt, du bist bei uns immer ~ gesehen* you know you're always welcome here; *er/es ist nicht ~ gesehen* he's not welcome around here *etc.* / it's frowned [up]on; *ein ~gesehener Gast* a welcome guest; *er sieht od. hat es nicht ~, wenn du ...* he doesn't like you (+ *Ger.*), he doesn't like it when you (+ *Inf.*); *~ geschehen!* you're welcome; *das haben wir ~!* *iro.* that's just great!; *du kannst mich mal ~ haben!* *umg.* you know what you can do; **2.** *Wunsch ausdrückend:* *ich hätte ~ Herrn X gesprochen* could I speak to Mr(.) X, please?; *ich möchte ~ wissen* I'd (really) like to know; *(auch ich frage mich)* I wonder; *ich wüsste gar ~ nur zu ~* I would be very glad (*od.* would very much like) to know; **3.** *billigend:* *das glaube ich ~* I can well believe it; *das kannst du ~ haben* you're welcome to it; *du kannst ~ kommen* you're welcome to come; **4.** *bes. umg. (häufig):* *nach dem Essen ging er ~ spazieren* he would go for a walk; *sie kommt ~ um diese Zeit* she usually comes (*od.* turns up) around this time; *... wird ~ gekauft ...* sells well, ... is in demand; → *gut* II 4, *hören* I 1, *Leben* 8, *liebend* III, *lieber* II

Gernegroß *m; -, -e; umg. hum.: das ist so ein kleiner ~ Kind:* he likes to act like a grown-up; *(Angeber)* he likes to act big

---

Geröchel *n; -s, kein Pl.* rattle (in the throat); *von einem Sterbenden* death rattle

gerochen *P.P.* → *riechen*

Geröll *n; -(e)s, -e* **1.** *am Berg:* debris, scree; *Geol.* detritus; **2.** *(Steinchen)* pebbles *Pl.; größeres:* boulders *Pl.;* **~feld** *n* scree (slope); **~halde** *f* scree

Gerontologe *m; -n, -n* gerontologist; **Gerontologie** *f; -, kein Pl.* gerontology; **Gerontologin** *f; -, -nen* gerontologist; **gerontologisch** *Adj.* gerontological

gerötet I. *P.P.* → *röten*; **II.** *Adj.* red(dened); *(entzündet)* inflamed; → *Augenrand* 1

Gerste *f; -, (Sorten:) -n* barley

Gersten|graupen *Pl.* pearl barley *Sg.;* **~grütze** *f* barley groats *Pl.; (Brei)* barley porridge; **~korn** *n* **1.** barleycorn; **2.** *Med., am Auge:* sty(e); **~saft** *m; nur Sg.; hum. (Bier)* beer

Gerte *f; -, -n* switch; *zum Reiten:* riding crop; **gertenschlank** *Adj.* very slender, willowy

Geruch *m; -(e)s, Gerüche* **1.** smell (*nach* of); *(Duft)* scent, fragrance; *übler ~* bad (*od.* unpleasant) smell *od.* odo(u)r; *stärker:* stench; *(Gestank)* reek; → *Körpergeruch, Mundgeruch;* **2.** *nur Sg.* → *Geruchssinn;* **3.** *nur Sg.; fig.* reputation; *in dem ~ stehen zu* (+ *Inf.*) be said to (+ *Inf.*); *allgemein: auch* have the reputation of (+ *Ger.*); *in schlechtem ~ stehen* be in bad odo(u)r (*bei* with)

geruchlos *Adj. Gas etc.:* odo(u)rless, inodorous; *Seife etc.:* unscented; *Blume:* scentless

Geruchsbelästigung *f* offensive smell

geruchs|bindend *Adj.* deodorant; **~empfindlich** *Adj.* sensitive to smell

Geruchs|filter *m* deodorizing filter; **⏣frei** *Adj.* odo(u)rless; **~nerv** *m Anat.* olfactory nerve; **⏣neutral** *Adj.* unscented, fragrance-free; **~sinn** *m; nur Sg.* sense of smell; **~stoff** *m* odorous substance

Gerücht *n; -(e)s, -e* rumo(u)r; *es geht das ~, dass ...* there's a rumo(u)r (going around) that ...; *rumo(u)r has it that ...;* *das halte ich für ein ~ umg.* I have my doubts about that; *stärker:* I don't believe that for one minute

Gerüchte|küche *f umg. pej.* rumo(u)r factory (*od.* mill); **~macher** *m, ~macherin** *f* rumourmonger, *Am.* rumormonger

geruchtilgend *Adj.* deodorizing

gerüchtweise *Adv.:* *~ verlautet, dass ...* rumo(u)r has it that ...; *ich habe es nur ~ gehört* I only know it from hearsay, I heard it on the grapevine *umg.*

gerufen *P.P.* → *rufen*

geruhen *v/i; -(e)s, kein Pl. umg.* → *röhren;* **II.** *Adj.* touched, moved; *zutiefst ~* deeply moved; *zu Tränen ~* moved to tears

geruhsam I. *Adj. (ruhig)* quiet, peaceful; *(gemütlich)* leisurely; **II.** *Adv.:* *~ frühstücken* have a leisurely breakfast

Gerümpel *n; -s, kein Pl.; pej.* junk

Gerundium *n; -s, Gerundien; Ling.* gerund

gerungen *P.P.* → *ringen*

Gerüst *n; -(e)s, -e* **1.** *am Bau:* scaffold(ing); *(Gestell)* trestle; *für Dach, Brücke:* truss; *Tech. (Arbeitsbühne)* stage, platform; **2.** *Bio.* stroma, reticulum; **3.** *fig.* framework; *(schriftlicher Entwurf)* outline; **~bau** *m; nur Sg.* scaf-

---

folding; **~bauer** *m*, **~bauerin** *f; -, -nen* scaffolder

gerüttelt I. *P.P.* → *rütteln*; **II.** *Adj. altm.: ein ~(es) Maß* a full measure (*an* + *Dat.* of)

ges, Ges *n; -, -; Mus.* G flat

Gesabber *n; -s, kein Pl.; umg. pej.* **1.** *Baby, Hund:* slobbering; **2.** *(Gerede)* drivel

Gesagte *n; -n, kein Pl.* what has been (*od.* s.o. has) said, s.o.'s words; *sie nahm das ~ zurück* she took back what she had said

Gesalbte *m, f; -n, -n; Reli, hist.* anointed; *der ~ (Jesus)* the Lord's Anointed, the Anointed One

gesalzen I. *P.P.* → *salzen*; **II.** *Adj. fig. Preis:* steep; *Rechnung: auch* hefty; *Brief etc.:* stiff; *Witz:* spicy

gesammelt I. *P.P.* → *sammeln*; **II.** *Adj.:* *~e Werke* complete works

gesamt *Adj. mst attr.* whole, entire; *(vollständig)* complete; *Summe etc.:* total, overall; *sein ~es Geld* all his money; → *auch ganz* I; **Gesamte** *n; -n, kein Pl.; the* whole, *the* total; → *auch insgesamt*

Gesamt|absatz *m Wirts.* total sales *Pl.;* **~ansicht** *f* general view; **~arbeitsvertrag** *m schw.* → *Tarifvertrag;* **~auflage** *f e-r Zeitung:* total circulation; *e-s Buchs:* total number of copies published; **~aufnahme** *f* **1.** *Film:* long shot; **2.** *Schallplatte:* complete (*od.* full-length) recording; **~ausfall** *m* total failure; **~ausgabe** *f* **1.** *e-s Buchs:* complete edition (*od.* works *Pl.*); **2.** *~n Wirts.* total expenditure *Sg.;* **~bedarf** *m* total requirements *Pl.;* **~betrag** *m* total (amount), grand total, sum total; **~bevölkerung** *f* total population; **~bild** *n* overall picture

gesamtdeutsch *Adj. Pol. hist.* all-German; **Gesamtdeutschland** *n Pol. hist.* all Germany

Gesamt|eigentum *n* joint property; **~eindruck** *m* general impression; **~einkommen** *n* total income; **~entwicklung** *f* general trend; **~erbe** *m*, **~erbin** *f* sole heir; **~erlös** *m* total revenue; **~ergebnis** *n* overall result; **~ertrag** *m* total proceeds *Pl.; Agr.* total yield

gesamteuropäisch I. *Adj. Pol.* Europe-wide, European-wide, pan-European, covering/affecting *etc.* the whole of Europe; *das ist ein ~es Problem* it is a problem that affects the whole of Europe; *wir streben e-e ~e Lösung an* we are trying to find a pan-European solution; **II.** *Adv.:* *~ betrachtet* looked at from a pan-European point of view

Gesamtfläche *f* total area

gesamtgesellschaftlich I. *Adj.* relating to society as a whole; *Aufgabe:* for society as a whole; *unter ~em Aspekt* from the point of view of society as a whole; **II.** *Adv.:* *~ betrachtet* looked at from the point of view of society as a whole

Gesamtgewicht *n* total weight

gesamthaft *schw.* **I.** *Adj.* → *gesamt*; **II.** *Adv.* → *insgesamt*

Gesamtheit *f; nur Sg.* **1.** totality; *(Ganzes)* the whole; *(Ganzheit)* the entirety; *die ~ der Lehrer etc.* all (the) teachers *etc.; in s-r od. i-r ~* in its entirety; **2.** *(Allgemeinheit)* general public

Gesamt|hochschule *f university-level institution combining academic and technical disciplines with teacher training and promoting interdisciplinary links and courses;* **~höhe** *f total (od.*

overall) height; **~katalog** *m* **1.** *mit allen Produkten*: complete catalog(ue); **2.** *mehrerer Bibliotheken*: union catalog(ue); **~konzept** *n*, **~konzeption** *f* overall plan (*od.* idea, design); master plan; **~kosten** *Pl.* total cost *Sg.*; **~kunstwerk** *n* total art work; **~lage** *f* general (*od.* overall) situation; **wirtschaftliche ~** state of the economy; **~länge** *f* overall length; **~leistung** *f Betrieb etc.*: total output; *Person, Maschine*: overall performance; **~note** *f Päd.* overall mark (*bes. Am.* grade); **~plan** *m* master plan; **~preis** *m* total price; **~produktion** *f* total output; **~regelung** *f* general arrangement; *Jur.* overall settlement; **~schaden** *m* total damage; *Verlust*: total loss

Gesamtschuld *f Wirts.* joint liability (*od.* debt); **~schuldner** *m*, **~schuldnerin** *f* co-debtor; *bei Bürgschaft*: joint guarantor

Gesamtschule *f Päd.*: (**integrierte**) **~** comprehensive (school)

Gesamt|sieger *m*, **~siegerin** *f* overall winner; **~summe** *f* → *Gesamtbetrag*; **~überblick** *m*, **~übersicht** *f* overall idea (*od.* picture); **~umsatz** *m* total turnover; **~unterricht** *m Päd.* integrated-curriculum teaching; **~urteil** *n* overall assessment (*od.* rating); **~verantwortung** *f* overall responsibility; **~verband** *m* general association; **~vermögen** *n* total assets *Pl.*; **~vollmacht** *f Jur.* joint power of attorney; **~weltcup** *m Sport, im Skisport etc.*: Overall World Cup; **~werk** *n* complete works *Pl.*; **~wert** *m* total value; *im ~ von ...* total(l)ing ... (in value); **~wertung** *f* overall placing(s *Pl.*); *in der ~ führen* have the overall lead; **~wetterlage** *f* overall (*od.* general) (weather) conditions *Pl.* (*od.* outlook); **~wirkung** *f* general effect

Gesamtwirtschaft *f* national (*od.* overall) economy; **gesamtwirtschaftlich I.** *Adj.* national (*od.* overall) economic ...; **II.** *Adv.*: **~** *gesehen* seen from the point of view of the economy as a whole

Gesamt|zahl *f* total number; **~zeit** *f bes. Sport* overall time

gesandt *P.P.* → *senden* II; **Gesandte** *m*, *f*; *-n*, *-n*; *Pol.* envoy; *rangmäßig*: minister; (*Botschafter*) ambassador; *päpstlicher ~r* (papal) nuncio; **Gesandtschaft** *f* legation; (*Botschaft*) embassy

Gesang *m*; *-(e)s*, *Gesänge* **1.** *nur Sg.*; (*Singen*) singing; *Mus.* vocal music; *von Vögeln*: song, singing; *von Grillen etc.*: chirping; **2.** *nur Sg.*; *Mus.*, *als Fach*: voice; **3.** *Mus.* (*Lied*) song; *gregorianische Gesänge* Gregorian chants; **4.** *Lit.*, *Teil e-r Dichtung*: canto, book; **~buch** *n* songbook; *kirchl.* hymnbook, hymnal; *dazu brauchst du das richtige ~ umg. iro.* for that you need the right (political, religious *etc.*) credentials; **~lehrer** *m*, **~lehrerin** *f* singing teacher

gesanglich *Adj.* singing ...; *~e Begabung* talent for singing, good voice; *~e Leistung* singing, vocal performance

Gesangprobe *f* audition

Gesangs|einlage *f* vocal number; **~lehrer** *m*, **~lehrerin** *f* singing teacher

Gesang(s)|stimme *f* singing voice; **~stück** *n* song, vocal number (*od.* piece)

Gesangstechnik *f* singing technique

Gesang(s)|unterricht *m* singing lessons (*od.* classes) *Pl.*; **~verein** *m* (*mst*

male) choir, *Am. auch* glee club

Gesäß *n*; *-es*, *-e* buttocks *Pl.*, behind *umg.*; *e-r Hose od. umg.*: seat; **~backe** *f* buttock; **~knochen** *m Anat.* ischium; **~muskel** *m Anat.* gluteal muscle; **~tasche** *f* back (*od.* hip) pocket

gesät I. *P.P.* → *säen*; **II.** *Adj.*: *dünn ~* few and far between

gesättigt I. *P.P.* → *sättigen*; **II.** *Adj.* full; *Chem.*, *Lösung*, *auch fig. Markt*: saturated

Gesaufe *n*; *-s*, *kein Pl.*; *umg. pej.* boozing

Gesäusel *n*; *-s*, *kein Pl.* **1.** *von Wind*, *Blättern etc.*: rustling; **2.** *umg. pej.* (*Schmeichelei*) blarney, *Brit. auch* flannel

gesch. *Abk.* (**geschieden**) divorced

Geschädigte *m*, *f*; *-n*, *-n*; *Jur.* injured party

geschaffen *P.P.* → *schaffen*[1]

geschafft I. *P.P.* → *schaffen*[2]; **II.** *Adj. umg.* (*erschöpft*) whacked, bushed

Geschäft *n*; *-(e)s*, *-e* **1.** business; (*Transaktion*) transaction, deal; *dunkles ~* racket *umg.*; *ein ~ abschließen od. tätigen* do (*od.* clinch) a deal, conclude a piece of business; *~e machen mit* (*j-m*) do business with; (*etw.*) deal in; *die ~e gehen gut/schlecht* business is good/slack; *die laufenden ~e* current business *Sg.*; *die ~e führen* (*für*) manage the affairs (of); (*groß*) *ins ~ kommen* make (a lot of) money (*mit out of*); *kommen wir miteinander ins ~?* can we do business?; **2.** *nur Sg.*; *Koll.*: *das ~* business; *an der Börse*: trading; (*Handel*) trade, business; *~ in Wolle etc.* wool *etc.* trading; *das ~ mit Abenteuerreisen blüht* business in adventure holidays (*Am.* vacations) is booming; **3.** (*Firma*) business, firm, company; (*Laden*) shop, *bes. Am.* store; *gut gehendes ~* thriving business; *ich muss jetzt ins ~* (*in die Arbeit*) I've got to go to work; **4.** (*Angelegenheit*) business, affair; (*Arbeit*) work; (*Beschäftigung*) trade, line, job; (*Aufgabe*) duty; *ein undankbares ~* a thankless task; *er versteht sein ~* he knows what he's doing; **5.** (*Gewinn*) profit; *sie hat damit ein* (*gutes*) */kein ~ gemacht* she made a (good) profit / didn't make a profit on that; *das wäre doch ein ~ für dich* you could make money out of that; *das ~ mit der Angst fig.* exploiting (*od.* playing on) people's fear and insecurity; **6.** *umg. euph.* (*Notdurft*): *sein ~ verrichten od.* *machen* do one's business; *kleines/ großes ~* small/big job

geschäftehalber *Adv.*: *~ unterwegs* away on business; *~ mit j-m zu tun haben* have business dealings with s.o.

Geschäftemacher *m pej.* profiteer, wheeler-dealer *umg.*; **Geschäftemacherei** *f*, *-*, *kein Pl.* profiteering, wheeling and dealing; **Geschäftemacherin** *f*; *-*, *-nen* profiteer, wheeler-dealer *umg.*

geschäftig *Adj.* busy, active; **Geschäftigkeit** *f*; *nur Sg.* activity; (*Unruhe*, *Betriebsamkeit*) bustle, bustling

geschäftlich I. *Adj.* **1.** business ...; *~e Angelegenheit* business matter; **2.** → *geschäftsmäßig* 1; **II.** *Adv.* on business; *~ unterwegs* away on business; *~ verhindert* prevented by business; *~ in Köln zu tun haben Köln betont*: have business (to do) in Cologne; *Geschäftszwecke betont*: be in Cologne on business; *~ geht es ihm gut/ schlecht* his business is doing well / is-

n't doing too well

Geschäfts|ablauf *m Wirts.* conduct of business; **~abschluss** *m* (business) transaction (*od.* deal); **~adresse** *f* business address; **~anteil** *m* share, business interest; *maßgeblicher ~* control(l)ing interest; **~aufgabe** *f*, **~auflösung** *f* closing of a business; *Räumungsverkauf wegen ~* closing-down (*Am.* going-out-of-business) sale; **~bank** *f*; *Pl.* -banken commercial bank; **~bedingungen** *Pl.* terms of business; **~bereich** *m* scope of business; *Jur.* jurisdiction; *Pol.* portfolio; *Minister ohne ~* minister without portfolio; **~bericht** *m* business report; *jährlicher ~* annual report; *über die Marktlage*: market report; **~beziehungen** *Pl.* business relations; **~brief** *m* business letter; **~bücher** *Pl.* account books

geschäftserfahren *Adj.* experienced (in business), ... with business experience

Geschäfts|eröffnung *f* **1.** *Laden*: opening of a shop (*Am.* store); **2.** *Firma*: starting-up of (*od.* starting up) a business; **~essen** *n* business lunch *etc.*

geschäftsfähig *Adj. Jur.*, *Wirts.* legally competent (*to* contract); *voll/beschränkt ~* with full/restricted legal capacity; **Geschäftsfähigkeit** *f*; *nur Sg.* legal (*od.* contractual) capacity

Geschäfts|frau *f* businesswoman; **~freund** *m* business friend

geschäftsführend... *Adj. nur attr.* **1.** managing, executive; **2.** (*stellvertretend*) acting; *~e Regierung Pol.* caretaker government; **Geschäftsführer** *m*, **Geschäftsführerin** *f e-s Ladens*: manager; *e-r GmbH*: managing director, *Am.* CEO (= chief executive officer); *e-s Vereins*: secretary; *e-r Partei*: party chairman; **Geschäftsführung** *f Personen und Tätigkeit*: management

Geschäfts|gang *m Wirts.* **1.** (*Ablauf*) (run of) business; business routine; **2.** (*Besorgung*) errand; *e-n ~ machen* run an errand; **~gebaren** *n* business policy (*od.* practices *Pl.*); *unlauteres ~* unfair dealing; **~geheimnis** *n* trade secret; **~grundlage** *f* basis of a (*od.* the) transaction; **~haus** *n* **1.** *Firma*: firm, company; *Gebäude*: business premises *Pl.* (*Am. auch* location); **2.** (*Bürogebäude*) office building; **~inhaber** *m*, **~inhaberin** *f* proprietor; **~interesse** *n* business interest; **~jahr** *n* financial year; *der Regierung*: *auch* fiscal year; **~jubiläum** *n* company anniversary; **~kosten** *Pl.* business expenses; *auf ~* on expense account; **~lage** *f* **1.** *Situation*: business situation; **2.** *räumlich*: location; *für Laden* position; *in guter ~* well situated (for business purposes); **~leben** *n* business; *ins ~ eintreten* go into business; **~leitung** *f* → *Geschäftsführung*; **~leute** *f* businessmen, business men and women; **~mann** *m*; *Pl. -leute* **1.** *beruflich*: businessman; **2.** *guter/schlechter ~* good/ bad businessman

geschäftsmäßig *Adj.* **1.** (*sachlich*) businesslike (*unpersönlich*) *auch* impersonal; **2.** → *geschäftlich* I 1; **Geschäftsmäßigkeit** *f*; *nur Sg.* buiness-like manner

Geschäfts|modell *n Wirts.* business model; **~moral** *f* business ethics *Pl.*; **~ordnung** *f* rules *Pl.* (of procedure); *Pol.*, *e-s Parlaments*: standing orders *Pl.*; (*Tagesordnung*) agenda; *Antrag/ Frage zur ~* point of order / question on a point of order

Geschäfts|papiere *Pl. Wirts.* business papers; **~politik** *f* company (*od.* corporate) policy; **~praktiken** *Pl.* business practices; **~räume** *f* business premises (*Am. auch* location *Sg.*)

Geschäfts|reise *f Wirts.* business trip; **~n** *auch* business travel *Sg.*; **~reisende** *m, f* business travel(l)er, person travel(l)ing on business

Geschäftsrückgang *m* decline in business

geschäftsschädigend *Adj.* bad for business; *Jur.* damaging to the interests of a company; **Geschäftsschädigung** *f* trade libel, injurious malpractice

Geschäfts|schluss *m Wirts.* closing time; **~sinn** *m; nur Sg.* business sense; **~sitz** *m* 1. *Ort:* place of business; 2. (*eingetragener ~*) registered office; **~sprache** *f* 1. *Fachsprache:* commercial language, commercialese *pej.*; 2. *Pol. der EU etc.:* official language

Geschäftsstelle *f Wirts.* office; *e-r Bank etc.:* branch; **Geschäftsstellenleiter** *m,* **Geschäftsstellenleiterin** *f Wirts.* office manager; *e-r Bank etc.:* branch manager

Geschäfts|straße *f Wirts.* shopping street; **~stunden** *Pl.* business (*od.* office) hours; **~tätigkeit** *f* business activity; **~teilhaber** *m,* **~teilhaberin** *f* partner; **~ton** *m:* (*im*) **~** (in a) businesslike tone; **~träger** *m,* **~trägerin** *f* 1. *Pol.* chargé d'affaires; 2. *Wirts.* representative

geschäftstüchtig *Adj.* efficient; (*gerissen*) smart; **Geschäftstüchtigkeit** *f* business acumen; (*Gerissenheit*) smartness

Geschäfts|übergabe *f Wirts.* handing over of a (*od.* the) business (**an** + *Akk.* to); **~umfang** *m* 1. volume of business; 2. scope of business

geschäftsunfähig *Adj. Jur.* legally incapacitated (*od.* incompetent); **Geschäftsunfähigkeit** *f* legal incapacity

Geschäfts|unkosten *Pl. Wirts.* business expenses; (*Gemeinkosten*) overheads, *Am.* overhead *Sg.*; **~unterlagen** *Pl.* business papers; **~verbindung** *f* business contacts *Pl.*; **in ~ stehen mit** do business with; **~verkehr** *m* business (dealings *Pl. od.* transactions *Pl.*); **~verlauf** *m* commercial fortunes *Pl.*; **~viertel** *n* 1. *mit Läden:* shopping area; 2. (*Gewerbegebiet*) commercial (*od.* business) district; **~vollmacht** *f* power of attorney; **~wagen** *m* company car; **~welt** *f* business world (*od.* community); **~wert** *m:* (*hoher*) **~** goodwill; **~zeichen** *n* reference (*od.* file) number; **~zeit** *f* → **Geschäftsstunden**, **~zentrum** *n* 1. shopping area; 2. *Stadt:* **X ist ein wichtiges ~** X is an important commercial (*od.* trading) cent|re (*Am.* -er); **~zimmer** *n* office; **~zweig** *m* line (of business)

geschah *Imperf.* → **geschehen**

Gescharre *n; -s, kein Pl.; umg. pej. von Menschen:* shuffling; scraping of feet; *von Hunden, Pferden etc.:* pawing; *von Hühnern:* scratching

geschätzt I. *P.P.* → **schätzen; II.** *Adj. fig.* respected; *förm.* esteemed; *Freund:* valued; (*beliebt*) well-liked

Geschaukel *n; -s, kein Pl.; umg. pej.* rocking; *im Bus etc.:* jolting; *im Boot etc.:* rocking, rolling

gescheckt *Adj. Hund, Pferd etc.:* piebald; *Kuh:* brindled; *Katze:* tabby

geschehen *v/i.; geschieht, geschah, ist*

---

geschehen 1. happen (*mit* to); (*sich ereignen*) *auch* occur; (*stattfinden*) take place; (*getan werden*) be done (*mit* with); **~ lassen** let *s.th.* happen, allow; (*wegschauen*) turn a blind eye to; *der Mord geschah aus Habgier* greed was the motive for the murder; *was soll damit ~?* what am I *etc.* supposed to do with it?; *es muss etwas ~* something must be done about it; *es geschieht in d-m Interesse* it's for your own good (*od.* sake); *es ~ noch Zeichen und Wunder!* *iro.* wonders will never cease!; *Dein Wille geschehe Reli.* Thy will be done; *es geschah, dass ... bibl.* it came to pass that; *~ ist ~* it's (*od.* there's) no use crying over spilt (*bes. Am.* spilled) milk; *Geschehenes kann man nicht rückgängig machen* you can't put (*od.* turn) the clock back; → *gern(e)* 1; 2. (*widerfahren*) happen (*j-m* to s.o.); *es wird dir nichts ~* nothing will happen to you, you'll be all right; *weitS.* they won't do anything to you; *er wusste nicht, wie ihm geschah* he didn't know what was happening to him; *das geschieht ihm (ganz) recht* it serves him right; → *Unrecht;* 3. *es ist um sie ~* (*sie ist verloren*) that's the end of her, she's done for *umg.*, she's had it *umg.*; (*sie ist verliebt*) she's lost

Geschehen *n; -s, -, mst Sg.* events *Pl.*; *in das ~ eingreifen* intervene; *das ~ auf der Straße faszinierte ihn* he was fascinated by what was going on in the street

...geschehen *n, im Subst.:* **Kriegs~** course of the war; **Wetter~** weather conditions *Pl.*

Geschehnis *n; -ses, -se; geh.* event, incident; *die ~se der letzten Tage* the events of the past few days, what has been happening in the past few days

gescheit I. *Adj.* 1. (*klug*) clever; (*aufgeweckt*) bright; (*vernünftig*) sensible; *das ist immer am ~esten* that's always the best policy; *du bist wohl nicht (ganz) ~!* you must be mad (*Am. auch* crazy); *ich werde nicht ~ daraus umg.* I can't make head(s) or tail(s) of it, I don't get it; *danach war ich so ~ wie vorher* it left me none the wiser, I was none the wiser for it; 2. *umg.* (*sinnvoll*) sensible, reasonable; (*ordentlich*) *Portion etc.:* decent; *nichts Gescheites* (*Lohnendes*) nothing (worth having/seeing etc.); *er weiß nichts Gescheites mit sich anzufangen* he doesn't know what to do with himself; *etwas Gescheites zu essen* (*Gutes*) something decent to eat, a decent meal; (*Gesundes*) some good healthy food; *etwas Gescheites zu trinken* something decent to drink; (*Gesundes*) a good healthy drink; *Alkohol: auch* a good stiff drink; 3. *südd. umg.* (*gehörige*) *Angst etc.:* proper; (*Ohrfeige, Tracht Prügel*) good; **II.** *Adv. südd. umg.* 1. (*sehr*) *sich ~ ärgern* get really angry; *wir haben es ihnen ~ gegeben* really gave it to them; 2. *~ machen* (*richtig*) do *s.th.* properly

gescheitelt I. *P.P.* → **scheiteln; II.** *Adj.:* *das Haar ~ tragen* have a parting (*Am.* part), part one's hair

gescheitert I. *P.P.* → **scheitern; II.** *Adj.:* **~er Versuch** unsuccessful (*od.* failed) attempt, failure; **~e Existenz** *Person:* (human) wreck, failure; *für ~ erklären* (*Verhandlungen etc.*) declare ... a failure

Geschenk *n; -(e)s, -e* present, gift; *zu*

Werbezwecken: give(-)away, free gift; (*Schenkung*) donation; **~ des Himmels** *fig.* godsend; *j-m etw. zum ~ machen* give s.o. s.th. as a present; *kleine ~e erhalten die Freundschaft Sprichw.* little presents keep friendships alive; **~abo** *n umg.,* **~abonnement** *n* gift subscription

Geschenkartikel *Pl.* gifts

Geschenk|gutschein *m* gift voucher; **~korb** *m* (gift) hamper; **~packung** *f* gift box; *in ~* gift-wrapped; **~papier** *n* (gift) wrapping paper; **~sendung** *f* gift parcel (*Am.* package)

Geschichte *f; -, -n* 1. (*Erzählung*) story (**über** + *Akk. od.* **von** about, of); (*Märchen etc.*) *auch* tale; *erzähl mir keine ~n!* *umg.* don't give me any of your nonsense; 2. *hist., Buch und Wissenschaft:* history; *weitS.* e-r *Person od. Sache: auch* story; *e-e ~ der Technik lesen* a history of technology; *in die ~ eingehen* go down in history; *damit hat er ~ geschrieben* in so doing (*od.* with that) he made history; *sie hat ~ studiert* she studied (*od.* took, *Brit. auch* read) history; 3. *umg. fig.* (*Angelegenheit, Sache*) affair, business; *e-e dumme ~* (such) a stupid business; *e-e schöne ~!* a fine mess; *e-e ~ mit j-m* (*haben*) (*Affäre*) (have) an affair with s.o.; *da haben wir die ~!* there you are; *keine langen ~n!* don't make a song and dance about it; *mach keine ~n!* (*zier dich nicht*) don't make such a fuss; (*lass das*) don't be a fool; *was machst du denn für ~n?* *tadelnd:* what are you playing at?, *Am. auch* what are you up to?; *zu Krankem:* what are you making such a fuss about?; *alte ~n aufwärmen pej.* rake over the ashes (*od.* coals); *immer die alte od. dieselbe ~!* it's the same old story every time

...geschichte *f, im Subst.* 1. *hist. etc.* history of ...; 2. *umg.* (*Problem*) problem; **Herz~** heart problem

Geschichten|buch *n* storybook; **~erzähler** *m,* **~erzählerin** *f* storyteller

geschichtlich I. *Adj.* historical; *bedeutsam:* historic; *von ~er Bedeutung* historically important, of historic(al) importance; **II.** *Adv.* historically; *es ist ~ belegt, dass ...* it is a historical fact that ...; **Geschichtlichkeit** *f; nur Sg.* historicity

Geschichts|atlas *m* historical atlas; **~auffassung** *f* view of history (*od.* the past); **~bewältigung** *f* coming to terms with history; **~bewusstsein** *n* sense of history (*od.* the past), historical awareness (*od.* consciousness); **~bild** *n* view of history; **~deutung** *f* interpretation (*od.* view) of history; **~drama** *n Lit.* historical play (*od.* drama); **~epoche** *f* period of history, historical period (*od.* era); **~fälschung** *f* falsification of history, corruption of historical fact(s); **~forscher** *m,* **~forscherin** *f* historian; **~forschung** *f* historical research; **~kenntnis** *f* (*~se*) knowledge *Sg.* of history; **~klitterung** *f* 1. bias(s)ed historical account; 2. → **Geschichtsfälschung**, **~lehrer** *m,* **~lehrerin** *f* history teacher

geschichtslos *Adj.* without (a) history; *Volk:* with no knowledge (*od.* consciousness) of its own history; *Bewusstsein:* ahistorical; **Geschichtslosigkeit** *f; nur Sg.* lack of (a) history; *e-s Volks:* lack of a sense of history; *des Bewusstseins* ahistoricity

Geschichts|philosophie *f; nur Sg.*

G

philosophy of history; **~schreiber** *m*, **~schreiberin** *f* historian; **~schreibung** *f*; *nur Sg.* historiography, *the* writing of history; **~stunde** *f* history class (*od.* lesson)

geschichtsträchtig *Adj. Ort, Stätte etc.*: steeped in history, (very) historical, historically important; *Moment, Ereignis etc.*: historic

Geschichts|unterricht *m* **1.** history class(es *Pl.*) *od.* lessons *Pl.*; **2.** *the* teaching of history; **~werk** *n* historical work; **~wissenschaft** *f* history; **~wissenschaftler** *m*, **~wissenschaftlerin** *f* historian

Geschick[1] *n*; *-(e)s, -e* **1.** (*Schicksal*) fate; *trauriges* **~** sad fate (*od.* lot); *schweres* **~** cruel fate; **2.** **~e** (*Belange*) destiny *Sg.*, fortunes

Geschick[2] *n*; *-(e)s, kein Pl.* **1.** (*Begabung*) talent (*zu* for), knack *umg.*; *er hat nicht das* **~** *dazu* he hasn't got the knack, he hasn't got what it takes; *ein* (*besonderes*) **~** *haben zu* (+ *Inf.*) *iro.* have the knack of (+ *Ger.*), have a (special) knack for (+ *Ger.*); **2.** → **Geschicklichkeit**

Geschicklichkeit *f*, *-, kein Pl.* skill; *bes. körperliche*: dexterity; *der Finger*: *auch* deftness

Geschicklichkeits|prüfung *f* test of skill; **~spiel** *n* game of skill; (*Puzzle*) puzzle; **~übung** *f* exercise in skill

geschickt I. *P.P.* → **schicken**; **II.** *Adj.* **1.** *Person*: skil(l)ful (*in* + *Dat.* at); (*fingerfertig*) *auch* dext(e)rous, deft; *geistig*: clever, quick; *er ist besonders* **~** *in* (+ *Dat*) he has a knack for (+ *Ger.*); **2.** *Frage, Schachzug etc.*: clever; **3.** *südd.* (*praktisch*) *Sache*: practical; (*passend*) *Zeitpunkt etc.*: suitable; **III.** *Adv.* skil(l)fully *etc.*; **~** *vorgehen* play one's cards well; → **Affäre** 1

Geschiebe *n*; *-s,* - **1.** *nur Sg.*; *umg.* pushing, shoving; (*Gedränge*) pushing and shoving; **2.** *Geol.* glacial drift

geschieden I. *P.P.* → **scheiden**; **II.** *Adj.*: **~er** *Mann od.* **~e** *Frau* divorcee; *ihr* **~er** *Mann* / *s-e* **~e** *Frau* her ex--husband / his ex-wife; *die Zahl der Geschiedenen* the number of divorced people; *wir sind* **~e** *Leute umg. fig.* we're through, I'm through with you (*od.* him *etc.*)

geschieht *Präs.* → **geschehen**

geschienen *P.P.* → **scheinen**[1], **scheinen**[2]

Geschimpfe *n*; *-s, kein Pl.*; *umg. pej.* ranting and raving; (*Fluchen*) cursing and swearing

Geschirr *n*; *-(e)s, -e* **1.** *nur Sg.*; (*Teller, Tassen etc.*) crockery, crocks *Pl. umg.*, *Am.* dishes, tableware; (*Porzellan*) china; *nimm das gute* **~** use the best china; **2.** *nur Sg.*; (*zu e-r Mahlzeit benutzte Dinge*) dishes *Pl.*; *für Tee etc.*: tea *etc.* things *Pl.*; *in der Küche*: kitchen things *Pl.*, pots and pans *Pl.*, *Am. auch* cookware; *Wirts.* kitchenware; *das* **~** *abräumen* clear the dishes away, clear the table; **3.** *für Pferde etc.*: harness; *e-m Pferd das* **~** *anlegen/abnehmen* harness/unharness a horse; *sich ins* **~** *legen* pull hard; *fig.* put one's back into it; **4.** *nur Sg.*; (*Ausrüstung*) tackle; **5.** *altm.* (*Gefäß*) vessel; **~macher** *m*, **~macherin** *f* harness-maker; **~schrank** *m* (china) cupboard, cupboard where the plates are kept *umg.*; **~spüler** *m*, **~spülmaschine** *f* dishwasher; **~spülmittel** *n* washing-up liquid, *Am.* dishwashing detergent; **~tuch** *n* tea towel, drying-up cloth,

Am. auch dish towel

geschissen *P.P.* → **scheißen**

geschlafen *P.P.* → **schlafen**

geschlagen I. *P.P.* → **schlagen**; **II.** *Adj.* **1.** *sich* **~** *geben* give in, admit defeat; *ein* **~er** *Mann geh.* a broken man; **2.** *geh.*: **~** *sein mit* (*leiden müssen unter*) be afflicted with (*od.* plagued by); **3.** *zwei* **~e** *Stunden* (*lang*) (for) two solid hours

geschlaucht I. *P.P.* → **schlauchen**; **II.** *Adj. umg.* whacked, bushed, dead beat

Geschlecht *n*; *-(e)s, -er* **1.** sex; *das andere* **~** the opposite sex; *das schwache/schöne* **~** the weaker/fair sex; *männlichen/weiblichen* **~s** (*sein*) (be) male/female; *beiderlei* **~s** of both sexes; **2.** (*Gattung*) species; *das menschliche* **~** the human race, humankind; **3.** (*Familie*) family; *von Fürsten etc.*: dynasty; (*Abstammung*) descent, lineage; **4.** (*Generation*) generation; **5.** *Ling.* gender; *welches* **~** *hat das Wort?* what gender is the word?; **6.** *nur Sg.*; *lit.* (*Geschlechtsteil*) sex

Geschlechter|kampf *m* battle of the sexes; **~trennung** *f* segregation of the sexes; **~verhältnis** *n* sex ratio

geschlechtlich I. *Adj.* sexual, sex …; *Bio. auch* (*gattungsmäßig*) generic; **II.** *Adv.*: *mit j-m* **~** *verkehren* have (sexual) intercourse with s.o.; **Geschlechtlichkeit** *f*; *nur Sg.* sexuality

Geschlechts|akt *m* sex(ual) act, coitus; **~bestimmung** *f* **1.** *Festlegung*: sex determination; **2.** *Feststellung*: sex determination, sex typing; *bei Tieren*: *auch* sexing; **~drüse** *f* gonad; **~genosse** *m*, **~genossin** *f* person (*od.* individual) of the same sex, same-sex …

geschlechtskrank *Adj.* having a sexually transmitted disease; **Geschlechtskranke** *m, f* person with a sexually transmitted disease; **Geschlechtskrankheit** *f* sexually transmitted disease, STD, venereal disease *altm.*

geschlechtslos *Adj.* **1.** sexless; *auch Bio.* asexual; **2.** *Ling.* neuter; **Geschlechtslosigkeit** *f*; *nur Sg.* sexlessness; *auch Bio.* asexuality

Geschlechts|lust *f*; *nur Sg.* libido; **~merkmal** *n*: *primäres/sekundäres* (primary/secondary) sex characteristic

geschlechtsneutral *Adj. Kleidung etc.*: unisex

Geschlechts|organ *n* sex(ual) organ; **~e** *auch* genitals; **~partner** *m*, **~partnerin** *f* (sexual) partner

geschlechtsreif *Adj.* sexually mature; **Geschlechtsreife** *f* sexual maturity

geschlechtsspezifisch *Adj.* sex-specific

Geschlechts|teil *n* (*auch* **~teile** *Pl.*) genitals *Pl.*, genitalia *Pl.*; **~trieb** *m* sex (-ual) drive; **~umwandlung** *f*: (*e-e*) **~** (*durchmachen*) (have a) sex change (operation); **~unterschiede** *Pl.* differences between the sexes; **~verkehr** *m* (sexual) intercourse, sex; **~wort** *n* *Ling.* article; **~zugehörigkeit** *f* sex

geschlichen *P.P.* → **schleichen**

geschliffen I. *P.P.* → **schleifen**[1]; **II.** *Adj. fig. Stil*: polished; *Umgangsformen*: refined; *Edelstein*: (*mit kleinen Flächen versehen*) facetted; **Geschliffenheit** *f*; *nur Sg.*; *fig.* polish; *der Umgangsformen*: refinement

geschlossen I. *P.P.* → **schließen**; **II.** *Adj.* **1.** *Gruppe, Einheit etc.*: cohesive; *Arbeit, Leistung*: well-rounded,

finished; (*einheitlich*) uniform; *Formation, Reihen*: closed, serried; (*vereint*) united; *in sich* (*Dat.*) **~** self-contained; **~e** *Ortschaft* built-up area; **~e** *Wolkendecke* overcast skies *Pl.*; *e-e* **~e** *Front bilden* form a united front; **2.** (*nicht öffentlich*) *Vorstellung etc.*: private; **~e** *Gesellschaft* private party; *in* **~er** *Sitzung Jur.* in camera; **3.** *Ling., Vokal*: closed; **4.** *Anhänger, Waggon*: covered; **~er** *Wagen Mot.* (*Ggs. Kabrio*) hardtop; (*Limousine*) saloon (car), *Am.* sedan; **III.** *Adv.* (*alle gemeinsam*) all together; (*einstimmig*) unanimously; **~** *hinter j-m stehen* be solidly behind s.o.; *sie waren* **~** *dafür/dagegen* they were unanimous in support of it / against it, they were unanimous in their support for it / opposition to it; **Geschlossenheit** *f*; *nur Sg.* **1.** (*Einheit*) unity, solidarity; **2.** (*Einheitlichkeit*) uniformity, homogeneity; **3.** (*Einstimmigkeit*) unanimity

geschlungen *P.P.* → **schlingen**[1], **schlingen**[2]

Geschlürfe *n*; *-s, kein Pl.*; *umg. pej.* (loud) slurping

Geschmack *m*; *-(e)s, Geschmäcke od. Geschmäcker umg. hum.* **1.** *von Essen etc.*: taste (*auch Empfindung*); (*Aroma*) *auch* flavo(u)r; *Gewürze* (*je*) *nach* **~** *hinzufügen* add spices to taste; **2.** *nur Sg.*; *Sinn*: (sense of) taste; **3.** (*ästhetisches Empfinden*) taste; (*Vorliebe*) taste, liking (*an* + *Dat.* for); **~** *haben* have (good) taste; *keinen* **~** *haben* have no (sense of) taste; *e-n teuren* **~** *haben* have expensive tastes; *der* **~** *von heute* today's tastes (*od.* fashions); *gegen den guten* **~** *verstoßen* offend (against) good taste; *es zeugt nicht gerade von* **~** it doesn't say much for his *etc.* taste(s); **~** *finden an* (+ *Dat.*) (get *od.* come to) like; *auf den* **~** *kommen* acquire a taste for it, get to like it, get hooked *umg.*; *j-n auf den* **~** *bringen* whet s.o.'s appetite (for s.th.); *wir werden dich schon auf den* **~** *bringen!* you'll get to like it soon enough; (*das ist*) *ein Mann nach m-m* **~***!* that's the kind of man I like, that's my kind of man; *jeder nach s-m* **~** everyone to his own taste; *ohne* **~** → *geschmacklos*; *mit* **~** → *geschmackvoll*

geschmäcklerisch *Adj. pej.* over-refined, rarefied

geschmacklich I. *Adj. nur attr.*: *zur* **~en** *Verfeinerung* to enhance the flavo(u)r; **II.** *Adv.* **1.** **~** *verschieden sein* taste different; **~** *verfeinern* improve the taste of; **2.** **~** *unmöglich Einrichtung etc.*: absolutely tasteless

geschmacklos *Adj.* **1.** *Essen etc.*: tasteless, bland; (*fad*) insipid; **2.** (*geschmacksneutral*) flavo(u)rless; **3.** *fig.* tasteless, in bad taste; *Kleidung*: *auch* tawdry; (*taktlos*) tactless; *das war* **~** that was in very bad taste; **Geschmacklosigkeit** *f* **1.** *nur Sg.*; tastelessness; *fig. auch* bad taste; **2.** (*Taktlosigkeit*) tactlessness; (*Verstoß gegen den guten Geschmack*) offen|ce (*Am.* -se) against good taste; (*geschmacklose Bemerkung*) tasteless remark

Geschmacksache *f* (a) matter of taste

geschmacksbildend *Adj.* aesthetically educative, helping to develop good taste

Geschmacks|empfindung *f* sense of taste; **~frage** *f* → **Geschmackssache**; **~knospe** *f* *Anat.* taste bud; **~muster** *n* *Jur.* registered design; **~nerv** *m* *Anat.* gustatory nerve

geschmacksneutral *Adj.* tasteless
Geschmacks|organ *n Bio.* organ of taste; **~probe** *f* **1.** *Vorgang:* tasting; **2.** *kleine Menge:* sample; **~richtung** *f* taste; *verschiedene ~en Lebensmittel etc.:* different flavo(u)rs; **~sache** *f* (a) matter of taste; **~sinn** *m; nur Sg.* (sense of) taste; **~stoff** *m* flavo(u)ring; **~störung** *f* impaired taste; **~verirrung** *f pej.* **1.** lapse in taste *sie leidet an ~* she has no taste; *du leidest doch an ~!* have you no respect for good taste?; **2.** *geschmackswidriger Gegenstand:* (definite) mistake; *das Kleid ist e-e ~* the dress is a mistake; **~verstärker** *m* flavo(u)r enhancer
geschmackswidrig *Adj.* in bad taste
Geschmackszusatz *m* flavo(u)r(ing); *mit ~* flavo(u)red
geschmackvoll I. *Adj. fig.* tasteful, in good taste; *(schick)* elegant, stylish; *das war nicht sehr ~ von ihm* that wasn't very tactful of him, that was in bad taste; **II.** *Adv.:* *er kleidet sich ~* he's very well dressed, he has good dress *(od.* fashion) sense
Geschmatze *n; -s, kein Pl.; umg. pej.* lip-smacking, noisy eating
Geschmeichel *n; -s, kein Pl.; umg. pej.* flattery
Geschmeide *n; -s, -; geh.* jewel(le)ry
geschmeidig *Adj.* **1.** *Bewegung, Körper:* supple, lithe; **2.** *(glatt)* Haar, Teig: smooth; *(elastisch)* elastic, pliant; *Leder:* soft; *Wachs:* pliable; **3.** *fig. Geist:* elastic; *(gewandt)* adroit; *(aalglatt)* smooth, slick *umg.; Zunge:* glib; **Geschmeidigkeit** *f; nur Sg.* **1.** *von Körper etc.:* suppleness, litheness; *von Haar etc.:* smoothness; *(Elastizität)* elasticity, pliancy; *(Weichheit)* softness; **2.** *fig., im Denken:* elasticity; *(Gewandtheit)* adroitness; *pej.* smoothness, slickness; *im Reden:* glibness
Geschmetter *n; -s, kein Pl.; umg. pej., von Trompeten etc.:* blare, blaring
Geschmier(e) *n; -s, kein Pl.; umg. pej.* **1.** *mit Creme, Matsch etc.:* smearing; **2.** *Schrift:* scribble, scrawl; *Gemaltes:* daub; *an Wänden etc.:* graffiti; **3.** *(Geschreibsel)* scribblings *Pl.; übles ~ (Machwerk)* vile piece of filth
geschmissen *P.P. → schmeißen*
geschmolzen I. *P.P. → schmelzen;* **II.** *Adj. Butter etc.:* melted; *Metall, Lava etc.:* molten
Geschmunzel *n; -s, kein Pl.; umg.* smirk(ing)
Geschmuse *n; -s, kein Pl.; umg.* (kissing and) cuddling; *Liebespaar: auch* smooching
Geschnarche *n; -s, kein Pl.; umg. pej.* snoring
Geschnatter *n; -s, kein Pl.; umg. pej.* **1.** *von Enten:* quacking; *von Gänsen:* cackling; **2.** *fig.* chatter(ing)
Geschnetzelte *n; -n, kein Pl.; Gastr. südd., österr., schw.* dish consisting of thin slices of meat stewed in a sauce
geschniegelt *Adj. umg. hum.:* **~** *(und gebügelt od. gestriegelt) (präd.* all) spruced up
geschnitten *P.P. → schneiden*
geschnoben *P.P. → schnauben*
Geschnüffel *n; -s, kein Pl.; umg. pej.* **1.** sniffling, sniffing; **2.** *fig.* snooping (around)
geschoben *P.P. → schieben*
gescholten *P.P. → schelten*
Geschöpf *n; -(e)s, -e* **1.** creature; *reizendes/armes* **~** lovely/poor creature *od.* thing; **2.** *(erdichtete Gestalt etc.)* creation (+ *Gen.* of)

geschoren *P.P. → scheren[1]*
Geschoss[1], *österr.* **Geschoß** *n; -es, -e;* *(Stockwerk)* stor(e)y, floor; *im ersten* **~** *on the first (Am.* second) floor; *im oberen/unteren* **~** upstairs/downstairs
Geschoss[2], *österr.* **Geschoß** *n; -es, -e* missile; *(Kugel)* bullet; *(Granate)* shell; **~bahn** *f* trajectory
geschossen *P.P. → schießen*
...geschossig, *österr.* **...geschoßig** *im Adj.* -stor(e)y ...; *dreizehn-*-stor(e)y ...; *viel~* multistor(e)y ..., high-rise ...
geschraubt I. *P.P. → schrauben;* **II.** *Adj.* **1.** *Tech.* screwed, bolted; **2.** *fig. Stil:* stilted, affected, artificial; **III.** *Adv.:* **~** *reden* talk like a book; **Geschraubtheit** *f; nur Sg. des Stils etc.:* affectation, artificiality
Geschrei *n; -s, kein Pl.; oft pej.* **1.** *(Schreien)* shouting; *stärker:* screaming; *anfeuerndes:* cheering; *von Baby:* crying; *von Esel:* braying; *von Möwen etc.:* screeching, screaming; **2.** *(Schreie)* shouts *Pl.,* screams *Pl.,* cheers *Pl.;* → 1; **3.** *umg. fig.* howls *Pl.* of protest, hue and cry; *(Aufheben)* huge *(od.* almighty) fuss; *ein großes ~ machen* raise a hue and cry; *(Getue)* make a huge fuss *(um od. wegen* about)
geschrieben *P.P. → schreiben*
geschrien *P.P. → schreien*
geschritten *P.P. → schreiten*
geschult I. *P.P. → schulen;* **II.** *Adj.* trained; *politisch:* indoctrinated
geschunden *P.P. → schinden*
geschuppt I. *P.P. → schuppen;* **II.** *Adj. Haut:* scaly; *Ziegel:* scalloped
Geschütz *n; -es, -e; Mil. schweres* **~** heavy gun; *Koll.* heavy artillery; *schweres ~ auffahren fig.* bring up the big guns *(gegen* against); **~donner** *m* roar *(od.* booming *od.* thunder) of gunfire; **~feuer** *n* gunfire, shelling
geschützt I. *P.P. → schützen;* **II.** *Adj.* protected; *(sicher)* safe, secure; *vor Wind etc.:* sheltered *(vor* from); **~e Tierart** protected species; *patentamtlich* **~** patented; *(gesetzlich)* **~es Warenzeichen** registered trademark; → *urheberrechtlich* II
Geschwader *n; -s, - 1. Naut.* squadron; *Flug.* group, wing; **2.** *umg. fig.* troop
Geschwafel *n; -s, kein Pl.; umg. pej.* drivel
Geschwätz *n; -es, kein Pl.; umg. pej., unnötiges:* talk, prattle; *unsinniges:* nonsense; *(Klatsch)* gossip; *leeres ~* hot air; **geschwätzig** *Adj. pej. (redselig)* talkative, garrulous; *(klatschsüchtig)* gossipy; *er ist ein ~er Typ* he talks an awful lot, he never stops talking, *Am. auch* he's a motor-mouth; **Geschwätzigkeit** *f; nur Sg.; pej.* talkativeness; gossiping
geschweift I. *P.P. → schweifen;* **II.** *Adj. Tischbein etc.:* curved; *Stern:* with a tail; **~e Klammern** braces
geschweige *Konj.:* **~** *denn* (*, dass ...*) let alone, never mind, much less
geschwiegen *P.P. → schweigen*
geschwind *südd.* **I.** *Adj.* fast; **II.** *Adv.* quickly; **~!** quick!
Geschwindigkeit *f* **1.** speed; *(Lauftempo etc.)* pace; *Phys.* velocity; *Maß der Fortbewegung:* rate; *(Schwung)* momentum; *mit e-r ~ von* at a rate *(od.* speed) of; *mit voller od. höchster ~* full speed, at top speed; *an ~ zunehmen Bewegungen:* speed up; *Lawine etc.:* gather speed; *Veränderungen etc.:* gather pace; *e-e ~ von 200 km/h erreichen* reach a speed of 200 kph; **2.** *nur*

Sg.; (Schnelligkeit) speed; **~** *ist keine Hexerei* there's nothing so wonderful about it
Geschwindigkeits|abfall *m* loss of speed; **~begrenzung** *f,* **~beschränkung** *f* speed limit; **~kontrolle** *f* speed check; **~messer** *m Mot.* speedometer; **~messung** *f* tachometry; **~rausch** *m* thrill of speed; *im ~* drunk with speed; **~regler** *m* governor; **~überschreitung** *f* speeding
Geschwirr *n; -s, kein Pl.; umg. pej.* whirring, buzz(ing); *von Pfeilen:* whizzing
Geschwister *n; -s, -, mst Pl.* sibling *förm.; Pl.* brother(s) and sister(s); *bes. förm.:* siblings, sibs *umg.; haben Sie noch ~?* have you any brothers or sisters?; *wir waren fünf ~* there were five of us (children) in the family; **Geschwisterchen** *n* little *(od.* baby) brother *od.* sister; *unsere Kinder freuen sich auf ihr ~* our children are looking forward to having a baby brother *od.* sister; **geschwisterlich** *Adj.* brotherly, sisterly
Geschwister|liebe *f* brotherly *(od.* sisterly) love; **~paar** *n* brother and sister; *zwei ~e* two sets of brother and sister
geschwollen I. *P.P. → schwellen[1];* **II.** *Adj.* **1.** swollen; **2.** *fig. pej. Rede:* pompous, inflated; **III.** *Adv., umg.:* **~** *daherreden* spout pompously
geschwommen *P.P. → schwimmen*
geschworen I. *P.P. → schwören;* **II.:** *Adj.:* **~er** *Gegner od. Feind* sworn enemy
Geschworene *m, f; -n, -n; Jur.* **1.** *in angelsächsischen Ländern:* juror, member of the jury; *die ~n* the jury *Sg.; e-n ~n ablehnen* challenge a juror; **2.** *altm.* lay judge
Geschworenen|bank *f Jur.: (auf der) ~* (in the) jury box; **~gericht** *n* jury court
Geschwulst *f, -, Geschwülste; Med.* growth, tumo(u)r; *(Knoten) auch* lump; **geschwulstartig** *Adj.:* **~e** *Gewebebildung* tumescent growth
geschwunden *P.P. → schwinden*
geschwungen I. *P.P. → schwingen;* **II.** *Adj. Augenbrauen etc.:* curved; *weit:* sweeping
Geschwür *n; -s, -e; Med.* ulcer; *auf der Haut:* sore; *(Furunkel)* boil; **geschwürartig** *Adj.* ulcerous
Ges-Dur *n Mus.* G flat major
gesegnet I. *P.P. → segnen;* **II.** *Adj.* **1.** *in Wünschen:* **~e** *Mahlzeit!* enjoy your meal; **~es** *neues Jahr!* Happy New Year!; **2.** *geh., oft iro.:* **~** *mit Talenten:* blessed with; *im ~en Alter von* at the ripe old age of; **3.** *umg.: e-n ~en Appetit/Schlaf haben* have a healthy appetite / sleep soundly
gesehen *P.P. → sehen*
Geselchte *n; -n, kein Pl.; Gastr. Dial.* smoked meat
Geselle *m; -n, -n* **1.** *Handwerker:* journeyman; **2.** *umg. (Bursche)* lad; *bes. pej. type:* *der Papagei war ein lustiger* **~** the parrot was great fun *(od.* a barrel of laughs *umg.)*
...geselle *m, im Subst.* journeyman ...; *Maler~* journeyman painter
gesellen *v/refl.: sich ~ zu* join *s.o.* etc.; *dazu gesellten sich noch andere Probleme fig.* and there were other problems beside that one; → *gleich* I 2
Gesellen|brief *m* apprenticeship diploma; **~prüfung** *f* (apprentices') final examination; **~stück** *n* **1.** *piece of work produced by an apprentice to*

G

qualify as a journeyman; **2.** *fig.* proof of proficiency

gesellig *Adj.* **1.** sociable; *auch Tiere*: gregarious; **~es Wesen** social being; **2. ~es Beisammensein** (little) get-together; **Geselligkeit** *f, nur Sg.* sociability; (*Umgang*) socializing

Gesellin *f, -, -nen* journeywoman

Gesellschaft *f, -, -en* **1.** society; *e-e* **klassenlose ~** a classless society; **2.** *nur Sg.*; (*Zusammensein mit anderen, Umgang*) company; **gute/schlechte ~** good/bad company; **in schlechte ~ geraten** get in with the wrong crowd, keep bad company; **j-m ~ leisten bei** join s.o. in (+ *Ger.*); **komm, leiste mir ein bisschen ~** come and talk to me; **hier hast du ~** here's someone to keep you company; **wir kriegen ~** look who's coming; **benimm dich, wir sind hier in ~!** (watch your manners -) we're not at home now; **sich in guter ~ befinden** *fig. iro.* (*unter Leidensgenossen etc.*) be in good company; **3.** *nur Sg.*; (*Oberschicht*): **die feine ~** high society; **sich in feiner** *od.* **guter ~ bewegen** move in high circles; **du bewegst dich ja nur in feiner ~!** *iro.* you don't mix with the hoi polloi, do you?; **4.** *nur Sg.*; *pej.* (*Personenkreis*) lot, bunch, crowd; **ihr seid ja e-e feine/langweilige ~!** what a mean/boring lot you are; **5.** *Veranstaltung*: social gathering; (*Party*) party; **e-e ~ geben** have (*od.* give) a party; **geschlossene ~** private party; **6.** (*Vereinigung*) society, association; *Wirts.* (*Firma*) company, *Am. auch* corporation; *von Partnern*: partnership; **~ des bürgerlichen Rechts** non-trading private company; **~ mit beschränkter Haftung** (*abgek.* **GmbH**) limited liability company (*abgek.* LLC), *Brit.* public limited company (*abgek.* plc); **~ Jesu** *kirchl.* Society of Jesus

Gesellschafter *m; -s, -* **1. er ist ein guter ~** he's good company; **2.** *Wirts.* partner, associate; *stiller* ~ sleeping (*Am.* silent) partner; → *auch* **Aktionär, Gesellschafterin** *f, -, -nen* **1.** *beruflich*: companion; *Hostess*: escort; **2.** *Wirts.* partner, associate; **Gesellschafterversammlung** *f Wirts.* corporate (*od.* general) meeting

gesellschaftlich I. *Adj.* social; **~e Entwicklung** development of society; **II.** *Adv.* socially; **~ gewandt** *od.* **sicher sein** have plenty of savoir-faire, move easily in society

Gesellschafts|abend *m* (dinner) party; **~anzug** *m* formal suit; **~ erbeten** black tie

gesellschaftsfähig *Adj. Verhalten*: socially acceptable; *Person, Kleidung*: presentable, respectable; *nicht ~ Witz etc.*: risqué, off-colo(u)r

Gesellschafts|fahrt *f* group tour; **Ofeindlich** *Adj. Einstellung etc.*: antisocial; **~ sein Entwicklungen etc.**: threaten (*od.* be a threat to) society; **~form** *f* social system; **~inseln** *Pl.; Geog.*: **die ~** the Society Islands; **~kapital** *n Wirts.* corporate capital; (*Grundkapital*) joint stock, share capital

Gesellschaftskritik *f* social criticism; **Gesellschaftskritiker** *m*, **Gesellschaftskritikerin** *f* social critic; **gesellschaftskritisch** *Adj.* sociocritical; *Person etc.*: socially critical, critical of society

Gesellschafts|kunde *f, nur Sg.* social studies *Pl.*; **~lehre** *f, nur Sg.* sociology;

~ordnung *f* social order

Gesellschaftspolitik *f* sociopolitics *Pl.* (*als Fach*: *V. im Sg.*); **gesellschaftspolitisch** *Adj.* sociopolitical

Gesellschafts|raum *m* function room; *im Hotel etc.*: lounge; **~recht** *n; nur Sg.; Wirts.* company law; **~reise** *f* group tour; **~roman** *m* social novel; **~schicht** *f* (social) class; **~spiel** *n* party (*od.* parlo[u]r) game; **~steuer** *f Wirts.* corporation tax; **~stück** *n* **1.** *Theat.* drawing-room comedy; **2.** *Kunst* genre painting; **~tanz** *m* ballroom dance; **~vermögen** *n Wirts.* company assets *Pl.*; **~vertrag** *m* **1.** *Pol.*, *Philos.* social contract; **2.** *Wirts.* articles *Pl.* of association

Gesellschafts|wissenschaften *Pl.* social sciences; **~zweck** *m Wirts.* company aim

gesengt I. *P.P.* → **sengen**; **II.** *Adj.* → **Sau** 3

gesessen *P.P.* → **sitzen**

Gesetz *n; -es, -e* **1.** *staatlich*: law; *Jur., Parl. auch* act; *als Vorlage*: bill; *das ~ Koll.* the law; **ein ~ erlassen/verabschieden** enact/pass a law; **auf dem Boden des ~es** within the law; **gegen das ~** against the law, illegal; **nach dem ~** under the law; **zum ~ werden** become law; **mit dem ~ in Konflikt geraten** come up against the law, get tangled up with the law *umg.*; **vor dem ~ sind alle gleich** everyone is equal before the law; **es steht im ~, dass ...** the law says (that) ...; **das steht nicht im ~** there's no law against it *umg.*; **ein die ~e achtender Bürger** a law-abiding citizen; → **Auge** 2, **Hüter** *etc.*; **2.** *der Natur etc.*: law; (*Regel, Prinzip*) rule, principle; **das ~ der Serie** the law of continuity; **sich** (*Dat.*) **etw. zum obersten ~ machen** make s.th. a cardinal rule; **das ist bei uns ein ehernes/ungeschriebenes ~** it's an iron rule / unwritten law as far as we're concerned; **~blatt** *n* law gazette; **~buch** *n Jur.* **1.** *System*: code (of law); **das Bürgerliche ~** the Civil Code; **2.** (*Gesetzessammlung in Buchform*) statute book; → **bürgerlich** 1; **~entwurf** *m Parl.* bill

Gesetzes|änderung *f* change in the law; **~hüter** *m*, **~hüterin** *f iro.* guardian of the law; **~initiative** *f Parl.* introduction of a bill; *schw.* (*Volksbegehren*) petition for a referendum; **Qkonform** *Adj. und Adv.* within the law; **~kraft** *f* legal force; **~ erlangen/haben** become/be law; **~lage** *f*: **wie ist die ~?** what is the legal position?; **~lücke** *f* legal loophole; **~novelle** *f Parl.* amendment; **~sammlung** *f* statute book; **~text** *m* wording of a law; **Qtreu** *Adj.* law-abiding; **~übertretung** *f* offen|ce (*Am.* -se); violation of the law; **~verstoß** *m* offen|ce (*Am.* -se); **~vorhaben** *n* proposed law; **~vorlage** *f Parl.* bill; **~werk** *n* body of law

gesetzgebend *Adj. Pol.* legislative; **~e Gewalt** legislature; **~e Körperschaft** legislative (body); **Gesetzgeber** *m* legislator, lawmaker; **Gesetzgebung** *f* legislation; **Gesetzgebungswerk** *n* body of law

gesetzlich I. *Adj.* **1.** legal; (*vorgeschrieben*) *auch* statutory; (*rechtmäßig*) lawful; *Forderung*: legitimate; **~es Mindestalter** legal age; **~es Rentenalter** compulsory retirement age; → **Feiertag**; **2.** (*gesetzgeberisch*) legislative; **II.** *Adv.* legally *etc.*; **~ geschützt** patented; *Warenzeichen etc.*: registered;

~ verboten prohibited (by law); **~ vorgeschrieben** prescribed by law; **~ zulässig** legal, lawful; **Gesetzlichkeit** *f; nur Sg.* legality; (*Rechtmäßigkeit*) legitimacy

gesetzlos *Adj.* lawless, anarchic(al); **Gesetzlosigkeit** *f* **1.** *nur Sg.*: lawlessness, anarchy; **2.** *Handlung*: lawless act

gesetzmäßig *Adj.* **1.** (*legal*) legal, lawful; *Anspruch etc.*: *auch* legitimate; **2.** *fig.* regular, following a set pattern; **Gesetzmäßigkeit** *f* **1.** (*Legalität*) legality, lawfulness; *von Anspruch etc.*: legitimacy; **2.** *Phys.* conformity with a natural law; **3.** *fig.* (inherent) law(s *Pl.*), regularity; (predetermined) pattern(s *Pl.*)

gesetzt I. *P.P.* → **setzen**; **II.** *Adj.* (*ruhig, ernsthaft*) staid; (*nüchtern*) sober; (*würdig, ernst*) dignified; (*älter, reif*) mature; **ein Herr in ~em Alter** of mature years; **III.** *Konj.*: **~ den Fall, (dass) ...** suppose ..., supposing ..., let's assume ...

Gesetztafel *f hist.* law tablet; **die ~n** *bibl.* the Tables of the Law

gesetzwidrig *Adj.* illegal; **Gesetzwidrigkeit** *f* unlawful (*od.* illegal) act

ges. gesch. *Abk.* (**gesetzlich geschützt**) reg. (= registered)

gesichert I. *P.P.* → **sichern**; **II.** *Adj.* **1.** *Schusswaffe*: at safe, *Am.* with the safety on; **2.** *Einkommen, Existenz*: secure, assured; **~e Untersuchungsergebnisse** *od.* **Erkenntnisse** solid (*od.* definite) findings

Gesicht¹ *n; -(e)s, -er* **1.** face (*auch fig. Person*); **über das ganze ~ strahlen** *umg.* beam all over one's face; **j-m (gerade) ins ~ sehen** look s.o. (straight) in the eye; **ich kann ihr nicht mehr ins ~ sehen** I can't look her in the face (*od.* eye) any more; **j-m ins ~ lachen/lügen** laugh in / lie to s.o.'s face; **e-r Gefahr etc. ins ~ sehen** *fig.* face up to a danger *etc.*; **den Tatsachen ins ~ sehen** *fig.* face the facts; **das springt einem doch ins ~** *umg.* it stares you in the face, it's so obvious; **ich hätte ihm ins ~ springen können** *umg.* I could have strangled him; **er ist s-m Vater wie aus dem ~ geschnitten** he's the spitting image (*od.* spit and image) of his father, he's a chip off the old block *umg.*; **2.** (*Miene*) face, expression; **~er machen** *od.* **schneiden** make (*od.* pull) faces; **ein böses ~ machen** scowl; **sie machte ein langes ~** *enttäuscht*: her face fell; *trotzig*: she pulled (*Am.* made) a face; **was machst du für ein ~?** what are you pulling (*Am.* making) (such) a face for?; **mach nicht so ein dummes ~!** don't look so stupid, wipe that stupid look off your face; **das sieht man ihr an ~** an you can tell by the look on her face; **es steht ihm im** *od.* **ins ~ geschrieben** it's written all over his face; **3.** *fig.* (*Aussehen*) look; *lit.* (*Charakter*) character; **das ~ e-r Stadt** the appearance of a town; **die vielen ~er Roms** the many faces of Rome; **ein anderes ~ bekommen** take on a new (*od.* different) look *od.* complexion; **4.** *äußerer Schein*: face; **das ~ verlieren** lose face; **das ~ wahren** save (one's) face; **sein wahres ~ zeigen** show its *etc.* true face; *Person*: *auch* show one's true colo(u)rs; **das steht e-m Staatsmann gut/schlecht zu ~(e)** it well/ill becomes a statesman *geh.*; **5.** *nur Sg.*; (*Sehen*): **das zweite ~ haben** have second sight; **zu ~ bekommen** (*erblicken*) catch sight of; *kurz*: catch a glimpse of; (*sehen*) set eyes (up)on, see; **aus dem ~ verlieren** lose sight of; **6.** (*Vorderseite*) face; *ein Blatt, Bild liegt mit dem ~ nach oben/unten* face up/down **Gesicht²** *n*; *-(e)s, -e*; (*Vision*) vision **Gesichts|ausdruck** *m* (facial) expression; **~erker** *m umg. hum.* hooter, *Am.* schnoz; **~farbe** *f* complexion; **~feld** *n Opt.* range of vision; **~haar** *n* facial hair; **~hälfte** *f*: (*die linke/rechte*) ~ (the left/right) side of the face; *die untere/obere ~* the lower/upper part of the face; **~kontrolle** *f umg., mst hum.* face check, *before being allowed into a night club*; **~kreis** *m* **1.** *fig.* (*Horizont*) horizon(s *Pl.*); *das liegt außerhalb ihres ~es* it's beyond her horizon; **2.** (*Blickfeld*) view; *in den ~ treten* come into view; *ich habe sie aus m-m ~ verloren fig.* I've lost touch with her, I've lost sight of her; **~lähmung** *f Med.* Bell's palsy **gesichtslos** *Adj.* **1.** faceless; **2.** (*nichts sagend*) characterless **Gesichts|maske** *f* **1.** mask; *des Chirurgen*: (face) mask; (*Schutzmaske*) face guard; *Fechten*: fencing mask; **2.** *kosmetisch*: face pack, facial; **~massage** *f* facial massage; **~muskel** *m* facial muscle; **~nerv** *m* facial nerve; **~operation** *f* plastic surgery; **~partie** *f* area (of the face); **~pflege** *f* skin (*od.* face) care; **~plastik** *f* plastic surgery; **~punkt** *m* point of view, angle; (*Faktor*) factor; *unter dem ~* (+ *Gen.*) *auch* in terms of; *unter diesem ~ gesehen* seen from this angle (*od.* point of view); *nach praktischen ~en gestaltet* designed for practicality; **~rose** *f Med.* facial erysipelas; **~sinn** *m*; *nur Sg.* sense of sight; **~straffung** *f* facelift; **~verlust** *m* loss of face; **~wasser** *n* face lotion; **~winkel** *m* **1.** *Opt.* visual angle; **2.** *fig.* angle; **~züge** *Pl.* features **Gesims** *n*; *-es, -e* **1.** *Archit.* (*Zierleiste*) mo(u)lding; *Kranz*: cornice; *am Kamin*: mantelpiece; *am Fenster*: sill; *am Dach*: cornice; **2.** *Geol.* ledge **Gesinde** *n*; *-s, -*; *altm., auf Bauernhof*: farm labo(u)rers, (farm) hands; *im Haushalt*: servants **Gesindel** *n*; *-s, kein Pl.*; *pej.* rabble, good-for-nothings *Pl.* **gesinnt** *Adj.* **1.** *liberal etc.*: ...-minded, ...-oriented; *anders ~ sein* have different views (*als* from); *fortschrittlich ~ sein* be (a) progressive, be in favo(u)r of progress; *wie ist sie politisch ~?* where does she stand politically?, what are her political leanings?; **2.** *freundschaftlich etc.*: ...-disposed (+ *Dat.* to[wards]), ...-meaning; *feindlich ~* hostile; *er war uns freundlich ~* he was friendly toward(s) us **Gesinnung** *f* mentality, mindset; (*Denkart*) way of thinking; (*Ansichten*) opinions *Pl.*, views *Pl.*; (*Einstellung*) attitude; (*Überzeugung*) conviction, persuasion; (*Charakter*) character; *von edler ~* noble-minded; *treue ~* loyalty; *s-e wahre ~ zeigen* show one's true colo(u)rs **Gesinnungs|genosse** *m*, **~genossin** *f* fellow-travel(l)er; *iro.* kindred spirit; *pej.* crony; (*Anhänger*) adherent, supporter **gesinnungslos** *Adj. pej.* unprincipled, lacking in character; (*treulos*) disloyal; **Gesinnungslosigkeit** *f*; *nur Sg.*; *pej.* lack of principles **Gesinnungs|schnüffelei** *f umg.* ideo-

logical snooping; **~täter** *m*, **~täterin** *f* *politically etc.* motivated offender; **⌀treu** *Adj.* loyal; **~treue** *f* loyalty; **~wandel** *m*, **~wechsel** *m* change of heart; *bes. Pol.* about-turn, volte-face, *Am.* U-turn **gesittet I.** *Adj.* civilized; (*moralisch*) moral; (*wohlerzogen*) well-mannered; (*höflich*) polite, courteous; **II.** *Adv.*: *sich ~ benehmen* behave in a civilized fashion; (*wohlerzogen*) show good manners, be well-mannered; *~ essen* have good table manners **Gesocks** *n*; *-es, kein Pl.*; *umg. pej.* rabble, shower **Gesöff** *n*; *-(e)s, -e*; *umg.* brew **gesoffen** *P.P.* → **saufen** **gesogen** *P.P.* → **saugen** **gesondert I.** *P.P.* → **sondern²**; **II.** *Adj.* separate **gesonnen I.** *P.P.* → **sinnen**; **II.** *Adj.* **1.** *~ sein zu* (+ *Inf.*) be inclined to (+ *Inf.*), be minded to (+ *Inf.*); **2.** *j-m ~ Person*: well-disposed to s.o.; *Schicksal etc.*: kindly disposed to s.o.; → *gesinnt 2* **gesotten I.** *P.P.* → **sieden**; **II.** *Adj.*: *hart ~* → *hart* II 1; *~ auch* **hartgesotten**; **Gesottene** *n*; *-n, kein Pl.*; *Dial.* boiled meat **gespalten** *Adj.*: *~er Gaumen Med.* cleft palate; *~er Huf Zool.* cloven hoof; *~e Persönlichkeit Psych.* split personality **Gespann** *n*; *-(e)s, -e* **1.** *Zugtiere*: team; **2.** (*Pferdegespann*) horse and cart; (*für Personen*) horse and carriage; (*Planwagen etc.*) wag(g)on and team; (*Hundeschlitten*) dog sled; *Mot.* (*Lkw mit Anhänger*) tractor-trailer, *Brit.* articulated lorry, *Am.* rig, semi; (*Motorrad mit Seitenwagen*) combination; **3.** *fig.* team; (*Paar*) pair, duo, tandem; *die beiden bilden ein ideales/merkwürdiges ~* make a perfect team / make strange bedfellows **gespannt I.** *P.P.* → **spannen**; **II.** *Adj.* **1.** *Seil*: taut; *Muskel*: tense; **2.** (*erwartungsvoll*) expectant; (*aufgeregt*) eager; (*neugierig*) curious; *ich bin ~ auf* (+ *Akk.*) I can't wait to see (*od.* find out *etc.*); *ich bin ~, ob ...* I wonder if (*od.* whether) ...; *etw. mit ~er Aufmerksamkeit verfolgen* follow s.th. closely (*od.* with keen interest); **3.** (*angespannt*) *Beziehungen*: strained; *Lage*: tense; **III.** *Adv.* (*aufmerksam, konzentriert*) intently; *~ zusehen* watch closely, be riveted; *er hörte ~ zu* he listened intently, he was all ears; **Gespanntheit** *f*; *nur Sg.* **1.** (*Erwartung*) expectation; *stärker*: excited anticipation; (*Aufmerksamkeit*) intentness; **2.** (*Spannungszustand*) tension **Gespenst** *n*; *-(e)s, -er* **1.** ghost; *wie ein ~ aussehen* look like a ghost; **2.** *fig.* (*Trugbild*) phantom; (*Gefahr*) spect|re (*Am. -er*); *das ~ der Anarchie etc.* **an die Wand malen** raise (*od.* conjure up) the spect|re (*Am. -er*) of anarchy *etc.*; *du siehst ja ~er!* *umg.* you're seeing (*od.* imagining) things **Gespenster|geschichte** *f* ghost story; **~glaube** *m* belief in ghosts **gespensterhaft** *Adj. Erscheinung*: ghostly; (*unheimlich*) uncanny **Gespensterstunde** *f* witching hour **gespenstisch** *Adj.* ghostly, eerie **gesperrt I.** *P.P.* → **sperren**; **II.** *Adv. Druck.*: **~gedruckt** spaced out **gespickt I.** *P.P.* → **spicken**; **II.** *Adj. umg. fig.*: *~ mit Fehlern* bristling with mistakes; *s-e Brieftasche war ~* his wallet (*od.* he) was loaded

Gespiele *m*; *-n, -n*, **Gespielin** *f*; *-, -nen*; *altm. und hum.* playmate **gespielt I.** *P.P.* → **spielen**; **II.** *Adj.*: *~e Gleichgültigkeit etc.* studied indifference *etc.*; *bei ihr ist alles nur ~* it's all play-acting (*od.* an act) with her; *es war alles nur ~ auch* it was all sham **gespien** *P.P.* → **speien** **Gespinst** *n*; *-(e)s, -e* **1.** spun yarn; (*Gewebe*) web, tissue; *der Raupe*: cocoon; *der Spinne*: web; **2.** *fig.*: *das ~ der Lügen* the tissue (*od.* web) of lies **gesplissen** *P.P.* → **spleißen** **gesponnen I.** *P.P.* → **spinnen**; **II.** *Adj. umg.*: *es ist alles ~* he's (*od.* she's) made it all up, it's a load of rubbish (*Am.* it's a crock) **Gespött** *n*; *-(e)s, kein Pl.* **1.** (*Spott*) mockery, ridicule; *sein ~ treiben mit* ridicule, make fun of; **2.** (*Gegenstand des Spottes*) laughing stock; *sich zum ~* (*der Leute*) *machen* make a fool of o.s., make o.s. a laughing stock **Gespräch** *n*; *-(e)s, -e* **1.** conversation (*über + Akk.* about, on; *mit* with; *zwischen* between); (*Diskussion*) discussion; *zu zweit*: dialog(ue); *Pol.* talks *Pl.*; *am Telefon*: telephone conversation; (*Anruf*) call; *ein ~ führen mit* have a conversation with; *~e führen mit* talk to; *bes. Pol.* have talks with; *ins ~ kommen mit* get into conversation with, get talking to; *fig.* make contact with; *es ist im ~* (*wird erwogen*) it's being considered, it's under discussion (*od.* consideration); (*wird beredet*) it's a talking point; *das ~ bringen auf* (+ *Akk.*) bring the conversation (a)round to; *mit j-m im ~ bleiben* keep in contact with s.o., keep up (the) contact with s.o.; *Gegenstand der ~e war ...* the subject under discussion was ...; **2.** *Thema*: talk; *das ~ des Tages sein* be the talking-point (*od.* topic) of the day **gesprächig** *Adj.* talkative; (*mitteilsam*) communicative; *der Alkohol / die Drohung machte ihn ~* the drink/threat loosened his tongue; **Gesprächigkeit** *f*; *nur Sg.* talkativeness **gesprächsbereit** *Adj.* **1.** *bes. Pol.* (*verhandlungsbereit*) ready for talks, prepared (*od.* willing) to have talks, ready (*od.* prepared, willing) to negotiate; **2.** *am Telefon*: free (*od.* available *od.* ready) (to talk to s.o.); **Gesprächsbereitschaft** *f*; *nur Sg.* (*Verhandlungsbereitschaft*) readiness for talks (*od.* negotiations), willingness to have talks **Gesprächs|dauer** *f Telef.* call time, call duration; *bei e-r ~ von fünf Minuten kostet es ...* a five-minute call will cost ...; **~einheit** *f* unit **Gesprächs|fetzen** *Pl.* snatches of (a *od.* the) conversation; **~form** *f*: *in ~* in the form of a conversation *od.* dialog(ue); **~gegenstand** *m* topic (*od.* subject) of conversation; **~grundlage** *f* basis for talks; **~klima** *n Pol.* atmosphere of the talks; **~kreis** *m* discussion group; **~leiter** *m*, **~leiterin** *f Radio, TV*: host; *bei Konferenzschaltung*: *auch* anchorman; *Frau*: anchorwoman; **~leitung** *f*: *die ~ hat ...* the discussion is chaired by ... **Gesprächspartner** *m*, **~in** *f*: *er ist ein guter ~* you can have good conversations with him; *mein ~ war ...* I was talking to ...; *unsere ~ heute Abend sind ...* taking part in this evening's discussion are ...; *sein ~ Pol.* his partner in the talks

Gesprächs|pause *f* lull in the conversation; **~runde** *f Pol.* round of talks; **~stoff** *m* topic(s *Pl.*) of conversation; → *ausgehen* 5; **~teilnehmer** *m*, **~teilnehmerin** *f* participant in a (*od.* the) discussion; *auf Podium, im Fernsehen*: panel(l)ist, panel member; **~thema** *n* topic (of conversation); *e-r Diskussion*: topic of discussion; **~ Nummer eins** the number one topic, the thing that everybody is talking about; *das ist für mich kein ~* that's not something I'm even prepared to discuss; **~therapie** *f Psych.* counsel(l)ing

gespreizt I. *P.P.* → *spreizen*; **II.** *Adj. fig. pej.* affected; *Stil: auch* stilted; **III.** *Adv.*: *sich ~ ausdrücken* speak affectedly; **Gespreiztheit** *f; nur Sg.* affectation

gesprenkelt I. *P.P.* → *sprenkeln*; **II.** *Adj.* speckled; (*gescheckt*) mottled

gespritzt I. *P.P.* → *spritzen*; **II.** *Adj. Getränk*: ... with soda; **~er Whisky** whisky with soda, *Am.* whiskey and soda; *sauer ~er Weißwein* dry white wine spritzer; *sauer/süß ~es Bier* beer with a dash of mineral water/lemonade; **Gespritzte** *m; -n, -n; Dial. Getränk*: spritzer

gesprochen *P.P.* → *sprechen*

gesprossen *P.P.* → *sprießen*

gesprungen I. *P.P.* → *springen*; **II.** *Adj. Scheibe, Lippen etc.*: cracked

Gespür *n; -s, kein Pl.* (*Gefühl*) feeling (*für* for); (*Wahrnehmungsvermögen*) sense (of); *sie hat ein ~ dafür* she picks that kind of thing up straightaway

gespurt I. *P.P.* → *spuren*; **II.** *Adj. Loipe*: tracked, prepared

Gestade *n; -s, -; lit. des Meeres*: shore; *flaches*: beach; *e-s Flusses*: bank

gestaffelt I. *P.P.* → *staffeln*; **II.** *Adj. Preise, Steuern, Zinsen*: graduated, sliding scale ...; **~e Arbeitszeiten** staggered working hours; **~er Zinssatz** progressive (interest) rate

Gestagen *n; -s, -e; Physiol.* progestin

Gestalt *f; -, -en* **1.** (*Form*) shape, form; (*feste*) **~ annehmen** take shape, materialize, be shaping up; *die ~ e-r Pyramide haben* be shaped like a pyramid; *in ~ von* (*od. + Gen.*) in the form (*od.* shape) of; **2.** *nur Sg.*; (*Körperbau*) build, frame; (*Körper*) figure, form; *s-e rundliche etc. ~* his chubby etc. figure; *sie hat e-e zierliche ~* she's petite; **3.** (*bes. undeutlich Wahrgenommenes*) form, shape; (*Person*) *auch* figure; *dunkle ~en im Nebel* dark shapes in the mist; **4.** (*Persönlichkeit*) personality, figure; *literarische*: figure, character; **5.** *umg., oft hum. od. pej.* (*Person*) character; *zerlumpte ~en* ragamuffins; *dunkle od. zwielichtige ~en* shady characters; **6.** (*Verkörperung*) shape, form; (*Tarnung*) *auch* guise; *in* (*der*) **~ von** (*od. + Gen.*) in the form (*od.* shape) of; (*verkleidet als*) *auch fig.* in the guise of, disguised as; *Zeus nahm die ~ e-s Schwanes an* Zeus took on the form of a swan; *sich in s-r wahren ~ zeigen* reveal one's true character; **7.** *Psych.* gestalt

gestaltbar *Adj.* formable

gestalten I. *v/t.* **1.** (*formen*) form, shape; *Bildhauerei etc.*: model; *kreatives Gestalten* creative expression; **2.** *schöpferisch*: create, produce, make; *ein Thema dramatisch/poetisch ~* give dramatic/poetic form to a subject, dramatize a subject / write a poem on a subject; **3.** (*entwerfen*) design (*auch Tech.*); (*Park etc.*) lay out; (*Raum etc.*) decorate; (*einrichten*) arrange; (*Schaufenster*) dress; **4.** (*Fest etc.*) arrange, organize; *e-e Feier etc. abwechslungsreich ~* bring some variety to the celebrations; *e-e Notlage etc. erträglich ~* not let a crisis etc. get out of hand; **II.** *v/refl.* take shape; (*sich entwickeln*) develop; *es gestaltete sich schwierig* it turned out to be difficult; **Gestalter** *m; -s, -*, **Gestalterin** *f; -, -nen* designer; (*Organisator*) organizer; (*Schöpfer*) creator; **gestalterisch** *Adj.* **1.** *Kräfte etc.*: formative; **2.** *Tätigkeit*: creative; (*künstlerisch*) artistic; (*formgebend*) design ...; (*organisatorisch*) organizational

gestaltlos *Adj.* shapeless, amorphous; **Gestaltlosigkeit** *f; nur Sg.* shapelessness

Gestalt|psychologie *f Psych.* gestalt psychology; **~therapeut** *m*, **~therapeutin** *f* gestalt therapist

Gestaltung *f* **1.** *mst Sg.*; (*Entwurf, Entwicklung*) design(ing); (*Schaffung*) creation, production; (*Formung*) formation; (*Formgebung*) shaping; *e-s Festes etc.*: organization, arrangement; (*Darbietung*) presentation; *e-s Raumes etc.*: decoration; *Hochschule für ~* college of design; **2.** (*Gestalt*) form, shape; (*Aufbau*) structure; (*Merkmale*) features *Pl.*; (*Stil, Zuschnitt*) style; *auch Tech.* design, lay(-)out

Gestaltungs|kraft *f* creative power; **~mittel** *n* artistic means; **~prinzip** *n* formal principle, principle on which s.th. is formed (*od.* organized *od.* based); **~wille** *m* will to create

Gestammel *n; -s, kein Pl.* **1.** stuttering, stammering; **2.** *oft pej.* (*unverständliche Wörter*) gobbledygook *umg.*

gestanden I. *P.P.* → *stehen*, *gestehen*; **II.** *Adj. bes. südd.*: *ein ~er Mann od. ein ~es Mannsbild männlich*: a manly man; *stattlich*: a fine figure of a man; *erfolgreich*: a man who's made it (*od.* got[ten] somewhere) in life; *ein ~er Politiker/Profi* a seasoned politician/pro

geständig *Adj.*: **~ sein** (*gestehen*) confess, own up; (*gestanden haben*) have confessed (*od.* owned up), have made a confession; *der ~e Entführer / Mörder etc.* the self-confessed kidnapper/murderer; **Geständnis** *n; -ses, -se* confession; (*Eingeständnis*) admission; (*Bekenntnis*) avowal; *ein ~ ablegen* make a confession, confess, *Am. umg.* fess up (*über etw.* [*Akk.*] s.th.); *ich muss dir ein ~ machen* there's something I have to tell (*od.* confess to) you

Gestänge *n; -s, -* **1.** struts; *e-s Bettes* frame(work); **2.** *Tech.* linkage

Gestank *m; -(e)s, kein Pl.* smell; *stärker*: stench, stink, reek

Gestapomethoden *Pl. pej.* Gestapo methods (*od.* tactics)

gestatten *v/t.* allow, permit; (*gewähren*) grant; (*dulden*) tolerate; *j-m etw. ~* allow s.o. to do s.th.; **~ Sie, dass ich rauche?** do you mind if I smoke?; *~ Sie?* may I?; *heute gestatte ich mir ...* geh. today I'm going to allow myself (*od.* treat myself to) ...; *wenn ich mir die Bemerkung ~ darf geh.* if I may be allowed (*od.* be permitted *od.* be so bold as) to say (so); *~ auch erlauben*, *gestattet*; **gestattet I.** *P.P.* → *gestatten*; **II.** *Adj.*: *Rauchen/Fotografieren nicht gestattet* smoking/photography prohibited

Geste *f; -, -n* gesture (*auch fig.*); *mit lebhaften ~n* gesticulating wildly; *als höfliche ~ fig.* as a matter of politeness; *es war e-e nette ~ von ihr zu* (+ *Inf.*) *fig.* it was kind of her to (+ *Inf.*)

Gesteck *n; -(e)s, -e* flower arrangement

gesteckt I. *P.P.* → *stecken*; **II.** *Adv. umg.*: *~ voll* jampacked, chock-a-block

gestehen *gesteht, gestand, hat gestanden* **I.** *v/t.* admit; *auch Jur.* confess; (*bekennen*) profess, avow; *j-m s-e Liebe ~* declare one's love to s.o.; *offen gestanden* to be quite honest; **II.** *v/i.* confess, make a confession (*auch Jur.*), own (*Am. auch* fess) up

Gestein *n; -s, -e* rock(s *Pl.*); *Bergb.* rock, stone

Gesteins|art *f* type of rock; **~bildung** *f* rock formation; **~brocken** *m* rock; **~kunde** *f; nur Sg.* petrology, mineralogy; **~masse** *f* rocky mass; **~mehl** *n* mineral powder; **~probe** *f* rock sample; **~schicht** *f* stratum

Gestell *n; -(e)s, -e* **1.** *zur Ablage*: rack; (*Regal*) shelves *Pl.*; (*Ständer*) stand; (*Stütze*) support; (*Bock*) trestle; *für Wäsche*: clothes(-)horse; **2.** *von Brille, Fahrrad etc.*: frame; *~ auch Bettgestell, Fahrgestell etc.*; **3.** *umg. hum.* (*Beine*) legs *Pl.*; (*Person*) beanpole; (*Körper*) lanky frame

gestellt I. *P.P.* → *stellen*; **II.** *Adj.* **1.** *Bild etc.*: posed; *Szene*: acted; *weitS.* (*unnatürlich*) artificial, unnatural; *es ist ~ Szene*: they're (just) acting; **2.** *gut/schlecht ~ sein* be well/badly off; *auf sich selbst ~ sein* have to fend for o.s., have to paddle one's own canoe

gestelzt I. *P.P.* → *stelzen*; **II.** *Adj. Ausdrucksweise*: affected; *Stil: auch* stilted, wooden; **III.** *Adv.*: *~ reden auch* talk like a book

gestern *Adv.* yesterday; *~ früh od. Morgen* yesterday morning; *~ Abend* last night; *~ Mittag* (at) midday yesterday; *~ vor e-r Woche* a week ago yesterday, *Brit. auch* yesterday week; *von ~* yesterday's ...; *er ist nicht von ~ fig.* he wasn't born yesterday, he's nobody's fool

gesteuert I. *P.P.* → *steuern*; **II.** *Adj. Tech.* controlled

gestiefelt I. *P.P.* → *stiefeln*; **II.** *Adj.* in boots; *der Gestiefelte Kater* Puss-in-Boots; *~ und gespornt umg. hum.* ready and waiting; *iro.* raring to go

gestiegen *P.P.* → *steigen*

gestielt *Adj. Vase etc.*: stemmed; *Bot.* stalked

Gestik *f; -, kein Pl.* gestures *Pl.*; (*Zeichen*) sign language; (*Körpersprache*) body language; *e-e lebhafte ~ haben* gesticulate a lot, use one's hands a lot

gestikulieren I. *v/i.* gesticulate, wave one's hands about (in the air); **II. Gestikulieren** *n; -s, kein Pl.* gesticulation

gestimmt I. *P.P.* → *stimmen*; **II.** *Adj.*: *fröhlich/traurig etc. ~* in a happy/sad mood

Gestirn *n; -(e)s, -e*;(*Stern*) star(s *Pl.*); (*Sternbild*) constellation; **gestirnt** *Adj. geh.* starry

gestisch *Adj.* gestural

gestoben *P.P.* → *stieben*; **Gestöber** *n; -s, -* (snow)drift, (snow) flurry

gestochen I. *P.P.* → *stechen*; **II.** *Adj. Handschrift*: (*wie*) *~* very neat (*od.* clear); **III.** *Adv.*: *~ scharf Fotos etc.*: pin-sharp

gestohlen I. *P.P.* → *stehlen*; **II.** *Adj. umg. fig.*: *der/das kann mir ~ bleiben* to hell with him/it *Sl.*

Gestöhn(e) *n*; *-s, kein Pl.*; *umg. pej.* moaning, moans *Pl.*

gestopft I. *P.P.* → *stopfen*; **II.** *Adv. umg.*: ~ **voll** jampacked, chock-a-block, chock-full

gestorben *P.P.* → *sterben*

gestört I. *P.P.* → *stören*; **II.** *Adj.* **1.** (*geistig*) ~ mentally disturbed (*od.* unbalanced); **der ist ja ~!** *umg. pej.* he's off his head (*Am.* rocker); **2. ~er Empfang** bad reception; **~e Verbindung** *Telef.* faulty line; **~er Schlaf** broken sleep; **~es Verhältnis** troubled (*od.* uneasy) relationship (**zu** with); **er hat ein ~es Verhältnis zu sich selbst** he finds it hard to come to terms with himself

gestoßen *P.P.* → *stoßen*

Gestotter *n*; *-s, kein Pl.*; *umg. mst pej.* stuttering

Gesträuch *n*; *-(e)s, -e* bushes *Pl.*, shrubbery

gestreckt I. *P.P.* → *strecken*; **II.** *Adj.*: **in ~em Galopp** at full gallop

gestreift I. *P.P.* → *streifen*; **II.** *Adj.* striped, strip(e)y *umg.*; **rotblau** ~ with red and blue stripes, red-and-blue striped ...

gestresst *umg.* **I.** *P.P.* → *stressen*; **II.** *Adj.* stressed

gestrichelt I. *P.P.* → *stricheln*; **II.** *Adj.*: **~e Linie** broken (*od.* dotted *umg.*) line

gestrichen I. *P.P.* → *streichen*; **II.** *Adj.* **1.** *Mus.* bowed; **2. drei ~e Teelöffel** three level teaspoons(ful); **III.** *Adv.*: ~ **voll** filled to the brim; **ich hab die Nase od. Schnauze ~ voll** *umg. fig.* I'm fed up to the back teeth (with it); **er hat die Hosen ~ voll** *umg. fig.* he's shitting himself (*Am.* his pants) *vulg.*

gestrickt I. *P.P.* → *stricken*; **II.** *Adj. umg.* **selbst ~** *oft pej.* home-made; **mit der heißen Nadel ~** *pej.* thrown together

gestriegelt I. *P.P.* → *striegeln*; **II.** *Adj.*: ~ (**und gebügelt**) (*präd.* all) spruced up

gestrig *Adj.* **1.** *nur attr.* yesterday's; **der ~e Tag** *od.* **am ~en Tage** yesterday; **der ~e Abend** *od.* **am ~en Abend** last night; **unser ~es Schreiben** our letter of yesterday; **2.** *geh.* (*rückständig*) *Ansichten*: outdated; → *Ewiggestrige*

gestritten *P.P.* → *streiten*

gestromt *Adj. Dogge, Fell, Katze*: brindled

Gestrüpp *n*; *-(e)s, -e* **1.** brushwood, scrub; (*Unterholz*) underbrush; (*Dickicht*) thicket; **2.** *fig.* jungle, maze

Gestühl *n*; *-(e)s, -e* chairs *Pl.*, seats *Pl.*, seating; *in der Kirche*: pews *Pl.*; *des Chors*: stalls *Pl.*

gestunken *P.P.* → *stinken*

Gestus *m*; *-, kein Pl.* **1.** (*Gestik*) gestures *Pl.*; **2.** (*Habitus*) air

Gestüt *n*; *-(e)s, -e* stud farm; **~buch** *n* studbook; **~hengst** *m* stallion; **~pferd** *n* horse at stud; **~stute** *f* stud mare

gestylt I. *P.P.* → *stylen*; **II.** *Adj.* (*zurechtgemacht*) styled; *Kleidung etc.*: designer ...; → *durchgestylt*

Gesuch *n*; *-(e)s, -e*; (*Bittschrift*) petition (**um** for); (*Antrag, Bewerbung*) application

gesucht I. *P.P.* → *suchen*; **II.** *Adj.* **1.** (*begehrt*) (much) sought-after; ~ **sein** *auch* be in demand; **sehr ~ sein** be in great demand, be very much in demand; **2.** *in Inseraten od. polizeilich*: wanted; **3.** *fig.* (*absichtlich*) studied; (*geziert, gekünstelt*) affected; *Ausdruck, Vergleich*: labo(u)red; **4.** *Math.*

Lösung, Wert: desired

Gesülze *n*; *-s, kein Pl.*; *umg. pej.* drivel, claptrap

Gesumm(e) *n*; *-s, kein Pl.*; *oft pej.* hum, humming (noise)

gesund I. *Adj.*; *gesünder, am gesündesten* **1.** (*Ggs. krank*) *Person*: healthy, präd. auch (very) well; (*fit*) fit; *Organ, Schlaf, Zähne*: sound, healthy; *Tier, Pflanze*: healthy; ~ **und munter** *umg.* as fit as a fiddle, in the pink; **körperlich und geistig ~** physically and mentally fit, sound in body and mind; **j-n ~ machen/pflegen** restore s.o. to / nurse s.o. back to health; (**wieder**) ~ **werden** get better, get well, recover; **wir machen dich schon wieder ~** we'll get you back on your feet again; **bleib** (**schön**) ~**!** look after yourself; **sonst bist du ~?** *iro.* but apart from that you're fine?, are you sure you're feeling all right?; **2.** *Nahrung etc.*: good (**für** for), wholesome; *Lebensweise*: healthy; *Obst ist ~* fruit is good for you; *Schokolade ist für die Zähne nicht ~* chocolate is bad for your teeth; **das ist ganz ~ für ihn** *fig.* it'll do him good; **3.** (*von Gesundheit zeugend*) *Bräune, Farbe*: healthy; **e-e ~e Farbe haben** have a healthy colo(u)r; **4.** *fig. Firma, Instinkt etc.*: sound; **5.** *fig.* (*natürlich, normal*) *Misstrauen etc.*: healthy; (*vernünftig*) *Ansichten*: sound, healthy; **~er Menschenverstand** (sound) common sense; **e-e ~e Einstellung haben zu** have a healthy attitude toward(s); **II.** *Adv.*: ~ **leben** have a healthy lifestyle; → *gesundschreiben etc.*

gesundbeten *v/t.* (*trennb. hat -ge-*) cure *s.o.* by faith healing; **Gesundbeter** *m*; *-s, -* faith healer; **Gesundbeterin** *f*; *-, -nen* faith healer

Gesundbrunnen *m* *fig.*: ... **ist der reinste ~** (**für mich**) ... does wonders (for me / my health), ... keeps you (keeps me) fit and healthy

Gesunde *m, f*; *-n, -n* healthy person

gesunden *v/i. geh.* recover (*auch fig.*), be restored to health

Gesundheit *f*; *nur Sg.* **1.** health; *des Geistes*: sanity; *von Organen, Zähnen etc.*: soundness; *von Pflanzen*: health; **bei bester/schlechter ~** in the best of health / in poor health; **e-e eiserne/schwache ~ haben** have an iron/weak constitution; **vor ~ strotzen** be the picture of health; **auf j-s ~ anstoßen** *od.* **trinken** drink to s.o.'s health; *~! beim Niesen*: bless you!, *Am. auch* gesundheit!; **auf Ihre ~!** your health!; **2.** (*Zuträglichkeit*) healthiness; **3.** *fig. e-r Firma etc.*: health

gesundheitlich I. *Adj.* health ...; **~er Zustand** state of health; **aus ~en Gründen** for health reasons; **II.** *Adv.* healthwise; ~ **geht es ihr gut/schlecht** she's well / not well, her health is good / not good

Gesundheits|amt *n* *e-r Stadt*: public health department; **~apostel** *m* health freak; **~artikel** *m* health product; **~attest** *n* health certificate

gesundheitsbewusst *Adj.* health-conscious

Gesundheits|dienst *m* public health service; **~fanatiker** *m*, **~fanatikerin** *f* health freak (*od.* fanatic); **⌷fördernd** *Adj.* healthy, good for one's health; **~fürsorge** *f* health care

Gesundheits|gefahr *f* health hazard; **⌷gefährdend** *Adj.* unhealthy, bad for one's health; **~gefährdung** *f* endan-

germent of health

Gesundheitsgründe *Pl.*: **aus ~n** → *gesundheitshalber*

gesundheitshalber *Adv.* for health reasons, for reasons of health

Gesundheits|industrie *f* health (*od.* healthcare) industry; **~minister** *m*, **~ministerin** *f* health minister, minister for health; *in GB*: Health Secretary, Secretary of State for Health; *in den USA*: Secretary of Health (and Human Services); **~ministerium** *n* health ministry (*od.* department); *in GB*: Health Department; *auch in den USA*: Department of Health and Human Services); **~pass** *m* *in GB*: medical card; *in US*: health chip card; **~pflege** *f* health care, *Am.* healthcare

Gesundheitspolitik *f* health policy; **gesundheitspolitisch** *Adj.* relating to health policy; **die ~e Sprecherin der Partei** the party's spokeswoman on health

Gesundheits|polizei *f* sanitary police; **~reform** *f* health service reform(s *Pl.*); **~risiko** *n* health hazard; **~schaden** *m* damage (*od.* injury) to one's health; **Gesundheitsschäden** damage *Sg.* to one's health

gesundheitsschädlich *Adj.* bad for one's health; *Gas etc.*: noxious; *Klima, Nahrung etc.*: unwholesome, unhealthy; *Verhältnisse*: unsanitary; **~e Auswirkungen** adverse health effects

Gesundheits|schuh *m* orthop(a)edic (*Am. auch* corrective) shoe; **~schutz** *m* health protection; **~system** *n* public health system; **~vorsorge** *f* health care, *Am.* healthcare; **~wesen** *n*; *nur Sg.*: (*öffentliches*) ~ public health system; **~zentrum** *n* health cent|re (*Am.* -er); **~zustand** *m* (state of) health, physical condition; *e-s Volkes*: *auch* standard of health

gesundschreiben *v/t.* (*unreg., trennb., hat -ge-*) certify *s.o.* as fit

gesundschrumpfen (*trennb., hat -ge-*) **I.** *v/t.* (*Firma etc.*) slim down, streamline; **II.** *v/refl.* slim down, downsize

gesundstoßen *v/refl.* (*unreg., trennb., hat -ge-*); *umg.* make a packet (*Am.* bundle) (**an** + *Dat.* on, with)

Gesundung *f*; *nur Sg.*; *geh.* recovery (*auch fig.*)

gesungen *P.P.* → *singen*

gesunken *P.P.* → *sinken*

getan I. *P.P.* → *tun*; **gesagt, ~** no sooner said than done; **II.** *Adj.*: **nach ~er Arbeit** when the day's work is done, after work

geteilt I. *P.P.* → *teilen*; **II.** *Adj.* divided; *Bot., Blatt*: parted; *Tech., Wirts.* split; **~er Meinung sein** disagree; **die Meinungen sind ~** opinions differ (*od.* are divided); **~es Leid ist halbes Leid** *Sprichw.* a sorrow shared is a sorrow halved; **~e Freude ist doppelte Freude** *Sprichw.* a joy shared is a joy doubled

Getier *n*; *-(e)s, kein Pl.*; *Koll.* animals *Pl.*; (*Insekten und Kleintiere*) creatures *Pl.*

getigert I. *P.P.* → *tigern*; **II.** *Adj.* striped; **~e Katze** tabby (cat)

Getöse *n*; *-s, kein Pl.* din, racket *umg.*; (*Krachen*) crash; *e-r Menge etc.*: uproar; *des Windes, der Wellen*: roaring; *e-s Kampfes*: roar, rage; *des Verkehrs*: roar, noise

getragen I. *P.P.* → *tragen*; **II.** *Adj.* **1.** *Kleidung*: (*benutzt*) second-hand; (*alt*) old; (*gebraucht gekauft*) second-hand; (*weitergereicht*) handed-down; **2.** *fig.* (*feierlich*) solemn; *Mus.* portato

G

(*auch Adv.*)

Geträller *n*; *-s*, *kein Pl.*; *umg. von Vögeln und Menschen*: trilling

Getrampel *n*; *-s*, *kein Pl.*; *umg. pej.* trampling about; *als Beifall etc.*: stamping (of feet)

Getränk *n*; *-(e)s*, *-e* drink, beverage *förm.*; **alkoholfreie** ⁓**e** non-alcoholic (*od.* soft) drinks; **für Speisen und** ⁓**e ist bestens gesorgt** there's plenty to eat and drink

Getränke|abholmarkt *m* drinks warehouse (*od.* cash-and-carry), *Am. etwa*: liquor superstore; ⁓**automat** *m* drinks machine (*od.* dispenser); ⁓**dose** *f* drinks (*Am.* aluminum) can; ⁓**industrie** *f* beverage industry; ⁓**karte** *f* list of beverages; wine list; ⁓**kellner** *m*, ⁓**kellnerin** *f* wine waiter; ⁓**markt** *m* drinks warehouse (*od.* cash-and -carry), *Am. etwa*: liquor superstore; ⁓**steuer** *f* beverage tax *on alcoholic beverages consumed in public*

Getrappel *n*; *-s*, *kein Pl. von Hufen*: clatter; *von Füßen*: patter; *lauter*: trampling

Getratsche *n*; *-s*, *kein Pl.*; *umg. pej.* gossip

getrauen *v/refl.* → **trauen**[1] II, III

Getreide *n*; *-s*, - grain, cereals *Pl.*, *Brit. auch* corn; ⁓**anbau** *m* growing of cereals, cereal agriculture; ⁓**art** *f* cereal, (type of) grain; ⁓**aussaat** *f* sowing of cereal crops; ⁓**börse** *f* *Fin.* grain exchange; *in England*: corn exchange; ⁓**ernte** *f* grain harvest; ⁓**feld** *n* cornfield, *Am.* grainfield; ⁓**flocken** *Pl.* *Gastr.* cereal *Sg.*; ⁓**händler** *m*, ⁓**händlerin** *f* grain merchant; ⁓**korn** *n* grain; ⁓**land** *n* grain-growing country; ⁓**lieferungen** *Pl.* grain supply *Sg.* (*od.* supplies) (**an** + *Akk.* to); ⁓**mehl** *n* flour; *grob*: meal; ⁓**mühle** *f* gristmill; ⁓**produkte** *Pl.* cereal products; ⁓**silo** *m*, *n*, ⁓**speicher** *m* granary; silo, *Am. auch* (grain) elevator; ⁓**stärke** *f* cereal starch; ⁓**vorrat** *m* grain supply (*od.* supplies *Pl.*)

getrennt I. *P.P.* → **trennen**; II. *Adj.* separate; **mit** ⁓**er Post** under separate cover; ⁓**e Kasse machen** go Dutch, go halves on s.th.; (*getrennte Konten haben*) have separate accounts; III. *Adv.* separately; ⁓ **leben** be separated (**von** from), live apart; ⁓ **schlafen** have separate bedrooms; *Begriffe* ⁓ **halten** distinguish between; *Wörter* ⁓ **schreiben** write as two words; **wir zahlen** ⁓ **im** *Restaurant*: could we have separate bills (*Am.* checks)?

Getrennt|sammlung *f von Abfällen*: separate collection; ⁓**schreibung** *f*: **die** ⁓ **findet man häufiger** it's usually written as two (*od.* three *etc.*) words

getreu *Adj.* 1. (*entsprechend*) true (+ *Dat.* to); ⁓**e Abschrift** true copy; ⁓**e Übersetzung** faithful translation; ⁓ **s-m Eid** *etc.*: true to his oath *etc.*; ⁓ **dem Motto** *od.* **der Devise**: ... true to the motto: ...; 2. *geh.* faithful, loyal (+ *Dat.* to); **er war stets ein** ⁓**er Freund** he never wavered in his friendship ...**getreu** *im Adj.* true to ...; *natur*⁓ true to life, natural; *Größe*; life-size

Getreue *m*, *f*; *-n*, *-n*; *geh.* follower, loyal supporter; **getreulich** *Adj.* 1. (*genau*) faithful; 2. *geh.* faithful, loyal

Getriebe *n*; *-s*, - 1. *Tech.* gear unit; *Mot. etc.* transmission; (*Räderkasten*) gearbox; (*Antrieb*) drive; *e-r Uhr etc.*: clockwork; 2. *fig.* machinery; → *Sand*; ⁓**gehäuse** *n*, *Mot.* gearbox

getrieben I. *P.P.* → **treiben**; II. *Adj.*

Metall: embossed; ⁓**e Arbeit** *auch* chased work; **Getriebenheit** *f*; *nur Sg.* (*innere Unruhe*) drivenness, restiveness

Getriebe|öl *n* *Mot.* gearbox oil; ⁓**rad** *n* gear wheel; ⁓**schaden** *m* transmission trouble (*totaler*: failure); ⁓**welle** *f* shaft

getrimmt I. *P.P.* → **trimmen**; II. *Adj. umg.*: (**sie ist**) **auf jugendlich** ⁓ (she's) mutton dressed up as lamb

getroffen[1] I. *P.P.* → **treffen**; II. *Adj.* 1. **auf dem Foto bist du gut** ⁓ it's a good photo of you; 2. **sich** ⁓ **fühlen** feel hurt

getroffen[2] *P.P.* (*selten*) → **triefen**

getrogen *P.P.* → **trügen**

Getrommel *n*; *-s*, *kein Pl.*; *umg. pej.* drumming

getrost *Adv.* (*sicher, ohne Risiko*) safely; (*leicht, ohne weiteres*) easily; (*vertrauensvoll*) confidently; **das kannst du** ⁓ **tun** there's no reason why you shouldn't do it; *Erlaubnis erteilend*: *auch* go ahead (and do it), feel free (to do so); **man kann** ⁓ **behaupten, dass ...** one can safely say that ...

getrunken *P.P.* → **trinken**

Getto *n*; *-s*, *-s*; *auch fig.* ghetto; **das** **Warschauer/Prager** ⁓ *hist.* the Warsaw/Prague Ghetto

gettoisieren *v/t. geh. pej.* ghettoize

Getue *n*; *-s*, *kein Pl.*; *umg. pej.* 1. (*Umstände*) fuss (**um** about, over); 2. *Benehmen*: **albernes** *od.* **dummes** ⁓ silly behavio(u)r; **affektiertes/vornehmes** ⁓ affectation / putting on airs

Getümmel *n*; *-s*, -, *mst Sg.* turmoil, tumult; **sich ins** ⁓ **stürzen** enter (*od.* throw o.s. into) the fray

getüpfelt, **getupft** I. *P.P.* → **tüpfeln**, **tupfen** I 1; II. *Adj.* spotted; *Kleid etc.*: with dots, polka-dot ...; **gelb** ⁓ with yellow dots (*od.* spots)

geübt I. *P.P.* → **üben**; II. *Adj.* practi|sed (*Am.* -ced) (**in** + *Dat.* in doing *s.th.*); (*erfahren*) skilled, experienced (at, in); (*geschult*) trained (*auch Auge*); **mit** ⁓**em Blick** with a practised (*Am.* practiced) eye; **Geübtheit** *f*; *mst Sg.* practice, experience

Gevatter *m*; *-s*, *-n*; *altm.* (*Pate*) godfather; (*Verwandte*) relative; *als Anrede*: friend; ⁓ **Tod** *lit.* the Grim Reaper; **Gevatterin** *f*; *-*, *-nen*; *altm.* (*Patin*) godmother; *als Anrede*: friend

Geviert *n*; *-(e)s*, *-e* 1. *Tech.* square; ... **im** ⁓ ... square; 2. *Druck.* quad; 3. *Astrol.* quartile

Gewächs *n*; *-es*, *-e* 1. (*Pflanze*) plant; 2. *Agr.* (*Erzeugnis*) produce; (*Wein*) wine; (*Jahrgang*) vintage; **ein edles** ⁓ (*Wein*) a choice wine; 3. *Med.* growth

gewachsen I. *P.P.* → **wachsen**[1]; II. *Adj.* 1. *Boden*: natural, undisturbed; *fig. Traditionen etc.*: deep-rooted; **wie aus dem Boden** ⁓ **erscheinen** appear (as if) from nowhere; **über die Jahre** ⁓**e soziale Kontakte** social contacts that have grown up over the years; 2. *fig.*: **j-m** ⁓ **sein** be a match for s.o.; **e-r Sache** ⁓ **sein / sich e-r Sache** ⁓ **fühlen** be/feel up to s.th.; **sich der Lage** ⁓ **zeigen** rise to the occasion

Gewächshaus *n* greenhouse, hothouse; ⁓**pflanze** *f* hothouse plant

Gewackel *n*; *-s*, *kein Pl.*; *umg. pej.* wobbling; (*Schaukeln*) rocking; **mit den Hüften**: wiggling

gewagt I. *P.P.* → **wagen**; II. *Adj.* 1. (*gefährlich*) risky; (*kühn*) daring; 2. *Kleid, Witz etc.*: risqué; **Gewagtheit** *f*; *nur Sg.* riskiness; (*Kühnheit*) daring

---

gewählt I. *P.P.* → **wählen**; II. *Adj.* *Sprache etc.*: refined; *Gesellschaft*: select; III. *Adv.*: **sich** ⁓ **ausdrücken** talk well, choose one's words well, be very articulate; **Gewähltheit** *f*; *nur Sg.*: ⁓ **des Ausdrucks** careful choice of words

gewahr *Adj. geh.*: ⁓ **werden** (+ *Gen.*) notice, become aware of; (*entdecken*) *auch* discover; *e-r Gefahr etc.*: realize; (*sehen*) catch sight of, see; (*wahrnehmen*) perceive

Gewähr *f*; *-*, *kein Pl.* 1. guarantee; ⁓ **bieten** *od.* **leisten für** guarantee; **alle Angaben ohne** ⁓ no responsibility is accepted for the correctness of this information; 2. *Jur.*, *Wirts.* (*Bürgschaft*) security

gewähren I. *v/t. geh.* 1. *Person*: (*bewilligen*) grant (*auch Bitte*); (*einräumen*) allow; **j-m Einlass** ⁓ let s.o. in, admit s.o.; 2. *Sache*: give, offer; **Schutz** ⁓ (*vor* + *Dat.*) give protection (from); **es gewährt e-n Einblick** it affords an insight (**in** + *Akk.* into); II. *v/i.*: **j-n** ⁓ **lassen** let s.o. have his way; (*in Ruhe lassen*) leave s.o. alone

gewährleisten *v/t.* (*untr.*, *hat*); (*garantieren*) guarantee; (*sichern*) ensure; **Gewährleistung** *f* guarantee; *auch Wirts.* warranty

Gewahrsam *m*; *-s*, *kein Pl.* 1. (*Obhut*) care; (*sichere Verwahrung*) safekeeping; **in** ⁓ **nehmen** take charge of; 2. (*Haft*) custody, detention; **in** ⁓ **nehmen** take into custody, place under detention

Gewährs|frau *f*, ⁓**mann** *m*; *Pl. auch* **-leute** authority, source; (*Bürge*) guarantor

Gewährung *f*; *mst Sg.* granting

Gewalt *f*; *-*, *-en* 1. *nur Sg.* violence; (*Zwang*) force; *Koll.* (*Gewalttätigkeiten*) violence; ⁓ **gegen Sachen** *Jur.* criminal damage; ⁓ **in der Familie** domestic violence; **brutale** *od.* **rohe** ⁓ brute force; **mit** ⁓ by force, using force, forcibly; ⁓ **anwenden** use force (*od.* violence); **j-m** ⁓ **androhen** threaten s.o. with violence; **j-m** ⁓ **antun** do violence to s.o.; *e-r Frau* ⁓ **antun** *geh. euph.* violate a woman; **sich** (*Dat.*) ⁓ **antun** lay hands (up)on o.s.; (*sich zwingen*) force oneself; **der Wahrheit** *etc.* ⁓ **antun** *fig.* do violence to the truth *etc.*; 2. *nur Sg.*; (*Krafteinsatz*) force; (*Kraft*) strength, might; **mit** ⁓ using force, forcibly; **mit sanfter** ⁓ gently but firmly; **mit** ⁓ **öffnen** force (*od.* break) open; (*Tür*) *auch* break down; 3. *nur Sg.*; *e-s Sturmes etc.*: violence, force; (*Stärke*) power; *e-r Explosion*: force; (*Wucht*) force, impact; 4. *nur Sg.*: ⁓ (**über** + *Akk.*) (*Macht*) power (over); *durch Amt etc.*: *auch* authority; (*Herrschaft*) control (of, over); **die elterliche/richterliche** ⁓ parental/judicial authority; **höhere** ⁓ *fig.* an act (*od.* acts) of God, force majeure; **in s-e** ⁓ **bringen** *od.* **bekommen** gain control of; (*Flugzeug etc.*) take command of; *weitS.* hijack; **in s-r** ⁓ **haben** (*j-n*) have s.o. under one's thumb (*od.* in one's power); (*etw.*) be in control of; **sich in** ⁓ **haben** have oneself under control; **die** ⁓ **verlieren über** (+ *Akk.*) *Fahrzeug*, *sich selbst etc.*: lose control of; *e-e Situation*: lose one's grip on; **hier geht** ⁓ **vor Recht** this is a case of might being right; 5. *mst Pl.*; *personifiziert*: force; *bes. Pol.* power; **die drei** ⁓**en** *Pol.* the three powers; 6. *umg.*: **mit (aller)** ⁓ (*unbedingt*) desperately, at all costs;

du willst wohl mit aller ~ unangenehm auffallen? *iro.* are you really so determined to make a bad impression?

Gewalt|akt *m* act of violence; *fig.* tour de force; **~anstrengung** *f:* **das war e-e enorme ~** it was an enormous effort; **~anwendung** *f* (use of) force; (*Gewalttätigkeit*) (use of) violence; **unter ~** by force, using force; **~ausbruch** *m* eruption of violence; **~bereitschaft** *f; nur Sg.* readiness to use force; **~darstellung** *f in Medien:* depiction of violence; **~einwirkung** *f:* **durch ~** by (an act of) violence; **ohne Anzeichen von ~** with no sign of violence being used

Gewalten|teilung *f,* **~trennung** *f Pol.* separation of powers

gewaltfrei *Adj. Protest etc.:* nonviolent; *Politik, Zeit:* peaceful; **Gewaltfreiheit** *f; nur Sg.* absence of violence

Gewalt|herrschaft *f* despotism, tyranny; **~herrscher** *m,* **~herrscherin** *f* despot

gewaltig I. *Adj.* **1.** (*ungeheuer*) enormous, immense, stupendous; (*riesig*) gigantic; *auch Gebiet, Anlage:* huge, vast, tremendous *umg.,* terrific *umg.; Unterschied, Zahl:* vast; *Menge: auch* huge; **~er Irrtum** big(, big) mistake; **~e Leistung** tremendous feat (*od.* achievement); **~e Lüge** great big lie, *Am.* whopper; **e-n ~en Eindruck hinterlassen** make a big (*od.* deep) impression (**bei** on); **2.** *Angst etc.:* terrible, violent, intense; *Hitze, Kälte:* intense; *Durst:* tremendous; *Sturm:* violent, tremendous; **3.** (*mächtig*) powerful; **die Gewaltigen der Industrie** *etc.:* the big names in industry *etc.;* **II.** *Adv.* enormously *etc.;* → I; **sich ~ anstrengen** make an enormous effort; **er hat sich ~ geärgert** he got terribly angry; **da irrst du dich aber** (*ganz*)**~!** you're very much mistaken!

Gewaltkriminalität *f* violent crime(s *Pl.*)

Gewaltkur *f* **1.** *Med. etc.* drastic cure; *zum Abnehmen:* crash diet; **2.** *fig.* drastic measures *Pl.*

gewaltlos *Adj. Politik:* nonviolent; *Übernahme etc.: auch* bloodless (*auch Revolution*); **Gewaltlosigkeit** *f; nur Sg.* absence of violence; *bes. als Prinzip:* nonviolence

Gewalt|lösung *f* drastic solution; **~marsch** *m* forced march; **~maßnahme** *f* drastic (*od.* violent) measure; **~mensch** *m* brutal person; **~opfer** *n* victim of violence; **~phantasien** *Pl.* violent fantasies

gewaltsam I. *Adj.* violent; (*drastisch*) drastic; (*erzwungen*) forcible; **e-s ~en Todes sterben** die a violent death; **~es Vorgehen** *der Polizei etc.:* use of force; **II.** *Adv.* violently; (*mit Gewalt*) by force; **~ öffnen** force open

Gewalt|schuss *m Sl. Fußball:* rocket; **~spirale** *f* spiral of violence (and counter-violence); **~streich** *m* coup de main; **~tat** *f* act of violence; → **terroristisch**

gewalttätig *Adj.* violent; **Gewalttätigkeit** *f* **1.** *nur Sg.;* brutality, violence; **2.** *Tat:* act of violence

Gewalt|verbrechen *n* violent crime; **~verbrecher** *m* violent criminal; **~verherrlichung** *f* glorification of violence; **~verzicht** *m* non-aggression; *Erklärung:* renunciation of force

Gewaltverzichts|abkommen *n Pol.* non-aggression pact; **~erklärung** *f* declaration renouncing the use of force; **~vertrag** *m* non-aggression

treaty

Gewand *n; -(e)s, Gewänder; geh. od. südd., österr., schw.* **1.** garment; *wallendes:* robe, gown; *kirchl.* robe, vestment; **2.** *fig.* look; **im ~** (+ *Gen.*) in the guise of; **die Zeitschrift etc. erscheint in neuem ~** has had a face(-)-lift (*od.* makeover)

gewandet *Adj.; altm., lit.* (*gekleidet*) dressed, apparel(l)ed (**als** as; **in** + *Akk.* in)

Gewand|haus *n hist.* cloth hall; **~meister** *m,* **~meisterin** *f Theat., TV etc.* wardrobe master, *weiblich:* wardrobe mistress

gewandt I. *P.P.* → **wenden** I 2, III 2; **II.** *Adj.* **1.** (*flink*) quick, agile, nimble; **2.** (*geschickt*) skil(l)ful (**in** + *Dat.* at), clever (*beide auch fig.*); (*tüchtig*) efficient; (*raffiniert*) clever, smart; **~ sein im Umgang mit** have a way with; **3.** *Umgangsformen, Stil etc.:* elegant; *auch pej.* smooth; *Redner:* fluent; **Gewandtheit** *f; nur Sg.* **1.** agility; **2.** skill; efficiency; smartness; **3.** elegance; smoothness; fluency; → **gewandt** II

gewann *Imperf.* → **gewinnen**

gewappnet I. *P.P.* → **wappnen**; **II.** *Adj.* armed (**gegen** against), prepared (for)

gewärtig *Adj. geh. präd.* prepared; **gewärtigen** *v/t. geh.* **1.** be aware of; (*erkennen*) realize; **2.** (*erwarten*) expect, reckon with; (*vorbereitet sein auf*) be prepared for

Gewäsch *n; -(e)s, kein Pl.; umg. pej.* twaddle, hogwash

gewaschen *P.P.* → **waschen**

Gewässer *n; -s, -* body of water; *Pl., im Binnenland:* lakes and rivers; *im Meer:* waters; **fließendes/stehendes ~** running/standing water; **~güte** *f* water quality; **~kunde** *f; nur Sg.* hydrology; **~reinhaltung** *f Öko.* water pollution control; **~reinigung** *f Öko.* cleaning up of rivers and lakes; **~schutz** *m Öko.* water conservation; **~verschmutzung** *f,* **~verunreinigung** *f* water pollution

Gewebe *n; -s, -.* **1.** (*Stoff*) fabric, textile; (*Webart*) texture; **2.** *Physiol.* tissue; **3.** *fig.* web; **~flüssigkeit** *f Physiol.* tissue (*od.* lymph) fluid; **~kultur** *f Med.* tissue culture; **~probe** *f Med.* tissue sample

gewebeschonend *Adj. Waschmittel etc.:* kind to fabrics; *Operationstechnik:* tissue-conserving

Gewebe|transplantation *f Med.* tissue transplant(s *Pl.*); **~verträglichkeit** *f Med.* tissue tolerance

Gewehr *n; -(e)s, -e allg.* gun; (*Büchse*) rifle; (*Schrotflinte*) shotgun; **~e** (*Feuerwaffen*) (fire)arms; **das ~ ab/über!** *Mil.* order/shoulder arms!; **präsentiert das ~!** *Mil.* present arms!; **~ bei Fuß stehen** *fig.* be ready for battle; **~feuer** *n* rifle fire; **~kolben** *m* (rifle) butt; **~kugel** *f* (rifle) bullet; **~lauf** *m* barrel; **~mündung** *f* muzzle (of a gun *od.* rifle); **~patrone** *f* cartridge; **~salve** *f* volley of gunfire; **~schloss** *n* gun lock; **~schrank** *m* gun cabinet; **~schuss** *m* rifle shot

Geweih *n; -(e)s, -e* antlers *Pl.;* **~ende** *n* tine, point of an antler

geweiht I. *P.P.* → **weihen**; **II.** *Adj.:* **dem Tode ~** doomed to die; **dem Untergang ~** doomed

Gewerbe *n; -s, -.* **1.** (*Erwerbszweig*) trade, business; (*Handwerk*) craft; (*Industriezweig*) branch of industry, trade; **ein ~ ausüben** practi|se (*Am.*

-ce) (*od.* carry on) a trade; **dunkles ~** shady business; **das älteste ~ der Welt** *euph. hum.* the oldest profession in the world; **2.** *nur Sg.; Wirts., Bereich:* trade, (branch of) industry, *bes. Am. auch* commerce; **Handel und ~** trade (*Am.* commerce) and industry; **mittelständisches ~** medium-sized industry; **3.** *Betrieb:* business, trade; **ein ~ anmelden/betreiben** register / carry on a business

Gewerbe|aufsicht *f* trade (*od.* industrial) supervision; *für Fabriken:* factory inspection; **~aufsichtsamt** *n* trade supervisory board; *für Fabriken:* factory inspectorate; **~betrieb** *m* business enterprise; **~erlaubnis** *f* licence to carry on a trade, *Am.* commercial license; **~freiheit** *f* freedom of trade; **~gebiet** *n* industrial estate (*od.* park); **~lehrer** *m,* **~lehrerin** *f* teacher in a trade (*Am.* vocational) school; **~ordnung** *f* trade regulations *Pl.;* **~recht** *n; nur Sg.* laws *Pl.* governing trade and industry, *Am.* commercial law; **~schein** *m* trading licence, *Am.* commercial license; **~schule** *f* trade (*Am.* vocational) school; **~steuer** *f* trade (*Am.* commercial) tax; **~tätigkeit** *f* commercial activity

gewerbetreibend *Adj.* engaged in a trade, trading; (*industriell*) industrial, manufacturing, *bes. Am.* commercial; **selbstständig ~** self-employed; **Gewerbetreibende** *m, f; -n, -n* businessman; (*Hersteller*) manufacturer; (*Handwerker*) craftsman, artisan

Gewerbezweig *m* trade, branch of industry; (*Industriezweig*) line (of business)

gewerblich I. *Adj.* industrial, commercial, trade ...; (*Geschäfts...*) business ...; **~e Einfuhr(en)** industrial imports; **~es Fahrzeug** commercial vehicle; **~e Räume** business premises; **~e Wirtschaft** trade (*Am.* commerce) and industry; **~e Schule(n)** (*Am.* vocational) school; **II.** *Adv. betreiben etc.:* commercially, on a commercial basis; **~ tätig sein** carry on (*od.* out) a trade (*Am.* business); **~ genutzt** (used) for commercial purposes

gewerbsmäßig I. *Adj.* professional (*auch Jur.*); **~er Diebstahl** theft; **~e Unzucht** prostitution; **II.** *Adv.* professionally, on a commercial basis

gewerbstätig *Adj.* → **gewerbetreibend**

Gewerkschaft *f* (trade) union, *Am.* labor union; **~ Erziehung und Wissenschaft** (*abgek.* **GEW**) Educators' Union

Gewerkschaft(l)er *m; -s, -,* **~in** *f; -, -nen* trade-unionist, *Am.* union member; (*Funktionär*) (trade, *Am.* labor) union official; **gewerkschaftlich I.** *Adj.* (trade, *Am.* labor) union ...; **II.** *Adv.:* (**sich**) **~ organisieren** form a union; (**nicht**) **~ organisiert** (not) unionized, (non-)union ...

Gewerkschafts|beiträge *Pl.* union dues; **~bewegung** *f; nur Sg.* trade (*Am.* labor) unionism, trade (*Am.* labor) union movement; **~boss** *m umg.* union leader; **~bund** *m* federation of trade (*Am.* labor) unions

gewerkschafts|eigen *Adj. Betrieb etc.:* union-owned; **~feindlich** *Adj.* anti-union *attr.*

Gewerkschafts|funktionär *m,* **~funktionärin** *f* (trade, *Am.* labor) union official; **~haus** *n* union headquarters *Pl.* (*auch Sg. konstr.*); **~jugend** *f* young members *Pl.* of the union; **~mitglied**

G

n (trade) union member; **~sekretär** *m*, **~sekretärin** *f* secretary of a (*od.* the) union; **~verband** *m* federation of trade (*Am.* labor) unions; **~vorsitzende** *m, f* president of a (*od.* the) union; **~wesen** *n* trade (*Am.* labor) unionism; **~zeitung** *f* union newsletter (*od.* magazine); **~zugehörigkeit** *f* union membership

gewesen I. *P.P.* → **sein**[1]; **II.** *Adj.*; *nur attr.* former, one-time; **Gewesene** *n*; *-n, kein Pl.* the past; **lass uns das ~ vergessen** let's forget the past, let bygones be bygones

gewichen *P.P.* → **weichen**[2]

Gewicht *n*; *-(e)s, -e* **1.** *nur Sg.* (*Schwere*) weight; (*Last, Belastung*) *auch* load; **fehlendes ~** short weight; **spezifisches ~** *Phys., Chem.* specific gravity; **zulässiges ~** maximum permitted weight, weight limit; *e-s Fahrzeugs mit Ladung*: maximum laden (*Am.* gross) weight; **nach ~** *verkaufen* by weight; **ein ~ von 100 kg haben** weigh 100 kg; **ein großes/geringes ~ haben** be heavy/light; **nicht das nötige ~ haben** be underweight; **er bringt momentan zu viel ~ auf die Waage** *Boxer, Ringer etc.*: he's over the weight limit at the moment; **2.** *e-r Waage, von Hanteln etc.*: weight; **~e heben/stemmen** do weight-lifting, lift weights; **3.** *nur Sg.*; *fig.* (*Bedeutung*) weight, importance, significance; **~ legen auf** (*wichtig nehmen*) set great store by; (*betonen*) place great emphasis on; *e-r Sache* **großes/wenig ~ beimessen** attach great/little importance to; **an ~ gewinnen/verlieren** gain/lose in importance (*od.* significance); **~ haben** carry weight (*bei* with); **das ~ hat sich verlagert** the emphasis has (*od.* the priorities have) shifted; **ins ~ fallen** count, matter (a lot); **so bekommt die Angelegenheit zu viel ~** that's making too much of the matter; **sein ganzes ~ in die Waagschale werfen** bring all one's weight to bear

gewichten *v/t.* **1.** *Statistik*: weight; **2.** *fig.* assess; **neu ~** reassess, have another look at

Gewichtheben *n*; *-s, kein Pl.* weight-lifting; **Gewichtheber** *m*; *-s, -*, **Gewichtheberin** *f*; *-, -nen* weight-lifter

gewichtig *Adj.* **1.** *altm. od. hum.* weighty, heavy; **2.** *fig.* weighty; *Entscheidung*: *auch* momentous; *Gründe*: *auch* important; (*einflussreich*) influential; *Auftreten, Person*: imposing; (*wichtigtuerisch*) self-important; *e-e ~ Person od. Persönlichkeit* an influential figure; *hum.* a person of some weight; **Gewichtigkeit** *f*; *nur Sg.* weightiness, importance

Gewichts|abnahme *f* loss of weight, weight loss; **~analyse** *f* gravimetric analysis; **~angabe** *f* *Wirts.* declared weight; *e-r Waage*: weight; **~einheit** *f* unit of weight; **~klasse** *f* **1.** *Sport* weight (class); **2.** *Wirts., von Eiern etc.*: weight (class); **~kontrolle** *f* weight check

gewichtslos *Adj.* weightless; **Gewichtslosigkeit** *f*; *nur Sg.* weightlessness

gewichtsmäßig *Adj.* in (terms of) weight

Gewichts|probleme *Pl.* weight problems; **~satz** *m* set of weights; **~unterschied** *m* difference in weight; **~verhältnis** *n* weight ratio; **~verlagerung** *f* **1.** shifting of weight; **2.** *fig.* shift of emphasis; **~zunahme** *f* weight gain

Gewichtung *f* **1.** *Statistik*: weighting; **2.** *fig.* assessment; (*Festlegen von Schwerpunkten*) prioritization, establishing priorities

gewieft *Adj. umg.* (*schlau*) smart, clever; (*gerissen*) shrewd; (*durchtrieben*) sly; (*erfahren*) experienced; *im täglichen Konkurrenzkampf*: streetwise, streetsmart; **er ist ein ~er Geschäftsmann** he's a shrewd businessman

gewiegt I. *P.P.* → **wiegen**[2]; **II.** *Adj. umg.* (*erfahren*) experienced; *im täglichen Konkurrenzkampf*: streetwise, streetsmart

Gewieher *n*; *-s, kein Pl.* **1.** *e-s Pferdes*: neigh(ing), whinny(ing); **2.** *umg. pej. Lachen*: horse laugh, guffaw(ing)

gewiesen *P.P.* → **weisen**

gewillt *Adj.* willing; (*bereit*) prepared; (*entschlossen*) determined; **sie war nicht ~ aufzugeben** *od.* **nicht zur Aufgabe ~** she was unwilling to give up

Gewimmel *n*; *-s, kein Pl.* swarming, bustle; (*Menge*) swarm, teeming crowd, mass of people; *von Insekten, Fischen etc.*: seething mass (*od.* swarm)

Gewimmer *n*; *-s, kein Pl.* whimpering

Gewinde *n*; *-s, -* **1.** *Tech., e-r Schraube*: thread; **2.** *Zool., e-s Schneckenhauses*: spire; *e-r Muschel*: whorl; **3.** *lit.* (*Girlande*) garland; (*Kranz*) wreath; **~bohrer** *m* tap; **~fräsen** *n* thread milling; **~gang** *m* (turn of a) thread

Gewinn *m*; *-(e)s, -e* **1.** *beim Spiel*: winnings *Pl.*; *Lotterie*: prize; **2.** *Wirts.* (*Profit*) profit; (*Ertrag*) yield, returns *Pl.*; (*Erlös*) proceeds *Pl.*; (*Verdienst*) earnings *Pl.*; **reiner ~** net profit; **~ abwerfen** *od.* **bringen** yield a profit; **mit ~ verkaufen/arbeiten** sell/work at a profit; **ein ~ bringendes Unternehmen** a profitable business, a going concern; **3.** *fig.* profit, gain; (*Vorteil, Nutzen*) advantage, benefit; (*Bereicherung*) improvement, enhancement; **~e bei e-r Wahl**: gains; **~ ziehen aus** profit from; **sie ist ein großer ~ für unseren Verein** she is a great addition to our organization

Gewinn|abführung *f* *Wirts.* transfer of profits; **~anteil** *m* *Wirts.* share in (the) profits; (*Dividende*) dividend; **~ausschüttung** *f* **1.** *in Lotterie*: prize draw; **2.** *Wirts.* declared payout; **~aussichten** *Pl.* **1.** *in Wettkampf etc.*: prospects of winning; **2.** *Wirts.* profit prospects; **~beteiligung** *f* *Wirts.* profit sharing

gewinnbringend I. *Adj.* profitable (*auch fig.*), lucrative; **II.** *Adv.*: **Geld ~ anlegen** invest money profitably

Gewinnchancen *Pl.* chances of winning; odds

gewinnen *gewinnt, gewann, hat gewonnen* **I.** *v/t.* **1.** (*Krieg, Prozess, Rennen, Spiel, Wahl, Wette etc.*) win; **2.** (*Geld etc.*) win, get, gain; (*Preis etc.*) win, fetch, carry off; **wie gewonnen, so zerronnen** *Sprichw.* easy come, easy go; **3.** (*Einblick, Eindruck, Vorteil, Vorsprung, j-s Zuneigung etc.*) gain; (*erwerben*) get, obtain; (*verdienen*) earn, make; **Zeit ~** (*einsparen*) save time; *bevor etw. passiert*: gain time; **damit ist schon viel gewonnen** that's already a great step forward, much has already been gained by that; **was ist damit gewonnen?** what good will it do?; **j-n für sich/etw. ~** win s.o. over (to s.th.); **j-n für s-e Pläne etc. ~** win s.o.'s support for one's plans *etc.*; → **Abstand** 3, **Oberhand** *etc.*; **4.** *geh.*, *räumlich*: reach, attain; **sie konnten**

das rettende Ufer ~ they succeeded in reaching dry land; **5.** **~** (*aus* from) (*Saft, Gummi, Sirup, Öl etc.*) get, obtain, extract; *Chem.* extract, derive; (*Kohle, Erdöl etc.*) win, obtain, extract; *aus Altmaterial*: recover, reclaim; **II.** *v/i.* **1.** win, be the winner(s); win the match *etc.*; **bei** *od.* **in etw.** (*Dat.*) **~** *bei Schach, Poker etc.*: win at s.th.; *in Lotterie etc.*: win a prize in s.th.; **~ gegen** beat; **knapp ~** *Sport* scrape home; **jedes dritte Los gewinnt!** every third ticket is a winner (*od.* wins a prize); → **spielend** II; **2. ~ an** (+ *Dat.*) an Bedeutung, Klarheit etc.: gain (in); **an Boden ~** gain ground; **3.** *durch Vergleich od. Kontrast etc.*: gain, improve; **~ durch** profit by, benefit from

gewinnend I. *Part. Präs.* → **gewinnen**; **II.** *Adj.* Lächeln, Art, Wesen etc.: winning, engaging; **III.** *Adv.*: **~ lächeln** smile winningly

Gewinner *m*; *-s, -*, **~in** *f*; *-, -nen* winner; **~straße** *f* *Sport umg.*: **auf der ~ sein** be on the way to (*od.* be heading for) victory

Gewinn|gemeinschaft *f* **1.** *Wirts.* profit pool; **2.** *bei Lotterie*: syndicate; **~klasse** *f* prize category; **~liste** *f* list of winners; **~los** *n* winning ticket (*od.* number), winner; **~nummer** *f* winning ticket (*od.* number), winner

gewinnorientiert *Adj. Wirts.* profit-oriented, for-profit …; **nicht ~e Organisation** non-profit(-making) (*od.* not-for-profit) organization

Gewinn|quote *f* **1.** *Lotterie etc.*: prize; *Fußballtoto*: dividend; **2.** *Wirts.* profit margin; **2reich** *Adj.* profitable; **~satz** *m* *Tennis etc.*: **der fünfte Satz war ihr ~** she won in the fifth set, she took the fifth set to win; **~schwelle** *f* *Wirts.* breakeven point; **~spanne** *f* profit margin; *im Handel*: *auch* trade margin; **~spiel** *n* prize game; **~strähne** *f* lucky streak; **~streben** *n* pursuit of gain (*od.* profit)

Gewinnsucht *f* profit-seeking; (*Habgier*) greed; **gewinnsüchtig** *Adj.* profit-seeking, grasping, profiteering; **in ~er Absicht** *Jur.* with the object of gain

gewinnträchtig *Adj.* profitable, lucrative; *Investition*: *auch* high-yield …

Gewinn-und-Verlust-Rechnung *f* *Wirts.* profit and loss account

Gewinnung *f*; *mst Sg.* production; *von Bodenschätzen etc.*: *auch* extraction; (*Fördermenge*) output; *von Neuland*: reclamation; *Chem.* preparation, extraction

Gewinn|warnung *Wirts., euph.* profit warning; **~zahl** *f* winning number; **~ziehung** *f* Lotto etc.: prize draw; **~zone** *f*: **in der ~ sein** be in profit; **in die ~ kommen** move into profit

Gewinsel *n*; *-s, kein Pl.*; *pej., von Hund, Person*: whining

Gewirr *n*; *-(e)s, kein Pl. von Schnüren, Haaren etc.*: tangle, snarl; *von Straßen etc.*: maze; (*Durcheinander*) jumble, confusion

gewiss I. *Adj.* **1.** (*sicher*) certain, positive, sure; **eins** *od.* **so viel ist ~** there's one thing for sure; **der Preis ist ihm ~** he's certain to win; **sich s-r Sache ~ sein** be sure of one's facts; **2.** *nur attr.*; (*nicht näher bezeichnet*) certain; **ein ~er Herr X** a certain (*od.* one) Mr(.) X; **das ~e Etwas haben** have a certain something; **3.** *nur attr.*; (*nicht sehr, aber immerhin*): **~e Ähnlichkeit haben** have (*od.* bear) a certain similarity;

bis zu e-m ~en Grad up to a (certain) point; in ~em Sinne in a sense (od. way); in ~er Hinsicht in a way, in some ways; in ~en Fällen in certain (od. some) cases; **II.** Adv. certainly; (zweifellos) no doubt; ~ nicht definitely not; ~! certainly; (verstärkend) yes, indeed; (aber) ~ (doch)! yes, of course
Gewissen n; -s, - conscience; ein gutes od. reines od. ruhiges ~ a clear conscience; ein schlechtes ~ a bad (od. guilty) conscience; kein ~ haben have no scruples; sein ~ regt sich his conscience is starting to trouble him; um sein ~ zu beruhigen (in order) to salve his conscience; j-m ins ~ reden have a serious talk with s.o.; j-n/etw. auf dem ~ haben have s.o./s.th. on one's conscience; das hast du auf dem ~ you've got to answer for that; das musst du mit d-m ~ ausmachen you'll have to settle that with your conscience; sich kein ~ machen aus have no scruples about (+ Ger.); kannst du das mit d-m ~ vereinbaren? can you reconcile that with your conscience?; ein gutes ~ ist ein sanftes Ruhekissen Sprichw. one can sleep easy with a clear conscience; → Ehre 3, Wissen
gewissenhaft Adj. conscientious; (zuverlässig) reliable; (gründlich) thorough; (übergenau) scrupulous; (sorgfältig) painstaking; **Gewissenhaftigkeit** f; nur Sg. conscientiousness; thoroughness; scrupulousness; → gewissenhaft
gewissenlos Adj. unscrupulous; (verantwortungslos) irresponsible; Tat: auch unconscionable; **Gewissenlosigkeit** f 1. nur Sg. unscrupulousness; irresponsibility; → gewissenlos; 2. Tat: unscrupulous act; irresponsible act
Gewissens|bisse Pl. pangs (od. pricks) of conscience (wegen about); ~ bekommen get a guilty conscience, start to feel guilty; er hat überhaupt keine ~ deswegen it doesn't bother (od. worry) him in the slightest; mach dir deswegen doch keine ~ don't lose any sleep over it; ~entscheidung f moral decision; ~erforschung f bes. kath., vor Beichte: examination of one's conscience; ~frage f matter of conscience; ~freiheit f freedom of conscience; ~gründe Pl.: aus ~n for reasons of conscience; Wehrdienstverweigerer aus ~n conscientious objector; ~konflikt m moral conflict; ~not f moral dilemma; ~pflicht f moral obligation (od. duty); ~prüfung f für Kriegsdienstverweigerer: examination of one's conscience; ~qualen Pl. terribly bad conscience Sg.; ~zwang m moral constraint; religiöser: religious despotism
gewissermaßen Adv. 1. (sozusagen) as it were, so to speak; 2. (in gewissem Maße) to a certain extent; (in gewissem Sinne) in a way
Gewissheit f; nur Sg. certainty; innere: assurance; mit ~ for certain, with certainty; zur ~ werden become certain (od. a certainty); sich ~ verschaffen über (+ Akk.) make sure about (od. of), find out for certain about; die ~ haben, dass ... know for sure (od. certain) that ...
Gewitter n; -s, - (thunder)storm; schweres/heftiges ~ heavy/severe (thunder)storm; wie ein reinigendes ~ wirken clear the air; ~fliege f thunderfly, Am. thrips Sg. und Pl.; ~front

f stormy front
gewitterig Adj. → gewittrig
gewittern v/impers.: es gewittert there's a storm on its way
Gewitter|neigung f possibility of thunderstorms; ~regen m, ~schauer m thundery shower; ~stimmung f: es herrscht ~ there's a storm in the air; fig. there's trouble brewing; ~störungen Pl. Radio: static Sg.; ~sturm m thunderstorm; ~wand f wall of thunderclouds; ~wolke f thundercloud
gewittrig Adj. thundery; es sieht ~ aus it looks as though we're in for a storm
Gewitzel n; -s, kein Pl. joking, (silly) jokes Pl.
gewitzt Adj. smart, clever, shrewd
gewoben P.P. → weben
gewogen I. P.P. → wägen, wiegen[1]; II. Adj. geh. well-disposed (+ Dat. to[wards]); bleiben Sie uns ~ please continue your good will toward(s) us; das Schicksal war ihm nicht ~ fig. destiny was not on his side; **Gewogenheit** f; nur Sg. goodwill (gegenüber towards); (Zuneigung) affection (for)
gewöhnen I. v/refl.: sich ~ an (+ Akk.) get used (od. accustomed) to; an ein Klima: become acclimatized (bes. Am. acclimated) to; sich daran ~ zu (+ Inf.) get used to (+ Ger.), get into the habit of (+ Ger.); man wird sich daran ~ müssen it'll take a bit of getting used to; man gewöhnt sich an alles you can get used to anything in time; **II.** v/t.: j-n ~ an (+ Akk.) get s.o. used to; (vertraut machen mit) familiarize s.o. with; an ein Klima: acclimatize (bes. Am. acclimate) s.o. to; → gewöhnt
Gewohnheit f habit; aus (alter) ~ out of habit; aus reiner od. lauter ~ out of sheer habit, from force of habit; die ~ haben zu (+ Inf.) be in the habit of (+ Ger.), have a habit of (+ Ger.); zur ~ werden become (od. grow into) a habit (j-m with s.o.); sich etw. zur ~ machen make s.th. (into) a habit; das macht die ~ (ist e-e ~) it's (a) habit; (richtet die ~ an) that's what habit can do (to you); → Macht 2
gewohnheits|gemäß I. Adj. usual; **II.** Adv. as is/was his/her etc. habit, habitually; (automatisch) automatically; ~mäßig **I.** Adj. 1. Trinker, Verbrecher etc.: habitual; 2. (üblich) usual; **II.** Adv. habitually, out of habit
Gewohnheits|mensch m creature of habit; ~recht n customary law; (ungeschriebenes Gesetz) common law; (traditionelles Recht) prescriptive right; weitS. established right; ~sache f matter of habit; ~tier n hum. creature (od. slave) of habit; ~trinker m, ~trinkerin f habitual drinker
gewöhnlich I. Adj. 1. (normal) normal; (alltäglich) ordinary, everyday; (durchschnittlich) average; (mittelmäßig) mediocre; (herkömmlich) conventional; (einfach) plain; unter ~en Umständen under ordinary (od. normal) circumstances; der ~e Sterbliche we ordinary mortals Pl.; im ~en Leben in everyday life; 2. (üblich) usual; 3. (unfein, ordinär) common, vulgar; ~ aussehen od. ein ~es Aussehen haben look (rather) common; **II.** Adv. usually etc.; für ~ usually, as a rule, generally, normally; wie ~ as usual; **Gewöhnlichkeit** f; nur Sg. commonness, vulgarity
gewohnt I. P.P. → wohnen; **II.** Adj. 1. usual; (vertraut) familiar; in ~er od.

auf ~e Weise (in) the usual way; zu ~er Stunde at the usual time; → Gang[1] 3; 2. etw. ~ sein be used (od. accustomed) to s.th. (od. + Ger.); ich bin (es) ~, früh aufzustehen I'm used to getting up early
gewöhnt I. P.P. → gewöhnen; **II.** Adj.: ~ sein an (+ Akk.) be used (od. accustomed) to; ich bin ja viel ~, aber ... I've seen a lot (of things) in my time, but ...
gewöhntermaßen Adv. usually
Gewöhnung f; nur Sg.: ~ (an) (+ Akk.) 1. getting used to; (Anpassung) adaptation (to); die ~ daran wird lange dauern it'll take a long time to get used to it; 2. Med. becoming habituated to; (Abhängigkeit) addiction (to); Kokain etc. führt zur ~ is a habit-forming drug; 3. an ein Klima: acclimatization (to), bes. Am. acclimation (to)
gewöhnungsbedürftig Adj. ... that needs getting used to, that takes (some) time to get used to
Gewölbe n; -s, - 1. bogenförmig: vault (auch fig. des Himmels); 2. Raum: vaults Pl.; ~bogen m arch (of a od. the vault)
gewölbt I. P.P. → wölben; **II.** Adj. vaulted, arched; Stirn etc.: domed; Tech. convex, curved
Gewölle n; -s, -; Zool., Jägerspr. pellet, cast
gewollt I. P.P. → wollen[1]; **II.** Adj. (absichtlich) deliberate; Höflichkeit etc.: studied; (gekünstelt) artificial; **III.** Adv. deliberately; ~ gelassen with studied calm; ~ ungezwungen with forced casualness
gewonnen P.P. → gewinnen
geworben P.P. → werben
geworfen P.P. → werfen
gewrungen P.P. → wringen
Gewühl n; -(e)s, kein Pl.; (Durcheinander) turmoil; (Menschenmenge) crowd, crush
gewunden I. P.P. → winden[1]; **II.** Adj. 1. Weg etc.: winding, twisting; 2. fig. Redeweise etc.: roundabout, tortuous; **III.** Adv.: sich ~ ausdrücken express o.s. in a roundabout way, beat about (od. around) the bush
gewunken P.P. → winken
gewünscht I. P.P. → wünschen; **II.** Adj. desired, wished-for; (erwartet) expected; (erhofft) hoped-for
gewürfelt I. P.P. → würfeln; **II.** Adj. Stoff: checked
Gewürm n; -(e)s, -e, mst Sg.; mst pej. 1. (mass of) worms Pl.; 2. fig. vermin
Gewürz n; -es, -e; Gastr. spice; als Zutat: seasoning; förm., Salz, Pfeffer, Ketchup: condiment; Kraut: herb; ~bord n spice rack; ~essig m aromatic vinegar; ~gurke f gherkin, Am. pickle; ~handel m spice trade; ~kraut n (pot) herb; ~mischung f mixed spices Pl.; ~nelke f clove; ~regal n, ~ständer m spice rack
gewürzt I. P.P. → würzen; **II.** Adj. fig. spiced, spicy
gewusst P.P. → wissen
Geysir m; -s, -e geyser
gez. Abk. (gezeichnet) sgd(.)
gezackt I. P.P. → zacken; **II.** Adj. jagged; bes. Bot., Tech. serrated
gezahnt I. P.P. → zahnen; **II.** Adj. toothed (auch Tech.); (gekerbt) notched; Bio., Bot. dentate; Briefmarke: perforated; **gezähnt** Adj. → gezahnt II
Gezänk n; -(e)s, kein Pl.; pej. squabbling, bickering

Gezappel n; -s, kein Pl.; umg., oft pej. fidgeting, wriggling (about)

gezeichnet I. P.P. → **zeichnen**; **II.** Adj. **1.** schön ~es Fell beautifully patterned fur; **2.** fig.: fürs Leben ~ scarred (als Krimineller etc.: branded) for life; vom Tod ~ bearing the stamp of death; sie ist von der Krankheit ~ the illness has left its mark (on her); **3.** ~ X (unterschrieben von) signed X

Gezeiten Pl. tide Sg.; den ~ unterworfen tidal; ~kraftwerk n tidal power plant; ~strom m, ~strömung f tidal current; ~wechsel m turn of the tide, changing tide

Gezerre n; -s, kein Pl.; pej. tugging

Gezeter n; -s, kein Pl.; pej. hue and cry

geziehen P.P. → **zeihen**

gezielt I. P.P. → **zielen**; **II.** Adj. **1.** Schuss: well-aimed; → **Todesschuss**; **2.** fig. selective; Frage: specific; Maßnahme: calculated; Werbung: targeted; Bemerkung: pointed; (absichtlich) Beleidigung, Versuch etc.: deliberate; e-e ~e Indiskretion a deliberate (od. calculated) indiscretion; durch e-n ~en Einsatz der Polizei through a concerted effort on the part of the police; **III.** Adv. **1.** ~ schießen shoot to kill; **2.** fig.: ~ fragen ask specifically, ask s.o. straight umg.; ~ handeln act purposefully; ~ vorgehen proceed according to plan

geziemen altm. **I.** v/i.: j-m ~ befit s.o.; **II.** v/refl.; unpers.: wie es sich geziemt as is proper (od. fitting) (für for); **geziemend** altm. **I.** Part. Präs. → **geziemen**; **II.** Adj. (anständig) decent; (gehörig) due, proper; Abstand: respectful

geziert I. P.P. → **zieren**; **II.** Adj. pej. affected; tu nicht so ~! stop putting it on; **Geziertheit** f; nur Sg.; pej. affectation

gezinkt I. P.P. → **zinken**; **II.** Adj. **1.** Holz: dovetailed; **2.** fig.: mit ~en Karten spielen play with marked cards (Am. auch a marked deck)

Gezisch(e) n; -s, kein Pl.; oft pej. **1.** von Schlange, Gans, Gas, Wasser: hiss(ing); **2.** wütendes: hiss

Gezischel n; -s, kein Pl.; pej. whispering

gezogen I. P.P. → **ziehen**; **II.** Adj. Waffe, Tech., Draht etc.: drawn; Gewehrlauf: rifled

gezuckert I. P.P. → **zuckern**; **II.** Adj. Fot.: ~e Leinwand glass-beaded screen

Gezwitscher n; -s, kein Pl. chirping, twittering

gezwungen I. P.P. → **zwingen**; **II.** Adj. **1.** (unnatürlich) unnatural; (geziert) affected; (steif) stiff; Lächeln etc.: forced; Gespräch etc.: strained; **2.** ~ sein od. sich ~ sehen, zu (+ Inf.) be (find o.s., feel) compelled od. constrained to (+ Inf.); **III.** Adv.: ~ lachen give a forced laugh, force a laugh; **gezwungenermaßen** Adv.: etw. (nur) ~ tun be forced to do s.th.; **Gezwungenheit** f; nur Sg. affectation; (Steifheit) stiffness

Ghana (n); -s; Geog. Ghana; **Ghanaer** m; -s, -, **Ghanaerin** f; -, -nen Ghanaian, weiblich auch Ghanaian woman (od. girl etc.); **ghanaisch** Adj. Ghanaian

Ghetto n → **Getto**

Ghostwriter ['goːstraɪtɐ] m; -s, -, ~in f; -, -nen ghostwriter

Gibbon m; -s, -s; Zool. gibbon

Gibraltar (n); -s; Geog. Gibraltar; **Gibraltarer** m; -s, -, **Gibraltarerin** f; -,

-nen Gibraltarian, weiblich auch Gibraltarian woman (od. girl etc.)

gibt Präs. → **geben**

Gicht[1] f; -, kein Pl.; Med. gout

Gicht[2] f; -, -en; Metall. furnace top; (Einsatz) furnace charge

Gichtanfall m Med. attack of gout

Gichtgas n Metall. blast furnace gas

gichtig Adj. Med. gout-ridden, gouty

Gichtknoten m Med. chalkstone, tophus

gichtkrank Adj.: ~ sein suffer from (od. have) gout

Giebel m; -s, - gable; (Ziergiebel) pediment; ~dach n gable(d) roof; ~feld n tympanum; ~seite f side, gable end, end wall

Gier f; -, kein Pl. greed (nach od. umg. auf + Akk. for); vorübergehende, bes. nach Essen: craving (for); voll(er) ~ → gierig II

gieren[1] v/i.: ~ nach crave, lust for (od. after)

gieren[2] v/i. Naut., Flug. yaw

gierig I. Adj. greedy (nach od. umg. auf + Akk. for); (gefräßig) auch gluttonous; **II.** Adv.: ~ essen eat greedily; ~ verschlingen bolt down, (auch fig. Buch) devour; ~ lesen read avidly; ~ in sich aufnehmen lap s.th. up umg.; ~ ansehen look at s.o./s.th. with lust in one's eyes (od. with lustful eyes)

Gießbach m torrent

gießen; gießt, goss, hat gegossen **I.** v/t. **1.** pour (in + Akk. into; aus out of; auf od. über + Akk. over); (verschütten) spill; sein Licht ~ über (+ Akk.) fig. shed its light over; **2.** (Blumen) water; **3.** Tech. (Glocke, Silber etc.) cast; (Kerzen) cast, mo(u)ld; **II.** v/i. unpers.; umg.: es gießt it's pouring

Gießer[1] m; -s, - von Kanne etc.: spout

Gießer[2] m; -s, -; Tech., Facharbeiter: caster, founder; **Gießerei** f; -, -en **1.** foundry; **2.** nur Sg.; Tätigkeit: casting; **Gießerin** f; -, -nen caster, founder

Gieß|form f Tech. mo(u)ld; Spritzguss: die; ~kanne f watering can

Gießkannen|kopf m rose; ~prinzip n principle of something for everyone (od. equal shares for all)

Gift n; -(e)s, -e **1.** poison, Chem., Bio. toxin; **2.** fig. poison; (Bosheit) venom; das ist das reinste ~ für ihn / für die Beziehung etc. that is the very worst thing (that could happen) for him / for the relationship; darauf kannst du ~ nehmen umg. you can bet your life (od. bottom dollar) on that; sein ~ verspritzen spit one's venom; er spuckte ~ und Galle umg. he was really fuming; ~ampulle f poison capsule; ~becher m cup of poison; ~beere f poisonberry; ~drüse f poison gland

giften umg. **I.** v/t. (ärgern) rile, (really) get to s.o.; **II.** v/i.: ~ über (+ Akk.) say (really) nasty things about; **III.** v/refl. get het up (od. mad) (über + Akk. about)

Gift|fass n toxic waste drum; ~flasche f bottle of poison

Giftgas n Mil. poison gas; ~anschlag m (poison) gas attack; ~granate f gas-filled (od. poison gas) artillery shell; ~opfer n victim of a poison gas attack; ~wolke f cloud of poison gas

gift|grün Adj. bright green; ~haltig Adj. toxic

giftig I. Adj. **1.** poisonous; Chem. toxic; Med. virulent, contagious; **2.** fig. (bösartig) vicious, (really) nasty; (wütend) vitriolic; Antwort etc.: vitriolic; **3.** umg. (grell) Farbe: poisonous;

II. Adv. fig. viciously; j-n ~ ansehen look daggers at; **Giftigkeit** f; nur Sg. **1.** poisonousness; **2.** fig. (Bosheit) viciousness

Gift|küche f umg. fig. hotbed of gossip (and intrigue); ~kunde f; nur Sg. toxicology; ~mischer m, ~mischerin f; -, -nen **1.** poison brewer; **2.** umg. fig. (Apotheker) poison peddler; ~mord m (murder by) poisoning; ~mörder m, ~mörderin f poisoner

Giftmüll m Öko. toxic waste; ~deponie f toxic waste dump; ~transport m transport(ation) of toxic waste

Gift|notruf m, ~notrufzentrale f poison information (od. control) cent|re (Am. -er); ~pfeil m poison arrow (Blasrohr: dart); ~pflanze f poisonous plant; ~pilz m poisonous mushroom (od. toadstool); ~schlange f **1.** poisonous snake; **2.** umg. pej. poison, Frau auch: bitch Sl.; ~schrank m poison cabinet; ~spinne f poisonous spider; ~spritze f **1.** umg., gegen Unkraut: pesticide spray; zur ~ greifen use pesticides; **2.** bei Hinrichtungen: lethal injection; ~stachel m poison sting; von Fischen: venomous spine

Giftstoff m poison(ous substance); Med. und Umwelt: toxin, toxic agent; (Abgas etc.) pollutant; ~beseitigung f disposal of toxic substances (od. wastes)

Gift|weizen m poisoned wheat; ~wirkung f effect of the (od. a) poison; ~zahn m poison fang; ~zettel m Jugendspr. school report, Am. report card; ~zwerg m umg. pej., Mann: poison dwarf; Kind: spiteful little beast, little terror

Giga|byte n; -s, -s; (abgek. GB) EDV gigabyte; ~hertz n; -, -, (abgek. GHz) Phys. gigahertz

Gigant m; -en, -en, ~in f; -, -nen **1.** geh. giant; **2.** fig. giant, heavyweight; ~en der Politik political giants (od. heavyweights); ~en der Landstraße/Meere juggernauts/leviathans; **gigantisch** Adj. **1.** huge, gigantic; Leistung etc.: tremendous; ~es Unternehmen huge (od. enormous, od. tremendous) undertaking; **2.** umg. (toll) stupendous; **Gigantismus** m; -, kein Pl.; Med. gigantism; **Gigantomanie** f; -, kein Pl.; geh. gigantomania; **gigantomanisch** Adj. geh. gigantomaniac

Gigue [ʒiːk] f; -, -n ['ʒiːgn̩] Mus. gigue; Tanz: jig

Gilde f; -, -n **1.** hist. guild; **2.** fig. (Vereinigung) fraternity; im Internet: guild; ~haus n guildhall; ~meister m guild master

gilt Präs. → **gelten**

Gimpel m; -s, - **1.** Orn. bullfinch; **2.** umg. pej. dimwit

Gin [dʒɪn] m; -s, - od. Sorten: -s gin

ging Imperf. → **gehen**

Gingerale, Ginger-Ale ['dʒɪndʒɐ 'eːl] n; -s, - ginger ale

Gink(g)o ['gɪŋko] m; -s, -s; Bot. ginkgo, gingko (Pl. -os od. -oes)

Ginseng m; -s, -s; Bot. ginseng; ~wurzel f ginseng root

Ginster m; -s, -; Bot. broom; mit Dornen: gorse; ~katze f Zool. genet

Gin Tonic [dʒɪn'tɔnɪk] m; - -(s), - -s gin and tonic, G&T umg.

Gipfel m; -s, - **1.** summit, (mountain) peak, mountain top; **2.** fig. (Höhepunkt) peak, height; e-r Kurve: peak; auf dem ~ (+ Gen.) at the peak (od. height) of; der ~ der Frechheit the height of impudence; das ist ja der ~!

umg. that really is the limit, *auch* that takes the biscuit (*Am.* cake); **3.** *Pol. umg.* summit; **4.** *altm.* (*Wipfel*) top; **~abkommen** *n Pol.* summit agreement; **~diplomatie** *f Pol.* summitry; **~höhe** *f:* **mit e-r ~ von ...** *Berg:* rising to a height of ... at the summit; *Flug., Ballistik:* with a ceiling of; **~konferenz** *f Pol.* summit (conference); **~kreuz** *n* cross on the peak of a mountain

gipfeln *v/i.* culminate (*in* + *Dat.* in); *Unruhen etc.:* auch escalate (into); *Karriere, Rede etc.:* climax (in), culminate (in)

Gipfel|punkt *m* **1.** *e-r Flugbahn, Kurve:* highest point, apex; **2.** *fig.* high point, culmination; **~stürmer** *m*, **~stürmerin** *f* **1.** mountaineering fanatic; **2.** *fig.* high flier; **~teilnehmer** *m*, **~teilnehmerin** *f Pol. umg.* summiteer; **~treffen** *n Pol.* summit (meeting)

Gips *m;* *-es, Arten: -e* **1.** *Min.* gypsum, calcium sulphate; **2.** *für Löcher, Abgüsse etc.:* plaster (of Paris); **~ anrühren** mix up some plaster (of Paris); **3.** *Med., Verband:* (plaster) cast; *e-n* **~ bekommen/haben** be put in / be in plaster; **~abdruck** *m* plaster cast; **~bein** *n:* **ein ~ haben** have one's leg in plaster (*Am.* in a cast); **~bett** *n Med.* plaster bed; **~büste** *f* plaster bust; **~decke** *f* plaster ceiling

gipsen *v/t.* plaster (*auch Wein und Agr.*); **Gipser** *m; -s, -,* **Gipserin** *f; -, -nen* plasterer

Gips|figur *f* plaster figure; **~kopf** *m umg. pej.* blockhead; **~korsett** *n Med.* plaster jacket; **~maske** *f* face mask; (*Totenmaske*) death mask; **~mörtel** *m* gypsum mortar; **~platte** *f* plasterboard, *Am. auch* drywall; **~verband** *m Med.* plaster cast; *j-m / e-m Bein* **e-n ~ anlegen** put s.o. / a leg in plaster (*Am.* in a cast)

Giraffe *f; -, -n; Zool.* giraffe

Girlande *f; -, -n* garland; *aus Papier:* paper chain

Giro ['ʒiːro] *n; -s, -s od. österr.* Giri; *Fin.* **1.** (*Überweisung*) bank (*od.* giro) transfer; **2.** *e-s Wechsels etc.:* endorsement, indorsement; **~abteilung** *f* giro (*Am.* transfer) department; **~auftrag** *m* credit transfer order; **~bank** *f; Pl. -banken* clearing bank; **~guthaben** *n* current account balance; **~konto** *n* current account; *bes. Post.* giro account; **~kunde** *m*, **~kundin** *f* current account customer (*od.* holder); **~überweisung** *f* giro (*Am. etwa* ACH) transfer; **~verband** *m* association of clearing banks, *Am.* automated clearinghouse system; **~verkehr** *m* clearing

gis, Gis *n; -, -; Mus.* G sharp

Gischt *m; -(e)s, -e, auch f; -, -en, mst Sg.* foam, froth; *von Wellen:* surf, spume; *in Tropfen:* spray

Gis-Dur *n Mus.* G sharp major

Giseh (*n*); *-s; Geog.:* **die Pyramiden von ~** the pyramids of Giza

gis-Moll *n Mus.* G sharp minor

Gitarre *f; -, -n; Mus.* guitar

Gitarren|konzert *n* guitar recital; *Stück:* guitar concerto; **~spieler** *m*, **~spielerin** *f* guitar player

Gitarrist *m; -en, -en,* **~in** *f; -, -nen* guitar player, guitarist

Gitter *n; -s, -* **1.** grating; *an Tür, Fenster:* auch grille; *feines, aus Draht:* mesh; *gegen Fliegen etc.:* screen; *aus Latten:* lattice; *für Pflanzen:* trellis; *aus parallelen Stäben:* bars *Pl.;* *Kindersicherung an Treppe etc.:* gate; *vor e-m Kamin:*

guard, *Am.* firescreen; (*Rost*) grate; (*Zaun*) fence; (*Geländer*) railing; **2.** *Math., Geog. für Kurven, Karten etc.:* grid; *Chem., Phys. von Kristallen etc.:* lattice; **3.** *Etron.* grid; **4.** *fig.:* **hinter ~** behind bars; **hinter ~ kommen** be locked up

gitterartig *Adj.* latticed

Gitter|bett *n* cot, *Am.* crib; **~draht** *m* **1.** wire netting; **2.** *Etech.* grid wire; **~fenster** *n* lattice window; *mit Eisenstangen:* window with iron bars; **~linien** *Pl. Computertabelle etc.:* gridlines; *auch in Karte:* grid; **~netz** *n Karte:* grid; **~rost** *m an Kellerfenster etc.:* grating; *im Backofen:* grill; *im Kamin:* grate; **~stab** *m* bar; **~tor** *n* iron gate; **~werk** *n* latticework; **~zaun** *m* palings *Pl.; gekreuzt:* lattice fence

Gizeh ['giːze] → *Giseh*

Glacé|handschuhe, Glaceehandschuhe [gla'seː-] *Pl.* kid gloves; *mit* **~n anfassen** *umg. fig.* handle *s.o.* with kid gloves

Gladiole *f; -, -n; Bot.* gladiola, gladiolus

Glamour ['glɛmɐ] *m, n; -s, kein Pl.* glamo(u)r

glamourös [glamu'røːs] *Adj.* glamorous

Glanz *m; -es, kein Pl.* **1.** shine, lust|re (*Am.* -er); *funkelnder:* brilliance, sparkle; *strahlender:* radiance, glow; (*Glitzern*) glitter; (*blendender Schein*) glare; *von Fußboden, Schuhen:* shine, polish; *des Haars:* shine; *auf Stoffen:* sheen; **2.** *fig.* splendo(u)r; (*Ruhm*) glory; (*Gepränge*) pomp; (*Flitter*) glitter, tinsel; *äußerer:* gloss; (*die Prüfung*) *mit* **~ (und Gloria) bestehen** *umg.* pass (the exam) with flying colo(u)rs

glänzen *v/i.* **1.** shine, gleam; *Hose, Nase etc.:* be shiny; (*funkeln*) glitter, sparkle, *Sterne: auch* twinkle; **die Augen der Kinder glänzten vor Freude** the children's eyes were shining with joy; **2.** *fig. durch Leistungen, Geist:* shine; **~ in** (+ *Dat.*) be brilliant at; **~ wollen** like (*od.* want) to impress; → *Abwesenheit* 1, *Gold* 1

glänzend I. *Part. Präs.* → *glänzen;* **II.** *Adj.* **1.** *Metall etc.:* shiny, bright; *Fell, Haar etc.:* glossy; *Fot.* glossy; **2.** *umg. fig.* brilliant, excellent; **~e Idee** brilliant (*iro. auch* bright) idea; *in* **~er Form** in top form; **III.** *Adv.* **1.** **~ schwarz** shiny black; **2.** *umg. fig.* brilliantly, extremely well; **~ aussehen** look great; **die Prüfung ~ bestehen** pass (the exam) with flying colo(u)rs, do brilliantly (in the exam); *ihm* **geht's ~** he's doing very well (*od.* just fine); *gesundheitlich: auch* he's in the pink; **sie verstehen sich ~** they get on (*Am.* along) like a house on fire

Glanz|foto *n* glossy print; **~lack** *m* brilliant varnish; **~leder** *n* patent leather; **~leistung** *f* brilliant feat (*od.* performance); **~licht** *n* **1.** reflected light; **2.** *Gemälde:* highlight (*auch fig.*); *e-r* **Sache ~er aufsetzen** *fig.* add a few highlights to s.th.

glanzlos *Adj.* **1.** dull; *bes. Augen: auch* lacklust|re (*Am.* -er); **2.** *fig.* (*ohne Höhepunkte*) lacklust|re (*Am.* -er); (*ruhmlos*) inglorious; (*langweilig*) dull

Glanz|nummer *f des Abends etc.:* highlight; *e-s Artisten etc.:* pièce de résistance, party piece *umg.;* **~papier** *n* glossy paper; **~parade** *f Sport* brilliant save; **~punkt** *m* highlight; (*Höhepunkt*) climax; **~rolle** *f Theat.* star role; (*erfolgreichste Rolle*) best role;

~seide *f* glossy silk; **~stück** *n* **1.** *e-r Sammlung etc.:* showpiece; **2.** → *Glanzleistung, Glanznummer*

glanzvoll *Adj. Fest, Karriere etc.:* glittering; → *auch glänzend*

Glanzzeit *f* heyday; (*Epoche*) golden age; *j-s* **~ ist vorüber** *s.o.* has had their day, s.o.'s heyday is over

Glas[1] *n; -es, Gläser od. als Mengenangabe: -* **1.** *nur Sg.; Substanz:* glass; **hinter ~** *Bild etc.:* behind glass; *Exponat etc.:* (*auch unter ~*) in a glass case; → *Glück* 2; **2.** *Gefäß:* glass; *ohne Fuß: auch* tumbler; *für Marmelade etc.:* jar; **zwei ~** *od.* **Gläser Wein** two glasses of wine; *bei e-m* **~ Wein besprechen** discuss over a glass of wine; **er hat ein ~ über den Durst getrunken** *od.* **zu tief ins ~ geguckt** *umg. hum.* he's had one (*od.* a drop) too many, *Brit. auch* he's had one over the eight; **3.** *Opt., e-r Brille:* lens; (*Fernglas*) binoculars *Pl.;* (*Opernglas*) opera glasses *Pl.;* **Gläser** (*Brille*) glasses

Glas[2] *n; -es, -en; Naut.* (½ *Stunde*) bell; **es schlägt acht ~en** it's eight bells

glasartig *Adj. Substanz etc.:* glassy

Glas|auge *n* glass eye; **~ballon** *m* demijohn; *Chem.* balloon (flask); **~bläser** *m* glass blower; **~bläserei** *f; -, -en* **1.** *nur Sg.; Gewerbe:* glass blowing; **2.** *Betrieb:* glassworks *Pl.* (*V. oft im Sg.*), glass factory; *kleinere:* glass blowing workshop; **~bläserin** *f* glass blower

Glasbodenboot *n* glass-bottom(ed) boat

Gläschen *n umg.:* **ein ~ zu viel** one too many; **sich ein ~ genehmigen** have a wee drop

Glascontainer *m für Altglas:* bottle bank, *Am.* glass recycling bin

Glaser *m; -s, -* glazier; **Glaserei** *f; -, -en* **1.** *Betrieb:* glazier's workshop; **2.** *nur Sg.; Handwerk:* glazing; **Glaserin** *f; -, -nen* glazier

Glasermeister *m*, **~in** *f* master glazier

gläsern *Adj.* **1.** (made of) glass; **2.** (*wie Glas*) *Augen:* glazed; *Klang:* tinkling; *Stimme:* brittle; **~er Blick** glassy stare; **3.** *fig. Abgeordnete, Bürger, Verbraucher etc.:* transparent, ... who has/have nothing to hide, ... who is/are an open book

Glasfaser *f* fibreglass, *Am.* fiberglass, glass fib|re (*Am.* -er); **~kabel** *n* fibre-optic (*Am.* fiber-optic) cable; **~optik** *f* fib|re (*Am.* -er) optics *Pl.* (*V. im Sg.*)

glasfaserverstärkt *Adj. Kunststoff:* fibreglass- (*Am.* fiberglass-)reinforced

Glasfenster *n* glass window

Glasfiber *f → Glasfaser;* **~boot** *n* fibreglass (*Am.* fiberglass) boat

Glas|flasche *f* glass bottle; **~flügler** *m Zool.* clearwing; **~geschirr** *n* glassware; **~glocke** *f für Käse etc.:* glass cover

glashart *Adj.* **1.** (as) hard as rock; **2.** *Sport umg., Schlag, Schuss:* cracking ...

Glas|haus *n* greenhouse; **wer im ~ sitzt, soll nicht mit Steinen werfen** *Sprichw.* people who live in glass houses shouldn't throw stones; **~hütte** *f* glassworks *Pl.* (*V. oft im Sg.*), glass factory

glasieren *v/t.* **1.** (*Keramik*) glaze; (*Metall*) enamel; **2.** *Gastr.* (*Kuchen*) frost, ice; (*Früchte*) candy; (*Fleisch*) glaze

glasig *Adj.* **1.** *Blick:* glassy; *Auge: auch* glazed; **2.** *Zwiebeln, Speck, beim Braten:* transparent; *Kartoffeln etc.:* waxy

Glaskasten *m* **1.** glass case, **2.** *umg.,*

G

oft pej. Gebäude, Raum: glass box
Glaskeramik *f für E-Herd etc.*: devitrified glass; **~kochfeld** *n*, **~platte** *f* glass hob (*Am.* cooktop)
glasklar *Adj.* crystal-clear (*auch fig.*)
Glas|knochenkrankheit *f Med.* brittle bone disease, osteoporosis, *als kongenitaler Zustand*: osteogenesis imperfecta *fachspr.*; **~kolben** *m* **1.** *Chem.* (glass) flask; **2.** *Etech.* (glass) bulb; **~körper** *m Anat.* vitreous body; **~kugel** *f* glass ball; **~maler** *m* glass painter, painter on glass; glass stainer; **~malerei** *f* painting on glass; *konkret*: stained glass (window [*s Pl.*]); **~malerin** *f* glass painter, painter on glass; *von Kirchenfenstern etc.*: stained glass artist; **~nudeln** *Pl. Gastr.* glass (*Am. auch* cellophane) noodles; **~palast** *m umg., oft pej.* glass box; **~perle** *f* (glass) bead; **~platte** *f* sheet of glass; (*Abdeckplatte*) glass top; **~reiniger** *m Reinigungsmittel*: glass cleaner; *Beruf*: window cleaner; **~röhrchen** *n* glass tube; *Pharm. auch* vial; **~scheibe** *f* pane (of glass); **~scherbe** *f* piece of (broken) glass, glass shard; **~n** broken glass *Sg.*, glass shards; **~schleifer** *m*, **~schleiferin** *f* glass grinder (*od.* cutter); **~schliff** *m* glass cutting; **~schneider** *m* glass cutter; *Diamant*: glazier's diamond; **~schneiderin** *f* glass cutter; **~schrank** *m* glass cabinet; **~schüssel** *f* glass bowl; **~splitter** *m* splinter of glass; **~tür** *f* glass door
Glasur *f*, -, -en **1.** *Keramik*: glaze; *auf Metall etc.*: enamel; **ohne ~** unglazed; **2.** *für Backwerk*: icing, *Am. auch* frosting; *für Obst*: sugar coating; *für Fleisch*: glaze
Glas|veranda *f* glass veranda, *Am.* sunroom, sun parlor, Florida room; **~versicherung** *f* glass insurance; **~vitrine** *f* glass (show)case; **~waren** *Pl.* glassware *Sg.*
glasweise *Adv.* by the glass
Glas|wolle *f* glass wool; **~ziegel** *m für Dach*: glass tile; *für Wand*: glass brick
glatt; *glatter od. glätter, am glattesten od. glättesten* **I.** *Adj.* **1.** *Fell, Haut, Teig etc.*: smooth; *Haut: auch* soft; *Haar*: (*nicht kraus*) straight; *Schnitt, Bruch*: clean; *Fläche etc.*: even; *Meer*: calm; (*poliert*) polished; **~ bügeln/schleifen** iron/polish; **~ bürsten** polish; (*Haar*) brush out; **etw. ~ feilen/hobeln** *etc.* file/plane *etc.* s.th. smooth; **~ rasiert** clean-shaven; **~ rühren** beat until smooth; **~ streichen** smooth out; (*Haar*) smooth down; **2.** (*rutschig*) slippery; *Straße: auch* icy; *Vorsicht*, **hier ist es ~!** mind (*Am.* watch out that) you don't slip (*Mot.* skid); **3.** *fig. Stil etc.*: smooth, polished; *oft pej. Person, Worte, Zunge*: glib; smooth; *Person: auch* slick; (*übermäßig höflich*) oily; **4.** *fig. Landung etc.*: smooth; *Niederlage, Sieg etc.*: outright, clear; *Zahl*: even, round; **~e Absage** flat refusal; **e-e ~e Eins** a straight A; **~ bügeln** (*Probleme*) iron out; **5.** *umg. fig., Lüge, Unsinn, Wahnsinn etc.*: downright; *Betrug*: outright; **das ist ~er Mord!** it's sheer (*od.* plain) murder!; **II.** *Adv.* **1.** smoothly; **~ anliegen** fit closely; **an der Wand** *etc.* **anliegen** be flush with the wall *etc.*; **~ rechts stricken** knit plain, do plain knitting; **2.** *fig.* (*ohne Probleme*) smoothly, without a hitch; **die Rechnung geht ~ auf** (*ohne Rest*) the sum (*Am.* total) works out exactly; **~ durchschneiden** cut clean through; **~ gehen** *od.* **verlaufen** *etc.* go

off smoothly (*od.* without a hitch); **3.** *umg.* (*völlig*) completely; **~ vergessen haben** have completely (*od.* clean) forgotten; **~ ablehnen/ableugnen** flatly refuse/deny; **4.** *umg.: er hat doch ~ behauptet, dass ...* he told me *etc.* to my *etc.* face that ...; **ich könnte ~ ...** (*sogar*) I've a good mind (*od.* half a mind) to (+ *Inf.*)
Glätte *f*, -, *kein Pl.* **1.** smoothness; (*polierte Oberfläche*) polish; **2.** (*Schlüpfrigkeit*) slipperiness; **3.** *fig. pej., e-r Person*: smoothness, slickness
Glatteis *n* **1.** *Mot. oft* black ice; **es ist ~** (*auf den Straßen*) the roads are icy (*od.* iced over); **2.** *fig.: j-n aufs ~ führen* put s.o. in a tricky situation
Glatteisgefahr *f*: (*auf den Straßen*) **~** icy roads (*od.* conditions) *Pl.*, ice on the roads
glätten I. *v/t.* **1.** smooth out; (*Haar etc.*) smooth (down); (*Falten*) take out; (*Hautfalten*) smooth away; *Tech.* smooth, give *s.th.* a smooth finish; (*polieren*) polish; (*Metall*) *auch* burnish; (*Holz*) plane; **2.** *fig.* polish; **die Wogen ~** pour oil on troubled waters; **3.** *schw. iron*; **II.** *v/refl.* **1.** smooth (itself) out; *Haut*: become smooth; *Gesicht*: relax; *Meer*: calm down; **die Wogen der Erregung haben sich geglättet** *fig.* the excitement has calmed down
glatthaarig *Adj.* straight-haired; *Hund etc.*: smooth-haired
Glattheit *f*; *nur Sg.* → **Glätte**
glattmachen *v/t.* (*trennb., hat -ge-*); *umg.* (*Rechnung etc.*) settle
glattstellen *v/t.* (*trennb., hat -ge-*); *Fin.* settle, square, even up
Glättung *f* smoothing
glattweg *Adv. umg.* just like that; (*rundheraus*) *auch* point-blank; (*völlig*) absolutely; **~ ablehnen** flatly refuse; **er hat ~ behauptet** he said straight out; **das hab ich ~ vergessen** I clean (*Am. auch* totally) forgot it
glattzüngig *Adj.* smooth-tongued, glib
Glatze *f*, -, -n bald head, bald pate *hum.*; (*kahle Stelle*) bald patch; **e-e ~ bekommen/haben** go/be bald; **sich** (*Dat.*) **e-e ~ schneiden lassen** have one's head shaved; **Glatzkopf** *m* **1.** bald head; **2.** *umg. fig.* baldie, slaphead, *Am. auch* cueball; **glatzköpfig** *Adj.* bald(-headed)
Glaube *m*; -ns, *kein Pl.* **1.** belief (**an** + *Akk.* in); (*festes Vertrauen*) faith (in), trust (in); (*Überzeugung*) conviction; **fester ~** firm belief; **in gutem ~n** *od.* **guten ~ns** *geh.* in good faith; **im ~n, dass ...** believing (that) ..., under the impression that ...; **~n schenken** (+ *Dat.*) believe; **des** (*festen*) **~ns sein, dass ...** *lit.* firmly believe (that) ...; **bei j-m ~n finden** be believed by s.o.; **j-n in dem ~n lassen, dass ...** let s.o. go on believing (that) ...; **sie lebte** *od.* **wiegte sich in dem ~n, dass ...** she lived in the belief that ...; *irrtümlich*: she clung to (*od.* cherished) the mistaken belief that ..., she labo(u)red under illusion that ...; **~ versetzt Berge** *Sprichw.* faith can move mountains; **2.** (*Religion*) (religious) faith *od.* belief (in), religion; (*Bekenntnis*) creed; **~, Liebe, Hoffnung** faith, hope and charity; **vom ~n abfallen** renounce one's faith
glauben I. *v/t.* **1.** (*Glauben schenken*) believe; **glaube es mir** believe me; **er glaubt alles** he'll believe anything; **es ist nicht zu ~** *umg.* it's incredible (*od.*

unbelievable); **ob du es glaubst oder nicht** believe it or not; **und das soll ich ~?** you don't expect me to believe that, do you?; **das glaubst du doch selbst nicht!** *umg.* tell me another one; **wer's glaubt, wird selig!** *umg.* that's a good one, a likely story!; **das glaube ich** (*dir*) **gern** I can (well) believe that; **2.** (*meinen, annehmen*) think; **ich glaubte, er sei Arzt** I thought he was a doctor; **sie glaubte sich unbeobachtet** she didn't think anyone was looking; **3.** *j-n etw.* **~ machen** make s.o. believe (*od.* think) s.th.; **II.** *v/i.* **1.** believe (**j-m** s.o.; **an** + *Akk.* in); **~ an** (+ *Akk.*) (*Vertrauen haben zu*) have faith in; **j-s Worten ~** believe what s.o. is saying; **ich glaube schon** *od.* **ja** I think so; **ich glaube kaum/nicht** I don't really think so / I don't think so (*od.* I think not); **sie ~ fest daran** they swear by it; **du kannst mir ~** take my word for it; **2.** *umg.*: **dran ~ müssen** *Person*: (*sterben*) kick the bucket, snuff it, *Am. auch* buy the farm; (*Unangenehmes erleiden*) come a cropper; *Auto etc.*: have had it; **e-s Tages müssen wir alle dran ~** we've all got to go one of these days
Glauben *m*; -s, *kein Pl.* → **Glaube**
Glaubens|bekenntnis *n* **1.** *Formel*: creed; **das ~ sprechen** *od.* **beten** say (*od.* recite) the creed; **2.** *Konfession*: denomination; *weitS.* religion; **3.** *Pol. etc.* creed; **sein politisches ~ ablegen** make a political profession of faith, declare one's political principles; **~bruder** *m* → **Glaubensgenosse**, **~eifer** *m* religious zeal; **~frage** *f* **1.** *nicht mit Verstand beantwortbar*: matter of faith; **2.** *in Bezug auf Religion*: religious question; **~freiheit** *f* religious freedom, freedom of religion; **~gemeinschaft** *f* religious community; **~genosse** *m*, **~genossin** *f* fellow Christian (*od.* Muslim, Socialist *etc.*), co(-)religionist; **~krieg** *m* religious war; *fig.* dispute *between people with differing opinions*, ideological conflict, war of words; **~lehre** *f* religious doctrine, dogma; *bes. kath.* dogmatics *Pl.* (*V. im Sg.*); **~richtung** *f* persuasion; **~sache** *f umg.* matter of faith; **~satz** *m* dogma; **~spaltung** *f* schism; **~streit** *m* religious controversy; **~treue** *f* (religious) faith; **~wechsel** *m* change of faith
glaubenswert *Adj.* credible
Glaubersalz *n Chem.* Glauber's salt
glaubhaft I. *Adj.* plausible; **~ machen** *Jur.* substantiate; **j-m etw. ~ machen** convince (*od.* persuade) s.o. of s.th.; **II.** *Adv.*: **~ nachweisen** satisfactorily show
gläubig *Adj.* **1.** religious; (*fromm*) *auch* devout; **2.** (*vertrauend*) trusting; *Anhänger*: faithful, loyal; (*naiv*) gullible
...gläubig *im Adj. pej.* trusting blindly in ...; **obrigkeits~** trusting blindly in authority
Gläubige *m*, *f*; -n, -n (true) believer; **die ~n** the faithful *Pl.*
Gläubiger *m*; -s, -; *Wirts.* creditor; *e-r Bürgschaft*: guarantor; *e-r Hypothek*: mortgagee; **~bank** *f*; *Pl. -banken* creditor bank; **~staat** *m* creditor country (*od.* nation); **~versammlung** *f* meeting of creditors
Gläubigkeit *f*; *nur Sg.* **1.** (*unquestioning*) faith; (*Frömmigkeit*) devoutness; **2.** (*Vertrauen*) trustfulness; **3.** *naive*: gullibility
glaublich *Adj.*: **kaum ~** hard to believe

glaubwürdig *Adj. Aussage etc.*: plausible; *Quelle etc.*: reliable; *Person*: (*zuverlässig*) trustworthy; **~er Zeuge** credible witness; **aus ~er Quelle** on good authority; **Glaubwürdigkeit** *f; nur Sg.* plausibility, credibility; reliability; trustworthiness; → *glaubwürdig*; **Mangel an ~** credibility gap

Glaubwürdigkeits|krise *f* credibility crisis; **~verlust** *m* loss of credibility

Glaukom *n; -s, -e; Med.* glaucoma

glazial *Adj. Geol.* glacial

gleich I. *Adj.* **1.** (*übereinstimmend*) same, *präd.* the same; (*identisch*) identical; *Bezahlung, Rechte etc.*: equal; (*einheitlich*) uniform; **fast ~** very similar; **in ~er Weise** (in) the same way; **zu ~en Teilen** equally; **zu ~er Zeit** at the same time, simultaneously; **~er Lohn für ~e Arbeit** equal pay for equal work; **das Gleiche** *od.* **Gleiches gilt für** the same applies to (*umg.* goes for); **es kommt** *od.* **läuft aufs Gleiche hinaus** *od.* **das bleibt sich ~** *umg.* it doesn't make any difference, it comes (*od.* boils) down to the same thing; **2.** (*ähnlich, vergleichbar*) similar, like, *präd.* alike; **Gleiches mit Gleichem vergelten** give s.o. tit for tat, pay s.o. back in kind, repay like with like; **Gleich und Gleich gesellt sich gern** *Sprichw.* birds of a feather (flock together); **3.** (*unverändert*) the same, unchanged; **~ bleiben** stay the same; **mit stets ~er Höflichkeit** with unfailing courtesy; **er ist nicht mehr der Gleiche** he's not the man I (*od.* we) used to know, he's really changed, you wouldn't recognize him any more; **4.** *Math., Winkel etc.*: equal; *Vorzeichen, Größe etc.*: same, like; *Phys., Ladung, Pole*: like; **in ~em Abstand voneinander** equidistant from each other; **x ist ~ y** x equals y; **7–2 ist ~ 5** 7–2 is (*od.* leaves) 5; **~ Null setzen** equate to zero; **x ist ungefähr ~ 10** x is approximately equal to 10; **x ist kleiner/größer (oder) ~ 10** x is equal to or less/greater than 10; **5.** (*egal*): **es ist mir ~** *umg.* it's all the same to me; **ganz ~ wann/wo** *etc.* whenever/wherever *etc.* (it is), no matter when/where *etc.* (it is); **das kann dir doch ~ sein** *umg.* why should you care?; **II.** *Adv.* **1.** alike, equally; **~ alt/groß** *etc.* the same age/size *etc.*; **sie stehen gleich** *Sport* they're drawing; *in der Tabelle*: they're level on points; **~ bleibend** always the same; (*unveränderlich*) constant, invariable; *Kurs, Barometer etc.*: steady; **~ geartet** of the same kind; (*ähnlich*) similar; **~ gerichtet** *Ziele, Interessen etc.*: similar, parallel; *Tech.* synchronous; *Etech.* unidirectional; **~ gesinnte Leute** people with the same kind of interest (*od.* outlook *etc.*); **~ gestellt** on an equal footing (+ *Dat.* with); *gesellschaftlich*: on the same social level; **~ gestimmt** *Instrumente*: tuned to the same pitch; *fig.* in tune (with one another); **~ gestimmte Seelen** kindred spirits; **~ lautend** *Text*: identical, with the same wording; *Inhalt*: to the same effect; *Wörter*: homonymic; *bei verschiedener Schreibung*: homophonic; **~ lautende Abschrift** true copy; **2.** (*unmittelbar*) right, straight, just, directly; (*sofort*) straightaway, immediately; **~ zu Beginn** right at the outset; (*als Anfang*) to start off with; **~ als** as soon as; **~ nach(dem)** right (*od.* straight) after; (*jetzt*) **~ now**, this minute; **~! hin-** *haltend*: just a minute, give us a chance *umg.*; (**ich komme**) **~!** (I'm) coming!, I'm on my way!; **ich ging ~ hin** I went straight there; **es muss nicht ~ sein** there's no hurry; **Kollege kommt ~** *im Restaurant*: you'll be served right away; **komme ~ wieder** *Schild*: will be right back, be back in a jiffy *umg.*; **bis ~!** see you in a minute (*od.* later); **das haben wir ~** *od.* **das ist ~ geschehen** it won't take a minute, we'll have that done (*od.* fixed) in no time; **es ist ~ zehn (Uhr)** it's nearly ten (o'clock); **3.** *umg., nachfragend*: **wie heißt er (noch) ~?** what's (*od.* what was) his name again?; **was wollte ich ~ sagen?** what was I going to say?; **4.** *umg.* (*auf einmal*) at a time, at once; **sie hat ~ drei Portionen gegessen** she ate three helpings at once; **er hat ~ zwei Freundinnen auf einmal** he has two girlfriends (on the go) at the same time; **5.** *umg., Gefühle od. Absicht ausdrückend*: **das hört sich ~ ganz anders an!** that's better, that's more like it; **~ passiert was!** *drohend*: there's going to be trouble!; **warum nicht ~ so?** *ungeduldig*: what's keeping you *etc.*?; **dann kann ich es ja ~ bleiben lassen!** *verärgert*: then I might as well forget it (*od.* give up now)!; **geh doch nicht ~ in die Luft!** there's no need to lose your temper; **das dachte ich mir doch ~!** I thought so (*od.* as much); **habe ich es nicht ~ gesagt?** what did I say?; **III.** *Präp.*: **~ e-m König** like a king; **e-m Wunder ~** as if by magic

gleichaltrig *Adj.* (of) the same age

gleichartig *Adj.* **1.** of the same kind; **2.** (*ähnlich*) similar; **Gleichartigkeit** *f; nur Sg.* **1.** homogeneity; **2.** (*Ähnlichkeit*) similarity

gleichauf *Adv. Sport*: **~ liegen** be on level pegging, *Am.* be tied

gleichbedeutend *Adj.* **1.** synonymous (*mit* with); **2.** equivalent (*mit* to); **das ist ~ mit e-r Annahme/Absage** it means you've *etc.* been accepted / turned down, it amounts (*od.* is tantamount) to an acceptance / a refusal

Gleichbehandlung *f; nur Sg.* equal treatment

gleichberechtigt I. *Adj.* equal; **~ sein** *auch* have equal rights; **II.** *Adv.*: **alle Menschen** *etc.* **~ behandeln** treat people *etc.* on an equal basis; **j-n ~ behandeln** *Vorgesetzter etc.*: treat s.o. as an equal; **~ nebeneinander stehen** *Möglichkeiten etc.*: be on an equal footing; **Gleichberechtigung** *f; nur Sg.* equality; **~ der Frau** *etc.* equal rights *Pl.* for women *etc.*

gleich bleiben → *gleich* I 3

gleich bleibend → *gleich* II 1

gleichen *v/i.; gleicht, glich, hat geglichen* **1.** (*ähnlich sein*) be (*od.* look) like, resemble (+ *Dat.* s.o./s.th.); **sich ~** be (*od.* look) alike, resemble one another; → *Ei* 1; **2.** (*nahe kommen*) come close to

Gleichenfeier *f österr.* → *Richtfest*

gleichen|orts *Adv. schw.* at (*od.* in) the same place; **~tags** *Adv. schw.* on the same day

gleicher|maßen *Adv.* **1.** equally; **2.** in the same way; **~weise** *Adv.* in the same way

gleichfalls *Adv.* likewise; **danke, ~!** thanks, and (the same to) you

gleichfarbig *Adj.* (of) the same colo(u)r

gleichförmig *Adj.* (*einheitlich*) uniform; *Bewegung etc.*: regular; *Beschleunigung etc.*: constant; (*unveränderlich*) steady, constant, unchanging; (*eintönig*) monotonous; **Gleichförmigkeit** *f; nur Sg.* uniformity; (*Unveränderlichkeit*) steadiness; (*Eintönigkeit*) monotony

gleich| geartet, ~ gelagert, ~ gerichtet → *gleich* II 1

gleichgeschlechtlich *Adj.* **1.** *Beziehung, Liebe*: homosexual; **2.** *Zwillinge*: (of) the same sex

gleich gesinnt → *gleich* II 1; **Gleichgesinnte** *m, f; -n, -n* kindred spirit

gleich| gestellt, ~ gestimmt → *gleich* II 1

Gleichgewicht *n; nur Sg.; auch fig.* balance, equilibrium; **~ der Kräfte** balance of power (*Phys.* of forces); **gestörtes ~** *fig.* unbalanced state, imbalance; **ökologisches ~** balance of nature, ecological balance; **seelisches ~** inner harmony; **im ~** balanced; **das ~ halten** (+ *Dat.*) counterbalance *s.o. od. s.th.*; **aus dem ~ kommen** *od.* **das ~ verlieren** lose one's balance; *fig.* be thrown (off balance); **aus dem ~ bringen** (*etw.*) unbalance; (*j-n*) put *s.o.* off balance; *fig. auch* throw *s.o.* (off balance); **sich wieder ins ~ bringen** steady o.s.; *fig.* get back on an even keel; **das ~ wiederherstellen** redress the balance

Gleichgewichts|gefühl *n* sense of balance; **~organ** *n Anat.* organ of equilibrium; **~sinn** *m; nur Sg.* sense of balance; **~störung** *f* imbalance; **sie leidet unter ~en** her sense of balance is upset

gleichgültig I. *Adj.* **1.** indifferent (*gegen* to); (*nachlässig*) careless; (*lässig*) *auch* casual; (*teilnahmslos*) apathetic (about), listless; (*gefühllos*) unfeeling, callous; **es ist mir (vollkommen) ~** it's all the same to me, I don't care (a bit, *stärker*: a damn *umg.*), I couldn't really care less; **er ist mir ~** he means nothing to me; **ich bin dir wohl ~** I don't suppose you care about me at all; **2.** (*belanglos*) unimportant, trivial; (*ganz*) **~, was du tust** whatever you do, no matter what you do; **II.** *Adv.*: **~ zusehen** (just) stand there and do nothing, (just) stand and watch; **sie reagierte ~** she didn't seem to care (*od.* be bothered); **Gleichgültigkeit** *f; nur Sg.* **1.** *e-r Person*: indifference (*gegen* to[wards]); (*Unbekümmertheit*) couldn't-care-less attitude; (*Teilnahmslosigkeit*) listlessness, apathy; (*Nachlässigkeit*) carelessness; (*Gefühllosigkeit*) callousness, lack of feeling; **2.** *e-r Sache*: unimportance, triviality

Gleichheit *f* **1.** equality; *völlige*: identity, identical nature; **~ vor dem Gesetz** equality before the law; **2.** (*Ähnlichkeit*) similarity; **3.** (*Einheitlichkeit*) uniformity; (*Übereinstimmung*) conformity; (*Gleichartigkeit*) homogeneity; (*Gleichwertigkeit*) equivalence; *von Flächen etc.*: evenness

Gleichheits|grundsatz *m,* **~zeichen** *n Math.* equal(s) sign

Gleichklang *m* **1.** unison; *Ling.* consonance; **2.** *fig.*: (*im*) **~** (in) harmony, unison; **~ der Herzen** (two) hearts that beat as one

gleichkommen *v/i.* (*unreg., trennb., ist -ge-*) (+ *Dat.*) **1.** (*erreichen*) come up to, compare with; **2.** (*hinauslaufen auf*) amount to; *negativ: auch* be nothing short of

Gleichlauf *m; nur Sg.; Tech., Etech.,*

TV synchronism, synchronized operation; *Math. etc.* parallelism; **gleichläufig** *Tech.* **I.** *Adj.* synchronous, synchronized; **II.** *Adv.*: *sie bewegen sich ~* their movement is synchronized

gleich lautend → gleich II 1

gleichmachen *v/t.* (*trennb., hat -ge-*) make equal (+ *Dat.* to), equalize (+ *Dat.* with); (*einebnen*) level (with *od.* to); (*vereinheitlichen*) standardize; *pej.* reduce to the same level, rob of its (*od.* their) individuality; *dem Erdboden ~* raze to the ground; *der Tod macht alle gleich* death is the great level(l)er (*od.* equalizer); **Gleichmacher** *m pej.* level(l)er, egalitarian; **Gleichmacherei** *f, -, -en; pej.* level(l)ing, egalitarianism; **Gleichmacherin** *f pej.* level(l)er, egalitarian

Gleichmaß *n; nur Sg.* **1.** (*Ebenmaß*) symmetry; (*Harmonie*) harmony; **2.** (*Regelmäßigkeit*) regularity; → *auch Gleichmäßigkeit*

gleichmäßig I. *Adj.* (*regelmäßig*) regular; (*ohne Schwankung*) *auch* steady, even; *Temperatur etc.*: constant; *Beschleunigung*: uniform; (*gleich bleibend*) consistent; (*wohlproportioniert*) well-proportioned; (*symmetrisch*) symmetrical; *Verteilung*: even; *Züge*: (very) regular; **II.** *Adv. verteilen etc.*: evenly; *~ gut* consistently good; **Gleichmäßigkeit** *f, nur Sg.* regularity; steadiness, evenness; consistency; symmetry; → *gleichmäßig*

Gleichmut *m, altm. und Dial. auch f, -, kein Pl.* equanimity; (*Unerschütterlichkeit*) imperturbability; (*Gelassenheit*) calmness, composure; (*Gleichgültigkeit*) indifference; *heiterer ~* serenity; *stoischer ~* stoicism; **gleichmütig** *Adj.* (*ruhig*) calm, composed; (*unerschütterlich*) imperturbable; (*gleichgültig*) indifferent

gleichnamig *Adj.* **1.** of the same name (*od. Buch etc.*: title); **2.** *Phys., Pole etc.*: like; *Math., Brüche*: with a common denominator; *~ machen* (*Brüche*) bring down (*od.* reduce) to a common denominator

Gleichnis *n; -ses, -se* **1.** *auch bibl.* parable; *das ~ vom verlorenen Sohn / barmherzigen Samariter bibl.* the parable of the prodigal son / good Samaritan; **2.** *Rhetorik*: simile; (*Bild*) image; **gleichnishaft I.** *Adj.* allegorical; (*symbolisch*) symbolic; **II.** *Adv.* symbolically

gleichpolig *Adj. Phys.* homopolar

gleichrangig *Adj. Mil. etc.* of equal rank; *leistungsmäßig*: on the same level, on a par; (*gleich wichtig*) equivalent, of equal importance (*od.* status); **Gleichrangigkeit** *f, nur Sg.* equality in rank; *leistungsmäßig*: parity; (*gleiche Wichtigkeit*) equality, equal status, equal importance

gleichrichten *v/t.* (*trennb., hat -ge-*); *Etech.* rectify; **Gleichrichter** *m* rectifier

gleichsam *Adv. geh.* (*sozusagen*) as it were, so to speak; *~ als wollte er sagen ...* as if (*od.* as though) he were trying to say ...

gleichschalten *v/t.* (*trennb., hat -ge-*) **1.** *Tech.* synchronize; **2.** *fig.* bring into line; *Pol. auch* impose political (and economic *etc.*) conformity on; **Gleichschaltung** *f* **1.** *Tech.* synchronization; **2.** *fig.* enforced (political *etc.*) conformity; *Pol. auch* gleichschaltung

gleichschenk(e)lig *Adj. Math.: ~es Dreieck* isosceles triangle

Gleichschritt *m; nur Sg.; Mil.: im ~* (marching) in step; *fig.* in step (*mit* with); *im ~, marsch!* forward, march!

gleichsehen *v/i.* (*unreg., trennb., hat -ge-*) **1.** resemble, look (*od.* be) like (+ *Dat.* s.o., s.th.); **2.** *umg.: das sieht ihm gleich* that's just like him

gleichseitig *Adj. Math.* equilateral

gleichsetzen *v/t.* (*trennb., hat -ge-*); *auch Math.* equate (+ *Dat. od. mit* with); (*vergleichen*) *auch* compare (with); (*auf dieselbe Ebene stellen*) identify, put on a level (with); **Gleichsetzung** *f* identification, equation; (*Vergleich*) comparison

Gleichstand *m; nur Sg.; Sport* tie; *Tennis*: deuce; *~ erzielen* level the score, draw level; **gleichstehen** *v/i.* (*unreg., trennb., hat / südd., öster., schw. ist -ge-*) *rangmäßig*: be on a par *od.* level (+ *Dat.* with)

gleichstellen *v/t.* (*trennb., hat -ge-*) equate (+ *Dat.* with), put in the same category (as); compare (with); *rechtlich etc.*: treat as equals, give equal treatment to; **Gleichstellung** *f* equation (+ *Dat.* with); *rechtlich etc.*: equality, equal treatment; *~ der Behinderten/Homosexuellen* equal rights (*bzw.* equal opportunities) for the disabled / for gays; **Gleichstellungsbeauftragte** *m, f Pol.* equal rights (*bzw.* opportunities) representative

Gleichstrom *m Etech.* direct current (*Abk.* DC); **Gleichstrom...** *im Subst.* direct-current ...; DC ...

gleichtun *v/t.* (*unreg., trennb., hat -ge-*): *es j-m ~* emulate s.o.; *in der Leistung*: match s.o.; *es j-m ~ wollen* vie with s.o.

Gleichung *f Math.* equation; *~ mit zwei Unbekannten* equation with two unknowns; *die ~ ging nicht auf* the equation didn't come out; *fig.* it (*od.* things) didn't work out

gleichviel *Adv.* all the same; *~, ob etc.* no matter whether *etc.*; *~!* it doesn't matter!, it makes no difference

gleichwertig *Adj. Qualität etc.*: equally good; *Ersatz*: of equal value *präd.*; *Leistung etc.*: equal (+ *Dat.* to), on a par (with), of the same standard (as); *Gegner*: ... who is a match for *s.o.*, well-matched; *Chem.* equivalent; **Gleichwertigkeit** *f; nur Sg.* equal value, parity; *von Qualität, Leistung etc.*: equal standard; *Chem.* equivalence

gleichwink(e)lig *Adj. Math.* with equal angles, equiangular *fachspr.*

gleichwohl I. *Adv.* (*dennoch*) nevertheless, all the same; yet; however; **II.** *Konj. altm.* (*obwohl*) although

gleichzeitig I. *Adj.* simultaneous; (*zusammenfallend*) concurrent; **II.** *Adv.* at the same time, simultaneously; **Gleichzeitigkeit** *f; nur Sg.* simultaneousness; concurrence

gleichziehen *v/i.* (*unreg., trennb., hat -ge-*); *Sport* (*einholen*) draw even, *Am.* tie (*mit* with), catch up (with) (*beide auch fig.*); (*ausgleichen*) equalize

Gleis *n; -es, -e* **1.** rails *Pl.*, track; (*Bahnsteig*) platform, *Am. auch* track; *ein totes ~* a disused line; *aus dem ~ springen* jump the rails; *Überschreiten der ~e verboten!* passengers must not cross the line; **2.** *fig.: sich in ausgefahrenen ~en bewegen* keep on in the same old way, keep to the well-trodden paths; *auf ein falsches ~ geraten* get onto the wrong track; *aus dem ~ werfen od. bringen* throw *s.o.* (completely); **~anlage** *f* track system;

~anschluss *m* works (*Am.* maintenance) siding; **~anzeige** *f* platform (*Am.* track) indicator; **~(bau)arbeiten** *Pl. Erneuerung*: track maintenance *Sg.*, track repairs; *Verlegung*: track laying; **~dreieck** *n* triangular junction, *Am.* Y-track; **~körper** *m* track

gleißen *v/i. poet.* gleam; (*blenden*) *Sonne etc.*: glare; **gleißend I.** *Part. Präs.* → *gleißen*; **II.** *Adj.: ~e Hitze* searing heat; *~es Licht* glaring (*stärker*: blinding) light, strong glare; **III.** *Adv.: ~ hell* glaring

Gleit|bahn *f* **1.** (*Rutschbahn*) slide; (*Rinne*) *auch* chute; *Naut.* slipway; **2.** *Flug.* glide path; **~boot** *n* hydroplane; **~creme** *f* lubricating cream, lubricant

gleiten *v/i.; gleitet, glitt, ist geglitten* **1.** *Schlange, Schlitten, Ski, Tänzer, Vogel etc.*: glide (*über + Akk.* across); *Boot*: auch skim (across); *Blick, Hände, Lächeln etc.*: pass (over); *Hände*: *auch* run (over); (*schlüpfen*) slip; *vom Pferd / ins Wasser ~* slip from the saddle (*od.* off the horse) / into the water; *die Hand ~ lassen über* (+ *Akk.*) run one's hand over; **2.** (*rutschen*) slide; (*ausrutschen*) slip; *Mot.* skid; *zu Boden ~* slip and fall; **gleitend I.** *Part. Präs.* → *gleiten*; **II.** *Adj. Wirts.: ~e Arbeitszeit* flexible working hours, flex(i)time

Gleit|flug *m* glide; **~flugzeug** *n* glider; **~klausel** *f Wirts.* escalator clause; **~komma** *n EDV* floating point; **~mittel** *n Tech., auch für Kondom etc.*: lubricant; **~schiene** *f* slide bar, guide; *Schreibmaschine*: carriage rail

Gleitschirm *m* paraglider; **~fliegen** *n* paragliding; **~flieger** *m*, **~fliegerin** *f* paraglider

Gleitschutz *m* **1.** anti-skid protection; **2.** *Vorrichtung*: anti-skid device

Gleitsegeln *n* hang-gliding; **Gleitsegler** *m* hang-glider

Gleit|tag *m Wirts.* flexiday; **~wachs** *n* gliding wax; **~zeit** *f Wirts.* flexible working hours *Pl.*, flexitime *Brit.*, flextime *Am.*

Gletscher *m; -s, -* glacier; **~bach** *m* glacial stream; **Ωbedeckt** *Adj.* glaciated; **~boden** *m* glacial soil; **~brille** *f*: (*e-e*) *~* (a pair of) snow goggles *Pl.*, glacier goggles *Pl.*; **~eis** *n* glacial ice; **~feld** *n* icefield, (surface of a) glacier; **~kunde** *f; nur Sg.* glaciology; **~mühle** *f Geol.* moulin; **~schmelze** *f* melting of glaciers; **~spalte** *f* crevasse; **~tor** *n Geol.* mouth of a (*od.* the) glacier; **~wanderung** *f* glacier tour; **~zunge** *f Geol.* glacier snout

Glibber *m; -s, kein Pl.; nordd.* slime; **glibb(e)rig** *Adj. nordd.* slimy; slippery

glich *Imperf.* → *gleichen*

Glied *n; -(e)s, -er* **1.** *Arm, Bein*: limb; *s-e ~er strecken* stretch (o.s.); *j-m tun alle ~er weh* s.o. is aching all over (*od.* in every limb); *an allen ~ern zittern* tremble in every limb (*od.* all over); *ich konnte kein ~ rühren* I couldn't move a muscle; *der Schreck fuhr ihm in die od. alle ~er* the shock made him tremble from head to foot; *weitS.* he got the shock of his life; **2.** *Anat., e-s Fingers etc.*: joint; **3.** (*Penis*) penis, (male) member; **4.** *e-r Kette etc.*: link (*auch fig.*); (*Teil*) member, part; (*Komponente*) component, element; *das fehlende ~ fig.* the missing link; **5.** *Ling.* → *Satzteil*; **6.** *Math., Logik*: term; **7.** *Mil.* rank; *aus dem ~ treten* fall out; *undiszipliniert*: break rank; *in*

Reih und ~ in rank and file, in formation; *fig.* in line; **8.** *geh. altm., bibl.* generation; *bis ins zehnte* ~ unto the tenth generation

Glieder|armband *n* adjustable bracelet; **~füßer** *m; -s, -; Zool.* arthropod; **~kaktus** *m Bot.* jointed cactus; **~kette** *f* link chain; **♀lahm** *Adj.* worn out; **~lähmung** *f* paralysis

gliedern I. *v/t.* (*anordnen*) arrange; (*aufbauen*) structure; *in Teile:* divide (*in* + *Akk.* into), (*unterteilen*) subdivide (into); *nach Sachgebieten etc.:* arrange, classify; *Mil.* organize, *taktisch:* deploy; **II.** *v/refl.:* **sich ~ in** (+ *Akk.*) (*bestehen aus*) be made up of; (*unterteilt sein in*) be divided into

Glieder|puppe *f* jointed doll; (*Marionette*) puppet; *für Maler:* lay figure; *für Kleider:* mannequin; **~reißen** *n umg.*, **~schmerzen** *Pl.* pains in one's arms *od.* legs (*od.* arms and legs); **~tier** *n Zool.* articulate

Gliederung *f* **1.** (*Anordnung*) arrangement; (*Plan*) plan; (*Muster*) pattern; (*Aufbau*) structure, organization; (*Einteilung*) division (*in* + *Akk.* into); *nach Sachgebieten etc.:* classification; *Mil.* organization; *Zool., Bot.* segmentation; **2.** *e-s Aufsatzes:* plan, *bes. Am.* outline; *e-e* ~ *schreiben* write (*od.* draw up) a plan (*bes. Am.* an outline)

Glied|maßen *Pl.* limbs; **~satz** *m Ling.* subordinate clause; **~staat** *m* member state

glimmen *v/i.*; glimmt, glimmte *od.* glomm, geglimmt *od.* geglommen **1.** *Feuer:* smo(u)lder (*auch fig.*); *Zigarette, Augen etc.:* glow; ~ *glimmend;* **2.** *lit.* (*schimmern*) glimmer, gleam; **3.** *fig.: ein Funken Hoffnung glomm noch in ihr* a glimmer of hope was still left in her; **Glimmen** *n; -s, kein Pl.* smo(u)ldering (*auch fig.*); faint glow; gleam, glimmer; **glimmend I.** *P.P.* → *glimmen;* **II.** *Adj.:* **~e Asche** embers *Pl.*

Glimmer *m; -s, -; Min.* mica
glimmern *v/i.* glimmer
Glimmstängel *m umg.* fag, *Am.* ciggie, smoke

glimpflich I. *Adj. Strafe, Urteil:* (relatively) mild; *Verluste:* (relatively) light; *Ausgang, Ende:* relatively happy, not too serious, with little harm done; **II.** *Adv.:* ~ *davonkommen* get off lightly

glissando *Mus.* **I.** *Adv.* glissando; **II. Glissando** *n; -s, -s od. Glissandi* glissando (*Pl.* glissandi *od.* glissandos)

glitschen *v/i. umg.* slip; **glitsch(r)ig** *Adj. umg.* slippery; (*schleimig*) slimy
glitt *Imperf.* → *gleiten*
Glitzer *m; -s, kein Pl., altm.* glitter; **glitzern** *v/i.* glitter; *Augen, Wasser etc.:* glisten; **Glitzerwelt** *f des Films etc.:* wonder world, magic; *abwertend:* glitzy world, glitz

global I. *Adj.* **1.** worldwide, global; *die Welt ist ein **~es** Dorf* global village; *die* **~e** *Erwärmung der Atmosphäre* global (atmospheric) warming; **2.** (*umfassend*) *Kontrolle, Steuerung:* overall; *Wissen:* exhaustive; *Ausbildung:* all-round; **3.** (*nicht detailliert*) general; **II.** *Adv.* **1.** worldwide, globally; ~ *gesehen* seen on a global scale; **2.** (*im Ganzen*) as a whole
Global|... *im Subst.* (*allgemein, umfassend*) overall ..., global ...; **~abkommen** *n* overall (*od.* global) agreement
globalisieren *v/t.* globalize; **Globalisierung** *f* globalization

Globalstrategie *f* global strategy
Globetrotter ['gloːbətrɔtɐ] *m; -s, -, ~in f; -, -nen* globetrotter
Globuli *Pl. Med.* globules
Globus *m; -(ses), -se od. Globen* globe; *sie ist um den ganzen ~ gereist* she's been all around the globe (*od.* all over the world)
Glöckchen *n* little bell
Glocke *f; -, -n* **1.** bell; *der Klingel:* gong; *etw. an die große ~ hängen fig.* tell the whole world about s.th., shout s.th. from the housetops (*Am.* rooftops); **2.** *e-r Lampe:* globe; *für Käse etc.:* cover; *Chem.* bell (jar); *Fechten:* guard; **3.** *fig. von Dunst etc.:* blanket, thick layer
Glockenblume *f Bot.* bellflower, campanula
glockenförmig *Adj.* bell-shaped; *Rock:* flared
Glocken|geläut *n* **1.** ringing of bells; **2.** bells *Pl.; abgestimmtes:* chime(s *Pl.*), chiming; **~gießer** *m; -s, -* bell founder; **~gießerei** *f; -, -en* bell foundry; **~gießerin** *f; -, -nen* bell founder
glockenhell *Adj. und Adv.* (as) clear as a bell
Glocken|hut *m* cloche; **~klang** *m* peal of bells; **~läuten** *n* ringing of bells
glockenrein *Adj. und Adv.* → *glockenhell*
Glocken|rock *m* flared skirt; **~schlag** *m* stroke of the clock; *mit dem od. auf den ~* (*pünktlich*) on the dot; **~spiel** *n* chime(s *Pl.*); *Mus., Instrument:* glockenspiel, carillon; **~stuhl** *m* bell cage; **~turm** *m* bell tower, belfry; **~zeichen** *n* bell signal
glockig *Adj.* bell-shaped; *Rock:* flared
Glöckner *m; -s, -, ~in f; -, -nen* bell ringer; (*Kirchendiener*) sexton; *der ~ von Notre-Dame* the hunchback of Notre Dame
glomm *Imperf.* → *glimmen*
Gloria *n; -s, -s* **1.** → *Glanz* 2; **2.** *Mus., kirchl.* Gloria
Glorie *f; -, -n* **1.** *geh.* glory; **2.** *geh. od. Astron.* halo; **Glorienschein** *m* halo
glorifizieren *v/t.* glorify
Gloriole *f; -, -n; geh.* halo
glorios, glorreich *Adj.* glorious; **~e Idee** *iro.* bright idea
Glossar *n; -s, -e* glossary (of terms)
Glosse *f; -, -n* **1.** *in der Presse:* commentary; *s-e ~n machen über* (+ *Akk.*) *fig.* (*spotten*) sneer (*od.* scoff) at; **2.** *Ling.* gloss; (*Texterläuterung*) commentary, marginal note; **glossieren** *v/t.* **1.** *in der Presse:* write (*Radio:* do) a commentary on; **2.** *fig.* make fun of; **3.** *Ling.* (*Text*) gloss
glottal *Adj. Ling.* glottal; **Glottallaut** *m* glottal (sound)
Glotzauge *n* **1.** *umg. pej.* goggle eye; **~n bekommen/machen** goggle; **2.** *Med.* exophthalmos; **glotzäugig** *Adj. umg. pej.* goggle-eyed
Glotze *f; -, -n; umg., oft pej.* the box, *Am. auch* (boob) tube, *Brit. auch* gogglebox
glotzen *v/i. umg., mst pej.* **1.** stare; *mit offenem Mund:* gawk; *glotz nicht so blöd!* stop gawking like an idiot; **2.** (*fernsehen*) watch the box (*Am.* boob tube)
Glotz|kasten *m umg. pej.* → *Glotze;* **~kopf** *m umg. pej.* gawper
Glubschaugen *Pl.* → *Glupschaugen*
gluck *Interj.* **1.** *beim Trinken:* glug (, glug); **~, ~, weg war er** *hum.* glug, glug, and down he went; **2.** *Henne:* cluck

Glück *n; -(e)s, kein Pl.* **1.** (*Ggs. Pech*) luck; (*Glücksfall, glücklicher Zufall*) (good) luck, stroke (*od.* piece) of (good) luck; ~ *auf! Bergb.* good luck!; *viel ~!* good luck!, best of luck! *umg.;* *zum ~* fortunately; ~ *bringender Talisman* lucky charm; *es soll ~ bringen* it's supposed to bring good luck; ~ *haben* be lucky, be in luck; *kein ~ haben* be out of luck; *das ~ haben zu* (+ *Inf.*) be lucky enough to (+ *Inf.*), have the good fortune to (+ *Inf.*); *damit wirst du bei ihr kein ~ haben* that won't get you anywhere with her, that won't cut any ice with her(, I'm afraid); *nochmal ~ gehabt! umg.* that was a close shave; *ich hatte ~ im Unglück* I was lucky things didn't turn out worse; *er/sie hat viel ~ bei den Frauen/Männern* he's/she's a great success with the ladies / (the) men; *mancher hat mehr ~ als Verstand* Fortune favo(u)rs fools; *dein ~!* lucky for you; *ein ~, dass ...* thank goodness (that) ...; *da kannst du von ~ reden od.* sagen you can count yourself lucky; ~ *verheißend Vorzeichen, Umstände:* auspicious, lucky; *sein ~ versuchen* try one's luck (*bei* with); *sie wusste noch nichts von i-m ~ iro.* she didn't know what was in store for her; *auf gut ~* on the off-chance; ~ *im Spiel, Pech in der Liebe Sprichw.* lucky at cards, unlucky in love; **2.** *Empfindung, Zustand:* happiness; *eheliches/häusliches ~* marital/domestic bliss; *junges ~ fig.* young lovers; *j-m ~ wünschen zum Geburtstag etc.:* congratulate s.o. (*zu* on); *sein ~ machen* make one's fortune; *sein ~ mit Füßen treten* spurn one's chance of happiness; *j-s ~ im Wege stehen* stand in the way of s.o.'s happiness; *das hat mir gerade noch zu m-m ~ gefehlt umg. iro.* that's all I wanted (*od.* needed); *jeder ist s-s ~es Schmied Sprichw.* everyone makes their own luck; ~ *und Glas, wie leicht bricht das Sprichw.* happiness is as brittle as glass; **3.** *personifiziert:* fortune; *ein Liebling des ~s sein* be born under a lucky star; *das ~ ist launisch* fortune is fickle; *das ~ ist auf j-s Seite od. das ~ ist j-m hold geh.* luck is on s.o.'s side
Glucke *f; -, -n* mother hen (*auch fig.*); *brütende:* sitting hen; *sie ist e-e richtige ~ umg. fig.* she's a real old mother hen; **glucken** *v/i.* **1.** (*hat*) *Henne:* (*Küken rufen*) cluck; (*brüten*) be broody; **2.** (*ist*); *umg.* (*hocken*) sit around; **3.** (*hat*); *umg. pej.:* ~ *über* (+ *Dat.*) (*behüten*) cluck over
glücken *v/i.* succeed, be successful, turn (*od.* work) out well, come off *umg.;* *nicht ~* not succeed, be unsuccessful, turn out badly, fall through; *es glückte ihm zu* (+ *Inf.*) he succeeded in (+ *Ger.*), he managed to (+ *Inf.*); *es ist ihm gut geglückt* he made a good job of it; *die Flucht ist (ihm) nicht geglückt* the (his) escape attempt failed; → *geglückt*
gluckern *v/i.* (*ohne Richtung:* hat; *mit Richtung:* ist) gurgle; **II.** *v/t.* (*hat*) (*Getränk*) *umg.* swill down
glücklich I. *Adj.* **1.** (*froh*) happy; ~ *sein* be (*od.* feel) happy; (*ein*) **~es neues Jahr!** Happy New Year!; *dem Glücklichen schlägt keine Stunde Sprichw.* time flies when you're having fun; **2.** (*erfolgreich, vom Glück begünstigt*) lucky, fortunate; *der ~e Aus-*

G

gang des Abenteuers a happy ending to the adventure; *e-e ~e Hand haben* have the right touch (*bei* for, when it comes to); *~e Reise!* bon voyage!; *~er Zufall* lucky (*od.* fortunate) chance; *du kannst dich ~ schätzen od.* preisen you can count yourself lucky; *du Glücklicher!* umg. you lucky thing; **3.** (*gut*) *Beispiel, Formulierung etc.*: most appropriate, happy; *Entscheidung, Wahl etc.*: good, fortunate; inspired; *ein ~er Wurf* a smart move; **II.** *Adv.* **1.** happily *etc.*; → I; (*gut*) well; (*erfolgreich*) successfully; *~ ankommen/landen etc.* arrive/land *etc.* safely; *~ enden* have a happy end(ing); *~ gewählter Augenblick* opportune moment; **2.** *umg. iro.* (*endlich*) finally; *jetzt hat er ~ auch noch ...* to cap it all (*Am.* top it all off) he's ...; **glücklicherweise** *Adv.* fortunately, luckily
Glückssache *f* → **Glückssache**
Glücksbringer *m; -s, -* Anhänger *etc.*: lucky charm; *Teddybär etc.*: mascot
glückselig *Adj.* blissful, happy, *präd. auch* overjoyed; **Glückseligkeit** *f; nur Sg.* bliss(fulness), happiness; *ewige ~* eternal bliss
glucksen *v/i.* **1.** *Henne*: cluck; **2.** *Wasser etc.*: gurgle; **3.** *fig. Baby*: gurgle; *~*(*d lachen*) chortle (*vor* with)
Glücks|fall *m* stroke of luck; (*glücklicher Umstand*) *auch* lucky coincidence; (*unerwarteter Gewinn*) windfall; **~fee** *f auch fig. hum.* fairy godmother, good fairy; **~gefühl** *n* feeling of happiness; *kurzes*: blissful sensation; **~göttin** *f*: *die ~* Fortune, Lady Luck; **~käfer** *m* ladybird, *Am. auch* ladybug; **~kind** *n*: *sie ist ein ~* she was born under a lucky star; **~klee** *m* four-leaf (*od.* four-leaved) clover; **~pfennig** *m* lucky penny; **~pille** *f umg.* get-happy pill; **~pilz** *m umg.* lucky devil; **~rad** *n* wheel of fortune; **~ritter** *m altm., auch pej.* soldier of fortune; **~sache** *f* a matter of luck; **~!** luck!; **~spiel** *n* **1.** game of chance; *Koll.* gambling; **2.** *fig.* gamble; **~spieler** *m*, **~spielerin** *f* gambler; **~stern** *m* lucky star; **~strähne** *f* streak *od.* run of (good) luck, lucky streak; **~tag** *m* lucky day
glückstrahlend *Adj.* radiant(ly happy), beaming all over one's face
Glücks|treffer *m* fluke, lucky shot (*auch Sport*); *fig.* stroke of luck; (*Geldgewinn*) windfall; **~zahl** *f* lucky number
glückverheißend → **Glück** 1
Glückwunsch *m* congratulations *Pl.* (*zu* on); good wishes *Pl.*; *herzlichen ~!* congratulations!; *bei Prüfung etc.*: *auch* well done! *umg.*; *zum Geburtstag*: happy birthday!, many happy returns (of the day); **~adresse** *f* message of congratulations; **~karte** *f* greeting(s) card
Glüh|birne *f* (light) bulb; **~draht** *m Etech.* filament
glühen I. *v/i.* **1.** glow; *Metall*: be red-hot; *zum Glühen bringen* heat *s.th.* till it glows (red-hot); **2.** *fig. Gesicht*: burn (*vor* + *Dat.* with); *Berge, Himmel etc.*: glow; *vor Eifer* ~ *geh. Person*: be flushed with enthusiasm; **II.** *v/t.* (*zum Glühen bringen*) make *s.th.* red-hot; (*Stahl*) anneal
glühend I. *Part. Präs.* → **glühen**; **II.** *Adj.* **1.** *Kohlen*: live; *Zigarette*: burning; **2.** *fig. Hitze, Sonne etc*: scorching; **3.** *fig. Hass, Wunsch etc.*: burning; *Anhänger etc.*: fervent, ardent; *in ~en Farben schildern* paint

s.th. in glowing colo(u)rs, paint a glowing picture of *s.th.*; → *Kohle* 1; **III.** *Adv.*: ~ *heiß od.* rot red-hot; *ein ~ heißer Tag* a (real) scorcher *umg.*
Glüh|kerze *f Mot.* glow plug; **~lampe** *f* electric light bulb; **~wein** *m* mulled wine, (glühwein), **~würmchen** *n umg.* glow(-)worm
Glukose *f; -, kein Pl.* glucose
Glupschaugen *Pl. nordd. umg. pej.* goggle eyes; **~ machen** goggle; **glupschäugig** *Adj. nordd. umg. pej.* goggle-eyed
Glut *f; -, -en* **1.** embers *Pl.*; **2.** *fig.* (*Hitze*) (scorching *od.* blazing) heat; (*Röte*) glow; *geh. der Leidenschaft etc.*: fervo(u)r, fire
Glutamat *n; -(e)s, -e; Chem.* glutamate; *Gastr.* monosodium glutamate, MSG
glutäugig *Adj. lit.* fiery-eyed
Gluten *n; -s, kein Pl.; Chem.* gluten; **~allergie** *f Med.* gluten allergy
glutenfrei *Adj. Gastr.* gluten-free; **glutenhaltig** *Adj.* gluten-containing
Gluthitze *f* searing (*od.* sweltering) heat
glutrot *Adj.* fiery red; *~ werden im Gesicht*: turn crimson
Glykol *n; -s, -e; Chem.* (ethylene) glycol
Glyzerin *n; -s, kein Pl.; Chem.* glycerine; **~salbe** *f* glycerine ointment
Glyzinie *f; -, -n; Bot.* wisteria
GmbH *f; -, -s; Abk.* (**Gesellschaft mit beschränkter Haftung**) → **Gesellschaft** 6
g-Moll *n; -, kein Pl.; Mus.* G minor; **~-Tonleiter** *f* G-minor scale
Gnade *f; -, -n* **1.** *nur Sg.*: (*Nachsicht, Barmherzigkeit*) mercy; *ohne ~* merciless(ly); ~ *vor od. altm. für Recht ergehen lassen* temper justice with mercy; **2.** (*Gunst*) favo(u)r; *bes. Gottes*: grace; (*Segnung*) blessing; *e-e ~ des Himmels* a blessing; ~ *finden vor* find favo(u)r with; *bei j-m in* (*hohen*) *~n stehen* be in s.o.'s good graces; *hättest du die ~ zu* (+ *Inf.*) *iro.* do you think you might condescend to (+ *Inf.*); *von Gottes ~n hist.* by the grace of God; **3.** *altm.*: *Euer od. Ihre, Ihro ~n* Your Grace
gnaden *v/i.*: *dann gnade dir etc.* Gott God help you *etc.*
Gnaden|akt *m* act of mercy (*od.* clemency); **~bezeigung** *f* show of favo(u)r (*od.* mercy, clemency); **~bild** *n kirchl.* miraculous image of the Virgin Mary *etc.*; **~brot** *n; nur Sg.*: *bei j-m das ~ bekommen Tier*: be looked after by s.o. in its old age; *altm. Person*: live on s.o.'s charity; **~erlass** *m* amnesty; **~frist** *f* reprieve; *e-e ~ von fünf Tagen / e-r Woche* five days' / one week's grace; **~gesuch** *n* plea for clemency
gnadenlos *Adj.* merciless, pitiless
gnadenreich *Adj. geh.* **1.** *Zeit*: happy; **2.** *kath. Maria*: full of grace
Gnaden|stoß *m* coup de grâce; **~tod** *m*: *der ~* euthanasia; *konkret*: mercy killing; **~weg** *m*: *auf dem ~* by means of a pardon
gnädig I. *Adj.* **1.** *oft iro.* (*gunstvoll*) gracious (*gegen|über*) to) (*auch im Titel*); *~e Frau od. ~es Fräulein altm. od.* **Gnädigste** *iro.* madam, *Am.* ma'am; *der ~e Herr altm.* the master; *~er Herr altm., Anrede*: sir; *wärst du wohl so ~ zu* (+ *Inf.*) *iro.* would you deign to (+ *Inf.*); **2.** (*barmherzig*) merciful; *Urteil*: lenient, mild; *Gott sei ihm ~!* God have mercy on him; **II.** *Adv.* graciously *etc.*; *noch ~ davonkommen* get off lightly; **gnädigerweise** *Adv. iro.*: *~ etw. tun* condescend to do s.th.

Gneis *m; -es, -e; Min.* gneiss
gneißen *v/t. österr. umg.* → **kapieren**
Gnom *m; -en od. -s, -e(n)* gnome; *umg. pej. auch* dwarf; **gnomenhaft** *Adj.* gnomish
Gnostik *f; -, kein Pl.* Gnosticism; **Gnostiker** *m; -s, -*, **Gnostikerin** *f; -, -nen* Gnostik; **gnostisch** *Adj.* Gnostic
Gnu *n; -s, -s; Zool.* gnu
Goal [goːl] *n; -s, -s; österr., schw.* goal; **~getter** *m; -s, -*, **~getterin** *f; -, -nen* goalscorer
Goa (*n*); -s; *Geog.* Goa; **Goanese** *m; -n, -n*, **Goanesin** *f; -, -nen* Goan, Goanese; **goanesisch** *Adj.* Goanese
Gobelin [gobə'lɛ̃ː] *m; -s, -s* tapestry, Gobelin
Gobi *f; -; Geog.*: *die Wüste ~* the Gobi desert
Gockel *m; -s, -; bes. südd.* cock, rooster; *eitler ~ fig. pej.* s.o. who is as vain as a peacock, fancy pants *umg.*
goethesch, goethisch *Adj.* Goethean; *Dramen, Verse etc.*: by Goethe
Go-go-Girl ['goːgogøːɐ̯l] *n* go-go-dancer
Go-in [goː'ʔɪn] *n; -(s), -s; Pol.* protest action in which demonstrators force an entry into a building in order to join in or disrupt discussions *etc.*; *ein ~ veranstalten* disrupt a meeting (*od.* discussion)
Gokart ['goːkart] *m; -(s), -s* go-kart
Golanhöhen *Pl. Geog.* Golan Heights
Gold *n; -(e)s, kein Pl.* **1.** gold (*auch Farbe, Münze, Medaille*); *flüssiges ~ fig.* (*Erdöl*) liquid gold; *schwarzes ~ fig.* (*Kohle*) black gold; ~ *schürfen/ waschen* prospect for / wash (*od.* pan) gold; *sie ist nicht mit ~ zu bezahlen od. aufzuwiegen* she's priceless, she's worth her weight in gold; *das ist ~(es geh.) wert fig.* it's worth its weight in gold; *sie hat ein Herz aus ~ fig.* she's got a heart of gold; ~ *in der Kehle haben fig.* have a golden voice; *es ist nicht alles ~, was glänzt Sprichw.* all that glitters (*Shakespeare*: glisters) is not gold; → *Herd* 2, *Morgenstunde etc.*; **2.** (*Goldmedaille*) gold (medal); ~ *gewinnen* win gold (*od.* a gold medal)
Gold|ader *f* vein of gold; **~ammer** *f Orn.* yellowhammer; **~anleihe** *f Wirts.* gold loan; **~auflage** *f* gold plating; **~barren** *m* gold ingot; *Wirts. Pl. mst* bullion *Sg.*; **~barsch** *m Zool.* rosefish, ocean perch; *Wirts.* Norway haddock; **~bestickt** *Adj.* embroidered with gold; **~blatt** *n* gold leaf
gold|blond *Adj.* golden(-haired); **~braun** *Adj.* golden-brown
Gold|brokat *m* gold brocade; **~buchstabe** *m* gold letter; *mit ~n* in gold lettering; **~deckung** *f Fin.* gold backing; **~devisenwährung** *f Fin.* gold exchange standard; **~doublé** ['-dublɛː], **~dublee** *n* gold plate
golddurchwirkt *Adj.* interwoven with gold
golden I. *Adj.* **1.** (of) gold; *Brille*: gold-rimmed; (*vergoldet*) golden; **2.** *fig. Haar, Herz, Regel, Zeitalter etc.*: golden; *das Goldene Buch* (+ *Gen.*) the visitors' book; *j-m ~e Brücken bauen* bend over backwards to make it easy for s.o.; *~e Hochzeit* golden wedding (anniversary); *im ~en Käfig sitzen* be a bird in a gilded cage; *das Goldene Kalb/Vlies* the Golden Calf/Fleece; *~er Mittelweg* golden mean; *~er Schnitt Math.* golden section; *die Goldenen Zwanziger* the roaring twenties; *sich* (*Dat.*) *e-e ~e Nase verdienen*

umg. make (*od.* earn) a fortune; **sich** (*Dat.*) **den ~en Schuss setzen** *Sl.* OD oneself; **II.** *Adv.*: **~ glänzen/schimmern** shine/glitter like gold

Gold|esel *m* **1.** *im Märchen:* etwa goose that lays the golden egg(s); **2.** *umg.:* **ich bin doch kein ~** I'm not made of money(, you know)

goldfarben, goldfarbig *Adj.* gold-colo(u)red, golden

Gold|fasan *m Orn.* golden pheasant; **~feder** *f e-s Füllers:* gold nib; **~fisch** *m Zool.* goldfish (*auch umg. hum.*); **~füllung** *f* gold filling; **~gehalt** *m* gold content; **2gelb** *Adj.* yellow(y)-gold; *Wein: auch* golden; **~gewicht** *n* troy (weight)

Goldgräber *m; -s, -,* **~in** *f; -, -nen* gold digger; **~stimmung** *f fig.* goldrush mood (*od.* mentality)

Gold|grube *f* goldmine; *umg. fig. auch* moneyspinner, *Am.* cash cow; **~grund** *m Kunst:* gold (back)ground; **2haltig** *Adj.* auriferous, gold-bearing; **~hamster** *m* golden hamster

goldig *Adj. umg.* lovely, cute; (*auch nett*) sweet

Gold|junge *m umg.* **1.** blue-eyed boy, golden boy; **2.** *Sport* golden boy, gold medal(l)ist; **~käfer** *m Zool.* rose chafer; **~kettchen** *n* gold chain; **~kind** *n* (little) darling; **~klumpen** *m* gold nugget; **~krone** *f* **1.** *e-s Königs etc.:* golden crown; **2.** *Dent.* gold crown; **3.** *Münze:* gold crown; **~kurs** *m* price of gold; **~küste** *f; nur Sg.; Geog.* Gold Coast; **~legierung** *f* gold alloy; **~mädchen** *n umg.* **1.** golden girl; **2.** *Sport* golden girl, gold medal(l)ist; **~medaille** *f* gold medal

Goldmedaillen|gewinner *m,* **~gewinnerin** *f,* **~inhaber** *m,* **~inhaberin** *f* gold medal(l)ist

Gold|mine *f* goldmine; **~münze** *f* gold coin; **~papier** *n* gold foil; **2plattiert** *Adj.* gold-plated; **~plombe** *f Dent.* gold filling; **~rahmen** *m* gold (*od.* gilt) frame; **~rand** *m* gilt edge; *mit ~* gilt-edged; **~rausch** *m* gold fever; *hist.* gold rush; **~regen** *m* **1.** *Bot.* laburnum; **2.** *fig. von Einnahmen:* bonanza; *von Goldmedaillen:* shower of gold, crop of gold medals; **~reif** *m geh.* gold ring; *Armband:* gold bracelet; *im Haar:* gold circlet; **~reserve** *f Fin., Wirts.* gold reserves *Pl.*

goldrichtig *umg.* **I.** *Adj.* exactly (*od.* just) right; *Sache: auch* spot (*Am.* right) on; **II.** *Adv.* exactly (*od.* just) right; **~ handeln** do just the right thing

Gold|ring *m* gold(en) ring; **~schatz** *m* **1.** treasure of gold; **2.** *umg. fig.* darling; **~schmied** *m* goldsmith

Goldschmiede|arbeit *f* goldwork, goldsmith|ery (*od.* -ing); *konkret* piece of goldwork (*od.* goldsmith's work); **~kunst** *f* goldsmith|ery (*od.* -ing)

Gold|schnitt *m Buch:* gilt edge; *mit ~* gilt-edged; **~standard** *m* gold standard; **~staub** *m* gold dust; **~stickerei** *f* gold embroidery; **~stück** *n* **1.** gold coin; **2.** *umg. fig. Person:* gem, treasure; **~sucher** *m,* **~sucherin** *f* gold prospector; **~ton** *m* golden colo(u)r; **~tresse** *f* gold(en) braid; **2umrandet** *Adj.* gilt-edged, edged in gold; **~vorkommen** *n* gold deposits *Pl.*; **~vorrat** *m* gold reserves *Pl.*; **~waage** *f* gold balance (*od.* scales *Pl.*); *jedes Wort auf die ~ legen fig.* (*genau überlegen*) weigh every word; (*zu ernst nehmen*) take everything to heart; **~währung** *f Fin.* gold standard; **~waren** *Pl.* gold

articles, jewellery *Sg., Am.* jewelry *Sg.*; **~wert** *m* value in gold; (*Goldpreis*) price of gold; **~zahn** *m umg.* gold tooth

Golf¹ *m; -(e)s, -e; Geog.* gulf; **~ von Bengalen/Biskaya** Bay of Bengal/Biscay

Golf² *n; -s, kein Pl.; Sport* golf; **~ball** *m* golf ball

golfen *v/i. umg.* play golf; **Golfer** *m; -s, -,* **Golferin** *f; -, -nen* golfer

Golfklub *m* golf club

Golf|krieg *m hist.* (Persian) Gulf War; **~krise** *f* Gulf crisis, crisis in the Persian Gulf

Golf|mütze *f* golfing (*od.* golfer's) cap; **~platz** *m* golf course; *bes. an der Küste:* golf links *Pl.*; **~schläger** *m* golf club; **~spiel** *n* **1.** golf; **2.** *Partie:* game of golf; **~spieler** *m,* **~spielerin** *f* golfer

Golf|staaten *Pl. Geog.* Gulf States; **~strom** *m; nur Sg.* Gulf Stream

Goliath *m; -s, -s* **1.** *nur Sg.; bibl.* Goliath; **2.** *fig.* giant

Gondel *f; -, -n* **1.** *Boot:* gondola; **2.** *e-r Seilbahn etc.:* cable car; *e-s Ballons:* basket; *e-s Luftschiffs:* gondola; **~bahn** *f* cable railway, gondola (ski) lift, bubble lift *umg.*

gondeln *v/i. umg.:* **~ durch** (*fahren*) cruise around in

Gondoliere [gɔndo'liɛːrə] *m; -s, Gondolieri* gondolier

Gong *m; -s, -s* gong; *Sport* bell; **gongen** *v/i.* sound the gong; *unpers.:* **es gongt** there's the gong; **Gongschlag** *m:* **beim ~ ist es 6 Uhr** etwa at the first stroke it will be 6 a.m.

gönnen *v/t.:* **j-m etw. ~ 1.** (*Ggs. neiden*) not (be)grudge s.o. s.th.; **ich gönne es ihm** (*von Herzen*) I'm really glad for him, he deserves it; *iro.* (it) serves him right; **2.** (*zukommen lassen*) allow s.o. s.th.; **er gönnt sich keine Pause** he never stops for a minute; **ich gönn mir jetzt e-e kleine Pause / ein Gläschen** I think I deserve a little break / a little liquid refreshment now; **gönn dir doch mal e-n Urlaub** treat yourself to a holiday (*Am.* vacation) (- you deserve it); **gönn's ihm doch!** (go on,) let him; (*sei nicht so streng*) don't be so hard (on him); **er gönnt ihr kein gutes Wort** he hasn't (got) a good word to say to her, *Am. auch* he won't give her the time of day

Gönner *m; -s, -* patron; (*Wohltäter*) benefactor; **gönnerhaft** *Adj. pej.* patronizing; **er tut so ~** he's so patronizing, he has such a patronizing manner; **Gönnerin** *f; -, -nen* patron, patroness; (*Wohltäterin*) benefactor, benefactress; **Gönnermiene** *f pej.:* (*mit*) **~** (with a) patronizing air

Gonokokken *Pl. Med.* gonococci; **Gonorrhö(e)** [gɔnɔ'røː] *f; -, Gonorrhöen* gonorrh(o)ea

Goodwillbesuch [ˈgʊdwɪl-] *m* goodwill visit

gor *Imperf.* → **gären**

Gör *n; -(e)s, -en; bes. nordd. umg.* **1.** (*Kind*) kid; *pej.* brat; **2.** (*Mädchen*) *pej.* little madam

gordisch *Adj.:* **~er Knoten** *Myth., fig.* Gordian knot; **den ~en Knoten zerhauen** cut the Gordian knot

Göre *f; -, -n* → **Gör**

Gorgonenhaupt *n* **1.** *Myth.* gorgon's head; *Kunst auch* gorgoneion *fachspr.,* gorgon head (*auch fig.*); **2.** *Zool.* giant basket star

Gorilla *m; -s, -s; Zool.* gorilla (*auch*

umg. pej. Leibwächter)

Gosch, Gosche, Goschen *f; -, Goschen; Dial., mst pej.* trap; **halt die ~!** shut up! *umg.*; **e-e große ~ haben** *fig.* have a big mouth

Gospel *n, m; -s, -s; Mus.* gospel; **~sänger** *m,* **~sängerin** *f* gospel singer

goss *Imperf.* → **gießen**

Gosse *f; -, -n* **1.** gutter; **2.** *fig. pej.* gutter; *in der ~ enden od. liegen* land (*od.* end up) in the gutter; *sich in der ~ wälzen* wallow in depravity; *j-n od. j-s Namen durch die ~ ziehen* drag s.o.'s name through the mud (*od.* mire)

Gote *m; -n, -n* Goth

Gotik *f; -, kein Pl.* **1.** *Stil:* Gothic (style); **2.** *Epoche:* Gothic period

Gotin *f; -, -nen* Goth

gotisch I. *Adj.* Gothic; **~e Schrift** *Druck.* Gothic (type), black letter; **II. Gotisch** *n; -en; Ling.* Gothic; **das Gotische** Gothic

Gott *m; -es, Götter* **1.** *ohne Art., nur Sg.; Reli.* God; **~ der Herr** the Lord God; **der liebe ~** the good Lord; **~ der Allmächtige** God (*od.* the) Almighty; **gebe ~, dass ...** please God ...; **~ segne dich!** (God) bless you!; **da sei ~ vor!** *umg.* God (*od.* heaven) forbid!; **so wahr mir ~ helfe!** so help me God; **wie es ~ gefällt** as God wills; **so ~ will** *umg.* God willing; **hier ruht in ~** *auf Grab:* here lies; **was ~ zusammengefügt hat, das soll der Mensch nicht scheiden** *bei Trauung:* those whom God hath joined, let no man put asunder; → **Gnade** 2, **helfen** 4; **2.** *in Redewendungen:* **ach ~, als Füllsel:** well; **ach du lieber ~!** *od.* **allmächtiger, großer, guter, mein ~!** *od.* **~ im Himmel!** *od.* **o ~!** oh (my) God!, oh no!; *milder:* good Lord!, goodness!; *heavens above!*; **um ~es willen!** for God's (*od.* heaven's) sake!; **~ sei Dank!** *umg.* thank God (*od.* goodness, God, heaven); (*glücklicherweise*) *auch* fortunately; **leider ~es** *umg.* unfortunately; **~ sei's geklagt!** *umg.* worst (*Am.* bad) luck, unfortunately, alas; **~ hab ihn selig** God rest his soul; **es ist weiß ~ nicht einfach** *etc.* God knows it isn't easy *etc.*; **~ weiß, wo er steckt** *od.* **er steckt weiß ~ wo** *umg.* God (*od.* heaven) knows where he is; **um ~es Lohn** for nothing; **den lieben ~ e-n guten Mann sein lassen** *umg.* live for the day; **den lieben ~ spielen** *umg.* play God; **dem lieben ~ den Tag stehlen** *umg.* laze away the day; **wie ~ in Frankreich leben** *umg.* live the life of Riley, live (*od.* be) in clover; **wie ~ ihn/sie geschaffen hat** *hum.* (*nackt*) naked as the day he/she was born; **er kennt ~ und die Welt** he knows everyone there is to know; **über ~ und die Welt reden** talk about everything under the sun; → **behüten** 2, **Gnade** 2, **gnaden, grüßen** 1, **helfen** 4, **Wort** 2, 5; **3.** (*Gottheit*) god, deity; **der ~ des Krieges** the god of war; **ein Geschenk der Götter** a gift from the gods; **wie ein junger ~ spielen, tanzen** *etc.*: supremely well, like an angel; **das wissen die Götter** *umg.* God knows, don't ask me; **ein Bild für die Götter** *umg.* a sight for sore eyes

gott|ähnlich *Adj.* godlike; **~begnadet** *Adj.* gifted, inspired; **~behüte** *österr.,* **~bewahre** *Interj.* God (*od.* heaven) forbid

Gotterbarmen *n umg.:* **zum ~** (*Mitleid erregend*) pitiful(ly); (*sehr schlecht*)

abysmally

Götter|bild n statue (od. picture etc.) of a god, idol; **~bote** m messenger of the gods; **der ~** (Merkur) Mercury; (Hermes) Hermes; **~dämmerung** f; nur Sg. twilight of the gods, Götterdämmerung; **~gatte** m umg. hum.: **j-s ~** s.o.'s lord and master

gottergeben Adj. resigned (to one's fate), meek; (fromm) pious

Götter|geschlecht n (race of) gods Pl.; **~glaube** m belief in (the) gods; **Ọgleich** Adj. godlike, ... like a god; **~sitz** m Myth. seat (od. home) of the gods; **~speise** f; nur Sg. **1.** Myth. ambrosia; **2.** Gastr. jelly, Am. Jell-O®; **~trank** m nectar; **~vater** m Myth. father of the gods; **2.** Koll. the gods Pl.

Gottes|anbeterin f, -, -nen; Zool. praying mantis; **~beweis** m proof of the existence of God

Gottesdienst m (church) service; **am ~ teilnehmen** take part in the service; weitS. go to church; **~besucher** m, **~besucherin** f worship(p)er, member of the congregation

Gottesfurcht f fear of God; (Frömmigkeit) piety; **gottesfürchtig** Adj. God-fearing; pious

Gottes|gabe f gift of God; unverhoffte: godsend; **~geißel** f scourge of God; **~gericht** n → **Gottesurteil**; **~glaube** m belief in God; **~haus** n house of God, church; **~lamm** n; nur Sg. lamb of God

Gotteslästerer m, **Gotteslästerin** f blasphemer; **Gotteslästerung** f blasphemy

Gottes|lohn m: **für** od. **um ~** for charity; **~mutter** f; nur Sg. Mother of God; **~sohn** m; nur Sg. Son of God; **~staat** m theocracy; **~urteil** n trial by ordeal; **~wort** n Word of God

gott|gefällig Adj. geh. Leben etc.: godly; **~geweiht** Adj. dedicated to God; Boden etc.: consecrated; **~gewollt** Adj. divinely-ordained; **~gleich** Adj. godlike

Gottheit f deity, divinity; (Gott/Göttin) god/goddess

Göttin f; -, -nen goddess

Gottkönig m god-king; **Gottkönigtum** n; -s, kein Pl. divine kingship

göttlich Adj. **1.** divine; (e-m Gott ähnlich) auch godlike; **das Göttliche** the divine; **~e Ordnung** divine order; **2.** umg. fig. (herrlich) divine, heavenly; **ein ~er Anblick** a sight for sore eyes; **Göttlichkeit** f; nur Sg. divinity

gottlob Adv. thank God (od. goodness)

gottlos Adj. **1.** (Gott leugnend) godless; **2.** (verwerflich) ungodly; (sündhaft) sinful, wicked; **Gottlosigkeit** f; nur Sg. ungodliness, irreligion; (Sündhaftigkeit) wickedness

Gottseibeiuns m; -, kein Pl.; umg. euph. Old Nick

Gottvater (m); nur Sg.: **~(, Sohn und der heilige Geist)** God the Father(, the Son and the Holy Ghost [od. Spirit])

gott|verdammt Adj. umg. damn(ed), Am. auch goddam; **~vergessen** Adj. **1.** → **gottlos**; **2.** → **gottverlassen**; **~verlassen** Adj. umg. godforsaken

Gottvertrauen n faith in God; **du hast vielleicht ~!** you really are a trusting soul!

Götze m; -n, -n idol (auch fig.)

Götzen|altar m altar to an idol; **~bild** n idol; **~diener** m, **~dienerin** f idola-

tor; fig. worship(p)er; **~dienst** m; nur Sg. idolatry; **~ treiben** worship idols

Götzzitat n: **er antwortete mit dem ~** umg. he told him etc. where to go (od. put it)

Gouache [gu̯aʃ] f; -, -en; Kunst gouache

Gourmand [gur'mãː] m; -s, -s gourmand, gormandizer

goutieren [gu'tiːrən] v/t. geh. appreciate

Gouvernante [guvɛr'nantə] f; -, -n governess; **gouvernantenhaft** Adj. pej. schoolmarmish

Gouvernement [guvɛrnə'mãː] n; -s, -s **1.** hist. (Regierung) government; (Verwaltung) administration (by a governor); **2.** frz. (Bezirk) district; **Gouverneur** [guvɛr'nøːɐ̯] m; -s, -e governor

Grab n; -(e)s, Gräber grave; lit. (auch Grabmal) tomb; (Gruft) sepulch|re (Am. -er); **das Heilige ~** the Holy Sepulchre; **am ~** at the graveside; **zu ~e tragen** auch fig. bury; **ins ~ sinken** geh. fig. (sterben) go to the grave; **ein nasses** od. **feuchtes ~** od. **ein ~ in den Wellen finden** geh. go to a watery grave; **er nahm sein Geheimnis mit ins ~** he took his secret with him to the grave, his secret died with him; **bis ans** od. **ins ~** unto (od. till) death; **über das ~ hinaus** beyond the grave; **er bringt mich noch ins ~** umg. he'll be the death of me yet; **mit einem Bein** od. **Fuß im ~(e) stehen** fig. have one foot in the grave; **sich** (Dat.) **sein eigenes ~ graben** od. **schaufeln** fig. dig one's own grave; **sich im ~(e) umdrehen** fig. turn in one's grave; **~beigabe** f burial object

Grabbeltisch m umg. bargain counter

Grabeinfassung f grave surround

graben; gräbt, grub, hat gegraben **I.** v/i. dig (**nach** for); Tier: burrow; **II.** v/t. **1.** dig; (Loch) auch burrow; (Brunnen, Schacht) sink; Archit. (Fundament) dig out, excavate; **der Kummer hat tiefe Falten in ihr Gesicht gegraben** fig. care has worn (od. made) deep furrows in her face; **2.** (schneiden) carve (**in** + Akk. into); Tech. engrave, cut; **III.** v/refl.: **sich ~ in** (+ Akk.) Krallen, Räder, Zähne etc.: dig into; Kugel etc.: bury itself in; **sich j-m ins Gedächtnis ~** fig. engrave itself on s.o.'s memory

Graben m; -s, Gräben **1.** ditch; bes. Mil. trench; zur Entwässerung: drain, culvert; um Burg: moat; **e-n ~ ziehen** dig a ditch; **der Streit riss tiefe Gräben auf** (zwischen + Dat.) fig. the quarrel opened up deep rifts (between); **2.** Geol. rift valley; im Meer: trench; **~bruch** m Geol. rift valley; **~krieg** m trench war(fare)

Gräber|feld n burial ground, necropolis; **~fund** m grave find

Grabes|dunkel n geh. sepulchral darkness; **es herrschte ~** it was as dark as the tomb; **~kirche** f; nur Sg.: **die ~ in Jerusalem** the Church of the Holy Sepulch|re (Am. -er); **~rand** m geh. fig.: **am ~** on the edge of the grave, at death's door; **~stille** f deathly silence; **~stimme** f; nur Sg.; umg. sepulchral voice

Grab|geläut(e) n (death) knell (auch fig.); **~gesang** m funeral song, dirge; fig. dirge; **~gewölbe** n burial vault, crypt; **~hügel** m burial mound; **~inschrift** f inscription (on a od. the gravestone); geh. epitaph; **~kapelle** f funeral chapel; **~kreuz** n grave cross; **~legung** f kirchl., Kunst: **~ (Christi)**

the Entombment (of Christ); **~licht** n candle on a grave; **~mal** n tomb; (Ehrenmal) monument; → auch **Grab**, **Grabstein**; **~pflege** f looking after (od. care of) a grave od. graves; **~platte** f ledger; aus Marmor: auch marble slab; **~rede** f funeral address (kirchl. sermon); **~relief** n tomb relief; **~schänder** m, **~schänderin** f **1.** entweihend: desecrator of graves; **2.** räuberisch: grave robber; **~schändung** f **1.** desecration of graves; **2.** grave robbery

grabschen → **grapschen**

Grab|stätte f burial place; (Grab) grave, tomb; **~stein** m gravestone, tombstone; **~stelle** f → **Grabstätte**; **~stichel** m Tech. graving tool, chisel

gräbt → **graben**

Grabtuch n shroud

Grabung f excavation, Archäol. auch dig

Grabungs|arbeiten Pl. excavations; **~leiter** m, **~leiterin** f dig leader; **~stätte** f arch(a)eological site

Graburne f (funeral) urn

Gracht f; -, -en canal in a Dutch town

Grad m; -(e)s, - od. -e, bei ~angaben: - **1.** Temperatur: degree; **bei acht ~** at (a temperature of) eight degrees; **es sind acht ~** it's eight degrees, the temperature is eight degrees; **zwei ~ Wärme/Kälte** od. **plus/minus** od. **über/unter Null** two degrees above/below zero; **39 ~** (Fieber) **haben** have a temperature of 39 (Celsius) bzw. 102.2 (Fahrenheit); **2.** Math., Phys., Geog. etc.: degree; **Gleichung zweiten ~es** quadratic equation, equation of the second degree; **sich um 180 ~ drehen** turn through 180 degrees; fig. do a complete about-turn (od. U-turn); **3.** (Maß) degree; (Ausmaß) auch extent; **ein geringer/hoher ~ an** (+ Dat.) a slight/high degree of; **in hohem ~e** to a high degree, highly; (weitgehend) largely, to a great extent; **im höchsten ~e** extremely, highly; **in geringem ~e** slightly; **in dem ~e, dass ...** to such a degree that...; **bis zu e-m gewissen ~(e)** up to a point, to some extent; **4.** (Stufe) stage; Mil. rank; Univ. degree; Druck. size (of type), pointsize; **Verbrennung zweiten ~es** second-degree burn; **Vetter ersten/zweiten ~es** first/second cousin

grad(e) umg. → **gerade**

Gradeinteilung f graduation, scale; Geog. graticule

gradieren v/t. graduate; **Gradierung** f graduation

gradlinig → **geradlinig**

Grad|messer m; -s, - yardstick, measure, indication (+ Gen. of); **~netz** n Landkarte: grid; **~strich** m graduation (mark)

graduell I. Adj. gradual; Unterschied etc.: ... of degree; **II.** Adv. gradually, by degrees; verschieden: in degree

graduieren I. v/t. **1.** Univ. confer a degree on; **2.** Tech. graduate; **II.** v/i. Univ. graduate; **Graduierte** m, f; -n, -n; Univ. graduate; **Graduiertenförderung** f Univ. funding for postgraduates (od. postgraduate studies)

Gradunterschied m difference in degree

gradweise Adv. by degrees

Graecum n; -s, kein Pl.: **das ~ haben/machen** have passed / take an examination in Greek, usually in order to gain entrance to a particular university faculty

G

Graf¹ *m*; *-en*, *-en* count; *als Titel*: Count; *in GB*: earl; *der Herr ~ umg. iro.* his lordship

Graf², **Grafem** *etc.* → **Graph²**, **Graphem** *etc.*

Grafen|geschlecht *n* line of counts (*in GB*: earls); **~krone** *f* count's (*in GB*: earl's) coronet

Graffito *m,n*; *-(s)*, *Graffiti*, *mst Pl.* graffiti *Sg. od. Pl.*

Grafik *f*; *-*, *-en* **1.** *nur Sg.*; *Fach*: graphic arts *Pl.* (*auch Koll. Kunst*); *Wirts.* commercial art; *EDV* graphics *Pl*; *moderne ~ sammeln* collect modern graphic art; **2.** (*grafische Gestaltung*) layout, artwork; **3.** (*grafische Darstellung*) graph, diagram; *Kunst* print; **~beschleuniger** *m EDV* graphics accelerator; **~-Design** *n*; *nur Sg. Fach*: graphic design

Grafiker *m*; *-s*, *-*, **~in** *f*; *-*, *-nen* graphic designer, commercial artist

grafikfähig *adj.* **~ sein** *EDV* have graphics capabilities, be graphics-enabled

Grafik|format *n EDV* graphics format; **~karte** *f* graphics card (*od.* board); **~modus** *m* graphics mode; **~programm** *n* graphics program; **~speicher** *m* graphics memory; **~tablett** *n* graphics (*od.* digitizing) tablet

Gräfin *f*; *-*, *-nen* countess

grafisch I. *Adj.* graphic; **~e Darstellung** graph, diagram; **~e Gestaltung** layout, artwork; **II.** *Adv.* graphically

gräflich *Adj.* count's, countess's; *in GB*: earl's; of a count(ess), of an earl

Grafschaft *f* county

Grahambrot *n* wheatmeal (*Am.* whole-wheat) bread

gräko... *im Adj.* Gr(a)eco-...

Gral *m*; *-s*, *kein Pl.*, *Myth.*: *der Heilige ~* the (Holy) Grail

Grals|burg *f Myth.* Castle of the Grail; **~hüter** *m*, **~hüterin** *f* keeper of the Grail; *fig. auch* guardian; **~ritter** *m* Knight of the Grail

Gram *m*; *-(e)s*, *kein Pl.*; *geh.* grief, sorrow; *vor ~ vergehen* pine away

gram *Adj.*; *präd.*; *geh.*: *j-m ~ sein* nachtragend: bear s.o. a grudge; *verärgert*: be angry with s.o.

grämen *geh.* **I.** *v/refl.* (*trauern*) grieve (*über* + *Akk.* over); (*sich sorgen*) fret (about); *sich zu Tode ~* pine away, die of a broken heart; **II.** *v/t.* trouble *s.o.* (deeply)

gram|erfüllt *Adj. geh. Person*: grief-stricken; *Leben*: full of grief; **~gebeugt** *Adj. geh.* bowed down with grief

grämlich *Adj.* morose, surly

Gramm *n*; *-s*, *-* gram(me), *Am.* gram; *100 ~ Salami* 100 grams of salami

Grammatik *f*; *-*, *-en* **1.** grammar; **2.** *Buch*: grammar (book); **grammatikalisch I.** *Adj.* grammatical; **II.** *Adv.*: **~ richtig/falsch** grammatically correct/incorrect; **Grammatiker** *m*; *-s*, *-*, **Grammatikerin** *f*; *-*, *-nen* grammarian

Grammatik|fehler *m* grammatical mistake, mistake in (one's) grammar; **~regel** *f* rule of grammar, grammatical rule

grammatisch I. *Adj.* grammatical, grammar ...; **II.** *Adv.*: **~ richtig/falsch** grammatically correct/incorrect

Grammel *f*; *-*, *-n*; *österr. Gastr.* crackling

Grammofon, Grammophon® *n*; *-s*, *-e*; *hist.* gramophone, *Am.* phonograph

gramvoll *Adj. geh.* grief-stricken, sorrowful

Gran *n*; *-(e)s*, *-*; *fig.*: *kein ~ zu viel/wenig* not a jot too much/little; *ein ~ Wahrheit* a grain of truth

Granat *m*; *-(e)s*, *-e od. -* **1.** *Pl. -e*; *Min.* garnet; **2.** *Pl. -*; *Zool.* shrimp, prawn

Granatapfel *m Bot.* pomegranate

Granate *f*; *-*, *-n* **1.** *Mil.* shell; (*Handgranate etc.*) grenade; **2.** *umg. fig.* (*Bombenschuss*) screamer, scorcher, tremendous shot

Granat|feuer *n Mil.* shellfire, shelling; **~splitter** *m* piece of shrapnel; *Pl.* shrapnel *Sg.*; **~werfer** *m* (trench) mortar

Grande *m*; *-n*, *-n*; *hist.* grandee

Grandezza *f*; *-*, *kein Pl.* grandeur

Grandhotel ['grã:hotɛl] *n* luxury (*od.* five-star) hotel

grandios *Adj.* grand, magnificent; *umg. fig.* brilliant; **~er Auftritt** *auch* heroic performance

Grand Prix [grã'pri:] *m*; *- -*, *- -* [grã'pri:s] *bes. Sport* Grand Prix

Grandseigneur [grãsɛn'jø:ɐ] *m*; *-s*, *-s od. -e*; *geh.* grand seigneur, great lord

Granit *m*; *-s*, (*Arten*:) *-e*; *Min.* granite; *hart wie ~* hard as granite, rock hard; *auf ~ beißen fig.* bang one's head against a brick wall

Granit|felsen *m* granite rock; **~gebirge** *n* granite mountains *Pl.*; **~gestein** *n* granite (rock)

Granne *f*; *-*, *-n*; *Bot.* awn, beard, arista *fachspr.*

Grant *m*; *-s*, *kein Pl.*; *Dial.* grumpiness, anger, the hump; *e-n ~ haben* be in a bad mood, be grumpy, have (got) the hump; **granteln** *v/i. Dial. pej.* (*schlechte Laune haben*) be in a bad mood, be grumpy, have the hump; (*meckern, murren*) grumble; **grantig** *Adj. Dial.* grumpy, grouchy, crabby; **Grantler, Grantlhuber** *m*; *-s*, *-*; *Dial. pej.* crosspatch, grouch

granulär *Adj. fachspr.* granular; **Granulat** *n*; *-(e)s*, *-e* granules *Pl.*; **granulieren** *v/t.* granulate

Grapefruit ['gre:pfru:t] *f*; *-*, *-s*; *Bot.* grapefruit; **~saft** *m* grapefruit juice

Graph¹ *m*; *-en*, *-en*; *Math., Phys.* graph

Graph² *m*; *-s*, *-e*; *Ling.* graph

Graphem *n*; *-s*, *-e*; *Ling.* grapheme

Graphik *etc.* → **Grafik** *etc.*

Graphit *m*; *-s*, *-e*; *Min.* graphite; **2farben** *Adj.* dark grey (*Am.* gray)

Graphologe *m*; *-n*, *-n* graphologist; **Graphologie** *f*; *-*, *kein Pl.* graphology; **Graphologin** *f*; *-*, *-nen* graphologist; **graphologisch** *Adj.* graphological

grapschen I. *v/i. umg.* **1.** grab (*nach* at); **2.** (*fummeln*) grope; **II.** *v/t.*: (*sich* [*Dat.*]) *j-n/etw. ~* grab s.o./s.th.; *fig.* (*j-n*) grab

Gras *n*; *-es*, *Gräser* **1.** grass; **~ fressend** *Zool.* grass-eating; **2.** *umg. fig.*: *ins ~ beißen* bite the dust; *wo er hinhaut, da wächst kein ~ mehr* (*er hat e-n harten Schlag*) he packs a terrific punch; (*er ist ein grober Kerl*) he's like a bull in a china shop; *er hört das ~ wachsen* he reads too much into things; *über etw.* (*Akk.*) *~ wachsen lassen* let the dust settle (on s.th.)

grasbewachsen *Adj.* grassy

Grasbüschel *n* tuft of grass

grasen *v/i.* graze (*auch ~ lassen*)

Gras|fläche *f* patch of grass; (*Rasen*) lawn; **~fresser** *m*; *-s*, *-*; *Zool.* grass-eater

grasgrün *Adj.* **1.** bright green; **2.** *umg.* (*völlig unreif*) green

Gras|halm *m* blade of grass; **~hüpfer** *m* grasshopper

grasig *Adj.* grassy

Gras|land *n* grassland; **~mücke** *f Orn.* warbler; **~narbe** *f* turf, sod; **~platz** *m Tennis*: grass court; **~samen** *m* grass seed(s *Pl.*)

grassieren *v/i.* rage; *bes. Verbrechen*: be rife, be rampant; *Unsitte*: take hold; *Gerücht*: spread; **grassierend I.** *Part. Präs.* → **grassieren**; **II.** *Adj.* widespread; *stärker*: raging, rampant

grässlich I. *Adj.* horrible, terrible, awful (*alle auch umg. fig.*); (*scheußlich*) hideous; *Verbrechen*: *auch* heinous, atrocious; **II.** *Adv. umg.*: **~ faul** *etc.* terribly (*od.* incredibly) lazy *etc.*; **Grässlichkeit** *f* **1.** *nur Sg.* awfulness, atrociousness; (*Scheußlichkeit*) hideousness; *e-s Verbrechens*: heinousness; **2.** (*Untat*) terrible thing to do; *stärker*: atrocity

Gras|sode *f bes. nordd.* turf, sod; **~steppe** *f* grassy plains *Pl.*; *in heißen Zonen*: savanna(h); *in Nordamerika*: prairie; *in Südamerika*: the pampas

grasüberwachsen, grasüberwuchert *Adj.* overgrown with grass

Grat *m*; *-(e)s*, *-e* **1.** (*Bergrücken*) ridge; **2.** (*Kante*) (sharp) edge; *Tech.* bur(r); *starker*: flash; (*Gussnaht*) fin; **3.** *Archit.*, *am Dach*: arris; *im Gewölbe*: groin

Gräte *f*; *-*, *-n* (fish)bone; *j-m/sich die ~n brechen umg.* beat s.o. to a pulp / get smashed up pretty badly; **grätenlos** *Adj.* boneless

Gratifikation *f*; *-*, *-en*; *Wirts.* gratuity; *zu Weihnachten etc.*: bonus

grätig *Adj.* **1.** *Fisch*: full of bones; **2.** *umg. fig.* grumpy, crabby

gratinieren *v/t.* gratiné, gratinate

gratis I. *Adj.*: **~ sein** be free; **II.** *Adv.* free (of charge); for nothing; *als Dreingabe*: into the bargain

Gratis|aktie *f Wirts.* bonus share; **~beilage** *f* free supplement; **~exemplar** *n* free copy; **~vorstellung** *f* free showing

Grätsche *f*; *-*, *-n* **1.** straddle; *in die ~ gehen* do the splits; **2.** (*Sprung*) straddle vault; **3.** *Fußball*: sliding tackle; **grätschen** *vt/i.* **1.** straddle (*über* + *Akk.* s.th.); *im Spagat*: do the splits; → **gegrätscht** II; **2.** *Fußball*: do a sliding tackle (on)

Gratulant *m*; *-en*, *-en*, **~in** *f*; *-*, *-nen* well-wisher; **Gratulation** *f*; *-*, *-en* congratulations *Pl.* (*zu* on); **Gratulationscour** *f*; *-*, *kein Pl. geh.* reception in s.o.'s hono(u)r; **gratulieren** *v/i.* congratulate (*j-m zu etw.* s.o. on s.th.); *j-m zum Geburtstag ~* wish s.o. a happy birthday; *ich gratuliere!* congratulations; *da kannst du dir ~! umg. fig.* you can count yourself lucky; *iro.* you'll regret it

Gratwanderung *f* **1.** ridge walk; **2.** *fig.* tightrope walk; *sich auf e-r ~ befinden* be walking a tightrope

grau *Adj.* **1.** grey, *Am.* gray; **~ in ~** *Wetter*: dismal; **~ gestreift** grey- (*Am.* gray-)striped; **~ meliert** *Haar*: greying, *Am.* graying; grizzled; *Stoff etc.*: mottled grey (*Am.* gray); **~ werden** turn *od.* go grey (*Am.* gray); *ich lass mir darüber keine ~en Haare wachsen fig.* I'm not going to lose any sleep over it; **2.** *fig.* (*trostlos*) dark, gloomy; **~er Alltag** the daily grind; **~er Markt** (*halb legal*) grey (*Am.* gray) market; *für Flugtickets*: bucket shop system; *e-e ~e Maus* a mousy person; **~er Star** *Med.* cataract(s); *das ist alles ~e Theorie* it's all theory; **~ ist alle Theorie**

Sprichw. theory is dull and boring, all things theoretical are dull and apathetical; *in ~er Vorzeit* in the dim and distant past; *die ~en Zellen umg.* the little grey (*Am.* gray) cells, one's grey (*Am.* gray) matter; *in ~er Zukunft od. Ferne* in the (far) distant future; *er sieht od. malt alles ~ in ~* he's so negative about everything

Grau *n; -s, - od. umg. -s* **1.** grey, *Am.* gray; *ganz in ~ gekleidet* dressed all in grey (*Am.* gray); **2.** *fig.* greyness (*Am.* grayness)

grauäugig *Adj.* grey- (*Am.* gray-)eyed

Graubart *m umg.* (*alter Mann*) greybeard, *Am.* graybeard

graublau *Adj.* greyish- (*Am.* grayish-)blue

Graubrot *n Gastr.* mixed-grain bread

Graubünden (*n*); *-s; Geog.* Graubünden, Grisons; **Graubündner** *m; -s, -,* **Graubündnerin** *f; -, -nen* inhabitant of Graubünden (*od.* the Grisons); **graubündnerisch** *Adj.* Graubünden ..., Grisons ...

Gräuel *m; -s, -* horror; *Tat:* atrocity, outrage; *er/es ist mir ein ~* I loathe him/it; *~geschichte f,* *~märchen n* horror story; *~propaganda f* horror stories *Pl.*; *~tat f* atrocity

grauen[1] *vt/i.; unpers.: es graut mir od. mir od. mich graut vor* I shudder at the thought of; *vor e-r Prüfung etc.:* I dread, I'm dreading

grauen[2] *v/i. geh. Tag:* dawn, be dawning

Grauen[1] *n; -s, kein Pl.* dread, horror (*vor + Dat.* of); *~ empfinden vor* be horrified of, shudder at the thought of; *j-m ~ einflößen* fill s.o. with horror; *~ erregend* horrifying, horrific, ghastly, grisly; *vom ~ gepackt* seized (*od.* filled) with horror; *ein Bild des ~s* (*bieten*) (be) a horrific sight *od.* scene, (be) a scene of horror

Grauen[2] *n; -s, kein Pl.: beim ~ des Tages* at daybreak

grauenhaft, grauenvoll *Adj.* horrific, ghastly, gruesome; *umg. fig.* dreadful, terrible

Graugans *f Orn.* greylag (goose), *Am.* graylag (goose)

grauhaarig *Adj.* grey-haired, *Am.* gray-haired

Grau|kopf *m umg.* **1.** grey (*Am.* gray) head; **2.** *fig. Person:* grey- (*Am.* gray-)haired man (*bzw.* woman)

graulen *v/refl.* be scared (*vor + Dat.* of), dread (s.th.); *unpers.* → *auch* **grauen**[2]; **II.** *v/t.: aus dem Haus ~* drive s.o. out of the house

gräulich[1] *Adj. Farbton:* greyish, *Am.* grayish

gräulich[2] *Adj.* → **grässlich**

Graumarktpreis *n Flug.* bucket-shop price

Graupe *f; -, -n* **1.** barley; **2.** *Bergb.* grain

Graupel *f; -, -n, mst Pl.; Met.* (soft) hail, *Am.* sleet (*beide auch Pl.*); **graupeln** *v/i. unpers.: es graupelt* it's hailing (*Am.* sleeting); **Graupelschauer** *m* hail, *Am.* sleet (*beide auch Pl.*)

Graureiher *m Orn.* grey (*Am.* gray) heron

Graus *m; -es, kein Pl.* horror, dread; *es ist ein ~* it's horrible; *das/er ist mir ein ~* I can't stand it/him

grausam I. *Adj.* **1.** cruel (*zu od. gegen*[*über*] to); **2.** *umg.* (*schlimm*) terrible, awful; **II.** *Adv.* cruelly *etc.;* → I; *~ zu Tode kommen* die a horrible death; **Grausamkeit** *f* **1.** *nur Sg.* cruelty;

2. (*Gräueltat*) atrocity

Grau|schimmel *m* **1.** *Pferd:* grey (horse), *Am.* gray (horse); **2.** *Pilz:* grey (*Am.* gray) rot; *~schleier m* **1.** *vor den Augen:* grey (*Am.* gray) haze; **2.** *in der Wäsche:* greyness, *Am.* grayness

grauschwarz *Adj.* grey(ish)-black, *Am.* gray(ish)-black

grausen I. *vt/i., unpers.: es graust mir od. mich od. mir graust vor* (+ *Dat.*) I shudder at the thought of; *vor e-r Prüfung etc.:* I dread, I'm dreading; *vor Schlangen etc.:* I'm terrified of; **II.** *v/refl.* → I

Grausen *n; -s, kein Pl.* horror; *sich mit ~ abwenden* turn away in horror; *da kann man das große od. kalte ~ kriegen umg.* it's enough to give you the creeps (*od.* heebie-jeebies)

grausig *Adj.* → **grauenhaft**

Grau|tier *n umg., hum.* donkey; *~ton m* shade of grey (*Am.* gray); *~wal m Zool.* (Californian) grey (*Am.* gray) whale; *~zone f fig.* grey (*Am.* gray) area, twilight zone

Graveur [gra'vøːɐ̯] *m; -s, -e, ~in f; -, -nen* engraver

gravieren *v/t.* engrave

gravierend I. *Part. Präs.* → **gravieren;** **II.** *Adj. geh. Fehler, Irrtum etc.:* serious, grave; *Unterschied etc.:* significant

Gravierung *f* engraving

Gravis ['graːvɪs] *m; -, -; Ling.* grave (accent)

Gravitation *f; -, kein Pl.; Phys.* gravitation, gravity

Gravitations|feld *n* gravitational field; *~gesetz n* law of gravity

gravitätisch I. *Adj. auch iro.* solemn, grave; **II.** *Adv.: ~* (*einher*)*schreiten* stride solemnly (into)

Gravur *f; -, -en* engraving

Grazie *f; -, -n* **1.** *nur Sg.* grace(fulness); *mit ~* → **graziös** II; **2.** *mst Pl.; Myth.: die drei ~* the three Graces; **3.** *fig. hum. od. iro.* (*Frau*) beauty, belle

grazil *Adj.* delicate(ly built); (*biegsam*) willowy; *Kunst etc.:* delicate; graceful

graziös I. *Adj.* graceful; **II.** *Adv.* gracefully; *auch fig.* elegantly

Greenpeace|-Aktion ['griːnpiːs-] *f* campaign by Greenpeace

Greenwicher ['grɪnɪdʒɐ] *Adj.: ~ Zeit* Greenwich (Mean) Time

gregorianisch *Adj.* **1.** *Mus.; Choräle, Gesänge:* Gregorian; **2.** *~er Kalender* Gregorian calendar

Greif *m; -(e)s, -e od. -en, -en* **1.** *Myth.* griffin; **2.** *Orn.* bird of prey, raptor *fachspr.*

Greif|arm *m Zool.* tentacle; *Tech.* grip(per) arm; *~bagger m* grab dredger

greifbar I. *Adj.* **1.** (*auch in ~er Nähe*) handy, within easy reach; **2.** *fig. Ergebnisse, Vorteile:* tangible; (*konkret*) *auch* concrete; (*offenkundig*) obvious; *er ist nie ~* you just can't get hold of him; *~e Gestalt annehmen* assume a definite form; *in ~e Nähe rücken Termin etc.:* get closer (and closer); (*möglich werden*) become a distinct possibility; *e-e Lösung schien in ~er Nähe* a solution seemed close at hand; **3.** (*verfügbar*) available; *Ware: auch* in stock; **II.** *Adv.: ~ nahe auch fig.* within reach, within touching distance

greifen; *greift, griff, hat gegriffen* **I.** *v/t.* **1.** take; *fest:* grasp; (*packen*) grab (hold of); *umg.* (*j-n*) grab; **2.** *Mus.* (*Ton, Akkord*) play; **3.** *fig.: aus dem Leben gegriffen* taken from life; *das ist* (*völlig*) *aus der Luft gegriffen*

that's something he's *etc.* just plucked out of the air, that's (completely) off the top of his *etc.* head; *das ist* (*fast*) *mit Händen zu ~* it's glaringly obvious; *sich* (*Dat.*) *j-n ~ umg.* (*bestrafen*) show s.o. what's what; (*tadeln*) tell s.o. what's what (*od.* a thing or two); *um ihm Aufgaben zu übertragen:* grab s.o., get hold of s.o.; *j-n ~ umg.* (*Dieb etc.*) nab (*Am. auch* nail) s.o.; **II.** *v/i.* **1.** reach (*in + Akk.* into; *hinter + Akk.* behind; *unter + Akk.* under); *an den Hut etc. ~* touch; *sich* (*Dat.*) *an die Stirn etc. ~* clutch one's brow (*od.* forehead *etc.*); *ins Leere ~* miss, grab thin air; *in die Saiten/Tasten ~ umg.* strike up a tune (on the guitar/piano *etc.*); *~ nach* reach for; *hastig:* snatch at; *klammernd:* clutch at; *mit beiden Händen ~ nach fig.,* nach e-r Gelegenheit *etc.:* jump at, grab *umg.;* *um sich ~* reach about ; *tastend:* grope (*od.* feel) around; *fig. Unsitte etc.:* spread, proliferate; *~ zu* reach for; *fig. zu List etc.:* resort to; *zu Alkohol, Droge etc.:* take to; *zu den Waffen ~* take up arms; *Volk: auch* rise in arms; *zu e-m Buch etc. ~* pick up a book *etc.;* *zum Äußersten ~ fig.* go to extremes; *es war zum Greifen nah* it was (*bzw.* seemed) so close you could almost touch it; *Erfolg etc.* it was within easy reach; → *Feder* 3, *Flasche* 1, *Strohhalm, Tasche* 2; **2.** *Bremse, Reifen, Zange etc:* grip; **3.** *fig.* (*zu wirken beginnen*) (begin to) take effect; (*wirksam sein*) be effective; (*ankommen*) catch on

Greifer *m; -s, -* **1.** *Tech.* gripping device; (*Klaue*) claw; *Bagger, Kran:* grab; **2.** *Sl.* (*Polizist*) cop *umg.*

Greif|fuß *m Zool.* prehensile foot; *~reflex m Med.* gripping reflex; *~vogel m* bird of prey, raptor *fachspr.*; *~werkzeuge Pl. Zool.* prehensile organs; *~zange f:* (*e-e*) *~* (a pair of) tongs *Pl.*

greinen *v/i. umg. pej., Kind:* grizzle, *Am.* whine; *Erwachsener:* whinge, *Am.* kvetch

Greis *m; -es, -e* old man

greis *Adj. geh.* old; (*grau*) grey, *Am.* gray; *er schüttelte sein ~es Haupt iro.* he shook his wise old head

Greisenalter *n: im ~* as an old man, at a ripe old age

greisenhaft *Adj.* aged, very old, geriatric *umg.;* (*altersschwach*) senile (*auch Med.*); *mit ~em Aussehen* with the look of an old (*od.* woman); **Greisenhaftigkeit** *f; -, kein Pl.* agedness, aged look; senility, dotage

Greisin *f; -, -nen* old woman (*od.* lady)

Greißler *m; -s, -, ~in f; -, -nen; österr.* grocer

grell I. *Adj.* **1.** *Farbe:* garish, loud, very bright; **2.** *Ton:* shrill, piercing; **3.** (*blendend hell*) dazzling, glaring; *Licht: auch* harsh; **4.** *fig. Kontrast etc.:* stark; **II.** *Adv.: ~ gegen etw. abstechen* form a glaring contrast to s.th., stick out like a sore thumb against s.th. *umg.;* *~ beleuchtet* blindingly bright, glaring; **grellbunt** *Adj.* gaudy; **Grellheit** *f; nur Sg.* **1.** *e-r Farbe:* garishness, loudness; **2.** *e-s Tons:* shrillness, piercing quality; **3.** *e-s Lichts:* glare, harshness; **grellrot** *Adj.* bright red

Gremium *n; -s, Gremien* committee; (*Körperschaft*) body

Grenz|abfertigung *f* passport control and customs clearance; *~abschnitt m* sector (of a frontier); *~aufsicht f* border surveillance; *~bahnhof m* frontier station; *~beamte m, ~beamtin f* border official; **~befestigungen** *Pl.* frontier fortifications; **~belastung** *f Tech.* critical load; **~bereich** *m* **1.** border area; **2.** (*Zwischenzone*) intermediate zone; **3.** (*äußerste Grenze*) limits *Pl.*; **~bereinigung** *f*, **~berichtigung** *f* frontier revision; **~bevölkerung** *f* borderers *Pl.*; **~bezirk** *m* border district

Grenze *f*; -, -n **1.** *zwischen Gebieten etc.*: boundary, border; *zwischen Ländern*: border (*zu od. nach* with), frontier; *e-e natürliche ~ bilden zwischen* (*Dat.*) form a natural frontier between; *Burghausen liegt an der österreichischen ~* Burghausen lies on the Austrian border; → *grün* 5; **2.** *fig.* (*Trennlinie*) border(line), (dividing) line; (*Begrenzung, Schranken*) limit(s *Pl.*); **~n** *der Bescheidenheit, des Möglichen etc.*: bounds; *obere/untere ~* upper/lower limit; *äußerste ~* furthest (*Am. auch* farthest) limit; *an der ~* on the borderline; *es ist hart od. noch an der ~ umg.* it's pushing it (a bit); *in ~n* within bounds; *in ~n bleiben od. sich in ~n halten* keep within (reasonable) bounds (*od.* limits); (*erträglich sein*) be tolerable; *alles hat s-e ~n* there's a limit to everything; *s-e ~n kennen* know one's limitations; *keine ~n kennen od. alle ~n übersteigen* know no bounds; *der Applaus kannte keine ~n* the applause just wouldn't stop; *~n setzen od. stecken* set limits (+ *Dat.* to); *dem sind nach oben keine ~n gesetzt* there's no upper limit, the sky's the limit *umg.*; *die ~n (des Erlaubten, Erträglichen) überschreiten* go too far, overstep the mark; *e-e (scharfe) ~ ziehen* draw a (sharp) line; *ohne ~n* → *grenzenlos*

grenzen *v/i.*: *~ an* (+ *Akk.*) **1.** border on; *Garten etc.*: *auch* be right next to, adjoin, abut (on); **2.** *fig.* border on, verge on, come close to, be little short of

grenzenlos I. *Adj.* **1.** *Ebene*: boundless, endless; *Weite*: immeasurable; **2.** *fig. Freude, Leid etc.*: boundless, unbounded, … that knows no bounds; (*unermesslich*) immeasurable; *Geduld*: infinite, limitless; *Macht, Reichtum*: unlimited; *Dummheit etc.*: incredible; *ins Grenzenlose gehen* be endless, be never-ending; **II.** *Adv.* (*unermesslich*) immeasurably; *~ glücklich* deliriously happy; *j-n ~ lieben* love s.o. with all one's being; **Grenzenlosigkeit** *f*; *nur Sg.* boundlessness, immensity

Grenzer *m*; -s, - **1.** *Beamte*: border guard; **2.** *Anwohner*: borderer

Grenzerin *f*; -, -nen; *umg.* → *Grenzer*

Grenz|fall *m* borderline case; **~fläche** *f* interface; **~fluss** *m* river forming a border; **~gänger** *m*, **~gängerin** *f* **1.** *Arbeiter, Schüler etc.*: cross-border commuter; *illegaler*: illegal border crosser; (*Schmuggler*) smuggler; **2.** *fig.* (*Musiker etc.*) crossover artist; **~gebiet** *n* **1.** border area; **2.** *zwischen Fachgebieten*: interdisciplinary subject; **~kämpfe** *Pl.* border fighting *Sg.*; **~konflikt** *m* border dispute; **~kontrolle** *f* border control; **~n** re-laxation of border controls; **~krieg** *m* border war(fare); **~land** *n* **1.** border area; *hist. in USA*: frontier; **2.** (*Nachbarland*) bordering country; **~lehre** *f Tech.* limit ga(u)ge; **~linie** *f* **1.** border; *Pol.* demarcation line; **2.** (*Trennlinie*) dividing line; **3.** *Sport* line; **~mauer** *f* boundary wall

grenznah *Adj.* close to the border

Grenz|öffnung *f* opening of a (*od.* the) border; **~ort** *m* border (*Am. hist.* frontier) town (*od.* village); **~pfahl** *m* boundary post; **~polizist** *m*, **~polizistin** *f* border policeman (*bzw.* policewoman); **~posten** *m* border guard; **~punkt** *m* limit

Grenz|schutz *m* **1.** *Schutz der Grenze*: frontier protection; **2.** *Koll., Truppen*: border guard(s); **~schützer** *m*, **~schützerin** *f umg.* border guard

Grenz|situation *f* borderline situation; **~stadt** *f* border (*Am. hist.* frontier) town; **~station** *f* frontier station; **~stein** *m* boundary stone; **~streitigkeiten** *Pl.* border disputes; **~übergang** *m* **1.** border crossing point; **2.** (*Übertritt*) border crossing

grenzüberschreitend *Adj.* **1.** *Handel, Verkehr etc.*: cross-border …; international; **2.** *Probleme etc.*: of international significance; **Grenzüberschreitung** *f*

Grenz|übertritt *m* border crossing; **~verkehr** *m*: (*kleiner*) ~ (local) border traffic; **~verlauf** *m* border(line); **~verletzung** *f* border violation; **~wache** *f* border guard; **~wert** *m* **1.** limit, threshold value; **2.** *Math.* limit; **~winkel** *m* critical angle; **~wissenschaft** *f* intermediate science; **~ziehung** *f*; *nur Sg.* setting (of) a boundary, drawing (of) a borderline; **~zoll** *m* customs duty; **~zwischenfall** *m* border incident

Gretchenfrage *f the* big question, *the* sixty-four thousand dollar question *umg.*

Greuel, greulich → *Gräuel, gräulich²*

Greyerzer ['grai̯ɛrtsɛ] *m*; -s, -; *Gastr., Käse*: Gruyère

Grieben *Pl. Gastr.* greaves, *bes. Am.* crackling *Sg.*

Grieche *m*; -n, -n **1.** Greek; **2.** *umg.* Greek restaurant; *zum ~n gehen* go to a Greek place; **Griechenland** (*n*); -s; *Geog.* Greece

Griechin *f*; -, -nen Greek, Greek woman (*od.* girl)

griechisch I. *Adj.* Greek; *Archit. und Kunst auch* Grecian; **II. Griechisch** *n*; -en, *kein Pl.*; *Ling.* Greek; *das Griechische* Greek

griechisch|-orthodox *Adj.* Greek Orthodox; **~römisch** *Adj.* Gr(a)eco-Roman

grienen *v/i. nordd.* → *grinsen*

Griesgram *m*; -(e)s, -e; *pej.* (old) grouch; **griesgrämig** *Adj. pej.* grumpy, grouchy, crabby

Grieß *m*; -es, *Sorten:* -e **1.** *Gastr.* semolina; **2.** (*Sand*) grit; **3.** *Med.* gravel; **4.** *TV* graininess; *bei m* semolina

grießig *Adj.* **1.** *TV, Bild:* grainy; **2.** *Med., Harn etc.:* sabulous

Grieß|kloß *m*, **~klößchen** *n*, **~nockerl** *n südd., österr., Gastr.* semolina dumpling

griff *Imperf.* → *greifen*

Griff *m*; -(e)s, -e **1.** *mit der Hand, zum Halten:* grip; *zum Ergreifen:* grasp (*nach* at); *schneller:* snatch (at); *klammernd:* clutch (at); (*Handgriff*) movement (of the hand); *Turnen:* grip; *Ringen etc.:* hold; *Bergsteigen:* (hand)hold; *Mus.* (*Fingerstellung*) fingering; *Blasinstrumente:* stop; (*Akkord*) chord; *fester ~* firm grip; *sicherer ~* sure touch; *mit einem ~* with one swift movement; *fig.* in no time; *e-n ~ in die Kasse tun umg.* put one's fingers (*od.* hand) in the till; *bei ihr sitzt jeder ~* she's good with her hands; **2.** *fig.*: *e-n guten ~ tun* make a good choice,

strike it lucky (*mit* with); *e-n schlechten ~ tun* make a bad choice, pick the wrong man *etc.*; *im ~ haben* have got-(ten *Am.*) the hang of; (*unter Kontrolle haben*) have *s.th.* under control; (*Person, Tier, Thema etc.*) *auch* have a good grip on; *~ nach der Macht* attempt to seize power; *der ~ zur Flasche/Droge* taking to the bottle / to drugs; **3.** *von Koffer, Messer etc.*: handle; (*Knauf, Knopf*) knob; *von Pistole:* butt; *von Schwert:* hilt; → *Türgriff etc.*; **4.** *von Stoff etc.*: feel

griffbereit I. *Adj.* handy; **II.** *Adv.*: *~ liegen* be (*od.* lie) ready to hand

Griffbrett *n Mus.* fingerboard

Griffel *m*; -s, - **1.** slate pencil; *hist., Tech.* stylus; **2.** *Bot.* pistil; **3.** *umg. pej.* (*Finger*): *nimm deine ~ weg* take your (dirty) paws (*od.* mitts) off

griffig *Adj.* **1.** *~ sein Werkzeug etc.*: handle (*od.* hold) well; *Reifen, Fahrbahn etc.*: have a good grip; *Stoff:* have a good feel; **2.** *Mehl:* coarse-grained; **3.** *fig. Schlagwort etc:* catchy; **Griffigkeit** *f*; *nur Sg.*; *Mot.* grip, traction

Griff|loch *n Mus.* fingerhole; **~wechsel** *m Turnen:* change of grip

Grill *m*; -s, -s **1.** grill; *im Freien* barbecue; *… vom ~* grilled …, barbecued …; **2.** → *Kühlergrill*

Grille *f*; -, -n **1.** *Zool.* cricket; **2.** *fig.* silly idea; *~n fangen* mope; *~n im Kopf haben* be full of silly ideas; *j-m ~n in den Kopf setzen* put ideas into s.o.'s head

grillen I. *v/t.* grill, *Am. auch* broil; *im Freien* barbecue; **II.** *v/i.* (have a) barbecue; **III.** *v/refl. umg.*: *sich in der Sonne ~* roast in the sun

grillenhaft *Adj.* **1.** (*seltsam*) strange; *Person: auch* eccentric; **2.** (*launisch*) moody; (*mürrisch*) grumpy *umg.*

Grill|fest *n* barbecue; **~fleisch** *n* **1.** (*Gegrilltes*) grilled meat; **2.** *zum Grillen:* meat for grilling; **~gut** *n*; *nur Sg.* grills *Pl.*; **~kohle** *f* charcoal; **~rost** *m* grill, rack; **~spieß** *m* spit

Grimasse *f*; -, -n grimace, face; **~n schneiden** pull (*Am.* make) faces; **Grimassenschneider** *m*, **Grimassenschneiderin** *f* face-puller; **grimassieren** *v/i.* grimace, pull (*Am.* make) a face

Grimm *geh. altm. m*; -(e)s, *kein Pl.* wrath, fury; **grimm** *Adj.* → *grimmig*; **Grimmdarm** *m Anat.* colon

Grimmen *n*; -s, *kein Pl.* im Bauch, Darm: colic, griping pains *Pl.*

grimmig I. *Adj.* **1.** *Blick, Gesicht, Lachen etc.*: grim; *Angriff, Blick, Gegner etc.*: fierce; (*schlecht gelaunt*) in a bad mood; **2.** *Kälte, Schmerzen etc.*: severe; **II.** *Adv.* grimly *etc.*; → I; *~ dreinschauen* look grim; *~ kalt* bitterly cold; **Grimmigkeit** *f*; *nur Sg.* **1.** e-r *Person*: grimness, fierceness; **2.** des *Winters etc.*: harshness, severity

grimmsch... *Adj.*; *nur attr.*: *~e Märchen* Grimm's fairy tales

Grind *m*; -(e)s, -e **1.** *Dial. auf Wunde*: scab; **2.** *umg. am Kopf etc.*: scurf; *Vet.* mange; *Bot.* scurf; **3.** *Sl.* (*Kopf*) nut; **grindig** *Adj.* scabby

grinsen I. *v/i.* grin; *spöttisch*: smirk; *stärker*: sneer (*über* + *Akk.* at); **II. Grinsen** *n*; -s, *kein Pl.* grin; *höhnisches*: sneer; *dir wird das Grinsen schon noch vergehen umg.* I'll *etc.* wipe that grin off your face(, don't you worry)

grippal *Adj. Med.*: *~er Infekt* influenza

Grippe f; -, -n; Med. influenza, flu; umg. (Erkältung) cold; **~epidemie** f flu epidemic; **~impfung** f flu vaccination; **~kranke** m, f flu-sufferer, person with (the) flu; **~mittel** n flu remedy; **~welle** f flu epidemic

Grips m; -es, nur Sg.; umg. brains Pl., Brit. auch nous; **streng d-n ~ an** use your brains (od. common sense)

Grisli, Grizzly ['grɪsli] m; -s, -s grizzly

grob; gröber, am gröbsten **I.** Adj. **1.** Feile, Filter, Gesichtszüge, Stoff etc.: coarse; (rau) auch rough; (unverarbeitet) raw, crude; (unfertig) unfinished; **2.** Kies, Sand etc.: coarse-grained; ~ **gemahlen** Kaffee, Mehl: coarse-ground; **3.** (ungefähr) Schätzung, Skizze: rough; **~e Entfernung** approximate distance; **in ~en Zügen** very roughly; **4.** Arbeit etc.: rough, heavy; **sie haben ein Mädchen fürs Grobe** they've got a girl (od. maid) to do the dirty jobs; **5.** pej. Person, Benehmen: coarse; (ungehobelt) uncouth; (roh) very rough, brutal; (unhöflich, beleidigend) rude; (geradeheraus) bluff, blunt; (ordinär) crude; ~ **sein** physisch: be rough; ~ **werden** be rude (**gegen** to), get offensive (toward[s]); **6.** (schlimm) serious, major; Jur. gross; **~e Fahrlässigkeit** gross negligence; **~er Fehler** od. Schnitzer grave mistake, blunder; **~e Lüge** downright (od. flagrant) lie; **~er Unfug** public nuisance, breach of the peace; → **gröber, gröbst...**; **II.** Adv. coarsely etc.; → I; ~ **gerechnet** roughly, at a rough estimate; ~ **geschätzt** at a rough guess; ~ **umreißen** give a rough outline of; **j-m ~ kommen** be rude to s.o., get offensive towards s.o.; ~ **fahrlässig** Jur. grossly negligent

gröber Komp. → **grob**

grobfaserig Adj. coarse-fibred (Am. fibered); Holz: coarse-grain(ed)

Grobheit f **1.** nur Sg. coarseness; roughness; crudeness; → **grob** I; **2.** fig. (grobes Benehmen) rudeness; **~en** abuse

Grobian m; -s, -e boor

grob|klotzig Adj. clumsy, hamfisted; **~knochig** Adj. big-boned

grobkörnig Adj. coarse-grained; Fot. grainy

gröblich geh. **I.** Adj.; nur attr. gross; **II.** Adv.: **j-n ~ beleidigen/vernachlässigen** grossly insult/neglect s.o.

grobmaschig Adj. wide-meshed

grobschlächtig Adj. pej. uncouth

Grobschnitt m Tabak: coarse cut

gröbst... Sup. coarsest; roughest; **der ~e Dreck** the worst of the dirt; **aus dem Gröbsten heraus sein** be out of the wood(s); bei Arbeit etc.: have broken the back of it; **j-n aufs Gröbste** od. **~e beleidigen/vernachlässigen** insult/neglect s.o. in the grossest possible way; → **grob**

Grog m; -s, -s hot grog

groggy ['grɔgi] Adj.; nur attr. umg. whacked, pooped

grölen vt/i. umg. pej. bellow; Menge: roar; (Lied) auch bawl out

Groll m; -(e)s, kein Pl.; geh. ranco(u)r, resentment; (eingewurzelter Hass) animosity; **e-n ~ gegen j-n hegen** bear a grudge against s.o.; **grollen** vli. geh. **1.** Donner etc.: rumble; **2.** j-m ~ bear s.o. a grudge; **er grollt seit Tagen** he's been like a bear with a sore head for days

Grönland (n); -s; Geog. Greenland

Grönländer¹ m; -s, -, **~in** f; -, -nen Greenlander

Grönländer², **grönländisch** Adj. Greenland ...; Greenlandic, from Greenland; **Grönlandwal** m Zool. Greenland whale

grooven ['gruːvn] v/i. Mus. umg.: **das groovt** it's grooving

Gros¹ [grɔs] n; -ses, -se; Wirts. gross; **fünf ~ Eier** five gross of eggs

Gros² [groː] m; - [groː], - [groːs], mst Pl.; the vast (od. great) majority

Groschen m; -s, - **1.** hist. österreichischer: groschen; **2.** hist. umg. deutscher: ten-pfennig piece, ten pfennigs Pl. (V. mst im Sg.); **3.** umg. fig.: **sich ein paar ~ dazuverdienen** earn a bit of pocket money (on the side); **der ~ ist gefallen!** the penny has dropped; → auch Pfennig; **~blatt** n umg. rag; **~grab** n hum. one-armed bandit; **~heft** n, **~roman** m penny dreadful, Am. dime novel

groß; größer, am größten **I.** Adj. **1.** big (bes. gefühlsbetont); Haus, Fläche etc.: large; Land: vast; Baum, Gebäude etc.: (hoch) tall; (riesig) huge; Person: tall; **Großer Bär** od. **Wagen** Astron. Great Bear, Ursa Major fachspr.; **ein ~es Gebäude** a big(, tall) building; **der Große Ozean** Geog. the Pacific (Ocean); **die Großen Seen** Geog. the Great Lakes; **~e Zehe** big toe; **~er Buchstabe** capital letter; **Gut mit ~em G** good with a capital G; ~ **machen/müssen** Kinderspr. do / have to do big jobs; **2.** an Ausmaß, Intensität, Wert etc.: great; Fehler, Lärm, Unterschied etc.: auch big; Entfernung: great, long; Geschwindigkeit: high; Hitze, Kälte, Schmerzen etc.: intense; Kälte: auch severe; Verlust: heavy; Wissen: extensive, wide; (tief) profound; Mus., Intervall, Terz: major; Angeber, Angsthase, Feigling etc.: terrible, dreadful; (auf) ~ **stellen** (Heizung, Herd etc.) set on high, turn up; **~es Bier** large one, Brit. etwa pint, Am. 16 ouncer; **wir waren zu Hause e-e ~e Familie** we were a large family; **~e Ferien** summer holiday(s), long vacation; **zu m-r ~en Freude** to my great joy (od. pleasure); **~es Geld** umg. (Scheine) notes Pl., Am. bills Pl.; (viel Geld) a lot of money; **~es Glück haben** be very lucky; **~en Hunger haben** be very hungry; stärker: be starving; **~e Pause** long (mid-morning) break; **ein Fest im ~en Rahmen** a celebration on the grand scale; **~e Schritte machen** make great progress; **zum ~en Teil** largely, for the most part; **x ist größer als 10** Math. x is greater than 10; → **Liebe** 2, **Mode** 1; **3.** mit Maßangabe: **wie ~ ist er?** how tall is he?; **er ist ...** he's ... (tall); **das Grundstück ist 600 m²** ~ is 600 met|res (Am. -ers) square; **das Zimmer ist drei mal fünf Meter ~** is five met|res (Am. -ers) square (od. each way); **gleich ~** Personen: the same height, as tall as each other; Flächen, Kleidungsstücke etc.: the same size; **so ~ wie ein Fußballfeld** the size of a football pitch (Am. soccer field); **x ist größer als 10** Math. x is greater than 10; **4.** (erwachsen) grown-up; (älter) big; ~ **werden** Kinder: grow up; **zu ~ werden für** outgrow s.th., get too big for; **er ist nur ein ~es Kind** he's just a big baby; **Groß und Klein** young and old; standesmäßig: high and low; **5.** fig. Augenblick, Entdeckung, Erfolg, Tag, Tat etc.: great; (bedeutend) major, important; (großartig) grand, magnificent; Pläne, Ziele: great, grand,

big; Künstler, Dichter etc.: great; **~e Politik** national (bzw. international) politics, the political big time umg.; **Friedrich der Große** Frederick the Great; **Karl der Große** Charlemagne; **~e Reden schwingen** iro. talk big; **6.** (allgemein, wesentlich) broad, general; **die ~e Linie verfolgen** follow the main lines, stick to the basic (od. broad) principles; **den ~en Zusammenhang erkennen** see the big picture; **im ~en Ganzen** overall; **7.** umg. (gut): **im Rechnen ist sie ganz ~** od. **~e Klasse** she's really good (od. she's brilliant) at arithmetic; **ich bin kein ~er Tänzer** etc. I'm not much of a dancer etc.; **ich bin kein ~er Freund von Partys/Suppe** I'm not a great one for parties/soup, I'm not particularly fond of parties/soup; **8.** (edel): **ein ~es Herz haben** have a noble (od. generous) heart; **9.** (aufwändig) Empfang, Fest etc.: big, lavish; **in ~er Aufmachung** Bericht etc.: prominently featured, splashed across the page; Person: in full dress; → **Auge** 2, **Bahnhof** 2, **Glocke** 1, **Große¹**, **Große²**, **größer**, **größt...**; **II.** Adv. **1.** big; ~ **gebaut** od. **gewachsen** Person: big; ~ **gedruckt** in large letters (od. print); ~ **gemustert** with a large pattern; ~ **kariert** large-checked; **er sah mich nur ~ an** he just stared at me; ~ **und breit dastehen** umg., unübersehbar: stand out, stärker: stick out like a sore thumb; ~ **geschrieben werden** fig. rank very high, be a high priority, be considered very important; (begehrt sein) be very much in demand; → **großschreiben**; **2.** (aufwändig): ~ **angelegt** Aktion etc.: large-scale, full-scale; ~ **ausgehen** umg. have a real night out; **j-n/etw. ~ herausbringen** umg. pull out all the stops for s.o./s.th., give s.o./s.th. a tremendous build-up; **3.** umg.: ~ **angeben** talk big; um einzuschüchtern: throw one's weight around (od. about); ~ **auftreten** act big; **4.** (edel) denken, handeln etc.: nobly; **5.** (gut): ~ **in Form** in great form; **ganz ~ dastehen** (Erfolg haben) do brilliantly; **6.** umg.: **er kümmert sich nicht ~ darum** he doesn't really bother about it; **was ist schon ~ dabei?** so what?, Am. auch (so) what's the big deal?; **was gibt's da noch ~ zu fragen?** is there really anything more we need to ask?; **was kann das schon ~ kosten?** it can't be very expensive, can it?

Groß-... im Subst., mit Städtenamen: Greater ...; **Groß-Berlin** Greater Berlin

Groß|abnehmer m Wirts. bulk buyer; **~aktion** f major (od. large-scale) campaign od. operation; **~aktionär** m, **~aktionärin** f major shareholder; **~alarm** m red (od. major) alert

groß angelegt → **groß** II 2

Großangriff m Mil. major offensive, all-out attack; Flug. major airraid

großartig **I.** Adj. **1.** tremendous, great; (ausgezeichnet) auch excellent; brilliant; (wunderbar) wonderful, magnificent; (spektakulär) grand; **du warst ~!** you were tremendous (od. just great); **~e Idee!** great idea!; **2.** pej. (großspurig) pompous; **II.** Adv. **1.** greatly; ~ **amüsieren** have a great time; **sie haben ~ gespielt** they played really well; **2.** pej.: ~ **tun** put on airs; **Großartigkeit** f; nur Sg. greatness; (Vortrefflichkeit) excellence, brilliance; (Prächtigkeit) splendo(u)r, magnificence

Groß|aufnahme f Fot., Film: close-up (shot); **~auftrag** m Wirts. large-scale order; **~äugig** Adj. big-eyed, wide-eyed; **~bank** f; Pl. -banken big (od. major) bank; **~bauer** m, **~bäuerin** f (big) farmer; **~baustelle** f major building site; **~betrieb** m large concern (Agr. farm)

Großbildkamera f large-format camera

Großbildschirm m large-format screen

groß|blätt(e)rig Adj. Pflanze: large-leaved, with large leaves; **~blumig** Adj. Muster: with large flowers

Großbrand m big fire, blaze, conflagration

Großbritannien (n); -s; Geog. Great Britain; **großbritannisch** Adj. British

Großbuchstabe m capital (letter); Druck. uppercase letter

Großbürger m, **~in** f member of the upper middle class; **großbürgerlich** Adj. upper middle class; **Großbürgertum** n upper middle class(es Pl.)

Großcomputer m mainframe (computer)

großdeutsch Adj. hist. pan-German; der **~e** Gedanke Pan-Germanism

Großdruckausgabe f large-print edition

Große¹ m, f; -n, -n 1. die **~n** der Welt / des Films the great ones of this world (od. oft iro. the great and the good) / the big names in the film industry (Am. in Hollywood od. motion pictures); 2. Pl. (Erwachsene) grown-ups; 3. (ältestes Kind) our etc. eldest, oldest; unser **~r** wird nächsten Monat zehn our eldest will be ten next month

Große² n; -n, kein Pl. 1. **~s** great things (od. deeds) Pl.; es hat sich nichts **~s** ereignet nothing important happened; 2. im **~n** (im großen Maßstab) on a large scale, large-scale ...; Wirts. kaufen etc.: wholesale, (in) bulk; im **~n** und Ganzen by and large, on the whole; im **~n** wie im Kleinen at all levels

Größe f; -, -n 1. size; (Fläche) area; (Ausdehnung) dimensions Pl.; (Geräumigkeit) spaciousness; (Weite) vastness; (Körpergröße, Höhe) height; e-s Gefäßes: capacity; (Rauminhalt) volume; der **~** nach aufstellen: according to height (bzw. size); sortieren: by size; von mittlerer **~** medium-sized; Person: of medium height; dieselbe **~** haben be the same size (Person: height); in voller **~** full-size, weitS. (as) large as life; 2. zahlen-, mengenmäßig: size; (Menge) quantity; (Größenordnung) order; (Ausmaß) extent; Astron. magnitude; 3. von Kleidung, Schuhen: size; welche **~** haben od. tragen Sie? what size do you take?; 4. e-s Künstlers, e-r Kultur etc.: greatness; (Bedeutsamkeit) significance; (Wichtigkeit) importance; e-s Vergehens: enormity; 5. charakterlich: greatness; (Edelhaftigkeit) nobility; **~** zeigen od. beweisen show greatness; 6. (berühmte Person) celebrity, important figure; bes. iro. worthy; Theat., Sport star; Wissenschaftler: authority; politische **~** political heavyweight; e-e vergangene **~** a has-been, a late great; 7. Math., Phys. quantity; (un)bekannte **~** (un)known quantity

Groß|einkauf m 1. e-n **~** machen do a big shop; 2. Wirts., Vorgang: bulk buying; Gekauftes: bulk purchase; **~einsatz** m large-scale (od. major) operation; **~** der Polizei large police deploy-

ment

Großeltern Pl. grandparents

Größenangabe f indication of size

Großenkel m, **~in** f great-grandson/ /great-granddaughter; Pl. great-grandchildren

Größen|klasse f size; **~ordnung** f order (of magnitude) (auch Astron.); Unternehmen etc. von dieser **~** of that scale

großenteils Adv. largely, to a great extent

Größen|unterschied m difference in size (bzw. height); **~verhältnis** n ratio; (Proportionen) proportions Pl., dimensions Pl.; (Maßstab) scale

Größenwahn(sinn) m pej. megalomania, delusions Pl. of grandeur; **größenwahnsinnig** Adj. megalomaniac

größer Komp. 1. bigger, larger; Person: taller; er ist um e-n Kopf **~** als sie he's a head taller than her; der **~e** Teil most of it (od. them); 2. (ziemlich groß) quite big, considerable, major; in **~em** Umfang on a larger (bzw. considerable) scale; es wird dir keine **~en** Probleme bereiten it won't present you with any major problems; → **groß**

größer(e)nteils Adv. largely, for the most part, to a large extent

Groß|erzeuger m, **~erzeugerin** f large-scale producer (od. manufacturer); **~fahndung** f dragnet operation; **~familie** f 1. kinderreich: large family; 2. Soziol. extended family

großflächig Adj. 1. extensive; 2. Gesicht: wide

Großflughafen m international (od. major) airport

Großformat n large size; Fot. etc. large format; **großformatig** Adj. large-format ...

Groß|fürst m grand duke; **~fürstentum** n grand duchy; **~fürstin** f grand duchess

großfüttern v/t. (trennb., hat); umg. bring up

Großgarage f 1. big garage; öffentliche: (underground) car park (Am. parking garage); 2. Werkstatt: major service station

groß| gedruckt, ~ gemustert, ~ gewachsen → **groß** II 1

Großgrund|besitz m large estate(s Pl.); **~besitzer** m, **~besitzerin** f big landowner

Großhandel m Wirts. wholesale trade (od. trading); (Großmarkt) wholesaler's, wholesale store; im **~** (ver)kaufen: wholesale, (in) bulk

Großhandels|geschäft n Wirts. 1. Vorgang, Firma: wholesale business; 2. Laden: wholesaler's, wholesale store; **~kauffrau** f, **~kaufmann** m wholesaler; **~rabatt** m bulk discount

Großhändler m, **~in** f Wirts. wholesaler

großherzig Adj. geh. magnanimous; **Großherzigkeit** f; nur Sg.; geh. magnanimity

Großherzog m, **Großherzogin** f grand duke/duchess; **großherzoglich** Adj. grand-ducal; **Großherzogtum** n grand duchy

Großhirn n Anat. cerebrum; **~rinde** f cerebral cortex

Groß|industrie f Wirts. big industry; **~industrielle** m, f Wirts. big industrialist, tycoon umg.; **~inquisitor** m kath. Grand Inquisitor, Inquisitor General

Grossist m; -en, -en, **~in** f; -, -nen Wirts. wholesaler

großkalibrig Adj. large-calib|re (Am. -er) ...

Groß|kampftag m umg. fig. tough (od. hard) day; **~kapital** n high finance, big business; Koll. big capitalists (od. financiers) Pl.

groß kariert → **groß** II 1

Groß|katze f Zool. big cat; **~kind** n schw. grandchild; **~klima** n macroclimate; **~konzern** m big concern

Großkopferte m, f; -n, -n; umg. pej. bigwig, bes. Am. big shot

großkotzig umg. pej. I. Adj. Person: full of o.s.; Sache: flashy; II. Adv.: **~** daherreden blow one's own trumpet; **Großkotzigkeit** f; nur Sg.; umg. pej. self-importance e-r Sache: flashiness

Groß|kraftwerk n large(-scale) power station (od. plant); **~kredit** m large-scale credit; **~küche** f large kitchen; weitS. canteen; **~kunde** m big customer; **~kundgebung** f mass rally; **~kundin** f big customer; **~leinwand** f im Kino: big screen

Großmacht f Pol. great power; (Supermacht) superpower

Großmacht|politik f Pol. superpower politics Pl.; **~stellung** f position of power

Großmama f Kinderspr. grandma, granny; als Anrede: Grandma, Granny

Großmannssucht f; er leidet unter **~** he desperately wants to be somebody (od. Mr Big od. a big shot)

Groß|markt m 1. für Wiederverkäufer etc.: wholesale market (od. store); 2. (großes Einkaufszentrum) large supermarket, Brit. auch hypermarket; **~maschig** Adj. wide-meshed; **~mast** m Naut. mainmast

Großmaul n umg. pej. loudmouth; **großmäulig** Adj. umg. pej. loud-mouthed

Groß|meister m, **~meisterin** f Schach: grand master; **~mogul** m hist. Grand (od. Great) Mogul

Großmut f; -, kein Pl. magnanimity, largess(e); **großmütig** Adj. magnanimous

Großmutter f 1. grandmother; sie ist (zum zweiten Mal) **~** geworden she's become a grandmother (for the second time); das kannst du d-r **~** erzählen! umg. you can tell that to the marines!; nach **~s** Art Gastr. like grandma (od. granny) used to make, grandmère ...; 2. (alte Frau) granny; **großmütterlich** Adj. 1. Erbe, Haus etc.: one's grandmother's; 2. fig. Güte etc.: grandmotherly

Groß|neffe m great-nephew; **~nichte** f great-niece; **~offensive** f major offensive; **~onkel** m great-uncle; **~packung** f large (od. economy) pack; **~papa** m Kinderspr. grandpa; als Anrede: Grandpa

großporig Adj. large-pored

Groß|rat m, **~rätin** f schw. member of the Grand Council of a canton

Großraum m metropolitan area, conurbation; der **~** München the Munich area, Munich and its surrounding areas; **~büro** n open-plan office; **~flugzeug** n wide-bodied jet, wide-body

großräumig Adj. 1. (geräumig) spacious; Flugzeug: wide-bodied; 2. Anbau, Planung etc.: extensive; 3. ortskundige Fahrer werden gebeten, den Stau **~** zu umfahren etwa motorists (Am. auch drivers) are advised to keep well away from the congested area

G

G

Großraum|limousine f Mot. stretch limousine; **~wagen** m Eisenb. open--plan carriage

Groß|razzia f large-scale raid (umg. swoop); **~rechner** m mainframe (computer); **~reinemachen** n umg. big clean-up, big cleaning-up session; bes. im Frühjahr: spring-clean(ing session); fig. purge

großschnauzig, großschnäuzig Adj. umg. pej. loudmouthed

großschreiben v/t. capitalize; **schreibt man das groß?** does that have a capital (letter)?; → auch **groß** II 1; **Großschreibung** f capitalization; **für Namen gilt (die) ~** names begin with capital letters

Groß|segel n Naut. mainsail; **~sender** m high-power transmitter (weitS. broadcasting station)

Großsprecher m pej. loudmouth; **Großsprecherin** f pej. loudmouth; **großsprecherisch** Adj. pej. loudmouthed

großspurig Adj. pej. boastful, full of o.s.; (überheblich) overbearing, high and mighty; (wichtigtuerisch) pompous, pretentious; **Großspurigkeit** f; nur Sg.; pej. boastfulness; (Überheblichkeit) overbearingness; (Wichtigtuerei) pomposity, pretentiousness

Großstadt f (big) city, Am. big city; (Weltstadt) metropolis; **Großstädter** m, **Großstädterin** f (big-)city dweller, city slicker pej.; **großstädtisch** Adj. urban, (big-)city …

Großstadt|dschungel m fig. urban jungle; **~kind** n 1. city child; 2. → **Großstadtmensch**; **~lärm** m big-city noise, noise (od. hubbub) of the (big) city; **~leben** n (big-)city life, life in the city; **~mensch** m (big-)city dweller, Am. auch urbanite, city slicker pej.; **~rummel** m bustling city life (od. life of the city), hubbub of the city; **~verkehr** m (big-)city traffic, traffic in the cities

größt… Sup. biggest, largest; Person: tallest; **der ~e Teil** the largest part; (Mehrheit) the majority; **mit dem ~en Vergnügen** with the greatest of pleasure; **~er gemeinsamer Teiler** Math. highest common denominator; **das ist für mich das Größte** umg. it's the greatest as far as I'm concerned; **du bist der/die Größte!** umg. you're the greatest!; → **groß**

Großtante f great-aunt

Groß|tat f great feat; **~teil** m a large part, the majority, the bulk (+ Gen. of); **ein ~** (+ Gen.) much of; **der ~** (+ Gen.) most of; **zum ~** for the most part; **zu e-m ~** largely

großteils Adv. largely

größtenteils Adv. mostly, for the most part; (hauptsächlich) mainly, chiefly; **die Anwesenden waren mir ~ unbekannt** the people there were unknown to me for the most part, I didn't know most of the people there

Größtmaß n 1. maximum (size); Passung: maximum limit; 2. → **Höchstmaß**

größtmöglich Adj. greatest possible; Sorgfalt, Vorsicht etc.: the utmost

Großtuer m; -s, -; umg. pej. show-off; **Großtuerei** f; -, kein Pl.; umg. pej. showing off; **Großtuerin** f; -, -nen; umg. pej. show-off; **großtuerisch** Adj. umg. pej. boastful; **großtun** (unreg., trennb., hat -ge-); pej. **I.** v/i. act big, show off; **II.** v/refl.: **sich mit etw. ~** show s.th. off; verbal: brag about s.th.

Groß|unternehmer m big businessman; **~unternehmerin** f big businesswoman

Großvater m 1. grandfather; **er ist (zum zweiten Mal) ~ geworden** he has become a grandfather (for the second time); 2. (alter Mann) old man; 3. **unsere Großväter** (Ahnen) our forebears; **großväterlich** Adj. 1. Erbe, Haus etc.: one's grandfather's; 2. fig. Güte etc.: grandfatherly; **Großvateruhr** f grandfather clock

Groß|veranstaltung f big event; bes. Pol. mass rally; **~verbraucher** m, **~verbraucherin** f bulk consumer; **~verdiener** m, **~verdienerin** f big (--income) earner; **~versuch** m large--scale test (od. experiment)

Großvieh n cattle and horses Pl.; **~einheit** f Agr. livestock unit

Großwetterlage f general weather situation; fig. general situation

Großwild n big game; **~jäger** m, **~jägerin** f big-game hunter

großziehen v/t. (unreg., trennb., hat) bring up, raise

großzügig I. Adj. 1. generous; **geh mit dem Geld/Platz etc. nicht zu ~ um** don't be too generous with the money/space etc.; 2. Ansichten, Charakter etc.: liberal, broadminded; (alles erlaubend) permissive; 3. Anlage, Planung etc.: large-scale, generous; (weiträumig) spacious; **II.** Adv. generously etc.; → I; **Großzügigkeit** f; nur Sg. (Freigebigkeit) generosity; (Toleranz) liberality, broadmindedness; (von Planung) bold conception (od. design)

grotesk Adj. grotesque; (extrem) auch gross; (lächerlich) absurd; **Groteske** f; -, -n 1. Lit. grotesque; 2. Archit., Kunst grotesque(rie); 3. fig. farce

Grotte f; -, -n grotto

grotten… im Adj. od. Adv. Sl. (sehr) mega; **~doof** thick (as two short planks, Am. as a board); **~schlecht** mega-bad(ly)

Groupie ['gru:pi] n; -s, -s; Sl. groupy

Growian m; -(e)s, -e od. f; -, -en; Abk. (große Windenergieanlage) wind farm

grub Imperf. → **graben**

Grubber m; -s, -; Agr. grubber

Grübchen n Wange etc.: dimple

Grube f; -, -n 1. pit; (Höhlung) hollow; (Loch) hole; Falle: trap, pitfall; **j-m e-e ~ graben** fig. set (up) a trap for s.o.; 2. Bergb. pit, mine; mit Kohle: auch colliery, Am. coal mine; **in die ~ einfahren** go down the pit (od. mine); 3. altm. (offenes Grab) grave; **in die ~ fahren** go to the grave

Grübelei f; -, -en; auch Pl. brooding; **grübeln** v/i. brood (über + Akk. over, about); **~ über ein akademisches Problem etc.:** brood over; **ins Grübeln kommen** start brooding

Gruben|arbeiter m, **~arbeiterin** f Bergb. miner; **~bahn** f pit railway, Am. mine railroad; **~gas** n mine gas, firedamp; **~lampe** f miner's lamp; **~schacht** m mineshaft; **~unglück** n mining accident (od. disaster), pit disaster; **~wehr** f mine rescue team

Grübler m; -s, -, **~in** f; -, -nen broody person; (Denker) reflective person; **grüblerisch** Adj. brooding, broody; (nachdenklich) introspective

grüezi Adv. schw. umg. hello, hi

Gruft f; -, Grüfte; geh. tomb; (Krypta) crypt; poet. grave; **Grufti** m; -s, -s; Jugendspr. 1. Person über 30: crumbly, wrinkly; 2. Jugendlicher: etwa goth

grummeln v/i. umg. 1. Person: mum-

ble; 2. Donner etc.: rumble

grün Adj. 1. green; **die Ampel ist ~** the lights are green, it's green; **die Grüne Insel** (Irland) the Emerald Isle; **~er Salat** lettuce; **~e Versicherungskarte** Mot. green card; **~e Weihnachten** snow-free Christmas; **~ und blau schlagen** umg. beat s.o. black and blue; → **Minna** 1, **Welle** 7; 2. (unreif) green, unripe; fig. Person: green, (still) wet behind the ears; **die Bananen etc. sind noch zu ~** aren't ripe yet; **~er Junge** greenhorn; 3. (nicht getrocknet) Holz: green, unseasoned; Erbsen etc. green, fresh; (nicht konserviert) Heringe etc.: fresh; **Aal** ~ stewed eel; 4. Pol. green, eco-friendly; **~er Punkt** green dot, on packaging to indicate that a charge for disposal has been paid; **~ wählen** vote green; 5. fig.: (noch) im **~en Bereich** umg. (still) all clear; **~e Grenze** open border; **~e Hölle** (Urwald) jungle; **j-m ~es Licht geben** give s.o. the green light (od. go-ahead od. umg. thumbs up); **~ vor Neid** green with envy; **ach du ~e Neune!** umg. well I'm blowed (Am. I'll be darned), strike me pink altm.; **~er Star** Med. glaucoma; **auf der ~en Wiese** greenfield …, on a greenfield site; **sich ~ und blau ärgern** umg. be livid, get really worked up; **ich komme auf keinen ~en Zweig** umg. I'm just not getting anywhere; **sie ist mir nicht ~** umg. she doesn't like me; → **Tisch** 4, **Witwe** 1

Grün n; -s, - od. umg. -s 1. green (auch Blätter, Golfplatz); **die Ampel steht auf ~** the lights are green; **bei ~** at green; **das ist dasselbe in ~** umg. fig. it's six of one and half a dozen of the other; 2. Kartenspiel, Spielfarbe: spades; Karte: spade **~ sticht** spades are trump(s)

grün-alternativ Adj. Pol. green alternative

Grünanlage f park; (Grünfläche) green

grün|äugig Adj. green-eyed; **~blau** Adj. greenish-blue

Grünbuch n Pol., der EU: green paper

Grund m; -(e)s, Gründe 1. nur Sg.; (Boden) ground; (Grundbesitz) land, property; (Bauplatz) plot, Am. lot; **~ und Boden** land, property; 2. nur Sg.; von Gewässern, Gefäßen etc.: bottom; lit. e-s Tales: floor; **auf ~ geraten** od. laufen run aground; **den ~ unter den Füßen verlieren** auch fig. get out of one's depth; **ein Glas bis auf den ~ leeren** geh. drain a glass (to the dregs); 3. nur Sg.; Archit. (Fundament) foundations Pl.; 4. nur Sg.; (Hintergrund) background; (Grundierung) priming (coat); **grün auf gelbem ~** green on a yellow ground; 5. nur Sg.; fig.: **den ~ legen für** od. **zu** lay the foundations of (od. for); **e-r Sache auf den ~ gehen** get to the bottom of s.th.; **im ~e s-s Herzens** at (the bottom of his) heart; **von ~ aus** od. **auf** completely, … through and through; **im ~e (genommen)** basically, (eigentlich) really; **in ~ und Boden reden, spielen:** into the ground; verdammen: outright; blamieren: utterly; schießen, stampfen: to pieces; 6. (Vernunftgrund) reason (zu + Inf. to + Inf., for + Ger.); (Ursache, Anlass) auch cause (für of); (Beweggrund) motive; (Argument) argument; **Gründe für und wider** arguments for and against, the pros and cons; **Gründe anführen** state one's case (für for); **aus diesem ~** that's (od. that was) why, for this reason; **aus**

G

welchem ~*?* why?; *mit* (*gutem*) ~ with good reason; *ohne jeden* ~ for no apparent reason; *nicht ohne* ~ not without reason; *ein* ~ *mehr zu* (+ *Inf.*) all the more reason to (+ *Inf.*); *ich habe m-e Gründe dafür* I have my reasons; *es besteht* (*kein* / *nicht der geringste*) ~ *zu der Annahme, dass ...* there is (no / not the slightest) reason to suppose that ...; *kein* ~ *zur Besorgnis* no need to get worried, there's no cause for concern; **7.** *auf* ~, *zu* ~*e* → *aufgrund, zugrunde*
Grund... *im Subst.* (*grundlegend*) basic ...
grund... *im Adj.* really ..., thoroughly ...
Grundakkord *m Mus.* basic chord
grundanständig *Adj.* thoroughly decent
Grund|anstrich *m* first coat(ing); ~**ausbildung** *f Mil.* basic training; ~**ausstattung** *f* basic equipment; ~**baustein** *m* **1.** basic component; **2.** *Phys. etc.* elementary particle; ~**bedarf** *m* basic needs (*od.* requirements) *Pl.*; ~**bedeutung** *f* primary (*od.* basic) meaning; ~**bedingung** *f* basic condition; ~**begriff** *m* **1.** basic concept; **2.** ~*e* (*Grundkenntnisse*) basics
Grund|besitz *m* property, real estate; (*Immobilien*) immovables *Pl.*; ~**besitzer** *m*, ~**besitzerin** *f* landowner
Grund|bestandteil *m* basic component; ~**betrag** *m* basic sum
Grundbuch *n Jur.* land register; ~**amt** *n* land registry; ~**eintrag** *m* entry in the land register
grundehrlich *Adj.* absolutely honest
Grund|eigenschaft *f* (*Charakteristikum*) basic (*od.* fundamental) characteristic; *wichtige Funktion etc.*: essential aspect (*od.* quality); ~**eigentum** *n* → *Grundbesitz*; ~**eigentümer** *m*, ~**eigentümerin** *f* → *Grundbesitzer*; ~**einheit** *f* fundamental unit; ~**einkommen** *n* basic income; ~**einstellung** *f* basic attitude (*od.* outlook)
gründeln *v/i. Ente etc.*: dabble
gründen I. *v/t.* **1.** (*Klub, Partei, Staat*) found; (*einrichten*) establish, set up; (*schaffen*) create; *Wirts.* (*Gesellschaft*) form, found; (*Geschäft*) start (up), set up; (*einleiten*) launch; *e-e Familie* ~ (marry and) settle down; (*Kinder haben*) start a family; *e-n* (*eigenen*) *Hausstand* ~ set up house; **2.** *etw.* ~ *auf* (+ *Akk.*) base (*od.* found) s.th. on; **II.** *v/i. Verdacht etc.*: ~ *auf* (+ *Dat.*) be based on; **III.** *v/refl.*: *sich* ~ *auf* (+ *Akk.*) be based on
Gründer *m*; -*s*, - founder; (*Schöpfer*) originator, creator; *Wirts.* founder, promoter
Grunderfahrung *f* basic experience
Gründerin *f*; -, -*nen* → *Gründer*
Gründer|jahre *Pl. hist.*, *the latter part of the nineteenth century in German history, from 1871 on, characterized by rapid industrial expansion and a grandiose and eclectic architectural style*; ~**vater** *m* founding father
Grunderwerb *m Jur.* acquisition of land; **Grunderwerb(s)steuer** *f* land transfer tax
grundfalsch *Adj.* absolutely (*od.* completely) wrong
Grund|farbe *f* **1.** primary colo(u)r; **2.** (*Grundanstrich*) first coat; ~**fehler** *m* basic *od.* fundamental mistake (*od.* error); ~**festen** *Pl. fig.* foundations; *an den* ~ *des Staates etc. rütteln* rock the foundations of the state *etc.*; ~**fläche** *f*

1. *e-r Wohnung etc.*: (floor) area; **2.** *Math.* base; ~**form** *f* **1.** (*Hauptform*) basic form; (*Urform*) original form; **2.** *Ling.* infinitive; ~**freiheiten** *Pl. Pol.* (basic) civil rights, basic freedoms
Grund|gebühr *f* basic charge, flat rate; ~**gedanke** *m* basic (*od.* fundamental) idea; ~**gefühl** *n* basic (*od.* essential) feeling
Grundgehalt[1] *m* basic content
Grundgehalt[2] *n* basic salary
Grund|gesetz *n* **1.** basic law; **2.** *Pol.*: *das* ~ (*abgek.* **GG**) the (German) constitution; ~**größe** *f* **1.** *Grundstück*: plot size; **2.** *Math., Phys.* fundamental quantity; ~**haltung** *f* basic attitude
Grundherr *m*, ~**in** *f hist.* lord of the manor; **Grundherrschaft** *f als Landbesitzsystem*: manorial system, manorialism; *die* ~ *ausüben* be (the) lord of the manor (*über* + *Akk.* of)
Grundidee *f* basic idea
Grundieranstrich *m* priming coat; *Farbe*: primer; **grundieren** *vt/i. Malerei*: ground; *Tech. mst* prime; (*Holz, Papier*) stain; **Grundierung** *f* **1.** *Anstrich*: priming coat; *Farbe*: primer; *Spachtelmasse*: filler; **2.** *nur Sg.*; (*das Grundieren*) priming
Grund|irrtum *m* fundamental error; ~**kapital** *n Wirts.* capital stock; ~**kenntnisse** *Pl.* basic knowledge *Sg.* (*in* + *Dat.* of), basics; ~**kosten** *Pl.* basic cost *Sg.*; ~**kurs** *m* basic (*od.* beginners') course
Grundlage *f* **1.** basis; *gesetzliche* ~ legal basis, basis in law; *auf der* ~ *von* (*od.* + *Gen.*) on the basis of; *die* ~ *bilden für* form the basis of, be (*od.* constitute) the basis for; *die* ~*n schaffen od. legen für* lay the foundations for; *jeder* ~ *entbehren* be completely unfounded; **2.** ~*n* (*Grundbegriffe*) fundamentals, basics; **3.** *umg., fig. für Alkohol etc.*: blotting paper, *Am.* stomach lining; **Grundlagenforschung** *f* basic research
Grundlasten *Pl.* **1.** *Jur.* property taxes; **2.** *hist.* feudal dues
grundlegend I. *Adj.* basic, fundamental; (*wichtig*) essential; *Änderungen*: fundamental, radical; **II.** *Adv.* fundamentally
gründlich I. *Adj.* **1.** thorough; (*sorgfältig*) *auch* careful; (*erschöpfend*) complete; *e-e* ~*e Arbeit* a thorough (*od.* painstaking) piece of work; ~*e Kenntnisse haben in* (+ *Dat.*) be well-grounded in; **2.** *Irrtum*: complete, total; **II.** *Adv.* **1.** thoroughly *etc.*; *sich* ~ *vorbereiten* prepare o.s. well; *er hat s-e Sache* ~ *gemacht* he's done a very thorough job; *iro.* he's made a thorough job of it; *j-m* ~ *die Meinung sagen* give s.o. a piece of one's mind; **2.** *umg.* (*sehr*) properly; *sich* ~ *blamieren* make a real (*umg.* right, proper, *Am.* complete, total) fool of oneself; ~ *danebengehen* go completely wrong; (*die Wirkung verfehlen*) fall totally flat; *da hast du dich* ~ *getäuscht* you're very much mistaken there; **Gründlichkeit** *f*; *nur Sg.* thoroughness; carefulness
Grundlinie *f* **1.** *Math.* base; **2.** *Sport* baseline
Grundlohn *m* basic wage(s *Pl.*)
grundlos I. *Adj.* **1.** (*unbegründet*) unfounded, groundless; **2.** *Meere, Tiefen*: bottomless; **3.** *Weg*: muddy; **II.** *Adv.* for no reason (at all)
Grund|mauer *f* foundation wall; *bis auf die* ~*n niederbrennen/niederrei-*

ßen burn to the ground / demolish completely; ~**modell** *n* standard model; ~**moräne** *f Geol.* ground moraine; ~**muster** *n* basic pattern; ~**nahrungsmittel** *n* staple, basic (*od.* staple) food; ~**netz** *n* **1.** *Fischerei*: ground net, bottom net; **2.** *e-s Systems*: main (*od.* basic) network; *von öffentlichen Verkehrsmitteln*: basic transport(ation) system, transport(ation) infrastructure
Gründonnerstag *m* Maundy Thursday
Grund|ordnung *f Pol., e-s Staates etc.*: fundamental order; ~**pfeiler** *m* **1.** main support; **2.** *fig.* mainstay, bedrock; ~**prinzip** *n* basic principle; ~**rechenart** *f*, ~**rechnungsart** *f* basic (arithmetical) operation; ~**recht** *n* basic (*od.* fundamental) right; ~**regel** *f* basic rule; *fürs Leben etc.*: maxim; ~**rente** *f* **1.** (*Mindestrente*) basic pension; **2.** *aus Immobilien*: ground rent; ~**richtung** *f* general tendency; ~**riss** *m* **1.** *Archit.* ground plan; (*Anlageplan*) layout; **2.** *fig.* outline, sketch; (*Abriss*) outline(s *Pl.*)
Grundsatz *m* principle; (*Lebensregel*) *auch* maxim; *bes. Philos.* axiom; (*Lehrsatz*) tenet; *nach dem* ~, *dass ...* on the principle that ...; *es sich* (*Dat.*) *zum* ~ *machen* make it a rule; ~**debatte** *f* debate on basic principles; *Pol.* policy debate; ~**entscheidung** *f* fundamental (*od.* basic) decision; *Jur.* landmark decision; ~**erklärung** *f* declaration of principle(s); ~**frage** *f* basic issue; (*Schlüsselfrage*) key question
grundsätzlich I. *Adj. Entscheidung, Frage etc.*: fundamental, basic; (*prinzipiell*) *Ablehnung, Gegner*: on principle (*nachgestellt*); *Übereinstimmung etc.*: in principle (*nachgestellt*); **II.** *Adv.* fundamentally; (*im Grunde*) basically; (*prinzipiell*) *übereinstimmen etc.*: in principle; *ablehnen etc.*: on principle, as a matter of principle; (*immer*) always, invariably; *weitS.* (*absolut*) absolutely
Grundsatz|programm *n Pol.* (basic) policy statement; (*bes. vor einem Wahlkampf*) manifesto; (*Plattform*) party platform; ~**rede** *f Pol.* keynote speech (*od.* address); ~**urteil** *n Jur.* judg(e)ment that establishes a principle, groundbreaking judg(e)ment; ~**vereinbarung** *f* agreement in principle
Grund|schein *m Schwimmen*: basic certificate (*in lifesaving*); ~**schlag** *m Mus.* beat; ~**schulbildung** *f* primary education; ~**schuld** *f Fin., Jur.* land charge; ~**schule** *f* primary school, *Am. auch* elementary (*od.* grade) school; ~**schüler** *m*, ~**schülerin** *f* primary pupil, *Am.* elementary (*od.* grade *od.* primary) school student
grundsolid(e) *Adj.* absolutely dependable, rock solid
Grundstein *m* foundation stone; *fig.* cornerstone; ~**legung** *f* laying of the foundation stone; *feierliche*: cornerstone ceremony
Grund|stellung *f Tanzen, Schach etc.*: starting position; *Ballett*: position; *Fechten, Boxen*: on-guard position; *Turnen*: normal position; *Mil.* position of attention; ~**steuer** *f Jur.* land tax; ~**stimmung** *f* general mood; *von Gesprächen etc.*: tenor; ~**stock** *m* basis; (*Kern*) core
Grundstoff *m* **1.** *Chem.* element; **2.** (*Rohstoff*) raw material; ~**industrie** *f* basic industry
Grundstück *n* piece (*od.* plot) of land,

Am. auch lot; (*Besitz*) property; (*Bauplatz*) (building) site; **bebautes ~** developed property

Grundstücks|eigentümer *m*, **~eigentümerin** *f* property owner; **~grenze** *f* site boundary; **~markt** *m* property market; **~spekulation** *f* land speculation

Grund|studium *n Univ.* basic studies *Pl.*, *Am.* core courses *Pl.*; **~stufe** *f* **1.** elementary stage; **2.** *Schule*: junior school; **3.** *Ling.* positive degree; **~tarif** *m* base (*od.* basic) rate; **~tendenz** *f* general tendency (*od.* direction); **~text** *m* original text; **~ton** *m* **1.** *Mus. e-r Tonleiter*: tonic, *e-s Dreiklangs*: root; **2.** *e-r Farbe*: ground colo(u)r; **3.** *fig.* general mood; **~tugend** *f* cardinal virtue; **~übel** *n* basic problem; **~überzeugung** *f* fundamental conviction; **~umsatz** *m* **1.** *Wirts.* basic turnover; **2.** *Physiol.* basal metabolic rate

Gründung *f* foundation; *Wirts. e-r Gesellschaft*: formation; (*Errichtung*) establishment, setting-up; *e-s Geschäfts*: *auch* opening, starting (up); *e-s Hausstandes*: setting up; **die ~ einer Familie** settling down (and starting a family)

Gründünger *m Agr.* green manure

Gründungs|feier *f* inaugural celebrations *Pl.* (*feierliche*: ceremony); **~jahr** *n* year of foundation, founding year; **~kapital** *n* initial capital stock; **~mitglied** *n* founder (*Am.* charter) member; **~urkunde** *f* corporate charter

Grund|unterschied *m* fundamental (*od.* basic) difference; **~ursache** *f* primary cause

grundverkehrt *Adj.* totally wrong

Grundvermögen *n* **1.** *Wirts.* basic assets *Pl.*; **2.** → *Grundbesitz*

grundverschieden *Adj.* totally (*od.* fundamentally) different; **~ sein** *Personen*: be totally different personalities, be poles apart *umg.*

Grund|versorgung *f* basic provision; **~voraussetzung** *f* basic (*od.* absolute) prerequisite

Grundwasser *n*; *nur Sg.* ground water; **~absenkung** *f* lowering of the water table; **~spiegel** *m*, **~stand** *m* water table; **~verbrauch** *m* ground water consumption

Grund|wehrdienst *m Mil.* basic military service, *Am.* selective service, *the* draft *umg.*; *Brit. hist.* national service; **~werte** *Pl.* fundamental values; **~wissen** *n* basic knowledge (**in** + *Dat.* of); **~wort** *n*; *Pl.* -wörter; *Ling.* primary word; *fachspr.* etymon; **~wortschatz** *m Ling.* basic vocabulary; **~zahl** *f Math.* **1.** cardinal number; **2.** *e-s Logarithmus*: base radix; *e-r Potenz*: base; **~zug** *m* characteristic (feature), main feature; **Grundzüge der Physik etc.**: fundamentals, outline; **in s-n Grundzügen** in outline

Grüne[1] *n*; -*n*, *kein Pl.* **1. im ~n** out in the open; **Häuschen im ~n** country cottage; **Fahrt ins ~** into the countryside; **2.** *umg.* → *Grünzeug*

Grüne[2] *m*, *f*; -*n*, -*n* **1.** *Pol.* Green; **die ~n** the Greens, the German ecology party; **2.** *umg.* (*Polizist*) cop; **die ~n** the cops, the boys in blue

grünen *v/i. geh.* **1.** be green (*od.* verdant); (*grün werden*) turn green; *unpers.*: **es grünt** (**und blüht**) everything's beginning to flower (again); **2.** *fig.* flourish, blossom

Grünen|-Abgeordnete *m*, *f* Green member of parliament; **~-Parteitag** *m* Green party congress

Grün|färbung *f* greening; green colo(u)ring; **~filter** *m Fot.* green filter; **~fink** *m* greenfinch; **~fläche** *f* green, lawn; **~n** green spaces; *größer*: unspoil|t (*Am.* -ed) countryside *Sg.*; **~futter** *n Agr.* green fodder; **⌾gelb** *Adj.* greenish-yellow, chartreuse; **~gürtel** *m* green belt; **~kern** *m* unripe spelt grain; **~kohl** *m* kale, **~land** *n*; *nur Sg.*; *Agr.* grassland

grünlich *Adj.* greenish

Grün|ordnung *f*: **Amt für ~** urban green space planning office, *Am. etwa* parks commission; **~pflanze** *f* non-flowering plant; **~phase** *f Ampel*: green phase; **~schnabel** *m fig.*, *oft pej.* little know-all (*Am.* know-it-all), *Mädchen auch* little madam; (*Neuling*) greenhorn; **~span** *m* verdigris; **~specht** *m* green woodpecker

Grünstich *m Fot.* green cast; **grünstichig** *Adj.*: **~ sein** have a green cast

Grün|stift *m* green pen (*od.* pencil); **~streifen** *m* grass strip; *Autobahn*: centre strip, *Am.* median (strip); **~tee** *m* green tea

grunzen I. *v/i.* grunt; **II.** *v/t/i. umg. fig.* grunt; **Grunzen** *n*; -*s*, *kein Pl.* grunt(ing)

Grünzeug *n*; *nur Sg.*; *umg.* (*Pflanzen*) greenery; (*Gemüse*) greens *Pl.*, (green) vegetables *Pl.*; (*Rohkost*) raw vegetables *Pl.*; (*Kräuter*) green (*od.* fresh) herbs *Pl.*; (*Blätter*) leaves *Pl.*

Grüppchen *n* small group, handful

Gruppe *f*; -, -*n* **1.** group; *von Häusern etc.*: *auch* cluster; *von Bäumen*: *auch* clump; *von Arbeitern etc.*: team, crew; **in ~n einteilen** divide into groups; **2.** (*Klasse*) group, category; **die ~ der schwachen Verben** the class (*od.* category) of weak verbs; **3.** *Mil.* section, *Am.* squad; *Flug. Brit.* wing, *Am.* group; **4.** *Wirts.* (*Konzern*) group, concern

Gruppen|abend *m* group get-together (*od.* meeting); **~akkord** *m Wirts.* group piecework; (*Lohnsatz*) group piece rate; **~arbeit** *f* teamwork; *Päd. auch* group work, work in groups

gruppenbewusst *Adj.* group-conscious; **Gruppenbewusstsein** *n* group consciousness (*od.* awareness), group (*od.* collective) identity

Gruppen|bild *n* group portrait (*od.* photo, shot), photo of the (*od.* a) group; **~bildung** *f* formation (*od.* forming) of groups, grouping

Gruppendynamik *f Psych.* group dynamics *Pl.* (*V. im Sg.*); **gruppendynamisch** *Adj.* group-dynamic

Gruppen|egoismus *m* sectional self-interest; **~foto** *n* group photo (*od.* shot), photo of the (*od.* a) group; **~führer** *m*, **~führerin** *f* group leader; *Mil. Brit.* section leader, *Am.* squad leader; **~leiter** *m*, **~leiterin** *f* group manager; **~praxis** *f* group (*od.* joint) practice; **~raum** *m* **1.** *für Gruppen*: seminar room; (*Aufenthaltsraum*) common room; **2.** *in Kindergarten*: classroom; **~reise** *f* group (*od.* organized) tour; **~sex** *m* group sex; **~sieg** *m Sport* victory in one's group; **~sieger** *m*, **~siegerin** *f Sport* group winner(s *Pl.*); **⌾spezifisch** *Adj.* group-specific; **~sprache** *f Ling.* jargon; **~stärke** *f*: **bei/mit e-r ~ von ...** in a group of ...

gruppenweise *Adv.* in groups

Gruppenzwang *m* (peer) group pressure

gruppieren I. *v/t.* group, arrange (in

groups); **neu ~** regroup; **II.** *v/refl.* form a group (*od.* groups), group (o.s.) (**um** [a]round); (*sich sammeln*) assemble; *Sport* line up; **Gruppierung** *f* **1.** (*das Gruppieren*) forming of groups; **2.** (*Anordnung*) grouping; **3.** (*Gruppe*[*n*]) group(s *Pl.*); *von Häusern etc.*: *auch* cluster; *Pol. etc.* group(ing)

Grusel *m*; -*s*, *kein Pl.* cold shivers *Pl.*, the creeps *Pl.*; **~**, **~!** *umg. hum.* shiver, shiver!, *bes. Am. auch* spooky!; **~effekt** *m* spine-chilling effect; **~film** *m* horror film, *Am. auch* splatter movie; (*Monsterfilm*) *auch* monster movie

gruselig *Adj.* creepy, scary *umg.*; *Geschichte*: *auch* spine-chilling

gruseln I. *v/t/i.*; *auch unpers.*: **mich** *od.* **mir gruselt** (**es**) *od.* **das macht mich ~** I'm scared, this is creepy, this is giving me the creeps; **II.** *v/refl.* be scared, get the creeps *umg.*; **sich ~ vor** (+ *Dat.*) have a horror of, get the creeps from *umg.*; **Gruseln** *n*; -*s*, *kein Pl.*; *the* creeps *Pl.*

Grusinien (*n*); -*s*; *Geog.* Grusinia; **Grusinier** *m*; -*s*, -, **Grusinierin** *f*; -, -*nen* Grusinian, *weiblich auch* Grusinian woman (*od.* girl *etc.*); **grusinisch I.** *Adj.* Grusinian; **II. Grusinisch** *n*; -*en* Grusinian; **das ~e** Grusinian

gruslig *Adj.* → *gruselig*

Gruß *m*; -*es*, *Grüße* **1.** greeting; *förm.* salutation; *Grüße übermittelte*: regards, *sehr vertraulich*: love (**an** + *Akk.* to); **schöne Grüße aus ...** greetings from ...; (**sag** *od.* **bestell ihm**) **e-n schönen ~ von mir!** give him my regards (*sehr vertraulich*: my love); *vertraulich*: *auch* say hello to him from me; **viele** *od.* **herzliche** *od.* **liebe Grüße** in *Briefen*: Kind regards, Best wishes; *sehr vertraulich*: (With) Love; **mit freundlichen Grüßen** (*abgek.* **MfG**) in *Geschäftsbriefen*: Yours sincerely; **als letzten ~ auf Grabschmuck**: a last goodbye; **er gab ihr** / **hob die Hand zum ~** / he shook hands with her / raised his hand in greeting; **deutscher ~** *hist.*, *im Nationalsozialismus*: Nazi salute, Heil Hitler *umg.*; → *Englisch*[2]; **2.** *Mil.* salute; **~adresse** *f*, **~botschaft** *f* message of greeting

grüßen *v/t/i.* **1.** greet, say hello (*od.* good morning *etc.*) to; *Mil. und feierlich*: salute; **grüß Gott** *od.* **dich** *od.* **euch!** *südd.*, *österr.* hello!, hi! *umg.*; **kannst du nicht ~?** *zu Kindern*: have you forgotten how to say hello?; **2.** (*Grüße senden*) send one's regards (*vertraulich*: love); **~ Sie ihn von mir!** give him my regards (*vertraulich*: my love); *vertraulich*: *auch* say hello to him from me; **er lässt** (**Sie**) **~** he sends his regards; **3.** *lit.* (*willkommen heißen*) hail (**als** as); **seid mir gegrüßt!** greetings!; *hum.* all hail!; **gegrüßet seist du, Maria** *Reli.* hail Mary; **4.** *fig.* greet

Gruß|formel *f* salutation (*auch am Briefbeginn*); *am Briefende*: complimentary close, ending; **welche ~n benutzt man in englischen Briefen?** how do you address people and sign off in English letters?; **~karte** *f* greeting(s) card

grußlos *Adv.* without a word (of greeting *od.* of goodbye), without (even) saying hello *od.* goodbye

Gruß|telegramm *n* greetings telegram; **~wort** *n*; *Pl.* -worte word(s *Pl.*) of welcome, opening words *Pl.*

Grütze *f*; -, *Sorten*: -*n* **1.** *Körner*: groats *Pl.*, *Am.* grits *Pl.*; *Brei*: porridge; **grü-**

ne/rote ~ dessert of semi-liquid green/red fruit; **2.** nur Sg.; umg. (Verstand) brains Pl.

GS Abk. (**geprüfte Sicherheit**) certified safe

G-Saite f Mus. G string

Gschaftlhuber m; -s, -; Dial.: **er ist ein richtiger** ~ he's a real busybody, he has to get his nose (od. hands) into everything

G-Schlüssel m Mus. treble clef

G7 Pl.; Abk. Pol. G7; ~**Staat** m G7 nation

Gspusi n; -s, -s; Dial. **1.** (Liebschaft) (love) affair; **2.** (Schatz) sweetheart

Gstanz(e)l n; -s, -n; Mus. südd., österr. (rude) song

GS-Zeichen n safety symbol, etwa Brit. kite mark, Am. seal of approval

Guatemala (n); -s; Geog. Guatemala; **Guatemalteke** m; -n, -n, **Guatemaltekin** f; -, -nen Guatemalan, weiblich auch Guatemalan woman (od. girl etc.); **guatemaltekisch** Adj. Guatemalan

Guayana (n); -s; Geog. Guyana

gucken umg. **I.** v/i. **1.** look; heimlich: auch peep; (starren) stare; **guck mal!** look!; **nicht** ~**!** no looking, no peeping; **lass mich mal** ~**!** let me (od. let's) have a look; **guck nicht so dumm!** stop staring!; **da hat er aber dumm geguckt!** he just stood there goggling at me etc.; (war überrascht) Brit. auch he was absolutely gobsmacked; (hat nichts verstanden) he looked completely blank; → **Glas¹** 2, **Mond** 1, **Röhre** 2; **2.** (sichtbar sein) show; peep (od. stick, od. bzw. hang) (**aus** out of); **II.** v/t.: **Fernsehen** ~ watch (the) television (od. TV, Brit. auch telly); **Gucker** m; -s, -; umg. **1.** (Fernglas) telescope; (Opernglas) opera glasses Pl.; **2.** Pl. (Augen) peepers; **3.** Person: peeper, rubberneck

Gucki m; -s, -s; umg. (Diabetrachter) (slide) viewer

Guckkasten m **1.** peep show (box); **2.** umg. (goggle) box, Am. boob tube; ~**bühne** f picture-frame stage, proscenium (stage)

Guckloch n peephole

Guerilla [geˈrɪlja] f; -, -s **1.** Gruppe: guer(r)illa unit; **2.** Krieg: guer(r)illa war

Guerilla|kämpfer m, ~**kämpferin** f guer(r)illa (fighter); ~**krieg** m guer(-r)illa warfare (konkret: war)

Guerillera [gerilˈjeːra] f; -, -s, **Guerillero** [gerilˈjeːro] m; -s, -s guer(r)illa in Latin America

Gugelhupf m; -(e)s, -e; südd., österr., Gastr., etwa ring (Am. auch Bundt) cake

Guillotine [gɪjoˈtiːnə] f; -, -n; hist. guillotine; **guillotinieren** v/t. guillotine

Gulasch n, auch m; -(e)s, -e od. -s; Gastr. goulash; ~**kanone** f Mil. field kitchen; ~**suppe** f goulash soup

Gulden m; -s, -; hist. guilder (ehemalige niederländische Währung)

Gülle f; -, kein Pl.; Agr. liquid manure

Gully m, auch n; -s, -s drain

gültig Adj. valid (auch fig.); (in Kraft) effective (**ab** od. **von** from; **bis** to, till), in force; (gesetzlich, zulässig) legal; Münze: good, legal tender; Fahrkarte: valid, good (**drei Tage** for three days); **nicht mehr** ~ expired, no longer valid (od. in force etc.); Fahrkarte: expired, out of date; **das ist auch heute noch** ~ fig. that still holds good (od. true) today; ~ **sein** → **gelten** I 1; **Gültigkeit**

f; nur Sg. validity (auch fig.); e-s Gesetzes: auch legal force; von Geld: currency; (Zulässigkeit) legality; ~ **erlangen** become valid (od. effective); **s-e** ~ **verlieren** cease to be valid; Vertrag, Pass etc.: expire; ~ **haben** → **gelten** I 1

Gültigkeitsdauer f (period of) validity; e-s Vertrags: mst term; e-s Patents etc.: life

Gummi¹ m, n; -s, (Arten:) -(s) **1.** rubber; **2.** Saft: gum; **3.** (Gummiring) rubber band; Band: elastic band; in Kleidung: elastic, **4.** (Kaugummi) gum

Gummi² m; -s, -s **1.** (Radiergummi) rubber, Am. eraser; **2.** umg. (Kondom) rubber, Brit. auch johnny

Gummi|arabikum n; -s, kein Pl. gum arabic; ℓ**artig** Adj. rubbery; ~**ball** m rubber ball; ~**bär** m, ~**bärchen** n gummy (od. jelly) bear; ~**baum** m rubber tree; Zierpflanze: rubber plant; ~**beine** Pl. umg.: ~ **haben** have wobbly knees (od. legs); ~**bonbon** m, n gumdrop; ~**boot** n rubber dinghy; ~**dichtung** f rubber seal

gummiert Adj. **1.** Briefmarke, Kuvert: gummed; **2.** Tech. rubberized

Gummi|geschoss m, österr. ~**geschoß** rubber bullet; ~**hammer** m rubber mallet; ~**harz** n gum resin; ~**knüppel** m (rubber) truncheon; ~**linse** f Fot. zoom lens; ~**mantel** m rubber coat; ~**paragraph** m umg. elastic (od. catch-all) clause; ~**puppe** f rubber doll; ~**reifen** m (rubber) tyre (Am. tire); ~**ring** m rubber band; für Einmachgläser: sealing ring; zum Spielen: rubber ring, quoit; ~**schlauch** m rubber tube; zum Spritzen: rubber hose; für Reifen: inner tube; ~**schuhe** Pl. galoshes, rubber overshoes, Am. auch rubbers; ~**schutz** m (Kondom) rubber, Brit. auch johnny; ~**sohle** f rubber sole; ~**stiefel** m wellington, rubber boot; ~**stöpsel** m rubber stopper; ~**strumpf** m elastic stocking; ~**tier** n rubber animal; zum Aufblasen: inflatable animal; ~**unterlage** f rubber sheet; ~**zelle** f padded cell; ~**zug** m elastic

Gunst f; -, kein Pl. **1.** (Wohlwollen) favo(u)r, goodwill; **j-m s-e** ~ **schenken** show favo(u)r to s.o.; **in j-s** ~ **stehen** be in s.o.'s good graces (umg. good books); **um j-s** ~ **werben** court (od. try to win) s.o.'s favo(u)r; im Wahlkampf etc.: woo s.o.; **die** ~ **des Augenblicks** od. **der Stunde nutzen** fig. make hay while the sun shines; **2.** (Gefallen) favo(u)r; **j-m e-e große** ~ **erweisen** do s.o. a big favo(u)r; **3.** **zu** ~**en** → **zugunsten**; **zu m-n** etc. ~**en** in my etc. favo(u)r

Gunst|beweis m, ~**bezeigung** f (mark of) favo(u)r

günstig I. Adj. favo(u)rable (**für** to); (positiv) auch positive; Moment: opportune; (viel versprechend) promising; (gut) good; Einfluss: beneficial; **j-n** ~ **stimmen** put s.o. in (od. get s.o. into) the right mood; **wäre das nicht** ~**er?** wouldn't that be better (od. more convenient)?; **e-n** ~**en Augenblick abwarten** wait for the right moment; **zu** ~**en Bedingungen** Wirts. on easy terms; **im** ~**sten Fall** at best; ~**e Gelegenheit** favo(u)rable opportunity, opportune moment; (Schnäppchen) bargain; **bei** ~**em Verlauf** if things go well; **II.** Adv. favo(u)rably; positively; ~ **abschneiden** come off well (**bei** in); **dort kann man** ~ **einkaufen** they're quite cheap; **sich** ~ **entwickeln für j-n**

work out well for s.o.; **...günstig** im Adj. low-; **verbrauchs**~ Auto: economical

günstig(st)enfalls Adv. at best; bei Geldbeträgen etc.: auch at (the) most

Günstling m; -s, -e; pej. favo(u)rite; **Günstlingswirtschaft** f; nur Sg.; pej. favo(u)ritism

Gurgel f; -, -n throat; **j-n bei der** ~ **packen** grab s.o. by the throat; **j-m an die** ~ **springen** od. **gehen** go for s.o.'s throat; **gurgeln I.** vt/i. Person: gargle; (gurgelnd sprechen) gurgle; **II.** v/i. Wasser: gurgle; **Gurgelwasser** n; Pl. Gurgelwässer gargle, mouthwash

Gürkchen n Gastr. small gherkin, cornichon, Am. mst pickle

Gurke f; -, -n **1.** (Salatgurke) cucumber; (kleine, Essiggurke) gherkin, Am. mst pickle; **saure** ~**n** pickled cucumbers, Am. pickles; **2.** umg. hum. (Nase) conk, beak

gurken v/i. umg.: (ziellos) **durch die Gegend** ~ wander around (aimlessly)

Gurken|kern m cucumber seed; ~**kraut** n; nur Sg. **1.** (Borretsch) borage; **2.** (Dill) dill; ~**salat** m cucumber salad

gurren vt/i. coo (auch fig.)

Gurt m; -(e)s, -e **1.** (Gürtel) belt; zum Binden, Tragen, an Sattel etc.: strap; (Hosengurt etc.) waistband; Mot., Flug. seatbelt; am Fallschirm: harness; **2.** Archit. flange

Gürtel m; -s, - **1.** belt (auch Judo); etw. am ~ **tragen** carry s.th. on one's belt; **den** ~ **weiter machen / enger schnallen** loosen/tighten one's belt (auch fig.); **2.** (Zone) belt; Geog. zone; **3.** aus Polizisten etc.: cordon; Sport belt; ~**linie** f waistline; **unter der** od. **die** ~ Boxen und fig.: below the belt; ~**reifen** m Mot. radial-ply tyre (Am. tire); ~**rose** f Med. shingles Sg., herpes zoster fachspr.; ~**schlaufe** f loop (of a od. the belt); ~**schnalle** f belt buckle; ~**tasche** f belt bag, pouch; ~**tier** n Zool. armadillo

gurten I. v/t. **1.** (anschnallen) strap; **2.** Archit. brace; **II.** v/i. Mot. put one's seatbelt on, strap o.s. in; **erst** ~, **dann starten** belt (Am. buckle) up then start up

gürten lit. **I.** v/refl. gird o.s.; **II.** v/t. **1.** (Schwert etc.) gird on; **2.** (Mantel etc.) don

Gurt|muffel m Mot., umg. seatbelt offender (Am. scofflaw); ~**pflicht** f Mot. compulsory wearing of seatbelts; ~**zeug** n am Fallschirm: harness; ~**straffer** m Mot. seatbelt tensioner; ~**zwang** m Mot.: **es besteht** ~ wearing a seatbelt is compulsory

Guru m; -s, -s; auch umg. fig. guru; **...guru** m, im Subst.; umg. fig. ... guru; **Medien**~ media guru

GUS f; -, kein Pl.; Pol., Abk. (**Gemeinschaft Unabhängiger Staaten**) CIS, C.I.S. (= Commonwealth of Independent States)

Guss m; -es, Güsse **1.** Tech. (Gießen) founding, casting (process); (Gussstücke) castings Pl.; Druck. fount, Am. font; **aus einem** ~ made in one casting; **es ist (wie) aus einem** ~ fig. it's all of a piece; **2.** Gastr. glaze; (Zuckerguss) icing; **3.** (Schwall) jet of water etc.; **kalte Güsse bekommen** be treated with cold affusions; → **Regenguss**; ~**asphalt** m poured asphalt; ~**beton** m cast concrete

Guss|eisen n; nur Sg. cast iron; ~**form** f mo(u)ld; ~**stahl** m cast steel; ~**stück**

n casting

Gusto *m*; *-s*, *-s*: *nach j-s ~ sein* be to s.o.'s taste (*od.* liking); *etw. nach s-m ~ machen* do s.th. (just) as one likes (*od.* fancies); *e-n ~ haben auf* feel like s.th.; *~stückerl n* österr. (*Leckerbissen*) delicacy; (*Attraktion*) star turn

gut; *besser, am besten* **I.** *Adj.* **1.** good; *Wetter:* auch fine; *Qualität, Wein etc.:* auch fine; *Stoff:* auch good-quality; *sehr ~!* very good!; *~ so!* good!, well done!; *~ finden* like; *~es Geschäft für Verkäufer:* good business; *für Käufer:* bargain; *ein ~es Ende nehmen* turn out well (*od.* all right); *sie spricht (ein) ~es Englisch* she speaks good English, she speaks English well; *er ist kein besonders ~er Tänzer* he's not much of a dancer; **2.** (*akzeptabel, in Ordnung*) good, all right, okay *umg.*; (*richtig*) right; (*angebracht*) fit, proper; *für ~ befinden* think s.th. to be good (*od.* a good thing); *~ und richtig sein* be right and proper; *das ist ja ~ und schön, aber …* that's all very well, but…; *noch ~ sein* be still good; *Kleidung:* auch be still wearable; *Nahrung:* auch be still fit to eat; *nicht mehr ~ sein Lebensmittel:* have gone off (*bes. Am.* bad); *Milch:* have gone off (*od.* sour), have turned sour; *ganz ~ (recht ~)* not bad; *das ist ganz od. auch ~ so* that's all right; (*wieder*) *~ werden* (*heilen*) get better; (*in Ordnung kommen, gelingen*) turn out all right *od.* well; *er hielt es für ~ zu schweigen* he thought it better (*od.* wise) to say nothing; **3.** (*körperlich wohl*) well; *mir ist nicht ~ od. ich fühle mich nicht ~* I don't feel well; *ist dir jetzt wieder ~?* are you better now?; *ist dir nicht ~?* don't you feel well?; (*du bist wohl verrückt!*) are you sure you're all right?; **4.** *mst gesprochen:* (*wie*) *~, dass od. es ist ganz ~, dass …* it's a good thing that …; *schon ~!* all right!; *auf Entschuldigung:* auch it's no problem; *verärgert, nachgebend:* auch okay, okay; (*es genügt*) auch that'll do; (*lass nur*) auch just leave it; *jetzt ist es aber ~ od. und damit ~!* *umg.* that'll do!; *lass (es) ~ sein (für dieses Mal)* let's leave it at that (for now); *so was ist immer ~* that's always useful; **5.** (*für besondere Anlässe*) *Anzug, Geschirr etc.:* good, best; **6.** (*wirksam*) *Mittel etc.:* good (*für, gegen* for); *wofür od. wozu soll das ~ sein?* what's that for (*umg.* in aid of)?; **7.** (*brav, edel, freundlich etc.*) good; *gegen die ~en Sitten verstoßen* offend against good manners; *e-e ~e Tat* a good deed; *mit etwas ~em Willen* with a bit of good will; (*bitte*) *sei so ~ und …* do me a favo(u)r and …, will you?; *wärst du bitte mal so ~, mir zu helfen?* would you be so kind (*od.* good) as to help me?; *bist du mir wieder ~?* (are we) friends again?; *dafür ist er sich zu ~* he thinks he's above that sort of thing, he thinks it would be beneath him (*od.* his dignity); *du bist (vielleicht) ~! iro.* I like that!; (*das soll wohl ein Witz sein*) you must be joking!; *Gut und Böse unterscheiden können* be able to tell right from wrong; → *jenseits* II; **8.** *Schulnote:* good; *sehr ~* very good; **9.** *in Grüßen, Wünschen:* good; *~en Tag!* good day (*bzw.* afternoon); *~es neues Jahr!* happy new year!; *auf ~e Nachbarschaft!* here's to good neighbourliness (*Am.* neighbors)!; → *Appetit, Besse-*

rung, Fahrt 1; **10.** *in Anreden:* good; *~er Freund* my dear fellow; **11.** (*Ggs. knapp*) *Meter, Pfund, Stunde etc.:* good; *ein ~(er) Teil* a good part; *das hat noch ~e Weile* there's still plenty of time for that; **12.** *so ~ wie* virtually, practically, as good as; *so ~ wie unmöglich* virtually impossible; *der Prozess ist so ~ wie gewonnen* as good as won; *so ~ wie nichts* next to nothing; **13.** *~ sein für* (*ausreichen für*) be enough for; *sie ist immer für e-n Witz ~* she's always good for a laugh; **14.** *zu ~er Letzt* finally; **II.** *Adv.* **1.** *mit Verb:* hören, sehen etc.: well; *riechen, schmecken etc.:* good; *das fängt ja ~ an!* that's a great start; *~ aussehen* look good; *Person, grundsätzlich:* be good-looking; *gesundheitlich:* look well; → 2; *es gefällt mir ~* I like it (very much); *das konnte nicht ~ gehen* it was bound to go wrong; *das kann ja nicht ~ gehen!* there's no way it's going to work; *wenn das nur ~ geht!* well, let's just hope for the best; *das ist noch einmal ~ gegangen* that was close (*od.* a close thing), talk about lucky *umg.*; *mir geht's gut* I'm fine; *geschäftlich etc.:* I'm doing fine; *es sich ~ gehen lassen* have a good time, enjoy o.s.; → 2; *dort hatte er es ~* he was doing all right (for himself) there; *da kennt sie sich ~ aus* she knows all about that; *in e-m Ort:* she really knows her way around there; *etw. ~ können* be good at s.th.; *es mit j-m ~ meinen* have s.o.'s interests at heart, mean well by s.o.; *j-m/etw. ~ tun* do s.o./s.th. good; *sehr ~ tun* do a lot of good; *das tut ~!* that's just what I need, that feels good; *bei Erleichterung:* that's better; *stärker:* what a relief; *j-m nicht ~ tun Arznei etc.:* disagree with s.o.; *das tut d-m Magen nicht ~* it's no good for your stomach, it won't do your stomach any good; *er täte ~ daran zu gehen* it would be a good idea if he went; **2.** *mit Partizip od. Adj.:* *~ aussehend* good-looking, attractive; *~ besetzt Stück:* well-cast; *Haus:* full; *~ besucht Vorstellung etc.:* well-attended; *~ betucht umg.* well-heeled; *~ bezahlt od. dotiert* well-paid; *~ erhalten* in good condition; *von alten Dingen:* well-preserved; *~ gebaut Haus:* well-made; *Person:* well-built; *~ gefedert Auto etc.:* well-sprung; *~ gehend Geschäft etc.:* flourishing, thriving; *Ware:* popular, … that is selling well; *~ gelaunt* in a good mood; *~ gemeint* well-meant; *~ gepflegt* well-looked-after, *Am.* auch well taken care of; *~ situiert* well-off, well-to-do, moneyed; *ein ~ sitzender Anzug* a well-fitting suit, a suit that fits properly; *wie aus ~ unterrichteten Kreisen verlautet* according to well-informed sources; *er ist ein ~ verdienender Mann* he earns a good (*od.* decent) salary; *~ verträglich Medikament etc.:* … with no side effects, mild-acting; (*hautverträglich*) gentle, gentle-action …; (*allergiegetestet*) hypoallergenic; **3.** (*leicht, mühelos*) easily; *das Auto fährt sich ~* the car is easy to drive; *das Buch liest sich ~* the book is a good read; *du hast ~ reden/lachen* you can talk/laugh (*od.* you may well laugh); *hinterher kann man immer ~ reden* it's easy with hindsight, hindsight is always 20/20; *das kann ~ sein od. es ist ~ möglich* that's quite possible, that may well be; *ich kann ihn nicht ~ darum bitten* I

can't very well (*od.* can't really) ask him; **4.** *~ (und gern)* (*mindestens*) at least, easily; *er ist ~ zwei Meter groß* he's a good two met|res (*Am.* -ers) tall; → *besser, best…*, *Gute¹*, *Gute²*, *zugute*

Gut *n*; *-(e)s*, *Güter* **1.** (*Besitz*) property; *Güter* goods, products; *Eisenb.* freight *Sg.*; (*Vermögensstücke*) assets; (*un)bewegliche Güter* (im)movables; *das höchste ~* the greatest good; *irdische Güter* worldly goods; → *Hab*; **2.** (*Landgut*) estate, farm

…gut *im Subst., nur Sg.* material; *Einmach~* fruit (*bzw.* vegetables *Pl.*) for preserving, *Am.* canning fruit etc.; *Versand~* goods *Pl.* for dispatch

Gutachten *n*; *-s*, - expert's opinion; (*Zeugnis*) certificate, testimonial; *ärztliches ~* medical certificate (*alle:* über + *Akk.* on); *ein ~ abgeben/einholen* give s.o. / get a certificate etc.; **Gutachter** *m*; *-s*, -, **Gutachterin** *f*; *-*, *-nen* expert; *Versicherung:* auch surveyor; (*Schätzer*) valuer; (*Berater*) consultant

gutartig *Adj.* bes. *Tier:* good-natured; auch *Krankheit:* harmless; *Med. Tumor etc.:* benign

gut| aussehend, **~ besetzt**, **~ betucht**, **~ bezahlt** → *gut* II 2

gutbürgerlich I. *Adj.* **1.** *Gastr., Essen etc.:* traditional, good plain; *~e Küche* home cooking, comfort food; *in Werbung:* auch traditional fare; **2.** middle-class …; **II.** *Adv.:* *~ essen/kochen* eat/cook good plain (*od.* homely *od.* traditional) food

gut dotiert → *gut* II 2

Gutdünken *n*; *-s*, *kein Pl.:* *nach (eigenem) ~* at one's own discretion, as one sees fit

Gute¹ *m*, *f*; *-n*, *-n* good man/woman; *die ~n* the good *Pl.*, the goodies (*Am.* auch goody-two-shoes) *umg.*; *bibl.* the righteous *Pl.*

Gute² *n*; *-n*, *kein Pl.:* *das ~ daran ist* the good thing about it is; *die Sache hat auch od. schon ihr ~s* there's a good side to it too; *des ~n zu viel tun* overdo it; *sich zum ~n wenden* change for the better; *mir schwant od. ich ahne nichts ~s* I have a strange feeling (something has gone wrong *od.* is going to go wrong); *alles ~!* all the best; *zum Geburtstag:* many happy returns; *etwas ~s (zu essen)* something nice to eat; *sie hat ~s und Böses im Leben erfahren* she has had her ups and downs; *er führt nichts ~s im Schild(e)* he is up to no good; *im ~n* amicably, on friendly terms; *im ~n wie im Bösen* for better, for worse

Güte *f*; *-*, *kein Pl.* **1.** goodness, kindness; (*Großzügigkeit*) generosity; *Gottes:* (God's) grace; *hätten Sie die ~ zu* (+ *Inf.*) *geh.* would you be so kind as to (+ *Inf.*); (*ach du*) *meine od. liebe ~!* *umg.* goodness me!, (my) goodness!; good God!; → *Vorschlag* 1; **2.** (*Qualität*) quality; (*Gütegrad*) auch grade, class; (*Vortrefflichkeit*) superior quality; (*von*) *erster ~* first-class, first-rate, top-quality …; *Idiot etc.* *erster ~ iro.* of the first order

Güte|grad *m* quality, grade; *~klasse f* class, grade; *~ 1* Grade A quality, prime …

Gutenacht|geschichte *f* bedtime story; *~kuss m* goodnight kiss; *j-m e-n ~ geben* kiss s.o. goodnight

Güter|abfertigung *f* **1.** *nur Sg.; Vorgang:* dispatch of goods; **2.** *Stelle:* goods (*Am.* freight) office; *~annahme*

f goods (*Am.* freight) office; **~bahnhof** *m* goods (*Am.* freight) station; **~fernverkehr** *m* long-haul transportation; **~gemeinschaft** *f Jur.* community of property; joint property; **~halle** *f* warehouse

gut erhalten → *gut* II 2

Güter|nahverkehr *m* short-haul transportation; **~transport** *m* transport(ation) of goods; **~trennung** *f Jur.* separation of property; **in ~ leben** have separate property; **~verkehr** *m* goods (*Am.* freight) traffic; **~versand** *m* goods shipment; **~wagen** *m Eisenb.* goods wag(g)on, *Am.* freight car; **~zug** *m* goods (*Am.* freight) train

Güte|siegel *n* seal of quality; **~stempel** *m* quality stamp; *Edelmetalle:* hallmark (*auch fig.*); **~zeichen** *n* quality label; *e-r Prüfstelle etc.:* scal of approval; *Edelmetalle:* hallmark (*auch fig.*)

gut| gebaut, ~ gefedert → *gut* II 2
gut gehen → *gut* II 1
gut| gehend, ~ gelaunt *etc.* → *gut* II 2
gutgläubig I. *Adj.* gullible, credulous; **II.** *Adv.* gullibly, credulously; **Gutgläubigkeit** *f; nur Sg.* gullibility, credulity

guthaben I. *v/t.* (*unreg., trennb., hat -ge-*) **1.** *Fin.* have credit for; **2.** *fig.: du hast bei mir noch ein Essen gut* I still owe you a meal; **II. Guthaben** *n; -s, -; Fin.* balance; (*Vermögen*) assets *Pl.*; *auf dem Konto ist ein Guthaben von 100 Euro* there is a credit balance of 100 euros on the account

gutheißen *v/t.* (*unreg., trennb., hat -ge-*) approve of, sanction

gutherzig *Adj.* kind(hearted)

gütig I. *Adj.* good, kind (*gegen* to); kindhearted; (*wohlmeinend*) well-meaning; *mit Ihrer ~en Erlaubnis geh. od. iro.* with your kind permission; *zu ~! iro.* too kind (of you); **II.** *Adv.* kindly

gütlich I. *Adj.* amicable; **II.** *Adv.: sich ~ einigen* come to (*od.* reach) a friendly agreement; *sich ~ einigen über* (+ *Akk.*) settle *s.th.* amicably; *sich ~ tun* have a good time, enjoy o.s.; *sich ~ tun an* (+ *Dat.*) eat (*od.* drink) one's fill of

gutmachen *v/t.* (*trennb., hat -ge-*) **1.** (*wieder*) **~** (*Fehler, Schaden, Versäumnis*) make up for, make good; (*Fehler*) *auch* correct; **2.** (*Hilfe, Gefallen*) repay; (*sich revanchieren*) repay, get even for; **3.** (*Abstand, Zeit*) make up (*gegenüber* on); **4.** (*Überschuss*) make (profit) (*bei* out of)

gutmütig *Adj.* good-natured; **Gutmütigkeit** *f; nur Sg.* good-naturedness

gutnachbarlich *Adj.* neighbo(u)rly

Gutsbesitzer *m, ~in f* estate owner; owner of the (*od.* an) estate; (*Grundbesitzer*) landowner

Gutschein *m* voucher, *Am. auch* coupon; *als Geschenk:* gift token (*Am.* certificate); **~heft** *n* book of vouchers (*Am.* coupons)

gutschreiben *v/t.* (*unreg., trennb., hat -ge-*) credit; *e-n Betrag e-m Konto ~* credit an account with an amount, credit an amount to an account; **Gutschrift** *f* **1.** credit entry; *zur ~ auf ihr Konto* to the credit of your account; **2.** *Beleg:* credit slip

Gutsel, Gutsle *n; -s, -; Dial.* (*Bonbon*) sweet, *Am.* candy; (*Keks*) biscuit, *Am.* cookie

Guts|haus *n* manor house; **~herr** *m,* **~herrin** *f* **1.** *hist.* lord/lady of the manor; **2.** estate owner; owner of the estate; **~herrenart** *f Gastr.: Schinken nach ~* ham *served in a traditional, local, but sumptuous style;* **~hof** *m* estate; (*Bauernhof*) farm

gut| situiert, ~ sitzend → *gut* II 2

Guts|verwalter *m,* **~verwalterin** *f* steward, estate manager; **~verwaltung** *f* stewardship, estate management

Guttempler *m; -s, -,* **~in** *f; -, -nen* Good Templar

gut tun → *gut* II 1

guttural I. *Adj.* guttural; **II. Guttural** *m; -s, -e; Ling.* guttural (sound)

gut| unterrichtet, ~ verdienend, ~ verträglich → *gut* II 2

gutwillig I. *Adj.* willing; (*gefällig*) obliging; (*freiwillig*) voluntary; **II.** *Adv.* willingly *etc.*; of one's own accord (*od.* free will); **Gutwilligkeit** *f; nur Sg.* willingness; (*Gefälligkeit*) obligingness

gymnasial *Adj. Oberstufe etc.:* etwa in a grammar (*Am.* high) school

Gymnasialbildung *f; nur Sg.* etwa grammar (*Am.* high) school education

Gymnasiast *m; -en, -en,* **~in** *f; -, -nen* etwa grammar (school) pupil, *Am.* high school student

Gymnasium *n; -s, Gymnasien* **1.** etwa grammar (*Am.* high) school; *humanistisches/musisches ~* etwa grammar (*Am.* high) school specializing in classics / the fine arts; *mathematisch-naturwissenschaftliches ~ mit neusprachlichem Zweig* etwa grammar (*Am.* high) school specializing in mathematics and sciences with a modern languages department; **2.** *hist.* gymnasium

Gymnastik *f; -, kein Pl.* exercises *Pl.*, cal(l)isthenics *Pl.*; *Disziplin:* gymnastics *Pl.* (*V. im Sg.*); *~ machen* (*Übungen machen*) do (one's) exercises; *als Diszplin:* do gymnastics; **~anzug** *m* leotard; **~lehrer** *m,* **~lehrerin** *f* PE (= physical education) teacher

gymnastisch *Adj.* gymnastic; *~e Übungen* physical exercises, cal(l)isthenics

Gynäkologe *m; -n, -n; Med.* gyn(a)ecologist, gyny *umg.*; **Gynäkologie** *f; -, kein Pl.* gyn(a)ecology; **Gynäkologin** *f; -, -nen* (woman) gyn(a)ecologist, gyny *umg.*; **gynäkologisch** *Adj.* gyn(a)ecological

G

H¹, h *n; -, - od. umg. -s* **1.** H, h; *H wie Heinrich* Buchstabieren: "h" for (*od.* as in) "hotel"; *stummes ~ Ling.* silent H, H mute; **2.** *Mus.* B

H² *Abk. Verk. auf Schild:* bus stop

h *Abk.* (*Stunde*) hr, hr.

ha¹ *Interj.* **1.** *bei Überraschung:* ah!, oh!; **2.** *bei Genugtuung:* ha!, aha!; **3.** *umg.: ~? erstaunt:* huh?

ha² *Abk.* (*Hektar*) ha, ha.

hä *Interj. umg.* **1.** *~? nicht verstehend:* eh?; *erstaunt:* huh?; **2.** *bei Schadenfreude:* heh(, heh)!

Haar *n; -(e)s, -e* **1.** hair (*auch Bot.*); *Koll.* (*Haare, Fell*) hair; *sie hat braunes ~ od. braune ~e* she has brown hair; *j-m/sich die ~e machen umg.* do s.o.'s/one's hair; *sich* (*Dat.*) *die ~e schneiden lassen* get a haircut; *du musst dir mal die ~e schneiden lassen* it's time you had a haircut; *j-n an den ~en ziehen* pull s.o.'s hair; *sich* (*Dat.*) *die ~e (aus)raufen auch fig.* tear one's hair (out); *ich könnte mir die ~e ausraufen auch* I could kick myself; **2.** *nur Sg.; fig.: aufs ~ umg.* to a T; *sich* (*Pl.*) *aufs ~ gleichen umg.* look absolutely identical; *Personen: auch* be as alike as two peas in a pod; *um ein ~ hätten wir uns verpasst umg.* we very nearly missed each other, we came so close to missing one another; *er hätte ums ~ gewonnen umg. etc.* he came within a whisker (*od.* hair) of winning *etc.*; *um kein ~ besser umg.* not a bit better; *j-m kein ~ krümmen umg.* not touch a hair on s.o.'s head; *er ließ kein gutes ~ an ihm umg.* he picked (*od.* pulled) him to pieces, he didn't have a good word to say about him; *an e-m ~ hängen umg.* hang by a thread; *ein ~ in der Suppe finden umg.* find something to criticize (*od.* quibble about); **3.** *mst Pl., fig.: ~e spalten pej.* split hairs; *sie hat ~e auf den Zähnen* she's a really tough nut (*Brit. auch* customer, *Am. auch* cookie); *sich in die ~e geraten umg.* get in each other's hair; *sich in den ~en liegen umg.* be at loggerheads (with each other); *heftiger* be at each other's throats; *an den ~en herbeigezogen umg.* far-fetched; *die ~e standen mir zu Berge od. mir sträubten sich die ~e umg.* it made my hair stand on end; *lass dir deshalb keine grauen ~e wachsen umg.* don't lose any sleep over it; *schwer ~e lassen* (*müssen*) *umg. finanziell etc.:* suffer heavy losses; (*auch leiden müssen*) pay dearly; (*eins abbekommen*) take a real beating, cop it hard *umg., Am.* get it *umg.*; *j-m die ~e vom Kopf fressen umg. hum.* eat s.o. out of house and home; *→ Haut 4*

Haar|ansatz *m* hairline; **~ausfall** *m* hair loss; *fachspr.* alopecia; **~band** *n* hairband; (*Schleife*) (hair) ribbon; **~boden** *m* scalp; **~breit** *n fig.: nicht*

ein ~ (*weichen/nachgeben*) not (give/budge) an inch; **~bürste** *f* hairbrush; **~büschel** *n* tuft of hair

haaren *v/i. und v/refl.* lose (*od.* shed) one's hair; *Pelz etc.:* lose (*od.* shed) hairs

Haar|entferner *m* depilatory (cream); *→ Epilierer,* **~ersatz** *m* false (*od.* artificial) hair; *Koll.* wigs and toupets *Pl.*

Haaresbreite *f: um ~* by a hair's breadth; *nicht um ~* not an inch

Haarewaschen *n; -s, kein Pl. → Haarwäsche*

Haarfarbe *f* hair colo(u)r; *was hat er für e-e ~?* what colo(u)r hair has he got?, what colo(u)r is his hair?

haarfein *Adj.* **1.** *Riss etc.:* hairline *attr.;* **2.** *fig.* subtle

Haar|festiger *m* setting lotion; (*Spray*) hair (setting) spray; **~gefäß** *n Anat.* capillary (vessel)

haargenau **I.** *Adj.* exact, (very) precise; **II.** *Adv.* exactly, (very) precisely; *to a T; das stimmt ~* that's exactly right, (that's) spot (*Am.* right) on *umg.;* **~ wissen/kennen** know *s.th.* absolutely precisely / know everything about *s.o./s.th.*

Haargummi *m, n* scrunchie, scrunchy

haarig *Adj.* **1.** hairy; hirsute *förm.; Bot.* pilous; **2.** *umg.* (*schlimm, gefährlich*) hairy

Haarklammer *f* hair clip, *Am.* bobby pin

haarklein *Adv. umg. beschreiben etc.:* down to the last detail; *berechnen:* down to the last cent

Haar|klemme *f → Haarklammer,* **~kranz** *m* **1.** *um e-e Glatze etc.:* (horseshoe-shaped) fringe of hair; **2.** *Zopf:* ring plait (*Am.* braid), plait (*Am.* braid) arranged in a ring around one's head; **~lack** *m* hair spray; **~locke** *f* curl; *bes. abgeschnittene od. herunterhängende:* lock

haarlos *Adj.* hairless; (*kahlköpfig*) bald

Haarmode *f* **1.** hairstyle; **2.** hair fashion(s *Pl.*)

Haarnadel *f* hairpin; **~kurve** *f* hairpin bend (*od.* curve)

Haar|netz *n* hairnet; **~öl** *n* hair oil

Haarpflege *f* hair care; **~mittel** *n* hair-care product

Haar|pinsel *m* fine (animal-hair) brush; **~pracht** *f etwa* crowning glory *hum.,* magnificent head of hair; **~riss** *m* hairline crack; *Keramik:* craze

haarscharf **I.** *Adj.* (*deutlich*) very clear; (*genau*) very precise; *Unterschied* very fine; **II.** *Adv.* **1.** *daneben, vorbei:* by a hair's-breadth, by (a fraction of) an inch; *der Wagen fuhr ~ an mir vorbei* missed me by an inch; *das ging ~ an e-r Niederlage vorbei fig.* he/she *etc.* came within an inch of being beaten; *~ e-m Unfall entgehen* just miss having an accident; **2.** *das hat er ~ erkannt* he spotted it right away;

das hast du ~ beobachtet very clever of you to notice that; *~ unterscheiden* make a very fine distinction (between)

Haar|schleife *f* (hair) ribbon, bow; **~schmuck** *m* hair accessories *Pl.; sie trägt nie ~* she never wears anything in her hair; **~schneider** *m Gerät:* hair clippers *Pl.,* hair trimmer; **~schnitt** *m* haircut; **~schopf** *m voller:* shock of hair; **~sieb** *n* hair sieve; **~spalterei** *f; -, -en; pej., auch Pl.* splitting hairs; *das ist reine ~* that's just splitting hairs; *~ treiben* split hairs; **~spange** *f* (hair) slide, *Am.* barrette; **~spitzen** *Pl.* hair-ends; *gespaltene ~* split ends; *bis in die ~ erröten umg. fig.* blush to the roots of one's hair; **~spray** *n, m* hair spray; **~strähne** *f* strand of hair

haarsträubend *Adj.* dreadful; (*unglaublich*) incredible; (*skandalös*) outrageous; *das ist ja ~* it's enough to make your hair stand on end

Haar|studio *n* hair stylist's; **~teil** *n* hairpiece; **~tracht** *f* hairstyle; **~trockner** *m* hairdryer; **~wäsche** *f* shampoo(ing); *beim Friseur:* shampoo, wash; *bei jeder ~* every time you wash your hair, with every shampoo; **~waschmittel** *n* shampoo; **~wasser** *n* hair tonic; **~wuchs** *m* growth of (the) hair; (*Haare*) hair; **~wuchsmittel** *n* hair restorer; **~wurzel** *f* root of a (*od.* the) hair; *bis zu den ~n erröten umg. fig.* blush to the roots of one's hair

Hab *n; ohne Art.; geh.:* (*all sein*) *~ und Gut* everything (he owns *od.* owned)

Habachtstellung *f bes. österr. Mil.* attention

Habe *f, -, kein Pl.; geh.* property, possessions *Pl.; persönliche:* personal effects *Pl.,* things *Pl. umg.; bewegliche ~* movables; *Jur.* chattels; *unbewegliche ~* immovables, real estate; *s-e ganze ~* everything he owns *od.* owned

haben; *hat, hatte, hat gehabt* **I.** *v/t.* **1.** (*Arbeit, Erfahrung, Geld, Zeit etc.*) have (got); (*besitzen*) *auch* possess, own; *~ wollen* (*wünschen*) want (to have); (*fordern*) want, demand; *die Erlaubnis / das Recht ~ zu* (+ *Inf.*) have permission / the right to (+ *Inf.*); *woher hast du das?* where did you get that (from)?; (*Nachricht etc.*) where did you hear that?; *kann ich mal das Salz ~? umg.* could I have the salt, please?; *da hast du's! umg.* there you are; *zu ~ Ware:* available; *Haus:* for sale; *ist es noch zu ~? auch* is it still going (*Am.* up for sale)?; *sie ist noch zu ~ umg. fig.* she's not spoken for, she's (still) available, she's (still) single; *dafür bin ich nicht zu ~ fig.* you can count me out; *generell:* that's not (really) my thing; *für ein Bier bin ich immer zu ~ fig.* I'm always game for a beer; *wer hat, der hat! umg. hum. od. iro.* if you've got it, flaunt it; *was man hat, das hat man* a bird in the hand (is worth two in the bush) *Sprichw.*, possession is nine points (*od.* tenths) of the law; *er hat's ja! umg.* he can afford it; *haste was, biste was Sprichw.* money makes a man; → *haste;* **2.** (*Eigenschaft, Krankheit, Unfall, Zustand etc.*) have (got); *welche Farbe ~ s-e Augen?* what colo(u)r are his eyes?; *Glück/Pech ~* be lucky/unlucky; *e-n Motorschaden ~* have engine trouble; *es im Hals ~ umg.* have a sore throat; *er hat Geburtstag* it's his birthday; *gestern hatten wir Regen* we had rain yesterday, it rained here yesterday; *hast du heute Dienst/Schule/frei?* are you on duty / have you got school / are you off today?; *Mathe ~ wir bei Herrn Hanel* Mr Hanel takes us for math(s), *We have math with Mr Hanel; in der vierten Stunde ~ wir Physik* we've got physics (in the) fourth period (*od.* lesson); *in Erdkunde ~ wir gerade China* we're doing China in geography at the moment; *da hast du's! (siehst du?)* I told you so; *das kann ich nicht ~! umg.* (*nicht ertragen, leiden*) I can't stand it; *auf etwas Spezifisches reagierend:* I'm not standing for that; **3.** (*fühlen*): *Angst/Durst etc. ~* be afraid/thirsty *etc.*; *Schmerzen ~* be in pain, have a pain *Sg.*; *was hast du denn? umg.* what's up (*od.* wrong)?; *hast du was? umg.* is something the matter?; **4.** (*bestehen aus*) comprise, be made up of, consist of; (*wiegen*) weigh; (*messen*) measure; *der Fisch hat zwei Kilo / zwanzig Zentimeter* the fish weighs two kilos / is 20 centimet|res (*Am.* -ers) long; *ein Kilogramm hat tausend Gramm* there are a thousand grams in a kilogram; *der Verein hat 20 Mitglieder* the club has 20 members; *Deutschland hat 16 Bundesländer* Germany is made up of 16 (federal) states; **5.** *Zeitangabe:* *wir ~ (jetzt) Montag, den 7.11.* it's Monday 7 November (*Am.* November 7th); *wie viel Uhr ~ wir?* what time is it?; *in New York ~ sie jetzt Nacht* it's nighttime in New York at the moment; **6.** *umg. als Brauch, Mode:* *das hat man jetzt so/wieder / nicht mehr Brauch:* it's what we do nowadays / we've gone back to doing it this way / we don't do it like that any more; *Mode:* it's the fashion / back in fashion / out of fashion now; **7.** *unpers., bes. südd., österr., schw:* *es hat* there is/are; *wie viel Grad hat es (draußen)?* what's the temperature (outside)?; *dieses Jahr hat es wenig Pilze* there aren't very many mushrooms this year; *was hat's bei euch für Wetter?* what sort of weather are you having?, what's the weather like where you are?; **8.** *umg.* (*beendet, bekommen, gemacht etc. haben*): *hast du den Abwasch schon?* have you finished washing up (yet)? (*Am.* finished the dishes [yet]?); *hat man den Dieb schon?* have they caught the thief yet?; *hab ich dich endlich!* (*erwischt*) got you!, gotcha! *umg.*; *das werden wir gleich ~!* no problem; *bei Reparatur etc.:* we'll have that done (*od.* fixed) in no time; *ich hab's bald* (I'm) nearly finished; *hast du's bald? ungeduldig:* how much longer are you going to take?; *ich hab's od. jetzt hab ich's!* (I've) got it!; *was hast du in Mathe? Note:* what did you get in math(s)?; *dich hat's wohl! od. hat's dich jetzt ganz?* (*spinnst du?*) you

must be mad (*Am.* crazy)!, you're off your head; **9.** *mit es und Adj.:* *du hast's gut* you've got it good *umg.*, everything's fine for you; *ich hab's eilig* I'm in a hurry; *schön habt ihr es hier* it's lovely for you here; *jetzt ~ wir's nicht mehr weit* not far to go now; *sie will es so ~* that's the way she wants it; *wie hätten Sie's denn gern(e)?* how would you like it?; **10.** *mit zu und Inf.:* *nichts/viel zu essen ~* have nothing / a lot to eat; *e-n Brief zu schreiben ~* have a letter to write; *ich habe noch Geld von ihr zu bekommen* I still have some money to come (*od.* coming) from her, she still owes me some money; *du hast hier/mir (gar) nichts zu befehlen etc.* it's not up to you to tell people/me what to do; *was hast du hier zu suchen?* (*verschwinde!*) what are you doing here?; **11.** *mit Verben:* *wo hast du dein Auto stehen?* where did you leave your car?; *e-n Läufer vor dem Bett liegen ~* have a rug in front of the bed; **12.** *mit Präp.:* *e-e Frau als od. zum Chef ~* have a woman as one's boss; *ich merke erst jetzt, was ich an ihr gehabt habe* it's only now that I can appreciate what I had in her (*bzw.* what an asset *od.* a treasure *od.* a wonderful woman she was); *er hat etwas Überspanntes an sich* there's something eccentric about him; *das ~ Katzen so an sich* that's just the way cats are; *was hat es damit auf sich?* what's it all about?, what does it mean?; *es hat nichts auf sich* (*damit*) it's nothing; *bei sich* (*Dat.*) *~* (*Geld, Ausweis etc.*) have on (*od.* with) one; (*Person*) have with one; *es hat viel für sich* there's a lot to be said for it; *was hast du gegen ihn?* what have you got against him?; *jetzt hätte ich nichts gegen ein Nickerchen* I wouldn't mind a little nap now; *sie hatte alle gegen sich* she had everyone against her; *hinter sich* (*Dat.*) *~* (*etw.*) have been through *s.th.*; (*j-n*) have behind one; *das hätten wir hinter uns* well, that's that; *e-n anstrengenden Tag hinter sich* (*Dat.*) *~* have had a tiring day; *die fünfzig hinter sich* (*Dat.*) *~* be over 50, be the wrong side of 50; *die Sache hat es in sich umg.* it's not easy, it's a tough one; *der Likör hat es in sich* it's a pretty strong liqueur; *hat sie was mit ihm? umg.* is there something going on between them?; *ich hab's nicht so mit ihr / mit Pizza umg.* I don't like (*od.* get on [*Am.* along] with) her / I don't go for (*od.* I'm not into) pizza; *die hat's vielleicht mit i-r Ordnung! umg.* she's got a real thing about tidiness; *unter sich* (*Dat.*) *~* be in charge of; (*befehligen*) command; *er hat viel von s-m Vater* he takes after his father; *er hat etwas von e-m Versager etc.* he's a bit of a quitter; *wenn du so viel arbeitest, ~ wir gar nichts mehr von dir* we'll never see anything of you; *wir ~ nicht viel von unserem Urlaub gehabt* we didn't get much out of our holiday; *was habe ich davon? umg.* what do I get out of it?, what for?; *das hast du jetzt davon! umg.* see?; *das hast du davon, wenn ... umg.* that's what you get when ... (*od.* from [+ *Ger.*]); *das ~ wir noch vor uns* that's still to come, we've still got that to come; *Sie wissen wohl nicht, wen Sie vor sich ~?* you obviously don't know who(m)

you're addressing; *j-n zum Feind/Freund ~* have s.o. as an enemy/friend; → *Anschein, Auge* 1, 2, *gehabt* II, *gern(e)* 1; **II.** *v/i. mit zu und Inf.:* *zu arbeiten/gehorchen etc. ~ (müssen)* have to work/obey *etc.*; *ich hab zu tun* I've got things to do; *du hast gut lachen/reden* you may well laugh/talk; **III.** *v/refl. umg.:* *hab dich nicht so!* don't make such a fuss; (*führ dich nicht so auf*) don't take (*Am.* carry) on like that; *der hat sich vielleicht mit s-n Büchern!* he makes such a fuss about his books!; *und damit hat sich's!* and that's that, and that's final; *es hat sich was damit* it's not that easy; *hat sich was!* some hope!; **IV.** *Hilfsv.* have; *hast du ihn gesehen?* have you seen him?; *ich habe bis jetzt gelesen* I have been reading up to now; *er hat uns gestern besucht* he visited us yesterday; *du hättest es mir sagen sollen* you should have told me; *er hätte es machen können* he could have done it

Haben *n*; *-s, kein Pl.*; *Fin.* credit (side); *Soll und ~* credit and debit

Habenichts *m*; *-(es)*, *-e*; *pej.* have-not (*Pl.* have-nots)

Haben|saldo *m Fin.* credit balance; **~seite** *f* credit side; **~zinsen** *Pl.* credit interest *Sg.*, interest *Sg.* on deposits

Haberer *m*; *-s, -*; *bes. österr.* **1.** (*Verehrer*) beau, boyfriend; **2.** (*Kumpel*) pal, *Brit. auch* mate, *Am. auch* buddy

Habgier *f pej.* greed, avarice; **habgierig** *Adj. pej.* greedy, grasping, avaricious

habhaft *Adj. geh.:* *~ werden* (+ *Gen.*) *e-r Sache:* get hold of; *e-s Verbrechers etc.: auch* seize, catch

Habicht *m*; *-s, -e*; *Orn.* hawk; **Habichtsnase** *f* hooked nose

habil. *Abk.:* *Dr. ~ degree entitling its holder to give lectures at university*; **Habilitation** *f*; *-, -en* habilitation; *qualification by means of a postdoctoral thesis for a senior position in a university department*; **habilitieren** *v/i. und v/refl.* habilitate; *obtain one's postdoctoral qualification*; *sie hat sich in Neurologie habilitiert* she did a postdoctoral thesis in neurology; **habilitiert I.** *P.P.* → *habilitieren*; **II.** *Adj.:* *~er Geisteswissenschaftler sein* be qualified for a senior academic post in the arts

Habit *m, n*; *-s, -e e-s Mönchs etc.*: habit

Habitat *n*; *-s, -e*; *Biol.* habitat

habituell *Psych. od. geh.* **I.** *Adj.* habitual; **II.** *Adv.* habitually, as a habit

Habitus *m*; *-, kein Pl.* **1.** bearing, deportment; *geistiger:* disposition; **2.** *Biol.* habit

Habsburg (*n*); *-s*; *hist.:* (*das Haus*) *~* (the house of) Hapsburg; **Habsburger** *m*; *-s, -*, **Habsburgerin** *f*; *-, -nen* Hapsburg; **habsburgisch** *Adj.* Hapsburg …

Habseligkeiten *Pl.* belongings, bits and pieces *umg.*

Habsucht *f*; *nur Sg.*; *pej.*, **habsüchtig** *Adj. pej.* → *Habgier, habgierig*

Hachse *f*; *-, -n* **1.** *Gastr.* knuckle (of pork, lamb *etc.*); **2.** *Zool.* hock; **3.** *~n umg. hum.* (*Beine*) pins, ham hocks

Hack *n*; *-s, kein Pl.*; *umg., bes. nordd.* mince, *Am.* ground beef *etc.*

Hack|beil *n* chopper; **~block** *m* chopping block; **~braten** *m* meat loaf; **~brett** *n* **1.** chopping board; **2.** *Mus.* dulcimer

Hacke[1] *f*; *-, -n* **1.** *Agr.* hoe; **2.** *bes. ös-*

terr. (*Picke*) pick, pickaxe, *Am.* pickax
Hacke² *f*; -, -*n*; (*Ferse*, *Absatz*) heel; *j-m auf die ~n treten* tread (*Am.* step) on s.o.'s heels; *j-m dicht auf den ~n sein* be hard (*od.* hot) on s.o.'s heels; *die ~n zusammenschlagen* click one's heels; → *ablaufen* II 1
Hackebeil *n umg.* chopper
hacken¹ *vt/i.* **1.** *mit Hacke*: hack; *Agr.* (*Kartoffeln*, *Rüben*) hoe; **2.** (*Holz Fleisch*, *Petersilie etc.*) chop; *klein od. in Stücke ~* chop (up) into little pieces; *ein Loch ins Eis ~* chop a hole in the ice; *sich* (*Dat.*) *ins Bein ~* cut one's leg; **3.** (*picken*) pick, peck (*nach* at); *j-m in den Finger ~* peck s.o.'s finger
hacken² ['hakn̩] *v/i. und v/refl. Computer*: hack (*in* + *Akk.* into)
Hacken *m*; -*s*, - → *Hacke²*
Hackentrick *m Fußball*: backheel
Hackepeter *m*; -*s*, *kein Pl.* **1.** → *Hackfleisch*; **2.** *Gastr.* raw minced pork mixed with chopped onions and spices
Hacker ['hakɐ] *m*; -*s*, -, *~in* *f*; -, -*nen Computer*: hacker
Hack|fleisch *n* minced (*Am.* ground) meat, mince(meat); *vom Rind*: *Am. auch* hamburger; *aus j-m ~ machen umg. fig., oft hum.* make mincemeat of s.o.; *~früchte Pl. Agr.* root crops; *~klotz* *m* chopping block; *~messer n* chopper; *~ordnung* *f Bio. und fig.* pecking order
Häcksel *m, n*; -*s*, *kein Pl.*; *Agr.* chaff, chopped straw; **häckseln** *vt/i. Stroh, Zweige etc.*: chop (up); **Häcksler** *m*; -*s*, - (garden) shredder; (*Häckselmaschine*) chaffcutter
Hacksteak *n Gastr. etwa* beefburger, hamburger
Hader¹ *m*; -*s*, *kein Pl.* quarrel(l)ing; (*Zwietracht*) discord; **hadern** *v/i.* (*streiten*) quarrel (*mit* with); *mit s-m Schicksal ~ fig.* wrestle with one's fate
Hades *m*; -, *kein Pl.*; *Myth.* Hades
Hadrianswall *m hist.* Hadrian's Wall
Hafen¹ *m*; -*s*, *Häfen* **1.** harbo(u)r; (*Handelshafen*) port; *Anlagen*: dock(s *Pl.*); **2.** *fig.* haven; *in den ~ der Ehe einlaufen hum.* be joined in holy matrimony
Hafen² *m*; -*s*, *Häfen* **1.** *südd., österr., schw.* (*Becher*) mug; (*Schüssel*) bowl; (*Topf*) pot; **2.** *nordd.* large glass container
Häfen *m*; -*s*, -; *österr., umg.* (*Gefängnis*) clink
Hafen|anlagen *Pl.* docks; *~arbeiter m*, *~arbeiterin* *f* docker, dock worker; *männlich*: *Am. auch* longshoreman; *~becken* *n* harbo(u)r basin, (wet) dock; *~behörde* *f* port authorities *Pl.*; *~damm* *m* pier, jetty; *~einfahrt* *f* harbo(u)r entrance; *~gebühren Pl.* harbo(u)r dues; *~kneipe* *f* dockland pub, *Am.* waterfront bar; *~meister m* harbo(u)r master; *~meisterei* *f*; -, -*en* harbo(u)r master's office; *~meisterin* *f* harbo(u)r mistress; *~mole* *f* mole; *~polizei* *f* harbo(u)r police; *~rundfahrt* *f* (boat) trip around a (*od.* the) harbo(u)r; *~schleuse* *f* dock gate(s *Pl.*); *~sperre* *f* barrage; (*Sanktion*) embargo; (*Blockade*) blockade; *~stadt* *f* (sea)port; *~viertel* *n* dock area, docklands *Pl.*
Hafer *m*; -*s*, *kein Pl.* oats *Pl.*; *dich sticht wohl der ~ fig.* you're full of beans; (*zu übermutig*) you're very full of yourself, *bes. Am.* you're obviously feeling your oats; *~brei* *m* porridge, *Am.* (cooked) oatmeal; *~brot* *n* oat-

(meal) bread; *~flocken Pl.* porridge (*Am.* rolled) oats, *Am. auch* oatmeal *Sg.*; *~grütze* *f* groats *Pl.*, grits *Pl.*; *~kleie* *f* oat bran; *~mehl* *n* oatmeal; *~sack* *m* *für Pferde*: nosebag; *~schleim* *m* gruel
Haff *n*; -(*e*)*s*, -*s od.* -*e* lagoon; *das Kurische ~ Geog.* the Kurisches Haff, the Courland Lagoon
Haflinger *m*; -*s*, - Haflinger
Haft *f*; -, *kein Pl.*; (*Gewahrsam*) custody; *bes. Pol.* detention; *im Gefängnis*: imprisonment; *strenge ~* close confinement; *in ~* under arrest, in custody; *zu drei Jahren ~ verurteilt werden* be sentenced to three years' imprisonment (*od.* three years in prison), be given a three-year (prison) sentence; *aus der ~ entlassen* release (from custody); *in ~ behalten* detain, hold in custody; *in ~ nehmen* take into custody; *bes. Pol.* place under detention
Haft|anstalt *f* prison; *~ausschließungsgrund* *m* grounds *Pl.* for not imposing a custodial sentence; *~aussetzung* *f* parole
haftbar *Adj.* responsible; *Jur.* liable (*für* for); *~ sein* (*für*) → *haften²*; *j-n ~ machen für* make s.o. liable for; (*verantwortlich*) hold s.o. responsible for; **Haftbarkeit** *f*; *nur Sg.* responsibility, liability
Haft|bedingungen *Pl.* prison conditions; *~befehl* *m* arrest warrant; *e-n ~ gegen j-n erlassen* issue a warrant for s.o.'s arrest; *~beschwerde* *f*: *~* (*einlegen*) (lodge *od.* make an) appeal against (a) remand in custody
Haftcreme *f* fixative cream
Haftdauer *f* term of imprisonment
haften¹ *v/i.* **1.** *~* (*bleiben*) *Geruch, Klette, Schmutz etc.*: cling (*an od. auf* + *Dat.* to); (*kleben*) stick (to); *Reifen etc.*: hold the road; **2.** *fig.*: *ein Makel haftet an* (+ *Dat.*) there is a stigma attached to; *im Gedächtnis ~ bleiben* stick (in one's mind)
haften² *v/i.* (*für* for) (*bürgen*) be liable, be responsible, answer; (*bei e-m Schaden etc. belangt werden*) be held responsible; *~ für* (*garantieren*) guarantee; *Sie ~ mir persönlich für etwaige Schäden* I shall hold you personally responsible for any damage
Haft|entlassene *m, f*; -*n*, -*n* released prisoner; *~entlassung* *f* release (from prison *od.* custody); *~entschädigung* *f* compensation for wrongful imprisonment; *~erleichterung* *f* remission
haftfähig *Adj.* **1.** adhesive; *~ sein auch* stick; **2.** *Jur.* fit to undergo detention; **Haftfähigkeit** *f*; *nur Sg.* **1.** adhesive power(s *Pl.*); **2.** *Jur.* fitness to undergo detention
Haftfrist *f* period of liability
Häftling *m*; -*s*, -*e* prisoner; *politischer ~ auch* political detainee
Häftlings|kleidung *f* prison clothes *Pl.*; *~revolte* *f* prison(ers') revolt
Haftpflicht *f*; *nur Sg.* **1.** *Jur.* liability; **2.** *umg. Versicherung*: personal liability insurance; *für KFZ*: third party (insurance); **haftpflichtig** *Adj.* liable (*für* for); **haftpflichtversichert** *Adj.* with personal liability cover; *Kraftfahrer*: with third party insurance; **Haftpflichtversicherung** *f* personal liability insurance; *für KFZ*: third party insurance
Haftprüfungs|termin *m Jur.* date for a review of a remand in custody (*Am.* a prisoner awaiting trial); *~verfahren* *n* review of a remand in custody (*Am.* a

prisoner awaiting trial)
Haft|pulver *n für Gebiss*: denture fixative; *~reifen* *m* traction tyre (*Am.* tire) (*with improved roadholding ability, especially for winter driving conditions*)
Haftrichter *m*, *~in* *f* magistrate
Haft|schale *f Opt.* contact lens; *~schicht* *f* adhesive surface
Haftstrafe *f* prison sentence
haftunfähig *Adj. Jur.* unfit to undergo detention; **Haftunfähigkeit** *f* unfitness to undergo detention
Haftung *f*; *mst Sg.* **1.** adhesion; *Chem.* absorption; **2.** *Jur.* liability; (*Bürgschaft*) guarantee; *beschränkte/persönliche ~* limited/personal liability; → *Gesellschaft* 6
Haftungs|ausschluss *m Jur.* exclusion of liability; *~beschränkung* *f* restriction of liability
Hafturlaub *m* parole
Haftvermögen *n* adhesive power(s *Pl.*)
Haft|verschärfung *f Jur.* increasing the severity of the terms of s.o.'s imprisonment; *~verschonung* *f* suspended sentence
Hagebutte *f*; -, -*n*; *Bot.* rose hip; **Hagebuttentee** *m* rose hip tea
Hagedorn *m*; *Pl.* -*e*; *Bot.* hawthorn
Hagel *m*; -*s*, -, *mst Sg.* **1.** hail; **2.** *fig.* hail, shower; *von Schimpfwörtern etc.*: volley, torrent; *~korn* *n* **1.** hailstone; **2.** *Med.* sty, chalazion *fachspr.*
hageln I. *v/i. unpers.*: *es hagelt* it's hailing; **II.** *v/t. fig.* hail; *die Schläge hagelten auf ihn nieder* the blows rained down on him; *es hagelte Vorwürfe* there was (*od. s.o./s.th.* was subjected to) a hail of reproaches; *es hagelte Vorwürfe auf ihn* he was showered with reproaches
Hagel|schaden *m* damage caused by hail; *~schauer* *m* hailstorm; *~schlag* *m* **1.** (heavy) hail(storm); **2.** damage caused by hail; *~sturm* *m* hailstorm; *~versicherung* *f* hail insurance; *~zucker* *m* sugar crystals *Pl.*
hager *Adj.* lean, gaunt; **Hagerkeit** *f*; *nur Sg.* leanness, gauntness
Hagestolz *m*; -*es*, -*e*; *altm.* old (*od.* confirmed) bachelor
haha(ha) *Interj.* ha ha!
Häher *m*; -*s*, -; *Orn.* jay
Hahn *m*; -(*e*)*s*, *Hähne* **1.** cock, *bes. Am.* rooster; *junger ~* cockerel; *der gallische ~* the Gallic (*od.* French) cockerel; *~ im Korb fig.* cock of the walk; *es kräht kein ~ danach umg. fig.* nobody cares two hoots about it; **2.** (*Wetterhahn*) weathercock; **3.** *Orn.* (*Vogelmännchen*) cock; **4.** *Pl. Tech. auch* -*en*; tap, *Am. auch* faucet; *am Fass*: spigot; (*Ventil*) valve; *den ~ aufdrehen/zudrehen od. öffnen/schließen* turn the tap (*Am.* faucet) on/off; *der ~ tropft* the tap (*Am.* faucet) is dripping; *fig.* → *Geldhahn*; **5.** *am Gewehr*: hammer; *den ~ spannen* cock the (*bzw.* a) gun
Hähnchen *n* chicken; *ein halbes ~* half a chicken
Hahnen|feder *f* cock feather; *~fuß* *m Bot.* crowfoot, buttercup; *~kamm* *m auch Bot.* cockscomb; *~kampf* *m* cockfight; *~schrei* *m* cockcrow; *beim od. mit dem ersten ~ fig.* at the crack of dawn; *~sporn* *m* cockspur; *~tritt* *m* **1.** *im Ei*: cock tread; **2.** *Muster*: dog's-tooth check; **3.** *beim Pferd*: stringhalt
Hahnrei *m*; -*s*, -*e*; *altm. pej.* cuckold; *zum ~ machen* cuckold

Hai *m*; -(e)s, -e; *Zool.* shark; **⁓fisch** *m* shark; **⁓fischflossensuppe** *f Gastr.* sharkfin soup

Hain *m*; -(e)s, -e; *poet.* grove; **⁓buche** *f Bot.* hornbeam

Hairstylist ['hɛːɐstailɪst] *m*; -en, -en hair stylist

Haiti(an)er *m*; -s, -, **⁓in** *f*; -, -nen Haitian, *weiblich auch* Haitian woman (*od.* girl *etc.*); **haiti(ani)sch** *Adj.* Haitian

Häkchen *n* **1.** small hook; *was ein ⁓ werden will, krümmt sich beizeiten Sprichw.* there's nothing like starting young; **2.** *beim Abhaken:* tick, *Am.* check; **3.** *umg. in Schrift:* diacritic(al mark); (*Apostroph*) apostrophe; (*Akzent*) accent; (*Cedille*) cedilla

Häkelarbeit *f* crochet (work); **Häkelei** *f*; -, -en crochet work; **Häkelgarn** *n* crochet thread *od.* yarn; **häkeln** *vt/i.* crochet; **Häkelnadel** *f* crochet needle (*od.* hook)

Haken *m*; -s, - **1.** hook; *für Kleider:* peg; **⁓ und Öse** hook and eye; *e-n ⁓ schlagen fig. Hase etc.:* make a (sideways) feint, dart sideways; **⁓ schlagen** *fig.* mehrere: zigzag, twist and turn, *Brit. auch* jink; **2.** *auf e-r Liste etc.:* tick, *Am.* check; **3.** *Boxen:* hook; *linker/rechter ⁓* left/right hook; **4.** *fig.* (*verborgene Schwierigkeit*) snag; (*Nachteil*) catch; *die Sache muss doch e-n ⁓ haben* there must be a catch (somewhere); *der ⁓ daran ist ...* the (only) snag *od.* problem *od.* thing is ...; *ohne ⁓* no strings attached

haken I. *v/t.* hook (*an* + *Akk.* onto *od.* into); **II.** *v/refl.:* **sich ⁓ an** (+ *Akk.*) catch (*od.* be caught) on *od.* in; **III.** *v/i.* (*klemmen*) get (*od.* be) stuck (*od.* jammed); *es hakt umg. fig.* we've *etc.* hit a snag, we *etc.* can't get any further

hakenförmig *Adj.* hooked

Haken|kreuz *n* swastika; **⁓nase** *f* hooked nose; **⁓wurm** *m* hookworm

Halali *n*; -s, -(s) *Jagd:* death halloo, mort; *das od. zum ⁓ blasen* sound the mort; *zum ⁓ auf od. gegen j-n blasen fig.* raise a hue and cry against s.o.

halb I. *Adj.* **1.** half; *⁓ Deutschland* half of Germany; *auf ⁓er Höhe* halfway (up); *⁓e Note Mus.* minim, *Am.* half note; *⁓e Pause Mus.* minim (*Am.* half note) rest; *zum ⁓en Preis* for half the price, (at) half-price; *die ⁓e Summe* half the amount; **2.** *bei Zeitangaben:* half; *e-e ⁓e Stunde* half an hour, a half hour; *⁓ drei* (*Uhr*) half past two; *fünf nach/vor ⁓* twenty-five to/past; **3.** (*teilweise, unvollständig*) half; *mit ⁓em Herzen* half-hearted(ly); *er hörte nur mit ⁓em Ohr zu* he was only half listening, he was listening with only half an ear; *sie ist nur noch ein ⁓er Mensch* she's only half the woman she was; *keine ⁓en Sachen machen* not do anything by halves; *j-m auf ⁓em Weg(e) entgegenkommen* meet s.o. halfway; *nur die ⁓e Wahrheit* only half the truth; *nichts Halbes und nichts Ganzes* neither one thing nor the other, neither fish nor fowl; **4.** *umg.* (*fast, so gut wie*) half; *sie ist ja noch ein ⁓es Kind* she's still half a child; *es dauert e-e ⁓e Ewigkeit* it's taking ages; *das weiß schon die ⁓e Stadt* half the town knows it already; **II.** *Adv.* **1.** leer, offen, voll: half-...; *präd.* half ...; *⁓ so viel* half as much; *die Zeit ist ⁓ vorbei* half the time has gone; *⁓ herausfordernd, ⁓ abwehrend*

half defiant(ly), half defensive(ly); *⁓ Mensch, ⁓ Tier* half-human, half-beast; *⁓ und ⁓ mischen etc.:* half and half; *umg. überzeugen, wollen etc.:* more or less; *⁓ und ⁓ machen mit j-m* go halves with s.o.; **2.** (*teilweise*) *bekleidet, nackt verdaut, wach etc.:* half-..., *präd.* half ...; *flüssig, offiziell etc.:* semi-...; *⁓ gar od. durch* half-done, half-cooked; *Steak:* medium; *⁓ verfault* rotting; *⁓ durchsichtig* translucent; *es war mir nur ⁓ bewusst* I was only half aware of it; *es ist ⁓ so schlimm od. wild umg.* it's not as bad as all that (*od.* as we *etc.* thought); **3.** *bes. umg. erfroren, tot, verdurstet etc.:* half; (*fast*) *auch* nearly, almost; (*so gut wie*) *auch* virtually; *⁓ blind vor Tränen* half blinded by tears; *⁓ verhungert* starving; *ich bin ⁓ erfroren* I'm nearly frozen to death; *wir sind da drin ⁓ erstickt* we nearly suffocated in there; *sich ⁓ totlachen* (nearly) kill o.s. laughing; *das ist ja ⁓ geschenkt* that's more or less a gift; *damit war die Sache schon ⁓ gewonnen* that was half the battle; *ich wünsche ⁓, dass ...* I half wish (that) ...; *ich dachte mir schon ⁓ ...* I half suspected, I had a feeling ...; **4.** *Fußball:* → *halblinks, halbrechts*

Halbaffe *m Zool.* prosimian

halb|amtlich *Adj.* semi-official; *Meldung:* unconfirmed; **⁓automatisch** *Adj.* semi-automatic

Halbbildung *f, nur Sg.; pej.* superficial education, smattering of education

halb|bitter *Adj. Schokolade:* plain; **⁓blind, ⁓ blind** *Adj.* nearly blind, partially blind

Halbblut *n* **1.** *Pferd:* half-breed; **2.** *neg! Person:* half-caste; **halbblütig** *Adj. Pferd:* half-breed

Halb|brille *f:* (*e-e*) *⁓* (a pair of) half-moon glasses *Pl.*; **⁓bruder** *m* half-brother; **⁓drehung** *f* half-turn

halbdunkel *Adj. draußen:* dusky; *Zimmer:* dimly-lit; **Halbdunkel** *n* semi-darkness, twilight

Halbe[1] *m, bes. südd. f*, -n, -n *Bier:* pint (of beer)

Halbe[2] *m*; -n, -n; *umg. Wein:* half (a) lit|re (*Am.* -er)

Halbedelstein *m* semi-precious stone

halbe-halbe *Adv.* fifty-fifty; *⁓ machen mit j-m* go halves with s.o.

halber *Präp.* (+ *Gen.*); *nachgestellt; geh.* (*wegen*) on account of, due to; (*um ... willen*) for the sake of; (*zwecks*) for

...halber *im Adv.* → *halber, deutlichkeitshalber* for the sake of clarity; *vergnügungshalber* for fun, for pleasure

halb| erfroren, ⁓ erstickt → *halb* II 3; **⁓erwachsen** *Adj.* almost grown-up; *⁓e Kinder auch* teenage children

Halb|esel *m Zool.* Asiatic wild ass; **⁓fabrikat** *n* semi-finished product

halb|fertig, ⁓ fertig *Adj.* **1.** half-done, half-finished; *Tech.* semi-finished; **2.** *fig. Person:* half-baked; **⁓fest, ⁓ fest** *Adj.* semi-solid; *Eis:* soft; **⁓fett** *Adj.* **1.** *Käse etc.:* medium-fat; **2.** *Druck.* semi-bold

Halbfettmargarine *f* half-fat margarine

Halb|finale *n Sport* semifinal; **⁓finalist** *m*, **⁓finalistin** *f Sport* semifinalist; **⁓fliegengewicht** *n Sport* light flyweight; **⁓fliegengewichtler** *m*, **⁓fliegengewichtlerin** *f* light flyweight; **⁓format** *n Fot.* half-frame

halbgar, halb gar *Adj.* underdone, rare

halbgebildet *Adj. pej.* half-educated,

semi-literate; **Halbgebildete** *m, f pej.* half-wit; *Pl. auch* bunch *Sg.* of half-wits, uneducated lot *Sg.*

Halb|gefrorene *n Gastr.* parfait, soft ice; **⁓geschwister** *Pl.* half-siblings; half-brother(s) and -sister(s); *er und sie sind ⁓* he's her half-brother; she's his half-sister; **⁓glatze** *f* receding hairline; **⁓gott** *m* demigod; *Halbgötter in Weiß umg. iro.* (*Ärzte*) medics; **⁓göttin** *f* demigoddess

Halbheit *f pej.* half measure; *er mag keine ⁓en* he doesn't like doing things by halves (*od.* in half measures)

halb|herzig *Adj.* half-hearted; **Halbherzigkeit** *f; nur Sg.* half-heartedness; **halbhoch** *Adj.* **1.** medium-high (*od.* -sized); *Tisch etc.:* low; **2.** *Sport, Schuss etc.:* hip-high; *Wurf:* shoulder-high

halbieren I. *v/t.* halve, cut in half, divide in half (*od.* in two), split in half (*od.* in two) *umg.*; *Kosten, Summe etc.:* halve, cut by (*od.* in) half; *Math.* bisect; **II.** *v/refl.* halve; **Halbierung** *f* halving; *Bot., Math.* bisection

Halb|insel *f* peninsula; **⁓invalide** *m*, **⁓invalidin** *f* semi-invalid; **⁓jahr** *n* half-year; (period of) six months *Pl.*

Halbjahres|... *im Subst. mst* half-yearly, six-monthly; **⁓bericht** *m Wirts.* half-yearly report; **⁓zeugnis** *n Päd.* half-yearly report

halb|jährig *Adj.* **1.** *Dauer:* six-month ..., *od.* of six months; **2.** *Alter:* six-month-old ...; **⁓jährlich I.** *Adj.* half-yearly, semi-annual, six-monthly; **II.** *Adv.* every six months, twice a year, semi-annually

Halb|kanton *m* demicanton; **⁓kreis** *m* semicircle

halbkreisförmig I. *Adj.* semicircular; **II.** *Adv.* in a semicircle

Halbkugel *f* hemisphere; **halbkugelig** *Adj.* hemispherical

halblang I. *Adj.* medium-length ...; *Rock, Hosen:* knee-length ...; *Laut:* half-long; **⁓er Ärmel** half-sleeve; **II.** *Adv. umg.:* nu' mach mal ⁓! hold on a minute!, hang about! *Sl.*

halblaut I. *Adj.* low, subdued; **II.** *Adv.* in an undertone, in undertones

Halbleder *n* half leather; *in ⁓ gebunden* half-leather ...

halb leer → *halb* II

halbleinen I. *Adj.* half-linen; **II. Halbleinen** *n* half-linen (cloth); *in Halbleinen gebunden* half-cloth

Halbleiter *m Etron.* semiconductor; **⁓technik** *f* semiconductor technology

halb|links, ⁓ links *Adv. bes. Fußball:* ⁓ spielen play inside left; **⁓mast** *Adv.:* (auf) ⁓ (at) half-mast (*auch umg. fig. Hose*); *auf ⁓ stehen* be (flying) at half-mast

Halb|messer *m Math.* radius; **⁓metall** *n Chem.* semi-metal

halbmilitärisch *Adj.* paramilitary

Halbmond *m* half-moon; (*auch Islamsymbol*) crescent; **halbmondförmig** *Adj.* crescent-shaped

halb nackt, halb offen → *halb* II

halbpart *Adv.:* ⁓ machen go halves, go fifty-fifty *umg.*

Halb|pension *f* half-board; **⁓profi** *m* semi-pro (*od.* -professional); **⁓profil** *n* three-quarters profile

halb|rechts, ⁓ rechts *Adv. bes. Fußball:* ⁓ spielen play inside right; **⁓reif, ⁓ reif** *Adj.* half-ripe

halbrund *Adj.* semicircular; **Halbrund** *n* semicircle

Halb|satz *m* half sentence; *bei amtli-*

chen Urkunden: clause; **~schatten** m half-shade; Astron., Kunst und fig.: penumbra (Pl. penumbrae od. penumbras); **~schlaf** m doze; **ich hab's im ~ gehört** I heard it just as I was dozing off (od. beginning to wake up); **~schranke** f Eisenb. half barrier; **~schuh** m (low) shoe; **~schwergewicht** n Sport light heavyweight; **~schwergewichtler** m, **~schwergewichtlerin** f Sport light heavyweight; **~schwester** f half-sister

halb|seiden Adj. **1.** half-silk; **2.** fig. pej. shady; **~seitig I.** Adj. **1.** Druck. half-page ...; **2.** Med. unilateral; **~e Lähmung** fachspr. hemiplegia; **II.** Adv. on one side; **~ gelähmt** paralysed on one side, hemiplegic fachspr.

halbstark Adj. umg. pej. loutish, hooliganesque, Brit. auch yobbish; **Halbstarke** m, f; -n, -n; umg. pej. lout, rowdy, hooligan, Brit. auch yob(bo)

Halb|stiefel m ankle boot; **~strauch** m subshrub

halb|stündig Adj. half-hour ...; **~stündlich I.** Adj. half-hourly; **II.** Adv. every half-hour

Halbtageskarte f half-day pass

halb|tägig I. Adj. half a day's ..., half-day ...; **II.** Adv. → **halbtags**; **~tags** Adv. (for) half the day; **~ arbeiten** work half-days, have a part-time job; **~ geöffnet** open in the mornings (od. afternoons)

Halbtags|arbeit f part-time job (od. employment); **~kraft** f part-time worker (od. employee), part-timer; **~stelle** f part-time job

Halbton m **1.** Mus. semitone, Am. half tone; **2.** Fot., Druck. half-tone

halb tot → **halb** II

halbtrocken Adj. Wein etc.: medium dry

halb verdaut, halb verfault, halb verhungert → **halb** II

Halbvokal m semivowel

halb voll, halb wach → **halb** II

Halb|wahrheit f half-truth; **~waise** f: **er ist ~** he('s) lost his father (od. mother), he('s) lost a parent

halbwegs Adv. fig. (leidlich) fairly, reasonably, halfway umg.; (in etwa) more or less; **ich möchte e-n ~ anständigen Wagen** I want a halfway decent car, I don't want just any old car; **kannst du dich nicht wenigstens ~ normal benehmen?** can't you try and behave at least a bit more normally?; **wie geht's? - so ~** how are things? - oh, so-so od. not so bad

Halbwelt f; nur Sg. demimonde; **~dame** f demimondaine

Halbwelter|gewicht n Boxen: light welterweight; **~gewichtler** m, **~gewichtlerin** f light welterweight

Halbwertszeit f Phys. half-life (period)

halbwild Adj. half-wild; Völker: semi-barbarian

Halbwissen n pej. superficial (od. bitty) knowledge

halbwüchsig Adj. teenage ...; **Halbwüchsige** m, f; -n, -n adolescent, teenager

Halbwüste f semi-desert

Halbzeit f Sport **1.** erste, zweite: half; **2.** Pause: half-time; **nach der ~** in the second half; **zur ~ steht es 2:1** the half-time score is 2-1, the score at half-time is 2-1; **~bilanz** f half-time score; **~pfiff** m half-time whistle; **~stand** m half-time score

Halbzeug n semi-finished product

Halde f; -, -n **1.** Bergb. slagheap, bes.

Am. tailings Pl.; **2.** von Kohlen: heap; fig. von Waren: pile; **auf ~ liegen** od. **sein** etc. Waren: be stockpiled; Wagen etc. be in the storage yard; **3.** geh. slope, hillside

half Imperf. → **helfen**

Halfpipe ['ha:fpaip] f; -, -s; Sport half-pipe

Hälfte f; -, -n **1.** half; **gib mir die ~** give me half (of it); **die ~ der Leute** half the people; **die ~ m-r Zeit** half my (od. the) time; **um die ~ teurer sein** cost half as much again; **die ~ zahlen** pay half(-price); **zur ~** half (of it od. them); **Kosten** etc. **zur ~ tragen** pay (od. bear) half the costs etc.; **sich je zur ~ beteiligen** go half-shares (**an** + Dat. in); **wir haben's zur ~ geschafft** we're halfway there; **m-e bessere ~** umg. hum. my better half; **2.** umg. (großer Teil) half; **davon kannst du die ~ abstreichen** you can discount half of it

Halfter[1] m, n; -s, - für Pferd: halter

Halfter[2] n; -s, - od. f; -, -n für Pistole: holster

halftern v/t. halter

Hall m; -(e)s, -e, mst Sg. **1.** geh. sound; **2.** Tech. (Widerhall etc.) echo

Halle f; -, -n **1.** Bahnhof, Markt etc.: hall; (Werkshalle) shop; für Flugzeuge: hangar; **2.** für Sport: sports hall; Turnen: gymnasium, gym; Reiten: indoor arena; Schwimmen: indoor pool; Tennis: covered court; **in der ~** (spielen etc.) (play etc.) indoors; **3.** (Saal) hall; (Vorhalle) auch entrance hall; Hotel: foyer, lobby; **die heiligen ~n** iro. the hallowed halls

Halleffekt f Etron. echo effect

halleluja Interj. hallelujah!; **Halleluja** n; -s, -s hallelujah

hallen v/i. **1.** (schallen) resound (**durch** through); **2.** (widerhallen) echo, resound (**von** with)

hallenartig Adj. Räume: hall-like, lofty and spacious

Hallen|bad n indoor (swimming) pool; **~fußball** m indoor football (Am. soccer), mst five-a-side football (Am. soccer); **~handball** m (indoor) handball; **~meisterschaft** f indoor championship(s Pl.); **~rekord** m indoor record; **~schwimmbad** n indoor (swimming) pool; **~sport** m indoor sports Pl. (od. athletics Pl.); **~tennis** n indoor tennis; **~turnier** n indoor tournament (Leichtathletik: auch meeting)

Hallig f; -, -en; Geog. Hallig, small island off Schleswig-Holstein

halli hallo Interj. hum. **1.** yoo hoo!; **2.** Begrüßung: well, hello there!

hallo Interj. **1.** um auf sich aufmerksam zu machen: hello; **~(, Sie)!** excuse me; **2.** freudig überrascht: well, well!, hello!; am Telefon: you bet!; **3.** umg. als Gruß: hi; am Telefon: Hallo n; -s, -s **1.** Ruf: hello; **2.** (Aufregung) fuss, hullabaloo; **es gab ein großes ~, als sie ankam** everyone made a big fuss (od. there was a great hullabaloo) when she arrived

Hallodri m; -s, -(s); Dial. scallywag umg., Am. scalawag umg.

Halluzination n; -, -en hallucination; **halluzinieren** v/i. hallucinate; **halluzinogen** Med. Adj. hallucinogenic; **Halluzinogen** n; -s, -e hallucinogen, hallucinogenic drug

Halm m; -(e)s, -e Gras: blade; Getreide: stalk; Stroh: straw (auch Trinkhalm)

Halogen Chem. n; -s, -e halogen; **halogen** Adj. halogenous

Halogen|lampe f halogen lamp; **~scheinwerfer** m Mot. halogen headlight (od. headlamp)

Hals m; -es, Hälse **1.** neck; (Rachen, Kehle) throat; **steifer ~** stiff neck; **j-m in den ~ schauen** (have a) look at s.o.'s throat; **ich hab's im ~** umg. I've got a sore throat; **sich** (Dat.) **den ~ brechen** break one's neck; **j-m um den ~ fallen** fling one's arms around s.o.'s neck; **bis an den ~** up to one's neck (fig. auch eyes, ears); **er hat es in den falschen ~ bekommen** it went down the wrong way; fig. he took it the wrong way; **aus vollem ~(e)** schreien: at the top of one's voice; lachen: roar with laughter; **2.** Tech. neck, collar; e-r Flasche, Geige etc.: neck; Mus., e-r Note: tail; **e-r Flasche den ~ brechen** fig. crack (open) a bottle; **3.** umg. fig.: **~ über Kopf** (hastig) headlong; **sich ~ über Kopf verlieben in** (+ Akk.) fall head over heels in love with; **ich hatte e-n dicken** od. **so 'nen ~** I was absolutely livid; **e-n langen ~ machen** crane one's neck; **am** od. **auf dem ~ haben** be lumbered with; **zu viel am ~ haben** have too much on one's plate; **sich** (Dat.) **auf den ~ laden** lumber o.s. with, get o.s. lumbered with; **j-m die Polizei** etc. **auf den ~ hetzen** get the police etc. onto s.o.; **sich j-m an den ~ werfen** throw o.s. at s.o.; **sich** (Dat.) **j-n/etw. vom ~ schaffen** get rid of s.o./s.th.; **das kann ihm den ~ brechen** that could cost him his neck; **s-n ~ riskieren** risk one's neck; **das Wort blieb mir im ~ stecken** the word stuck in my throat; **es hängt mir zum ~ heraus** I'm fed up to the back teeth with it, I'm sick (and tired) of it; **bis zum ~ stecken in** (+ Dat.:) in Arbeit, Schulden etc.: be up to one's neck in; **sie kann den ~ nicht voll kriegen** she can't get enough (of it); **schaff ihn** etc. **mir vom ~ räumlich:** get him etc. out of here (od. out of my sight); weitS. I don't want to have anything to do with him etc., get him etc. off my back umg.; **bleib mir damit vom ~!** I don't want to know about it; → **Herz**[1] 8

Halsabschneider m; -s, -, **~in** f; -, -nen; pej. shark; **halsabschneiderisch** Adj. pej. attr. cutthroat ...; Preis etc.: extortionate, exorbitant; Zinssatz: usurious

Hals|ansatz m base of the neck; **~ausschnitt** m am Kleid: neckline; **tiefer ~** low neck(line); **~band** n; Pl. -bänder necklace; fest um den Hals getragen: choker; für Hunde: collar

halsbrecherisch Adj. hair-raising, highly dangerous; Tempo etc.: break-neck

Hals|entzündung f Med. sore throat; **~grat** m Gastr., bes. südd. neck; **~kette** f necklace; **~krause** f **1.** von Clown, Vogel etc.: ruff; **2.** Med. neck brace; **~länge** f: **um e-e ~** by a neck

Hals-Nasen-Ohren|-Arzt m, **~-Ärztin** f Med. ear, nose and throat (od. ENT) specialist, otolaryngologist

Hals|partie f neck (area), throat (area); throat and neck Pl.; **~schlagader** f carotid (artery); **~schmerzen** Pl. sore throat Sg.; **~ haben** have a sore throat; **~schmuck** m necklace; kollektiv decorative neckwear, necklaces Pl.

halsstarrig Adj. pej. stubborn; **Halsstarrigkeit** f; nur Sg.; pej. stubbornness

Hals|tuch *n* neckerchief; (*Schal*) scarf; **~- und Beinbruch** *Interj. umg.* break a leg!; **~weh** *n* → **Halsschmerzen**; **~weite** *f* collar size; **was haben Sie für e-e ~?** what size collar do you take?, what's your collar size?; **~wirbel** *m* Anat. cervical vertebra (*Pl.* vertebrae)

Halt *m*; -(e)s, -e *od.* -s **1.** *nur Sg.*; *für Hände, Füße*; *für die Füße*: auch foothold; (*Stütze*) support; **keinen** (**richtigen**) **~ finden** find no (secure) hold; **~ suchen** try to get (*od.* find) a hold; **den ~ verlieren** lose one's hold (*bzw.* footing); **2.** *nur Sg.*, *fig.* (*innere Festigkeit*) (moral) stability; (*Unterstützung*) support; **ohne ~** (*schwach*) weak, unstable; (*hilflos*) helpless, disoriented; **j-m ~ geben** *od.* **ein ~ sein** be a (great) support to s.o.; **3.** (*Aufenthalt, Pause*) stop; **ohne ~** non-stop, without stopping; **~ gebieten** (+ *Dat.*) *geh.* call a halt to, halt, stop; **~ machen** (make a) stop; **er/es macht vor nichts** (**und niemandem**) **~** *fig.* he'll stop at nothing (and for nobody) / it won't stop for anything (or anybody)

halt *Präs.* → **halten**

halt I. *Interj.* **1.** stop!, don't move!; *bes. Mil.* halt!; (*warte!*) wait!; **~, wer da?** halt, who goes there?; **2.** (*es genügt*) that'll do; **3.** (*Moment mal!*) wait a minute; **II.** *Adv. bes. südd., österr., schw.* (*eben*) just; you know; **das ist ~ so** that's just the way it is; **da kann man ~ nichts machen** there's nothing you can do (about it); **dann tu's ~** do it then(, if you must)

haltbar *Adj.* **1.** *Lebensmittel*: non-perishable; *Milch etc.*: long-life ...; **~ sein** *mst* keep (for a long time); **~ machen** preserve; **mindestens ~ bis ...** best before ...; **2.** *Material*: hardwearing, durable; (*fest, stabil*) strong, solid; *Tech. auch* wear-resistant; *Farbe*: fast; **3.** *fig.* lasting; *Argument etc.*: tenable, valid; **sich als nicht ~ erweisen** prove untenable; **Haltbarkeit** *f von Ware*: shelf life; *von Material*: durability; stability (*auch Chem.*); *Tech. auch* resistance to wear; service life; *von Farbe*: fastness

Haltbarkeits|datum *n* best-by (*od.* best-before) date, *Am.* pull (*od.* sell--by) date; **~dauer** *f*: **mit e-r ~ von ...** to be used within ...; **was hat das für e-e ~?** how long will it keep?

Halte|bogen *m Mus.* tie; **~bucht** *f Verk.* lay-by, *Am.* rest stop; **~griff** *m* strap

halten; *hält, hielt, gehalten* **I.** *v/t.* **1.** (*festhalten*) hold; **j-n an** *od.* **bei der Hand ~** hold s.o.'s hand; **im Arm ~** hold in one's arms; **sie hielt sich den Bauch** (**vor Schmerzen**) she was holding her stomach (in pain); → **Daumen**; **2.** (*stützen*) hold (up), support; **das Bild wird von zwei Nägeln gehalten** the picture is held up by two nails; **das Seil hat nicht viel zu ~** (*wird wenig belastet*) there isn't very much weight on the rope; **3.** *in e-r Lage*: hold; **ans Licht ~** hold to the light; **den Kopf gesenkt/hoch ~** keep one's head down / hold one's head up; **die Hand ins/unters Wasser ~** put one's hand in the water / hold one's hand under the tap (*Am. auch* faucet); **sich** (*Dat.*) **beim Gähnen die Hand vor den Mund ~** put one's hand in front of one's mouth when yawning; **4.** *in e-m Zustand*: keep; **frisch/warm ~** keep fresh/warm; **in Gang ~** keep s.th. going; **in Ordnung ~** keep in order; **auf Lager ~** (keep in)

stock; → **bereit** 1, **bereithalten**, **gefangen etc.**, **gehalten** II 3; **5.** (*enthalten, fassen*) hold, contain; **das Fass hält 20 Liter** the barrel holds 20 lit|res (*Am.* -ers); **6.** (*zurückhalten, behalten*) keep, hold; (*Festung, Stellung, Rekord, Titel*) hold; (*aufhalten*) stop; *Sport* (*Schuss*) hold, stop, save; **das Wasser nicht ~ können** be incontinent, not be able to hold one's water (*od.* control one's bladder); **den Ball in den eigenen Reihen ~** hold onto the ball, keep possession (of the ball); **s-n Vorsprung ~ können** retain one's lead; **er war nicht zu ~** there was no stopping (*od.* holding) him, you couldn't hold him back; **was hält mich hier noch?** what is there to keep me here?; **haltet den Dieb!** stop thief!; → **Klappe** 4, **Mund etc.**; **7.** (*Geschwindigkeit, Kurs, Niveau, Preise etc.*) hold, maintain; (*Richtung*) continue in, keep going in; *Mus.* (*Ton*) *lange*: hold; (*nicht abweichen*) keep to; **Ordnung ~** keep order; **Kontakt ~** keep in contact (**mit** *od.* **zu** with); **haltet jetzt bitte Ruhe/Frieden** *umg.* keep quiet now, please / no more arguing, please; **diese Theorie lässt sich nicht ~** this theory is untenable; **8.** (*Versprechen, sein Wort etc.*) keep; **was ich verspreche, halte ich auch** my word is my bond; **das Buch hält nicht, was es verspricht** the book doesn't live up to its promise(s); **9.** (*sich* [*Dat.*]) **j-n/etw. ~** (*Haustiere, Personal, Wagen*) keep; (*Zeitung*) take; **sie hält sich e-n Liebhaber** she keeps a lover; **10.** (*behandeln*) (*Person, Tier, Pflanze, Sache*) treat; **die Kinder knapp/streng ~** not give the children much money / be strict with the children; **11.** (*Sitzung, Versammlung etc.*) hold; (*Hochzeit, Messe*) *auch* celebrate; (*Mahlzeit, Schläfchen etc.*) have, take; (*Rede, Vortrag etc.*) give; **Winterschlaf ~** hibernate; **12.** **~ für** consider (to be), think *s.o./s.th.* is; *irrtümlich*: (mis)take for; **sie hält ihn für den Besitzer** *mst* she thinks he's the owner; **ich halte es für richtig, dass er absagt** I think he's right to refuse, I think it's right that he should refuse; **tu, was du für richtig hältst** do what you think is right; **ich hielte es für gut, wenn wir gingen** I think we should go, I think it would be a good idea if we went; **für wie alt hältst du ihn?** how old do (*od.* would) you think he is?; **wofür ~ Sie mich?** *empört*: who do you think I am?; **13.** **~ von** think of; **viel/wenig ~ von** think highly (*stärker*: the world) / not think much of; **was hältst du von ...?** what do you think of ...?; *auffordernd*: how about ...?; **ich halte nicht viel davon** I don't think much of it; *von Idee, Gemälde etc.*: *auch* I'm not keen on it; **sie hält nichts vom Sparen** she doesn't believe in saving; **14.** **wie hältst du es mit ...?** what do you usually do about ...?; (*was denkst du über ...?*) what do you think of (*od.* about) ...?; **das kannst du ~, wie du willst** please (*bes. Am.* suit) yourself; **ich halte es mit m-m Lehrer, der immer sagte ...** I go by what my teacher always used to say ...; → **gehalten**; **II.** *v/i.* **1.** (*fest sein*) *Knoten, Schnur, Schraube etc.*: hold; *Eis*: be (frozen) solid enough to walk on; *Brücke*: stand the weight of *s.th./s.o.*; (*kleben bleiben*) stick; **2.** (*Bestand haben*) last; *Lebensmittel etc.*: keep; *Wetter*: hold;

3. (*Halt machen*) stop; *Fahrzeug*: *auch* draw up, pull up; **der Zug hält hier zehn Minuten** the train stops here for ten minutes; **er ließ ~** he called a halt; → **halt** I; **4.** *Sport, Torwart etc.*: save; **sie hält gut** she's good in goal, she's a good goalkeeper; **5.** *in Zustand*: **das hält gesund/jung!** it keeps you healthy/young; **6.** *Richtung, mit Waffe*: aim (**auf** + *Akk.* at); *Schiff etc.*: head (**nach** for; **nach Norden etc.** north etc.); **7.** **an sich** (*Akk.*) **~** control o.s.; **ich musste an mich ~, um nicht zu** (+ *Inf.*) it took great self-control not to (+ *Inf.*), I could hardly stop (*od.* keep) myself (from) (+ *Ger.*); **8.** **zu j-m ~** stand by s.o.; *Partei nehmend*: side with s.o.; **III.** *v/t./i.* **1.** (**viel/wenig**) **~ auf** (+ *Akk.*) (*achten auf*) pay (a lot of/little) attention to; (*Wert legen auf*) set (great/little) store by; **2.** **etwas/viel auf sich** (*Akk.*) **~** take pride / a lot of pride in o.s.; *äußerlich*: be particular / very particular about one's appearance; *gesundheitlich*: look after / take great care of one's health; **kein Handwerker, der** (**etwas**) **auf sich hält** no self-respecting craftsman; **IV.** *v/refl.* **1.** *Lebensmittel etc.*: keep; *Schuhe etc.*: last; *Wetter*: hold; *Preis, Kurs etc.*: hold; *Geschäft, Mode, Restaurant etc.*: last; **sich gut ~** *Lebensmittel etc.*: keep well; **sie hat sich gut gehalten** (*ist wenig gealtert*) she looks good for her age, she's well preserved; **2.** (*bleiben*) *fit, warm etc.*: keep, stay; **sich in Form ~** keep in form; *körperlich*: *auch* keep fit; **sich bereit ~** be ready; *Truppen etc.*: be on standby; **sich verborgen** *od.* **versteckt ~** remain hidden *od.* in hiding; **3.** (*standhalten*) hold out; **sich gut** *od.* **wacker ~** hold one's own (*gegen* against), do well; **sich ~ als** maintain one's position as; **sich auf e-m Posten ~** (**können**) last; **4.** **sich ~ an** (+ *Akk.*) keep to, stick to; *an Vorschriften etc.*: comply with; *an j-n*: (*sich verlassen auf*) rely on; *wegen Schadenersatz*: hold *s.o.* liable; **sich an das Gesetz ~** comply with (*od.* abide by) the law; **der Film hält sich eng an die Vorlage** the film keeps very close to the original; **möchten Sie e-n Sherry? - nein, ich halte mich lieber an alkoholfreie Getränke** I'd rather stick to (*od.* with) something non-alcoholic; **5.** *Haltung, Lage, Richtung*: **sich links/rechts ~** keep to the left/right; **sich südlich ~** keep on south, keep going in a southerly direction; **sich sehr gerade** *od.* **aufrecht ~** hold o.s. very straight *od.* erect; **sich kaum noch auf den Beinen ~ können** hardly be able to stand; **sich oft abseits ~** often keep (o.s.) to o.s.; **halt dich immer dicht hinter mir** keep very close behind me; **6.** (*beherrschen*) **sich nicht** *od.* **kaum mehr ~ können** not be able to contain o.s.; **sie konnte sich nicht mehr ~ vor Freude etc.** she was so happy etc. that she could no longer contain herself; **sich vor Lachen nicht mehr ~ können** *umg.* not be able to keep a straight face, not be able to stop o.s. (*od.* keep from) laughing; **7.** **sich ~ für** think o.s. *sth.*, consider (*od.* hold geh.) o.s. to be *sth.*; **sie hält sich mal wieder für besonders schlau** she thinks she's been terribly clever again; → *auch* I 12

Halten *n*; -s, *kein Pl.*: **zum ~ bringen** stop, bring to a halt (*od.* stop); **~ verboten!** no stopping; **da gab es kein ~**

H

mehr there was no holding them *etc.* (back)

Halte|platz *m* stopping place; **~punkt** *m* **1.** (*Haltestelle*) stop; **2.** *Phys.* critical point; **3.** *beim Schießen*: point of aim

Halter[1] *m; -s, -* *Vorrichtung*: holder; (*Griff*) handle

Halter[2] *m; -s, -,* **~in** *f; -, -nen;* (*Eigentümer*) owner

Halterung *f* fixture

Halte|seil *n* safety rope; **~signal** *n Eisenb.* stop signal; **~stange** *f* supporting rod; **~stelle** *f* stop; **~verbot** *n Verk.*: (*absolutes*) *auf Schild*: no stopping; *eingeschränktes ~* no waiting; *im ~ stehen etwa* be parked on a double yellow line, be parked in a no-stopping (*Am. auch* tow-away) zone; *das ~ missachten* disregard the no-stopping sign; **~verbotsschild** *n Verk.* no-stopping sign; **~vorrichtung** *f Tech.* (clamping *od.* holding) fixture

...haltig *im Adj.* containing; *Chem., Geol., etc.* -iferous; *brom~* bromine-containing; *granit~* granitiferous; *Vitamin-B-~* containing vitamin B; **...hältig** *im Adj. österr.* → **...haltig**

haltlos I. *Adj.* **1.** *Mensch*: disoriented, (completely) insecure, completely adrift; *stärker*: floundering; **2.** *Theorie etc.*: untenable; *Anschuldigung, Verdacht etc.*: unfounded; **II.** *Adv.* schluchzen, weinen: uncontrollably; **Haltlosigkeit** *f; nur Sg.* **1.** lack of orientation; **2.** lack of foundation, untenable nature (+ *Gen.* of)

Halt machen → *Halt* 3

Haltung *f* **1.** *mst Sg.; des Körpers*: posture; (*Stellung*) *auch Sport* position; (*Pose*) pose; *e-e schlechte ~ haben* have bad posture; *e-e drohende etc. ~ einnehmen* adopt (*od.* assume) a threatening posture; *in gebückter ~* bent over, stooping; *~ annehmen Mil.* stand to attention; **2.** *mst Sg.;* (*Grundeinstellung*) outlook (*zu* on), approach (to); *zu etw. Bestimmtem*: attitude (*gegenüber* toward[s]); *politische ~* political outlook (*od.* views *Pl.*); *e-e konservative etc. ~ einnehmen* take a conservative *etc.* approach (*od.* line); **3.** *mst Sg.;* (*Auftreten*) bearing, manner; *ihre ganze ~ auch* the way she comes (*od.* came) across; **4.** *nur Sg.;* (*inneres Gleichgewicht*) poise, composure; (*Selbstbeherrschung*) self-possession; *~ bewahren* keep a stiff upper lip; *im Zorn etc.*: retain one's composure, keep one's cool *umg.; um ~ ringen* struggle to keep one's composure (*od.* one's cool *umg.*); *die ~ verlieren* lose one's composure (*od.* one's cool *umg.*); **5.** *nur Sg.; von Tieren etc.*: keeping

Haltungs|fehler *m* **1.** *Med.* bad posture; **2.** *Sport* style fault; **~note** *f Sport* style mark; **~schaden** *m Med.* postural impairment

Halunke *m; -n, -n,* **Halunkin** *f; -, -nen* **1.** *pej.* rogue; **2.** *hum.* (*Schlingel*) rascal

Hämatom *n; -s, -e; Med.* h(a)ematoma (*Pl.* h(a)ematomas *od.* h(a)ematomata)

Hamburger[1] *m; -s, -; Gastr.* hamburger

Hamburger[2] *m; -s, -,* **~in** *f; -, -nen* Hamburger; *gebürtig*: native of Hamburg; *Einwohner*: citizen of Hamburg

Hamburger[3]**, hamburgisch** *Adj.* Hamburg ...

Häme *f; -, kein Pl.* malice; **hämisch I.** *Adj.* malicious; *~e Bemerkung* snide remark; **II.** *Adv.* maliciously; *~ grinsen*

sneer (*über* + *Akk.* at)

Hammel *m; -s, -* **1.** *Zool.* (*Schafbock*) wether; **2.** *Gastr. Fleisch*: mutton; **3.** *umg. pej.* dumm und grob: oaf; *dumm*: idiot, dolt; *grob*: lout, boor; *blöder ~* blithering idiot; **~beine** *Pl. umg.: j-m die ~ lang ziehen* haul s.o. over the coals, give s.o. a dressing-down; **~braten** *m Gastr.* joint of mutton; *gebraten*: roast mutton; **~fleisch** *n* mutton; **~keule** *f Gastr.* leg of mutton; **~kotelett** *n Gastr.* mutton chop; **~sprung** *m Parl.* (vote by) division

Hammer *m; -s, Hämmer* **1.** hammer (*auch Mus., Sport und Auktion*); *aus Holz*: mallet; *Parl. etc.* gavel; *unter den ~ kommen/bringen fig.* come under the hammer / (bring to) auction; **2.** *umg. fig.* (*Fehler*) boo-boo, gaffe; (*Ungeheuerlichkeit*) scandal, disgrace; (*Knüller*) sensation; *das ist ein od. der ~! (ist toll)* that's great; (*ist unerhört*) that's incredible, that really takes the biscuit (*Am.* cake); *und jetzt kommt der ~: ... das Beste*: and this is the best bit (*Am.* part): ...; *das Schlimmste*: and this is the worst bit (*Am.* part): ...; *die große Sensation*: and the absolute cream of it is: ...; *du hast wohl 'n ~! you must be off your nut* (*Am.* head); **3.** *Sport umg., Fußball*: hammer

Hammerhai *m Zool.* hammerhead (shark)

Hammerklavier *n hist.* pianoforte, *a type of piano popular in Germany in the early nineteenth century*

hämmern I. *v/i.* **1.** hammer; **2.** *fig.* hammer (*gegen* on, against); *mit Faust auch*: pound; *auf Klavier etc.*: pound, hammer; *Blut, Herz, Puls*: pound; *Specht*: hammer; *Maschine, Motor*: hammer; **II.** *v/t* **1.** hammer; (*Gefäß, Schmuck etc.*) beat; (*schmieden*) forge; **2.** *fig.* hammer; *j-m etw. in den Kopf ~* hammer s.th. into s.o.

Hammer|schlag *m* hammer blow, blow of the hammer; *die Nachricht traf sie wie ein ~* the news hit her like a hammer; **~werfen** *n; -s, kein Pl.; Sport* throwing the hammer; **~werfer** *m,* **~werferin** *f Sport* hammer thrower; **~wurf** *m Sport* **1.** *einzelner*: hammer throw; **2.** *Disziplin*: (throwing) the hammer; **~zeh** *m,* **~zehe** *f Med.* hammer toe

Hammondorgel [ˈhɛmənt-] *f Mus.* Hammond organ

Hämoglobin *n; -s, kein Pl.; Physiol.* h(a)emoglobin

hämorrhagisch *Adj. Med.: ~es Fieber* h(a)emorrhagic fever

Hämorrhoiden [hɛmɔroˈiːdṇ]**, Hämorriden** *Pl. Med.* h(a)emorrhoids, piles *umg.*

Hampelmann *m* **1.** *Spielzeug*: jumping jack; *Gymnastikübung*: jumping jack; **2.** *umg. pej.* (*Waschlappen*) wimp; (*Marionette*) puppet; *j-n zum ~ machen* have s.o. on a string, get s.o. under one's thumb; *ich bin doch nicht dein ~!* I'm not your puppet on a string!, I don't jump every time you say "jump"!; **hampeln** *v/i. umg.* jump around; (*zappeln*) fidget

Hamster *m; -s, -; Zool.* hamster; **~backen** *Pl. umg.* pudgy cheeks; **~fahrt** *f* foraging trip; **~käufe** *Pl.* hoarding *Sg.; in Panik*: panic buying *Sg.; ~ machen* hoard (food *etc.*), stock up (on food *etc.*)

hamstern *vt/i.* **1.** (*horten*) hoard; *in Panik*: panic-buy; **2.** (*in Notzeiten eintau-*

schen) barter goods for food

Hand[1] *f; -, Hände* **1.** hand; *auf/mit der flachen ~* in/with the palm of one's hand; *in der hohlen ~* in the hollow of one's hand; *Hände hoch (oder ich schieße)!* hands up (or I'll shoot)!; *Hände weg!* hands off!; *an der/j-s ~ gehen* walk holding hands / holding s.o.'s hand; *sie hatte ihr Kind an der ~* she was holding her child's hand, she had her child by the hand; *j-n an die od. bei der ~ nehmen* take s.o.'s hand; *auf Händen und Füßen kriechen* on all fours, on one's hands and knees; *aus der ~ legen od. geben* put aside; *j-m aus der ~ lesen* read s.o.'s hand; *bei der ~ od. zur ~* at hand, handy; *durch (Heben der) ~ abstimmen* by a show of hands; *in Händen halten geh.* hold in one's hands; *~ in ~ gehen* walk hand in hand; *in die od. zur ~ nehmen* pick s.th. up; *mit Händen und Füßen reden* gesticulate, talk with one's hands; *sich mit Händen und Füßen wehren umg. auch fig.* fight tooth and nail; *mit der ~ machen etc.*: by hand; *mit der od. von ~ gemacht/ gemalt etc.* handmade/handpainted *etc.; zu Händen auf Brief*: c/o (= care of); *amtlich*: att., Attention; *zur linken/rechten od. linker/rechter ~* on the left-hand/right-hand side; *~ anlegen* (*an* + *Akk.*) take s.th. in hand; (*mit*) *~ anlegen* lend a hand; *~ an sich* (*Akk.*) *legen* euph. commit suicide; *letzte ~ an etw.* (*Akk.*) *legen* add the finishing touches to s.th.; *j-m die ~ auflegen segnend*: lay one's hand on s.o.; *j-m die ~ geben od. reichen od. schütteln* shake hands with s.o.; (*gib mir die*) *~ drauf!* (let's) shake on it!; **2.** *fig. Wendungen, mit Adj.*: *die öffentliche ~* the authorities, the state; *j-s rechte ~* s.o.'s right-hand man (*od.* woman); *aus erster ~* first-hand; *ich hab's aus erster ~* I got it straight from the horse's mouth; *ein Gebrauchtwagen aus erster ~* a used car from the first owner; *aus privater ~* privately; *aus zweiter ~ kaufen etc.*: second-hand; *Erlebnis, erleben*: vicarious(ly); *e-e feste ~ brauchen* need a firm hand; *sie ist in festen Händen umg.* she's accounted for, she's booked; *j-m freie ~ lassen* give s.o. a free hand; *in guten Händen sein* be in good hands; *e-e glückliche od. geschickte ~ haben* have the right touch (*mit* for); *sie hat e-e* (*glückliche*) *~ mit* she knows how to handle; *mit Menschen, Pflanzen etc.*: she has a way with; *alle Hände voll zu tun haben umg. generell*: have a lot on one's plate; *mit j-m/etw.*: have one's hands full *with s.o./s.th.; mit beiden Händen zugreifen* jump at the chance; *von langer ~* long beforehand; *mit leeren Händen dastehen* be left empty-handed; *j-m etw. zu treuen Händen geben geh.* give s.th. to s.o. for safekeeping; (*aber*) *zu treuen Händen! geh. hum.* (but) I want it *etc.* back!; *mit vollen Händen* liberally; *sein Geld mit vollen Händen ausgeben* throw one's money about (*Am.* around); *hinter vorgehaltener ~ sprechen etc.*: off the record; → *link...* 1; **3.** *fig. Wendungen, mit Präp.: j-m etw. an die ~ geben* (*Argumente, Informationen etc.*) hand s.o. s.th., pass s.th. on to s.o., make s.th. available to s.o.; *an der ~ haben umg.* know of, know where to find, be able to get hold of; (*Person*) *auch* have contacts with *s.o.; (bar) auf die ~* cash in hand; *es liegt* (*klar*) *auf der* ~ it's (so) obvious; *j-n auf Händen tragen* wait on s.o. hand and foot; ~ *aufs Herz!* (*ich lüge nicht*) cross my heart; (*sei ehrlich*) be honest; *j-m aus der* ~ *fressen umg.* eat out of s.o.'s hand; *aus der* ~ *geben* part with; (*Posten etc.*) *auch* give up; *er gibt od. lässt es nicht aus der* ~ *auch* he won't let go of it, he won't let anyone else have it (*od.* take it from him); *mit Kritik ist er immer schnell bei der* ~ *umg.* he's always very quick to criticize; *durch j-s Hände gehen* go through s.o.'s hands; *schon durch viele Hände gegangen sein* have been through several hands; ~ *in* ~ *arbeiten* work together, cooperate (closely); *das geht* ~ *in* ~ *mit ...* it goes hand in hand with ..., it goes together with ...; *j-m in die Hände arbeiten* play into s.o.'s hands; *in die Hände bekommen* (*etw., j-n*) get one's hands on; *j-m in die Hände fallen* fall into s.o.'s hands; *j-n in der* ~ *haben* have s.o. in one's grip; *etw. gegen j-n in der* ~ *haben* have s.th. on s.o.; *sich in der* ~ *haben* have everything under control, have a firm grip on o.s.; *du hast es in der* ~ *od. es liegt in d-r* ~ it's up to you; *in j-s* ~ *sein Person*: be in s.o.'s hands, be up to s.o.; *in die Hände spucken umg. fig.* roll up one's sleeves; *j-m etw. in die* ~ *versprechen* promise s.o. s.th. (*od.* s.th. to s.o.); *s-e* ~ *ins Feuer legen für* put one's hand into the fire for; *die Hände in den Schoß legen* (*nicht arbeiten*) take it easy; (*sich untätig verhalten*) sit on one's hands; *s-e* ~ *od. Hände im Spiel haben* have a hand in it; *etw. in die* ~ *nehmen Aufgabe etc.*: take charge of s.th.; *die Sache in die* ~ *nehmen* take the initiative; *j-m* (*etw.*) *in die Hände spielen* play (s.th.) into s.o.'s hands; *es ist mit Händen zu greifen* it sticks out a mile (*od.* like a sore thumb) *umg.*; *s-e* ~ *über j-n halten* take s.o. under one's wing, shield (*od.* protect) s.o.; *die Hände über dem Kopf zusammenschlagen umg.* throw up one's hands in horror; *um j-s* ~ *anhalten od. bitten* ask for s.o.'s hand; *unter der* ~ (*nicht offiziell*) unofficially; (*privat*) *kaufen etc.*: privately; (*heimlich, illegal*) under the counter; (*nebenbei*) on the side; *j-m unter den Händen zerrinnen Geld etc.*: go through s.o.'s fingers like water; *die Arbeit geht ihm flott von der* ~ he's a fast worker; *von der* ~ *in den Mund leben* live from hand to mouth; *von der* ~ *weisen* (*verwerfen, abtun*) dismiss; (*leugnen*) deny; *es ist nicht von der* ~ *zu weisen* it can't be denied, there's no denying (*od.* getting away from) it; *von j-s* ~ *sterben etc. geh.* die by s.o.'s hand; *von* ~ *zu* ~ *gehen* go (*od.* be passed) from hand to hand; *j-m zur* ~ *gehen* lend s.o. a hand; *sie hat immer e-e Antwort zur* ~ *auch* she's always got an answer pat (*Am.* ready), she's never at a loss for words; → *anhand*; **4.** *fig. sonstige Wendungen*: ~ *und Fuß haben Plan etc.*: make sense, hold water; *was er macht, hat* ~ *und Fuß* he doesn't do things in (*od.* by) half measures; *die* ~ *aufhalten umg., mst pej.* hold out one's hand; *einander die* ~ *geben Ereignisse etc.*: follow hard on each other's heels, happen in close succession; *die Ereignisse gaben einander die* ~ *auch* one thing led to another; *j-m die* ~ *zur Versöhnung reichen* of-

fer s.o. one's hand as a sign of reconciliation; *die beiden können einander die* ~ *reichen* they're two of a kind; *im negativen Sinne*: *auch* they're as bad as each other, one's as bad as the other; (*sie sind in der gleichen Lage*) they're in the same boat; *sich* (*Dat.*) *die Hände reiben* vor heimlicher Freude: rub one's hands; *e-e* ~ *wäscht die andere Sprichwort* you scratch my back and I'll scratch yours, one hand washes the other *altm.*; *ich wasche m-e Hände in Unschuld geh.* I wash my hands in innocence; → *ausrutschen* 2, *gebunden* II 2, *küssen*; **5.** (*Schrift*) hand; **6.** *Kartenspiel*: hand; *auf der* ~ in one's hand; (*aus der*) ~ *spielen* play from one's hand (*Skat*: without picking up the discard); **7.** *Fußball*: (*das war*) ~! handball!

Hand² *f; -, - od. Hände Maßangabe*: *zwei* ~ *breit etwa* a foot wide; *e-e* ~ *voll konkret*: a handful; (*wenige*) a handful

Hand|abwehr *f Fußball*: save (with the hand), parry; *Boxen*: parry with the open hand; ~**apparat** *m Bibliothek*: (set of) reference works *Pl.*

Handarbeit *f* **1.** handicrafts *Pl.*; *textile*: needlework; (*Gegenstand*) *auch Pl.* handiwork; (*Handanfertigung*) handmade article; *feine* ~ skilled handiwork; *in* ~ *hergestellt* made by hand; **2.** *nur Sg.*: *Schulfach*: needlework; **3.** (*manuelle Arbeit*) manual work; **Handarbeiter** *m*, **Handarbeiterin** *f* **1.** manual worker; **2.** (*Handwerker*) craftsman

Handarbeits|geschäft *n* wool and needlework shop; ~**heft** *n* needlework book; ~**unterricht** *m* needlework (classes *Pl.*)

Hand|aufheben *n; -s, kein Pl.; Parl.*: *durch* ~ *abstimmen*: by a show of hands; ~**auflegen** *n; -s, kein Pl.; kirchl.* laying on of hands; ~**ball** *m* **1.** *nur Sg.*; *Spiel*: handball; **2.** *Ball*: handball (ball); ~**ballen** *m Anat.* ball of the thumb

Handballer *m; -s, -,* ~**in** *f; -, -nen; umg.* handball player

Handball|spiel *n* game of handball; ~**spieler** *m*, ~**spielerin** *f* handball player

Hand|bedienung *f; nur Sg.* manual operation; ~**beil** *n* hatchet; ~**besen** *m* (hand)brush

Handbetrieb *m; nur Sg.* manual operation; *mit* ~ manually operated, hand-operated; **handbetrieben** *Adj.* hand-operated

Hand|bewegung *f* movement (*schwungvolle*: sweep) of the hand, gesture; *durch e-e* ~ *auffordern* motion (*zu + Inf.* to + *Inf.*); → *auch Handgriff*; ~**bibliothek** *f* reference library; ~**bohrer** *m Tech.* gimlet; ~**bohrmaschine** *f* hand drill; ~**brause** *f* shower handset, hand-held showerhead

handbreit *Adj. a* hand's breadth; ~ *offen stehen Tür*: be ajar; **Handbreit** *f; -, - hand's breadth*; → *auch Hand²*

Hand|bremse *f Mot.* hand brake, *Am.* emergency (*od.* parking) brake; ~**buch** *n* textbook; (*Anweisungen*) manual, handbook; ~**bürste** *f* nail-brush

Händchen *n; -s, -* (little) hand; ~ *halten* hold hands; *bei j-m od. j-m das* ~ *halten* hold s.o.'s hand; ~ *haltend* hand in hand, holding hands; *sie hat ein* ~ *dafür umg.* she's got the knack

Hand|creme *f* handcream; ~**dusche** *f* shower handset, hand-held showerhead

Hände|druck *m*; *Pl. Händedrücke* handshake; *etw. mit e-m* ~ *bekräftigen* shake hands on s.th.; ~**klatschen** *n* clapping, applause

Handel¹ *m; -s, kein Pl.; Wirts.* **1.** trade, commerce; *bes. Börse*: trading (*mit* in); (*Markt*) market; ~ *und Gewerbe* trade (*bes. Am.* commerce) and industry; ~ *und Wandel altm.* business and social life; *im* ~ on the market; *im* ~ (*erhältlich od. zu haben*) *sein auch* available; *nicht mehr im* ~ off the market, no longer available; *in den* ~ *bringen/kommen* put on / come onto the market; *aus dem* ~ *ziehen* take off the market; ~ *treiben* trade; ~ *treiben mit mit etw.*: deal in s.th.; *mit j-m*: do business with s.o.; ~ *treibend* trading; **2.** (*Geschäft*) (business) transaction, deal; (*Tauschhandel*) barter; (*Vereinbarung*) deal; *ich lasse mich auf keinen* ~ *mit dir ein fig.* I don't want to get involved with you at all

Handel² *m; -s, Händel, mst Pl.; altm., geh.* quarrel, argument; **Händel suchen** be looking for trouble, be trying to pick a quarrel

handelbar *Adj. Wirts.*: *an der Börse / frei* ~ negotiable on the stock exchange / freely negotiable

Handelfmeter *m Fußball*: penalty for handball

handeln¹ I. *v/i.* **1.** act; (*in Aktion treten*) take action; (*verfahren*) proceed; (*sich verhalten*) behave; *die* ~**den Personen** *in e-m Buch, Film etc.*: the characters; *eigenmächtig/selbstsüchtig etc.* ~ act on one's own authority, take the law into one's own hands / act selfishly; *gut/ schlecht etc. an j-m* ~ treat s.o. well/badly, behave well/badly toward(s) s.o.; *nicht reden,* ~! stop talking and do something!; *sie hat in Notwehr gehandelt* she acted in self-defen|ce (*Am.* -se); *rasches Handeln ist nötig* swift action is necessary; **2.** (*Handel treiben*) trade (*mit* with s.o., in s.th.), deal (in s.th.); (*feilschen*) bargain (*um ein Objekt*: for; *e-n Preis*: over), haggle (over) *pej.*; *mit sich* (*Dat.*) ~ *lassen* be open to offers; *fig.* be prepared to discuss things, be open to persuasion; **3.** ~ *von od. über* (+ *Akk.*) be about; *sachlich*: *auch* deal with; **4.** *unpers.*: *es handelt sich um* it's a question (*od.* matter) of, it concerns; *es handelt sich um Folgendes* the thing (*od.* situation etc.) is (this); *es handelt sich darum, ob/wann etc.* the question is whether/where etc.; *gerade darum handelt es sich ja* that's (just) the point; *wenn es sich darum handelt zu helfen etc.* when it comes to helping etc.; *worum handelt es sich? bei der Sache etc.*: what's it about?; (*was willst du*) what's the problem?; **II.** *v/t.*: *an der Börse gehandelt werden* be traded (*od.* listed) on the stock exchange; *zu od. für 10 Dollar gehandelt werden Waren*: be selling for 10 dollars; *Aktien*: be trading (*od.* be being traded) at 10 dollars; *sie wird als neue Direktorin gehandelt fig.* she's being talked about as the new director, her name is being mentioned in connection with a directorship

handeln² ['hɛndln] *v/t. Sl.*: *wie wird das gehandelt?* what do you do with it?, how do you use it?; *der neue Dru-*

H

cker ist einfach zu ~ the new printer is easy to handle
Handels|... *im Subst. Wirts. siehe auch* **Wirtschafts...**; **~abkommen** *n Pol.* trade agreement
Handels|akademie *f österr., Päd.* business school, commercial college; **~akademiker** *m,* **~akademikerin** *f österr.* business school graduate
Handels|bank *f; Pl. -banken; Wirts.* commercial (*od.* merchant) bank; **~bericht** *m* trade (*od.* market) report; **~beschränkungen** *Pl.* trade restrictions; **~betrieb** *m* commercial enterprise, business; **~bezeichnung** *f* trade name; **~beziehungen** *Pl.* trade relations; **~bilanz** *f* balance of trade; **~blatt** *n* trade journal; **~buch** *n* account book; **~defizit** *n* trade deficit
handelseinig, handelseins *Adj.:* ~ *werden* come to (*od.* reach) an agreement (*mit* with)
Handelsembargo *n Pol.* trade embargo
handelsfähig *Adj.* negotiable
Handels|flagge *f Naut.* merchant flag; **~flotte** *f Naut.* merchant fleet; **~freiheit** *f Wirts.* freedom of trade, *weitS.* free trade
handelsgängig *Adj. Fin.* marketable
Handels|gericht *n Jur.* commercial court; **~gesellschaft** *f Wirts.* (trading) company, *bes. Am.* (business) corporation
Handelsgesetz *n Jur.* commercial law; **~buch** *n* (*abgek.* **HGB**) commercial code
Handels|gewerbe *n Wirts.* trade, business; **~gut** *n →* **Handelsware**; **~hafen** *m* commercial port; **~haus** *n altm.* firm; **~hochschule** *f* business school, commercial college; **~kammer** *f* chamber of commerce; **~kette** *f* chain (of stores); **~klasse** *f* grade; *Eier der* ~ *1* grade 1 (*Am.* A) eggs; **~kontor** *n hist.* branch; **~korrespondenz** *f* commercial correspondence; **~krieg** *m* trade war(fare); **~lehrer** *m,* **~lehrerin** *f* teacher of business studies; **~macht** *f* trading nation; **~marine** *f* merchant navy; **~marke** *f* trademark; **~metropole** *f* commercial capital, cent|re (*Am.* -er) of commerce
Handels|minister *m,* **~ministerin** *f Pol.* minister (*Am.* secretary) of commerce; *in GB:* Secretary of State for Trade and Industry, *ehemals:* President of the Board of Trade; *in den USA:* Secretary of Commerce; **~ministerium** *n* department of commerce; *in GB:* Department of Trade and Industry; *in den USA:* Department of Commerce
Handels|monopol *n Wirts.* trade monopoly; **~name** *m* trade name; **~nation** *f* trading nation; **~niederlassung** *f* **1.** business establishment; **2.** *Jur.* registered seat; **3.** (*Zweigstelle*) branch; **~organisation** *f* **1.** trading organization; **2.** (*abgek.* **HO**) *hist., ehem. DDR: state enterprise in the former GDR that ran shops, hotels, etc.;* **~partner** *m,* **~partnerin** *f* trading partner; **~platz** *m* trading cent|re (*Am.* -er)
Handelspolitik *f Pol.* commercial policy; **handelspolitisch** *Adj.* trade ...
Handelsrecht *n Jur.* commercial (*Am. auch* business) law; **handelsrechtlich I.** *Adj.* in accordance with (*od.* relating to) commercial (*Am. auch* business) law; **II.** *Adv.* under (*od.* according to) commercial (*Am. auch* busi-

ness) law
Handels|register *n Wirts.* commercial (*od.* trade, *Am.* company) register; *e-e Firma ins* ~ *eintragen* register a firm; **~reisende** *m, f* travel(l)ing salesman
Handelsschiff *n Naut.* merchant ship, trading vessel; **~fahrt** *f* merchant shipping
Handelsschranken *Pl. Wirts., Pol.* trade barriers, barriers to trade; *der Abbau der* ~ the removal of trade barriers
Handels|schule *f Päd.* commercial school; **~schüler** *m,* **~schülerin** *f* student at a commercial school
Handels|spanne *f* profit margin, markup; **~sprache** *f* business language; *mst pej.* commercialese; **~stadt** *f* commercial cent|re (*Am.* -er); **~straße** *f* trade route; **~stützpunkt** *m* trading base; **~überschuss** *m* trade surplus
handelsüblich *Adj.* usual in the trade; *Verpackung, Größe:* standard commercial ...; *Qualität:* commercial; **~e Bezeichnung** trade name
Handels|unternehmen *n Wirts.* commercial enterprise; **~verbindung** *f* **1.** *räumlich:* trade route; **2.** *~en (Beziehungen)* trade relations; **~verkehr** *m* trading; *in großem Maßstab:* commerce; **~vertrag** *m* trade agreement; **~vertreter** *m,* **~vertreterin** *f* travel(l)ing salesman; **~vertretung** *f* commercial agency; *Pol.* trade mission; **~volumen** *n* volume of trade; **~ware** *f* commodity; **~n** merchandise *Sg.;* **~weg** *m* trade route; **~wert** *m* market value; **~zentrum** *n* commercial cent|re (*Am.* -er); **~zweig** *m* line of business
Handel treibend → *Handel*[1]; **Handeltreibende** *m, f; -n, -n* trader; *weitS.* businessman (*bzw.* businesswoman)
hände|reibend *Adv.* gleefully; **~ringend** *Adv.* (*flehentlich*) imploringly; (*verzweifelt*) despairingly; *j-n* ~ *anflehen* implore s.o.
Hände|schütteln *n; -s, kein Pl.* shaking of hands, handshake; **~trockner** *m* dryer; **~waschen** *n* washing one's hands; *vor dem Essen* ~ *nicht vergessen hum.* don't forget to wash your hands before the meal
Hand|feger *m* (hand)brush; **~fertigkeit** *f* manual skill, dexterity; **~fesseln** *Pl.* manacles; (*Handschellen*) handcuffs
handfest *Adj.* **1.** *Person:* sturdy, strong; **2.** *Essen:* substantial; **~e Mahlzeit** good, square meal; **3.** *fig. Beweise etc.:* tangible, concrete; *Argument, Vorschlag etc.:* serious, solid; *Drohung:* serious; *Skandal, Konflikt etc.:* full-blown; **~e Lüge** out and out lie
Hand|feuerwaffe *f* portable firearm; *Pl. mst* small arms; **~fläche** *f* palm (of one's hand)
hand|gearbeitet *Adj.* handmade; **~geknüpft** *Adj.* handwoven
Hand|geld *n* **1.** *hist.* earnest money; **2.** *Sport* signing(-on) fee; **~gelenk** *n* **1.** wrist; **2.** *umg. fig.: aus dem* ~ off the cuff; (*leicht*) just like that; *ich kann keine Rede so einfach aus dem* ~ *schütteln* I can't come up with a speech just like that
hand|gemacht *Adj.* handmade; **~gemalt** *Adj.* handpainted; **~gemein** *Adj.:* ~ *werden* come to blows (*mit* with)
Handgemenge *n* brawl, scuffle; *es kam zu e-m* ~ scuffling (*od.* scuffles) broke out
handgenäht *Adj.* hand-sewn

Hand|gepäck *n* hand luggage (*Am. auch* baggage), carry-on luggage (*Am. auch* baggage); **~gerät** *n* handtool
hand|gerecht *Adj.* handy; (*praktisch*) *auch* practical; **~geschnitzt** *Adj.* hand-carved; **~geschrieben** *Adj.* handwritten; **~gesteuert** *Adj.* hand-operated; **~gestickt** *Adj.* hand-embroidered; **~gestrickt** *Adj.* **1.** hand-knitted; **2.** *umg. fig.* homemade; **~gewebt** *Adj.* hand-woven
Handgranate *f* hand grenade
handgreiflich I. *Adj.* **1.** *Auseinandersetzungen etc.:* violent; ~ *werden* turn (*od.* get) violent, lash out, get rough *umg.; mehrere: auch* come to blows; *umg. sexuell:* get physical; **2.** *fig.* palpable; (*offensichtlich*) evident, manifest; **~e Lüge** out and out (*od.* blatant *od.* bald-faced) lie; **II.** *Adv.: j-m etw.* ~ *vor Augen führen* show s.o. s.th. quite plainly; **Handgreiflichkeiten** *Pl.: es kam zu* ~ they came to blows, blows were exchanged
Handgriff *m* **1.** *Hebel etc.:* grip, handle; **2.** *Handlung:* movement, manipulation; **~e im Haushalt etc.:** mechanical jobs; *mit e-m* ~ with a flick of the wrist; (*schnell*) in no time, just like that; *mit wenigen* **~en** without any trouble; (*schnell*) in a brace of shakes, in next to no time, *Am. auch* before you can (*od.* could) say Jack Robinson; *er tut keinen* ~ he doesn't lift a finger, he won't do a hand's turn; *da muss jeder* ~ *sitzen* every move has to be exactly right
handgroß *Adj.* hand-sized, *nachgestellt:* the size of a hand; *e-e* **~e Wunde** a wound the size of a hand
handhabbar *Adj.: leicht/schwer* ~ easy/difficult to manage, handy/unwieldy; **Handhabbarkeit** *f; nur Sg.* manageability
Handhabe *f; -, -n* grounds *Pl.* (*um etw. zu tun* for doing s.th.); (*Beweise*) proof, evidence; *gesetzliche* ~ legal grounds; *e-e gesetzliche* ~ *haben gegen* have a case against *s.o.; keinerlei* ~ *gegen j-n haben* have nothing on s.o. *umg.; er hat keinerlei* ~ he hasn't got a leg to stand on
handhaben *v/t.* (*untr., hat ge-*) **1.** (*Werkzeug etc.*) use, handle, manage; (*Maschine*) operate; **2.** *fig.* handle, deal with; (*anwenden*) apply; *das wurde immer so gehandhabt* it's always been done like that; **Handhabung** *f* **1.** use; *e-r Maschine etc.:* operation; **2.** *fig.* handling
Handicap, Handikap ['hɛndikɛp] *n; -s, -s* handicap; (*Nachteil*) *auch* drawback; **handicappen, handikappen** ['hɛndikɛpn̩] *v/t.* handicap
Handkamera *f* handheld camera
Handkante *f* side of the hand; **Handkantenschlag** *m* chop
Hand|karren *m* handcart; **~käse** *m* small, round, hand-formed, curd cheese *flavo(u)red with caraway seeds; mit Musik Dial. Handkäse served with a sauce;* **~katalog** *m* ready-reference catalog(ue); **~koffer** *m* small suitcase; **~kreissäge** *f* portable circular saw; **~kuss** *m* kiss on the hand; *j-m e-n* ~ *geben* kiss s.o.'s hand; *er hat es mit* ~ *genommen fig.* he was only too glad to have (*od.* accept) it
Handlanger *m; -s, -,* **~in** *f; -, -nen* **1.** odd-job man; **2.** *pej.* dogsbody, *bes. Am.* gofer; (*Komplize*) accomplice; *Pol. etc.* henchman, stooge, lackey *umg.; den* ~ *machen umg.* do the don-

key (*od.* dirty) work; **für j-n den ~ ma-chen** fetch and carry for s.o.; **~diens-te** *Pl. pej.* donkey (*od.* dirty) work *Sg.*; **j-m ~ leisten** fetch and carry for s.o.; *bei Verbrechen etc.*: do the dirty work (for s.o.)

Handlauf *m* handrail

Händler *m*; *-s, -,* **~in** *f*; *-, -nen* trader, merchant; (*Einzelhändler*) retailer, dealer; (*Ladenbesitzer*) shop|keeper (*Am. auch* store-); **fliegender ~** street trader (*Am.* vendor) *...händler m, im Subst.* ... dealer; *Ge-müse~* greengrocer; *Schallplatten~* re-cord dealer

Händler|preis *m* trade (*Am.* whole-sale) price; **~rabatt** *m* trade discount

Handlesekunst *f* palmistry; **Handleser** *m,* **~in** *f* palmist

Handleuchte *f* (portable) lamp

handlich *Adj. Gerät, Format, Form, Größe etc.*: handy; (*angenehm*) con-venient; (*praktisch*) *auch* practical; (*kompakt*) compact; *Auto etc.*: easy to handle; **Handlichkeit** *f; nur Sg.* handi-ness; convenience; practicality

Handling ['hɛndlɪŋ] *n*; *-s, kein Pl.* han-dling

Handlung *f* 1. (*Tat*) act, action; **krie-gerische ~** act of war; **strafbare ~** criminal act; 2. *e-s Romans etc.*: ac-tion, story; *im Grundriss*: plot (*auch Theat.*); *Ort der ~* scene (of action); **Ort der ~ ist ...** the scene (*od.* story *etc.*) is set in ..., the action (*od.* story *etc.*) takes place in ...; 3. → **Geschäft** 3

...handlung f, im Subst. 1. (*Geschäft*) business, shop, *bes. Am.* store; **Auto-zubehör~** car accessories shop, *Am.* automotive (*od.* auto parts) store; *Süßwaren~* sweetshop, *Am.* candy store, confectioner *geh.*; 2. *in Buch, Film*: plot; *e-e typische Krimi~* a typi-cal detective story plot

Handlungsablauf *m* sequence (*od.* course) of events; *Theat. etc.* plot

handlungsarm *Adj.*: **ein ~er Roman** *etc.* a novel etc. without much action (*bzw. auf die Fabel bezogen*): without much [of a] plot); **Handlungsarmut** *f* lack of action; lack of plot, thinness of the plot

Handlungs|bedarf *m*: **es besteht kein/dringender ~** there's no/urgent call for action; **ich sehe ~** I think there's a need for action; **~bevollmächtigte** *m, f* (authorized) agent, proxy

handlungsfähig *Adj. Jur.* capable of acting; *Mehrheit*: working; *Regierung*: able to govern; **Handlungsfähigkeit** *f; nur Sg.* 1. capacity to act; 2. *Jur.* le-gal capacity

Handlungsfreiheit *f* freedom of action; **j-m ~ geben** *auch* give s.o. a free hand

handlungsreich *Adj. Geschichte etc.*: full of action, action-packed

Handlungs|reisende *m, f* travel(l)ing salesperson (*männlich*: *mst* salesman); **~schema** *n* plot; **~spielraum** *m* room for manoeuvre (*Am.* maneuver); **~strang** *m* strand (of the plot)

handlungsunfähig *Adj. Jur.* incapable of acting; *weitS. Regierung etc.*: unable to govern *etc.*; **Handlungsunfähigkeit** *f* 1. *bes. Pol.* inability to act; 2. *Jur.* le-gal incapacity

Handlungs|verlauf *m* sequence (*od.* course) of events; *Theat. etc.* plot; **~vollmacht** *f* limited authority to act and sign; **~weise** *f* (*Verhalten*) behavi-o(u)r, conduct; (*Verfahren*) procedure; (*Methoden*) methods *Pl.*

Handmehr *n*; *-s, kein Pl.*; *schw.* show of hands

Hand-out, Handout ['hɛndaut] *n*; *-s, -s* handout

Hand|pflege *f* hand care, care of the hands; (*Maniküre*) manicure; **~presse** *f* hand press; **~pumpe** *f* hand pump; **~puppe** *f* (hand) puppet; **~reichung** *f* *auch Pl.* help; (*Empfehlung*) tip, sug-gestion; *Papier zu e-m Thema*: paper; **~en** *Päd., zum Lehrplan etc.*: (*Hinwei-se*) teacher's notes; (*Materialien*) back-up materials; (*j-m*) **~en machen** help (s.o.) out; **~rücken** *m* back of the (*od.* one's) hand; **~säge** *f* hand saw

handsam *Adj. Dial.* (*umgänglich*) amenable

Hand|schalter *m* hand switch; **~schel-le** *f* handcuff; **j-m ~n anlegen** handcuff s.o.; **~schaltung** *f Mot.* manual gear change; **~schlag** *m* 1. (*Einschlagen*) handshake; **durch ~ bekräftigen** shake hands on; 2. *umg.*: **keinen ~ tun** not do a hand's turn, not lift a finger

Handschrift *f* 1. handwriting, hand; **e-e gute ~** good (*od.* nice) handwriting, a nice hand; **es trägt i-e ~** *fig.* it carries her trademark; 2. (*Manuskript*) manu-script; **handschriftlich I.** *Adj.* 1. *Le-benslauf, Notiz etc.*: handwritten; 2. *Quelle, Text etc.*: manuscript ...; **II.** *Adv.* in writing

Handschuh *m* glove; (*Fäustling*) *auch* mitten; *fig.* → **Fehdehandschuh**; **~fach** *n* glove compartment; **~num-mer** *f* glove size

Hand|schutz *m*; *-es, -e* protective glove; **handsigniert** *Adj.* auto-graphed, signed (*Gemälde etc.*: by the artist); **~skizze** *f* rough sketch; **~spie-gel** *m* hand mirror; **~spiel** *n Fußball*: hand ball, hands

Handstand *m* handstand; **e-n ~ ma-chen** do a handstand; **~überschlag** *m* handspring

Hand|staubsauger *m* upright vacuum cleaner; **~steuerung** *f Tech.* manual control; **~streich** *m* surprise attack; (*Staatsstreich*) coup; **im ~ nehmen** take in a surprise attack; **durch ~ an die Macht kommen** come to power in a coup; **~tasche** *f* handbag, *Am. auch* purse; **~taschenraub** *m* bag-snat-ching; **~teller** *m Anat.* palm (of one's hand)

Handtuch *n*; *Pl.* Handtücher towel; **das ~ werfen** *umg.* Boxen *und fig.*: throw in the towel; (*schmales*) *~ umg. hum. Person*: beanpole; *Grundstück*: pocket handkerchief; **~automat** *m* towel dis-penser; **~halter** *m* towel rack; **~spen-der** *m* towel dispenser

Handumdrehen *n*: **im ~** in no time

Hand- und Spanndienste *Pl. hist.* feu-dal services

handverlesen *Adj.* handpicked (*auch fig.*)

Hand voll → **Hand²**

Handwagen *m* handcart

handwarm *Adj.* lukewarm

Hand|waschbecken *n* hand basin; **~wäsche** *f* hand wash(ing)

Handwerk *n*; *-(e)s, -e* 1. craft, trade; **ein ehrliches ~** an honest trade; **ein ~ ler-nen** learn a trade; 2. *das ~* (*Berufs-stand, auch Koll.*) the craft, the trade; **Industrie und ~** trade and industry; 3. *fig. des Politikers etc.*: trade; **sein ~ verstehen** know one's business (*umg.* stuff); **j-m das ~ legen** throw a span-ner (*Am.* [monkey] wrench) into the works, put a stop to s.o.('s game); **j-m ins ~ pfuschen** meddle in s.o. else's affairs; **ich möchte Ihnen nicht ins ~ pfuschen** I wouldn't like to tread (*Am.* step) on your toes; **Handwerker** *m*; *-s, -,* **Handwerkerin** *f*; *-, -nen* 1. workman; *weiblich*: workwoman; **morgen kommen die ~** we're having (the) workmen in tomorrow; 2. *künst-lerischer*: craftsman; *weiblich*: crafts-woman; **handwerklich** *Adj.* (handi)-craft ...; *Beruf*: skilled

Handwerks|betrieb *m* workshop; **~bursche** *m hist.*, **~geselle** *m*, **~ge-sellin** *f* journey|man (*weiblich*: -wom-an); **~kammer** *f* small business trade group, *Am. etwa* Small Business Asso-ciation; **~mann** *m*; *Pl. -leute* crafts-man; **~meister** *m*, **~meisterin** *f* mas-ter crafts|man (*weiblich*: -woman); **~rolle** *f* register of qualified craftspeo-ple; **in die ~ eintragen** register as a qualified craftsperson; **~zeug** *n* tools *Pl.*; *fig.* tools *Pl.* of the trade, stock--in-trade

Handwörterbuch *n etwa* concise dic-tionary

Handwurzel *f Anat.* wrist; carpus *fachspr.*; **~knochen** *m* wristbone; car-pal bone *fachspr.*

Handy ['hɛndi] *n*; *-s, -s*; *Telef.* mobile (-phone), cell(ular) phone

handzahm *Adj.* 1. *Tier*: tame enough to be handled; 2. *fig. Person*: biddable

Hand|zeichen *n* (*Signal*) sign, signal; *e-s Autofahrers*: hand signal; *Parl.* show of hands; *e-s Analphabeten*: cross; *e-s Künstlers*: signature; *Kürzel etc.*: mark; **~zeichnung** *f* sketch; **~zet-tel** *m* leaflet

hanebüchen *Adj. geh. altm.* outra-geous

Hanf *m*; *-(e)s, kein Pl.*; *Bot.* hemp

Hänfling *m*; *-s, -e* 1. *Orn.* linnet; 2. *pej.* (*schwächlich aussehende Person*) weed

Hanf|öl *n* hempseed oil; **~samen** *m* hempseed; **~seil** *n* hemp rope

Hang *m*; *-(e)s, Hänge* 1. slope; **am ~ Haus etc.**: on a slope (*od.* hill); (*beim Schifahren*) on the slopes; 2. *nur Sg.*; *fig.* (*Neigung*) (natural) inclination (**zu** to *s.th.*, to + *Inf.*), bent (**zu** for *s.th.*, for + *Ger.*), tendency (**zu** toward[s] *s.th. od.* + *Ger.*, to + *Inf*), propensity (**zu** to *s.th. od.* + *Inf.*, for + *Ger.*), pen-chant (for *s.th.*); (*Vorliebe*) partiality (**zu** for *s.th.*); (*auch Zuneigung*) fond-ness (for, of *s.th.*); (*Anfälligkeit*) proneness (**zu** to *s.th.*); 3. *nur Sg.*; *Tur-nen*: hang; **in den ~ gehen** hang from the bar

hangabwärts *Adv.* downhill

Hangar *m*; *-s, -s*; *Flug.* hangar

Hänge|arsch *m vulg.* 1. drooping but-tocks *Pl.*; 2. (*Hose*) droopy drawers *Pl. umg.*; **~backen** *Pl.* flabby cheeks; **~bahn** *f* suspension railway

Hängebauch *m* paunch, pot belly, flabby stomach, *Am. auch* beer gut *umg.*; **~schwein** *n Zool.* pot-bellied pig

Hänge|birke *f Bot.* weeping birch; **~boden** *n* 1. (*Zwischendecke*) false ceiling; 2. *Raum*: ceiling loft; **~brücke** *f* suspension bridge; **~brust** *f* sagging breasts *Pl.*; **~gleiter** *m*; *-s, -* hang glider; **~lampe** *f* hanging lamp

hangeln *v/i.* (*ist gehangelt*) *und v/refl.* (*hat*) work one's way along *s.th.* (with one's hands); **sich aufwärts** *od.* **nach oben ~** climb up hand over hand

Hänge|mappe *f* hanging file; **~matte** *f* hammock

hängen¹ *v/i.*; *hängt, hing, hat* / *südd., österr., schw. ist gehangen* 1. (*befestigt* *sein*) hang (*an* + *Dat.* on; *von* from); *an der Decke*: be suspended (from); *an e-m Fahrzeug*: be attached (to); *es hängt schief* it's not (hanging) straight; *die Waggons* ~ *aneinander* the wagons are coupled; ~ *lassen* (*Wäsche*) leave on the line; (*vergessen*) leave (hanging); (*j-n*) *umg. fig.* leave *s.o.* in the lurch; **2.** (*sich festhalten*) hang; *das Kind hing an i-r Hand / i-m Hals* the child was hanging onto her hand / around her neck; *sie hing aus dem Fenster umg.* (*lehnte sich hinaus*) she was hanging out of the window; **3.** *durch sein Gewicht etc.*: droop, hang down; (*durchhängen*) sag; (*sich zur Seite neigen*) be inclined, lean over (*nach* to[ward(s)]); (*nicht waagrecht sein*) slope; *die Köpfe der Blumen* ~ the heads of the flowers are drooping; *die Beine ins Wasser* ~ *lassen* dangle one's legs in the water; *den Kopf/Schwanz* ~ *lassen* hang one's head / let its tail hang down; *lass den Kopf nicht* ~*! fig.* keep your head up; *sich* ~ *lassen fig.* (*sich gehen lassen*) let o.s. go; *lässig im Sessel* ~ loll in the armchair; *die Kleider hingen mir nur so am Leib* the clothes were hanging off me *umg.*; → *hängend* II; **4.** *geh.* (*unbeweglich schweben*) float, hover; *Rauch, Wolken*: hang; ~ *über* (+ *Dat.*) *Schicksal, Schwert etc.*: hang over; **5.** (*haften*) cling, stick (*an* + *Dat.* to); *Tech.* catch, stick; (*festsitzen*) be caught; *Computer*: hang; **6.** ~ *bleiben* get (*od.* be) caught (*an* + *Dat.* on), catch (on, in); get (*od.* be) stuck (*in* + *Dat.* in); *Tech.* jam, stick; *Computer, Programm, Schallplatte*: hang; *umg. fig.* (*nicht weiterkommen*) be stuck; *fig.* stick (*im Gedächtnis* in one's mind); *umg. bei Freunden, in Kneipe etc.*: get stuck; (*aufgehalten werden*) *Sport*: be stopped (*an* + *Dat.* by); *umg., in der Schule*: be kept down (*Am.* held back); *er blieb mit der Hose am Zaun* ~ he caught his trousers (*Am.* pants) on the fence; *ihr Blick / ein Verdacht blieb an ihm* ~ her eyes / a suspicion rested on him; *von dem Vortrag ist bei mir nicht viel* ~ *geblieben* I can't remember much of (what was said in) the talk; *an mir bleibt alles* ~ *umg.* I get lumbered with everything, I end up having to do everything; *wo(ran) hängt's? umg.* what's the problem?; *sie hängt in Latein umg.* she's behind in Latin; **7.** *umg.* (*sich aufhalten, sein*) hang around (*in* + *Dat.* in; *bei* at); *er hängt dauernd am Telefon* he's on the phone all day, he's never off the phone; *sie hängt den ganzen Tag vor dem Fernseher* she's glued to the TV all day; **8.** (*voll sein*): *voller Bilder* ~ *Wand*: be covered in paintings; *Haus*: be full of paintings; *der Baum hängt voller Früchte* the tree is laden with fruit; **9.** (*angeschlossen sein*) be connected (up) (to); *der Computer hängt am Netz* the computer is connected to the net(work), the computer is networked; *sie hängt am Tropf / an der Herz-Lungen-Maschine* she's on a drip (*Am.* IV) /heart-lung machine; **10.** *fig.*: ~ *an* (+ *Dat.*) *an e-m Brauch, am Leben etc.*: cling to; *an j-m*: be very attached (*stärker*: devoted) to; *am Geld, an Besitz*: love, be fond of; (*abhängen von*) depend on; (*verbunden sein mit*) be involved; *du weißt ja nicht, was für*

mich alles daran hängt you've no idea how much is hanging on this as far as I'm concerned, you just don't know what this means for me; → *auch Faden*[1] 3, *Lippe* 1
hängen[2] **I.** *v/t.*; *hängt, hängte, hat gehängt* **1.** (*Bild, Wäsche etc.*) hang (*an die Leine, Wand* [up] on; *an die Decke* from), suspend (from); **2.** *an Fahrzeug etc.*: fix, fasten, attach (*an* + *Akk.* to); (*anhaken*) hook (on[to]); **3.** (*hängen lassen*) dangle; *die Beine ins Wasser* ~ dangle one's legs in the water; *den Kopf aus dem Fenster* ~ stick one's head out of the window; **4.** (*j-n*) hang; *gehängt werden* be hanged; *er soll* ~*!* he ought to be hanged (*od.* hung *umg.*)!; → *Brotkorb, Glocke* 1, *Herz*[1] 8, *Nagel* 1; **II.** *v/refl.*: *sich* ~ *an* (+ *Akk.*) hang on to; *auch gefühlsmäßig*: cling to; *Laufsport*: drop in behind *s.o.*; *sich ans Telefon* ~ *umg.* get on the telephone; *sich an j-s Fersen* ~ (*j-n verfolgen*) follow close on s.o.'s heels; *sich aus dem Fenster* ~ hang out of the window; *sich in etw.* (*Akk.*) ~ *umg. fig.* (*sich engagieren*) get involved in s.th.; (*sich einmischen*) meddle in s.th.
Hängen *n*; *-s, kein Pl.* **1.** *e-r Person*: hanging; **2.** *umg.*: *mit* ~ *und Würgen* by the skin of one's teeth; *die Prüfung mit* ~ *und Würgen bestehen* scrape through (the exam)

hängen bleiben → *hängen*[1] 6
hängend I. *Part. Präs.* → *hängen*[1]; **II.** *Adj. Lampe etc.*: hanging; *Brüste*: sagging; *Schultern etc.*: drooping; *die Hängenden Gärten der Semiramis* the Hanging Gardens of Babylon; *mit* ~*em Kopf/Schwanz* with his (*od.* her) head hanging / with its tail hanging down; *mit* ~*er Zunge* gasping for breath
hängen lassen → *hängen*[1] 3
Hänge|ohren *Pl.* drooping (*od.* floppy) ears; ~**partie** *f Schach*: adjourned game; ~**pflanze** *f* hanging plant
Hänger *m*; *-s, -* **1.** *Kleid*: loose dress; (*Kittel*) smock; *Mantel*: loose coat; **2.** *umg.* (*Anhänger*) trailer; **3.** *umg., beim Vortragen etc.*: dry
Hänge|schloss *n* padlock; ~**schrank** *m* wall cupboard
Hanglage *f* hillside location
Hannover (*n*); *-s* Hanover
Hannoveraner[1] *m*; *-s, - Pferd*: Hanoverian
Hannoveraner[2] *m*; *-s, -*, ~**in** *f*; *-, -nen* Hanoverian
Hannoveranisch[3] *Adj.* Hanoverian
Hans *m*; *-, Hänse* Jack; *der Blanke* ~ *lit.* the North Sea in stormy weather; ~ *im Glück* Lucky Jim; *ich will* ~ *heißen, wenn ...* I'll be a Dutchman if ..., *Am.* if ..., I'll eat my hat
Hansaplast® *n*; *-(e)s, nur Sg.* Elastoplast®, *Am.* Band-Aid®
Hänschen: *was* ~ *nicht lernt, lernt Hans nimmermehr Sprichw.* what you don't learn as a child, you'll never learn as an adult, *etwa* you can't teach an old dog new tricks
Hansdampf *m*; *-(e)s, -e*; *umg.*: *er ist ein richtiger* ~ (*in allen Gassen*) he's a jack-of-all-trades; *weitS.* he's got his finger in every pie
Hanse *f*; *-, kein Pl.*; *hist.* Hansa, Hanseatic League; **Hanseat** *m*; *-en, -en* **1.** *hist.* merchant belonging to the Hanseatic League); **2.** (*Einwohner e-r Hansestadt*) inhabitant of a Hanseatic town; **Hanseatin** *f*; *-, -nen* (*Einwohne-*

rin e-r Hansestadt) inhabitant of a Hanseatic town; **hanseatisch** *Adj.* Hanseatic
Hänselei *f*; *-, -en* teasing; **hänseln** *v/t.* tease
Hansestadt *f* Hansa (*od.* Hanseatic) city; *die* ~ *Hamburg* the Hanseatic city of Hamburg
Hanswurst *m*; *-(e)s, -e, hum. auch Hanswürste* **1.** clown; *Theat.* pantaloon; **2.** (*Hampelmann*) fool, idiot, buffoon; *den* ~ *machen für* do the donkey work for
Hantel *f*; *-, -n* dumbbell; ~*n stemmen* exercise with the dumbbells
hantieren *v/i.* bustle around (*od.* about); *gemütlich*: potter around (*od.* about); ~ *mit* work with, handle; *mit Werkzeug etc., gefährlich*: wave *s.th.* around; ~ *an* (+ *Dat.*) work on, fiddle with *pej.*, tinker with *pej.*
hapern *v/i. unpers.*: *es hapert mit od. bei* there are problems with; *es hapert an* (+ *Dat.*) the problem is ..., *auch* there isn't (*od.* aren't) enough ...; *bei uns hapert's am Geld* the problem (with us) is money; *im Englischen hapert's bei ihm* English is his weak point
Häppchen *n* **1.** → *Happen* 1; **2.** (*Imbiss*) small snack; **häppchenweise** *Adv.* bit by bit, *bes. Am.* little by little
Happen *m*; *-s, -* **1.** bite (*to eat*); (*Bissen*) gobbet; *kleiner*: morsel; *leckerer*: tit|bit (*Am.* tid-); *großer* ~ hunk; *e-n* ~ *essen* have a bite to eat; **2.** *fig.* (*Beute*) catch; *fetter* ~ good catch (*od.* haul)
Happening ['hɛpənɪŋ] *n*; *-s, -s* (*art*) happening
happig *Adj. umg. Preis, Ansprüche etc.*: steep; *Prüfung etc.*: stiff; *das ist ganz schön* ~ *auch* that's a bit much
happy ['hɛpɪ] *Adj. umg.* (as) pleased as Punch, over the moon, high; **Happyend, Happy End** *n*; *-(s), -s* happy ending
Harakiri *n*; *-(s), -s*: ~ (*machen*) (commit) hara-kiri
Härchen *n* little (*od.* tiny) hair; *Bio.* cilium (*Pl.* cilia); → *auch Haar*
Hardcoreporno ['haːɐtkoːɐ-] *m* hard-core porn
Hardcover, Hard Cover ['haːɐtkavɐ] *n*; *-s, -s* hard cover
Hardliner ['haːɐtlaɪnɐ] *m*; *-s, -* hardliner
Hardrock, Hard Rock ['haːɐtrɔk] *m Mus.* hard rock
Hardware ['haːɐtvɛːɐ] *f*; *-, -s Computer etc.*: hardware
Harem *m*; *-s, -s* harem; **Haremsdame** *f* concubine, odalisque, harem girl
Häresie *f*; *-, -n*; *kath. od. geh.* heresy; **Häretiker** *m*; *-s, -*, **Häretikerin** *f*; *-, -nen* heretic; **häretisch** *Adj.* heretical
Harfe *f*; *-, -n*; *Mus.* harp; **Harfenspieler** *m*, **Harfenspielerin** *f* harpist; *Volksmusik*: harper
Harke *f*; *-, -n* rake; *j-m zeigen, was e-e* ~ *ist fig.* tell s.o. what's what; **harken** *v/t.* rake
Harlekin *m*; *-s, -e* harlequin
härmen *v/refl. geh.* → *grämen* I
harmlos I. *Adj.* harmless; (*unschädlich*) *auch* innocuous; *Medizin etc.*: *auch* (perfectly) safe; **1.** *Miene*: innocent; *Vergnügen etc.*: *auch* harmless; (*ohne Bosheit*) guileless; *er ist ein* ~*er Typ* he's harmless, you needn't worry about him; **2.** *Prüfung etc.*: easy; (*unbedeutend*) insignificant; *der Film ist eher* ~ it's a harmless sort of film; *das*

ist ja noch ~*!* that's nothing; **II.** *Adv.:* ~ *verlaufen Krankheit etc.:* take its normal course; *ganz* ~ *fragen* ask in all innocence; **Harmlosigkeit** *f* **1.** *nur Sg.* harmlessness: (*Unschädlichkeit*) *auch* innocuousness; **2.** *Verhalten:* innocence; (*ohne Bosheit*) guilelessness; *in aller* ~ in all innocence

Harmonie *f; -, -n* harmony (*auch fig.*); ~**bedürfnis** *n* need for peace and harmony; *pej.* need to conciliate and appease people; ~**lehre** *f* harmony

harmonieren *v/i.* **1.** *Mus.* harmonize (*mit* with); **2.** go (*well*) together; *Personen:* get on (*Am.* along) well (together); *Paar: auch* make a good couple

harmoniesüchtig *Adj.* peace-loving; *pej.* afraid of conflict, wanting peace at any price

Harmonika *f; -, -s od. Harmoniken; Mus.* accordion; *kleinere:* concertina; (*Mundharmonika*) mouth organ (*od.* harp), harmonica; *er spielt* ~ he plays the accordion *etc.*

harmonisch I. *Adj. Mus.* harmonic (*auch Math.*); *auch fig.* harmonious; *Wein:* well-balanced, harmonious; ~*e Schwingungen* harmonics; **II.** *Adv.:* (*vollkommen*) ~ *zusammenleben etc.:* in (perfect) harmony; ~ *ablaufen* go (off) smoothly (*od.* without a hitch)

harmonisieren *v/t.* harmonize; **Harmonisierung** *f* harmonization

Harmonium *n; -s, Harmonien od. -s; Mus.* harmonium

Harn *m; -(e)s, -e; Physiol., Med.* urine; ~ *lassen* pass water; ~**blase** *f* bladder; ~**drang** *m* urge to urinate

Harnisch *m; -s, -e* **1.** *hist.* (suit of) armo(u)r, harness *altm.;* **2.** *fig.: j-n in* ~ *bringen* infuriate s.o., raise s.o.'s hackles; *in* ~ *geraten/sein* get/be (really) furious

Harn|**leiter** *m Anat.* ureter; ~**probe** *f* urine sample; ~**röhre** *f Anat.* urethra; ~**säure** *f Physiol.* uric acid; ~**stein** *m Med.* urinary calculus; ~**stoff** *m Physiol.* urea

harntreibend *Adj. Med.* (*auch* ~*es Mittel*) diuretic

Harnwege *Pl. Anat.* urinary tract *Sg.*

Harpune *f; -, -n* harpoon; **harpunieren** *v/t.* harpoon

harren *v/i. geh.* wait (+ *Gen. od. auf* + *Akk.* for); (*hoffen*) hope (for); ~ (+ *Gen. od. auf* + *Akk.*) *auch* await; *der Dinge* ~*, die da kommen* wait and see what happens, await events

harsch *Adj.* **1.** *Schnee:* crusted; **2.** *geh. Stimme, Worte etc.:* harsh; **3.** *Wind:* biting; **Harsch** *m; -(e)s, kein Pl.* crusted snow

hart; *härter, am härtesten* **I.** *Adj.* **1.** *allg., auch Bleistift, Wasser:* hard; *Brot:* stale; *Ei:* hard-boiled; (*fest*) firm, solid; (*steif*) rigid; ~ *wie Stahl/Stein* hard as steel / a rock, ~ *werden* harden; *Zement etc.: auch* set; *der Reis ist noch ganz* ~ the rice is still quite hard; **2.** *Landung etc.:* hard; *Schlag: auch* heavy; *Aufprall: auch* violent; *Ruck:* sharp; **3.** (*abgehärtet*) hardened; (*zäh*) tough; ~*er Bursche* hard man; ~ *im Nehmen sein* be able to take it, be tough; *gelobt sei, was* ~ *macht etwa* when the going gets tough, the tough get going, treat them rough, make them tough; **4.** *fig. seelisch:* hard; (*gefühllos*) *auch* hard-hearted, unfeeling; (*streng*) severe, tough *umg.;* (*unerbittlich*) relentless; *Stimme, Strafe etc.:* severe, harsh; *Worte:* harsh; *Sport Spiel:*

rough; *zu j-m* ~ *sein* be hard on s.o.; *er blieb* ~ he was adamant, he wouldn't relent; ~*e Auseinandersetzung* violent argument; ~*es Urteil von Gericht:* heavy sentence; *weitS.:* harsh judg(e)ment; *die Enttäuschungen hatten ihn* ~ *gemacht* he was a man hardened by disappointments; **5.** *fig.* (*schwer*) hard, tough *umg.; Winter: auch* severe; *Arbeit, Kampf, Zeiten:* hard; *Schlag, Verlust:* heavy; ~*es Los* hard lot; *auf e-e* ~*e Probe stellen* put severely to the test; *e-n* ~*en Stand haben* have a hard time (of it); *das war* ~ *für sie schwierig:* it was hard for her; *bes. unverdient:* it was hard on her; *das ist ganz schön* ~ *umg.* (*schwer*) it's tough (going); (*gewagt*) that's pretty strong stuff; *durch e-e* ~*e Schule gegangen sein fig.* have learn|t (*Am.* -ed) the hard way; **6.** *fig. Drogen, Konsonant, Strahlen, Tatsachen, Währung:* hard; *Licht, Ton, Aussprache, Gegensätze etc.:* harsh; *Kontrast, Konturen, Negativ etc.:* sharp; *Krimi, Western etc.:* hard-bitten; *Porno:* hard(-core); *die* ~*en Sachen* (*Alkohol*) *umg.* the hard stuff *Sg.;* → *Brocken* 1, *Kern* 3, *Nuss* 1; **II.** *Adv.* **1.** ~ *gefroren* frozen; *präd. auch* frozen solid (*od.* hard); ~ *gekocht* hard-boiled; ~ *gesotten Ei:* hard-boiled; *ich schlafe gerne* ~ I like sleeping on a hard mattress; **2.** *arbeiten, bestrafen, treffen etc.:* hard; *bestrafen: auch* severely; ~ *aneinander geraten* come to blows, go at each other hammer and tongs *umg.; j-n* ~ *anfassen* be firm (*umg.* tough) with s.o.; *es kommt ihn* ~ *an* it's hard on him, he's finding it hard; ~ *aufsetzen Flug. etc.* make a hard landing, land with a bump; *j-n* ~ *bedrängen od. j-m* ~ *zusetzen* put s.o. under a lot of pressure; ~ *durchgreifen* take stern (*od.* tough) measures; *wenn es* ~ *auf* ~ *geht od. kommt* when it comes to the crunch; *sich* ~ *tun südd., österr.* have a hard time (*mit* with); ~ *umkämpft* hotly contested; **3.** ~ *an* (+ *Dat.*) (*dicht, nah an*) hard by, close to; ~ *an der Grenze des Erlaubten/Machbaren etc.* very close to the limit of what is permissible/feasible; ~ *an der Grenze zur Beleidigung etc.* very close to being an insult; ~ *am Wind segeln* sail close to the wind; ~ *zuhalten auf* (+ *Akk.*) *Naut.* hold a steady course for

Härte *f; -, -n* **1.** hardness; *des Stahls: auch* temper; *Bleistifte in verschiedenen* ~*n* pencils of varying degrees of hardness; **2.** (*Wucht*) force; **3.** *fig.* (*Zähigkeit, Brutalität, Aggressivität*) toughness; *Sport* tough play; (*Strenge*) severity; *e-s Verlusts etc.:* severity; (*Belastung, Ungerechtigkeit*) hardship; *soziale* ~ social hardship; *unbillige* ~ *Jur.* undue hardship; *mit aller* ~ extremely hard; (*verbissen*) fiercely; (*erbarmungslos*) relentlessly; (*drastisch*) drastically; *es traf sie in s-r ganzen* ~ it hit her with all its force; *das ist die* ~*! Jugendspr.* that's not on!, *Am.* no way!; **4.** *fig. der Währung:* stability; *Fot.* contrast; *der Aussprache, des Tons etc.:* harshness; *e-s Konsonanten:* hardness; *Phys., von Strahlung etc.:* degree of penetration; ~**ausgleich** *m* hardship allowance; ~**bad** *n Tech.* hard-treating (*Metall.* tempering) bath; ~**bereich** *m des Wassers:* degree of hardness

Härtefall *m* **1.** case of hardship; **2.** *Person:* hardship case; ~**regelung** *f* provi-

sion for cases of hardship

Härte|**fonds** *m* hardship fund; ~**grad** *m* degree of hardness; *von Stahl:* temper; ~**klausel** *f Jur.* hardship clause

härten I. *v/t.* harden; (*Stahl*) temper; **II.** *v/i.* harden, grow hard

härter *Komp.* harder; → *hart*

Härter *m; -s, -* hardener

Härteskala *f* scale of hardness

härtest... *Sup.* hardest; → *hart*

Härte|**stufe** *f* degree of hardness; ~**test** *m* endurance test; ~**verfahren** *n* hardening process

Hartfaserplatte *f* hardboard, *Am.* fiberboard

hart gefroren, hart gekocht, hart gesotten → *hart* II 1

Hartgeld *n* hard cash, coins *Pl.*

hartgesotten *Adj. fig.* hard-boiled; *Verbrecher etc.:* hardened

Hart|**glas** *n; nur Sg.* hard(ened) glass; ~**gummi** *n, m* hard rubber; *Wirts.* vulcanite

hartherzig *Adj.* hard-hearted, unfeeling, callous; **Hartherzigkeit** *f* **1.** *nur Sg.* hard-heartedness, callousness; **2.** *Handlung:* callous act

Hartholz *n* hardwood; (*Schichtholz*) laminated wood

harthörig *Adj.* **1.** *altm.* (*schwerhörig*) hard of hearing; **2.** *fig.* unresponsive

Hartkäse *m* hard cheese

hart|**leibig** *adj. altm.* constipated; ~**löten** *vt/i.; nur Inf. und PP.* (*hat hartgelötet*) *Tech.* hard-solder

Hartmetall *n* hard metal; *Tech.* cutting metal

hartnäckig *Adj.* **1.** stubborn; (*beharrlich*) persistent; *Versuch etc.: auch* dogged; **2.** *Schnupfen etc.:* stubborn; *Problem etc.:* intractable; **Hartnäckigkeit** *f; nur Sg.* stubbornness; persistence, doggedness; intractability; → *hartnäckig*

Hart|**pappe** *f für Koffer etc.:* board; ~**platz** *m Tennis:* hard court; ~**riegel** *m Bot.* cornel; ~**schalenkoffer** *m* hard-shell case

hart umkämpft → *hart* II 2

Härtung *f* hardening; *Stahl: auch* tempering

Hartweizen *m* durum wheat; ~**grieß** *m* semolina

Hartwurst *f* dry sausage

Harz[1] *n; -es, -e* **1.** resin; *in festem Zustand:* (*auch Mus. für Bogen*) rosin; **2.** *Mot.* (*Benzinrückstand*) gum

Harz[2] *m; -es, kein Pl.; Geog.* Harz (Mountains)

harzen I. *v/i. Baum, Holz:* secrete resin; **II.** *v/t.* **1.** (*Wein*) resinate; **2.** (*Segel, Stoff*) resin; (*Heftklammern etc.*) resin-coat

Harzer *Adj.:* ~ *Roller od. Käse Gastr.* type of skim-milk cheese from the Harz Mountains often packaged in roll form

harzig *Adj.* resinous

Hasard [ha'zart] *n; -s, kein Pl.:* ~ *spielen* gamble; **Hasardeur** [hazar'døːʁ] *m; -s, -e*, **Hasardeurin** *f; -, -nen* gambler (*auch fig.*); **Hasardspiel** *n* **1.** game of chance; **2.** *fig.* gamble

Hasch *n; -s, kein Pl.; umg.* hash, pot

Haschee *n; -s, -s; Gastr.* hash

haschen[1] **I.** *v/t. altm.* catch; *sich od. einander* ~ *Spiel:* play catch; **II.** *v/i.* ~ *nach* **1.** grasp at, try to catch; **2.** *fig.* strive after; *nach Anerkennung/Komplimenten* ~ strive for recognition / fish for compliments

haschen[2] *v/i. umg.* (*Haschisch rauchen*) smoke pot

Häschen n **1.** young hare, leveret; umg. (Kaninchen) bunny; **~ in der Grube** Kinderspiel: etwa ring-a-ring o' roses, Am. ring-around-the-rosey; **2.** umg.; von Playboy: bunny (girl); **3.** Kosename: bunny, sweetie-pie

Hascher m; -s, -; umg. (Haschischraucher) pothead

Häscher m; -s, -; pej. bloodhound

Hascherin f; -, -nen pothead

Hascherl n; -s, -(n); Dial.: **armes ~** poor little thing (od. mite)

haschieren v/t. Gastr. hash

Haschisch n; -(s), kein Pl. hashish, cannabis; **~rausch** m high; **im ~** on a high; **~zigarette** f joint

Hase m; -n, -n **1.** Zool. hare; **junger ~** leveret; **männlicher ~** buck (hare); **2.** umg. od. Dial. (Kaninchen) rabbit; **3.** Gastr.: **falscher ~** meat loaf; **4.** umg. fig.: **alter ~** old hand; **wie der ~ läuft** which way the wind blows; **da liegt der ~ im Pfeffer** that's the heart (od. crux) of the matter, that's the real problem; **mein Name ist ~(, ich weiß von nichts!)** search me!, I don't know anything about anything; **5.** Sport umg. (Tempomacher) pacemaker, Am. auch rabbit; Hunderennen: hare

Hasel f; -, -n; Bot. hazelnut (tree), hazel; **~huhn** n Orn. hazel grouse; **~maus** f Zool. dormouse; **~nuss** f Bot. **1.** hazelnut; **2.** → Hasel

haselnuss|braun Adj. hazel; **~groß** Adj. nachgestellt: the size of a hazelnut

Hasel(nuss)strauch m → Hasel

Hasen|braten m Gastr. roast hare; umg. und Dial. (Kaninchenbraten) roast rabbit; **~fell** n hare pelt; umg. und Dial. (Kaninchenfell) rabbit fur

Hasen|fuß m, **~herz** n fig. pej. coward, chicken; **~jagd** f hare hunt(ing); **~klein** n → Hasenpfeffer, **~panier** n: **das ~ ergreifen** take to one's heels; **~pfeffer** m Gastr. etwa jugged hare, Am. has(s)enpfeffer; **~pfote** f als Glücksbringer: rabbit's foot

hasenrein Adj. umg.: **nicht ganz ~** a bit fishy, not quite kosher

Hasen|rücken m Gastr. saddle of hare; **~scharte** f Med. harelip

Häsin f; -, -nen; Zool. female hare, doe

Haspel f; -, -n **1.** für Garn etc.: reel; **2.** bes. Bergb. (Winde) windlass, winch; Naut. capstan; **haspeln I.** v/t. (Garn) reel; **II.** vt/i. (hastig sprechen) splutter (out)

Hass m; -es, kein Pl. hatred, hate (**auf** + Akk. od. **gegen** for); (Erbitterung) animosity; (Abscheu) loathing; (Feindschaft) enmity; **aus ~** out of hatred; **e-n ~ haben auf** (+ Akk.) umg. really hate; **e-n ~ kriegen** umg. see red, go wild

...hass m, im Subst. -phobia, hatred of ...; **Ausländer~** xenophobia; **Bruder~** hatred of one's brother; hatred between brothers

hassen v/t. hate; (verabscheuen) auch loathe, detest; **sie hasst es zu verlieren / ausgelacht zu werden** she hates losing / being ridiculed; **ich hasse es, wenn er raucht** I hate it when he smokes; → Pest, **hassenswert** Adj. hateful; stärker: odious

...hasser m; -s, -, **~in** f; -, -nen; im Subst. -phobe, -hater; **Ausländerhasser** xenophobe; **Männerhasserin** man-hater

hasserfüllt I. Adj. full of hatred; Person: auch seething with hatred; **II.** Adv.: **j-n ~ anblicken** give s.o. a

look of hatred, look daggers at s.o.

Hassgefühle Pl. feelings of hatred, ranco(u)r Sg.

hässlich I. Adj. **1.** allg. ugly; Mensch, Tier: Am. auch homely; (scheußlich) hideous; (unschön) unsightly; **~er Anblick** ugly sight, (real) eyesore; **~es Entchen** ugly duckling (auch fig.); **~ wie die Nacht (finster)** as ugly as sin; **2.** fig. Benehmen, Wetter, Wunde etc.: nasty; (unangenehm) ugly, unpleasant; **~ (zu j-m) sein** be nasty (to s.o.); **das war sehr ~ von dir!** that was very nasty of you; **II. Adv. 1.** sich kleiden etc.: unattractively; **2. sich ~ benehmen** be nasty, behave nastily; **~ über j-n reden** say nasty things about s.o.; **Hässlichkeit** f **1.** nur Sg. ugliness; **2.** mst Pl.: sich (Pl.) **~en an den Kopf werfen** hurl insults (od. vicious remarks) at each other

Hass|liebe f love-hate relationship (**für** j-n with); **mit e-r Art ~ an j-m hängen** have a (kind of) love-hate relationship with s.o.; **~objekt** n (object of) hate; **bevorzugtes ~** umg. pet hate; **~tirade** f vitriolic attack

hassverzerrt Adj. contorted with hate

Hast f; -, kein Pl. hurry(ing), haste; des Lebens: mad rush; **ohne ~** without hurrying (od. rushing); **sich ohne ~ fertig machen** auch take one's time getting ready; **in großer ~** in a great hurry, in great haste lit.; **nur keine ~!** no need to rush

hast Präs. → haben; **haste** umg. (hast du) → haben; **~ was, biste was** Sprichw. money makes a man

hasten v/i. hurry; (rennen) auch rush, race

hastig I. Adj. hasty, hurried, rushed; (voreilig) rash; (schlampig) slapdash; **II. Adv.** quickly, in a hurry; **nicht so ~!** just a minute!, not so fast!

hat Präs. → haben

Hätschelkind n pampered child, Mummy's (Am. mama's) boy (od. girl)

hätscheln v/t. **1.** oft pej. (verwöhnen) pamper, mollycoddle, spoil; **2.** (liebkosen) (kiss and) cuddle; (Tier) pet; **sie hätschelt das Kind dauernd** auch she smothers that child, she's all over that child

hatschen v/i. Dial. (gehen) stroll, amble; schleppend: trudge, Brit. auch trog umg.

hatschi Interj. a(h)choo!, atishoo!

hatte P.P. → haben

Hattrick ['hɛttrɪk] m; -s, -s; Sport hat trick

Hatz f; -, -en hunt, chase

Haube f; -, -n **1.** bonnet; südd., österr. (Mütze) cap; (Kapuze) hood; hist. coif; e-r Krankenschwester etc.: cap; e-r Nonne: cornet, coif; für Falken: hood; **unter die ~ bringen** find a husband for, get s.o. married; **unter die ~ kommen** fig. get married; gezwungenermaßen: be married off; **2.** fig. aus Schnee, Sahne, Schaum etc.: covering; (Abdeckung) cover; am Plattenspieler etc.: dust cover; über Speisen: topping; für Kaffeekanne etc.: lid; Tech. cover, cap, dome; (Abzugshaube) hood; **3.** Mot. bonnet, Am. hood; Flug. cowling; **4.** (Trockenhaube) hair drier; **unter der ~ sitzen** sit under the drier; **5.** Orn. (Federbüschel) crest; **6.** Mil. hist. coif; (Sturmhaube) helmet

Hauben|lerche f Orn. crested lark; **~meise** f Orn. crested tit(mouse); **~taucher** m Orn. (great) crested grebe

Haubitze f; -, -n; Mil. howitzer; **voll wie e-e ~** umg. fig. drunk to the gills, plastered

Hauch m; -(e)s, -e; geh. **1.** breath; von Luft: breath (of wind), breeze; von Duft: whiff; **2.** fig. (Anflug) trace, touch; auch von Farbe: tinge, hint; (dünne Schicht) (thin) film; (Atmosphäre) air; **ein ~ von Ironie** a touch of irony; **nicht der leiseste ~ von** not a trace of

hauchdünn Adj. **1.** wafer-thin; Gewebe: flimsy; Strumpf, Kondom: sheer; Porzellan: eggshell ...; **~ schneiden** cut into very fine (od. wafer-thin) slices; **2.** fig. Mehrheit, Vorsprung: very slim, wafer-thin; Sieg: knife-edge attr.

hauchen I. v/i. breathe; (sich [Dat.]) **in die Hände ~** blow on one's hands; **II.** v/t. **1.** geh.: **j-m e-n Kuss auf die Stirn ~** kiss s.o. very lightly on the forehead etc., brush s.o.'s forehead etc. with one's lips; **2.** (flüstern) breathe, whisper; **3.** Ling. aspirate

hauchfein Adj. **1.** wafer-thin; Gewebe: flimsy; **2.** fig. Unterschied: very fine, subtle

Hauchlaut m Ling. aspirate

hauchzart Adj. very delicate

Haudegen m fig.: **alter ~** Soldat: old trooper; Politiker etc.: old warhorse

Haue[1] f; -, -n; südd., österr., schw. (Hacke) hoe

Haue[2] f; -, kein Pl.; Kinderspr.: **~ kriegen** get a smack (od. spanking); **jetzt gibt's ~!** you'll get a smack!, I'll smack your bottom (bes. Am. behind!)

hauen; haut, haute od. hieb, hat/ist gehauen od. Dial. gehaut **I.** v/t. (hat) **1.** (haute) umg. (j-n) (schlagen) hit; (Kind) smack; (prügeln) beat; **haut ihn!** let him have it!; **j-n zu Brei od. Mus** etc. **~** make mincemeat of s.o.; → Lukas 2, Ohr, 2. (mst haute) (schlagen) hit, bang; (zerschlagen) smash; mit Werkzeug: (hacken) chop; (meißeln) (Statue etc.) hew, make (**aus** from); (Loch etc.) cut, make; Bergb. (Erz) cut, (Kohle) auch break; Dial. (Bäume) chop down; (Gras etc.) cut, mow; (Fleisch, Holz) chop; **j-m etw. auf den Kopf ~** hit s.o. over the head with s.th.; **e-n Nagel in die Wand ~** umg. bang a nail into the wall; **etw. / die Wohnung kurz und klein ~** smash s.th. to pieces / tear the place apart; → Ohr 1,2; **3.** (hieb) geh., mit Waffe: thrust (at); **4.** (haute); umg. (stoßen) knock; (werfen) chuck; **auf den Tisch** etc.: bang (down); **das haut den stärksten Mann vom Hocker** etc. umg. it really knocks you sideways (Am. knocks your socks off); **das haut mich nicht vom Hocker** etc. umg. I'm not exactly bowled over by it; → Pfanne 1; **II.** v/i. **1.** (mst haute; hat); umg.: **~ nach** lash out at; **um sich ~** hit out in all directions; **j-m auf die Schulter ~** clap s.o. on the shoulder; **j-m ins Gesicht ~** hit (od. slap) s.o. in the face; **auf den Tisch ~** bang (one's fist on) the table; **auf od. in die Tasten ~** pound the keys; **nicht ~!** don't hit me (od. him etc.)!; → Pauke; **2.** (hieb; hat); mit Waffe: thrust, strike; **3.** (haute; ist); umg. unabsichtlich: **mit dem Kopf an die Tür ~** (stoßen) knock (od. bang) one's head against the door; **in den Dreck ~** (fallen) fall slap in the mud; **III.** v/refl. (haute; hat); umg. **1. sich mit j-m ~** (have a) fight with s.o.; **sie ~ sich** they're fighting; **2. sich aufs Bett** od.

in die Falle etc. **~** hit the sack

Hauer[1] *m; -s, - des Keilers*: tusk

Hauer[2] *m; -s, -,* **~in** *f; -, -nen* **1.** *Bergb.* face worker; **2.** *südd., österr. (Winzer[in])* vintner, wine grower

Häufchen *n umg.* **1.** (small) pile (*od.* heap); *Kot:* (pile of) dog's *etc.* muck; **2.** (*kleine Gruppe*) handful; **3.** *wie ein* **~** *Elend* the picture of misery

häufeln *v/t.* **1.** (*Erde etc.*) heap up; **2.** *Agr.* (*Kartoffeln etc.*) hill *od.* earth up; **3.** *Pol.: Stimmen* **~** give several votes to the same candidate

Haufen *m; -s, -* **1.** pile; *mst größer:* heap; (*Ansammlung, Häufung*) mass; *Holz etc.:* stack; *auf e-n* **~** *legen/werfen* put on / throw on(to) a pile; *zu e-m* **~** *aufschichten/zusammenkehren* stack up / sweep (up) into a pile; *e-n* **~** *machen umg. euph.* do (*od.* take *od.* have) a dump; *j-n über den* **~** *rennen/schießen umg. fig.* (nearly) knock s.o. flying / bump s.o. off; *über den* **~** *werfen umg. fig.* (*Theorie etc.*) upset; *stärker:* explode; (*Pläne etc.*) (*durcheinander bringen*) mess up; (*zunichte machen*) *Unvorhergesehenes etc.:* put paid to, *Am.* do away with; (*Vorhaben, Pläne*) scupper; (*eigene Pläne*) throw overboard; **2.** *umg.: ein* **~** (*große Menge*) piles (of), masses (of); *ein* **~** *Arbeit* a pile (*od.* piles) of work; *ein* **~** *Geld* heaps (*od.* stacks) of money; *e-n* **~** (*Geld*) *verdienen* rake it in; *einmalig:* make a pile; *es hat e-n* **~** *Geld gekostet* it cost a packet (*Am.* bundle); **3.** (*Schar, Menge*) swarm, crowd; *in* **~** in droves; *auf e-m* **~** *sitzen etc.:* in a big group; *so viel(e) ... auf e-n* **~** so much/many ... in one place; **4.** *Mil.* (*Trupp*) troop; *umg. fig.* (*Gruppe*) bunch, crowd; **5.** *Astron.* cluster

häufen I. *v/t.* pile up, heap up; **~** *auf* (+ *Akk.*) pile (up) on, pile onto; → *gehäuft* II; **II.** *v/refl.* (*sich anhäufen*) pile up, accumulate, mount; (*sich mehren*) multiply, increase; (*sich verbreiten*) spread; (*öfter vorkommen*) happen (*od.* occur) more and more often, be on the increase; *die Beschwerden* **~** *sich* more and more complaints are being made (*od.* are coming in); *die Todesfälle* **~** *sich* the number of deaths (*od.* the death toll) is going up (*od.* is on the increase); *die Hinweise* **~** *sich* evidence is mounting; → *gehäuft* III

Haufendorf *n* Haufendorf, cluster village, *a village that has grown up haphazardly and is not arranged along a street*

haufenweise *Adv. umg.* in piles; (*scharenweise*) in droves; *wir kriegen* **~** *Beschwerden* we get an endless stream of complaints; *CDs hat er* **~** he's got masses (*od.* piles) of CDs

Haufenwolke *f* cumulus (*Pl.* cumuli) (cloud)

häufig I. *Adj.* frequent; (*verbreitet*) widespread; *ein* **~***er Fehler* a common mistake; **~***er werden* (be on the) increase, be increasing; **II.** *Adv.* frequently, (quite) often, a lot *umg.; das ist* **~** *so* that's often the case; **Häufigkeit** *f* frequency; *von Verbrechen, Krankheit etc.:* incidence

Häufigkeits|verteilung *f* frequency distribution; **~zahl** *f* frequency

Häuflein *n; -s, -* → *Häufchen*

Häufung *f* accumulation (+ *Gen.* of); (*Verbreitung*) spread(ing) (of); (*Wiederholung*) increase (in, of), increased number (of)

Haupt *n; -(e)s, Häupter; geh.* **1.** head; *erhobenen* **~***es* with head erect; *zu Häupten* (+ *Gen.*) at the head (of); → *Asche* 1; **2.** *fig.* head (+ *Gen.* of); *bemooste/gekrönte Häupter* perpetual students / crowned heads; *an* **~** *und Gliedern reformieren* reform root and branch

Haupt|... *im Subst. mst* main, chief, principal; **~abnehmer** *m Wirts.* biggest buyer (*od.* importer); **~abschnitt** *m Eisenb. etc.* main stretch; **~absicht** *f* main intention (*od.* purpose); **~abteilungsleiter** *m,* **~abteilungsleiterin** *f* (senior) head of department; **~achse** *f* **1.** main axis; **2.** *fig.* (*Straße*) main thoroughfare; **~aktionär** *m,* **~aktionärin** *f Wirts.* principal shareholder (*Am.* stockholder); **~akzent** *m* **1.** *Ling.* primary stress; **2.** *fig.* main emphasis; *der* **~** *liegt auf* the main emphasis is on; **~altar** *m* high altar

hauptamtlich I. *Adj.* full-time; **II.** *Adv. auch* on a full-time basis

Haupt|angeklagte *m, f* principal defendant; **~angriffsziel** *n* main (*od.* chief) target; **~anliegen** *n* main (*od.* chief) concern; **~anschluss** *m Telef.* main line; **~anteil** *m* **1.** *Wirts.* principal share; **2.** *fig.* lion's share (*an* + *Dat.* of); **~arbeit** *f* **1.** *die* **~** most (*od.* the main part) of the work; **2.** → *Hauptaufgabe;* **~argument** *n* main (*od.* chief) argument; **~artikel** *m Wirts., Jur.* main article; *e-r Zeitung:* leader, lead story; **~attraktion** *f* main (*od.* chief) attraction; *bei Veranstaltung etc.: auch* big draw; **~aufgabe** *f* main (*od.* chief) task; **~augenmerk** *n: sein* **~** *richten auf* (+ *Akk.*) focus (one's) attention on; **~ausgang** *m* main exit; **~aussage** *f* main statement (*od.* point); **~ausschuss** *m* central committee; **~bahnhof** *m* main (*od.* central) station; **~bedeutung** *f* **1.** *Ling.* primary meaning; **2.** *fig. e-s Ereignisses etc.:* main (*od.* primary) significance; **~bedingung** *f* main (*od.* principal) condition; **~belastungszeuge** *m,* **~belastungszeugin** *f* chief witness for the prosecution

Hauptberuf *m* main job; **hauptberuflich I.** *Adj.* full-time ...; **II.** *Adv.* as one's main job; *arbeiten, tätig sein:* full-time; **~** *ist er Lehrer* his main job is teaching; *was machen Sie* **~***?* what's your main job?

Haupt|beschäftigung *f* main occupation; **~bestandteil** *m* main constituent (*bes. Tech.* component); **~beteiligte** *m, f* principal party (*od.* person) concerned; *aktiv: auch* chief protagonist; **~betrieb** *m* **1.** main office(s *Pl.*) *od.* plant; **2.** *zeitlich:* peak period; **~buch** *n Wirts.* ledger; **~büro** *n* head office; **~darsteller** *m* leading man; **~darstellerin** *f* leading lady; → *auch Hauptrolle;* **~datei** *f Computer:* master file; **~deck** *n Naut.* main deck; **~eigenschaft** *f* chief characteristic; **~einfahrt** *f,* **~eingang** *m* main entrance; **~einkaufszeit** *f* peak shopping hours *Pl.;* **~einnahmequelle** *f* chief (*od.* main) source of income; **~einwand** *m* main objection

Häuptelsalat *m südd., österr.* lettuce

Haupt|entlastungszeuge *m,* **~entlastungszeugin** *f* chief witness for the defen|ce (*Am.* -se); **~erbe** *m,* **~erbin** *f* principal heir; **~erzeugnis** *n* main product

Haupteslänge *f geh.: um* **~** *überragen* be a head taller than

Haupt|fach *n* main subject, *Am.* major; *was hast du als* **~***?* what's your main subject?, (*Am.* your major)?; **~faktor** *m* main factor; **~fehler** *m* chief mistake; *Schwäche:* main fault; **~feind** *m,* **~feindin** *f* chief enemy, archenemy; **~feldwebel** *m Mil. etwa* staff sergeant, *Am.* sergeant major; **~figur** *f* main (*od.* central) figure; *Theat. etc.* main character; *männlich:* hero; *weiblich:* heroine; (*Protagonist[in]*) protagonist; **~film** *m* main feature; **~forderung** *f* main *od.* principal demand; **~frage** *f* main question (*od.* issue); **~funktion** *f* main function (*od.* purpose); **~gang** *m* **1.** *Gastr.* main course; **2.** main corridor; *im Fuchsbau etc.:* main passage; **~gebäude** *n* main building; **~gedanke** *m* main idea; **~gefahr** *f* main (*od.* primary) danger; **~gefreite** *m, f Mil.* lance corporal, *Am.* private 1st class; **~gericht** *n Gastr.* main course; **~geschäft** *n* **1.** head office; **2.** *Zeit:* peak business hours *Pl.;* → **Haupteinkaufszeit;** **~geschäftsstelle** *f* head office; **~geschäftsstraße** *f* main shopping street; **~geschäftszeit** *f* → **Hauptgeschäft** 2; **~gesprächsthema** *n* main topic of conversation, conversation topic number one; **~gewicht** *n fig.* main emphasis; **~gewinn** *m* **1.** *Lotterie:* first prize; **2.** *Wirts.* main profit; **~grund** *m* main reason

Haupthaar *n; nur Sg.; geh.* hair (on one's *od.* s.o.'s head)

Haupt|hahn *m* main tap (*Am.* faucet); **~handlung** *f Theat. etc.* main plot; **~hindernis** *n* main obstacle (*od.* hurdle); **~inhalt** *m* essence; **~interesse** *n* main interest; *sein* **~** *gilt ...* he's mainly (*od.* primarily) interested in ...; **~kasse** *f* main cash desk; *Theat.* box office; **~katalog** *m* main catalog(ue); **~kläger** *m,* **~klägerin** *f* principal plaintiff; **~last** *f* main burden; brunt (of it); *die* **~** *zu tragen haben* have to bear the brunt (of it); **~leidtragende** *m, f* main victim; *der* **~** *auch* the one to suffer most; *die* **~***n* those who suffer most; **~leitung** *f* main(s *Pl. Brit.*); **~leute** *Pl. Mil.* → **Hauptmann;** **~lieferant** *m* main (*od.* chief) supplier

Häuptling *m; -s, -e* **1.** headman; *des Stammes: auch* tribal chief; *von Indianern:* (Indian) chief; **2.** *hum. od. iro.* (*Anführer, Chef*) boss

Haupt|macht *f Mil.* main force; **~mahlzeit** *f* main meal (of the day); **~mangel** *m* main fault (*Schwäche:* weakness); **~mann** *m; Pl. -leute; Mil.* captain; (*Anführer*) leader; **~masse** *f* bulk, main body; **~menü** *n Computer:* main menu; **~merkmal** *n* main feature, chief characteristic; **~mieter** *m,* **~mieterin** *f* main tenant; **~motiv** *n* **1.** *Beweggrund:* main motive (*od.* motivation); **2.** *Kunst, Fot.* central motif (*od.* theme); **~nachricht** *f* **1.** lead story; **2.** *Pl.* main news *Sg.;* **~nahrung** *f,* **~nahrungsmittel** *n* staple (food); *Pl. auch* staple diet *Sg.;* **~nenner** *m Math. und fig.* common denominator; *um es auf e-n* **~** *zu bringen fig.* to bring it down (*od.* reduce it) to a common denominator; **~niederlassung** *f Wirts.* head (*od.* central) office, headquarters *Pl.* (*auch V. im Sg.*); **~person** *f* → **Hauptfigur**, *er will immer die* **~** *sein* he always wants to be number one (*od.* the cent|re [*Am.* -er] of attention); **~platine** *f Computer:* motherboard; **~portal** *n* main entrance (+ *Gen.* of, to), main door(way) (of, into); **~post** f, **~postamt** n main (*Am.* general) post office; **~probe** f *Theat.*, *Oper.* last rehearsal before the (*public*) dress rehearsal; *Mus.* general rehearsal; **~problem** n main problem; **~punkt** m main point (*od.* issue); **~quartier** n headquarters *Pl.* (*auch V. im Sg.*); **~quelle** f main *od.* primary source; **~rechner** m *Computer:* mainframe (computer); **~redner** m, **~rednerin** f main speaker; **~regel** f principal (*od.* most important) rule, rule number one; **~reisezeit** f (peak) tourist season; **~revier** n main police station; **~richtung** f 1. main (*od.* general) direction; 2. (*Trend*) major (*od.* main) trend; **~rolle** f leading role, main part, lead; (*Titelrolle*) title role; **die ~ spielen** *Theat. etc.* play the lead(ing role) *od.* main part; *fig. Person:* be the central figure; *auch:* be the chief protagonist; *Sache:* play the most important role, be the most important thing; **~runde** f *Sport* (main) round, *a round that is not a preliminary round*

Hauptsache f 1. main (*od.* most important) thing; **das ist die ~** *auch* that's what matters most (**für mich** to me); **~, sie gewinnt** *umg.* the main thing is that she wins (*od.* is for her to win); **in der** *od.* **zur ~** mainly, in the main, for the main part; 2. *Jur.* main issue; **hauptsächlich I.** *Adj.* main ..., most important, essential; **II.** *Adv.* mainly, chiefly, essentially; (*vor allem*) above all; **worauf es ~ ankommt, ist** ... what matters most is ..., the most important thing is ...

Haupt|saison f peak (*od.* high) season; **~satz** m 1. *Ling.* main clause; 2. *Phys. etc.* first principle (*od.* law); 3. *Mus.* first (*od.* main) subject; **~schalter** m 1. *Etech.* main (*od.* master) switch; 2. *Bank etc.:* main desk (*od.* counter); *Eisenb. etc.* main booking (*Am.* ticketing) office (*od.* ticket desk, ticket counter); **~schiff** n *Archit.* nave; **~schlagader** f *Anat.* aorta; **~schlüssel** m master key; **~schulabschluss** m qualification obtained on completion of a student's education at a *Hauptschule*, *etwa* leaver's certificate, *Am.* diploma; **~schuld** f; *nur Sg.* 1. **er trägt die ~ daran** it's mainly his fault, he's mostly to blame (for it); 2. *Wirts.* principal debt; **~schuldige** m, f major offender; **~schule** f *etwa* secondary school, *a school that takes students through the last five years of their compulsory period of education*; **~schullehrer** m, **~schullehrerin** f teacher in a *Hauptschule*; **~schüler** m, **~schülerin** f student at a *Hauptschule*; **~schwierigkeit** f main (*od.* chief, major) difficulty; **~seminar** n *Univ.* (advanced) seminar; **~sendezeit** f *TV* peak viewing hours *Pl.*, prime time; **~sicherung** f *Etech.* main fuse; **~sitz** m *Wirts.* head office, headquarters *Pl.* (*auch V. im Sg.*); **~sorge** f main (*od.* chief) concern, main worry; **~speicher** m *Computer:* main memory; **~speise** f main course

Hauptstadt f capital (city); **Hauptstädter** m, **Hauptstädterin** f citizen of the (*od.* a) capital; **hauptstädtisch** *Adj.* metropolitan

Haupt|straße f main street; *in der Innenstadt: Brit. mst* High Street, *Am. mst* Main Street; → *auch* **Hauptverkehrsstraße**; **~strecke** f main route; *Eisenb.* main line; **~streitpunkt** m main issue (*od.* point of contention);

~studium n *Univ.* main course; **~stütze** f *fig.* mainstay; **~täter** m, **~täterin** f *Jur.* principal offender; **~tätigkeit** f main job; *Pflicht:* main duty (*od.* function); **~teil** m main part; (*das meiste*) most of it, the greater part; **~thema** n main subject; *Mus.* principal theme; **~ton** m main stress; *Mus.* keynote; **~tor** n main gate; **~treffer** m first prize, jackpot *umg.*; **den ~ gewinnen** hit the jackpot; **~treppe** f main (*od.* grand) staircase; **~tribüne** f grandstand; **~tugend** f cardinal virtue; **~unterschied** m main difference; **~ursache** f main cause; **die ~ ist ...** *auch* what's at the bottom of it is ...; **~verantwortliche** m, f person chiefly responsible; **~verantwortung** f chief (*od.* prime) responsibility; **die ~ übernehmen** take chief (*od.* prime) responsibility (**für** for)

Hauptverdienst[1] m main income

Hauptverdienst[2] n major (*od.* greatest) achievement

Haupt|verfahren m *Jur.* main proceedings *Pl.*; **~verhandlung** f *Strafprozess:* trial, hearing; *Zivilprozess:* main proceedings *Pl.*; **~verkehr** m 1. rush-hour traffic; 2. **der ~** *Großteil:* most of the traffic

Hauptverkehrs|straße f main road; *in Stadt:* main thoroughfare; *Fernverkehr:* arterial (*Brit. auch* trunk) road, *Am.* principal highway; **~zeit** f peak traffic hours *Pl.*; *bes. Berufsverkehr:* rush hour

Haupt|versammlung f *Wirts.* general meeting; **~verwaltung** f head office, headquarters *Pl.* (*auch V. im Sg.*); **~verzeichnis** n *EDV* root directory; **~vorstand** m governing board; **~wachtmeister** m, **~wachtmeisterin** f 1. *etwa* (police) sergeant; 2. *Mil. hist.* → **Hauptfeldwebel**; **~wäsche** f, **~waschgang** m main wash; **~werk** n 1. *e-s Künstlers:* major work; 2. *Fabrik:* main plant; **~wohnsitz** m main (place of) residence; **~wort** n *Ling.* noun; **~zeuge** m, **~zeugin** f chief witness; **~ziel** n 1. main objective; 2. *e-s Angriffs:* main target; **~zollamt** n chief customs office; **~zweck** m main (*od.* chief, primary) purpose

hau ruck *Interj.* heave-ho!; **Hauruckverfahren** n *pej.* railroading; **im ~** by railroading it through

Haus n; *-es, Häuser* 1. house; (*Gebäude*) building; **im ~** inside, indoors; **im nächsten ~** *od.* **ein ~ weiter** *bei Einfamilienhäusern:* next door; *bei größeren:* in the next block (of flats) (*Am.* the next [apartment] building); **zwei Häuser weiter** *bei Einfamilienhäusern:* next door but one, *Am.* two houses down (*od.* up); *bei größeren:* two blocks (*Am.* buildings) (further) down (*od.* up); **~ an ~ wohnen** live next door to each other, be next-door neigh-bo(u)rs; **~ an ~ mit j-m wohnen** live next door to s.o.; **von ~ zu ~ gehen** *etc.:* from door to door; **j-n durchs ~ führen** show s.o. (a)round (the house); **~ und Hof** *od.* **~ und Herd** house and home; **er hat an der Börse ~ und Hof verspekuliert** he lost everything he had speculating on the stock exchange; **ihm steht e-e Versetzung ins ~** *fig.* he's got a posting (*Am.* transfer) coming up, he's due for a posting (*Am.* transfer); **es** *od.* **uns stehen Neuwahlen ins ~** *fig.* elections are coming up, there are elections ahead (*od.* on the doorstep); 2. (*Zuhause*)

home, house, place *umg.*; (*Haushalt*) household; **das väterliche ~** one's father's home; **außer ~ essen** eat out; **er ist außer ~(e)** he's out, he's not in, he's gone out; **im ~ m-r Tante** at my aunt's (house); **im ~e Müller** at the Müllers' (house); **ein großes ~ führen** entertain lavishly; **ein offenes ~ haben** keep open house; **~ halten** (*wirtschaften*) economize; **~ halten mit** be economical with; (*sehr sparsam sein*) economize on; **mit s-r Zeit/Energie ~ halten** (*müssen*) (have to) divide one's time/energies up sensibly; **das ~ hüten** (*müssen*) (have to) stay at home (*od.* indoors); **j-m das ~ verbieten** not allow s.o. in the (*od.* one's) house; **zu j-m ins ~ kommen** *Friseur, Lehrer etc.:* come to the (*od.* one's) house; **das/der kommt mir nicht ins ~!** I'm not having that in the (*od.* my) house / he will never be welcome in this family; → **frei** I 10, **Herr** 3, **schneien** *etc.*; 3. **nach ~e** home; **j-n nach ~e bringen** take (*od.* see) s.o. home; **komm du mir nur nach ~e!** *drohend:* just wait till I get you home!; **komm mir ja nicht mit e-r kaputten Hose / e-m Kind nach ~e!** don't come home with your trousers torn / pregnant; 4. **zu ~e** at home (*auch Sport*); **zu ~e sein** *auch* be in; **wieder zu ~e sein** be back home again; **er ist in X zu ~e** his home is (in) X, he comes from X; **bei uns zu ~e** (*in m-m Heim*) in my family, at our place *umg.*; (*in m-r Heimat etc.*) where I come from; **fühlt euch ganz zu ~e** make yourselves at home; **diese Arbeit kann ich von zu ~e aus machen** this is a job I can do from home; **in etw.** (*Dat.*) **zu ~e sein** *fig.* (*sich auskennen*) be well up (*od.* at home) in s.th.; 5. **für Firma etc.:** house; **im ~e auf Briefen:** in house; **ist Frau X schon im ~e?** is Ms (*od.* Ms.) X in yet?; **außer ~ geben** *Wirts.* contract out, *bes. Am.* outsource; **ich möchte mich im Namen unseres ~es bedanken** I'd like to thank you on behalf of the firm (*bes. Am.* company); **das erste ~ am Platz(e)** the best hotel (*od.* restaurant, store) in town, the number one hotel *etc.* around here; **Empfehlung des ~es** *Gericht etc.:* our recommendation, the house special; *fig. bei Geschenk an e-n Kunden:* compliments of the management; 6. *Theat.* house; **ausverkauftes** *od.* **volles ~** *Theat.* full house; **immer volle Häuser haben** always be sold out; **vor leeren Häusern spielen** play to empty houses; 7. (*Familie, Herkunft*) family, home; (*Herrscherhaus*) house; (*Geschlecht*) dynasty; **das ~ Hannover** the House of Hanover; **aus gutem ~ sein** come from a good family; **von ~ aus** by birth; *fig.* (*eigentlich*) actually; (*ursprünglich*) originally; (*seit jeher*) always; (*von Natur her*) by nature; **er ist von ~ aus Chirurg** *fig.* (*eigentlich*) he's (actually) a qualified surgeon; (*ursprünglich*) he was originally a surgeon; (*seit jeher*) he's always been a surgeon; **du meinst wohl, du hast von ~ aus Recht?** *umg. fig.* I suppose you think you're always bound to be right; 8. *in Eigennamen etc.:* **das Weiße ~** *Pol., in Washington:* the White House; **wie aus dem Weißen ~ verlautet ...** according to White House sources; **das ~ Gottes** *Reli., geh.* the House of God *od.* the Lord; **das ~ des Sports/Handwerks** *etc.* the sports/craft cent|re

(*Am.* -er); **9.** *Parl.* House; *Hohes ~!* hono(u)rable members (of the House)!; *die beiden Häuser des Parlaments* both houses of Parliament; **10.** *umg. Koll.*: *das halbe ~ war auf dem Fest* (*viele Bewohner*) half the building was at the party; *das (ganze) ~ tobte im Theater etc.*: the (whole) audience went wild, they nearly brought the house down; **11.** *umg. hum.* (*Person*) *fideles, gelehrtes etc.*: type; *altes ~* old chap; **12.** *Astrol.* house; **13.** *der Schnecke etc.*: shell; *ohne ~* naked

Haus|altar *m* family altar; **~angestellte** *f, m* domestic (servant); *weiblich*: maid; *männlich*: manservant; **~antenne** *f* roof aerial (*od.* antenna); **~anzug** *m* leisure suit; **~apotheke** *f* medicine cabinet (*od.* chest); **~arbeit** *f* **1.** housework; **2.** *Päd. auch Pl.* homework; **3.** *Univ.* piece of course work (*usually counting towards the class of degree* [*Am.* grade]); **~arrest** *m* **1.** *für Kinder*: grounding, being kept in; *in Internat*: gating, *Am.* campusing; *sie hat ~* she's been grounded; **2.** *Jur.* house arrest; **~arzt** *m*, **~ärztin** *f* family doctor, *in GB*: *etwa* GP (= general practitioner); *Am.* family practitioner; **~aufgabe** *f* auch *Pl.* homework; (*s-e*) **~n machen** do (one's) homework; *fig.* (*sich gut auf etw. vorbereiten etc.*) do one's homework; *sie hat i-e ~n gemacht fig.* (*aus Fehlern gelernt*) she's learn|t (*Am.* -ed) her lesson

Hausaufgaben|betreuung *f Päd.* homework supervision; **~heft** *n* (*Merkheft*) homework book (*od.* diary); → *Hausheft*

Hausaufsatz *m Päd.* essay (to be done as homework)

hausbacken *Adj.* **1.** *fig. Person*: homely, *Am.* homey; *Sache*: plain, prosaic, boring *umg.*; **2.** *altm.* homemade

Haus|ball *m* private ball, dinner and dance; **~bank** *f; m-e etc. ~* my etc. bank; **~bar** *f* **1.** *Fach, Möbelstück*: cocktail (*Am.* liquor) cabinet; **2.** *mit Theke*: bar; **3.** *Koll. Getränke*: (stock of) drinks *Pl. od.* liquor; **~bau** *m; Pl. -ten, mst Sg.* house building; **~bedarf** *m* household requirements *Pl.*; *für den ~* for the home, *weitS.* for (your etc. own) private use; **~berg** *m umg. e-r Stadt*: local mountain; *e-s Sportlers*: home slopes *Pl.*, *the area where a skier etc. usually trains*; **~besetzer** *m*, **~besetzerin** *f* squatter; **~besetzung** *f* squatting; **~besitzer** *m*, **~besitzerin** *f* homeowner; (*Vermieter*) landlord/ landlady; **~besorger** *m*, **~besorgerin** *f österr.* housekeeper; **~besuch** *m des Arztes etc.*: home visit, house call; **~e machen** auch be on (*od.* doing) one's rounds; **~bewohner** *m*, **~bewohnerin** *f* occupant; (*Mieter*) tenant; **~boot** *n* houseboat; **~brand** *m* **1.** *Unglück*: house fire; **2.** *nur Sg. Material*: domestic fuel; *Vorgang*: domestic heating

Häuschen *n* **1.** *Pl. auch Häuserchen* small house; (*Wochenend-, Ferienhaus*) cottage, *bes. Am.* cabin, bungalow; *für Pförtner, Jagd*: lodge; → *Hütte*; **2.** *umg.* (*Abort*) loo, *Am.* john; *außerhalb des Hauses*: privy, outside loo, *Am.* outhouse; **3.** *umg. fig.*: (*ganz*) *aus dem ~ geraten* flip, go mad, go berserk; *ganz aus dem ~ sein* be wildly excited, *vor Glück*: auch be over the moon

Haus|dach *n* roof (of the house); **~dame** *f* housekeeper; **~detektiv** *m*, **~de-**

tektivin *f* store detective; *im Hotel*: house detective; **~diener** *m* domestic servant; *im Hotel*: page, *Am.* bellhop; *Gepäckträger*: auch porter; **~drachen** *m umg. pej.* battleax(e); **~durchsuchung** *f* house search; **~ecke** *f* corner of a (*bzw.* the) house

hauseigen *Adj. attr.* ... belonging to the establishment (*bzw.* hotel, firm, etc.); *mit ~em Strand* with its own private beach

Haus|eigentümer *m*, **~eigentümerin** *f* → *Hausbesitzer*; **~eingang** *m* entrance (to a *od.* the house), front door (*od.* entrance)

Häusel *n; -s, -n; bes. österr.* loo, *Am.* john

hausen *v/i. umg.* **1.** *hum. od. pej.* (*wohnen*) live; **2.** *pej.* wreak havoc; *sie haben dort wie die Wandalen gehaust* auch they wrecked the place

Häuser|block *m* block (of houses); **~front** *f* **1.** housefront; **2.** row of houses; **~kampf** *m* **1.** *Mil.* house-to-house fighting; **2.** *Pol.* squatting action; **~meer** *n* sea of houses; *ein ~* auch houses as far as the eye can see; **~zeile** *f* row of houses

Haus|flur *m* hall(way); **~frau** *f* **1.** housewife; *Am. auch* homemaker; **2.** *weitS.* lady of the house; (*Hauswirtin*) landlady

Hausfrauen|art *f*: *nach od. auf ~* home-made-style ..., *etwa* ... just like mother used to make; **~dasein** *n* life of a housewife; *das ~ satt haben* be fed up of being (just) a housewife

hausfraulich *Adj.* housewifely; (*häuslich*) domestic; **~e Pflichten** duties of a housewife; *ich habe keine ~en Fähigkeiten* I'm (*od.* I'd be) no good as a housewife

Hausfreund *m* **1.** friend of the family; **2.** *hum. euph.* boyfriend, man *umg.*; **Hausfreundin** *f* **1.** friend of the family; **2.** *hum. euph.* girlfriend, lady friend

Hausfriede(n) *m* domestic peace; **Hausfriedensbruch** *m Jur.* illegal entry of *s.o.'s* house, *Am.* breaking and entering

Haus|gans *f Orn.* domestic goose; **~garten** *m* (back) garden, *Am.* backyard; **~gast** *m Gastr.* (house)guest; **~gebrauch** *m*: *für den ~* for use in the home, *umg. fig.* for (one's own) pleasure; *für den ~ reichen umg. fig.* be enough to get by on, be good enough for one's own simple needs (*od.* requirements); **~geburt** *f* home birth; **~gehilfin** *f* maid

hausgemacht *Adj.* homemade (*auch umg. fig.*)

Haus|gemeinschaft *f* **1.** *Koll.* (*Bewohner*) tenants *Pl.*; **2.** community, household; *wir haben e-e nette ~* we have nice neighbo(u)rs, we all get on (*Am.* along) with each other (in our block of flats [*Am.* in our building]); **~genosse** *m*, **~genossin** *f* housemate; *Mitmieter*: fellow tenant; *Untermieter*: lodger; **~götter** *Pl.* household gods

Haushalt *m; -(e)s, -e* **1.** household; (*Haushaltung*) housekeeping; *den ~ führen od. machen* run the household; *j-m den ~ führen od. besorgen* auch keep house for s.o.; *im ~ helfen* help (out) in (*od.* around) the house; **2.** *Pol.* budget; **3.** *Koll. Personen*: household; **~haushalt** *m, im Subst. des Körpers etc.*: balance; *Eiweiß~* protein balance; *Fett~* fat balance

haushalten *v/i.* → *Haus* 2; **Haushälter**

m; -s, -, **Haushälterin** *f; -, -nen* housekeeper; **haushälterisch** *Adj.* economical

Haushalts|artikel *m* household article; **~auflösung** *f* house clearance; *wegen ~ in Verkaufsanzeige*: from house clearance; **~ausschuss** *m Parl.* budget(ary) committee; **~buch** *n* housekeeping (*od.* account) book; **~debatte** *f Parl.* budget(ary) debate, debate on the budget; **~defizit** *n Pol.* budget deficit; **~entwurf** *m Pol.* budget proposals *Pl.*; **~führung** *f* housekeeping; **~geld** *n* housekeeping money; **~gerät** *n* household appliance; **~gesetz** *n Pol.* budget law; **~hilfe** *f* **1.** *Person*: home help; **2.** *Gerät etc.*: domestic appliance, labo(u)r-saving device; **~jahr** *n Pol.* fiscal (*od.* financial) year; **~kasse** *f* **1.** *nur Sg.; Geld*: housekeeping (money); *etw. aus der ~ zahlen* pay s.th. out of the housekeeping; **2.** *Behälter*: container where the housekeeping money is kept; **~loch** *n Pol.* budget deficit; **~mitglied** *n* member of a (*od.* the) household; **~mittel** *Pl. Pol.* budgetary means; *gebilligte*: appropriations; **~packung** *f* economy pack; **~plan** *m Pol.* budget; **~planung** *f Pol.* budgeting

Haushaltspolitik *f Pol.* budgetary policies *Pl.*; **haushaltspolitisch** *Adj.* budgetary

Haushalts|posten *m Pol.* item in a (*bzw.* the) budget; **~reiniger** *m* household cleaner; **~überschuss** *m Pol.* budget surplus; **~volumen** *n Pol.* total budget; **~vorstand** *m* head of a (*od.* the) household; **~waage** *f* kitchen scale(s *Pl. Brit.*); **~waren** *Pl.* household articles

Haushaltung *f* **1.** housekeeping; **2.** (*Haushalt*) household; **Haushaltungskosten** *Pl.* household expenses

Hausheft *n Päd.* exercise book (*for homework in a particular subject*)

Hausherr *m* **1.** (*Familienvorstand*) head of a (*od.* the) household; **2.** (*Gastgeber*) host (*auch Sport*); (*Wirt*) landlord; **3.** *südd., österr.* → *Hausbesitzer*, **Hausherrin** *f* **1.** lady of the house; **2.** (*Gastgeberin*) hostess; (*Wirtin*) landlady; **3.** *südd., österr.* → *Hausbesitzer*

haushoch I. *Adj.* **1.** very high, huge; **2.** *fig.* vast, enormous; *Niederlage*: shattering, crushing; *haushoher Sieg* walkover, *Am.* walkaway; **II.** *Adv.*: *~ gewinnen* win hands down; *~ schlagen* trounce; *Sport auch* play *s.o.* into the ground; *~ überlegen sein* (+ *Dat.*) be more than a match for; *bes. Einzelperson*: auch be head and shoulders above; *in Wissen, Erfahrung etc.*: be streets (*Am.* miles) ahead of; *zahlenmäßig*: outnumber by far; *sie ist ihm ~ überlegen* auch he's no match for her, he can't hold a candle to her; *~ verlieren* suffer a crushing defeat, be thrashed *umg.*

Haus|hofmeister *m hist.* chamberlain; **~huhn** *n* domestic fowl; **~hund** *m* (domestic) dog

hausieren *v/i.* hawk; *auch fig.* peddle (*mit etw.* s.th.); *Betteln und Hausieren verboten!* no beggars, no hawkers, *bes. Am.* no solicitors; *~ gehen mit e-r Geschichte etc. fig.* tell the whole world (about); **Hausierer** *m; -s, -,* **Hausiererin** *f; -, -nen* hawker, peddler; door-to-door salesperson

hausintern *Adj.* internal, in-house

Haus|jurist *m*, **~juristin** *f* company

H

(*od.* corporate) lawyer; ~**kapelle** f **1.** private chapel; **2.** *Mus.* resident band (*od.* orchestra); ~**katze** f (domestic) cat; ~**kauf** m house purchase; ~**käufer** m, ~**käuferin** f house buyer; ~**klingel** f (front) doorbell; ~**konzert** n private (*od.* house) concert

Häusl → **Häusel**

Häuslebauer m; *mst Pl.*; *umg.* private developer

Hauslehrer m, ~**in** f private tutor

häuslich I. *Adj.* **1.** *Frieden, Glück, Pflichten etc.*: domestic; (*der Familie gehörend*) household ...; family ...; *Arbeitszimmer, Pflege etc.*: home ...; *der ~e Herd* one's own fireside; *weitS.* the family home; **2.** (*gern zu Hause bleibend*) domesticated; *er ist ein ~er Typ auch* he's quite happy to be at home (with the family) *od.* around the house, he's a homebody; **II.** *Adv.*: *sich ~ einrichten od. niederlassen* make o.s. at home (*bei j-m* in s.o.'s flat *etc.*), camp down (at s.o.'s place) *umg.*; **Häuslichkeit** f; *nur Sg.*; (*Liebe zum Haus*) domesticity

Hausmacherart f: *nach ~* traditional home-made-style ...

Haus|macht f; *nur Sg.* **1.** *hist.* allodium; **2.** *fig.* power base; ~**mädchen** n maid

Hausmann m house husband; **Hausmannskost** f good plain cooking, *Am.* home cooking

Haus|marke f own (*Am.* house) brand; (*Wein*) house wine; *umg. weitS.* one's favo(u)rite brand; ~**maus** f house mouse; ~**meister** m, ~**meisterin** f caretaker, *Am.* janitor; ~**mitteilung** f **1.** *für Mitarbeiter*: internal memo; **2.** *für Kunden*: company newsletter; ~**mittel** n household (*od.* home) remedy; ~**müll** m household waste; ~**musik** f music-making in the home; ~**mutter** f matron, housemother; ~**mütterchen** n *umg. hum. od. pej.* homebody; ~**nummer** f house number, number of the house; ~**ordnung** f house rules *Pl.*; *die ~ besagt, dass ... iro.* the rules in this house say that ...; ~**personal** n domestic staff (*mst V. im Pl.*) *od.* servants *Pl.*; ~**pflege** f *Med.* home nursing; *Sozialwesen*: home care; ~**post** f internal (*od.* in-house) mail; ~**putz** m spring-clean(ing); *~ machen* give the house a spring-clean(ing *Am.*), do the spring-cleaning

Hausrat m; *nur Sg.* household effects *Pl.*; ~**versicherung** f household contents insurance

Haus|recht n *Jur.* householder's rights *Pl.* (*to forbid entry to his or her home*); *von s-m Gebrauch machen* show *s.o.* the door; refuse to let *s.o.* in; ~**sammlung** f door-to-door collection; ~**schlachtung** f home slaughtering; ~**schlüssel** m (front) doorkey, key to the (front) door; ~**schuh** m (house) slipper; ~**schwamm** m dry rot; ~**schwein** n (domestic) pig

Hausse ['hoːs] f; -, -n; *Fin., Börse*: bull market; *auf ~ spekulieren* bull the market

Haussegen m *umg. hum.*: *der ~ hängt* (*bei ihnen*) *schief* there's a bit of an atmosphere in the house, they've been having a row

Haussier [ho'sieː] m; -s, -s; *Fin.* bull operator

Haussprechanlage f intercom; *über die ~* on the intercom

Hausstand m household; *e-n ~ gründen* set up house

Hausstaub m house dust; ~**allergie** f *Med.* house dust allergy; ~**milbe** f dust mite

Haussuchung f house search; **Haussuchungsbefehl** m search warrant

Haus|telefon n intercom; ~**tier** n **1.** domestic animal; **2.** (*Heimtier*) pet; ~**tochter** f girl living with a family in order to learn domestic skills

Haustür f front door, main entrance *weitS.*; *vor j-s ~ fig.* on s.o.'s doorstep; ~**geschäft** n door-to-door transaction; ~**schlüssel** m front door key

Haus|tyrann m household tyrant; ~**vater** m warden, *Am.* housefather; ~**verbot** n ban on entering the house (*od.* premises); *Jur.* restraining order; *er hat bei ihnen ~* he's not allowed to enter their house (*od.* premises), he's banned from the premises; ~**verwalter** m, ~**verwalterin** f **1.** property manager, *Am.* superintendent; **2.** (*Hausmeister*) caretaker, *Am.* janitor; ~**verwaltung** f property management; ~**wand** f outside wall, (outer) wall of a (*od.* the) house; ~**wart** m *Dial.*, ~**wartin** f; -, -nen; *schw.* caretaker, *Am.* janitor; ~**wirt** m landlord; ~**wirtin** f landlady

Hauswirtschaft f housekeeping; *als Lehrfach*: home economics *Pl.* (*V. im Sg.*), domestic science; **hauswirtschaftlich** *Adj.* domestic, household ...; *~e Schule* school of home economics, school of domestic science; **Hauswirtschaftslehre** f home economics *Pl.* (*V. im Sg.*), domestic science *altm.*

Haus|wurfsendung f mailshot, *Am.* direct mail advertisement *etc.*; ~**zelt** n ridge tent

Haus-zu-Haus-... im *Subst.* door-to-door; ~**Service** *von Transportunternehmen*: door-to-door service

Haut f; -, *Häute* **1.** *mst Sg.* skin; *helle/dunkle ~ haben* have a fair/dark skin; *nass bis auf die ~* soaked to the skin; *auf bloßer ~ tragen* wear next to one's skin; *er trägt die Jacke auf der bloßen ~ auch* he's got nothing on under his jacket; *sich* (*Dat.*) *die ~ aufschürfen* graze o.s.; *sich* (*Dat.*) *die ~ an den Knien etc. aufschürfen* skin (*od.* graze) one's knees *etc.*; *viel ~ zeigen umg. hum. Person*: show a lot of bare flesh, be scantily clad; *Kleidung*: be very revealing; **2.** *abgezogene, von kleinem Tier*: skin; *von großem Tier*: hide; *abgeworfene, e-r Schlange etc.*: slough; *auf Braten*: skin; *e-m Tier die ~ abziehen* skin an animal; **3.** *e-r Frucht*: skin; *mst entfernt*: peel; *e-r Wurst, auf der Milch*: skin; *auf Flüssigkeiten*: film; (*Membran*) membrane; *um Organe*: tunic; *am Fingernagel*: cuticle; *Tech., e-s Ballons, Flugzeugs etc.*: skin; (*Überzug*) sheathing; **4.** *nur Sg.*; *umg. fig.*: *e-e ehrliche/gute ~* an honest / a good soul; *mit ~ und Haar(en)* completely, hook, line and sinker; *aus der ~ fahren* go through (*od.* hit) the roof, go ballistic; *es ist zum Aus-der-~-Fahren!* it's enough to drive you up the wall!; *e-e dicke ~ haben* have a thick skin, be thick-skinned; *s-e ~ retten* save one's skin (*umg. hum.* bacon); *sich s-r* (*Gen.*) *~ wehren* defend o.s. (with all one's might); *ihr ist od. sie fühlt sich nicht wohl in ihrer ~* she feels (rather) uncomfortable (*od.* uneasy); *ich möchte nicht in s-r ~ stecken* I wouldn't like to be in his shoes; *er ist nur noch ~ und Knochen* he's just skin and bones; *es kann eben*

keiner aus s-r ~ a leopard can't change its spots; *das geht einem unter die ~* it gets under your skin; *s-e ~ zu Markte tragen* (*sein Leben riskieren*) risk one's neck; (*sich verkaufen*) sell o.s.; *Frau*: sell one's body; *s-e ~ teuer verkaufen* sell one's life dearly; → *faul* I 2, *heil*

Haut|abschürfung f abrasion, graze; ~**arzt** m, ~**ärztin** f dermatologist, skin specialist; ~**atmung** f cutaneous respiration; ~**ausschlag** m (skin) rash

Häutchen n (*Überzug*) thin coat(ing); *auf Flüssigkeiten*: film; *Anat., Bot.* membrane

Haut|creme f skin cream; ~**drüse** f cutaneous gland

Haute Couture [oːtkuˈtyːɐ] f; - -, *kein Pl.*: (*die*) ~ haute couture

häuten I. *v/t.* skin, flay; **II.** *v/refl.* **1.** shed one's skin; *Schlange etc.*: slough off, mo(u)lt; **2.** *umg. nach Sonnenbrand*: peel

hauteng *Adj. Kleidung*: skintight, body-hugging

Hautentzündung f inflammation of the skin; (*Ausschlag*) skin rash

Hautevolee [oːtvoˈleː] f; -, *kein Pl.*; *oft iro. od. pej.* upper crust; top knobs *Pl.*

Haut|falte f skin fold; *kleine*: wrinkle; ~**farbe** f colo(u)r (of one's skin); (*Teint*) complexion

hautfarben *Adj.* flesh-colo(u)red; *Kosmetik*: skin-colo(u)red

Haut|fetzen m piece of skin; ~**flügler** m; -s, -; *Zool.* hymenopteron

hautfreundlich *Adj.* kind to the skin; → *auch* **hautverträglich**

Haut|jucken n itching, irritation of the skin; *stärker*: pruritus *fachspr.*; ~**klinik** f dermatological clinic; ~**kontakt** m skin contact; ~**krankheit** f skin disease, dermatitis *fachspr.*; ~**krebs** m *Med.* skin cancer

hautnah I. *Adj.* **1.** *fig. Beschreibung etc.*: graphic, vivid; **2.** *Sport* close, tight; **II.** *Adv.* **1.** *fig.*: *j-n berühren* affect s.o. directly; *emotional*: go straight to the core (of s.o.), get under s.o.'s skin; *wir haben es ~ miterlebt* it happened right in front of our eyes; *durch das Fernsehen kann man das Weltgeschehen ~ miterleben* television brings world events right into your living room; **2.** *Sport* closely

Hautöl n skin oil

Hautpflege f skin care; ~**mittel** n skin-care product; ~**serie** f skin-care range

Haut|pilz m *Med.* **1.** *Erreger*: skin (*od.* cutaneous) fungus; **2.** *Erkrankung*: fungal infection; ~**reizung** f skin irritation; ~**rötung** f red (patch of) skin; ~**salbe** f skin ointment; ~**schere** f cuticle scissors *Pl.*

hautschonend *Adj.* kind to the (*od.* one's) skin

Haut|transplantation f *Med.* skin graft(ing); ~**typ** m skin type; *was für ein ~ ist sie od. was für e-n ~ hat sie?* what type of skin has she got?

Häutung f **1.** *der Schlange etc.*: sloughing, mo(u)lting; **2.** *von Jagdbeute etc.*: skinning, dressing

Haut|unreinheit f (skin) blemish; (*Pickel*) spot, pimple; ~**en** *auch* spots (*od.* pimples) and blackheads; ~**verletzung** f superficial wound, (skin) lesion

hautverträglich *Adj.* non-irritant, hypoallergenic

Hautwunde f → **Hautverletzung**

Havanna f; -, -s, **Havannazigarre** f Havana (cigar)

Havarie f; -, -n **1.** *bes. Naut.* (*Schaden*)

damage, average; **2.** (*Unfall*) *Naut.* collision; *Flug.* crash; *in Kraftwerk*: accident; **3.** *bes. österr.*, *mit Auto*: accident

Havarist *m*; *-en*, *-en*; *Naut.* **1.** *Schiff*: damaged vessel; **2.** *Besitzer*: owner of a damaged vessel; **Havaristin** *f*; *-*, *-nen*; *Naut.* owner of a damaged vessel

Hawaii (*n*); *-s*; *Geog.* Hawaii; **Hawaiianer** *m*; *-s*, *-*, **Hawaiianerin** *f*; *-*, *-nen* Hawaiian; *weiblich auch* Hawaiian woman (*od.* girl *etc.*)

Hawaii|gitarre *f* Hawaiian (*bes. Am.* steel) guitar; **~hemd** *n* Hawaiian shirt; **hawaiisch** *Adj.* Hawaiian

Haxe *f*; *-*, *-n*; *südd.* → *Hachse*

Hbf. *Abk.* → *Hauptbahnhof*

H-Bombe *f* H-bomb

h.c. *Abk.* (*honoris causa*) h.c.

H-Dur *n*; *-*, *kein Pl.*; *Mus.* B major

he *Interj. umg.* **1.** *Zuruf*: hey!, oy!; **~ du!** hey, you!; **2.** *empört etc.*: hey!, oy!; **~, was soll das!** hey, what's going on?'; **3.** *nach Frage*: eh?

Headhunter ['hɛthantɐ] *m*; *-s*, *-*; *Wirts.* headhunter

Hearing ['hiːrɪŋ] *n*; *-(s)*, *-s*; *bes. Pol.* hearing

Heavymetal, Heavy Metal ['hɛvi'mɛtl] *n*; *-(s)*, *kein Pl.*; *Mus.* heavy metal

Hebamme *f* midwife

Hebe|arm *m*, **~baum** *m* lever; **~bühne** *f Mot.* hydraulic lift; **~figur** *f Eiskunstlauf etc.*: overhead lift; **~kran** *m* hoist(ing crane)

Hebel *m*; *-s*, *-*. **1.** *Phys.* lever; **2.** *am Automat etc.*: handle; (*Kurbel*) crank; **3.** *fig.* lever; **den ~ ansetzen** *umg.* get things moving; **wo willst du den ~ ansetzen?** *umg.* where are you going to start?, how are you going to set about it?; **alle ~ in Bewegung setzen** *umg.* do everything in one's power, move heaven and earth, leave no stone unturned; **am längeren ~ sitzen** have the whip (*od.* upper) hand; **an den ~n der Macht sitzen** be at the levers of power; **~arm** *m Phys.* lever arm; **~gesetz** *n Phys.* lever law; **~kraft** *f Phys.* leverage

hebeln *v/t. fig.*: **j-n aus dem Amt ~** lever s.o. out

Hebel|punkt *m Phys.* fulcrum (*Pl.* fulcra *od.* fulcrums); **~wirkung** *f* leverage; **e-e ~ haben** have a levering effect

heben; *hebt, hob, hat gehoben* **I.** *v/t.* **1.** (*Last, Gewichte etc.*) lift (*auch Sport*); (*schwere Last*) heave; (*höher bewegen*) (*auch Augen, Hand, Glas*) raise; **einen ~** *umg.* hoist one; **2.** *Tech.* (*hochwinden*) hoist; (*aufbocken*) (*Auto*) jack up; **3.** (*Schatz, Wrack*) raise; (*ausgraben*) dig up; **4.** *sich* (*Dat.*) **e-n Bruch ~** *Med.* rupture o.s. (by lifting heavy objects); **heb dir bloß keinen Bruch** *iro.* don't strain yourself!; **5.** *fig.* (*Niveau, Qualität, Stimme etc.*) raise; (*vermehren*) increase; (*verbessern*) improve; (*Moral, Selbstvertrauen etc.*) boost; (*Wirkung etc.*) add to; **6.** *Dial.* → *halten* I 1; **II.** *v/refl.* **1.** rise, go up; *Vorhang, Nebel etc.*: lift; **sich ~ und senken** rise and fall; **j-m hebt sich der Magen** s.o.'s stomach turns over, s.o. feels sick; → *Angel²* 1, *Himmel* 3; **2.** *Stimme*: rise; **3.** *fig.* (*sich verbessern*) improve; **4.** *geh.* (*emporragen*) rise; **5.** *Dial.* → *festhalten* III; **III.** *v/i. Dial.* → *halten* II 1,2

Heben *n*; *-s*, *kein Pl.*; *Sport* (*Gewichtheben*) weightlifting

Heber *m*; *-s*, *-*. **1.** *bes. Chem., zum Saugen*: siphon; (*Pipette*) pipette; (*Spritze*)

syringe; **2.** *Sport* (*Gewichtheber*) weightlifter; **3.** *umg*; *Fußball*: lob

...heber *m*, *im Subst. Tech.* ...-lifter, ...-raiser; *Mot.* jack

Hebe|satz *m für Steuern*: rate of assessment; **~schiff** *n* salvage ship; **~vorrichtung** *f* lifting gear, hoisting apparatus; *an Werkzeugmaschinen*: elevating mechanism; (*hydraulische Hebeflasche*) hydraulic jack; **~zeug** *n* lifting gear, hoist

...hebig *im Adj. Lit., Metrik*: -beat; **vierhebig** four-beat; **sechshebig** six-beat

Hebräer *m*; *-s*, *-*, **~in** *f*; *-*, *-nen* Hebrew; *weiblich: auch* woman (*od.* girl *etc.*); **hebräisch** *Adj.* Hebrew, Hebraic; **Hebräisch** *n*; *-en*; *Ling.* Hebrew; **das ~e** Hebrew

Hebriden *Pl. Geog.*: **die ~** the Hebrides; **hebridisch** *Adj.* Hebridean

Hebung *f* **1.** *Handlung*: lifting, raising; **2.** *des Geländes*: elevation, rise; **3.** *fig.* improvement; increase; **4.** *Lit., Metrik*: stress; (*Silbe*) stressed syllable

Hechel *f*; *-*, *-n* hackle, flax comb; **hecheln I.** *v/i.* **1.** *Hund etc.*: pant; **2.** *umg. pej.* (*klatschen*) gossip; **II.** *v/t.* (*Flachs, Hanf*) hackle, heckle, comb

Hecht *m*; *-(e)s*, *-e* **1.** *Zool.* pike; **2.** *umg. fig.*: **ein toller ~** some guy; **er ist der ~ im Karpfenteich** he really stirs things up; **3.** *umg.* → *Hechtsprung*; **4.** *umg.* (*Tabakqualm*) fug

hechten *v/i. Schwimmen*: do a racing dive; *Turnen*: do a long-fly; *Fußball etc.*: dive (full-length) (**nach** at)

Hecht|rolle *f Turnen*: long-fly and forward roll; *Fußball etc.*: flying dive; **~sprung** *m Schwimmen*: racing dive; *Turnen*: long-fly; *Fußball etc.*: (flying) dive; **~suppe** *f umg.*: **hier zieht's wie ~** there's a gale-force wind blowing in here, there's a terrible draught (*Am.* draft) in here

Heck¹ *n*; *-(e)s*, *-e od.* *-s*; *Naut.* stern; *Mot.* rear; *Flug.* tail

Heck² *n*; *-(e)s*, *-e*; *nordd.* **1.** (*Weide, Pferch*) paddock; **2.** (*Gattertür*) gate

Heckantrieb *m Mot.* rear-wheel drive

Hecke *f*; *-*, *-n* hedge (*auch Reitsport*); *an Feld, Straße*: hedgerow

Hecken|rose *f Bot.* dogrose; **~schere** *f*: (*e-e*) (a pair of) hedge clippers *Pl.*; **~schütze** *m Mil.* sniper; **~zaun** *m* hedge(s *Pl.*), hedge fencing

Heck|fenster *n Mot.* rear window; **~flosse** *f Mot.* tailfin; **~klappe** *f Mot.* tailgate

hecklastig *Adj. Flug., Mot.* tail-heavy

Hecklicht *n Flug., Mot.* tail-light

Heckmeck *m*; *-s*, *kein Pl.*; *umg. pej.* **1.** (*Umstände*) fuss; **mach keinen ~** stop making such a fuss; **2.** (*dummes Zeug*) rubbish

Heck|motor *m Mot.* rear engine; **~scheibe** *f Mot.* rear window

Heckscheiben|heizung *f Mot.* rear-window heater; **~wischer** *m* rear (window) wiper

Heck|spoiler *m Mot.* back spoiler; **~tür** *f Mot., nach oben öffnend*: hatch; *nach unten öffnend*: tailgate; **Modell mit ~** hatchback; **~welle** *f Naut.* wake

heda *Interj.* hey(, you there)!

Hedgefonds ['hɛtʃfɔː] *m Fin.* hedge fund

Hedonismus *m*; *-*, *kein Pl.*; *Philos.* hedonism; **Hedonist** *m*; *-en*, *-en*, **Hedonistin** *f*; *-*, *-nen* hedonist; **hedonistisch I.** *Adj.* hedonistic; **II.** *Adv.* hedonistically

Heer *n*; *-(e)s*, *-e* **1.** *Mil.* (*Streitkräfte*)

armed forces; *für Kampf an Land*: army; **stehendes ~** standing army; **2.** *fig.* army, huge crowd; **das ~ der Arbeitslosen** the ranks of the unemployed

Heeres|bestände *Pl.* military stores; **~leitung** *f* army command; **Oberste ~** the Supreme Command; **~macht** *f* (military) forces *Pl.*, army

Heer|fahrt *f hist.* expedition; **~führer** *m*, **~führerin** *f* **1.** military leader; **2.** commander (of the army); **~lager** *n* army camp; **~schar** *f*, *mst Pl.* host; *himmlische ~en bibl.* heavenly hosts; **ganze od. wahre ~en von Mücken etc.** *umg.* absolute hosts of midges; **~straße** *f* military road; **~wesen** *n*; *nur Sg.* the army; **das römische ~ zur Zeit Caesars** the Roman army machine in the time of Caesar

Hefe *f*; *-*, *Arten*: *-n* yeast; *Bäckerei*: (baker's) yeast; *Brauerei*: (brewer's) yeast; (*Bodensatz*) dregs *Pl.*; **~extrakt** *m* yeast extract; **~gebäck** *n* yeast pastries *Pl.*; **~kloß** *m bes. nordd.*, **~knödel** *m bes. südd., österr. Gastr.* yeast dumpling; **~kranz** *m Gastr.* savarin; **~kuchen** *m Gastr.* yeast cake; **~pilz** *m* yeast fungus; **~teig** *m* yeast dough; **~zopf** *m Gastr.* plaited (*Am.* braided) yeast bun

hefig *Adj.* yeasty; *Wein*: full of dregs

Heft¹ *n*; *-(e)s*, *-e* **1.** *zum Schreiben*: notebook; *zum Üben*: *bes. Brit.* exercise book; **2.** (*Zeitschrift*) magazine; (*Lieferung*) number; (*Exemplar*) copy; *e-r Zeitung*: number, issue; *geheftete Druckschrift, Büchlein*: booklet; (*Broschüre*) brochure; **Fortsetzung in ~ 3** continued in issue 3; **3.** *von Briefmarken, Fahrscheinen, Zündhölzern etc.*: book

Heft² *n*; *-(e)s*, *-e*; *geh.* **1.** (*Griff*) *von Messer etc.*: handle, hilt; *von Schwert*: hilt; **das Messer bis zum ~ hineinstoßen** drive the knife in up to the hilt; **2.** *fig.*: **das ~ fest in der Hand haben** have things firmly under control; **das ~ aus der Hand geben** hand over control (*od.* the controls *od.* the reins); **j-m das ~ aus der Hand nehmen** seize control from s.o.

Heftchen *n* **1.** notebook; **2.** *oft pej., Comics etc.*: comic; (*Groschenroman*) pulp novel; **3.** *von Briefmarken, Fahrscheinen, Zündhölzern etc.*: book

heften I. *v/t.* **1.** (**an** + *Akk.* to); fix, attach; *mit Stecknadeln, Reißzwecken etc.*: pin; *mit Klammern*: staple; *Näherei*: baste, tack; (*auch Buch*) stitch, sew; **j-m e-n Orden an die Brust ~** pin a medal on s.o.'s chest; **2.** *fig.*: **s-e Augen / s-n Blick ~ auf** (+ *Akk.*) fix one's eyes / gaze on; **II.** *v/refl. fig.*: **sich ~ auf** (+ *Akk.*) *Augen*: fix (themselves) on; *stärker*: be glued to; **sich an j-s Fersen ~** fix hard on s.o.'s heels; **Hefter** *m*; *-s*, *-* **1.** (*Ordner*) file; **2.** (*Heftmaschine*) stapler

Heft|faden *m*, **~garn** *n* tacking thread

heftig I. *Adj.* **1.** *Kampf, Streit, Sturm, Zorn*: violent, vehement; (*wild, erbittert*) fierce; (*leidenschaftlich*) passionate; (*wütend*) furious; (*stark*) intense, intensive; *Abneigung*: strong; *Sehnsucht*: intense, passionate; *Hass, Verlangen*: burning; *Kälte*: numbing, severe; *Erkältung*: bad, severe; *Fieber*: raging; *Worte*: angry; *Regen, Schneefälle etc.*: heavy; *Kopfweh*: severe, splitting; **~er Aufprall** violent impact; „*Wie war die Prüfung?* " – „**Heftig!**" "It was a brute!"; **2.** (*reizbar*) hot-tempered; **~ werden** *Person*: lose one's

temper; **sei doch nicht gleich so ~** calm down, no need to get upset; **II.** *Adv.* violently *etc.*; → I; **es stürmt ~** there's a real storm going (*od.* outside); **der Wind bläst ~** there's a strong wind blowing; **die Meldung wurde von e-m Unternehmenssprecher ~ dementiert** the announcement was strongly denied by a company spokesperson; **Heftigkeit** *f* **1.** *nur Sg.* violence; (*Wildheit*) fierceness; (*Stärke*) intensity; (*Schärfe*) severity; **2.** *nur Sg.*; *Temperament*: hot temper, violent temperament; (*Ungezügeltheit*) lack of self-control; **3.** *Äußerung*: cutting remark
Heft|klammer *f* **1.** *der Heftmaschine*: staple; **2.** (*Büroklammer*) paper clip; **~naht** *f* basted seam; **~pflaster** *n* (sticking) plaster, *Am.* bandage
Heftroman *m* limp-bound *light fiction* novel, *etwa* airport novel, *Am.* dime novel
heftweise *Adv. Buch*: in fascicles
Heftzwecke *f* drawing pin, *Am.* thumbtack
Hege *f*, -, *kein Pl.* care, preservation
Hegemonie *f*, -, *-n* hegemony, supremacy
hegen *v/t.* **1.** look after; (*Pflanzen, Garten*) *auch* tend; (*Wild, Wald*) preserve, maintain; (*schützen*) protect; (*Künste, Beziehungen*) cultivate; **~ und pflegen** take great care of, look after *s.th.* well; (*j-n*) attend to *s.o.'s* every need; **2.** *geh.* (*Gefühle, Hoffnung*) cherish, entertain; (*Verdacht, Wunsch, Zweifel etc.*) have; (*Hass*) harbo(u)r (*gegen* against); (*Groll*) bear (*gegen* against); **die Absicht ~ zu** (+ *Inf.*) harbo(u)r the intention of (+ *Ger.*), be intending to (+ *Inf.*); **ich hege schon lange den Verdacht, dass ...** I have long suspected that ...
Hehl *n*, *m*: **kein(en) ~ machen aus** make no secret of, make no bones about
Hehler *m*; -s, -; *Jur.* receiver of stolen goods, fence *umg.*; **Hehlerei** *f*, -, *-en* receiving (of) *od.* accepting stolen goods; **Hehlerin** *f*, -, *-nen Jur.* receiver of stolen goods, fence *umg.*
hehr *Adj. geh. Augenblick, Ideal, Ziel*: sublime, noble
heia *Kinderspr.*: **~ machen** go bye-bye(s); **Heia** *f*, -, *-(s)*: **in die ~ gehen** go to beddy-bye(s) (*od.* go bye-bye[s])
Heide[1] *m*; -n, -n heathen; *bes. in der klassischen Antike*: pagan; *bibl.* (*Nichtjude*) gentile
Heide[2] *f*, -, *-n* **1.** heath(land); (*Moor*) *auch* moor(land); **2.** *Pflanze*: heather; **~kraut** *n Bot.* heather
Heidelbeere *f Bot.* bilberry, blueberry
Heidelerche *f Orn.* wood lark
Heiden|angst *f*; *nur Sg.*; *umg.*: **e-e ~ haben** be scared to death, be scared stiff (*vor* + *Dat.* of); **~arbeit** *f*; *nur Sg.*; *umg.*: **e-e ~** a huge (*Sl.* hell of a) job; **das war e-e ~** *auch* that was a real sweat; **~geld** *n*; *nur Sg.*; *umg.*: **ein ~** a packet (*Am.* bundle), pots (*od.* stacks, *bes. Am.* loads) of money; **~lärm** *m* *umg.* dreadful racket (*od.* din); **ihr macht ja e-n ~!** *auch* you'll bring the roof down in a minute; **~respekt** *m* *umg.*: **e-n ~ haben vor** have a healthy respect for; *stärker*: be scared to death of; **sie haben e-n ~ vor ihm** *auch* they wouldn't dare put a foot wrong when he's around; **~schreck** *m* *umg.* the fright of *s.o.'s* life; **j-m e-n ~ einjagen** scare *s.o.* to death, put the fear of God into *s.o.*; **~spaß** *m*; *nur Sg.*; *umg.*:

e-n ~ haben have a whale of a time (**an** + *Dat.* with)
Heidentum *n*; -s, *kein Pl.* **1.** heathenism; *mst klassisch*: paganism; **2.** *Koll.* (**die Heiden**) the heathen; *mst klassisch*: the pagans *Pl.*
Heideröschen *n Bot.* briar-rose
Heidin *f*, -, *-nen* → **Heide**[1]; **heidnisch** *Adj.* heathen; *klassisch*: pagan; **~e Bräuche** pagan customs (*od.* rites)
Heidschnucke *f Zool.* (North German) moorland sheep
heikel *Adj.* **1.** *Angelegenheit etc.*: awkward; *auch Problem*: tricky; *Thema*: delicate; **2.** *Dial.* (*wählerisch*) fussy, hard to please; (*anspruchsvoll*) choosy; *beim Essen*: fussy about one's food (*od.* what one eats), a fussy eater
heil *Adj.* (*unversehrt*) *Person*: unhurt, unharmed, safe and sound; *Sache*: undamaged, intact; (*geheilt*) healed, cured; *Welt*: intact, ideal, sugarcoated *iro.*; **etw. ~ überstehen** come through (s.th.) unscathed; **da bist du noch mal mit ~er Haut davongekommen** *iro.* you got off lightly this time; **wieder ~ machen** fix, mend; *Kinderspr.* (**e-n verletzten Finger etc.**) make *s.th.* better; **die Vase etc. ist ~ geblieben** didn't break, is still intact (*od.* in one piece)
Heil *n*; -s, *kein Pl.* **1.** welfare, well-being; *kirchl.* salvation; **sein ~ bei j-m / in etw.** (*Dat.*) **versuchen** try one's luck with *s.o.* / *s.th.*; **sein ~ in der Flucht / im Alkohol suchen** take flight / take to drink; **~ bringend** *Reli., Botschaft etc.*: saving, redemptive, bringing salvation; *Med., Kur, Wirkung*: therapeutic; **2.** *Gruß*: *altm.* hail (+ *Dat.* to); **~ Hitler!** *hist., im Nationalsozialismus*: Heil Hitler!; → **Petri Heil**
Heiland *m*; -(e)s, *kein Pl.*; *kirchl.* Savio(u)r
Heil|anstalt *f* sanatorium; *psychiatrische*: (mental) home; **~anzeige** *f Med.* indication; **~bad** *n Med.* **1.** (*Kurort*) health resort, spa; **2.** (*Bad*) therapeutic bath
heilbar *Adj. Med.* curable; **nicht ~** incurable; **es ist nicht ~** *auch* it can't be cured
Heilberuf *m* healing profession
heilbringend *Adj.* → **Heil** 1
Heilbrunnen *m* mineral spring
Heilbutt *m Zool.* halibut
heilen I. *v/t.* (*hat geheilt*) **1.** *Med.* (*Krankheit, j-n*) cure (**von** of); (*Wunde*) heal; *auch Hände, Wirkung etc.*: healing; **als geheilt entlassen werden** be discharged with a clean bill of health; **2.** *fig.*: **j-n ~ von** cure *s.o.* of; **II.** *v/i.* (*ist*) *Med.* heal; *Wunde*: *auch* heal up; **Heiler** *m*; -s, -, **Heilerin** *f*; -, *-nen*; *geh.* healer
Heil|erde *f Med.* fuller's earth; **~erfolg** *m* successful cure (*od.* treatment), success; **damit hat man gute ~e erzielt** it has proved a successful cure; **~fasten** *n* **1.** fasting (cures *Pl.*); **2.** (*Kur*) fasting cure
heilfroh *Adj. umg.* really glad; (*erleichtert*) *auch* relieved; **ich war ~, als ich wegkam** I was glad (*od.* relieved) to get away
Heilgymnast etc. → **Krankengymnast etc.**
heilig *Adj.* **1.** *kirchl.* holy; (*geheiligt, geweiht*) sacred, hallowed; *vor Eigennamen*: Saint (*Abk.* St, St.); **~ sprechen** canonize; **der ~e Antonius** St (*od.* St.) Anthony; **der Heilige Abend** Christmas Eve; **der Heilige Geist/Stuhl/Vater** the Holy Spirit *od.* Ghost/See/-

Father; **das Heilige Grab/Land** the Holy Sepulch|re (*Am.* -er) /Land; **die Heilige Jungfrau** the Blessed Virgin; **die Heilige Schrift** the Bible, the Holy Scriptures *Pl.*; **die Heiligen Drei Könige** the Three Kings, the Three Wise Men; **2.** (*fromm*) *altm.* pious, devout; **~ tun** *umg. pej.* act the saint; **3.** *geh.* (*unantastbar*) sacred, inviolable, sacrosanct; (*ehrwürdig*) venerable; (*feierlich*) solemn; *Kuh, Pflicht*: sacred; **das ist mein ~er Ernst** I'm in deadly earnest; **ihn erfasste ein ~er Zorn** he was seized with righteous anger; **ihm ist nichts ~** nothing is sacred to him; **den Sonntag ~ halten** keep the Sabbath holy, observe the Sabbath; **4.** *umg.* (*groß*) *Angst, Respekt*: tremendous; **s-e ~e Not haben mit** have terrible trouble with; **5.** *umg. in Ausrufen*: **~er Bimbam** *od.* **Strohsack** *etc.!* holy smoke!, ye gods!
Heiligabend *m* Christmas Eve
Heilige *m*, *f*; -n, -n saint; **sie ist e-e wahre ~** *hum.* she's a real saint; **wie ein ~r leben** live a saintly life; **den ~n** *od.* **die ~ spielen** *pej.* play the saint
heiligen *v/t.* **1.** *Reli.* hallow, sanctify; **geheiligt werde dein Name** *im Gebet*: hallowed be thy name; **2.** (*heilig halten*) hold *s.th.* sacred, observe; → **geheiligt, Zweck**
Heiligen|bild *n* image (*od.* picture *od.* statue) of a saint; **~figur** *f* figure (*od.* statue) of a saint; **~leben** *n* life of a saint; **~legende** *f* life (*od.* legend) of a saint; **~schein** *m* halo, gloriole, Heiligenschein *Am. lit.*; **sich mit e-m ~ umgeben** *iro.* be holier-than-thou; **s-n ~ einbüßen** *iro.* lose one's halo; **~verehrung** *f* veneration of the saints
heilig halten → **heilig** 3
Heiligkeit *f*; *nur Sg.* **1.** holiness, sanctity, sacredness; *e-r Person*: saintliness; **2.** *Papst*: **Eure/Seine ~** Your/His Holiness
heilig sprechen → **heilig** 1; **Heiligsprechung** *f* canonization
Heiligtum *n*; -s, *Heiligtümer* **1.** *Stätte*: (holy) shrine; *Gegenstand*: (sacred) relic; **2.** *fig.* something sacred; *umg. hum.* (*Zimmer*) sanctum
Heiligung *f*; *mst Sg.*; *geh.* hallowing, sanctification (*auch fig.*)
Heilklima *n* healthy climate; **heilklimatisch** *Adj. Kurort*: with a climate that has curative properties
Heilkraft *f* healing power(s *Pl.*); **heilkräftig** *Adj.* curative
Heilkraut *n* medicinal herb
Heilkunde *f*; *nur Sg.* medicine, therapeutics *Pl.* (*V. im Sg.*); **heilkundig** *Adj.* skilled in medicine (*od.* the art of healing)
Heilkunst *f* healing
heillos I. *Adj.* dreadful, unholy *umg.*; **dort herrscht ein ~es Durcheinander** the place is an absolute shambles *umg.*, it's absolute chaos (in) there *umg.*; **II.** *Adv.* hopelessly; **~ verschuldet** up to one's neck in debt
Heil|methode *f* (method of) treatment, therapy, cure; **~mittel** *n* remedy, cure (*gegen* for) (*auch fig.*); (*Arznei*) medicine; **~pädagoge** *m*, **~pädagogin** *f* remedial teacher; **~pflanze** *f* medicinal plant (*od.* herb); **~praktiker** *m*, **~praktikerin** *f* non-medical practitioner; **~quelle** *f* mineral spring
Heilrufe *Pl.* acclamations
Heilsalbe *f Med.* healing ointment
heilsam *Adj. fig.* salutary; **das wäre sehr ~ für ihn** *iro.* that would do him

good, he could do with (something like) that

Heils|armee f; nur Sg.; Reli. Salvation Army; **~botschaft** f gospel, message of salvation (auch fig.); **~erwartung** f expectation of salvation; **~geschichte** f kirchl. Heilsgeschichte, the history of the world interpreted as showing forth the working of God's grace; **~lehre** f kirchl. doctrine of salvation

Heil|stätte f Med. sanatorium, Am. auch sanitarium; **~trank** m medicinal potion; **~ und Pflegeanstalt** f altm. 1. sanatorium, Am. auch sanitarium; 2. mental home (od. institution)

Heilung f Med. cure; (das Heilen) curing; von Wunden: healing; (Genesung) recovery

Heilungs|aussichten Pl., **~chancen** Pl. Med. chances of recovery; **~prozess** m healing process; (Genesung) recovery

Heil|verfahren n Med. (medical) treatment, therapy; **~wasser** n healing water(s Pl.); **~wirkung** f therapeutic effect; **~zweck** m: zu **~en** for medicinal purposes; **~en dienen** be medicinal

heim Adv. home

Heim n; -(e)s, -e 1. nur Sg.; (Zuhause) home; ein ~ gründen set up (a) home; **~ und Herd** lit. hearth and home; → traut; 2. (Anstalt) home; ins ~ kommen Kind: be taken into care (od. a home); → Altenheim, Kinderheim etc.

...heim n, im Subst. 1. (Anstalt) ... home; 2. (Unterkunft) ... hostel; 3. (Zentrum) ... cent|re (Am. -er)

Heim|abend m social (evening); **~arbeit** f homework, outwork; weitS. cottage industry; **~arbeiter** m, **~arbeiterin** f homeworker, outworker; **~arbeitsplatz** m: die Zahl der Heimarbeitsplätze the number of jobs as homeworkers

Heimat f; -, -en, mst Sg. 1. home (auch fig.); Land: auch home country, homeland; Stadt: auch home town; in der ~ at home; die alte ~ e-s Auswanderers: the old country, one's homeland; zweite ~ second home, home (away) from home umg.; 2. Bot., Zool. habitat; 3. (Ursprungsland) country of origin; **~adresse** f, **~anschrift** f home address; **~boden** m native soil; **~dichter** m, **~dichterin** f regional writer; **~dorf** n home village; **~erde** f native soil; **~film** m (sentimental) film with a regional setting and characters; **~forscher** m, **~forscherin** f local historian; **~forschung** f local heritage studies Pl.; **~front** f hist. home front; **~hafen** m home port

Heimatkunde f Päd. local (Am. area) studies Pl., mst. local history; **heimatkundlich** Adj. relating to local history (and other distinctive characteristics of the area)

Heimatland n home country, homeland

heimatlich Adj. home ...; (~ anmutend) like home, Am. hom(e)y; **~er Boden** one's native soil; Klänge: familiar; das sind **~e Klänge** auch it sounds just like home

Heimat|liebe f love of one's homeland (od. home town od. local area); **~lied** n song of the homeland

heimatlos Adj. homeless; (ausgestoßen) outcast; (entwurzelt) uprooted; **Heimatlose** m, f; -n, -n homeless person

Heimat|museum n local heritage museum; **~ort** m home town (od. village); **~pfleger** m, **~pflegerin** f enthusiast

for local history and heritage; **~recht** n right of abode; **~roman** m novel set in a regional background; **~staat** m native country, country of origin; **~stadt** f home town; **~urlaub** m Mil. home leave; **~verband** m homeland association; association of people from a particular area of Germany's former eastern territories

heimatverbunden Adj. tied to one's roots

Heimatvertriebene m, f displaced person, expellee (from one of Germany's former eastern territories)

Heim|aufenthalt m stay in (od. period spent in) a home; **~bewohner** m, **~bewohnerin** f resident (of a home)

heimbringen v/t. (unreg., trennb., hat -ge-) see (od. take) s.o. home

Heimchen n; -s, - 1. Zool. (house) cricket; 2. umg. pej.: ein ~ am Herd (just a) housewife, an ordinary housewife

Heimcomputer m EDV home computer

heimdürfen v/i. (unreg., trennb., hat -ge-): darf ich jetzt heim? can I go home now?

heimelig Adj. cosy, Am. cozy, hom(e)y

Heimen n; -s, -; schw. farm

Heim|erzieher m, **~erzieherin** f counsel(l)or for children in care (Am. in foster care); **~erziehung** f upbringing in (foster) care od. a home od. an institution, institutional upbringing

Heimet n; -s, -; schw. homestead

heimfahren (unreg., trennb.) I. v/i. (ist heimgefahren) go home; nach Urlaub: auch go back; mit Auto: drive home (od. back); II. v/t. (hat) drive home (od. back); **Heimfahrt** f ride (länger: journey) back od. home, return journey (länger: auch trip); auf der ~ on the (od. our etc.) way back

Heimfall m; nur Sg.; Jur. reversion, escheat; **heimfallen** v/i. (unreg., trennb., ist -ge-) revert (an + Akk. to)

heim|finden v/i. (unreg., trennb., hat -ge-) find one's way home; **~fliegen** v/i. (unreg., trennb., ist -ge-) fly home; **~führen** v/t. (trennb., hat -ge-) 1. take s.o. home; 2. altm.; j-n als Frau: marry

Heim|gang m; mst Sg.; geh. euph. (Tod) death, decease; **~gegangene** m, f; -n, -n; geh. euph. departed, deceased

heim|gehen v/i. (unreg., trennb., ist -ge-) 1. go home; 2. geh. euph. (sterben) die, pass away; 3. unpers., umg.: jetzt geht's heim it's time to go home, home, James! hum.; **~geigen** v/i. (trennb., hat -ge-); umg. → heimleuchten; **~holen** v/t. (trennb., hat -ge-) fetch home; heimgeholt werden geh. euph. (sterben) be called to one's Maker

Heimindustrie f cottage industry

heimisch Adj. 1. home ...; Bot. etc. native, indigenous; ~ sein in (+ Dat.) be indigenous to; (wohnen, leben) live in, be at home in; ~ machen (Pflanze, Tier) naturalize; am **~en Herd** by one's own fireside; an den **~en Herd zurückkehren** return home; 2. (wie zu Hause): sich ~ fühlen feel at home; auch nach 5 Jahren fühlte er sich nicht ~ auch he didn't feel he belonged (there), he felt no sense of belonging; ~ werden acclimatize o.s. (in + Dat. to); bist du auf dem Gebiet **~?** fig. are you well versed in the subject?

Heimkehr f; -, kein Pl. return, homecoming; **heimkehren** v/i. (trennb., ist

-ge-) come (od. return) home, come back; **Heimkehrer** m; -s, -, **Heimkehrerin** f; -, -nen homecomer; aus Krieg, Exil etc.: returnee

Heim|kind n child brought up in (foster) care od. in a home; **~kino** n 1. Gerät: cine-projector, movie-projector; 2. Vorführung: movie night; 3. umg. hum. (Fernseher) the box

heimkommen v/i. (unreg., trennb., ist -ge-) → heimkehren; **Heimkunft** f → Heimkehr

Heim|leiter m, **~leiterin** f director (of a home); Internat: headmaster/headmistress, head, Am. principal; Studentenwohnheim: warden, Am. houseparent

heimleuchten v/i. (trennb., hat -ge-); umg. fig.: j-m ~ (j-n zurechtweisen) tell s.o. what's what; (j-n abweisen) tell s.o. where to go

heimlich I. Adj. (geheim) secret; (verborgen) auch hidden; (verstohlen) surreptitious, furtive; (verboten) clandestine; (getarnt) undercover ...; **~e Machenschaften** secret machinations; ~ tun pej. be very secretive (mit about), make a mystery (out of); II. Adv. secretly etc.; → I; (innerlich) lächeln etc.: inwardly; j-n ~ anblicken steal a (furtive) glance at s.o.; sich ~ entfernen sneak (od. slip) away; ~ lauschen eavesdrop; ~, still und leise umg. on the quiet; **Heimlichkeit** f 1. secrecy; in aller ~ in strictest secrecy; 2. **~en** secrets

Heimlichtuer m; -s, -; pej. mysterymonger; **Heimlichtuerei** f; -, -en; pej. secretiveness, mysteriousness; **Heimlichtuerin** f; -, -nen; pej. mysterymonger; **heimlich tun** → heimlich I

Heimmannschaft f Sport home team

heimmüssen v/i. (unreg., trennb., hat -ge-) have to go home

Heim|mutter f warden, housemother; **~niederlage** f Sport home defeat; **~orgel** f Mus. electric organ

Heimreise f journey home, return trip (od. journey); auf der ~ auch on the (od. our etc.) way home; die ~ antreten set off (for) home; **heimreisen** v/i. (trennb., ist -ge-) go (od. drive, fly etc.) home

heimschicken v/t. (trennb., hat -ge-) send home

Heim|sieg m Sport home win; **~spiel** n home game; **~statt** f geh., **~stätte** f home; (Land) auch homeland

heimsuchen v/t. (trennb., hat -ge-) hit, strike, visit bibl.; (zerstören) ravage; Geister: haunt; Ungeziefer, auch hum. Besucher: descend on; heimgesucht von struck etc. by; heimgesucht werden von auch suffer s.th., be afflicted with; von e-r Krankheit: come down with; von Dürre/Krieg heimgesucht drought-stricken/war-torn; **Heimsuchung** f disaster; ~ Gottes divine retribution; ~ Mariä kath. the Visitation

Heim|tier n pet; **~trainer** m Gerät: home exerciser; Person: personal trainer

heimtrauen v/refl. (trennb., hat -ge-) dare to go home

Heimtücke f; nur Sg. 1. (Hinterlist) insidiousness; (Boshaftigkeit) malice, maliciousness; (Verrat) treachery; 2. e-r Krankheit: insidiousness; **heimtückisch** Adj. 1. insidious; (boshaft) malicious; Tat: treacherous; 2. fig. Krankheit: insidious; Straße etc.: treacherous

Heim|unterbringung f: Kosten für ~ cost of accommodation in a home;

~vorteil m Sport, auch fig. home advantage

heimwärts Adv. homeward(s), home

Heimweg m way home; **auf dem ~** on the (od. my etc.) way home; **sich auf den ~ machen** set off (for) home

Heimweh n homesickness; **~ haben** be homesick; **~ haben nach** auch pine for (od. after); **auch nach j-m**: yearn for s.th.

Heimwerker m, **~in** f do-it-yourselfer, DIYer, handyman

heimzahlen v/t. (trennb., hat -ge-): **j-m etw. ~** get one's own back on s.o. for s.th.

Hein m → **Freund** 1

Heini m; -s, -s; umg. pej.: (**blöder** etc.) **~** idiot, twerp; **komischer ~** queer customer, Am. oddball

...heini m, im Subst.; umg. pej. → **...fritze**

Heinzelmännchen n brownie; **die ~ etwa** the little people, the fairies

Heirat f; -, -en marriage; **heiraten** vt/i. marry, get married (to); **Geld ~** umg. pej. marry money; **nach Italien** etc. **~** marry and go to live in Italy etc.

Heirats|absichten Pl. marriage plans; **~ haben** od. **sich mit ~ tragen** be thinking of getting married, be planning to get married, Am. auch be altar bound umg.; **~alter** n: (**durchschnittliches**) **~** (average) age at marriage; **~annonce** f advertisement for a potential marriage partner; **~antrag** m (marriage) proposal; **j-m e-n ~ machen** propose to; **~anzeige** f 1. Mitteilung: marriage announcement; 2. → **Heiratsannonce**

heiratsfähig Adj. marriageable; **in ~em Alter** of marriageable age

Heirats|kandidat m 1. groom-to-be; 2. eligible young man; **~kandidatin** f 1. bride-to-be; 2. marriageable young woman

heiratslustig Adj. keen (Am. eager) to get married

Heirats|markt m 1. Zeitung: marriage ads Pl.; 2. marriage (pej. umg. cattle) market; **~schwindel** m marriage fraud; **~schwindler** m, **~schwindlerin** f person who defrauds s.o. by means of a spurious marriage proposal; **~urkunde** f marriage certificate; **~vermittler** m, **~vermittlerin** f marriage broker; **~vermittlung** f marriage brokerage (od. bureau)

heiratswillig Adj. ready to get married

heischen v/t. geh. 1. (fordern) demand; **Aufmerksamkeit/Zustimmung ~d** Blick, Räuspern: demanding attention/ agreement; 2. altm. (erbitten) ask for

heiser Adj. hoarse; (belegt) husky; (krächzend) croaky; **sich ~ schreien** shout o.s. hoarse; **Heiserkeit** f; mst Sg. hoarseness; huskiness; **~ heiser**

heiß I. Adj. 1. hot; Land, Wüste: torrid; Stirn etc., bei Fieber: hot; **glühend ~** red-hot; Sand, Sonne etc.: scorching; **siedend ~** boiling hot; **~ machen** heat (up); **mir ist ~** I'm hot; **mir wird ~** I'm getting hot; **das Kind ist ganz ~** the baby feels hot; **ihm wurde ~ und kalt (vor Angst)** he went hot and cold (with fear); **~e Spur** fig. hot trail; → **Draht** 2, **Nadel** 1; 2. fig. (heftig) vehement, fierce; (leidenschaftlich) fiery; Liebesaffäre: auch passionate; (inbrünstig) fervent; **~es Blut** hot blood (od. temper); **~es Blut haben** be hot-blooded; **~en Dank!** umg. thanks a lot; **~er Krieg** shooting war; **~e Tränen weinen** weep bitterly; **was ich nicht weiß, macht mich nicht ~** umg. ignorance is

bliss, what you don't know can't hurt you; **ganz ~ sein auf** umg. be wild about; 3. (erregend) Musik, Rhythmen: hot; **~es Höschen** hot pants; 4. (gefährlich) Geld, Ware etc.: hot; **das Land steht vor e-m ~en Herbst** things are likely to get pretty hot in the country this autumn; **~es Thema** (highly) controversial issue, Am. auch hot-button topic; → **Eisen** 3; 5. Phys. (radioaktiv) hot; 6. umg. (sexuell erregt) Tier: on (Am. in) heat; Person: hot; **j-n machen** turn s.o. on; 7. umg. (mit guten Aussichten) Favorit, Tipp: hot; **ein ~er Anwärter auf den Posten** a hot prospect for the post; 8. Sl. (toll) hot; **~er Typ** hunk; **echt ~!** brill!, Am. awesome!; II. Adv. 1. **die Sonne brennt ~ herunter** the sun is burning down; **(sich) ~ laufen** Motor, Maschine: overheat, run hot; **der Motor ist ~ gelaufen** the engine has overheated; **sie haben sich die Köpfe ~ geredet** they talked themselves silly, they talked till they were blue in the face; (haben sich gestritten) they went at it hammer and tongs; **den haben sie als Kind wohl zu ~ gebadet!** umg. they must have dropped him on his head when he was a baby; **es wird nichts so ~ gegessen, wie es gekocht wird** Sprichw. things are never as bad as they look; 2. fig. (leidenschaftlich) fervently, ardently; **~ begehrt** coveted; **~ begehrt sein** auch be in great demand; **~ ersehnt** longed-for; Brief etc.: auch long-awaited; **~ geliebt** dearly (stärker: passionately) loved; **m-e ~ geliebte Frau** my dearly beloved wife; **~ (und innig) lieben** love s.o. madly; (auch Sache) adore, be wild about umg.; **~ umkämpft sein** be fiercely fought over, be the object of fierce fighting; fig. Wahlkreis, Sieg: be hotly (od. fiercely) contested; **die Stadt ist ~ umkämpft** fierce battles are being fought over the town; **~ umstritten** highly controversial; (Thema etc.) auch hotly debated; → **hergehen** 2

heißblütig Adj. (impulsiv) hot-blooded; (leidenschaftlich) passionate, fiery

heißen[1]; heißt, hieß, hat geheißen, umg. auch geheißen I. v/i. 1. mit Name, Bezeichnung: be called; **ich heiße ...** my name is ...; **wie heißt du?** what's your name?; **sie heißt (Gertrud) nach ihrer Tante** she's called (Gertrude) after her aunt; **früher hat sie anders geheißen** she used to have a different name, she used to be called something else; **so wahr ich ... heiße** as sure as my name's ...; **wenn das stimmt, will ich ... ~** then I'm ...; **... und wie sie alle ~** and so on, and all that sort of thing; **wie heißt das?** what's that called?; **wie heißt die Straße?** what's the name of this street?, what street is this?; 2. (bedeuten) mean; **wie heißt das auf Englisch?** what's that (called) in English?; **was heißt ... auf Englisch?** what's ... in English?, what's the English (word od. expression) for ...?; **das heißt** (abgek. d.h.) einschränkend od. erläuternd: that is (to say) (Abk. i.e.); **das hieße** od. **würde ~** that would mean; **das will etwas ~** that's saying something; **das will nicht viel ~** that doesn't mean much; **was heißt das schon?** so?, that doesn't mean a thing; **das soll nicht ~, dass ...** that doesn't mean (to say) that ...; **was soll das denn ~?** what's that supposed to mean?; **was soll das eigentlich ~?**

what's this all about?, what's the big idea? umg.; **was heißt hier: „gleich?"** what do you mean, "straight away"?; 3. unpers.; (gesagt werden): **es heißt, dass ...** they say that ..., apparently ...; **es soll nachher nicht ~, dass ...** I don't want it to be said that ...; **damit es nicht heißt, ...** so that nobody can say ...; **es hieß doch (ausdrücklich), dass ...** it was (specifically od. expressly) stated that ...; **es heißt in dem Brief** it says in the letter, the letter says; **wie heißt es doch gleich bei Schiller?** what does it say in Schiller?, what does Schiller say?; 4. unpers.: **nun heißt es handeln** etc. the situation calls for action etc., it's time to act etc.; **da heißt es aufpassen!** then you'd etc. better watch out!; II. v/t. 1. (nennen) call; **das heiße ich e-e gute Nachricht** that's what I call good news; 2. **j-n willkommen ~** welcome s.o.; 3. geh. (auffordern zu): **er hieß sie schweigen** he bade her be silent; **wer hat dich denn kommen ~?** verärgert: who invited you?

heißen[2] v/t. Naut. hoist

heiß| ersehnt, **~ geliebt** → **heiß** II 2

Heißhunger m (sudden) craving (**auf** + Akk., **nach** for); **heißhungrig** Adj. ravenous; bes. fig. voracious

heißlaufen v/i. (unreg., trennb., ist -ge-) und v/refl. (hat) → **heiß** II 1

Heißluft f hot air; Einstellung am Backofen: convection; **~ballon** m hot-air balloon; **~herd** m convection oven

Heiß|mangel f rotary iron, Am. mangle; **~sporn** m fig. hothead

heiß| umkämpft, **~ umstritten** → **heiß** II 2

Heißwasser|bereiter m water heater, Brit. auch geyser; **~speicher** m hot-water tank

heiter Adj. 1. Wetter: bright; Himmel: sunny; **~ bis wolkig** fair to cloudy; **~(er) werden** brighten up; **(wie) aus ~em Himmel** fig. completely out of the blue; 2. (fröhlich) cheerful; **j-n ~ stimmen** cheer s.o. up; **das ist ja ~!** umg. iro. that's just (od. really) great; **das kann ja ~ werden!** umg. iro. looks like we're in for some fun and games; 3. (amüsant) amusing, funny; Geschichte etc.: humorous; 4. (abgeklärt, gelassen) serene; **~e Gelassenheit** serenity; 5. Mus. bright, cheerful; **heiter-besinnlich** Adj. Film etc.: serio-comic, amusing but thought-provoking; **~er Film** auch serious (od. thoughtful) comedy; **Heiterkeit** f; nur Sg. cheerfulness; (Belustigung) amusement; (Gelächter) auch mirth; **zur allgemeinen ~** to everybody's amusement

Heiz|anlage f heating system; **~apparat** m heater

heizbar Adj. heatable; Zimmer: with heating; **~e Heckscheibe** Mot. heated rear window; **das Haus ist schlecht ~** the house is difficult to heat

Heiz|decke f electric blanket; **~draht** m heating wire; **~element** n heating element

heizen I. v/t. 1. heat; 2. (Ofen) fire; II. v/i. 1. put (od. have) the heat(ing) on; **letztes Jahr mussten wir schon im September ~** last year we had to put the heating on as early as September, last year we already had the heating on in September; 2. der Ofen **heizt gut** heats well, gives off plenty of heat; 3. **~ mit** use s.th. for heat(ing); III. v/refl.: **sich gut ~** Zimmer, Haus:

get warm quickly

Heizenergie f energy used for heating

Heizer m; -s, -, ~in f; -, -nen boilerman, Am. stoker; Eisenb. etc. stoker, Am. fireman

Heiz|fläche f heating surface; ~gas n gas (used for heating); ~gerät n heating appliance, heater; ~kessel m boiler; ~kissen n electric pad; ~körper m heater; (Radiator) radiator

Heizkosten Pl. heating costs; ~abrechnung f heating bill; ~pauschale f charge for heating

Heiz|kraftwerk n thermal power station; ~lüfter m fan heater; ~material n fuel; ~ofen m stove; transportabler: (electric, oil etc.) heater; ~öl n heating (Am. fuel) oil; ~periode f heating period; ~platte f hotplate; ~raum m boiler room, furnace room; ~strahler m (heater-)reflector; ~strom m heating current

Heizung f 1. (central) heating; 2. (Heizkörper) radiator; 3. nur Sg.; Kosten: heating (costs)

Heizungs|anlage f heating system; ~bauer m, ~bauerin f; -, -nen heating engineer; ~keller m boiler room; ~monteur m, ~monteurin f heating engineer; ~rohr n heating pipe; ~technik f heating engineering

Heiz|werk n boiler plant (for district heating system); ~wert m Phys. thermal (od. calorific) value

Hektar n od. bes. schw. m; -s, -e, bei Mengen: - hectare

Hektik f; -, kein Pl. des Lebens: mad rush, frantic pace; im Büro etc.: commotion, hectic atmosphere; e-r Person: nervousness; **in der ~** habe ich m-e Tasche lassen: in the general rush; **nur keine ~!** (just) take your time, take it easy umg.; **wozu die ~?** what's the rush?; **sie bringt viel ~ hinein** she makes everybody nervous; **das ist e-e ~ heute!** it's one of those days, it's all go

Hektiker m; -s, -, ~in f; -, -nen hyperactive person, person who is always on the go; (Hysteriker[in]) hysteric; **er ist ein absoluter Hektiker** he's always rushing around like a madman

hektisch I. Adj. hectic; Betriebsamkeit: frantic; Atmosphäre: excited; stärker: frenzied; Person: nervous; **~es Treiben** hustle and bustle; stärker: frantic activity; **ein paar ~e Stunden** a few frantic hours; **sei nicht so ~!** calm down, take it easy!; **II.** Adv. hectically; frantically; **~ hin und her laufen** dash backwards and forwards; **ihr Alltag verläuft ziemlich ~** their daily routine is pretty hectic

Hektoliter m, n hectolit|re (Am. -er)

helau Interj. Dial. greeting or cheer used during Carnival

Held m; -en, -en hero (Pl. heroes); Theat., e-s Romans etc.: protagonist; (Vorkämpfer) champion; **~ des Tages** man of the moment (od. hour); **~ der Arbeit** hist., ehemalige DDR: hero of labo(u)r; **er ist kein ~ in Mathematik** umg. hum. he's not the greatest mathematician in the world; **den ~en spielen** Theat. play the hero; iro. be a hero; **das ist vielleicht ein ~!** iro. some hero he is; **na, ihr** (zwei etc.) **~en?** umg. hum. zu Kindern: now then you two etc.?

Helden|dichtung f epic poetry; ~epos n epic (poem); ~friedhof m war cemetery; ~gestalt f hero (Pl. heroes)

heldenhaft I. Adj. heroic; **II.** Adv. her-

oically

Heldenlied n Lit. epic, heroic song

Heldenmut m bravery, heroism; **heldenmütig I.** Adj. heroic; **II.** Adv. heroically

Helden|rolle f Theat. part of a (od. the) hero; ~sage f saga; ~stück n heroic deed; **da hast du dir ja ein ~ geleistet!** umg. you've really covered yourself with glory!; → auch **Heldentat**, ~tat f heroic deed; **nicht gerade e-e ~** umg. nothing to write home about; ~tenor m heroic tenor, heldentenor; ~tod m heroic death; Mil. death in action; **den ~ sterben** die a hero's death; Mil. be killed in action

Heldentum n; -s, kein Pl. heroism

Heldenverehrung f hero worship

Heldin f; -, -nen heroine (auch Theat.)

helfen v/i.; hilft, half, hat geholfen **1.** allg. help (j-m s.o.; bei with); (behilflich sein) auch lend s.o. a hand; **j-m etw. tun ~** help s.o. (to) do s.th.; **kann ich irgendwie ~?** is there anything I can do?, can I (be of any) help?; **im Haushalt ~** help (out) with the housework; **j-m über die Straße ~** help s.o. across the road; **j-m aus dem / in den Mantel ~** help s.o. off/on with his (od. her) coat; **j-m aus e-r Verlegenheit ~** help s.o. out of a difficulty; **j-m bei der Arbeit ~** help s.o. with his (od. her) work; **da ist nicht zu ~** there's nothing you can do (about it); **2.** (nutzen) help, be of use; **damit ist mir wenig geholfen** that's not much help; **hat's was geholfen?** was it any use?; **es hat nichts geholfen** it was no good; auch Mittel, Tadel etc.: it didn't help, it didn't do any good; **es hilft nichts** it's no use; **da hilft kein Jammern** it's no use complaining; **da hilft nur eins** there's only one thing for it; **was hilft es, wenn ...** what's the use of (+ Ger.); **es hilft alles nichts, wir müssen gehen** we've got to go whether we like it or not; **3.** Medikament: help; **das hilft bei** od. **gegen Müdigkeit/Schnupfen** etc. is good for tiredness/ a cold; **haben die Tropfen geholfen?** did the drops help?, did the drops do any good?; **4.** fig., in Wendungen: **das half** that worked, that did the trick umg.; **ich kann mir nicht ~** I can't help it; **ich kann mir nicht ~, ich muss einfach lachen** I can't help laughing (about it); **ihm ist nicht (mehr) zu ~** there's no hope for him, he's beyond help; iro. auch he's hopeless, he's a dead loss (Am. a write-off) umg.; **ich werd' ihm schon ~!** iro. I'll show him; **dir werd' ich ~!** warnend: just you try; **er weiß sich zu ~** he can cope, he can look after (Am. take care of) himself; **er weiß sich immer zu ~** he's never at a loss as to what to do; **er weiß sich nicht (mehr) zu ~** he's at a loss as to what to do; stärker: he's at his wits' end; **ich wusste mir nicht anders zu ~ (als zu + Inf.)** it was the only thing I could do (the only thing I could do was to [+ Inf.]); **hilf dir selbst, dann hilft dir Gott** Sprichw. God helps those who help themselves; **so wahr mir Gott helfe** so help me God

Helfer m; -s, -, ~in f; -, -nen **1.** helper; (Gehilfe) assistant; bei Verbrechen: accomplice; **ein Helfer in der Not** a friend in need; **2.** Gerät etc.: help

Helfershelfer m, ~in f accomplice, stooge umg.

Helfer|syndrom n Psych. (helpless)

helper syndrome, Am. compassion fatigue (a psychological condition, afflicting over-altruistic people in the caring professions, which can lead to career burnout); ~zelle f Physiol. T-helper cell

helfgott Interj. südd., österr. bless you!

Helgoland (n); -s; Geog. Heligoland, bes. Am. Helgoland

Helikopter m; -s, -; Flug. helicopter

heliozentrisch Astron. **I.** Adj. heliocentric; **II.** Adv. heliocentrically

Helium n; -s, kein Pl.; Chem. helium

Helix f; -, -Helices; Chem. helix (Pl. helices od. helixes)

hell I. Adj. **1.** Licht, Himmel: bright; (leuchtend) shining; Zimmer etc.: bright; **es wird ~ morgens:** it's getting light; nach Regen etc.: it's brightening up (again); **es ist schon ~** it's light (already), the sun's up (already); **es bleibt lange ~** it stays light for a long time; **in ~en Flammen** burning brightly; **2.** Farbe: light (auch Haarfarbe); Hautfarbe: fair; Kleidung: light-colo(u)red; Soße: white; **~es Bier** etwa lager; **3.** Klang: clear; Vokal: bright; Lachen: ringing; Stimme, Ton: high and clear; **4.** fig. (klug) bright, clever; (geistig klar) lucid; **er ist ein ~er Kopf** he's a bright young spark umg.; **er ist nicht gerade der Hellste** he's not (one of) the brightest; **5.** fig. (groß) Unsinn, Verzweiflung: sheer, utter; Neid: pure; **er hatte s-e ~e Freude daran** he really enjoyed it; **an ihm wirst du noch deine ~e Freude haben** iro. you're really going to have fun with him; **die Zuschauer strömten in ~en Scharen** the spectators came in droves; **das ist ja ~er Wahnsinn!** that's (sheer) madness, that's (absolutely) crazy umg.; **II.** Adv. **1.** leuchten, Lampe etc.: brightly; Mond etc.: bright; **~ erleuchtet** brightly lit; **~ glänzend** od. **leuchtend** bright(ly shining); **~ lodernd** blazing; **2.** klingen, tönen: bright and clear; **~ klingend** clear-sounding; **3.** → **hellauf**

hellauf Adv.; **sie waren ~ begeistert** they thought it was tremendous; von e-r Idee etc.: they were all for it; **~ lachen** laugh out loud

hellblau Adj. light blue; **Hellblau** n light blue

hell|blond Adj. very fair; ~braun Adj. light brown

Helldunkel n Kunst: chiaroscuro

helle Adj. umg. bright, clever

Helle[1] f; -, kein Pl.; geh. (bright) light; brightness

Helle[2] n; -n, -n Bier: etwa lager; **ein kleines ~s, bitte** etwa a half of lager, please; **wir hätten gerne zwei ~** we'd like two lagers, please

Hellebarde f; -, -n; hist. halberd, halbert

Hellene m; -n, -n; hist. Hellene, (ancient) Greek; **Hellenentum** n; -s, kein Pl. Hellenism, Hellenic culture; **Hellenin** f; -, -nen Hellene (woman), (ancient) Greek (woman); **Hellenismus** m; -, kein Pl. Hellenism; **Hellenistik** f; -, kein Pl. ancient (od. classical) Greek, Greek studies Pl.; **hellenistisch** Adj. Hellenistic

Heller m; -s, - **1.** hist. heller, small German or Austrian coin of little value; **2.** umg. fig.: **es ist keinen roten ~ wert** it's not worth a cent; **er besitzt keinen roten ~** he hasn't got a penny to his name, Am. auch he doesn't have a red cent; **auf ~ und Pfennig** down to the last penny (od. cent)

hell|gelb *Adj.* pale (*od.* straw) yellow; **~grau** *Adj.* light grey (*Am.* gray); **~grün** *Adj.* light green; **~haarig** *Adj.* fair-haired; **~häutig** *Adj.* light-skinned, fair-skinned

hellhörig *Adj.* **1.** *Person:* (*empfänglich*) sensitive (**für** to); (*aufmerksam*) alert (to); **~ sein** *auch* have keen senses; **~ werden** prick up one's ears; **da wurde er ~** that made him sit up and take notice (*od.* prick up his ears); **sie ist für solche Dinge sehr ~** she picks that kind of thing up very quickly; **2.** *Wand:* wafer-thin; *Haus etc.:* badly sound-proofed; **das Haus ist sehr ~** *auch* the house has got very thin walls, you can hear (virtually) everything in this house

Helligen *Pl.* → **Helling**

Helligkeit *f* brightness (*auch TV*); *Phys.* light intensity

Helligkeits|regler *m TV* brightness control; *Etech., für Beleuchtung:* dimmer; **~stufe** *f* degree of brightness

Helling *f;* -, -*en od. Helligen, auch m;* -*s, -e; Naut.* slip(way); *Flug.* (assembly) cradle

hell| klingend → **hell** II 2; **~ leuchtend** → **hell** II 1

helllicht *Adj.:* **am ~en Tage** in broad daylight; **es ist schon ~er Tag** it's already broad daylight

hell lodernd → **hell** II 1

hell|rosa *Adj.* pale pink; **~rot** *Adj.* light red

hellsehen *v/i.;* nur im Inf. have second sight (*od.* psychic powers), be clairvoyant, be psychic; **Hellsehen** *n* clairvoyance; **Hellseher** *m*, **Hellseherin** *f* clairvoyant, psychic; **ich bin doch kein Hellseher!** *umg.* I'm not clairvoyant!, I'm not a mind reader!; **hellseherisch** *Adj.* clairvoyant, psychic

hellsichtig *Adj.* perceptive; (*klug*) shrewd; **Hellsichtigkeit** *f; nur Sg.* perceptiveness; (*Klugheit*) shrewdness

hellwach *Adj.* wide-awake (*auch fig.*)

Helm *m;* -(*e*)*s, -e* **1.** helmet; (*Schutzhelm*) bes. *auf Baustellen:* hard hat; **2.** *Archit.* cap; *spitzer. auch* spire; *Helmdach:* helm roof; **~busch** *m* plume; **~pflicht** *f*, **~zwang** *m:* **es besteht ~** you have to wear a helmet (*bzw.* hard hat), wearing a helmet (*bzw.* hard hat) is compulsory

Helvetismus *m;* -, *Helvetismen; Ling.* Helveticism

Hemd *n;* -(*e*)*s, -en* **1.** shirt; (*Unterhemd*) vest, *Am.* undershirt; **nass bis aufs ~** wet through; **j-m sein letztes ~ geben** give s.o. the shirt off one's back; **sein letztes ~ verlieren** lose one's shirt; **j-n bis aufs ~ ausziehen** fleece s.o.; **das ~ ist mir näher als der Rock** *od.* **die Jacke** *Sprichw.* near is my kirtle but nearer is my smock, near is my shirt but nearer is my skin; **2.** *fig.:* **halbes** *od.* **schmales ~** *umg.* half pint

Hemd|bluse *f* shirt; **~brust** *f* shirt front; **~knopf** *m* shirt button; **~kragen** *m* shirt collar

Hemdsärmel *m* shirt sleeve; **in ~n** *umg.* in one's shirt sleeves; **hemdsärmelig** *Adj.* **1.** shirt-sleeved; **2.** *umg. fig.* casual, shirt-sleeve …; **er hat so e-e ~e Art** he has a very casual manner

Hemdzipfel *m* shirt tail

Hemisphäre *f;* -, -*n* hemisphere

hemmen *v/t.* **1.** (*verlangsamen*) slow (down); (*aufhalten*) stop, check; (*verzögern*) delay; *Med.* (*Blutfluss*) sta(u)nch; (*Entwicklung*) hold back; (*behindern*) impede, hamper; **sich gegenseitig ~** hold each other back; **2.** *seelisch:* inhibit; → **gehemmt**; **hemmend I.** *Part. Präs.* → **hemmen**; **II.** *Adj.* obstructive; (*behindernd*) hampering, impeding; *Psych. etc.* inhibitory

...hemmer *m;* -*s, -; im Subst.; Bio., Physiol. etc.* … inhibitor

Hemmnis *n;* -*ses, -se* obstacle

Hemm|schuh *m* **1.** *für Fahrzeug:* brake shoe; **2.** *fig.* obstacle (**für** to), impediment (to); **~schwelle** *f Psych.* inhibition threshold; **e-e ~ überwinden** overcome one's inhibitions

Hemmung *f* **1.** (*Scheu*) inhibition; (*Skrupel*) scruple; **~en haben** be inhibited; **ohne ~en** uninhibited(ly); **nur keine ~en!** don't be shy!; **~en haben zu** (+ *Inf.*) have inhibitions (*od.* scruples) about (+ *Ger.*); (*sich genieren*) feel awkward about (+ *Ger.*); **keine ~en haben zu** (+ *Inf.*) have no compunction (*od.* inhibitions *od.* scruples) about (+ *Ger.*); **die haben überhaupt keine ~en** *umg.* they don't give a damn; **2.** *nur Sg.; Vorgang:* hampering; checking *etc.;* → **hemmen**; **3.** *Tech.* stop, catch; *e-r Uhr:* escapement; (*Ladehemmung*) jam, stoppage

hemmungslos *Adj.* (*skrupellos*) unscrupulous; (*ungezügelt*) unrestrained; **~ sein** (*ohne Skrupel*) *auch* have no scruples; (*ohne Scham*) have no sense of shame; **Hemmungslosigkeit** *f* **1.** *nur Sg.;* shamelessness; **2.** *Verhalten:* shameless behavio(u)r (*auch Pl.*)

Hendiadyoin *n;* -*s, -; Lit.* hendiadys

Hendl *n;* -*s, -(n); Dial.* chicken; **~braterei** *f;* -, -*en Restaurant:* chicken grill (*od.* place)

Hengst *m;* -(*e*)*s, -e* **1.** *Zool., Pferd:* stallion; *Esel:* jack, jackass; *Kamel, Zebra etc.:* male …; **2.** *umg. fig.* stud; **~fohlen** *n* colt

Henkel *m;* -*s, -* handle; **~glas** *n* glass with a handle; **~korb** *m* basket (with a handle); **~krug** *m* jug

henkellos *Adj.* without a handle

Henkelmann *m; Pl. -männer; umg.* (*Topf*) canteen

henken *v/t. altm.* hang; **Henker** *m;* -*s, -* hangman; (*Scharfrichter*) executioner; **geh** *od.* **scher dich zum ~!** *umg. altm.* go to hell!; **zum ~!** *umg. altm., erstaunt:* what the hell?; *verärgert:* in hell's name!; **was/wer etc. zum ~?** *umg. altm.* what/who etc. the hell?

Henkers|beil *n* executioner's axe; **~knecht** *m* executioner's assistant; *fig.* henchman; **~mahlzeit** *f* **1.** *hist.* condemned man's breakfast (*od.* last meal); **2.** *fig. hum.* final binge

Henna *f;* -, *kein Pl.; od. n;* -(*s*), *kein Pl.* henna; **sich** (*Dat.*) **die Haare** *etc.* **mit ~ färben** henna one's hair *etc.;* **hennarot** *Adj.* henna(-colo[u]red), hennaed

Henne *f;* -, -*n; Orn.* hen

Hepatitis *f;* -, *Hepatitiden; Med.* hepatitis

her *Adv.* **1.** *räumlich:* **um mich ~** around me, about me; **von … ~** from; **von oben/links ~** from above / the left; **der Wind weht vom Meer ~** the wind is blowing off the sea; **er ist von weit ~ gekommen** he's come a long way; **wo ist er her?** where is he from?, where does he come from?; **2.** *zeitlich:* **j-n von früher ~ kennen** know s.o. from before; **es ist drei Tage ~** it was three days ago, it's three days now; **es ist drei Tage ~, dass …** it's three days since …, it was three days ago that …; **wie lange ist es schon ~?** how long ago was it?, how long has it been now?; **das ist lange ~** that was a long time ago; **3.** *in Aufforderungen:* **zu mir ~!** come here!; **Bier ~!** bring me a beer!; **~ damit!** give it to me!, hand it over!; **immer ~ damit!** keep it coming!; **4.** *fig.:* **von … ~** from the point of view of; **vom Technischen ~** from a technical point of view, technically (speaking); **vom Inhalt ~** as far as the content goes, contentwise *umg.;* **hinter** *j-m od. etw.* **~ sein** *umg.* be after (*auch Frau, Mann*), be trying to get hold of; **mit ihm / dem Roman ist es nicht weit her** *umg.* he's / the novel's no great shakes

herab *Adv. geh.* down; **von oben ~** from above; *fig.* from on high, condescendingly; → *auch* **herunter**

herab... *im V.; mst …* down; → *auch* **herunter...**

herab|blicken *v/i.* (*trennb., hat -ge-*) → **herabsehen**; **~fließen** *v/i.* (*unreg., trennb., ist -ge-*) *geh.* → **herunterfließen**; **~gesetzt I.** *P.P.* → **herabsetzen**; **II.** *Adj. Preise:* reduced, cut-rate …; *Ware:* reduced, cut-price …, *Am. auch* on sale; **zu ~en Preisen** at reduced prices, cut-price …, *Am. auch* on sale; **~hängen** *v/i.* (*unreg., trennb., ist -ge-*) *geh.* → **herunterhängen**

herablassen (*unreg., trennb., hat -ge-*) **I.** *v/t. geh.* let down, lower; **II.** *v/refl. fig.* lower o.s.; **sich zu e-m Gespräch ~** *od.* **sich dazu ~, mit j-m zu sprechen** deign (*od.* condescend *od.* stoop) to talk to s.o.; **herablassend I.** *Part. Präs.* → **herablassen**; **II.** *Adj.* condescending; **~e Art** condescending attitude (*od.* approach); **III.** *Adv.* condescendingly; **j-n ~ behandeln** patronize s.o., be (very) patronizing towards s.o.

herabmindern *v/t.* (*trennb., hat -ge-*) **1.** reduce, diminish; **2.** (*Wert, Leistung etc.*) belittle; (*bagatellisieren*) minimize; **Herabminderung** *f* **1.** reduction, diminution; **2.** (*von Wert, Leistung etc.*) belittling; (*Bagatellisieren*) minimization

herab|regnen *v/i.* (*trennb.*): **~ auf** (+ *Akk.*) **1.** *unpers.* (*hat herabgeregnet*) rain on; **2.** (*ist*): *Bonbons, Steine, Schläge, Vorwürfe etc.:* rain down on; **~sehen** *v/i.* (*unreg., trennb., hat -ge-*) *geh.* look down (**auf** + *Akk.* on) (*auch fig.*); **~senken** *v/refl.* (*trennb., hat -ge-*); *lit. Dunkelheit, Nacht, Nebel etc.* descend (**auf** + *Akk.* on)

herabsetzen *v/t.* (*trennb., hat -ge-*) **1.** (*verringern*) reduce, lower; *Wirts.* reduce (in price); (*kürzen*) cut (back); → **herabgesetzt**; **2.** *fig.* (*j-n*) disparage, run down; (*Leistung*) belittle; **herabsetzend I.** *Part. Präs.* → **herabsetzen**; **II.** *Adj. fig.* disparaging; **Herabsetzung** *f* **1.** lowering, reduction (*auch Wirts.*); (*Kürzung*) *auch* cut (**von** in); **2.** *fig.* disparagement

herab|sinken *v/i.* (*unreg., trennb., ist -ge-*) **1.** *geh.* sink down; **2.** *lit. Nacht, Nebel etc.:* descend; **3.** *fig.:* **auf das Niveau** (+ *Gen.*) **~** sink to the level of s.th.; **~steigen** *v/i.* (*unreg., trennb., ist -ge-*) descend, walk (*od.* climb, come) down; *vom Pferd, Fahrrad etc.:* dismount; *von Baum etc.:* climb down (**von** from); **~stürzen** (*trennb., ist -ge-*) → **herunterstürzen**; **~tropfen** *v/i.* (*trennb., ist -ge-*) drip (onto the ground *od.* floor *etc.*); **von e-m Baum ~** drip from a tree

herabwürdigen *v/t. und v/refl.* (*trennb.*, *hat -ge-*) degrade (*sich* o.s.), lower (o.s.); **herabwürdigend I.** *Part. Präs.* → *herabwürdigen*; **II.** *Adj.* disparaging; **III.** *Adv.* disparagingly; **~ behandeln** *auch* treat *s.o.* with disdain; **Herabwürdigung** *f* degradation
herabziehen → *herunterziehen*
Heraldik *f*, -, *kein Pl.* heraldry; **heraldisch** *Adj.* heraldic
heran *Adv.* near, close; (*bis*) **~ an** (+ *Akk.*) up (*od.* close, next) to; **mehr links ~** more (*od.* closer) to the left; **immer** *od.* **nur ~!** come closer!
heran... *im V. siehe auch* **an...**, **ran...**
heranarbeiten *v/refl.* (*trennb.*, *hat -ge-*): **sich ~ an** (+ *Akk.*) work one's way forward to (*od.* through toward[s], *fig.* toward[s])
heran|bilden (*trennb.*, *hat -ge-*) **I.** *v/t.* (*Fachkräfte etc.*) train (*zu* to be); *in Schule etc.*: educate; **II.** *v/refl.* **1.** *Sache*: be in the making; **2.** *Person*: train (*zu* to be); **~bringen** *v/t.* (*unreg.*, *trennb.*, *hat -ge-*) **1.** bring (*an* + *Akk.* [up] to; *zu* to); **2.** *fig.* → *heranführen*; **~drängen** *v/refl.* (*trennb.*, *hat -ge-*) push forward (*an* + *Akk.* toward[s]); **~fahren** *v/i.* (*unreg.*, *trennb.*, *ist -ge-*) *Person*, *mit Auto*: drive up (*an* + *Akk.* to); *mit Rad*: ride up; *Fahrzeug*: drive up; **~führen** *v/t.* (*trennb.*, *hat -ge-*) **1.** (*Person*, *Tier*) lead, take (*an* + *Akk.* to); **2.** (*Werkzeug etc.*) bring (to); **3.** *fig.*: *j-n an etw.* (*Akk.*) **~** introduce *s.o.* to *s.th.*
herangehen *v/i.* (*unreg.*, *trennb.*, *ist -ge-*) **1.** go up closer; **~ an** (+ *Akk.*) go up to; **geh nicht so nah heran** don't go (*od.* get) too close; **2.** *fig.*: **~ an** (+ *Akk.*) approach, tackle; **Herangehensweise** *f* approach
heran|holen *v/t.* (*trennb.*, *hat -ge-*) **1.** fetch, get; **2.** *Fot.*: (*näher*) **~** zoom in on; **~kämpfen** *v/refl.* (*trennb.*, *hat -ge-*); *Sport* close in (*an* + *Akk.* on), pull up (*to*); **~kommen** *v/i.* (*unreg.*, *trennb.*, *ist -ge-*) **1.** come up (*zu* to), approach; **2.** **~ an** (+ *Akk.*) come up to; *mit der Hand*: reach, get hold of; (*Zugang haben zu*) an *Stelle etc.*: be able to get (through) to; *an j-n, etw.*: be able to get at (*od.* get hold of); **3.** *fig.*: **~ an** (+ *Akk.*) an *Vorbild etc.*: come up to, equal; *an e-e Zahl etc.*: come near (*od.* close to), approach; **sie kommt längst nicht an ihn heran** she can't touch him, she can't hold a candle to him; **der Film kommt lange nicht an s-n letzten heran** the film (*Am. auch* movie) isn't nearly as good as his last one (*od.* isn't a patch on his last one); → *auch* **heranlassen**; **~lassen** *v/t.* (*unreg.*, *trennb.*, *hat -ge-*): **näher ~** allow to get closer; **~ an** (+ *Akk.*) let *s.o.* get at; **er lässt niemanden an sich / s-e Bücher heran** he won't let anyone (come) near him / touch his books; **sie ließ den Schmerz nicht an sich heran** *umg.* she wouldn't let the pain get to her; **~machen** *v/refl.* (*trennb.*, *hat -ge-*): **sich ~ an** (+ *Akk.*) an *etw.*: set to work on, get going on; *an j-n*: sidle up to; *fig.* approach; *schmeichelnd*: make up to; *beeinflussend*: start working on
herannahen *v/i.* (*trennb.*, *ist -ge-*); *geh.* approach, draw near; **die ~de Gefahr** the approaching (*od.* imminent) danger; **das ~de Gewitter** the gathering storm; **Herannahen** *n*; -s, *kein Pl.* approach
heran|pirschen *v/refl.* (*trennb.*, *hat*

-ge-): **sich ~ an** (+ *Akk.*) stalk (up on); *an j-n*: stalk (*od.* creep, sneak) up on; **~reichen** *v/i.* (*trennb.*, *hat -ge-*): **~ an** (+ *Akk.*) **1.** *Person*: reach; **2.** *Gelände*, *Weg etc.*: reach (up to); *Gras*, *Wasser etc.*: *auch* come up to; **3.** *fig.* → *herankommen* 3; **~reifen** *v/i.* (*trennb.*, *ist -ge-*) **1.** *Früchte etc.*: ripen; **2.** *fig. Plan etc.*: mature; *Person*: grow up (*zu* into); **er reift zu e-m wahren Profi heran** he's fast becoming a real professional; **~rücken** (*trennb.*) **I.** *v/t.* (*hat herangerückt*) move (*od.* push) nearer; (*Stuhl*) pull up; **II.** *v/i.* (*ist*): *räumlich*, *zeitlich*: approach, draw near; **~ an ~** move up (close) to *s.o.*; **~schaffen** *v/t.* (*trennb.*, *hat -ge-*) get, bring in; (*liefern*) provide, supply; **~schleichen** *v/refl.* (*unreg.*, *trennb.*, *hat -ge-*) sneak (*od.* creep) up (*an* + *Akk.* to; *j-n*: on)
heran|tasten *v/refl.* (*trennb.*, *hat -ge-*): **sich ~ an** (+ *Akk.*) **1.** grope one's way towards; **2.** *fig.* feel one's way towards; *an ein Problem etc.*: cautiously approach; **~tragen** *v/t.* (*unreg.*, *trennb.*, *hat -ge-*) **1.** bring (over); **2.** *fig.*: *etw.* **an j-n** (*Bitte*, *Wunsch etc.*) approach *s.o.* with *s.th.*; **er ignoriert an ihn herangetragene Wünsche meist** he usually ignores any requests that are made to him
herantrauen *v/refl.* (*trennb.*, *hat -ge-*) dare to go near (*od.* approach); **sich ~ an** (+ *Akk.*) dare to go near; *an Hund etc.*: *auch* dare to go up to; **sich nicht ~ an** (+ *Akk.*) *auch fig.* be scared of; **ich trau mich an die Maschine nicht heran** I wouldn't like to tinker with the machine; *stärker*: I daren't (*Am.* dare not) touch the machine; **ich trau mich an das Projekt nicht heran** *fig.* I don't think I can handle the project; **er hat sich schon an schlimmere Probleme herangetraut** *fig.* he's tackled (*od.* had to deal with) worse problems than that
herantreten *v/i.* (*unreg.*, *trennb.*, *ist -ge-*) approach (*an j-n/etw.* s.o./s.th.) (*auch fig.*); **~ an** (+ *Akk.*) go (*od.* step) up to; **näher ~** get closer to
heranwachsen *v/i.* (*unreg.*, *trennb.*, *ist -ge-*) grow up; **~ zu** grow (up) into; **die ~de Jugend** the youth of today, today's youth; **Heranwachsende** *m*, *f*; -*n*, -*n* adolescent; *Jur.* young person
heran|wagen *v/refl.* (*trennb.*, *hat -ge-*) → *herantrauen*; **~winken** *v/t.* (*auch unreg.*, *trennb.*, *hat -ge-*) wave *s.o.* over; *aus der Nähe*: motion *s.o.* to come nearer; (*Taxi*) hail; **~ziehen** (*unreg.*, *trennb.*) **I.** *v/t.* (*hat herangezogen*) **1.** pull up (*an* + *Akk.* to); **näher ~** bring closer; **sich** (*Dat.*) ~ draw toward(s) one; **2.** *fig.* (*aufziehen*) raise; (*Pflänzchen*) rear, grow; **3.** *fig.* (*Nachwuchs etc.*) train; **sich** (*Dat.*) **j-n als Nachfolger ~** train s.o. up as one's successor; **4.** *fig. zu Diensten, zur Unterstützung*: call on (*zu* for), enlist *s.o.*(*'s* services) (for, as); (*Arzt*, *Fachmann*) consult, call in; (*Arbeitskräfte etc.*, *auch Mil.*) mobilize, recruit (*zu* for); *j-n zur Zahlung von ... ~* make s.o. pay, get s.o. to pay ...; **5.** *fig.* (*verwenden*) use; (*Gelder etc.*) *auch* draw on; (*berücksichtigen*) consider; (*Literatur*) consult; (*sich berufen auf*) cite, quote; *zum Vergleich ~* use as a comparison; **II.** *v/i.* (*ist*) approach, draw near; *Mil. auch* advance; *Wolken*: gather, thicken
herauf *Adv.* up, upwards; (*hierherauf*) up here; **den Berg ~** up the hill, uphill;

den Fluss ~ up the river, upstream; **die Treppe ~** up the stairs, upstairs; **vom Keller/Tal ~** up from the cellar/valley; (*von*) **unten ~** from below
herauf... *im V. mst* up; → *auch* **empor..., hoch...**
herauf|beschwören *v/t.* (*unreg.*, *trennb.*, *hat*) **1.** (*verursachen*) bring on, provoke; **wir wollen es nicht ~** let's not tempt fate; **2.** (*Vergangenes*) evoke, recall, conjure up; **~bringen** *v/t.* (*unreg.*, *trennb.*, *hat -ge-*) bring up(stairs); **~dämmern** *v/i.* (*trennb.*, *ist -ge-*); *geh.* **1.** *Tag*: dawn; *Morgen*: break; **2.** *fig. Zeit*, *Zukunft*: dawn; **~dringen** *v/i.* (*unreg.*, *trennb.*, *ist -ge-*) *Duft*: waft up; **der Lärm drang von unten herauf** the noise was coming up from below; **~fahren** (*unreg.*, *trennb.*) **I.** *v/i.* (*ist heraufgefahren*) go up; (*mit Auto*: *auch* drive up; *mit Rad*: cycle up; **II.** *v/t.* (*hat*) **1.** (*Wagen*, *Waren etc.*) drive *s.th.* up; **2.** *umg.* (*Computer etc.*) boot up; (*Reaktor*) start up; **~führen** (*trennb.*, *hat -ge-*) **I.** *v/t.* take up; (*Besucher*) *auch* show up; (*Gefangene*, *Hund etc.*) lead up; **II.** *v/i.* *Straße etc.*: lead up; **~kommen** *v/i.* (*unreg.*, *trennb.*, *ist -ge-*) come up; *in Stockwerk*: come up(stairs); **die Straße ~** come up (*od.* along) the street; **komm zu mir auf die Dachterrasse herauf** come up here to me on the roof terrace; **~reichen** (*trennb.*, *hat -ge-*) **I.** *v/t. Person*: reach up; **das Wasser reicht schon fast bis zu uns herauf** the water is almost up to us already; **II.** *v/t.* pass up; **~schalten** *v/i.* (*trennb.*, *hat -ge-*) *Mot.* change (*Am.* shift) up, (*in* + *Akk.* to); **~sehen** *v/i.* (*unreg.*, *trennb.*, *hat -ge-*) look up (*zu* at)
heraufsetzen *v/t.* (*trennb.*, *hat -ge-*) raise (*auf* + *Akk.* to), put up; **Heraufsetzung** *f*; *nur Sg.* raising, increase
herauf|steigen *v/i.* (*unreg.*, *trennb.*, *ist -ge-*) **1.** go (*od.* climb) up; **2.** *Dämpfe*, *Nebel etc.*: rise; **3.** *Unwetter*: come up, be brewing; → *auch* **heraufdämmern**; **~ziehen** (*unreg.*, *trennb.*) **I.** *v/t.* (*hat heraufgezogen*) pull up; **II.** *v/i.* (*ist*) **1.** *Unwetter*: come up, be brewing; **das ~de Unheil erkannte ich nicht** *fig.* I was unaware of the storm that was about to break; **2.** (*nach oben umziehen*) move upstairs
heraus *Adv.* **1.** *räumlich*: out; **~** (*aus*) out of; **da ~** out (of) there; **zum Fenster ~** out of the window, *Am. und Brit. umg. auch* out the window; **nach vorn ~ wohnen**: at the (*od.* in) front; **~ mit ihm!** out with him; **von innen ~** from inside; *fig.* (*durch und durch*) through and through; **von innen ~ frieren** be chilled to the bone; **~ sein** *umg. Zahn*, *Nagel etc.*: be out; **warte, bis wir aus der Stadt ~ sind** wait until we're out of the town; **aus dem dicksten Trubel ~ sein** *umg.* have got(ten *Am.*) through the worst of the hustle and bustle; **2.** *verstärkend*: **aus ... ~** out of ...; **aus einem Gefühl der Verlassenheit etc. ~** from (*od.* out of) a sense of ...; **aus e-r Notlage ~** out of necessity; **3.** *fig.*: **aus sich** (*Dat.*) **~** on one's own initiative; **frei** *od.* **gerade** *od.* **offen** *od.* **rund ~** openly; (*schonungslos*) bluntly, point-blank; **~ damit** *od.* **mit der Sprache!** *umg.* (come on,) out with it; **~ sein** *umg.* (*bekannt*, *veröffentlicht*, *ausgesprochen sein*) be out; *Gesetz*: be in force; **jetzt ist es ~!** *umg. auch* now the secret's out, now the cat's out of the bag; **es ist noch nicht ~, ob ...**

umg. it's still open as to whether ...; ~ **sein aus** *umg.* (*hinter sich haben*) have got(ten *Am.*) over; **aus der Schule ~ sein** *umg.* have finished school; **aus dem Alter bin ich ~** *umg.* I'm past that age; → **fein** II 2, **gröbst...** *etc.*

heraus... *im V.*; *mst* ... out; *siehe auch* **aus..., hinaus..., raus...**

herausarbeiten (*trennb., hat -ge-*) **I.** *v/t.* **1.** *aus Stein, Holz*: carve out; **2.** (*Aspekte, Details, Unterschiede*) bring out; (*Gedanken*) work out; *kunstvoll, umständlich*: elaborate; **II.** *v/refl.* **1.** work one's way out (*aus* of), struggle out (of); **2.** *fig.* manage to get out (of); **Herausarbeitung** *f; nur Sg.* **1.** carving out; **2.** *fig.* bringing out; working out

heraus|bekommen *v/t.* (*unreg., trennb., hat*) **1.** *Fleck, Nagel etc.*: get out (*aus* of); **2.** *fig.*: *etw. aus j-m ~* get s.th. out of s.o.; *kein Wort ~ aus j-m*: not get a word out of s.o.; *ich bekomme keine vernünftige Antwort aus ihr heraus* I can't get a sensible answer out of her; *sie bekam kein Wort / keinen Ton heraus* she couldn't get a word out / utter a sound, she was completely tongue-tied; **3.** *umg.* (*Aufgabe, Lösung*) get s.th. (to come) out; get the answer to; (*Geheimnis*) find out; (*Rätsel etc.*) work out, solve; (*den Sinn*) make (*od.* figure) out; *was hast du bei Aufgabe 2 ~?* what (answer) did you get for question 2?; **4.** (*zurückbekommen*): *sein Geld wieder ~* get one's money back; *etwas ~* get some change; *Sie bekommen zwei Euro heraus* you get two euros change

heraus|bilden *v/t. und v/refl.* (*trennb., hat -ge-*) develop, form; *~boxen* *v/t.* (*trennb., hat -ge-*); *umg. fig.* (*j-n*) get s.o. out (*aus* of), bail s.o. out; *~brechen* (*unreg., trennb.*) **I.** *v/t.* (*hat herausgebrochen*) knock out, break out; *mit Gewalt*: wrench out; **II.** *v/i.* (*ist*) **1.** *aus der Tasse ist ein Stück herausgebrochen* there's a chip out of the cup; *größeres Stück*: a piece has broken off the cup; **2.** *fig. Ärger, Frust, Hass etc.*: burst out, erupt (*aus j-m* from s.o.); *~bringen* *v/t.* (*unreg., trennb., hat -ge-*) **1.** bring out (*aus* of); (*herausbegleiten*) show out; *bring mich bitte hier heraus* please show me the way out of here; *dringender*: get me out of here, please; **2.** *umg.* → *herausbekommen* 1, 2; **3.** *fig.* (*Fabrikat*) bring out, *bes. Am.* come out with; (*Buch*) *auch* publish; (*Schallplatte*) release; *Theat.* produce; *groß ~* give s.o. *od.* s.th. a big buildup; *~drehen* *v/t.* (*trennb., hat -ge-*); (*Glühbirne, Schraube*) unscrew; *~drücken* *v/t.* (*trennb., hat -ge-*) **1.** squeeze out (*aus* of); **2.** (*Brust*) stick out; *~fahren* (*unreg., trennb.*) **I.** *v/i.* (*ist herausgefahren*) **1.** come out (*aus* of); (*mit*) *Auto*: *auch* drive out (of); *Zug*: *auch* leave; *sie kam zu schnell aus der Einfahrt herausgefahren* she drove out of the driveway too fast; **2.** *fig. Worte*: slip out; **II.** *v/t.* (*hat*) **1.** drive out (*aus* of); **2.** *Sport*: *e-e gute Zeit ~* record a good *od.* fast time; *~fallen* *v/i.* (*unreg., trennb., ist -ge-*) **1.** fall out; *Sache*: *auch* drop out; **2.** *fig. aus Kategorie, Liste etc.*: drop out, be dropped from; *~filtern* *v/t.* (*trennb., hat -ge-*) filter out (*auch fig.*); *~finden* (*unreg., trennb., hat -ge-*) **I.** *v/t.* **1.** (*Geheimnis, Täter*) find out; (*Fehler, Ursache etc.*)

find; *~, warum/wie etc. ...* find out why/how etc. ...; **2.** *aus e-m Haufen / unter Tausenden etc. ~* discover among (*od.* unearth from among) a pile of things / pick out from a crowd of thousands etc.; **II.** *v/i. und v/refl.* **1.** find one's way out (*aus* of); **2.** *fig.* get out (of); *~fischen* *v/t.* (*trennb., hat -ge-*); *auch fig.* fish out (*aus* of); *~fliegen* (*unreg., trennb.*) **I.** *v/i.* (*ist herausgeflogen*) **1.** fly out (*aus* of); **2.** *umg. fig.* → *herausfallen* 1, 2; **3.** *umg. fig.*; *aus Team etc.* → *fliegen* I 6; **II.** *v/t.* (*hat*) fly out (*aus* of); *~fließen* *v/i.* (*unreg., trennb., ist -ge-*) flow out (*aus* of)

Herausforderer *m; -s, -,* **Herausforderin** *f; -, -nen* challenger; *Pol.* rival candidate, opponent; **herausfordern** (*trennb., hat -ge-*) **I.** *v/t.* challenge (*zu* to); (*provozieren*) provoke (into + *Ger.*); *das Unglück ~* court disaster; *sein Glück od. das Schicksal ~* tempt fate; **II.** *v/i.*: *zur Kritik ~* invite criticism; *das fordert geradezu heraus zu ...* that's an open invitation to; **herausfordernd I.** *Part. Präs.* → *herausfordern*; **II.** *Adj.* challenging; (*trotzig*) defiant; (*aufreizend*) provocative; (*anmaßend*) arrogant; (*lockend*) inviting; *er Blick* (*einladend*) come-hither look *umg.*; **III.** *Adv.*: *j-n ~ ansehen* give s.o. a challenging look; **Herausforderung** *f* challenge (*auch fig. Aufgabe etc.*); (*Provokation*) provocation

herausführen (*trennb., hat -ge-*) **I.** *v/t.* bring out, lead out; *Besucher*: show out; *Gefangene*: lead out; *aus e-r Krise ~* lead out of a crisis; **II.** *v/i. Straße etc.*: lead out

Herausgabe *f; nur Sg.* **1.** *Jur.* surrender; (*Auslieferung*) delivery; **2.** *e-s Buches*: publication; **herausgeben** (*unreg., trennb., hat -ge-*) **I.** *v/t.* **1.** (*herausreichen*) pass *od.* hand out; **2.** (*zurückgeben*) give back, return; (*Gefangene etc.*) hand over; **3.** (*j-m*) *zwei Euro ~* give (s.o.) two euros change; **4.** (*Buch etc.*) publish; *als Bearbeiter*: edit; (*Briefmarken, Vorschrift etc.*) issue; **II.** *v/i. Geld s.o.* change; *~ auf* (+ *Akk.*) give change for; *können Sie ~?* can you change this?; **Herausgeber** *m,* **Herausgeberin** *f* publisher; (*Redakteur[in], Verfasser[in]*) editor

heraus|gehen *v/i.* (*unreg., trennb., ist -ge-*) **1.** go out; **2.** *umg., Fleck etc.*: come out; **3.** *fig.*: *aus sich* (*Dat.*) *~* come out of one's shell; **4.** *unpers.*: *geht es da heraus?* is that the way out?; *~greifen* *v/t.* (*unreg., trennb., hat -ge-*) pick out; (*Beispiele*) cite; *sich* (*Dat.*) *ein Opfer etc. ~* single out; *~haben* *v/t.* (*unreg., trennb., hat -ge-*); *umg.* **1.** have got s.th. out; *j-n/etw. ~ wollen aus* want to get s.o./s.th. out of, *mit großer Mühe*: want to winkle (*Am.* wrangle) s.o./s.th. out of; **2.** (*festgestellt haben*) have found s.th. out; (*Rätsel etc.*) have solved (*od.* got) s.th.; *als Lösung*: get s.th. (as an answer to s.th.), make it s.th.; *jetzt hat er es heraus* (*kapiert*) he's got (the hang of) it now; → *Dreh* 1; **3.** (*wieder*) *~* (*Ausgaben, Kosten etc.*) have recovered, have got back; *~halten* (*unreg., trennb., hat -ge-*) **I.** *v/t.* **1.** hold s.th. out (*aus dem od. zum Fenster* [of] the window); **2.** *umg.* (*fern halten von*): *~ aus* keep s.o. *od.* s.th. out of; **II.** *v/refl.* keep out of it; *halt dich da heraus* Ratschlag: don't get involved; *Drohung*: stay (*od.* keep) out of it

heraushängen¹ *v/i.* (*unreg., trennb., hat / südd., österr., schw. ist -ge-*) **1.** hang out (*aus* of); → *Hals* 3; **2.** *umg. pej.*: *du musst* (*es dir*) *nicht so ~ lassen, dass du das besser kannst* you oughtn't to show off (*od.* parade) the fact that ... so much

heraushängen² *v/t.* (*trennb., hat -ge-*) **1.** hang out (*aus* of); **2.** *umg. pej.* → **herauskehren** 2

heraus|hauen *v/t.* (*auch unreg., trennb., hat -ge-*) **1.** remove (by striking, cutting etc.); (*Steine, Stücke etc.*) knock out (*aus* of); (*Bäume*) chop down; **2.** (*meißeln*) carve out (of); **3.** *fig., umg.*: *j-n ~* get s.o. out (*aus* of), get s.o. off the hook *umg.*; *~heben* (*unreg., trennb., hat -ge-*) **I.** *v/t.* **1.** lift (*od.* take) out; **2.** *fig.* → *hervorheben*; **II.** *v/refl.* stand out; *~helfen* *v/i.* (*unreg., trennb., hat -ge-*): *j-m ~* help s.o. out (*auch fig.*) (*aus* of); *~holen* *v/t.* (*trennb., hat -ge-*) **1.** get out (*auch retten*) (*aus* of); (*herausbringen*) bring (*od.* fetch) out; **2.** *umg. fig.* (*Gewinn, Vorteil etc.*) gain, notch up *umg.*; (*Sieg*) win, notch up *umg.*, chalk up *umg.*; (*Zeit*) achieve, record, notch up *umg.*; *~ aus* get out of; *wie viel / was hast du herausgeholt?* how much did you get out of it? / what did you manage to achieve?; *300 Sachen aus dem Wagen ~* get 300 ks out of the car; *alles aus sich* (*Dat.*) *~* give everything one has got; → *Letzte* 2; *~hören* *v/t.* (*trennb., hat -ge-*) **1.** hear; **2.** *fig.* detect (*aus* in); *es war deutlich herauszuhören* it was obvious to anyone with ears, you couldn't ignore it; *~kehren* *v/t.* (*trennb., hat -ge-*) **1.** sweep out (*aus* of); **2.** *fig.* (*betonen*) emphasize; (*s-e Intelligenz, Überlegenheit etc.*) show, display; *stärker*: parade; (*den Experten etc.*) act, play; *~kitzeln* *v/t.* (*trennb., hat -ge-*); *umg.*: *etw. aus j-m ~* worm s.th. out of s.o.; *~klamüsern* *v/t.* (*trennb., hat*); *umg.* figure out, work out; *~klettern* *v/i.* (*trennb., ist -ge-*) climb *od.* clamber out (*aus* of)

herauskommen *v/i.* (*unreg., trennb., ist -ge-*) **1.** come out (*aus* of); (*erscheinen*) appear, emerge (from); (*wegkommen*) get out (of); *aus den nassen Kleidern ~* get out of (*od.* take off) one's wet clothes; *sie ist noch nie aus i-m Dorf herausgekommen* she's never been out of (*od.* away from) her home village yet; **2.** *umg. fig. aus e-r Situation*: get out (of) (*heil* safely, unscathed); *aus Schwierigkeiten, Sorgen*: get over; *aus den roten Zahlen ~* get out of the red; *wir kamen aus dem Lachen/Staunen nicht mehr heraus* we just couldn't stop laughing / we couldn't believe our eyes; **3.** *fig.* (*deutlich werden*) *Details, Farben, Unterschiede etc.*: come out, emerge; *Bässe, Höhen*: be clear; **4.** *umg. fig., Äußerung*: come out; **5.** *Erzeugnis*: come out; *Buch etc.*: *auch* be published, appear; *Briefmarken etc.*: be issued; **6.** *umg. fig.* (*bekannt werden*) come out; **7.** *umg. fig., als Ergebnis*: be the result; *bei Aufgabe*: *auch* be the answer; *~ bei* (*resultieren*) come (out) of s.th.; *es kommt nichts dabei heraus* it's not worth it, it doesn't pay; *was ist dabei herausgekommen?* what was the outcome?; *als Entscheidung*: *auch* what was decided?; *ist irgendetwas dabei herausgekommen?* was it any good?, did you *etc.* get anywhere?; *es kommt aufs Gleiche od. auf das-*

selbe heraus it boils (*od.* comes) down to the same thing; → *auch* **herausspringen** 2; **8.** *umg. fig.*: **~ mit** (*äußern*) come out with; (*gestehen*) admit; **9.** *umg. fig., beim Kartenspiel*: **~ mit** lead with; **wer kommt heraus?** who leads?, whose turn is it to lead?; **10.** *umg. fig.*: **groß ~** (*erfolgreich sein*) be a great success; **11.** *umg. fig., aus dem Rhythmus etc.*: lose it, get out of the rhythm *etc.*; *beim Nachdenken, Gedichtaufsagen etc.*: lose it, lose the thread; (*aus der Übung kommen*) get out of practice

heraus|können *v/i.* (*unreg., trennb., hat -ge-*) *umg.* be able to get out (**aus** of); **ich kann nicht heraus** I can't get out; (*hänge fest*) *auch* I'm stuck; **~kriegen** *v/t.* (*trennb., hat -ge-*); *umg.* → **herausbekommen**; **~kristallisieren** (*trennb., hat*) **I.** *v/refl.* crystallize (**zu** into; **aus** out of, *auch fig.* from); **II.** *v/t.* **1.** crystallize (**aus** out of, from); **2.** *fig.* distil(l), extract (from); **~lassen** *v/t.* (*unreg., trennb., hat -ge-*) **1.** let out; **e-e blöde Bemerkung ~** *umg. fig.* come out with a stupid remark; **2.** *umg.* (*weglassen*) leave out; **~laufen** (*unreg., trennb.*) **I.** *v/i.* (*ist herausgelaufen*) run out (**aus** of); *Wasser*: *auch* pour out; **II.** *v/t.* (*hat*) *Sport* (*Vorsprung*) gain, build up; (*Zeit*) achieve, run; (*Sieg*) win; (*zweiten etc. Platz*) take; **~legen** *v/t.* (*trennb., hat -ge-*) put out (+ *Dat.* for); **~lesen** *v/t.* (*unreg., trennb., hat -ge-*) **1.** (*entnehmen*) gather (**aus** from); (*hineindeuten*) read (into); **2.** *umg., sortierend*: pick out; **~locken** *v/t.* (*trennb., hat -ge-*) **1.** lure out (**aus** of); **2.** *fig.*: **etw. aus j-m ~** worm s.th. out of s.o.; **j-n aus s-r Reserve ~** draw s.o. out of his (*od.* her) shell; **~machen** (*trennb., hat -ge-*) **I.** *v/t.* take out (**aus** of); (*Fleck*) get out; **II.** *v/refl. umg. fig.* be coming along well, improve; *nach e-r Krankheit*: be doing nicely; **~müssen** *v/i.* (*unreg., trennb., hat -ge-*); *umg. Zahn etc.*: have to come out; *aus e-r Wohnung etc.*: have to get out; *nach draußen*: have to go out(side); *aus dem Bett*: have to get up; **das musste noch heraus** (*musste gesagt werden*) it had to be said, I *etc.* had to say it

herausnehmbar *Adj.* removable, detachable; **herausnehmen** *v/t.* (*unreg., trennb., hat -ge-*) **1.** take out (**aus** of); *weitS.* (*entfernen*) remove (from); **sich** (*Dat.*) **den Blinddarm etc. ~ lassen** have one's appendix *etc.* (taken) out; **den Gang ~** *Mot.* go into neutral, put the car *etc.* in neutral; **j-n aus der Mannschaft / dem Spiel ~** *Sport* drop s.o. from the team / take s.o. off; **2.** *fig.*: **sich** (*Dat.*) **etw. ~** (*sich anmaßen*) arrogate s.th. (to o.s.); **sich** (*Dat.*) **Freiheiten ~** take liberties (**j-m gegenüber** with s.o.); **sich** (*Dat.*) **das Recht ~ zu** (+ *Inf.*) take the liberty of (+ *Ger.*); **sich** (*Dat.*) **zu viel ~** go too far, overstep the mark

heraus|pauken *v/t.* (*trennb., hat -ge-*); *umg.* bail s.o. out (**aus** of); **~picken** *v/t.* (*trennb., hat -ge-*) **1.** *Vogel*: peck out; **2.** *umg. fig.* pick s.o./s.th. out; **~platzen** *v/i.* (*trennb., hat -ge-*) *umg.* burst out (*lachend*: laughing); **mit der Wahrheit etc. ~** blurt out the truth *etc.*; **~pressen** *v/t.* (*trennb., hat -ge-*) **1.** press (*od.* squeeze) out (**aus** of); **2.** *pej.* (*Geständnis, Lösegeld etc.*) extort, screw out *umg.* (**aus** from); **~putzen** *v/t. und v/refl.* (*trennb., hat -ge-*)

spruce (**sich** o.s.) up; **~quetschen** *v/t.* (*trennb., hat -ge-*) squeeze out (*auch fig.*)

herausragen *v/i.* (*trennb., hat -ge-*) **1.** jut out; *Haus etc.*: tower, rise (**aus** above); **2.** *fig.* stand out; **herausragend I.** *Part. Präs.* → **herausragen**; **II.** *Adj. fig.* outstanding

heraus|reden *v/refl.* (*trennb., hat -ge-*) talk one's way out of it, wriggle out of it; **sich ~ aus** talk one's way out of, wriggle out of; **~reißen** *v/t.* (*unreg., trennb., hat -ge-*) **1.** pull out; (*Papier etc.*) tear out; **2.** *umg. fig.* (*j-n*) tear s.o. (*aus* from); (*befreien*) get s.o. out (of); (*aufrütteln*) shake s.o. out (of); (*retten*) save; **~ aus** (*unterbrechen*) drag s.o. out of; **das reißt es auch nicht mehr heraus** that doesn't make up for it

herausrücken (*trennb.*) **I.** *v/t.* (*hat herausgerückt*) **1.** push (*od.* move) out (**aus** of); **2.** *umg. fig.* (*hergeben*) → II; **II.** *v/i.* (*ist*); *umg.*: **~ mit** come out with; *mit Geld*: fork out, cough up; **mit der Sprache ~** talk; (*gestehen*) come out with it; **jetzt rück mal heraus damit** come on, out with it

heraus|rutschen *v/i.* (*trennb., ist -ge-*) slip out (*auch umg. fig.*) (**aus** of); **das ist mir so herausgerutscht** *umg. fig.* it just slipped out; **~schaffen** *v/t.* (*trennb., hat -ge-*) take (*od.* move, carry) out (**aus** of); **~schälen** (*trennb., hat -ge-*); *fig.* **I.** *v/t.* (*Idee etc.*) sift out; **II.** *v/refl.* **1.** *umg.*: **sich aus s-r Kleidung ~** peel one's clothes off; **2.** *Sache*: emerge; **~schauen** *v/i.* (*trennb., hat -ge-*); *bes. südd., österr.* **1.** look out (**aus** of); **2.** (*zu sehen sein*) peep out (**aus** of); **3.** *umg. fig.* → **herausspringen** 2; **~schießen** (*unreg., trennb.*) **I.** *v/t.* (*hat herausgeschossen*) shoot out (**aus** of); **II.** *v/i.* (*ist*); *Person, Fahrzeug etc.*: shoot out; *Blut etc.*: spurt out; **~schinden** *v/t.* (*unreg., trennb., hat -ge-*); *umg.* → **herausschlagen** I 2

herausschlagen (*unreg., trennb.*) **I.** *v/t.* (*hat herausgeschlagen*) **1.** knock out (**aus** of); **2.** *umg. fig.* get (**aus** out of); **Geld ~ aus** make money out of; **möglichst viel ~** get as much as one can (**aus** out of); **e-n Vorteil ~** wangle an advantage (**aus** out of); **II.** *v/i.* (*ist*); *Flamme*: leap out (**aus** of)

heraus|schleudern *v/t.* (*trennb., hat -ge-*) **1.** throw (*od.* hurl, catapult) out (**aus** of); **2.** (*Worte, Anklage etc.*) burst out with; **~schlüpfen** *v/i.* (*trennb., ist -ge-*) slip out (**aus** of); **~schmecken** *v/t.* (*trennb., hat -ge-*) taste (**aus** in); **~schrauben** *v/t.* (*trennb., hat -ge-*) unscrew (**aus** from); **~schreiben** *v/t.* (*unreg., trennb., hat -ge-*) copy (**aus** from, out of); **~schreien** *v/t.* (*unreg., trennb., hat -ge-*); *umg.*: **s-e Gefühle / s-n Hass ~** shout out; *heftiger*: scream out; **~sehen** *v/i.* (*unreg., trennb., hat -ge-*) look out (**aus** of. from); **~ sein** → **heraus** 1, 3; **~sickern** *v/i.* (*trennb., ist -ge-*) seep (**aus** out of); (*tröpfeln*) trickle (out of)

heraußen *Adv. südd., österr.* out here

heraus|springen *v/i.* (*unreg., trennb., ist -ge-*) **1.** jump out (**aus** of); **aus den Schienen ~** jump the rails, derail; **2.** *umg. fig.*: **was springt für mich dabei heraus?** what's in it for me?; **~spritzen** *v/i.* (*trennb., ist -ge-*) squirt out (**aus** of, from); **~sprudeln** (*trennb.*) **I.** *v/i.* (*ist herausgesprudelt*) **1.** bubble out (**aus** of); **2.** *fig. Worte*:

come spluttering out; **II.** *v/t.* (*hat*); *fig.* splutter out; **~stechen** *v/i.* (*unreg., trennb., hat -ge-*); (*sich abheben*) stand out; **~stehen** *v/i.* → **hervorstehen**

herausstellen (*trennb., hat -ge-*) **I.** *v/t.* **1.** put out(side); **2.** *Sport* (*Spieler*) send off; **3.** *fig.* (*betonen*) emphasize, underline, bring out (clearly); (*an die Öffentlichkeit bringen*) publicize; *in der Werbung etc.*: highlight, feature (*auch Theat.*), bring out; (*abheben*) set off, throw into (sharp) relief; **etw. klar und deutlich ~** make s.th. quite clear; **II.** *v/refl.*: **sich ~ als** turn out (to be); *unpers.*: **es wird sich schon** (*noch*) **~, ob/wann etc.** we shall find out (eventually) whether/when *etc.*; **das muss sich erst** (*noch*) **~** that remains to be seen; **es hat sich herausgestellt, dass ...** it turned out (that)...; **es hat sich herausgestellt, dass er ein Drogenschmuggler ist** he turned out to be (*od.* it turned out he was, *od.* he proved to be) a drug smuggler

heraus|strecken *v/t.* (*trennb., hat -ge-*); (*Kopf etc.*) stick out (**aus** of); → **Zunge** 1; **~streichen** (*unreg., trennb., hat -ge-*) **I.** *v/t.* **1.** cross out (**aus** of), delete (from); **2.** *fig.* (*betonen*) point out; *pej.* praise to the skies; **II.** *v/refl. pej.* blow one's own trumpet; **~strömen** *v/i.* (*trennb., ist -ge-*); *auch fig.* pour out (**aus** of); **~stürzen** *v/i.* (*trennb., ist -ge-*) **1.** fall out (**aus** of); **2.** (*eilen*) rush (*od.* storm) out (of), come rushing (*od.* storming) out (of); **~suchen** *v/t.* (*trennb., hat -ge-*) **1.** (*hervorsuchen*) find, look for; *mit Mühe*: dig out (**j-m** for s.o.); **2.** (*auswählen*) choose, pick out; **~trennen** *v/t.* (*trennb., hat -ge-*) detach, remove (**aus** from); **~treten** *v/i.* → **hervortreten**; **~trommeln** *v/t.* (*trennb., hat -ge-*); *umg.* get s.o. out (*by hammering on the door*) (**aus** of); *Brit. auch, bes. nachts*: knock s.o. up; **~wachsen** *v/i.* (*unreg., trennb., ist -ge-*): **~ aus** grow out of; *aus den Kleidern*: *auch* outgrow; **~waschen** *v/t.* (*unreg., trennb., hat -ge-*) wash out (**aus** of); **~winden** *v/refl.* (*unreg., trennb., hat -ge-*); *fig.* wriggle out of it; **sich ~ aus** wriggle out of; **~winken** (*auch unreg., trennb., hat -ge-*) **I.** *v/t.* (*Auto*) flag down; (*dirigieren*) gesture *od.* signal to s.o. to come (*out od.* over); **II.** *v/i.*: **aus dem** *od.* **zum Fenster etc. ~** wave from the window *etc.*; **~wirtschaften** *v/t.* (*trennb., hat -ge-*) make (**aus** out of); **e-n Gewinn ~** make a profit (**aus** out of); **~wollen** *v/i.* (*trennb., hat -ge-*); *umg.* **1.** want to get out; **2. er will nicht mit der Sprache heraus** he won't come out with it, he's clammed up

herausziehen *v/t.* (*unreg., trennb., hat -ge-*) **1.** pull out (**aus** of); (*Zahn*) *auch* extract (from); (*schleppen*) drag out (of); **2.** *Mil.* (*Truppenteil*) withdraw (from), pull out (of); **3.** *Chem.* extract (from); **4.** (*Inhalt*) extract (from); (*Notizen*) **aus Büchern etc.**: cull (from)

herb *Adj.* **1.** *geschmacklich*: sour, tart; *Wein*: dry; **2.** *Duft*: tangy; **3.** *fig. Gesichtszüge, Kritik, Worte*: harsh, severe; *Enttäuschung, Niederlage etc.*: bitter; *Schönheit, Stil*: austere

Herbarium *n*; *-s, Herbarien* herbarium (*Pl.* herbaria)

herbei *Adv.* here; **nur ~, ~!** just come here

herbei... *im V.* → *auch* **heran...**

herbei|bringen *v/t.* (*unreg., trennb., hat -ge-*) **1.** *räumlich*: bring (over); **2.** (*Be-*

H

weise etc.) produce; **~eilen** v/i. (trennb., ist -ge-) come running (up); Feuerwehr etc.: rush to the scene; **~führen** v/t. (trennb., hat -ge-) (verursachen) cause, bring about; (bewirken) lead to; (erzwingen) force; bes. Med. induce; **~reden** v/t. (trennb., hat -ge-); (Krise etc.) provoke; **wir wollen es nicht ~** let's not tempt fate, we don't want to bring it on ourselves (od. make it happen) by talking about it; **~rufen** v/t. (unreg., trennb., hat -ge-) call over; (Arzt etc.) call (od. send) for; **~schaffen** v/t. (trennb., hat -ge-) fetch; (besorgen) provide, get; (Beweise etc.) produce; **~sehnen** v/t. (trennb., hat -ge-) long for; **sie sehnt den Frühling / i-e Kinder herbei** auch she can't wait for spring / she wishes her children were there od. with her; **~strömen** v/i. (trennb., ist -ge-) flock to the scene; massenweise: come in droves; **~ zu** flock to; **die Menschen sind herbeigeströmt** auch crowds of people came; **~stürzen** v/i. (trennb., ist -ge-) rush up (to the scene); **~wünschen** v/t. (trennb., hat -ge-): (sich [Dat.]) etw. **~** long for s.th.; sich (Dat.) j-n **~** wish s.o. were (od. was) there; → auch herbeisehnen; **~zaubern** v/t. (trennb., hat -ge-) conjure up; **~ziehen** v/t. (unreg., trennb., hat -ge-) pull near; (Stuhl) pull up; fig. → Haar 3; **~zitieren** v/t. (trennb., hat) send for, ask s.o. to come and see one

her|bekommen v/t. (unreg., trennb., hat) get (hold of); **~bemühen** I. v/t. (trennb., hat): j-n **~** ask s.o. to come (there od. here); II. v/refl. take the trouble to come; **Sie haben sich leider umsonst herbemüht** I'm afraid you've come all this way for nothing; **~beordern** v/t. (trennb., hat) summon

Herberge f; -, -n; (Gasthaus) inn; (Jugendherberge etc.) (youth etc.) hostel; (Obdach) shelter (auch fig.), hostel

Herbergs|eltern Pl. wardens, Am. houseparents; **~mutter** f, **~vater** m warden, Am. housemother, housefather

her|bestellen v/t. (trennb., hat) ask s.o. to come; send for; (Taxi) order; **~beten** v/t. (trennb., hat -ge-) pej. reel (od. rattle) off

Herbheit f; -, kein Pl. **1.** sourness; Wein: dryness, dry quality; **2.** fig. severity; e-r Enttäuschung etc.: bitterness; Schönheit, Stil: austerity; → **herb**

herbitten v/t. (unreg., trennb., hat -ge-) ask s.o. to come

Herbizid n; -(e)s, -e herbicide

herbringen v/t. (unreg., trennb., hat -ge-) bring (along)

Herbst m; -(e)s, -e autumn, Am. auch fall; **im ~** in autumn (Am. auch fall od. the fall); **im ~ des Lebens** lit. fig. in the autumn of (one's) life; **~anfang** m beginning of autumn (Am. auch fall); **~ferien** Pl. autumn (Am. auch fall) break Sg.; **~kollektion** f autumn (Am. auch fall) collection; **~laub** n autumn leaves

herbstlich I. Adj. autumn(al), Am. auch fall ...; **II.** Adv.: **~ kühles Wetter** etc. cool autumn (Am. auch fall) weather etc.

Herbst|mode f fashion for autumn (Am. auch fall); Koll. autumn (Am. auch fall) fashions; **~monat** m autumn month; **~nebel** m autumn mist; **~sturm** m autumnal (Am. auch fall) storm; **~tag** m autumn (Am. auch fall) day; **~wetter** n autumn (Am. auch

fall) weather; **~zeitlose** f; -n, -n; Bot. meadow saffron, naked lady

Herd m; -(e)s, -e **1.** stove, cooker; Am. und aus Eisen: auch range; (Backofen) oven; **auf den ~ stellen** put on the stove (od. cooker, Am. flame); **vom ~ nehmen** take off the stove (od. cooker, Am. flame); **den ganzen Tag am ~ stehen** stand in the kitchen all day long; **2.** fig. hearth, home; **am heimischen** od. **häuslichen ~** at home; **eigener ~ ist Goldes wert** Sprichw. there's no place like home; **3.** fig. (Ausgangspunkt) cent|re (Am. -er); focus (Pl. focuses od. foci) (auch Med.); e-s Erdbebens: epicent|re (Am. -er)

Herdbuch n für Rinder etc.: herd book; für Pferde: stud book

Herde f; -, -n **1.** herd (+ Gen. of); von Schafen: flock; **in der ~ leben** Tierart: live in herds; **2.** fig. pej. herd, masses Pl.; geh. des Priesters: flock; **mit der ~ laufen** (just) follow the herd (Am. auch pack); **aus der ~ ausbrechen** break away from the others, go one's own way

Herden|instinkt m herd instinct; **~tier** n **1.** gregarious animal; **2.** fig. pej. sheep; **~trieb** m fig. auch herd instinct

herdenweise Adv. in herds (auch fig.)

Herd|feuer n fire in a cooking range; **~platte** f hotplate

herein Adv. in; **von draußen ~** from outside; **~!** come in!

herein... im V. → auch hinein..., rein...

herein|bekommen v/t. (unreg., trennb., hat); umg. **1.** (Waren) get in; **2.** (Radiosender) pick up; **3.** (Außenstände, Unkosten) recover; **~bitten** v/t. (unreg., trennb., hat -ge-): **~ (in + Akk.)** ask s.o. (to come) in(to); **~brechen** v/i. (unreg., trennb., ist -ge-) **1. ~ (in + Akk.)** Wassermassen etc.: burst in(to); **2.** geh. fig., Nacht: fall; Sturm: break; Winter: set in; **~ über (+ Akk.)** hit, strike; Unglück, Schicksal etc.: auch befall; **~bringen** v/t. (unreg., trennb., hat -ge-) **1. ~ (in + Akk.)** bring in(to); **2. ~ (in + Akk.)** umg., mit Mühe: get in(to); **3.** umg. fig. (Kosten etc.) recover; (verlorene Zeit etc.) make up for; **~dringen** v/i. (unreg., trennb., ist -ge-): **~ (in + Akk.)** Person: force one's way (into); Geräusch, Licht, Wasser etc.: penetrate, come in, get through; **kein Laut drang zu uns herein** not a sound came through to us; **~dürfen** v/i. (unreg., trennb., hat -ge-); umg.: **~ (in + Akk.)** be allowed in(to); **darf der Hund mit herein?** do you mind if the dog comes in too?; **~fahren** (unreg., trennb.) **I.** v/i. (ist hereingefahren): **~ (in + Akk.)** come in(to); (mit) Auto: auch drive in(to); Schiff, Zug: come in(to); mit Fahrrad: cycle in(to); **II.** v/t. (hat): **~ (in + Akk.)** (Waren, Personen etc.) bring in(to); **~fallen** v/i. (unreg., trennb., ist -ge-) **1. ~ (in + Akk.)** fall in(to); Licht etc.: come in(to); **2.** umg. fig. be taken in (**auf** + Akk. by); (darauf) **~** fall for it; **~ auf** (+ Akk.) auch fall for; **bei dem Kauf / mit dem neuen Auto bin ich schwer hereingefallen** I made a big mistake when I bought that / with the new car; **~fliegen** v/i. (unreg., trennb., ist -ge-) **1. ~ (in + Akk.)** fly in(to); **2.** umg. fig. → hereinfallen 2; **~führen** v/t. (trennb., hat -ge-): **~ (in + Akk.)** (Gast) show in(to); (Gefangenen, Hund etc.) lead in(to); **~holen** v/t. (trennb., hat -ge-) **1. ~ (in + Akk.)**

fetch (od. bring) in(to); **2.** Wirts. (Aufträge) get (in); **3.** fig. (Verluste etc.) recoup; (aufholen) make up for

hereinkommen v/i. (unreg., trennb., ist -ge-) **1. ~ (in + Akk.)** come in(to) (od. inside); Person: auch walk in(to); (hereingelangen) get in(to); **komm doch kurz herein** come in for a minute; **2.** Wirts. (Ware) come in; **3.** umg. fig., Geld: come in; **wieder ~** Geld, Zeit: be made up; **mehr Geld ausgeben als wieder ~ konnte** spend more money than one was able to get back

herein|kriegen v/t. (trennb., hat -ge-); umg. → hereinbekommen; **~lassen** v/t. (unreg., trennb., hat -ge-): **~ (in + Akk.)** let in(to); **~laufen** v/i. (unreg., trennb., ist -ge-): **~ (in + Akk.)** Person, Wasser etc.: run in(to); **hereingelaufen kommen** come running in; **~legen** v/t. (trennb., hat -ge-); umg., mit Scherz: take s.o. for a ride; auch finanziell: take s.o. in; **man hat mich hereingelegt** I was (od. got) taken for a ride; **~nehmen** v/t. (unreg., trennb., hat -ge-): **~ (in + Akk.) 1.** (auch fig. Schutzbedürftigen) take in(to); **2.** in Liste etc.: include (in), put (on od. in); **~platzen** v/i. (trennb., ist -ge-) umg.: **~ (in + Akk.)** in ein Zimmer: burst in(to); **~regnen** v/i. (trennb., hat -ge-) unpers.: **es regnet herein (in + Akk.)** it's raining in(to), the rain's coming in(to) (od. through the roof etc.); **~reichen** (trennb., hat -ge-) **I.** v/t.: j-m etw. **~** pass od. hand s.th. in to s.o.; **II.** v/i.: **~ (in + Akk.)** reach in(to); **~ bis** reach as far as; **~reißen** v/t. (unreg., trennb., hat -ge-); umg. → hereinreiten II; **~reiten** (unreg., trennb.) **I.** v/i. (ist hereingeritten): **~ (in + Akk.)** ride in(to); **II.** v/t. (hat); umg. fig. get (od. land) s.o. in a (real) mess; **j-n in etw. (Akk.) ~** land s.o. in s.th., drag s.o. into s.th.

hereinschauen v/i. (trennb., hat -ge-); bes. südd., österr. **1. ~ (in + Akk.)** look in(to); **zur Tür ~** pop one's head around the door; **die Sonne schaute zum Fenster herein** fig. the sun was shining in through the window; **2.** umg. fig. (vorbeischauen) look in, drop by (**bei** at); **er schaute zu uns herein** he looked in on us, he dropped by

hereinschneien v/i. (trennb.) **1.** unpers.; (hat hereingeschneit): **es schneit herein (in + Akk.)** it's snowing in(to), the snow's coming in(to) (od. through the door etc.); **2.** (ist); umg. fig.: **~ (in + Akk.)** blow in(to), breeze in(to); **plötzlich kam der Chef hereingeschneit** all of a sudden the boss came breezing in; **ja, wer kommt denn da hereingeschneit?** überrascht: look who's coming!

herein|sehen v/i. (unreg., trennb., hat -ge-) → hereinschauen; **~spazieren** v/i. (trennb., ist) umg.: **~ (in + Akk.)** stroll in(to), walk in(to); **hereinspaziert kommen** come waltzing (od. strolling) in; **hereinspaziert kam ... in** strolled ..., in walked ..., who should walk in but ...; **hereinspaziert!** come in!, come in!; **~stecken** v/t. (trennb., hat -ge-): **~ (in + Akk.)** stick s.th. in(to); **den Kopf zur Tür ~** poke od. pop one's head (a)round the door; **~strömen** v/i. (trennb., ist -ge-): **~ (in + Akk.)** pour in(to) (auch fig.); **~stürzen** v/i. (trennb., ist -ge-): **~ (in + Akk.)** rush in(to); **~tragen** v/t. (unreg., trennb., hat -ge-): **~ (in + Akk.)** carry in(to), bring in(to); (Schmutz) an

Schuhen: bring in(to), walk in(to); **~treten** *v/i.* (*unreg., trennb., ist -ge-*): ~ (*in + Akk.*) come in(to), walk in(to), enter; **~werfen** *v/t.* (*unreg., trennb., hat -ge-*): ~ (*in + Akk.*) throw in(to); *sie warf e-n Blick zum Fenster herein* she cast an eye through the window, she looked in through the window; **~wollen** *v/i.* (*unreg., trennb., hat -ge-*); *umg.*: ~ (*in + Akk.*) want to come in(to); **~ziehen** (*unreg., trennb.*) **I.** *v/t.* (*hat hereingezogen*) ~ (*in + Akk.*) **1.** pull in(to) (*od.* inside); **2.** *umg. fig.* → *hineinziehen*; **II.** *v/i.* (*ist*) **1.** in *Wohnung*: move in(to); **2.** *Soldaten etc.*: march in(to); **3.** *unpers.*: be a draught (*Am.* draft) in; *hier zieht es herein* there's a draught (*Am.* draft) in here

herfahren (*unreg., trennb.*) **I.** *v/t.* (*hat hergefahren*) bring (*od.* drive) here, bring by car *etc.*; **II.** *v/i.* (*ist*) **1.** come by car *etc.*; *mit Auto*: drive (here); *mit Rad*: cycle (here); **2.** *hinter j-m od. etw.* ~ drive behind; follow; *vor j-m od. etw.* ~ drive in front (*od.* ahead) of; *neben j-m od. etw.* ~ drive beside od. alongside; **Herfahrt** *f* journey (*od.* trip) here; *auf der* ~ on the (*od.* my *etc.*) way here

her|fallen *v/i.* (*unreg., trennb., ist -ge-*): ~ *über* (+ *Akk.*) **1.** pounce on, attack; **2.** *umg. fig., mit Fragen*: besiege *with* questions *etc.*; (*kritisieren*) have a (real) go at, *Am.* tear into; *über Essen*: go for, pitch into; *über Geschenke etc.*: pounce on; **~finden** *v/i.* (*unreg., trennb., hat -ge-*) find one's way here; **~führen** (*trennb., hat -ge-*) **I.** *v/t.* bring here; *was führt Sie her?* what brings you here?; **II.** *v/i.*: *Straße etc.*: lead here; *neben etw.* ~ run *od.* go along-(side) s.th.

Hergang *m*; *mst Sg.* sequence of events; (*Umstände*) circumstances *Pl.*, details *Pl.*; *den* ~ *schildern* describe exactly what happened

hergeben (*unreg., trennb., hat -ge-*) **I.** *v/t.* **1.** (*zurückgeben*) give (*od.* hand) back; (*weggeben*) give away; *gib her!* give it to me, hand it over; *gib mal her!* (*lass mich mal sehen*) let me have a look; *ich gebe es nicht gerne her* I don't like to part with it; **2.** *s-n Namen* ~ *für od. zu* associate o.s. with; **3.** *fig.*: *e-e Menge od. viel* ~ be pretty good *umg.*, *weitS.* be well worth the effort; *es gibt nichts od. wenig her* it's not much use; (*lohnt sich nicht*) it's not worth it; *Buch, Thema etc.*: there isn't much to it; *schreien, was die Stimme hergibt* shout at the top of one's voice; *sie lief, was die Beine hergaben* she ran as fast as her legs would carry her; **II.** *v/refl.*: *sich für od. zu etw.* ~ get involved in s.th.; *stärker*: stoop to s.th.; *sich dazu* ~ *zu* (+ *Inf.*) lower o.s. to (+ *Inf.*), stoop to (+ *Ger.*); *dazu gebe ich mich nicht her auch* I'm not going to have anything to do with that (*od.* be a party to that)

hergehen *v/i.* (*unreg., trennb., ist -ge-*) **1.** *hinter j-m od. etw.* ~ follow, walk behind; *vor j-m od. etw.* ~ walk in front (*od.* ahead) of; *neben j-m od. etw.* ~ walk beside *od.* alongside; **2.** *unpers.*; *umg.*: *es ging heiß od.* **hoch her** things got pretty lively; *Party*: they were having a great time; *hier geht es hoch her* there's plenty of action (*od.* plenty going on) around here; *es ging laut/ lustig her* things got pretty noisy / it

was great fun; **3.** *südd., österr.* (*herkommen*) come here; ~ *und etw. tun* *umg.*, *ohne Zögern, Skrupel etc.*: go and do s.th.

hergeholt I. *P.P.* → *herholen*; **II.** *Adj.*: *weit* ~ far-fetched

her|gehören *v/i.* (*trennb., hat*) → *hierher*; **~gelaufen I.** *P.P.* → *herlaufen*; **II.** *Adj. pej.*: *jeder* ~*e Kerl* any (old) Tom, Dick or Harry; *du kannst doch nicht diesen* ~*en Kerl heiraten* you can't possibly marry this Johnny--come-lately that no one knows anything about; **~haben** *v/t.* (*unreg., trennb., hat -ge-*); *umg.*: *wo hast du das her?* where did you get that (from)?; *diese Neuigkeit*: where did you hear that?; **~halten** (*unreg., trennb., hat -ge-*) **I.** *v/t.* hold out; **II.** *v/i.*: ~ *müssen* have to take the rap (*für* for) *umg.*; ~ *müssen als* be called on to serve as (*j-m* for s.o.); *das wird als Ersatz* ~ *müssen* it will have to do as a substitute; **~holen** *v/t.* (*trennb., hat -ge-*) fetch, get; ~ *lassen* send for; → *hergeholt*; **~hören** *v/i.* (*trennb., hat -ge-*) listen; *alle(s) mal* ~*!* listen, everyone

Hering *m*; *-s, -e* **1.** *Zool.* herring; *wie die* ~*e zusammengedrängt* packed like sardines; **2.** (*Zeltpflock*) tent peg; **3.** *umg. fig.* (*dünner Mensch*) match-stick, beanpole

Herings|milch *f Zool.* herring milt; **~salat** *m Gastr.* pickled herring salad; **~topf** *m Gastr.* pickled herring(s) in sour cream

herinnen *Adv. südd., österr.* in here

her|jagen (*trennb.*) **I.** *v/i.* (*ist herge-jagt*): ~ *hinter j-m*: chase after; *hinter e-r Sache*: *auch* try to chase up; **II.** *v/t.* (*hat*): *ein Tier etc. vor sich* (*Dat.*) ~ drive an animal *etc.* along in front of one; **~kommen** *v/i.* (*unreg., trennb., ist -ge-*) **1.** come (here); (*sich nähern*) approach; *komm mal her* (*zu mir*)*!* come (over) here (to me); **2.** ~ *von auch fig.* come from; *wo kommt er her?* where does he come from?; *ich weiß nicht, wo der Fleck / m-e Unruhe herkommt* I don't know what caused the stain / why I feel uneasy, I don't know where the stain / my uneasiness came from

herkömmlich *Adj.* (*gebräuchlich, üblich*) customary; *Brauch*: traditional; *Waffen etc.*: conventional

herkriegen *v/t.* (*trennb., hat -ge-*); *umg.* get (hold of)

Herkules *m*; *-, -se*; *Myth. und fig.* Hercules; **~arbeit** *f fig.* Herculean task, labo(u)r of Hercules; **~säulen** *Pl. Geog. hist.* Pillars of Hercules

herkulisch *Adj.* Herculean

Herkunft *f*; *-, Herkünfte* origin; *e-r Person*: *auch* background; *e-s Wortes*: origin, derivation; *der* ~ *nach* by origin; *er ist chinesischer* ~ he's of Chinese origin (*od.* descent); *es ist kanadischer* ~ it comes from Canada

Herkunfts|angabe *f*, **~bezeichnung** *f Wirts.* mark of origin; **~land** *n Wirts.* country of origin; **~ort** *m Wirts.* place of origin

her|laufen *v/i.* (*unreg., trennb., ist -ge-*) **1.** *schnell*: run (here); *umg.* walk (here); **2.** *hinter j-m od. etw.* ~ run (*od.* chase) after; *neben/vor j-m od. etw.* ~ run along beside / ahead of; → *herge-laufen*; **~leiern** *v/t. pej.* reel off; **~leihen** *v/t.* (*unreg., trennb., hat -ge-*) *umg.* lend; *ich leihe nichts her* I never lend anything

herleiten (*trennb., hat -ge-*) **I.** *v/t.* (*ab-*

leiten) derive (*von* from); *logisch*: deduce (from), infer (from); **II.** *v/refl.*: *sich* ~ *von* derive (*od.* be derived) from; go back to; *genealogisch*: descend (*od.* be descended) from; **Herleitung** *f e-s Wortes etc.*: derivation

hermachen (*trennb., hat -ge-*); *umg.* **I.** *v/refl.*: *sich* ~ *über* (+ *Akk.*) *über Arbeit, Buch etc.*: tackle, get one's teeth (*Brit. auch* get stuck) into; *über Essen etc.*: go for, pitch into; *über j-n*: have a (real) go at, *Am.* tear into; → *auch herfallen*; **II.** *v/i.* **1.** *etwas/viel* ~ be quite/very impressive; *Kleidung etc.*: look good/great; *es macht nicht viel od. nichts her* it's not up to much, it's not much to look at; **2.** *Aufheben*: *viel* ~ *von* make a lot of fuss about, make a big thing of; *viel/nichts von sich* (*Dat.*) ~ be full of oneself / be modest

Hermaphrodit *m*; *-en, -en*; *Bio., Med.* hermaphrodite

Hermelin[1] *n*; *-s, -e*; *Zool.* ermine, stoat

Hermelin[2] *m*; *-s, -e Pelz*: ermine

Hermeneutik *f*; *-, kein Pl.* hermeneutics *Pl.* (*V. im Sg.*); **hermeneutisch** *Adj.* hermeneutic

Hermesbürgschaft *f Wirts.* government export credit guarantee

hermetisch I. *Adj.* hermetic, airtight; **II.** *Adv.* hermetically; ~ *abgeschlossen od. abgeriegelt* hermetically sealed

hermüssen *v/i.* (*unreg., trennb., hat -ge-*); *umg.* have to come (here); *das Buch muss her!* we must get hold of (*od.* get our hands on) that book; *da muss ein Fachmann her!* what we *etc.* need is an expert!

hernach *Adv. Dial.* (*danach*) afterwards; (*später*) later (on)

hernehmen *v/t.* (*unreg., trennb., hat -ge-*) **1.** get (*von* from), find; **2.** *umg.* (*stark fordern*) put s.o. through the mill; **3.** *umg.* (*schelten*) give s.o. a good talking-to; (*verprügeln*) give s.o. a good going over; *den muss ich mir mal* ~ I'll have to have a little word with him; **4.** *Dial.* (*nehmen, benutzen*) use, take (*für od. zu* for *od.* to); ~ *als* use (*od.* take) as

Hernie *f*; *-, -n* **1.** *Med.* hernia (*Pl.* hernias *od.* herniae), rupture; **2.** *Bot.* club root

hernieder *Adv. geh.* down

hernieder... *im Verb, geh.* → *herunter...*

heroben *Adv. südd., österr.* up here

Heroe *m*; *-n, -n*; *geh.* hero

Heroin[1] *n*; *-s, kein Pl.* heroin; ~ *spritzen* shoot heroin

Heroin[2] *f*; *-, -nen*, **Heroine** *f*; *-, -n*; *bes. Theat.* heroine

Heroinsucht *f* heroin addiction; **heroinsüchtig** *Adj.* addicted to heroin; **Heroinsüchtige** *m, f* heroin addict; **Herointote** *m, f* heroin victim; *die Zahl der* ~*n auch* the number of heroin deaths

heroisch *geh.* **I.** *Adj.* heroic; **II.** *Adv.* heroically; **heroisieren** *v/t. geh.* make a hero of; **Heroismus** *m*; *-, kein Pl.*; *geh.* heroism

Herold *m*; *-(e)s, -e*; *hist.* herald; *fig.* (*Vorbote*) *auch* harbinger

Heros *m*; *-, Heroen*; *Myth. und fig.* hero

Herpes *m*; *-, Herpetes, mst Sg.*; *Med.* herpes; **~bläschen** *n* herpes blister

Herr *m*; *-n, -en* **1.** (*Mann*) *auch* vornehmer *etc.*: gentleman; *als Tanzpartner etc. e-r Frau*: partner; ~*en Toilette*:

Gentlemen, Men; *Sport* men; *bei den ~en Sport* in the men's event; *Alte ~en Sport* veterans; *Studentenverbindung*: old members; *mein Alter* ~ *umg. hum.* my old man; *ein feiner od. sauberer* ~ *iro.* a fine one; *die ~en der Schöpfung umg. hum.* the lords of creation; *den (großen od. feinen) ~n spielen* play lord of the manor, act the big shot *umg.*; **2.** *vor Namen*: Mr, *Am.* Mr.; *vor Titeln: mst nicht übersetzt; die ~en N. und M.* Messrs N and M; ~ *Doktor/ Professor etc.* doctor/professor *etc.*; ~ *Präsident!* Mr (*od.* Mr.) Chairman; *im Unterhaus*: Mr (*od.* Mr.) Speaker; *zum Präsidenten der USA*: Mr. President; *der* ~ *Präsident* the Chairman *etc.*; *meine (Damen und) ~en!* (ladies and) gentlemen!; *Sehr geehrter* ~ *N. in Briefen*: Dear Sir; *vertraulicher*: Dear Mr (*od.* Mr.) N; *Ihr* ~ *Vater geh.* your father; ~ *Ober, ein Bier bitte!* waiter, a beer, please; *bitte schön, der ~! beim Servieren*: here you are, sir; *umg. hum. od. iro.* for you, kind sir; *'meine ~en! umg. als Ausruf*: would you believe it; **3.** (*Gebieter*) master (*auch e-s Hundes*); *bes. Adliger*: lord; (*Herrscher*) ruler; *mein* ~ *und Gebieter* my lord and master; *s-n ~n und Meister finden in* (+ *Dat.*) meet one's match in; *aus aller ~en Länder* from the four corners of the earth; *sein eigener* ~ *sein* be one's own boss; ~ *im eigenen Hause sein* be master (*od.* have the say) in one's own house; ~ *der Lage sein* have everything under control, be master of the situation; ~ *über Leben und Tod sein* have power over life and death; ~ *werden* (+ *Gen.*) *od. über* (+ *Akk.*) get *s.th.* under control; *Problemen*: get on top of; *e-s Gegners*: get the upper hand over; *s-r Gefühle* ~ *werden* get a grip of oneself; *nicht mehr* ~ *s-r selbst sein* be unable to contain oneself; *wie der* ~, *so's Gscherr Sprichw.* like master, like man; **4.** *der* ~ (*Gott, Christus*) Lord; *Gott, der* ~ the Lord God; *der* ~ *Jesus* the Lord Jesus; *im Jahre des* ~*n* in the year of our Lord; *Brüder und Schwestern im ~n* in the Lord; *er ist ein großer Angeber etc. vor dem ~n umg.* he's a mighty show-off *etc.* before the Lord; ~ *des Himmels! umg.* Lord above!, God in heaven!

Herrchen *n e-s Hundes*: master; *komm zu ~!* come to Daddy (*od.* Papa)!

Herren|abend *m* stag party; **~anzug** *m* man's suit; **~artikel** *Pl.* men's accessories; **~ausstatter** *m* men's outfitter (*Am.* clothier), *Am. auch* haberdasher *altm.*; **~begleitung** *f*: *in* ~ accompanied by a man, in male company, with a man; **~bekanntschaft** *f* **1.** (*Bekannter*) male acquaintance, man friend; *euph.* gentleman friend; **2.** *e-e* ~ *machen* make the acquaintance of a man; **~bekleidung** *f* men's clothing, menswear; **~besuch** *m* male visitor(s *Pl.*); **~doppel** *n Sport, Tennis, Badminton etc.*: men's doubles *Pl.* (*Match*: V. *im Sg.*); **~einzel** *n Sport, Tennis, Badminton etc.*: men's singles *Pl.* (*Match*: V. *im Sg.*); **~fahrrad** *n* men's bicycle; **~friseur** *m* men's hairdresser, barber; (*Geschäft*) men's hairdresser's, barber's, barber('s) shop; *Am.* barbershop; **~gesellschaft** *f* **1.** (*Herrenabend*) stag party; **2.** → *Herrenbegleitung*; **~größe** *f* men's size; **~haus** *n* **1.** manor house; **2.** *hist.* upper house; **~hemd** *n* man's shirt; **~hof** *m* manor; **~hose** *f*: (*e-e*) ~ (a pair of) men's trou-

sers (*Am.* pants *od.* slacks) *Pl.*; **~hut** *m* men's hat; **~jahre** *Pl.* → *Lehrjahr*; **~leben** *n* life of luxury; *ein* ~ *führen* live like a lord

herrenlos *Adj.* abandoned; *Tier*: stray; *~e Güter* unclaimed property *Sg.*

Herren|magazin *n* men's magazine; **~mannschaft** *f Sport* men's team; **~mensch** *m iro. od. rassistisch*: member of the master race; *weitS.* masterful person; **~mode** *f* men's fashion(s *Pl.*); **~oberbekleidung** *f* menswear; **~pilz** *m österr.* (*Steinpilz*) cep, *bes. Am.* porcini; **~rad** *n* men's bike; **~rasse** *f iro. od. rassistisch*: master race; **~reiter** *m Sport* amateur jockey; **~salon** *m* men's hairdresser's, barber's; **~schirm** *m* men's umbrella; **~schneider** *m*, **~schneiderin** *f* men's tailor; **~schuh** *m* man's shoe; **~sitz** *m* **1.** (*Gut*) manor; **2.** *im ~ reiten Reitsport*: ride astride; **~toilette** *f* men's lavatory (*od.* toilet, *Am.* restroom); *Aufschrift*: Gentlemen, Men; **~torte** *f* not very sweet torte with alcohol flavo(u)ring; **~witz** *m* dirty joke

Herrgott *m* God, *the* Lord (God); ~ (*noch mal*)! *umg.* good Lord!

Herrgotts|frühe *f*: *in aller* ~ at the crack of dawn, at an (*od.* some) unearthly hour; **~winkel** *m südd., österr.* corner of a room with a crucifix (*and often other devotional objects*)

herrichten (*trennb., hat -ge-*) **I.** *v/t.* (*bereiten*) get ready; (*ordnen*) tidy up; (*renovieren*) do up; **II.** *v/refl. Dial.* get ready; *fein*: smarten o.s. up, get all spruced up

Herrin *f*; -, -nen **1.** *hist., Anrede*: mistress, lady; **2.** (*Herrscherin*) ruler

herrisch *Adj. Person, Benehmen*: domineering, imperious (*auch Ton*); *stärker*: dictatorial; *Stimme etc.*: commanding; (*hochmütig*) arrogant, overbearing

herrje(mine) *Interj. umg.* jeepers!

herrlich I. *Adj.* wonderful, marvel(l)ous; *Wetter: auch* beautiful, glorious; (*prächtig*) splendid; **II.** *Adv.* marvel(l)ously *etc.*; **Herrlichkeit** *f* **1.** *nur Sg.* magnificence; (*Pracht*) splendo(u)r; *der Landschaft etc.*: (great) beauty; *das war schon die ganze* ~ *umg.* that was it; *morgen ist es vorbei mit der weißen* ~ tomorrow will see the end of the winter wonderland; **2.** **~en** wonders; (*Schätze*) treasures; **3.** *hist., Anrede*: *Ihre/Seine* ~ her ladyship / his lordship

Herrschaft *f* **1.** *nur Sg.* rule (*über + Akk.* over); (*Macht*) power; (*Regierung*) government; *e-s Fürsten*: reign; (*Vorherrschaft*) supremacy; *unter j-s* ~ *fallen/kommen* fall/come under s.o.'s sway; *die* ~ *ausüben od. innehaben über* (+ *Akk.*) exercise (*od.* hold) sovereignty over; **2.** *fig.* (*Kontrolle*) control (*über + Akk.* of); *die* ~ *verlieren über* (+ *Akk.*) lose control of; **3.** *mst Pl.; Personen*: *j-s* ~ *altm.* s.o.'s master and mistress; *ältere* ~*en* senior citizens, seniors *Am. umg.*; *umg. iro.* nobs; *meine od. hohe verehrte etc.* ~*en!* ladies and gentlemen; *was darf ich den* ~*en bringen?* what can I bring you ladies and gentlemen?; *so geht das nicht weiter,* ~*en!* *zu Schulklasse etc.*: ladies and gentlemen, this has got to stop; **4.** *umg.*: ~ (*noch mal*)! damnation!; **herrschaftlich** *Adj. Haus etc.*: manorial; *Rechte*: territorial; (*erstklassig, vornehm*)

grand

Herrschafts|anspruch *m* claim to power (*od.* the throne); *e-n* ~ *geltend machen auf Gebiet*: make a territorial claim (*auf + Akk.* on); *auf Thron*: lay claim to the throne; **~bereich** *m* **1.** sphere of control; **2.** *Gebiet*: territory; *e-n* ~ *form* *f* form (*od.* system) of rule; **~gewalt** *f* authority; **~instrument** *n* instrument of power; **~ordnung** *f* power structure; **~struktur** *f* power structure; **~system** *n* system of rule (*od.* government); **~verhältnisse** *Pl.* power relationships, relationships between rulers and ruled

herrschen *v/i.* **1.** rule (*über + Akk.* over); *Monarch*: reign (over); (*regieren*) govern (*über e-n Staat etc.* a state *etc.*); **2.** *fig. Geld, Gewalt etc.*: rule *s.th. od. s.o.*, be in control (of); ~ *über* (+ *Akk.*) *auch* control; **3.** (*vorhanden sein*) be; (*vorherrschen*) prevail; *Krankheit*: be raging, be rife; *Stille, Schweigen*: reign; (*in Mode sein*) be the fashion; *es herrscht ... oft* there is ...; *bei uns herrscht ...* we have ..., we're having ..., we've got ...; *es herrschte große Hitze* it was very hot; *daran herrscht kein Mangel* there is no lack (*od.* shortage) of that; *es herrschte e-e gute Stimmung* everyone was in good spirits, the general mood was positive; *in den Regalen herrschte Ordnung* everything on the shelves was in its proper place; *in unserem Betrieb herrscht Ordnung* our company is run along orderly lines; *in vielen Betrieben herrscht die Angst vor Entlassungen* the fear of redundancy (*Am.* layoffs *Pl.*) is to be found in many companies

herrschend I. *Part. Präs.* → *herrschen*; **II.** *Adj.* **1.** ruling, in power; *die Herrschenden* the rulers, those in power; **2.** (*vorherrschend*) prevailing, prevalent, current; (*gegenwärtig*) present; *Mode*: current, latest; *nach der ~en Meinung ...* current opinion has it that ...; *unter den ~en Verhältnissen* under the present circumstances, conditions being as (*od.* what) they are

Herrscher *m*; -s, -, **~in** *f*; -, -nen ruler (*über + Akk. od. von* of); (*Monarch*) monarch, sovereign; **~geschlecht** *n* dynasty; **~gewalt** *f* sovereign power; **~haus** *n* **1.** dynasty; **2.** *regierendes*: ruling house

Herrschsucht *f*; *nur Sg.* **1.** lust (*od.* thirst) for power; **2.** *fig.* domineering (*stärker*: tyrannical) nature; **herrschsüchtig** *Adj.* **1.** power-mad, *präd.* on a power trip; **2.** *fig.* domineering; *stärker*: tyrannical

her|rufen (*unreg., trennb., hat -ge-*) **I.** *v/t. hierher*: call (over); **II.** *v/t/i.: hinter j-m* ~ call out after s.o.; **~rühren** *v/i.* (*trennb., hat -ge-*): ~ *von* come (*od.* stem, result, derive) from, be due to; **~sagen** *v/t.* (*trennb., hat -ge-*) recite; (*Gebet, Aufgabe*) say; (*herunterleiern*) reel off; **~schauen** *v/i.* (*trennb., hat -ge-*); *bes. südd., österr.* → *hersehen*; *da schau her!* (*wer hätte das gedacht*) well I never!; **~schenken** *v/t.* (*trennb., hat -ge-*); *umg.* give away; **~schicken** *v/t.* (*trennb., hat -ge-*) **1.** *hierher*: send here (*od.* over); **2.** *hinter j-m* ~ send after s.o.; **~schieben** *v/t.* (*unreg., trennb., hat -ge-*) **1.** *hierher*: push over (here), push this way; **2.** *vor sich* (*Dat.*) ~ push (along); *fig.* keep putting off; **~schleppen** *v/t.* (*trennb., hat -ge-*) **1.** *hierher*: drag *od.* lug over (here); *über größere Entfernung*: drag (*od.* lug) all the way here; **2.** *hinter sich* (*Dat.*) ~ drag along behind here; **~sehen** *v/i.* (*unreg., trennb., hat -ge-*) **1.** *hierher*: look (here *od.* this way); *sie sah zu mir her* she looked in my direction (*od.* over at me); **2.** ~ *hinter* (+ *Dat.*) follow *s.o./s.th.* with one's eyes; **~sein** → **her**

hersetzen (*trennb., hat -ge-*) **I.** *v/t.* put (*od.* place) here; **II.** *v/refl.*: *sich zu j-m* ~ sit (down) next to (*od.* beside) s.o.; *setz dich zu mir her!* come and sit down next to (*od.* beside) me; **III.** *v/i.*: *hinter j-m* ~ go (*od.* run) after s.o., chase (after) s.o.

her|spionieren *v/i.* (*trennb., hat*): *hinter j-m* ~ spy on s.o.; **~stammen** *v/i.* (*trennb., hat -ge-*) **1.** ~ *von* come from; **2.** → **herrühren**

herstellbar *Adj.*: *leicht/schwer* ~ easy/difficult to make *od.* produce; **herstellen** (*trennb., hat -ge-*) **I.** *v/t.* **1.** *hierher*: put here; **2.** (*erzeugen*) produce, make; *industriell*: manufacture; (*bauen*) build; *Chem.* prepare; **3.** (*schaffen, zustande bringen*) establish; (*Kontakt, Verbindung*) make; **II.** *v/refl.* **1.** *hierher*: come and stand over here; *stell dich her zu mir!* come and stand over here (*od.* next to me, beside me); **2.** (*zustande kommen*) come about, be established

Hersteller *m; -s, -,* **~in** *f; -, -nen* **1.** manufacturer; **2.** *im Verlag*: production manager; **~angabe** *f* **1.** (*Nennung des Herstellers*) manufacturer's details *Pl.*; **2.** *mst Pl.*; (*Produktinformation*) product information *Sg.*

Herstellung *f* **1.** *nur Sg.* production; **2.** *nur Sg.*; *von Beziehungen etc.*: establishment; **3.** *mst Sg.*; *Abteilung*: production (department)

Herstellungs|fehler *m* manufacturing fault (*od.* defect); **~kosten** *Pl.* production costs (*od.* cost *Sg.*); (*Selbstkosten*) prime cost *Sg.*; **~land** *n* producer country; (*Ursprungsland*) country of origin; **~preis** *m* production price, cost of manufacture; **~verfahren** *n* manufacturing process

her|tragen *v/t.* (*unreg., trennb., hat -ge-*) **1.** *hierher*: carry here; **2.** *hinter/neben/vor j-m* ~ carry along behind/beside/in front of s.o.; **~trauen** *v/refl.* (*trennb., hat -ge-*) dare to come here; **~treiben** (*unreg., trennb.*) **I.** *v/t.* (*hat hergetrieben*) **1.** *hierher*: bring here; *was treibt dich her?* what brings you here?; **2.** *vor sich* (*Dat.*) ~ drive along (in front of one); *Wind*: blow along; *hinter/neben/vor j-m od. etw.* ~ drive (*Wind*: blow) along behind/beside/in front of s.o. (*od.* s.th.); **II.** *v/i.* (*ist*); *mit der Strömung*: be washed here; *mit dem Wind*: be blown here

Hertz *n; -, -; Phys.* hertz, cycle per second

herüben *Adv. südd., österr.* over here, (over) on this side

herüber *Adv.* (over) here; *über Grenze, Fluss etc.*: across; ~ *und hinüber* to and fro

herüber... *im V. mst ...* over, *...* across; → *auch hinüber...*

herüber|bringen *v/t.* (*unreg., trennb., hat -ge-*) bring over (*od.* [a]round); *über e-e Grenze etc.* ~ take (*od.* carry) across; → **rüberbringen**; **~fahren** (*unreg., trennb.*) **I.** *v/i.* (*ist herübergefahren*) come over (*od.* across) (*über etw.* [*Akk.*] *s.th.*); (*mit*) *Auto*: *auch* drive over (*od.* across); *mit Rad*: ride over

(*od.* across); **II.** *v/t.* (*hat*); (*Auto*) drive over (*od.* across) (*über etw.* [*Akk.*] *s.th.*); (*Personen, Sachen*) bring over (*od.* across); **~holen** *v/t.* (*trennb., hat -ge-*) fetch (over); **~kommen** *v/i.* (*unreg., trennb., ist -ge-*) come over (*od.* round); ~ *über* (+ *Akk.*) *über e-e Straße etc.*: get across; → *rüberkommen*; **~reichen** (*trennb., hat -ge-*) **I.** *v/t.* hand over, pass across (*über etw.* [*Akk.*] *s.th.*); **II.** *v/i. auch Person*: reach (across); *die Schnur etc. reicht nicht herüber* won't reach, isn't long enough; **~retten** *v/t.* (*trennb., hat -ge-*) → *hinüberretten*; **~sehen** *v/i.* (*unreg., trennb., hat -ge-*) *Richtung*: look (*od.* glance) over *od.* across (*zu* to); *über Zaun etc.*: look across (*über* + *Akk.* *s.th.*); *er sah zu mir herüber auch* he looked my way; **~wehen** (*trennb., hat -ge-*) **I.** *v/i. Duft etc.*: waft over (*od.* across) (*zu* to); *Papier etc.*: be blown over (*od.* across); **II.** *v/t.* blow over (*od.* across) (*über etw.* [*Akk.*] *s.th*)

herum *Adv.* **1.** *Richtung, Lage, ziellos od. verstreut*: (a)round, about; *im Bogen, Kreis*: (a)round about, (all) around; *im Kreis* ~ (a)round in a circle; ~ *um* (a)round; *falsch od. verkehrt /richtig* ~ (*nach links statt rechts*) (a)round the wrong/right way, the wrong/right way (a)round; (*Rückseite nach vorn*) back to front, *Am.* backwards / the right way (a)round; (*Oberseite unten*) upside down / the right way up, *Am.* right side up; *links /rechts* ~ (a)round to the left/right; *oben/unten* ~ *fahren*: (a)round the top/bottom; (*nördlich/südlich*) (a)round the northern/southern end; *am Körper*: (a)round the top/bottom; *gleich um die Ecke* ~ just (a)round the corner; *sie ist immer um ihn* ~ she is always around him; *sie fuhr immer im Kreis / um den Platz* ~ she drove round and round in a circle / the square; *er nahm nicht mehr wahr, was um ihn* ~ *vorging* what was going on around him; **2.** *um ... ~* (*ungefähr*) about; in the region of; *er ist um die vierzig* ~ he's about forty, he's fortyish; (*so*) *um zehn Uhr* ~ (at) about ten o'clock; *um Weihnachten* ~ round about Christmas (time); *hier* ~ *muss es sein*: somewhere (*od.* round) here; **3.** (*vorbei*) over; *die Zeit ist* ~ time's up

herum... *im V. mst ...* round, *Am.* around; *siehe auch* **umher...**

herum|albern *v/i.* (*trennb., hat -ge-*) fool around; **~ärgern** *v/refl.* (*trennb., hat -ge-*); *umg.*: *sich* ~ *mit* battle with; *dauernd*: be having a constant battle with; *sich* ~ *müssen mit* be plagued by; **~ballern** *v/i.* (*trennb., hat -ge-*); *umg.* fire in all directions; **~basteln** *v/i.* (*trennb., hat -ge-*); *umg.* tinker around; ~ *an* (+ *Dat.*) tinker *od.* fiddle (around) with; *fig. an Gesetz etc.*: tinker with; **~blättern** *v/i.* (*trennb., hat -ge-*): ~ *in* (+ *Dat.*) leaf through; **~blödeln** *v/i.* (*trennb., hat -ge-*); *umg.* mess (*od.* fool) about (*bes. Am.* around); **~brüllen** *v/i.* (*trennb., hat -ge-*); *umg.* shout one's head off, yell; *was brüllt der so herum?* what's he shouting (his head off) about?; **~bummeln** *v/i.* (*trennb.*); *umg.* **1.** (*ist herumgebummelt*); (*schlendern*) stroll around; (*sich herumtreiben*) gad about (the place); **2.** (*hat*); (*trödeln*) mess around; **~deuteln** (*trennb., hat -ge-*); *umg.* **I.** *v/i.*: ~ *an* (+ *Dat.*) quibble (*od.* split hairs)

over; **II.** *v/t. unpers.*: *daran ist nichts herumzudeuteln* it's perfectly plain; **~doktern** *v/i.* (*trennb., hat -ge-*); *umg.*: ~ *an* (+ *Dat.*) *an Sache, Krankheit*: tinker *od.* fiddle (around) with; *an j-m*: tinker around with, treat *s.o.* like a guinea pig; **~drehen** (*trennb., hat -ge-*) **I.** *v/t. und v/refl.* turn (a)round; (*Schlüssel*) turn; (*Liegendes*) *auch* turn over; *sich im Kreis* ~ turn right (a)round; *fig. bei Diskussion*: go (a)round in a circle; → *Grab*; **II.** *v/i. umg.*: ~ *an* (+ *Dat.*) fiddle about with

herumdrücken (*trennb., hat -ge-*) **I.** *v/refl. umg.* **1.** *sich* ~ hang (a)round (*in* + *Dat.* in); **2.** *sich* ~ *um* try to get out of; *sich um das wahre Problem* ~ (try to) avoid the issue; **II.** *v/i.*: ~ *an* (+ *Dat.*) squeeze; **III.** *v/t.* (*Hebel etc.*) turn

herum|drucksen *v/i.* (*trennb., hat -ge-*); *umg.* hum (*Am.* hem) and haw; **~erzählen** *v/t.* (*trennb., hat*) spread around; **~experimentieren** *v/i.* (*trennb., hat*); *umg.* experiment (*mit* with); *pej.* experiment around (with)

herumfahren (*unreg., trennb.*) *v/i.* **1.** (*ist herumgefahren*) go (*od.* travel) (a)round; (*mit*) *Auto*: drive (a)round; *mit Rad/Schiff*: ride/sail (a)round; *um die Stadt* ~ drive (a)round the outskirts of the town; *in der Stadt* ~ drive around (the) town; *um e-e Ecke* ~ drive (a)round (*od.* turn) a corner; **2.** (*ist*): (*sich schnell umdrehen*) turn (a)round; **3.** (*hat od. ist*): (*sich* [*Dat.*]) *mit den Fingern in den Haaren / mit der Hand im Gesicht* ~ run one's fingers through one's hair / brush at one's face (with one's hand); **II.** *v/t.* (*hat*): *j-n in der Stadt* ~ drive s.o. (a)round the town

herum|fingern *v/i.* (*trennb., hat -ge-*); *umg.*: ~ *an* (+ *Dat.*) fiddle around with; (*betasten*) touch, finger; **~fliegen** (*unreg., trennb.*) **I.** *v/i.* (*ist herumgeflogen*) **1.** fly (a)round (*um etw.* s.th.); **2.** *umg.* (*herumliegen*) lie around (*od.* about); (*herumgeworfen werden*) be thrown around; *ich weiß nicht, wo der Schlüssel wieder herumfliegt* I don't know where the key has got(ten *Am.*) to again; **II.** *v/t.* (*hat*); (*j-n*) fly (a)round; **~fragen** *v/i.* (*trennb., hat -ge-*); *umg.* ask (a)round (*bei* among); **~fuchteln** *v/i.* (*trennb., hat -ge-*); *umg.* gesticulate; *mit etw.* ~ wave *s.th.* around; *drohend*: brandish, wield

herumführen (*trennb., hat -ge-*) **I.** *v/t.* **1.** (*Besucher*) show *s.o.* (a)round (*in der Stadt etc.* the town *etc.*); *um etw.* ~ (*j-n, Tier*) *an Hand, Leine etc.*: lead (a)round s.th.; (*dirigieren*) direct (a)round s.th.; → *Nase*[1] 5; **2.** *e-n Graben etc.* ~ *um* run a ditch *etc.* (a)round; **II.** *v/i. Straße etc.*: ~ *um* go (*od.* run) (a)round; *da führt kein Weg drum herum umg. fig.* there's no getting (a)round it

herum|fuhrwerken *v/i.* (*trennb., hat -ge-*); *umg.* bustle about (*Am. auch* around); *mit etw.* ~ wield s.th. about; **~fummeln** *v/i.* (*trennb., hat -ge-*); *umg.*: ~ *an* (+ *Dat.*) fiddle (*od.* mess) around with; (*herumbasteln*) tinker with; *an Person, Kleidung, ordnend etc.*: fiddle around with; *sexuell*: touch *s.o.* up, *Am.* diddle with; **~gammeln** *v/i.* (*trennb., hat -ge-*); *umg.* loaf around

herumgehen *v/i.* (*unreg., trennb., ist -ge-*) **1.** walk (*od.* go) (a)round (*um j-n/etw.* s.o./s.th.); *im Zimmer etc.* ~

H

walk around the room *etc.*; **2.** (*herumgereicht werden*) be passed (a)round; ~ *lassen* pass *s.th.* (a)round; **3.** (*verlaufen*) *Graben etc.*: run (a)round; **4.** *umg. Zeit*: pass; **5.** *fig.*: *j-m im Kopf* ~ go round and round in one's head

herumgeistern *v/i.* (*trennb., ist -ge-*); *umg.* flit around (*im Haus* the place); *in j-s Kopf* ~ dart about (*bes. Am.* around) in s.o.'s head; *stärker*: haunt s.o.; *in den Köpfen* ~ be on people's minds

herum|hacken *v/i.* (*trennb., hat -ge-*); *umg.*: *auf j-m* ~ pick on s.o., browbeat s.o.; *auf dem Klavier* ~ bang away at the piano; ~**hängen** *v/i.* (*unreg., trennb., hat / südd., österr., schw. ist -ge-*); *umg., auch fig.* hang (a)round (*in + Dat.* in); ~**hantieren** *v/i.* (*trennb., hat*): ~ *mit* fiddle around with; ~**horchen** *v/i.* (*trennb., hat -ge-*); *umg., bes. südd., österr.* keep one's ears open, ask around (*ob* to see whether, in case); ~**irren** *v/i.* (*trennb., ist -ge-*); *umg.* wander around (*od.* about) lost (*od.* like a lost soul); *im Wald* ~ wander around (*od.* about) the forest; ~**kauen** *v/i.* (*trennb., hat -ge-*): ~ *an* (+ *Dat.*) *od. auf* (+ *Dat.*) chew away on; ~**klettern** *v/i.* (*trennb., ist -ge-*): *auf od. in e-m Baum / in den Klippen* ~ climb about in a tree / around the rocks; ~**kommandieren** *v/t.* (*trennb., hat*); *umg.* boss around (*od.* about)

herumkommen *v/i.* (*unreg., trennb., ist -ge-*) **1.** (*auch* ~ *um*) *um Ecke, Kurve etc.*: come (a)round *s.th.*; *umg. aus dem Nachbarhaus*: come (a)round (*od.* over); **2.** *erfolgreich*: *um etw.* ~ get (a)round *s.th.* (*auch fig.*); *viel od. weit* ~ get around; *du kommst um die Tatsachen nicht herum fig.* there's no getting away from the facts; **3.** *fig. Gerücht*: spread

herum|krabbeln *v/i.* (*trennb., hat -ge-*); *umg.* crawl around (*od.* about); ~**kramen** *v/i.* (*trennb., hat -ge-*); *umg.*: ~ *in* (+ *Dat.*) rummage around (*od.* about) in; ~**krebsen** *v/i.* (*trennb., hat -ge-*); *umg.* struggle along; ~**kriechen** *v/i.* (*unreg., trennb., ist -ge-*); *umg.* crawl around (*od.* about)

herumkriegen *v/t.* (*trennb., hat -ge-*); *umg.* **1.** (*j-n*) get (*od.* talk, bring) s.o. (a)round; *j-n dazu* ~ *zu* (+ *Inf.*) get s.o. to (+ *Inf.*), get s.o. round to (+ *Ger.*), talk s.o. into (+ *Ger.*); **2.** (*Zeit*) pass; *wie kriegen wir den Abend / die Stunde herum?* what are we going to do all evening / for the next hour?; **3.** *räumlich*: ~ *um* be able to get *s.th.* (a)round *s.th.*

herum|kritisieren *v/i.* (*trennb., hat*), ~**kritteln** *v/i.* (*trennb., hat -ge-*); *umg.* find fault; ~ *an* (+ *Dat.*) keep finding fault with, pick (*od.* keep picking) holes in; ~**kurven** *v/i.* (*trennb., ist -ge-*); *umg.* cruise around (*in etw.* [*Dat.*] s.th.); ~**kutschieren** (*trennb.*); *umg.* **I.** *v/t.* (*hat herumkutschiert*) cart *s.o.* around (*in etw.* [*Dat.*] s.th.); **II.** *v/i.* (*ist*) drive (*od.* cart people) around (*in etw.* [*Dat.*] s.th.); ~**laufen** *v/i.* (*unreg., trennb., ist -ge-*) **1.** *ziellos*: run (a)round; *um etw.* ~ run (a)round *s.th.*; **2.** *umg.*: *mit kurzen Hosen etc.* ~ go (*od.* run) around in; *mit e-m Schnurrbart* ~ be sporting a m(o)ustache; *so kann ich doch nicht* ~*!* I can't go around looking like this!; *wie läuft der denn herum?* what does he look like!, *Am.* what is he 'wearing?';

~**liegen** *v/i.* (*unreg., trennb., hat / südd., österr., schw. ist -ge-*) **1.** *um etw.* ~ surround; **2.** *umg. pej.* lie around; *faul* ~ laze around (*od.* about); *lass die Wurst nicht draußen* ~ don't leave the sausage lying around (*od.* about) outside; ~**lümmeln** *v/i.* (*trennb., ist -ge-*); *umg.* loll about; ~**lungern** *v/i.* (*trennb., hat od. ist -ge-*); *umg.* hang (a)round

herummachen (*trennb., hat -ge-*); *umg.* **I.** *v/i.* **1.** ~ *an* (+ *Dat.*) (*fingern*) fiddle around with; *sexuell*: carry on with; *fig.* (*nörgeln*) *an j-m*: go on at; *an e-r Sache*: go on about; **2.** (*überlegen*): *mach nicht so lang herum* (*trödel nicht*) stop dawdling; (*entscheide dich*) make up your mind; **II.** *v/t.* (*Band, Schnur, Zaun etc.*) put around (*um etw. s.th.*)

herum|mäkeln *v/i.* (*trennb., hat -ge-*); *umg.* → *herumkritisieren*; ~**meckern** *v/i.* (*trennb., hat -ge-*); *umg.* moan (about everything), keep moaning, whinge; ~**nörgeln** *v/i.* (*trennb., hat -ge-*); *umg.* → *herumkritisieren*; ~**pfuschen** *v/i.* (*trennb., hat -ge-*); *umg.* mess around; ~ *an* (+ *Dat.*) fiddle around with; *unerlaubt*: tamper with; ~**plagen**, ~**quälen** *v/refl.* (*trennb., hat -ge-*); *umg.*: *sich* ~ *mit* struggle with; *stärker*: be plagued by, have a hard time with; *mit Krankheit etc.*: *auch* go around with, try to fight off; ~**rasen** *v/i.* (*trennb., ist -ge-*); *umg.* rush around (like a madman *od.* an idiot); ~**rätseln** *v/i.* (*trennb., hat -ge-*); *umg.* rack one's brains (*an + Dat.* over); *an etw.* (*Dat.*) ~ *auch* try to figure (*od.* work) s.th. out; ~**reden** *v/i.* (*trennb., hat -ge-*); *umg.*: *um etw.* ~ talk (a)round *s.th.*; *darum* ~ beat around (*od.* about) the bush, avoid the issue; → *Brei* 1

herumreichen (*trennb., hat -ge-*) **I.** *v/t. von einem zum andern*: hand (*od.* pass) round; **II.** *v/i. umg.*: (*um j-n/etw.*) ~ *mit Armen*: reach (a)round (s.o./s.th.); *Schnur etc.*: reach round (s.o./s.th.)

herum|reisen *v/i.* (*trennb., ist -ge-*); *umg.* travel around (*in e-m Land etc.* a country *etc.*); ~**reißen** (*unreg., trennb., hat -ge-*) **I.** *v/t.* (*Auto, Pferd*) pull round; (*Steuer*) pull hard over; **II.** *umg.*: ~ *an* (+ *Dat.*) keep pulling; ~**reiten** *v/i.* (*unreg., trennb., ist -ge-*) **1.** *auch ziellos*: ride around (*um etw. s.th.*); **2.** *fig.*: ~ *auf* (+ *Dat.*) harp (*od.* go) on about *s.th.*; ~**rennen** *v/i.* (*unreg., trennb., ist -ge-*); *umg.* → *herumlaufen*; ~**rutschen** *v/i.* (*trennb., ist -ge-*); *umg.*: *auf den Knien* ~ slide around on one's knees; *nervös auf dem Stuhl* ~ shift about nervously in one's seat; ~**scharwenzeln** *v/i.* (*trennb., ist -ge-*); *umg.*: ~ *um* suck up to; ~**schlagen** *v/refl.* (*unreg., trennb., hat -ge-*): *sich* ~ *mit* scuffle with; *fig.* grapple with; ~**schleichen** *v/i.* (*unreg., trennb., ist -ge-*); *umg.* creep around (*od.* about); ~**schleppen** *v/t.* (*trennb., hat -ge-*); *umg.* drag around; *mit sich* ~ lug (*Am. auch* schlep) around with one; *fig.* (*Sorgen etc.*) be troubled by; (*Krankheit etc.*) be going around with; ~**schnüffeln** *v/i.* (*trennb., hat -ge-*); *umg. pej.* snoop around (*in j-s Sachen* in s.o.'s things); ~**schrauben** *v/i.* (*trennb., hat -ge-*); *umg.*: ~ *an* (+ *Dat.*) fiddle about with, tinker with; ~**schreien** *v/i.* (*unreg., trennb., hat -ge-*); *umg.* keep on screaming; (*brül-*

len) keep on shouting; ~**schubsen** *v/t.* (*trennb., hat -ge-*); *umg. pej.* push *s.o.* around; ~**schwänzeln** *v/i.* (*trennb., ist -ge-*); *umg.*: ~ *um* suck up to; ~**schwenken** (*trennb.*) **I.** *v/t.* (*hat herumgeschwenkt*); (*Fahne etc.*) wave around; *das Ruder od. Steuer* ~ change course; *fig.* change tack; **II.** *v/i.* (*ist*) swing (a)round; ~**schwimmen** *v/i.* (*unreg., trennb., ist -ge-*) **1.** *Fisch etc.*: swim around; **2.** ~ *um* swim (a)round; *im Kreis* ~ swim (a)round in a circle

herumschwirren *v/i.* (*unreg., trennb., ist -ge-*) **1.** (*auch* ~ *um*) buzz around; *lautlos*: fly around; ~ *um auch* circle; **2.** *fig. Menschen*: mill around *od.* about (*in + Dat.* in); *einzelne Person*: flit around (the place)

herum sein → *herum* 1, 3

herum|sitzen *v/i.* (*unreg., trennb., hat / südd., österr., schw. ist -ge-*) **1.** *umg.* sit around (doing nothing); **2.** ~ *um* sit (a)round; ~**spazieren** *v/i.* (*trennb., ist*); *umg.* walk around; ~**spielen** *v/i.* (*trennb., hat -ge-*); *umg.* play around (*mit, an* + *Dat.* with); ~**spionieren** *v/i.* (*trennb., hat*); *umg.* snoop around; ~**sprechen** *v/refl.* (*unreg., trennb., hat -ge-*) get around; *es sprach sich herum* auch word got out; ~**springen** *v/i.* (*unreg., trennb., ist -ge-*); *umg.*: *im Garten* ~ romp (a)round the garden; ~**stehen** *v/i.* (*unreg., trennb., hat / südd., österr., schw. ist -ge-*) **1.** ~ *um* stand (a)round; **2.** *umg.* stand (a)round; *Geschirr etc.*: be lying around; *steh mir nicht im Weg herum* don't stand around in my way; ~**stöbern** *v/i.* (*trennb., hat -ge-*); *umg.* poke around; ~ *in* (+ *Dat.*) dig around in; (*herumschnüffeln*) nose around in; ~**stochern** *v/i.* (*trennb., hat -ge-*); *umg.*: ~ *in* (+ *Dat.*) poke around in; *im Essen* ~ pick at one's food; ~**stolzieren** *v/i.* (*trennb., ist*); *umg.* strut around (*in etw.* [*Dat.*] s.th.); ~**stoßen** *v/t.* (*unreg., trennb., hat -ge-*); *umg. auch fig.* push *s.o.* around; ~**streichen** *v/i.* (*unreg., trennb., ist -ge-*), ~**streifen** *v/i.* (*trennb., ist -ge-*) prowl (*in den Straßen* the streets), roam around (*in etw.* [*Dat.*] s.th.); ~**streiten** *v/refl.* (*unreg., trennb., hat -ge-*); *umg.* argue; *ich will mich mit dir nicht* ~ *auch* I don't want to waste time arguing with you; ~**streunen**, ~**stromern** *v/i.* (*trennb., ist -ge-*); *umg. Hund, Kind etc.*: roam around, wander around (*the streets etc.*); ~**suchen** *v/i.* (*trennb., hat -ge-*); *umg.* look (*stärker*: hunt) around (*nach* for); ~**tanzen** *v/i.* (*trennb., ist -ge-*) dance around (*um etw. s.th.*); ~**tappen** *v/i.* (*trennb., ist -ge-*), ~**tasten** *v/i.* (*trennb., hat -ge-*); *umg.* grope (*od.* feel) around (*nach* for); ~**telefonieren** *v/i.* (*trennb., hat*); *umg.* ring (*Am.* call) up all over the place; *den ganzen Tag* ~ spend the whole day on the phone (*od.* ringing [*Am.* calling] people up); ~**toben** (*trennb.*) **1.** (*hat od. ist herumgetobt*) romp around (*im Garten etc.* the garden); **2.** *umg. wütend*: rage about; ~**tollen** *v/i.* (*trennb., ist -ge-*) → *herumtoben*; ~**tragen** *v/t.* (*unreg., trennb., hat -ge-*) **1.** (*mit sich*) ~ carry (a)round; **2.** *fig.* (*Nachrichten*) spread; *mit sich* ~ (*Kummer etc.*) nurse; ~**trampeln** *v/i.* (*trennb., hat -ge-*); *umg. pej.* **1.** trample around (*auf + Dat.* on); *laut*: stamp around (on); **2.** *fig.*: ~ *auf j-s Gefühlen etc.*: trample on; *auf j-m*: treat *s.o.* like a doormat

herumtreiben v/refl. (unreg., trennb., hat -ge-); umg. pej. roam around (**in etw.** [Dat.] s.th.); in Lokalen etc.: hang out (in); **sich** (**mit j-m**) ~ (gammeln) hang around (od. about) (with s.o.); **wo hast du dich wieder herumgetrieben?** what have you been up to then?; **Herumtreiber** m, **Herumtreiberin** f umg. pej. loafer; (Vagabund) tramp

herum|trödeln v/i. (trennb., hat -ge-); umg. dawdle (**mit** over); ~**turnen** v/i. (trennb., ist -ge-); umg. Kinder, Affen etc.: clamber about; ~**wälzen** (trennb., hat -ge-) **I.** v/t. turn (od. roll) over; **II.** v/refl. turn (a)round; schlaflos: toss and turn; ~**wandern** v/i. (trennb., ist -ge-) wander (a)round (**in etw.** [Dat.] s.th.)

herumwerfen (unreg., trennb., hat -ge-) **I.** v/t. **1.** umg. achtlos: throw (od. toss) around; **2.** schnell: (Kopf) turn quickly; (Steuer etc.) pull (a)round quickly; **II.** v/refl. schnell: roll over quickly; im Schlaf: toss and turn; **III.** v/i. umg.: ~ **mit** (Geld) throw about; (Worten) bandy about

herum|wickeln v/t. (trennb., hat -ge-) wrap (Schnur: tie) (a)round (**um etw.** s.th.); ~**wirbeln** (trennb.) v/t. (hat herumgewirbelt) und v/i. (ist) spin od. whirl (s.o.) (a)round; ~**wühlen** v/i. (trennb., hat -ge-) **1.** rummage (**in** + Dat. [around] in); **2.** fig. in j-s Vergangenheit etc.: dig around (in); ~**wurs(ch)teln** v/i. (trennb., hat -ge-); umg. pej. mess around (**an** + Dat. with); ~**zeigen** v/t. (trennb., hat -ge-); umg. show (s.o.); ~**zerren** (trennb., hat -ge-); umg. **I.** v/t.: (**mit sich**) ~ drag (a)round; **II.** v/i.: ~ **an** (+ Dat.) tug at

herumziehen (unreg., trennb.) **I.** v/t. (hat herumgezogen) **1.** umg.: (**mit sich**) ~ drag around; **2.** ~ **um** (Linie) draw (a)round; (Zaun, Mauer) put up (a)round, surround s.th. with; **II.** v/i. (ist) **1.** umg. wander about (bes. Am. around); ~ **mit** fig. hang around with; **2.** ~ **um** go around; **III.** v/refl.: **sich** ~ **um** Zaun etc.: go around; **herumziehend I.** Part. Präs. → **herumziehen**; **II.** Adj. umg., Volk: nomadic; Händler: itinerant; ~**er Musikant** wandering minstrel

herunten Adv. südd., österr. down here

herunter Adv. **1.** down; **die Treppe** ~ down the stairs, downstairs; **den Fluss** ~ downriver; **die Straße** ~ down the street; **vom Himmel** ~ down from the sky; ~ **damit!** mit Tablette: swallow (od. down with) it!; mit Kleidung: take it off!; ~ **mit dir!** get down!, down with you!; ~ **vom Bett!** get off the bed!; **2.** fig.: ~ **sein** gesundheitlich, auch Betrieb etc.: be run-down; **er ist mit den Nerven völlig** ~ his nerves are shot

herunter... im V. → auch herab..., hinunter..., runter...

herunter|bekommen v/t. (unreg., trennb., hat); umg. **1.** get s.th. down; **2.** (wegbekommen) get s.th. off; **3. ich bekomm's nicht herunter** (Essen etc.) I can't eat (od. drink) it, I can't get it down; **keinen Bissen** ~ not be able to eat a thing; ~**beten** v/t. (trennb., hat -ge-); umg. reel off, rattle off; ~**beugen** v/refl. (trennb., hat -ge-): **sich** ~ **zu** bend down to; ~**blicken** v/i. (trennb., hat -ge-) look down (**auf** +Akk. od. **zu** at); ~**brennen** v/i. (unreg., trennb.) **1.** (hat heruntergebrannt): **die Sonne brannte heiß vom Himmel / auf uns herunter** the sun was blazing down from the sky / on us; **2.** Kerze,

Feuer: burn down; **bis auf die Grundmauern** od. **völlig** ~ Haus: burn down to the ground; ~**bringen** v/t. (unreg., trennb., hat -ge-) **1.** bring down (auch fig. Preise, Temperatur etc.); (begleiten) bring down; **2.** umg. → **herunterbekommen**; **3.** umg. fig. (j-n, Wirtschaft etc.) ruin; ~**drücken** v/t. (trennb., hat -ge-) **1.** press down; (Taste) **2.** fig. (Löhne, Preise) bring (stärker: force) down

herunterfahren (unreg., trennb.) **I.** v/i. (ist heruntergefahren) come down; (mit) Auto: auch drive down; mit Rad: ride down; **II.** v/t. (hat) **1.** (Personen, Waren) bring down; (Wagen) drive down; **2.** fig. (Kapazität, Leistung) scale down; (Reaktor) (schließen) shut down; (Leistung reduzieren) scale down; EDV (Computer, Programm) shut down

herunter|fallen v/i. (unreg., trennb., ist -ge-) fall (down); ~ **von** fall (od. drop) off s.th.; **die Treppe** ~ fall down the stairs/steps; **fall nicht herunter!** mind (Am. be careful) you don't fall; **der Teller ist mir heruntergefallen** I dropped the plate; **etw.** ~ **lassen** drop s.th.; ~**fließen** v/i. (unreg., trennb., ist -ge-) flow down

heruntergehen v/i. (unreg., trennb., ist -ge-) **1.** go down; Person: auch walk down; **2.** Weg etc.: go down (**zu** to); **3.** umg. (herunterkommen) vom Bett etc.: get off (**von etw.** s.th.); **4.** umg. (mit) Flugzeug: descend; **mit dem Kopf** ~ bend down; **5.** umg. fig. Temperatur etc.: go down, drop (**bis auf** + Akk. to); Preise: auch fall; ~ **mit den Preisen, der Geschwindigkeit** etc.: reduce, lower s.th.

heruntergekommen I. P.P. → **herunterkommen**; **II.** Adj. **1.** Person: (schäbig) dowdy, down-at-heel, scruffy; sittlich: dissolute; gesundheitlich: in bad shape; **2.** Bauernhof etc.: run-down, neglected; (verfallen) dilapidated; Betrieb etc.: run-down; ~ **sein** Haus, Betrieb etc.: auch be going to rack and ruin

herunter|handeln v/t. (trennb., hat -ge-) (Preis, j-n) beat down (**auf** + Akk. to); **e-e Summe um ...** ~ get ... knocked off (**vom Preis** the price); **etw. um 20 Euro** ~ get 20 euros knocked off s.th., (manage to) get s.th. 20 euros cheaper; ~**hängen** v/i. (unreg., trennb., hat / südd., österr., schw. ist -ge-) hang down; baumelnd: dangle (**von** from); **die Beine/Flügel** ~ **lassen** let one's legs dangle / wings hang down

herunterholen v/t. (trennb., hat -ge-) **1.** fetch (od. get) down (**von** from); **2.** umg. (Flieger, Vogel) (abschießen) bring (od. shoot) down; **3.** umg. fig.: **sie ist so begeistert davon, wie können wir sie da bloß wieder** ~? she is so enthusiastic about it, how on earth can we get her feet back on the ground?; **4.** vulg. → **runterholen**

herunter|klappen v/t. (trennb., hat -ge-); (Kragen) turn down; (Sitz) fold down; (Deckel) close; ~**klettern** v/i. (trennb., ist -ge-) climb down (**von** from)

herunterkommen v/i. (unreg., trennb., ist -ge-) **1.** come down; kletternd etc.: get down (**von** from); **die Treppe** ~ auch come downstairs; ~ **von** e-m Bett etc.: auch get off; **2.** umg. fig. go downhill; stärker, Betrieb, Wirtschaft etc.: go to rack and ruin; Person, wirt-

schaftlich: come down in the world; sittlich: go to the dogs, sink low; gesundheitlich: get run down; ~ → **heruntergekommen**; **3.** umg. fig.: **vom Alkohol** ~ give up alcohol, stop drinking, get on the wagon; **von den Drogen** ~ give up drugs, kick the habit; **ach, komm herunter von dem Trip!** (sei nicht so naiv etc.) oh, open your eyes!

herunter|kriegen v/t. → **herunterbekommen**; ~**kurbeln** v/t. (trennb., hat -ge-) wind down; ~**laden** v/t. (unreg., trennb., hat -ge-); EDV download (**aus** od. **von** off, from; **auf** + Akk. onto); ~**lassen** v/t. (unreg., trennb., hat -ge-) **1.** let down, lower (**an** + Dat. on); (Hose) drop; **2.** umg.: **bitte lass mich herunter** please let me come down; ~**laufen** v/i. (unreg., trennb., ist -ge-) **1.** run down; umg. go (od. walk down) (+ Akk. s.th.); **2.** Wasser etc.: run down (**an der Wand** etc. the wall etc.); ~**leiern** v/t. (trennb., hat -ge-) rattle off, reel off

heruntermachen v/t. (trennb., hat -ge-); umg. **1.** fig. (schlecht machen) run down, pull to pieces; (tadeln) haul over the coals; **2.** (entfernen) remove; **3.** niedriger: lower; (Kragen) turn down

herunter|nehmen v/t. (unreg., trennb., hat -ge-) take down; (Arme) lower; ~ **von** take down from, take off; ~**putzen** v/t. (trennb., hat -ge-); umg.: **j-n** ~ tear a strip off s.o., haul (od. rake) s.o. over the coals; ~**rasseln** (trennb.); umg. **I.** v/i. (ist heruntergerasselt); Rollladen etc.: come rattling down; **II.** v/t. (hat) rattle off; ~**reichen** (trennb., hat -ge-) **I.** v/i. umg. reach down (**bis** to, as far as); **II.** v/t. hand (od. pass) s.th. down

herunterreißen v/t. (unreg., trennb., hat -ge-) **1.** nach unten: pull down (**von** from, off); **2.** (Tapete) pull off; (Plakat) tear down; **3.** umg. fig.: **er hat seinen Vortrag heruntergerissen** he just went through the motions when he gave his talk; **4.** umg. fig. (Zeit) get through; **5.** fig. → **heruntermachen** 1

herunter|rinnen v/i. (unreg., trennb., ist -ge-) run down; ~**rollen** (trennb.) **I.** v/i. (ist heruntergerollt) roll down; **vom Tisch** ~ roll off the table; **II.** v/t. (hat) roll down (auch umg. Ärmel); ~**rutschen** v/i. (trennb., ist -ge-) slide (od. slip) down; → **Buckel** 2; ~**schalten** v/i. (trennb., hat -ge-); Mot. change (Am. shift) down, Am. auch downshift; ~**schlagen** v/t. (unreg., trennb., hat -ge-) **1.** knock down; Kastanien etc. vom Baum ~ knock chestnuts etc. down from the tree; **2.** (Kragen etc.) turn down; ~**schlingen** v/t. (unreg., trennb., hat -ge-); umg. bolt (od. wolf) down; ~**schlucken** v/t. (trennb., hat -ge-) swallow (auch fig.); ~**schneiden** v/t. (unreg., trennb., hat -ge-); umg.: (**sich** [Dat.]) **etwas** ~ vom Schinken, Brot etc. cut off (od. cut o.s.) a piece (Scheibe: slice) of ham, bread etc.; ~**schrauben** v/t. **1.** turn down; **2.** fig. (Erwartungen etc.) lower

herunter sein → **herunter** 2

herunter|setzen v/t. (trennb., hat -ge-) → **herabsetzen** 1; ~**spielen** v/t. (trennb., hat -ge-); umg. **1.** Mus. rattle off, rush through; **2.** fig. (bagatellisieren) play down; ~**springen** v/i. (unreg., trennb., ist -ge-) **1.** jump down; **2.** umg.: **die Treppe** ~ rush down the stairs (od. steps); ~**spülen** v/t. (trennb., hat -ge-) **1.** wash off (**von**

s.th.), wash down (from); **2.** *fig.*: **~n Kummer** (**mit Alkohol**) **~** drown one's sorrows in drink; **~steigen** *v/i.* (*unreg., trennb., ist -ge-*) climb down (**von** off, from); **die Treppe ~** *auch* come down the stairs, come downstairs; **~stoßen** *v/t.* (*unreg., trennb., hat -ge-*) knock down (**von** off, from); **~stufen** *v/t.* (*trennb., hat -ge-*) downgrade

herunterstürzen (*trennb.*) **I.** *v/i.* (*ist heruntergestürzt*) **1.** (*fallen*) fall down; *heftig*: come crashing down, crash to the floor (*od.* ground); *fig.* plummet; **~ von** fall off; **vom Fenster**: fall out of; **2.** *umg.* (*heruntereilen*) rush (*od.* run) down(stairs *od.* down the stairs); **II.** *v/t.* (*hat*); *umg.* (*Bier etc.*) knock (*Am. auch* toss) back; (*Kaffee etc.*) gulp down

herunter|tragen *v/t.* (*unreg., trennb., hat -ge-*) carry *od.* take down(stairs); **~werfen** *v/t.* (*unreg., trennb., hat -ge-*) **1.** *absichtlich*: throw down (**von** from); **2.** *umg. unabsichtlich*: drop; (*umstoßen*) knock down; **~wirtschaften** *v/t.* (*trennb., hat -ge-*); *umg.* mismanage, run down; **~würgen** *v/t.* (*trennb., hat -ge-*); *umg.* choke (*od.* force) down

herunterziehen (*unreg., trennb.*) **I.** *v/t.* (*hat heruntergezogen*) **1.** pull down (**von** from; **zu sich** to one); (*Bettbezug, Tischdecke*) pull off; **die Mundwinkel ~** draw down the corners of one's mouth; **2.** *fig. pej.* drag *s.o.* down (**auf niedrigeres Niveau** to); **j-n zu sich ~** drag s.o. down to one's own level; **II.** *v/i.* (*ist*) move down; **III.** *v/refl.* (*hat*): **der Wald/Weg zieht sich bis zum Tal herunter** the forest/path reaches / runs down to the valley

hervor *Adv. geh.* out; **~ aus** out of; **hinter/unter** (+ *Dat.*) **~** from behind/under …

hervor… *im V. mst* out

hervor|brechen *v/i.* (*unreg., trennb., ist -ge-*) **1.** burst out (*od.* through) (**aus etw.** s.th.); *Mil.* rush forward; **2.** *fig. Hass, Zorn etc.*: burst out; **~bringen** *v/t.* (*unreg., trennb., hat -ge-*) produce (*auch Nachkommen*); (*schaffen*) create; (*bewirken*) cause, give rise to; (*Worte*) utter; **~dringen** *v/i.* (*unreg., trennb., ist -ge-*); *geh.* come out (**von** of); **~ aus** *Geräusche etc.*: come (*od.* penetrate) from

hervorgehen *v/i.* (*unreg., trennb., ist -ge-*): **~ aus** (*stammen aus*) come (*od.* emerge) from; (*sich entwickeln aus*) develop (*od.* arise) from; (*sich als Folge ergeben aus*) result from; **als Sieger ~ aus** emerge victorious from; **aus i-r Ehe sind keine Kinder hervorgegangen** the marriage did not produce any children; **daraus geht hervor, dass …** it follows that, this shows that …; **aus dem Brief geht nicht hervor, ob …** the letter doesn't indicate whether …; **wie aus der Umfrage hervorgeht** the survey shows that …

hervorgucken *v/i.* (*trennb., hat -ge-*); *umg.* → **hervorschauen**

hervorheben (*unreg., trennb., hat -ge-*); *fig.* **I.** *v/t.* emphasize, underline, stress; (*Schrift etc.*) set off, bring out; **lobend ~** single out for praise; **II.** *v/refl.* stand out (**aus** against); **Hervorhebung** *f* emphasis; **unter** (**besonderer**) **~** (+ *Gen.*) with (special) emphasis on

hervor|holen *v/t.* (*trennb., hat -ge-*) produce; take (*od.* pull) out (**aus** of); **~kehren** *v/t.* (*trennb., hat -ge-*); *geh.* → **herauskehren** 2; **~kommen** *v/i.* (*unreg., trennb., ist -ge-*) come out

(*hinter/unter* + *Dat.* from behind/under); (*auftauchen*) appear, emerge (**aus** from); **~kramen** *v/t.* (*trennb., hat -ge-*); *umg.* **1.** fish out, dig up; **2.** *fig.* (*Erinnerungen etc.*) dredge up; **~locken** *v/t.* (*trennb., hat -ge-*) lure out

hervorquellen *v/i.* (*unreg., trennb., ist -ge-*) **1.** *Flüssigkeit etc.*: well up (**aus** out of, from); *stärker*: gush out (of); **~ aus** *auch* well (*od.* gush) from; **2.** *Rauch etc.*: pour (**aus** from); **3.** *Augen, Bauch etc.*: bulge, protrude

hervorragen *v/i.* (*trennb., hat -ge-*) **1.** jut (*od.* stick) out (**aus** of; **hinter/unter** + *Dat.* from behind/under); project (from); **~ aus** (*sich erheben*) rise (*od.* tower) above; **2.** *fig.* stand out (**durch** by); **hervorragend I.** *Part. Präs.* → **hervorragen**; **II.** *Adj.* excellent, outstanding, first-rate; **sie hat Hervorragendes geleistet** she has achieved some outstanding things; **III.** *Adv.* extremely well, outstandingly

hervorrufen *v/t.* (*unreg., trennb., hat -ge-*) **1.** *fig.* (*bewirken*) cause, give rise to; (*Ärger, Protest etc.*) provoke; (*Eindruck*) create; **bei j-m Gelächter/ e-e Reaktion** etc. **~** make s.o. laugh/react etc.; **2.** *Theat.* call for

hervor|schauen *v/i.* (*unreg., trennb., hat -ge-*); *bes. südd., österr. auch* (*sichtbar sein*) peep out (**hinter, unter** + *Dat.* of); **hinter e-m Baum** etc. **~** peep from behind a tree etc.

hervorspringen *v/i.* (*unreg., trennb., ist -ge-*) **1.** jump out (**aus** of); **das Kind sprang hinter dem Auto hervor auf die Fahrbahn** the child jumped out from behind the car into the road; **2.** *Felsen, Kinn*: jut out; **~der Felsen** protruding rock; **~des Kinn / ~de Nase** prominent chin/nose; **sie hat ein Kinn** *auch* her chin juts out; **3.** *fig.* → **hervorstechen**

hervorstechen *v/i.* (*unreg., trennb., hat -ge-*); *fig.* stand out (**aus** against); *Kennzeichen*: be prominent; (*auffallen*) be striking; **hervorstechend I.** *Part. Präs.* → **hervorstechen**; **II.** *Adj.* prominent; (*auffallend*) striking; (*vorherrschend*) (pre)dominant

hervor|stehen *v/i.* (*unreg., trennb., hat / südd., österr., schw. ist -ge-*) jut (*od.* stick) out; *Augen*: protrude, bulge; *Ohren*: stick out; **~de Backenknochen** high cheekbones; **~de Zähne** buck teeth; **~suchen** *v/t.* (*trennb., hat -ge-*) look out

hervortreten *v/i.* (*unreg., trennb., ist -ge-*) **1.** come out (**aus** of; **hinter** + *Dat.* from behind); **aus e-m Versteck** etc.: *auch* emerge (from); **2.** *fig. Augen*: bulge, protrude; (*sich abheben*) stand out; *Farben*: stand out, be striking; (*in Erscheinung treten*) emerge; *Person*: make s.o. a name (**als** as); **hervortretend I.** *Part. Präs.* → **hervortreten**; **II.** *Adj.* striking, prominent; *Augen*: protruding

hervor|tun *v/refl.* (*unreg., trennb., hat -ge-*) **1.** distinguish o.s.; **2.** (*angeben*) show off; **sich mit etw. ~** *auch* flaunt s.th.; **~wagen** *v/refl.* (*trennb., hat -ge-*) venture out, dare to appear; **~zaubern** *v/t.* (*trennb., hat -ge-*) conjure up (**aus** out of, from) (*auch fig.*); **~ziehen** *v/t.* (*unreg., trennb., hat -ge-*) pull out (**aus** of; **hinter/unter/zwischen** + *Dat.* from behind/under/between); **zum Vorzeigen**: *auch* produce (out of, from)

herwagen *v/refl.* (*trennb., hat -ge-*) dare to come (*od.* put in an appearance) here

Herweg *m*: **auf dem ~** on the way here

Herz[1] *n*; *-ens, -en* **1.** *Anat. als Organ*: heart; **Operation am offenen ~** open-heart surgery; **er hat's am ~en** *umg.* he has heart trouble (*od.* a heart condition); **2.** *poet.* (*Brust*) breast; **j-n ans ~ drücken** clasp s.o. to one's breast; **komm an mein ~** come to my arms; **3.** *bes. geh.* (*Gemüt*) heart; (*Seele*) *auch* soul; (*Mut*) *auch* courage; **ein gutes/hartes/weiches ~ haben** be good-/hard-/soft-hearted; **kein ~ haben** be heartless; **ein ~ aus Stein** a heart of stone; **es tut dem ~en wohl** it does you good; **etw. fürs ~** s.th. to warm the heart; **j-m das ~ schwer machen** sadden s.o.'s heart; **4.** *Person*: soul; *Kosewort*: **mein ~** my love, my dear; **einsame ~en** lonely hearts; → **Herzchen**; **5.** *fig. von Salat, Stadt etc.*: heart, core, cent|re (*Am.* -er); **6.** *kath.*: **~ Jesu** Sacred Heart; **7.** *Bot.*: **Tränendes ~** bleeding heart, dicentra; **8.** *Redewendungen*: **ein Kind unter dem ~en tragen** *poet.* be with child; **j-m stockt das ~ vor Schreck** *geh.* s.o.'s heart skips a beat (in fright); **mir schlug das ~ bis zum Hals** my heart was in my mouth; **sein ~ schlug höher** his heart leapt; **er/es lässt die ~en höher schlagen** he makes the ladies swoon (*od.* go weak in the knees) / it makes your heart swell; **mir blutet das ~** my heart bleeds; **es bricht** *od.* **zerreißt mir das ~** *geh.* it breaks my heart; **mir rutschte das ~ in die Hose** *umg.* my heart sank; **j-m sein ~ ausschütten** pour one's heart out to s.o.; **alles, was das ~ begehrt** everything your heart desires, everything you could possibly wish for; **sagen, was sein ~ bewegt** unburden one's heart; **j-s ~ brechen/gewinnen/stehlen** break/win/steal s.o.'s heart; **sich** (*Dat.*) **ein ~ fassen** pluck (*umg.* screw) up some courage; **mein ~ gehört ihr / der Malerei** *geh.* my heart belongs to her / painting is my true love; **s-m ~en e-n Stoß geben** go for it; **ein ~ und eine Seele sein** be inseparable; **sein ~ an etw.** (*Akk.*) **hängen** set one's heart on s.th.; **sein ganzes ~ hängt daran** it means the world to him; **es liegt mir am ~en** it means a lot to me (**zu** + *Inf.* to be able to + *Inf.*); **es liegt mir am ~en zu** (+ *Inf.*) *auch* I'm (very) anxious to (+ *Inf.*); **j-m etw.** (*besonders*) **ans ~ legen** (*nahe legen*) urge s.o. to do s.th.; (*anvertrauen*) entrust s.o. with the task of doing s.th.; **sein ~** (**an j-n**) **verlieren** lose one's heart (to s.o.); **es ist mir ans ~ gewachsen** I have grown fond of it; **auf ~ und Nieren prüfen** *umg.* (*Person*) grill *s.o.*; (*Sache*) put *s.th.* through its paces; **etw. auf dem ~en haben** have s.th. on one's mind; **sein ~ auf der Zunge tragen** *geh.* wear one's heart on one's sleeve; **aus tiefstem ~en** *geh.* from the bottom of one's heart; **ein ~ für Kinder** etc. a place in one's heart for children *etc.*; **sein ~ für … entdecken** discover a fondness (*od.* liking) for …; **j-n in sein** *od.* **ins ~ schließen** grow very fond of s.o., become very attached to s.o.; **da lacht mir das ~ im Leibe!** it makes my heart leap for joy!; **mit ganzem/halben ~en** *dabei sein etc.*: heart and soul, wholeheartedly / halfheartedly; **er ist mit ganzem ~en bei der Arbeit** his heart's in his work; **ein Mann etc. nach m-m ~en** after my own heart; **ich kann es nicht übers ~ bringen** I can't bring myself to do it, I haven't got the heart (to do it); **mir wurde warm ums** ~ I felt all warm inside; **es war ihr leicht/ schwer ums** ~ she felt relieved / heavy-hearted; **er weiß, wie mir ums** ~ **ist** he knows how I feel; **von** ~**en** sincerely; **von** ~**en froh** heartily pleased; **von** ~**en gern** gladly, with great pleasure; **es kommt von** ~**en** it comes from the heart; **von** ~**en kommend** sincere, heartfelt; **von ganzem** ~**en** with all one's heart; **ich bedanke mich von ganzem** ~**en** I'm deeply grateful (to you); **j-m zu** ~**en gehen** move s.o.; **sich etw. zu** ~**en nehmen** take s.th. to heart; → **Fleck** 3, **gebrochen** II, **Hand**[1] 3, **leicht** I 3, **Mördergrube**, **schwer** I 2, **Stein** I, 2

Herz[2] *n*; -, - **1.** *nur Sg.*; *Kartenfarbe*: hearts *Pl.*; **2.** *Einzelkarte*: heart

Herz... *im Subst. Kartenspiel*: ... of hearts

Herzallerliebste *m*, *f altm*. darling

Herz|anfall *m Med.* heart attack; ~**ass** *n* ace of hearts; ~**attacke** *f Med.* heart attack

herzaubern *v/t.* (*trennb., hat -ge-*) conjure up

Herzbeschwerden *Pl.* heart trouble *Sg.*

Herzbeutel *m Anat.* pericardium (*Pl.* pericardia); ~**entzündung** *f Med.* pericarditis

herzbewegend *Adj.* (deeply) moving, heartrending

Herz|blatt *n* **1.** *Pl.*, *von Salat etc.*: heart *Sg.*; **2.** *Bot.* grass-of-Parnassus; **3.** *umg.* sweetheart; ~**blut** *n geh. fig.* one's lifeblood; **etw. mit s-m** ~ **schreiben** *etc.* put one's entire heart into s.th.; ~**bube** *m* jack of hearts

Herzchen *n* **1.** little heart; **2.** *Kosewort*: darling, sweetheart; **3.** *iro.* (*naiver Mensch*) simple soul; **du bist mir vielleicht ein** ~**!** you're a real simple Simon!

Herz|chirurg *m Med.* heart surgeon; ~**chirurgie** *f* heart (*od.* cardiac) surgery; ~**chirurgin** *f* heart surgeon; ~**dame** *f auch fig.* queen of hearts

Herzegowina *f*; -; *Geog.* Herzegovina; **herzegowinisch** *Adj.* Herzegovinian

herzeigen *v/t.* (*trennb., hat -ge-*) show, let s.o. see *s.th.*; **zeig mal her!** *auch* let's have a look; **so kann man dich ja nicht** ~**!** you can't be seen like that!; **solche Erfolge lassen sich** ~**!** such results are worth showing off (about)!

Herzeleid *n geh.* heartache

herzen *v/t. geh.* hug, cuddle

Herzens|angelegenheit *f* **1.** matter of the heart; **2.** something close to one's heart; ~**brecher** *m* lady-killer, heartbreaker; ~**brecherin** *f*; -, -nen heartbreaker; ~**grund** *m*: **aus tiefstem** ~ from the bottom of one's heart

herzensgut *Adj.* very kind(hearted); **ein** ~**er Mensch** *auch* a good soul; **Herzensgüte** *f geh.* kindheartedness

Herzens|lust *f*: **nach** ~ to one's heart's content; ~**wunsch** *m* great desire; (*größter Wunsch*) one's dearest wish

Herzentzündung *f Med.* carditis

herz|erfrischend *Adj.* heartwarming, very refreshing; ~**ergreifend** *Adj.* deeply moving; ~**erwärmend** *Adj.* heartwarming; ~**erweichend** *Adj.* heartrending

Herz|erweiterung *f Med.* dilatation of the heart; ~**fehler** *m Med.* heart defect; ~**flattern** *n Med.* **1.** *umg. fig.* palpitations *Pl.*; **dabei kriege ich** ~ *auch umg.* it makes my heart go pitter-pat-

ter; **2.** → **Herzflimmern**; ~**flimmern** *n Med.* heart flutter; (*Kammerflimmern*) ventricular fibrillation; **ich habe** ~ *fig.* my heart is going pitter-patter

Herzform *f*: **in** ~ in the shape of a heart; **herzförmig** *Adj.* heart-shaped

Herz|gegend *f* cardiac region; **in der** ~ *auch* around the heart; ~**geräusch** *n Med.* cardiac murmur

herzhaft I. *Adj.* **1.** good, decent; *Essen*: substantial, robust; (*Ggs. süß*) savo(u)ry; *Händedruck*: firm; *Wein*: hearty; ~**er Kuss** big kiss, smack on the cheek (*od.* lips) *umg.*; **2.** *altm.* (*mutig*) bold, brave; **II.** *Adv.* **gähnen**: hugely, cavernously; ~ **lachen** have a good laugh; ~ **schmecken** be hearty and tasty; ~ **zulangen** dig in *umg.*

herziehen (*unreg., trennb.*) **I.** *v/t.* (*hat hergezogen*) **1.** *umg.* hierher: pull (*od.* draw) up (**zu** to); **2. hinter sich** (*Dat.*) ~ pull along; **II.** *v/i.* **1.** (*ist*): **hinter** (+ *Dat.*) ~ follow; **neben/vor** (+ *Dat.*) ~ walk beside/in front of; **2.** (*ist*); *umg.* hierher: come to live here, move here (*od.* to this place); **3.** (*hat od. ist*); *umg. fig.*: ~ **über** (+ *Akk.*) run down, pull to pieces

herzig *Adj.* cute

Herz|infarkt *m Med.* heart attack, coronary, *fachspr.* cardiac infarction; ~**insuffizienz** *f Med.* heart failure, *fachspr.* cardiac insufficiency; ~**jagen** *n* tachycardia

Herz-Jesu-Bild *n kath.* Sacred Heart picture

Herz|kammer *f Anat.* ventricle; ~**katheter** *m Med.* cardiac catheter

Herzkirsche *f Bot.* heart cherry

Herzklappe *f Anat.* (heart) valve; **Herzklappenfehler** *m Med.* valvular defect

Herz|klopfen *n* **1.** *Med.* palpitations *Pl.*; **2. mit** ~ **ging ich hinein** my heart was thumping when I went in; ~**kollaps** *m Med.* heart failure; ~**könig** *m* king of hearts

herzkrank *Adj.*: ~ **sein** suffer from a heart disease (*od.* condition); **Herzkranke** *m*, *f* heart (*od.* cardiac) patient; **Herzkrankheit** *f* heart disease (*od.* complaint, condition)

Herzkranzgefäß *n Anat.* coronary vessel

Herz-Kreislauf-Erkrankung *f* cardiovascular disease (*od.* complaint); ~**-System** *n* cardiovascular system

Herzleiden *n* heart disease (*od.* complaint); **herzleidend** *Adj.* → **herzkrank**

herzlich I. *Adj.* **1.** *Empfang, Freundschaft etc.*: warm; (*innig empfunden*) heartfelt, sincere; (*liebevoll*) affectionate; *im Brief*: ~**e Grüße** best regards; *vertraulich*: love; ~**en Dank** many thanks indeed, I'm much obliged; ~**en Glückwunsch!** congratulations! (**zu** on); ~**es Beileid** I'm so sorry (to hear about your father *etc.*); **ich habe e-e** ~**e Bitte an dich** I wonder if you could do me a big favo(u)r; **2.** *Lachen*: hearty; **II.** *Adv.* **1.** warmly *etc.*; ~ **empfangen werden** be given a warm welcome; **ich gratuliere** ~**!** congratulations! (**zu** on); **ich danke Ihnen** ~ many thanks indeed, I'm much obliged to you; ~ **willkommen!** welcome!; **ihr seid uns jederzeit** ~ **willkommen** you are always very welcome; **2.** (*sehr*) very; (*ziemlich*) quite, pretty; ~ **gern** gladly, with pleasure; ~ **wenig** not very much at all; ~ **wenig verdienen** earn a pittance; ~ **wenig Zeit haben** have very

little time; **damit kann ich** ~ **wenig anfangen** that's very little good to me; ~ **lachen** have a good laugh; **es tut mir** ~ **Leid** I'm terribly (*od.* awfully) sorry; **Herzlichkeit** *f* warmth; sincerity

Herzlinie *f* **1.** *Med.* cardioid; **2.** *Handlesen*: heart line

herzlos *Adj.* heartless, unfeeling; **Herzlosigkeit** *f* heartlessness

Herz-Lungen-Maschine *f Med.* heart--lung machine

Herz|massage *f Med.* cardiac massage; ~**mittel** *n* cardiac stimulant

Herzmuskel *m Anat.* cardiac muscle; ~**entzündung** *f Med.* myocarditis; ~**schwäche** *f Med. Insuffizienz*: myocardial insufficiency; *Schaden*: myocardiac lesion

Herzog *m*; -s, *Herzöge* duke; **Herzogin** *f*; -, -nen duchess; **herzoglich** *Adj.* ducal; **Herzogswürde** *f*: **j-m die** ~ **verleihen** bestow the duchy on s.o.; **Herzogtum** *n*; -s, *Herzogtümer* duchy

Herz|operation *f Med.* heart surgery (*od.* operation); ~**patient** *m*, ~**patientin** *f* heart (*od.* cardiac) patient; ~**rhythmusstörungen** *Pl. Med.* irregular heartbeat *Sg.*, cardiac arrhythmia (*od.* dysrhythmia) *Sg.*; ~**schaden** *m* heart (*od.* cardiac) defect; ~**scheidewand** *f Anat.* septum of the heart; ~**schlag** *m* **1.** heartbeat; *weitS.* pulse; **der** ~ **der Großstadt** *fig.* the pulse of the city; **2.** *Med.* (*Herztod*) heart failure; ~**schmerz** *m*; *mst Pl.* pains (*od.* pain *Sg.*) in the chest; ~**schrittmacher** *m* pacemaker; ~**schwäche** *f Med.* cardiac insufficiency; *momentane*: syncope; ~**spezialist** *m*, ~**spezialistin** *f* heart specialist, cardiologist

herzstärkend *Adj.* cardiotonic; ~**es Mittel** cardiac stimulant

Herz|stillstand *m Med.* cardiac arrest; ~**stück** *n fig.* heart, core; ~**tätigkeit** *f* cardiac activity; **Aussetzen der** ~ cardiac arrest; ~**tod** *m* cardiac (*od.* heart--related) death; **den** ~ **sterben** die of heart failure; ~**töne** *Pl.* cardiac sounds; ~**transplantation** *f* heart transplant; ~**tropfen** *Pl.* heart drops

herzu... → **herbei...**, **hinzu...**

Herz|verfettung *f* fatty degeneration of the heart; ~**vergrößerung** *f* cardiac enlargement; ~**verpflanzung** *f* heart transplant; ~**versagen** *n* heart failure; ~**vorkammer** *f* atrium (*Pl.* atria *od.* atriums); ~**wand** *f* cardiac wall; ~**zentrum** *n Klinik*: heart cent|re (*Am.* -er)

herzzerreißend *Adj.* heartrending

Hesse *m*; -n, -n Hessian; ~ **sein** *auch* come from Hesse; **Hessen** (*n*); -s; *Geog.* Hesse; **Hessin** *f*; -, -nen Hessian (woman *od.* girl *etc.*); **hessisch** *Adj.* Hessian

hetero *Adj. umg.* straight; **Hetero** *m*; -s, -s *und f*; -, -s het

heterogen *Adj. geh.* heterogeneous; **Heterogenität** *f*; -, kein *Pl.*; *geh.* heterogeneity

Heterosexualität *f* heterosexuality; **heterosexuell** *Adj.* heterosexual; **Heterosexuelle** *m*, *f* heterosexual

Het(h)iter *m*; -s, -, ~**in** *f*; -, -nen; *hist.* Hittite

Hetz *f*; -, -en, *mst Sg.*; *österr. umg.* laugh

Hetz|artikel *m pej.* inflammatory article; ~**blatt** *n pej.* smear(-)sheet, scandal rag

Hetze *f*; -, -n, *mst Sg.* **1.** (*Eile*) rush, *des Lebens*: *auch* rat race *umg.*; **was soll die** ~**?** what's the big rush?; **2.** *nur Sg.*; *pej.* smear campaign; (*Aufhet-*

H

zung) agitation; ~ *gegen die Juden etc.* Jew- baiting *etc.*; **3.** → *Hetzjagd* 1; **hetzen I.** *v/t.* (*hat gehetzt*) **1.** (*antreiben*) rush; *j-n* ~ *bei der Arbeit: auch* breathe down s.o.'s neck; *ich lasse mich nicht* ~ I won't be rushed; *gehetzt werden* (*von*) be under pressure (from); *von Person, absichtlich:* be put under pressure (by); **2.** (*Tiere*) hunt (with hounds), chase; *fig.* (*verfolgen, jagen*) chase, hunt; *zu Tode* ~ hound to death; *weitS.* (*Witz etc.*) flog to death; **3.** *j-n od. ein Tier* ~ *auf* (+ *Akk.*) set on(to); **II.** *v/i.* **1.** (*ist*); (*eilen*) rush; *hetz nicht so!* not so fast!; **2.** (*hat*); (*sich beeilen*) be in a rush; *du brauchst nicht zu* ~ there's no (great) rush; **3.** (*hat*); *fig. pej.* (*Hetzreden führen*) stir (things up); ~ *gegen* stir up hatred against; *zum Krieg* ~ engage in warmongering; **III.** *v/refl.* (*hat*) → II 2; **Hetzer** *m*; *-s*, *-*; *pej.* agitator, rabble--rouser; **Hetzerei** *f* → *Hetze* 1, 2; **Hetzerin** *f*; *-*, *-nen* agitator, rabble-rouser; **hetzerisch** *Adj. pej.* inflammatory; *Rede: auch* rabble-rousing

Hetz|jagd *f* **1.** *das Jagen:* hunting with hounds; *einzelne Jagd:* hunt (*with hounds*); **2.** *fig.* (*Verfolgung*) hunt, chase; **3.** *fig.* (*Eile*) (mad) rush; **4.** *pej.*, *in den Medien:* smear campaign; ~**kampagne** *f pej.* smear campaign; ~**parole** *f pej.* demagogic slogan; ~**rede** *f pej.* inflammatory (*od.* rabble-rousing) speech; ~**tirade** *f pej.* inflammatory harangue

Heu *n*; *-(e)s, kein Pl.* hay; *Geld wie* ~ *haben umg. fig.* have money to burn; ~**ballen** *m* bale of hay, hay bale; ~**boden** *m* hay loft

Heuchelei *f*; *-*, *-en*; *pej.* **1.** *nur Sg.* hypocrisy; (*Verstellung*) dissimulation; (*Unaufrichtigkeit*) insincerity; (*Falschheit*) deceit; **2.** *Äußerung:* hypocritical remark; **heucheln I.** *v/i.* (*scheinheilig sein od. tun*) be hypocritical; (*unaufrichtig sein*) be insincere; (*scheinheilig reden*) cant; (*sich verstellen*) (dis)simulate, dissemble; **II.** *v/t.* feign, affect; **Heuchler** *m*; *-s*, *-*, **Heuchlerin** *f*; *-*, *-nen* hypocrite; **heuchlerisch** *Adj.* hypocritical; (*falsch*) deceitful, insincere

heuer *Adv. südd., österr., schw.* this year

Heuer *f*; *-*, *-n*; *Naut.* **1.** *Bezahlung:* pay; **2.** *Anstellung:* position (*on a ship*)

heuern *v/t.* **1.** *Naut.* (*Schiff*) charter; (*Matrosen*) sign on, *Am.* enlist, sign up *umg.*; **2.** *umg. weitS.* (*auch sich* [*Dat.*] *j-n* ~) hire

Heuernte *f* hay harvest, haying; *Zeit:* haymaking season

Heuervertrag *m Naut.* seaman's work contract

Heu|fieber *n* hay fever; ~**gabel** *f* pitchfork; ~**haufen** *m* haystack

Heulboje *f* **1.** whistling buoy; **2.** *umg. pej. Kind:* bawler; *Sänger:* caterwauler

heulen *v/i.* **1.** *Wolf, Wind etc.:* howl; *Eule:* hoot; *Sirene:* wail; *Bombe etc.:* scream; **2.** *umg.* (*weinen*) cry; *laut:* howl; ~ *um* cry over (*od.* about); *er heulte vor Wut* he wept with rage; *es ist zum Heulen umg.* it's enough to make you weep; **Heuler** *m*; *-s*, *-* **1.** *umg.: das ist ja der letzte* ~*! kritisierend:* would you believe it; *anerkennend:* it's (absolutely) brill *Sl.*, *Am.* it's (totally) awesome; **2.** (*junger Seehund*) baby seal, seal pup; **3.** *umg.* → *Heulton*; **4.** *Feuerwerkskörper:* banshee, screamer, howler; **Heulerei** *f*; *-*,

-en, *mst Sg.*; *pej.* crying, howling; *hör auf mit der* ~*!* stop howling!

Heul|suse *f*; *-*, *-n*; *umg. pej.* crybaby; ~**ton** *m* wailing sound; *e-r Sirene:* sound of a siren

Heupferd *n Zool.* grasshopper; *schädliches:* locust

heureka *Interj. geh.* eureka

heurig *Adj. südd., österr., schw.* this year's (*od.* season's), new; **Heurige** *m*; *-n*, *-n* **1.** new wine; **2.** *Lokal:* (*Austrian*) wine tavern (*selling new wine*)

Heuristik *f*; *-*, *kein Pl.* heuristics *Pl.* (*V. im Sg.*); **heuristisch** *Adj.* heuristic

Heu|schnupfen *m* hay fever; ~**schober** *m südd., österr.* haystack

Heuschrecke *f*; *-*, *-n*; *Zool.* grasshopper; *schädliche:* locust

Heuschrecken|plage *f* plague of locusts; ~**schwarm** *m* swarm of locusts

Heu|stadel *m südd., österr.* barn; ~**stock** *m südd., österr.* (*gesamter Heuvorrat*) stock of hay

heute *Adv.* **1.** today; ~ *Abend* this evening, tonight; ~ *früh od.* **Morgen** this morning; ~ *Nacht kommende:* tonight; *vergangene:* last night; ~ *in einem Jahr* a year from today; ~ *in acht Tagen* a week (from) today, *Brit. auch* today week *umg.*; ~ *vor acht Tagen* a week ago (today); *von* ~ *an od.* *ab* ~ from today, as of today; *von* ~ *auf morgen* overnight, from one day to the next; *lieber* ~ *als morgen* the sooner the better; (*noch*) *bis* ~ to this day; *er hat bis* ~ (*noch*) *nicht bezahlt* he hasn't paid to this day, I'm *etc.* still waiting for him to pay (up); *die Ausgabe von* ~ today's issue; **2.** (*heutzutage*) these days, nowadays, today; *das Amerika von* ~ present-day America, America today; *die Frau von* ~ today's women, the women of today; *das Heute* the present, today

heutig *Adj.* today's; (*gegenwärtig*) *auch* present(-day...), of today, modern; *der* ~*e Tag* today; *bis zum* ~*en Tag* to this day; *in der* ~*en Zeit* → *heutzutage; die* ~*e Zeitung* today's paper

heutzutage *Adv.* these days, nowadays, today

Heu|wagen *m* haycart, haywag(g)on; ~**wender** *m*; *-s*, *-* tedder

hexadezimal *Adj. Math., EDV* hexadecimal, hex *umg.*

Hexadezimal|system *n Math., EDV* hexadecimal system; ~**zahl** *f* hexadecimal number

Hexaeder *n*; *-s*, *-*; *Math.* hexahedron (*Pl.* hexahedra *od.* hexahedrons)

Hexagon *n*; *-s*, *-e*; *Math.* hexagon

Hexagramm *n*; *-s*, *-e*; *Math.* hexagram

Hexameter *m Lit.* hexameter

Hexe *f*; *-*, *-n* **1.** witch; **2.** *fig. pej.:* (*alte*) ~ old hag; *so e-e kleine* ~*!* what a little minx!; **hexen I.** *v/i.* practi|se (*Am.* -ce) witchcraft; *ich kann doch nicht* ~ *umg.* I can't perform miracles; **II.** *v/t.* conjure up; ~, *dass ...* cast a spell so that ...

Hexen|einmaleins *n* magic square; ~**glaube** *m* belief in witches; ~**häuschen** *n* **1.** *verzaubertes:* witch's cottage; **2.** *aus Lebkuchen:* gingerbread house; ~**jagd** *f auch fig. pej.* witch--hunt(ing); ~**kessel** *m* **1.** witch's (*od.* witches') cauldron; **2.** *fig.* pandemonium; *das Stadion glich e-m* ~ the stadium was like bedlam; ~**küche** *f fig.* witches' kitchen; ~**kunst** *f auch Pl.* witchcraft; ~**meister** *m* wizard, sorcerer; ~**prozess** *m* witch('s) trial; ~**sabbat** *m* **1.** witches' sabbath; **2.** *geh., fig.*

pandemonium; *es war ein wahrer* ~ it was pure pandemonium; ~**schuss** *m Med.* lumbago; ~**verbrennung** *f* burning of witches (*od.* of a witch); ~**verfolgung** *f* witch-hunt; ~**wahn** *m* witch-hunting mania

Hexer *m*; *-s*, *-* warlock; (*Hexenmeister*) wizard, sorcerer

Hexerei *f*; *-*, *-en*, *mst Sg.* **1.** witchcraft, sorcery; **2.** (*Zauberei*) magic

HG *Abk.* → *Handelsgesellschaft*

hg. *Abk.* (*herausgegeben von*) ed.

Hg. *Abk.* (*Herausgeber*) ed.

hibbelig *Adj. nordd. umg.* (*zappelig*) fidgety; (*nervös*) jittery

Hibiskus *m*; *-*, *Hibisken; Bot.* hibiscus

Hickhack *n*, *m*; *-s*, *-s*; *umg.* wrangling, squabbling

hicks *Interj. umg.* hic; **hicksen** *v/i. Dial.* hiccup

hie *Adv.:* ~ *und da zeitlich:* now and then; *räumlich:* here and there

hieb *Imperf. geh.* → *hauen*

Hieb *m*; *-(e)s, -e* **1.** (*Schlag*) blow; *mit der Faust: auch* punch; *mit der Peitsche:* lash; *Fechten:* cut; ~*e* (*Prügel*) beating; *j-m e-n* ~ *versetzen auch fig.* deal s.o. a blow; **2.** *Wunde:* cut, gash; **3.** *fig.* (*Anspielung*) dig (*auf* + *Akk.* at); *der* ~ *saß* that hit home; ~*e bekommen* (*kritisiert werden*) get a tongue-lashing

hieb- und stichfest *Adj. Argumente etc.:* watertight; *Beweise, Garantie etc.:* cast-iron ...

hielt *Imperf.* → *halten*

hier *Adv.* **1.** here; (*an diesem Ort*) *auch* in this place; ~ (*drüben*) over here; ~ *draußen/drinnen* out/in here; ~ *entlang* this way; *das Haus* ~ this house; ~ *behalten/bleiben/lassen/sein etc.* keep/stay/leave/be here; ~*! bei Appell:* present!, here!; ~*! geblieben!* don't you move!, you just stay put!; ~ (*spricht*) *John B. am Telefon:* (this is) John B. speaking; *sind Sie von* ~*?* are you from around here?, are you local?; *ich bin auch nicht von* ~ I'm a stranger here myself; *wann sollte er* ~ *sein?* when was he supposed to come (*od.* be here)?; ~ *und da räumlich:* here and there; *zeitlich:* now and then; ~ *und jetzt od.* *heute* here and now; *im Hier und Jetzt od. Heute* in the here and now; *es steht mir bis* ~ *umg. fig.* I'm fed up to the back teeth with it; *du stehst mir bis* ~*! umg.* I've had it up to here with you!; **2.** (*in diesem Fall*) here, in this case; (*zu diesem Zeitpunkt*) at this point; ~ *ist nichts mehr zu machen* there's nothing more we can do

hieran *Adv.* at (*od.* by, in, on, to) this; *halt dich* ~ *fest, nicht daran* hold on here, not there; *wenn ich* ~ *denke* when I think of this; *er wird sich* ~ *erinnern* he'll remember this

Hierarchie *f*; *-*, *-n* hierarchy; **hierarchisch** *Adj.* hierarchical

hierauf *Adv.* **1.** on this (*od.* that), here; **2.** *zeitlich:* then, thereupon *geh.*

hieraus *Adv.* from (*od.* out of) this; ~ *geht hervor, dass ...* it follows (*od.* would appear) from this that ...

hier behalten → *hier* 1

hierbei *Adv.* **1.** (*bei dieser Gelegenheit*) here, on this occasion; (*in diesem Zusammenhang*) in this connection; (*in diesem Fall*) in this case; **2.** (*währenddessen*) during this, while doing so

hier bleiben → *hier* 1

hierdurch *Adv.* **1.** *räumlich:* through here, this way; **2.** *ursächlich:* this way;

(*deswegen*) because of this; *am Satzanfang*: *auch* that's how; (*hiermit*) hereby

hierein *Adv.* in here

hierfür *Adv.* for this (*od.* it)

hiergegen *Adv.* **1.** against this (*od.* it); **2.** (*im Vergleich*) in comparison

hierher *Adv.* here; *in Richtung*: this way, over here; (*komm*) *~!* come here (*od.* hither *altm. und hum.*)!; *bis ~* up to here, this far; *bis ~ und nicht weiter* this far and no (*od.* not a step) further; *er gehört ~* this is where he belongs; *das gehört nicht ~* (*ist unangebracht*) it's out of place; (*ist abwegig*) it's irrelevant; *~ passen* fit, look right; *fig. auch* be appropriate; *es passt nicht ~ auch* it looks out of place; *wie kannst du dich ~ wagen?* how dare you come near this place?

hier|herauf *Adv.* up here; *~heraus* *Adv.* out of here, from here; *~herein* *adv.* in here

hierher| gehören, ~ kommen, ~ passen → *hierher*

hier|herüber *Adv.* over here, hither *altm.*; *~herunter* *Adv.* down here; *~herum* *Adv.* this way (a)round; (*ungefähr hier*) somewhere (a)round here

hierher wagen → *hierher*

hier|hin *Adv.* here, this way; *leg es ~, nicht dahin* lay it down here, not there; *~ und dorthin* here and there; *~hinab* *Adv.* down here; *~hinauf* *Adv.* up here; *~hinaus* *Adv.* out here; *~hinein* *Adv.* in here; *~hinter* *Adv.* behind here; *~hinüber* *Adv.* over here, hither *altm.*; *~hinunter* *Adv.* down here

hierin *Adv.* **1.** in here, in it; **2.** (*in diesem Punkt*) here, in this

hier lassen → *hier* 1

hiermit *Adv.* with this; (*mit diesen Worten*) with these words, with this, saying this; *~ ist die Sache erledigt* that settles that; *~ bin ich einverstanden* I'll agree to that, that's all right by me; *~ wird bescheinigt* this is to certify; *~ geht unsere Sendung zu Ende* that brings us to the end of our program(me); *~ möchte ich mich verabschieden* and that's all from me (for today *etc.*)

hiernach *Adv.* **1.** *zeitlich*: after this; **2.** *Bezug*: *~ kannst du dich richten* you can use this to guide you; **3.** (*demzufolge*) according to this

Hieroglyphe *f;* -, -*n* hieroglyph; **Hieroglyphenschrift** *f* hieroglyphic writing (*od.* script); **hieroglyphisch** *Adj.* hieroglyphic

hier sein → *hier* 1

hierüber *Adv.* **1.** *räumlich*: over here; over this (*od.* it); **2.** *thematisch*: about this (*od.* it), on this (*od.* it), on this (*od.* the) subject; **3.** *geh.* (*währenddessen*) in the process

hierum *Adv.* **1.** *räumlich*: (a)round here; **2.** *thematisch*: about this (*od.* it); *~ geht es nicht* that's not the point

hierunter *Adv.* **1.** *räumlich*: under(neath) this (*od.* it); **2.** (*unter dieser Menge*) (included) among them (*od.* these); **3.** *verstehen etc.*: by that; *~ verstehe ich* by that I mean

hiervon *Adv.* **1.** of *od.* from this (*od.* it, these, them); **2.** *thematisch*: about it (*od.* this)

hiervor *Adv.* → *davor*

hierzu *Adv.* **1.** (*dazu*) to this (*od.* these); *gleichzeitig, als Ergänzung, Beilage etc.*: with this; (*hierfür*) for this (*od.* it); **2.** (*zu diesem Zweck*) for this

(*purpose*); **3.** (*zu diesem Punkt*) concerning this, on this score

hierzulande, **hier zu Lande** *Adv.* in this country, in these parts, around here, (over) here

hierzwischen *Adv.* between them (*od.* these, the two), in between

hiesig *Adj.* local, ... (around) here; **Hiesige** *m, f; -n, -n* local

hieß *Imperf.* → *heißen*[1]

hieven *v/t. Naut. od. umg.* heave, hoist

Hi-Fi ['haifai] *Abk.* hi-fi; *~-Anlage* *f* stereo (system), hi-fi (system); *~-Gerät* *n* piece of hi-fi equipment; *~e* hi-fi equipment *Sg.*

high [hai] *Adj. umg.* **1.** *euph.* high; **2.** (*in Hochstimmung*) high

Highlife ['hailaif] *n; -(s), kein Pl.; umg.*: *~ machen* live it up; *bei uns war gestern ~* we were living it up at our house yesterday

Highlight ['hailait] *n; -(s), kein Pl.; umg.* highlight

highlighten ['hailaitn] *v/t. EDV* highlight; **High Society**, **Highsociety** ['haisə'saiəti] *f, -, kein Pl.* high society

Hightech, **High Tech** ['haitɛk] *n; -(s), kein Pl. od. f; -, kein Pl.* high tech, hi tech; **Higtechindustrie**, **High-Tech-Industrie** *f* high-tech industry

hihi(hi) *Interj.* teehee

Hilfe *f; -, -n* **1.** help; (*Beistand*) *auch* finanziell etc.: *auch* aid, assistance; (*Unterstützung*) support; (*Mitwirkung*) co-operation; (*zu*) *~!* help!; *mit j-s ~* with s.o.'s help; *ohne (fremde) ~* (*selbstständig*) without any help, single-handed, (*by*) himself *etc.*; *erste ~* (*leisten*) (give) first aid; *j-m ~ leisten* help s.o.; *~ suchen* seek help; *~ suchend nachgestellt*: seeking help; *Blick*: beseeching; *um ~ bitten* ask for help; *j-n um ~ bitten* ask s.o. to help one, ask for s.o.'s help; *um ~ rufen* call (*od.* shout) for help; *j-m zu ~ kommen* come to s.o.'s assistance (*od.* aid); *etw. zu ~ nehmen* make use of; *mit ~* → *mithilfe*; *~ zur Selbsthilfe* helping people to help themselves; **2.** *mst Pl.*; (*Hilfsmittel*) aid *Pl.*; *Handlung, Reiten*: aids *Pl.*; *Turnen*: support *Sg.*; *mechanische ~n* mechanical aids; **3.** *Person*: help; *du bist mir e-e schöne ~ iro.* you're a great help(, I must say)

Hilfe|funktion *f EDV* help function; *~gesuch* *n* request for help; *~leistung* *f* help; *auch finanzielle*: assistance, aid; *unterlassene ~ Jur.* failing to render assistance in an emergency; *~menü* *n Computer*: help menu; *~ruf* *m, ~schrei* *m* call (*od.* cry) for help (*auch fig.*); *~stellung* *f Turnen*: support; *Person*: support; *j-m ~ leisten* support s.o., give s.o. support; *fig. auch* back s.o. up

Hilfe suchend → *Hilfe*

Hilfe|suchende *m, f; -n, -n* person seeking (*od.* in need of) help; *Pl.* those seeking (*od.* in need of) help; *~taste* *f Computer*: help key

hilflos I. *Adj. auch fig.* helpless; (*schutzlos*) *auch* defen|celess (*Am.* -seless); *j-m od. e-r Sache gegenüber völlig ~ sein* be at a complete loss as to what to do with (*od.* about); **II.** *Adv.*: *j-m od. e-r Sache ~ ausgeliefert sein* be at the mercy of; **Hilflosigkeit** *f; nur Sg.* helplessness

hilfreich I. *Adj.* helpful; (*Unterstützung bietend*) supportive; *es wäre ~, wenn wir wüssten ...* it would be helpful to know ..., it would help if we knew ...;

II. *Adv.*: *j-m ~ zur Seite stehen* help s.o. out; *in Krise etc.*: *auch* support s.o.

Hilfs... *im Subst.* **1.** (*Ersatz..., Not...*) auxiliary, emergency; *vorübergehend*: temporary; **2.** *beruflich*: assistant, junior; *siehe auch Behelfs..., Not...*

Hilfs|aktion *f* relief campaign; *~arbeiter* *m, ~arbeiterin* *f* unskilled worker (*od.* labo[u]rer); *Pl.* unskilled labo(u)r *Sg.*; *~assistent* *m, ~assistentin* *f Univ.* research (*od.* tutorial) assistant

hilfsbedürftig *Adj.* in need of help; (*Not leidend*) needy; **Hilfsbedürftigkeit** *f; nur Sg.* need of help, neediness

hilfsbereit *Adj.* (very) helpful; *im Dienst*: *auch* cooperative; **Hilfsbereitschaft** *f; nur Sg.* helpfulness; cooperativeness

Hilfs|bremse *f* auxiliary brake; *~dienst* *m* auxiliary service; (*Notdienst*) emergency service; *~fonds* *m* relief fund; *~gelder* *Pl.* subsidies; *~zahlen an* subsidize; *~güter* *Pl.* relief aid *Sg.*; *~ für das Katastrophengebiet* relief aid for the disaster area; *~kasse* *f* relief fund; *~komitee* *n* action committee; *~konstruktion* *f* **1.** *Math.* auxiliary construction; **2.** (*Idee*) constructive idea; *~kraft* *f* temporary worker; (*bes. Sekretärin*) temp *umg.*; *wissenschaftliche etc.*: assistant; *~lehrer* *m, ~lehrerin* *f* supply (*Am.* substitute) teacher; *~linie* *f Mus.* leger line; *Math. etc.* auxiliary line; *~maßnahmen* *Pl.* aid *Sg.*; *im Notfall*: *auch* emergency measures

Hilfsmittel *n* aid; (*Maßnahme*) measure; (*Notbehelf*) expedient; *finanzielle ~* financial aid *Sg.*; *~ Pl. für den Unterricht* teaching aids

Hilfs|motor *m* auxiliary engine (*Etech.* motor); *Fahrrad mit ~* motor-assisted bicycle; *~organisation* *f* relief organization, aid agency; *~paket* *n* aid package; *~personal* *n* ancillary staff; *~polizei* *f* auxiliary police; *~polizist* *m, ~polizistin* *f* special constable (*Am.* officer); *~prediger* *m, ~predigerin* *f* curate; *~programm* *n* aid program(me); *~quelle* *f* **1.** (*natural*) resource; **2.** *Wirts.* financial resources *Pl.*; **3.** *wissenschaftliche*: source; *~schule* *f altm.* (*Sonderschule*) special school; *~schüler* *m, ~schülerin* *f altm., pej.* pupil (*Am.* student) at a special school; *~schwester* *f* auxiliary nurse; *~sheriff* *m* deputy sheriff (*auch fig., iro.*); *~stoff* *m* in Waschmittel etc.: aid; *~tätigkeit* *f* auxiliary work; *e-e ~ ausüben* help out; *~transport* *m* transport of relief aid; *~truppen* *Pl. Mil.* reinforcements; *~verb* *n Ling.* auxiliary (verb)

hilfsweise *Adv.* (*ersatzweise*) alternatively, as an alternative; (*als zusätzliche Hilfe*) as an additional aid

Hilfswerk *n* welfare (*od.* relief) organization

hilfswillig *Adj. präd. und nachgestellt*: willing to help

Hilfs|wissenschaft *f* auxiliary science; *~zeitwort* *n* auxiliary (verb)

hilft *Präs.* → *helfen*

Himalaja, **Himalaya** *m; -(s); Geog.: der ~* the Himalayas *Pl.*

Himbeere *f Bot.* raspberry

Himbeer|eis *n* raspberry ice cream; *~geist* *m* raspberry brandy; *~geschmack* *m* raspberry flavo(u)r; *~marmelade* *f* raspberry jam

himbeerrot *Adj.* raspberry-colo(u)red

Himbeerstrauch *m* raspberry bush

H

Himmel *m*; *-s*, - (*Pl. selten, mst poet.*) **1.** sky; *Met. auch* skies *Pl.*; *lit.* heavens *Pl.*; *am ~* in the sky; *unter freiem ~* in the open air; *unter südlichem ~* under southern skies; *der Rauch steigt zum ~ (auf)* the smoke is rising up into the sky; *der ~ lacht* fig. (*die Sonne scheint*) the sun has got his hat on; **2.** *Reli.* heaven; *im ~* in heaven; *in den ~ kommen* go to heaven; *zum od. in den ~ auffahren od. gen ~ fahren* bibl. ascend into heaven; *im ~ sein* euph. be with the angels; *~ und Hölle in Bewegung setzen* fig. move heaven and earth; *~ und Hölle Hüpfspiel*: hopscotch; **3.** *fig.* heaven, paradise; *der ~ auf Erden* geh. heaven on earth; *den ~ auf Erden haben* geh. live in paradise; *aus heiterem ~* (completely) out of the blue; *in den ~ heben* umg. praise to the skies; *im sieb(en)ten ~ sein od. sich [wie] im sieb[en]ten ~ fühlen* umg. be on cloud nine, be walking on air, be in the seventh heaven; *ihm hängt der ~ voller Geigen* geh. he thinks life's a bed of roses; *das schreit od. umg. stinkt zum ~* it's a scandal; *vom ~ fallen* appear from nowhere; *... fallen nicht (einfach) vom ~ ...* don't grow on trees; *Erfolge, Fortschritte etc.*: don't (just) happen by themselves; *Wolken am politischen ~* clouds on the political horizon; → *Meister* 2; **4.** *in Ausrufen*: *dem ~ sei Dank!* thank heavens!; *der ~ ist od. sei mein Zeuge!* altm. as God is my witness!; *gütiger od. du lieber ~!* umg. my goodness!, good Heavens!; *um ~s willen!* for Heaven's (od. God's) sake!; *weiß der ~!* umg. God knows!; *~ (noch mal od. Herrgott, Sakrament)!* umg. for heaven's sake!; *~, Arsch und Zwirn od. Wolkenbruch* Sl. bloody hell, *Am.* holy smoke; **5.** *vom Bett etc.*: canopy; *im Auto*: roof; *umg. (Gaumen)* roof of one's mouth

himmelangst *Adj.* umg.: *mir ist/wurde ~* I am/was scared to death

Himmelbett *n* four-poster (bed)

himmelblau *Adj.* sky-blue, azure

Himmel|donnerwetter *Interj.* umg. damnation!; *~fahrt* f; nur Sg.; kirchl. **1.** (*Christi*) *~* the Ascension (of Christ); *Mariä ~* the Assumption (of the Blessed Virgin); **2.** *Feiertag*: Ascension Day

Himmelfahrts|kommando *n* **1.** *Auftrag*: suicide mission; **2.** *Personen*: suicide squad; *~nase* f umg. hum. snub nose; *~tag* m: *der ~* Ascension Day

Himmelherrgott *Interj.* umg.: *~ noch (ein)mal* for heaven's sake

himmelhoch I. *Adj.* sky-high, soaring; **II.** *Adv.* **1.** high in the sky; **2.** *fig.*: *j-m ~ überlegen sein* be better than s.o. by far; *~ jauchzend, zu Tode betrübt* up one moment, down the next

Himmel|hund *m* umg. **1.** *pej.* (*Schuft*) scoundrel; **2.** (*Draufgänger*) daredevil; *~reich* *n* (Kingdom of) Heaven

Himmels|... *im Subst. oft* heavenly (*bes. Reli.*); *Astron.* celestial; *~äquator* m *Astron.* celestial equator; *~bote* m *lit.* angel

Himmelschlüssel *m Bot.* cowslip

himmelschreiend *Adj. Ungerechtigkeit etc.*: outrageous; *Unsinn etc.*: blatant; *Dummheit*: appalling

Himmels|erscheinung f celestial phenomenon; *~gabe* f geh. gift from heaven; *~globus* m *Astron.* celestial globe; *~karte* f star chart, map of the night sky; *~körper* m celestial body;

~kugel f sphere; *~kunde* f; nur Sg. astronomy; *~leiter* f Jacob's ladder (*auch Bot.*); *~macht* f lit.: *die Liebe ist e-e ~* love is a power sent from heaven; *~pforte* f lit. gates *Pl.* of Heaven, pearly gates *Pl.* umg.; *~pol* m *Astron.* celestial pole

Himmelsrichtung f **1.** point of the compass, cardinal point; *in die vier ~en deuten* point north, south, west and east; **2.** *allg.* direction; *aus allen ~en* from everywhere, from all four corners of the earth; *in alle ~en zerstreut werden* be scattered to the four winds

Himmels|schlüssel *m Bot.* cowslip; *~stürmer* m, *~stürmerin* f geh. idealist; *~tor* n, *~tür* f lit. → *Himmelspforte*; *~zelt* n; nur Sg.; lit. firmament

himmelwärts *Adv.* geh. heavenward(s)

himmelweit umg. fig. **I.** *Adj.* vast, enormous; *das ist ein ~er Unterschied* that is a vast difference; **II.** *Adv.* → I; *~ voneinander entfernt* worlds apart; *~ von der Wahrheit entfernt* miles away from the truth

himmlisch I. *Adj.* **1.** *Reli.* heavenly; (*göttlich*) divine; *~er Vater* Our Father in Heaven (*od.* Heavenly Father); *e-e ~e Fügung* divine providence; *~e Geduld* fig. the patience of Job; **2.** umg. fig. (*herrlich*) (absolutely) wonderful; *Kleid etc.*: *auch* gorgeous; **II.** *Adv.* umg. fig. wonderfully

hin *Adv.* **1.** *räumlich*: *an ... (Dat.) ~* (*entlang*) along; *auf (+ Akk.) od. zu ... ~* toward(s), to; (*bis*) *zu ... ~* as far as, up to; *nach außen ~* fig. outwardly; *der Wald erstreckt sich über viele Quadratkilometer ~* the forest stretches over many square kilomet|res (*Am.* -ers); *wo ist er ~?* where has he gone?; (*wo hat er sich versteckt?*) *auch* where has he got(ten *Am.*) to?; *nichts wie ~!* what are we waiting for?; *~ und zurück* there and back; *zweimal Kiel, ~ und zurück / nur ~* two returns (*Am.* round-trip tickets) / two singles to Kiel; **2.** *zeitlich*: *über Jahre ~* for years; *gegen od. zum Abend ~* toward(s) evening; *bis ... ist noch / nicht mehr lange ~* ... is still a long way off / isn't far away now; *bis Weihnachten sind noch einige Wochen ~* we've still got a few weeks to go before Christmas, Christmas is still a few weeks off; **3.** *ziellos*: *~ und her gehen, laufen etc.*: to and fro, back and forth; *auf dem Stuhl ~ und her rutschen* fidget around on one's seat; *von den Wellen ~ und her geworfen werden* be tossed around by the waves; *wir haben ~ und her geredet od. überlegt etc.* fig. we to-ed and fro-ed, *Am.* we went here and there; *etw. ~ und her überlegen* fig. turn s.th. over in one's mind; *~ und her gerissen sein* fig. be torn (*zwischen* between); *begeistert*: be absolutely delighted (*von* with, by) umg.; *gebannt*: be entranced *od.* mesmerized (*von* by); *~ bin ... und her gerissen* auch I just can't decide; *ein Hin und Her* (*Kommen und Gehen*) coming and going, to-ing and fro-ing; *fig. in Diskussion*: to-ing and fro-ing, *Am.* going back and forth; (*Wenn und Aber*) ifs and buts; *nach langem Hin und Her* fig. (*Verhandeln*) after much discussion (*od.* talk[ing], bargaining); (*Herumprobieren*) after many attempts, after much experimentation; (*Überlegen*) after a lot of to-ing and fro-ing (*Am.*

a lot of hemming and hawing); **4.** umg.: *Freundschaft ~ oder her od. Freundschaft ~, Freundschaft ~* friendship or no; *ein paar Euro ~ oder her* give or take a couple of euros; *ein paar Euro ~ od. her machen nichts* a few euros more or less aren't going to make any difference; **5.** *~ und wieder* (*manchmal*) now and then; (*stellenweise*) here and there; **6.** *vor sich ~ murmeln, weinen etc.*: to o.s.; *starren, stieren etc.*: straight ahead; *vor sich ~ brüten / dämmern od. dösen / träumen* brood/doze/daydream; **7.** *auf etw. (Akk.) ~ als Folge*: as a result of, following; *als Antwort*: in reply to, on; (*hinsichtlich*) concerning; *auf die Gefahr ~ zu (+ Inf.)* at the risk of (+ Ger.); *auf s-n Rat ~* on his advice; *auf e-e Zielgruppe etc. ~ konzipiert* designed for ..., with ... in mind; *j-n auf Krebs ~ untersuchen* test s.o. for cancer; *auf den bloßen Verdacht ~* purely on suspicion; **8.** umg.: *~ sein* (*kaputt*) be broken; (*zerschlagen*) *auch* be smashed; (*verloren*) be gone (*od.* lost); (*ruiniert*) be done for; (*erschöpft*) be done in, be all in, *Am.* be wiped out; (*tot*) be dead and gone; *er/es ist ~ auch* he's/it's had it; *ich war ganz ~ (und weg) von ihr* I was completely mad about (*od.* besotted with) her

hin... *im V. siehe auch* dahin..., nieder...

hinab... → herab..., hinunter...

hinarbeiten (*trennb., hat -ge-*) **I.** *v/i.*: *auf (+ Akk.)* work toward(s); *darauf ~ zu (+ Inf.)* work toward(s) (+ Ger.); *angestrengt*: strive to (+ Inf.); **II.** *v/refl.*: *sich ~ zu* work one's way toward(s)

hinauf *Adv.* up, upward(s); up there; *bis ~ zu* up to; *den Berg ~* up the hill; *die Treppe ~* up the stairs, upstairs

hinauf... *im V. mst* ... up; → *auch* herauf..., hoch...

hinauf|begleiten *v/t.* (*trennb., hat*) accompany up(stairs); *~blicken* *v/i.* (*trennb., hat -ge-*) look up (*zu* at, fig. to); *~bringen* *v/t.* (*unreg., trennb., hat -ge-*) bring (*od.* carry, take) up(stairs); *~fahren* (*unreg., trennb.*) **I.** *v/i.* (*ist hinaufgefahren*) go up; (*mit*) *Auto*: auch drive up; *mit Rad*: ride up; **II.** *v/t.* (*hat*) take (*od.* drive) up

hinaufführen (*trennb., hat -ge-*) **I.** *v/t.* (*Besucher etc.*) take *s.o.* up(stairs); (*Gefangene, Hund etc.*) lead up(stairs); **II.** *v/i. Weg etc.*: lead (*od.* go) up (there); *den Berg ~* lead (*od.* go) up the mountain

hinaufgehen (*unreg., trennb., ist -ge-*) *v/i.* **1.** go (*od.* walk) up; *die Treppe ~* go upstairs; **2.** → *hinaufführen* II; **3.** *Flugzeug*: *~ auf (+ Akk.)* climb to; **4.** *fig. Fieber, Löhne, Preise etc.*: go up, rise

hinauf|helfen *v/i.* (*unreg., trennb., hat -ge-*) *j-m ~* help s.o. up (*auf + Akk.* onto); *~klettern* *v/i.* (*unreg., trennb., ist -ge-*) climb up (*auf + Akk.* s.th.)

hinaufkommen *v/i.* (*unreg., trennb., ist -ge-*) **1.** come up; (*es schaffen*) make it; *wie ist die Katze die Leiter / auf das Dach hinaufgekommen?* how did the cat manage to get up the ladder / onto the roof?; **2.** *fig. beruflich etc.*: *wie ist er so weit hinaufgekommen?* how did he make it this far?

hinauf|laufen *v/i.* (*unreg., trennb., ist -ge-*) run up (*s.th.*); *~reichen* (*trennb., hat -ge-*) **I.** *v/t.* pass *s.th.* up (*j-m* to s.o.); **II.** *v/i.* reach (*bis zu* as far as, up to), reach up (to); **~schrauben** v/t. (*trennb., hat -ge-*); (*Preise etc.*) push (*od.* force) up; (*Produktion etc.*) step up; **~sehen** v/i. (*unreg., trennb., hat -ge-*) look up (**zu** at); **~setzen** v/t. (*trennb., hat -ge-*); (*Preis etc.*) put up; **~steigen** v/i. (*unreg., trennb., ist -ge-*) climb up; (**auf**) *etw.* (*Akk.*) **~** climb (up) s.th.; **die Treppe ~** *auch* go up the stairs; **~tragen** v/t. (*unreg., trennb., hat -ge-*) carry *od.* take up(stairs)

hinauftreiben v/t. (*unreg., trennb., hat -ge-*) **1.** (*Vieh*) drive up (**den Berg** the mountain; **zur Alm** to the mountain [*od.* high] pasture; **2.** *fig.* (*Kurs, Preis*) push (*od.* force) up

hinaufziehen (*unreg., trennb.*) **I.** v/t. (*hat hinaufgezogen*) pull up; *unpers.*: **es zieht mich in die Berge hinauf** I am drawn to go up into the mountains; **II.** v/i. (*ist*) move up; **in den 3. Stock ~** move up to the third (*Am.* fourth) floor; **III.** v/refl. (*hat*) **1.** pull o.s. up (**zu** to; **an e-m Seil** with a rope; **2. sich ~ bis** (*erstrecken*) stretch up to

hinaus *Adv.* **1.** *räumlich*: out, out there; (*nach außen*) outside; **~!** get out!; **~ mit ihm!** throw him out!; **~ damit!** out with it; **aufs Meer ~** out to sea; **~ aus** out of; **nach hinten/vorn ~** *wohnen*: at the back/front; **über ...** (*Akk.*) **~** (*weiter als*) beyond, past; (*höher als*) above, more than; **zum** *od.* **durchs Fenster ~** out of the window, *Am. und Brit. umg. auch* out the window; **ein Zimmer zur Straße / zum Hof ~** a room facing (*od.* overlooking) the street / overlooking (*od.* looking into) a *od.* the courtyard; **er ist hinten / zur Hintertür ~** *umg.* he went out the back / the back door; **2.** *zeitlich*: **auf Jahre ~** for years (to come); **über die nächste Woche ~** till (at least) the week after next; **über das Alter ist sie ~** she's grown out of it; **über die vierzig ~ sein** be over forty; **3.** *fig.*: **über etw.** (*Akk.*) **~** (*zusätzlich zu*) over and above s.th., in addition to s.th.; **über das normale Maß ~** beyond the norm; **über etw.** (*Akk.*) **~ sein** be past s.th.; **ich bin längst darüber ~ zu** (+ *Inf.*) I'm long past (+ *Ger.*); **darüber ist er ~** he's got over that; → **darüber** 5

hinaus... *im V. mst.* ... out; → *auch* **heraus..., raus...**

hinaus|befördern v/t. (*trennb., hat*) **1.** move out; **2.** *umg. fig.* kick s.o. out; **~begleiten** v/t. (*trennb., hat*) see (*od.* show) *s.o.* out (*od.* to the door); **~beugen** v/refl. (*trennb., hat -ge-*) lean out (**aus dem** *od.* **zum Fenster** of the window; **zu ihr** toward[s] her)

hinausbringen v/t. (*unreg., trennb., hat -ge-*) **1.** bring (*od.* take) out(side); **2.** → **hinausbegleiten**; **3.** *erfolgreich*: get out (**aus** of); **4.** *unpers.*: **er hat es nie über die Grundbegriffe hinausgebracht** he has never got(ten *Am.*) any further than (*od.* beyond) the basic principles

hinaus|dürfen v/i. (*unreg., trennb., hat -ge-*) *umg.*: **er darf nicht hinaus** he is not allowed to go out; **~ekeln** v/t. (*trennb., hat -ge-*); *umg.* freeze out

hinausfahren (*unreg., trennb.*) **I.** v/i. (*ist hinausgefahren*) go out (**aus** of); (*mit*) *Auto*: drive out (of); (*mit*) *Schiff*: sail out, put to sea; *mit Rad*: ride out (of); *Zug*: pull out (of); **aufs Land ~** go out into the countryside; **aufs** (*offene*) **Meer ~** go out to sea; **über die Markierung ~** go beyond (*od.* past) the

marker; **II.** v/t. (*hat*) take out (**aus** of); (*mit*) *Auto*: drive out (of)

hinaus|fallen v/i. (*unreg., trennb., ist -ge-*) **1.** fall out (**aus, zu** of); **2.** *Licht*: come out (**aus** of); **3.** *fig. aus Kategorie, Liste, Programm etc.*: be removed (**aus** from); **~finden** v/i. (*unreg., trennb., hat -ge-*) find one's way out (**aus** of); **allein ~** find one's own way out

hinausfliegen (*unreg., trennb.*) **I.** v/i. (*ist hinausgeflogen*) **1.** fly out (**aus** of); **über das Ziel ~** fly past the target; **2.** *umg.* be kicked out; *aus e-r Stellung*: *auch* get the sack, *Am.* get fired; **II.** v/t. (*hat*) fly out (**aus** of)

hinausführen (*trennb., hat -ge-*) **I.** v/t. **1.** take out (**aus** of); (*Gäste etc.*) lead out (of); **2.** *fig.*: **die Firma aus der Krise ~** lead the company out of the crisis; **II.** v/i. *Weg etc.*: lead out (**aus** of); **~ auf** (+ *Akk.*) *Tür*: open onto, lead to; **über etw.** (*Akk.*) **~** go beyond s.th.

hinausgehen v/i. (*unreg., trennb., ist -ge-*) **1.** go (*od.* walk) out (**aus** of; **auf die Straße** into the street), leave (**aus** s.th.); *ins Freie*: *auch* go outside; **2.** *Weg etc.*: lead out (**aus** of); **~ auf** (+ *Akk.*) *Tür*: open onto, lead to; *das Fenster/Zimmer geht auf den Park / nach Süden hinaus* looks out onto the park / faces south; **3.** (*gesandt werden*) go out, be sent out (**an** + *Akk.* to; **in alle Welt** all over the world); **4.** *unpers.*: **hier geht es nicht hinaus** there is no way out here, you can't get out here; **5. ~ über** (+ *Akk.*) go beyond; *Sache*: *auch* surpass

hinaus|halten v/t. (*unreg., trennb., hat -ge-*) hold out (**aus, zu** of); (*Hand, Kopf etc.*) put (*od.* stick) out (of); **~jagen** v/t. (*trennb., hat -ge-*); *auch fig.* chase out; *fig.* (*entlassen*) kick out *umg.*

hinauskommen v/i. (*unreg., trennb., ist -ge-*) **1.** come out (**aus** of); (*hinauskönnen*) get out (of); **er ist nie aus s-m Dorf hinausgekommen** he has never been out of his village; **mach, dass du hinauskommst!** *umg.* get out!; **2.** *fig.* → **hinauslaufen** 2; **3.** *fig.*: **~ über** (+ *Akk.*) get beyond, get further than; *in der Leistung*: manage (*od.* do)

hinaus|komplimentieren v/t. (*trennb., hat*); *iro.* get rid of, see *s.o.* off the premises; **~können** v/i. (*unreg., trennb., hat -ge-*); *umg.* be able to go out; **~lassen** v/t. (*unreg., trennb., hat -ge-*) let out

hinauslaufen v/i. (*unreg., trennb., ist -ge-*) **1.** run (*od.* rush) out (**aus, zu** of; **auf die Straße** into the street); **2.** *fig.*: **~ auf** (+ *Akk.*) (*bedeuten*) come (*od.* boil) down to; (*enden in*) end up in; **es läuft auf dasselbe** *od.* **eins hinaus** it comes (*od.* amounts) to the same thing

hinaus|lehnen v/refl. (*trennb., hat -ge-*) lean out (**aus, zu** of); **Nicht ~!, Hinauslehnen verboten!** *Aufschrift im Zug*: do not lean out (of the window); **~müssen** v/i. (*unreg., trennb., hat -ge-*); *umg.* have to go out; **ich muss mal hinaus** *euph.* (*auf die Toilette*) I need to pay a visit; **~posaunen** v/t. (*trennb., hat*); *umg., mst pej.* broadcast *s.th.*; **~ragen** v/i. (*trennb., hat -ge-*) *horizontal*: jut out (**über** + *Akk.* over); **~ über** (+ *Akk.*) *vertikal und fig.*: tower above; **~reden** v/refl. (*trennb., hat -ge-*) **1.** → **herausreden**; **2. sich auf etw.** (*Akk.*) **~** (*wollen*) (want to) use

s.th. as an excuse

hinausreichen (*trennb., hat -ge-*) **I.** v/t. reach (*od.* hand) *s.th.* out (**aus, zu** of); **II.** v/i. **1.** reach, stretch (**bis** as far as); **2. ~ über** (+ *Akk.*) reach (*od.* stretch) beyond; *zeitlich*: last more than; *fig.* go beyond

hinaus|schaffen v/t. (*trennb., hat -ge-*) **1.** take (*od.* get) out; **2.** → **schaffen**[2] I 1; **~schauen** v/i. (*trennb., hat -ge-*) look out (**aus, zu** of); **~schicken** v/t. (*trennb., hat -ge-*) send out; **~schieben** v/t. (*unreg., trennb., hat -ge-*) **1.** push out (**aus** of); **2.** *fig.* put off, postpone; (*verzögern*) delay

hinausschießen v/i. (*unreg., trennb.*) **1.** (*hat hinausgeschossen*) shoot (*od.* fire) out (**aus** of); **2.** (*ist*); (*schnell fliegen, rennen etc.*) shoot out; **über das Ziel ~** *auch fig.* overshoot the mark

hinaus|schmeißen v/t. (*unreg., trennb., hat -ge-*); *umg.* → **hinauswerfen**; **~schreien** (*unreg., trennb., hat -ge-*) **I.** v/i. shout out (**aus, zu** of); **II.** v/t. *geh.*: **s-n Hass/Schmerz ~** give vent to one's hatred/pain; **~schwimmen** v/i. (*unreg., trennb., ist -ge-*) swim (*Gegenstand*: float) out (**aus** of; **aufs Meer** to sea); **~sehen** v/i. (*unreg., trennb., hat -ge-*) look out (**aus, zu** of); **~ sein** → **hinaus**; **~springen** v/i. (*unreg., trennb., ist -ge-*) **1.** jump out (**aus, zu** of); **2.** *umg.* (*hinauslaufen*) run out (of); **~steigen** v/i. (*unreg., trennb., ist -ge-*): **zum Fenster ~** climb out of the window; **~stellen** v/t. (*trennb., hat -ge-*) **1.** put out(side); **2.** *Sport* send off; **~stoßen** v/t. (*trennb., hat -ge-*) push out (**aus** of); **~strecken** v/t. (*trennb., hat -ge-*): **den Kopf zum Fenster ~** put (*od.* stick) one's head out (of) the window

hinausstürzen (*trennb.*) **I.** v/i. (*ist hinausgestürzt*) **1.** (*fallen*) fall out (**aus, zu** of); **2.** (*eilen*) rush out (of); **II.** v/refl. (*hat*): **sich** (**zum Fenster**) **~** jump out *od.* throw o.s. out ([of] the window)

hinaustragen v/t. (*unreg., trennb., hat -ge-*) **1.** carry out (**aus, zu** of); **der Schwung trug ihn über das Ziel hinaus** his/its momentum carried him/it past the target; **2.** *fig.*: **e-e Botschaft in alle Welt ~** spread a message throughout the world

hinaustreiben (*unreg., trennb.*) **I.** v/t. (*hat hinausgetrieben*) drive out (**aus** of); (*verjagen*) chase away; *unpers.*: **es treibt mich hinaus** I've got to get out of (*od.* away from) here; **II.** v/i. (*ist*): **aufs Meer ~** drift out to sea

hinaus|trompeten v/t. (*trennb., hat*); *umg., mst pej.* broadcast *s.th.*; **~wachsen** v/i. (*unreg., trennb., ist -ge-*): **~ über** (+ *Akk.*) grow bigger than; *fig.* (*reifer werden*) outgrow *s.th.*; (*übertreffen*) surpass *s.o.*; **über sich selbst ~** *fig.* rise above o.s.; **der Baum ist über die Garage hinausgewachsen** the tree's taller than the garage now; **~wagen** v/refl. (*trennb., hat -ge-*) venture out; **~weisen** (*unreg., trennb., hat -ge-*) **I.** v/t. show *s.o.* the door; *höflicher*: ask *s.o.* to leave; **II.** v/i.: **~ über** (+ *Akk.*) (*Augenblicksprobleme etc.*) point (*od.* go, reach) beyond

hinauswerfen v/t. (*unreg., trennb., hat -ge-*) **1.** throw (*od.* cast) out (**aus** of); **2. e-n Blick** (**zum Fenster**) **~** glance out (of the window); **3.** *umg. fig.* throw (*od.* chuck) out; (*j-n*) (*entlassen*) *auch* (give the) sack, *bes. Am.*

fire; *Geld zum Fenster* ~ squander; *das ist hinausgeworfenes Geld* that's a waste of money, that's money down the drain

hinauswollen *v/i.* (*unreg., trennb., hat -ge-*) **1.** *umg.* want to get out (*aus* of); **2.** *fig.:* ~ *auf* (+ *Akk.*) drive at; *worauf will er hinaus? auch* what's he getting at?; *hoch* ~ aim high, be ambitious; *höher* ~ *als* have set one's sights further than

Hinauswurf *m umg.:* *e-n* ~ *riskieren* risk getting thrown (*od.* kicked) out; *j-m mit dem* ~ *drohen* threaten to throw (*od.* kick) s.o. out

hinausziehen (*unreg., trennb.*) **I.** *v/t.* (*hat hinausgezogen*) **1.** pull out (*aus* of); *sie zog ihn am Arm mit sich hinaus* she took him by the arm and dragged him outside; **2.** *fig.* (*verzögern*) draw (*od.* drag) out; **3.** *mst unpers.:* *es zog ihn hinaus in die Welt* he felt he had to go out into the big wide world; *bei dem Wetter zieht mich nichts hinaus* nothing can persuade me to go outside in this weather; **II.** *v/i.* (*ist*) move out (*aus* of); *Soldaten:* withdraw (*aus* from); *aufs Land* ~ move out into the country; *in die Welt* ~ go out into the world; *der Rauch zieht zum Kamin hinaus* the smoke goes out of the chimney; **III.** *v/refl.* (*hat*) drag on; (*sich verzögern*) be delayed

hinauszögern (*trennb., hat -ge-*) **I.** *v/t.* (*verschieben*) put off; (*in die Länge ziehen*) drag (*umg.* spin) out; **II.** *v/refl.* be delayed, take longer than expected

hin|bauen *v/t.* (*trennb., hat -ge-*): *da haben sie jetzt ... hingebaut* they have built ... there now; **~bekommen** *v/t.* (*unreg., trennb., hat -ge-*) → *hinkriegen*; **~bemühen** (*trennb., hat -ge-*) *förm.* **I.** *v/t.* ask *s.o.* to go there; **II.** *v/refl.* take the trouble to go there; **~biegen** *v/t.* (*unreg., trennb., hat -ge-*) *umg.* **1.** (*wieder in Ordnung*) put straight (*od.* right), straighten out; **2.** → *hindrehen*; **~blättern** *v/t.* (*trennb., hat -ge-*); *umg.* (*Geld*) shell out

Hinblick *m:* *im* ~ *auf* (+ *Akk.*) in view of; (*hinsichtlich*) regarding; (*vorausschauend auf*) with the prospect of, with ... in mind (*od.* view)

hin|bringen *v/t.* (*unreg., trennb., hat -ge-*) **1.** take there; *wo darf ich Sie* ~? where would you like to go to?; **2.** (*Zeit*) spend, pass (away); **3.** *umg.* (*fertig bringen*) manage; *wieder* ~ → *hinbiegen* 1; **~denken** *v/i.* (*unreg., trennb., hat -ge-*); *umg.:* *wo denkst du hin?* say that again?, you've got to be joking

hinderlich *Adj.* obstructive (+ *Dat.* to); (*lästig*) troublesome; (*unbequem*) inconvenient (to); *er war mir bei der Arbeit* ~ (*störend*) he was in my (*od.* the) way while I was working; *sich* ~ *auswirken* prove to be a hindrance; *das ist m-n Plänen od. für m-e Pläne eher* ~ that is rather going to get in the way of my plans

hindern **I.** *v/t.* **1.** *j-n an etw.* (*Dat.*), *j-n* (*daran*) ~ *zu* (+ *Inf.*) stop (*od.* prevent) s.o. from (+ *Ger.*); **2.** (*j-n*) hinder (*bei* in); (*Verkehr*) block, obstruct; **II.** *v/i.* (*stören*) be a hindrance (*bei* to)

Hindernis *n; -ses, -se* **1.** *im Weg:* obstacle, barrier; *Laufsport:* hurdle; *Reitsport:* fence; *ein unüberwindliches* ~ an insurmountable hurdle (*od.* obstacle); **2.** *fig.* obstacle (*für* to); (*Schwierigkeit*) difficulty; (*Behinderung*) hin-

drance; *kein* ~ *für* no obstacle to; *Kinder kein* ~ in *Kontaktanzeige:* children no obstacle, kids OK *umg.*; *auf* ~*se stoßen* run into difficulties; *j-m* ~*se in den Weg legen* throw obstacles into s.o.'s path; *Familienglück mit* ~*sen* happy family life with a few hitches along the way

Hindernis|lauf *m,* ~**rennen** *n Sport* steeplechase

Hinderung *f* obstruction; *ohne* ~ unhindered; **Hinderungsgrund** *m* reason (*for not coming etc.*); (*Argument dagegen*) argument (*for not coming etc.*); (*Ausrede*) excuse; *das ist für mich kein* ~ *auch* that's not going to stop me

hindeuten *v/i.* (*trennb., hat -ge-*): ~ *auf* (+ *Akk.*) point to (*od.* at); *fig.* point to, indicate

Hindi *n; -; Ling.* Hindi

hindrängen (*trennb., hat -ge-*) **I.** *v/refl.:* *sich* ~ *zu* push (one's way) toward(s); **II.** *v/i.* **1.** ~ *zu od. nach* push (one's way) toward(s); **2.** *fig.:* *auf Reformen* ~ urge (*od.* press for) reforms; *alles in ihm drängte zum Film hin* everything in him was urging him to go into films (*Am.* into movies *od.* to Hollywood); **III.** *v/t.:* ~ *zu* push toward(s)

hindrehen *v/t.* (*trennb., hat -ge-*); *umg.* **1.** *etw. so* ~, *dass ...* twist s.th. so that ...; *er dreht alles so hin, wie's ihm gerade passt* he twists everything to suit his purposes; **2.** → *hinbiegen* 1

Hindu *m; -(s), -(s)* Hindu; **Hinduismus** *m; -, kein Pl.* Hinduism; **hinduistisch** *Adj.* Hindu

Hindukusch *m; -(s); Geog.* Hindu Kush

hindurch *Adv.* **1.** *räumlich:* through; *durch etw.* ~ through s.th.; *mitten* ~ right *od.* straight through (the middle); *quer/schräg* ~ straight/diagonally across; **2.** *zeitlich:* through(out), during; *den ganzen Tag* ~ all day (long); *das ganze Jahr* ~ all year round, the whole year; *mein ganzes Leben* ~ all my life

hindurch... *im V. siehe auch* **durch...**

hin|dürfen *v/i.* (*unreg., trennb., hat -ge-*); *umg.* be allowed to go (there); *darf ich hin?* may I go?; ~**eilen** *v/i.* (*trennb., ist -ge-*) hurry there

hinein *Adv.* in; ~ *in* (+ *Akk.*) into, in(side); *bis od. mitten* ~ *in* (+ *Akk.*) right into (the middle of); *bis in die Nacht* ~ well (*od.* right) into the night; *bis tief in die Nacht* ~ till the (wee) small hours; *nur* ~! go on in; ~ *mit dir!* in you go!

hinein... *im V. mst ...* in; ~ *in* (+ *Akk.*) ... into; *siehe auch* **ein...,** **herein...,** **rein...**

hinein|beißen *v/i.* (*unreg., trennb., hat -ge-*): ~ *in* (+ *Akk.*) bite into; take a bite of; ~**bekommen** *v/t.* (*unreg., trennb., hat*); *umg.:* ~ (*in* + *Akk.*) get s.th. in(to); *ich bekomme nichts mehr hinein* (*bin satt*) I couldn't eat another thing; ~**blasen** *v/i.* (*unreg., trennb., hat -ge-*): ~ *in* (+ *Akk.*) blow into; ~**bringen** *v/t.* (*unreg., trennb., hat -ge-*): ~ (*in*) (+ *Akk.*) **1.** take *od.* bring in(to); **2.** *umg.* → *hineinbekommen*

hinein|denken *v/refl.* (*unreg., trennb., hat -ge-*): ~ *in* (+ *Akk.*) *in j-n:* put o.s. in s.o.'s place (*od.* position); *in ein Problem etc.:* think one's way into; *in Zeit, Umgebung etc.:* imagine one is in; *in Vergangenes:* think back to; ~**deuten** *v/t.* (*trennb., hat -ge-*): *etw.* ~ *in* (+ *Akk.*) read s.th. into; *das deu-*

test du nur hinein you're just reading that into it

hineindrängen (*trennb., hat -ge-*) **I.** *v/t.:* ~ (*in* + *Akk.*) (*etw.*) squeeze *od.* force in(to); (*j-n*) force *od.* push in(to); (*Menge*) *auch* herd in(to); **II.** *v/i. und v/refl.:* (*sich*) ~ (*in* + *Akk.*) push one's way in(to)

hineindürfen *v/i.* (*unreg., trennb., hat -ge-*); *umg.* be allowed in; *in die Soße darf ruhig ein Schluck Wein hinein* a dash of wine can be added to the sauce if desired

hineinfahren (*unreg., trennb.*) **I.** *v/i.* (*ist hineingefahren*) **1.** ~ (*in* + *Akk.*) go in(to); (*mit*) *Auto:* drive in(to); *mit Rad:* ride in(to); *Zug:* pull in(to); *Schiff:* sail in(to); **2.** *Unfall:* *in j-s Auto* ~ run into s.o.'s car; *j-m hinten* ~ run into the back of s.o.; **3.** *in die Schuhe etc.* ~ slip into one's shoes *etc.*; **II.** *v/t.* (*hat*): ~ (*in* + *Akk.*) drive in(to)

hineinfallen *v/i.* (*unreg., trennb., ist -ge-*) **1.** ~ (*in* + *Akk.*) fall in(to); **2.** *fig.* → *hereinfallen*

hineinfinden (*unreg., trennb., hat -ge-*) **I.** *v/i./i.:* ~ (*in* + *Akk.*) find one's way in(to); **II.** *v/refl. fig.:* *sich* ~ *in* (+ *Akk.*) get into; *sich in sein Schicksal* ~ come to terms with one's fate

hineinfressen (*unreg., trennb., hat -ge-*) **I.** *v/refl.:* *sich* ~ *in* (+*Akk.*) **1.** *Raupe etc.:* eat into; **2.** *Säure etc.:* eat into; **II.** *v/t.:* *in sich* ~ (*Akk.*) ~ **1.** *umg. pej.* (*hineinschlingen*) gobble s.th. up; **2.** *umg. fig.* (*Kummer etc.*) bottle s.th. up; *jahrelang hat sie alles in sich hineingefressen* she's been bottling everything up for years

hineingeheimnissen *v/t.* (*trennb., hat*): *etw. in etw.* (*Akk.*) ~ try to read s.th. into s.th., try to find a hidden meaning in s.th.; *viel in etw.* (*Akk.*) ~ read all sorts of things into s.th., try to find all sorts of things in s.th.

hineingehen (*unreg., trennb., ist -ge-*): ~ (*in*) (+ *Akk.*) **1.** go in(to), enter; *lass uns* ~ let's go in; **2.** (*passen*) go in(to); *in den Kanister gehen ... hinein auch* the container holds ...; *in den Saal gehen ... hinein auch* the hall seats ...

hinein|geraten **I.** *v/i.* (*unreg., trennb., ist -ge-*): ~ (*in* + *Akk.*) get in(to); (*verwickelt werden in*) *auch* get (o.s.) involved (in); (*Unangenehmes etc.*) *auch* get caught up in it (*od.* in s.th.); **II.** *P.P.* → I; ~**halten** *v/t.* (*unreg., trennb., hat -ge-*): ~ (*in* + *Akk.*) put s.th. in(to)

hineinhängen[1] *v/i.* (*unreg., trennb., hat / südd., österr. schw. ist -ge-*) hang (*in* + *Akk.*)

hineinhängen[2] (*trennb., hat -ge-*) **I.** *v/t.:* ~ (*in* + *Akk.*) hang *s.th.* in(to) *od.* inside; **II.** *v/refl. umg.:* *sich* ~ *in* (+ *Akk.*) **1.** → *hineinknien*; **2.** (*sich einmischen*) stick one's nose into

hinein|horchen *v/i.* (*trennb., hat -ge-*); *geh. fig.:* *in sich* (*Akk.*) ~ do some soul-searching; ~**interpretieren** *v/t.* (*trennb., hat*): *etw.* ~ *in* (+ *Akk.*) read s.th. into; ~**knien** *v/refl.* (*trennb., hat -ge-*) put one's back into it; *sich in etw.* (*Akk.*) ~ get down to s.th.

hineinkommen *v/i.* (*unreg., trennb., ist -ge-*): ~ (*in*) (+ *Akk.*) **1.** come in(to), enter; **2.** (*gelangen, geraten*) get in(to); **3.** *umg.* (*hineingehören, hineingetan werden etc.*) go in(to); **4.** *fig., in Aufgabe etc.:* get in(to)

hinein|kriechen *v/i.* (*unreg., trennb., ist -ge-*): ~ (*in* + *Akk.*) creep in(to); ~**la-**

chen v/i. (trennb., hat -ge-): **in sich** (Akk.) ~ laugh (od. chuckle) to o.s.; **~lassen** v/t. (unreg., trennb., hat -ge-): ~ (**in** + Akk.) let in(to)

hineinlaufen v/i. (unreg., trennb., ist -ge-) **1.** Person, Wasser, Farbe etc.: run inside (od. in there); ~ **in** (+ Akk.) run inside (od. into); **2.** unachtsam: **in j-n** ~ run (od. bump) into s.o.; **in ein Auto** ~ run into a car

hineinlegen v/t. (trennb., hat -ge-) **1.** ~ (**in** + Akk.) put in(to) od. inside; **2.** fig.: **viel Gefühl in s-e Worte** ~ put lots of feeling into one's words; **etw. in j-s Worte** ~ read s.th. into s.o.'s words; **3.** umg. fig. → **hereinlegen**

hinein|lesen v/t. (unreg., trennb., hat -ge-): **etw.** ~ **in** (+ Akk.) read s.th. into; **~manövrieren** v/t. (trennb., hat): ~ (**in** + Akk.) man|oeuvre (Am. -euver) in(to) od. inside; **~passen** v/i. (trennb., hat -ge-): ~ (**in** + Akk.) fit in(to); platzmäßig: auch go in(to); **es passt nicht hinein** it won't fit (in) od. go in; **~pfuschen** v/i. (trennb., hat -ge-) meddle (**in** + Akk. in, with), interfere (in, with); **~platzen** v/i. (trennb., ist -ge-): ~ (**in** + Akk.) burst in(to); **~pressen** v/t. (trennb., hat -ge-) **1.** ~ (**in** + Akk.) press in(to); **2.** fig.: **in ein Schema** ~ force s.o./s.th. into a mould; **~projizieren** v/t. (trennb., hat): ~ **in** (+ Akk.) project onto; **~pumpen** v/t. (trennb., hat -ge-): ~ **in** (+ Akk.) pump in(to) (auch umg. fig.); **~quetschen** v/t. und v/refl. (trennb., hat -ge-): (sich) ~ (**in** + Akk.) squeeze in(to)

hineinreden (trennb., hat -ge-) **I.** v/i. **1.** ~ (**in** + Akk.) (dazwischenreden) interrupt; **2.** pej. → **dreinreden**; **II.** v/refl.: **sich in Begeisterung/Wut** ~ talk o.s. into being enthusiastic / work o.s. up into a rage

hinein|reichen (trennb., hat -ge-) **I.** v/t. pass in; **II.** v/i. reach in(side); **~schaufeln** v/t. (trennb., hat -ge-); umg. fig.: **etw. in sich** (Akk.) ~ stuff one's face with s.th., Am. auch pig out (on s.th.); **~schlittern** v/i. (trennb., ist -ge-): ~ (**in**) (+ Akk.) **1.** slide in(to); **2.** umg. fig. drift in(to), get involved (in); **~schnuppern** v/i. (trennb., hat -ge-); umg. fig.: ~ **in** (+ Akk.) Firma etc.: take a look at; in e-e Arbeit etc.: have a go at, Am. give it a try; **~schütten** v/t. (trennb., hat -ge-); umg.: **etw. in sich** (Akk.) ~ knock (Am. auch toss) s.th. back

hineinsehen v/i. (unreg., trennb., hat -ge-) **1.** ~ (**in** + Akk.) look in(to); **man kann in niemanden** ~ one cannot tell what is (od. you can't tell what's umg.) going on in other people's minds; **2.** umg., flüchtig: **ich hab nur mal kurz in den Film / die Kneipe hineingesehen** I only saw a small part of the film / I was just in the pub (Am. bar) for a few minutes

hineinsetzen (trennb., hat -ge-) **I.** v/refl.: **sich** ~ (**in** + Akk.) in Sessel etc.: sit down (in); in Zimmer: sit down (in); in Fahrzeug etc.: get in(to); **II.** v/t.: ~ (**in** + Akk.) put in(to)

hinein|spielen v/i. (trennb., hat -ge-); fig. be involved, play a role (od. part), figure (**in** + Akk. in); **~stecken** v/t. (trennb., hat -ge-) **1.** ~ (**in** + Akk.) put in(to); **2.** fig. (Mühe, Zeit etc.) put in(to); **Geld** ~ **in** (+ Akk.) put (Wirts. sink) money into; → **Nase**[1] 5

hineinsteigern v/refl. (trennb., hat -ge-): **sich** ~ (**in** + Akk.) in Wut etc.:

---

work o.s. up (into); in Problem etc.: get all worked up (over); in Arbeit etc.: get completely wrapped up (in); in Idee etc.: go completely overboard (for); in Rolle etc.: get completely involved (od. caught up) (in); in Kummer, Schmerz: become completely overwhelmed (by)

hinein|stopfen v/t. (trennb., hat -ge-) **1.** ~ (**in** + Akk.) stuff in(to) (auch umg. fig.); **2.** umg.: Schokolade etc. **in sich** (Akk.) ~ stuff o.s. with, feed one's face with Sl., Am. auch pig out on; **~stoßen** v/t. (unreg., trennb., hat -ge-) **1.** ~ (**in** + Akk.) push in(to); (Messer etc.) thrust (into); **2.** Mus.: ~ **in** (+ Akk.) blow into

hineinstürzen (trennb.) **I.** v/i. (ist hineingestürzt): ~ (**in** + Akk.) **1.** fall in(to); **2.** in ein Zimmer etc.: burst in(to); **II.** v/t. (hat): ~ (**in** + Akk.) **1.** push s.o. in(to); **2.** fig. in e-e unangenehme Lage etc.: plunge s.o. into; **III.** v/refl. (hat) **1.** **sich** ~ (**in** + Akk.) jump in(to), plunge in(to); **sich ins Treiben** ~ throw o.s. into the fray; **2.** fig.: **sich in die Arbeit** ~ throw o.s. into one's work

hinein|tappen v/i. (trennb., ist -ge-): ~ **in** (+ Akk.) in Falle, Pfütze etc.: walk into (auch fig.); **~tragen** v/t. (unreg., trennb., hat -ge-): ~ (**in**) (+ Akk.) **1.** carry in(to); **2.** fig. Unfrieden, Unruhe etc.: bring in(to); **~tun** v/t. (unreg., trennb., hat -ge-): ~ (**in** + Akk.) put in(to); **2.** fig.: **e-n Blick** ~ **in** (+ Akk.) take a look at; **~versetzen** v/refl. (trennb., hat) → **versetzen** II; **~wachsen** v/i. (unreg., trennb., ist -ge-): ~ **in** (+ Akk.) grow in(to) (auch fig.); **~wagen** v/refl. (trennb., hat -ge-): **sich** ~ (**in** + Akk.) venture in(to); **ich wagte mich nicht hinein** I didn't dare (to) go in; **~werfen** v/t. (unreg., trennb., hat -ge-) **1.** ~ (**in** + Akk.) throw in(to); **2.** fig.: **e-n Blick** ~ (**in** + Akk.) take od. have a quick look (at); **e-n Blick in ein Buch** etc. ~ auch glance at a book etc.; **~wählen** v/t. (trennb., hat -ge-): **in den Bundestag** etc. ~ vote s.o. into the Bundestag etc.; **~wollen** v/i. (unreg., trennb., hat -ge-); umg.: ~ **in** (+ Akk.) want to go (od. get) in(to); **das will mir nicht in den Kopf hinein** I just can't understand it; **~ziehen** v/t. (unreg., trennb., hat -ge-) **1.** ~ (**in** + Akk.) pull in(to); **2.** fig.: **j-n** (**in etw.** [Akk.]) ~ (verwickeln) drag s.o. in(to s.th.); **~zwängen** v/t. und v/refl. (trennb., hat -ge-): ~ (**in** + Akk.) squeeze (od. force) in(to)

hinfahren (unreg., trennb.) **I.** v/t. (hat hingefahren) **1.** take (mit Auto: drive) s.o. od. s.th. there; ~ **nach** od. **zu** take (od. drive) to; **II.** v/i. (ist) **1.** go there (by car/train etc.); (mit) Auto: drive there; mit Rad: ride there; (mit) Schiff: sail there; ~ **nach** od. **zu** go (od. drive etc.) to; **Hinfahrt** f journey there; Naut. voyage out; **auf der** ~ on the (od. our etc.) way there

hinfallen v/i. (unreg., trennb., ist -ge-) fall (down); Person: (stürzen) auch fall over; **etw.** ~ **lassen** drop s.th.; **sich** ~ **lassen** let o.s. fall; **vor j-m** ~ geh. throw o.s. at s.o.'s feet

hinfällig Adj. **1.** (gebrechlich) frail; **2.** (ungültig) invalid; **~machen** invalidate; **damit wird die Sache** ~ that disposes of that (od. the matter); **Hinfälligkeit** f; nur Sg. **1.** (Gebrechlichkeit) frailty; **2.** (Ungültigkeit) invalidity

hin|finden v/i. (unreg., trennb., hat -ge-) find the way (od. one's way

---

there); **~flegeln** v/refl. (trennb., hat -ge-); umg. sprawl all over the place; **sich** ~ **auf** (+ Akk.) sprawl all over

hinfliegen (unreg., trennb.) **I.** v/i. (ist hingeflogen) **1.** fly there; **2.** über **j-n/etw.** ~ Ball etc.: fly over s.o./s.th.; **das Pferd flog wie ein Pfeil über die Ebene hin** the horse flew like an arrow across the plain; **3.** umg. (stürzen) come a cropper, fall; **II.** v/t. (hat) fly there; **Hinflug** m outward flight; **auf dem** ~ auch on the way there

hinfort Adv. geh. henceforth

hinführen (trennb., hat -ge-) **I.** v/t. take there; **II.** v/i. **1.** Straße etc.: go (od. lead) there; ~ **nach** od. **zu** go (od. lead) to; **2.** fig.: **wo soll das** ~**?** where will it all end?; **wo soll** od. **würde das** ~, **wenn ...** where would we all be if ...

hing Imperf. → **hängen**[1]

Hingabe f; nur Sg. **1.** devotion (an + Akk. to); **mit** od. **voller** ~ → **hingebungsvoll** II; **2.** geh. euph., sexuell: surrender; **3.** geh. (das Opfern) sacrificing; **unter** ~ **s-s Lebens** by laying down one's life

hingeben (unreg., trennb., hat -ge-) **I.** v/refl.: **sich** ~ (+ Dat.) (widmen) devote (od. dedicate) o.s. to; Lastern etc.: indulge in; Hoffnungen, Illusionen etc.: cherish; der Verzweiflung etc.: surrender to; **sie gab sich ihm hin** euph. she gave herself to him; **sich s-m Schmerz** etc. ~ abandon o.s. to one's grief etc.; **II.** v/t. **1.** (weggeben) give away; **2.** geh. (opfern) sacrifice; **sein Leben** ~ lay down one's life; **Hingebung** f → **Hingabe** 1; **hingebungsvoll I.** Adj. devoted; **II.** Adv. devotedly; (begeistert) auch passionately; (selbstvergessen) with abandon

hingegen Konj. geh. however, on the other hand

hingegossen Adj. umg. hum.: **wie** ~ **auf der Couch liegen** lie draped over the settee

hingehen v/i. (unreg., trennb., ist -ge-) **1.** go there; (weggehen) go; **zu j-m** ~ go up to s.o.; (besuchen) go to see s.o., go and see s.o.; **wo gehst du hin?** where are you going?; **wo kann man hier** ~**?** umg. (ausgehen) what sort of places can you go to around here?; **gehet hin in Frieden** kirchl. go in peace; **2.** Straße etc.: go (od. lead) there; unpers.: **wo soll's denn** ~**?** in den Urlaub etc.: where to?; Taxifahrer: where to?; **3.** fig. Jahre, Zeit: pass (by); **darüber gingen viele Jahre hin** in the meantime many years passed; **4.** geh. euph. (sterben) pass away; **5.** fig. (durchgehen) pass (als as); ~ **lassen** let s.th. pass; (übersehen) overlook; **das mag ja noch** ~, **aber ...** that may just about pass, but ...

hin|gehören v/i. belong; **wo gehört das hin?** where does that belong (od. go)?; **~gelangen** v/i. (trennb., ist -ge-) geh. get there; ~ **nach** od. **zu** get to; **~geraten** v/i. (unreg., trennb., ist -ge-); umg. land, end up; **wo ist sie** ~**?** auch what became of her?

hingerissen I. P.P. → **hinreißen**; **II.** Adj. fascinated, enthralled; Lächeln etc.: enraptured; **III.** Adv. lauschen: with rapt attention; zusehen: enthralled; ~ **der Musik lauschen** auch be transported (od. carried away) by the music

hin|geworfen I. P.P. → **hinwerfen**; **II.** Adj. Bemerkung etc.: casual; **~ha-**

H

ben v/t. (unreg., trennb., hat -ge-); umg.: **wo hast du den Schlüssel hin?** where have you put the key?; **wo willst du das ~?** where do you want this?

hinhalten v/t. (unreg., trennb., hat -ge-) **1.** hold out (+ Dat. to); **2.** fig. (j-n) put off; (warten lassen) keep s.o. hanging; Mil. hold off; **~de Politik** delaying tactic; **Hinhaltetaktik** f delaying (od. stalling) tactics Pl.

hinhängen v/t. (trennb., hat -ge-) **1.** hang up; **wo hast du es hingehängt?** where have you hung it?; **2.** umg. fig.: **j-n ~** (anschwärzen) blacken s.o.'s name (**bei** with)

hinhauen (unreg., trennb., hat -ge-); umg. **I.** v/i. **1.** hit; → **Gras** 2; **2.** fig. (klappen) work; (stimmen) work out (just) right; **hat es hingehauen?** auch did you manage it?; **es wird schon ~!** it'll be okay!; **das haut hin** (klappt) that's working; (reicht) that's enough; (stimmt) that's right; **wenn es hinhaut, wollen wir im Mai in Urlaub fahren** if things work out; **II.** v/t. **1.** (hinwerfen) slam od. bang down (**auf** + Akk. on); fig. (aufgeben) chuck in; **2.** fig., schnell und schlampig: (erledigen) knock off; (schreiben) reel off; **3.** unpers.: **j-n haut es hin** (j-d stürzt) s.o. comes a cropper; **III.** v/refl. (schlafen gehen) hit the sack (od. hay); **ich hau mich jetzt für eine Stunde hin** I'm going to lie down now and have an hour's kip (Am. nap); **sich aufs Bett ~** flop down on the bed

hinhocken v/refl. (trennb., hat -ge-) **1.** squat (down); **2.** umg. **hock dich hin!** plonk yourself down; **wenn du die Prüfung schaffen willst, musst du dich endlich mal ~** (**und büffeln**) you'll just have to get down to it finally (and do some swotting [Am. cramming])

hinhören v/i. (trennb., hat -ge-) listen

Hinkebein n umg. **1.** gammy (Am. bum) leg; **2.** fig. Person: person with a gammy (Am. bum) leg, Am. gimp neg!

Hinkelstein m menhir

hinken v/i. **1.** (hat gehinkt) (have a) limp; **auf dem linken Bein ~** limp with one's left leg; **der Vergleich hinkt** fig. the metaphor doesn't work; **2.** (ist) irgendwohin: limp

hinknallen umg. (trennb.) **I.** v/t. (hat hingeknallt) slam (od. bang) down (**auf** + Akk. on); **... und dann hab ich dem Chef m-e Kündigung hingeknallt** and then I hit the boss between the eyes with my notice (wörtl. I slammed my notice down in front of the boss); **II.** v/i. (ist) → **hinfliegen** I 3; **III.** v/refl. (hat) → **hinhauen** III

hinknien (trennb.) v/i. (ist hingekniet und hat) (hat) kneel down

hinkommen v/i. (unreg., trennb., ist -ge-) **1.** come (od. get) there; **2.** (hingeraten) go; **wo ist das Buch hingekommen?** where has the book gone (od. got [ten Am.] to)?; **wo kämen od. kommen wir (denn da) hin, wenn ...** fig. where would we be if ...; **3.** umg. (hingehören) go, belong; **wo kommen die Blumen hin?** where do you want the flowers?; **4.** umg. (auskommen) manage, get along (**mit** with); zeitlich: make it; **5.** umg. (stimmen) Rechnung, Schätzung etc.: be right; **19,85 Euro – das kommt in etwa hin** 19.85 euros – that's about right; **6.** umg. (in Ordnung kommen) turn out okay

hinkriegen v/t. (trennb., hat -ge-); umg.

1. (fertig bringen) do, manage; **das hast du gut hingekriegt** you've done a good job of it; iro. you've made a fine mess of that; **wie hast du das denn wieder hingekriegt?** iro. how on earth did you manage that?; **ich krieg das nicht mehr hin**, wie war das noch? it's gone right out of my head; **2.** (wieder) **~** (reparieren) fix; (heilen) (j-n, etw.) put right; notdürftig: patch up; (wieder gutmachen) put right (od. straight); **das werden wir wieder ~** (reparieren) auch we'll have that fixed again, no problem

hinkritzeln v/t. (trennb., hat -ge-) scribble down; **hastig hingekritzelte Zeilen** hastily scribbled lines

Hinkunft f, nur Sg.; österr.: **in ~** in (the) future; **hinkünftig** Adj. österr. future

hinlangen v/i. (trennb., hat -ge-) **1.** (anfassen) touch; (greifen) grab, grasp; Versuch: reach out (**nach** for); **2.** umg. fig. (sich an die Arbeit machen) get one's teeth into it, Brit. auch get stuck in; (tüchtig arbeiten) put one's shoulder to the wheel (od. one's nose to the grindstone); (tüchtig zugreifen) take what one can get; (viel essen) auch tuck in; (viel Geld verlangen) auch be asking a lot; (fest zuschlagen) take a swipe; (hart kämpfen, spielen) play rough; **er hat ganz schön hingelangt** he didn't exactly hold back; **3.** (ausreichen) be enough

hinlänglich I. Adj. sufficient, adequate; **II.** Adv. → I; **~ bekannt** sufficiently well-known

hinlassen v/t. (unreg., trennb., hat -ge-); umg. let s.o. go (there)

hinlaufen v/i. (unreg., trennb., ist -ge-) **1.** run (there); **~ zu** run to; **2.** umg. (hingehen) walk (there); **~ zu** walk to; **3.** umg. pej.: **musst du denn wegen jeder Kleinigkeit zum Chef ~?** do you have to go running to the boss for every little thing?; **4.** (verlaufen) run (**über/unter** + Akk. over/under; **nach** od. **zu** to); (fließen) flow

hin|legen (trennb., hat -ge-) **I.** v/t. **1.** lay (od. put) down; (Kind) put to bed; **j-m e-n Zettel ~** leave s.o. a note; **j-m frische Wäsche ~** put out clean underwear (Bettwäsche: linen od. sheets) for s.o.; **wo hab ich nur den Schlüssel hingelegt?** where on earth have I put the key?; **2.** umg. (bezahlen) fork out; **3.** umg., gekonnt: **sie hat e-n tollen Auftritt/Vortrag hingelegt** she turned in a fantastic performance / gave a fantastic talk; **II.** v/refl. **1.** lie down; zum Schlafen: lie down; **sich lang** od. **der Länge nach ~** umg. fall flat on one's face; **er hat sich für ein paar Minuten hingelegt** he went to have a lie down (Am. went to lie down) for a few minutes; **~lümmeln** v/refl. (trennb., hat -ge-) → **hinflegeln**

hinmachen (trennb.) **I.** v/t. (hat hingemacht) **1.** umg. put (there); **2.** umg. → **kaputtmachen**; **3.** Sl. (töten) bump off, take out; **II.** v/i. **1.** (hat); umg., Hund etc.: do something; **2.** (hat); umg. (sich beeilen) hurry up; **mach mal hin!** get a move on!; **3.** (ist); Dial. (hinbegeben) go there; **~ nach** go to; **III.** v/refl. (hat); umg. burn o.s. out

hinmüssen v/i. (unreg., trennb., hat -ge-); umg. have to go (there); **da muss ich unbedingt hin!** I simply have to go there!

Hinnahme f; -, kein Pl. acceptance

hinnehmbar Adj. acceptable; **nicht mehr ~** no longer acceptable

hinnehmen v/t. (unreg., trennb., hat -ge-) **1.** accept, take; (dulden) take; put up with; widerstandslos: take s.th. lying down; **e-e Niederlage ~ müssen** have to accept a defeat; → **selbstverständlich** I; **2.** umg.: (mit) **~** (zu) take (with one) (to)

hinneigen (trennb., hat -ge-) → **neigen**

hinnen Adv. altm. geh.: **von ~** (from) hence; **von ~ (nach dannen)** from here (to there)

hin|passen v/i. (trennb., hat -ge-); umg. fit (in); platzmäßig: fit; **~pfeffern** I. (trennb., hat -ge-); umg. → **hinknallen** I; **~pflanzen** (trennb., hat -ge-) **I.** v/t. **1.** plant; **2.** umg. (etw.) plonk down (**vor** + Dat. in front of); **II.** v/refl. umg. plonk o.s. down (**vor** + Dat. in front of); **~raffen** v/t. (trennb., hat -ge-); geh., Tod: snatch away; **~reiben** v/t. (unreg., trennb., hat -ge-); südd.: **j-m etw. ~** rub s.o.'s nose in s.th.

hinreichen (trennb., hat -ge-) **I.** v/t. hand, give; **II.** v/i. (genügen) be enough, do; **~ bis** reach to (od. as far as); **hinreichend I.** Part. Präs. → **hinreichen**; **II.** Adj. enough, sufficient; (angemessen) adequate; (reichlich) ample; **III.** Adv. sufficiently, enough; adequately

Hinreise f outward journey (mit dem Schiff: voyage); umg. trip there; **auf der ~** on the way there; **Hin- und Rückreise** journey there and back; **die ~ nach Köln** the journey to Cologne; **hinreisen** v/i. (trennb., ist -ge-) travel (od. go) there

hinreißen v/t. (unreg., trennb., hat -ge-) **1.** Person: **zu sich ~** pull to one; Fluss etc.: **mit sich ~** carry s.th. away; **2.** fig. (begeistern) enthral(l); **sich ~ lassen** let o.s. be carried away (**von** by); **sich (dazu) ~ lassen, etw. zu tun** let o.s. be carried away and do s.th.; **das Stück riss (das Publikum) zu Beifallsstürmen hin** the play received rapturous applause; → **hingerissen**; **hinreißend I.** Part. Präs. → **hinreißen**; **II.** Adj. Anblick, Schönheit: stunning; Redner etc.: thrilling, marvel(l)ous; (faszinierend) fascinating; (großartig) marvel(l)ous; **III.** Adv. schön: stunningly; **sie hat ~ gespielt** she played beautifully, it was a wonderful performance

hinrichten v/t. (trennb., hat -ge-) **1.** execute, put to death; auf dem elektrischen Stuhl: electrocute; durch den Strang: hang; **2.** umg. (herrichten) get ready; (bereitlegen) put out (ready); **Hinrichtung** f execution

Hinrichtungs|befehl m orders Pl. for execution; **~kommando** n execution squad; **~stätte** f place of execution

Hinrunde f Sport **1.** first half of the season; **2.** (Hinspiel) corresponding match (Am. game) in the first half of the season

hin|sagen v/t. → **dahinsagen**; **~schaffen** v/t. (trennb., hat -ge-) **1.** take (od. get) there; **~ zu** take to; **2.** unpers.; umg.: **es ~ (zu)** make it (to); **~schauen** v/i. (trennb., hat -ge-); bes. südd., österr. → **hinsehen**; **~schicken** v/t. (trennb., hat -ge-) send (there); **~ zu** send to

Hinschied m; -(e)s, -e; schw., geh. demise

hin|schlachten v/t. (trennb., hat -ge-) slaughter; **~schlagen** v/i. (unreg., trennb.) **1.** (hat hingeschlagen) strike, hit; **2.** (ist); (heftig stürzen) fall over; **lang** od. **der Länge nach ~** fall flat on one's face

hinschleppen (*trennb., hat -ge-*) **I.** *v/t. auch fig.* drag along; **~ zu** drag along to; **II.** *v/refl.* **1.** drag o.s. along; *sich ~ zu* drag o.s. along to; **2.** *fig. Zeit, Verhandlungen, Prozess etc.*: drag (on)

hin|schludern *v/t.* (*trennb., hat -ge-*); *umg.* dash off; **~schmeißen** *v/t. und v/refl.* (*unreg., trennb., hat -ge-*); *umg.* → *hinhauen* II 2, *hinwerfen* I 3; **~schmieren** *v/t.* (*trennb., hat -ge-*); *umg.* (*schreiben*) scribble, scrawl; (*malen*) daub; **~schreiben** *v/t.* (*unreg., trennb., hat -ge-*) **1.** *an j-n*: write; **2.** (*aufschreiben*) write down; **~schwimmen** *v/i.* (*unreg., trennb., ist -ge-*) swim (there); **~ zu** swim to; **~schwinden** → *dahinschwinden*

hinsehen *v/i.* (*unreg., trennb., hat -ge-*) look (*zu* at); *ich mag od. kann gar nicht ~* I can't bear to look; *bei genauerem Hinsehen* on closer inspection

hin sein → *hin* 1, 2, 8

hinsetzen (*trennb., hat -ge-*) **I.** *v/t.* put (down); (*Person*) *auch* seat; (*Baby*) sit down; **II.** *v/refl.* sit down; *sich zu j-m ~* sit with s.o.; *sich ~ und lernen* sit down and study; *ich hätte mich fast hingesetzt, als ich das gehört habe umg.* I nearly fell off my chair

Hinsicht *f; mst Sg.*: *in dieser ~* on that score; *in einer ~* in one sense; *in doppelter ~* in two respects; *in der e-n ~ ... in der anderen ~* in one respect ... in another respect; *in gewisser ~* in a way; *in mancher/vieler ~* in some/many ways; *in jeder ~* in every respect; *in keiner ~* in no respect (*od.* way); *in politischer/wirtschaftlicher ~* politically/economically; *in beruflicher ~* in terms of my *etc.* job; *in ~ auf* (+ *Akk.*) → *hinsichtlich*; **hinsichtlich** *Präp.* (+ *Gen.*) concerning, regarding, with regard to, as to

hinsollen *v/i.* (*trennb., hat*); *umg.*: *wo soll das/ich hin?* where does this / do I go?

Hinspiel *n Sport* **1.** first leg; **2.** away leg (*od.* tie)

hinstellen (*trennb., hat -ge-*) **I.** *v/t.* **1.** (*absetzen*) put down; *an bestimmte Stelle*: put; (*hinbauen*) put up; *ich hab dir das Essen hingestellt auf Tisch*: I've put your food on the table; *auf Herd*: I've put your meal on (to warm up); **2.** *fig.*: *~ als* make out (*od.* appear) to be; *etw. als falsch/richtig ~* make s.th. out to be false/true; *j-n als Vorbild ~* hold s.o. up as an example; **II.** *v/refl.* **1.** (*aufstehen*) stand up; *an bestimmte Stelle*: stand; *mit Auto*: park; *sich aufrecht/gerade ~* stand upright / up straight; *sich ~ vor* (+ *Akk.*) *etc.* stand in front of *etc.*; **2.** *fig.*: *sich ~ als* make o.s. out to be, pose as

hinsteuern (*trennb., hat -ge-*) **I.** *v/i.* **1.** *nach od. zu* steer toward(s), make (*od.* head) for (*auch fig.*); *wo steuerst du hin?* where are you heading for?, where are you off to?; **2.** *fig.*: *auf ein Ziel ~* be aiming at; **II.** *v/t.*: *~ nach od. zu* steer toward(s)

hinstreben *v/i.* (*trennb., hat -ge-*): *~ zu od. nach* make (*od.* head) for; *fig.* strive for (*od.* after); *Phys. und fig.* gravitate toward(s)

hinstrecken (*trennb., hat -ge-*) **I.** *v/t.* **1.** (*Hand*) stretch *od.* hold out (+ *Dat.* to); **2.** *altm. geh.* (*j-n*) fell; **II.** *v/refl.* **1.** *Person, Tier*: lie down, stretch out; **2.** (*sich erstrecken*) stretch (out), extend (*über Meilen* for miles)

hin|streuen *v/t.* (*trennb., hat -ge-*): *den Hühnern Futter ~* scatter food for the chickens; **~strömen** *v/i.* (*trennb., ist -ge-*) **1.** *Fluss, Wasser etc.*: flow; **2.** *Menschen*: throng there; **~stürzen** *v/i.* (*trennb., ist -ge-*) **1.** fall; **2.** *~ nach od. zu* rush to

hintan|setzen *v/t.* (*trennb., hat -ge-*); *geh.* (*zuletzt berücksichtigen*) put last; (*vernachlässigen*) neglect; (*ignorieren*) disregard, ignore; **~stehen** *v/i.* (*unreg., trennb., hat / südd., österr., schw. ist -ge-*); *geh.* come last (*od.* second); **~stellen** *v/t.* (*trennb., hat -ge-*); *geh.* → *hintansetzen*

hinten *Adv.* **1.** at the back; (*am Ende*) *auch* at the end; *Naut., Flug.* aft; (*im Hintergrund*) in the background; *~ in* (+ *Dat.*) in (*od.* at) the back of; *nach ~* (to the) back; *Naut., Flug.* aft; *nach ~ gelegenes Zimmer* room at the back; *nach ~ hinausgehen Zimmer etc.*: be at (*od.* face) the back; *nach ~ umkippen* tip up backwards; *von ~* from behind; *anfangen*: at the end; *der Zweite von ~* the second from the back; *von ~ nach vorne lesen, sortieren*: from back to front, backwards; *ziehen, kämpfen*: from the back to the front, toward(s) the front; *~ anfügen* add; *sich ~ anstellen* join (*od.* go to the back of) the queue (*Am.* line); **2.** (*im Rückstand*): *ziemlich weit ~ sein* be a long way behind; *fig., in Entwicklung*: be quite far behind; *~ bleiben* lag behind; **3.** (*weit entfernt*): *dort ~* back there; *ganz weit ~* far away in the distance; *weit ~ im Wald / in Sibirien* in the depths of the forest / far away in Siberia; **4.** *umg. euph.* (*am Gesäß*) on one's behind (*od.* backside); *~ wund sein* have a sore behind; *j-m ~ reinkriechen fig., vulg.* suck up to s.o., lick s.o.'s arse (*Am.* ass); **5.** *umg., in Wendungen*: *~ und vorn(e) betrügen*: left, right and cent|re (*Am.* -er); *bedienen*: hand and foot; *es reicht/stimmt ~ und vorn(e) nicht od. weder ~ noch vorn(e)* it's nowhere near enough / it's totally wrong; *ich weiß nicht mehr, wo ~ und vorn(e) ist* I don't know whether I'm coming or going; *von ~ durch die Brust ins Auge hum.* in a roundabout way; *ich sehe sie am liebsten von ~* I'm always glad to see the back of her; *er kommt ~ nicht mehr hoch* (*ist gebrechlich*) he is very frail; (*ist in verzweifelter Lage*) he is in a desperate situation; *da heißt es Herr Professor ~, Herr Professor vorn* Professor this and Professor that

hintenan *Adv.* behind, at the back

hintenan... → *hintan...*

hinten|dran *Adv. umg.* **1.** *räumlich*: at the back; **2.** (*im Rückstand*) behind; **~drauf** *Adv. umg.* on the back; *von Lastwagen*: in the back; *eins od. ein paar ~ bekommen* get a smacked bottom; *j-m eins od. ein paar ~ geben* smack s.o.'s bottom; **~drein** *Adv.* → *hinterher*; **~heraus** *Adv.*: *die Zimmer ~* the rooms at the back; **~herum** *Adv. umg.* **1.** round the back, *Am.* around back; **2.** *euph.* (*am Gesäß*) around one's posterior; **3.** *fig., erfahren von*: through the grapevine; *beschaffen*: under the counter; **~hin** *Adv.* to the back; **~nach** *Adv. bes. südd., österr.* afterwards; **~raus** *Adv.* → *hintenheraus*; **~rum** *Adv.* → *hintenherum*; **~über** *Adv.* backwards

hintenüber|fallen *v/i.* (*unreg., trennb., ist -ge-*), **~kippen** *v/i.* (*trennb., ist -ge-*)

topple over backwards

hinter **I.** *Präp.* **1.** (+ *Dat.*) behind, at the back of; *Naut.* aft of, astern of; (*nach*) after; *~ ... her* behind ...; *~ ... hervor* from behind ...; *~ m-m Rücken auch fig.* behind my back; *e-r ~ dem anderen* one behind the other; *sie kommt gleich ~ mir* she is right behind me; *zehn Kilometer ~ Köln / der Grenze* ten kilomet|res (*Am.* -ers) after Cologne / beyond the border; *sich lassen* (*Ort etc.*) leave behind; (*j-n*) *in Wettrennen etc.*: leave behind, outdistance; *fig.* (*übertreffen*) leave behind, outstrip; **2.** (+ *Akk.*) behind; *~ das Haus gehen* go behind the house; **3.** (+ *Dat.*); *zeitlich*: *weit zurückreichen* ~ go way back to before; *zehn Minuten ~ der Zeit sein Dial.* be ten minutes late; **4.** *fig.*: *~ etw. (Akk.) kommen* find out about s.th., find s.th. out; (*verstehen*) get the hang of; *~ j-m/etw. her sein* be after s.o./s.th.; *~ etw. (Dat.) stecken* be at the bottom of (*od.* behind); *~ etw. (Dat.) stehen* be behind; (*unterstützen*) *auch* back; *sich ~ j-n/etw. stellen* get behind, support; *~ sich (Akk.) bringen* get s.th. over (and done) with; (*Strecke*) cover; *j-n ~ sich (Dat.) haben* have s.o. behind one; *etw. ~ sich (Dat.) haben* (*erledigt haben*) have got s.th. out of the way (*od.* over [and done] with); (*mitgemacht haben*) have been through s.th.; *viel ~ sich (Dat.) haben* have been through a lot; *er hat gerade e-e Niereninfektion ~ sich* (*Dat.*) he's just got over a kidney infection; *das Schlimmste haben wir ~ uns* we've got over the worst part (of it), we're out of the wood(s) now; *sich ~ etw. (Akk.) machen* get down to; *nicht zurückstehen ~* (+ *Dat.*) be just as good as; *zurückstehen müssen ~* (+ *Dat.*) have to take second place to; *Person*: *auch* have to play second fiddle to; → *dahinter*; **II.** *Adv. bes. südd., österr.* (*nach hinten*) to the back; (*herunter*) down

hinter...[1] *Adj.*; *nur attr.* rear, back; *Beine, Hufe, Pfoten etc.*: hind; *Naut., Luke etc.*: aft; *fachspr.* posterior; *Ende*: far; *die ~en Bänke* the back benches; *die ~en Räume etc. auch* the rooms etc. at the back (*od.* rear); *die ~en Wagen Eisenb.* the rear coaches; → *hinterst...*

hinter...[2] *im V.*; *trennb.*; *bes. südd., österr. umg.* **1.** (*nach hinten*) to the back; (*herunter*) down; **2.** → *hinunter...*

Hinterachsantrieb *m Mot.* rear-axle drive; **Hinterachse** *f* rear axle

Hinter|ansicht *f* rear view; **~ausgang** *m* rear (*od.* back) exit; **~backe** *f umg.* buttock; *Pl.* backside; **~bänkler** *m*; *-s, -, *~bänklerin** *f*; *-, -nen*; *Parl.* backbencher; **~bein** *n* hind leg; *sich auf die ~e stellen Tier*: stand on its hind legs; *umg. fig.* put up a fight, not take it (*od.* things) lying down

Hinterbliebene *m, f*; *-n, -n* dependant, *bes. Am.* dependent; *die ~n in Traueranzeigen*: the bereaved; **Hinterbliebenenrente** *f* survivor's pension (*od.* benefit [s *Pl.*])

hinterbringen *v/t.* (*unreg., untr., hat*): *j-m etw. ~* inform s.o. about s.th.

Hinterdeck *n Naut.* afterdeck

hinterdrein... *altm. siehe auch hinterher...*

hintereinander *Adv. aufstellen, fahren, gehen, stehen etc.*: one behind the other; (*in Einerreihe*) in single file; (*nach-*

einander) one after the other, one by one; (*ohne Pause*) in a row, at a stretch; **dicht** ~ close together; **drei Tage** ~ three days running (*od.* in a row); **an drei Tagen** ~ on three consecutive days; ~ **hergehen/herrennen** *etc.* follow/chase *etc.* each other; **Geräte** ~ **schalten** *Etech.* connect pieces of equipment in series; *Zahlen etc.* ~ **schreiben** write one after the other; **etw.** ~ **tun** do s.th. one by one; (*abwechselnd*) do s.th. in turns, take turns (to do s.th.); (*ohne Pause*) do s.th. non-stop; ~**her** *Adv.* one behind the other; ~**weg** *Adv.* umg. (*ohne Pause*) one after the other

Hintereingang *m* back (*od.* rear) entrance

hinterfotzig *Adj. Dial. pej.* two-faced

hinterfragen *v/t.* (*untr., hat*) question; *stärker:* scrutinize; (*ergründen*) try to get to the bottom of

Hinter|fuß *m* hind foot; *von Hund, Katze:* hind paw; ~**gebäude** *n* back building; ~**gedanke** *m negativer:* ulterior motive; **ohne** ~**n** *auch* quite innocently; **mein** ~**n dabei war ...** what was at the back of my mind was ...

hinter'gehen[1] *v/t.* (*unreg., untr., hat*) **1.** (*j-n*) deceive, go (*od.* do s.th.) behind s.o.'s back; (*Ehepartner etc.*) deceive, be unfaithful to; **er fühlt sich von s-m Bruder hintergangen** he thinks his brother should have come to him about it (and not done it behind his back); **2.** (*etw.*) (*umgehen*) avoid

'hintergehen[2] *v/i.* (*unreg., trennb., ist -ge-*) *umg.* (*nach hinten gehen*) go to the back

Hinterglasmalerei *f* painting on the back of glass; *fachspr.* verre églomisé painting (*Bild*), verre églomisé technique (*Maltechnik*)

Hintergrund *m* background (*auch Kunst und fig.*); (*hinterer Teil e-s Raumes*) back; *Theat. und fig.* backdrop; **die Hintergründe** *fig.* the background (+ *Gen.* of), what's behind *s.th.*; **die Tat hat politische Hintergründe** the act is politically motivated; **sich vor dem** ~ **e-s Krieges** *etc.* **abspielen** take place against a backdrop of war *etc.*; **in den** ~ **treten** *od.* **geraten** *umg.* take a back seat; **in den** ~ **rücken** *Problem, Aspekt etc.:* be pushed into the background; **sich im** ~ **halten** *od.* **im** ~ **bleiben** keep out of the way; *beobachtend:* watch from the sidelines; **j-n in den** ~ **drängen** push s.o. into the background, force s.o. onto the sidelines; **etw. im** ~ **haben** (*geheimen Plan etc.*) have s.th. up one's sleeve; **im** ~ **stehen** (*kaum beachtet werden*) be in the background; ~**bericht** *m* background report; ~**gespräche** *Pl.* briefings

hintergründig *Adj. fig.* (*rätselhaft*) enigmatic; (*fein, subtil*) subtle; (*tief*) profound; (*heimlich*) hidden

Hintergrund|information *f* background information; ~**musik** *f* background music; ~**rauschen** *n Hi-Fi etc.:* background noise; ~**wissen** *n* background knowledge

Hinterhalt *m* **1.** ambush; (*Falle*) trap; **aus dem** ~ **angreifen** *od.* **überfallen** waylay, ambush; **im** ~ **liegen** *od.* **lauern** lie in ambush; **2.** *umg.:* **etw. im** ~ **haben** have s.th. up one's sleeve; **hinterhältig** *Adj.* underhanded; *Methoden: auch* underhand; (*tückisch*) insidious; **Hinterhältigkeit** *f nur Sg. Art:* underhandedness

Hinter|hand *f* **1.** *Pferd etc.:* hindquarters *Pl.*; **2.** *Kartenspiel:* youngest hand; **in der** ~ **sein** be the youngest hand; **in der** ~ **haben** *fig.* have *s.th.* up one's sleeve; ~**haus** *n* **1.** *Teil:* back (part) of the house; **2.** *im Hinterhof:* house at the back

hinterher *Adv.* **1.** *räumlich:* after, behind; **j-m** ~ **sein** (*verfolgen*) be after s.o.; **2.** *zeitlich:* afterwards; ~ **ist man immer klüger** you're always wise 'after the event; **3.** *fig.:* ~ **sein in** (+ *Dat. od. mit*) *in Entwicklung, mit Arbeit etc.:* be behind with; (*sehr*) ~ **sein, dass ...** (*achten auf*) see (to it) that ..., make sure that ...

hinterher|fahren *v/i.* (*unreg., trennb., ist -ge-*) follow; *mit Auto:* drive behind; *mit Rad:* ride behind; ~**gehen** *v/i.* (*unreg., trennb., ist -ge-*) follow; ~**hinken** *v/i.* (*trennb., ist -ge-*) **1.** limp along behind; **2.** *fig.* lag behind; ~**kommen** *v/i.* (*unreg., trennb., ist -ge-*) **1.** *räumlich:* follow behind; *zeitlich:* come later; *als Letzter:* bring up the rear; **2.** *umg. fig.:* **j-m/ der Arbeit nicht** ~ not keep up (*od.* pace) with s.o. / the work; ~**laufen**, ~**rennen** *v/i.* (*unreg., trennb., ist -ge-*) **1.** run behind; **j-m** ~ run (*bes. fig.* chase) after s.o.; **2.** *fig.:* **e-r Sache** ~ chase after s.th.; ~**rufen** *vt/i.* (*unreg., trennb., hat -ge-*): **j-m** (*etw.*) ~ call (s.th.) out after s.o.; ~**schicken** *v/t.:* **j-n j-m** ~ send s.o. after s.o.; ~**sehen** *v/i.* (*unreg., trennb., hat -ge-*): **j-m/etw.** ~ gaze after s.o./s.th.

hinterher sein → **hinterher** 1-3

hinterher|spionieren *v/i.* (*trennb., hat*) spy on; ~**tragen** *v/t.* (*unreg., trennb., hat -ge-*): **j-m etw.** ~ (*Vergessenes*) run after s.o. with s.th.; ~**werfen** *v/t.* → **nachwerfen**

Hinter|hirn *n Anat.* hind brain; ~**hof** *m* backyard; ~**huf** *m* hind hoof; ~**indien** (*n*) *Geog.* South-East Asian peninsula; ~**kopf** *m* back of the head; **etw. im** ~ **haben/behalten** *fig.* have/keep s.th. at the back of one's mind; ~**lader** *m; -s, -* breech-loader; ~**land** *n; nur Sg.* hinterland

hinter'lassen *v/t.* (*unreg., untr., hat*) (*Kratzer, Spuren etc.*) leave (behind); (*Eindruck, Nachricht, Testament etc.*) leave; (*Person*) *nach eigenem Tod:* leave behind, be survived by; **j-m etw.** ~ (*vererben*) leave s.th. to s.o.; **sie hinterließ, dass ...** she left word that ...; ~**e Werke** posthumous works; **Hinterlassenschaft** *f* **1.** *geh.* (*Zurückgelassenes*): **die übel riechende** ~ **von Hunden** the foul-smelling deposits left by dogs; **2.** (*Erbe*) estate; *fig.* bequest; **j-s literarische** ~ s.o.'s literary legacy; **j-s** ~ **antreten** (*j-n beerben*) inherit s.o.'s estate; (*j-m nachfolgen*) take over from s.o.; **Hinterlassung** *f geh.:* **unter** ~ **von** leaving

Hinterlauf *m Jägerspr.* hind leg

hinter'legen *v/t.* (*untr., hat*) deposit (*bei* with); *als Pfand:* leave (*bei* with); **Hinterlegung** *f:* **gegen** ~ (+ *Gen.*) on depositing *s.th.*; (*Bezahlung*) *auch* against payment of

Hinterleib *m Zool.* hindquarters *Pl.*; *von Insekten etc.:* abdomen

Hinterlist *f; nur Sg.*; (*Verschlagenheit*) cunning, deceit; (*Tücke*) underhandedness; **hinterlistig** *Adj.* cunning, deceitful; underhanded; *Methoden: auch* underhand

hinterm *Präp. + Art. umg.* → **hinter**

Hinter|mann *m; Pl.* **Hintermänner**
1. person behind (me, him *etc.*); **2.** *fig.* wirepuller, *the* brains behind it; ~**mannschaft** *f Sport* defen|ce (*Am. -se*)

hintern *Präp. + Art. umg.* → **hinter**

Hintern *m; -s, -; umg.* **1.** backside, bottom, behind, *Am. auch* butt, rear end; **du kriegst gleich ein paar auf den** ~ you'll get your bottom (*bes. Am.* behind) smacked; **2.** *fig.:* **j-m in den** ~ **treten** give s.o. a kick up the backside; **j-m in den** ~ **kriechen** *pej.* suck up to s.o., lick s.o.'s arse (*Am.* ass) *vulg.*; **sich auf den** ~ **setzen** (*fleißig arbeiten, lernen*) knuckle down; (*erstaunt sein*) fall off one's chair; **ich hätte mich in den** ~ **beißen können** I could have kicked myself

Hinterpfote *f* hind paw

Hinterrad *n Mot.* back (*od.* rear) wheel; ~**achse** *f* rear axle; ~**antrieb** *m* rear-wheel drive; ~**aufhängung** *f* rear suspension; ~**bremse** *f* rear-wheel brake

Hinter|reifen *m Mot.* back (*od.* rear) tyre (*Am.* tire); ~**rhein** *m Geog.* Rhine hinterland

hinterrücks *Adv.* **1.** from behind; **2.** *fig.* behind s.o.'s back

hinters *Präp. + Art. umg.* → **hinter**

Hinter|sasse *m; -n, -n* **1.** *hist.* villein; **2.** *schw.* inhabitant who does not enjoy civil rights; ~**schiff** *n Naut.* stern; ~**seite** *f* back; *von Blatt, Münze etc.:* reverse

Hintersinn *m* deeper (*od.* hidden) meaning; **hintersinnig** *Adj. Geschichte etc.:* with a deeper (*od.* hidden) meaning; ~**e Absicht** ulterior motive; → **hintergründig**

Hinter|sitz *m* back seat; ~**spieler** *m*, ~**spielerin** *f Sport* backrow player

hinterst... *Adj.* (very) last; ~**e Reihe** *auch* back row; **der** ~**e Baum** *etc. auch* the tree *etc.* right at the back; **das** ~**e Ende** the tail end; **die Hintersten** those (*od.* the ones) (right) at the back

Hinter|stübchen *n:* **etw. im** ~ **haben** have s.th. at the back of one's mind; ~**teil** *n* **1.** back (part); **2.** *umg.* → **Hintern**; ~**treffen** *n:* **im** ~ **sein** be at a disadvantage; (*nachhinken*) lag behind; **im** ~ **sein** *auch* have fallen behind with; **ins** ~ **geraten** *od.* **kommen** fall behind

hintertreiben *v/t.* (*unreg., untr., hat*) obstruct, thwart, prevent *s.th.* (from being carried out *od.* taking place *etc.*); *durch Gegenlist:* counteract; (*torpedieren*) torpedo; **Hintertreibung** *f* obstruction

Hintertreppe *f* back stairs *Pl.*

Hintertupfingen *n; -s, kein Pl.; umg.:* (*aus*) ~ (from) the back of beyond

Hinter|tür *f* back door; *fig. auch* loophole; **sich** (*Dat.*) **e-e** ~ **offen halten** *fig.* leave o.s. a way out; **durch die** ~ **wieder hereinkommen** *fig.* come back in through the back door; ~**türchen** *n fig.* → **Hintertür**

Hinterwäldler *m; -s, -,* ~**in** *f; -, -nen* country bumpkin (*od.* yokel), *Am. auch* hick; **hinterwäldlerisch** *Adj.* yokelish

Hinterwand *f* back wall

hinterziehen *v/t.* (*unreg., untr., hat*); (*Steuern*) evade; **Hinterziehung** *f von Steuern:* tax evasion

Hinterzimmer *n* back room

hin|tragen *v/t.* (*unreg., trennb., hat -ge-*) carry (*od.* take) there; ~ **zu** carry (*od.* take) to; ~**treiben** (*unreg., trennb.*) **I.** *v/t.* (*hat hingetrieben*); *Per-*

son *etc.*: drive there; *Strömung*: carry there; *Wind*: blow there; *fig. Neugier, Sehnsucht etc.*: drive there; **~ zu** drive/carry/blow to; **II.** *v/i.* (*ist*): **wo treiben wir hin?** mit *Boot, Ballon etc.*: where are we drifting to?; *fig.* where are we going?; **~treten** (*unreg., trennb.*) **I.** *vt/i.* (*hat hingetreten*) tread; (*stoßen*) kick; **pass auf, wo du hintrittst** watch where you step; **II.** *v/i.* (*ist*); *geh.*: **vor j-n ~** go up to s.o.; *fig.* stand before s.o.; **zum od. ans Fenster ~** go over to the window; **~tun** *v/t.* (*unreg., trennb., hat -ge-*) *umg.* **1.** put (there); **wo soll ich es ~?** where shall I put it?; **2.** *fig.*: **ich weiß nicht, wo ich ihn ~ soll** I can't place him

hinüber *Adv.* **1.** over (there); (*auf die andere Seite*) to the other side; *über Grenze, Straße etc.*: across; **über ...** (*Akk.*) **~** over, across; **~ und herüber** back and forth; **nach links/rechts ~** over to the left/right; **2.** *umg fig.*: **~ sein** (*verdorben*) be bad, be off; (*kaputt*) be broken; (*zerschlagen*) *auch* be smashed; (*erschöpft*) be done in, be all in (*Am.* wiped out); (*tot*) be dead; (*ohnmächtig*) be out; **er ist hinüber** *auch* he's had it

hinüber... *im V.* → *auch* **herüber...**, **rüber...**

hinüber|gehen *v/i.* (*unreg., trennb., ist -ge-*) **1.** **~** (**über** + *Akk.*) go over, walk across; **~ über** (+ *Akk.*) cross; **2.** *euph.* pass away; **~retten** *v/t.* (*trennb., hat -ge-*) save, salvage; **~ in** (+ *Akk.*) (*Werte*) ensure the survival of *s.th.* into; **j-n über die Grenze ~** get s.o. over the border

hinüber sein → *hinüber* 2

hin- und her|... *im V.* back and forth, to and fro, backwards and forwards; **~bewegen** *v/t. und v/refl.* (*trennb., hat*) move back and forth; **~gehen** *v/i.* (*unreg., trennb., ist -ge-*) **1.** *Person*: go (*od.* walk) up and down; **2.** *Sache*: go back and forth; *Gespräch*: go backwards and forwards

Hinundhergerede *n mst pej.* talk; **was soll das ganze ~?** all this talk isn't going to get you *etc.* anywhere

hin- und hergerissen *Adj. fig.*: **~ sein** be in a terrible dilemma, be torn (**zwischen** between)

Hinundherüberlegen *n; -s, kein Pl.* indecision, humming (*Am.* hemming) and hawing

Hin- und Rück|fahrt *f* journey (*bes. Am.* trip) there and back; *Fahrkarte*: return (ticket), *Am.* round trip; **~flug** *m* flight there and back

hinunter *Adv.* down; **die Treppe ~** down the stairs; **~ damit!** *umg. mit Getränk etc.*: get it down you!; (**von ...**) **bis ~ zu** *Hierarchie*: (from...) down to

hinunter... *im V. mst ...* down; → **herab...**, **herunter...**, **runter...**

hinunter|blicken *v/i.* look (*od.* glance) down (**auf** at); **~bringen** *v/t.* take *s.th.* down; **~fahren** *v/i.* drive (*od.* go) down); **~fallen** *v/i.* fall down; **~führen** **I.** *v/i. Treppe etc.*: lead down; *Straße*: *auch* run down; **II.** *v/t.* take *s.o.* down (*auf die Treppe*: downstairs); **~gehen** *v/i.* **1.** go (*od.* walk) down; **2.** (*hinunterführen*) go (*od.* lead) down (**zu** to); **~lassen** *v/t.* let down, lower; **~schlingen** *v/t.* (*Essen*) bolt (*od.* wolf) down; **~schlucken** *v/t.* swallow (*auch fig*); **~sehen** *v/i.* → **hinunterblicken**; **~springen** *vt/i.* jump down; **~spülen** **I.** *v/i. Toilette*: flush (the toilet); **II.** *v/t. mit Spülung*: flush *s.th.* down; *Regen*,

Fluss: wash *s.th.* down; **s-n Kummer mit Alkohol ~** drown one's sorrows in drink

hinunterstürzen **I.** *v/i.* **1.** fall down; *schwerer Gegenstand*: crash down; *auch* crash to the ground (*od.* floor); *schnell, Bergsteiger etc.*.: plummet down; **~ von** fall off; **2.** (*hinunterrasen*) rush down (*die Treppe*: downstairs, down the stairs); **II.** *v/t.* **1.** (*hinunterrasen*) → I 2; **den Berg ~** fall down the mountainside; **2.** *umg.*: (*Glas Bier etc.*) knock back; (*Tasse Tee etc.*) gulp down

hinunter|tragen *v/t.* carry (*od.* take) down (*die Treppe*: downstairs); **~werfen** *v/t.* throw *s.th.* down; **~würgen** *v/t.* choke (*od.* force) down; **~ziehen** **I.** *v/t.* (*hat*) pull down; **II.** *v/i.* (*ist*) (*umziehen*) move down

hinwagen *v/refl.* (*trennb., hat -ge-*): **sich ~ zu** dare to go to (*od.* near), venture near

hinwärts *Adv.* on the way there

Hinweg *m*: **auf dem ~** on the way there

hinweg *Adv.* **1.** *geh.* away; **~ damit!** away with it!; **2.** **über** (+ *Akk.*) **~** over (*od.* across); **3.** *fig.*: **über Jahre ~** for years (and years); **über alle Unterschiede ~** despite (*stärker*: transcending) all differences; **über j-s Kopf ~** over s.o.'s head; **~ sein über** (+ *Akk.*) *über Stadium*: be past *s.th.*; *über ein Erlebnis etc.*: have got(ten *Am.*) over *s.th.*; *über j-n*: have got(ten *Am.*) over *s.o.*

hinweg|gehen *v/i.* (*unreg., trennb., ist -ge-*): **~ über** (+ *Akk.*) **1.** pass over *od.* across; **2.** *fig.* pass over *s.o. od. s.th.*; (*auslassen*) skip; (*ignorieren*) ignore; *lachend*: laugh *s.th.* off; *gleichgültig*: shrug *s.th.* off; **~helfen** *v/i.* (*unreg., trennb., hat -ge-*): **j-m ~ über** (+ *Akk.*) help s.o. (to) get over *s.th.*; *auch finanziell*: tide s.o. over; **~kommen** *v/i.* (*unreg., trennb.*): **~ über** (+ *Akk.*) get over; **ich komme nicht darüber hinweg, dass ...** I can't get over the fact that ...; *weitS.* I can't get it into my head that ...; **~raffen** *v/t.* (*trennb., hat -ge-*); *geh.* snatch away; **~sehen** *v/i.* (*unreg., trennb., hat -ge-*): **~ über** (+ *Akk.*) **1.** see over; (*blicken*) look over; **2.** *fig.* overlook, turn a blind eye to; (*ignorieren*) ignore

hinweg sein → *hinweg* 3

hinwegsetzen (*trennb.*) **I.** *v/i.* (*ist hinweggesetzt*): **~ über ein Hindernis** jump (over); **II.** *v/refl.* (*hat*); *fig.*: **sich ~ über** (+ *Akk.*) ignore; *gleichgültig*: shrug *s.th.* off; *über j-n*: ignore; *rücksichtslos*: ride roughshod over *s.th.*

hinwegtäuschen (*trennb., hat -ge-*) **I.** *v/t.*: **j-n ~ über** (+ *Akk.*) mislead s.o. as to; **sich nicht darüber ~ lassen, dass ...** not to have any illusions about (*od.* as to) the fact that ...; **II.** *vt/i.*: **über etw.** (*Akk.*) **~** obscure the fact

hinwegtrösten (*trennb., hat -ge-*) **I.** *v/t.*: **j-n ~ über** (+ *Akk.*) help s.o. get over *s.th.*; **das kann (mich) nicht darüber ~** that's no consolation (to me), that doesn't make up for it; **II.** *v/refl.*: **sich ~ über** (+ *Akk.*) (try to) get over

Hinweis *m; -es, -e* **1.** (*Rat*) tip, piece of advice; (*Verweis*) reference; (*Bemerkung*) remark; (*Anleitung*) instruction; (*Fingerzeig, Wink*) hint; (*Anspielung*) allusion; **anonymer/sachdienlicher ~ an die Polizei**: anonymous tip-off / useful lead; **~e für den Benutzer** instructions for use; **mit dem (ausdrück-**

lichen) ~, dass ... with the (specific) emphasis that ...; **mit od. unter ~ auf** (+ *Akk.*) referring to; **ich erlaube mir den ~, dass ...** I might point out that ...; **2.** (*Anhaltspunkt*) clue, pointer (**für** to); (*Andeutung*) indication; **es gibt handfeste ~e dafür, dass ...** there are definite indications that ...

hinweisen (*unreg., trennb., hat -ge-*): **~ auf** (+ *Akk.*) **I.** *vt/i.* point *s.th.* out (to s.o.); **ich möchte Sie nochmals auf die Gefahren ~** I'd like to remind you once again of the dangers; **ich möchte (Sie) darauf ~, dass ...** may I point out that ...; *nachdrücklich*: I'd like to stress (*od.* emphasize, underline) that ...; **II.** *v/i.* **1.** *Sache*: point to; (*anspielen*) allude to; (*verweisen*) refer to; **2.** *mit dem Finger etc.*: point to (*od.* out)

Hinweis|schild *n*, **~tafel** *f* sign

hinwenden (*auch unreg., trennb., hat -ge-*) **I.** *v/refl.* **1.** **sich ~ zu** turn toward[s], turn (a)round to; **2.** *fig.*: **sich ~ an** (+ *Akk.*) turn to; **an e-e Dienststelle**: *auch* go to; **ich wusste nicht, wo ich mich ~ sollte** I didn't know which way to turn; **II.** *v/t.*: **den Kopf ~ zu** turn (one's head) (a)round to; **die Augen ~ zu** turn to look at; **Hinwendung** *f fig.*: **~ zu** change of direction toward(s); **das spiegelt die ~ der Anleger zu neuen Technologien** this reflects the way in which investors are turning to new technologies

hinwerfen (*unreg., trennb., hat -ge-*) **I.** *v/t.* **1.** throw down; *umg., unabsichtlich*: drop; **e-m Hund etw. ~** throw a dog s.th., throw s.th. to a dog; **wo hast du es hingeworfen?** where did you throw it?; **2.** (*Blick*) cast (**auf** + *Akk.* at); **3.** *fig.* (*Bemerkung etc.*) (casually) drop, throw in; **hastig ein paar Zeilen ~** dash off a few hasty lines; → **hingeworfen**; **4.** *umg. fig.* (*aufgeben*) chuck in; **~ Kram**; **II.** *v/refl.* throw o.s. down (*od.* onto the floor *od.* ground)

hinwieder(um) *Adv. altm.* on the other hand, in turn

hin|wirken *v/i.* (*unreg., trennb., hat -ge-*): **~ auf** (+ *Akk.*) work toward(s); **darauf ~, dass j-d etw. tut** try and bring s.o. to do s.th.; **~wollen** *v/i.* (*unreg., trennb., hat -ge-*); *umg.* want to go (there); **wo willst du hin?** where do you want to go?; (*wohin gehst du*) where are you going?

Hinz *m*: **~ und Kunz** every (*od.* any old) Tom, Dick and Harry; **von ~ zu Kunz** from pillar to post

hin|zählen *v/t.* (*trennb., hat -ge-*) count out (+ *Dat.* to); **~zaubern** *v/t.* (*trennb., hat -ge-*); *umg.* conjure up; (*bes. Essen*) *auch* whip up; **~zeigen** *v/i.* (*trennb., hat -ge-*) point there; **~ auf** (+ *Akk.*) *od.* **zu** point at; **wo zeigt der Pfeil hin?** where is the arrow pointing?

hinziehen (*unreg., trennb.*) **I.** *v/t.* (*hat hingezogen*) **1.** pull there; **sich hingezogen fühlen zu** *fig.* be drawn toward[s]; **2.** *fig.* (*verzögern*) draw (*od.* drag) out; **II.** *v/refl.* (*hat*) **1.** *zeitlich*: drag on; **sich ~ bis** (*zu*) *auch* go on until (*od.* till); **sich über Jahre ~** go on for years (and years); **die Entscheidung wird sich noch ~** it will be some time (yet) before a decision is reached; **2.** *räumlich*: stretch (**bis** to, as far as); **sich an der Küste etc. ~** stretch along; **III.** *v/i.* (*ist*) move; *Zugvögel*: migrate; *Rauch, Wolken etc.*: drift; **wo zieht ihr hin?** where are you

H

moving (to)?

hinzielen v/i. (trennb., hat -ge-): ~ **auf** (+ Akk.) aim at; Bemerkung: be directed at, be meant for; Maßnahmen, Pläne etc.: be aimed at

hinzu Adv. **1.** (dazu) in addition; **2.** räumlich: there

hinzu... im V. siehe auch **dazu..., zu...**

hinzu|bekommen v/t. (unreg., trennb., hat) get s.th. on top of it (od. into the bargain); ~**denken** v/t. (unreg., trennb., hat -ge-) (try to) imagine (there is od. are), (try to) visualize; **das Übrige können Sie sich ~** I'm sure you can fill in (bes. visuell: imagine) the rest, I'll leave the rest to your imagination

hinzufügen v/t. (trennb., hat -ge-) add (+ Dat. to); (beilegen) enclose; als Nachtrag: append; **Hinzufügung** f addition; **unter ~ von** (by) adding

hinzu|geben v/t. (unreg., trennb., hat -ge-); geh. add (+ Dat. od. **zu** to); ~**ge-sellen** v/refl. (trennb., hat): **sich ~** (**zu** od. + Dat.) join the group (od. us, them etc.); ~**gewinnen** v/t. (unreg., trennb., hat -ge-) gain in addition (**zu** to); ~**kommen** v/i. → **dazukommen**; ~**nehmen** v/t. (unreg., trennb., hat -ge-) add (**zu** to); (Person) auch include (in); ~**stoßen** v/i. (unreg., trennb., ist -ge-); geh. join (**zu** s.o. od. s.th.); ~**treten** v/i. (unreg., trennb., ist -ge-) **1.** Person: come up to join s.o.; **2.** Sache: ensue; ~**zählen** v/t. (trennb., hat -ge-) add (**zu** to)

hinzuziehen v/t. (unreg., trennb., hat -ge-) **1.** (Arzt etc.) call in; (auch Hilfsmittel etc.) consult; **2.** (mit einbeziehen) include; **Hinzuziehung** f; nur Sg. consultation; **unter ~ von** with the help of

Hiob m; -s; bibl. Job; **Hiobsbotschaft** f bad news Sg.

hipp, hipp, hurra Interj. hip, hip, hooray; **Hipphipphurra** n; -s, -s: **ein dreifaches ~** three cheers

Hippie m; -s, -s hippie, hippy

hippokratisch Adj. Med. Hippocratic

Hirn n; -(e)s, -e **1.** brain; Gastr. brains Pl.; **2.** fig. (Kopf) mind; (Verstand) brains Pl.; → auch **Gehirn...**; ~**anhang(s)drüse** f Anat. pituitary (gland); ~**funktion** f function(ing) of the brain

hirngeschädigt Adj. brain-damaged

Hirn|gespinst n pej. crazy idea; (Einbildung) delusion; (Utopie) pipe dream; ~**hälfte** f: **rechte/linke ~** right/left half of the brain

Hirnhaut f Anat. cerebral membrane; ~**entzündung** f Med. meningitis

Hirni m; -s, -s; umg. pej. screwball

hirnlos Adj. pej. brainless; ~**er Mensch** auch moron, cretin; **Hirnlosigkeit** f pej. **1.** nur Sg. brainlessness; **2.** Handlung: crazy thing to do

Hirnmasse f cerebral matter

hirnrissig Adj. umg. pej. crazy, whacky

Hirn|schaden m Med. brain damage; ~**schale** f Anat. cranium (Pl. craniums od. crania); ~**substanz** f Anat. cerebral matter; **graue/weiße ~** grey (Am. gray) /white matter

Hirntod m Med. brain death; **hirntot** Adj. brain dead

Hirntrauma n Med. brain (od. cerebral) trauma

hirnverbrannt Adj. pej. crazy, cracked

Hirsch m; -(e)s, -e **1.** Zool. (red) deer; männlich: stag; **ein kapitaler ~** a royal deer, Am. etwa 12-point buck; **2.** Gastr. venison; **3.** pej. od. hum. (Idiot) clod;

~**fänger** m hunting knife; ~**geweih** n (stag's) antlers Pl.

Hirschhorn n; nur Sg. Substanz: stag-horn, buckhorn; ~**salz** n Gastr. ammonium carbonate

Hirsch|käfer m Zool. stag beetle; ~**kalb** n fawn, calf; ~**kuh** f hind

Hirschleder n buckskin; **hirschledern** Adj. buckskin (...)

Hirse f; -, (Arten:) -n millet; ~**brei** m millet gruel; ~**korn** n **1.** millet (seed); **2.** Med. whitehead, milium (Pl. milia) fachspr.

Hirt m; -en, -en; altm., **Hirte** m; -n, -n herdsman; für Schafe: shepherd (auch fig. und bibl.)

Hirten|amt n kath. pastorate; ~**brief** m kath. pastoral letter; ~**dichtung** f Lit. pastoral poetry; ~**hund** m sheepdog; ~**junge** m shepherd boy; ~**lied** n pastoral song; ~**mädchen** n (young) shepherdess; ~**spiel** n Lit. pastoral play; ~**stab** m shepherd's crook; kirchl. crosier, crozier; ~**täschel** n; -s, kein Pl., ~**täschelkraut** n Bot. shepherd's purse; ~**volk** n pastoral tribe

Hirtin f; -, -nen shepherdess

his, His n; -, -; Mus. B sharp

Hisbollah f; -, kein Pl. Hezbollah, Hizbollah

Hispanist m; -en, -en, ~**in** f; -, -nen Hispanist, Hispanicist

hissen v/t. Naut. hoist (up), raise

Histamin n; -s, -e; Physiol. histamine

Histologie f; -, kein Pl.; Med. histology; **histologisch** Adj. histological, histologic

Histörchen n anecdote, little story; **Historie** f; -, -n; altm. **1.** nur Sg.; (Weltgeschichte) history; **2.** (Erzählung) tale, story; **Shakespeares ~n** Shakespeare's histories

Historien|bild n historical painting; ~**malerei** f historical painting; ~**schinken** m umg. pej., Bild: vast historical painting; Buch: historical tome; Film: historical epic

Historiker m; -s, -, ~**in** f; -, -nen historian

historisch I. Adj. **1.** historical; ~**es Verständnis** sense (od. understanding) of history; **2.** (geschichtlich bedeutsam) historic; **II.** Adv.: ~ **bedeutend sein** be historically significant, be of historical significance; ~**kritisch** Adj. historico-critical

historisieren v/t./i. geh. historicize; **Historismus** m; -, Historismen historicism

Hit m; -s, -s; umg. hit

Hitler|gruß m Nazi salute; ~**jugend** f hist. Hitler Youth; ~**junge** m hist. member of the Hitler Youth; ~**zeit** f hist. Hitler era; **in der ~** auch at the time of Hitler, in Hitler's time

Hit|liste f charts Pl.; **auf Platz 1 der ~ sein** be number one in the charts, top the charts; ~**parade** f altm. hit parade etc.; → **Hitliste**

hitverdächtig Adj.: **ein ~es Lied** a potential hit

Hitze f; -, kein Pl. heat (auch fig. und Zool.); **fliegende ~** Med. hot flushes Pl.; ~ **abweisend** heat-repellent; **das ist heute e-e ~!** it's sweltering (od. really hot) today; **hier drinnen ist aber e-e ~!** it's like an oven in here; **bei dieser ~** in this heat; **in ~ geraten** fig. get all worked up; **in der ~ des Gefechts** in the heat of the moment

hitzebeständig Adj. heat-resistant, heat-proof; Glas: auch oven-proof

Hitze|bläschen Pl. heat blisters; ~**ein-**

~**wirkung** f effect of (the) heat

hitzeempfindlich Adj. heat-sensitive, sensitive to heat

hitzefrei Adj., **Hitzefrei** n: ~ **bekommen/haben** be given a day / be off school because of the heat

Hitze|grad m temperature; ~**periode** f hot spell; ~**schild** m Raumfahrt: heat shield; ~**stau** m accumulation of heat; ~**wallung** f Med. hot flush; ~**welle** f **1.** heat wave; **2.** ~**n** Med. hot flushes

hitzig Adj. quick-tempered; (vorschnell) rash; (heftig) violent; Debatte: heated; ~ **werden** flare up; **nicht so ~!** don't get excited

Hitzkopf m hothead; **hitzköpfig** Adj. hotheaded

Hitzschlag m Med. heatstroke

HIV|-Infektion f Med. HIV infection; ~**-infiziert** Adj. attr. HIV-infected; präd. infected with HIV; ~**-negativ** Adj. HIV-negative; ~**-positiv** Adj. HIV-positive; ~**-Positive** m, f; -n, -n HIV-carrier, person with HIV; ~**-Test** m AIDS test

Hiwi m; -s, -s; umg. **1.** Univ. assistant; **2.** (Handlanger) dogsbody, Am. gofer

HJ f; -, kein Pl.; Abk. → **Hitlerjugend**

hl Abk. (**Hektoliter**) hl

hl. Abk. (**heilig**) St.

hm Interj. **1.** überlegend: um; **2.** zustimmend: mm; **3.** zweifelnd: hmm; **4.** verwundert: huh?

H-Milch f long-life (od. UHT) milk

h-Moll n; -, kein Pl.; Mus. B minor

HNO-Arzt m, **HNO-Ärztin** f ear, nose and throat doctor, bes. Am. ENT specialist

Hoax [ho:ks] m; -, -es Internet: hoax virus warning, hoax email

hob Imperf. → **heben**

Hobby n; -s, -s hobby, pastime

Hobby... im Subst. amateur ...; ~**gärtner** amateur gardener; **er ist ~gärtner** gardening is his hobby

Hobby|keller m workshop (in the cellar); ~**koch** m, ~**köchin** f keen (Am. avid) cook; ~**raum** m hobby room

Hobel m; -s, - **1.** für Holz: plane; **2.** Küchengerät: slicer; **3.** Mot., Sl. (Motorrad) (set of) wheels; (Auto) (set of) wheels, motor; ~**bank** f, Pl. -bänke carpenter's bench, workbench; ~**maschine** f planer, planing machine

hobeln I. v/t./i. Tech. plane; **wo gehobelt wird, da fallen Späne** Sprichw. you can't make an omelet(te) without breaking some eggs; **II.** v/t. Gastr. (Gurken etc.) slice

Hobelspäne Pl. (wood) shavings; Stahl: facings

hoch; höher, am höchsten **I.** Adj. **1.** räumlich: high; Gestalt, Baum, Haus etc.: tall; Leiter etc.: long; Schnee, Wasser etc: deep; **ein zwei Meter hoher Zaun** a two-met|re (Am. -er) -high fence; **hohe Schuhe** (mit hohen Absätzen) (high) heels; **hoher Seegang** heavy (od. rough) seas; **der hohe Norden** fig. the far north; fig. → **Kante, Ross, 2.** Ton, Stimme etc.: high; **zu ~** Mus. sharp; **das hohe C** top C; **3.** Druck, Einkommen, Fieber, Miete, Preis, Temperatur, Tempo etc.: high; Einkommen, Profit, Verlust: auch big; Lotteriegewinn: big; Betrag, Menge, Summe: large; Alter, Gewicht, Tempo: great; Gewicht, Strafe: heavy; Strafe, Verlust etc.: auch severe; **ein hohes Alter erreichen** auch live to be very old (od. to a ripe old age); **trotz seines hohen Alters** despite his (advanced od. great) age, despite his advanced years; *in hohem Maße* highly, greatly; *es ist hohe Zeit* (*es eilt*) it's high time; **4.** *fig.* (*schwierig*): *das ist mir zu ~ umg. fig.* (*zu schwierig*) that's above my head (*od.* beyond me); *s-e Rede war zu ~ für sie umg. fig.* he was talking over their heads; **5.** *Geburt, Politik, Posten etc.*: high; *Geburt: auch* noble; *Rang: auch* superior; *Diplomatie, Politik: auch* high-level; *Beamter, Offizier:* high-ranking, senior; *Besuch, Feiertag, Jubiläum etc.*: important; *hoher Adel* nobility, *in GB auch* peerage; *hoher Gast* distinguished guest, VIP; *hohes Gericht* high court; *Anrede*: Your Lordship (*Am.* Your Honor), Members of the Jury; *der Hohe Priester* the high priest; *der hohe Herr umg. iro.* the great lord; → *Haus* 9, *Tier.* **6.** *Ehre, Konzentration*: great; *Anspruch, Meinung etc.*: high; *Favorit*: hot; *e-e hohe Meinung haben von* think very highly of; *das Hohe Lied bibl.* Song of Solomon, Song of Songs; *fig.* hymn (+ *Gen.* in praise of); → *Ansehen, Schule* 4; **7.** (*auf Höhepunkt*): *in hoher Blüte stehen* be in full bloom; *künstlerische Bewegung*: be at its height; *das hohe Mittelalter* the High Middle Ages; **II.** *Adv.* **1.** (*Ggs. niedrig*) high; *~ oben* high up; (*weit*) a long way up; *~ oben im Norden* far up in the north; *~ über dem Boden* high above the ground; *ein ~ beladener Wagen* a heavily-laden cart; *~ fliegen* (*weit oben*) fly high (up); *3000 m ~ fliegen* fly at a height of 3000 m; *~ gelegen* high-up, high up in the mountains; *~ liegen Ort*: be situated high up; *Schnee*: be deep; *die Sonne steht ~* (*am Himmel*) the sun is high (in the sky); *zwei Treppen ~ wohnen* live on the second (*Am.* third) floor, live two floors up; *den Kopf / die Nase ~ tragen fig.* hold one's head up high / go around with one's nose in the air; *wer ~ steigt, wird tief fallen Sprichw.* the higher you climb, the further you have to fall; *fig.* → *hergehen* 2, *hinauswollen* 2; **2.** (*nach oben*) up; *~ aufgeschossen od. gewachsen* lanky; *~ aufragen* tower (up), soar; *Hände ~!* hands up!; *Kopf ~!* chin up!; **3.** *Tonlage*: high; *zu ~ singen, spielen*: sharp; **4.** *bezahlt, dotiert, versichert etc.*: highly; *besteuert, verlieren*: heavily; *gewinnen*: by a large margin; *~ besteuert* heavily taxed; *~ bezahlt* highly payed; *~ dosiert* in large doses; *~ dotiert* highly paid; *~ in den Achtzigern sein* be well into one's eighties; *zu ~ einschätzen* overestimate, overrate; *das ist zu ~ gegriffen* (*überschätzt*) that's a bit high; (*übertrieben*) that's an exaggeration; *~ pokern od. spielen* play (for) high (stakes) (*auch fig.*); *~ verschuldet* heavily (*od.* deep) in debt; **5.** *in Wendungen mit Adjektiven wie angesehen, begabt, geachtet, geehrt, industrialisiert, konzentriert, motiviert, qualifiziert, spezialisiert, zivilisiert etc.*: highly; *beglückt, erfreut, zufrieden*: very; (*überaus, äußerst*) *auch* extremely; *~ angesehen* highly regarded, very distinguished; *~ begabt* highly gifted (*od.* talented); *~ dekorierter Offizier* highly-decorated officer; *~ empfindlich Instrument, Material*: highly sensitive; *Gleichgewicht*: extremely delicate; *Film*: high-speed ..., fast; *umg. Person*: hypersensitive; (*leicht reizbar*) *auch* very touchy; *~ entwickelt* highly developed, sophisticated; *Technik etc.*: auch

very advanced; *~ favorisiert sein* be a great favo(u)rite; *~ geachtet* highly esteemed; *~ gebildet* very learned, erudite; *~ geehrt* highly hono(u)red; *~ geschätzt* highly esteemed; *~ gestecktes Ziel* ambitious aim; *~ gestellt Person*: high-ranking; *~ industrialisiert* highly industrialized; *~ konzentrierte Säure* highly-concentrated acid; *~ qualifiziert* highly qualified; *~ spezialisiert* highly specialized; *qualitativ ~ stehende Erzeugnisse* products of superior quality; *~ stehende Persönlichkeit* leading figure, distinguished personality, VIP; *~ technisiert* sophisticated; high-tech ...; *~ zivilisiert* highly civilized; **6.** *in Wendungen mit Verben*: highly, greatly; *~ achten* greatly respect, hold in high esteem; *j-m etw. ~ anrechnen* respect s.o. for (doing) s.th.; *er rechnet dir das ~ an auch* that really impressed him *umg.*; *j-n ~ schätzen* regard s.o. highly; *~ und heilig versprechen* promise solemnly, swear; → *hochleben;* **7.** *umg*: *drei Mann ~* three of them (*od.* us, you); *wenn es ~ kommt* at (the) most, at best; **8.** *Math.*: *drei ~ zwei/drei* three squared/cubed, three (raised) to the power (of) two/three; *drei hoch vier/fünf etc.* three (raised) to the power (of) four/five *etc.*; *das ist doch Schwachsinn ~ drei! umg.* that's totally stupid!; → *höher, höchst...*

Hoch *n*; *-s, -s* **1.** (*Hochruf*) cheers *Pl.* (*auf* + *Akk. od.* + *Dat.* for); *ein ~ auf j-n ausbringen* give three cheers for s.o.; **2.** *Stand*: high, peak; *... hat ein vorläufiges ~ erreicht* ... has reached a temporary high, ... has peaked temporarily; **3.** *Met.* high(-pressure area)

hoch...; *im V. siehe auch auf..., hinauf...*

hoch achten → *hoch* II 6

Hochachtung *f* (great) respect (*vor* + *Dat.* for); (*Bewunderung*) admiration (for); *bei aller ~ vor* (+ *Dat.*) with all respect to; *mit vorzüglicher ~ Briefschluss*: Yours faithfully, *bes. Am.* Yours sincerely; **hochachtungsvoll** *Adv. altm. Briefschluss*: Yours sincerely, *bes. Am.* Yours truly

Hochadel *m* higher nobility

hoch|aktuell *Adj.* highly topical; *Informationen etc.*: up-to-the-minute; *präd.* very much in the news; **~alpin** *Adj.* alpine

Hoch|altar *m* high altar; **~amt** *n kath.* high mass

hoch| angesehen → *hoch* II 5; **~anständig** *Adj.* very decent; **~arbeiten** *v/refl.* (*trennb., hat -ge-*) work one's way up; **~auflösend** *Adj. Fot.* high--resolution; *TV* high-definition; **~es Fernsehbild** high-definition TV (screen), HDTV

Hochbahn *f* elevated railway (*Am.* railroad), *Am. auch* el *umg.*

Hochbau *m* building construction; → *Hoch- und Tiefbau;* **~amt** *n* municipal building department

Hochbeet *n* raised bed

hochbefriedigt *Adj.* very (*od.* extremely) satisfied

hochbegabt, hoch begabt *Adj.* → *hoch* II 5; **Hochbegabte** *m, f* highly--gifted person; **Hochbegabtenförderung** *f* assistance for highly-gifted students

hoch|beglückt *Adj.* extremely (*od.* blissfully) happy; **~beinig** *Adj.* **1.** *Person, Tier*: long-legged; *Möbel*: ... with long legs; **2.** *Mot., Auto*: high off the

road; *~ beladen* → *hoch* II 1; **~berühmt** *Adj.* very famous; *~ besteuert* → *hoch* II 4

hochbetagt *Adj.* (very) advanced in years; *~ sterben* die at a very old age, die a very old man (*od.* woman); **Hochbetagte** *m, f*; *-n, -n* very old person

Hochbetrieb *m* **1.** *es herrscht od. wir etc. haben ~* things are really busy (*Am. auch* hopping), it's all go *umg.*; **2.** (*Stoßzeit*) rush hour, peak hours *Pl.*; **3.** (*Hochsaison*) peak season

hoch bezahlt → *hoch* II 4

hoch|biegen *v/t. und v/refl.* (*unreg., trennb., hat -ge-*) bend upwards; **~binden** *v/t.* (*unreg., trennb., hat -ge-*) tie up

Hochblüte *f*; *nur Sg.*; *fig. kulturelle etc.*: golden age; (*Glanzzeit*) heyday; *die ~ der italienischen Malerei etc.* the flowering of Italian painting *etc.*; *e-e/s-e ~ erleben* experience a peak / have its heyday; *e-e wirtschaftliche ~ erleben* go through a period of economic power (*od.* prosperity, expansion)

hochbringen *v/t.* (*unreg., trennb., hat -ge-*) **1.** bring up; **2.** *umg.* → *hochkriegen;* **3.** (*großziehen*) bring up, raise; **4.** *fig.*: *wieder ~* get s.th./s.o. back on its/ his (*od.* her) feet; **5.** *umg. fig.*: *j-n ~* (*ärgern*) get s.o.'s back up

hochbrisant *Adj.* highly charged, explosive

Hochburg *f fig.* stronghold

hoch dekoriert → *hoch* II 5

hochdeutsch *Adj. Ling.* standard (*engS.* High) German; **Hochdeutsch** *n* standard (*engS.* High) German; *das ~e* standard (*engS.* High) German

hochdienen *v/refl.* (*trennb., hat -ge-*) work one's way up

hoch| dosiert, ~ dotiert → *hoch* II 4

hochdrehen *v/t.* (*trennb., hat -ge-*); (*Fenster*) wind up; (*Motor*) rev up; (*Heizung etc.*) turn up

Hochdruck¹ *m*; *nur Sg.* **1.** high pressure (*auch Met.*); **2.** *Med.* high blood pressure, hypertension *fachspr.*; **3.** *umg. fig.*: *mit od. unter ~ arbeiten* work flat out (*Am.* at full speed)

Hochdruck² *m*; *Pl. -e*; *Druck.* **1.** *nur Sg.*; *Verfahren*: letterpress (printing), relief printing; **2.** *Erzeugnis*: letterpress, relief print

hochdrücken (*trennb., hat -ge-*) **I.** *v/t.* press *od.* push up(wards); **II.** *v/refl.* push o.s. up(wards)

Hochdruck|gebiet *n Met.* high(-pressure area); **~kranke** *m, f* person with high blood pressure, person suffering from hypertension; **~reiniger** *m* high--pressure water blaster; **~zone** *f Met.* high(-pressure area)

Hochebene *f* plateau

hoch|elegant *Adj.* very elegant; *~ empfindlich* → *hoch* II 5; *~ entwickelt* → *hoch* II 5; **~erfreut** *Adj.* delighted (*über* + *Akk.* at); **~erhoben** *Adj.*: *~en Hauptes* with one's head (*od.* nose) in the air; **~explosiv** *Adj.* highly explosive

hoch|fahren (*unreg., trennb.*) **I.** *v/i.* (*ist hochgefahren*) **1.** go up; (*mit*) *Auto*: drive up; *mit Rad*: ride up; **2.** *erschreckt*: start; *zornig*: flare up; *aus dem Schlaf ~* wake with a start; **II.** *v/t.* (*hat*) **1.** drive s.o. *od.* s.th. up (there); **2.** (*Computer*) boot up; **3.** (*Atomkraftwerk, Reaktor, Hochofen*) *von Null*: start up; (*Leistung erhöhen*) ramp up; **4.** (*Produktion etc.*) raise; **~fahrend**

H

I. *Part. Präs.* → **hochfahren**; **II.** *Adj.* (*überheblich*) overbearing, arrogant
hoch|fein *Adj.* first-class, top quality; **~fest** *Adj. Tech., Kunststoff, Verbindung etc.:* high tenacity …
Hochfinanz *f* high finance
hoch|fliegen *v/i.* (*unreg., trennb., ist -ge-*) **1.** *nach oben:* soar (up); **2.** (*hochgeschleudert werden*) be thrown up; *umg.* (*explodieren*) blow up; **~fliegend I.** *Part. Präs.* → **hochfliegen**; **II.** *Adj. fig.* ambitious; (*übertrieben*) high-flown; **~florig** *Adj. Teppich etc.:* deep-pile …
Hoch|flut *f* **1.** high tide; **2.** *fig.* flood, deluge; **~form** *f:* **in ~** in top form; **~format** *n* upright format; **Foto im ~** upright photo
hochfrequent *Adj.* high-frequency … (*auch Ling., Wort*)
Hochfrequenz *f Etech.* high frequency; radio frequency; **~bereich** *m* high-frequency (*bzw.* radio frequency) range; **~technik** *f* high-frequency (*bzw.* radio frequency) engineering
Hoch|frisur *f:* **eine ~ haben** wear one's hair up; **~garage** *f* multi-stor(e)y car park, *Am.* (multistory) parking garage
hoch| geachtet → **hoch** II 5; **~gebildet, ~ gebildet** *Adj.* → **hoch** II 5
Hochgebirge *n* high mountain region(s *Pl.*); **Hochgebirgs...** *im Subst.* high mountain, alpine
hoch geehrt → **hoch** II 5
Hochgefühl *n* feeling of elation; **das ist ein ~** it's a wonderful feeling; **im ~ des Erfolges** *etc.* elated by success *etc.*
hochgehen *v/i.* (*unreg., trennb., ist -ge-*) **1.** go up, *Vorhang, Preise etc.: auch* rise; **2.** *umg. fig.* (*explodieren*) blow up; (*wütend werden*) hit the roof; **~ lassen** (*Sprengsatz etc.*) blow up; (*Bande etc.*) bust
hoch|geistig *Adj.* (highly) intellectual; *iro.* highbrow; **~ gelegen** → **hoch** II 1; **~gelehrt** *Adj.* very learned, erudite
Hochgenuss *m* absolute delight, real treat
hoch| geschätzt → **hoch** II 5; **~geschlossen** *Adj. Kleidung:* high-necked, with a high neckline; **~geschraubt** *Adj. Erwartungen:* high, exaggerated; *Ambitionen:* high-flown
Hochgeschwindigkeits|modem *n Computer:* high-speed modem; **~strecke** *f,* **~trasse** *f* high-speed rail link; **~zug** *m* high-speed train
hochgespannt *Adj. Tech.* **1.** (*unter hohem Druck*) high-pressure …; **2.** *Etech.* high-voltage …; → **hoch gespannt**
hoch gespannt *Adj. fig. Erwartungen:* great, high; *Pläne:* ambitious; → **hochgespannt**
hoch| gesteckt → **hoch** II 5; **~gestellt** *Adj. Math.* (*Zahl*) superior; **~ gestellt** *Person:* → **hoch** II 5; **~gestochen** *Adj. umg. pej. Art, Redeweise:* high(-)falutin; *Buch etc.:* highbrow; *Person:* jumped-up; → **gewachsen, ~ gewachsen** *Adj.* → **hoch** II 2; **~gezüchtet** *Adj.* high-bred; *Tech.* sophisticated; *Rennwagen etc.:* souped up *umg.;* **~giftig** *Adj.* highly toxic
Hochglanz *m* high polish; **auf ~ polieren** give s.th. a high polish; **auf ~ bringen** *fig.* spruce up; **~abzug** *m Fot.* glossy print; **~magazin** *n* glossy (*bes. Am.* slick) magazine; **~papier** *n Fot.* glossy paper
hoch|gradig I. *Adj.* **1.** extreme; intense; *Unsinn:* utter; **2.** *Chem.* highly concentrated; **II.** *Adv.* extremely, to a high degree; **~gucken** *v/i.* (*trennb.,*

hat -ge-) look up (**von** from; **zu** at); **~hackig** *Adj.* high-heeled
hoch|halten *v/t.* (*unreg., trennb., hat -ge-*) **1.** hold up; **2.** (*Niveau, Preise etc.*) keep up; **3.** *fig.* hono(u)r; (*Andenken, Gefühl*) cherish; (*Traditionen etc.*) uphold, preserve; (*Ehre*) uphold; **~hangeln** *v/refl.* (*trennb., hat -ge-*) climb up hand over hand (**an** + *Dat.* on)
Hochhaus *n* high-rise, tower block; **~siedlung** *f* high-rise estate
hoch|heben *v/t.* (*unreg., trennb., hat -ge-*) lift up; **durch Hochheben der Hände** *Parl.* by show of hands; **~herrschaftlich I.** *Adj.* grand; **II.** *Adv.:* **dort geht es ~ zu** they live in grand style; **~herzig** *Adj.* high-minded; (*großzügig*) magnanimous
Ho-Chi-Minh-Stadt (*n*); *-s; Geog.* Ho Chi Minh City
hoch| industrialisiert → **hoch** II 5; **~intelligent** *Adj.* very (*od.* highly) intelligent; **~interessant** *Adj.* very (*od.* most) interesting; **~jagen** *v/t.* (*trennb., hat -ge-*) **1.** *aus dem Schlaf:* rouse; **2.** *Sl.* (*Motor*) rev up; **3.** *Sl.* (*sprengen*) blow up
hochkant *Adv.* **1.** on end; **~ stellen** upend; **2.** *umg. fig.:* **~ hinausfliegen** be turned out on one's ear; *aus e-m Job etc.: auch* get the boot; **j-n ~ hinauswerfen** kick s.o. out, give s.o. the boot; **hochkantig** *Adv.* → **hochkant** 2
hochkarätig *Adj.* **1.** high-carat …; **2.** *fig.* high-calib|re (*Am.* -er), top-flight …
Hochkirche *f; nur Sg. in GB:* High Church
hochklappbar *Adj.* tip-up …; *Bett:* folding …; **hochklappen** (*trennb.*) **I.** *v/t.* (*hat hochgeklappt*); (*Kragen*) turn up; (*Bett*) fold up; (*Sitz*) *auch* tip up; **II.** *v/i.* (*ist*) (*Bett*) fold up; (*Sitz*) *auch* tip up
hoch|klettern *v/i.* (*trennb., ist -ge-*) climb up (*auch fig.*); **~ an** (+ *Dat.*) climb (up) *s.th.;* **langsam ~** *fig. Zinsen etc.:* creep up; **~kochen** *v/i.* (*trennb., ist -ge-*) **1.** *Milch etc.:* boil up; **2.** *fig. Emotionen:* run high; *Gerücht:* spread
hochkommen *v/i.* (*unreg., trennb., ist -ge-*) **1.** *nach oben:* come up; **2.** (*aufstehen*) get up, get on one's feet; → **hinten** 5; **3.** *fig.* get on (*od.* ahead) *nach Schwierigkeiten etc.:* get back on one's feet; **niemanden neben sich ~ lassen** not allow any competition; **4.** *umg. fig.:* **mir kam alles wieder hoch** I brought everything up again; *Erinnerungen etc.:* it all came (flooding) back; → *auch* **hoch** II 7
hochkompliziert *Adj.* highly complicated
Hochkonjunktur *f Wirts.* (economic) boom; **~ haben** be going through (*od.* experiencing) an economic boom
hoch|konzentriert I. *Adj. Zuhörer etc.:* highly concentrated; **II.** *Adv. lesen etc.:* with great concentration, very concentratedly; **~ konzentriert** → **konzentriert** → **hoch** II 5
hoch|krempeln *v/t.* (*trennb., hat -ge-*) roll up; **die Ärmel ~** *fig.* roll up one's sleeves, get down to it *umg.;* **~kriegen** *v/t.* (*trennb., hat -ge-*); *umg.* **1.** get *s.o. od. s.th.* up; **2.** *vulg.:* **einen ~** (*e-e Erektion haben*) get (*od.* have) a hard-on; **er kriegt keinen hoch** he can't get it up
Hochkultur *f* advanced civilization
hoch|kurbeln *v/t.* (*trennb., hat -ge-*) wind up; **~laden** *v/t.* (*unreg., trennb.,*

hat -ge-); *EDV* upload; **~lagern** *v/t.* (*trennb., hat -ge-*): **die Beine ~** put one's legs up; **j-s Kopf ~** prop s.o.'s head up
Hochland *n Geog.* uplands *Pl.*, highlands *Pl.*; (*Gebirge*) mountains *Pl.*; **das schottische ~** the Scottish Highlands
hoch|leben *v/i. nur in:* **j-n ~ lassen** give s.o. three cheers; **er** *od.* **sie lebe hoch!** three cheers!; **hoch lebe …!** three cheers for …!; **hoch lebe der König!** long live the King!; **~legen** *v/t.* (*trennb., hat -ge-*) (*Bein, Füße*) put *s.th.* up; (*hinauflegen*) put *s.th.* up high
Hochleistung *f* top performance; *Tech. auch* high output
Hochleistungs|... *im Subst. Tech.* high-capacity, high-output, high-performance, high-power(ed); **~rechner** *m* supercomputer; **~sport** *m* high-performance sport(s *Pl.*); **~sportler** *m,* **~sportlerin** *f* top athlete, top sportsman, *weiblich:* top sportswoman
Hoch|leitung *f Etech.* overhead wire; **~lohnland** *n Wirts.* high-wage country; **~mittelalter** *n hist.* High Middle Ages *Pl.*
hoch|modern I. *Adj.* very modern, ultramodern; **II.** *Adv.:* **sich ~ kleiden** wear the latest fashions; **e-e ~ eingerichtete Küche** a kitchen with all the latest mod cons (*Am.* with cutting-edge appliances); **~modisch I.** *Adj.* highly (*od.* very) fashionable; **II.** *Adv.:* **sich ~ kleiden** wear the latest fashions; **~molekular** *Adj. Chem.* macromolecular
Hochmoor *n* high-moor bog
Hochmut *m* arrogance, pride; **~ kommt vor dem Fall** *Sprichw.* pride goes before a fall; **hochmütig** *Adj.* haughty, arrogant
hochnäsig *Adj. umg. pej.* stuck-up, snooty, snotty-nosed; **Hochnäsigkeit** *f; nur Sg.; umg. pej.* snootiness
Hochnebel *m* low stratus; **~decke** *f* extended low stratus
hoch|nehmen *v/t.* (*unreg., trennb., hat -ge-*) **1.** *in die Höhe:* lift up; *vom Boden etc.:* pick up; **mit ~** take up with one; **2.** *umg. fig.* (*aufziehen*) pull *s.o.*'s leg; (*übervorteilen*) fleece, do *umg., Am.* con *umg.;* (*Verbrecherbande etc.*) bust; **~notpeinlich** *Adj. altm.* **1.** *hist. nachgestellt:* involving torture; **2.** *hum.* (*streng*) severe; (*genau*) scrutinizing
Hochofen *m Tech.* blast furnace
hoch|offiziell *Adj.* highly (*od.* extremely) formal; **~päppeln** *v/t.* (*trennb., hat -ge-*) → **aufpäppeln**
Hoch|parterre *n* raised ground floor; **~phase** *f im Leben:* highpoint; *e-s Künstlers:* most creative period; *der Wahlkampf tritt jetzt in s-e ~* the election campaign now entered its most intense phase; *während der ~ des Kalten Krieges* at the height of the Cold War; **~plateau** *n* high plateau
hochprozentig *Adj. Alkohol:* high-proof; **Hochprozentiges** hard liquor, schnapps
hoch| qualifiziert → **hoch** II 5; **~ragen** *v/i.* (*trennb., hat -ge-*) tower *od.* rise (up); **~rangig** *Adj. nur attr. Funktionär, Politiker, Offizier etc.:* high-ranking; **~ranken** *v/refl.* (*trennb., hat -ge-*) climb (up); **sich ~ an** (+ *Dat.*) climb (*od.* creep) up *s.th.*
hochrechnen (*trennb., hat -ge-*) **I.** *v/t.* project; **II.** *v/i.* make a projection; **Hochrechnung** *f* projection; *bei Wahlen:* computer prediction; *aufgrund*

von Umfrage: exit poll; *die ersten ~en haben ergeben …* early indications point to …

hoch|reichen (*trennb., hat -ge-*) **I.** *v/t.* pass *s.th.* up; **II.** *v/i.* reach up; **~reißen** *v/t.* (*unreg., trennb., hat -ge-*) jerk (*od.* throw) *s.th.* up

Hochrelief *n* high relief

hochrot *Adj.* bright red, crimson

Hochruf *m* cheer; *die Menge brach in ~e aus* the crowd burst out cheering

hoch|rüsten *etc.* → *aufrüsten etc.*; **~rutschen** *v/i.* (*trennb., ist -ge-*) **1.** *Kleid etc.*: ride up; **2.** *fig.* (*aufrücken*) move up

Hochsaison *f*: (*in der*) **~** (in the) peak season, (at the) height of the season; **~ haben** be at one's busiest; *während der Urlaubszeit haben Einbrecher ~* burglars have their busiest time during the holiday (*Am. auch* vacation) period

hochschalten *v/i.* (*trennb., hat -ge-*) *Mot.* go (*od.* move) up a gear (*in + Akk.* into)

hoch schätzen *v/t.* → *hoch* II 6; **Hochschätzung** *f*; *nur Sg.* high regard

hoch|schauen *v/i.* (*trennb., hat -ge-*); *bes. südd., österr.* look up (*von* from; *zu* at, *fig.* to); **~schaukeln** (*trennb., hat -ge-*) **I.** *v/t.* play up; **II.** *v/refl.*: *sich* (*gegenseitig*) *~* get each other (all) worked up; **~schieben** *v/t.* (*unreg., trennb., hat -ge-*) push up; **~schlagen** (*unreg., trennb.*) **I.** *v/t.* (*hat hochgeschlagen*); (*Kragen etc.*) turn up; **II.** *v/i.* (*ist*) **1.** *Wellen*: be high; **2.** *fig. Gefühle*: run high; **~schnellen** *v/i.* (*trennb., ist -ge-*) **1.** jump up; **2.** *fig. Preise etc.*: soar, go sky-high *umg.*, skyrocket *umg.*

Hochschrank *m* tall cupboard

hoch|schrauben (*trennb., hat -ge-*) **I.** *v/t.* **1.** (*Drehstuhl etc.*) screw *s.th.* upwards; **2.** *fig.* (*Preise etc.*) push (*od* force) up; (*Erwartungen*) raise; **II.** *v/refl.* **1.** *Flugzeug etc.*: twist upwards; **2.** *fig.*: *die Lohn-Preis-Spirale schraubt sich hoch* prices and wages are spiral(l)ing upwards (*od.* are on an upward spiral); **~schrecken** → *aufschrecken*[1,2]

Hochschul|abschluss *m Univ.* (university *od.* college) degree; **~absolvent** *m*, **~absolventin** *f* (university *od.* college) graduate; **~bildung** *f*; *nur Sg.* (university *od.* college) education

Hochschule *f Univ.* university; (*Akademie*) college; *technische ~* college of advanced technology, *Am.* institute of technology, polytechnic; *pädagogische ~* college of education; **Hochschüler** *m*, **Hochschülerin** *f* university (*od.* college) student

Hochschul|gesetz *n Univ. legislation governing higher education*; **~lehrer** *m*, **~lehrerin** *f Univ.* (university *od.* college) lecturer; **~reform** *f* higher education reforms *Pl.*; **~reife** *f* university entrance qualification(s *Pl.*); *allgemeine/fachgebundene ~* general entrance qualification / *entrance qualification restricted to certain subjects*; *sie hat 2001 die ~ erworben in GB etwa*: she's got her A-levels in 2001; *in USA etwa*: she's graduated from high school in 2001; → *auch* **Abitur**, **~studium** *n* university (*od.* college) studies *Pl.*

hochschwanger *Adj.* heavily pregnant; *~ sein auch* be in an advanced stage of pregnancy

Hochsee *f*; *nur Sg.* high sea(s *Pl.*),

open sea; **~fischerei** *f* deep-sea fishing; **~flotte** *f* **1.** deep-sea fishing fleet; **2.** *Mil.* navy fleet; **~jacht** *f* ocean yacht

hochsehen *v/i.* (*unreg., trennb., hat -ge-*) look up (*von* from; *zu* at)

Hochseil *n* tightrope, high wire; **~akt** *m* **1.** tightrope (*od.* high-wire) act; **2.** *fig.* tightrope walk

Hochsicherheits|gefängnis *n* top-security prison; **~trakt** *m* security wing; **~verwahrung** *f* high-security detention, close custody

Hochsitz *m für Jäger*: raised hide (*Am.* blind)

Hochsommer *m* middle of summer; **hochsommerlich** *Adj.* summery; *~e Temperaturen* temperatures in the (high) eighties

Hochspannung *f* **1.** *Etech.* high voltage; **2.** *fig.* great suspense; *es herrscht ~* things are very tense

Hochspannungs|leitung *f Etech.* high-tension power line; **~mast** *m Etech.* pylon

hoch spezialisiert → *hoch* II 5

hochspielen *v/t.* (*trennb., hat -ge-*) (*Sache*) play up; *stärker*: blow up; (*Film etc.*) build up

Hochsprache *f*: *die deutsche ~* standard German; **hochsprachlich** *Adj.* standard (German *etc.*) …

hochspringen *v/i.* (*unreg., trennb., ist -ge-*) **1.** jump up (in the air); *an j-m ~* jump up at s.o.; *vom Stuhl / auf den Tisch ~* jump up from one's chair / onto the table; **2.** *als Sport betreiben*: do the high jump; **Hochspringer** *m*, **Hochspringerin** *f Sport* high jumper; **Hochsprung** *m Sport* high jump

hochspülen *v/t.* (*trennb., hat -ge-*) **1.** wash up to the surface; **2.** *fig.* bring to the surface

höchst *Adv.* (*äußerst*) highly, greatly, extremely, most

höchst… *Sup.* **1.** highest; *~er Punkt* peak; *wenn die Sonne am ~en steht* when the sun is at its highest; **2.** *aufs ~e od.* **Höchste** → *höchst*, **3.** *fig. Ansprüche etc.*: highest; (*größt…*) greatest, utmost; *mit ~er Diskretion* with the greatest discretion; *im ~en Fall* at (the) most; *in ~er Gefahr* in the greatest of danger; *~e Vollkommenheit* peak of perfection; *das ~e Wesen* (*Gott*) the Supreme Being; *von ~er Wichtigkeit* extremely important; *Verhandlungen auf ~er Ebene* top-level negotiations; *in den ~en Tönen loben* praise to the skies; *es ist ~e Zeit* (*ins Bett zu gehen*) it's high time (you/we *etc.* went to bed); *das ist das ~e der Gefühle umg.* (*ist das Äußerste*) that's the (absolute) limit; *das ist ja das Höchste! Äußerste*: that's the limit!; *Beste*: that's absolutely brilliant!; → *hoch*

Höchstalter *n* age limit; *das ~ überschritten haben* be over the age limit, be too old

hochstämmig *Adj. Baum*: tall; *Blume*: long-stemmed, standard

Hochstapelei *f*, *-*, *-en* **1.** *Jur.* confidence trickery, swindling; *Einzelfall*: confidence trick; **2.** *fig.* (*Übertreibung*) overstatement, exaggeration; (*Angeberei*) boasting; *geistige ~* intellectual fraud; **hochstapeln** *v/i.* (*trennb., hat -ge-*) **1.** *Jur.* swindle (s.o. *od.* people); **2.** *fig.* (*übertreiben*) exaggerate, overstate things (*od.* the case *etc.*); (*angeben*) boast; **Hochstapler** *m*; *-s*, *-*, **Hochstaplerin** *f*, *-*, *-nen* **1.** *Jur.* fraud,

confidence trickster; *männlich*: con man, *weiblich*: con woman *umg.*; **2.** *fig.* fake

Höchstarbeitszeit *f* maximum working hours *Pl.*

Hochstart *m Sport* standing start

Höchst|belastung *f* **1.** *Tech.* peak stress (*auch Etech.* load); **2.** *steuerlich etc.*: maximum burden; **~betrag** *m* maximum (amount), limit; **~bietende** *m*, *f*, *-n*, *-n* highest bidder; **~dauer** *f* maximum duration; **~dosis** *f* maximum dose

hoch|stecken *v/t.* (*trennb., hat -ge-*): *sich* (*Dat.*) *die Haare ~* put one's hair up; **~stehen** *v/i.* (*unreg., trennb., hat / südd., österr., schw. ist -ge-*) *Kragen*: be turned up; *Rand*: stick up; *Haare*: stick up; **~stehend** → *hoch* II 5; **~steigen** *v/i.* (*unreg., trennb., ist -ge-*) **1.** climb up; *die Treppe ~* climb (up) the ladder; **2.** *Preise, Rakete, Rauch, Zahlen etc.*: go up, rise; **3.** *fig. Wut etc.*: well up (*in j-m* inside s.o.)

höchsteigen… *Adj.*; *attr.*; *altm. od. hum.*: *in ~er Person* in person; *der Präsident in ~er Person auch* the president himself(, no less)

hochstellen *v/t.* (*trennb., hat -ge-*) **1.** put *s.th.* up; **2.** (*hochkant stellen*) stand *s.th.* upright (*od.* on end); → *auch* *hochklappen* I; **3.** (*Heizung etc.*) turn up; **Hochstelltaste** *f Schreibmaschine, Computer*: shift key

hochstemmen (*trennb., hat -ge-*) **I.** *v/t.* lift (*od.* heave) up; **II.** *v/refl.* push o.s. up

höchstenfalls *Adv.* → *höchstens*

höchstens *Adv.* **1.** at (the) most, at the outside; *er ist ~ zwanzig* he can't be more than twenty; *es ist ~ neun Uhr* it can't be later than nine o'clock; *ich trinke ~ mal ein Bier* very occasionally I might have a beer; *das gibt es ~ noch in …* the only place you might find it is (in) …; *das gibt es ~ im Fachhandel* you might find it at a specialist's (*Am.* specialist store *od.* shop); *~ ein Wunder würde …* only (*od.* nothing short of) a miracle would …, it would take a miracle to …; **2.** (*außer*) only; *~, wenn …* unless …; *ich esse kein Fleisch, ~ Fisch* I don't eat meat, and fish only at a push

Höchst|fall *m*; *nur Sg.*: *im ~* → *höchstens*; **~form** *f*; *nur Sg.*: *in ~* in top form; *zur ~ auflaufen* achieve top form; **~gebot** *n* highest offer; *Rennpferd gegen ~ zu verkaufen Annonce*: offers invited in the sale of racehorse; **~geschwindigkeit** *f* maximum (*od.* top) speed; *zulässige ~* speed limit; *wegen Überschreiten der ~* for exceeding the speed limit, for speeding; **~gewicht** *n* maximum weight; **~gewinn** *m* maximum win(nings *Pl.*); **~grenze** *f* limit, ceiling; *e-e ~ festsetzen für* put a ceiling on

hochstilisieren *v/t.* (*trennb., hat*) build up; *~ zu* turn s.o. *od.* s.th. into, make s.o. *od.* s.th. out to be

Hochstimmung *f* high spirits *Pl.*; *in ~ sein auch* be excited

Höchst|kurs *m Fin.* peak price; **~last** *f* maximum load; **~leistung** *f* top performance; *Tech. auch* maximum output; *Sport* record (performance); *wissenschaftliche ~*: great achievement; **~lohn** *m* maximum wage(s *Pl.*) (*od.* salary); **~marke** *f*: *der Wasserstand hat die ~ erreicht* the water level has reached the highest mark; **~maß** *n* maximum (*an + Dat.* of); *an Geduld*

H

etc.: great deal (of); **~menge** *f* maximum (amount)

höchstmöglich... *Adj. attr.* highest possible

Höchstnote *f Sport* top score, top marks *Pl.*

höchstpersönlich I. *Adj.* strictly personal; **II.** *Adv.* himself *bzw.* herself, in person, personally

Höchstpreis *m* top (*od.* maximum) price, price ceiling

Hochstraße *f* **1.** *im Gebirge*: mountain road; **2.** *erhöht*: elevated highway

hochstrecken *v/t.* (*trennb., hat -ge-*); (*Arm etc.*) stretch up (into the air)

höchstrichterlich *Adj.*: **~e Entscheidung** decision by the supreme court

Höchst|satz *m* maximum rate; **~stand** *m* highest level, all-time high; *Wasser*: high-water mark; **~strafe** *f* maximum penalty (*od.* sentence); **~summe** *f* maximum sum (*od.* amount); **~temperaturen** *Pl.* maximum temperatures

Hochstuhl *m für Kleinkind*: highchair

höchstwahrscheinlich *Adv.* very probably (*od.* likely), in all probability

Höchstwert *m* maximum value

hochstylen *v/t.* (*trennb., hat -ge-*); *umg.* tart (*Am.* doll) up; **ein hochgestyltes Auto** *etc.* a stylish car *etc.*

Höchstzahl *f* maximum (figure)

höchstzulässig... *Adj.; attr.* maximum (permitted)

Hochtal *n Geog.* high-lying valley

hoch technisiert → **hoch** II 5

Hochtemperaturreaktor *m Tech.* high-temperature reactor

Hochtöner *m; -s, -* Hi-Fi: tweeter

Hochtouren *Pl.*: **auf ~ laufen** *od.* **arbeiten** *Maschine*: be running at full power (*Mot.* speed); *Sache*: be in full swing; *bes. Projekt etc.*: be going full steam ahead; *Person*: be working flat out (*Am.* at top speed); **auf ~ bringen** (*Maschine*) bring (*od.* get) up to full power; (*Sache*) get into full swing; **Kaffee bringt mich auf ~** coffee gets me going; **hochtourig** *Adv.*: **~ fahren** run at high revs

hoch|trabend *Adj.* pompous, high(-)falutin, high-sounding; **~treiben** *v/t.* (*unreg., trennb., hat -ge-*) **1.** (*Vieh*) drive up; **2.** *Kosten, Löhne, Preise etc.*: force up

Hoch- und Tiefbau *m* structural and civil engineering

hoch|verdient *Adj.* **1.** *Sieg etc.*: well-deserved, well-earned; **2.** *Person*: meritorious, of great merit; **sich ~ machen um** serve *s.th.* well; **~verehrt** *Adj.* esteemed, greatly respected; *in der Anrede*: dear

Hoch|verrat *m* high treason; **~verräter** *m*, **~verräterin** *f* traitor

hochverzinslich *Adj. Fin.* ... yielding high interest, high-interest-bearing ...; **~e Wertpapiere/Anlageformen** high-yield securities / forms of investment

hochwachsen *v/i.* (*unreg., trennb., ist -ge-*): **~ an** (+ *Dat.*) grow up *s.th.*; → **hochgewachsen**

Hochwald *m* timber forest

Hochwasser *n; -s, -* *-s Flusses*: high water; *der See*: high tide; (*Überschwemmung*) flood(s *Pl.*); **~ haben** *od.* **führen** be swollen; **~gefahr** *f; nur Sg.* danger of flooding; **~katastrophe** *f* flood disaster; **~marke** *f* high-water mark; **~schaden** *m* flood damage; **~stand** *m* high-water level

hochwerfen *v/t.* (*unreg., trennb., hat -ge-*) throw up (in the air)

hochwertig *Adj.* high-grade ..., high-quality ...; **~e Nahrungsmittel** highly nutritive (*Am.* nutritious) food

Hochwild *n Jägerspr.* big game

hoch|willkommen *Adj.* most welcome; **~wirksam** *Adj.* highly effective

Hoch|wohlgeboren *m, f altm.*: **Euer** *od.* **Eure ~!** Sir *od.* Madam; **Seine/Ihre ~** the Hono(u)rable + *Name*; **hochwuchten** *v/t.* (*trennb., hat -ge-*); *umg.* heave up; *mit Hebel*: lever up

Hochwürden *m; -(s), altm.; kirchl.* Reverend (Father); **Eure** *od.* **Euer ~!** Reverend (Father); **Seine ~** the Most Reverend (*mit Titel und vollem Namen*)

Hochzahl *f Math.* exponent

Hochzeit[1] [ˈhɔxtsaɪt] *f* wedding; **silberne/goldene/diamantene/eiserne ~** silver/golden/diamond/65th wedding anniversary; **~ feiern** *od.* **halten** *Paar*: get married; *Gesellschaft*: have a wedding; **wann feiert ihr denn ~?** *auch iro.* when's the wedding (*od.* big) day then?

Hochzeit[2] [ˈhoːxtsaɪt] *f geh.* (*Blütezeit*) golden age

Hochzeiter *m; -s, -, ~in f; -, -nen; südd., österr., schw.* bridegroom, *weiblich*: bride; *Pl.* (*Paar*) bride and groom

Hochzeits|feier *f*, **~fest** *n* wedding (reception); **~flug** *m Zool.* nuptial flight; **~foto** *n* wedding photo; **~gast** *m* wedding guest; **~geschenk** *n* wedding present; **~gesellschaft** *f* wedding party; **~kleid** *n* wedding dress; **~kutsche** *f* (horsedrawn) wedding carriage; **~nacht** *f* wedding night; **~paar** *n* bride and groom, happy couple *umg.*; **~reise** *f* honeymoon; **auf ~ sein** be on one's honeymoon, be honeymooning *umg.*; **~tag** *m* **1.** wedding day; **2.** *Jahrestag*: (wedding) anniversary; **~torte** *f* wedding cake

hochziehen (*unreg., trennb.*) **I.** *v/t.* (*hat hochgezogen*) **1.** pull up; (*Hose*) hitch up; (*Beine*) draw up; (*Augenbrauen*) raise; **2.** *Flug.* pull up; **3.** *die Nase ~* sniff; **4.** (*Mauer etc.*) build, erect; **II.** *v/refl.* (*hat*) **1.** pull o.s. up (*an + Dat.* by); **2.** *umg. fig.*: *sich ~ an* (+ *Dat.*) positiv: get a thrill out of; *negativ*: make a fuss about; **III.** *v/i.* (*ist*) *Gewitter*: come up

Hochzins|phase *f Fin.* period of high interest rates; **~politik** *f* policy of high interest rates

hoch zivilisiert → **hoch** II 5

Hocke *f; -, -n* **1.** *Turnen etc.*: crouch, squatting position; **in die ~ gehen** crouch down, squat (down); **e-e ~ machen über** (+ *Akk.*) perform a squat vault over; **2.** *nordd., aus Getreide*: shock

hocken I. *v/i.* **1.** (*hat / südd., österr., schw. ist gehockt*) squat, crouch; *Huhn, Vogel*: perch; **2.** (*hat / südd., österr., schw. ist*); *umg.* (*sitzen*) sit; *untätig*: sit around; **über den Büchern ~** be poring over one's books; **~ bleiben** *Schüler*: have to repeat a year; **3.** (*ist*); *springen*: perform a squat vault (*über + Akk.* over); **über den Kasten ~** *Sport* perform a squat vault over the box; **II.** *v/refl.* (*hat*) **1.** squat down; **2.** *umg.* (*sich setzen*) plonk (*Am.* plop) o.s. down

Hocker *m; -s, -* stool; **das reißt mich nicht vom ~** *umg. fig.* that doesn't exactly bowl me over

Höcker *m; -s, -* **1.** *Kamel*: hump; **2.** *auf Nase etc.*: bump; *auf Schnabel*: knob; (*Hügel*) hump; *umg.* (*Buckel*) hump

höckerig *Adj.* bumpy

Höckerschwan *m Zool.* mute swan

Hockey [ˈhɔki] *n; -s, kein Pl.* hockey; **~schläger** *m* hockey stick

Hockstellung *f* squatting position

Hode *m; -n, -n und f; -, -n* → **Hoden**

Hoden *m; -s, -; Anat.* testicle; **~bruch** *m Med.* scrotal hernia; **~sack** *m Anat.* scrotum (*Pl.* scrota *od.* scrotums)

Hof *m; -(e)s, Höfe* **1.** yard; (*Innenhof*) courtyard; (*Hinterhof*) backyard; *Schule*: playground; *Kaserne*: barrack square; **2.** *e-s Herrschers*: court; **bei** *od.* **am ~e** at court; **~ halten** hold court; **am ~** (+ *Gen.*) **verkehren** move in court circles; **j-m den ~ machen** *fig.* court *s.o.*; **3.** (*Bauernhof*) farm; (*Gutshof*) estate; *Gebäude*: farmhouse; **in e-n ~ einheiraten** marry a farmer (*od.* the owner of an estate); **4.** *im Namen von Gasthöfen*: inn; *von Hotels*: hotel; **5.** *um Sonne, Mond*: halo, corona (*Pl.* coronae); *Anat.* areola (*Pl.* areolae); *Opt., Med.* halo; **~dame** *f* lady-in-waiting; **~dichter** *m in GB*: Poet Laureate; **~einfahrt** *f* entrance to a courtyard (*Bauernhof*: farm; *Landgut*: estate); **~erbe** *m*, **~erbin** *f* heir to a farm (*od.* estate)

hoffähig *Adj.* socially acceptable; *engS.* presentable

Hoffart *f; -, kein Pl.; geh. pej.* haughtiness, pride; **hoffärtig** *Adj. geh. pej.* haughty, proud

hoffen *vt/i.* hope (*auf + Akk.* for); **~ auf** (+ *Akk.*) *auch* set (*od.* pin) one's hopes on; **es steht** *od.* **ist zu ~** it's to be hoped; **ich hoffe es** (*sehr*) I (sincerely *od.* certainly) hope so; **ich hoffe nicht** I hope not; **ich hoffe doch,** (*dass*) **er** *etc.* I do hope (that) he *etc.*; **ich will nicht ~, dass ich es tun muss** I hope I don't have to do it; **das will ich doch ~!** *drohend*: you'd (*od.* he'd *etc.*) better!; **verzweifelt ~** hope against hope; **~ wir das Beste!** let's hope for the best; **zwischen Hoffen und Bangen** between hope and fear

hoffentlich *Adv.* hopefully, I hope ...; *in Antworten*: I hope so, let's hope so; **~ nicht** I hope not, let's hope not

Hoffnung *f* hope (*auf + Akk.* for, of); (*Erwartung*) *auch* expectation; (*Aussicht*) prospect; **in der ~ zu** (+ *Inf.*) in the hope of (+ *Ger.*), hoping to (+ *Inf.*); **die ~ verlieren** lose hope; **die ~ aufgeben** give up (*od.* abandon) hope; **man darf die ~ nie aufgeben** *auch* never say die; **sich der ~ hingeben, dass ...** cherish the hope that ...; **j-m ~(en) machen** *od.* **in j-m ~(en) erwecken** raise s.o.'s hopes; **sich ~en machen** be hopeful, be hoping; **sich falsche ~en machen** have false hopes; **j-m ~ machen, dass ...** lead s.o. to believe (*od.* expect) that ...; **j-m ~en auf etw.** (*Akk.*) **machen** hold out the prospect of s.th. to s.o.; **mach dir keine allzu großen ~en** don't be too hopeful, don't expect too much; **s-e ~en setzen auf** *od.* **in** (+ *Akk.*) pin one's hopes on, place one's hopes in, bank on; **es besteht noch ~** there's still hope, there's hope yet; **ist** *od.* **besteht noch ~?** is there any hope (left)?; **er/es ist unsere letzte ~** he's/it's our last hope; **guter ~ sein** *geh. euph. altm.* (*schwanger sein*) be expecting

hoffnungsfroh *Adj. geh.* hopeful

Hoffnungslauf *m Sport* repechage

hoffnungslos *Adj.* hopeless (*auch umg. fig.*); (*verzweifelt*) desperate; **ein ~er Fall** *umg.* a hopeless case; **Hoffnungslosigkeit** *f; nur Sg.* hopelessness; despair

Hoffnungs|schimmer *m geh.* glimmer of hope; **~strahl** *m geh.* ray of hope; **~träger** *m,* **~trägerin** *f the* great white hope *umg.*

hoffnungsvoll *Adj.* **1.** hopeful; *j-n ~ stimmen* give s.o. cause to hope; **2.** (*viel versprechend*) promising

Hof halten → **Hof** 2

Hofhund *m* guard dog

hofieren *v/t.: j-n ~* court s.o.'s favo(u)r; *pej.* curry favo(u)r with s.o.

höfisch *Adj.* courtly

Hof|kapelle *f* **1.** court chapel; *königliche:* chapel royal; **2.** *Mus.* court orchestra; **~knicks** *m* formal curtsy; **~leute** *Pl.* courtiers

höflich I. *Adj.* polite, courteous (*zu* to[wards]); **~,** *aber bestimmt* polite but firm; **II.** *Adv.* politely *etc.*; *wir bitten Sie ~ zu* (+ *Inf.*) may we ask you to (+ *Inf.*) (*od.* request that you ...); **Höflichkeit** *f* **1.** *nur Sg.* politeness, courtesy; **2.** (*Kompliment*) compliment; *~en austauschen* exchange pleasantries

Höflichkeits|besuch *m* courtesy call; **~bezeigung** *f* mark of respect; **~floskel** *f,* **~formel** *f* polite phrase; *im Briefschluss:* complimentary close

höflichkeitshalber *Adv.* out of politeness (*od.* courtesy)

Hoflieferant *m* purveyor to the court (*in GB:* to His *od.* Her Majesty)

Höfling *m; -s, -e* courtier

Hof|maler *m* court painter; **~marschall** *m* chamberlain, major-domo; **~narr** *m* court jester; **~rat** *m* **1.** *altm. in GB:* Privy Councillor; **2.** *österr.* Hofrat; **~sänger** *m hist.* court minstrel; **~schranzen** *Pl. pej.* fawning courtiers; **~staat** *m* royal (*od.* princely) household (*Gefolge:* retinue); **~statt** *f; -, -en od. -stätten; schw.* farm; **~tor** *n* courtyard (*od.* yard) gate; **~zeremoniell** *n* court etiquette

HO-Geschäft *n hist., ehem. DDR:* state-owned store; *Pl. Koll.* state-owned store chain *Sg.*

hoh... *Adj.; attr.* → **hoch**

Höhe *f; -, -n* **1.** height; *Astron., Geog., Flug., Math.* altitude; *von Schnee, Wasser etc.:* depth; *lichte ~ Tech.* headroom, clearance; *auf halber ~ machen wir Rast* we'll stop for a rest when we're halfway up; *die ~ des Turms beträgt 100 Meter* the tower is 100 m high (*od.* tall); *in e-r ~ von 1000 Metern* at a height (*Flug.* an altitude) of; *aus der ~* from above; *an ~ gewinnen Flug.* gain height (*od.* altitude); *in die ~* up, upwards, in the air; *etw. in die ~ heben* lift s.th. up (into the air); *in die ~ wachsen Pflanze etc.:* grow upwards; *Gebäude:* grow taller; *in die ~ mit Verb* → *auch* **hoch...**; **2.** (*Anhöhe*) hill, elevation; (*Gipfel*) summit, top; *Täler und ~n* hills and valleys; **3.** *von Geschwindigkeit, Miete, Preis, Temperatur etc.:* level; *von Gewicht, Geldstrafe, Gewinn, Verlust etc.:* size, amount; *von Druck, Wert:* amount; (*Ausmaß*) extent; (*Grad*) degree; (*Intensität*) intensity; *in ~ von Summe:* (to the amount) of; *Bevölkerungszuwachs etc.:* at the rate of; *e-e Strafe bis zu e-r ~ von ...* up to a maximum of ...; *in die ~ gehen* go up, increase; *in die ~ treiben* force up; *e-e gewaltige ~ erreichen* reach great heights; **4.** *Mus.* (*Tonhöhe*) pitch; *~n* (*hohe Töne*) treble *Sg.*; **5.** *horizontal: auf gleicher ~ mit* on a level with; *auf gleicher ~ lie-*

gen *od.* sein bei Rennen etc.: be level; *Pferde:* be neck and neck; *Geog.* be on (*Am. auch* at) the same latitude; *auf der ~ von Dover Geog.* on (*Am.* at) the same latitude as Dover; *Naut.* off Dover; **6.** *fig.* (*Niveau*) level; (*Bedeutung, Größe*) importance, magnitude; (*Höhepunkt*) height, peak; *die ~n und Tiefen des Lebens* the ups and downs of life; *auf der ~ s-s Ruhms etc.:* at the height (*od.* peak) of; *auf der ~ der Zeit* up to date; *auf der ~ sein* be in good form; *sich nicht ganz auf der ~ fühlen* not feel quite up to the mark; *in die ~ gehen umg.* hit the roof; *das ist ja wohl die ~! umg.* that really is the limit!

Hoheit *f; -, -en* **1.** *nur Sg.; Pol.* sovereignty; **2.** *Titel: His etc.* Highness; *Anrede:* Your Highness; *Seine/Ihre Königliche ~* His/Her Royal Highness; **3.** *nur Sg.; geh. e-r Person:* dignity; *von Bergen etc.:* grandeur, majesty; **hoheitlich** *Adj.* sovereign

Hoheits|akt *m* sovereign act; **~bereich** *m* **1.** jurisdiction (*of the state etc.*); **2.** → **Hoheitsgebiet**; **~gebiet** *n* (sovereign) territory; *deutsches ~* German territory; **~gewalt** *f* sovereignty; **~gewässer** *Pl.* territorial waters; **~recht** *n* sovereign right

hoheitsvoll I. *Adj.* majestic; (*gebieterisch*) imperious; **II.** *Adv.* majestically

Hoheitszeichen *n* national emblem

Hohelied *n* → **hoch** I 6

Höhen|angabe *f im Flugzeug:* altitude reading; *auf Karte:* altitude marking; **~angst** *f* fear of heights, vertigo; **~flosse** *f Flug.* stabilizer; **~flug** *m* **1.** high-altitude flight; **2.** *fig.: geistiger ~* flight of fancy; *der ~ des Dollars* the soaring dollar

höhengleich I. *Adj.* level; **II.** *Adv.* at the same level

Höhen|klima *n* mountain climate; **~krankheit** *f Med.* altitude sickness; **~lage** *f* altitude; *in ~n* at high altitudes; **~leitwerk** *n Flug.* horizontal tail; **~linie** *f Geog., auf Karte:* contour (line); **~luft** *f; nur Sg.* mountain air; **~messer** *m* altimeter; **~messung** *f* measurement of altitude, altimetry; **~meter** *m: die letzten 20 ~* the last 20 met|res (*Am.* -ers) in height; **~rausch** *m Med.* high-altitude euphoria; **~regler** *m Radio etc.:* treble control; **~rücken** *m Geog.* high ridge; **~ruder** *n Flug.* elevator; **~sonne** *f* **1.** *nur Sg.* mountain sun; **2.** *Lampe:* sun-ray lamp, *Am.* sunlamp; **3.** *nur Sg.; Behandlung:* sun-ray treatment; **~strahlung** *f* cosmic radiation; **~unterschied** *m* difference in altitude; **~verlust** *m Flug.* loss of altitude

höhenverstellbar *Adj.* height-adjustable

Höhen|weg *m am Gebirgskamm:* ridge path; *am Höhenzug entlang:* path running along a mountain range; **~wind** *m* upper wind; **~zug** *m Geog.* (*Hügelkette*) range of hills; (*Bergkette*) mountain range

Hohepriester → **hoch** I 5

Höhepunkt *m* **1.** highest point; (*Zenith*) zenith; *e-r Kurve:* vertex (*Pl.* vertices *od.* vertexes); **2.** *fig. des Glücks, e-r Karriere, der Macht etc.:* height, peak; *der Spannung, e-r Geschichte, auch sexuell:* climax; (*Orgasmus*) *auch* orgasm; *e-s Festes etc.: auch* highlight; *e-r Entwicklung etc.:* summit, peak; (*entscheidende Phase*) critical stage; *e-r Epoche, Kultur etc.:* heyday; *auf*

dem ~ (+ *Gen.*) at the height of; *s-n ~ erreichen* culminate (*in* + *Dat.* in), climax (*in*); *Verkaufszahlen etc.:* peak, reach its (*od.* their) peak; *Krankheit:* reach a crisis; *den ~ überschritten haben* have passed its peak; *e-n ~ haben sexuell:* climax, have an orgasm

höher I. *Komp.* **1.** higher; **2.** *fig. Bildung, Instanz, Mathematik, Wesen etc.:* higher; *Alter, Geschwindigkeit, Gewicht etc.:* greater; *Gewinn, Verlust etc.:* higher, greater; *~es Dienstalter* seniority; *in ~em Maße* to a greater extent; *~en Ortes* higher up; *~e Weihen* major orders; *sich zu Höherem berufen fühlen* feel called to greater (*od.* higher) things; → **Gewalt** 4, **Schule** 1, **Tochter** 1; **II.** *Adv.* higher; *entwickelt, qualifiziert etc.:* more highly; (*weiter* [*nach*] *oben*) higher up; *immer ~* higher and higher; *~ besteuert* more heavily taxed; *~ bezahlt* better (*od.* more highly) paid; *~ gelegen od. liegend* higher, *präd. und nachgestellt:* *auch* situated higher (*od.* further) up; *~ gruppieren* upgrade; *das lässt die Herzen ~ schlagen* this makes the heart beat faster; *~ schrauben* (*Fenster, Stuhl*) screw s.th. up higher; *fig.* (*steigern, anheben*) increase; (*Preise etc.*) push up; (*Ansprüche*) step up; *~ stehend Person:* higher(-ranking); *Bio.* more highly developed; *~ stufen* upgrade

Höhergruppierung *f* upgrading

höherwertig *Adj.* **1.** quality ...; *Material etc.:* of higher quality; **2.** *Chem.* of higher valence value

hohl *Adj.* **1.** hollow (*auch Zahn*); *Nuss:* empty; *das ist was für den ~en Zahn umg. fig.* that's not enough to keep a sparrow alive; **2.** *Augen, Wangen:* hollow, sunken; *Hand:* cupped; *Opt.* concave; *e-e ~e Hand machen* cup one's hand; *etw. in der ~en Hand halten* hold s.th. cupped in one's hand (*od.* in the hollow of one's hand); **3.** *Klang:* hollow; *~ klingend* hollow-sounding; **4.** *fig. pej. Pathos, Phrasen etc.:* hollow, empty; *Schwätzer:* empty-headed; *e-n ~en Kopf haben umg.* have nothing but sawdust in one's head; **~äugig** *Adj.* hollow-eyed

Hohlblock(stein) *m* hollow block

Höhle *f; -, -n* **1.** cave; (*Grotte*) grotto; **2.** (*Höhlung*) hollow; *in Baum etc.:* hole; *Anat.* cavity; *der Augen:* socket; **3.** *von Bären:* cave; *von Raubtieren:* den, lair (*beide auch fig.*); (*Bau*) hole, burrow; *sich in die ~ des Löwen wagen fig.* venture into the lion's den; *sich in s-r ~ verkriechen umg. fig.* retreat into one's den; **4.** *pej.* (*feuchte etc. Wohnung*) hole, hovel

Hohleisen *n* gouge; (*Meißel*) spoon chisel

höhlen *v/t.* → **Tropfen**

Höhlen|bär *m* cave bear; **~bewohner** *m* **1.** *Mensch:* cave-dweller, caveman; *bes. prähistorischer: auch* troglodyte; **2.** *Tier:* hole-dweller; *in Felsenhöhlen:* cave-dweller; **~brüter** *m Zool.* bird that nests in holes; **~forscher** *m,* **~forscherin** *f* cave explorer, spel(a)eologist, *Am., als Hobby:* spelunker; *unterirdisch: auch* potholer; **~fund** *m* cave find; **~malerei** *f* cave painting; **~mensch** *m* caveman

Hohl|form *f* hollow mo(u)ld; **~glas** *n* hollow glass(ware)

Hohlheit *f; nur Sg.* hollowness; *fig. auch* emptiness

Hohlkopf *m pej.* num(b)skull; **hohl-**

H

köpfig *Adj. pej.* empty-headed
Hohl|körper *m* hollow body; **~kreuz** *n* hollow back; **ein ~ machen** bend over backwards; **~kugel** *f* hollow sphere; **~maß** *n* measure of capacity; *für Korn etc.*: dry measure; **~meißel** *m* gouge; **~nadel** *f Med.* cannula (*Pl.* cannulae *od.* cannulas); **~raum** *m* hollow (space); *auch Anat., Med., Metall.* cavity; **~raumversiegelung** *f Mot.* vacuum sealing; **~saum** *m* hemstitch; **~schliff** *m* hollow grinding; **~spiegel** *m* concave mirror; **~tier** *n Zool.* zoophyte, coelenterate
Höhlung *f* hollow; *auch Anat.* cavity
hohlwangig *Adj.* hollow-cheeked
Hohl|weg *m* hollow; (*Schlucht*) ravine, gorge; (*Engpass*) narrow pass; **~ziegel** *m* hollow brick; *für Dach*: hollow tile
Hohn *m*; -(e)s, *kein Pl.*; (*Verachtung*) scorn, disdain; (*Verspottung*) mockery, derision, scoffing, sneering; (*Sarkasmus*) sarcasm; **der blanke** *od.* **reinste ~** sheer mockery; **zum ~(e)** (+ *Gen.*) in defiance of; **wie zum ~** as if in mockery; **nur ~ und Spott ernten** be(come) a laughing stock; **~ lachen** laugh derisively (**über** *j-n*: at, *etw.*: about); *e-r Sache ~ **lachen** *od.* **sprechen** *geh. fig.* make a mockery (+ *Dat.* of)
höhnen *vt/i. geh.* sneer, mock, scoff (*alle* + *Akk.* at *od.* **über** + *Akk.* at)
Hohngelächter *n* derisive laughter
höhnisch *Adj.* (*geringschätzig*) disdainful; (*spöttisch*) sneering, mocking, derisive; (*hämisch*) gloating; **~es Lächeln** sneer
hohnlächeln *v/i. nur Inf. und Part. Präs.* sneer (**über** + *Akk.* at); **sich ~d abwenden** turn away with a sneer; **Hohnlächeln** *n* sneer
hohnlachen, Hohn lachen *v/i. nur Inf. und Part. Präs.* → *Hohn*
hohnsprechen, Hohn sprechen *v/i.* → *Hohn*
hoi *Interj. erstaunt*: hey!
Hokuspokus *m*; -, *kein Pl.* **1.** *Zauberformel*: abracadabra; **~ Fidibus** (**dreimal schwarzer Kater**) *hum.* abracadabra; **2.** *pej.* (*Zaubertrick*) trick; (*fauler Zauber*) mumbo-jumbo (*auch fig.*); *fig.* (*Schwindel*) eyewash; **3.** (*Unfug*) nonsense
hold I. *Adj.* **1.** *poet. altm.* (*lieblich*) lovely, sweet, fair; **2.** *geh.*: **j-m/etw. ~ sein** be well-disposed towards s.o./s.th.; **das Glück war ihm ~** fortune smiled upon him, he was in luck; **II.** *Adv. lächeln etc.*: sweetly
Holding ['hoːldɪŋ] *f*; -, -s *Wirts.* holding company
holen *v/t.* **1.** (*Sache, Polizei, Hilfe*) get, fetch; (*nehmen*) take; *gehen*: go for, go and get; (*einkaufen*) go and buy; **aus der Tasche / vom Regal ~** take out of one's pocket / from the shelf; **j-m etw. ~** fetch (*od.* get) s.th. for s.o.; **~ lassen** send for, call *s.o.*; **j-n ans Telefon ~** get s.o. (to come) to the phone; **j-n aus dem Bett ~** get s.o. out of bed, wake s.o. up; **nach i-m Tod holte er i-e Kinder zu sich** he took in her children after her death; **2.** (*abholen*) call for, pick up; *euph. Polizei, Sanitäter etc.*: take away; **sie kommen ihn ~** they are coming to pick him up (*euph.* to take him away); **3.** (*bekommen*) get; **sich** (*Dat.*) **etw. ~** (*Anregungen, Rat, Trost*) seek s.th.; (*Preis*) get s.th., win s.th., take s.th.; (*Titel, Sieg*) win s.th.; *umg. fig.* (*Abreibung, Schnupfen, Standpauke etc.*) catch s.th.; **sich bei j-m Rat ~** ask s.o.'s advice; **hier / bei ihr ist**

nichts zu ~ there's nothing going here / you won't get anything out of her; **du holst dir noch den Tod!** you'll catch your death (of cold)!; → *Atem, Geier, Luft* 2, *Teufel* 1
holistisch I. *Adj.* holistic; **II.** *Adv.* holistically
Holland (*n*); -s *Geog.* **1.** Holland; → *Niederlande*; **2.** *umg.* Holland; **Holländer** *m*; -s, - **1.** Dutchman; **die ~** the Dutch; **der Fliegende ~** *Myth.* the Flying Dutchman; **2.** Dutch cheese; **Holländerin** *f*; -, -nen Dutchwoman, Dutch girl *etc.*; **holländisch** *Adj.* Dutch; **Holländisch** *n*; -en; *Ling.* Dutch; **das ~e** Dutch
Hollandrad *n* (heavy-duty) town bike
Hölle *f*; -, -n **1.** *nur Sg.* hell; **in der ~** in hell; **in die ~ kommen** go to (*od.* end up in) hell; **zur ~ fahren** *kirchl.* go to hell; **2.** *mst Sg.*; *fig.* hell; **grüne ~** jungle; **durch die ~ gehen** go through hell; **j-m die ~ heiß machen** *umg.* (*Angst machen*) put the fear of death into s.o.; (*j-m zusetzen*) give s.o. a hard time, make things unpleasant for s.o.; **j-m die ~ heiß machen, damit er etw. tut** *umg.* keep on at s.o. to do s.th., put s.o. under pressure to do s.th.; **j-m das Leben zur ~ machen** make life hell for s.o.; **da ist die ~ los** it is sheer pandemonium; **zur ~ wünschen** *geh.* curse *s.o./s.th.* to hell
Höllen|angst *f umg.*: **e-e ~ haben** be scared stiff; **j-m e-e ~ machen** scare s.o. stiff; **~brut** *f*; *nur Sg.*; *pej.* infernal rabble; **~fahrt** *f kirchl.* Christ's Descent into Hell; **~feuer** *n* hellfire; **~hund** *m Myth. umd fig.* hellhound; **~lärm** *m umg.* terrible racket, almighty din; **~maschine** *f* **1.** *altm.* time bomb; **2.** *umg.* infernal machine; **~qual** *f umg.* terrible agony; **~en ausstehen** go through hell; **~schlund** *m poet.* mouth of hell; **~stein** *m zum Verätzen* *od.*: lunar caustic, lapis infernalis, silver nitrate
Holler *m*; -s, -; *südd., österr.* → *Holunder*
höllisch I. *Adj.* **1.** infernal; (*teuflisch*) devilish; **2.** *umg. fig.* hellish; (*extrem*) incredible; **~e Angst / ~en Durst haben** be scared stiff / terribly thirsty; **e-n ~en Lärm machen** make a terrible racket; **II.** *Adv. umg. fig.* **heiß, kalt, laut, schwer**: hellishly; **es tut ~ weh** it hurts like hell *Sl.*; **du musst ~ aufpassen** you've really got to watch out
Hollywood|schaukel ['hɔlivʊt-] *f* swing hammock; **~star** *m* Hollywood star
Holm *m*; -(e)s, -e **1.** *Barren*: bar; *Leiter*: side rail, upright; *Ruder*: shaft; **2.** *Tech., von Kfz*: spar; *von Dach*: crossbeam; *Flug.* spar
Holocaust *m*; -(s), -s; *hist. und fig.*: (*atomarer*) ~ (nuclear) holocaust; **~opfer** *n* victim of the holocaust
Hologramm *n*; -s, -e hologram; **Holografie, Holographie** *f*; -, *kein Pl.* holography; **holografisch, holographisch I.** *Adj.* holographic; **II.** *Adv.* holographically
Holozän *n*; -s, *kein Pl.*; *Geol.* Holocene
holperig → *holprig*; **holpern** *v/i.* **1.** (*ist geholpert*); *fortbewegen*: bump (along); **2.** (*hat*) (*wackeln*) shake, jolt; **3.** (*hat*); *Flug. Vers etc.*: be clumsy; *Person*: stumble (along); **holprig I.** *Adj.* **1.** rough; *Weg*: *auch* bumpy; **2.** *fig. Stil*: clumsy; **sie spricht ein ~es Englisch** her English is very shaky; **II.** *Adv.* (*stockend*) haltingly; (*unge-*

schickt) clumsily; **etw. ~ vorlesen** *od.* **vortragen** stumble through s.th.
Holstein (*n*); -s; *Geog.* Holstein; **Holsteiner I.** *m*; -s, - **1.** *Einwohner*: inhabitant of Holstein; **2.** *Pferd*: Holsteiner; **II.** *Adj.* of (*od.* from) Holstein; **Holsteinerin** *f*; -, -nen inhabitant of Holstein; **holsteinisch** *Adj.* of (*od.* from) Holstein
holterdiepolter *Adv. umg.* (*überstürzt*) helter-skelter
Holunder *m*; -s, -; *Bot.* elder; **~beere** *f* elderberry; **~blüte** *f* elderflower; **~saft** *m* elderberry juice; **~strauch** *m* elder
Holz *n*; -es, Hölzer **1.** *mst Sg.*; *Material*: wood; *zum Bauen etc.*: timber, *Am.* Bäume und Baumstämme, *auch* timber; *Bretter und geschnittene Stücke*: lumber; **aus ~** made of wood, wooden; **edle Hölzer** precious (*od.* fine) woods; **~ verarbeitende Industrie** wood-processing industry; **ich bin doch nicht aus ~** I've got feelings too, you know; **2.** *fig.*: **er ist aus dem ~, aus dem man Spitzensportler macht** he is cut out to be a top sportsman; **sie sind / er ist aus demselben ~ geschnitzt** they're two of a kind / he's a chip off the old block; **aus anderem ~ geschnitzt sein** be made of different stuff; **aus härterem/grobem ~ geschnitzt** made of sterner stuff / rough and insensitive; **~ sägen** *umg.* (*schnarchen*) saw wood; **wie ein Stück ~ dastehen** *umg.* stand there (*od.* around) like a lemon; **viel ~ vor der Hütte haben** *umg. fig. hum., Frau*: be well-stacked; **das ist viel ~!** *umg.* that's a lot!; **3.** *mst Pl.; Stamm, Scheit*: log; *Pfahl etc.*: (wooden) post, stake; *Pflock*: (wooden) peg; *Stöckchen, Brettchen*: piece of wood; (*Streichholz*) match; **~ treffen** *Fußball etc.*: hit the woodwork; *Tennis etc.*: hit the wood; **4.** *nur Sg.; Mus.* woodwind; **5.** *nur Sg.; altm.* (*Wald*) wood, woods *Pl.*
Holz|apfel *m* crab apple; **~art** *f* (kind of) wood; **~asche** *f* wood ashes *Pl.*; **~auge** *n umg. hum.*: **~, sei wachsam!** keep your eyes peeled; **~balken** *m* wooden beam; **~bank** *f*; *Pl. -bänke* wooden bench; **~bau** *m*; *Pl. -ten* **1.** wooden structure; **2.** *nur Sg.; Bauweise*: timber (*Am.* woodframe) construction; **~bauweise** *f* timber (*Am.* woodframe) construction; **~bein** *n* wooden leg; **~bläser** *m*, **~bläserin** *f Mus.* woodwind player; **die Holzbläser** the woodwind (section); **~blasinstrument** *n* woodwind (instrument); **~block** *m* **1.** block of wood; **2.** *Mus.* woodblock; **~bock** *m* **1.** *Zool.* (*Zecke*) wood tick, sheep tick; *Käfer*: wood-boring longhorn; **2.** (*Sägebock*) sawhorse, *Am. altm. auch* sawbuck; **~boden** *m* wooden floor; **~bohrer** *m* **1.** wood drill; (*Handbohrer*) gimlet; **2.** *Zool., Falter*: carpenter (*od.* leopard) moth; (*Borkenkäfer*) bark beetle; **~brett** *n* **1.** wooden board; *großes*: wooden plank; **2.** (*Schneidbrett*) wooden chopping board; (*Holzteller*) wooden plate; **~brücke** *f* wooden (*od.* timber) bridge
Hölzchen *n* small piece of wood; (*Streichholz*) match
Holz|decke *f* wooden ceiling; **~druck** *m*; *Pl. -e* woodblock print(ing); **~dübel** *m* wooden dowel; **~einschlag** *m* tree-felling, cutting down of trees, *Am. auch* timber harvesting
holzen *v/i. umg. pej. Fußball*: kick everything above the grass, play dirty;

Holzerei *f umg. pej.* dirty game

hölzern *Adj.* **1.** wooden; **2.** *fig. Bewegung, Interpretation etc.*: wooden; (*ungeschickt*) awkward

Holzfällen *n*; *-s, kein Pl.* tree-felling, cutting down of trees, *Am. auch* timber harvesting; **Holzfäller** *m* woodcutter, *bes. Am.* lumberjack

Holzfaser *f* wood fib|re (*Am.* -er); (*Struktur*) grain; **~platte** *f* wood fibreboard (*Am.* fiberboard), *Am. auch* Masonite®

Holz|fäule *f* dry rot; **~figur** *f* wood carving, wooden figure; **~floß** *n* (wooden) raft

holzfrei *Adj. Papier*: wood-free

Holzfußboden *m* wooden floor

holzgetäfelt *Adj.* wood-panel(l)ed, wainscot(t)ed

Holz|hacken *n* wood chopping, chopping wood; **~hacker** *m* **1.** woodchopper; → *auch* **Holzfäller**, **2.** *Sl. pej., Fußball*: butcher; **ein ~ sein am Klavier**: be hamfisted

holzhaltig *Adj.* ligneous; *Papier*: woody

Holzhammer *m* mallet; **j-m etw. mit dem ~ beibringen** *od.* **einbläuen** *umg. fig.* hammer s.th. into s.o.; **~methode** *f umg. pej.* sledge-hammer method

Holz|handel *m* wood (*od.* timber, *Am.* lumber) trade; **~händler** *m*, **~händlerin** *f* timber merchant, *Am.* lumber dealer; **~haufen** *m* woodpile, stack of wood; **~haus** *n* wooden house; **~hütte** *f* wooden hut

holzig *Adj.* **1.** *Pflanze, Teile*: woody; **2.** *Rettich, Spargel etc.*: stringy

Holz|industrie *f* wood (*od.* timber, *Am. auch* lumber) industry; **~kiste** *f* wooden box (*od.* crate); **~kitt** *m* plastic wood; **~klotz** *m* **1.** block of wood; **sitz nicht da wie ein ~!** *umg.* don't just sit there (like a lemon)!; **2.** *Spielzeug*: wooden brick; **~klötzchen** *n* wooden brick

Holzkohle *f* charcoal; **Holzkohlengrill** *m* charcoal grill

Holz|konstruktion *f* **1.** *Technik*: wood (*od.* timber) construction; **2.** *konkret*: wooden structure; **~kopf** *m umg. pej.* blockhead; **~lager** *n* timber yard, *Am.* lumberyard; **~latte** *f* wooden slat; **~leim** *m* wood glue; **~leiste** *f* strip (*od.* thin piece) of wood; **~löffel** *m* wooden spoon; **~maserung** *f* wood grain, grain of the wood; **~nagel** *m* wooden nail (*od.* peg)

Holzofen *m* wood-burning stove; **Holzofen…** *im Subst. Gastr. …* bread etc. baked in a wood-burning oven

Holz|pantoffeln *Pl.* clogs; **~pfahl** *m* wooden post, stake; **~pflock** *m* wooden peg; **~platte** *f* wooden board; **~rahmen** *m* wooden frame; **~schädling** *m* wood pest; **~scheit** *n* piece of wood

Holzschnitt *m* woodcut; **holzschnittartig** *Adj. fig.* simplistic

Holz|schnitzer *m* wood carver; **~schnitzerei** *f* **1.** *nur Sg.*; *Handwerk*: wood carving, woodwork; **2.** *konkret*: piece of woodwork; (*Figur*) wood carving, wooden figure; **~schnitzerin** *f* wood carver; **~schraube** *f* wood screw; **~schuh** *m* clog, wooden shoe; **~schuppen** *m* **1.** wooden shed; **2.** *für Holz*: woodshed; **~schutzmittel** *n* wood preserver; **~schwamm** *m* dry rot; **~span** *m* small stick; *vom Hobeln*: wood shaving; **~splitter** *m* splinter (of wood); **~stapel** *m* woodpile, pile of wood; **~stich** *m* wood engraving; **~stift** *m* wooden peg; **~stock** *m*

1. *Block*: woodblock; **2.** *Dial. Stapel*: woodpile, pile of wood; **~stoß** *m* pile of wood; **~täfelung** *f* wood panel(l)ing, wainscot(t)ing; **~teller** *m* wooden plate; **~treppe** *f* wooden staircase; **~tür** *f* wooden door; **~ verarbeitend** → *Holz* 1; **~verarbeitung** *f* **1.** woodworking; **2.** *Veredelung*: wood processing; **~veredelung** *f* wood processing; **~verkleidung** *f* wood panel(l)ing, wainscot(t)ing; **~verschalung** *f* timber facing, boarding; **~verschlag** *m* wooden shed; *pej.* wooden shack; **~waren** *Pl.* wooden articles; *pej.* logger's (*od.* logging) path; **auf dem ~ sein** *fig.* be barking up the wrong tree, be very much mistaken; **~wirtschaft** *f* wood (*od.* timber, *Am. auch* lumber) industry; **~wolle** *f* wood-wool, excelsior; **~wurm** *m* woodworm; **~zaun** *m* wooden fence; *aus Brettern*: hoarding

Home|banking ['hoːmbɛŋkɪŋ] *n*; *-s, kein Pl.* home banking, online banking; **~page** ['-peːdʒ] *f EDV* home page

Hominide *m*; *-n, -n*; *Bio.* hominid

Hommage [ɔ'maːʃ] *f*; *-, -n*; *geh.* homage (**an** + *Akk.* to)

homo *Adj. Sl.* gay, *pej.* queer; **Homo** *m*; *-s, -s*; *umg. altm.* gay, *pej.* queer, *Am. auch* fag; **homo…** *im V. und Adj.* homo…

Homoehe *f* gay marriage, same-sex marriage

Homoerotik *f geh.* homoeroticism; **homoerotisch** *Adj. geh.* homoerotic

homogen *Adj. geh.* homogeneous; **homogenisieren** *v/t. geh.* homogenize; **Homogenisierung** *f geh.* homogenization; **Homogenität** *f*; *-, kein Pl.*; *geh.* homogeneity

Homograph *n*; *-s, -e*, **Homograf** *n*; *-s, -e Ling.* homograph

homonym *Ling. Adj.* homonymic, homonymous; **Homonym** *n*; *-s, -e* homonym

Homöopath *m*; *-en, -en*; *Med.* homöopath; **Homöopathie** *f*; *-, kein Pl.* hom(o)eopathy; **Homöopathin** *f*; *-, -nen* hom(o)eopath; **homöopathisch I.** *Adj.* hom(o)eopathic; **in ~en Dosen** *fig.* in hom(o)eopathic doses; **II.** *Adv.* hom(o)eopathically

homophil *Adj. geh.* homophile

homophob *Adj. geh.* (*stark bzw. krankhaft gegen Homosexualität eingestellt*) homophobic

Homophon *n*; *-s, -e*, **Homofon** *n*; *-s, -e* homophone

Homosexualität *f* homosexuality; **homosexuell** *Adj.* homosexual; **Homosexuelle** *m, f*; *-n, -n* homosexual

Honduraner *m*; *-s, -*, **~in** *f*; *-, -nen* Honduran, *weiblich auch*: Honduran woman (*od.* girl etc.); **honduranisch** *Adj.* Honduran; **Honduras** (*n*); *-*; *Geog.* Honduras

honett *Adj. geh.* (*rechtschaffen*) honest, upright; (*anständig*) decent

Hongkong (*n*); *-s*; *Geog.* Hong Kong

Honig *m*; *-s, -e* honey; **türkischer ~** Turkish delight; **j-m ~ um den Bart** *od.* **ums Maul schmieren** *umg. fig.* butter s.o. up; **~biene** *f* honeybee; **~brot** *n* piece of bread and honey

honigfarben, honiggelb *Adj.* honey-colo(u)red

Honig|klee *m* sweet clover; **~kuchen** *m* honey cake; **~kuchenpferd** *n umg. hum.*: **grinsen** *od.* **strahlen** *etc.* **wie ein ~** grin like a Cheshire cat; **~lecken** *n umg.*: **das ist kein ~** it's no bed of roses; **~melone** *f* sugar (*od.* honey-

dew) melon; **~schlecken** *n* → *Honiglecken*; **~schleuder** *f* honey extractor

honigsüß I. *Adj.* honey-sweet, as sweet as honey; **II.** *Adv.* as sweet as honey

Honig|tau *n von Pflanze, Blattlaus*: honeydew; **~wabe** *f* honeycomb; **~wein** *m* mead

Honneurs [ɔ'nøːɐs] *Pl.* **1.** *altm.* hono(u)r *Sg.*; **die ~ machen** *geh.*, *auch iro.* do the hono(u)rs; **2.** *Bridge, Whist*: hono(u)rs, high cards

Honorar *n*; *-s, -e* fee; *e-s Autors etc.*: royalties *Pl.*; **~abrechnung** *f Schlussrechnung*: settlement of a fee; *Aufstellung*: fee statement; **~basis** *f*: **auf ~** on a fee-paying basis; **~forderung** *f* charge; **eine ~ stellen** charge a fee; **e-e ~ an j-n haben** be owed a fee by s.o.

honorarfrei *Adj.* free of charge

Honorar|konsul *m*, **~konsulin** *f* honorary consul; **~professor** *m*, **~professorin** *f* honorary professor

Honoratioren *Pl.* local dignitaries

honorieren *v/t.* **1.** (*etw.*) pay for; (*j-n*) pay, remunerate *geh.* (**für** for); **2.** *Fin.* (*Wechsel*) hono(u)r; **3.** *fig.* (*anerkennen*) acknowledge; (*belohnen*) reward; **es wird überhaupt nicht honoriert** you get no credit (*od.* thanks) for it; **Honorierung** *f* **1.** remuneration, payment; **2.** *fig.* acknowledg(e)ment; (*Belohnung*) reward

honorig *Adj. altm. od. iro.* (*ehrenhaft*) hono(u)rable; (*Respekt verdienend*) respectable

honoris causa *Adv.* (*abgek.* **h.c.**): **Dr. ~** honorary doctor

Hopfen *m*; *-s, -*; *Bot.* hop; *Agr. Koll.* hops *Pl.*; **an ihm ist ~ und Malz verloren** *umg. fig.* he's a dead loss (*Am.* a lost cause *od.* a write-off); **~ernte** *f* hop picking; *Saison*: hop-picking time (*od.* season); **~stange** *f* hop pole

hopp *Interj.* jump!; (*schnell*) quick!; **nun mal ~!** *umg.* get a move on!, chop, chop!; **~, raus aus dem Bett!** come on, up you get!

hoppe *Kinderspr.*: **~, ~ Reiter** nursery rhyme recited while bouncing child on one's knee; **~, ~ Reiter machen** *etwa* have a ride-a-cock-horse (on s.o's knee)

hoppeln *v/i.* **1.** hop; **2.** *Wagen etc.*: jolt (along), bump along

hopphopp I. *Interj.* chop, chop!; **II.** *Adv. umg.*: **bei ihr muss alles ~ gehen** she wants everything done in double-quick time; **das ist alles ~ gemacht** (*schludrig*) it's all been sloppily done

hoppla I. *Interj. beim Stolpern etc.*: (wh)oops(-a-daisy)!; **1.** *überrascht*: **~, was ist denn das?** hello, what's this?; **~, jetzt komm ich!** look out, here I come!; **II.** *Adv. umg.*: **aber ein bisschen ~!** (*schnell*) chop chop!, jump to it!

hopplahopp *Adv. umg.* (*schlampig*) slapdash; (*schnell-schnell*) chop-chop; **so ~ geht das nicht** you can't rush these things, it takes time

hops *Adj. umg.*: **~ sein** (*tot sein*) have snuffed it, have popped one's clogs; (*verloren sein*) be lost; *Geld*: be down the drain; (*entzwei sein*) be broken

hopsa, hopsala, hopsassa *Interj. Kinderspr.* (wh)oops(-a-daisy)!

hopsen *v/i. umg.* hop, skip, hop and skip; **Hopser** *m*; *-s, -*; *umg.* hop; **e-n ~ machen** give a little hop

hops|gehen *v/i.* (*unreg., trennb., -ist -ge-*); *umg.* (*sterben*) snuff it, pop one's clogs, (*verloren gehen*) get lost;

Geld etc.: go down the drain; (*verhaftet werden*) get nabbed; **~nehmen** *v/t.* (*unreg.*, *trennb.*, *hat -ge-*); *umg.* (*festnehmen*) nab

Hörapparat *m* hearing aid

hörbar *Adj.* audible; **sich ~ machen** make o.s. heard; **Hörbarkeit** *f*; *nur Sg.* audibility

hörbehindert *Adj.* partially deaf; **Hörbehinderte** *m*, *f* person who is hard of hearing; **Hörbehinderung** *f* impaired hearing; partial deafness

Hör|bereich *m* auditory range; *e-s Senders*: broadcasting range; **~bibliothek** *f* audio library; **~bild** *n* radio feature; **~brille** *f* hearing aid glasses *Pl.*; **~buch** *n* talking book

horchen *v/i.* listen (**auf** + *Akk.* to); *heimlich*: *auch* eavesdrop; **an der Tür ~** listen at the door; **horch!** listen!

Horchposten *m Mil. und hum.* listening post; **auf ~ sein** be on duty at the listening post; *fig.* be listening out

Horde[1] *f*; *-*, *-n* **1.** *pej.* horde, mob; **wahre ~n von ...** absolute hordes of ...; **2.** *Völkerkunde*: horde

Horde[2] *f*; *-*, *-n Gestell*: rack

hören I. *vt/i.* **1.** hear; (*zufällig mit anhören*) overhear; **gut ~** have good ears (*od.* hearing); **schwer od. schlecht ~** be slightly deaf, be hard of hearing; **ich hör dich so schlecht** I can't hear you very well; **du hörst wohl schlecht?** *iro.* are you (going) deaf?; **ich glaub, ich hör nicht recht!** *umg.* did I hear (you) right?, say that again; **das lässt sich ~!** that doesn't sound too bad at all; **j-n kommen/lachen ~** hear s.o. coming/laughing; **er hört sich gerne reden** he likes the sound of his own voice; **ich habe sagen ~** I've heard it said; **ihm verging Hören und Sehen** *umg.* he almost passed out; **..., dass dir Hören und Sehen vergeht** *umg. drohend*: ... that you'll wish you were never born; **ich hörte an Ihrer Stimme, dass etwas faul war** I could tell by her voice that something fishy was going on; **2.** (*zuhören*) listen; **Radio ~** listen to the radio; **hör mal!** listen, *bes. Am.* listen up!; **na hör mal, so geht das aber nicht!** now listen here, now just a minute; **hört, hört!** *Zwischenruf*: well, well!; **man höre und staune** would you believe it; **3.** (*erfahren*) hear (**von** of *od.* about); **ich hab's von ihr gehört** I heard it from her, she told me; **ich habe von ihm gehört** (*kenne den Namen*) I've heard of him; (*habe e-n Brief etc. bekommen*) I've heard from him; **ich habe schon viel von ihm gehört** I've heard a lot about him; **man hörte nie mehr etwas von ihm** he was never heard of again; **ich habe gehört, dass ...** they say (that) ...; **wie ich höre, sie krank** I hear she's ill; **nach allem, was ich höre** from what I've heard; **was muss ich da ~?** what's this you're (*od.* they're *etc.*) telling me?; **das will ich nicht gehört haben!** I'll pretend I didn't hear that!; **er hat nichts von sich ~ lassen** he hasn't written (*od.* phoned), we *etc.* haven't heard from him at all; **lasst mal von euch ~** keep in touch; **ich lasse von mir ~** I'll let you know; **Sie werden noch von mir ~!** you haven't heard the last of this!; **II.** *v/t.* **1.** (*anhören*) (*Beschuldigten, Zeugen etc.*) hear; **die Beichte ~** hear confession; **2.** *Univ.*: **bei Professor B. Geschichte ~** go to Professor B's history lectures; **Politologie ~**

go to (*od.* attend) lectures in political science; **III.** *v/i.* **1.** **~ auf** (+ *Akk.*) listen to; **auf den Namen ... ~** answer to the name of ...; **nicht auf j-s Flehen ~** not heed s.o.'s pleas; **2.** *umg.* (*gehorchen*) obey, listen; **alles hört auf mein Kommando!** I am in command!; (*was ich sage, wird gemacht*) you will all do what I say!; **willst du wohl ~?** I wish you'd listen!; **wer nicht ~ will, muss fühlen** *Sprichw.* that's what you get for not listening; → **Ohr** 2

Hörensagen *n*: **vom ~** by hearsay

hörenswert *Adj. präd. und nachgestellt*: worth listening to

Hörer *m*; *-s*, *-* **1.** (*Zuhörer*) listener, auditor *geh.*; **liebe ~innen und ~!** *zum Sendebeginn*: hello everybody, hello to our listeners everywhere; *im Satz, verstärkend*: dear listeners; **2.** *Univ.* student; **3.** *Telefon*: receiver; **den ~ abnehmen** pick up (*wenn es klingelt*: *auch* answer) the phone; **den ~ auflegen** put the phone down

Hörerin *f*; *-*, *-nen* **1.** (*Zuhörerin*) listener; **2.** *Univ.* student

Hörer|kreis *m*, **~schaft** *f* listeners *Pl.*, audience; **~wunsch** *m* request (from a listener); *Pl.* (listeners') requests

Hör|fähigkeit *f* hearing ability; **~fehler** *m* **1.** misunderstanding; *Med.* hearing disorder, auditory defect; **~funk** *m* radio; *als technischer Begriff*: sound broadcasting; **~genuss** *m* pleasurable listening; **~gerät** *n* hearing (*od.* deaf) aid; **~geräteakustiker** *m*, **~geräteakustikerin** *f* hearing aid specialist

hörgeschädigt *Adj.* hard of hearing, partially deaf; **Hörgeschädigte** *m*, *f* person who is hard of hearing, hearing-impaired person

Hör|grenze *f* limit of hearing, audible limit; **~hilfe** *f* → **Hörgerät**

hörig *Adj. auch sexuell*: dependent (+ *Dat.* on); **j-m ~ sein** *hist.*, *als Sklave*: be in bondage to s.o.; **Hörige** *m*, *f*; *-n*, *-n* serf, *männlich*: bondsman, *weiblich*: bondswoman; **Hörigkeit** *f*; *nur Sg.* (total) dependence (*gegenüber* on); *auch hist.* bondage (to)

Horizont *m*; *-(e)s*, *-e* **1.** horizon; **am ~** on the horizon; **die Sonne sank unter den ~** the sun sank (*od.* disappeared) behind the horizon; **2.** *fig.* horizon; **beschränkter od. enger ~** narrow horizons *Pl.*; **weiter ~** broad view (*od.* horizon); **s-n ~ erweitern** broaden one's horizons *Pl.*; **das erweitert den ~** it broadens your horizons *Pl.* (*od.* the mind); **das geht über s-n ~** that's beyond him; **3.** *Geol.* horizon

horizontal *Adj.* horizontal; **das ~e Gewerbe** *umg. hum.* the oldest profession in the world; **Horizontale** *f*; *-*, *-n* horizontal; **sich in die ~ begeben** *umg. hum.* (go and) recline; **Horizontallage** *f* horizontal position

Hormon *n*; *-s*, *-e*; *Physiol.* hormone; **hormonal** *Adj.* hormonal

Hormon|behandlung *f Med.* hormonal treatment; *e-e* ~ a course of hormone treatment; **~drüse** *f Physiol.* hormone gland

hormonell I. *Adj.* hormonal, hormone ...; **II.** *Adv. behandeln etc.*: with hormones

Hormon|haushalt *m* hormone balance; **~mangel** *m* lack of hormones; **~präparat** *n* hormone preparation; **~spiegel** *m* hormone level

Hörmuschel *f Telef.* earpiece

Horn[1] *n*; *-(e)s*, *Hörner* **1.** *Zool.* horn; *der Schnecke*: feeler; **auf die Hörner**

nehmen Stier etc.: toss; *umg. fig. mit Auto*: knock up into the air; **j-m Hörner aufsetzen** *fig.* cuckold s.o.; **sich** (*Dat.*) **die Hörner abstoßen** *fig.* sow one's wild oats; → **Stier** 1; **2.** *Mus.* (French) horn; *Mil.* bugle; **ins ~ stoßen** blow one's horn; **ins gleiche ~ stoßen** *fig.* play the same tune, be of one mind (in the matter); **mit j-m ins gleiche ~ stoßen** *fig.* chime in with s.o., go along with s.o. (wholeheartedly); **3.** *Mot.* (*Hupe*) horn; **4.** *umg.* (*Beule*) bump (on one's head)

Horn[2] *n*; *-(e)s*, *-e*, *mst Sg. Substanz*: horn

Hornberger *Adj.*: **ausgehen wie das ~ Schießen** come to nothing

Horn|bläser *m*, **~bläserin** *f* horn player; **~blende** *f Min.* hornblende; **~brille** *f*: (*e-e*) ~ (a pair of) horn-rimmed glasses *Pl. od.* spectacles *Pl.*

Hörnchen *n* **1.** (*Gebäck*) croissant; **2.** *Zool.* squirrel

Hörnerklang *m* sound of horns

Hörnerv *m* auditory nerve

Hornhaut *f* **1.** callus(es *Pl.*); **2.** *des Auges*: cornea; **~entzündung** *f im Auge*: inflammation of the cornea, keratitis; **~trübung** *f* nebula (*Pl.* nebulae *od.* nebulas); **~verletzung** *f* injured cornea

hornig *Adj. Haut*: horny

Hornisse *f*; *-*, *-n*; *Zool.* hornet; **Hornissennest** *n* hornets' nest

Hornist *m*; *-en*, *-en*, **~in** *f*; *-*, *-nen* (French) horn player

Horn|klee *m Bot.* bird's foot trefoil; **~ochse** *m umg. pej.* idiot, clod; **~signal** *n Mil.* bugle call; *von Auto*: blast on the horn; *in Fabrik*: hooter, *Am.* whistle; **~vieh** *n Tier*: horned cattle *Pl.*

Hörorgan *n* organ of hearing

Horoskop *n*; *-s*, *-e* horoscope; **j-m das ~ stellen** do (*od.* cast) s.o.'s horoscope

Hör|probe *f* audition; *bei Tonaufnahme*: test recording; **~prüfung** *f Med.* hearing test

horrend *Adj. Preis etc.*: shocking, ridiculous

Hörrohr *n* **1.** ear trumpet; **2.** *Med.* stethoscope

Horror *m*; *-s*, *kein Pl.* horror (**vor** + *Dat.* of); **e-n ~ haben vor** (+ *Dat.*) *umg.* have a thing about (*od.* **vor** *j-m*, *e-r Prüfung*, *Spinnen etc.*): be terrified of; **ich habe e-n ~ vor Spinnen** *etc. auch* I can't stand spiders *etc.*; **es ist der reinste ~** it's excruciating, it's sheer hell *umg.*; **~film** *m* horror film (*od.* movie); **~geschichte** *f* horror story; **~szene** *f* scene of horror; *im Film*: horror (*od.* horrific) scene; **~szenario** *n* horror scenario; **~trip** *m umg.* **1.** *durch Droge*: bad trip; **2.** *fig. Erlebnis*: nightmare; *Reise auch*: nightmare trip; **~video** *n* video nasty, *Am.* splatter video; **~vision** *f* nightmare vision

Hör|saal *m* lecture hall, auditorium; **~schaden** *m* hearing defect (*od.* impairment), impaired hearing; **~schärfe** *f* hearing acuity; **~schwelle** *f* auditory threshold

Horsd'œuvre [ɔr'dœːvrə] *n*; *-s*, *-s* [ɔr'dœːvrəs] *Gastr. geh.* hors d'œuvre, starter, *Am. auch* appetizer

Hörspiel *n* radio play

Horst *m*; *-(e)s*, *-e* **1.** nest; *von Adler*: eyrie; **2.** *Flug.* air base; **3.** (*Gehölz*) thicket; **4.** *Bot.*, *von Blumen*: cluster; *von Gräsern etc.*: tuft; **5.** *Geol.* horst

Hörsturz *m Med.* acute hearing loss, sudden deafness

Hort *m*; -(*e*)*s*, -*e* **1.** *poet.* (*Schatz*) treasure; **2.** *geh.* (*sicherer Ort*) safe retreat, refuge; *ein ~ der Freiheit* a stronghold of liberty; **3.** *für Kinder*: after-school care cent|re (*Am.* -er); **horten** *v/t.* hoard; (*Rohstoffe*) stockpile

Hortensie *f*, -, -*n*; *Bot.* hydrangea

Hör|test *m* hearing test; *e-n ~ machen lassen* have one's ears tested; **~vermögen** *n* hearing; **~weite** *f*: *außer/in ~ out* of / within earshot

Höschen *n* **1.** (*ein*) *~* (*Slip*) (a pair of) panties *Pl.*; *für Kinder*: (a pair of) (short) trousers *Pl.*; *heiße ~* hot pants; **2.** *Zool., bei Bienen*: pollen load; **~windel** *f* disposable nappy (*Am.* diaper)

Hose *f*, -, -*n* **1.** (*e-e*) *~* (a pair of) trousers (*Am.* pants *od.* slacks) *Pl.*; *kurze ~(n)* (pair of) shorts *Pl.*; *in die ~ machen* (*urinieren*) wet o.s. (*auch umg. fig.*); (*einkoten*) fill (*od.* make a mess in) one's pants; **2.** *umg. fig.*: *die ~(n) anhaben* wear the trousers (*Am.* pants); *die ~n runterlassen* admit it, come clean, *Am. auch* fess up; *die ~(n)* (*gestrichen*) *voll haben* be in a blue funk; *die ~(n) voll kriegen* get (*od.* be given) a good hiding; *es ist in die ~ gegangen* (*war ein Misserfolg*) it was a flop (*od.* washout); (*ist schief gegangen*) it didn't work out, it was a bit of a disaster; (*ist nicht angekommen*) *Witz etc.*: nobody got it, it didn't come over; *tote ~ sein* be a washout; *Ort etc.*: a dump

Hosen|anzug *m* trouser (*Am.* pants) suit; **~band** *n*; *Pl. -bänder* kneeband; **~bandorden** *m* Order of the Garter; **~bein** *n* trouser (*Am.* pant) leg; **~boden** *m* seat of the *od.* one's trousers (*bes. Am.* pants); *sich auf den ~ setzen* (*stillsitzen*) sit down (and shut up); *umg. fig.* (*fleißig lernen*) knuckle under; *den ~ voll kriegen umg. fig.* get a smacked bottom (*bes. Am.* behind); *j-m den ~ strammziehen umg. fig.* tan s.o.'s hide; **~bügel** *m* trouser (*Am.* pants) hanger; **~bund** *m*, **~gurt** *m* waistband; **~klammer** *f zum Radfahren*: (bi)cycle clip; **~laden** *m umg.* flies *Pl.*, fly; **~latz** *m* flies *Pl.*, fly; **~matz** *m umg. hum.* little tot; **~rock** *m*: (*ein*) *~* (a pair of) culottes *Pl.*; **~scheißer** *m umg. pej.* scaredy-pants, scaredy-cat; **~schlitz** *m* flies *Pl.*, fly; **~stall** *m umg. hum.* flies *Pl.*, fly; **~tasche** *f* trouser (*Am.* pant) pocket; *etw. wie s-e ~ kennen umg.* know s.th. like the back of one's hand; **~träger** *m*: (*ein* [*Paar*]) *~* (a pair of) braces (*Am.* suspenders) *Pl.*

hosianna *Reli. Interj.* hosanna; **Hosianna** *n*; -*s*, -*s* hosanna

Hospital *n*; -*s*, -*e od.* Hospitäler; *altm.* **1.** (*Krankenhaus*) hospital; **2.** (*Altenheim*) old people's home; (*Pflegeheim*) care home

Hospitalismus *m*; -, *kein Pl.*; *bes. Psych.* hospitalism

Hospitant *m*; -*en*, -*en*, *~in f*; -, -*nen*; *geh.* auditor; **hospitieren** *v/i. geh.* sit in (*bei* on); *Lehrerausbildung*: sit in on classes; *Univ. Am.* audit a course *etc.*

Hospiz *n*; -*es*, -*e* **1.** *kirchl.* hospice; **2.** *für Sterbende*: hospice; **3.** *christliche Pension*: Christian-run hotel

Hostcomputer *m* host computer

Hostess *f*, -, -*en* hostess (*auch euph.*); *Flug.* air hostess, *Am.* (female) flight attendant, stewardess *altm.*

Hostie *f*, -, -*n*; *kirchl.* host

Hotdog, Hot Dog [ˈhɔtˈdɔk] *m*, *n*; -*s*, -*s*; *Gastr.* hot dog

Hotel *n*; -*s*, -*s* hotel; *~ garni* bed and breakfast hotel; *in welchem ~ seid ihr?* which hotel are you (staying) at?; *e-e Woche ~ mit Frühstück umg.* a week's stay in a hotel with bed and breakfast; **~angestellte** *m*, *f* hotel employee; **~anlage** *f* hotel complex; **~bar** *f* hotel bar; **~besitzer** *m*, **~besitzerin** *f* hotel owner, hotelier; **~bett** *n* hotel bed; *hier gibt es wenig ~en* hotel accommodation here is limited; **~direktor** *m*, **~direktorin** *f* hotel manager; **~fach** *n*; *nur Sg.* hotel business; **~fachschule** *f* school for hotel management; **~führer** *m* hotel guide; **~gast** *m* hotel guest; **~gewerbe** *n* hotel trade (*od.* industry); **~halle** *f* foyer, (hotel) lobby

Hotelier [hoteˈljeː] *m*; -*s*, -*s* hotelier

Hotel|kette *f* hotel chain; **~küche** *f* **1.** hotel kitchen; **2.** *nur Sg.*; *Speisen*: hotel food

Hotellerie *f*, -, *kein Pl.* hotel trade (*Am.* industry)

Hotel|nachweis *m* **1.** *Service*: hotel information service; **2.** *Liste*: list of hotels; **~pension** *f* residential hotel, boarding house; **~personal** *n* hotel staff (*V. mst im Pl.*); **~portier** *m* (hotel) doorman; **~rechnung** *f* hotel bill; **~schiff** *n* floating hotel; **~ und Gaststättengewerbe** *n* catering trade; **~verzeichnis** *n* list of hotels; **~zimmer** *n* hotel room

Hot|key [ˈhɔtkiː] *m*; -(*s*), -*s*; *EDV* hot key; **~line** [ˈhɔtlaɪn] *f*; -, -*s*; *Telek.* hotline; *e-e ~ einrichten* set up a hotline

Hotpants, Hot Pants [ˈhɔtpɛnts] *Pl.* hot pants

hott *Interj.* gee!; → *hü*

Hottentotte *m*; -*n*, -*n*, **Hottentottin** *f*; -, -*nen* Hottentot; *hier geht's zu wie bei den Hottentotten umg. pej.* it's like bedlam in here

Hr. *Abk.* (**Herr**) Mr, *Am.* Mr.

Hrn. *Abk.* (**Herrn**) Mr(.)

hrsg. *Abk.* (**herausgegeben** [**von**]) ed.

Hrsg. *Abk.* (**Herausgeber**) ed.

HTML *Abk. EDV* HTML (= hypertext markup language)

http *Abk. EDV* http (= hypertext transfer protocol)

hu *Interj.* **1.** *bei Ekel*: ugh!; **2.** *bei Furcht*: ooh!; **3.** *bei Hitze etc.*: whew!; **4.** *bei Kälte*: brrr!; **5.** *zum Erschrecken*: boo!

hü *Interj.* **1.** (*vorwärts*) gee up!, *Am.* giddyap!; (*links*) wo hi!; *~ hott* gee up!, *Am.* giddyap!; **2.** *fig.*: *was nun, ~ oder hott?* make up your mind; *einmal sagt er ~, einmal hott* first he says one thing and then he says something completely different

Hub *m*; -(*e*)*s*, *Hübe*; *Tech., Mot.* stroke; *des Ventils*, *e-s Krans*: lift

Hubbel *m*; -*s*, -; *Dial.* bump; **hubbelig** *Adj. Dial.* bumpy

Hubbrücke *f* lift bridge

hüben *Adv.* on this side; *~ und od. wie drüben* on either side

Hub|höhe *f* lift; **~kraft** *f* lifting capacity; *Mot.* output per unit of displacement; **~raum** *m* cubic capacity

hübsch I. *Adj.* **1.** pretty; *Junge*: nice-looking; *Mann*: good-looking, handsome; *sich ~ machen* make o.s. look nice; *na, ihr zwei Hübschen? umg.* well, my lovelies?; **2.** *weitS. auch umg. iro.* nice; *e-e ganz ~e Leistung* a fine performance; *~e Aussichten umg. iro.* nice prospects; *e-e ~e Bescherung*

umg. iro. a fine state of affairs; **3.** *umg. fig.* (*beträchtlich*) nice; *ein ~es Sümmchen* a tidy sum; *ein ~es Stück Weg* quite a way; **II.** *Adv.* **1.** nicely; *sie kann ganz ~ singen* she can sing very well; **2.** *umg.* (*ziemlich, sehr*) pretty; *ganz ~ kalt hier!* it's freezing here!; **3.** *umg.*: *das wirst du ~ sein lassen! drohend*: you'll do nothing of the sort; *sei ~ artig!* be a good boy (*od.* girl); *immer ~ langsam!* take it nice and slowly!; *immer ~ der Reihe nach!* one after the other, please

Hubschrauber *m*; -*s*, -; *Flug.* helicopter; **~landeplatz** *m* heliport; **~pilot** *m*, **~pilotin** *f* helicopter pilot

Hubstapler *m* forklift truck

huch *Interj.* ooh!

Hucke *f*; -, -*n*; *umg.*: *j-m die ~ voll hauen/lügen* give s.o. a good hiding / tell s.o. a pack of lies; *die ~ voll kriegen* get a good hiding; *sich* (*Dat.*) *die ~ voll saufen* get plastered

huckepack *Adv.* piggyback; *j-n ~ nehmen od. tragen* give s.o. a piggyback (ride); **Huckepackverkehr** *m* piggyback transport (*od.* traffic), piggybacking

Hudelei *f*; -, -*en*; *bes. südd., österr. umg. pej.* sloppiness; *konkret*: sloppy work; **hudeln** *v/i.* be sloppy; do a sloppy job

Huf *m*; -(*e*)*s*, -*e* hoof

Hufeisen *n* horseshoe; **hufeisenförmig** *Adj.* horseshoe ..., horseshoe-shaped

Huf|lattich *m Bot.* coltsfoot; **~nagel** *m* horseshoe nail; **~schlag** *m* **1.** *Geräusch*: hoofbeat; **2.** *Tritt*: (horse's) kick; **~schmied** *m*, **~schmiedin** *f* blacksmith; **~spur** *f* hoof mark

hüftbetont *Adj.*: *ein ~es Kleid* a dress that emphasizes the hips

Hüfte *f*; -, -*n* hip; *von Tieren*: haunch; *mit wiegenden ~n* with hips swaying; *sich in den ~n wiegen* sway one's hips; *mit den ~n wackeln* wiggle one's hips; *die Arme in die ~n stemmen* put one's hands on one's hips; *die Arme od. mit den Armen in den ~n auch* (with) arms akimbo; *aus der ~ schießen* shoot from the hip; *ich stand bis an die ~n im Wasser/Schilf* I was standing waist-deep (*od.* up to my waist) in water / waist-high (*od.* up to my waist) in reeds

Hüft|gelenk *n* hip joint; **~gürtel** *m*, **~halter** *m* suspender belt

hüfthoch *Adj.* waist-high; *Wasser*: waist-deep; **Hüfthöhe** *f*: *in ~* at waist height

Huftier *n Zool.* hoofed animal

Hüft|knochen *m* hip-bone; **~schwung** *m* **1.** *nur Sg.*; *beim Gehen*: swinging of one's hips; **2.** *Turnen*: hip swing; **3.** *Ringen*: cross-buttock; **~umfang** *m*, **~weite** *f* hip measurement

Hügel *m*; -*s*, - **1.** *kleiner*: hillock; **2.** (*Erdhaufen*) mound; **~grab** *n Archäol.* burial mound; *in GB*: barrow, *in Schottland*: cairn; *in Europa*: tumulus (*Pl.* tumuli); *in den USA*: (burial) mound

hügelig *Adj.* hilly

Hügel|kette *f* range of hills; **~land** *n* hill(y) country

Hugenotte *m*; -*n*, -*n*, **Hugenottin** *f*; -, -*nen* Huguenot; **hugenottisch** *Adj.* Huguenot

hüglig *Adj.* hilly

Huhn *n*; -(*e*)*s*, *Hühner* **1.** *Orn.* chicken; (*Henne*) hen; **2.** *Gastr.* chicken; *Koll.* poultry; **3.** *Jägerspr.* partridge; **4.** *umg. fig.*: *verrücktes ~* (real) nutcase; *dum-*

mes ~ stupid fool; **5.** in Wendungen: **mit den Hühnern zu Bett gehen / aufstehen** hum. go to bed early / get up at the crack of dawn; **da lachen ja die Hühner!** umg. don't make me laugh!; **ich sah aus wie ein gerupftes ~** my hair was all standing on end; **herumlaufen wie ein aufgescheuchtes ~** run around like a headless chicken

Hühnchen n chicken; gebraten: roast chicken; **mit j-m ein ~ zu rupfen haben** umg. fig. have a bone to pick with s.o.

Hühnerauge n Med. corn; **j-m auf die ~n treten** umg. fig. (j-n beleidigen) tread (Am. step) on s.o.'s toes (od. corns); (j-n antreiben) give s.o. a subtle reminder; **Hühneraugenpflaster** n corn plaster

Hühner|bein n chicken leg; **~brühe** f chicken broth; **~brust** f 1. Gastr. chicken breast; 2. Med. pigeon chest; **e-e ~ haben** umg. be pigeon-chested; **~dreck** m umg. pej. 1. chicken dirt (Am. poop); 2. fig. chicken shit vulg.; **~ei** n hen's egg

hühnereigroß Adj. the size of an (od. a chicken's) egg

Hühner|farm f poultry (od. chicken) farm; **~fleisch** n chicken; **~frikassee** n chicken fricassee; **~futter** n chickenfeed; **~habicht** m Orn. goshawk; **~haus** n henhouse; **~haut** f österr., schw. fig. → Gänsehaut; **~hof** m 1. chicken run; 2. → Hühnerfarm; **~hund** m pointer; **~klein** n -s, kein Pl.; Gastr. chicken giblets Pl.; **~leber** f chicken liver (Gastr. livers Pl.); **~leiter** f chicken ladder; **~pest** f fowl pest; **~schlag** m chicken coop; **~schlegel** m Gastr. chicken leg; **~stall** m chicken coop; **~stange** f perch, (chicken) roost; **~suppe** f Gastr. chicken soup; **~vogel** m; mst Pl.; Zool. gallinaceous bird; **~zucht** f 1. chicken farming; 2. Farm: chicken farm; 3. Koll. chickens Pl., hens Pl.

huhu Interj. 1. Zuruf: yoo-hoo!; 2. lautmalerisch, für Weinen: boo hoo!; für Eule: tu-whit tu-whoo!; für Gespenst: woooh!

hui Interj. 1. lautmalerisch, für Wind: whoosh!; für schnelle Bewegung: whoosh!; 2. erstaunt: ooh!; beeindruckt: wow!; **außen ~, innen pfui** it's all right until you take the wrappings off

Huld f, -, kein Pl.; geh. altm. od. iro. grace, favo(u)r; (Güte) benevolence; **in j-s ~ stehen** be in s.o.'s good graces; **j-m s-e ~ schenken** bestow one's favo(u)r on s.o.; **huldigen** v/i. 1. hist. od. geh. altm. (j-m) pay tribute (od. homage) to; 2. geh., oft iro. (e-r Anschauung etc.) subscribe to; (e-m Laster etc.) indulge in; (e-m Glauben etc.) hold; (der Mode etc.) follow, worship; **Huldigung** f 1. hist. (Treueeid) homage, fealty; 2. geh. altm. (Verehrung) homage; (Ehrung) tribute; (Beifall) applause; **~en entgegennehmen** receive tributes; **huldreich, huldvoll** Adj. geh. altm. od. iro. gracious

Hülle f, -, -n 1. cover; für Ausweis, Buch etc.: auch jacket; für Schallplatte: auch (record) sleeve (bes. Am. jacket); für Schirm etc.: sheath; (Futteral, Gehäuse) case; (Schleier) veil; (Überzug) coat; **die letzten ~n fallen lassen** umg. hum. strip off the remaining layer; 2. Phys., des Atoms: shell; 3. Bot. (Hochblätter) involucre; 4. Anat. (Deckhaut) integument; (Membran) membrane; 5. fig.: **... in ~ und Fülle**

... galore, plenty of ...; **sterbliche ~** lit. mortal remains

hüllen v/t.: **in etw.** (Akk.) **~** wrap (up) in s.th.; **gehüllt In** (+ Akk.) in Flammen: enveloped in; in Dunkel, Nebel: shrouded in; in Wolken: covered in; **sich in Schweigen ~** fig. remain silent (über + Akk. about); **er hüllt sich in Schweigen** auch his lips are sealed

hüllenlos Adj. naked; umg. hum. stark (Am. auch buck) naked, starkers

Hülse f, -, -n 1. Bot. von Getreide: husk; (Schote) pod; (Schale) shell; (Kapsel) capsule; 2. e-r Patrone: case; e-s Füllhalters: cap; (Etui) case; (Röhre) tube; **nur noch e-e leere ~ sein** be just an empty shell; **Hülsenfrucht** f 1. Pflanze: legume; 2. Frucht: pulse

human Adj. 1. humane; (anständig) decent; (verständnisvoll) sympathetic; (nachsichtig) considerate; 2. Bio., Med. human

Human|biologie f human biology; **~genetik** f human genetics Pl. (V. im Sg.); **~insulin** n human insulin

humanisieren v/t. humanize, make more human

Humanismus m; -, kein Pl. 1. humanism; 2. Lit., Ling. Humanism; **Humanist** m; -en, -en, **Humanistin** f; -, -nen 1. humanist; 2. (Altphilologe) classicist; **humanistisch** Adj. 1. humanist; 2. **~e Bildung** classical education; **~es Gymnasium** grammar school (emphasizing the study of the classics)

humanitär Adj. humanitarian

Humanität f, -, kein Pl. humanitarianism

Human|medizin f human medicine; **~mediziner** m, **~medizinerin** f doctor (of medicine); **~wissenschaften** Pl. human sciences (od. studies)

Humboldtstrom m Geog. Humboldt (bes. Am. Peru) Current

Humbug m; -s, kein Pl.; umg. pej. nonsense; (Schwindel) humbug

humid(e) Adj. Geog. humid; **Humidität** f; -, kein Pl. humidity

Hummel f; -, -n; Zool. bumblebee; **wilde ~** fig. hum. real tomboy; **~n im Hintern haben** umg. fig. have ants in one's pants

Hummer m; -s, -; Zool. lobster; **~krabben** Pl. king prawns; **~schere** f lobster claw; **~suppe** f Gastr. lobster bisque

Humor m; -s, -e, mst Sg. humo(u)r; (Sinn für **~**) sense of humo(u)r; **schwarzer ~** black humo(u)r; **er hat keinen ~** he has no sense of humo(u)r; (versteht keinen Spaß) auch he can't take a joke; **etw. mit ~ tragen** od. **nehmen** take s.th. in good humo(u)r; **du hast (vielleicht) ~!** iro. you've got a nerve!; **~ ist, wenn man trotzdem lacht** Sprichw. it's not the end of the world

Humoreske f; -, -n 1. Lit. humorous sketch (od. story); 2. Mus. humoresque

humorig Adj. humorous

Humorist m; -en, -en, **~in** f; -, -nen humorous writer; (Komiker[in]) comedian; **humoristisch** Adj. humorous

humorlos Adj. humo(u)rless, unfunny; **~ sein** have no sense of humo(u)r; **sei doch nicht so ~!** don't take everything so seriously; can't you take a joke?; **Humorlosigkeit** f; nur Sg. lack of humo(u)r; **an ~ leiden** have no sense of humo(u)r

humorvoll Adj. humorous, funny

humos Adj. attr. Boden: humus ...; (reich an Humus) präd. und nachge-

stellt: rich in humus

humpeln v/i. (ist / ohne Richtung auch hat gehumpelt) hobble; (hinken) limp; permanent: have a limp

Humpen m; -s, - tankard

Humus m; -, kein Pl. humus; **~boden** m humus soil; **~erde** f humus; **~schicht** f humus layer

Hund m; -(e)s, -e 1. dog; (Jagdhund) auch hound; Zool. canine; **junger ~** puppy; **streunender ~** stray (dog); → **bissig** 1; 2. (Rüde) dog, male; 3. umg. fig., armer, schlauer, fauler: devil; (gemeiner) **~** pej. (rotten) swine Sl.; **blöder ~!** pej. idiot!, cretin!; **so ein blöder ~!** pej. auch what a stupid bastard vulg.; **krummer ~** Zigarre: culebras (cigar); (zwielichtiger Kerl) crafty devil; **scharfer ~** (strenger Lehrer) strict bastard vulg.; (harter Trainer) demanding sod Sl., Am. slavedriver; **sturer ~** stubborn bastard vulg.; **verrückter ~** crazy sod (Am. bastard) Sl.; 4. Zool.: **Fliegender ~** flying fox; 5. Astron.: **Großer/Kleiner ~** Great/Little (od. Lesser) Dog, Canis Major/Minor; 6. Gastr.: **Kalter ~** cake made out of layers of biscuits (Am. cookies) and chocolate; 7. Bergb. tub; 8. in Wendungen: **auf den ~ bringen/kommen** umg. ruin / go to pot; **auf dem ~ sein** umg. be in a real mess; gesundheitlich: auch be a wreck; **mit den Nerven auf dem ~ sein** umg. be a nervous wreck; **vor die ~e gehen** umg. go to the dogs; **da liegt der ~ begraben** umg. that's why; **er ist mit allen ~en gehetzt** umg. he knows all the tricks of the trade; **er ist bekannt wie ein bunter ~** everybody knows him; **das ist ein dicker ~!** umg. (e-e Frechheit) that's a bit thick!, Am. what nerve!; (grober Fehler) that's a real boo-boo!; **wie ein geprügelter ~** like a whipped cur; **wie ~ und Katze sein** umg. fight like cat and dog; **damit kann man keinen ~ hinter dem Ofen hervorlocken** umg. who's interested in that?; **den/die Letzten beißen die ~e** Sprichw. the devil take the hindmost; **bei diesem Wetter würde man keinen ~ auf die Straße jagen** you wouldn't turn a dog out in weather like this; **da wird ja der ~ in der Pfanne verrückt!** umg. it's unbelievable!; **schlafende ~e weckt man nicht** Sprichw. let sleeping dogs lie; **~e, die bellen, beißen nicht** barking dogs seldom bite; **viele ~e sind des Hasen Tod** Sprichw. the one stands little chance against the many

Hundchen, Hündchen n 1. kleiner: little (Am. auch lap) dog; 2. junger: puppy

Hunde|arbeit f umg.: **das war e-e ~** that was an awful job; **~augen** Pl. fig.: **treue ~** big faithful eyes; **j-n mit traurigen ~ ansehen** give s.o. a hangdog look; **~ausstellung** f dog show; **~biss** m dog bite; **~blick** m → Hundeaugen; **~dreck** m umg. dog's muck, Am. dog poop, doggy doo; **~dressur** f dog training

hundeelend Adj. umg.: **sich ~ fühlen** feel lousy

Hunde|fänger m, **~fängerin** f dogcatcher; **~führer** m, **~führerin** f dog handler; **~futter** n dogfood; **~gebell** n (sound of) barking dogs (od. a dog barking), barking; **~haare** Pl. einzelne: dog's hairs; **allergisch gegen ~** allergic to dog's hair; **~halsband** n dog collar; **~halter** m, **~halterin** f dog owner; **~hütte** f (dog) kennel, Am. doghouse

Hunde|kälte f umg.: *es ist od. herrscht e-e ~* it's absolutely freezing; **~kot** m dog('s) dirt, Am. dog poop; **~krankheit** f dog's disease; **~kuchen** m dog biscuit; **~leben** n; nur Sg.; umg. pej.: *ein ~ führen* lead a dog's life; **~leine** f lead, bes. Am. leash; **~liebhaber** m, **~liebhaberin** f dog lover; **~marke** f dog tag (auch Mil. umg. etc.); **~meute** f pack of dogs

hundemüde Adj. umg. dog-tired, Sl. zonked

Hunde|nahrung f dogfood; **~narr** m, **~närrin** f umg. dog freak; *er ist ein ~* he's crazy about dogs; **~pflege** f dog care; **~rasse** f breed (of dog); **~rennen** n dog (od. greyhound) racing (konkret: race)

hundert Zahlw. **1.** a (betont one) hundred; umg. fig. → **hundertachtzig** 2; **2.** umg. hundreds of; *~ Kleinigkeiten* hundreds of little details; *~e von Menschen* hundreds of people; *ein paar ~ Menschen* etc. a couple of hundred people etc.; *die paar ~, die das kostet* the small amount (od. the pennies) that it costs; *zu ~en* by the (od. in their) hundreds; *in die ~e gehen Kosten* etc.: run into hundreds

Hundert¹ n; -s, - od. -e **1.** Pl. nur -; hundred; *fünf vom ~* (abgek. **v.H.**) five per cent (od. percent); *das macht das ~ voll* that makes up a hundred; **2.** umg. *~e von Menschen, in die ~e gehen* etc. → **hundert** 2

Hundert² f, -, -en Zahl: hundred

hundert|achtzig Zahlw. **1.** a (od. one) hundred and eighty; **2.** umg. fig.: *auf ~ sein* be hitting the roof, be freaking out Sl.; *j-n auf ~ bringen* make s.o. wild (with anger), really get s.o. going; **~ein**, **~eins** Zahlw. a (od. one) hundred and one

Hunderter m; -s, - **1.** mst Pl.; Math., Stelle: the hundred; (dreistellige Zahl) three-digit number; **2.** umg. Geldschein: hundred-euro etc. note (Am. bill)

hunderterlei Adj. umg. hundreds of different ...

Hunderterstelle f Math. hundred's place

Hunderteuroschein m (one-)hundred--euro note

hundertfach I. Adj. a hundredfold; *die ~e Summe* a hundred times the sum; *in ~er Vergrößerung* enlarged (od. magnified) a hundred times; **II.** Adv. a hundred times; **Hundertfache** n: um *das ~ zunehmen* increase a hundredfold; → **Achtfache**

Hundertfrankenschein m Schweiz: (one-)hundred-franc note

hundertfünfzigprozentig Adj. umg. iro. ultra ..., unreconstructed ...; *so ein Hundertfünfzigprozentiger* one of those fanatics

Hundertfüßer m; -s, -; Zool. centipede

Hundertjahrfeier f centenary, Am. centennial

hundertjährig Adj. Person etc.: a hundred-year-old ..., präd. und nachgestellt: a hundred years old; Zeitraum: a hundred years of ...; *~es Jubiläum* centenary, Am. centennial; *der Hundertjährige Krieg* hist. the Hundred Years' War; *~er Kalender* hundred--year calendar; **Hundertjährige** m, f; -n, -n centenarian

hundertmal Adv. a hundred times; **hundertmalig** Adj.: *nach ~er Wiederholung* after having been repeated a hundred times; → **achtmalig**

Hundertmarkschein m hist. hundred--mark note (Am. bill)

Hundertmeter|hürdenlauf m the (one-)hundred-met|res (Am. -er) hurdles; **~lauf** m Sport the 100 met|res (Am. -ers)

hundertpro Adv. umg.: *ich bin mir ~ sicher* I'm absolutely certain; *aber ~!* of course!

hundertprozentig I. Adj. **1.** a hundred per cent (Am. percent); Alkohol: pure; *~e Tochtergesellschaft* wholly--owned subsidiary; **2.** fig. Engländer, Kommunist etc.: one hundred per cent (Am. percent) ..., out-and-out ...; (völlig) total; Unsinn: absolute; *das wird mit ~er Sicherheit geschehen* that's absolutely bound to happen; **II.** Adv. a (od. one) hundred per cent (Am. percent); (vollkommen) auch absolutely; *das weiß ich ~ auch* I know that for sure; *ich stimme ~ mit Ihnen überein* I couldn't agree with you more

Hundertsatz m percentage

Hundertschaft f contingent of a hundred police etc., hundred-strong police etc. contingent; *mehrere ~en* several hundred police etc.

Hundertschillingschein m hist. Österreich: (one-)hundred-schilling note

hundertst... Zahlw. hundredth; *wir kamen vom Hundertsten ins Tausendste* fig. one thing led to another; engS. we just got talking and couldn't stop; *das geht vom Hundertsten ins Tausendste* fig. it just goes on forever, there's no end to it

hundertstel Adj.: *e-e ~ Sekunde* a hundredth of a second; **Hundertstel** n; -s, - hundredth; *sie hat zwei ~ Vorsprung* Sport she leads by two hundredths of a second; *etw. mit e-m ~ belichten* Fot. use an exposure time of one hundredth of a second for s.th.; **Hundertstelsekunde** f hundredth of a second

hunderttausend Zahlw. a (od. one) hundred thousand; *~e od. Hundertausende von Exemplaren* hundreds of thousands of copies

hundertundein, **hundertundeins** Zahlw. a (od. one) hundred and one

hundertzehn Zahlw. **1.** a (od. one) hundred and ten; **2.** umg. fig. → **hundertachtzig** 2

hundertweise Adv. by the hundred, in (their) hundreds

Hunde|salon m dog (umg. poodle) parlo(u)r; **~scheiße** f vulg. dog shit; **~schlitten** m dogsled; **~schnauze** f dog's nose; *kalt wie e-e ~* umg. fig. (as) cold as a fish; **~sohn** m pej. bastard Sl., bes. Am. Sl. son of a bitch; **~staffel** f dog team (od. squad); **~steuer** f dog licen|ce (Am. -se) fee; **~wetter** n; nur Sg.; umg. nasty weather; **~zucht** f **1.** nur Sg. dog breeding; **2.** (Zwinger) kennel (of dogs); **~züchter** m, **~züchterin** f dog breeder; **~zwinger** m (dog) kennel(s Pl.)

Hündin f; -, -nen bitch

hündisch fig. pej. **I.** Adj. servile; *~e Ergebenheit* abject devotion; **II.** Adv.: *~ ergeben* abjectly (od. utterly) devoted (+ Dat. to)

Hundsfott m; -(e)s, -e od. Hundsfötter; vulg. pej. pile of shit, fucking scum; **hundsföttisch** Adj. vulg. pej. fucking awful

hundsgemein umg. **I.** Adj. really mean; auch Lüge, Bemerkung etc.: nasty; *~er Kerl* auch bastard Sl.; *er/sie*

kann ~ werden he can be a real bastard / she can be a real bitch Sl.; **II.** Adv. **1.** nastily; **2.** (sehr, verdammt) damn, bloody Sl.; *es tut ~ weh* it hurts like hell Sl.; **Hundsgemeinheit** f; nur Sg.; umg. **1.** nastiness; **2.** konkret: dirty trick

Hundskamille f Bot. dog fennel, (stinking) mayweed

hundsmiserabel Adj. umg. lousy

Hunds|rose f Bot. dogrose; **~stern** m Astron. Sirius, the Dog Star; **~tage** Pl. dog days

Hüne m; -n, -n giant; *er ist ein ~* auch he's gigantic (od. huge); **Hünengrab** n megalithic grave, dolmen; **hünenhaft** Adj. giant, gigantic

Hunger m; -s, kein Pl. **1.** hunger; umg. (Esslust) appetite; *~ haben/bekommen* be/get hungry (umg. auf + Akk. for); *ich habe keinen richtigen ~* I'm not really hungry; *ich habe ~ auf* (+ Akk.) umg. auch I feel like ..., Brit. auch I (could just) fancy ..., Am. auch I could go for ...; *ich habe ~ wie ein Bär od. Wolf* I could eat a horse; *~ leiden* starve; *vor ~ sterben* die of starvation, starve to death; *ich sterbe vor ~* umg. fig. I'm famished, I'm ravenous; *~ ist der beste Koch* Sprichw. hunger is the best sauce; **2.** (Hungersnot) famine; **3.** geh. fig. hunger, thirst (nach for); **~blockade** f hunger blockade; **~gefühl** n hungry feeling; *starkes ~* hunger pangs, gnawing hunger; **~hilfe** f relief aid; **~jahr** n year of famine; Pl. lean years; **~künstler** m, **~künstlerin** f professional faster; **~kur** f starvation diet; **~leider** m; -s, -; umg. pej. pauper; **~lohn** m pittance

hungern I. v/i. **1.** go hungry; stärker: starve; (fasten) fast; **2.** fig.: *~ nach* hunger (od. long) for; **II.** v/refl.: *sich gesund/schlank ~* get fit/slim by going on a starvation diet; *sich zu Tode ~* starve o.s. to death; **III.** v/t. unpers.; lit.: *j-n hungert (es)* s.o. is hungry; **hungernd I.** Part. Präs. → **hungern**; **II.** Adj. hungry, starving

Hunger|ödem n Med. nutritional (od. famine) (o)edema; **~ration** f umg. starvation rations Pl.; **~revolte** f hunger revolt

hungers geh.: *~ sterben* starve to death

Hungersnot f famine; *es herrscht ~ in ...* there is a (od. there is widespread) famine in ...

Hunger|streik m hunger strike; *in den ~ treten* go on hunger strike; **~tod** m (death from) starvation; *den ~ sterben* die of starvation, starve to death; **~tote** m, f person who has died of starvation; **~tuch** n umg. hum.: *am ~ nagen* be on the breadline; **~turm** m hist. prison often in a tower in which prisoners were left to starve to death

hungrig Adj. **1.** hungry (nach for); (ausgehungert) starving, famished; *ich bin ~ wie ein Bär od. Wolf* (I'm so hungry) I could eat a horse; Holzhacken etc. *macht ~* chopping wood etc. gives you an appetite (od. is hungry work); **2.** geh. fig. hungry (auch Blick etc.), starved (nach for)

Hunne m; -n, -n Hun; **Hunnenkönig** m king of the Huns

Hunni m; -s, -s; umg. **1.** hist. (Hundertmarkschein) (one-)hundred-mark note; **2.** (Hunderteuroschein) (one-)-hundred-euro note

Hunnin f; -, -nen Hun; **hunnisch** Adj. Hunnic, Hunnish

Hunsrück *m*; *-s*; *Geog.* Hunsrück mountains *Pl.*

Hupe *f*; *-*, *-n*; *Mot.* horn; **auf die ~ drücken** sound (*umg.* toot, beep, *Am.* honk) one's horn; **hupen** *v/i.* hoot, honk, sound (*umg.* toot, beep) one's horn; **Huperei** *f*; *-*, *kein Pl.*; *umg.* honking, tooting

Hüpfburg *f* bouncy castle

hupfen *v/i. bes. südd., österr.* → **hüpfen**; **das ist gehupft wie gesprungen** *umg.* it's six of one and half a dozen of the other

hüpfen *v/i.* hop; (*springen*) jump (*vor Freude* for joy); **ihm hüpfte das Herz vor Freude** *fig.* his heart leapt for joy

Hupfer *m*; *-s*, *-*; *südd., österr.* **1.** *ein junger ~* a greenhorn; **2.** → **Hüpfer, Hüpfer** *m*; *-s*, *-* hop, (little) jump; **e-n ~ machen** give a hop (*od.* little jump)

Hup|konzert *n umg.* barrage of honking; **~signal** *n* hoot; **j-m ein ~ geben** hoot (*Am.* honk) (*od.* toot one's horn) at s.o.; **~ton** *m* sound of a horn; **ein anhaltender ~** prolonged tooting; **~verbot** *n Hinweis:* no horns (to be sounded)

Hürde *f*; *-*, *-n* **1.** *Sport* hurdle; **e-e ~ nehmen** take (*od.* clear) a hurdle; **400 m ~n** *Wettkampf:* the 400 m hurdles; **sie siegte über 400 m ~n** she came first in the 400 m hurdles; **2.** (*Pferch, Viehzaun*) fold, pen; **3.** *fig.* (*Hindernis*) hurdle, obstacle; **wir standen vor schier unüberwindlichen ~n** we were faced with virtually insurmountable obstacles

Hürden|lauf *m* hurdles *Pl.*; → **Hürde** 1; **~läufer** *m*, **~läuferin** *f* hurdler; **~rennen** *n für Pferde:* hurdle race

Hure *f*; *-*, *-n*; *pej.* whore; **huren** *v/i. pej.* whore around

Huren|bock *m pej.* lecher; **~kind** *Druck. Sl.* widow; **~sohn** *m pej.* son of a bitch, bastard *Sl.*; **~viertel** *n umg.* red-light district

Hurerei *f*; *-*, *-en*; *pej.* whoring

hurra *Interj.* hooray!; **Hurra** *n*; *-s*, *-s* hooray, cheer

Hurra|geschrei *n* cheering; **~patriot** *m umg. pej.* jingoist, flag-waver; **~patriotismus** *m umg. pej.* jingoism; **~ruf** *m* cheer(s *Pl.*), cheering

Hurrikan ['harikən] *m*; *-s*, *-s* hurricane

hurtig *Adj.* swift, quick; (*flink und gewandt*) nimble

Husar *m*; *-en*, *-en* hussar

Husaren|ritt *m* act of daring; **~streich** *m*, **~stück(chen)** *n* daring surprise attack

husch I. *Interj.* **1.** *verscheuchend:* shoo!; **2.** *lautmalerisch:* whoosh!; **~**, **~**, **weg waren sie** with a whoosh! they were gone; **II.** *Adv. umg.* (*schnell*) quick; **~ ins Bett!** off to bed with you!; **so ~**, **~ geht das nicht** you can't do it so quickly, it doesn't work that quickly; **bei ihm muss immer alles ~**, **~ gehen** he always needs everything doing pronto (*od.* pdq = pretty damn quick); **huschen** *v/i.* dart, flit; *lautmalerisch:* whiz(z) *umg.*, whoosh *umg.*

hüsteln *v/i.* give a little cough; (*e-n leichten Husten haben*) have a slight cough; **Hüsteln** *n*; *-s*, *kein Pl.* slight cough(ing)

husten I. *v/i.* **1.** cough; **stark ~** have a bad cough; **2.** *Motor:* splutter; **II.** *v/t.* **1.** (*Schleim etc.*) cough (*od.* bring) up; **Blut ~** spit blood; **sich** (*Dat.*) **die Seele aus dem Leib ~** *umg.* cough one's heart out, cough one's guts up *Sl.*; **2.** *umg. fig.:* **ich werde dir was** *od.*

eins ~ you'll be lucky, you know what you can do

Husten *m*; *-s*, *-*, *mst Sg.* cough; (**e-n schlimmen** *od.* **bösen**) **~ haben** have a (bad *od.* nasty) cough

Husten|anfall *m* coughing fit; **~bonbon** *m*, *n* cough sweet (*Am.* drop); **~mittel** *n* cough medicine; **~reiz** *m* tickle in one's throat; **~saft** *m*, **~sirup** *m* cough mixture (*Am.* syrup); **~tee** *m* bronchial tea; **~tropfen** *Pl.* cough drops

Huster *m*; *-s*, *-*; *umg.* cough

Hut¹ *m*; *-(e)s, Hüte* **1.** *des Pilzes:* cap; **3.** *fig.:* (**das ist doch**) **ein alter ~** *umg.* (that's) old hat; **~ ab!** *umg.* I take my hat off (*vor* to); **vor j-m den ~ ziehen** take one's hat off to s.o.; **unter einen ~ bringen** *umg.* (*Meinungen etc.*) reconcile; (*Personen*) *auch* get people to agree (*od.* cooperate *etc.*); (*koordinieren*) coordinate, sort out; (*Termine, Pläne etc.*) fit in; **s-n ~ nehmen** (**müssen**) *umg.* (have to) leave one's job; **mit Politik** *etc.* **habe ich nichts am ~** *umg.* politics *etc.* isn't my cup of tea, I'm not very politically-minded *etc.*; **da geht einem doch der ~ hoch!** *umg.* it's enough to make your blood boil!; **das kannst du dir an den ~ stecken!** *umg.* you can stick that *Sl.*

Hut² *f*; *-*, *kein Pl.*; *geh.* **1.** (*Obhut*) care, keeping; (*Schutz*) protection; **bei j-m in bester ~ sein** be in the best hands with s.o.; **2.** **auf der ~ sein** be on one's guard (*vor + Dat.* against), look (*od.* watch) out (for), be on the lookout (for), be careful (**davor, dass ...** not to + *Inf.*); **nicht auf der ~ sein** be off one's guard

Hut|ablage *f* hat rack; **~band** *n*; *Pl.* **-bänder** hatband

Hütchen *n* **1.** little hat; **2.** *Spielfigur:* counter used in the boardgame 'Fang-den-Hut'

Hüte|hund *m* sheepdog; **~junge** *m* shepherd boy

hüten I. *v/t.* **1.** (*Vieh*) tend; (*Kind*) look after; **2.** (*schützen*) guard, protect (**vor** + *Dat.* from); (*bewachen*) watch (over); (*Geheimnis*) keep, guard; **hüte d-e Zunge!** watch your tongue!; **3.** *das Bett/Haus ~* (**müssen**) (have to) stay in bed / at home; **II.** *v/refl.* be on one's guard (**vor** + *Dat.* against), look (*od.* watch) out (for), be on the lookout (for); **hüte dich vor ihm** *auch* be careful of him; **sich ~ zu** (+ *Inf.*) be careful not to (+ *Inf.*), take care not to (+ *Inf.*); **ich werd mich ~!** *umg.* I'll be blowed (*Am.* darned) if I do; *auf Frage:* not likely!; **hüte dich** (**davor**), **etwas zu verraten** take care not to give anything away; **er soll sich ~(, das zu tun)** he'd better not (try)

Hüter *m*; *-s*, *-*; **~in** *f*; *-*, *-nen*; *geh.* custodian; **bin ich m-s Bruders ~?** *bibl.* am I my brother's keeper?; **die ~ des Gesetzes** *hum.* the arm of the law

Hut|geschäft *n* hat shop (*Am. auch* store); **für Damen:** *auch* milliner's (shop); **~größe** *f* hat size; **welche ~ haben Sie?** what size hat do you take?; **~krempe** *f* brim (of a *od.* the hat); **~macher** *m*, **~macherin** *f* hat maker; **für Damen:** *auch* milliner; **~nadel** *f* hatpin; **~schachtel** *f* hatbox; **~schnur** *f* hat string; **das geht mir über die ~** *umg. fig.* that's a bit much; **~ständer** *m* hat stand

Hütte *f*; *-*, *-n* **1.** hut; (*Blockhütte*) cabin; *elende:* hovel, shack; (*Berghütte*) al-

pine hut; (*Schutzhütte*) refuge; (*Jagdhütte*) hunting lodge; (*Baracke*) hut, barracks *Pl.*; *hum.* (*Haus*) humble abode; (*Hundehütte*) kennel; **2.** *Metall.* steelworks *Pl.* (*V. auch im Sg.*); (*Schmelzhütte*) smelting works *Pl.* (*V. auch im Sg.*); (*Glashütte*) glassworks *Pl.* (*V. auch im Sg.*)

Hütten|abend *m sociable evening spent in an alpine hut*; **~arbeiter** *m*, **~arbeiterin** *f* (iron-and-)steelworker; **~betrieb** *m* metal plant (*od.* factory); **~industrie** *f* iron and steel industry; **~käse** *m Gastr.* cottage cheese; **~kunde** *f*; *nur Sg.* metallurgy; **~ruhe** *f*: **um 11 Uhr ist ~** it's lights out at 11 o'clock; **~schuhe** *Pl.* slipper socks; **~wesen** *n*; *nur Sg.* metallurgy; **~zauber** *m party held in an alpine hut*

hutz(e)lig *Adj.* shrivel(l)ed, withered; *Person: auch* wizened

Hyäne *f*; *-*, *-n* **1.** *Zool.* hyena; **2.** *fig. pej. Person:* demon, hellcat

Hyazinthe *f*; *-*, *-n*; *Bot.* hyacinth

hybrid *Adj.* **1.** *fachspr.* hybrid; **2.** *geh.* hubristic, arrogant; **Hybride** *f*, *m*; *-n*, *-n* hybrid

Hybrid|antrieb *m Tech.* hybrid propulsion; **~fahrzeug** *n Mot.* hybrid vehicle; **~züchtung** *f Bio., Verfahren:* hybridization, cross-breeding, crossing; *Ergebnis:* hybrid, cross-breed, cross

Hybris *f*; *-*, *kein Pl.* hubris

Hydra *f*; *-*, *Hydren*; *Myth., Zool.* hydra

Hydrant *m*; *-en*, *-en* fire hydrant

Hydrat *n*; *-(e)s*, *-e*; *Chem.* hydrate

Hydraulik *f*; *-*, *kein Pl.*; *Tech.* hydraulics *Pl.* (*V. mst im Sg.*); *Anlage: auch* hydraulic system; **~öl** *n* hydraulic fluid

hydraulisch I. *Adj.* hydraulic; **~es Getriebe** hydrodynamic drive; **II.** *Adv.* hydraulically

Hydrid *n*; *-(e)s*, *-e*; *Chem.* hydride

hydrieren *v/t. Chem.* hydrogenate

Hydro... *im Subst.* hydro...; *siehe auch* **Wasser...**

Hydrographie, Hydrografie *f*; *-*, *kein Pl.* hydrography

Hydrokultur *f Agr.* **1.** *nur Sg.* hydroponics *Pl.* (*V. im Sg.*); **2.** *umg. Pflanze:* hydroponic plant

Hydrolyse *f*; *-*, *-n*; *Chem.* hydrolysis; **hydrolytisch** *Adj.* hydrolytic

hydrophil *Adj. Bio.* hydrophilous

hydrophob *Adj. Bio.* hydrophobic

Hydrotherapie *f Med.* hydrotherapy

Hygiene *f*; *-*, *kein Pl.* hygiene; **mangelnde ~** lack of hygiene, unhygienic conditions; **~artikel** *Pl.* toiletries; **~papier** *n* tissue; (*Toilettenpapier*) toilet paper; **~vorschriften** *Pl.* rules of hygiene

hygienisch I. *Adj.* hygienic; **II.** *Adv.* hygienically

Hygrometer *n*; *-s*, *-*; *Met.* hygrometer

hygroskopisch *Adj. Chem.* hygroscopic

Hymen *n*, *m*; *-s*, *-*; *Anat.* hymen

Hymne *f*; *-*, *-n* hymn (**an** + *Akk.* to); (*Gedicht*) *auch* ode (to); (*Nationalhymne*) national anthem; **hymnisch** *Adj.* **1.** hymnic; **2.** *fig.* eulogistic, panegyrical

Hype [haip] *m*; *-s*, *-s*; (*spektakuläre Werbung bzw. Publicitytrick*) hype

hyper... *im Adj.*, **Hyper...** *im Subst.* hyper...

hyperaktiv *Adj. Med. Kind:* hyperactive

Hyperbel *f*; *-*, *-n* **1.** *Math.* hyperbola (*Pl.* hyperbolas *od.* hyperbolae); **2.** *Ling.* hyperbole; **~funktion** *f Math.* hyperbolic function

hyperkinetisch *Adj. Med.*: ~**es Syndrom** hyperkinesis; **hyperkorrekt** *Adj.*: ~**er Mensch** stickler for etiquette (*od.* form)

Hyperlink [ˈhaipɐlɪŋk] *n*; *-s, -s*; *EDV* hyperlink; *e-n* ~ *setzen* set up (*od.* establish *od.* make) a hyperlink

hyper|modern *Adj.* ultramodern, hypermodern; ~**sensibel** *Adj.* hypersensitive; *auf nervöse Art*: highly strung

Hypertonie *f*; *-, -n*; *Med., Blutdruck*: hypertension; *Muskel, Auge*: hypertonia; **Hypertoniker** *m*; *-s, -*, **Hypertonikerin** *f*; *-, -nen* hypertension sufferer

hypertroph *Adj. Med.* hypertrophied; *fig.* exaggerated; **Hypertrophie** *f*; *-, -n*; *Med.* hypertrophy

Hypnose *f*; *-, -n* hypnosis; *in* ~ *versetzen* hypnotize, put under hypnosis; *unter* ~ in a state of hypnosis, in a hypnotic state; *aus der* ~ *erwachen* come out of one's hypnosis, wake up again *umg.*; ~**behandlung** *f* hypnotherapy

hypnotisch **I.** *Adj.* hypnotic (*auch* *fig.*); **II.** *Adv.* hypnotically

Hypnotiseur [hypnotiˈzøːɐ] *m*; *-s, -e*, ~**in** *f*; *-, -nen* hypnotist; **hypnotisieren** *v/t.* hypnotize; *fig.* mesmerize

Hypochonder *m*; *-s, -* hypochondriac; **Hypochondrie** *f*; *-, -n* hypochondria; **hypochondrisch** *Adj.* hypochondriac

Hypophyse *f*; *-, -n*; *Anat.* pituitary (gland)

Hypostase *f*; *-, -n*; *Ling., Philos.* hypostasis (*Pl.* hypostases)

hypotaktisch *Adj. Ling. Satz*: hypotactic; **Hypotaxe** *f*; *-, -n* hypotaxis

Hypotenuse *f*; *-, -n*; *Math.* hypotenuse

Hypothalamus *m*; *-, kein Pl.*; *Anat.* hypothalamus (*Pl.* hypothalami)

Hypothek *f*; *-, -en* **1.** mortgage; *e-e* ~ *aufnehmen* take out a mortgage (*auf* + *Akk.* on); *mit e-r* ~ *belasten* mortgage; **2.** *fig.* burden; *mit e-r* ~ *belastet sein* be carrying a burden; **hypothekarisch** **I.** *Adj.* mortgage ...; **II.** *Adv.*: ~ *belasten* mortgage; ~ *belastet* mortgaged; ~ *belastbar* mortgageable; ~ *gesichert* secured by a mortgage

Hypotheken|bank *f* mortgage bank; ~**brief** *m* mortgage (deed); ~**darlehen** *n* mortgage loan

hypothekenfrei *Adj.* unencumbered

Hypotheken|gläubiger *m*, ~**gläubigerin** *f* mortgagee; ~**pfandbrief** *m* mortgage bond; ~**schuld** *f* mortgage debt; ~**schuldner** *m*, ~**schuldnerin** *f* mortgagor; ~**zinsen** *Pl.* mortgage interest *Sg.*

Hypothese *f* hypothesis (*Pl.* hypotheses), supposition; **hypothetisch** *Adj.* hypothetical

Hypotonie *f*; *-, -n*; *Med., Blutdruck*: hypotension; *Muskel, Auge*: hypotonia

Hysterie *f*; *-, -n*; *bes. Psych.* hysteria; **Hysteriker** *m*; *-s, -*, **Hysterikerin** *f*; *-, -nen* hysterical person; **hysterisch** *Adj.* hysterical; *e-n* ~**en Anfall bekommen** *od.* ~ *werden* *umg. fig.* go hysterical, go into hysterics; *werd nicht gleich* ~! *umg.* keep your hair (*Am.* shirt) on

Hz *Abk. Phys.* (*Hertz*) Hz

H

I, i I. *n*; -, - *od. umg.* -s I, i; *I wie Ida Buchstabieren*: "i" for (*od.* as in) "India"; → *Tüpfelchen*; **II.** *Interj. i! bei Ekel*: ugh!; *umg. i wo!* no way!, not likely!

i. A. *Abk.* (*im Auftrag*) pp, p.p.

iah *Interj.* hee-haw; **iahen** *v/i.* go hee--haw, hee-haw

i. Allg. *Abk.* (*im Allgemeinen*) in general

Iambus → *Jambus*

ib., ibd. *Abk.* → *ibidem*

Iberer *m*; -s, -, **~in** *f*; -, -nen Iberian, *weiblich auch*: Iberian woman (*od.* girl *etc.*); **Iberien** (*n*); -s; *Geog., hist.* Iberia

iberisch *Adj.* Iberian; *die Iberische Halbinsel Geog.* the Iberian Peninsula

Iberoamerika (*n*); -s; *Geog.* Latin America; **iberoamerikanisch** *Adj.* Latin-American

ibid. *Abk.* → *ibidem*

ibidem *Adv.* ibidem

Ibis *m*; -ses, -se; *Orn.* ibis

Ibiza (*n*); -s; *Geog.* Ibiza; **Ibizenker** *m*; -s, -, **Ibizenkerin** *f*; -, -nen Ibizan, *weiblich auch*: Ibizan woman (*od.* girl *etc.*); **ibizenkisch** *Adj.* Ibizan

IC® *m*; -s, -s; *Abk.* (*Intercity*) *Eisenb.* intercity (train); *mit dem ~ fahren* travel (*od.* go) by intercity, go intercity

ICE® *m*; -, -s; *Abk.* (*Intercity Express*) *Eisenb.* intercity express

ich *pers. Pron.* I; *~ bin's!* it's me; *wer, ~?* who, me?; *~ nicht* not me, not I *förm.; wer will es? – ~!* me!, I do!; *immer ~!* why (always) me?; *~ Idiot!* I'm so stupid!; *hier bin ~!* here I am!; *eingebildet und iro.:* hey, people, it's me!; *Menschen od. Leute wie du und ~* people like you and me (*od.* I)

Ich *n*; -(s), -(s) self; *Psych., Philos.* ego; *mein zweites od. anderes ~* my second (*od.* other) self; (*guter Freund*) my alter ego; *sein besseres ~* his better self

Ichbewusstsein *n* self-awareness, awareness of the self

ichbezogen *Adj.* egocentric, self-cent|red (*Am.* -ered); **Ichbezogenheit** *f* self-cent|redness (*Am.* -eredness)

Icherzähler *m*, **~in** *f Lit.* first-person narrator; **Icherzählung** *f* first-person narrative

Ichform *f*: *ein Roman in der ~* a novel written in the first person (singular)

Ichlaut *m Phon.* palatal fricative, ich--laut

Ichmensch *m* self-cent|red (*Am.* -ered) person

Ichsucht *f*; -, *kein Pl.; geh.* egoism; **ichsüchtig** *Adj. geh.* egoistic

Ichthyologie *f*; -, *kein Pl.* ichthyology; **ichthyologisch** *Adj.* ichthyological

Ichthyosaurier *m*; -s, -, **Ichthyosaurus** *m*; -, *Ichthyosaurier; Zool.* ichthyosaurus

Icing ['aisiŋ] *n*; -(s), -s *beim Eishockey*: icing

IC-Zuschlag *m* intercity supplement

Icon ['aikən] *n*; -s, -s; *EDV* icon

ideal *Adj.* **1.** ideal, perfect; *Ehemann etc.* (*vorbildlich*) *auch* model ...; **2.** *Philos.* ideal; (*gedanklich*) conceptual; **3.** (*ideell*) idealistic

Ideal *n*; -s, -e ideal; *umg.* (*Wunsch*) *auch* dream

Ideal|besetzung *f in Film*: ideal casting; *in einer Mannschaft od. Firma usw.*: ideal person; *zwei oder mehr Personen*: ideal people, dream team; **~bild** *n* ideal; **~fall** *m* ideal case, ideal conditions *Pl.* (*od.* circumstances *Pl.*); *im ~* ideally; **~figur** *f* **1.** *the* perfect figure; **2.** *fig.* ideal; **~gestalt** *f fig.* ideal; **~gewicht** *n* optimum weight

idealisch *Adj. geh., altm.* idealized

idealisieren *v/t.* idealize; **Idealisierung** *f* idealization

Idealismus *m*; -, *kein Pl.* idealism; **Idealist** *m*; -en, -en, **Idealistin** *f*; -, -nen idealist; **idealistisch I.** *Adj.* idealistic; **II.** *Adv.* idealistically; **Idealität** *f*; -*kein Pl.* ideality

Ideal|linie *f bes. Sport* ideal line; **~maß** *n* optimum amount (*od.* degree)

Ideal|staat *m* ideal state; *konkret:* model state; **~typ** *m* **1.** *der ~ des Lehrers* the ideal teacher; *konkret:* a model teacher; **2.** → *Idealtypus* 1

idealtypisch *Adj.* idealized; **Idealtypus** *m* **1.** *Soziol.* ideal type; **2.** → *Idealtyp* 1

Ideal|vorstellung *f* ideal; (*Illusion*) idealistic view; **~zustand** *m* ideal (state of affairs)

Idee *f*; -, -n **1.** idea; (*Gedanke*) *auch* thought; (*Begriff*) concept; *gute ~* good idea; *ich habe keine ~* (I've) no idea; *ich kam auf die ~ zu* (+ *Inf.*) it occurred to me to (+ *Inf.*) (*od.* that I could ...), I (suddenly) hit on the idea of (+*Ger.*); *wie kamst du auf die ~?* what made you think of it?, what made you decide that?; *wie kamst du auf die ~ zu* (+ *Inf.*)? what made you think of (+ *Ger.*) (*od.* decide to [+ *Inf.*])?; *das bringt mich auf eine ~* that's given me an idea; *das ist die ~!* that's it, that's the answer; *ein Mann mit ~n* a man of ideas; *die hat (vielleicht) ~n! umg.* she's got some fancy ideas!; *ich hab so 'ne ~, dass ... umg.* I have an idea (*od.* a feeling) that ...; → *fix* I 1; **2.** *umg.:* *eine ~* (*ein bisschen*) just a bit (*od.* wee bit *od.* shade *od.* touch) *darker etc.*; *an der Soße fehlt (noch) eine ~ Pfeffer* the sauce needs just a little bit of (*od.* a little bit more) pepper

ideell *Adj.* **1.** (*Ggs. materiell*) non-material(istic), idealistic; *Werte:* *auch* spiritual; (*ethisch*) moral, ethical; *~er Wert e-s Gegenstandes:* sentimental value; **2.** *der ~e Gehalt e-s Buches etc.* the ideas in (*od.* behind) a book *etc.*; **3.** *Philos., Math.* ideal

ideenarm *Adj.* lacking in ideas; (*ohne Fantasie*) unimaginative; **Ideenarmut**

f lack of ideas (*od.* imagination)

Ideen|austausch *m* exchange of ideas; **~drama** *n Lit.* drama of ideas; **~flug** *m* flight of fancy; **~geber** *m*, **~geberin** *f* ideas (*Am.* idea) man *bzw.* woman; **~gehalt** *m* the ideas in (*od.* behind) *s.th.*

Ideengeschichte *f; kein Pl.* history of ideas; **ideengeschichtlich** *Adj.* relating to the history of ideas

Ideen|gut *f; kein Pl.* ideas *Pl.*, stock of ideas; **~lehre** *f Philos.* concept (*od.* theory) of ideas; (*Ideologie*) ideology

ideenlos *Adj.* → *ideenarm*; **Ideenlosigkeit** *f* → *Ideenarmut*

ideenreich *Adj.* full of ideas, very (*od.* highly) imaginative; *Person: auch* inventive; **Ideenreichtum** *m* wealth of ideas; (*Fantasie*) inventiveness

Ideenwelt *f* (world of) ideas *Pl.*

Ideenwettbewerb *m* competition (*in which people are invited to submit ideas, plans, etc. for tackling a specific project*)

Iden *Pl.; hist.:* *die ~* the Ides

Identifikation *f*; -, -en **1.** *e-r Person:* identification; **2.** *Psych.* identification; **Identifikationsfigur** *f* role model

identifizierbar *Adj.* identifiable; **identifizieren I.** *v/t.* identify (*auch gleichsetzen*) (*mit* with); **II.** *v/refl.:* *sich ~ mit* identify with, relate to; **Identifizierung** *f* identification

identisch *Adj.* identical (*mit* with); **Identität** *f* identity

Identitäts|findung *f bes. Psych.* discovery of (one's) identity; **~karte** *f schw.* identity card; **~krise** *f* identity crisis, crisis of identity; **~nachweis** *m* proof of (one's) identity; **~papiere** *Pl. Jur.* identity documents; **~verlust** *m* loss of identity

Ideologe *m*; -n, -n ideologist; *pej.* ideologue

Ideologie *f*; -, -n ideology

ideologie|frei *Adj.* unaffected by (*od.* free from) ideology; **~gebunden** *Adj.* bound by ideology

Ideologiekritik *f* criticism of ideologies

Ideologin *f*; -, -nen → *Ideologe*; **ideologisch** *Adj.* ideological; **ideologisieren** *v/t.* ideologize; **Ideologisierung** *f* ideologization

Idioblast *m*; -en, -en; *Bio.* idioblast

Idiolatrie *f*; -, *kein Pl.* idiolatry

Idiolekt *m*; -(e)s, -e; *Ling.* idiolect

Idiom *n*; -s, -e; *Ling.* (*Spracheigenheit und Wortprägung*) idiom; (*Sprache*) language; **Idiomatik** *f*; -, *kein Pl.* idioms (and phrases) *Pl.*; (*Phraseologie*) phraseology; **idiomatisch I.** *Adj.* idiomatic; **~e Wendung** idiom, idiomatic phrase (*od.* expression); **II.** *Adv.* idiomatically

Idiosynkrasie *f*; -, -n; *Med., Psych.* idiosyncrasy; **idiosynkratisch** *Adj.* idiosyncratic

Idiot *m*; -en, -en idiot

Idiotenarbeit *f umg.* donkeywork,

mindless work (*od.* job), drudgery

Idioten|hang *m*, **~hügel** *m umg.* Skisport: nursery slope, *hum.* dope slope, *Am.* bunny slope

idiotensicher *Adj. umg.* foolproof

Idiotentest *m umg. psychological test to prove a person's fitness to drive*

Idiotie *f*, -, -n **1.** *umg.*: **e-e ~** (sheer) lunacy; (*Dummheit*) a totally stupid thing to do; **2.** *Med.* idiocy *altm.*

Idiotikon *n*; -s, *Idiotiken*; *Ling.* dialect dictionary

idiotisch *Adj.* **1.** *umg.* idiotic, ridiculous; **2.** *Med.* idiotic *altm.*

Idiotismus *m*; -, *Idiotismen* **1.** *Med.* idiotism *altm.*; **2.** *Ling.* idiom

Idol *n* idol; (*der Jugend*) *auch* hero, *weiblich:* heroine; **ein ~ der sechziger Jahre** *auch* an icon of the sixties; **Idolatrie** *f*, -, -n idolatry

idolisieren *v/t.* idolize

Idyll *n*; -s, -e idyll; **Idylle** *f*, -, -n idyll; *in der Malerei: auch* pastoral scene; (*Hirtengedicht*) pastoral poem; **idyllisch** *Adj.* idyllic

i. e. *Abk.* (**id est**) i.e.

IG *f*, -, -s; *Abk.* **1.** (**Industriegewerkschaft**) industrial trade (*Am.* labor) union; **2.** (**Interessengemeinschaft**) interest group

Igel *m*; -s, -; *Zool.* hedgehog

Igel|fisch *m Zool.* porcupine fish; **~frisur** *f umg., hum.* crew (*od.* buzz) cut

Igel|kaktus *m Bot.* hedgehog cactus; **~schnitt** *m umg. hum.* crew (*od.* buzz) cut

igitt, igittigitt *Interj.* ugh!, yuk!

Iglu *m, n*; -s, -s igloo

ignorant *Adj.* ignorant; **Ignorant** *m*; -en, -en, **Ignorantin** *f*, -, -nen ignorant person, ignoramus; **Ignorantentum** *n* ignorance; **Ignoranz** *f* ignorance

ignorieren *v/t.* ignore, take no notice of; (*j-n schneiden*) *auch* cut *s.o.* dead

ihm *pers. Pron.* **1.** (to) him; *von Dingen, Tieren:* (to) it; (*für ihn*) for him; **ich hab's ~ gesagt/gegeben** I told him / I gave it to him, I gave it him; **wie geht's ~?** how is he?; **2.** *nach Präp.:* him; **von ~** from him; **ein Freund von ~** a friend of his, one of his friends

ihn *pers. Pron.* him; *von Dingen:* it

ihnen *pers. Pron.* **1.** (to) them; **ich hab's ~ gesagt/gegeben** I told them / I gave it to them, I gave it them; **wie geht's ~?** how are they?; **2.** *nach Präp.:* them; **bei ~** with them; *in ihrer Wohnung etc.:* at their place; **3. Ihnen** (*Dat. von* **Sie**) (to) you

ihr I. *pers. Pron.* **1.** (to) her; *von Dingen, Tieren:* (to) it; (*für sie*) for her; **ich hab's ~ gesagt/gegeben** I told her / I gave it to her, I gave it her; **wie geht's ~?** how is she?; **2.** (*Nom. Pl. von* **du**) you; **3.** (*Nom. Pl. von* **du**) *altm.*, *Anrede:* thou; **II. Poss. Pron.** (→ *auch* **sein²** I) **1.** *adjektivisch: Sg.* her; *von Dingen, Tieren:* its; *Pl.* their; **einer ~er Verwandten** one of her (*Pl.* their) relatives, a relative of hers (*Pl.* theirs); **2.** *substantivisch: der* (*die, das*) **ihr(ig)e** (*od.* **Ihr[ig]e**) hers, *Pl.* theirs; *Anrede: der* (*die, das*) **Ihr(ig)e** yours

ihrer *pers. Pron.*; *geh.* of (*od.* about) her; **sie gedachten ~** they remembered her

ihrerseits *Adv.* as far as she's (*Pl.* they're) concerned; *Anrede:* as far as you're concerned

ihresgleichen *Pron.* people like her (*Pl.* them); *pej.* the likes of her (*Pl.* them), her (*Pl.* their) sort; *Anrede:*

people like you; *pej.* the likes of you, your sort

ihret|halben *altm.* → **ihretwegen**; **~wegen** *Adv.* **1.** (*wegen ihr etc.*) because of her (*Pl.* them), on her (*Pl.* their) account; *Anrede:* because of you, on your account; **2.** (*ihr etc. zuliebe*) because of her (*Pl.* them), for her (*Pl.* their) sake; *Anrede:* because of you, for your sake; **3.** (*in ihrer etc. Sache*) on her (*Pl.* their) behalf; *Anrede:* on your behalf; **~willen** *Adv.:* **um ~** a) for her (*Pl.* their) sake, b) (*in ihrer Sache*) on her (*Pl.* their) behalf; *Anrede:* **um Ihretwillen**, c) for your sake, d) (*in Ihrer Sache*) on your behalf

ihrige → **ihr** II 2

Ikarier *m*; -s, - *Artist:* Icarian

Ikarus *m*; -s; *Myth.* Icarus

Ikone *f*, -, -n; *Kunst* icon; **Ikonenmalerei** *f* **1.** icon painting; **2.** *Bild:* icon; **Ikonenwand** *f* iconostasis (*Pl.* iconostases)

Ikonographie *f* iconography; **ikonographisch** *Adj.* iconographic

Ikonoklasmus *m*; -, *Ikonoklasmen* iconoclasm; **Ikonoklast** *m*; -en, -en iconoclast; **ikonoklastisch** *Adj.* iconoclastic

Ikonostas *m*; -, -e, **Ikonostase** *f*; -, -n iconostasis (*Pl.* iconostases)

Ikterus *m*; -, *kein Pl.*; *Med.* icterus

Iktus *m*; -, - **1.** *Lit.* ictus; **2.** *Med.* ictus

Ileus *m*; -s, *Ileen*; *Med.* ileus

Ilias *f*, -, *kein Pl.*; *Myth.*, *Lit.* Iliad

ill. *Abk.* (**illustriert**) ill.

illegal *Adj.* illegal; **Illegalität** *f*, -, -en **1.** *nur Sg.* illegality; **2.** *nur Sg.*; (*Zustand*) illegal status; **3.** (*Handlung*) illegal act

illegitim *Adj.* illegitimate; **Illegitimität** *f*, -, *kein Pl.* illegitimacy

illiberal *Adj.* illiberal; **Illiberalität** *f*, -, *kein Pl.* illiberality

illiquid *Adj. Wirts.* illiquid; **Illiquidität** *f*, -, *kein Pl.*; *Wirts.* illiquidity

illoyal *Adj.* disloyal; **Illoyalität** *f*, -, *kein Pl.* disloyalty

Illumination *f* **1.** illumination; **2.** *konkret:* illuminations *Pl.*, lights *Pl.*; **Illuminator** *m*; -s, -en illuminator; **illuminieren** *v/t.* illuminate; **Illuminierung** *f* illumination

Illusion *f* illusion; (*Wahn*) *auch* delusion; **das ist e-e reine ~** that's an illusion, that's pure illusion; **sich** (*Dat.*) **~en machen** delude o.s., fool o.s.; **mach dir keine ~en!** don't fool (*umg.* kid) yourself!; **sich** (*Dat.*) **~en machen über** *auch* be under an illusion about; **darüber mache ich mir keine ~en** I have no illusions about that; **illusionär** *Adj.* illusory; **Illusionismus** *m*; -, *kein Pl.*; *Kunst, Philos. etc.:* illusionism

Illusionist *m*; -en, -en, **~in** *f*; -, -nen **1.** *geh.* (*Träumer*) illusionist; fantasist; **2.** (*Zauberkünstler*) illusionist

illusionistisch *Adj.* illusionistic; **illusionslos** *Adj.* **1.** free from illusions; *Einschätzung etc.:* realistic, sober; **~ sein** *auch* have no illusions; **2.** (*desillusioniert*) disillusioned; **Illusionslosigkeit** *f* freedom from illusions, realism; **illusorisch** *Adj.* illusory; **das ist doch ~!** that's an illusion, you're *etc.* fooling yourself *etc.*

illuster *Adj. geh.* illustrious

Illustration *f*, -, -en illustration, picture; **zur ~** by way of illustration, to illustrate (what I mean); **illustrativ** *Adj.* illustrative; **Illustrator** *m*; -s, -en, **Illustratorin** *f*, -, -nen illustrator; **illustrie-**

ren *v/t.* illustrate; *fig. auch* demonstrate; **illustriert** *Adj.* illustrated; **Illustrierte** *f* (glossy, *Am. auch* slick) magazine, glossy *umg.*, *Am. auch* slick *umg.*

Illyrer *m*; -s, -, **~in** *f*, -, -nen; *hist.* Illyrian, *weiblich auch:* Illyrian woman (*od.* girl *etc.*); **Illyrien** (*n*); -s; *hist.* Illyria; **Illyrier** *m*; -s, -, **Illyrierin** *f*; -, -nen → **Illyrer**, **illyrisch I.** *Adj.* Illyrian; **II. Illyrisch** *n*; -en; *Ling.* Illyrian; **das Illyrische** Illyrian

Iltis *m*; -ses, -se; *Zool.* polecat

im *Präp. + Art.* **1.** → **in¹**; **2.** *bei Monatsnamen:* **~ Mai** in May; *bei Zeiträumen:* **~ Herbst** in autumn (*bes. Am.* fall); **~ Mittelalter** in the Middle Ages; *in festen Verbindungen:* **~ Grunde** basically; **~ Bau** under construction; **~ Gegenteil** on the contrary; **3. ~ Kommen sein** be coming; **~ Wachsen sein** be growing (*od.* developing); **sie war schon ~ Gehen** going, on her way

Image *n*; -(s), -s image; **~beratung** *f* image counsel(l)ing; **~broschüre** *f* promotional pamphlet; **~kampagne** *f* *bes. Wirts.* image-building (*od.* image- -rebuilding) campaign; **~pflege** *f* image building; **~verlust** *m* loss of image, damage to one's image

imaginär *Adj.* imaginary

Imagination *f*, -, -en **1.** *nur Sg.* (*Vorstellungskraft*) imagination; **2.** (*Vorstellung*) notion; **imaginativ** *Adj.* imaginative

Imago *f*, -, *Imagines*; *Psych.*, *Zool.* imago (*Pl.* imagos *od.* imagines)

Imam *m*; -s, -s *od.* -e; *Reli.* imam; **Imamit** *m*; -en, -en imamite

Imbiss *m*; -es, -e **1.** snack, *umg.* bite to eat; **2.** → **Imbissstand**, **Imbissstube**; **~bude** *f* → **Imbissstand**, **~halle** *f* → **Imbissstand**, **Imbissstube**; **~stand** *m* *etwa* hot-dog stand (*od.* stall); **~stube** *f* snack bar

Imitat *n*; -(e)s, -e imitation; **Imitation** *f*; -, en imitation; (*Nachbildung*) *auch* copy; (*Fälschung*) fake; **imitativ** *Adj.* imitative; **Imitator** *m*; -s, -en, **Imitatorin** *f*, -,-nen imitator; *von Personen:* impersonator, impressionist; **imitatorisch** *Adj.* imitative; **imitieren** *v/t.* **1.** imitate; (*Politiker etc.*) impersonate; **2.** (*nachbilden*) copy

Imker *m*; -s, - bee(-)keeper, apiarist *förm.*; **Imkerei** *f* **1.** bee(-)keeping; **2.** (*Betrieb*) apiary; **Imkerin** *f*, -, -nen → **Imker**

immanent *Adj.* inherent (+ *Dat.* in); *Philos.* immanent; **Immanenz** *f*; -, *kein Pl.* immanence

immateriell *Adj.* immaterial

Immatrikulation *f*; -, -en; *Univ.* enrol(l)ment; **immatrikulieren** *v/t. und v/refl.* enrol(l), register (**an** + *Dat.* at); **Immatrikulierung** *f* enrol(l)ment

immens *Adj.* tremendous, vast

immer *Adv.* **1.** always; (*jedesmal*) *auch* every time; (*fortwährend*) *auch* constantly, all the time; **~ während Freundschaft** eternal friendship; **wie ~** as always; **~ noch, noch ~** still; **er ist ~ noch** (*immerhin*) **dein Chef** he is your boss after all, he's still your boss (when all's said and done); **~ wenn** every time, whenever; **für ~ weggehen** *etc.*: for good; **~ wieder** over and over again, time and again; **etw. ~ wieder tun** (*zum wiederholten Mal*) do s.th. over and over again; (*dauernd*) keep (on) doing s.th.; **es ist ~ wieder dasselbe** it's the same (thing) every time; **~ weiter reden** keep (on) talking; *umg.*

go on and on; **~ und ewig** for evermore; **~ zu!** *umg.* (*mach weiter*) don't stop!; **~ mit der Ruhe!** *umg.* (take it) easy now; **er soll nur ~ kommen!** *umg. einladend*: there's no reason for him not to come; *drohend*: (just) let him come!; **2.** *vor Komp.*: **~ besser** better and better; **~ schlimmer** worse and worse; **~ größer werdend** ever-increasing; **3.** *umg.* (*jeweils*) at a time; **~ den dritten Tag** every third day; **~ zu zweit** (always *od.* usually …) in twos; **4.** *verallgemeinernd*: **wann auch ~** whenever; **was auch ~** whatever; **wer auch ~** whoever; **wie lang** *etc.* **auch ~** however long *etc.*; **wie auch ~ du es machen willst** *etc.* whichever way you choose *etc.*; **wo auch ~** wherever; **wann/wo** *etc.* **auch ~ ich …** *auch* it doesn't matter when/where *etc.* I …, no matter when (where *etc.*) I …

immerdar *Adv. geh.* (for) evermore; **jetzt und ~** now and evermore; **immerfort** *altm. Adv.* continually, all the time

immergrün *Adj.* evergreen; **Immergrün** *n Bot.* evergreen

immerhin *Adv. einräumend*: still; *am Satzende*: though; (*doch*) after all; (*wenigstens*) at least; **~!** *lobend*: not bad, considering; *relativierend*: well, that's something at least; **das ist ~ etwas** it's better than nothing, it's something, I suppose; **es war ~ das zweitbeste Ergebnis** it was still the second--best score; **er ist ~ dein Chef** he is your boss after all, don't forget he's your boss, he's still your boss (when all's said and done)

immerzu *Adv.* all the time; **etw. ~ tun** *auch* keep (on) doing s.th.

Immigrant *m; -en, -en,* **~in** *f; -, -nen* immigrant; **Immigration** *f; -, -en* immigration; **Immigrationsbestimmungen** *Pl.* immigration laws; **immigrieren** *v/i.* immigrate

Immission *f; -, -en; Öko., Umweltverschmutzung*: pollutant input; *der Luft*: (input of) air-borne pollution, *von Lärm*: (input of) noise pollution; **Immissionsschutz** *m* protection against pollution, *etwa* environmental protection; **Immissionsschutzgesetz** *n law governing protection against pollution, etwa* environmental protection legislation

immobil *Adj.* immovable, immobile; **~es Vermögen** immovable property, real estate

Immobiliarkredit *m Wirts.* mortgage credit (*od.* loan)

Immobilie *f; -, -n* property, piece of real estate; **mit ~n handeln** deal in property (*od.* real estate); **~n Zeitungsrubrik**: property

Immobilien|besitz *m Wirts.* property (*od.* real estate) holdings; **~fonds** *m* real estate fund; **~handel** *m Wirts.* property dealing, dealing in real estate; **~händler** *m,* **~händlerin** *f → Immobilienmakler*; **~makler** *m,* **~maklerin** *f* estate agent, *Am.* real estate agent, Realtor®; **~markt** *m* property market

immobilisieren *v/t. Med.* immobilize; **Immobilisierung** *f; -, kein Pl.; Med.* immobilization

Immobilität *f; -, kein Pl.* immobility

Immortalität *f; -, kein Pl.; geh.* immortality

Immortelle *f; -, -n; Bot.* everlasting (flower), immortelle

immun *Adj.* **1.** *Med., auch fig.* immune

(**gegen** to); **~ machen** → **immunisieren**; **2.** *Pol., Jur.* immune; **~ sein** *auch* have immunity

Immunbiologie *f Biol.* immunobiology

Immundefizienz *f; -, kein Pl.; Med.* immunodeficiency

immunisieren *v/t.* make immune (**gegen** against, to), immunize (against); **Immunisierung** *f* immunization (against)

Immunität *f; -, -en, mst. Sg.* **1.** *Med., fig.* immunity (**gegen** to, against); **2.** *Pol., Jur.* immunity; *Parl. auch* (parliamentary) privilege

Immunkörper *m Physiol.* antibody

Immunologe *m; -n, -n* immunologist; **Immunologie** *f; -, kein Pl.* immunology; **Immunologin** *f; -, -nen* immunologist; **immunologisch** *Adj.* immunological

Immun|reaktion *f Med.* immunological reaction, immunoreaction; **~schwäche** *f* immunodeficiency; **~serum** *n* immune serum; **~system** *n* immune system; **~therapie** *f* immunotherapy

Impala *f; -, -s; Zool.* impala

Impedanz *f; -, -en; Etech.* impedance

imperativ *Adj.* imperative; **~es Mandat** *Pol.* imperative mandate

Imperativ *m; -s, -e; Ling.* imperative (mood); **kategorischer ~** *Philos.* categorical imperative; **imperativisch** *Adj.* imperative; **Imperativsatz** *m Ling.* sentence in the imperative

Imperator *m; -s, -en* imperator; **imperatorisch** *Adj.* imperatorial; **Imperatrix** *f; -, Imperatrices* imperatrix (*Pl.* imperatrices)

Imperfekt *n; -s, -e; Ling.* imperfect (tense); **imperfektisch** *Adj. Ling.* imperfect

imperial *Adj.* imperial; **Imperialismus** *m; -, -men, mst Sg.; Pol.* imperialism; **Imperialist** *m; -en, -en,* **Imperialistin** *f; -, -nen; Pol.* imperialist; **imperialistisch** *Adj. Pol.* imperialist(ic)

Imperium *n; -s, Imperien* empire (*auch fig.*)

impermeabel *Adj. Med.* impermeable; **Impermeabilität** *f; -, kein Pl.* impermeability

Impersonale *n; -s, Impersonalia und Impersonalien; Ling.* impersonal (verb)

impertinent *Adj.* impertinent, insolent; **Impertinenz** *f; -, -en* **1.** *nur Sg.* impertinence; **2.** *konkret: auch* impertinent remark (*od.* thing to do)

Impetus *m; -, kein Pl.* impetus

Impf|aktion *f* vaccination programme (*Am.* program); **~ausweis** *m* vaccination card

impfen *v/t.* **1.** *Med.* vaccinate, inoculate (*auch Biol. und Agr.*); **sich ~ lassen** be vaccinated (*od.* inoculated); **2.** *umg. fig.* (*beeinflussen*) influence; **mein Anwalt hat mich vor der Verhandlung geimpft** my lawyer coached me (in what to say) before the trial; → *einimpfen*

Impfling *m; -s, -e; Med. person who has been vaccinated or who is to be vaccinated*

Impf|narbe *f Med.* vaccination scar; **~pass** *m* vaccination card; **~pflicht** *f* compulsory vaccination (*od.* inoculation); **~pistole** *f* vaccination gun; **~schein** *m* vaccination certificate; **~schutz** *m* protection given by vaccination; **~stoff** *m* vaccine, serum

Impfung *f Med.* vaccination, inoculation

Impfzwang *m; nur Sg.* compulsory vac-

cination

Implantat *n; -(e)s, -e; Med.* implant; **Implantation** *f; -, -en* implantation; **implantieren** *v/t.* implant

implementieren *v/t. EDV, Jur., Pol.* implement; **Implementierung** *f* implementation

Implikation *f; -, -en; geh.* implication; **implizieren** *v/t.* imply; **dies impliziert, dass …** *auch* this would indicate *od.* suggest that …

implizit *Adj. geh.* implicit

implodieren *v/i.* implode; **Implosion** *f* implosion

Imponderabilien *Pl.* imponderables; **Imponderabilität** *f; -, kein Pl.* imponderability

imponieren *v/i.* (*j-m*) impress; (*Achtung einflößen*) command *s.o.*'s respect; **imponierend** *Adj.* impressive; **~es Auftreten** commanding presence; → *imposant;* **Imponiergehabe** *n* **1.** showing off, posturing, exhibitionism; *konkret*: attempt to impress; **2.** *Zool.* display behavio(u)r

Import *m; -(e)s, -e; Wirts.* **1.** *nur Sg.* import(ing); **2.** *konkret*: import; → *auch Einfuhr*, **~abhängigkeit** *f* dependence on imports; **~artikel** *m* import, imported article; *Pl. auch* imported goods; **~beschränkung** *f* import restriction

Importeur *m; -s, -e; Wirts.* importer

Import|firma *f Wirts.* importer, importing company; **~geschäft** *n* **1.** import trade; **2.** → *Importfirma*; **~handel** *m* import trade

importieren *v/t. Wirts.* import

Import|kontingent *n Wirts.* import quota; **~stopp** *m* ban on imports; **~überschuss** *m* import surplus; **~ware** *f Wirts.* imported goods *Pl.*; **~zoll** *m* import duty

imposant *Adj.* impressive; *Gebäude, Figur etc.*: imposing; (*auffallend*) striking

impotent *Adj.* impotent; **Impotenz** *f; -, kein Pl.* impotence

Imprägnation *f; -, -en* **1.** *von Stoffen etc.*: proofing, treatment; *gegen Wasser*: waterproofing; **2.** *Geol.* impregnation; **3.** *Biol.* impregnation

imprägnieren *v/t.* impregnate, treat; (*bes. Webstoffe*) waterproof; **Imprägniermittel** *n* impregnating agent; **Imprägnierung** *f* impregnation; waterproofing

impraktikabel *Adj.* impracticable

Impresario *m; -s, -s* impresario, agent

Impression *f; -, -en, mst Pl.* impression

Impressionismus *m; -, kein Pl.* Impressionism; **Impressionist** *m; -en, -en* Impressionist; **impressionistisch** *Adj.* impressionist(ic); *Kunstrichtung*: Impressionist

Impressum *n; -s, Impressen; Druck.* imprint; *e-r Zeitung: auch* masthead

Imprimatur *n; -s, kein Pl.; Druck.* imprimatur; **das ~ erteilen für** pass *s.th.* for press; **imprimieren** *v/t. Druck.* pass *s.th.* for press

Impromptu *n; -s, -s; Mus.* impromptu

Improvisation *f; -, -en* improvisation; **Improvisationstalent** *n* talent for improvisation

Improvisator *m; -s, -en,* **~in** *f; -, -nen* improviser

improvisieren *vt/i.* improvise (*auch fig.*); *Mus., beim Reden etc.: auch* ad--lib, extemporize; **improvisiert I.** *P.P.* → *improvisieren;* **II.** *Adj.* improvised; *Rede: auch* off-the-cuff, *Am. auch* on the fly; (*schnell zusammengestellt*) improvised; *umg.* instant ..., *präd.* thrown together

Impuls *m; -es, -e* **1.** impulse; (*Idee*) *auch* idea; *auch Pl.* inspiration *Sg.*; **e-r Sache neue ~e geben** give a fresh impetus to s.th.; **2.** (*Drang*) impulse; *aus e-m ~ heraus* on an (*od.* a sudden) impulse; **3.** *Etron.* impulse

Impulsgeber *m* **1.** *Etron.* pulse generator; **2.** *fig.* initiator

impulsiv I. *Adj.* impulsive; *Entscheidung etc.*: spur-of-the-moment ...; **II.** *Adv.*: **~ handeln** act on impulse (*od.* on the spur of the moment); **Impulsivität** *f; -, kein Pl.* impulsiveness

Impulssatz *m Phys.* momentum conservation law (*od.* theorem)

imstande, im Stande *Adj.; nur präd.*: **~ sein zu** (+ *Inf.*) be capable of (+ *Ger.*), be in a position to (+ *Inf.*); **nicht ~ zu** (+ *Inf.*) unable to (+ *Inf.*), incapable of (+ *Ger.*); **sie ist durchaus ~, das zu tun** she's perfectly capable of doing it, there's nothing to stop her doing it; **dazu ist er glatt ~** *iro.* I wouldn't put it past him; **er ist ~ und ...** he's quite capable of (+ *Ger.*); **sie ist zu allem ~** she'll stop at nothing

in¹ *Präp.* **1.** *räumlich*: (*wo?*) in, at; *e-r Stadt*: in; *e-m kleineren Ort*: *auch* at; (*innerhalb*) within; **im Haus** in(side) the house, indoors; **im ersten Stock** on the first (*Am.* second) floor; **~ der Kirche/Schule** at (*Am. auch* in) church/school; *Gebäude*: in the church/school; **im Theater** at the theat|re (*Am. auch* -er); **~ England** in England; **waren Sie schon ~ England?** have you ever been to England?; **ich habe ~ München studiert** I studied at (*Am.* in) Munich; **2.** *räumlich*: (*wohin?*) into, in; **in die Kirche/Schule** (*hinein*: into the) church/school; **~ die Schweiz** to Switzerland; **gehen wir ~s Haus** let's go indoors (*od.* inside); **3.** *zeitlich*: in; (*während*) during; (*innerhalb*) within; *Dauer*: **~ drei Tagen** in three days; **~ diesem / im letzten/ nächsten Jahr** this/last/next year; **heute ~ acht Tagen** a week (from) today; **im Jahr 2009** in (the year) 2009; **im** (**Monat**) **Februar** in (the month of) February; **im Frühling/Herbst** in (the) spring / autumn (*bes. Am.* fall); **~ der Nacht** at night, during the night; **~ letzter Zeit** lately; **4.** *Art und Weise*: **ich bin ~ Eile** I'm in a hurry; **~ tiefer Trauer** (*in Todesanzeigen*) sadly missed by; **wir sind ~ Sorge, dass ...** we are worried (*od.* concerned) that ...; **5.** *e-e Situation bezeichnend*: **im Alter von** at the age of; **~ Behandlung sein** be having treatment; **~ e-m Klub etc. sein** be in a club *etc.*, belong to a club *etc.*; **~ Biologie ist er schwach** he's not very good at biology; **6.** *Wirts.* in; **er macht ~ Textilien** *umg.* he's in textiles (*od.* in the textile business)

in² *Adj.; nur präd.*: **~ sein** *umg.* be in, be the fashion

inadäquat *Adj. geh.* inadequate; **Inadäquatheit** *f* inadequacy

inaktiv *Adj.* inactive; *Chem. auch* inert; *Mitglied*: *auch* non-active; **inaktivieren** *v/t.* inactivate; **Inaktivierung** *f* inactivation; **Inaktivität** *f; -, nur Sg.* inactivity; *Chem. auch* inertness

inakzeptabel *Adj. geh.* unacceptable

Inangriffnahme *f; -, -n e-s Projekts etc.*: launching; *e-r Arbeit*: tackling; **seit ~ des Projekts** since the project was launched (*od.* started)

Inanspruchnahme *f; -, -n* (laying)

---

claim (+ *Gen.* to); (*Benutzung*) use (of), utilization (of); (*Zuhilfenahme*) *e-s Rechtes etc.*: resort (to); (*Beanspruchung*) demands *Pl.* (on); *zeitliche*: claims *Pl.* on *s.o.'s* time; (*Belastung*) strain (on); **~ von Kredit** *Wirts.* making use (*od.* taking advantage) of credit (facilities)

Inaugenscheinnahme *f; -, -n; Amtsspr.* inspection

Inauguraldissertation *f; -, -en; Univ.* thesis, dissertation; **Inauguration** *f; -, -en* inauguration; **inaugurieren** *v/t.* inaugurate; **Inaugurierung** *f* inauguration

Inbegriff *m* model, perfect example; *geh.* embodiment, epitome (*alle* + *Gen.* of); **der ~ von Qualität** *etc.* a byword for quality *etc.*

inbegriffen I. *Adj. präd.* included; **Mahlzeiten ~** meals included, including meals; **II.** *Präp.* including, inclusive of

Inbesitznahme *f* appropriation, seizure; *von Land, Gebäude*: *auch* occupation

Inbetriebnahme *f; -, -n*, **Inbetriebsetzung** *f e-r Fabrik etc.* opening; *e-r Maschine etc.*: starting up; (*Einschalten*) switching on; **vor ~** (+ *Gen.*) before starting (*od.* switching on) ...

Inbild *n geh.* quintessence, personification

Inbrunst *f; -, kein Pl.; geh.* ardo(u)r, fervo(u)r; **inbrünstig** *geh.* **I.** *Adj.* ardent, fervent; **II.** *Adv.*: **~ hoffen, dass ...** *auch* hope and pray that ...

Inbus|schlüssel® *m Tech.* Allen key®, *Am. auch* hex wrench (*od.* key); **~schraube®** *f Tech.* Allen screw®

Incentivereise [ɪnˈsɛntɪv-] *f* incentive trip, *Am.* junket

indanthren *Adj.* colo(u)r-fast; **Indanthren®** *n; -s, -e* indanthrene (*type of colo[u]r-fast dye*); **Indanthrenfarbe** *f*, **Indanthrenfarbstoff** *m →* **Indanthren**

indefinit *Adj. bes. Ling.* indefinite; **Indefinitpronomen** *n Ling.* indefinite pronoun

indeklinabel *Adj.* indeclinable

indelikat *Adj.* indelicate; (*taktlos*) tactless

indem I. *Konj.* **1.** *Gleichzeitigkeit*: as, while; **~ er mich ansah, sagte er** looking at me he said; **2.** *Mittel*: by (+ *Ger.*); **er gewann, ~ er mogelte** he won by cheating; **II.** *Adv. altm.* (*unterdessen*) in the meantime

Indemnität *f; -, kein Pl.* indemnity

Inder *m; -s, -* **1.** *Person*: Indian; **2.** *umg.* (*Restaurant*) Indian restaurant; **zum ~ gehen** *umg.* go to an Indian; **Inderin** *f; -, -nen* Indian woman (*od.* girl *etc.*)

indes, indessen I. *Adv.* (*mittlerweile*) meanwhile, in the meantime; (*dennoch*) nevertheless; (*dessen ungeachtet*) still; **II.** *Konj. geh.* **1.** (*wohingegen*) whereas; **2.** (*während*) while, as

indeterminabel *Adj. Philos.* indeterminable; **Indeterminismus** *m; -, kein Pl.; Philos.* indeterminism

Index¹ *m; -, Indices; allg.* index (*Pl.* indexes *od.* indices); *Math. auch* exponent

Index² *m; -, -e; kirchl. hist.* Index; *Bücher auf den ~ setzen* put on the Index

Index|lohn *m Wirts.* index-linked wages *Pl.*; **~zahl** *f*, **~ziffer** *f* index (number)

indezent *Adj.* indecent; **Indezenz** *f; -, kein Pl.* indecency

Indian *m; -s, -e; österr.* turkey

Indianer *m; -s,* American Indian, Na-

---

tive American; **~geschichte** *f* story about (*cowboys and*) Indians; **~häuptling** *m* Indian chief

Indianerin *f; -, -nen* (American) Indian woman (*od.* girl *etc.*), squaw *neg!*

Indianer|krapfen *m österr., Gastr.* small, ball-shaped sponge cake filled with cream and covered in chocolate; **~reservat** *n*, **~reservation** *f* Indian reservation; **~sprache** *f* American Indian (*od.* Native American, Amerindian *fachspr.*) language; **~stamm** *m* Indian (*od.* Native American) tribe; **~zelt** *n* wigwam, tepee

indianisch *Adj.* Indian, Native-American, Amerindian *fachspr.*

Indien (*n*); *-s; Geog.* India

Indienstnahme *f; -, -n; Amtsspr.* commissioning, taking into service; **Indienststellung** *f Amtsspr.* commissioning, putting into service

indifferent *Adj.* indifferent (*gegenüber* to); *Phys., Chem. auch* neutral; *Gas*: inert; **Indifferenz** *f; -, kein Pl.* indifference (*gegenüber* to)

indigniert *Adj.* indignant (*über* + *Akk.* at)

Indignität *f; -, kein Pl.; Jur.* disqualification from inheritance

Indigo *m, n; -s, -s* indigo; **indigoblau** *Adj.* indigo; **Indigoblau** *n Chem.* indigo

Indigopflanze *f Bot.* indigo (plant)

Indikation *f; -, -en; Med.* indication; **medizinische/soziale** *etc.* **~ für e-e Abtreibung**: medical/social *etc.* grounds for an abortion; **Indikationenmodell** *n*, **Indikationsmodell** *n etwa* model grounds *Pl.* for legal abortion

Indikativ¹ *m; -s, -e; Ling.* indicative (mood)

Indikativ² *m; -s, -s* (*Erkennungsmelodie*) signature tune

Indikator *m; -s, -en* indicator; **~en** *auch* indications; **Indikatrix** *f; -, kein Pl.; bes. Math., Geog.* indicatrix

Indio *m; -s, -s* (*South American*) Indian

indirekt I. *Adj.* indirect; *Antwort, Anspielung etc.*: *auch* oblique; (**die**) **~e Rede** indirect (*od.* reported) speech; **II.** *Adv.* indirectly; *antworten etc.*: *auch* obliquely; *ausdrücken*: *auch* in a roundabout way

indisch *Adj.* Indian; **der Indische Ozean** *Geog.* the Indian Ocean

Indischrot *n Farbe*: Indian red

indiskret *Adj.* indiscreet; (*taktlos*) tactless; **Indiskretheit** *f* **1.** *nur Sg.; Eigenschaft*: indiscretion; (*Taktlosigkeit*) tactlessness; **2.** *konkret*: indiscretion; tactless remark (*od.* thing to do); **Indiskretion** *f; -, -en* **1.** *nur Sg.; Eigenschaft*: indiscretion; **2.** *konkret*: *auch* tactless remark (*od.* thing to do); **durch gezielte ~en wurde bekannt, dass ...** it became known, as a result of calculated indiscretion, that ..., it was deliberately allowed to leak out that ...

indiskutabel *Adj.* not worth considering; *Theorie etc.*: out of court; (*nicht in Frage kommend*) out of the question; (*unmöglich*) appalling, impossible

indisponiert *Adj.* indisposed; **Indisponiertheit** *f* indisposition

Indium *n; -s, kein Pl.; Chem.* indium

Individualbereich *m* personal sphere

individualisieren *v/t.* individualize; **Individualisierung** *f* individualization

Individualismus *m; -, kein Pl.* individualism

Individualist *m; -en, -en*, **~in** *f; -, -nen*

individualist; **individualistisch** *Adj.* individualist(ic)

Individualität *f*, -, *-en* **1.** *nur Sg.* individuality; **2.** *Persönlichkeit*: individual character, personality

Individualpsychologie *f* individual psychology; **individualpsychologisch** *Adj.* of (*od.* in) individual psychology

Individual|recht *n* right(s *Pl.*) of an (*od.* the) individual; **~verkehr** *m* private vehicle traffic; *Fahrzeuge*: private vehicles

individuell I. *Adj.* individual; (*persönlich*) personal; (*originell*) original; *die* *~e Note* the personal touch; **II.** *Adv.*: *~ gestalten* do (*od.* arrange *etc.*) according to one's own tastes *etc.*; (*e-e persönliche Note geben*) individualize, personalize; *das ist ~ verschieden* that varies from person to person; *man kann es sich* (*Dat.*) *~ zusammenstellen* you can arrange it whichever way you like (*od.* as it suits you best)

Individuum *n*; -s, *Individuen* individual (*auch fig. pej.*)

Indiz *n*; -es, *-ien* **1.** indication, sign; **2.** *Jur.* piece of circumstantial evidence; *Pl. auch* circumstantial evidence *Sg.*

Indizien|beweis *m Jur. auch Pl.* circumstantial evidence; **~kette** *f* chain of evidence; **~prozess** *m* trial based on circumstantial evidence

indizieren *v/t.* **1.** indicate; **2.** (*Buch etc.*) index; *kirchl.* put on the Index; **indiziert** *Adj. Med. und fig.* indicated; **Indizierung** *f* indication

Indochina (*n*); -s; *Geog.* Indo-China, *Am.* Indochina

Indoeuropäer *m* Indo-European; **indoeuropäisch** *Adj.* Indo-European

Indogermane *m* Indo-European; **indogermanisch** *Adj.* Indo-European

Indogermanische *n*; -en, *kein Pl.*; *Ling.* Indo-European; **Indogermanistik** *f* Indo-European studies *Pl.*

Indoktrination *f*, -, *-en*; *bes. Pol., pej.* indoctrination; **indoktrinieren** *v/t.* indoctrinate; **Indoktrinierung** *f* indoctrination

indolent *Adj.* indolent, idle; **Indolenz** *f*, -, *kein Pl.* indolence

Indologie *f*; -, *kein Pl.* Indology; **indologisch** *Adj.* Indological

Indonesien (*n*); -s; *Geog.* Indonesia

Indonesier *m*; -s, -, **~in** *f*; -, *-nen* Indonesian, *weiblich: auch* Indonesian woman (*od.* girl *etc.*); **indonesisch** *Adj.* Indonesian

Indossament *n*; -(e)s, -e; *Fin.* endorsement; **Indossant** *m*; -en, -en; *Fin.* endorser; **Indossat** *m*; -en, -en; *Fin.* endorsee; **Indossatar** *m*; s, -e; *Fin.* endorsee; **indossieren** *v/t. Fin.* endorse; **Indossierung** *f Fin.* endorsement

Induktion *f*, -, *-en*; *Philos. und Etech.* induction

Induktions|beweis *m Philos.* inductive proof; **~motor** *m Etech.* induction motor; **~ofen** *m Tech.* induction furnace; **~spule** *Etech. f* induction coil; **~strom** *m Etech.* induced current

induktiv *Adj.* inductive; **Induktivität** *f*; -, *-en* inductivity, inductance

industrialisieren *v/t.* industrialize; **industrialisiert I.** *P.P.* → **industrialisieren; II.** *Adj.* industrialized; **Industrialisierung** *f* industrialization; **Industrialismus** *m*; -, *kein Pl.* industrialism

Industrie *f*; -, *-n* industry; *einzelne*: (branch of) industry; *in die ~ gehen* umg. go into industry; *in der ~ (tätig)*

---

sein be (employed) in industry; **~abgase** *Pl.* industrial emissions (*od.* waste gases); **~abwässer** *Pl.* industrial sewage (*od.* effluent) *Sg.*; **~aktie** *f Fin.*, *Wirts.* industrial share; **~anlage** *f* industrial plant; **~anleihe** *f* → **Industrieobligation; ~ansiedlung** *f* setting-up (*od.* establishment) of industries; **~arbeiter** *m*, **~arbeiterin** *f* industrial worker; **~bau** *m* industrial construction; *Gebäude* industrial building, plant; **~berater** *m*, **~beraterin** *f* industrial consultant; **~betrieb** *m* industrial concern; (*Anlage*) industrial plant; **~brache** *f* industrial wasteland, brown-field site; **~denkmal** *n* industrial monument; **~erzeugnis** *n* industrial product; **~gebiet** *n* **1.** industrial area; **2.** *e-s Ortes*: industrial estate (*Am.* park); **~gelände** *n* industrial estate (*Am.* park); **~geschichte** *f hist.* industrial history; **~gesellschaft** *f* industrial society; **~gewerkschaft** *f* industrial (*od.* industry-wide) union; *~ Metall* Metal Workers' Union; **~kauffrau** *f* woman white-collar worker in an industrial company; **~kaufmann** *m* white-collar worker in an industrial company; **~komplex** *m* industrial complex; **~konzern** *m* industrial group (of companies); **~land** *n* industrial (*od.* developed) nation; **~landschaft** *f* industrial landscape

industriell *Adj.* industrial; *die ~e Revolution hist.* the Industrial Revolution; **Industrielle** *m, f*; -n, -n industrialist

Industrie|magnat *m* industrial magnate, captain of industry, tycoon; **~mechaniker** *m*, **~mechanikerin** *f* industrial mechanic; **~metropole** *f* major industrial city; **~müll** *m* industrial waste; **~nation** *f* industrialized nation; *die ~en auch* the developed world; **~norm** *f* industrial standard; *Deutsche ~* German Standard Specification; **~obligation** *f Wirts.* industrial debenture; **~produkt** *n* industrial product; **~produktion** *f* industrial production; **~revier** *n* industrial belt; **~roboter** *m* industrial robot; **2schwach** *Adj.* under-industrialized; **~spionage** *f* industrial espionage; **~staat** *m* industrial nation; **~stadt** *f* industrial town (*od.* city); **~standort** *m* site of major industries, (heavily) industrialized area; *~ und Handelskammer f* Chamber of Industry and Commerce; **~unternehmen** *n* industrial company; **~verband** *m* confederation of industries; **~viertel** *n* industrial area (*od.* part of town); **~werte** *Pl.* industrials; **~wirtschaft** *f* industry; **~zeitalter** *n* industrial age; **~zentrum** *n* industrial centre (*Am.* -er); **~zweig** *m* (branch of) industry

induzieren *v/t.* induce (*auch Phys.*)

ineffektiv *Adj.* ineffective

ineffizient *Adj. geh.* **1.** (*unwirksam*) ineffective; **2.** (*unwirtschaftlich*) uneconomical; *Methode etc.*: inefficient; **Ineffizienz** *f*; -, *-en* ineffectiveness, inefficiency

ineinander *Adv.* in(to) one another; *zwei*: in(to) each other; *in Verbindungen mit Verben*: *auch* inter...; *~ verliebt* in love (with each other); *~ fließen* merge (into one another); *Farben*: *auch* run; *~ fügen* fit together, fit ... into each other, join; (*sich*) *~ schieben* telescope; *~ flechten* intertwine, *~ greifen* interlock; *fig. Tatsachen etc.*: be interconnected

inexakt *Adj.* inaccurate

---

inexistent *Adj. geh.* non(-)existent

infam *Adj.* disgraceful, shameless; *umg. fig.* awful; *~e Lüge auch* disgusting lie; **Infamie** *f*; -, *-n* **1.** *nur Sg.* disgrace; **2.** disgraceful thing to do (*bzw.* say)

Infant *m*; -en, -en infante

Infanterie *f*; -, *-n*; *Mil.* infantry; **~regiment** *n* infantry regiment; **Infanterist** *m*; -en, -en infantryman, infantry soldier

infantil *Adj.* childish, infantile, puerile; **Infantilismus** *m*; -, *Infantilismen*; *Med., Psych.* **1.** *nur Sg.* infantilism; **2.** infantile trait; **Infantilität** *f*, -, *kein Pl.* childishness; childish (*od.* infantile, puerile) behavio(u)r

Infantin *f*; -, *-nen* infanta

Infarkt *m*; -(e)s, -e; *Med.* **1.** infarct; **2.** (*Herzinfarkt*) heart attack, coronary, *fachspr.* cardiac (*od.* myocardial) infarction; **infarktgefährdet** *Adj.* Patient etc.: coronary-risk ...; **Infarktpersönlichkeit** *f* coronary-risk type

Infekt *m*; -(e)s, -e, **Infektion** *f*; -, *-en*; *Med.* infection

Infektions|abteilung *f* isolation ward; **~erreger** *m* pathogen; **~gefahr** *f* risk of infection; **~herd** *m* focus of infection; **~krankheit** *f* infectious disease; **~risiko** *n* risk of infection; **~träger** *m* (infection) carrier; **~weg** *m* path of infection

infektiös *Adj.* infectious; *durch Kontakt*: *auch* contagious

inferior *Adj.* inferior; **Inferiorität** *f*; -, *kein Pl.* inferiority

infernalisch *Adj.* **1.** (*teuflisch*) infernal; *Gelächter*: fiendish; **2.** (*unangenehm*) *Geruch etc.*: dreadful; *~er Lärm* terrible din; **Infernalität** *f*; -, *kein Pl.*; *altm.* dreadfulness *allg.*

Inferno *n*; -s, -s inferno (*auch fig.*)

infertil *Adj. Med.* infertile; **Infertilität** *f*; -, *kein Pl.*; *Med.* infertility

Infiltrant *m*; -en, -en, **~in** ; -, *-nen* infiltrator; **Infiltration** *f* infiltration (*auch fig.*); **Infiltrationsanästhesie** *f Med.* an(a)esthesia by infiltration; **infiltrieren** *vt/i.* infiltrate (*auch fig.*); **Infiltrierung** *f* infiltration

infinit *Adj. Ling.* non(-)finite

infinitesimal *Adj. Math.* infinitesimal; **Infinitesimalrechnung** *f* infinitesimal calculus

Infinitiv *m*; -s, -e; *Gram.* infinitive; **~konjunktion** *f* conjunction coupled with the infinitive; **~satz** *m* infinitive clause

Infix *n*; -es, -e; *Ling.* infix

infizieren I. *v/t.* infect; *j-n* (*mit etw.*) *~ auch* pass s.th. on to s.o.; **II.** *v/refl.*: *sich ~* get an infection; *sich bei etw. ~* infect o.s. doing s.th.; **Infizierung** *f* infection

in flagranti *Adv.*: *~ ertappt werden* be caught in the act (*od.* in flagrante) (*Dieb*: *auch* red-handed)

inflammabel *Adj.* (*entzündlich*) inflammable, flammable

Inflation *f*; -, *-en*; *Wirts.* inflation; **inflationär** *Adj.* inflationary; **inflationieren I.** *v/i.* pursue inflationary policies; **II.** *v/t.* devalue through inflation; **Inflationierung** *f* pursuing inflationary policies; **inflationistisch** *Adj.* inflationary

Inflations|ausgleich *m* inflationary adjustment; *als ~* to compensate for inflation; **~bekämpfung** *f* fight against inflation; **~gefahr** *f* risk of inflation; **~politik** *f* inflationary policies *Pl.*; **~rate** *f* rate of inflation, inflation rate; **~rückgang** *m* easing-off of inflation, drop in the inflation rate

inflations|sicher *Adj.* inflation-proof; **~treibend** *Adj.* inflationary

Inflationszeit *f* time of inflation, inflationary period

inflatorisch *Adj.* inflationary

inflexibel *Adj.* inflexible; *Ling.* invariable; **Inflexibilität** *f; -, kein Pl.* inflexibility; *Ling.* invariability

Influenz *f; -, -en; Etech.* electrostatic induction

Info[1] *n; -s, -s; umg.* (*Informationsblatt*) *umg.* info sheet, *Am.* flier, handbill

Info[2] *f; -, -s; umg.* info; *Informationsveranstaltung*: briefing, info session

Infoblatt *n umg.* → *Informationsblatt*

infolge I. *Präp.* (+ *Gen.*) as a result of; **~** *starker Windböen* as a result of high winds; **II.** *Adv.*: **~** *von Betriebsstörungen* as a result of breakdowns

infolgedessen *Adv.* as a result (of this), consequently

Infomobil *n; -s, -e* travel(l)ing information cent|re (*Am.* -er)

informal *Adj. bes. Soziol.* informal

Informant *m; -en, -en* **1.** *allg.* source; *in der Forschung: auch* informant (*auch für die Regierung etc.*); **2.** (*Denunziant*) informer

Informatik *f; -, kein Pl.* computer science, informatics *Pl.* (*V. im Sg.*)

Informatiker *m; -s, -, ~in* *f; -, -nen* computer scientist

Information *f -, -en* **1.** *auch Pl.* information (*über* + *Akk.* on, about); *zu Ihrer* **~** for your information; **2.** (*Stelle*) information (*od.* inquiry) desk

Informations|abend *m* (evening) briefing session; **~austausch** *m* exchange of information; **~bedürfnis** *n* need for information; **~besuch** *m* fact-finding mission; **~blatt** *n* information sheet; news sheet; **~büro** *n* inquiry office; **~dienst** *m* information service; **~fluss** *m* flow of information; **~flut** *f* information explosion; **~gehalt** *m* informational content; **~gesellschaft** *f* informed society; **~gespräch** *n* exchange of information; **~⌀hungrig** *Adj.* starved for information; **~material** *n* information; (*Prospekte etc.*) literature; **~netz** *n* information network; **~politik** *f* information policy; **~quelle** *f* source (of information); **~recht** *n* right to be informed; **~reise** *f* fact-finding tour (*od.* mission); **~schalter** *m* information desk; **~stand** *m* **1.** *nach dem neuesten* **~** according to the latest information (available); **2.** *auf e-r Messe etc.*: information stand (*od.* desk)

Informationstechnik *f* information technology, IT; **informationstechnisch** *Adj.* relating to information technology; using information technology; **Informationstechnologie** *f* information technology

Informations|träger *m* (data) storage medium; **~veranstaltung** *f* briefing; **~verarbeitung** *f* information processing; **~wert** *m* informational value; **~wissenschaft** *f* information science; **~wissenschaftler** *m*, **~wissenschaftlerin** *f* information scientist; **~zentrum** *n* information cent|re (*Am.* -er)

informativ *Adj.* informative, instructive

informatorisch *Adj.* informational

informell *Adj.* **1.** informal; **~e** *Malerei Kunst* abstract expressionism; **2.** → *informatorisch*

informieren I. *v/t.* **1.** (*in Kenntnis setzen*) let *s.o.* know (*über* + *Akk.* about), tell *s.o.* (about), *offiziell: auch*

notify *s.o.* (of), inform *s.o.* (about); *falsch* **~** misinform; **2.** (*belehren*) inform (*über* + *Akk.* about, of); **3.** (*anweisen*) instruct; *bes. Mil.* brief; **II.** *v/refl.*: *sich* **~** find out, inform o.s.; *generell*: keep informed (*alle über* + *Akk.* about); *sich* **~** *über* (+ *Akk.*) *durch Lesen: auch* read up on; **informiert I.** *P.P.* → *informieren*; **II.** *Adj.* informed; *über Sachverhalt: auch* in the picture; **~e** *Kreise* well-informed circles; *er ist gut* **~** he knows a lot (*über* + *Akk.* about), *er ist gut* **~** *über* (+ *Akk.*) *auch* he's well up on; *ich bin darüber* **~** I've been told (*od.* I know) about it; **Informiertheit** *f* (extent of) knowledge

Infostand *m* information stand

Infotainment *n; -s, kein Pl.* infotainment

Infothek *f; -, -en* information cent|re (*Am.* -er)

infrage, in Frage *Adv.*: **~** *kommen* be a possibility; **~** *stellen* call into question; **Infragestellung** *f* questioning, calling into question; (*Gefährdung*) jeopardizing

infrarot *Adj.* infrared; **Infrarot** *n* infrared

Infrarot|bestrahlung *f* infrared heat treatment; **~film** *m* infrared film; **~fotografie** *f* infrared photography; **~grill** *m* infrared grill; **~lampe** *f* infrared lamp; **~strahl** *m* infrared ray; **~strahler** *m* infrared heater

Infraschall *m* infrasound

Infrastruktur *f* infrastructure; **infrastrukturell** *Adj.* infrastructural

Infusion *f; -, -en; Med.* infusion, intravenous drip, *Brit. umg. auch* the drip

Infusions|flasche *f Med.* drip bag, *Am.* IV (bag); **~lösung** *f* drip (*Am.* IV) solution; **~schlauch** *m* drip (*Am.* IV) tube; **~ständer** *m* dripstand, *Am.* IV stand; **~therapie** *f* infusion (*Am.* IV) therapy

Infusionstierchen *Pl.*, **Infusorien** *Pl. Biol.* infusoria

Inganghaltung *f Amtsspr.* maintenance, keeping going; **Ingangsetzung** *f* starting (up)

Ingebrauchnahme *f; -, kein Pl.; Amtsspr.* taking into use

Ingenieur *m; -s, -e* engineer; **~bau** *m* **1.** *nur Sg.* civil engineering; **2.** *Pl. -bauten* (civil) engineering construction; **~biologie** *f* use of biology to measure and modify the environmental impact of civil engineering projects; **~büro** *n* consulting engineers *Pl.*; engineering office; **~geologie** *f* engineering geology

Ingenieurin *f; -, -nen* engineer

Ingenieur|schule *f* school of engineering; **~wissenschaft** *f mst Pl.* engineering (science)

Ingrediens *n; -, Ingredienzien, mst Pl.*, **Ingredienz** *f; -, -en, mst Pl.* **1.** *Gastr.* ingredient; **2.** *Pharm. etc.* constituent, component, constituent part

Ingression *f; -, -en; Geol.* ingression

ingressiv *Adj. Ling.* ingressive

Ingrimm *m; -s, kein Pl.; altm.* (terrible) wrath

Ingroup ['ɪngruːp] *f; -, -s; Soziol.* in-group

Ingwer *m; -s, kein Pl.; Bot., Gastr.* ginger; **~bier** *f* ginger beer; **~stäbchen** *n* ginger stick

Inhaber *m; -s, -* owner, proprietor; *e-r Urkunde, e-s Titels, e-s Amts etc., auch Sport* holder; *e-s Wechsels, Wertpapiers etc.*: holder, bearer

Inhaberaktie *f Wirts.* bearer share

Inhaberin *f; -, -nen* → *Inhaber*

Inhaber|papier *n Wirts.* bearer share; **~scheck** *m* cheque (*Am.* check) to bearer; **~schuldverschreibung** *f* bearer bond

inhaftieren *v/t.* arrest, take into custody; **Inhaftierte** *m, f; -n, -n* person in custody; **Inhaftierung** *f* imprisonment, detention; **Inhaftnahme** *f; -, -n; Amtsspr.* taking into custody; (*Haft*) imprisonment, detention

Inhalation *f; -, -en; Med.* inhalation; **Inhalationsapparat** *m* inhaler; **Inhalatorium** *n; -s, Inhalatorien* inhalation room, inhalatorium *fachspr.*; **inhalieren** *vt/i.* inhale

Inhalt *m; -(e)s, -e* **1.** *e-s Pakets etc.*: contents *Pl.*; **2.** (*eines Raumes*) capacity; (*von Körpern*) volume; (*einer Fläche*) area; **3.** (*gedanklicher* **~**) content; (*Handlungsablauf*) plot, (*auch behandelter Stoff*) contents *Pl.*; (*Thematik*) subject matter; (*das Wesentliche*) essence, substance; **4.** (*des Lebens etc.*) meaning; *ein Leben ohne* **~** a meaningless life

inhalt... *im Adj. siehe* **inhalts...**

inhaltlich I. *Adj.* (*den Text betreffend*) textual; **~e** *Zusammenfassung* summary of the contents (*Handlung*: plot); **II.** *Adv.* in content; as far as the content (*Handlung*: plot) is concerned

Inhaltsangabe *f* summary, synopsis; *e-e* **~** *machen von* summarize

inhaltsarm *Adj.* lacking in substance, shallow; *handlungsmäßig*: thin on plot

Inhaltserklärung *f Warensendung*: description of contents

inhalts|gleich *Adj. Math.* equal; **~leer**, **~los** *Adj. auch Leben*: empty, meaningless; *Buch etc.*: lacking in substance, shallow; **~reich** *Adj. Buch etc.*: substantial, *umg.* meaty; (*bedeutsam*) weighty, momentous; *Leben*: full, rich; **~schwer** *Adj.* fraught with meaning; (*bedeutsam*) momentous

Inhalts|stoff *m* content (material); **~übersicht** *f* **1.** summary, synopsis; *e-r wissenschaftlichen Arbeit: mst* abstract; **2.** → *Inhaltsverzeichnis*; **~verzeichnis** *n* list (*Buch*: table) of contents; *EDV* directory

inhärent *Adj.* inherent (+ *Dat.* in); **Inhärenz** *f; -, kein Pl.* inherence

inhomogen *Adj.* inhomogeneous; **Inhomogenität** *f* inhomogeneity

inhuman *Adj.* inhuman; **Inhumanität** *f; -, -en* **1.** *nur Sg.* inhumanity; **2.** (*Tat*) inhuman act, act of inhumanity (*od.* cruelty)

Initial *n; -s, -e* → *Initiale*; **Initialbuchstabe** *m* initial letter; **Initiale** *f; -, -n auch Buchmalerei*: initial

Initial|sprengstoff *m* initiator (explosive); **~wort** *n Ling.* acronym; **~zünder** *m* booster; **~zündung** *f* **1.** booster; **2.** *fig.* (*zündende Idee*) initial (*od.* original) idea

Initiation *f; -, -en* initiation; **Initiationsritus** *m* initiation rite, rite of initiation

initiativ *Adj.* with initiative, self-starting; **~** *werden* take the initiative

Initiativ|antrag *m Parl.* notice of motion; **~begehren** *n schw. Parl.* petition for the implementation of a referendum; **~bewerbung** *f* unsolicited application, job application made on one's own intitiative, *Am. umg.* cold (*od.* over-the-transom) application

Initiative *f; -, -n* **1.** initiative; *die* **~** *ergreifen* take the initiative; *aus eigener*

~ on one's own initiative, of one's own accord; **2.** (*Bürgerinitiative etc.*) action group; **Initiativgruppe** *f* action group

Initiator *m*; *-s, -en*, **~in** *f*; *-, -nen* initiator

initiieren *v/t.* initiate, start *s.th.* off

Injektion *f*; *-, -en*; *Med.* injection, *Brit. umg.* jab, *Am. umg.* shot

Injektions|lösung *f Med.* injection solution; *nach Injektion*: injected solution; **~nadel** *f* hypodermic needle; **~spritze** *f* hypodermic syringe

injizieren *v/t.* inject

Injurie *f*; *-, -n* (*Beleidigung*) injury

Inka *m*; *-(s), -(s), (-s); hist.* Inca; **~bein** *n*, **~knochen** *m Anat.* incarial bone; **~reich** *n* Inca Empire

Inkarnation *f*; *-, -en*; *kirchl.* incarnation; *fig. auch* embodiment

Inkassant *m*; *-en, -en*, **~in** *f*; *-, -nen*; *österr.* collector (of money due)

Inkasso *n*; *-s, -s od. österr. -i*; *Wirts.* collection; **2bevollmächtigt** *Adj.* authorized to collect; **~büro** *n* collection agency; **~verfahren** *n* collection procedure; **~vollmacht** *f* authority to collect

Inkaufnahme ; *-, kein Pl.* acceptance

inkl. *Abk.* (*inklusive*) incl.

Inklusion *f*; *-, -en*; *Math., Med., Min.* inclusion

Inklusivangebot *n* all-in (*Am.* all-inclusive) package

inklusive I. *Präp.* including, inclusive of; **~ Verpackung** *Wirts.* packing included; **II.** *Adv.*: *bis zum 3. Mai* **~** up to and including May 3rd; *Montag bis* **~** *Freitag* Monday to Friday, *Am.* Monday through Friday

Inklusivpreis *m* inclusive (*od.* all-in) price

inkognito I. *Adv. reisen etc.*: incognito; **II. Inkognito** *n*; *-s, -s* disguise; *sein In-kognito wahren* remain incognito, preserve one's disguise; *sein Inkognito lüften* reveal one's (true) identity, drop one's mask

inkohärent *Adj.* incoherent; **Inkohärenz** *f*; *-, -en* incoherence

inkompatibel *Adj.* incompatible; **Inkompatibilität** *f*; *-, -en* incompatibility

inkompetent *Adj.* incompetent; **Inkompetenz** *f*; *-, -en* incompetence

inkongruent *Adj. Math.* incongruent; *fig.* incongruous; **Inkongruenz** *f*; *-, -en*; *Math.* incongruence; *fig.* incongruity

inkonsequent *Adj.* **1.** *im Verhalten etc.*: inconsistent; **2.** (*unlogisch*) inconsequential, illogical; **Inkonsequenz** *f*; *-, -en* **1.** inconsistency; **2.** inconsequentiality, illogicality

inkonsistent *Adj.* inconsistent; **Inkonsistenz** *f*; *-, kein Pl.* inconsistency

Inkontinenz *f*; *-, -en*; *Med.* incontinence

inkonvertibel *Adj. Wirts.* inconvertible

Inkorporation *f*; *-, -en* incorporation, uptake; **inkorporieren** *v/t.* incorporate (*in* + *Akk.* into)

inkorrekt *Adj.* (*unrichtig*) incorrect; (*ungenau*) inaccurate; *Benehmen, Kleidung etc.*: inappropriate, *stärker*: improper; **Inkorrektheit** *f* **1.** *kein Pl.* (*Unrichtigkeit*) incorrectness; (*Ungenauigkeit*) inaccuracy; *des Benehmens etc.* inappropriateness, *stärker*: impropriety; **2.** mistake; inaccuracy; *im Benehmen*: breach of etiquette, gaffe, faux pas; *stärker* impropriety

Inkraftsetzung *f Amtsspr. e-s Gesetzes*: introduction, enactment; **In-Kraft-Treten** *n*: *-s, kein Pl.*: *bei* **~** *des Gesetzes*

etc. when the law *etc.* comes into effect (*od.* is introduced); *Tag des* **~s** effective date

Inkreis *m Geom.* inscribed circle

Inkrement *n*; *-(e)s, -e*; *Math., Phys.* increment

inkriminieren *v/t.* incriminate; **inkriminiert I.** *P.P.* → *inkriminieren*; **II.** *Adj.* illegal, banned

Inkubation *f*; *-, -en* incubation; **Inkubationszeit** *f* incubation (*Med. auch* latency) period

Inkubator *m*; *-s, -en* incubator

Inkubus *m*; *-, Inkuben* incubus (*Pl.* incubi)

Inkunabel *f*; *-, -n* incunabulum (*Pl.* incunabula); early printed book

Inland *n*; *-(e)s, kein Pl.*; (*Ggs. Ausland*) home; *im In- und Ausland* at home and abroad; *im* **~** *hergestelltes Erzeugnis etc.* domestic product *etc.*; *für das* **~** *bestimmt* for home consumption; **Inland...** *im Subst. mst* home ..., internal ..., domestic ...; **Inlandeis** *n Geol.* ice sheet

Inländer *m*; *-s, -*, **~in** *f*; *-, -nen* resident; (*Staatsbürger*) national

Inlandflug *m* domestic (*od.* internal) flight

inländisch *Adj. mst* home ..., domestic ..., internal ...

Inlands|absatz *m Wirts.* domestic sales *Pl.*; **~auftrag** *m* domestic order; **~brief** *m* inland (*Am.* ordinary) letter; **~geschäft** *n* domestic trade; **~gespräch** *n* inland (*Am.* domestic) call; **~markt** *m* home (*od.* domestic) market; **~porto** *n* inland (*Am.* domestic) postage; **~presse** *f* domestic press; **~tarif** *m* inland (*Am.* domestic) rate; **~telegramm** *n* inland (*Am.* domestic) telegram

Inlaut *m Ling.* medial sound; **inlautend** *Adj. Ling.* medial

Inlay ['ɪnleɪ] *n*; *-s, -s* inlay

Inlett *n*; *-(e)s, -e od. -s* ticking

inliegend *Adj. Amtsspr.* enclosed

Inliner ['ɪnlaɪnɐ] *m*; *-s, -s* **1.** (*Skate*) in-liner; **2.** (*Skater*) in-liner; **Inlineskate** ['ɪnlaɪnskeɪt] *n*; *-s, -s* in-line skate; **inlineskaten** *v/i.* (*untr., hat -ge-*) go (*od.* be) in-line skating (*Am. auch* roller-blading); **Inlineskater** *m*; *-s, -* **1.** *Rollschuh*: in-line skate; **2.** *Person*: in-line skater; **Inlineskaterin** *f*; *-, -nen* → **Inlineskater** 2

in medias res: **~** *gehen geh.* get straight to the point, plunge in medias res *förm.*

inmitten I. *Präp.* in the middle (*lit.* midst) of; **II.** *Adv.*: **~** *von* (*umgeben von*) in the middle (*lit.* midst) of, among(st), surrounded by

in natura *Adv.* in real life; *Person: auch* in the flesh

inne *adj.*: *e-r Sache* **~** *sein geh.* be aware of *s.th. allg.*

inne|haben *v/t.* (*unreg., trennb., hat -ge-*) (*Amt, Stelle, Rekord*) hold; **~halten** *v/i.* (*unreg., trennb., hat -ge-*) stop, pause

innen *Adv.* **1.** (on the) inside; **~** *und außen* inside and out(side); *nach* **~** *tragen etc.*: inside, *nach* **~** (*zu*) inward(s); *nach* **~** *gekehrt Mantel*: inside-out; *Pelzfutter etc.*: on the inside, facing inwards; *fig. Person*: introspective, *stärker*: introverted; *von* **~** from (the) inside; *hast du das Haus von* **~** *gesehen?* have you been inside the house?; **2.** *österr.* (*hier drinnen*) inside; *hier* **~** in here

Innen|abmessungen *Pl.* inside mea-

surements (*od.* dimensions); **~ansicht** *f* interior view; **~arbeiten** *Pl. beim Bau*: indoor work *Sg.*; **~architekt** *m*, **~architektin** *f* interior designer; **~architektur** *f* interior design; **~aufnahme** *f Fot.* indoor (*Film*: studio) shot; **~ausbau** *m* interior conversion (work), *Am.* remodeling, rehabbing; **~ausstattung** *f e-r Wohnung*: décor; *Mot.* interior fittings *Pl.*; *Flug.* inside furnishings *Pl.*; **~bahn** *f Sport* inside lane (*od.* track); **~beleuchtung** *f* interior lighting; **~bezirk** *m e-r Stadt etc.*: central area (*od.* district); **~dienst** *m* office work; *im* **~** *tätig sein* work in the office (*umg.* at base); **~druck** *m* interior pressure; **~durchmesser** *m* inside diameter; **~einrichtung** *f* → **Innenausstattung**; **~fläche** *f* inside surface; *der Hand*: palm; **~hand** *f Boxsport* palm (*od.* inside) of the hand; **~hof** *m* (inner) courtyard; **~kante** *f* inside (*od.* inner) edge; **~kurve** *f* inside bend

Innenleben *n* **1.** inner life; **2.** *fig. e-r Uhr etc.*: internal *od.* inner mechanism (*od.* workings *Pl.*), *umg.* insides *Pl.*; → *auch* **Innereien** 2

Innenleuchte *f Mot.* courtesy light

Innen|minister *m*, **~ministerin** *f Pol.* minister of the interior; *in GB*: Home Secretary; *in den USA*: etwa Secretary of the Interior; **~ministerium** *n* interior ministry; *in GB*: Home Office; *in den USA*: etwa Department of the Interior

Innen|ohr *n Anat.* inner ear; **~pfosten** *m Sport* inside of the post

Innenpolitik *f Pol.* domestic policy (*od.* policies *Pl.*); **innenpolitisch I.** *Adj.* domestic (political), internal; **~e Ereignisse** *auch* home affairs; **II.** *Adv.* on the domestic front; **~** *gesehen* as far as domestic policy is (*od.* home affairs are) concerned

Innen|raum *m* interior; **~rist** *m Anat.* inside of the foot; **~rolle** *f* piece of hair curled under (*as in a pageboy cut*); **~seite** *f* inside; **~ski** *m* inside ski; **~spiegel** *m Mot.* inside mirror; **~stadt** *f* town (*od.* city) cent|re (*Am.* -er), inner city, *Am. auch* downtown; *in der* **~** *leben* live in the cent|re (*Am.* -er) of town (*od.* in the inner city), *Am.* live downtown; **~stürmer** *m*, **~stürmerin** *f Sport* inside forward (*Fussball: auch* central striker); **~tasche** *f* inside pocket; **~temperatur** *f* inside (*im Haus etc.*: indoor) temperature; **~tür** *f* inside door; **~verkleidung** *f* inside (*od.* interior) lining; **~wand** *f* inside wall; **~welt** *f* inner world; **~winkel** *m Math.* internal angle

inner... *Adj.* (*auf der Innenseite*) inside; *Pol.* internal, domestic; (*seelisch*) inner; (*geistig*) mental; *Med., Blutung, Medizin etc.*: internal; *das* **~e** *Auge* one's mind's eye; *ohne* **~en** *Halt* very insecure; **~er Konflikt** inner conflict; **~er Monolog** interior monolog(ue); **~e Ordnung** internal order; **~e Unruhe** agitation; **~e Uhr** body clock, *fachspr.* circadian rhythms; **~e Ruhe** peace of mind; **~e Stimme** inner voice, voice inside (*od.* within) one; **~er Wert** intrinsic value

inner|betrieblich *Adj. Wirts.* internal; **~e Ausbidung** *etc.* in-house training *etc.*; **~deutsch** *Adj.* **1.** German, domestic, internal; **2.** *hist.* (*deutsch-deutsch*) German-German, inter-German; **~dienstlich** *Adj.* internal, in-house

Innere¹ *n*; *-n und Innern, kein Pl.* **1.** *örtlich:* interior (*auch Geog.*), inside; (*Mitte*) heart, core, cent|re (*Am.* -er); *im ~n* inside; *e-s Landes:* in the interior; *Pol.* on the home front; *Minister des ~n* → *Innenminister.* **2.** *fig. e-s Menschen:* inner being, (*Geist*) mind, heart, soul; *im ~n* at heart, secretly; *tief im ~n fig.* deep down (inside); *ich würde gern wissen, was in s-m ~n so vor sich geht* what's going on inside him, what's going through his mind (*od.* head)

Innere² *f*; *-n, -n; Med. umg.* **1.** internal medicine; **2.** *in der ~n arbeiten/liegen umg.* work in internal medicine / be in an internal ward

Innereien *Pl.* **1.** innards; *von Geflügel: auch* giblets; *von Fisch:* guts; **2.** *umg. fig.* insides, innards, entrails

innereuropäisch *Adj.* European, ... within Europe

innerhalb I. *Präp.* inside, within (*auch fig.*); *zeitlich:* within, in; (*während*) within, during; *~ e-r Woche* within a week; **II.** *Adv.: ~ von* within; *zeitlich: auch* within a period of

innerkirchlich *Adj.* within the Church

innerlich I. *Adj.* **1.** *Med.* internal; **2.** *Gefühle etc.:* inner; (*~ veranlagt*) introspective; (*gefühlsmäßig, gefühlsbetont*) emotional; **II.** *Adv.* **1.** *Med.* internally; *~ (anzuwenden) Pharm.* for internal use (only); **2.** *betroffen etc.:* inwardly; (*deep down*) inside; (*insgeheim*) secretly; *~ lachen* laugh to o.s.; **Innerlichkeit** *f* sensitivity; (*Tiefe*) depth; (*nach Innen gekehrtes Wesen*) introspection

inner|örtlich *Adj.* local; *~orts Adv. bes. österr., schw.* locally; (*in der Stadt*) in the town; *~parteilich Adj. Pol.* inner-party ..., internal; *~e Kämpfe* (party) infighting

innerst... *Adj.* innermost; *fig. auch* inmost; *die ~en Gedanken* one's most secret thoughts

innerstaatlich *Adj.* internal

Innerstadt *f schw.* town cent|re (*Am.* -er), inner city, *Am auch* downtown; **innerstädtisch** *Adj.* urban, inner-city ..., intra-city ...

Innerste *n*; *-n, kein Pl.* the innermost part; (*Mittelpunkt*) heart, core; *bis ins ~ fig.* to the heart (*od.* core); *in s-m ~n* deep down (inside), in his heart of hearts

innert *Präp. österr., schw.* (*binnen, innerhalb*) *~ e-s Jahres od. e-m Jahr* within a year

inne|werden *v/i.* (*unreg., trennb., ist -ge-*) *geh.: e-r Sache ~* become aware of s.th.; *~wohnen v/i.* (*trennb., hat -ge-*): *e-r Sache ~* be inherent in s.th.; *~wohnend Adj.* inherent (+ *Dat.* in), innate (in)

innig I. *Adj.* (*zärtlich*) tender, affectionate; (*glühend*) ardent, fervent; (*herzlich*) heartfelt, sincere; *Freundschaft etc.:* close; **II.** *Adv.* tenderly etc.; → *heiß* II; **Innigkeit** *f* tenderness; ardo(u)r; sincerity; closeness; → *innig* I; **inniglich** *Adv.* → *innig* II; **innigst I.** *Adj.: mein ~er Wunsch* my greatest desire; **II.** *Adv.: ~ wünschen* wish fervently (*od.* with all one's heart)

Innovation *f*; *-, -en* innovation; **innovationsfeindlich** *Adj.* hostile to (any form of) innovation, unwilling to adapt (to the times), Luddite; **innovationsfreudig** *Adj.* innovative; **innovativ** *Adj.* innovative; **innovatorisch** *Adj.* innovational

Innung *f* (trade) guild; *die ganze ~ blamieren umg. fig.* let the side down

Innungs|krankenkasse *f health insurance scheme* (*Am. plan*) run by a guild; *~meister m, ~meisterin f* guild master; *~verband m* association of trade guilds; *~versammlung f* guild meeting; *~wesen n; -s, kein Pl.* guild system

inoffiziell *Adj.* unofficial; (*zwanglos*) *Gespräche etc.:* informal; *~e Erklärung* off-the-record statement; **inoffiziös** *Adj.* unofficial

inoperabel *Adj. Med.* inoperable

inopportun *Adj.* inopportune; **Inopportunität** *f* inopportunity

in petto *Adv.: etw. ~ haben* have s.th. up one's sleeve

in puncto *Präp.* when it comes to, where (*od.* as far as) ... is (*od.* are) concerned, in matters of, as regards

Input *m*, *n*; *-s, -s; EDV, Wirts.* input

Inquilin *m*; *-en, -en; Zool.* inquiline

Inquisition *f*; *-,-en* **1.** *nur Sg.: hist.* Inquisition; **2.** *fig.* inquisition; **Inquisitionsgericht** *n hist.* Court of Inquisition; **Inquisitor** *m*; *-s, -en; hist.* inquisitor; **inquisitorisch** *Adj.* inquisitorial

ins *Präp. + Art.* **1.** → *in¹*; **2.** *in festen Verbindungen: bis ~ Einzelne* down to the last detail; *~ Leben rufen* bring s.th. into being; **3.** *mit subst. Inf.: ~ Schleudern geraten od. kommen* go into a skid; *~ Schwimmen kommen* start to flounder

Insasse *m*; *-n, -n e-s Autos etc.:* passenger; *e-s Gefängnisses:* inmate; **Insassenversicherung** *f Mot.* passenger insurance (cover); **Insassin** *f*; *-, -nen* → *Insasse*

insbesondere, insbesondre *Adv.* particularly, (e)specially, in particular

Inschrift *f* inscription; *auf Gräbern etc.: auch* epigraph

Insekt *n*; *-s, -en; Zool.* insect, *Am. umg.* bug; *~en fressend* insectivorous

Insekten|bekämpfung *f* insect (*od.* pest) control; *~bekämpfungsmittel n* insecticide; *~forscher m, ~forscherin f* entomologist; *~fraß m* insect damage; *~fresser m* insectivore, insect-eater; *~gift n* **1.** *von Insekten:* insect poison; **2.** *gegen Insekten:* insecticide; *~kunde f* entomology; *~plage f* plague of insects; *~spray m, n* insect (*Am. umg.* bug) spray; *~staat m* insect colony; *~stich m* insect (*Am. umg.* bug) bite; *~vertilgungsmittel n* insecticide

Insektizid *n*; *-s, -e* insecticide

Insel *f*; *-, -n* island (*auch fig. und Verkehrsinsel*); *poet.* isle; *die ~ Wight* the Isle of Wight; *die Britischen ~n* the British Isles

Insel|berg *m Geol.* inselberg; *~bewohner m, ~bewohnerin f* islander

Inselchen *n* islet

Insel|gruppe *f* group of islands, archipelago; *~kette f* string of islands; *~lage f* island position; *~paradies n* island (*od.* tropical) paradise; *~reich n* island kingdom; *~republik f* island republic; *~staat m* island state; *~volk n* (nation of) islanders *Pl.*; *~welt f* (group of) islands *Pl.*

Insemination ; *-, -en; Med., Zool.* insemination; **inseminieren** *v/t.* inseminate

Inserat *n*; *-(e)s, -e* advertisement, ad, *Brit. auch* advert; *ein ~ aufgeben* → *inserieren* II; **Inseratenteil** *n* the advertisements, advertisement (*od.* advertising, *Am. auch* classified) section,

Inserent *m*; *-en, -en,* **Inserentin** *f*; *-, -nen* advertiser; **inserieren I.** *v/i.* advertise; **II.** *v/i.* advertise, place an advertisement (in the *od.* a paper); put an ad in the paper *umg.*

insgeheim *Adv.* secretly; behind *s.o.'s* back

insgesamt *Adv.* altogether, in all; (*als Ganzes*) as a whole; *~ gesehen* on the whole, all in all; *er erhielt ~ 500 Briefe* he received a total of 500 letters; *s-e Schulden betragen ~ ...* his debts total ...

Inside ['ɪnsaɪd] *m*; *-(s), -s schw. Sport* inside forward

Insider ['ɪnsaɪdɐ] *m*; *-s, -* insider; *~geschäft n* insider dealing; *~e* insider trading *Sg.*, insider dealings (*od.* dealing *Sg.*); *~kreise Pl.* the inner circle, those (*od.* people) in the know; *~wissen n* inside knowledge

Insignien *Pl.* insignia

insignifikant *Adj.* insignificant

insistieren *v/i.* insist (*auf + Akk.* on); *darauf ~, dass ...* insist that ...

inskribieren *österr. Univ.* **I.** *v/i.* register, enrol(l); **II.** *v/t.* register *s.o.,* enrol(l) *s.o.;* **Inskription** *f*; *-, -en; österr.* registration, enrol(l)ment

inskünftig *Adv. schw.* in (the) future

insofern I. *Adv.* (*in dieser Hinsicht*) as far as that goes (*od.* is concerned), from that point of view; **II.** *Konj.: ~ (als)* in so far as, insofar as, inasmuch as, in that; (*wenn, falls*) if; *er hat ~ Recht, als ...* he's right in so far as ...

insolent *Adj.* insolent; **Insolenz** *f*; *-, -en* insolence

insolubel *Adj. Chem.* insoluble

insolvent *Adj. Wirts.* insolvent; **Insolvenz** *f*; *-, -en* insolvency; → *Bankrott*

insoweit *Adv. und Konj.* → *insofern*

in spe *Adj.* ...-to-be, future ...; *ein Arzt ~ auch* a doctor in the making

Inspekteur *m*; *-s, -e* inspector; *Mil.* Chief of Staff

Inspektion *f*; *-, -en* **1.** inspection; **2.** *Mot.* service; *den Wagen zur ~ bringen* put the car in for a service; **3.** (*Amt*) inspectorate

Inspektions|gang *m* inspection round; *~reise f* tour of inspection

Inspektor *m*; *-s, -en,* *~in f*; *-, -nen* inspector

Inspiration *f*; *-, -en* inspiration; **inspirieren** *v/t.* inspire; *j-n zu e-m Gedicht / e-m Gemälde etc. ~* inspire s.o. to write a poem / paint a picture *etc.*; *sich ~ lassen von* draw inspiration from

Inspizient *m*; *-en, -en,* *~in f*; *-, -nen Theat.* stage manager

inspizieren *v/t.* inspect; examine

instabil *Adj.* unstable; *Konstruktion: auch* not stable; **Instabilität** *f*; *-, -en mst Sg.* instability

Installateur *m*; *-s, -e,* *~in f*; *-, -nen* plumber; *für Gasanlagen:* gas (*Am.* pipe) fitter; *Etech.* electrician; **Installation** *f*; *-, -en* **1.** (*das Installieren*) installation; **2.** (*Anlage*) installation; (*Wasserleitungen*) plumbing; **installieren I.** *v/t.* put in, fit, instal(l); **II.** *v/refl.: sich ~* instal(l) o.s.

instand, in Stand *Adv.: ~ halten* keep in good condition (*od.* repair); maintain, service; *~ setzen* repair, (*renovieren*) renovate, (*Gerät etc.*) recondition; *j-n ~ setzen zu* (+ *Inf.*) enable s.o. to (+ *Inf.*), put s.o. in a position to (+ *Inf.*); *~ besetzen* (*Haus*) occupy (*od.* squat) and refurbish

Instandbesetzung *f* squatter-renova-

tion
Instandhaltung *f* upkeep, maintenance; *Tech., Mot.* servicing; **Instandhaltungskosten** *Pl.* maintenance costs
inständig I. *Adj.* urgent; **II.** *Adv.: j-n ~ bitten* implore; **Inständigkeit** *f e-r Bitte etc.*: urgency
Instandsetzung *f* repair; (*Renovierung*) renovation; **Instandsetzungsarbeit** *f* repair work, repairs *Pl.* (*an + Dat.* on); **Instandstellung** *f schw.* repair; (*Renovierung*) renovation
Instant|getränk ['instant-] *n* instant drink; **~kaffee** *m* instant coffee
Instanz *f*, -, -en (*Dienststelle*) authority; *Jur.* instance; **höhere ~en** higher authorities (*Jur.* courts); **in erster ~** *Jur.* at first instance; **Gericht erster ~** court of first instance, (*Strafgericht*) *auch* trial court; **in letzter ~** without further appeal; **in letzter ~ entscheiden** make the final decision; *fig.* have the final say, ultimately decide; **Instanzenweg** *m Jur.* (successive) stages *Pl.* of appeal; → *auch* **Dienstweg**; **auf dem ~** through the prescribed channels
Instinkt *m*; -(e)s, -e instinct; *weitS. auch* feeling; **s-m ~ folgen** follow one's instincts (*umg.* one's nose); **mein ~ sagt mir** my instinct tells me, I have an instinctive feeling; **sich an die niederen ~e richten** appeal to the baser human instincts; **instinkthaft** *Adj.* instinctive; **Instinkthandlung** *f* instinctive act (*od.* reaction); **instinktiv I.** *Adj.* instinctive, intuitive; *Reaktion: auch* visceral; *Angst etc.*: instinctive, innate; **II.** *Adv.* instinctively, intuitively; **instinktlos** *Adj.* lacking in instinct; *weitS.* (*taktlos*) tactless, insensitive; **Instinktlosigkeit** *f* lack of (an *od.* the) instinct; *weitS.* tactlessness, insensitivity; **instinktmäßig I.** *Adj.* instinctive; **II.** *Adv.* instinctively, on (an) instinct; **instinktsicher I.** *Adj.: ~ sein* have a good (*od.* an unerring) instinct, *umg.* have a good nose; **II.** *Adv.: ~ handeln* rely on one's instincts
Institut *n*; -(e)s, -e institute; **Institution** *f*, -, -en institution (*auch fig.*); **institutionalisieren** *v/t.* institutionalize; **Institutionalisierung** *f* institutionalization; **institutionell** *Adj.* institutional
Instituts|bibliothek *f* institute library; **~leiter** *m*, **~leiterin** *f* head of an (*od.* the) institute
instruieren *v/t.* instruct *s.o.*, give *s.o.* instructions (**über** + *Akk.* on); *auch Mil.* brief (on); (*unterrichten*) inform (about); **Instruktion** *f*; -, -en instruction; (*Anweisung*) *auch* directions *Pl.*; **instruktiv** *Adj.* instructive
Instrument *n*; -(e)s, -e instrument; (*Gerät*) *auch* tool, implement; **instrumental** *Adj.* instrumental
Instrumental *m*; -s, -e; *Ling.* (*Kasus*) instrumental
Instrumental|aufnahme *f* instrumental version; **~begleitung** *f* instrumental accompaniment
Instrumentalis *m*; -, *Instrumentales*; *Ling.* → *Instrumental*
instrumentalisieren *v/t.* **1.** *fig.* instrumentalize; (*ausnutzen*) exploit; **2.** *Mus.* arrange for instruments; **Instrumentalisierung** *f* **1.** *fig.* instrumentalization; (*Ausnutzung*) exploitation; **2.** *Mus.* arrangement for instruments; **Instrumentalist** *m*; -en, -en, **Instrumentalistin** *f*; -, -nen instrumentalist

Instrumental|musik *f* instrumental music; **~satz** *m* **1.** *Ling.* instrumental clause; **2.** *Mus.* instrumental movement; **~stück** *n* instrumental piece; *modernes*: instrumental
Instrumentarium *n*; -s, *Instrumentarien*; *Mus. und fig.* instruments *Pl.*; **Instrumentation** *f*; -, -en; *Mus.* instrumentation, orchestration
instrumentell *Adj.* **1.** (*mit Instrumenten*) instrumental, using instruments; **2.** (*funktional*) instrumental
Instrumenten|bau *m* instrument making; **~bauer** *m*, **~bauerin** *f* instrument maker; **~beleuchtung** *f Mot.* dashboard lighting; **~brett** *n* instrument panel; *Mot. auch* dashboard; *Flug. auch* control panel; **~flug** *m* instrument flying (*od.* flight); **~macher** *m*, **~macherin** *f* instrument maker
instrumentieren I. *v/t.* **1.** *Mus.* arrange (for instruments), instrument, orchestrate; **2.** instrument, equip with instruments; **II.** *v/i. Med.* assist at a surgical operation by passing the instruments; **Instrumentierung** *f* arrangement (for instruments), instrumentation
Insubordination *f*; -, -en insubordination
insuffizient *Adj. bes. Med.* insufficient; *Organ: auch* defective; **Insuffizienz** *f*; -, -en; *bes. Med.* insufficiency
Insulaner *m*; -s, -, **~in** *f*; -, -nen islander; **insular** *Adj.* insular
Insulin *n*; -s, kein *Pl.* insulin; **~mangel** *m Med.* insulin deficiency; **~schock** *m Med.* insulin (*od.* hypoglyc[a]emic) shock; **~spritze** *f* insulin injection (*umg.* jab, *Am.* shot)
inszenatorisch *Adj.* directorial; **inszenieren** *v/t. Theat.* stage, put on stage, produce, (*auch Sendung*) mount, *als Regisseur* direct; (*Film*) produce, *als Regisseur:* direct; *fig.* (*Aufruhr, Streik etc.*) stage; *pej.* stage-manage; (*Intrige*) conduct, (*Kampagne etc.*) *auch* orchestrate; **e-n Streit ~** *umg. auch* kick up a row; **Inszenierung** *f* production; **~: X** directed by X
intakt *Adj.* intact (*auch Verhältnis*); *Organe etc.: auch* in good shape; *Motor etc.: auch* in good working order
Intarsien *Pl.* intarsia *Sg.*, inlaid work *Sg.*, marquetry *Sg.*
integer *Adj.: integre Persönlichkeit* person of integrity; **~ sein** have integrity
integral *Adj.* integral; **Integral** *n*; -s, -e; *Math.* integral
Integral|gleichung *f Math.* integral equation; **~helm** *m* full-face helmet; **~rechnung** *f Math.* integral calculus; **~zeichen** *n Math.* integral sign
Integration *f*; -, -en integration; **Integrationsfigur** *f* unifying figure; **Integrationsprozess** *m* process of integration; **integrativ** *Adj.* integrative
integrierbar *Adj.* integrable
integrieren I. *v/t. Math. und fig.* integrate (**in** + *Akk.* into); **II.** *v/refl.: sich ~** integrate (o.s.), become integrated (**in** + *Akk.* into); **Integrierung** *f* integration
Integrität *f*; -, kein *Pl.* integrity (*auch e-s Staates*)
Intellekt *m*; -(e)s, kein *Pl.* intellect
Intellektualität *f* ; -, kein *Pl.* intellectualism
intellektuell *Adj.* intellectual, *umg.* highbrow; *Stoff, Person:* (*durchgeistigt*) *auch* cerebral; **Intellektuelle** *m, f*; -n, -n intellectual, *umg.* highbrow
intelligent *Adj.* intelligent, bright

Intelligenz *f*, -, -en **1.** *nur Sg.* intelligence; **künstliche ~** artificial intelligence; **2.** *nur Sg.*; (*Intelligenzschicht*) intelligentsia; **3.** *mst Pl.*: **gibt es außerirdische ~en?** is there intelligent life in the rest of the universe?; **~bestie** *f umg.* egghead, brain(box); **~grad** *m* level of intelligence
Intelligenzija *f*; -, kein *Pl.* intelligentsia
Intelligenzleistung *f* feat of (human) intelligence
Intelligenzler *m*; -s, -, **~in** *f*; -, -nen *umg.* egghead
Intelligenz|quotient *m* intelligence quotient, IQ; **~test** *m* intelligence test
Intendant *m*; -en, -en, **~in** *f*; -, -nen; *Theat. etc.* (artistic and business) director, business manager and artistic director; **Intendantur** *f*; -, -en → **Intendanz** 1,2; **Intendanz** *f*; -, -en **1.** (artistic and business) directorship; **2.** (*Büro*) manager and artistic director's office(s *Pl.*)
intendieren *v/t.* (*beabsichtigen*) intend; (*hinarbeiten auf*) aim at, plan
Intensität *f*; -, -en, *mst Sg.* intensity; **intensiv I.** *Adj.* intensive; *Gefühl, Interesse, Schmerz etc.*: intense; (*gründlich*) intensive, thorough; **II.** *Adv.* intensively; (*stark*) intensely; **sich ~ bemühen** try very hard, make a great (*od.* tremendous) effort; **~ nachdenken** think hard; **j-n ~ ansehen** give s.o. a long, hard look
...intensiv im *Adj.* **1.** *in hohem Maß aufweisend: gefühls~* emotionally intense; (*empfindlich*) (highly) sensitive; (*Kondom*) extra sensitive; **lärm~** (extremely) noisy; **2.** *in hohem Maß erfordernd: arbeits~* labo(u)r-intensive; **bewegungs~** *Kinder, Tiere* (very) lively, (very) active; *Trainingsform* very active, involving continual movement; **zeit~** time-consuming
Intensiv|anbau *m Agr.* intensive cultivation; **~bildung** *f Ling.* intensive form; **~haltung** *f Agr.* intensive rearing
intensivieren *v/t.* intensify; (*Bemühungen*) *auch* step up; **Intensivierung** *f* intensification; **~ von Bemühungen** *auch* stepping up of efforts
Intensiv|kurs *m* crash course; **~medizin** *f* intensive care; **~station** *f Med.* intensive care unit, *abgek.* ICU
Intention *f*; -, -en intention; **intentional** *Adj.* intentional
interagieren *v/i.* interact; **Interaktion** *f*; -, -en interaction; **interaktiv** *Adj.* interactive; **Interaktivität** *f*; -e, kein *Pl.* interactivity
Intercity *m*; -s, -s intercity (train); → *auch IC*; **Intercity-Expresszug** *m* intercity express (train); → *auch ICE*; **Intercity-Zug** *m* intercity (train); → *auch IC*
interdependent *Adj.* interdependent; **Interdependenz** *f* interdependence
Interdikt *n kirchl.* interdict
interdisziplinär *Adj.* interdisciplinary
interessant I. *Adj.* interesting; *Geschäft etc.*: attractive; **das Interessante daran** the interesting thing about it; **er will sich bei ihr bloß ~ machen** he's just trying to impress her; **II.** *Adv.: er kann ~ erzählen** he's a good story(-) teller; **interessanterweise** *Adv.* interestingly (enough), it's interesting that ...; **Interessantheit** *f* interest, interestingness
Interesse *n*; -s, -n interest (**an** + *Dat.*, **für** in); **das ~ verlieren** lose interest; **~ zeigen** show an (*od.* some) interest

I

(*für* in); **~ haben an** (+ *Dat.*) *od. für* be interested in; *es ist für mich nicht von ~* it's of no interest to me; *sein besonderes ~ gilt* he's particularly interested in, his special area of interest is; *in j-s ~ sein* be in s.o.'s interest; *ich tat es in d-m ~* for your sake; *im öffentlichen ~* in the public interest; *j-s ~n wahrnehmen/vertreten* look after/represent s.o.'s interests; *es besteht kein ~ an* (+ *Dat*) nobody's interested in; (*e-m Artikel etc.*) there's no demand for; **interessehalber** *Adv.* out of interest, as a matter of interest

interesselos *Adj.* uninterested, indifferent; **Interesselosigkeit** *f* indifference; *stärker:* apathy

Interessen|ausgleich *m* balancing of interests; **~gebiet** *n* field (*od.* area) of interest; **~gegensatz** *m* conflict of interests; **~gemeinschaft** *f* interest group; *Wirts.* (*Vereinbarung*) pooling agreement; (*Vereinigung*) combine, pool; (*Kartell*) syndicate; **~gruppe** *f* interest group; *Pol.* lobby; **~konflikt** *m* conflict of interests; **~lage** *f: die ~ erforderte es, dass* it was in their etc. interests to (+ *Inf.*); **~schwerpunkt** *m* focus of interest; **~sphäre** *f* sphere of influence

Interessent *m; -en, -en* **1.** *für e-e Ware etc.:* prospective buyer; *wir haben schon drei ~en auch* there are already three people interested, three people have already shown (an) interest; **2.** *für e-n Kurs etc.:* interested person; *~en sollen sich melden etc.:* anyone (*od.* those) interested; **3.** (*Bewerber*) applicant; **4.** *für e-e Sache:* interested party; **Interessentenkreis** *m* group of interested people, those *Pl.* interested; *Wirts.* prospective buyers *Pl.*, market; **Interessentin** *f; -, -nen* → *Interessent*

Interessen|verband *m* pressure group, lobby; **~vertreter** *m* representative, spokesman, spokesperson; **~vertreterin** *f* representative, spokeswoman; **~vertretung** *f* representation (of *s.o.'s* interests); (*Interessenvertreter*) body (*od.* group) representing (the interests of) *s.o.* (*od. s.th.*)

interessieren I. *v/refl.: sich ~ für* be interested in; *sich gar nicht ~ für auch* take no interest in; **II.** *v/t.* **1.** *das Buch etc. interessiert mich nicht* I'm not interested in the book *etc.*, the book *etc.* doesn't interest me; *das interessiert mich überhaupt nicht* I'm not in the least bit interested, I couldn't care less; *es wird dich ~ zu erfahren* you'll be interested to know; *das hat dich nicht zu ~!* that's none of your business!, that's no concern of yours; **2.** (*Interesse wecken*) *j-n für etw. ~* interest s.o. in s.th., get s.o. interested in s.th.; **III.** *v/i.: das interessiert nicht* that's of no interest, that's irrelevant; **interessiert I.** *P.P.* → *interessieren;* **II.** *Adj.* interested (*an* + *Dat.* in); *politisch etc. ~* interested in politics *etc.*, politically aware; *musikalisch Interessierte* the musically minded, music lovers; *sehr daran ~ sein, dass es klappt etc.* be keen (*Am.* eager) to see it work out *etc.*; **III.** *Adv.: ~ zuhören etc.* listen *etc.* intently; **Interessiertheit** *f* interest

Interferenz *f; -, -en* **1.** *Phys. und Med.* interference; **2.** *geh.* (*Überschneidung*) overlapping; **~erscheinung** *f* interference phenomenon

Interferon *n; -s, -e; Med.* interferon
interfraktionell *Adj. Pol.* inter-party

intergalaktisch *Adj. Astron.* intergalactic

interglazial *Adj. Geol.* interglacial; **Interglazial** *n; -s, -e; Geol.* interglacial (period)

Interieur [ɛ̃te'ri̯øːɐ̯] *n; -s, -s* interior

Interim *n; -s, -s* **1.** (*Übergangsregelung*) temporary arrangement, interim solution; **2.** (*Zwischenzeit*) interim; **interimistisch** *Adj.* interim ...

Interims|lösung *f* interim (*od.* stopgap) solution; **~regelung** *f* → *Interim* 1; **~regierung** *f* caretaker (*od.* interim, transitional) government

Interjektion *f; -, -en* interjection

interkantonal *Adj. schw.* intercantonal

interkommunal *Adj.* intercommunal

Interkommunion *f; -, -en; kirchl.* intercommunion

interkonfessionell *Adj.* interdenominational

interkontinental *Adj.* intercontinental

Interkontinental|flug *m* intercontinental flight; **~rakete** *f* intercontinental ballistic missile, *abgek.* ICBM

interkulturell *Adj.* intercultural, between (different) cultures

interlinear *Adj. Ling., Lit.* interlinear; **Interlinear...** *Ling., Lit. im Subst.:* interlinear

Interludium *; -s, Interludien; Mus.* interlude

intermenstrual, intermenstruell *Adj. Med.* intermenstrual

Intermezzo *n; -s, -s; Mus.* intermezzo, interlude (*auch fig.*)

interministeriell *Adj.* interministerial

intermittierend *Adj. fachspr.* intermittent; **~es Hinken** intermittent claudication

intermolekular *Adj. Chem., Phys.* intermolecular

intern I. *Adj.* internal; *das ist e-e ~e Sache auch* that's something that concerns us (*od.* them *etc.*); **II.** *Adv.* internally; (*unter uns etc.*) among ourselves (*od.* themselves *etc.*)

...intern *im Adj.:* *e-e schul~e Regelung* a school regulation, a regulation affecting only the school; *universität~e Angelegenheiten* a (*od.* the) university's internal affairs; *eine Sache vereins~ klären* settle *s.th.* within the club

internalisieren *v/t.* internalize
Internat *n; -(e)s, -e* boarding school
international I. *Adj.* international; **II.** *Adv.: ~ bekannt* internationally known, world-renowned
Internationale *f; -, -n* **1.** (*Zusammenschluss, Arbeiterbewegung*) Internationale(e); **2.** (*Lied*) Internationale
internationalisieren *v/t.* internationalize; **Internationalisierung** *f* internationalization
Internationalismus *m; -, Internationalismen* internationalism
Internationalität *f; -, kein Pl.* internationality, international character; *e-r Gemeinde etc.: auch* mix of nationalities, international mix

Internats|schule *f* boarding school; **~schüler** *m*, **~schülerin** *f* boarder
Interne *m, f; -n, -n* boarder
Internet *n; -(s), kein Pl.; EDV* Internet; *im ~* on the Internet; *im ~ surfen umg. fig.* surf the Internet; **~adresse** Internet address; **~anschluss** *m* connection to the Internet; **~café** *n* Internet café, cybercafé
internieren *v/t.* intern; *Med.* isolate; **Internierte** *m, f; -n, -n* internee; **Internierung** *f* internment; **Internierungs-**

lager *n* detention camp
Internist *m; -en, -en, ~in** *f; -, -nen Med.* internist; **internistisch** *Adj.* internal(-medical)
Internum *n; -s, Interna, mst Pl.* internal matter
interparlamentarisch *Adj.* interparliamentary
Interpellation *f; -, -en* (parliamentary) question; **interpellieren** *v/i.* ask (*od.* put) a question (in parliament)
interplanetar, interplanetarisch *Adj.* interplanetary
Interpol *f; -, kein Pl.* Interpol
Interpolation *f; -, -en; Math.* interpolation; **interpolieren** *v/t./i.* interpolate
Interpret *m; -en, -en* **1.** interpreter; *e-r Theorie etc.: auch* exponent; **2.** *Mus.* performer; (*Sänger*) singer; **Interpretation** *f* interpretation; *Mus., Gedicht etc.: auch* rendering; **interpretatorisch** *Adj.* interpretive; **interpretierbar** *Adj.* interpretable; **interpretieren** *v/t.* interpret (*auch Mus.*); (*auffassen*) *auch* understand; *Jur.* construe; *etw. als Beleidigung etc. ~* take s.th. as an insult *etc.*; **Interpretin** *f; -, -nen* → *Interpret*
Interpunktion *f* punctuation
Interpunktions|fehler *m* punctuation mistake; **~regel** *f* rule of punctuation; **~zeichen** *n* punctuation mark, mark of punctuation
Interregio *m; -s, -s,* **Interregiozug** *m Eisenb.* fast train running a regular service
interrogativ *Adj. Ling.* interrogative
Interrogativ|adverb *n* interrogative adverb; **~pronomen** *n* interrogative pronoun; **~satz** *m* interrogative clause
Interruptus *m; -, kein Pl.; umg.* coitus interruptus *fachspr.*, withdrawal
intersexuell *Adj. Biol.* intersexual
interstellar *Adj. Astron.* interstellar
Intervall *n; -(e)s, -e* interval (*auch Mus.*); **~training** *n Sport* interval training
intervenieren *v/i.* intervene; **Intervention** *f; -, -en* intervention; **Interventionismus** *m; -, kein Pl.* interventionism
Interventions|krieg *m* war of intervention; **~recht** *n* right to intervene, right of intervention
Interview ['ɪntɐvjuː] *n; -s, -s* interview; **interviewen** *v/t.* interview; **Interviewer** *m; -s, -,* **Interviewerin** *f; -, -nen* interviewer
interzellular, interzellulär *Adj. Biol., Med.* intercellular; **Interzellulare** *f; -, -n,* **Interzellularraum** *Biol., Med.* intercellular space
Interzonen|handel *m hist.* trade between the former East and West Germany; **~zug** *m hist.* train running between the former East and West Germany
Inthronisation *f; -, -en* enthronement; **inthronisieren** *v/t.* enthrone; **Inthronisierung** *f* enthronement
Intifada *f; -, kein Pl.* Intifada
intim *Adj.* intimate (*auch Kenntnisse*); *Raum: auch* cosy, *Am.* cozy; *Freundschaft:* close; (*plump-vertraulich*) chummy *umg.*; (*sexuell*) intimate, sexual; *im ~en Kreis* with close friends (and relatives); *ich bin mit ihnen nicht so ~* I don't know them that well; *~er Kenner* → *Intimkenner;* *mit j-m ~ sein sexuell:* sleep with s.o. *umg.*, be intimate with s.o. *euph.*; *miteinander ~ sein* sleep together (*od.* with each other); be intimate *euph.*
Intim|bereich *m* **1.** genitals *Pl.*; *Pflege*

des **~s** intimate hygiene; *bei Frauen:* *auch* feminine hygiene; **2.** → **Intimsphäre**; **~feind** *m*, **~feindin** *f* pet hate (*Am.* peeve); bosom (*od.* dearest) toe *lit.*; **~hygiene** *f* → **Intimpflege**

Intimität *f*; -, *-en* **1.** *nur Sg.*; (*Vertraulichkeit*) familiarity; *e-r Freundschaft:* closeness; *e-s Raums etc.*: intimacy; **2. ~en** liberties; *es kam zu ~en sexuell:* they became intimate

Intim|kenner *m*, **~kennerin** *f* expert (+ *Gen.* on), connoisseur (of); **~kontakt** *m* sexual contact; **~leben** *n* sex (*od.* love) life; **~pflege** *f* intimate hygiene; *bei Frauen: auch* feminine hygiene; **~sphäre** *f* private sphere, privacy; *in j-s ~ eindringen* invade (*od.* encroach on) s.o.'s privacy; **~spray** *m*, *n* vaginal (*od.* feminine hygiene) spray

Intimus *m*; -, *Intimi*; *mst hum.* best buddy

Intimverkehr *m* intercourse

intolerabel *Adj.* intolerable; **intolerant** *Adj.* intolerant (**gegen**[**über**] towards, *Sache: auch* of); **Intoleranz** *f* intolerance (**gegen**[**über**] towards, *Sache: auch* of)

Intonation *f Mus., Ling.* intonation; **intonieren** *v/t.* **1.** *Mus.* intone; start to play/sing; **2.** *Ling.* intonate

intrakardial *Adj. Med.* intracardiac

intrakutan *Adj. Med.* intracutaneous, intradermal

intramolekular *Adj. Chem.* intramolecular

intramuskulär *Adj. Med.* intramuscular

Intranet *n*; *-(s)*, *-s*; *EDV* intranet

intransitiv *Adj. Ling.* intransitive; **Intransitiv** *n*; *-s*, *-e*, **Intransitivum** *n*; *-s*, *Intransitiva*; *Ling.* intransitive verb

intrauterin *Adj. Med.* intrauterine; **Intrauterinpessar** *n* intrauterine device, IUD

intravaginal *Adj. Med.* intravaginal

intravenös *Adj. Med.* intravenous, IV

intrazellular, intrazellulär *Adj. Biol., Med.* intracellular

intrigant *Adj.* scheming; **Intrigant** *m*; *-en, -en*, **Intrigantin** *f*; -, *-nen* schemer, intriguer; **Intrige** *f* intrigue, scheme; **~n spinnen** intrigue, weave plots; **Intrigenspiel** *n* intrigue; **Intrigenwirtschaft** *f* plotting and scheming; *intern: auch* infighting; **intrigieren** *v/i.* intrigue, scheme

intrinsisch *Adj. Päd., Psych.* intrinsic

Introduktion *f*; -, *-en* introduction

Introitus *m*; -, - **1.** *kirchl.* introit; **2.** *Anat., Med.* introitus

introspektiv *Adj. Psych.* introspective

Introversion *f*; -, *-en*; *Psych.* introversion; **introvertiert** *Adj.* introverted; **~er Mensch** introvert; **Introvertiertheit** *f* introversion

Intrusion *f*; -, *-en*; *Geol.* intrusion; **intrusiv** *Adj.* intrusive; **Intrusivgestein** *n* intrusive rock

Intubation *f*; -, *-en*; *Med.* intubation; **intubieren** *v/t.* intubate

Intuition *f*; -, *-en* **1.** *nur Sg.*; *Fähigkeit:* intuition; **2.** (*plötzliches Erfassen*) (sudden) intuition; (*Eingebung*) (flash of) inspiration; **intuitiv** *Adj.* intuitive

intus *Adv. umg.*: **~ haben** (*Essen*) have put away, (*Getränke*) have downed, (*Alkohol*) *auch* have knocked back; *e-n ~ haben* have had one too many (*od.* had a few); *jetzt hab ich's ~ fig.* (*Grammatikregel etc.*) it's finally sunk in, I've got it now

Inuit *Pl. Indianervolk:* Inuit

invalid(e) *Adj.* disabled, *attr. auch* inva-

lid; **Invalide** *m*; *-n, -n* invalid

Invaliden|rente *f* disability pension (*od.* benefit); **~versicherung** *f schw.* disability insurance

Invalidin *f*; -, *-nen* invalid; **Invalidität** *f*; -, *kein Pl.* disablement, disability, invalidity

invariabel *Adj.* invariable

invariant *Adj.* invariant; **Invarianz** *f*; -, *kein Pl.* invariance

Invasion *f*; -, *-en* invasion (*auch fig.*); **Invasionskrieg** *m* war of invasion; **invasiv** *Adj. Med.* invasive; **Invasoren** *Pl.* invaders, invading forces

Invektive *f*; -, *-n* (*beleidigende Äußerung*) invective

Inventar *n*; *-s, -e*; (*Verzeichnis*) inventory; (*Gegenstände*) stock; **~ aufnehmen** → **inventarisieren**; **zum ~ gehören** *umg. fig. Person:* be a fixture; **Inventaraufnahme** *f*, **Inventarisation** *f*; -, *-en* stock-taking, making (*od.* taking) (an) inventory; **inventarisieren I.** *v/i.* take inventory (*od.* stock); **II.** *v/t.* take an inventory of; **Inventarisierung** *f* stock-taking, making (*od.* taking) (an) inventory

Inventar|liste *f* inventory; **~recht** *n Jur.* right of inventory; **~verzeichnis** *n* inventory

Inventur *f*; -, *-en*; *Wirts.* inventory, stocktaking; **~ machen** take inventory (*od.* stock); **~ausverkauf** *m*, **~verkauf** *m* stocktaking (*Am.* inventory) sale

invers *Adj.* inverse; **Inversion** *f*; -, *-en* inversion; **Inversionswetterlage** *f Met.* temperature inversion

Inverter *m*; *-s, -*; *Etron.* inverter; **invertieren** *v/t. fachspr.* invert; **invertiert** *Adj.* inverted

Invertzucker *m* invert sugar

investieren I. *v/t.* invest (*in + Akk.* in); *fig.* (*Zeit, Mühe etc.*) put (into), invest (in); *Geld ~ in* (+ *Akk.*) *auch umg.* sink money into; **II.** *v/i.* invest; **Investierung** *f* investment

investigativ *Adj.* investigative; **~er Journalismus** investigative journalism

Investition *f*; -, *-en*; *Wirts.* investment; (*Kapitalaufwand*) capital expenditure

Investitions... *im Subst. mst* investment ...

Investitions|anreiz *m* investment incentive; **~bank** *f* investment bank; **~bereitschaft** *f* willingness to invest; **~güter** *Pl.* capital goods; **~kosten** *Pl.* investment costs, cost *Sg.* of investment; **~lenkung** *f* investment control; **~programm** *n* investment program(me); **~spritze** *f umg.* shot in the arm; **~tätigkeit** *f* investment activity; **~zulage** *f* capital investment bonus

Investitur *f*; -, *-en* investiture; **~streit** *m hist.: der ~* the Investiture Controversy

investiv *Adj. Wirts.* investment ...; **Investivlohn** *m* portion of wages invested in share-option program(me)s

Investment *n*; *-s, -s* investment; **~anteil** *m* investment share; **~bank** *f* investment bank; **~fonds** *m* unit trust, *Am.* mutual fund; **~gesellschaft** *f* investment company; **~papier** *n* investment fund certificate; **~sparen** *n* saving through an investment trust; **~zertifikat** *n* investment trust certificate

Investor *m*; *-s, -en*, **~in** *f*; -, *-nen*; *Wirts.* investor

In-vitro-Fertilisation *f*; -, *-en*; *Med.* in vitro fertilization

involvieren *v/t.* involve

inwendig I. *Adj.* inner, inside; **II.** *Adv.* inside; → *auch* **auswendig**

inwiefern I. *Konj.* in what way, how;

→ *auch* **inwieweit**; **II.** *Interr. Adv.* in what way, in what respect, how

inwieweit I. *Konj.* to what extent; **II.** *Interr. Adv.* to what extent

Inzahlungnahme *f*; -, *-n*; *Wirts.* part exchange, trade-in

inzentiv *Adj.* providing an incentive; **Inzentiv** *n*; *-s, -e* incentive

Inzest *m*; *-(e)s, -e* incest; **inzestuös** *Adj.* incestuous

inzidentell *Adj.* incidental

Inzucht *f*; -, *-en*; *auch Zool.* inbreeding; **~schaden** *m* damage caused by inbreeding; *konkret:* defect caused by inbreeding

inzwischen *Adv.* **1.** (*in der Zwischenzeit*) in the meantime, meanwhile; (*bis dahin*) *auch* before (*od.* till, until) then; (*bis spätestens dann*) by then; *ich mache ~ das Mittagessen* (meanwhile) I'll be getting on with (the) lunch; **2.** (*nunmehr*) now; (*schon*) already; *ich habe ~ an die 600 Münzen* I've managed to collect about 600 coins so far

IOK *n*; *-s, kein Pl.*; *Abk.* (*Internationales Olympisches Komitee*) IOC

Ion *n*; *-s, -en*; *Phys.* ion

Ionen|austausch *m Chem., Phys.* ion exchange; **~austauscher** *m* ion(ic) exchanger; **~beschleuniger** *m Etron.* ion accelerator; **~bindung** *f Chem., Phys.* ionic bond; **~gitter** *n Chem.* ionic lattice; **~strahl** *m Chem., Phys.* ionic beam; **~triebwerk** *n Etron.* ion engine

Ionien (*n*); *-s*; *hist.* Ionia; **Ionier** *m*; *-s, -*, **Ionierin** *f*; -, *-nen* Ionian

Ionisation *f*; -, *-en*; *Chem., Phys.* ionization

Ionisator *m*; *m*; *-s, -en*; *Chem., Phys.* ionizer

ionisch *Adj. Archit., Ling., Lit., Philos.* Ionic; *Geog., Mus.* Ionian

ionisieren *v/t.* ionize; **Ionisierung** *f* ionization; **Ionosphäre** *f* ionosphere

i-Punkt *m* dot over the i; *bis auf den ~ fig.* down to the last detail

IQ *m*; *-(s), -(s)*; *Abk.* (*Intelligenzquotient*) IQ; **IQ-Test** *m* IQ test

IR *Abk.* → **Interregio**

i. R. *Abk.* (*im Ruhestand*) retd, retd.

IRA *f*; -, *kein Pl.*; *Abk.* (*Irisch-Republikanische Armee*) IRA

Irak *m*; *-s*; *Geog.*: (*im*) *~* (in) Iraq; **Iraker** *m*; *-s, -*, **Irakerin** *f*; -, *-nen* Iraqi, *weibl. auch*: Iraqi woman (*od.* girl); **irakisch** *Adj.* Iraqi

Iran *m*; *-s*; *Geog.*: (*im*) *~* (in) Iran; **Iraner** *m*; *-s, -*, **Iranerin** *f*; -, *-nen* Iranian, *weibl. auch*: Iranian woman (*od.* girl); **iranisch** *Adj.* Iranian; **Iranistik** *f*; -, *kein Pl.* Iranian studies

Irbis *m*; *-ses, -se*; *Zool.* snow leopard, ounce

irden *Adj. attr.* earthenware ...

Irden|geschirr *n* earthenware (crockery); **~ware** *f* earthenware

irdisch *Adj.* earthly; (*zeitlich*) temporal; (*weltlich*) worldly; (*sterblich*) mortal; **Irdische** *n*; *-n, kein Pl.*: *den Weg alles ~n gehen* go the way of all flesh

Ire *m*; *-n, -n* Irishman; *die ~n* the Irish *Pl.*

Irenik *f*; -, *kein Pl.* irenics *Pl.* (*V. im Sg.*)

irgend *Adv.* **1.** (*überhaupt*) at all; *wenn es ~ geht* if (it's) at all possible, if I etc. possibly can; *wann/wo es ~ geht* whenever/wherever it might be possible; *wer nur ~ geeignet ist* anyone who is even remotely qualified; *so rasch wie ~ möglich* as soon as at all possible; **2.** *Beliebigkeit ausdrückend*: **~ so ein Politiker** one of those politicians, some politician or other; *Verdunklungsgefahr, Fluchtgefahr - ~ so etwas war es* it was something of that kind

irgendein... *unbest. Pron.* some ... (or other); *in Fragen, Verneinungen und die Beliebigkeit betonend*: any; **~e Tasse** a cup; (*egal welche*) any cup; any old cup *umg.*; **nimm ~e Tasse** take any cup(, it doesn't matter what sort [of cup]); **~ anderer** someone else, *in Fragen/Verneinungen*: *auch* anyone else; (*egal wer*) anyone else; **besteht ~e Hoffnung?** is there any hope at all?

irgendeine... *unbest. Pron.* **1.** (*Person*) somebody, someone; *in Fragen/Verneinungen*: *auch* anybody, anyone; (*egal welche[r, -s]*) anybody, anyone; **2.** (*Ding*) something, *in Fragen/Verneinungen*: *auch* anything; (*egal welche[r, -s]*) anything; *was für einen Wein möchten Sie? - irgendeinen* any (will do)

irgend|einmal *Adv.* → **irgendwann**; **~eins** *unbest. Pron. umg.* → **irgendeine...**; **~etwas** *unbest. Pron.* something; *in der Frage/Verneinung*: *auch* anything; (*egal was*) anything; **nicht ~!** not just anything; **~jemand** *unbest. Pron.* somebody, someone; *in Fragen/Verneinungen*: *auch* anybody, anyone; (*egal wer*) anybody, anyone; **er ist ja** (**schließlich**) **nicht ~** (I mean,) he isn't just anybody; **~wann** *Adv.* sometime (or other); (*egal wann*) *auch* any time, whenever you like *etc.*, whenever it suits you *etc.*; **~was** *unbest. Pron. umg.* → **irgendetwas**; **~welche...** *unbest. Pron.* any; **~n Unsinn erzählen** any old nonsense, any old thing; **~wer** *unbest. Pron.* somebody, someone; *in Fragen/Verneinungen*: *auch* anybody, anyone; (*egal wer*) anybody, anyone; **er ist ja** (**schließlich**) **nicht ~** (I mean,) he isn't just anybody; **ich habe es irgendwem gegeben** I gave it to somebody or other; **~wie** *Adv.* somehow (or other); (*egal wie*) any old how; **~ kann ich mir das nicht vorstellen** I can't somehow imagine that (*od.* imagine that somehow); **~wo** *Adv.* somewhere (or other); *in Fragen/Verneinungen*: *auch* anywhere; (*egal wo*) anywhere; **~ anders** somewhere else, *in Fragen/Verneinungen*: *auch* anywhere else; **~woher** *Adv.* from somewhere (or other); *in Fragen/Verneinungen*: *auch* from anywhere; (*egal woher*) from anywhere; **~wohin** *Adv.* somewhere (or other); *in Fragen/Verneinungen*: *auch* anywhere; (*egal wohin*) anywhere; **~ müssen** *euph.*, *umg.* (*zur Toilette müssen*) have got to go somewhere

Iridium *n*; *-s, kein Pl.* iridium

Irin *f*; *-, -nen* Irishwoman; Irish girl, girl from Ireland; **sie ist ~** she's Irish (*od.* from Ireland)

Iris *f*; *-, - od. Iriden, Irides* **1.** *Pl. -*; *Bot.* iris; **2.** *Pl. - od. Iriden, Irides, mst Sg.*; *Anat.* iris; **Irisblende** *n Fot.* iris (diaphragm)

irisch *Adj.* Irish; **die Irische Republik** the Irish Republic, Eire; **~-römisches Bad** Turkish bath

irisieren *v/i.* iridesce, be iridescent; **irisierend** *Adj.* iridescent

IRK *Abk.* (**Internationales Rotes Kreuz**) International Red Cross, IRC

Irland (*n*); *-s; Geog.* Ireland; **Irländer** *m*; *-s, -* → **Ire**; **Irländerin** *f*; *-, -nen* →

Irin; **irländisch** *Adj.* Irish

Irokese *m*; *-n, -n* Iroquois (Indian); **Irokesenschnitt** *m* (*Frisur*) Mohican (*Am.* mohawk) (haircut)

Ironie *f*; *-, -n, mst Sg.* irony (**des Schicksals** of fate); **Ironiker** *m*; *-s, -*, **Ironikerin** *f*; *-, -nen* ironist; **ironisch** **I.** *Adj.* ironic; **II.** *Adv.* ironically; **ironisieren** *v/t.* treat with irony; **Ironisierung** *f* ironical treatment

irr *Adj.* → **irre**

irrational *Adj.* irrational; **Irrationalismus** *m*; *-, Irrationalismen* **1.** *nur Sg.* irrationalism; **2.** *Element.*: irrational element; *Geschehen*: irrational occurrence; **Irrationalität** *f*; *-, kein Pl.* irrationality, irrational nature (+ *Gen.* of); **irrationell** *Adj.* irrational

irre **I.** *Adj.* **1.** (*verrückt, geistesgestört wirkend*) mad, *umg.* crazy; *Blick*: wild, crazed *look*; *Lachen*: mad, *umg.* crazy; **~s Lächeln** crazy grin, wild sneer; **~s Zeug reden** *umg.* talk *wie* **~ schuften** *etc. umg.* work *etc.* like mad (*od.* like a madman, *Sl.* like crazy); **in e-m ~n Tempo fahren** drive like a maniac; **2.** *Med.* (*geisteskrank*) mad, insane, demented; **3.** *umg.* (*sagenhaft, ungewöhnlich*) incredible, *Brit. auch* magic, *Am. auch* awesome; **ein ~r Typ** *auch* an amazing guy; **es ist ~** *auch* it's unreal; **4.** (*verwirrt*) (totally) confused; → *auch* **irremachen**, **irrewerden**; **II.** *Adv. umg. verstärkend*: incredibly; *schwitzen etc.*: like mad (*Sl.* crazy, hell)

Irre¹ *f*: **in die ~ führen** lead *s.o.* astray; → *auch* **irreführen**; **in die ~ gehen** go astray

Irre² *m*, *f*; *-n, -n* madman (*f* madwoman); *umg. fig.* lunatic; **wie ein ~r** *umg.* like an idiot (*od.* a maniac)

irreal *Adj.* **1.** unreal; **2.** unrealistic; **Irreal** *m*; *-s, -e*, **Irrealis** *m*; *-, Irreales*; *Ling.* hypothetical subjunctive; **Irrealität** *f*; *-, kein Pl.* unreality

Irredenta *f*; *-, Irredenten* irredenta; **Irredentismus** *m*; *-, kein Pl.* irredentism

irreduzibel *Adj.* irreducible; **Irreduzibilität** *f*; *-, kein Pl. Philos.* irreducibility

irreführen *v/t.* (*trennb., hat -ge-*) mislead; (*täuschen*) *auch* deceive; **sich ~ lassen** be deceived (**von** by); **irreführend** *Adj.* misleading; **Irreführung** *f* (*Täuschung*) deception, *umg.* pulling the wool

irregehen *v/i.* (*unreg., trennb., ist -ge-*) *geh.* **1.** (*sich täuschen*) be mistaken; **gehe ich irre in der Annahme, dass ...?** am I wrong in assuming that ...?; **2.** (*in die Irre gehen*) go astray

irregeleitet **I.** *P.P.* → **irreleiten**; **II.** *Adj.*: misguided

irregulär *Adj.* irregular; **Irreguläre** *m*; *-n, -n*; *Mil.* irregular; **Irregularität** *f*; *-, -en* irregularity

irreleiten *v/t.* (*trennb., hat -ge-*) misguide, *stärker*: lead astray

irrelevant *Adj.* irrelevant (**für** to); **Irrelevanz** *f*; *-, -en* irrelevance

irreligiös *Adj.* irreligious; **Irreligiosität** *f*; *-, kein Pl.* irreligiousness

irremachen *v/t.* (*trennb., hat -ge-*) **1.** totally confuse, *umg.* throw; **2.** **j-n in etw. ~** cause s.o. to have doubts about s.th., put s.o. off s.th.; → *auch* **beirren**

irren **I.** *v/i.* **1.** (*hat geirrt*) wander (*auch Blick*), roam; **2.** (*hat*) (*im Irrtum sein*) be wrong, be mistaken; *Sprichw.* **Irren ist menschlich** to err is human; **II.** *v/refl.* (*hat*) be wrong, be mistaken;

sich in *j-m od. etw.* **~** be wrong about, *engS. im Datum etc.*: get *s.th.* wrong, **sich in der Tür** *etc.* **~** go to the wrong door *etc.*; **sich um tausend Euro ~** be out (*Am. auch* off) by a thousand euros, be a thousand euros out (*Am. auch* off); **ich kann mich** (**auch**) **~** I may be wrong; **wenn ich mich nicht irre** if I'm not mistaken, I think I'm right in saying (that); **da irrst du dich aber gewaltig** you couldn't be more wrong, that's where you make your big mistake; *wenn sie glaubt, dass ich das mache etc.*, **dann irrt sie sich gewaltig** she's making a big mistake, she's got another think (*Am.* thing) coming

Irren|anstalt *f altm.* mental asylum; **~haus** *n umg.* madhouse, nuthouse; **hier geht's zu wie im ~** it's like a madhouse (here), it's (sheer) bedlam; **er ist reif fürs ~** he ought to be certified (*Am.* committed)

irreparabel *Adj.* irreparable; **Irreparabilität** *f*; *-, kein Pl.* irreparability

irrereden *v/i.* (*trennb., hat -ge-*) rave; **Irresein** *n altm.* insanity

irreversibel *Adj.* irreversible; **Irreversibilität** *f*; *-, kein Pl.* irreversibility

irrewerden *v/i.* (*trennb., unreg., ist -ge-*) lose one's faith, have doubts; **~ an** (+ *Dat.*) begin to have one's doubts about; **Irrewerden** *n*; *-s, kein Pl.* process of becoming insane

Irr|fahrt *f* wandering(s *Pl.*); *längere*: odyssey; (*aussichtslose Suche*) wild goose chase; **~flug** *m* odyssey (in the air); **~gang** *m* path in a maze, *etwa* blind alley; **~garten** *m* maze, labyrinth; **~gast** *m Zool.* casual migrant

Irrglaube(n) *m* misconception, delusion; (*Ketzerei*) heresy; **irrgläubig** *Adj.* deluded; (*ketzerisch*) heretical

irrig *Adj.* wrong, mistaken, erroneous; **~e Ansicht** *auch* misconception

irrigerweise *Adv.* wrongly, erroneously; **Irrigkeit** *f* mistakenness, erroneousness

Irritation *f*; *-, -en* irritation; **irritierbar** *Adj.*: **leicht ~** (*verärgert*) easily annoyed; (*verwirrt*) easily put off (*umg.* thrown); (*abgelenkt*) easily distracted; **irritieren** *v/t.* irritate, get on *s.o.'s* nerves, (*ärgern*) *auch* annoy; (*ablenken*) irritate, distract; (*unsicher machen*) put *s.o.* off (**bei** s.th.), *umg.* throw; **sich ~ lassen** be put off, *umg.* be thrown (**durch** by); *altm.* (*erregen*) be annoyed; **Irritierung** *f* irritation

Irr|läufer *m* **1.** *Brief etc.*: stray (*od.* misdirected) letter *etc.*; **2.** (*Satellit*) rogue satellite; **~lehre** *f* false doctrine, heresy; **~licht** *n* will-o'-the-wisp (*auch fig.*)

irrlichtern *v/i.* (*untr., hat ge-*) flit about

Irrsein *n* → **Irresein**

Irrsinn *m*; *nur Sg.* madness (*auch fig.*); **irrsinnig** **I.** *Adj.* insane, mad; *umg. fig.* crazy, mad; *umg.* (*toll*) → **irre** I 3; **II.** *Adv. umg.* → **irre** II; **Irrsinnige** *m*, *f*; *-n, -n* → **Irre²**

Irrsinns|hitze *umg.* terrific (*od.* incredible) heat; **~kälte** *f umg.* terrible (*od.* incredible) cold; **~tempo** *n umg.* terrific (*od.* tremendous) speed

Irrtum *m*; *-s; Irrtümer* mistake; (*Missverständnis*) misunderstanding; **im ~ sein, sich im ~ befinden** be mistaken, be wrong, be in the wrong (**über** + *Akk.* about); **~ vorbehalten** errors (and omissions) excepted; **irrtümlich** **I.** *Adj.* wrong; **II.** *Adv.* wrongly; **ich war ~ der Meinung** I was wrong in thinking; **irrtümlicherweise** *Adv.* by mistake, mistakenly

Irrweg *m*; -(e)s, -e *fig.*: **auf e-n ~ geraten sein** bc on the wrong track completely; **j-n auf e-n ~ führen** lead s.o. astray

irrwerden *v/i.* (*unreg.*, *trennb.*, *ist -ge-*) → **irrewerden**; **Irrwerden** *n* → **Irrewerden**

Irrwisch *m*; -(e)s, -e **1.** will-o'-the-wisp; **2.** (*Kind*) jack-in-the-box; **er ist ein richtiger ~** *auch* he's up and down like a yo-yo, he can't sit still for one minute

Irrwitz *m*; -es, *kein Pl.* madness, craziness; (*Absurdität*) absurdity; **irrwitzig** *Adj.* ridiculous, absurd, *umg.* crazy, hare-brained

Isabelle *f*; -, -n; *Zool.*, *Pferd*: light bay, *Am.* claybank; **isabellfarben**, **isabellfarbig** *Adj.* Isabella, Isabelline

ISBN *f*; -, -s; *Abk.*, **ISBN-Nummer** *f* (**Internationale Standardbuchnummer**) ISBN

Ischialgie *f*; -, -n; *Med.* ischialgia; **Ischias** *m, n, f*; -, *kein Pl.*; *Med.* sciatica; **Ischiasnerv** *m* sciatic nerve

ISDN *n*; -, *kein Pl.*; *mst kein Art.*; *Abk.*, **ISDN-Anschluss** *m* ISDN

Isegrim *m*; -s, -e **1.** *nur Sg.* Ise(n)grim; *Kinderspr.* the big bad wolf; **2.** *pej.* sourpuss

Islam *m*; -(s), *kein Pl.*; *Rel.* Islam; **Islamisation** *f*; -, -en Islamization; **islamisch** *Adj.* Islamic; **islamisieren** *v/t.* convert to Islam, Islamize; **Islamisierung** *f* Islamization; **Islamismus** *m*; -, *kein Pl.* Islamism; *Pol. auch* Islamic fundamentalism; **Islamist** *m*; -en, -en, **Islamistin** *f*; -, -nen **1.** (*Islamforscher*) Islamist; **2.** (*islamischer Fundamentalist*) Islamic fundamentalist, Islamist; **islamistisch** *Adj.* Islamic fundamentalist, Islamist

Island (*n*); -s; *Geog.* Iceland; **Isländer** *m*; -s, -, **Isländerin** *f*; -, -nen Icelander, *weiblich auch*: Icelandic woman (*od.* girl); **isländisch I.** *Adj.* Icelandic; **Isländisch(es) Moos** Iceland moss; **II. Isländisch** *n*; -(s); *Ling.* Icelandic; **das ~e** Icelandic; **Islandtief** *n* *Met.* Icelandic depression

Ismus *m*; -, *Ismen*; *umg.* ism

Isobare *f*; -, -n; *Met.* isobar

Isobutan *n*; -s, *kein Pl.*; *Chem.* isobutane

isochrom *Adj.* → **isochromatisch**; **Isochromasie** *f*; -, *kein Pl.*; *Fot.* isochromatism; **isochromatisch** *Adj.* *Fot.* isochromatic

Isogamie *f*; -, -n; *Biol.* isogamy

Isoglosse *f*; -, -n; *Ling.* isogloss

Isogon *n*; -s, -e; *Math.* isogon; **isogo-**

nal *Adj.* isogonic

Isohyete ; -, -n; *Met.* isohyet

Isohypse *f*; -, -n; *Geog.* contour line

Isolation *f*; -, -en **1.** *auch Pol.* isolation; → **Isolationshaft**; **2.** *Etech.*, *Tech.* insulation

Isolationismus *m*; -, *kein Pl.*; *Pol.* isolationism; **Isolationist** *m*; -en, -en, **Isolationistin** *f*; -, -nen isolationist; **isolationistisch** *Adj.* isolationist

Isolations|folter *f* (torture by) solitary confinement; **~haft** *f* solitary confinement

Isolator *m*; -s, -en insulator

Isolierband *n* insulating tape

isolieren I. *v/t.* **1.** *auch Pol. etc.* isolate (*auch Chem.*); **2.** *Etech.*, *Tech.* insulate; **II.** *v/refl.*: **sich ~** isolate o.s., cut o.s. off; **III.** *v/i.*: **gut ~** insulate well, be a good insulator

Isolier|glas *n* insulating glass; **~haft** *f* solitary confinement; **~kanne** *f* Thermos® (jug), *umg.* thermos; **~masse** *f* insulating compound; **~material** *n* insulating material; **~schicht** *f* insulating layer; **~schutz** *m* (thermal) insulation; **~station** *f* *Med.* isolation ward

isoliert I. *P.P.* → **isolieren**; **II.** *Adj.* **1.** isolated, cut off; *Med.*, *Häftling*: isolated, in isolation; **~e Fälle** isolated cases; **2.** *Etech.*, *Tech.* insulated; **III.** *Adv.*: **~ betrachten** view s.th. in isolation; **man darf es nicht ~ betrachten** *auch* you've got to see it in context; **Isoliertheit** *f* isolation

Isolierung *f* **1.** isolation; **2.** *Etech.*, *Tech.* insulation

Isolierwirkung *f* *Tech.* insulating action

Isolinie *f* *Geog.*, *Met.* isoline

isomer *Adj.* isomeric; **Isomer** *n*; -s, -e, **Isomere** *n*; -n, -n; *Chem.* isomer; **Isomerie** *f*; -, *kein Pl.* isomerism

Isometrie *f*; -, *kein Pl.* isometry; **isometrisch** *Adj.* isometric

isomorph *Adj.* isomorph; **Isomorphie** *f*; -, *kein Pl.* isomorphism; **Isomorphismus** *m*; -, *kein Pl.*; *Chem.*, *Math.* isomorphism

Isopren *n*; -s, *kein Pl.*; *Chem.* isoprene

Isostasie *f*; -, *kein Pl.*; *Geog.* isostasy

Isothermie *f*; -, *kein Pl.*; *Met.* isothermal state

Isoton *n*; -s, -e; *Phys.* isotone; **isotonisch** *Adj.* *Chem.*, *Physiol.* isotonic

Isotop *n*; -s, -e isotope

Isotopen|batterie *f* *Etech.* isotope battery; **~diagnostik** *f* *Med.* isotope diagnosis; **~therapie** *f* *Med.* isotope radiotherapy

isotrop *Adj.* isotropic; **Isotropie** *f*; -, *kein Pl.*; *Chem.*, *Phys.* isotropy

isozyklisch *Adj.* *Chem.* isocyclical

Israel (*n*); -s; *Geog.* Israel

Israeli *m*; -(s), -(s), *f*; -, -(s) Israeli, *weiblich auch*: Israeli woman (*od.* girl); **israelisch** *Adj.* Israeli

Israelit *m*; -en, -en, **~in** *f*; -, -nen Israelite; **israelitisch** *Adj.* Israelite

Ist|aufkommen *n* actual yield (*od.* revenue); **~bestand** *m* *Wirts.* actual stock

Istgleichzeichen *n* *Math.* equal(s) sign

Isthmus *m*; -, *Isthmen*; *Geog.* isthmus

Ist|leistung *f* *Wirts.* actual output; **~stärke** *f* *Mil.* effective (*od.* actual) strength; **~wert** *m* actual (*od.* true) value; **~zustand** *m* actual state (*od.* status)

Itaker *m*; -s, -, **~in** *f*; -, -nen *umg.*, *neg!* dago, wop, Eyetie

italianisieren *v/t.* → **italienisieren**; **Italianismus** *m*; -, *Italianismen*; *Ling.* Italianism, Italicism; **Italianist** *m*; -en, -en, **Italianistin** *f*; -, -nen Italianist; **italianistisch** *Adj.* Italianist

Italien (*n*); -s; *Geog.* Italy; **Italiener** *m*; -s, -, **1.** Italian; **er ist ~** *auch* he's from Italy; **2.** *umg.* (*Restaurant*) Italian place; **lass uns zum ~ gehen** *umg.* let's go to an Italian (restaurant); **um die Ecke ist ein ~** *umg.* there's an Italian (place) round the corner; **Italienerin** *f*; -, -nen Italian (woman *od.* girl); **sie ist ~** *auch* she's from Italy; **italienisch I.** *Adj.* Italian; **die ~e Schweiz** Italian-speaking Switzerland; **II. Italienisch** *n*; -(s); *Ling.* Italian; **das Italienische** Italian; **italienisieren** *v/t.* Italianize

italisch *Adj.* italic

Italo|amerikaner *m*, **~amerikanerin** *f* Italian-American; **~western** *m* *umg.* spaghetti western

Item ['aitəm] *n*; -s, -s item

iterativ *Adj.* iterative; **Iterativ** *n*; -s, -e, **Iterativbildung** *f*, **Iterativum** *n*; -s, *Iterativa* *Ling.* iterative (verb)

Itinerar *n*; -s, -e, **Itinerarium** *n*; -s, *Itinerarien* itinerary

i. Tr. *Abk.* (**in der Trockenmasse**) (in) dry measure

IT-Spezialist *m*, **IT-Spezialistin** *f* *Informationstechnologie*: IT specialist

i-Tüpfelchen *n* → **i-Punkt**; **i-Tüpferl** *n*; -s, -n; *österr.* → **i-Punkt**; **i-Tüpferl-Reiter** *m*, **i-Tüpferl-Reiterin** *f* *österr. umg.* nit-picker

Iwan *m*; -s, -s; *umg. hum.*, *neg!* Ivan, Russky; **der ~** the Russkies *Pl.*

IWF *m*; -(s), *kein Pl.*; *Abk.* (**Internationaler Währungsfonds**) IMF

Iwrit(h) *n*; -(s), *kein Pl.*; *Ling.* (modern) Hebrew

J, j [jɔt] *n*; -, -*s* J, j; *J wie Julius Buch-stabieren:* "j" for (*od.* as in) "Juliet"

ja *Adv.* **1.** yes; *umg.* yeah, yep; *Parl.* aye, *Am.* yea; *bei der Trauung:* I do; *beim Nachdenken, als Pausenfüller:* um, er; (*na ja*) well; **~?** (*tatsächlich?*) really?, *umg.* oh yeah?; *Telef.* (*hallo?*) hello?; *wenn* **~** if so; **~ sagen** say yes; (*zustimmen*) *auch* agree (**zu** to); *wird er kommen? – ich glaube* **~** I think so; *aber* **~!** *beruhigend:* yes, of course; *ungeduldig:* yes, yes; *zum Ehepartner etc.:* yes, dear *mst iro.;* **~ sicher** *od.* *gern* yes, of course; **2.**; **3.** (*schließlich*) *er ist* **~** *mein Freund* I mean, he's a friend (after all); *dazu ist es* **~** *da* that's what it's (there) for (after all); *es ist* **~** *nicht so schlimm* it's not that bad; *du kennst ihn* **~** you know what he's like; **4.** *einleitend:* **~,** *wissen Sie* well, you know; **5.** *feststellend:* *da bist du* **~!** there you are!; *ich komme* **~** *schon* I'm (just) coming; *da haben wirs* **~!** there we are, isn't that (just) what I said?; *ich sagte es dir* **~** didn't I tell you?; *das ist* **~** *unglaublich* that's really incredible; *das kann* **~** *heiter werden* that sounds like fun; **6.** *einschärfend:* *sags ihm* **~** *nicht* don't you tell (*od.* go telling) him; *lass sie* **~** *in Ruhe* just (*od.* you'd better) leave her alone; *bring es* **~** *mit* make sure you bring it up!; **7.** *überrascht:* **~,** *weißt du denn nicht, dass* you mean to say you really don't know (that); **~** *wer kommt denn da?* look who's coming (*od.* who's here)!; **8.** *einschränkend:* *ich würde es* **~** *gern tun, aber ...* I'd really like to do it, but ...; **9.** *verstärkend:* *du weißt* **~** *gar nicht ...* you have no idea ...; *das sag ich* **~** that's what I mean; **10.** *steigernd:* *er genießt Filme,* **~** *verschlingt sie* he enjoys films (*Am.* movies), in fact he can't get enough of them; *schwer,* *sogar unmöglich* difficult, or even (*od.* if not) impossible; **11.** *nachgestellt:* *du kommst doch später,* **~?** you 're coming later on, aren't you?; *gibst du's mir,* **~?** will you give it to me (, please)?; *Zusicherung erhoffend:* are you going to give it to me then?

Ja *n*; -(s), -(s) yes; *Parl.* aye, *Am.* yea; *mit* **~** *oder Nein antworten* answer yes or no; **~** *zu etw. sagen* say yes to s.th.; *mit* **~** *stimmen* vote yes (*od.* in favo[u]r); → *auch Jawort*

Jab [dʒɛp] *m*; -s, -s; *Boxsport* jab

Jabo *m*; -s, -s; *Abk.* → *Jagdbomber*

Jacht *f*; -, -en yacht; **~hafen** *m* marina; **~klub** *m* yacht club

Jäckchen *n* little (*od.* short) jacket; *für Baby:* baby jacket, *Brit. auch* matinée coat; **Jacke** *f*; -, -n jacket, *Am. auch* coat; (*gestrickt*) cardigan; *das ist* **~** *wie Hose umg.* it's much of a muchness, it's (a case) of six of one and half a dozen of the other; *j-m die* **~** *voll hauen umg.* give s.o. a good hiding

Jacken|kleid *n* (*woman's*) two-piece (suit, outfit), *Brit. auch* costume *altm.;* **~tasche** *f* jacket pocket

Jacketkrone ['dʒɛkɪt-] *f* jacket crown

Jackett [ʒa'kɛt] *n*; -s, -s jacket, *Am. auch* coat

Jackpot ['dʒɛkpɔt] *m*; -s, -s jackpot

Jacquard [ʒa'ka:r] *m*; -(s), -s jacquard; **~gewebe** *n* jacquard weave

Jade *m, f*; -, *kein Pl.*; *Min.* jade; **jade-grün** *Adj.* jade(-green)

Jagd *f*; -, -en **1.** a) (*Jagen*) hunt(ing); *mit der Flinte: auch* shoot(ing); *auf* (*die*) **~** *gehen* go hunting; *auf der* **~** *sein* be hunting; *ein Tiger etc.* *bei der* **~** hunting for prey; *die hohe/niedere* **~** hunting for larger/smaller game; *die* **~** *auf Schwarzwild etc.* hunting for wild boar, b) (*Gesellschaft*) hunting (*od.* shooting) party; *die Wilde* **~** the Wild Hunt, c) (*Revier*) shoot, *Am.* hunt; **2.** *fig.* (*Verfolgung*) chase, pursuit; *die* **~** *auf Terroristen etc.* the hunt for terrorists *etc.;* **~** *machen auf* (+ *Akk.*) chase (after), hunt for, try to track down; **3.** *fig.* (*Streben*) pursuit (*nach* of); *die* **~** *nach Geld etc.* chasing after money *etc.;* *e-e wilde* **~** a mad scramble *od.* rush (*nach* for); *die* **~** *hat begonnen* the race (*od.* chase) is on; **~aufseher** *m* gamekeeper

jagdbar *Adj. präd. und nachgestellt:* allowed to be hunted; **~es Wild** game, fair game

Jagd|beute *f* bag; **~bomber** *m Mil.* fighter bomber; → *auch Jabo;* **~fieber** *n* hunting fever; **~flieger** *m,* **~fliegerin** *f Mil.* fighter pilot; **~flugzeug** *n Mil.* fighter (jet, plane, aircraft); (*Abfangjäger*) interceptor (aircraft); **~frevel** *m* poaching; **~gebiet** *n* hunting ground; **~gerechtigkeit** *f altm.* → *Jagdrecht;* **~geschwader** *n Mil.* fighter squadron; **~gesellschaft** *f* hunting party; **~gewehr** *n* hunting rifle; (*Schrotflinte*) shotgun; **~glück** *n* good hunting; **~kein** **~** *haben* have good luck / no luck when hunting, have good/poor hunting; **~gründe** *Pl.* hunting grounds; *in die ewigen* **~** *eingehen* go to the happy hunting grounds; **~haus** *n* (hunting) lodge; **~horn** *n* hunting horn, bugle; **~hund** *m* hound; (*Rasse*) short-haired pointer; **~hütte** *f* (hunting) lodge; **~leidenschaft** *f* passion for hunting

jagdlich *Adj.* hunting

Jagd|lied *n* hunting song; **~messer** *n* hunting knife; **~panzer** *m Mil.* anti--tank vehicle, tank destroyer; **~pächter** *m,* **~pächterin** *f* tenant of a shoot (*Am.* hunt)

Jagdrecht *n* **1.** hunting rights *Pl.;* **2.** (*Gesetz*) game law; **jagdrechtlich** *Adj.* in (*od.* of) game law

Jagd|rennen *n Sport* steeplechase; **~revier** *n* hunting ground; **~ruf** *m* hunting call; **~schein** *m* shooting licence, *Am.* hunting license; **~schloss**

n hunting lodge; **~springen** *n Sport* show jumping; **~staffel** *f Mil.* fighter squadron; **~szene** *f Kunst:* hunting scene; **~tasche** *f* game bag; **~trophäe** *f* hunting trophy; **~waffe** *f* hunting weapon; **~wesen** *n nur Sg.* hunting; **~wild** *n* game, game animal(s *Pl.*); **~wurst** *f Gastr.* chasseur sausage; **~zeit** *f* hunting (*od.* shooting) season

jagen I. *v/t.* **1.** hunt; (*treiben*) drive; (*verfolgen*) chase; *mit Hunden:* hound; (*schießen*) shoot; **2.** *fig.* (*verfolgen*) chase (after); (*suchen*) hunt for; *aus dem Bett etc.* **~** chase out of bed *etc.;* *in die Luft* **~** blow up, *umg.* blow *s.th.* sky-high; *j-m ein Messer in den Leib* **~** *umg.* stick a knife into s.o.; *j-m/sich e-e Kugel durch den Kopf* **~** *umg.* put a bullet through s.o.'s/one's head; *Sl.* blow s.o.'s/one's brains out; *ein Ereignis jagte das andere* it was one thing on top of another, things were happening really fast; *damit kannst du mich* **~!** *umg.* I wouldn't touch it with a bargepole (*Am.* a ten-foot pole); **II.** *v/i.* **1.** (*auf die Jagd gehen*) go hunting, go shooting, hunt; **2.** *fig.* (*rasen*) race, tear; *Wind etc.:* sweep; *Wolken:* scud across the sky; **~** *nach* chase after

Jagen[1] *n*; -s, *kein Pl.* hunt(ing), shooting; → *auch Jagd*

Jagen[2] *n*; -s, -; (*Waldgebiet*) *marked section of forest,* compartment *fachspr.*

Jäger *m*; -e, - **1.** hunter, huntsman; (*Förster*) ranger; (*Wildhüter*) gamekeeper; *Völkerkunde:* hunter; *der Wilde* **~** *Myth.* the Wild Huntsman; **2.** *Mil.* rifleman; **3.** *Mil., Flug.* fighter (jet, plane, aircraft); **Jägerei** *f*; -, *kein Pl.* hunting

Jägerhut *m* Tyrolean hat; **Jägerin** *f*; -, *-nen* huntswoman; *lit.* huntress

Jäger|latein *n* cock-and-bull story (*od.* stories *Pl.*); **~prüfung** *f* examination to qualify for a hunting licence

Jägerschnitzel *n Gastr.* escalope chasseur

Jägersmann *m* huntsman

Jäger|sprache *f* hunting terms *Pl.;* *auch pej.* hunting jargon; **~zaun** *m* wooden lattice fence

Jaguar *m*; -s, -e; *Zool.* jaguar

jäh I. *Adj.* **1.** (*plötzlich*) sudden, abrupt; (*ungestüm*) impetuous; (*vorschnell*) rash; *er Aufbruch* abrupt departure; *es Erwachen auch fig.* rude awakening; *er Tod* sudden death; **2.** (*abschüssig*) steep; *er Abhang* sheer drop, precipice; **II.** *Adv.* **1.** (*plötzlich*) all of a sudden, abruptly; (*kopfüber*) headlong; **2.** (*steil*) precipitously; *abfallend* precipitous; *dort fällt die Straße* **~** *nach rechts ab* at that point the road turns right and drops away steeply; **Jähheit** *f* **1.** (*Plötzlichkeit*) suddenness, abruptness; **2.** (*Steilheit*) steepness; **jählings** *Adv.* **1.** suddenly, abruptly; **2.** steeply;

precipitously

Jahr *n*; -(*e*)*s*, -*e* **1.** *Zeitspanne*: year; *ein halbes* ~ six months; *anderthalb* ~*e* a year and a half, eighteen months; *ein drei viertel* ~ nine months; *im* ~ *2011* in (the year) 2011; *bis zum 31. Dezember d. J.* (= *dieses* ~*es*) until December 31st of this year; *Anfang der achtziger* ~*e* in the early eighties; *das ganze* ~ all year; *alle* ~*e* every year; *auf* ~*e hinaus* for years to come; *im Lauf der* ~*e* through (*od.* over) the years; *in diesem / im nächsten* ~ this/next year; *nach* ~*en* after (many) years; *nach* ~ *und Tag* after a very long time, (many) years later; *seit* ~ *und Tag* for a long time, for many years; *heute vor einem* ~ a year ago today; *von* ~ *zu* ~ from year to year; *weitS.* as the years go by; ~ *für* ~ year after year; **2.** *Alter*: *mit* ~. *im Alter von 20* ~*en* at the age of twenty; *in den besten* ~*en sein* be in the prime of life; *in die* ~*e kommen* be getting on (a bit), be getting a bit long in the tooth *hum.*, *Am.* be getting up there; (*noch*) *jung an* ~*en sein* be (still) young (*od.* in one's youth); *mit den* ~*en lernt man das* over the years, as the years go by; → *Buckel 2*

jahraus *Adv.*: ~, *jahrein* year in, year out

Jahrbuch *n* yearbook; (*Almanach*) almanac

Jährchen *n umg.* year; *ein paar* ~ *noch* another year or two, another couple of years

jahrein *Adv.* → *jahraus*

jahrelang I. *Adj.* longstanding; ~*e Erfahrung* years of experience; *ein* ~*er Kampf auch* years of struggle (*od.* struggling); **II.** *Adv.* for years (and years), for years on end

jähren *v/refl.*: *2015 jährt sich die Erfindung des ... zum 200. Mal* 2015 will see the 200th anniversary (*od.* the bicentennial) of the invention of ...; *heute/morgen jährt sich sein Todestag* it's a year today since he died, it's a year ago today that he died /it'll be a year ago tomorrow that he died

Jahres|... *im Subst. mst* annual, yearly; ~**abonnement** *n* annual subscription; *Theat. etc.* yearly season ticket; ~**abrechnung** *f*, ~**abschluss** *m Wirts.* annual (statement of) accounts *Pl.*; ~**anfang** *m*: → *Jahresbeginn*; ~**ausgleich** *m* annual tax adjustment; ~**ausklang** *m* end of the year; ~**ausstoß** *m Wirts.* annual output; ~**beginn** *m* beginning of the year; *zu* ~ at the beginning of the year; ~**beitrag** *m* annual subscription (*od.* contribution); ~**bericht** *m* annual report; ~**bestzeit** *f Sport* best time for the year (*od.* [so far] this year); ~**bilanz** *f Wirts.* annual balance (sheet); ~**durchschnitt** *m* annual (*od.* yearly) average; ~**einkommen** *n* yearly income; ~**ende** *n* end of the year; ~**frist** *f*: *binnen* ~ within a year; *nach* ~ after one year; *vor* ~ *zukünftig*: in less than a year, within a year; *vergangen*: a year ago; ~**gehalt** *n* annual salary; ~**gespräch** *n zwischen Chef(in) und Mitarbeiter(in)*: annual (performance) review; ~**hälfte** *f*: *erste/zweite* ~ first/second half of the year; ~**hauptversammlung** *f Wirts.* annual general meeting, AGM; ~**karte** *f* yearly season ticket; ~**mitte** *f* middle of the year; ~**mittel** *n* yearly average; ~**produktion** *f* annual production; ~**ring** *m Bot.* annual (*od.* growth *od.* tree) ring; ~**rückblick** *m* review of (*od.* a look back at)

the year's events; ~**schluss** *m* end of the year; ~**tag** *m* anniversary; ~**tagung** *f* annual meeting (*od.* conference); ~**temperatur** *f*: *mittlere* ~ annual mean temperature; ~**überschuss** *m Wirts.* net earnings *Pl.*; ~**umsatz** *m Wirts.* annual turnover; ~**urlaub** *m* annual holiday (allowance), *Am.* annual vacation (allowance); ~**verlauf** *m*: *im* ~ in the course of the year; ~**versammlung** *f* annual meeting; ~**vertrag** *m* one-year contract; ~**wagen** *m* employee('s) car; ~**wechsel** *m f* turn of the year; (*Fest*) New Year; ~**wende** *f* turn of the year; *um die* ~ *2003/04* about the end of 2003 or the beginning of 2004; ~**wirtschaftsbericht** *m Pol.* annual economic report; ~**zahl** *f* date, year

Jahreszeit *f* season, time of the year; *zu jeder* ~ (in) any season, in all seasons; **jahreszeitlich I.** *Adj.* seasonal; **II.** *Adv.* seasonally; ~ *bedingt* seasonal

Jahrgang *m* **1.** (*Altersklasse*) age group, *fachspr.* cohort; *der* ~ *1998* those born in 1998, *wir sind derselbe* ~ we're the same age, we were born in the same year; *was ist er für ein* ~? what year was he born (in)?; *ich bin* ~ *72* I was born in (19)72; **2.** *Päd.* year; *sie ist mein* ~ we were in the same year; **3.** *Wein*: vintage (*auch fig.*), year; *der* ~ *1998* the 1998 vintage; **4.** *Zeitschriften*: volume, year

Jahrhundert *n* century; *das 16.* ~ the 16th century; *im 17. und 18.* ~ in the 17th and 18th centuries; *seit* ~*en bewohnen Bergbauern das Tal* the valley has been home to hill farmers for centuries

jahrhunderte|alt *Adj.* centuries-old; (*uralt*) ancient; ~**lang I.** *Adj.* centuries of ...; **II.** *Adv.* for centuries, for hundreds of years

Jahrhundert|ereignis *n* **1.** *the* event (*od.* happening) of the century; **2.** once-in-a-lifetime event; ~**feier** *f* centenary, *Am.* centennial; ~**hochwasser** *n nur alle Jahrhunderte vorkommend*: once-in-a-century high tide; *dieses Jahrhunderts*: *the* high tide of the century; ~**sommer** *m the* summer of the century; ~**wein** *m* vintage of the century; *einer*: rare vintage; ~**wende** *f*: (*um die*) ~ (around the) turn of the century

jährlich I. *Adj.* yearly, annual; **II.** *Adv.* every year, yearly, once a year; *1000 Dollar* ~ 1,000 dollars a year (*od.* per annum)

Jährling *m*; -*s*, -*e*; *Zool.* yearling

Jahrmarkt *m* fair; ~ *der Eitelkeiten fig.* Vanity Fair; **Jahrmarktsbude** *f* booth *od.* stall (at a fairground, *Am. auch* carnival); **Jahrmarktstreiben** *n* fairground (hustle and) bustle

Jahrmillionen *Pl.*: *vor* ~ millions of years ago; *seit* ~ for millions of years (now)

Jahrtausend *n* millennium; **jahrtausendealt** *Adj. präd.* thousands of years old; **jahrtausendelang I.** *Adj. nachgestellt*: lasting thousands of years; *nicht unterbrochen*: over thousands of years, thousands of years of ...; **II.** *Adv.* for thousands of years

Jahrtausend|feier *f* millenary; ~**wende** *f* turn of the millennium

Jahrzehnt *n*; -(*e*)*s*, -*e* decade, ten years *Pl.*; **jahrzehntealt** *Adj. etwa* twenty-/thirty-*etc.* -year-old; **jahrzehntelang I.** *Adj. nachgestellt*: lasting decades; *nicht unterbrochen*: over dec-

ades, decades of ...; **II.** *Adv.* for decades

Jähzorn *m* **1.** (*Eigenschaft*) violent temper; **2.** (*Anfall von* ~) sudden (outburst of) rage; **jähzornig I.** *Adj.* hot-tempered; *er ist ein* ~*er Mensch auch* he's got a violent temper, he tends to flare up; **II.** *Adv.* angrily, in a temper

jaja *Adv. umg. seufzend*: oh well; *irritiert*: OK, OK!

Jak *m*; -*s*, -*s* yak

Jakob *m*; -*s* Jacob (*auch bibl.*); *entsprechender Vorname*: *auch* James; *nicht gerade der wahre* ~ *umg.* not quite right; *nicht das Echte*: not the real McCoy; *billiger* ~ *umg. altm.* cheapjack

Jakobiner *m*; -*s*, - *hist. Pol.* Jacobin; ~**mütze** *f hist.* liberty cap; **Jakobinertum** *n*; -*s*, *kein Pl.* Jacobinism; **jakobinisch** *Adj.* Jacobin(ical)

Jakobs|leiter *f Naut. und bibl.*: (*die*) ~ Jacob's ladder; ~**muschel** *f* scallop

Jakobus *m*; -; *bibl.* James; *Brief des* ~ → *Jakobusbrief*; ~**brief** *m*: *bibl. der* ~ (the Epistle of St[.]) James

Jalousette [ʒalu'zɛtə] *f*; -, -*n* Venetian blind(s *Pl.*)

Jalousie [ʒalu'ziː] *f*; -, -*n* (Venetian) blind(s *Pl.*)

Jamaika (*n*); -*s*; *Geog.* Jamaica; **Jamaikaner** *m*; -*s*, -, **Jamaikanerin** *f*; -, -*nen* Jamaican, *weiblich auch*: Jamaican woman (*od.* girl); **jamaikanisch** *Adj.* Jamaican; **Jamaikarum** *m* Jamaica rum

Jambe *f*; -, -*n* → *Jambus*; **Jambendichtung** *f Lit.* iambic poetry; poem in iambics; **jambisch** *Adj.* iambic

Jambus *m*; -, *Jamben*; *Lit.* iamb, iambus (*Pl.* iambuses *od.* iambi)

Jammer *m*; -*s*, *kein Pl.*; (*Elend*) misery; (*Verzweiflung*) despair; (*Wehklagen*) lamentation; *es ist ein* ~ it's such a shame; ~**bild** *n* pitiful sight, (*Person*) *auch* picture of misery; ~**geschrei** *n* wailing; ~**gestalt** *f* miserable wretch (*auch fig. pej.*); ~**lappen.** *m umg.* wimp

jämmerlich I. *Adj.* miserable, wretched, pitiful (*alle auch fig. pej.*); (*verächtlich*) deplorable; (*herzzerreißend*) heart-rending; ~ *aussehen* look wretched; *ihm war* ~ *zumute* he felt utterly miserable; **II.** *Adv.*: ~ *weinen* weep bitterly; *bes. Kind*: cry one's eyes out; ~ (*schlecht*) *singen etc.*: miserably; ~ *frieren* be dreadfully cold, be freezing, freeze; **Jämmerlichkeit** *f* wretchedness, pitifulness; (*Verächtlichkeit*) deplorableness; *Zustand auch* miserable (*od.* wretched *etc.*) state (*od.* nature)

jammern I. *v/i.* **1.** moan; *laut*: *auch* wail; (*wimmern*) whimper; ~ *nach* (*der Mutter etc.*) cry for; **2.** (*sich beklagen*) moan, *umg.* bellyache; **II.** *v/t. geh.*, *altm.*: *es jammert mich zu sehen ...* it breaks my heart to see ...; *er jammert mich* I feel sorry for him

Jammern *n*; -*s*, *kein Pl.* moaning, wailing; → *jammern* I

jammerschade *Adj.*: *es ist* ~ it's such a shame (*um* about), *umg.* it's too bad (about)

Jammertal *n*; -*s*, *kein Pl.*; *lit.* vale of tears; **jammervoll** *Adj.* miserable, wretched; (*verächtlich*) deplorable; (*herzzerreißend*) heart-rending

Jamswurzel *f Bot.* yam

Jan. *Abk.* (*Januar*) Jan.

Janitschar *m*; -*en*, -*en*; *hist.* janissary

Janker *m*; -*s*, -; *südd.*, *österr.* Alpine

Janker jacket

Jänner *m*; *-s*, *-*; *österr*. January

Januar *m*; *-(s)*, *-e*, *mst Sg*.; (*abgek*. **Jan.**) January; → **April**

Januskopf *m* Janus face; **janusköpfig** *fig*. two-faced, Janus-faced

Japan (*n*); *-s*; *Geog*. Japan; **Japaner** *m*; *-s*, *-*, **Japanerin** *f*; *-*, *-nen* Japanese, *weibl. auch*: Japanese woman (*od*. girl *etc*.); **japanisch I.** *Adj*. Japanese; **II. Japanisch** *n*; *-(s)*; *Ling*. Japanese; *das Japanische* Japanese

Japanologe *m*; *-n*, *-n* Japanologist; **Japanologie** *f*; *-*, *kein Pl*. Japanese studies *Pl*., Japanology; **Japanologin** *f*; *-*, *-nen* → **Japanologe**

Japan|papier *n* rice paper; **~seide** *f* Japanese silk

Japs *m*; *-es*, *-e und -en*; *umg., neg!* Jap, Nip

japsen *v/i*. *umg*. gasp (*nach Luft* for breath), pant; **Japser** *m*; *-s*, *-* *umg*. gasp

Jargon [ʒar'gõː] *m*; *-s*, *-s* jargon; slang

Jasager *m*; *-s*, *-* yes(-)man; **Jasagerin** *f*; *-*, *-nen* yes(-)woman

Jasmin *m*; *-s*, *-e*; *Bot*. jasmin(e); **~tee** *m* jasmine tea

Jaspis *m*; *-* *od. -se*, *-se* (*Pl. nur bei Arten*) *Min*. jasper

Jass *m*; *-es*, *kein Pl*.; *schw. popular Swiss card game*, jass; **jassen** *v/i*. *schw*. play jass

Jastimme *f* yes vote; vote in favo(u)r; *Parl*. aye, *Am*. yea

jäten I. *v/t*. weed (out); (*Beet etc*.) weed; *Unkraut* ~ pull out (the) weeds; **II.** *v/i*. weed (the garden), pull out (the) weeds

Jauche *f*; *-*, *-n* liquid manure, slurry; *umg. fig*. swill; **~grube** *f* manure (*od*. slurry) pit; *für Abwässer* cesspit

jauchen *vt/i*. manure, dung; **Jauchewagen** *m* dung cart

jauchzen *v/i*. cheer; *vor Freude* ~ shout for joy, whoop with joy; **Jauchzen** *n*; *-s*, *kein Pl*. cheers *Pl*.; *lit*. jubilation; **jauchzend I.** *Part. Präs*. → **jauchzen**; **II.** *Adj*. (*laut jubelnd*) cheering; (*sehr froh*) exultant, jubilant; **Jauchzer** *m*; *-s*, *-* (loud) whoop, shout of joy

jaulen *v/i*. howl; *Gitarre: auch* whine, scream

Jause *f*; *-*, *-n* *österr*. snack

Jausen|brot *n* *österr*. snack sandwich; **~station** *f* *österr*. snack bar

jausnen I. *v/t*. snack on *s.th*.; **II.** *v/i*. have a snack

Java (*n*); *-s*; *Geog*. Java

jawohl *Adv*. yes; (*mache ich*) will do; *Mil. etc., auch iro*. yes, Sir!, yessir!; **jawoll** *Adv. umg. iro*. → **jawohl**

Jawort *n*: *sie gab ihm das* ~ she said yes

Jazz [dʒɛs] *m*; *-*, *kein Pl*.; *Mus*. jazz; **~band** *f* jazz band; **~besen** *m* *Mus*. (wire) brushes *Pl*.

jazzen ['dʒɛsn̩] *v/i*. *Mus*. jazz; **Jazzer** *m*; *-s*, *-*, **Jazzerin** *f*; *-*, *-nen* jazz musician, *männlich auch* jazzman

Jazz|fan ['dʒɛsfɛn] *m* jazz fan; **~gymnastik** *f* pop mobility, *Am*. jazzercise

jazzig ['dʒɛsɪç] *Adj*. jazzy

Jazz|kapelle *f* jazz band; **~keller** *m* jazz cellar; **~musik** *f* jazz (music); **~musiker** *m*, **~musikerin** *f* jazz musician; **~trompete** *f* jazz trumpet; **~trompeter** *m*, **~trompeterin** *f* jazz trumpeter

je¹ *Interj*.: *ach od*. *o* ~! oh no!, oh dear!

je² **I.** *Adv. und Konj*. **1.** → *eh* I 2; **2.** (*jemals*) ever; *ohne ihn* ~ *gesehen zu haben* without ever having seen him;

hast du ~ *so etwas gehört?* did you ever hear (of) such a thing?; **3.** ~ *sechs* six each; *sie kosten* ~ *einen Dollar* they cost a dollar each; *er gab den Jungen* ~ *einen Apfel* he gave each of the boys an apple, he gave the boys an apple each; *in Schachteln mit* ~ *zehn Stück* in boxes of ten; ~ *zwei und zwei* in twos; **4.** ~ *nach* according to; ~ *nachdem als Adv*.: it (all) depends, *als Konj*.: according to; ~ *nachdem was er sagt etc*. depending on what he says *etc*.; **5.** *mit Komp*.: ~ *... desto ...* the ... the ...; ~ *länger*, ~ *lieber* the longer the better; **II.** *Präp*.: *3 Euro* ~ (*angefangene*) *Stunde* Parkgebühren 3 euros per hour (or part of an hour)

Jeans [dʒiːnz] *Pl*., *umg. auch f*; *-*, *-*: (*e-e*) ~ (a pair of) jeans *Pl*.; **~anzug** *m* denim suit

jeansfarben *Adj*. denim(-colo[u]red)

Jeans|hemd *n* denim shirt; **~hose** *f* → *Jeans*; **~jacke** *f* denim jacket; **~laden** *m* shop specializing in denims; **~rock** *m* denim skirt; **~stoff** *m* denim

jeck *Adj*. *Dial*. mad; *umg*. crazy; *bist du* ~? *auch* have you gone mad?; **Jeck** *m*; *-s*, *-en*; *Dial*. fool, nut(case); *Fastnacht* (carnival) clown

jede|... *unbest. Pron*. **1.** *adjektivisch*: (*insgesamt*) every; (*alle einzeln*) each; *betonend*: each and every; (*beliebige*) any; *von zweien*: either; (*alle, jegliche*) all; ~*s Mal* every time; (*immer*) always; ~*s Mal, wenn* every time, whenever; ~*r einzelne ...* every single ...; ~*r zweite ...* every other ...; ~ *Hilfe kam zu spät* there was nothing anyone could do, he/she *etc*. was beyond help; *hier ist* ~*s Wort zu viel* there's nothing (any)one can say; *ohne* ~*n Zweifel* without (any) doubt; (*zu*) ~*r Zeit* (at) any time; *sie kann* ~*n Moment da sein* she could be here any minute; *um* ~*n Preis* whatever the cost, at any price; *bei* ~*m Wetter* in any weather; → *Fall²* 1; **2.** *substantivisch*: (*Personen*) everyone; (*jeder Einzelne*) every single one (*od*. person); (*jeder Beliebige*) anyone, any (of them); (*Dinge*) every (*od*. each) one; *für Personen* → *auch jedermann*; ~*r von ihnen* all (*od*. each) of them; *alles und* ~*s* everything (under the sun); ~*r hat seine Fehler* we all have our faults

jedenfalls *Adv*. **1.** (*wie besprochen*) anyway, in any case, at any rate; **2.** (*was immer auch sei*) at any rate, at all events; **3.** (*wie dem auch sei*) be that as it may; **4.** (*wenigstens*) at least, at any rate; *ich bin es* ~ *nicht* it's not me, anyway; (*nicht überrascht etc*.) I for one am not

jederart *Adj*. any kind (*od*. sort) of; **jederlei** *Adj*. all sorts (*od*. kinds) of ...

jedermann *unbest. Pron*. everyone, everybody; (*jeder Beliebige*) anyone, anybody; *nicht* ~*s Sache* not everybody's cup of tea; *Jedermann Theat*. Everyman

jeder|zeit *Adv*. **1.** any time, always; **2.** (*jeden Moment*) any minute (now); (*jeden Tag*) any day (now); **~zeitig** *Adj*.: *mit e-r* ~*en Änderung rechnen* expect things to change at any time

jedesmal → *Mal¹*

jedoch *Adv*. however, still; *nachgestellt*: though

jedwede *unbest. Pron*. every single; *Freude, Bedauern etc*.: all; *ohne* ~*n ...* without a trace of, bar all, devoid of (all); *ihm fehlt* ~*r Sinn für Humor etc*.

he hasn't got (*bes. Am*. doesn't have) the slightest sense of humo(u)r *etc*.; ~*r kann teilnehmen* anyone can join in (*od*. take part)

Jeep® [dʒiːp] *m*; *-s*, *-s* jeep®

jegliche *unbest. Pron*. → *jedwede*

jeher *Adv*.: *von* ~ always; all along; (*seit alters*) from time immemorial, ever since I *etc*. can remember

Jehova (*m*); *-s*; *Reli*.: *die Zeugen* ~*s* Jehovah's Witnesses

jein *Adv. hum., oft iro*. yes and no

jemals *Adv*. ever; → *je²* I 2

jemand *unbest. Pron*. somebody, someone; *fragend: auch* anybody, anyone; *verneinend*: anybody, anyone; *es kommt* ~ somebody's coming; *ist da* ~? is anybody there?; ~ *anders* somebody (*od*. anybody) else; *sonst noch* ~? anyone else (*iro*. while I'm at it)?; → *irgendjemand*; **Jemand** *m* *hum., iro*.: *ein gewisser* ~ a certain somebody

Jemen (*m*); *-s*; *Geog*. Yemen; **Jemenit** *m*; *-en*, *-en*, **Jemenitin** *f*; *-*, *-nen* Yemeni, *weibl. auch*: Yemeni woman (*od*. girl *etc*.); **jemenitisch** *Adj*. Yemeni

jemine *Interj*.: *ach* ~ oh dear

jener *Dem. Pron. m*, **jene** *f*, **jenes** *n*, **jene** *Pl*. **1.** *adjektivisch*: that, of this, those; *seit jenem Tag* from that day on; **2.** *substantivisch*: that one, *Pl*. those; (*der, die, das vorher Erwähnte*) the former; → *dieser* 2

jenseitig *Adj*. **1.** on the other side; *am* ~*en Ufer* on the opposite bank; **2.** *fig*. otherworldly

jenseits I. *Präp*. on the other side of, across, beyond; **II.** *Adv*. on the other side; ~ *von* beyond; ~ *von Gut und Böse umg*. past it

Jenseits *n*; *-*, *kein Pl*. the hereafter; *ins* ~ *befördern umg*. send *s.o*. to meet his (*od*. her) Maker; **~glaube** *m* belief in life after death

Jeremia *m*; *-s*; *bibl*. Jeremiah; *das Buch* ~ (the Book of) Jeremiah

Jersey¹ ['dʒøːɐzi] *m*; *-(s)*, *-s Stoff*: jersey

Jersey² *n*; *-s*, *-s*; *Sport* jersey

Jesaja *m*; *-s*; *bibl*. Isaiah

Jesses *Interj*. (*auch* ~ *Maria!*) good Lord!, *umg*. Jesus (Christ)!, *bes. Am*. *auch* gee!

Jesuit *m*; *-en*, *-en*; *Reli*. Jesuit

Jesuitenorden *m* Jesuit Order, Order of Jesuits; Jesuits *Pl*.

jesuitisch *Adj*. Jesuit ..., Jesuitic(al); *pej*. jesuitical

Jesus (*m*); *-* Jesus; ~ *Christus* Jesus Christ; *der Herr* ~ the Lord Jesus; ~ (*Maria und Josef*)! *Interj*. Jesus (Mary and Joseph)!; **~kind** *n*: *das* ~ the infant Jesus, *Kinderspr*. (the) baby Jesus; **~latschen**. *Pl. umg*. Jesus sandals; (*Zehensandalen*) (leather) thongs

Jet [dʒɛt] *m*; *-(s)*, *-s*; *Flug*. jet

Jetlag ['dʒɛtlɛg] *m*; *-s*, *-s*; *Flug*. jet lag

Jetliner ['dʒɛtlainɐ] *m*; *-s*, *-*; *Flug*. jetliner

Jeton [ʒə'tõː] *m*; *-s*, *-s* chip

Jetset ['dʒɛtsɛt] *m*; *-s*, *-s* jet set

Jetstream ['dʒɛtstriːm] *m*; *-(s)*, *-s*; *Met*. jet stream

jetten ['dʒɛtn̩] *v/i. umg*.: ~ *nach* jet off to

jetzig *Adj*. present, current; (*bestehend*) existing; (*vorherrschend*) prevailing; *in der* ~*en Zeit* these days, nowadays

jetzt *Adv*. **1.** now; (*heutzutage*) these days, nowadays; *er fehlt* ~ *schon drei Tage* he's been missing (*od*. absent) now for three days; *erst* ~ only now; ~

J

gleich ~ right now; *ich habe* ~ *keine Zeit* I haven't got (any) time right now; **2.** *bei lebhafter Erzählung:* ~ *(da) erhob er sich* then he got up; **3.** *nach Präp.:* *bis* ~ so far, *bei Verneinung:* *auch* as yet; *von* ~ *an* from now on; **4.** *wo hab ich's* ~ *hingetan?* where did I put it now?; ~ *reicht es aber!* that's enough!; ~ *oder nie!* now or never; **Jetzt** *n*; -, *kein Pl.* → *hier* 1

Jetzt|mensch *m* person alive today; **~zeit** *f* present (time)

Jeunesse dorée [ʒœnɛsdɔ're:] *f*; -, -; *lit.* jeunesse dorée, gilded youth

jeweilen *Adv. schw.* → *jeweils*

jeweilig *Adj.* respective; *(gegeben, spezifisch)* particular; *(relevant)* relevant; *(vorherrschend)* prevailing; *der* ~*e Präsident* the president in office, the sitting president; *der* ~*e Abteilungsleiter* the head of the department in question; *den* ~*en Umständen entsprechend* according to the circumstances (at the time)

jeweils *Adv.* **1.** *(gleichzeitig)* ~ *zwei etc.* two *etc.* at a time; **2.** *(jedesmal)* always; *sie kommt* ~ *am Montag* she comes every Monday *(od.* on Mondays)*; **3.** *(je)* each; *Übungen mit* ~ *20 Fragen* with twenty questions each; **4.** *(zu diesem Zeitpunkt)* at the time; *die* ~ *erforderlichen Maßnahmen* the relevant *(od.* appropriate) measures

jiddisch I. *Adj.* Yiddish; **II. Jiddisch** *n*; -(s), *kein Pl.; Ling.* Yiddish; *das Jiddische* Yiddish; **Jiddistik** *f*; -, *kein Pl.* Yiddish studies

Jingle [dʒɪŋgl] *m*; -(s), -(s) *in Werbespot:* jingle

Jiu-Jitsu ['dʒiːu'dʒɪtsu] *n*; -(s), *kein Pl.; altm.* → *Jujutsu*

Job [dʒɔp] *m*; -s, -s job; **jobben** *v/i.* job around; *Student:* work during the vac *(Am.* summer); *umg. (e-n Beruf ausüben)* work, have a job; **Jobber** *m*; -s, -, **Jobberin** ; -, -nen jobber

Job|hopping *n*; -s, -s job hopping; **~killer** *m umg.* job killer; **~rotation** *f*; -, -en job rotation; **~sharing** ['-ʃɛːrɪŋ] *n*; -(s), *kein Pl.* job sharing; **~suche** *f* job hunting; **~ticket** *n* reduced rate ticket for travel to work; **~vermittlung** *f* job finding

Joch *n*; -(e)s, -e, *als Maß:*- **1.** yoke *(auch fig.);* *Ochsen ins* ~ *spannen* yoke oxen; *das* ~ *der Diktatur abschütteln fig.* shake/throw off the yoke of dictatorship; **2.** *e-s Bergs:* saddleback; **3.** *Archit.* bay; → *auch Jochbalken;* **4.** *österr., Flächenmaß:* unit of area equal to 575.54 square met|res *(Am. -ers)*

Joch|balken *m* crossbeam, girder; **~bein** *n Anat.* cheekbone; **~bogen** *m Archit.* bay

Jockei *m*; -s, -s, **Jockey** ['dʒɔke] *m*; -s -s jockey

Jod *n*; -(e)s, *kein Pl.; Chem.* iodine; **jodeln** *v/t./i.* yodel

jodhaltig *Adj.:* ~ *sein* contain iodine

Jodid *n*; -(e)s, -e; *Chem.* iodide; **jodieren** *v/t. Chem.* iodinate; *Med. und Fot.* iodize

Jodler *m*; -s, - **1.** *(Person)* yodel(l)er; **2.** *(Ruf)* yodel; *(Lied)* yodel(l)ing song; **Jodlerin** *f*; -, -nen → *Jodler* 1

Jodmangel *m* iodine deficiency

Jod|präparat *n* iodine preparation; **~salz** *n* iodized salt; **~tinktur** *f* iodine tincture, tincture of iodine

Joga *m, n*; -(s), *kein Pl.* yoga; **~übung** *f* yoga exercise

joggen ['dʒɔgn] *v/i.* jog, go jogging;

Jogger ['dʒɔgɐ] *m*; -s, -, **Joggerin** *f*; -, -nen jogger

Jogging ['dʒɔgɪŋ] *n*; -s, *kein Pl.* jogging; **~anzug** *m* tracksuit, jogging suit; **~hose** *f*: *(e-e)* ~ (a pair of) jogging bottoms *Pl., Am.* sweat pants *Pl.;* **~schuhe** *Pl.* running shoes

Joghurt *m, n*; -(s), -s yog(h)urt; **~becher** *m* yog(h)urt pot

Jogurt → *Joghurt*

Johannes[1] *m*; -; *bibl.* John; ~ *der Täufer* John the Baptist; → *Offenbarung* 2; *der 1./2. Brief des* ~ the 1st/2nd Epistle of St *(od.* St.) John, John I/II

Johannes[2] *m*; -, -se; *umg. (Penis) Brit.* willy, *Am.* johnson

Johannes|brief *m*: *der 1./2./3.* ~ the 1st/2nd/3rd Epistle of St *(od.* St.) John, John I/II/III; **~evangelium** *n*: *das* ~ (the Gospel according to) St *(od.* St.) John, St *(od.* St.) John's Gospel; **~passion** *f*: *die* ~ the St *(od.* St.) John Passion

Johannisbeere *f Bot.:* *Rote* ~ redcurrant; *Schwarze* ~ blackcurrant; **Johannisbeerstrauch** *m* currant bush

Johannis|brot *n Bot.* carob; **~brotbaum** *m Bot.* carob tree; **~feuer** *n* Midsummer Eve bonfire; **~käfer** *m Dial.* glow-worm; **~kraut** *n Bot.* St *(od.* St.) John's wort; **~tag** *m* St *(od.* St.) John the Baptist's Day *(June 24th);* **~trieb** *m* **1.** *Bot.* lammas shoot; **2.** *umg. fig.* late love

Johanniter *m*; -s, -; *Reli.* Knight of St *(od.* St.) John of Jerusalem; **~orden** *m* Order of (the Knights of) St *(od.* St.) John of Jerusalem; **~unfallhilfe** *f* St *(od.* St.) John's Ambulance

johlen I. *v/i.* bawl, yell; **II. Johlen** *n*; -s, *kein Pl.* bawling, yelling

Joint [dʒɔynt] *m*; -s, -s joint

Jointventure ['dʒɔynt'ventʃɐ] *n*; -(s), -s; *Wirts.* joint venture

Jo-Jo *n*; -s, -s yoyo

Jojoba *f*; -, *Bot.* jojoba

Joker *m*; -s, - joker; *fig.* trump card

Jokus *m*; -, -se *umg.* fun

Jolle *f*; -, -n; *Naut.* dinghy

Jom Kippur *m*, -; *Reli.* Yom Kippur

Jona *m*; -s; *bibl.* Jonah

Jongleur *m*; -s, -e, **~in** *f*; -, -nen juggler; **jonglieren** *v/t/i.* juggle *(mit* [with] *s.th.) (auch fig.)*

Joppe *f* jacket

Jordan *m*; -s; *Geog.* (River) Jordan; *über den* ~ *gehen fig.* cross over Jordan, go to meet one's Maker, pass on

Jordanien *(n)*; -s; *Geog.* Jordan; **Jordanier** *m*; -s, -, **Jordanierin** *f*; -, -nen Jordanian, *weiblich auch:* Jordanian woman *(od.* girl); **jordanisch** *Adj.* Jordanian

Josephsehe *f* unconsummated marriage

Josua *m*; -s; *bibl.* Joshua; *das Buch* ~ (the Book of) Joshua

Jot *n*; -, - J, j

Jota *n*; -(s), -s; *fig.:* *kein* ~ not one jot (or tittle)

Joule [dʒuːl] *n*; -(s), -; *Phys.* joule

Journaille [ʒʊr'naljə] *f*; -, *kein Pl.; pej.* gutter press

Journal [ʒʊr'naːl] *n*; -s, -e **1.** *Zeitschrift:* journal, magazine; **2.** *Wirts.* daybook; **3.** *(Schiffstagebuch)* log

Journalismus *m*; -, *kein Pl.* journalism; **Journalist** *m*; -en, -en journalist; **Journalistik** *f*; -, *kein Pl.* journalism; **Journalistin** *f*; -, -nen → *Journalist;* **journalistisch I.** *Adj.* journalistic; **II.** *Adv.* journalistically

jovial *Adj.* genial, affable; **Jovialität** *f*;

-, *kein Pl.* geniality; *(Umgänglichkeit)* affability

Joystick *m*; -s, -s *Computerspiele:* joystick

jr. *Abk. (junior)* Jr

Jubel *m*; -s, *kein Pl.* cheering, cheers *Pl.;* *(Freude)* rejoicing; *es herrschte allgemeiner* ~ there was general rejoicing; *es herrschte* ~*, Trubel, Heiterkeit* there was much merrymaking; **~feier** *f*, **~fest** *n* anniversary (celebration [s *Pl.*]); **~geschrei** *n* cheering; **~greis** *m umg.* sprightly old fellow; **~jahr** *n* jubilee year; *alle* ~*e einmal umg.* once in a blue moon

jubeln *v/i.* cheer, shout for joy; *(sich freuen)* rejoice; *zu früh* ~ celebrate too soon *(od.* prematurely), count one's chickens before they're hatched; *j-m etw. unter die Weste* ~ *umg. (andrehen)* fob s.th. off on s.o.; *(aufhalsen)* land s.o. with s.th.

Jubel|paar *n* couple celebrating a major wedding anniversary; **~ruf** *m* cheer, shout of joy; **~schrei** *m* cheer, shout of joy

Jubilar *m*; -s, -e, **~in** *f*; -, -nen person celebrating an anniversary; *umg. am Geburtstag:* birthday boy, *weiblich:* birthday girl

Jubiläum *n*; -s, Jubiläen anniversary, *nach 25, 50 od. 60 Jahren* jubilee; ~ *haben* have *(od.* celebrate) an anniversary/jubilee

Jubiläums|ausgabe *f* anniversary/jubilee edition; **~feier** *f* anniversary *(od.* jubilee) celebration(s *Pl.*); **~jahr** *n* anniversary *(od.* jubilee) year

jubilieren *v/i.* **1.** rejoice *(über + Akk.* over), *schadenfroh: auch* gloat (over); **2.** *Vogel:* trill, carol

juchhe *Interj.* whoopee!

juchten *Adj.* Russia-leather ..., *nachgestellt:* made of Russia leather; **Juchten** *n*; -s, *kein Pl.* Russia leather *(auch Duft);* **Juchtenleder** *n* Russia leather; **Juchtenstiefel** *m* Russia-leather boot

juchzen *v/i.* → *jauchzen;* **Juchzer** *m*; -s, - → *Jauchzer*

juckeln *v/i. umg.* **1.** *(hat)* fidget *(od.* twitch) around; **2.** *(ist) Auto:* chug along

jucken I. *v/t/i.* **1.** itch; *mich juckt's* I'm itching; *es juckt mich am Arm* my arm's itching; *der Pullover juckt* the pullover's scratchy *(od.* itchy); **2.** *fig.:* *es juckt(e) mich zu (+ Inf.)* I'd love to *(+ Inf.)* (I was tempted *od.* itching to *+ Inf.);* *dich/dir juckt wohl das Fell* what's got into you all of a sudden?; *das juckt mich nicht* why should I care?; *es scheint ihn nicht zu* ~ it doesn't seem to bother him (in the slightest); *wen juckt's?* who cares?; *das juckt niemanden* nobody could care less *(umg.* give a damn); *lass* ~*!* (come on,) get on with it!; **II.** *v/refl. umg. (sich kratzen)* scratch o.s.

Jucken *n*; -s, *kein Pl.* itch(ing)

Juck|pulver *n* itching powder; **~reiz** *m* itch(ing), itchiness

Judäa *(n)*; -s; *hist.* Jud(a)ea

Judaika *Pl.* Judaica

Judaismus *m*; -, *kein Pl.* Judaism; **Judaist** *m*; -en, -en Judaist; **Judaistik** *f*; -, *kein Pl.* Jewish *(od.* Judaic) studies *Pl.;* **Judaistin** *f*; -, -nen → *Judaist*

Judas *m*; -, -se; *bibl.* Judas; *fig. auch* traitor; *Brief des* ~ → *Judasbrief;* **~baum** *m Bot.* Judas tree; **~brief** *m bibl.: (der)* ~ (the Epistle of) Jude; **~kuss** *m* Judas kiss; *der* ~ *Kunst* the Betrayal; **~lohn** *m* traitor's reward;

sein etc. ~ his *etc.* thirty pieces of silver

Jude *m*; *-n, -n* Jew

Juden|christ *m* Jud(a)eo-Christian; **~christentum** *n*: *das* ~ Jud(a)eo--Christians *Pl.*; **~christenheit** *f* Jud(a)eo-Christianity; **~kirsche** *f Bot.* ground cherry; **~stern** *m im Nationalsozialismus*: Star of David, Magen David

Judentum *n*; *-s, kein Pl.* **1.** *das* ~ Judaism; **2.** (*das Volk*) the Jews *Pl.*, the Jewish people; *das moderne etc.* ~ modern *etc.* Jewry

Juden|verfolgung *f* persecution of the Jews; **~viertel** *n* Jewish quarter

Judikative *f*; *-, -n* judiciary; **judikatorisch** *Adj. Jur. altm.* judicatory *allg.*

Jüdin *f*; *-nen* Jew, Jewish woman (*od. girl etc.*), Jewess *neg!*; **jüdisch** *Adj.* Jewish

judizieren *v/i. Jur.* administer justice; **Judizium** *n*; *-s, Judizien; Jur.* judg(e)ment

Judo *n*; *-(s), kein Pl.* judo; **~anzug** *m* judo outfit; **~griff** *m* judo hold

Judoka *m*; *-(s), -(s) und f*; *-, -s* judoka

Jugend *f*; *-, kein Pl.* **1.** youth; (*Kindesalter*) childhood; *in m-r* ~ when I was young; *von* ~ *auf* since I was (*od.* you were *etc.*) young *od.* a child; *seit frühester* ~ from when I was (*od.* you were *etc.*) very young, from my (*od.* your *etc.*) earliest youth *geh.*; **2.** (*Jugendlichkeit*) youth(fulness); **3.** *Koll.*: *die* ~ young people, the younger generation, *heutige: auch* the youth of today, today's youth; *die deutsche* ~ the young Germans (of today); *die reifere* ~ *hum.* the over-forties; **4.** *Sport* (*Jugendmannschaft*) youth team; **~alter** *n*: (*im*) ~ (in) adolescence; **~alkoholismus** *m* alcoholism among the young; **~amt** *n* youth welfare office; **~arbeit** *f*; *nur Sg.* **1.** youth employment; **2.** *Soziol.* youth work; **~arbeitslosigkeit** *f* youth unemployment; **~arbeitsschutzgesetz** *n* law governing the protection of young people at work; **~arrest** *m Jur.* short-term detention for young offenders; **~bande** *f* gang of youths; **~betreuer** *m*, **~betreuerin** *f* youth leader (*adult supervisor who looks after young people*)

Jugend|bewegung *f* youth movement; **~bild** *n*, **~bildnis** *n*: *ein* ~ *von X* a portrait of X as a young man (*od.* woman); → *Jugendfoto*; **~blüte** *f poet.* youthful bloom; **~buch** *n* book for young people (*od.* adolescents); **~bücherei** *f* junior library, library for young people; **~elf** *f Fußball* youth team; **~erinnerungen** *Pl.* memories of one's youth; **~eselei** *f umg.* youthful prank; **~foto** *n*: *ein* ~ *von X* a photo of X as a young man (*bzw.* woman), a photo of X when he (*bzw.* she) was young

jugendfrei *Adj. Film*: suitable for all ages, U-certificate, *Am.* G-rated; *nicht* ~ for adults only

Jugendfreund *m*, **~in** *f* friend from (*od.* of) one's youth; *er ist ein* ~ *von mir oft* we've been friends ever since we were young

jugendfrisch *Adj. geh.* youthful; **Jugendfrische** *f* youthfulness

jugendgefährdend *Adj.* harmful (to young people)

Jugend|gericht *n* juvenile court; **~gerichtsbarkeit** *f* jurisdiction over juveniles; **~gottesdienst** *m* young people's service; **~gruppe** *f* youth group;

~heim *n* youth cent|re (*Am.* -er); **~herberge** *f* youth hostel; **~hilfe** *f* youth welfare (services *Pl.*); **~jahre** *Pl.*: *die* ~ one's youth; *in m-n* ~*n* in my youth, when I was young, when I was a young lad (*od.* girl); **~kammer** *f Jur.* juvenile division; **~klasse** *f Sport* youth class; **~klub** *m* youth club; **~kriminalität** juvenile delinquency; **~lager** *n* youth camp

jugendlich *Adj.* youthful (*auch Aussehen, Kleidung etc.*); (*jung*) young; *Jur. auch* juvenile; **~er Leichtsinn** youthful abandon (*Ahnungslosigkeit*: innocence); ~ *aussehen* look young; ~ *wirken auch* come across as quite young; **Jugendliche** *m, f*; *-n, -n* young person, *m auch* youth, *Jur. auch* juvenile; **Jugendlichkeit** *f* youthfulness

Jugend|liebe *f* **1.** (*Person*) old flame; **2.** puppy love; **~literatur** *f* books *Pl.* for young people, young adult literature; **~mannschaft** *f* youth team; **~meister** *m*, **~meisterin** *f* youth champion; **~meisterschaft** *f* youth championships *Pl.*; **~organisation** *f* youth organization; **~pfarrer** *m*, **~pfarrerin** *f* priest (*od.* minister) with special responsibility for young people; **~pflege** *f* youth welfare; **~pfleger** *m*, **~pflegerin** *f* youth welfare worker; **~psychologie** *f* adolescent psychology; **~recht** *n* juvenile law (*od.* legislation); **~richter** *m*, **~richterin** *f* juvenile court judge; **~schöffengericht** *n* juvenile court presided over by a judge and two lay assessors who usually have experience in youth work

Jugendschutz *m* legal protection for children and young persons; **~gesetz** *n* laws *Pl.* protecting young people; *in GB*: Children and Young Persons Act

Jugend|spieler *m*, **~spielerin** *f* player in a youth team; **~sprache** *f* teenage slang; **~stadium** *n* youth; **~stil** *m* art nouveau, *bes. in Deutschland*: Jugendstil; **~strafanstalt** *f* young offender institution, remand centre, *Am.* juvenile correction facility, reform school *altm.*; **~strafe** *f* detention in a young offender institution (*Am.* reform school); **~strafrecht** *n* law governing young offenders; **~streich** *m* youthful escapade (*od.* exploit); **~sünde** *f* sin (*od.* transgression) of one's youth; **~torheit** *f* youthful indiscretion, folly of one's youth; **~traum** *m* childhood dream (*od.* ambition); **~treff** *m* youth club (*od.* centre *od. Am.* center); **~verbot** *n*: *der Film hat* ~ is for adults only; **~weihe** *f* dedication ceremony for children or young people; **~werk** *n* e-s Künstlers etc.*: early work; **~zeit** *f* → *Jugend* 1; **~zentrum** *n* youth cent|re (*Am.* -er)

Jugoslawe *m*; *-n, -n* **1.** Yugoslav; **2.** *umg.* (*Restaurant*) *umg.* Yugoslavian place; **Jugoslawien** (*n*); *-s*; *Geog.* Yugoslavia; **Jugoslawin** *f*; *-, -nen* Yugoslav woman (*od.* girl); **jugoslawisch** *Adj.* Yugoslav

juhu *Interj.* **1.** *Ausruf*: hooray, yippee; **2.** *Zuruf*: yoohoo

Jujutsu *n*; *-(s); kein Pl.* j(i)ujitsu

Jukebox ['dʒuːkbɔks] *f*; *-, -es* jukebox

Jul *n*; *-(s), kein Pl.* (*Wintersonnenwende bzw. skandinavisches Weihnachtsfest*) Yule

Julei *m*; *-(s), -s*; *aus Gründen der Deutlichkeit gesprochene Form von* → *Juli*

Juli *m*; *-(s), -s, mst Sg.*; (*abgek. Jul.*) July; → *April*

julianisch *Adj.*: *der* ~*e Kalender* the

Julian calendar

Julienne [ʒyˈljɛn] *f*; *-, kein Pl.*; *Gastr.* julienne; **~suppe** *f Gastr.* julienne

Jumbo *m*; *-s, -s*, **Jumbo-Jet** *m Flug.* jumbo (jet)

Jumelage [ʒymˈlaːʒ] *f*; *-, -n* (town-)twinning

Jump [dʒamp] *m*; *-s, -s beim Dreisprung*: jump (stage)

jun. *Abk.* (*junior*) Jr

jung *Adj.*; *jünger, am jüngsten* young; (*jugendlich*) youthful; **~es Unternehmen** new company; **~er Wein** new wine; **~es Glück** new-found happiness; *von* ~ *auf* from childhood; ~ *heiraten/sterben etc.* marry/die *etc.* young (*od.* at an early age); *so* ~ *kommen wir nicht mehr zusammen mst. hum.* you're only young once; *sie ist* ~ *geblieben* she has stayed young; (*sieht noch jung aus*) *auch* she has kept her looks; ~ *verheiratet* newly-wed; *Jung und Alt* young and old; *die Jungen* the young ones, the young(er) generation; → *jünger, jüngst..., Gemüse, Hund* 1

Jung|akademiker *m*, **~akademikerin** *f* recent graduate; **~bauer** *m*, **~bäuerin** *f* young farmer; **~brunnen** *m* fountain of youth; **~bürger** *m*, **~bürgerin** *f österr., schw.* junior citizen; **~demokrat** *m*, **~demokratin** *f* Young Democrat

Junge[1] *m*; *-n, -n od. umg. Jungs* boy; *umg.* (*junger Mann*) *umg.* lad, *Am. auch* kid; *umg.* (*Spielkarte*) jack; *dummer* ~ silly little boy; *armer* ~ poor lad (*Am.* kid); *umg.* ~, ~! *umg.* boy oh boy; *hallo Jungs!* hi guys!; *die blauen Jungs* the sailor boys; → *schwer* I 4

Junge[2] *n*; *-n, -n*; *Zool. umg.* baby; (*Hund*) puppy; (*Kätzchen*) kitten; *von Raubtier*: oft cub; (*Kalb, Elefant, Robbe*) calf; *ein* ~*s haben* have a puppy *od.* kitten *od.* cub *etc.*; *Junge werfen od. bekommen* have young (*od.* a litter), *Hündin*: have puppies, *Katze*: have kittens, *Kuh etc.*: calve, *Reh, Rotwild*: fawn

Jüngelchen *n umg. pej.* lad

jungen *v/i.* have young (*od.* a litter); *Hündin*: have puppies; *Katze*: have kittens; *Kuh etc.*: calve; *Reh, Rotwild*: fawn

Jungengesicht *n* boy's face; (*jungenhaftes*) boyish face

jungenhaft *Adj.* boyish; **Jungenhaftigkeit** *f* boyishness

Jungen|klasse *f* boys' class; **~schule** *f* boys' school; **~streich** *m* schoolboy prank

jünger *Adj.* younger; *weitS.* (*ziemlich jung*) youngish; (*zeitlich näher*) more recent, later; *der Jüngere* (*d. J.*) the Younger; **~en Datums** more recent; *sie sieht* ~ *aus als sie ist* she looks younger than her age, she doesn't look her age

Jünger *m*; *-s, -*, **~in** *f*; *-, -nen* disciple; *fig. auch* follower; **Jüngerschaft** *f* (body of) followers *Pl. od.* disciples *Pl.*

Jungfer *f*; *-, -n*; *altm.*: *alte* ~ old maid

Jungfern|fahrt *f* maiden (*od.* inaugural) voyage; (*od.* inaugural) flight; **~flug** *m* maiden (*od.* inaugural) flight; **~häutchen** *n Anat.* hymen; **~kranz** *m altm.* bridal bouquet; **~rede** *f* maiden speech; **~schaft** *f altm.* virginity; **~zeugung** *f Bio.* parthenogenesis

Jungfilmer *m*; *-s, -*, **~in** *f*; *-, -nen* young film(-)maker

Jungfrau *f* **1.** virgin; *sie ist noch* ~ she's still a virgin; *die* ~ *Maria* the Virgin Mary; *die Heilige* ~ the Blessed (*od.* Holy) Virgin; *eiserne* ~ Iron Maiden; *die* ~ *von Orleans* the Maid of Orleans, Joan of Arc; *umg.* **er ist dazu gekommen wie die** ~ **zum Kind** it just (*umg.* sort of) fell into his lap; **2.** *nur Sg.*; *Astrol.* (*Sternzeichen*) Virgo; **3.** *Astrol.* (*e-e*) ~ *sein* be (a) Virgo; **Jungfrauengeburt** *f* *bibl.* Virgin Birth; **jungfräulich** *Adj.* (*keusch*) chaste; (*unberührt*) virginal; *fig.* virgin …; **Jungfräulichkeit** *f* virginity; (*Keuschheit*) chasteness

Junggeselle *m* bachelor, single man; *eingefleischter* (*alter*) ~ confirmed (old) bachelor; **er ist noch** ~ he's still a bachelor, he's still single

Junggesellen|bude *f* *umg.* bachelor pad; ~**dasein** *n* life of a bachelor, bachelor life; ~**haushalt** *m* bachelor household; ~**leben** *n* → **Junggesellendasein**; ~**wirtschaft** *f* bachelor household; ~**wohnung** *f* bachelor flat (*Am.* apartment); ~**zeit** *f* bachelor years (*od.* days) *Pl.*

Junggesellin *f* single girl (*od.* woman), unmarried woman; *Amtsspr.* spinster

Jung|holz *n*; *kein Pl.* young growth; ~**lehrer** *m*, ~**lehrerin** *f* student teacher; ~**liberale** *m*, *f* Young Liberal (*young member of the F.D.P.*)

Jüngling *m*; *-s, -e* youth; *pej.* stripling; **jünglinghaft** → **jünglingshaft**, **Jünglingsalter** *n*: (*im* ~ *in* one's) youth, (*in*) adolescence; **jünglingshaft** *Adj.* youthful, *nachgestellt*: of youth

Jung|pflanze *f* seedling, young plant; ~**sozialist** *m*, ~**sozialistin** *f* Young Socialist (*young member of the SPD*)

jüngst *Adv.* *geh.* recently; (*neulich*) the other day

jüngst… *Adj.* youngest; *zeitlich*: latest; **Jüngster Tag** Day of Judg(e)ment; **Vorgänge der** ~**en Vergangenheit** recent events; **sein** ~**es Werk** his latest work; *umg.* **sie ist auch nicht mehr die Jüngste** she's not getting any younger; *umg.* she's no spring chicken any more; **unser Jüngster** *od.* **unsere Jüngste** our youngest (one *od.* child); **in** ~**er Zeit** recently; (*neulich*) the other day

Jungsteinzeit *f* Neolithic Age

jüngstens *Adv.* *altm.* → **jüngst**

Jung|tier *n* young animal; *Jagd*: young deer (*od.* doe); ~**unternehmer** *m*, ~**unternehmerin** *f* young entrepreneur (*od.* businessman, *weiblich auch*: businesswoman); ~**verheiratete** *m*, *f*; *-n*, *-n*, ~**vermählte** *m*, *f*; *-n*, *-n*: **die** ~**n** the newly(-)weds, the young couple *Sg.*; ~**vieh** *n* young stock; ~**vogel** *m* young bird, fledgling; ~**volk** *n*; *nur Sg.* **1.** *altm.* young folk; **2.** *hist.*, *im Nationalsozialismus*: young people; ~**wähler** *m*, ~**wählerin** *f* *Pol.* young voter

Juni *m*; *-(s), -s, mst Sg.*; (*abgek.* **Jun.**) June; → **April**; ~**käfer** *m* *Zool.* June bug, garden chafer

junior *Adj.* junior; **X** ~ X junior (*od.* Junior), young X

Junior *m*; *-s, -en* **1.** *Sport und umg.* e-r *Familie etc.*: junior; **2.** *Wirts.* owner's (*od.* boss's) son; → *auch* **Juniorchef**

Junior|chef *m*, ~**chefin** *f* *Wirts.* m boss's son/daughter

Junioren… *im Subst. Sport* junior …

Juniorin *f*; *-, -nen* **1.** → **Junior** 1; **2.** *Wirts.* owner's (*od.* boss's) daughter

Juniorpartner *m*, ~**in** *f* *Wirts.* junior partner

Junker *m*; *-s, -* **1.** (young) nobleman; (*Landjunker*) (country) squire; **2.** *hist. in Preußen*: Junker; **Junkertum** *n* *hist. in Preußen*: Junkerdom

Junkie *m*; *-s, -s*; *Sl.* junkie

Junktim *n*; *-s, -s*; *Pol.* package (deal)

Juno *m*; *-(s)*; *aus Gründen der Deutlichkeit gesprochene Form von* → *Juni*

Junta *f*; *-, Junten*; *Pol.* junta

Jupe [ʒyːp] *m*; *-s, -s*; *schw.* skirt

Jupiter *m*; *-s, kein Pl.*; *Astron, Myth.* Jupiter; **Jupiterlampe®** *f* klieg light

Jura¹ (*Pl.*) law; ~ *studieren* study (*od.* read *od.* do) law

Jura² *m*; *-s, kein Pl.*; *Geog.*: *der Schweizer* ~ the Swiss Jura; *der Kanton* ~ the canton of Jura

Jura³ *m*; *-s, kein Pl.*; *Geol.* Jurassic (period); ~**formation** *f* Jurassic system

jurassisch *Adj.* **1.** *Geol.* Jurassic; **2.** *schw.* of (*od.* from, *od.* in) (the canton of) Jura

Jura|student *m*, ~**studentin** *f* law student; ~**studium** *n* law studies *Pl.*, study of law; *abgeschlossenes*: law degree

Jurisdiktion *f*; *-, -en* jurisdiction; **Jurisprudenz** *f*; *-, kein Pl.* jurisprudence

Jurist *m*; *-en, -en* jurist; (*Student*) law student

Juristen|deutsch *n*, ~**sprache** *f* oft *pej.* legalese

Juristerei *f*; *-, kein Pl.*; *hum.* law

Juristin; *-, -nen* → **Jurist**

juristisch **I.** *Adj.* legal; ~**e Fakultät** faculty of law, law school; ~**e Person** legal entity; **II.** *Adv.*: ~ *argumentieren* argue from a (purely) legal point of view (*od.* on [purely] legal grounds *od.* legalistically)

Juror *m*; *-s, -en*, ~**in** *f*; *-, -nen* → **Jurymitglied** 1

Jurte *f*; *-, -n* yurt

Jury [ʒyˈriː] *f*; *-, -s* **1.** jury, (panel of) judges *Pl.*; *Ausstellung*: selection committee; **2.** *Jur.* jury; **juryfrei** *Adj.* without a selection committee

Jurymitglied *n* **1.** panel(l)ist; **2.** *Jur.* member of the jury, juror

Jus¹ *n*; *-, kein Pl.*; *österr., schw.* law

Jus² [ʒyː] *m*, *n*; *-, -* **1.** juices from the meat; gravy, *Am. auch* jus; **2.** *schw.* fruit juice

Juso *m*; *-(s), -s*; *Abk.* → **Jungsozialist**

Jusstudium *n* *österr., schw.* → **Jurastudium**

just *Adv.* *altm., auch hum.* just; ~ *als* just as; ~ *in dem Moment* at that very moment, just then

Justage [jʊsˈtaːʒə] *f*; *-e, -n*; (*Justie-*

rung) adjustment; *Druck.* justification

justierbar *Adj.* adjustable; **justieren** *v/t.* adjust, set; (*Gewehr etc.*) true (up); (*eichen*) calibrate; *Druck.* justify; **Justierer** *m*; *-s, -*, **Justiererin** *f*; *-, -nen* adjuster; (*Eicher[in]*) calibrator; **Justierung** *f* adjustment; (*Eichung*) calibration; **Justierwaage** *f* adjusting balance

Justitia *f*; *-, kein Pl.* Justice; *Darstellung*: goddess of justice

justitiabel, Justitiar, Justitiariat, Justitiarin, Justitium → **justiziabel** *etc.*

Justiz *f*; *-, kein Pl.*; *Jur., Prinzip*: justice; *Behörden*: the law, judiciary; ~**angestellte** *m*, *f* judicial authority employee; ~**beamte** *m*, ~**beamtin** *f* judicial officer; ~**behörde** *f* legal authority; ~**gebäude** *n* law courts *Pl.*; ~**gewalt** *f* judiciary (power)

justiziabel *Adj.* *Jur.* litigable; **Justiziar** *m*; *-s, -e*, **Justiziarin**; *f*; *-, -nen* legal adviser

Justiz|irrtum *m* error of justice; ~**minister** *m* justice minister; *in GB: etwa* Lord Chancellor; *in den USA: etwa* Attorney General; ~**ministerin** *f* justice minister; ~**ministerium** *n* ministry of justice; *in den USA: etwa* Department of Justice; ~**mord** *m* judicial murder; ~**palast** *m* (central) law courts *Pl.*; ~**verwaltung** *f* **1.** administration of justice; **2.** *konkret*: legal administrative body; ~**vollzugsanstalt** *f* prison; ~**vollzugsbeamte** *m*, ~**vollzugsbeamtin** *f* (prison) warder, *weiblich*: wardress, *Am.* prison guard; ~**wesen** *n* judicial system, judiciary

Jute *f*; *-, kein Pl.* jute

Jute|faser *f* jute fib|re (*Am.* -er); ~**pflanze** *f* jute plant; ~**sack** *m* (gunny) sack; ~**spinnerei** *f* **1.** *nur Sg.* jute spinning; **2.** jute spinning mill; ~**tasche** *f* jute (*od.* burlap) bag

Jütland (*n*); *-s*; *Geog.* Jutland; **jütländisch** *Adj.* Jutland …, … of Jutland

Juwel¹ *n*; *-s, -en* jewel (*auch fig. Bauwerk etc.*); ~**en** jewellery, *Am.* jewelry; (*Edelsteine*) precious stones

Juwel² *n*; *-s, -e*; *fig.* (*Person*) gem; (*Bauwerk etc.*) jewel

Juwelen|händler *m*, ~**händlerin** *f* jewel(l)er

Juwelier *m*; *-s, -e* jewel(l)er; **Juweliergeschäft** *n*, ~**laden** *m* jewel(l)er's shop; **Juwelierin** *f*; *-, -nen* → **Juwelier**

Jux *m*; *-es, -e Pl. selten*; *umg.* (practical) joke; *aus* ~ for fun, for a laugh, *umg.* for (*od.* as) a lark; *umg.* *aus* (*lauter*) ~ *und Tollerei* just for the (sheer) hell of it; *sich e-n* ~ *machen* have a lark; *sich e-n* ~ *daraus machen zu Inf.* have a bit of fun *Ger.*; **juxen** *v/i.* *umg.* joke

Juxta *f*; *-, Juxten*; *Wirts.* counterfoil

Juxtaposition *f* *Ling.* juxtaposition

Juxte *f*; *-, -n*; *österr.* → **Juxta**

jwd *Adv.* *umg. hum.*: ~ *wohnen* *umg.* live at the back of beyond, live out in the sticks (*Am. auch* boondocks)

K, k n; -, - K, k; *K wie Kaufmann Buch-stabieren*: "k" for (*od.* as in) "kilo"
Kabale f; -, -n; *altm.* cabal
Kabarett n; -s, -e **1.** (political) satirical revue, cabaret; *Veranstaltungsort*: cabaret; **2.** *Servierplatte*: serving dish (divided into sections); *rotierbar*: lazy Susan; **Kabarettist** m; -en, -en, **Kabarettistin** f; -, -nen (political) satirist; **kabarettistisch** *Adj.* (satirical) revue ...
Kabäuschen n; -s, -; *umg.* (*Pförtnerlo-ge*) (gatekeeper's) hut; (*Zimmer*) cubbyhole; (*Kommentatorenbox*) commentary box; (*Glaskabine*) booth
Kabbala f; -, *kein Pl.* cabbala, kabbala; **Kabbalistik** f; -, *kein Pl.* cabbalism; **kabbalistisch** *Adj.* cabbalistic
Kabbelei f; -, -en; *nordd.* squabble
kabbelig *Adj. Naut.*: **~e See** choppy water (*od.* seas)
kabbeln I. v/i. *Naut.* be choppy; **II.** v/refl. *nordd.* squabble
Kabel n; -s, - **1.** *Etech., Tech.* cable; **2.** *umg.* (*Kabelfernsehen*) cable (TV); (*Kabelanschluss*) cable connection; **habt ihr ~?** have you got cable?; **~ader** f cable core; **~anschluss** m cable connection; **~baum** m *Etech.* cable harness; **~brand** m: **das Feuer entstand durch ~** the fire was caused by an electrical fault; **~fernsehen** n cable TV; **~gatt** n *Naut.* cable room
Kabeljau m; -s, -e *und* -s; *Zool.* cod
Kabel|klemme f *Etech. etc.* (*Anschluss-stück*) cable terminal; **~kran** m cable crane; **~leger** m; -s, -, - cable layer; **~mantel** m cable sheath(ing)
Kabel|netz n cable network; **~rolle** f cable drum; **~rundfunk** m cable broadcasting; **~schuh** m *Etech.* cable terminal; **~trommel** f cable drum; **~tuner** m cable decoder (*od.* tuner); **~verbindung** f cable link
Kabine f; -, -n cabin; *Naut.* (*Luxuska-bine*) stateroom (*auch Am. Eisenb.*); *im Schwimmbad, beim Arzt*: cubicle; *Sport* dressing (*Am. auch* locker) room; *Seilbahn*: car; *Telef.* telephone booth; *im Sprachlabor etc.*: booth
Kabinen|bahn f cable railway; **~roller** m *Mot.* bubble car
Kabinett[1] n; -s, -e *Pol.* cabinet
Kabinett[2] m; -(s), *Kabinettweine Wein*: Kabinett (*Am. auch* cabinet) wine, Kabinettwein
Kabinett[3] n; -s, -e; *österr.* (*kleines Zimmer*) boxroom *Brit.*, small room
Kabinetts|beschluss m *Pol.* cabinet decision; **~bildung** f formation of a (*od.* the) cabinet; **~chef** m, **~chefin** f head of the cabinet; **~liste** f list of cabinet members; **~mitglied** n cabinet member; **~sitzung** f cabinet meeting; **~tisch** m: (**mit**) **am ~ sitzen** have a seat (*od.* seats) in the cabinet
Kabinettstück n **1.** *Kunst*: showpiece; **2.** *fig.* masterstroke; (*brillanter Einfall*) flash of genius, *Sport* piece of skill, *umg.* party piece; **Kabinettstückchen**

n → **Kabinettstück** 2
Kabinettsumbildung f *Pol.* cabinet reshuffle
Kabinettwein m Kabinett (*Am. auch* cabinet) wine
Kabrio n; -s, -s, **Kabriolett** n; -s, -s; *Mot.* convertible; **Kabriolimousine** f open-topped limousine
Kabuff n; -s, -s; *umg.* cubbyhole
Kachel f; -, n glazed tile; **kacheln I.** v/t. (*hat gekachelt*) tile; **II.** v/i. (*ist*) *umg.* (*rasen*) race (along); **über die Straße** etc. **~** tear along the road etc.
Kachel|ofen m tiled stove; **~wand** f tiled wall
kackbraun *Adj. vulg.* shit-colo(u)red
Kacke f; -, *kein Pl.*; *vulg.* shit; **die ~ ist am Dampfen** *vulg.* the shit's really flying now; **kacken** v/i. *vulg.* shit
Kadaver m; -s, - (*Aas*) carcass (*auch fig.*); (*Leiche*) corpse; **~gehorsam** m slavish obedience; **~verwertung** f animal waste processing
Kadenz f; -, -en; *Ling., Mus.* cadence; **kadenzieren I.** v/t. *Mus.* cadence; **II.** v/i. *Ling.* cadence
Kader m; -s, -; *Mil., Pol. etc.* cadre; *Sport* pool of players *etc.*; **~abteilung** f *ehem. DDR* personnel department; **~schmiede** f cadre training unit; *weitS.* elite training cent|re (*Am.* -er)
Kadett m; -en, -en **1.** *Mil.* cadet; **2.** *umg.* guy, fellow
Kadetten|anstalt f; *hist.* cadet school; **~korps** n cadet corps
Kadi m; -s, -s; *altm.* cadi; **j-n vor den ~ schleppen** *od.* **bringen** *umg.* have (*od.* bring) s.o. up (**wegen** for)
kadmieren v/t. cadmium-plate
Kadmium n; -s, *kein Pl.*; (*abgek.* **Cd**) *Chem.* cadmium
Kadmiumlegierung f cadmium alloy
kaduzieren v/t. *Wirts.* cancel; **kaduzier-te Aktie** forfeited share
Käfer m; -s, - **1.** *Zool.* beetle (*auch umg.* VW); **2.** *umg.* (*junges Mädchen*) chick, *Brit. auch* bird; **ein flotter ~** *altm.* nice bit of stuff *Sl.*
Kaff n; -s, -e *und* **Käffer**; *umg.* hole, dump
Kaffee m; -s, - *od. bei Sorten* -s coffee; **~ machen** *od.* **kochen** make (some *od.* the) coffee; **e-e Tasse ~** (**trinken**) (have) a cup of coffee; **~ mit Milch** coffee with milk, *Brit. auch* white coffee; **kalter ~** *Dial.* lemonade and cola; **das ist kalter ~** *umg. fig.* that's old hat; **~anbau** m coffee growing; **~automat** m coffee machine; **~bohne** f coffee bean
kaffeebraun *Adj.* coffee-colo(u)red
Kaffee|ernte f (*die geernteten Bohnen*) coffee crop; **~ersatz** m coffee substitute, ersatz coffee; **~extrakt** m coffee essence; **~fahrt** f excursion involving a stop for afternoon coffee and sales promotion; **~filter** m **1.** coffee filter; **2.** (*Papierfilter*) filter, paper cone
Kaffeehaus n café, coffee house; **~lite-**

rat m coffee-house writer; *Pl.* coffee-house literati; **~musik** f palm-court music
Kaffee|kanne f coffee pot; **~klatsch** *umg.* m coffee party, *Am. umg.* coffee klat(s)ch; **~kränzchen** n ladies' afternoon coffee party (*Am.* klat[s]ch); **~löffel** m teaspoon, coffee spoon; **~maschine** f coffee maker; **~mühle** f coffee grinder; **~pause** f coffee break; **~sahne** f (coffee) cream; **~satz** m coffee grounds *Pl.*; **~service** n coffee service; **~sieb** n coffee strainer; **~sorte** f type of coffee; **~strauch** m coffee bush; **~tante** *umg.* f *umg.* coffee freak (*od.* addict); **~tasse** f coffee cup; **~tisch** m table laid for (afternoon) coffee; *Brit. etwa* tea table; **am ~ sitzen** be having (afternoon) coffee; *Brit. etwa* be having (afternoon) tea; **~trinker** m, **~trinkerin** f: **ich bin (kein) Kaffetrinker** I (don't) drink coffee; **~wasser** n: **das ~ aufsetzen** put the kettle on for some coffee; **~wärmer** m; -s, - coffee pot cosy (*Am.* cozy); **~weißer** m; -s, - coffee whitener (*Am.* creamer)
Kaffein n; -s, *kein Pl.* → **Koffein**
Kaffer m; -s, -n Kaffir *neg!*
Kaffernbüffel m *Zool.* Cape buffalo
Käfig m; -s, -e cage (*auch Etech., Tech.*); *fig.* **im goldenen ~ sitzen** be a bird in a gilded cage
Käfighaltung f caging of animals
kafkaesk *Adj.* Kafkaesque
Kaftan m; -s, -e caftan
kahl I. *Adj.* bald; (*geschoren*) shorn; *fig. Felsen etc.*: bare; *Baum*: bare, leafless; *Landschaft*: barren, bleak; *Wand*: bare; (*schmucklos*) plain; (*leer*) empty; **~ werden** go bald; **~ fressen** strip (of its *od.* their leaves); **II.** *Adv.*: **~ geschoren** *od.* **rasiert** shaven
Kahlfraß m complete defoliation
Kahlheit f baldness; *von Felsen, Bäumen etc.* bareness; *einer Landschaft* barrenness, bleakness; (*Schmucklosig-keit*) plainness; (*Leere*) emptiness
Kahlkopf m bald head; *umg.* (*Person*) *umg.* baldy, slaphead, *Am. auch* cue ball; **kahlköpfig** *Adj.* bald(-headed); **Kahlköpfigkeit** f baldness
Kahlschlag m complete deforestation; (*Stelle*) clearing, deforested area; *weitS.* (*Zerstörung*) eradication; *fig.* wiping the slate clean; **~sanierung** f wholesale redevelopment
Kahl|weiden n; -s, *kein Pl.* overgrazing; **~wild** n *Jägerspr.* (*hornloses Wild*) does *Pl.*; (*Junge*) fawns *Pl.*
Kahm m; -(e)s, *kein Pl.*; *Biol.* mo(u)ld; **Kahmhaut** f film of mo(u)ld
Kahn m; -s, **Kähne 1.** (*rowing od.* fishing) boat; (*Lastkahn*) barge; *umg.* (*altes Schiff*) *umg.* tub; **2.** *umg.* (*Bett*): **in den ~ gehen** turn in; **3.** *Pl. umg.* (*Schuhe*) beetle-crushers, *Am.* clodhoppers; **~fahrt** f boat trip
Kai m; -s, -s quay(side), wharf; **~anlage**

f wharf, wharves *Pl.*; **~arbeiter** *m* docker, *Am.* longshoreman, stevedore

Kaiman *m*; *-s*, *-e*; *Zool.* cayman

Kaimauer *f* quayside

Kains|mal *n*, **~zeichen** *n* mark of Cain

Kaiser *m*; *-s*, - emperor; *der deutsche* **~** the German Emperor; *(1871-1918) auch* the Kaiser; *fig.* **sich um des ~s Bart streiten** squabble over little things; **gebt dem ~, was des ~s ist** render unto Caesar the things that are Caesar's; **hingehen, wo auch der ~ zu Fuß hingeht** *umg. hum.* visit the throneroom, pay a call; **~adler** *m* imperial eagle; **~brötchen** *n südd.* bread roll (*with a raised pattern on top*), *Am.* kaiser roll; **~haus** *n* imperial dynasty

Kaiserin *f*; *-*, *-nen* empress; **~mutter** *f* dowager empress

Kaiser|krone *f* **1.** imperial crown; **2.** *Bot.* crown imperial; **~krönung** *f* coronation (as emperor)

kaiserlich *Adj.* imperial; **kaiserlich--königlich** *Adj.*: **die ~e Monarchie** *hist.* the Dual Monarchy (*of Austria-Hungary from 1867 to 1918*); → *auch* **k. u. k.**

Kaiserling *m*; *-s*, *-e Bot.* golden agaric, *Am.* caesar's mushroom

Kaiser|palast *m* imperial palace; **~pfalz** *f hist.* imperial palace; **~reich** *n* empire; **~schmarr(e)n** *m Gastr.* shredded pancake with sugar and raisins; **~schnitt** *m Med.* C(a)esarean (section), *Am. auch* C-section; **~semmel** *f österr.*, *südd.* → **Kaiserbrötchen**; **~stadt** *f* imperial city

kaisertreu *Adj.* loyal to the emperor

Kaisertum *n*; *-s*, *Kaisertümer* **1.** *nur Sg.* (*Staatsform*) imperial rule; **2.** (*Kaiserwürde*) imperial status

Kaiser|wetter *n* glorious weather; **~würde** *f*; *nur Sg.* imperial status; **~zeit** *f* period of imperial rule (*od.* empire); **in der (römischen) ~** at the time of the (Roman) Empire, under the (Roman) empire

Kajak *m*, *n*; *-s*, *-s* kayak; **~einer** *m Rudersport* single kayak; **~zweier** *m Rudersport* double kayak

Kajal *n*; *-(s)*, *kein Pl.* kohl; **~stift** *m* kohl pencil

Kajüte *f*; *-*, *-n*; *Naut.* cabin

Kakadu *m*; *-s*, *-s*; *Orn.* cockatoo; *umg. fig.* chatterbox

Kakao *m*; *-s*, *-s* **1.** cocoa; *umg.* **durch den ~ ziehen** (*hänseln*) make fun of *allg.*, kid *umg.*, (*schlecht machen*) pull to pieces; **2.** (*Kakaobaum*) *Bot.* cocoa tree, cacao tree; **~baum** *m* → **Kakao 2**; **~bohne** *f* cocoa bean; **~butter** *f* cocoa butter; **~masse** *f* cocoa paste; **~pulver** *n* cocoa (powder)

Kakerlak *m*; *-s und -en*, *-en*, **Kakerlake** *f*; *-n*, *-n*; *Zool.* cockroach, *Am. umg.* roach

Kakophonie *f*; *-*, *-n* cacophony

Kaktee *f*; *-*, *-n*, **Kaktus** *m*; - *und -ses*, *Kakteen und -se*; *Bot.* cactus (*Pl.* cacti, cactuses)

Kalabreser *m*; *-s*, - slouch hat

Kalamität *f*; *-*, *-en* difficulty

Kalander *m*; *-s*, - *Tech.* calender, roller; **kalandern**, **kalandrieren** *v/t.* calender, roll

Kalaschnikow *f*; *-*, *-s* Kalashnikov, AK-47

Kalauer *m*; *-s*, - (*Wortspiel*) low pun; (*dummer Witz*) corny joke; **kalauern** *v/i.* pun; (*Witze machen*) tell corny jokes

Kalb *n*; *-(e)s*, *Kälber* calf; (*Fleisch*) veal; *fig.* **der Tanz um das Goldene ~**

the pursuit of mammon; *umg.* **dummes ~** *umg.* silly goose; **Kälbchen** *n* little calf; **Kalbe** *f*; *-*, *-n* (*Färse*) heifer; **kalben** *v/i.* calve

Kälbermast *f Agr.* calf fattening

Kalb|fell *n* calfskin; **~fleisch** *n* veal; **~leder** *n* calf (leather)

Kalbs|braten *m Gastr.* joint of veal; *gebraten:* roast veal; **~bries** *n* sweetbread; **~brust** *f* breast of veal; **~frikassee** *n* veal fricassee; **~hachse** *f*, **~haxe** *f südd.* knuckle of veal; **~keule** *f* leg of veal; **~kopf** *m* **1.** calf's head; **2.** *umg. fig.* (*dummer Mensch*) *umg.* stupid oaf (*od.* twit); **~leber** *f* calf's liver; **~leberwurst** calf's liver sausage

Kalbsleder *n* calf (leather); **kalbsledern** *Adj.* calfskin ...

Kalbs|medaillon *n Gastr.* veal medallion; **~milch** *f* sweetbread; **~schlegel** *m* leg of veal; **~schnitzel** *n* veal escalope; **~vögerl** *n*; *-s*, *-n*; *österr.* piece of knuckle of veal

Kaldaunen *Pl. Gastr.* tripe *Sg.*

Kalebasse *f*; *-*, *-n* **1.** calabash; **2.** *Bot.* (*bottle*) gourd

Kaleidoskop *n*; *-s*, *-e* kaleidoscope; **kaleidoskopisch** *Adj.* kaleidoscopic

kalendarisch *Adj.* calendrical, calendar ...; (*nach dem Kalender*) according to the calendar

Kalender *m*; *-s*, - calendar (*auch weitS.*); **etw. rot im ~ anstreichen** mark s.th. down as a red-letter day, *iro.* put s.th. on the record; **der hundertjährige ~** the Hundred Years' calendar; **~blatt** *n* page of a (*od.* the) calendar; **~block** *m* calendar pad, day--by-day calendar; **~geschichte** *f Lit.* (*edifying*) *story printed on a page of a calendar*; **~jahr** *n* calendar year; **~spruch** *m* motto, quotation etc. *printed on a page of a calendar*, **~tag** *m* calendar day; **~woche** *f* calendar week

Kalesche *f*; *-*, *-n*; *hist.* barouche, calash

Kalfakter *m*; *-s*, *-*, **Kalfaktor** *m*; *-s*, *-en* handyman, odd-job man; *im Gefängnis:* trusty

kalfatern *v/t. Naut.* caulk

Kali *n*; *-s*, *-s*; *Chem.* potash (*auch Agr.*); (*kohlensaures*) **~** potassium carbonate; **salpetersaures ~** potassium nitrate

Kaliber *n*; *-s*, - **1.** *Gewehr:* calib|re (*Am.* -er) (*auch fig.*), bore; **2.** *Tech.* ga(u)ge; **3.** *fig. auch* type, sort; **kleineren/größeren ~s** *Ausmaß:* small-scale/ /large-scale; *Bedeutung:* low-calib|re (*Am.* -er) /high-calib|re (*Am.* -er)

Kalibergwerk *n* potassium mine

kalibrieren *v/t. Tech.* calibrate, ga(u)ge

Kalidünger *m* potash fertilizer

Kalif *m*; *-en*, *-en*; *hist.* caliph; **Kalifat** *n*; *-(e)s*, *-e*; *hist.* caliphate

Kalifornien (*n*); *-s*; *Geog.* California; **Kalifornier** *m*; *-s*, *-*, **Kalifornierin** *f*; *-*, *-nen* Californian, *weiblich auch:* Californian woman (*od.* girl *etc.*); **kalifornisch** *Adj.* Californian

Kaliko *m*; *-s*, *-s* calico; *Buch:* cloth (binding)

Kali|lauge *f Chem.* potash lye; **~salpeter** *m* potassium nitrate, saltpet|re (*Am.* -er); **~salz** *n* potash salt

Kalium *n*; *-s*, *kein Pl.*; (*abgek.* **K**) *Chem.* potassium; **~karbonat** *n* potassium carbonate; **~nitrat** *n* potassium nitrate; **~permanganat** *n* potassium permanganate

Kalk *m*; *-(e)s*, *-e*; *Chem.* lime; (*Kalkstein*) limestone, chalk; *Med.* calcium; **gelöschter ~** slaked lime; *umg. fig.* **bei ihm rieselt schon der ~** he's past it;

~ablagerung *f* **1.** *Geol.* lime deposit; (*in Kaffeemaschine etc.*); scale; **2.** *Med.* calcification, calcium deposit; **2arm** *Adj.* deficient in lime (*Med.* calcium); **~boden** *m* chalky soil; **~brennerei** *f* limekiln; **~dünger** *m* lime (fertilizer)

kalken *v/t. Agr.* lime; (*tünchen*) whitewash

Kalkgebirge *n* limestone mountains *Pl.*

kalkhaltig *Adj. Wasser:* hard; *Erde:* chalky

kalkig *Adj.* **1.** → **kalkhaltig**, **2.** *Farbe:* chalky

Kalk|mangel *m Med.* calcium deficiency; **~ofen** *m* limekiln; **~präparat** *n Med.*, *Pharm.* calcium preparation; **~sinter** *m* travertine, calc(-)sinter; **~spat** *m* calcite, calcspar; **~stein** *m* limestone

Kalkül[1] *n*; *-s*, *-e* calculation; (*mit*) **ins ~ ziehen** take into consideration (*od.* account)

Kalkül[2] *m*; *-s*, *-e*; *Math.* calculus

Kalkulation *f*; *-*, *-en* calculation; (*Kostenberechnung*) estimate; **Kalkulationsfehler** *m* miscalculation; **Kalkulator** *m*; *-s*, *-en*, **Kalkulatorin** *f*; *-*, *-nen* cost accountant; **kalkulatorisch** *Adj.* calculatory; **kalkulierbar** *Adj.* calculable; *Wirts.* **~e Risiken** insurable risks; **kalkulieren** *v/t/i.* calculate

kalkweiß *Adj.* chalky white; *Haut*, *Gesicht: auch* deathly pale

Kalligraph *m*; *-en*, *-en* calligrapher; **Kalligraphie** *f*; *-*, *kein Pl.* calligraphy; **Kalligraphin** *f*; *-*, *-nen* calligrapher; **kalligraphisch** *Adj.* calligraphic

Kalme *f*; *-*, *-n*; *Met.* calm; **Kalmengürtel** *m Geog.* calm belt; **äquatorialer ~** the doldrums *Pl.*; **Kalmenzone** *f Geog.* calm belt

Kalorie *f*; *-*, *-n* calorie

kalorienarm *Adj.* low-calorie ..., low in calories

Kalorienbedarf *m* calorie requirement

kalorienbewusst *Adj.* calorie-conscious

Kalorien|bombe *f umg.* dietary disaster, slimmer's nightmare; **~gehalt** *m* calorie content

kalorien|reduziert *Adj.* low-calorie ..., low in calories; **~reich** *Adj.* high-calorie ..., high in calories

Kalorien|tabelle *f* calorie chart; **~wert** *m* calorific value

Kalorik *f*; *-*, *kein Pl.*; *Phys.* theory of heat

Kalorimeter *n Phys.* calorimeter; **Kalorimetrie** *f*; *-*, *kein Pl.*; *Phys.* calorimetry; **kalorimetrisch** *Adj.* calorimetrical; **kalorisch** *Adj.* caloric

kalt I. *Adj.* **1.** cold; *Wetter etc.: auch* chilly; **mir ist ~** I'm cold; **mir wird ~** I'm getting cold; **~ werden** get cold, (*sich abkühlen*) cool down; **2.** *Psych. und Zone:* frigid; **3.** *fig. Person*, *Farbe etc.:* cold; *Blick*, *Empfang:* cool; **~l im Spiel:** cold; **j-m die ~e Schulter zeigen** give s.o. the cold shoulder; **j-n ~ erwischen** *umg.* catch s.o. with his (*od.* her) pants down; → **Dusche**, **Fuß[1] 1**, **Küche 2; II.** *Adv.* coldly; **~ stellen** put in a cool place, *in den Kühlschrank:* put in the fridge; **wir zahlen ~ 500 Euro** we pay 500 euros without heating; **~ bleiben** *fig. Person* keep cool; **~ lächelnd** without turning a hair; **das lässt mich ~** that leaves me cold; → **Rücken 1**

Kaltblut *n Zool.* draught (*Am.* draft) horse; **Kaltblüter** *m*; *-s*, *-*; *Zool.* cold--blooded animal

kaltblütig I. *Adj. Zool. und fig. Mord etc.*: cold-blooded; *fig.* (*ruhig*) cool; **II.** *Adv. umbringen etc.*: in cold blood; (*gelassen*) calmly; **Kaltblütigkeit** *f* cold-bloodedness; (*Beherrschtheit*) calmness, sangfroid
Kälte *f*; -, *kein Pl.* **1.** cold; *drei Grad ~* three degrees below zero; *draußen in der ~* (out) in the cold; *vor ~ zittern* shiver with cold; **2.** *Psych.* frigidity; **3.** *fig. e-r Person, Farbe etc.*: coldness; **~behandlung** *f Med.* cryotherapy; **◌beständig** *Adj.* cold-resistant; **~chirurgie** *f* cryosurgery; **~einbruch** *m* cold snap, sudden cold spell; **◌empfindlich** *Adj.* sensitive to (the) cold; **~gefühl** *n* cold feeling; **~grad** *m* temperature (below zero); **~maschine** *f* refrigerating machine; **~mittel** *n* refrigerant; **~periode** *f* cold spell
Kalter *m*; -*s*, -; *südd., österr.* fish tank
Kälte|schauer *m* cold shiver; **~starre** *f Zool.* torpor; **~steppe** *f Geogr.* tundra; **~technik** *f* refrigeration engineering; **~therapie** *f Med.* cryotherapy; **~welle** *f* cold spell
Kaltfront *f Met.* cold front
kalt|gepresst *Adj. Öl*: cold-pressed; **~geschlagen** *Adj. Öl*: cold-pressed
Kalthaus *n* cold house
kaltherzig *Adj.* cold-hearted, unfeeling; **Kaltherzigkeit** *f* cold-heartedness
Kaltleim *m* wood glue, cold-setting adhesive
Kaltluft *f Met.* cold air; **~einbruch** *m* cold snap; **~masse** *f* cold air mass
kalt|machen *v/t.* (*trennb., hat -ge-*) (*töten*) *umg.* bump off, *Am. auch* ice
Kaltmiete *f* basic rent (without heating)
Kaltnadel *f Kunst* dry point; **~radierung** *f Kunst* dry point (engraving)
Kaltschale *f Gastr.* iced fruit soup
kaltschnäuzig *Adj. umg.* callous; (*frech*) cheeky; **Kaltschnäuzigkeit** *f umg.* callousness; (*Frechheit*) cheekiness
kaltschweißen *v/t.* (*trennb., hat -ge-*) *nur im Inf. und P.P.; Metall.* cold-weld
Kaltstart *m* **1.** *Mot.* cold start; **2.** *EDV* (*Booten*) cold start
kaltstellen *v/t.* (*trennb., hat -ge-*) *umg. fig.* sideline; → *auch* **kalt** II, **stellen** I 1; **Kaltstellung** *f umg. fig* sidelining
Kaltverpflegung *f* cold dishes *Pl.*
kaltwalzen *v/t.* (*trennb., hat -ge-*) cold-roll
Kaltwasser|behandlung *f Med.* cold-water treatment, hydrotherapy; **~kur** *f* cold-water therapy (*od.* cure)
Kalt|welle *f* (*Dauerwelle*) cold wave; **~zeit** *f* (*Kälteperiode der Eiszeit*) glacial period
Kalvarienberg *m Reli.*: *der ~* Calvary
kalvinisch *Adj. Reli.* Calvinist; **Kalvinismus** *m* Calvinism; **Kalvinist** *m*; -*en*, -*en*, **Kalvinistin** *f*; -, -*nen* Calvinist; **kalvinistisch** *Adj.* Calvinist(ic)
Kalzit *m*; -*s*, -*e* calcite
Kalzium *n*; -*s*, *kein Pl.*; (*abgek.* **Ca**) *Chem.* calcium; **~chlorid** *n* calcium chloride; **~karbonat** *n* calcium carbonate; **~mangel** *m Med.* calcium deficiency; **~spiegel** *m* calcium level
kam *Imperf.* → **kommen**
Kamaldulenser *m*; -*s*, -; *kath.* Camaldolese, Camaldolite
Kamarilla *f*; -, *Kamarillen pej.* camarilla
Kambium *n*; -*s*, *Kambien*; *Bot.* cambium
Kambodscha (*n*); -*s*; *Geog.* Cambodia; **Kambodschaner** *m*; -*s*, -, **Kambod-**

schanerin *f*; -, -*nen* Cambodian, *weiblich auch*: Cambodian woman (*od.* girl *etc.*); **kambodschanisch** *Adj.* Cambodian
kambrisch *Adj. Geol.* Cambrian; **Kambrium** *n*; -*s*, *kein Pl.*; *Geol.* the Cambrian (period)
Kamee *f*; -, -*n* cameo
Kamel *n*; -*s*, -*e*; *Zool.* camel; *umg. fig.* idiot; *eher geht ein ~ durchs Nadelöhr* it's easier for a camel to go through the eye of a needle; **Kamelhaar** *n*, **Kamelhaar...** *im Subst.* camelhair
Kamelie *f*; -, -*n*; *Bot.* camellia
Kamellen *Pl.*: *olle ~ umg.* old hat, (*Witze, Geschichten*) *umg.* old chestnuts; *das sind doch olle ~ Witze etc.*: *auch* they're as old as the hills
Kameltreiber *m* camel driver
Kamera *f*; -, -*s* camera; *vor laufender ~* with the camera running, live to camera; *vor der ~ stehen* be on camera
Kamerad *m*; -*en*, -*en* comrade, companion; (*Freund*) friend; *umg.* pal, *Brit. auch* mate; → **Schulkamerad**, **Spielkamerad**
Kameraden|diebstahl *m bes. Mil.* theft from a comrade; **~schwein** *n umg. pej.* back-stabber
Kameraderie *f*; -, *kein Pl.*; *pej.* cliquishness; **Kameradin** ; -, -*nen* comrade, companion; (*Freundin*) (girl)friend; *umg.* pal, chum, *Brit. auch* mate
Kameradschaft *f* comradeship; loyalty; **kameradschaftlich I.** *Adj.* friendly; *rein ~* purely platonic; *unser Verhältnis ist rein ~ auch* we're just good friends; *das war nicht sehr ~ von dir* that wasn't very nice of you, a fine friend you are; **II.** *Adv.* as a friend; **Kameradschaftlichkeit** *f* friendliness
Kameradschafts|ehe *f* companionate marriage; **~geist** *m*; *nur Sg.* esprit de corps, team spirit
Kamera|einstellung *f* **1.** camera position (*od.* angle); *Film: lange etc. ~ auch* long *etc.* shot; **2.** *der Blende etc.*: camera setting; **~fahrt** camera movement; **~frau** *f* camerawoman; **~führung** *f Film*: camera work, photography
Kameralistik *f*; -, *kein Pl.* **1.** *Wirts.* governmental accounting; **2.** *altm.* finance; **kameralistisch** *Adj.* **1.** *altm.* (*staatswissenschaftlich*) relating to political science; **2.** *Wirts.* cameralistic
Kamera|mann *m* cameraman; **~rekorder** *m* camcorder; **◌scheu** *Adj.* camera-shy; **~schwenk** *m* pan; *vertikal*: tilt; **~tasche** *f* camera case (*größere*: holdall); **~team** *n* camera crew
kameraüberwacht *Adj.* under video surveillance
Kamera|verschluss *m* shutter; **~wagen** *m* dolly
Kamerun (*n*); -*s*; *Geog.* Cameroon; **Kameruner** *m*; -*s*, -, **Kamerunerin** *f*; -, -*nen* Cameroonian, *weiblich auch*: Cameroonian woman (*od.* girl *etc.*); **kamerunisch** *Adj.* Cameroonian
Kamikaze *m*; -, - *hist.* kamikaze pilot
Kamikaze|flieger *m* → **Kamikaze**; **~unternehmen.** *n fig.* suicide mission, kamikaze operation
Kamille *f*; -, -*n Bot.* camomile; **Kamillentee** *m* camomile tea
Kamin *m*; -*s*, -*e innen*: fireplace; *bes. südd.* (*Schornstein*) chimney (*auch Geol.*); *am ~ sitzen* sit in front of the fire; *fig. in den ~ schreiben* write *s.th.* off; **~feger** *m*; -*s*, -, **~fegerin** *f*; -, -*nen südd., schw.* chimney sweep; **~feuer** *n*

(open) fire; *am ~* by the fireside; **~kehrer** *m*; -*s*, -, **~kehrerin** *f*; -, -*nen* chimney sweep; **~sims** *m* mantelpiece
Kamm *m*; -(*e*)*s*, *Kämme* comb; (*eines Gebirges*) ridge; (*einer Welle*) crest; *orn.* comb, crest; (*vom Rind etc.*) neck; *fig. man kann nicht alle(s) über e-n ~ scheren* you can't just lump them all (*od.* lump everything) together; *ihm schwoll der ~* it went to his head; *da schwillt mir/einem doch der ~* it really gets my/one's back up, *Am.* it really gets on my/your nerves
kämmen *v/t.* comb; *sich* (*Dat.*) *~* comb one's hair; *j-m die Haare ~* comb s.o.'s hair
Kammer *f*; -, -*n* **1.** small room; (*Abstellraum*) cubbyhole; **2.** *Pol.* chamber; *Jur.* division; **3.** *Anat.* (*im Herzen etc.*) ventricle, chamber; **4.** *Bot.* valve; **~chor** *m* chamber choir; **~diener** *m* valet
Kämmerei *f* finance department; **Kämmerer** *m*; -*s*, -, **Kämmerin** *f*; -, -*nen* treasurer
Kammer|flimmern *n*; -*s*, *kein Pl.*; *Med.* ventricular fibrillation; **~frau** *f*, **~fräulein** *n hist.* lady-in-waiting; **~gericht** *n Jur.* Court of Appeal (in Berlin); **~herr** *m hist.* chamberlain; **~jäger** *m* pest controller; **~konzert** *n Mus.* chamber concert; (*Musikstück*) chamber concerto
Kämmerlein *n*: *umg. im stillen ~* in private
Kammer|musik *f Mus.* chamber music; **Kammermusiker** *m*, **Kammermusikerin** *f* chamber musician; **~orchester** *n* chamber orchestra
Kammerpräsident *m*, **~in** *f Jur.* president of a division (*of a court*)
Kammer|sänger *m*, **~sängerin** *f Mus.* title conferred on singer of outstanding merit; **~spiel** *n Theat.* **1.** small-scale play (*suitable for a studio theatre*); **2.** *Pl.* (*Theater*) studio theat|re (*Am. auch* -er); **~ton** *m Mus.* concert pitch; **~zofe** *f* lady's maid
Kamm|garn *n* worsted; **~lagen** *Pl.*: *in den ~* on the peaks
Kämmmaschine *f* comber
Kamm|muschel *f Zool.* scallop; **~stück** *n Gastr. vom Rind etc.*: neck; **~weg** *m* ridgeway
Kampagne [kam'panjə] *f*; -, -*n* **1.** campaign (*für* for; *gegen* against); *e-e ~ starten* launch a campaign; **2.** *Archäol.* stage (*od.* phase) (of an excavation); **3.** (*Hochbetriebszeit*) busy season
Kampanile *m*; -, - *Archit.* campanile
Kämpe *m*; -*n*, -*n* (old) campaigner *od.* soldier
Kampf *m*; -(*e*)*s*, *Kämpfe* fight; (*Schlacht*) battle; *fig.* fight, battle; *schwerer*: struggle (*alle um* for; *gegen* against); (*Konflikt*) conflict (*auch Pol.*); (*Fehde*) feud; (*Rivalität*) rivalry; (*innerer, seelischer ~*) struggle, battle (with o.s.), inner conflict; (*sportlicher Wettstreit*) contest; (*Spiel*) match; (*Boxen*) fight; *~ ums Dasein* fight for survival; *~ dem Hunger etc.* war on hunger *etc.*; *~ auf Leben und Tod* life-and-death struggle; *j-m / einer Sache den ~ ansagen* declare war on s.o./s.th.; *es kam zum ~* fighting broke out; *im ~ fallen* die in battle, be killed in action; *auf in den ~! hum.* once more unto the breach!
Kampf|abschnitt *m Mil.* combat zone; **~abstimmung** *f Pol.* crucial vote; *Gewerkschaft*: strike ballot; **~ansage** *f* challenge (*an* + *Akk.* to); **~anzug** *m*

Mil. battle dress; **~ausbildung** *f Mil.* combat training; **~ausrüstung** *f der Polizei:* riot gear

kampfbereit *fig. Adj. Mil.* battle-ready; *auch fig.* ready for the fray (*od.* for a fight); **Kampfbereitschaft** *f Mil.* combat-readiness; *auch fig.* readiness for the fray (*od.* for a fight)

kampfbetont *Adj. Sport* tough, hard

Kampf|bund *m,* **~bündnis** *n* pressure (*od.* action) group; **~einheit** *f Mil.* combat unit; **~einsatz** *m Mil.* operational mission

kämpfen I. *v/i.* fight (**für, um** for) (*auch fig.*); (*ringen, auch fig.*) struggle (**mit** with; **gegen** against), wrestle (**mit** with); **~ gegen** fight (against); *fig.* **~ mit** *auch* fight (against), contend (*od.* grapple) with, (*Schwierigkeiten*) be up against, (have to) face; **mit dem Schlaf ~** struggle to stay awake; **mit den Tränen ~** fight back one's tears; **zu ~ haben** have to contend with s.th.; (*lange*) **mit sich ~** have a (long) struggle with o.s.; **II.** *v/t.:* **e-n schweren Kampf ~** *auch fig.* fight a hard battle; **III.** *v/refl.:* **sich durch etw. ~** *auch fig.* fight (*od.* battle) one's way through s.th.; *fig.* **sich nach oben ~** fight (*od.* claw) one's way to the top

Kämpfen *n; -s, kein Pl.* → *Kampf*
Kampfer *m; -s, kein Pl.* camphor
Kämpfer *m; -s, -* **1.** *Mil.* combatant; **2.** *fig.* champion (**für** of), fighter (for); **3.** *Sport* contestant, (*Boxer*) fighter, (*Ringer*) wrestler; **4.** *Archit., Bauw.* impost; *im Fensterrahmen* transom

kampferfahren *Adj.* battle-hardened; *fig.* seasoned, *auch Sport* veteran …

Kämpferin *; -, -nen* → *Kämpfer* 1-3
kämpferisch I. *Adj.* combative; (*aggressiv*) belligerent, aggressive; *Pol. etc.* militant; *Sport* physically strong; **II.** *Adv.:* **~ stark sein** have a lot of (fighting) spirit; **~ eine gute Leistung bieten** give a good account of s.o.

Kämpfernatur *f:* **e-e ~ sein** be a born fighter

kampferprobt *Adj.* → *kampferfahren*
Kampfes|lärm, ~lust, ~mut, ~wille → *Kampflärm, Kampflust, Kampfmut, Kampfwille*

kampffähig *Adj. Mil.* fit for action, *auch Sport* fighting fit

Kampf|fahrzeug *n Mil.* combat vehicle; **~fisch** *m Zool.* fighting fish; **~flieger** *m,* **~fliegerin** *f Mil.* combat pilot; fighter pilot; **~flugzeug** *n Mil.* fighter aircraft; *hist.* bomber; **~gas** *n Mil.* (poison) gas; **~gebiet** *n Mil.* conflict area; **~gefährte** *m,* **~gefährtin** *f* comrade-in-arms; **~geist** *m* fighting spirit; **~ zeigen** put up a good fight; **~gemeinschaft** *f* activist group; **~gericht** *n Sport:* the judges *Pl.;* **~geschehen** *n* fighting, action; **Ort des ~s** scene of the fighting; **ins ~ eingreifen** enter the fray; **~geschwader** *n Mil.* tactical group; **~getümmel** *n* fighting; **sich ins ~ stürzen** throw o.s. into the fray; **~gewicht** *n Sport* fighting weight; **sein ~ ist 70 kg** *bei Wettkampf:* he has weighed in at 70 kilos; **~hahn** *m* **1.** fighting cock; **2.** *umg. fig.* (*Person*) *umg.* pugnacious so-and-so; **guck dir die zwei Kampfhähne an** look at those two fighting like cat(s) and dog(s); **~handlung** *f Mil. auch Pl.* action, fighting; **~hubschrauber** *m Mil.* (helicopter) gunship; **~hund** *m* fighting dog, killer dog

Kampfkraft *f* (fighting) strength; **kampfkräftig** *Adj.* strong, powerful

Kampf|kunst *f* art of self-defence; (*Kampfsportarten*) martial arts *Pl.;* **~lärm** *m* noise of battle; **~läufer** *m Orn.* ruff; *Weibchen* ree(ve); **~lied** *n* **1.** battle song; **2.** revolutionary song

kampflos *Adj. und Adv.* without a fight; **~ e-e Runde weiterkommen** reach the next round by default

Kampflust *f* aggressiveness, pugnacity; **kampflustig** *Adj.* belligerent

Kampf|maßnahme *f Mil. auch Pl.* military (*Pol.* militant) action; **~mittel** *n* weapon; *Pl. auch* munitions; **~mittelräumdienst** *m* battlefield clearance unit; **~moral** *f* morale (of the soldiers *od.* troops); **2müde** *Adj.* battle-weary; **~mut** *m* fighting spirit; **~panzer** *m Mil.* battle tank; **~pause** *f* lull in the fighting; **~platz** *m* battleground; *Sport* arena; *fig.* scene of the action; **~preis** *m Wirts.* cut-rate price; **~richter** *m,* **~richterin** *f* judge; (*Schiedsrichter*) referee, *Tennis, Schwimmen:* umpire; **~schrift** *f* pamphlet, political broadside; **~schwimmer** *m Mil.* frogman; **~sport** *m* **1.** *Koll.* combative sports *Pl.;* (*Judo, Karate etc.*) martial arts *Pl.;* **2.** *Sportart:* combative sport; *Judo, Karate etc.:* martial art

kampfstark *Adj. Mil. und Sport* strong; **Kampfstärke** *f* strength

Kampf|stier *m* fighting bull; **~stoff** *m Mil.:* **chemischer** (**biologischer**) **~** chemical (biological) weapon; **~truppe** *f* combat troops *Pl.*

kampfunfähig *Adj.* out of action; **~ machen** *auch Sport* put out of action; **Kampfunfähigkeit** *f* unfitness of action (*od.* a fight)

Kampf|verband *m Mil.* combat unit; **~weise** *f Mil.* tactics *Pl.,* strategy; **~wille** *m* will to fight; **~zone** *f Mil.* fighting zone

kampieren *v/i.* camp; **bei j-m ~** *umg. fig.* sleep (*umg.* crash out) on s.o.'s floor (*od.* sofa)

Kamuffel *n; -s, -; umg.* fool

Kanada (*n*); *-s; Geog.* Canada
Kanadier¹ *m; -s, -,* **~in** *f; -, -nen* Canadian; *weiblich auch:* Canadian woman (*od.* girl *etc.*)

Kanadier² *m; -s, -; Sport* Canadian (canoe); **~-Einer** (**-Zweier**) Canadian single (double)

kanadisch *Adj.* Canadian

Kanaille [ka'naljə] *f; -, -n; pej.* **1.** *altm.* (*Pack*) mob, rabble; **2.** (*Schuft*) *Sl.* swine

Kanake *m; -n, -n* **1.** *wörtlich:* Kanaka; **2.** *umg. pej.* (*Ausländer*) bloody (*Am.* damn) foreigner, wog *Sl.;* **Kanaker** *m; -s, - umg. pej.* → *Kanake* 2

Kanal *m; -s, Kanäle* canal; *natürlicher:* channel (*auch fig.*); *für Abwasser:* drain, sewer; *Anat.* duct; *Radio, TV:* channel; *der ~* (*Ärmelkanal*) the (English) Channel; **den ~ voll haben** *umg.* be fed up to the back teeth; *von Alkohol:* be full to the gills; **~arbeiter** *m,* **~arbeiterin** *f* **1.** sewage worker; **2.** *umg. fig. Pol.* backroom boy; **~bau** *m* canal construction; *für Abwasser:* construction of sewers; **~bett** *n* canal bed; **~deckel** *m* manhole cover; **~gas** *n* sewer gas; **~gebühren** *Pl.* canal dues; **~inseln** *Pl. Geog.:* **die ~** the Channel Islands

Kanalisation *f; -, -en* **1.** sewerage (*Am.* sewer) system; **2.** *e-s Flusses:* canalization; **Kanalisationsnetz** *n* sewerage (*Am.* sewer) system; network of sewers

kanalisieren *v/t.* (*Stadt*) provide with

sewers; (*Fluss*) canalize; *fig.* channel; **Kanalisierung** *f* installation of sewers; *e-s Flusses* canalization

Kanal|netz *n* sewerage (*Am.* sewer) system; **~räumer** *m; -s, -,* **~räumerin** *f; -, -nen* sewer worker; **~reiniger** *m; -s, -,* **~reinigerin** *f; -, -nen* sewer worker; **~rohr** *n* sewage pipe; **~schwimmen** *n; -s, kein Pl.* (cross-)Channel swimming; **~schwimmer** *m,* **~schwimmerin** *f* (cross-)Channel swimmer; **~system** *n zur Bewässerung:* irrigation system; *zur Entwässerung:* drainage system; **~tunnel** *m* (*Ärmelkanal*) Channel tunnel, *umg.* Chunnel

Kanapee *n; -s, -s* **1.** *Gastr.* canapé; **2.** (*Sofa*) sofa

Kanaren *Pl. Geog.: die ~* the Canaries

Kanari *m; -s, -; südd., österr. umg.* (*Kanarienvogel*) canary

kanariengelb *Adj.* canary yellow; **Kanarienvogel** *m Orn.* canary

Kanarische Inseln *Pl. Geog.: die Kanarischen Inseln* the Canary Islands

Kandare *f; -, -n* bit; *fig.* **j-n an die ~ nehmen** keep a tighter rein on s.o., bring s.o. to heel (*od.* into line); **j-n an der ~ haben** keep s.o. on a tight rein

Kandelaber *m; -s, -* candelabra

Kandidat *m; -en, -en* candidate (*auch fig.*), contender; *Pol.* **vorgeschlagener ~** nominee; *Univ.* (*Student in höherem Semester*) candidate; **Kandidatenliste** *f* list of candidates; *e-r Partei: Am.* party ticket; **Kandidatin** *; -, -nen* → *Kandidat;* **Kandidatur** *f; -, -en* candidature; **kandidieren** *v/i.* stand *od.* run for election (*od.* an office *etc.*); **für das Amt des Präsidenten** (**Bürgermeisters**) **~** run for the presidency (the office of mayor); **gegen j-n ~** run against s.o.; **erneut ~** run for re-election, stand (for election) again

kandieren *v/t.* crystallize; **kandiert** *Adj.* candied, glacé

Kandis *m; -, kein Pl.,* **~zucker** *m* sugar (*od.* rock) candy

Kanditen *Pl. österr.* a) (*kandierte Früchte*) crystallized fruits, b) (*Süßigkeiten*) sweets, *Am.* candy *Sg.*

Kaneel *m; -s, -e* cinnamon

Kanevas *m; - und –ses, - und –se* canvas; **kanevassen** *Adj.* canvas

Känguru *n; -s, -s; Zool.* kangaroo

Kanin *n; -s, -e fachspr.* rabbit (fur)

Kaninchen *n; -s, -; Zool.* rabbit; **~bau** *m* burrow; **~stall** *m* rabbit hutch

Kanister *m* canister, can

kann *Präs.* → *können*

Kannbestimmung *f Jur.* discretionary clause

Kännchen *n* jug; **ein ~ Kaffee** *etc.* a pot of coffee *etc.*

Kanne *f; -, -n* (*Krug*) jug; (*für Kaffee etc.*) pot; (*für Öl etc.*) can; (*große Milchkanne*) churn, *Am.* milk can

kanneliert *Adj.* fluted; **Kannelierung** *f* fluting

kannenweise *Adv.* **1.** in cans; **2. ~ Kaffee trinken** *umg.* drink pots of coffee, drink coffee by the gallon

Kannibale *m; -n, -n* cannibal; *fig.* savage; **kannibalisch I.** *Adj.* cannibal …; *fig.* brutal, savage; **II.** *Adv.:* **sich ~ wohl fühlen** *umg. fig. hum.* feel terrific (*od.* on top of the world); **Kannibalismus** *m; -, kein Pl.* cannibalism

kannte *Imperf.* → *kennen*

Kannvorschrift *f Jur.* discretionary clause

Kanon *m; -s, -s* **1.** (*Maßstab, Regel*) canon, code; **2.** *bibl., kirchl., Jur., auch*

Math. canon; **3.** *Mus.* canon, round

Kanonade *f; -, -n* cannonade; **~ von Schimpfwörtern** volley (*od.* salvo) of abuse

Kanone *f; -, -n* **1.** *allg.* gun; (*Geschütz*) *auch* cannon; *Sl.* (*Revolver*) iron, *Am. Sl.* rod; → **Spatz** 1; **2.** *umg. fig.* (*Könner*) wizard, *bes. Sport* ace; **3.** *unter aller ~ umg. fig.* lousy, *Sl.* the pits

Kanonenboot *n hist.* gunboat; **~politik** *f* gunboat diplomacy

Kanonen|donner *m* (rumble of) gunfire; **~futter** *n fig.* cannon fodder; **~kugel** *f* cannonball; **~ofen** *m* cylindrical stove; **~rohr** *n* gun barrel; (*ach du*) *heiliges ~! umg.* good grief!; **~schlag** *m* (*Feuerwerk*) cannon cracker; **~schuss** *m* cannon shot

Kanonier *m; -s, -e* gunner

Kanoniker *m; -s, -,* **Kanonikus** *m; -,* *Kanoniker* canon; **Kanonisation** *f; -, -en; kirchl.* canonization; **kanonisch** *Adj.* canonical; **~es Recht** canon law; **kanonisieren** *v/t.* canonize; **Kanonisierung** canonization

Kanonistik *f; -, kein Pl.* theory of canon law

Kanossa *n: fig. nach ~ gehen* pocket one's pride, eat humble pie; **~gang** *m: es war für ihn ein ~* he had to pocket his pride

Känozoikum *n Geol.* Cenozoic (era); **känozoisch** *Adj.* Cenozoic

kantabel *Adj. Mus.* cantabile; *Komposition:* songlike; (*sangbar*) singable; **Kantabilität** ; *-, kein Pl. Mus.* cantabile (*od.* songlike) quality; (*Sangbarkeit*) singable quality

Kantate¹ *f; -, -n Mus.* cantata

Kantate² *kein Art.; kirchl.* fourth Sunday after Easter; **am Sonntag ~** on the fourth Sunday after Easter

Kante *f; -, -n* **1.** edge; (*Webkante*) selvage; *umg. fig.* **etwas auf die hohe ~ legen** put something aside (*od.* away *od.* by) for a rainy day; **etwas auf der hohen ~ haben** have something put away (somewhere); **2.** *Dial.* (*Gegend*) part of the world

Kantele *f; -, -n; Mus.* Finnish zither

Kanten *m; -s, -; Dial. Brot:* crust

kanten I. *v/t.* tilt; (*Ski*) carve; *auf Paket:* **nicht ~!** this side up; **II.** *v/i. Skisport:* carve

Kantenlänge *f* length of an (*od.* the) edge (*od.* side)

Kanter *m; -s, -* **1.** *Reiten* canter; **2.** *Vorrichtung:* tipping device; **kantern** *v/i. Reiten* canter; **Kantersieg** *m Sport* runaway victory, walkover, *Am.* walkaway

Kant|haken *m: umg. fig. j-n am/beim ~ kriegen umg.* give s.o. a good going-over; **~holz** *n* squared timber

Kantianer *m; -s, -; Philos.* Kantian

kantig *Adj.* **1.** squared; *Gesicht:* angular; *Kinn:* square; **2.** *fig. Mensch:* difficult, awkward

Kantilene *f; -, -n Mus.* cantilena

Kantine *f; -, -n* canteen

Kantinen|essen *n* canteen meal(s *Pl.*), canteen food; **~fraß** *m umg. pej.* canteen slop, swill; **~wirt** *m,* **~wirtin** *f* canteen manager

Kanton *m; -s, -e* canton; **kantonal** *Adj.* cantonal

Kantonalbank *f schw.* cantonal bank

kantonalisieren *v/t. schw.* bring *s. th.* under cantonal control; **Kantonalwahl** *f schw.* cantonal election

Kantonist *m; -en, -en: unsicherer ~ umg.* fly-by-night

Kantons|... *im Subst. schw.* cantonal

...; **~bürgerrecht** *n schw.* civic rights *Pl.* in a canton; **~rat** *m* **1.** cantonal council; **2.** (*Kantonsratsmitglied*) member of a cantonal council; **~rätin** *f → Kantonsrat* 2; **~regierung** *f schw.* cantonal government

Kantor *m; -s, -en; Mus.* choirmaster; **Kantorei** *f; -, -en* (church) choir; **Kantorin** *f; -, -nen* choirmistress

Kantstein *m nordd.* kerb|stone (*Am.* curb-)

Kanu *n; -s, -s* canoe

Kanüle *f; -, -n; Med.* can(n)ula, (drain) tube

Kanusport *m* canoeing; **Kanute** *m; -n, -n,* **Kanutin** *f; -, -nen* canoeist

Kanzel *f; -, -n* **1.** pulpit; **auf der ~** in the pulpit; **2.** *Flug.* cockpit; **3.** *Bergsteigen* (*Vorsprung in Felswand*) spur; **4.** *Jägerspr.* raised hide (*Am.* blind); **~rede** *f* sermon; **~wort** *n* word from the pulpit

kanzerogen *Adj. Med.* carcinogenic; **Kanzerologie** *f; -, kein Pl.* study of cancer, oncology; **kanzerös** *Adj.* cancerous

Kanzlei *f; -, -en* (*Amt, Büro*) office; **~deutsch** *n* officialese

Kanzler *m; -s, -; Pol.* chancellor; *Univ.* vice-chancellor, *Am.* (university) president; *hist.* **der Eiserne ~** (*Bismarck*) the Iron Chancellor; **~amt** *n* **1.** chancellorship; **2.** (*Einrichtung*) chancellor's office, chancellery; **~amtsminister** *m,* **~amtsministerin** *f* chancellery minister

Kanzlerin *f; -, -nen → Kanzler*

Kanzler|kandidat *m,* **~kandidatin** *f Pol.* candidate for the chancellorship; **~kandidatur** *f* candidacy for the chancellorship

Kanzlerschaft *f Pol.* chancellorship, term as chancellor; **während Helmut Kohls zweiter ~** during Helmut Kohl's second term as Chancellor

Kanzone *f; -, -n; Lit.* canzone (*Pl.* canzoni); *Mus.* canzona

Kaolin *n; -s, -e,* **~erde** *f Min.* kaolin

Kap *n; -s, -s; Geog.* cape; **das ~ der Guten Hoffnung** the Cape of Good Hope; **~ Hoorn** Cape Horn

Kap. *Abk.* (*Kapitel*) chap.

Kapaun *m; -s, -e* capon

Kapazitanz *f; -, -en Etech.* capacitance; **Kapazität** *f; -, -en Phys., Tech., Etech. und fig.* capacity; *fig.* (leading) authority (**auf dem Gebiet** *Gen.* on, in the field of)

Kapazitäts|abbau *m* cutback(s *Pl.*) in capacity; **~auslastung** *f,* **~ausnutzung** *f* capacity utilization; **~erweiterung** *f* increase in capacity; **~grenze** *f* limit of capacity

Kapelle *f; -, -n* **1.** *kirchl.* chapel; **2.** *Mus.* band; (*Orchester*) orchestra; **3.** *fachspr.* (*Tiegel*) cupel

Kapell|meister *m,* **~meisterin** *f Mus.* **1.** director of music; **2.** (*Dirigent*) conductor; **3.** *beim Chor:* chorusmaster, choral director; **4.** *Mil.* bandmaster

Kaper¹ *f; -, -n Bot.* caper

Kaper² *m; -s, -; hist Naut.* privateer

Kaperei *f; -, -en; hist.* privateering; **Kaperfahrt** *f hist.* privateering expedition

kapern *v/t.* capture, seize; *umg. fig. umg.* nab

Kapern|soße *f Gastr.* caper sauce; **~strauch** *m Bot.* caper (shrub)

Kaperschiff *n → Kaper²*

kapieren *umg.* **I.** *v/t. umg.* get, twig, *Am.* catch on (to); **ich kapier das nicht!** I (just) don't get it; **II.** *v/i.* catch

---

on, *umg.* twig; *bei Drohung etc.:* auch get the message; **kapiert?** got it?, *bei Drohung etc.:* do you read me?

kapillar *Adj.* capillary; **Kapillare** *f; -, -n; Med., Phys.* capillary; **Kapillargefäß** *n Anat.* capillary ([blood]vessel); **Kapillarnetz** *n* capillary network

kapital *Adj.* **1.** *umg.* major; **ein ~er Fehler** a major (*od.* colossal) blunder; **e-e ~e Dummheit/Schlamperei** an extraordinarily stupid thing to do / a dreadfully sloppy piece of work; **2.** *Jägerspr.* large and strong; **~er Hirsch** royal stag, *Am. etwa* 12-point buck

Kapital *n; -s, -e* **1.** *Fin., Wirts.* capital; (*Geldmittel*) *auch* funds *Pl.*; (*Grundkapital*) share capital, capital stock; **flüssiges ~** available capital (*od.* funds); **mit 25% am ~ des Betriebs beteiligt sein** have a 25% stake in the business; **wir müssen ~ aufnehmen** we need an injection of capital; **2.** *fig.* asset; **~ aus etw. schlagen** capitalize on s.th., cash in on s.th.; **3.** *nur Sg.; Koll.* (*Kapitalisten*) capital; **4.** *Druck.* headband

Kapital|abwanderung *f* capital outflow; **~anlage** *f Fin., Wirts.* (capital) investment; **~anlagegesellschaft** *f* investment trust; **~anleger** *m,* **~anlegerin** *f Fin., Wirts.* investor; **~aufstockung** *f* capital increase

Kapitalband *m Druck.* headband

Kapital|bedarf *m Fin., Wirts.* capital requirements *Pl.*; **~beschaffung** *f* raising of funds, fund-raising; **~besitz** *m* capital holdings *Pl.*; **~beteiligung** *f* **1.** participation; **2.** *konkret:* stake; **~bildung** *f* accumulation of capital

Kapitalbuchstabe *m Druck.* capital (*od.* uppercase) letter; **Kapitälchen** *n* small capital (*umg.* cap)

Kapitaldecke *f Fin., Wirts.* capital resources *Pl.*

Kapitale *f; -, -n; altm.* capital (city)

Kapital|eigner *m,* **~eignerin** *f Fin., Wirts.* shareholder, stockholder; **~einlage** *f* capital contribution; **~erhöhung** *f* capital increase

Kapitalertrag *m Fin., Wirts.* return on capital; **~(s)steuer** *f* investment income tax

Kapital|flucht *f Fin., Wirts.* capital flight; **~fluss** *m* flow of capital; **~geber** *m,* **~geberin** *f* investor; **~gesellschaft** *f etwa* joint-stock company; **~gewinn** *m Fin., Wirts.* capital gains *Pl.*; **~güter** *Pl. Fin., Wirts.* capital goods; **~hilfe** *f* financial aid

kapitalintensiv *Adj.* capital-intensive

Kapitalinvestition *f* capital investment

kapitalisieren *v/t. Fin., Wirts.* capitalize; **Kapitalisierung** *f* capitalization

Kapitalismus *m; -, Kapitalismen, mst Sg.; Wirts.* capitalism; **Kapitalist** *m; -en, -en,* **Kapitalistin** *f; -, -nen* capitalist; **kapitalistisch** *Adj.* capitalist(ic)

Kapitalkraft *f* financial strength; **kapitalkräftig** *Adj.* well-funded, (financially) powerful

Kapital|mangel *m* lack of capital; **~markt** *m* capital (*od.* money) market; **~rücklage** *f* capital reserve(s *Pl.*); **~spritze** *f* cash injection, (fiscal) shot in the arm

Kapital|verbrechen *n* serious crime (*od.* offen|ce, *Am.* -se); **~verbrecher** *m,* **~verbrecherin** *f* dangerous criminal

Kapital|verflechtung *f* interlacing of capital interests; **~verkehr** *m* turnover of capital; **~vermögen** *n* capital assets *Pl.*; **~wert** *m* capital value; **~zins** *m*

interest on capital

Kapitän *m*; *-s*, *-e* **1.** *Naut.*, *Flug.* captain; *bes. auf kleinem* (*Handels*)*Schiff*: skipper; **~** *der Landstraße fig.* king of the road; **2.** *Sport* captain, *umg.* skipper; **~leutnant** *m Mil.* lieutenant commander

Kapitänspatent *n Naut.* master's certificate

Kapitel *n*; *-s*, *-* **1.** chapter (*auch kirchl.*); **2.** *fig. der Geschichte etc.*: chapter; *des Lebens*: *auch* period; (*Sache*) story; *das ist ein* **~** *für sich* that's another story (*od.* another matter altogether)

Kapitell *n*; *-s*, *-e Archit.* capital

Kapitelsaal *m kirchl.* chapter house

Kapitular *m*; *-s*, *-e*; *kirchl.* capitulary

Kapitulation *f*; *-*, *-en* capitulation, surrender; **kapitulieren** *v/i.* capitulate, surrender; *fig.* give in (*od.* up) (*vor* + *Dat.* in the face of. to)

Kaplan *m*; *-s*, *Kapläne*; *kath.* chaplain; (*Hilfsgeistlicher*) curate

Kapo *m*; *-s*, *-s* **1.** *Mil.* NCO; **2.** (*Aufseher*) (prisoner acting as) overseer; **3.** *südd. umg.* (*Vorarbeiter*) foreman, *Brit. auch* gaffer, *Am. auch* strawboss

Kapodaster *m*; *-s*, *-*; *Mus.* capo (tasto)

Kapok *m*; *-s*, *kein Pl.* kapok; **~baum** *m Bot.* kapok (tree)

Kaposi-Sarkom *n Med.* Kaposi's sarcoma

Käppchen *n* little cap; **Kappe** *f*; *-*, *-n* cap; (*Verschluss*) *auch* top; *des Schuhs*: (toe)cap; (*Abdeckung*) cover; *etw. auf s-e* **~** *nehmen fig.* take (the) responsibility for s.th., *Brit. umg. auch* carry the can for s.th.; *auf j-s* **~** *gehen/kommen* be down to s.o.

kappen *v/t.* **1.** (*Tau*) cut; (*Baum*) lop, top; (*Verbindungen*) cut off; **2.** (*kastrieren*) caponize

Kappen|abend *m*, **~sitzung** *f Dial.* carnival party (*at which funny caps are worn*)

Kappes *m*; *-*, *kein Pl.*; *Dial.* **1.** (*Unsinn*) rubbish, *umg.* rot, *bes. Am. umg.* garbage; **2.** (*Weißkohl*) white cabbage

Käppi *n*; *-s*, *-s* cap; *Mil.* forage (*Am.* garrison) cap

Kapp|messer *n* jack-knife; **~naht** *f* flat-felled (*od.* French) seam

Kappung *f* **1.** cutting; *von Baum*: lopping, topping; *von Verbindungen*: cutting off; **2.** (*Kastrieren von Hahn*) caponizing, castration; **Kappungsgrenze** *f Pol.* cap

Kaprice [ka'priːsə] *f*; *-*, *-n geh.* caprice, whim

Kapriole *f*; *-*, *-n* **1.** (*Luftsprung*) caper; **~n schlagen** cut capers; **2.** (*Streich*) prank; **3.** *Reitsport*: capriole

kaprizieren *v/refl.*: *sich auf etw.* (*Akk.*) **~** insist (doggedly) on s.th.; *sich darauf* **~**, *etw. zu tun* be intent on doing s.th.

kapriziös *Adj.* capricious

Kapsel *f*; *-*, *-n* **1.** *Anat.*, *Bot.*, *Pharm.* capsule; (*Raumkapsel*) *auch* module; (*Behälter*) case; **2.** (*Kappe*, *Deckel*) cap; (*Sprengkapsel*) detonator

kapselförmig *Adj.* capsule-shaped

Kapselfrucht *f Bot.* capsule, capsular fruit

kapseln *v/t. Tech.* encase, enclose; *Kernphysik*: jacket

Kapstadt (*n*); *-s*; *Geog.* Cape Town

kaputt *Adj. umg.* **1.** (*entzwei*) broken, bust, *Am. auch* kaput; *Kleidungsstück*: (*zerrissen*) torn; (*abgetragen*) worn out; (*außer Betrieb*) not working; *es ist* **~** *ganz*: it's had it; *funktioniert nicht*: it's not working, *Am. auch* it's

kaput; *Gerät*: *auch* it's given up; *Auto*, *Maschine*: it's broken down, *Am. auch* it's kaput; *Birne*, *Sicherung*: it's gone; *was ist denn jetzt schon wieder* **~**? *fig.* what's wrong (*od.* up) now?; **2.** *Firma*: failed; *Ehe*: failed, broken; *die Firma ist* **~** the firm's gone bust (*od.* belly up); **3.** *Organ*, *Glied etc.*: bad; *Leber*, *Gesundheit*: *auch* ruined; *ein* **~es** *Bein* a bad (*Brit. altm.* gammy, *Am.* gimp) leg; *gebrochen*: a broken leg; **4.** (*erschöpft*) shattered, *Brit. auch* knackered, *Am.* wiped out; **~er** *Typ* (human) wreck; *Mann*: *auch* broken man; *krankhaft*: seriously sick personality; *ich bin nervlich* **~** I'm a nervous wreck, my nerves are shot

kaputt|arbeiten *v/refl.* (*trennb.*, *hat -ge-*) *umg.* work o.s. to death; **~ärgern** *v/refl.* (*trennb.*, *hat -ge-*) *umg.*: *ich hab mich kaputtgeärgert* I was hopping mad; *über mich selbst*: I could have kicked myself; **~fahren** *v/t.* (*unreg.*, *trennb.*, *hat -ge-*) *umg.* (*Auto*) drive into the ground; *bei e-m Unfall*: smash up, wreck; **~gehen** *v/i.* (*unreg.*, *trennb.*, *ist -ge-*) *umg.* get broken, break; *fig. Ehe*, *Freundschaft*: break up; *Person*: go to pieces, crack up; (*Bankrott gehen*) *Firma*: go bust; **~kriegen** *v/t.* (*trennb.*, *hat -ge-*) *umg.* manage to break; **~lachen** *v/refl.* (*trennb.*, *hat -ge-*) *umg.* kill o.s. laughing

kaputt|machen *umg.* (*trennb.*, *hat -ge-*) **I.** *v/t.* break; *heftig*: (*Teller etc.*) *auch* smash; (*Kleider*, *Gerät*, *Reifen etc.*) ruin; *fig.* (*Person*) destroy; (*Ehe*) wreck; *Wirts.* (*Betrieb*) put out of business, ruin; *der ganze Stress macht ihn noch kaputt* all this stress will finish him off (*od.* will be the death of him); **II.** *v/refl.*: *sich* (*bei etw.*) **~** wear o.s. out (*od.* kill o.s.) (doing s.th.); **~reden** *v/t.* (*trennb.*, *hat -ge-*) *umg.*: *ein Thema* **~** flog a subject to death; **~schlagen** *v/t.* (*unreg.*, *trennb.*, *hat -ge-*) *umg.* smash

Kapuze *f*; *-*, *-n* hood; *von Mönch*: cowl

Kapuzenmantel *m* hooded coat

Kapuziner *m*; *-s*, *-* **1.** *kath.* Capuchin (monk); **2.** *Zool.* Capuchin monkey; **3.** *österr. Kaffee*: cappuccino; **~affe** *m Zool.* Capuchin monkey; **~kresse** *f Bot.* nasturtium; **~mönch** *m kath.* Capuchin monk; **~orden** *m kath.* Capuchin order

Kar *n*; *-s*, *-e*; *Geol.* cirque

Karabiner *m*; *-s*, *-* **1.** *Gewehr*: carbine; **2.** *österr.* (*Haken*) karabiner, snaplink; **~haken** *m* karabiner, snaplink

Karacho *n*; *-s*, *kein Pl.*; *umg.*: *mit* **~** like a bomb

Karaffe *f*; *-*, *-n* carafe, *für Wein*: *auch* decanter

Karakulschaf *n Zool.* karakul (sheep)

Karambolage *f*; *-*, *-n* **1.** *Billard*: cannon, *Am.* carom; **2.** *umg.* (*Zusammenstoß*) collision, crash; **Karambole** *f*; *-*, *-n Billard*: red (ball); **karambolieren** *v/i. Billard*: cannon, *Am.* carom

Karamell *m*; *-s*, *kein Pl.* caramel; **Karamellbonbon** *m*, *n*, **Karamelle** *f*; *-*, *-n* (caramel) toffee; **karamellfarben** *Adj.* caramel(-colo[u]red); **karamellieren** *v/i.* caramelize; **karamellisieren** *v/t.* caramelize

Karamell|pudding *m Gastr.* crème caramel; **~zucker** *m* caramelized sugar

Karaoke *n*; *-(s)*, *kein Pl.* karaoke

Karat *n*; *-(e)s*, *-e*, *mit Zahl*: *-* carat

Karate *n*; *-(s)*, *kein Pl.* karate

Karateka *m*; *-(s)*, *-(s) und f*; *-*, *-(s)* kar-

ateka

Karate|kämpfer *m*, **~kämpferin** *f* karate exponent, karateka; **~schlag** *m* karate chop

...karäter *m*, *im Subst.* ...-carat; *Zwei~* two-carat stone (*bes.* diamond)

...karätig *im Adj.* ...-carat; *achtzehn~es Gold* 18-carat gold

Karausche *;* *-*, *-n*; *Zool.* crucian carp

Karavelle *f*; *-*, *-n*; *hist.* caravel

Karawane *f*; *-*, *-n* caravan; *e-e* **~** *von Autos fig.* a long line (*Brit. auch* queue) of cars

Karawanenstraße *f* caravan route

Karawanserei *f*; *-*, *-en* caravanserai

Karbid *n*; *-(e)s*, *-e*; *Chem.* carbide

Karbid|lampe *f*, **~licht** *n* carbide lamp

Karbol *n*; *-s*, *kein Pl.*; *Chem.* carbolic acid

Karbolineum *n*; *-s*, *kein Pl.* carbolineum

Karbol|säure *f Chem.* carbolic acid; **~seife** *f* carbolic soap

Karbon *n*; *-s*, *kein Pl.*; *Geol.* Carboniferous (period)

Karbonado *m*; *-s*, *-s*; *Min.* carbonado, black diamond

Karbonat[1] *n*; *-(e)s*, *-e*; *Chem.* carbonate

Karbonat[2] *m*; *-(e)s*, *-e*; *Min.* carbonado

karbonisch *Adj. Geol.* Carboniferous

Karbonsäure *f Chem.* carbonic acid

Karbunkel *m*; *-s*, *-*; *Med.* carbuncle

Kardamom *m*, *n*; *-s*, *-e(n)* cardamom

Kardan|antrieb *m Tech.* cardan drive; **~gelenk** *n* universal joint

kardanisch *Adj.* cardan(ic); **~e Aufhängung** *Naut.* cardan suspension

Kardan|tunnel *m Mot.* transmission tunnel; **~welle** *f* cardan shaft; *zwischen Motor und Achse*: propeller shaft

Kardätsche *f*; *-*, *-n* body brush

Karde *f*; *-*, *-n* **1.** *Bot.* teasel; **2.** *beim Spinnen*: card

Kardeel *n*; *-s*, *-e*; *Naut.* (rope, *stärker*: hawser) strand

karden *v/t. beim Spinnen*: card

kardial *Adj. Med.* cardiac

kardinal *Adj. Fehler*: cardinal; *e-e* **~e** *Frage* a cardinal (*od.* crucial) question

Kardinal... *im Subst.* cardinal ...

Kardinal *m*; *-s*, *Kardinäle* **1.** *kath.* cardinal; **2.** *Orn.* cardinal (bird)

Kardinalbischof *m kath.* cardinal bishop

Kardinal|fehler *m* cardinal error; **~problem** *n* cardinal (*od.* crucial) problem

Kardinals|hut *m kath.* cardinal's (*od.* red *od.* scarlet) hat; **~kollegium** *n kath.* College of Cardinals, Sacred College

Kardinalstaatssekretär *m* Papal Secretary of State

Kardinal|tugend *f* cardinal virtue; **~zahl** *f* cardinal number

Kardiogramm *n*; *-s*, *-e*; *Med.* cardiogram; **Kardiograph** *m*; *-en*, *-en* cardiograph

Kardiologe *m*; *-n*, *-n* heart specialist, cardiologist; **Kardiologie** *f*; *-*, *kein Pl.* cardiology; **Kardiologin** *f*; *-*, *-nen* → *Kardiologe*; **kardiologisch** *Adj.* cardiological

Karenz *f*; *-*, *-en* → *Karenzzeit*; **~frist** *f* waiting (*od.* qualifying) period; **~tag** *m* first day of illness for which no benefit is paid; **~zeit** *f* **1.** *Versicherung*: waiting (*od.* qualifying) period; **2.** *Wirts.*, *Konkurrenzklausel*: period of restriction; **3.** *Med.* period of rest

Karettschildkröte *f Zool.* hawksbill (turtle)

Karfiol *m*; *-s*, *kein Pl*.; *österr*. cauliflower

Karfreitag *m* Good Friday

Karfunkel *m*; *-s*, *-*; *Min*., *Med*. carbuncle; **Karfunkelstein** *m Min*. carbuncle (stone)

karg I. *Adj*. **1.** *mengenmäßig*: meag|re (*Am*. -er); *stärker*: paltry; *Essen*, *Leben*: frugal; *Möblierung*: sparse, scanty; **mit Lob ~ sein** be sparing (*od*. grudging) with one's praise; **2.** (*unfruchtbar*) *Boden*: poor, infertile; *Landschaft*: barren; **3.** (*schmucklos*) *Raum*: bare; **II.** *Adv*. **~ bemessen sein** be meag|re (*Am*. -er) (*umg*. stingy); *Vorrat*: be scanty; **~ ausgestattet sein** be scantily equipped; (*wenig besitzen*) have few possessions

Kargadeur [karga'dø:ɐ̯] *m*; *-s*, *-e*, **Kargador** *m*; *-s*, *-e Wirts*. supercargo

kargen *v/i*. *geh*.: **~ mit** be sparing (*od*. grudging) with; *mit Geld*: be mean with; **mit Worten ~** say little, be a person of few words, be taciturn *geh*.; **Kargheit** *f* **1.** meagreness, *Am*. meagerness; *stärker*: paltriness; *von Essen*, *Leben*: frugality; *der Möblierung*: sparseness, scantiness; **2.** *des Bodens*: poorness, infertility; *der Landschaft*: barrenness; **3.** *e-s Raums*: bareness

kärglich *Adj*. → **karg**; **die ~en Reste** the paltry remains; **Kärglichkeit** *f* → **Kargheit**

Kargo *m*; *-s*, *-s* cargo

Karibe *m*; *-n*, *-n* Caribbean, Carib; **Karibik** *f*; *-*; *Geog*., *Meer*, *Raum*: Caribbean; **Karibin** *f*; *-*, *-nen* → **Karibe**; **karibisch** *Adj*. Caribbean; **die Karibischen Inseln** the islands of the Caribbean

Karibu *m*, *n*; *-s*, *-s*; *Zool*. caribou

kariert I. *Adj*. **1.** checked; *Papier*: squared; **2.** *umg*.: **~es Zeug reden** talk crap *Sl*.; **II.** *Adv*.: **~ daherreden** *umg*. talk crap *Sl*.

Karies *f*; *-*, *kein Pl*.; *Med*. tooth decay, caries

Karikatur *f*; *-*, *-en* caricature (*auch fig*.); (*Witzzeichnung*) *mst* cartoon; **karikaturartig** *Adj*. *und Adv*. in the manner of a caricature; **Karikaturist** *m*;, *-en*, *-en*, **Karikaturistin** *f*; *-*, *-nen* caricaturist; *witzig*: cartoonist; **karikaturistisch** *Adj*.: **~e Darstellung** *witzig*: cartoon; *verzerrt*: caricature; **karikieren** *v/t*. caricature

kariös *Adj*. *Med*., *Zähne*: decayed; *stärker*: rotten

karitativ I. *Adj*. charitable; **es dient ~en Zwecken** it's for charity (*od*. a good cause); **II.** *Adv*.: **sich ~ betätigen/engagieren** do/involve o.s. in charity work

Karkasse *f*; *-*, *-n* **1.** *Gastr*. bones *Pl*., *Geflügel*: *auch* (chicken) carcass; **2.** *e-s Reifens*: casing

Karl *m*; *-s*, *kein Pl*. Charles; **~ der Große** *hist*. Charlemagne

Karma *n*; *-s*, *kein Pl*. karma

Karmeliter *m*; *-s*, *-*; *kath*. Carmelite (monk); **Karmeliterin** *f*; *-*, *-nen* Carmelite (nun); **Karmeliterorden** *m* Carmelite order

Karmesin *n*; *-s*, *kein Pl*. crimson; *mit Purpurstich*: carmine; **karmesinrot** *Adj*. crimson; *mit Purpurstich*: carmine

Karmin *n*; *-s*, *kein Pl*. crimson; *mit Purpurstich*: carmine; **karminrot** *Adj*. crimson; *mit Purpurstich*: carmine

Karneol *m*; *-s*, *-e*; *Min*. carnelian

Karneval *m*; *-s*, *-s od*. *-e* carnival; **an ~** at carnival time, in the carnival sea-

son; **Karnevalist** *m*; *-en*, *-en*, **Karnevalistin** *f*; *-*, *-nen* carnival participant; **karnevalistisch** *Adj*. carnival ...

Karnevals|... *im Subst*. carnival ..., → *auch* **Faschings...**; **~kostüm** *n* carnival costume; **~orden** *m* carnival medal; **~prinz** *m* carnival prince; **~prinzessin** *f* carnival princess; **~schlager** *m* popular carnival song; **~sitzung** *f* meeting of the carnival convention (*with funny speeches*, *singing and dancing*); **~treiben** *n*; *nur Sg*. carnival goings-on (*od*. festivities) *Pl*.; **~umzug** *m* carnival procession; **~verein** *m* carnival association; **~zeit** *f* carnival time (*od*. season)

Karnickel *n*; *-s*, *-* **1.** *Dial*. rabbit; **2.** *umg*.: **immer bin ich das ~** (*der Sündenbock*) I'm always the one (*Brit*. *auch* it's always muggins) who gets the blame

karnisch *Adj*. *Geol*. Karnic; **die Karnischen Alpen** the Karnic Alps

karnivor *Adj*. *Zool*., *Bot*. carnivorous

Karnivore¹ *m*; *-n*, *-n*; *Zool*. carnivore

Karnivore² *f*; *-*, *-n*; *Bot*. carnivorous plant, carnivore

Kärnten (*n*); *-s*; *Geog*. Carinthia; **Kärnt(e)ner** *m*; *-s*, *-*, **Kärnt(e)nerin** *f*; *-*, *-nen* Carinthian, *weiblich auch*: Carinthian woman (*od*. girl *etc*.); **kärntnerisch** *Adj*. Carinthian

Karo *n*; *-s*, *-s* **1.** *im Stoff*: check, square; **2.** (*Kartenfarbe*) diamonds *Pl*.; (*Einzelkarte*) diamond

Karo... *im Subst*.: ... of diamonds; **~ass** ace of diamonds; **~sechs** six of diamonds

Karolinger *m*; *-s*, *-*; *hist*. Carolingian; **karolingisch** *Adj*. *hist*. Carolingian; **~e Minuskel** Caroline minuscule

Karomuster *n* check(ed) pattern

Karosse *f*; *-*, *-n* **1.** state coach; **2.** *umg*. → **Karosserie**

Karosserie *f*; *-*, *-n*; *Mot*. bodywork, *Brit*. *auch* coachwork; *konkret*: *auch* body; **~bau** *m*; *nur Sg*. body production; *mst früher*, *bei exklusiven Autos*: coachbuilding; **~bauer** *m* body builder; *mst früher*, *bei exklusiven Autos*: coachbuilder

Karotin *n*; *-s*, *kein Pl*. carotin

Karotte *f*; *-*, *-n* carrot; **Karottensaft** *m* carrot juice

Karpaten *Pl*. *Geog*.: **die ~** the Carpathians

Karpfen *m*; *-s*, *-*; *Zool*. carp; **~teich** *m* carp pond; → **Hecht 2**

Karre¹ *f*; *-*, *-n* → **Karren**

Karre² *f*; *-*, *-n*; *Geol*. channel (in limestone)

Karree *n*; *-s*, *-s* square; (*Wohnblock*) block, *Am*. (apartment) building; **ums ~ gehen** go for a walk (a)round the square

Karren *m*; *-s*, *-* **1.** cart; **ein ~ voll Äpfel** a cartload of apples; **den ~ in den Dreck fahren** *fig*. mess things up; **den ~ aus dem Dreck ziehen** *fig*. straighten things out; **der ~ ist total verfahren** things are in a hopeless mess; **den ~ (einfach) laufen lassen** let things go; **j-n vor s-n ~ spannen** *umg*. rope s.o. in; **2.** *alter* ~ *umg*. old banger (*Am*. beater), old jalopy

karren I. *v/t*. (*hat gekarrt*) *auch umg*. *fig*. cart; **j-n (mit dem Auto) nach Hause ~** *umg*. run s.o. home (in the car); **II.** *v/i*. (*ist*) *umg*. drive (around)

Karrette *f*; *-*, *-n*; *schw*. handcart; (*Einkaufswagen*) shopping trolley (*Am*. cart); (*Schubkarren*) wheelbarrow

Karriere *f*; *-*, *-n* **1.** career; **~ machen**

have a successful career, get on (in life); (*nach oben kommen*) get to the top; **2.** *Reitsport*: full gallop; **karrierebewusst** *Adj*. career-minded; **karriereredienlich** *Adj*. ... useful for one's career, furthering one's carrer

Karriere|frau *f* career girl (*od*. woman); **~knick** *m* downturn *od*. setback (in one's career), bad patch; **~leiter** *f* ladder of success; **ganz oben auf der ~ stehen** be at the top of the ladder (*od*. tree); **~typ** *m* careerist

Karrierist *m*; *-en*, *-en*, **~in** *f*; *-*, *-nen* careerist; **karrieristisch** *Adj*. careerist

Kärrnerarbeit *f pej*. hard labo(u)r; *undankbare*: donkey work

Karsamstag *m* Easter Saturday

Karst¹ *m*; *-(e)s*, *-e*; *Dial*. (two-pronged) hoe

Karst² *m*; *-(e)s*, *-e*; *Geol*. karst; **~boden** *m* karstic soil; **~höhle** karst cave

karstig *Adj*. karstic; **Karstlandschaft** *f* (area of) karst; *größeres Gebiet*: karst country

Kart *m*; *-(s)*, *-s* kart, go-cart; **~bahn** *f* kart track; **~fahren** *n*; *-s*, *kein Pl*. karting

kart. *Abk*. → **kartoniert**

Kartätsche *f*; *-*, *-n*; *hist*. case-shot

Kartäuser *m*; *-s*, *-*; *kath*. Carthusian (monk); **Kartäuserin** *f*; *-*, *-nen* Carthusian (nun)

Kartäuser|likör *m* chartreuse; **~orden** *m kath*. Carthusian order

Kärtchen *n* little card

Karte *f*; *-*, *-n* **1.** *allg*. card; **gelbe/rote ~** *Sport* yellow/red card; **j-m die gelb-rote ~ zeigen** show s.o. the yellow and red cards; **die grüne ~** *Kfz-Versicherungsnachweis*: green card; **2.** (*Kreditkarte*) card; **kann ich mit ~ zahlen?** can I pay with a card (*umg*. with plastic)?; **3.** (*Landkarte*) map; (*Seekarte*) chart; **4.** (*Eintritts-*, *Fahrkarte*) ticket; **5.** (*Speisekarte*) menu; (*Weinkarte*) wine list; **nach der ~ essen** eat à la carte; **6.** *Spielkarte*: card; **~n spielen** play cards; **~n geben** deal; **j-m die ~n legen** tell s.o.'s fortune (from the cards); **mit gezinkten ~n spielen** play with marked cards; **gute/schlechte ~n haben** have a good/bad hand; *fig*. be well/badly placed; **bei ihr habe ich schlechte ~n** *fig*. she's got it in for me, I'm in her bad books (*Am*. on her blacklist); **sich** (*Dat*.) **nicht in die ~n sehen lassen** not let anyone see one's cards; *fig*. play one's cards close to one's chest; **mit offenen ~n spielen** *fig*. put one's cards on the table; **mit verdeckten ~n spielen** *fig*. play one's cards close to one's chest; **alles auf e-e ~ setzen** *fig*. put all one's eggs in one basket; **auf die falsche ~ setzen** *fig*. back the wrong horse

Kartei *f*; *-*, *-en* card file (*od*. index); **e-e ~ führen über** (+ *Akk*.) keep a file on; **~karte** *f* file card, index card; **~kasten** *m* card file (*od*. card-index) box; **~leiche** *f umg*. *hum*. inactive member

Kartell *n*; *-s*, *-e*; *Wirts*. cartel; *Pol*. (loose) coalition (*for fighting an election*); *Univ*. action group (*of student bodies*); **~absprache** *f* cartel agreement; **~amt** *n* Federal Cartel Office; **~gesetz** *n* monopolies law, *bes. Am*. antitrust law

kartellieren *v/t*. *Wirts*. cartelize; **Kartellierung** *f* cartelization

Kartellrecht *n Jur*., *Wirts*. monopolies law, *bes. Am*. antitrust law; **kartellrechtlich** *Adj*. relating to monopolies (*bes. Am*. antitrust) law; **Kartellver-**

bot *n Wirts.* ban on cartels
karten *v/i. umg.* play cards
Karten|bestellung *f* ticket reservation; **~block** *m* block of tickets; **~brief** *m* letter card; **~gruß** *m* postcard greeting (*od.* message); **~haus** *n* **1.** house of cards; *wie ein ~ einstürzen od. in sich zusammenfallen fig.* fold up (*od.* collapse) like a house of cards; **2.** *Naut.* chart house; **~kunde** *f* cartography; **~kunststück** *n* card trick; **~legen** *n*; *-s, kein Pl.* reading the cards; **~leger** *m*; *-s, -*, **~legerin** *f*; *-, -nen* fortune teller (*who reads the cards*); **~lesen** *n* map reading; **~raum** *m* map room; **~skizze** *f* sketch map; **~spiel** *n* **1.** card game, game of cards; **2.** (*Karten*) pack of cards; **~spieler** *m*, **~spielerin** *f* card player; **~ständer** *m* map stand; **~telefon** *n* cardphone; **~tisch** *m* **1.** card table; **2.** *für Landkarten:* map table; *für Seekarten:* chart table; **~verkauf** *m* **1.** sale of tickets; **2.** (*Stelle*) box office; **~vorverkauf** *m* **1.** advance booking (*bes. Am.* reservations *Pl.*); **2.** (*Stelle*) box office; **~zahlung** *f* payment by credit card; **~zimmer** *n* map room
kartesianisch, kartesisch *Adj.* Cartesian
kartieren *v/t.* map; *Naut.* chart; **Kartierung** *f* mapping; *Naut.* charting
Karting *n*; *-s, kein Pl.* karting
Kartoffel *f*; *-, -n* **1.** potato, *Am. umg.* spud, tater; *j-n wie e-e heiße ~ fallen lassen umg. fig.* drop s.o. like a hot potato; *rein in die ~n, raus aus die ~n umg.* first it's do one thing, then it's do the other; **2.** *umg. hum.* (*dicke Nase*) conk, *Am.* schnoz(zle); **3.** *umg. hum.* (*Loch im Strumpf*) gaping hole; **~acker** *m* potato field; **~brei** *m Gastr.* mashed potatoes *Pl.*; **~chips** *Pl.* potato crisps (*Am.* chips); **~ernte** *f Agr.* potato harvest; (*Ertrag*) potato crop; **~fäule** *f Agr.* potato rot; **~feld** *n* potato field; **~feuer** *n* fire for burning potato tops; **~gratin** *n Gastr.* gratiné(e) potatoes *Pl.*; **~käfer** *m Zool.* Colorado (potato) beetle; **~kloß** *m*, **~knödel** *m südd. Gastr.* potato dumpling; **~kraut** *n* potato tops *Pl.*; **~mehl** *n* potato flour; **~presse** *f* potato press; **~puffer** *m Gastr.* potato fritter; **~püree** *n Gastr.* mashed potatoes *Pl.*; **~sack** *m* potato sack; **~salat** *m Gastr.* potato salad; **~schalen** *Pl.* potato peel(ing)s; **~schäler** *m*; *-s, -* potato peeler; **~schnaps** *m* potato spirit (*Am.* liquor); **~stampfer** *m* potato masher; **~stock** *m*; *nur Sg.; schw., südd.* mashed potatoes *Pl.*; **~suppe** *f Gastr.* potato soup; **~teig** *m* potato dough
Karto|graph *m*; *-en, -en* cartographer; **~graphie** *f*; *-, kein Pl.* cartography; **~graphin** *f*; *-, -nen* (female) cartographer
kartographieren *v/t.* (*Land etc.*) map; **kartographisch I.** *Adj.* cartographic; **II.** *Adv.* cartographically
Karton [kar'tɔŋ, kar'to:n] *m*; *-s, -s* **1.** (*Pappe*) cardboard, *stärker:* pasteboard; **2.** (*Schachtel*) cardboard box; **3.** (*Skizze*) cartoon
Kartonagen [karto'na:ʒn] *Pl.* (cardboard) packaging materials; **~fabrik** *f* cardboard box factory
kartoniert *Adj.* (bound) in paper boards; **~e Ausgabe** (stiff) paper cover edition
Kartothek *f*; *-, -en* card index
Kartusche *f*; *-, -n* **1.** *Archit.* cartouche; **2.** *Mil. etc.* cartridge
Karussell *n*; *-s, -e od. -s* roundabout,

merry-go-round, *Am.* carousel; *fig.* merry-go-round; *~ fahren* have a ride on a roundabout (*od.* merry-go-round, *Am.* carousel)
Karwoche *f* (*auch die ~*) Holy Week
Karyatide *f*; *-, -n; Archit.* caryatid
Karzer *m*; *-s, -; Päd. hist.* **1.** detention room; **2.** (*Strafe*) detention
karzinogen I. *Adj. Med.* carcinogenic; **II. Karzinogen** *n*; *-s, -e; Med.* carcinogen
Karzinologie *f*; *-, kein Pl.* oncology
Karzinom *n*; *-s, -e; Med.* carcinoma
Kasache *m*; *-n, -n*, **Kasachin** *f*; *-, -nen* Kazakh, *weiblich auch:* Kazakh woman (*od.* girl); **kasachisch I.** *Adj.* Kazakh; **II. Kasachisch** *n*; *-(s); Ling.* Kazakh; *das Kasachische* Kazakh; **Kasachstan** (*n*); *-s; Geog.* Kazakhstan
Kasack *m*; *-s, -s* (*überlange Bluse*) casaque, tunic
Kaschemme *f*; *-, -n; umg. pej.* (low) dive
kaschen *v/t. umg.* **1.** (*verhaften*) nab; **2.** (*klauen*) pinch
kaschieren *v/t.* **1.** (*verdecken*) hide, cover up; **2.** (*Bucheinband*) *mit Papier:* line; *mit Folie* laminate; **3.** *Theat.* (*Bühnendekoration*) mo(u)ld; **Kaschierung** *f* **1.** (*Verdeckung*) hiding; **2.** *Buchbinderei:* lining (with paper); *mit Folie:* lamination; **3.** *Theat.* mo(u)lding
Kaschmir¹ (*n*); *-s; Geog.* Kashmir
Kaschmir² *m*; *-s, -e* cashmere; **~wolle** *f* cashmere wool; **~ziege** *f* Kashmir goat
Käse *m*; *-s, -* **1.** cheese; *weißer ~ Dial.* quark, *Am.* farmer('s) cheese; *~ schließt den Magen* cheese rounds off the meal; **2.** *umg. fig.* (*Unsinn*) rubbish, *Am.* garbage; (*dumme Sache*) stupid business; **~aufschnitt** *m* assorted cheese slices *Pl.*; **~blatt** *n umg.* (local) rag; **~brot** *n* (open) cheese sandwich; **~ecke** *f* cheese triangle; **~fondue** *n Gastr.* cheese fondue; **~füße** *Pl.; umg.* smelly (*od.* cheesy) feet; **~gebäck** *n* cheese savouries (*Am.* crackers) *Pl.*; **~glocke** *f* cheese cover
Kasein *n*; *-s, kein Pl.; Chem.* casein
Käsekuchen *m* cheesecake
Kasematte *f*; *-, -n; hist.* casemate
Käsemesser *n* cheese knife
käsen *v/i.* **1.** make cheese; **2.** *Milch:* go cheesy, curdle
Käseplatte *f* cheese platter
Käser *m*; *-s, -* cheesemaker; **Käserei** *f* **1.** *nur Sg.* cheesemaking; **2.** (*Betrieb*) cheese dairy; **Käserin** *f*; *-, -nen* cheesemaker; **Käserinde** *f* cheese rind
Kaserne *f*; *-, -n; Mil.* barracks *Pl.*
Kasernenhof *m* barrack square; (*Exerzierplatz*) parade ground; **~ton** *m* parade-ground tone (of voice), *Am.* drill sergeant's bark
Kasernentor *n* barracks gate
kasernieren *v/t.* quarter in barracks; **Kasernierung** *f* quartering in barracks
Käse|schmiere *f bei Neugeborenen:* vernix caseosa; **~stange** *f* cheese straw; **~torte** *f* cheesecake
käseweiß *Adj.* (as) white as a sheet
Käsewürfel *Pl.* diced cheese *Sg.*
käsig *Adj.* **1.** cheesy; **2.** (*blass*) pale
Kasino *n*; *-s, -s* **1.** *Mil.* officers' mess; **2.** (*Speiseraum*) canteen, cafeteria; **3.** (*Spielkasino*) casino
Kaskade *f*; *-, -n* **1.** cascade (*auch Phys., Etech.*); **2.** *Sprung:* acrobatic leap (*with a pretended fall*); **Kaskaden-**

schaltung *f Etech.* cascade connection
Kaskadeur [kaska'dø:ɐ] *m*; *-s, -e*, **~in** *f*; *-, -nen* (circus) acrobat
Kasko¹ *m*; *-s, -s; Naut.* hull
Kasko² *f*; *-, -s; Abk. umg.* → **Kaskoversicherung**
Kaskoschaden *m* own damage, *Am.* damage to one's own vehicle *etc.*
kaskoversichern *v/t.* (*untr., hat*) *nur Inf. und P.P.* insure against own damage, *etwa* insure comprehensively; *kaskoversichert sein etwa* have comprehensive insurance; **Kaskoversicherung** *f* **1.** *Mot.* insurance against damage to one's own vehicle, *etwa* comprehensive (*Am.* collision) insurance; **2.** *Naut.* hull insurance
Kasper *m*; *-s, -* **1.** *etwa* Punch; **2.** *umg. fig.* clown; **Kasperei** *f*; *-, -en* clowning, fooling around; **Kasperl** *m*; *-s, -(n) österr.*, **Kasperle** *n, m*; *-s, -; südd. etwa* Punch; **Kasperlepuppe** *f südd. etwa* Punch puppet; **Kasperletheater** *n südd. etwa* Punch and Judy show; **Kasperli** *m*; *-s, -; schw. etwa* Punch; **kaspern** *v/i. umg.* clown (*od.* fool) around
Kasper|puppe *f etwa* Punch puppet; **~theater** *n etwa* Punch and Judy show
kaspisch *Adj.*: *das Kaspische Meer Geog.* the Caspian Sea
Kassa *f*; *-, Kassen; österr.* → **Kasse**
Kassa|geschäft *n Wirts.* spot transaction; **~kurs** *m* spot price; **~markt** *m Wirts.* spot market
Kassandra *f*; *-, Kassandren* Cassandra; **Kassandraruf** *m* words *Pl.* of warning; *Prophezeiung:* prophecy of doom
Kassation *f*; *-, -en; Jur.* annulment
Kassations|beschwerde *f schw. Jur.* appeal process; **~gericht** *n schw. Jur.* (cantonal) court of appeal; **~hof** *m Jur.* court of cassation (*od.* appeal)
Kassazahlung *f Wirts.* cash payment
Kasse *f*; *-, -n* **1.** (*Ladenkasse*) till, (*Registrierkasse*) cash register; *die ~ klingelt od. die ~n klingeln umg.* the cash tills are ringing; *in die ~ greifen od. e-n Griff in die ~ tun* help o.s. to the takings (*Am.* the take), have a hand in the till; **2.** (*Zahlstelle*) (*Kassentisch*) cash desk; *Supermarkt:* checkout (counter); *e-r Bank:* counter (for payments); *Büro:* cashier's office; *Theat. etc.:* box office; *Sport* ticket window; *zahlen Sie bitte an der ~* please pay at the cash desk (*Am.* pay the cashier); *j-n zur ~ bitten umg.* present s.o. with the bill; **3.** *Kartenspiel etc.:* pool; **4.** (*Krankenkasse*) health (insurance) scheme (*Am.* plan); *bei welcher ~ sind Sie?* which health scheme (*Am.* plan *od.* company) are you with?; **5.** (*Sparkasse*) savings bank; (*örtliche Bank*) local (bank) branch; **6.** (*Einnahmen*) takings *Pl.*, receipts *Pl.*, *Am. auch* take; *~ machen* cash up; **7.** (*Bargeld*) cash; *gut/knapp bei ~ sein umg.* be flush / be hard up; *etw. reißt ein Loch in j-s ~* s.th. makes a big hole in s.o.'s finances; *~ machen umg.* (*sehr viel verdienen*) be raking it in; → *getrennt II*
Kasseler *n*; *-s, -; Gastr.* (smoked and) cured pork; *~ Rippchen od. Rippenspeer* cured spare rib
Kassenarzt *m*, **Kassenärztin** *f* doctor treating patients belonging to a health (insurance) scheme; *in GB etwa* NHS doctor; *in den USA etwa* preferred provider, HMO doctor; **kassenärztlich** *Adj.*: *~e Behandlung* treatment

by a health scheme doctor (*Am.* a preferred provider)

Kassen|automat *m* cash dispenser, *Am.* automatic teller, ATM; **~beleg** *m* till (*Am.* sales) receipt; **~bericht** *m* cash report; **~bestand** *m* cash balance, cash in hand; **~bon** *m* till (*Am.* sales) receipt; **~brille** *f* (pair of) glasses supplied by a health insurance scheme (*Am.* plan); *in GB etwa:* (pair of) National Health glasses *Pl.*; **~buch** *n* cashbook; **~erfolg** *m* box-office hit; **~gestell** *n umg.* glasses frame supplied by a health insurance scheme; *etwa in GB:* National Health frame; **~magnet** *m* crowd puller, box-office draw (*Am.* bonanza); **~obligation** *f Wirts.* medium-term bond; **~patient** *m*, **~patientin** *f* health scheme (*Am.* plan) patient, non-private patient; *in GB:* NHS patient; *in den USA:* insured patient; **~prüfer** *m*, **~prüferin** *f* auditor; **~prüfung** *f* cash audit; **~schalter** *m Bank:* counter; **~schlager** *m* 1. → **Kassenerfolg**; 2. *Produkt:* money spinner; **~stand** *m* cash in till; **~stunden** *Pl. Bank etc:* business hours; **~sturz** *m umg.:* ~ **machen** count one's cash; **~wart** *m* treasurer; **~zettel** *m* (till) receipt

Kasserolle *f*; -, -n casserole

Kassette *f*; -, -n 1. *für Geld:* cashbox; *für Schmuck:* (jewel|lery, *Am.* -ry) case; *für Bücher:* slipcase; *mit Schallplatten:* box; 2. *Tonband:* cassette; *Fot.* cassette, cartridge; 3. *Archit.* coffer

Kassetten|deck *n* cassette deck; **~decke** *f Archit.* coffered ceiling; **~fach** *n* cassette holder (*od.* compartment); **~recorder, ~rekorder** *m* cassette recorder

Kassia *f*; -, *Kassien; Bot.* cassia

Kassiber *m*; -s, -; *Sl.* (prisoner's) secret message, *Am. auch* stiff *Sl.*

Kassier *m*; -s, -e; *südd., österr., schw.* → **Kassierer**

kassieren I. *v/t.* 1. (*Miete, Geld etc.*) collect; 2. *umg.* (*verlangen*) charge; (*einstecken*) take, pocket; (*verdienen*) make; (*erhalten*) receive; *fig.* (*Lob, Anerkennung*) earn; *bei dem Geschäft kassierte sie ein Vermögen* she made a fortune on the deal; 3. *umg.* (*hinnehmen müssen*) (*Schlag*) take, receive; (*blaues Auge, Strafpunkte etc.*) get; (*Niederlage*) suffer; *die Mannschaft kassierte die siebte Niederlage in Folge* (*od.* the team recorded (*od.* went down to) their seventh successive defeat; 4. *umg.* (*wegnehmen*) take away, confiscate; (*verhaften*) pick up, nab *umg.*; 5. *Jur.* (*Urteil*) quash; (*Erlass, Anordnung*) revoke; **II.** *v/i.* take (*od.* collect) the money; *bei j-m* ~ give s.o. the bill (*Am., im Restaurant* check); *dürfte ich jetzt* ~*? im Lokal:* do you mind if I give you the bill (*Am.* check) now?, can I settle up with you now?; *ganz schön* ~ *umg.* be raking it in; *bei e-m Geschäft:* clean up, make a bomb (*Am.* a fortune)

Kassierer *m*; -s, -, **~in** *f*; -, -nen 1. cashier; *Bank:* teller; 2. (*Kassenwart*) treasurer; **Kassierin** *f*; -, -nen; *südd., österr., schw. siehe* **Kassiererin**

Kassler *n*; -s, - → **Kasseler**

Kastagnette [kastan'jɛtə] *f*; -, -n castanet

Kastanie *f*; -, -n; *Bot.* chestnut; *Baum:* chestnut (tree); (*Rosskastanie*) (horse) chestnut; *(für j-n) die* ~*n aus dem Feuer holen umg. fig.* pull the chestnuts out of the fire (for s.o.); **Kastanien-**

baum *m Bot.* chestnut (tree); **kastanienbraun** *Adj.* chestnut (brown)

Kästchen *n* small box; *in Zeitung, Formular:* box; *auf Rechenpapier:* square

Kaste *f*; -, -n caste

kasteien *v/refl.* chastise o.s.; (*sich enthalten*) deny o.s.; **Kasteiung** *f* self-chastisement; (*Enthaltung*) self-denial

Kastell *n*; -s, -e fortress, castle; (*römisches Lager*) castell; **Kastellan** *m*; -s, -e castle warden; *hist.* castellan

Kasten *m*; -s, *Kästen* 1. box (*auch Turnen, in Zeitungen etc.*); (*Behälter, Kiste*) case; (*Bierkasten etc.*) crate; (*Briefkasten*) letterbox, *Am.* mailbox; (*Schaukasten*) showcase; *südd., österr., schw.* (*Schrank*) wardrobe; 2. *umg.:* *im* ~ *sein Film:* be in the can; *e-e Szene/ ein Bild im* ~ *haben* have a scene/picture in the can; 3. *umg. pej.* (*Auto, Flugzeug*) crate; (*Gebäude*) barn (*od.* barracks) of a building, pile, heap; 4. *umg.* (*Fernseher*) box; 5. *Mil. Sl.* (*Gefängnis*) cooler, clink; 6. *umg.* (*großer Mensch*) great big hulk; 7. *umg.:* *er hat was auf dem* ~ he's not daft; 8. *Sport Sl., bei Ballspielen* (*Tor*) goal; **~brot** *n* tin loaf; **~form** *f* rectangular baking tin

kastenförmig *Adj.* box-shaped

Kastengeist *m* caste spirit

Kastenwagen *m Mot.* box van, *bes. Am.* panel truck

Kastenwesen *n; nur Sg.* caste system

Kastilien *n*; -s; *Geog.* Castile; **kastilisch** *Adj.* Castilian

Kastrat *m*; -en, -en 1. eunuch; 2. *Mus. hist.* castrato; **Kastratenstimme** *f* 1. *Mus.* castrato (voice); 2. *pej.* high, piping voice

Kastration *f*; -, -en castration; *von männlichen Tieren: auch* neutering; *von Pferd: auch* gelding; *weitS. von weiblichen Tieren:* spaying

Kastrations|angst *f Psych.* fear of castration; **~komplex** *m Psych.* castration complex

kastrieren *v/t.* castrate; (*männliches Tier*) *auch* neuter; (*Pferd etc.*) *auch* geld; *weitS.* (*weibliches Tier*) spay;

Kastrierung *f* → **Kastration**

Kasuar *m*; -s, -e; *Zool.* cassowary

Kasuistik *f* casuistry; **kasuistisch I.** *Adj.* casuistic; **II.** *Adv.* casuistically

Kasus *m*; -, -; *Ling.* case; **~endung** *f Ling.* case ending

Kat *m*; -s, -s; *Abk.* (*Katalysator*) *Mot.* cat

Katafalk *m*; -s, -e catafalque

Katakombe *f*; -, -n catacomb

Katalane *m*; -n, -n, **Katalanin** *f*; -, -nen Catalan, *weiblich auch* Catalan woman (*od.* girl); **katalanisch I.** *Adj.* Catalan; **II. Katalanisch** *n*; -(s); *Ling.* Catalan; *das Katalanische* Catalan

Katalog *m*; -(e)s, -e catalog(ue); *fig. von Maßnahmen etc.:* package; *ein ganzer* ~ *von Fragen fig.* a long list of questions; **katalogisieren** *v/t.* catalog(ue); **Katalogisierung** *f* catalog(u)ing

Katalog|nummer *f* catalog(ue) number; **~preis** *m* catalog(ue) (*od.* list) price

Katalonien (*n*); -s; *Geog.* Catalonia

Katalonier *m*; -s, -, **Katalonierin** *f*; -, -nen Catalan; **katalonisch** *Adj.* → *katalanisch*

Katalysator *m*; -s, -en catalyst (*auch fig.*); *Mot.* catalytic converter; **~auto** *n* car with a catalytic converter, cat car *umg.*

Katalyse *f*; -, -n; *Chem.* catalysis; **kata-**

lysieren *v/t.* cata|lyse (*bes. Am.* -lyze); **katalytisch** *Adj. auch fig.* catalytic

Katamaran *m*; -s, -e; *Naut.* catamaran

Katapult *n*; -s, -e catapult; **~flugzeug** *n* catapult takeoff aircraft; **katapultieren I.** *v/t.* catapult; (*Piloten*) eject; *fig. auch* propel (*in, auf* + *Akk.* [in]to); **II.** *v/refl. fig.:* *sich an die Spitze* ~ shoot to the top

Katapultstart *m* catapult takeoff

Katar (*n*); -s; *Geog.* Qatar

Katarakt¹ *m*; -(e)s, -e (*Wasserfall*) cataract; (*Stromschnelle*) rapids *Pl.*

Katarakt² *f*; -, -e; *Med.* cataract

Katarr *m*, **Katarrh** *m*; -s, -e; *Med.* catarrh

Kataster *m, n*; -s, - land register, cadastre; **~amt** *n* land registry; **~auszug** *m* land register entry; **~karte** *f* land register map, cadastral map

katastrieren *v/t.* enter in the land register

katastrophal I. *Adj. auch fig.* disastrous; *stärker:* catastrophic; *Zustände:* appalling; **II.** *Adv.* disastrously; *stärker:* catastrophically; ~ *enden* end in disaster; *sich* ~ *auswirken* have a disastrous effect (*od.* disastrous consequences); ~ *aussehen* look appalling

Katastrophe *f*; -, -n disaster (*auch fig.*); *stärker:* catastrophe

Katastrophen|alarm *m* red alert; **~dienst** *m* (disaster) relief organization; **~fall** *m* disaster situation, emergency; *im* ~ in the event of a disaster; **~gebiet** *n* disaster area; **~medizin** *f* medical care for disaster victims; **~schutz** *m* disaster control; **~stimmung** *f* doomsday mood; **~theorie** *f*; *nur Sg. Geol.* catastrophism

Katauto *n Mot. umg.* cat car

Kate *f*; -, -n small cottage; *aus Holz:* shack

Katechese *f*; -, -n; *kirchl.* catechesis; **Katechet** *m*; -en, -en, **Katechetin** *f*; -, -nen catechist; **Katechismus** *m*; -, *Katechismen* catechism

Katechumene *m*; -n, -n; *kirchl.* catechumen

kategorial *Adj.* categorical; **Kategorie** *f*; -, -n category; *diese* ~ *Mensch / von Menschen* this sort (*od.* type) of person/people; **kategorisch** *Adj.* categorical; → *Imperativ*; **kategorisieren** *v/t.* categorize; **Kategorisierung** *f* categorization

Katen|brot *n Gastr.* coarse dark bread; **~wurst** *f* coarse smoked salami-type sausage

Kater¹ *m*; -s, -; *Zool.* tom(cat); *der Gestiefelte* ~ Puss-in-Boots

Kater² *m*; -s, -; *umg.* hangover; *fig. auch* the morning after; **~frühstück** *n umg.* breakfast usually including pickled herrings and gherkins (*Am.* pickles) as a hangover cure; **~stimmung** *umg. f* morning-after feeling

Katharsis *f*; -, *kein Pl.; Lit., Psych.* catharsis

Katheder *n, m*; -s, - *Univ.* lectern; *Schule:* teacher's desk; **~weisheit** *f* academic (*od.* bookish) knowledge

Kathedrale *f*; -, -n cathedral

Kathete *f*; -, -n; *Math.* cathetus, *short side of a right-angled triangle*

Katheter *m*; -s, -; *Med.* catheter

Kathode *f*; -, -n; *Etech.* cathode; **Kathodenstrahlen** *Pl.* cathode rays

Kathole *m*; -n, -n; *umg.* papist

Katholik *m*; -en, -en (*Roman*) Catholic; **Katholikentag** *m* (*Regional*) Catholic Assembly; **Katholikin** *f*; -, -nen (*Ro-*

man) Catholic; **katholisch** *Adj.* (Roman) Catholic; **Katholizismus** *m*; -, *kein Pl.* Catholicism

Kation ['katio:n] *n*; -s, en; *Phys.* cation

Kattun *m*; -s, -e calico; *weitS.* (*Baumwolle*) cotton; *grob*: dungaree, denim

Katz *f fig.*: **~ und Maus spielen mit** play cat and mouse with; **für die ~ sein** be wasted, be for nothing; (*alles*) **für die ~!** a complete waste of time!, I don't know why I bothered!

katzbalgen *v/refl.* (*untr., hat -ge-*) *umg.* **1.** (*raufen*) scrap, tussle; **2.** (*streiten*) squabble; **Katzbalgerei** *f*; -, -en scrapping; (*Streiterei*) squabbling

Katz|buckelei *f*; -, *kein Pl.* bowing and scraping; **katzbuckeln** *v/i.* (*untr., hat -ge-*) bow and scrape (**vor** + *Dat.* before)

Kätzchen *n* kitten; *Bot.* catkin

Katze *f*; -, -n **1.** *Zool.* cat; **die ~ aus dem Sack lassen** *umg.* blow the gaff; *allg.* disclose *a secret or plan*; **die ~ im Sack kaufen** buy a pig in a poke; **die ~ lässt das Mausen nicht** a leopard can't change its spots; **wenn die ~ aus dem Haus ist, tanzen die Mäuse** (**auf dem Tisch**) when the cat's away the mice will play; **bei Nacht sind alle ~n grau** everything looks the same in the dark; → *Katz*; **2.** *Jägerspr.* female

katzenartig I. *Adj.* catlike, feline; **II.** *sich bewegen etc.*: like a cat

Katzen|auge *n* **1.** cat's eye (*auch Min.*); **sie hat ~n** *fig.* she has eyes like a cat; **2.** (*Rückstrahler*) reflector; **~buckel** *m*: **e-n ~ machen** arch one's back; **~dreck** *m* cat's droppings *Pl.*; **ein ~** *umg. fig.* (*Kleinigkeit*) a mere nothing; (*Geld*) chickenfeed; **~fell** *n* cat skin

Katzenfreund *m*, **~in** *f* cat-lover

Katzen|futter *n* catfood; **~gold** *n Min.* yellow mica; *Pyrit*: iron pyrites, fool's gold

katzenhaft I. *Adj.* catlike, feline; **II.** *Adv.* like a cat

Katzen|hai *m Zool.* dogfish; **~jammer** *m* (*Kater*) hangover (*auch fig.*); (*depressive Stimmung*) black mood; **~klo** *n umg.* litter tray (*Am.* box) (for a cat *od.* for cats); **~kopfpflaster** *n* cobbles *Pl.*; **~musik** *f* caterwauling; **~mutter** *f* mother cat; **~nahrung** *f* catfood; **~pfötchen** *n* cat's paw; *Bot.* cat's foot; **~sprung** *m fig.*: **nur ein ~** only a stone's throw, no distance; **~streu** *f* cat litter; **~tisch** *m umg.*: **am ~ essen müssen** have to eat at the side table; **~toilette** *f* **1.** → *Katzenklo*,; **2.** → *Katzenwäsche*; **~wäsche** *f umg.* a lick and a promise; **~ machen** give o.s. a lick and a promise, (just) splash o.s.; **~zunge** *f Süßigkeit*: langue de chat

Kätzin *f*; -, -nen female cat

Katz-und-Maus-Spiel *n* cat-and-mouse game

Kaubewegung *f* chewing movement

Kauderwelsch *n*; -(e)s, *kein Pl.* gibberish, jabberwocky; (*unverständliche Fachsprache*) incomprehensible jargon; **kauderwelschen** *v/i.* talk gibberish

kauen *vt/i.* chew; **an den Nägeln ~** bite one's nails; **an e-m Problem ~** *fig.* chew over a problem; → *Backe* 1

kauern *vi./refl.*: (*sich*) **~** crouch (*od.* squat) (down)

Kauf *m*; -(e)s, *Käufe* purchase; (*das Kaufen*) purchasing, buying; **günstiger ~** bargain, good buy; **zum ~ anbieten** offer for sale; **zum ~ stehen** be for sale; (*mit*) **in ~ nehmen** *fig.* accept;

(*Unannehmlichkeiten, Nachteile*) *auch* put up with; **~anreiz** *m* incentive to buy; **~brief** *m* bill of sale; **~auftrag** *m Wirts.* buying order

kaufen I. *v/t.* **1.** buy; **j-m etw. ~** buy s.th. for s.o.; **es wird gern gekauft** it's a popular item, it sells well; **dafür kann ich mir nichts ~** *umg. fig.* that's no use to me; *stärker*: that's a fat lot of use (to me); → *teuer* I 1; **2.** (*bestechen*) bribe, buy; **3. den werde ich mir ~** *umg.* I'll tell him what's what; **II.** *v/i.* (*einkaufen*) shop; **~ bei gewohnheitsmäßig**: shop at, go to

Kaufentscheidung *f* decision to buy

Käufer *m*; -s, - buyer; (*Kunde*) customer

Käuferkreis *m* group of customers *od.* buyers

Käuferin *f*; -, -nen → *Käufer*

Käuferschicht *f* class of customer, spending group

Kauffahrer *m hist. Naut.* merchant ship, merchantman

Kauf|frau *f Wirts.* businesswoman; (*Händlerin*) trader, *Am.* dealer; (*Einzelhändlerin*) retailer; **~gewohnheiten** *Pl.* buying habits

Kaufhaus *n* department store; **~detektiv** *m*, **~detektivin** *f* store detective; **~kette** *f* chain of (department) stores; **~konzern** *m* (department) stores group

Kauf|interesse *n* (buyer) demand; **~interessent** *m*, **~interessentin** *f* prospective purchaser (*od.* buyer)

Kaufkraft *f Wirts.* purchasing power; *des Käufers*: *auch* spending power; **kaufkräftig** *Adj.* *Kunden etc.*: affluent, … with money to spend; *Währung*: strong; **Kaufkraftschwund** *m* dwindling purchasing power

Kaufläche *f Zahnmedizin*: biting surface

Kauf|laden *m* **1.** *altm.* shop, *bes. Am.* store; **2.** *für Kinder*: toy (grocer's) shop (*Am.* store); **~leute** *Pl.* → *Kaufmann*

käuflich I. *Adj.* präd. for sale; (*bestechlich*) open to bribery; **~e Liebe** venal love; **~es Mädchen** prostitute, working girl; **II.** *Adv.*: **~ erwerben** purchase; **Käuflichkeit** *f* (*Bestechlichkeit*) corruptibility, venality *förm.*

Kauflust *f* urge to spend; *Wirts.* demand for consumer goods; **kauflustig** *Adj.* eager to buy; **~ sein** be in a buying mood

Kaufmann *m*; *Pl. Kaufleute* **1.** *Wirts.* businessman; (*Händler*) trader, *Am.* dealer; (*Einzelhändler*) retailer; **2.** *altm., Dial.* (*Ladenbesitzer*) shopkeeper, *Am.* storekeeper; **kaufmännisch I.** *Adj.* commercial; *Geschick, Erfahrung, Ausbildung etc.*: business …; **~er Angestellter** business employee; **~es Personal** sales and marketing staff; **e-n ~en Beruf ergreifen** go into business; **II.** *Adv.*: **~ ausgebildet sein** have business training; **~ denken** think in business terms

Kaufmannssprache *f Ling.* commercial language, *Am. pej.* commercialese

Kauf|objekt *n* article (*od.* item) for sale; *Gebäude*: property (for sale); **~preis** *m* purchase price; **~rausch** *m* oft hum. spending spree

Kaufunlust *f* disinclination to buy; *Wirts.* lack of demand (for consumer goods); **kaufunlustig** *Adj.*: **~ sein** have no desire to buy

Kauf|verhalten *n Wirts.* buying patterns *Pl.*; **~vertrag** *m* bill of sale;

~wert *m* purchase value; **~zwang** *m*: **kein ~** no obligation (to purchase)

Kaugummi *m, n*; -s, -s chewing gum

Kaukasier *m*; s, , **~in** *f*; , nen Caucasian, *weiblich auch*: Caucasian woman (*od.* girl *etc.*); **kaukasisch** *Adj.* Caucasian; **Kaukasus** *m*; -; *Geog.* Caucasus

Kaul|barsch *m Zool.* ruff(e); **~quappe** *f* tadpole

kaum *Adv.* **1.** hardly; (*nur gerade*) scarcely, barely, *Brit. auch* only just; **~ hatte er angefangen, als** *od.* **da …** he had hardly (*od.* only just, *Am.* barely) started when …, no sooner had he started than …; **es ist ~ zu sehen** it is scarcely (*od.* barely) visible, you can hardly see it; **wir haben ~ noch Milch** we've hardly (*Am.* we hardly have) any milk left; **2.** *unwahrscheinlich*: (**wohl**) **~!** hardly, I doubt it very much; **ich glaube ~** I hardly think so; **er wird es wohl ~ überleben** he is unlikely to survive; **jetzt wird sie ~ noch kommen** she's hardly (*od.* she's not) likely to come now; **3.** (*selten*) **er ist ~ zu Hause** he is hardly ever at home; **4.** *mit Zahlen*: barely, just under; **ich bekomme ~ 2000 Euro** *auch* I'm lucky if I get 2,000 euros

Kaumuskel *m Anat.* masticatory muscle

Kaurischnecke *f Zool.* cowrie

kausal *Adj.* causal

Kausal|adverb *n Ling.* causal adverb; **~beziehung** *f Philos.* causal connection; **~gesetz** *n*; *nur Sg.*; *Philos.* law of causality, law of cause and effect

Kausalität *f*; -, -en causality

Kausal|kette *f Philos.* causal chain, chain of cause and effect; **~prinzip** *n Philos.* principle of causality; **~satz** *m Ling.* causal clause; **~zusammenhang** *m* causal connection

Kausativ *n*; -s, -e, **~bildung** *f Ling.* causative (verb)

Kaustik *f*; -, *kein Pl.*; *Opt.* caustic; **kaustisch** *Chem. und fig.* **I.** *Adj.* caustic; **II.** *Adv.* caustically

Kautabak *m* chewing tobacco

Kauterisation *f*; -, -en; *Med.* cauterization

Kaution *f*; -, -en **1.** *Wirts.* security; *Jur.*, *für Freilassung*: bail; **~ für j-n stellen** stand security (*Jur.* bail) for s.o.; **gegen ~ freilassen** release on bail; **gegen ~ freigelassen werden** be granted bail; **j-n gegen ~ freibekommen** bail s.o. out; **2.** *für Wohnung etc.*: deposit

Kautionssumme *f* (amount of) security (*Jur.* bail)

Kautschuk *m*; -s, -e (india) rubber; **~baum** *m* rubber tree; **~milch** *f* latex; **~plantage** *f* rubber plantation

Kauwerkzeuge *Pl.* masticatory organs

Kauz *m*; -es, *Käuze* **1.** *Zool.* small owl; (*Waldkauz*) tawny owl; (*Steinkauz*) little owl; **2.** *umg. fig.*: **komischer ~** odd customer, oddball; *stärker*: weirdo; **Käuzchen** *n* → *Kauz* 1; **kauzig** *Adj.* strange, odd

Kavalier *m*; -s, -e **1.** gentleman; **ein ~ der alten Schule** a (*od.* the) perfect gentleman, a gentleman of the old school; **der ~ genießt und schweigt** a gentleman never boasts about his conquests; **2.** *altm., hum.* (*Begleiter, Freund*) cavalier, beau; **3.** *hist.* (*Edelmann*) nobleman; **kavaliermäßig** *Adj.* gentlemanly; (*ritterlich*) chivalrous

Kavaliersdelikt *n umg.* peccadillo, trivial offen|ce (*Am.* -se); **es gilt als ~** *auch* it's considered a harmless sport;

kavaliersmäßig *Adj.* → *kavaliermäßig*

Kavalier(s)start *m Mot.* racing start

Kavallerie *f*; -, -*n*; *Mil.*, *hist.* cavalry; **~regiment** *n* cavalry regiment; **Kavallerist** *m*; -*en*, -*en*; *Mil.*, *hist.* cavalryman

Kaventsmann *m Dial.* (*Mann*) great hulk; (*Fisch etc.*) whopper

Kaverne *f*; -, -*n* **1.** (*artificial*) underground storage cave; **2.** *Med.* cavern; **kavernös** *Adj. Geol.*, *Med.* cavernous

Kaviar *m*; -*s*, *Sorten*: -*e* caviar(e); **~brötchen** *n* caviar(e) (half-)roll; *auf Weißbrotscheibe*: caviar(e) open sandwich; *kleiner*: caviar(e) canapé

Kavität *f*; -, -*en*; *Med.* cavity

Kebab *m*; -(*s*), -*s*; *Gastr.* kebab

keck I. *Adj.* **1.** (*frech*) cheeky, saucy, *Am. auch* fresh; (*forsch*) pert, cocky *umg.*; **2.** (*auffällig*, *flott*) *Hut*, *Bart*: jaunty, saucy; **II.** *Adv.*: **~** **antworten** give a pert (*frech*: cheeky, saucy) reply; *sich ~ über etw. hinwegsetzen* airily disregard s.th.; *ein ~ aufgesetzter Hut* a hat worn at a jaunty (*od.* rakish) angle

Keckheit *f* **1.** cheekiness, sauciness; (*Forschheit*) pertness, cockiness *umg.*; **2.** (*Auffälligkeit*, *Flottsein*) jauntiness, sauciness

Keeper [ˈkiːpɐ] *m*; -*s*, -; *bes. österr.*, *schw. Fußball*: keeper, goalie

Kefir *m*; -*s*, -; *Gastr.* kefir

Kegel *m*; -*s*, - **1.** *zum Spiel*: skittle; *auch Bowling*: pin; *~ schieben Dial.* play skittles (*od.* ninepins) *allg.*; **2.** *bes. Math. und Tech.* cone; (*sich verjüngendes Teil*) taper; **3.** (*Lichtkegel*) light cone; *von Scheinwerfer*: beam; **4.** (*Bergkegel*) (conical) peak; **5.** *Druck.* body (size); → *Kind* 1; **~abend** *m* skittles evening; *Bowling*: bowling evening; **~bahn** *f* skittle alley; *Bowling*: bowling alley; **~bruder** *m umg.* **1.** *Kamerad*: skittles club (*Bowling*: bowling club) mate (*Am.* buddy, partner); **2.** (*begeisterter Kegler*) skittles/bowling freak

kegelförmig *Adj.* conical

Kegel|klub *m* skittles club; *Bowling*: bowling club; **~kugel** *f* skittles ball; *Bowling*: bowling ball; **~mantel** *m Math.* (lateral) surface of a cone

kegeln I. *v/i.* play skittles; *Bowling*: bowl; (*~ gehen*) go bowling; **II. Kegeln** *n*; -*s*; *kein Pl.* (playing) skittles; (*Bowling*) bowling

Kegel|projektion *f* conic projection; **~rad** *n* bevel gear; **~schnitt** *m Math.* conic section; **~sport** *m* skittles (*V. im Sg*); (*Bowling*) bowling; **~stumpf** *m Math.* truncated cone

Kegler *m*; -*s*, -, **~in** *f*; -, -*nen* skittles player; *Bowling*: bowler

Kehldeckel *m Anat.* epiglottis

Kehle *f*; -, -*n* **1.** *Anat.* throat; (*Luftröhre*) windpipe; *aus voller ~* at the top of one's voice; *sich* (*Dat.*) *die ~ aus dem Hals schreien* shout one's head off; *j-m das Messer an die ~ setzen* put a knife to s.o.'s throat; *fig.* point a gun at s.o.'s head; *j-m die ~ durchschneiden* cut s.o.'s throat; *er hat es in die falsche ~ bekommen* it went down the wrong way; *umg. fig.* he got the wrong end of the stick; *j-m in der ~ stecken bleiben* get stuck in s.o.'s throat; *ihm gehts an die ~* his number's up now; (*immer*) *e-e trockene ~ haben umg.* have an unquenchable thirst, be a serious drinker; *sich* (*Dat.*) *die ~ anfeuchten umg.* have a little

drink, wet one's whistle *altm.*; → *zuschnüren* 2; → *auch Hals*; **2.** *Archit.* groove, channel, *als Dekoration*: flute; (*Dachkehle*) valley

kehlig I. *Adj.* throaty; *Laute etc.*: guttural; *ein ~er Alt* a full-throated contralto; **II.** *Adv.* in a throaty voice

Kehlkopf *m Anat.* larynx (*Pl.* larynges); **~entzündung** *f Med.* laryngitis; **~krebs** *m Med.* cancer of the larynx; **~mikrofon** *n* throat microphone; **~schnitt** *m Med.* laryngotomy; **~spiegel** *m Med.* laryngoscope; **~spiegelung** *f Med.* laryngoscopy

Kehl|laut *m Ling.* guttural (sound); **~sack** *m Zool.* laryngeal air sac; *Orn.* throat pouch

Kehlung *f Archit.* mo(u)lding

Kehraus *m*; -, *kein Pl.* last dance; *fig.* (grand) finale; *den ~ machen* bring down the curtain, call it a day; (*aufräumen*) clear up

Kehr|besen *m südd.* broom; **~blech** *n südd.* dustpan

Kehre *f*; -, -*n* **1.** (*Kurve*) (sharp) bend; (*Haarnadelkurve*) hairpin (bend *od.* turn); **2.** (*Wendeplatz*) turning space; loop (*auch Eisenb.*); **3.** *Turnen*: rear vault; (*beim Abgang*) back dismount; **4.** *Flug.*, *Skisport*: turn

kehren[1] *v/i. bes. südd.* sweep

kehren[2] **I.** *v/t.* (*hat gekehrt*) turn; *j-m den Rücken ~ auch fig.* turn one's back on s.o.; *in sich gekehrt fig.* withdrawn, introspective; (*gedankenverloren*) lost (*od.* wrapped) in thought; **II.** *v/refl.* (*hat*) *sich ~ gegen* turn against; *sich nicht ~ an* (+ *Akk.*) pay no attention to; (*sich nicht kümmern um*) not care about; **III.** *v/i.* **1.** (*hat*) (*umdrehen*) turn (a)round; *kehrt! Mil.* about turn!, *Am.* about face!; **2.** (*hat/ist*) *Turnen*: perform a back vault

Kehricht *m*, *n*; -*s*, *kein Pl.* **1.** dirt; *das geht dich e-n feuchten ~ an umg.* that's none of your damned business; **2.** *schw.* (*Müll*) refuse, *Am.* garbage, trash; **~deponie** *f schw.* → *Mülldeponie*; **~eimer** *m schw.* rubbish bin, *Am.* trashcan; **~schaufel** *f südd.* dustpan

Kehr|maschine *f* **1.** road sweeper; **2.** (*für Teppiche*) carpet sweeper; **~ordnung** *f schw.* rota (*Am.* roster) for the use of communal facilities; **~reim** *m* refrain; **~seite** *f* **1.** other side, back; *von Münze*: reverse; *die ~ der Medaille fig.* the other side of the coin; **2.** *umg.* (*Hintern*) backside; (*Rücken*) back; *j-m s-e ~ zuwenden* turn one's back on s.o.

kehrtmachen *v/i.* (*trennb.*, *hat* -*ge*-) turn (a)round (*and go back*), turn back; *plötzlich*, *zu Fuß*: turn on one's heels; *auch Mot.* turn in one's tracks, do an about-turn (*fig. auch* about-face)

Kehrtwendung *f*: *e-e ~ machen* do an about-turn (*od.* a U-turn, *fig. auch* an about-face)

Kehrwert *m Math.* reciprocal

Kehrwoche *f südd.* week when the tenant of an apartment building is responsible for cleaning the stairs and (*in winter*) clearing the pavement outside

keifen *v/i.* nag, scold; *Paar*: bicker; **Keiferei** *f*; -, -*en* nagging, scolding; *Paar*: bickering

Keil *m*; -(*e*)*s*, -*e* **1.** wedge (*auch Met.*); (*Bremskeil*) chock; *e-n ~ treiben zwischen* (+ *Akk.*) *fig.* drive a wedge between; **2.** (*Zwickel*) gusset; **3.** *Mil.* V-formation; *e-s Vormarsches*: spearhead; **~absatz** *m* wedge heel; **~bein** *n*

Anat. sphenoid bone

Keile *f*; -, *kein Pl.*; *umg.*: *~ kriegen* get a hiding

keilen I. *v/t.* **1.** (*spalten*) split (with a wedge); (*hineintreiben*) drive (*in* + *Akk.* into); (*festkeilen*) wedge; **2.** *umg.* (*gewinnen*) rope in (*für* for); **II.** *v/refl. umg.* fight, tussle, scrap (*um* over)

Keiler *m*; -*s*,-; *Zool.* wild boar

Keilerei *f*; -, -*en*; *umg.* fight, brawl, tussle, scrap

keilförmig *Adj.* wedge-shaped; *Buchstabe*, *Schrift*: cuneiform

Keil|hose *f*: (*e-e*) (*a pair of*) stretch trousers *Pl.* (*Am.* pants *Pl.*); (*Skihose*) ski pants *Pl.*; **~kissen** *n* (wedge-shaped) bolster; **~riemen** *m Tech.* V-belt; **~schrift** *f* cuneiform (script)

Keim *m*; -(*e*)*s*, -*e* **1.** *Med.* germ; **2.** *Bot.* (*Schössling*) shoot; (*Trieb*) sprout; **~e treiben** germinate; **3.** *Bio.* (*befruchtete Eizelle*) embryo; **4.** *fig.* seed(*s Pl.*); *etw. im ~ ersticken* nip s.th. in the bud; (*Gerücht*) scotch; *den ~ zu etw. legen* sow the seeds of s.th.; **~blatt** *n* **1.** *Bot.* cotyledon; **2.** *Bio.* germ layer

Keim|drüse *f Anat.* gonad; **~drüsenhormon** *n Physiol.* sex hormone

keimen *v/i.* **1.** germinate; (*treiben*) sprout; (*knospen*) bud; **2.** *fig. Gedanke etc.*: (*begin to*) form; *Gefühle*, *Hoffnung*: stir; **~de Liebe** awakening love

keimfähig *Adj.* capable of germinating, viable

keimfrei I. *Adj.* sterile; *~ machen* sterilize; **~e Milch** sterilized milk; **II.** *Adv.*: *~ verpackt* in sterile packaging; **Keimfreiheit** *f*; *nur Sg.* sterility

Keimling *m*; -*s*, -*e* **1.** seedling; **2.** *Bio.*, *Med.* (*befruchtete Eizelle*) embryo

Keimöl *n* germ oil, seed oil

keimtötend *Adj. Bio.*, *Med.* germicidal, antiseptic

Keimträger *m Med.* (germ) carrier

Keimung *f* germination

Keimzelle *f Bio.* germ cell, gamete; *fig.* embryo, nucleus

kein *unbest. Pron.* **1.** *adj.*: *~(e*) no; *Sg. auch* not a; *abstrakt od. Pl. auch* not any; *er hat ~ Auto* he hasn't got a car, he doesn't have a car, he has no car; *sie hat ~e Freunde* she hasn't got any friends, she doesn't have any friends, she has no friends; *ich habe jetzt ~e Zeit* I have no (*od.* I don't have any) time at the moment; *ich kann ~ Russisch* I don't know any Russian; *~ anderer als* none other than; *~ anderer als er kann es gewesen sein* it can't (*od.* couldn't) have been anybody other than him (*od.* anybody else); *~ Einziger ist gekommen* not a single person came; *ich bin ~ großer Schwimmer* (*ich schwimme schlecht*) I'm not the best of swimmers, I'm not a great swimmer; **2.** *umg. mit Zahlen*, *Mengen*: less than; *es ist ~e fünf Minuten her* it was less than five minutes ago; *es kostet ~e 20 Euro* it's not even as much as (*Am.* it doesn't even cost) 20 euros; **3.** *substantivisch*: *~er*, *~e*, *~(e)s von Sachen*: none, not any; *von Personen*: no one, nobody; *hast du welche gesehen? - nein, ~e* did you see any? - no, I didn't (see any); *ich habe ~en gefunden, der es wusste* I didn't find anybody (*od.* anyone) who knew; *~er* (*~e*, *~s*) *von beiden* neither (of them); *~er von uns* none of us; *betont*: not one of us; *~er von uns beiden* neither of us; **4.** *nachgestellt*: *Geld hab ich ~s* (*mehr*) *umg.* I haven't got any money (left); *Lust habe ich ~e umg.* I'm not keen, *Am.* I'm not that hot

keinerlei *Adj.* no … at all; **~ Schmerzen** *etc. auch* no pain *etc.* whatsoever; **auf ~ Weise** in no way

keines|falls *Adv.* under no circumstances, on no account; *(auf keine Weise)* in no way; *als Antwort*: certainly not, *umg.* no way; **~wegs** *Adv.* not at all; *(alles andere als)* anything but

keinmal *Adv.* not once, never; → *einmal* 1

Keks *m, n*; *-(es), - und -e* biscuit, *Am.* cookie; *j-m auf den ~ gehen umg.* get in s.o.'s hair, *Brit. auch* get on s.o.'s wick; *e-n weichen ~ haben umg.* be a bit soft in the head; **~riegel** *m* chocolate biscuit bar

Kelch *m*; *-(e)s, -e* **1.** goblet; *kirchl.* chalice, communion cup; *der ~ ist noch einmal an uns vorübergegangen* we've been spared, that was close *umg.*; **2.** *Bot.* calyx (*Pl.* calyces *od.* calyxes); **~blatt** *n Bot.* sepal

kelchförmig *Adj.* cup-shaped; *Bot.* calyciform; **Kelchglas** *n* (crystal *od.* glass) goblet

Kelle *f*; *-, -n* **1.** *(Schöpflöffel)* ladle; *(des Maurers)* trowel; **2.** *(Signalkelle)* signalling disc, *Am.* signal disk; **3.** *umg.* *(Tennisschläger)* tennis racket

Keller *m*; *-s, -* cellar; *bewohnt*: basement; *in den ~ fallen fig.* hit rock bottom; *Kurs: auch* go through the floor; *im ~ sein umg.* have reached rock bottom; *Kurs: auch* have gone through the floor; *Sport* be bottom of the league; **~abfüllung** *f*, **~abzug** *m* bottling at source; *Aufschrift auf Etikett*: bottled at source; **~assel** *f Zool.* woodlouse; **~bar** *f* cellar bar

Kellerei *f*; *-, -en* winery; *Räume*: wine cellars *Pl.*

Keller|fenster *n* cellar window; *e-s Kellergeschosses*: basement window; **~geschoss** *n* basement; **~gewölbe** *n* (underground) vault, cellar; **~kind** *n* **1.** deprived child; **2.** **~er** *Pl. Sport* bottom-of-the-table team(s), *Am.* cellar dweller(s *Pl.*); **~loch** *n* dark, musty little basement; **~meister** *m*, **~meisterin** *f* cellarer; **~raum** *m* basement room; *unbewohnt*: cellar room; **~temperatur** *f* cellar temperature; **~treppe** *f* cellar steps (*aus Holz*: stairs) *Pl.*; **~tür** *f* cellar door; **~wohnung** *f* basement apartment (*Brit. auch* flat)

Kellner *m*; *-s, -* waiter; **Kellnerin** *f* waitress; **kellnern** *v/i. umg.* work (*od.* job around) as a waiter (*od.* waitress)

Kelte *m*; *-n, -n* Celt

Kelter *f*; *-, -n* wine press; *andere Obstarten*: fruit press; **Kelterei** *f*; *-, -en* press house; **keltern** *v/t.* press

Keltin *f*; *-, -nen* Celt; **keltisch I.** *Adj.* Celtic; **II. Keltisch** *n*; *-(s)*; *Ling.* Celtic; *das Keltische* Celtic

Kelvin *n*; *-s, -*; *Phys.* kelvin

Kemenate *f*; *-, -n* **1.** *hist.* ladies' apartment; **2.** *umg. (kleiner Raum)* den

Kendo *n*; *-(s), kein Pl.* kendo

Kenia (*n*); *-s; Geog.* Kenya; **Kenianer** *m*; *-s, -*, **Kenianerin** *f*; *-, -nen* Kenyan, *weiblich auch*: Kenyan woman (*od.* girl *etc.*); **kenianisch** *Adj.* Kenyan

Kenn|buchstabe *m* identification (*od.* code) letter; *Mot., Flug.* registration letter

kennen *v/t.*; *kennt, kannte, hat gekannt* **1.** know; *(erkennen)* recognize (*an + Dat.* by); *das ~ wir!* we know all about that!; *wir ~ uns schon* we 've met; *wir ~ uns schon seit zehn Jahren* we have known one another for ten years;

du kennst mich schlecht you don't know me (at all) yet; *so kenne ich dich gar nicht* I've never known (*od.* seen) you like this; *kennst du mich noch?* remember me?; *er kannte sich nicht mehr vor Wut* he was beside himself with anger; *kennst du den (Witz) vom …* do you know the one about …?; *die ~ keine Rücksicht* they're absolutely ruthless; *da kenne ich nichts* nothing's going to stop me; **2.** **~ lernen** get to know; *(begegnen)* meet; *als ich ihn ~ lernte* when I first met him; *j-n/etw. näher ~ lernen* get to know s.o./s.th. better; *der soll mich noch ~ lernen!* *umg.* he hasn't seen anything yet; *j-n von einer ganz anderen Seite ~ lernen* see quite a different side of s.o.; **3.** *(haben)* know; *keine Angst ~* know no fear; *hier kennt man keinen Winter* they don't have any real winter here

Kenner *m*; *-s, -* bes. *Wein, Speisen, Antiquitäten*: connoisseur; *(Fachmann)* expert (*+ Gen.* on), authority (on)

Kennerblick *m*: *mit ~* with an expert eye (*od.* the eye of an expert)

kennerhaft I. *Adj.* discerning; *Blick: auch* expert, of an expert; **II.** *Adv.* *lächeln, nicken*: with the air of an expert (*od.* a connoisseur)

Kennerin *f*; *-, -nen* → *Kenner*; **kennerisch** *Adj.* → *kennerhaft*

Kennermiene *f*: *mit ~* with the air of an expert (*od.* a connoisseur)

Kennerschaft *f* expertise

Kennlinie *f Math., Phys.* characteristic curve

kenntlich *Adj.* recognizable (*an + Dat.* by); *(unterscheidbar)* distinguishable (by); *(wahrnehmbar)* discernible (from); *(bezeichnet)* marked; *weithin ~ sein* be visible from a long way off; *~ machen* mark, *(etikettieren)* label

Kenntnis *f*; *-, -se* **1.** *nur Sg.* knowledge (*+ Gen. od. von* of); *~ haben von* know (about), be aware of; *j-n von etw. in ~ setzen* inform s.o. of s.th., bring s.th. to s.o.'s attention; *~ nehmen von* take note of; *das entzieht sich m-r ~* I have no knowledge of it; **2.** **~se** *Pl.* *(Wissen)* knowledge (*+ Gen. od. in + Dat.* of); *(Erfahrung)* experience (*in*); *(Verständnis)* understanding (of); *gute ~se haben in (+ Dat.)* have a good knowledge of, be well grounded in; **Kenntnisnahme** *f*; *-, kein Pl.*; *Amtsspr.*: *zu Ihrer ~* for your information (*od.* attention); *mit der Bitte um ~* please take note; *nach ~ der Akten* after perusing the files; **kenntnisreich** *Adj.* knowledg(e)able, well-informed; **Kenntnisstand** *m* state of knowledge (*od.* information)

Kennung *f* identification (signal *od.* code); *Funk. auch* call sign; *Naut., Flug.* route marking

Kenn|wort *n* password, *auch Wirts. etc.* code word; *Inserat*: reference; *Zuschriften unter dem ~ X* mark your letters (*od.* envelopes) X; **~zahl** *f* **1.** *Telef.* (area) code; **2.** → *Kennziffer*

Kennzeichen *n* **1.** *(distinguishing)* feature, characteristic; *besondere ~ Pass*: distinguishing marks; *ein sicheres ~, dass …* a sure sign that …; **2.** *(Abzeichen)* badge, emblem; *(Eigentumszeichen)* brand; *Flug.* aircraft marking; *(polizeiliches)* ~ *Mot.* registration (*Am.* license) number; *ein Auto mit Münchner ~* a car with a Munich registration (*Am.* with Munich plates); **kennzeichnen I.** *v/t.* **1.** mark, identify;

(etikettieren) label; *(Weg)* signpost; *(Tiere, Vögel)* tag; *mit Brandzeichen*: *(Vieh)* brand; **2.** *(charakteristisch sein für)* be typical of, typify; *j-n als ~* show s.o. to be, mark s.o. out as; **3.** *(charakterisieren)* characterize; *(darstellen)* describe, *(j-n) auch* portray; **II.** *v/refl.* be characterized *(durch* by); **kennzeichnend I.** *Part. Präs.* → *kennzeichnen*; **II.** *Adj.* characteristic, typical *(für* of); *(unterscheidend)* distinguishing

Kennzeichnung *f* **1.** marking; *mit Etiketten*: label(l)ing; *von Wegen*: signposting; *von Tieren, Vögeln*: tagging; *von Vieh*: branding; **2.** *(Charakterisierung)* characterization; *(Darstellung)* description: *e-r Person: auch* portrayal; **3.** *(charakteristisches Merkmal)* characteristic; **Kennzeichnungspflicht** *f* obligation to label goods (*Am.* products) precisely; **kennzeichnungspflichtig** *Adj.* subject to the requirement to label goods (*Am.* products) precisely

Kennziffer *f* **1.** code number, reference number; *Statistik*: index (number); *Inserat*: box number; **2.** *Math.* characteristic, index (of a logarithm)

kentern *v/i.* capsize

Keramik *f*; *-, -en* **1.** *nur Sg.* *(Ware, Handwerk)* ceramics *Pl.*, pottery; **2.** *(Stück)* piece of pottery; **Keramiker** *m*; *-s, -*, **Keramikerin** *f*; *-, -nen* potter; **keramisch** *Adj.* ceramic

Kerbe *f*; *-, -n* notch; *(Nut)* groove; *in dieselbe ~ hauen fig.* do (*sagen*: say) exactly the same thing

Kerbel *m*; *-s, kein Pl.*; *Bot.* chervil

kerben *v/t.* notch; *(Muster etc.)* carve

Kerb|holz *n*: *etwas auf dem ~ haben fig.* have blotted one's copybook, *Am.* spoil one's record, shoot o.s. in the foot *umg.*; *einiges auf dem ~ haben* have quite a record; **~tier** *n* insect

Kerbung *f* **1.** *nur Sg.* notching; **2.** *Stelle*: notch

Kerker *m*; *-s, -* **1.** *hist. (Gefängnis)* jail, *Brit. auch* gaol, prison; *(Verlies)* dungeon; **2.** *österr. Jur. hist.*, *Strafe*: imprisonment; **~meister** *m hist.* jailer, *Brit. auch* gaoler

Kerl *m*; *-s, -e*, *nordd. umg. auch*: *-s*; *umg.* guy, *Brit. auch* chap, bloke, *Am. auch* fellow, dude *Sl.*; *armer ~* poor devil; *ein ganzer ~* a real man; *ein anständiger ~* a decent sort; *sie ist ein feiner ~* she's a good sort; *blöder ~* idiot

Kern *m*; *-(e)s, -e* **1.** *von Kernobst*: pip, seed; *von Steinobst*: stone; *der Nuss*: kernel; **2.** *Tech.*, *in Gießform, Etech.*, *e-r Spule, Phys.*, *e-s Reaktors etc.*: core; *Phys., des Atoms, Bio., der Zelle*: nucleus; **3.** *fig.* core, *(das Wichtigste) auch* essence; *(Stadtkern etc.)* cent|re (*Am.* -er); heart; *der ~ des Problems* the heart (*od.* nub, crux) of the problem; *der harte ~* the hard core; *sie hat e-n guten ~* she's good at heart; *ein Tief mit ~ über der Nordsee Met.* a depression cent(e)red over the North Sea; **4.** *(eines Baumstamms)* heartwood

Kern… *im Subst. Phys.* nuclear …

Kern|beißer *m*; *-s, -*; *Orn.* hawfinch; **~bereich** *m e-r Stadt etc.*: central area; *e-s Erdbebens*: epicent|re (*Am.* -er); **~arbeitszeit** *f* core time; **~brennstoff** *m* nuclear fuel; **~energie** *f* nuclear energy

Kerner *m*; *-s, - Rebsorte, Wein*: kerner

Kern|explosion *f* nuclear explosion;

~fach *n Päd.* core subject
Kernforschung *f* nuclear research; **Kernforschungsanlage** *f* nuclear research facility
Kern|frage *f* core issue, central question; **~frucht** *f Bot.* pome; **~fusion** *f Phys.* nuclear fusion; **~gebiet** *n* central area; (*Hauptgebiet*) core area; **~gedanke** *m* central idea; **~gehäuse** *n* core; **~geschäft** *n Wirts.* core (business) activity
kerngesund *Adj.* (as) fit as a fiddle
Kernholz *n fachspr.* heartwood
kernig *Adj.* **1.** *Obst:* full of pips (*Am.* seeds); **2.** *fig.* (*markig*) pithy; (*kraftvoll*) robust, vigorous; (*derb*) earthy; **3.** *Wein:* full-bodied, robust; **4.** *Leder:* full
Kernkraft *f* nuclear power (*od.* energy); **~gegner** *m*, **~gegnerin** *f* antinuclear protester (*od.* campaigner); **~werk** *n* nuclear power plant
Kernladung *f Phys.* nuclear charge; **Kernladungszahl** *f* atomic number
kernlos *Adj. Bot.* seedless
Kern|modell *n Phys.* nuclear model; **~obst** *n* pomaceous fruit, pome(s *Pl.*)
Kernphysik *f* nuclear physics *Pl.* (*V. im Sg.*); **kernphysikalisch** *Adj.* nuclear physics ...; **Kernphysiker** *m*, **Kernphysikerin** *f* nuclear physicist
Kern|problem *n* central (*od.* core) problem; **~punkt** *m* essential (*od.* central) point; **~reaktion** *f Phys.* nuclear reaction; **~reaktor** *m* nuclear reactor; **~satz** *m* **1.** (*wichtigster Satz*) crucial (*od.* key) sentence; **2.** *Ling.* basic (form of the) sentence; **~schatten** *m* deepest shadow; *Astron.* umbra; **~schmelze** *f; nur Sg.* core meltdown; **~seife** *f* hard (*od.* washing) soap; **~spaltung** *f Phys.* nuclear fission
Kernspin|tomograph *m Med.* MRI scanner; **~tomographie** *f Med.* magnetic resonance imaging, MRI
Kern|strahlung *f* nuclear radiation; **~stück** *n* main item; *e-r Rede, Politik, Argumentation etc.:* main (*od.* central) point; *e-r Sammlung etc.:* centrepiece, *Am.* centerpiece; (*Glanzstück*) pièce de résistance
Kerntechnik *f* nuclear technology; **kerntechnisch** *Adj.* of (*od.* relating to) nuclear technology; **~e Anlage** nuclear plant
Kern|teilung *f Biol.* nuclear division; **~umwandlung** *f Phys.* nuclear transformation; *Zerfall:* nuclear disintegration; **~verschmelzung** *f Biol., Phys.* nuclear fusion
Kernwaffe *f Mil.* nuclear weapon; **kernwaffenfrei** *Adj.:* **~e Zone** nuclear-free zone
Kernwaffen|gegner *m*, **~gegnerin** *f* opponent of nuclear weapons, nuclear protester; **~versuch** *m* nuclear test; **~verzicht** *m* abandonment of nuclear weapons
Kern|zeit *f* core time; **~zone** *f* cent|re (*Am.* -er), central area
Kerosin *n; -s, kein Pl.* kerosene
Kerze *f; -, -n* **1.** candle (*auch Etech., Lampe und Messeinheit*); **2.** (*Zündkerze*) spark plug, *Brit. auch* sparking plug; **3.** *Turnen:* shoulder stand; **4.** *beim Fußball:* **e-e ~ schießen** sky the ball
Kerzen|beleuchtung *f* candlelight; **~flamme** *f* candle flame
kerzengerade *Adj. und Adv.* (as) straight as a die (*Am.* an arrow); *Person:* (as) straight as a ramrod; (*aufrecht*) bolt upright

Kerzen|halter *m am Baum:* candleholder; **~leuchter** *m* candelabrum; *für eine Kerze:* candlestick; *an der Wand:* sconce; **~licht** *n* candlelight; **bei ~** by candlelight; **Essen bei ~** *auch* a candlelight dinner; **~schein** *m* candlelight; **~schlüssel** *m Mot.* plug spanner (*Am.* ratchet *od.* wrench); **~ständer** *m → Kerzenleuchter*; **~stecker** *m Mot.* (spark)plug connector; **~stummel** *m* stump of a (*od.* the) candle, candle end
Kescher *m; -s, - für Krebse, Insekten:* net; *für Fische:* landing net
kess I. *Adj. Mädchen, Antwort:* pert; (*etwas frech*) saucy; (*flott*) *Hut:* jaunty; *Kleid:* rather daring; **II.** *Adv.:* **~ antworten** give a pert (*frech:* saucy) reply
Kessel *m; -s, -* **1.** (*Wasserkessel*) kettle; (*Topf*) pot; *großer, auf offenem Feuer:* ca(u)ldron; (*Waschkessel*) copper; *in Färberei, Brauerei etc.:* vat; **2.** (*Dampfkessel*) boiler; **3.** (*Vertiefung*) hollow; (*Talkessel*) basin-shaped valley; **4.** *Mil.* pocket, encircled area; **~fleisch** *n Dial.* boiled belly pork; **~flicker** *m altm.* tinker; **sich streiten wie die ~** *umg.* fight like cat(s) and dog(s); **~haus** *n* boiler house (*od.* room); **~mundstück** *n Mus.* cup-shaped mouthpiece; **~pauke** *f* kettledrum; **~schlacht** *f Mil.* battle of encirclement; **~stein** *m* fur, scale; **~treiben** *n Jagd:* battue; *fig. Pol.* witch-hunt (*gegen* against); **~wagen** *m Eisenb.* tank wagon (*Am.* car)
Kessheit *f* pertness; *etwas frech:* sauciness; (*Flottsein*) *von Hut:* jauntiness; *von Kleid:* rather daring style
Ketchup *m, n; -(s), -s* (tomato) ketchup, *Am. auch* catsup, *umg. auch* tomato sauce
Keton *n; -s, -e; Chem.* ketone
Kettcar® *n; -s, -s* pedal car (*with chain drive*)
Kettchen *n* fine (neck) chain; *für den Arm:* bracelet; *am Fuß:* anklet
Kette *f; -, -n* **1.** chain (*auch Chem., Wirts.*); *auch fig.* **~n** (*Fesseln*) chains, fetters; **in ~n legen** (*Gefangenen*) put in chains; **an die ~ legen** (*Hund*) put on the chain, chain up; *fig.* (*j-n*) keep on a tight rein (*od.* short leash); *Sport* (*genau decken*) mark very closely (*stärker:* out of the game); **2.** (*Halskette*) *mst* necklace, (*für den Arm*) chain, bracelet; (*am Fuß*) anklet; **3.** *e-s Kettenfahrzeugs:* track; **4.** *Weberei:* warp; **5.** *von Bergen etc.:* chain, range; *von Seen:* series, string; *von Autos:* line; *fig. von Ereignissen etc.:* chain, series, der Beweisführung, von Gedanken etc.: chain; (*Absperrung*) cordon; **e-e ~ bilden** form a cordon; *zum Weiterreichen, auch Demonstration:* form a human chain
ketteln *v/t.* loop, link
ketten *v/t.* chain (**an** + *Akk.* to) (*auch fig.*)
Ketten|antrieb *m Tech.* chain drive; **~brief** *m* chain letter; **~bruch** *m Math.* continued fraction; **~fahrzeug** *n Mot.* tracked vehicle; **~förderer** *m Tech.* chain conveyor
kettenförmig *Adj. Chem.* aliphatic
Ketten|gebirge *n Geol.* mountain range; **~gelenk** *n* chain link; *von Gleisketten:* track link; **~glied** *n* chain link; **~hemd** *n hist.* coat of chain mail; **~hund** *m* watchdog; **~karussell** *n* chairoplane; **~panzer** *m hist.* coat of chain mail; *Hemd:* coat of chain mail; **~rad** *n Tech.* sprocket (wheel)

Ketten|rauchen *n; -s, kein Pl.* chain-smoking; **~raucher** *m*, **~raucherin** *f* chain-smoker
Ketten|reaktion *f Phys. und fig.* chain reaction; **~restaurant** *n* chain restaurant; **~säge** *f* chainsaw; **~schaltung** *f am Fahrrad:* dérailleur gears *Pl.*, derailleurs *Pl.*; **~schluss** *m Philos.* chain syllogism, sorites; **~schutz** *m am Fahrrad:* chain guard; **~stich** *m* chain stitch; **~vertrag** *m* chain contract
Kett|faden *m*, **~garn** *n* warp
Ketzer *m; -s, -*, **~in** *f; -, -nen* heretic; **Ketzerei** *f; -, -en* heresy; **Ketzergericht** *n hist.* (court of) inquisition; **ketzerisch** *Adj.* heretical; **Ketzerverfolgung** *f* persecution of heretics
keuchen *v/i.* pant; *pfeifend:* wheeze; *vor Schreck, Erregung etc.:* gasp; *Dampflok etc.:* puff, chug
Keuchhusten *m Med.* whooping cough
Keule *f; -, -n* **1.** club, cudgel; *hist.* mace; *e-s Mörsers:* pestle; *Gymnastik:* (Indian) club; **2.** *Zool.* haunch; *Gastr.* leg; *Reh, Hase:* haunch; *Geflügel:* leg, drumstick; **3.** *chemische ~* Mace®
keulen *v/t. Vet.* cull
keulenförmig *Adj.* club-shaped
Keulen|gymnastik *f* club-swinging exercises *Pl.*; **~schlag** *m* cudgel blow; **es traf ihn wie ein ~** *fig.* it came as a tremendous blow to him
Keulung *f Vet.* contiguous cull
Keuper *m; -s, kein Pl.; Geol.* Keuper
keusch I. *Adj.* chaste; (*jungfräulich*) virginal; **II.** *Adv.:* **~ leben** live a chaste life; **Keuschheit** *f* chastity
Keuschheits|gelübde *n* vow of chastity; **~gürtel** *m* chastity belt
Keyboard ['kiːbɔːɐ̯t] *n; -s, -s; EDV, Mus.* keyboard
Kfz *n → Kraftfahrzeug*, **~....** *im Subst. siehe auch Kraftfahrzeug...*
Kfz|-Kennzeichen *n* car registration (*Am.* license) number; **~-Mechaniker** *m*, **~-Mechanikerin** *f*, **~-Schlosser** *m*, **~-Schlosserin** *f* (car) mechanic; **~-Steuer** *f* road (*Am.* motor vehicle) tax; **~-Werkstatt** *f* car repair shop, garage; **~-Versicherung** *f* car insurance; **~-Zulassungsstelle** *f* vehicle registration office (*Am.* center)
kg *Abk.* kg, kg.
KG *f; -, -s; Abk. → Kommanditgesellschaft*
Khaki¹ *m; -(s), kein Pl.* (*Farbe*) khaki
Khaki² *n; -(s), kein Pl.* (*Stoff*) khaki
khaki|farben, **~farbig** *Adj.* khaki
Khaki|hose *f* (*e-e*) **~** (a pair of) khaki trousers (*Am.* pants) *Pl.*; **~uniform** *f* khaki uniform
Khmer¹ *m; -s, -* Khmer; **die ~** the Khmer (people); **die Roten ~** the Khmer Rouge
Khmer² *n; -s, kein Pl.; Ling.* Khmer
kHz *Abk.* (*Kilohertz*) kHz
Kibbuz *m; -, -e und Kibbuzim* kibbutz; **Kibbuznik** *m; -s, -s* kibbutznik
Kiberei *f; -, kein Pl.; österr. umg. pej.* fuzz, cop; **Kiberer** *m; -s, -; österr. umg. pej.* flatfoot, *Brit. auch* rozzer, *Am. auch* pig
Kicher *f; -, -en* giggling
Kichererbse *f Bot.* chickpea, *Am. auch* garbanzo
kichern I. *v/i.* giggle; *spöttisch:* snigger; **dass nicht kichere!** don't make me laugh!; **II. Kichern** *n; -s, kein Pl.* giggling; *spöttisch:* sniggering, *Am.* snickering
Kick *m; -(s), -s; umg.* **1.** *beim Fußball:* kick; **2.** *fig.* (*Nervenkitzel*) kick; **Kickboxen** *n* kick-boxing

Kick-down [kɪkˈdaʊn] *m*, *n*; *-s*, *-s*; *Mot.* kick(-)down

kicken *umg.* **I.** *v/t.* kick; **II.** *v/i.* play football; **Kicker** *m*; *-s*, *-*, **Kickerin** *f*; *-*, *-nen umg.* (*Spieler*) (football) player

Kickstarter *m Mot.* kickstarter

Kid *n*; *-s*, *-s*; *mst Pl.*; *umg.* (*Jugendlicher*) kid

kidnappen [ˈkɪtnɛpn̩] *v/t.* kidnap; **Kidnapper** *m*; *-s*, *-*, **Kidnapperin** *f*; *-*, *-nen* kidnapper; **Kidnapping** *n*; *-s*, *-s* kidnapping

Kiebitz *m*; *-es*, *-e* **1.** *Orn.* peewit, lapwing; **2.** *umg.* (*Zuschauer*) nosy onlooker at cards, *Am.* kibitzer; **kiebitzen** *v/i. umg.* sneak a look; *Kartenspiel etc.: Am.* kibitz

Kiefer[1] *m*; *-s*, *-*; *Anat.* jaw; *Knochen*: jawbone; (*Unterkiefer*) mandible

Kiefer[2] *f*; *-*, *-n*; *Bot.* pine (tree); (*Holz*) pine(wood)

Kiefer|bruch *m Med.* fractured jaw; **~chirurgie** *f* oral surgery

Kieferhöhle *f Anat.* (maxillary) sinus; **Kieferhöhlenentzündung** *f Med.* (maxillary) sinusitis

Kiefer|klemme *f* lockjaw; **~knochen** *m* jawbone

kiefern *Adj.* pine(wood)

Kiefern|holz *n* pine(wood); **~nadel** *f* pine needle; **~öl** *n* pine oil; **~spanner** *m Zool.* geometrid pine moth; **~wald** *m* pinewood; *sehr großer*: pine forest; **~zapfen** *m* pine cone

Kiefer|orthopäde *m* orthodontist; **~orthopädie** *f* orthodontics *Pl.* (*V. im Sg.*); **~orthopädin** *f* (female) orthodontist

kieken *v/i. Dial. umg.* → *gucken*; **Kieker** *m*; *-s*, *-* **1.** *bes. nordd.* binoculars *Pl.*; **2.** *umg.*: *j-n auf dem ~ haben auch misstrauisch*: have one's eye on s.o., (*es auf j-n abgesehen haben*) have it in for s.o.

Kiekser *m*; *-s*, *-*; *umg.* (half-suppressed) squeal

Kiel *m*; *-s*, *-e* **1.** *Naut.* keel; *auf ~ legen* (*Schiff*) lay down; **2.** (*Federkiel*) quill; **~feder** *f* quill feather

kielholen *v/t.* (*untr.*, *hat ge-*) *Naut.* **1.** (*Schiff*, *Boot*) careen; **2.** (*Mann*) keelhaul

Kiellinie *f Naut.* **1.** (*in*) **~ fahren** sail in line ahead; **2.** *e-s Schiffs*: keel line

kieloben *Adv. Naut.* bottom up

Kiel|raum *m Naut.* bilge; **~schwert** *n Naut.* centre|board (*Am.* center-); **~wasser** *n* wake; *in j-s ~ segeln auch fig.* follow in s.o.'s wake

Kieme *f*; *-*, *-n*; *Zool.* gill; *sich* (*Dat.*) *etw. zwischen die ~n schieben umg.* get s.th. down one; *etw. zwischen die ~n bekommen umg.* get s.th. to eat

Kiemen|atmer *m*; *-s*, *-*; *Zool.* gill breather, gill-breathing animal; **~atmung** *f* gill breathing; **~deckel** *m* gill cover; **~spalte** *f* gill slit

Kien *m*; *-(e)s*, *-e* resinous wood, *mst* resinous pinewood; **~holz** *n* pine(-wood); **kienig** *Adj.* (highly) resinous; **~span** *m* pine(wood) chip

Kiepe *f*; *-*, *-n*; *bes. nordd.* pannier

Kies *m*; *-es*, *-e* **1.** gravel; (*für Wege*, *Straßen*) auch grit; *grober*, *auf dem Strand*: shingle; **2.** *Min.* pyrites; **3.** *nur Sg.*; *umg.* (*Geld*) dough, bread, *Brit. auch* dosh, *altm.* lolly; **~boden** *m* gravelly soil

Kiesel *m*; *-s*, *-* pebble; **~alge** *f* diatom; **~erde** *f* silica

kieselsauer *Adj. Chem.* silicic; **~es Natrium** silicate of sodium

Kiesel|säure *f* silicic acid; **~stein** *m*

pebble

kiesen *v/t.* spread with gravel, gravel; *gekieste Wege* gravel paths

Kiesgrube *f* gravel pit

kiesig *Adj.* gravelly

Kies|strand *m* shingle beach; **~weg** *m* gravel path

Kiez *m*; *-es*, *-e* **1.** *Dial.* district, quarter; **2.** *Sl.* (*Bordellviertel*) red-light district

kiffen *v/i. umg.* smoke pot; **Kiffer** *m*; *-s*, *-*, **Kifferin** *f*; *-*, *-nen*; *umg.* pot smoker, pothead

kikeriki *Interj.* cock-a-doodle-doo

Kikeriki[1] *n*; *-s*, *-s* cock-a-doodle-doo

Kikeriki[2] *m*; *-s*, *-s*; *Kinderspr.* (*Hahn*) cock, *bes. Am.* rooster

Kilimandscharo *m*; *-(s)*; *Geog.*: *der ~* (Mount) Kilimanjaro

killekille *Interj. umg.* tickle-tickle; (*bei j-m*) **~ machen** tickle (s.o.)

killen *v/t. umg.* bump s.o. off; **Killer** *m*; *-s*, *-*; *umg.* killer; *im Auftrag e-s anderen*: hit man

Killer... *im Subst. mst* killer ...

...killer *m*, *im Subst.* killer, destroyer; *mit erwünschter Wirkung*: *auch* eliminator; *Job~* killer (*od.* destroyer) of jobs; *Ozon~* ozone destroyer; *Schmutz~* dirt eliminator

Killer|kommando *n umg.* hit squad; **~satellit** *m Mil.* hunter-killer satellite; **~wal** *m* killer whale, orca; **~zelle** *f Med. Sl.* killer cell; *fachspr.* cytotoxic cell

Kilo *n*; *-s*, *-(s)* kilo; **~bit** *n EDV* kilobit; **~byte** *n EDV* kilobyte; **~gramm** *n* kilogram; **~hertz** *n* kilohertz; **~joule** *n* kilojoule; **~kalorie** *f* kilocalorie

Kilometer *m* kilomet|re (*Am.* -er); *60 ~ (in der Stunde) fahren* do 60 kilomet|res (*Am.* -ers) an hour (*etwa* 40 miles an hour); **~fresser** *m umg.* driver who covers long distances at high speeds; **~geld** *n etwa* mileage allowance

kilometerlang I. *Adj.* ... stretching for miles; *Sandstrand*, *Baustellen etc.*: *auch* miles (and miles) of ...; **II.** *Adv.* for miles (and miles)

Kilometer|pauschale *f etwa* flat mileage rate; **~stand** *m Mot. etwa* mileage, mileometer (*bes. Am.* odometer) reading; **~stein** *m* kilomet|re (*Am.* -er) stone

kilometerweit *Adj.* → *kilometerlang*

Kilometerzähler *m bes. Am.* odometer, *Brit. etwa* mileometer

Kiloohm *n Elektr.* kilohm, (a) thousand ohms *Pl.*

Kilopond *n Phys.*, *altm.* kilogram weight; **~meter** *n Phys.* kilogram-met|re (*Am.* -er)

Kilo|preis *m* price per kilo; **~tonne** *f* kiloton

Kilovolt *n Elektr.* kilovolt; **~ampere** *n* kilovolt-ampere

Kilowatt *n Elektr.* kilowatt; **~stunde** *f* kilowatt hour, *abgek.* kwh

kiloweise *Adv.* by the kilo

Kilt *m*; *-(e)s*, *-s* kilt

Kimber *m*; *-s*, *-n hist.* Cimbrian; *die ~n* the Cimbri; **kimbrisch** *Adj.* Cimbrian

Kimm *f*; *-*, *kein Pl.*; *Naut.* **1.** visual horizon; **2.** (*Schiffsbauch*) bilge

Kimme *f*; *-*, *-n* **1.** *zum Zielen*: (sight) notch; → *Korn*[1] **2.** *umg.* (*Gesäßspalte*) anal cleft

Kimmung *f Naut.* visual horizon; (*Luftspiegelung*) loom

Kimono *m*; *-s*, *-s* kimono

Kind *n*; *-(e)s*, *-er* **1.** child; (*Baby*) *auch* baby; *ein ~ bekommen* be pregnant, be expecting (a baby); *sie bekommt*

ein Kind she's expecting a baby, she's going to have a baby; *ein ~ / ~er in die Welt setzen* bring a child / children into the world; *j-m ein ~ machen umg.* make s.o. pregnant, put s.o. in the club *Sl.*, *Am.* knock s.o. up *vulg.*; *j-n an ~es statt annehmen* adopt s.o.; *eure ~er und Kindeskinder* your children and children's children; *sie sind mit ~ und Kegel losgezogen* they went off with their whole clan; *von ~ auf* (ever) since I was (*od.* you were *etc.*) a child; *das ist nichts für kleine ~er umg.* you're too young for that; *sie ist kein ~ mehr* she's not a child any more; *ein großes ~* a big baby; *das ~ im Manne* the child in him, his childish side; *sich freuen wie ein ~* be as pleased as punch; *das weiß doch jedes ~!* any child knows that; → *Leute* 1; **2.** *fig.*: *wie sag ich's m-m ~e? umg.* I'm not sure how to put this; *schonend*: how am I going to break it gently?; *wir werden das ~ schon schaukeln umg.* we'll work it out (somehow); *das ~ mit dem Bade ausschütten* throw out the baby with the bathwater; *(ein) gebranntes ~ scheut das Feuer Sprichw.* once bitten, twice shy; *sich lieb ~ machen bei j-m* try to get into s.o.'s good books; *das ~ beim rechten Namen nennen* call a spade a spade; *kein ~ von Traurigkeit sein* know how to enjoy o.s.; *ein Berliner ~* a Berliner born and bred; **3.** *fig. des Geistes*: product; *j-s liebstes ~ sein* be s.o.'s first love; *Thema*: be s.o.'s pet subject; **4.** *Anrede*: *~er, hört mal! an Erwachsene*: listen to this, folks (*Am.* you guys); *~er, ~er!* my goodness!

Kindbett *n*; *mst Sg.*; *altm.* childbed; *im ~ liegen* be confined (*od.* in confinement), *Am. auch* be lying-in

Kindchen *n* (little) child, *umg.* kid

Kinderarbeit *f* child employment; *bes. manuelle*: child labo(u)r

Kinder|arzt *m*, **~ärztin** *f* p(a)ediatrician; **~augen** *pl.* children's eyes; *etw. mit ~ ansehen* look at s.th. with the eyes of a child; **~beihilfe** *f österr.* child benefit; **~bekleidung** *f* children's clothes *Pl.*; *Abteilung*: children's wear; **~betreuung** *f* childcare; **~betreuungskosten** *Pl. Amtsspr.* childcare costs; **~bett** *n* cot, *Am.* crib; **~buch** *n* children's book

Kinderchen *Pl.* (little) children, toddlers, *umg.* kids

Kinder|chor *m* children's choir; **~dorf** *n* children's village; → *SOS-Kinderdorf*

Kinderei *f*; *-*, *-en*; *auch Pl.* childishness, childish behavio(u)r; *e-e ~ Spaß*: a childish prank

Kinder|ermäßigung *f* reduction for children, children's rate; **~erziehung** *f* bringing up children; **~fahrkarte** *f* child's ticket; **~fahrrad** *n* children's bicycle

kinderfeindlich *Adj.* hostile to children, anti-children; *Planung*: failing to meet the needs of children; *e-e ~e Gesellschaft/Hausverwaltung* a society hostile to children/an apartment block (*Am.* building) management that does not welcome children; *~ sein Mensch*: hate children; **Kinderfeindlichkeit** *f* hostility to children; *bei Planung*: failure to meet the needs of children

Kinder|fernsehen *n* children's television (*od.* TV); **~fest** *n* children's party; **~film** *m* children's film; **~frau** *f* nanny; **~freibetrag** *m* child allowance

Kinderfreund m: *ein ~ sein* be fond of children; **kinderfreundlich I.** *Adj.* **1.** *Mensch:* fond of children; **2.** *Umgebung etc.:* child-friendly, child-orientated; *ein ~es Hotel etc. auch* a hotel *etc.* that welcomes children, *Am.* a family-friendly hotel *etc.*; **II.** *Adv.* in a child-friendly way; *~ geplant* planned with children in mind; **Kinderfreundlichkeit** f **1.** *e-s Menschen:* fondness of children; **2.** *von Umgebung etc.:* child--friendliness, orientation towards children

Kinder|funk m *Radio, TV* children's program(me)s *Pl.*; **~garten** m kindergarten; *in GB, USA:* nursery school; **~gärtnerin** f kindergarten teacher; *in GB, USA:* nursery school teacher; **~geld** n child benefit, *Brit. auch* children's allowance; **~geschrei** n children's screaming; *e-s Kindes:* a child's screaming; **~gesicht** n child's face; *e-s Erwachsenen:* babyface; **~glaube** m childlike faith; **~gottesdienst** m children's service; *(Sonntagsschule)* Sunday school; **~grab** n child's grave; *Archäol.* child burial; **~hand** f a child's hand; *e-e Zeichnung von ~* a child's drawing; **~heilkunde** f p(a)ediatrics *Pl.* (*V. im Sg.*); **~heim** n children's home; **~herz** n child's heart; *~en erfreuen* make children happy; **~jahre** *Pl.* childhood years; **~hort** m after--school day care cent|re (*Am.* -er); **~karussell** n roundabout, merry-go--round, *Am. auch* carousel; **~kleidung** f children's clothes *Pl.*; *Abteilung:* children's wear; **~klinik** f children's hospital, p(a)ediatric clinic

kinderkopfgroß *Adj.* ... the size of a baby's head, *etwa* grapefruit-size(d)

Kinder|kram m *umg.* kids' stuff; **~krankenhaus** n children's hospital; **~krankenschwester** f p(a)ediatric nurse, (sick) children's nurse; **~krankheit** f *Med.* childhood illness; *~en fig.* teething troubles; **~kreuzzug** m *hist.* Children's Crusade; **~kriegen** n; -s, *kein Pl.*; *umg.* having children; *es ist zum ~ fig.* it's enough to drive you up the wall; **~krippe** f crèche, day nursery, *Am.* daycare center; **~laden** m **1.** children's shop (*bes. Am.* store); **2.** *Kindergarten:* antiauthoritarian playgroup; **~lähmung** f *Med.* polio, poliomyelitis *fachspr.*

kinder|leicht *Adj. umg.* really (*Brit. auch* dead) easy; *es ist ~ auch* it's a pushover (*od.* cinch); **~lieb** *Adj.* very fond of children

Kinder|liebe f love of children; **~lied** n children's song; *Reim:* nursery rhyme; **kinderlos** *Adj.* childless; **Kinderlosigkeit** f childlessness

Kinder|mädchen n nanny; **~mode** f children's fashions *Pl.*; (*Kleidung*) children's wear; **~mord** m child murder; *Jur.* infanticide; *der ~ zu Bethlehem bibl.* the Massacre of the Innocents; **~mörder** m, **~mörderin** f child murderer; **~mund** m child's mouth; *fig. Gerede:* child talk; **~nahrung** f baby food; **~narr** m, **~närrin** f: *ein Kindernarr sein umg.* be crazy about children, go potty over children; **~pflegerin** f children's nurse; **~popo** m *umg.*: *glatt wie ein ~* (as) smooth as a baby's bottom; **~pornographie** f child pornography; **~prostitution** f child prostitution; **~psychologie** f child psychology; **~puder** m baby powder

kinderreich *Adj.* ... with many children; *eine ~e Familie* a large family;

Kinderreichtum m; *nur Sg.* large number of children

Kinder|reim m nursery rhyme; **~sachen** *Pl.*; *umg.* children's things (*Kleidung:* *auch* clothes); **~sarg** m **1.** child's coffin; **2.** *umg. hum:* **Kindersärge** huge shoes, clodhoppers; **~schänder** m child abuser; **~schar** f crowd of children; **~schreck** m; *nur Sg.* bogeyman; **~schuhe** *Pl.* children's shoes; *sie ist den ~n entwachsen* she's not a child any more; *das Unternehmen steckt noch in den ~n fig.* the enterprise is still in its infancy, it's still early days for this enterprise; **~schutzbund** m child welfare association; **~schwester** f children's nurse; **~segen** m *mst hum.*: *e-e Familie mit reichem ~* blessed with many children; **~sendung** f children's program(me)

kindersicher *Adj.* childproof

Kinder|sicherung f child lock; **~sitz** m child seat; **~spiel** n children's game; *fig.* pushover; *das ist für ihn ein ~ auch* that's child's play for him; **~spielplatz** m children's playground; **~spielzeug** n children's toys *Pl.*; *eines:* child's toy; **~sprache** f; *nur Sg.* children's language; *von Erwachsenen:* baby talk; **~star** m child star; **~station** f children's ward, p(a)ediatric ward; **~sterblichkeit** f child (*jünger:* infant) mortality; **~stimme** f child's voice; *Pl.* children's voices; **~stube** f; *nur Sg.*; *fig.* upbringing; *er hat keine / e-e gute ~* he's got no manners / good manners, he's been badly/well brought up; **~stuhl** m child's chair; *hoher:* high chair; **~stunde** f *TV etc.* children's program(me); **~tage** *Pl.* childhood days; *e-e Erinnerung an ferne ~* a memory of childhood (days) long ago; **~tagesstätte** f day nursery, day care cent|re (*Am.* -er); **~taufe** f infant baptism; **~teller** m *im Restaurant:* children's menu; **~theater** n children's theat|re (*Am.* -er); **~vorstellung** f *Theat. etc.* children's performance (*od.* show); **~wagen** m pram, *Am.* baby carriage; (*Sportwagen*) pushchair, *Am.* stroller; **~wunsch** m *von Frau, Paar:* desire for a child (*Pl.* children); **~zahl** f number of children; **~zeit** f childhood; **~zimmer** n **1.** children's room; *für Kleinkinder:* nursery; **2.** *Mobiliar:* nursery furniture and furnishings *Pl.*; **~zulage** f child benefit

Kindes|alter n childhood; *frühes:* infancy; *im ~* in childhood, when (still) a child; (*schon früh*) at an early age; **~aussetzung** f abandoning of a child (*Pl.* children); **~beine** *Pl.*: *von ~n an* from childhood; **~entführung** f child kidnapping; **~kind** n *altm.* grandchild; → *Kind 1*; **~liebe** f *geh.* filial love; **~missbrauch** m (sexual) child abuse; **~misshandlung** f child abuse; **~mord** m child murder; *am eigenen Kind:* infanticide; **~mörder** m, **~mörderin** f child murderer; *des eigenen Kindes:* infanticide; **~mutter** f child's mother; **~raub** m child kidnapping; *von Kleinkindern:* baby-snatching; **~tötung** f *Jur.* infanticide; **~vater** m child's father

Kindfrau f **1.** *frühreif:* nymphet; **2.** *sie ist e-e ~* (*Mädchenfrau*) she's a mere slip of a girl

kind|gemäß I. *Adj.* suitable for children (*od.* a child); **II.** *Adv.*: *etw. ~ ausdrücken* express s.th. in children's terms; **~gerecht** *Adj.* suitable for children (*od.* a child)

kindhaft *Adj.* childlike

Kindheit f childhood; *frühe:* infancy; *von ~ an* from childhood

Kindheits|erinnerung f childhood memory; **~erlebnis** n childhood experience

kindisch I. *Adj.* childish; *Benehmen, stärker:* infantile; **II.** *Adv.*: *sich ~ freuen* take a childish pleasure (*an + Dat.* in)

kindlich I. *Adj.* childlike; (*unschuldig*) *auch* innocent; (*naiv*) naive; **II.** *Adv.* in a childlike manner; **Kindlichkeit** f childlike nature

Kinds|... *im Subst. siehe auch* **Kind(es)...**; **~bewegung** f *Med.* f(o)etal movement

Kindschaft f parentage, filiation *förm.*

Kindskopf m *umg.* overgrown child, big baby; **kindsköpfig** *Adj.* childish

Kinds|lage f *Med.* presentation; f *Dial.* → *Kindtaufe*; **~tod** m: *plötzlicher ~* cot (*Am.* crib) death; *fachspr.* sudden infant death syndrome (*abgek.* SIDS)

Kindtaufe f *kirchl.* christening, baptism

Kinematographie f; -, *kein Pl.* cinematography; **kinematographisch I.** *Adj.* cinematographic; **II.** *Adv.* cinematographically

Kinetik f; -, *kein Pl.*; *Phys.* kinetics *Pl.* (*V. im Sg.*); **kinetisch I.** *Adj.* kinetic; **II.** *Adv.* kinetically

King m; -(s), -s; *umg.* top dog, boss

Kinkerlitzchen *Pl. umg.* (*Kleinigkeiten*) odds and ends, knicknacks; (*Flausen*) fooling around *Sg.*

Kinn n; -(e)s, -e chin; **~backe** f, **~backen** m *südd.* jaw; **~bart** m chin beard; (*Spitzbart*) goatee; **~haken** m (left *od.* right) hook to the chin; **~lade** f jaw; **~spitze** f point of the chin

Kino n; -s, -s **1.** (*Gebäude*) cinema, *Am.* movie theater; *ins ~ gehen* go to the cinema (*Am.* movies), go and see a film (*Am.* movie); *dieser Film kommt jetzt in die ~s* this film (*Am.* movie) is going on general release; **2.** (*Institution*) cinema, *bes. Am. auch* the movies *Pl.*, Hollywood; **~...** *im Subst. siehe auch* **Film...**; **~besuch** m visit to the cinema (*Am.* movies); *allg.* cinemagoing, *Am.* moviegoing; **~besucher** m, **~besucherin** f cinemagoer, *Am.* moviegoer; **~center** n multi--screen cinema, multiplex (cinema); **~film** m (cinema) film, *bes. Am.* movie film; **~hit** m hit film (*bes. Am.* movie), screen hit; **~karte** f cinema (*Am.* movie) ticket; **~kasse** f cinema (*Am.* theater) box office; **~programm** n cinema (*Am.* movie) program(me); *Vorschau:* film (*bes. Am.* movie) guide; **~publikum** n cinema (*Am.* movie) audience(s *Pl.*); **~saal** m hall where films (*bes. Am.* movies) are shown; **~vorstellung** f film (*bes. Am.* movie) showing; **~werbung** f cinema (*od.* screen, *Am.* movie) advertising

Kintopp m, n; -(e)s, -s; *umg.* → *Kino* 1, 2

Kiosk m; -(e)s, -e kiosk; (*Zeitungsstand*) *auch* newsstand

Kipfel n; -s, -, **Kipferl** n; -s, -n; *südd., österr.* croissant

kippbar *Adj.* tiltable; *Wagen, Anhänger:* tipping

Kippe f; -, -n **1.** *umg.* (*Zigarettenstummel*) cigarette butt (*od.* end), *Brit. auch* fag end; **2.** *auf der ~ stehen Tasse, Flasche etc.:* be precariously balanced; *der Kranke/die Firma steht auf der Kippe fig.* it's touch and go with the patient/company; *sie steht in Ma-*

K

the und Chemie auf der ~ she's very borderline in math(s) and chemistry, math(s) and chemistry could be her downfall; **3.** (*Müllkippe*) dump, *Brit. auch* tip; *Bergb., Halde*: slag heap, tailings *Pl.*; **4.** *Turnen*: upstart

kippelig *umg. Adj.* wobbly

kippeln *umg. v/i.* **1.** *Stuhl etc.*: be wobbly; **2.** *auf e-m Stuhl*: rock backwards and forwards (*mit dem Stuhl* on one's chair)

kippen I. *v/i.* tip (*od.* topple) over; *Fahrzeug*: roll over; *Boot*: turn on its side, keel over; (*kentern*) capsize; *vom Stuhl* ~ fall off one's chair; → *Latschen*; **II.** *v/t.* **1.** tip up; (*Fenster*) tilt; *nicht* ~*!* *Aufschrift*: (please) keep upright; **2.** (*schütten*) (*Sand etc.*) tip, dump, (*Wasser etc.*) *auch* pour (*aus* out of); *einen* ~ *umg.* (*trinken*) have a quick one; → *auch umkippen*; **3.** *umg.* (*zurückziehen*) (*Plan*) give the chop; (*absetzen*) (*Person*) dump

Kipper *m*; *-s*, - **1.** *Tech., Vorrichtung*: tipper, *Am.* dumper; **2.** → *Kippwagen*

Kipp|fenster *n* bottom-hinged (*od.* tilting) window; ~**hebel** *m* **1.** tilting lever; **2.** *Mot.* rocker (arm); ~**lore** *f* tipping truck (*Am.* car); ~**schalter** *m* toggle (*od.* tumbler) switch; ~**schaltung** *f* *Etech.* trigger circuit

kippsicher *Adj.* stable

Kipp|vorrichtung *f* tipping device; ~**wagen** *m* **1.** *Mot.* tipper lorry, *Am.* dump truck; **2.** *Eisenb.* tipping wagon, *Am.* dumping car

Kirche *f*, -, -*n* church; (*Gottesdienst*) *auch* service; *in der* ~ at (*bes. Am.* in) church; *in die od. zur* ~ *gehen* go to church; *wir wollen die* ~ *im Dorf lassen fig.* let's not get carried away

Kirchen|älteste *m*, *f* elder; ~**amt** *n* **1.** *Posten*: ecclesiastical office; **2.** *Stelle*: (administrative) church offices *Pl.*; ~**austritt** *m* leaving the church; *Pl.* cases of people leaving the church; ~**bank** *f* pew; ~**bann** *m* excommunication; ~**bau** *m* **1.** *nur Sg.*; *das Bauen*: building of churches; **2.** *Gebäude*: church (building); ~**besuch** *m* **1.** church attendance; **2.** → *Kirchgang*; ~**besucher** *m*, ~**besucherin** *f* churchgoer; ~**buch** *n* parish register; ~**chor** *m* church choir; ~**diener** *m*, ~**dienerin** *f* sexton

kirchenfeindlich *Adj.* anti-Church, anticlerical

Kirchen|fenster *n* church window; ~**funk** *m* religious broadcasting; ~**fürst** *m* high church dignitary; *kath.* (*Kardinal*) Prince of the Church; ~**gemeinde** *f* parish; *in der Kirche*: congregation; ~**geschichte** *f* church history; ~**glocke** *f* church bell; ~**jahr** *n* ecclesiastical year; ~**kampf** *m* struggle between Church and state; ~**konzert** *n* church concert; ~**latein** *n* Church Latin; ~**lehre** *f* church doctrine; ~**licht** *n*: *kein / nicht gerade ein* (*großes*) ~ *sein umg. hum.* be no genius / not exactly a genius; ~**lied** *n* hymn; ~**mann** *m* churchman; ~**maus** *f fig.*: *arm wie e-e* ~ (as) poor as a church mouse; ~**musik** *f* sacred (*od.* church) music; ~**patron** *m*, ~**patronin** *f* (church's) patron saint

Kirchenpolitik *f* policy toward(s) the Church, church policy; **kirchenpolitisch** *Adj.* concerning policy toward (-s) the Church (*od.* church policy)

Kirchen|präsident *m*, ~**präsidentin** *f ev.* regional church leader; ~**provinz** *f* Archbishop's province; ~**rat** *m ev.*

1. *Organ*: regional church council; **2.** *Mitglied*: member of the regional church council; ~**rätin** *f* (female) member of the regional church council; ~**raub** *m* theft from a church (*Pl.* churches)

Kirchenrecht *n* canon law; **kirchenrechtlich** *Adj.* canonical

Kirchen|schändung *f* desecration (of a church); ~**schiff** *n* nave; ~**spaltung** *f* schism; ~**staat** *m*: *der* ~ **1.** *hist.* the Papal States *Pl.*; **2.** (*Vatikanstaat*) the Vatican City; ~**steuer** *f* church tax; ~**tag** *m* church congress; ~**ton** *m*, ~**tonart** *f Mus.* church mode; ~**tür** *f* church door; ~**übertritt** *m* change of confession; ~**vater** *m hist.* Father of the Church, church father; *die Kirchenväter* the Early Fathers (of the Church); ~**verfolgung** *f* persecution of the church; ~**vorstand** *m* parochial church council

Kirch|gang *m*: *der* ~ *am Sonntag war Familientradition/Pflicht* going to church on Sundays was a family tradition / everyone had to go to church on Sundays; ~**gänger** *m*; *-s*, -, ~**gängerin** *f*; -, -*nen* churchgoer

Kirchhof *m* churchyard

Kirchhofsruhe *f* → *Friedhofsruhe*

kirchlich I. *Adj.* church ... (*auch Trauung etc.*); (*Gesetz, Bau etc.*) ecclesiastical; (*Geistliche betreffend*) clerical; (~ *gesinnt*) religious, devout; **II.** *Adv.*: *sich* ~ *trauen lassen* have a church wedding

Kirch|platz *m* church square; ~**spiel** *n*, ~**sprengel** *m* parish; ~**tag** *m südd., österr.* → *Kirchweih*

Kirchturm *m* (church) steeple, spire; *ohne Spitze*: church tower; ~**politik** *f* parish-pump politics *Pl.*; ~**spitze** *f* (top of a) church spire; ~**uhr** *f* church clock

Kirchweih *f*; -, -*en* annual fair (*commemorating the consecration of the local church*)

Kirchweihe *f* consecration of a church; **Kirchweihfest** *n* → *Kirchweih*

Kirgise *m*; -*n*, -*n* Kyrgyz, Kirghiz; **Kirgisien** (*n*); -*s*; *Geog.* Kyrgyzstan, Kirghizia; **Kirgisin** *f*; -, -*nen* Kyrgyz (*od.* Kirghiz) woman (*od.* girl); **kirgisisch** *Adj.* Kyrgyz, Kirghiz

Kirmes *f*; -,-*sen*; *Dial.* → *Kirchweih*

kirre *Adj. umg.* (*auch* ~ *machen*) tame

Kirsch *m*; -(*e*)*s*, -; (*Kirschwasser*) kirsch; ~**baum** *m Bot.* cherry tree; *Holz*: cherry wood; ~**blüte** *f* cherry blossom

Kirsche *f*; -, -*n*; *Bot.* **1.** cherry; *saure* ~ sour cherry, morello; *mit ihm ist nicht gut* ~ *n essen umg. fig.* it's best to steer clear of him, he's a difficult customer (to deal with); **2.** (*Kirschbaum*) cherry (tree)

Kirschenmund *m poet.* full, cherry-red lips *Pl.*

Kirschentkerner *m* cherry stoner (*Am.* pitter)

kirschgroß *Adj.* cherry-size

Kirsch|kern *m* cherry stone (*bes. Am.* pit); ~**kuchen** *m Gastr.* cherry cake; ~**likör** *m* cherry brandy

kirschrot *Adj.*, **Kirschrot** *n* cherry red, cerise

Kirsch|saft *m* cherry juice; ~**torte** *f Gastr.* cherry gateau; *Schwarzwälder* ~ Black Forest gateau (*Am.* cake); ~**wasser** *n* kirsch

Kismet *n*; -*s*, *kein Pl.* kismet, fate, destiny

Kissen *n*; -*s*, - cushion; (*Kopfkissen*)

pillow; ~**bezug** *m* cushion cover; *des Kopfkissens*: pillowcase, pillowslip; ~**füllung** *f* cushion (*Kopfkissen*: pillow) stuffing; ~**schlacht** *f* pillow fight; ~**überzug** *m* → *Kissenbezug*

Kiste *f*; -, -*n* **1.** box; (*Truhe*) chest; *Wirts., bes. Wein*: case; *aus Latten*: crate; **2.** *umg. Mot., Flug.* crate, *bes. Am.* rustbucket; (*Boot*) tub; *alte* ~ old crate, jalopy, *Brit. auch* banger, *Am. auch* beater; **3.** *umg.* (*Bett*) bed; *ab in die* ~*!* off to bed with you!; **4.** *umg.* (*Sarg*) coffin; *in der* ~ *liegen* be five (*Am.* six) feet under; **5.** *umg.* (*Sache*) business, job; *faule* ~ fishy business

Kistenbrett *n* slat of a crate

kistenweise *Adv.* (*in Kisten verpackt*) in crates; *Wein*: in cases; (*in großen Mengen*) by the crate(ful); *Wein*: by the case

Kita *f*; -, -*s*; *Abk.* → *Kindertagesstätte*

Kitchenette [kɪtʃə'nɛt] *f*; -, -*s* kitchenette

Kithara *f*; -, -*s und Kitharen* cithara

Kitsch *m*; -(*e*)*s*, *kein Pl.* kitsch; (*Waren etc.*) trash, junk; **kitschig** *Adj.* kitschy, tacky; *Roman etc.*: trashy; **Kitschroman** *m* trashy novel

Kitt *m*; -(*e*)*s*, -*e*; (*Fensterkitt*) putty; *zum Kleben*: cement; (*Dichtmasse*) sealing compound; (*Füllmasse*) filler, filling compound

Kittchen *n*; -*s*, -; *umg.* clink; *im* ~ *sitzen* be in clink (*od.* in the slammer), be inside, be doing time

Kittel *m*; -*s*, - **1.** overall, *Am.* smock; (*des Arztes, Laboranten etc.*) white coat; *(Bluse)* smock; **3.** *südd.* jacket; ~**schürze** *f* sleeveless overall

kitten *v/t.* **1.** cement; *mit Klebstoff*: glue (*an + Akk.* to; *aneinander* together); *Glaserei*: fix with putty; **2.** *umg. fig.* (*Ehe, Freundschaft*) patch up

Kitz *n*; -*es*, -*e*, **Kitze** *f*; -, -*n*; *Zool.* kid; (*Rehkitz*) fawn

Kitzel *m*; -*s*, - **1.** *Gefühl*: tickle, tickling; *fig. bei Gefahr etc.*: thrill; *umg.* kick; **2.** (*Verlangen*) itch (*nach* for); **kitz(e)lig** *Adj.* ticklish (*auch fig. heikel*); **kitzeln** *v/t/i.* tickle (*auch fig.*); *mich kitzelt's am Fuß / im Hals* my foot's tickling / I've got a tickle in my throat; *es kitzelte ihn zu* (+ *Inf.*) *fig.* he was itching to (+ *Inf.*)

Kitzler *m*; -*s*, -; *Anat.* clitoris

Kiwi[1] *m*; -*s*, -*s*; *Zool.* kiwi

Kiwi[2] *f*; -, -*s*; (*Frucht*) kiwi (fruit)

kJ *Abk.* (*Kilojoule*) kJ

k.k. *Abk.* → *kaiserlich-königlich*

KKW *n*; -*s*, -*s*; *Abk.* → *Kernkraftwerk*

Kl. *Abk.* → *Klasse*

Klabautermann *m* hobgoblin

klack *Interj.* click; *bei Tropfen*: drip; *bei breiiger Masse*: splat; **klacken** *v/i. umg.* click; *Tropfen*: drip; *breiige Masse*: splash

klackern *v/i. Dial.* clatter

Klacks *m*; -*es*, -*e*; *umg.* blob; *Sahne etc.*: dollop, splosh; *das ist* (*für sie*) *doch nur ein* ~ *fig.* that's a cinch (*Brit. auch* doddle) (for her/them)

Kladde *f*; -, -*n* **1.** (rough) notebook; scribbling pad; *Wirts.* waste book; **2.** (*Entwurf*) rough draft

kladderadatsch *umg.* **I.** *Interj.* crash, bang, wallop!; **II.** **Kladderadatsch** *m*; -(*e*)*s*, -*e*; *umg.* unholy mess, a (complete) shambles; *Wirts.* crash, collapse; (*Skandal*) rumpus, to-do *umg.*

klaffen *v/i. Loch Wunde etc.*: gape; *Abgrund, Spalte*: yawn; *vor ihnen klaffte ein Abgrund* a yawning gulf opened in front of them

kläffen v/i. yap, yelp; umg. fig., Person: bark; **Kläffer** m; -s, - Hund: yapping dog, yelper; umg. fig., Person: loud-mouth

Klafter m, n; -s, - hist., Naut. fathom (auch Holzmaß)

klagbar Adj. Jur. actionable; Anspruch: enforceable

Klage f, -, -n **1.** geh. (Ausdruck des Schmerzes) complaint; (Wehklage) lament (um for); **2.** (Beschwerde) complaint; (keinen) **Grund zur ~ haben** have (no) cause (od. grounds) for complaint; **über etw. ~ führen** lodge a complaint about s.th.; **3.** Jur. suit, action; **~ erheben gegen** file a suit against, sue (wegen for); **eine ~ auf Schadenersatz** an action for damages; → auch Anklage; **~erhebung** f Jur. filing of an action, institution of legal proceedings; **~geschrei** n wailing, lamentation; **~laut** m plaintive cry, moan; **~lied** n lament; um e-n Toten: dirge; fig. lamentation; **ein ~ (über j-n/etw.) anstimmen** fig. start moaning (about s.o./s.th.); **~mauer** f: **die ~** the Wailing Wall

klagen I. v/i. **1.** complain (über + Akk. about, of; bei to); (wehklagen) wail, lament; **~ über** (+ Akk.) (leiden an) complain of; **ich kann nicht ~** umg. I can't complain; **2.** Jur. bring an action (gegen against; auf + Akk., wegen for), go to court (auf + Akk., wegen about), sue (for); → auch **Klage 3; II.** v/t. **1.** j-m sein Leid ~ pour one's heart out to s.o.; **2.** j-n ~ österr. → ver-klagen

Klagepunkt m Jur. particular of a (od. the) charge

Kläger m; -s, -, **~in** f; -, -nen Jur. plaintiff; bes. in der Berufung: complainant; in Scheidungssachen: petitioner; **Klägerschaft** f bes. schw. Jur. **1.** die ~ (Kläger) the plaintiffs Pl.; **2.** (Anklage) charge

Klage|schrift f Jur. particulars Pl. of the charge(s); Zivilrecht: statement of claim; **~weg** m Jur. litigation; auf dem ~ by taking legal action; **~weib** n professional mourner

kläglich I. Adj. Blick etc.: pitiful; (elend) Dasein, Lage, Anblick etc.: auch miserable, wretched; (geringwertig) Ergebnis, Leistung,Gehalt etc.: auch pathetic; **e-e ~e Miene machen** look pitiful (od. pathetic); **II.** Adv.: **~ weinen** cry pitifully; **~ umkommen** die a miserable death; **~ versagen** fail miserably; **die Gehaltserhöhung ist ~ ausgefallen** the pay rise (Am. raise) was a pathetic amount (od. a mere pittance)

klaglos Adv. **1.** without complaining; **2.** österr. without any problems; verlaufen: auch smoothly

Klamauk m; -s, kein Pl. **1.** umg. (Lärm). row, racket; (Getue). rumpus, to-do; **2.** Theat. etc. slapstick

klamm Adj. **1.** clammy; Bett: damp; (erstarrt) numb; **~ vor Kälte** stiff with cold; **2.** umg.: **~ sein** (Geldprobleme haben) be hard up (pleite: broke, Brit. auch skint)

Klamm f; -, -en; Geol. gorge

Klammer f; -, -n **1.** (Büro-, Hosenklammer, Med. Wundklammer etc.) clip; (Heftklammer) staple; (Wäscheklammer) peg, Am. clothes pin; (Zahnklammer) brace(s Pl.); (Haarklammer) (hair)grip, Am. bobby pin; Tech. clamp; (Bauklammer) cramp; **2.** Druck. (runde Klammer) bracket,

Am. parenthesis, (Pl. parentheses); (eingeklammerter Text) (words in) parentheses; **runde ~n** round brackets; Am. parentheses; **eckige ~n** square brackets, Am. (square) brackets; **geschweifte ~n** braces; **spitze ~n** angle od. pointed od. broken brackets; **~auf/zu** open/close brackets (Am. parentheses); **3.** fig. (Klammergriff) tight grip, clinch; **~affe** m **1.** Zool. spider monkey; **2.** EDV Sl. @ sign, at sign; **~beutel** m clothes peg (Am. pin) bag; **mit dem ~ gepudert sein** umg. fig. be off one's head; **~griff** m tight grip, clinch

klammern I. v/t. clip (an + Akk. to); fest: clamp (to); mit Heftmaschine: staple (to); **die Hand um etw. ~** grasp s.th. tightly; **II.** v/refl.: **sich ~ an** (+ Akk.) auch fig. cling to; **III.** v/i. Boxen: clinch

klammheimlich umg. **I.** Adj. Freude, Genugtuung etc.: quiet, secret; **II.** Adv. on the quiet; verschwinden: without a word

Klamotte f, -, -n; umg. **1.** ~n (Kleider) things, gear Sg.; **2.**; **3.** ~n (Sachen) things, stuff Sg.; **4.** (alter Film) oldie; pej. trashy old film (bes. Am. movie)

Klamottenkiste f box of old clothes; **aus der ~, aus Omas ~** umg. fig. ancient, out of the ark

Klampe f; -, -n Naut. cleat; für Rettungsboote: chock

Klampfe f; -, -n **1.** umg. guitar; **2.** österr. (Bauklammer) cramp

klang Imperf. → **klingen**

Klang m; -(e)s, Klänge **1.** sound; von Gläsern: auch clinking; heller: tinkling; von Geld: chinking; von Metall: clanking; **2.** (Tonfarbe) tone; (eigener, e-s Instruments, e-r Stimme) timbre; fig. ring; **sein Name hat e-n guten ~** fig. he's got a good reputation; **3.** Mus.: **Klänge** strains, sounds; **zu den Klängen e-s Walzers / der Nationalhymne** to the strains of a waltz / the national anthem; **~bild** n sound; **~effekt** m sound effect; **~farbe** f tone quality; charakteristische: timbre; **~fülle** f (rich) sonority, richness of sound; **~körper** m orchestra; **~lehre** f acoustics Pl. (V. im Sg.)

klanglich I. Adj. tonal; Fülle, Schönheit etc.: auch of sound; Qualität: auch sound …; **II.** Adv. as far as the sound is concerned; **die Aufnahme könnte ~ voller sein** the recording could have a richer sound

klanglos Adj. toneless; → sang- und ~

Klang|qualität f e-s Tones: tonal quality; der Wiedergabe: sound quality; **~regler** m tone control

klangrein Adj. … with a pure sound (od. tone); **~ sein** have a pure sound (od. tone); **Klangreinheit** f purity of sound (od. tone)

klangschön Adj. … with a beautiful sound (od. tone); **~ sein** have a beautiful sound (od. tone); **Klangschönheit** f; nur Sg. beauty of sound (od. tone)

Klangspektrum n range of sound(s), tonal palette

klangvoll Adj. sonorous; Musik: melodious; fig. (berühmt) illustrious

Klangwirkung f effect produced by a sound

Klapp|bett n folding bed; **~brücke** f bascule bridge; **~deckel** m hinged lid

Klappe f; -, -n **1.** lose: flap (auch am Briefumschlag, an Tasche etc.); (Deckel) lid; am Ofen: door; am Lastwa-

gen: tailboard; seitlich: drop side; am Kombi: tailgate; am Tisch: leaf; (Ventil) flap valve; **bei mir ist die ~ runtergegangen** umg. I don't want to hear any more about it; **2.** Anat. des Herzens: valve; **3.** Mus., am Blasinstrument: key:; **4.** umg. (Mund) gob, Am. trap; **halt die ~!** umg. shut up!, Am. auch shut your trap!; (immer) **die ~ aufreißen, e-e große ~ haben** umg. have a big mouth; **5.** beim Film: clapper board(s Pl.); **nach der letzten ~** Film: after the final take (od. shoot), when shooting finishes (Vergangenheit: finished); **6.** umg. (Bett) bed; **in die ~ gehen** hit the hay; **7.** Sl. (Treffpunkt von Homosexuellen) gay haunt

klappen I. v/t. fold; **der Sitz lässt sich nach hinten ~** the seat folds back; **nach oben/unten ~** (Deckel) raise (od. lift) /lower, open/close; (Kragen etc.) turn up/down; **II.** v/i. **1.** Tür etc.: bang (an + Akk. against); **mit den Türen ~** bang (od. slam) the doors; **2.** umg. (gut gehen) work; go off well; **es klappt nicht** it won't work; **wenn alles klappt** if all goes well; **(es) wird schon ~!** it'll work out OK (od. all right), it'll be fine

Klappen|fehler m Med. valvular defect; **~text** m im Buch: blurb

Klapper f; -, -n rattle

klapperdürr Adj.: **~ sein** umg. be all skin and bone (od. a bag of bones)

Klappergestell n umg. **1.** (Person) umg. bag of bones; **2.** → **Klapperkasten**

klapperig Adj. → **klapprig**

Klapper|kasten m umg., **~kiste** f Mot. umg. rattletrap; Flug. umg. old crate

klappern v/i. rattle; Geschirr, Maschine etc.: clatter; Hufe, Holzschuhe: auch go clip-clop; Stricknadeln: click; **mit etw. ~** rattle (od. clatter) s.th.; **er klapperte (vor Kälte) mit den Zähnen** his teeth were chattering (with cold); **vor Angst klapperten mir die Zähne** my teeth were chattering with fear; **mit dem Schnabel ~** Storch: make a clattering noise with its beak

Klappern n; -s, kein Pl. rattling, rattle; von Geschirr, Maschine etc.: clatter(ing); von Stricknadeln: clicking; von Zähnen: chattering; **~ gehört zum Handwerk** puff(ery) is part of the trade

Klapper|schlange f Zool. rattlesnake; **~storch** m Kinderspr. stork (that brings babies); **er glaubt noch an den ~** he doesn't know about the birds and the bees yet; iro. a uch: he still thinks the earth is flat

Klapp|fahrrad n folding bicycle; **~fenster** n top-hinged window; **~laden** m folding shutter; **~leiter** f folding ladder; **~messer** n jack-knife; **~pult** n folding desk; **~rad** n folding bicycle

klapprig Adj. shaky; bes. ältere Person: umg. doddery; Stuhl etc.: rickety; Wagen: rattly

Klapp|schute f Naut. (dredging) hopper barge, Am. auch dump scow; **~sitz** m folding seat; **~stuhl** m folding chair; **~tisch** m folding table; mit Seitenteilen: drop-leaf table; im Zug etc.: foldaway table; **~ventil** n flap valve; **~verdeck** n Mot. (folding) hood, soft top

Klaps m; -es, -e **1.** smack, slap; **2.** umg.: **e-n ~ haben** have a screw loose; **~mühle** f umg. funny farm, loony bin, nuthouse, Am. altm. auch booby hatch

klar I. *Adj.* **1.** clear (*auch Himmel, Stimme, Suppe etc.*); *Schnaps*: colo(u)rless, white; **~er Blick** open, honest look; **2.** (*deutlich*) clear; (*offenkundig*) *auch* plain; **bei ~em Bewusstsein sein** be fully conscious; **er hat e-n ~en Blick** he is clear-sighted; (*denkt nüchtern*) he knows what he's doing; **e-n ~en Kopf behalten** keep a clear head; (*nicht in Panik geraten*) keep one's wits about one; (*nicht mehr*) **~ im Kopf sein** be (no longer) thinking clearly; **3.** *Entscheidung, Ziel etc.*: clear(-cut), definite; (*geordnet*) clear, straight; **~e Verhältnisse schaffen** get things straight; **zwischen ihnen ist alles ~** they've settled everything; **4.** *Sport etc.*: *Sieg, Vorsprung*: clear; **5.** *Wendungen*: **es ist ~, dass** it's clear (*od.* obvious) that; **es ist mir ~, dass, ich bin mir darüber ~, dass** it's clear to me that, I realize that; **ich bin mir nicht ~ (darüber), was ich tun soll** I'm not quite sure what to do; **j-m etw. ~ machen** make s.th. clear to s.o., explain s.th. to s.o., clarify s.th. for s.o.; **sich** (*Dat.*) **etw. ~ machen** get s.th. clear (*od.* straight) in one's own mind; **sich** (*Dat.*) **über etw. ~ werden** come to realize s.th.; **dir sollte endlich ~ werden, dass ...** you should have realized by now that ...; **ist das ~?** is that clear?, *bes. drohend*: have you got that?; **alles ~?** *umg.* got it?; (*alles in Ordnung?*) everything OK?; **jetzt ist mir alles ~!** now I understand!; **sich** (*Dat.*) **über etw. im Klaren sein** realize s.th., be aware of s.th.; → **Klärchen, Kloßbrühe**; → *auch* **klarkommen, klarmachen** etc.; **6.** *Naut., Flug.* clear, ready; **~ zum Gefecht** ready for action, *als Kommando*: clear the decks (for action); **II.** *Adv.* **1.** clearly; **jetzt sehe ich endlich ~** at last it's clear to me, at last I understand; **ein ~ denkender Mensch** a clear-headed person; **~ und deutlich** quite clearly; **~ zutage treten** be obvious; **die Mannschaft hat ~ gewonnen** *Sport* the team had a clear win; **2.** *umg.* (*natürlich*) **(na) ~!** of course, oh yes

Klar *n; -s, -; österr.* egg white

Kläranlage *f* sewage (*e-r Fabrik*: waste water) treatment plant

Klärbecken *n* clearing tank

Klar|blick *m* clear-sightedness; **klarblickend** *Adj.* clear-sighted

Klärchen: **klar wie ~ sein** *umg.* be crystal clear

Klare *m; -n, -n* schnapps; **e-n ~n / zwei ~ bestellen** order one/two schnapps

klären I. *v/t.* **1.** (*reinigen*) purify; (*Abwässer*) treat; **2.** (*Sache, Missverständnis*) clear up; (*Sache, Tatbestand*) clarify; (*Frage*) settle; **II.** *v/i. Sport* clear; **III.** *v/refl.* **1.** *Himmel etc.*: clear (up); **2.** *Frage*: be settled; *Problem*: be solved

klargehen *v/i.* (*unreg., trennb. ist -ge-*) *umg.*: **(es) geht klar!** it's OK (*od.* okay); **ist alles klargegangen?** did it all go smoothly (*od.* OK)?

Klärgrube *f* cesspit

Klarheit *f* **1.** *des Himmels, der Sicht etc.*: clearness; *strahlende*: brightness; (*Durchsichtigkeit*) transparency; **2.** *fig. geistig*: clarity; *des Stils etc.*: *auch* lucidity; **sich** (*Dat.*) **~ verschaffen** get s.th. clear in one's mind; **alle ~en restlos beseitigt** *umg. hum.* now everything's as clear as mud

Klarinette *f; -, -n; Mus.* clarinet; **Klarinettist** *m; -en, -en*, **Klarinettistin** *f; -,* -nen clarinet(t)ist

Klarisse *f, -, -n*, **Klarissin** *f; -, -nen; kath.* nun of the order of St (*od.* St.) Clare

klarkommen *v/i.* (*unreg., trennb., ist -ge-*) *umg.*: (*mit etw.*) ~ manage (s.th.), cope (with s.th.); (*verstehen*) understand (s.th.); **mit j-m ~** get along with s.o.

klarkriegen *v/t.* (*trennb., hat -ge-*) *umg.* sort out

Klarlack *m* clear varnish

klarlegen *v/t.* (*trennb., hat -ge-*): **j-m etw. ~** explain s.th. to s.o., clarify s.th. for s.o.; **Klarlegung** *f* explanation, clarification

klarmachen (*trennb., hat -ge-*) **I.** *v/t. Naut. etc.* get ready (*zu* for); **II.** *v/i. Naut.* make ready; **zum Gefecht ~** clear the decks for action; → **klar** I 5

Klärschlamm *m* (sewage) sludge

Klarschriftleser *m Computer*: (optical) character reader

Klarsicht|folie *f* cling film, *Am.* plastic (*od.* Saran®) wrap; **~hülle** *f* plastic cover; *mit zwei offenen Seiten*: plastic wallet; **~packung** *f* transparent pack

Klar|spüler *m; -s, -,* **~spülmittel** *n* (liquid) rinse

klarstellen *v/t.* (*trennb., hat -ge-*): **etw. ~** get s.th. straight; **Klarstellung** *f* clarification

Klartext *m* text in clear; **im ~** *fig.* in plain English; **mit j-m ~ reden** *umg.* level with s.o., talk turkey with s.o.

Klärung *f* **1.** purification; *Abwässer*: treatment; **2.** *e-r Sache etc.*: clearing up, clarification

klasse I. *indekl. Adj. umg.*: **e-e ~ Idee** a terrific (*od.* great, brilliant) idea; **das Buch ist ~** the book is brilliant; **~!** *Ausruf*: super!; **II.** *Adv.*: **~ gemacht** brilliantly done; **du siehst ~ aus** you look fantastic

Klasse *f; -, -n* **1.** *Päd.* class, *Brit. auch* form, *Am. auch* grade; *in Klassenbezeichnungen*: *Brit. mst* form; (*Stufe*) year, *Am.* grade; (*Klassenzimmer*) classroom; **2.** *Soziol.* class; **die herrschende ~** the ruling class; **3.** *Wirts.* grade, quality; **4.** *Sport* class; *bes. Fußball*: division, league, *Am. auch* conference; **5.** (*Gehalts-, Steuerklasse*) bracket; **6.** *Qualitätsstufe*: class; **~karte erster ~** first-class ticket; **erster ~ reisen** travel first-class; **man behandelte uns wie Menschen zweiter ~** we were treated as second-class citizens; **er ist e-e ~ für sich** he's in a class of his own; **das war (ganz große) ~!** *umg.* that was (really) great (*od.* fantastic); **7.** (*Fahrzeug-, Führerscheinklasse*) category; **Führerschein ~ B** category B driving licence (*Am.* driver's license) (*for cars and light commercial vehicles up to 3,500 kg and 8 seats*); **8.** *Bio.* class

Klasse... *im Subst. umg.* super ..., great ..., brilliant ...; **~auto** brilliant (*od.* super) car; **~mannschaft** brilliant (*od.* terrific) team; **~spiel** great (*od.* brilliant) game

Klassefrau *f umg.*: **das ist e-e ~** she's a real looker, she's quite stunning

Klassemannschaft *f* brilliant (*od.* terrific) team

Klassement [klasə'mãː] *n; -s, -s; Sport* rankings *Pl.*, ranking list

Klassen|arbeit *f* (class) test; **~ in Mathematik etc.** maths (*Am.* math) *etc.* test; **~ausflug** *m* class outing, *Am. auch* field trip; **~beste** *m, f*: **~(r) sein** be top of the class (*Brit. auch* form)

klassenbewusst *Adj.* class-conscious; **Klassenbewusstsein** *n* class-consciousness

Klassen|buch *n Päd.* (class) register; **~durchschnitt** *m* class average; **~erhalt** *m Sport* staying up; **um den ~ kämpfen** fight to stay up, fight against relegation; **~fahrt** *f* class trip; **~feind** *m* class enemy; **~gesellschaft** *f* class society; **~justiz** *f* class justice; **~kamerad** *m*, **~kameradin** *f* classmate; **~kampf** *m* class struggle; **~keile** *f Jugendspr.* beating up by classmates; **~lehrer** *m*, **~lehrerin** *f*, **~leiter** *m*, **~leiterin** *f* class teacher, *Brit. auch* form teacher; *Am. Highschool*: homeroom teacher

klassenlos *Adj.* classless

Klassen|lotterie *f* lottery in which draws with separate tickets are held on different days; **~raum** *m* classroom; **~satz** *m von Büchern etc.*: class set; **~schranken** *Pl.* class barriers; **~sprecher** *m*, **~sprecherin** *f* class spokesperson, *etwa* form captain, *bes. Am.* class president; **~stärke** *f* class size; **~treffen** *n* class reunion; **~unterschied** *m Soziol.* class difference; *Sport* difference in class; **~verbleib** *m Sport* → **Klassenerhalt**; **~vorstand** *m österr.* (*Klassenlehrer[in]*, *-leiter[in]*) class teacher; *Brit. auch* form teacher; *Am. Highschool*: homeroom teacher

Klassen|ziel *n* required standard for the school year; **das ~ erreichen** *auch* complete the school year successfully, *Am.* pass, *fig.* make the grade; **~zimmer** *n* classroom

Klassespiel *n* great (*od.* brilliant) game

Klassifikation *f; -, -en* classification; **klassifizierbar** *Adj.* classifiable; **klassifizieren** *v/t.* classify; **Klassifizierung** *f* classification

Klassik *f; -, kein Pl.* **1.** classical period (*od.* age); **die deutsche ~** the classical period of German literature; *Mus.* **die Wiener ~** the Viennese classical period (in music); **2.** (*Musik*) classical music

Klassiker *m; -s, -.* **1.** classical author; *Komponist*: classical composer; **die antiken ~** the classical authors (*Künstler*: artists) of antiquity; **2.** *fig.* (*großer Künstler, Autor etc.*) great artist (*Autor*: author, *Komponist*: composer *etc.*) with classic status; **3.** *fig.* (*Werk*) classic; **„Zwölf Uhr mittags" - ein ~ des Westerns** High Noon, a classic western; **~ausgabe** *f* edition of a classic; *Pl.* editions of classics

Klassikerin *; -, -nen* → **Klassiker** 2

klassisch *Adj.* **1.** classical (*auch Mus.*); **~es Werk** classic; **2.** *fig.* (*mustergültig*) classic (*auch Fehler, Beispiel etc.*); **3.** (*herkömmlich*) classical

Klassizismus *m; -, Klassizismen* classicism; **klassizistisch** *Adj.* classical; **Klassizität** *f; -, kein Pl.* classical nature

Klasslehrer *m*, **~in** *f südd., österr.* → **Klassenlehrer**

...klässler *m; -s, -,* **~in** *f; -, -nen im Subst. südd., schweiz.*: **Erst-/Dritt~** first-/third-year (pupil), *Am.* first-/third-grader

klatsch *Interj.* slap!, smack:!; *Brei etc.*: splat!; *ins Wasser*: splash!

Klatsch *m; -(e)s, -e* **1.** *Geräusch*: *Brei etc.*: splat; *ins Wasser*: splash; *Buch etc.*: slap, smack; **2.** *umg. pej. nur Sg.* (*Geschwätz*) gossip, tittle-tattle; (*Plauderei*) chat, chinwag; **~base** *f umg. pej.* gossipmonger, *stärker*: scandalmonger; **~blatt** *n umg.* gossipy rag, scandal sheet

Klatsche *f*; -, -*n* **1.** (*Fliegenklatsche*) fly swat(ter); **2.** *umg.* (*Petze*) sneak; **3.** *Dial. Jugendspr.* (*Hilfsmittel*) crib; **4.** *Sport Sl.* hammering *inf.*

klatschen I. *v/i.* **1.** slap, smack (**gegen** against); *Regen etc.*: splash; *Tuch etc.*: flap; **sich** (*Dat.*) **auf die Schenkel ~** slap one's thigh; **2.** (*Beifall spenden*) clap, applaud; **in die Hände ~** clap one's hands; **lautes Klatschen** loud applause; **3.** *umg. fig.* (*schwatzen*) gossip (**über** + *Akk.* about); **4.** *Dial.* (*verraten*) sneak; **II.** *v/t.* **1.** (*Fliege*) swat; **2.** (*schmeißen*) slap (**an, auf** + *Akk.* on); **3. Beifall ~** clap, applaud; **Klatscherei** *f*; -, -*en*; *umg.* gossiping

Klatschgeschichte *f* piece of gossip, titbit, *Am.* tidbit

klatschhaft *Adj.* gossipy

Klatsch|kolumne *f* gossip column; **~kolumnist** *m*, **~kolumnistin** *f* gossip columnist; **~maul** *n umg.* gossipmonger, *stärker*: scandalmonger; **~mohn** *m Bot.* corn poppy

klatschnass *Adj. umg.* soaking (*od.* sopping) (wet); *Person*: *auch* drenched, soaked (to the skin)

Klatschspalte *f umg. pej.* gossip column

Klatschsucht *f*; *nur Sg.* obsession with gossip; **klatschsüchtig** *Adj.* compulsively gossipy

Klatschtante *f umg.*, **Klatschweib** *n umg.* (old) gossipmonger, *stärker*: scandalmonger

klauben *v/t. Dial.* (*sammeln*) gather, (*Beeren etc.*) *auch* pick; (*sortieren*) pick out

Klaue *f*; -, -*n* **1.** claw, *der Raubvögel*: *auch* talon; (*Pfote*) paw (*auch pej.* Hand); *der Füchse, Wölfe etc.*: foot; **in j-s ~n geraten** *fig.* fall into s.o.'s clutches; **die ~n des Todes** the jaws of death; **2.** *umg.* (*schlechte Handschrift*) scrawl; **was ist denn das für e-e ~?** what a dreadful scrawl; **3.** *Tech.* claw

klauen *umg.* **I.** *v/t.* steal, pinch, snitch, swipe; **II.** *v/i.* steal (things)

Klauenfuß *m* claw foot

Klause *f*; -, -*n* **1.** (*Einsiedelei*) retreat, hermitage; (*Zelle*) cell; *umg.* (*Bude*) den; **2.** (*Bergpass*) defile, pass

Klausel *f*; -, -*n*; *Jur.* clause; (*Vorbehalt*) proviso; (*Bedingung*) stipulation

Klausner *m*; -*s*, -, **~in** *f*; -, -*nen* hermit, recluse

Klaustrophobie *f* claustrophobia

Klausur *f*; -, -*en* **1.** *Univ., Päd.* written test, exam(ination); **e-e Klausur schreiben** do a written test (*od.* examination under examination conditions); **2.** *kirchl., Ort*: enclosure; (*Abgeschlossenheit*) seclusion; **in ~ tagen** meet in private; **~arbeit** *f* exam(ination) paper; **~tagung** *f* closed conference (*od.* meeting); **dreitägige ~** three-day retreat

Klaviatur *f*; -, -*en* **1.** *Mus.* keyboard; (*Tasten*) keys *Pl.*; *Orgel*: *auch* manual; **2.** *fig.* (*ganze Skala*) whole range (*od.* gamut)

Klavichord *n*; -(*e*)*s*, -*e*; *Mus.* clavichord

Klavier *n*; -*s*, -*e*; *Mus.* **1.** piano; **~ spielen** (**können**) play the piano; **am ~:** ... with ... at the piano, accompanied by ...; **2.** *hist., fachspr.* (*Tasteninstrument*) keyboard instrument; **das Wohltemperierte ~** *hist.* the Well-Tempered Clavier; **~abend** *m* piano recital; **~auszug** *m* piano score; **~bauer** *m*, **~bauerin** *f*; -, -*nen* piano maker; **~begleitung** *f* piano accompaniment; **~duo** *n* piano

duet; **~hocker** *m* piano stool; **~konzert** *n* piano recital; (*Stück*) piano concerto; **~lehrer** *m*, **~lehrerin** *f* piano teacher; **~musik** *f* piano music; **~quartett** *n* piano quartet; **~saite** *f* piano string; **~schule** *f Übungsbuch*: piano tutor; **~sonate** *f* piano sonata; **~spiel** *n* piano playing; **~spieler** *m*, **~spielerin** *f* piano player; (*Pianist[in]*) pianist; **~stimmer** *m*, **~stimmerin** *f*; -, -*nen* piano tuner; **~stück** *n* piano piece, piece for piano; **~stuhl** *m* piano stool; **~stunde** *f* piano lesson; **~unterricht** *m* piano lessons *Pl.*

Klebe *f*; -, -*n* **1.** *umg.* glue; **2.** *Fußball Sl.*: **e-e starke linke/rechte ~ haben** have a powerful left/right foot

Klebe|band *n* adhesive (*od.* sticky) tape; **~bindung** *f Druck.* perfect binding; **~folie** *f* adhesive foil; **~mittel** *n* adhesive

kleben I. *v/i.* **1.** stick, *altm. und geh.* cleave (**an** + *Dat.* to); **an j-m ~** *fig.* cling to s.o. (like a leech), *Sport* mark (*Am.* guard) s.o. very closely; **an s-m Posten / am Geld ~** cling to one's job/ money; **am Buchstaben ~** stick to the letter (of the law); **sie klebte den ganzen Abend an i-m Stuhl** she didn't budge from her chair all evening; **an j-s Stoßstange ~** tailgate s.o., stick on s.o.'s tail; **~ bleiben** get stuck (*auch fig.*); stay stuck (**an** + *Dat.* to); *umg. Schüler*: stay down, repeat a year, *Am.* flunk; **das wird an ihm ~ bleiben** he won't be allowed to forget that for a long time; **2.** (*klebrig sein*) be sticky; **m-e Haare ~ vor Schweiß** my hair's (all) sticky with sweat; **m-e Schuhe ~ vor Dreck** my shoes are plastered with mud; **3.** *umg. altm.* (*Sozialversicherung bezahlen*) get one's national insurance stamps; **II.** *v/t.* **1.** stick; *mit Klebstoff*: glue; (*Film*) splice; **2.** *j-m e-e ~* *umg.* give s.o. a belt (*od.* clout), land s.o. one

Kleber *m*; -*s*, - **1.** glue; **2.** *Bot.* gluten

Klebe|stelle *f* → **Klebstelle**; **~stift** *m* glue stick; **~streifen** *m* → **Klebstreifen**; **~verband** *m* adhesive dressing; **~zettel** *m* adhesive label

Kleb|festigkeit *f* adhesive strength, sticking power; **~mittel** *n* adhesive

klebrig *Adj.* sticky

Kleb|stelle *f* joint; *Film*: splice; **~stoff** *m* glue; (*Kleister*) paste; **~streifen** *m* **1.** sticky (*od.* adhesive) tape; *Brit., durchscheinender*: Sellotape®; **2.** *auf Umschlag etc.*: adhesive strip

Kleckerei *f*; -, -*en*; *umg.* making a mess; *beim Essen*: messy eating

Kleckerfritze *m*; -*n*, -*n*; *umg.* mucky pup, *Am.* slob

Kleckerkram *m umg. pej.* dribs and drabs *Pl.*

kleckern *umg.* **I.** *v/i.* **1.** (*hat gekleckert*) make a mess; **2.** (*ist*) *Farbe*: drip (**auf** + *Akk.* on); *Suppe etc.*: spill (on); **3.** (*hat*) *fig. Arbeit*: go (*od.* come) in fits and starts; **4.** → **klotzen**; **II.** *v/t.* (*hat*) (*Suppe etc.*) spill (**auf** + *Akk.* on); (*Farbe*) splash (on); (*Eiscreme etc.*) drip (on)

kleckerweise *Adv.* in dribs and drabs; *arbeiten etc.*: in fits and starts

Klecks *m*; -*es*, -*e* **1.** (*Fleck*) mark, stain, blotch; (*Tintenfleck*) blot; **2.** *umg.* (*kleine Menge*) blob; **~bild** *n Psych.* inkblot

klecksen I. *v/i.* **1.** make a mess (*Fleck*: stain); *durch Schütten*: spill something; *Füller*: make a blot; **2.** *umg.* (*schlecht malen*) daub; **II.** *v/t.* splash; (*Farbe*)

daub; (*Marmelade, Butter etc.*) slap (**auf** + *Akk.* on); **Kleckser** *m*; -*s*, -; *umg.* **1.** *pej.* (*Mensch*) mucky pup, *Am.* slob; (*Maler*) dauber; **2.** → **Klecks**; **Kleckserei** *f*; -, -*en*; *umg.* **1.** *nur Sg.* making a mess (*Flecke*: stains, *mit Tinte*: blots); *mit Farbe*: daubing; **2.** mass of stains (*mit Tinte*: blots, *mit Farbe*: daubs); **3.** (*schlechte Malerei*) daub

Klee *m*; -*s*, *kein Pl.* clover; **über den grünen ~ loben** *umg.* praise to the skies

Kleeblatt *n* **1.** cloverleaf; *irisches Nationalzeichen*: shamrock; **vierblättriges ~** four-leaf(ed) (*od.* -leaved) clover; **2.** *fig.* threesome, trio; **3.** (*Straßenkreuzung*) cloverleaf (junction)

Klee|feld *n* field of clover; **~salz** *n* salt of sorrel

Klei *m*; -(*e*)*s*, *kein Pl.*; *Dial.* clay

Kleiber *m*; -*s*, - *Orn.* nuthatch

Kleid *n*; -(*e*)*s*, -*er* **1.** dress; **die Natur trägt ein weißes ~** *fig.* nature is wearing a mantle of snow *lit.*; **2.** **~er** (*Kleidung*) clothes; **~er machen Leute** clothes make the man; what you wear says who you are; **3.** *Jägerspr.* (*Gefieder*) plumage; (*Fell*) coat; **Kleidchen** *n* little dress; *umg. leichtes*: simple sleeveless dress

kleiden I. *v/t.* **1.** dress; **sie ist immer korrekt gekleidet** she always wears the right clothes (for the occasion); **j-n** (**gut**) **~** suit s.o.; **2. in Worte ~** *fig.* put into words, express; **etw. in schöne Worte ~** express s.th. in fine language; **II.** *v/refl. dress*; **sich modern/leicht** *etc.* **~** wear fashionable/thin *etc.* clothes

Kleider|ablage *f* coat rack, (*Ständer*) coat stand; (*Raum*) cloakroom, *Am.* checkroom; **~bad** *n* basic dry clean(ing); **~bügel** *m* clothes (*od.* coat) hanger; **~bürste** *f* clothes brush; **~haken** *m* coat hook; **~kammer** *f bes. Mil.* clothing store; **~kasten** *m südd., österr.* wardrobe; **~laus** *f Zool.* clothes louse; **~motte** *f Zool.* clothes moth; **~ordnung** *f hist.* dress regulations *Pl.*; **~sack** *m* garment bag; **~sammlung** *f* old clothes collection; **in die ~ geben** give to the people collecting old clothes for charity, *Am. etwa* give to Goodwill; **~schrank** *m* wardrobe; *umg. fig.* (*großer Mann*) gorilla, great hulk (of a man); **~ständer** *m* coat stand; *im Kaufhaus*: clothes rack

kleidsam *Adj.* becoming; **der Hut/die Frisur ist sehr ~** *auch* the hat looks really good on you/the hairstyle really suits you; **ein ~er Mantel** a coat that really does something for you

Kleidung *f* clothes *Pl.*; *lit. mst iro.* garb; *förm.* attire; *für e-n bestimmten Zweck*: *auch* gear; **Nahrung und ~** food and clothing; **warme ~** warm clothing (*od.* clothes); **schützende ~** protective clothing (*od.* gear); **Kleidungsstück** *n* piece (*od.* article) of clothing; *Pl. auch* clothing *Sg.*

Kleie *f*; -, -*n* bran

klein I. *Adj.* **1.** small (*auch ~gewachsen*); *bes. attr. und gefühlsbetont*: little; (*winzig*) tiny; *Finger, Zehe*: little; *Buchstabe*: small; **ein rundlicher ~er Mann** a chubby little man; **sie ist von uns allen die Kleinste** she is the smallest of us; **als ich noch ~ war** when I was a little boy (*od.* girl); **er ist doch noch ~** he's only small (*od.* a child); *zu e-m Kind*: he's much smaller than you, remember; **von ~ auf** from an early age, since childhood, since I was *etc.* a child; **~e Augen haben** (*müde aussehen*) look tired; **da wurde er ganz ~** *fig.* that cut him down to size; (*er schwieg dann*) that shut him up; **könnt ihr euch ~ machen?** *fig.* can you make yourselves thin (*od.* squeeze up a bit)?; **2.** (*unbedeutend*) small (*auch Stimme*); *Fehler, Vergehen etc.*: little, minor; **~e Rolle** small (*od.* bit) part; **~er Geschäftsmann** small businessman; **der ~e Mann** the man in the street; **~e Leute** ordinary people; **aus ~en Verhältnissen stammen** come from a humble background; **3.** (*jünger*) little, younger; **meine ~e Schwester** my little (*od.* younger) sister; **4.** *Pause, Unterbrechung etc.*: short, brief; **5.** (*gering*) small; **auf ~er Flamme kochen** cook on a low flame; **x ist kleiner als 10** *Math.* x is less than 10; **6.** **im Kleinen** on a small scale, *engS.* in miniature; **bis ins Kleinste** down to the last detail; **7.** *Mus.*: **~e Terz** *etc.* minor third *etc.*; **8.** *in Wendungen*: *umg.*: **es ~ haben** (*Betrag*) have the right change; **~, aber fein** good things come in small packages; **~, aber oho!** *umg.* a mighty midget, *Person: auch* a pocket dynamo; → **Geschäft** 6, **Übel**; **II.** *Adv.* **1.** small; **~ gedruckt** in small print; → *auch* **Kleingedruckte**; **~ gehackt** finely chopped; **~ hacken** chop (up) fine; **~ machen** (*Holz*) chop up; (*Geldschein*) change; **~ schneiden** (*Holz, Fleisch etc.*) cut up into small pieces; (*auf*) **~ drehen/stellen** (*Herd etc.*) turn down, put on low; **2.** *fig.*: **~ anfangen** start off small, start from small beginnings; **Höflichkeit etc. wird bei ihr klein geschrieben** politeness *etc.* is not one of her priorities; → **kleinschreiben**; **~ machen** *Kinderspr.* do number one

Klein|aktionär *m*, **~aktionärin** *f* small shareholder; **~anzeige** *f* small (*od.* classified) advertisement; **~arbeit** *f* finicky work; **in mühevoller ~** painstakingly

kleinasiatisch *Adj.* of (*od.* from) Asia Minor; **Kleinasien** (*n*) *Geog.* Asia Minor

Klein|bahn *f* light rail(way); *schmalspurig*: narrow-gauge railway (*Am.* railroad); **~bauer** *m* small farmer

kleinbekommen *v/t.* → **kleinkriegen**

Klein|betrieb *m* small business; **landwirtschaftlicher ~** smallholding; **~bildfilm** *m* 35 mm film; **~bildkamera** *f* 35 mm camera, miniature camera; **~buchstabe** *m* small (*Druck.* lower case, *Am.* lowercase) letter

Kleinbürger *m*, **~in** *f* petty (*od.* petit) bourgeois; **kleinbürgerlich** *Adj.* petty (*od.* petit) bourgeois; **Kleinbürgertum** *n* petty bourgeoisie

Kleinbus *m* minibus

Kleindarsteller *m*, **~in** *f* bit part actor

kleindeutsch *Adj. hist. Reich, Lösung*: without Austria

Kleine¹ *m*, *f*, *-n*, *-n* **1.** **der/die ~** the little boy/girl; **die ~n** the little ones; *allg.* (*Kinder*) the children, *umg.* the kids; **unser ~r / unsere ~** our little boy/girl; (*jüngster/jüngste*) our little son/ daughter; **2.** *umg. Erwachsene(r)*: **m-e ~** (*Freundin*) my girl; **e-e süße ~** a sweetie; **na, ~(r)!** hi, darling!

Kleine² *n*; *-n*, *-n umg.* little thing; *bes. mitleidig*: little mite

Kleineleutemllieu *n* kitchen-sink (*Am.* homespun) setting

kleinerentells *Adv.* to a smaller extent

Klein|familie *f* nuclear family; **~format** *n*: **... im ~** small-size ...; *Buch, Foto*:

small-format ...; fig. Veranstaltung etc.: small-scale, mini-...; **~garten** *m* (separate) garden plot (*with a hut*), *Brit. etwa* allotment; **~gärtner** *m*, **~gärtnerin** *f etwa* allotment holder; **~gebäck** *n* (fancy) biscuits *Pl., Am.* cookies *Pl.*; **~gedruckte** *n*: **das ~** the small (*bes. Am.* fine) print

Kleingeist *m* small-minded person, small mind; **kleingeistig** *Adj.* small-minded, petty

Kleingeld *n* (small) change; **das nötige ~ haben** *iro.* größere Summe: have the necessary, *hum.* have enough pennies

kleingewachsen *Adj.* small, short; → **kleinwüchsig**

Kleingewerbe *n* small trade; *Koll.* small-scale industries *Pl.*

kleingläubig *Adj.* faint-hearted; (*zweifelnd*) doubting, scep|tical (*Am.* skep-); **Kleingläubigkeit** *f* faint-heartedness; (*zweifelnde Art*) scep|tical (*Am.* skep-) nature

Kleingolf *n* minigolf, *Am.* miniature golf

klein hacken → **klein** II 1

Kleinhandel *m* retail trade

Kleinheit *f* smallness

Klein|hirn *n Anat.* cerebellum; **~holz** *n* firewood; **aus etw./j-m ~ machen** *umg. fig.* smash s.th. to pieces / beat s.o. to a pulp

Kleinigkeit *f*; *-, -en* **1.** (*kleine Sache*) little thing, trifle; (*Einzelheit*) (mere) detail; (*Geschenk, Imbiss*) little something; **musst du bei jeder ~ heulen?** do you have to cry about every little thing?; **ich habe e-e ~ für dich** I've got a little something for you; **e-e ~ essen** have a little something (*od.* a bite) to eat; **2.** **e-e ~ zu lang** a little bit (*od.* a tad, a smidgin/smidgen) too long, a little bit on the long side; **es kostet die ~ von zwei Millionen Dollar** *iro.* it costs a little matter (*od.* the mere trifle) of two million dollars; **3.** (*etwas Leichtes*) **das ist e-e ~ (für dich)** that's a simple matter (for you), you can easily manage that; **das war für sie keine ~** that was no small matter (*od.* quite something) for her

Kleinigkeitskrämer *m*, **~in** *f* pettifogging (*od.* pedantic) fusspot (*Am.* fussbudget)

Kleinkaliber *n* small bore; **~gewehr** *n* small-bore rifle; **~schießen** *n* small-bore shooting

kleinkalibrig *Adj.* small-bore ...

kleinkariert *fig. Adj. umg.* small-minded, pettifogging; **Kleinkariertheit** *f* small-mindedness

Kleinkind *n* toddler, small child; *förm.* infant

Kleinkleckersdorf *ohne Art.*: **in ~** *umg.* out in the sticks, at the back of beyond, *Am. auch* in hicksville

klein-klein *Adv.*: **~ spielen** *Fußball Sl.* play pretty-pretty stuff, pussyfoot (around); **Klein-Klein** *n*; *-s, kein Pl.*; *Fußball Sl.* pretty-pretty stuff, pussyfooting (around)

Klein|klima *n* microclimate; **~kraftrad** *n Mot.* lightweight motorcycle; **~kraftwagen** *m Mot.* small car; **~kram** *m umg.* **1.** (*kleine Dinge*) odds and ends *Pl.*; *pej.* bits *Pl.* of junk; **2.** (*unwichtige Sachen*) trivial matters *Pl.*, trivia *Pl.*; (*Kleinigkeiten*) minor details *Pl.*; **~kredit** *m* small cash loan (*repayable over two years*); **~krieg** *m* **1.** guerrilla war; *Kriegsführung*: guerrilla warfare; **2.** *fig. Streit*: (constant) bickering

kleinkriegen *v/t. umg.* **1.** (*Sache*)

break; (*Person*) cut down to size; **ich lasse mich nicht ~** I won't allow myself to be pushed about (*Am.* around) (*od.* sat on); **nicht kleinzukriegen sein** *Sache*: be indestructible; *Person*: refuse to lie down, keep bouncing back; **2.** (*verbrauchen*) gobble up, get through; (*Geld*) *auch* blow; (*Kuchen etc.*) *auch* demolish *hum.*

Klein|kriminalität *f Jur.* minor offences *Pl., Am.* petty crime; **~kriminelle** *m*, *f* petty offender

Kleinkunst *f* **1.** (*Kabarett*) cabaret; **2.** *handwerklich*: craftwork; **~bühne** *f* cabaret theat|re (*Am. auch* -er)

Kleinlaster *m* pickup truck

kleinlaut I. *Adj.* subdued; *Antwort, Entschuldigung etc.*: meek, sheepish; **da wurde er ganz ~** he became all meek and mild; (*da schwieg er*) that shut him up; **II.** *Adv.* meekly, sheepishly

Kleinlebewesen *n Biol.* microorganism

kleinlich *Adj.* petty; (*sehr genau*) pedantic, nit-picking *umg.*; (*umständlich*) pernickety *umg., Am.* persnickety, fussy; (*geizig*) stingy; **Kleinlichkeit** *f* pettiness; (*Übergenauigkeit*) pedantic attitude; (*Umständlichkeit*) fussiness; (*Geiz*) stinginess

klein|machen *v/t. umg.* (*Vermögen etc.*) gobble up, get through; **~maßstäbig** *Adj.*, **~maßstäblich** *Adj. Landkarte*: small-scale

Kleinmöbel *Pl.* small pieces of furniture

Kleinmut *m* faint-heartedness, timidity; (*Niedergeschlagenheit*) despondency; **kleinmütig** *Adj.* faint-hearted, timid; (*niedergeschlagen*) despondent; **Kleinmütigkeit** *f* → **Kleinmut**

Kleinod *n*; *-(e)s, -e od. -ien*; (*Schmuckstück*) piece of jewel|lery (*Am.* -ry); *fig.* jewel, gem

Klein|plastik *f Kunst* small sculpture; (*Statuette*) statuette; **~rentner** *m*, **~rentnerin** *f* person on a small pension

kleinschreiben *v/t.* (*unreg., trennb., hat -ge-*) (*Wort*) write with a small letter; → **klein** II 2; **Kleinschreibung** *f* use of small initial letters; → **Großschreibung**

Kleinsparer *m*, **Kleinsparerin** *f* small saver

Kleinstaat *m* small state; **Kleinstaaterei** *f*; *-, kein Pl.*; *hist.* particularism

Kleinstadt *f* small town; **Kleinstädter** *m*, **Kleinstädterin** *f* small-town dweller; *Pl.* small-town people; **kleinstädtisch** *Adj.* small-town ...; *von der Provinz*: provincial

Kleinst|kind *n* small child (*under two years old*); **~lebewesen** *n* microorganism

kleinstmöglich *Adj.* smallest possible

Kleinteile *Pl.* small parts

Kleintier *n* small (farm) animal; **~haltung** *f* keeping of small livestock

Klein|transporter *m* pickup (truck); **~verdiener** *m*, **~verdienerin** *f* low earner; *Pl. Koll.* low income bracket *Sg.*; **~vieh** *n* small livestock; **~ macht auch Mist** *fig.* every little thing helps; **~wagen** *m* small car; **~wohnung** *f* small apartment, *Brit.* flatlet

Kleinwuchs *m* stunted growth, *fachspr.* hyposomia; **kleinwüchsig** *Adj.* ... of small stature, short, *präd.* small in stature; **Kleinwüchsige** *m*, *f*; *-n, -n* person of small stature, short person

Kleinzeug *n*; *nur Sg.*; *umg. pej.* small

odds and ends *Pl.*; *Gerümpel*: bits *Pl.* of junk; *fig.* minor matters *Pl.*, trivia *Pl.*

Kleister *m*; *-s*, - paste; *umg. fig.* (*Brei*) goo, *pej.* gooey mess

kleistern *v/t.* **1.** paste (**an, auf** + *Akk.* on); **2.** *umg. fig.*: *j-m e-e* ~ paste s.o. one; (*j-n ohrfeigen*) box s.o.'s ears

Klementine *f*; *-*, *-n Obst*: clementine

Klemme *f*; *-*, *-n* **1.** clamp; *Etech.* terminal; → *auch* **Haarklemme**; **2.** *umg. fig.*: *in der* ~ *sein od.* *sitzen* be in a fix (*od.* tight spot); *j-m aus der* ~ *helfen* help s.o. out of a tight spot

klemmen I. *v/t.* **1.** (*quetschen*) squeeze; (*zwängen*) wedge, jam (**hinter** + *Akk.* behind); (*stecken*) stick, tuck (**unter den Arm** *etc.* under one's arm *etc.*); *sich* (*Dat.*) *den Finger* ~ get one's finger jammed (*od.* pinched), jam one's finger; **2.** *umg.* (*stehlen*) swipe, pinch; **II.** *v/i.* stick, be stuck, be jammed; **III.** *v/refl. umg. fig.*: *sich hinter etw.* (*Akk.*) ~ get stuck (*Am.* get one's teeth) into s.th., put one's back into s.th.; *sich hinter j-n* ~ get to work on s.o.

Klemmer *m*; *-s*, -; *Dial. altm.* pince-nez

Klemm|lampe *f* clamp-on lamp; ~**mappe** *f* spring binder; ~**zange** *f Med.* blunt (*od.* clamp) forceps

Klempner *m*; *-s*, - metal worker; *umg.* (*Installateur*) plumber; **Klempnerei** *f*; *-*, *-en* **1.** *nur Sg.* metalworker's trade; *umg.* (*Installieren*) plumbing; **2.** *Werkstatt*: metalworker's (*umg., des Installateurs*: plumber's) workshop; **Klempnerhandwerk** *n* metalworker's trade; *umg., des Installateurs*: plumbing; **Klempnerin** *f*; *-*, *-nen* metalworker; *umg.* (*Installateurin*) plumber; **Klempnerladen** *m umg. fig* (whole) row of gongs, *Am.* chest full of medals; **klempnern** *v/i. umg.* do some (amateur) plumbing

Klepper *m*; *-s*, - broken-down (old) nag

kleptoman *Adj.* kleptomaniac; **Kleptomane** *m*; *-n*, *-n*, **Kleptomanin** *f*; *-*, *-nen* kleptomaniac, *umg.* klepto; **Kleptomanie** *f*; *-*, *kein Sg.* kleptomania; **kleptomanisch** *Adj.* kleptomaniac; *umg.* klepto

klerikal *Adj.* clerical; **Klerikalismus** *m*; *-*, *kein Pl.* clericalism; **Kleriker** *m*; *-s*, - clergyman, cleric; **Klerus** *m*; *-*, *kein Pl.* clergy

Klette *f*; *-*, *-n* burr; *sich wie e-e* ~ *an j-n hängen fig.* cling to s.o. like a leech

Klettenverschluss *m* → **Klettverschluss**

Kletterei *f*; *-*, *-en* climbing; **Kletterer** *m*; *-s*, - climber

Kletter|garten *m* mountain-climbing (*bes.* rock-climbing) school; ~**gerüst** *n* climbing frame

Kletterin *f*; *-*, *-nen* (female) climber

Klettermaxe *m*; *-n*, *-n*: *er ist ein richtiger* ~ *umg. hum. Kind*: he climbs all over the place

klettern I. *v/i.* climb (*auch Bot. und fig.*); ~ *auf* (+ *Akk.*) (*Baum etc.*) climb (up); (*Berg*) climb; *mit Mühe*: clamber (*od.* scramble) up; **II. Klettern** *n*; *-s, kein Pl.* climbing

Kletter|pflanze *f* climbing plant; ~**seil** *n* climbing rope; ~**stange** *f Turnen*: climbing pole; ~**tau** *n Turnen*: climbing rope; ~**tour** *f* climbing tour; ~**wand** *f Turnen*: climbing wall

Klettverschluss *m* Velcro® fastening

klick *Interj.* click; ~ *machen* (go) click; *bei j-m* ~ *machen umg. fig.* click with

s.o., dawn on s.o.; **Klick** *m*; *-s*, *-s* click (*auch EDV*)

klicken I. *v/i.* click (*auch EDV*); **II. Klicken** *n*; *-s, kein Pl.* click; *wiederholt*: clicking

Klicker *m*; *-s*, - *Dial.* (*Murmel*) marble; (*Murmelspiel*) marbles *Pl.*

Klient *m*; *-en*, *-en* client; **Klientel** *f*; *-*, *-en* clientele; **Klientin** *f*; *-*, *-nen* client

klietschig *Adj. bes. nordd.* not cooked right (*Am.* all the way) through, soggy

Kliff *n*; *-(e)s*, *-e* cliff

Klima *n*; *-s*, *-s und Klimate* climate; *fig. auch* atmosphere; ~**änderung** *f* change in climate; ~**anlage** *f* (*Klimatisierung*) air conditioning; *Gerät*: air conditioner; ~**forscher** *m*, ~**forscherin** *f* climatologist; ~**forschung** *f* climatology; ~**gipfel** *m Öko. Pol.* climate conference; ~**kammer** *f* climatic chamber; ~**katastrophe** *f* climatic disaster; *aktuelle*: global warming

klimakterisch *Adj. Med.* climacteric, menopausal; **Klimakterium** *n*; *-s*, *kein Pl.* climacteric, menopause, change of life

Klima|schwankung *f* climatic variation; ~**technik** *f*; *nur Sg.* air-conditioning technology

klimatisch I. *Adj.* climatic; **II.** *Adv.* climatically; ~ *verschieden* different in climate; ~ *günstig* … with a favo(u)rable climate; **klimatisieren** *v/t.* air-condition; **klimatisiert I.** *P.P.* → *klimatisieren*; **II.** *Adj.* air-conditioned; *der Raum ist* ~ *auch* the room has air conditioning (*Am. auch* A/C); **Klimatologie** *f*; *-*, *kein Pl.* climatology

Klima|veränderung *f* climate change; ~**wechsel** *m* change in climate (*auch fig.*)

Klimax *f*; *-*, *-e*; *geh.* climax

Klimazone *f* climatic zone

Klimbim *m*; *-s*, *kein Pl.*; *umg.* **1.** (*Kram*) rubbish, junk; **2.** (*Getue*) fuss; (*auch lautes Treiben*) to-do

klimmen *v/i.*; *klimmt*, *klimmte od. klomm*, *ist geklimmt od. geklommen*; *geh.* climb

Klimmzug *m* pull-up, *Am. auch* chin-up; *geistige Klimmzüge machen umg. fig.* perform mental gymnastics, go into mental contortions

Klimperei *f*; *-*, *-en*; *umg. pej. mit Schlüsseln, Münzen*: jingling; *auf Klavier*: tinkling; *auf Gitarre*: strumming; **Klimperkasten** *m umg.* honky-tonk; *Brit. Sl.* joanna

klimpern I. *v/i.* jingle, jangle; *auf Klavier*: plonk (*schneller*: tinkle) (away); *auf Gitarre*: strum (away); *mit den Schlüsseln etc.* ~ jingle (*od.* jangle) one's keys *etc.*; *mit den Wimpern* ~ *umg. hum.* flutter one's eyelashes; **II.** *v/t. auf Klavier*: plonk (*schneller*: tinkle) through; *auf Gitarre*: strum out

kling *Interj. Gläser*: clink; *Metall*: ting; *Glocke*: ding

Klinge *f*; *-*, *-n* blade; *mit j-m die* ~*n kreuzen fig.* cross swords with s.o.; *über die* ~ *springen lassen* get rid of; (*ruinieren*) ruin, destroy; *Sport Sl.* (*foulen*) take out; *e-e scharfe* ~ *führen geh.* be a hard-hitting opponent

Klingel *f*; *-*, *-n* bell; ~**beutel** *m* collection bag

klingeling *Interj.* tingaling!

Klingelknopf *m* bell push

klingeln I. *v/i.* ring; *es hat geklingelt* there's the doorbell, there's somebody at the door; *in der Schule etc.*: the bell's gone (*Am.* rung); *umg. fig.* the penny's dropped; **II.** *v/t.*: *j-n aus dem*

Schlaf ~ wake s.o. by ringing the bell, get s.o. out of bed; **Klingeln** *n*; *-s*, *kein Pl.* ring; *anhaltend*: ringing; *er hat das* ~ *nicht gehört* he didn't hear the bell (ringing)

Klingel|putzen *n umg.* ringing doorbells and running away, *Am.* (playing) devil-on-the-doorstep; ~**zeichen** *n* ring; ~**zug** *m* bell pull

klingen *v/i.*; *klingt, klang, hat geklungen* **1.** sound; *Metall, Glocke*: (*auch* ~ *lassen*) ring; *Glas*: clink; *die Gläser* ~ *lassen* clink glasses; *mir* ~ *die Ohren* my ears are ringing; **2.** (*sich anhören*) sound; *es klingt verrückt* it sounds crazy; *das klingt wie ein Vorwurf* it sounds like a reproach; *das Gedicht klingt nach Yeats* the poem sounds like Yeats; *das klingt schon besser* that's more like it

klingend I. *Part. Präs.* → *klingen*; **II.** *Adj. Stimme etc.*: ringing, sonorous; *schön* ~*e Worte* nice-sounding words; ~*er Reim* feminine rhyme; → *Münze* 1

kling, klang *Interj. Gläser*: clink, clink; *Glocke*: ding, dong

Klinik *f*; *-*, *-en* **1.** clinic, (specialized) hospital; (*Universitätsklinik*) teaching hospital; **2.** *nur Sg.* (*klinisches Studium*) (practical) hospital training, *Brit. etwa* houseman's (*Amtsspr.* house officer's) training, *Am.* internship; **Kliniker** *m*; *-s*, -, **Klinikerin** ; *-*, *-nen* **1.** (*Arzt, Ärztin*) clinician; **2.** (*Student*[*in*]) houseman, *Amtsspr.* house officer, *Am.* intern; **Klinikum** *n*; *-s*, *Klinika und Kliniken* **1.** *Krankenhaus*: (teaching) hospital (*comprising a group of clinics*); **2.** (*klinisches Studium*) (practical) hospital training, *Brit. etwa* houseman's (*Amtsspr.* house officer's) training, *Am.* internship; **klinisch I.** *Adj.* clinical; *ein* ~*es Semester* a term of (practical) hospital training; **II.** *Adv.*: ~ *tot* clinically dead

Klinke *f*; *-*, *-n* **1.** (door) handle; *die Bewerber gaben sich die* ~ *in die Hand umg. fig.* there was a steady stream of applicants; ~*n putzen umg.* (*hausieren, Vertreterbesuche machen*) sell from door to door; **2.** *Tech.* (*Sperrklinke*) pawl, catch

Klinkenputzer *m*; *-s*, -, ~**in** *f*; *-*, *-nen* (*Hausierer*[*in*]) hawker; (*Vertreter*) door-to-door salesman

Klinker *m*; *-s*, - clinker brick; ~**bau** *m*; *Pl. -bauten* **1.** clinker brick building; **2.** *nur Sg.*; *Naut.* clinker construction; ~**stein** *m* clinker brick

Klinomobil *n* mobile clinic

klipp I. *Interj.*: ~, *klapp* click-clack, *Hufschlag*: clip-clop; **II.** *Adv.*: ~ *und klar* very clearly; *bei Zurechtweisung*: in no uncertain terms; (*schonungslos*) point-blank, straight out

Klipp *m*; *-s*, *-s* clip; (*am Ohr*) earclip

Klippe *f*; *-*, *-n*; (*Fels*) rock; *fig.* obstacle; *alle* ~*n umschiffen fig.* (*Schwierigkeiten überwinden*) negotiate all the obstacles, clear all the hurdles; (*Heikles vermeiden*) steer clear of any difficult topics

Klippenrand *m* rock edge

Klipper *m*; *-s*, - clipper

Klippfisch *m* dried fish, *mst* dried cod

klirr *Interj. Gläser*: clink; *Metall*: clank; *heller*: jingle; *Teller etc.*: clatter

klirren *v/i. Gläser*: clink; *Ketten etc.*: clank, jangle; *Schlüssel etc.*: jingle, *schwere*: jangle; *Teller, Fensterscheiben etc.*: rattle; *Waffen*: clash; *mit den Ketten/Schlüsseln* ~ clank one's chains/ jingle (*od.* jangle) one's keys; **klirrend**

I. *Part. Präs.* → **klirren**; **II.** *Adj. fig.*: ~e Kälte icy (*od.* bitter) cold; ~er Frost sharp (*od.* biting) frost; **heute ist e-e** ~e Kälte *auch* it's bitterly cold (*umg.* brass monkey weather) today; **III.** *Adv.*: **es ist** ~ **kalt** it's bitterly cold

Klirrfaktor *m Etron.* harmonic distortion

Klischee *n*; *-s*, *-s* **1.** *Figur, Vorstellung*: stereotype, *Wort, Mode etc.*: cliché; **2.** *Druck.* (printing) block; ~figur *f* stereotype

klischeehaft *Adj.* stereotyped; *Vorstellung, Wendung*: hackneyed

Klischeevorstellung *f* hackneyed (*od.* stereotyped) idea, stereotype

klischieren *v/t.* **1.** *Druck.* make a block of; **2.** *fig. pej.* make a slavish copy of

Klistier *n*; *-s*, *-e*; *Med.* enema; **klistieren** *v/t.* give an enema to

klitoral *Adj.* clitoral; **Klitoris** *f*, *-*, *- und Klitorides*; *Anat.* clitoris

Klitsche *f*, *-*, *-n*; *umg.* **1.** *Hof*: dilapidated, rundown farm; *Betrieb*: small-time, rundown outfit; **2.** (*Schmierentheater*) shoddy little theat|re (*Am. auch* -er)

klitsch(e)nass *Adj.* → **klatschnass**

klitschig *Adj. Dial.* → **klietschig**

klittern *v/t.* throw together; *Tatsachen* ~ lump facts together (indiscriminately); **Klitterung** *f* lumping together; *Ergebnis*: hotchpotch, *Am.* hodgepodge

klitzeklein *Adj. umg.* tiny (little …); *bes. Kindersprache*: teeny weeny; *hum.* itsy-bitsy, *bes. Am. auch* itty-bitty

Klo *n*; *-s*, *-s*; *umg.* loo, *Am.* john; **aufs / auf dem** ~ to/in the loo (*Am.* john)

Kloake *f*, *-*, *-n* **1.** *Kanal*: sewer; **2.** *Zool.* cloaca (*Pl.* cloacae)

Klobecken *n umg.* loo(*Am.* john) bowl

Kloben *m*; *-s*, *-* **1.** (*Holzklotz*) log; **2.** *fig. Mann*: (uncouth) hunk, boorish type; **3.** (*Eisenhaken*) iron hook; **4.** *Dial.* (*Pfeife*) pipe

klobig *Adj.* **1.** bulky; *Schmuck*: chunky; *Schuhe, Möbel etc.*: *auch* (heavy and) clumsy; ~e Schuhe *auch* clodhoppers *umg.*; **2.** (*ungeschickt*) clumsy; (*grob*) rough, uncouth

Klo|brille *f umg.* loo (*Am.* toilet) seat; ~bürste *f umg.* loo (*Am.* toilet) brush; ~deckel *m umg.* lid of the loo (*Am.* toilet); ~fenster *n umg.* loo (*Am.* bathroom) window; ~frau *f umg.* loo (*Am.* toilet) attendant

klomm *Imperf.* → **klimmen**

Klon *m*; *-s*, *-e*; *Gnt.* clone; **klonen** *vt/i.* clone (**aus** from); **Klonen** *n*; *-s*, *kein Pl.*; *Med.* cloning; **das** ~ **von Menschen** reproductive cloning

klönen *v/i. Dial.* (have a) chat (*Brit. umg. auch* natter)

klonieren *vt/i.*; *Gnt.* clone

Klopapier *n umg.* loopaper, *Am.* TP; *Rolle*: loo roll, *Am.* roll of TP

klopfen I. *v/i.* **1.** knock (*auch Mot.*); *sanft*: tap (**an, auf** + *Akk.* at, on); **es klopft** there's somebody (knocking) at the door; *Bühnenanweisung*: there is a knock (at the door); **j-m auf die Schulter** ~ *anerkennend*: pat s.o. (*od.* give s.o. a pat) on the back; **2.** *Herz*: beat; *stark*: thump (**vor** + *Dat.* with); **II.** *v/t.* (*Fleisch, Kleider, Teppich*) beat; (*Fleisch*) *auch* tenderize; (*Steine*) break; **e-n Nagel in die Wand** ~ knock a nail into the wall; **Schnee vom Mantel** ~ beat (*leichter*: pat) the snow off one's coat; **Beifall** ~ applaud by rapping on the table (*Univ.* desk); **Klopfen** *n*; *-s*, *kein Pl.* knock(ing) (*auch Mot.*); *leises*: tap(ping)

Klopfer *m*; *-s*, *-*; (*Türklopfer*) knocker; (*Teppichklopfer*) (carpet) beater; (*für Fleisch*) mallet

klopffest *Adj. Mot.* antiknock …; **Klopffestigkeit** *f Mot.* antiknock rating

Klopf|käfer *m* deathwatch beetle; ~sauger *m* vacuum cleaner (*with beating action*); ~zeichen *n* tap (signal), knock

Klöppel *m*; *-s*, *-* **1.** *e-r Glocke*: tongue; **2.** (*Spitzenklöppel*) (lacemaking) bobbin; **Klöppelarbeit** *f* **1.** *nur Sg.* (*od.* pillow) lacemaking; **2.** *Erzeugnis*: piece of bobbin (*od.* pillow) lace; **Klöppelei** *f*; *-*, *-en* → **Klöppelarbeit** 2

klöppeln I. *v/i.* make bobbin (*od.* pillow) lace; **II.** *v/t.* make s.th. in bobbin (*od.* pillow) lace; **Klöppelnadeln** *Pl.* lacemaking bobbins; **Klöppelspitzen** *Pl.* bobbin (*od.* pillow) lace *Sg.*

kloppen *Dial* **I.** *v/t.* hit; **II.** *v/refl.* brawl, scrap; **Klopperei** *f*; *-*, *-en*; *Dial.* **1.** hitting; **2.** (*Prügelei*) brawl, scrap

Klöpplerin *f*; *-*, *-nen* bobbin (*od.* pillow) lacemaker

Klops *m*; *-es*, *-e* **1.** *Dial.* meatball; **Königsberger** ~e *Gastr.* meatballs boiled in caper sauce; **2.** *Pl. auch* Klöpse; *umg.* howler, *Am.* blooper

Kloschüssel *f umg.* loo (*Am.* toilet) bowl

Klosett *n*; *-s*, *-s und -e* toilet, *Am.* bathroom, *formeller*: lavatory, WC; ~becken *n* toilet bowl (*od.* pan); ~brille *f* toilet seat; ~bürste *f* toilet brush; ~deckel *m* toilet lid; ~frau *f* toilet (*od.* lavatory) attendant; ~papier *n* toilet paper; ~spülung *f* toilet flush; ~umrandung *f* toilet surround, pedestal mat

Klo|spruch *m umg.* example of (public) toilet graffiti; ~spülung *f* toilet flush

Kloß *m*; *-es*, *Klöße* **1.** clump, clod (of earth); **2.** *Gastr.* dumpling; *aus Fleisch*: meatball; **e-n** ~ **im Hals haben** *fig.* have a lump in one's throat; ~brühe *f*: **klar wie** ~ *umg.* crystal clear

Klößchen *n* dumpling

Kloster *n*; *-s*, *-*; *Reli.* monastery, cloister *lit.*; (*Nonnenkloster*) convent; **ins** ~ **gehen** go into a monastery (*od.* convent); *Nonne*: *auch* take the veil; ~anlage *f* monastery (*Nonnenkloster*: convent) complex (*od.* grounds *Pl.*); ~bibliothek *f* monastery (*Nonnenkloster*: convent) library; ~bruder *m* lay brother; *altm.* (*Mönch*) monk; ~frau *altm.* nun; ~garten *m* monastery (*Nonnenkloster*: convent) gardens *Pl.*; ~kirche *f* monastery (*Nonnenkloster*: convent) church

klösterlich *Adj.* monastic; *fig. auch* secluded, cloistered

Kloster|mauer *f* monastery (*Nonnenkloster*: convent) wall; ~pforte *f* monastery (*Nonnenkloster*: convent) gateway; ~schule *f* monastery (*von Nonnen geführt*: convent) school

Klotür *f umg.* toilet (*od.* loo, *Am.* bathroom) door

Klotz *m*; *-es*, *Klötze* **1.** block of wood; (*Baumstumpf*) stump; **j-m ein** ~ **am Bein sein** *fig.* be a millstone round s.o.'s neck; **2.** *umg.* (*großes Gebäude*) massive lump; **3.** *umg.* (*Rüpel*) lout

Klötzchen *n* small wooden block; *für Kinder*: building block

klotzen *v/i. umg.* **1.** go the whole hog, go all out; (*viel Geld ausgeben*) lash (*Am.* splash) out; ~, **nicht kleckern!** think big!, no half measures!; **2.** (*hart*

arbeiten) slog away, put in some hard graft, *Am.* use some elbow grease

klotzig I. *Adj. Möbelstück etc.*: unwieldy; (*hässlich*) clumsy(-looking); **II.** *Adv.*: ~ **viel Geld** *umg.* stacks of money

Klub *m*; *-s*, *-s* **1.** club; **2.** *österr. Parl.* → **Fraktion** 1

klubeigen *Adj.* … belonging to the club, club's own …

Klub|haus *n* clubhouse; ~jacke *f* blazer; ~mitglied *n* (club) member; ~obfrau *f*, ~obmann *m österr. Parl.* → **Fraktionsvorsitzende**; ~raum *m* clubroom; ~sessel *m* comfortable armchair, club chair; ~urlaub *m* club holidays; ~zwang *m österr. Parl.* → **Fraktionszwang**

Kluft[1] *f*, *-*, *Klüfte* **1.** (*Spalt*) cleft, crevice, fissure; (*Abgrund*) chasm, abyss; **2.** *fig. zwischen Menschen*: gulf; (*Feindschaft*) rift

Kluft[2] *f*, *-*, *Kluften*; *umg.* (*Kleidung*) gear, get-up; **s-e beste** ~ one's glad rags

klug I. *Adj.* clever; *auch Gesicht etc.*: intelligent; (*aufgeweckt*) bright; (*schlau*) clever, smart; (*weise*) wise; *Geschäftsmann, Politiker*: shrewd, astute; (*verständig*) sensible; *Rat*: *auch* sound; **sie ist ein** ~**er Kopf** she's got brains, she's no fool; **es wäre das Klügste zu** … (+ *Inf.*) the best idea would be to … (+ *Inf.*); **so** ~ **wie vorher** *od.* **zuvor sein** be none the wiser; **daraus wird man nicht** ~ it's impossible to make head(s) or tail(s) of it; **ich werde aus ihm nicht** ~ I can't make him out; **der Klügere gibt nach** *Sprichw.* discretion is the better part of valo(u)r; **der** ~**e Mann baut vor** *Sprichw.* the wise man is always prepared; → *auch* **schlau**; **II.** *Adv.*: ~ **daherreden** *umg.* talk as if you know it all, pretend to know all the answers

klugerweise *Adv.* sensibly

Klugheit *f* cleverness, intelligence; (*Weisheit*) wisdom; (*Gewitztheit*) shrewdness, astuteness; (*gesunder Menschenverstand*) good sense; (*Schläue*) smartness

klugscheißen *v/i.* (*unreg., trennb., hat*) *vulg.* shoot one's mouth off *Sl.*; **Klugscheißer** *m*, **Klugscheißerin** *f vulg.* smart arse (*Am.* ass); **Klugschwätzer** *m*, **Klugschwätzerin** *f umg.* know-all, *Am.* know-it-all

Klump *m umg.*: **in** *od.* **zu** ~ **fahren** reduce to a pile of scrap, write off, *Am.* total

Klumpatsch *m*; *-(e)s*, *kein Pl.*; *umg. pej.* junk

Klümpchen *n* little lump; **klumpen** *v/i.* go lumpy

Klumpen *m*; *-s*, *-* **1.** lump; (*Blutklumpen*) clot; (*Goldklumpen*) nugget; ~ **Erde** clod of earth; **2.** *umg.* (*Haufen*) heap; **3.** *Dial.* (*Holzschuh*) clog

Klumpfuß *m Med.* clubfoot; **klumpfüßig** *Adj.* clubfooted

klumpig *Adj.* lumpy

Klüngel *m*; *-s*, *-* **1.** clique, crowd; **2.** *Dial. Bot.* panicle; **Klüngelei** *f*; *-*, *-en* cronyism; (*Vetternwirtschaft*) nepotism; **klüngeln** *v/i.* band together, form a clique (*mehrere*: cliques)

Klunker *m*; *-s*, *- und f*; *-*, *-n*; *mst. Pl.*; *umg.* (*Schmuckstein*) rock; *Pl. auch* ice

Klupperl *n*; *-s*, *-(n)*; *österr., südd.* (*Wäscheklammer*) clothes peg, *Am.* clothespin

Klus *f*; *-*, *-en*; *schw.* (narrow) gorge, ravine

Klüse *f*; -, -*n* **1.** *Naut.* hawse; **2.** *nur Pl.*; *umg. hum (Augen)* peepers

Klüver *m*; -*s*, -; *Naut.* jib; **~baum** *m* jib boom

km *Abk.* (**Kilometer**) km

km² *Abk.* (**Quadratkilometer**) sq km

km/h *Abk.* (**Stundenkilometer**) kph

kn *Abk. Naut.* (**Knoten**) kt

Knabberei *f*; -, -*en* **1.** *nur Sg.* (constant) nibbling; **2.** *mst Pl.*; *zu essen*: nibbles *Pl.*

knabbern *vt/i.* nibble (**an** + *Dat.* at); **daran wird er noch lang zu ~ haben** *fig.* that'll keep him busy for a long time; *noch lange leiden müssen*: it'll take him a long time to get over that

Knabe *m*; -*n*, -*n* **1.** *geh., Amtsspr.* boy; **2.** *umg.* (*Mann*) chap, *bes. Am.* guy; **alter ~** *umg.* old chap

Knaben|alter *n* boyhood; **im ~** as a boy; **~chor** *m* boys' choir

knabenhaft *Adj.* boyish

Knaben|kraut *n Bot.* wild orchid; **~liebe** *f altm.* pederasty; **~stimme** *f* boy's voice, *Mus.* auch treble

knack *Interj.* crack; **Knack** *m*; -(*e*)*s*, -*e* crack

Knäckebrot *n* crispbread; **ein ~** a piece of crispbread

knacken I. *v/i.* **1.** crack; *Fußboden etc.*: creak; *wiederholt: Feuer, Radio, Telefon*: crackle; *metallisch*: click; **mit den Fingern ~** crack one's fingers; **2.** *umg.* (*zerbrechen*) *Zweig, Ast etc.*: snap; **3.** *umg.* (*schlafen*) snooze; **eine Runde ~** get a bit of shuteye; **II.** *v/t.* **1.** (*Nüsse*) crack; **j-m e-e harte Nuss zu ~ geben** *fig.* give s.o. a hard nut to crack; **daran wird er noch lange zu ~ haben** that'll keep him hard at it for a long time; **2.** *umg.* (*Geldschrank etc.*) crack (open); (*Auto*) break into; (*Schloss*) break open; (*Laus etc.*) (*zerdrücken*) squash; *fig.* (*Geheimcode etc.*) crack; (*Rätsel*) solve; **knackend I.** *Part. Präs.* → **knacken**; **II.** *Adv. umg.* extremely; **~ voll** packed, full to bursting

Knacker *m*; -*s*, -; *umg.* **1.** **alter ~** old fogey; **2.** → **Knackwurst**

Knacki *m*; -*s*, -*s*; *Sl.* con, jailbird

knackig *Adj.* **1.** (*knusprig*) *Brötchen etc.*: crisp, crunchy; **2.** *umg. fig.* (*jugendlich frisch*) *Mädchen*: luscious; *Hose, Po*: sexy; **Knackigkeit** *f von Mädchen*: lusciousness; *von Hose, Po*: sexiness

Knack|laut *m Ling.* glottal stop; **~punkt** *m umg.* sticking point, crunch

knacks *Interj.* crack; **Knacks** *m*; -*es*, -*e* **1.** crack, cracking sound; **2.** *umg.* (*Riss*) crack; **3.** *umg. fig.* (*Defekt*) **er hat e-n ~ weg** *gesundheitlich*: his health has taken a bad knock (*Am.* a beating); *seelisch*: he's had a breakdown; **e-n leichten ~ haben** *umg.* be slightly crazy, have a screw loose; **ihre Ehe hat e-n ~** their marriage is on the rocks, there's a rift between them

Knackwurst *f short fat sausage of the frankfurter type, Am.* knackwurst, knockwurst

Knäkente *f Zool.* garganey

Knall *m*; -(*e*)*s*, -*e* **1.** bang; (*Schuss*) *auch* shot; *Korken*: pop; (*beim Überschallflug*) (sonic) bang (*Am.* boom); (*Aufprall*) thud; (*auf*) **~ und Fall** *fig.* just like that, without a word of warning; **du hast wohl 'nen ~** *umg.* you must be off your nut (*Am.* rocker); **2.** *umg. fig.* (*Streit*) big row, flare-up; **~bonbon** *m, n* cracker

knallbunt *Adj.* brightly colo(u)red, *pej.*

gaudy, garish

Knalleffekt *m umg.* sensation; *e-r Geschichte*: amazing part

knallen I. *v/i.* **1.** (*hat geknallt*) bang; *Feuerwerk etc.*: go bang; *Korken*: (go) pop; **mit der Peitsche ~** crack one's whip; **plötzlich knallte es** suddenly there was a loud bang (*Schuss: auch* shot, *Zusammenstoß*: crash); **2.** (*hat geknallt*) *mit e-r Schusswaffe*: fire, shoot; **er knallte wild um sich** he opened fire (*od.* shot out) wildly in all directions; **3.** (*ist geknallt*) **gegen etw. ~** *umg.* crash into s.th.; **ins Schloss ~** *Tür*: bang shut; **4.** (*hat*) *umg.*: **hör auf, sonst knallt's!** stop it, or else (you'll cop it)!; **5.** (*hat*) *umg. Sonne*: **vom Himmel ~** blaze down; **II.** *v/t.* (*hat*) (*schießen*) fire, shoot; (*werfen*) fling; (*hauen*) slam, bang; **den Ball ins Tor ~** slam the ball home; **er knallte ihm eine** *umg.* he gave him a wallop

knalleng *Adj. umg.* pencil-thin; *eng anliegend*: skintight

Knaller *m*; -*s*, -; *umg.* **1.** banger; **2.** (*Pistole*) gun; **3.** *fig.* sensation; (*Sonderpreis*) fantastic (*od.* incredible) price; → *auch* **Knüller**

Knallerbse *f etwa* cap bomb

Knallerei *f*; -, -*en*; *umg.* (*Schüsse, Feuerwerk*) banging; (*Korken*) popping

Knall|frosch *m* jumping jack; **~gas** *n Chem.* oxyhydrogen

knall|gelb *Adj. umg.* vivid yellow; **~hart** *umg.* **I.** *Adj.* (as) hard as rock; *Mensch*: (as) hard as nails; (*brutal*) ruthless; *Gegner, Geschäft, Arbeit etc.*: really tough; *Schlag*: crushing, knockout; *Aufschlag*: scorching; *Kritik etc.*: ruthless, unsparing; **~er Bursche** real tough guy; **der Film** *etc.* **ist ~** the film *etc.* doesn't pull any punches; **II.** *Adv.*: *schießen, aufschlagen* with great ferocity; **~ fragen** put searching (*od.* penetrating) questions; **j-m etw. ~ sagen** put s.th. to s.o. starkly (*od.* in unsparing terms); **~heiß** *Adj. umg.* scorching (hot)

knallig *umg.* **I.** *Adj. Farbe*: glaring, loud; *Musik*: blaring; **II.** *Adv. gelb, rot etc.*: glaring …; *heiß*: scorching …

Knall|kopf *m umg.* blockhead; **~körper** *m* banger

knallrot *Adj.* bright (*stärker*: glaring) red; **e-n ~en Kopf bekommen** turn bright scarlet

Knalltüte *f umg.* twerp

knallvoll *Adj. umg.* **1.** jam-packed, chock-a-block; **2.** (*betrunken*) completely sloshed, *Brit.* auch paralytic, pissed (*Am.* drunk) out of one's mind

knapp I. *Adj.* **1.** *Kleider*: (*zu eng*) tight; (*eng anliegend*) tight-fitting; **2.** *Stil*: concise, terse; **mit ~en Worten** in a few words, briefly; **3.** (*kärglich*) mea-g|re (*Am.* -er); (*beschränkt*) limited; *Ware*: scarce; *Gelder*: auch tight; **~ bei Kasse** short of cash, *umg.* hard up; **~ sein** *Lebensmittel etc.*: be in short supply, be scarce; **~ werden** auch run short; **4.** *nicht ganz*: just under; **vor e-r ~en Stunde** barely an hour ago; **5.** (*gerade noch erreicht*) *Vorsprung, Sieg, Niederlage*: narrow; *Ergebnis, Ausgang*: close; **~e Mehrheit** slim (*od.* narrow) majority; **mit ~er Not** only just, *Am.* just barely; **er ist mit ~er Not entkommen** auch *umg.* it was a close shave; **II.** *Adv.* **1.** *bei Kleidung*: **~/zu sitzen** be a tight fit/be too tight; **~ sitzend** tight-fitting; **2.** *formulieren etc.*: concisely, succinctly; *antworten*: tersely; **kurz und ~ gesagt** put briefly, in

a few choice words; **3.** (*kärglich*) **etw. ~ bemessen** give short measure of s.th.; (*Dosis, Ration etc.*) be stingy with s.th.; **das ist ~ bemessen** *od.* **berechnet** that's a bit on the short (*od.* low) side; **m-e Zeit ist ~ bemessen** I'm short of (*od.* pushed for) time; **etw. ~ halten** (*Ware*) keep s.th. in short supply, create a scarcity of s.th.; **j-n ~ halten** keep s.o. short (**mit** of); **4.** *mit Zeit- und Zahlenangaben*: **er starb ~ 65-jährig** he died when he was barely 65; **in/vor ~ vier Wochen** in barely (*od.* just under) four weeks/barely (*od.* just under) four weeks ago; **es dauerte ~ zwei Stunden** it took just under (*od.* not quite) two hours; **der Computer kostet ~ 1500 Euro** the computer costs just on 1500 euros; **5.** (*gerade eben*) only just; *gewinnen, verlieren, entkommen*: narrowly; **der Schuss ging ~ vorbei** the shot only just (*Am.* just barely) missed; **6.** *am Wochenende haben wir gefeiert etc.* **und nicht zu ~!** *umg.* …, and how!

Knappe *m*; -*n*, -*n* **1.** *hist.* squire; **2.** *Bergb.* miner

Knappheit *f* **1.** *an Vorräten*: shortage (**an** + *Dat.* of); **2.** *des Ausdrucks*: conciseness; *e-r Antwort*: terseness

Knappschaft *f Bergb.* miners *Pl.* (*of an area*); *Organisation*: miners' guild; **knappschaftlich** *Adj.* miners' …

Knappschaftsrente *f* miner's disability pension

knapsen *v/i. umg.* skimp, be stingy (**mit** with)

Knarre *f*; -, -*n* **1.** (*Rassel*) rattle; **2.** *umg.* (*Gewehr*) shooter, shooting iron

knarren *v/i.* creak; **~de Stimme** grating (*od.* rasping) voice

Knast *m*; -(*e*)*s*, -*e und* **Knäste**; *umg.* **1.** (*Gefängnis*) clink, *bes. Am.* the slammer; **im ~ sitzen** be in clink (*od.* the slammer); **2.** *nur Sg.* (*Haftstrafe*) time, *Brit. Sl.* auch porridge; **zwei Jahre ~ bekommen** get two years inside, be put away for two years; **~ schieben** do time, *Brit. Sl.* auch do porridge; **~bruder** *m umg.* jailbird

Knaster *m*; -*s*, -; *umg.* cheap(, smelly) tobacco

Knatsch *m*; -(*e*)*s*, *kein Pl.*; *umg.* rumpus; (*Streit*) row, *Am.* dispute; **es gab ~** there was big trouble; **knatschen** *v/i. Dial.* **1.** (*quengeln*) whine; **2.** (*schmatzen*) smack one's lips; **knatschig** *Adj. Dial* grumpy

knattern *v/i. Maschinengewehr*: chatter, go rat-a-tat-tat; *Motorrad*: hammer; *Radio*: crackle; *Fahne, Segel*: flap noisily, drum

Knäuel *m, n*; -*s*, - ball; **ein ~ Wolle** *etc.* a ball of wool *etc.*

knäueln I. *v/refl.* form a solid knot; *Verkehr*: reach gridlock; **II.** *v/t.* wind into a ball

Knauf *m*; -(*e*)*s*, **Knäufe 1.** knob; (*des Degens*) pommel; **2.** *Archit.* capital

Knauser *m*; -*s*, -; *umg.* scrooge, skinflint; **Knauserei** *f*; -, -*en*; *umg. pej.* miserly behavio(u)r, stingy ways *Pl.*; **knauserig** *Adj.* stingy, mean; **~ mit** auch tight with; **Knauserigkeit** *f* stinginess, meanness; **knausern** *v/i.* be stingy, be mean; **mit dem Geld ~** auch be tight with one's money, be tight-fisted

Knaus-Ogino-Methode *f*; *nur Sg.*; *Med.* rhythm method

knautschen *vt/i. umg.* crumple up,

crease

knautschig *Adj. umg.* creased, *Am.* wrinkled; *(zerknautscht)* crumpled (up); **∼er Stoff** material that creases *(bes. Am.* wrinkles) easily

Knautsch|lack *m,* **∼lackleder** *n* patterned wet-look leather; **∼zone** *f Mot.* crumple zone

Knebel *m; -s, -* **1.** *(zum Knebeln)* gag; **2.** *Tech. (Hebel)* lever; *am Dufflecoat etc.:* toggle; **∼bart** *m* Vandyke beard; *Schnurrbart:* waxed *(od.* twisted) moustache

knebeln *v/t.* gag; **Knebelung** *f* gagging

Knebel|verband *m* tourniquet; **∼vertrag** *m* severely restrictive *(od.* draconian) contract *(that is difficult to cancel)*

Knecht *m; -(e)s, -e* **1.** *altm.* farmhand; *(Stallknecht)* stableboy; **2.** *mst pej.* *(Diener)* servant; *(Unfreier)* slave *(auch fig.); hist. (Leibeigener)* serf; → **Ruprecht; knechten** *v/t.* reduce to servitude, enslave; *(unterjochen)* subjugate, oppress; **knechtisch** *Adj. geh. pej.* servile; **Knechtschaft** *f* servitude, slavery, bondage

kneifen; *kneift, kniff, hat gekniffen* **I.** *v/t.i.* *(zwicken)* pinch; *j-m od. j-n in den Po* **∼** pinch s.o.'s bottom; **II.** *v/i.* **1.** *Kleidung:* be too tight, pinch; **2.** *umg. (sich drücken)* back out *(vor + Dat.* of); *feige:* chicken out (of); *vor e-r Aufgabe* **∼** shirk *(od.* duck) a task; *du willst wohl* **∼?** I suppose you want out?

Kneifer *m; -s, -* **1.** *(Zwicker)* pince-nez; **2.** *umg. (Drückeberger)* shirker, *Brit. auch* skiver, *Am. auch* goldbrick; *(Feigling)* chicken

Kneifzange *f:* **(e-e)** **∼** (a pair of) pincers *Pl.*

Kneipe *f; -, -n* **1.** *umg. etwa* pub, *Am.* bar; **2.** *altm. von Studentenverbindung:* drinking evening; **Kneipenwirt** *m,* **Kneipenwirtin** *f umg. etwa* publican, *Am.* barowner; **Kneipier** [knaɪˈpieː] *m; -s, -s; umg.* → **Kneipenwirt**

kneippen *v/i. umg.* take a Kneipp cure; **Kneippkur** *f* Kneipp cure

Knete *f; -, kein Pl.* **1.** *umg. (Knetmasse)* plastic model(l)ing material, Plasticine®, *Am.* Play-Doh®; **2.** *umg. (Geld)* dough, *Brit. auch* dosh; **kneten** *v/t.* *(Teig, Körper)* knead; *(Wachs etc.)* mo(u)ld, work

Knet|gummi *m, n,* **∼masse** *f* plastic model(l)ing material, Plasticine®, *Am.* Play-Doh®

Knick¹ *m; -(e)s, -e* **1.** *(Kurve)* (sharp) bend; *in Draht, Rohr etc.:* kink; *(Falte)* crease; *(Eselsohr)* dog-ear; *im Metall:* buckle; *(Winkel)* angle *(auch Archit.); in graphischer Kurve:* blip; *e-n* **∼** *machen* bend sharply; **2.** *fig. in der Karriere etc.:* downturn *(in + Dat.* in); *vorübergehend:* blip; *im Selbstbewusstsein etc.:* dent; *die hat wohl e-n* **∼** *in der Optik umg. hum.* she must be blind

Knick² *m; -(e)s, -s; nordd.* earthwork surmounted by a hedge

knicken I. *v/i.* **1.** bend; *Knie, Metall:* buckle, give way; **2.** *(brechen)* break, snap; **II.** *v/t.* **1.** bend; *(Papier)* fold;,,*Bitte nicht* **∼**" *auf einem Umschlag:* "Do not bend"; **2.** *(brechen)* break, snap; **3.** *fig. (j-s Selbstbewusstsein, Stolz etc.)* dent, *stärker: (auch j-n)* crush; **4.** *umg. (entjungfern)* ravish; → **geknickt**

Knicker *m; -s, -* **1.** *umg.* scrooge, skinflint; **2.** *nordd.* marble

Knickerbocker(s) [ˈnɪkɐbɔkɐ(s)] *Pl.* plus fours; *kürzer:* knickerbockers

Knickerei *f; -, -en; umg. pej.* miserly behavio(u)r, stingy ways *Pl.;* **knickerig** *Adj. umg.* stingy, mean; **Knickerigkeit** *f* stinginess, meanness; **knickern** *v/i. umg.* → **knausern**

Knick|festigkeit *f Tech.* buckling strength; **∼flügel** *m Flug.* cranked wing; *nach unten geknickt: auch* gull wing; **∼fuß** *m Med.* skew foot

knickrig *Adj.* → **knickerig, Knickrigkeit** *f* → **Knickerigkeit**

Knicks *m; -es, -e* curts(e)y; **e-n** **∼** *machen* curts(e)y *(vor + Dat.* to)

knicksen *v/i.* curts(e)y *(vor + Dat.* to)

Knie *n; -s, -* **1.** *Anat.* knee; *j-n auf den* **∼***n bitten* beg s.o. on bended knees; *auf die* **∼** *fallen* fall to one's knees; *in die* **∼** *gehen* sink to one's knees; *tiefer:* crouch on one's knees; *fig.* go to the wall; *j-n auf/in die* **∼** *zwingen fig.* force s.o. to his *(od.* her) knees; *j-n übers* **∼** *legen umg.* put s.o. across one's knee, give s.o. a good hiding; *etw. übers* **∼** *brechen* do s.th. in a rush, rush s.th.; *mit weichen* **∼***n umg.* with knees knocking; **2.** *(Biegung)* bend; *Tech. (Rohrstück)* elbow, knee

Knie|beuge *f* **1.** *Turnen:* knee bend; **2.** *kirchl.* genuflection; **∼bundhose** *f:* **(e-e)** **∼** (a pair of) knee breeches *Pl.*

Kniefall *m: e-n* **∼** *vor j-m machen auch fig.* go down on one's knees before s.o.; **kniefällig** *altm.* **I.** *Adj.* ... on one's knees; **II.** *Adv.: j-n* **∼** *bitten* beg s.o. on one's knees *(hum.* on bended knee)

kniefrei *Adj.:* **∼er Rock** skirt that ends above the knee *(od.* of less than knee length)

Knie|geige *f Mus.* viola da gamba; **∼gelenk** *n Anat.* knee joint

kniehoch I. *Adj.* knee-high; *Schnee, Wasser:* knee-deep; **II.** *Adv.* up to one's knees

Knie|hose *f:* **(e-e)** **∼** (a pair of) knee breeches; **∼kehle** *f* hollow of the knee; *in der* **∼** *auch* at the back of one's knee

knielang *Adj.* knee-length ...

knien I. *v/i.* kneel, be on one's knees; **II.** *v/refl. (niederknien)* kneel down, go down on one's knees; *sich in die Arbeit* **∼** *umg. fig.* knuckle down (to work), get stuck *(Am.* get one's teeth) in(to one's work)

Knie|reflex *m* knee jerk; **∼rohr** *n* elbow pipe

Knies *m; -es, kein Pl.; umg.* subdued animosity, aggro *(Am.* trouble) under the surface

Knie|scheibe *f Anat.* kneecap; **∼schoner** *m,* **∼schützer** *m* knee pad; **∼sehnenreflex** *m Med.* knee jerk; **∼strumpf** *m* knee sock; **∼stück** *n Tech.* bend, elbow

knietief I. *Adj.* knee-deep; **II.** *Adv.* up to one's knees

Knie|umschwung *m,* **∼welle** *f Turnen:* knee circle

Kniff *m; -(e)s, -e* **1.** *(Kneifen)* pinch; **2.** *(Falte)* crease; *im Papier:* fold; *im Hut:* dent; **3.** *fig. (Kunstgriff)* trick, dodge; *den* **∼** *(dabei) heraushaben* have got(ten) the hang *(od.* knack) of it

kniffelig *Adj. umg.* tricky; *(umständlich)* fiddly; **knifflig** *Adj.* → **kniffelig**

Knilch *m; -s, -e; umg.* creep

knipsen I. *v/i.* take snaps *(od.* photos); **II.** *v/t.* **1.** take a snap *(od.* shot) of; **2.** *(Fahrkarte etc.)* punch; **Knipser** *m;*

-s, - umg. **1.** *Gerät:* click switch; *(Zange)* punch; *(Entwerter)* ticket-cancel(-l)ing machine; **2.** *Person:* ticket-puncher

Knirps *m; -es, -e* **1.** *umg. (kleiner Junge)* little lad, titch, *Am.* nipper; **2.** *pej. (kleiner Mann)* little squirt; **3.** *Knirps®* *(Taschenschirm)* folding umbrella

knirschen *v/i.* Kies, Sand etc.: crunch; *mit den Zähnen* **∼** grind one's teeth

knistern *v/i.* Papier etc.: rustle; *Feuer:* crackle; *mit Papier* **∼** rustle paper; *es herrschte e-e* **∼***de Spannung fig.* the atmosphere was electric; → **Gebälk; Knistern** *n; -s, kein Pl.* rustling; *Feuer:* crackling

Knittelvers *m* doggerel

Knitter *m; -s, -* crease, *bes. Am.* wrinkle

knitterarm *Adj.* low-crease *(Am.* -wrinkle)

Knitterfalte *f* crease, *bes. Am.* wrinkle

knitter|fest *Adj.* crease- *(Am.* wrinkle-)resistant; **∼frei** *Adj.* non-crease, *Am.* wrinkle-free

knitt(e)rig *Adj.* creased, crumpled, *bes. Am.* wrinkled; **knittern** *v/t.i.* crease, *bes. Am.* wrinkle

Knobelbecher *m* **1.** dice cup; **2.** *Pl. umg. (Stiefel)* jackboots

knobeln *v/i.* throw dice *(um* for); **∼** *an + Dat. fig.* puzzle over

Knoblauch *m; -(e)s, kein Pl.; Bot.* garlic; **Knoblauch...** *im Subst.* garlic ...; **∼pille** *f* garlic pill; **∼presse** *f* garlic press; **∼pulver** *n* garlic powder; **∼zehe** *f* clove of garlic

Knöchel *m; -s, -* **1.** *(Fußknöchel)* ankle; **2.** *(Fingerknöchel)* knuckle

knöchel|lang *Adj. Kleid etc.:* ankle-length; **∼tief I.** *Adj.* ankle-deep; **II.** *Adv.* up to one's ankles

Knochen *m; -s, -* **1.** bone; *Fleisch mit/ohne* **∼** meat on/off the bone; *sich (Dat.) die* **∼** *brechen* break something; *mir tun sämtliche* **∼** *weh* every bone in my body is aching; *die od. s-e* **∼** *(für etw.) hinhalten müssen* have to risk one's neck (for s.th.); *j-m sämtliche* **∼** *(einzeln) brechen umg.* break every bone in s.o.'s body; **∼** *bildend Medikament etc.:* bone-building; **2.** *fig., in Wendungen: es ist ihm in die* **∼** *gefahren* it really got to him; *es sitzt mir noch in den* **∼** I still haven't got over it (completely); *sich bis auf die* **∼** *blamieren* make an absolute fool of o.s.; *fauler* **∼** *umg.* lazybones; *harter* **∼** *umg.* toughie; **3.** *umg., Werkzeug:* double-ended ring spanner *(Am.* box wrench)

Knochen|arbeit *f umg.* hard labo(u)r, back-breaking work; **∼bau** *m; nur Sg.* bone structure; **∼bildung** *f* bone formation; **∼bruch** *m Med.* fracture; **∼entzündung** *f Med.* inflammation of the bones; *fachspr.* ostitis; **∼erweichung** *f Med.* softening of the bones; *fachspr.* osteomalacia; **∼fisch** *m Zool.* bony fish; **∼fraß** *m Med.* bone decay, caries; **∼gerüst** *n* skeleton; **∼gewebe** *n* bone tissue

knochenhart I. *Adj. umg.* rock-hard; *fig. Sport* tough as old boots; **II.** *Adv. gefroren etc.:* rock-hard; *fig. trainieren:* very hard

Knochen|haut *f Anat.* periosteum *(Pl.* periostea); **∼krebs** *m Med.* bone cancer; **∼leim** *m* bone glue; **∼mann** *m umg. (künstliches Skelett)* model skeleton; *fig. (der Tod)* (figure of) Death

Knochenmark *n Anat.* bone marrow; **∼spender** *m,* **∼spenderin** *f* bone-marrow donor; **∼transplantation** *f Med.*

bone-marrow transplant

Knochen|mehl *n* bonemeal; **~mühle** *f* *umg.* **1.** sweatshop; **2.** (*Auto*) rattletrap; **~säge** *f* butcher's (*od.* bone) saw; **~schinken** *m* ham on the bone; **~schwund** *m* *Med.* atrophy of the bone(s), osteoporosis; **~splitter** *m* bone fragment, piece of bone; **~substanz** *f* bony substance

knochentrocken *Adj. umg.* bone-dry

knöchern *Adj.* bony, osseous *fachspr.*; *aus Knochen*: made of bone, bone …

knochig *Adj. Person, Gesicht etc.*: bony; **Knochigkeit** *f* boniness

Knock-out *m*; *-(s)*, *-s* knockout; → **K. o.**; **Knock-out-Schlag** *m* knockout blow; **Knock-out-Sieg** *m* win by a knockout

Knödel *m*; *-s*, *-*; *Gastr.*, *bes. südd.*, *österr.* dumpling

knödeln *v/i. umg.* sing (*sprechen*: speak) in a strangled voice

Knofel *m*; *-s*, *kein Pl.*; *umg.* garlic

Knöllchen *n* **1.** small lump; **2.** *umg.* (parking) ticket

Knolle *f*; *-*, *-n* **1.** *Bot.*, *Kartoffel etc.*: tuber; *Zwiebel etc.*: bulb; *Baum*: node; **2.** *umg.* (*dicke Nase*) big fat conk *Sl.* (*Am.* schnozzle); **3.** *umg.* (parking) ticket

Knollen *m*; *-s*, *-*; *Dial.* **1.** lump; → *auch* **Knolle**, **2.** (parking) ticket; **~blätterpilz** *m* amanita; **~fäule** *f* *Bot.* potato blight (*od.* rot)

knollenförmig *Adj.* tuberous

Knollen|nase *f* bulbous nose; **~sellerie** *m* celeriac

knollig *Adj.* bulbous; (*knotig*) knotty; (*klumpig*) lumpy; *Bot.* tuberous

Knopf *m*; *-(e)s*, *Knöpfe* **1.** button (*auch Schalterknopf*); (*Türknopf*, *Knauf etc.*) knob; *auf den ~ drücken* press the button; *etw. an den Knöpfen abzählen hum.* decide s.th. by counting buttons; **2.** *umg.* (*Kerl*) chap, *Am.* guy; **3.** *südd.*, *österr.*, *schw.* (*Knospe*) bud; **~augen** *Pl.* big round eyes; **~druck** *m*: *auf ~* at the touch of a button; *fig. auch* at the flick of a switch

knöpfen *v/t.* button (up); *falsch geknöpft* buttoned up the wrong way; *vorne/seitlich geknöpft Rock etc.* buttoned at the front/side

Knopfleiste *f* button facing; *ein Jackett mit verdeckter ~* a jacket with a fly (*Am.* button-down) front

Knopfloch *n* buttonhole; *aus allen Knopflöchern platzen umg. fig.* be bursting at the seams; *ihm scheint die Neugier aus allen Knopflöchern* he's just bursting with curiosity; *aus allen Knopflöchern stinken umg.* stink to high heaven; *mit e-r Träne im ~ iro.* with a tear in my *etc.* eye

Knopfzelle *f Etech.* round cell battery

knorke *Adj. Dial.*, *umg. altm.* great; *Brit. auch* brill, *Am. auch* awesome

Knorpel *m*; *-s*, *-* cartilage; *in Wurst etc.*: gristle; **Knorpelfisch** *m Zool.* cartilaginous fish; **knorpelig** *Adj.* gristly; *Anat.* cartilaginous

Knorren *m*; *-s*, *-*; *Dial.* knot; **knorrig** *Adj.* **1.** *Baum*: knotty, gnarled; **2.** (*Person*: cantankerous, crabbed; (*mürrisch*) gruff, surly

Knospe *f*; *-*, *-n*; *Bot.* bud (*auch fig.*); *~n treiben* bud; *weitS.* (*sprießen*) sprout; *fig. auch* burgeon; *e-e* (*zarte*) *~ fig. der Liebe*: a tender bud; **knospen** *v/i.* bud, *weitS.* (*sprießen*) sprout; *fig. auch* burgeon; **Knospung** *f* budding

Knötchen *n* small knot; *Med.* nodule

knoten *v/t.* knot; (*Seil etc.*) make a

knot in; *mehrmals*: make knots in; (*Krawatte*, *Schnürsenkel*) tie; *etw. um etw. ~* tie s.th. to/(a)round s.th.

Knoten *m*; *-s*, *-* **1.** knot; (*Haarknoten*) *auch* bun; *e-n ~ ins Taschentuch machen* tie a knot in one's handkerchief; *bei j-m ist der ~ geplatzt fig. umg.* the penny has dropped (for s.o.); **2.** *Bot.* (*Astknoten*) joint; **3.** *Med.*, *in Gewebe*: lump; **4.** *Lit.*, *im Drama etc.*: plot; *der ~ schürzt sich* the plot thickens; **5.** (*Knotenpunkt*) *von Straßen etc.*: junction, intersection; *Handel etc.*: cent|re (*Am.* -er); (*Mittelpunkt*) hub; **6.** *Naut.*, *Geschwindigkeit*: knot; → **gordisch**

Knoten|punkt *m von Straßen etc.*: junction, intersection, *allg.* crossing of the ways; *Math.*, *Opt.*, *Phys.* nodal point; *Handel etc.*: cent|re (*Am.* -er); (*Mittelpunkt*) hub; **~schrift** *f* quipu

Knöterich *m*; *-s*, *-e*; *Bot.* knotgrass

knotig *Adj.* knotty; *Med.* nodular

Know-how [nou'hau] *n*; *-(s)*, *kein Pl.* know-how, expertise, savvy *umg.*; *geschäftliches/technisches etc. ~ Fertigkeiten*: *auch* business/technical *etc.* skills

Knubbel *m*; *-s*, *-*; *Dial.* small lump; **knubbelig** *Adj. Dial.* podgy, *Am.* pudgy

knuddelig *Adj. umg.* (*niedlich*) cuddly; **knuddeln** *v/t. umg.* (*umarmen*, *küssen etc.*) cuddle; *einfach zum Knuddeln* really cuddly (*hum.* cuddlesome)

Knuff *m*; *-(e)s*, *Knüffe*; *umg.* poke; **knuffen** *v/t* poke

Knülch *m*; *-s*, *-e*; *umg.* creep

knülle *Adj. umg.* (*betrunken*) tight

knüllen **I.** *v/i.* (*knittern*) crumple, crease, *bes. Am.* wrinkle; **II.** *v/t.* crease, *bes. Am.* wrinkle; (*Papier*) screw (*Am. auch* crumple) up

Knüller *m*; *-s*, *-*; *umg.* sensation (*auch Meldung*); *Zeitungsmeldung*: *auch* scoop; *Film*, *Buch etc.*: *auch* blockbuster; *Theat. etc.* crowd-puller; *Schlager*: smash hit

Knüpfarbeit *f* (piece of) knotwork

knüpfen **I.** *v/t.* (*Knoten*, *Netz*) tie, make; (*Teppich*) knot; (*befestigen*) tie, fasten (*an* + *Akk.* to); *e-e Freundschaft ~* form a friendship; *s-e Hoffnungen an etw.* (*Akk.*) *~* pin one's hopes on s.th.; *große Erwartungen an etw.* (*Akk.*) *~* have great expectations of s.th.; *Bedingungen an etw.* (*Akk.*) *~* attach conditions to s.th.; **II.** *v/refl.*: *sich ~ an* (+ *Akk.*) *Vorstellungen etc.*: be connected (*od.* associated, tied up) with; *Bedingungen*: be attached to; (*folgen aus*) arise from

Knüpf|technik *f* knotwork technique; **~teppich** *m* hand-knotted carpet

Knüppel *m*; *-s*, *-* **1.** (heavy) stick, club; (*Schlagstock*) truncheon; *mit dem ~ dreinschlagen umg.* use the big stick; *j-m e-n ~ zwischen die Beine werfen fig.* put a spoke in s.o.'s wheel, *Am.* put s.o.'s nose out of joint; **2.** *Flug.* (*Steuerknüppel*) control stick, *umg.* joystick; *Mot.* (*Schaltknüppel*) gear lever, *Am.* gearshift (lever); **3.** *Dial. Brötchen*: long roll; **4.** *vulg.* (*Penis*) willy, *Am.* dick; **~damm** *m* log (*od.* corduroy) road

knüppeldick *umg.* **I.** *Adj.*: *~e Überraschung* real whammy; **II.** *Adv.*: *es kommt immer gleich ~* it never rains but it pours; *when it rains it pours*; *dann kam's ~* then it came thick and fast, then things started happening with a vengeance, then it was just one

thing after another; *er hat's ~ hinter den Ohren* he knows all the tricks of the trade

knüppeldickevoll *Adj. umg.* chock-a--block, jampacked, *bes. Am.* chock-full

knüppelhart *Adj.* rock-hard

knüppeln **I.** *v/t.* beat (with a stick/club/truncheon); **II.** *v/i.* **1.** (*prügeln*) wield a club (*Polizist*: truncheon); *muss die Polizei immer gleich ~?* do the police always have to go straight in with truncheons?; **2.** *Sport Sl.* (*foul spielen*) play dirty

Knüppelschaltung *f Mot.* floor gearchange, *Am.* stick shift

knüppelvoll *Adj. umg.* chock-a-block, jampacked, *bes. Am.* chock-full

knurren *v/i.* **1.** *Tier*: growl; *lauter*: snarl; *fig. Magen*: rumble; *mir knurrt der Magen* my stomach's rumbling; **2.** (*grunzen*) grunt; (*murren*) grumble (*über* + *Akk.* at)

Knurrhahn *m Zool.* (*Fisch*) gurnard

knurrig *Adj. umg.* grumpy

Knusperhäuschen *n* gingerbread house

knuspern *vt/i. umg.* crunch (*an* + *Dat.* at); **knusprig** *Adj.* **1.** crunchy; *Brötchen*, *Braten*: crisp; **2.** *umg.*: (*jung und*) *~* (young and) sprightly, bright--eyed and bushy-tailed

Knute *f*; *-*, *-n*; (*russische Peitsche*) knout *hist.*; *allg.* lash; *unter j-s ~ stehen fig.* be under s.o.'s thumb (*des Unterdrückers*: heel); **knuten** *v/t. fig.* oppress brutally

knutschen *umg.* **I.** *v/i.* neck, *Brit. auch* snog, *Am. auch* make out; **II.** *v/t.* neck (*Brit. auch* snog, *Am. auch* make out) with; *sie knutschten sich in einer dunklen Ecke* they were smooching (*Brit. auch* snogging) in a dark corner; **Knutscherei** *f*; *-*, *-en*; *umg.* necking, smooching, *Brit. auch* snogging, *Am. auch* making out; **Knutschfleck** *m umg.* lovebite, *Am.* hickey

Knüttelvers *m* → **Knittelvers**

k. o. **I.** *Adj.* **1.** knocked out, k.o.; **2.** *umg.* (*erschöpft*) whacked, bushed, *Brit. auch* knackered, *Am. auch* wiped out; **II.** *Adv.*: *j-n ~ schlagen* knock s.o. out, k.o. s.o.; **K. o.** *m*; *-(s)*, *-(s)* knockout, k.o.; *Sieger durch ~* winner by a knockout

Koagulation *f*; *-*, *-en*; *Chem.* coagulation; **koagulieren** *Chem.* **I.** *v/t.* (*hat koaguliert*) coagulate; **II.** *v/i.* (*ist*) coagulate

Koala *m*; *-s*, *-s*, **~bär** *m Zool.* koala (bear)

koalieren *v/i. Pol.* form a coalition (*mit* with)

Koalition *f*; *-*, *-en*; *Pol.* coalition; *große ~* grand coalition; **Koalitionär** *m*; *-s*, *-e*, **Koalitionärin** *f*; *-*, *-nen* member of a (*od.* the) coalition, coalition partner; *Partei*: *auch* coalition party

Koalitionsabsprache *f Pol.* coalition agreement

koalitionsfähig *Adj.* in a position to form a coalition; *~e Partei* possible coalition party

Koalitions|freiheit *f*; *nur Sg.*; *Jur.* freedom of association; **~gespräch** *n Pol.* talk(s *Pl.*) with a view to forming a coalition; **~partei** *f Pol.* coalition party; **~partner** *m*, **~partnerin** *f* coalition partner; **~politiker** *m*, **~politikerin** *f* member of a coalition party; **~regierung** *f Pol.* coalition government; **~vereinbarung** *f* coalition agreement; **~wechsel** *m* change of coalition

Koautor *m*, **~in** *f* co-author

K

koaxial *Adj. Tech.* coaxial; **Koaxialkabel** *n Etech.* coaxial cable

Kobalt *n*; *-s, kein Pl.*; (*abgek.* **Co**) *Chem.* cobalt; **Kobalt...** *im Subst.* cobalt ...

kobaltblau *Adj.* cobalt blue; **Kobaltblau** *n* cobalt blue

Kobalt|blüte *f Min.* cobalt bloom, erythrite; **~glanz** *m Min.* cobalt glance, cobaltite; **~kanone** *f Med.* cobalt bomb

Koben *m*; *-s,* - (pig)sty

Kobold *m*; *-(e)s, -e* (hob)goblin; *umg. fig. imp;* **~maki** *m Zool.* tarsier

Kobolz *m*: ~ *schlagen bes. nordd.* turn a somersault; *mehrmals:* turn somersaults

Kobra *f*; *-, -s; Zool.* cobra

Koch *m*; *-(e)s, Köche* cook; *im Restaurant: auch* chef; (*Küchenchef*) chef; *viele Köche verderben den Brei Sprichw.* too many cooks spoil the broth

Koch|anleitung *f* cooking instructions *Pl.*; **~beutel** *m: Reis etc. im* ~ boil-in-the-bag rice *etc.*; **~buch** *n* cookery book, *Am.* cookbook; **~dunst** *m* haze from cooking

kochecht *Adj. Stoff, Kleidungsstück:* washable in boiling water; *Farbe:* fast in boiling water

Kochecke *f* kitchenette

köcheln *v/i.* 1. simmer; 2. *umg. hum.* have a go at cooking

Köchelverzeichnis *n Mus.* Köchel catalog(ue); ~ *421* (*Abk.* **KV 421**) Köchel (number *od.* listing) 421 (*Abk.* K.421)

kochen I. *v/i.* 1. cook; *für die Familie etc.:* do the cooking; *Speise:* be cooking, *er kocht gut* he's a good cook; *sie kocht zu fett* she uses too much fat (in her cooking); 2. (*sieden*) boil; *gerade:* be boiling; *10 Minuten ~ lassen* boil for 10 minutes; **~d heiß** boiling hot, scalding; 3. (*vor Wut*) *umg. fig.* be seething with rage; *es kochte in mir* I was seething inwardly; **II.** *v/t.* (*Gemüse, Fleisch*) cook; *im Ggs. zu braten etc.:* boil; (*Eier, Wasser, Wäsche*) boil; (*Kaffee, Tee, Suppe*) make; *das Essen ~* get (*od.* cook) the meal; → *gekocht*; **Kochen** *n*; *-s, kein Pl.* 1. cooking, cookery; 2. (*Sieden*) *etw. / fig. j-n zum ~ bringen* bring s.th. to the boil / *fig.* make s.o.'s blood boil

Kocher *m*; *-s,* - stove, (small) cooker, *Am.* range; (*Kessel*) boiler

Köcher *m*; *-s,* - quiver; *Fot.* lens case

Kocherei *f*; *-, kein Pl.*; *umg., mst pej.* (endless) cooking

koch|fertig *Adj.* ready to cook, (ready) prepared; (*ofenfertig*) oven-ready; *in Vakuumtüte etc.:* boil-in-the-bag ...; **~fest** *Adj.* washable in boiling water, boil-wash ...

Koch|flasche *f Chem.* boiling flask; **~gelegenheit** *f* cooking means; *e-e/keine* ~ *haben* have something/ nothing to cook on; **~geschirr** *n* cooking (*od.* kitchen) utensils *Pl. od.* things *Pl.*; *Mil.* mess kit; **~herd** *m* cooker, stove, *Am. auch* range

Köchin *f*; *-, -nen* cook; *im Restaurant: auch* chef; (*Küchenchefin*) chef

Koch|käse *m* soft cheese made of quark (*Am.* farmer cheese), *salt and spices*; **~kunst** *f* cookery, (art of) cooking, cuisine; **~kurs** *m,* **~kursus** *m* cookery (*Am.* cooking) course; **~löffel** *m* wooden spoon; *den ~ schwingen hum.* do the cooking; **~mulde** *f fachspr.* hob unit, *Am.* cooktop; **~müt-**

ze *f* chef's hat; **~nische** *f* kitchenette; **~platte** *f* hot plate; (*Kocher*) small (electric) stove; **~rezept** *n* recipe

Kochsalz *n* common salt; *Chem.* sodium chloride; **kochsalzarm I.** *Adj.* low in salt; **II.** *Adv.:* ~ *kochen* use little salt in one's cooking; **Kochsalzlösung** *f* saline solution

Koch|schinken *m* boiled ham; **~stelle** *f* 1. *im Freien:* campfire hearth; 2. (*Kochplatte*) hot plate; **~topf** *m* saucepan; **~wäsche** *f; nur Sg.* boil wash; **~wasser** *n; nur Sg.* cooking water; **~wurst** *f* cooked sausage (*which is reheated before eating*); **~zeit** *f* cooking time

Koda *f*; *-, -s; Mus.* coda

Kode *m*; *-s, -s* code

Kodein *n*; *-s, kein Pl.*; *Pharm.* codeine

Köder *m*; *-s,* - bait (*auch fig.*); **Köderfisch** *m* bait fish; **ködern** *v/t.* bait; *fig.* lure, entice; **Köderwurm** *m* lugworm, lobworm

Kodex *m*; *-es und -, -e und Kodizes* 1. *hist.* codex, manuscript; 2. *Jur.* code; (*Ehrenkodex etc.*) code (of hono[u]r *etc.*)

Kodiakbär *m Zool.* kodiak bear

kodieren *v/t.* (en)code; **Kodierung** *f* (en)coding

Kodifikation *f*; *-, -en* codification; **kodifizieren** *v/t.* codify; **Kodifizierung** *f* codification

Koedukation *f*; *-, kein Pl.*; *Päd.* coeducation; **koedukativ** *Adj. Päd.* coeducational

Koeffizient *m*; *-en, -en* coefficient

Koexistenz *f*; *-, kein Pl.*; *bes. Pol.* coexistence; **koexistieren** *v/i.* coexist

Koffein *n*; *-s, kein Pl.* caffeine

koffein|frei *Adj.* decaffeinated; **~er Kaffee** *auch* decaf *umg.*; **~haltig** *Adj.* containing caffeine, caffeinated

Koffer *m*; *-s,* - 1. suitcase; (*Instrumentenkoffer etc.*) case; *Pl. auch* baggage, luggage; *s-e packen* pack one's bags (*auch fig.*); *die ~ packen müssen umg.* have to pack one's bags, get one's marching orders; *aus dem ~ leben* live out of a suitcase; 2. *Straßenbau:* roadbed; **~anhänger** *m* address tag

Köfferchen *n* small suitcase; *für Kosmetik:* vanity case

Koffer|kuli *m* baggage trolley, *Am.* luggage cart; **~radio** *n* portable radio; **~raum** *m* boot, *Am.* trunk

Kogel *m*; *-s, -; südd., österr.* conical peak

Kogge *f*; *-, -n; hist. Naut.* cog

Kognak *m* brandy; → *Cognac*; **~bohne** *f* brandy-filled liqueur chocolate; **~schwenker** *m* brandy balloon

kognitiv *Adj. Päd., Psych.* cognitive

Kohabitation *f*; *-, -en* cohabitation

kohärent *Adj. Phys.* coherent; **Kohärenz** *f Phys., geh.* coherence

Kohäsion *f*; *-, kein Pl. Phys., geh.* cohesion; **Kohäsionskraft** *f Phys.* cohesive force; **kohäsiv** *Adj.* cohesive

Kohl *m*; *-(e)s, -e* 1. *Bot.* cabbage; *fig., in Wendungen: alten ~ aufwärmen umg.* dig up old stories; *das macht den ~ (auch) nicht fett umg.* that doesn't make things any better; 2. *nur Sg.; umg. fig.* (*Unsinn*) rubbish, crap, *Am. auch* garbage; *red keinen ~! umg.* stop talking nonsense; → *auch Kraut* 3; **~dampf** *m umg.:* ~ *haben umg.* be starving (*od.* famished); ~ *schieben* have to be hungry

Kohle *f*; *-, -n* 1. coal; ~ *führende Schichten Bergb.* coal-bearing strata;

(*wie*) *auf* (*glühenden*) **~n sitzen** be on tenterhooks; 2. *Chem., Etech.* carbon; 3. (*Holzkohle, Zeichenkohle*) charcoal; 4. *umg.* (*Geld*) cash, *Am. auch* dough, *Brit. auch* readies *Pl.*; *ich mach das nur gegen ~* I'm only doing it for cash; *Hauptsache, die ~ stimmt umg.* the main thing is the money's right

Kohle|... *im Subst. siehe auch Kohlen...*; **~bürste** *f Etech.* carbon brush; **~filter** *m, n* charcoal filter

kohlehaltig *Adj.* carbonaceous

Kohle|herd *m* coal (cooking) stove; **~hydrat** *n Chem.* carbohydrate; **~hydrierung** *f Chem.* hydrogenation of coal; **~kraftwerk** *n* coal(-fired) power station; **~lager** *n* coal deposit

kohlen¹ *v/i.* (*schwelen*) smo(u)lder

kohlen² *v/i. umg.* (*schwindeln*) tell tall stories

Kohlen|becken *n* 1. *Geol.* coal basin; 2. *Behälter:* brazier; **~bergbau** *m* coal-mining (industry); **~bergwerk** *n* coalmine, colliery; **~bunker** *m bes. Naut.* coal bunker; **~dioxid** *n* carbon dioxide; **~feuerung** *f* coal firing; **~flöz** *n* coal seam; **~förderung** *f* extraction of coal; (*Produktionsvolumen*) coal output; **~grube** *f* coal pit; **~grus** *m* (coal) slack; **~halde** *f* coal dump; **~handlung** *f* coal merchant's (*bes. Am.* dealer); **~heizung** *f* coal-fired heating; **~herd** *m* coal (cooking) stove; **~hydrat** *n Chem.* carbohydrate; **~keller** *m* coal cellar; **~lager** *n Wirts.* coal deposit; **~meiler** *m* charcoal pile; **~monoxid** *n Chem.* carbon monoxide; **~monoxidvergiftung** *f Med.* carbon monoxide poisoning; **~ofen** *m* coal(--burning) stove; **~pott** *m umg.: der ~* the Ruhr coalfield; **~revier** *n* coalfield

kohlensauer *Adj. Chem.* carbonic; *kohlensaures Salz* carbonate; **Kohlensäure** *f* carbonic acid; *ohne ~ Getränke:* still, *bes. Am.* non-carbonated; *mit ~* fizzy, sparkling, *bes. Am.* carbonated; **kohlensäurehaltig** *Adj.* fizzy, sparkling, *bes. Am.* carbonated

Kohlen|schaufel *f* coal shovel; **~schicht** *f* coal bed; **~schippe** *f* → **Kohlenschaufel**; **~staub** *m* coal dust; **~stift** *m Etech.* carbon electrode; **~stoff** *m; nur Sg.; Chem.* carbon; **~stoffverbindung** *f* hydrocarbon compound; **~waggon** *m Eisenb.* coal wag(g)on (*Am.* car)

Kohlenwasserstoff *m Chem.* hydrocarbon

Kohlenzeche *f Bergb.* coalmine

Kohle|ofen *m* coal(-burning) stove; **~papier** *n* carbon paper; **~präparat** *n Med.* medicinal charcoal

Köhler *m*; *-s,* - 1. charcoal burner; 2. (*Fisch*) coalfish; **Köhlerei** *f*; *-, -en* 1. *Ort:* charcoal-burning site; 2. *nur Sg.* charcoal-burning; **Köhlerin** *f*; *-, -nen* charcoal burner

Kohle|stift *m* 1. *zum Zeichnen:* piece of charcoal; 2. *Etech.* carbon rod; **~tablette** *f Pharm.* charcoal tablet; **~verflüssigung** *f Chem.* hydrogenation of coal; **~vergasung** *f Chem.* gasification of coal; **~vorkommen** *n* coal deposit(s *Pl.*); **~zeichnung** *f* charcoal drawing

Kohl|kopf *m* (head of) cabbage; **~meise** *f Orn.* great tit

kohlrabenschwarz *Adj.* coal-black; *von Schmutz: Hände, Gesicht:* black as soot; *jet-black; Himmel, Nacht:* pitch-black

Kohl|rabi *m*; *-(s), -(s)* kohlrabi; **~roulade** *f Gastr.* stuffed cabbage leaves *Pl.*;

~rübe f swede, Am. rutabaga

kohlschwarz Adj. → **kohlraben-schwarz**

Kohl|sprossen Pl. österr. Brussels sprout; ~**strunk** m cabbage stalk; ~**weißling** m Zool. cabbage white (butterfly)

Kohorte f; -, -n; Soziol., hist. cohort

koitieren I. v/i. have sexual intercourse, copulate; **II.** v/t. have sexual intercourse with; **Koitus** m; -, - und -se sexual intercourse, fachspr. coitus

Koje f; -, -n 1. Naut. bunk, berth; umg. hum. (Bett) bed; 2. (Ausstellungsstand) exhibition stand

Kojote m; -n, -n; Zool. coyote

Koka f; -, -; Bot. coca

Kokain n; -s, kein Pl. cocaine

kokainsüchtig Adj. addicted to cocaine; **Kokainsüchtige** m, f cocaine addict

Kokarde f; -, -n cockade; **Kokarden-blume** f Bot. gaillardia

Kokastrauch m Bot. coca

kokeln v/i. umg. play with fire

Kokerei f; -, -en coking plant

kokett Adj. coquettish; Mädchen auch flirtatious, umg. flirty; **Koketterie** f; -, kein Pl. coquettishness; **kokettieren** v/i. auch fig. flirt (**mit** with)

Kokke f; -, -n; Biol., Med. coccus (Pl. cocci)

Kokolores m; -, kein Pl.; umg. rubbish, crap, Am. auch garbage

Kokon [ko'kõː] m; -s, -s cocoon

Kokos|faser f coconut fib|re (Am. -er); ~**fett** n coconut oil bzw. butter; ~**flocken** Pl. desiccated coconut Sg.; ~**makrone** f macaroon; ~**matte** f coconut mat(ting), coir; ~**milch** f coconut milk; ~**nuss** f coconut; ~**öl** n coconut oil; ~**palme** f coconut palm (od. tree); ~**raspel** Pl. desiccated coconut Sg.; ~**teppich** m coconut (od. coir) matting

Kokotte f; -, -n; altm. cocotte

Koks m; -es, -e 1. (Brennstoff) coke; 2. nur Sg.; Sl. (Kokain) coke; 3. nur Sg.; umg. (Unsinn) rubbish, crap, Am. auch garbage

koksen v/i. 1. Sl. take coke; 2. umg. (schlafen) snooze, Brit. auch kip; **Kokser** m; -s, -, **Kokserin** f; -, -nen; Sl. coke addict

Koksheizung f coke-fired heating

Kolabaum m Bot. cola (tree)

Kolani m; -s, -s; Naut. thick dark blue jacket with brass buttons

Kolanuss f cola nut

Kolben m; -s, - 1. Tech. piston; 2. (des Gewehrs) butt; 3. (Flasche, bes. Chem.) flask; Etech. (Birne) bulb; 4. (Tauchkolben) plunger; 5. Bot. spike; (Maiskolben) cob; 6. umg. (Nase) conk, Am. schnoz(zle); ~**blitz** m Fot. flash bulb; ~**fresser** m Mot., umg. piston seizure; **ich hatte e-n** ~ I had a piston seize on me; ~**hieb** m blow with a rifle butt; ~**hirse** f Italian (Am. German od. foxtail) millet; ~**hub** m Tech. piston stroke; ~**motor** m Tech. piston engine; ~**ring** m Tech. piston ring; ~**stange** f Tech. piston rod

Kolchos|bauer m, ~**bäuerin** f hist. collective farmer; **Kolchose** f; -, -n; hist. kolkhoz, collective farm

Kolibakterien Pl. Bio. coliform bacteria

Kolibri m; -s, -s; Orn. hummingbird

Kolik f; -, -en; Med. colic

Kolk m; -(e)s, -e; Geol. pothole

Kolkrabe m Orn. (common) raven

kollabieren v/i. Med. collapse

Kollaborateur [kɔlabora'tøːɐ̯] m; -s, -e, ~**in** f; -, -nen Pol. collaborator; **Kollaboration** f; -, -en collaboration; **kollaborieren** v/i. collaborate

Kollagen n; -s, -e; Bio., Med. collagen

Kollaps m; -es, -e; Med. collapse; **e-n** ~ **erleiden** (suffer a) collapse

Kollateralschaden m Mil. euph. collateral damage

kollationieren v/t. Druck. collate

kollaudieren v/t. österr., schw. Amtsspr. inspect (and approve)

Kolleg n; -s, -s 1. Univ. (Lehrveranstaltung) lecture; Reihe: course of lectures; **ein** ~ **belegen/besuchen** enrol (-l) for/attend a course of lectures; 2. college where mature students can gain university entrance qualification; 3. kath. theological college

Kollege m; -n, -n 1. (Arbeitskollege) colleague; Arbeiter: workmate; Student, Radler etc.: fellow student (od. cyclist etc.); im gleichen Klub: clubmate; 2. umg. als Anrede: mate, Am. buddy, pal

Kollegen|kreis m: **im** ~ among colleagues; **im** ~ **behauptet man** etc. colleagues maintain etc.; ~**rabatt** m trade discount (in publishing)

kollegial I. Adj. helpful and considerate (towards colleagues); (loyal) loyal (to one's colleagues); **das war nicht sehr** ~ **von dir** that was no way to treat your colleague(s); **II.** Adv.: **sich** ~ **verhalten** be helpful and considerate to one's colleagues; **Kollegialität** f; -, kein Pl. helpfulness and consideration (toward[s] colleagues); (Loyalität) loyalty (to one's colleagues)

Kollegiat m; -en, -en, ~**in** f; -, -nen college student on a course for university entrance qualification

Kollegin f; -, -nen → **Kollege**

Kollegium n; -s, Kollegien 1. (Gruppe) group; (Gremium) committee; 2. (Lehrkörper) teaching staff (mst V. im Pl.)

Kolleg|mappe f document case; ~**stufe** f Päd. etwa sixth-form college, Am. junior college

Kollekte f; -, -n; (Sammlung) collection

Kollektion f; -, -en; Wirts. collection, range

kollektiv Adj. collective

Kollektiv n; -s, -e group; (sozialistische Arbeitsgemeinschaft) collective; **im** ~ in a group (od. team); ~**arbeit** f joint effort; ~**bedürfnis** n collective need; ~**bildung** f Ling. collective noun; ~**eigentum** n collectively owned (od. common) property; ~**geist** m; nur Sg. collective spirit, esprit de corps

kollektivieren v/t. collectivize; **Kollektivierung** f collectivization

Kollektivismus m; -, kein Pl. collectivism; **kollektivistisch** Adj. collectivist

Kollektivität f; -, kein Pl. collectivity, collectiveness

Kollektivschuld f collective guilt

Kollektivum n; -s, Kollektiva; Ling. collective noun

Kollektiv|urteil n general verdict, generalization; ~**vertrag** m collective agreement (Pol. treaty); ~**wirtschaft** f (Kolchose) collective farm

Kollektor m; -s, -en 1. Etech. collector; (Stromwender) commutator; 2. → **Sonnenkollektor**

Koller m; -s, - 1. Vet. staggers Sg.; 2. umg. fig. (outburst of) rage; **e-n** ~ **kriegen** lose one's rag, hum. flip one's lid

kollern v/i. 1. Dial. (rollen) roll; 2. Puter: gobble; Taube: coo; Magen: rumble

kollidieren v/i. collide; fig. clash

Kollier [kɔ'lieː] n; -s, -s necklace; (Pelz) necklet

Kollision f; -, -en collision; fig. clash; auch Jur. conflict; **Kollisionskurs** m: **auf** ~ **sein** auch fig. be on a collision course

Kollo n; -s, -s und Kolli; fachspr. item of freight

kolloid Adj. Chem. colloidal; **Kolloid** n; -(e)s, -e; Chem. colloid; **kolloidal** Adj. → **kolloid**

Kollokation f; -, -en; Ling. collocation; **Kollokator** m; -s, -en; Ling. collocator

Kolloquium n; -s, Kolloquien; Univ. 1. colloquium, seminar; 2. (Prüfung) test

Köln (n); -s; Geog. Cologne

Kölner¹ m; -s, - inhabitant (gebürtiger: native) of Cologne; **er ist** ~ he comes from Cologne; **die** ~ the people (od. citizens) of Cologne; **ich fühle mich nicht als** ~ I don't feel I belong in Cologne

Kölner² Adj. Cologne ..., ... of (od. in) Cologne; **der** ~ **Dom** Cologne Cathedral; **der** ~ **Karneval** the Cologne carnival; **die** ~ **Kirchen** Cologne's churches, the churches of (od. in) Cologne

Kölnerin f; -, -nen inhabitant (gebürtige: native) of Cologne; **sie ist** ~ she comes (od. is) from Cologne

kölnisch Adj. Cologne ..., ... of Cologne; **Kölnischwasser** n eau de cologne

Kolombine f; -, -n Columbine

Kolon n; -s, -s und Kola; Ling., Anat. colon

kolonial Adj. colonial (auch Bio., Zool.)

Kolonial|... ** im Subst. colonial; ~besitz** m colonial possessions Pl.; ~**herren** Pl. colonial masters; ~**herrschaft** f; nur Sg. colonial rule

kolonialisieren v/t. colonialize; **Kolonialisierung** f colonialization

Kolonialismus m; -, kein Pl. colonialism; **kolonialistisch** Adj. colonialist

Kolonial|krieg m colonial war; ~**macht** f colonial power; ~**reich** n colonial empire; ~**stil** m Archit. colonial style; ~**warengeschäft** n altm. grocer's shop, Am. grocery store; ~**zeit** f colonial age; **in der** ~ auch in colonial times (od. days)

Kolonie f; -, -n colony (auch Bio.); **Kolonisation** f; -, -en colonization; **Kolonisator** m; -s, -en, **Kolonisatorin** f; -, -nen colonizer; **kolonisatorisch** Adj. colonizing; **kolonisieren** v/t. colonize; (urbar machen) clear and cultivate; (besiedeln) settle; **Kolonisierung** f colonization; (Urbarmachung) clearing and cultivation; (Besiedlung) settlement; **Kolonist** m; -en, -en, **Kolonistin** f; -, -nen colonist; (Siedler) settler

Kolonnade f; -, -n colonnade

Kolonne f; -, -n 1. column; (von Arbeitern) gang; **die fünfte** ~ Pol. the fifth column; 2. von Fahrzeugen: line, stream; (Schlange) Brit. auch queue; Mil. convoy; ~ **fahren** Mot. drive in a queue (od. stream, Am. auch line) of traffic

Kolonnen|springen n Mot. umg. queue-jumping, Am. cutting in (front); ~**springer** m umg. queue-jumper, Am. etwa hotdog; ~**verkehr** m queue(s Pl.) (od. stream[s], Am.

line[s]) of traffic

Kolophonium n; -s, kein Pl. rosin; fachspr. colophony

Koloratur f; -, -en; Mus. coloratura; **~sängerin** f coloratura (soprano)

kolorieren v/t. colo(u)r; (Film) colo(u)rize; **Kolorierung** f colo(u)ring; Film: colo(u)rization

Kolorit n; -(e)s, -e colo(u)r(ing); fig. e-s Orts etc.: local colo(u)r, atmosphere

Koloss m; -es, -e colossus; fig. auch giant

kolossal I. Adj. **1.** colossal, gigantic; Aufgabe etc.: mammoth ...; **2.** umg. Glück, Schrecken etc.: terrific, tremendous; **das war e-e ~e Dummheit** that was incredibly stupid; **II.** Adv. umg.: **~ reich sein** be enormously wealthy; **es gab ~ viel Schnee** there was a collossal amount of of snow

Kolossal|film m screen epic, huge (Hollywood) spectacular; **~gemälde** n gigantic painting; **~schinken** m umg. pej. **1.** → **Kolossalfilm**; **2.** gigantic painting; **~statue** f giant statue

Kolosser m; -s, -; hist. Colossian

Kolostrum n; -s, kein Pl.; Med. colostrum, foremilk, first milk

Kolportage [kɔlpɔrˈtaːʒə] f; -, -n **1.** in der Presse: cheap sensationalism; konkret: sensationalized trash; **2.** von Gerüchten: rumo(u)r-mongering; **~roman** m trashy (sensational) novel

Kolporteur [kɔlpɔrˈtøːɐ] m; -s, -e, **~in** f; -, -nen **1.** rumo(u)r-monger; **2.** österr. (Zeitungsausträger) newspaper boy (weiblich: girl), Am. auch news|boy (-girl); **kolportieren** v/t. geh. (Nachricht, Gerücht) spread, circulate

Kölsch n; -(s), - **1.** nur Sg.; Dialekt: Cologne dialect; **2.** Bier. non-fizzy top-fermented wheat beer brewed in Cologne

Kolumbianer m; -s, -, **~in** f; -, -nen Colombian, weiblich auch: Colombian woman (od. girl etc.); **kolumbianisch** Adj. Colombian; **Kolumbien** (n); -s; Geog. Colombia; **Kolumbier** m; -s, -, **Kolumbierin** f; -, -nen → **Kolumbianer**, **kolumbisch** Adj. → **kolumbianisch**

Kolumbus m; -, kein Pl.; hist.: **Christoph** → Christopher Columbus

Kolumne f; -, -n; Druck. column; **Kolumnentitel** m running title (od. headline)

Kolumnist m; -en, -en, **~in** f; -, -nen columnist

Koma n; -s, -s und -ta; Med. coma; **im ~ liegen** be in a coma

Komantsche m; -n, -n, **Komantschin** f; -, -nen Comanche

Kombi m; -s, -s estate car, Am. (station) wagon

Kombinat n; -(e)s, -e; ehem. DDR collective combine

Kombination f; -, -en **1.** combination (auch Schach, Math., Tech. etc., auch e-s Schlosses); **alpine/nordische ~** Alpine/Nordic combination; **2.** Ballspiele: (concerted) move; (Ballpassage) sequence (od. string) of passes; **e-e tolle ~** a lovely move; **3.** (Kleidung) matching jacket and trousers (Am. pants) (od. skirt etc.) Pl., ensemble, bes. Am. outfit; (Fliegerkombination) flying suit; (Arbeitsanzug) overalls Pl., Am. coverall; **4.** (Folgerung) deduction; **~en anstellen** make deductions, put two and two together

Kombinations|gabe f; nur Sg powers Pl. of deduction; **~möglichkeit** f possible combination; **~präparat** n

Pharm. compound preparation Sg.; **~schloss** n combination lock; **~spiel** n teamwork; **~vermögen** n; nur Sg. powers Pl. of deduction

kombinatorisch Adj. deductive; Logik: combinatory

kombinierbar Adj. combinable; Kleidungsstücke: auch mix-and-match; **kombinieren I.** v/t. combine (mit with); **das lässt sich gut miteinander ~ Kleidung** etc.: they go together very well, Termine etc.: we etc. could combine that very nicely; **II.** v/i. (folgern) deduce; **schnell/richtig ~** make a rapid deduction / come to the right conclusion; **1.** Sport, Ballspiele: **gut ~** play well together; (Pässe aneinander reihen) string together passes, put together good moves

Kombi|wagen m estate car, Am. (station) wagon; **~zange** f: (e-e) ~ (a pair of) combination pliers Pl.

Kombüse f; -, -n; Naut. galley

Komet m; -en, -en; Astron. comet

kometenhaft Adj.: **~er Aufstieg** meteoric rise

Kometenschweif m tail of a (od. the) comet

Komfort [kɔmˈfoːɐ] m; -s, kein Pl. conveniences Pl.; (Luxus) luxury; **mit allem ~ Wohnung:** with every possible convenience, Brit. umg. auch with all mod cons; Auto etc.: with every possible extra

komfortabel Adj. luxurious, luxury ...; Wohnung: auch well-appointed, Hotel: auch good

Komfortklasse f luxury class

Komik f; -, kein Pl. comedy, comic effect; (das Komische an e-r Sache) comic aspect, funny side (an + Dat. of); **voller ~** very funny; **Sinn für ~** sense of the comic (od. of comedy)

Komiker m; -s, - **1.** comedian, comic (beide auch fig.); (Schauspieler) comic actor; **2.** umg. fig. pej. clown; **Komikerin** f; -, -nen **1.** comedian, comedienne altm.; (Schauspielerin) comic actress; **2.** umg. fig. pej. clown; **Komikerpaar** n comedy duo

komisch Adj. **1.** funny; Wirkung, Rolle, Oper etc.: comic; **das finde ich aber gar nicht!** umg. I don't think that's at all funny; **2.** (merkwürdig) funny, odd, strange; **das Komische daran** the funny (od. odd) thing about it; **das kommt mir ~ vor** that seems odd (od. strange) to me; **~er Vogel** umg. oddball type; **mir ist so ~** I feel really funny; **komischerweise** Adv. funnily (od. strangely) enough

Komitee n; -s, -s committee

Komma n; -s, -s und -ta **1.** Ling., Satzzeichen: comma; **ein ~ setzen** put a comma; **kommt hier ein ~ (hin)?** should there be a comma here?; **hier fehlt ein ~** there's a comma missing (od. needed) here; **2.** Math., im Dezimalbruch: (decimal) point; **sechs ~ vier** six point four; **null ~ fünf** (nought) point five; **bis auf drei Stellen hinter** od. **nach dem ~ ausrechnen** calculate to three decimal places; **~fehler** m mistake in the use of a comma

Kommandant m; -en, -en, **~in** f; -, -nen Mil. commander; e-r Einheit: commanding officer (Abk. CO); e-r Festung: commandant; **Kommandantur** f; -, -en commandant's office; e-r Garnison: garrison headquarters Pl. (auch V. im Sg.)

Kommandeur [kɔmanˈdøːɐ] m; -s, -e,

~in f; -, -nen Mil. commander

kommandieren I. v/t. **1.** (befehligen, führen) command, be in command of; (befehlen) (Rückzug etc.) order; **j-n ~ zu** detach (od. detail) s.o. to; **2.** umg. (herumkommandieren) boss about; **II.** v/i. give the orders; **er kommandiert gern** umg. he likes bossing people about (Am. around); **Kommandierender General** Mil. Corps commander

Kommanditgesellschaft f Wirts. limited partnership

Kommanditist m; -en, -en, **~in** f; -, -nen limited partner

Kommando n; -s, -s **1.** (Befehl) command, order; **auf ~** on command; **wie auf ~** as if by command; **ich kann nicht auf ~ lachen** I can't laugh to order (od. just turn on the laughs); **~ zurück!** hold it!; **2.** (Befehlsgewalt) command; **das ~ führen** od. **haben** be in command; **das ~ übernehmen** assume command; **3.** (Abteilung) detachment; (Kommandoeinheit, mit Sonderauftrag) commando (unit); **4.** Behörde: (command) headquarters Pl. (auch V. im Sg.); **~brücke** f Naut. bridge; **~gewalt** f power of command; **~kapsel** f Raumfahrt: command module; **~sache** f: **geheime ~** military secret; **~sprache** f Computer: command language; **~stelle** f command post; **~ton** m commanding (od. peremptory) tone; **im ~** auch in one's sergeant-major's (Am. drill sergeant's) voice hum.; **~wirtschaft** f pej. command economy; **~zentrale** f Mil. command headquarters Pl. (auch V. im Sg.)

Komma|setzung f (rules Pl. for the) use of commas; **~zahl** f decimal (number)

kommen v/i.; kommt, kam, ist gekommen **1.** come; (ankommen) auch arrive; (gelangen) get (bis to); **durch e-e Stadt** etc. **~** pass through a town etc.; **nach Hause ~** come (od. get) home; **wie komme ich zum Bahnhof/nach Linz?** how do I get to the (Am. train) station/to Linz?; **ich komme gerade von der Arbeit** I've just got back from work; **komm schon!** come on!, hurry up!; **ich komme schon!** I'm coming; **na komm schon!** umg. come on(, now)!; **er wird bald ~** he'll be here (od. with you) soon, he won't be long; **da kommt jemand** there's somebody coming; **es ist Post für dich gekommen** there's some post (Am. mail) for you; **spät ~** come (od. be) late; **zu spät ~** be late; und etwas versäumen: be too late; **du kommst an die Reihe** it's your turn; **zuerst** od. **als Erster / zuletzt** od. **als Letzter ~** come first/last; **wer zuerst kommt, mahlt zuerst** Sprichw. first come, first served; **angelaufen** etc. **~** come running etc. along (od. up); **der soll mir nur ~!** (od. **er soll nur ~!** drohend: (just) let him come; **j-n ~ lassen** send for s.o.; **etw. ~ lassen** (bestellen) send for (od. order) s.th.; **wie weit bist du gekommen?** how far did you get?; **es kam mir (der Gedanke), dass** it occurred to me that; **mir kommt e-e Idee** I've got an idea, I know what we can do; **mir ~ die Tränen** tears come to my eyes, my eyes fill with tears; iro. don't make me weep; **das wird teuer ~ / dich teuer ~** umg. it'll come expensive / it'll cost you; → auch **Reihe** 5, **spät** II; **2.** (herannahen) be coming; Gewitter etc.: auch be coming up; Flut: be coming in; *der Morgen kommt* it's nearly morning, it's starting to get light; *da vorn kommt gleich eine Kreuzung* there's a junction (*Am.* intersection) coming up, we're just coming to a junction (*Am.* intersection); *das kommt* (*steht*) *auf Seite 12* that comes (*od.* is) on page 12; **3.** (*geschehen*) *auch* happen; *etw.* ~ *sehen* (*voraussehen*) see s.th. coming; *das kommt mir gelegen/ungelegen* it's a good/bad time (*od.* the right/wrong moment) for me; *wie kommt das?* how does that come about?, how is that possible?; *wie od. woher kommt es, dass* how is it that, how come *umg.*; *das kommt daher, dass* it's because; *das durfte jetzt nicht* ~ it shouldn't happen (now), it shouldn't be possible; *umg.* (*das hättest du nicht sagen sollen*) you shouldn't have said that; *was auch* (*immer*) ~ *mag ...* whatever happens, ...; *komme, was da wolle* come what may; *es wird noch ganz anders* ~ there's worse to come (yet); *das musste ja so* ~ it had to (*od.* was bound to) happen; *es kam, wie es* ~ *musste* the inevitable happened; *es ist so weit gekommen, dass* things have got to the stage where; *es wird noch so weit* ~, *dass er rausgeschmissen wird* he'll be thrown out one of these days; **4.** *umg.*: *wenn Sie mir so* ~ if you talk to me like that; *komm mir ja nicht so frech!* don't be so cheeky, *Am.* don't be such a smart-aleck, I don't want any of your cheek; *komm mir nur nicht mit diesen Ausreden* spare me your excuses; *damit kannst du mir nicht* ~ you don't expect me to believe that, do you?; *komm mir nicht dauernd mit dieser Geschichte* I wish you wouldn't keep going on (*od.* I wish you'd stop pestering me) about that business; **5.** (*e-n Orgasmus haben*) come; *ich komme* I'm coming; *auch unpers.*: *es kommt ihr* she's coming; **6.** (*sich entwickeln*) develop; *wie kommt dein neues Projekt?* how is your new project coming on?; **7.** ~ *an* (+ *Akk.*) (*gelangen zu*) come (*od.* get) to, arrive at; (*bekommen*) come by s.th., get hold of s.th.; (*j-m zukommen*) go (*od.* fall) to; *an j-s Stelle* ~ take s.o.'s place; **8.** ~ *auf* (+ *Akk.*) (*herausfinden*) think of, hit upon; (*sich erinnern an*) think of, remember; *auf eine Summe* ~ come to (*od.* total) an amount; *auf die Rechnung* ~ go (*od.* be put) on the bill (*Am. auch* tab); *auf etw. zu sprechen* ~ get onto the subject of s.th.; *wie kommst du darauf?* what makes you say that?, what gives you that idea?; *darauf wäre ich nie gekommen* it would never have occurred to me; *ich komme nicht darauf!* I just can't think of it; *darauf komme ich gleich* I'll be coming to that; *auf 100 Einwohner kommt ein Arzt* there's a (*od.* one) doctor for every 100 inhabitants; *ich lasse nichts auf ihn* ~ I won't have anything said against him; **9.** *hinter etw.* (*Akk.*) ~ find s.th. out; **10.** *in etw.* (*Akk.*) ~ *in Gefahr, e-e Situation etc.*: get into s.th.; *ins Rutschen* ~ get into a slide (*od.* skid); *das Buch kommt ins oberste Regal / ins Arbeitszimmer* the book goes on the top shelf / belongs in the study; **11.** *über e-n Zaun etc.* ~ get over a fence *etc.*; *über j-n* ~ *Gefühl etc.*: come over s.o.; *Fluch*: come upon s.o.; **12.** *um etw.* ~ lose

s.th.; *durch fremdes Mitwirken*: be done out of s.th.; *ums Leben* ~ lose one's life, die; (*getötet werden*) *auch* be killed; **13.** ~ *unter* (+ *Akk.*) (*e-e Überschrift etc.*) go under; (*ein Auto etc.*) be run over by; **14.** ~ *von Ergebnis*: be a result of (*od.* due to); *das kommt davon!* see what happens?, what did I tell you?; *das kommt davon, wenn du so viel trinkst* that's what happens when you drink so much; **15.** ~ *vor* (+ *Akk.*) come (*od.* go) before; *vors Gericht* ~ *Sache*: come up before the court; **16.** *zu etw.* ~ come (*od.* get) to s.th.; (*bekommen*) come by s.th., get hold of s.th.; *zu Geld* ~ (*erben*) come into money; *zur Ansicht* ~, *dass* come to the conclusion that, decide that; *zur Sprache* ~ come up (for discussion); (*wieder*) *zu sich* ~ come to (*od.* [a]round), regain consciousness; *wie kamst du bloß dazu(, das zu tun)?* what on earth made you do that?; *es kam zum Streit* a quarrel developed; *es kam zu Kämpfen zwischen ...* fighting broke out between ...; *zum Stehen* ~ come to a standstill; *ich komme einfach nicht zum Lesen* I just don't get (*od.* find) the time to read anything; *ich komme aber erst morgen dazu* I won't get (a)round to it (*od.* manage it) before tomorrow; *wie* ~ *Sie dazu?* how dare you?; → *auch* **Kraft** 1, **Sache** 2

Kommen *n*; *-s, kein Pl.* arrival; *es ist ein ständiges* ~ *und Gehen* people are in and out all day, there's a constant stream of of people coming and going; *im* ~ *sein Ideologie etc.*: be in the ascendant; *breitere Schlipse etc. sind wieder im* ~ wide ties *etc.* are coming in again; *dieser Dirigent ist im* ~ he's an up-and-coming conductor

kommend I. *Part. Präs.* → **kommen**; **II.** *Adj.* coming; (*zukünftig*) *auch* future; (*bevorstehend*) next; (*baldig*) forthcoming; *im ~en Jahr* next year; *in* (*den*) *~en Jahren* in (the) years to come; *die ~e Generation* the rising (*od.* up-and-coming) generation

Kommentar *m*; *-s, -e* commentary; (*Stellungnahme*) comment; *TV etc.* (*Reportage*) running commentary; *e-n* ~ *zu etw. geben* comment on s.th.; *er muss ständig s-n* ~ *abgeben* he always has to have his say (*Am. auch* put in his two cents worth); *kein ~!* no comment; ~ *überflüssig* no comment needed; **kommentarlos** *Adv.* without comment; **Kommentator** *m*; *-s, -en* commentator; **Kommentatorenbox** *f im Stadion etc.*: commentary box; **Kommentatorin** *f*; *-, -nen* (female) commentator; **kommentieren** *v/t.* comment on; *ausführlich*: give (*od.* write) a commentary on; (*mit Anmerkungen versehen*) annotate; *ein Spiel etc.* (*live*) ~ *TV etc.* give a running commentary on a game *etc.*

Kommers *m*; *-es, -e*; *altm.* (student fraternity's) evening drinking session

Kommerz *m*; *-es, kein Pl.* commerce; *reiner* ~ pure commercialism; *nur auf* ~ *aus sein* have purely commercial interests, be out for profit; **kommerzialisieren** *v/t.* commercialize; **Kommerzialisierung** *f* commercialization; **Kommerzialrat** *m österr.* → **Kommerzienrat**; **kommerziell** *Adj.* commercial; **Kommerzienrat** *m hist.* honorary title conferred on distinguished financiers or industrialists

Kommilitone *m*; *-n, -n*, **Kommilitonin**

f; *-, -nen* fellow student; *m-e Kommilitonen auch* the other students

Kommiss *m*; *-es, kein Pl.*; *umg.* army; *beim* ~ in the army

Kommissar *m*; *-s, -e* **1.** commissioner; *hist. in Russland*: commissar; **2.** (*bei der Polizei*) (police) superintendent; (*Kriminalkommissar*) (detective) superintendent; **Kommissär** *m*; *-s, -e*; *südd., österr., schw.* → **Kommissar** 2; **Kommissariat** *n*; *-s, -e* **1.** (*Amt*) commissionership; (*Behörde*) commissioner's office; *Polizei*: superintendent's office; **2.** *österr.* (*Polizeirevier*) police station; **Kommissarin** *f*; *-, -nen* → **Kommissar**

kommissarisch *Adj.* (*vorübergehend*) provisional, temporary

Kommissbrot *n* coarse brown bread

Kommission *f*; *-, -en*; (*Ausschuss, Wirts.: Auftrag, Provision*) commission; *in* ~ *geben* commission; **Kommissionär** *m*; *-s, -e*, **Kommissionärin** *;-, -nen Wirts.* commission agent

Kommissions|basis *f*: *auf* ~ on commission; ~**buchhandel** *m* wholesale book trade; ~**gebühr** *f* commission; ~**geschäft** *n* commission business; ~**lager** *n* consignment stock; ~**ware** *f* goods *Pl.* on commission

kommissionsweise *Adv.* on commission

Kommisskopp *m*; *-s, -köppe*; *umg. pej.* sergeant-major (*Am.* drill sergeant) type

kommod *Adj. bes. österr.* comfortable

Kommode *f*; *-, -n* chest of drawers, *Am. auch* bureau, commode *altm.*

Kommodore *m*; *-s, -n und -s* commodore

kommunal *Adj.* community..., local; *e-r städtischen Gemeinde*: municipal; *auf ~er Ebene* at local level

Kommunal|abgaben *Pl.* local rates and taxes; *in GB*: council tax *Sg.*; ~**anleihe** *f* municipal loan; ~**bank** *f* municipal bank; ~**beamte** *m*, ~**beamtin** *f* municipal civil servant, *Am. auch* city (*od.* town) employee; ~**behörde** *f* local authority; ~**obligation** *f* municipal loan; ~**politik** *f* local (government) politics *Pl.*

kommunalpolitisch *Adj.* relating to local (government) politics

Kommunal|steuer *f* → **Kommunalabgaben**; ~**verwaltung** *f* local government; ~**wahl** *f* local elections *Pl.*

Kommunarde *m*; *-n, -n* **1.** *hist.* Communard; **2.** commune member; ~ *sein* live in a commune; **Kommunardin** *f*; *-, -nen* → **Kommunarde**

Kommune *f*; *-, -n* **1.** (*Gemeinde*) community; (*Wohngemeinschaft*) commune; **2.** *hist.*: *die Pariser* ~ the Paris Commune

Kommunikant *m*; *-en, -en*, ~**in** *f*; *-, -nen*; *kath.* communicant

Kommunikation *f*; *-, -en* communication

kommunikationsfähig *Adj.* able to communicate; **Kommunikationsfähigkeit** *f* ability to communicate; *bes. fremdsprachlich*: communicative skills *Pl.*

Kommunikations|fluss *m* flow of communications, intercommunication; ~**gestörter** communications breakdown; ~**mittel** *n* means *Sg.* (*od.* channel) of communication; *die* ~ (*Radio, TV etc.*) the (communications) media; ~**satellit** *m* communications satellite; ~**schwierigkeiten** *Pl.*, ~**störungen** *Pl.* difficulties in communication; *es*

gab ~ we *etc.* had difficulty communicating; **~system** *n* communications system; **~technik** *f* communications technology; *Ausrüstung*: communications equipment; **~technologie** *f* communications technology; **~wissenschaft** *f* communication(s) science; **~zentrum** *n* (central) meeting place; *städtisches etc.*: community cent|re (*Am.* -er)

kommunikativ *Adj.* communicative

Kommunion *f*; -, -en; *kath.* (Holy) Communion; **~kind** *n* first communicant; **~kleid** *n* first communicant's (white) dress; **~unterricht** *m* preparation for first communicants

Kommuniqué [kɔmyni'keː] *n*; -s, -s communiqué

Kommunismus *m*; -, *kein Pl.* communism; **Kommunist** *m*; -en, -en, **Kommunistin** *f*; -, -nen communist; (*Parteimitglied*) Communist; **kommunistisch I.** *Adj.* communist; *Partei, Regierung, Manifest etc.*: Communist; **II.** *Adv.*: ~ *regiert etc.* Communist-ruled *etc.*

kommunizieren *v/i.* 1. *geh., fachspr.* communicate; 2. *kath.* receive Holy Communion

Komödiant *m*; -en, -en 1. actor; *er ist ein echter* ~ he's a full-blooded actor; 2. *fig. pej.* play-actor; (*Heuchler*) hypocrite; **Komödiantin** *f*; -, -nen 1. actress; 2. → *Komödiant* 2; **komödiantisch** *Adj.* acting ..., theatrical

Komödie *f*; -, -n 1. comedy; *fig.* farce; 2. (*Verstellung*) play-acting; ~ *spielen* put on an act

Komödien|dichter *m*, **~dichterin** *f* comedy writer

komödienhaft *Adj.* theatrical, histrionic

Komödien|schreiber *m*, **~schreiberin** *f* comedy writer

Komoren *Pl.*; *Geog.*: *die* ~ the Comoro Islands

Komp. *Abk. Wirts.* (**Kompanie**) Co.

Kompagnon [kɔmpan'jõː] *m*; -s, -s; *Wirts.* partner

kompakt *Adj.* compact; (*fest*) compressed; *umg. Mensch*: stocky

Kompakt|anlage *f* compact system; **~auto** *n* small family car, *Am.* subcompact; **~bauweise** *f* compact construction (method)

Kompaktheit *f*; *nur Sg.* compactness; *umg. von Mensch*: stockiness

Kompakt|kamera *f* compact camera; **~klasse** *f Mot.* small family (*Am.* subcompact) class; **~ski** *m* compact ski; **~wagen** *m* small family car, *Am.* subcompact

Kompanie *f*; -, -n; *Mil.* company (*auch Wirts. altm.*); **~chef** *m* company commander; **~stärke** *f* company strength

Komparation *f*; -, -en; *Ling.* comparison (of adjectives)

Komparatistik *f*; -, *kein Pl.* comparative studies *Pl.*, comparative literature and linguistics; **komparatistisch** *Adj.* comparatist

komparativ *Adj. Ling.* comparative; **Komparativ** *m*; -s, -e; *Ling.* comparative

Komparse *m*; -n, -n *Film*: extra; *Theat.* super, *Am.* extra; **Komparsin** *f*; -, -nen *Film*: extra; *Theat.* (female) super (*Am.* extra)

Kompass *m*; -es, -e compass; **~nadel** *f* compass needle

kompatibel *Adj.* compatible; **Kompatibilität** *f*; -, -en compatibility

Kompendium *n*; -s, *Kompendien* com-

pendium (*Pl.* compendiums *od.* compendia)

Kompensation *f*; -, -en; *auch Etech., Med., Psych.* compensation

Kompensations|geschäft *n* barter transaction; **~zahlung** *f* compensation payment

kompensatorisch *Adj.* compensatory

kompensieren *v/t.* compensate for (*auch Psych.*) (*mit, durch* by); *bes Wirts.* offset

kompetent *Adj.* competent; *Urteil*: authoritative; (*befähigt*) qualified; *~er Sprecher Ling.* someone with native-speaker competence; *für solche Fälle nicht* ~ *sein* not have the authority to deal with such cases; *Gericht auch*: not have jurisdiction in such cases; *der dafür ~e Kollege* the colleague responsible for (*od.* who deals with) these matters

Kompetenz *f*; -, -en; (*Sachverstand*) competence (*auch Ling.*); (*Zuständigkeit*) authority, responsibility; *e-s Gerichts*: auch jurisdiction; *in die* ~ (+ *Gen.*) *fallen* be the responsibility of; *e-s Gerichts*: come within the jurisdiction of; *s-e ~en überschreiten* exceed one's authority *Sg.* (*od.* powers); **~bereich** *m* area (*od.* sphere) of authority; **~erweiterung** *f* extension of (*s.o.'s*) powers; **~gerangel** *n umg.*, **~streitigkeiten** *Pl.* conflict *Sg.* of powers; *Gewerkschaft*: demarcation dispute; *Jur.* jurisdictional dispute; **~überschreitung** *f* exceeding of (*s.o.'s*) authority (*od.* powers); **~verlust** *m* loss of authority (*od.* powers); **~verteilung** *f* distribution of powers

Kompilation *f*; -, -en compilation; **Kompilator** *m*; -s, -en, **Kompilatorin** *f*; -, -nen compiler; **kompilieren** *v/t. geh., fachspr.* compile, put together

komplementär *Adj.* complementary; **Komplementär** *m*; -s, -e; *Wirts.* general partner

Komplementärfarbe *f* complementary colo(u)r

Komplementärin *f*; -, -nen → *Komplementär*

komplementieren *v/t.* complement; **Komplementierung** *f* complementing

Komplet¹ [kõ'pleː] *n*; -(s), -s matching dress and coat (*od.* jacket), suit

Komplet² *f*; -, -e; *kirchl.* (*Abendgebet*) compline

komplett I. *Adj.* 1. complete; *ich bin / wir sind jetzt* ~ now I've got everything / we're all here; 2. *umg. pej.* Unsinn, Wahnsinn etc.: (complete and) utter; **II.** *Adv. überholen*: completely; *eingerichtet, ausgerüstet, möbliert*: fully; *abgeben, aufführen*: in full; **komplettieren** *v/t.* complete; **Komplettierung** *f* completion

Komplett|lösung *f* complete solution; **~preis** *m* all-in (*Am.* all-included) price

komplex I. *Adj.* 1. complex (*auch Math.*); 2. (*umfassend*) comprehensive; **II.** *Adv.* 1. in a complex manner; ~ *aufgebaut* with a complex structure; 2. (*umfassend*) *renovieren*: completely; *vorbereiten, durchdenken*: thoroughly; **Komplex** *m*; -es, -e complex (*auch Psych., Math., Chem. etc.*); (*Gebäudekomplex*) *auch* group of buildings; *voller ~e Psych.* complex-ridden, full of complexes; **komplexbeladen** *Adj. Psych.* full of complexes; **Komplexität** *f*; -, *kein Pl.* complexity

Komplikation *f*; -, -en complication; **komplikationslos I.** *Adj.* straightfor-

ward, uncomplicated; **II.** *Adv. ablaufen etc.*: without a hitch

Kompliment *n*; -(e)s, -e compliment; (*mein*) ~*!* congratulations!; *j-m ~e machen* pay s.o. compliments (*für, über* + *Akk.* on); **komplimentieren** *v/t. geh. in ein Zimmer etc.*: escort, usher; *j-n zur Tür* ~ *euph.* show s.o. out

Komplize *m*; -n, -n accomplice; **Komplizenschaft** *f*; *nur Sg.* involvement as an accomplice

komplizieren I. *v/t.* complicate; *das kompliziert die Sache* that complicates matters; **II.** *v/refl.* become more complicated; *die Lage kompliziert sich immer mehr* the situation is becoming more and more complicated (*od.* involved); **kompliziert I.** *P.P.* → *komplizieren*; **II.** *Adj.* complicated; complex; (*verwickelt*) *Gerät*: auch intricate; *Problem, Lage*: auch involved; *~er Bruch Med.* compound fracture; **Kompliziertheit** *f*; *nur Sg.* complexity; *e-s Geräts*: auch intricacy

Komplizin *f*; -, -nen (female) accomplice

Komplott *n*; -(e)s, -e plot, conspiracy; *ein* ~ *schmieden* plot, conspire (*gegen* against), hatch a plot; *in ein* ~ *zum Sturz der Regierung verwickelt sein* be involved in a conspiracy to overthrow the government

Komponente *f*; -, -n component; (*Aspekt*) aspect, element

komponieren *vt/i.* compose (*auch Farben etc.*); (*Lied*) auch write; **Komponist** *m*; -en, -en, **Komponistin** *f*; -, -nen composer

Komposition *f*; -, -en composition (*auch e-s Gemäldes etc.*); *e-e ~ erlesener Düfte* a blend of exquisite fragrances; **Kompositionslehre** *f Mus.* (theory of) composition; **kompositorisch** *Adj.* compositional; *sein ~es Werk* his (musical) compositions

Kompositum *n*; -s, *Komposita*; *Ling.* compound

Kompost *m*; -(e)s, -e compost; **~erde** *f* compost; **~haufen** *m* compost heap

kompostierbar *Adj.* suitable for composting, compostable; **kompostieren** *v/t.* compost; (*Erde, Beet*) put compost on, add compost to; **Komposterer** *m*; -s, - compost-maker; **Kompostierung** *f* composting; **Kompostierungsanlage** *f* composting station (*größer*: plant)

Kompott *n*; -(e)s, -e stewed fruit; **~schale** *f*, **~schüssel** *f* dessert (*od.* fruit) bowl

Kompresse *f*; -, -n compress

Kompression *f*; -, -en; *Tech.* compression

Kompressions|strumpf *m Med.* support stocking; **~verband** *m* pressure bandage

Kompressor *m*; -s, -en; *Tech.* compressor; *Mot.* supercharger

komprimierbar *Adj.* compressible; **komprimieren** *v/t.* compress; *fig.* (*Buch etc.*) auch condense; **komprimiert I.** *P.P.* → *komprimieren*; **II.** *Adj.* (*knapp*) condensed; *Stil*: concise; **III.** *Adv.*: *etw.* ~ *ausdrücken* put s.th. concisely; **Komprimierung** *f* compression; *e-s Buchs*: auch condensing

Kompromiss *m*; -es, -e compromise; *bei Verhandlungen*: auch tradeoff; *e-n* ~ *schließen* (make a) compromise (*über* + *Akk.* on); *zu keinem* ~ *bereit sein* be unwilling to compromise; **kompromissbereit** *Adj.* willing to compromise; **Kompromissbereit-**

schaft *f; nur Sg.* willingness to compromise; **kompromissfähig** *Adj.* able to compromise

Kompromissler *m; -s, -,* **~in** ; *-, -nen; pej.* compromiser; **kompromisslerisch** *Adj.* (too) ready to make compromises (*Zugeständnisse:* concessions); **~e Haltung** *bes. Pol.* accommodating (*vorsichtig:* softly-softly) approach

kompromisslos *Adj.* uncompromising; *Pol. auch* hard-line ...; (*unerbittlich*) relentless; **Kompromisslosigkeit** *f; nur Sg.* uncompromising attitude, *Pol. auch* hard-line approach; (*Unerbittlichkeit*) relentlessness

Kompromiss|lösung *f* compromise solution; **~papier** *n* compromise document; **~vorschlag** *m* compromise proposal

kompromittieren *v/t. und v/refl.:* (**sich**) **~** compromise (o.s.)

Komsomol *m; -, kein Pl.; hist.* Komsomol; **Komsomolze** *m; -n, -n,* **Komsomolzin** *f; -, -nen; hist.* Komsomol member

Komtess *f; -, -en,* **Komtesse** *f; -, -n* countess

Kondemnation *f; -, -en; Jur., Naut.* writing-off (*of a damaged ship*)

Kondensat *n; -(e)s, -e; Chem., Phys.* condensate

Kondensation *f; -, -en; Chem., Phys.* condensation; **Kondensationspunkt** *m* condensation temperature; *der Luft:* dew point

Kondensator *m; -s, -en; Etech.* capacitor, *bes. Tech., Chem.* condenser

kondensieren I. *v/t.* (*hat kondensiert*) condense; **II.** *v/i.* (*ist und hat*) condense

Kondens|milch *f* evaporated (*od.* condensed) milk; **~streifen** *m Flug.* vapo[u]r trail; **~wasser** *n* condensation

konditern *v/i. umg.* make patisserie

Kondition *f; -, -en* **1.** *mst Pl.; Wirts.* condition; **zu besonders günstigen ~en** on particularly favo(u)rable terms; **2.** *nur Sg.* (*Verfassung*) condition, fitness; **e-e gute/schlechte ~ haben** be in good/poor shape, be very fit / not at all fit; **keine ~ haben** (*keine Ausdauer haben*) have no stamina

konditional *Adj. Ling.* conditional; **Konditional** *m; -s, -e; Ling.* conditional; **Konditionalsatz** *m* conditional clause

konditionell I. *Adj.* with regard to fitness; **~e Schwächen haben** be in poor shape, lack fitness; **II.** *Adv.* fitness-wise; **~ am Ende** in extremely poor shape, on one's last legs *umg.;* **~ ganz oben** in perfect shape, in top form

konditionieren *v/t.* condition; **Konditionierung** *f* conditioning

Konditionsmangel *m →* **Konditionsschwäche; konditionsschwach** *Adj.* very unfit; **Konditionsschwäche** *f* lack of fitness; **an ~ leiden** be very unfit; **konditionsstark** *Adj.* very fit; **Konditionstraining** *n* fitness training

Konditor *m; -s, -en* patissier, pastry cook; (*Zuckerbäcker*) confectioner, *Am. auch* candy maker; **Konditorei** *f; -, -en* **1.** cake (*od.* pastry) shop, patisserie; (*Café*) café, coffee house (*selling cakes and pastries*); **2.** *nur Sg.* patissier's trade; **Konditorin** *f; -, -nen →* **Konditor**

Kondolenz|besuch *m* visit of condolence; **~brief** *m* letter of condolence; **~buch** *n:* **sich ins ~ eintragen** sign the condolences book; **~karte** *f* condo-

lence card; **~schreiben** *n* letter of condolence

kondolieren *v/i.:* **j-m ~** express one's condolences to s.o. (**zu** on)

Kondom *n, m; -s, -e* condom; **~automat** *m* condom dispenser

Kondor *m; -s, -e; Zool.* condor

Kondukteur [kɔndʊkˈtøːɐ̯] *m; -s, -e,* **~in** *f; -, -nen; schw.* Straßenbahn: conductor; *Eisenb.* guard, *Am.* conductor; (*Fahrkartenkontrolleur*) ticket inspector

Konfekt *n; -(e)s, -e* **1.** (*Pralinen*) chocolates *Pl.;* (*Süßigkeiten*) confectionery, *Am. auch* candy; **2.** *bes. südd., österr., schw.* (*Teegebäck*) fancy biscuits (*Am.* cookies)

Konfektion *f; -, -en* **1.** *nur Sg.* (factory) clothing production, manufacture of ready-to-wear clothing; **2.** *Kleidung:* ready-to-wear clothing; **Konfektionär** *m; -s, -e* manufacturer of ready-to--wear clothing

konfektionieren *v/t.* manufacture, produce in series; **konfektioniert** *Adj.* factory-made, *Kleidung:* off-the-peg, *Am.* off-the-rack; **Konfektionierung** *f* manufacture, series (*od.* assembly--line) production

Konfektions|anzug *m* ready-to-wear (*od.* off-the-peg, *Am.* off-the-rack) suit; **~geschäft** *n* (ready-to-wear) clothes shop; **~größe** *f* standard (clothing) size; **~n** standard clothing sizes; **~ware** *f* ready-made (*Br. auch* off-the-peg) clothes *Pl.*

Konferenz *f; -, -en* conference; **~beschluss** *m* conference resolution; **~dolmetscher** *m,* **~dolmetscherin** *f* conference interpreter; **~ort** *m* conference venue (*bes. Am.* location); **~raum** *m,* **~saal** *m* conference room (*größer:* hall); **~schaltung** *f* conference circuit (*od.* hookup); **~sendung** *f* hookup broadcast; **~sprache** *f* conference language; **~teilnehmer** *m,* **~teilnehmerin** *f* conference participant (*Delegierte:* delegate); **~tisch** *m* conference table; **am ~** *auch fig.* at the round table

konferieren I. *v/i.* **1.** confer (**über** + *Akk.* on); **2.** *Theat., TV* act as compère (*Am.* MC, emcee); **II.** *v/t.* compère, *Am.* emcee

Konfession *f; -, -en* religion, (religious) denomination; **welcher ~ gehören Sie an?** what (religious) denomination (*od.* religion) are you?, what is your religion?; **konfessionell** *Adj.* denominational; **konfessionslos** *Adj.* non--denominational; **Konfessionsschule** *f* denominational school

Konfetti *n; -(s), kein Pl.* confetti; **~parade** *f* ticker-tape parade

Konfident *m; -en, -en,* **~in** *f; -, -nen; österr.* (police) informer

Konfiguration *f; -, -en* configuration

Konfirmand *m; -en, -en; kirchl.* confirmation candidate, confirmand *fachspr.*

Konfirmanden|blase *f umg. hum* leaky bladder; **~unterricht** *m* confirmation classes *Pl.*

Konfirmandin *f; -, -nen* confirmation candidate, confirmand *fachspr.*

Konfirmation *f; -, -en; kirchl.* confirmation

konfirmieren *v/t.* confirm

Konfiserie *f; -, -n; schw.* **1.** (*Geschäft*) cake shop, confectioner's; **2.** (*Gebäck*) confectionery

konfiszieren *v/t.* confiscate, seize; **Konfiszierung** *f* confiscation

Konfitüre *f; -, -n* jam, *Am. auch* pre-

serves *Pl.*

Konflikt *m; -(e)s, -e* conflict; *bes. Pol., Wirts.* dispute; **ein bewaffneter ~** an armed conflict (*od.* struggle); **in ~ geraten** come into conflict, clash (**mit** with); **das bringt mich mit m-m Gewissen in ~** I can't square that with my conscience; **ein innerer ~** *Psych.* a state of inner (*od.* emotional) conflict; *→* **Gesetz** 1; **~bewältigung** *f* conflict management

konfliktfähig *Adj.* able to handle conflict situations; **Konfliktfähigkeit** *f; nur Sg.* ability to handle conflict situations

Konfliktfall *m* (case of) conflict, dispute; **im ~** should a conflict occur, if there is a dispute

konflikt|frei *Adj.* peaceful; **~freudig** *Adj.* belligerent, combative; **~geladen** *Adj.* ridden with conflict; *Situation:* explosive

Konflikt|herd *m* cent|re (*Am.* -er) of conflict; trouble spot; **~kommission** *f ehem.* DDR commission for settling disputes in the workplace; **~region** *f* area of conflict

konflikt|reich *Adj.* conflict-ridden; **~scheu** *Adj.:* **er ist ~** he avoids any sort of conflict (*od.* confrontation)

Konflikt|situation *f* conflict situation; **~stoff** *m* seeds *Pl.* of conflict

konfliktträchtig *Adj. Situation:* (potentially) explosive; **die Situation ist ~** *auch* the least thing could spark off a conflict

Konföderation *f; -, -en* confederation; (*Bündnis*) confederacy; **konföderieren** *v/i. und v/refl.:* (**sich**) **~** form a confederation (*Bündnis:* confederacy) (**mit** with); **Konföderierte** *m, f; -n, -n; hist.* confederate

konform *Adj.* conforming (**mit** *od.* **+** *Dat.* to), in conformity (with); **~ gehen** *od.* **sein** be in agreement, concur (**mit** with); **wir** (*od.* **unsere Meinungen**) **sind da ~** we see eye to eye on this; **...konform** *im Adj.* in conformity with ...; **partei~** in conformity with party policy, toeing the party line; **regel~** in conformity with the rules

Konformismus *m; -, kein Pl.* conformism; **Konformist** *m; -en, -en,* **Konformistin** *f; -, -nen* conformist; **konformistisch** *Adj.* conformist; **Konformität** *f; -, kein Pl.* conformity

Konfrontation *f; -, -en* confrontation; **Konfrontationskurs** *m; nur Sg.* collision course; **auf ~ gehen** aim deliberately for confrontation; **sich auf e-m ~ befinden** be on a collision course; **konfrontieren** *v/t.* confront (**mit** with); **er sah sich mit s-m Erzfeind konfrontiert** he found himself confronted (*od.* face to face) with his arch enemy

konfus *Adj.* confused, *Gedanken etc.: auch* muddled; **~es Zeug reden** *umg.* come out with confused nonsense; **Konfusion** *f; -, -en* confusion, muddle

Konfuzianismus *m; -, kein Pl.; Philos.* Confucianism; **Konfuzius** *m; -; Philos.* Confucius

kongenial *Adj. geh. zwei Sachen, Personen:* perfectly matched; *Partner, Übersetzung: auch* ideal; *Interpretation etc.:* very sensitive; **~er Geist** kindred spirit, (spiritual) soulmate; **Kongenialität** *f; -, kein Pl.* perfectly matched quality (*Person:* character); *von Interpretation:* great sensitivity

Konglomerat *n; -(e)s, -e* **1.** *Wirts., Geol.* conglomerate; **2.** *flg.* (*Gemisch*)

K

conglomeration

Kongo[1] *m*; -(*s*); *Geog.* Congo (River)

Kongo[2] (*m*); -*s*; *Geog.*: *der* ~ the Congo; *Republik* ~ Republic of the Congo; *Demokratische Republik* ~ Democratic Republic of the Congo; **Kongolese** *m*; -*n*, -*n*, **Kongolesin** *f*; -, -*nen* Congolese, *weiblich auch*: Congolese woman (*od.* girl *etc.*); **kongolesisch** *Adj.* Congolese

Kongregation *f*, -, -*en*; *kath.* congregation; **Kongregationalist** *m*; -*en*, -*en*, **Kongregationalistin** *f*, -, -*nen* Congregationalist

Kongress *m*; -*es*, -*e* congress; (*Fachkongress*) conference; *bes. Am.* (*auch einer Partei etc.*) convention; *der* ~ *Am. Pol.* Congress; ~**abgeordnete** *m*, *f Am. Pol.* Congressman; *weiblich*: Congresswoman; ~(*r*) *sein* be a Congressman/Congresswoman; ~**gebäude** *n* conference building, *Am. auch* convention building; ~**halle** *f*, ~**saal** *m* congress (*od.* conference) hall, *Am. auch* convention hall; ~**stadt** *f* (frequent) congress (*od.* conference, *Am. auch* convention) venue (*bes. Am.* location), city of congresses (*od.* conferences, *Am. auch* conventions); ~**teilnehmer** *m*, ~**teilnehmerin** *f* m congress (*od.* conference) participant; ~**wahl** *f Am. Pol.* election to Congress; ~**zentrum** *n* conference cent|re (*Am.* -er), *Am. auch* convention center

kongruent *Adj. Math.*, *Ling.* congruent; *fig. geh.* (*identisch*) identical; **Kongruenz** *f*; -, -*en Math.*, *Ling.* congruence, congruency

K.-o.-Niederlage *f* defeat by a knockout

Konifere *f*; -, -*n*; *Bot.* conifer

König *m*; -*s*, -*e* king; *j-n zum* ~ *machen* make s.o. king; *die Heiligen Drei* ~*e bibl.* the Three Wise Men, the Magi; → *Kunde*[1] 1

Königin *f*, -, -*nen* queen (*auch Ameisen-, Bienenkönigin*); *sie war die* ~ *des Festes* she was the belle of the ball; ~**mutter** *f* queen mother; ~**pastete** *f Gastr.* chicken vol-au-vent; ~**witwe** *f* dowager queen

königlich I. *Adj.* **1.** *Haltung etc.*: regal, kingly; *Seine/Ihre* ~*e Hoheit* His/Her Royal Highness; **2.** (*großzügig*) *Geschenk, Belohnung etc.*: princely, handsome; *Bewirtung*: lavish; *Mahl*: sumptuous; **3.** *umg.* tremendous; **II.** *Adv.*: **1.** *j-n* ~ *bewirten* entertain s.o. lavishly; *er wurde* ~ *belohnt/beschenkt* he was handsomely (*od.* richly) rewarded / was showered with presents; **2.** *umg.* tremendously, immensely; *sich* ~ *amüsieren* have a marvel(l)ous time; *sich* ~ *freuen* be as pleased as Punch

Königreich *n* kingdom (*auch kirchl.*), *lit.* realm

Königs|adler *m* golden eagle; ~**bauer** *m Schach*: king's pawn

königsblau *Adj.* royal blue

Königs|burg *f* royal castle; ~**haus** *n* royal dynasty; ~**hof** *m* royal court; ~**kerze** *f Bot.* mullein; ~**kind** *n* royal child, little prince (*Prinzessin*: princess); ~**klasse** *f Sport* elite class (*Liga*: division); ~**kobra** *f Zool.* king cobra; ~**krone** *f* royal crown; ~**kuchen** *m* loaf-shaped fruit cake; ~**macher** *m* kingmaker; ~**paar** *n* royal couple; ~**palast** *m* royal palace; ~**schießen** *n* competition to decide who is the champion marksman; ~**schloss** *n* royal pal-

ace; ~**sohn** *m* king's son; ~**thron** *m* royal throne; ~**tiger** *m Zool.* Bengal tiger; ~**tochter** *m* king's daughter

königstreu *Adj.* loyal (to the king); *allg.* royalist

Königs|wasser *n*; *nur Sg.*; *Chem.* aqua regia, nitrohydrochloric acid; ~**weg** *m* ideal solution; ~**würde** *f* regal dignity

Königtum *n*; -*s*, *Königtümer* monarchy

konisch *Adj.* conical; (~ *zugespitzt*) *Werkzeug etc.*: tapering, tapered

Konj. *Abk.* → **Konjunktion, Konjunktiv**

Konjugation *f*, -, -*en* conjugation; **konjugieren** *v/t.* conjugate (*auch Math., Med., Etech.*)

Konjunktion *f*, -, -*en* conjunction (*auch Astrol., Astron., Logik*); **konjunktional** *Adj. Ling.* conjunctional; **Konjunktionaladverb** *n Ling.* adverbial conjunction; **Konjunktionalsatz** *m Ling.* conjunctional (*od.* conjunctive) clause

Konjunktiv *m*; -*s*, -*e*; *Ling.* subjunctive; ~ *I* present subjunctive; ~ *II* imperfect subjunctive; **konjunktivisch I.** *Adj.* subjunctive; **II.** *Adv.* in the subjunctive; **Konjunktivsatz** *m* subjunctive clause

Konjunktur *f*, -, -*en*; *Wirts.* **1.** (*Wirtschaftslage*) economic situation; (*Wirtschaftstätigkeit*) business activity; (*Konjunkturzyklus*) trade (*bes. Am.* business) cycle; *rückläufige/steigende* ~ decreasing/increasing business activity, downward/upward economic trend; *die* ~ *dämpfen/beleben* slow down / stimulate the economy; **2.** (*Hochkonjunktur*) boom; ~ *haben fig.* Ware, Handwerker etc.: be in great demand, Kleidung etc.: be in fashion, *umg.* be in; *dieses Modell hat im Moment* ~ *auch* everyone's buying this model now; **konjunkturabhängig** *Adj.* dependent on economic trends; (*zyklisch*) cyclical

Konjunktur|abschwächung *f*, ~**abschwung** *m Wirts.* downward trend (*od.* downturn, downswing) in the economy; ~**aufschwung** *m* upward trend (*od.* upturn, upswing) in the economy, business revival; ~**aussichten** *Pl.* economic outlook *Sg.*; ~**barometer** *n* economic barometer

konjunkturbedingt *Adj. Wirts.* driven by economic trends; (*zyklisch*) cyclical

Konjunktur|belebung *f Wirts.* business revival; *das Beleben*: stimulation of the economy; ~**bewegung** *f* cyclical movement; ~**bremse** *f umg.* brake on the economy

konjunkturell *Wirts.* **I.** *Adj.* economic; *Entwicklung, Zyklus etc.*: *auch* business ...; *dem Konjunkturzyklus entsprechend*: cyclical; ~*e Arbeitslosigkeit* unemployment driven by economic trends; **II.** *Adv.* ~ *bedingt* driven by economic trends; (*zyklisch*) cyclical

Konjunktur|entwicklung *f Wirts.* economic (*od.* business) trends *Pl.*; ~**flaute** *f* economic slowdown; *ernsthafte*: slump, recession; ~**klima** *n* economic (*od.* business) climate; ~**krise** *f* economic crisis (*von Dauer*: depression); ~**lage** *f* economic situation; ~**phase** *f* phase of a trade (*bes. Am.* business) cycle; ~**politik** *f* trade (*bes. Am.* business) cycle policy (*aimed at stabilization*), economic (stabilization) policy; ~**prognose** *f* economic (*od.* business) forecast; ~**programm** *n* program(me) of measures for the stimulation of the economy; ~**ritter** *m pej.* business opportunist; ~**rückgang** *m* (economic)

recession (*od.* slump); ~**schwankungen** *Pl.* cyclical (*od.* business) fluctuations; ~**spritze** *f umg.* shot in the arm for the economy; ~**tief** *n* eonomic low point, depth of recession; ~**verlauf** *m* trade (*bes. Am..* business) cycle; economic trends *Pl.*; ~**zuschlag** *m* economic stabilization surcharge; ~**zyklus** *m* trade (*bes. Am.* business) cycle

konkav *Adj.* concave; *Tastatur*: sculptured

Konkav|linse *f* concave lens; ~**spiegel** *m* concave mirror

Konklave *n*; -*s*, -*n*; *kath.* conclave

Konkordanz *f*; -, -*en* concordance

Konkordat *n*; -(*e*)*s*, -*e* concordat

konkret I. *Adj.* concrete (*auch Kunst, Musik etc.*); (*greifbar*) *auch* tangible; (*genau*) specific, definite; (*bestimmt*) actual; *er hat nichts Konkretes gesagt* he didn't say anything definite; **II.** *Adv.* in concrete terms; *was willst du* ~ *damit sagen?* (*od. wie soll man das* ~ *verstehen?*) what do you actually mean by that?; *könntest du dich etwas* ~*er ausdrücken?* could you be a bit less vague (*od.* more specific)?

konkretisieren I. *v/t.* put in concrete terms; **II.** *v/refl.* take shape, materialize; *Idee*: be realized; **Konkretisierung** *f* expression in concrete terms

Konkubinat *n*; -(*e*)*s*, -*e*; *Jur.* concubinage; **Konkubine** *f*; -, -*n* concubine

Konkurrent *m*; -*en*, -*en*, ~**in** *f*; -, -*nen* competitor, rival; *die/keine* ~*en auch* the/no competition *Sg.*

Konkurrenz *f*; -, -*en* **1.** *nur Sg.* (*Wettbewerb*) competition, rivalry; (*Wettbewerb*) competition, *stärker*: rivalry; *j-m/sich* ~ *machen* compete with s.o./one another; *mit j-m in* ~ *stehen/ treten* be in / enter into competition with s.o.; *außer* ~ *stehen* be unrival(l)ed; **2.** (*Konkurrent, mst Koll. die Konkurrenten*) competitor(s *Pl.*), rival(s *Pl.*), *Koll.* competition; **3.** *Sport*: (*Wettkampf*) event, competition, contest; *außer* ~ *teilnehmen* take part as a non-official competitor; **4.** *Jur.* concurrence; ~**angebot** *n* rival offer; ~**blatt** *n* rival newspaper; ~**denken** *n* competitive mentality; ~**druck** *m* competitive pressure; ~**erzeugnis** *n* rival product

konkurrenzfähig *Adj.* competitive, able to compete; **Konkurrenzfähigkeit** *f*; *nur Sg.* competitiveness

Konkurrenzfirma *f* rival firm (*bes. Am.* company)

konkurrenzieren *v/t.* *südd.*, *österr.*, *schw.* compete *with* (*each other*); **Konkurrenzierung** *f südd.*, *österr.*, *schw.* competition

Konkurrenz|kampf *m* competition; *stärker*: rivalry; *es war ein harter* ~ competition was tough; ~**klausel** *f* non-competition (*od.* restraint) clause

konkurrenzlos *Adj.* unrival(l)ed, unequal(l)ed; *Preise*: unmatched; ~ *sein Firma*: have no competitors

Konkurrenz|neid *m* professional jealousy; ~**produkt** *n* rival product; ~**unternehmen** *n* rival concern; ~**verbot** *n* (agreement on) restraint of trade; ~**waren** *Pl.* competing goods (*bes. Am.* products)

konkurrieren *v/i.* compete (*mit* with; *um* for); **konkurrierend I.** *Part. Präs.* → **konkurrieren**; **II.** *Adj.* competing, rival ...; ~*e Gesetzgebung Jur.* concurrent legislation

Konkurs *m*; -*es*, -*e Wirts.* bankruptcy; ~ *anmelden* file for bankruptcy; *in* ~ *gehen od.* ~ *machen* go bankrupt; *vor*

dem ~ stehen be on the brink of bankruptcy (*od.* ruin); **~antrag** *m* petition for bankruptcy; **~ausfallgeld** *n* amount paid by the department of employment to employees of an insolvent employer; **~erklärung** *f* declaration of insolvency; **~eröffnung** *f* opening of bankruptcy proceedings; **~masse** *f* bankrupt's estate (*od.* assets *Pl.*); **~verfahren** *n* bankruptcy proceedings *Pl.*; **~verwalter** *m*, **~verwalterin** *f* receiver, liquidator; *von Gläubigern eingesetzter*: trustee (in bankruptcy)

können I. *Hilfsv.*; *kann, konnte, hat können* **1.** (*vermögen*) be able to (+ *Inf.*), (*fähig sein zu*) be capable of (+ *Ger.*); be in a position to (+ *Inf.*); *kannst du nicht aufpassen?* can't you look (at) what you're doing?; *er hätte es tun ~* he could have done it; *du kannst machen, was du willst, es nützt nichts* whatever you do it doesn't make any difference, it's like banging your head on a brick wall; *ich kann das nicht mehr hören* I can't take it any more; *er tut, was er kann* he does his best; *man kann nie wissen* you never know; **2.** (*dürfen*) be allowed to (+ *Inf.*); *er kann gehen* he can go; *Sie ~ es mir glauben* you take my word for it; *kannst du machen!* *umg.* go ahead; I don't mind; *das kannst du doch nicht machen!* you can't (*od.* mustn't) do that!; **3.** *Möglichkeit, Wahrscheinlichkeit*: *das kann (schon) sein* it's possible; (*es kann stimmen*) that may be true; *kann sein umg.* maybe, perhaps; *das kann nicht sein* (that's) impossible; *wer kann es gewesen sein?* who could it have been?; *ich kann mich auch täuschen* I may be wrong, of course; *du könntest Recht haben* you may (well) be right; *es kann od. könnte etwas länger dauern* it could (*od.* might) take a while longer; *sie kann jeden Augenblick kommen* she could be here any moment; *die Idee könnte von mir sein* that idea could have been mine; **4.** *er kann schwimmen* he can (*od.* knows how to) swim; *kannst du Schach spielen?* can you (*od.* do you) play chess?; **5.** *du kannst mich mal!* *umg.* you know what you can do; (*erst einmal*) *~ vor Lachen!* wouldn't that be nice (if I could)!; **II.** *v/t.* (*hat gekonnt*) **1.** *ich kann es (nicht)* I can('t) do it; *er kann es (gut)* he can do it (well); *er kann gar nichts* he's useless; *sie kann was umg.* she can do a lot of things, she's very capable; *das habe ich früher alles gekonnt* I used to be able to do all that; *man kann alles, wenn man will* you can do anything if you put your mind to it; *ich kann nichts dafür* I can't help it; *er kann nichts dafür, dass er …* he can't help (+ *Ger.*); *er kann's mit ihm umg.* he gets on (*Am.* along) all right with him; **2.** (*Sprache*) speak, know; (*Gedicht etc.*) know; *sie kann gut Englisch* she speaks good English; *kannst du das Gedicht auswendig?* do you know the poem by heart?; **III.** *v/i.* (*hat gekonnt*): *wir ~ nicht ins Haus* we can't go (*od.* get) into the house; *so schnell sie konnte* as fast as she could; *ich kann nicht mehr* (*bin erschöpft*) I can't go on, I'm whacked (*Am.* wiped out); (*bin satt*) I can't eat any more; *betont*: I couldn't eat another thing; *psychisch*: I can't take any more; *wir konnten nicht mehr (vor La-*

chen) umg. we were helpless with laughter; *wie konntest du!* how could you!; **Können** *n*; *-s, kein Pl.* ability; (*Fertigkeit[en]*) skill(s *Pl.*); *sportliches ~* sporting ability (*od.* prowess)

Könner *m*; *-s, -, ~in f*; *-, -nen* expert; **Könnerschaft** *f nur Sg.* expertise

Konnossement *n*; *-(e)s, -e*; *Wirts.* bill of lading

Konnotation *f*; *-, -en*; *Ling.* connotation

konnte *Imperf.* → **können**

Konquistador *m*; *-en, -en*; *hist.* conquistador (*Pl.* conquistadores *od.* conquistadors)

Konrektor *m* deputy head(master), *Am.* deputy principal; **Konrektorin** *f* deputy head(mistress), *Am.* deputy principal

Konsekration *f*; *-, -en*; *kirchl.* consecration; **konsekrieren** *v/t.* *kirchl.* consecrate

konsekutiv *Adj.* consecutive

Konsekutiv|dolmetschen *n*; *-s, kein Pl.* consecutive interpreting; **~dolmetscher** *m*, **~dolmetscherin** *f* consecutive interpreter; **~satz** *m Ling.* consecutive clause

Konsens *m*; *-es, -e* **1.** consensus; **2.** *altm.* (*Einwilligung*) consent

konsequent I. *Adj.* (*folgerichtig*) logical; (*beständig*) consistent; (*kompromisslos*) uncompromising; (*beharrlich*) firm; (*entschlossen*) resolute, single-minded; (*gründlich*) rigorous, thorough; *Sport, Decken*: close, tight; *~ bleiben* remain firm, *umg.* stick to one's guns; **II.** *Adv. denken*: logically; *handeln*: consistently; *etw. verfolgen*: single-mindedly; *untersuchen*: rigorously, thoroughly; *Sport, decken*: closely; *~ schweigen* remain resolutely silent, refuse to utter a word; **konsequenterweise** *Adv.* logically, to be consistent

Konsequenz *f*; *-, -en* **1.** (*Zielstrebigkeit*) persistence; (*Entschlossenheit*) determination, firmness; *mit eiserner ~* with absolute determination (*od.* single-mindedness), doggedly; *wenn er sich etw. in den Kopf gesetzt hat, tut er es bis zur äußersten ~* to the logical extreme, to the bitter end; (*ohne Rücksicht auf die Folgen*) with complete disregard for the consequences; **2.** (*Folge, Ergebnis*) consequence; *die ~en tragen* bear (*od.* take) the consequences; *die ~en ziehen* draw the obvious conclusions (*aus* from); (*folgerichtig handeln*) take the necessary steps; *er zog die ~en und trat zurück* he realized he had no alternative and resigned; *als letzte od. in letzter ~ blieb ihr nur der Rücktritt* the only logical step left for her was to resign; *ich werde daraus meine ~en ziehen* I will come to my own conclusions about this (and act accordingly)

Konservatismus *m*; *-, kein Pl.*; *Pol.* conservatism; *Brit.* Conservatism; **konservativ** *Adj. auch weitS.* conservative; *Partei(mitglied) etc.*: Conservative, *in GB: auch* Tory; **Konservative** *m, f*; *-n, -n* conservative; *Parteimitglied*: Conservative, *in GB: auch* Tory; **~(r) sein** be a Conservative; **Konservativismus** *m*; *-, kein Pl.*; *Pol.* conservatism; *Brit.* Parteipolitik: Conservatism; **Konservativität** *f*; *-, kein Pl.* conservativeness

Konservator *m*; *-s, -en, ~in f*; *-, -nen* curator

konservatorisch *Adj. Kunst, Archit.*

conservational; **~e Maßnahmen** conservation measures

Konservatorium *n*; *-s, Konservatorien*; *Mus.* conservatoire, *bes. Am.* conservatory; *in GB*: music academy

Konserve *f*; *-, -n* **1.** (*Dose*) can, *Brit. auch* tin; **2.** *Pl. L ebensmittel*: canned (*Brit. auch* tinned.) foods; *von ~n leben* live on canned food, *Brit. umg. auch* live out of tins; **3.** (*Blutkonserve*) unit of (stored) blood; **4.** *TV* repeat; *Musik aus der ~ umg.* canned music

Konserven|büchse *f*, **~dose** *f* can, *Brit. auch* tin; **~fabrik** *f* canning factory, *bes. Am.* cannery; **~glas** *n* preserving (*Am.* canning *od.* Mason) jar; **~öffner** *m* can (*Brit. auch* tin) opener

konservieren I. *v/t.* preserve (*auch Blut, Leiche, Holz etc.*); (*Gebäude, Kunstwerk*) *auch* conserve; *in Büchsen*: can, *Brit. auch* tin; (*Traditionen etc.*) preserve, uphold; **II.** *v/refl.* preserve (itself); *umg. fig. Person*: look after o.s.

Konservierung *f* preservation; *von Gebäude, Kunstwerk*: conservation

Konservierungs|maßnahmen *Pl.* conservation measures; **~mittel** *n*, **~stoff** *m* preservative; **~verfahren** *n* conservation process

Konsiliar|arzt *m*, **~ärztin** *f Med.* consultant

Konsilium *n*; *-s, Konsilien* **1.** consultation; **2.** (*Beratergruppe*) group giving consultation

konsistent *Adj.* **1.** (*fest*) solid; **2.** (*konsequent*) consistent; **3.** (*logisch*) logical; *die Argumentation war in sich ~* the line of argument was inherently logical; **Konsistenz** *f*; *-, kein Pl.* consistency

Konsole *f*; *-, -n*; *Archit.* console, bracket; *tischartig*: console (table)

konsolidieren I. *v/t.* consolidate; **II.** *v/refl.* be consolidated, consolidate; **Konsolidierung** *f* consolidation; **Konsolidierungsphase** *f* consolidation phase

konsonant *Adj. Mus.* consonant; **Konsonant** *m*; *-en, -en*; *Ling.* consonant; **konsonantisch** *Adj. Ling.* consonantal; **Konsonanz** *f*; *-, -en*; *Mus.* consonance, concord

Konsorte *m*; *-, -n* **1.** *nur Pl.*: **Lehmann und ~n** *umg. pej.* Lehmann and co., Lehmann and his lot (*Am. auch* his cohorts); **2.** *Wirts.* consortium (*od.* syndicate) member

Konsortialbank *f Wirts.* consortium bank

Konsortium *n*; *-s, Konsortien* consortium (*Pl.* consortia *od.* consortiums), syndicate

Konspiration *f*; *-, -en* conspiracy; **konspirativ** *Adj.* conspiratorial; **~e Wohnung** apartment used by conspirators, safe house; *von Terroristen*: terrorist hideout; **~es Treffen** meeting of conspirators; **konspirieren** *v/i.* conspire (*mit* with; *gegen* against)

konstant I. *Adj.* constant, steady; *Kosten, Einkommen*: fixed; *Phys.* constant; *Leistung: auch Sport* consistent; **~e Größe** *Math.* constant (quantity); *~ halten* maintain at a consistent level; **II.** *Adv.* consistently; **Konstante** *f*; *-(n), -n*; *Math., Phys.* constant; *fig.* constant factor

Konstantinopel (*n*); *-s*; *Geog. hist.* Constantinople

Konstanz[1] (*n*); *-*; *Geog.* Constance

Konstanz[2] *f*; *-, kein Pl.* constancy; **~ zeigen** display consistency

konstatieren *v/t.* **1.** *(wahrnehmen)* note; *(ermitteln)* ascertain, discover; **2.** *(erklären)* state

Konstellation *f; -, -en* **1.** *Astron., Med.* constellation; **2.** *(Gesamtlage)* combination of circumstances

konsterniert *Adj.* alarmed; *(erstaunt)* taken aback, flabbergasted

konstituieren I. *v/t.* constitute; *(gründen) auch* establish; **~de Sitzung** organizational *(od.* procedural) session; **die ~de Versammlung** *Pol.* the constituent assembly; **II.** *v/refl. Parl.* assemble, convene; *(gegründet werden)* become established

Konstitution *f; -, -en* **1.** *Pol.* constitution; **2.** *Med.* constitution; **sie hat eine eiserne/zarte ~** she has an iron / a delicate constitution; **konstitutionell I.** *Adj.* **1.** *Pol. Monarchie etc.:* constitutional; **2.** *Med.* constitution; **er hat s-m Gegner gegenüber ~e Vorteile** he has a stronger constitution *(od.* physique) than his opponent; **II.** *Adv.* **1.** *Pol.* constitutionally; **2.** *Med.* constitutionally; **die Mannschaft war ~ unterlegen** the team was inferior in terms of physical strength

konstitutiv *Adj.* constitutive

konstruieren *v/t.* **1.** *(bauen)* construct *(auch Math., Philos., Ling. etc.)*; *(herstellen)* create; *(entwerfen)* design; **mit dem Dativ konstruiert werden** take the dative *(od.* a dative construction); **2.** *pej. (erfinden)* fabricate; **konstruiert I.** *P.P.* → **konstruieren**; **II.** *Adj. pej. (gezwungen)* contrived; *Fall:* hypothetical; **das Beispiel klingt** *od.* **wirkt ~** the example seems contrived

Konstrukt *n; -(e)s, -e* working model; *(Erfindung)* creation

Konstrukteur [kɔnstrʊkˈtøːɐ̯] *m; -s, -e, ~in f; -, -nen* designer, design engineer

Konstruktion *f; -, -en* construction *(auch Ling.)*; *(Entwurf, Bauart)* design

Konstruktions|büro *n* drawing office; **~fehler** *m* structural *(im Entwurf:* design) fault; **~merkmal** *n* constructional *(od.* design) feature; **~plan** *m* structural plan

konstruktionstechnisch *Adj.* constructional

Konstruktions|teil *n* structural component; **~zeichner** *m* draughtsman, *Am.* draftsman; designer; **~zeichnerin** *f* draughtswoman, *Am.* draftswoman; designer; **~zeichnung** *f* design drawing

konstruktiv I. *Adj.* **1.** *Kritik etc.:* constructive; *Beitrag etc.:* positive, useful; **~es Misstrauensvotum** *Pol.* constructive vote of no confidence; **von dir kam bis jetzt wenig Konstruktives** you haven't had much to say for yourself of any use, you haven't really made a positive contribution; **2.** *Tech.* constructional, design ...; **II.** *Adv.* **1.** constructively; **du hast sehr ~ mitgearbeitet** you made a very positive *(od.* useful) contribution; **2.** *Tech.* constructionally, design-wise; **Konstruktivismus** *m; -, kein Pl.; Kunst, Philos.* constructivism

Konsul *m; -s, -n; hist., Pol.* consul

Konsular|... *im Subst.* consular; **~abkommen** *n* consular convention; **~beamte** *m*, **~beamtin** *f* consular official

konsularisch *Adj. Pol.* consular

Konsulat *n; -(e)s, -e; Pol.* consulate

Konsulats|gebäude *n* consulate; **~gebühren** *Pl.* consular fees

Konsulin *f; -, -nen* consul

Konsultation *f; -, -en* consultation; **konsultativ** *Adj.* consultative; **konsultieren** *v/t.* consult; *(Arzt) auch* see

Konsum *m; -s, -s* **1.** *nur Sg.* consumption *(auch fig.)*; *von Alkohol: auch* intake; **der ~ von Drogen nimmt zu** drug-taking is on the increase; **2.** *österr., ehem. DDR (Geschäft)* consumer co-operative shop *(Am.* store), co-op *umg.*; **~artikel** *m* consumer article; *Pl.* consumer goods

Konsumation *f; -, -en; österr., schw.* consumption

Konsumdenken *n* consumer mentality; consumerism

Konsument *m; -en, -en, ~in f; -, -nen* consumer; **Konsumentenkredit** *m Wirts.* consumer credit

Konsum|forschung *f* consumer research; **~genossenschaft** *f* consumers' cooperative; **~gesellschaft** *f* consumer society; **~gewohnheiten** *Pl.* consumer habits; **~güter** *Pl.* consumer *(Am. auch* end-user) goods

konsumierbar *Adj.* consumable; **konsumieren** *v/t.* consume *(auch fig.)*; **Konsumierung** *f; -, -en* consumption

Konsum|klima *n* consumer demand; **das ~ ist gut/schlecht** buyer demand is up/down; **~terror** *m* → **Konsumzwang**; **~verein** *m* consumers' cooperative; **~verhalten** *n* consumption pattern; **umweltbewusstes ~** green *(od.* eco-)consumerism; **~verweigerer** *m* anti-consumerist; **~verzicht** *m* non-consumption; **~ üben** practise *(Am.* practice) non-consumption, refuse to consume; **~zwang** *m* pressure to consume *(od.* buy), aggressive marketing *(pressurizing the consumer to buy more)*

Kontakt *m; -(e)s, -e* contact *(auch Etech.)*; **enger ~** close contact(s *Pl.*); **mit j-m ~ aufnehmen** *od.* **in ~ treten** get in touch with s.o.; **mit j-m in ~ stehen** be in contact *(od.* touch) with s.o.; **mit j-m in ~ bleiben** keep in touch with s.o.; **mit j-m keinen ~ bekommen** not have any contact with s.o., be unable to get to know s.o.; **die ~e abbrechen** *Pol.* break ties *(mit* with); **keinen ~ haben** *Etech.* Drähte etc. not be making contact

Kontakt|abzug *m Fot.* contact print; **~adresse** *f* contact address; **~anzeige** *f* personal ad; **~n** *Rubrik:* personal column

kontaktarm *Adj.:* **er ist ~** he's not a mixer, he finds it difficult to mix with people *(od.* make friends); *(hat wenig Freunde)* he hasn't *(Am.* doesn't have) many friends; **Kontaktarmut** *f* difficulty in making friends; *(Mangel an Freunden)* lack of friends

Kontakt|aufnahme *f: bei der ersten ~ verallgemeinernd:* when first making contact; *bestimmter Fall:* when I etc. first took up contact *(od.* got in touch); **~bereichsbeamte** *m*, **~bereichsbeamtin** *f* community policeman; **~bildschirm** *m Computer:* touch screen; **~büro** *n Pol.* liaison mission

kontakten *v/t.* contact, get in touch with; **würden Sie bitte Herrn X bei der Firma Y ~** would you please get in touch with Mr *(od.* Mr.) X of the Y company; **II.** *v/i.* make contacts; **Kontakter** *m; -s, -, Werbung:* contact man, *bes. Am.* frontman; **Kontakterin** *f; -, -nen Werbung:* contact woman, *bes. Am.* frontwoman

kontaktfähig *Adj.* able to make contact *(od.* mix) easily; **~ sein** be a good mixer; **Kontaktfähigkeit** *f; nur Sg.* ability to make contact *(od.* mix) easily

Kontakt|fläche *f* contact area; **~frau** *f (Agentin etc.)* contact

kontaktfreudig *Adj.* sociable, gregarious; **Kontaktfreudigkeit** *f* sociability, gregariousness

Kontakt|gespräche *Pl.* initial talks; **~gift** *n* contact poison

kontaktieren *v/t.* contact, get in touch with

Kontakt|linse *f* contact lens; **~mangel** *m* lack of social contact; **sie leidet unter ~** she hasn't got many friends; **~mann** *m (Agent etc.)* contact; **~nahme** *f; -, -n* → **Kontaktaufnahme**; **~person** *f bes. Med.* contact; **~pflege** *f* social interaction; **~ betreiben** mix with people; **~schalter** *m* contact switch

kontaktscheu *Adj.* shy; **er ist ~ auch** he shies away from social contact; **Kontaktscheu** *f* shyness, avoidance of social contact

Kontakt|schwierigkeiten *Pl.:* **~ haben** find it hard to make friends, have problems mixing with people; **~sperre** *f Jur.* incommunicado confinement; **~stelle** *f* contact point; **~störung** *f Psych.* social contact dysfunction; **~studium** *n* refresher course *(covering new developments in a field)*

kontaktunfähig *Adj.* unable to mix with people *(od.* make friends); **Kontaktunfähigkeit** *f* inability to mix with people *(od.* make friends)

Kontaktverbot *n Jur.* ban on contact *(with a child/children), Am.* denial of visitation rights

Kontamination *f; -, -en* contamination; **kontaminieren** *v/t.* contaminate

Kontemplation *f; -, -en* contemplation; *religiöse etc.:* meditation; **kontemplativ** *Adj.* contemplative, meditative

kontemporär *Adj.* contemporary

Konten|plan *m Wirts.* classification of accounts; **~rahmen** *m Wirts.* uniform accounting system

Konter *m; -s, -* **1.** *Boxen:* counter(-punch); *Ballspiele:* counterattack, break; **2.** *umg., fig. Handlung:* counter move; *Äußerung:* rejoinder, parry; → **Konterschlag**

Konteradmiral *m; Naut., Mil.* rear admiral

Konter|angriff *m*, **~attacke** *f österr.* counterattack; **~bande** *f* contraband; **~chance** *f Sport* opportunity to counterattack *(Fußball: auch* break)

Konterfei *n; -s, -s; hum.* likeness; *Gemälde:* portrait; *auf Münzen:* effigy

konterkarieren *v/t.* go against; *(durchkreuzen)* thwart

kontern *vt/i. Boxen, fig.:* counter; *Fußball:* counterattack, break; **er versteht es immer wieder zu ~** *fig.* he's never at a loss for a reply; **gut gekontert!** touché!

Konterrevolution *f Pol.* counter-revolution; **konterrevolutionär** *Adj.* counter-revolutionary

Konterschlag *m* counterpunch; *fig. auch* counterattack

Kontext *m; -(e)s, -e* context; **im ~** in context; **aus dem ~ gerissen** (taken) out of context; **kontextuell** *Adj. Ling.* contextual

kontieren *v/t. Wirts.* allocate to an account

Kontinent *m; -(e)s, -e; Geog.* continent; **der (europäische) ~** the Continent

kontinental *Adj.* continental; **Kontinentaldrift** *f* continental drift

Kontinentaleuropa (*n*) continental Europe; **kontinentaleuropäisch** *Adj.* Continental

Kontinental|klima *n* continental climate; **~macht** *f hist.* Continental power; **~sockel** *m* continental shelf; **~sperre** *f*; *nur Sg.*; *hist.*: **die ~** the Continental System; **~verschiebung** *f* continental drift

Kontingent *n*; *-(e)s, -e*; *bes. Mil.* contingent; *Wirts. auch* quota; **kontingentieren** *v/t.* impose a quota/quotas on, subject to quota; (*Waren*) *auch* ration; (*nicht*) *kontingentierte Einfuhren* (non-)quota imports; **Kontingentierung** *f* quota fixing, imposition of a quota/quotas (+ *Gen.* on)

kontinuierlich I. *Adj.* continuous; (*beständig*) steady; *Politik*: consistent; **II.** *Adv.* continuously; (*beständig*) steadily; *arbeiten: auch* without interruption; **Kontinuität** *f*; *-, kein Pl.* continuity; **Kontinuum** *n*; *-s, Kontinua und Kontinuen* continuum (*Pl.* continua)

Konto *n*; *-s, Konten, auch: -s und Konti* **1.** *Fin., Wirts.* account; **auf ~ von** chargeable to the account of; **2.** *fig.*: **die Getränke gehen auf mein ~** the drinks are on me; **das geht auf sein ~** *fig.* he's to blame (for that), that's his doing; **dieser Fehler geht auf dein ~** you're responsible for this mistake, this mistake is down to you

Konto|abschluss *m Fin., Wirts.*, **~ausgleich** *m* balancing of an (*od.* the) account; **~auszug** *m* (bank) statement; **~bewegung** *f* account movement, transaction; **~eröffnung** *f* opening of an account; **~führung** *f* account management; **~führungsgebühr** *f* service charge; *Pl.* bank charges; **~inhaber** *m*, **~inhaberin** *f* account holder

Kontokorrent *n*; *-s, -e*; *Fin., Wirts.* current account; **~kredit** *m* current account credit; (*Überziehungskredit*) overdraft facility

Kontonummer *f* account number

Kontor *n*; *-s, -e*; *Wirts.* (*Niederlassung*) branch (office); **das war ein Schlag ins ~** *fig.* it was (*od.* came as) a nasty shock (*umg.* bombshell); **Kontorist** *m*; *-en, -en*, **Kontoristin** *f*; *-, -nen* clerk

Kontostand *m* balance (of account); **wie ist der ~?** how does the account stand?

kontra I. *Präp.* against; *bes. Jur. und fig.* versus (*Abk.* vs.); **II.** *Adv.*: **er ist immer ~** (*eingestellt*) he always has to take the opposite line; **III. Kontra** *n*; *-s, -s*: *Kontra sagen od.* **geben** *Kartenspiel*: double; **j-m Kontra geben** *fig.* flatly contradict s.o.; *Selbstverteidigung*: hit back at s.o.; → **Pro**

Kontra|alt *m Mus.* contralto; **~bass** *m* double bass, bass viol, contrabass; **~bassist** *m*, **~bassistin** *f* double bass etc. player, bassist

Kontrahent *m*; *-en, -en*, **~in** *f*; *-, -nen* **1.** *Jur.* contracting party; **2.** *Sport etc.* (*Gegner*) opponent

kontrahieren *vt/i. Bio., Med.* contract

Kontraindikation *f Med.* contraindication; **kontraindiziert** *Adj. Med.* contraindicated

Kontrakt *m*; *-(e)s, -e*; *Wirts.* contract **e-n ~** (*ab*)*schließen* make (*od.* conclude) a contract; **j-n in ~ nehmen** contract s.o.; **~abschluss** *m* conclusion of a (*od.* the) contract

Kontraktbruch *m* breach of contract; **kontraktbrüchig** *Adj.* in breach of contract

Kontraktion *f*; *-, -en* contraction

kontraproduktiv I. *Adj.* counterproductive; **II.** *Adv.*: **~ wirken** have a counterproductive effect

Kontrapunkt *m Mus.* counterpoint; **kontrapunktierend** *Adj.*, **kontrapunktisch** *Adj.* contrapuntal

konträr I. *Adj.* opposing, antithetical; *Charaktere*: (completely) opposite; *Ziele*: contrary; **II.** *Adv.* sich entwickeln: in opposite ways

Kontrast *m*; *-(e)s, -e* contrast; **e-n ~ bilden zu / im** *od.* **in ~ stehen mit** (be in) contrast with

kontrastarm *Adj. Fot.* lacking in contrast, low-contrast ...

Kontrast|brei *m Med.* test meal, *mst* barium meal; **~farbe** *f* contrasting colo(u)r; **~figur** *f* foil

kontrastieren *vt/i.*: **~ mit** contrast with, form a contrast to; **etw. mit etw. ~** contrast s.th. with s.th.; **~de Farben** contrasting colo(u)rs

kontrastiv *Adj. Ling.* contrastive

Kontrast|mittel *n Med.* contrast medium; **~programm** *n* alternative program(me); **~regler** *m* contrast control

kontrastreich *Adj.* rich in contrast; (*abwechslungsreich*) varied; *Fot. etc.* high-contrast ..., contrasty

kontrazeptiv *Adj. Med.* contraceptive; **Kontrazeptiv** *n*; *-s, -e*, **Kontrazeptivum** *n*; *-s, Kontrazeptiva*; *Med.* contraceptive

Kontribution *f*; *-, -en* contribution

Kontroll|abschnitt *m* counterfoil, *bes. Am.* stub; **~apparat** *m* **1.** surveillance apparatus; **2.** *Behörde*: supervisory body; **~ausschuss** *m Pol.* supervisory committee; **~befugnis** *f* authority to carry out a check; **~behörde** *f* supervisory body; **~datum** *n* control date

Kontrolle *f*; *-, -n* **1.** (*Aufsicht*) supervision; (*Prüfung*) *auch von Gepäck etc.*: check(ing); *Tech. und von Lebensmitteln etc.*: inspection; (*Überwachung, auch Beherrschung*) control; **unter ärztlicher ~** under medical supervision; **außer ~ geraten** get out of control; **unter ~ bringen, haben, halten**: under control; **die Inflation** *etc.* **unter ~ halten** *auch* keep the lid on inflation *etc. umg.*; **die ~ verlieren über** (+ *Akk.*) lose control of; **er verlor die ~ über s-e Leute** *auch* his men got out of hand; **er verliert leicht die ~ über sich** he's quick to lose his temper, he tends to flare up (very quickly); → **Qualitätskontrolle**; **2.** (*Kontrollpunkt*) checkpoint; (*Passkontrolle*) passport control; (*Zollkontrolle*) customs *Sg.* (control)

Kontrolleur *m*; *-s, -e*, **~in** *f*; *-, -nen* inspector

Kontroll|frage *f* control question; **~funktion** *f* monitoring function; **~gang** *m* round (of inspection); *Polizei*: patrol; **~gerät** *n* monitor; **~gruppe** *f bes. Med.* control group

kontrollierbar *Adj.* **1.** checkable, verifiable; **schwer ~** difficult to check (*od.* to keep a check on); **2.** (*steuerbar*) controllable; **Kontrollierbarkeit** *f*; *nur Sg.* **1.** checkability, verifiability; **2.** (*Steuerbarkeit*) controllability

kontrollieren *v/t.* **1.** (*beaufsichtigen*) supervise; (*Fortschritt, Verlauf*) monitor; *punktuell*: check; *Tech.* (*Qualität*) control; (*Tatsachen*) *auch* verify; (*j-n*) *auch* check up on; **hör auf, mich dauernd zu ~!** you'll stop checking up on me all the time!; **2.** (*nachprüfen, auch Gepäck etc.*) check; *Tech.* (*auch*

Lebensmittel etc.) inspect; **auf etw.** (*Akk.*) (*hin*) **kontrolliert werden** be checked for s.th.; **an der Grenze wurde streng kontrolliert** there was a strict customs inspection (*od.* control) at the border; **3.** (*beherrschen, regeln, steuern*) control

Kontroll|instanz *f* supervisory authority; **~karte** *f* time card; **~kommission** *f* control commission; **~lampe** *f*, **~leuchte** *f*, **~licht** *n* pilot light; (*Warnlampe*) warning light; **~liste** *f* checklist; **~maßnahmen** *Pl.* controlling measures; **~mechanismus** *m* control mechanism; **die Kontrollmechanismen des demokratischen Systems** the checks and balances of the democratic system; **~möglichkeit** *f* opportunity for inspection (*od.* checking); **~nummer** *f* control number

Kontrollor *m*; *-s, -e*; *österr.* → **Kontrolleur**

Kontroll|organ *n Pol.* governing (*od.* controlling) body; **~punkt** *m* checkpoint; *Mot. bei Rallye*: control; **~rat** *m hist.*: **der Alliierte ~** the Allied Control Commission; **~schild** *n schw. Mot.* number plate, *Am.* license plate; **~schirm** *m* monitor; **~stelle** *f* checkpoint; **~stempel** *m* inspection stamp; **~system** *n* monitoring system; **~turm** *m* control tower; **~uhr** *f* timer; (*Stechuhr*) time clock; **~untersuchung** *f* (medical) checkup; **~waage** *f für Waren auf Transportband etc.*: checkweigher; **~zentrum** *n* control cent|re (*Am. -er*); **~zettel** *m* check slip

kontrovers I. *Adj.* controversial; *Frage: auch* contentious; **II.** *Adv.*: **~ diskutieren** dispute; **Kontroverse** *f*; *-, -n* controversy; (*Streit*) dispute (**über** + *Akk.*, **um** about)

Kontur *f*; *-, -en* **1.** **~en** contours, outlines; **2.** *fig.*: **an ~ gewinnen/verlieren** (begin to) take shape / fade away; **als Politiker etc.**: (begin to) make a name for o.s. (*od.* make one's mark) / fade from view

konturen|los *Adj.* shapeless, flat; **~reich** *Adj.* well-defined, clear-cut

Konturen|schärfe *f Fot.* definition; **~stift** *m* lip pencil

konturieren *v/t.* outline, draw in outline; **konturlos** *Adj.* → **konturenlos**

Konus *m*; *-, -se und Konen* cone; *Tech.* (*Verjüngung*) taper

Konvaleszent *m*; *-en, -en*, **~in** *f*; *-, -nen* convalescent; **Konvaleszenz** *f*; *-, kein Pl.* convalescence

Konvektion *f*; *-, -en* convection; **Konvektor** *m*; *-s, -en* convector, convection heater

Konvent *m*; *-(e)s, -e* **1.** convention; **2.** (*Kloster*) monastery; (*Frauenkloster*) convent

Konvention *f*; *-, -en* convention; *gesellschaftliche: auch Pl.* (social) convention

Konventionalstrafe *f* penalty for failing to fulfil(l) a contract, default penalty

konventionell I. *Adj.* **1.** conventional (*auch Waffen*); **2.** (*steif*) stiff, formal; **II.** *Adv.*: **hier geht es sehr ~ zu** it's all very stiff and formal here

konvergent *Adj.* convergent; **Konvergenz** *f*; *-, -en* convergence; **konvergieren** *v/i.* converge

Konversation *f*; *-, -en* conversation; **~ machen** make conversation

Konversations|lexikon *n altm.* encyclop(a)edia; **~stück** *n Theat.* comedy of manners; **~ton** *m, nur Sg.* conversational tone

Konversion f; -, -en conversion; (*Entmilitarisierung*) demilitarization, conversion to civilian use

Konverter m; -s, - converter

konvertibel *Adj.*, **konvertierbar** *Adj. Wirts.*, *EDV* convertible; **frei konvertierbare Währungen** freely convertible currencies; **Konvertierbarkeit** f convertibility

konvertieren I. v/t. (*hat konvertiert*); *Wirts.*, *EDV* convert (**zu** to); **II.** v/i. (*ist*); *Reli.* convert; **zum Protestantismus** etc. ~ convert (*od.* be converted) to Protestantism *etc.*, become a Protestant *etc.*; **Konvertit** m; -en, -en, **Konvertitin** f; -, -nen; *Reli.* convert

konvex *Adj. Opt.* convex

Konvex|linse f convex lens; **~spiegel** m convex mirror

Konvikt n; -(e)s, -e **1.** *Reli.* seminary; **2.** *österr.* (*Internat*) Catholic boarding school

Konvoi m; -s, -s convoy; **im** ~ **fahren** drive in convoy

Konvolut n; -(e)s, -e bundle of documents

Konvulsion f; -, -en; *Med.* convulsion; **konvulsiv** *Adj.* **konvulsivisch** *Adj.* convulsive

konzedieren v/t. concede (*j-m* to s.o.)

Konzentrat n; -(e)s, -e concentrate; *fig.* résumé

Konzentration f; -, -en concentration; **konzentrationsfähig** *Adj.* able to concentrate

Konzentrations|fähigkeit f; *nur Sg.* powers *Pl.* of concentration; **~lager** n concentration camp; **~mangel** m: **unter** ~ **leiden** have difficulty concentrating; **~schwäche** f lack of concentration

konzentrieren I. v/t. concentrate (**auf** + *Akk.* on); (*Aufmerksamkeit*) *auch* focus (on); **II.** v/refl. concentrate (**auf** + *Akk.* on); **Ruhe bitte - ich muss mich auf meine Arbeit** ~ quiet, please - I've got to concentrate on my work; **konzentriert I.** *P.P.* → **konzentrieren**; **II.** *Adj.* concentrated; **III.** *Adv.*: ~ **arbeiten** work with great concentration, concentrate on one's work; **Konzentriertheit** f; *nur Sg.*, **Konzentrierung** f concentration

konzentrisch I. *Adj.* concentric; **II.** *Adv.* concentrically

Konzept n; -(e)s, -e (rough) draft, *für e-e Rede: auch* notes *Pl.*; (*Plan*) plan(s *Pl.*); **aus dem** ~ **kommen** *od.* **geraten** lose the thread; **j-n aus dem** ~ **bringen** put s.o. off his (*od.* her) stride; **j-m das** ~ **verderben** thwart s.o.'s plans; **das passt ihr nicht ins** ~ it doesn't fit in with her plans; (*gefällt ihr nicht*) she doesn't like it

Konzeption f; -, -en **1.** (*Begriff*) (basic) concept; (*Entwurf*) plan; **2.** *Med.* conception; **konzeptionell** *Adj.* conceptual; **konzeptionslos** *Adj.* haphazard; ~ **sein** have no clear idea; **Konzeptionslosigkeit** f haphazardness

Konzept|kunst f conceptual art; **~künstler** m, **~künstlerin** f conceptual artist; **~papier** n rough paper

konzeptualisieren v/t. conceptualize; **konzeptuell** *Adj.* conceptual

Konzern m; -(e)s, -e; *Wirts.* group (of companies), combine; **die multinationalen** ~e the multinationals; **~leitung** f **1.** *nur Sg.* (central) management of a group of companies; **2.** group management; **~spitze** f top-flight management (of a group of companies)

Konzert n; -(e)s, -e; *Mus.* **1.** concert (*auch fig.*); (*Solovortrag*) recital; **ein ~ geben** give a concert (*Solo:* recital); **ins ~ gehen** go to a concert; **2.** (*Musikstück*) concerto; **~agentur** f concert agency

konzertant *Adj.* concertante; **~e Aufführung** e-r *Oper:* concert performance; **~e Sinfonie** sinfonia concertante

Konzert|besucher m, **~besucherin** f concertgoer; **die** ~ **waren begeistert** the (concert) audience was delighted; **~flügel** m concert grand; **~führer** m guide to the concert repertoire; **~gitarre** f classical guitar; **~halle** f concert hall

konzertiert *Adj.*: **~e Aktion** concerted action

Konzertina f; -, -s; *Mus.* concertina

Konzert|meister m, **~meisterin** f *Mus.* leader, first violin, *Am.* concertmaster; **~pianist** m, **~pianistin** f concert pianist; **~programm** n **1.** (*auch Heft*) (-concert) program(me); **2.** e-r *Saison:* program(me) of concerts; **~publikum** n concert audience; **~reihe** f series of concerts; **~reise** f concert tour; **~saal** m concert hall; **~sänger** m, **~sängerin** f m concert singer; **~tournee** f concert tour; **auf** ~ (on a concert) tour; **~veranstalter** m, **~veranstalterin** f concert promoter; **~veranstaltung** f concert

Konzession f; -, -en **1.** (*Gewerbeerlaubnis*) licen|ce (*Am.* -se); *für die Produkte e-s Unternehmens:* franchise; *Bergb.* (*auch für Ölbohrungen etc.*) concession; **2.** (*Zugeständnis*) concession (**an** + *Akk.* to); **~en machen** make concessions (+ *Dat. od.* **an** + *Dat.* to); **Konzessionär** m; -s, -e, **Konzessionärin** f; -, -nen licensee; *für ein Produkt:* franchisee; *Bergb. etc.* concessionaire, *Am. auch* concessioner; **konzessionieren** v/t. grant a licen|ce (*Am.* -se) (*für ein Produkt:* franchise, *Bergb. etc.* concession) to

konzessionsbereit *Adj.* willing to make concessions, conciliatory; **Konzessionsbereitschaft** f conciliatory attitude

Konzessionsinhaber m, **~in** f licensee; *für ein Produkt:* franchisee; *Bergb. etc.* concessionaire, *Am. auch* concessioner

konzessionspflichtig *Adj.* requiring a licen|ce (*Am.* -se)

konzessiv *Adj. Ling.* concessive; **Konzessivsatz** m concessive clause

Konzil n; -s, -e und -ien **1.** *kirchl.* council; **2.** *Univ.* etwa senate

konziliant *Adj.* conciliatory

Konzilsvater m *kirchl.* council member with voting rights

konzipieren v/t. plan, conceive; *Tech.* design; (*Schriftliches*) draft, prepare a draft for; **konzipiert für/als** designed for/as; **Konzipierung** f conception, *Tech.* design(ing); *schriftlich:* drafting

Kooperation f; -, -en cooperation

kooperationsbereit *Adj.* ready to cooperate, cooperative; **Kooperationsbereitschaft** f readiness to cooperate, cooperative attitude

Kooperationsvertrag m cooperative agreement

kooperativ I. *Adj.* cooperative; **II.** *Adv.*: **wir können es nur** ~ **lösen** we can only solve it by working together; **Kooperative** f; -, -n cooperative, co-op *umg.*; **kooperieren** v/i. cooperate

Koordinate f; -, -n; *Geog.*, *Math.* coordinate

Koordinaten|achse f *Math.* coordinate axis; **~kreuz** n *Math.* coordinate axes *Pl.*; **~netz** n *Geog.* grid of parallels and meridians, map grid; **~system** n *Math.* system of coordinates

Koordination f; -, -en coordination; **Koordinationsstörungen** *Pl. Med.* impaired coordination *Sg.*; **Koordinator** m; -s, -en, **Koordinatorin** f; -, -nen coordinator; **koordinieren** v/t. coordinate; **Koordinierung** f coordination

Kopeke f; -, -n kope(c)k; **~n** *umg. fig.* (*Geld*) cash, dough

Kopenhagen (n); -s; *Geog.* Copenhagen

Köper m; -s, - twill; *für Jeans:* denim

kopernikanisch *Adj.*; *nur attr.* Copernican

Kopf m; -(e)s, Köpfe **1.** head (*auch von Sachen und Tech.*); (*Briefkopf*) letterhead; e-r *Seite etc.*: top; e-r *Pfeife:* bowl; ~ **an** ~ closely packed; *bei Rennen etc.*: neck and neck; ~ **stehen** stand on one's head; *Flug.* nose over; *umg. fig.* go mad (*bes. Am.* crazy) (*wegen* over); **es steht auf dem** ~ it's upside down; **etw. auf den** ~ **stellen** turn s.th. upside down; **die Bude auf den** ~ **stellen** *umg.* (*durchsuchen, in Unordnung bringen*) turn the place upside down; (*ausgelassen feiern*) have a wild fling; **die Tatsachen auf den** ~ **stellen** turn the facts on their head, twist things (*od.* the facts); **und wenn du dich auf den** ~ **stellst** *umg.* you can do what you like, you can talk until you're blue in the face; **von** ~ **bis Fuß** from head to foot, from top to toe; **den** ~ **hängen lassen** hang one's head; ~ **hoch!** *umg.* chin up!; **e-n dicken** ~ **haben** have a headache (*umg.* a thick head); *vom Alkohol:* have a hangover; **e-n roten** ~ **bekommen** go red, blush; **j-m den** ~ **waschen** wash s.o.'s hair; **2.** (*Sinn, Verstand, Urteil*) head, mind; (*Willen*) head; (*Gedächtnis*) memory; **aus dem** ~ **aufsagen:** from memory, by heart; **im** ~ **ausrechnen** work out in one's head; **ich habe andere Dinge im** ~ I've got other things on my mind (*od.* to think about); **er hat nur Fußball im** ~ all he ever thinks about is football; **er ist nicht ganz richtig im** ~ *umg.* he's got a screw loose; **wo hatte ich nur meinen** ~? what was I thinking of?; **den** ~ **voll haben** have a lot (*od.* too much) on one's mind; **das kannst du dir aus dem** ~ **schlagen** you can forget (about) that; **das will mir nicht aus dem** ~ I can't get it out of my mind; **sich** (*Dat.*) **etw. durch den** ~ **gehen lassen** think s.th. over; **j-m im** ~ **herumgehen** go (a)round and (a)round in s.o.'s mind; **er hat es sich in den** ~ **gesetzt, es zu tun** he's determined to do it, *umg.* he's dead set on doing it; **geht das nicht in d-n** ~? can't you get that into your head?; **j-m in den** ~ *od.* **zu** ~ **steigen** go to s.o.'s head; **sich** (*Dat.*) **den** ~ **zerbrechen** rack one's brains; **s-n eigenen** ~ **haben** have a mind of one's own; **mir steht der** ~ **nicht danach** I don't really feel like it; **3.** *fig.* (*Geist, Denker*) (great) thinker; (*Führer*) head, leader; (*treibende Kraft*) mastermind, driving force; **der** ~ **von etw. sein** mastermind s.th.; **4.** (*einzelne Person*) person, head; (*Stück*) piece; **pro** ~ a head, per person, each; **5.** *fig* (*Leben*) **s-n** ~ **retten** save one's skin; ~ **und Kragen riskie-**

ren risk one's neck; *das wird ihn den ~ kosten!* it'll cost him his life; **6.** *sonstige Wendungen*: *er wird dir schon nicht gleich den ~ abreißen* he won't bite your head off; *den ~ in den Sand stecken* hide one's head in the sand; *den ~ (nicht) verlieren* (not) lose one's head; *den ~ aus der Schlinge ziehen* wriggle out of it, *bes. Am.* auch beat the rap *umg.*; *sich* (*Dat.*) *e-n ~ machen umg.* worry; *er ist nicht auf den ~ gefallen umg.* he's no fool; *ich weiß nicht, wo mir der ~ steht umg.* I don't know whether I'm coming or going; *j-m den ~ verdrehen umg.* turn s.o.'s head; *j-m den ~ zurechtrücken umg.* bring s.o. to his (*od.* her) senses, sort s.o. out; *sein Geld auf den ~ hauen umg.* blow one's money; *immer mit dem ~ durch die Wand wollen umg.* be pigheaded; *bis über den ~ in Schulden stecken* be up to one's neck (*umg.* eyeballs) in debt; *j-m über den ~ wachsen umg.* outgrow s.o., *Arbeit etc.*: get too much for s.o.; *über s-n ~ hinweg* over his head, without consulting him; *j-n vor den ~ stoßen umg.* put s.o.'s nose out of joint; *j-m Beleidigungen an den ~ werfen* hurl insults at s.o.; *Köpfe werden rollen* heads will roll; *da fasst man sich doch an den ~* it really makes you wonder; **7.** *ein ~ Salat/Blumenkohl* a (head of) lettuce/ cauliflower

Kopf-an-Kopf-Rennen *n* neck-and--neck race

Kopf|arbeit *f* brainwork; **~arbeiter** *m*, **~arbeiterin** *f* brainworker; **~bahnhof** *m* terminus

Kopfball *m Fußball*: header; **~spiel** *n* heading of the ball, play in the air

kopfballstark *Adj.* strong in the air; *ein ~er Spieler* a good header of the ball

Kopfballtor *n* headed goal

Kopf|bedeckung *f* headgear; *mit ~* with something on one's head; *ohne ~* bareheaded; **~bewegung** *f* movement of the head

Köpfchen *n* little head; *~, ~! umg.* it's brains you need; *~ haben* have brains; *vernünftig*: have one's head screwed on; *mit ~ arbeiten* use one's brains

köpfeln *südd., österr., schw.* **I.** *v/t.* → *köpfen* I 3; **II.** *v/i.* dive (headfirst)

köpfen I. *v/t.* **1.** *j-n ~* behead s.o., decapitate s.o., cut (*od.* chop) off s.o.'s head; **2.** (*Ei*) slice the top off (*Blume etc.*) decapitate; (*Bäume*) top; (*Flasche*) crack open; **3.** *Fußball*: (*Ball*) head; (*Tor*) score with a header; **II.** *v/i. Fußball*: head the ball

Kopfende *n* head; *Eisenb.* front

Köpfer *m; -s, -; umg.* → *Kopfball*, *Kopfsprung*

Kopf|form *f* shape of head; *runde etc. ~* round(-shaped) *etc.* head; **~füßer** *m; -s, -; Zool.* cephalopod; **~geburt** *f fig.* figment of the imagination, impossible idea; **~geld** *n* (*Belohnung*) reward (*for s.o.'s capture*), head money, bounty; *weitS.* blood money; **~grippe** *f* cold with a bad headache; **~haar** *n* hair (on one's head); **~haltung** *f* head posture; *e-e gerade ~ haben* hold one's head straight; **~haut** *f* scalp; **~höhe** *f*: *in ~* at head height; **~hörer** *m*: (*ein*) ~ (a pair of) headphones *Pl.*

...köpfig *im Adj.* **1.** *...-headed*; *rund~* round-headed; *kahl~* bare-headed; *drei~* three-headed; **2.** *Zahl der Mitglieder*: *e-e fünf~e Familie* a family of five; *ein sieben~es Gremium* a com-

mittee of seven; **3.** *Art von Haarwuchs*: *...-haired*; *grau~* grey-haired, *Am.* gray-haired (*od.* -headed); *locken~* curly-haired

Kopf|jäger *m* headhunter (*auch fig.*); **~jucken** *n; -s, kein Pl.* itching of the scalp; *~ haben* have an itchy scalp; **~keil** *m wedge-shaped ridge in the end of a mattress*

Kopfkissen *n* (bed) pillow; **~bezug** *m* pillowcase, pillowslip

Kopf|lage *f bei Geburt*: head presentation; **~länge** *f*: *um e-e ~* by a head

kopflastig *Adj.* **1.** *Flug.* nose-heavy; *Naut.* bow-heavy; **2.** *fig. Betrieb*: top--heavy; *Buch, Film etc.*: over-intellectual, *Am. umg. auch* eggheaded; **Kopflastigkeit** *f; nur Sg.* **1.** *Flug.* nose--heaviness; *Naut.* bow-heaviness; **2.** *fig. e-s Betriebs*: top-heaviness; *von Buch, Film etc.*: excessive intellectual weight, *Am. umg. auch* eggheadedness

Kopf|laus *f* head louse; **~leiste** *f Druck.* headpiece

Köpfler *m; -s, -; südd., österr. Fußball*: header

kopflos I. *Adj.* **1.** headless; **2.** *fig.* (*erschreckt*) panic-stricken; **~e Flucht** stampede; **II.** *Adv.*: **~ davonrennen** flee in panic; **Kopflosigkeit** *f; nur Sg.; fig.* panic; (*Übereiltheit*) rashness

Kopf|massage *f* scalp massage; **~mensch** *m* cerebral person; **~nicken** *n; -s, kein Pl.* nod(ding); **~nuss** *f umg.* **1.** rap on the head; **2.** (*Denkaufgabe*) brainteaser

kopfrechnen I. *v/i. nur Inf.* do sums in one's head, do mental arithmetic; *gut ~ können* be good at mental arithmetic; **II. Kopfrechnen** *n* mental arithmetic

Kopfsalat *m* cabbage lettuce

kopfscheu *Adj.* timid; *j-n ~ machen* intimidate s.o.

Kopfschmerzen *Pl.* headache *Sg.*; *~ haben* have a headache; *j-m ~ bereiten umg. fig.* give s.o. a headache; *was mir am meisten ~ bereitet* my biggest headache; *mach dir deswegen keine ~ umg.* don't let that worry you, don't lose any sleep over it; **Kopfschmerztablette** *f* headache pill (*od.* tablet)

Kopf|schmuck *m* headdress; **~schuppe** *f* flake of dandruff; *Pl.* dandruff; **~schuss** *m* shot in the head

Kopfschütteln *n; -s, kein Pl.* shaking (*od.* shake) of the head; *allgemeines ~* general disapproval; **kopfschüttelnd** *Adv.* shaking one's head; *verneinen etc.*: with a shake of the head

Kopf|schutz *m* protective headgear; (*Helm*) helmet; **~sprung** *m*: *e-n ~ machen* dive head(-)first; **~stand** *m* headstand; *Flug.* nose-over; *e-n ~ machen* stand on one's head

kopfstark *Adj. umg.* brainy

kopfstehen → *Kopf* 1

Kopf|steinpflaster *n* cobblestones *Pl.*; **~steuer** *f hist.* poll tax; **~stimme** *f* head voice; *weitS.* falsetto; **~stoß** *m Boxen*: butt; *Fußball*: header; **~stütze** *f* headrest; *Mot. auch* head restraint; **~teil** *n, m des Betts*: headboard; **~tuch** *n* (head)scarf

kopfüber *Adv.* head-first (*auch fig.*); *sich ~ in die Arbeit stürzen fig.* plunge headlong into one's work

Kopf|verband *m* head bandage; **~verletzung** *f* head injury; **~wäsche** *f* hairwash; *beim Friseur*: shampoo; *umg. fig.* dressing down; **~weh** *n umg.* → *Kopfschmerzen*; **~weide** *f Bot.* pollarded willow; **~wunde** *f* head wound;

~zahl *f* number of persons; **~zerbrechen** *n*: *es hat uns viel ~ bereitet* we really had to rack our brains (over it), it gave us quite a headache; *mach dir kein ~ darüber* don't lose any sleep over it

Kopie *f; -, -n* copy (*auch fig.*); (*Zweitschrift*) *auch* duplicate; (*Fotokopie*) photocopy; *Fot.* (*Abzug*) print; *Kunst*: copy, *Gemälde: auch* reproduction, *Plastik: auch* replica; **kopieren** *v/t.* copy; (*nachahmen*) *auch* imitate; *Fot.* (*Abzüge machen*) print; **Kopierer** *m; -s, -* (photo)copier

Kopier|gerät *n* (photo)copier; **~papier** *n* (*zum Fotokopieren*) photocopying paper; (*Fotopapier*) printing paper; **~schutz** *m EDV* copy protection

Kopilot *m*, **~in** *f Flug.* copilot; *Mot.* co--driver

Kopist *m; -en, -en*, **~in** *f; -, -en* copyist; (*Nachahmer*) copier, imitator

Koppel¹ *f; -, -n* **1.** (*Pferdegehege*) paddock; (*Einfriedung*) enclosure; **2.** (*Riemen*) leash; **3.** (*~ Hunde*) pack

Koppel² *n; -s, -; Mil.* belt

koppeln *v/t.* **1.** (*Teile, Fahrzeuge*) couple; (*Anhänger*) hitch up (*an + Akk.* to); (*Raumschiffe*) *auch* dock; **2.** (*Tiere*) leash together; **3.** (*Sache*) link, connect (*an + Akk.* to); associate (*mit* with)

Kopp(e)lung *f* coupling; *Raumfahrt*: docking; *von Tieren*: leashing; *von Sachen*: linking, association

Kopplungs|geschäft *n* package deal, *Am. auch* tie-in (deal); **~manöver** *n Raumfahrt*: docking

Kopra *f; -, kein Pl.* copra

Koproduktion *f* coproduction, joint production; **Koproduzent** *m*, **Koproduzentin** *f* coproducer

Kopte *m; -n, -n*, **Koptin** ; *-, -en Reli.* Copt; **koptisch** *Adj.* Coptic

Kopulation *f; -, -en* **1.** copulation; **2.** *Gartenbau*: whip graft(ing); **kopulieren I.** *v/t. Bot.* splice-graft; **II.** *v/i.* (*koitieren*) copulate

kor *Imperf.* → *küren*

Koralle *f; -, -n* coral

Korallen|bank *f* coral reef; **~insel** *f* coral island; **~kette** *f* coral necklace; **~riff** *n* coral reef

korallenrot *Adj.* coral red

Korallentier *n Zool.* coral polyp

Koran *m; -s, -e* Koran; **~schule** *f* Koranic school; **~schüler** *m* student of the Koran

Korb *m; -(e)s, Körbe* **1.** basket; *j-m e-n ~ geben umg. fig.* turn s.o. down, give s.o. the brush-off; *e-n ~ bekommen / sich* (*Dat.*) *e-n ~ holen* be turned down, be given the brush-off; **2.** *Sport, Basketball*: basket; *Korbball*: net; **3.** (*Bienenkorb*) hive; **4.** (*Förderkorb*) cage; **~ball** *m* netball; **~blütler** *m; -s, -; Bot.* composite (flower)

Körbchen *n* **1.** (*für Hunde etc.*) basket; *ab ins ~! umg. fig.* off to bed with you; **2.** *von BH*: cup; **~größe** *f von BH*: cup size

körbeweise *Adv.* by the basketful; *etw. ~ pflücken auch* pick basketfuls of s.th.

Korb|flasche *f* wicker bottle; *sehr groß*: demijohn; **~flechter** *m*, **~flechterin** *f* basket maker (*bes. Am.* weaver); **~geflecht** *n* wickerwork; **~macher** *m*, **~macherin** *f* basket maker (*bes. Am.* weaver); **~möbel** *Pl.* wicker furniture *Sg.*; **~sessel** *m*, **~stuhl** *m* wicker chair; **~wagen** *m für Kinder*: wicker pram; **~waren** *Pl.* wickerwork

Sg.; **~weide** *f* osier, basket willow; **~wurf** *m Basketball*: basket shot

Kord *m*; *-(e)s*, *-e od. -s* corduroy; **~anzug** *m* corduroy suit

Kordel *f*; *-*, *-n* cord

Kordhose *f*: *(e-e)* ~ (a pair of) corduroy trousers (*Am.* pants *od.* slacks), cords *umg. Pl.*

Kordilleren [kɔrdɪlˈjeːrən] *Pl. Geog.*: **die** ~ the Cordilleras

Kord|jacke *f* corduroy jacket; **~jeans** *f*: *(e-e)* ~ (a pair of) cord(uroy) jeans *Pl.*

Kordon *m*; *-s*, *-s*, *österr.* *-e* cordon; *e-n* ~ **ziehen um** form a cordon around, cordon off

Kordsamt *m* cord velvet

Korea *(n)*; *-s; Geog.* Korea; **Koreakrieg** *m hist.* Korean War; **Koreaner** *m*; *-s*, *-*, **Koreanerin** *f*; *-*, *-nen* Korean, *weiblich auch*: Korean woman (*od.* girl *etc.*); **koreanisch I.** *Adj* Korean; **II. Koreanisch** *n*; *-en; Ling.* Korean; **das Koreanische** Korean

kören *v/t. fachspr.* choose for breeding

Korfu *(n)*; *-s; Geog.* Corfu

Körhengst *m* breeding stallion

Koriander *m*; *-s*, *-* coriander, *Am. auch* cilantro

Korinth *(n)*; *-s; Geog.* Corinth

Korinthe *f*; *-*, *-n* currant; **Korinthenkacker** *m*; *-s*, *-*; *umg. pej.* nitpicker; **Korinthenkackerei** *f*; *-*, *kein Pl.*; *umg. pej.* nitpicking

Korinther *m*; *-s*, *-* Corinthian; **korinthisch** *Adj.* Corinthian

Kork *m*; *-(e)s*, *-e; Bot.* cork; *nach* ~ **schmecken** *Wein etc.*: be corked; **~eiche** *f Bot.* cork oak

Korken *m*; *-s*, *-* cork

Korkenzieher *m*; *-s*, *-* corkscrew; **~locken** *Pl.* corkscrew curls

Kork|geschmack *m*: *e-n* ~ **haben** *Wein etc.*: be corked; **~gürtel** *m* cork belt

korkig *Adj.* corky; *Wein*: corked

Korksohle *f* cork sole

Kormoran *m -s*, *-e; Orn.* cormorant

Korn[1] *n*; *-(e)s*, *Körner* **1.** *von Sand, Getreide*: grain; *(Samen)* seed; *(Pfefferkorn)* (pepper)corn; **2.** *(Getreide)* grain, cereal, *Brit. auch* corn; *(Roggen)* rye; *(Weizen)* wheat; *das* ~ *steht gut* the grain harvest is coming on well; **3.** *Leder, Fot.* grain; **4.** *Pl. -e*; *(an Handfeuerwaffen)* front sight; *über Kimme und* ~ *anvisieren* line up the sights to take aim; *j-n/etw. aufs* ~ *nehmen* take aim at s.o./s.th.; *fig. (beobachten)* keep a close watch on s.o. / *(angreifen)* attack s.th.

Korn[2] *m*; *-(e)s*, *-*; *umg. (Kornbranntwein)* (corn) schnapps

Korn|ähre *f* ear of corn; **~blume** *f* cornflower; **Ɔblumenblau** *Adj.* cornflower (blue); *umg. fig.* pissed as a newt *Sl., Am.* three sheets to the wind *Sl.*; **~branntwein** *m* corn schnapps

Körnchen *n* small grain; ~ *Wahrheit fig.* grain of truth

körnen I. *v/i. Salz, Zucker etc.*: granulate; **II.** *v/t. Metall.* granulate; *(auch Leder, Schießpulver)* grain

Körner|fresser *m* **1.** *Zool.* seed-eating bird, granivore; **2.** *umg. pej.* muesli freak; **~fresserin** *f umg. pej.* → **Körnerfresser** 2; **~frucht** *f* cereal; **~futter** *n* grain feed

Kornett *n*; *-(e)s*, *-e und -s*; *Mus.* cornet

Korn|fäule *m* bunt, stinking smut; **~feld** *n* cornfield, *Am.* grainfield

körnig *Adj.* granular, grainy (*auch Fot.*); *Gastr., Reis etc.*: al dente; **…körnig** *im Adj.* …-grained

kornisch I. *Adj.* Cornish; **II. Kornisch**

---

n; *-en; Ling.* Cornish; *das Kornische* Cornish

Korn|käfer *m Zool.* corn weevil; **~kammer** *f* granary (*auch fig.*); **~rade** *f Bot.* corn cockle; **~speicher** *m* granary

Körnung *f* grain

Korona *f*; *-*, *Koronen* **1.** *Astron., Etech.* corona (*Pl.* coronae); **2.** *umg. (Personenkreis)* crowd, bunch

Koronar|erkrankung *f Med.* coronary disease; **~gefäß** *n Anat.* coronary vessel; **~insuffizienz** *f Med.* coronary insufficiency (*od.* failure)

Körper *m*; *-s*, *-* **1.** body (*auch von Farbe, Wein*); *am ganzen* ~ *zittern* tremble all over; **2.** *Phys., Math.* body; *fester*: solid; **3.** *(Körperschaft)* body; **~ausdünstung** *f* body odo(u)r; **~bau** *m*; *nur Sg.* build, physique; **~behaarung** *f* body hair; **~beherrschung** *f* body control

körperbehindert *Adj.* (physically) disabled, handicapped, *Am. auch* physically challenged; **Körperbehinderte** *m*, *f* handicapped (*Am. auch* physically challenged) person; *Pl.* the handicapped, handicapped people; **~(r) sein** be handicapped (*Am. auch* physically challenged); **Körperbehinderung** *f* (physical) disability *od.* handicap

körperbetont I. *Adj.* **1.** *Sport* (very) physical; **2.** *Mode*: figure-hugging, emphasizing the figure; **II.** *Adv.*: ~ *geschnitten* cut so as to emphasize the figure

Körperbewegung *f* (body) movement; **~en** *Gymnastik*: motions

körpereigen *Adj.* endogenic; *die* ~*en Abwehrkräfte etc.* the body's own (*od.* inbuilt) defen|ces (*Am. -ses etc.*)

Körper|einsatz *m Sport* use of physical strength; *Fußball etc.*: physical play; **~ertüchtigung** *f* physical training

körperfeindlich *Adj.* anti-physical

Körper|flüssigkeit *f* bod(il)y fluid; **~form** *f* body shape

körperfremd *Adj.* foreign

Körper|fülle *f* corpulence; **~funktion** *f* bodily function

körpergerecht *Adj. Sitz etc.*: contoured

Körper|geruch *m* body odo(u)r, BO *umg.*; **~gewicht** *n* (body) weight; **~größe** *f* height; **~haare** *Pl.* body hair *Sg.*; **~hälfte** *f*: *die rechte/linke* ~ the right/left half (*od.* side) of the body; *die obere/untere* ~ the upper/lower part (*od.* half) of the body; **~haltung** *f* posture; *e-e gute/schlechte* ~ good/bad posture; **~hygiene** *f* personal hygiene; **~kontakt** *m* physical (*od.* bodily) contact; *Sport* body contact; **~kraft** *f* physical strength; **~länge** *f Mensch*: height; *Schlange etc.*: length

körperlich I. *Adj.* **1.** physical; *(fleischlich)* carnal; *Appetite*: *auch* corporeal; ~*e Arbeit* physical (*od.* manual) work, manual labo(u)r; ~*e Betätigung* physical exercise; ~*e Genüsse* physical (*od.* carnal) pleasures, pleasures of the flesh; ~*e Züchtigung* corporal punishment; **2.** *Math.* solid; **II.** *Adv.* physically; ~ *im Vorteil/Nachteil sein* have a physical advantage / be at a physical disadvantage; ~ *hart arbeiten* do hard physical work

körperlos *Adj.* **1.** bodiless, disembodied; **2.** *Sport* without body contact

Körper|maße *Pl.* (body) measurements; **~öffnung** *f* (body) orifice; **~organ** *n* bodily organ; **~pflege** *f* person-

---

al hygiene; **~pflegemittel** *n* personal hygiene product; **~puder** *m* talcum powder

körperreich *Adj. Wein*: full-bodied

Körpersäfte *Pl.* body juices

Körperschaft *f* corporation, corporate body; *gesetzgebende* ~ legislative body; ~ *des öffentlichen Rechts* public corporation; **körperschaftlich** *Adj.* corporate; **Körperschaft(s)steuer** *f* corporation tax

Körper|sprache *f* body language, non-verbal communication *förm.*; **~spray** *m*, *n* deodorant spray; **~stärke** *f* physical strength; **~stelle** *f* place on the body; **~teil** *m* part of the body; *e-r Leiche, abgetrennt*: body part; **~temperatur** *f* body temperature; **~verletzung** *f* (physical) injury; *schwere/leichte* ~ *Jur.* grievous/actual bodily harm; *fahrlässige* ~ bodily harm caused by negligence; **~wärme** *f* body heat; **~zelle** *f Biol.* body cell

Korporal *m*; *-s*, *-e und Korporäle*; *Mil.* corporal

Korporation *f*; *-*, *-en* **1.** *(Körperschaft)* corporation; **2.** *Univ.* fraternity, *Am. auch* frat *umg.*; **korporativ** *Adj.* corporate; **korporiert** *Adj. Univ. altm.* belonging to a fraternity; **Korporierte** *m*; *-n*, *-n Univ. altm.* fraternity member

Korps [koːɐ̯] *n*; *-*, *-* **1.** *Mil.* corps; → *diplomatisch*; **2.** *Univ.* duel(l)ing fraternity; **~geist** *m*; *nur Sg.* esprit de corps; **~student** *m Univ.* student member of a duel(l)ing fraternity

korpulent *Adj.* corpulent, stout; **Korpulenz** *f*; *-*, *kein Pl.* corpulence

Korpus[1] *m*; *-*, *-se* **1.** *umg. (Körper)* body; **2.** *Kunst (Christusfigur)* figure of Christ crucified; **3.** *fachspr. bei Möbeln* basic shell (*od.* frame); **4.** *nur Sg.*; *Mus.* resonance box

Korpus[2] *n*; *-*, *Korpora* **1.** *(Werksammlung, EDV Datensammlung)* corpus (*Pl.* corpora *od.* corpusses); **2.** *Mus.* resonance box

korpusbasiert *Adj. EDV, Ling.* corpus-based

Korreferat *n Univ.* supplementary (seminar) paper; **Korreferent** *m*, **Korreferentin** *f* **1.** reader of the supplementary paper; **2.** *(Prüfer)* coexaminer

korrekt I. *Adj.* *(richtig)* correct; *(angemessen) auch* appropriate, proper; *(fair)* fair; *(ehrlich)* honest, ~*es Benehmen* correct (*od.* proper) behavio(u)r; *j-m* ~*es Benehmen beibringen auch* teach s.o. etiquette (*od.* good manners); *er ist sehr* ~ *im Benehmen*: he is very correct (*od.* proper), he's a stickler for etiquette; *er ist* ~ *wie ein Beamter* he's a stickler for the rules; **II.** *Adv.* **1.** correctly; *sich kleiden, sich benehmen*: *auch* appropriately, properly; *behandeln*: *auch* fairly; *sich* ~ *verhalten* do the right thing; **2.** *Jugendspr.*: *echt voll* ~ good and proper; **korrekterweise** *Adv.* as is right and proper; *(um höflich zu sein)* as a matter of courtesy; so as not to offend anyone; **Korrektheit** *f*; *nur Sg.* correctness; *von Kleidung, Benehmen*: *auch* appropriateness, properness

Korrektiv *n*; *-s*, *-e* corrective

Korrektor *m*; *-s*, *-en*, **~in** *f*; *-*, *-nen Druck.* proofreader; **Korrektorat** *n*; *-(e)s*, *-e* proofreading department

Korrektur *f*; *-*, *-en* **1.** correction; *Druck. (Korrekturlesen)* proofreading; **2.** *(Fahne)* proof; ~*(en) lesen* proofread, read (the) proofs, do (the) proofreading; **~abzug** *m* (galley) proof; **~band** *n* correction tape; **~bogen** *m* page proof; **~fahne** *f* galley (proof); **~lesen** *n* proofreading; **~vorschriften** *Pl.* rules for proofreading; **~taste** *f* correction key; **~zeichen** *n* proofreader's mark, proof-correction mark

Korrelat *n*; *-(e)s*, *-e* correlate; **Korrelation** *f*; *-*, *-en* correlation; **korrelieren** *v/i.* (*auch miteinander ~*) correlate

korrepetieren *v/i. Mus., Theat.* act as repetiteur, coach opera singers; **~ mit** coach; **Korrepetitor** *m*, **Korrepetitorin** *f* repetiteur

Korrespondent *m*; *-en*, *-en* correspondent; **Korrespondentenbericht** *m* correspondent's report; **Korrespondentin** *f*; *-*, *-en* correspondent

Korrespondenz *f*; *-*, *en* correspondence

korrespondieren *v/i.* **1.** correspond (*mit* with); **miteinander ~** write to one another, correspond, exchange letters; **2.** *Sache(n)*: correspond (*mit* to)

Korridor *m*; *-s*, *-e* corridor (*auch fig.*); (*Flur*) hall

korrigierbar *Adj.* correctable; **korrigieren** *v/t.* **1.** *allg.*: correct; (*Druckfahnen*) *auch* read; **2.** (*Klassenarbeiten etc.*) mark, *bes. Am.* grade; **3.** (*justieren*) adjust; **4.** (*s-e Meinung*) revise

korrodieren *v/t/i.* corrode; **Korrosion** *f*; *-*, *-en* corrosion

korrosions|beständig *Adj.*, **~fest** *Adj.* non-corroding, corrosion-resistant

Korrosions|mittel *n* corrosive; **~schutz** *m* corrosion protection

korrosionsverhütend *Adj.* anti-corrosive

korrumpierbar *Adj.* corruptible; **korrumpieren** *v/t.* corrupt

korrupt *Adj.* corrupt; **Korruptheit** *f*; *nur Sg.* corruptness

Korruption *f*; *-*, *-en* corruption; (*Bestechung*) bribery; **Korruptionsaffäre** *f*, **Korruptionsskandal** *m* corruption scandal

Korsage [kɔr'zaːʒə] *f*; *-*, *-n* corsage

Korsar *m*; *-en,-en* corsair

Korse *m*; *-n*, *-n* Corsican

Korsett *n*; *-s*, *-s und -e* corset (*auch Med.*); **~stab** *m*, **~stange** *f* corset bone

Korsika (*n*); *-s*; *Geog.* Corsica; **Korsin** *f*; *-*, *-en* Corsican woman (*od.* girl); **korsisch** *Adj.* Corsican

Korso *m*; *-s*, *-s* **1.** (*Umzug*) parade, procession; **2.** (*Prachtstraße*) boulevard

Kortikoid *n*; *-(e)s*, *-e*; *Bio., Med.* corticosteroid, corticoid

Kortison *n*; *-s*, *-e*; *Med., Pharm.* cortisone

Korvette *f*; *-*, *-n*; *Naut.* corvette; **Korvettenkapitän** *m Mil.* lieutenant-commander

Koryphäe *f*; *-*, *-n* luminary (+ *Gen.* of); great authority (*auf e-m Gebiet* on a subject)

Kosak *m*; *-en*, *-en* Cossack; **Kosakenmütze** *f* (Cossack) fur hat

koscher I. *Adj.* kosher (*auch fig.*); **II.** *Adv.* kochen, schlachten etc.: using kosher methods

K.-o.-Schlag *m* knockout blow

Koseform *f* affectionate form

kosen *v/t/i. poet.* caress; (*miteinander*) ~ kiss and cuddle

Kose|name *m* pet name; **~wort** *n* term of affection

K.-o.-Sieg *m* win by a knockout

Kosinus *m*; *-*, *- und -se*; *Math.* cosine

Kosmetik *f*; *-*, *kein Pl.* **1.** (*Kosmetika*) cosmetics *Pl.*, makeup; **2.** (*Schönheitspflege*) beauty treatment; *viel Zeit für ~ brauchen* need a lot of time to put on one's makeup; **3.** *fig.* cosmetic effect, appearances *Pl.*; *geschickte ~* skil(l)ful patching-up; *die Maßnahme beschränkt sich auf ~* the measure is purely cosmetic; **Kosmetika** *Pl.* cosmetics, makeup *Sg.*

Kosmetik|abteilung *f* cosmetics department; **~artikel** *m* cosmetic (product)

Kosmetiker *m*; *-s*, *-*, **~in** *f*; *-*, *-nen* beautician

Kosmetik|koffer *m* vanity case; **~salon** *m* beauty parlo(u)r (*od.* salon, *Am. auch* shop); **~tasche** *f* makeup bag

kosmetisch I. *Adj.* cosmetic; **~es Mittel** cosmetic; **~e Behandlung** beauty treatment; *bloß ~ sein fig.* be just for show (*od.* effect); **II.** *Adv.* cosmetically; *j-n ~ behandeln* give s.o. beauty treatment

kosmisch I. *Adj.* cosmic; *Station, Zeitalter etc.*: space; **~e Flugkörper** spacecraft *Pl.*; **II.** *Adv.* cosmically

Kosmobiologie *f* cosmobiology

Kosmologie *f*; *-*, *-n* cosmology; **kosmologisch** *Adj.* cosmological

Kosmonaut *m*; *-en*, *-en*, **~in** *f*; *-*, *-nen Raumf.* cosmonaut; **kosmonautisch** *Adj.* (Russian) space travel …

Kosmopolit *m*; *-en*, *-en* cosmopolitan; **kosmopolitisch** *Adj.* cosmopolitan

Kosmos *m*; *-*, *kein Pl.* cosmos; (*Weltall*) *auch* universe

Kosovare *m*; *-n*, *-n* Kosovar; **Kosovarin** *f* -, *-nen* Kosovar woman (*od.* girl)

Kosovo (*n*);*-s*; *Geog.* Kosovo; **~albaner** *m*; *-s*, *-*, **~albanerin** *f*; *-*, *-nen* Kosovar Albanian

Kost *f*; *-*, *kein Pl.* food; *lit. und fig.* fare; (*Verpflegung*) board; *magere ~* a low-fat diet; *fig.* a meag|re (*Am. -er*) offering; *leichte ~* light food; *auch fig.* light fare; (*Lektüre*) light reading; *das Buch etc. ist schwere ~ fig.* the book etc. is heavy-going; *geistige ~* intellectual nourishment; → *Logis 1*

kostbar *Adj.* precious, valuable (*auch fig. Zeit etc.*); (*teuer*) expensive; **Kostbarkeit** *f* **1.** *konkret:* precious object, treasure; **2.** *nur Sg.*; (*Wert*) (great) value

kosten[1] *v/t.* **1.** (*Speisen*) taste; (*probieren*) *auch* try, sample (*beide auch fig.*); **2.** *fig. geh.* (*genießen*) savo(u)r; (*Negatives*) get a taste of

kosten[2] *v/t/i.* cost (*j-n* s.o.); (*Mühe, Zeit*) *auch* take; *was kostet es?* what (*od.* how much) does it cost?, how much is it?; *es kostete ihn sein Leben od. den Kopf* it cost him his life, he paid for it with his life; *er ließ es sich viel ~* he spent a lot of money on it; *koste es, was es wolle* whatever it costs; *das kostet! umg.* that'll cost him etc.!

Kosten *Pl.* cost(s *Pl.*) *Sg.*; (*Spesen*) expenses; (*Gebühren*) fees, charges; *Jur.* costs; *hohe ~* considerable expense *Sg.*; *~ sparende Maßnahmen* cost-saving measures; *auf anderer Leute / eigene ~ auch fig.* at other people's / one's own expense; *auf ~ der Allgemeinheit* at the public expense, out of the public purse; *auf s-e ~ kommen* cover one's expenses; *fig.* get one's money's worth; *das geht auf ~ der Gesundheit fig.* it'll take its toll on your health; *ohne ~* at no cost (*für* to); *die ~ tragen* bear (*od.* pay) the costs; *kei-*

ne ~ scheuen spare no expense; *sie scheuen die ~* they're not prepared to spend the money (*od.* pay that kind of money)

Kosten|anschlag *m* estimate, quotation; **~anstieg** *m* increase in costs; **~anteil** *m* share of the costs; **~aufwand** *m* expenditure; *mit e-m von ~* at a cost of; **~berechnung** *f* costing; **~beteiligung** *f* cost-sharing

kostenbewusst *Adj.* cost-conscious; **Kostenbewusstsein** *n* cost-consciousness

Kostendämpfung *f* curbing (of) costs; *die ~ im Gesundheitswesen* keeping healthcare costs down

kostendeckend I. *Adj.* cost-covering; *Preise:* that cover costs; **II.** *Adv.:* **~ arbeiten** break even, cover one's costs; **Kostendeckung** *f* breaking even, covering costs

Kosten|druck *m Wirts.* pressure of rising costs; **~entwicklung** *f* cost trend; **~ersparnis** *f* cost saving; **~erstattung** *f* refund (of expenses); **~explosion** *f* runaway costs *Pl.*; **~faktor** *m* cost factor; **~festsetzung** *f Jur.* fixing of costs; **~frage** *f* question of cost

kosten|frei *Adj.* free (of cost); **~günstig I.** *Adj.* (very) reasonable; (*billig*) cheap; **II.** *Adv.* at (*od.* for) a reasonable price; (*billig*) cheaply; **~intensiv** *Adj.* cost-intensive

Kostenlawine *f* spiral(l)ing (*od.* escalating) costs *Pl.*

Kosten-Leistungs-Verhältnis *n* cost-performance ratio

kostenlos *Adj. und Adv.* free (of charge); *bekommen: auch* for nothing

Kosten-Nutzen|-Analyse *f* cost-benefit analysis; **~Verhältnis** *n* cost-benefit ratio

kostenpflichtig I. *Adj. Person:* liable to pay (the) costs; **II.** *Adv. abschleppen etc.:* at the owner's expense; *e-e Klage ~ abweisen Jur.* dismiss a case with costs

Kosten|planung *f* expense budgeting; **~preis** *m Wirts.* cost (*Am.* wholesale) price; *unter dem ~ verkaufen etc.:* below cost, at a loss; **~punkt** *m* **1.** → **Kostenfrage; 2.** *umg.:* **~?** how much?, what's the damage?; **~ 7000 Euro** it costs (*Pl.* they cost) 7000 euros; **~rechnung** *f* cost accounting; **~schraube** *f umg. fig.* cost spiral; *an der ~ drehen* (try to) cut down on costs

kostensenkend, **Kosten senkend** *Adj.* cost-cutting; **Kostensenkung** *f auch Pl.* reduction in costs

kostensparend, **Kosten sparend** *Adj.* cost-saving

kostensteigernd *Adj.* cost-increasing; **Kostensteigerung** *f* increase in costs; **Kostenstelle** *f* cost cent|re (*Am. -er*)

kostenträchtig *Adj.* costly

Kosten|voranschlag *m* estimate, quotation; **~vorschuss** *m* advance on costs

Kost|gänger *m*; *-s*, *-*, **~gängerin** *f*; *-*, *-nen* boarder, lodger; **~geld** *n* payment for one's keep

köstlich I. *Adj.* delicious; (*erlesen*) exquisite; (*reizend*) delightful; (*sehr unterhaltsam*) hilarious, priceless; **II.** *Adv.: sich ~ amüsieren* enjoy o.s. immensely, *umg.* have a brilliant time; **Köstlichkeit** *f Gastr.* **1.** delicacy; *auch fig.* delicious tit|bit (*Am.* tid-); **2.** *nur Sg.*; *geh.* (*Köstlichsein*) deliciousness; (*Erlesenheit*) exquisiteness; (*reizende Art*) delightfulness; (*Unterhaltsamkeit*)

K

hilariousness

Kostprobe f sample; fig. auch taste

kostspielig Adj. expensive, costly; durch Aufwand: sumptuous

Kostüm n; -s, -e **1.** costume; beim Kostümfest: Brit. auch fancy dress; hist. dress (auch Pl.), costume; **2.** (Damenkostüm) suit; **~ball** m fancy-dress (Am. costume) ball; **~bildner** m; -s, -, **~bildnerin** f; -, -nen costume designer; **~fest** n fancy-dress (Am. costume) ball; **~film** m costume film; **~fundus** m Theat. etc. wardrobe

kostümieren I. v/refl. dress o.s. up (als as); kostümiert erscheinen come in fancy dress (Am. in costume); sich merkwürdig ~ umg. wear a strange get-up; **II.** v/t. dress up; **Kostümierung** f **1.** nur Sg. dressing up; **2.** Verkleidung: fancy dress, Am. costume

Kostüm|probe f Theat. dress rehearsal; **~verleih** m costume hire firm, Am. costume rental

Kostverächter m: umg. er ist kein ~ he enjoys his food, he likes to tuck in; (ist ein richtiger Genießer) he believes in enjoying life to the full; (mag Frauen) he's one for the ladies

K.-o.-System n Sport knockout system

Kot m; -(e)s, -e, mst Sg. excrement, f(a)eces Pl.; von Tieren: auch droppings Pl., umg. muck

Kotangens m; -, -; Math. cotangent

Kotau m; -s, -s: vor j-m e-n ~ machen kowtow to s.o.

Kotelett n; -s, -s; Gastr. chop, cutlet

Koteletten Pl. (Backenbart) sideburns

koten v/i. Zool. defecate

Köter m; -s, -; pej. cur

Kotflügel m Mot. mudguard, Am. fender

kotig Adj. mucky

Kotzbrocken m vulg. nasty piece of work, bastard, swine

Kotze f; -, kein Pl.; vulg. puke umg.; **kotzelend** Adj. vulg.: sich ~ fühlen feel like death warmed up (Am. over) umg.; **kotzen** v/i. vulg. throw up, puke umg., Am. auch hurl umg.; es ist doch zum Kotzen it's absolutely sickening; da kann man das (große) Kotzen kriegen (angewidert sein von etw.) it makes you want to puke (od. throw up od. Am. hurl)

kotz|langweilig Adj. vulg. boring as hell, Brit. auch dead boring; **~übel** Adj. vulg.: mir ist ~ I think I'm going to puke (od. throw up, Am. auch hurl)

kp Abk. → **Kilopond**

KPD f; -, kein Pl.; Abk. (Kommunistische Partei Deutschlands) hist. German Communist Party

Kraal m; -s, -e → **Kral**

Krabbe f; -, -n **1.** Zool. crab; **2.** (Garnele) shrimp, größere: prawn; **3.** umg. Kind: süße kleine ~ little cutie

Krabbelalter n crawling age; im ~ at the crawling stage; **krabbeln I.** v/i. (ist gekrabbelt) crawl; **II.** v/t. (hat) umg. (kitzeln) tickle; (kratzen) scratch

Krabbencocktail m prawn cocktail

krach Interj. crash!, bang!; **Krach** m; -(e)s, Kräche **1.** nur Sg. (Lärm) noise; stärker: row, Am. ruckus, racket umg.; (Knall, Schlag) crash; ~ machen make a row (umg. und Am. racket, din); **2.** umg. (Streit) row; ~ schlagen kick up a fuss, cause an uproar; ~ bekommen mit get into trouble with; bei denen gibt's ständig ~ they're always having rows (od. rowing), Am. they never stop squabbling; **3.** Wirts. crash

krachen I. v/i. **1.** (hat gekracht) crash (auch Donner); Feuer, Radio: crackle; Tür etc.: bang, slam; (bersten) burst, explode; Eis: crack; auf der Straße kracht es dauernd there's one crash after another on that road; du tust, was ich dir sage, sonst kracht's umg. you'll do as I tell you, or there'll be trouble; dass es nur so krachte umg. like crazy; **2.** (hat); Wirts. crash; **3.** (ist); (krachend zusammenstoßen mit) crash (gegen od. in + Akk. into); er ist mit 100 Sachen gegen den Baum gekracht he crashed (od. slammed) into the tree at 60 mph; **II.** v/refl. (hat); umg. (sich streiten) have a row (Am. an argument); (mehrmals) have rows (Am. arguments); er hat sich mit ihr gekracht he's had a bust-up with her

Kracher m; -s, -; umg. (Knallkörper) banger, Am. firecracker

Krachmacher m umg. noisy type, rowdy

krächzen v/i. Krähe: caw; Papagei: squawk; fig. Person: croak; Lautsprecher: crackle; ~de Stimme croaking voice; **Krächzer** m; -s, -; umg. croak

kracken ['krɛkn] v/t. Chem. crack

Krad n; -(e)s, Kräder; Abk. bes. Mil.. → **Kraftrad**; **~fahrer** m, **~fahrerin** f bes. Mil. motorcyclist; **~melder** m Mil. des|patch (bes. Am. dis-) rider

kraft Präp. (+ Gen.) by virtue of; on the strength of; ~ Gesetzes by law

Kraft f; -, Kräfte **1.** körperlich: strength; (Tatkraft) energy; fig. auch power; am Ende s-r Kräfte at the end of one's strength, at one's last gasp; aus eigener ~ by one's own efforts, under one's own steam; mit aller ~ with all one's might; mit frischen Kräften with renewed strength (od. vigo[u]r); mit letzter ~ with one's last ounce of strength; nach besten Kräften to the best of one's ability; das geht über od. übersteigt m-e Kräfte that's more than I can handle; Kräfte sammeln gather strength; an den Kräften zehren sap one's strength (od. energy); wieder bei Kräften sein have regained one's strength (od. energy); (gesund sein) be back on one's feet; wieder zu Kräften kommen regain one's strength (od. energy); (gesund werden) get back on one's feet; ~ verleihen give strength (+ Dat. to), fig. e-r Argumentation etc.: lend force (to); → Spiel 7, vereint II; **2.** (Naturkraft, auch Phys.) force; (Energie) energy; überirdische Kräfte supernatural forces; heilende ~ healing power; treibende ~ driving force; fig. auch powerhouse; Arbeit ist ~ mal Weg Phys. work is force times distance; **3.** (Macht, auch Tech., Etech.) power; volle ~ voraus Naut. full speed ahead; mit voller/halber ~ at full/half speed; **4.** (Arbeitskraft) employee, Pl. auch staff, personnel Pl.; wir müssen noch e-e ~ fürs Lager einstellen we need to take on another member of staff (Am. to hire somebody) for the warehouse; **5.** (politische Kraft, Machtgruppe) force, power; dritte ~ third force; revolutionäre Kräfte revolutionary forces; **6.** (Geltung, Rechtsgültigkeit): in ~ sein be in force, be effective; in ~ setzen put into force, enforce; in ~ treten come into effect (od. force), become effective; außer ~ setzen annul; (Gesetz) repeal; (Vertrag etc.) cancel; (Regel) auch overrule; zeitweilig: suspend; außer ~ sein/treten no longer be in force / cease to be

in force, expire

Kraft|akt m strong-man act; fig. great feat, tour de force; **~anstrengung** f effort, exertion; **~antrieb** m power drive; mit ~ power-driven; **~aufwand** m (expenditure of) energy, effort; **~ausdruck** m expletive, swearword; **~brühe** f Gastr. beef tea (Am. bouillon)

Kräfteausgleich m Pol. etc. balance of power

kräftemäßig Adv. physically; ~ geht's mir gut I feel quite strong (od. fit)

Kräfte|messen n; -s, kein Pl. trial of strength; **~spiel** n interplay of forces; **~verfall** m loss of strength; **~verhältnis** n relative strength; **~verschleiß** m energy wastage

kräftezehrend Adj. energy-sapping

Kraftfahrer m, **~in** f driver, motorist; **~gruß** m iro. driver's tapping of the forehead (indicating annoyance at bad driving)

Kraftfahrstraße f Amtsspr. road restricted to motor vehicles, motor road, Am. highway

Kraftfahrzeug n Mot. motor vehicle; → auch Auto, Kfz...; **~bau** m; nur Sg. **1.** motor manufacturing; Fach: automotive engineering; **2.** motor (Am. automotive) industry; **~brief** m vehicle title (document); **~halter** m, **~halterin** f Amtsspr. (registered) keeper (of a motor vehicle); **~industrie** f motor (Am. automotive) industry; **~kennzeichen** n (motor vehicle) registration (Am. license) number; **~mechaniker** m, **~mechanikerin** f motor mechanic; **~papiere** Pl. (motor vehicle) registration documents; **~schein** m car licen|ce (Am. -se); **~steuer** f road (Am. automobile) tax; **~steuermarke** f road (Am. automobile) tax sticker; **~versicherung** f motor vehicle insurance

Kraft|feld n Phys. field (of force); **~futter** n concentrated feed

kräftig I. Adj. **1.** strong; Motor etc.: powerful; Schlag: hefty, hard, powerful; Händedruck: firm, hearty; Wuchs, Pflanze: vigorous; ~en Durst/Hunger haben be really thirsty/hungry; ~er Schluck good swig umg.; e-e ~e Tracht Prügel a sound thrashing, a good hiding; **2.** (~ gebaut) strongly (od. powerfully) built; ein ~es Kind a robust child; Kleinkind: a healthy (hum. bouncing) baby; **3.** (nahrhaft) nourishing; Mahlzeit: substantial; Wein: strong, powerful; etwas Kräftiges essen eat something substantial; **4.** Farbe: bright, strong; **5.** Met.: ein ~es Hoch/Tief an area of very high pressure / a deep depression; **6.** (grob) Sprache: strong; ~er Fluch hearty curse; **II.** Adv. schlagen, drucken, schieben: hard; wachsen: vigorously; fluchen: heartily; ~ gebaut strongly (od. powerfully) built; bes. Kind: sturdily built, sturdy; ~ schütteln shake vigorously, give a good shake; als Anweisung: shake well; j-m ~ die Hand schütteln give s.o. a firm handshake; ~ zuschlagen hit out hard; fig. beim Essen: tuck in with a will, get stuck in umg., Am. chow down umg.; ~ regnen rain heavily, pour

kräftigen v/t. strengthen, fortify (auch fig.); (beleben) invigorate; (stählen) harden, steel; (erfrischen) refresh, revive; **kräftigend I.** Part. Präs. → **kräftigen; II.** Adj. fortifying; (erfrischend) refreshing; (belebend) invigorating; Luft: auch bracing; (nahrhaft) nour

ishing; **~es Mittel** tonic; **das wirkt ~** that'll give you strength
Kräftigung f strengthening; (*Nahrung*) nourishment; **Kräftigungsmittel** n *Med.* tonic
Kraft|leistung f feat of strength; *fig.* great feat, tour de force; **~linien** *Pl. Phys.* lines of force
kraftlos *Adj.* weak (*auch fig.*); *Glieder: auch* limp; **Kraftlosigkeit** f; *nur Sg.* lack of energy; **sie klagt über ~** she complains that she has no energy (*od.* strength)
Kraftmaschine f engine
Kraftmeier m; *-s, -; umg.* muscleman; **Kraftmeierei** f; *kein Pl.; umg.* display of strength; *fig.* strongarm tactics *Pl.*, acting tough
Kraft|mensch m *umg.* strongman; **~paket** n *umg.* muscleman; *Frau:* musclewoman; *allg. Sport* powerhouse; *fig.* (*leistungsstarkes Fahrzeug, Gerät etc.*) powerhouse, muscle machine; **~probe** f trial of strength; **~protz** m *umg.* muscleman; *stark abwertend:* gorilla; **~rad** n *Amtsspr.* motorcycle; **~raum** f *Sport* power training gym; **~reserven** *Pl.* reserves of strength, energy reserves; **~sport** m strength events *Pl.*
Kraftstoff m fuel; → *auch Benzin;* **~anzeige** f, **~anzeiger** m fuel ga(u)ge
kraftstoffsparend, Kraftstoff sparend *Adj.* fuel-saving, fuel-efficient
Kraftstrom m power current
kraftstrotzend *Adj.* bursting with energy
Kraft|training n *Sport* power training; **~übertragung** f power transmission; **~verkehr** m *Amtsspr.* motorized traffic; **~verschwendung** f waste of energy
kraftvoll *Adj.* strong, powerful (*auch Stil*)
Kraft|wagen m *Mot.* motor vehicle; **~werk** n *Etech.* power station
Kraftwerk(s)|bau m; *nur Sg.* power station construction; **~betreiber** m, **~betreiberin** f power station operator
Kraftwort n; *Pl. -e od. -wörter* swear word
Kragen m; *-s, -, südd. und schw. Krägen* collar (*auch Tech.*); **j-n am ~ packen** *fig.;* **jetzt geht's ihm an den ~** he's in for it now; **j-m den ~ umdrehen** wring s.o.'s neck; **da platzte mir der ~** then I blew my top; (*das war der Gipfel*) that was the last straw; **~bär** m *Zool.* (Himalayan) black bear; **~knopf** m collar stud; (*oberster Hemdknopf*) top button; **~weite** f collar size; **das ist nicht m-e ~** *umg. fig.* it's not my cup of tea
Kragstein m *Archit.* console, corbel
Krähe f; *-, -n* crow; (*Saatkrähe*) rook; **e-e ~ hackt der anderen kein Auge aus** dog does not eat dog
krähen v/i. crow; *fig. Baby:* coo
Krähen|füße *Pl. umg.* **1.** (*Fältchen*) crow's feet; **2.** (*Schrift*) scrawl *Sg.*; **~nest** n crow's nest (*auch Naut.*)
Krähwinkel (*n*); *-s; iron.* (sleepy) provincial backwater, *Am. umg.* hick (*od.* podunk) town
Krakau (*n*); *-s; Geog.* Cracow
Krakauer f; *-, -; Gastr.* spicy smoked beef and pork sausage
Krake m; *-n -n* **1.** *Zool.* octopus; **2.** *Myth.* kraken
Krakeel m; *-s, kein Pl.; umg.* row, *Am.* ruckus; (*Lärm*) *auch* racket; **krakeelen** v/i. *umg. pej.* (*streiten*) row, have a row (*Am.* squabble); (*Lärm machen*) make a row (*od.* racket); **Kra-**

keeler m; *-s, -; umg. pej.* rowdy; (*Schläger*) brawler; **Krakeelerin** f; *-, -en; umg. pej.* (rowing, *Am.* ornery) fishwife (*od.* shrew), termagant *lit.*
Krakelei f; *-, -en; umg. pej.* spidery scrawl(ing); **krakelig** *Adj. umg. pej.:* **~e Schrift** spidery scrawl; **krakeln** vt/i. *umg. pej.* scrawl
Kral m; *-s, -e und -s* kraal
Kralle f; *-, -n* **1.** claw (*auch fig. und Tech.*); (*von Raubvogel*) talon; (*bar*) **auf die ~** *Sl.* cash on the barrelhead (*od.* nail); **etw. in die ~n kriegen** *fig.* get one's hands on s.th.; **die ~n zeigen** *fig.* bare one's teeth; **j-n fest in den ~n haben** *fig.* have s.o. in one's clutches; **j-n aus den ~n des Todes retten** *geh.* rescue s.o. from the jaws of death; **2.** (*Parkkralle*) wheel clamp, *Am.* (Denver) boot; **krallen I.** v/refl.: **sich an etw.** (*Akk.*) **~** *Tier:* dig its claws (*Raubvogel:* talons) into s.th.; *Mensch:* cling to (*od.* grasp, clutch) s.th; **sich in etw.** (*Akk.*) **~** dig one's fingers (*Zehen:* toes) into s.th.; **II.** v/t.: **die Finger/ Nägel in etw.** (*Akk.*) **~** dig one's fingers/ nails into s.th.; (**sich** [*Dat.*]) **j-n ~** *umg. fig.* collar s.o.; (*verhaften*) nab (*Am. auch* nail) s.o.; *als Sexpartner:* hook s.o.
Kram m; *-(e)s, kein Pl.; umg.* **1.** (*Zeug*) stuff; *wertlos:* junk, rubbish; **der ganze ~** the whole caboodle; **den ganzen ~ hinschmeißen** chuck the whole thing; **2.** (*Sache*) business; **das passt mir überhaupt nicht in den ~** that's the last thing I want; **soll er s-n ~ alleine machen** let him get on with it (then)
kramen I. v/i. rummage (about) (*in, unter + Dat.* in; *nach* for); **in s-n Erinnerungen ~** *fig.* take a trip down memory lane, (*schwelgen*) wallow in memories; **II.** v/t.: **etw. aus etw. ~** dig s.th. out of s.th.
Krämer m; *-s, -* **1.** *Dial.* small trader (*Am.* dealer); (*Ladeninhaber*) shopkeeper; **2.** *pej. engstirnig:* small-minded person; *eigennützig:* mean, selfish person; **Krämergeist** m *pej.* **1.** *nur Sg.* small-mindedness; **2.** small-minded person; **Krämerin** f; *-, -nen; Dial.* → *Krämer* 1; **Krämerseele** f *pej.* **1.** *nur Sg.* petty-mindedness; **2.** petty-minded person
Kramladen m *umg. pej.* junk shop
Krampe f; *-, -n; Tech.* staple
Krampf m; *-(e)s, Krämpfe* **1.** *Med.* (*Muskel-, Magenkrampf etc.*) cramp, *bes. Am.* cramps *Pl.*; (*Zuckung*) spasm, convulsion; (*Anfall*) fit; **e-n ~ im Bein bekommen** get cramp(s) (*Am. umg.* a charley horse) in one's leg; **epileptische Krämpfe** epileptic fits; (*einzelner Anfall*) an epileptic fit (*Am.* seizure); **2.** *umg.* (*Unsinn*) crap; **so ein ~ Aufgabe etc.:** what a bind; **das Konzert war der reinste ~** the concert was absolutely diabolical
Krampfader f *Med.* varicose vein; **~verödung** f *Med.* varicosclero|sation (*od.* -tization)
Krampfanfall m attack of cramp(s); (*Zuckungen*) convulsive fit; **epileptischer ~** epileptic fit (*Am.* seizure)
krampfartig *Adj.* spasmodic, convulsive
krampfen I. v/refl. **1.** *Bein etc.:* cramp up; **ihr Magen krampfte sich** she had stomach cramps; **2.** *Finger etc.:* **sich um etw. ~** grip s.th. tightly; **II.** v/t. **1. die Finger/Hände um etw. ~** clutch s.th. tightly; **2.** *Dial., umg* (*klauen*) **sich** (*Dat.*) **etw. ~** pinch s.th.; **III.** v/i.

1. *Med.* (*e-n Krampfanfall haben*) have a spasm (*od.* convulsion); **2.** *schw. umg.* (*schuften*) slave away
krampfhaft I. *Adj.* **1.** convulsive (*auch Lachen, Schluchzen*); **2.** (*gezwungen*) forced; (*verbissen*) *Anstrengung etc.:* desperate; **II.** *Adv. lachen, schluchzen etc.:* convulsively; *festhalten, nachdenken etc.:* desperately; **sich ~ anstrengen** *od.* **bemühen** make desperate efforts
Krampfhusten m whooping cough
krampflösend, krampfstillend I. *Adj.* antispasmodic; **II.** *Adv. Mittel:* **~ wirken** have an antispasmodic effect, *bei Muskelkrampf:* ease cramp(s)
Krampus m; *-(ses), -se; österr., südd.* (*Knecht Ruprecht*) helper to Santa Claus
Kran m; *-(e)s, -e und Kräne* **1.** *Tech.* crane; **2.** *Dial.* (*Wasserhahn*) tap; **~arm** m jib; **~brücke** f gantry; **~führer** m, **~führerin** f crane driver
Kranich m; *-s, -e; Orn.* crane
krank *Adj.; kränker, am kränksten* sick (*auch psychisch*); *präd. auch* ill, not well; *Organe und Bot.:* diseased; *Zahn, Mandeln:* bad; *fig. Geist:* sick; *Wirtschaft etc.:* sick, ailing; *Jägerspr.* (*angeschossen*) *Tier:* wounded; **~e Fantasie** sick mind; **~ werden** fall ill, *bes. Am.* get sick; **kränker werden** get worse; **~ spielen** malinger, pretend to be ill (*bes. Am.* sick); **j-n ~ machen** make s.o. ill; *fig.* get s.o. down; *Lärm etc.:* get on s.o.'s nerves; **er macht mich ~** *umg.* he's driving me (a)round the bend; **~ vor Sorge/Heimweh** *fig.* sick with worry / really homesick; → **krankmelden, krankschreiben** *etc.*; **Kranke** m, f; *-en, -en* sick person; *im Krankenhaus, beim Arzt etc.:* patient; **die ~n** the sick *Pl.*; **die unheilbar ~n** the terminally ill *Pl.*
kränkeln v/i. be poorly, *Am.* be not too well; *allg.* be sickly, suffer from poor health; **sie kränkelt seit einiger Zeit / schon immer** she hasn't been in the best of health lately / she's never been the healthiest of people
kranken v/i. *fig.:* **~ an** (+ *Dat.*) suffer from
kränken vt/i.: **j-n ~** hurt s.o., hurt s.o.'s feelings; **j-n in s-r Eitelkeit / s-m Stolz ~** wound s.o.'s vanity/pride; **das kränkt** that hurts; **es kränkt mich, dass** I am hurt (*od.* it upsets me) that; **e-e Bemerkung** *etc.* **als ~d empfinden** find a remark *etc.* hurtful, feel hurt by a remark *etc.*; → *auch gekränkt*
Kranken|anstalt f *Amtsspr.* (large) hospital, hospital complex; **~bahre** f stretcher; **~bericht** m medical report; *offiziell:* (health) bulletin; **~besuch** m visit (to the hospital); *des Arztes:* (home) visit, *Pl.* rounds; **~bett** n sickbed; **am ~** at the bedside; **~blatt** n doctor's notes *Pl.*, medical record; **~geld** n sickness benefit; **~geschichte** f medical history; **~gymnast** m physiotherapist; **~gymnastik** f physiotherapy; **~gymnastin** f physiotherapist
Krankenhaus n hospital; **im ~ liegen** be in hospital (*Am.* in the hospital); **ins ~ gebracht/ eingeliefert werden** be taken/admitted to (the) hospital; **~arzt** m, **~ärztin** f hospital doctor; **~aufenthalt** m stay in (the) hospital; **~behandlung** f hospital treatment; **~bett** n hospital bed; **~kosten** *Pl.* hospital fees
krankenhausreif *Adj.:* **j-n ~ schlagen** *umg.* hospitalize s.o., beat s.o. to pulp

Krankenhaustagegeld *n* (hospital) daily benefit; **~versicherung** *f* (hospital) daily benefits insurance

Krankenkasse *f* health (insurance) scheme (*Am.* plan); **Krankenkassenbeitrag** *m* payment to a (*od.* the) health (insurance) scheme (*Am.* plan)

Kranken|kost *f* light foods *Pl.*; *weitS.* convalescent diet; **~lager** *n geh.* (*Krankenbett*) sickbed; **sich vom ~ erheben** (*wieder gesund sein*) rise from one's sickbed; **~pflege** *f* nursing; **~pfleger** *m* staatlich ausgebildet: male nurse; *Pflegehelfer*: nursing auxiliary, *Am.* nurse's aid; **~pflegerin** *f* nurse; *Pflegehelferin*: nursing auxiliary, *Am.* nurse's aid; **~pflegeschule** *f* nurses' training school (*od.* college); **~revier** *n Mil.* sickbay; **~saal** *m* ward; **~salbung** *f kirchl.* extreme unction; **~schein** *m* **1.** health scheme membership certificate, *Am.* certificate of insurance; **2.** *Dial. umg.* sick note; **e-n ~ machen** organize a sick note; **~schwester** *f* nurse; **~stand** *m* number of staff away sick; **e-n hohen/niedrigen ~ haben** have a lot of people / only a few people away sick; **im ~ sein** *österr.* be off work due to illness; **~trage** *f* stretcher; **~träger** *m* stretcher bearer, ambulance man; **~transport** *m* ambulance service(s *Pl.*)

krankenversichern *v/t.* take out medical insurance for; **II.** *v/refl.* take out medical (*od.* health) insurance; **krankenversichert I.** *P.P.* → **krankenversichern; II.** *Adj.* medically insured; **sind Sie ~?** do you have medical (*od.* health) insurance?; **Krankenversichertenkarte** *f* health insurance scheme membership card, *Am.* insurance card; **Krankenversicherung** *f* health insurance; **krankenversicherungspflichtig** *Adj.* obliged to join a health insurance scheme (*Am.* plan)

Kranken|wagen *m* ambulance; **~wärter** *m*, **~wärterin** *f altm.* (medical) orderly; **~zimmer** *n* sickbay

krankfeiern *v/i.* (*trennb., hat -ge-*); *umg.* skive (pretending to be ill), go (*Am.* play) sick, take a sickie (*Am.* a princess day)

krankhaft *Adj.* **1.** *Med., Organ*: diseased; *Zustand, Wuchs*: morbid; *Veränderung*: pathological; **2.** *bes. Psych.* (*übertrieben, anormal*) pathological, obsessive

Krankheit *f* illness, sickness; *bestimmte*: disease (*auch Bot. und fig.*); (*Leiden*) complaint; (*Störung*) disorder; **psychische ~** mental illness; **während meiner ~ hat sie mich oft besucht** she often came to see me while I was ill; **das ist kein Computer, das ist e-e ~!** *umg.* this computer is an absolute pest; **krankheitsbedingt I.** *Adj.* ... due to illness; **II.** *Adv.* due to illness

Krankheitsbild *n* (clinical) syndrome

krankheitserregend *Adj.* pathogenic; **Krankheitserreger** *m* germ; *fachspr.* pathogen

Krankheitsfall *m einzelner*: case (of illness); **im ~** in the event of illness

krankheitshalber *Adv.* owing (*od.* due) to illness

Krankheits|herd *m* focus of a (*od.* the) disease; **~keim** *m* germ; **~symptom** *n* symptom; **~tag** *m* day of illness; **~träger** *m*, **~überträger** *m* carrier (of a disease); **~übertragung** *f* transmission of a (*od.* the) disease; **~ursache** *f* cause of a (*od.* the) disease; **~verlauf** *m* course of an (*od.* the) disease.

the) illness; **~zeichen** *n* symptom

kranklachen *v/refl.* (*trennb., hat -ge-*); *umg.* kill o.s. (laughing), laugh one's head off

kränklich *Adj.* sickly; (*gebrechlich*) frail; **Kränklichkeit** *f; nur Sg.* sickliness, infirmity; (*Gebrechlichkeit*) frailty

krankmachen *v/i.* (*trennb., hat -ge-*); *umg.* → **krankfeiern**

krankmelden (*trennb., hat -ge-*) **I.** *v/t.*: **j-n ~** notify s.o.'s employer that he (*od.* she) is sick; **II.** *v/refl.* report sick; *telefonisch*: phone (*Am.* call) in sick; **Krankmeldung** *f* notification of sickness

krankschreiben *v/t.* (*unreg., trennb., hat -ge-*): **j-n ~** give s.o. a medical (*Am.* doctor's) certificate (*weniger formell*: sick note); **Krankschreibung** *f* medical (*Am.* doctor's) certificate; *weniger formell*: sick note

Kränkung *f* wounding, hurting (of s.o.'s feelings); (*Beleidigung*) insult; **etw. als ~ empfinden** feel hurt (*beleidigt*: insulted) by s.th.

Kran|wagen *m* **1.** crane truck; **2.** (*Abschleppwagen*) breakdown truck, *Am.* tow truck; **~winde** *f Tech.* crane winch

Kranz *m; -(e)s, Kränze* **1.** garland, wreath (*auch Grabschmuck, Siegerkranz*); **2.** *Archit.* cornice; **3.** *Tech.* (*Radkranz*) rim; (*Scheibenkranz*) face; **4.** (*Haarkranz*) fringe, *Am.* bangs *Pl.*; *von Zöpfen*: chaplet; **5.** *Dial.* (*Kranzkuchen*) ring cake; **6.** *fig. von Seen, Bergen etc.*: ring; *von Leuten*: circle; **7.** *schw.* place; **in die Kränze kommen** be placed

Kränzchen *n* circle (of women); *zum Kaffeetrinken*: coffee circle; (*Gesellschaft*) hen party

kränzen *v/t. geh.* crown (with a wreath, garland *etc.*)

Kranz|gefäß *n Anat.* coronary artery; **~jungfer** *f Dial.* bridesmaid; **~kuchen** *m* ring cake; **~niederlegung** *f* (ceremonial) laying of a wreath, wreath-laying ceremony; **~schleife** *f* wreath ribbon (with an inscription); **~spende** *f* wreath, floral tribute; **es wird gebeten, von ~n abzusehen** no flowers please

Krapfen *m; -s, -; Gastr.* **1.** fritter; **2.** *südd.* (*Berliner*) doughnut, *Am.* *umg. auch* donut

krass *Adj.* **1.** (*unverblümt*) crass (*auch Beispiel*); *Widerspruch, Fehler*: auch glaring, flagrant; *Unterschied, Gegensatz etc.*: auch stark; *Fall, Lüge*: blatant; *Unrecht*: flagrant; *Übertreibung etc.*: gross; **dazwischen ist ein ~er Unterschied** auch there's a world of difference (between them); **~er Außenseiter** rank outsider; **2.** *Jugendspr.* (*toll, gut*) cool; **der Film ist voll ~** the film is really great (*bes. Am.* totally cool); **ein ~er Typ** a dishy type

Krater *m; -s, - crater; **~landschaft** *f* crater landscape; **~see** *m* crater lake

Kratzbürste *f umg. hum.* prickly character; **sie ist e-e richtige ~** she's got a really vicious temper, she'll bite your head off; **kratzbürstig** *Adj. umg.* prickly, vicious

Krätze *f; -, kein Pl.; Med.:* **die ~** scabies; **sich (Dat.) die ~ an den Hals ärgern** *umg.* be hopping mad

kratzen I. *v/t.* **1.** scratch; (*schaben*) scrape (*aus/von* out of / off); **sich (Dat.) die Nase ~** scratch one's nose; **2.** *umg. fig.* (*stören*) bother; **das kratzt**

mich nicht that doesn't bother (*od.* worry) me; **was kratzt mich das?** what do I care (about that)?; **II.** *v/i.* **1.** scratch; (*scharren*) scrape; **auf der Geige ~** *umg.* scrape away on the violin; **2.** *Rauch etc.*: get to one's throat, be rough on the throat; *Pullover etc.*: be prickly (*od.* itchy, scratchy); **mir kratzt der Hals** I've got a tickle in my throat; **III.** *v/refl.* scratch o.s.; **sich am Ohr etc. ~** scratch one's ear *etc.*; **sich blutig ~** scratch (o.s.) until one bleeds; **IV. Kratzen** *n; -s, kein Pl.* **1.** *Geräusch*: scratching (noise); **2. ein Kratzen im Hals** a tickle in one's throat

Kratzer *m; -s, -* **1.** scratch; **2.** (*Gerät*) scraper

kratzfest *Adj.* non-scratch, scratch-proof

Kratzfuß *m umg.*: **e-n ~ machen** bow and scrape

kratzig *Adj.* **1.** scratchy, prickly; **2.** *umg.* vicious

Krätzmilbe *f* itch mite

Kratz|putz *m* **1.** plaster with scratchwork; **2.** *Kunst*: sgraffito; **~spur** *f* scratch (mark); **~wunde** *f* scratch

krauchen *v/i.* **1.** *Dial.* crawl; **2.** *umg.* move with great difficulty; **kaum noch ~ können** be barely able to drag o.s. along

Kraul *n; -s, kein Pl.; Sport* (*Schwimmstil*) crawl

kraulen[1] **I.** *v/i.* (*ist gekrault*); (*Schwimmstil*) do the crawl; **über den See ~** swim across the lake doing the crawl; **II.** *v/t.* (*hat/ist*); (*Strecke*) swim … doing the crawl; **e-n neuen Weltrekord ~** set up a new world record for the crawl

kraulen[2] *v/t.*: **e-n Hund etc. ~** ruffle a dog's *etc.* fur (*od.* neck); **j-m das Haar ~** run one's fingers through s.o.'s hair; **sich (Dat.) den Bart ~** finger one's beard

Krauler *m; -s, -, ~in f; -, -nen* crawl swimmer

Kraul|schwimmen *n Sport* (the) crawl; **beim ~** when swimming the crawl; **~stil** *m* crawl

kraus *Adj.* **1.** *Haar*: very curly; *stärker*: frizzy; *umg.* fuzzy; *Kleidung etc.*: crinkly; (*mit Falten*) creased, *Am.* wrinkled; **die Stirn ~ ziehen** knit (*od.* wrinkle) one's brow; **2.** (*verworren*) *Gedanken etc.*: muddled, confused

Krause *f; -, -* **1.** ruffle; (*Halskrause*) ruff; **2.** *der Haare*: frizz(iness); **e-e ~ haben** *Person*: have frizzy hair; *Haare*: be frizzy

Kräusel *m; -s, - und f; -, -n im Kleid*: gather, fold; *auf dem Wasser*: ripple; **~band** *n* ruffle tape, *Am.* (decorative) ribbon; **~garn** *n* stretch yarn

kräuseln *v/t.* (*Haar*) frizz; *mit Lockenstab*: crimp; (*Stoff*) gather; (*Nase*) wrinkle, screw up; (*Lippen*) pucker; (*Wasser, Oberfläche*) ruffle, ripple; **ein Lächeln kräuselte ihre Lippen** a smile creased her lips; **II.** *v/refl. Wasser*: ripple; *Rauch*: curl up; *Haar*: curl; **sich vor Lachen ~** *umg. fig.* crease o.s. (*Am.* double over) (with laughter)

krausen I. *v/t.* → **kräuseln** I; **II.** *v/refl.*: **s-e Stirn kraust sich** his brow is wrinkled; *missmutig*: he's frowning

Kraus|haar *n Haar*: frizzy hair; **~kopf** *m* **1.** (head of) frizzy hair; *Person*: man (*od.* girl *etc.*) with frizzy hair; **2.** *fig. pej.* muddle-headed person

Kraut *n; -(e)s, Kräuter* **1.** *Blätter bestimmter Pflanzen*: leaves *Pl.*; *von Gemüse*: top(s *Pl.*); **ins ~ schießen** run to leaf, bolt; *fig.* run riot; **2.** *Gastr., Med.* herb; **dagegen ist kein ~ gewachsen** there's no cure for that yet; **3.** *bes. südd., österr. (Kohl)* cabbage; **wie ~ und Rüben** *(durcheinander)* in a complete muddle *(od.* mess); **4.** *(Unkraut, umg. Tabak)* weed

Kräuter|buch *n* herbal (book); **~butter** *f Gastr.* herb-butter; **~essig** *m* aromatic vinegar; **~garten** *m* herb garden; *am Fensterbrett etc.:* potted herbs *Pl.;* **~hexe** *f umg. hum.* herbwoman; **~käse** *m* herb-flavo(u)red cheese, cheese with herbs; **~likör** *m* herb liqueur; **~quark** *m* quark *(Am.* farmer cheese) with herbs; **~tee** *m* herb(al) tea

krautig *Adj.* herbaceous

Kraut|kopf *m südd., österr.* (head of) cabbage; **~salat** *m etwa* coleslaw; **~wickel** *m südd., österr.* stuffed cabbage

Krawall *m; -s, -e* **1. ~e** riot(s *Pl.*), rioting; **2.** *umg. (Krach)* row, *Am.* ruckus, racket; **~ machen** make a racket *(od.* din); **~ schlagen** kick up a row, cause an uproar; **was soll dieser ~?** what's all this racket in aid of?, *Am.* what's all this noise about?; **~macher** *m*, **~macherin** *f umg.* rowdy

Krawatte *f; -, -n* tie, *bes. Am.* necktie; *fig (Würgegriff)* headlock

Krawatten|knoten *m* knot (of a tie); **~muffel** *m umg.:* **er ist ein ~** he hates wearing a tie; **~nadel** *f* tie-pin, *Am.* tie tack; **~zwang** *m; nur Sg.* collar and tie compulsory

Kraxe *f; -, -n; südd., österr.* basket carried on the back

Kraxelei *f; -, -en; südd., österr. umg.* (endless) climbing; **kraxeln** *v/i. südd., österr. umg.* **1.** climb; *als Tätigkeit:* go climbing; **2.** *mühsam:* clamber *(auf + Akk.* up)

Kreation *f; -, -en* creation, design

kreativ *Adj.* creative; **Kreativität** *f; -, kein Pl.* creativity

Kreatur *f; -, -en* creature; *fig. pej. Mensch:* minion, lackey

Krebs *m; -es, -e* **1.** *Zool.* crustacean; *Gastr.* crayfish, *Am. auch* crawfish, crawdad *umg.; (Taschenkrebs)* crab; **2.** *Med.* cancer; **~ erregend** cancer-causing, carcinogenic; **~ erregend sein** cause cancer, be carcinogenic; **3.** *Sternzeichen:* Cancer; **(ein) ~ sein** be (a) Cancer, be a Cancerian; **~behandlung** *f* treatment of cancer; **~bekämpfung** *f* fight against cancer

krebsen *v/i.* **1.** *(Krebse, Krabben fangen)* catch cray|fish *(Am. auch* craw-)/crabs; **2.** *umg. (mühsam kriechen)* crawl

krebserregend, Krebs erregend *Adj.* → *Krebs* 2; **Krebserreger** *m* carcinogen

Krebs|forschung *f Med.* cancer research; **~früherkennung** *f* early cancer diagnosis

Krebsgang *m* **1.** retrogression; **den ~ gehen** be going downhill; **2.** *Mus.* retrograde movement

Krebs|geschwulst *f Med.* carcinoma *(Pl.* carcinomas *od.* carcinomata); **~geschwür** *n* cancerous ulcer; *fig.* cancer

krebsig *Adj. Med.* cancerous

Krebs|klinik *f Med.* cancer clinic; **~knoten** *m* cancerous lump

krebskrank *Adj.:* **er ist ~** he's got cancer; **~e Kinder** children with *(od.* suffering from) cancer; **Krebskranke** *m, f* cancer patient

Krebs|leiden *n Med.* cancer(ous dis-

ease); **~nachsorge** *f* aftercare for (former) cancer patients; **~patient** *m*, **~patientin** *f* cancer patient; **~risiko** *n* risk of cancer

krebsrot *Adj.* (as) red as a lobster; **~ werden** *auch* blush scarlet

Krebs|schere *f* cray|fish *(Am. auch* craw-) claw; **~schwanz** *m Gastr.* cray|fish *(Am. auch* craw-) tail

Krebs|spezialist *m*, **~spezialistin** *f Med.* cancer specialist; **~station** *f* cancer ward

Krebssuppe *f Gastr.* cray|fish *(Am. auch* craw-) soup

Krebstherapie *f Med.* cancer therapy

Krebstier *n Zool.* crustacean

Krebs|tod *m Med.* death from cancer; **~tote** *m, f* person who has died from cancer, cancer victim; **~verdacht** *m:* **es besteht ~** cancer is suspected, (there are fears) it may be cancer; **~vorsorge** *f* cancer prevention; *(Untersuchung)* cancer screening (test); **~vorsorgeuntersuchung** *f* cancer screening (test), *Pl. Koll.* cancer screening *Sg.;* **~zelle** *f* cancer(ous) cell

Kredenz *f; -, -en; altm.* sideboard, *Am. auch* credenza

kredenzen *v/t. geh.:* **j-m ein Getränk ~** offer s.o. a drink

Kredit *m; -(e)s, -e* **1.** *Wirts.* credit; *(Darlehen)* loan; **auf ~** on credit, *umg.* on tick, *Am. umg.* on a tab; **e-n ~ aufnehmen** take out a loan; **j-m e-n ~ gewähren** grant s.o. a loan; **2.** *fig.* standing; **du hast bei mir keinen ~ mehr** *umg.* I'm through with you

Kredit|anstalt *f Wirts.* credit bank; **~antrag** *m* loan application; **~aufnahme** *f* borrowing; **~auszahlung** *f* loan payout; **~bank** *f* credit bank; **~bedarf** *m* borrowing requirement(s *Pl.*); **~bedingungen** *Pl.* credit terms; **~beschränkungen** *Pl.* lending restrictions; **~betrug** *m* loan fraud

kreditfähig *Adj. Wirts.* sound, solvent; *(kreditwürdig)* creditworthy

Kredit|finanzierung *f Wirts.* credit-financing, financing by loans; **~geber** *m*, **~geberin** *f* lender; **~genossenschaft** *f* credit cooperative; **~geschäft** *n* **1.** credit transaction; **2.** *Koll.* lending business; **~gewährung** *f* granting *(od.* extension) of credit; **~hai** *m umg.* loan shark

kreditieren *v/t. Wirts.:* **j-m e-n Betrag ~** give s.o. an amount on credit, advance s.o. an amount; *(gutschreiben)* credit s.o. *(od.* s.o.'s account) with an amount; **Kreditierung** *f* advancing; *(Gutschrift)* crediting; *(Anzeige)* credit advice; *(Aufgabe)* credit note

Kredit|institut *n Wirts.* credit institute *(od.* bank); **~karte** *f* credit card; **~kauf** *m* credit sale; **~knappheit** *f* shortage of credit, credit tightness; **~laufzeit** *f* credit period; **~limit** *n* credit limit; *Bankkonto:* overdraft limit; **~linie** *f* credit line; **~markt** *m* credit market; **~nehmer** *m*, **~nehmerin** *f* borrower

Kreditor *m; -s, -en; Wirts.* creditor; *Pl. auch* accounts payable; **Kreditorenkonto** *n* accounts payable account

Kredit|rahmen *m Wirts.* credit framework; **~rückzahlung** *f* repayment of a loan; **~sperre** *f* credit freeze; **~vereinbarung** *f* credit agreement; **~volumen** *n* lending volume, total lending; **~wesen** *n; nur Sg.* lending business; **~wirtschaft** *f* paper economy

kreditwürdig *Adj. Wirts.* creditworthy; *fig.* credible; **Kreditwürdigkeit** *f* creditworthiness, credit rating; *fig.* credi-

bility

Kreditzins *m Wirts.* lending rate

Kredo *n; -s, -s; kirchl. und fig.* creed; *Messe:* Credo

kregel *Adj. Dial.* lively

Kreide *f; -, -n* **1.** chalk; **mit ~ geschrieben** written in chalk; **2.** *umg. fig.:* **tief in der ~ sitzen** be up to one's ears *(od.* eyes, *umg.* eyeballs) in debt, **bei j-m (tief) in der ~ sein** owe s.o. (a pile of) money; **~ gefressen haben** be all meek and mild; **3.** *Geol. (Kreidezeit)* Cretaceous period; **kreidebleich** *Adj.* (as) white as a sheet; **Kreidefels(en)** *m* chalk cliff; **kreidehaltig** *Adj.* chalky, cretaceous *fachspr.*

Kreide|küste *f Geol., Geog.* coastline of chalk cliffs; **~stift** *m* (piece of) chalk; *(Malkreide)* crayon; **~strich** *m* chalk line

kreideweiß *Adj.* → *kreidebleich*

Kreide|zeichnung *f* chalk drawing; **~zeit** *f Geol.* Cretaceous period

kreidig *Adj.* chalky; *Geol. auch* cretaceous

kreieren *v/t.* create; *Mode:* design; **Kreierung** *f* creation; *Mode:* design(ing)

Kreis *m; -es, -e* **1.** *Math., fig.* circle; *(Ring)* ring; *Astron.* orbit; **im ~** in a circle; **mir dreht sich alles im ~** my head's spinning; **e-n ~ schließen um** form a circle around; **sich im ~ drehen** revolve, rotate; *Kind:* spin (a)round (in circles); *Diskussion etc.:* go (a)round in circles; **~e ziehen** *Vogel etc.:* circle; **immer weitere ~e ziehen** *Gerücht:* spread further and further (afield); *Affäre etc.:* have far-reaching implications; **in weiten ~en** widely; **der ~ schließt sich** we've come full circle; **2.** *Etech. (Stromkreis)* circuit; **3.** *(Kreislauf)* cycle; **4.** *(Gruppe)* circle; *(Wirkungskreis)* sphere; **der ~ seiner Anhänger** the circle of his supporters; **in den besten ~en verkehren** move in the best circles; **im kleinen** *od.* **engsten ~** with a few close friends *(der Familie:* relatives); **5.** *(Bezirk)* district; **der ~ Unna** the Unna district

Kreis|abschnitt *m Math.* segment (of a *od.* the circle); **~amt** *n* district administration; **~ausschnitt** *m Math.* sector (of a circle); **~bahn** *f Astron.* orbit; *Math.* circular path; **~behörde** *f* district authority; **~bewegung** *f* rotation, circular motion; **~bogen** *m Math.* arc of a circle

kreischen *vt/i.* screech *(auch Bremsen etc.);* **vor Vergnügen** *etc.* **~** squeal with pleasure *etc.;* **kreischend I.** *Part. Präs.* → *kreischen;* **II.** *Adj. Stimme:* shrill

Kreis|diagramm *n* circular *(od.* pie) chart; **~durchmesser** *m Math.* diameter

Kreisel *m; -s, -* **1.** (spinning) top; *Tech.* gyroscope; *Naut., Flug.* gyrostabilizer; **2.** *Verkehrswesen:* (traffic) roundabout, *Am.* traffic circle; **~bewegung** *f* gyration; **~kompass** *m* gyrocompass

kreiseln *v/i.* **1.** play with a top; **2.** *(sich drehen)* spin (around)

kreisen I. *v/i. (hat/ist gekreist)* circle *(um* around, *über + Dat.* above, over); *Satellit etc.:* orbit *(um s.th.); (sich drehen)* *Planet etc.:* revolve, rotate, *schnell:* spin; *Blut, Geld:* circulate; **~ lassen** *(Flasche etc.)* pass (a)round; **die Arme ~ lassen** describe circles with one's arms, move one's arms in circles; **~ um** *fig. Gedanken:* revolve around, **II.** *v/t. (hat); Turnen:* **die Arme**

K

K

~ describe circles with one's arms, move one's arms in circles; **III. Kreisen** n; kein Pl. circling; (Drehen) rotation; der Gestirne: revolution
Kreisfläche f Math. area of a (od. the) circle
kreis|förmig I. Adj. circular; **II.** Adv.: ~ **angeordnet** arranged in a circle; ~**frei** Adj. Amtsspr. Stadt: administered as an independent district
Kreis|inhalt m → **Kreisfläche**; ~**krankenhaus** n district hospital; ~**lauf** m Bio., des Lebens etc.: cycle; (des Blutes, auch von Geld etc.) circulation; ~**läufer** m, ~**läuferin** f Hallenhandball: pivot player
Kreislauf|kollaps m Med. circulatory failure (od. breakdown, collapse); **ich hatte e-n ~** umg. I fainted (od. passed out); ~**mittel** n circulatory preparation; ~**schwäche** f circulatory weakness, poor circulation; ~**störungen** Pl. circulatory (od. cardiovascular) trouble Sg., problems Pl. with one's circulation; ~**versagen** n circulatory failure (od. breakdown, collapse)
Kreis|linie f (line describing a od. the) circle, circumference; ~**meister** m, ~**meisterin** f Sport district champion
kreisrund Adj. circular
Kreis|säge f circular saw; ~**segment** n → **Kreisabschnitt**; ~**sektor** m → **Kreisausschnitt**; ~**sparkasse** f district savings bank; ~**spieler** m, ~**spielerin** f Hallenhandball: pivot player
Kreißsaal m delivery room
Kreis|stadt f chief town of a (od. the) district; **Große ~** chief town with district administration; ~**tag** m district assembly; ~**umfang** m Math. circumference (of a od. the circle); ~**verkehr** m (traffic) roundabout, Am. traffic circle; **im ~** in a roundabout (Am. traffic circle); ~**verwaltung** f district administration; Behörde: district (bes. Brit. local) authority; ~**wehrersatzamt** n district recruiting office; ~**zahl** n; nur Sg.; Math. pi (3.14159)
Krem f → **Creme**
Krematorium n; -s, Krematorien crematorium, Am. auch crematory
Kreme f → **Creme**
kremig Adj. → **cremig**
Kreml m; -s, kein Pl.; Pol.: **der ~** the Kremlin; ~**chef** m Pol. Kremlin boss
Krempe f; -, -n brim
Krempel m; -s, kein Pl.; umg. → **Kram** 1
krempeln v/t.: **die Ärmel** etc. **nach oben** ~ roll up one's sleeves etc.
Kren m; -(e)s, kein Pl.; südd., österr. horseradish
Kreole m; -n, -n, **Kreolin** f; -, -nen Creole, weiblich auch: Creole woman (od. girl); **kreolisch I.** Adj. Creole; **II. Kreolisch** n; -en; Ling. Creole; **das Kreolische** Creole
krepieren v/i. **1.** umg. Tier, Person: die (a wretched death); **2.** Geschoss: burst, explode
Krepp m; -s, -s und -e crepe; ~**papier** n crepe paper; ~**seide** f crepe de Chine; ~**sohle** f crepe sole
Kresse f; -,-n; Bot., Gastr. cress
Kreta (n); -s; Geog. Crete; **Kreter** m; -s, -, **Kreterin** f; -, -nen Cretan, weiblich auch: Cretan woman (od. girl etc.); **ich bin ~** auch I'm from Crete
Krethi und Plethi Pl. pej. every Tom, Dick and Harry
Kretin [kre'tɛː] m; -s, -s cretin; pej. auch moron; **Kretinismus** m; -, kein Pl.; Med. cretinism

kretisch Adj. Cretan
kreucht Präs. altm. → **kriechen**; **alles, was da ~ und fleucht** all creatures on land and in the air
kreuz Adv.: ~ **und quer parken/liegen** etc. be parked/lying etc. all over the place; ~ **und quer durch die Stadt gehen** walk this way and that all through the town
Kreuz n; -es, -e **1.** cross; (Kruzifix) crucifix; **über ~** crosswise; **das ~ schlagen** make the sign of the cross; **über sich:** auch cross o.s. (auch fig.); **das Eiserne ~** the Iron Cross; ~ **des Südens** Astron. Southern Cross; **2.** fig., in Wendungen: **sein ~ auf sich nehmen / tragen** take up / bear one's cross; **zu ~e kriechen** eat humble pie, Am. auch eat crow; **er ist mit ihm über(s) ~** they've fallen out (with each other); **es ist ein ~ mit ihm** he tries one's patience, he's a real pain umg.; **ich hab drei ~e gemacht** I was glad to see (od. hear) the last of that, I heaved a sigh of relief; **3.** Anat. lower back, small of the back; **ich hab's wieder im ~** umg. my back's playing me up (Am. playing up on me) again; **aufs ~ legen** vulg. (Frau) lay; umg. fig. (betrügen) take s.o. for a ride; **beinahe aufs ~ fallen** be flabbergasted, be knocked sideways; **4.** (Autobahnkreuz) intersection; **rund um das ~ München-Nord werden Staus gemeldet** there are jams all around the Munich North intersection; **5.** Kartenfarbe: clubs Pl., Einzelkarte: club; ~ **sticht** od. **ist Trumpf** clubs are trump(s); **6.** Mus. sharp; **7.** Druck. dagger
Kreuz... im Subst. (Spielkarte) … of clubs
Kreuz|abnahme f Kunst descent from the Cross; ~**ass** n ace of clubs; ~**band** n **1.** Anat. crucial ligament; **2.** (Streifband) wrapper; ~**bandriss** m Med. torn crucial ligament; ~**bein** n Anat. sacrum; ~**blütler** m; -s, -; Bot. crucifer
kreuzbrav Adj. umg. bes. Kind: (as) good as gold; **ein ~er Mensch** a fine upstanding person
Kreuz|bube m jack of clubs; ~**dame** f queen of clubs
kreuzen I. v/t. **1.** (Linie, Straße etc.) cross, intersect; **die Beine ~** cross one's legs; **die Arme ~** fold one's arms; **2.** Bio. cross(breed), interbreed; **II.** v/refl. cross; Briefe: cross in the post (Am. mail); fig. Interessen etc.: clash; **unsere Wege/Blicke kreuzten sich** our paths crossed / our eyes met; **III.** v/i. **1.** Naut., Flug. cruise; **2.** Naut., im Zickzackkurs: tack
Kreuzer m; -s, - **1.** Mil. cruiser; (Jacht) cruising yacht; **2.** hist. (Münze) kreuzer
Kreuzestod m (death by) crucifixion; **den ~ sterben** die on the cross
Kreuz|fahrer m hist. crusader; ~**fahrt** f **1.** cruise; **2.** hist. (Kreuzzug) crusade; ~**fahrtschiff** n cruise ship; großer: cruise liner; ~**feuer** n crossfire (auch fig.); **ins ~ geraten** fig. come under fire from all sides, umg. come in for a roasting; **im ~ der Kritik stehen** be attacked by the critics
kreuz|fidel Adj. umg. very chirpy (Am. chipper), happy as a sandboy (Am. a clam); ~**förmig** Adj. cross-shaped, cruciform
Kreuz|gang m Archit. cloisters Pl.; ~**gelenk** n Tech. universal joint; ~**gewölbe** n Archit. cross (od. groined) vault

kreuzigen v/t. crucify (auch fig.); **Kreuzigung** f crucifixion
Kreuz|knoten m Naut. reef (Am. auch square od. flat) knot; ~**könig** m king of clubs; ~**kümmel** m cumin
kreuzlahm Adj. umg.: **jetzt bin ich aber ~** my back's killing me; (ich bin k.o.) I'm shattered (Am. wiped out)
Kreuz|otter f Zool. adder; ~**probe** f Med. cross-matching; **die ~ machen** cross-match; ~**reim** m Lit. alternate rhyme; ~**rippengewölbe** n Archit. ribbed vault
Kreuzritter m hist. **1.** crusader; **2.** des Deutschen Ordens: knight of the Teutonic Order, Teutonic Knight; ~**orden** m Teutonic Order of Knights
Kreuz|schiff n **1.** cruise ship; großes: cruise liner; **2.** e-r Kirche: transept; ~**schlitzschraube** f cross-head screw, mst Phillips screw; ~**schlitzschraubendreher** m crosshead screwdriver, mst Phillips screwdriver; ~**schlüssel** m spider wheelbrace; ~**schmerzen** Pl. backache Sg.; ~**schnabel** m Orn. crossbill; ~**spinne** f cross (od. garden) spider; ~**stich** m cross-stitch
Kreuzung f **1.** (road) junction, crossroads Pl. (V. im Sg.), bes. Am. intersection; **in die ~ einfahren / über die ~ fahren** enter/cross the junction (Am. intersection); **2.** Bio. (Züchtung) cross-breeding; (Produkt) cross(-breed)
Kreuzungsbereich m area of a (od. the) junction (Am. intersection); **im ~** at or near the junction (Am. intersection); **kreuzungsfrei** Adj. without any junctions (Am. intersections), non-intersecting; **Kreuzungspunkt** m point of intersection
Kreuz|verband m **1.** Med. crossed bandage; **2.** Archit. English cross bond; ~**verhör** n Jur. cross-examination; weitS. interrogation, umg. grilling; **j-n ins ~ nehmen** cross-examine s.o.; weitS. umg. give s.o. a grilling; ~**verweis** m cross-reference; ~**weg** m **1.** crossroads Pl. (V. im Sg.) (auch fig.); **am ~ stehen** bes. fig. be at the crossroads; **2.** kath. stations Pl. of the Cross; **den ~ beten** pray at all the stations of the Cross; ~**wegstation** f kath. station of the Cross; ~**weh** n umg. backache
kreuzweise I. Adj. crossways, bes. Am. crosswise; **die ~ Anordnung der Balken** etc. the crossways (od. crosswise) arrangement of the beams etc.; **II.** Adv. **1.** crossways, crosswise, across; **2.** Sl.: **du kannst mich mal ~** you know what you can do (with yourself), you can get lost
Kreuz|worträtsel n crossword (puzzle); ~**zeichen** n kirchl. sign of the cross; ~**zug** m hist. crusade (auch fig.)
Krevette f; -, -n shrimp (Am. auch Pl.)
kribbelig Adj. edgy, umg. jittery; präd. on edge; **das macht mich ganz ~** auch umg. it gives me the jitters
kribbeln v/i. **1.** (prickeln) prickle, tingle; (jucken) itch, tickle; **es kribbelt mir** od. **mich auf der Haut / in der Nase** I've got a prickling (od. tingling) sensation on my skin / a tickle in my nose; **mir kribbelt's in den Fingern** I've got pins and needles in my fingers; fig. I'm itching to do it; **ein ~des Gefühl** a tingling sensation (od. pins and needles) (in + Dat. in); **2.** **es kribbelt von Ameisen** etc. the place is crawling with ants etc.; **Kribbeln** n; -s, kein Pl. tingling, pins and needles Pl.;

(*Jucken*) itching, tickling; **kribblig** *Adj.* → **kribbelig**

Krickelkrakel *n*; *-s*, *kein Pl.*; *umg.* scribble, scrawl

Krickente *f Orn.* teal

Kricket *n*; *-s*, *kein Pl.*; *Sport* cricket; **~spieler** *m*, **~spielerin** *f* cricketer

kriechen *v/i.*; *kriecht*, *kroch*, *ist gekrochen* **1.** crawl; *verstohlen*, *Schutz suchend*: creep; *Schlange*: *auch* slither; **2.** (*sich langsam fortbewegen*) crawl; *Mot. auch* creep; *kaum noch / nicht mehr ~ können* be barely / no longer able to get about (*Am.* around); **3.** (*hat od. ist gekrochen*) *fig. vor j-m ~ umg.* toady to s.o., suck up to s.o.; **kriechend I.** *Part. Präs.* → **kriechen**; **II.** *Adj.*: **~e Pflanze** creeper

Kriecher *m*; *-s*, *-*; *pej.* toady; **Kriecherei** *f*, *-*, *en*; *pej.* toadying; **Kriecherin** *f*; *-*, *-nen*; *pej.* toady; **kriecherisch** *Adj. pej.* servile, *attr. auch* bootlicking; *ich kann s-e ~e Art nicht ausstehen umg.* I can't stand the way he sucks up to people

Kriech|pflanze *f Bot.* creeper; **~spur** *f* **1.** *Mot.* slow lane; **2.** *Zool.* trail; **~strom** *m Etech.* (surface) leakage current; **~tempo** *n*: *sich im ~ fortbewegen* crawl along; **~tier** *n Zool.* reptile

Krieg *m*; *-(e)s*, *-e* war (*auch fig.*); (*Kriegführung*) warfare; (*Fehde*, *auch fig.*) feud; *der Kalte ~ hist.* the Cold War; *totaler ~* total warfare; *im ~* in the war; (*im Kriegszustand*) at war (*mit* with); *sie sind ständig im ~ miteinander fig.* they are constantly feuding; *vom ~ verwüstet* war-torn; *~ führen gegen* make (*od.* wage) war on; (*im Kriegszustand sein mit*) be at war with; *die ~ führenden Staaten* the belligerent states; *den ~ erklären* (+ *Dat.*) declare war on (*auch fig.*); *in den ~ ziehen* go to the war

kriegen *v/t. umg.* **1.** (*bekommen*) get; *ich habe noch Geld von ihm zu ~* I've still got some money to come from him; *Besuch ~* get visitors; *am Ende des Films kriegen sie sich* at the end of the film boy gets girl; *er kriegt was von mir zu hören!* I'll have something to say to him; *gleich kriegst du was!* *drohend*: just watch your step; *~ auch bekommen*; **2.** (*erwischen*) get, catch (*auch Verbrecher*, *Zug etc.*); **3.** (*Krankheit*) get, come down with; *ansteckende Krankheit*: *auch* catch (*Herzinfarkt etc.*) have; (*e-n*) *Schnupfen ~* get (*od.* catch) a cold; **4.** (*dazu bringen*) persuade; *j-n dazu ~*, *etw. zu tun* get s.o. to do s.th.; *j-n dazu ~*, *etw. zu tun* get s.o. to do s.th.; *bei dem Wetter ist er nicht aus dem Haus zu ~* you can't persuade him to go out (*od.* there's no getting him out) in this weather; **5.** (*schaffen*) manage; *das werden wir schon ~!* we'll sort that out, don't you worry; *ich kriege es nicht über mich zu* (+ *Inf.*) I can't bring myself to (+ *Inf.*)

Krieger *m*; *-s*, *-* warrior; (*Soldat*) soldier; *alter ~ hum.* old campaigner; *kalter ~ Pol.* cold war exponent; **~denkmal** *n* war memorial

Kriegerin *f*; *-*, *-nen* (female) warrior, Amazon *lit.*; **kriegerisch** *Adj.* **1.** warlike; *auch fig.* belligerent; **2.** *Konflikt etc.*: military, armed; **~e Auseinandersetzung(en)** armed conflict

Kriegerwitwe *f* war widow

kriegführend → *Krieg*

Kriegführung *f* military strategy; *bestimmter Fall*: conduct of the war; *bio-*

logische etc. ~ biological *etc.* warfare

Kriegs|anleihe *f* war loan; **~ausbruch** *m* outbreak of (the) war; *bei ~* at the outbreak of war, when (the) war broke out; *Zukunft*: when war breaks out; **~auszeichnung** *f* war decoration; **~begeisterung** *f* war fever; **~beginn** *m* beginning of a (*od.* the) war; **~beil** *n* tomahawk; *das ~ ausgraben fig.* (re)start hostilities; *das ~ begraben* bury the hatchet; **~bemalung** *f* war paint; *in voller ~ umg. fig.* with all her war paint on; **~bericht** *m* war report; **~berichterstatter** *m* war correspondent

kriegsbeschädigt *Adj.* war-disabled; **Kriegsbeschädigte** *m*, *f* (war-)disabled veteran; **~(r) sein** be war-disabled

Kriegs|beute *f* spoils *Pl.* of war; **~blinde** *m*, *f* person blinded in the war; *er ist ~r* he was blinded in the war; **~braut** *f* war bride

Kriegsdienst *m* military service; *kämpfend*: active service; **~gegner** *m*, **~verweigerer** *m* conscientious objector; **~verweigerung** *f* conscientious objection

Kriegs|drohung *f* threat of war; **~eintritt** *m* entry into the war; **~einwirkung** *f* military action; *durch ~ verursachte Zerstörungen* war damage; **~ende** *n* end of the war; *bei/nach/vor ~* auch when/after/before the war ended; **~entschädigung** *f* reparations *Pl.*

kriegsentscheidend *Adj.* decisive for the outcome of the war; *die ~e Schlacht* the battle that decided the war

Kriegs|erklärung *f* declaration of war; **~erlebnis** *n* wartime experience; **~fall** *m*: *im ~* in the event of (a) war; **~film** *m* war film; **~flagge** *f Mil.* naval ensign; **~flotte** *f Mil.* navy, (fighting) fleet; **~folge** *f* consequence of the war; **~freiwillige** *m*, *f* war volunteer; **~führung** *f* → *Kriegführung*; **~fuß** *m hum.*: *mit j-m/etw. auf ~ stehen* be at loggerheads with s.o. / be having a hard time (*od.* a real struggle) with s.th.; *mit der Rechtschreibung steht er schon immer auf ~* he's always been completely lost when it comes to spelling; **~gebiet** *n* war zone; **~gefahr** *f* threat of war; **~gefangene** *m*, *f* prisoner of war (*Abk.* POW); **~gefangenenlager** *n* prisoner-of-war camp, POW camp; **~gefangenschaft** *f* captivity (as a prisoner of war); *in ~ geraten* be taken prisoner; *in ein Lager kommen*: be put into (*od.* interned in) a prisoner-of-war camp; *aus der ~ heimkehren* return from captivity as a prisoner of war; **~gegner** *m*, **~gegnerin** *f* **1.** (*Feind*) (wartime) enemy; **2.** (*Pazifist*) opponent of war, pacifist; **~generation** *f* war generation; **~gerät** *n* military equipment, matériel; **~gericht** *n* court martial, courts martial *Pl.*; *vor ein ~ gestellt werden* be tried by court martial, be court-martial(l)ed; **~geschrei** *n* battle cry, war cry; **~gesetz** *n* martial law; **~gewinnler** *m*; *-s*, *-*; *pej.* war profiteer; **~gott** *m* god of war; **~göttin** *f* goddess of war; **~gräberfürsorge** *f* War Graves Commission; **~gräuel** *Pl.* wartime atrocities; **~hafen** *m* naval port; **~handwerk** *n geh.* art of warfare; **~held** *m* war hero; *hist.* great warrior; **~herr** *m* **1.** *oberster ~* commander-in-chief, supreme commander; **2.** *im Mittelalter*: warlord; **~hetze** *f* warmongering; **~hetzer** *m*

warmonger; **~hinterbliebene** *m*, *f* surviving dependant; *Witwe*: war widow; *Waisenkind*: war orphan; *Pl.* war widows and orphans; **~industrie** *f* war industry; **~invalide** *m*, *f* disabled veteran; **~jahr** *n* year of (the) war; **~kamerad** *m* wartime comrade, comrade in arms; *wir sind ~en auch* we fought together in the war; **~kasse** *f hist.* war chest (*auch fig.*); *die ~ der Gewerkschaft ist gefüllt* the union's coffers are filled ready for a long fight; **~kunst** *f altm.* art of warfare; **~list** *f* (military) stratagem; *fig.* cunning ruse; **~marine** *f* navy; **~maschine** *f* **1.** *hist.* engine of war; **2.** *pej.* (*militärische Möglichkeiten*) war machine; **~maschinerie** *f* machinery of war; **~material** *n* military equipment, matériel; **~minister** *m hist.* minister of war; **~ministerium** *n* war ministry; *in GB*: War Office; *in den USA bis 1947*: War Department

kriegsmüde *Adj.* war-weary

Kriegsopfer *n* war victim; **~rente** *f* war pension

Kriegs|pfad *m*: *auf dem ~ sein* be on the warpath; **~propaganda** *f* war propaganda; **~rat** *m*: *~ halten fig.* have a conference (*od.* pow-wow); **~recht** *n*; *nur Sg.* **1.** *Jur.* den Krieg regelnd: laws *Pl.* of war; **2.** *Mil.*, *im Krieg geltend*: martial law; **~roman** *m* war novel; **~schaden** *m* war damage; **~schauplatz** *m* theat|re (*Am. auch* -er) of war; **~schiff** *n* warship; *hist.* man-of--war; **~schuld** *f* war guilt; **~schulden** *Pl.* war debts; **~spiel** *n* **1.** *Mil.* war game; **2.** *fig. von Kindern*: game of soldiers; **~spielzeug** *n* war toys *Pl.*; **~stärke** *f* wartime strength; **~tanz** *m* war dance; **~teilnehmer** *m* (*Soldat*) combatant; *ehemaliger*: (war) veteran; (*Land*) warring nation, belligerent; **~treiber** *m* warmonger; **~treiberei** *f* warmongering; **~verbrechen** *n* war crime

Kriegsverbrecher *m* war criminal; **~prozess** *m* war crimes trial; **~tribunal** *n* war crimes tribunal

Kriegsverletzung *f* war wound (*od.* injury)

kriegsversehrt *Adj.* war-disabled; **Kriegsversehrte** *m*, *f* disabled veteran; **~(r) sein** be war-disabled

Kriegs|veteran *m* war veteran; **~waffe** *f* weapon of war; **~wagen** *m hist.* war chariot; **~waise** *f* war orphan

kriegswichtig *Adj.* strategically important; **~e Güter** materials essential to the war effort

Kriegs|wirren *Pl.* chaos *Sg.* of war; **~wirtschaft** *f* war economy; **~zeit** *f* wartime; *in ~en* in times of war; **~ziel** *n* war aim; **~zug** *m altm.* campaign; **~zustand** *n* state of war; *im ~* at war

Krill[1] *m*; *-(e)s*, *-e*; *Zool.* krill

Krill[2] *n*; *-(e)s*, *kein Pl.* krill plankton

Krim *f*; *-*; *Geog.*: *die ~* the Crimea

Krimi *m*; *-s*, *-s*; *umg.* **1.** *Roman*: detective story, *Am. umg.* gumshoe; (*Mordgeschichte*) whodun(n)it, (murder) mystery; *spannend*: crime thriller; **2.** *Film*: crime film (*bes. Am.* movie) (*spannend*: thriller); *Sendereihe*: crime series; **3.** *umg. fig.* (*spannendes Fußballspiel etc.*) nailbiter, cliffhanger; **~autor** *m*, **~autorin** *f* author of detective fiction, crime writer

Kriminalbeamte *m*, **Kriminalbeamtin** *f* (plain-clothes) detective; **Kriminaler** *m*; *-s*, *-*; *umg.* detective, *Am. umg.* gumshoe

K

K

Kriminal|film m crime film (bes. Am. movie) (spannend: thriller); **~geschichte** f **1.** nur Sg. history of crime; **2.** → Krimi 1; **~inspektor** m, **~inspektorin** f detective inspector

kriminalisieren v/t. criminalize; Jugendliche ~ make young people turn to crime; **Kriminalisierung** f criminalization

Kriminalist m; -en, -en detective, Am. umg. gumshoe; (Kriminologe) criminologist; **Kriminalistik** f; -, kein Pl. criminalistics Pl. (als Fach mit V. im Sg.); **Kriminalistin** f; -, -nen → Kriminalist; **kriminalistisch** Adj. criminal investigation …; Fähigkeiten: crime-solving; **~e Untersuchung** criminal investigation

Kriminalität f; -, kein Pl. crime; hohe ~ high crime rate

Kriminal|kommissar m, **~kommissarin** f detective superintendent; **~komödie** f crime comedy; **~polizei** f criminal investigation department (Am. division), Brit. auch CID; Personal: plain-clothes police Pl.

kriminalpolizeilich I. Adj. plain-clothes (police) …, CID …; II. Adv. ermitteln etc.: by the CID

Kriminal|polizist m, **~polizistin** f plain-clothes policeman; **~psychologie** f psychology of crime, criminal psychology; **~roman** m detective novel, (murder) mystery, Am. umg. gumshoe; spannend: crime thriller; Pl. Koll. crime (od. detective) fiction Sg.; **~schriftsteller** m, **~schriftstellerin** f crime writer; **~soziologie** f sociology of crime; **~statistik** f crime statistics Pl.; engS. crime figures Pl.; **~stück** n Theat. detective play, crime thriller

Kriminaltechnik f forensic science; **kriminaltechnisch** Adj. forensic

kriminell Adj. criminal; **Kriminelle** m, f; -n, -n criminal

Kriminologe m; -n, -n criminologist; **Kriminologie** f; -, kein Pl. criminology; **Kriminologin** f; -, -nen criminologist; **kriminologisch** Adj. criminological

Krimiserie f umg. crime series

Krim|krieg m; nur Sg.; hist. Crimean War; **~sekt** m Crimean sparkling wine

Krimskrams m; -(e)s; umg. junk, odds and ends Pl.; (Einzelstück) piece of junk

Kringel m; -s, - ring (auch Gebäck); Schrift: (circular) squiggle; **kringelig** Adj. curly; sich ~ lachen umg. crease o.s. (with laughter); **kringeln** v/refl. curl (up); sich (vor Lachen) ~ umg. crease o.s. (Am. double over) (with laughter); das ist ja zum Kringeln umg. that's a hoot

Krinoline f; -, -n crinoline

Kripo f; -, -s; Abk. umg. (Kriminalpolizei) Brit. CID

Krippe f; -, -n; auch bibl. **1.** für Futter: manger; **2.** (Weihnachtskrippe) crib, Am. crèche; **3.** (Kinderkrippe) crèche, bes. Am. day nursery

Krippen|figur f nativity figure; **~platz** m place in a day nursery (Brit. mst crèche); **~spiel** n nativity play

Krise f; -, -n crisis (Pl. crises) (auch Med.); in e-e ~ geraten get into a state of crisis; sich in e-r ~ befinden be in (a state of) crisis; die ~ kriegen umg. have a fit, Brit. auch throw a wobbly

kriseln v/i. unpers.: es kriselt all's not well; es droht etwas: there's trouble brewing; in ihrer Ehe etc. kriselt es their marriage etc. is in trouble (umg.)

going through a sticky patch), all is not well in their marriage etc.

krisenanfällig Adj. unstable, crisis-prone

Krisen|beschwörer m alarmist; **~bewältigung** f crisis management; **~erscheinung** f crisis symptom

krisenfest Adj. stable

Krisengebiet n crisis area

krisen|geschüttelt Adj. crisis-ridden; **~haft** I. Adj. critical; die ~e Entwicklung auf dem Arbeitsmarkt the incipient crisis in the labo(u)r market; II. Adv. sich entwickeln: into a crisis; sich ~ zuspitzen Entwicklung etc.: reach crisis proportions

Krisen|herd m trouble spot, flashpoint; **~management** n crisis management; **~plan** m contingency plan; **~region** f trouble area

krisensicher Adj. → krisenfest

Krisen|situation f crisis (situation); **~sitzung** f crisis meeting; **~stab** m crisis management group, umg. troubleshooting team; **~stimmung** f crisis mood; **~zeit** f time of crisis

Kristall¹ m; -s, -e crystal

Kristall² n; -s, kein Pl. Glasware: crystal

Kristallbildung f crystallization

kristallen Adj. crystal; fig. Wasser etc.: crystal clear

Kristall|gitter n Chem. crystal lattice; **~glas** n **1.** nur Sg. crystal; **2.** (Gefäß) crystal glass

kristallin Adj. crystalline

Kristallisation f; -, -en crystallization; **kristallisieren** vt/i. und v/refl. crystallize (auch fig.)

kristallklar Adj. crystal clear

Kristall|kugel f crystal ball; **~leuchter** m crystal chandelier; **~nacht** f hist., euph. kristallnacht, Night of the Broken Glass (in 1938, when Nazis instigated an anti-Jewish pogrom); **~schale** f crystal bowl; **~waren** Pl. crystal(ware) Sg.; **~zucker** m (refined) sugar crystals Pl.

Kriterium n; -s, Kriterien **1.** criterion (Pl. criteria); **2.** Sport race with many competitors; Radsport: circuit race won on a points system

Kritik f; -, -en **1.** (das Kritisieren) criticism, criticizing; einzelne: criticism (an + Dat. of); (Tadel) auch censure; unter aller ~ umg. completely hopeless; ~ üben (an + Dat.) criticize; **2.** (Rezension) review, write-up; gute ~en haben get good reviews, have a good press; was sagt die ~? what do the critics say?; **3.** (kritische Abhandlung, Rede etc.) critique (+ Gen. of)

Kritikaster m; -s, - pej. faultfinder; (Rezensent) cavil(l)ing critic

Kritiker m; -s, -, auch f; -, -en critic; (Rezensent) auch reviewer

kritikfähig Adj. **1.** aktiv: capable of (constructive) criticism; **2.** passiv: capable of taking criticism; **Kritikfähigkeit** f; nur Sg. **1.** critical faculties Pl.; (Unterscheidungsvermögen) powers Pl. of discernment; **2.** ability to take criticism

kritiklos Adj. uncritical; **Kritiklosigkeit** f; nur Sg. uncriticalness; (mangelndes Unterscheidungsvermögen) lack of discrimination

Kritikpunkt m point of criticism; es gibt noch einen weiteren ~ and there is another point which is open to criticism

kritikwürdig Adj. … deserving criticism

kritisch I. Adj. **1.** critical (gegenüber of); (fein urteilend) auch discriminating, discerning; Fernsehen: investigative; **2.** (bedenklich) Augenblick, Punkt etc.: critical (auch Phys., Tech.); ~ werden become critical; Reaktor: go critical; II. Adv. critically; ~ eingestellt sein have a critical attitude (od. turn of mind); e-r Sache ~ gegenüberstehen have a critical attitude to s.th.; sich ~ zu etw. äußern be critical of s.th.

kritisieren v/t. criticize; (rezensieren) review; er hat an allem etwas zu ~ he always finds something to criticize, he finds fault in everything

Krittelei f; -, -en; pej. carping, nitpicking umg.; **krittelig** Adj. carping, nitpicking umg.; **kritteln** v/i. find fault (an + Dat. with), carp (at); sie hat immer etwas zu ~ she's forever finding fault; **Krittler** m; -s, -, **Krittlerin** f; -, -nen carper, nitpicker umg.

Kritzelei f; -, -en; umg. pej. **1.** nur Sg. (Kritzeln) scribbling; **2.** (Gekritzeltes) scribble; malend: doodle; **kritzelig** Adj. umg. pej. scribbly; **kritzeln** v/i. scribble; malend: doodle

Kroate m; -n, -n Croatian; **Kroatien** (n); -s; Geog. Croatia; **Kroatin** f; -, -nen Croatian woman (od. girl); **kroatisch** Adj. Croatian; **Kroatisch** n; -en; Ling. Croatian; das ~e Croatian

kroch Imperf. → kriechen

Krocket n; -s, kein Pl.; Sport croquet

Krokant m; -s, kein Pl. cracknel

Krokette f; -, -n; Gastr. croquette

Kroko n; -(s), -s; Abk. umg. → Krokodilleder

Krokodil n; -s, -e; Zool. crocodile; **~leder** n crocodile leather (od. skin)

Krokodilstränen Pl. umg. fig. crocodile tears; ein paar ~ weinen shed crocodile tears

Krokus m; -, - und -se; Bot. crocus (Pl. crocuses od. croci)

Krönchen f small crown, coronet

Krone f; -, -n **1.** crown; (Adelskrone) coronet; die päpstliche ~ the papal tiara; brich dir keinen Stein od. Zacken aus der ~! fig. iro. don't put yourself out!; → Zacken 2; **2.** fig. (Vollendung, Gipfel) climax; das Lebenswerks etc.: crowning glory; die ~ der Schöpfung the summit of creation; die ~ des Widersinns the height of absurdity; e-r Sache mit etw. die ~ aufsetzen crown s.th. with s.th.; das setzt allem die ~ auf that beats everything; **3.** fig. e-s Baums: top; Bot., e-r Blume: corolla; (Zahnkrone) crown; e-s Deichs: top; e-r Welle: crest (Mauerkrone) coping; e-r Uhr: winding button, Am. stem; (ganz schön) e-n in der ~ haben umg. have had one too many; **4.** Währungseinheit: hist. crown; Dänemark, Norwegen: krone; Schweden, Island: krona; Tschechien: koruna

krönen v/t. **1.** crown; j-n zum König ~ crown s.o. king; **2.** fig. (vollenden) crown, cap; (Veranstaltung etc.) round off; → gekrönt

Kronen|korken m crown cork (od. cap); **~mutter** f castle nut

Kron|erbe m, **~erbin** f heir to the throne (od. crown); **~gut** n crown estate; **~juwelen** Pl. crown jewels; **~kolonie** f crown colony; **~korken** m crown cork; **~land** n crown estate; **~leuchter** m chandelier; mir geht ein ~ auf umg. it's dawned on me; **~prätendent** m, **~prätendentin** f pretender to the throne; **~prinz** m crown prince; *in GB*: Prince of Wales; **~prinzessin** *f* crown princess; *in GB*: Princess Royal; **~rat** *m* ministerial council presided over by the monarch; **~schatz** *m* crown treasure

Krönung *f* coronation; *fig.* climax, high point; crowning moment (*od.* event, *Leistung*: achievement); **zur ~ des Ganzen** *fig.* to crown (*od.* top) it all

Krönungs|eid *m* coronation oath; **~feier** *f* coronation (ceremony)

Kronzeuge *m Jur.* chief witness; (*geständiger Mittäter*) state witness, accomplice witness; **als ~ auftreten** testify as a state witness; *in GB*: turn Queen's (*od.* King's) evidence; *in den USA*: turn state's evidence; **Kronzeugenregelung** *f Jur.* regulation guaranteeing a state witness from a terrorist background immunity from prosecution or a lenient sentence; **Kronzeugin** *f* → **Kronzeuge**

Kropf *m*; *-(e)s*, *Kröpfe*; *Med.* goit|re (*Am.* -er); *Orn.* crop; **überflüssig wie ein ~** *umg.* as useful as a hole in the head

Kroppzeug *n*; *nur Sg.*; *umg.* **1.** (*Gesindel*) dregs *Pl.*, scum, peasants *Pl.*; **2.** *oft hum.* (*Kinder*) brats *Pl.*; **3.** (*Kram*) junk

kross *Adj.* crisp

Krösus *m*; *- und -ses*, *-se*; *fig.*: **ich bin doch kein ~!** I'm not made of money

Kröte *f*; *-*, *-n* **1.** *Zool.* toad; **2.** *umg. fig* (*Person*): **giftige ~** spiteful (*od.* venomous) creature, nasty piece of work; (*Kind*): (**freche**) **kleine ~** (cheeky) little devil (*od.* rascal); **3.** *Pl. umg.* (*Geld*): **m-e letzten ~n** my last few pennies; **Krötenwanderung** *f* migration of toads

Krs. *Abk.* → **Kreis** 5

Krücke *f*; *-*, *-n* **1.** crutch; (*Griff*) handle; **an ~n gehen** walk on crutches; **2.** *umg. fig.* (*Versager*) dead loss, washout, *bes. Am.* write-off; (*Gegenstand*) heap of junk

Krückstock *m* walking stick

krud(e) *Adj.* rough, crude

Krug *m*; *-(e)s*, *Krüge* **1.** jug, *bes. Am.* pitcher; (*Bierkrug*) beer mug, *mst Am.* stein; *aus Metall*: tankard; (*Vase*) vase; **der ~ geht so lange zum Brunnen, bis er bricht** *Unrecht*: you *etc.* won't get away with that forever; *Geduld*: there's a limit to everything; *drohend*: you do that one more time; **2.** *nordd.* (*Wirtshaus*) inn

Krügerrand ['kry:gərant] *m*; *-s*, *-s* krugerrand

Kruke *f*; *-*, *-n*; *nordd.* (large) jug, pitcher

Krümchen *n fig.* tiny bit

Krume *f*; *-*, *-n* **1.** crumb; **2.** *Agr.* topsoil

Krümel *m*; *-s*, *-* **1.** crumb; **es ist kein ~ Salz mehr im Haus** *umg.* we haven't got a grain of salt in the house; **2.** *umg., mst hum.* (*Kind*) little mite; **krümelig** *Adj.* crumbly; (*voller Krümel*) full of crumbs; **krümeln** *v/i.* be crumbly; **bitte nicht ~!** no crumbs (on the floor), please

krumm *Adj. und Adv.* **1.** crooked (*auch Nase*); (*verbogen*) bent; (*gewunden*) winding; (*verdreht*) twisted; **~e Haltung** bent posture, stoop; **~ gehen** stoop; **~ biegen** bend; **alt und ~** bowed down with age; **sich ~ legen** *umg. fig.* (*eisern sparen*) scrimp and save; (*sich sehr einschränken müssen*) have to count every penny; **2.** *umg. fig.*: **(j-m) etw. ~ nehmen** take offen|ce (*Am.* -se) at s.th. (from s.o.); **sie hat es mir ~ ge-**

---

nommen, dass ich ... she was offended (*od.* took it amiss) that I...; **3.** *umg. fig.* (*unrechtmäßig*) crooked, shady; **~e Finger machen** walk off with s.th.; **~e Sachen machen** have shady dealings; (*mit dem Gesetz in Konflikt geraten*) get onto the wrong side of the law; **es auf die ~e Tour versuchen** try to do it by underhand(ed) means, try to pull a fast one; **~beinig** *Adj.* bandy- (*od.* bow-)legged

krümmen I. *v/t.* bend; *Katze etc.*: (*den Rücken*) arch; → **Finger** 2, **Haar** 2; **II.** *v/refl. Straße*: curve, bend; *Fluss*: bend; *über längere Strecke*: be very windy, wind its way, *Fluss*: *auch* meander; *Holz, Blech*: warp; *Wurm*: wriggle; **sich ~ vor** (+ *Dat*) *fig. Schmerzen, Lachen*: double up (*Am.* over) with; *Zustand*: be doubled up (*od.* convulsed) with; **sich vor Verlegenheit ~** squirm with embarrassment; → **gekrümmt**

Krümmer *m*; *-s*, *-*; *Tech.* elbow, bend; *Mot.* manifold

Krummhorn *n Mus.* crumhorn

krumm|legen, **~nehmen** → **krumm**

krumm|linig *Adj. Math.* curvilinear; **~nasig** *Adj.* crooked-nosed, ... with a crooked nose

Krumm|säbel *m* scimitar; **~stab** *m* *kirchl.* (bishop's) crook, crozier, crosier

Krümmung *f* curve; (*e-r Straße, e-s Flusses*) *auch* bend; *Math., Med., Phys.* curvature; (*Windung*) twist

krumpelig *Adj. Dial.* creased, *Am.* wrinkled; **krumpeln** *v/i. Dial.* crease, *bes. Am.* wrinkle

Krupp *m*; *-s*, *kein Pl.*; *Med.* croup

Kruppe *f*; *-*, *-n des Pferdes*: croup

Krüppel *m*; *-s*, *-* cripple; **zum ~ machen** cripple, maim; **zum ~ werden** be crippled; **krüppelig** *Adj.* deformed, crippled; *Baum*: stunted

Krupphusten *m Med.* croupy cough

Krustazee *f*; *-,-n*; *Zool.* crustacean

Kruste *f*; *-*, *-n*; *auch Geol.* crust; *von Braten*: crisp; *von Schweinebraten*: pork rind; *gebraten*: crackling; *von Wunde*: scab

Krustentier *n Zool.* crustacean

krustig *Adj.* crusty; *Wunde*: scabby

Kruzifix *n*; *-es*, *-e* crucifix

Krypta *f*; *-*, *Krypten* crypt

kryptisch I. *Adj.* cryptic; **e-e ~e Ausdrucksweise** a cryptic way of expressing o.s.; **II.** *Adv.* cryptically; **sich ~ ausdrücken** express o.s. cryptically

Krypton *n*; *-s*, *kein Pl.*; *Chem.* krypton (*abgek.* **Kr**)

KSZE *f*; *-*, *kein Pl.*; *Abk.* (**Konferenz über Sicherheit und Zusammenarbeit in Europa**) CSCE

Kuba (*n*); *-s*; *Geog.* Cuba; **Kubaner** *m*; *-s*, *-*, **Kubanerin** *f*; *-*, *-nen* Cuban, *weiblich auch*: Cuban woman (*od.* girl); **kubanisch** *Adj.* Cuban

Kübel *m*; *-s*, *-* bucket; *größerer, für Pflanzen*: tub; (*Toiletteneimer*) (latrine) bucket; **es gießt wie aus ~n** *umg.* it's bucketing (down), it's coming down in buckets; **~pflanze** *f* tub plant; **~wagen** *m* **1.** *Mil.* open cross-country vehicle, *etwa* jeep®; **2.** *Eisenb.* (rail) bucket car

kübelweise *Adv.* by the bucket(load)

kubieren *v/t. Math.* cube

Kubik (*m*); *Abk. umg.* → **Kubikzentimeter**, **der Wagen hat 2300 ~** the car has a 2.3 lit|re (*Am.* -er) engine

Kubik|... *im Subst.* cubic ...; **~dezimeter** *m* cubic decimet|re (*Am.* -er);

~maß *n* cubic measure; **~meter** *m* cubic met|re (*Am.* -er); **~zentimeter** *m* cubic centimet|re (*Am.* -er); **~wurzel** *f Math.* cube root; **~zahl** *f Math.* cube number

kubisch *Adj.* cubic

Kubismus *m*; *-*, *kein Pl.*; *Kunst* cubism; **kubistisch** *Adj.* cubist

Kubus *m*; *-*, *Kuben*; *Math.* cube

Küche *f*; *-*, *-n* **1.** kitchen (*auch Kücheneinrichtung*); *Naut.*, *Flug.* galley; (*Kochnische*) kitchenette; **was ~ und Keller zu bieten haben** the best food and wine in the house; **das Restaurant hat eine gut geführte ~** they really know how to cook at this restaurant; **ein Fachgeschäft für ~n** a specialist kitchen supplier; **2.** (*Kochart*) cooking, cuisine; **kalte ~** cold dishes; **warme ~** hot meals; **französische ~** French cuisine; → **gutbürgerlich** I 1, **Teufel** 3

Kuchen *m*; *-s*, *-* **1.** cake; (*Torte*) gateau, *Am.* cake; (*Obstkuchen*) flan, *Am.* pie; **2.** (*Rückstand*) cake

Küchen|abfälle *Pl.* kitchen waste *Sg.*; (*Essensabfälle*) kitchen scraps; **~benutzung** *f*: **mit ~** *in Anzeige*: use of kitchen

Kuchenblech *n* baking tin (*Am.* pan) (*od.* tray)

Küchen|büfett *n*, **~buffet** *n* kitchen cupboard; **~bulle** *m Mil. Sl.* cookhouse wallah (*Am.* chef); **~chef** *m*, **~chefin** *f* chef; **~dienst** *m*: **du hast heute ~** today it's your turn in the kitchen; **~einrichtung** *f* (fitted) kitchen; **~fee** *f umg. hum.* kitchen lady; **~fenster** *n* kitchen window

küchenfertig *Adj. Gemüse etc.*: pre--cooked

Kuchen|form *f* cake tin (*Am.* pan); **~gabel** *f* pastry (*od.* cake) fork

Küchen|gerät *n allg.* kitchen utensil; *elektrisches*: kitchen appliance; **~Hängeschrank** *m* kitchen wall-cupboard; **~herd** *m* (electric *od.* gas) cooker (*Am.* stove *od.* range); **~hilfe** *f* kitchen help; **~kabinett** *n Pol.* group of advisers; **~latein** *n* dog Latin; **~maschine** *f* food processor; **~meister** *m*, **~meisterin** *f* chef; **~messer** *n* kitchen knife; **~personal** *n* kitchen staff *Sg.* (*mst V. im Pl.*)

Kuchenplatte *f* cake plate

Küchenschabe *f Zool.* cockroach, *Am. umg.* roach

Küchenschlacht *f umg. hum.* (*Kuchenessen*) cake-eating orgy

Küchen|schrank *m* kitchen cupboard; **~schürze** *f* kitchen apron; **~stuhl** *m* kitchen chair

Kuchen|teig *m* cake batter (*od.* dough); **~teller** *m* cake plate; **mit Kuchen darauf**: plate of cakes; **~theke** *f* cake counter

Küchen|tisch *m* kitchen table; **~tuch** *n* (*Geschirrtuch*) tea towel, *Am. auch* dish towel; (*Papiertuch*) (piece of) tissue; **~uhr** *f* kitchen clock; **~waage** *f* (**e-e**) (a pair of) kitchen scales *Pl.*, *Am.* (a) kitchen scale; **~wecker** *m* timer; **~zeile** *f* kitchen units *Pl.*; **~zettel** *m* menu

kucken *v/i. Dial.* → **gucken**

kuckuck *Interj.* cuckoo; **Kuckuck** *m*; *-s*, *-e* **1.** *Orn.* cuckoo; **2.** *umg.*: **zum ~!** damn it!; **wo/wie** *etc.* **zum ~ ...?** where/how *etc.* on earth ...?; **mein ganzes Geld ist zum ~** all my money's down the drain; **der ~ soll dich holen!** go to blazes!, *Am.* get lost!; (*das*) **weiß der ~** heaven only knows; **3.** *umg. des*

Gerichtsvollziehers: bailiff's seal
Kuckucks|ei *n* **1.** *Orn.* cuckoo's egg; **2.** *umg. fig. Geschenk*: gift of dubious value; *Aufgabe*: dubious hono(u)r; *j-m ein ~ ins Nest legen* land s.o. with a liability; **~uhr** *f* cuckoo clock
Kuddelmuddel *m, n*; *-s, kein Pl.*; *umg.* muddle; *von Dingen*: jumble, mess
Kufe *f*; *-, -n* **1.** (*e-s Schlittens*) runner; *Flug.* skid; **2.** *Dial.* (*Bottich*) vat; (*Kübel*) tub
Küfer *m*; *-s, -*, **~in** *f*; *-, -nen* **1.** *südd., schw.* cooper; **2.** (*Kellermeister*) cellarman
Kugel *f*; *-, -n* **1.** *Math.* sphere; *die Erde ist e-e ~* the earth is a sphere; **2.** *für Spiele*: ball (*auch Billardkugel, Lederkugel*); *beim Kegeln, Bowling*: bowl; *beim Kugelstoßen*: shot; *e-e ruhige ~ schieben* *umg. fig.* have a cushy job (*od.* number); **3.** *Fußball Sl.* ball; **4.** *Anat., e-s Knochens*: head; **5.** (*Geschoss*) bullet; *sich* (*Dat.*) *e-e ~ in den Kopf schießen od. jagen* put a bullet through one's head, shoot o.s. in the head; *ich gebe mir die ~* I'm going to shoot myself; *fig. resignierend*: that's the end, I might as well give up; **6.** (*Weihnachtskugel*) bauble; **~blitz** *m* ball lightning
Kügelchen *n* small ball; (*Schrot-, Papierkügelchen*) pellet
Kugelfang *m* butt; *j-n als ~ benutzen* use s.o. as a shield
kugelfest *Adj.* bulletproof
Kugelfisch *m Zool.* puffer, globefish
Kugelform *f* spherical shape; **kugelförmig** *Adj.* spherical
Kugel|gelenk *n Anat., Tech.* ball-and-socket joint; **~hagel** *m* hail of bullets
kugelig *Adj.* spherical
Kugelkopf *m Schreibmaschine*: golfball; **~maschine** *f* golfball typewriter
Kugellager *n Tech.* ball bearing
kugeln I. *v/i.* roll; **II.** *v/refl.* roll around (*Am.* around); *sich ~ vor Lachen umg.* double up with laughter, fall about (*Am.* down) laughing; **III.** *Kugeln n*: *-s, kein Pl.*: *es war zum Kugeln umg.* it was a scream
Kugelregen *m* hail of bullets
kugelrund *Adj.* perfectly round; *hum.* (*dick*) rotund, like a balloon; *Baby*: chubby
Kugel|schreiber *m* ballpoint (pen), *Brit. auch* biro ®; **~segment** *n Math.* spherical segment
kugelsicher *Adj.* bulletproof; **~e Weste** bulletproof vest
kugelstoßen *v/i. nur Inf.*; *Sport* put the shot; **Kugelstoßen** *n* shot-put; **Kugelstoßer** *m*; *-s, -*, **Kugelstoßerin** *f*; *-, -nen* shot-putter
Kuh *f*; *-, Kühe* **1.** cow; (*Hirschkuh*) hind; *heilige ~ auch fig.* sacred cow; **2.** *pej.* (*Frau*) *blöde ~* silly cow; **~augen** *Pl. umg.* goggle eyes; **~dorf** *n umg.* one-horse town, backwater, *Am.* hick town; **~dung** *m* cow dung; **~euter** *n* cow's udder; **~fladen** *m* cowpat, *Am.* cow pie; **~glocke** *f* cow bell; **~handel** *m umg. fig., bes. Pol.* horse-trading; **~haut** *f* cowhide; *das geht auf keine ~ umg. fig.* it's just incredible; **~hirt(e)** *m* cowherd
kühl I. *Adj.* **1.** cool; *Wetter, Raum etc.*: *auch* chilly; *mir ist ~* I feel a bit chilly; **~es Bier** cold beer; **~ werden** cool (down); **~ stellen** (*Wein etc.*) chill; (*Speisen*) leave to cool; **2.** *fig.* cool; *e-n ~en Kopf bewahren* keep a cool head; (*nicht zornig werden*) keep one's cool *umg.*; **II.** *Adv.* coolly; **~ auf-**

bewahren *od. lagern!* keep in a cool place
Kühl|aggregat *n* refrigeration unit; **~anlage** *f* cold-storage (*od.* refrigeration) plant; *Mot. etc.* cooling system; **~box** *f* cool box
Kuhle *f*; *-, -n*; *umg.* hollow
Kühle *f*; *-, kein Pl.* coolness (*auch fig.*); *die ~ der Nacht* the cool of the night
kühlen I. *v/t.* cool; (*erfrischen*) refresh; (*Lebensmittel*) cool; *im Kühlschrank*: refrigerate; (*Wein etc.*) chill; **II.** *v/i.* have a cooling effect
Kühler *m*; *-s, -*. **1.** cooler; **2.** *Mot.* radiator; (*Kühlerhaube*) bonnet, *Am.* hood; **~figur** *f* radiator emblem (*od.* mascot, *Am.* ornament); **~grill** *m* radiator grille; **~haube** *f* bonnet, *Am.* hood
Kühl|fach *n* freezing compartment; **~flüssigkeit** *f* coolant; **~haus** *n* cold store; **~kette** *f* cold chain; **~lagerung** *f* cold storage; **~luft** *f* cooling air; **~mittel** *n* coolant; **~raum** *m* cold room (*od.* store); **~rippen** *Pl.* cooling fins (*od.* ribs); **~schiff** *n* refrigerator ship; **~schlange** *f* cooling coil; **~schrank** *m* refrigerator, *umg.* fridge; **~system** *n* cooling system; **~tasche** *f* cool(er) bag; **~truhe** *f* (deep) freeze, (chest) freezer; **~turm** *m* cooling tower
Kühlung *f* **1.** cooling; *Tech. von Lebensmitteln*: refrigeration; **2.** (*Anlage*) cooling system; *für Lebensmittel*: refrigeration system; **3.** (*Kühle*) coolness
Kühl|wagen *m Eisenb.* refrigerator van (*Am.* car); *Mot.* refrigerator van (*bes. Am.* truck); **~wasser** *n* coolant
Kuh|milch *f* cow's milk; **~mist** *m* cow dung
kühn *Adj.* bold (*auch Entwurf etc.*); (*riskant*) daring; (*verwegen*) audacious; *j-s ste Träume übertreffen* go beyond s.o.'s wildest dreams; **Kühnheit** *f* boldness; (*Gewagtheit*) daring; (*Verwegenheit*) audacity
Kuh|schelle *f Bot.* pasque flower; **~stall** *m* cowshed; **~weide** *f* cow pasture
kujonieren *v/t. umg. pej.* bully
k. u. k. *Abk.* (*kaiserlich und königlich*) *hist.* Austrian imperial and royal
Küken *n*; *-s, -* **1.** *Orn.* chick; **2.** *umg. fig.* (*Kind*) little chap; (*Mädchen*) young thing; **3.** *Tech.* plug
Ku-Klux-Klan *m*; *-s, kein Pl.* Ku Klux Klan
Kukuruz *m*; *-(es), kein Pl.*; *bes. österr., Bot.* maize, *bes. Am.* corn
kulant *Adj. Wirts.* accommodating, obliging; *Preis, Bedingungen*: fair, reasonable; **Kulanz** *f*; *-, kein Pl.* readiness to oblige; (*Bereitwilligkeit*) goodwill; *von Preis, Bedingungen*: fairness; *die Reparatur geht auf ~* the repair will be carried out at the firm's expense
Kuli[1] *m*; *-s, -s* coolie; *fig.* slave
Kuli[2] *m*; *-s, -s*; *Abk. umg.* → **Kugelschreiber**
kulinarisch *Adj.* culinary; **~e Genüsse** culinary delights
Kulisse *f*; *-, -n* **1.** *Theat.* set; *einzelne*: flat; (*Hintergrund*) backdrop; *Pl.* scenery *Sg.*; *seitliche*: wings *Pl.*; **~n schieben** *umg.* change the scenery; *als Beruf*: work as a scene-shifter; *die ~n aufbauen/abbauen* build/strike the set; *hinter die/den ~n* backstage, *bes. fig.* behind the scenes; **2.** *fig.* background (*auch Mus.*); (*Rahmen*) setting; (*Fassade*) façade; *die ~ für etw.* **bilden** provide the backdrop (*od.* set-

ting) for s.th.; *das ist doch alles nur ~* this is all a facade (*od.* a mere pretence [*Am.* -se]); **3.** *Wirts.* unofficial market
Kulissen|schieber *m umg. hum.* scene-shifter; **~wechsel** *m* scene change
Kulleraugen *Pl. umg.* big wide eyes, bulging eyes; **~ machen** goggle
kullern I. *v/i.* (*ist gekullert*) roll; **II.** *v/t.* (*hat*) roll
Kulmination *f*; *-, -en* culmination; **Kulminationspunkt** *m Astron., fig.* culminating point, culmination, *fig. auch* apex; **kulminieren** *v/i. auch Astron.* culminate (*in* + *Dat.* in)
Kult *m*; *-(e)s, -e* **1.** *Reli.* cult; (*Anbetung*) *auch* worship; **2.** *übersteigerte Verehrung*: cult; *mit j-m/etw. e-n treiben* make a cult figure of (*od.* idolize) s.o. / make a cult of s.th.; **~ sein** *umg. Person*: be a cult figure, have cult status; *Sache*: be very fashionable; **~band** *f Mus.* cult band; **~bau** *m* place of worship; **~bild** *n* cult image; *christlich*: devotional image; **~buch** *n* cult book; **~figur** *f* **1.** cult (*od.* ritual) image; **2.** *Pop-, Filmstar etc.*: cult figure; **~film** *m* cult film (*Am. auch* movie); **~handlung** *f* rite, ritual act; *christlich*: act of worship
kultig *Adj. umg.*: *voll ~*: *die neue CD von X* a real cult object: X's new CD; *gefärbte Achselhaare sind zurzeit voll ~* dyed armpit hair is the latest craze
kultisch I. *Adj.* ritual; **~e Gegenstände** cult objects; *die Mannschaft genießt bei ihren Fans ~e Verehrung* the team is idolized by the fans; **II.** *Adv.* ritually; *sie wird ~ verehrt* she is idolized
kultivieren *v/t.* cultivate (*auch fig.*); **kultiviert I.** *P.P.* → **kultivieren**; **II.** *Adj. Sprache, Atmosphäre etc.*: cultivated; (*vornehm*) refined; *Person*: *auch* cultured; *Volk, Land etc.*: civilized; **Kultiviertheit** *f*; *nur Sg.* culture, refinement; *Art*: cultured manner; **Kultivierung** *f* cultivation
Kult|stätte *f* place of cult (*od.* ritual) worship; **~tanz** *m* ritual dance
Kultur *f*; *-, -en* **1.** *Kunst, Wissenschaft etc.*: culture; (*Zivilisation*) civilization; *die griechische ~* (ancient) Greek civilization, the civilization of (ancient) Greece; *er ist von der ~ unbeleckt umg.* he hasn't got a vestige of culture, he's a real philistine; **2.** (*Bildung, Kultiviertheit*) culture; *er hat ~* he's a cultured person; *etwas für die ~ tun umg.* get some culture; *die ~ des Wohnens* a cultivated lifestyle; **3.** *n ur Sg.*; *Agr.* (*das Anbauen*) cultivation; **4.** *Bio.* (*Bakterienkultur*) culture; *Agr.* (*Bestand*) plantation
Kultur|abkommen *n* cultural agreement; **~amt** *n* cultural affairs department; **~angebot** *n* program(me) of cultural events, cultural scene; *Münchens vielfältiges ~* auch Munich's rich and varied cultural life; **~arbeit** *f* cultural activities *Pl.*; **~attaché** *m Pol.* cultural attaché
kulturbeflissen *Adj.* (very) culturally-minded; *sie ist sehr ~* she's a real culture vulture *umg.*
Kultur|betrieb *m*; *nur Sg.* cultural scene; **~beutel** *m* toilet bag (*Am.* kit); **~denkmal** *n* (*Gebäude etc.*) cultural monument; (*Gemälde etc.*) work of art; *Pl. e-s Landes etc.*: *auch* cultural heritage *Sg.*; *die Kulturdenkmäler Ägyptens* auch the Egyptian antiqui-

ties, *(Bauten etc.) auch* the ancient Egyptian monuments; **~dezernent** *m*, **~dezernentin** *f* head of cultural affairs; **~einrichtung** *f* cultural institution

kulturell *Adj.* cultural

Kulturerbe *n* cultural heritage

kulturfeindlich *Adj.* philistine; *Haltung, Politik etc.*: hostile to culture

Kultur|flüchter *m*; *-s, -*; *Bot., Zool.* animal or plant that only does well in areas untouched by civilization; **~folger** *m*; *-s, -*; *Bot., Zool.* animal or plant that even does well close to civilization; **~förderung** *f* (state) promotion of the arts; **~führer** *m* cultural guide

Kulturgeschichte *f* **1.** *des Menschen*: history of civilization *(auch Buch)*; **2.** *e-s Landes etc.*: cultural history; **3.** *(Wissenschaft)* history of culture; **kulturgeschichtlich I.** *Adj.* cultural-historical, relating to cultural history; *zivilisationsbedingt*: relating to the history of civilization; **II.** *Adv.* from the point of view of cultural history *(zivilisationsbedingt*: the history of civilization)

Kultur|güter *Pl.* cultural assets; **~hauptstadt** *f*: **~** *Europas* European capital of culture; **~hoheit** *f* cultural and educational autonomy; **~kampf** *m*; *nur Sg.*; *hist.* struggle between state and church *(in Prussia 1872-87), Am. auch* Kulturkampf; **~kreis** *m* **1.** *Verein*: arts society; *heimatgeschichtlich*: local history society; **2.** *Gebiet*: cultural area *(od.* environment); **~kritik** *f*; *nur Sg.* critique of contemporary civilization; **~land** *n* **1.** *Agr.* cultivated land; **2.** *(Land mit einer bedeutenden Kultur)* (country with a) great civilization; **~landschaft** *f* **1.** man-made *(od.* -built) landscape; *fachspr. (Agrargebiet)* area under cultivation; **2.** *(Kulturszene)* cultural scene; **~leben** *n* cultural life

kulturlos *Adj.* uncultured; **Kulturlosigkeit** *f*; *nur Sg.* lack of culture

Kultur|magazin *n* arts journal; *TV* arts program(me); **~management** *n* arts management; **~metropole** *f* cultural capital; **~nation** *f* nation with a great cultural history; **~papst** *m umg.* cultural guru; **~pessimismus** *m* pessimistic view of civilization; **~pflanze** *f* *Agr.* cultivated plant

Kulturpolitik *f* cultural and educational policy; **kulturpolitisch** *Adj.* politico-cultural

Kultur|programm *n* program(me) of cultural events; **~raum** *m* area of culture; *im südostasiatischen* **~** in the Southeast Asian cultural area; **~redakteur** *m*, **~redakteurin** *f* arts (features) editor; **~redaktion** *f von Zeitung, TV-Sender etc.*: arts section; *für Nachrichten*: cultural news department; **~referat** *n e-r Stadtverwaltung etc.*: cultural affairs department; **~referent** *m*, **~referentin** *f* head of cultural affairs; **~ressort** *n* cultural affairs portfolio; *Abteilung*: cultural affairs department; **~revolution** *f* cultural revolution; **~schaffende** *m, f; -n, -n*; *ehem. DDR* creative artist; **~schock** *m* culture shock; **~sprache** *f* language of a civilized people; **~steppe** *f* steppe created by cultivation; **~stufe** *f* level of civilization; **~szene** *f* cultural scene; **~träger** *m*, **~trägerin** *f* transmitter of cultural values; **~veranstaltung** *f* cultural event; **~volk** *n* civilized

race *(od.* people); **~zentrum** *n* **1.** cultural cent|re *(Am.* -er); **2.** *(Einrichtung)* arts cent|re *(Am.* -er)

Kultus *m*; *-, kein Pl.* **1.** → *Kult*; **2.** *Amtsspr.* cultural affairs; **~minister** *m*, **~ministerin** *f* minister *(Am.* secretary) of education and cultural affairs; **~ministerium** *n* ministry of education and cultural affairs

Kumarin *n*; *-s, kein Pl.*; *Pharm.* coumarin

Kümmel *m*; *-s, -* **1.** *Samen*: caraway (seed); *Pflanze*: caraway (plant); **2.** *Branntwein*: kümmel; **~brot** *n* caraway-seed bread; **~schnaps** *m* kümmel; **~türke** *m umg. pej. neg!* bloody *(Am.* damn) Turk

Kummer *m*; *-, kein Pl.*; *(Sorgen)* worry, worries *Pl. (um* about); *(Leid)* grief *(um* for); *(Schwierigkeiten)* problems *Pl.*, trouble; **~** *haben* have problems *(um* with); *j-m* **~** *machen od.* bereiten cause s.o. a lot of worry; *du machst mir* **~** I'm worried about you; *s-n* **~** *hinunterspülen* drown one's sorrows; *das ist mein geringster* **~** that's the least of my worries; *ich bin* **~** *gewöhnt! umg.* I always have to put up with this sort of thing, I'm used to it

Kummer|bund *m*; *-(e)s, -e* cummerbund; **~falten** *Pl.* worry lines; **~kasten** *m umg.* complaints box

kümmerlich *Adj.* **1.** *(ärmlich, gering)* miserable; *Lohn etc.*: paltry, *umg.* measly; *Wissen, Essen*: meagre, scanty; **2.** *(verkümmert)* stunted; *(schwächlich)* puny

Kümmerling *m*; *-s, -e* pathetic little specimen; *Tier*: weakling; *Pflanze*: stunted plant *(od.* specimen)

Kummermiene *f umg.* sorrowful *(bes. hum.* woebegone) expression

kümmern I. *v/refl.*: *sich* **~** *um (versorgen, pflegen)* look after, take care of, see to; *(sich Gedanken machen über)* worry about; *(beachten)* pay attention to; *pej. (sich einmischen in)* poke one's nose into; *sich nicht* **~** *um* not bother about, ignore; *(vernachlässigen)* neglect; *ich muss mich um alles* **~** I have to see to everything; *du musst dich um Karten* **~** you'll have to see to *(od.* take care of) the tickets; *ich kümmere mich nicht um solche Sachen* I don't (have time to) worry about *(od.* bother with) that sort of thing; *kümmere dich um d-e eigenen Angelegenheiten!* mind your own business; **II.** *v/t.*: *was kümmert's mich?* what's that to me?, what do I care?, it's not my problem *(umg.* pigeon); *das braucht dich nicht zu* **~** it doesn't concern you, it's none of your business; → *Dreck* 3

Kümmernis *f*; *-, -se*; *geh.* tribulations *Pl. förm.*, worries *Pl.*

Kummer|speck *m umg.*: **~** *ansetzen* put on weight with overeating due to worry; **~tante** *f umg.* agony aunt; **~telefon** *n* helpline

kummervoll *Adj.* sorrowful; *Miene*: *auch* woebegone *bes. hum.*

Kummet *n*; *-s, -e* (horse) collar

Kumpan *m*; *-s, -e*; *umg.* **1.** mate, chum, *bes. Am.* buddy; **2.** *(Mittäter)* partner; **Kumpanei** *f*; *-, -en*; *umg.* **1.** *(Gruppe)* crowd, *umg.* lot; **2.** *(Kameradschaft)* chumminess; **Kumpanin** *f*; *-, -nen*; *umg.* → *Kumpan*

Kumpel *m*; *-s, -* **1.** *Bergb.* miner; **2.** *umg. (Kamerad)* mate, chum, *bes. Am.* buddy; **kumpelhaft** *Adj. umg.* pally, chummy

Kumpen *m*; *-s, -*; *nordd.* bowl, basin

Kumquat *f*; *-s, -s*; *Bot. (kleine Orangenart)* kumquat

Kumulation *f*; *-, -en* accumulation; **kumulativ** *Adj.* cumulative; **kumulieren** *vt/i.* accumulate

Kumulonimbus *m*; *-, -se*; *Met.* cumulonimbus

Kumulus *m*; *-, Kumuli, ~wolke* *f Met.* cumulus (cloud) *(Pl.* cumuli)

kündbar *Adj. Vertrag*: terminable; *Anstellung, Miete etc.*: subject to notice; *Wirts., Kapital*: callable; *Anleihe*: redeemable; *wir sind jederzeit* **~** we can be given notice at any time; *sie ist nicht* **~** she cannot be dismissed

Kunde[1] *m*; *-n, -n* **1.** customer; *für Dienstleistungen*: client; *(e-s Ladengeschäfts) auch* patron *form.*; *fester* **~** regular customer; *„Nur für* **~***n"* For Patrons Only; *Dienst am* **~***n* free service to customers; *der* **~** *ist König* the customer is always right, the customer is king; **2.** *umg. (Kerl)* customer; *übler* **~** nasty piece of work

Kunde[2] *f*; *-, -n*; *geh., altm. (Kenntnis)* knowledge; *(Nachricht)* tidings *Pl.*; **~** *geben von* bring news of; *frohe* **~** good news *Sg.*, glad tidings

Kunde[3] *f*; *-, -n*; *österr.* → *Kundschaft* 1

künden *geh.* **I.** *v/t.* proclaim, announce *(+ Dat.* to); *(auf Künftiges hindeuten)* herald; **II.** *v/i.*: **~** *von* tell of, bear witness to *förm.*

Kunden|berater *m*, **~beraterin** *f* customer advis|er *(Am.* -or); *euph.* sales assistant, sales person; **~beratung** *f* customer advisory service *(Stelle*: office); **~besuch** *m* (customer) call; **~betreuer** *m*, **~betreuerin** *f* personal shopping attendant; **~betreuung** *f* customer care *(od.* service); **~dienst** *m* **1.** (customer) service; *(Wartungsdienst)* after-sales service; *das gehört zum* **~** it's (all) part of the service; **2.** *Stelle*: service department; *Person(en)*: man *(Pl.* men) from the service department; *morgen kommt der* **~** *wegen m-s Kühlschranks* they're sending someone *(od.* someone's coming) from the service department to have a look at my fridge tomorrow; **~fang** *m pej.* touting for custom *(Am.* for patronage *od.* customers)

kundenfreundlich *Adj.* convenient (for customers); **~e** *Öffnungszeiten* opening times to suit the customer

Kunden|gespräch *n* customer pitch; **~kartei** *f* customer file; **~kredit** *m* consumer credit; **~kreis** *m* customers *Pl.*, clientele; **~parkplatz** *m* customer car park *(Am.* parking lot); **~profil** *n* client *(od.* customer) profile; **~stamm** *m* regular customers *Pl.*; **~werbung** *f* advertising (to attract customers); *durch direktes Ansprechen*: canvassing for customers

kundgeben *v/t. (unreg., trennb., hat -ge-) (bekannt geben)* make known *(+ Dat.* to); *(ankündigen)* announce (to); *(erklären)* declare, proclaim *form.*; **Kundgebung** *f Pol.* rally; *(Demonstration)* demonstration

kundig *Adj.* (well-)informed, knowledg(e)able; *(sachverständig)* expert *(+ Gen.* on); *(geschickt)* skil(l)ful; *e-r Sache (Gen.)* **~** *sein* be knowledg(e)able about s.th., know about s.th.

kündigen I. *v/i.* dem *Arbeitgeber*: hand *(od.* give) in one's notice; *dem Vermieter*: give notice *(bei* to; *zum* for); *e-m Arbeitnehmer*: give s.o. notice *(Brit. umg.* the sack, *Am. umg.* his/her pink slip); *e-m Mieter*: give *s.o.* (his *etc.*) notice (to quit); **II.** *v/t.* (*Vertrag etc.*) cancel; *formell*: terminate; (*Anleihe, Geldeinlage etc.*) call in; **er hat uns die Wohnung gekündigt** he's given us notice (*od.* told us we have) to leave the flat (*Am.* apartment); **wir haben die Wohnung gekündigt** (we've given notice that) we're moving out of the flat (*Am.* apartment); **j-m die Stellung ~** *altm.* dismiss s.o.; **sie ist gekündigt worden** *umg. seitens des Arbeitgebers*: she's been given the sack (*Am.* been given her pink slip); **j-m die Freundschaft ~** *umg. fig.* end a friendship with s.o.

Kündigung *f* notice; (*Entlassung*) dismissal; *e-r Anleihe etc.*: calling in; *e-s Vertrags*: termination; **s-e ~ erhalten** be given notice (*umg.* the sack); **mit monatlicher ~** at (*od.* subject to) a month's notice; **ich habe vierteljährliche ~** I'm on three months' notice; **die ~ erfolgte fristgerecht** notice was given on time

Kündigungs|frist *f* period of notice; **mit halbjähriger ~** at six months' notice; **~grund** *m* grounds *Pl.* for giving notice (*od.* for dismissal); **~recht** *n* right to give notice; **~schreiben** *n* written notice; *des Arbeitgebers*: letter of dismissal; **~schutz** *m für Arbeitnehmer*: protection against unlawful dismissal; *für Mieter*: protection against unwarranted eviction; **~termin** *m* (last) date for giving notice

Kundin *f*; *-, -nen* (female) customer *etc.*; → *Kunde*[1]

Kundschaft *f* **1.** *Wirts.* customers *Pl.*, clientele; *bei Dienstleistungen*: clients *Pl.*; *Stammkundschaft*: regular customers *Pl.*; *umg.* (*Kunde*) customer; **hallo - ~!** how about some service?; **2. auf ~ gehen** *altm.* go scouting; **3.** *altm.* (*Botschaft*) news *Sg.*, tidings *Pl.*

Kundschafter *m*; *-s, -*, **~in** *f -, -nen* scout, spy

kundtun *v/t.* (*unreg., trennb., hat -ge-*) *geh.* → *kundgeben*

künftig I. *Adj.* future; *Generationen etc.*: *auch* (up-and-)coming, *nachgestellt*: ... to come; **s-e ~e Frau** his future wife, his bride-to-be; **in ~en Zeiten** in times to come; **in e-m** *od.* **im ~en Leben** in a future life, in the next life; **II.** *Adv.* in future (*Am.* the future), from now on

Kungelei *f*; *-, -en*; *umg. pej.* wheeling and dealing, fiddling; **kungeln** *v/i. umg. pej.* fiddle (things); **es wurde häufig gekungelt** there was frequent wheeling and dealing

Kung-Fu *n*; *-(s), kein Pl.* kung fu

Kunst *f*; *-, Künste* **1.** *Kunst* art; **die schönen/freien Künste** the fine/liberal arts; **die griechische ~** Greek art; **die bildende ~** the fine arts *Pl.*; **was macht die ~?** *umg.* how's things?; → *brotlos* etc; **2.** (*Fertigkeit*) art; (*Geschicklichkeit*) *auch* skill; (*Kniff*) trick; **die ~ des Reitens** the art of riding; **jetzt bin ich mit m-r ~ am Ende** I give up, I've tried everything; **nach allen Regeln der ~** *umg.* good and proper; **das ist keine ~!** *umg.* that's no big deal, there's nothing to it; **die schwarze ~ Magie**: the black art; *Druck.* the art of printing

Kunst|akademie *f* academy of arts, art college (*bes. Am.* school); **~auge** *n* artificial eye; *aus Glas*: *auch* glass eye; **~auktion** *f* art auction; **~ausstellung**

f art exhibition; **~banause** *m pej.* philistine; **er ist ein ~ auch** he doesn't know the first thing about art; **~blume** *f* artificial flower; **~buch** *n* art book; **~darm** *m* (artificial) sausage skin; **~denkmal** *n* art monument, (great) work of art; **~dieb** *m*, **~diebin** *f* art thief; **~diebstahl** *m* art theft; **~druck** *m* **1.** art reproduction; **2.** art printing; **~papier** *n* art paper; **~dünger** *m Agr.* artificial fertilizer; **~eis** *n* artificial ice; **~eisbahn** *f* artificial ice rink; **~erzieher** *m*, **~erzieherin** *f* art teacher; **~erziehung** *f* art education; **~experte** *m*, **~expertin** *f* art connoisseur; **~fälschung** *f* art forgery, fake; **~faser** *f* man-made (*od.* synthetic) fib|re (*Am.* -er); **~fehler** *m Med.* professional (*ärztlich*: medical) blunder; *Pl. auch* medical malpractice *Sg.*

kunstfertig *Adj.* (*geschickt*) skilled; (*gekonnt*) skil(l)ful; (*fachmännisch*) expert; **Kunstfertigkeit** *f* (artistic *od.* technical) skill; *von Handwerker*: *auch* craftsmanship

Kunst|flieger *m*, **~fliegerin** *f* aerobatic pilot; *für den Film, für e-e Schau etc.*: stunt pilot; **~flug** *m* aerobatics *Pl.* (*V. mst im Sg.*); *für den Film, für e-e Schau etc.*: stunt flying; **~form** *f* art form; **~freund** *m*, **~freundin** *f* art lover; **~führer** *m* art guide; **~galerie** *f* art gallery; **~gattung** *f* art form, genre; **~gegenstand** *m* art object, objet d'art; **~genuss** *m* **1.** *Freude an der Kunst*: enjoyment of art; **2.** *Konzert, Theateraufführung etc.*: aesthetic treat

kunstgerecht *Adj.* expert, professional

Kunstgeschichte *f* history of art, art history; *Buch*: (book on) art history; **kunstgeschichtlich** *Adj.* art-historical, ... of art history; *Museum, Studium*: of art history; *Forschung, Arbeit, Buch etc.*: on art history

Kunst|gewerbe *n*; *nur Sg.* arts and crafts *Pl.*; (*angewandte Kunst*) applied art(s *Pl.*); **kunstgewerblich** *Adj. Produkte, Gegenstände, Fertigkeiten etc.*: craft ...

Kunst|griff *m* (clever) trick; *durch e-n ~* (*Täuschungsmanöver*) *auch* by sleight of hand; **~halle** *f* art gallery; **~handel** *m* art trade; **~händler** *m*, **~händlerin** *f* art dealer; **~handlung** *f* art dealer('s); **~handwerk** *n* arts and crafts *Pl.*; **~handwerker** *m* arttist-craftsman; **~handwerkerin** *f* artist-craftswoman; **~harz** *n* synthetic resin; **~herz** *n Med.* artificial heart

Kunst|historiker *m*, **~historikerin** *f* art historian; **kunsthistorisch** *Adj.* art-historical; *Museum, Studium*: of art history; *Forschung, Arbeit, Buch etc.*: on art history

Kunst|hochschule *f* art academy (*od.* college, *bes. Am.* school); **~honig** *m* artificial honey

kunstinteressiert *Adj.* interested in art, keen on (*Am.* enthusiastic about) art; **Kunstinteressierte** *m, f*; *mst Pl.* art enthusiast; **zur Documenta kommen ~ aus aller Welt** the Documenta exhibition attracts art enthusiasts from all over the world

Kunst|kalender *m* art calendar; **~kenner** *m*, **~kennerin** *f* (art) connoisseur; **~kritik** *f* art criticism; (*die Kunstkritiker*) art critics *Pl.*; **~kritiker** *m*, **~kritikerin** *f* art critic; **~lauf** *m* figure skating; **~leder** *n* imitation leather

Künstler *m*; *-s, -* **1.** artist; *Mus., Theat.* oft performer; *im Zirkus etc.*: artiste; **2.** (*besonders fähiger Mensch*) genius

(*im* at); **ein ~ der Improvisation** a brilliant improviser; **~hand** *f*: **wie von ~ gemalt/gezeichnet** as if painted/drawn by an artist; **mit ~** with the hand of an artist

Künstlerin *f*; *-, -nen* → *Künstler*

künstlerisch I. *Adj.* artistic; **~e Form** art form; **~er Leiter** art director; **~e Ader** artistic vein; **II.** *Adv.* artistically; **ein ~ wertvoller Film** a film of artistic merit

Künstler|kneipe *f* bar popular with artists; **~kolonie** *f* artists' colony; **~leben** *n* the life of an artist; **ein ~** an artist's life; **~name** *m* stage name; *e-s Schriftstellers*: pseudonym, pen name, nom de plume; **~pech** *n umg.* bad luck

Künstlertum *n*; *-s, kein Pl.* **1.** artistry; **2.** *Koll.*: **das ~** the art world

Künstler|viertel *n* artists' quarter; **~werkstatt** *f* studio; **~zimmer** *n* artists' room, green room

künstlich I. *Adj.* artificial (*auch Beatmung, Blume, Befruchtung, Ernährung, Licht, See etc.*); *Zähne etc.*: *auch* false; *Leder etc.*: imitation ...; (*unecht*) fake; (*~ hergestellt*) synthetic; man-made; *Lächeln etc.*: forced; **~e Niere** kidney machine; **II.** *Adv.* artificially; **~ in die Länge ziehen** (deliberately) stretch out; **sich ~ aufregen** *umg.* get worked up over nothing; **Künstlichkeit** *f* artificiality

Kunst|licht *n* artificial light; **~liebhaber** *m* **~liebhaberin** *f* art lover; **~lied** *n Mus.* art song

kunstlos *Adj.* simple, unsophisticated

Kunst|maler *m*, **~malerin** *f* painter, artist; **~markt** *m* art market; **~objekt** *n* art object, objet d'art; **~pause** *f* pause for effect; *iro. stockend*: awkward pause; **e-e ~ machen** pause for effect; **~postkarte** *f* postcard reproduction; **~preis** *m* art award (*od.* prize); **~radfahren** *n Sport* trick cycling; **~rasen** *m* artificial turf; **~raub** *m* art theft; **~räuber** *m*, **~räuberin** *f* art thief

kunstreich *Adj.* (very) artistic; (*reich verziert*) elaborate, ornate

Kunst|reiter *m*, **~reiterin** *f* trick rider; **~richtung** *f* style (of painting *etc.*); *Bewegung*: art movement, art school; **~sammler** *m*, **~sammlerin** *f* art collector; **~sammlung** *f* art collection; **~schätze** *Pl.* art treasures; **~schmied** *m*, **~schmiedin** *f* ornamental ironworker, craftsman blacksmith; **~schnee** *m* artificial snow; **~schütze** *m*, **~schützin** *f* marksman, *weiblich*: markswoman, *bes. Am.* sharpshooter

Kunstseide *f* rayon; **kunstseiden** *Adj.* rayon; **~e Strümpfe** artificial silk stockings *altm.*

kunstsinnig *Adj. geh.* artistically inclined; **ein ~er Monarch** a monarch with a feeling for art

Kunst|sprache *f Ling.* artificial language; **~springen** *n Sport* (springboard) diving; **~springer** *m*, **~springerin** *f Sport* (springboard) diver

Kunststoff *m* plastic; **aus ~** (made of) plastic; **kunststoffbeschichtet** *Adj.* plastic-coated

Kunststoff|faser *f* synthetic fib|re (*Am.* -er); **~folie** *f* plastic foil; **~industrie** *f* plastics industry; **~verpackung** *f* plastic (*mst* polystyrene, *bes. Am.* Styrofoam®) packing material

kunststopfen *v/t.* (*untr., hat -ge-*) *nur Inf. und P.P.* repair by invisible mending; **ich muss das Jackett ~ lassen** I

must get this jacket invisibly mended
Kunst|stück *n* **1.** *e-s Zauberers etc.*: trick; **2.** *fig.*: *das ist schon ein ~* that takes some doing; *das ist kein ~* (there's) nothing to it; *wie er wohl dieses ~ fertig gebracht hat? iro.* how on earth did he manage that?; *~! umg. iro.* big deal!; *~student m*, *~studentin f* art student; *~szene f* art scene; *~tischler m*, *~tischlerin f* cabinet--maker; *~turnen n* gymnastics *Pl.* (*auch V. im Sg.*); *~turner m*, *~turnerin f* gymnast; *~verein m* arts society; *~verlag m* (fine) art publisher; *~verstand m*, *~verständnis n* **1.** knowledge of art; **2.** *Sinn*: (a)esthetic sense, feeling for art
kunstvoll *Adj.* very artistic; (*reich verziert*) elaborate, ornate; (*geschickt*) skil(l)ful
Kunst|werk *n* work of art; *~wissenschaft f* theory and history of art; (*Ästhetik*) (a)esthetics *Pl.* (*mst V. im Sg.*); *~wissenschaftler m*, *~wissenschaftlerin f* expert on the theory of art; *~wort n* artificial coinage, made--up word; *~zeitschrift f* art journal (*od.* magazine)
kunterbunt I. *Adj.* **1.** (*sehr bunt*) colo(u)rful; (*mehrfarbig*) multicolo(u)red; **2.** (*liederlich*) untidy, jumbled; *ein ~es Durcheinander* a (real) mess, a complete jumble; **3.** *Leben*: chequ|ered (*Am.* check-), very varied; *~e Mischung* very mixed bag; *es gab ein ~es Programm* the program(me) was a very mixed bag, there were all sorts of things going on (*od.* being shown *etc.*); **II.** *Adv.*: *alles ~ durcheinander werfen* jumble everything up; *fig. auch* lump everything together; *hier geht's ja ~ zu!* things are really chaotic here
Kupfer *n*; *-s*, *-* **1.** *nur Sg.*; copper; *in ~ gestochen* engraved on copper, copper-engraved; **2.** → *Kupferstich*; *~bergwerk n* copper mine; *~blech n* sheet copper; *ein ~* a copper sheet; *~dach n* copper roof; *~draht m* copper wire
kupferfarben *Adj.* copper-colo(u)red
Kupfergeld *n*; *nur Sg.* copper coins *Pl.*, *Brit. auch* coppers *Pl.*
kupferhaltig *Adj.* containing copper
Kupfer|kessel *m* copper kettle; *~münze f* copper coin
kupfern *Adj.* (made of) copper
kupferrot *Adj.* copper-colo(u)red
Kupfer|schmied *m*, *~schmiedin f* coppersmith; *~stecher m* **1.** copperplate engraver; **2.** *Zool.* pityogenes chalcographus, six-dentated bark beetle; *~stecherin f*; *-*, *-nen* → *Kupferstecher* 1; *~stich m Kunst* copperplate engraving; *~vergiftung f* copper poisoning; *~vitriol n* blue vitriol, cupric sul|-phate (*Am.* -fate)
kupieren *v/t.* (*Tier, Ohren etc.*) crop; (*Schwanz*) dock; (*Flügel*) clip; (*Hecke, Strauch*) trim
Kupon *m* → *Coupon*
Kuppe *f*; *-*, *-n* **1.** (*Bergkuppe*) mountain top; *e-s Hügels*: hilltop; **2.** (*Fingerkuppe*) fingertip; **3.** *Tech.*, *e-es Nagels*: head
Kuppel *f*; *-*, *-n* dome; *kleine*: cupola; *~bau m* domed building; *~dach n* domed roof
Kuppelei *f*; *-*, *-en* **1.** *Jur.* procuration; **2.** *altm.* (*Heiratsvermittlung*) matchmaking
kuppelförmig *Adj.* dome-shaped
kuppeln I. *v/t.* → *koppeln*, **II.** *v/i.*

1. *Mot.* operate the clutch, (*einkuppeln*) depress the clutch; (*auskuppeln*) let out the clutch; **2.** *altm.* (*Kuppelei betreiben*) act as a matchmaker; **Kuppler** *m*; *-s*, *-* *allg.*: matchmaker; *Jur.* procurer; *pej.* pimp; **Kupplerin** *f*; *-*, *-nen allg.*: matchmaker; *Jur.* procuress
Kupplung *f* **1.** *Tech.* coupling (*auch Eisenb.*, *Etech.*); **2.** *Mot.* clutch (*auch Pedal*); *die ~ schleifen lassen* slip the clutch; *die ~ kommen lassen* let the clutch in gently; *die ~ treten* step on the clutch, depress the clutch pedal *förm.*
Kupplungs|pedal *n Mot.* clutch pedal; *~scheibe f* clutch disc (*Am.* disk)
Kur *f*; *-*, *-en* (course of) treatment; *am Kurort*: cure; *e-e ~ machen* (*od.* *zur ~ gehen*) go for (*od.* take) a cure
Kür *f*; *-*, *-en*; *Sport, Eislauf*: free program(me); *Turnen*: free exercises *Pl.*; → *auch Kürlauf*
Kürassier *m*; *-s*, *-e*; *hist.* cuirassier
Kurat *m*; *-en*, *-en*; *kirchl.* curate
Kuratel *f*; *-*, *-en*; *Jur. altm.* guardianship; *unter ~* under the care of a guardian; *j-n unter ~ stellen fig.* keep a close eye on s.o.; (*bevormunden*) keep s.o. on a close rein
Kurator *m*; *-s*, *-en*, *~in f*; *-*, *-nen*; *Jur.* trustee; *Museum, Univ.* curator; **Kuratorium** *n*; *-s*, *Kuratorien* board of trustees
Kur|aufenthalt *m* stay at a health resort (*Badeort*: spa); *~bad n* spa
Kurbel *f*; *-*, *-n* winder; *Tech.* crank (handle); *Mot. zum Anlassen*: starting handle; **kurbeln I.** *v/t.* **1.** wind (*od.* crank) up *etc.*; **2.** *umg.* (*filmen*) film, shoot; **II.** *v/i.* **1.** wind the handle; **2.** *Mot.* (*ankurbeln*) crank the engine; *mit dem Lenkrad*: work away (at the steering); *ich musste beim Einparken ganz schön ~ umg.* I had to wind away at the steering (*Am.* steer like crazy) to get into the parking space
Kurbel|stange *f Tech.* connecting rod; *~welle f Tech.* crankshaft
Kürbis *m*; *-*, *-se* **1.** *Bot.* pumpkin; (*Flaschenkürbis*) gourd; **2.** *umg.* (*Kopf*) nut; *~kern m* pumpkin seed
Kurde *m*; *-n*, *-n*, **Kurdin** *f*; *-*, *-nen* Kurd, *weiblich: auch* Kurd woman (*od.* girl)
Kurdirektor *m*, *~in f* spa director
kurdisch I. *Adj.* Kurdish; **II. Kurdisch** *n*; *-en*; *Ling.* Kurdish; *das Kurdische* Kurdish; **Kurdistan** (*n*); *-s*; *Geog.* Kurdistan
kuren *v/i. umg.* take (*gerade*: be on) a cure
küren *v/t. geh.* choose, select (*zu* as)
Kürettage [kyrɛ'taːʒə] *f*; *-*, *-n*; *Med.* curettage; **Kürette** *f*; *-*, *-n* curette; **kürettieren** *v/t.* curette
Kurfürst *m hist.* (prince) elector; **Kurfürstentum** *n* electorate; **Kurfürstin** *f* electress; **kurfürstlich** *Adj.* electoral
Kur|gast *m* patient at a health resort (*od.* spa); *Besucher*: spa visitor; *~haus n* spa rooms *Pl.*, assembly rooms *Pl.* (of a health resort *od.* spa); *~hotel n* health-resort hotel, spa hotel
Kurie *f*; *-*, *-n*; *kath.* Curia; **Kurienkardinal** *m kath.* cardinal of the (Roman) Curia
Kurier *m*; *-s*, *-e* courier, messenger; *auf Motorrad*: courier, *Mil.* dispatch rider; *~dienst m* courier service
kurieren *v/t. auch fig.* cure (*von* of); *davon bin ich kuriert fig.* I've had enough of that
Kurier|gepäck *n* diplomatic baggage;

~post f mail sent by courier
kurios *Adj.* strange, funny; **kurioserweise** *Adv.* strangely enough, remarkable though it may seem
Kuriosität *f*; *-*, *-en* **1.** *nur Sg.* oddness; **2.** → *Kuriosum*; **3.** (*Sammlungsstück*) curio, curiosity; **Kuriosum** *n*; *-s*, *Kuriosa* oddity, odd thing (*od.* fact); *konkret*: curiosity
Kur|kapelle *f* spa orchestra; *~karte f* ticket received by a spa visitor on payment of the Kurtaxe, giving access to certain places and events; *~klinik f* sanatorium; *private: auch* health farm; *~konzert n* spa concert
Kurkuma *n*; *-(s)*, *kein Pl.* (*Gewürz*) turmeric, curcuma
Kurlaub *m*; *-(e)s*, *-e* holiday-cum-cure, *Am.* health spa vacation
Kür|lauf *m Eissport*: free skating (program[me]); *~läufer m*, *~läuferin f* free skater
Kur|mittel *n* spa therapy; *~mittelhaus n* spa treatment cent|re (*Am.* -er); *~ort m* health resort, spa; *~packung f* für die Haare*: conditioner; *Großpackung e-s Medikaments*: complete treatment; *~park m* spa gardens *Pl.*
Kurpfalz *f hist.*: *die ~* the Electoral Palatinate; **kurpfälzisch** *Adj. hist.* ... of the Electoral Palatinate
Kurpfuscher *m* charlatan, quack *umg.*; **Kurpfuscherei** *f*; *-*, *-en* charlatanism; **Kurpfuscherin** *f* → *Kurpfuscher*
Kurpromenade *f* spa promenade

Kurs *m*; *-es*, *-e* **1.** *Wirts.* price; (*Notierung*) quotation; *von Devisen*: exchange rate; *der ~ des Euro* the euro exchange rate; *zum ~ von* at the rate of; *hoch im ~ stehen* be at a premium; *fig.* rate highly (*bei* with); *in ~ setzen* circulate; *außer ~ setzen* take out of circulation; *außer ~ kommen fig.* lose its popularity; **2.** *Naut., Flug.* course; (*Radarkurs*) track; (*Strecke*) route; *fig. Pol.* course, line, policy; *~ halten* stay on course; *vom ~ abweichen* go off course; *~ nehmen auf* (+ *Akk.*) head for (*auch fig.*); *e-n neuen/härteren ~ einschlagen fig.* take a new/harder line; **3.** *Sport, für Rad-, Autorennen, Skirennen etc.*: course; *der anspruchsvolle ~ wurde vom Schweizer Trainer gesteckt* the demanding course was set by the Swiss coach; **4.** (*Lehrgang*) course; (*die Teilnehmer*) course participants; *der ganze ~* all those on the course; → *Kursus*
Kursaal *m* kursaal, spa assembly room
Kurs|abschlag *m Wirts.* markdown; *~abschwächung f Wirts.* easing off of (market) prices; *~abweichung f Naut. etc.* deviation (from the course); *~änderung f* change of course; *fig. auch* policy change; *~anstieg m Wirts.* rise in (market) prices; *~aufschlag m Wirts.* markup; *~bewegung f Wirts.* movement of prices; *~blatt n Wirts.* stock market report; *~buch n Eisenb.* (railway) timetable, *Am.* train schedule(s *Pl.*)
Kurschatten *m umg. hum.* companion of the opposite sex picked up while on a cure
Kürschner *m*; *-s*, *-* furrier; **Kürschnerei** *f*; *-*, *-en* **1.** *nur Sg.* furrier's trade; **2.** furrier's (work)shop; **Kürschnerin** *f*; *-*, *-nen* furrier
Kurs|einbruch *m Wirts.* sudden fall in prices; *~einbuße f* price decline; *~entwicklung f* trend in prices; *~erholung f* rally in prices; *~festsetzung f* fixing of the exchange rate (*Börse*:

K

price); **~gewinn** *m* price gain
kursieren *v/i.* circulate; *Gerüchte*: go (a)round
Kursindex *m Wirts.* share prices (*Am.* stock market) index
kursiv *Druck.* **I.** *Adj.* italic ..., in italics; **II.** *Adv.* in italics
Kursiv|druck *m; nur Sg. Druck.* italics *Pl.*; **~schrift** *f* italics *Pl.*; **in ~ setzen** italicize
Kurs|korrektur *f* course correction; *Börse*: price adjustment; *fig. auch* shift in policy; **~leiter** *m,* **~leiterin** *f Päd.* course leader (*od.* instructor); **~makler** *m,* **~maklerin** *f Wirts.* official (*od.* inside) broker; **~notierung** *f Wirts.* (price *od.* market) quotation
kursorisch *Adj.* cursory
Kurs|rückgang *m Wirts.* decline in prices; **~schwankungen** *Pl.* price fluctuations; **~stabilität** *f* price stability; **~steigerung** *f* price increase; **~sturz** *m* sharp fall in prices; **~stützung** *f* price pegging; **~system** *n Päd.* streaming, *Am.* tracking; **~teilnehmer** *m,* **~teilnehmerin** *f Päd.* course participant; **~treiberei** *f Wirts.* rigging the market
Kursus *m; -, Kurse* course; (*Klasse*) *auch* class
Kurs|verlust *m* loss in price; **~wagen** *m Eisenb.* through coach; **~wechsel** *m* change of course (*fig. auch* policy); **~wert** *m* market value; **~zettel** *m* stock exchange list
Kurtaxe *f* spa (*od.* health resort) tax
Kurtisane *f; -, -n; hist.* courtesan
Kür|turnen *n Sport* free exercises *Pl.*; **~übung** *f* free exercise
Kurve *f; -, -n* **1.** (*Bogen, auch Math. und grafische* ~) curve; **in großen ~n fahren** *Skifahrer*: ski in wide sweeps; **in die ~ gehen** *Flug.* start to turn; *Querlage*: bank; **e-e weite ~ fliegen** fly in a wide arc; **2.** *e-r Straße etc.*: bend, *bes. Am.* curve; *scharfe*: corner; *allmähliche*: curve; **e-e ~ schneiden** cut a corner; **zu schnell in die ~ gehen** take a (*od.* the) corner too fast; **e-e ~ nach rechts/links machen** *Straße*: bend to the right/left; **die ~ kratzen** *umg. fig.* make a quick getaway; **ich hab die ~ nicht gekriegt** *umg.* I didn't quite make it; **sie hat gerade noch die ~ gekriegt** *umg.* she just scraped by, she did it by the skin of her teeth; **3.** *Pl., umg. hum. e -r Frau*: curves; **kurven** *v/i.* **1.** make a turn; (*sich schlängeln*) wind about; *Flug.* circle; **um die Ecke ~ come** (a)round the corner; **2.** *umg.*: (*durch die Gegend*) **~ schnell**: bomb around; *ziellos*: potter (*Am.* putter) around
kurvenförmig *Adj.* curved
Kurven|lage *f Mot.* roadholding (on bends, *Am.* on curves), cornering (ability); **e-e gute ~ haben** hold the road well (on bends, *Am.* on curves), corner well; **~lineal** *n* curve
kurvenreich *Adj.* **1.** *Straße*: winding, twisting, full of bends (*Am.* curves); *Schild*: „**~ auf 3 km**" "bends for 2 miles", *Am.* "winding road next 2 miles"; **2.** *umg. hum Frau*: curvaceous
Kurvenschreiber *m* plotter
kurvensicher *Adj.*: **~ sein** hold the road well (on bends, *Am.* on curves), corner well
Kurven|star *m* curvaceous (*od.* sexy) star; **~verhalten** *n Mot.* → *Kurvenlage*; **~vorgabe** *f Sport* stagger
Kurverei *f; -, -en; umg.* (endless) series of corners

Kurverwaltung *f* spa administration
kurvig *Adj. Straße*: winding, twisting
kurz **I.** *Adj.; kürzer, am kürzesten* **1.** *räumlich*: short; **~ und dick** dumpy; **~e Hose** shorts *Pl.*; **mit ~en Ärmeln** short-sleeved; **sie trägt ~es Haar** she's got short hair; **sich** (*Dat.*) **die Haare ~ schneiden lassen** have one's hair cut short; **hinten und an den Seiten ~** *Haarschnitt*: short back and sides; **die Hose ist ihm zu ~ geworden** he's grown too tall for those trousers (*Am.* pants); **kürzer machen** shorten; **~ und klein schlagen** *umg.* smash to pieces; **alles ~ und klein schlagen** *umg.* wreck the place; **den Kürzeren ziehen** *fig.* come off worst, lose out; **2.** *zeitlich od. in der Abfassung*: short, brief; (*schroff*) short, curt (*gegen* with); **~e Zusammenfassung** (brief) summary; **~er Blick** quick glance; **in ~en Worten** in a few words, briefly; **binnen ~em** shortly; **seit ~em geht es ihm besser** he's been feeling better lately; **er ist erst seit ~em in Prag** he's only been in Prague for a short time; **vor ~em** recently, not long ago; **die Tage werden kürzer** the days are getting shorter; → *Prozess* 2; **II.** *Adv.* **1.** *räumlich*: **er sprang zu ~** he jumped too short, he didn't jump far enough; **~ vor Lissabon** just before (we *etc.* got to) Lisbon; **es liegt ~ hinter der Post®** it's a little way (*od.* just) past the post office; **~ geschnitten** *Haar*: short; **~ geschoren** very short, close-cropped; **die Röcke werden dieses Jahr ~ getragen** hemlines are high this year; **zu ~ kommen** *fig.* not get one's fair share; **das Problem ist viel zu ~ gekommen** the problem didn't get the attention it deserved; **kürzer treten** *fig. finanziell*: tighten one's belt; *aus Gesundheitsgründen*: slow down, take things more easily; **ich muss mit dem Essen etwas kürzer treten** I must (*bes. Am.* I have to) cut down a bit on eating; **j-n ~ halten** *umg. fig.* keep s.o. on a tight rein (*od.* short leash); **mit Geld etc.*: umg.* keep s.o. short of money *etc.*, stint s.o. of money *etc.*; **2.** *zeitlich od. in der Abfassung, im Ausdruck*: briefly; (*vorübergehend*) for a while; (*flüchtig*) for a moment; **könntest du ~ herüberkommen?** could you come over for a moment (*od.* minute)?; **~ darauf** shortly after (this); **~ zuvor** shortly before (this); **über ~ oder lang** sooner or later; **~** (*gesagt*), **um es ~ zu sagen** *od.* **zu machen** to cut a long story short; **~** (**und bündig**) briefly; (*schroff*) curtly; (*schonungslos*) bluntly, point-blank; *ablehnen*: flatly; **~ und schmerzlos** *umg.* quickly and without any fuss; **~ angebunden** short, curt (*gegen* with); **~ gesagt** very briefly, in a word, in short; **j-m ~ schreiben** drop s.o. a line; **~ nicken** give a brief (*od.* quick) nod; **lass mich mal ~ überlegen** let me have a quick think, *Am.* let me think about that for a minute; **ich will ihn nur ~ anrufen** I just want to give him a quick call; **fasse dich ~!** (try to) be brief (*od.* make it short); **~ gefasst** *Brief, Bericht*: brief; **er wird ~ Will genannt** he's called Will for short; **~ gebraten** *Gastr.* fried on high heat for a very short time; → *abfertigen* 2
Kurzarbeit *f* short-time work; **kurzarbeiten** *v/i.* (*trennb., hat -ge-*) work (*od.* be on) short time; **Kurzarbeiter** *m* short-time worker; **~ sein** *auch* be on short time; **Kurzarbeitergeld** *n*

short-time worker's supplement; **Kurzarbeiterin** *f* → *Kurzarbeiter*
kurz|ärm(e)lig *Adj.* short-sleeved; **~atmig** *Adj.* short of breath, short-winded
Kurzausgabe *f* abridged edition
kurzbeinig *Adj.* short-legged
Kurz|bericht *m* brief report; (*Zusammenfassung*) summary; **~beschreibung** *f* brief description; **~besuch** *m* brief (*od.* flying) visit; **~biografie**, **~biographie** *f* profile
Kurze *m; -n, -n; umg.* **1.** *Elektr., Kurzschluss*: **in der Leitung ist ein ~r** there's a short in the lead (*Am.* cord); **2.** (*Schnaps*) shot of schnapps *etc.*; **wir kriegen drei ~** we'll have three (shots of) schnapps *etc.*
Kürze *f; -, -n* shortness; *e-s Berichts etc.*: *auch* brevity; *des Stils*: conciseness; **in ~** shortly, soon; **in aller ~** very briefly; **in der ~ liegt die Würze** brevity is the soul of wit
Kürzel *n; -s, -* **1.** (*Abkürzung*) abbreviation (*für* of); **2.** (*Stenozeichen*) shorthand symbol; **das ist ein ~ für ...** *fig.* that's shorthand for ...
kürzen *v/t.* **1.** shorten (*um* by); (*Buch*) *auch* abridge; (*Film etc.*) cut; (*Arbeitszeit, Gehalt*) reduce, cut; (*drastisch* *auch* slash *umg.*); **wir zeigen die gekürzte Version des Films** we are showing the cut version of the film (*Am. auch* movie); **2.** *Math.* (*Bruch*) reduce
Kurzentschlossene *m, f; -n, -n* person who decides to do something at the last moment; **ein Schnäppchen für ~** a bargain for last-minute (*od.* impulse) bookers (*Am.* vacationers)
kurzerhand *Adv.* unceremoniously; *umg.* just like that; (*plötzlich*) *auch* there and then; **~ leugnen** flatly deny; **etw. ~ abweisen** reject s.th. out of hand
kürzer treten → *kurz* II 1
Kurz|fassung *f* abridged version; **~film** *m* short film; (*Vorfilm*) short *umg.*; **~form** *f* short(ened) form; **~formel** *f*: **etw. auf e-e ~ bringen** put s.th. in a nutshell
kurzfristig **I.** *Adj.* short-term ...; (*plötzlich*) ... at short notice, sudden; (*sofortig*) immediate; **II.** *Adv.* at short notice; *absagen*: *auch* at the last minute; (*rasch*) quickly
kurz| gebraten, ~ gefasst → *kurz* II 2
Kurzgeschichte *f* short story
kurz| geschnitten, ~ geschoren → *kurz* II 1
Kurzhaar|dackel *m Zool.* short-haired dachshund; **~frisur** *f* short hairstyle
kurzhaarig *Adj.* short-haired
Kurzhaarschnitt *m* short haircut
kurz|halsig *Adj.* short-necked; **~ halten** → *kurz* II 1
Kurz|information *f* information summary; *Blatt*: information sheet; **~kommentar** *m* brief commentary (*od.* analysis)
kurzlebig *Adj.* short-lived (*auch fig. und Phys.*), *Bot., Zool., fig. auch* ephemeral; *Konsumgüter*: non-durable; *Lebensmittel*: perishable; **es war ziemlich ~** *auch* it didn't last very long
Kurzlehrgang *m* short course; *sehr intensiv*: crash course
kürzlich *Adv.* recently, the other day; **erst ~** just the other day
Kurz|meldung *f* news flash; **~nachricht** *f auf Handy*: (SMS) text message; **~en** news *Sg.* in brief, summary *Sg.* of the news.; **~parker** *m; -s, -**

short-term parker; **~parkzone** *f* short-
-term (*Brit. auch* short-stay) parking
zone; **~prosa** *f Lit.* short prose works;
~referat *n* short talk (*Univ.* paper);
ein ~ halten über give a short talk
(*Univ.* paper) on; **~reise** *f* short trip
kurzschließen *v/t.* (*unreg., trennb., hat
-ge-*); *Elektr.* short-circuit; *Mot.* (*Auto*)
hotwire
Kurzschluss *m* **1.** *Elektr.* short circuit,
umg. short; **2.** *seelischer:* moment of
madness; **~handlung** *f*, **~reaktion** *f*
panic reaction
Kurzschrift *f* shorthand, stenography
kurzsichtig *Adj.* shortsighted (*auch
fig.*); *Med.* myopic; **Kurzsichtigkeit** *f;
nur Sg.* shortsightedness (*auch fig.*);
Med. myopia
Kurz|ski *m* short ski; **~start** *m Flug.*
short takeoff; **~strecke** *f* short distance; *Leichtathletik:* sprint distance
Kurzstrecken|flug *m* short-haul flight;
~flugzeug *n* short-haul aircraft; **~lauf**
m sprint; **~läufer** *m*, **~läuferin** *f*
sprinter; **~rakete** *f* short-range missile
Kurztrip *m umg.* short trip
kurzum *Adv.* in a word, to cut a long
story short
Kürzung *f e-s Buches etc.:* abridg(e)-
ment; *von Gehältern etc.:* cut, cutback
(+ *Gen.* in); *Math.* reduction; **~en vornehmen in** (+ *Dat.*) */bei in Film etc.:*
cut, shorten; *beim Personal etc.:* cut
down on
Kurz|urlaub *m* short break; **~urlauber**
m, **~urlauberin** *f* holidaymaker (*Am.*
vacationer) on a short break; **~wahl** *f
Telef.* abbreviated dial(l)ing, quick dial, *Am.* speed dial
Kurzwaren *Pl.* haberdashery *Sg., Am.*
notions, dry goods; **~abteilung** *f* haberdashery (*Am.* notions) department;
~geschäft *n* haberdasher's (shop),
Am. notions (*od.* dry goods) store
kurzweg *Adv.* → *kurzerhand*
Kurzweil *f*, -, *kein Pl.; altm.* amusement, entertainment; *etw. aus ~ tun*
do s.th. for fun; **kurzweilig** *Adj.* entertaining
Kurzwelle *f Phys., Funk.* short wave
Kurzwellen|bereich *m Phys., Funk.*
short-wave band; **~empfänger** *m
Funk.* short-wave receiver; **~sender** *m
Funk.* short-wave radio station (*od.*
transmitter)
Kurzwort *n; Pl.* -*wörter* abbreviation;
(*Akronym*) acronym
Kurzzeitgedächtnis *n* short-term
memory
kurzzeitig I. *Adj.* short, brief; (*kurzlebig*) short-lived; **II.** *Adv.* for a short

time, briefly
Kurzzeitwecker *m* timer
Kuschelecke *f* cosy (*Am.* cozy) corner
kuschelig *Adj.* soft and cuddly; *Sessel
etc.:* cosy, *Am.* cozy; **kuscheln
I.** *v/refl.: sich an j-n/etw. ~* snuggle
(*od.* cuddle) up to s.o. / snuggle
against s.th.; **II.** *v/t.: s-n Kopf an/in
etw.* (*Akk.*) *~* nestle one's head against
/ bury one's head in s.th.; **III.** *v/i.* cuddle
Kuscheltier *n* soft (*od.* cuddly) toy
kuschelweich *Adj.* soft and cuddly
kuschen *v/i. Hund:* lie down; *fig.
Mensch:* knuckle under (*vor + Dat.*
to)
kuschlig *Adj.* → *kuschelig*
Kusine *f*, -, -*n* cousin
Kuskus *m, n;* -, -; *Gastr.* couscous
Kuss *m;* -*es*, *Küsse* kiss; *Gruß und ~ als
Briefschluss:* love and kisses
Küsschen *n* (little) kiss; *auf die Wange:* peck (on the cheek); *~! umg.* give
us a kiss; *ein ~ in Ehren kann niemand verwehren* there can be no objection to a friendly kiss
kussecht *Adj.* kiss-proof
küssen *v/t.* kiss; *sie küssten sich* they
kissed (each other); *j-n zum Abschied
~* kiss s.o. goodbye; *j-n auf den Mund
~* kiss s.o.'s lips, kiss s.o. on the lips;
j-m die Hand ~ kiss s.o.'s hand; *küss
die Hand österr.* (*Guten Tag*) hallo,
how are you?; (*auf Wiedersehen*)
goodbye; **Küsserei** *f*, -, *kein Pl.; umg.*
constant kissing
Kusshand *f: j-m e-e ~ zuwerfen* blow
s.o. a kiss; *mit ~ fig.* gladly, with pleasure; *ich würde es mit ~ nehmen auch*
I'd take it like shot, *Am.* I'd take it in
a heartbeat
Küste *f*, -, -*n* coast, shore
Küsten|bewohner *m*, **~bewohnerin** *f*
coastal inhabitant; *die friesischen ~*
those living on the Frisian coast;
~dampfer *m Naut.* coaster; **~ebene** *f*
coastal plain; **~fischerei** *f* inshore
fishing; **~frachter** *Naut.* coastal
freighter; **~gebiet** *n* coastal area; **~ge-
birge** *n* coastal range (of mountains);
~gewässer *n* coastal waters *Pl.;* **~mo-
torschiff** *n* (*abgek. Kümo*) *Naut.*
coastal motor vessel, coaster
küstennah *Adj.* coastal, offshore ...,
near the coast; **Küstennähe** *f: in ~*
near the coast
Küsten|region *f* coastal area; **~schiff-
fahrt** *f* coastal shipping; **~schutz** *m*
coastal protection (*od.* preservation);
~staat *m* littoral state; **~stadt** *f* coast-
(al) town; **~straße** *f* coast(al) road,

road along the coast; **~streifen** *m*,
~strich *m* coastal strip; *bestimmte
Strecke:* stretch of coast; **~wache** *f*
coastguard station; *Dienst:* coastguard
(service); **~wachschiff** *n* coastal patrol vessel; **~wacht** *f → Küstenwache*
Küster *m;* -*s*, - sexton, sacristan
Kustode *m;* -*n*, -*n*, **Kustos** *m;* -, *Kusto-
den im Museum:* curator, keeper
Kutschbock *m* coach box
Kutsche *f;* -, -*n* coach; *alte ~ Mot.
umg.* old banger (*Am.* beater)
Kutscher *m;* -*s*, - coachman; **~sitz** *m*
coach box
kutschieren I. *v/i.* (*ist kutschiert*)
1. drive (*od.* ride) in a coach; (*selbst
fahren*) drive (a coach); **2.** *Mot. umg.*
drive; **II.** *v/t.* (*hat*) drive; *ich habe keine Lust, sie durch die Gegend zu ~
umg.* I've no desire to chauffeur her
all over the place, I don't see why I
should be her private taxi service
Kutschkasten *m* coach body
Kutte *f*, -, -*n* **1.** (monk's) habit; **2.** *Jugendspr.* (*Mantel*) coat; (*Parka*) parka,
Brit. auch anorak
Kutteln *Pl.; südd., österr., schw., Gastr.*
tripe *Sg.*
Kutter *m;* -*s*, -; *Naut.* cutter
Kuvert [ku'veːɐ] *n;* -*s*, -*s* **1.** *mst südd.,
österr.* (*Briefumschlag*) envelope;
2. *geh.* (*Gedeck*) cover
Kuvertüre *f*, -, -*n*; *Gastr.* (chocolate)
coating
Kuwait (*n*); -*s*; *Geog.* Kuwait; **Kuwaiter**
m; -*s*, -, **Kuwaiterin** *f*, -, -*nen* Kuwaiti,
weiblich auch: Kuwaiti woman (*od.*
girl); **kuwaitisch** *Adj.* Kuwaiti
kV *Abk.* (*Kilovolt*) kV
kW *Abk.* (*Kilowatt*) kW
KW *Abbr.* (*Kalenderwoche*) calendar
week
kWh *Abk.* (*Kilowattstunde*) kWh
Kybernetik *f*, -, *kein Pl.* cybernetics *Pl.*
(*V. im Sg.*); **Kybernetiker** *m;* -*s*, -, **Ky-
bernetikerin** *f*, -, -*nen* cybernetician,
cyberneticist; **kybernetisch I.** *Adj.* cy-
bernetic; **II.** *Adv.* cybernetically
Kykladen *Pl. Geog.: die ~* the Cyclades
Kyrie *n;* -, -*s*, **Kyrieeleison** *n;* -*s*, -*s*;
kirchl. Kyrie (eleison)
kyrillisch *Adj.* Cyrillic
KZ *n;* -(*s*), -*s*; *Abk.* (*Konzentrationslager*) concentration camp; **~Aufseher**
m, **~Aufseherin** *f* concentration camp
guard; **~Gedenkstätte** *f* concentration camp memorial; **KZ-Häftling** *m*
concentration camp internee (*od.* prisoner)
KZler *m;* -*s*, -, **Kzlerin** *f*, -, -*nen; umg.*
→ *KZ-Häftling*

K

L

L, l *n*; -, - *od. umg.* -s L, l; **L wie Ludwig** *Buchstabieren*: "l" for (*od.* as in) "Lima"

la *Interj., Mus.* la

Lab [la:p] *n*; -(e)s, -e; *Bio., Zool., Enzym*: rennin; *Produkt*: rennet

labb(e)rig *Adj. umg.* **1.** (*geschmacklos*) tasteless, wishy-washy; *Brot, Pudding etc.*: mushy; (*wässerig*) *Getränk, Suppe etc.*: watery; *Salat etc.*: soggy; *das schmeckt total ~* it tastes of nothing at all, it has no taste; *dieses ~e Zeug kann ich nicht essen* I can't eat this tasteless mush; **2.** *Kleidung*: sloppy, shapeless; *Hose: auch* baggy; *Gummi etc.*: slack; **3.** *Händedruck*: limp

Labeflasche *f am Rennrad*: water bottle; *mit Schlauch*: sipper bottle

Label ['le:bl] *n*; -s, -s label

laben I. *v/refl.* refresh o.s., revive o.s. (*an + Dat.* with); *sich ~ an* (+ *Dat.*) *fig.* relish; *mit Schadenfreude*: gloat over; *fig. an e-m Anblick*: feast one's eyes on; **II.** *v/t.* refresh, revive; *das Auge ~ fig.* delight the eye

Laberdan *m*; -s, -e; *Gastr.* salt cod

labern *umg.* **I.** *v/i.* blather; **II.** *v/t.* babble; *was laberst du da?* what are you babbling about (*Brit. auch* rabbiting) on about?

labial *Adj. Ling.* labial; **Labial** *m*; -s, -e labial; **Labiallaut** *m* labial

labil *Adj. Psych., Phys.; Lage, Person, Gleichgewicht etc.*: unstable; *Psych. auch* labile; (*beeinflussbar*) *auch* easily influenced, impressionable; (*anfällig*) susceptible; *Kreislauf*: fluctuating; *~e Gesundheit* weak constitution; **Labilität** *f*; -, -en instability; *Psych. auch* lability; (*Anfälligkeit*) susceptibility

Lab|kraut *n Bot.* bedstraw; *~magen m Zool.* fourth stomach; *fachspr.* abomasum (*Pl.* abomasa)

Labor *n*; -s, -s *und* -e laboratory, *umg.* lab; **Laborant** *m*; -en, -en, **Laborantin** *f*; -, -nen lab(oratory) assistant; **Laboratorium** *n*; -s, *Laboratorien* laboratory; **Laborbefunde** *Pl.* (laboratory) test results; **laborgeprüft** *Adj.* laboratory-tested

laborieren *v/i. umg.*: *~ an* (+ *Dat.*) **1.** *an e-r Krankheit*: be struggling with; *ich laboriere schon seit Wochen an e-r Erkältung auch* I've been trying to shake off a cold for weeks; *er laboriert noch an der Verletzung* his injury is still giving him trouble; **2.** (*sich abmühen*) toil away at, struggle with

Labor|platz *m* laboratory place; *~techniker m, ~technikerin f* lab(oratory) technician; *~tier n* lab(oratory) animal; *~test m, ~untersuchung f* lab(oratory) test; *~versuch m* lab(oratory) experiment

Labrador *m*; -s, -e; *Zool., Hund*: Labrador

Labsal *n*; -(e)s, -e, *und südd., österr. f*; -, -e; *geh.* (*Erfrischung*) refreshment; *fig.* (*Genuss*) delight; (*Trost*) solace, comfort; *es war ein ~* it was very refreshing; *fig.* it was a great delight/solace

Labskaus *n*; -, *kein Pl.; Gastr.* seaman's beef stew, lobscouse

Labyrinth *n*; -(e)s, -e; *Antike und Anat.*: labyrinth; (*Irrgarten*) maze; *fig.* maze, warren; **labyrinthisch** *Adj.* labyrinthine

Lachanfall *m* laughing fit, fit of laughter; *e-n ~ kriegen* go into fits (of laughter)

Lache¹ *f*; -, -n; *umg.* laugh; *dreckige ~* dirty laugh

Lache² *f*; -, -n pool; *nach Regen*: puddle

lächeln *v/i.* smile (*über + Akk.* at); *spitzbübisch*: grin (at); *höhnisch*: sneer (at); *immer nur ~!* keep smiling!; *über das ganze Gesicht ~* be all smiles, be grinning from ear to ear; *ihm lächelte das Glück lit. fig.* fortune smiled (up)on him; **Lächeln** *n*; -s, *kein Pl.* smile; grin; *höhnisches*: sneer

lachen *vt/i.* laugh (*über + Akk.* at); (*lächeln*) smile; *laut ~* laugh out loud; *leise vor sich hin ~* chuckle (to o.s.); *sich* (*Dat.*) *e-n Ast ~ umg.* nearly die laughing, kill o.s. (laughing), crease (*Am.* double) up (with laughter); *du hast gut ~* it's all very well for you to laugh, you can laugh; *dass ich nicht lache! od. da kann ich nur ~! umg.* don't make me laugh; *lach* (*du*) *nur! umg.* just you wait and see; *es wäre doch gelacht, wenn ... umg.* it would be ridiculous if ...; *da gibt's nichts zu ~* it's not funny; *formeller*: this is no laughing matter; *was gibt's da zu ~?* what's so funny about that?; *es darf gelacht werden iro.* you can laugh now; *bei ihm hat sie nichts zu ~* he really gives her a hard time; *er hat nicht viel zu ~* life's no bed of roses for him; *du wirst ~, aber ...* you won't believe this, but ...; *wer zuletzt lacht, lacht am besten Sprichw.* he who laughs last, laughs loudest; *lach doch mal!* (*lächle*) come on, give us a smile; *die Sonne lacht fig.* the sun is shining brightly; *ihm lachte das Glück lit.* fortune smiled (up)on him; → *Fäustchen etc.*

Lachen *n*; -s, *kein Pl.* laugh(ing), laughter; *j-n zum ~ bringen* make s.o. laugh; *ich konnte ihn nicht zum ~ bringen* I couldn't make him laugh (*od.* get him to laugh); *in lautes ~ ausbrechen* burst out laughing, *Am. auch* crack up; *sich biegen od. ausschütten od. kugeln etc. vor ~ umg.* kill o.s. (laughing), split one's sides (laughing); *das ist nicht zum ~!* it's no joke!; *das ist zum ~!* that's ridiculous!; *ich werde dir das ~ schon abgewöhnen!* I'll wipe that smile off your face!; *ihm wird das ~ schon noch vergehen!* he'll be laughing on the other side of his face before he knows it!; *~ ist gesund od. die beste Medizin* laughter is the best medicine; → *verbeißen I 1, zumute*

lachend I. *Part. Präs.* → *lachen*; **II.** *Adj.* laughing; *fig. Sonne*: smiling; *die ~en Erben* the laughing heirs; *der ~e Dritte* the real winner

Lacher *m*; -s, - **1.** (*Lachender*) laugher; *er hatte die ~ auf seiner Seite* he got everybody to laugh with him; **2.** (*Lachen*) laugh; **Lacherfolg** *m*: *es war ein großer ~ umg.* it was a scream; *~e ernten* have everybody laughing; **Lacherin** *f*; -, -nen → *Lacher* 1

lächerlich I. *Adj.* **1.** ridiculous; (*unsinnig*) laughable, absurd; *~ machen* ridicule; *sich ~ machen* make a fool of o.s.; *das Lächerliche daran* the ridiculous thing about it; *ins Lächerliche ziehen* make fun of, ridicule; **2.** (*unbedeutend, geringfügig*) piddling; *Summe: auch* ridiculously small, derisory; *Preis*: ridiculously low; *~e Kleinigkeit* ridiculously trivial matter, piddling little affair, *Pl. auch* piffling trivia; **II.** *Adv.*: *~ wenig etc.* ridiculously little *etc.*, a ridiculously small amount *etc.*; **lächerlicherweise** *Adv.* ridiculous though it may seem; **Lächerlichkeit** *f* **1.** ridiculousness; *der ~ preisgeben* make s.o./s.th. look ridiculous; **2.** (*etw. Lächerliches, Unbedeutendes*) merest trifle, piddling little affair; *umg., Pl. auch* piffling trivia

Lach|fältchen *Pl.*, *~falten Pl.* laughter (*Am.* laugh) lines; *~gas n* laughing gas

lachhaft *Adj. pej.* ridiculous, laughable

Lach|krampf *m* laughing fit; *e-n ~ bekommen od. kriegen* start laughing uncontrollably, get the giggles, have a laughing fit; *ich bekam e-n ~ auch* I couldn't stop laughing; *ich krieg e-n ~! umg. iro.* you're kidding!; *~möwe f Orn.* laughing gull; *~muskel m* laughing muscle, risorius *fachspr.*; *etw. strapaziert j-s ~n hum.* s.th. makes s.o. laugh fit to bust; *~nummer f, ~platte f umg. pej.* (bad) joke; *Person, Mannschaft: auch* laughing stock; *die ~ des Jahres* the biggest flop of the year; *~reiz m* (sudden) urge to laugh

Lachs *m*; -es, -e; *Zool.* salmon

Lach|sack *m* **1.** *Scherzartikel*: laughing bag; **2.** *umg. hum. Person*: jovial type; *~salve f* peal (*od.* burst) of laughter

Lachs|brötchen *n* smoked salmon (*Am.* lox) roll; *~ersatz m* (thinly sliced) rock salmon; *~fang m* salmon fishing

lachsfarben, lachsfarbig *Adj.* salmon(-colo[u]red), salmon pink

Lachsforelle *f Zool.* salmon trout

lachsrosa *Adj.* salmon pink, salmon-colo(u)red

Lachsschinken *m smoked, rolled, lean ham*

Lack *m*; -(e)s, -e **1.** paint; (*farblos*) lacquer; (*Holzlack*) varnish; (*Emaille-*

lack) enamel; **2.** (*Lackschicht*) *auch Mot.* paintwork, *umg.* paint job; **3.** *fig.* veneer; **der ~ ist ab** *umg.* the novelty has worn off, the thrill is gone; **~affe** *m umg.* fop

Lackel *m*; *-s, -*; *südd., österr.*; *umg., pej.* peasant; *ungeschickter:* clumsy oaf *umg.*

lacken *v/t.* → **lackieren** 1

lackglänzend *Adj.* brilliantly glossy (*od.* shiny)

Lackgürtel *m* patent leather belt

lackieren *v/t.* **1.** paint; *farblos:* lacquer; (*Holz*) varnish; *Mot.* spray; **sich** (*Dat.*) **die Fingernägel ~** put some nail varnish on, paint one's nails; **2.** *umg. fig.* (*hereinlegen*): **j-n ~** take s.o. in, take s.o. for a ride; **der Lackierte sein** → **gelackmeiert** II; **Lackierer** *m*; *-s, -*, varnisher; *Mot.* body painter; **Lackiererei** *f*; *-, -en* **1.** *Werkstatt:* paint shop; **2.** *nur Sg.*; *umg. pej.* (constant) painting; **Lackiererin** *f*; *-, -nen* → **Lackierer**, **Lackierung** *f* **1.** *nur Sg.* (*das Lackieren*) painting; *farblos:* lacquering; *mit Holzlack:* varnishing; *Mot.* spraying; **2.** (*Lackschicht*) paint(work); *farblos:* lacquer; *für Holz:* varnish; (*Emaille*) enamel; *Mot.* paintwork, *umg.* paint job

Lack|kratzer *m Mot.* scratch (on the paintwork); **~leder** *n* patent leather; **~mantel** *m* patent leather coat

lackmeiern *v/t.* → **gelackmeiert**

Lackmöbel *Pl.* lacquered furniture

Lackmus *m*, *n*; *-, kein Pl.*; *Chem.* litmus; **~papier** *n*; *nur Sg.* litmus paper

Lack|pflege *f* care of the paintwork; **~schaden** *m Mot.* damage to the paintwork, paint damage; **~schuh** *m* patent leather shoe; **~stiefel** *m* patent leather boot

Lade *f*; *-, -n* **1.** *altm.* (*Truhe*) chest; **2.** *Dial.* (*Schublade*) drawer

Lade|baum *m Naut.* derrick boom; **~brücke** *f* loading bridge; **~bucht** *f* loading bay; **~bühne** *f* loading platform; **~fähigkeit** *f*; *nur Sg.* loading capacity; (*Schiff*) tonnage; *Etech., Batterie:* storage capacity; **~fläche** *f* load(-ing) space, *Wirts.* payload area; **~gerät** *n Etech.* battery charger; **~geschirr** *n Naut.* loading tackle; **~gewicht** *n* maximum load; **~gut** *n* cargo, load; **~hemmung** *f* jam, stoppage; **~haben** *Gewehr etc.:* be jamming; *umg. fig. Person:* have a mental block; *engS.* not be able to get a word out; **~kapazität** *f* → **Ladefähigkeit**; **~klappe** *f Mot.* tailboard, tailgate; **~kran** *m* loading crane; **~linie** *f Naut.* load line, Plimsoll line; **~liste** *f* manifest, cargo list; **~luke** *f* hatch(way)

laden¹; *lädt, lud, hat geladen* **I.** *v/t.* **1.** load; **das Schiff hat Getreide geladen** the ship has taken on a load of grain; *Zustand:* the ship is carrying a cargo of grain; **der Lkw hat Kies geladen** the truck has been loaded with gravel; *Zustand:* the truck has a load of gravel; **die Kisten aus dem Wagen ~** unload the crates from the car (*Lieferwagen:* van, *Pferdewagen:* cart); **die Säcke vom Lkw auf Lasttiere ~** load the sacks from the truck onto pack animals; **auf sich ~** *fig.* saddle o.s. with; (*Hass, Schuld etc.*) incur; (*Verantwortung*) shoulder; **2.** *Etech.* (*Akku*) charge; **die Atmosphäre war mit Spannung/Hass geladen** *fig.* the atmosphere was charged with tension / filled with hatred; **3.** *Mot.* (*Motor*) supercharge, boost; **4.** (*Computer*) boot

(*up*) **5.** (*Gewehr etc.*) load; **II.** *v/i.* **1.** load; **der Lkw hat schwer geladen** the truck has a heavy load; **schwer geladen haben** *umg. hum. fig.* be plastered (*od.* tanked up, *bes. Am.* loaded), be three sheets to the wind, *Brit. auch* have had one over the eight *altm.*; **2.** *EDV* load; **der Rechner lädt sehr langsam** the computer loads very slowly; → **geladen**

laden² *v/t.*; *lädt* (*Dial.* ladet), *lud, hat geladen* **1.** *geh.* (*einladen*) invite; **2.** *Jur.:* **vor Gericht ~** summon before a court; *unter Strafandrohung:* subpoena

Laden *m*; *-s, Läden* **1.** shop, *bes. Am.* store; **2.** *umg.* (*Unternehmen*) business; **den ~ schmeißen** run the show; *fig.* (*es schaffen*) **den ~ dichtmachen** shut (*Am.* close) up shop; (*scheitern*): *auch* fold; **der ~ läuft geschäftlich:** business is good; *allg.* everything's hunky-dory; **wie ich den ~ kenne** if you ask me; **3.** *umg., fig.* (*Sache*) business; **den ~ hinschmeißen** *umg.* give up the whole thing, chuck (*Am.* pack) it in; **4.** (*Fensterladen*) shutter(s *Pl.*)

Laden|besitzer *m*, **~besitzerin** *f* shop (*Am. auch* store) owner, proprietor; **~detektiv** *m*, **~detektivin** *f* store detective; **~dieb** *m*, **~diebin** *f* shoplifter; **~diebstahl** *m* shoplifting; **~einbruch** *m* shopbreaking; **~einrichtung** *f* shop fittings *Pl.*, *Am.* store fixtures *Pl.*; **~fenster** *n* shop (*Am.* store) window; **~fläche** *f* sales area; **~front** *f* shop front, *Am.* storefront; **~geschäft** *n* retail business; **~hüter** *m umg.* slow seller; *gar nicht absetzbar:* non-seller; **~inhaber** *m*, **~inhaberin** *f* → **Ladenbesitzer**, **~kasse** *f* till; **~kette** *f* chain (of stores); **~lokal** *n* shop (*Am.* store) premises *Pl.*; **~miete** *f* shop (*Am.* store) rent

ladenneu *Adj.* brand new, new, unused

Laden|passage *f* shopping cent|re (*Am.* -er); *bes. Am. große:* (shopping) mall; **~preis** *m* retail price; *Bücher:* cover price; **~schild** *n* shop (*Am.* store) sign; *über dem Schaufenster:* fascia

Ladenschluss *m* closing time; **nach ~** after the shop (*Am.* store) has closed, after hours; **~gesetz** *n* shop (*Am.* store) closing laws *Pl.*; **~zeit** *f* shop (*Am.* store) closing time

Laden|straße *f* shopping street; **~theke** *f*, **~tisch** *m* counter; **unter dem Ladentisch** *fig.* under the counter; **~tochter** *f schw. altm.* shop assistant, *Am.* sales clerk; **~verkauf** *m* retail (sale)

Ladeplatz *m* loading area

Lader *m*; *-s, -* **1.** (*Mensch, Maschine*) loader,; **2.** *Mot.* (*Gebläse*) supercharger, blower; **3.** *Etech.* battery charger

Lade|rampe *f* loading ramp; **~raum** *m* **1.** *e-s Autos etc.:* load space; *Naut., Flug.* (cargo) hold; **2.** *Naut.* (*Kapazität*) tonnage; **~schein** *m Naut.* bill of lading, manifest; **~strom** *m Etech.* charging current; **~zone** *f* loading area (*od.* bay)

lädieren *v/t.* (*beschädigen*) damage; (*verletzen*) injure; **lädiert I.** *P.P.* → **lädieren; II.** *Adj.* **1.** (*beschädigt*) damaged; *Person:* injured; **leicht ~** rather the worse for wear; **er sah ziemlich ~ aus** he looked as if he'd taken quite a beating (*od.* had a rough time); **2.** *fig. Ruf, Ansehen, Image etc.:* damaged; *Stolz:* injured; **Lädierung** *f* damage;

(*Verletzung*) injury

Ladiner *m*; *-s, -*, **~in** *f*; *-, -nen* Ladin, *weiblich auch:* Ladin woman (*od.* girl); **ladinisch** *Adj.* Ladin; **Ladinisch** *n*; *-en*; *Ling.* Ladin; **das ~e** Ladin

lädt *Präs.* → **laden¹,²**

Ladung¹ *f* **1.** *Wirts.* (*Fracht*) load, *Naut. Flug.* cargo; (*Lieferung*) shipment; (*Wagenladung*) truckload; **2.** *Mil.* (*Sprengladung*) (explosive) charge; **e-e geballte ~ von Vorwürfen** *fig.* a volley of criticism; **3.** *Etech., auch Phys., e-s Atomkerns:* charge; **4.** *umg.* (*große Menge*): **e-e** (*ganze*) **~ Sand/Wasser** *etc. umg.* a (whole) load (*od.* pile) of sand / mass of water *etc.*

Ladung² *f Jur.* summons; *unter Strafandrohung:* subpoena

Lady ['leːdi] *f*; *-, -s*; (*Dame*) (real) lady; **Ladykiller** *m umg. hum.* ladykiller

Lafette *f*; *-, -n*; *Mil.* (gun) carriage, mount

Laffe *m*; *-n, -n*; *umg.* fop

lag *Imperf.* → **liegen**

Lage *f*; *-, -n* **1.** *räumlich:* position (*auch des Körpers*); *e-s Gebäudes etc.:* auch situation, location; *genauer:* site; *Haus in schöner ~* beautifully situated; *in höheren ~n* on high ground, higher up; **2.** (*Weinanbaugebiet*) site; (*Weinberg*) vineyard; (*Wein*) wine from a particular site; **3.** *fig.* (*Lebenslage, finanziell, wirtschaftlich etc.*) situation; (*Umstände*) *auch* circumstances *Pl.*; *mst unbefriedigend:* state of affairs; (*Zustand*) condition, state; *rechtliche ~* legal position; *in allen ~n* in any situation; *nach ~ der Dinge* as matters stand; *die ~ der Dinge erfordert es, dass er zurücktritt* the situation calls for his resignation; (*nicht*) *in der ~ sein zu* (+ *Inf.*) (not) be in a position to (+ *Inf.*), be (un)able to (+ *Inf.*); *ich bin nicht in der ~ zu* (+ *Inf.*) I'm in no position to (+ *Inf.*); *j-n in die ~ versetzen zu* (+ *Inf.*) enable s.o. to (+ *Inf.*), make it possible for s.o. to (+ *Inf.*); *in der glücklichen ~ sein zu* (+ *Inf.*) be in the fortunate position (*od.* be fortunate enough) to (be able to) (+ *Inf.*); *in derselben ~ sein* auch be in the same boat; *in e-r unangenehmen/unglücklichen ~ sein* be in an unpleasant/unfortunate position (*od.* situation); *wenn ich in d-r ~ wäre* if I were you, (if I were) in your position; *Herr der ~ sein/bleiben* be/remain in control of the situation (*od.* of things); *wie ist die ~?* how are things?, how's it going?; *j-n in die ~ versetzen zu* (+ *Inf.*) enable s.o. to (+ *Inf.*), make it possible for s.o. to (+ *Inf.*); *versetzen Sie sich in m-e ~* put yourself in my place (*od.* position); → *peilen* I; **4.** (*Schicht*) layer; *Geol. auch* stratum; *im Stapel:* tier; *Tech., von Werkstoff:* ply; *Farbe:* coat; *von Wurst etc.:* layer; **5.** *Buchwesen, von Papier:* quire; **6.** *Mus.* (*Ton-, Stimmlage*) register; *von Akkorden:* position; *die höheren ~n* the upper registers; **7.** *umg.:* *e-e ~ Bier ausgeben* buy (*od.* stand) a round of beer; **~bericht** *m* progress report; **~besprechung** *f* briefing

Lagen *Pl. Sport, Schwimmen:* **400 m ~** 400 met|res (*Am.* -er) individual medley; *4 x 100 m ~* 4 x 100 met|res (*Am.* -er) medley relay; **~schwimmen** *n* individual medley; **~staffel** *f Schwimmen:* medley relay; (*Mannschaft*) medley relay team

lagenweise *Adv.* in layers

Lageplan *m* layout (plan)

Lager n; -s, - **1.** Wirts. warehouse; (Raum) storeroom; Mil. depot; **ab ~** ex warehouse; **2.** (Warenbestand) stock, stores Pl.; **auf od. am ~ haben** have in stock; **das haben wir nicht auf ~** we haven't got it in stock, it's out of stock; **auf ~ haben** fig. have up one's sleeve; **e-e Überraschung** etc. **für j-n auf ~ haben** fig. have a surprise etc. in store for s.o.; **3.** Mil. (auch Ferien-, Flüchtlingslager etc.) camp; (geheimes Waffenlager etc.) cache; **4.** fig. (Partei) camp; **im feindlichen ~** in the enemy camp; **ins andere ~ überwechseln** change sides; **5.** Tech. (Widerlager, Unterlage) support; (Kugellager etc.) bearing; **6.** Geol. layer, deposit; **7.** altm. (Bett) bed; Jägerspr. (Ruheplatz) resting place; **~apfel** m apple for storing, (good) keeping apple; **~arbeiter** m, **~arbeiterin** f warehouse employee, warehouser, warehouseman; im Betrieb: storekeeper, storeman, Am. stockman; **~aufseher** m, **~aufseherin** f camp warden; **~bestand** m stock (on hand); **den ~ aufnehmen** take stock, do the stocktaking (od. inventory); **~bier** n lager; **~buch** n stock book, stores ledger

lagerfähig Adj. suitable for storage; **Lagerfähigkeit** f; nur Sg. suitability for storage, shelf life

Lagerfeuer n campfire; **~romantik** f campfire romanticism

Lager|fläche f Wirts. storage area; e-s Lagerhauses: warehouse area; **~gebühren** Pl. storage charges, storage Sg.

Lagerhaft f detention in a (prison) camp; **nach sieben Jahren ~** after seven years in a prison camp

Lager|halle f warehouse; **~haltung** f storage; Verwaltung: storekeeping, stockkeeping; **~haus** n warehouse

Lager|insasse m, **~insassin** f camp inmate

Lagerist m; -en, -en, **~in** f; -, -nen stockkeeper, storekeeper, männlich auch: storeman, weiblich auch: storewoman

Lager|koller m camp psychosis; **~kosten** Pl. storage charges, storage Sg.; **~kommandant** m camp commandant; **~leben** n camp life; **~leiter** m, **~leiterin** f e-s Ferienlagers etc.: camp leader; e-s Flüchtlingslagers: camp warden; **~liste** f stock list

lagern I. v/t. **1.** store; trocken etc.: auch keep; **Wein in Holzfässern ~** keep (od. lay down) wine in wooden barrels; → **kühl** II; **2.** (ablagern) (Holz etc.) season; **3.** (betten) put, lay; bes. Med. (Bein etc.) rest; **e-e bewusstlose Person wird seitlich gelagert** an unconscious person should be laid on their side; **4.** Tech. mount; (abstützen) support; (in e-e bestimmte Lage bringen) position; → **gelagert**; II. v/i. **1.** (rasten) camp; **~ auf** (+ Dat.) auf provisorischem Bett: camp down on; **ein guter Platz zum Lagern** a good place to camp; **2.** Waren: be stored; Wein: be kept, be laid down; **3.** (ausreifen) mature; **den Wein ~ lassen** let the wine age; **4.** Tech. (sich stützen) rest, be supported; **5.** Geol. be found; III. v/refl. settle (down)

Lager|obst n fruit for storing, (good) storing fruit; **~platz** m **1.** über Nacht: place to spend the night; **2.** Wirts. storage place; **~raum** m storeroom; **~schuppen** m storage shed; **~statt** f geh. couch, bed; **~stätte** f **1.** Geol. de-

posit; **2.** geh. couch, bed

Lagerung f **1.** Wirts. storage; (Alterung, Reifung) seasoning; von Wein: ag(e)ing; **2.** (Ruhen) resting, support(-ing); Tech. mounting; **3.** Geol. deposit

Lager|verwalter m, **~verwalterin** f Wirts. storekeeper, stockkeeper; **~verzeichnis** n stock list; **~vorrat** m stock, supply; **~zeit** f period of storage; (Dauer der Reifung) maturing period; beim Wein: auch ag(e)ing period

Lageskizze f sketch map

Lagune f; -, -n; Geol., Geog. lagoon

lahm Adj. **1.** lame; (steif) stiff; Med. (gelähmt) paraly|sed (Am. -zed); (verkrüppelt) crippled; **auf e-m Bein ~ sein** od. **ein ~es Bein haben** be lame in one leg; **~ legen** fig. paraly|se (Am. -ze), cripple; (Verkehr etc.) bring to a standstill (od. halt); Tech. (Gerät, Anlage) knock out; **2.** umg. (kraftlos) limp; fig. Ausrede etc.: lame, feeble; **3.** umg. fig. (träge) slow, sluggish; (langweilig) dull; Witz, Abenteuer etc.: tame, feeble; **~e Ente** Person: slowcoach, Am. slowpoke; (Wagen) feeble performer; **~er Verein** umg. useless bunch, hopeless lot

Lahmarsch m Sl. pej. drip, useless character; **diese Lahmärsche!** what a bunch of drips, what a bloody useless bunch; **komm, du ~!** come on, get off that butt of yours!; **lahmarschig** Adj. Sl. pej. hopelessly lethargic, utterly feeble

Lähme f; -, kein Pl.; Vet. lameness

lahmen v/i. Tier: be lame (**auf** + Dat. in)

lähmen v/t. paraly|se (Am. -ze) (auch fig.); fig. auch cripple; (Verkehr etc.) bring to a standstill (od. halt); → **gelähmt**; **lähmend** I. Part. Präs. → **lähmen**; II. Adj. paraly|sing (Am. -zing) (auch fig. Angst); Müdigkeit: crippling

Lahmheit f; nur Sg. **1.** lameness; (Steifheit) stiffness; Med. paralysis (Pl. paralyses); (Verkrüppeltsein) crippled state; **2.** umg. (Kraftlosigkeit) limpness; fig. von Ausrede etc.: lameness; **3.** umg. fig. (Trägheit) slowness, sluggishness; (Langweiligkeit) dullness; von Witz, Abenteuer etc.: tameness, feebleness

Lahmlegung f paraly|sing (Am. -zing), crippling

Lähmung f Med. paralysis (Pl. paralyses); fig. paraly|sing (Am. -zing); **einseitige/doppelseitige ~** paralysis on (od. down) one side/both sides of the body; fachspr. hemiplegia/paraplegia; **Lähmungserscheinung** f symptom of paralysis

Lahnung f low dam (for land reclamation in the Watt)

Laib m; -(e)s, -e loaf; **Laiberl** n österr. (bread) roll; **faschiertes ~** rissole

Laibung f Archit. inner face; vom Bogen: intrados

Laich m; -(e)s, -e; Zool. spawn; **laichen** v/i. spawn; **Laichplatz** m Zool. auch Pl. spawning ground

Laie m; -n, -n **1.** kirchl. layman; (Frau) laywoman; **die ~n** lay people, the laity Sg.; **2.** (Ggs. Fachmann) layman; **da bin ich absoluter ~** I don't know the first thing about it; **da staunt der ~ (und der Fachmann wundert sich)** umg. hum. that's unbelievable, the mind boggles

Laien|bruder m lay brother; **~bühne** f amateur theat|re (Am. auch -er) group; allg., auch Gebäude: amateur theat|re (Am. auch -er); **~chor** m am-

ateur choir; **~darsteller** m amateur actor; **~darstellerin** f amateur actress

laienhaft I. Adj. (Arbeit, Aufführung etc.) unprofessional; (stümperhaft) amateurish; (Urteil) layman's, inexpert; II. Adv. inexpertly; (stümperhaft) amateurishly; **~ ausgedrückt** (put) in layman's terms

Laien|kelch m kirchl. offering of the chalice to the laity; **~prediger** m, **~priester** m lay preacher; **~richter** m, **~richterin** f Jur. lay judge; **~schauspieler** m amateur actor; **~schauspielerin** f amateur actress; **~spiel** n Theat. **1.** nur Sg. amateur dramatics Sg.; **2.** Stück: play for amateurs; **~spielgruppe** f Theat. amateur theat|re (Am. auch -er) group; Verein: amateur dramatic society; **~sprache** f layman's language; **~stand** m; nur Sg.; kirchl. lay status; Koll. (Laien) laity; **e-n Priester in den ~ zurückversetzen** defrock a priest; **~theater** n amateur theat|re (Am. auch -er) group

Laientum n; -s, kein Pl. **1.** Koll. laity; **2.** (das Laiesein) lay status

Laienverstand m layman's way of thinking, lay mind; **das sagt mir schon mein ~** even I as a layman realize (od. know) that

laisieren v/t. kirchl. defrock

Laisser-faire [lese'fɛːr] n; -, kein Pl.; Wirts., geh. laisser-faire, laissez-faire

Laizismus m; -, kein Pl.; Pol. laicism; **laizistisch** Adj. laicist

Lakai m; -en, -en **1.** hist. lackey, footman; **2.** pej. lackey, minion; **lakaienhaft** Adj. pej. servile, cringing

Lake f; -, -n brine, pickle

Laken n; -s, - sheet

lakonisch I. Adj. laconic; II. Adv. laconically

Lakritz m, n; -es, -e; Dial., **Lakritze** f; -, -n liquorice

Laktation f; -, -en; Bio., Med. lactation

Laktose f; -, kein Pl.; Bio., Chem. lactose

lala Adj.; nur präd. und Adv. umg.: **so ~** so-so

lallen v/i. Baby: babble; Betrunkener: blabber; unverständlich: mumble

Lama¹ n; -s, -s; Zool. llama

Lama² m; -(s), -s Buddhismus: lama; **Lamaismus** m; -, kein Pl. Lamaism; **Lamakloster** n lamasery

Lamäng f: **aus der ~** umg. off the top of one's head, just like that

Lambdasonde f Mot. oxygen sensor, lambda probe

Lamé m; -(s), -s lamé

Lamelle f; -, -n **1.** Tech. lamella (Pl. lamellae); Etech. (commutator) segment; Mot., des Kühlers: fin, gill; Fot., der Blende: blade, leaf; **2.** e-r Jalousie: slat; **3.** Bot., der Pilze: gill; **lamellenförmig** Adj. lamellar

Lamellenverschluss m Fot. diaphragm shutter, bladed shutter

lamentieren v/i. umg. pej. complain, moan; **Lamento** n; -s, -s **1.** umg. pej. (Gejammer) howl of complaint; **ein großes ~ anstimmen** make (od. send up) a howl of complaint (über + Akk. about), kick up a great fuss (about) umg.; **2.** Mus. lament

Lametta n; -s, kein Pl. **1.** lametta; **2.** umg. fig. (Orden) fruit salad

Laminat n; -(e)s, -e; Tech. laminate

laminieren v/t. Tech. **1.** (Werkstoffe, Einbände) laminate; **2.** (Textilien) draw

Lamm n; -(e)s, Lämmer; Zool. lamb (auch fig.); **das ~ Gottes** the Lamb of

God, Agnus Dei; **~braten** *m Gastr.* roast lamb

Lämmchen *n* little lamb

lammen *v/i. Vet., Zool.* lamb

Lämmergeier *m Orn.* lammergeyer, bearded vulture

Lammfell *n* lambskin; **~jacke** *f* lambskin (*od.* sheepskin) jacket; **~mantel** *m* lambskin (*od.* sheepskin) coat

Lammfleisch *n* lamb

lammfromm *Adj. und Adv.* (as) meek as a lamb (*od.* lambs), like a little lamb (*od.* little lambs)

Lamm|keule *f Gastr.* leg of lamb; **~kotelett** *n* lamb chop

Lämmlein *n* little lamb

Lamm|rücken *m Gastr.* saddle of lamb; **~wolle** *f* lamb's wool

Lämpchen *n* (small) lamp

Lampe *f; -, -n* lamp; *weitS.* light; (*Glühlampe*) bulb

Lampen|fassung *f* bulb socket; **~fieber** *n* stage fright; *bei der Premiere: auch* first-night nerves *Pl.*; **~licht** *n* lamplight; **~schein** *m* lamplight, light of the lamp; **~schirm** *m* lampshade

Lampion [lam'pi̯oː] *m; -s, -s* Chinese lantern

lancieren [lãˈsiːrən] *v/t.* **1.** (*Produkt, Buch etc.*) launch; (*Nachricht*) put about, broadcast; *j-n ~* (pull strings to) get s.o. promoted (*in + Akk.* to); *etw. auf den Markt ~* put s.th. on the market; **2.** *Wirts.* (*Anleihe*) float; **Lancierung** *f* **1.** launch(ing); *von Nachricht:* broadcasting; *i-e ~ in den Vorstand* her elevation to the board; **2.** *Wirts., von Anleihen:* flotation

Land *n; -(e)s, Länder und -e* **1.** *nur Sg.*; (*Grund und Boden*) land; (*Ackerboden*) land, soil; *10 Hektar ~* 10 hectares of land; *das ~ bebauen* farm the land, till the soil *lit.*; **2.** *nur Sg.*; (*Ggs. Wasser*) land; *~ in Sicht Naut.* land ahead; *an ~* ashore; *an ~ gehen* go ashore, disembark; *etw. an ~ ziehen* land s.th., pull s.th. ashore; *umg. fig.* land o.s. s.th.; *wieder (festes) ~ unter den Füßen haben* be back on terra firma (*od.* dry land); *~ sehen* see land; (*wieder*) *~ sehen umg. fig.* see the light at the end of the tunnel; *ich sehe noch kein ~ fig.* there's no end in sight yet; *kein ~ mehr sehen fig.* be completely at sea, be floundering; → *unter* I 1; **3.** *nur Sg.*; (*Ggs. Stadt*) country; countryside; *auf dem ~* in the country; *aufs ~ fahren* go (*od.* drive) out into the country(side); *aufs ~ ziehen* move to the country(side); (*draußen*) *auf dem flachen od. platten ~ umg.* out in the sticks, in the middle of nowhere; **4.** *Pl. altm. od. hum. -e*; (*Gegend*) region; (*Landschaft*) country; *hügeliges ~* hilly (stretch of) country; *durch die ~e reisen* travel widely; *in deutschen ~en altm., hum.* in Germany; *ins ~ gehen od. ziehen fig. Zeit:* pass, elapse; **5.** *Pl. Länder*, *geographisch:* country; *politisch:* auch nation, state; *lit., fig.* land; (*Territorium, Lebensraum*) territory, land; *dieses Gebiet war das ~ der Apachen* this area was Apache territory (*od.* land); *das ~, wo Milch und Honig fließt hum.* the land of milk and honey; *das ~ m-er/s-er etc. Väter geh.* the land of my/his *etc.* fathers; *das ~ meiner Träume* the land of my dreams; *das ~ der unbegrenzten Möglichkeiten* the land of limitless opportunity; *das ~ der aufgehenden Sonne* the land of the rising sun; *das ~ der tausend Seen* the land of a thousand lakes; *andere Länder, andere Sitten Sprichw.* when in Rome, do as the Romans do; *~ und Leute kennen lernen* get to know the country and its people; *aus aller Herren Länder* from all four corners of the earth; *sich außer ~es befinden* be abroad; *wieder im ~e sein umg. fig.* be back again; (*unter den Leuten*) be back in circulation; *bist du wieder mal im ~e? umg. nach langer Abwesenheit:* returned from your wanderings, have you?, *iro.* hello (there), stranger!; *zu e-m Ausländer etc.:* come to see us again, have you?; *bei uns zu ~e* in our country, where we live; → *gelobt, heilig* 1; **6.** *Pl. Länder*; *Pol., innerhalb Deutschlands:* (federal) state, Land (*Pl. Länder*); *in Österreich:* province; *die Länder der Bundesrepublik Deutschland* the states (*od.* Länder) of the Federal Republic of Germany; *das ~ Bayern* the state of Bavaria; *das ~ Kärnten* the province of Carinthia

landab *Adv.* → *landauf*

Land|adel *m* (landed) gentry; **~ammann** *m schw.* head of a Swiss cantonal government; **~arbeit** *f* farming; **~arbeiter** *m*, **~arbeiterin** *f* farm worker; *besitzloser:* peasant

Landart ['lɛndʔɑːt] *f; -, kein Pl.; Kunst* Land Art

Land|arzt *m*, **~ärztin** *f* country doctor

landauf *Adv.: ~, landab* up and down the country

Landaufenthalt *m* stay in the country

landaus *Adv.: ~, landein* all over the place; *ziehen etc.:* from country to country

Land|bau *m; nur Sg.* agriculture, farming; **~besitz** *m* **1.** *Land:* landed property; *Jur.* real estate; **2.** *das Besitzen:* land ownership; **~besitzer** *m*, **~besitzerin** *f* landowner; **~bevölkerung** *f* rural population; **~bewohner** *m*, **~bewohnerin** *f* country dweller; *Pl. auch* country people, rustics *umg.*; **~brot** *n* farm bread; **~brücke** *f Geol.* land bridge; **~butter** *f* farm butter

Lande|anflug *m Flug.* landing approach (*auf + Akk.* to); **~bahn** *f Flug.* auf e-m Flugplatz: runway; *primitive:* landing strip; **~brücke** *f Naut.* landing stage, pier, jetty; **~erlaubnis** *f Flug.* landing clearance, permission to land; *~ erhalten* be given permission to land; **~fähre** *f Raumf.* lunar module

Landei *n* **1.** farm egg; **2.** *umg. hum.* country wench

landein *Adv.* → *landaus*

landeinwärts *Adv.* (further) inland

Lande|klappe *f Flug.* landing flap; **~kopf** *m Mil.* beachhead; **~manöver** *n* landing man|oeuvre (*Am.* -euver), approach

landen I. *v/i.* **1.** *Flug.* land, touch down; *Raumkapsel:* land; *im Wasser:* splash down; *fig. Mensch, auf dem Boden etc.:* land; **2.** *Schiff:* dock; (*sich ausschiffen*) disembark, go ashore; *umg.* (*ankommen*) arrive; **3.** *umg.* (*geraten*) land (up), end up, wind up; *im Graben ~ Fahrzeug:* end up in the ditch; *im Papierkorb ~ Briefe etc.:* be consigned to the wastepaper basket; *auf dem dritten Platz ~ Sport* come in third; *bei ihm kannst du* (*damit*) *nicht ~* you won't get (*od.* that won't get you) anywhere with him; **II.** *v/t.* **1.** (*Truppen etc.*) disembark; **2.** *e-n Schlag ~* land a blow; → *Coup*

Landen *n; -s, kein Pl.* landing; *beim ~* when (*od.* during) landing; *Vergangen-*

heit: as we *etc.* (*od.* the plane) landed

Landenge *f Geog.* isthmus

Lande|piste *f Flug.* landing strip; **~platz** *m* **1.** *Flug.* airstrip; **2.** *Naut.* landing place; *ausgebaut:* quay

Länderchefs *Pl. Pol.* (*die Ministerpräsidenten*) prime ministers of the Länder, *Am. etwa* state governors

Ländereien *Pl.* estates, landed property *Sg.*

Länder|kammer *f; nur Sg.; Pol.* (*der Bundesrat*) second chamber comprising representatives of the Länder; **~kampf** *m Sport* international competition; *Fußball etc.:* international match; **~kennzahl** *f Telef.* national (*od.* country) code; **~kunde** *f* regional geography; **~name** *m* name of a country; *Pl.* names of countries; **~parlamente** *Pl. Pol. innerhalb Deutschlands:* parliaments of the Länder, *Am. etwa* state legislatures; **~spiel** *n Sport* international match

länderübergreifend *Adj.* **1.** *in der BRD:* at federal level; **2.** (*international*) at international level

Landes|amt *n Pol. innerhalb e-s Bundeslandes:* Land office; *das ~ für Denkmalpflege* the Land Bureau for the Conservation of Historic Monuments; **~bank** *f Fin.* regional bank; **~behörde** *f* Land (*od.* regional) authority; **~bischof** *m*, **~bischöfin** *f ev.* bishop of a Landeskirche, Land bishop

Lande|scheinwerfer *m Flug.* landing light; **~schleife** *f Flug.* circuit; **~n ziehen** be in a holding pattern, be circling (above an *od.* the airport)

Landesebene *f: auf ~* on a regional level; *BRD:* at Land level

Landes|erzeugnis *n* domestic product; *Pl. auch* home produce *Sg.*; **~farben** *Pl.* national colo(u)rs; *e-s Bundeslandes:* state colours; **~flagge** *f* national flag; *e-s Bundeslandes:* state flag; **~fürst** *m* sovereign prince; **~fürstin** *f* sovereign princess; **~gebiet** *n* national territory; **~gericht** *n österr., Jur.* Provincial Court; **~geschichte** *f* regional history; **~gesetz** *n Pol.* Land law; **~grenze** *f* national (*e-s Bundeslandes:* state) frontier (*od.* border); **~gruppe** *f Parl.* regional parliamentary party group (*from a particular Land*); **~hauptfrau** *f*, **~hauptmann** *m österr., Pol.* head of a (*od.* the) provincial government; **~hauptstadt** *f* capital; *e-s Bundeslandes:* Land (*od.* state) capital; *in Österreich:* provincial capital

Landesherr *m*, **~in** *f hist.* sovereign, monarch

Landes|hoheit *f* sovereignty; **~hymne** *f* national anthem; *e-s Bundeslandes: BRD:* Land (*od.* state) anthem; *Österreich:* provincial anthem, *Am. etwa* state song; **~innere** *n* interior (of the country); **~kind** *n*; *mst Pl.* citizen (of the country), native; **~kirche** *f* national church; *evangelische:* regional (*mst* Land) church

Landeskunde *f* cultural studies *Pl.*; *britische/amerikanische ~* British/ American studies *Pl.*; **landeskundig** *Adj.* knowledgeable about a (*od.* the) country

Landes|liste *f Pol.* party's list of parliamentary candidates for a particular Land; **~meister** *m*, **~meisterin** *f Sport* national champion; **~meisterschaft** *f Sport* national championship; **~minister** *m*, **~ministerin** *f Pol.* Land minister; **~mittel** *Pl. Pol.* Land funds; **~mutter** *f* 1. *hist., auch hum.* sovereign lady, mother of the nation; 2. *Bundesland*: wife of the prime minister (*österr.* Landeshauptmann); **~natur** *f* character of a (*od.* the) country; **~parlament** *n Pol.* Land Parliament; **~parteitag** *m* regional party conference; **~planung** *f Pol., Wirts.* regional planning

Landespolitik *f* state (*od.* regional) politics *Pl.*; **landespolitisch** *Adj.* relating to regional (*od.* provincial) politics

Landes|produkt *n* → *Landeserzeugnis*; **~rat** *m*, **~rätin** *f österr.* member of a (*od.* the) provincial government; **~recht** *n Pol., BRD*: Land law; *Österreich*: provincial law; **~regierung** *f BRD*: Land government; *in Österreich*: provincial government; **~rekord** *m Sport* national record; **~schulrat** *m österr.* (*oberste Schulbehörde e-s Bundeslandes*) education authority (of a/the federal state), *Am.* state school board; **~sitte** *f* national custom; **~sprache** *f* (national) language, language of a (*od.* the) country; *offizielle*: official language

Landesteg *m Naut.* landing stage

Landes|theater *n* Landestheater, *BRD*: the Land's (*Österreich*: the province's) main theat|re (*Am. auch* -er); **~tracht** *f* national costume; *regional*: regional costume

landes|üblich *Adj.* customary (in a *od.* in the country); **~typisch** *Adj.* typical (for a *od.* for the country)

Landes|vater *m* 1. *hist, auch hum.* sovereign lord, father of the nation; 2. *Bundesland*: prime minister, *österr.* Landeshauptmann; **~verrat** *m* treason; **~verräter** *m*, **~verräterin** *f* traitor; **~versicherungsanstalt** *f* (*abgek.* **LVA**) *etwa* National Insurance Authority; **~verteidigung** *f* national defen|ce (*Am.* -se); **~verweis** *m schw.*, **~verweisung** *f österr., schw.* expulsion (from the country); **~währung** *f* national (*od.* local) currency

landesweit *Adj.* nationwide

Landeszentralbank *f* (*abgek.* **LZB**) Land (*od.* Regional, State) Central Bank

Lande|trupp *m Mil.* landing party; **~verbot** *n Flug.*: *e-r Maschine ~ erteilen* refuse an aircraft permission to land; *wegen starken Nebels herrschte am Flughafen ~* the airport was closed due to thick fog; **~zeit** *f Flug.* landing time; *Raumkapsel im Wasser: auch* splashdown time

Landfahrer *m*, **~in** *f Jur.* vagrant

landfein *Adj.*: *sich ~ machen Naut., auch umg. hum.* get spruced up (for going ashore)

Landflucht *f* rural exodus, drift to the cities; **Landfrau** *f* countrywoman

landfremd *Adj.* foreign

Landfriede(n) *m hist.* King's peace; **Landfriedensbruch** *m Jur.* breach of the peace

Landfunk *m Funk.* farming program(me)

Landgang *m Naut.* shore leave

Landgericht *n Jur.* Land (*od.* regional) court

landgestützt *Adj.*: *~e Rakete* land-based missile

Land|gewinnung *f* land reclamation; **~gut** *n* country estate; **~haus** *n* country house, *kleines*: cottage; **~jäger** *m*; *mst. Pl.*; *Gastr.* small flat sausage con-

taining highly seasoned, well smoked meat; **~jugend** *f* young rural population, rural youth; **~karte** *f* map; **~kreis** *m* rural district

landläufig I. *Adj.* (*üblich*) current, common; (*Ansicht etc.*) generally accepted; (*volkstümlich*) popular; *im ~en Sinn* in the generally accepted (*od.* conventional) sense (of the word); *der ~en Meinung nach* according to popular opinion (*od.* belief), as conventional wisdom has it; *entgegen ~er Meinung* contrary to popular opinion (*od.* belief); II. *Adv.* commonly, in popular usage; *~ verbreitete Meinung* commonly held opinion

Ländle *n*; *-s, kein Pl.*: *das ~ in BRD*: Swabia; *in Österreich*: Vorarlberg

Landleben *n*; *nur Sg.* country life, life in the country

Ländler *m*; *-s, -; Mus.* ländler, country waltz

Landleute *Pl.* country people, rustics *umg.*

ländlich *Adj.* 1. rural, country …; 2. (*einfach, bäuerlich*) rustic

Land|luft *f* country air; **~macht** *f* country with powerful land forces; **~mann** *m altm.* peasant; **~marke** *f* landmark; **~maschine** *f* piece of agricultural machinery, farm machine; **~n** *Pl.* agricultural machinery *Sg.*, farming equipment *Sg.*; **~masse** *f* landmass; **~mine** *f* landmine; **~nahme** *f*; *-, nur Sg.* (conquest and) settlement of land; **~partie** *f altm.* country outing (*mst* picnic); **~pfarrer** *m* country parson; **~plage** *f* 1. serious plague, scourge; 2. *umg. iro.* nuisance, pest; **~pomeranze** *f umg. iro., auch pej.* country miss

Landrat *m* 1. district administrator; 2. *schw. in einigen Kantonen*: cantonal parliament; 3. *schw. in einigen Kantonen*: member of the (*od.* a) cantonal parliament

Landrätin *f* 1. district administrator; 2. *schw. in einigen Kantonen*: member of the (*od.* a) cantonal parliament

Landratsamt *n* district administration

Land|ratte *f umg.* landlubber; **~regen** *m* continuous steady rainfall; **~rücken** *m* ridge of land

Landschaft *f* 1. scenery; *aus der Ferne gesehen, auch Geol.*: landscape; *Geog.* topography; (*das Land*) countryside; *fig., politische etc.*: scene, landscape; *das passt nicht in die ~ umg. fig.* it doesn't fit into the general scheme of things; 2. *Gemälde*: landscape; 3. (*Gegend*) region

landschaftlich I. *Adj.* 1. (*Schönheit etc.*) scenic; *~e Unterschiede* differences in the landscape; *Geog.* topographical variation; 2. *Wort, Aussprache, Brauch etc.*: regional; II. *Adv.*: *e-e ~ sehr schöne Gegend* an area with beautiful scenery, a scenically beautiful area; *dort ist es ~ sehr schön auch* the countryside around there is really beautiful; *~ schöne Strecke* scenic route

Landschafts|architekt *m*, **~architektin** *f* landscape architect; **~bild** *n* 1. *Kunst, Gemälde*: landscape (painting), *Zeichnung*: landscape (drawing), *Foto*: landscape photograph; 2. *An-*

blick: (piece of) scenery; *dieser Betonklotz passt überhaupt nicht ins ~* this concrete monstrosity is completely out of character with its surroundings (*stärker*: is a blot on the landscape); **~gärtner** *m*, **~gärtnerin** *f* landscape gardener; **~maler** *m*, **~malerin** *f* landscape painter (*od.* artist); **~malerei** *f* landscape painting; **~pflege** *f*, **~schutz** *m* landscape conservation, conservation of the countryside; **~schutzgebiet** *n* landscape conservation area, nature reserve

Land|schildkröte *f Zool.* (land) tortoise; **~schulheim** *n* school's field cent|re (*Am.* -er) *in the country*

Landsitz *m* country seat

Landsknecht *m hist.* lansquenet; (*Söldner*) mercenary

Landsmann *m* (fellow) countryman, compatriot; *was sind Sie für ein ~?* where (*od.* which part of the world, *altm. in Deutschland auch*: what part of Germany) do you come from?; **Landsmännin** *f* (fellow) countrywoman, compatriot; **Landsmannschaft** *f* homeland association (*for refugees from one of Germany's former eastern territories*)

Land|spitze *f* point, promontory, headland; **~straße** *f* (*nicht Autobahn*) (ordinary) main road; *auf dem Lande*: country road; *wir sind über die ~ gefahren auch* we took the (ordinary) cross-country road

Landstreicher *m* vagrant, tramp; **Landstreicherei** *f*; *-, kein Pl.*; *Jur.* vagrancy; **Landstreicherin** *f* vagrant, tramp

Land|streitkräfte *Pl.* land forces; (*Ggs. Flug.*) ground forces; **~strich** *m* region, area; *offener*: tract of land

Landtag *m Pol. BRD*: Land (*od.* state) parliament, Landtag; *Österreich*: provincial parliament (*jeweils auch Gebäude*)

Landtags|abgeordnete *m, f*; *-n, -n*; *Pol. BRD*: member of the Land (*od.* state) parliament (*Österreich*: the provincial parliament); **~fraktion** *f* party group in the Land (*od.* state) parliament (*Österreich*: the provincial parliament); **~präsident** *m*, **~präsidentin** *f* president of the Land (*od.* state) parliament (*Österreich*: the provincial parliament); **~wahl** *f* elections *Pl.* for the Land (*od.* state) parliament (*Österreich*: the provincial parliament)

Land|tier *n* terrestrial animal; **~transport** *m* overland transport; **~truppen** *Pl. Mil.* land forces; (*Ggs. Flug.*) ground troops

Landung *f* landing; (*Ausschiffung*) disembarkation; *zur ~ ansetzen Flug.* come in to land; *zur ~ zwingen Flug.* force down

Landungs|boot *n Mil.* landing craft; **~brücke** *f*, **~steg** *m Naut.* landing stage, jetty; **~trupp** *m Mil.* landing party; **~truppen** *Pl. Mil.* landing force *Sg.*

Land|urlaub *m Naut.* shore leave; **~vermesser** *m*, **~vermesserin** *f* (land) surveyor; **~vermessung** *f* (land) surveying; **~volk** *n*; *nur Sg.* country people *Pl.*, rustics *umg. Pl.*; *das ~ auch* the rural population

landwärts *Adv.* landward(s)

Land|weg *m* 1. country lane; (*Feldweg*) track; 2. *Route*: overland route; *auf dem ~* by land, overland; **~wehr** *f hist.* territorial reserve; **~wein** *m* vin ordinaire, table wine; **~wind** *m* offshore wind

Landwirt *m*, **~in** *f* farmer; **Landwirt-schaft** *f* **1.** agriculture, farming; **2.** (*Anwesen*) (small) farm, smallhold-ing; **landwirtschaftlich I.** *Adj.* agri-cultural; **~er Betrieb** farm; **~e Maschi-nen** agricultural machinery *Sg.*, farm equipment *Sg.*; **II.** *Adv.*: **~ genutzte Flächen** areas in agricultural use

Landwirtschafts|... *im Subst.* agricul-tural; **~ausstellung** *f* agricultural ex-hibition (*od.* show); **~minister** *m*, **~ministerin** *f* minister (*Am.* secretary) of agriculture; **~ministerium** *n* minis-try (*od.* department) of agriculture; **~politik** *f* agricultural policy; **~schule** *f* agricultural college; **~woche** *f* agri-cultural show

Landzunge *f* promontory

lang¹; *länger, am längsten* **I.** *Adj.* **1.** *räumlich*: long; *Mensch*: tall; *ein Hemd mit ~en Ärmeln* a long-sleeved shirt; *e-n Rock länger machen* length-en (*od.* let down) a skirt; *zehn Meter ~ und vier Meter breit* ten met|res (*Am.* -res) (long) by four (other); *e-e 20 cm lange Kette* a chain 20 cm long (*od.* in length); *sie sind gleich ~* they're the same length; *e-n ~en Hals machen* umg. crane one's neck, *Am.* rubberneck; *sich des Langen und Breiten über etw. auslassen* fig. expa-tiate at great length on s.th., go on and on about s.th.; → *Bank¹* 1, *Ge-sicht¹* 2; **2.** *zeitlich*: long; **~e Jahre** for years; *seit ~em* for a long time; *vor nicht allzu ~er Zeit* not so long ago; *in nicht allzu ~er Zeit* before long; *mir wird die Zeit ~* the days are beginning to drag; *das wird e-e ~e Nacht* it's go-ing to be a long night; *die Tage wer-den länger* the days are getting longer (*od.* drawing in); **3.** *zur Angabe der Dauer*: lasting; *e-e drei Wochen ~e Reise* a trip lasting three weeks, a three-week trip; **II.** *Adv.* **1.** *räumlich*: *das Haar ~ tragen* wear one's hair long; *~ gestreckt* extended; *Form*: elongated; *Gebäude*: long; *auch Mensch*: stretched out; *Gebirgszug etc.*: stretching for miles; *~ und breit* fig. at great length; **2.** *zeitlich*: for a long time; *mit P.P.*: long-...; *~ anhal-tend* prolonged, long-lasting; *~ ent-behrt od. vermisst* sorely missed; *~ er-hofft* long-hoped-for; *~ ersehnt od. er-wartet* long-awaited; *~ gehegt* Hoff-nung etc.: long-cherished (*od.* -nourish-hed); *~ gezogen* Ton etc.: long-drawn--out; **3.** *nachgestellt, zur Angabe der Dauer*: for; *drei Jahre ~* for three years; *die ganze Woche ~* all week long, (for) the whole week; *e-e Sekun-de etc. ~* for a second etc.; **4.** umg. → *lange*; → *dauern¹, kurz* II 2, *länger, längst, Leitung* 2, *Lulatsch etc.*

lang² Dial. **I.** *Präp.* (entlang) along; *die Straße ~* along (*od.* down) the street; **II.** *Adv.*: *wir müssen hier ~* we must go along here (*od.* this way)

lang|ärm(e)lig *Adj.* long-sleeved; **~at-mig** *Adj.* long-winded; *Schriftliches*: *auch* wordy; **~beinig** *Adj.* long-legged, umg. leggy

lange *Adv.* **1.** *zeitlich*: for a long time; *nicht ~ danach* not long after-(ward[s]); *er braucht immer ~* it always takes him a while; *pej.* he's very slow; *das ist schon ~ her* that was a long time ago; *es ist schon ~ her, dass* it's been a long time since, it's ages since umg.; *wie ~ lernen Sie schon Eng-lisch?* how long have you been learn-

ing English?; *so ~ wie* as long as; *so ~ bis* till, until; *da kannst du ~ warten* umg. you can wait till the cows come home; *du brauchst nicht ~ zu fragen* you don't need to ask; *er fragte nicht erst ~* he didn't stop to ask; **2.** *verstär-kend*: *~ nicht* (bei weitem nicht) not nearly ...; umg. not by a long chalk (*Am.* shot), nowhere near ...; **(noch) ~ nicht fertig / gut genug** etc. not nearly ready / good enough etc.; *ist er fertig? - noch ~ nicht* umg. has he finished? - nowhere near (*od.* nothing like, iro. you must be joking); *das ist noch ~ kein Grund, um aufzugeben* that's ab-solutely no reason for giving up, that certainly doesn't mean you've got to give up; *deswegen brauchst du dir noch ~ nichts einzubilden* you mustn't go getting any ideas just because of that, don't imagine that's anything at all special

Länge *f*, -, *-n* **1.** length (*auch zeitlich*); (*Größe*) height; *20 Meter in der ~ od. mit e-r ~ von 20 Metern* 20 met|res (*Am.* -ers) (*od.* in length), with a length of 20 met|res (*Am.* -ers); *der ~ nach* lengthwise; *der ~ nach hinfallen* fall flat on one's face, go sprawling; *in s-r vollen ~ senden* etc. broadcast etc. in full; *in die ~ ziehen* fig. draw (*od.* drag) out; (*Erzählung*) spin out; *sich in die ~ ziehen* drag on; **2.** *Sport* length; *mit einer ~ gewinnen* win by a length; *um ~n gewinnen* win by a mile; *um ~n geschlagen werden* be beaten out of sight; **3.** (*langweilige Stelle*) longueur; *der Film hatte ~n* the film (*Am* auch movie) had its dull patches; **4.** *Ling.* long vowel; *Metrik*: long syllable; **5.** *Geog., Astron., Math.* longitude; *auf od. unter 10 Grad west-licher ~ liegen* have a longitude of 10 degrees West, lie at 10 degrees West longitude

längelang *Adv.* umg.: *~ hinfallen* go sprawling (*od.* flying)

langen umg. **I.** *v/i.* **1.** (ausreichen) be enough (*für* for); *das langt uns für die nächsten Tage* auch that'll last us for the next few days; *langt das?* is that enough?, will that do?; *mir langt's* I've had enough; *jetzt langt's mir aber!* I've had enough of this (busi-ness), that's it umg.; **2.** (auskommen) *damit lange ich e-e Woche* that'll last me a week; **3.** *~ nach* reach for, *~ in* (+ Akk.) reach into; **4.** *~ bis räumlich*: reach to (*od.* as far as); **II.** *v/t.*: *j-m etw. ~* (reichen) hand s.o. s.th.; *j-m e-e ~* (*j-n ohrfeigen*) give s.o. a clout

Längen|einheit *f* unit of length; **~grad** *m* Geogr. degree of longitude; **~kreis** *m* Geogr. meridian; **~maß** *n* linear measure; *Einheit*: unit of length; **~wachstum** *n* Bio. linear growth

länger I. *Adj.* **1.** (*Komp. von lang*) longer; *je ~, je lieber* the longer, the better; *~ machen* make s.th. longer, lengthen; (*Kleid etc.*) auch let down; **2.** (ziemlich lang) fairly long; *~e Zeit* auch (for) quite a while, (for [quite]) some time; *über ~e Zeiträume* for (*od.* over) prolonged periods; **II.** *Adv.* long-er; *es wird etwas ~ dauern* it'll take a little longer; *ich kann es nicht ~ ertra-gen* I can't stand (*od.* take) it any longer

längerfristig I. *Adj.* long(er)-term, for the long(er) term; **II.** *Adv.* planen etc.: for the long(er) term, for the future; anlegen etc.: on a long(er)-term basis; *~ gesehen* taking the longer-term

view

Langerhans-Inseln *Pl.* Med. islets of Langerhans

Langeweile *f*, -, *kein Pl.* boredom; *aus od. vor ~* out of (sheer) boredom; *~ haben* be (*od.* feel) bored; *länger*: suf-fer from boredom; *sich* (*Dat.*) *die ~ vertreiben* while away the time

Langfinger *m* umg. thief; (*Taschen-dieb*) pickpocket; **langfing(e)rig** *Adj.* long-fingered; umg. fig. (diebisch) light-fingered

langfristig I. *Adj.* long-term; **~er Wechsel** Wirts. long(-dated) bill; **II.** *Adv.* in the long term; *~ gesehen* taking the long(-term) view; *~ inves-tieren* etc. invest etc. long term

langgehen *v/i.* (unreg., trennb., ist -ge-); umg. **1.** → *entlanggehen*; **2.** fig.: *wissen, wo's langgeht* know what's what; *j-m zeigen, wo's langgeht* show s.o. what's what, tell s.o. a few home truths

Langhaar|dackel *m* long-haired dachs-hund; **~frisur** *f* long hairstyle; *e-e ~ haben* wear one's hair long

langhaarig *Adj.* long-haired

Langhaarkatze *f* long-haired cat

langhalsig *Adj.* long-necked

Lang|haus *n* **1.** Archit. nave and side aisles; *ohne Seitenschiffe*: nave; **2.** hist., *der Indianer*: longhouse; **~holz** *n*; *nur Sg.* long timber

langjährig *Adj.* longstanding; **~e Frei-heitsstrafe** long prison sentence; **~e Erfahrung** (many) years of experience

Langkornreis *m* long-grain rice

Langlauf *m*; *nur Sg.*: *Sport* cross-coun-try skiing; **Langläufer** *m*, **Langläufe-rin** *f* cross-country skier

Langlauf|loipe *f* Ski: cross-country trail (*od.* course); **~schuhe** *Pl.* Sport cross-country skiing boots; **~ski** *m* cross-country ski

langlebig *Adj.* long-lived (*auch Tech. und fig.*); Wirts. durable; *Erscheinung etc.*: lasting, long-lived; *es war ~* it lasted (*od.* was around) for a long time; **~e Verbrauchsgüter** consumer durables; **Langlebigkeit** *f*; *nur Sg.* longevity; Wirts. durability

langlegen *v/refl.* (trennb., hat -ge-); umg. have a lie-down (*Am.* a rest), stretch out (on the bed *od.* couch etc.)

langliegen *v/i.* (unreg., trennb., hat /südd., österr. schw. ist -ge-); umg. be having a lie-down (*Am.* a rest)

länglich *Adj.* long; *Kasten etc.*: oblong; *~ rund* oval

langmähnig *Adj.* Tier: long-maned; umg. (langhaarig) long-haired

Langmut *f*; -, *kein Pl.* patience, for-bearance; **langmütig I.** *Adj.* patient, longsuffering; **II.** *Adv.* patiently; **Langmütigkeit** *f* geh. → *Langmut*

langnasig *Adj.* long-nosed

Langobarde *m*; -n, -n, **Langobardin** *f*; -, *-nen*; hist. Lombard; **langobardisch** *Adj.* Lombard

Langohr *n* umg., Kindersprache: (Ha-se) Mister Hare; (Kaninchen) bunny rabbit; (Esel) Neddy

längs I. *Präp.* along(side); *die Bäume ~ der Straße* the trees lining the road; **II.** *Adv.* longwise; *~ gestreift* Kleid: with vertical stripes; *~ gerichtet* longi-tudinal

Längsachse *f* longitudinal axis

langsam I. *Adj.* **1.** slow; (allmählich) gradual; *~er werden* get slower; Fahr-zeug: slow down; *bei der Arbeit etc.*: auch let up; *geht's noch ~er?* umg. iro. can't you make it any slower?;

L

2. (*träge*) sluggish; (*schwerfällig*) heavy, plodding; **3.** *geistig*: slow-witted; **er ist ein bisschen ~** he's a bit slow on the uptake; **4.** (*Sport*) *Platz, Bahn etc.*: slow; **II.** *Adv.* slowly; (*allmählich*) gradually; **~, aber sicher** slowly but surely; **~, aber sicher nähern wir uns dem Ziel** we're getting there (slowly but surely); **immer ~!** not so fast, easy does it *umg.*; **~ fahren!** *Mot., Schild*: slow; **es wird ~ Zeit, dass er anruft** it's about time he rang up (*Am.* called); **es wird ~ Zeit, dass du gehst** you'd better be thinking about going; **es wird mir ~ zu viel** it's gradually getting too much for me, it's beginning to get on top of me; **~/~er treten** *umg. fig.* take things easy / more easily, slow down; **Langsamkeit** *f; nur Sg.* **1.** slowness; **2.** (*Trägheit*) sluggishness; *geistig*: slow-wittedness

Längsbalken *m* longitudinal beam, stringer (*Am. auch* string)

Lang|schiff *n Archit., e-r Kirche*: nave; **~schläfer** *m*, **~schläferin** *f* late riser; **~seite** *f Archit.* long side

Langspielplatte *f* (*abgek.* **LP**) long-playing record, LP

Längs|richtung *f* longitudinal direction; **in** (*der*) **~** lengthways, lengthwise; **~schnitt** *m* longitudinal section; (*Bauzeichnung*) sectional elevation; **~seite** *f* long side

längsseits *Adv. und Präp.* (+ *Gen.*) alongside

Längsstreifen *m* lengthways (*od.* longitudinal) stripe

längst *Adv.* **1.** (*seit langem*) long ago, long since; **ich weiß es ~** I've known that for a long time; **das solltest du ~ wissen** you really ought to know that by now; **er sollte ~ hier sein** he should have been here long ago; **das ist ~ vorbei/vergessen** that's long past/forgotten; **als ich ankam, war er ~ weg** when I arrived he had long since left; **2. ~ nicht** (*bei weitem nicht*) not nearly ..., *umg.* not by a long chalk (*Am.* shot), nowhere near ...; **das ist ~ nicht so gut** that's not nearly (*od.* nowhere near) as good; **er ist ~ nicht fertig** he hasn't nearly finished (yet), *umg.* he's nowhere near finished (yet), he's still got a long way to go; **3. am ~en** longest

längstens *Adv.* (*höchstens*) at (the) most; (*spätestens*) at the latest

langstielig *Adj. Werkzeug*: long-handled; *Bot.* long-stemmed (*auch Glas*)

Langstrecke *f* long distance

Langstrecken|flug *m* long-haul flight; **~flugzeug** *n* long-haul aircraft; **~lauf** *m* (long-)distance run *od.* race; **~läufer** *m*, **~läuferin** *f* (long-)distance runner; **~rakete** *f* long-range missile; **~schwimmer** *m*, **~schwimmerin** *f* long-distance swimmer

Languste *f; -, -n; Zool.* spiny (*od.* rock) lobster

Langweile *f* → **Langeweile**

langweilen (*untr., hat*) **I.** *v/t.* bore (*zu Tode* to death, to tears, stiff); **II.** *v/refl.* be (*od.* feel) bored; **sich zu Tode ~** be bored to death (*od.* to tears, stiff, out of one's mind); **Langweiler** *m; -s, -*, **Langweilerin** *f; -, -nen; umg.* **1.** bore, boring type; **2.** (*langsamer Mensch*) slowcoach, *Am.* slowpoke; **langweilig** *Adj.* **1.** boring, tedious; (*eintönig: Leben etc.*) humdrum; **es war mir sehr ~** I found it very boring, I was very bored; **~er Verein** *umg.* dull (*od.* boring) lot; **es war so was von ~** *umg.* it

was an absolute (*od.* a crushing, *Am.* crashing) bore; **2.** *umg.* (*langsam, Zeit raubend*) slow; **e-e ~e Sache** a tedious business, a drag; **~er Betrieb** dozy outfit; **nicht so ~!** get a move on!; **Langweiligkeit** *f; nur Sg.* tediousness, tedium

Langwelle *f Radio*: long wave

Langwellen|bereich *m* long-wave band; **~sender** *m* long-wave radio station (*od.* transmitter)

langwierig *Adj.* lengthy, prolonged, protracted; (*Prozess, Vorgang*) *auch* long-drawn-out; (*mühselig*) laborious; **es war e-e ~e Sache** *auch* it dragged on for a long time; **Langwierigkeit** *f; nur Sg.* lengthiness, protracted nature; **mit der ~ dieses Prozesses hat niemand gerechnet** no one expected this trial to be so protracted (*od.* would go on forever *umg.*)

Langzeit|arbeitslose *m, f* long-term unemployed person; *Pl.* the long-term unemployed; **~arbeitslosigkeit** *f* long-term unemployment; **~EKG** *n Med.* long-term ECG (*Am.* EKG); **~gedächtnis** *n* long-term memory; **~prognose** *f* long-term (*od.* long-range) forecast; **~programm** *n* long-term program(me); **~studie** *f* long-term study; **~therapie** *f Med.* long-term therapy; **~untersuchung** *f* long-term study; **~versuch** *m* long-term trial; **~wirkung** *f* long-term effect(s *Pl.*)

Lanolin *n; -(s), kein Pl.* lanolin

Lanze *f; -, -n* lance; (*zum Werfen*) spear; **e-e ~ brechen für** *fig.* take up the cudgels for

Lanzen|spitze *f* lancehead; *e-r Wurflanze*: spearhead; **~stechen** *n hist.* joust(ing); **~stoß** *m* lance thrust; *der Wurflanze*: spear thrust

Lanzette *f; -, -n; Med.* lancet

Lanzettfischchen *n Zool.* lancelet

La-Ola-Welle *f Sport* Mexican wave

Laos (*n*); *-; Geog.* Laos; **Laote** *m; -n, -n*, **Laotin** *f; -, -nen* Laotian, *weiblich auch* Laotian woman (*od.* girl); **Laote** *od.* **Laotin sein** *auch* come from Laos; **laotisch** *Adj.* Laotian, from Laos

lapidar *Adj.* terse, succinct

Lapislazuli *m; -, -; Min.* lapis lazuli

Lappalie *f; -, -n* trivial matter, trifle

Lappen *m; -s, -* **1.** (*zum Putzen*) cloth; (*Fetzen*) rag; (*Waschlappen*) flannel, *Am.* washcloth; *umg. fig.* (*Kleid etc.*) rag; *Sl.* (*Geldschein*) note, *Am.* bill; **j-m durch die ~ gehen** *umg. fig. Person*: give s.o. the slip, *Person, Sache*: slip through s.o.'s fingers; **2.** *Anat., Bot.* lobe; **3.** *Med.* (*Stück Haut*) flap; **4.** *Zool., des Hahns*: wattle

läppern *v/refl. umg.*: **es** *od.* **das läppert sich** it all adds up

lappig *Adj.* **1.** (*schlaff*) limp; *Haut*: flabby; **2.** *Anat., Bot.* lobed

Lappin *f; -, -nen* Sami woman (*od.* girl); *neg!* Lapp woman (*od.* girl)

läppisch *Adj.* silly; (*lächerlich*) ridiculous; **wegen ~er zehn Euro regt er sich auf** *umg.* he makes a fuss about a measly ten euros

Lappland (*n*); *-s; Geog.* Lapland; **Lappländer** *m; -s, -*, **Lappländerin** *f; -, -nen* Sami, *weiblich auch*: Sami woman (*od.* girl); *neg!* Laplander, *weiblich auch*: Lapp woman (*od.* girl); **lappländisch** *Adj.* Sami; *neg!* Lapp, from Lapland

Lapsus *m; -, -; geh.* slip; *in Gesellschaft*: faux pas; **e-n ~ begehen** make

a slip; commit a faux pas; **mir ist ein ~ unterlaufen** I slipped up (there)

Laptop ['lɛptɔp] *m; -s, -s; EDV* laptop

Lärche *f; -, -n; Bot.* larch

large [larʒ] *Adj. schw.* (*großzügig*) generous; (*nachsichtig*) lenient

Largo *n; -(s), -s und Larghi; Mus.* largo

larifari *Interj. umg.* rubbish; **Larifari** *n; -s, kein Pl.; umg.* nonsense, rubbish

Lärm *m; -(e)s, kein Pl.* noise; (*Radau*) racket, din; **macht nicht so e-n ~** *auch* keep the noise down; **bei dem ~ kann ich nicht schlafen** I can't sleep with all this noise (going on); **~ am Arbeitsplatz** workplace noise; **viel ~ um nichts** *fig.* a lot of fuss (*lit.* much ado) about nothing; **viel ~ um nichts machen** *fig.* make a lot of fuss (*od.* a big to-do) about nothing, make a big thing out of nothing (*od.* a mountain out of a molehill); **~ schlagen** make a racket (*od.* din); *fig.* make a lot of noise, kick up a fuss; **~bekämpfung** *f* noise abatement (*od.* control); **~belästigung** *f* noise pollution, noise nuisance; **~belastung** *f* noise pollution

lärmempfindlich *Adj.* sensitive to noise; **sie ist sehr ~** *auch* she's got very sensitive ears (*od.* hearing)

lärmen *v/i.* make a (lot of) noise; *Radio, Musik*: blare (away); **lärmend I.** *Part. Präs.* → **lärmen**; **II.** *Adj.* noisy

lärmgeplagt *Adj.* plagued by noise

lärmig *Adj. altm., schw.* noisy

larmoyant [larmoa'jant] *Adj.* maudlin, mawkish; (*auch Stimme, Ton*) lachrymose; (*Stil*) *auch* tear-jerking; **Larmoyanz** *f; -, kein Pl.* maudlin (*od.* mawkish) nature; *Ton*: lachrymose tone

Lärm|pegel *m* noise level; **~quelle** *f* noise source

Lärmschutz *m* noise protection; **~wall** *m*, **~wand** *f* noise barrier, acoustic insulation

Larve *f; -, -n* **1.** *Zool.* larva (*Pl.* larvae); **2.** *altm.* (*Maske*) mask; *fig. pej.* (*Gesicht*) face

las *Imperf.* → **lesen**[1], **lesen**[2]

Lasagne [la'zanjə] *Pl., umg. auch f; -, -; Gastr.* lasagne

lasch *Adj.* **1.** (*schlaff*) limp; (*lässig, disziplinlos*) slack, lax; *Maßnahme*: inadequate, feeble; **~e Anschauungen haben** *fig.* have woolly ideas; **~er Typ** *umg.* lethargic type, wimp; **2.** *Dial. Essen*: tasteless, insipid

Lasche *f; -, -n* strap; *im Schuh*: tongue; (*Schlaufe*) loop; *am Umschlag*: flap; *Tech.* butt strap; *Eisenb., an Schienen*: fishplate

Laschheit *f* (*Schlaffheit*) limpness; (*Lässigkeit*) slackness, laxness; *von Maßnahmen*: inadequacy, feebleness; *e-s Menschen*: lethargy

Laser ['le:zɐ] *m; -s, -; Phys.* laser; **~abtastung** *f* laser scanning; **~chirurgie** *f* laser surgery; **~drucker** *m EDV* laser printer

lasern ['le:zɐn] *vt/i. Med.* treat with laser beams

Laser|pistole *f* laser gun; **~strahl** *m* laser beam; **~technik** *f* laser technology

lasieren *v/t.* (*Bild*) glaze; (*Holz*) varnish; **Lasierung** *f* glazing; (*Lasur*) glaze; *von Holz*: varnish(ing)

Läsion *f; -, -en; Med.* lesion

Lassafieber *n Med.* Lassa fever

lassen I. *Modalv.; lässt, ließ, hat lassen* **1.** (*erlauben, zulassen*) let; **j-n gehen/schlafen etc. ~** let s.o. go/sleep etc.; **fallen ~** drop (*auch fig.: Bemerkung, j-n*); **sehen ~** show; **das Licht brennen ~**

leave the light(s) on; *lass* (*die*) *Arbeit Arbeit sein* *umg.* you can leave your work, it won't run away; *lass mich mal sehen!* let me see (*od.* have a look); *lass ihn nur kommen!* just let him come; *lass mich nur machen!* (just) leave it to me; *er lässt sich nichts sagen* he won't listen (to anyone); *sie ließ alles mit sich geschehen* she put up with everything he (*od.* they *etc.*) did to her; *lass ihn doch ausreden* let him finish (what he's saying); *ich lass mich so nicht anreden* I won't be spoken to like that, I won't have anyone speak to me like that; *ich lass mich doch nicht verarschen!* *umg.* I won't be made a fool of!, what sort of a fool do they *etc.* take me for?; *einen fahren ~* *vulg.* let off; → *bieten* I 6, *einfallen* 1, *gefallen*[1] 2, *hören* I, *laufen* I 1, *schmecken* I 1, II 1, *sehen* II 5, *stören* I 1, *träumen* 1; **2.** (*veranlassen*): *j-n etw. tun ~* get s.o. to do s.th.; *stärker*: make s.o. do s.th.; *er ließ sich e-n Anzug machen* he had a suit made (for himself); *sich* (*Dat.*) *etw. schicken ~* have s.th. sent; *sich* (*Dat.*) *e-n Zahn ziehen ~* have a tooth (taken) out; *er ließ den Arzt kommen* he sent for (*od.* called) the doctor; *er ließ mich warten* he kept me waiting, he made me wait; *~ Sie mich wissen ...* let me know ...; → *auch laufen* I 1, 5, 7; **3.** (*auffordern*): *lass*(*t*) *uns gehen!* let's go; *lasst od. lasset uns beten* let us pray; → *Sorge* 2; **4.** (*unterlassen*): *lass es sein* leave it, don't bother; *ich kann's nicht ~* I can't stop, I can't help it; *er kann das Streiten nicht ~* he can't stop arguing, he 'will go on arguing; *tu, was du nicht ~ kannst* you must do what you think best (*od.* what you have to do); → *tun* I 1; **5.** (*zugestehen*) grant (+ *Dat.* to); *das muss man ihm ~* one must grant him that; **6.** *mit „sich" + Möglichkeit*: *das lässt sich* (*schon*) *machen/einrichten* (I'm sure) it can be done / we can manage that; *das Wort lässt sich nicht übersetzen* this word can't be translated (*od.* is untranslatable); *der Schrank lässt sich leicht öffnen* the cupboard is easy to open; *die Tür lässt sich nicht öffnen grundsätzlich*: the door can't be opened, the door doesn't open; *im Moment*: the door won't open; *es lässt sich nicht leugnen, dass ...* there's no denying that; *es lässt sich gut mischen/drehen* it mixes well / turns easily; *der Wein lässt sich trinken umg.* this wine's very drinkable (*od.* not bad at all); **II.** *v/i.*; *P.P. lassen* **1.** *umg.*: *lass nur, ich mach das schon* you can leave that to me; *lass doch, das geht auch so* leave it, it's OK as it is; **2.** *ich habe mir sagen ~* I've heard (*od.* been told); *ich lasse bitten* *geh.* please bring our visitor(s) in; **3.** *geh.* (*sich trennen*): *von j-m/etw. ~ altm.* leave s.o. / give up s.th.; *sie können nicht voneinander ~* they cannot be parted, they are inseparable; **III.** *v/t.*; *P.P. gelassen* **1.** *er ließ ihn ins Haus* he let him in(to the house); *Wasser in die Wanne ~* run ([the] water into) the bath; *einen ~* *vulg.* let off; **2.** (*unterlassen*) stop; *lass das!* don't!; (*hör auf*) *auch* stop it!; *lass das Weinen* (do) stop crying; *lass es* (*sein*) leave it, don't bother; *~ wir das* enough of that; → *Vortritt, Wille, Zeit etc.*; **3.** (*in e-m Zustand belassen*)

leave; *alles so ~, wie es ist* leave things as they are; *die Tür offen ~* leave the door open; *hinter sich* (*Dat.*) *~* leave *s.th./s.o.* behind; *das kann man* (*so*) *~! umg.* (mm,) not bad; → *Ruhe* 4, 5; **4.** *an e-m Ort etc.*: leave; *wo habe ich* (*bloß*) *m-n Schirm gelassen?* where can I have left (*od.* put) my umbrella?; *lass mir noch e-n Schluck in der Flasche* leave a drop for me in the bottle; *viel Geld ~ umg. fig. beim Glücksspiel etc.*: lose a packet (of money); **5.** (*überlassen, gewähren*) give; (*vermachen*) leave; *j-m etw. ~* leave s.o. s.th.; *fig.* leave s.th. to s.o.; *ich lasse Ihnen das Bild für 400 Dollar* you can have the picture for $400; *j-m fünf Minuten ~* give s.o. five minutes; → *Vortritt, Wille, Zeit etc.*; **6.** *poet.* (*verlassen, aufgeben*) (*Land, Frau etc.*) leave; *sein Leben ~* lose one's life, be killed, die; *sein Leben für etw. ~* lay down one's life for s.th.

lässig I. *Adj.* casual (*auch Kleidung*); (*unbekümmert*) *auch* nonchalant; *er ist total ~ umg.* he's so totally laid-back; **II.** *Adv.* **1.** *~ gekleidet* casually dressed, in casual dress; **2.** *umg.* (*mühelos*) easily, *Am.* no problem; *wir haben's ~ geschafft* we did it easy as pie; it was a cinch; **Lässigkeit** *f; nur Sg.* casualness; (*Unbekümmertheit*) nonchalance, offhandedness; *die ~, mit der sie es macht auch* the offhand way (in which) she does it

lässlich *Adj.*: *kirchl.*: *~e Sünde* venial (*od.* pardonable) sin

Lasso *m, n; -s, -s* lasso, *Am. auch* lariat, rope

lässt *Präs.* → *lassen*

Last *f; -, -en* **1.** load (*auch Naut., Flug.*); (*Gewicht*) *auch* weight; *nur für ~en* (for) goods (*Am.* freight) only; **2.** *fig.* (*Bürde*) burden; *j-m zur ~ fallen/werden* be/become a burden to s.o.; *belästigend*: bother s.o.; *ich will Ihnen nicht zur ~ fallen* I don't want to be a nuisance; *damit war ihr e-e schwere ~ vom Herzen genommen* it was great load off her mind; *j-m etw. zur ~ legen* charge s.o. with s.th., accuse s.o. of s.th.; **3.** *mst Pl.*; *Fin.* costs; *soziale ~en* welfare costs; *wir buchen es zu Ihren ~en* we will debit (*od.* charge) it to your account; **4.** *Etech.* load; **5.** *Naut., Raumf.* hold; **6.** *zu ~en* (+ *Gen. od.* **von**) → *zulasten*

Last|arm *m Phys.* load arm; *~auto* → *Lastkraftwagen*

lasten *v/i.* **1.** *~ auf* (+ *Dat.*) *Schnee, auch fig. Sorgen etc.*: be a great weight on, weigh down; *die Verantwortung lastet auf ihr* the (burden of) responsibility rests on her (shoulders), she bears the (burden of) responsibility; **2.** *auf dem Grundstück lastet e-e Hypothek* the property is mortgaged (*förm.* encumbered by a mortgage), there is a mortgage on the property

Lasten|aufzug *m* goods lift, *Am.* freight elevator; *~ausgleich* *m Wirts.* equalization of burdens (*compensating for losses suffered during and just after World War II*)

lastend I. *Part. Präs.* → *lasten*; **II.** *Adj.* *Schwüle, Stille etc.*: oppressive

lastenfrei *Adj.* unencumbered; (*Haus*) not mortgaged, owned outright

Lasten|segler *m Flug.* transport glider; *~verteilung* *f fig.* burden-sharing

Laster[1] *m; -s, -; umg.* truck, *Brit. auch* lorry

Laster[2] *n; -s, -* **1.** vice; *sich e-m ~ hin-*

geben *od.* *e-m ~ frönen* indulge in a vice; → *Müßiggang*; **2.** *umg.*: *langes ~* beanpole

Lästerei *f; -, -en* negative (*boshaft*: malicious) remarks *Pl.* (*über + Akk.* about); → *Lästerer*

Lästerer *m; -s, -* **1.** (*Gotteslästerer*) blasphemer; **2.** → *Lästermaul* 2

lasterhaft *Adj.* (*ausschweifend, haltlos*) depraved, dissolute; (*unmoralisch*) immoral, profligate *förm.*; (*verdorben*) corrupt; **Lasterhaftigkeit** *f; nur Sg.* depravity; (*Unmoral*) immorality, profligacy *förm.*; (*Verdorbenheit*) corruptness

Lasterhöhle *f* den of iniquity

Lästerin *f; -, -nen* → *Lästerer*

Lasterleben *n; nur Sg.* life of sin (*od.* depravity)

lästerlich *Adj.* malicious, malevolent; (*gotteslästerlich*) blasphemous; **Lästermaul** *n umg.* **1.** vicious (*od.* malicious) tongue; **2.** *Person*: *er ist ein ~* he's got a vicious (*od.* malicious) tongue, he's always saying malicious things about people, *Am. auch* he's always bad-mouthing people; **lästern** *v/i. pej.* (*abfällig reden*) criticize (*über j-n/etw. s.o./s.th.*); (*sich den Mund zerreißen*) gossip (about s.o./s.th.), spread gossip (about s.o./s.th.); *über j-n ~ auch* take s.o. to pieces *umg.*, *Am.* pick s.o. apart *umg.*; *bösartig*: say nasty (*stärker*: malicious) things about s.o. (behind his *od.* her back), bitch about s.o. *umg.*, *Am. auch* bad-mouth s.o. *umg.*; **II.** *v/t. altm.* blaspheme against; *Gott ~* blaspheme; **Lästerung** *f* calumny; (*Gotteslästerung*) blasphemy

Lastesel *m* (pack) mule; *fig.* workhorse

Lastex® *n; -, kein Pl.* (type of) stretch fabric, Lastex®; *~hose* *f* stretch trousers (*bes. Am.* pants)

lästig *Adj.* (*ärgerlich*) annoying, irksome; *Krankheit*: troublesome; *Pflicht*: tiresome; *j-m ~ sein auch* be a nuisance (for s.o.); *ein ~er Mensch* a pest; *er ist einfach ~ auch* he's just a nuisance, he just gets in the way; *es wird mir langsam ~* it's getting to be a nuisance, it's beginning to get on my nerves; *ist dir die Musik ~?* does the music bother you (*stärker*: get on your nerves)?; *ich will euch nicht ~ fallen* I don't want to be a nuisance

Last|kahn *m* barge; *~kraftwagen* *m* (*abgek.* **Lkw, LKW**) truck, *Brit. auch* lorry

Last-Minute-Flug *m Touristik*: late-availability (*od.* last-minute) flight

Last|pferd *n* pack horse; *~schiff* *n* freighter

Lastschrift *f Wirts.* **1.** *Anzeige*: debit note; *Eintrag*: debit entry; **2.** *Buchung*: direct debit; *~verfahren* *n*, *~verkehr* *m* direct debiting

Last|spitze *f Etech.* peak load; *~tier* *n* pack animal, beast of burden

Lastwagen *m* truck, *Brit. auch* lorry; *~anhänger* *m* truck trailer; *~fahrer* *m*, *~fahrerin* *f* truck (*Brit. auch* lorry) driver, *Am. auch* trucker, teamster

Lastzug *m Mot.* truck trailer, *Am. auch* rig

Lasur *f; -, -en* glaze; *für Holz*: varnish

lasziv *Adj.* lascivious; **Laszivität** *f; -, kein Pl.* lasciviousness

Lätare *kein Art.*; *indekl.*; *ev.*: *an ~ od. am Sonntag ~* on Laetare (*od.* Mid-Lent) Sunday, on the fourth Sunday in Lent

Latein *n; -s, kein Pl.*; *Ling.* Latin; *mit s-m ~ am Ende sein* *fig.* be at one's

wits' end, be at a loss as to what to do (next); *ich bin mit m-m ~ am Ende auch* I give up; → *Lateinisch*
Lateinamerika (*n*); *-s; Geog.* Latin America; **Lateinamerikaner** *m*, **Lateinamerikanerin** *f* Latin American; **lateinamerikanisch** *Adj.* Latin American
Lateiner *m; -s, -, ~in f; -, -nen Experte:* Latin scholar, Latinist; *Schüler/Schülerin:* boy/girl doing (*Am.* taking) Latin
lateinisch *Adj.* Latin; *die ~e Schrift* the Latin alphabet; **Lateinisch** *n; -en; Ling.* Latin; *auf ~* in Latin; *das ~e* Latin
latent I. *Adj.* latent; II. *Adv.: ~ vorhanden sein* be latent; **Latenz** *f; -, kein Pl.* latency; **Latenzzeit** *f* latency period
lateral *Adj.* lateral
Lateran *m; -s, kein Pl.* Lateran Palace; **Lateranverträge** *Pl. hist.* Lateran Treaties
Laterne *f; -, -n* lantern; (*Straßenlaterne*) streetlamp, *Am. auch* streetlight; *die rote ~ übernehmen/abgeben Sport* drop to / move off the bottom of the table
Laternen|garage *f umg. hum.* kerb|side (*Am.* curb-) garage; *sein Auto in der ~ parken* keep one's car in the street; **~licht** *n* light of the stree-t|lamps (*Am. auch* -lights); **~pfahl** *m* lamppost, *Am. auch* lightpole; **~umzug** *m* lantern procession
Latex *m; -, Latizes* latex (*Pl.* latexes *od.* latices)
Latifundienwirtschaft *f; nur Sg.; Agr.* latifundium system; **Latifundium** *n; -s, Latifundien; hist.* latifundium (*Pl.* latifundia)
latinisiert *Adj. Ling.* Latinized
Latin Lover ['lɛtɪn 'lavɐ] *m; -(s), -s* Latin lover
Latino *m; -s, -s* Latino
Latin Rock ['lɛtɪn 'rɔk] *m; -(s), kein Pl.; Mus.* Latin rock
Latinum *n; -s, kein Pl.; Päd.: Großes ~* Latin qualifying examination; *Kleines ~* intermediate Latin qualifying examination
Latrine *f; -, -n* latrine; **Latrinenparole** *f umg.* empty rumo(u)r
Latsche[1] *f; -, -n; Bot.* dwarf pine
Latsche[2] *f; -, -n; umg.* → *Latschen*
latschen *umg.* I. *v/i.* (*ist gelatscht*) trail along; *schwerfällig:* trudge along; *schlurfend:* shuffle along; *nachlässig:* slouch along; *latsch nicht so!* don't drag your feet like that, walk properly!; II. *v/t.* (*hat*): *j-m eine ~* slap s.o. one
Latschen *m; -s, -; umg.* (*Hausschuh*) (old) slipper; (*Schuh*) old (worn-out) shoe; *aus den ~ kippen fig.* (*ohnmächtig werden*) keel over; *ich bin fast aus den ~ gekippt vor Überraschung etc.:* I nearly fell over backwards
Latschen|kiefer *f Bot.* dwarf pine; **~kiefernöl** *n* pine needle oil
Latte *f; -, -n* 1. slat; *dünne:* batten; *Sport* (cross)bar; *Fußball etc.: ~!* it's hit the bar; 2. *umg. fig.: lange ~* (*Person*) beanpole; 3. *umg. fig.: e-e* (*lange*) *~ von Fragen etc.* a whole string (*Am.* slew) of questions *etc.; nicht alle auf der ~ haben* have a screw loose (somewhere); *j-n auf der ~ haben* have it in for s.o.; 4. *vulg.* (*Penis*) hard-on, boner
Latten|gestell *n* slatted frame; **~kiste** *f* crate; **~kreuz** *n Fuß-, Handball:* angle between the bar and the post; **~rost**

m duckboards *Pl.; Tech.* grid; *Bett:* slatted (bed)frame; **~schuss** *m*, **~treffer** *m Fußball:* shot against the bar; **~zaun** *m* paling (fence)
Lattich *m; -s, -e; Bot.* lettuce
Latz *m; -es, Lätze* 1. *für Kleinkinder:* bib; (*Schürzchen*) pinafore; 2. (*an Hose, Rock od. Schürze*) bib; *j-m eine od. einen od. eins vor den ~ knallen od. ballern umg.* sock (*od.* thump) s.o. one; 3. *Dial.* (*Hosenlatz*) flies *Pl.*, fly
Lätzchen *n* bib
Latzhose *f:* (*e-e*) *~* (a pair of) dungarees *Pl.*
lau I. *Adj.* 1. (*Flüssigkeit*) lukewarm; *nicht warm genug: auch* tepid; *Luft, Wetter:* mild; *Abend, Wind etc.:* balmy; *das Badewasser sollte ~ sein* the bathwater should be lukewarm; 2. *fig.* (*halbherzig*) half-hearted; *Applaus, Freundschaft etc.: auch* lukewarm; (*dürftig*) (*Geschäfte, Nachfrage*) slack; *die Umsätze sind zurzeit ~* turnover is slow at the moment; 3. *Dial.: für ~* for nothing, free; II. *Adv.* 1. *der Wind weht ~ aus Südwest* a balmy wind is blowing from the southwest; 2. *fig.* half-heartedly; *die Geschäfte gehen ~* business is slack
Laub *n; -(e)s, kein Pl.* foliage; leaves *Pl.; ~ tragend* leafy, leafed; *im ~ stehen* be in leaf; **~baum** *m* deciduous tree; **~dach** *n* canopy of leaves
Laube *f; -, -n* 1. arbo(u)r, bower; (*Gartenhäuschen*) summer house; (*und*) *fertig ist die ~! umg. fig.* and Bob's your uncle!; 2. *Archit.* (*Vorhalle*) porch; (*Säulengang*) portico; (*Bogengang*) arcade
Lauben|gang *m* 1. pergola; 2. *Archit.* (*Bogengang*) arcade; *am Haus:* loggia; **~kolonie** *f* allotment area, collection of allotments; **~pieper** *m; -s, -; Dial. hum.* allotment gardener
Laub|fall *m; nur Sg.* leaf fall, fall of the leaves; *vor/nach dem ~* before the leaves fall / after the leaves have fallen; **~frosch** *m Zool.* tree frog; **~holz** *n* hardwood; (*Baum*) deciduous tree
Laubhüttenfest *n Reli.* Feast of Tabernacles
Laubsäge *f* fretsaw; **~arbeit** *f* fretwork
Laub|sänger *m Zool.* wood warbler; **~wald** *m* deciduous forest; *Pl. auch* deciduous woodland *Sg.;* **~werk** *n* foliage; *Kunst: auch* leafwork
Lauch *m; -(e)s, -e; Bot.* allium; (*Porree*) leek; *Gastr.* leeks *Pl.*
Laudatio *f; -, Laudationes* panegyric, eulogy; **Laudator** *m; -s, Laudatoren*, **Laudatorin** *f; -, -nen* panegyrist
Laudes *Pl. kirchl.* (*Gebetsstunde*) lauds *Pl.* (*auch V. im Sg.*)
Lauer *f: auf der ~ liegen* be lying in wait; *sich auf die ~ legen* settle down to lie in wait; *auf der ~ sein nach* be on the lookout (*od.* be watching out) for; **lauern** *v/i.* lie in wait (*auf + Akk.* for); (*Ausschau halten*) be on the lookout (for); *Gefahr:* lurk; *auf e-e Gelegenheit etc. ~* watch out for an opportunity *etc.; ungeduldig:* wait impatiently for an opportunity *etc.;* **lauernd** I. *Part. Präs.* → *lauern;* II. *Adj. Gefahr etc.:* lurking; *Blick:* furtive, shifty
Lauf *m; -(e)s, Läufe* 1. run; (*Wettlauf*) race; (*Durchgang*) run; (*Vorrunde*) heat, *der 100-Meter-~* the 100 met|res (*Am.* -ers); *e-n ~ haben Sport Sl.* have a run of great form, be on a roll; 2. *nur Sg.;* (*Laufen*) running; *sich in ~ setzen* break into a run, start running;

im ~ anhalten/innehalten stop running / stop running for a moment; *in vollem ~ umg.* (at) full tilt; 3. *nur Sg.;* (*Bewegung*) movement, motion; *des Wassers:* flow; *Tech.* running, operation; *die Maschine hat e-n leisen ~* the machine (*Mot.* engine) is very quiet (*od.* quiet-running, quiet in operation); 4. *nur Sg.; fig.* (*Verlauf, Entwicklung*) course; *der ~ der Geschichte* the course (*od.* tide) of history; *das ist der ~ der Dinge* that's the way things are, that's life; *den ~ der Dinge aufhalten* stop the course of events; *den Dingen freien* (*od. ihren*) *~ lassen* let things take their course; *s-r Fantasie* / *s-n Gefühlen freien ~ lassen* give free rein to one's emotions/imagination; *stärker:* let one's emotions/imagination run wild; *s-m Zorn freien ~ lassen* give vent to one's anger; *s-n ~ nehmen* take its course; *im ~e des Monats/Gesprächs etc.* in the course of (*od.* during) the month/conversation *etc.; im ~e der nächsten Woche etc.* some time next week *etc.; im ~e der Jahre* over the years; *im ~e der Zeit* in the course of time; *Vergangenheit: auch* as time went on; 5. *nur Sg.;* (*Verlauf e-s Wegs, Flusses*) course; *von Gestirnen:* orbit; *am oberen/unteren ~ des Indus* along the upper/lower reaches of the Indus; *dem ~ der Straße folgen* follow the (course of the) road; 6. *Mus.* run; *Koloratur: auch* roulade; 7. (*von Schusswaffen*) barrel; *mit zwei Läufen* double-barrel(l)ed; *etw. vor den ~ bekommen Jagd und fig.:* get s.th. in one's sights; 8. *Jägerspr.* (*Bein*) leg
Lauf|arbeit *f; nur Sg.; Sport* running, legwork; **~bahn** *f* 1. career; *gehobene ~ oft* profession; *e-e ~ einschlagen* choose (*od.* take up) a career; 2. *Sport, Leichtathletik:* running track; **~band** *n* 1. (*Transportband*) travelator, moving walkway (*Am. auch* sidewalk); 2. *zum Training:* treadmill; **~brett** *n* plank; **~bursche** *m mst pej.* errand boy (*auch fig.*), *auch umg.* gofer; *für j-n den ~n machen od.* spielen *mst fig., pej.* run errands for s.o., fetch and carry for s.o.; **~disziplin** *f Sport* running event
laufen; *läuft, lief, gelaufen* I. *v/i.* (*ist*) 1. run, *in Eile: auch* rush, race; *gelaufen kommen* come running along; *lauf!, quick!; ein Pferd ~ lassen im Rennen:* run a horse; *ein Schiff auf ein Riff etc. ~ lassen* run a ship onto a reef *etc.; j-n ~ lassen* let s.o. go; *straflos:* let s.o. off; *ein Tier ~ lassen* let an animal go, set an animal free; → *auch 7;* → *Arm 1, Grund 2, Strand 2.* (*gehen*) walk, go (on foot); *viel ~* do a lot of walking; *gern ~* like walking; *~ lernen Kind:* learn to walk; *noch nicht sicher ~ Kind:* still be unsteady on its legs; *es sind nur fünf Minuten zu ~* it's only five minutes' walk (*od.* five minutes on foot); *wegen jeder Kleinigkeit zum Arzt ~ umg. pej.* run to the doctor with every little twinge; *gegen etw. ~* walk into s.th.; *er ist in ein Auto gelaufen* he walked into a car; 3. *Tech., Mot. etc.* run; (*funktionieren*) *Fahrzeug, Uhr:* go; *Gerät:* work; *auf Schienen* / *über Rollen ~* run on rails/rollers; *vom Fließband ~* come off the production line; *den Motor ~ lassen vor Bahnschranke etc.:* leave the engine running; (*anschalten*) turn on the engine; → *warmlaufen;* 4. (*sich bewe-*

gen) move; *um die Sonne etc.* ~ *Gestirn etc.*: revolve (*od.* move) around the sun *etc.*; **5.** *Linie, Weg etc.*: run, pass (*durch* through); *Flüssigkeit, auch Schweiß, Blut etc.*: run; *Tränen: auch* stream (*über j-s Gesicht* down s.o.'s face); *Wasser in etw.* ~ *lassen* run water into s.th.; *ein Raunen lief durch die Menge fig.* a murmur went (*od.* passed) through the crowd; → *Rücken* 1; **6.** (*sich erstrecken*) run, stretch (*von ... bis* from ... to); **7.** *fig.* (*im Gang sein*) be under way; *Film:* run, *im Programm: auch* be on, be showing; ~ *bis / über ... Jahre auch* run until / for ... years; *der Antrag läuft* the application is being considered (*od.* is under consideration); *das Stück lief drei Monate* the play ran (*od.* was on) for three months, the play had a three-month run; *die Dinge* ~ *lassen* let things ride; *die Sache ist gelaufen vorbei:* it's all over (*od.* settled); *gut:* everything's all right; (*kann nicht mehr geändert werden*) there's nothing anyone can do about it (now); *wie läuft es so? umg.* how are things?, how are you getting on (*Am.* along)?; *wissen, wie's läuft umg.* know what gives; *was läuft hier eigentlich? umg.* what's doing (*Am.* going on) here?; *da läuft* (*bei mir, ihm etc.*) *nichts! umg.* nothing doing!; *das läuft nicht! umg.* it's just not on, you can forget it, *Am.* no way; **8.** (*gelten*) *Vertrag etc.*: be valid; *das Abonnement läuft noch drei Monate* the subscription runs (*od.* is valid) for another three months; **9.** *Nase, Augen etc.*: run; *Wunde:* weep; *Kerze:* drip; *Gefäß:* leak; *Butter, Schokolade, Eis etc.*: melt; *Käse:* be runny; **II.** *v/t.* (*hat*) **1.** (*Strecke, Geschwindigkeit*) run; (*Rekord*) run, set (up); *einige Runden / (die) 5000 m* ~ run several laps / run in the 5000 met|res (*Am.* -ers); **2.** *sich* (*Dat.*) *ein Loch in die Socken* ~ wear a hole into one's sock; *sich* (*Dat.*) *Blasen* ~ get blisters from walking; → *Gefahr, Sturm* 3, *wund etc.*; **III.** *v/refl.* (*hat*) *sich müde* ~ wear o.s. out (with) running; *sich warm* ~ warm up; *Sport auch* do a warm-up run; **IV.** *v/refl., unpers.* (*hat*): *es läuft sich schlecht hier* it's difficult to walk (*od.* run *etc.*) along here, it's hard going along here *umg.*; *es läuft sich gut/schlecht in diesen Schuhen* these shoes are comfortable/uncomfortable (to walk in); *in der Gruppe läuft es sich besser als alleine* it's better to run in a group than on your own

Laufen *n; -s, kein Pl.* running; (*Gehen*) walking

laufend I. *Part. Präs.* → *laufen*; **II.** *Adj.* **1.** *Motor etc.*: running; *bei od. mit ~em Motor* with the engine running; **2.** (*jetzig*) current; *~en Monats* of this month; **3.** (*ständig*) continuous; (*regelmäßig*) regular; (*in Gang befindlich*) ongoing; *~e Berichterstattung* running commentary; *~e Nummer* (serial) number; *~e Nummern* consecutive numbers; *~e Wartung/Prüfung* routine maintenance/check; *~er Meter 12,50 Euro* 12.50 euros per met|re (*Am.* -er) from the piece; **4.** *Wirts., Kredit:* outstanding; (*in Umlauf befindlich*) in circulation; *Patent:* pending; *~e Kosten* overheads, running costs; *~e Rechnung* current account; **5.** *auf dem Laufenden sein* be up to date (*über +Akk.* on), be in the picture (about); *j-n/sich auf dem Laufenden halten*

keep s.o./o.s. informed (*od.* posted), keep up with things; **III.** *Adv.* (*ständig*) continually; (*zunehmend*) increasingly; ~ *besser werden* get better and better all the time, be continually improving; ~ *zunehmen/abnehmen an Gewicht:* be forever (*od.* constantly) putting on / losing weight, put on / lose more and more weight; *wir haben* ~ *zu tun* there's always plenty of work to do, there's never any shortage of work

laufen lassen → *laufen* I 1, 3

Läufer *m; -s, -* **1.** *Sport:* runner; **2.** *Schach:* bishop; **3.** (*Teppich*) rug; (*Tischläufer*) runner; *auf Treppen:* stair carpet; **4.** *Tech.* rotor; **5.** *Archit.* stretcher

Lauferei *f; -, -en; umg.* running around, legwork; *j-m ~en bereiten fig.* cause s.o. a lot of bother (*od.* trouble)

Läuferin *f; -, -nen; Sport* runner

läuferisch I. *Adj. Können:* as a runner; *Pl.* as runners; *beim Eislaufen:* skating ...; **II.** *Adv.* as a runner; *Pl.* as runners; *Eislaufen:* as a skater, *Pl.* as skaters; *die Mannschaft war dem Gegner* ~ *überlegen Fußball etc.*: the team's work rate was better (than their opponents')

Lauf|feuer *n* brush fire; *sich wie ein* ~ *verbreiten fig.* spread like wildfire; *~fläche f Reifen:* tread; *Ski:* running surface, sole; **lauffreudig** *Adj. Sport* keen on (*Am.* wild about) running; ~ *sein* do a lot of running

Lauf|gang *m* **1.** (*Gangway*) gangway; **2.** *für Raubtiere:* passage (between cages); **3.** *hist., hinter Befestigungsmauern:* walk(way); **4.** *Archit.* triforium (*Pl.* triforia); *~geräusch n* noise (made while running); *~geschwindigkeit f Tech.* running speed; *~gitter n* playpen

läufig *Adj.*: *~e Hündin* bitch on (*Am.* in) heat

Lauf|kran *m* travel(l)ing crane; *~kundschaft f* casual customers *Pl.*; passing trade; *~leistung f Mot.* (useful) life; *~en von mehr als 500.000 km haben Motoren:* cover more than 300,000 miles (without overhaul); *~masche f* ladder, *Am.* run; *~pass m umg.: j-m den* ~ *geben* give s.o. his (*od.* her) marching orders; (*kündigen*) *auch* give s.o. the boot, *Am.* give s.o. the pink slip; *dem Freund, der Freundin:* ditch (*od.* drop) s.o.; *den* ~ *bekommen* get one's marching orders; (*entlassen werden*) *auch* get the boot; *Freund(in):* be ditched (*od.* dropped); *~pensum n Sport* amount of running; *sie absolvierte ein enormes* ~ she got through a huge amount of running; *~planke f* gangplank; *~rad n* **1.** *Tech.* (non-driven) wheel, running wheel; *Pumpe:* impeller; *Turbine:* rotor; **2.** *hist.* (*Draisine*) dandy-horse, *Am.* velocipede; *~richtung f* direction (of movement); *~rolle f Tech.* roller; *an Möbeln:* castor; *~schiene f* rail, track; (*Leitschiene*) guide rail; *~schrift f Werbung:* moving letters *Pl.*; *~schritt m* run, jog; *Mil.:* double; *im* ~ *ins Büro eilen etc.* run to the office *etc.*; *~schuh m* **1.** walking shoe; **2.** *Sport* trainer, *Am.* running shoe; *~sohle f* (outer) sole, outsole; *~sport m* running; *~stall m* playpen

laufstark *Adj. Sport* good at running; *er ist sehr* ~ he's a strong runner, there's a lot of running in him

Lauf|steg *m* catwalk (*auch Mode*);

~stil m Sport running style; *~stuhl m* (baby) walker

läuft *Präs.* → *laufen*

Lauf|training *n Sport* running (in training); (*Joggen*) jogging; *beim* ~ on a training run; *~treff m Sport* running and jogging meet, *Am.* track meet; *~vogel m Orn.* flightless bird, ratite *fachspr.*; *~werk n* **1.** *Tech.* (*Antrieb*) drive; *Computer: auch* disk drive; *für Kassette, Magnetband, Film:* transport; (*Mechanismus*) mechanism; *e-r Uhr:* movement; **2.** *Eisenb. etc.*: running gear; *e-r Seilbahn:* pulley cradle; **3.** *umg. hum.* (*Beine*) pins *Pl.*; *~wettbewerb m Sport* running (*Am.* foot) race; *~zeit f* **1.** *e-s Vertrages:* term, life; *e-r Anleihe:* repayment period; **2.** *Film etc.*: run; (*Spieldauer*) length, *auch CD etc.*: running time; **3.** *Tech.* hours *Pl.* of operation; (*Lebensdauer*) (service) life; **4.** *Sport* time (for a [*od.* the] distance); *im Triathlon, Zehnkampf:* running time; *~zettel m* **1.** (*Rundschreiben*) circular; *Büro:* memo; **2.** *für Akten:* distribution slip; *an Werkstücken:* control slip

Lauge *f; -, -n* **1.** *Chem.* lye, alkaline solution; **2.** (*Salzlake*) brine; (*Seifenlauge*) suds *Pl.*

Laugen|bad *n* alkaline bath; *~brezel f Dial.* salt pretzel; *~brötchen n Dial.* salt roll

laugig *Adj.* alkaline

Lauheit *f; nur Sg.; bes. fig.* lukewarmness; *Wetter etc.*: mildness

Laune *f; -, -n* **1.** mood; *gute/schlechte* ~ *haben od. guter/schlechter* ~ *sein* be in a good/bad mood; *bester* ~ in a very good (*umg.* a great) mood; *stärker: on* top of the world; *hat die heute e-e ~!* she's in a terrible mood today; *im Urlaub nur Regen – das macht ~! umg. iro.* if it rains non-stop on holiday (*Am.* vacation), it gets you down; *~n haben* be moody, be subject to moods; *er hat* (*so*) *s-e ~n* he has his little moods; *j-n bei ~ halten* keep s.o. in a good (*od.* in the mood, keep s.o. happy; (*j-s Launen nachgeben*) humo(u)r s.o.; *du hast mir die ~ gründlich verdorben* you've really spoil|t (*Am.* -ed) my day; → *Lust*; **2.** plötzliche: whim; *aus e-r ~ heraus* on a whim; *aus e-r ~ heraus haben wir den Wagen gekauft auch* we just decided on the spur of the moment to buy the car; *es war nur so e-e ~ von mir* it was just one of my (little) whims; *die ~n des Schicksals etc.* the vagaries of fortune *etc.*; ~ *der Natur* freak of nature

launenhaft *Adj.* **1.** moody, subject to moods; (*unberechenbar*) temperamental; **2.** *fig. Wetter:* changeable; **Launenhaftigkeit** *f; nur Sg.* moodiness; (*Unberechenbarkeit*) temperamental nature

launig *Adj.* witty; (*humorvoll*) humorous

launisch *Adj. pej.* **1.** moody; **2.** (*unbeständig, sprunghaft*) capricious; (*unberechenbar*) temperamental; **3.** *fig. Glück:* fickle; *Wetter:* changeable

Laus *f; -, Läuse; Zool.* louse (*Pl.* lice); *dem ist wohl e-e ~ über die Leber gelaufen umg. fig.* I wonder what's eating him; *j-m/sich e-e ~ in den Pelz od. ins Fell setzen umg.* create trouble for s.o./o.s., land s.o./o.s. in it

Lausbub(e) *m umg.* rascal; **lausbubenhaft** *Adj. umg. Gesicht etc.*: impish, mischievous, **Lausbubenstreich**

m roguish prank; **lausbübisch** *Adj. umg. Blick etc.*: mischievous

Lausch|aktion *f*, **~angriff** *m* bugging operation, *auch Pl.* electronic eavesdropping

lauschen *v/i.* listen (+ *Dat. od. auf* + *Akk.* to); *angestrengt*: strain one's ears (for); *heimlich*: eavesdrop (on), listen (in on); **an der Wand ~** put one's ear to the wall to eavesdrop

Lauscher *m*; *-s, -* **1.** eavesdropper; *der ~ an der Wand hört seine eigene Schand! Sprichw.* people who eavesdrop never hear any good of themselves; **2.** *Jägerspr.* ear; *jetzt stell mal deine ~ auf umg.* now pin back your lugholes!, *Am.* listen up!

Lauscherin *f*; *-, -nen* → *Lauscher* 1

lauschig *Adj.*: **~es Plätzchen / ~er Winkel** nice quiet spot / nice cosy corner

Läusebefall *m* lice infestation

Lause|bengel *m umg.*, **~junge** *m umg.* rascal, (little) rogue; *stärker*: (little) devil

lausekalt *Adj. umg.* absolutely freezing

lausen *vt/refl.*: **j-n/sich ~** pick s.o.'s/one's lice, delouse s.o./o.s.; → *Affe*

Lauser *m*; *-s, -*; *Dial. umg.* → *Lausejunge*

lausig *umg.* **I.** *Adj.* lousy, dreadful; *wegen ~en 10 Euro!* for the sake of a measly 10 euros (*od.* 10 measly euros); *e-e ~e Kälte* a perishing (*Am.* nasty) cold; **II.** *Adv.*: **~ kalt** absolutely freezing, *Brit. auch* bloody cold

laut¹ I. *Adj.* (*Ggs. leise*) *Musik, Stimme, Gelächter etc.*: loud; (*lärmend, Ggs. ruhig*) *Straße, Person, Auto etc.*: noisy; *fig. Farbe*: loud; *mit ~er Stimme* in a loud voice; **~es Geräusch** loud noise; **~e Nachbarn** noisy neighbo(u)rs; *seid nicht so ~!* don't make so much noise; **~ werden** (*zornig werden*) raise one's voice; *stärker*: start shouting; *fig. Wünsche etc.*: be expressed; *Proteste*: be heard; *Geheimnis etc.*: get out; *es wurden Gerüchte ~, dass ...* *fig.* it was rumo(u)red that ...; *muss ich erst ~ werden, bevor ...?* do I have to shout before ...?; *lass das ja nicht ~ werden* don't spread it about (*Am.* around), keep that to yourself; **II.** *Adv.* **1.** loud(ly); (*geräuschvoll*) noisily; *reden etc.*: in a loud voice, loud; **~ und deutlich** loud and clear; (*offen*) openly; **~er, bitte!** speak up, please; **~er stellen** (*Musik, Radio etc.*) turn up; *er schrie, so ~ er konnte* he shouted at the top of his voice; **2.** (*nicht für sich*) *lesen, denken*: aloud; *das kannst du ~ sagen fig.* you can say that again; *das darfst du nicht ~ sagen* you can't mention that, don't say that too loudly

laut² *Präp.* according to; *Wirts.* as per; **~ Befehl** as ordered; **~ Befehl** (+ *Gen.*) by order of; **~ Vorschrift** *od.* **Verordnung** in accordance with the regulations; **~ Vorschrift** *od.* **Verordnung** (+ *Gen.*) as prescribed by

Laut *m*; *-(e)s, -e* sound (*auch Ling.*); *keinen ~ von sich geben* not say a word (*od.* utter a sound); *er gab keinen ~ mehr von sich auch umg.* there wasn't another peep from him, he shut up like a clam; **~ geben** *Jagdhund*: give tongue; *umg.* (*etwas sagen*) say something; *stärker*: speak up (*od.* out); (*reagieren*) react; (*sagen, was man will*) say what one wants

Laut|äußerung *f Zool.* sound (utter-

ance); (*Ruf*) call; **~bildung** *f Ling.* articulation

Laute *f*; *-, -n*; *Mus.* lute

lauten *v/i. Text*: read, run; *Zeile etc.*: go; *Antwort, Bitte, Meinung etc.*: be; (*klingen*) sound; *wie lautet die Antwort?* what's the answer?; *der Pass lautet auf m-n Namen* the passport is in my name; *das Urteil lautet auf ein Jahr Gefängnis* the sentence is one year's imprisonment (*od.* one year in prison)

läuten I. *v/i.* **1.** *Glocke*: ring (**zu** for); (*feierlich*) toll; *Glöckchen*: tinkle; *Wecker*: go off; *es läutet zu Mittag* the midday bells are ringing; *ich habe davon ~ hören od. gehört fig.* I heard something to that effect; *ich habe etwas ~ hören, dass ...* I have heard rumo(u)rs that ...; **2.** *südd., österr., schw.* (*klingeln*) ring; (*nach*) *j-m ~* ring for s.o.; *oft unpers.*: *es läutet an der Tür*: the doorbell's ringing, there's the doorbell; *Schule etc.*: the bell's ringing; **II.** *v/t.* ring; *12 Uhr/Mittag ~* strike twelve/midday (*Am.* noon)

Läuten *n*; *-s, kein Pl.* ringing

Lauten|spiel *n Mus.* lute playing; **~spieler** *m*, **~spielerin** *f* lute player, lutenist

lauter¹ *Adj.* **1.** *altm.* (*rein*) pure; **2.** *fig.* (*aufrichtig, ehrlich*) sincere, genuine; *die ~e Wahrheit* the plain truth

lauter² *Adv.* (*nichts als, nur*) nothing but; **~ Unsinn** a lot of nonsense; *aus ~ Bosheit* out of sheer spite; *aus ~ Dankbarkeit ließ er ihn gehen* he was so grateful (that) he let him go; *vor ~ Aufregung habe ich s-n Namen vergessen* in (*od.* with) all the excitement I forgot his name; *das sind ~ Lügen* it's all lies

Lauterkeit *f*; *nur Sg.*; *fig.* sincerity, integrity

läutern *v/t.* purify; *die Erfahrung hat ihn geläutert geh. fig.* he was purged by the experience; *weitS.* it was a salutary experience for him; **Läuterung** *f* purification; *geh. fig.* purging; **Läuterungsprozess** *m* purification process; *geh. fig.* purging (*od.* cleansing) process

Lautgesetz *n Ling.* phonetic law, law of phonetics

lautgetreu *Ling.* **I.** *Adj.* phonetically accurate; (*Wiedergabe*) faithful; **II.** *Adv.* with phonetic accuracy; *wiedergeben*: faithfully

lauthals *Adv.*: **~ lachen/schreien** roar with laughter / scream at the top of one's voice

Lautheit *f*; *nur Sg.* loudness

Lautlehre *f* phonetics *Pl.* (*V. im Sg.*); *in e-r bestimmten Sprache*: phonology

lautlich I. *Adj.* phonetic; **II.** *Adv.* phonetically

lautlos I. *Adj.* silent (*auch fig. wortlos, widerspruchslos*); (*geräuschlos*) *auch* noiseless, soundless; *Stille*: complete (*od.* absolute); **II.** *Adv.* silently; (*geräuschlos*) *auch* noiselessly, without a sound; *er brach ~ zusammen* he collapsed without a sound; **Lautlosigkeit** *f*; *nur Sg.* silence; (*Geräuschlosigkeit*) noiselessness, soundlessness

Lautmalerei *f* onomatopoeia; **lautmalerisch** *Adj.* onomatopoe(t)ic

Lautschrift *f Ling.* **1.** phonetic alphabet (*od.* script); *die internationale ~* the international phonetic alphabet, IPA; **2.** *Umschrift*: phonetic transcription, phonetics *Pl.* (*V. im Sg.*)

Lautsprecher *m* loudspeaker; **~anlage**

f: **öffentliche ~** public address (system), PA; **~box** *f* speaker; **~durchsage** *f* announcement over the public address; **~stimme** *f* voice over the public address; **~wagen** *m* loudspeaker van (*PKW*: car)

lautstark I. *Adj. Protest, Forderung etc.*: loud; *stärker*: strident, vehement; *auch Person, Minderheit*: vociferous; **II.** *Adv.* loudly; *sprechen etc.*: *auch* in a loud voice; (*unüberhörbar*) so that everyone can (*od.* could) hear; (*heftig*) vehemently, vociferously; **~ schimpfen** rant and rave; *die Mannschaft ~ unterstützen* give the team vociferous support

Lautstärke *f* volume; **~messer** *m*; *-s, -* (*volume*) level meter; **~regelung** *f* volume control; **~regler** *m* volume control

Laut|symbol *n Ling.* phonetic symbol (*od.* character); **~system** *n* phonetic (*od.* phonological) system

Lautung *f Ling.* pronunciation

Laut|verschiebung *f Ling.* sound shift; **~wandel** *m Ling.* (general) phonetic change

lauwarm *Adj.* lukewarm; (*nicht warm genug*) *auch* tepid; → *auch lau*

Lava *f*; *-, Laven; Geol.* lava

Lavabo *n*; *-(s), -s* **1.** *schw.* washbasin; **2.** *kath.* lavabo

Lava|gestein *n* lava rock; **~strom** *m* stream of (molten) lava

Lavendel *m*; *-s, -; Bot.* lavender

lavendel|blau, **~farben** *Adj.* lavender (blue)

lavieren¹ I. *v/i.* manoeuvre, *Am.* maneuver; **~ zwischen** (+ *Dat.*) steer a course between; **II.** *v/refl.*: *sich aus e-r schwierigen Lage etc.* **~** extricate o.s. from a tricky position *etc.*

lavieren² *v/t. Kunst*: wash (over); *lavierte Zeichnung* wash drawing

Lawine *f*; *-, -n* avalanche, snowslide; *fig. von Fragen etc.*: *auch* torrent; *von Protesten*: flood; *e-e ~ lostreten fig.* provoke a storm

...lawine *f*, *im Subst. fig.*, *oft pej.* avalanche, torrent; *Besucher~* avalanche (*od.* deluge) of visitors; *Kosten~* tidal wave of costs; *Prozess~* whole spate of trials

lawinenartig *Adj. und Adv.* avalanche-like; **~ anwachsen** *od.* **anschwellen** snowball

Lawinengefahr *f* danger of avalanches; **lawinengefährdet** *Adj.*: **~es Gebiet** avalanche-prone area, area exposed to avalanches

Lawinen|hund *m* avalanche (search) dog; **~katastrophe** *f* avalanche disaster; **~opfer** *n* avalanche victim; **~schutz** *m* avalanche protection

lawinensicher I. *Adj.* safe from avalanches; **II.** *Adv.*: **~ gebaut** built with avalanche protection

Lawinen|verbauung *f* avalanche barrier; **~warnung** *f* avalanche warning

lax *Adj.* lax; **Laxheit** *f* laxness, laxity

Layout ['le:?aʊt] *n*; *-s, -s; Druck.* layout; **layouten** *v/i.* **1.** do a (*od.* the) layout; **2.** *allg.* do layout; **Layouter** *m*; *-s, -* layout artist (*od.* man); **Layouterin** *f*; *-, -nen* layout artist

Lazarett *n*; *-(e)s, -e* (military) hospital; **~flugzeug** *n* air ambulance; **~schiff** *n* hospital ship

LCD-Anzeige *f* LCD, liquid crystal display

Lead|gitarre [li:d-] *f Mus.* lead guitar; **~sänger** *m*, **~sängerin** *f* lead singer

leasen ['li:zn] *v/t.* lease

Leasing ['li:zɪŋ] *n*; *-s*, *-s* leasing; **~firma** *f* leasing company; **~rate** *f* leasing payment
Lebe|dame *f pej.* demi(-)mondaine; **~hoch** *n* cheer(s *Pl.*), three cheers *Pl.*; **ein ~ ausbringen** give three cheers; **~mann** *m pej.* man about town, playboy
leben I. *v/i.* **1.** (*am Leben sein*) live; (*nicht tot sein*) be alive; **lebt er noch?** is he still alive?; **er wird nicht mehr lange ~** he hasn't got much longer to live, his days are numbered; **so wahr ich lebe!** I swear it; **lebst du noch?** *umg. hum. iro.* well, hello stranger; **ich habe alles, was ich zum Leben brauche** I have all I need to keep body and soul together; **wir ~ nicht mehr im 19. Jahrhundert** *iro.* this isn't the 19th century(, you know); **wie gehts? - man lebt (so eben)** *umg.* how are things? - surviving; **2.** *e-e bestimmte Lebensweise haben*: **~ von** *von Nahrung*: live on (*od.* off); *von Tätigkeit etc.*: live from (*od.* off), make a living with (*od.* by *+ Ger.*); *von Verdienst, Rente*: live on; **vegetarisch ~** be a vegetarian; **makrobiotisch ~** live on macrobiotic food(s); **gesund/ungesund ~** lead a healthy / an unhealthy life; *in gesunden/ungesunden Verhältnissen*: live in healthy/unhealthy conditions; **sie ~ ganz gut** they don't do too badly (for themselves); **nach e-m Grundsatz ~** live in accordance with a principle, stick to a principle; **~ und ~ lassen** live and let live; **3.** (*wohnen*) live; **wie lange ~ Sie schon hier?** how long have you been living here?; **4.** *fig., Andenken etc.*: live on; **die Statue lebt** the statue is very (*od.* so) lifelike; **das Stück lebt nicht** there's no life in the play; **5. lebe ...!** three cheers for ...!; **es lebe der König / die Königin!** long live the King/Queen!; **~ Sie wohl** *altm.* farewell; → **Tag¹** 4; **II.** *v/t.*: **ein angenehmes/bequemes** *etc.* **Leben ~** lead a pleasant/comfortable *etc.* life, have a pleasant/comfortable (*od.* an easy) *etc.* lifestyle; **sein Leben noch einmal ~** live one's life (over) again; **sein eigenes Leben ~** lead an independent life, go one's own way; **s-n Glauben ~** geh. live according to one's faith (*od.* beliefs); **III.** *v/refl. unpers.*: **es lebt sich ganz angenehm/bequem** *etc.* life's quite pleasant/comfortable *etc.*; **hier lebt es sich gut** it's not a bad life here, life's not bad here
Leben *n*; *-s*, *-* **1.** life; (*Dasein*) *auch* existence; (*Sein*) being; **so ist das ~ (nun einmal)** that's life, such is life, *umg.* that's the way the cookie crumbles; **am ~ sein** be alive; **am ~ bleiben** stay alive, survive; **am ~ erhalten** keep alive; **er lebt am ~** he really enjoys life; *Todkranker*: he's not ready to die yet; **mit dem ~ davonkommen** survive, escape; **sein ~ teuer verkaufen** sell one's life dearly; **j-m das ~ schenken** spare s.o.'s life; **e-m Kind das ~ schenken** geh. (*gebären*) bring a child into the world; **~ spendend** geh. life-giving; **sich** (*Dat.*) **das ~ nehmen** take one's (own) life; **s-m ~ ein Ende machen** od. **setzen** put an end to one's life; (*freiwillig*) **aus dem ~ scheiden** geh. euph. die by one's own hand; **ums ~ kommen** be killed; **es geht um ~ und Tod** it's a matter of life and death; **um sein ~ laufen** od. **rennen** run for dear life; **2.** (*Lebenszeit*) life(time); **das ~ vor/ hinter sich** (*Dat.*) **haben** have one's

whole life ahead of one / have done with life; **mein ganzes ~** (*lang*) all my life; **das Geschäft m-s/s-s** *etc.* **~s** the best deal I have / he has *etc.* ever done, the deal of a lifetime; **3.** (*Lebensweise*) (way of) life, *auch pej.* lifestyle; **das ~ in Australien** life in Australia; **ein ~ in Armut / im Überfluss** a life of poverty/luxury; **das einfache ~** the simple life; **das süße ~** la dolce vita; **das ~ genießen** enjoy life; **das ~ ist schon schwer** it's a hard life; **j-m das ~ sauer machen** make s.o.'s life a misery; **sich mühsam durchs ~ schlagen** have a hard struggle through life; **das Stück ist aus dem ~ gegriffen** the play is a slice of life; **ein Stück nach dem ~** a play taken from real life, a slice of life; **4.** (*Lebenskraft, Lebendigkeit*) life, vitality; (*geschäftiges Treiben*) activity, bustle; *im Gesichtsausdruck*: animation; **~ in e-e Sache bringen** put some life into s.th.; **~ ins Haus bringen** *Kinder*: liven up the place; **~ in die Bude bringen** umg. liven things up; **das Stück hat kein ~** the play lacks vitality, there's no life in the play; **voll(er) ~** full of life (*umg.* full of activity (*od.* bustle); Straßen: full of activity (*od.* bustle); **5.** (*Lebensbeschreibung*) life, biography; **~ des Galilei** Titel: The Life of Galileo; **aus seinem ~ erzählen** recount stories from one's life; **6.** (*Geschehen*) kulturelles *etc.*: life; **im öffentlichen ~ stehen** be active in public life; **7.** (*Lebewesen Pl.*) life; **auf dem Mond ist kein ~** there's no life on the moon; **8.** *in Wendungen*: **etw. für sein ~ gern tun** love doing s.th.; **ich würde für mein ~ gern dorthin fahren** I'd give anything to go there, I'd love to go there; **nie im ~!** umg. never; (*auf gar keinen Fall*) auch not on your life; **je im ~** ever; **ins ~ rufen** call into being, start (up); **ins ~ treten** step into the big, wide world; **wie das ~ so spielt** life is full of surprises; **nicht ums ~ möchte ich das**: not for anything (in the world); → **abschließen** II 2, **blühend** II, **erwecken** 2, **ewig** I 1, **froh** 1, **lassen** III 6, **nackt**, **trachten**
lebend I. *Part. Präs.* → **leben**; **II.** *Adj.* (*lebendig*) living (*auch Sprache*); *Bio.* live; **~es Inventar** livestock; **~er Schild** human shield; **~e Ziele** live targets; **kein ~es Wesen** not a living soul; **der größte ~e Künstler** the greatest living artist; **ein noch ~er Zeuge** a witness who is still alive, a surviving witness; **III.** *Adv.* **gefangen, geborgen werden** *etc.*: alive; **~ gebärend** Zool. viviparous; **Lebende** *m, f*; *-n*, *-n* living person; **die** (*noch*) **~n** the survivors; **die ~n und die Toten** the living and the dead; **nicht mehr unter den ~n weilen** geh. no longer be in the land of the living; **er nimmt's von den ~n** he'd have the shirt off your back
Lebendgewicht *n* live weight
lebendig I. *Adj.* **1.** (*lebend*) living, präd. alive; **bei ~em Leibe** od. **~en Leibes verbrannt werden** be burnt alive; **wieder ~ machen/werden** bring/come back to life; **~ bleiben** Erinnerung *etc.*: be kept alive, survive; **~es Museum** working museum; **2.** *fig.* (*lebhaft*) lively; Schilderung: auch vivid; Geist: alert; Fantasie: lively; Farbe: cheerful; Glaube *etc.*: living; **~ werden** come to life, liven up; **II.** *Adv.* **1.** (*lebend*) alive; **~ begraben** buried alive; **sehr ~ wirken** be very lifelike; **2.** (*lebhaft*) in a lively manner; schildern: vividly; **sehr**

~ berichten give a very vivid report; → *auch* **lebend**; **Lebendigkeit** *f*; *nur Sg.* → **Lebhaftigkeit**
Lebens|abend *m* old age, the twilight years *lit.*; (*Ruhestand*) retirement; *lit.* evening of (one's) life; **~abschnitt** *m* stage of (one's) life, period in one's life; **~abschnittspartner** *m*, **~abschnittspartnerin** *f* oft hum. companion for a while; **~ader** *f* vital line of communication, lifeline; **~alter** *n* age; (*Lebensstufe*) stage of life; **ein hohes ~ erreichen** live to a ripe old age; **~angst** *f* angst, existential fear (*od.* anxiety); **~anschauung** *f* approach to life; philosophy (of life); **~arbeitszeit** *f* working life; **~art** *f* **1.** (*Lebensweise*) way of life, lifestyle; **2.** (*gute Umgangsformen*) manners; **feine ~** savoir-vivre; **er hat keine ~** he has no style; **~auffassung** *f* view (*od.* philosophy) of life; **~aufgabe** *f* life's work; *Zweck*: purpose in life; **es sich** (*Dat.*) **zur ~ machen zu** (*+ Inf.*) make it one's purpose in life to (*+ Inf.*), dedicate one's life to (*+ Ger.*); **~äußerung** *f* sign of life; **~baum** *m* **1.** tree of life; **2.** Bot. arbor vitae; **~bedingungen** *Pl.* living conditions
lebensbedrohend *Adj.*, **lebensbedrohlich** *Adj* life-threatening; **Lebensbedrohung** *f* threat to (one's) life
Lebens|bedürfnisse *Pl.* necessities of life; **~beichte** *f lit.* confessions *Pl.* (of one's past)
lebensbejahend *Adj.* life-affirming, positive(-minded)
Lebens|berechtigung *f* right to live (*od.* exist); **~bereich** *m* sphere (of life); **~beschreibung** *f* life, biography; **~bund** *m geh.* lifelong union; **~chancen** *Pl.* chances of survival; **~daten** *Pl.* biographical data, biodata; **~dauer** *f* lifespan; *fig., Tech. etc.* (*Haltbarkeit*) useful life; *Maschine*: auch working life; **auf ~ gebaut** built for longevity (*od.* durability); **~drang** *m* life force, vital instinct
lebensecht I. *Adj.* true to life, realistic; **II.** *Adv.* realistically
Lebens|einstellung *f* attitude to life; **~elixier** *n* elixir of life; **~ende** *n* end of one's life; **bis an sein ~** till the end of one's days; **~energie** *f* vitality
lebenserfahren *Adj.* experienced; **er ist sehr ~** he has much experience of life; **Lebenserfahrung** *f* experience of life; **aus m-r ~ heraus kann ich sagen ...** experience (of life) has taught me that ...
lebenserhaltend *Adj. Medikamente etc.*: life-saving; **~e Maßnahmen** measures to prolong life
Lebens|erinnerungen *Pl.* memoirs; **~erwartung** *f* life expectancy; **er/es hat keine hohe ~** he cannot be expected to live long / it cannot be expected to last long; **~faden** *m*: **j-m den ~ abschneiden** geh. cut the thread of s.o.'s life
lebensfähig *Adj. auch fig.* capable of surviving, viable; **Lebensfähigkeit** *f*; *nur Sg.* viability; *fig. auch* ability to survive
lebensfeindlich *Adj.* hostile to life
lebensfern *Adj.* remote from reality, unrealistic; **Lebensferne** *f*; *nur Sg.* remoteness from reality
Lebens|form *f* **1.** (*Lebensart*) way of life; **2.** Bio. life form, form of life; **~frage** *f* vital issue
lebensfremd *Adj.* out of touch (with

everyday life); unrealistic

Lebensfreude f joie de vivre

lebensfroh Adj. full of the joys of life, full of joie de vivre

Lebens|führung f life(style), way of life; **~funke(n)** m vital spark, spark of life; **~funktion** f vital function

Lebensgefahr f mortal danger; **~!** danger!; **in ~ schweben** be in a critical condition; **außer ~ sein** be out of danger; **im Krankenhaus:** be in a stable condition, be off the critical list; **sie hat ihn unter ~ gerettet** she risked her life to save him; **lebensgefährlich I.** Adj. extremely dangerous; Krankheit etc.: very serious, life-threatening; **II.** Adv.: **~ verletzt** very seriously injured

Lebens|gefährte m, **~gefährtin** f partner, companion for life; Jur. common law husband (Frau: wife); **~gefühl** n **1.** experience (od. awareness) of life; **es steigerte mein ~** it made me more keenly aware of being alive; **es war ein völlig neues ~** it was a completely new feeling (for me etc.), I etc. felt a different person; **2.** (Lebenseinstellung) attitude towards life; **~geister** Pl.: **j-s ~ wecken** put some life (back) into s.o., umg. get s.o. going (again); **nach dem Kaffee erwachten m-e ~ wieder** after the coffee I felt revived, the coffee got me going again; **~gemeinschaft** f **1.** (Zusammenleben) partnership; **2.** Bio. symbiosis (Pl. symbioses); **~genuss** m enjoyment of life; **~geschichte** f life story; **~gewohnheiten** Pl. **1.** way Sg. of life, (everyday) habits; **2.** e-s Volkes: way Sg. of life, customs; **~gier** f lust for life; **~glück** n happiness

lebensgroß Adj. life-size(d); **Lebensgröße** f: **in ~** bei Person, Tier: life-size(d); bei Sache: actual-size; **in doppelter ~** twice life-size/actual-size; **Gemälde in ~** life-size painting (od. portrait); **in voller ~** umg. fig. (höchstpersönlich) as large as life

Lebens|grundlage f (basis for one's) livelihood; **das ist keine ~** that's not enough to live on; **~hälfte** f: **in der ersten/zweiten ~** in the first/second half of one's life; **~haltung** f standard of living; (Kosten) cost of living

Lebenshaltungskosten Pl. cost Sg. of living

Lebenshilfe f Beratung: counsel(l)ing; Unterstützung: social support; Organisation: counsel(l)ing and support organization

Lebenshunger m appetite for life; **lebenshungrig** Adj. eager to live life to the full

Lebens|inhalt m purpose in life; **sie hat keinen ~** auch she's got nothing to live for; **sich** (Dat.) **etw. zum ~ machen** make s.th. the focal point of one's life, dedicate one's life to s.th.; **s-e Tiere sind sein einziger od. ganzer ~** he only lives for his animals, his whole life revolves around his animals; **~jahr** n: **im / in s-m 50. ~** at the age of 50 / when he was 50; **die ersten/letzten ~e** the first/last years of one's life; → **vollendet**; **~kampf** m struggle (od. fight) for survival

lebensklug Adj. worldly-wise

Lebens|kraft f vitality (auch Med.); **~krise** f personal (od. existential) crisis; **~kunst** f art of survival, making the best of things; **~künstler** m, **~künstlerin** f survivor, person who makes the best of things; **~lage** f situation (in life); **in allen ~n kommt er zurecht** he can cope (od. deal) with anything life throws at him

lebenslang Adj. lifelong ..., lifetime ...; **lebenslänglich I.** Adj. lifelong ..., lifetime ...; **~e Freiheitsstrafe** life sentence (od. imprisonment); **~ bekommen od. kriegen** umg. get life; **II.** Adv. all one's life; Jur. etc. for life; **Lebenslängliche** m, f; -n, -n; umg. prisoner serving a life sentence, umg. lifer; **~(r) sein** be serving a life sentence

Lebens|lauf m **1.** schriftlicher: curriculum vitae, CV, Am. résumé; (Kurzbiographie) biodata Pl.; **2.** life (story); **~linie** f in der Hand: lifeline; **~lüge** f grand delusion (on which s.o.'s life is based), sustaining delusion

Lebenslust f; nur Sg. joie de vivre, zest for life; **lebenslustig** Adj. full of joie de vivre (od. the joy of living); **er ist sehr ~** auch he's somebody who really enjoys life

Lebens|maxime f maxim (of life); principle (by which s.o. lives); **~mitte** f middle (od. mid-point) of one's life

Lebensmittel Pl. food Sg., formeller: foodstuffs, foods; **~abteilung** f food department; groß angelegt: food hall; **~chemie** f food chemistry; **~chemiker** m, **~chemikerin** f food chemist (od. analyst); **~geschäft** n food shop, Am. grocery store; **~gesetz** n food (purity) law; weitS. food regulations Pl.; **~händler** m, **~händlerin** f grocer; **~industrie** f food industry; **~karte** f (food) ration card; **~kette** f chain of food shops (Am. grocery stores); **~knappheit** f food shortage(s Pl.); **~kontrolle** f food quality control; **~paket** n food parcel (Am. package); **~vergiftung** f food poisoning; **~versorgung** f food supply; **~vorrat** m food supplies, provisions Pl.

Lebensmonat m: **in den ersten ~en** in (od. during) the first few months of life

lebensmüde Adj. tired of life; weitS. world-weary; **~ sein** auch have lost the will to live (od. go on living); **du bist wohl ~!** umg. are you trying to kill yourself?

Lebensmut m courage to face life; weitS. will to live; **er hatte keinen ~ mehr** auch he had lost all interest in life

lebensnah I. Adj. Darstellung etc.: true to life, lifelike; auch weitS. realistic; **II.** Adv. realistically; **Lebensnähe** f realism

Lebensnerv m fig. nerve cent|re (Am. -er); **ein Land in seinem ~ treffen** hit a country's vital nerve

lebensnotwendig Adj. vital, essential; **Lebensnotwendigkeit** f essential (for life), vital necessity

Lebenspartner m, **~in** f → **Lebensgefährte**; **Lebenspartnerschaft** f partnership for life

Leben spendend → **Leben** 1

Lebens|philosophie f philosophy of life; **~planung** f career planning

lebensprühend Adj. brimming over with life

Lebens|qualität f quality of life; **~raum** m **1.** living space; Pol. lebensraum; **2.** Bio. habitat; **~recht** n right to live (auf unabhängiges Leben: an independent life); **~regel** f rule of life, guiding principle

lebensrettend Adj. lifesaving; **Lebensretter** m, **~in** f rescuer, lifesaver; **mein ~** auch the man who saved my life, my

savio(u)r

Lebensrettungs|maßnahmen Pl. lifesaving measures; **~medaille** f lifesaving medal

Lebens|rhythmus m rhythm of life; **~saft** m poet. lifeblood; **~sinn** m; nur Sg. meaning of life; **~spanne** f lifespan; **~standard** m standard of living, living standard; **~stellung** f permanent post (Am. position), job for life; **~stil** m lifestyle; **~traum** m great dream of one's life; **mein ~** auch my life's dream

lebenstüchtig Adj. able to cope (od. deal) with life; **sehr ~ sein** cope very well with life; **Lebenstüchtigkeit** f ability to cope (od. deal) with life

Lebensumstände Pl. circumstances of one's life

lebensunfähig Adj. non-viable; auch fig. unfit for life; **Lebensunfähigkeit** f non-viability; auch fig. inability to survive

Lebensunterhalt m livelihood, living; (sich [Dat.]) **s-n ~ verdienen** earn (od. make) a living

lebensuntüchtig Adj. unable to cope (od. deal) with life

Lebens|verhältnisse Pl. **1.** living conditions; **2.** → **Lebensumstände**

lebensverlängernd I. Adj. life-prolonging; **II.** Adv.: **~ wirken** have the effect of prolonging life

Lebens|versicherung f life insurance; **~ auf den Erlebensfall** endowment insurance; **~wandel** m way of life; **e-n liederlichen ~ führen** lead a dissolute life; **~weg** m (path through) life; **~weise** f way of life; (Gewohnheiten) habits Pl.; **sitzende ~** sedentary life(style); **~weisheit** f **1.** nur Sg. worldly wisdom; **2.** (Spruch) maxim, (wise) aphorism; **~werk** n life's work

lebens|wert Adj. Leben: präd. und nachgestellt: worth living; **das Leben ~ machen** make life worth living; verbessern: improve the quality of life; **~wichtig** Adj. essential; Med., auch Frage etc.: vital; **~e Güter** essentials

Lebens|wille(n) m will to live; **~zeichen** n sign of life; (Nachricht) auch news Sg.; **kein ~ von sich geben** fig. show (od. give) no sign of life; **wir haben seit Wochen kein ~ von ihr (bekommen)** fig. auch we haven't heard a thing from her (od. had a peep out of her) for weeks umg.; **~zeit** f life(time); **auf ~** for life; **Mitglied auf ~** life member; **~ziel** n aim in life; **~zweck** m purpose (od. aim) in life

Leber f; -, -n; Anat., Gastr. liver; **frei od. frisch von der ~ weg reden** od. **sprechen** umg. fig. speak one's mind, not mince one's words; → **Laus**; **~blümchen** n Bot. hepatica, liverleaf; **~fleck** m mole; **~käse** m Gastr. type of meat loaf made of pork or veal, sometimes including liver

Leberknödel m südd., österr. Gastr. liver dumpling; **~suppe** f Gastr. liver dumpling soup

leberkrank Adj. suffering from a liver complaint; **~ sein** have (od. suffer from) a liver complaint

Leber|leiden n liver complaint (od. disease); **~moos** n Bot. liverwort; **~pastete** f Gastr. liver pâté; **~punktion** f Med. liver puncture; **~schaden** m Med. damaged liver; **~tran** m cod-liver oil; **~verfettung** f Med. fatty degeneration of the liver; **~werte** Pl. Med. liver count Sg.; **~wurst** f Gastr. liver sausage, Am. auch liverwurst,

Braunschweiger; → **beleidigt** II 2; **~zirrhose** f Med. cirrhosis of the liver

Lebewesen n living being; kleines: living organism; **menschliches ~** human being

Lebewohl n; -(e)s, -s und -e; lit. farewell; **j-m ~ sagen** bid s.o. farewell

lebhaft I. Adj. **1.** lively (auch Interesse, Fantasie etc.); Diskussion: auch animated; (hitzig) heated; Beifall: enthusiastic; Widerstand: vigorous; Straße: busy, bustling; Stadt: lively, bustling; stärker: vibrant; Verkehr: busy; Nachfrage: brisk; **~er Handel** brisk (od. buoyant) trading (Am. business); **~e Börse** buoyant (Am. active) trading on the stock market; **es herrschte ~es Treiben** there was a lot of activity (od. hustle and bustle); **~en Anteil nehmen** show a lively (od. keen) interest (**an** + Dat. in); **2.** (deutlich) Schilderung, Erinnerung etc.: vivid; (kräftig) Farbe: bright, vivid; **in ~er Erinnerung haben** have a vivid recollection (od. memory) of, remember vividly; **II.** Adv. **1.** in a lively manner; diskutieren: animatedly; (hitzig) heatedly; **~ begrüßen** give a warm welcome to; **sich ~ unterhalten** have a lively (od. an animated) conversation; **2.** (deutlich) darstellen, sich erinnern: vividly; **das kann ich mir ~ vorstellen** I can just imagine; **3.** (intensiv) sich interessieren: keenly; bedauern: greatly, deeply; **Lebhaftigkeit** f: nur Sg. **1.** liveliness; des Gesprächs: auch animation; e-r Straße, Stadt: auch bustling activity; des Handels: briskness; des Beifalls: enthusiasm; des Widerstands: vigo(u)rousness; **2.** e-r Schilderung, Erinnerung, Farbe etc.: vividness

Lebkuchen m etwa gingerbread

leblos Adj. lifeless (auch fig.); Materie, Gegenstand: inanimate; Augen, Gesicht: expressionless; **die Gegend ist ~** the place is dead, there's no life in the place; **~ liegen bleiben** od. **daliegen** lie there motionless; **Leblosigkeit** f; nur Sg. lifelessness; der Materie: inanimate nature; von Augen, Gesicht: expressionlessness; e-r Gegend: dead state, lack of life (+ Gen. in)

Lebtag m: **mein/dein** etc. **~ (nicht)** umg. (never in) all my/your etc. life; **so was hatte er sein ~ nicht gesehen** never in all his life (od. in all his born days) had he seen anything like it; **das wirst du dein ~ nicht vergessen** you won't forget it as long as you live, you'll remember it to your dying day

Lebzeiten Pl.: **zu s-n ~** in his time (od. day); (als er noch lebte) when he was still alive; **er war schon zu ~ als Genie anerkannt** he was already recognized as a genius in his own lifetime

lechzen v/i.: **~ nach** geh. thirst after

leck Adj. leaking, leaky; **~e Stelle** leak; **~ sein** auch leak, have a leak

Leck n; -(e)s, -e; Naut. leak; **ein ~ bekommen** spring a leak

lecken¹ v/i. (undicht sein) leak, have a leak

lecken² v/t/i. lick (auch **~ an** + Dat.); **die Katze leckte mir die Hand** the cat licked my hand; **sich** (Dat.) **die Finger ~ nach** umg. fig. drool after; **leck mich** (**doch**)! vulg. piss off!; → **Arsch** 1, **Blut** 1, **geleckt**

lecker I. Adj. **1.** (gut schmeckend) tasty; stärker: delicious, umg. scrumptious, delish, yummy; **2.** umg. fig. Mädchen etc.: gorgeous; **II.** Adv. deli-

---

ciously; **hier riecht's aber ~** there's a delicious (od. an appetizing) smell; **das schmeckt ~** it tastes really good (stärker: delicious, umg. scrumptious, yummy)

Leckerbissen m tasty titbit (Am. tidbit) (od. morsel); delikat: delicacy; fig. (real) treat, something to savo(u)r; **Leckerei** f; -, -en **1.** nur Sg. (constant) licking; **2.** titbit (Am. tidbit); (Süßigkeit) sweetie, Am. candy

Lecker|maul n, **~mäulchen** n: **ein ~ sein** (Feinschmecker sein) be a gourmet; (Süßes lieben) have a sweet tooth

leckschlagen v/i. (unreg., trennb., ist -ge-); Naut. be holed

led. Abk. → **ledig**

LED-Anzeige f LED display, light--emitting diode

Leder n; -s, Sorten: - **1.** leather; **die ~ verarbeitende Industrie** the leather (-working) industry; **in ~ gebunden** (Buch) leather(-)bound; **aus ~** (made of) leather; **vom ~ ziehen** fig. let fly; umg. let rip (**gegen** against); **j-m ans ~ gehen** umg. (angreifen) go for s.o.; **er wollte seinem Nebenbuhler ans ~** he was out to get his rival; → **zäh** I 1; **2.** (Fensterleder etc.) (chamois) leather; **3.** umg. (Fußball) ball

lederartig Adj. leathery; Stoff: leather--like

Lederball m leather ball

Lederband¹ m leather(-)bound book (od. volume)

Lederband² n leather strap

Leder|couch f leather sofa; **~einband** m leather binding

leder|farben Adj., **~farbig** Adj. buff(--colo[u]red)

Leder|garnitur f Möbel: (three-piece) leather suite; **~gurt** m leather strap; **~gürtel** m leather belt; **~handschuh** m leather glove; **~haut** f Anat. corium; Auge: sclera; **~hose** f (**e-e**) (a pair of) leather trousers (Am. pants) Pl.; mst Pl., kurze: lederhosen Pl.; **~imitat** n imitation leather; **~jacke** f leather jacket; Wildleder: suede jacket; **~koffer** m leather suitcase; **~mantel** m leather coat; **~mappe** f leather briefcase; **~montur** f Motorradfahrer: **in ~** in his (od. her) leathers (od. leather gear) umg.

ledern¹ Adj. leather ..., made of leather; fig. (fest, zäh) leathery; (langweilig) dull

ledern² v/t. (trockenwischen) wipe dry (polieren: go over) with a leather, leather down

Leder|nacken m umg. fig. leatherneck; **~polster** n leather cushion; **~riemen** m leather strap (od. belt); **~schuh** m leather shoe; **~sessel** m leather armchair; **~sohle** f leather sole; **~stiefel** m leather boot; **~tasche** f leather bag; **~tuch** n (chamois) leather; **~waren** Pl. leather goods

ledig Adj. **1.** (unverheiratet) single; auch Mutter, Vater: unmarried; **2.** geh.: **e-r Sache ~ sein** be free (od. rid) of s.th.; **Ledige** m, f; -n, -n single (person)

lediglich Adv. merely, only; **ich habe ~ gesagt** auch all I said was

ledrig Adj. leathery

Lee f, n; -s, kein Pl.; Geog., Naut. lee; **nach** od. **in ~** leeward

leer I. Adj. **1.** empty (auch fig.); Stelle: vacant; Blatt etc.: blank; **~es Gerede** hot air, empty talk; **~e Menge** Math. null set; **die Batterie ist ~** the battery is flat (Mot. und Am. dead); **mit ~en**

Händen empty-handed; **vor ~em Haus** / **vor ~en Bänken spielen** play to an empty theat|re (Am. auch -er) /stadium; **~ machen** umg. (Kiste, Packung etc.) empty, finish; **sein Glas ~ trinken** empty one's glass; **s-n Teller ~ essen** empty (od. clean) one's plate; **~ kaufen** (Geschäft etc.) buy out, empty the shelves of; **~ fahren** (Tank) run dry; **~ bleiben** Platz, Sitz: remain empty (od. unoccupied); **~ stehen** be empty, be unoccupied; **ein ~ stehendes Haus** an unoccupied (od. empty) house; **~ lassen** (Zeile, Seite) leave blank; **~ laufen** Tank etc.: run dry; **~ laufen lassen** (Fass, Teich etc.) drain; **~ pumpen** pump out (od. dry); **~ gefegt Straßen**: empty, deserted; Regale: empty; → **ausgehen** 8, **Stroh**; **2.** (unmöbliert) unfurnished; **3.** (ausdruckslos) empty, blank; Augen, Blick: expressionless; **4.** (unbegründet) unfounded; Drohung, Versprechen: empty, idle; **II.** Adv. Tech.: **~ laufen** od. **drehen** idle, be idling; → **Leerlauf**

Leere¹ n; -n, kein Pl.; (leerer Raum) empty space; **ins ~ starren** stare into space; **ins ~ greifen** clutch at thin air; **j-n ins ~ laufen lassen** (Gegner, Angreifer etc.) sidestep s.o. (auch fig.); Ballspiele: send s.o. the wrong way, sell s.o. a dummy, Am. fake s.o. out; **ins ~ gehen** guter Rat etc.: fall on deaf ears

Leere² f; -, kein Pl. **1.** (Leersein) emptiness (auch fig.); **geistige ~** mental vacuum; **2.** Raum: empty space; luftleerer: vacuum; innere: void; → **gähnend**

leeren I. v/t. **1.** empty; (räumen) clear out, von Menschen: clear, evacuate; **2.** Dial. (ausschütten) pour out; **II.** v/refl. empty; Straße: grow empty

Leer|fahrt f von Bus, Lkw: empty trip; **~formel** f empty formula; weitS. empty phrase; **~gang** m Tech. idle running, idling; Mot., bei der Schaltung: neutral (gear); **~gewicht** n dead weight; Behälter, Fahrzeug etc.: tare (weight); **~gut** n Wirts. empty containers, empties Pl.; **bitte ~ zurück** please return empty containers (Flaschen: bottles); **~kassette** f blank tape (od. cassette)

Leerlauf m **1.** Tech., Motor: idling; Maschine: idle running; **im ~ sein** Motor: be idling; Maschine: be running idle; **2.** Mot., Schaltung: neutral (gear); Fahrrad: freewheel; **im ~ fahren** coast, freewheel; **in den ~ schalten** go into neutral, put the car into neutral; **3.** fig. in Betrieb: unproductive phase, slack (od. idle) period(s Pl.); Sport etc.: boring patch(es Pl.); **~ haben** be having (od. going through) a slack (od. an idle) period; Person: have nothing to do; **es gab viel ~ im Betrieb** there were a lot of slack periods at work; in der Arbeitsweise: the firm had a lot of slack in the system

Leer|packung f Wirts. dummy; **~schritt** m Maschinenschreiben: space; **~stelle** f blank (space); **~takt** m Mot. idle stroke; **~taste** f space bar (Computer: auch key)

Leerung f emptying; Briefkasten: collection

Leer|zeichen n Computer: blank (character), space (character), spaceband; **~zeile** f empty line; **zwei ~n lassen** leave two lines free (od. blank)

Leeseite f Geog., Naut. lee(ward); **leewärts** Adv. leeward

Lefze f; -, -n, mst. Pl.; Zool. lip; Pl. von

Bluthund etc.: flews

legal *Adj.* legal; *auf ~em Weg erwerben* obtain by legal means; **legalisieren** *v/t.* legalize; **Legalisierung** *f* legalization; **Legalität** *f*; -, *kein Pl.* legality; *das ist am Rande der ~* that borders on the illegal, that's stretching the law

Legasthenie *f*; -, -*n* dyslexia; **Legastheniker** *m*; -*s*, -, **Legasthenikerin** *f*; -, -*nen* dyslexic; **legasthenisch** *Adj.* dyslexic

Legat[1] *m*; -*en*, -*en*; *kath.* legate

Legat[2] *n*; -(*e*)*s*, -*e*; *Jur.* legacy

Legato *n*; -*s*, -*s und Legati*; *Mus.* legato

Lege|batterie *f für Hennen*: laying battery; **~henne** *f* layer; **~leistung** *f von Hennen*: laying (performance)

legen I. *v/t.* **1.** (*auch Eier*) lay; (*bes. stellen, setzen*) put; (*hinstrecken*) lay down; (*flach hinlegen*) lay flat; *e-e Tischdecke auf den Tisch ~* spread (*od.* put) a tablecloth on the table; *ein Tuch um die Schultern ~* wrap a scarf around one's shoulders; *j-m den Arm um die Schultern ~* put one's arm (a)round s.o.'s shoulders; *sich* (*Dat.*) *die Haare ~ lassen* have a set (*Am.* perm *od.* permanent); *den Kopf ~ an* (+ *Akk.*) rest one's head against; **2.** (*Teppich*) put down, lay; (*Kabel etc.*) lay; **3.** (*Bombe*) plant, (*Mine*) lay; *Feuer ~ an* (+ *Akk.*) set fire to; *e-n Brand ~* start a fire, commit arson; **4.** *Sl.*, *beim Ringen*: *j-n ~* pin s.o. to the floor; *beim Fußball etc.*: floor s.o.; → *beiseite*, *Hand*[1] 1, 3, *Handwerk* 2; **II.** *v/refl.* **1.** lie down; *sich schlafen od. ins Bett ~* go to bed; *sich auf etw.* (*Akk.*) *~ Mensch, Tier*: lie on s.th.; *Staub, Nebel etc.*: settle on s.th.; *sich aufs Gemüt ~ fig.* get one down, be depressing; **2.** *fig.* (*nachlassen*) *Sturm, Wind, Lärm, auch Begeisterung, Aufregung etc.*: die down; *Skandal, Streit etc.*: blow over; *Spannung*: ease off; *Schmerz*: ease; *völlig*: go away; **III.** *v/i.* *Huhn etc.*: lay (eggs)

legendär *Adj.* legendary (*auch fig.*); **Legende** *f*; -, -*n* **1.** legend (*auch fig.*); *wie die ~ berichtet* as legend has it; *er war schon zu Lebzeiten e-e ~ fig.* he was a legend in his own (life)time; **2.** *Landkarte etc.*: legend; (*Schlüssel*) key; **Legendenbildung** *f* myth-making

leger [leˈʒɛːɐ̯] *Adj.* casual; *Ton, Benehmen etc.*: *auch* informal; *auch Person*: relaxed; *umg.* laid-back

Leggings *Pl.*, **Leggins** *Pl.* leggings

Leghenne *f* layer

legieren *v/t.* **1.** *Metall.* alloy; **2.** *Gastr.* thicken; **legiert I.** *P.P.* → *legieren*; **II.** *Adj.* **1.** *Metall.* alloy ..., alloyed; **2.** *Gastr.* thickened; *Suppe, Sauce*: cream *attr.*; **Legierung** *f* alloy

Legion *f*; -, -*en*; *Mil.* legion; *~en von fig.* myriads of; *ihre Zahl war ~* their number was legion; **Legionär** *m*; -*s*, -*e* **1.** *hist.* legionary; **2.** *der Fremdenlegion*: legionnaire (*auch fig. Sport*); **Legionärskrankheit** *f*; *nur Sg.*; *Med.* legionnaire's disease

Legislative *f*; -, -*n*; *Pol.* legislature, legislative assembly (*od.* body)

Legislatur *f*; -, -*en*; *Pol.* legislation; *~periode f* **1.** legislative period; *die erste/zweite Hälfte der ~* the first/second session of parliament (*Am.* legislative session); **2.** *Amtsdauer*: term of office

legitim *Adj.* legitimate; *fig. auch* (perfectly) justified; **Legitimation** *f*; -, -*en*

legitimation; (*Identitätsnachweis*) proof of identity, credentials *Pl.*; (*Berechtigung*) authority; **legitimieren I.** *v/t.* legitimize; (*berechtigen*) authorize; (*rechtfertigen*) justify; **II.** *v/refl.* prove one's identity; *mit Dokumenten etc.*: show one's credentials; **Legitimierung** *f* legitimizing; (*Berechtigung*) justification

Legitimität *f*; -, *kein Pl.* legitimacy

Leguan *m*; -*s*, -*e*; *Zool.* iguana

Leguminose *f*; -, -*n*, *mst Pl.*; *Bot.* leguminous plant, legume

Lehen *n*; -*s*, -; *hist.* fief; *j-m Land zu ~ geben* give s.o. land in fee, enfeoff s.o.; **Lehens...** *siehe Lehns...*

Lehm *m*; -(*e*)*s*, -*e* loam; (*Ton*) clay; (*Dreck*) mud; *~bau m* **1.** *nur Sg.* → *Lehmbauweise*; **2.** *Pl.* -*bauten* clay (*od.* adobe) building; *~bauweise f* building with clay; *mit Flechtwerk*: wattle and daub construction; *~boden m* loamy soil; (*Tonerde*) clay(ey) soil

lehmfarben *Adj.* clay-colo(u)red

Lehmgrube *f* clay pit

lehmhaltig *Adj.*: *~er Boden* soil containing loam

Lehmhütte *f* mud (*aus Ziegeln*: adobe) hut

lehmig *Adj.* loamy; (*tonartig*) clayey

Lehm|klumpen *m* lump of clay; *~ziegel m* clay brick; *luftgetrocknet*: adobe

Lehne *f*; -, -*n* **1.** (*Rückenlehne*) back; (*Armlehne*) arm(rest); **2.** *südd., österr., schw.* (*Hang*) slope

lehnen I. *v/i. und v/refl.* (*sich*) *~* lean (*an* + *Akk.* against; *auf* + *Akk.* on; *über* + *Akk.* over); *sich aus dem Fenster ~* lean out of (*Am. auch* out) the window; **II.** *v/t.* lean, rest (*gegen* + *Akk.* against, on); (*stützen*) prop (against)

Lehngut *n* **1.** *hist.* estate held in fee, fee; **2.** *Ling.* loan vocabulary

Lehnsessel *m* easy chair

Lehns|herr *m*, *~herrin f hist.* feudal lord; *~mann m Pl.* -*leute* vassal, liege man; *~recht n* feudal law; *subjektives*: right of investiture

Lehnstuhl *m* armchair, easy chair

Lehnswesen *n*; *nur Sg.*; *hist.* feudal system

Lehn|übersetzung *f Ling.* loan translation; *~wort n* loanword

Lehramt *n Päd.* teaching profession; *Stelle*: teaching post

Lehramtsanwärter *m*, *~in f Päd.* trainee (*Am.* student) teacher

Lehr|angebot *n Univ.* range of courses offered, teaching program(me), *Am. auch* curriculum; *~anstalt f förm.* educational establishment, school; *~auftrag m* teaching assignment; *Univ.* part-time lectureship (without full status), *Am. auch* adjunct status

lehrbar *Adj.* teachable

Lehr|beauftragte *m, f* **1.** *Univ.* part-time lecturer (without full status), *Am.* adjunct (professor, *etc.*); *~(r) sein Am.* teach as an adjunct; **2.** (*Fachleiter[in]*) teacher trainer; *~befähigung f* (school) teaching qualification; *~beruf m* **1.** *Päd.* teaching profession; **2.** *altm.* job requiring apprenticeship; *Tischler ist ein klassischer ~* carpentry is a classic case of a job for which one has to serve an apprenticeship; *~betrieb m*, *nur Sg.*; *Univ. etc.* teaching activity; *~brief m* certificate (of apprenticeship); *~bub m südd., österr., schw.* apprentice; *~buch n* textbook

Lehre[1] *f*; -, -*n* **1.** (*Erfahrung*) lesson;

e-r Geschichte: moral; *das war mir e-e ~* that was a lesson (for me); *lass dir das e-e ~ sein* let that be a lesson to you; *e-e ~ ziehen aus* draw a lesson from, take a warning from; *weitS.* learn from; *wir müssen aus dieser Panne unsere ~n ziehen* we must learn (the lessons) from this failure; **2.** *Berufsausbildung*: apprenticeship; *bei j-m in die ~ gehen* be apprenticed (*od.* an apprentice) to s.o.; *bei dem kannst du noch in die ~ gehen umg. fig.* he can teach you a thing or two; *bei j-m in die ~ gegangen sein fig.* have learn|t (*Am.* -ed) a lot from s.o.; *e-e harte ~ durchmachen* (*müssen*) (have to) learn the hard way; **3.** (*Weltanschauung*) teaching, doctrine; *nach der marxistischen ~* according to Marxist doctrine; **4.** (*Wissenschaft*) science; (*Theorie*) theory; **5.** (*Ratschlag*) (piece of) advice

Lehre[2] *f*; -, -*n*; *Tech.* ga(u)ge

lehren *vt/i.* teach; *j-n etw. ~* teach s.o. (how to do) s.th.; *j-n lesen ~* teach s.o. to read; *die Erfahrung lehrt, dass ...* experience teaches us (*od.* shows [us], tells us) that ...; *ich werd dich ~, so frech zu lügen!* I'll teach you to tell such barefaced (*bes. Am.* bald-faced) lies!; **Lehrende** *m, f*: -*n*, -*n* teacher; *die ~n* the teaching staff

Lehrer *m*; -*s*, -; *Päd.* teacher; (*Fahr-, Skilehrer etc.*) instructor; (*Privatlehrer*) tutor; *ist er noch ~?* does he still teach?, is he still in teaching?; *er ist ~ für Englisch und Geschichte* he is a teacher of English and history, he teaches English and history; *~ausbildung f* teacher training; *~beruf m* teaching profession

lehrerhaft *Adj. pej.* teacherly; *Mann*: *Brit. auch* schoolmasterly; *Frau*: schoolmarmish

Lehrerhandreichungen *Pl. Päd.* teachers' notes

Lehrerin *f*; -, -*nen* → *Lehrer*

Lehrer|kollegium *n Päd.* teaching staff (*mst V. im Pl.*), *Am. auch* faculty; *~konferenz f* staff (*Am.* faculty) meeting; *~mangel m* shortage of teachers, teacher shortage

Lehrerschaft *f Päd.* teachers *Pl.*; *e-r einzigen Schule*: *auch* teaching staff (*mst V. im Pl.*), *Am. auch* faculty

Lehrer|schwemme *f umg.* glut (*od.* surplus) of teachers; *~stelle f* teaching post (*Am.* position); *~zimmer n* staff room, *Am. auch* teachers' lounge

Lehr|fach *n* **1.** (*Unterrichtsfach*) subject; **2.** *als Beruf*: teaching profession; *~film m* educational film; *~gang m* course; *~gebäude n* system of theories; *~gegenstand m* **1.** subject (of instruction); **2.** *österr.* subject; *~geld n früher*: apprenticeship premium; *teures od. schwer ~ bezahlen* (*müssen*) *für etw. fig.* (have to) pay (dearly) for s.th.; *engS.* (have to) learn s.th. the hard way

lehrhaft *Adj.* instructive; *pej.* (*belehrend*) *umg.* know-(it-)all

Lehr|herr *m hist.* (apprentice's) master; *~jahr n* year of one's apprenticeship; *die ~e* one's (period of) apprenticeship; *harte ~e fig.* a school of hard knocks; *~e sind keine Herrenjahre* we've all got to work our way up from the bottom; *~junge m* apprentice; *~körper m Päd.* teaching staff (*mst V. im Pl.*), *Am. auch* faculty; *~kraft f Päd.* (qualified) teacher

Lehrling *m*; -*s*, -*e* apprentice, trainee

Lehr|mädchen *n altm.* (female) apprentice; **~material** *n* teaching material; **~meinung** *f* school of thought; **~meister** *m*, **~meisterin** *f* **1.** *auch hist. e-s Lehrlings*: master; **2.** *fig.* (*Person*) teacher, mentor; **~methode** *f* teaching method; **~mittel** *Pl.* teaching materials; **~mittelfreiheit** *f; nur Sg.* free provision of teaching materials; **~personal** *n* teaching staff (*mst V. im Pl.*)
Lehrplan *m Päd.* syllabus; *über mehrere Jahre*: curriculum; **~entrümpelung** *f* curricular streamlining
Lehrprobe *f Päd.* demonstration lesson
lehrreich *Adj.* instructive, informative; *das war für mich sehr ~* I found it very instructive (*od.* informative), I learnt a lot from it
Lehr|saal *m Univ.* lecture hall; **~satz** *m* doctrine; *Math., Philosophie*: theorem, proposition; *Rel. auch* dogma; **~schwimmbecken** *n* beginners' pool; **~stelle** *f* apprenticeship, position as an apprentice; *kaufmännisch*: trainee place; **~stoff** *n Päd.* material; **~stück** *n Lit.* didactic play
Lehrstuhl *m Univ.* chair (*für* of); **~inhaber** *m*, **~inhaberin** *f*: *sie ist Lehrstuhlinhaberin an der Universität X* she has (*od.* holds) a chair at the University of X (*od.* at X University)
Lehr|stunde *f fig.*: *das Endspiel war e-e ~ in brasilianischer Fußballkunst* the final was a demonstration lesson in (*od.* demonstration of) Brazilian footballing skill; **~tätigkeit** *f Päd., Univ.* (*Unterrichten*) teaching; (*Stelle*) teaching post (*od.* job); *e-e ~ ausüben* teach; **~tochter** *f schw.* (girl) apprentice; **~veranstaltung** *f* (*Vorlesung*) lecture; (*Seminar*) seminar; *die ~en in diesem Semester* this semester's courses (and lectures); **~vertrag** *m altm.* articles *Pl.* of apprenticeship; **~werk** *n* (school) textbook; **~werkstatt** *f* training workshop; **~zeit** *f* apprenticeship; *harte ~ fig.* school of hard knocks; **~zeugnis** *n* apprentice's diploma
Leib *m; -(e)s, -er* **1.** (*Körper*) body; *~ und Seele* body and soul; *mit ~ und Seele* heart and soul; *der ~ Christi od. des Herrn kirchl.* the body of Christ, corpus Christi; *e-e Gefahr für ~ und Leben* a risk to life and limb; *am ganzen ~ zittern* tremble from head to toe; *sie besaß nur noch, was sie auf dem ~ trug* she only had what she was standing up in; *etw. am eigenen ~ erfahren* experience s.th. oneself (*od.* first-hand); *am eigenen ~ erfahren, was Armut heißt* learn from experience (*od.* the hard way) what it means to be poor; *ich hab's am eigenen ~ erfahren od.* gespürt *auch* I know that only too well (from my own experience); *j-m* (*hart*) *auf den ~ rücken umg.* start breathing down s.o.'s neck; *j-m/ e-r Sache zu ~e rücken* tackle s.o./s.th.; *j-m auf den ~ geschnitten sein* be tailor-made for s.o.; *die Rolle ist ihm auf den ~ geschrieben* he was made for the part; *sich* (*Dat.*) *j-n vom ~(e) halten umg.* keep s.o. at arm's length; *sich* (*Dat.*) *etw. vom ~(e) halten umg.* steer clear of s.th.; *halt ihn mir bloß vom ~(e)! umg.* just don't let him come near me; *bleib mir damit vom ~(e)! umg.* I don't want to hear about it; → *lebendig* I 1, *Lunge etc.*; **2.** *geh.* (*Bauch*) abdomen (*auch fachspr.*); (*Rumpf*) trunk; (*Mutterleib*) womb; (*noch*) *nichts Ordentliches im ~ haben umg.* have had nothing proper to eat
Leib|arzt *m*, **~ärztin** *f* private (*od.* personal) physician; **~binde** *f* **1.** waistband, sash; **2.** *Med.* truss
Leibchen *n* **1.** *altm.* (*Mieder*) bodice; **2.** *österr., schw.* (*Unterhemd*) vest, *Am.* undershirt; (*Trikot*) singlet
leibeigen *Adj.* in bondage; **Leibeigene** *m, f; -n, -n* serf; *~(r) sein auch* be in bondage; **Leibeigenschaft** *f* serfdom
leiben *v/i.*: *das ist Petra, wie sie leibt und lebt* (*zum Verwechseln ähnlich*) that's Petra to a T, she's the spitting image of Petra; (*typisch für sie*) that's Petra all over
Leibes|erziehung *f Amtsspr.* physical education; **~frucht** *f Med.* f(o)etus; *poet.* fruit of the womb; **~fülle** *f; nur Sg.* corpulence, portliness; **~kräfte** *Pl.*: *aus ~n* with all one's might, *lit.* with might and main; *schreien*: at the top of one's voice; **~übungen** *Pl. Amtsspr. Schulfach*: physical education, PE; (*Fülle*) corpulence; **~umfang** *m* waist(line); **~visitation** *f* body search; *j-n e-r ~ unterziehen* body-search (*od.* frisk *umg.*) s.o.
Leib|garde *f* bodyguard; *e-s Monarchen*: Royal Guard; **~gericht** *n* favo(u)rite food; *Spaghetti sind mein ~ auch* I could live off spaghetti; **~getränk** *n* favo(u)rite drink
leibhaftig **I.** *Adj.* **1.** (*wirklich*) real; *umg.* real live; *ein ~es Gespenst* a real ghost, a ghost as real as you are; **2.** (*personifiziert*) in person; *der ~e Teufel* the devil incarnate; *sie war die ~e Faulheit* she was laziness in person (*od.* the epitome of laziness); *er sah aus wie mein ~er Bruder* he was the spitting image of my brother; *wie der ~e Tod aussehen* look like death warmed up (*Am.* over), look like a corpse; **II.** *Adv.*: *da stand er ~ vor mir* there he was, as large as life; *ich seh ihn noch ~ vor mir* (*stehen*) I can see him now, I can still see him in my mind's eye; **Leibhaftige** *m; -n, kein Pl.*: *der ~* the devil, Satan
Leib|koch *m*, **~köchin** *f* personal cook
leiblich **I.** *Adj.* bodily (*auch Adv.*), physical; (*irdisch*) worldly; *Eltern, Erbe*: natural; *Mutter*: *auch* biological, birth; *Bruder, Schwester*: blood; *ihr ~er Sohn* her own son; *~e Genüsse* physical pleasures; *sinnliche*: pleasures of the flesh; *~es Wohl*(*ergehen*) physical well-being; *weitS.* (*Genüsse*) creature comforts; *wir werden schon für dein ~es Wohl sorgen hum.* we'll make sure you don't go hungry; **II.** *Adv.* bodily
Leib|rente *f* life annuity; **~schmerzen** *Pl.* stomache-ache *Sg.*; **~speise** *f* favo(u)rite food; **~-und-Magen-Gericht** *n* → *Leibgericht*; **~wache** *f* bodyguard(s *Pl.*); **~wächter** *m*, **~wächterin** *f* bodyguard; **~wäsche** *f* underwear
Leiche *f; -, -n* **1.** corpse, (dead) body; *e-s Tiers*: carcass, cadaver; *sie sieht aus wie e-e wandelnde od. lebende ~ umg. fig.* she looks like death warmed up (*Am.* over) (*immer*: like a corpse); *er geht über ~n pej.* he'll stop at nothing; *nur über m-e ~! umg.* over my dead body!; *e-e ~ im Keller haben umg. fig.* have a skeleton in the cupboard; → *fleddern* 1; **2.** *Dial.* (*Begräbnis*) funeral; (*Leichenschmaus*) funeral reception; **3.** *Druck.* omission
Leichen|beschau *f* postmortem (examination); **~beschauer** *m*, **~be-**
schauerin *f* pathologist (performing a postmortem), *Am.* medical examiner; **~bestatter** *m*, **~bestatterin** *f* undertaker, *Am. auch* mortician; *förm.* funeral director; **~bittermiene** *f umg. iro.* doleful expression
leichenblass *Adj.* deathly pale, (as) white as a sheet (*od.* ghost); **Leichenblässe** *f* deathly pallor
Leichen|feier *f* funeral reception; **~fleck** *m* livor mortis; *mst Pl.* cadaveric lividity; **~fledderei** *f; -, -en; Jur.* robbing of the dead (*od.* unconscious), body-stripping; **~fledderer** *m* robber of the dead (*od.* unconscious), body-stripper; **~fund** *m* discovery of a corpse; **~geruch** *m* smell of (decaying) corpses (*od.* a [decaying] corpse); **~gift** *n* ptomaine
leichenhaft *Adj.* corpse-like, cadaverous; *~e Blässe* deathly pallor
Leichen|halle *f*, **~haus** *n* mortuary; **~hemd** *n* burial garment, shroud; **~mahl** *n geh.* funeral meal; **~öffnung** *f* postmortem (examination), autopsy; **~raub** *m* **1.** body-snatching; **2.** → *Leichenfledderei*; **~räuber** *m* **1.** body-snatcher; **2.** → *Leichenfledderer*; **~rede** *f* funeral oration; *e-e ~ halten umg. fig.* hold a postmortem; **~redner** *m*, **~rednerin** *f* funeral orator; **~reste** *Pl.* bodily remains; **~sack** *m* body bag; **~schänder** *m*, **~schänderin** *f* necrophiliac; **~schändung** *f* necrophilia; **~schau** *f Jur.* postmortem (examination); **~schauhaus** *n* morgue; **~schmaus** *m hum.* funeral reception (*od.* party), wake; **~starre** *f* rigor mortis; **~teil** *m* part of a dead body; **~tuch** *n altm.* shroud (*auch fig.*), winding sheet; **~verbrennung** *f* cremation; **~wagen** *m* hearse; **~wäscher** *m*, **~wäscherin** *f* washer of corpses; **~zug** *m* funeral procession, cortège
Leichnam *m; -s, -e; geh.* corpse, (dead) body; *der ~ Christi* the body of Christ, corpus Christi; → *auch Leiche*
leicht **I.** *Adj.* **1.** *Gewicht*: light; *Kleidung*: *auch* thin, cool; *Anzug*: lightweight; *das Kind ist für sein Alter zu ~* this child is underweight for his age; *danach war ich um hundert Euro ~er umg. fig.* I came away a hundred euros lighter; *gewogen und zu ~ befunden fig.* tried and found wanting; **2.** (*bekömmlich*) *Essen, Lektüre, Musik, Wein etc.*: light; *Zigarre*: mild; *abends esse ich meist etwas Leichtes* I usually have a light meal in the evening; *er hat e-n ~en Schlaf* he's a light sleeper; → *Kost*; **3.** (*unbeschwert*) light-hearted; *~en Herzens* happily; (*erleichtert*) relieved; (*ohne weiteres*) readily; *jetzt ist mir ~er* (*ums Herz*)! what a relief!, that's a load off my mind; *~en Fußes* lightfootedly, nimbly; *fig.* with a spring in one's step; **4.** (*nicht schwierig*) easy; *Aufgabe etc.*: *auch* simple; *~er Sieg walkover, Am.* walkaway; *nichts ~er als das!* nothing could be simpler, no problem, it's a cinch (*Am. auch* snap) *umg.*; *er nimmt es auf die ~e Schulter* he's making light of it, he's pretty casual about it; *keinen ~en Stand haben* be in a difficult (*od.* tricky) position; *es ist ihm ein Leichtes zu* (+ *Inf.*) it's a simple matter (*umg.* no big deal) for him to (+ *Inf.*); → *Spiel* 2; **5.** (*sanft*) *Brise, Berührung etc.*: light, gentle; **6.** (*geringfügig*) slight (*auch Erkältung*); *Entzündung, Gehirnerschütterung*: *auch* mild; *Strafe*: mild; *Verletzung, Verge-*

L

hen: minor; *Fehler*: minor, little; *Kratzer*: *Mot.* surface, *auch am Körper*: little; **~er Regen/Schnee** light rainfall/snowfall; **ein ~er Fall** (*Krankheit*) a mild case, nothing serious; (*Kranker*) a straightforward case; **er hat e-e ~e Bronchitis** he has a mild case of (*umg.* a touch of) bronchitis; **7.** *umg.*: **ein ~es Mädchen** a bit of a tart (*Am.* slut); **II.** *Adv.* **1.** (*geringfügig*) slightly; **~ berühren** touch gently (*od.* carefully); *versehentlich*: brush against; **es regnete ~** it was raining slightly, there was a light rain falling; **das ist ~ übertrieben** that's a slight (*od.* a bit of an) exaggeration; **~ bedeckter Himmel** slightly overcast skies, slight cloud cover; **~ bekleidet** lightly dressed; *spärlich*: scantily dressed (*iro.* clad); **~ beschwingt Melodie**: lilting, with a gentle lilt; **~ bewaffnet** lightly armed; **~ geschürzt** *hum.* scantily clad; **~ verletzt** slightly hurt (*od.* injured); **~ verwundet** slightly wounded; **2.** (*mühelos*) *mit Adj.* easily; **~ beweglich** easily transportable; (**~ verstellbar**) easily adjustable **~ entzündlich** *Gas, Flüssigkeit etc.* highly inflammable (*bes. Am. und Tech.* flammable); **~ löslich** easily (*od.* readily) soluble; **~ verdaulich** (easily) digestible; *auch fig.* light; **~ verderblich** perishable; **~ verderbliche Waren** perishables; **~ verdientes Geld** easy money; **~ verkäuflich** *Artikel*: easy to sell, fast-selling; **~ verständlich** easy to understand (*od.* follow); *Sprache*: *auch* (very) straightforward; **~ verständliche Lektüre** easy reading; **in ~ verständlicher Form** in comprehensible (*od.* accessible) form; **3.** (*einfach*) *mit Verb*: **es geht ganz ~** it's really easy; **~er gesagt als getan** *od.* **das ist ~ gesagt** easier said than done; **du hast ~ reden** it's all right for you, 'you can talk; **j-m ~ fallen** be easy for s.o.; **es fällt ihm nicht ~** it isn't easy for him (*zu + Inf.* to + *Inf.*), he doesn't find it easy (+ *Ger. od.* to + *Inf.*); **so etwas fällt ihm ~** he finds that sort of thing easy, that sort of thing comes easily to him, he has no difficulty with that sort of thing; **es ~ haben** have an easy time (of it); **mit ihm hat sie's nicht ~** she has a difficult time with him, he gives her a hard time; **j-m etw. ~ machen** make s.th. easy for s.o.; **es sich** (*Dat.*) **~ machen** take the easy way out; **du machst es dir zu ~** you're making life too easy for yourself; *in diesem Fall*: it's not that simple; **sich** (*Dat.*) **mit etw. ~ tun** *umg.* have no difficulties with s.th., have no difficulty doing s.th.; *auch grundsätzlich*: find it easy to do s.th.; **mit so etwas tut er sich ~** *auch* that sort of thing comes easily (*od.* easy) to him; **4.** (*nicht ernst*): **etw. ~ nehmen** take s.th. lightly; **er nimmt es zu ~** he doesn't take it seriously enough; **das Leben ~ nehmen** take life as it comes; **nimm's ~!** *umg.* don't worry about it; **5.** (*schnell*) easily; **er erkältet sich ~** he catches cold very easily, he's always catching cold; **so etwas passiert ~** that (sort of thing) can happen very easily (*od.* before you know it); **das wird so ~ nicht wieder passieren** it's not likely to happen again; **das wird mir so ~ nicht wieder passieren** I'll make sure that doesn't happen again in a hurry; **das wird er so ~ nicht vergessen** I('ll) bet he won't forget that in a hurry; **es ist ~ möglich** that could well be, that's quite possi-

ble; **du kannst dir ~ denken ...** you can well imagine

Leichtathlet m, **~in** f (track *od.* field) athlete; *Pl.* (track-and-field) athletes; **Leichtathletik** f (track-and-field) athletics *Pl.* (*oft V. im Sg.*); **leichtathletisch** *Adj.* athletic, track-and-field

Leicht|bauweise f lightweight construction; **~benzin** n benzine

leichtern *v/t. Naut.* unload (partially)

leichtfertig I. *Adj.* **1.** (*unbedacht, gedankenlos*) careless, thoughtless; *Versprechen, Entscheidung*: ill-considered, rash; (*fahrlässig*) irresponsible; **~es Gerede** careless (*od.* loose) talk; **2.** *altm.* (*frivol*) frivolous, easygoing; *Mädchen*: flighty, ... of easy virtue; **II.** *Adv.*: **etw. ~ abtun** shrug s.th. off; **etw. ~ aufs Spiel setzen** gamble with s.th.; **Leichtfertigkeit** f **1.** carelessness, thoughtlessness; *von Versprechen, Entscheidung*: rashness; (*Fahrlässigkeit*) irresponsibility; **2.** *altm.* (*Frivolität*) frivolity; *e-s Mädchens*: flightiness

Leicht|flugzeug n light aircraft; **~fuß** m *umg. hum.*, *mst pej.* devil-may-care (*od.* happy-go-lucky) type; (*Abenteurer*) adventurer; (*Frauenheld*) ladykiller; **du bist ein Bruder ~** you're really easy come, easy go

leichtfüßig *Adj.* nimble, *lit.* fleet-footed; **Leichtfüßigkeit** f, *nur Sg.* nimbleness, *lit.* fleetness of foot

leichtgängig *Adj. Tech.*, *Lenkung, Steuerung*: light; *Kupplung, Schaltung*: smooth

Leichtgewicht n **1.** *Sport* lightweight (*auch Sportler*); **2.** *umg.* (*leichte Person*) featherweight; **Leichtgewichtler** m; -s, -, **Leichtgewichtlerin** f; -, -nen lightweight

leichtgläubig *Adj.* gullible, credulous; **Leichtgläubigkeit** f gullibility, credulity

Leichtheit f; *nur Sg.* lightness

leichtherzig *Adj.* lighthearted, carefree; *auch pej.* happy-go-lucky; **Leichtherzigkeit** f lightheartedness, carefree (*auch pej.* happy-go-lucky) attitude (*od.* outlook)

leichthin *Adv.* straight out (without thinking), *umg.* just like that; (*lässig*) casually

Leichtigkeit f; *nur Sg.* **1.** (*Mühelosigkeit*) easiness, ease; **mit** (*größter*) **~** with (the greatest of) ease, effortlessly; **es ist für ihn e-e ~** it's no problem (*umg.* big deal, great shakes) for him; *stärker*: it's the easiest thing in the world for him; **2.** (*Leichtheit*) lightness

leichtlebig *Adj.* easygoing; (*unbekümmert*) happy-go-lucky; **Leichtlebigkeit** f; *nur Sg.* easygoing (*od.* happy-go-lucky) attitude (*od.* nature

Leichtlohngruppe f *Wirts.* low-wage group

Leichtmatrose m *Naut.* ordinary seaman

Leichtmetall n light metal; *mst Alulegierung*: (light) alloy; **~rad** n *Mot.* alloy wheel

Leichtöl n light oil, low-viscosity oil

Leichtschwergewicht n *Sport, Gewichtsklasse, auch Sportler(in)*: light heavyweight; **Leichtschwergewichtler** m; -s, -, **Leichtschwergewichtlerin** f; -, -nen light heavyweight

Leichtsinn m; *nur Sg.* carelessness; *gefährlich*: recklessness; **sträflicher ~** criminal negligence; **jugendlicher ~** youthful abandon; **purer ~** sheer recklessness; **leichtsinnig I.** *Adj.* careless;

(*gefährlich*) reckless; **II.** *Adv.*: **~ umgehen mit** be careless with; → *auch* **leichtfertig II**; **leichtsinnigerweise** *Adv.* carelessly; (*gefährlich*) recklessly; (*voreilig*) rashly, unthinkingly; **Leichtsinnigkeit** f carelessness; *gefährlich*: recklessness; **Leichtsinnsfehler** m careless mistake, slip

Leichtverletzte m, f minor casualty; slightly injured person; **~(r) sein** be slightly injured

Leichtverwundete m, f minor casualty; **~(r) sein** be slightly wounded

Leichtwasserreaktor m *Kerntechnik*: light water reactor

leid *Adj.*; *nur präd.*; *umg.*: **j-n/etw. ~ sein/werden** be/get tired (*od.* fed up) with s.o./s.th.; **ich bin es ~** *auch* I've had enough of it; *stärker*: I'm sick and tired of it; **ich habe es so ~** *auch* I can't take it any more

Leid n; -(e)s, kein Pl. **1.** suffering; (*Trauer*) sorrow, grief; **j-m großes ~ zufügen** cause s.o. great suffering; **j-m sein ~ klagen** pour one's heart out to s.o.; **~ tragen** *lit.* mourn (**um** for); **2.** (**es**) **tut mir ~** (I'm) sorry; **das tut mir aber ~** *mitfühlend*: I'm sorry to hear that; **es tut mir ~, aber ... bei Absage etc.*: I'm afraid ..., much as I'd like to, ...; **es tut mir ~ um ihn** I feel sorry for him; **es tut mir um die Möbel ~** it's the furniture I'm worried about; **es wird dir** (**noch**) **~ tun** you'll be sorry (you did this), you'll (live to) regret it; → **geteilt II**; **3.** (*Schaden*) harm; (*Unrecht*) wrong; **j-m ein ~ zufügen** *od.* **tun** do s.o. harm (*Unrecht*: wrong), *handgreiflich*: do s.o. an injury; **es wird ihm kein ~ geschehen** he won't come to any harm

Leideform f *Ling.* passive (voice)

leiden; *leidet, litt, hat gelitten* **I.** *v/i.* **1.** suffer (**an, unter** + *Dat.* from); (**sehr**) **~** (*Schmerzen haben*) be in (considerable) pain; **er leidet an e-r Leberkrankheit** *etc.* he has a liver *etc.* complaint; **s-e Gesundheit litt darunter** it took its toll on his health; **der Motor hat stark gelitten** the engine has suffered considerably (*od.* suffered considerable damage); **2.** *fig. nach Kränkung etc.* suffer (**unter** + *Dat.* from); **II.** *v/t.* **1.** (*Hunger, Not etc.*) suffer; *weitS.* (*ertragen*) put up with; **2.** (*aushalten*) stand, endure; **j-n gut können** *od.* **mögen** like s.o., have a soft spot for s.o.; **ich kann ihn/es nicht ~** I can't stand him/it; **ich hab ihn/es nie ~ können** I've never liked him/it; *stärker*: I could never stand him/it; **3.** (*dulden*): **er war dort nur gelitten** he was only tolerated there; **sie ist überall / bei ihren Freunden** *etc.* **gut gelitten** she is popular (*od.* well liked) everywhere / among her friends *etc.*

Leiden n; -s, - suffering(s *Pl.*); (*Krankheit*) illness, complaint; **sie starb nach langem, schwerem ~** she died after a long and painful illness; **das ~ Christi** the Passion; **aussehen wie das ~ Christi** *umg. fig.* look like death warmed up (*Am.* over)

...leiden n, *im Subst.* condition, complaint; *Asthma~* asthmatic complaint; *Haut~* skin condition (*od.* complaint)

leidend I. *Part. Präs.* → **leiden**; **II.** *Adj.* **1.** (*kränklich*) ailing, in poor health; **~ aussehen** look ill; **2.** *Blick etc.*: woeful; **~e Miene** martyred (*od.* pained *od.* long-suffering) expression; **III.** *Adv.*: **j-n ~ ansehen** give s.o. a woeful look

Leidenschaft f; -, -en passion; (*heftiges Gefühl*) (powerful) emotion; (*intensive Begeisterung*) ardo(u)r; (*Hingabe*) zeal, fervo(u)r; **von e-r heftigen ~ für j-n** od. **zu j-m ergriffen werden** be consumed with a passion (od. passionate love) for s.o.; **mit ~ sprechen, verteidigen** etc.: passionately; **Musik ist s-e ~** music is his passion; **aktiv:** auch he's a passionate musician; **Nörgeln ist bei ihr e-e ~** complaining is her favo(u)rite pastime, complaining is a fine art with her; **Gärtner aus ~ sein** be a really devoted gardener, really love one's garden; **leidenschaftlich I.** Adj. passionate; *Mensch. auch* very emotional; (*aufbrausend*) hotheaded; *Rede, Appell* etc.: impassioned; *Sehnsucht, Wunsch:* ardent; (*begeistert*) wildly enthusiastic; (*heftig*) violent; **er ist ein ~er Skifahrer** he has a passion for skiing; **II.** Adv. *lieben, hassen* etc.: passionately; **etw. ~ gern tun** absolutely love (*stärker:* adore) doing s.th.; **ich esse ~ gern Schokolade** I absolutely love chocolate, I'm a total chocolate addict (*umg.* chocoholic); **Leidenschaftlichkeit** f; nur Sg. passionateness; (*Begeisterung*) ardo(u)r, wild enthusiasm; (*Vehemenz*) vehemence; **leidenschaftslos** Adj. unemotional, dispassionate; (*gefühllos*) impassive; **Leidenschaftslosigkeit** f; nur Sg. lack of emotion; dispassionateness; (*Gefühllosigkeit*) impassiveness

Leidensdruck m; nur Sg.; Psych. level of suffering (od. pain)
leidensfähig Adj. able to cope with suffering; **Leidensfähigkeit** f; nur Sg. capacity for suffering
Leidens|genosse m, **~genossin** f fellow sufferer; **~geschichte** f 1. sad story; iro. tale of woe; 2. nur Sg.; kirchl.: **die ~** the Passion Story; **~miene** f woeful (od. martyred, pained) expression; **... sagte er mit ~** ... he said, looking pained; **~weg** m 1. long ordeal; *Leben:* life of suffering; 2. kirchl.: **der ~** (**Christi**) the Way of the Cross; **~zeit** f period of suffering
leider Adv. unfortunately; **~ müssen wir jetzt gehen** auch I'm afraid we have to go now; **~ ja!** I'm afraid so; **~ nicht** od. **nein!** I'm afraid not; **~** (**Gottes**)! unfortunately(, yes)
leid|erfüllt Adj. grief-stricken; **~gebeugt** Adj. bowed down with grief; **~geprüft** Adj. sorely tried; **das ist e-e ~e Familie** that family has suffered severely
leidet Präs. → leiden
leidig Adj. (*ärgerlich*) annoying; (*lästig*) tiresome; (*verwünscht*) wretched; **das ~e Geld** filthy lucre; **wenn nur das ~e Geld nicht wäre** if only it weren't for (the) blasted money umg.
leidlich I. Adj. bearable; (*halbwegs gut*) passable; **sein Englisch ist ~** his English is fair to middling; **II.** Adv. (*halbwegs*) vor Adj.: passably, tolerably, reasonably; **~** (**gut**) not too badly, reasonably well; **er spielt ~ gut Gitarre** auch he's a passable guitar player; **wie geht's? - ~** how are you? - fair to middling, so-so umg.
Leidtragende m, f; -n, -n victim; **der** od. **die ~** the one who suffers; **die ~n** the ones who suffer; **er ist immer der ~** auch he's always at the receiving end
leidvoll Adj. geh. Miene: sorrowful; Erfahrung: painful; **ein ~es Leben** a life

of suffering (*Trauer:* sorrow)
Leidwesen n: **zu m-m** (**großen**) **~** much to my regret; **zum ~** (+ Gen.) to the disappointment (*stärker:* chagrin) of
Leier f; -, -n 1. Mus. (*Drehleier*) barrel organ; hist. (*Kithara*) lyre; 2. umg. (*Kurbel*) crank; **immer die alte** od. **dieselbe ~** fig. pej. (it's) always the same old story, umg. can't he etc. change his tune?; 3. nur Sg.; Astron. Lyra
Leierkasten m umg. barrel organ; **~mann** m organ grinder
leiern umg. **I.** v/t. 1. **nach oben ~** crank up, wind up; **nach unten ~** wind down, lower; 2. (*Text*) schnell: rattle off; eintönig: drone out; **II.** v/i. 1. wind away (**an** + Dat. at); 2. (*eintönig vortragen*) drone (on)
Leierschwanz m Zool. lyrebird
Leih|amt n pawnshop; **~arbeit** f subcontracted work; **~arbeiter** m, **~arbeiterin** f subcontracted worker; **~bibliothek** f, **~bücherei** f lending library
leihen v/t.; leiht, lieh, hat geliehen 1. (*verleihen*) lend (out); (*Geld*) loan; (*Gemälde* etc.) loan (**e-m Museum** to a museum); **j-m etw. ~** lend (*bes. Am. auch* loan) s.o. s.th. (od. s.th. to s.o.); **kannst du mir dein Auto ~?** could you lend me your car?; **j-m sein Ohr ~** geh. fig. give s.o. one's attention; 2. (*entleihen*) borrow; **sich** (Dat.) **etw. von** od. **bei j-m ~** borrow (*mieten:* hire, Am. rent) s.th. from s.o.; **es ist** (**nur**) **geliehen** (it's not mine,) I've only borrowed it; Ausstellungsstück etc.: it's (only) on loan
Leih|frist f loan period; Buch: lending period; Auto, Boot, Frack etc.: hire (*bes. Am.* rental) period; **~gabe** f Ausstellung etc.: item on loan, loan (**von** od. **+** Gen. from); **~gebühr** f hire charge, Am. rental fee; für Bücher: lending fee; **~haus** n pawnshop; **~mutter** f surrogate mother; **~mutterschaft** f surrogate motherhood, surrogacy; **~schein** m 1. pawn ticket; 2. Bücherei: borrowing slip; **~skier** Pl. hire (Am. rental) skis; geliehene: auch hired (Am. rented) skis; **~stimme** f Pol. tactical vote; **wir haben keine ~n zu vergeben** we don't want to give away any votes, we don't want any tactical voting; **~wagen** m hire (Am. rental) car
leihweise I. Adv. on loan; (*gegen Miete*) on hire, Am. rented; **j-m etw. ~ überlassen** lend (*bes. Am.* loan) s.o. s.th.; **könnten Sie es mir ~ geben?** auch could I borrow it (for a while)?; **II.** Adj.: **bei ~r Überlassung** when loaned, where a loan is made
Leim m; -(e)s, -e glue; **aus dem ~ gehen** umg. auch fig. Beziehung etc.: fall apart, come apart at the seams; (*dick werden*) put on weight, lose one's figure; **j-m auf den ~ gehen** umg. fall for s.o.'s line, be taken in by s.o.; **leimen** v/t. glue (together); **geleimt werden** umg. fig. be taken in (od. for a ride), umg. be had; **ich bin der Geleimte** umg. I'm the mug (Am. dupe od. fallguy) in this case
Leim|farbe f distemper; **~ring** m grease band; **~rute** f lime(d) twig
Lein m; -(e)s, -e; Bot. flax
Leine f; -, -n 1. (*Tau*) (thin) rope; (*Wäscheleine*) (clothes) line; **die ~n losmachen** Naut. cast off; **zieh ~!** umg. fig. push off!; 2. (*Hundeleine*) lead, bes. Am. leash; „**Hunde sind an der ~ zu führen**" "Dogs must be kept on a lead (Am. leash)"; **j-n an der** (**kurzen**) **~**

haben od. halten umg. fig. keep s.o. on a short (od. tight) rein; **j-m ~** / **mehr ~ lassen** umg. give s.o. some/more leeway (od. scope)
leinen Adj. linen
Leinen n; -s, - linen; **in ~** (**gebunden**) Buch: clothbound; **~band** m (Buch) clothbound book; **~einband** m cloth binding; **~sack** m burlap bag; **~schuhe** Pl. canvas shoes; **~tuch** n (Stoff, Tischtuch) linen cloth; (Betttuch) linen sheet; **~weber** m, **~weberin** f linen weaver
Leinenzwang m für Hunde: mandatory leashing of dogs; **dort herrscht ~** dogs have to be kept on a lead (od. leash) there
Lein|kraut n Bot. toadflax; **~öl** n linseed oil; **~saat** f; nur Sg., **~samen** m linseed
Leintuch n linen; (Betttuch) (linen) sheet
leinwand Adj. österr., mst wienerisch umg. fabulous, fantastic
Leinwand f 1. nur Sg. (Gewebe) canvas; 2. (des Malers) canvas; **auf ~ malen** paint on canvas; 3. Film: screen; **die Helden der ~** the heroes of the silver screen; **auf die ~ bringen** od. **bannen** make a film of, commit to celluloid; **~größe** f hum. screen celebrity, umg. film great; **~held** m hum. screen hero, hero of the silver screen; **~heldin** f hum. screen heroine, heroine of the silver screen
leise I. Adj. 1. (*ruhig*) quiet; Ton, Stimme, Musik etc.: soft; Geräusch: faint; **mit ~r Stimme** in a low voice; **seid bitte ~!** quiet, please; not so loud, please; umg. iro. can you turn the volume down, please; **~r stellen** turn down; **wir müssen ~ sein** we'll have to be quiet; (*leise sprechen*) we'll have to keep our voices down; 2. (*gering*) Hoffnung: faint; Bewegung, Verdacht: slight; Schlaf, Berührung, Regen, Wind: gentle; **ich habe nicht die ~ste Ahnung** I haven't the faintest (od. slightest) idea; **nicht im Leisesten** not in the slightest; **ich glaube nicht im Leisesten daran, dass ...** I don't believe for a moment that ...; **II.** Adv. 1. (*ruhig*) quietly; singen, klopfen etc.: softly; sprechen: auch in a low voice; **sprich ~(r)** not so loud, keep your voice down (a bit); **~ vor sich hin murmeln** mumble away to oneself; **~** (*auf*)**treten** tread softly; 2. (*sanft, sacht*) gently
leisetreten v/i. (unreg., untr., ist -ge-) mst Inf. u. P.P.; pej. pussyfoot (around) umg.; **Leisetreter** m pej. pussyfooter umg.; **Leisetreterin** f pej. pussyfooter umg.
Leiste f; -, -n 1. (*Umrandung*) border; (*Latte*) lath; **mit quadratförmigem Schnitt:** batten; **mit Profil:** mo(u)lding; (*Tapetenleiste*) picture rail (Am. molding); (*Fußbodenleiste*) skirting board, Am. baseboard; Maschine etc.: (guide) rail; Buch: edge; (*Knopfleiste*) facing; Weberei: selvage; (*Zierleiste*) trim; 2. Anat. groin
leisten v/t. 1. do; (*schaffen*) auch manage; (*vollbringen*) achieve, accomplish; Tech. do; **ich habe schon einiges geleistet** I've done quite a bit, I haven't been idle; **was leistet der Wagen?** what will (od. can) the car do?; **der Motor leistet 200 PS** the engine produces (od. delivers, develops) 200 bhp; **gute Arbeit ~** do a good job; **da musst du schon was ~** you've got to

L

show what you can do; **er hat Großes geleistet** he has some remarkable achievements to his name; *bei e-r Aufführung etc.*: it was a great performance; **2.** *mit Subst.*: **Zahlungen ~** make payments; **e-e Anzahlung ~** pay a deposit; → *Abbitte, Beistand* 1, *Dienst* 1, *Eid, Folge* 4, *Hilfe* 1; **3.** *auch* (*Dat.*) *etw. ~* (*sich gönnen*) treat o.s. to s.th.; *umg.* (*Blödes tun*) get up to s.th.; **leiste dir doch mal etwas** give yourself a treat; **was hast du dir da wieder geleistet?** *fig. umg.* what have you been up to this time?; **er leistet sich dauernd Frechheiten** he's forever coming out with these cheeky remarks; **da haben wir uns wirklich was Schönes geleistet** *umg.* we've really (gone and) done it now; *iro.* we've really excelled ourselves this time; **4.** *sich* (*Dat.*) *etw. ~ können finanziell, auch fig.*: be able to afford s.th.; **ich kann es mir** (*nicht*) **~, Urlaub zu machen** I can('t) afford to go on holiday; **sie könnte sich wirklich neue Vorhänge ~** she could really run to some new curtains; **du kannst dir keine weiteren Fehler ~** you can't afford to make (*od.* won't get away with) any more mistakes
Leisten *m*; *-s, -*; (*für e-n Schuh*) shoe tree; *beim Schuster*: last; **alles über e-n ~ schlagen** *fig.* tar everything with the same brush; → *Schuster*
Leisten|bruch *m Med.* hernia (*Pl.* hernias *od.* herniae); **~gegend** *f Anat.* groin; **~zerrung** *f mst* groin injury; **e-e ~ haben** *auch* have pulled a groin muscle
Leistung *f* **1.** (*Errungenschaft*) achievement; (*Großtat*) (great) feat; *einmalige, e-s Künstlers, Sportlers, Examenskandidaten etc.*: performance; **e-e hervorragende ~!** an excellent job!; *Sport, Theater, Mus.* an outstanding performance!; **e-e bemerkenswerte technische ~** a remarkable technical feat (*od.* achievement); **reife ~!** *umg.* not bad!; **2.** *nur Sg.*; (*allg. e-s Schülers, Angestellten etc.*) performance; (*geleistete Arbeit*) work; (*Resultat*) results *Pl.*; **nach ~ bezahlt werden** be paid by results (*od.* according to performance, *Industrie*: according to productivity; **Bezahlung nach ~** performance-related pay; **unter/über der üblichen ~** below/above average; **schwache ~!** poor show; **s-e schulischen ~en lassen nach** his school work is getting worse; **3.** *mst Sg.*; (*Leistungsvermögen*) (*Kapazität, auch des Hirns etc.*) capacity; *Tech., Wirts.* performance; (*Kraft*) power (output); (*Ausstoß, Produktion*) output; *Etech.* power, *abgegebene*: output, *aufgenommene*: input; **4.** (*Dienstleistung*) service; **die ~en des Reisebüros** the services provided by the travel agency; **5.** (*Zahlung*) payment, *e-r Krankenkasse, Versicherung*: benefit; (*Beitrag*) contribution; **soziale ~en** fringe benefits; **6.** *nur Sg.*; (*das Leisten*) completion; *bes. Jur.* performance; *e-s Eides*: swearing
Leistungs|abfall *m* **1.** *Päd.* deterioration (*od.* slipping) in his *etc.* work; *e-s Sportlers*: drop in (*od.* loss of) performance; *Med.* loss of energy; **2.** *Tech. Motor*: drop in power (*od.* output); *Etech.* power drop; *Fahrzeug*: drop in (*od.* loss of) performance; **3.** *Wirts.* drop in productivity (*od.* output); **~angabe** *f Tech.* power rating; **~abzeichen** *n Sport* proficiency badge; **~angebot** *n* range of services (offered);

~anspruch *m* entitlement to benefits; **~anstieg** *m* **1.** *Päd. etc.* improvement in his *etc.* work (*Sport* performance); **2.** *Tech., Motor*: increase in power (*od.* output); *Fahrzeug*: improvement in performance; **3.** *Wirts.* increase in productivity (*od.* output); **~ausfall** *m* **1.** *Jur.* failure to fulfil(l) a (contractual) obligation, non-performance, breach of contract; **2.** *Psych., Päd.* loss of performance
leistungsberechtigt *Adj. bei Versicherung etc.*: entitled to benefits; **Leistungsberechtigung** *f* entitlement to (receive) benefits
leistungsbereit *Adj.* willing to work (*Sportler*: to perform); **Leistungsbereitschaft** *f* willingness to work (*Sportler*: to perform)
leistungsbezogen *Adj.* performance--related
Leistungs|bilanz *f* balance of trade; **~denken** *n* performance orientation, competitive thinking; **~druck** *m* pressure to perform; *Päd. auch* pressure (to get higher marks [*Am.* grades]); **~empfänger** *m*, **~empfängerin** *f* beneficiary
leistungsfähig *Adj.* efficient (*auch Tech., Wirts.*); *Motor*: powerful; *Mensch, körperlich*: fit, able-bodied; *Päd. etc.* capable; (*zahlungsfähig*) solvent; **Leistungsfähigkeit** *f; nur Sg.* efficiency; *Tech. auch* performance; *Motor*: power(fulness); *Maschine*: capacity; *Mensch, körperliche*: fitness; *Päd. etc.* ability
leistungsgerecht *Adj.* performance-related; **~e Bezahlung** *auch* adequate pay in relation to performance
Leistungs|gesellschaft *f* achievement- (*od.* performance-)oriented society, competitive society; **~grenze** *f* maximum potential (*bes. Sport* performance); *bei Produktion, Motor*: maximum output; **~gruppe** *f* ability group; **~kontrolle** *f* (student) assessment; *Prüfung*: (achievement) test; *Pl. auch* testing; **~kraft** *f →* **Leistungsfähigkeit; ~kurs** *m Päd.* special subject; **ich bin im ~ Geschichte** I'm taking history as a special subject; **~kurve** *f* performance chart; **~kürzung** *f* reduction of benefit (*od.* of a payment); **~lohn** *m* performance-related pay; **~nachweis** *m* certificate (*showing academic achievement*); **~niveau** *n Sport* standard (of performance); *Päd.* achievement level
leistungsorientiert *Adj.* achievement--oriented
Leistungspflicht *f Jur.* obligation to perform; *Wirts.* liability to pay; **leistungspflichtig** *Adj. Jur.* obliged to perform; *Wirts.* liable to pay
Leistungs|prämie *f* productivity bonus; **~prinzip** *n; nur Sg.* achievement principle; **~prüfung** *f* performance (*Päd.* achievement) test; **~reserve** *f* reserves *Pl.* of performance; **~rückgang** *m →* **Leistungsabfall; ~schau** *f Wirts.* industrial exhibition; *Agr.* agricultural show
leistungsschwach *Adj.* **1.** *Tech.* low--performance …; *Motor, Fahrzeug*: low-powered; **2.** *Sport, Päd.* low-achieving; *Mannschaft*: weak; **~er Schüler** low-ability pupil (*Am.* student), underachiever; **Leistungsschwäche** *f* **1.** *Tech.* low performance; *Motor, Fahrzeug*: *auch* low power, lack of power; **2.** *Sport, Päd.* low achievement, low ability; *Mannschaft*: weak-

ness
Leistungs|soll *n* performance target; **~sport** *m* competitive sport; **~sportler** *m*, **~sportlerin** *f* competitive sportsperson (*Mann*: *auch* sportsman, *Frau*: *auch* sportswoman; **~stand** *m* performance level; *Produktion*: level of output; *Päd.* standard of work
leistungsstark *Adj.* **1.** *Tech.* high-performance; *Motor, Fahrzeug*: *auch* powerful, high-powered; **2.** *Sport, Päd.* high-performing, high-achieving; *Mannschaft*: strong; **~er Schüler** *auch* high achiever; **Leistungsstärke** *f; nur Sg.* **1.** *Tech.* high performance; *Motor, Fahrzeug*: *auch* (high) power, high output; **2.** *Sport, Päd.* high achievement, high ability; *Mannschaft*: strength
leistungssteigernd *Adj. Mittel*: performance-enhancing; **Leistungssteigerung** *f* improvement in performance; *im Betrieb*: increase in efficiency; *Produktion*: increase in productivity; *Tech. Motor, Fahrzeug*: increase in power (*od.* output)
Leistungs|test *m* performance (*Päd.* achievement) test; **~tief** *n bes. Sport* (patch of) bad form, *Am.* slump; **~vermögen** *n →* **Leistungsfähigkeit; ~verweigerung** *f* **1.** *Päd.* rejection of the requirement to do well (at [*Am.* in] school); *Soziol.* rejection of the competitive society; **2.** *Jur.* refusal to fulfil (-l) the contract; **~zulage** *f*, **~zuschlag** *m* bonus for extra work; **~zwang** *m* compulsion to perform; *→* **Leistungsdruck**
Leit|antrag *m bes. Pol.* framework motion (*put forward by the party leadership etc.*); **~artikel** *m* leader, leading article (*Am.* editorial); **~artikler** *m*; *-s, -*, **~artiklerin** *f*; *-, -nen* leader (*Am.* editorial) writer; **~bild** *n* (role) model; **~ der Mode** leader of fashion
leiten I. *v/t.* **1.** (*führen*) lead; *hinweisend, steuernd*: guide, steer; (*Verkehr*) direct, route; *fig.* (*lenken*) guide; **sich von anderen Beweggründen / s-n Gefühlen ~ lassen** be guided by other motives / governed by one's emotions; **2.** (*anführen*) head; (*Staat*) govern; (*Betrieb etc.*) manage, run; (*Schule*) be head of; (*Projekt*) be in charge of, head (up); (*beaufsichtigen*) supervise; (*Versammlung, Diskussion*) chair; **wer leitet die Delegation?** who is leading (*od.* heading) the delegation?; **3.** *Mus.* (*Orchester, Chor*) conduct; (*kleineres Ensemble*) direct; **e-e Kapelle ~** be leader of a (*od.* the) band, be (the) bandleader; **4.** (*Fußballspiel etc.*) referee; **5.** *Phys., Physiol. etc.* (*Wärme, Strom, Schall*) conduct; **6.** (*Öl, Gas*) *in Röhren*: pipe; **7.** (*Brief etc.*) pass on (*an + Akk.* to), direct (to); **II.** *v/i.* *Phys. etc.*: **gut/schlecht ~** be a good/ bad conductor
leitend I. *Part. Präs. →* **leiten; II.** *Adj.* **1.** leading; **~e Stellung** managerial post; **~er Angestellter** executive, *Pl.* managerial (*od.* senior) staff *Sg.(mst V. im Pl.*), *Am.* senior management; **~er Beamte** senior civil servant; **~er Ingenieur** chief engineer; **es fehlt die ~e Hand** there is no proper control, no one is really in charge; **~er Gedanke** *fig. →* **Leitgedanke; 2.** *Phys.* conductive; **nicht ~** non-conductive
Leiter¹ *m*; *-s, -*; **1.** *e-r Firma etc.*: manager, director; *e-s Instituts*: director; *e-r Schule*: head (teacher), *Am.* principal; *e-r Abteilung*: head; *Wirts. auch* man-

ager; *e-s Projekts, e-r Delegation etc.*: head, leader; *e-r Gruppe, e-r Partei etc.*: leader; *e-r Versammlung*: chair(person), chairman; *e-s Orchesters, e-s Chors*: conductor; *e-s kleineren Ensembles*: director; *e-r Kapelle, Band*: leader; **technischer/künstlerischer ~** technical/artistic director; **~ sein von** *auch* be in charge of, head (up); **2.** *Phys., Etech.* conductor

Leiter² *f;* -, -n ladder (*auch fig.*); (*Stehleiter*) stepladder

Leiterin *f;* -, -nen → **Leiter¹**; *e-r Firma etc. auch* manageress; *e-r Versammlung: auch* chairwoman

Leiter\|sprosse *f* rung (of a ladder); **~wagen** *m* wooden open-framed (hand)cart

Leitfaden *m* **1.** main thread (*od.* theme) (*running through s.th.*), leitmotif; **2.** (*Buch*) guide (+ *Gen.* to); (*Einführung*): introduction (to); *Lehrgang*: basic course (in)

leitfähig *Adj. Phys., Etech.* conductive; **Leitfähigkeit** *f* conductivity

Leit\|feuer *n Naut.* (*Richtfeuer*) leading light; **~figur** *f* role model; **~gedanke** *m* central (*od.* dominant) theme; (*Prinzip*) guiding principle; **~hammel** *m* **1.** *Tier*: bellwether; **2.** *umg. fig.* (*Führer*) leader of the pack, boss figure, alpha male *etc.*; **manche Leute brauchen immer e-n ~** some people always have to play follow-my-leader; **~hund** *m* leader of the pack, alpha male; **~idee** *f* central theme; **~kegel** *m Mot.* traffic cone; **~kultur** *f* (*od.* guiding) culture; **~linie** *f* **1.** (*Richtlinie*) guideline; **2.** *Mot.* lane marking, white line; **~motiv** *n Mus., Lit., fig.* leitmotif; **~pfosten** *m Mot.* reflector post; **~planke** *f Mot.* crash barrier, *Am.* guardrail; **~satz** *m* guiding principle; **~spruch** *m* motto; **~stelle** *f* central office; *der U-Bahn etc.*: control cent\|re (*Am.* -er); **~stern** *m* lode star; *fig. auch* guiding star; **~strahl** *m* **1.** *Flug., Mil.* radio guidance beam; **2.** *Math.* radius vector; **~studie** *f* pilot study; **~system** *n* (traffic) guidance system; **~thema** *n* main theme; leitmotif; (*Anliegen*) key issue; **~tier** *n* leader (of the herd), alpha male; **~ton** *m Mus.* leading note

Leitung *f* **1.** *e-r Firma*: management; (*Verwaltung*) administration; *Arbeit, Projekt etc.*: (*Führung*) direction; (*Beaufsichtigung*) control, supervision; (*Organisation*) organization; (*Vorsitz*) chairmanship; *als Einrichtung*: management, *bei Veranstaltungen*: management committee; **die ~ haben** be in charge (**von** of); *Mus.* be the conductor (of), be conducting; **unter der ~ stehen von** (*od.* + *Gen.*) be directed (*od.* headed, supervised, *Mus.* conducted) by; **... wurde ausgeführt unter der ~ von X** ... was carried out under the direction of X; **das Orchester spielt unter der ~ von X** *Mus.* the orchestra is conducted by X; **2.** (*Kabel*) lead, *Am.* cord; (*Draht*) wire; (*Stromkreis*) circuit; (*Rohrleitung*) pipes *Pl.*, (*Überlandleitung*) pipeline; (*für Gas, Wasser, Strom*) main(s *Pl.*); (*Wasseranschluss*) tap; (*Leitkanal*) duct; **in der ~ bleiben** *Telef.* hold the line; **die ~ ist besetzt/tot** the line is engaged (*od.* busy) /dead; **die ~ steht** you're through; **da ist jemand in der ~** the lines are crossed, I've got a crossed line; **e-e lange ~ haben** *umg. fig.* be slow on the uptake; **du stehst wohl**

auf der ~ *umg.* you're not quite with it today

Leitungs\|draht *m* (electrical) wire; **~mast** *m* (electricity) pylon; *Telef.* telegraph pole; **~netz** *n* supply network; *öffentliches*: mains system; **~rohr** *n Wasser*: water pipe; *Gas*: gas pipe; (*Hauptleitung*) main; **~wasser** *n*; *nur Sg.* tap water; **~widerstand** *m Etech.* line resistance

Leit\|vermerk *m bei Akten etc.*: distribution (list); **~währung** *f* base currency; **~werk** *n* **1.** *Flug.* tail (unit); **2.** *EDV* (*Steuerwerk*) control unit; **~wert** *m Etech.* conductance; **~wolf** *m Zool., fig.* leader of the pack, alpha male; **~zins** *m Wirts.* base rate, (central bank) discount rate, *Am.* prime rate

Lektion *f;* -, -en *im Lehrbuch*: unit, lesson (*auch fig.*); **j-m e-e ~ erteilen** *fig.* teach s.o. a lesson

Lektor *m*; *-s, -en* **1.** *Univ. teacher or instructor giving mainly supplementary or practical classes; in Fremdsprachen*: (foreign) language assistant, lector; **2.** *im Verlag*: editor; **Lektorat** *n; -(e)s, -e* **1.** *Univ.* post as Lektor; *in Fremdsprachen*: (foreign) language assistant's post; lector's (*weiblich*: lectrice's) post; **2.** *im Verlag*: (editorial) department; **lektorieren I.** *v/t.* edit, prepare for press; **II.** *v/i.* work as an editor; **Lektorin** *f;* -, -nen **1.** → **Lektor** 1; *in Fremdsprachen*: *auch* lectrice; **2.** → **Lektor** 2

Lektüre *f;* -, -n **1.** reading (matter); (*Bücher*) books *Pl.*; *leichte/schwere ~* light/heavy reading; **e-e unterhaltsame ~ suchen** look for something entertaining to read; **das ist keine ~ für dich** that's not the right (kind of) reading for you, that's not the sort of thing you should be reading; **sich** (*Dat.*) **etw. als ~ mitnehmen** take s.th. to read; **2.** *nur Sg.* (*das Lesen*) reading; **bei der ~ des Buchs** when (*od.* while) reading the book; **3.** *Päd.* reader

Lemma *n; -s, -ta; Ling., Math.* lemma (*Pl.* lemmas *od.* lemmata)

Lemming *m; -s, -e; Zool.* lemming

Lemur *m;* -en, -en, **Lemure** *m; -n, -n* **1.** *Zool.* lemur; **2.** *Myth.*: **die Lemuren** the lemures

Lende *f;* -, -n **1.** *Anat.* lumbar region, lower back; **2.** *Gastr.* loin; **3.** *lit. Pl.* loins

Lenden\|braten *m Gastr.* roast loin; *vom Rind*: sirloin; **~gegend** *f Anat.* lumbar region; **~schurz** *m* loincloth; **~steak** *n* sirloin steak; **~stück** *n* (piece of) tenderloin; **~wirbel** *m Anat.* lumbar vertebra (*Pl.* vertebrae)

Leninismus *m*; *-, kein Pl.* Leninism; **Leninist** *m; -en, -en*, **Leninistin** *f; -, -nen* Leninist; **leninistisch** *Adj.* Leninist

Lenkachse *f* steering axle; *Eisenb.* pivoted axle

lenkbar *Adj.* **1.** *Tech.* steerable; (*steuerbar*) controllable; *leicht ~* easy to control, manoeuvrable, *Am.* maneuverable; **2.** *Person, mst Kind*: controllable, pliable; *leicht ~* tractable, manageable; **Lenkbarkeit** *f; nur Sg.* **1.** *Tech.* steerability; (*Steuerbarkeit*) controllability; *leichte*: manoeuvrability, *Am.* maneuverability; **2.** *e-r Person*: controllability; *leichte*: manageability

lenken I. *v/t.* **1.** *Mot.* steer; (*fahren, auch Pferdewagen*) drive; *Flug.* pilot, be at the controls of; (*Rakete, Tier*)

guide; (*wenden*) steer, turn (**nach** towards, to); **2.** *fig.* (*richten*) (*Person, Gedanken, Gespräch etc.*) guide, direct; *geschickt*: steer; **die Aufmerksamkeit auf etw./sich** (*Akk.*) **~** draw attention to s.th. / draw attention to o.s., attract attention; **s-n Blick auf j-n/etw. ~** turn one's gaze on s.o. / to(wards) s.th.; **das Gespräch / die Diskussion ~ auf** (+ *Akk.*) steer (*od.* bring) the conversation/discussion [a]round to; **s-e Schritte heimwärts** *etc.* **~** *geh.* head for home *etc.*, turn (*od.* direct) one's steps towards home *etc. lit.*; → **Verdacht**; **3.** (*kontrollieren*) (*Person, Wirtschaft, Presse etc.*) control; (*Staat*) govern; **das Kind lässt sich schwer ~** the child is difficult to manage; **ihm fehlt die ~de Hand** he has no one to keep him under control; → **gelenkt**; **II.** *v/i. Mot.* steer; (*fahren*) drive; (*mehr*) **nach links ~** steer (a bit more) to the left; *Anweisung*: left hand down (a bit more); **mit einer Hand ~** drive with one hand; **darf ich mal ~?** can I (have a) drive?; → **denken** I 1

Lenker *m*; *-s, -* **1.** (*Lenkrad*) steering wheel; *Motorrad, Fahrrad*: handlebars *Pl.*; **2.** (*Fahrer*) driver; *lit. fig., e-s Staats etc.*: *allg.* ruler; *des Schicksals*: controller, arbiter; **Lenkerin** *f;* -, -nen → **Lenker** 2

Lenkflugkörper *m* guided missile

Lenkrad *n* steering wheel; **~schaltung** *f* steering-column gearchange (*Am.* gearshift); **~schloss** *n* steering (--wheel) lock

Lenk\|säule *f Mot.* steering column; **~stange** *f* **1.** *e-s Fahrrads*: handlebars *Pl.*; **2.** *Mot.* draglink

Lenkung *f* **1.** *Mot.* steering; **2.** (*Kontrolle*) control (*auch der Wirtschaft, Presse etc.*); *hinweisend*: guidance (*auch e-r Person*); *e-s Staats*: rule, government

Lenkwaffe *f Flug., Mil.* guided missile

Lenkzeit *m Mot. Amtsspr. tatsächliche*: time spent at the wheel; *zulässige*: permissible driving time

Lenz *m; -es, -e; poet.* spring(tide); **er zählte zwanzig ~e** he was twenty years of age; **sie zählte gerade zwanzig ~e** she had just turned twenty; **sich** (*Dat.*) **e-n faulen** *etc.* **~ machen** *umg.* take things easy, put one's feet up

Leopard *m; -en, -en; Zool.* leopard; **Leopardenfell** *n* leopardskin

Leporello *n; -s, -s Druck.* concertina folder

Lepra *f;* -, *kein Pl.; Med.* leprosy; **~kolonie** *f* lepers' colony

leprakrank *Adj. Med.*: **~ sein** have (*od.* be suffering from) leprosy; **Leprakranke** *m, f* leper

leprös *Adj. Med.* leprous

leptosom *Adj. Fachspr.* leptosome; **Leptosome** *m, f; -n, -n* leptosome

Lerche *f;* -, -n; *Zool.* lark

lernbar *Adj.* learnable; *leicht/schwer ~* easy/difficult to learn

Lernbegier(de) *f* eagerness to learn, thirst for knowledge; **lernbegierig** *Adj.* eager (*od.* keen) to learn; *Schüler*: keen

lernbehindert *Adj. Päd., Psych.* ... with learning difficulties, educationally subnormal; **~ sein** have learning difficulties; **Lernbehinderte** *m, f* child with learning difficulties, educationally subnormal child; **Lernbehinderung** *f* learning difficulties *Pl.*, learning disability

Lerneifer *m* eagerness to learn; *e-s Schülers*: *auch* keenness; **lerneifrig**

Adj. eager to learn; *Schüler: auch* keen

lernen I. *v/t.* **1.** learn; *(aufschnappen)* pick up; *lesen* ~ learn to read; *Englisch* ~ learn English; *Klavier* ~ learn to play the piano; *das Autofahren* ~ learn to drive a car; *du wirst es nie* ~ you'll never learn; *das will gelernt sein!* it's something that has to be learn|t (*Am.* -ed), it's not as easy as it looks; *gelernt ist gelernt* once learn|t (*Am.* -ed) never forgotten; **2.** *(ausgebildet werden als):* **Tischler(in)** ~ train to be (*od.* train as) a carpenter; *er hat Kaufmann gelernt* he qualified in business studies; **3.** *j-n schätzen* ~ come to appreciate s.o.; *j-n lieben* ~ grow (*od.* learn) to love s.o.; **4.** *umg.* *(lehren)* teach; *mein Vater hat mir das Schwimmen gelernt* my father taught me to swim; **II.** *v/i.* **1.** learn; *aus Fehlern / aus der Geschichte* ~ learn from one's mistakes / from history; *schnell/leicht* ~ be a fast/good learner; *langsam/schwer* ~ be a slow/poor learner; **2.** *(studieren)* study; *für die Schule:* do (one's) homework; *(Stoff wiederholen) auch* revise, do one's revision; *(in der Ausbildung sein)* be a trainee; *die Mutter hat jeden Tag mit ihr (für die Prüfung) gelernt* her mother worked with her every day (*od.* helped her every day with her work) (preparing for the exam); *fleißig* ~ work (*od.* study) hard; → *gelernt*; **III.** *v/refl.: das lernt sich leicht/schwer* that's easy/hard to learn *od.* remember; *das lernt sich schnell* you'll learn that (*od.* pick that up) in no time

Lernen *n; -s, kein Pl.;* *Päd.* learning; *(Studieren)* studying; *er tut sich mit dem* ~ *schwer* he's not a good (*od.* he's a poor) learner; *ihr macht das* ~ *Spaß* she enjoys her schoolwork; *j-m beim* ~ *helfen* help s.o. with his (*od.* her) schoolwork (*Hausaufgaben:* homework)

Lerner *m; -s, -,* ~**in** *f; -, -nen;* *Päd.* learner

Lern|erfolg *m* *Päd.* success of the learning process; ~**fabrik** *f pej.* cramming factory

lernfähig *Adj.* capable of learning; **Lernfähigkeit** *f; nur Sg.* learning ability (*od.* capacity)

Lern|hilfe *f* *Päd.* **1.** *j-m eine* ~ *geben* help s.o. with his (*od.* her) (school)work; **2.** *(Buch mit Hinweisen)* study aid (*od.* guide); ~**inhalt** *m* course content

Lernmittel *n* learning aid; *Pl.* teaching materials; ~**freiheit** *f* free provision of teaching materials

Lern|programm *n* **1.** *Päd.* programmed learning scheme (*Am.* plan); **2.** *EDV* learning program; *für Software:* tutorial (program); ~**prozess** *m* learning process; ~**psychologie** *f* psychology of learning; ~**schritt** *m* *Päd.* step in the learning process; ~**schwester** *f* trainee (*od.* student) nurse; ~**schwierigkeiten** *Pl.* learning difficulties; ~**stoff** *m* *Päd.* material to be learn|t (*Am.* -ed)

lernwillig *Adj.* willing to learn

Lernziel *n* *Päd.* (learning) objective; ~**kontrolle** *f* monitoring of achievement (of objectives)

Lesart *f* reading, version; *verschiedene* ~**en** variants, variant readings

lesbar *Adj.* readable; *(leserlich) auch* legible; **Lesbarkeit** *f; nur Sg.* readabil-

ity; *(Leserlichkeit)* legibility

Lesbe *f; -, -n; umg.* lesbian, *Sl.* dike; **Lesbierin** *f; -, -nen* lesbian; **lesbisch** *Adj.* lesbian

Lese *f; -, -n; (Weinlese)* vintage; *(Ernte)* harvest

Lese|abend *m* **1.** *(Ggs. Fernsehabend)* evening of reading; *ich freue mich auf e-n gemütlichen* ~ I'm looking forward to spending the evening reading in comfort (*od.* curled up with a book); **2.** *(Autorenlesung)* evening of readings *(given by an author)*; *ein* ~ *mit Uwe Timm als Ankündigung:* Uwe Timm reads from his own works; ~**brille** *f: (e-e)* ~ (a pair of) reading glasses *Pl.*; ~**buch** *n* reader; ~**drama** *n Lit.* closet drama; ~**ecke** *f* reading corner; ~**exemplar** *n* proof copy; *gebunden:* reading copy; ~**gerät** *n Computer:* scanner; *für Mikrofilme, Bankbelege etc.:* reader; ~**geschwindigkeit** *f EDV* reading speed; ~**gewohnheiten** *Pl.* reading habits *Pl.*; ~**hunger** *m* appetite for reading; ~**lampe** *f* reading lamp; ~**lupe** *f* reading glass; ~**mappe** *f* selection of periodicals *(sent out to subscribers by a magazine reading circle)*

lesen[1]; *liest, las, hat gelesen* **I.** *v/t.* **1.** read *(auch Computer)*; *(mühsam entziffern)* make out; *falsch* ~ misread; *in i-n Augen war Enttäuschung zu* ~ *fig.* you could tell from her eyes she was disappointed; → *Gedanke* 1, *Korrektur* 2; **2.** *Univ.:* *Geschichte etc.* ~ lecture on *(ständig:* teach) history etc.; **3.** *kirchl.:* *die Messe* ~ say Mass; **4.** *Parl.:* *e-n Gesetzentwurf* ~ give a bill a reading; **II.** *v/i.* **1.** read *(in + Dat.* s.th.); *viel* ~ read a lot, do a lot of reading; *in der Zeitung war od. stand zu* ~, *dass ...* it said in the paper that ...; *ich habe drei Wochen an diesem Buch gelesen* I have been reading this book for three weeks; **2.** *(deuten):* *in j-s Augen* ~ gaze into s.o.'s eyes and read his (*od.* her) thoughts; *aus der Hand* ~ read palms; → *Zeile* 1; **3.** *Univ.:* ~ *über (+ Akk.)* lecture on *(ständig:* teach); **III.** *v/refl.:* *sich gut* ~ be very readable, be a good read; *(leserlich sein)* be easy to read, be very legible; *Gedrucktes:* read well; *sich schlecht* ~ *(auch unleserlich sein)* be difficult to read, be tough going *umg.*; *es liest sich wie ein Roman* it's like reading a novel; *in diesem Licht liest es sich schlecht* this light isn't good for reading; **Lesen** *n; -s, kein Pl.* reading

lesen[2] *v/t./i.; liest, las, hat gelesen;* *(aufsammeln)* gather; *(pflücken)* pick; *(Trauben) auch* harvest

lesenswert *Adj.* worth reading

Lese|probe *f* **1.** *Theat.* first rehearsal, read-through; **2.** *aus e-m Buch:* extract; ~**pult** *n* lectern; *auf e-m Schreibtisch:* bookstand

Leser *m; -s, -* reader *(auch EDV)*

Leseratte *f umg. hum.* bookworm

Leser|brief *m* reader's letter; ~**e** readers' letters; *Zeitungsrubrik:* letters to the editor, *Am. auch* mailbag *umg.*; ~**echo** *n* reader(s') response

Lese-Rechtschreib-Schwäche *f* dyslexia

Leserin *f; -, -nen* reader

Leserkreis *m* (circle of) readers *Pl.*; *e-n weiten od. großen* ~ *haben* be widely read

leserlich I. *Adj.* legible, readable; *fein* ~ nice and neat; **II.** *Adv.* legibly; **Le-**

serlichkeit *f; nur Sg.* legibility

Leserschaft *f; -, -en, mst Sg.* readership, readers *Pl.*

Leser|schicht *f* class of readers, readership (range); ~**schwund** *m* declining circulation, drop in circulation; ~**stamm** *m* regular readers *Pl.*; ~**stimmen** *Pl.* readers' opinions; ~**umfrage** *f* reader survey; ~**wunsch** *m* reader's request; *auf vielfachen* ~ in response to many readers' requests (*od.* requests from readers); ~**zuschrift** *f* reader's letter; *Pl.* readers' letters

Lese|saal *m* reading room; ~**stoff** *m* reading (matter); ~ *mitnehmen* take something to read; ~**übung** *f* reading exercise; ~**wut** *f* reading mania; ~**zeichen** *n* bookmark *(auch Computer)*; ~**zirkel** *m* (magazine) reading circle

Lesung *f* **1.** *Parl.* reading; *in zweiter* ~ on second reading; *zur dritten* ~ *kommen* come up for the third reading; **2.** *(Autorenlesung)* reading; *e-e* ~ *halten* give a reading; **3.** *kirchl.* lesson, reading

letal *Adj.* lethal; **Letaldosis** *f* lethal dose; **Letalität** *f; -, kein Pl.* lethality *fachspr.,* mortality

Lethargie *f; -, kein Pl.* lethargy *(auch Med.)*; **lethargisch** *Adj.* lethargic

Lette *m; -n, -n* Latvian

Letter *f; -, -n; Druck.* letter; *(Schriftzeichen)* character

Lettin *f; -, -nen* Latvian woman (*od.* girl); **lettisch** *Adj.* Latvian, Lettish; **Lettisch** *n; -en; Ling.* Latvian, Lettish; *das* ~**e** Latvian, Lettish; **Lettland** (*n*); *-s; Geog.* Latvia

Lettner *m; -s, -; Archit.* rood screen

Letzt *f: zu guter* ~ *(endlich)* finally, at long last; *(doch noch)* in the end; *(als Letzter, Letztes)* last but not least

letzt... *Adj.* **1.** last; *(endgültig)* final; *als* ~**er Ausweg** as a last resort; *... vom* ~**en Monat** last month's ...; *(am)* ~**en Sonntag** last Sunday; *im* ~**en Sommer** last summer; *und nun die* ~**en Nachrichten vom Tage** and now here is the last news of the day (*od.* the late-night news); *die* ~**en Stunden der Tagung** the last (*od.* final) hours of the conference; *das ist mein* ~**es Angebot** that's my final offer; *im* ~**en Augenblick** at the last moment (*od.* minute); *(gerade rechtzeitig)* just in time; *Änderungen im* ~**en Augenblick** last-minute changes; *an* ~**er Stelle liegen** be last, be in last place; *in e-r Tabelle:* be bottom; *bis auf den* ~**en Platz gefüllt** filled down to the last seat, filled to capacity; *m-e* ~**en Ersparnisse** the last of my savings; *das ist mein* ~**es Geld** that's all the money I have (left); ~**en Endes** in the end, when all is said and done, ultimately; *beim* ~**en Mal** the last time; *zum* ~**en Mal** for the last time; *die Ausgabe* ~**er Hand** *Lit.* the last edition supervised by the author; **2.** *(gerade vergangen)* recent; *in den* ~**en Jahren** in recent years; *in* ~**er** *od.* in der ~**en Zeit** lately; *die* ~**en Tage waren sehr hektisch** the last few days were very hectic; **3.** *(neuest)* latest; *die* ~**en Nachrichten vom Unfallort** the latest news *Sg.* from the scene of the accident; → *Ehre* 1, *Loch* 1, *Ölung* 2

Letzte *m, f, n; -n, -n* **1.** last; *die, die, das* ~ the last (one); *das* ~ *auch* the last thing; *der* ~ *des Monats* the last day of the month; *als* ~(r) *etw. tun* be the last to do s.th.; *als* ~ *ins Ziel kommen* come in last; **2.** *das* ~ *(das Äußerste)* the most (I can do *etc.*), one's utmost;

es geht ums ~ it's a case of do or die, everything's at stake; **sein ~s hergeben** od. **das ~ aus sich herausholen** do one's utmost, make an all-out (od. a supreme) effort; **bis ins ~** down to the last detail, in the utmost detail; **bis zum ~n** (sehr) to the utmost; sich bemühen etc.: as far as is (humanly) possible; **bis zum ~n gehen** (konsequent sein) go all the way, go the whole hog umg.; (vor nichts Halt machen) stop at nothing; **3.** umg. (Schlechteste): **das ist ja wohl das ~!** that really takes the biscuit (Am. cake), that really is the limit; **er ist doch der ~!** he really is the pits!

letztendlich Adv. in the end

letztens Adv. **1.** lastly, finally; **2.** (neulich) the other day, recently

letzter... Adj. latter; **im ~en Fall** in the latter case, where the latter is the case; **der, die, das Letztere** the latter; **Letztere(r) fehlt** the last-named (person) is missing; **Letzteres** od. **das Letztere muss noch geprüft werden** this last point still has to be checked

letztgeboren Adj.; nur attr. lastborn, youngest; **Letztgeborene** m, f, n; -n, -n lastborn (od. youngest) child

letztgenannt Adj. last-mentioned; Person: auch last-named

letzthin Adv. **1.** (neulich) recently; **2.** (schließlich) in the end

letztjährig Adj. last year's

letztlich Adv. **1.** (letzten Endes) in the end; (nach reiflicher Überlegung) in the final analysis; **2.** → letztens 2

letztmalig Adj. last; (endgültig) auch final; **letztmals** Adv. (zum letzten Mal) for the last time

letztmöglich Adj. last (od. latest) possible ..., last (od. latest) ... possible

letztwillig Jur. **I.** Adj. testamentary, by will; **~e Verfügung** last will and testament; **II.** Adv.: **~ verfügen** state in one's last will and testament (**dass** that)

Leu m; -en, -en; poet. lion

Leucht|anzeige f LED display; **~bake** f Naut. beacon light; **~boje** f Naut. light buoy; **~bombe** f Flug. flare; **~buchstaben** Pl. neon letters

Leuchtdiode f light-emitting diode, LED; **Leuchtdiodenanzeige** f LED display

Leuchte f **1.** light; (Lampe) lamp; **2.** umg. fig.: **e-e große ~** a genius; auf s-m od. i-m Gebiet: a leading light; **er ist keine große ~** he's no genius; **sie ist e-e / keine ~ in Physik** she's brilliant / not exactly brilliant at physics

leuchten v/i. **1.** Himmelskörper etc.: shine; (glühen) glow; Kerze: burn; **die Kerze leuchtet nur schwach** the candle doesn't give much light; **golden ~** have a golden glow; **die Sterne ~ am Himmel** the stars are out, the sky is lit with stars; **in der Sonne ~** Meer, Haar: gleam in the sunshine; **2.** fig. Augen: shine; (aufleuchten) light up; **i-e Augen leuchteten / ihr Gesicht leuchtete vor Freude** her eyes/face lit up with joy, she beamed with joy; **3.** **j-m ~** shine a light for s.o.; den Weg erhellen: light the way for s.o.; **leuchte mir bitte mal** can I have some light here?; **mit e-r Taschenlampe** etc. **~** shine a torch (Am. flashlight etc.); **unter das Bett / j-m ins Gesicht ~** shine a light under the bed / into s.o.'s face

leuchtend I. Part. Präs. → **leuchten**; **II.** Adj. **1.** Farben: vivid, brilliant; Rot, Orange: auch glowing; **~e Augen**

gleaming (od. shining) eyes; **2.** fig.: **~es Beispiel** od. **Vorbild** shining example; **etw. in ~en Farben schildern** paint s.th. in glowing colo(u)rs; **III.** Adv.: **~ blau** bright blue

Leuchter m; -s, - candlestick; (Kronleuchter) chandelier; (Armleuchter) candelabr|um (od. -bra, auch Pl.)

Leucht|farbe f luminous paint; **~feuer** n (flashing) beacon; **~käfer** m glow-worm; männlich: firefly; **~körper** m light source; **~kraft** f (Helligkeit) brightness, bes. Astron. luminosity; e-r Farbe, e-s Edelsteins etc.: brilliance; **~kugel** f flare; **~munition** f flare cartridges Pl.; **~patrone** f flare cartridge; **~pistole** f flare pistol; **~rakete** f rocket flare, signal rocket; **~reklame** f neon (advertising) sign; **~röhre** f neon tube; **~schirm** m fluorescent screen (auch Med.); **~schrift** f neon letters Pl.; (Leuchtreklame) neon sign; **~signal** n flare signal; **~skala** f luminous dial; **~spurmunition** f tracer ammunition; **~stärke** f candlepower; **~stift** m highlighter, marker pen

Leuchtstoff m fluorescent substance; **~lampe** f, **~röhre** f fluorescent lamp (od. tube)

Leuchtturm m lighthouse; **~wärter** m, **~wärterin** f lighthouse keeper

Leucht|uhr f luminous clock (Armbanduhr: watch); **~zeiger** m luminous hand; **~zifferblatt** n luminous dial; **~ziffern** Pl. luminous figures

leugnen I. v/t. deny; **~, etw. getan zu haben** deny having done s.th. (od. that one has done s.th.); **es ist nicht zu ~(,** **dass)** it can't be denied (that), it's undeniable (that); **II.** v/i. deny it, deny having done it; **Leugnen** n; -s, kein Pl. denying; (Leugnung) denial; **da half kein ~** it was no use denying it; **Leugnung** f denial

Leukämie f; -, -n; Med. leuk(a)emia

Leukoplast ® n; -(e)s, -e sticking plaster, Am. Band-Aid®

Leukozyt m; -en, -en; Med. leuc|ocyte (bes. Am. leuk-); **Leukozytenzählung** f white cell count

Leumund m; -(e)s, kein Pl.; geh. reputation, name; **ihr ~ ist gut/schlecht** she has a good/bad reputation; **Leumundszeugnis** n character reference

Leutchen Pl. umg. people, folks

Leute Pl. **1.** people; einzelne: auch persons, individuals; **m-e ~** (Familie) my people, bes. Am. umg. my kin; **die ~ sagen** people (od. they) say; **es gibt manche ~, die ...** some people ...; (ganz bestimmte) there are those (people) who ...; **unter die ~ bringen** umg. (erzählen) tell the world about; (Gerücht) spread; (sein Geld) succeed in getting rid of; **unter die ~ gehen** od. **kommen** mix with people, socialize; **vor allen ~n** in front of everyone (od. everybody); **kleine ~** fig. ordinary people (od. folk); **die jungen ~** (die Jugend) young people; (das junge Ehepaar) the young couple; **aus Kindern werden ~** von e-m jungen Menschen: he's (od. she's) not a child any longer, he's (od. she's) quite grown up; → **geschieden** II; **2.** umg. Anrede: **hört mal zu, ~!** listen, everyone (od. everybody, Brit. auch you lot, Am. you guys!); **aber, liebe ~!** oh, come on, now; **3.** umg. (Personal) people, staff Sg.(mst V. im Pl.); (Arbeiter) auch workers; **der Offizier und s-e ~** the officer and his men

...leute Pl., im Subst. **1.** Pl. zu Wörtern

auf ...**mann**: **Berg~** miners; **Fach~** specialists, experts; **Lands~** fellow-countrymen; **2.** bestimmte Gruppe: **Nachbars~** people next door; **Wirts~** landlord and landlady

Leuteschinder m pej. slave-driver; **Leuteschinderei** f pej. slave-driving; **Leuteschinderin** f slave-driver

Leutnant m; -s, -s und -e; Mil. second lieutenant (Am. auch Flug.); Brit. Flug. pilot officer; **~ zur See** Brit. sub-lieutenant, Am. ensign

leutselig Adj. affable; **Leutseligkeit** f; nur Sg. affability

Levante f; -; altm.: **die ~** the Levant; **Levantiner** m; -s, -, **Levantinerin** f; -, -nen Levantine; **~(in) sein** auch come from the Levant

Level [levl] m; -s, -s level

Leviat(h)an m; -s, kein Pl.; bibl. leviathan

Leviten Pl.: **j-m die ~ lesen** umg. read s.o. the riot act

Levkoje f; -, -n; Bot. stock

Lew m; -(s), Lewa Währung: lev

Lexem n; -s, -e; Ling. lexeme

Lexik f; -, kein Pl.; Ling. lexis; **lexikalisch** Adj. lexical

Lexikograph m; -en, -en lexicographer; **Lexikographie** f; -, kein Pl. lexicography; **Lexikographin** f; -, -nen lexicographer; **lexikographisch** Adj. lexicographic(al)

Lexikologe m; -n, -n lexicologist; **Lexikologie** f; -, kein Pl. lexicology; **Lexikologin** f; -, -nen lexicologist; **lexikologisch** Adj. lexicological

Lexikon n; -s, Lexika und Lexiken **1.** umfangreiches: encyclop(a)edia; einbändig, für ein Sachgebiet: dictionary (+ Gen., für of); **~ der** od. **zur Musik** Dictionary of Music; → **wandeln** III; **2.** umg. (Wörterbuch) dictionary; **3.** Ling. (Wortbestand e-r Sprache) lexicon

Lezithin n; -s, -e; Bio., Chem. lecithin

lfd. Abk. → **laufend**

Liaison [liɛ'zõː] f; -, -s liaison (auch Ling.); (Affäre) auch affair; **e-e ~ der Firmen** a liaison (od. tie-up) between the firms

Liane f; -, -n; Bot. liana

Libanese m; -n, -n, **Libanesin** f; -, -nen Lebanese, weiblich auch: Lebanese woman (od. girl etc.); **libanesisch** Adj. Lebanese; **Libanon** (m); -s; Geog. Lebanon; **der ~** Gebirge: the Lebanon Mountains

Libelle f; -, -n **1.** Zool. dragonfly; **2.** Tech. bubble tube; (Wasserwaage) spirit level

liberal I. Adj. liberal; (tolerant) auch tolerant; Pol. Liberal; **II.** Adv. denken, erziehen: along liberal lines; **~ eingestellt sein** have liberal attitudes; **Liberale** m, f; -n, -n; Pol. Liberal; **liberalisieren** v/t. liberalize; **die Einfuhr/Zollpolitik ~** remove import controls / customs barriers; **Liberalisierung** f liberalization; **Liberalismus** m; -, kein Pl. liberalism; Pol. Liberalism; **Liberalität** f; -, kein Pl. liberality

Liberia f; -s; Geog. Liberia; **Liberianer** m; -s, -, **Liberianerin** f; -, -nen Liberian, weiblich auch: Liberian woman (od. girl); **liberianisch** Adj. Liberian; **unter ~er Flagge** under a Liberian flag

Libero m; -s, -s Fußball: sweeper, libero

libertär Adj. geh. libertarian

Libertinismus m; -, kein Pl.; geh. libertinism

libidinös *Adj. Psych.* libidinous; **Libido** *f; -, kein Pl.* libido

Librettist *m; -en, -en,* **~in** *f; -, -nen; Mus.* librettist; **Libretto** *n; -s, -s und Libretti* libretto (*Pl.* libretti *od.* librettos)

Libyen (*n*); *-s; Geog.* Libya; **Libyer** *m; -s, -,* **Libyerin** *f; -, -nen* Libyan, *weiblich auch:* Libyan woman (*od.* girl); **libysch** *Adj.* Libyan

licht *Adj.* **1.** *geh.* (*hell*) light, bright; *Farbe:* light; **~er werden** become lighter (*od.* brighter); **~er Augenblick** *od.* **Moment** *fig.* lucid moment (*auch iro.*); **2.** (*spärlich*) *Haar, Wald:* thin, sparse; (*kahl*) *Stelle:* bare; *am Kopf:* auch bald; *im Wald:* clear; **~(er) werden** thin (out); **3.** *Tech.:* **~e Breite/Höhe** clear breadth / clear height, headroom; **~e Weite** inside width; *Durchfahrt:* clearance width

Licht *n; -(e)s, -er* **1.** light; (*Helle*) brightness; (*Beleuchtung*) lighting; (*Lampe*) lamp; (*Verkehrslicht*) light; (*Tageslicht*) daylight; **bei ~** in daylight; **offenes ~** an open flame; **~ machen** turn on the light(s); **gegen das ~ halten** hold up to the light; **j-m im ~ stehen** stand in the (*od.* s.o.'s) light; **j-m aus dem ~ gehen** get out of the (*od.* s.o.'s) light; **es werde ~** *bibl. und hum.* let there be light; **das ewige ~** *kath.* the Eternal Light; **wo ~ ist, ist auch (viel) Schatten** *Sprichw.* there's no joy without sorrow; **2.** *fig. in Wendungen:* **ans ~ bringen /kommen** bring/come to light; **das ~ der Welt erblicken** see the light of day; **im ~e dieser Tatsachen** *etc.* in the light of (*bes. Am.* in light of) these facts *etc.*; **~ bringen in** (+ *Akk.*) *od.* **ein ~ werfen auf** (+ *Akk.*) shed (*od.* throw) light on; **ein schlechtes ~ werfen auf** (+ *Akk.*) throw a bad light on, reflect badly on; **in e-m schlechten ~ zeigen** show in a bad light; **ein neues ~ werfen auf** (+ *Akk.*) show in a new light, put a new complexion on; **etw. ins rechte ~ rücken** *vorteilhaft:* put (*od.* show) s.th. in a favo(u)rable light; *richtig:* put (*od.* show) s.th. in its true light; **etw. in e-m günstigen/ungünstigen ~ erscheinen lassen** show s.th. in a favo(u)rable / an unfavo(u)rable light; **etw. in ein schiefes** *od.* **falsches ~ rücken** *od.* **ein schiefes ~ auf etw. werfen** put a wrong complexion on s.th., show s.th. in the wrong light; **bei ~e besehen** *geh.* (*bei näherer Betrachtung*) on closer inspection; (*nüchtern betrachtet*) (seen) in the cold light of day; **das ~ scheuen** have something to hide; **j-n hinters ~ führen** pull the wool over s.o.'s eyes, lead s.o. up the garden path; **in X gehen die ~er aus** things are beginning to look pretty grim in X; **es ging mir ein ~ auf** the truth began to dawn on me; **j-m ein ~ aufstecken** *umg.* put s.o. in the picture; **sein ~ leuchten lassen** not hide one's light under a bushel; → **grün** 5, **Scheffel**; **3.** *umg.* (*Strom*) electricity; **~ legen** put in electric wiring; **4.** *Lichter Pl. Jägerspr.* eyes

Lichtanlage *f* lighting system

licht|arm *Adj.* badly lit, dingy; **~beständig** *Adj.* light-resistant; *Stoff:* non-fading

Lichtbild *n* **1.** *Amtsspr.* (*Passbild*) (passport) photo(graph); **2.** *altm.* (*Fotografie*) photograph; (*Diapositiv*) slide; **Lichtbildervortrag** *m* slide talk (*od.* lecture)

Lichtblick *m* bright spot (on the horizon), ray of sunshine *fig.*; **der einzige ~ in m-m Leben** the only bright spot in my life

Lichtbogen *m Etech.* arc; **~schweißung** *f Tech.* arc welding

lichtbrechend *Adj. Opt.* refractive; **Lichtbrechung** *f* refraction (of light)

Lichtbündel *n* light beam, pencil of rays

licht|dicht *Adj.* lightproof; **~durchflutet** *Adj.* flooded with light, bathed in light

lichtdurchlässig *Adj.* translucent; *völlig:* transparent; **Lichtdurchlässigkeit** *f* translucency; *völlige:* transparency

Lichte *f; -, kein Pl.; Tech.* inside width; *Durchfahrt:* clearance width

lichtecht *Adj.* light(-)fast; *Stoff:* non-fading; **Lichtechtheit** *f* light-fastness; *Stoff:* non-fading quality

Licht|effekt *m* light effect; *Theat. etc.* lighting effect; **~einfall** *m* **1.** incidence of light; **2.** (*Eindringen*) light leakage; **~einstrahlung** *f* incidence of light; **~einwirkung** *f* action of light

lichtempfindlich *Adj.* sensitive to light; *Phys.* photosensitive; *Fot., Papier:* sensitized; *Sonnenbrille:* photochromic; **~ machen** sensitize; **Lichtempfindlichkeit** *f* (light-)sensitivity; *Phys.* photosensitivity; *Fot., e-s Films:* speed

lichten¹ I. *v/t.* (*Wald*) clear; *fig.* thin out; **II.** *v/refl.* thin out (*auch fig.*); (*heller werden*) clear up; → **Reihe** 5

lichten² *v/t.: Naut.:* **den Anker ~** weigh anchor

Lichter|baum *m* Christmas tree; **~fest** *n Reli.* Hanukkah, Festival of Lights

lichterfüllt *Adj. lit.* suffused with light

Lichter|glanz *m* bright lights *Pl.*, blaze of lights; **~kette** *f* chain of lights (*auch von Menschen*); *umlaufend blinkende:* chasing rope lights *Pl.*, running lights *Pl.*

lichterloh *Adv.:* **~ brennen** be blazing fiercely; **es brannte ~ in der Abwehr** *Sport* the defen|ce (*Am.* -se) was subjected to a barrage of attacks

Lichtermeer *n* sea of lights

Licht|filter *m, n* (light) filter; **~geschwindigkeit** *f* speed of light; **~gestalt** *f geh.* gleaming form; **~griffel** *m EDV* light pen

lichtgrün *Adj.* light green

Lichthof *m* **1.** *Archit.* light well, atrium; **2.** *Fot.* halo; *Pl. auch* halation

lichthungrig *Adj.* needing a lot of (sun)light

Licht|hupe *f Mot.* (headlamp) flasher; **die ~ betätigen** flash one's lights; **~jahr** *n* light year; **~kegel** *m* beam (of light); *Phys.* cone of light; **~kreis** *m* circle of light; **~kuppel** *f* light dome, domed roof light; **~leitung** *f umg.* electrical cable

lichtlos *Adj.* (completely) dark; without daylight

Licht|mangel *m* lack of light; **~maschine** *f Mot.* dynamo, *Am.* generator; (*Drehstromlichtmaschine*) alternator

Lichtmast *m* lamp standard

Lichtmess (*n*); *kein Art.: kath.:* (*Mariä*) **~** Candlemas

Licht|messer *m* light meter; **~messung** *f* photometry; **~nelke** *f Bot.* campion; **~orgel** *f* light keyboard; **~pause** *f* photocopy; (*Blaupause*) blueprint; **~punkt** *m* spot of light; *fig.* bright spot; → *auch* **Lichtblick**; **~quelle** *f* light source; **~reflex** *m* light re-

flection, reflection of light; **~reiz** *m* light stimulus; **~reklame** *f* neon (advertising) sign; **~schacht** *m* light well; **~schalter** *m* light switch; **~schein** *m* (beam of) light

lichtscheu *Adj.* **1.** *fig.:* **~er Mensch** shady character; **~es Gesindel** shady characters (*od.* riff-raff); **2.** (*lichtempfindlich*) sensitive to light; *Pflanze:* shade-loving; **~e Tiere** *etc.* animals *etc.* that avoid (*od.* shun) the light

Licht|schimmer *m* glimmer of light; **~schranke** *f* light barrier, photoelectric beam

Lichtschutz *m* protection against the light (*od.* sun); **~faktor** *m* (sun) protection factor

lichtschwach *Adj.* **1.** *Lichtquelle:* dim, low-powered; **2.** *Opt., Fernglas etc.:* with a slow lens; *Objektiv:* slow, low-speed

Licht|seite *f fig.* bright side; **~signal** *n* light signal; (*Verkehrsampel*) *auch* traffic light; *Mot., Lichthupe:* flash(ing) (of one's lights); **ein ~ geben** flash one's lights; **~spalt** *m* crack of light; **~spektrum** *n* light spectrum

Lichtspiel|haus *n altm.,* **~theater** *n altm.* cinema, *Am.* movie theater

lichtstark *Adj.* **1.** *Lichtquelle:* powerful; **2.** *Opt., Fernglas:* with a fast lens; *Objektiv:* fast, high-speed ...; **Lichtstärke** *f* brightness; *e-s Objektivs:* F-number, speed

Licht|stift *m EDV* light pen; **~strahl** *m* ray (*od.* beam) of light; **~technik** *f* light technology; (*Lichtmessung*) photometry; **~therapie** *f Med.* phototherapy

lichtundurchlässig *Adj.* opaque; **Lichtundurchlässigkeit** *f* opacity, opaqueness

lichtunempfindlich *Adj.* insensitive to light; **Lichtunempfindlichkeit** *f* insensitivity to light

Lichtung *f* clearing

Licht|verhältnisse *Pl.* lighting conditions, lighting *Sg.*; **~welle** *f Phys.* light wave; **~wert** *m Fot.* light value; **~zeichen** *n* light signal; **~zeichenanlage** *f Mot. Amtsspr.* traffic light(s *Pl.*)

Lid *n; n; -(e)s, -er* eyelid; **~rand** *m* eyelid margin; **~sack** *m* baggy skin under the eyes; **~schatten** *m* eye shadow; **~spalte** *f Anat.* palpebral fissure; **~strich** *m* (eye)lid line

lieb I. *Adj.* **1.** (*liebevoll*) *Brief, Worte:* kind; (*gütig*) kind, good; *in Briefen:* (*viele*) **~e Grüße** (much) love (**an** + *Akk.* to); **sei so ~ und ...** would you be so kind as to ..., would you be a dear (*od.* do me a favo[u]r) and ...; **sei so ~** could you?, do you mind?; **das ist ~ von dir** that's very kind (*stärker:* sweet) of you; **~ sein zu** be kind (*od.* nice) to; **2.** (*nett, freundlich*) nice; (*goldig*) sweet; **er/sie ist ein ~er Kerl** he's/she's a dear; **ein ~es Ding** a darling, a sweetie *umg.*; **er hat eine ~e Frau** his wife is a dear; **sie hat ein ~es Gesicht** she has a sweet face; **3.** (*brav*) good; **sei (schön) ~!** be good!; **warst du auch ~?** have you been a good boy (*Mädchen:* girl)?; **4.** (*geschätzt, geliebt*) dear; **die ~e Sonne scheint wieder** the good old sun has come out again; **alles, was ihr ~ war** all that was dear to her; **diese alte Uhr ist mir ~ und teuer** this old clock is very precious (to me); **wenn dir dein Leben ~ ist** if you value your life; **~ behalten** still be fond of; **~ gewinnen** grow fond of, come to like; **~ haben** like; *stärker:* love; **~ gewor-**

den cherished; **~er Herr N.** *im Brief*: Dear Mr (*od.* Mr.) N; *in der Anrede*: **~e Anwesende** *od.* **meine ~en Anwesenden** *etwa* ladies and gentlemen; **mein ~er Mann!** *umg.* I tell you!; **das ~e Geld** *umg.* the wretched money; → **bisschen** III, **Himmel** 4, **Gott** 1, 2, **Not** 3, **Schwan** 1, **Tag**[1] 2; **5.** (*angenehm, willkommen*) welcome; **~er Besuch** *eine Person*: a welcome visitor; *mehrere Personen*: welcome visitors; **das ist mir gar nicht ~** I don't like this at all; **es wäre mir ~, wenn** I'd appreciate it (*od.* be glad) if; **mehr, als ihm ~ ist** more than he really wants; → **lieber, liebst...**; **II.** *Adv.* **1.** (*liebevoll*) lovingly, fondly; (*freundlich*) kindly; (*nett*) nicely; (*zärtlich*) tenderly, (*sanft*) gently; **er hat es so ~ hergerichtet** *etc.* he took such a lot of care over it; **2.** (*brav*): **er/sie hat es ganz ~ aufgegessen** he/ she ate it all up like a good boy/girl; **III.** *substantivisch*: **mein Lieber!** *Frau zu Mann*: my dear; *Mann zu Mann*: my dear fellow; **meine Liebe!** my dear (girl); **meine Lieben** my dears; **meine Lieben!** dear people!; **Liebes** *Anrede*: (my) love; **etwas Liebes** something nice; **j-m etwas Liebes tun** *od.* **erweisen** do s.o. a favo(u)r, be very kind to s.o.; **kann ich dir irgendetwas Liebes tun?** is there anything I can do for you?; → **Liebste**

liebäugeln *v/i.* (*untr., hat ge-*): **mit etw. ~** have one's eyes on s.th.; **mit dem Gedanken** *od.* **der Idee ~ zu** (+ *Inf.*) toy with the idea of (+ *Ger.*)

Liebchen *n altm.* sweetheart

Liebe *f*, -, *-n* **1.** *nur Sg.* love (**zu** *j-m*: *mst* for, *e-r Sache*: *mst* of); (*Zuneigung*) liking (for); (*Liebschaft*) love affair, romance; **~ auf den ersten Blick** love at first sight; **~ machen** *umg.* make love; **er ist gut in der ~** he is good at making love; **m-e ganze ~ gehört der See** I really love the sea; **aus ~** for love; **aus ~ zu** for (the) love of; **in ~** *Briefschluss*: with (all my) love; **bei aller ~** much as I'd like to; **bei Kritik**: look here; **mit ~ gemacht** *etc.* made (*od.* done) *etc.* with loving care; **die ~ geht durch den Magen** the way to a man's heart is through his stomach; **alte ~ rostet nicht** old friendships never die; **wo die ~ hinfällt** love finds some strange objects, there's no accounting for tastes where love is concerned; → **blind** I 2; **2.** (*Geliebte[r]*) sweetheart, beloved; (*Angebetete[r]*) idol; **m-e große ~** the great love of my life; (*Hobby etc.*) my great passion; **e-e alte ~** *umg.* an old flame; **3.** *nur Sg.* → **Gefallen**[1]

liebe|bedürftig *Adj.*: **~ sein** need (*stärker*: crave) love and affection; **unsere Katze ist sehr ~** (*will immer gestreichelt werden*) our cat always needs lots of strokes (*od.* stroking); **~dienerisch** *Adj. pej.* toadying, sycophantic *förm.*

Liebelei *f*, -, *-en* little affair

lieben I. *v/t.* love; (*etw. gern haben*) *auch* (really) like; *sexuell*: make love to; **er liebt es zu** (+ *Inf.*) he loves (+ *Ger. od.* to + *Inf.*); **er liebt es nicht zu** (+ *Inf.*) he doesn't like (+ *Ger. od.* to + *Inf.*); **er liebt es nicht, wenn man zu spät kommt** he doesn't like people arriving late, he doesn't like it when people arrive late; **sich** (*Pl.*) **~** love each other (one another), be in love (with each other); *sexuell*: make love; **was sich liebt, das neckt sich**

lovers are always teasing one another; → **lernen** I 3; **II.** *v/i.* love; *sexuell*: make love

liebend I. *Part. Präs.* → **lieben**; **II.** *Adj.* loving; **e-e ~e Frau** a woman in love; *Ehefrau*: a loving wife; **III.** *Adv.*: **~ gern** gladly; **ich würde ~ gern** I'd simply love to; **er spielt ~ gern Schach** he really loves playing chess; **ich esse ~ gern Kartoffeln** I (just) love potatoes, I have a passion for (*od.* I'm wild about) potatoes; **Liebende** *m, f*, *-n*, *-n* lover; **die ~n** the lovers

liebenswert *Adj. Mensch*: lovely; *Art, Eigenschaft*: endearing; **ein ~er Mensch** *auch* such a nice person

liebenswürdig *Adj.* (very) kind; (*gewandt und höflich*) charming; **wären Sie so ~ zu** (+ *Inf.*) would you be so kind as to (+ *Inf.*), would you be kind enough to (+ *Inf.*); **liebenswürdigerweise** *Adv.* (very) kindly; **er hat es mir ~ geliehen** *auch* he was kind enough to lend it to me; **Liebenswürdigkeit** *f* kindness; (*Eigenschaft*) charm, charming nature; **hätten Sie die ~ zu** (+ *Inf.*) would you be so kind as to (+ *Inf.*), would you be kind enough to (+ *Inf.*)

lieber I. *Adj. Komp. von* → **lieb** I; **II.** *Adv.*: **... ~ haben** *od.* **mögen** like ... better, prefer ...; **ich möchte ~ nicht** I'd rather not; **ich bleibe ~ zu Hause** I'd rather (*od.* I'd prefer to) stay at home; **du solltest ~ gehen** you'd (*od.* you had) better go, it would be better if you left; **das hättest du ~ nicht machen sollen** you shouldn't (really) have done that; **lass es ~ better not** (do that); **machen wir es ~ gleich** let's do it now, I think we should do it now; **was wäre dir ~?** what would you prefer?; **mir wäre ~, wenn ...** I'd prefer it if ..., I'd prefer us *etc.* to (+ *Inf.*); **mir wäre nichts ~ als das** I'd like nothing better, there's nothing I'd rather do (*od.* have *etc.*)

Liebes|abenteuer *n* amorous adventure (*od.* escapade); **~affäre** *f* love affair; **~akt** *m geh.* act of love, sexual act

Liebesbedürfnis *n* need for love and affection; **liebesbedürftig** *Adj.* → **liebebedürftig**

Liebes|beziehung *f* love affair (*od.* relationship); *engS.* sexual relationship; **~brief** *m* love letter; **~dichtung** *f* love poetry; **~dienst** *m* favo(u)r; **j-m e-n ~ erweisen** do s.o. a good turn; **~entzug** *m Psych.* withdrawal of love (and affection); **j-n mit ~ bestrafen** punish s.o. by withdrawing one's love (and affection); **~erklärung** *f* declaration of love; (**j-m**) **e-e ~ machen** declare one's love (to s.o.); **~erlebnis** *n* love affair

liebesfähig *Adj. Psych.* capable of love; **Liebesfähigkeit** *f*; *nur Sg.* capacity for love

Liebes|film *m* (filmed) love story, screen romance; **~freuden** *Pl.* pleasures of love; **~gedicht** *n* love poem; **~geschichte** *f* love story; **~glück** *n* joy(s *Pl.*) of love; (*glückliche Liebe*) happy love affair; **~gott** *m* love god; **~göttin** *f* love goddess; **~heirat** *f* love match; **~knochen** *m Dial.* eclair

liebeskrank *Adj.* lovesick

Liebes|kummer *m* lovesickness; **~ haben** be lovesick; **~kunst** *f* art of love; **~laube** *f hum.* love nest; **~leben** *n* love life; **~lied** *n* love song; **~lyrik** *f Lit.* love poetry; **~müh(e)** *f*: **das ist vergebliche ~** that's a waste of time

(and effort); **~nacht** *f* night of love; **~nest** *n* love nest; **~objekt** *n* object of love; **~paar** *n*, **~pärchen** *n* (courting) couple, (pair of) lovers *Pl.*; **~perlen** *Pl.* hundreds and thousands; **~roman** *m* love story; (*Romanze*) romantic novel; **~schwur** *m* lover's oath; **~spiel** *n* loveplay; *Zool.* mating ritual; **~szene** *f* love scene

liebestoll *Adj.* love-crazed; *lit.* love-stricken

Liebes|töter *Pl. umg.* bloomers; **~tragödie** *f* tragedy of love; **~trank** *m* love potion

liebestrunken *Adj.* besotted

liebesunfähig *Adj. Psych.* incapable of love; **Liebesunfähigkeit** *f Psych.* incapacity for love

Liebes|verhältnis *n* (sexual) relationship, love affair; **~verlust** *m Psych.* love deprivation; **~werben** *n*; *-s, kein Pl.*; *geh.* wooing, courtship; **~zauber** *m* spell of love; **~zeichen** *n* token of love

liebevoll I. *Adj.* loving, (*herzlich*) very kind; **II.** *Adv.* lovingly; **~ zubereitet** *auch* prepared with loving care; **er wird ~ umsorgt** he's well looked after; **j-n ~ ansehen** give s.o. a loving glance (*od.* a look of affection)

Liebhaber *m*; *-s, -* **1.** lover; (*Verehrer*) admirer; **jugendlicher ~** *Theat.* juvenile lead; **er ist ein guter/schlechter ~** he's good / not very good at lovemaking; **2. ~ der Kunst/Musik** *etc.* art/music *etc.* lover; **3.** (*Kenner*) connoisseur; **~ausgabe** *f* de luxe (*od.* collector's) edition

Liebhaberei *f*, -, *-en* hobby; **aus ~** as a hobby, for pleasure

Liebhaberin *f*, -, *-nen* → **Liebhaber**

Liebhaber|preis *m* collector's price; **~stück** *n* collector's item; **~wert** *m* value as a collector's item

liebkosen *v/t.* (*untr., hat*) *geh.* caress; (*bes. Kind*) *auch* kiss and cuddle; **Liebkosung** *f* caress

lieblich I. *Adj.* lovely; *Mädchen, Gesicht*: *auch* sweet; *Landschaft, Gesicht*: charming, delightful; (*sanft*) gentle; *Duft*: sweet; *Wein*: (medium) sweet; **II.** *Adv.*: **~ duften/klingen** *etc.* have a sweet fragrance/sound *etc.*, smell/ sound *etc.* lovely; **Lieblichkeit** *f*; *nur Sg.* loveliness; *von Duft, Wein, fig. Gesicht etc.*: sweetness; *von Landschaft*: charm; (*Sanftheit*) gentleness

Liebling *m*; *-s, -e* darling; *als Anrede*: *auch* (my) love; (*Bevorzugte[r]*) favo(u)rite; **der ~ der Damen** the ladies' darling; **er war ein ~ der Götter** he was beloved of the gods *lit.*

Lieblings|... *im Subst. mst* favo(u)rite ...; **~buch** *n* favo(u)rite book; **~kind** *n* favo(u)rite child; *fig.* baby; **~schauspieler** *m*, **~schauspielerin** *f* favo(u)rite actress; **~schüler** *m*, **~schülerin** *f* favo(u)rite pupil (*Am.* student), teacher's pet; **er ist ihr ~** he's the teacher's pet; **~speise** *f* favo(u)rite food; **~thema** *n* favo(u)rite (*od.* pet) subject; **er ist wieder bei s-m ~** he's onto his favo(u)rite (*od.* pet) subject again, he's on his hobby-horse again

lieblos I. *Adj.* unkind; (*gefühllos*) cold; *Eltern etc.*: uncaring; *Behandlung*: harsh; **II.** *Adv.*: **sie geht sehr ~ mit ihm um** she treats him very harshly; **~ zubereitet** *Essen*: prepared without any care (*umg.* any old how); **Lieblosigkeit** *f* unkindness; (*Kälte*) coldness; *von Eltern etc.*: lack of love; *von Behandlung*: harshness; (*Interesselosig-*

keit) lack of care, couldn't-care-less attitude

liebreich *Adj. geh.* loving

Liebreiz *m; nur Sg. geh.* charm, attractiveness

Liebschaft *f* (love) affair

liebst... **I.** *Adj. Komp. von* → **lieb** I; *m-e* ~**e Pflanze** *etc.* my favo(u)rite plant *etc.*; *Liebste Christine! Briefanfang:* Dearest Christine; **II.** *Adv.:* **am** ~**en schwimme ich** I like swimming best; **am** ~**en würde ich bleiben / ihm eine runterhauen** I'd really prefer to stay / I had an overwhelming desire to punch him; **am** ~**en wäre mir, wenn ...** I'd really like to ...

Liebste *m, f; -n, -n:* **meine** ~**, mein** ~**r** darling, my love

Liebstöckel *m, n; -s, -; Bot.* lovage

Lied *n; -(e)s, -er* song; (*Melodie*) tune; (*deutsches Kunstlied*) lied; (*Gedicht*) poem; (*Ballade*) ballad; **es ist immer das alte** ~ *umg. fig.* it's the same old story every time; **er kann dir ein** ~ **davon singen** *umg. fig.* he can tell you a thing or two about that; **das Ende vom** ~ *fig.* the upshot (of the whole affair); **und das war das Ende vom** ~ *fig.* and that was that; **das Hohe** ~ (*Salomo[n]s*) *bibl.* the Song of Solomon, the Song of Songs

Lieder|abend *m* song recital; *mit deutschen Kunstliedern:* lieder recital; ~**buch** *n* songbook

liederlich *Adj.* **1.** untidy, messy; (*schlampig*) sloppy, slovenly; *Arbeit: auch* slipshod; **2.** *pej.* (*verwerflich*) dissolute; **Liederlichkeit** *f* **1.** untidiness, messiness; (*Schlampigkeit*) sloppiness, slovenliness; **2.** (*Verwerflichkeit*) dissipation, dissolution

Lieder|macher *m,* ~**macherin** *f* singer-songwriter; ~**sänger** *m,* ~**sängerin** *f Mus., Schubert etc.:* lieder singer; ~**zyklus** *m* song cycle

Lied|gut *n; nur Sg.* song literature, body of song; **das bayerische** ~ Bavarian song; ~**text** *m* lyrics *Pl. od.* words *Pl.* (of a *od.* the song)

lief *Imperf.* → **laufen**

Lieferant *m; -en, -en; Wirts.* supplier; **Lieferanteneingang** *m* tradesman's (*od.* goods, *Am.* service) entrance; **Lieferantin** *f; -, -nen* supplier

Lieferauftrag *m Wirts.* order

lieferbar *Adj. Wirts.* available, in stock; **nicht** ~ not available; (*nicht mehr vorrätig*) out of stock; **sofort** ~**e Waren** goods available from stock, *fachspr.* spot goods

Lieferbedingungen *Pl. Wirts.* terms of delivery

lieferbereit *Adj.* ready for delivery

Liefer|engpass *m* supply shortage; ~**firma** *f* supplier(s *Pl.*); ~**frist** *f* delivery deadline; ~**kosten** *Pl.* delivery charges, shipping costs; ~**menge** *f* quantity delivered (*od.* ordered)

liefern *vt/i.* **1.** *Wirts.* deliver (+ *Dat. od.* **an** + *Akk.* to); (*beschaffen*) supply (*j-m etw.* s.o. with s.th.); **bis wann können Sie** ~**?** when can you deliver?; **wir** ~ **frei Haus** we offer free delivery (to the door); (*Waren*) **ins Ausland** ~ supply goods abroad (*od.* to the foreign market); **2.** (*erzeugen*) produce; (*Ertrag*) yield; *fig.* (*Beweise etc.*) supply, provide, furnish; **es lieferte uns genug Gesprächsstoff** it gave us plenty to talk about; **3.** (*austragen*): **sich** (*Dat.*) **e-e Schlacht/ein Duell** ~ fight a battle/duel; **er lieferte e-n harten Kampf / ein gutes Spiel** he put up a good fight / he played well; → **geliefert**

Liefer|ort *m Wirts.* place of delivery; ~**preis** *m* contract price; ~**schein** *m* delivery note; ~**schwierigkeiten** *Pl.* delivery problems; ~**sperre** *f* cessation of deliveries; **e-e** ~ **verhängen** stop all deliveries; ~**tag** *m* delivery date; ~**termin** *m* **1.** delivery deadline; **2.** delivery date

Lieferung *f* **1.** *Wirts.* (*das Liefern*) delivery, *bes. Am. auch* shipment; (*Belieferung*) supply; (*Sendung*) *auch* consignment, shipment; (*Teillieferung*) instal(l)ment; **2.** (*e-s Buchs*) instal(l)ment; *e-s Wörterbuchs:* fascicle

Lieferungs|vertrag *m* supply contract; ~**verzug** *m* delay in delivery; **bei** ~ in cases of late delivery

Liefer|verkehr *m* delivery activity; **für den** ~ **frei** open for deliveries; ~**vertrag** *m Wirts.* supply contract; ~**wagen** *m Mot.* delivery van; *offener:* pickup (truck); ~**zeit** *f Wirts.* delivery period; **die** ~ **einhalten** deliver on time

Liege *f; -, -n* daybed; *für den Garten:* sun lounger; (*Campingliege*) campbed

Liege|bank *f* reclining bench; ~**deck** *n Naut.* sun deck; ~**kur** *f Med.* rest cure

liegen; *liegt, lag, hat (südd., österr., schw.: ist) gelegen v/i.* **1.** lie; **die Flaschen müssen** ~ the bottles have to lie flat; **der Boden lag voller Zeitungen** the floor was strewn with newspapers; **der Schnee lag meterhoch** the snow was piled up to a height of several met|res (*Am.* -ers); **es lag viel Schnee** there was a lot of snow (on the ground); **liegt mein Haar richtig?** is my hair all right?; **der Griff liegt gut in der Hand** the grip sits nicely in your hand; **2.** *Person:* lie; **im Gras / auf dem Bett** ~ lie in the grass / on the bed; ~ **bleiben** (*nicht aufstehen*) not get up; **im Bett:** *auch* stay in bed; *Boxen:* stay down; **er blieb verletzt** ~ he was unable to get up because he was injured; **3.** *Kranker:* be in bed; *weitS.* (*krank sein*) be laid up; ~ **müssen** *Kranker:* have to stay in bed; *flach:* have to lie flat; **er hat drei Wochen gelegen** he was in bed (*od.* was laid up) for three weeks; **4.** (*gelegen sein*) *Stadt etc.:* lie, be (situated); *Gebäude:* be (situated *od.* located); ~ **nach** *Haus:* face, *Zimmer: auch* look out on, overlook; **das Dorf liegt hoch über dem Tal** the village is (situated) high above the valley; **5.** *Naut., Schiff:* lie; **im Hafen liegt seit gestern eine Segelyacht** there's been a yacht in (the) harbo(u)r since yesterday; **6.** *fig.:* **es liegt hinter uns** it's behind us; **da liegt noch einiges vor uns** we've got quite a lot coming up; **in ihrer Stimme lag leise Ironie** there was a hint of irony in her voice; **das lag nicht in m-r Absicht** that was not my intention; **die Schwierigkeit liegt darin, dass ...** the problem is that ...; **da liegt der Fehler** that's where the trouble lies; **wie die Sache jetzt lag** as matters (now) stand, as things are at the moment; **7.** ~ **bleiben** *Sachen:* be left (**auf** + *Dat.* on); *Schnee:* settle; (*vergessen werden*) be left (behind); *auch fig.* be forgotten; *fig. Arbeit:* be left unfinished; *Wirts. Waren:* be left unsold, *umg.* be left on the shelf; *Auto:* have a breakdown (on the way); **das kann** ~ **bleiben** *fig.* that can wait; ~ **geblieben** (*vergessen*) forgotten; *Auto etc.:* stranded; (*aufgegeben*) abandoned; ~

gebliebene Bücher *etc.* books etc. left behind; **8.** ~ **lassen** (*vergessen*) leave behind, forget; (*in Ruhe lassen*) leave alone; (*Arbeit*) leave (unfinished); **die Arbeit** ~ **lassen** (*unterbrechen*) stop work; *plötzlich:* drop everything; *Fabrikarbeiter:* down tools, *Am.* walk out; **alles** ~ **lassen** (*nicht aufräumen*) leave everything lying around, not clean up; **lass es liegen!** don't touch it!; → **links** I 1; **9.** (*gemäß sein*): **das liegt mir nicht** it's not my thing; **er liegt mir überhaupt nicht** he's not my type of person; *als Mann:* he's not my type; **nichts liegt mir ferner** nothing could be further from my mind; **10.** **mit Präp.:** ~ **an** (+ *Dat.*) be near; **an e-r Straße, e-m Fluss:** be on; (*dicht an*) be next to; *fig. Ursache:* be because of; **an der Spitze** *etc.* ~ be in front *etc.*; **es liegt an dir** it's your fault; *etw. zu tun:* it's up to you; **an mir soll's nicht** ~ I'll certainly do my best; (*ich werde dir nicht im Weg stehen*) I won't stand in the way; **11.** **mit Präp.:** **es liegt daran, dass ...** it's because ...; **es liegt mir daran zu** (+ *Inf.*) I'm keen (*Am.* eager) to (+ *Inf.*); **es liegt mir sehr viel daran** it means a lot to me; **es liegt mir viel an ihr** she means a lot to me; **mir liegt viel an deiner Mitarbeit** your cooperation is very important to me; **es liegt mir nichts daran** it doesn't mean much to me; **es liegt mir nichts daran zu gewinnen** it doesn't make any difference to me whether I win or not; **12.** **mit Präp.:** ~ **auf** (+ *Akk.*) lie on; *Akzent:* be on; **der Wagen liegt gut (auf der Straße)** the car holds (the road) well; **es liegt Nebel auf den Feldern** mist is hanging over the fields; → **Hand**[1] 3, **Seele** 1; **13.** **mit Präp.:** **der Gewinn liegt bei fünf Millionen** there is a profit of five million; **die Temperaturen** ~ **bei 30 Grad** temperatures are (*im Wetterbericht:* will be) around 30 degrees (centigrade); **die Entscheidung liegt bei dir** it's your decision, it's up to you; → **Blut** 2, **Magen** etc.

Liegen *n; -s, kein Pl.* lying; (*Stellung*) lying (*od.* horizontal) position; **im** ~ lying down; **das** ~ **bekommt ihm nicht** he can't take all this lying down

liegend I. *Part. Präs.* → **liegen**; **II.** *Adj.* **1.** (*ruhend*) resting; *Position:* horizontal; *Figur, Haltung:* recumbent; *bes. Kunst* reclining; **auf dem Rücken** ~ lying on one's back; **Liegende** *Kunst* reclining figure; **2.** (*gelegen*) situated; **III.** *Adv.:* ~ *aufbewahrt* stored flat; ~ **transportieren** (*Kranke etc.*) move in a recumbent position

Liegenschaften *Pl.* real estate *Sg.*; **Liegenschaftsamt** *n* local authority real estate office

Liege|platz *m Naut., Verk.* mooring; ~**rad** *n* recumbent bicycle, recumbent, bent *umg.*; ~**sitz** *m* reclining seat, recliner; ~**statt** *f; -, Liegestätten; geh.* resting place; (*Bett*) bed; ~**stuhl** *m* deckchair; *mit Polsterung:* lounger; ~**stütz** *m Gymnastik:* press-up, *auch Am.* push-up; **20** ~**e machen** do 20 press-ups; ~**terrasse** *f* sun terrace; ~**wagen** *m Eisenb.* couchette car; ~**wiese** *f* sunbathing lawn; ~**zeit** *f Naut., Verk.* time spent in harbo(u)r

lieh *Imperf.* → **leihen**

Lieschen *n; -s, -* **1.** *umg.:* ~ **Müller** the average woman, *umg.* Mrs (*od.* Mrs.) Average (*od.* Jones); (*ach*) **du liebes** ~**!** good grief!, good heavens!; **2.** *umg.*

(*Frau, Mädchen*) female; **3.** *Bot.* → **fleißig** I 1

Liese *f*; -, -*n*; *umg. pej.* female; **dumme** ~ stupid female (*stärker*: cow)

ließ *Imperf.* → **lassen**

liest *Präs.* → **lesen**[1],[2]

Lifestyle ['laifstail] *m*; -*s, kein Pl.* lifestyle

Lift *m*; -(*e*)*s, -s und -e* lift, *Am.* elevator; (*Skilift*) (ski) lift

liften *v/t. Gesichtshaut*: tighten; *Busen*: lift; **sich ~ lassen** have a facelift; **Lifting** *n*; -*s, -s* facelift

Liftkarte *f Skifahren*: lift ticket

Liga *f*; -, *Ligen* league (*auch Sport*); **erste/zweite ~** First/Second Division; **~spiel** *n Sport* league match (*od.* game)

Ligatur *f*; -, -*en*; *Anat., Druck.* ligature; *Mus.* tie

light [lait] *indekl. Adj. Werbesprache*: **Beck's Light®** Beck's Light; **Cola ~** diet cola

Lightshow ['laitʃoː] *f* light show

...ligist *m, im Subst.* member of the ... league; **Erst~/Zweit~** member of the first/second division; *Mannschaft*: first/second division team

Lignit *m*; -*s, -e*; *Min.* lignite

Ligurien (*n*); -*s*; *Geog.* Liguria; **ligurisch** *Adj.* Ligurian; **das Ligurische Meer** the Ligurian Sea

Liguster *m*; -*s, -*; *Bot.* (common) privet; **~hecke** *f* privet hedge

liieren I. *v/refl.* **1.** *Paar*: get together, become an item, start a relationship; (*fest*) *liiert sein* have a (stable) relationship (*mit* with), be an item; **2.** *Wirts. etc.* establish links (*mit* with); **II.** *v/t. bes. Wirts.* establish links between; *der Plan, beide Autohersteller zu ~, scheiterte* the planned association between the two car makers (*Am.* carmakers) came to nothing; *die Verlage sind seit fast 30 Jahren liiert* the publishing houses have been working together for nearly 30 years

Likör *m*; -*s, -e* liqueur; **~glas** *n* liqueur glass; **~wein** *m* liqueur wine

lila *indekl. Adj.* mauve, *bes. Am.* purple; *hell*: lilac; **Lila** *n*; -*s, -* mauve, *bes. Am.* purple; *hell*: lilac; **lilafarben** *Adj.* mauve, *bes. Am.* purple; *hell*: lilac

Lilie *f*; -, -*n*; *Bot.* lily; *Her. auch* fleur-de-lis; *gelbe* ~ gold lily; *blaue* ~ iris; **Liliengewächs** *n Bot.* member of the lily family; *die* ~*e* the lily family, the liliaceae; **lilienweiß** *Adj.* lily-white

Liliputaner *m*; -*s, -*, **~in** *f*; -, -*nen*; *umg. neg.!* midget, Lilliputian

Liliput|bahn *f* miniature rail|way (*Am.* -road) (*used as a people-mover on an exhibition site*); **~format** *n*: **in** *od.* **im ~** in a miniature format

Limburger *m*; -*s, -*, **~ Käse** *m Gastr.* Limburger (cheese)

Limerick ['lɪmərɪk] *m*; -(*s*), -*s*; *Lit.* limerick

Limes *m*; -, - **1.** *hist.* limes; **2.** *Math.* limit

Limette *f*; -, -*n*; *Bot.* lime; **Limettensaft** *m* lime juice

Limit ['lɪmɪt] *n*; -*s, -s* limit; *Wirts. auch* ceiling; *Auktion*: reserve (price); **limitieren** *v/t.* limit; *Wirts. auch* put a ceiling on; **limitiert I.** *P.P.* → **limitieren**; **II.** *Adj.* limited; **nicht ~** unlimited, open-ended; **Limitierung** *f* limitation; *Wirts. auch* ceiling

limnisch *Adj. Bio., Geol.* limnic; **Limnologie** *f*; -, *kein Pl.* limnology

Limo *f, n*; -, -(*s*); *umg.*, **Limonade** *f*; -, -*n* fizzy drink, *Am.* soda, pop, soda

pop; (*Zitronenlimonade*) lemonade; (*Orangenlimonade*) orangeade

Limone *f*; -, -*n* **1.** (*Limette*) lime; **2.** *altm.* (*Zitrone*) lemon

Limousine *f*; -, -*n*; *Mot.* saloon, *Am.* sedan; *luxuriöse, mit Trennwand*: limousine

lind *Adj. geh.* gentle, mild

Linde *f*; -, -*n*; *Bot.* **1.** *Baum*: lime, *Am.* linden; **2.** *nur Sg.*; *Holz*: limewood, *Am. auch* linden

Linden|baum *m* lime (*Am.* linden) tree; **~blatt** *n* lime tree leaf, *Am.* linden leaf; **~blütentee** *m* lime (*Am.* linden) blossom tea; **~holz** *n* limewood, *Am. auch* linden

lindern *v/t.* alleviate; (*Schmerzen*) *auch* ease, relieve; (*Fieber*) bring down; (*Armut*) relieve; **Linderung** *f* alleviation; *von Schmerzen*: *auch* easing, relief; **~ verschaffen** *od.* **bringen** bring relief (*j-m* to s.o.)

lindgrün *Adj.* lime green

Lindwurm *m Myth., Her.* (wingless) dragon, lindworm

Lineal *n*; -*s, -e* ruler

linear *Adj.* linear; *Wirts.* flat-rate; *Lohnerhöhung*: across-the-board

Linearbeschleuniger *m Phys.* linear accelerator

Linearität *f*; -, *kein Pl.* linearity

Linearschrift *f* linear script

Liner ['laɪnə] *m*; -*s, -* **1.** *Kosmetik*: eyeliner; **2.** *Naut.* liner; **3.** *Flug.* airliner

Lingerie [lɛ̃ʒəˈriː] *f*; -, -*n*; *schw.* lingerie

Linguist *m*; -*en, -en* linguist; **Linguistik** *f*; -, *kein Pl.* linguistics *Pl.* (*V. im Sg.*); **Linguistin** *f*; -, -*nen* linguist; **linguistisch I.** *Adj.* linguistic; **II.** *Adv.* linguistically

Linie *f*; -, -*n* **1.** line (*auch Reihe, im Gesicht, Mil., Sport etc.*); **in ~ antreten** *od.* **sich in e-r ~ aufstellen** line up; *Mil.* fall in; **in erster ~** *fig.* first of all, in the first place; **in vorderster ~ stehen** *Mil.* be in the front line; *fig.* be at the forefront (*od.* in the front line); **auf der ganzen ~** *fig.* (right) down the line; *Sieg*: across the board; **2.** (*Strecke*) route; **die ~ 20** (*Bus*) bus number 20, the number 20 (bus); **auf der ~ Köln-Hamburg** on the Cologne-Hamburg line (*od.* route); **3.** (*Fluglinie*) airline; **4.** (*Tendenz*) trend; *Pol.* course; (*Parteilinie*) party line; *e-r Zeitung*: editorial policy; **e-e klare ~ haben** (*fest umrissen sein*) be clear-cut; (*konsequent sein*) be consistent; **e-e klare ~ einhalten** follow a consistent line, stay consistent; **5.** (*Taille*) figure, waistline; **ich muss auf m-e** (*schlanke*) **~ achten** *auch* I've got to watch what I eat; **6.** (*Stamm, Geschlecht*) line; **in direkter ~ abstammen von** be a direct descendant of

Linien|ball *m Tennis*: ball (right) on the line; **~blatt** *n* (sheet of) lined paper; **~bus** *m* public service bus; **~dienst** *m* scheduled service(s *Pl.*); *Flug. auch* regular flights *Pl.*; **~flug** *m* scheduled flight; **~flugzeug** *n* scheduled aircraft; **linienförmig** *Adj.* linear

Linien|führung *f Zeichnen etc.*: line (work), use of line; **~maschine** *f* scheduled aircraft; **~netz** *n* (rail *etc.*) network; **~papier** *n* ruled (*od.* lined) paper; **~richter** *m Sport* linesman; **~richterin** *f* (female) linesman; **~schiff** *n* ship operating a regular service; *früher*: liner; **~schifffahrt** *f* (operation of) regular sailings *Pl.*; **~system** *n Mus.* staff, stave

linientreu *Adj. Pol.* loyal (to the party

line); **~ sein** *auch* toe the line

Linientreue[1] *f* loyalty to the party line

Linientreue[2] *m, f*; -*n, -n* party liner

Linienverkehr *m* scheduled services *Pl.*; *Flug.* scheduled air traffic

lin(i)ieren *v/t.* rule, line; **lin(i)iert I.** *P.P.* → **lin(i)ieren**; **II.** *Adj.* ruled, lined; **Lin(i)ierung** *f* ruling; *Linien*: (system of) ruled lines *Pl.*; *Kunst* (*Linienführung*) line (work)

link *Adj. umg.* (*gemein, niederträchtig*) dirty, mean, nasty; (*hinterhältig*) underhand(ed); (*falsch*) two-faced; **~e Tour** underhand(ed) (*stärker*: dirty, mean) trick; (*auch Pl.*) underhand(ed) (*od.* fishy) dealings *Pl.*; **j-m auf die ~e Tour kommen** (*j-n für dumm verkaufen*) try and play s.o. for a sucker; (*reinlegen*) do the dirty on s.o., *Am.* take s.o. for a ride; **komm mir ja nicht auf die ~e Tour!** *auch* just don't try it on with me; **~er Hund** *vulg.* two-faced swine *Sl.* (*vulg.* bastard)

Link *m, n*; -*s, -s Internet*: link

link... *Adj.* **1.** (*Ggs. recht...*) left; **~e Seite** left-hand side, left; **~er Hand** on the left; **zwei ~e Hände haben** *fig.* have two left hands; **das mache ich mit der ~en Hand** I can do that with my hands tied; **er ist wohl mit dem ~en Fuß** *od.* **Bein zuerst aufgestanden** he must have got out of the wrong side of the bed this morning; **2.** *Pol.* left-wing, leftist; *Flügel*: **~e Positionen vertreten** have left-wing views; **die Parteien des ~en Spektrums** the parties encompassing the spectrum of left-wing opinion; → **links** I; **3.** (*umgedreht*) reverse; **ein Hemd auf der ~en Seite bügeln** iron a shirt on the inside; **e-e ~e Masche stricken** purl one

Linke[1] *f*; -*n, -n Hand*: left hand; *Boxen*: left; *Pol.* the left; *e-r Partei*: left wing; **zur ~n** to (*od.* on) the left; **zu s-r ~n** to (*od.* on) his left

Linke[2] *m, f*; -*n, -n*; *Pol.* leftist, left-winger; *umg.* leftie

linken *v/t. umg.* (*hereinlegen*): *j-n* do the dirty on s.o., *Am.* take s.o. for a ride

linkerseits *Adv.* (on the) left

linkisch *Adj.* clumsy, gauche; *Bewegung etc.*: *auch* awkward

links I. *Adv.* **1.** *Lage*: on the left(-hand side); *Richtung*: (to the) left; **~ von** to the left of; **~ von ihm** on (*od.* to) his left; **~ oben/unten** at the top/bottom left; **drittes Regal ~** third shelf on the left; **~ abbiegen** turn left; **sich ~ halten** (*od.* **~ fahren** *od.* **gehen**) keep to the left; **das mache ich mit ~** *umg. fig.* I can do that with my hands tied; **~ liegen lassen** *umg. fig.* completely ignore; (*j-n*) give *s.o.* the cold shoulder; **ich weiß nicht mehr, was ~ und was rechts ist** I'm totally confused, I don't know which way to turn; **2.** *Pol.* on the left; **~ stehen** be on the left, be a left-winger; **die ~ stehenden Abgeordneten** the left-wing members; **~ von der Mitte** to the left of cent|re (*Am.* -er); **3.** *umg. auf, von der Innenseite*: inside out; *bügeln*: on the inside; **4. ~ stricken** purl; **5. mit ~** *fig.* without any trouble, really easily; **II.** *Präp.* **1.** (*mit Gen.*) on (*od.* to) the left of; **~ der Spree** on the left bank of the Spree; **2.** *Pol.*: **~ der Mitte** left of cent|re (*Am.* -er); **III.** *Adj.*; *nur präd.*; *umg.* (*linkshändig*) left-handed

Links|abbiegen *n Verk.*: **~ verboten** no left turn; **~abbieger** *m*; -*s, -*, **~abbiegerin** *f*; -, -*nen* vehicle turning left; *Pl.*

L

auch traffic *Sg.* turning left; **~abbiegerspur** *f*, **~abbiegespur** *f* left-hand turning (*Am.* turn) lane

Links|abweichler *m*, **~abweichlerin** *f Pol.* left-wing deviationist; **~außen** *m* **1.** *Fußball*: outside left, left wing; **2.** *Pol.* extreme left-winger

linksbündig *Adj. Druck.* flush left

Linksdrall *m* left-hand twist; *fig. Pol.* leftist tendencies *Pl.*

linksdrehend *Adj.* **1.** *Tech., Gewinde*: left-hand; **2.** *Chem., Phys.* l(a)evorotatory, *Am. auch* levorotary; **Linksdrehung** *f* anti|clockwise (*Am.* counter-)rotation

Linksextremismus *m Pol.* left-wing extremism; **Linksextremist** *m*, **Linksextremistin** *f* left-wing extremist; **linksextremistisch** *Adj.* (of the) extreme left

Linksfüßler *m*; *-s*, *-*, **~in** *f*; *-*, *-nen Fußball*: left-footed player

linksgängig *Adj. Tech., Gewinde*: left-hand

linksgerichtet *Adj. Pol.* ... with left-wing orientation

Linksgewinde *n Tech.* left-hand thread

Linkshänder *m*; *-s*, *-*, **~in** *f*; *-*, *-nen* left-hander, *Am. umg.* lefty, leftie; **er ist ~** he's left-handed; **linkshändig** *Adj.* left-handed; *Schlag etc.*: left hand ...; **Linkshändigkeit** *f* left-handedness

linksherum *Adv.* anticlockwise, *Am.* counterclockwise; (*nach links*) (to the) left

Links|intellektuelle *m*, *f* left-wing intellectual; **~katholizismus** *m* left-wing Catholicism; **~koalition** *f Pol.* left-wing coalition, coalition of the left; **~kurs** *m* left-wing policy; **~kurve** *f* left turn (*Flug.* bank); *in der Straße*: left-hand bend

linkslastig *Adj.*: **~ sein** lean to the left, *Pol. fig.* lean toward(s) the left, have left-wing tendencies (*od.* leanings)

linksläufig *Adj. Gewinde*: left-hand; *Schrift*: running from right to left

Linkslenker *m Mot.* left-hand drive vehicle

linksliberal *Adj. Pol.* left-wing liberal; **Linksliberale** *m*, *f* left-wing liberal

linksorientiert *Adj. Pol.* leftist; **Linksorientierung** *f* leftist tendencies *Pl.*

Linkspartei *f Pol.* left-wing party

linksradikal *Adj. Pol.* left-wing extremist; **Linksradikale** *m*, *f* left-wing extremist; **Linksradikalismus** *m* left-wing extremism

linksrheinisch *Adj, Adv. Geog.* on the left bank of the Rhine; → *auch* **rechtsrheinisch**

Linksruck *m Pol.* swing to the left

linksrum *Adv. umg.* → **linksherum**

Linksrutsch *m Pol.* swing to the left

linksseitig I. *Adj.* left; on the left (--hand) side; **II.** *Adv.* → **gelähmt**

Linkssteuerung *f Mot.* left-hand drive

linksum *Adv. bes. Mil.* to the left; **~ kehrt!** to the left about turn!

Links|verkehr *m Verk.*: **in Großbritannien ist ~** in Britain traffic drives on the left(-hand side)

Linnen *n*; *-s*, *-*; *altm.* linen

Linoleum *n*; *-s, kein Pl.* linoleum, *Brit. umg.* lino

Linol|säure *f* linoleic acid; **~schnitt** *m* linocut

Linse *f*; *-*, *-n* **1.** *Bot.* lentil; **2.** *Anat. und Opt.* lens; **j-n vor die ~ kriegen** *umg.* get s.o. into one's viewfinder

linsen *v/i. umg.* peek, peep

linsenförmig *Adj.* lenticular

Linsen|suppe *f Gastr.* lentil soup;

~trübung *f Med.* cataract

Liparische Inseln *Pl. Geog.*: **die Liparischen Inseln** the Lipari Islands

Lipgloss *n*; *-*, *- Kosmetik*: lip gloss

Lipizzaner *m*; *-s*, *-*; *Zool.* Lippizaner

Lipom *n*; *-s*, *-e*; *Med.* lipoma, skin tag, *Am.* fatty tumor

Lippe *f*; *-*, *-n* **1.** lip; *Anat. auch* labium (*Pl.* labia); **von den ~n lesen** lip(-)read; **ein Lied / e-n Fluch auf den ~n haben** sing a song / utter a curse; **sich** (*Dat.*) **auf die ~n beißen** *fig.* bite one's tongue; **an j-s ~n hängen** hang on s.o.'s every word; **das bringe ich nicht / nur schwer über die ~n** I can't / I can hardly bring myself to say it; **e-e große od. dicke ~ riskieren** *umg.* shoot one's mouth (off); **2.** *Bot.* labellum (*Pl.* labella)

Lippenbekenntnis *n* lip service; **ein ~ ablegen** pay lip service

Lippenblütler *m*; *-s*, *-*; *Bot.* labiate

Lippen|lesen *n* lip(-)reading; **~pomade** *f Med.* lip salve (*Am.* balm); **~stift** *m* lipstick

lippensynchron *Adj. Film*: lip-syn-c(h)ed

Lippfisch *m Zool.* labrid, wrasse

liquid(e) *Adj. Wirts.* (*flüssig*) *Geldmittel*: liquid; (*zahlungsfähig*) solvent

Liquidation *f*; *-*, *-en*; *Wirts. e-r Firma*: liquidation, *bes. Brit.* winding-up, *bes. Am.* closing out; *Börse*: settlement; **liquidieren** *v/t. Wirts.* liquidate (*auch fig. j-n*), *Brit.* wind up, *Am.* close out;

Liquidierung *f* liquidation (*auch fig.*)

Liquidität *f*; *-, kein Pl.* liquidity; (*Zahlungsfähigkeit*) solvency; **Liquiditätsreserve** *f* liquidity reserve; *Pl.* liquid reserves

Lira[1] *f*; *-*, *Lire*; *Fin.* (*frühere italienische Währung*) lira (*Pl.* lire)

Lira[2] *f*; *-*, *-*; *Fin.* (*türkische Währungseinheit*) lira (*Pl.* lire)

lispeln I. *v/i.* (have a) lisp; **II.** *v/t.* lisp; (*flüstern*) whisper

Lissabon (*n*); *-s*; *Geog.* Lisbon

List *f*; *-*, *-en* cunning; (*Trick*) ruse, trick, ploy; **zu e-r ~ greifen** use (*od.* employ, resort to) a trick, use a bit of cunning; **mit ~ und Tücke** with a great deal of cunning

Liste *f*; *-*, *-n* **1.** *allg.* list; *amtliche*: register; **schwarze ~** blacklist; **auf die schwarze ~ setzen** blacklist; **Rote ~** *Pharm.* list of medications, *Amtsspr.* pharmacop(o)eia; *Öko.* list of endangered species; → **Wahlliste**; **2.** *von Geschworenen, Kassenärzten*: list, panel

listen *v/t. Wirts.* list, *Am.* carry, stock; **diese Größe haben wir nicht gelistet** we don't list (*Am.* carry) (*od.* stock) this size

Listen|führer *m*, **~führerin** *f* **1.** compiler of a (*od.* the) list; **2.** *bes. Pol.* leading candidate; **~platz** *m bes. Pol.* place on the list of candidates; **~preis** *m Wirts.* list price

listenreich *Adj.* full of cunning; **der ~e Odysseus** wily Odysseus

Listenwahl *f Pol.* election using the list system

listig *Adj.* cunning, crafty, wily; *auch Blick*: sly

Litanei *f*; *-*, *-en*; *kirchl., fig.* litany; **die ganze ~** *auch umg. fig.* the whole spiel; **immer dieselbe ~** *umg.* the same old story every time

Litauen (*n*); *-s*; *Geog.* Lithuania; **Litauer** *m*; *-s*, *-*, **Litauerin** *f*; *-*, *-nen* Lithuanian, *weiblich auch*: Lithuanian woman (*od.* girl); **litauisch** *Adj.* Lithuanian; **Litauisch** *n*; *-en*; *Ling.* Lithuani-

---

an; **das ~e** Lithuanian

Liter *m*, *n*; *-s*, *- lit|re* (*Am.* -er)

literarisch I. *Adj.* literary; **II.** *Adv.*: **~ gebildet** literate, well-read; **~ tätig sein** be a writer, write

Literat *m*; *-en,-en* **1.** *Lit.* man of letters; (*Schriftsteller*) writer, *bekannter: auch* literary figure; *Pl.* literati, literary establishment *Sg.*; **2.** *pej.* (*Schreiberling*) scribe

Literatenkreise *Pl.*: **in ~n** in (*od.* among) literary circles

Literatin *f*; *-*, *-nen* lady of letters, literary lady; (*Schriftstellerin*) (woman) writer; *bekannter: auch* literary figure

Literatur *f*; *-*, *-en*; *Lit.* literature; **~agent** *m*, **~agentin** *f* (literary) agent; **~angabe** *f* bibliographical reference; *Pl.* bibliography *Sg.*; **~beilage** *f* literary supplement; **~betrachtung** *f* reflection on literature; **~betrieb** *m* literary scene; **~epoche** *f* period of literature; **~gattung** *f* literary genre; **~geschichte** *f Lit.* history of literature, literary history; **~hinweise** *Pl.* recommendations for further reading; *als Überschrift*: further reading *Sg.*; **~kritik** *f Lit.* literary criticism; **~kritiker** *m*, **~kritikerin** *f* literary critic; **~lexikon** *n Lit.* dictionary (*od.* encyclop[a]edia) of literature; **~nachweis** *m* bibliography; **~papst** *m iro.* literary guru; **~preis** *m* literary prize (*od.* award); **~sprache** *f* written language; **~verzeichnis** *n* bibliography

Literaturwissenschaft *f Lit.* study of literature, literary studies *Pl.*; **Literaturwissenschaftler** *m*, **Literaturwissenschaftlerin** *f* literary scholar; **literaturwissenschaftlich** *Adj.* relating to the study of literature

Literaturzeitschrift *f* literary journal (*od.* review)

Liter|flasche *f* lit|re (*Am.* -er) bottle; **~leistung** *f Mot.* bhp per lit|re (*Am.* -er)

literweise *Adv.* by the lit|re (*Am.* -er); **sie saufen das Zeug ~** *umg. fig.* they knock back bottle after bottle of the stuff

Litfaßsäule *f* advertising column

Lithium *n*; *-s, kein Pl.*; *Chem.* lithium

Lithographie *f*; *-*, *-n* **1.** *nur Sg.* lithography; **2.** (*Bild*) lithograph

Lithotripter *m*; *-s*, *-*, *Med.* lithotripter, lithotriptor

Litotes *f*; *-*, *-*; *Rhet.* litotes

Litschi *f*; *-*, *-s Bot.* lychee, litchi

litt *Imperf.* → **leiden**

Liturgie *f*; *-*, *-n*; *kirchl.* liturgy; **liturgisch** *Adj.* liturgical

Litze *f*; *-*, *-n* **1.** cord, braid; **2.** *Etech.* flex, *Am.* cord, cable

live [laif] *Adj. und Adv.* live

Live|aufnahme *f* live recording; **~auftritt** *m* live performance; **~aufzeichnung** *f* live recording; **~mitschnitt** *m* live recording; **~musik** *f* live music; **~reportage** *f* on-the-spot report; **~schaltung** *f Radio, TV* live transmission; **~sendung** *f* live broadcast; **~show** *f* live show; **~übertragung** *f* live transmission

Livland (*n*); *-s*; *hist.* Livonia

Livree *f*; *-*, *-n* livery; **livriert** *Adj.* liveried

Lizenz *f*; *-*, *-en* licen|ce (*Am.* -se); **j-m die ~ erteilen zu** (+ *Inf.*) give s.o. a licen|ce (*Am.* -se) to (+ *Inf.*), license s.o. to (+ *Inf.*); **in ~** under licen|ce (*Am.* -se); **~ausgabe** *f Buchwesen*: licensed edition; **~geber** *m*, **~geberin** *f* licensor; **~gebühr** *f* licen|ce (*Am.* -se)

fee; *für geistiges Eigentum*: royalty
lizenzieren *v/t.* license
Lizenz|inhaber *m*, **~inhaberin** *f* licensee; **~nehmer** *m*, **~nehmerin** *f* recipient of a licen|ce (*Am.* -se); **~spieler** *m*, **~spielerin** *f* *Sport* licensed professional, *umg.* pro
Lkw, LKW *m*; -(s), -; *Abk.* → **Lastkraftwagen** *m*, **~-Fahrer** *m*, **~-Fahrerin** *f* → **Lastwagenfahrer**
Lob¹ [loːp] *n*; -(e)s, -e praise; (*Beifall*) approval; **j-m ein ~ aussprechen** praise s.o.; **j-m ein ~ zollen** geh. bestow praise on s.o., extol s.o. *förm.*; **großes ~ ernten** earn a great deal of praise; **des ~es voll über j-n/etw. sein** geh. be full of praise for s.o./s.th., sing s.o.'s praises / the praises of s.th.; **über alles ~ erhaben** geh. beyond praise
Lob² [lɔp] *m*; -(s), -s *Tennis, Volleyball*: lob; **lobben** *vt/i.* lob
Lobby *f*; -, -s lobby; **Lobbyismus** *m*; -, *kein Pl.*; *Pol.* lobbyism, lobbying; **Lobbyist** *m*; -en, -en, **Lobbyistin** *f*; -, -nen lobbyist
Lobelie *f*; -, -n; *Bot.* lobelia
loben *vt/i.* praise; *gegenüber anderen*: *auch* speak very highly of; (*rühmen*) extol *förm.*; **da lobe ich mir ...** give me ... any time; **das lob ich mir!** that's what I like to see!; **gut gemacht, lobte sie** well done, she said approvingly; **man darf nicht nur tadeln, man muss auch ~** you can't only criticize(, you must [*Am.* have to] be positive sometimes); → **Abend** 1; **lobend I.** *Part. Präs.* → **loben; II.** *Adj. Erwähnung*: positive, favo[u]rable; **~es Wort** word of praise; **III.** *Adv.*: **~ erwähnen** give s.o. (*od.* s.th.) a positive (*od.* a favo[u]rable) mention, mention favo(u)rably; **~ sprechen über** (+ *Akk.*) be full of praise for; **lobenswert** *Adj.* commendable, praiseworthy; *stärker*: laudable; **lobenswerterweise** *Adv.* laudably
Lobeshymne *f* hymn (*od.* song) of praise; **e-e ~ / ~n auf j-n/etw. singen** *od.* anstimmen *fig.* praise s.o./s.th. to the skies
Lobgesang *m* song of praise; *fig.* → **Lobeshymne**
Lobhudelei *f auch Pl. pej.* adulation, sycophantic flattery; **lobhudeln** *vt/i.* (*untr., hat ge-*) **j-m** *od.* **j-n ~** heap flattery on s.o., adulate s.o. sycophantically
löblich *Adj.* commendable, creditable; *stärker*: laudable; *iro.* brilliant
lobpreisen *v/t.*; *lobpreist, lobpreiste od. lobpries, hat gelobpreist od. lobgepriesen* praise, extol; (*verherrlichen*) glorify; *überschwänglich*: praise to the skies; **Lobpreisung** *f* praise; (*Verherrlichung*) glorification
Lobrede *f* eulogy, panegyric *förm.*
Loch *n*; -(e)s, Löcher **1.** *allg.* hole (*auch fig. elende Behausung, Stadt etc.*); (*Öffnung*) opening; (*Lücke*) gap; *Billard*: pocket; **schwarzes ~** *Astron.* black hole; **auf** *od.* **aus dem letzten ~ pfeifen** *umg. fig.* be on one's last legs; **j-m Löcher in den Bauch fragen/reden** *umg. fig.* bombard s.o. with questions / go on and on at s.o.; **Löcher in die Luft starren** *umg.* stare into space; **etw. reißt j-m ein großes ~ in den Geldbeutel** *umg.* s.th. makes a big hole in s.o.'s pocket; **ein ~ mit dem anderen zustopfen** *umg.* rob Peter to pay Paul; **er säuft wie ein ~** *umg.* he drinks like a fish; **2.** *umg. fig.* (*Gefängnis*) (the) clink, *Sl.* the slammer;

3. *vulg.* (*Vagina*) cunt, hole
Loch|band *n EDV* punched tape, control tape; **~billard** *n* pocket billiards, *bes. Am.* pool; **~eisen** *n Tech.* punch
lochen *v/t.* punch a hole (*mehrmals*: holes) in; (*Fahrkarten, Band*) punch; **Locher** *m*; -s, - punch
löcherig *Adj.* **1.** full of holes (*auch fig.*), *umg.* holey; **2.** *Med.* perforated
löchern *v/t. umg. mit Fragen etc.*: go on (*Am.* hammer) at, pester; **sie löchert mich seit Tagen, wann wir wegfahren** she's been pestering me (*od.* going on at me, *Am.* hammering me) for days about when we're going away
Loch|kamera *f Fot.* pinhole camera; **~karte** *f EDV* punchcard
Löchlein *n* little hole
löchrig *Adj.* → **löcherig**
Loch|säge *f* keyhole saw; **~stickerei** *f Handarbeit*: broderie anglaise, *Am. auch* Madeira embroidery; **~streifen** *m EDV* punched tape
Lochung *f* punching; (*Perforierung*) perforation
Loch|verstärker *m* paper reinforcement ring; **~zange** *f*: (*e-e*) **~** (a pair of) punch pliers *Pl.*; *für Fahrkarten*: punch; **~ziegel** *m Archit.* air brick
Löckchen *n* little curl, ringlet
Locke *f*; -, -n curl; *bes. abgeschnittene od. herunterhängende*: lock; **blonde/ schwarze ~n** have curly blond/ black hair; **das Haar in ~n legen** put curlers in one's hair
locken¹ *v/t. und v/refl.* curl; → **gelockt**
locken² *v/t.* **1.** (*Tier*) lure; (*rufen*) call; (*Fisch*) bait; **2.** *fig.* lure; tempt, entice (**mit** with); **~ in** (+ *Akk.*) **/aus** lure (*od.* entice) into/out of; **es lockt mich** I feel tempted; **das lockt mich sehr /** *gar nicht* I'm very tempted / it doesn't interest me at all, *umg.* it doesn't grab me; **mich würde Portugal ~** I quite fancy (*Am.* I like the idea of) Portugal; **j-m das Geld aus der Tasche ~** entice s.o. into spending his (*od.* her) money; *betrügerisch*: cheat s.o. out of his (*od.* her) money; → **Reserve** 3; **lockend I.** *Part. Präs.* → **locken¹, locken²; II.** *Adj. fig.* attractive; *stärker*: enticing; *Angebot*: tempting
Locken|haar *n* curly hair; **~kopf** *m* (*Haar*) curly hair; (*Kopf*) curly head; (*Person*) curly head, *umg.* curly; **~stab** *m* curling tongs *Pl.*; **~wickler** *m* curler
locker I. *Adj.* **1.** *Boden*: *auch* friable; (*nicht straff*) slack; *Teig etc.*: light; **~ machen** → **lockern** I; **~ werden** → **lockern** II; **e-e ~e Hand haben** *umg. fig.* be quick to lash out, have a short fuse; **2.** *fig.* relaxed; *Haltung, Regelung etc.*: *auch* lenient; *Person*: (*leger*) easygoing; *Verhältnis*: (very) casual; *Moral etc.*: loose, lax; **ein ~er Lebenswandel** loose living; → **Mundwerk; II.** *Adv.* **1.** loosely; **~ sitzen** be loose; **die Pistole sitzt ihm ~** *fig.* he's trigger-happy; **(bei) ihm sitzt das Geld ziemlich ~** he is very free with his money, he doesn't think twice when it comes to spending money; **2.** *umg. fig.* (*mit Leichtigkeit*) (as) easy as pie; **das schafft er ~** *auch terminlich*: *auch* he'll manage it no problem; **3.** (*ungezwungen*): **~ handhaben** handle very casually; (*Gesetz*) interpret leniently, not enforce strictly; **es geht sehr ~ zu** it's all very relaxed; **das musst du etwas ~er sehen** you mustn't take such a narrow view; **vom Hocker** *umg.* as cool as a cucumber, without batting an eyelid; **das machen wir ~ vom Ho-**

cker we can do it, no problem, that'll be a piece of cake; **Lockerheit** *f*; *nur Sg.* **1.** looseness; *von Seil etc.*: slackness; *von Teig etc.*: lightness; **2.** *fig.* relaxed nature; *von Haltung, Regelung etc.*: *auch* leniency; *von Verhältnis*: casualness; *von Lebenswandel, Moral*: looseness
lockerlassen *v/i.* (*unreg., trennb., hat -ge-*); *umg.*: **nicht ~** keep at it, keep going; **nicht ~!** don't give up!; (*nicht nachlassen*) no slacking now!; **er ließ nicht locker, bis ...** he wouldn't give up until ...
lockermachen *v/t.* (*trennb., hat -ge-*); *umg.* (*Geld*) fork out, cough up; **bei j-m 20 Euro ~** get s.o. to fork out 20 euros
lockern I. *v/t.* loosen; (*Seil etc.*) slacken; (*Griff*) *auch* relax (*auch fig. Disziplin, Vorschriften etc.*); (*Muskeln etc.*) loosen up; **II.** *v/refl.* loosen, come loose; (*sich loslösen*) come off; *Seil etc.*: slacken; *körperlich*: loosen up; *Sport* limber up; *fig. Person, Moral etc.*: relax; **die Sitten haben sich gelockert** *fig.* morals have become lax (*od.* slack); **Lockerung** *f* loosening; *von Seil etc.*: slackening; *von Griff, Disziplin, Vorschriften etc.*: relaxation; *körperliche*: loosening up, *Sport* limbering up; → **lockern; Lockerungsübung** *f* loosening-up (*Sport etc.*: limbering-up) exercise
lockig *Adj.* curly
Lock|mittel *n* enticement; (*Köder*) bait; **~ruf** *m Zool.* mating call; **~spitzel** *m* stool pigeon; *Pol.* agent provocateur
Lockung *f auch Pl.* lure; (*Versuchung*) temptation
Lockvogel *m auch fig.* decoy; **~angebot** *n Wirts.* loss leader
Loddel *m*; -s, -; *umg.* (*Zuhälter*) pimp
Loden *m*; -s, - loden; **~mantel** *m* loden coat
lodern *v/i.* (*mit Richtungsangabe auch*: ist gelodert) blaze; *fig.* (*leuchten*) *auch* glow; *Augen, Leidenschaft*: burn; **die Flammen loderten zum Himmel** the flames blazed up into the sky; **lodernd I.** *Part. Präs.* → **lodern; II.** *Adj.*: *Flammen*: blazing; *fig. Begeisterung etc.*: fervent, ardent
Löffel *m*; -s, - **1.** spoon; **ein ~ für Oma etc. beim Füttern von Kindern**: a spoonful for granny etc.; **den ~ abgeben** (*sterben*) *umg. fig.* kick the bucket, *Brit. auch* pop one's clogs, *Am. auch* buy the farm; **er hat die Weisheit nicht mit ~n gefressen** *umg. pej.* he's not over-endowed with brains; **der glaubt, er hat die Weisheit mit ~n gefressen** *umg. pej.* he thinks he knows it all; **2.** *umg. fig. Pl.* (*Ohren*) ears, *Brit. hum.* lugholes; **schreib dir das hinter die ~** *umg.* and don't you forget it; **du kriegst gleich eins hinter die ~** you'll get one (a)round the ear in a minute!; **3.** *Med.*: spoon; (*Kurette*) curet(te); **4.** *Tech.* scoop, shovel (*auch eines Löffelbaggers*); **~bagger** *m Tech.* mechanical shovel; **~biskuit** *m*, *n* sponge finger, *Am.* ladyfinger
löffeln *vt/i.* spoon; *mit der Kelle*: ladle; (*mit dem Löffel essen*) spoon up; **sie löffelten alle aus einer Schüssel** they were all spooning it up from the same bowl
Löffel|reiher *m Orn.* spoonbill; **~stiel** *m* spoon handle
löffelweise *Adv.* in spoonfuls, by the spoonful

L

Löffler *m; -s, -; Zool.* spoonbill
Lofoten *Pl. Geog.: die* ~ the Lofoten Islands
Loft *m; -(s), -s* (luxury) loft conversion, attic apartment
log *Imperf.* → **lügen**
Logarithmentafel *f Math.* log(arithmic) tables *Pl.*; **logarithmieren I.** *v/t.* take the logarithm of; **II.** *v/i.* do logarithms; **logarithmisch** *Adj.* logarithmic; **Logarithmus** *m; -, Logarithmen* logarithm
Logbuch *n Naut.* log(book)
Loge ['loːʒə] *f; -, -n* **1.** *Theat.* box; **2.** (*Pförtnerloge*) (porter's) lodge; **3.** *Freimaurer:* lodge
Logen|bruder *m* fellow mason; ~**platz** *m* box seat
Loggia ['lɔdʒa] *f; -, Loggien; Archit.* loggia; (*Balkon*) recessed balcony
logieren [loˈʒiː-] *v/i.* stay (*bei* with; *in* + *Dat.* at); **Logiergast** *m altm.* house guest
Logik *f; -, -en* **1.** *nur Sg.* logic; *was du sagst, entbehrt jeglicher* ~ there is no logic in what you say; *wo ist denn da die* ~? where is the logic in that?; **2.** *nur Sg.; Philos.* logic; *formale* ~ formal logic; **3.** *EDV* logic; **Logiker** *m; -s, -,* **Logikerin** *f; -, -nen* logician; (*logisch Denkender*) logical thinker
Logis [loˈʒiː] *n; -s, -* **1.** lodgings *Pl.*; *Kost und* ~ board and lodgings, *Am.* room and board; **2.** *Naut.* crew's quarters *Pl.*
logisch *Adj.* logical; *es ist doch völlig* ~ *auch* it stands to reason; *ist doch* ~! but that's logical (*od.* obvious), that's just what you'd expect; ~! *umg.* (*selbstverständlich*) of course!; (*na klar*) you bet!; **logischerweise** *Adv.* logically; obviously; ~ *muss er ... auch* it's obvious (*od.* only logical) that he has to ...
Logistik *f; -, -en; Math.* mathematical logic; *Wirts., Mil.* logistics *Pl.* (*mst V. im Sg.*); **logistisch I.** *Adj.* logistic; **II.** *Adv.* logistically
logo *indekl. Adj. nur präd.; Sl.:* (*ist doch*) ~! sure thing!; *zustimmend: auch umg.* you bet!
Logo *m, n; -s, -s; Wirts.* logo
Logopäde *m; -n, -n; Med.* speech therapist; **Logopädie** *f; -, kein Pl.* speech therapy; **Logopädin** *f; -, -nen* speech therapist; **logopädisch** *Adj.* relating to speech therapy
Logotherapie *f Med.* speech therapy
Lohe¹ *f; -, -n Gerberei:* tanbark
Lohe² *f; -, -n; geh.* blaze; *Flamme:* leaping flame
Lohn *m; -(e)s, Löhne* **1.** *Wirts.* (*Arbeitslohn*) wage(s *Pl.*), pay; (*Bezahlung*) payment; *Löhne und Gehälter* wages and salaries; *der tarifliche* ~ *beträgt ...* the fixed wage rate is ...; *bei j-m in* ~ *stehen* be in s.o.'s pay (*od.* service); *in* ~ *und Brot stehen* have a job and income; *j-n um* ~ *und Brot bringen* deprive s.o. of his (*od.* her) livelihood, take the bread out of s.o.'s mouth; **2.** (*Belohnung*) reward; *zum* ~ as a reward (*für* for); *fig. auch* in return (for); *er hat s-n* (*gerechten*) ~ *bekommen iro.* he got his just deserts; ~**abbau** *m Wirts.* wage cuts *Pl.*
lohnabhängig *Adj. Wirts.* wage-earning ...; **Lohnabhängige** *m, f; -n, -n* wage-earner
Lohn|abkommen *n Wirts.* wage agreement; ~**abrechnung** *f* pay slip; (*Vorgang*) payroll accounting; ~**abschluss** *m* wage agreement, pay settlement;

~**abzug** *m* wage (*od.* salary) deduction; ~**angleichung** *f* wage adjustment; ~**anstieg** *m* rise (*Am.* raise) in wages; ~**arbeit** *f* paid labo(u)r; ~**auftrag** *m* farming-out contract; *e-n* ~ *vergeben* farm out a job (to a subcontractor); ~**ausfall** *m* loss of earnings; ~**ausgleich** *m: bei vollem* ~ without cuts in payment; ~**auszahlung** *f* payment of wages
Lohnbuchhalter *m,* ~**in** *f Wirts.* payroll clerk; **Lohnbuchhaltung** *f* **1.** *nur Sg.; Tätigkeit:* payroll accounting; **2.** *Abteilung:* payroll department
Lohn|büro *n Wirts.* payroll office; ~**differenz** *f* wage gap, wage differential; ~**diktat** *n* imposed pay settlement; ~**drift** *f Wirts.* wage drift; ~**drückerei** *f; -, -en* downward pressure on wages; ~**empfänger** *m,* ~**empfängerin** *f* wage-earner; *Lohn- und Gehaltsempfänger Pl.* salaried and wage-earning employees
lohnen I. *v/refl.* be worthwhile, be worth one's while; *bes. materiell:* auch pay; *es lohnt sich* it's worth it; *es lohnt sich, zu* (+ *Inf.*) it's worth (+ *Ger.*); *generell: auch* it pays to (+ *Inf.*); *es lohnt sich nicht* it's not worth it; (*es bringt nichts*) it's no use; *der Film lohnt sich* the film's worth seeing, you should go and see the film; *ein Versuch lohnt sich* it's worth a try; *die Mühe lohnt sich* it's worth (making) the effort *od.* (taking) the trouble; **II.** *v/t.* **1.** *die Ausstellung lohnt e-n Besuch* the exhibition is worth seeing; *j-m etw.* ~ repay (*od.* reward) s.o. for s.th.; **2.** *es lohnt die Mühe* it's worth the effort
löhnen *v/t./i. umg.* (*bezahlen*) cough up; *fig.* (*die Zeche bezahlen*) pick up the tab; *sie hat für die neue Frisur 100 Euro gelöhnt* she forked out 100 euros for her new hairdo
lohnend I. *Part. Präs.* → **lohnen**; **II.** *Adj.* worthwhile; (*dankbar*) rewarding; (*sehenswert*) worth seeing
lohnenswert *Adj.* rewarding, worthwhile
Lohn|erhöhung *f Wirts.* wage increase, pay rise, *Am.* raise; ~**folgekosten** *f* non-wage labo(u)r costs; ~**forderung** *f* wage claim; ~**fortzahlung** *f* continued pay (in case of sickness); ~**gefälle** *n* wage differential, wages gap; ~**gruppe** *f* wage bracket
lohnintensiv *Adj.* wage-intensive
Lohnkosten *Pl. Wirts.* wage costs; ~**zuschuss** *m* allowance toward(s) wage costs paid to the employer of a long-term unemployed
Lohn|kürzung *f Wirts.* cut in wages, pay cut; ~**leitlinie** *f; mst Pl.* guideline for pay settlements; ~**liste** *f* payroll; *auf j-s* ~ *od. bei j-m auf der* ~ *stehen* be on s.o.'s payroll; *auch fig. pej.* be in the pay of s.o.; ~**nachzahlung** *f auch Pl.* back pay; ~**nebenkosten** *Pl. Wirts.* additional (*od.* non-wage) labo(u)r costs; ~**niveau** *n Wirts.* wage level; ~**pause** *f* temporary wage freeze; ~**pfändung** *f* garnishment (of wages); ~**politik** *f* wages policy; ~**Preis-Spirale** *f* wages-price spiral; ~**runde** *f* round of wage talks; ~**senkung** *f* cut in wages; ~**sklave** *m,* ~**sklavin** *f pej.* wage slave; ~**staffelung** *f* graduated salary
Lohnsteuer *f Wirts.* income tax; ~**jahresausgleich** *m* annual adjustment of income tax; *s-n* ~ *machen* do one's tax return (*Am. auch* one's income

tax); ~**karte** *f* tax card
Lohn|stopp *m Wirts.* wage freeze, pegging of wages; ~**streifen** *m* pay slip; ~**stückkosten** *Pl. Wirts.* unit wage costs; ~**summe** *f Wirts.* payroll, wages bill; ~**tarif** *m* wage rate; ~**tüte** *f mst fig.* wage packet, *Am.* pay package
Löhnung *f* (*Auszahlung*) payment of wages; (*Lohn, Sold*) pay
Lohn|vereinbarung *f Wirts.* wage (*od.* pay) agreement; ~**verhandlungen** *Pl.* wage negotiations (*od.* talks); ~**verzicht** *m* renunciation of pay; ~**vorsprung** *m* wage differential; ~**zettel** *m* pay slip; ~**zurückhaltung** *f* pay (*od.* wage) restraint; ~**zuwachs** *m* pay increase
Loipe *f; -, -n Ski:* cross-country trail (*od.* course)
Lok *f; -, -s* loco *umg.*, engine
lokal I. *Adj.* **1.** local (*auch Med.*); ~*e Schauer* local showers; *ein* ~*es Netzwerk EDV* a local area network; **2.** *nur attr.; Ling.:* ~*e Adverbien* adverbs of place; **II.** *Adv.* locally; *j-n* ~ *betäuben Med.* give s.o. a local an(-a)esthetic
Lokal *n; -s, -e;* (*Gaststätte*) restaurant; (*Kneipe*) bar, *Brit.* pub, *umg. hum.* watering hole; *ich kenne ein gutes* ~ *auch umg.* I know a good place
Lokal|anästhesie *f Med.* local an(a)esthetic; ~**anzeiger** *m* free (local) paper, local freesheet (*od.* advertiser); ~**augenschein** *m österr. Jur.* → **Lokaltermin**; ~**ausgabe** *f Zeitung:* local edition; ~**bahn** *f Eisenb.* branch line; ~**bericht** *m* local report; ~**blatt** *n* local paper; ~**derby** *n Sport* local derby
Lokale *n; -n, kein Pl. Zeitung:* ~*s* local news *Sg.*
Lokalfernsehen *n; -s, kein Pl.; TV* local television (*od.* TV)
lokalisierbar *Adj.* locatable; **lokalisieren** *v/t.* **1.** locate; *genau: auch* pinpoint; **2.** (*beschränken, eingrenzen*) localize
Lokalität *f; -, -en* **1.** place, locality; *wo sind denn hier die* ~*en? umg. euph.* where are the facilities?; **2.** *umg. hum.* → **Lokal**
Lokal|kolorit *n* local colo(u)r; ~**matador** *m* local hero; ~**nachrichten** *Pl.* local news *Sg.*; ~**patriotismus** *m* local (*od.* regional) patriotism; ~**presse** *f* local (*od.* regional) press; ~**redakteur** *m,* ~**redakteurin** *f* local (*od.* regional) news editor; ~**redaktion** *f* local newsroom; ~**runde** *f: e-e* ~ *ausgeben od. umg. schmeißen* buy drinks (*od.* a round) for everyone (in the house); ~**seite** *f* local news page (*od.* section); ~**sender** *m Radio, TV* local station; ~**sport** *m* local sport(s *Am.*); ~**teil** *m* local news pages *Pl.* (*od.* section); ~**termin** *m Jur.* visit to the scene of the crime; ~**verbot** *n:* ~ (*erteilt*) *bekommen* be barred from the premises; *er hat* (*hier*) ~ he's been barred from the premises; ~**zeitung** *f* local paper
Lokativ *m; -s, -e; Ling.* locative
Lokführer *m,* ~**in** *f* → **Lokomotivführer**
Loko... *im Subst. Wirts.* spot (*goods, price, transaction, etc.*)
Lokomotive *f; -, -n; Eisenb.* engine, *formeller:* locomotive
Lokomotiv|führer *m,* ~**führerin** *f Eisenb.* engine driver, *Am.* engineer; ~**schuppen** *m* engine shed
Lokus *m; - und -ses, - und -se; umg.* loo, *Am.* john; *er ist auf dem* ~ he's on (*od.* he's gone to) the loo (*Am.* john)
Lombard *m, n; -(e)s, -e; Wirts.* collater-

al loan

Lombardei *f*; -; *Geog.* Lombardy

Lombardgeschäft *n Wirts.* collateral loan transaction

lombardieren *v/t.* grant on collateral securities

Lombard|kredit *m* collateral loan; **~satz** *m* Lombard rate

London (*n*); -s London; **Londoner I.** *Adj.* London; **die ~ City** the City of London; **II.** *m*; -s, -, **Londonerin** *f*; -, -nen Londoner; **er ist Londoner** *auch* he's from London

Longdrink *m* long (*Am.* tall) drink

Longe ['lōːʒə] *f*; -, -n; *Sport, beim Reiten*: lunge; *beim Schwimmen, Turnen*: harness; **longieren** [lõˈʒiːrən] *v/t. Pferd*: lunge

Longseller *m*; -s, - *Buchhandel etc.*: steady long-term seller

Looping ['luːpɪŋ] *m, n*; -s, -s; *Flug.* loop; **e-n ~ drehen** loop the loop

Lorbeer *m*; -s, -en **1.** *Bot.* bay; *nicht aromatisch*: laurel; **2.** *Gewürz*: bay leaf (*od.* leaves *Pl.*); **3.** *Pl. fig.* laurels; **sich auf s-n ~en ausruhen** rest on one's laurels; **die ersten ~en ernten** win one's first laurels; **damit wird sie keine ~en ernten** that won't win her any laurels; **~baum** *m* bay (tree); *nicht aromatisch*: laurel; **~blatt** *n* bay leaf; **~kranz** *m* laurel wreath (*auch fig.*); **~zweig** *m* sprig of laurel (*aromatisch*: bay)

Lord *m*; -s, -s lord; *als Titel*: Lord; **Lordschaft** *f*; -, -en Lordship

Lore *f*; -, -n **1.** *Bergb. etc.* wagon; *kippbar*: tipper (truck), *Am.* dump truck; **2.** *Eisenb.* goods wagon, *Am.* open freight car

Lorgnette [lɔrnˈjɛtə] *f*; -, -n lorgnette

Lorgnon [lɔrnˈjõː] *n*; -s, -s lorgnon

Lori *m*; -s, -s **1.** *Orn.* lory; *in Australien*: lorikeet; **2.** *Zool.* loris

los I. *präd. und Adv.* **1.** → **lose** I 1; **2.** (*ab, weg*) off; *Hund etc.*: loose, off the leash (*od.* lead); **der Knopf ist ~** the button has come off; **3.** *umg.*: **ich bin's immer noch nicht ~** I haven't got(ten) rid of it yet; *negatives Erlebnis*: I still haven't got(ten) over it; **den wären wir endlich ~!** thank goodness he's gone!; **den Auftrag bist du ~** you can say goodbye to that job; **sie ist ihr ganzes Geld ~** she has lost all her money; **4.** *umg.*: **was ist (mit ihm) ~?** what's wrong (with him)?, what's the matter (with him)?; **was ist denn schon wieder ~?** what's the matter this time (*od.* now)?; **was ist denn hier ~?** what's going on here?, what's up?; **da ist etwas ~** there's something going on; (*etwas stimmt nicht*) there's something wrong; (*es ist etwas passiert*) something has happened; **da war (schwer) was ~** *Ärger, Streit*: the sparks were (really) flying; *Stimmung, Trubel etc.*: things were really happening; **wenn deine Mutter das hört, dann ist aber was ~!** if your mother hears of this all hell will break loose; **da ist immer was ~** there's always something going on there; **hier ist nichts ~** there's nothing doing around here; **wo ist hier was ~?** where's the action around here?; **mit ihm ist nicht viel ~** he isn't up to much; **heute ist mit ihr nichts ~** you won't get any joy from her today, she's a dead (*Am.* total) loss today; → **losgehen, Teufel** 3; **5.** *umg.* (*gegangen*) gone; **er ist schon ~** he's gone (*od.* left) already; **sie ist mit dem Auto ~** she's gone off in her

car; **6.** *hist.*: **~ von Rom / vom Reich!** *etc.* independence from Rome / from the empire! *etc.*; **II.** *Interj.*: **~! go on!**; *beim Wettkampf etc.*: go!; (*mach schnell*) let's go!, come on!; **Achtung, fertig, ~!** ready, steady (*Am.* set), go!; **auf die Plätze, fertig, ~!** *Sport, Startkommando*: on your marks, get set, go!; **jetzt aber ~!** let's go!, *umg.* go for it!; **nichts wie ~!** *umg.* let's get going!

Los *n*; -es, -e **1.** (*Lotterielos*) (lottery) ticket; **das große ~ ziehen** win first prize; *fig.* hit the jackpot; **2.** *etw.* **durch(s) ~ entscheiden** *etc.* decide *etc.* s.th. by drawing lots; **ihm fiel das ~ zu, zu** (+ *Inf.*) *fig.* it fell to his lot to (+ *Inf.*); **das ~ fiel auf mich** it has fallen on me *to do s.th.*; *iro.* I was the lucky one; **3.** (*Schicksal*) fate; **ein schweres ~** a hard lot; **es war mein ~ zu** (+ *Inf.*) it was my lot (*od.* fate, destiny) to (+ *Inf.*); **4.** *Wirts.* lot

los|arbeiten *v/i.* (*trennb., hat -ge-*) (*anfangen zu arbeiten*) start working, set to work; (*darauf ~*) work away (*auf* + *Akk.* at); **auf etw. ~** (*hinarbeiten*) start work(ing) on s.th.; **~ballern** *v/i.* (*trennb., hat -ge-*) *umg.* start banging (*stärker*: blazing) away

lösbar *Adj.* **1.** (*löslich*) soluble; **2.** *Frage, Problem etc.*: solvable (*auch Math. etc.*); **das ist e-e ~ / kaum ~e Aufgabe** this problem can be solved / is almost insoluble; **Lösbarkeit** *f*; *nur Sg.* solubility; *von Frage etc.*: solvability

los|beißen (*unreg., trennb., hat -ge-*) **I.** *v/i.* *Hund etc.*: start biting; **II.** *v/t.* bite off (*od.* through); **III.** *v/refl.* bite o.s. free; **~bekommen** *v/t.* (*unreg., trennb., hat*) get off (*od.* out); **~bellen** *v/i.* (*trennb., hat -ge-*) start barking; **~binden** *v/t.* (*unreg., trennb., hat -ge-*) untie; (*Gefangenen*) *auch* free; (*Hund etc.*) take off the lead (*Am.* leash); (*wildes Tier*) set free; **~brausen** *v/i.* (*trennb., ist -ge-*); *umg.* zoom off; **~brechen** (*unreg., trennb. -ge-*) **I.** *v/t.* (*hat*) break off; **II.** *v/i.* (*ist*); *fig. Sturm*: break; *Gelächter etc.*: break out; **~brüllen** *v/i.* (*trennb., hat -ge-*) start shouting (*stärker*: screaming)

Losbude *f umg.* lottery ticket stall

Lösch|anlage *f* fire-fighting equipment; **~arbeiten** *Pl.* fire-fighting operations (*od.* operation *Sg.*); **die ~ dauern noch an** firemen are still fighting (*od.* trying to put out) the blaze

löschbar *Adj.* **1.** *Daten, Tonband etc.*: erasable; **2.** *schwer ~ Feuer*: difficult to put out

Lösch|blatt *n* (piece of) blotting paper; **~boot** *n* fire boat; **~eimer** *m* fire bucket

löschen I. *v/t.* **1.** (*Feuer*) put out, extinguish; (*Kerze*) *auch* snuff out; *blasend*: blow out; *mit Wasser*: (*Glut, Flamme etc.*) *auch* douse; **2.** (*Licht*) put out, switch off; (*den Durst*) quench one's thirst; **4.** (*Geschriebenes*) delete; (*ausstreichen*) (*Eintrag in e-m Verzeichnis etc.*) cross out; (*Namen e-r Firma etc.*) strike (*od.* cross) off; **5.** *Computer.* erase, delete; (*Tonband*) erase, wipe everything off; (*Aufgenommenes*) erase, wipe off; **6.** (*Erinnerungen, Spuren etc.*) wipe out (*aus of*), erase (*from*); **aus dem Gedächtnis ~** wipe (*od.* erase) from one's memory; **7.** (*tilgen*) cancel; (*Hypothek, Schuld etc.*) clear, pay off; (*Konto*) close; **8.** *Wirts.* (*ausladen*) unload; **II.** *v/i.* put out a (*od.* the) fire; **die**

Feuerwehr hat mit Schaum gelöscht the fire brigade (*Am.* firemen) used foam to put out the fire; **Löscher** *m*; -s, - **1.** (*Feuerlöscher*) fire extinguisher; **2.** (*Tintenlöscher*) blotter

Lösch|fahrzeug *n* fire engine, *Am. auch* fire truck; **~gerät** *n* fire extinguisher; *Koll.* fire-fighting equipment; **~kalk** *m* slaked lime; **~kommando** *n* fire-fighting squad, *Am. auch* fire brigade; **~kopf** *m Etron.* erase head; **~mannschaft** *f* fire-fighting team, fire brigade; **~papier** *n* blotting paper; **~schaum** *m* fire-extinguishing foam; **~taste** *f Tonband etc.*: erase (*od.* record) button; *Computer.* delete key; *Schreibmaschine*: erase key; *Radio, CD-Spieler etc.*: clear button; **~teich** *m* static water tank; **~trupp** *m* fire-fighting team (*od.* squad)

Löschung *f* **1.** *e-s Eintrags*: deletion; *Wirts., e-r Forderung*: cancel(l)ation; *e-r Hypothek*: *auch* discharge; *e-r Firma*: striking off the register; **2.** *von Waren*: unloading

Lösch|wagen *m* fire engine; **~wasser** *n* water for fire-fighting; **~zug** *m* fire brigade unit

los|donnern *v/i.* (*trennb. -ge-*); *umg.* **1.** (*ist*) start thundering; *Lastwagen etc.*: roar off; **2.** (*hat*) (*schimpfen*) explode; **~drehen** *v/t.* (*trennb., hat -ge-*) twist off; (*Schraube*) *auch* unscrew

lose I. *Adj.* **1.** (*locker, unbefestigt*) loose; (*nicht straff*) *auch* slack; (*beweglich*) movable; **2.** *Wirts.* (*unverpackt*) loose; **~ Blätter** loose leaves; **~ Teile** separate parts; **3.** *fig.* (*locker, unverbindlich*) *Kontakt etc.*: loose; **in ~r Folge** sporadically, at (varying) intervals; **4.** *fig.* (*zügellos*) loose; (*boshaft*) malicious; *hum.* (*schelmisch*) naughty, mischievous; **~s Maul** *od.* **Mundwerk** *od.* **~ Zunge** *umg.* loose (*od.* nasty, malicious) tongue; **~ Sitten** loose morals; **II.** *Adv.* loosely; **die Haare ~ tragen** wear one's hair down; **etw. ~ verkaufen** sell s.th. loose (*od.* unpacked)

Loseblattausgabe *f* loose-leaf edition

Lösegeld *n* ransom (money)

loseisen (*trennb., hat -ge-*); *umg.* **I.** *v/t.* (*befreien*) get s.o./s.th. away (*von* from); (*herauskriegen*) get (*stärker*: prise) s.o./s.th. out (of); **etw. von j-m ~** get s.th. from (*Geld*: out of) s.o.; **II.** *v/refl.* get away (*von* from); (*herauskommen*) get out (of)

Lösemittel *n* solvent

losen *v/i.* draw lots (*Am. auch* straws) (*um* for); *mit e-r Münze*: toss (for); **beim Losen gewinnen/verlieren** win/lose the toss

lösen I. *v/t.* **1.** (*losbinden*) untie; (*aufbinden*) *auch* undo; **2.** (*lockern*) loosen; (*Bremse, Griff*) release (*auch Spannung*); (*Husten*) loosen (up); **den Blick** *od.* **s-e Blicke von etw. nicht ~ können** be unable to take one's eyes off s.th.; **j-m die Zunge ~** *fig.* loosen s.o.'s tongue; → **gelöst**; **3.** (*entfernen*) remove; (*trennen*) separate (*von* from); **4.** (*auflösen*) dissolve; **5.** (*entwirren*) disentangle; *auch fig.* unravel; **6.** *fig.* (*Aufgabe, Rätsel, Schwierigkeit*) solve; (*Frage*) answer; (*Konflikt*) resolve, settle; **7.** *fig.* (*Verbindung, auch Verlobung*) break off; (*Ehe*) dissolve; **8.** (*Vertrag*) cancel; **9.** (*Fahrkarte etc.*) buy; **II.** *v/refl.* **1.** *Knoten etc.*: come undone; **2.** (*sich lockern*) come loose; *Husten*; *fig. Zunge*: loosen up; *Spannung*: ease; **3.** (*sich loslösen*) come off; *Schuss*: go off, **4.** *fig.*: **sich ~ von**

(verlassen) leave; *(ausbrechen aus)* break away from; *(e-r Vorstellung, Verpflichtung etc.)* free *(od.* rid) o.s. of; **5.** *(sich auflösen)* dissolve; **6.** *Problem etc.:* be solved; *Konflikt:* be settled; **sich von alleine ~** solve *(od.* resolve) itself

Losentscheid *m* drawing lots *(Am. auch* straws); **die Gewinner werden durch ~ ermittelt** the winners are established by drawing lots

losfahren *v/i. (unreg., trennb., ist -ge-)* leave *(auch Eisenb.),* drive off; **~ auf** *(+ Akk.)* make *(od.* head) (straight) for; **auf j-n ~** *fig.* let fly at s.o., go for s.o.

losgehen *v/i. (unreg., trennb., ist -ge-)* **1.** go, leave; **ich geh jetzt los** *auch* I'm off now; **~ auf** *(+ Akk.)* go up to; **geh mir los mit Mallorca!** *umg.* you can keep *(od.* I've had enough of) your wretched Majorca!; **2.** *(angreifen)* go for *(auch fig.);* **aufeinander ~** go for each other('s throats); **3.** *umg. (beginnen)* start; **jetzt geht's los!** here we go!, this is it (now)!; **jetzt geht's schon wieder los!** here we go again!; **es kann ~** we're *(od.* I'm *etc.)* ready; **wann geht es endlich los?** when is it going to start?; *(wann gehen wir?)* when are we going?; **4.** *Gewehr etc.:* go off; *(explodieren) auch* explode; **die Pistole ist nicht losgegangen** the pistol didn't fire; **nach hinten ~** *umg. fig.* backfire (on one)

los|gelassen I. *P.P.* → **loslassen; II.** *Adj. Dial.:* **wie ~** like mad *(umg.* crazy); **~gelöst I.** *P.P.* → **loslösen; II.** *Adj. auch fig.* detached *(von* from); *(einzeln)* separate, isolated *(from);* **III.** *Adv. fig. betrachten, behandeln:* separately, in isolation; **~haben** *v/t. (unreg., trennb., hat -ge-); umg.:* **er hat was los** he's got what it takes; *(weiß etwas)* he knows a thing or two; *fachlich etc.: auch* he's on the ball *umg.;* **er hat in Physik viel/nichts los** he's very good at *(od.* knows a lot about) physics / he's no good at physics; **~haken** *v/t. (trennb., hat -ge-)* unhook; **~hauen** *v/i. (unreg., trennb., hat -ge-) (auch drauf ~)* start hitting out *(auf + Akk.* at); **~heulen** *v/i. (trennb., hat -ge-); umg.* start *(od.* burst out) crying; *Baby: auch* start screaming; **~kaufen** *v/t. und v/refl. (trennb., hat -ge-)* → **freikaufen; ~ketten** *v/t. (trennb., hat -ge-) (Hund etc.)* take off the chain; **~kommen** *v/i. (unreg., trennb., ist -ge-)* get away *(von* from); *(freikommen)* get free; *mit Mühe:* tear o.s. away; **von Drogen / vom Alkohol ~** get off drugs / give up alcohol; **ich komme nicht los davon** *von e-r Angewohnheit:* I can't stop doing it; *vom Alkohol etc.:* I can't kick the habit; *von e-m Gedanken:* I can't get it out of my mind; **~kriegen** *v/t. (unreg., trennb., hat -ge-); umg. (wegkriegen)* get off; *(herauskriegen)* get out; *(loswerden)* get rid of *(auch verkaufen);* **~lachen** *v/i. (trennb., hat -ge-)* burst out laughing

loslassen *v/t. (unreg., trennb., hat -ge-)* **1.** let go *(auch freilassen);* **lass mich los!** let go!; **nicht ~!** hold tight!, hang on!; **der Gedanke lässt mich nicht los** I can't get it out of my mind; **2.** **den Hund / j-n auf j-n ~** set the dog on / let s.o. loose on s.o.; **j-n auf die Menschheit ~** *umg.* let s.o. loose on an unsuspecting world; **3.** *umg. (e-n Brief etc.)* send off; *(Bemerkung)* come out with; *(e-n Witz)* crack;

4. *vulg.:* **einen ~** let off

los|laufen *v/i. (unreg., trennb., ist -ge-)* start running *(auf + Akk.* toward[s]); *(weglaufen)* run off; **~ auf** *(+ Akk.) (zulaufen auf)* run toward(s); **ich lauf schon mal los** I'll go on ahead; **lauf schon mal los!** go on ahead; **~legen** *v/i. (trennb., hat -ge-) umg. (anfangen)* get cracking; **dann legte er los** *(redete, schimpfte)* then he really got going; *stärker:* then he let rip; **leg los!** fire away!; **~ gegen** → **losziehen**

löslich *Adj. Chem.* soluble; **leicht ~** readily soluble; **Löslichkeit** *f; nur Sg.* solubility

loslösen *(trennb., hat -ge-)* **I.** *v/t.* remove, detach *(von* from); **II.** *v/refl.* come off; *(sich abschälen) auch* peel off; *fig.* free o.s. *(von* of), cut o.s. loose *(von* from), break away *(from);* → **losgelöst; Loslösung** *f* removal; *fig.* breaking away *(von* from)

losmachen *(trennb., hat -ge-)* **I.** *v/t.* **1.** *(abnehmen)* take off; *(entfernen)* take away; *(Strick etc.)* untie; *(Knoten) auch* undo; *(Hund etc.)* take off the chain *(od.* lead); **2.** *Naut. (Boot etc.)* cast off; **3.** *umg.:* **einen** *od.* **was ~** *(feiern)* live it up; **II.** *v/refl.* get free, free o.s. *(von* from); *fig.* get away *(from);* **sich von j-m ~** break away from s.o.; **III.** *v/i.* **1.** *umg.:* **mach jetzt endlich los!** get a move on!; **2.** *Naut. (ablegen)* cast off

Losnummer *f* (lottery) ticket number

los|platzen *v/i. (trennb., ist -ge-); umg.* **1.** *lachend:* burst out laughing; **2.** **mit etw. ~** blurt s.th. out; **~rasen** *v/i. (trennb., ist -ge-)* zoom *(od.* race, tear) off; **~reißen** *(unreg., trennb., hat -ge-)* **I.** *v/t.* tear *(od.* rip) off; **II.** *v/refl.* break loose; free o.s.; *fig.* tear o.s. away *(von* from); **~rennen** *v/i. (unreg., trennb., ist -ge-)* → **loslaufen**

Löss *m; -es, -e,* **Löß** *m; -es, -e; Geol.* loess

lossagen *v/refl. (trennb., hat -ge-)* **sich ~ von** renounce; *Familie: auch* disown; **Lossagung** *f* renunciation *(von* of), break (with)

Lössboden *m,* **Lößboden** *m Geol.* loess soil

los|schicken *v/t. (trennb., hat -ge-)* send; *(Brief)* send off; **~schießen** *v/i. (unreg., trennb., hat -ge-)* **1.** start shooting, fire away *(auf + Akk.* at), open fire (on); **2.** *(losrennen etc.) umg.* shoot off; **3.** *(zu reden anfangen)* **schieß los!** *umg.* fire away!, open fire!; **~schimpfen** *v/i. (trennb., hat -ge-)* start cursing and swearing; **~schlagen** *(unreg., trennb., hat -ge-)* **I.** *v/t. Wirts. (Waren)* sell off; *Auktion:* knock down; **II.** *v/i. im Krieg:* strike; **auf j-n ~** start hitting out at s.o., let fly at s.o.; **~schnallen** *(trennb., hat -ge-)* **I.** *v/t.* unstrap; **II.** *v/refl.* unstrap o.s.; *Flug., Mot. etc.* undo one's seatbelt

lössig, lößig *Adj. Geol.* loessial

lossprechen *v/t. (unreg., trennb., hat -ge-):* **~ von** release from; *kirchl.* absolve from; *(Lehrling)* → **freisprechen; Lossprechung** *f kirchl.* absolution

Lössschicht *f,* **Lößschicht** *f Geol.* lo-

ess stratum

los|steuern *v/i. (trennb., ist -ge-):* **~ auf** *(+ Akk.)* make for, head for; *fig. (ein Ziel)* have set one's sights on; *(ein Examen etc.)* be working toward(s); *(e-e Katastrophe)* be heading for; **~stürmen, ~stürzen** *v/i. (trennb., ist -ge-)* tear *(od.* dash) off; **auf j-n/etw. ~** make a rush toward(s) s.o. / for s.th.; **~treten** *v/t. (unreg., trennb., hat -ge-)* **1.** kick away; **2.** *fig.* kick off, get going; → **Lawine**

Lostrommel *f* lottery ticket drum

Losung¹ *f* watchword; *(Erkennungswort)* password

Losung² *f Jägersprache:* droppings *Pl.*

Lösung *f* **1.** solution; *(Antwort) auch* answer *(+ Gen.* to); **zur ~ des Konflikts** *etc.* to (help) resolve the dispute *etc.;* **zur ~ des Problems beitragen** help solve the problem; **2.** *Chem.* solution; *(das Sichauflösen)* dissolution; **3.** *(Loslösung)* separation; **4.** *(Auflösen) e-r Ehe etc.:* breakup; *e-r Verlobung:* breaking off; *e-s Vertrags, Arbeitsverhältnisses:* termination

Lösungs|ansatz *m* attempt at a solution; **~mittel** *n* solvent; *für Lacke etc.:* thinner; **~möglichkeit** *f* possible solution; **~versuch** *m* attempt at a solution; **~vorschlag** *m* suggested solution; *bei Rätsel etc.:* suggested answer; **~weg** *m* way to reach a solution

Losungswort *n* password

Lösungswort *n* answer

Los|verfahren *n* decision by lot; **etw. im ~ entscheiden** decide s.th. by drawing lots *(Am. auch* straws); **~verkäufer** *m,* **~verkäuferin** *f* lottery ticket seller, *Am.* lottery vendor

los|werden *v/t. (unreg., trennb., ist -ge-)* get rid of; *(verlieren)* lose; *(ausgeben)* spend; **ich bin dabei viel Geld losgeworden** *umg.* it put me back a pretty penny, it really cost me; **ich werde den Gedanken / das Gefühl nicht los, dass** I can't help thinking/ feeling that; **e-e Frage ~** *umg.* manage to ask a question; **ich muss das endlich ~** *umg. (aussprechen)* I have to get it off my chest (at last); **~wollen** *v/i. (unreg., trennb., hat -ge-) umg.* want to leave; **willst du schon los?** are you going already?; **~ziehen** *v/i. (unreg., trennb., ist -ge-); umg.* set off; **~ gegen** *fig.* lash out at, have a real go at, *Am.* pounce on

Lot *n; -(e)s, -e* **1.** *(Senkblei)* plumbline; **aus dem ~** out of plumb; **im ~** perpendicular; *fig.* all right; **aus dem ~ geraten** *fig.* come unstuck; *Person: auch* be thrown (off balance); **wieder ins ~ bringen** straighten out; **wieder ins ~ kommen** straighten itself out; *Person:* get o.s. sorted out; *auch gesundheitlich:* get back on one's feet again; **2.** *Math.* perpendicular; **das ~ von Punkt C auf die Strecke AB fällen** drop a perpendicular from C on the line AB; **3.** *Naut.* sounding line; **4.** *(Lötzinn)* solder

loten *v/t.* **1.** plumb; **2.** *Naut.* sound

löten *v/t.* solder

Lothringen *(n); -s; Geog.* Lorraine

Lothringer¹ *m; -s, -,* **~in** *f; -, -nen* **1.** *hist.* Lotharingian; **2.** inhabitant of Lorraine; *Lothringer(in) sein auch* be *(od.* come) from Lorraine

Lothringer² *indekl. Adj.,* **lothringisch** *Adj.* Lotharingian *(auch hist.);* from Lorraine

Lotion *f; -, -en* lotion

Löt|kolben *m* soldering iron; **~lampe** *f*

blowlamp, blowtorch; **~metall** *n* solder

Lotos *m*; -, -, **~blume** *f Bot*. lotus; **~sitz** *m Joga etc*.: lotus position

Lötpistole *f* soldering gun

lotrecht *Adj*. perpendicular; **Lotrechte** *f* perpendicular

Lotse *m*; -*n*, -*n*; *Naut*. pilot; *Mot*. guide; → **Fluglotse, Schülerlotse**; **lotsen** *v/t*. guide; *Naut*. pilot; *Flug*., *per Funk*: talk down; *fig*. (*j-n*) steer; *umg*. ins Kino *etc*.: drag to; *durch e-e Schwierigkeit, Prüfung*: see through

Lotsen|boot *n* pilot boat; **~dienst** *m Mot*. driver-guide service

Löt|spitze *f* (soldering) bit; **~stelle** *f* (soldered) joint

Lotterbett *n altm*., *hum*. comfy old bed (*used by lovers*)

Lotterie *f*; -, -*n* lottery; **~gewinn** *m* win in the lottery; (*Preis*) lottery prize; **~los** *n* lottery ticket; **~spiel** *n* lottery; *fig*. gamble

Lotterleben *n pej*. dissolute life(style)

Lotto *n*; -*s*, -*s* **1**. (national) lottery; (*im*) **~** spielen play the lottery; **2**. (*Gesellschaftsspiel*) bingo; **~annahmestelle** *f* (local) lottery counter *od*. kiosk; **~gewinn** *m* **1**. win in the lottery; **2**. (*Summe*) lottery winnings *Pl*.; **~könig** *m*, **~königin** *f umg*. jackpot winner; **~schein** *m* lottery coupon; **~spieler** *m*, **~spielerin** *f* lottery player (*od*. participant); **~zahlen** *Pl*. (winning) lottery numbers; **~zettel** *m* lottery coupon

Lötung *f* soldering

Lotus *m*; -, - → **Lotos**

Lötzinn *n* solder

Löwe *m*; -*n*, -*n* **1**. *Zool*. lion; → **Höhle** 3; **2**. (*Sternzeichen*) Leo; (*ein*) **~** sein be a Leo

Löwen|anteil *m* lion's share; **sich** (*Dat*.) **den ~ sichern** make sure one gets the lion's share; **~bändiger** *m*, **~bändigerin** *f* lion tamer; **~grube** *f hist*., *bibl*. lion's den; **~junge** *n* lion cub; **~käfig** *m* lion's cage; **~mähne** *f* lion's mane; *fig*. (*wallendes Haar*) flowing mane; **~maul** *n*, **~mäulchen** *n*; *nur Sg*.; *Bot*. snapdragon; **~mut** *m geh*. bravery (*od*. courage) of a lion; **~zahn** *m*; *nur Sg*.; *Bot*. dandelion

Löwin *f*; -, -*nen*; *Zool*. lioness

Loxodrome *f*; -, -*n*; *Geogr*., *Math*. loxodrome, rhumb

loyal [loa'ja:l] *Adj*. loyal (*gegenüber* to); **Loyalität** *f*; -, *kein Pl*. loyalty (*gegenüber* to)

LP *f*; -, -(*s*); *Abk*. (**Langspielplatte**) LP (= long-playing record)

LPG *f*; -, -(*s*); *Abk*.; *ehem*. DDR (**Landwirtschaftliche Produktionsgenossenschaft**) collective farm

LSD *n*; -(*s*); *Abk*. LSD; **~süchtig** *Adj*. addicted to LSD; **~Süchtige** *m*, *f* LSD addict

lt. *Abk*. → **laut²**

Lt. *Abk*. (**Leutnant**) Lt

Luchs *m*; -*es*, -*e*; *Zool*. lynx; **Augen wie ein ~** eyes like a hawk; **aufpassen wie ein ~** watch like a hawk; **~augen** *Pl*. *umg*. eagle eyes; **~ haben** have eyes like a hawk

Lücke *f*; -, -*n* gap (*auch Wissenslücke etc*.); (*schwache Stelle*) im Gesetz *etc*.: loophole; (*leere Stelle, auch Parklücke*) space; *fig*. (*Bedürfnis*) need; (*Leere*) void; **e-e ~ ausfüllen** *od*. **schließen** fill a gap; *fig*. *auch* supply a need; *Person*: *auch* step into the breach; **e-e ~ reißen** create a gap; **e-e ~ hinterlassen** leave a gap; *stärker*:

leave a void

Lückenbüßer *m*, **~in** *f* stopgap; (*Person auch*) stand-in

lückenhaft *Adj*. full of gaps; *fig*. *auch* incomplete; *Wissen, Erinnerung*: sketchy; (*fragmentarisch*) fragmentary; *Beweiskette etc*.: full of holes; *Gesetz etc*.: full of loopholes; **ein ~es Gebiss haben** have gappy teeth, be gap-toothed

lückenlos *Adj*. complete; *Reihe etc*.: *auch* unbroken; *Alibi*: watertight; **~er Lebenslauf** complete CV (*Am*. résumé); **e-e ~e Beweisführung/Beweiskette** a watertight case / an unbroken chain of evidence

Lücken|springer *m Mot*. lane-hopper; **~test** *m Päd*., *Psych*. completion test; **~text** *m Päd*. completion exercise

lud *Imperf*. → **laden¹,²**

Lude *m*; -*n*, -*n*; *Sl*. pimp

Luder *n*; -*s*, - **1**. *umg*. so-and-so; *freches ~* cheeky thing (*jünger*: brat); *armes ~* poor thing; **2**. *Jägerspr*. bait

Lues *f*; -, *kein Pl*.; *Med*. lues, syphilis

Luft *f*; -, *Lüfte* **1**. *Atmosphäre*) atmosphere; *im Bauch*: wind; *frische ~ schnappen umg*. *od*. **an die frische ~ gehen** get some fresh air; **er kommt zu wenig an die ~** he doesn't get enough fresh air, he doesn't get out enough; **den ganzen Tag an der frischen ~ sein** be out in the open all day; *etw*. **an die ~ hängen** hang s.th. out (to air); **in der ~** (*über dem Boden*) schwebend *etc*.: in mid-air; **die Aufnahmen sind aus der ~ gemacht** the photographs were taken from the air; **sich in die Lüfte schwingen** *geh*. glide high in the air; **in der ~ liegen** *Gewitter*: be coming; **es liegt etwas in der ~** *fig*. there's something in the air; **die ~ herauslassen aus** let the air out of; *Reifen etc*.: *auch* let down; *umg*. *fig*. uncork; **aus etw**. **ist die ~ raus** *umg*. *fig*. s.th. has fizzled out (*od*. gone phut); **die ~ ist rein** *umg*. *fig*. the coast is clear; **j-n an die ~ setzen** *umg*. *fig*. throw (*od*. kick) s.o. out; **j-n wie ~ behandeln** act as if s.o. wasn't there; **sie ist für mich ~** she doesn't exist as far as I'm concerned; **vor Freude in die ~ springen** jump for joy; **in die ~ fliegen** *umg*. blow up, explode; **in die ~ jagen** *umg*. blow up; **in die ~ gehen** *umg*. *fig*. hit the roof, go ballistic; **leicht in die ~ gehen** be quick to lose one's temper, have a short fuse; **sich in ~ auflösen** *umg*. disappear into thin air; *Pläne etc*.: go up in smoke; **das hängt** *od*. **schwebt alles** (*noch*) **in der ~ umg**. *fig*. it's all up in the air; → **dick** I 6, **greifen** I 3, **Loch** 1; **2**. (*Atem*) breath; (*Atempause*) breathing space; **~ holen** take a (*od*. draw) breath; *beim Sprechen*: pause for breath; *tief* **~ holen** take a deep breath; *fig*. *vor Erstaunen*: swallow hard; **keine ~ haben** be out of breath; **ich bekam keine ~ mehr** I couldn't breathe properly, I felt I was going to suffocate; **nach ~ schnappen** *umg*. gasp for breath; **wieder ~ bekommen** get one's breath back (*auch fig*.); **mir blieb die ~ weg** *umg*. *fig*. it took my breath away, I just stood gaping; **halt** (*mal*) **die ~ an!** *umg*. *fig*. give us a break, *Brit*. *auch* put a sock in it(, will you); **von ~ und Liebe leben** *umg*. live on air; → **ausgehen** 5; **3**. (*Luftbewegung*) light breeze, breath of air; **j-m/sich ~ zufächeln** fan s.o./o.s.; **4**. *umg*. *fig*. (*Raum*) space; (*Spielraum*) room to move; *zeit-

lich: leeway; *Tech*. clearance; **s-r Wut ~ machen** let out one's anger, vent one's wrath; **sich** (*Dat*.) *od*. **s-n Gefühlen ~ machen** let out one's pent-up feelings; **seine Gefühle machten sich ~** his feelings all came pouring out; **jetzt hab ich endlich wieder ~** I can breathe again at last, I've got some space again; **sobald ich etwas ~ habe** as soon as I've got a breathing space (*od*. a moment to spare); **wir haben genügend ~** there's plenty of time

Luftabschluss *m*: *unter ~* airtight

Luftabwehr *f* air defen|ce (*Am*. -se); **~rakete** *f* anti(-)aircraft missile; → *auch* **Flugabwehr**...

Luft|abzug *m Tech*. air vent; **~akrobatik** *f* **1**. trapeze act(s *Pl*.); *auf dem Seil*: high-wire act(s *Pl*.); **2**. *Flug*. aerobatics *Pl*.; **~alarm** *m* air alert; **~angriff** *m Mil*. air attack (*od*. strike); **~ansicht** *f* aerial view; **~aufklärung** *f Mil*. aerial reconnaissance; **~aufnahme** *f* aerial photograph (*Ansicht*: view); **~aufsicht** *f Flug*. air traffic control; **~austausch** *m Met*. exchange of air masses; **~ballon** *m* balloon; **~befeuchter** *m*; -*s*, - humidifier; **~bereifung** *f Mot*. pneumatic tyres (*Am*. tires) *Pl*.; **~bewegung** *f* movement of air; **schwache ~** light breeze(s)

Luftbild *n* aerial photograph (*Ansicht*: view); **~karte** *f* map made up of aerial photographs

Luft|bläschen *n*, **~blase** *f* air bubble; **~-Boden-Rakete** *f* air-to-surface missile; **~bremse** *f Tech*. air brake; **~brücke** *f Flug*. airlift

Lüftchen *n* breeze, breath of air (*od*. wind); **es weht** *od*. **es regt sich kein ~** there's not a breath of wind

luftdicht I. *Adj*. airtight; **II**. *Adv*.: **~ verschließen** seal hermetically, airseal; **~ verschlossen** airtight, hermetically sealed; **~ verpackt** vacuum-packed

Luftdichte *f Phys*. atmospheric density

Luftdruck *m*; *nur Sg*. **1**. *Met*. atmospheric pressure; **2**. (*Explosionsdruck*) blast; **3**. *Tech*. air pressure; **~messer** *m* barometer

luftdurchlässig *Adj*. pervious to air; *Stoff*: cellular, breathable ...; **Luftdurchlässigkeit** *f* air permeability; *von Stoff*: breathability

Luftdüse *f* air nozzle, air jet

lüften *v/t*. **1**. (*Raum*) air; *ständig*: ventilate; (*Kleidung etc*.) air; *Mot*. (*Bremsen*) bleed; **hier muss mal gelüftet werden** this place needs airing; **das Zimmer ist gut gelüftet** the room is well ventilated; **2**. (*heben*) lift; (*Hut*) raise; (*Geheimnis*) reveal, take the wraps off; **sein Inkognito ~** drop one's mask; **das Geheimnis ist gelüftet** the secret is out; **Lüfter** *m*; -*s*, - fan

Luftfahrt *f*; *nur Sg*.; *Flug*. **1**. aviation; **2**. *Wissenschaft*: aeronautics *Pl*. (*V*. *im Sg*.); **~behörde** *f*: zivile **~** civil aviation authority; **~gesellschaft** *f* airline (company); **~industrie** *f* aviation industry

Luft|fahrzeug *n Flug*. aircraft; **~federung** *f Tech*. air cushioning; *Mot*. air (*od*. pneumatic) suspension

Luftfeuchte *f fachspr*., **Luftfeuchtigkeit** *f* humidity; **Luftfeuchtigkeitsmesser** *m* hygrometer

Luft|filter *m*, *n* air filter; **~flotte** *f Flug*. air fleet

Luftfracht *f Flug*. air freight; *einzelne*: air cargo; **per ~** by air freight; **per ~ schicken** *auch* airfreight; **~brief** *m* air waybill

Luftgeist *m* aerial spirit

luft|gekühlt *Adj.* air-cooled; **~geschützt** *Adj.* sheltered; **~gestützt** *Adj.*: **~e Rakete** air-launched missile; **~getrocknet** *Adj.* air-dried

Luft|gewehr *n* airgun; **~hauch** *m* breath of air; **~herrschaft** *f*; *nur Sg.*; *Mil.* air supremacy, control of the air; **~hoheit** *f* air sovereignty; **~holen** *n*; *-s, kein Pl.* breathing; **zum ~ an die Oberfläche kommen** come up for air; **~hülle** *f* atmosphere

Lufthunger *m* craving for fresh air; **lufthungrig** *Adj.* hungry for fresh air

luftig I. *Adj.* airy; *Platz etc.*: breezy; *Kleidung etc.*: light, cool; **in ~er Höhe** at a dizzy height; **II.** *Adv.*: **~ gekleidet sein** be wearing light clothes

Luftikus *m*; *-(ses), -se*; *umg. pej.* happy-go-lucky sort; **er ist ein ~** *auch umg.* he's easy come, easy go

Luftkampf *m Mil.* air (*od.* aerial) combat; *zwischen Jägern*: dogfight

Luftkissen *n* air cushion (*auch Tech.*); **~boot** *n*, **~fahrzeug** *n* hovercraft

Luft|klappe *f Tech. etc.* air flap; *Mot.* choke; **~korridor** *m Flug.* air corridor

luftkrank *Adj.* airsick; **Luftkrankheit** *f*; *nur Sg.* airsickness

Luft|krieg *m Mil.* aerial warfare (*od.* war); **~kühlung** *f Tech.* air cooling; **~kurort** *m* (climatic) health resort

Luftlande|truppen *Pl. Mil.* airborne troops, paratroops; **~unternehmen** *n Mil.* airborne operation

luftleer *Adj.* (completely) airless; **~ sein** *auch* **be a vacuum; ~er Raum** vacuum

Luftlinie *f*: **500 km** *≈* 500 km (*od.* 300 miles) as the crow flies

Lüftlmalerei *f Kunst* painting(s *Pl.*) on external walls, outdoor mural(s *Pl.*)

Luft|loch *n Flug.* air hole, vent; *Flug.* air pocket; **~Luft-Rakete** *f Mil.* air--to-air missile; **~mangel** *m* lack of air; **~masche** *f Häkeln*: chain stitch; **~masse** *f* air mass; **~matratze** *f* air mattress, *Brit. auch* lilo®; **~mine** *f Mil.* aerial mine; **~not** *f*: *Flugzeug in ~* aircraft in distress; **~pirat** *m* hijacker, *bes. Am. auch* skyjacker; **~piraterie** *f* hijacking (of aircraft), *bes. Am. auch* skyjacking; **~piratin** *f* → **Luftpirat**; **~polster** *n* air cushion

Luftpost *f* airmail; **mit** *od.* **per ~** (by) airmail; **~brief** *m* airmail letter; **~papier** *n* airmail paper

Luft|pumpe *f* air (*od.* pneumatic) pump; *für Fahrrad*: bicycle pump; **~qualität** *f* air quality

Luftraum *m* airspace; **~überwachung** *f* air traffic control

Luft|reifen *m* pneumatic tyre (*Am.* tire); **~reinhaltung** *f Öko.* air pollution control; **~reinhaltungsgesetz** *n Öko.* air quality (*od.* clean air) law (*Pl.* legislation *Sg.*); **~reinheit** *f* air cleanliness; **~reiniger** *m* air purifier; *Filter*: air filter; *Raumspray*: deodorizing spray; **~reinigung** *f* air purification; **~reklame** *f* aerial advertisement (*od.* advertising); *mit Rauch*: skywriting; **~rettungsdienst** *m* air rescue service; **~röhre** *f Anat.* windpipe

Luftröhrenschnitt *m Med.* tracheotomy

Luft|sack *m* **1.** *Mot.* air bag; **2.** *Zool.* air sac; **~sauerstoff** *m* atmospheric oxygen; **~säule** *f*; *nur Sg.*; *Phys.* air column; **~schacht** *m* ventilation (*od.* air) shaft; **~schadstoff** *m Öko.* air pollutant; **~schaukel** *f Dial.* boat-shaped swing seating several at a carnival, *Brit.* swingboat; **~schicht** *f* air layer,

layer of the atmosphere; **~schiff** *n Flug.* airship; **~schlacht** *f Mil.* air battle; **~schlange** *f* streamer; **~schlauch** *m* inner tube; **~schleuse** *f Tech.* air lock; **~schloss** *n* pipedream; **Luftschlösser bauen** build castles in the air; **~schneise** *f* air lane

Luftschutz *m ziviler*: (civil) air defen|ce (*Am.* -se); **~bunker** *m* air-raid shelter; **~keller** *m* underground air--raid shelter; **~raum** *m* air-raid shelter

Luft|sicherung *f* air traffic control; **~sog** *m* air suction; *nach Explosion*: vacuum; **~spediteur** *m* air carrier; **~spiegelung** *f* mirage; **~sprung** *m*: **e-n ~ machen** jump in the air; *vor Freude*: jump for joy

Luftstrahl *m* air jet; **~triebwerk** *n* jet engine

Luft|strecke *f* air route; **~streitkräfte** *Pl. Mil.* air combat forces; **~strom** *m* **1.** stream of air; **2.** *Met.* air current, airstream; **~strömung** *f Met.* air current, airstream; **~stützpunkt** *m Mil.* air base; **~taxi** *n* air taxi; **~temperatur** *f* air temperature; **~transport** *m* air transport(ation *Am.*)

lufttrocknen *v/t.* (*untr., hat -ge-*) air-dry

lufttüchtig *Adj. Flug.* airworthy; **Lufttüchtigkeit** *f* airworthiness

Luft|überlegenheit *f Mil.* air superiority; **~überwachung** *f* air surveillance

Luft- und Raumfahrtindustrie *f* aerospace industry

Lüftung *f* **1.** airing; *künstliche*: ventilation; **2.** *Anlage*: ventilation (system)

Lüftungs|anlage *f* ventilation (system); **~klappe** *f* ventilation flap; **~rohr** *n* vent pipe; **~schacht** *m* ventilation (*od.* air) shaft

Luft|ventil *n* air valve; **~veränderung** *f* change of air; **~verdichter** *m* (air) compressor; **~verkehr** *m Flug.* air traffic; **~verkehrsgesellschaft** *f* airline (company); **~verpestung** *f*, **~verschmutzung** *f Öko.* air pollution; **~ durch Abgase** exhaust pollution; **~verunreinigung** *f* → **Luftverpestung**; **~waffe** *f Mil.* air force; **~warnung** *f* air(-raid) warning; **~wechsel** *m* change of air; **~weg** *m* **1.** *Flug.* air route; *Am.* auch airways; **auf dem ~ by** air; **2.** *Pl.* (*Atemwege*) air passages, respiratory tract *Sg.*; **~widerstand** *m* air resistance, drag; **~wirbel** *m* air eddy; **~wurzel** *f Bot.* aerial root; **~ziegel** *m* air brick; **~zufuhr** *f* air supply; **~zug** *m* draught, *Am.* draft; (*Brise*) gentle breeze

Lug *m*: **~ und Trug** *geh.* lies and deception; **es war alles ~ und Trug** *auch* it was all lies (*umg.* a pack of lies)

Lüge *f*; *-, -n* lie; **alles ~** all lies; **j-n/etw. ~n strafen** show s.o. to be a liar / show s.th. to be a lie (*od.* untrue); **j-n bei e-r ~ ertappen** catch s.o. lying; **~n haben kurze Beine** *Sprichw.* your lies will always catch up with you, the truth will out

lugen *v/i. Dial.* peer; *durch etw.*: *auch* peep; **~ nach** look out for, *fig.* have an eye on

lügen; *lügt, log, hat gelogen* **I.** *v/i.* lie, tell a lie (*mehrmals*: lies); **er lügt** he's lying; *prinzipiell*: he's a liar; **ich müsste ..., wenn ...** I'd be lying (*od.* telling a lie) if ...; **wer einmal lügt(, dem glaubt man nicht, und wenn er auch die Wahrheit spricht)** *Sprichw.* a liar is not believed forsooth, even when a liar tells the truth; → **Balken** 1, **gedruckt**; **II.** *v/t.*: **das ist gelogen!** that's

a lie; **alles gelogen!** (it's) all lies, *umg.* it's a pack of lies *umg.*; **Lügen** *n*; *-s, kein Pl.* lying

Lügen|bold *m*; *-(e)s, -e*; *Dial., sonst altm.* habitual liar; **~detektor** *m* lie detector; **~gebäude** *n* tissue of lies; **~geschichte** *f* cock and bull story; **~gespinst** *geh.* tissue of lies

lügenhaft *Adj. Geschichte etc.*: untrue, false, untruthful

Lügen|kampagne *f* campaign of lies; **~märchen** *n* cock and bull story; **~maul** *n umg. pej.* lying toad; **~propaganda** *f* untrue propaganda

Lügerei *f*; *-, -en*; *pej.* constant lying

Lügner *m*; *-s, -*, **~in** *f*; *-, -nen* liar; **lügnerisch** *Adj.* Rede etc.: full of lies; *Behauptung*: untrue; *Mensch*: lying

Luk *n*; *-(e)s, -e*; *Naut.* hatch

Lukas *m*; *- *1. Luke; **2.** *auf dem Jahrmarkt*: try-your-strength machine; **hau den ~!** *Ausruf*: sock him one!

Lukasevangelium *n bibl.*: **das ~** the Gospel of (*od.* according to) St (*od.* St.) Luke (*od.* St.) Luke's Gospel

Luke *f*; *-, -n*; (*Dachluke*) skylight; (*zum Ein- und Ausstieg, Ladeluke*) hatch; → **dichtmachen** I 2

lukrativ *Adj.* lucrative

lukullisch *Adj.* epicurean; *Gericht*: *auch* exquisite; (*üppig*) sumptuous

Lulatsch *m*; *-(e)s, -e*; *umg.* lanky type; **langer ~** beanpole

lullen *v/t.*: **in den Schlaf ~** lull to sleep

Lumineszenz *f*; *-, -en*; *Phys.* luminescence

Lumme *f*; *-, -n*; *Zool. Vogel*: guillemot

Lümmel *m*; *-s, -* **1.** (*Flegel*) lout; *umg.* (*Bengel*) rascal; **2.** *Sl.* (*Penis*) willy, *Am.* dick; **Lümmelei** *f*; *-, -en*; *pej.* **1.** (*Verhalten*) loutishness; **2.** *nur Sg.* (*Herumlümmeln*) lounging around (all day), lolling about; **lümmelhaft** *Adj. pej.* loutish; **lümmeln** *v/i. und v/refl. umg. pej.*: (**sich**) ~ loll about; **auf dem Sofa ~** lie sprawled across the sofa

Lump *m*; *-en, -en*; *pej.* rogue, scoundrel, *umg.* louse

lumpen *umg.* **I.** *v/i.* (*ausgiebig feiern*) live it up, go out on the tiles, *Am.* paint the town red; **II.** *v/t.*: **sich nicht ~ lassen** do things (*od.* it) in style, splash out; **wir wollen uns nicht ~ lassen** *auch* we don't want it to be said that we're stingy

Lumpen *m*; *-s, -* **1.** *Pl.* rags (*auch fig. Kleidung*); **2.** *Dial.* (*Lappen*) rag; (*Putzlappen*) cloth

Lumpen|bande *f umg. pej.* bunch of troublemakers; **~gesindel** *n umg. pej.* riff-raff; **~händler** *m*, **~händlerin** *f* rag-and-bone man, junk dealer; **~pack** *n umg.* → **Lumpenbande**; **~proletariat** *n Pol. hist.* lumpenproletariat; **~sammler** *m* **1.** *altm.* rag-and-bone man; **2.** *umg. fig.* last bus (*Straßenbahn*: tram, *U-Bahn*: underground, *Am.* subway etc.); **~sammlerin** *f altm.* rag-and-bone woman

Lumperei *f*; *-, -en*; *pej.* mean (*od.* dirty) trick

lumpig I. *Adj.* **1.** *Gesinnung, Tat etc.*: mean; **2.** (*heruntergekommen*) shabby; **3.** *umg.* (*kümmerlich*) paltry; **wegen ~er zehn Euro** because of a measly ten euros; **II.** *Adv.*: **~ gekleidet** etc. shabbily dressed etc.

lunar *Adj.* lunar

Lunch [lantʃ] *m*; *-(e)s und -, -(e)s und -e* lunch; **lunchen** *v/i.* (have) lunch; **Lunchpaket** *n* packed (*Am.* box) lunch

Lüneburger Heide *f*: **die ~** Lüneburg

Heath

Lünette *f*; -, -*n* **1.** *Archit.* lunette; **2.** *Tech.* steadyrest

Lunge *f*; -, -*n*; *Anat. als Organ*: lungs *Pl.*; (*Lungenflügel*) lung; **auf ~ rauchen** inhale (when smoking); **eiserne ~** *Med.* iron lung; **e-e gute ~ haben** *umg. hum.* have a powerful pair of lungs; **er hat es auf der ~** he's got lung trouble; **sich** (*Dat.*) **die ~ aus dem Leib schreien** *umg. fig.* scream one's head off

Lungen|atmer *m*; -*s*, -; *Zool.* lung breather; **~atmung** *f Med., Zool.* pulmonary respiration; **~bläschen** *n Med.* (pulmonary) alveolus (*Pl.* alveoli); **~braten** *m österr. Gastr. vom Rind*: sirloin; **~embolie** *f Med.* embolism of the lung, pulmonary embolism; **~emphysem** *n Med.* pulmonary emphysema; **~entzündung** *f Med.* pneumonia; **~fisch** *m Zool.* lungfish; **~flügel** *m Anat.* (lobe of the) lung; **rechter/linker ~** right/left lung; **~haschee** *n Gastr.* hash of lung; **~heilanstalt** *f* sanatorium (*Am. auch* sanitarium) for lung patients; *bes. früher*: tuberculosis sanatorium (*Am. auch* sanitarium)

lungenkrank *Adj. Med.*: **~ sein** have a lung disease; **Lungenkranke** *m*, *f* lung patient; **Lungenkrankheit** *f* lung disease

Lungen|kraut *n Bot.* lungwort; **~krebs** *m Med.* lung cancer; **~leiden** *n* lung disease; **~ödem** *n Med.* pulmonary (o)edema; **~spitze** *f Anat.* apex of the lung; **~tuberkulose** *f Med.* tuberculosis (of the lung), pulmonary tuberculosis; **~zug** *m*: **e-n ~** *od.* **Lungenzüge machen** inhale (when smoking)

lungern *v/i.* hang around

Lunte *f*; -, -*n* **1.** fuse; **~ riechen** *umg. fig.* (*Gefahr wittern*) sense danger, (*Verdacht schöpfen*) smell a rat; **die ~ ans Pulverfass legen** *fig.* trigger the explosion; **2.** *Jägerspr. e-s Fuchses, Marders*: brush

Lupe *f*; -, -*n* magnifying glass; *für Juweliere und Uhrmacher*: loupe; **unter die ~ nehmen** *fig.* have a good look at, scrutinize; **so etwas kann** *od.* **muss man mit der ~ suchen** there aren't many of them around, they're pretty thin on the ground; *stärker*: they're like hen's teeth; **lupenrein** *Adj. Edelstein*: flawless; *fig.* (*perfekt*) perfect; **es ist ~** *fig. auch* you can't fault it; **nicht ganz ~** *umg.* (*verdächtig*) not quite kosher

lupfen *v/t. südd., österr. schw.*, **lüpfen** *v/t.* lift; (*Hut*) raise

Lupine *f*; -, -*n*; *Bot.* lupin

Lurch *m*; -(e)*s*, -*e*; *Zool.* amphibian

Lurex® *n*; -, *kein Pl. Textilindustrie*: lurex®

Lusche *f*; -, -*n*; *umg.* worthless card; *fig. Mensch*: no-hoper, useless type

Lust *f*; -, **Lüste** **1.** (*Wunsch, Verlangen*) desire; (*Appetit*) an appetite (**auf +** *Akk.* for); *stärker*: (*Verlangen*) craving (for); **ich habe** (**keine**) **~ zu** (+ *Inf.*) I (don't) feel like it (+ *Ger.*); **ich hätte ~ zu** (+ *Inf.*) I wouldn't mind (+ *Ger.*); **ich hätte große ~ zu** (+ *Inf.*) I'd love to (+ *Inf.*); **ich hätte ~ auf ein Bier** I wouldn't mind (*od.* I feel like) a beer; **ich habe keine ~** I don't feel like it, I'm not in the mood; **ich habe keine ~ mehr zu arbeiten** I don't feel like doing any more work, I've had enough (of work); **ich hätte gute ~ zu** (+ *Inf.*) I've a good mind (*od.* half a mind) to

(+ *Inf.*); **alle ~ an etw.** (*Dat.*) **verlieren** lose all interest in s.th.; **sie haben mir ~ gemacht** they've whet my appetite; **dabei kann einem die ~ vergehen** it can really put you off; **mir ist die ~ vergangen** I don't feel like it any more; (**je**) **nach ~ und Laune** as the mood takes you, just as you fancy; **dort kannst du nach ~ und Laune schwimmen/malen** you can go swimming there whenever you feel like it *od.* as often as you like / you can paint whenever and whatever you like there; **er kann schlafen, so lange er ~ hat** he can sleep as long as he likes; **2.** (*Genuss*) pleasure; **es ist e-e wahre ~, ihr zuzusehen** it's a real pleasure to watch her; **das ist für mich die höchste ~** that for me is sheer bliss (*od.* the ultimate); **mit ~ und Liebe** heart and soul; **3.** (*sexuelle Begierde*) sexual appetite, lust *pej.*; (*sexuelles Vergnügen*) sensual (*od.* sexual) pleasure

Lustbarkeit *f altm*; *mst Pl.* festivities, merrymaking *Sg.*

lustbetont I. *Adj.* hedonistic; *Mensch*: fun-loving, pleasure-seeking; **II.** *Adv.* hedonistically

Lustempfinden *n* pleasurable sensation

Luster *m*; -*s*, -; *österr.* chandelier

Lüster *m*; -*s*, - **1.** (*Kronleuchter*) chandelier; **2.** (*Glasur, Stoff*) lust|re (*Am.* -er); **~klemme** *f Etech.* strip connector

lüstern I. *Adj.* (*begierig*) greedy (**nach** for); *sexuell*: lascivious, lecherous; **~ auf Kirschen sein** have a craving for cherries; **~e Blicke** greedy eyes; *sexuell*: lustful (*od.* lascivious) glances; **nach j-m ~ sein** (*umg.* lech) after s.o.; **II.** *Adv.*: **~ schauen nach** cast lustful (*od.* lascivious) glances in the direction of; *begehren*: lust (*umg.* lech) after s.o./s.th.; **Lüsternheit** *f*; *nur Sg.* greed; *sexuelle*: lasciviousness, lecherousness

lustfeindlich *Adj.* opposed to carnal pleasures; **Lustfeindlichkeit** *f*; *nur Sg.* opposition to carnal pleasures

Lust|garten *m Archit. hist.* pleasure grounds *Pl.*; **~gefühl** *n* **1.** pleasurable sensation; **das ist ein ~!** what a delightful sensation; **2.** (feeling of) sexual pleasure(*od.* enjoyment); **~gewinn** *m* (experience of) pleasure; **nach ~ streben** seek only pleasure; **~greis** *m umg. pej.* old lecher, dirty old man

lustig I. *Adj.* (*komisch*) funny; (*unterhaltend*) amusing; (*fröhlich*) jolly; **es war sehr ~** it was great fun; **ein ~er Abend** a jolly (*umg.* fun) evening; **er ist ein ~er Typ** he's good (*bes. Am.* a lot of) fun; **das ist ja ~!** (*merkwürdig*) that's funny; **das kann ja ~ werden!** *iro. umg.* it looks like we're in for some fun and games; **du bist ~!** *iro. umg.* you're a right one (*Am.* a case); **bei naiver Bemerkung**: **~ umg.** don't make me laugh; **sich ~ machen über** (+ *Akk.*) laugh at; *offen*: *auch* make fun of; **ihr fällt immer etwas Lustiges ein** she always comes up with a fun idea; **II.** *Adv.* **1.** (*komisch*) funnily; (*unterhaltend*) amusingly; (*fröhlich*) merrily; **~ erzählen** tell amusing stories; **hier geht's ja ~** everyone seems to be having a good time; *iro.* we're having a good time, aren't we?; **die Fahnen flatterten ~ im Wind** the flags were fluttering merrily in the wind; **2.** (*sorglos*) blithely; **er spielte ~ weiter** (*unbekümmert*) he carried on

playing as if nothing had happened; **~ drauflossingen/draufloshämmern** *etc.* sing/hammer *etc.* away

...lustig *im Adj.* fond of ...; (*eifrig*) eager to ...; **aggressions~** eager to seek confrontation, confrontational; **schreib~** fond of writing; **trink~** fond of drinking

Lustigkeit *f*; *nur Sg.* **1.** *Stimmung*: fun atmosphere; **2.** *e-r Person*: jolliness, joviality; *Persönlichkeit*: amusing personality; (*Humor*) *auch* sense of humo(u)r; **3.** (*lustige Art*) funniness; (*lustige Seite*) funny side (of it)

Lustknabe *m altm.* (gay's) young boyfriend, boy toy, catamite *lit.*

Lüstling *m*; -*s*, -*e*; *pej.* lecher

lustlos I. *Adj.* **1.** listless; (*desinteressiert*) uninterested; **er ist völlig ~** he doesn't take any interest in (*od.* he can't be bothered with) anything; **2.** *Wirts., Börse*: inactive; *Tendenz*: dull, sluggish; **II.** *Adv.* listlessly; (*halbherzig*) half-heartedly; (*ohne Begeisterung*) without any enthusiasm; **Lustlosigkeit** *f*; *nur Sg.* **1.** listlessness; (*Desinteresse*) lack of interest (*od.* enthusiasm); **2.** *Wirts.* dullness, slackness

Lust|molch *m umg.* lecher; *iro. umg.* sex-fiend; **~mord** *m* sex murder; **~mörder** *m*, **~mörderin** *f* sex killer; **~objekt** *n* sex object, object of sexual desire; **~prinzip** *n Psych.* pleasure principle; **~schloss** *n* summer residence; **~schrei** *m* cry of pleasure; **~seuche** *f* **1.** *altm.* syphilis; **2.** *geh.* sexual disease; **~spiel** *n Lit.* comedy

lustvoll I. *Adj.* joyful; *Seufzer etc.*: of pleasure; (*wollüstig*) voluptuous; **II.** *Adv. verspeisen etc.*: with relish

lustwandeln *v/i.* (*untr., ist/hat*) *altm., hum.* stroll

Lutheraner *m*; -*s*, -, **~in** *f*; -, -*nen Reli.* Lutheran

Lutherbibel *f Reli.* Luther (translation of the) Bible

lutherisch I. *Adj.* Lutheran; (*von Luther*) Luther's; **II.** *Adv. erziehen etc.*: as a Lutheran

Luthertum *f*; -*s*, *kein Pl.* Lutheranism

lutschen *vt/i.* suck; **am Daumen ~** suck one's thumb; **er ist dauernd am Lutschen** *umg. auch* he's always got something in his mouth; **Lutscher** *m*; -*s*, - **1.** lollipop, lolly *umg., Am.* sucker; **2.** *umg.* (*Schnuller*) dummy, *Am.* pacifier

lütt *Adj. nordd. umg.* small; **unsere Lütte macht jetzt auch schon Abitur** our little girl is already taking her school-leaving exam

Lüttich (*n*) -*s*; *Geog.* Liège

Lutz *m*; -, - *Eis-, Rollkunstlauf*: lutz

Luv *f*, *n*; -*s*, *kein Pl.*; *Geogr., Naut* windward side; **nach ~** to windward; **luven** *v/i.* luff; **Luvseite** *f* windward side

Lux *n*; -, -; *Phys.* lux

Luxemburg (*n*) -*s*; *Geog.* Luxembourg

Luxemburger[1] *Adj.* Luxembourg; **die ~ Regierung** the government of Luxembourg, the Luxembourg government

Luxemburger[2] *m*; -*s*, -, **~in** *f*; -, -*nen* Luxembourger, *weiblich auch*: Luxembourger woman (*od.* girl); **sie ist Luxemburgerin** *auch* she's from Luxembourg; **luxemburgisch** *Adj.* Luxembourgian, from Luxembourg

luxuriös *Adj.* luxurious; *Auto etc.*: *auch* luxury ...; **~es Leben** life of luxury, lush life

Luxus *m*; -, *kein Pl.* luxury; **im ~ leben** live in luxury, live a life of luxury; **das**

L

ist reiner ~ that's sheer extravagance; **sich** (*Dat.*) **den ~ erlauben zu** (+ *Inf.*) allow o.s. the luxury of (+ *Ger.*); **den ~ kann ich mir nicht erlauben** I can't afford that kind of luxury; *weitS.* I can't afford the luxury of (+ *Ger.*); **~apartment** *n*, **~appartement** *n* luxury apartment; **~artikel** *m* luxury article; *Pl. auch* luxury goods; **~ausführung** *f* de luxe (*bes. Am.* deluxe) model; **~ausgabe** *f* de luxe (*bes. Am.* deluxe) edition; **~auto** *n* luxury car; **~dampfer** *m* luxury liner; **~geschöpf** *n mst pej.* pampered female (*accustomed to luxury*); **~güter** *Pl.* luxury goods; **~herberge** *f umg. hum.* top hotel; **~hotel** *n* five-star (*od.* luxury) hotel; **~jacht** *f* luxury yacht; **~kabine** *f* de luxe (*bes.*

Am. deluxe) cabin; **~klasse** *f*: ... **der ~** de luxe ..., *Am.* deluxe, luxury ...; **~limousine** *f* de luxe saloon, *Am.* luxury sedan; *große, mit Chauffeur:* limousine; **~restaurant** *n* top-class restaurant; **~steuer** *f* luxury tax; **~villa** *f* luxury mansion; **~wagen** *m* luxury car; **~ware** *f* → **Luxusartikel**

Luzern (*n*); *-s*; *Geog.* Lucerne

Luzerne *f*; *-, -n*; *Bot.* lucerne, *bes. Am.* alfalfa

Luzifer *m*; *-s, kein Pl.*; *kirchl.* Lucifer

LVA *f*; *-, -(s)*; *Abk.* → **Landesversicherungsanstalt**

LW *Abk.* (**Langwelle**) LW

Lycra® ['laikra] *n*; *-s, kein Pl.* Lycra®

Lymph|bahn *f Anat.* lymph vessel; **~drainage** *f* lymph drainage; **~drüse**

f altm. lymph node, lymph gland

Lymphe *f*; *-, -n*; *Med.* lymph; (*Impfstoff*) lymph vaccine

Lymph|gefäß *n Med.* lymph vessel; **~knoten** *m Med.* lymph node, lymph gland; **~system** *n* lymphatic system

lynchen *v/t.* lynch

Lynch|justiz *f* mob law; **~mord** *m* lynching

Lyoner *f*; *-, -*; *Gastr.* bologna (sausage)

Lyra *f*; *-, Lyren* **1.** *Mus.* lyre; **2.** *nur Sg.*; *Astron.* Lyra

Lyrik *f*; *-, kein Pl.* **1.** *Lit.* (lyric) poetry; **2.** (*lyrische Beschaffenheit*) lyricism; **Lyriker** *m*; *-s, -*, **Lyrikerin** *f*; *-, -nen* (lyric) poet; **lyrisch** *Adj.* lyrical

Lyzeum *n*; *-s, Lyzeen*; *altm.* girls' high school

M, m *n*; -, -, *umg. auch* -s M, m; **M wie Martha** *Buchstabieren*: "m" for (*od. as in*) "Mike" (*Am. auch* "Mary")

M.A. *Abk.* (**Magister Artium**) MA, *Am. auch* M.A.; → *auch* **Magister**

Mäander *m*; -s, -; *Geog., Kunst* meander

mäandern, mäandrieren I. *v/i. Geog.* meander; **II.** *v/t. Kunst* decorate with meanders

Maar *n*; -(e)s, -e; *Geog.* maar; *mit Wasser gefüllt*: crater lake

Maas *f*; -; *Geog.*: **die ~** the Meuse; *in Holland*: the Maas

Maat *m*; -(e)s, -e(n) **1.** *Naut.* (ship's) mate; **2.** *Mil., Dienstgrad*: petty officer

Macchia ['makja] *f*, -, *Macchien*, **Macchie** *f*, -, *Macchien*; *Bot.* maquis

Mach *n*; -(s), -; *Phys.* Mach

Machart *f* style, design

machbar *Adj.* feasible; *umg.* doable; *es müsste ~ sein* it ought to be possible; **Machbarkeit** *f* feasibility; **Machbarkeitsstudie** *f* feasibility study

Mache *f*, -, *kein Pl.*; *umg.* **1.** show; *Vortäuschung*: sham; *das ist alles nur ~* it's all show (*od.* sham); *Person*: *auch* it's all put on (*od.* just an act); **2.** *etw. in der ~ haben* have s.th. in the pipeline (*od.* on the stocks); (*Pläne etc.*) *auch* be hatching s.th. *umg.*; *etw./j-n in die ~ nehmen* take s.th. in hand/give s.o. a good going over; **3.** *umg.* (*Machart*) style

machen I. *v/t.* **1.** (*tun*) do; *was machst du?* what are you doing?; *beruflich*: what do you do (for a living)?; *so was macht man nicht* that isn't done, you just don't do that; *da kann man nichts ~* there's nothing you can do (about it), it's (just) one of those things; *er macht es nicht unter 500 Euro umg.* he won't do it for less than 500 euros; *was macht die Familie?* how's the family (getting on [*Am.* along])?; *mach's gut!* see you; (*alles Gute*) all the best; *gut gemacht!* well done!, good show!; *das lässt sich schon ~* that can be arranged, that's no problem; *mit mir könnt ihr's ja ~! umg. iro.* the things I put up with; *die Festplatte wird es wohl nicht mehr lange ~ umg.* (*wird bald defekt sein*) the hard disk is on its last legs (*od.* has just about had it); **2.** (*herstellen, schaffen*) make; (*Essen*) make, prepare; (*Bett*) make; *ein Foto ~* take a photograph; *Hausaufgaben ~* do one's homework; *e-e Prüfung ~* take (*erfolgreich*: pass) an exam; *e-n Spaziergang ~* go for a walk; *e-n Fehler ~* make a mistake; *e-n Kurs ~* do (*od.* take) a course; *e-e unangenehme Erfahrung ~* have an unpleasant experience; *j-n zum General ~* make s.o. a general; *zu od. für etw.* (*nicht*) *gemacht sein* (not) be cut out for s.th.; *er ist nicht zur Arbeit gemacht iro.* work doesn't agree with him *hum.*; *den Schiedsrichter ~* be

(*od. act as*) umpire (*od.* referee); *das macht das Wetter* it's the weather that causes it; *das macht Durst* it makes you thirsty; *der Wagen macht 160 km/h umg.* the car does 100 mph; → *Ferien, Hoffnung, Krach* 1, *Licht* 1; **3.** (*ergeben*) *beim Rechnen*: be, come to, amount to; *4 mal 5 macht 20* four times five is twenty, four fives are twenty; *was macht das? Rechnung etc.*: how much does that come to?, what's the damage? *umg.*; *das macht dreißig Euro* that's (*od.* that'll be) thirty euros; **4.** (*ausmachen*): *was macht das schon?* what does it matter?, what difference does it make?; *umg.* so what?; *das macht nichts* it doesn't matter, never mind; *es macht mir nichts* I don't mind; *sie macht sich nichts / nicht viel aus Geld* she doesn't care / doesn't care much about money, money doesn't mean anything / doesn't mean much to her, she's not bothered / not really bothered about money *umg.*; *er macht sich nicht viel aus Kuchen etc.* he doesn't particularly like cake *etc.*, he's not particularly keen on (*Am.* not wild about) cake *etc.*; *mach dir nichts draus!* don't worry about it, don't take it to heart; **5.** *Sl. euph.*: *es ~* (*Sex haben*) have it off (*Am.* get it on) (*mit* with); *es j-m ~* give it to s.o. (*II. v/refl.* **1.** *sich* (*gut*) *~ Person*: be coming along (*well od.* fine), be getting on (*Am.* along) fine; *sich gut ~ Sache*: (*gut aussehen*) look good (*bei j-m* on s.o.); (*gern gesehen werden*) make a good impression; *er macht sich gut als ...* he makes a good ...; *wie macht sich Vincent als Chef?* what sort of a boss is Vincent?; *wie macht sich der Kleine?* how's the little one doing (*od.* getting on [*Am.* along])?; **2.** *sich an etw. ~* get down to (work on) s.th.; → *Arbeit* 1, *Weg* 1; **III.** *v/i.* **1.** *macht, dass ihr bald zurück seid!* be sure to be back (*od.* you get back) soon!; *mach, dass du wegkommst!* get out of here!; *mach schon!* (*beeile dich!*) hurry up!, get a move on! *umg.*; **2.** *lass ihn nur ~* (*lass ihm s-n Willen*) let him if he wants to, let him have his way; (*red ihm nichts ein*) just let him do it (*od.* get on with it); (*verlass dich auf ihn*) leave it to him; *lass mich nur ~* (*red mir nichts ein*) let me do it my way; (*verlass dich auf mich*) just leave it to me; **3.** *~ in* (+ *Dat.*) *Wirts.* deal in, sell; *in Politik ~ umg.* be in politics; **4.** *auf etw. ~ umg.* (*etw. spielen*) act (*od.* play) s.th., pretend to be s.th.; *auf unschuldig/doof ~ umg.* act (*od.* play) the innocent / the fool; *sie macht neuerdings auf jung* her latest fad is to act all girlish; **5.** *Schokolade macht dick* chocolate makes you fat; *Querstreifen machen dick* horizontal stripes make you look fat; **6.** *umg.*

euph. (*die Notdurft verrichten*): (*klein*) *~* wee; (*groß*) *~* shit; *sich* (*Dat.*) *vor Angst in die Hosen ~* wet o.s. (*Am.* wet one's pants) from fear; *der Hund hat auf den Teppich gemacht* the dog made a mess on the carpet; **7.** (*hat od. ist*) (*sich begeben*) go; *wir haben od. sind 1966 in den Westen gemacht* (*sind aus der DDR in die BRD geflüchtet*) in 1966 we made it to West Germany; → *gemacht*

Machenschaften *Pl.* wheelings and dealings, machinations, intrigues; *heimliche od. dunkle ~* underhand dealings

Macher *m*; -s, - man of action, doer

...macher *m*; -s, - **1.** *allg. im wörtl. Sinn in Berufszeichnungen etc.*: maker; *Korb~* basketmaker; *Filme~* film maker, *Am.* filmmaker, moviemaker; **2.** *nach dem, was j-d gerne und oft macht*: *Witze~* joker; **3.** *nach dem, was j-s Verhalten bei anderen hervorruft*: *Angst~* cause of fear; *Stimmungs~* creator of atmosphere; **4.** *nach dem, was eine Sache bei j-m od. etw. bewirkt*: *Dick~* thing that makes you fat; *Süchtig~* source of addiction; *Droge*: addictive drug

Macherin *f*; -m, -nen woman of action, doer

...macherin *f*; -m, -nen → *...macher* 1-3

Machete *f*; -, -n machete

Machiavellismus [makjaveˈlɪsmʊs] *m*; -, *kein Pl.* Machiavellianism; **machiavellistisch** *Adj.* Machiavellian

Macho ['matʃo] *m*; -s, -s macho

Macht *f*, -, *Mächte* **1.** *nur Sg.* (*Kraft*) power; (*Stärke*) strength; *bes. lit.* might; *mit aller ~* with all one's might; *lit.* with might and main; **2.** *nur Sg.* (*Einfluss, Herrschaft*) power; (*Machtbefugnis*) *auch* authority; *es steht nicht in m-r ~* it's not within my power; *~ der Gewohnheit* force of habit; *die ~ ergreifen* seize power; *an die ~ kommen od. zur ~ gelangen* come (in)to power; *an der ~ sein* be in power; **3.** *Pol.* (*Staat*) power; (*einflussreiche Gruppe*) *auch* force; **4.** *metaphysische*: power, force; *die ~ des Schicksals* the force of destiny; *die Mächte der Finsternis* the powers of darkness; *~ablösung* *f* transfer of power; *~anhäufung* *f* accumulation (*od.* concentration) of power; *~anspruch* *m* claim to power; *~ausübung* *f* exercise of power; *~befugnis* *f* authority; *Pl. mst* powers; *~bereich* *m* sphere of influence

machtbesessen *Adj.* power-crazed; **Machtbesessene** *m*, *f* megalomaniac; **Machtbesessenheit** *f* megalomania, obsession with power

machtbewusst *Adj.* conscious of one's power

Machtblock *m Pol.* power bloc

Mächtegruppe *f Pol.* group of powers

Macht|entfaltung f development (*od.* expansion) of power, growth in power; **Ära der** ~ period of political growth (*od.* expansion); **~ergreifung** f **1.** seizure of power; **2.** *nur Sg.*; *hist.* Hitler's seizure of power; **~erhalt** m retention of power; **~faktor** m power factor; **~frage** f question of who is (the) more powerful, question of superior strength; **~fülle** f great power; **~gewinn** m gain in power

Machtgier f lust for power; **machtgierig** *Adj.* power-hungry

Machthaber m; -s, -, **~in** f; -, -nen ruler; **die** ~ those in power; *iro.* the powers that be

Machthunger f lust for power; **machthungrig** *Adj.* power-hungry

mächtig I. *Adj.* **1.** (*einflussreich, stark*) powerful; *lit.* mighty (*auch Stimme, Schlag etc.*); **2. e-r Sprache** ~ **sein** geh. be able to speak (*od.* have a good command of) a language; **der Sprache** ~ **sein** geh. be able to speak; **s-r selbst / s-r Sinne nicht mehr ~ sein** have lost control of oneself / be out of one's senses; **3.** (*gewaltig, sehr groß*) huge, enormous, *lit.* mighty; *umg.* (*schrecklich*) terrific, terrible; **~en Hunger/ Durst haben** be terribly hungry/ thirsty; **ich hatte ~en Bammel** I was scared stiff; **4.** *Bergb., Geol.* thick; **II.** *Adv. umg.* verstärkend: incredibly, tremendously, *Am. auch* mighty; ~ **groß** (really) huge, massive; **sich ~ anstrengen** make a terrific effort; **Mächtige** m, f; -n, -n powerful figure; **die ~n dieser Erde** the rulers of this world, those who wield the power on earth; **Mächtigkeit** f **1.** *nur Sg.* powerfulness, *lit.* mightiness; (*beeindruckende Größe*) enormous size; **2.** *Bergb., Geol.* thickness; **3.** *Math.* cardinality

Macht|instrument n instrument of power; **~kampf** m power struggle, struggle for power

machtlos *Adj.* powerless (**gegen** in the face of); (*hilflos*) *auch* helpless; **da ist man** ~ *umg.* there's nothing you can do (about it); **Machtlosigkeit** f powerlessness, impotence (**gegen** in the face of); (*Hilflosigkeit*) *auch* helplessness

Macht|mensch m power-seeker; **~missbrauch** m abuse of power; **~mittel** n instrument of power; means *Sg.* of enforcing power; **~monopol** n monopoly of power

Machtpolitik f power politics *Pl.*; **Machtpolitiker** m, **Machtpolitikerin** f power politician; **machtpolitisch** *Adj.* power-political

Macht|position f position of power; **~probe** f test (*od.* trial) of strength; *umg.* showdown, *Am.* face-off; **~stellung** f position of power; **~streben** n striving for power; **~struktur** f power structure; **~übernahme** f assumption of power; **~verhältnisse** *Pl.* balance *Sg.* of power; *zwischen Individuen:* hierarchy *Sg.* of power, *umg.* pecking order *Sg.*; **~verlust** m loss of power; **~verteilung** f distribution of power; **machtvoll** *Adj.* powerful (*auch fig.*)

Macht|vollkommenheit f absolute power; **aus eigener** ~ on one's own authority, at one's own discretion; **~wechsel** m changeover of power; **~wille** m will to power; **~wort** n: **ein** ~ **sprechen** *umg.* put one's foot down; **~zentrum** n cent|re (*Am.* -er) of power, powerhouse

Machwerk n pej. (auch **elendes** ~) mis-

erable effort (*od.* piece of work); *umg.* lousy (*od.* botched-up) job, botch

Machzahl f *Phys.* Mach number

Macke f; -, -n; *umg.* **1.** (*Defekt*) fault, defect; *im Blech:* dent; (*Sprung*) crack; **2. e-e ~ haben** (*Person*) *umg.* have a screw loose; **sie hat so ihre ~n** (*ist eigenwillig*) she has her little fads

Macker m; -s, - **1.** *Sl.* (*Mann*) guy *umg., Brit. auch* bloke *umg.*; (*Freund*) fella, *Brit. auch* bloke *umg.*; **2.** *Sl.:* **den großen** ~ **spielen** throw one's weight around, act as if one owns the place; **3.** *nordd. umg.* workmate; *beim Skat:* partner

MAD m; -(s), *kein Pl.*; *Abk.* (**Militärischer Abschirmdienst**) Military Counter-Intelligence

Madagaskar (n); -s; *Geog.* Madagascar; **Madagasse** m; -n, -n, **Madagassin** f; -, -nen Madagascan, *weiblich auch:* Madagascan woman (*od.* girl); **madagassisch** *Adj.* Madagascan

Madam f; -, -s und -en; *umg.* **1.** *altm.* (*Hausherrin*) lady of the house, *the* mistress; **2.** *Dial.* (*Ehefrau*) *the* missus; **3.** (*ältere Frau*) old dame

Mädchen n; -s, - **1.** girl; **2.** (*Dienstmädchen*) maid; **~ für alles** *umg. fig.* maid of all work, (general) dogsbody, *Am.* gofer; *bes. im Büro:* girl Friday; **~alter** n: (**schon**) **im** ~ as a girl

mädchenhaft *Adj.* girlish

Mädchen|handel m white slave trade; **~händler** m white slave trader; **~herz** n: **diese Boygroup lässt alle ~en höher schlagen** this boy band wows the girls; **~klasse** f girls' class; **~kleidung** f girls' clothes; **~name** m girl's name; *e-r Frau:* maiden name; **~schule** f girls' school

Made f; -, -n; *Zool.* maggot; **wie die ~ im Speck leben** be (*od.* be living) in clover

Madeira [ma'de:ra] m; -s, -s; *Geog.* Madeira; **~wein** m Madeira

Mädel n; -s, - und -s; *umg.* girl, lass

madig *Adj.* **1.** *Lebensmittel:* full of maggots, *umg.* maggoty; **2.** *j-n od. etw.* ~ **machen** *umg. fig.* run down, knock; (*j-m*) *etw.* ~ **machen** *umg.* spoil s.th. (for s.o.), take the fun out of s.th. (for s.o.)

Madjar m; -en, -en, **~in** f -, -nen Magyar

Madonna f; -, Madonnen **1.** *nur Sg.*; *Reli.:* **die** ~ the Virgin Mary, Our Lady; **2.** *Kunst* Madonna; **e-e** ~ **mit Kind** a Madonna (*od.* Virgin) and Child

Madonnenbild n *Kunst* picture of the Virgin (Mary), Madonna; **madonnenhaft** *Adj.* Madonna-like; **Madonnenkult** m worship of the Virgin Mary; *pej.* Mariolatry

Madrigal m; -s, -e; *Lit. und Mus.* madrigal; **~chor** m madrigal choir

Maestro m; -s, -s und Maestri; *Mus.* maestro (*Pl.* maestri *od.* maestros)

Maf(f)ia [~fia] f; -; *Mafia; fig.* mafia

...maf(f)ia f, *im Subst.* **1.** *Verbrecherorganisation auf einem bestimmten Gebiet:* mafia, ring; **Kokain~** cocaine ring; **2.** *pej. einflussreiche Interessengruppe:* mafia, clique; **Pharma~** pharmaceutical industry pressure group

Mafia|boss m Mafia boss; *e-r bestimmten Mafia: auch* head of the Mafia, *Am.* capo; **~methoden** *Pl.* Mafia (--type) methods

Mafioso m; -(s), Mafiosi member of the Mafia, Mafioso (*Pl.* Mafiosi)

mag *Präs.* → **mögen**

Mag. *Abk. österr.* → **Magister**

Magazin n; -s, -e **1.** (*Lager*) warehouse; (*Depot*) depot; (*Lagerraum*) storeroom; *in der Bibliothek:* stacks *Pl.*; **2.** *Tech., auch in Schusswaffen:* magazine; (*Fülltrichter*) hopper; (*für Dias*) magazine; **3.** (*Illustrierte*) magazine; *TV, Radio:* magazine program(me); **Magaziner** m; -s, -, **Magazinerin** f; -, -nen; *schw.* (*Lagerverwalter[in]*) *Wirts.* storekeeper, stockkeeper; **Magazineur** m; -s, -e, **Magazineurin** f; -, -nen; *österr. Wirts.* storekeeper, stockkeeper; **magazinieren** v/t. put into storage

Magd f; -, Mägde; *lit.* maiden; (*Bauernmagd*) farmgirl; *altm.* (*Dienstmagd*) maid(servant)

Magen m; -s, - und Mägen stomach, *umg.* tummy; **mit leerem** ~ *od.* **auf nüchternen** ~ on an empty stomach; **ich habe noch nichts im** ~ I haven't eaten anything; **ich habe mir den** ~ **verdorben** (*umg.* verkorkst) I've got an upset stomach; **es liegt mir schwer im** ~ I'm having trouble digesting it; *fig.:* it's really bothering me, it's really getting to me *umg.*; **dabei drehte es ihr den** ~ **um** it turned her stomach, it made her feel sick; **j-m auf den** ~ **schlagen** *Erkältung etc.:* settle on s.o.'s stomach; *stärker:* (begin to) give s.o. stomach ulcers; *fig. Sorgen etc.:* get to s.o.; → **knurren** 1, **Liebe** 1; **~beschwerden** *Pl.* stomach trouble *Sg.*; **~bitter** m bitters *Pl.*; **~blutung** f *Med.* gastric h(a)emorrhage

Magen-Darm-Katarrh m *Med.* gastroenteritis

Magen|drücken n; -s, *kein Pl.* stomach pains *Pl.*; **~durchbruch** m *Med.* perforation of the stomach; **~eingang** m *Anat.* cardiac orifice, cardia; **~gegend** f stomach area; **~geschwür** n *Med.* stomach (*od.* peptic) ulcer; **~grube** f pit of one's stomach; **~knurren** n; -s, *kein Pl.* rumbling stomach, *umg.* tummy rumbles *Pl.*; **ich habe** ~ my stomach's (*umg.* tummy's) rumbling; **~krämpfe** *Pl.* stomach cramps

magenkrank *Adj.:* ~ **sein** suffer from a stomach complaint; **Magenkrankheit** f stomach complaint (*od.* disorder)

Magen|krebs m *Med.* stomach cancer; **~leiden** n stomach complaint (*od.* disorder); **~operation** f stomach operation; **~reizung** f gastric irritation

Magen|saft m *Physiol.* gastric juices *Pl.*; **~säure** f gastric (*od.* stomach) acid

Magenschleimhaut f *Anat.* stomach lining; **~entzündung** f *Med.* gastritis

Magen|schmerzen *Pl.* stomachache *Sg.*; **~sonde** f *Med.* stomach probe; **~spiegel** m *Med.* gastroscope; **~spiegelung** f gastroscopy; **~spülung** f *Med.* gastric irrigation

Magen|verstimmung f upset stomach; **~wand** f *Anat.* wall of the stomach; **~weh** n *umg.* stomachache

mager *Adj.* **1.** *Person:* thin, *umg.* skinny; **2.** *Fleisch:* lean; *Diät, Joghurt etc.:* low-fat; *Mot., Kraftstoffgemisch:* lean; *unerwünscht:* weak; **3.** (*dürftig*) mea-g|re (*Am.* -er), poor; (*Ernte*) *auch* lean; **~e Jahre** lean years; **~es Lob** scant praise; **4.** *Druck.:* **~e Schrift** light-face(d) type

Mager|joghurt m *Gastr.* low-fat yoghurt; **~käse** m low-fat cheese

Magerkeit f **1.** *von Person:* thinness, *umg.* skinniness; **2.** *von Fleisch:* leanness; *von Diät, Joghurt etc.:* low fat content; *Mot., von Gemisch:* leanness; *unerwünscht:* weakness; **3.** (*Dürftigkeit*)

meagreness, *Am.* meagerness, poorness; *von Zeit:* leanness

Mager|milch *f* skimmed milk; **~motor** *m* lean-burn engine; **~quark** *m* low-fat curd cheese

Magersucht *f nur Sg.; Med.* anorexia (nervosa); **magersüchtig** *Adj.* anorexic

Maggi® *n*; -(*s*), *kein Pl. fluid flavo(u)ring for food, especially soups;* **Maggikraut** *n Bot.* lovage

Maghreb *m*; -; *Geog.* Maghrib; **maghrebinisch** *Adj.* Maghrib

Magie *f*, -, *kein Pl.* magic; **schwarze/ weiße ~** black/white magic; **Magier** *m*; -*s*, -, **Magierin** *f*, -, -*nen* magician; (*Zauberkünstler[in]*) *auch* conjuror; **magisch I.** *Adj.* magic; *Anziehungskraft, Atmosphäre etc.:* magical; **II.** *Adv.* magically; (*durch Magie*) by magic; **j-n ~ anziehen** have a magical attraction for s.o.

Magister *m*; -*s*, - *etwa* Master's degree; **~ Artium** *etwa* Master of Arts (*Abk.* MA, *Am. auch* M.A.); **den ~ machen** take a (*od.* one's) MA *od.* Master's degree; **~arbeit** *f etwa* MA (*od.* Master's) thesis

Magistrale *f*; -, -*n*; *Verk.* main thoroughfare

Magistrat¹ *m*; -(*e*)*s*, -*e* City Council

Magistrat² *m*; -*en*, -*en*; *schw.* Federal Council(l)or

Magistrats|beschluss *m* City Council decision; **~mitglied** *n* City Council(-l)or

Magma *n*; -*s*, *Magmen; Geol.* magma; **magmatisch** *Adj.* magmatic

Magna Charta *f*, -, *kein Pl.; hist.* Magna C(h)arta

magna cum laude *Univ.* with great distinction (*second highest grade awarded to doctoral candidates*), *Am.* magna cum laude

Magnat *m*; -*en*, -*en* magnate, tycoon

Magnesia *f*; -, *kein Pl.; Chem.* magnesia

Magnesium *n*; -*s*, *kein Pl.; Chem.* magnesium; **~legierung** *f Metall.* magnesium alloy; **~oxid** *n* magnesium oxide

Magnet *m*; -*en und* -(*e*)*s*, -*e*(*n*) magnet (*auch fig.*), *natürlicher:* lodestone; **~band** *n* magnetic tape; **~eisenstein** *m Min.* magnetite; **~feld** *n Phys.* magnetic field

magnetisch I. *Adj.* magnetic (*auch fig*); **II.** *Adv.* magnetically

magnetisieren *v/t.* magnetize; (*j-n, hypnotisieren*) *auch fig.* mesmerize; **Magnetisierung** *f* magnetization; **Magnetismus** *m*; -, *kein Pl.* magnetism (*auch fig.*); (*Heilmagnetismus*) mesmerism

Magnet|karte *f Computer:* magnetic card; **~kern** *m Phys.* magnet core; **~kompass** *m* magnetic compass; **~kopf** *m Etron., EDV* magnetic head; **~nadel** *f* magnetic (*od.* compass) needle

Magnetosphäre *f* magnetosphere

Magnet|platte *f EDV* magnetic disk; **~pol** *m Phys.* magnetic pole

Magnet|schalter *m Mot.* solenoid switch; **~Schnellbahn** *f* magnetic railway (*Am.* railroad); **~schwebebahn** *f* magnetic levitation system, maglev system; *Zug:* maglev train; **~spule** *f Etech.* electromagnet coil; **~streifen** *m EDV* magnetic strip; **~wirkung** *f* magnetic effect (*od.* attraction); **~zünder** *m Mot.* magneto; **~zündung** *f Mot.* magneto ignition

Magnolie *f*, -, -*n*; *Bot.* magnolia; **Mag-**

noliengewächs *n* member of the magnolia family

mäh *Interj.* baa; **~ machen** bleat

Mahagoni *n*; -*s*, *kein Pl.* mahagony; **~baum** *m Bot.* mahogany (tree); **~holz** *n* mahogany; **~möbel** *Pl.* mahogany furniture

Maharadscha *m*; -*s*, -*s* maharaja(h); **Maharani** *f*, -, -*s* maharanee

Mahd *f*; -, -*en*; *Dial. Agr.* **1.** (*Mähen*) mowing, hay harvest; **2.** (*Gemähtes*) cut grass, grass cuttings *Pl.*

Mähdrescher *m* combine (harvester)

mähen¹ I. *v/t.* (*Rasen*) mow; (*Gras*) *auch* cut; (*Getreide*) *auch* reap; **II.** *v/i.* mow (the lawn *od.* grass); *Agr.* reap (the corn *etc.*)

mähen² *v/i.* (*blöken*) bleat

Mäher *m*; -*s*, - **1.** *für Gras:* mower; *für Getreide:* reaper; **2.** → **Mähmaschine**; **Mäherin** *f*, -, -*nen* → **Mäher** 1

Mahl *n*; -(*e*)*s*, *Mähler; geh.* meal; **ein festliches ~** a banquet

mahlen I. *v/t.* grind; (*Getreide*) *auch* mill; → **gemahlen; II.** *v/i.* **1.** grind; **wer zuerst kommt, mahlt zuerst** *Sprichw.* first come first served; **2.** *Räder:* spin

Mahlgut *n* grist

mählich *Adv. geh.* gradually

Mahlstein *m* grinding stone

Mahlstrom *m Naut.* maelstrom

Mahl|werk *n Tech.* grinding apparatus; **~zahn** *m Anat.* molar

Mahlzeit *f* meal; **nur zu den ~en erscheinen** only appear at mealtimes; **~!** *ugs.* (*guten Appetit*) bon appétit, enjoy your meal; (*Gruß*) afternoon!; (**na dann**) **prost ~!** *umg.* that's (just) great!; *iro.* that's the end!

Mähmaschine *f für Gras:* mower; *für Getreide:* reaper

Mahn|bescheid *m Jur.* default summons; **~brief** *m* reminder

Mähne *f*; -, -*n* mane (*auch fig. iro.*)

mahnen I. *v/t.* **1.** (*auffordern*) urge, exhort; *warnend:* admonish; **j-n zur Vorsicht** *etc.* **~** urge s.o. to be careful *etc.*; **2.** (*erinnern*) remind (**an** + *Akk.* of) (*auch Schuldner etc.*); **j-n schriftlich ~** send s.o. a (written) reminder; **II.** *v/i.:* **zur Vorsicht/Geduld** *etc.* **~** urge caution/patience *etc.*; **zum Aufbruch ~** insist that it's time to leave; **mahnend I.** *Adj.* admonishing, warning; **~es Wort** word of admonishment (*od.* warning); **II.** *Adv.* in admonishment, in (*od.* as a) warning; **~ den Finger heben** raise a warning (*od.* an admonitory) finger

Mahner *m*; -*s*, -, **~in** *f*; -, -*nen*; *geh.* admonisher

Mahn|gebühr *f* reminder fee; **~mal** *n* memorial; **~ruf** *m auf;fordernd:* exhortation; *warnend:* warning cry; *auch schriftlich:* admonition; **~schreiben** *n* reminder; *an Schuldner: auch* demand for payment, dun(ning notice); **~stätte** *f* memorial site

Mahnung *f* **1.** (*Warnung*) warning, admonition; (*Aufforderung*) exhortation; **2.** (*Erinnerung*) reminder; *Bibliothek: auch* overdue notification

Mahn|verfahren *n Jur.* collection proceedings *Pl.* (*for a debt*); **~wache** *f* vigil

Mähre¹ *f*; -, -*n*; *pej.* (old) nag

Mähre² *m*; -*n*, -*n Moravian;* **Mähren** (*n*); -*s*; *Geog.* Moravia; **Mährin** *f* Moravian (girl *od.* woman); **mährisch** *Adj.* Moravian

Mai *m*; -(*e*)*s*, -*e*, *mst Sg.* May; **der Erste ~** *Feiertag:* May Day; → **April; ~andacht** *f kath.* May Devotions *Pl.;*

~baum *m* maypole; **~blume** *f Bot.* **1.** (*Maiglöckchen*) lily of the valley; **2.** (*Waldmeister*) woodruff; **3.** (*Löwenzahn*) dandelion

Maid *f*; -, -*en*; *altm., noch iro.* maiden

Maidemonstration *f* May Day demonstration

Maiensäß *n*; -*es*, -*e*; *schw. Agr.* springtime (mountain) pasture

Mai|feier *f* May Day celebrations *Pl.;* **~feiertag** *m* May Day; **~glöckchen** *n Bot.* lily of the valley; **~käfer** *m* cockchafer, maybug; **~kundgebung** *f* May Day rally

Mail [meːl] *f*; -, -*s Computer:* e(-)mail

Mailand (*n*); -*s*; *Geog.* Milan

Mailänder¹ *indekl. Adj.* Milanese; **der ~ Dom** Milan Cathedral

Mailänder² *m*; -*s*, -, **~in** *f*; -, -*nen* Milanese

Mailbox ['meːlbɔks] *f Computer, Telef.* mailbox; **mailen** ['meːlən] *vt/i.* e(-)mail

Mailing ['meːlɪŋ] *n*; -(*s*), *kein Pl.; Wirts.* mailing

Mainstream ['meːnstriːm] *m*; -(*s*), *kein Pl.; mst pej.* mainstream

Maiparade *f* May Day parade

Mais *m*; -*es*, -*e*, *mst Sg.; Bot.* maize, *Am.* corn; **~brei** *m* maize (*Am.* corn) porridge; **~brot** *n* cornbread

Maische *f*; -, -*n Bier, Branntwein:* mash; *Wein:* must; **maischen** *v/t. Brauerei, Branntweinherstellung:* mash; *Weinherstellung:* crush

maisfarben *Adj.* corn-colo(u)red

Mais|feld *n* field of maize, *Am.* cornfield; **~flocken** *Pl.* cornflakes

maisgelb *Adj.* corn-colo(u)red

Mais|keimöl *n Gastr.* corn oil; **~kolben** *m* corncob; *Gastr.* corn on the cob; **~korn** *n* grain of maize, *Am.* corn kernel; **~mehl** *n* Indian meal, *Am.* cornmeal

Maison(n)ette [mɛzo'nɛt] *f*; -, -*s*, **~wohnung** *f* maisonette, *bes. Am.* duplex (apartment)

Mais|stärke *f* cornflour, *Am.* cornstarch; **~stroh** *n* corn straw

Maître de Plaisir ['metrə də plɛ'ziːɐ] *m*; -, *Maîtres de Plaisir; hum.* master of ceremonies

Majestät *f*; -, -*en* majesty (*nur Sg. auch fig.*); **Seine/Ihre/ Eure** *od.* **Euer** His/ Her/Your Majesty; **majestätisch I.** *Adj.* majestic; **II.** *Adv.* majestically; **Majestätsbeleidigung** *f bes. iro.* lèse-majesté

Major *m*; -*s*, -*e*; *Mil.* major

Majoran *m*; -*s*, -*e*; *Bot.* marjoram

Majorin *f*; -, -*nen* **1.** *Heilsarmee:* major; **2.** *altm.* major's wife

majorisieren *v/t.* outvote; **Majorisierung** *f* outvoting

Majorität *f*; -, -*en* majority; **die ~ haben** have a majority

Majoritäts|beschluss *m* majority decision; **~prinzip** *n* principle of majority rule; **~wahl** *f* election by a simple majority, *Brit. auch* first-past-the-post election

Majorsrang *m*; *nur Sg.; Mil.* rank of major

Majorz *m*; -*es*, *kein Pl.; schw.* → **Majoritätswahl**

Majuskel *f*; -, -*n*; *Druck.* capital (letter)

MAK *f*; -, -(*s*); *Abk.* (**Maximale Arbeitsplatzkonzentration**); → **MAK-Wert**

makaber *Adj.* macabre; *Witz: auch umg.* sick

Makak *m*; -*s und* -*en*, -*en*; *Zool.* macaque

Makedonien (*n*); -*s*; *Geog.* Macedonia;

M

Makedonier *m*; *-s*, *-*, **Makedonierin** *f*; *-*, *-nen* Macedonian; **makedonisch** *Adj.* Macedonian

Makel *m*; *-s*, *-* **1.** *e-r Ware etc.*: flaw, defect, imperfection, fault; *an Haut, Lackierung, Obst etc.*: blemish; **2.** (*Charakterfehler*) flaw, blemish, taint; **3.** (*Schande*) stigma

Mäkelei *f*, *-*, *-en*; *pej.* fault-finding (*an* + *Dat.* with), carping (at); **mäkelig** *Adj. pej.* fussy, finicky

makellos I. *Adj.* flawless, perfect; *Aussehen*: immaculate; *Aussprache*: *auch* impeccable; *fig. Ruf*: unblemished, spotless; **~e Vergangenheit** blameless past; **II.** *Adv.*: **~ sauber** spotlessly clean; **Makellosigkeit** *f* flawlessness; *im Aussehen*: immaculateness; *Sauberkeit, auch fig. des Rufs*: spotlessness; *fig. des Lebens etc.*: blamelessness

makeln *Wirts. Sl.* **I.** *v/t.* sell as an agent (*Börse*: a broker); **II.** *v/i.* **1.** work as an agent; *an der Börse*: act as a broker; **2.** *Telef.* act as a go-between (*relaying information on the telephone provided by a third person*)

mäkeln *v/i.* find fault (*an* + *Dat.* with)

mäkelsüchtig *Adj.*: **~ sein** be forever finding fault

Make-up [meːkˈʔap] *n*; *-s*, *-s* makeup; **~Unterlage** *f* makeup base

Maki *m*; *-s*, *-s*; *Zool.* true lemur

Makkaroni[1] *Pl.*; *Gastr.* macaroni *Sg.*

Makkaroni[2] *m*; *-(s)*, *-s*, **~fresser** *m*; *-s*, *-*; *umg. pej., neg!* wop, *Am. auch* dago

Makler *m*; *-s*, *-*; *Wirts.* broker; (*Börsenmakler*) stockbroker; (*Grundstücksmakler*) estate agent, *Am.* realtor

Mäkler *m*; *-s*, *-*; *pej.* fault-finder, carper, caviller *förm.*

Makler|büro *n Börse*: broker's office; *von Grundstücksmakler*: estate agent's (*Am.* realtor's) office; **~firma** *f Börse*: (firm of) brokers *Pl.*, brokerage company (*od.* concern); *Grundstücksmakler*: (firm of) estate agents (*Am.* realtors); **~gebühr** *f Börse*: broker's commission; *von Grundstücksmakler*: estate agent's (*Am.* realtor's) fee; **~geschäft** *n Börse*: broker's business, brokerage; *von Grundstücksmakler*: estate agent's (*Am.* realtor's) business

Maklerin *f*, *-*, *-nen* → **Makler**

Mäklerin *f*, *-*, *-nen* → **Mäkler**

Maklerprovision *f Börse*: broker's commission

Makramee *n*; *-(s)*, *-s* macramé

Makrele *f*; *-*, *-n*; *Zool.* mackerel

Makro *m*, *n*; *-s*, *-s* **1.** *Computer*: macro; **2.** *Fot.* macro (lens); **~aufnahme** *f* macro shot; **~befehl** *m Computer*: macro command

Makrobiotik *f* macrobiotics *Pl.* (*V. im Sg.*); **makrobiotisch** *Adj.* macrobiotic

Makro|fotografie *f* macrophotography; **~kosmos** *m* macrocosm

makromolekular *Adj.* macromolecular

Makrone *f*, *-*, *-n*; *Gastr.* macaroon

Makroobjektiv *n Fot.* macro lens

Makroökonomie *f Wirts.* macroeconomics *Pl.* (*V. im Sg.*); **makroökonomisch** *Adj.* macroeconomic

makroskopisch *Adj.* macroscopic

Makro|struktur *f* macrostructure; **~virus** *n*, *m EDV* macro virus

Makulatur *f*, *-*, *-en* **1.** (*Altpapier*) waste paper; *Druck.* spoilage; *weitS.* useless stuff; *umg. fig.* (*Unsinn*) rubbish, *bes. Am.* garbage, trash; *der Produktionsplan für das laufende Jahr ist bereits jetzt* **~** you can already forget about this year's planned output; **2.** *beim Tapezieren*: paper pulp; **~ streichen**

apply a preparatory coat of paper pulp before wallpapering

makulieren *v/t. Druck.* pulp

MAK-Wert *m fachspr.* highest permissible level of pollutants in the workplace

mal *Adv.* **1.** *beim Multiplizieren*: times, multiplied by; *bei Maßangaben*: by; *ein ~ eins ist eins* one times one is one; *zwei ~ sechs ist* (*gleich*) *zwölf* two times (*Brit. auch* twice) six is (*od.* equals, are) twelve; *vier ~ zehn* (*ist ...*) *auch* four tens (are ...); *das Zimmer ist sechs ~ vier Meter / sechs ~ vier* the room is six met|res (*Am.* -ers) by four / six by four; **2.** *umg.*: *guck ~* look; *die Aufmerksamkeit auf etw. lenkend*: here, have a look at this; *komm ~ her* come here a minute(, will you?); *wenn das ~ gut geht* if we're lucky; → *auch einmal*; **3.** *umg.* (*manchmal*) sometimes; *er macht es ~ so, ~ so* he does it differently every time; → *auch einmal*

Mal[1] *n*; *-(e)s*, *-e* time; *dieses eine ~* this once; *jedes ~* every time; *ein paar ~* a few (*umg.* a couple of) times; *ein anderes ~* some other time; *mehrere ~e* several times; *beim ersten ~* the first time; *etw. schaffen etc.*: (*a*) first time (a)round; *beim letzten ~ od. letztes ~* (the) last time; *das nächste ~* next time ([a]round); *zum ersten/zweiten ~* for the first/second time; *das eine oder andere ~* now and then, now and again; *zum wiederholten ~* repeatedly; *von ~ zu ~* every time, all the time; *~ für ~* time after time; *ein einziges ~* just once; *kein einziges ~* not once; *für dieses ~* for now, for the time being; *ein für alle ~(e)* once and for all; *mit einem ~(e)* all of a sudden

Mal[2] *n*; *-(e)s*, *-e und Mäler* **1.** *Pl. mst -e*; (*Kennzeichen*) mark, sign; (*Hautfleck*) mark; (*Muttermal*) birthmark; *fig.* stigma; **2.** *Pl. mst Mäler* (*Ehrenmal*) monument, memorial; **3.** *Pl. -e*; *Spiel*: (*Ablaufpunkt*) start; (*Ziel*) base, home; *Rugby*: (*Tor*) goal; (*Malfeld*) in-goal (area)

Malachit *m*; *-s*, *-e*; *Min.* malachite

Malaie *m*; *-n*, *-n*, **Malaiin** *f*; *-*, *-nen* Malay, *weiblich auch*: Malay(an) woman (*od.* girl); **malaiisch** *Adj.* Malay(an); *die Malaiische Halbinsel* the Malay Peninsula; **Malaiisch** *n*; *-en*; *Ling.* Malay; *das ~e* Malay

Malaise [maˈlɛːzə] *f*; *-*, *-n*, *schw. n*; *-s*, *-s* malaise; *Lage*: unfortunate situation

Malaria *f*; *-*; *kein Pl.*; *Med.* malaria; **~anfall** *m* attack of malaria; **~erreger** *m* malaria parasite; **~gebiet** *n* malaria(l) (*od.* malaria-infested) territory

malariakrank *Adj.*: **~ sein** be suffering from (*od.* have) malaria; **Malariakranke** *m*, *f* malaria patient (*od.* victim)

Malaria|mücke *f* malaria mosquito, anopheles *fachspr.*; **~prophylaxe** *f Medikament*: malaria prophylaxis; *Therapie*: course of malaria tablets

Malaysia (*n*); *-s*; *Geog.* Malaysia; **Malaysier** *m*; *-s*, *-*, **Malaysierin** *f*; *-*, *-nen* Malaysian, *weiblich auch*: Malaysian woman (*od.* girl); **malaysisch** *Adj.* Malaysian

Malbuch *n* colo(u)ring book

Malediven *Pl. Geog.*: *die ~* the Maldives, the Maldive Islands

Malefizkerl *m südd. umg. altm.* **1.** (*Draufgänger*) daredevil; **2.** (*Mistkerl*) wretched fellow

malen I. *v/t.* **1.** paint (*umg. auch Fingernägel etc.*); (*zeichnen*) draw (with

crayons); *fig.* (*beschreiben*) portray, paint, depict; *wie gemalt* like a painting; *etw. rosig ~ fig.* paint a rosy picture of s.th.; **2.** (*wie malend schreiben*) write carefully; **II.** *v/i.* paint; (*zeichnen*) draw; **III.** *v/refl. geh. fig.*: *sich ~* (*sich spiegeln*) be reflected, be mirrored; (*sich zeigen*) show (*auf j-s Gesicht* in s.o.'s face)

Maler *m*; *-s*, *-* painter (*auch Anstreicher*); *Künstler auch*: artist; **~arbeiten** *Pl.* painting *Sg.* (jobs), decorating *Sg.*; **~betrieb** *m* firm of painters and decorators

Malerei *f*, *-*, *-en* **1.** *nur Sg.* painting; **2.** *mst Pl.* painting

Malerfarbe *f* **1.** (*Anstrichfarbe*) house paint; **2.** (*Künstlerfarbe*) artists' colo(u)r

Malerin *f*; *-*, *-nen* (woman) painter (*od.* artist)

malerisch I. *Adj.* **1.** **~e Tätigkeit** work as a painter, artistic work; **~es Talent** artistic (*od.* painterly) talent, talent as a painter (*od.* an artist); **2.** (*pittoresk*) picturesque; **II.** *Adv.* **1.** artistically; **2.** (*pittoresk*) picturesquely; *die Kapelle, ~ in einem Seitental liegend, ...* the chapel, picturesquely situated (*od.* in a picturesque situation) in a side valley, ...

Maler|leinwand *f* artist's canvas; **~meister** *m*, **~meisterin** *f* master painter and decorator

malern *v/i. umg.* go in for painting; *gern ~* like to do a bit of painting

Malgrund *m Kunst* (*Fläche*) grounding; (*Grundiermasse*) *auch* primer

Malheur [maˈløːɐ] *n*; *-s*, *-e und -s*; *umg.*: (*kleines*) *~* (slight) mishap, (little) accident; *das ist doch kein ~!* it's not exactly a disaster, it's not the end of the world

maligne *Adj. Med.* malign

maliziös *Adj.* malicious, spiteful; *~e Bemerkung abfällig*: *auch* snide remark

Mal|kasten *m* paintbox; **~klasse** *f* painting class; **~kreide** *f* artist's chalk; **~kunst** *f* art of painting

Mall[1] *n*; *-(e)s*, *-e*; *Naut., Tech.* template, pattern

Mall[2] [moːl] *f*; *-*, *-s* shopping arcade; (*Einkaufszentrum*) shopping mall

mallen *v/i. Naut.* veer (constantly), keep on changing

Mallorca [maˈjɔrka] (*n*); *-s*; *Geog.* Majorca; **mallorquinisch** [majɔrˈkiːnɪʃ] *Adj.* Majorcan

malnehmen *vt/i.* (*unreg., trennb., hat -ge-*); *Math.* multiply (*mit* by)

Maloche *f*; *-*; *kein Pl.*; *Sl.* (hard) graft, grind *umg.*; *auf ~ sein od. gehen* be slaving (*od.* slogging) away; **malochen** *v/i. Sl.* slave (*od.* slog) away *umg.*; **Malocher** *m*; *-s*, *-*, **Malocherin** *f*; *-*, *-nen*; *umg.* grafter, workhorse

Malpinsel *m* paintbrush

Malstange *f Rugby*: (*Torpfosten*) goal post; (*Querlatte*) crossbar

Malstift *m* crayon

Malstrom *m* → **Mahlstrom**

Malta (*n*); *-s*; *Geog.* Malta

Maltechnik *f* painting technique

Malteser *m*; *-s*, *-*, **~in** *f*; *-*, *-nen* Maltese

Malteser-Hilfsdienst *m etwa* St (*od.* St.) John Ambulance Brigade, *Am. etwa* (voluntary) ambulance service

Malteser|kreuz *n* Maltese cross; **~orden** *m* order of the Knights of St (*od.* St.) John; **~ritter** *m* Knight of St (*od.* St.) John, Knight Hospitaller

maltesisch *Adj.* Maltese; **Maltesisch**

n; -en; Ling. Maltese
malträtieren *v/t.* ill-treat, maltreat; (*Sache*) *auch* treat (*od.* handle) roughly
Malus *m; - und -ses, - und -se* **1.** *Versicherungswesen*: excess (imposed as a result of heavy claims); **2.** *Schulwesen, Sport*: penalty for a better initial position, handicap
Malutensilien *Pl.* painting utensils
Malve *f; -, -n; Bot.* mallow; **malvenfarben** *Adj.* mauve; **Malvengewächs** *n Bot.* plant of the mallow family
Malwinen *Pl. Geog.* Falkland Islands, Falklands
Malz *n; -es, kein Pl.* malt; **~bier** *n* (low-alcohol) malt beer; **~bonbon** *n* malt(-flavo[u]red) sweet (*Am.* candy)
Malzeichen *n Math.* multiplication sign
mälzen *v/i.* malt; **Mälzer** *m; -s, -* maltster; **Mälzerei** *f; -, -en* malthouse; **Mälzerin** *f; -, -nen* maltster
Malz|kaffee *m* malt coffee, coffee substitute (*made from malt*); **~zucker** *m* malt sugar, maltose
Mama *f; -, -s* mummy, *Am.* mommy, momma; *in der Anrede*: Mummy, *Am.* Mommy, Momma; *sagen Sie Ihrer Frau ~ ...* tell your mother (*altm. auch* mama) ...; *als Eigenname*: *an ~s Geburtstag* on Mama's birthday
Mamakind *n* mummy's (*Am.* mommy's) (little) darling
Mamba *f; -, -s; Zool.* mamba; *Schwarze ~* black mamba; *Grüne ~* West African mamba
Mami *f; -, -s → Mama*
Mammographie *f; -, -n; Med.* mammography
Mammon *m; -s, kein Pl.; mst pej.* mammon; *der schnöde ~* filthy lucre
Mammoplastik *f Med.* mammaplasty
Mammut *n; -s, -e und -s; Zool.* mammoth
Mammut|... *im Subst. mst* mammoth, giant; (*von sehr langer Dauer*) marathon; **~bau** *m* mammoth building; **~baum** *m* sequoia; **~film** *m* huge screen epic (*od.* spectacular); **~knochen** *m* mammoth bone; **~konzert** *n* marathon concert; **~programm** *n* huge program(me); *sehr lang*: marathon program(me); **~prozess** *m* marathon trial; **~skelett** *n* mammoth skeleton; **~unternehmen** *n* giant (*od.* mammoth) enterprise
mampfen *vt/i. umg.* munch, chomp
man[1] *unbest. Pron.* **1.** one, you; *~ weiß nie od. ~ kann nie wissen* you never know, you never can tell; *so etwas tut ~ nicht* that isn't done, you just don't do that; *~ darf ja wohl noch fragen* there's no harm in asking, is there?; *ehe man sich's versah* before we knew what was happening; **2.** (*die Leute*) they, people; (*irgendjemand*) somebody; *hat mir gesagt* I've been told, somebody told me; *~ sagt* they say, people say; *~ holte ihn* he was fetched; *~ trägt wieder ... ...* are in again, ... are back in fashion; *heute ist ~ toleranter* there is more tolerance nowadays; **3.** *in Anweisungen*: *~ nehme* take; *~ lasse sich nicht täuschen* don't be deceived; **4.** *statt direkter Anrede*: *hat ~ sich gut erholt?* I hope you're feeling better?
man[2] *Adv. nordd. umg.*: *lass ~ gut sein* forget it!; *denn ~ los!* we'd better be off then
Management ['mɛnɛdʒmənt] *n; -s, -s* **1.** management; **2.** (*das Managen*) management; *e-r Kampagne etc.*: *auch* running; **~beratung** *f* management

consulting
Management-Buy-out ['mɛnɛdʒmənt 'baɪaut] *n; -s, -s; Wirts.* management buyout
managen ['mɛnɛdʒn̩] *v/t.* **1.** *umg.* (*schaffen*) manage, fix; (*deichseln*) *auch* wangle; **2.** *umg.* (*Kampagne etc.*) run; **3.** (*Sportler, Musiker etc.*): *j-n ~* be s.o.'s manager; **Manager** *m; -s, -, * **Managerin** *f; -, -nen* **1.** executive; (*Geschäftsführer[in], Direktor[in]*) manager; *weiblich: altm. auch* manageress; **2.** *Sport, Mus.* manager
Manager|krankheit *f umg.* executive stress; **~typ** *m* management (*od.* executive) type
Manati *m; -s, -s; Zool.* manatee
manch *unbest. Pron.* **1.** *unflektiert*: many a; *~ eine(r)* many (people), many a person; *~ ein Lehrer* many a teacher, quite a few teachers *Pl*; **2.** *adjektivisch*: many, a number of; (*einige*) some; *in ~er Beziehung* in many respects *Pl.*; **3.** *substantivisch* (*Sachen*): (*so*) *~es* a thing or two, (quite) a few things; *in ~em hat er recht* he's right about some things; **4.** *substantivisch* (*Personen*): (*so*) *~er* a number of people, quite a few (people); **manche** *Pl.* a number of people, quite a few (people); (*einige*) some (people)
mancherlei *Adj.* **1.** (*viele*) many, quite a few; (*verschiedene*) various; (*verschiedenartige*) many sorts (*od.* kinds) of; **2.** *substantivisch*: a number of (*od.* quite a few, various) things, many sorts (*od.* kinds) of things
mancherorten, mancherorts *Adv. geh.* in a number of places, in various places
manchmal *Adv.* sometimes; (*gelegentlich*) occasionally
Mandant *m; -en, -en, ~in f; -, -nen; Jur.* client
Mandarin *m; -s, -e; hist.* mandarin
Mandarine *f; -, -n; Bot.* mandarin (orange); *tieforangene Frucht*: tangerine
Mandarinenbaum *m Bot.* mandarin tree; *mit tieforangenen Früchten*: tangerine tree
Mandat *n; -(e)s, -e* **1.** (*Auftrag*) mandate; *Jur., des Anwalts*: brief; **2.** *Parl.* (*Sitz*) seat; *sein ~ niederlegen* resign one's seat
Mandatar *m; -s, -e* **1.** *Jur.* mandatary; **2.** *österr.* (*Abgeordnete*) member of parliament
Mandats|gebiet *n Pol.* mandate, mandated territory; **~macht** *f* mandatory power; **~träger** *m,* **~trägerin** *f* (political) representative; **~verzicht** *m* resignation of a (*sein*: one's) seat
Mandel *f; -, -n* **1.** *Bot.* almond; **2.** *Anat.* tonsil
mandeläugig *Adj.* almond-eyed
Mandel|baum *m Bot.* almond (tree); **~entzündung** *f* tonsillitis
mandelförmig *Adj.* almond-shaped
Mandel|gebäck *n* almond biscuits (*Am.* cookies) *Pl.*; **~kern** *m* almond (kernel); **~kleie** *f* almond meal; **~öl** *n* almond oil
Mandeloperation *f Med.* tonsillectomy; *sich e-r ~ unterziehen* have one's tonsils out, have a tonsillectomy
Mandelsplitter *Pl.* chopped almonds
Mandoline *f; -, -n; Mus.* mandolin
Mandrill *m; -s, -e; Zool.* mandrill
Mandschurei *f; -; Geog.* Manchuria; **mandschurisch** *Adj.* Manchurian
Manege [ma'ne:ʒə] *f; -, -n* (circus) ring
Manen *Pl. Myth.*: *die ~* the manes
mang *Präp. nordd.* among(st)

Mangan *n; -s, kein Pl.; Chem.* manganese; **Manganat** *n; -s, -e; Chem.* manganate
Mangan|erz *n* manganese ore; **~knollen** *Pl.* manganese nodules
mangansauer *Adj. Chem.* manganic; *mangansaures Salz* manganate
Mangel[1] *m; -s, Mängel* **1.** (*Fehler*) defect, fault, flaw; (*Unzulänglichkeit*) shortcoming, imperfection; (*Schwäche*) weakness; *Mängel aufweisen* be flawed, have (its) faults (*od.* shortcomings *od.* imperfections); *e-n ~ beseitigen* remedy a fault (*od.* defect); **2.** *nur Sg.* (*Knappheit*) lack, shortage; *lit.* dearth (*alle*: *an* + *Dat.* of); *auch Med.* deficiency (*an* + *Dat.* in); *aus ~ an* (+ *Dat.*) for lack (*od.* want) of; *~ leiden* suffer hardship (*od.* privation); *→ auch Not*
Mangel[2] *f; -, -n* mangle; *j-n durch die ~ drehen od. in die ~ nehmen umg. fig.* put s.o. through the mill; *bes. bei Prüfungen*: give s.o. a grilling
Mängelanzeige *f* notification of defects
Mangelberuf *m* undermanned profession
Mängelbeseitigung *f* correction of faults
Mangel|ernährung *f Med.* malnutrition; **~erscheinung** *f Med.* deficiency symptom
mangelfrei *Adj.* faultless, free from faults (*od.* defects)
mangelhaft *Adj. Waren*: faulty, defective; *Gedächtnis, Beleuchtung, Qualität*: poor, inadequate; *Leistung, Note etc.*: unsatisfactory, poor; *Wissen*: imperfect, insufficient, inadequate; **Mangelhaftigkeit** *f von Waren*: faultiness, defectiveness; (*schlechte Qualität*) poor quality; *von Beleuchtung, Wissen*: inadequacy; *von Leistung, Note etc.*: unsatisfactory nature
Mängelhaftung *f Wirts., Jur.* liability for defects
Mangelkrankheit *f Med.* deficiency disease
Mängelliste *f* list of faults (*weitS.* complaints)
mangeln[1] **I.** *v/i. unpers.*: *es mangelt an* (+ *Dat.*) there's a lack (*od.* shortage) of; *es mangelt mir an Geld etc.* I'm short of money *etc.*; *es mangelt ihm an Mut* he lacks (*od.* is lacking in) courage; *~des Selbstvertrauen* lack of self-confidence; *wegen ~der Nachfrage* due to inadequate (*od.* lack of) demand; **II.** *v/i. geh.*: *dir mangelt der erforderliche Ehrgeiz etc.* you lack the necessary ambition *etc.*
mangeln[2] *v/t.* (*Wäsche*) mangle
Mängelrüge *f Wirts., Jur.* notification of defects, complaint
mangels *Präp.* for lack (*od.* want) of; *bes. Jur.* in default of; *~ Beweisen auch* in the absence of evidence; *~ Masse Jur.* for lack of assets; *umg.* for lack of money
Mangelware *f* scarce commodity; *~ sein auch umg. fig.* be scarce, be in short supply, be hard to come by; *weitS.* (*selten sein*) be rare
Mangelwäsche *f* laundry for mangling
Mangelwirtschaft *f* economy characterized by constant shortages
Mango *f; -, -s und -onen; Bot.* mango; **~baum** *m* mango tree
Mangold *m; -(e)s, -e, mst Sg.; Bot.* (Swiss) chard
Mangrove *f; -, -n; Geog.* mangrove
Mangrove(n)|küste *f Geog.* mangrove

coastline; **~sumpf** *m* mangrove swamp

Manguste *f*; -, -*n*; *Zool.* mongoose

Manichäer *m*; -*s*, -; *Reli.* Manich(a)ean; **manichäisch** *Adj.* Manich(a)ean; **Manichäismus** *m*; -, *kein Pl.* Manich(a)eism

Manie *f*; -, -*n*; *auch Psych.* mania; (*Besessenheit*) obsession; **zur ~ werden** become an obsession (*bei* with)

Manier *f*; -, -*en* **1.** *mst Sg.* manner; (*Weise*) *auch* way; (*Kunststil*) style; **in gewohnter/bewährter ~** in the usual/well-tried fashion; **in rembrandtscher ~** in the style (*od.* manner) of Rembrandt; → **altbewährt**; **2.** *mst Pl.*; (*Benehmen*) manner(s *Pl.*); **gute/ schlechte ~en haben** have good/bad manners, be well-mannered/bad-mannered; **das sind doch keine ~en!** *umg.* that's no way to behave

maniert I. *Adj.* mannered; (*affektiert*) affected; **II.** *Adv.* in a mannered way; **Manieriertheit** *f e-s Stils*: mannerism; (*Verhaltensart*) mannered behavio(u)r; (*Affektiertheit*) affectation

Manierismus *m*; -, *kein Pl.*; *Kunst, Lit.* mannerism; **Manierist** *m*; -*en*, -*en* mannerist; **manieristisch** *Adj.* mannerist(ic)

manierlich I. *Adj.* well-behaved, well-mannered; *fig. Preise etc.*: decent, acceptable; **II.** *Adv.* properly, decently

manifest *Adj.* manifest; **an etw.** (*Dat.*) **~ werden** be made manifest in s.th.; **Manifest** *n*; -(*e*)*s*, -*e* manifesto; **Manifestant** *m*; -*en*, -*en*, **Manifestantin** *f*; -, -*nen*; *österr., schw.* demonstrator; **Manifestation** *f*; -, -*en* **1.** *Med., Psych.* manifestation; **2.** *österr., schw.* (*Kundgebung*) demonstration; **manifestieren** *v/refl.* manifest itself, become manifest; (*in den Vordergrund treten*) come to the fore; **II.** *v/t.* manifest, show, display

Maniküre *f*; -, -*n* **1.** *nur Sg.* manicure; **2.** (*Person*) manicurist; **maniküren** *vt/i.* manicure

Maniok *m*; -*s*, -*s*; *Bot.* cassava, manioc

Manipulation *f*; -, -*en* manipulation; **manipulativ I.** *Adj.* manipulative; **II.** *Adv.* by manipulation; **Manipulator** *m*; -*s*, -*en* **1.** *Person*: manipulator, fixer; **2.** *Tech., Gerät*: manipulator; **manipulierbar** *Adj.* manipulable; **Manipulierbarkeit** *f* manipulability; **manipulieren** *v/t.* manipulate (*auch Pol.*); (*beeinflussen*) influence; (*Markt, Wahlen etc.*) rig; (*Zahlen, Bericht*) massage; **an dem Gerät ist manipuliert worden** somebody has fiddled with the device; **Manipulierung** *f* manipulation; (*Beeinflussung*) influencing; *von Markt, Wahlen etc.*: rigging; *von Zahlen, Bericht*: massaging

manisch I. *Adj.* manic; **~-depressiv** manic-depressive, *Am. auch* bipolar; **II.** *Adv.* manically

Manitu *m*; -*s*, *kein Pl.* Manitou

Manko *n*; -*s*, -*s* **1.** *Wirts.* deficiency, shortage; (*Fehlbetrag*) deficit, shortfall; **2.** *fig.* (*Nachteil*) shortcoming, drawback; **ein entscheidendes ~** a decisive negative factor

Mann *m*; -(*e*)*s*, *Männer* **1.** man (*Pl.* men); **~ für ~** one after the other; **ein Gespräch von ~ zu ~** unter Männern a man-to-man talk; **ein Kampf gegen ~** a man-to-man (*od.* hand-to-hand) fight; **wie ein ~** (*geschlossen*) as one; *sprechen etc.*: with one voice; **bis auf den letzten ~** to a man; **der dritte ~** *Skat*: the third player; **er ist ein ~**

der Tat he's a man of action; **ein ~ von Welt** a man of the world; → **Bord**[1] **2**, **lieb** I **4**, **selbst** I **1**, **schwarz** I **2**, **stark** I **1**, **tot** 1 b; **2.** *Pl. Mann*; *bes. Naut. und nach Zahlen*: **alle ~ an Deck!** *Naut.* all hands on deck; **mit ~ und Maus untergehen** *Naut.* go down with all hands; **die Maschine hat fünf ~ Besatzung** the aircraft has a crew of five; **alle ~ hoch** *umg.* the whole lot of us (*od.* them); **alle ~ mitmachen!** come on, everyone!; **wir brauchen drei ~** we need three men (*od.* people); **3.** (*Ehemann*) husband; **als od. wie ~ und Frau leben** live as husband and wife; **~ und Frau werden** *geh.* become husband and wife; **4.** *Sport* (*Spieler*) player, man; **freier ~** *Fußball*: free man; **den freien ~ anspielen/suchen** pass to / look for the player in space; **~ decken** *Ballspiele*: mark (*Am.* guard) man-to-man; **5.** *fig., in Wendungen*: **der ~ auf der Straße** the man in the street, the ordinary man; **~s genug sein für etw.** be man enough for (*od.* to do) s.th.; **an den ~ bringen** (*Ware*) find a buyer for; *umg.* (*Witz etc.*) find an audience for; (*Meinung*) get *s.th.* across; **s-n ~ stehen** (*sich behaupten*) hold one's own, stand one's ground; (*ganze Arbeit leisten*) do a fine job; **ein ~, ein Wort** a promise is a promise; **einen kleinen ~ im Ohr haben** *umg.* be off one's rocker; **~ Gottes!** *umg.* for God's sake!; **~!** *umg.* wow!; *auch sich beschwerend: umg.* hey!

Manna *n*; -(*s*), *kein Pl. und f*, -, *kein Pl.*; *bibl. und fig.* manna (from heaven)

Männchen *n*; -*s*, - **1.** little man, manikin; **~ malen** *umg.* draw matchstick men; **2.** *Zool.* male; (*Vogel*) cock; **~ machen** *Tier*: stand on its hind legs; *Hund*: *auch* sit up and beg; *Mil. umg.* snap to attention; *umg. Person*: grovel, bow and scrape

Manndeckung *f* man-to-man marking, *Am.* one-on-one defense; **e-n Spieler in ~ nehmen** mark (*Am.* guard) a player man-to-man (*od.* closely)

Mannen *Pl. hist.* (*Gefolgsleute*) vassals; **seine ~ um sich scharen** *umg. hum.* get the troops to rally (a)round

Mannequin ['manəkɛ̃] *n*; -*s*, -*s* (fashion) model

Männer *Pl.* men; *WC*: Gentlemen, *bes. Am.* Men

Männer|... *im Subst.* men's ..., male ...; **~arbeit** *f* a man's work (*od.* job); **~bekanntschaft** *f* male (*od.* man) friend, boyfriend; **~beruf** *m* male profession; *bei dem Männer vorherrschen*: male-dominated profession; **~chor** *m Mus.* male(-voice) choir; **~fang** *m umg. hum. od. pej.*: **auf ~ ausgehen / aus sein** go after men

männerfeindlich *Adj.* anti-male, *präd. auch* anti-men; **sie ist ~** *auch* she's hostile toward(s) men, she hates men; **Männerfeindlichkeit** *f* hostility toward(s) men, anti-male attitude

Männer|freundschaft *f* friendship between men; **~gesangverein** *m* male choral society; *Chor*: male-voice choir; **~geschichte** *f mst Pl.*; *umg.* affair (with a man); *Pl.* affairs (with men); **~gesellschaft** *f* male(-dominated) society; **~hand** *f* man's hand; **in ~** (*von Männern kontrolliert*) in the hands of men, male-dominated; **~hass** *m* hatred towards men; **~herrschaft** *f*; *nur Sg.*; *mst pej.* male domination, androcracy; **~herz** *n fig.* man's heart; *Pl.*

men's hearts; **~en höher schlagen lassen** set male pulses racing; **~kleider** *Pl.* men's clothes

männerlos *Adj.* ... without (any) men

Männermagazin *n* men's magazine, male-interest magazine

männermordend *Adj. umg. hum.* man-eating

Männer|orden *m* male order; **~rolle** *f* **1.** *Soziol.* man's role; **2.** *Theat. etc.* male part; **~runde** *f* male circle; **~sache** *f* a man's business, men's business; **~station** *f* men's ward; **~stimme** *f* man's voice, *bes. Mus.* male voice; *Pl.* men's voices, *bes. Mus.* male voices; **~überschuss** *m* surplus of men; **~welt** *f*; *nur Sg.* **1.** *e-e* ~ a man's world; **2.** *die* ~ men *Pl.*, the male population; **~wirtschaft** *f umg.* **1.** (all-)male setup; **2.** male household; **~wohnheim** *n* men's hostel

Mannes|alter *n* manhood; **im besten ~** in one's (*od.* his *etc.*) prime, in the prime of life; **~jahre** *Pl.* years (*od.* period *Sg.*) of manhood; **~kraft** *f* manly strength; *bes. sexuell*: virility; **~würde** *f geh.* hono(u)r as a gentleman

mannhaft *Adj.* manly, (*tapfer*) *auch* brave, courageous; (*entschlossen*) resolute; **Mannhaftigkeit** *f* manliness; (*Tapferkeit*) *auch* braveness, courageousness; (*Entschlossenheit*) resoluteness

mannigfach I. *Adj.* (many and) varied, manifold; (*verschiedener Art*) diverse; **II.** *Adv.* in many different ways

mannigfaltig *Adj. geh.* multifarious, manifold; **Mannigfaltigkeit** *f* great diversity

männiglich *unbest. Pron. schw.* everyone

Männlein *n* little man; **~ und Weiblein** *Pl. umg.* men and women; (*Jungen und Mädchen*) boys and girls

männlich *Adj.* male (*auch Bio., Bot.*); *Wesen, Auftreten etc.*, *auch Frau und Ling.*: masculine; (*mannhaft*) manly; **~e Entsprechung** male equivalent; **Männlichkeit** *f* **1.** masculinity; (*Mannhaftigkeit*) manliness; (*auch Potenz*) virility; **2.** *hum.* (*Geschlechtsteile*) private parts *Pl.*, manhood; **Männlichkeitswahn** *m* machismo

Mannomann *Interj. umg.* boy, oh boy

Mannsbild *n bes. südd., österr. umg.* man; **ein stattliches ~** a fine figure of a man

Mannschaft *f*; -, -*en* **1.** *Sport* team, side; **2.** (*Besatzung*) crew; **3.** *fig.* (*Arbeitsteam etc.*) *auch Pol.* team; (*Gruppe*) group (of people); **4.** *Mil.* (*Einheit*) unit; **vor versammelter ~** in front of all the men; *auch fig.* in front of everyone; **~en** enlisted men, other ranks

mannschaftlich *Adj. Sport* ... as a team; **Schalkes Stärke ist die ~e Geschlossenheit** Schalke's strength is that they play together as a team

Mannschafts|arzt *m*, **~ärztin** *f Sport* team doctor; **~aufstellung** *f Sport* (team) line-up; **~dienstgrad** *m Mil.* non-commissioned rank; *Brit. Pl. auch* other ranks; **~fahren** *n*; -*s*, *kein Pl. Radsport*: team racing; **~führer** *m*, **~führerin** *f* (team) captain, *umg.* skipper; **~geist** *m* team spirit; **~kamerad** *m*, **~kameradin** *f Sport* teammate; **~kantine** *f Mil.* other ranks' (*Am.* noncom's) canteen; **~kapitän** *m Sport* (team) captain; *umg.* skipper; **~leistung** *f Sport* team performance; **~messe** *f Naut.* crew's messroom; **~raum** *m Naut.* crew's quarters; **~ren-**

nen *n Radsport*: team race; **~sieger** *m Sport* winning team; **~spiel** *n Sport* **1.** team game; **2.** (*Zusammenspiel*) team play, teamwork; **~sport** *m* team sport; **~stärke** *f* **1.** *Sport* team strength; **2.** *Mil.* personnel; **in ~ ausrücken** march out at full strength; **~wagen** *m* personnel carrier; *der Polizei*: police van; **~wertung** *f Sport* team classification; **~wettbewerb** *m Sport* team event

mannshoch *Adj. und Adv.* as tall as a man, *etwa* six-foot (high)

mannstoll *Adj. umg.* oversexed, nymphomaniac; **Mannstollheit** *f umg.* nymphomania

Mannweib *n pej.* butch type; *sehr stark*: amazon

Manometer I. *n*; *-s, -*; *Tech.* pressure ga(u)ge; **II.** *Interj. umg.* wow!

Manöver *n*; *-s, -* **1.** manoeuvre, *Am.* maneuver; **ein geschicktes ~** *fig.* a clever move; **2.** *Mil.* manoeuvre, *Am.* maneuver, exercise; **ins ~ ziehen** go on manoeuvres (*Am.* maneuvers) *Pl*; **~gelände** *n* area for manoeuvres (*Am.* maneuvers), exercise area; **~kritik** *f fig.* postmortem; **~schaden** *m* damage caused by manoeuvres (*Am.* maneuvers)

manövrierbar *Adj.* → **manövrierfähig**; **manövrieren** *vt/i.* manoeuvre, *Am.* maneuver (*auch Mot. und fig.*); **manövrierfähig** *Adj.* maneuverable; **Manövrierfähigkeit** *f*; *nur Sg.* manoeuvrability, *Am.* maneuverability; **Manövriermasse** *f Geldsumme*: transferable sum; *fig. Menschen*: pawns *Pl.* (*od.* chattels *Pl.*) who can be shoved around; **zur ~ der Politiker werden** *Thema*: become a political football; **manövrierunfähig** *Adj.* unmanoeuvrable, *Am.* unmaneuverable; *durch Beschädigung*: disabled

Mansarde *f* attic; → **Mansardenwohnung, Mansardenzimmer**

Mansarden|dach *n* mansard roof; **~fenster** *n* dormer window; **~wohnung** *f* attic flat (*bes. Am.* apartment); **~zimmer** *n* attic room

Mansch *m*; *-(e)s, kein Pl.; umg. pej.* (*breiiges Essen*) mush; (*Schlamm*) mud; (*Schneematsch*) slush; **manschen** *v/i. umg. pej.* slosh about

Manschette *f*; *-, -n* **1.** cuff; *Tech.* sleeve, collar; *um Blumentöpfe etc.*: frill; **2.** *Sport* (*Würgegriff*) stranglehold; **3.** *umg. fig.*: **~n haben vor** (+ *Dat*) be scared of; **~n bekommen** get the wind up; (*es sich anders überlegen*) get cold feet; **Manschettenknopf** *m* cufflink

Mantel *m*; *-s, Mäntel* **1.** coat; (*Umhang*) cloak; **im ~** in a (*od.* one's) coat, wearing a coat; **gib mir d-n ~ zum Aufhängen**: let me take your coat; **zum Anziehen**: let me help you on with your coat; **2.** *fig.* cloak, mantle; **den ~ des Schweigens über etw. breiten** *od.* **decken** observe a strict silence about s.th.; **den ~ nach dem Wind hängen** swim with the tide, trim one's sails to the wind, *Am.* auch go with the flow; → **Verschwiegenheit**; **3.** *Tech.*, *e-s Rohrs*: jacket; (*Geschossmantel, Reifenmantel*) casing; (*Kabelmantel*) sheath; *einer Glocke*: cope; **4.** *Wirts.* share (*Am.* stock) certificate; **5.** *Math.* curved surface

Mäntelchen *n fig.*: **e-r Sache ein ~ umhängen** gloss over s.th., cover s.th. up; **sich** (*Dat.*) **ein frommes ~ umhängen** play the saint, pretend to be holier than thou

Mantel|futter *n* coat lining; **~gesetz** *n* skeleton law (*providing guidelines for more specific legislation*); **~kleid** *n* coat dress; **~pavian** *m Zool.* hamadryas (baboon), sacred baboon; **~tarif(vertrag)** *m* collective agreement on working conditions; **~tasche** *f* coat pocket; **~tier** *n Zool.* tunicate

Mantel-und-Degen-Stück *n* cloak-and-dagger play

Mantisse *f*; *-, -n*; *Math.* mantissa

Mantsch *m*; *-(e)s, kein Pl.*, **mantschen** *v/i. umg.* → **Mansch, manschen**

Manual¹ *n*; *-s, -e*, **Manuale** *n*; *-(s), -(n)*; *Mus.* manual, keyboard

Manual² ['mɛnjəl] *n*; *-s, -s* (user) manual

manuell I. *Adj.* manual; **II.** *Adv.*: **~ begabt sein** be skilled with one's hands

Manufaktur *f*; *-, -en* **1.** (*Fabrik*) factory; **2.** (*Herstellung*) manufacture, manufacturing; **~waren** *Pl.* piece goods, *Am.* yard goods

Manus *n*; *-, -*; *Abk. österr., schw.* → **Manuskript**

Manuskript *n*; *-(e)s, -e* **1.** *e-s Buches etc.*: manuscript; **2.** *Film, Radio, TV etc.*: script; **3.** *Notizen für Vortrag etc.*: notes *Pl.*; **ohne ~ sprechen** speak without notes; *aus dem Stegreif*: speak extempore (*od.* off the cuff, off the top of one's head); **~abgabe** *f* delivery of the manuscript; **Termin für ~** date for delivery (of manuscript)

Maoismus *m*; *-, kein Pl.*; *Pol.* Maoism; **Maoist** *m*; *-en, -en*, **Maoistin** *f*; *-, -nen* Maoist; **maoistisch** *Adj.* Maoist

Maori¹ *m*; *-(s), -(s)*, *f*; *-, -(s)* Maori, *weiblich auch*: Maori woman (*od.* girl)

Maori² *n*; *-, kein Pl.*; *Ling.* Maori

Mäppchen *n* case; (*Federmäppchen*) pencil case

Mappe *f*; *-, -n* (*Aktentasche*) briefcase; (*Schulmappe*) *auch* school bag; (*Aktenmappe*) folder, file; *große, für Zeichnungen etc.*: portfolio

Mär *f*; *-, -en* **1.** *umg. hum.* (*unwahre Erzählung*) (tall) story, fable; **2.** *altm.* (*Märchen*) fairy tale (*od.* story); **nur e-e fromme ~** *umg.* just an old fairy tale

Marabu *m*; *-s, -s*; *Orn.* marabou

Marabut *m*; *-(s), -(s)* marabout

Maracuja *f*; *-, -s*; *Bot.* passion fruit

Maraschino [maras'ki:no] *m*; *-s, -s*, **~likör** *m* maraschino

Marathon¹ *m*; *-s, -s*; *Sport* marathon

Marathon² *n*; *-s, -s*; *umg.* marathon

Marathon... *im Subst.* marathon ... **...marathon** *n, im Subst.* ... marathon; *Sitzungs~* marathon session; *Verhandlungs~* negotiations *Pl.* of marathon length

Marathon|lauf *m* marathon (race); **~läufer** *m*, **~läuferin** *f* marathon runner; **~radrennen** *n* cycling marathon; **~sitzung** *f* marathon session (*od.* meeting); **~strecke** *f* **1.** marathon route; **2.** marathon distance; **~veranstaltung** *f* event of inordinate length, marathon

March *f*; *-, -en*; *schw.* boundary of a village holding; (*Grenzzeichen*) boundary mark; → **Mark²**

Märchen *n*; *-s, -* **1.** fairy tale (*od.* story); **2.** *fig.* (tall) story, yarn; **erzähl doch keine ~!** *umg.* don't give me that crap!; **~buch** *n* book of fairy tales; **~dichter** *m*, **~dichterin** *f* author of fairy tales; **~dichtung** *f*; *nur Sg.*; *Lit.* fairy tale literature; **~erzähler** *m*, **~erzählerin** *f* teller of fairy tales; *umg.*

fig. storyteller; **~figur** *f* → **Märchengestalt**; **~film** *m* fairy tale film; **~forschung** *f* research into fairy tales; **~gestalt** *f* fairy tale character (*od.* figure)

märchenhaft I. *Adj.* **1.** ... as in a fairy tale, fairytale ...; (*zauberhaft*) magical; *Schönheit*: bewitching; **2.** *umg. fig.* (*toll*) fantastic; **~e Aussichten** fabulous prospects; **II.** *Adv.* ... as in a fairy tale; (*zauberhaft*) magically, bewitchingly; **2.** *umg.* (*toll*) fantastically, fabulously

Märchen|land *n*; *nur Sg.* fairyland, land of fairy tales; **~motiv** *n Lit.* fairytale motif; **~onkel** *m* teller of fairy tales, *TV, Radio*: fairy story presenter; **~prinz** *m* fairytale prince, Prince Charming (*auch fig.*); **~prinzessin** *f* fairytale princess; **~sammlung** *f* **1.** collection of fairy tales; **2.** → **Märchenbuch**; **~schloss** *n* fairytale castle; **~stunde** *f* fairy story time; **~tante** *f* (female) teller of fairy tales, *TV, Radio*: fairy story presenter; **~wald** *m* fairytale forest, magic forest; **~welt** *f* **1.** → **Märchenland**; **2.** *fig.* fairytale world

Marder *m*; *-s, -*; *Zool.* marten; **~fell** *n* marten skin; **~pelz** *m* marten fur

Margarine *f*; *-, kein Pl.* margarine; **~becher** *m* margarine tub

Marge ['marʒə] *f*; *-, -n*; *bes. Wirts.* margin

Margerite *f*; *-, -n*; *Bot.* oxeye daisy; *kultiviert*: marguerite

marginal *Adj.* marginal; **Marginalie** *f*; *-, -n* marginal note; **marginalisieren** *v/t.* marginalize; **Marginalisierung** *f* marginalization

Maria (*f*); *-s od. Mariens, Reli. auch Mariä* (*mit Art. -*), *-s* **1.** *Vorname*: Maria; *englische Entsprechung*: Mary; **2.** *ohne Art.*; *nur Sg.*; *Reli.* (the Virgin) Mary; **Mariä Himmelfahrt** Assumption of the Virgin Mary; (**Jesus,**) **~ und Josef!** *od.* **Jesses ~!** *umg.* good heavens!, *Am. auch* Jesus, Mary and Joseph!

Marianen *Pl. Geog.*: **die Marianen** the Mariana Islands

marianisch *Adj. kirchl.* Marian

Marien|bild *n* picture of the Virgin Mary; **~dichtung** *f Lit.* Marian literature; **~käfer** *m Zool.* ladybird, *Am. auch* ladybug; **~kult** *m mst pej.* → **Marienverehrung**; **~leben** *n Lit. und Kunst* life of the Virgin Mary; **~statue** *f* statue of the Virgin Mary; **~verehrung** *f* worship of the Virgin Mary; *pej.* Mariolatry

Marihuana *n*; *-s, kein Pl.* marijuana; *Sl.* pot, weed

Marille *f*; *-, -n*; *österr., Bot.* apricot

Marillen|geist *m* apricot brandy; **~knödel** *m österr., Gastr.* apricot dumpling; **~konfitüre** *f*, **~marmelade** *f* apricot jam

Marimba *f*; *-, -s*; *Mus.* marimba

marin *Adj.* marine

Marinade *f*; *-, -n*; *Gastr.* marinade

Marine *f*; *-, -n*; *Naut.* (*Kriegsmarine*) navy; (*Handelsmarine*) merchant navy (*Am.* marine); **~artillerie** *f Mil.* naval artillery; **~attaché** *m* Naval Attaché; **~basis** *f Mil.* naval base

marineblau *Adj.*, **Marineblau** *n* navy (blue)

Marine|flieger *m Mil.* naval pilot; **~infanterie** *f* marines *Pl.*; **~infanterist** *m* marine; **~luftwaffe** *f* naval air force; *in GB*: Fleet Air Arm; *in den USA*: Navy Air Force; **~offizier** *m* naval officer; **~soldat** *m Mil.* marine, member of the marines; **~streitkräfte** *Pl.* naval forces; navy *Sg.*; **~stützpunkt** *m* naval base; **~truppen** *Pl.* marines; **~uniform** *f* naval uniform

marinieren *v/t. Gastr.* marinate

Marionette *f*; -, -*n*; *auch fig.* marionette, puppet; **marionettenhaft I.** *Adj.* puppet-like; **II.** *Adv.* like a puppet

Marionetten|regierung *f* puppet government; **~spiel** *n* puppet show; **~spieler** *m*, **~spielerin** *f* puppeteer; **~theater** *n* puppet theat|re (*Am.* -er)

maritim *Adj.* maritime

Mark[1] *n*; -(*e*)*s*, *kein Pl.*; (*Knochenmark*) marrow; *von Früchten etc.*: pulp; *im Stängel etc.*: pith; *fig.* (*Innerstes*) *auch* core; **kein ~ in den Knochen haben** be feeble (*umg.* wimpish), have no get--up-and-go; **j-m das ~ und Bein gehen** *fig.* set s.o.'s teeth on edge; **j-n bis ins ~ treffen** cut s.o. to the quick; **faul** *od.* **verderbt bis ins ~** rotten to the core

Mark[2] *f*; -, -*en*; *hist.* march; **die ~ Brandenburg** the Mark (of) Brandenburg; **die ~en** (*Landschaft in Italien*) the Marches

Mark[3] *f*; -, - *und umg. hum. Märker*; *hist.* (*Münze und Währung*) mark; **Deutsche ~** German mark, deutschmark; **zehn ~** ten marks; **jede ~ umdrehen** (*müssen*) *umg. fig.* (have to) count every penny; → **müde I**

markant *Adj.* (*auffallend*) striking (*auch Gesichtszüge, Persönlichkeit, Beispiel etc.*); (*hervorstechend*) prominent; (*klar umrissen, ausgeprägt*) *Stil etc.*: clear-cut; (*eigenwillig*) distinctive; (*markig*) pithy; (*charaktervoll*) full of character

markdurchdringend I. *Adj. Schrei etc.*: bloodcurdling; **II.** *Adv.*: **~ schreien** let out a bloodcurdling scream (*od.* bloodcurdling screams)

Marke *f*; -, -*n* **1.** (*Fabrikat*) make, type; *bes.* (*Automarke*) *auch* marque; (*Sorte*) brand, sort; (*früher: Warenzeichen*) trademark; **2.** (*Zettel*) ticket; (*Bon für Essen etc.*) voucher; (*Lebensmittelmarke*) coupon; (*Briefmarke, Rabattmarke*) stamp; (*Erkennungsmarke*) (identification) tag (*e-s Polizisten*: badge); **3.** (*Messpunkt*) mark; (*Menge, Entfernung etc.*) figure; (*Rekord*) record; **4.** *umg.* (*Person*) odd character; **du bist mir e-e ~!** you're a fine one!

Märke *f*; -, -*n*; *österr.* laundry mark; **märken** *v/t. österr.* (*Wäsche*) mark

Marken|album *n* stamp album; **~artikel** *m* branded (*Am.* brand-name) article; *Pl.* branded (*Am.* brand-name) goods; **~artikler** *m Wirts.* branded company, seller of branded (*Am.* brand-name) goods; **~bewusstsein** *n* brand awareness; **~butter** *f* best quality butter; **~erzeugnis** *n*, **~fabrikat** *n* branded (*Am.* brand-name) product; **~heftchen** *n umg.* stamp book; **~name** *m* trade (*od.* brand) name; **~piraterie** *f* brand-name piracy; **~produkt** *n* branded (*Am.* brand-name) product; **~sammlung** *f* stamp collection; **~schutz** *m Jur.* trademark protection; **~treue** *f* brand loyalty; **~ware** *f* branded (*Am.* brand-name) article (*Pl.* goods); **~zeichen** *n auch fig.* trademark

Marker *m*; -*s*, - **1.** *Ling.*, *Gnt.* marker; **2.** (*Stift*) marker pen

markerschütternd *Adj.* bloodcurdling

Marketender *m*; -*s*, -; *hist.* sutler; **Mar-**

ketenderin *f*; -, -*nen*; *hist.* (woman) sutler

Marketing *n*; -(*s*), *kein Pl.*; *Wirts.* marketing; **~abteilung** *f* marketing department; **~instrument** *n* marketing tool; **~konzept** *n* marketing concept; **~strategie** *f* marketing strategy

Markgraf *m hist.* margrave; **Markgräfin** *f* margravine; **markgräflich** *Adj.* ... of a (*od.* the) margrave; **Markgrafschaft** *f* margrav(i)ate

markieren I. *v/t.* **1.** (*kennzeichnen*) mark; **2.** (*hervorheben*) accentuate, underline; **3.** (*vortäuschen*) act, play, pretend to be; (*Krankheit etc.*) feign; **den starken Mann ~** (try to) act tough; **den Dummen ~** play the fool; **4.** *Sport* (*decken*) mark; (*e-n Treffer*) score; **5.** *österr.* (*entwerten*) cancel; **II.** *v/i.* (*vortäuschen*) pretend, act, pose; **sie markiert nur** she's putting it on; **Markierstein** *m* → **markieren**; **markiert I.** *P.P.* → **markieren**; **II.** *Adj.* **1.** *auch Wanderweg etc.*: marked; **bitte die ~en Wege nicht verlassen!** *Schild in Naturschutzgebiet*: please remain on the marked paths; **2.** (*gestellt*) put-on, sham; **Markierung** *f* marking; (*Zeichen*) mark

Markierungs|fähnchen *n Sport* (course) marker; **~linie** *f* (marked) line; **~punkt** *m* mark

markig *Adj.* pithy; *Worte: auch* strong; *Stimme, Wein*: powerful; **~e Sprüche machen** use strong words

märkisch *Adj.* ... of the Mark (of) Brandenburg; *Mensch, Gericht*: ... from the Mark (of) Brandenburg

Markise *f*; -, -*n* awning, *Brit. auch* sun blind

Mark|klößchen *n Gastr.* bone marrow dumpling; **~knochen** *m* marrowbone

Markscheide *f Bergb.* (mining area) boundary

Markstein *m* boundary stone; *fig.* landmark, milestone

Markstück *n hist.* (one-)mark piece

Markt *m*; -(*e*)*s*, *Märkte* **1.** *Verkaufsveranstaltung*: market; (*Marktplatz*) marketplace; *bestimmten Platz*: market square; **auf dem ~** at the market; **auf den ~ gehen** go to the market; **morgen ist ~** there's a market tomorrow, tomorrow is market day; **2.** *Wirts.* (*Absatzgebiet, Wirtschaftsbereich*) market; **freier/inländischer/schwarzer ~** free/home/black market; **auf dem ~** in (*od.* on) the market; **auf den ~ bringen** (put on the) market; **auf den ~ kommen** come on(to) the market; **der ~ für Elektrowaren** the market in electrical goods, the electrical goods market; → **gemeinsam I 1; 3.** *Fin.* (*Geldmarkt etc.*) market; **4.** (*Supermarkt*) supermarket; **5.** (*Jahrmarkt*) fair; **~absprache** *f Wirts.* marketing agreement; **~analyse** *f* market analysis; **~anteil** *m* share of the market, market share

marktbeherrschend *Adj. Wirts.* dominant in the market, market-dominant; **~ sein** *auch* control the market; **~e Stellung** dominant market position; **Marktbeherrschung** *f* control of the market, market control

Markt|beobachter *m*, **~beobachterin** *f Wirts.* market observer (*od.* analyst); **~bereinigung** *f* market cleansing; **~bericht** *m Wirts.* market report; **~bude** *f* market stall; **~chancen** *Pl. Wirts.* sales opportunities; **~entwicklung** *f Wirts.* market trend; **~erfolg** *m Wirts.* success on the market, sales success

marktfähig *Adj. Wirts.* marketable, sal(e)able

Markt|fahrer *m*, **~fahrerin** *f österr.*, *schw.* itinerant market trader, *Am.* hawker; **~flecken** *m* (small) market town

Marktforscher *m*, **~in** *f Wirts.* market researcher; **Marktforschung** *f* market research

Marktfrau *f* market woman, (woman) market trader (*Am.* vendor)

marktführend *Adj.* market-leading; **Marktführer** *m*, **Marktführerin** *f Wirts.* market leader; **Marktführerschaft** *f Wirts.* market leadership

markt|gängig *Adj.* **1.** *Wirts.* marketable, sal(e)able; *Preis*: current; **2.** (*üblich*) usual; **~gerecht I.** *Adj.* geared to market requirements; **~er Preis** right price for the market; **II.** *Adv.* in line with market requirements

Markt|halle *f* covered market; **~händler** *m*, **~händlerin** *f* market trader (*Am.* vendor); **~lage** *f Wirts.* market conditions *Pl.*; **~leiter** *m*, **~leiterin** *f* supermarket *etc.* manager; **~lücke** *f Wirts.* gap in the market; **~nische** *f Wirts.* (market) niche; **~ordnung** *f Wirts.* market regulations *Pl.*

marktorientiert *Adj. Wirts.* geared to market conditions

Markt|platz *m* marketplace, market square (*auch als Anschrift*); **~preis** *m* market price; *Tarif*: market rate; **~recht** *n hist.* right to hold a market

marktreif *Adj. Wirts.* ready to launch; (*marktfähig*) marketable; **Marktreife** *f* marketability

Marktschreier *m*, **~in** *f* oft pej. stallholder crying his *bzw.* her wares; *fig.* (*Propagandamacher[in]*) strident propagandist; **marktschreierisch** *Adj. fig. pej.* vociferous, loud

Markt|schwankungen *Pl. Wirts.* market fluctuations; **~segment** *n Wirts.* market sector; **~stand** *m* market stall; **~stellung** *f* market position; **~studie** *f Wirts.* market study (*od.* analysis); **~tag** *m* market day; **~übersicht** *f Wirts.* market survey

marktüblich *Adj. Wirts.* customary in the market; **~e Mieten/Preise** rents at the market rate / (customary) market prices

Markt|weib *n umg.*, *mst pej.* market woman; **schreien wie ein ~** shout like a fishwife; **~wert** *m Wirts.* (current) market value, commercial value

Marktwirtschaft *f* market economy; **freie ~** free market; *als Prinzip: auch* free enterprise; **soziale ~** social market economy; **marktwirtschaftlich I.** *Adj.* free-market ...; **II.** *Adv.* on free-market lines

Markusevangelium *n bibl.*: **das ~** (the Gospel of *od.* according to) St (*od.* St.) Mark, St (*od.* St.) Mark's Gospel

Marmarameer *n Geog.* Sea of Marmara

Marmelade *f*; -, -*n* jam; *von Zitrusfrüchten*: marmalade

Marmelade(n)|brot *n* jam (*Am. auch* jelly) sandwich, *Brit. Dial. auch* jam butty; **~glas** *n* jam (*Am. auch* jelly) jar

Marmor *m*; -*s*, -*e* marble

Marmor|bild *n* marble statue; **~block** *m* block of marble; **~bruch** *m* marble quarry

marmorieren *v/t.* marble; **Marmorierung** *f* marbling, marbled pattern

Marmorkuchen *m Gastr.* marble cake

marmorn *Adj. geh.* marble ... (*auch*

fig.); (*aus Marmor hergestellt*) (made) of marble; **~e Blässe** *fig.* ashen pallor

Marmor|platte *f* marble slab; (*Tischplatte*) marble top; **~säule** *f* marble column; **~statue** *f* marble statue; **~tisch** *m* marble-top table; **~treppe** *f* marble staircase; *vor der Haustür:* marble steps *Pl.*

marode *Adj.* **1.** *Wirtschaft etc.:* ailing; *Gesellschaft:* degenerate, rotten (to the core) (*von* with); **2.** (*erschöpft*) washed out, whacked, *Am.* bushed

Marodeur [maroˈdøːɐ̯] *m; -s, -e; Mil.* marauding looter; **marodieren** *v/i.* maraud and loot

Marokkaner *m; -s, -, ~in f; -, -nen* Moroccan, *weiblich auch:* Moroccan woman (*od. girl etc.*); **marokkanisch** *Adj.* Moroccan; **Marokko** (*n*); *-s; Geog.* Morocco

Marone *f; -, -n; Bot.* **1.** (*Esskastanie*) (sweet) chestnut; **2.** *Pilz:* cep

Maronenröhrling *m Bot.* cep

Maroni *f; -, -; südd., österr.* → **Marone** 1; **Maronibrater** *m; -s, -,* **Maronibraterin** *f; -, -nen; österr.* chestnut roaster

Marotte *f; -, -n;* (*Eigenart*) (strange) quirk; *vorübergehende:* fad

Marquis [marˈkiː] *m; -, -* marquis; **Marquise** [marˈkiːzə] *f; -, -n* marquise

Marroni *f; -, -; schw.* → **Marone** 1

Mars *m; -, kein Pl.; Astron. und Myth.* Mars

Marsbewohner *m* Martian

marsch *Interj. Mil.:* **vorwärts, ~!** forward march!; **~!** (*mach schnell!*) hurry up!; *umg.* get a move on!, chop, chop!; **~ ins Bett!** *umg.* off to bed with you!; **~ an die Arbeit!** *umg.* come on, get cracking!

Marsch¹ *m; -(e)s, Märsche* **1.** *Mil.* march; *weitS.* (hard) walk; *längerer:* hike, trek; **2.** (*das Marschieren*) marching; **sich in ~ setzen** march (*od.* move) off; *fig. auch* set out (*od.* off); *j-n/etw.* **in ~ setzen** *fig.* get s.o./s.th. moving; **3.** *Mus.* march; **j-m den ~ blasen** *umg. fig.* haul s.o. over the coals

Marsch² *f; -, -en; Geog.* (*Land*) *fertile, low-lying land behind the dikes, etwa* fen, Marsch

Marschall *m; -s, Marschälle; hist. und Mil.* marshal; **~stab** *m* (field) marshal's baton

Marschbefehl *m Mil.* marching orders *Pl.*

marschbereit *Adj. Mil.* ready to march; **Marschbereitschaft** *f:* **in ~ sein** be ready to march

Marschboden *m Geol., Geog.* fertile soil of the Marsch

Marschflugkörper *m Mil.* cruise missile

Marschgepäck *n Mil.* field kit

marschieren *v/i.* **1.** *Mil.* march (*auch ~ lassen*); **2.** (*spazieren*) walk; *über längere Strecke:* hike, trek; (*entschlossen schreiten*) stride, march (**nach, zu** off to); **3.** *umg. fig.:* **die Sache marschiert** things are moving along nicely

Marschierer *m; -s, -, ~in f; -, -nen* marcher

Marschkolonne *f Mil.* marching column

Marschland *n Geog.* → **Marsch²**

Marschlied *n* marching song

marschmäßig I. *Adj.* **1.** *Ausrüstung etc.:* for a march, for marching; **2.** *Mus.* march(-)like; **II.** *Adv. Mil.:* **~ ausgerüstet sein** be kitted out (*Am.* be outfitted) for a march

Marsch|musik *f* military marches *Pl.*; **~ordnung** *f Mil.* march formation;

~rhythmus *m Mus.* march rhythm; **~richtung** *f* **1.** *Mil.* direction of march; **2.** *fig.* line of approach; **~route** *f* **1.** *Mil.* route of the march; **2.** *fig.* line of approach; **~schritt** *m* marching step; **~tempo** *n* **1.** marching pace; **2.** *Mus.* march tempo; **~verpflegung** *f Mil.* marching rations *Pl.*; *fig.* provisions *Pl.* (for the road); **~ziel** *n Mil.* destination of the march

Mars|männchen *m umg.*, **~mensch** *m* Martian; **~sonde** *f Raumf.* Mars probe

Marstall *m* (royal) stables *Pl.*

Marter *f; -, -n; geh.* torture; *fig. auch* ordeal, torment; **Marterinstrument** *n* instrument of torture

Marterl *n; -s, -n; südd., österr.* wayside shrine

martern *v/t. geh.* torture; *fig. auch* torment

Marter|pfahl *m* stake; **am ~ sterben** die at the stake; **~tod** *m geh.* death by torture; (*Märtyrertod*) martyr's death; **~werkzeug** *n* instrument(s *Pl.*) of torture

martialisch *Adj.* martial

Martins|fest *n* Martinmas; **~gans** *f* Martinmas goose; **~horn** *n* siren (*of an emergency service vehicle*); **~tag** *m* St (*od.* St.) Martin's Day, Martinmas

Märtyrer *m; -s, -, ~in f; -, -nen* martyr; **j-n/sich zum Märtyrer machen** *auch iro.* make a martyr of s.o./o.s.

Märtyrertod *m* martyr's death; **den ~ sterben** die a martyr's death, die a martyr

Märtyrertum *n; -s, kein Pl.* martyrdom

Märtyrin *f; -, -nen* (female) martyr

Martyrium *n; -s, Martyrien* martyrdom; **ein einziges ~** *fig.* one long torment (*od.* ordeal), hell on earth

Marxismus *m; -, kein Pl.* Marxism; **Marxismus-Leninismus** *m* Marxism-Leninism; **Marxist** *m; -en, -en,* **Marxistin** *f; -, -nen* Marxist; **marxistisch** *Adj.* Marxist

März *m; -(es), -e, mst Sg.* March; → **April**

Märzbecher *m Bot.* → **Märzenbecher**

Märzen *n; -, -; Abk.* → **Märzenbier**

Märzen|becher *m Bot.* spring snowflake; **~bier** *n* strong dark beer

Marzipan *n; österr. m; -s, -e* marzipan; **~brot** *n* marzipan loaf; **~kartoffel** *f* marzipan ball; **~torte** *f* cake with a filling and topping of marzipan

März|revolution *f nur Sg.; hist.:* **die ~** the March Revolution (of 1848); **~sonne** *f; nur Sg.* March sunshine

Mascara [masˈkaːra] *f; -, -s Kosmetik:* mascara

Masche *f; -, -n* **1.** (*beim Stricken*) stitch; *im Netz:* mesh; (*Laufmasche*) ladder, *bes. Am.* run; **durch die ~n des Gesetzes schlüpfen** *fig.* find a loophole in the law; **j-m durch die ~n gehen** slip through s.o.'s hands (*od.* fingers), give s.o. the slip; **2.** *umg.* (*Trick*) trick, ploy; (*Modeerscheinung*) fad, craze; **es mit der sanften ~ versuchen** try a bit of soft soap (**bei j-m** with s.o.); **komm mir nicht mit 'der ~!** don't try that one on me; **das ist 'die ~!** that's the way; **die ~ raushaben** have got the hang of it; **3.** *österr., schw.* (*Schleife*) bow

Maschendraht *m* wire netting; **~zaun** *m* wire-netting fence

Maschen|netz *n* network; **~werk** *n* netting

Mascherl *n; -s, -n; österr.* (*Fliege oder Zierschleife als Krawattenalternative*)

bow tie

Maschine *f; -, -n* **1.** *Tech.* machine; **2.** *umg.* (*Motor*) engine; **3.** *umg.* (*Motorrad*) machine; **4.** *Flug.* (*Flugzeug*) plane; **5.** (*Schreibmaschine*) typewriter; **~ schreiben** type; **gut/schlecht ~ schreiben** be a good/bad (*od. umg.* hopeless) typist, be good / not very good (*od. umg.* hopeless) at typing → **Nähmaschine, Waschmaschine**

maschinegeschrieben *Adj.* typewritten, typed

maschinell I. *Adj.* machine ...; **II.** *Adv.* by machine, machine-...; **~ bearbeiten** machine; **~ hergestellt** machine-made

Maschinenantrieb *m* machine drive; **mit ~** machine-driven

Maschinenbau *m; nur Sg.; Tech.* mechanical engineering; **Maschinenbauingenieur** *m*, **Maschinenbauingenieurin** *f* mechanical engineer

Maschinen|fabrik *f Tech.* engineering works *Pl.* (*auch V. im Sg.*); **~führer** *m*, **~führerin** *f* machine operator

maschinen|geschrieben *Adj.* typewritten, typed; **~gestrickt** *Adj.* machine-knitted

Maschinen|gewehr *n* machine gun; **~halle** *f* machine shop; **~haus** *n* engine (*od.* power) house; *e-s Kraftwerks:* turbine house (*od.* room); *Naut., e-s Schiffes:* engine room; **~laufzeit** *f Tech.* running time for machinery

maschinenlesbar *Adj. EDV* machine-readable

Maschinen|meister *m*, **~meisterin** *f* machine minder (*Am.* tender); *Theat.* stage machinist; **~öl** *n* machine (*od.* lubricating) oil; **~park** *m Tech., Koll.* machinery; **~pistole** *f* submachine gun; **~raum** *m Tech.* engine room; **~schaden** *m Tech.* mechanical breakdown; *Mot., Naut., Flug.* engine trouble; **~schlosser** *m*, **~schlosserin** *f* machine fitter; *für Motoren:* engine fitter

Maschinenschreiben *n; kein Pl.* typewriting, typing; *als Fähigkeit:* typing ability, typewriting skills *Pl.*

Maschinenschrift *f* typescript; **in ~** typewritten; **maschinenschriftlich I.** *Adj.* typewritten; **II.** *Adv.* in typewritten form, in typescript

Maschinen|stürmer *m hist., fig.* machine wrecker; **~stürmerei** *f; -, kein Pl.; hist., fig.* machine wrecking; **~wäsche** *f* **1.** *das Waschen:* washing in the washing machine; **2.** *Wäsche:* machine-washed laundry; **~zeitalter** *n* machine age

Maschinerie *f; -, -n* machinery (*auch fig.*)

Maschinist *m; -en, -en, ~in f; -, -nen* **1.** machine operator (*od.* minder); **2.** *Naut.* chief engineer; *Eisenb.* engine driver, *Am.* engineer

maschinschreiben *v/i* (*unreg., untr., hat -ge-*); *österr.* type; **maschinschriftlich** *Adj. österr.* → **maschinenschriftlich**

Maser¹ *f; -, -n im Holz:* vein; **feine ~n** fine grain *Sg.*

Maser² [ˈmeːzɐ] *m; -s, -; Phys.* maser

Maserholz *n* veined wood

masern *v/t.* grain; vein

Masern *Pl. Med.* measles *Sg.*

Maserung *f im Holz:* grain; *in Marmor:* veins *Pl.*

Maske *f; -, -n* **1.** mask (*auch Med., Fot., Computer, Schutzmaske, Maskierter*); *fig.* mask, guise; **ihr Gesicht**

wurde zur ~ *fig.* her face became inscrutable; *in od. hinter der* ~ (+ *Gen.*) in the guise of; *die* ~ *fallen lassen* show one's true face, drop one's mask; **2.** *Theat.* make-up; *in* ~ (fully) made up; ~ *machen auch umg. hum.* (*sich schminken*) put on (one's) make-up; **3.** *bes. TV* (*Schminkraum*) make-up room

Masken|ball *m* masked ball; (*Kostümball*) fancy-dress (*Am.* costume) ball; ~**bildner** *m; -s, -,* ~**bildnerin** *f; -, -nen* make-up artist

maskenhaft *Adj.* mask(-)like; (*starr, ausdruckslos*) inscrutable, expressionless

Masken|spiel *n Theat.* masque; ~**verleih** *m* fancy dress (*Am.* costume) hire; ~**zug** *m* fancy dress (*Am.* costume) procession; *beim Karneval:* carnival procession; ~**zwang** *m; nur Sg.* requirement to wear a mask; *auf Einladung etc.:* „~" masks will be worn

Maskerade *f; -, -n* **1.** (*Verkleidung*) costume; **2.** (*Fest*) masquerade, masked ball; **3.** *fig.* masquerade; ~ *sein* be a preten|ce (*Am.* -se)

maskieren I. *v/t.* (*verkleiden*) dress up; (*verdecken*) disguise, conceal; **II.** *v/refl.* dress up; (*sich unkenntlich machen*) disguise o.s.; (*e-e Maske aufsetzen*) put on a mask; **Maskierung** *f* **1.** (*Vorgang*) dressing up; **2.** *konkret:* disguise; (*Gesichtsmaske*) mask

Maskottchen *n* mascot

maskulin *Adj.* masculine; **Maskulinum** *n; -s, Maskulina; Ling.* masculine

Masochismus *m; -, kein Pl.* masochism; **Masochist** *m; -en, -en,* **Masochistin** *f; -, -nen* masochist; **masochistisch I.** *Adj.* masochistic; **II.** *Adv.* masochistically

maß *Imperf.* → *messen*

Maß¹ *n; -es, -e* **1.** (*Maßeinheit*) measure, unit of measurement; ~*e und Gewichte* weights and measures; **2.** *Pl.* (*Körpermaße*) measurements; *e-s Zimmers, Kartons etc.:* auch dimensions; *j-m* ~ *nehmen* take s.o.'s measurements; *etw. nach* ~ *anfertigen lassen Kleidung:* have s.th. made to measure; *Möbel etc.:* have s.th. made to fit (*od.* custom-made); **3.** *fig.: das* ~ *ist voll* enough is enough; *stärker:* I've had just about all I can take; *um das* ~ *voll zu machen* to cap it all; *das* ~ *aller Dinge lit.* the measure of all things; *das* ~ *überschreiten* overstep (*od.* overshoot) the mark; → *zweierlei;* **4.** (*Ausmaß*) extent, degree; *ein gerüttelt* ~ (*an*) *geh.* a fair measure of; *ein hohes* ~ *an* (+ *Dat.*) *od.* von a high degree (*od.* measure) of; *in hohem* ~*e* to a great (*od.* high) degree, highly; *in gleichem* ~*e* to the same extent; *in zunehmendem* ~*e* increasingly, to an increasing extent; *in dem* ~*e, dass ...* to such an extent that ...; *in dem* ~*e, wie sich die Lage verschlechtert, steigt die Zahl der Flüchtlinge* as the situation worsens, the number of refugees rises accordingly; *in besonderem* ~*e* especially; *in beschränktem* ~*e* to a limited extent (*od.* degree); *auf ein vernünftiges* ~ *reduzieren* reduce to an acceptable level; *über alle* ~*en* exceedingly, ... beyond all measure; **5.** (*Mäßigung*) moderation; ~ *halten* be moderate; *im Essen/Trinken etc.* ~ *halten* be a moderate eater/drinker *etc.*, eat/drink *etc.* in moderation; *ohne* ~ *und Ziel* immoderately; *weder* ~ *noch Ziel kennen* know no bounds; *in*

~*en trinken etc.* drink *etc.* in moderation (*od.* moderately); → *Messbecher, Metermaß etc.*

Maß² *f; -, -(e)*; *bayrisch, österr.* litre (*Am.* liter) (of beer); *drei* ~ (*Bier*) three litres (*Am.* liters) of beer

Massage [ma'saːʒə] *f; -, -n* massage; ~**gerät** *n* massager; ~**praxis** *f* masseur's practice; ~**salon** *m auch euph.* massage parlo(u)r; ~**stab** *m* vibrator

Massaker *n; -s, -* massacre; *ein* ~ *anrichten* carry out a massacre; **massakrieren** *v/t.* massacre, slaughter

Maß|anfertigung *f* **1.** *nur Sg.; von Kleidung:* making to measure, (custom) tailoring; *von Möbeln etc.:* custom construction; *das Hemd ist* ~ the shirt is made to measure (*Am.* custom-made); **2.** (*Kleidungsstück*) made-to-measure (*od.* tailor-made, *Am.* custom-made) item; (*Möbel etc.*) specially-made (*od.* custom-made *od.* custom-built) item; ~**angabe** *f* measurements *Pl.* given; *Anzeige:* indication of size, measurements *Pl.*; ~**anzug** *m* made-to-measure (*od.* tailor-made, *Am.* custom-made) suit; ~**arbeit** *f* **1.** → *Maßanfertigung;* **2.** *fig. sehr genau:* precision work (*od.* job)

Masse *f; -, -n* **1.** (*Materie, ungeformter Stoff*) mass; **1.** *umg.* (*große Menge von*) masses (*od.* loads) *Pl.* of; *von Dingen:* auch umg. heaps (*od.* piles) of; *sie kommen in* ~*n* they come in droves; *... in* ~*n* masses of ..., *Dinge:* auch loads (*od.* heaps, piles) of ...; *die* ~ *bringt's* it's quantity that counts; **3.** (*Großteil*) bulk, majority; **4.** (*Menschenmasse*) crowd, mass of people; *die breite* ~ the great mass of the population; *die arbeitende* ~ the working masses *Pl.*; **5.** *Etech.* earth, *Am.* ground; *etw. an* ~ *legen* earth (*Am.* ground) s.th.; **6.** (*Brei*) mixture, (*Mischung*) compound; **7.** *Phys.* mass; **8.** *Jur.* → *Erbmasse, Konkursmasse etc.*; → *mangels*

Maß|einheit *f* unit of measure (*od.* measurement); ~**einteilung** *f* calibrations *Pl.*

Massekabel *n* earth (*Am.* ground) cable

Massel *m; -s, kein Pl.; Sl.* (good) luck; (*e-n*) ~ *haben* be dead lucky

masselos *Adj.* **1.** *Etech.* unearthed, *Am.* ungrounded; **2.** *Phys.* without mass

Massen|abfertigung *f mst pej.* mass (*od.* wholesale) processing; ~**abfütterung** *f umg. pej.* feeding of the masses; ~**absatz** *m* bulk selling; ~**andrang** *m* **1.** (*Ansturm*) great rush (of people); **2.** (*Menschenmenge*) huge crowd, masses *Pl.* of people; ~**arbeitslosigkeit** *f* mass unemployment; ~**artikel** *m Wirts.* mass-produced article; ~**aufgebot** *n* huge force (*an* +*Dat.* of); *Mil.* levy en masse; ~ *an Polizisten* auch massive police presence; ~**auflage** *f e-r Zeitung:* mass circulation; *e-s Buchs:* huge edition

Massenbedarf *m* mass demand; **Massenbedarfsartikel** *m* mass market commodity

Massen|beförderung *f* mass transportation; ~**bewegung** *f* mass movement; ~**blatt** *n* mass-circulation paper; ~**entlassung** *f* mass redundancy (*Am.* layoff); ~**fertigung** *f* mass production; ~**flucht** *f* mass exodus; *panikartige:* mass stampede; ~**grab** *n* mass grave

Massengüter *Pl.* bulk goods; ~**transport** *m* bulk haulage (*Am. auch* car-

riage)

massenhaft I. *Adj.* ... in masses; *das* ~*e Auftreten von ...* the appearance of vast numbers of ...; **II.** *Adv.* ... in masses; *etw.* ~ *haben umg.* have masses (*od.* heaps, piles) of s.th.; *es gibt* ~ *...* there are masses of ...; *es entstanden* ~ *neue Siedlungen* vast numbers of new settlements sprang up

Massen|hinrichtung *f* mass execution; ~**hysterie** *f* mass hysteria; ~**karambolage** *f Mot.* massive pile-up; ~**keulung** *f* mass cull; ~**kundgebung** *f* mass demonstration, huge rally; ~**medien** *Pl.* mass media; ~**mord** *m* mass murder; ~**mörder** *m,* ~**mörderin** *f* mass murderer; ~**organisation** *f* mass organization; ~**produktion** *f* mass production; ~**psychologie** *f* crowd psychology; ~**psychose** *f* mass hysteria; ~**schlachtung** *f* mass slaughter; ~**schlägerei** *f* wholesale punch-up; *größere:* riot; ~**sport** *m* popular (*od.* mass-participation) sport; ~**sterben** *n* deaths *Pl.* in huge numbers; *es begann ein* ~ *von Tieren* huge numbers of animals began to die off; *das* ~ *von Kinos etc. fig.* the innumerable closures *Pl.* of cinemas (*Am.* movie theaters *etc.*); ~**szene** *f Film etc.:* crowd scene; ~**tierhaltung** *f* animal husbandry on a massive scale; ~**tourismus** *m* mass tourism; ~**veranstaltung** *f* huge event; ~**musikalische** ~ mammoth concert; ~**verhaftung** *f* mass arrest; ~**verkehrsmittel** *n* means *Sg.* of mass transportation

Massenvernichtung *f* mass extermination; **Massenvernichtungswaffen** *Pl.* weapons of mass destruction

Massen|versammlung *f* mass meeting; ~**wahn** *m* mass hysteria; ~**ware** *f* mass-produced goods (*od.* articles) *Pl.*

massenweise *Adj. und Adv.* → *massenhaft*

massenwirksam *Adj.:* ~ *sein* have mass appeal

Massen|wirkung *f* mass impact; ~**zahl** *Phys.* mass number

Masseur [ma'søːɐ] *m; -s, -e,* ~**in** *f; -, -nen* masseur; **Masseuse** [ma'søːzə] *f; -, -n; euph.* masseuse

Maßgabe *f: nach* ~ (+ *Gen.*) according to, in accordance with; *mit der* ~, *dass ...* provided that ...; *mit der* ~ *zu* (+ *Inf.*) with instructions to ...

maßgearbeitet *Adj. Kleidung:* made to measure, tailor-made, *Am.* custom-made; *Möbel etc.:* custom-made

maßgebend *Adj.* (*wichtig*) important; *Meinung etc.:* definitive, authoritative; *Werk:* auch standard ...; *Persönlichkeit:* important, influential; *das ist nicht* ~ (*kein Maßstab*) that is no criterion; *Ihre Meinung ist hier nicht* ~ your opinion is of no consequence (*od.* carries no weight) in this case

maßgeblich I. *Adj.* (*entscheidend*) decisive; (*zuständig*) relevant, competent; *sie hat* ~*en Anteil am Erfolg des Projekts* she is playing a crucial role in the success of the project; **II.** *Adv.:* ~ *beteiligt sein* play a decisive (*od.* crucial) role (*an* + *Dat.* in)

maßgerecht *Adj.* **1.** true to size; **2.** true to scale; ~*es Modell* accurate scale model

maßgeschneidert *Adj.* made-to-measure, tailor-made (*auch fig.*), *Am.* custom-made

Maßhalteappell *m bes. Pol.* appeal for restraint

massieren¹ *v/t.* massage; *kannst du*

mir mal den Rücken ~? can you massage my back (*od. umg.* give my back a rub)?

massieren² I. *v/t.* **1.** *Mil.* (*Truppen*) mass; **2.** *Sport* (*Abwehr*) pack; **II.** *v/refl. Mil., Truppen:* mass

Massieren *n; -s, kein Pl.* **1.** *Heilbehandlung:* massages *Pl.;* **2.** *von Truppen:* massing; *auch von Waffen:* buildup; **Massierung** *f* → **Massieren** 2

massig I. *Adj.* massive; *Person, Gegenstand: auch* bulky; **II.** *Adv. umg.* masses (*od.* heaps) of

mäßig I. *Adj.* **1.** *Genuss, Tempo etc.:* moderate; *Ansprüche, Preise etc.: auch* modest; *Trinken: auch* temperate; **2.** (*nicht gut*) *Leistungen:* mediocre, indifferent; *Befinden: umg.* (fair to) middling; (*mittelmäßig*) indifferent, (rather) poorly; **II.** *Adv.:* **~ trinken** *etc.* drink *etc.* moderately (*od.* in moderation)

mäßigen I. *v/t.* (*Meinungen, Ansprüche etc.*) moderate; (*Zorn, Hass etc.*) curb; (*Kritik, Worte*) tone down; **das Tempo ~** slow down, reduce (one's) speed; **~d auf j-n einwirken** have a moderating (*od.* restraining) influence on s.o.; **II.** *v/refl.* **1.** (*maßvoller werden*) *Person:* restrain (*od.* control) o.s.; **sich beim Essen** *etc.* **~** cut down on food *etc.;* **sich in s-n Worten ~** moderate one's language; **2.** (*sich abschwächen*) *Wind:* moderate, slacken; *Hitze:* grow less intense; → **gemäßigt**

Massigkeit *f* massiveness, bulkiness

Mäßigkeit *f* **1.** moderation; **2.** (*Mittelmäßigkeit*) mediocrity

Mäßigung *f* moderation; *stärker:* restraint

massiv I. *Adj.* **1.** *Metall, Holz etc.:* solid; **2.** (*stabil gebaut, wirkend*) solidly built; (*wuchtig*) massive, heavy; **3.** *fig. Widerstand, Angriff etc.:* heavy, massive; *Drohung, Kritik etc.:* severe, vehement; *Beleidigung, Vorwurf etc.:* grave; *Druck:* severe; *Forderungen:* excessive; **~ werden** *umg.* cut up rough, *Am.* get rowdy; **II.** *Adv.* **1.** **~ gebaut** massively (*od.* solidly) built; **2.** *fig. protestieren, angreifen, drohen:* vehemently; *kritisieren:* severely; *beleidigt:* gravely, grossly; **~ angreifen** *Mil.* launch a heavy (*od.* massive) attack

Massiv *n; -s, -e; Geol.* massif

Massivbau *m* **1.** massive structure; **2.** *nur Sg.* (*Bauweise*) massive construction

Massivität *f; -, kein Pl.* **1.** *e-s Baus etc.:* solidity, solid nature; (*Wuchtigkeit*) massiveness; **2.** *fig. von Widerstand, Angriff etc.:* massiveness; *von Drohung, Kritik, Druck etc.:* severity; *von Beleidigung:* gravity; *von Forderung:* excessiveness

Maß|kleidung *f* made-to-measure (*od.* tailor-made, *Am.* custom-made) clothes *Pl.*

Maßkrug *m* lit|re (*Am.* -er) beer mug; *aus Keramik:* stein

maßlos I. *Adj.* **1.** *Person, Gewohnheit:* immoderate; *mit Geld:* extravagant; *im Trinken, in der Sprache:* intemperate; *Gefühle, Ehrgeiz, Gier:* boundless; **2.** (*übertrieben*) excessive, inordinate; **das ist ja e-e ~e Frechheit!** this cheek (*Am.* impertinence) is beyond everything!; **II.** *Adv.* **1.** (*unmäßig*) immoderately; (*übertrieben*) *trinken, rauchen etc.:* excessively, to excess; (*rückhaltlos*) without restraint; **2.** (*äußerst*) extremely, terribly; **~ empört** boiling (*od.* seething) with indignation; **~ übertrie-**

---

ben grossly exaggerated; **~ enttäuscht** desperately disappointed; **Maßlosigkeit** *f* (*Unmäßigkeit*) immoderateness, lack of moderation; *im Trinken, in der Sprache:* intemperance; (*Übertriebenheit*) excessiveness; (*Unbeherrschtheit*) lack of restraint; (*Grenzenlosigkeit*) boundlessness

Maßnahme *f; -, -n* measure, step; **~n ergreifen** *od.* **treffen gegen** take measures (*od.* steps, action *Sg.*) against

Maßnahmen|katalog *m,* **~paket** *n* package of measures

Maßregel *f* (*Richtlinie*) rule, guideline; (*Vorschrift*) regulation; **strenge ~n treffen** establish strict guidelines; **maßregeln** *v/t.* (*untr., hat -ge-*) reprimand, take to task (**wegen** for, about); (*strafen*) punish, discipline; **Maßreg(e)lung** *f* reprimand; (*Bestrafung*) disciplinary action

Maßschneider *m,* **~in** *f Männerkleidung:* bespoke (*Am.* custom) tailor; *Frauenkleidung:* dressmaker

maßschneidern *v/t.* (*untr., hat -ge-*) make to measure, tailor; **sie ist für diese Rolle maßgeschneidert** *umg. fig.* this part is tailor-made for her (*od.* fits her like a glove), she is perfect for this part

Maßstab *m* **1.** (*Richtlinie*) standard; (*Prüfstein*) yardstick, criterion (*Pl.* criteria), benchmark; **e-n ~ setzen** set a (*od.* the) standard; **e-n strengen ~ anlegen** apply a strict standard (**an** + *Akk.* to); **j-n/etw. als ~ nehmen** take s.o./s.th. as one's yardstick (*od.* model), model o.s. on s.o./s.th.; **das ist (für mich) kein ~** that's no criterion (as far as I'm concerned); **2.** *e-r Landkarte etc.:* scale; **ein Modell im ~ 1:5** a model to a scale of 1:5, a one-fifth scale model; **in verkleinertem/vergrößertem ~ zeichnen** draw to (*od.* on) a reduced / an enlarged scale; **maßstab(s)gerecht, maßstab(s)getreu , maßstäblich I.** *Adj.* (true) to scale; **II.** *Adv.:* **~ vergrößern/verkleinern** scale up/down accurately; **~ nachbilden** make a true-to-scale copy of

maßvoll I. *Adj. Verhalten:* moderate, restrained; *Wünsche etc.:* moderate, reasonable; **II.** *Adv.* moderately, with (*od.* in) moderation

Mast¹ *m; -(e)s, -e(n); Naut.* mast (*auch für Antenne*); (*Stange, Flaggenmast, Telegrafenmast*) pole; *Etech.* pylon

Mast² *f; -, -en* **1.** (*das Mästen*) fattening; **2.** (*Mastfutter*) (fattening) feed

Mastbaum *m Naut.* mast

Mastbulle *m* **1.** *gemästet:* fattened bull; **2.** *zum Mästen:* fattening bull

Mastdarm *m Anat.* rectum (*Pl.* rectums *od.* recta)

mästen I. *v/t.* fatten (*auch umg. fig.*); **II.** *v/refl. umg. fig.* stuff o. s., gorge o.s.

Mästerei *f; -, -en* **1.** *nur Sg.* fattening; **2.** *Betrieb:* fattening station

Mast|futter *n* (fattening) feed; **~gans** *f* **1.** *gemästet:* fattened goose; **2.** *zum Mästen:* fattening goose

mastig *Adj. Dial.* **1.** *Speise:* fatty; **2.** *Pflanzen, Wiese:* lush

Mastixstrauch *m Bot.* mastic shrub

Mastkorb *m Naut.* crow's nest

Mast|kur *f umg.* fattening diet; **~ochse** *m* **1.** *gemästet:* fattened ox; **2.** *zum Mästen:* fattening (*od.* feeder) ox

Mast|rind *n* beef cow (*od.* steer); *Pl.* beef cattle; **~schwein** *n* **1.** *gemästet:* fattened pig, porker; **2.** *zum Mästen:* fattening (*od.* feeder) pig

---

Mastspitze *f* masthead

Mästung *f* fattening (process)

Masturbation *f; -, -en* masturbation; **masturbieren** *vt/i.* masturbate

Mastvieh *n* **1.** fat stock; **2.** *zum Mästen:* fattening stock

Masuren (*n*); *-s; Geog.* Masuria; **masurisch** *Adj.* Masurian

Matador *m; -s und -en, -e und -en,* **~in** *f; -, -nen* **1.** matador; **2.** *fig.* (*Held*) hero, star

Match [mɛtʃ] *n, schw. m; -(e)s, -e(s) Sport* match, game; **~ball** *m Tennis, Tischtennis, Badminton:* match point; **~beutel** *m,* **~sack** *m* duffle (*od.* duffel) bag

Material *n; -s, -ien* **1.** material; *Koll.* materials *Pl.; Geräte:* equipment; *Mil.* materiel; **2.** (*Beweismaterial*) evidence; → *auch* **Büromaterial** *etc.;* **~aufwand** *m* cost of materials; **~ausgabe** *f* **1.** (*Raum*) stores *Pl., Am.* stockroom; **2.** (*Vorgang*) issue of stores, *Am.* requisition; **~bedarf** *m* material requirements *Pl.;* **~beschaffung** *f* obtaining (*od.* getting hold of) materials; *durch Kauf:* purchase of materials; *weitS. Verfügbarkeit:* availability of materials; **~ermüdung** *f* material fatigue; **~fehler** *m* material fault

materialisieren *v/t. und v/refl. Phys.* materialize

Materialismus *m; -, kein Pl.* materialism (*auch pej.*); **Materialist** *m; -en, -en,* **Materialistin** *f; -, -nen* materialist; **materialistisch** *Adj.* materialist(ic); **~es Weltbild** materialistic outlook

Material|knappheit *f* shortage (*od.* scarcity) of materials; **es herrscht ~** materials are in short supply; **~kosten** *Pl.* cost *Sg.* of materials, material costs; **~krieg** *m Mil.* war of materiel; *fig. Sport* rivalry between equipment manufacturers; **~lager** *n* stores *Pl., Am.* inventory; **~prüfung** *f* materials testing; **~sammlung** *f* gathering of material (*od.* information); **~schaden** *m* material defect; **~schlacht** *f Mil. battle where equipment is the deciding factor; fig. Sport* event where the result often depends on the equipment used; **~wert** *m* material value; *von Münzen, Schmuck etc.: auch* intrinsic value

Materie *f; -, -n* **1.** *nur Sg.; Phys., Philos.* matter; **2.** (*Thema*) subject (matter); **die ~ beherrschen** be on top of one's subject, know one's stuff; **materiell I.** *Adj.* material; *pej.* (*materialistisch*) materialistic; **II.** *Adv.:* **sie ist ~ abgesichert** her material needs are covered; **~ eingestellt** materially-minded, materialistic

Mate|strauch *m Bot.* maté bush; **~tee** *m* maté

Mathe *f* (*mst ohne Art.*); *-, kein Pl.; umg., bes. Schülersprache* maths *Pl.* (*V. im Sg.*), *Am.* math; **~arbeit** *f Schülersprache:* math(s) test

Mathematik *f; -, kein Pl.* mathematics *Pl.* (*V. im Sg.*), maths *Pl.* (*V. im Sg.*), *Am.* math; **das ist höhere ~ für mich** *hum. fig.* that's higher mathematics as far as I'm concerned

Mathematiker *m; -s, -,* **~in** *f; -, -nen* mathematician

Mathematik|lehrer *m,* **~lehrerin** *f* math(s) teacher; **~unterricht** *m* math (-s) teaching; *Stunden:* math(s) lessons *Pl.*

mathematisch *Adj.* mathematical

Matinee *f; -, -n; Theat.* morning performance

Matjes *m; -, -,* **~hering** *m Gastr.* matjes

herring; **~filet** *n* filleted matjes herring

Matratze *f*; -, -en **1.** *für Bett*: mattress; **2.** *umg. hum. fig. Bart*: thick beard; *Brustbehaarung*: very hairy chest

Matratzenlager *n* doss-down, *Am.* crash pad *umg.* (*with a mattress on the floor*)

Mätresse *f*; -, -n; *hist., altm. pej.* mistress

matriarchalisch *Adj.* matriarchal; **Matriarchat** *n*; -(*e*)*s*, -*e* matriarchy

Matrikel *f*; -, -n **1.** *Univ.* matriculation register; **2.** *österr.* register of births, marriages and deaths

Matrix *f*; -, *Matrizen und Matrizes*; *Bio., Ling., Math.* matrix (*Pl.* matrices *od.* matrixes); **~drucker** *m Computer.* dot matrix printer

Matrize *f*; -, -n **1.** *Tech., Druck.* matrix (*Pl.* matrices *od.* matrixes); **2.** (*Folie*) stencil; **etw. auf ~ schreiben** stencil s.th.

Matrone *f*; -, -n matron; **matronenhaft** *Adj.* matronly

Matrose *m*; -n, -n sailor, seaman; (*Dienstgrad*) ordinary sailor, *Am.* seaman recruit

Matrosen|anzug *m* sailor suit; **~lied** *n* (sea) shanty; **~mütze** *f* sailor's cap

Matsch *m*; -(*e*)*s*, *kein Pl.*; *umg.* **1.** (*Brei*) mush; **2.** (*Schlamm*) mud; (*Schneematsch*) slush; **matschen** *v/i. umg.* slosh about (*Am.* around); **matschig** *Adj. umg.* **1.** *Obst etc.*: mushy, squashy, *Am.* squishy; **2.** (*schlammig*) muddy; *Schnee*: slushy; **Matschwetter** *n umg.* (weather giving) mucky (*od.* muddy, *mit Schneematsch*: slushy) conditions

matt *I. Adj.* **1.** (*glanzlos*) dull; *Papier, Foto, Lack etc.*: matt, *bes. Am.* matte; *Glas*: frosted; *Glühbirne*: pearl, opal; **2.** *Licht*: dim, faint; **3.** *Person*: (*erschöpft*) exhausted, worn out; *Glieder*: weary; (*schwach*) feeble, weak; **4.** (*geistlos*) dull; (*farblos*) colo(u)rless, insipid; *Ausrede, Witz etc.*: feeble, lame; **5.** *Stimme*: faint, weak; *Lächeln*: faint, wan; **6.** *Wirts.* dull, slack; **7.** *Schachspiel*: (**Schach und**) **~!** checkmate; **j-n ~ setzen** checkmate s.o. (*auch fig.*); **II. Adv. 1.** (*glanzlos*) dully; **~ vergoldet** dead-gilt; *Glas*: **~ schleifen** frost (*Opt.* grind) glass; **2.** (*schwach*) weakly; *lächeln, scheinen*: faintly, wanly; *winken, applaudieren*: feebly

Matt *n*; -s, -s *Schach*: checkmate

mattblau *Adj.* pale blue

Matte¹ *f*; -, -n mat; **bereits um 7 Uhr stand er bei mir auf der ~** at 7 am he was already standing on my doorstep; **j-n auf die ~ legen** *Sport* floor s.o.

Matte² *f*; -, -n; *schw. und poet.* (alpine) meadow

Matt|glanz *m* matt(e) finish; **~glas** *n* frosted glass; *Opt., Fot.* ground glass

Mattgold *n* dull (*od.* dead) gold

Matthäi: **bei ihm ist ~ am Letzten** *umg.* he's done for; (*er hat kein Geld*) he's stony (*Am.* stone) broke

Matthäusevangelium *n bibl.*: **das ~** (the Gospel of *od.* according to) St (*od.* St.) Matthew, St (*od.* St.) Matthew's Gospel

Mattheit *f* **1.** dullness; *von Licht*: dimness; **2.** (*Energielosigkeit*) lack of energy; (*Müdigkeit*) weariness, tiredness; (*Erschöpfung*) exhaustion

mattieren *v/t.* matt(e), give a matt(e) finish to; (*Glas*) frost; **Mattierung** *f* **1.** (*Vorgang*) matting; *von Glas*: frosting; **2.** *konkret*: matt(e) finish; *von Glas*: frosting

Mattigkeit *f* lack of energy ; (*Müdigkeit*) weariness, tiredness; (*Erschöpfung*) exhaustion

Mattscheibe *f* **1.** *umg.* (*Fernseher*) telly, box, *bes. Am.* tube; **2.** *Fot.* ground glass (focus[s]ing) screen; **3.** *umg. fig.*: **ich hab ~** I'm not with it; *momentan*: *auch* I've got a mental block

mattschwarz *Adj.* matt(e) black; **Mattschwarz** *n* matt(e) black

mattweiß *Adj.* matt(e) white; **Mattweiß** *n* matt(e) white

Matura *f*; -, *kein Pl.*; *österr., schw.* → **Abitur**

Maturand *m*; -en, -en, **Maturandin** *f*; -, -nen; *schw.*, **Maturant** *m*; -en, -en, **Maturantin** *f*; -, -nen; *österr.* → **Abiturient**

maturieren *v/i. österr., schw.* pass the Matura; **Maturität** *f*; -, *kein Pl.*; *schw.* → **Abitur**

Maturitätsprüfung *f schw.* → **Abitur**

Matz *m*; -es, -e und **Mätze**; *umg.*: **kleiner ~** little lad (*od.* man)

Mätzchen *Pl. umg.* **1.** (*Unsinn*) nonsense *Sg.*; **~ machen** fool (*od.* mess) around; **2.** (*Kniffe*) tricks; **mach keine ~!** none of your tricks!

Matze *f*; -, -n, **Matzen** *m*; -s, -; (*ungesäuertes Fladenbrot*) matzo

mau *I. Adj. umg.* bad; **die Wirtschaft ist ~** the economy is in a bad way; **mir ist ~** I feel funny (*od.* queasy); **II. Adv.: die Geschäfte gehen ~** business is slack, there's not much doing (*Am.* happening) on the business front

Mauer *f*; -, -n wall (*auch fig. und Sport*); **die** (**Berliner**) **~** *hist.* the (Berlin) Wall; **~absatz** *m* ledge; **~assel** *f Zool.* woodlouse; **~bau** *m*; *nur Sg.*; *hist.* building of the Berlin Wall; **~blümchen** *n umg. fig.* wallflower; **~fall** *m*; *nur Sg.*; *hist.* fall of the Berlin Wall; **~haken** *m* wall hook; **~kelle** *f* trowel; **~krone** *f Archit.* coping (of a wall)

mauern *I. v/t.* build (with bricks); **ein gemauerter Kamin** a bricked-in fireplace; **II. v/i. 1.** build masonry, lay bricks; **2.** *Sport* play defensively, close the game down; *Kartenspiel*: hold back; **3.** *fig.* stonewall, stall

Mauer|pfeffer *m Bot.* stonecrop; **~schütze** *m hist.* East German border guard who shot at those trying to escape over the Berlin Wall; **~schwalbe** *f Zool.* swift; **~schwamm** *m* dry rot; **~segler** *m Zool.* swift; **~stein** *m* (building) brick; **~vorsprung** *m* wall projection, ledge; **~werk** *n* **1.** *aus Stein*: masonry; *aus Ziegeln*: brickwork; **2.** (*Mauern*) walls *Pl.*; **~ziegel** *m* (building) brick

Maul *n*; -(*e*)*s*, *Mäuler* **1.** *Zool.* mouth; (*Kiefer*) jaws *Pl.*; (*Schnauze*) muzzle, snout; **2.** *Sl. Von Menschen*: trap, gob; **ein großes ~ haben** have a big mouth, be a big-mouth; **ein böses/loses ~ haben** have a malicious/loose tongue; **das ~ halten** keep one's mouth shut; **halt's ~!** shut up!; **sich** (*Dat.*) **das ~ zerreißen** gossip (*über* + *Akk.* about); **j-m das ~ stopfen** *umg.* shut s.o. up; **er hat sechs Mäuler zu stopfen** *umg. fig.* he's got six hungry mouths to feed; **j-m übers ~ fahren** cut s.o. short; **dem Volk aufs ~ schauen** listen to what people are saying; → *auch* **Mund**

Maulaffen *Pl. umg.*: **~ feilhalten** stand around gaping

Maulbeerbaum *m Bot.* mulberry tree; **Maulbeere** *f* mulberry

Mäulchen *n* little mouth; **ein ~ machen**

pout

Maulesel *m Zool.* mule; *fachspr.* hinny

maulfaul *Adj. umg.* too lazy to talk; *generell*: uncommunicative

Maul|held *m umg.* big-mouth; **~korb** *m* muzzle; **e-m Hund** / *fig.* **j-m e-n ~ anlegen** muzzle a dog/s.o.

Maul|sperre *f* **1.** *bei Tieren*: lockjaw; **2.** *umg. hum.*: **die ~ kriegen** *fig.* gape open-mouthed; **da kriegt man ja die ~** it gives you lockjaw; **~taschen** *Pl. Gastr.* pasta case filled with forcemeat, cheese or vegetables and served in soup; **~tier** *n Zool.* mule; **~trommel** *f Mus.* Jew's harp

Maul-und-Klauenseuche *f Vet.* foot-and-mouth disease

Maulwurf *m Zool.* mole (*auch Sl. fig.*)

Maulwurfs|haufen *m*, **~hügel** *m* molehill

maunzen *v/i. umg. Katze*: miaow, *Am.* meow

Maure *m*; -n, -n Moor

Maurer *m*; -s, - bricklayer, *Am. auch* mason; *Brit. umg.* brickie; **~arbeit** *f* bricklaying; **~geselle** *m*, **~gesellin** *f* journeyman bricklayer; **~handwerk** *n* bricklaying

Maurerin *f*; -, -nen (female) bricklayer

Maurer|kelle *f* trowel; **~meister** *m*, **~meisterin** *f* master bricklayer; **~polier** *m* foreman bricklayer; **~polierin** *f* forewoman bricklayer; **~zunft** *f* bricklayers' guild

Mauretanien (*n*); -s; *Geog.* Mauretania; **Mauretanier** *m*; -s, -, **Mauretanierin** *f*; -, -nen Mauretanian, *weiblich auch*: Mauretanian woman (*od.* girl); **mauretanisch** *Adj.* Mauretanian

maurisch *Adj.* Moorish

Maus *f*; -, *Mäuse* **1.** *Zool., auch Computer.* mouse (*Pl.* mice, *Computer auch* mouses); **weiße Mäuse sehen** *umg.* etwa see pink elephants; **graue ~** *umg. pej.* nondescript person, nonentity; *Frau*: mousy woman; **da beißt die ~ keinen Faden ab** *umg.* there's no way (a)round it, that's the way things are; **2.** *umg. fig.*: **Mäuse** (*Geld*) dough, *Brit. auch* lolly; → **Katz**, **Katze**; → *auch* **Mäuschen** 2

Mauschelei *f*; -, -en; *umg. pej.* wheeling and dealing; **mauscheln** *v/i.* **1.** *umg. pej.* fiddle; (*schummeln*) cheat; **2.** *Dial.* (*undeutlich reden*) mumble; **3.** *Kartenspiel*: cheat; **Mauscheln** *n*; -s, *kein Pl. Kartenspiel*: cheat

Mäuschen *n* **1.** *Dim. von Maus* little mouse; **da möchte ich ~ sein** *umg.* I'd like to be a fly on the wall there; **2.** *umg. als Kosewort*: love, pet, *Am.* honey, hon

mäuschenstill *Adj. und Adv. umg. Person*: (as) quiet as a mouse; **es war ~** there wasn't a sound, you could have heard a pin drop

Mäusebussard *m Orn.* (common) buzzard

Mausefalle *f* mousetrap; *fig.* death-trap

Mäuse|fang *m* mousing; **auf ~ sein** *Katze*: be mousing, be after mice; **~fraß** *m* damage (done) by mice; **~gift** *n* mouse poison

Mauseloch *n* mousehole; **am liebsten hätte ich mich in ein ~ verkrochen** *fig.* I just wished the ground would open and swallow me up

Mäusemelken *n*: **es ist ja zum ~!** *umg.* it's enough to drive you spare (*Am.* crazy)

mausen *v/t. I. v/i.* **1.** *altm., Dial. Katze*:

M

mouse, go mousing; *die Katze lässt das Mausen nicht Sprichw.* he/she will never change; **2.** *Dial. vulg.* (*koitieren*) have a screw; **II.** *v/t. umg. hum.* (*stibitzen*) pinch

Mauser *f*; -, *kein Pl.*; *Zool.* mo(u)lt, mo(u)lting period; *in der ~* (*sein*) (be) mo(u)lting

Mäuserich *m*; *-s*, *-e*; *umg.* (male) mouse

mausern I. *v/i. und v/refl. Zool.* mo(u)lt; **II.** *v/refl. umg. fig.* shape up nicely; *sich ~ zu* turn out; (*sich verwandeln in*) be transformed into; *bes. Mädchen*: blossom (out) into

mausetot *Adj. umg.* stone dead, *präd. auch* (as) dead as a doornail

maus|gesteuert *Adj. Computer*: mouse-controlled; **~grau** *Adj.* mouse-grey (*Am.* -gray), mouse-colo(u)red

mausig *Adj.*: *sich ~ machen umg.* get cheeky (*bes. Am.* fresh)

Mausklick *m Computer*: click of the mouse

Mausoleum *n*; *-s*, *Mausoleen* mausoleum

Maus|pad ['maʊspɛt] *n*; *-s*, *-s Computer*: mouse mat (*Am.* pad); **~taste** *f* mouse button

Maut *f*; -, *-en*, **~gebühr** *f* toll; **mautpflichtig** *Adj.* subject to a toll, toll …; **Mautstelle** *f* toll gate, *Am. auch* toll booth; **Mautstraße** *f* toll road, *Am. auch* turnpike

Max: *strammer ~ Gastr.* ham and fried egg on bread

max. *Abk.* → *maximal*

Max. *Abk.* → *Maximum*

Maxi¹ *n*; *-s*, *-s* **1.** *nur Sg.*; *Modestil*: maxi; **2.** *Abk. umg.* → *Maxikleid*

Maxi² *m*; *-s*, *-s*; *Abk. umg.* → *Maxirock*

Maxikleid *n* maxi dress

maximal I. *Adj.* maximum; **II.** *Adv.* at (the) most; *~ … erreichen/betragen* reach/amount to a maximum of …; *~ zulässiges Gewicht* maximum permitted weight

Maximal|… *im Subst. mst* maximum; *siehe auch Höchst*…; **~betrag** *m* maximum (amount); **~forderung** *f* maximum demand; **~geschwindigkeit** *f* maximum (*od.* top) speed; *zulässige ~* maximum permitted speed; **~strafe** *f* maximum penalty (*od.* sentence)

Maxime *f*; -, *-n* maxim

maximieren *v/t.* maximize; **Maximierung** *f* maximization

Maximum *n*; *-s*, *Maxima* maximum (*Pl.* maxima *od.* maximums) (*an* + *Dat.* of); *ein ~ an Arbeit erfordern* require the maximum conceivable amount of work

Maxirock *m* maxi skirt

Maya *m*; *-(s)*, *-(s)* Maya

Mayonnaise [majo'nɛːzə] *f*; -, *-n*; *Gastr.* mayonnaise, *Am. auch* mayo *umg.*

MAZ *f*; -, *kein Pl.*; *Abk.*; *TV* VTR

Mazedonien (*n*); *-s*; *Geog.* Macedonia; **Mazedonier** *m*; *-s*, -, **Mazedonierin** *f*; -, *-nen* Macedonian, *weiblich auch* Macedonian woman (*od.* girl); **mazedonisch** *Adj.* Macedonian; **Mazedonisch** *n*; *-en*; *Ling.* Macedonian; *das ~e* Macedonian

Mäzen *m*; *-s*, *-e* patron; **Mäzenatentum** *n*; *-s*, *kein Pl.* patronage; **Mäzenin** *f*; -, *-nen* (female) patron

mbH *Abk.* (*mit beschränkter Haftung*) *Wirts.* Ltd, Ltd.

MByte, Mbyte *Abk.* → *Megabyte*

M. d. B., MdB *Abk.* (*Mitglied des Bundestags*) Member of the Bundestag,

Brit. etwa MP, *Am. etwa* Sen. *od.* Rep.

M. d. L., MdL *Abk.* (*Mitglied des Landtags*) Member of the Landtag

Mechanik *f*; -, *-en*, *mst. Sg.* **1.** *Phys.* mechanics *Pl.* (*als Fach V. im Sg.*); **2.** *Tech.* (*Mechanismus*) mechanism; **Mechaniker** *m*; *-s*, -, **Mechanikerin** *f*; -, *-nen* mechanic; **mechanisch I.** *Adj.* mechanical (*auch fig.*); *~es Auswendiglernen fig.* rote learning; **II.** *Adv.* mechanically; *~ herunterleiern fig.* reel (*od.* rattle) off mechanically (*od.* like an automaton)

mechanisieren *v/t.* mechanize; **Mechanisierung** *f* mechanization

Mechanismus *m*; -, *-en* mechanism (*auch fig. und Psych., Philos.*); → *Uhrwerk*; **Mechanismen** *fig. auch* workings; **mechanistisch I.** *Adj.* mechanistic; **II.** *Adv.* mechanistically

Meckerecke *f umg.* complaints column

Meckerei *f*; -, *-en*; *umg. pej.* grousing, griping; **Meckerer** *m*; *-s*, -; *umg. pej.* grouser; **Meckerfritze** *m*; *-n*, *-n*; *umg. pej.* grouser, bellyacher, grumbleguts *hum.*; **meckern** *v/i.* **1.** *Ziege*: bleat; *ein ~des Lachen umg. fig.* a billy goat laugh; **2.** *umg. Person*: grouse, gripe, bellyache

Mecklenburg ['meːklənbʊrk] (*n*); *-s*; *Geog.* Mecklenburg; **mecklenburgisch** *Adj.* Mecklenburg …; **Mecklenburg-Vorpommern** (*n*); *-s*; *Geog.* Mecklenburg - Western Pomerania

Mecki *m*; *-s*, *-s*; *umg.*, **~frisur** *f umg.* crew cut

Medaille [me'daljə] *f*; -, *-n* medal; → *Kehrseite* 1

Medaillen|gewinner *m*, **~gewinnerin** *f Sport* medal(l)ist; **~spiegel** *m Sport* medals table

medaillenträchtig *Adj.*: *~ sein* be a medal prospect (*od. umg.* hopeful)

Medaillon [medal'jõː] *n*; *-s*, *-s* medallion (*auch Kunst und Gastr.*); (*Kapsel mit Andenken*) locket

Media|abteilung *f* (media) publicity department; **~fachfrau** *f*, **~fachmann** *m* media publicity expert

medial I. *Adj.* **1.** *Parapsychologie, Fähigkeit etc.*: as a medium, mediumistic; **2.** *Med.* medial; **3.** *Ling.* middle; **4.** *von den Medien*: media …; **II.** *Adv.* **1.** *Parapsychologie, begabt*: as a medium; **2.** *in den Medien*: aufarbeiten, ausnutzen etc.: in the media

Mediation *f*; -, *-en*; (*Vermittlung*) mediation

Mediävist *m*; *-en*, *-en*, **~in** *f*; -, *-nen* medi(a)evalist, medi(a)eval scholar; **Mediävistik** *f*; -, *kein Pl.* medi(a)eval studies *Pl.*

Medien *Pl.* media (*V. auch im Sg.*); **~forschung** *f* media research (*od.* studies *Pl.*)

medien|geil *Adj. umg.* greedy for media exposure; **~gerecht** *Adj.* adapted to the needs of the media

Medien|kompetenz *f* media competence; **~konzern** *m* group of media firms (*Am.* companies); **~landschaft** *f* media scene (*od.* world); **~mogul** *m*, **~zar** *m* media mogul

Medienpolitik *f* media politics *Pl.* (*auch V. im Sg.*); **medienpolitisch** *Adj.* media-political; *der ~e Sprecher der SPD-Fraktion* the SPD party spokesman on media policy

Medien|präsenz *f* media coverage (*od.* exposure); **~referent** *m*, **~referentin** *f Pol.* spin doctor *umg.*; **~rummel** *m* media circus; **~schelte** *f umg.* media-

-bashing; *~ betreiben* knock the media; **~spektakel** *n* media circus; **~verbund** *m Päd.* multimedia system; *Unterricht im ~* multimedia teaching

medienwirksam *Adj.* effective in the media

Medienzentrum *n* multimedia information cent|re (*Am.* -er)

Medikament *n*; *-(e)s*, *-e* medicine; (*Droge*) drug; (*Pille*) *auch* tablet, pill; *Pl. auch* medication *Sg.*; **medikamentenabhängig** *Adj.* dependent on drugs, drug-dependent; **Medikamentenmissbrauch** *m* drug abuse; **medikamentös I.** *Adj.* medicinal; *~e Behandlung* medication, *auch* course of drugs; **II.** *Adv.*: *~ behandeln* treat with drugs; **Medikation** *f*; -, *-en* medication; **Medikus** *m*; -, *Medizi und hum. -se*; *hum.* medic (*auch Student*), quack (*auch pej.*)

medioker *Adj. geh.* mediocre

Mediothek *f*; -, *-en* multimedia resource cent|re (*Am.* -er)

Meditation *f*; -, *-en* meditation; **Meditationsübung** *f* meditation exercise; **meditativ I.** *Adj.* meditative; **II.** *Adv.*: *~ veranlagt sein* have a meditative disposition, *umg.* be the meditative type

mediterran *Adj.* Mediterranean

meditieren *v/i.* meditate (*über* + *Akk.* on)

medium *indekl. Adj. Gastr.* medium

Medium *n*; *-s*, *Medien und Media* **1.** medium (*Pl.* media *od.* mediums); → *Medien*; **2.** *Pl. Media*; *Ling.* middle voice; **3.** *Pl. Medien*; *Parapsychologie*: medium (*Pl.* mediums)

Medizin *f*; -, *-en* medicine (*auch Heilmittel*); → *auch Medikament*; *Doktor der ~* doctor of medicine (*Abk.* MD)

Medizinal|assistent *m* houseman, house officer, *Am.* intern; **~assistentin** *f* house officer, *Am.* intern; **~rat** *m*, **~rätin** *f Amtsspr. etwa* senior medical officer; **~wesen** *n*; *nur Sg.* medical world

Medizinball *m* medicine ball

Mediziner *m*; *-s*, -, **~in** *f*; -, *-nen* **1.** (*Student*) medical student; *umg.* medic; **2.** (*Arzt*) doctor; *umg.* medic

Medizingeschichte *f* history of medicine

medizinisch *Adj.* medical; (*arzneilich*) medicinal; **~technische Assistentin** *f* medical laboratory assistant

Medizin|mann *m* witch-doctor; *bes. bei Indianern*: medicine man; *umg. hum.* (*Arzt*) quack; **~schränkchen** *n* medicine cabinet; **~student** *m*, **~studentin** *f* medical student; *umg.* medic; **~studium** *n* medical studies *Pl.*

Meduse *f*; -, *-n* **1.** *Myth.* Medusa; **2.** *Zool.* medusa (*Pl.* medusae *od.* medusas), *mst* jellyfish

Meer *n*; *-(e)s*, *-e* sea (*auch fig.*); (*Weltmeer*) ocean; *am ~* by the sea; *Urlaub*: *auch* at the seaside; *ans ~ fahren* go to the seaside; *auf dem ~* (out) at sea; *über dem ~* (*Meeresspiegel*) above sea level; **~blick** *m* → *Meeresblick*; **~busen** *m altm.*, *in Namen*: gulf; **~enge** *f* strait(s *Pl.*)

Meeres|algen *Pl.* marine algae; **~arm** *m* arm of the sea, inlet; **~biologie** *f* marine biology; **~blick** *m* sea (*Am. auch* ocean) view; *Zimmer mit ~* room with (a) sea (*Am. auch* ocean) view (*od.* a view of the sea *od.* ocean); **~boden** *m* → *Meeresgrund*; **~bucht** *f* bay; **~forschung** *f* marine research; **~früchte** *Pl. Gastr.* seafood *Sg.*;

~grund *m* sea (*Am. auch* ocean) floor, bottom of the sea; **~klima** *n* maritime climate

Meereskunde *f* oceanography; **Meereskundler** *m*; *-s*, *-*, **Meereskundlerin** *f*; *-*, *-en* oceanographer; **meereskundlich** *Adj.* oceanographic

Meeres|leuchten *n*; *-s*, *kein Pl.* marine phosphorescence; **~luft** *f* **1.** sea air; **2.** *Met.* maritime air; **~oberfläche** *f* surface of the sea; **~säuger** *m Zool.* marine mammal; **~schildkröte** *f Zool.* turtle; **~spiegel** *m* sea level; **600 m über/unter dem ~** 2,000 ft above/below sea level; **~strand** *m geh.* seashore; **~straße** *f* strait(s *Pl.*); **~strömung** *f* ocean current; **~tiefe** *f* depth (of the sea); **~tier** *n* marine animal; **~verschmutzung** *f* marine pollution

Meergott *m* sea god

meergrün *Adj.* sea-green

Meer|jungfrau *f* mermaid; **~katze** *f Zool.* long-tailed monkey; **~rettich** *m Bot.* horseradish; **~salz** *n* sea salt

Meerschaum *m* meerschaum; **~pfeife** *f* meerschaum pipe

Meer|schildkröte *f Zool.* turtle; **~schweinchen** *n Zool.* guinea pig

meerumschlungen *Adj. poet.* sea-girt

meerwärts *Adv.* toward(s) the sea

Meer|ungeheuer *n* sea monster; *lit.* monster of (*od.* from) the deep; **~wasser** *n* seawater

Meeting ['mi:tɪŋ] *n*; *-s*, *-s* meeting; *Sport auch* meet

mega... *im Adj. umg., mst Jugendspr., verstärkend:* mega

Mega... *im Subst.* **1.** *in Maß- und Mengenangaben:* mega...; **2.** *umg., mst Jugendspr., verstärkend:* mega

Mega|bit *n EDV* megabit; **~byte** *n* megabyte

Megaevent ['megaʔi'vɛnt] *n umg.* mega event

megageil *Adj. umg.* mega brilliant

Megahertz *n Phys.* megahertz

mega-in *Adj. umg. präd.* mega in, mega cool

Megalith *m*; *-s und -en*, *-e(n)*; *Archäol.* megalith; **~grab** *n* megalithic tomb

megalithisch *Adj.* megalithic

Megalithkultur *f Archäol.* megalithic culture

megaloman *Adj.* megalomaniac; **Megalomanie** *f* megalomania

Megalopolis *f*; *-*, *Megalopolen* megalopolis

mega-out *Adj. präd.* completely out

Megaparty *f umg.* mega party, huge party

Megaphon *n*; *-s*, *-e* megaphone

Megatonne *f* megaton

megatrendy *Adj. Jugendspr.* super trendy

Mega|volt *n Etech.* megavolt; **~watt** *n Etech.* megawatt

Mehl *n*; *-(e)s*, *-e* flour; *gröberes:* meal; (*Staub*) dust, powder

mehlig *Adj.* **1.** *Äpfel etc.:* mealy; **2.** (*mit Mehl bedeckt*) floury

Mehl|käfer *m Zool.* meal beetle; **~kloß** *m*, **~knödel** *m* dumpling; **~sack** *m* flour bag; *gefüllt:* sack of flour; **wie ein ~** *umg.* like a sack of potatoes; **~schwalbe** *f Zool.* house martin; **~schwitze** *f Gastr.* roux; **~speise** *f Gastr.* **1.** batter pudding; **2.** *österr.* (*Nachtisch*) pudding, dessert; **~staub** *m* dusting of flour; **~tau** *m Bot.* mildew; **~wurm** *m Zool.* mealworm

mehr I. *unbest. Pron.* more; **~ als genug** more than enough; **~ als 20** more than (*od.* over) 20; **und dergleichen ~**

and so on, and the like; **das ist ein Grund ~, um zu** (+ *Inf.*) that's one more (*od.* another) reason to (+ *Inf.*); **was will er ~?** what more does he want?; **je ~ ..., desto besser** the more ..., the better; **II.** *Adj.* more; **~ und ~** *od.* **immer ~ Tiere** more and more animals; **III.** *Adv.* **1.** more; **das sagt mir ~ zu** that's more to my liking; **er ist ~ ein praktischer Mensch** he's more of a practical man; **~ oder weniger** *od.* **minder** more or less; **das war ein grober Fehler, nicht ~ und nicht weniger** it was a serious mistake, there are no two ways about it; **der Hahn tropft immer ~** the tap is dripping more and more; **je ~ er sich isoliert, desto ~ leidet er** the more he shuts himself away, the more he suffers; **um so ~** all the more; → **schmecken** II 1; **2.** *mit Negation:* **nicht ~** *zeitlich:* no longer, not any longer (*od.* more); **nie ~** never again; **ich habe keins** *od.* **keine Pl. ~** I haven't got any more; **ich habe nichts ~** I've got nothing left; **kein Wort ~** not another word; **ich habe keine Lust ~** I no longer want to, I don't want to any more; **ich kann nicht ~** *umg. beim Essen:* I couldn't eat another thing; (*bin erschöpft*) I can't go on; (*ertrage es nicht mehr*) I can't take it any more; **ich werd nicht ~!** *umg.* I don't believe it!; **3.** *südd., österr.:* **ich habe nur ~ 10 Euro** I've only got 10 euros (left)

Mehr *n*; *-(s)*, *kein Pl.* **1. ein ~ an Zeit/ Erfahrung** *etc.* more (*od.* extra) time/ experience *etc.*; **2.** *schw.* (*Mehrheit*) majority

Mehrarbeit *f* extra work; (*Überstunden*) overtime

mehratomig *Adj.* polyatomic

Mehr|aufwand *m* extra *od.* additional time (*Kosten:* cost, *Mühe:* effort); **~ausgaben** *Pl.* additional *od.* extra expenditure *Sg.*

mehrbändig *Adj.* multivolume ..., in several volumes

Mehr|bedarf *m* extra (*od.* increased) demand; **~belastung** *f* additional (*od.* extra) load (*fig.* burden); **~bereichsöl** *n Mot.* multigrade oil; **~betrag** *m* surplus; (*Zuschlag*) extra charge

mehrdeutig *Adj.* ambiguous; **Mehrdeutigkeit** *f* ambiguity

mehrdimensional *Adj.* multidimensional; **Mehrdimensionalität** *f*; *-*, *kein Pl.* multidimensionality, multidimensional nature (*Gen.* of)

Mehr|ehe *f* polygamous marriage; **~einnahmen** *Pl.* additional *oder* extra earnings

mehren I. *v/t. geh.* increase, add to, augment *förm.*; **II.** *v/refl.* increase, grow; *momentan:* be on the increase; **die Fälle** *etc.* **~ sich** there are an increasing number of cases *etc.*; **die Anzeichen ~ sich, dass ...** there is mounting evidence that ...; **seid fruchtbar und mehret euch** *bibl.* be fruitful and multiply

mehrere I. *unbest. Pron.* several; **sie standen zu ~n im Hof** several (*od.* a number) of them were standing in the courtyard; **~s** several (*od.* a number of) things; **II.** *Adj.* several

mehrerlei I. *unbest. Pron.* several different (*od.* nur various) things; **II.** *Adj.* several (*od.* various) (kinds of)

Mehr|erlös *m* additional revenue; **~ertrag** *m* additional (*od.* surplus) yield

mehrfach I. *Adj.* (*wiederholt*) repeat-

ed; **~e Verletzungen** multiple injuries; **in ~er Hinsicht** in several respects; **er ist ~er deutscher Meister** he has been German champion several times; **ein ~er Millionär** a multimillionaire, a millionaire several times over; **II.** *Adv.* (*mehrmals*) several times; (*wiederholt*) repeatedly; **~ vorbestraft sein** have had several previous convictions; → **ungesättigt**

Mehrfach... *im Subst. mst* multiple

mehrfachbehindert *Adj.* multiple--handicap ...; **~ sein** have more than one handicap (*od.* disability), have multiple handicaps (*od.* disability)

Mehrfach|belichtung *f Fot.* multiple exposure; **~besteuerung** *f* multiple taxation

Mehrfache *n*; *-n*, *kein Pl.:* **das ~** (+ *Gen.*) *od.* **ein ~s** (+ *Gen.*) several times the ...; **das ~** *od.* **ein ~s absolut:* several times as much, several times over

Mehrfach|impfstoff *m Med.* polyvalent vaccine; **~nennung** *f in Fragebogen etc.:* more than one answer; **~sprengkopf** *m Mil.* multiple warhead; **~steckdose** *f* multiple socket; **~talent** *n* multitalented person, man (*od.* woman) of many talents

Mehrfamilienhaus *n* house divided into flats; *Am.* apartment house; *amtlich:* multiple dwelling (unit), *Am.* multifamily house

Mehrfarbendruck *m* **1.** *Bild:* multicolo(u)r print; **2.** *Vorgang:* multicolo(u)r printing

mehrfarbig *Adj.* multicolo(u)r ..., multicolo(u)red

Mehrgebot *n Versteigerung etc.:* higher bid

mehrgeschossig *Adj.* multistor(e)y ..., multistoried

Mehr|gewicht *n* excess weight; **~gewinn** *m* additional (*od.* surplus) profits *Pl.*

mehrgleisig *Adj.* multitrack ..., multitracked

mehrglied(e)rig *Adj.* **1.** *Tech.* multisectional; **2.** *Math.* polynomial

Mehrheit *f* majority; **in der ~ sein** be in the majority; **mit knapper/großer ~** *bes. Parl.* by a narrow/large majority; **mit zehn Stimmen ~** by a majority of ten; **die ~ auf sich vereinigen** be supported by the majority, secure a majority; → **schweigend** II; **mehrheitlich I.** *Adj. Entscheidung etc.:* majority ...; **II.** *Adv.* by a majority (of votes); **~ getroffener Beschluss** majority decision

Mehrheits|aktionär *m*, **~aktionärin** *f* majority shareholder; **~beschaffer** *m*; *-s*, *-*, **~beschafferin** *f*; *-*, *-nen*; *bes. Pol. small party whose votes are needed by another party to obtain a majority; bei e-r Koalition:* junior partner; **~beschluss** *m* majority decision; **~beteiligung** *f Wirts.* majority holding; **~entscheidung** *f* majority decision

mehrheitsfähig *Adj.* capable of obtaining a majority

Mehrheits|meinung *f* majority opinion; **~prinzip** *n* principle of majority rule; **~verhältnis** *n* majority; *Pl. auch* distribution of power; **~wahlrecht** *n Pol.* first past the post electoral system

mehrjährig *Adj.*; *nur attr. Aufenthalt etc.:* ... of (*od.* lasting) several years; **mit ~er Erfahrung** with several years' (*od.* several years of) experience

Mehr|kampf *m Sport* multiple event competition; **~kämpfer** *m*, **~kämpfe-**

rin f multiple event athlete
mehrköpfig Adj.: ~e Delegation etc. delegation etc. consisting of several members
Mehr|kosten Pl. additional od. extra cost Sg. (od. costs, expenses); (Zuschlag) extra charge Sg.; ~leistung f increased performance; → Leistung
Mehrlingsgeburt f multiple birth
mehrmalig Adj.; nur attr. repeated; nach ~er Warnung after repeated warnings, after being warned several times; **mehrmals** Adv. several times
mehrmonatig Adj.; nur attr. Aufenthalt etc.: ... of (od. lasting) several months; mit ~er Erfahrung with several months' experience
mehrmotorig Adj. multi-engined
Mehrparteiensystem n Pol. multiparty system
Mehrpersonenhaushalt m multiperson household
Mehrphasenstrom m Etech. multiphase current
mehrphasig Adj. multiphase ...
mehrpolig Adj. multipole ...
Mehrpreis m extra charge
mehrschichtig Adj. auch fig. multilayered
mehrseitig Adj. 1. polygonal; 2. Pol., Abkommen etc.: multilateral
mehrsilbig Adj. polysyllabic
mehrspaltig Adj. multicolumn ...; in several columns
mehrsprachig I. Adj. multilingual; Person: auch polyglot; II. Adv.: ~ aufwachsen grow up speaking several languages, have a multilingual upbringing
mehrspurig Adj. 1. Tonband(aufnahme): multitrack ...; 2. Mot. multilane ...
mehrstellig Adj. Zahl: multidigit
mehrstimmig Mus. I. Adj. for several voices, polyphonic; ~er Gesang part singing; II. Adv.: ~ singen/spielen sing/play in harmony; etw. ~ setzen set s.th. for several parts; homophon: auch harmonize s.th.; **Mehrstimmigkeit** f Mus. polyphony
mehrstöckig Adj. multistorey ..., Am. multistoried
Mehrstufenrakete f Raumf. multistage rocket
mehrstufig Adj. Rakete: multistage
mehrstündig Adj.; nur attr. Treffen etc.: of (od. lasting) several hours; Aktivität: several hours' ..., several hours of ...
mehrtägig Adj.; nur attr. Treffen etc.: of (od. lasting) several days; Aktivität: several days' ..., several days of ...
Mehrteiler m umg. 1. Kleidungsstück: combination; einheitlich: suit; 2. TV series; Film etc.: serial; **mehrteilig** Adj. 1. Gerät etc.: consisting of several parts; 2. Sendung: in several parts; Film etc.: auch serialized
Mehrverbrauch m increased consumption
Mehrweg|flasche f Öko. returnable bottle; ~geschirr n reusable crockery (Am. dishes); ~verpackung f reusable packaging
Mehrwert m; nur Sg.; Wirts. increase in value, appreciation; nach Marx: surplus value; ~steuer f VAT, value-added tax, bes. Am. sales tax
mehrwöchig Adj.; nur attr. Aufenthalt etc.: of (od. lasting) several weeks; Aktivität: several weeks' ..., several weeks of ...
Mehrzahl f 1. nur Sg. (Mehrheit) ma-

jority; 2. Ling. plural
mehrzeilig Adj. (consisting) of several lines
mehrzellig Adj. multicellular, polycellular
Mehrzweck|... im Subst. multipurpose; ~fahrzeug n multipurpose vehicle, MPV; ~halle f multipurpose (public) building
meiden v/t.; meidet, mied, hat gemieden avoid, steer clear of; (bes. Person) auch shun
Meierei f; -, -en 1. hist. feudal manor; 2. Dial. (Molkerei) dairy
Meile f; -, -n mile; man riecht es drei ~n gegen den Wind umg. fig. you can smell it a mile off; → Seemeile; **Meilenstein** m milestone; fig. auch landmark; **meilenweit** I. Adj. miles and miles of; Entfernung: of many miles; in ~er Entfernung many miles away; II. Adv. for miles (and miles); ~ voneinander entfernt miles apart; fig. auch worlds apart
Meiler m; -s, - 1. charcoal pile; 2. (Atommeiler) (atomic) pile
mein I. Poss. Pron. 1. adjektivisch: my; e-r ~er Wagen one of my cars; e-r ~er Freunde a friend of mine, one of my friends; ~e Damen und Herren ladies and gentlemen; ich trinke so ~e fünf Tassen Tee am Tag umg. I regularly drink about five cups of tea a day; Mein und Dein verwechseln od. nicht unterscheiden können umg. euph. be no respecter of other people's property; 2. substantivisch: mine; ~er, ~e, ~(e)s, der (die, das) ~e od. Meine mine; ich habe das ~e od. Meine getan I've done my share (umg. bit); (mein Möglichstes) I've done my best (od. all I can); die ~en od. Meinen (meine Familie) my family, bes. Am. my folks; II. pers. Pron. poet. (Gen. von ich) of me; gedenke ~ remember me; → meiner
Meineid m perjury; e-n ~ schwören swear a false oath, commit perjury; **meineidig** Adj. perjured; ~ werden perjure o.s., Jur. commit perjury
meinen I. v/t. 1. (e-r Ansicht sein) think; was ~ Sie dazu? - ich meine überhaupt nichts what do you think? - I have no opinion, it's all the same to me; ~ Sie (wirklich)? do you (really) think so?; das will ich ~! I should (jolly well) think (od. hope) so; das sollte man ~ you'd think so; 2. (sagen wollen, beabsichtigen) mean; wie ~ Sie das? how do you mean?; schärfer: what do you mean by that?; ~ Sie das ernst? do you really mean it (od. that)?; so war es nicht gemeint I (od. he, she etc.) didn't mean it like that; er hat es nicht böse gemeint he meant no harm; sie meint es gut she means well; es war gut gemeint it was well-meant; sie meint es gut mit dir she's only thinking of what's good for you, she has your best interests at heart; das Wetter meint es gut mit uns the weather is being kind to us; 3. (j-n od. etw. im Sinn haben) mean; (sprechen von) auch refer to, speak of; er meinte mich he meant me, he was referring to me; 4. (sagen) say; was ~ Sie? what did you say?, höflicher: I beg your pardon?; II. v/i. 1. wenn du meinst if you say so; (ganz) wie Sie ~ as you wish; ich meine ja nur umg. it was just a thought; 2. wie ~ Sie? I beg your pardon?
meiner pers. Pron. of me; gedenke ~

remember me; erbarme dich ~ have mercy upon me; → mein II
meinerseits Adv. for my part, as far as I'm (od. I was) concerned; ganz ~ the pleasure is (od. has been) all mine
meinesgleichen Pron. people like me; iro. my sort, the likes of me
meinethalben Adv. altm. → meinetwegen
meinetwegen Adv. 1. (wegen mir) because of me, on my account; (mir zuliebe) because of me, for my sake; 2. (von mir aus) I don't care, it's all right by (od. with) me, please yourself; 3. (zum Beispiel) let's say, shall we say; **meinetwillen** Adv.: (um) ~ for my sake; (in meiner Sache) on my behalf
meinige poss. Pron.: der, die, das ~ od. Meinige mine, my one; die ~n od. Meinigen (Angehörigen) my people, bes. Am. my folks
Meinung f opinion (über + Akk. of, about, on); meiner ~ nach od. nach meiner ~ in my opinion; der ~ sein, dass ... think (od. believe od. be of the opinion) that ...; e-e ~ äußern express (od. put forward) an opinion; derselben/anderer ~ sein think the same / think differently, agree/disagree; ganz meine ~! I quite (Am. totally) agree; s-e ~ ändern change one's opinion; (es sich anders überlegen) change one's mind; sich (Dat.) e-e ~ bilden form an opinion (über + Akk. on, about); e-e hohe/schlechte ~ von j-m/etw. haben have a high/low opinion of s.o./s.th.; ich habe dazu e-e dezidierte ~ my mind is quite made up on the subject; j-m (gehörig) die ~ sagen give s.o. a piece of one's mind; → öffentlich I 1, vorgefasst
Meinungs|änderung f change of opinion; ~äußerung f expression of (one's) opinion; freie ~ freedom of expression (od. speech); ~austausch m exchange of views (über + Akk. on); ~befragung f opinion poll, survey
meinungsbildend I. Adj. opinion-forming; II. Adv.: ~ wirken help to shape public opinion; **Meinungsbildung** f forming of an opinion; öffentliche: opinion-forming, shaping of public opinion
Meinungsforscher m, ~in f (opinion) pollster; **Meinungsforschung** f opinion polling (od. research); **Meinungsforschungsinstitut** n opinion research institute, polling institute
Meinungs|freiheit f freedom of (opinion and) expression; ~führer m, ~führerin f leader of opinion
meinungslos Adj. devoid of (all) opinion; ~e Masse unthinking masses
Meinungs|mache f manipulation of public opinion; ~macher m, ~macherin f opinion-maker; ~monopol n pej. monopolistic influence on public opinion; ~streit m conflict of views (od. opinions), controversy, dispute; ~umfrage f (public) opinion poll, survey; ~umschwung m shift in (od. swing of) opinion; ~unterschied m; mst Pl. difference of opinion; ~verschiedenheit f; mst Pl. (auch Streit) difference of opinion, disagreement
Meise f; -, -n; Orn. tit(mouse); du hast wohl 'ne ~? umg. you must be nuts
Meißel m; -s, - chisel; **meißeln** vt/i. chisel; (Statue etc.) carve
Meißener indekl. Adj.: ~ Porzellan Dresden china, fachspr. auch Meissen (china)

M

meist *Adv.* → **meistens**

meist... **I.** *Adj.* most; (*der größte Teil von*) most of; **die ~en Leute** most people; **er hat das ~e Geld** he's got (the) most money; **die ~e Zeit** most of the time; **II.** *unbest. Pron.* **1. das ~e** (the) most; (*der größte Teil davon*) most of it; **2. die ~en** most (of them); (*die größte Zahl*) (the) most; **sie ist ruhiger als die ~en** she's quieter than most; **die ~en** (*davon*) **kenne ich** I know most of them; **wer die ~en hat, gewinnt** whoever has the (the) most, wins; **III.** *Adv.:* **am ~en** (*Superlativ von viel*) (the) most; (*Superlativ von sehr*) most (of all), the most; *weitS.* (*am besten*) best (of all); **er hat am ~en** he's got (the) most; **das hat mich am ~en geärgert** that annoyed me (the) most (*od.* most of all); **das am ~en verkaufte Buch** the best-selling book

meistbegünstigt *Adj.* most-favo(u)red; **~es Land** most-favo(u)red nation, MFN; **Meistbegünstigung** *f* most-favo(u)red nation treatment

meistbietend **I.** *Adj.:* **~er Interessent** highest bidder; **II.** *Adv.:* **~ verkaufen** sell to the highest bidder; **~ abzugeben:** ... best offer (accepted); **Meistbietende** *m, f; -n, -n* highest bidder

meistdiskutiert *Adj.:* **~es Thema** most popular topic of discussion, topic number one

meistens *Adv.* usually; (*die meiste Zeit*) most of the time; (*zum größten Teil*) mostly, for the most part; **es sind ~ Italiener** they are mostly Italians

meistenteils *Adv.* for the most part

Meister *m; -s, -* **1.** (*im Handwerk*) master (craftsman); **ein ~ im Bäckerhandwerk** a master baker; **s-n ~ machen** take one's master craftsman's diploma; **2.** (*Künstler, Könner*) master (*auch fig., iro.*); **alter ~** *Mus., Kunst etc.:* old master; **ein ~ im Lügen** a master at (*od.* in the art of) lying; **s-n ~ finden** *fig.* find (*od.* meet) one's match; **Übung macht den ~** *Sprichw.* practice makes perfect; **früh übt sich, was ein ~ werden will** *Sprichw.* you can't start too young; **es ist noch kein ~ vom Himmel gefallen** *Sprichw.* you can't expect to get it right first time; **3.** *Sport etc.:* champion; (*Mannschaft*) champions *Pl.*; **4.** *im Betrieb:* foreman; **5.** *als Anrede, vertraulich: Sl.* guv, chief, *Am.* Mac; **6.** *in Märchen:* **~ Lampe** Master Hare; **~ Petz** Master Bruin (the Bear)

Meister|brief *m* master craftsman's diploma; **~detektiv** *m,* **~detektivin** *f* master detective; **~elf** *f Fußball:* champion team

meisterhaft **I.** *Adj.* masterly; **II.** *Adv.* in masterly fashion, brilliantly; **es ~ verstehen zu mogeln** be a past master at cheating; **Meisterhaftigkeit** *f* masterliness

Meisterhand *f* master's touch; **ein Werk von ~** the work of a master

Meisterin *f* **1.** (*Handwerksmeisterin*) master craftswoman; *Frau e-s Meisters:* master craftsman's wife; **2.** *Sport* (women's) champion; **die deutsche ~ im Hochsprung** the German women's high jump champion

Meister|klasse *f Mus., Kunst* master class; **~koch** *f,* **~köchin** *f* master cook (*beruflich:* chef); **~kurs** *m Mus., Kunst* master class course; → **Meisterschule**; **~leistung** *f* superb feat; *Sport, Theat. etc.* masterly performance; (*Meisterwerk*) masterpiece; **technische ~** re-

markable technical feat; **musikalische ~** masterly feat of musicianship

meisterlich *Adj. altm.* → **meisterhaft**

meistern *v/t.* master; (*Gefühle*) *auch* control; (*Schwierigkeit, Herausforderung*) overcome; **sein Leben ~** cope with life

Meisterprüfung *f* examination for the master craftsman's diploma

Meisterschaft *f* **1.** *nur Sg.* (*Können*) mastery; **es** (*bis*) **zur ~ bringen in** become a master in, *förm.* attain mastery in; **2.** *Sport* championship; (*Titel*) title; **e-e ~ gewinnen** win a championship (*od.* title)

Meisterschafts|feier *f Sport* title-winners' celebration; **~spiel** *n* championship game (*Fußball, Tennis etc.: auch* match); *e-r Liga:* league match; **~wettbewerb** *m* championship competition

Meister|schule *f* vocational school (*preparing for the master craftsman's diploma*), **~schüler** *m,* **~schülerin** *f* **1.** *Mus., Kunst etc.:* master-class pupil (*od.* student); **2.** *in der Schule:* model (*od.* prize) pupil (*Am.* student); **~singer** *m; -s, -; Lit., hist.* mastersinger, *bes. Am.* Meistersinger; **~stück** *n* **1.** (*Meisterleistung*) masterpiece; *Handlung:* masterstroke; **das war** (*wahrlich*) **kein ~ von dir** that wasn't exactly brilliant on your part; **2.** *work submitted for the master craftsman's diploma;* **~titel** *m* **1.** *Sport* championship title; *der Liga:* league title; **2.** *im Handwerk:* master craftsman's title

Meisterung *f* mastery

Meisterwerk *n* masterpiece

Meistgebot *n* highest bid

meist|gebräuchlich *Adj.* most widely (*od.* frequently) used; **~gefragt** *Adj.* most popular, most sought-after, *nachgestellt:* most in demand; **~gehasst** *Adj.* most hated; **~gekauft** *Adj.* best-selling; **~gelesen** *Adj.* most widely read; **~geliebt** *Adj.* best-loved; **~genannt** *Adj.* most frequently cited

meistverkauft *Adj.* best-selling

Mekka **1.** (*n*); *-s; Geog.* Mecca; **2.** *n; -s, -s, mst Sg.; fig.* Mecca (+ *Gen., für* for)

Melancholie *f; -, -n* melancholy; *Psych.* melancholia; **Melancholiker** *m; -s, -,* **Melancholikerin** *f; -, -nen* melancholic; **melancholisch** *Adj.* melancholy

Melanesien (*n*); *-s; Geog.* Melanesia; **Melanesier** *m; -s, -,* **Melanesierin** *f; -, -nen* Melanesian, *weiblich auch:* Melanesian woman (*od.* girl); **melanesisch** *Adj.* Melanesian

Melange [me'lã:ʒə] *f; -, -n* **1.** *fachspr.* (*Gemisch*) mixture; *Gastr.* blend; **2.** *österr.* [me'lã:ʒ] latte (coffee)

Melanin *n; -s, -e; Bio.* melanin

Melanom *n; -s, -e; Med.* melanoma

Melanzani *f; -, -; österr. Bot.* aubergine, *Am.* eggplant

Melasse *f; -, -n; fachspr.* molasses

Melatonin *n; -s, kein Pl.; Med.* melatonin

Melde *f; -, -n; Bot.* orache

Melde|amt *n,* **~behörde** *f* → **Einwohnermeldeamt;** **~frist** *f* registration period; **~gänger** *m; -s, -; Mil.* messenger

melden **I.** *v/t.* **1.** (*berichten*) report; **wie soeben gemeldet wird** as has just been reported; *vorangestellt:* according to reports just received, ...; **2.** (*ankündigen, bekannt geben*) announce; **würden Sie mich bei ihm ~?** would you tell him I'm here?; **3.** *amtlich:* notify the authorities of; (*Geburt etc.*) register; (*Unfall, Vergehen etc.*) report

(*der Polizei etc.* to the police *etc.*); *j-n* **als vermisst ~** report s.o. (as) missing; *j-m etw.* **~** notify s.o. of s.th.; **nichts zu ~ haben** *umg. fig.* have no say (in the matter); **du hast hier nichts zu ~!** *umg. fig. iro.* this is none of your business; **II.** *v/refl.* **1.** *dienstlich:* report (**bei** to; **zur Arbeit / zum Dienst** for work/duty); **2.** *polizeilich:* register with the police; **3.** *Telef.* answer (the [tele]-phone); **4.** *freiwillig:* volunteer (**zu etw.** for s.th.); **sich zum Militär ~** join the armed forces (*bes. Am.* enlist) as a volunteer; **5.** *Leiden etc.:* make its presence felt; **mein Weisheitszahn meldet sich wieder** my wisdom tooth is sending messages again; **6.** *in der Schule:* put one's hand up; **7.** *zum Lehrgang etc.:* enrol(l), sign up (**zu** for); *zum Examen, Wettbewerb:* enter (**zu** for); **8. sich auf ein Inserat ~** answer an advertisement; **9. er wird sich schon ~** (*von sich hören lassen*) he'll be in touch; (*sich bemerkbar machen*) he'll make noises; **wenn du mich brauchst, melde dich** just let me know (*od. umg.* just give me a shout) if you need me; → **anmelden, krankmelden;** **III.** *v/i.* **1.** *Hund* (*Laut geben*) give tongue; **2.** *Sport* (*sich anmelden*) enter; **sie hat für Wimbledon gemeldet** she has entered for Wimbledon

Meldepflicht *f* **1.** *Verwaltung:* obligation to register (with the authorities); **es besteht ~** registration is obligatory; **2.** *Med., bei Krankheit:* duty of notification; **meldepflichtig** *Adj.* subject to registration; *Med. Krankheit:* notifiable

Melder *m; -s, -; Mil.* messenger

Melde|register *n* register (of residents); **~schluss** *m* closing date (for entries); **~stelle** *f* registration office; **~wesen** *n; nur Sg.* registration system; **~zettel** *m* registration form

Meldung *f* **1.** (*Mitteilung*) announcement; **2.** (*Pressemeldung*) report; (*Nachricht*) news item; (*Bekanntmachung*) announcement; **letzte ~en des Tages** late news broadcast *Sg.*; *Kurznachrichten:* final news headlines; **3.** (*Anzeige*) report; **~ machen** report (**bei** to); **4.** *bei e-r Behörde:* registration (**bei** with); **5.** *Sport etc.* entry

meliert *Adj.* mixed; *in der Farbe:* mottled

Melioration *f; -, -en; Agr.* soil improvement

Melisse *f; -, -n; Bot.* balm, melissa; **Melissengeist®** *m; nur Sg.* melissa extract

Melk|anlage *f Agr.* milking plant; **~eimer** *m* milk(ing) pail

melken *vt/i.; melkt, melkte od. molk, hat gemelkt od. gemolken* **I.** *v/t.* milk (*auch fig.*); **II.** *v/i.* give milk; **~de Kuh** → **Melkkuh; Melker** *m; -s, -,* **Melkerin** *f; -, -nen* milker; *weiblich auch* milkmaid

Melk|kuh *f* dairy cow; *fig.* milch cow; **~maschine** *f* milking machine; **~schemel** *m* milking stool

Melodie *f; -, -n; Mus.* melody; (*Weise*) *auch* tune; **~instrument** *n Jazz:* melodic instrument

Melodienfolge *f* medley of tunes

Melodik *f; -, kein Pl.; Mus.* **1.** melody, melodic character; **2.** (*Lehre*) theory of melody; **melodiös** *Adj.* melodious; **melodisch** **I.** *Adj.* melodic; **II.** *Adv.* melodically

Melodram *n; -s, Melodramen,* **Melodrama** *n* melodrama (*auch umg. fig.*);

Melodramatik *f mst iro.* melodramatic character; **melodramatisch I.** *Adj.* melodramatic; **II.** *Adv.* melodramatically

Melone *f; -, -n* **1.** (*Frucht*) melon; **2.** *umg. hum.* (*Hut*) bowler (hat), *Am.* derby; **Melonenbaum** *m Bot.* papaya

Melos *n; -, kein Pl.* **1.** *Mus.* melody; **2.** (*Sprachmelodie*) speech melody, intonation

Membran *f; -, -en*, **Membrane** *f; -, -n*; *Anat., Phys.* membrane; *Tech.* diaphragm

Memento *n; -s, -s* **1.** *geh.* warning, admonition *förm.*; **2.** *kath., in der Messe:* Memento

Memme *f; -, -n*; *altm., pej.* coward, sissy *umg.*; **memmenhaft** *Adj. altm., pej.* cowardly, sissy *umg.*

Memo *n; -s, -s; umg.* memo

Memoiren [me'mŏaːrən] *Pl.* memoirs

Memorandum *n; -s, Memoranden* memorandum (*Pl.* memoranda *od.* memorandums) *förm.*, memo

memorieren *v/t. altm.* memorize, learn by heart

Menage [me'naːʒə] *f; -, -n; Gastr.* cruet stand

Menagerie [menaʒə'riː] *f; -, -n; altm., noch hum. fig.* menagerie

mendelsch *Adj.:* ~*e Regeln* Mendel's laws

Menetekel *n; -s, -; lit.: das ~ ist an der Wand* the writing is on the wall; *etw. als ~ deuten* see s.th. as a portent

Menge *f; -, -n* **1.** quantity; amount; **2.** (*große ~*) lot (of); *umg.* lots (of); *e-e ~ Autos* a lot (*umg.* lots) of cars; *e-e ~ zu essen* a lot (*umg.* lots) to eat; *... in ~n ...* in abundance, plenty of ...; *... in großen ~n ...* in large quantities, large quantities of ...; *stärker:* vast amounts of ...; *Menschen etc.:* a large number of ..., crowds of ...; *jede ~ Geld od. Geld in rauen ~n umg.* piles (*od.* stacks *od.* heaps) of money; *Arbeit gibt es jede ~* there is any amount (*od. umg.* masses) of work; **3.** (*Menschenmenge*) crowd; *mit der ~ laufen fig.* follow the crowd; **4.** *Math.* set

mengen I. *v/t. Dial.* mix; *etw. in etw. ~* mix s.th. with (*od.* into) s.th.; **II.** *v/refl.* **1.** *sich mit etw. ~ Sachen:* be mixed (*od.* mingle) with s.th.; *sich unter die Leute ~ umg. Person:* mingle (*od.* mix) with the crowd; **2.** *umg.: sich in etw. ~* (*sich einmischen*) interfere in s.th.

Mengen|angabe *f* indication of quantity; ~**begrenzung** *f* restriction (of quantity); ~**bezeichnung** *f* term of quantity; ~**lehre** *f Math.* set theory

mengenmäßig I. *Adj.* quantitative; **II.** *Adv.* quantitatively, in terms of quantity

Mengen|preis *m Wirts.* bulk price; ~**rabatt** *m* bulk (*od.* quantity) discount

Menhir *m; -s, -e; Archäol.* menhir, standing stone

Meningitis *f; -, Meningitiden; Med.* meningitis

Meniskus *m; -, Menisken; Anat., Opt.* meniscus (*Pl.* menisci); *am ~ operiert werden* have a cartilage operation; ~**linse** *f Opt.* meniscus (lens); ~**operation** *f Med.* cartilage operation; ~**riss** *m Med.* torn meniscus (*od.* cartilage)

Menjoubart ['mɛnʒu-] *m* pencil moustache

Mennige *f; -, kein Pl.* red lead (paint), minium *fachspr.*

Mennonit *m; -en, -en,* ~**in** *f; -, -nen* Mennonite; **mennonitisch** *Adj.* Mennonite

Menopause *f; -, -n; Med.* menopause

Menorca (*n*); *-s; Geog.* Minorca, Menorca

Menorrhö *f; -, -en Med.* menorrh(o)ea

Mensa *f; -, -s und Mensen; Univ.* refectory, canteen, *Am. auch* commons *Pl.* (*V. im Sg.*), cafeteria; ~**essen** *n* meal (*allg.* food) in the (university) canteen (*Am. auch* commons *od.* cafeteria)

Mensch[1] *m; -en, -en* **1.** *als Gattung:* human being; *der ~* man, homo sapiens; (*die Menschheit*) mankind; *die ~en* man *Sg.*, humans; *ich bin auch nur ein ~* I'm only human; *das sind doch keine ~en mehr!* they're no longer human, they're just animals; *e-e Seele von ~ sein* have a heart of gold; *sich anstellen wie der erste ~ umg.* act as if one hasn't a clue, pretend to be stupid; ~*en fressende Tiere* man-eating animals; → *denken* I 1; **2.** (*Person*) person, man, *weiblich:* woman; (*die*) ~*en* people; *mit j-m von ~ zu ~ reden* have a heart-to-heart (talk) with s.o.; *Mann auch:* talk to s.o. man to man; *gern unter ~en sein* enjoy company, be the sociable type; *kein ~* nobody, not a soul; *ein neuer ~ werden* (*sich wandeln*) become a different person; *des ~en Wille ist sein Himmelreich Sprichw.* do what you like if it makes you happy; **3.** *umg., als Interj., erstaunt:* goodness!, gosh!; *vorwurfsvoll:* for goodness' (*Sl.* Christ's) sake!; *begeistert:* wow!; ~*, pass doch auf!* hey, look what you're doing!; *~ Meier!* good grief!

Mensch[2] *n; -(e)s, -er; Dial., mst pej.* female

Mensch ärgere dich nicht® *n; -, kein Pl. Spiel:* ludo

menscheln *v/i., unpers.; umg.* **1.** *hier menschelt es aber sehr* (*hier sind e-e Menge Leute*) there are crowds of people here; **2.** (*menschliche Schwächen zeigen*) *auch in der Behörde menschelt es* they're only human at the local authority

Menschenaffe *m* anthropoid ape

menschenähnlich *Adj.* manlike, anthropoid *fachspr.*

Menschen|alter *n* generation; (*Lebensspanne*) lifetime; ~**ansammlung** *f* crowd (of people); *kleinere:* cluster of people

menschenarm *Adj.* thinly populated

Menschen|artige *m; -n, -n, mst Pl.: Biol.* hominid; ~**auflauf** *m* crowd of people; ~**bild** *n* view of man (*des Mittelalters etc.* in the Middle Ages *etc.*)

Menschenfeind *m,* ~**in** *f* misanthropist; **menschenfeindlich I.** *Adj.* **1.** misanthropic; **2.** *Lebensbedingungen etc.:* hostile (to man); *Haus:* inhospitable, unwelcoming; (*unmenschlich*) inhuman; **II.** *Adv.* **1.** misanthropically; **2.** (*unmenschlich*) inhumanly; *konzipiert:* creating a hostile environment; **Menschenfeindlichkeit** *f* **1.** misanthropy; **2.** *von Lebensbedingungen etc.:* hostility (to man); (*Unmenschlichkeit*) inhumanity

Menschen|fleisch *n* human flesh; ~**fresser** *m* cannibal; (*Tier*) man-eater

Menschenfreund *m,* ~**in** *f* philanthropist; **menschenfreundlich I.** *Adj.* **1.** philanthropic; **2.** *Umwelt, Haus etc.:* hospitable, welcoming; *Städteplanung:* on a human scale; **II.** *Adv.* **1.** philanthropically; **2.** *konzipiert:* on a human scale; (*menschlichen Bedürfnissen ent-*

sprechend) to cater for human needs; **Menschenfreundlichkeit** *f* **1.** philanthropy; **2.** *der Umwelt etc.:* hospitable nature; *der Städteplanung:* human scale

Menschen|führung *f* leadership; *er versteht einiges von ~* he's a good leader, he has leadership qualities; ~**gedenken** *n: seit ~* (*seit undenklichen Zeiten*) from (*od.* since) time immemorial; (*so weit man sich zurückerinnern kann*) within living memory; ~**geschlecht** *n: das ~* the human race, mankind; ~**gestalt** *f: in ~* in human form; *ein Teufel in ~* a devil incarnate; ~**haar** *n* human hair; ~**hai** *m* man-eating shark; ~**hand** *f: von ~ geschaffen* made (*od.* created) by human hand (*od.* by the hand of man); *es liegt nicht in ~* it is beyond the control of man

Menschenhandel *m* slave trade; *mit Prostituierten:* white slave trade; **Menschenhändler** *m,* **Menschenhändlerin** *f* slave trader; *mit Prostituierten:* white slaver

Menschenhass *m* misanthropy, hatred of people; **Menschenhasser** *m,* **Menschenhasserin** *f* misanthropist, hater of people

Menschen|jagd *f pej.* manhunt; *das Jagen:* manhunting; ~**kenner** *m,* ~**kennerin** *f:* (*guter*)/*schlechter ~* good/bad judge of character (*od.* human nature); ~**kenntnis** *f* knowledge of (*od.* insight into) human nature; ~**kette** *f* human chain; ~**kunde** *f; nur Sg.* anthropology; ~**leben** *n* **1.** (human) life; *~ sind nicht zu beklagen* there were no fatalities; **2.** (*Lebenszeit*) lifetime; *weitS.* (*Leben*) life

menschenleer *Adj.* deserted

Menschen|liebe *f* love of one's fellow men, human kindness; ~**los** *n: das ~* the human lot; ~**masse** *f* mass of people, huge crowd; ~**material** *n; nur Sg.* human resource (*Mil.* material); ~**menge** *f* crowd (of people)

menschenmöglich *Adj.* humanly possible; *das od. alles Menschenmögliche* everything humanly possible

Menschen|opfer *n* **1.** *bei e-m Unfall etc.:* death, fatality; *Pl. auch* death toll *Sg.*; *zahlreiche ~ fordern* cost many lives; **2.** *rituelles:* human sacrifice; ~**pflicht** *f* duty as a human being; ~**rasse** *f* race (of people); ~**raub** *m* kidnapping, abduction

Menschenrecht *n; mst Pl.* human right; **Menschenrechtler** *m; -s, -,* **Menschenrechtlerin** *f; -, -nen* human rights activist

Menschenrechts|abkommen *n* agreement on human rights; → *auch Menschenrechtskonvention*; ~**katalog** *m* catalog(ue) of human rights; ~**kommission** *f* human rights commission; *Europäische ~* European Commission for Human Rights; ~**konvention** *f* Human Rights Convention; ~**verletzung** *f* violation of human rights

menschenrechtswidrig *Adj.* contrary to human rights, in violation of human rights

menschenscheu *Adj.* shy; (*ungesellig*) unsociable; **Menschenscheu** *f* shyness; (*Ungeselligkeit*) unsociableness

Menschenschinder *m* slavedriver; **Menschenschinderei** *f* slavedriving; **Menschenschinderin** *f* slavedriver

Menschen|schlag *m* breed of people; ~**schlange** *f* queue (*Am.* line) of people; ~**seele** *f* human soul; *keine ~* not

M

a living soul

Menschenskind *Interj. erstaunt*: goodness!, good heavens!; *vorwurfsvoll*: for goodness' sake!

Menschen|sohn *m kirchl.* Son of Man; **~strom** *m* stream (*od.* flood) of people; **~traube** *f* cluster of people

Menschentum *n; nur Sg.* humanity

Menschen|typ *m* **1.** type (*od.* sort) of person; **2.** *fachspr.* anthropological type; **~typus** *m* → *Menschentyp* 2

menschenunwürdig I. *Adj. Behandlung*: degrading, inhumane; *Zustände*: unfit for human beings; *Unterkunft*: unfit for human habitation; **II.** *Adv.*: *j-n ~ behandeln* treat s.o. in a degrading manner

menschenverachtend *Adj.* contemptuous of one's fellow men; *Politik*: showing contempt for humanity; (*zynisch*) cynical; **Menschenverächter** *m*, **Menschenverächterin** *f* misanthropist, *lit.* despiser of men; (*Zyniker*) cynic; **Menschenverachtung** *f* contempt for human beings (*od.* humanity); (*Zynismus*) cynicism

Menschen|verstand *m* human intellect; *gesunder ~* common sense; *das sagt einem schon der gesunde ~* common sense will tell you that; **~versuch** *m* experiment on a human being, human experiment; **~werk** *n geh.* the work of man; **~wesen** *n geh.* human being

Menschenwürde *f* (*auch die ~*) human dignity; **menschenwürdig I.** *Adj. Behandlung*: humane; *Zustände*: fit for human beings; *Verhalten*: befitting a human being; **II.** *Adv.*: *j-n ~ behandeln* treat s.o. in a manner befitting a human being

Menschheit *f*: *die ~* mankind, humanity, the human race, man; **menschheitlich** *Adj.* human

Menschheits|entwicklung *f; nur Sg.* human evolution; **~geschichte** *f; nur Sg.* history of man(kind) (*od.* of the human race); **~traum** *m* dream of mankind

menschlich I. *Adj.* **1.** human; (*human*) *auch* humane; *die ~e Natur* human nature; *nach ~em Ermessen* as far as one can possibly judge; → *irren* I 2, *Rühren*; **2.** *umg.* (*erträglich*) tolerable; (*wieder*) *ganz ~ aussehen umg.* look halfway civilized (again); **II.** *Adv.* **1.** (*als Mensch*) as a person; *sich ~ benehmen* behave like a normal human being; *sich ~ näher kommen* get to know one another on a personal level; **2.** *etw. ~ betrachten* consider s.th. in human terms; *rein ~ gesehen* seen in purely human terms; **Menschliche** *n*; *-n, kein Pl.*: *das ~* human nature, human characteristics *Pl.*; *alles ~* every human characteristic, every aspect of human nature; **Menschlichkeit** *f* **1.** (*menschliche Art*) human nature; *Schwäche*: human frailty; **2.** (*Humanität*) humaneness, humanity; *Verbrechen gegen die ~* crime against humanity

Menschwerdung *f; -, kein Pl.* **1.** *kirchl.* incarnation; **2.** *Bio.* evolution into man

Menstruation *f; -, -en; Med.*: (*die*) *~* menstruation

Menstruations|beschwerden *Pl.* **1.** (*Schmerzen*) period pains, *Am.* menstrual cramps; **2.** (*Spannung etc.*) PMT, premenstrual tension, *Am.* PMS (premenstrual syndrome) *Sg.*; **~zyklus** *m* menstrual cycle

menstruieren *v/i.* menstruate

Mensur *f; -, -en* **1.** (*Fechtabstand*) (fencing) distance; **2.** *Verbindungswesen*: (student's) duel, fencing bout; **3.** *Mus., von Orgelpfeife*: scale; *von Blasinstrument*: bore; *von Streichinstrument*: stop; **4.** *Mus.* (*Notenwert*) time value

mental *Adj.* mental; **Mentalität** *f; -, -en* mentality; *sich in j-s ~ hineinzuversetzen suchen* try to understand s.o. else's way of thinking

mentalitäts|bedingt *Adj.* governed by (their *etc.*) mentality; **~mäßig** *Adj.* in (their *etc.*) mentality, in their *etc.* way of thinking

Menthol *n; -s, kein Pl.* menthol; **~zigarette** *f* menthol(ated) cigarette

Mentor *m; -s, -en, ~in** *f; -, -nen* mentor; *Univ.* supervisor, tutor; *Schule*: supervisor

Menu [me'ny:] *n; -s, -s; schw.,* **Menü** *n; -s, -s* **1.** (*Speisenfolge*) menu; *Mahlzeit*: set meal; *mittags*: *auch* set lunch; **2.** *Computer*: menu

Menuett *n; -s, -e; Mus.* minuet

Menüleiste *f Computer*: menu bar

Meran (*n*); *-s Geog.* Merano

Mercerie [mɛrsə'ri:] *f; -, -n; schw.* **1.** *nur Sg.* haberdashery, *Am.* notions *Pl.*; **2.** *Geschäft*: haberdasher's (*Am.* notion) shop

Merchandising ['mœrtʃəndaizɪŋ] *n; -s, kein Pl.; Wirts.* merchandising

Mergel *m; -s, -; Geol.* marl

Meridian *m; -s, -e; Astron., Geog.* meridian; **~kreis** *m* meridian circle

meridional *Adj. Astron., Geog.* meridional

Meringe *f; -, -n,* **Meringue** [me'rɛ̃:k] *f; -, -s; schw.* meringue

Merino *m; -s, -s Gewebe*: merino; **~schaf** *n Zool.* Merino sheep; **~wolle** *f* Merino wool

Meriten *Pl. geh.* merits; *ein Mann mit zahlreichen ~* a man of great merit (*od.* of many merits); *sich* (*Dat.*) *große ~ erwerben um* render great services to

merkantil *Adj. geh.* mercantile; **Merkantilismus** *m; -, kein Pl.; hist.* mercantilism; **Merkantilist** *m; -en, -en* mercantilist; **merkantilistisch** *Adj.* mercantilist(ic)

merkbar *Adj.* **1.** → *merklich*; **2.** (*leicht zu behalten*): *leicht od. gut ~* easily remembered, *präd. od. nachgestellt*: easy to remember; *schwer ~ präd. od nachgestellt*: difficult to remember

Merk|blatt *n* leaflet; *mit Erläuterungen*: instruction leaflet; **~buch** *n* notebook

merken *v/t.* **1.** (*wahrnehmen*) notice; (*fühlen*) feel, sense; (*erkennen*) realize, see; (*sich e-r Sache bewusst sein*) be aware of, know; *merkt man es?* is it noticeable?, does it show?; *man merkte es an s-r Stimme* you could tell by his voice; *ich habe nichts gemerkt* I didn't notice anything, nothing struck me as unusual; *~ lassen, dass* show that, make it clear that; *er ließ nicht ~, dass* he gave no sign that; *du merkst* (*aber*) *auch alles iro.* you don't miss a thing, do you?; *merkst du was? umg.* haven't you noticed anything?; **2.** *sich* (*Dat.*) *etw. ~* (*im Gedächtnis behalten*) remember s.th.; (*notieren*) make a mental note of s.th.; *Namen kann ich mir einfach nicht ~* I'm hopeless at remembering names, I have no memory for names; *~ Sie sich das!* (and) don't you forget it!; *das werde ich mir ~!* I shan't (*Am.* won't)

forget that (in a hurry); *merke: ...* please note …

Merk|fähigkeit *f* (powers *Pl.* of) memory; **~heft** *n* notebook; **~hilfe** *f* mnemonic (aid)

merklich I. *Adj.* noticeable; *stärker*: distinct, marked; (*sichtbar*) *auch* visible; (*beträchtlich*) considerable, appreciable; **II.** *Adv.* noticeably; *stärker*: distinctly, markedly; (*sichtbar*) visibly

Merk|mal *n* (*characteristic*) feature; (*Symptom*) symptom; (*Zeichen*) sign; *unterscheidendes ~* distinctive mark (*od.* feature); *besondere ~e* distinguishing marks (*od.* features); **~satz** *m* **1.** mnemonic (phrase); **2.** (*Lebensweisheit*) maxim; **~spruch** *m* **1.** mnemonic (rhyme); **2.** (*Lebensweisheit*) maxim

Merkur *m; -s; Astron., Myth.* Mercury

Merkvers *m* mnemonic rhyme

merkwürdig *Adj.* strange, odd; *stärker*: curious, peculiar; **merkwürdigerweise** *Adv.* strangely (*od.* oddly) enough; **Merkwürdigkeit** *f* **1.** strangeness, oddness; *stärker*: curiousness, peculiarity; **2.** *Erscheinung*: curiosity; *Eigenschaft*: (strange) quirk

Merk|zeichen *n* mark(er); **~zettel** *m* note

Merowinger *m; -s. -, ~in** *f; -, -nen; hist.* Merovingian; **merowingisch** *Adj.* Merovingian

merzerisieren *v/t.* (*Baumwolle*) mercerize

meschugge *Adj. umg.* crazy, off one's head, nuts, *Am. auch* meshug(g)a

Meskalin *n; -s, kein Pl.; Pharm.* mescaline

Mesner *m; -s, -, ~in** *f; -, -nen; Dial. kath.* sexton, verger

Mesolithikum *n; -s; kein Pl.; Geol.* Mesolithic (period); **mesolithisch** *Adj.* Mesolithic

Mesopotamien (*n*); *-s; hist.* Mesopotamia

Mesosphäre *f; nur Sg.; Met.* mesosphere

Mesozoikum *n; -s, kein Pl.; Geol.* Mesozoic (period); **mesozoisch** *Adj.* Mesozoic

Message ['mɛsɪtʃ] *f; -, -s* message

Messband *n* tape measure

messbar *Adj.* measurable; **Messbarkeit** *f* measurability

Mess|becher *m* measuring cup (*größer*: jug); **~bereich** *m* measuring range

Messbild *n Kartographie*: photogram; **~verfahren** *n* photogrammetry

Messbuch *n kath.* missal

Messdaten *Pl.* measuring data, measurements

Messdiener *m, ~in** *f kath.* server

Messe¹ *f; -, -n; kath.* mass (*auch Mus.*); (*die*) *~ lesen* say Mass; *für j-n e-e ~ lesen lassen* have a Mass said for s.o.; *zur ~ gehen* go to Mass

Messe² *f; -, -n; Mil., Naut.* mess

Messe³ *f; -, -n* **1.** (*Ausstellung*) (trade) fair; *auf e-r ~ ausstellen* exhibit at a trade fair; **2.** *Dial.* (*Jahrmarkt*) fair; **~ausweis** *m* fair pass; **~bau** *m; nur Sg.* exhibition stand construction; **~besucher** *m*, **~besucherin** *f* visitor to a (*od.* the) fair; **~gelände** *n* exhibition site; **~halle** *f* exhibition hall; **~hostess** *f* hostess (at a fair); **~katalog** *m* exhibition catalog(ue); **~leitung** *f* fair management

messen; *misst, maß, hat gemessen* **I.** *v/t.* **1.** measure; *fig. mit Blicken*: size up; *die Zeit ~* do the timing; *die Zeit ~*

bei *e-m Wettlauf*: time; **nach Litern/ Metern** ~ measure in litres (*Am.* liters) /metres (*Am.* meters); **es wurden 40° (Wärme) gemessen** a temperature of 40° was recorded; → **Blutdruck, Fieber, Temperatur, 2.** *fig.* judge (*nach* by); (*vergleichen*) compare; **du kannst s-e Leistung nicht an i-r** ~ you can't compare his performance with (*od.* to) hers; **s-e Kräfte mit j-m** ~ pit one's strength against s.o.; **II.** *v/refl. fig.*: **sich mit j-m** ~ match o.s. against s.o.; *geistig*: pit one's wits against s.o.; *Sport* compete against s.o.; **sich mit j-m/etw. nicht** ~ **können** be no match for s.o. / not bear comparison with s.th.; **III.** *v/i.* **1.** *Maßangabe*: measure …(long *od.* high, wide *etc.*); *Person*: be … (tall); **das Zimmer misst 3 m mal 4 m** the room measures (*od.* is) 10ft by 13ft; **2.** *Person*: measure, take measurements; → **gemessen**

Messe|neuheit *f* new product (launched) at the fair; ~**pavillon** *m* trade fair pavilion

Messer *n; -s,* - **1.** knife; **Kampf bis aufs** ~ *fig.* fight to the death (*od.* finish); **auf (des)** ~**s Schneide stehen** be hanging in the balance, be on a knife edge; **es steht auf** ~**s Schneide, ob …** it's touch and go whether …; **j-n ans** ~ **liefern** *umg. fig.* put s.o.'s head on the block; (*verraten*) blow the whistle on s.o.; **ins offene** ~ **rennen** *umg. fig.* fall straight into the trap; → **Kehle** 1; **2.** *Tech.* cutter; (*Klinge*) blade; **3.** *Med.* scalpel, knife; **unters** ~ **kommen** come under the (surgeon's) knife, have an operation

Messergebnis *n* measurement; *abgelesen*: reading

Messer|griff *m* knife handle; ~**haarschnitt** *m* razor cut; ~**held** *m* knifer; ~**klinge** *f* knife blade; ~**rücken** *m* back of a (*od.* the) knife

messerscharf I. *Adj.* razor-sharp; *fig.* (*scharfsinnig*) *auch* incisive; *Kritik*: trenchant; ~**er Verstand** *fig.* razor-sharp intellect; **II.** *Adv. iro.*: **das war** ~ **geschlossen!** that was good thinking

Messer|schmied *m,* ~**schmiedin** *f* cutler; ~**schnitt** *m* **1.** knife cut (*od.* wound); **2.** (*Haarschnitt*) razor cut; ~**spitze** *f* knife point; **e-e** ~ **Salz** a pinch of salt

Messerstecher *m* knifer; **Messerstecherei** *f; -, -en* stabbing; *Kampf*: knife fight; **Messerstich** *m* stab; (*Wunde*) stab wound

Messe|schlager *m* highlight of the exhibition (*od.* trade fair); ~**stadt** *f* trade fair mecca; **die** ~ **Frankfurt** Frankfurt, the scene of many trade fairs; ~**stand** *m* exhibition stand; ~**teilnehmer** *m,* ~**teilnehmerin** *f* trade fair exhibitor; ~**zentrum** *n* exhibition cent|re (*Am.* -er)

Messfeier *f kath.* celebration of Mass

Mess|fühler *m Tech.* sensor; ~**gerät** *n* measuring instrument; (*Lehre*) ga(u)ge; (*Zähler*) meter

Messgewand *n kath.* chasuble

Mess|glas *n* measuring jug; ~**größe** *f Messtechnik, gemessen*: measured quantity; *zu messen*: quantity to be measured

messianisch *Adj.* messianic; **Messias** *m; -, -se* **1.** *nur Sg.; kirchl.*: **der** ~ the Messiah; **2.** *fig.* (*Erlöser*) messiah

Messie *m; -s, -s; umg.* (*krankhaft unordentlicher Mensch*) messy fellow

Messing *n; -s, -e* brass; ~**bett** *n* brass bed; ~**blech** *n* sheet brass; ~**draht** *m*

---

brass wire; ~**griff** *m* brass handle; ~**schild** *n* brass (name)plate

Messinstrument *n* → **Messgerät**

Messkelch *m kath.* (Communion) chalice

Mess|latte *f Landvermessung*: surveyor's pole; *fig.* yardstick, standard; **die** ~ **höher legen** *fig.* raise one's standards, demand more; ~**methode** *f* measuring method

Messner *m; -s, -,* ~**in** *f; -, -nen* → **Messner**

Messopfer *n kath.* Sacrifice of the Mass

Mess|schnur *f* measuring cord; ~**stab** *m* **1.** *Mot.* dipstick; **2.** → **Messlatte**; ~**station** *f* survey (control) station; ~**strecke** *f* distance to be measured; *gemessene*: distance measured; ~**technik** *f; nur Sg.* technology of measurement, metrology *fachspr.*

Messtisch *m Kartographie*: plane table; ~**blatt** *n* map produced by the plane table method

Mess|trupp *m* measuring unit; ~**uhr** *f Tech.* meter, dial ga(u)ge; ~ -**und-Regel-Technik** *f; nur Sg.* regulation by repeated measurements

Messung *f* measurement; (*Ablesung*) reading

Mess|verfahren *n* measuring method; ~**wagen** *m* (pollution- *etc.*) measuring vehicle

Messwein *m kath.* altar (*od.* communion) wine

Mess|werk *n Tech.* measuring device; ~**wert** *m* measurement; *abgelesen*: reading; ~**zahl** *f,* ~**ziffer** *f* reading; *Statistik*: relative, index (*Pl.* indices *od.* indexes), index number

Mestize *m; -n, -n,* **Mestizin** *f; -, -nen* mestizo

MESZ *Abk.* (**Mitteleuropäische Sommerzeit**) Central European Summer Time

Met *m; -(e)s, kein Pl.* mead

Metabolismus *m; -, Metabolismen*; *Physiol.* metabolism

Metalinguistik *f Ling.* metalinguistics *Pl.* (*V. im Sg.*)

Metall *n; -s, -e* metal; ~ **verarbeitend** metal-processing; *Industrie etc*: metalworking; ~**arbeit** *f* piece of metalwork; *Pl.* metalwork *Sg.*; ~**arbeiter** *m,* ~**arbeiterin** *f* metalworker; ~**bearbeitung** *f* metalworking; ~**beruf** *m* job in metalworking; ~**beschlag** *m* metal fitting (*od.* mounting); ~**börse** *f* metal exchange; ~**detektor** *m* metal detector

metallen I. *Adj.* (*aus Metall*) metal; *wie Metall*: metallic (*auch Stimme etc.*); **II.** *Adv.*: ~ **klingen/glänzen** have a metallic sound/gleam

Metaller *m; -s, -,* ~**in** *f; -, -nen; umg.* metalworker

Metall|ermüdung *f* metal fatigue; ~**geld** *n* metallic currency; (*Münzen*) coins *Pl.*

metallhaltig *Adj.* metalliferous

Metall|hütte *f* metalworking plant

metallic *indekl. Adj.* metallic; **ein Auto in Blau** ~ / **in** ~ **Blau** a metallic blue car

Metalliclackierung *f* metallic paintwork (*od.* finish)

Metallindustrie *f* metal(working) industry

metallisch I. *Adj.* metallic (*auch Stimme etc.*); **II.** *Adv.*: ~ **klingen/glänzen** have a metallic sound/gleam

metallisieren *v/t. Tech.* metal(l)ize

Metall|kleber *m Tech.* metal-bonding adhesive; ~**kunde** *f; nur Sg.* metallur-

---

gy; ~**legierung** *f* metal alloy

Metall|oxid *n Chem.* metallic oxide; ~**säge** *f* hacksaw; ~**schnitt** *m Kunst* metal engraving; ~**stift** *m* metal pin; ~**überzug** *m* metal coating

Metallurgie *f; -, kein Pl.* metallurgy; **metallurgisch** *Adj.* metallurgical

Metall verarbeitend → **Metall**

Metall|verarbeitung *f* metal processing, metalworking; ~**waren** *Pl.* metal goods; *bes. Utensilien*: metalware; ~**wert** *m* von *Münzen, Schmuck etc*.: metallic (*od.* intrinsic) value; ~**zaun** *f* metal fence; ~**zeit** *f; nur Sg.; Archäol.* Metal Age, Age of Metals

metamorph *Adj. fachspr.* metamorphic

Metamorphose *f; -, -n* metamorphosis (*Pl.* metamorphoses); *fig. auch* transformation; **e-e** ~ **durchmachen** *fig.* undergo a metamorphosis (*od.* transformation)

Metapher *f; -, -n; Ling., Rhet.* metaphor; **Metaphorik** *f; -; kein Pl.* (use of) metaphor; **metaphorisch** *Adj.* metaphorical

Metaphysik *f* metaphysics *Pl.* (*V. im Sg.*); **Metaphysiker** *m,* **Metaphysikerin** *f* metaphysician; **metaphysisch** *Adj.* metaphysical

Metasprache *f Ling.* metalanguage; **metasprachlich** *Adj.* metalinguistic

Metastase *f; -, -n; Med.* metastasis (*Pl.* metastases); **metastasieren** *v/i.* metastasize

Meteor *m; -s, -e; Astron.* meteor; **meteorhaft** *Adj. fig.* meteoric

Meteorit *m; -en und -s, -e(n); Astron.* meteorite; **Meteoritenkrater** *m* meteor(ite) crater; **meteoritisch** *Adj.* meteoric

Meteorologe *m; -n, -n; Met.* meteorologist; *beim Wetterbericht*: weatherman *umg.*; **Meteorologie** *f; -, kein Pl.* meteorology; **Meteorologin** *f; -, -nen* meteorologist; *beim Wetterbericht*: weatherlady *umg.*; **meteorologisch** *Adj.* meteorological

Meteorstein *m* meteorite

Meter *m, n; -s,* - met|re (*Am.* -er); **Vorhangstoffe** *etc.* **am laufenden** ~ **verkaufen** sell curtain materials *etc.* by the met|re (*Am.* -er)

meter|dick *Adj.* a met|re (*Am.* -er) thick, metre- (*Am.* meter-)thick …, three feet (and more) thick; (*mehrere Meter dick*) (several) met|res (*Am.* -ers) thick; ~**hoch** *Adj.* metre- (*Am.* meter-)high …, three feet (and more) high …; (*mehrere Meter hoch*) several met|res (*Am.* -ers) high; *Schnee*: waist-deep, … three feet (and more) deep; ~**lang** *Adj.* metre- (*Am.* meter-)long …, *nachgestellt*: … just over three feet long; *fig.* very long *umg.* great long …

Metermaß *n* (*Bandmaß*) tape measure, yardstick; (*Stab*) measuring rod, rule; (*Zollstock*) folding rule

meter|stark *Adj.* → met|re, ~**tief** *Adj.* a met|re (*Am.* -er) deep, three feet (and more) deep, why the me-

Meterware *f* goods *Pl.* … t|re (*Am.* …) … met|re (*Am.* …)

meterweise *Adv.* b … -er)

Methadon *n; -s,* … *Chem., Med.* methadone; ~**… f** *Med.* methadone treatmen …

Methan *n;* … *Pl.; Chem.* methmethane …

Methanol … method; **etw. mit** ~

Method …

machen do s.th. methodically; *es hat* ~ there's method in (*od.* behind) it; *er hat* ~ he's very methodical, he's a man of method; **2.** ~**n** (*Verhalten*) ways; *er hat so s-e* ~**n** he has his own way of doing things; **Methodik** *f*; -, -*en* **1.** *Lehre*: methodology; **2.** (*Verfahrensweise*) method; **Methodiker** *m*; -*s*, -, **Methodikerin** *f*; -, -*nen* methodical person; *Päd.* methodologist; *guter/erfahrener* **Methodiker** methodologically sound/experienced teacher; **methodisch I.** *Adj.* methodical; *Päd.* methodological; **II.** *Adv.* methodically; *Päd.* methodologically; ~ *geschickt/falsch Päd.* methodologically astute/incorrect

Methodist *m*; -*en*, -*en* Methodist; **Methodistenkirche** *f* Methodist church; **Methodistin** *f*; -, -*nen* Methodist; **methodistisch** *Adj.* Methodist

Methodologie *f*; -, -*n* methodology; **methodologisch** *Adj.* methodological

Methusalem *m*; -(*s*), -*s* **1.** *nur Sg.*; *bibl.* Methuselah; **2.** *umg.*: *die Band bestand nur aus* ~*s* the members of the band were all ancient, the band was entirely made up of doddery old men

Methyl *n*; -*s*, *kein Pl.*; *Chem.* methyl; ~**alkohol** *m* methyl alcohol, methanol; **Methylen** *n*; -*s*, *kein Pl.*; *Chem.* methylene

Metier [me'tie:] *n*; -*s*, -*s* profession, job; (*Handwerk*) trade; *das ist nicht mein* ~ *fig.* that's not my line

Metrik *f*; -, -*en*; *Lit.* **1.** *Lit., Lehre*: metrics *Pl.* (*V. im Sg.*); *Mus.* met|re (*Am.* -*er*); **2.** (*Metrum*) met|re (*Am.* -*er*); **metrisch** *Adj.* **1.** *Maß etc.*: metric; **2.** *Lit., Mus.* metrical

Metro *f*; -, -*s* Metro

Metronom *n*; -*s*, -*e*; *Mus.* metronome

Metropole *f*; -, -*n* **1.** metropolis; **2.** *hist.* (*Mutterland*) metropole

Metropolit *m*; -*en*, -*en*; *kirchl.* metropolitan; **Metropolitankirche** *f kirchl.* metropolitan church

Metrostation *f* underground station; *bes. in Paris*: Metro station

Metrum *n*; -*s*, *Metren* (*Versmaß*) met|re (*Am.* -*er*)

Mett *n*; -(*e*)*s*, *kein Pl.*; *Gastr.* minced (*Am.* ground) pork

Mett|brot *n* minced (*Am.* ground) pork open sandwich; ~**brötchen** *n Gastr.* minced (*Am.* ground) pork roll

Mette *f*; -, -*n*; *kirchl.* → **Christmette**, *Frühmette*, *Nachtmette*

Mettwurst *f Gastr.* smoked sausage (*made from minced pork or beef*); *zum Streichen*: smoked sausage spread

Metzelei *f*; -, -*en*; *pej.* slaughter, butchery; **metzeln** *v/t.* **1.** → *niedermetzeln*; **2.** *südd.* slaughter

Metzg... *m*; -*s*, -; *bes. südd.* butcher; *zum* ~ *gehen* go to the butcher's; **Metzgerei** *f*; -, -*en*; *bes. südd.* butcher['s] *(shop)*; **Metzgermeister** *m*, ~**in** *f bes. südd.* master butcher; **Metzgetcher**

Schlac... -, -*n*; *bes. schw.* **1.** → *schüssel*; **2.** *Gastr.* → *Schlacht*-

Meuchel... ~**mörde...** *m* dastardly killing; murderer, **mörderin** *f* dastardly **meucheln** ...*iter[in]*: assassin) *tentat*: assa...*pej.* murder (*bei Attion* ... a dastardly fashion **meuchlerisc...** *risch*) treach... **meuchlings** ... stardly; (*verräterisch) geh. pej.* mur...

~ *umbringen* ... a dastardly

(*verräterisch*: treacherous) fashion

Meute *f*; -, -*n* **1.** pack (of hounds); **2.** *fig.* mob; (*Gruppe von Freunden etc.*) *umg.* gang

Meuterei *f*; -, -*en* mutiny; **Meuterer** *m*; -*s*, -, **Meuterin** *f*; -, -*nen* mutineer; **meutern** *v/i.* mutiny; *umg. fig.* rebel

Mexikaner *m*; -*s*, ~**in** *f*; -, -*nen* Mexican, *weiblich auch*: Mexican woman (*od.* girl); **mexikanisch** *Adj.* Mexican; **Mexiko** (*n*); -*s*; *Geogr., Land*: Mexico; (*auch* ~-*Stadt*) Mexico City

MEZ *Abk.* (**Mitteleuropäische Zeit**) CET

Mezzanin *m*, *n*; -*s*, -*e*; *Archit.* mezzanine; *unter dem Dach*: attic

Mezzosopran *m* mezzo-soprano

mg *Abk.* (**Milligramm**) mg

MG *n*; -(*s*), -(*s*); *Abk.* (**Maschinengewehr**) MG

MG|-Salve *f* burst of machine-gun fire; ~**Schütze** *m*, ~**Schützin** *f* machine-gunner

MHz *Abk.* (**Megahertz**) MHz

miau *Interj.* miaow!, *Am.* meow; **miauen** *v/i.* miaow, *Am.* meow

mich I. *pers. Pron.* (*Akk. von ich*) me; **II.** *refl. Pron.* myself; *nach Präp.* me; *hinter* ~ behind me; *oft unübersetzt*: *ich setzte* ~ I sat down

Micha (*m*); -*s*; *bibl.* Micah

Michaelis (*n*); -, ~**tag** *m* Michaelmas

Michel *m*; -*s*, -; *umg.* (*Deutscher*) German; *der deutsche* ~ your typical dreamy, apolitical German

mick(e)rig *Adj. umg. Sache*: measly, pathetic, *stärker*: lousy; *Person*: puny, (*kränklich*) sickly

Mickymaus *f*; -, *kein Pl.* Mickey Mouse; ~**Stimme** *f umg. pej.* squeaky voice

Midi[1] (*n*); -*s*, *kein Pl. Mode*: midi-(length); *Kleidung*: midi(-length) clothing

Midi[2] *m*; -*s*, -*s* midi skirt; ~**kleid** *n* midi dress; ~**rock** *m* midi skirt

Midlifecrisis ['mɪdlaɪfˈkraɪsɪs] *f*; -, *kein Pl.* midlife crisis, male menopause

mied *Imperf.* → **meiden**

Mieder *n*; -*s*, - bodice; ~**hose** *f* panty girdle; ~**waren** *Pl.* foundation garments, *Am. auch* foundations

Mief *m*; -(*e*)*s*, *kein Pl.*; *umg. pej.* fug, stuffiness; (*Gestank*) stink; *fig.* stuffy (*od.* claustrophobic) atmosphere; **miefen** *v/i. umg. pej.* pong, stink, stench; *hier mieft es* there's a pong (*Am.* stench) in here; **miefig** *Adj. umg.* stuffy (and smelly), *Brit. auch* frowsty, *Am. auch* funky

Miene *f*; -, -*n* expression; (*auch Gesicht*) face; (*auch* ~*unschuldsvolle* ~) innocent expression (*od.* air); *e-e ernste* ~ *aufsetzen* look serious; *gute* ~ *zum bösen Spiel machen* put on a brave face, make the best of it, *umg.* grin and bear it; ~ *machen, etw. zu tun* make as if to do s.th.; *ohne e-e* ~ *zu verziehen* without batting an eyelid, without turning a hair; *bei Schmerz etc.*: *auch* without flinching; **Mienenspiel** *n* facial expressions *Pl.* (*od.* play)

mies I. *Adj. umg.* lousy, rotten; (*e-e*) ~*e Laune haben* be in a foul mood; *er hat* ~*e Arbeit geleistet* he made a lousy job of it; *j-n/etw.* ~ *machen* run s.o./s.th. down, slag s.o./s.th. off; **II.** *Adv.* dreadfully; *ihr geht es* ~ she's in a bad way

Miese *Pl. umg.*: *in den* ~*n sein auf dem Konto*: be in the red; *beim Kartenspiel*: be down on points

Miesepeter *m*; -*s*, -; *umg.* (old) grouch,

---

sourpuss; **miesepet(e)rig** *Adj. umg.* grumpy; **Miesmacher** *m*, **Miesmacherin** *f umg.* (*Meckerer*) whinger, moaner, *Am. auch* whiner; (*Beckmesser*) fault-finder; (*Spielverderber*) killjoy

Miesmuschel *f Zool.* mussel

Miet|anstieg *m* rent increase; ~**ausfall** *m* loss of rent; ~**auto** *n* hire(d) (*Am.* rented *od.* rental) car; ~**beihilfe** *f* rent allowance; ~**dauer** *f* (period of) tenancy

Miete[1] *f*; -, -*n* rent; *in od. zur* ~ *wohnen* live in a rented flat (*Am.* apartment) (*od.* house); *als Untermieter*: live in lodgings, rent a room; *das ist (ja schon) die halbe* ~ *umg. fig.* that's half the battle

Miete[2] *f*; -, -*n* (*Lager für Feldfrüchte*) *unter der Erde*: pit; *über der Erde*: stack

Mieteinnahme *f*, ~**n** *Pl.* rental income *Sg.*

mieten *v/t.* (*Haus*) rent; (*Sachen*) hire, *Am. mst* rent; **Mieter** *m*; -*s*, -, **Mieterin** *f*; -, -*nen* tenant; (*Untermieter*) lodger, *Am. auch* roomer

Mieterhöhung *f* rent increase

Mieterschutz *m* protection of tenants' rights; ~**bund** *m* tenants' (rights) association; ~**gesetz** *n* law protecting tenants' rights; *in GB*: *etwa* Rent Act

Mieter|verein *m* tenants' association; ~**versammlung** *f* tenants' meeting

Mietforderung *f* rent demand

mietfrei *Adj. und Adv.* rent-free; **Mietfreiheit** *f*; *nur Sg.* rent exemption

Miet|gesetz *n* tenancy law; ~**kauf** *m Wirts.* lease-purchase agreement (*with option to buy at the end of the lease period*); ~**kaution** *f* deposit

mietmindernd I. *Adj. Wirkung*: ... (of) reducing the rent; **II.** *Adv.*: *sich* ~ *auswirken* have the effect of reducing the rent; **Mietminderung** *f* rent reduction

Miet|objekt *n* rented property; ~**partei** *f* tenant

Mietpreis *m* rent; *für Sachen*: rental (fee, *Am.* rate), *Brit. auch* hire charge; ~**bindung** *f* rent control

Miet|recht *n*; *nur Sg.* laws *Pl.* governing tenancy; ~**rückstand** *m* rent arrears *Pl.*; ~**schuld** *f* back rent; ~**schulden** *Pl.* rent arrears

Miets|haus *n* block of (rented) flats, *Am.* apartment house; ~**kaserne** *f* tenement block (*Am.* building)

Mietspiegel *m* rental table

mietsteigernd I. *Adj. Wirkung*: ... of increasing the rent; **II.** *Adv.*: *sich* ~ *auswirken* have the effect of inreasing the rent

Miet|streitigkeiten *Pl.* tenancy disputes; ~**verhältnis** *n* tenancy; ~**verlängerung** *f* extension of one's (*od.* the) lease; ~**vertrag** *m* lease; *für Sachen*: hire (*Am.* rental) agreement; ~**vorauszahlung** *f* advance payment of rent, rent in advance

Mietwagen *m Mot.* hire(d) (*Am.* rented, rental) car; ~**verleih** *m* car rental (*Am. auch* rent-a-car) (service)

mietweise *Adj. und Adv.* on a rental basis, for rent

Miet|wert *m* rental value; ~**wohnung** *f* rented flat (*bes. Am.* apartment); ~**wucher** *m* rent racketeering, rack renting; ~**zahlung** *f* payment of rent; ~**zins** *m südd., österr., schw.* rental (fee); ~**zuschuss** *m* rent allowance

Miez *f*; -, -*en*; *umg., Kinderspr.* pussy(-cat); **Mieze** *f*; -, -*n* **1.** *umg., Kinderspr.* pussy(cat); **2.** *umg. fig.* (*Mädchen*) bird, *Am.* chick; **Miezekatze** *f* Kin-

derspr. pussy(cat)

Mignonzelle [mɪnˈjõ:-] *f Etech.* AA battery

Migräne *f; -, -n; Med.* migraine; **~anfall** *m* migraine (attack)

Migrant *m; -en, -en; Zool., Soziol.* migrant; **Migrantin** *f; -, -nen; Soziol.* (female) migrant; **Migration** *f; -, -nen; Zool., Soziol.* migration

Mikado[1] *n; -s, -s* spillikins *Sg., Am.* pick-up-sticks

Mikado[2] *m; -s, -s* **1.** spillikin (*Am.* pick-up-stick) with the highest value; **2.** *hist.* mikado

Mikro *n; -s, -s; Abk. umg.* mike; → *Mikrofon*

Mikro|... *im Subst.* micro...; **~ananlyse** *f Chem.* microanalysis

Mikrobe *f; -, -n* microbe; **mikrobiell** *Adj.* microbial

Mikrobiologie *f* microbiologymicrobiologist; **mikrobiologisch** *Adj.* microbiological

Mikro|chip *m Etron.* microchip; **~chirurgie** *f Med.* microsurgery; **~computer** *m* microcomputer; **~elektronik** *f* microelectronics *Pl.* (*V. im Sg.*); **~farad** *n Phys.* microfarad; **~faser** *f Stoff:* microfib|re (*Am.* -er); **~fiche** *m, n* microfiche; **~film** *m* microfilm

Mikrofon *n; -s, -e* microphone; **~buchse** *f* microphone jack

Mikrofotografie *f* microphotography

Mikrogramm *n* microgram

Mikroklima *n Met.* microclimate

Mikrokosmos *m* microcosm

mikrokristallin *Adj. Geol., Min.* microcrystalline

Mikrometer *n; -s, -* micron

Mikronesien (*n*); *-s; Geog.* Micronesia

Mikroorganismus *m Bio.* microorganism

Mikrophon → *Mikrofon*

Mikroprozessor *m* microprocessor

Mikroskop *n; -s, -e* microscope; **Mikroskopie** *f; -, kein Pl.* microscopy; **mikroskopieren** *v/i.* work with the microscope; **mikroskopisch I.** *Adj.* microscopic; **II.** *Adv.* microscopically; *etw.* **~** *untersuchen* examine s.th. under the microscope; **~** *klein* microscopic

Mikro|struktur *f* microstructure; **~welle** *f* (*auch umg. Herd*) microwave

Mikrowellen|behandlung *f* microwave treatment; **~gerät** *n,* **~herd** *m* microwave oven

Mikrozensus *m Statistik:* quarterly population count

Milan *m; -s, -e; Orn.* kite

Milbe *f; -, -n; Zool.* mite

Milch *f; -, -e(n), Pl. nur fachspr.* **1.** milk (*auch fig. Reinigungsmilch etc.*); **~** *geben Kuh, Ziege etc.:* give milk; **2.** *Bot.* milk; (*Latex*) latex; **3.** *e-s Fisches:* (soft) roe, milt; **~auto** *n umg.* milk tanker; **~bar** *f* milk bar; → *Eisdiele*; **~bart** *m pej.* greenhorn, callow youth; **~brei** *m Gastr.* milk pudding; **~brötchen** *n* milk roll; **~drüse** *f Anat.* mammary gland; **~eis** *n Gastr.* milk-based ice cream; **~eiweiß** *n* lactoprotein; **~ersatzfutter** *n Agr.* milk substitute feed; **~fett** *n* milk fat; **~flasche** *f* milk bottle; *für Babys:* (feeding) bottle, baby's bottle; **~frau** *f umg.* dairywoman

milchfrei *Adj.* non-milk ...

Milch|gebiss *n* milk teeth *Pl.*; **~geschäft** *n* dairy, creamery; **~gesicht** *n umg. pej.* babyface; **~glas** *n* **1.** *Tech.* milk glass; **2.** (*Trinkglas für Milch*) milk beaker (*Am.* glass); **~glasschei-**

be *f Tech.* milk glass pane

milchig *Adj.* milky

Milch|kaffee *m* milky coffee; *italienischer Art:* latte; **~kalb** *n* sucking calf; **~kännchen** *n* milk jug; **~kanne** *f* milk churn; *kleine:* milk can; **~kuh** *f* dairy cow, milch cow; **~leistung** *f e-r Kuh:* milk yield

Milchmädchen *n* milkmaid; **~rechnung** *f umg.* naive expectation

Milch|mann *m* milkman; **~mixgetränk** *n* milkshake

Milchner *m; -s, -;* (*männlicher Fisch*) milter

Milch|produkt *n; mst Pl.* dairy product; **~pulver** *n* powdered milk; **~pumpe** *f* breast pump; **~reis** *m Gastr.* rice pudding; **~säure** *f Chem.* lactic acid; **~säurebakterien** *Pl. Bio., Chem.* lactic acid bacteria; **~schaf** *n* milk sheep; **~schokolade** *f* milk chocolate; **~schorf** *m Med.* milk crust

Milchstraße *f; nur Sg.; Astron.* (*Galaxie*) galaxy; *die* **~** the Milky Way, the Galaxy; **Milchstraßensystem** *n* galactic system, galaxy

Milch|tüte *f* milk tetrapack®; **~vieh** *n* dairy cattle *Pl.*

milchweiß *Adj.* milk-white

Milch|wirtschaft *f* dairy farming; **~zahn** *m* milk tooth; **~zentrifuge** *f* (cream) separator; **~zucker** *m* milk sugar, lactose

mild I. *Adj. auch Klima, Essen etc.:* mild; *Strafe, Richter etc.: auch* lenient; *Lächeln:* gentle, *ironisches:* wan; *Spirituosen:* smooth; *Wein:* mellow; (*lieblich*) (medium) sweet; *Licht, Farbe:* soft; *e-e* **~e** *Gabe* a charitable donation; (*Almosen*) alms *Pl.*; *j-n* **~** *stimmen* put s.o. in a lenient mood; **II.** *Adv.:* **~e** *gesagt* to put it mildly; *da kann ich nur* **~e** *lächeln iro.* you must be joking

milde → *mild*

Milde *f; -, kein Pl.* mildness; *e-s Lächelns:* gentleness; (*Nachsichtigkeit*) leniency; → *mild;* **~** *walten lassen* be lenient, show leniency

mildern I. *v/t.* (*Schmerz*) soothe, ease, alleviate; (*Urteil*) moderate; (*Strafe*) reduce; (*Aussage etc.*) qualify; (*Wirkung etc.*) reduce, soften; **~de** *Umstände Jur.* extenuating (*od.* mitigating) circumstances; **II.** *v/refl. Schmerz:* ease; *Emotionen:* cool off; *Wetter:* turn milder; **Milderung** *f von Schmerz:* alleviation; *e-r Strafe:* reduction; *e-r Aussage etc.:* qualification; *e-r Ansicht:* moderation; *e-e* **~** *des Wetters herbeiführen:* cause the weather to become milder; **Milderungsgrund** *m Jur.* extenuating (*od.* mitigating) factor

mildherzig *Adj. geh.* kind-hearted

mildtätig *Adj.* charitable; **Mildtätigkeit** *f* charity

Milieu [miˈljøː] *n; -s, -s* **1.** (*Umwelt*) environment (*auch Bio.*), surroundings *Pl.*; *Soziol.* milieu; (*soziale Herkunft*) background; **2.** (*Dirnenwelt*) world of prostitution; (*Rotlichtdistrikt*) red light district, *Am. auch* combat zone

milieu|bedingt *Adj.* due to environmental factors; (*wegen sozialer Herkunft*) due to social background; **~geschädigt** *Adj.* maladjusted due to environmental factors

Milieu|schaden *m bes. Psych.* maladjustment due to environmental factors; **~studie** *f bes. Lit.* background [description]; **~theorie** *f Psych.* environmentalism

militant *Adj.* militant; **Mili...**

kein Pl. militancy

Militär[1] *n; -, kein Pl.; Mil.* **1.** armed forces *Pl.*, military; (*Heer*) army; *beim* **~** *sein* be in the forces; *zum* **~** *müssen* have to do military service; **2.** (*Soldaten*) military personnel, soldiers *Pl.*; **~** *einsetzen* (*gegen j-n*) use troops (against s.o.)

Militär[2] *m; -s, -s; Mil.* (high-ranking) officer

Militär|abkommen *n Mil.* military agreement (*od.* pact); **~akademie** *f* military academy; **~aktion** *f* military action; **~arzt** *m,* **~ärztin** *f* medical officer; **~attaché** *m* military attaché; **~basis** *f* military base; **~berater** *m* military adviser; **~bündnis** *n* military alliance; **~dienst** *m* military service; **~diktatur** *f* military dictatorship; **~einsatz** *m* **1.** (*Einsatz von Militär*) use of troops; **2.** (*Kampfhandlung*) military action; **~fahrzeug** *n* military vehicle

Militärflug *m Mil., Flug.* military flight; **~platz** *m* military airfield; **~zeug** *n* military aircraft

Militär|gefängnis *n Mil.* military prison; **~gelände** *n* area used by the military, military property; **~gericht** *n* military court, court martial; **~gerichtsbarkeit** *f* military jurisdiction; **~herrschaft** *f; nur Sg.* military regime; *Diktatur:* military dictatorship; **~hoheit** *f* military authority; **~hubschrauber** *m* military helicopter

Militaria *Pl.* militaria; **~händler** *m,* **~händlerin** *f* dealer in militaria

militärisch I. *Adj.* military; *Gebaren etc.:* martial; *mit allen* **~en** *Ehren* with full military hono(u)rs; **II.** *Adv.:* **~** *grüßen* give a military salute, salute (in military style); **~** *stark sein* have considerable military strength

Militarisierung *f* militarization

Militarismus *m; -, kein Pl.; pej.* militarism; **Militarist** *m; -en, -en,* **Militaristin** *f; -, -nen pej.* militarist; **militaristisch** *Adj. pej.* militaristic

Militär|junta *f Mil.* military junta; **~kapelle** *f* military band; **~konvoi** *m* convoy (of military vehicles); **~krankenhaus** *n* military hospital; **~lastwagen** *m* army lorry (*Am.* truck); **~macht** *f* military power; **~marsch** *m Mus.* military march; **~maschine** *f* military aircraft; **~musik** *f* military marches *Pl.* (*od.* music); **~parade** *f* military parade; **~pfarrer** *m,* **~pfarrerin** *f* forces chaplain; *im Heer:* army chaplain; **~polizei** *f* military police; **~polizist** *m* military policeman; **~polizistin** *f* military policewoman; **~putsch** *m* military putsch; **~regierung** *f* military government; **~regime** *n* military [re]gime; **~schlag** *m* military st[w.] action; **~seelsorge** *f* pastor[le] *f* forces personnel; **~sp[i]cher** marching (military) ba[   ]White military (*od.* forces)[   ]**~spre-** *m:* (*des Weiß*[   ]ase; **~taug-** House) milit[   ]tary service; cherin [   ]ary affairs *Pl.*; **~stützpu[   ]**ary science lichkei[   ]eiter *-s Reitsport:* **~wes[   ]**[   ]iter *m* three-day wi[   ]military service; *wäh-* M[   ] when I was in the ar- [etc.)

[   ] *Mil.* militia [   ]*; -s, -e,* **~in** *f; -, -nen; Mil.*

member of a militia; *männlich: auch* militiaman

Milizparlament *n schw. federal assembly composed of part-time politicians*

Miliz|soldat *m Mil.* militiaman; **~soldatin** *f* (female) member of a militia

Mille *n*; *-*; *umg.* grand, K; **25 ~** 25 grand, 25 K

Millennium *n*; *-s*, *Millenien* millennium (*Pl.* millennia *od.* millenniums)

Milliampere *n Etech., Phys.* milliampere

Milliardär *m*; *-s*, *-e*, **~in** *f*; *-*, *-nen* billionaire

Milliarde *f*; *-*, *-en* billion, *Brit. altm. auch* thousand million; *in die* **~n** *gehen* run into billions (of pounds, dollars *etc.*)

Milliarden|betrag *m* sum of a billion (*mehrere Milliarden*: billions of) pounds (*od.* dollars *etc.*); *es sind Milliardenbeträge* the amounts run into billions; **~gewinn** *m* (multi)billion profit; **~höhe** *f*: ... *in ~* amounting to a billion (*mehrere Milliarden*: billions); → *auch* **Millionenhöhe**

milliardenschwer *Adj. umg.* ... worth a billion (*mehrere Milliarden*: billions)

Milliardenvermögen *n* fortune amounting to a billion (*mehrere Milliarden*: running into billions)

milliardst... *Adj.* billionth, *Brit. altm. auch* thousand millionth; **Milliardstel** *n*; *-s*, *-* billionth (part), *Brit. altm. auch* thousand millionth (part)

Milli|bar *n Met.* millibar; **~gramm** *n* milligram; **~liter** *m, n* millilit|re (*Am.* -er)

Millimeter *n, m* millimet|re (*Am.* -er); **Millimeterarbeit** *f*; *nur Sg.*: *das ist ~* it's an ultra-precision (*umg.* terribly fiddly) job; *Manöver*: you have to get it exactly right; **millimetergenau** *Adj.* ultra-precise; **Millimeterpapier** *n* graph paper

Million *f*; *-*, *-en* **1.** million; *fünf* **~en** *Dollar* five million dollars; *der Neubau kostet* **~en** the new building will cost millions; **2.** *Pl. umg. übertreibend: e-e große Zahl:* **~en** *Menschen waren da* there were thousands of people there

Millionär *m*; *-s*, *-e*, **~in** *f*; *-*, *-nen* millionaire, *weiblich auch* millionairess

Millionen|anleihe *f* loan of a million; *von mehreren Millionen:* loan running into millions, multimillion loan; **~auflage** *f Zeitung:* circulation of over a million (*von mehreren Millionen:* of several million); *das Buch hat inzwischen e-e ~ erreicht* the book has sold over a million copies; **~auftrag** *m* order worth a million (*mehrere Millionen:* millions); **~betrag** *m* sum of a million (*mehrere Millionen:* millions of pounds (*od.* dollars, euros *etc.*); *es sind Millionenbeträge* the amounts ... millions; **~ding** *n umg.* million... (*od.* -pound, -euro *etc.*) ... chen: job); *von mehreren* ... job)... multimillion dollar (*od.* ...tc.) deal (*Verbrechen:* ... million... multimil... *Adj.* ... millionfold; ...etc.) bus...s (over) ...-pound (o...*Unternehmen:* ...gewinn *m* ...dollar, -euro running into ...ultimillion over a milli...(.) deal; ...beitslosen thc... profit ploye... **~höhe** J. ...army ...-Ar-

a million (*mehrere Millionen:* millions); *die Explosion verursachte e-n Schaden in ~* the explosion caused damage running into millions of dollars *etc.*; **~loch** *n*: *das ~ im Haushalt* the million-dollar *etc.* budget deficit; **~schaden** *m* damage running into millions of dollars *etc.*

millionenschwer *Adj. umg.* ... worth millions

Millionen|stadt *f* city of over a million inhabitants; **~verlust** *m* loss of a million; *von mehreren Millionen:* loss running into millions; **~vermögen** *n* fortune running into millions

millionst... *Adj.* millionth; **Million(s)-tel** *n*; *-s*, *-* millionth (part)

Milz *f*; *-*, *kein Pl.; Anat.* spleen

Milzbrand *m Vet., Med.* anthrax; **~an-schlag** *m* anthrax attack; **~erreger** *m* anthrax bacillus

Mime *m*; *-en*, *-en; Theat.* actor; **mimen** *v/t.* act (*auch fig. pej.*); (*Rolle*) *auch* play; *Überraschung etc. ~* act (*od.* pretend to be) surprised *etc.*, feign surprise *etc.*

Mimese *f*; *-*, *-n*; *Zool.* mimicry, mimesis

Mimik *f*; *-*, *kein Pl.* facial expression (and gesture); *darstellerisch:* mime

Mimikry *f*; *-*, *kein Pl.; Bio.* mimicry (*auch fig.*)

Mimin *f*; *-*, *-en* actress

mimisch I. *Adj.; nur attr.* mimic, of facial expression (and gesture); *Begabung:* for facial expression (and gesture) (*od.* mime); **II.** *Adv.: etw. ~ ausdrücken* express s.th. by facial expression (and gesture)

Mimose *f*; *-*, *-en* **1.** *Bot.* mimosa; **2.** *fig. pej.* hypersensitive creature; **mimosenhaft** *Adj. fig., mst pej.* hypersensitive

mimsen *vt/i. umg. Handy:* send *s.o.* an MMS

Minarett *n*; *-s*, *-e* minaret

minder *Adv.* less; *nicht ~* no less

minder... *Adj.; nur attr.* less(er); (*kleiner*) smaller; *an Ausmaß, Bedeutung: auch* minor; *an Güte:* inferior; *Waren* **~er** *Güte* inferior (*od.* low-quality) goods

Minder|ausgaben *Pl.* reduced expenditure *Sg.*; **~bedarf** *m* reduced demand, drop in demand

minderbegabt *Adj.* less gifted; *Schüler: auch* lower-ability ...; **Minderbegabte** *m, f* less gifted person; *Schule:* lower-ability pupil (*Am.* student)

minderbemittelt *Adj.* less well-off, needy; *geistig ~ umg.* mentally less well endowed, not very bright; **Minderbemittelte** *m, f* needy person

Minder|betrag *m* deficit; **~bewertung** *f* undervaluation; **~einnahme** *f* shortfall in receipts; **~ertrag** *m* reduced yield (*Wirts.* profit); **~gebot** *n bei Auktion:* bid below estimate; **~gewicht** *n* short weight

Minderheit *f* minority

Minderheiten|frage *f* minorities question; **~recht** *n; mst Pl.* minority rights *Pl.*; **~schutz** *m* protection of minorities

Minderheits|regierung *f Pol.* minority government; **~votum** *n* minority vote

minderjährig *Adj.* under age; *attr.* under-age; **Minderjährige** *m, f*; *-n*, *-n* minor; **Minderjährigkeit** *f* minority

mindern I. *v/t.* diminish, lessen, decrease; (*herabsetzen*) reduce, lower; (*Wert*) depreciate; **II.** *v/refl.* diminish, decrease; *Begeisterung etc.: auch* abate; **Minderung** *f* decrease, reduc-

tion; *des Wertes:* depreciation

minderwertig *Adj.* inferior, of inferior quality; *Wirts. auch* low-grade ...; **Minderwertigkeit** *f* inferiority; *Wirts.* inferior quality

Minderwertigkeits|gefühl *n* feeling of inferiority; **~komplex** *m Psych.* inferiority complex

Minderzahl *f*; *nur Sg.*: minority; *in der ~ sein* be in the minority

mindest... *Adj.* least, slightest, minimum ...; *nicht im Mindesten* not in the least, not at all; *nicht die ~e Chance* not the slightest chance; *ich habe nicht die ~e Ahnung davon* I don't know the first thing about it; *zum Mindesten* at least; *das Mindeste* the very minimum (*od.* least)

Mindest|... *im Subst.* minimum ...; **~abstand** *m* minimum distance (*od.* gap); **~alter** *n* minimum age; **~anforderung** *f* minimum requirement; **~ausstattung** *f* basic minimum equipment; **~beitrag** *m* minimum contribution (*Mitgliedsbeitrag:* subscription); **~besteuerung** *f* lowest tax rate; **~betrag** *m* minimum amount

mindestens *Adv.* at least

Mindest|forderung *f* minimum (wage) demand; **~gebot** *n* lowest bid; *Auktion:* reserve (price)

Mindestgehalt¹ *n Entlohnung:* minimum wage

Mindestgehalt² *m Anteil:* minimum content

Mindest|geschwindigkeit *f* minimum speed; **~größe** *f* minimum size; **~haltbarkeitsdatum** *n* best-before date, *Am.* pull date; **~lohn** *m* minimum wage; **~maß** *n* minimum (*Pl.* minima *od.* minimums); **~preis** *m* minimum price; **~reserve** *f Wirts.* minimum reserve (deposit); **~rente** *f* minimum pension; **~satz** *m* minimum rate; **~strafe** *f* minimum penalty; **~umtausch** *m* minimum currency exchange; **~wortschatz** *m* minimum vocabulary; **~zeit** *f* minimum period

Mine *f*; *-*, *-n* **1.** *Bergb.* mine; **2.** *Mil., Naut.* mine; **~n legen** lay mines; *auf e-e ~ laufen* hit a mine; **3.** *e-s Bleistifts:* lead; *e-s Kugelschreibers:* cartridge, (*Ersatzmine*) refill

Minen|arbeiter *m*, **~arbeiterin** *f Bergb.* mineworker, miner; **~feld** *n* minefield; **~leger** *m*; *-s*, *-*; *Mil., Naut.* minelayer; **~räumboot** *n* minesweeper; **~sperre** *f Naut.* mine barrier; *auf einer Straße:* mine roadblock; **~suchboot** *n* minehunter; **~suchgerät** *n* mine detector

minenverseucht *Adj.* mine-infested

Mineral *n*; *-s*, *-e und Mineralien* mineral; **~bad** *n* mineral bath; (*Kurort*) spa; **~brunnen** *m* mineral spring; **~dünger** *m* mineral fertilizer

Mineralisation *f*; *-*, *-en; Chem., Geol.* mineralization; **mineralisieren** *vt/i.* mineralize

mineralisch *Adj.* mineral ...

Mineraloge *m*; *-en*, *-en* mineralogist; **Mineralogie** *f*; *-* mineralogy; **Mineralogin** *f*; *-*, *-nen* (female) mineralogist; **mineralogisch** *Adj.* mineralogical

Mineralöl *n* mineral oil

Mineralöl|... *im Subst.* → *auch* **Erdöl...**; **~erzeugnis** *n* petroleum product; **~gesellschaft** *f* oil company; **~industrie** *f* oil industry; **~konzern** *m* oil company; **~steuer** *f* tax on oil

Mineral|quelle *f* mineral spring; **~salz** *n* mineral salt; **~stoff** *m* inorganic mineral salt, mineral nutrient; **~vorkommen** *n* mineral deposit(s *Pl.*);

M

~wasser *n* mineral water
Mini[1] *n*; *-s*, *-s* **1.** *nur Sg.* mini(-length); *Kleidung*: mini(-length) clothing; **2.** *Abk. umg. Kleid*: minidress
Mini[2] *m*; *-s*, *-s* **1.** *Abk. umg. Rock*: miniskirt; **2.** *Mot.*, *Auto*: mini
Mini... *im Subst.* mini...
Miniatur *f*, *-*, *-en* miniature; *in Handschriften*: *auch* illumination; **~ausgabe** *f* miniature edition
miniaturisieren *v/t. Etron., Etech.* miniaturize; **Miniaturisierung** *f* miniaturization
Miniatur|maler *m* miniaturist; **~malerei** *f* miniature painting; **~malerin** *f* (female) miniaturist
Mini|bar *f* minibar; **~car** *m* minicab; **~format** *n* mini format, tiny format; **... in ~** mini-format ...
Minigolf *n* crazy golf, *Am.* miniature golf; **~platz** *m* crazy golf course, *Am.* miniature golf course
Minikleid *n* minidress
minim *Adj. schw.* → **minimal**
minimal *Adj.* minimal; *(unwesentlich)* insignificant, negligible
Minimal|betrag *m* minimal (*od.* insignificant) amount; **~forderung** *f* minimum requirement
minimal-invasiv *Adj. Med.*: **~e Chirurgie** minimally invasive surgery
minimalisieren *v/t.* minimalize
Minimalist *m*; *-en*, *-en*, **~in** *f*; *-*, *-nen* minimalist; **minimalistisch** *Adj.* **1.** *Mus., Kunst* minimalist; **2.** *(sehr gering) Beschreibung*: very brief
Minimal|konsens *m bes. Pol.* minimum amount of common ground; **~lösung** *f* minimal solution
Minimal|programm *n* (basic) policy plan; **~wert** *m* minimum value
minimieren *v/t.* minimize; **Minimierung** *f* minimization
Minimum *n*; *-s*, *Minima* minimum (*Pl.* minima *od.* minimums)
Mini|pille *f* minipill; **~rock** *m* miniskirt; **~slip** *m*: (*ein*) **~** (a pair of) bikini briefs *Pl.*
Minister *m*; *-s*, *-*; *Pol.* minister (+ *Gen.* of, for); *e-s Hauptministeriums, in GB*: Secretary of State (for), *in den USA*: Secretary (of)
Minister|amt *n Pol.* ministerial office; *Geschäftsbereich*: portfolio; **~anklage** *f* impeachment of a minister; **~bank** *f* government front bench; **~ebene** *f*: **auf ~** at cabinet level
Ministerial|beamte *m*, **~beamtin** *f m Pol.* ministry (*Am.* department) official; **~bürokratie** *f* departmental red tape (*od.* bureaucracy); **~direktor** *m*, **~direktorin** *f* head of department (*in a ministry*); **~dirigent** *m*, **~dirigentin** *f* head of section (*in a ministry*), *in GB*: principal; *in den USA*: undersecretary
Ministerial|erlass *m Pol.* ministerial decree; **~rat** *m*, **~rätin** *f etwa Brit.* principal, *Am.* undersecretary
ministeriell *Adj. Pol.* ministerial; **Ministerin** *f*; *-*, *-nen* → **Minister**, **Ministerium** *n*; *-s*, *Ministerien* ministry, (government) department
Ministeriums|sprecher *m Pol.* ministerial spokesman, spokesman for the ministry; **~sprecherin** *f* ministerial spokeswoman, spokeswoman for the ministry
Minister|konferenz *f Pol.* ministerial conference; **~posten** *m* ministerial post; **~präsident** *m*, **~präsidentin** *f* prime minister (*auch e-s Bundeslandes*), premier; **~rat** *m EU, Frankreich etc.*: Council of Ministers; **~riege** *f*

Pol. Sl. ministerial line-up; **~sessel** *m umg.* ministerial (*od.* cabinet) post
Ministrant *m*; *-en*, *-en*, **~in** *f*; *-*, *-nen*; *kath.* server; **ministrieren** *v/i.* act as server, serve
Minivan ['mınıvæn] *m Mot.* people carrier
Minna *f*, *-*, *-s*; *umg.* **1. grüne ~** green police van, *früher in GB*: *etwa* Black Maria, *Am.* paddy wagon; **2. j-n zur ~ machen** give s.o. a roasting, bawl (*Am. auch* chew) s.o. out
Minne *f*; *-*, *kein Pl.*; (*auch* **hohe ~**) courtly love; **~dienst** *m hist.* service of a knight to his lady; **~lied** *n Lit.* minnelied, courtly love song; **~sang** *m* minnesang; **~sänger** *m* minnesinger
minoisch *Adj. hist.* Minoan
Minorität *f*, *-*, *-en* minority; **Minoritätenfrage** *f* question of minorities
Minstrel *m*; *-s*, *-s*; *hist.* minstrel
Mintsoße *f Gastr.* mint sauce
Minuend *m*; *-en*, *-en*; *Math.* minuend
minus I. *Präp.* minus; **II.** *Adv.*: **~ 10 Grad** 10 (degrees) below zero; **III.** *Konj.* minus; **neunzehn ~ elf ist** (*gleich*) *acht* nineteen minus eleven is (*od.* equals) eight
Minus *n*; *-*, *kein Pl.* **1.** (*Fehlbetrag*) deficit; *auf dem Konto*: overdraft; **~ machen** make a loss; **ins ~ kommen** *od.* **geraten** get into the red; **2.** *fig.* (*Nachteil*) disadvantage, drawback
Minusbetrag *m* deficit
Minuskel *f*; *-*, *-n*; *Druck.* small (*od.* lower case) letter, minuscule *fachspr.*; **~schrift** *f* lower case type
Minus|pol *m Etech.* negative pole; **~punkt** *m* **1.** penalty point; *Sport* point against; **2.** (*Nachteil*) minus point (*od.* factor), disadvantage, drawback, downside; **~rekord** *m* record (*od.* all-time) low; **~seite** *f Wirts. und fig.*: (*auf der*) **~** (on the) debit side; **~stunde** *f* minus hour; **~temperaturen** *Pl.* temperatures below zero; **bei ~** in freezing temperatures, when the temperature is below zero; **~zeichen** *n Math.* minus (sign)
Minute *f*; *-*, *-n* minute (*auch Astron., Math.*); **auf die ~** (*genau*) on the dot; **es klappte auf die ~** (*genau*) it was perfectly timed, the timing was perfect; **in letzter ~** at the last minute; **bis zur letzten ~** right up to the last minute; **jede freie ~ nutzen** use every free moment; **hast du ein paar ~n Zeit für mich?** can you spare me a few minutes?; → **ruhig** I 2, **zwölf**; **minutenlang I.** *Adj.* lasting several minutes; *Beifall, Schweigen etc.*: *auch* several minutes of ...; **II.** *Adv.* for (several) minutes
Minuten|schnelle *f*: **in ~** in a matter of minutes; **~takt** *m*: **im ~** *Telefongebühren*: (charged) per minute; *fig.* (*schnell, häufig*) one a minute; **~zeiger** *m* minute hand
...minütig *im Adj.* ...-minute, of ... minutes; **ein fünf~er Aufenthalt** a stop of five minutes, a five-minute stop; **mit zehn~er Verspätung** ten minutes late
minutiös *Adj.* minutely detailed; (*äußerst genau*) scrupulously precise; (*sorgfältigst*) meticulous
minuziös *Adj.* → **minutiös**
Minze *f*; *-*, *-n*; *Bot.* mint
Mio. *Abk.* → **Million**
Miozän *n*; *-s*, *kein Pl.*; *Ge...*
mir *pers. Pron.* (*Dat. ...* (*auch* **~ selbst**) mys... denken können I s...

(that); **ich dachte bei ~:** ... I thought to myself: ...; **er gab es ~** he gave it to me, he gave me it; **~ ist kalt** I feel cold; **ein Freund von ~** a friend of mine; **du bist ~ ein schöner Freund** a fine friend you are; **lass ~ m-e Ruhe** leave me alone; **dass ihr ~ ja nichts verratet!** *Drohung*: and don't you dare breathe a word of it!; **von ~ aus** it's OK by me, (go ahead,) I don't mind; **wie du ~, so ich dir** an eye for an eye, tit for tat; **ich putzte ~ die Zähne** I brushed my teeth; **das verbitte ich ~!** I won't have it!; → **nichts** 1
Mirabelle *f*, *-*, *-n*; *Bot.* yellow plum, mirabelle (plum)
Mirabellen|baum *m Bot.* mirabelle (plum) tree; **~schnaps** *m* mirabelle plum brandy
Misanthrop *m*; *-en*, *-en* misanthropist; **Misanthropie** *f*; *-*, *kein Pl.* misanthropy; **Misanthropin** *f*; *-*, *-nen* (female) misanthropist; **misanthropisch I.** *Adj.* misanthropic; **II.** *Adv.* misanthropically
mischbar *Adj.* mixable; **gut ~ sein** mix well
Misch|batterie *f* mixer tap, *Am.* mixing faucet; **~becher** *m* shaker; **~brot** *n* (mixed) wheat and rye bread; **~ehe** *f* mixed marriage
mischen I. *v/t.* **1.** *allg.* mix; (*Kaffee, Tabak etc.*) blend; **etw. in** *od.* **unter etw. ~** mix s.th. into s.th., add s.th. to s.th.; *Gift* **~** concoct (*od.* mix) a poison; **2.** (*Karten*) shuffle; **3.** (*Tonaufnahmen etc.*) mix; **II.** *v/refl.* **1. sich ~** (*gut etc.*) **~** mix (well *etc.*); **2. sich ~ unter** (+ *Akk.*) mix (*od.* mingle) with; **sich ~ in** (+ *Akk.*) interfere (*od.* meddle) in; (*dazwischenreden*) butt in on; **sich in ein Gespräch ~** join in a conversation; **III.** *v/i. beim Kartenspiel*: shuffle; → **gemischt**; **Mischer** *m*; *-s*, *-* mixer (*auch Radio etc.*)
Mischfarbe *f* compound colo(u)r; **mischfarbig** *Adj.* of mixed (*od.* various) colo(u)rs
Misch|finanzierung *f Wirts.* mixed financing; **~form** *f* mixture; *bes. Ling., Kunst* hybrid (form); **e-e ~ zwischen** (*od.* **aus** + *Dat.*) **... und ...** a mixture (*od.* fusion) of ... and ...; **~futter** *n Agr.* mixed feed; **~gemüse** *n Gastr.* mixed vegetables *Pl.*; **~gewebe** *n* mixed fabric, mixture; **~kalkulation** *f Wirts.* compensatory pricing; **~konzern** *m Wirts.* conglomerate; **~kost** *f* mixed diet; **~kultur** *f* **1.** *soziologisch*: mixed(-race) culture; **2.** *Agr.* mixed cultivation
Mischling *m*; *-s*, *-e* hybrid (*auch Bot.*); *Mensch*: half-caste, *bes. pej.* ha~-breed; *Tier*: crossbreed
Mischmasch *m*; *-(e)s*, *-e*; *um...* potch, *Am.* hodgepodge, *...nixing pej. auch* jumble ~~ *... mixed*
Mischmaschine *f* (*...rossbreed;*
Misch|pult *n Ra...ge;* **~trom-** desk (*od. ...auch fig.*); *von* race; *Ti...nd;* *von Gebäck,* **~spra...ment; e-e ~ aus** a me...chungsverhältnis *n*

M... mixed woodland (*com-* ...duous *and* coniferous ...ort *n* hybrid (*od.* portman- *...el Adj.* **1.** terrible, dreadful, *umg.* lousy; *Wetter: auch* rotten *umg.*; **2.** (*gemein*) beastly

Misere *f; -, -n* dreadful situation, plight

misogyn *Adj.* misogynous; **Misogyn** *m; -s und -en, -(e)*; *Psych.* misogynist; **Misogynie** *f; -, kein Pl.* misogyny

Mispel *f; -, -n*; *Bot.* medlar (tree)

missachten *v/t.* (*untr., hat*) (*nicht beachten*) ignore, disregard; (*gering schätzen*) disdain, despise; **Missachtung** *f* disregard (+ *Gen.* of); (*Verachtung*) disdain (for); **~ des Gerichts** *Jur.* contempt of court

missbehagen *v/t.* (*untr., hat*); *geh.:* **es missbehagt mir** I don't feel happy about it, I don't like the idea; **Missbehagen** *n; -s, kein Pl.* feeling of unease, uncomfortable feeling; (*Bedenken*) misgivings *Pl.*; (*Missfallen*) displeasure, discontent

Missbildung *f* deformity

missbilligen *v/t.* (*untr., hat*) disapprove (of)

missbilligend I. *Part. Präs.* → **missbilligen**; **II.** *Adj.* disapproving; **III.** *Adv.* disapprovingly

Missbilligung *f* disapproval; **Missbilligungsantrag** *m Pol.* motion of censure

Missbrauch *m* abuse; (*falsche Anwendung*) misuse; *vorsätzlicher: auch* improper use; **der ~ von Medikamenten** drug abuse; **unter ~ von** by abusing (*od.* misusing); **~ treiben mit** abuse; (*falsch anwenden*) misuse, put *s.th.* to improper use; **missbrauchen** *v/t.* (*untr., hat*) abuse (*auch sexuell*); (*falsch anwenden*) misuse; **missbräuchlich I.** *Adj.:* **~e Verwendung** improper use, misuse; **II.** *Adv.:* **~ benutzen** misuse

missdeuten *v/t.* (*untr., hat*) misinterpret, misconstrue; → *auch* **missverstehen**; **Missdeutung** *f* misinterpretation

missen *v/t.* (*auskommen ohne*) do without; **das möchte ich nicht ~** I wouldn't like to do (*od.* be) without it; (*Erlebnis etc.*) I wouldn't like to miss out on it; (*Vergangenes*) I wouldn't like to have done (*od.* been) without it; (*Erlebnis etc.*) I wouldn't like to have missed out on it

Miss|erfolg *m* failure; *e-s Buchs etc.:* auch flop; **~ernte** *f* bad harvest, crop failure

Missetat *f geh.* misdeed; **Missetäter** *m*, **Missetäterin** *f geh.* malefactor *förm.*, miscreant *mst hum.*; *auch Jur.* offender

missfallen *v/i.* (*unreg., untr., hat*): **er/es missfällt ihr** she doesn't like him/it; **Missfallen** *n; -s, kein Pl.* displeasure, disapproval; → **Missvergnügen**; **Missfallensäußerung** *f* expression of disapproval; **missfällig I.** *Äußerung*: disapproving; (*abschätzig*) disparaging; **II.** *Adv.:* **sich ~ äußern über** (*other*) disapprovingly (*abparagingly*) about (*od.* of) Tier *Adj.* Person: deformed; freak: misshapen **2.** *fig.* deformed child; **3.** *umg.* (*extreme ~*) sonofabitcal; monstrosity; **missgelaun** ...lure, flop; **Missgeschick** ...re, *Am.* fortune; (*Unfall* ...ered **missgestaltet** formed

missgestimmt *Adj.* → **missgelaunt**

missglücken *v/i.* (*untr., ist*) fail, be a failure, be unsuccessful, not come off; **der Kuchen ist mir missglückt** the cake didn't turn out; **missglückt** *Adj. Versuch:* unsuccessful

missgönnen *v/t.* (*untr., hat*): **j-m etw. ~** begrudge s.o. s.th.; **sie missgönnte mir, dass ...** she held it against me that ...

Missgriff *m* mistake; (*Fauxpas*) gaffe, wrong move; (*schlechte Wahl*) mistake, bad choice; (*Fehleinschätzung*) misjudgment; **e-n ~ tun** make a mistake (*od.* wrong move *od.* bad choice)

Missgunst *f* (*Missgönnen, Neid*) envy, jealousy; (*böser Wille*) ill will, malevolence; **missgünstig** *Adj.* (*neidisch*) envious, jealous; (*böswillig*) malevolent

misshandeln *v/t.* (*untr., hat*) ill-treat, maltreat; **misshandelt I.** *P.P.* → **misshandeln**; **II.** *Adj.:* **~es Kind** battered child; **Misshandlung** *f* ill-treatment, maltreatment; *Jur.* (*Körperverletzung*) assault

Misshelligkeiten *Pl.* (*Unstimmigkeiten*) differences (of opinion), disagreement *Sg.*

Mission *f; -, -en* **1.** *kirchl.* mission; **in der ~ tätig sein** do missionary work; **2.** *Pol.* (*diplomatische Vertretung*) mission; **3.** (*Abordnung*) mission, delegation; **4.** *geh.* (*Auftrag*) mission; **in geheimer ~ unterwegs sein** be (travel[-]l]ing) on a secret mission; **Missionar** *m; -s, -e*, **Missionarin** *f; -, -nen kirchl.* missionary; **missionarisch I.** *Adj.* missionary; **mit ~em Eifer** *fig.* with missionary zeal; **II.** *Adv.:* **~ tätig sein** do missionary work; **Missionarsstellung** *f umg.* missionary position; **missionieren I.** *v/i.* do missionary work; (*bekehren*) make conversions; *bes. fig.* proselytize *oft pej.*; **II.** *v/t.* (*Land*) do missionary work in, take the Gospel *etc.* to; (*Volk*) do missionary work among, preach the Gospel *etc.* to; (*bekehren*) convert

Missions|arbeit *f; nur Sg.* missionary work; *bes. fig.* proselytizing *oft pej.*; **~haus** *n kirchl.* mission (house); **~schule** *f* mission school; **~schwester** *f* missionary sister; **~station** *f kirchl.* mission station; *entlegene: auch* missionary outpost

Miss|klang *m* discordant note, *auch Pl.* dissonance, discord; *fig. auch* note of discord; **~kredit** *m* discredit, disrepute; **in ~ bringen** bring discredit upon, bring into disrepute; **in ~ kommen** *od.* **geraten** fall into disrepute, get (o.s. *od.* itself) a bad name

misslang *Imperf.* → **misslingen**

misslaunig *Adj.* → **missgelaunt**

Misslaut *m* harsh (*od.* ugly) sound

misslich *Adj.* (*unangenehm*) disagreeable, awkward; (*schwierig*) difficult, awkward; (*unerfreulich*) unfortunate; **~e Lage** awkward (*od.* unpleasant) situation, predicament; **Misslichkeit** *f der Lage etc.:* disagreeable nature, awkwardness; (*missliche Lage*) awkward (*od.* unpleasant) situation, predicament; **~en** unpleasant things (*od.* aspects)

missliebig *Adj.* unpopular; **Missliebigkeit** *f* unpopularity

misslingen *v/i.* (*untr.; misslingt, misslang, ist misslungen*) fail, be unsuccessful, turn out (to be) a failure, flop *umg.*; **es misslang ihr, zu** (+ *Inf.*) she ...led (in her attempt) to (+ *Inf.*), she

was unsuccessful in (+ *Ger.*); **misslingt** *Präs.* → **misslingen**; **misslungen I.** *P.P.* → **misslingen**; **II.** *Adj. Versuch:* unsuccessful; **~er Staatsstreich** abortive coup

Missmanagement *n; nur Sg.*; *Wirts.* mismanagement

Missmut *m* disgruntled state, bad mood; **missmutig** *Adj.* bad-tempered, sullen, *präd. auch* in a bad mood; (*unzufrieden*) disgruntled

missraten I. *v/i.* (*unreg., untr., ist*) *Versuch etc.:* fail; *Kuchen etc.:* turn out a failure, go wrong; **es ist mir ~** I've made a mess of it; **II.** *P.P.* → **missraten I**; **III.** *Adj.:* **ein ~es Kind** a difficult (*od.* problem) child

Missstand *m* (serious) anomaly; *auch Pl.* deplorable state of affairs; *bei der Verwaltung:* irregularity; (*Missbrauch*) abuse; **Missstände** (*Misswirtschaft*) mismanagement; **e-n ~ anprangern** denounce an irregularity (*Unrecht:* injustice, *Missbrauch:* abuse *etc.*); **Missstände abschaffen** *od.* **beseitigen** remedy abuses *etc.*

Missstimmung *f* bad (*od.* ill) feeling, note of discord; (*Unstimmigkeit*) (note of) disagreement

misst *Präs.* → **messen**

Misston *m* discordant note; *kratzender:* grating note; *fig.* sour note, note of discord; **misstönend** *Adj.* discordant; (*kratzend*) grating

misstrauen *v/i.* (*untr., hat*) (*j-m, e-r Sache*) distrust, mistrust; have no confidence in

Misstrauen *n; -s, kein Pl.* distrust, mistrust (*gegen* of); (*Verdacht*) suspicion (of); (*Zweifel*) doubt(s *Pl.*) (concerning); **voller ~ sein** be very distrustful (*od.* suspicious *od.* doubtful)

Misstrauens|antrag *m bes. Parl.* motion of no confidence; **e-n ~ stellen** propose a motion of no confidence; **~votum** *n* vote of no confidence

misstrauisch *Adj.* distrustful; (*argwöhnisch*) suspicious, wary; (*skeptisch*) sceptical, *Am.* skeptical

Missvergnügen *n; nur Sg.*; *geh.* annoyance, displeasure (*über* + *Akk.* at); (*Unzufriedenheit*) discontent(ment) (-at, about); **sehr zu seinem ~** much to his annoyance; **missvergnügt** *Adj. geh.* annoyed, disgruntled (*über* + *Akk.* at, about), not (exactly) pleased (about); *stärker:* upset (at, about); (*unzufrieden*) discontented (at, about); (*schlecht gelaunt*) sullen, grumpy *umg.*

Missverhältnis *n* imbalance, disproportion; (*Diskrepanz*) discrepancy, disparity; **in e-m ~ stehen** be out of proportion (*zu* to)

missverständlich *Adj.* misleading, unclear; (*zweideutig*) ambiguous; **Missverständlichkeit** *f* **1.** *e-r Äußerung:* misleading nature; (*Zweideutigkeit*) ambiguity; **2.** *konkret:* misleading (*od.* ambiguous) statement; **Missverständnis** *n* misunderstanding; (*Streit*) *auch* disagreement; **missverstehen** *v/t.* (*unreg., untr., hat*) misunderstand; (*falsch auslegen*) misinterpret, misconstrue; (*j-s Absichten*) *auch* mistake

Misswahl *f* beauty contest

Missweisung *f Phys.* declination

Misswirtschaft *f* mismanagement, bad management

Mist¹ *m; -(e)s, kein Pl.* **1.** (*Kuh-, Pferdemist*) dung; (*Tierkot*) droppings *Pl.*; (*Dünger*) manure; (*Misthaufen*) dung heap, *mit Dünger:* manure heap; **das ist nicht auf m-m ~ gewachsen** *umg.*

fig. I had nothing to do with it; **2.** *umg.* (*Plunder*) junk, rubbish; **3.** *umg.* (*Unsinn*) rubbish, *bes. Am.* crap, garbage; **~ machen** *od.* **bauen** (make a) boob, make a mess of things, botch (*od.* cock) it up; **~ verzapfen** talk rubbish (*bes. Am.* crap); (**so ein**) **~!** damn (it)!

Mist² *m; -s, -e; Naut., nordd.* mist

Mistbeet *n* forcing bed, hotbed

Mistel *f; -, -n; Bot.* mistletoe; **~zweig** *m* sprig of mistletoe

misten I. *v/t.* **1.** (*düngen*) manure; **2.** (*ausmisten*) muck out; II. *v/i. umg. fig.* → **ausmisten** II

Mist|fink *m umg.* dirty slob *Sl.;* **~gabel** *f* pitchfork; **~haufen** *m* dung heap; *mit Dünger:* manure heap

mistig *Adj.* **1.** mucky; **2.** *umg. Wetter:* lousy, foul; **3.** *Naut., nordd.* misty

Mist|käfer *m Zool.* dung beetle, *mst* scarab; **~kerl** *m umg. pej.* swine, bastard *Sl.;* **~kübel** *m österr., schw.* dustbin, *Am.* trashcan

Mist|schaufel *f österr.* dustpan; **~stock** *m schw.* → **Misthaufen; ~stück** *n,* **~vieh** *n umg. pej.* (*Mann, Kind*) rascal; *stärker:* bastard; (*Frau*) wretched woman; *stärker:* bitch; **~wetter** *n umg.* lousy (*od.* foul) weather; **~zeug** *n umg. pej.* → **Mist¹** 2, 3

mit I. *Präp.* **1.** *Gemeinsamkeit, Zugehörigkeit od. Beteiligung ausdrückend:* with; **ein Mann ~ Hund** a man with a dog; **Whisky ~ Eis** whisky with ice (*od.* on the rocks); **Zimmer ~ Frühstück** bed and breakfast; **ein Korb ~ Obst** a basket of fruit; **ein Gespräch ~ dem Nachbarn** a conversation with the neighbo(u)r; **e-e Bluse ~ Streifen** a blouse with stripes on it, a striped blouse; **eine Flasche ~ Schraubverschluss** a bottle with a screw top, a screw-top bottle; **~ Fieber im Bett liegen** be in bed with a temperature; **Körperverletzung ~ Todesfolge** *Jur.* grievous bodily harm resulting in death; **2.** (*mit Hilfe von*) with; **~ Bleistift/Kugelschreiber schreiben** write with a (*od.* in) pencil/ballpoint; **sie brät alles ~ Butter** she fries everything in butter; **~ Gewalt** by force; **~ Bargeld/Scheck/Kreditkarte bezahlen** pay in cash (*Am.* check) / by credit card; **~ der Bahn/Post®** *etc.* by train/post *etc.;* **~ dem nächsten Bus ankommen/fahren** come on the next bus / take the next bus; → **List; 3.** *Art und Weise beschreibend:* with; **~ Absicht** intentionally; **~ Bestürzung** to one's consternation; **~ lauter Stimme** in a loud voice; **~ Appetit essen** enjoy one's food; **nur ~ Mühe** only with (some) difficulty; **~ Verlust** at a loss; **~ einem Mal** all of a sudden, suddenly; **~ einem Wort** in a word; **~ 8 zu 11 Stimmen beschließen** decide by 8 votes to 11; **~ e-r Mehrheit von** by a majority of; *Regierung:* with a majority of; **~ Einwilligung ihrer Eltern** with her parents' consent; **~ (e-r Geschwindigkeit von) 80 km/h** *od.* **~ 80 Sachen** *umg.* at a speed of 50 mph; → **Abstand** 4, **Nachdruck¹; 4.** *j-n od. etw. betreffend:* **was ist ~ ihm?** what's the matter with him?; **wie steht es ~ Ihrer Arbeit?** how's your work getting on?; **wie steht's ~ dir?** how about you?; **wie wär's ~ ...?** how about ...?; **~ mir nicht!** don't (*od.* they *etc.* needn't) try it on with (*Am.* try that on) me; **du ~ deiner ewigen Unkerei** *umg.* you and your constant gloom and doom; **raus**

~ euch! *umg.* out with you!, out you go!; **Schluss ~ dem Unsinn!** that's enough of this nonsense!; **~ der Arbeit beginnen** start work; **~ Weinen aufhören** stop crying; **es ist einfach schlimm ~ dir** you're hopeless, what are we to do with you?; **5.** (*einschließlich*): **~ ihr waren zehn Personen anwesend** there were ten people there including her; **die Miete beträgt 1000 Euro ~ Nebenkosten** the rent is 1000 euros with all extras (*od.* all-inclusive); **die Fahrkarte kostet ~ Zuschlag 60 Euro** the ticket is 60 euros including (*od.* with) the supplement; **6.** *zeitlich:* **~ 20 Jahren** at (the age of) twenty; **~ dem 3. Mai** as of May 3rd; **~ dem heutigen Tag** as of today; **~ Einbruch der Dunkelheit** at nightfall; → **Zeit** 1; **7.** *gleichlaufende Bewegung kennzeichnend:* **~ dem Wind im Rücken spielen** play with one's back to the wind; **~ der Strömung schwimmen** swim with the current; → **Strom** 3, **Zeit** 1; II. *Adv.* **1.** also, too; **das gehört ~ zu deinen Aufgaben** this is another of your tasks; **~ dabei sein** be there too; **wer war außer dir noch ~?** *umg.* who else was there (apart from you)?; **etwas ~ ansehen** watch (*od.* witness) something; *fig.* (*dulden*) (*auch* **es ~ ansehen**) sit back and watch; **das muss man ~ bedenken** you have to consider that too; **2.** *mit Superlativ:* **er war ~ der Beste** he was one of the (very) best; **das ist ~ das Schönste** this is one of (*od.* among) the most beautiful; → **mitgehen, mitkommen** *etc.;* → **dazugehören**

Mitangeklagte *m, f Jur.* codefendant

Mitarbeit *f; nur Sg.* **1.** collaboration (**bei** on); (*Zusammenarbeit*) cooperation; (*Hilfe*) *auch* assistance (**bei** in); *weitS.* (*Arbeit*) work; **unter ~ von** with the collaboration (*od.* assistance) of; **ihre langjährige ~ bei ...** her many years of service with (*od.* for) ...; **2.** (*Beteiligung*) participation (**in, an** + *Dat.* in); **mitarbeiten** *v/i.* (*trennb., hat -ge-*) **1.** collaborate (**an** + *Dat.,* **bei** on); (*mitmachen*) cooperate (on); (*mithelfen*) help out (with); **2.** (*sich beteiligen*) participate (**in, an** + *Dat.* in); **im Unterricht ~** play an active part in the lesson

Mitarbeiter *m* **1.** (*Angestellter*) employee; **2.** (*Arbeitskollege*) colleague; *Arbeiter:* workmate; *bei e-m Projekt:* collaborator; *freier ~* freelance(r); *e-r Zeitung:* contributor (+ *Gen. od.* **bei** to); **er war ~ an dem Projekt** he worked on (*od.* was involved in) the project; **Mitarbeiterin** *f -, -nen* → **Mitarbeiter, Mitarbeiterstab** *m* staff (*mst V. im Pl.*), *umg.* team; **sie gehört zu s-m engsten ~** she's one of his closest collaborators; **Mitarbeiterzahl** *f* number of employees (*od.* staff)

Mitautor *m,* **~in** *f* co-author

Mitbegründer *m,* **~in** *f* co-founder

mitbekommen *v/t.* (*unreg., trennb., hat*) **1.** *etw. ~* get (*od.* be given) s.th. (to take with one); *für unterwegs:* get (*od.* be given) s.th. for the road; *als Mitgift:* get s.th. as a dowry; **2.** (*wahrnehmen*) take in; (*hören*) hear; (*schnappen*) catch; (*verstehen*) understand; **ich habe kaum etwas ~** *Film* mitbekommen (*Am. auch* movie) (*nicht verstanden*) any of the fi... **hast du das n...**

not get it?; → **mithören** I 1

mitbenutzen *v/t.* (*trennb., hat*) share the use of; **Mitbenutzer** *m,* **Mitbenutzerin** *f* co-user; **Mitbenutzung** *f* joint (*od.* shared) use

Mitbesitzer *m,* **~in** *f* co-owner, joint owner

mitbestimmen (*trennb., hat*) I. *v/t. Sache:* have an influence on, influence; II. *v/i.:* (*bei e-r Sache*) **~** have a say (in a matter); **über etw.** (*Akk.*) **~** have a say in the decision about s.th.; **Mitbestimmung** *f* co-determination; *der Arbeitnehmer:* auch worker participation

Mitbestimmungsgesetz *n* law on co-determination; **mitbestimmungspflichtig** *Adj.* subject to the agreement of the workforce; **Mitbestimmungsrecht** *n* right of co-determination

mitbetreuen *v/t.* (*trennb., hat*) share in the care of, help to look after; **einen Aufgabenbereich ~** share an area of responsibility

Mitbewerber *m,* **~in** *f* fellow competitor; *für e-e Stellung:* other applicant

Mitbewohner *m,* **~in** *f* fellow occupant; *Brit. e-r Wohnung:* flatmate; *e-s Zimmers, Am. auch e-r Wohnung:* roommate

mitbezahlen *v/t.* (*trennb., hat*) help (to) pay for; **bei diesem Produkt bezahlt man den Namen mit** *umg.* with this product you have to pay (*od.* you're paying) for the name

mitbieten *v/i.* (*unreg., trennb., hat -ge-*) *bei e-r Au ktion:* bid (as well)

mitbringen *v/t.* (*unreg., trennb., hat -ge-*) bring (*od.* take) along (with one); *fig.* (*Fähigkeiten*) have, be endowed with; **hast du mir was mitgebracht?** have you got (*od.* brought) anything for me?; **für das Museum solltest du genügend Zeit ~** *fig.* you need to allow enough time for going (a)round the museum; **Mitbringsel** *n; -s, -* little present, *umg.* pressie; (*Andenken*) souvenir

Mitbürger *m,* **~in** *f* fellow citizen; **unsere ausländischen Mitbürger** our fellow citizens from abroad; **die älteren Mitbürger** the senior citizens

mitdenken *v/i.* (*unreg., trennb., hat -ge-*) **1.** (*mit Überlegung vorgehen*) think things through; **2. denk mal mit!** help me (*od.* us) think; **ich muss immer für andere ~** I have to do all the thinking; **3.** (*mitkommen*) follow the argument

mitdürfen *v/i.* (*unreg., trennb., hat -ge-*) *umg.* be allowed to go (*od.* com (with s.o.); **darf ich mit?** can I, (*od.* go) too?

Miteigentümer *m,* **~in** *f* (*zu... one;* ... another; *co-owner*

miteinander *Adv.* ...know each sammen) toget... they've ...n; -s, kein Pl. **verheiratet** ...men) getting **sie sind**...

other... (*...reg., trennb., hat*) f...orries/pain *etc.* **~** know what s.o. is going ...mpathize with s.o.; II. *v/i.:* ...s, kein Pl. empathy **Mitemp**-... m, weiblich: **Miterbin** *f* co-heir, joint ...leben *v/t.* co-heiress, joint heiress **(*trennb., hat*)** see s.th.

(with one's own eyes); *sie hat den Krieg noch miterlebt* she was still alive during the war; *das wird er nicht mehr* ~ he won't live (*od.* be around) to see that; *ich musste* ~*, wie er an Krebs starb* I had to watch him die of cancer

mitessen (*unreg., trennb., hat -ge-*) **I.** *v/i.* eat with us *etc.*; *bei Freunden* ~ eat with friends (at their house); *die Augen essen mit fig.* the food must also appeal to the eye; **II.** *v/t.*: *kann man die Schale etc.* ~*?* can you eat the peel *etc.* (too)?

Mitesser *m* **1.** *Med.* blackhead; **2.** *umg. hum.* person eating with other people; *wir haben zwei* ~ we have two people coming to eat with us, we have two dinner *etc.* guests

mitfahren *v/i.* (*unreg., trennb., ist -ge-*) go (*od.* ride) as a passenger, get a lift; *auf Motorrad:* ride pillion; (*mitkommen*) come along (too); *j-n* ~ *lassen* give s.o. a lift (*Am. auch* ride); **Mitfahrer** *m*, **Mitfahrerin** *f* passenger; *auf Motorrad:* pillion rider; *Mitfahrer gesucht für Fahrgemeinschaft:* person wanted to join car-sharing group

Mitfahr|gelegenheit *f* lift, *Am. auch* ride; *biete* ~ *nach Köln* lift (*Am. auch* ride) offered to Cologne; ~**zentrale** *f* car pool service (offering lifts)

Mitfahrt *f* ride, trip (as passenger); (*Begleitung*) accompanying

mitfeiern *v/i.* (*trennb., hat*) join in on the celebrations

mitfinanzieren *v/t.* (*trennb., hat*) help to finance

mitfliegen *v/i.* (*unreg., trennb., ist -ge-*) fly with us *etc.*; (*mit derselben Maschine*) ~ be on the same flight

mitfreuen *v/refl.* (*trennb., hat -ge-*) be (very) pleased too

mitfühlen *vt/i* (*trennb., hat -ge-*) → *mitempfinden*; **mitfühlend I.** *Part. Präs.* → *mitfühlen*; **II.** *Adj.* (*Mitgefühl zeigend*) sympathetic, compassionate; (*verständnisvoll*) understanding

mitführen *v/t.* (*trennb., hat -ge-*) **1.** *Person:* take with one; (*bei sich haben*) have (*od.* carry) with (*od.* on) one; **2.** *Fluss etc.*: carry along (with it)

mitgeben *v/t.* (*unreg., trennb., hat -ge-*) *j-m etw.* ~ give s.o. s.th. (to take with him *od.* her); *fig.* (*Ratschlag etc.*) give s.o. s.th. along the way; *j-m j-n* ~ send s.o. along with s.o.

mitgefangen *Adj.* ~*, mitgehangen* in for a penny (*Am. auch* dime) (, in for a pound, *Am. auch* dollar); **Mitgefangene** *m, f* fellow prisoner; *die* ~*n* the other prisoners

Mitgefühl *n*; *nur Sg.* sympathy; *j-m* ~ *ausdrücken* offer one's sympa- (*förm. bei Todesfall:* condo-) ~ s.o.; *du hast mein* ~ *bes. iro.* ~ize, you have my (deepest)

~s.o.),

~mit~

I'll c*unreg., trennb., ist -ge-*)
you); ~along (*mit j-m* with
walk off~*in Stückchen mit*
spiel: *ich* ~~ ~ the way (with
Zuhörer
play along, ~*g.* (*stehlen*)
wholehearted~~ *Glücks-*
werden) be car*n* **I. 2.** *fig.*
mitgenommen *elen*)
II. *Adj.* in a sorry~ nd
(*ramponiert*) *auch* ~d
(*erschöpft*) exhausted

Mitgesellschafter *m*, ~**in** *f Wirts.* fellow partner

mitgestalten *v/t.* (*trennb., hat -ge-*) help to create; **Mitgestaltung** *f* involvement in the creation (+ *Gen.* of)

Mitgift *f*; -, -*en* dowry; ~**jäger** *m altm. pej.* fortune-hunter

Mitglied *n* member; *ordentliches/förderndes/zahlendes* ~ full/supporting/ subscribing member; ~ *sein von od. in* be a member of, belong to

mitgliederschwach *Adj.* ... with a small membership

Mitgliederschwund *m* serious drop in membership

mitgliederstark *Adj.* ... with a large membership

Mitglieder|versammlung *f* general meeting; ~**verzeichnis** *n* list of members, membership list; ~**werbung** *f* canvassing for new members; ~**zahl** *f* membership

Mitglieds|ausweis *m* membership card; ~**beitrag** *m* (membership) subscription (*Am.* dues *Pl.*)

Mitgliedschaft *f* membership

Mitgliedskarte *f* membership card

Mitglied(s)|land *n* member country; ~**staat** *m* member state

Mitgründer *m*, ~**in** *f* co-founder

mithaben *v/t.* (*unreg., trennb., hat -ge-*) *umg.*: *etw.* ~ have (got) s.th. with one; (*Scheckkarte etc.*) have s.th. on (*od.* with) one

mithaften *v/i. Jur.* be jointly liable

Mithäftling *m* fellow prisoner

mithalten *v/i.* (*unreg., trennb., hat -ge-*) keep up, keep pace; ~ *mit auch fig.* keep abreast of

mithelfen *v/i.* (*unreg., trennb., hat -ge-*) → *helfen*; **Mithelfer** *m*, **Mithelferin** *f pej.* accomplice

Mitherausgeber *m*, ~**in** *f* co-editor

mithilfe I. *Präp.* + *Gen.* with the help (*od.* aid) of; **II.** *Adv.*: ~ *von* with the help (*od.* aid) of

Mithilfe *f*; *nur Sg.* help, assistance; (*Zusammenarbeit*) cooperation

mithin *Adv.* consequently, therefore, thus

mithören (*trennb., hat -ge-*) **I.** *v/t.* **1.** *absichtlich:* listen in on; *heimlich:* auch eavesdrop on; *zufällig:* overhear; *ich hab's zufällig mitgehört* I happened to hear it; *ungewollt:* I couldn't help overhearing it; **2.** (*abhören*) monitor, listen in on; (*Funkverkehr*) intercept; **3.** (*Radiosendung etc.*) listen to, hear; **II.** *v/i.* **1.** listen in; *heimlich: auch* eavesdrop; **2.** (*abhören*) tap the wire

Mitinhaber *m*, ~**in** *f* joint owner (*od.* proprietor); *Wirts.* partner

mitkämpfen *v/i.* (*trennb., hat -ge-*) take part in the fighting; *mit j-m* ~ fight at s.o.'s side; **Mitkämpfer** *m*, **Mitkämpferin** *f Mil.* fellow combatant; *lit.* comrade-in-arms; *fig. bei e-r Aktion etc.*: fellow campaigner (*für, in Sachen* + *Gen.* of); *Sport* (*Mannschaftskamerad*) teammate

Mitkläger *m*, ~**in** *f Jur.* co-plaintiff

mitklingen *v/i.* (*unreg., trennb., hat -ge-*) → *mitschwingen*

mitkommen *v/i.* (*unreg., trennb., ist -ge-*) **1.** come (along) too; *sie kann nicht* ~ she can't come (with us); **2.** (*Schritt halten*) keep up; *geistig:* be able to follow; *da komme ich* (*einfach*) *nicht mit geistig:* it's above my head, I can't make head or tail of it; *der Schule gut* ~ / *nicht* ~ get along ~ lag behind at (*Am.* in) school; ~*rricht gut* ~ make good pro-

gress in class

mitkönnen *v/i.* (*unreg., trennb., hat -ge-*); *umg.* **1.** be able to come (*gehen:* go) too; *sie kann nicht mit mit uns:* she can't come with us; *mit ihnen:* she can't go with them; **2.** *fig.* → *mitkommen* 2

mitkriegen *v/t.* (*trennb., hat -ge-*) *umg.* → *mitbekommen*

mitlassen *v/t.* (*unreg., trennb., hat -ge-*) *umg.*: *j-n* ~ let s.o. go (*kommen:* come) along (too)

mitlaufen *v/i.* (*unreg., trennb., ist -ge-*) **1.** run (*od.* go) along too; ~ *mit* run (along) with; **2.** *Wettläufer:* **beim Rennen** ~ run in the race; **3.** *umg. fig. Aufgabe:* *nebenher* ~ get done on the side, be fitted in as and when; **4.** *ein Tonband* ~ *lassen* keep a tape recorder switched on; **II.** *v/t.* (*Rennen*) take part in; **Mitläufer** *m*, **Mitläuferin** *f pej.* hanger-on; *Pol., kommunistisch:* fellow travel(l)er; *in Nazideutschland etc.*: tacit supporter, non-resister

Mitlaut *m Ling.* consonant

Mitleid *n*; *nur Sg.* pity; (*Mitgefühl*) sympathy; *aus* ~ *für* out of pity for; *mit j-m* ~ *haben* feel sorry for s.o.; (*Erbarmen haben*) have (*od.* take) pity on s.o.

mitleiden *v/i.* (*unreg., trennb., hat -ge-*) suffer as well (in sympathy); *mit j-m* ~ suffer with s.o.

Mitleidenschaft *f*: *in* ~ *ziehen* (begin to) affect, spread to; (*die Bevölkerung etc.*) take its toll on ... (as well)

mitleiderregend, Mitleid erregend *Adj.* pitiful, pitiable, piteous *lit.*; **mitleidig** *Adj.* compassionate, sympathetic; *ein* ~*es Lächeln* a pitying smile; **mitleid(s)los** *Adj.* unfeeling, pitiless, heartless; **mitleid(s)voll** *Adj.* full of pity, compassionate

mitlesen *v/t.* (*unreg., trennb., hat -ge-*) read too; *etw. mit j-m* ~ *leise:* read s.th. along with s.o.

mitliefern *v/t.* (*trennb., hat -ge-*) deliver with the rest (of the order)

mitmachen (*trennb., hat -ge-*) **I.** *v/i.* **1.** (*teilnehmen*) join in, take part (*bei* in); *umg.* (*mitspielen*) play along, go along with it; *da mach' ich nicht mit* you can count me out (as far as that's concerned); (*bin nicht einverstanden*) I'm not going along with that; **2.** (*zusammenarbeiten*) cooperate; *wenn das Wetter mitmacht fig.* if the weather cooperates, weather permitting; **3.** *umg.*: *m-e Beine machen nicht mehr mit* my legs are giving up (on me); *der Motor macht nicht mehr mit* the engine has packed up; **II.** *v/t.* **1.** (*teilnehmen bei*) take part in, join in; (*anwesend sein bei*) be at; *die Mode* ~ follow (*od.* go with) the fashion; **2.** (*erleben*) live through; (*erleiden*) go through, suffer; *sie hat einiges mitgemacht* she's been through (*od.* seen) a thing or two; *da machst du* (*vielleicht*) *od. da macht man was mit! umg.* it's a hard life; **3.** *umg.* (*billigen*) go along with; *diesen Blödsinn mache ich nicht länger mit* I'm not putting up with this nonsense a moment longer

mitmarschieren *v/i.* (*trennb., ist*) march along (too)

Mitmensch *m*; *mst Pl.* fellow human being, fellow creature; *die lieben* ~*en! iro.* people!

mitmischen *v/i.* (*trennb., hat -ge-*) *umg.* **1.** be involved, be in; **2.** (*sich an e-m Wettbewerb beteiligen*) compete; *in der Spitzengruppe kräftig*

~ be up there among the leaders
mitmüssen *v/i. (unreg., trennb., hat -ge-); umg.* have to go (*kommen:* come) too

Mitnahme *f; -, kein Pl.; bes. Amtsspr.:* **die ~ von Getränken in den Saal ist nicht gestattet** patrons are not permitted to take drinks into the auditorium; **~artikel** *m Wirts.* impulse purchase article; **~preis** *m* cash and carry price

mitnehmen *v/t. (unreg., trennb., hat -ge-)* **1.** take along (*od.* with one); (*fortnehmen*) take away; *j-n* (*im Auto*) ~ give s.o. a lift (*Am. auch* ride); **das Postschiff nimmt auch Passagiere mit** the mail boat also carries passengers; **zum Mitnehmen** *Schild:* please take one; **Pizza** *etc.* **zum Mitnehmen** takeaway pizza, *bes. Am.* carryout pizza, pizza to go; **2.** *umg. fig. (streifen):* take with one (*Sache:* with it) (as well); **wolltest du die Tür noch ~?** *iro.* are you taking the whole door with you?; **3.** *umg. (stehlen)* make (*od.* walk) off with; **4.** (*erschöpfen*) exhaust, wear out; *auch emotional:* take it out of one; **das hat ihn ziemlich mitgenommen** it hit him hard; → *mitgenommen;* **5.** *umg. (nebenbei erledigen)* do on the side; (*kaufen*) snap up; (*Ort etc. besuchen*) take in (on the way); **6.** *umg. (ausnützen, Gelegenheit)* make the most of; **jede Gelegenheit ~** grab every opportunity, never miss a chance; **sie nimmt jede Party mit** she never misses a party; **7.** (*lernen*): **ich habe aus dem Seminar einiges mitgenommen** I got one or two things out of the seminar; **8.** *Fin., Wirts.* (*Gewinne*) take

mitnichten *Adv. altm., noch hum.* certainly not, not at all

Mitochondrium *n; -s, Mitochondrien; Bio.* mitochondrion (*Pl.* mitochondria)

Mitose *f; -, -n; Bio.* mitosis (*Pl.* mitoses)

Mitra *f; -, Mitren; kirchl.* mitre, *Am.* miter

mitrauchen (*trennb., hat -ge-*) **I.** *v/i. als Passivraucher:* inhale (other people's) tobacco smoke; **II.** *v/t.* **1.** (*Rauch*) inhale; **2.** *umg.:* **rauchst du eine mit?** (want to) have a cigarette with me?, want a smoke too?; **Mitrauchen** *n; -s, kein Pl.* passive smoking; **Mitraucher** *m* passive smoker

mitrechnen *v/t. (trennb., hat -ge-)* **1.** include, count (as well), count in; ... **nicht mitgerechnet** not counting ...; **2.** (*gleichzeitig rechnen*) do the calculation at the same time (*od.* as well)

mitreden (*trennb., hat -ge-*) **I.** *v/i.* **1.** join in (the conversation), make a worthwhile comment; **da kann ich nicht ~** I don't know enough about that to comment; **2.** (*mitbestimmen*) have a say; **II.** *v/t.:* **etwas** *od.* **ein Wörtchen mitzureden haben** have a say (*bei* in)

mitregieren *v/t/i. (trennb., hat)* have a share in government; **~der Koalitionspartner** coalition partner with a share in government

mitreisen *v/i. (trennb., ist -ge-)* go (*kommen:* come) on the trip too; *mit Zirkus, Schaustellern etc.:* travel with the group; *mit j-m* ~ travel (*od.* go, come) with s.o.; **junger Mann zum Mitreisen gesucht** *Schild, von Zirkus etc.:* young man wanted to come on the road with us; **Mitreisende** *m, f* fellow passenger (*od.* travel[l]er); *e-r Grup-*

penreise: (other) tour member; **alle ~n** all the other passengers; *e-r Gruppenreise:* all the other tour members, the rest of the party

mitreißen *v/t. (unreg., trennb., hat -ge-)* **1.** carry (*od.* sweep) along; (*mitschleifen*) drag along; **2.** *fig.* (*begeistern*) carry (*od.* sweep) away; **mitreißend I.** *Part. Präs.* → *mitreißen;* **II.** *Adj. fig. Musik, Rede:* rousing; *Rhythmus, Applaus etc.:* infectious; *Spiel etc.:* exciting, thrilling

mitsammen *Adv. bes. österr.* together

mitsamt *Präp.* together (*od.* along) with

mitschicken *v/t. (trennb., hat -ge-)* send (along); *in Briefen etc.:* enclose

mitschleifen *v/t. (trennb., hat -ge-)* (*auch umg. fig. j-n*) drag along (with one)

mitschleppen *v/t. (trennb., hat -ge-); umg.* (*Gepäck etc.*) cart along (with one); (*Schweres*) *auch* hump (*Am.* schlep) along; *fig.* (*j-n*) drag (*Am. auch* schlep) along (with one); **sie will mich unbedingt in die Oper ~** she's dead set on getting me to go to the opera with her (*od.* on dragging me to the opera)

mitschneiden *v/t. (unreg., trennb., hat -ge-); Radio, TV* (*Sendung etc.*) record; **Mitschnitt** *m* recording

mitschreiben (*unreg., trennb., hat -ge-*) **I.** *v/t.* **1.** write (*od.* take) down; (*Vorlesung etc.*) make notes on; **2.** (*Prüfung*) take part in, *umg.* do; **II.** *v/i.* make notes; **Mitschrift** *f* written record

Mitschuld *f; nur Sg.* share of the blame; *bes. Jur.* partial responsibility; **ihn trifft e-e ~** he is partly to blame (*an* + *Dat.* for), he is partly responsible (for), he has a share in the blame (for); **mitschuldig** *Adj.:* ~ **sein** be partly responsible (*an* + *Dat.* for), be partly to blame (for); **Mitschuldige** *m, f* accomplice (*an* + *Dat.* in)

Mitschüler *m, ~in* *f* schoolmate; *ältere Jahrgänge: auch* fellow student; (*Klassenkamerad*) classmate

mitschwimmen (*unreg., trennb., ist -ge-*) **I.** *v/t.* (*Rennen etc.*) swim in; **II.** *v/i.* **1.** take part, swim (*bei* in); *in der Staffel* ~ swim in (*od.* be a member of) the relay team; **2.** *umg.* (*mitmachen*) participate; **auf der neuesten Modewelle ~** go in for the latest fashion trend

mitschwingen *v/i. (unreg., trennb., ist -ge-)* resonate; **darin schwingt ... mit** *fig.* it has overtones of ...

mit sein → *mit* II

mitsingen *v/i. (unreg., trennb., hat -ge-)* join in the singing, sing along; *in e-m Chor* ~ sing in a choir

mitsollen *v/i. (trennb., hat -ge-); umg.* be supposed to go (*mitkommen:* come) too

mitspielen (*trennb., hat -ge-*) **I.** *v/i.* **1.** join in (the game); **darf ich ~?** can I play with you?; **2.** *Sport* play (*bei* for); *in der Mannschaft* ~ be in the team; **3.** (*mitwirken*) *Theat. etc.* play a role (*od.* part) (*bei* in) (*auch fig.*); *im Orchester* ~ play in the orchestra; **der Zufall hat hier mitgespielt** *fig.* it was partly coincidence; **4.** (*etw. unterstützen*) play along, cooperate; **d[...] ist, ob das Finanzamt mi[...]** it all depends whether [...] are amenable (*od.* c[...] **übel** *od.* **böse** ~ b[...] tough) on s.o.; *au[...]* really hard time; [...]

übel mitgespielt he's had a hard life; **II.** *v/t.* (*unterstützen*) play along with; **dieses Spiel spiele ich nicht länger mit** I've had enough of this game; **Mitspieler** *m,* **Mitspielerin** *f* player; *Sport, in e-r Mannschaft:* team-mate; *Theat.* member of the (supporting) cast; **die ~** the other players (*Theat.* actors)

Mitsprache *f; nur Sg.* share in decisions, say; **~recht** *n; nur Sg.* right to a say (*bei* in); **wir haben kein ~** we have no say (whatsoever)

mitsprechen (*unreg., trennb., hat -ge-*) **I.** *v/t.* join in saying; **alle sprachen den Eid mit** they all said the oath together; **II.** *v/i.* **1.** → *mitreden*

mitstenografieren (*trennb., hat*) **I.** *v/t.* take down in shorthand; **II.** *v/i.* make shorthand notes

Mitstreiter *m,* **~in** *f* fellow campaigner (*für, in Sachen* + *Gen.* of); *lit.* comrade-in-arms

Mitt|achtziger *m* man in his mid-eighties; **~achtzigerin** *f* woman in her mid-eighties

Mittag¹ *m; -s, -e* **1.** *Uhrzeit:* midday, noon; (*Zeit zum Mittagessen*) lunchtime; **heute ~** at noon (*od.* midday) today; **es schlägt ~** it's striking noon (*od.* twelve midday); **gegen ~** around noon, at lunchtime; **wir haben über ~ geschlossen** we close for lunch, we're closed at lunchtime; **zu ~ essen** have lunch; **etw. zu ~ essen** have s.th. for lunch; **2.** *bes. südd.* (*Nachmittag*) afternoon; **3.** *umg.* (*Mittagspause*) lunch hour, lunch break; **es ist ~** it's my lunch hour; **~ machen** have one's lunch hour (*od.* break); **4.** *nur Sg.; poet. altm.* south

Mittag² *n; -s, kein Pl.; umg.* lunch; **~ essen** have lunch; **was gibt's zu ~?** what's for lunch?

Mittag|brot *n; nur Sg.; Dial.* lunch; **~essen** *n* lunch; **beim ~ sitzen** be having lunch

mittägig *Adj.; nur attr.* midday

mittäglich *Adj.* midday; *Hitze etc.: auch* noonday; *Pause etc.:* lunchtime; **mittags** *Adv.* **1.** at midday (*od.* noon), at lunchtime; (*um*) **12 Uhr ~** at 12 noon, at 12 o'clock midday; **von/bis ~** from/until noon; **dienstags ~** on Tuesdays at lunchtime, Tuesday lunchtimes; **2.** *bes. südd.* → *nachmittags*

Mittags|hitze *f* midday heat; **~mahlzeit** *f* lunch; *als Hauptmahlzeit: auch* dinner; **~pause** *f* lunch hour, lunch break; **~ruhe** *f* **1.** afternoon quiet hour; **2.** → *Mittagsschlaf;* **3.** *von 12-14h ~ Schild:* closed for lun[...] noon-2 pm; **~schicht** *f* midday[...] **~schlaf** *m,* **~schläfchen** *n* [...] nap, siesta; **~sonne** *f; nu[...]* mid-sun; **~sperre** *f* österr. [...] break); **~tempe-** *von 12-14h ~ Schi[...]tures (im* noon-2 pm; **~s[...]ghs);** **~tisch** day; **2.** *Dia[...]* ~ **decken** lay **~tafel** *f[...] altm.* lunch; **ratu[...]** **2.** → *Mittagspau-* **So[...]** [...]accomplice; *Jur. auch* [...]plicity the crime); **Mittäter-** [...]eißigerin *f* woman in her [...] *m* man in his mid-thir-

M

Mitte *f*; -, -*n* **1.** (*mittlerer Teil*) middle; (*Mittelpunkt*) cent|re (*Am.* -er); *wir nahmen ihn in die ~* we took him between us; *beim Sitzen*: we sat down on either side of him; *in unserer ~* with us, in our midst; *jemand aus unsrer ~* someone from our midst, one of our close friends; *er wurde aus unserer ~ gerissen euph.* he was taken from our midst; *in der ~ zwischen* half-way between; *die goldene ~ fig.* the golden mean, a (*od.* the) happy medium; *ab durch die ~! umg.* off you go!; **2.** *nur Sg.* (*Zeitpunkt*): *~ Juli* in the middle of July, (in) mid-July; *~ des Jahres* halfway through the year; *~ der Woche* midweek, in the middle of the week; *in der ~ des 18. Jahrhunderts* in the mid-18th century; *~ dreißig* in one's mid-thirties; **3.** *nur Sg.; Pol.*: *die ~* the cent|re (*Am.* -er); *e-e Politik der ~* a policy of moderation

mitteilbar *Adj.* communicable

mitteilen (*trennb., hat -ge-*) **I.** *v/t.* **1.** *j-m etw. ~* inform s.o. of s.th., tell s.o. s.th.; *amtlich*: notify s.o. of s.th.; *Wirts.* advise s.o. of s.th.; *er teilte ihr die Nachricht schonend mit* he broke the news to her gently; **2.** *geh.* (*Wissen etc.*) communicate (+ *Dat.* to), impart *förm.* (to); (*auch Stimmung*) convey; **3.** *Phys.* (*Energie, Schwingung etc.*) convey, impart *förm.* (+ *Dat.* to); **II.** *v/refl.* **1.** *geh.*: *sich j-m ~* (*anvertrauen*) confide in s.o., open up to s.o.; **2.** *geh.*: *sich j-m ~* (*übertragen*) *Stimmung etc.*: communicate itself to s.o.; **3.** *Phys.* be conveyed (*förm.* imparted) (+ *Dat.* to)

mitteilenswert *Adj.* worth telling; *~e Nachricht* interesting piece of news

mitteilsam *Adj.* communicative, forthcoming; (*redselig*) talkative

Mitteilung *f amtliche*: communication; (*Benachrichtigung*) notification; (*Bekanntgabe*) announcement; (*in der Presse*) report; (*Nachricht*) message; (*Erklärung*) statement; *j-m ~ machen* inform s.o. (*von, über + Akk.* of); *amtlich*: notify s.o. (of); *ich muss Ihnen e-e vertrauliche ~ machen* I've (got) something to tell you in confidence

Mitteilungs|bedürfnis *n; nur Sg.* need to communicate; *er hat ein großes ~* auch he always has to tell someone everything (*od.* open up to someone)

mittel *Adj.; nur präd.; umg.* (*mäßig*) (fair to) middling, so-so; *in der Schule war ich nur (so) ~* I wasn't better than average at school

Mittel *n; -s, -* **1.** (*Hilfsmittel*) means *Sg.* (*zu, um zu + Inf.* of + *Ger.*); (*Verfahren*) method (for + *Ger.*), way (of + ...); (*Ausweg*) expedient; *fig.* (*Werk...*) tool, device; (*Waffe*) weapon; *~s ~, wenn alle ~ versagen* as ... if all else fails; *ihm ist jedes ... me...'ll stop at nothing, he'll ke...* ...(s); *~ und Wege finden* look for ways and means; *...one* ... *Inf.* to + *Inf.*); *versucht ... → Zweck ... sen* try every ... (*gegen ...*) ...e), leave no (*Tabletten*) ... o... *allen* ... reiben an ... *ossible*); *ein ~ gegen* a he...emedy thing for a medic...ne; *~ a strong medic...*

... *tel, chemisches ~ etc.*) agent; (*Putzmittel*) *auch* cleaner; *ein ~ gegen Schädlingsbefall* a pesticide; *ein ~ zum Entfernen von Teer/Haaren* a tar remover / a depilatory agent; **4.** *Pl.* (*Reserven*) *auch geistige*: resources; (*Geldmittel, Kapital*) means, funds; *Geld aus öffentlichen ~n* money from the public purse, public money; *m-e ~ erlauben es nicht* it's beyond my means; **5.** (*Durchschnitt*) average; (*Mittelwert*) mean; *im ~* on average; *arithmetisches Mittel Math.* arithmetic mean

Mittelachse *f* central axis

Mittelalter *n; nur Sg.* **1.** *hist.*: *das ~* the Middle Ages *Pl.*; *das finstere ~* the Dark Ages; *das sind Zustände wie im ~!* this is positively medieval; **2.** *umg. e-r Person*: middle age; *er ist ~* he's middle-aged; **mittelalterlich** *Adj.* medieval (*auch fig.* rückständig)

Mittelamerika (*n*); *Geog.* Central America; **Mittelamerikaner** *m*, **Mittelamerikanerin** *f* Central American; **mittelamerikanisch** *Adj.* Central American

mittelbar *Adj.* indirect

Mittel|bau *m* **1.** *Pl.* -*ten*; *Archit.* central part (of a building), central block; **2.** *Pl.* -*e*; *Wirts., Personal*: middle range, middle-range positions *Pl.*; *Univ.* non-professorial (*Am. auch* support) staff *Sg.* (*V. im Pl.*); *~betrieb m* medium-size(d) business

Mittelchen *n umg.* cure; (*Kniff*) (little) trick

mitteldeutsch *Adj.* **1.** *Geog.* Central German; **2.** *Ling.* Central (*od.* Middle) German; **3.** *hist. Pol.* East German; **Mitteldeutsch** *n; -en; Ling.* Central (*od.* Middle) German; **Mitteldeutschland** (*n*) **1.** *Geog.* Central Germany; **2.** *hist. Pol.* East Germany

Mittelding *n* cross; *ein ~ zwischen A und B* a cross between A and B, something (in) between A and B

Mitteleuropa (*n*); *Geog.* Central Europe; **Mitteleuropäer** *m*, **Mitteleuropäerin** *f* Central European; **mitteleuropäisch** *Adj.* Central European; *~e Zeit* (*abgek.* **MEZ**) Central European Time (*abgek.* CET)

mittelfein I. *Adj. Wirts., Gewinde, Sandpapier etc.*: medium-fine; **II.** *Adv.*: *~ gemahlen* medium ground

Mittelfeld *n Sport* **1.** *nur Sg.; Baseball*: centrefield, *Am.* center field; *Fußball*: midfield; *das ~* (*die Mittelfeldspieler*) the midfield (players *Pl.*); **2.** *nur Sg.* (*Gruppe*): *im ~ fahren beim Rennen*: be in the middle of the field; *im ~ sein od. stehen in der Tabelle*: be in mid-table; *~spieler m, ~spielerin f* midfield player

Mittelfinger *m* middle finger; *j-m den* (*ausgestreckten*) *~ zeigen* raise one's middle finger at s.o., *Brit. etwa* give s.o. the V sign, *Am.* give s.o. the finger

mittelfristig I. *Adj. Kredit etc.*: medium-term ...; *~e Anleihe* medium-term bond; *~es Ziel* medium-range (*od.* intermediate) target; **II.** *Adv.*: *~* (*gesehen*) (seen) in the medium term; *~ planen* plan for the medium term

Mittelfuß *m Anat.* metatarsus (*Pl.* metatarsi); *~knochen m* metatarsal

Mittel|gang *m* (cent|re, *Am.* -er) aisle; *~gebirge n Geog.* minor mountain range under 3,000 ft; high hills *Pl.*

Mittelgewicht *n* (*Sport*) middleweight ...uch *Sportler*); **Mittelgewichtler** *m*; **Mittelgewichtlerin** *f*; -, -*nen* mid-

... dleweight

Mittelglied *n* middle (*od.* connecting) joint

mittelgroß *Adj.* medium-sized

Mittelgrund *m Kunst* middle ground

Mittelhand *f* **1.** *Anat.* metacarpus (*Pl.* metacarpi); **2.** *Zool.* (*Rumpf*) barrel; **3.** *Skat*: *in der ~ sitzen od. sitzen* sit next to the lead player (and play second)

Mittelhirn *n Anat.* midbrain; *fachspr.* mesencephalon

mittelhochdeutsch *Ling. Adj.* Middle High German; **Mittelhochdeutsch** *n* Middle High German

Mitte-links|-Bündnis *n*, *~-Koalition f Pol.* centre-left (*Am.* center-left) coalition; *~-Regierung f* centre-left (*Am.* center-left) government

Mittelklasse *f* **1.** *Wirts.* medium price range; **2.** (*Mittelstand*) middle classes *Pl.*; *~hotel n* mid-price hotel; *~wagen m* middle-of-the-range car; *von mittlerer Größe*: medium-sized car, *Am.* compact

Mittellage *f* central position, mid-position; *Mus.* middle voice

mittelländisch *Adj.*: *das Mittelländische Meer* the Mediterranean Sea

Mittellatein *n Ling.* medieval Latin

Mittel|lauf *m e-s Flusses*: middle reaches *Pl.*; *~läufer m Fußball*: cent|re (*Am.* -er) back, cent|re (*Am.* -er) half; *~linie f auch Sport* cent|re (*Am.* -er) line; *Fußball*: halfway line; *Tennis*: cent|re (*Am.* -er) service line; *Math.* median line; *Mot.* white (cent|re, *Am.* -er) line

mittellos *Adj.* penniless, destitute; (*verarmt*) impoverished; **Mittellosigkeit** *f; nur Sg.* impoverishment, destitution

Mittelmacht *f* **1.** *Pol.* middle-size power; **2.** *Pl.*: *die Mittelmächte hist.* the Central Powers

Mittelmaß *n* (*Durchschnitt*) average; *pej.* (*Mittelmäßigkeit*) mediocrity; *gutes ~* above average; *ein gesundes ~* a (*od.* the) happy medium; **mittelmäßig** *Adj. Leistung, Person*: mediocre, indifferent; (*durchschnittlich*) average; *umg.* (*weder gut noch schlecht*) middling; **Mittelmäßigkeit** *f* mediocrity; mediocre standards *Pl.* (+ *Gen.* of)

Mittelmeer *n; nur Sg.; Geog.* Mediterranean (Sea); **Mittelmeer... im Subst.** Mediterranean; *~länder Pl.* Mediterranean countries; *~raum m* Mediterranean area; **mittelmeerisch** *Adj.* Mediterranean

Mittelmotor *m Mot.* mid-engine

mitteln *v/t.* take the mean of; → *gemittelt*

Mittelohr *n Anat.* middle ear; *~entzündung f Med.* inflammation of the middle ear

Mittelpfosten *m am Fenster*: mullion

mittelprächtig *umg.* **I.** *Adj.* **1.** (*mittelmäßig*) middling, not too good; **2.** (*beträchtlich*) quite a ...; **II.** *Adv.*: *wie geht's? - ~* how are you? - so-so, (fair to) middling

Mittelpunkt *m* cent|re (*Am.* -er); *e-r Stadt etc.*: *auch* heart; *fig.* cent|re (*Am.* -er) of interest (*od.* attention); (*Brennpunkt*) focus; *der Welt, e-s Landes*: hub; *sie will immer im ~ stehen fig.* she always wants to be the focus of attention; *etw. in den ~ e-r Rede etc. stellen* focus on s.th. in a speech *etc.*, make s.th. the focal point of a speech *etc.*; *in den ~ rücken* move cent|re (*Am.* -er) stage; *~schule f* (rural) school cent|re (*Am.* -er)

mittels *Präp.* by means of, with the help of

Mittel|scheitel *m* middle (*od.* centre) parting, *Am.* center part; **~schicht** *f Soziol.* middle classes *Pl.*; **~schiff** *n Archit.* nave; **~schule** *f* **1.** *in Deutschland:* → **Realschule**; **2.** *in der Schweiz, früher auch in Österreich:* (*Gymnasium*) secondary school, *Am.* high school

mittelschwer *Adj.* **1.** *an Gewicht:* moderately heavy; *Stoff:* medium-weight; **2.** *Schwierigkeitsgrad:* moderately difficult, ... *of* medium difficulty; **3.** (*ziemlich ernst*) *Unfall, Verletzung etc.:* fairly serious

Mittelschwergewicht *n Sport* middle heavyweight (*auch Sportler*); **Mittelschwergewichtler** *m; -s, -*, **Mittelschwergewichtlerin** *f; -, -nen* middle heavyweight

Mittels|mann *m*, **~person** *f* intermediary, go-between; *mst Pol.* mediator

Mittelstadt *f* medium-sized town

Mittelstand *m; nur Sg.* middle classes *Pl.*; **mittelständisch** *Adj.* **1.** middle-class; **2. ~e Betriebe** small and medium-size(d) businesses; **Mittelständler** *m; -s, -*, **Mittelständlerin** *f; -, -nen* member of the middle classes

Mittelstands|... *im Subst.* middle-class; **~bürger** *m* middle-class citizen, member of the middle classes

Mittel|station *f von Bergbahn:* halfway station, mid-station; **~steinzeit** *f* Mesolithic period; **~stellung** *f* midway position; **e-e ~ einnehmen zwischen** be halfway between; *fig. auch* be a cross between; **~stimme** *f Mus.* middle voice

Mittelstrecke *f Sport* middle distance

Mittelstrecken|flugzeug *n* medium--haul aircraft; **~lauf** *m Sport* middle--distance race; **~läufer** *m*, **~läuferin** *f* middle-distance runner; **~rakete** *f Mil.* medium-range missile

Mittel|streifen *m Autobahn:* central reservation, *Am.* median strip; **~stück** *n* middle (*od.* central) part; *umg.* middle bit; *von Fleisch etc.:* middle; **~stufe** *f* **1.** intermediate stage; **2.** *Päd. etwa* middle school, *Am. auch* junior high; **~stürmer** *m Sport* cent|re (*Am.* -er) forward; **~weg** *m fig.* middle course; **der goldene ~** the golden mean; **~welle** *f Radio:* medium wave

Mittelwellen|bereich *m Radio:* medium-wave band; **~sender** *m* medium--wave radio station (*Anlage:* transmitter)

Mittelwert *m* average, mean (value)

Mittelwort *n Ling.* participle; **~ der Gegenwart** present participle

mitten *Adv.:* **~ in** (+ *Dat.*) in the middle (*od.* midst) of; *betont: auch* right in (the middle [*od.* midst] of); (*im Gewühl*) in the thick of; **~ unter uns** in our (very) midst; **~ durch** (right) through the middle of; **~ in etw.** (*Akk.*) (*hinein*) right into s.th.; **~ ins Herz** straight into the heart; **~ im Winter** in the middle (*lit.* depth) of winter; **~ in der Nacht** in the middle of the night; **~ am Tag** (*am helllichten Tag*) in broad daylight; **er stand ~ im Leben** he was in the prime of life; *bei Verstorbenem: auch* he was cut off in his prime; **~ im Satz** in mid-sentence; **~ auf dem Meer** in mid-ocean

mittendrin *Adv. umg.* right in the middle (of it [*od.* them], *in einer Tätigkeit:* of doing it)

mittendurch *Adv.* right (*od.* straight)

through the middle; *brechen, schneiden etc.: auch* clean through

Mitternacht *f; nur Sg.:* (**um**) **~** (at) midnight

mitternächtlich *Adj.* midnight ...; **mitternachts** *Adv.* at (*od.* around) midnight

Mitternachts|gottesdienst *m*, **~messe** *f* midnight mass; **~sonne** *f* midnight sun; **~stunde** *f* midnight hour; **zur ~** (at) around midnight

Mittfünfziger *m* man in his mid-fifties; **Mittfünfzigerin** *f* woman in her mid--fifties

mittig I. *Adj. Tech.* centred, *Am.* centered; *präd. auch* O.C., on cent|re (*Am.* -er); **II.** *Adv.:* **~ geteilt** divided in the middle

Mittler *m; -s, -; geh.* mediator

mittler... *Adj.* **1.** middle, central; **sie ist das ~e von drei Kindern** *umg.* she is the middle one (*od.* second) of three children; **Mittlerer Osten** part of south central Asia comprising Afghanistan and the Indian subcontinent; → **Reife**; **2.** (*durchschnittlich*) average; *Math., Phys., Tech.* mean; *Größe, Qualität, Wert:* medium; (*mittelmäßig*) middling; **von ~em Alter** middle-aged; **~er Beamter** lower-grade administrative civil servant; **~es Einkommen** middle income; **von ~er Größe** medium-sized; **~es Management** middle management

Mittlerfunktion *f* mediating role, role as (a) mediator

Mittlerin *f; -, -nen; geh.* mediator

Mittler|rolle *f* mediating role, role as (a) mediator; **~sprache** *f Ling.* lingua franca

mittlerweile *Adv.* meanwhile, (in the) meantime; (*seitdem*) since (then)

mittragen (*unreg., trennb., hat -ge-*) **I.** *v/t.* **1.** help (to) carry; **2.** *fig.* (*Verantwortung etc.*) share, bear (*od.* carry) one's share of; **II.** *v/i.* help carrying, help with (the) carrying

mittrinken *vt/i.* (*unreg., trennb., hat -ge-*) join in the drinking; **trinkst du e-n** (**mit uns**) **mit?** will you have a drink with us (*od.* join us for a drink)?

mittschiffs *Adv. Naut.* amidships

Mittsechziger *m* man in his mid-sixties; **Mittsechzigerin** *f* woman in her mid-sixties

Mittsiebziger *m* man in his mid-seventies; **Mittsiebzigerin** *f* woman in her mid-seventies

Mittsommer *m* midsummer; **~nacht** *f* midsummer night

mittun *v/i.* (*unreg., trennb., hat -ge-*); *Dial.* → **mitmachen I**

Mittvierziger *m* man in his mid-forties; **Mittvierzigerin** *f* woman in her mid--forties

Mittwinter *m* midwinter

Mittwoch *m* Wednesday; → **Dienstag**; **~abend** *m* Wednesday evening

mittwochs *Adv.* on Wednesdays; → **dienstags**

Mittzwanziger *m* young man in his mid-twenties; **Mittzwanzigerin** *f* young woman in her mid-twenties

mitunter *Adv.* now and then, sometimes, occasionally

mitunterzeichnen *v/t.* (*trennb., hat*) co-sign; (*gegenzeichnen*) countersign; **Mitunterzeichner** *m*, **Mitunterzeichnerin** *f* cosignatory, cosigner

Mitveranstalter *m*, **~in** *f* co-organizer; *von Konzert etc.:* co-promoter

mitverantwortlich *Adj.* jointly responsible; (*teilweise verantwortlich*) partly

responsible; **Mitverantwortlichkeit** *f* share of the responsibility; **Mitverantwortung** *f* joint responsibility

mitverdienen *v/i.* (*trennb., hat*) be earning as well; **Mitverdiener** *m*, **Mitverdienerin** *f* second (*od.* extra) earner

Mitverfasser *m*, **~in** *f* co-author

Mitvergangenheit *f; nur Sg.; Ling. österr.* past (tense)

mitverschulden *v/t.* (*trennb., hat*) be partly responsible for; **Mitverschulden** *n* part of the blame (*Jur.* guilt) (**an** + *Dat.* for); *durch Fahrlässigkeit:* contributory negligence (regarding)

Mitverschwörer *m*, **~in** *f* fellow conspirator

mitversichern *v/t.* (*trennb., hat*) *Versicherungswesen:* include in the insurance; **Mitversicherte** *m, f* jointly insured party; **Mitversicherung** *f* coinsurance; *e-r Person:* joint insurance

mitverursachen *v/t.* (*trennb., hat*) be partly responsible for; **von etw. mitverursacht sein** be partly caused by s.th.

Mitwelt *f; nur Sg.* society in which one lives; (*Zeitgenossen*) one's contemporaries *Pl.*

mitwirken *v/i.* (*trennb., hat -ge-*) **1.** (*mithelfen*) help, assist (**bei, an** + *Dat.* in); (*teilnehmen*) take part (in), be involved (in); **2.** (*e-e Rolle spielen*) play one's (*Sache*[*n*]: its *od.* their) part (**bei** in), play (*od.* have) a part (in); **3.** *Theat. etc.* take part (**bei** in), appear (in); *Musiker:* perform (in); (*spielen*) play (in); (*singen*) sing (in); **Mitwirkende** *m, f; -n, -n* participant; (*Ausführende*[*r*]) performer; *Theat. auch* actor; *weiblich:* actress; **die ~n** the cast; **Mitwirkung** *f* cooperation, collaboration; (*Mithilfe*) assistance; (*Teilnahme*) participation; **unter ~ von** ... assisted by ..., with the collaboration of; *Theat. etc.* starring (*od.* featuring) ...; **die ~ der Länder bei der Gesetzgebung** the involvement of the Länder in the legislation

Mitwirkungs|pflicht *f; nur Sg.* duty to cooperate; **~recht** *f; nur Sg.* right of participation

Mitwissen *n* knowledge; (*Einverständnis*) connivance; **Mitwisser** *m; -s, -*, **Mitwisserin** *f; -, -nen* someone who is in the know; (*Vertraute*[*r*]) confidant, *Frau:* confidante; *Jur.* accessory; **es gibt zu viele Mitwisser** too many people know about it; **Mitwisserschaft** *f* connivance; **er leugnete s-e ~** he denied all knowledge of the matter

mitwollen *v/i.* (*unreg., trennb., hat -ge-*); *umg.* want to go (*kommen:* come) too

mitzählen (*trennb., hat -ge-*) **I.** *v/i.* **1.** count along, count as well; **ich hab nicht mitgezählt** I wasn't counting; **2.** (*von Belang sein*) count, be important; **das zählt nicht mit** (*gilt nicht*) that doesn't count; **II.** *v/t.* count (in), include; (*berücksichtigen*) take into account

mitziehen (*unreg., trennb., -ge-*) **I.** *v/i.* (*hat*) **1.** help (to) pull, help pulling; **2.** (*ist*) (*mitreisen*) travel (*od.* go) too; **mit j-m ~** travel (*od.* go) along with s.o.; **3.** (*hat*) (*sich anschließen*) follow suit; *umg.* (*mitmachen*) play along; **II.** *v/t.* (*hat*) **1.** help (to) pull; **2.** (*nach sich ziehen*) pull (*od.* drag) along behind one

Mix *m; -, -e; fachspr., Sl.* mixture; **Mixbecher** *m* cocktail shaker

Mixed ['mɪkst] *n*; -(s), -(s); *Sport* (*Spiel*) mixed doubles *Sg.*; (*Mannschaft*) mixed doubles pair

mixen *v/t.* mix; **Mixer** *m*; -s, - **1.** (*Barmixer*) bartender, mixologist *hum.*; **2.** *TV etc. auch Person*: mixer; **3.** (*Mixgerät*) blender, liquidizer; **Mixerin** *f*; -, -nen **1.** barmaid; **2.** → *Mixer* 2

Mix|gerät *n* mixer; **~getränk** *n* mixed drink; *alkoholisches*: cocktail

Mixtur *f*; -, -en mixture

MKS *f*; -, *kein Pl.*; *Vet. Abk.* (**Maul- und Klauenseuche**) FMD (foot and mouth disease)

MKS-System *n*; *nur Sg.* mks system

ml *Abk.* (**Milliliter**) ml

mm *Abk.* (**Millimeter**) mm

MMS *f*; -, -(e); *Abk.* (**Multimedia Messaging Service**) *Handy*: MMS

Mnemotechnik *f* mnemonics *Pl.* (*V. im Sg.*); **Mnemotechniker** *m*, **Mnemotechnikerin** *f* mnemonist; **mnemotechnisch I.** *Adj.* mnemonic; **II.** *Adv.* mnemonically

Mob *m*; -s, *kein Pl.*; *pej.* mob

mobben *v/t.* harass, bully; *j-n aus der Firma* ~ keep on harassing s.o. until he/she leaves the firm, *Am.* hound s.o. out of the company; **Mobbing** *n*; -s, *kein Pl.* bullying, harassment at work

Möbel *n*; -s, -; (*Möbelstück*) piece of furniture; ~ *Pl.* furniture *Sg.*; **~geschäft** *n* furniture shop (*bes. Am.* store); **~händler** *m*, **~händlerin** *f* furniture dealer; **~haus** *n* → *Möbelgeschäft*; **~lager** *n* furniture warehouse; *für Altmöbel*: furniture repository; **~packer** *m* removal man, *Am.* mover; **~politur** *f* furniture polish; **~schreiner** *m*, **~schreinerin** *f* cabinet-maker; **~spediteur** *m* removal man, *Am.* mover; *Firma*: removal firm, *Am.* movers *Pl.*, van line; **~spedition** *f* removal firm, *Am.* movers *Pl.*, van line; **~stoff** *m* furnishing fabric; **~stück** *n* piece of furniture; **~tischler** *m*, **~tischlerin** *f* cabinet-maker; **~wagen** *m* furniture (*od.* removal) van, *Am.* furniture truck

mobil I. *Adj.* **1.** mobile; *Jur., Besitz*: movable; *~es Kapital Fin.* floating capital; ~ *machen Mil.*, *fig.* mobilize; **2.** *umg.* (*munter*) active; (*rüstig*) sprightly; **II.** *Adv. Telef.*: ~ **telefonieren** (*mit dem Mobiltelefon telefonieren*) use the mobile phone (*Am.* cellphone), make a call on the mobile (*Am.* on a cellphone)

Mobile ['moːbilə] *n*; -s, -s mobile

Mobilfunk *m Telek.* mobile (*Am.* cell) telephony; **~netz** *n Telek.* mobile (*Am.* cell) telephone network

Mobiliar *n*; -s, -e furniture, furnishings *Pl.*

Mobilien *Pl. Jur., Wirts.* movables, chattels, movable property *Sg.*

mobilisieren I. *v/t.* **1.** *Mil., Med., fig.* mobilize; *alle Kräfte* ~ summon up all one's strength; **2.** *Wirts.* realize; **II.** *v/i. Wirts.* realize assets (*od.* capital); **Mobilisierung** *f* mobilization; *Wirts.* realization

Mobilität *f*; -, *kein Pl.* mobility; *geistig-seelische*: mental agility

Mobilmachung *f*; -, -en; *Mil., fig.* mobilization

Mobil|netz *n Telek.* mobile (*Am.* cell) telephone network, cellular network; **~telefon** *n* mobile (tele)phone, *Am.* cellphone; **~toilette** *f* portable toilet, *Am.* portable rest room

möblieren *v/t.* furnish; *neu* ~ refurnish; **möbliert I.** *P.P.* → *möblieren*; **II.** *Adj.*

furnished; *~es Zimmer* furnished room, *Brit. auch* bedsit(ter); **III.** *Adv.*: ~ **wohnen** live in furnished accommodation

mochte *Imperf.* → *mögen*

möchte(n) → *mögen*

Möchtegern... *im Subst.* would-be

modal *Adj. Ling.* modal

Modaladverb *n Ling.* adverb of manner

Modalität *f*; -, -en **1.** *Ling., Logik*: modality; **2.** (*Umstand*) circumstance; *~en e-s Vertrags etc.*: details; (*Bedingungen*) (precise) terms, conditions

Modal|logik *f* modal logic; **~satz** *m Ling.* modal sentence (*od.* phrase); **~verb** *n Ling.* modal (verb)

modd(e)rig *Adj. nordd. umg.* muddy

Mode *f*; -, -n **1.** fashion; *die neueste* ~ the latest fashion; ~ *sein* be in fashion, *umg.* be in; (*die*) *große* ~ *sein* be all the rage; *in* ~ *kommen* come into fashion; *aus der* ~ *kommen* go (*od.* fall) out of fashion; *mit der* ~ *gehen* follow (*od.* keep up with) the (latest) fashion; *es ist* (*nicht*) ~ *zu* (+ *Inf.*) it's (not) the fashion to (+ *Inf.*), it's (not) considered fashionable to (+ *Inf.*); **2.** *Pl.* (*modische Kleidung*): *die neuesten* ~*n vorführen* present the latest fashions; **~artikel** *m* fashionable article; *engS.* (*Neuigkeit*) novelty; **~ausdruck** *m* vogue expression (*Wort*: word); *Am. auch* the latest jargon *Sg.*; **~beruf** *m* fashionable career

modebewusst *Adj.* fashion-conscious, *umg.* trendy

Mode|branche *f* fashion trade (*od.* industry), *umg.* rag trade; **~designer** *m*, **~designerin** *f* fashion illustrator (and designer); **~droge** *f* fashionable drug, *umg.* in drug; **~erscheinung** *f* vogue, (passing) fashion; **~farbe** *f* fashionable colo(u)r, *umg.* in colo(u)r; *der Saison*: this season's colo(u)r; **~fotograf** *m*, **~fotografin** *f* fashion photographer; **~geck** *m pej.* dandy; **~geschäft** *n* fashion store; *kleines*: boutique; **~haus** *n* **1.** *Unternehmen*: fashion house; **2.** *Laden*: fashion store; **~journal** *n* fashion magazine; **~krankheit** *f* fashionable complaint (*od.* illness)

Model¹ ['moːdl] *m*; -s, - **1.** *Dial.* (*Backform*) decorated (wooden) baking mo(u)ld; **2.** *Druck*: printing block (for fabrics)

Model² ['mɔdl] *n*; -s, -s (photographic) model

Modell *n*; -s, -e **1.** (*Muster, Vorbild, Modellkleid*) model; (*Nachbildung*) mock-up; **2.** *Kunst etc.* model; ~ *stehen* work as a model; *j-m* ~ *sitzen od. stehen* model (*od.* pose) for s.o.; *für ein Bild* ~ *stehen* model for a painting; **3.** (*Ausführung, Typ*) model; (*Konstruktion*) design; **4.** (*Entwurf*) draft; **5.** *euph.* (*Prostituierte*) call girl, model; **~bau** *m*; *nur Sg.* model-making; **~bauer** *m*; -s, -, **~bauerin** *f*; -, -nen model-maker; **~baukasten** *m* model-making kit, construction kit; **~charakter** *m*; *nur Sg.*: ~ *haben* serve as a model; **~eisenbahn** *f* model railway (*Am.* railroad); **~fall** *m* **1.** model case; **2.** (*typischer Fall*) classic (*od.* textbook) case; **~flugzeug** *n* model aeroplane (*Am.* airplane)

modellhaft *Adj.* model, exemplary

Modellierbogen *m* model-making pattern

modellieren *vt/i.* (*Figur etc.*) model; (*Ton, Wachs etc.*) *auch* mo(u)ld

Modellier|masse *f* model(l)ing materi-

al; **~ton** *m* model(l)ing clay

Modell|kleid *n* model (dress); **~projekt** *n* pilot project; **~puppe** *f* dummy; *im Schaufenster*: *auch* mannequin; **~schreiner** *m*, **~schreinerin** *f* pattern maker; **~tischler** *m*, **~tischlerin** *f* pattern maker; **~versuch** *m* **1.** pilot experiment (*od.* scheme); **2.** *Phys. etc.* experiment on (*od.* with) a model; **~zeichnung** *f Kunst* drawing (*od.* sketch) of a model

modeln¹ ['moːdln] *v/t.* model (*nach* on); *etw. nach s-n Wünschen* ~ mo(u)ld (*ändern*: change) s.th. to conform to one's wishes

modeln² ['mɔdln] *v/i. umg.* (*als Fotomodell arbeiten*) model

Modem *m*, *n*; -s, -s; *EDV, Telek.* modem; **~anschluss** *m* modem connection

Modemacher *m*, **~in** *f umg.* fashion designer

Modenschau *f* fashion show

Modepuppe *f umg. pej.* dolled up young bird (*Am.* chick)

Moder *m*; -s, *kein Pl.* mo(u)ld (*Fäulnis*) decay; *stärker*: putrefaction

moderat I. *Adj. Preiserhöhung etc.*: moderate, reasonable; *e-e ~e Haltung zu e-m Thema einnehmen* adopt a moderate (*od.* middle-of-the-road) attitude on an issue; **II.** *Adv.* moderately; *die Krankenkassenbeiträge sollen* ~ *erhöht werden* there are to be moderate increases in health insurance contributions

Moderation *f*; -, -en **1.** *TV* presentation, *Am.* moderation; **2.** *bei Seminar, Diskussion etc.*: chairing

Moderator *m*; -s, -en **1.** *TV* presenter, host, *Am. auch* moderator; *bei Nachrichtensendung*: newsreader, *Am.* anchor; **2.** *bei Seminar, Diskussion etc.*: chairman, chair(person); **3.** *ev.* synodal committee member; **Moderatorin** *f*; -, -nen **1.** *TV* presenter, host, *Am. auch* moderator, anchor; **2.** *bei Seminar, Diskussion etc.*: chairwoman, chair(person); **3.** *ev.* synodal committee member

Modergeruch *m* mo(u)ldy (*od.* musty) smell; (*Fäulnisgeruch*) smell of decay (*stärker*: putrefaction)

moderieren I. *v/t.* **1.** *TV* present, *Am.* anchor, moderate; **2.** (*Seminar, Diskussion etc.*) chair; **II.** *v/i.* **1.** *TV* act as presenter (*Am.* moderator); **2.** *bei Seminar, Diskussion etc.*: be in the chair

moderig *Adj.* mo(u)ldy; *Geruch*: *auch* musty; (*faulend*) decaying, putrid

modern¹ ['moːdɐn] *v/i.* mo(u)lder, go mo(u)ldy; (*verwesen*) decay, rot (*away*)

modern² [moˈdɛrn] **I.** *Adj.* **1.** modern; (*fortschrittlich*) progressive; *pej.* newfangled; (*auf dem Laufenden*) up-to-date ...; *präd.* up to date; *er ist ein ~er Mensch* he's very up to date (*umg.* with it), he has modern ideas; **2.** (*modisch*) fashionable; *im Trend liegend*: trendy; *lange Röcke sind* ~ long skirts are in *umg.*; **II.** *Adv.* in a modern style; ~ *denken* be a progressive thinker, have modern ideas; **Moderne** *f*; -, *kein Pl.* **1.** modern age; **2.** *Kunst etc. der* ~ modern art etc.

modernisieren I. *v/t.* modernize; (*auf den neuesten Stand bringen*) update, bring up to date; **II.** *v/i.* introduce modern methods; *in großem Umfang* ~ undertake large-scale modernization; **Modernisierung** *f* modernization, updating; **Modernismus** *m*; -,

Modernismen modernism; **modernistisch I.** *Adj.* modernistic; **II.** *Adv.* in a modernistic style; **Modernität** *f*; -, -*en* modernity

Mode|sache *f*: *das ist* (*reine*) ~ it's (just) the fashion; ~**salon** *m* fashion house; *kleiner*: boutique; ~**schau** *f* fashion show; ~**schmuck** *m* costume jewellery (*Am.* jewelry); ~**schöpfer** *m*, ~**schöpferin** *f* creator of fashion, couturier, *weiblich*: couturière; ~**schriftsteller** *m*, ~**schriftstellerin** *f* fashionable writer (*od.* author); ~**tanz** *m* latest thing in dances, newest dancing craze; ~**torheit** *f* crazy fashion; ~**trend** *m* fashionable trend; ~**welt** *f* world of fashion; ~**wort** *n* vogue word, buzzword; ~**zar** *m*, ~**zarin** *f umg. hum.* fashion mogul; ~**zeitschrift** *f* fashion magazine

Modifikation *f*; -, -*en* modification; (*Einschränkung*) *auch* qualification; **modifizierbar** *Adj.* modifiable; **modifizieren** *v/t.* modify; (*Ausdruck*) *auch* qualify

modisch *Adj.* fashionable; *umg.* in ...; *bes. pej.* trendy; (*schick*) stylish

Modistin *f*; -, -*nen* milliner

Modul[1] *n*; -*s*, -*e*; *Etech.*, *Computer*: module (*auch fig.*)

Modul[2] *m*; -*s*, -*n*; *Phys.*, *Tech.* module

modular *Adj. fachspr.* modular

Modulation *f*; -, -*en* modulation; **modulieren** *v/t.* modulate

Modus *m*; -, *Modi* **1.** (*Art und Weise*) procedure, method; **2.** *Mus.* mode; **3.** *Ling.* mood; **Modus Vivendi** *m*; - -, *Modi* -; *geh.* modus (*Pl.* modi) vivendi

Mofa *n*; -*s*, -*s*; *Mot.* (low-powered) moped (*not capable of more than 25 kph*)

Mogelei *f*; -, -*en*; *umg.* cheating; **mogeln** *umg.* **I.** *v/i.* cheat; *beim Kartenspiel* ~ cheat at cards; **II.** *v/t.* slip, smuggle (*in + Akk.* into, *unter + Akk.* among); **III.** *v/refl.*: *sich ins Konzert* ~ wangle one's way into the concert; **Mogelpackung** *f* **1.** *Wirts.* deceptive packaging *Sg.*; **2.** *umg. fig. Maßnahme*: cosmetic measure (*Änderung*: improvement, change)

mögen I. *Modalv.*; *möchte, mag, mochte, hat ... mögen* **1.** *Wunsch ausdrückend*: *ich möchte* (*Dial.* mag) *gehen* I want to go; *Bier hat sie noch nie trinken* ~ she never liked drinking beer; *ich möchte Tee trinken* I'd like to drink tea; *darüber möchte ich nicht reden* I don't want to talk about that; *ich möchte ihn sehen* I want (*höflicher*: I'd like) to see him; *ich möchte wissen* I'd like to know; (*ich frage mich*) I wonder; *ich möchte lieber ins Kino gehen* I'd rather go to the cinema (*Am.* movies); *das möchte ich doch einmal sehen!* I'd like to see that; *man möchte meinen ...* you might think ...; **2.** *Vermutung ausdrückend*: *das mag* (*wohl*) *sein* that may be (so); *das mag sein, dass ...* perhaps ..., maybe ...; *wo er auch sein mag* wherever he may be; *wie dem auch sein mag* be that as it may; *was mag das bedeuten?* what can it mean?; *man mag das bedauern, aber ...* it may be regrettable, but ...; *Müller, Maier und wie sie alle heißen* ~ Müller, Maier and whatever their names are; *sie mochte 30 Jahre alt sein* she must have been (*od.* she looked) about 30; **3.** *einräumend*: *mag er sagen, was er will* he can say what he wants; *was ich*

auch tun mag whatever I do, no matter what I do; **4.** *auffordernd*: *Zeugen möchten sich bitte melden* would any witnesses please come forward; *sag ihr, sie möge od. möchte zu mir kommen* tell her she should come and see me; **II.** *v/t.* (*hat gemocht*) **1.** (*wünschen*) want; *was möchtest du denn?* (*was ist?*) what is it you want?; **2.** (*gern* ~) like, be fond of; *nicht* ~ not like; *stärker*: dislike; *Milch mag ich nicht besonders* I'm not particularly keen on (*Am.* not crazy about) milk; *Tee mag ich lieber als Kaffee* I prefer tea to coffee; *am liebsten* ~ like best; **III.** *v/i* (*hat gemocht*) (*wollen*) want; *ich mag nicht* I don't want to; (*ich habe keine Lust*) I don't feel like it; *ich möchte schon, aber ...* I'd like to, but ...; *sie möchte noch nicht nach Hause* she doesn't want to go home yet; *magst / möchtest du noch?* *zum Essen/Trinken*: do you want / would you like some more?; *weitermachen*: do you want / would you like to go on?

Mogler *m*; -*s*, -, ~**in** *f*; -, -*nen*; *umg.* cheat

möglich *Adj.* **1.** possible (*j-m* for s.o.); (*durchführbar*) *auch* practicable, feasible; *alle* ~*en* ... all sorts of ...; *alles Mögliche* all sorts of things; *alles Mögliche tun* do everything possible; *sein Möglichstes tun* do one's best (*od.* utmost), do everything in one's power; *im Bereich des Möglichen* within the realm (*od.* bounds) of possibility; *es* (*j-m*) ~ *machen zu* (+ *Inf.*) make it possible (for s.o.) to (+ *Inf.*); → *auch* **ermöglichen**; *nicht* ~*!* I don't believe it!; *umg.* no kidding!; *das ist* (*gut*) ~ that's (quite) possible; *schon* ~ *umg.* could be; *das ist eher* ~ that's more likely; *es ist* ~, *dass er kommt* he may come; *es ist mir nicht* ~ *zu* (+ *Inf.*) I can't ...; *stärker*: I can't possibly ..., there's no way I can ...; *es war mir nicht* ~ I wasn't able to do it, I didn't manage (to do) it; *wenn es mir* (*irgendwie*) ~ *ist* if I can (possibly) manage it; *wenn irgend* ~ if at all possible; *man sollte es nicht für* ~ *halten* would you believe it; *so bald etc. wie* ~ as soon etc. as possible; → **möglichst**; **2.** (*eventuell*) potential; (*denkbar*) conceivable; *alle* ~*en Einwände* every conceivable objection

möglichenfalls *Adv.* if possible; **möglicherweise** *Adv.* possibly, it is possible that; (*vielleicht*) *auch* perhaps; *ist er schon da* he may already be there

Möglichkeit *f* **1.** possibility; (*Gelegenheit*) opportunity; (*Aussicht*, *Chance*) chance, possibility; ~*en* (*Entwicklungsmöglichkeiten*, *Potenzial*) potentialities; *nach* ~ as far as possible; (*wenn möglich*) if possible; *es besteht die* ~, *dass ...* there is a possibility that ..., it's possible that ...; *ich sehe keine* ~ *zu* (+ *Inf.*) I don't see any chance of (+ *Ger.*); *ist das die* ~*!* would you believe it!; **2.** *nur Pl.* (*Mittel*) means; (*Fähigkeiten*) abilities; *das übersteigt m-e* (*finanziellen*) ~*en* that's beyond my means, that's more than I can afford; *s-e darstellerischen* ~*en sind begrenzt* his acting ability is limited; **Möglichkeitsform** *f Ling.* subjunctive

möglichst *Adv.* **1.** *mit Adj.* (*so ... wie möglich*): ~ *bald etc.* as soon etc. as possible; ~ *klein* as small as possible, *attr. the* smallest possible ...; ~ *wenig* as little (...) as possible, a minimum

of ...; *ich brauche e-n* ~ *schnellen Wagen* I need the fastest car available (*od.* you've got); **2.** *mit Verb*: as much as possible; *sich* ~ *zurückhalten* restrain o.s. as far as possible; **3.** (*wenn möglich*) if (at all) possible; *Zimmer gesucht,* ~ *am Stadtrand* room wanted, preferably on the outskirts

Mogul *m*; -*s*, -*n*; *hist.* Mogul

...mogul *m*, *im Subst. fig.*: *Film*~ film magnate (*od.* tycoon); *Medien*~ media mogul

Mohair [mo'hɛːɐ̯] *m*; -*s*, -*e Stoff*: mohair

Mohammedaner *m*; -*s*, -, ~**in** *f*; -, -*nen*; *umg.* Muslim, Moslem; **mohammedanisch** *Adj. umg.* Muslim, Moslem

Mohär → **Mohair**

Mohikaner *m*; -*s*, - Mohican; *der letzte* ~ *umg. fig. hum.* the last of the Mohicans

Mohn *m*; -(*e*)*s*, -*e*; *Bot.* poppy; (*Mohnkörner*) poppy seed; ~**beugel** *m* österr., *Gastr.* croissant with a poppy-seed filling; ~**blume** *f Bot.* poppy; ~**brötchen** *n Gastr.* roll sprinkled with poppy seeds; ~**korn** *n* poppy seed; ~**kuchen** *m Gastr.* poppy-seed cake; ~**saft** *m* poppy juice; *weitS.* opium; ~**samen** *m* poppy seed; ~**strudel** *m südd. Gastr.* strudel with a poppy-seed filling

Mohr *m*; -*en*, -*en*; *altm.* Moor; *der* ~ *hat s-e Schuldigkeit getan, der* ~ *kann gehen fig.* now that I'm (*od.* he's *etc.*) not needed any more, I'm (*od.* he's *etc.*) simply discarded

Möhre *f*; -, -*n*; *Bot.* carrot

Mohrenkopf *m Gastr.* **1.** spherical, chocolate-coated cream cake; **2.** (*Negerkuss*) chocolate marshmallow

Möhrensaft *m* carrot juice

Mohrrübe *f Bot.* carrot

Moiré [mɔa'reː] *m*, *n*; -*s*, -*s* moiré

mokant I. *Adj.* mocking; *höhnisch*: sneering, sardonic; **II.** *Adv.* mockingly; *höhnisch*: sneeringly, sardonically

Mokassin *m*; -*s*, -*s* moccasin; (*bequemer Halbschuh*) *auch* slip-on

Mokick *n*; -*s*, -*s*; *Mot.* small motorcycle (*with a kickstarter and a maximum of 40 kph*)

mokieren *v/refl.*: *sich* ~ *über* (+ *Akk.*) *geh.* make fun of; *stärker*: sneer at

Mokka *m*; -*s*, -*s* mocha (coffee); ~**löffel** *m* (small) coffee spoon; ~**tasse** *f* (small) coffee cup, demitasse

Mol *n*; -*s*, -*e*; *Chem.* mole

Molar *m*; -*s*, -*en*, ~**zahn** *m Dent.* molar

Molasse *f*; -, *kein Pl.*; *Geol.* molasse

Molch *m*; -(*e*)*s*, -*e* **1.** *Zool.* newt; **2.** *Tech.* pipe-clearing and -cleaning device

Moldau *f*; -; *Geog.* Vltava, Moldau

Moldawien (*n*); -*s*; *Geog.* Moldavia; **Moldawier** *m*; -*s*, -, **Moldawierin** *f*; -, -*nen* Moldavian, *weiblich auch*: Moldavian woman (*od.* girl); **moldawisch** *Adj.* Moldavian

Mole *f*; -, -*n* (harbo[u]r) mole

Molekül *n*; -*s*, -*e*; *Chem.* molecule

molekular *Adj. Chem.*, **Molekular...** *im Subst.* molecular; **Molekularbiologie** *f* molecular biology

Moleskin ['moːlskɪn] *m*, *n*; -*s*, -*s Stoff*: moleskin

molk *Prät.* → **melken**

Molke *f*; -, *kein Pl.*, whey

Molkerei *f*; -, -*en* dairy; ~**butter** *f* standard (quality) butter; ~**genossenschaft** *f* dairy cooperative; ~**produkt** *n* dairy product

Moll *n*; -, *kein Pl.*; *Mus.* minor (key);

M

a~ A minor; *auf ~ gestimmt sein* fig. be down in the dumps *umg.*; ~**akkord** *m* minor chord; ~**dreiklang** *m* minor triad

Molle *f*; -, -*n*; *Dial.* glass of beer

mollert *Adj. österr. umg.* → *mollig* I 1

Molli *m*; -*s*, -*s*; *Sl.* Molotov cocktail

mollig I. *Adj.* **1.** *Person*: plump; *Mode für Mollige* fashion for the fuller figure; **2.** (*behaglich*) cosy, *Am.* cozy; (*warm*) *auch* snug (*auch Pullover etc.*); **II.** *Adv.*: ~ *warm* warm and cosy (*Am.* cozy)

Moll|tonart *f* minor key; ~**tonleiter** *f* minor scale

Molluske *f*; -, -*n*; *Zool.* mollusc, *Am.* mollusk

Moloch *m*; -*s*, -*e*; *geh.* fig. Moloch

Molotowcocktail *m* Molotov cocktail

Molybdän *n*; -*s*, *kein Pl.*; *Chem.* molybdenum

Moment[1] *m*; -(*e*)*s*, -*e* moment; (*e-n*) ~*!* just a moment (*od.* minute)!; ~ *mal!* just a moment!, wait a minute!, *umg.* hang on (a minute)!; *im* ~ at the moment, right now; *im* ~ *nicht* not at the moment, not just now; *im ersten* ~ for a moment, at first; *im letzten* ~ at the last minute; *im richtigen* ~ just in time; *jeden* ~ any minute *od.* moment (now), *Am. auch* momentarily; → *auch Augenblick*

Moment[2] *n*; -(*e*)*s*, -*e* **1.** (*Beweggrund*) motive; (*Faktor*) factor; *das auslösende* ~ *für etw. sein* trigger s.th. off; **2.** *Phys., Tech.*, e-r *Kraft, Bewegung*: moment; ~ *der Trägheit* moment of inertia

momentan I. *Adj.* **1.** (*vorübergehend*) momentary; *Übelkeit etc.*: *auch* passing; *Besserung*: temporary; **2.** (*gegenwärtig*) present, current; **II.** *Adv.* **1.** (*jetzt*) at the moment; *ich habe* ~ *keine Zeit* I have no time just at the moment (*od.* at present); **2.** (*vorübergehend*) for the time being; (*flüchtig*) momentarily

Momentaufnahme *f* Fot. snapshot (*auch* fig.)

Monaco (*n*); -*s*; *Geog.* Monaco

Monade *f*; -, -*n*; *Philos.* monad

Monarch *m*; -*en*, -*en* monarch; **Monarchie** *f*; -, -*n* monarchy; **Monarchin** *f*; -, -*nen* monarch; **monarchisch I.** *Adj.* monarchic(al); **II.** *Adv.*: ~ *regiert* ruled by a monarch; **Monarchist** *m*; -*en*, -*en*, **Monarchistin** *f*; -, -*nen* monarchist; **monarchistisch** *Adj.* monarchist

monastisch *Adj.* monastic

Monat *m*; -(*e*)*s*, -*e* month; *der* ~ *Januar* the month of January; *... im* ~ *verdienen etc.*: earn etc. *... a* (*od.* per) month (*od.* monthly); *im dritten* ~ (*schwanger*) *sein* be three months pregnant, be in the third month; *Ihr Schreiben vom 20. dieses* ~*s* your letter of the 20th (*altm.* 20th instant); *auf* ~*e hinaus ausverkauft etc.* sold out etc. for months ahead; *er bekam acht* ~*e umg.* he got eight months; **monatelang I.** *Adj.* months (and months) of ..., ... lasting for months; **II.** *Adv.* for months (on end); **...monatig** *im Adj.* **1.** (*... Monate dauernd*) ...-month, lasting ... months; *ein drei*~*er Aufenthalt* a three-month stay, a stay of three months; **2.** (*... Monate alt*) ...-month-old; **monatlich I.** *Adj.* monthly; **II.** *Adv.* monthly, a month

Monats|anfang *m* beginning of the month; ~**beitrag** *m* monthly contribution; *Abonnement*: monthly subscription; ~**binde** *f* sanitary towel (*Am.*

napkin); ~**einkommen** *n* monthly income; ~**ende** *n* end of the month; ~**erste** *m* first (day) of the month; ~**frist** *f* term (*od.* period) of one month; *binnen/nach* ~ within/after a period of a month; ~**gehalt** *n* monthly salary (*od.* pay); *ein* ~ a (*od.* one) month's pay (*od.* salary); *ein dreizehntes* ~ an additional month's pay (*od.* salary) (*paid at Christmas*); ~**hälfte** *f* half of the month; ~**karte** *f* monthly (season) ticket; ~**letzte** *m* last day of the month; ~**lohn** *m* monthly wage(s *Pl.*); ~**miete** *f* monthly rent; *eine* ~ *als Kaution* a (*od.* one) month's rent in advance (as a deposit); ~**mitte** *f* middle of the month; ~**mittel** *n* monthly average; ~**rate** *f* monthly instal(l)ment; ~**schrift** *f* monthly journal (*od.* periodical); ~**temperatur** *f*: *durchschnittliche* ~ average monthly temperature

monat(s)weise *Adv.* monthly; *auch attr.*: ~ *Abrechnung* monthly statement (of account)

Mönch *m*; -(*e*)*s*, -*e* **1.** monk; (*Bettelmönch*) friar; **2.** *Archit.* over tile (*of a Spanish-tiled roof*); **3.** *Tech.*, am *Fischteich*: box sluice; **mönchisch** *Adj.* monastic; *wie ein Mönch*: monkish

Mönchs|geier *m* Orn. black vulture; ~**grasmücke** *f* Orn. blackcap; ~**kloster** *n* monastery; ~**kutte** *f* monk's habit; ~**leben** *n* life of a monk, monastic life; ~**orden** *m* monastic order

Mönch(s)tum *n*; -*s*, *kein Pl.* **1.** monasticism, monkhood; **2.** (*Mönchsleben*) monastic life, life of a monk

Mönchszelle *f* monk's cell

Mond *m*; -(*e*)*s*, -*e* **1.** moon; *hinter dem* ~ *leben umg.* fig. be way behind the times; *du lebst wohl hinter dem* ~*! umg.* where have you been (all your life)?; *ich könnte ihn auf den* ~ *schießen! umg.* I could wring his neck; *etw. in den* ~ *schreiben umg.* write s.th. off; *in den* ~ *gucken umg.* be left (*od.* come away) empty-handed; **2.** *poet. altm.* (*Monat*) month, moon *hum.*

mondän *Adj.* fashionable, chic; ~*e Frau* smart (*Am.* fashionable) society woman

Mond|aufgang *m* moonrise; ~**bahn** *f* lunar (*od.* moon's) orbit

mondbeschienen *Adj. poet.* moonlit; *präd. und nachgestellt*: *auch* bathed in moonlight

Mondenschein *m*; *nur Sg.*; *poet.* moonlight

Mondesfinsternis *f* österr. → *Mondfinsternis*

Mond|fähre *f* Raumf. lunar module; ~**finsternis** *f* Astron. eclipse of the moon, lunar eclipse; ~**flug** *m* Raumf. flight to the moon; ~**gebirge** *n* lunar mountain range; ~**gesicht** *n umg.* moonface; ~**gestein** *n* lunar rock(s *Pl.*), rocks *Pl.* from the moon

mondhell *Adj. Nacht*: moonlit

Mond|jahr *n* lunar year; ~**kalb** *n umg.* simpleton, dumbo, mooncalf; ~**karte** *f* map of the moon, moon chart; ~**krater** *m* lunar crater, crater on the moon; ~**landschaft** *f* lunar landscape, moonscape; ~**landung** *f* moon (*od.* lunar) landing, landing on the moon; ~**licht** *n*; *nur Sg.* moonlight

mondlos *Adj. Nacht*: moonless

Mond|mobil *n*; -*s*, -*e*; *Raumf.* moon buggy; ~**nacht** *f* moonlit night; ~**oberfläche** *f* surface of the moon; ~**orbit** *m* Raumf. lunar orbit; ~**phase** *f* phase of the moon; ~**rakete** *f* moon rocket; ~**schatten** *m* Astron. shadow of the

moon

Mondschein *m* moonlight; *du kannst mir im* ~ *begegnen! umg.* you can get lost; ~**tarif** *m* Telef. night rate

Mond|sichel *f* crescent (of the moon); ~**sonde** *f* Raumf. lunar probe; ~**staub** *m* lunar dust; ~**stein** *m* Min. moonstone

mondsüchtig *Adj.* somnambulist ..., somnambulistic; ~ *sein mst* sleepwalk, walk in one's sleep; **Mondsüchtige** *m, f* sleepwalker, somnambulist

Mond|umkreisung *f* Raumf. lunar orbiting; ~**umlaufbahn** *f* Raumf. lunar orbit; ~**untergang** *m* moonset; *e-n* ~ *beobachten* watch the moon set

Monegasse *m*; -*n*, -*n* Monégasque; **Monegassin** *f*; -, -*nen* Monégasque (woman *od.* girl); **monegassisch** *Adj.* Monégasque

monetär *Adj.* monetary

Monetarismus *m*; -, *kein Pl.*; *Wirts.* monetarism; **monetaristisch** *Adj.* monetarist

Moneten *Pl. umg.* dough *Sg.*, shekels *hum.*

Mongole *m*; -*en*, -*en* Mongolian; **Mongolei** *f*; -; *Geog.* Mongolia; *die Innere/ Äußere* ~ Inner/Outer Mongolia

mongolid *Adj.* Mongoloid; **Mongolide** *m, f*; -*n*, -*n* Mongoloid

Mongolin *f*; -, -*nen* Mongolian (woman *od.* girl); **mongolisch** *Adj.* Mongolian

Mongolismus *m*; -, *kein Pl.*; *Med.* Down's syndrome; *oft pej.* mongolism

mongoloid *Adj.* **1.** *Anthropologie*: Mongoloid; **2.** *Med.*, *neg!* affected with Down's syndrome; *oft pej.* mongoloid; **Mongoloide** *m, f*; -*n*, -*n* **1.** *Anthropologie*: Mongoloid; **2.** *Med.*, *neg!* person with Down's syndrome; *oft pej.* mongoloid

monieren *v/t. geh.* complain about, criticize; (*Rechnung*) query; (*Sendung etc.*) make a complaint about

Monierzange *f* Tech. tower pincers *Pl.*

Monismus *m*; -, *kein Pl.*; *Philos.* monism; **monistisch** *Adj.* monistic

Monitor *m*; -*s*, -*en und -e*; *TV, Med. etc.* monitor

mono *Adv.* in mono

Monoaufnahme *f* mono recording

monochrom *Adj. Kunst, Fot.* monochrome

monocolor *Adj. österr. Pol.* single-party

Monoempfänger *m* Radio: mono receiver

monogam *Adj.* monogamous; ~*er Mann* monogamist; **Monogamie** *f*; -, *kein Pl.* monogamy

Monografie *etc.* → *Monographie etc.*

Monogramm *n* monogram; *... mit* ~ monogrammed ...

Monographie *f*; -, -*n* monograph; **monographisch I.** *Adj.* monographic; **II.** *Adv.* in monographic form

Monokel *n*; -*s*, - monocle

Monokultur *f* Agr. monoculture

Monolith *m*; -*s und -en*, -*en* monolith; **monolithisch** *Adj.* monolithic

Monolog *m*; -(*e*)*s*, -*e* monolog(ue); *Theat. auch* soliloquy; **monologisch** *Adj.* monological; **monologisieren** *v/i.* talk in monolog(ue)s, talk to o.s.; *Theat. mst* soliloquize

monoman *Adj. Psych., Med.* monomaniac, monomaniacal; **Monomane** *m*; -*n*, -*n* monomaniac; **Monomanie** *f*; -, -*n* monomania; **Monomanin** *f*; -, -*nen* monomaniac (woman *od.* girl); **monomanisch** *Adj.* → *monoman*

monomer *Adj. Chem.* monomeric

monomisch *Adj. Math.* monomial
monophon *Adj.* monophonic
Monophthong *m*; *-s*, *-e*; *Ling.* monophthong; **monophthongisch** *Adj.* monophthongal
Monoplatte *f* mono record
Monopol *n*; *-s*, *-e* monopoly (*auf* + *Akk.*, *für* of, in); **~inhaber** *m*, **~inhaberin** *f* owner of a monopoly
monopolisieren *v/t. Wirts.* monopolize; **Monopolismus** *m*; *-*, *kein Pl.* monopolism; **Monopolist** *m*; *-en*, *-en*, **Monopolistin** *f*; *-*, *-nen* monopolist; **monopolistisch I.** *Adj.* monopolistic; **II.** *Adv.*: **~ beherrschter Markt** captive market
Monopolkapital *n*; *nur Sg.*; *Wirts.* monopoly capital
Monopol|kommission *f*; *nur Sg.* monopolies commission; **~partei** *f* dominant party; **~presse** *f* monopoly press; **~stellung** *f* position of monopoly; **e-e ~ innehaben** have a monopoly (*für* in)
Monopoly® *n*; *- Gesellschaftsspiel*: Monopoly®
Monosendung *f Radio*: mono broadcast
Monostruktur *f* monolithic structure; **monostrukturell** *Adj.* ... with a monolithic structure
Monotheismus *m* monotheism; **Monotheist** *m*, **Monotheistin** *f* monotheist; **monotheistisch** *Adj.* monotheistic
monoton *Adj.* monotonous; **Monotonie** *f*; *-*, *-n* monotony
Monotypie *f*; *-*, *-n Grafik*: monotype
Monowiedergabe *f Radio*: mono reproduction
Monoxid *n Chem.* monoxide
Monozelle *f Etech.* single-cell battery
monozyklisch *Adj. Chem.* monocyclic
Monsignore [mɔnzɪn'joːrə] *m*; *-*, **Monsignori**; *kath.* Monsignor (*Pl.* Monsignori)
Monster *n*; *-s*, *-* monster
Monster... *im Subst. mst* mammoth
Monster|film *m* **1.** *über Monster*: monster film (*Am.* movie), horror film (*Am. auch* movie) with monsters; **2.** *Großproduktion*: mammoth screen epic; **~truck** *m Mot.* giant truck, *Brit. auch* juggernaut; **~veranstaltung** *f* mammoth event
Monstranz *f*; *-*, *-en*; *kath.* monstrance
monströs *Adj.* monstrous; *Gebäude etc.*: gigantic, monster ...; (*hässlich*) huge and hideous; **Monstrosität** *f*; *-*, *-en* monstrosity
Monstrum *n*; *-s*, *Monstren* monster; *ein ~ von einem Kleiderschrank hum.* a hulking great wardrobe
Monsun *m*; *-s*, *-e*; *Geog.* monsoon; **~regen** *m* monsoon rain(s *Pl.*); **~wald** *m* monsoon forest; **~zeit** *f* monsoon (period)
Montag *m*; *-s*, *-e* Monday; → *Dienstag*; → *blau* 2; **~abend** *m* Monday evening
Montage [mɔn'taːʒə] *f*; *-*, *-n* **1.** *Tech.* (*Anbringung*) mounting, fitting; (*Aufstellung*) erection; *e-r Anlage*: installation; (*Zusammenbau*) assembly; *auf ~ sein umg.* be away on a construction job; **2.** *Fot.*, *Film etc.*: montage; **3.** *Druck.* make-up; **~anleitung** *f* assembly instructions *Pl.*; **~band** *n Tech.* assembly line; **~bau** *m* construction from prefabricated parts; **~bauweise** *f* prefabricated construction method; **~halle** *f* assembly shop; **~werk** *n* assembly plant
montags *Adv.* on Mondays; → *dienstags*

Montags|auto *n umg.*, *mst pej.* Friday car, *Am.* lemon; **~stimmung** *f* Monday(-morning) blues
montan *Adj. Geog.*, *Bot.*, *Zool.* mountain ...
Montan|industrie *f* coal and steel industry; **~union** *f*; *-*, *kein Pl.* European Coal and Steel Community
Monteur *m*; *-s*, *-e*; *Tech.* fitter; *Mot.*, *Flug.* mechanic; *Etech.* electrician; **~anzug** *m* overalls *Pl.*
Monteurin *f*; *-*, *-nen* → *Monteur*
Montgolfiere [mõgɔl'fieːrə] *f*; *-*, *-n* (*Heißluftballon*) hot-air balloon
montieren *v/t.* **1.** *Tech.* (*anbringen*) mount, fit (*an* + *Akk.*, *Dat.* to, *auf* + *Akk.*, *Dat.* on); (*aufstellen*) set up, put up; (*zusammenbauen*) assemble; (*Anlage etc.*, *einrichten*) instal(l); **2.** *Fot.* (*Film etc.*) put together; **3.** *Druck.* make up; **Montierer** *m*; *-s*, *-*, **Montiererin** *f*; *-*, *-nen* assembly worker
Montur *f*; *-*, *-en* **1.** *umg.* (*Arbeitskleidung etc.*) gear; (*Aufmachung*) *auch* get-up; *in voller ~* in all one's gear, wearing the complete outfit, in full regalia *hum.*; **2.** *altm.* (*Uniform*) uniform
Monument *n*; *-(e)s*, *-e* monument (*für* to); **monumental I.** *Adj.* monumental; **II.** *Adv.* on a monumental scale
Monumental|... *im Subst. mst* monumental; (*riesig*) mammoth; **~bau** *m* monumental structure; **~film** *m umg.* (screen) epic, (Hollywood) spectacular; **~gemälde** *n* massive canvas
Monumentalität *f*; *-*, *kein Pl.* monumental nature, massiveness; *Ausmaß*: monumental scale
Monumental|schinken *m umg.* **1.** (*Film*) (screen) epic, (Hollywood) spectacular; **2.** (*Gemälde*) massive canvas; **~werk** *n* monumental work; *Lit. auch* epic work
Moonboots ['muːnbuːts] *Pl.* moon boots
Moor *n*; *-(e)s*, *-e* (*Sumpf*) bog, marsh; (*Flachmoor*) fen; (*Hochmoor*) (high) moor; **~bad** *n* mudbath; **~boden** *m* marshy ground; *Erde*: bog soil; **~eiche** *f Möbelindustrie*: bog oak; **~erde** *f* bog soil; *zu Heilzwecken*: therapeutic mud
Moorhuhn *n Orn.* grouse; **~jagd** *f* grouse shoot (*Am.* hunt); *Tätigkeit*: grouse shooting; *Computerspiel*: moorhen-chicken chase
moorig *Adj.* marshy, boggy
Moor|kolonie *f* fenland community; **~kultur** *f*; *mst. Sg.* marshland (reclamation and) cultivation; **~land** *n* bog, marshland; (*Flachmoor*) fenland; **~landschaft** *f* marshland, marshy landscape; **~leiche** *f* body found in a bog, bog man; **~packung** *f* mudpack
Moos¹ *n*; *-es*, *-e*; *Bot.* moss; **~ ansetzen** *umg. fig.* be getting a bit past it
Moos² *n*; *-es*, *-e*, *südd.*, *österr.*, *schw. auch Möser* (*Sumpf*) bog, marsh
Moos³ *n*; *-es*, *kein Pl.*; *Sl.* (*Geld*) dough
moosbedeckt *Adj.* moss-covered
Moosbeere *f Bot.* cranberry
moosgrün *Adj.* moss-green; **moosig** *Adj.* **1.** mossy; **2.** *südd.*, *österr.*, *schw.* marshy
Moos|pflanze *f* (variety of) moss; **~röschen** *n*, **~rose** *f Bot.* moss rose
Mop *m*; *-s*, *-s* mop
Moped *n*; *-s*, *-s*; *Mot.* moped
Mopp *m*; *-s*, *-s* mop
Moppel *m*; *-s*, *-*; *umg. hum.* (little) podge (*Am.* pudge)
moppen I. *v/t.* (*Parkettboden etc.*)

mop; **II.** *v/i.* mop the floor
Mops *m*; *-es*, *Möpse* **1.** *Hund*: pug(-dog); **2.** *umg.* (*dicke Person*) podge, *Am.* pudge, fatso; **3.** *Pl.*; *Sl.* (*Geld*) dough; **4.** *Pl.*; *Sl.* (*Brüste*) boobs
mopsen *umg.* **I.** *v/t.* pinch, snitch; **II.** *v/refl.* be bored
mopsfidel *Adj. umg.* jolly, jovial
mopsig *Adj.* **1.** *umg.* dumpy, tubby; **2.** *umg.* (*langweilig*) tedious; **3.** *Dial.*: *sich ~ machen* get cheeky, *bes. Am.* get fresh
Moral *f*; *-*, *kein Pl.* **1.** morals *Pl.*, moral standards *Pl.*; *gegen die herrschende ~ verstoßen* offend against the accepted moral code; *doppelte ~* double standards; *~ predigen pej.* moralize (*j-m* to s.o.); **2.** (*Sittenlehre*) morality, ethics *Pl.* (*als Wissenschaft V. auch im Sg.*); **3.** (*Lehre*) moral; **4.** (*Kampf-, Arbeitsmoral, Stimmung*) morale; *die ~ der Mannschaft ist gut/schlecht* the team's morale is high/low, morale in the team is high/low; *die Mannschaft hat eine tolle ~ bewiesen* the team showed (a) fantastic spirit; **~apostel** *m umg. pej.* moralizer; **~begriff** *m* concept of morality; *persönlicher*: *auch* moral (*od.* ethical) standards *Pl.*
Moralin *n*; *-s*, *kein Pl.*; *pej.*, *auch hum.* priggish moralizing; (*Selbstgerechtigkeit*) self-righteousness; **moralinsauer** *Adj.* priggishly moralizing; (*selbstgerecht*) self-righteous
moralisch I. *Adj.* **1.** moral; *~e Skrupel haben* have moral scruples; *aus ~en Gründen* on moral grounds; *~er Sieger* moral victor; *den od. e-n Moralischen haben umg.* (*deprimiert sein*) have the blues, be feeling down; (*Gewissensbisse haben*) have pangs of remorse (*od.* conscience); **2.** (*die Kampfmoral etc. betreffend*): *gute/ schlechte ~e Verfassung* high/low morale; *ein ~er Zusammenbruch* a breakdown in morale; **II.** *Adv.* morally; *e-e ~ hoch stehende Persönlichkeit* a person of high moral standing; *du bist dazu ~ verpflichtet* you are morally obliged to do it
moralisieren *v/i.* moralize; *pej. auch* sermonize; **Moralismus** *m*; *-*, *kein Pl.* **1.** sense of morality; **2.** *übertrieben*: high moral tone; **Moralist** *m*; *-en*, *-en*, **Moralistin** *f*; *-*, *-nen* moralist; **moralistisch I.** *Adj.* moralistic; **II.** *Adv.* moralistically; **Moralität** *f*; *-*, *kein Pl.* morality
Moral|kodex *m* moral code; *persönlicher*: *auch* moral standards *Pl.*; **~lehre** *f* moral philosophy
Moral|prediger *m*, **~predigerin** *f pej.* moralizing prig, sermonizer; **~predigt** *f iro.*, *oft pej.* sermon, lecture; *j-m e-e ~ halten* lecture s.o. on morals, preach at s.o.; **~en halten** sermonize
Moral|theologie *f* moral theology; **~vorstellung** *f*; *mst Pl.* → *Moralbegriff*
Moräne *f*; *-*, *-n*; *Geol.* moraine
Morast *m*; *-(e)s*, *-e und Moräste* bog; (*Schlamm*) mire (*auch fig.*); *im ~ waten fig.* wallow in the mire; **morastig** *Adj.* muddy; *Wiese*: *auch* marshy
Moratorium *n*; *-s*, *Moratorien*; *Wirts.*, *Pol.* moratorium (*Pl.* moratoriums *od.* moratoria)
morbid *Adj. geh.* **1.** (*dekadent*) decadent; *Geschlecht etc.*: degenerate; **2.** (*kränklich*) sickly, ailing; *Blässe*: sickly, deathly
Morbidität *f*; *-*, *kein Pl.* **1.** (*Dekadenz*) decadence; (*Degeneration*) degenera-

cy; **2.** *Med.* (*Kränklichsein*) sickly nature, sickliness; (*Häufigkeit der Erkrankungen*) morbidity (rate)

Morbus *m*; -, *Morbi*; *Med.* disease; ~ **Crohn** Crohn's disease

Morchel *f*; -, -*n*; *Bot.* morel (mushroom)

Mord *m*; -(*e*)*s*, -*e* murder (**an** + *Dat.* of); *durch Attentat*: assassination; *Jur.* (first-degree) murder, *bes. Am.* homicide; *e-n ~ begehen* commit (a) murder; *wegen ~es angeklagt werden* be accused of (first-degree) murder; *das gibt ~ und Totschlag umg. fig.* all hell will be let loose; *es ist glatter ~ umg. fig.* it's sheer murder (*Blödsinn*: lunacy); ~**anklage** *f Jur.* charge of (first-degree) murder; ~ *erheben* bring a charge of murder; *j-n unter ~ stellen* charge s.o. with murder; ~**anschlag** *m* attempted murder (**auf** + *Akk.* of); (*Attentat*) *auch* assassination attempt (against, on); *e-n ~ auf j-n verüben* carry out a murderous attack (*Attentat*: assassination attempt) on s.o., make an attempt on s.o.'s life; ~**befehl** *m* order to carry out a murder; ~**brenner** *m altm.* arsonist with murderous intent; ~**dezernat** *n* murder (*od.* homicide) squad, *Am.* homicide (department); ~**drohung** *f* death threat; ~ *gegen j-n auch* threat on s.o.'s life

morden I. *v/i.* commit murder, kill; **II.** *v/t.* murder; *allg.* (*töten*) kill; **Morden** *n*; -*s*, *kein Pl.* murder(ing); (*Töten*) killing; *stärker*: slaughter(ing)

Mörder *m*; -*s*, - murderer, killer; (*Attentäter*) assassin; ~**bande** *f* gang of murderers; ~**biene** *f* killer bee; ~**grube** *f*: *aus s-m Herzen keine ~ machen* speak openly (*od.* freely); ~**hand** *f*: *durch od. von ~ sterben geh.* die at the hands of a murderer

Mörderin *f*; -, -*nen* murderer, killer; *altm. auch* murderess; (*Attentäterin*) assassin

mörderisch I. *Adj.* murderous; *fig. auch* deadly; *fig. Geschwindigkeit*: breakneck; *Konkurrenz, Preise*: cutthroat; *es herrschte e-e ~e Kälte umg.* it was fiendishly cold; **II.** *Adv. umg. fig., verstärkend*: dreadfully, incredibly; ~ *heiß auch umg.* fiendishly hot, hot as hell

Mörderwal *m Zool.* killer whale, orca

Mord|fall *m* murder case; ~**gier** *f* lust for murder (*od.* to kill); ~**instrument** *n* murder weapon; *umg. fig. Gegenstand* murderous-looking device; ~**kommando** *n* death squad; ~**kommission** *f* murder (*od.* homicide) squad, *Am.* homicide (department)

Mordlust *f* → *Mordgier*, **mordlustig** *Adj.* out to kill *präd.*; (*blutgierig*) bloodthirsty

Mord|nacht *f* night of the murder; ~**prozess** *m* murder trial

Mords|... *im Subst. umg.* (*enorm*) great, terrific, fantastic; (*schrecklich*) dreadful, terrible; ~**angst** *f*: *e-e ~ haben umg.* be in a flat panic (**vor** + *Dat.* about), be scared stiff (of); ~**arbeit** *f umg.*: *e-e ~* a hell of a job; ~**ding** *n umg.* whopper, humdinger; ~**durst** *m*: *e-n ~ haben umg.* be dying of thirst, be thirsty as hell; ~**gaudi** *f südd. umg.* → *Mordsspaß*, ~**glück** *n umg.* fantastic stroke of luck; ~**hitze** *f umg.* scorching heat; *es ist e-e ~ heute!* it's a real scorcher today; ~**hunger** *m*: *e-n ~ haben* be famished, be dying of hunger; ~**kerl** *m umg.* great (*od.* terrific) guy; ~**krach** *m umg.* **1.** *Lärm*:

frightful din, incredible racket, *Am.* ruckus; *e-n ~ machen* kick up a hell of a racket (*od.* din); **2.** *Streit*: great rumpus (*od.* row), *Am.* ruckus; ~**lärm** *m umg.* → *Mordskrach* 1

mordsmäßig *umg.* **I.** *Adj.* terrific; **II.** *Adv.* like crazy (*od.* hell); *ich habe mich ~ gefreut* I was thrilled to bits (*Am.* pieces), I was over the moon

Mords|schreck(en) *m umg.* terrible fright; *e-n ~ bekommen* get one hell of a fright, be scared out of one's wits; ~**skandal** *m umg.* full-blown scandal; ~**spaß** *m umg.*: *das war ein ~!* that was terrific fun; *e-n ~ haben* have a great time; ~**spektakel** *m umg.* **1.** (*Getue*) great palaver (*od.* fuss); **2.** (*Lärm*) frightful din, incredible racket (*Am. auch* ruckus); ~**wut** *f umg.*: *e-e ~ (im Bauch) haben* be seething with rage, be ready to explode

Mord|tat *f* (act of) murder; ~**verdacht** *m* suspicion of murder; *unter ~ stehen* be suspected of murder; ~**versuch** *m* attempted murder; ~**waffe** *f* murder weapon

Morelle *f*; -, -*n*; *Bot.* morello cherry

Mores *Pl.*: *j-n ~ lehren umg.* teach s.o. what's what

morgen *Adv.* tomorrow; ~ *früh/Abend* tomorrow morning/evening (*od.* night); ~ *in acht Tagen* a week (from) tomorrow, *Brit. auch* tomorrow week; ~ *vor acht Tagen* a week ago tomorrow; ~ *um diese Zeit* (by) this time tomorrow; *bis ~!* see you tomorrow; *die Technik von ~* tomorrow's technology; ~ *ist auch noch ein Tag* tomorrow is another day; ~, ~, *nur nicht heute, sagen alle faulen Leute Sprichw. etwa* don't put off till tomorrow what you can do today

Morgen¹ *n*; -*s*, *kein Pl.* future

Morgen² *m*; -*s*, - **1.** morning; *am ~* in the morning; (*jeden ~*) *auch* (in the) mornings; *heute/gestern ~* this/yesterday morning; (*guten*) ~*!* (good) morning!; *es wird ~* dawn is breaking, it's getting light; *bis in den ~ feiern* go on celebrating into the early hours; *schön od. frisch wie der junge ~ geh. hum* fresh as a daisy; → *auch morgen*; **2.** *geh. altm.* (*Osten*) east

Morgen³ *m*; -*s*, -; *altm.* unit of measurement equal to between 2,500 and 2,800 square met|res (*Am. -ers*), *etwa* acre

Morgen|andacht *f kirchl.* morning service; ~**ausgabe** *f* morning edition; ~**dämmerung** *f* dawn, daybreak

morgendlich *Adj.* (early) morning ..., ... of (early) morning

Morgen|frische *f* fresh morning air; ~**frühe** *f* early morning; ~**gabe** *f hist.* husband's gift to his new bride on the morning after the wedding; morning gift; ~**grauen** *n*: *beim od. im ~* at dawn, at daybreak; *aufstehen etc.*: *auch* at the crack of dawn *umg.*; ~**gymnastik** *f* morning exercises *Pl.*, *umg.* daily dozen *Pl.*; ~**kaffee** *m* breakfast coffee; *vor dem Frühstück*: early morning coffee; *Frühstück*: light breakfast (with coffee)

Morgenland *n*; *nur Sg.; altm.* Orient, East; **morgenländisch I.** *Adj.* eastern, oriental; **II.** *Adv.* in an oriental manner (*od.* style)

Morgen|licht *n*; *nur Sg.* morning light; *im ersten ~* in the first light of day; ~**luft** *f* morning air; ~ *wittern umg. fig.* see an opportunity coming up, see one's chance; ~**mantel** *m* dressing gown; ~**muffel** *m*: *er ist ein ~ umg.*

he's not at his best in the mornings; ~**post** *f* morning post (*Am.* mail); ~**rock** *m* dressing gown; ~**rot** *n* (red) dawn, sunrise; *fig.* dawn(ing)

morgens *Adv.* in the morning; (*jeden Morgen*) *auch* (in the) mornings, every morning; ~ *in aller Frühe* at an early hour (of the morning); ~ *als Erstes* first thing in the morning; *von ~ bis abends* from morning till night, all day long, from dawn to dusk *lit.*

Morgen|sonne *f*; *nur Sg.* (early) morning sun; ~**spaziergang** *m* (early) morning walk; ~**stern** *m* **1.** *nur Sg.* morning star; **2.** *hist. Waffe*: spiked mace; ~**stunde** *f*: *in den ~n* in the morning(s); *bis in die frühen ~n* into the small (*od.* wee) hours; *Morgenstund hat Gold im Mund Sprichw.* the early bird catches the worm; ~**toilette** *f*; *nur Sg.*; *geh.* morning toilet; ~**zeitung** *f* morning paper

morgig *Adj.* tomorrow's; *der ~e Tag* tomorrow; *die ~e Konferenz* tomorrow's meeting, the meeting tomorrow

Moriske *m*; -*n*, -*n*; *hist.* Morisco

Moritat *f*; -, -*en* street ballad (*relating a usually horrific event*); **Moritatensänger** *m*, **Moritatensängerin** *f* street ballad singer

Moritz *m*: *wie sich der kleine ~ das (so) vorstellt umg. hum.* as some simple soul might imagine it

Mormone *m*; -*n*, -*n*, **Mormonin** *f*; -, -*nen Reli.* Mormon; **mormonisch** *Adj.* Mormon

Morphem *n*; -*s*, -*e*; *Ling.* morpheme

Morpheus: *in ~' Armen ruhen od. liegen geh. hum.* be in the land of Nod; *lit.* rest in the arms of Morpheus

Morphin *n*; -*s*, *kein Pl.*; *Chem., Med.* morphine

Morphinismus *m*; -, *kein Pl.*; *Med.* morphine addiction; **Morphinist** *m*; -*en*, -*en*, **Morphinistin** *f*; -, -*nen* morphine addict

Morphium *n*; -*s*, *kein Pl.* morphine; ~**spritze** *f* morphine injection

Morphiumsucht *f*; *nur Sg.* morphine addiction; **morphiumsüchtig** *Adj.* addicted to morphine; **Morphiumsüchtige** *m, f* morphine addict

Morphogenese *f Bio.* morphogenesis

Morphologie *f* morphology; **morphologisch** *Adj.* morphological

morsch *Adj.* rotten; (*verwesend*) rotting; (*spröde*) brittle; *Gestein*: crumbling; ~ *werden* (start to) rot; **Morschheit** *f* rottenness; (*Brüchigkeit*) brittleness

Morsealphabet *n*: *das ~* Morse alphabet (*od.* code); **morsen I.** *v/t.* send in Morse; **II.** *v/i.* send a message (*od.* communicate) in Morse

Mörser *m*; -*s*, - mortar (*auch Mil.*)

Morsezeichen *n* Morse signal

Mortadella *f*; -, -*s*; *Gastr.* mortadella, *Am.* baloney, *Am.* bologna

Mortalität *f*; -, *kein Pl. Med.* mortality (rate)

Mörtel *m*; -*s*, - mortar; ~**kelle** *f* trowel

mörteln *v/t.* mortar; (*verputzen*) render

Mörteltrog *m* mortar trough

Mosaik *n*; -*s*, -*en und* -*e* mosaic (*auch fig.*); ~**arbeit** *f* **1.** mosaic (*regelmäßig*: tessel[l]ated) work; **2.** *konkret*: mosaic

mosaikartig *Adj.* tessel(l)ated, mosaic-like

Mosaik|bild *n* mosaic; ~**fußboden** *m* mosaic (*regelmäßig*: tessel[l]ated) floor; ~**stein** *m*, ~**steinchen** *n* **1.** mosaic piece (*od.* stone); *regelmäßig*: tessera (*Pl.* tesserae); **2.** piece of (*od.*

from a) mosaic; **3.** *fig.* piece of a *od.* the (jigsaw) puzzle

mosaisch *Adj.* Mosaic; *das ~e Gesetz* Mosaic law

Mosaizist *m*; *-en, -en, ~in f*; *-, -nen*; *Kunst* mosaicist

Mosambik (*n*); *-s*; *Geog.* Mozambique

Moschee *f*; *-, -n* mosque

Moschus *m*; *-, kein Pl.* musk

moschusartig *Adj.* musky

Moschus|beutel *m Zool.* musk bag; **~geruch** *m* musky odo(u)r; **~hirsch** *m Zool.* musk deer; **~ochse** *m Zool.* musk ox; **~ratte** *f Zool.* muskrat

Möse *f*; *-, -n*; *vulg.* cunt, *Sl.* pussy, *Brit. auch* fanny

Mosel¹ *f*; *-*; *Geog.* Moselle

Mosel² *m*; *-s, -*, **~wein** *m* Moselle

mosern *v/i. umg.* gripe, grumble (*über + Akk.* about)

Moses (*m*); *-e od. Mosis*; *bibl.* Moses; *das 1./2./3./4./5. Buch ~* the Book of Genesis/Exodus/Leviticus/Numbers/Deuteronomy; *die 5 Bücher Mosis* the Five Books of Moses, the Pentateuch

Moskau (*n*); *-s*; *Geog.* Moscow

Moskauer¹ *m*; *-s, -* Muscovite

Moskauer² *indekl. Adj.* Moscow ..., ... of Moscow

Moskauerin *f*; *-, -nen* Muscovite (woman *od.* girl)

Moskito *m*; *-s, -s*; *Zool.* mosquito; **~netz** *n* mosquito net; **~stich** *m* mosquito bite

Moskwa *f*; *-*; *Geog.* Moskva (river)

Moslem *m*; *-s, -s, ~in f*; *-, -nen* Muslim, Moslem; **moslemisch** *Adj.* Muslim, Moslem

Most *m*; *-(e)s, -e* **1.** (*aus Weintrauben*) (freshly-pressed) grape juice; *zur Weiterverarbeitung für Wein*: must; *Dial.* (*Federweißer*) new wine; **2.** (*Süßmost*) fruit juice; *von Äpfeln*: apple juice; *von Birnen*: pear juice; **3.** *südd., österr., schw., vergorener*: fruit wine; *engS.* (*Apfelmost*) (rough, *Am.* hard) cider; (*Birnenmost*) perry; **~apfel** *m* cider apple; **~birne** *f* perry pear

mosten I. *v/i.* **1.** make fruit juice (*aus Trauben*: grape juice, *aus Äpfeln*: apple juice, *aus Birnen*: pear juice); *zur Weiterverarbeitung für Wein*: make must; *Dial.* (*Federweißen machen*) make new wine; **2.** *südd., österr., schw. aus Äpfeln*: make (rough, *Am.* hard) cider; *aus Birnen*: make perry; **II.** *v/t.* **1.** (*Trauben*) make into grape juice (*für Wein*: must, *Federweißen*: new wine); (*Äpfel*) make into apple juice; (*Birnen*) make into pear juice; **2.** *südd., österr., schw.* (*Äpfel*) make into (rough, *Am.* hard) cider; (*Birnen*) make into perry; **Mosterei** *f*; *-, -en* **1.** fruit-juice producing plant; **2.** *südd., österr., schw.* (rough) cider-making plant; *für Birnenmost*: perry-making plant; **Mostobst** *n* fruit for making Most

Mostrich *m*; *-s, kein Pl.*; *Dial.* mustard

Motel *n*; *-s, -s* motel

Motette *f*; *-, -n*; *Mus.* motet

Motion *f*; *-, -en* **1.** *schw. Parl.* motion; **2.** *Ling.* inflection according to gender

Motiv *n*; *-s, -e* **1.** motive (*zu* for); *aus welchem ~ heraus hat sie es getan?* what was her motive for doing it?, what made her do it?; **2.** *Kunst, Literatur, Mus.*: motif; *Film etc.*: *auch* theme; *Fot.* subject

Motivation *f*; *-, -en*; *Päd., Psych.* motivation; **Motivationskünstler** *m*, **Motivationskünstlerin** *f umg.* brilliant motivator; **Motivationsseminar** *n*

Wirts. motivational seminar

Motivator *m*; *-s, -en* (*Person*) motivator; (*Anreiz*) motivating factor

Motivforschung *f* motivation research; **motivieren** *v/t.* **1.** (*anregen*) motivate; (*Tat*) *auch* be behind; *was hat dich dazu motiviert?* what was your motive for doing it?, what made you do it?; *ich konnte ihn nicht dazu ~* I couldn't spur him on to do it; **2.** (*begründen*) explain, account for; **motiviert I.** *P.P.* → *motivieren*; **II.** *Adj.* motivated; *sehr ~* highly motivated; **Motiviertheit** *f* (degree of) motivation; **Motivierung** *f* motivation

motivisch *Adj.* relating to motifs

Motiv|sammler *m*, **~sammlerin** *f Philatelie*: collector of stamps according to the subjects shown; **~wagen** *m bei Festumzügen etc.*: commemorative float

Motocross *n*; *-, -e Motorsport*: motocross

Motodrom *n*; *-s, -e Motorsport*: motor racing circuit

Motor *m*; *-s, -en, auch*: *-e* **1.** engine; *bes. Etech.* motor; **2.** *fig.* driving force, powerhouse (*des Unternehmens* behind the enterprise)

Motor|... *im Subst.* engine; *bes. Etech.* motor; **~block** *m Mot.* engine block, cylinder block; **~boot** *n* motorboat; **~bremse** *f Mot.* engine brake

Motoren|bau *m*; *nur Sg.* engine-building; **~geräusch** *n* sound of engines; **~lärm** *m* noise (*stärker*: roar) of engines; **~öl** *n* engine oil; **~werk** *n* engine-building plant

Motor|fahrzeug *n bes. schw.* motor vehicle; **~geräusch** *n* engine noise; **~haube** *f Mot.* bonnet, *Am.* hood; *Flug.* (engine) cowl (*Am.* cowling)

...motorig *im Adj.*: *ein zwei~es Flugzeug* a twin-engined aircraft

Motorik *f*; *-, kein Pl.*; *Physiol.* motor functions *Pl.* (*od.* activity); **motorisch I.** *Adj.* **1.** *Physiol., Nerv etc.*: motor ...; **2.** *Mot.* with regard to the engine, in the engine department; **II.** *Adv.* **1.** *Physiol.* with regard to motor functions; *~ gestört sein* have impaired motor functions; **2.** *Mot.* with regard to the engine, in the engine department

motorisieren I. *v/t.* motorize; (*Betrieb, auch Mil.*) mechanize; *ein Boot ~* fit a boat with an engine; **II.** *v/refl.* buy (o.s.) a car (*Motorrad*: motorbike), *umg.* get o.s. some wheels; **motorisiert I.** *P.P.* → *motorisieren*; **II.** *Adj.* motorized; *sind Sie ~?* (*haben Sie ein Auto?*) have you got any (motorized) transport(ation)?, *umg.* have you got any wheels?; *sind Sie mit dem Auto hier?* did you come with your own transport(ation)?; **Motorisierung** *f* motorization; (*e-s Betriebs, auch Mil.*) mechanization

Motor|jacht *f Naut.* motor yacht; **~leistung** *f Tech.* engine output (*od.* power); **~öl** *n Mot.* engine oil; **~pumpe** *f* power pump

Motorrad *n Mot.* motorbike, *formeller*: motorcycle; **~ fahren** ride a motorbike (*od.* motorcycle); **~braut** *f umg. hum.* biker's girl (*Am. auch* chick); **~fahrer** *m*, **~fahrerin** *f* motorcyclist, biker; **~helm** *m* motorcyclist's helmet; **~rennen** *n* **1.** motorcycle race; **2.** (*Sportart*) motorcycle racing

Motor|raum *m Mot.* engine compartment; **~roller** *m Mot.* (motor) scooter; **~säge** *f* power saw; **~schaden** *m*

Mot. engine damage; *Panne*: engine breakdown (*od.* failure); **~schiff** *n Naut.* motor vessel, *Am.* motor ship; **~schlitten** *m* snowmobile; **~segler** *m Flug.* powered glider; **~sport** *m* motor sport; **~spritze** *f* power hose; **~wäsche** *f Mot.* engine clean

Motte *f*; *-, -n*; *Zool.* moth; *von ~n zerfressen* moth-eaten; *ach, du kriegst die ~n! umg.* well, I'll be blowed (*Am.* darned); *Bestürzung*: that's all I (*od.* we) need!

Motten|fraß *m* moth damage; **~kiste** *f umg.*: *e-e Geschichte/ein Witz etc. aus der ~* a hoary old (*od.* an ancient) story/joke *etc.*; *das gehört in die ~* that should be consigned to oblivion (*hum.* given a decent burial); **~kugel** *f* mothball; **~pulver** *n* moth powder

motten|sicher *Adj.* mothproof; **~zerfressen** *Adj.* moth-eaten

Motto *n*; *-s, -s* **1.** motto; *das ~ des Balles ist „Südseezauber"* the theme of the dance will be "South Sea Magic"; *unter dem ~ ... stehen* have as a motto ...; **2.** (*Prinzip*) principle; *nach dem ~ leben ...* live according to the principle ...

motzen *v/i.* **1.** *umg.* gripe, beef, bellyache; **2.** *Dial.* (*schmollen*) sulk; **Motzerei** *f*; *-, -en*; *umg.* griping, bellyaching; **motzig** *Adj.* **1.** *umg.* grouchy, *Brit. auch* ratty; **2.** *Dial.* (*schmollend*) sulky, sulking

Mountainbike ['maʊntn̩baɪk] *n*; *-s, -s* mountain bike

Mousse [mʊs] *f*; *-, -s*; *Gastr.* mousse

moussieren [mʊ'siːrən] *v/i.* sparkle, be sparkling; **moussierend I.** *Part. Präs.* → *moussieren*; **II.** *Adj. Wein*: sparkling

Möwe *f*; *-, -n*; *Orn.* (sea)gull; **Möwenvogel** *m* gull, one of the laridae

mozartisch *Adj.* Mozartian

Mozartkugel *f chocolate-covered marzipan and nougat truffle*

Mozzarella *m*; *-s, -s*; *Gastr.* mozzarella

MP *f*; *-, -(s)*; *Abk.* **1.** → *Maschinenpistole*; **2.** (*Militärpolizei*) MP

MP3-Player *m*; *-s, -* MP3 player

Mrd. *Abk.* (*Milliarde*) bn

MS *Abk.* **1.** (*Motorschiff*) MV, *Am.* MS; **2.** (*multiple Sklerose*) MS

Ms. *Abk.* (*Manuskript*) MS

MS-Kranke *m, f* MS patient

MTA *f*; *-, -(s)*; *Abk.* (*medizinisch-technische Assistentin*) medical laboratory assistant

Mucke *f*; *-, -n* **1.** *Mus. Sl.* moonlighting gig; **2.** *Dial.* → *Mücke*

Mücke *f*; *-, -n* **1.** *Zool.* mosquito; (*kleine*) midge; *aus e-r ~ e-n Elefanten machen umg. fig.* make a mountain out of a molehill; **2.** *Pl.*; *Sl.* (*Geld*) dough; **3.** *Dial.* (*Fliege*) fly

Muckefuck *m*; *-s, kein Pl.*; *umg.* disgustingly weak coffee, *Brit. auch* kiddies' coffee; (*Ersatzkaffee*) coffee substitute; **mucken** *v/i. umg.* grumble; *ohne zu ~* without a murmur

Mucken *Pl. umg.* e-r *Person*: whims; (*Launen*) moods; *die Sache hat ihre ~* it's got its snags; *j-m s-e ~ austreiben* sort s.o. out

Mücken|dreck *m* fly droppings *Pl.*; *sich über jeden ~ aufregen umg. fig. pej.* get worked up about every little detail; **~plage** *f* plague of mosquitoes (*od.* midges); **~schwarm** *m* swarm of mosquitoes (*od.* midges); **~spray** *m, n* mosquito spray (*od.* repellent); **~stich** *m* mosquito bite

Mucker *m*; *-s, -*; *pej.* **1.** *umg.* (*Duck-*

mäuser) chicken; **2.** *Dial.* (*griesgrämiger Typ*) grouch

Muckis *Pl. umg. hum.* (bulging) muscles

Mucks *m*; *-es, -e*; *umg.*: **keinen ~ tun** be as quiet as a mouse; (*sich nicht bewegen*) not budge (*od.* stir)

mucksen *v/i. und v/refl.*: (**sich**) **~** stir, move, budge; **Muckser** *m*; *-s, -*; *umg.* → **Mucks**

mucksmäuschenstill *Adj. umg.* → **mäuschenstill**

muddeln *v/i. nordd. umg.* **1.** (*wühlen*) wallow; **2.** (*pfuschen*) make a mess (**bei** of)

müde I. *Adj.* tired; (*matt*) weary; (*erschöpft*) exhausted; (*schläfrig*) sleepy; **~s Lächeln** weary smile; **keine ~ Mark** *umg. fig.* not a penny (*od.* cent); **e-r Sache ~ werden** grow weary (*od.* tired) of s.th.; *umg.* (*satt haben*) get fed up with s.th.; **nicht ~ werden zu** (+ *Inf.*) never tire of (+ *Ger.*); **II.** *Adv.* wearily, in a tired way; **~ lächeln** smile wearily, give a weary smile; **~ abwinken** give a weary gesture of refusal

...müde *im Adj.* tired of ...; **ehe.~** tired of (*od.* disillusioned with) married life; **kriegs.~** war-weary

Müdigkeit *f* tiredness, weariness; (*Erschöpfung*) fatigue, exhaustion; **keine ~ vorschützen!** *umg.* it's no use pretending to be tired; *fig.* (*mach schon*) come on, get on with it!

...müdigkeit *f*, *im Subst.*: **Ehe.~** disillusionment with married life; **Kriegs.~** war-weariness

Mudschahed *m*; *-*, *Mudschaheddin* member of the mujaheddin; *Pl.* mujaheddin

Müesli *n*; *-s, -*; *schw., Gastr.* muesli

Muezzin *m*; *-s, -s* muezzin

Muff¹ *m*; *-(e)s, -e zum Händewärmen*: muff

Muff² *m*; *-(e)s, kein Pl.*; *nordd.* musty smell

Muffe *f*; *-, -n* **1.** *Tech.* sleeve; (*Fassung*) socket; (*Kupplungsmuffe*) coupling (sleeve); **2.** *nur Sg.*; *Sl.*: **~ haben** (*Angst haben*) be in a funk

Muffel¹ *m*; *-s, -*; *umg.* **1.** (*Griesgram*) sourpuss, misery-guts *Sl.*; **2.** (*gleichgültiger Mensch*): **er ist ein schrecklicher ~** you can't get him interested in anything; → **Krawattenmuffel, Partymuffel** etc.

Muffel² *f*; *-, -n*; *Tech.* crucible

...muffel *m im Subst. umg. Person, die einer Sache gleichgültig od. ablehnend gegenübersteht*: **Ehe.~** anti-marriage type

muffelig *Adj. umg. pej.* **1.** *Geruch*: musty; (*faulig*) mo(u)ldy; **2.** (*mürrisch*) grumpy, grouchy

muffeln I. *v/i. umg.* **1.** *Dial.* (*riechen*) smell musty; *faulig*: smell mo(u)ldy; **2.** (*mürrisch sein*) have the grumps; (*eingeschnappt sein*) be in a huff; **II.** *vt/i. Dial. umg.* (*kauen*) munch away

müffeln *v/i. Dial.* → **muffeln** I 1

Muffelwild *n Jägerspr.* mouf(f)lon

Muffensausen *n umg.*: **~ kriegen** get the wind up; **~ haben** have the wind up; *stärker*: be in a flat (*Am.* complete) panic

muffig *Adj.* **1.** *Luft*: musty; (*miefig*) stuffy; *Keller etc.*: musty-smelling, *Am. auch* funky; **2.** *fig. pej.* (*spießig*) stuffy; **3.** *umg. pej.* (*mürrisch*) *umg.* grumpy; **Muffigkeit** *f* **1.** *der Luft*: mustiness; (*Mief*) stuffiness; **2.** *fig. pej.* stuffiness; **3.** *umg.* (*Mürrischkeit*) grumpiness

mufflig *Adj.* → **muffelig**

Mufflon *m*; *-s, -s*; *Zool.* mouf(f)lon

Mugel *m*; *-s, -(n)*; *österr.* hillock; *Skifahren*: mogul; **mug(e)lig** *Adj.* **1.** *österr.* humpy; *Piste*: full of moguls; **2.** *fachspr. Schmuckstein*: ... en cabochon

muh *Interj.* moo!; **~ machen** go moo

Mühe *f*; *-, -n* trouble; (*Anstrengung*) effort; **viel ~ kosten** cost a lot of effort; **spar dir die ~** you can save yourself the trouble; **nur mit ~** only with (great) difficulty; (*gerade noch*) just about; (**nicht**) **der** *od.* **die ~ wert** (not) worth the effort, (not) worth it; **die ~ lohnt sich** it's worth the effort; **sich** (*Dat.*) **~ geben** (**mit j-m/etw.**) go to great trouble (*od.* pains) (over s.o./s.th.); **gib dir doch etwas ~!** (you could) make some sort of an effort!; **sich** (*Dat.*) **die ~ machen zu** (+ *Inf.*) go to the trouble of (+ *Ger.*); **er machte sich nicht einmal die ~ zu** (+ *Inf.*) he couldn't even be bothered to (+ *Inf.*); **keine ~ scheuen** spare no effort *od.* pains (*zu* + *Inf.* in + *Ger.*); **wenn es Ihnen keine ~ macht** if it's no trouble (for you); **alle** *od.* **s-e** (**liebe**) **~ haben, j-n zu überreden** have a hard time persuading s.o.

mühelos I. *Adj.* effortless, easy; **II.** *Adv.* easily, with ease, effortlessly; **Mühelosigkeit** *f* effortlessness, lack of effort; (*Leichtigkeit*) (great) ease, facility

muhen *v/i.* moo, low

mühen *v/refl. geh.* make an effort, try hard, take pains (*zu* + *Inf.* to + *Inf.*)

mühevoll *Adj.* laborious; *Arbeit*: *auch* painstaking; (*schwierig*) difficult, hard; *Weg* arduous

Mühlbach *m* mill stream

Mühle *f*; *-, -n* **1.** mill (*auch Gebäude*); → **Kaffeemühle** etc., **Wasser~**. **2.** *fig.* (*monotone Tätigkeit*) treadmill; **in die ~ der Justiz geraten** get caught up in the machinery of the law; **j-n durch die ~ drehen** *umg.* put s.o. through the mill (*Am. auch* wringer); **3.** *kein Art., nur Sg.* (*Spiel*) nine men's morris; *Figur*: mill; **4.** *umg., mst pej.* (*Auto*) heap, pile of junk; (*auch Flugzeug*) (old) crate; (*auch Fahrrad*) rattletrap

Mühlenflügel *m* sail of a (*od.* the) windmill

Mühlespiel *n* nine men's morris

Mühl|rad *n* mill wheel; **~stein** *m* millstone; **~werk** *n* mill machinery

Mühsal *f*; *-, -e*; *geh.* (*Schufterei*) drudgery, toil (and trouble); (*Ungemach*) hardship; (*Strapaze*) tribulation

mühsam I. *Adj.* (*schwierig*) difficult; (*anstrengend*) strenuous; (*ermüdend*) tiring; (*gezwungen*) *Gespräch etc.*: labo(u)red; *Lächeln*: forced; **~e Kleinarbeit** painstaking detail work; **II.** *Adv.* with difficulty, after a lot of effort; **sich ~ erheben** struggle to one's feet; **~ verdientes Geld** hard-earned money; **Mühsamkeit** *f* effort, strain (+ *Gen.* of, involved in)

mühselig I. *Adj.* laborious; *Leben, Reise etc.*: arduous, hard; **II.** *Adv.* laboriously; (*mit äußerster Sorgfalt*) painstakingly; **Mühseligkeit** *f* laboriousness; *von Leben, Reise etc.*: arduousness

Mukoviszidose *f*; *-, -n*; *Med.* cystic fibrosis

Mulatte *m*; *-n, -n*, **Mulattin** *f*; *-, -nen* mulatto

Mulch *m*; *-(e)s, -e*; *Agr. etc.* mulch; **mulchen** *v/t.* mulch

Mulde *f*; *-, -n* **1.** (*Vertiefung*) hollow;

Geol. auch depression; *Skifahren*: bowl; **2.** *Dial.* (*Trog*) trough

Muli *n*; *-s, -s*; *südd., österr.* mule

Mull¹ *m*; *-(e)s, -e Gewebe*: gauze

Mull² *m*; *-(e)s, -e*; *nordd.* (*Humus*) mull

Müll *m*; *-s, kein Pl.* **1.** *allg.* waste (*auch Sonder-, Industriemüll*), *förm.* refuse; (*bes. Hausmüll*) rubbish, *bes. Am.* garbage, trash; **radioaktiver ~** radioactive waste; **etw. in den ~ werfen** throw s.th. in(to) the dustbin (*Am.* trashcan, garbage can); **das kommt** *od.* **kann in den ~** that can be thrown out; **2.** *umg. fig.* (*unnützes Zeug*) rubbish, *bes. Am.* garbage, trash; **~abfuhr** *f* **1.** refuse (*Am.* garbage) collection; **2.** (*Müllmänner*) dustmen *Pl.*, *Am.* garbage men (*od.* collectors) *Pl.*; **~abladeplatz** *m* rubbish tip, *Am.* (garbage) dump, landfill

Mullah *m*; *-s, -s* mullah

Müll|aufbereitung *f* refuse (*od.* waste, *Am.* garbage) treatment; **~auto** *n* → **Müllwagen**; **~berg** *m* **1.** pile of rubbish (*Am.* garbage); *großer*: mountain of rubbish (*Am.* garbage); **2.** (*künstlicher Berg*) artificial hill; **~beseitigung** *f* waste disposal (*od.* management); **~beutel** *m* bin liner, *Am.* garbage bag

Mullbinde *f* gauze bandage

Müll|container *m* rubbish (*od.* refuse) skip, *Am.* (garbage) dumpster; **~deponie** *f* rubbish tip (*od.* dump), *Am.* (garbage) dump, landfill; *Gelände*: waste disposal site; **~eimer** *m* rubbish (*od.* waste) bin, *Am.* garbage can; **~entsorgung** *f* waste disposal

Müller *m*; *-s, -* miller; **Müllerin** *f*; *-, -nen*; *altm.* miller's wife

Müllerinart *f*.. **Forelle** etc. **auf** *od.* **nach ~** *Gastr.* trout etc. meunière

Müll|fahrer *m* dustman, *Am.* garbage man (*od.* collector), sanitation worker; **~fahrerin** *f* (female) refuse (*Am.* garbage) collector, sanitation worker; **~gebühr** *f* refuse (*Am.* garbage) collection charge; **~grube** *f* refuse (*Am.* garbage) pit; **~halde** *f* rubbish (*Am.* garbage) dump; **~haufen** *m* rubbish (*Am.* garbage) heap; *fig.* scrapheap; **~kippe** *f* rubbish tip (*od.* dump), *Am.* (garbage) dump; **~kutscher** *m Dial.*, *umg.* → **Müllfahrer**

Müll|mann *m umg.* → **Müllfahrer**; **~sack** *m* **1.** *ohne Inhalt*: rubbish (*od.* waste) bag, *Am.* garbage bag; **2.** *mit Inhalt*: sack of rubbish (*Am.* garbage); **~schlucker** *m* rubbish (*Am.* garbage) chute, waste disposal unit; **~tonne** *f* dustbin, *Am.* trashcan, garbage can; **~trennung** *f* waste separation, separation of waste; **~verbrennung** *f*; *nur Sg.* refuse (*Am.* waste) incineration; **~verbrennungsanlage** *f* refuse (*Am.* waste) incinerator, waste incineration plant; **~vermeidung** *f* waste prevention; **~verwertung** *f* waste recycling; **~wagen** *m* dustcart, *Am.* garbage (*od.* trash) truck; **~zerkleinerung** *f* waste maceration; (*Zusammenstampfen*) waste compaction

Mullwindel *f* muslin nappy (*Am.* diaper)

mulmig *Adj.* **1.** *umg.* (*bedrohlich*) threatening; (*gefährlich*) nasty; **es sieht ziemlich ~ aus** things aren't looking too good; **mir ist** *od.* **wird ganz ~ zumute** I feel weak at the knees; (*übel*) I feel a bit queasy; (*unbehaglich*) I've got an uneasy feeling in the pit of my stomach; **2.** *fachspr. Boden*: powdery; *Dial.* (*morsch*) rotten

Multi *m*; *-s, -s*; *umg.* multinational (concern)

multidimensional *Adj.* multidimensional

multifunktional *Adj.* multifunctional

Multifunktions|anzeige *f Mot.* multifunctional display; **~taste** *f* multifunction button

multikausal *Adj.*: **~ sein** have multiple causes

multikulti *indekl. Adj.; nur präd.; umg.* multicultural

Multikulti *n*; *-, -; umg.* (*Multikulturalität*) multicultural mix

Multikulturalität *f*; *kein Pl.* multiculturalism

multikulturell *Adj.* multicultural

multilateral *Adj.* multilateral

Multimedia *n*; *-(s), kein Pl.* multimedia; **multimedial** *Adj.* multimedia ...; *Verwendung*: with multimedia; **Multimediaveranstaltung** *f* multimedia show (*od.* event); **Multimedienzentrum** *n* multimedia cent|re (*Am.* -er)

Multimillionär *m*, **~in** *f* multimillionaire, *weiblich auch* multimillionairess

multinational *Adj.* multinational

Multipack *n, m*; *-s, -s; Wirts.* multiple pack

multipel *Adj.* multiple; → **Sklerose**

Multiple-Choice-Verfahren *n* ['mʌltɪpl-'tʃɔʏs] *n* multiple choice method

Multiplexkino *n* multiplex (cinema, *bes. Am.* movie theater)

Multiplikand *m*; *-en, -en; Math.* multiplicand; **Multiplikation** *f*; *-, -en* multiplication; **Multiplikationsspunkt** *m Math.* multiplication dot; **Multiplikationszeichen** *n Math.* multiplication sign; **Multiplikator** *m*; *-s, -en; Math.* multiplier; *fig. von Information etc.*: disseminator; **Multiplikatorin** *f*; *-, -nen; fig.* disseminator; **multiplizieren I.** *v/t. Math.* multiply (*mit* by); *fig. auch* increase (several times); *13 multipliziert mit 12 ist (gleich) 156* 13 multiplied by 12 is (*od.* equals) 156; **II.** *v/refl. fig.* multiply, increase several times

Multi|talent *n umg.* many-talented person, all-round talent; **~tasking** *n*; *-(s), kein Pl. Computer*: multitasking; **~vision** *f; nur Sg.* multiple projection system (for slides)

Mumie *f*; *-, -n* mummy; **mumienhaft** *Adj.* mummy-like; **mumifizieren I.** *v/t.* (*hat mumifiziert*) mummify; **II.** *v/i.* (*ist*) *Med.* mummify; **Mumifizierung** *f* mummification

Mumm *m*; *-s, kein Pl.; umg.* **1.** (*Schneid*) spunk, guts *Pl., Brit. auch* bottle; **2.** (*Schwung*) get-up-and-go, oomph; *als ständige Eigenschaft*: drive, verve; (*Kraft*) muscle

Mummelgreis *m umg. pej.* old dodderer

Mümmelmann *m umg. hum.* hare

mummeln *Dial. umg.* **I.** *vt/i.* **1.** (*undeutlich reden*) mumble (into one's beard); **2.** → **mümmeln** 1; **II.** *v/t. und v/refl.* (*einwickeln*): *j-n/sich* (*in etw. Akk.*) **~** wrap s.o./o.s. up (in s.th.)

mümmeln *vt/i. Dial.* **1.** (*knabbern*) nibble (away) at; (*kauen*) chew away at, chew on; **2.** → **mummeln** I 1

Mummenschanz *m*; *-es, kein Pl.; altm.* masquerade

Mumpitz *m*; *-es, kein Pl.; umg. pej.* (*Unsinn*) rubbish, *bes. Am.* garbage

Mumps *m, Dial. f*; *-, kein Pl.; Med.* mumps *Sg.*

München (*n*); *-s; Geog.* Munich

Münch(e)ner¹ *m*; *-s, -, ~in* *f*; *-, -nen* inhabitant (*gebürtige[r]*: native) of Munich; → **Kölner¹, Kölnerin**

Münch(e)ner² *indekl. Adj.* Munich ..., ... of (*od.* in) Munich

Mund *m*; *-(e)s, Münder* mouth; *den ~ aufmachen* open one's mouth; *umg. fig.* speak up; *mit vollem ~ sprechen* talk with one's mouth full; *aus dem ~ riechen* have bad breath; *sie küsste seinen ~* she kissed him on the lips; *ein ~ voll fig.* a mouthful; *Flüssigkeit*: *auch* a gulp; *von ~ zu ~ beatmen* give mouth-to-mouth resuscitation; *es ist in aller ~e* everyone's talking about it, it's the talk of the town; *~ und Nase aufsperren od. aufreißen umg.* fig gape open-mouthed (in astonishment); *halt den ~!* *umg.* shut up!; *den ~ nicht aufmachen od. auftun umg. fig.* not utter a word; *sie hat den ~ nicht aufgekriegt umg. fig.* she didn't say a word; *den ~ voll nehmen umg. fig.* talk big, shoot one's mouth off; *j-m den ~ verbieten fig.* stop s.o. saying anything, silence s.o.; *j-m etwas in den ~ legen fig.* put words into s.o.'s mouth; *j-m das Wort aus dem ~ nehmen umg. fig.* take the words (right) out of s.o.'s mouth; *j-m das Wort im ~ umdrehen* twist s.o.'s words; *j-m nach dem ~(e) reden fig.* echo s.o.'s words; *um zu gefallen*: say what s.o. wants to hear; *j-m über den ~ fahren umg. fig.* cut s.o. short; *nicht auf den ~ gefallen sein umg. fig.* have the gift of the gab; *sich (Dat.) den ~ verbrennen umg. fig.* put one's foot in it; *von ~ zu ~ gehen Neuigkeit*: be passed on from one person to the next, *umg.* do the rounds; *in Redewendungen* → *auch Maul*; → *berufen IV 1, Blatt 1, fransig 2, stopfen II 1, wässrig etc.*

Mundart *f* dialect; **~dichter** *m*, **~dichterin** *f* dialect writer (*Lyriker*: poet); **~dichtung** *f* dialect literature (*Gedichte*: poetry); **~forschung** *f* dialectology, dialect research

mundartlich I. *Adj.* dialect ..., dialectal; *Schriften*: in dialect; **II.** *Adv.* in dialect; *beeinflusst, gefärbt*: by dialect

Mundart|sprecher *m*, **~sprecherin** *f* dialect speaker; **~wörterbuch** *n* dialect dictionary

Mundatmung *f* oral respiration

Mündchen *n* little mouth

Munddusche *f* dental water jet, water pick

Mündel *n*; *-s, -; Jur.* ward; **~geld** *n Jur.* money held in trust (*for a ward*)

mündelsicher *Adj. Wirts. etwa* gilt-edged; **~e Wertpapiere** gilt-edged securities, gilts; **Mündelsicherheit** *f; nur Sg.; Wirts.* suitability for investment of trust money, trustee status

munden *v/i. geh.* taste good; *es mundet mir* I like (the taste of) it; *stärker*: I find it delicious; *sich (Dat.) etw. ~ lassen* savo(u)r s.th., relish s.th.

münden *v/i.*: *~ in* (+ *Akk.*) lead to (*auch fig.*); *Fluss*: flow (*od.* empty) into; *Straße*: lead into

mundfaul *Adj. umg.* too lazy to open one's mouth; → *auch maulfaul*

Mund|fäule *f Med.* stomatitis; **~flora** *f* (bacterial) flora of the mouth

mundgeblasen *Adj. Glas*: (mouth-)blown

mundgerecht I. *Adj.* bite-sized; *j-m etw. ~ machen fig.* make s.th. easily digestible for s.o.; **II.** *Adv. schneiden, servieren etc.*: in bite-sized pieces; *fig. präsentieren*: in an easily digestible form

Mund|geruch *m* (*auch übler ~*) bad breath, halitosis; **~harmonika** *f Mus.* mouth organ, harmonica; **~höhle** *f* oral cavity; **~hygiene** *f* oral hygiene

mündig *Adj.* **1.** *Jur.* of age; *~ werden* come of age, attain one's majority; **2.** (*urteilsfähig*) responsible (adult), mature; *~er Bürger* responsible adult citizen; **Mündige** *m, f*; *-n, -n* major; **Mündigkeit** *f Jur.* (age of) majority; *fig.* maturity

mündlich I. *Adj. Aussage etc.*: verbal; *Prüfung*: oral; *~e Überlieferung* oral tradition; **II.** *Adv.* orally, verbally; *etw. ~ weitergeben* pass s.th. on by word of mouth; *alles Weitere ~* I'll tell you the rest when I see you

Mund|partie *f* area around the mouth; *mouth and lips Pl.*; **~pflege** *f* oral hygiene; **~propaganda** *f*: (*durch ~* by) word-of-mouth recommendation, *Am. umg. auch* buzz; **~raub** *m Jur. altm.* petty larceny of food; **~schenk** *m*; *-en, -en; hist.* cupbearer; **~schleimhaut** *f* mucous membrane of the mouth; **~schutz** *m* **1.** *Med.* mask; **2.** *Boxen etc.*: gumshield

M-und-S-Reifen *m* snow tyre (*Am.* tire)

Mundstück *n* **1.** *Mus.* mouthpiece; *e-r Zigarette*: tip; **2.** *des Zaumzeugs*: bit

mundtot *Adj.*: *~ machen* (*Person*) silence, *umg.* shut up; *Pol.* (*auch Presse etc.*) gag, muzzle

Mündung *f* **1.** *e-s Flusses*: mouth; *den Gezeiten unterworfene*: estuary; *e-r Straße*: (T-)junction; *die ~ e-s Flusses in e-n anderen* the confluence of two rivers; *an der ~ der Goethestraße in die Hauptstraße* at the junction (*Am.* intersection) of the Goethestrasse and the Hauptstrasse, at the point where the Goethestrasse joins the Hauptstrasse; **2.** *e-r Röhre, auch Anat.*: mouth, orifice; *e-r Feuerwaffe*: muzzle

Mündungs|feuer *n* muzzle flash; **~gebiet** *n e-s Flusses*: estuary (area)

Mund|verkehr *m Sex*: oral sex; **~vorrat** *m* provisions *Pl.*; **~wasser** *n* mouth wash, gargle; **~werk** *n; nur Sg.; umg.* mouth; *ein loses od. lockeres ~ haben* have a loose tongue; **~werkzeuge** *Pl. Zool.* mouth parts; **~winkel** *m* corner of one's mouth; *die ~ verziehen* grimace

Mund-zu-Mund-Beatmung *f Med.* mouth-to-mouth resuscitation, *bes. Brit. auch* kiss of life; **Mund-zu-Nase-Beatmung** *f* mouth-to-nose resuscitation

Mungo *m*; *-s, -s; Zool.* mongoose

Munition *f*; *-, -en* ammunition (*auch fig.*); *s-e ~ verschießen* use up one's ammunition; *fig.* shoot one's bolt (*Am.* wad); *j-m ~ liefern fig.* provide s.o. with (plenty of) ammunition; **munitionieren** *v/t.* supply with ammunition

Munitions|depot *n* → **Munitionslager**, **~fabrik** *f* munitions factory; **~lager** *n* ammunition depot (*Stapelplatz*: dump)

Munkelei *f*; *-, -en; umg.* talk, gossip; (*Gerüchte*) rumo(u)rs *Pl.*; **munkeln** *umg.* **I.** *v/i.* talk, gossip; **II.** *v/t.* say, whisper; *man munkelt od. es wird gemunkelt, dass ...* people are saying (that) ..., there's a rumo(u)r (going round) that ...

Münster¹ *n*; *-s, -,* minster; (*Kathedrale*) cathedral

Münster² *m*; *-s, -,* **~käse** *m Gastr.* Münster cheese

munter I. *Adj.* **1.** (*wach*) awake; (*auf*)

M

up (and about); ~ **werden** wake up, perk up; **Kaffee macht** ~ coffee gets you going; **2.** (*lebhaft*) lively; (*vergnügt*) cheerful; *umg.* chirpy, *Am. auch* chipper *umg.*; ~ **werden** cheer up; → **gesund** I 1; **II.** *fig. Adv.* (*unbekümmert*) blithely; **Munterkeit** *f* (*Lebhaftigkeit*) liveliness; (*Vergnügtheit*) cheerfulness, high spirits *Pl.*; **Muntermacher** *m umg.* stimulant; (*Aufputschtablette*) pep pill

Münz|anstalt *f* mint; **~automat** *m* slot machine; *in e-r Parkgarage:* pay station

Münze *f*; -, -*n* **1.** coin; **klingende** ~ *geh. fig.* hard cash; **etw. für bare** ~ **nehmen** *fig.* take s.th. at face value; **j-m mit gleicher** ~ **heimzahlen** *fig.* pay s.o. back in his (*od.* her) own coin; **2.** (*Münzanstalt*) mint

Münz|einheit *f* monetary unit; **~einwurf** *m* coin slot

münzen *vt/i.* coin, mint; **auf j-n gemünzt sein** *fig.* be meant for s.o.

Münz|fernrohr *n* coin(-operated) telescope; **~fernsprecher** *m* payphone, pay phone; **~gaszähler** *m* gas slot meter; **~geld** *n; nur Sg.* coins *Pl.*, change; **~gewicht** *n* (standard) weight of a coin (*od.* coins); **~hoheit** *f* (state's) coining prerogative; **~kunde** *f; nur Sg.* numismatics *Pl.* (*V. im Sg.*); **~recht** *n* **1.** *nur Sg.* coining prerogative; **2.** coinage legislation; **~sammler** *m*, **~sammlerin** *f* coin collector, numismatist *förm.*; **~sammlung** *f* coin collection; **~stätte** *f* mint; **~tank(automat)** *m* coin-operated (petrol, *Am.* gas) pump; **~tankstelle** *f* coin-operated petrol (*Am.* gas) station; **~telefon** *n* payphone, pay phone; **~wäscherei** *f* laund(e)rette, *bes. Am.* Laundromat®; **~wechsler** *m* change machine; **~wesen** *n; nur Sg.* minting and distribution of coinage; **~zähler** *m* slot meter

Muräne *f*; -, -*n; Zool.* moray

mürbe *Adj.* **1.** *Obst:* soft, very ripe; *Fleisch:* tender, *gekochtes: auch* well-cooked; *Kuchen:* crumbly; *Holz:* soft, rotten; *Gewebe:* threadbare; **Fleisch** ~ **machen** tenderize meat; **2.** *fig.* (*erschöpft*) worn-out, *präd.* worn out; **j-n** ~ **machen** wear s.o. down, wear down s.o.'s resistance; **j-n** ~ **kriegen** *umg.* break s.o.'s resistance *allg.*

Mürbeteig *m* short(-crust) pastry

Mürbheit *f von Obst etc.:* softness; *von Fleisch:* tenderness; *von Kuchen:* crumbliness; *von Holz:* softness, rottenness; *von Gewebe:* threadbare state

Mürbteig *m österr.* short(-crust) pastry

Mure *f*; -, -*n* (Alpine) mudflow; **murig** *Adj. Geog., Geol.* subject to regular mudflows

Murks *m*; -*es, kein Pl.*; *umg.* botch-up; ~ **machen** (*pfuschen*) make a mess of things; **murksen** *v/i. umg.* mess around (**an** + *Dat.* with); (*pfuschen*) make a mess of things

Murmel *f*; -, -*n* marble; **~n spielen** play with marbles

murmeln *vt/i.* murmur, mutter; **etw. vor sich hin** ~ mutter s.th. to o.s.; **Murmeln** *n*; -*s, kein Pl.* murmur

Murmeltier *n Zool.* marmot, *Am. auch* woodchuck; **schlafen wie ein** ~ *fig.* sleep like a log (*od.* top)

murren *v/i.* grumble (**über** + *Akk.* about); **ohne zu** ~ without complaining; **Murren** *n*; -*s, kein Pl.* grumbling

mürrisch *Adj.* grumpy, surly; (*wortkarg*) sullen

Mus *n, Dial. auch m*; -*es, -e*; (*Brei*)

mush; *aus Früchten etc.:* puree; (*Pflaumenmus*) (plum) jam; **zu** ~ **schlagen** *od.* **machen** *umg. fig.* beat to a pulp, make mincemeat of

Muschel *f*; -, -*n* **1.** *Zool.* (*Miesmuschel*) mussel; (*Schale*) shell; → **Jakobsmuschel, Perlmuschel** *etc.*; **2.** *Telef.* (*Hörmuschel*) earpiece, (*Sprechmuschel*) mouthpiece; **3.** (*Ohrmuschel*) outer ear; **4.** *österr.* (*Toilettenbecken*) lavatory pan; (*Waschbecken*) washbasin; **~bank** *f* mussel bank

muschelförmig *Adj.* shell-shaped

Muschel|kalk *m* muschelkalk; **~schale** *f* (mussel *etc.*) shell; **~seide** *f* byssus (*Pl.* byssuses *od.* byssi); **~tier** *n Zool.* mollusc, *Am.* mollusk

Muschi *f*; -, -*s* **1.** *Kinderspr.* (*Katze*) pussy(-cat); **2.** *umg.* (*Vulva*) pussy

Muse *f*; -, -*n; Myth.* Muse; **von der** ~ **geküsst werden** *hum.* be inspired by the muses; **die leichte** ~ *fig.* light entertainment

museal *Adj.* museum ...; *fig. pej.* (*museumsreif*) antiquated

Muselman *m*; -*en, -en, ~in f*; -, -*nen; altm.* Muslim, Moslem; **muselmanisch** *Adj. altm.* Muslim, Moslem

Musen|sohn *m altm., noch hum.* son of the Muses, poet; **~tempel** *m altm., noch hum.* temple of the Muses

Museum *n*; -*s, Museen* museum; *für Kunst, bes. in Namen: auch* gallery

Museums|aufseher *m*, **~aufseherin** *f* museum attendant; **~besuch** *m* museum visit; **~besucher** *m*, **~besucherin** *f* visitor to a museum; **~direktor** *m*, **~direktorin** *f* museum director, curator (of a [*od.* the] museum); **~führer** *m* **1.** museum guide, *Am.* docent; **2.** (*Buch*) guide to a (*od.* the) museum; **~führerin** *f* museum guide, *Am.* docent; **~katalog** *m* museum catalog(ue); **~pädagogik** *f* museum's educational program(me)

museumsreif *Adj. umg.* fit for a museum; (*altertümlich*) positively archaic (*od.* antiquated); **Museumsstück** *n* museum piece; **Museumswert** *m*: ~ **haben** be a museum piece, *pej.* belong in a museum

Musical ['mju:zikl] *n*; -*s, -s* musical, musical comedy

Musik *f*; -, -*en* **1.** music; ~ **machen** play music; **etw. in** ~ **setzen** set s.th. to music; **die** ~ **schreiben zu etw.** write the music (*Film etc.: auch* score) for *od.* to s.th.; **im Blut haben** *fig.* be a born musician; **das ist** ~ **in m-n Ohren** *umg. fig.* that's music to my ears; → **Handkäse; 2.** *umg.* (*Musikkapelle*) band; **~akademie** *f* → **Musikhochschule**

Musikalien *Pl.* **1.** (printed) music *Sg.*; **2.** *Instrumente etc.:* musical instruments and accessories; **~handlung** *f* music shop

musikalisch *Adj.* musical; **~er Akzent** *Ling.* pitch accent; **Musikalität** *f*; -, *kein Pl.* musicality

Musikant *m*; -*en, -en* musician

Musikantenknochen *m umg.* funny bone

Musikantin *f*; -, -*nen* musician; **musikantisch I.** *Adj.* ... full of brio; **II.** *Adv. spielen:* with (*od.* con) brio

musikbegeistert *Adj.* very keen on (*Am.* wild about) music; **Musikbegeisterung** *f* love of music

Musik|begleitung *f* (musical) accompaniment; **~berieselung** *f pej.* piped (*Am.* canned) music, Muzak®; **~bibliothek** *f* music library; **~box** *f* jukebox; **~direktor** *m*, **~direktorin** *f* musical di-

rector; **~drama** *n* music drama

Musiker *m*; -*s, -*, **~in** *f*; -, -*nen* musician

Musik|erzieher *m*, **~erzieherin** *f* music teacher; **~erziehung** *f* musical education (*od.* training); **~festspiele** *Pl.* music festival *Sg.*; **~freund** *m*, **~freundin** *f* music lover; **~geschäft** *n* **1.** *Laden:* music shop; **2.** *nur Sg.* **das** ~ the music business

Musikgeschichte *f* history of music; **musikgeschichtlich I.** *Adj.* musico-historical; *Bedeutung etc.:* in musical history; **II.** *Adv.* in terms of musical history

Musik|hochschule *f* academy of music, college of music; (*Konservatorium*) conservatoire, *bes. Am.* conservatory; **~instrument** *n* musical instrument; **~kanal** *m* TV music channel; **~kapelle** *f* band; **~kassette** *f* music cassette; **~konserve** *f; umg. auch Pl. Koll.* canned music

Musikkritik *f* **1.** *nur Sg.* music criticism; **2.** *Rezension:* music review; **Musikkritiker** *m*, **Musikkritikerin** *f* music critic

Musik|leben *n; nur Sg.* musical life; **~lehrer** *m*, **~lehrerin** *f* music teacher; **~lexikon** *n* dictionary of music; *mit längeren Einträgen zu bestimmten Themen:* encyclop(a)edia of music; **~liebhaber** *m*, **~liebhaberin** *f* music lover

Musikologe *m*; -*en, -en* musicologist; **Musikologie** *f*; -, *kein Pl.* musicology; **Musikologin** *f*; -, -*nen* musicologist

Musikpädagoge *m* **1.** music teacher; **2.** *Wissenschaftler:* expert on the theory of music teaching; **Musikpädagogik** *f* (theory of) music teaching; **Musikpädagogin** *f* → **Musikpädagoge**

Musik|pavillon *m* bandstand, music pavilion; **~preis** *m* music prize; **~professor** *m*, **~professorin** *f* professor of music; **~saal** *m* music room; **~schule** *f* music school; **~stück** *n* piece of music; **~student** *m*, **~studentin** *f* music student, student of music; **~stunde** *f* music lesson; **~theater** *n* musical theat|re (*Am.* -er); **~theorie** *f* musical theory; **~truhe** *f altm.* radiogram; **~unterricht** *m* music lesson(s *Pl.*)

Musikus *m*; -, *Musizi und -se; altm., noch hum. od. iro.* musician; *bes. hum.* man of music

Musik|verein *m* music society; **~verlag** *m* music publisher(s *Pl.*); **~video** *n* music video; **~werk** *n* musical work (*od.* composition), piece of music

Musikwissenschaft *f* musicology; **Musikwissenschaftler** *m*, **Musikwissenschaftlerin** *f* musicologist; **musikwissenschaftlich** *Adj.* musicological

Musik|wunsch *m bes. Radio:* listener's request (*for a piece of music*); **~zeitschrift** *f* musical journal

musisch I. *Adj. Person, Begabung:* artistic; **~e Fächer** fine arts (subjects); **II.** *Adv.:* ~ **veranlagt sein** have an artistic bent

musiv *Adj. Kunst(handwerk):* mosaic; **Musivgold** *n* mosaic gold

musizieren *v/i.* play music; *in kleinem Rahmen, bei sich zu Hause:* mst make music; **das Musizieren** music-making; **Musizierweise** *f* style of playing

Muskat *m*; -(*e*)*s, -e; Bot.* nutmeg; **~blüte** *f* mace

Muskateller *m*; -*s, -*; (*Wein*) muscatel (wine); **~traube** *f* muscat (*od.* muskat) grape

Muskat|nuss *f Bot.* nutmeg; **~reibe** *f* nutmeg grater

Muskel *m*; -*s, -n; Anat.* muscle; **s-e ~n spielen lassen** *umg. fig.* flex one's muscles; **~arbeit** *f* muscular activity; **~bündel** *n Anat.* muscle bundle; **~faser** *f Anat.* muscle fib|re (*Am.* -er); **~faserriss** *m Med.* torn muscle fib|re (*Am.* -er); **~fleisch** *n* meat composed of muscle tissue; **~geschwulst** *f Med.* myoma (*Pl.* myomas *od.* myomata); **~kater** *m* sore (*od.* stiff) muscles *Pl.* (*after violent exercise*); **~ haben** have got sore muscles, be stiff and sore; **~kraft** *f* muscle power, *umg.* beef; **~krampf** *m* cramp, *Med.* muscle spasm; **~mann** *m umg.* muscleman; **~paket** *n umg.* **1.** *Muskeln:* bulging muscles *Pl.;* **2.** muscleman; **~protz** *m umg.* Mr (*od.* Mr.) Muscles, Tarzan (type); **~riss** *m Med.* torn muscle; **~schwund** *m Med.* muscular atrophy; **~spiel** *n auch fig.* flexing of muscles; **~training** *n* muscle exercises *Pl.;* **~zerrung** *f Med.* pulled muscle; *sich* (*Dat.*) *e-e ~ zuziehen* pull a muscle

Muskete *f; -, -n; Mil. hist.* musket; **Musketier** *m; -s, -e* musketeer

muskulär *Adj.* muscular

Muskulatur *f; -, -en* muscular system, muscles *Pl.*

muskulös *Adj.* muscular

Müsli *n; -s, -; Gastr.* muesli

Muslim *m; -s, -e usw.* → **Moslem**

Müsliriegel *m* cereal bar

muss *Präs.* → **müssen**

Muss *n: es ist ein/kein ~* it's a (*stärker:* an absolute) must / it's not essential; **~bestimmung** *f Jur.* mandatory provision

Muße *f; -, kein Pl.* leisure; (*Freizeit*) leisure time; *mit od. in ~* at (one's) leisure; *dazu habe ich nicht die ~* I don't have the time (or the relaxed frame of mind) for that kind of thing; *Zeit und ~ finden* (*zu* + *Inf.*) find the time to relax (in order to … + *Inf.*)

Mussehe *f umg.* involuntary marriage; → *auch* **Mussheirat**

Musselin *m; -s, -e* muslin

müssen I. *Modalv.; muss, musste, hat … müssen* **1.** *bes. bei äußerer Notwendigkeit, Verpflichtung:* have to, have got to; *bes. bei innerer Überzeugung:* must; *ich muss* I have to, I've got to, I must; *ich muss unbedingt* I really must; *ich musste* I had to; *ich werde ~* I'll have to; *ich müsste* (*eigentlich*) I ought to; *er muss nicht hingehen von außen bestimmt:* he doesn't have to go; *weil ich es so bestimme:* he needn't go; *er hätte nicht gehen ~* (*brauchen*) he needn't have gone; *er hätte hier sein ~* he ought to (*od.* should) have been here; *was sein muss, muss sein* that's just the way it is, that's life; *muss das sein?* is that really necessary?; (*hör doch auf*) do you have to?; *wenn es* (*unbedingt*) *sein muss* if there's no other way, if you *etc.* (absolutely) must; *das muss man gesehen haben* you've got to see it, you mustn't miss it; *man glaubt es sonst nicht:* you've got to see it to believe it; **2.** *bei innerem Zwang: ich musste* (*einfach*) *lachen* I couldn't help laughing, I just had to laugh; *ich musste sie immerzu ansehen* I just had to go on looking at her, I couldn't take my eyes off her; *er muss immer alles wissen* he's always got to know about everything; **3.** *bei* (*sicherer*) *Annahme, in logischer Konsequenz:* must; *Vergangenheit:* must have; *er muss verrückt sein* he must be mad; *er muss es gewesen sein* it must have been him; *es muss nicht stimmen* it

doesn't have to be right; *ich muss es vergessen haben* I must have forgotten; *sie ~ bald kommen* they're bound to be here soon; *der Zug müsste längst hier sein* the train should have arrived long ago; *das musste ja passieren* that was bound to (*od.* just had to) happen; **4.** *im Konj. um e-n Wunsch auszudrücken: man müsste mehr Zeit haben* there ought to be more time, we ought to have more time (for that sort of thing); *Geld müsste man haben* if only we had plenty of money; *so müsste es immer sein* it should always be like this; *das müsste sie eigentlich wissen* she really ought to know that; **5.** *umg. verneint* (*dürfen*) *du musst doch nicht gleich die Wut kriegen* there's no need to go straight into a rage; *du musst nicht traurig sein* you mustn't be sad; **II.** *v/i.* **1.** (*hat gemusst*) have to; (*gezwungen werden*) *auch* be forced to; *bei innerer Überzeugung:* must; *ich muss!* I've got no choice; *muss ich* (*wirklich*)? do I (really) have to?; *er muss zur Schule* he has to go to school; *sie hat zum Chef gemusst* she had to go and see the boss; *ich muss mal* (*aufs Klo*) *umg.* I must go to the loo, *Am.* I have to go to the bathroom; *Kinderspr.* I need to do a wee; **2.** *umg.* (*an der Reihe sein*) *wer muss heute?* whose turn is it today?

Mußestunde *f* leisure hour; *in e-r ~* in a moment of leisure

Mussheirat *f umg.* shotgun wedding

müßig *geh.* **I.** *Adj.* idle; (*sinnlos*) useless, futile; (*Gedanken, Gerede*) idle; *es ist ~ zu* (+ *Inf.*) it's no use (+ *Ger.*), it's useless (+ *Ger.*); **II.** *Adv.:* **~ dabeistehen** stand idly by (and watch); **~ gehen** idle about, idle away one's time

Müßiggang *m; nur Sg.; geh.* idleness; *~ ist aller Laster Anfang Sprichw.* the devil finds work for idle hands, idle hands are the devil's tools; **Müßiggänger** *m; -s, -,* **Müßiggängerin** *f; -, -nen geh.* idler; **müßiggängerisch** *Adj. geh.* idle; **müßig gehen** → **müßig I**

musste *Prät.* → **müssen**

Mussvorschrift *f* mandatory provision

Mustang *m; -s, -s; Zool.* mustang

Muster *n; -s, -* **1.** (*Vorlage, Zeichnung*) pattern; *nach e-m ~ arbeiten* work from a pattern; **2.** *Wirts.* (*Probe*) sample, specimen; **3.** (*Verzierung*) pattern, design; **4.** (*Vorbild*) model; (*Beispiel*) example; *ein ~ an Tugend* a paragon of virtue; *nach dem ~ von* following the example of; *ein Justizwesen nach angelsächsischem ~* a justice system model(l)ed on the English one (*od.* along English lines); **~beispiel** *n* classic example (*für* of); **~betrieb** *m* model plant; **~brief** *m* specimen letter; **~buch** *n* **1.** *Wirts.* pattern book; *mit Proben:* samples folder; **2.** *Kunst hist.* artist's sketchbook; **~ehe** *f* perfect (*od.* ideal, model) marriage; **~exemplar** *n* **1.** sample, specimen; **2.** *Druck.* specimen copy; **3.** *bes. iro.* perfect example; **~fall** *m* model case; *weitS.* perfect (*od.* classic) example

mustergültig *Adj. und Adv.* → **musterhaft; Mustergültigkeit** *f* → **Musterhaftigkeit**

musterhaft I. *Adj.* exemplary, model …; **II.** *Adv.: sich ~ benehmen* behave impeccably, be on one's best behavio(u)r; **Musterhaftigkeit** *f* exemplari-

ness, model nature (+ *Gen.* of)

Muster|haus *n* showhouse, *Am auch* model (home); **~knabe** *m bes. iro.* paragon; *pej. umg.* goody-goody, goody-two-shoes; **~koffer** *m* sample case; **~kollektion** *f Wirts.* sample collection; **~land** *n* model country; **~leistung** *f auch iro.* brilliant achievement

mustern *v/t.* **1.** study, scrutinize; (*Truppen*) inspect, review; *j-n* (*von oben bis unten od. von Kopf bis Fuß*) *~* look s.o. up and down; **2.** (*Rekruten*) muster; *j-n ~* (*untersuchen*) examine s.o. for suitability, screen s.o.; *ärztlich:* give s.o. a medical; **3.** (*Stoff*) pattern; → **gemustert**

Muster|prozess *m Jur.* test case; **~schüler** *m,* **~schülerin** *f* model pupil (*Am.* student); (*Streber*) *umg.* swot, *Am.* grind; **~schutz** *m Jur., Wirts.* protection of registered designs; **~sendung** *f* package of samples

Musterung *f* **1.** inspection, scrutiny; *altm. von Truppen:* review; **2.** *von Rekruten:* mustering; (*Untersuchung*) screening; *ärztlich:* medical (examination); **3.** → **Muster** 3

Musterungsbescheid *m* notice to attend a recruiting board (*including a medical*)

Muster|vertrag *m* specimen contract; **~zeichnung** *f* pattern drawing

Mut *m; -(e)s, kein Pl.* **1.** (*Tapferkeit*) courage, bravery; (*Schneid*) pluck, *umg.* guts *Pl.;* (*Verwegenheit*) daring; *~ fassen* take heart; *für etw.:* pluck up courage; *j-m ~ machen* boost s.o.'s courage; (*auch j-m ~ zusprechen*) give s.o. a few words of encouragement; *j-m den ~ nehmen* dishearten s.o.; *den ~ verlieren od. sinken lassen* lose heart; *es gehört schon ~ dazu* it takes a bit of courage; *nur ~!* chin up!; *umg.* keep your pecker (*Am.* chin) up!; → **antrinken; 2.** *geh.:* **guten** *od.* **frohen ~es sein** be in good spirits; *mit frohem od. frischem ~* cheerfully; → **zumute**

mutabel *Adj. Bio., Genetik:* mutable

Mutagen [muta'ge:n] *n; -s, -e; Bio.* mutagen; **Mutant** *m; -en, -en,* **Mutante** *f; -, -en; Bio.* mutant; **Mutation** *f; -, -en* **1.** *Bio.* mutation; **2.** *Med.* (*Stimmwechsel*) breaking of the voice

Mütchen *n: sein ~ kühlen* let off steam; *sein ~ an j-m kühlen* take it out on s.o.

mutieren *v/i.* **1.** *Bio.* mutate; **2.** *er mutiert* (*gerade*) (*ist im Stimmbruch*) his voice is breaking

mutig *Adj.* brave, courageous; *umg.* gutsy; (*kühn*) bold; (*verwegen*) daring

mutlos *Adj.* disheartened; (*verzagt*) despondent; **Mutlosigkeit** *f* despondency; (*Verzweiflung*) despair

mutmaßen *vt/i.* (*untr., mutmaße, mutmaßte, hat gemutmaßt*) speculate, conjecture; (*vermuten*) surmise (*dass … that …*); **mutmaßlich** *Adj.* (*wahrscheinlich*) probable; *Täter:* suspected; *auch Vater:* presumed; *~er Terrorist auch* terrorist suspect; **Mutmaßung** *f auch Pl.* speculation, conjecture; (*Verdacht*) suspicion; *~en anstellen* speculate (*über* + *Akk.* about, on)

Mutprobe *f* test of courage

Muttchen *n* **1.** *in der Anrede:* Mummy, *Am.* Mommy; *iro.* Mummy dear, *Am.* Mommy dear; **2.** (*alte Frau*) little old lady, *umg.* old biddy

Mutter¹ *f; -, Mütter* **1.** mother (*auch Muttertier*); *werdende ~* expectant mother; *sie wird ~* she's expecting (*od.*

going to have) a baby; **~ sein** be a mother; **X, ~ von zwei Kindern, ...** X, a mother of two, ...; **als Frau und ~** as a wife and mother; *als Eigenname*: **wie bei ~(n)** *umg.* just like home; **es schmeckt wie bei ~(n)** *umg.* it tastes like mother's (*Am.* Mom's) cooking; **~ Gottes** *kirchl.* Mother of God; → *auch* **Muttergottes**; **~ Erde** *geh. fig.* mother earth; **~ Natur** *geh. fig.* mother nature; **2.** *Wirts.* parent (company)

Mutter² *f*; -, -*n*; *Tech.* (*Schraubenmutter*) nut

Mütterberatung *f* counsel(l)ing for expectant and nursing mothers; **Mütterberatungsstelle** *f* mother and baby clinic, *Am.* maternity center

Mutter|bild *n* *Psych.* mother image; **~bindung** *f* *Psych.* attachment (*od.* ties *Pl.*) to one's mother; **~boden** *m* *Agr.* topsoil; **~brust** *f* *geh.* mother's breast

Mütterchen *n* **1.** *Anrede*: mother (dear); **2.** *altes ~* little old lady, *umg.* old biddy

Mutter|erde *f* topsoil; **~ersatz** *m* substitute mother; **~freuden** *Pl.*: **~ entgegensehen** *geh.* be looking forward to becoming a mother; **~gefühle** *Pl.* motherly (*od.* maternal) feelings

Müttergenesungsheim *n* mothers' convalescent home

Mutter|gesellschaft *f* *Wirts.* parent company; **~gestein** *n* *Geol.* bedrock; **~gewinde** *n* *Tech.* female thread; **~glück** *n* joy(s *Pl.*) of motherhood

Muttergottes *f* *kath.* (Mary the) Mother of God; *m* (*Abbild*) Madonna

Mutterhaus *n* **1.** *kirchl.* training cent|re (*Am.* -er) for nurses and deaconesses; **2.** *Kloster*: mother house; **3.** *Wirts.* parent company

Mütterheim *n* maternity home

Mutter|herrschaft *f* matriarchy; **~herz** *n* motherly feelings *Pl.*; **~instinkt** *m* maternal (*od.* motherly) instinct(s *Pl.*); **~komplex** *m* *Psych.* mother fixation; **~konzern** *m* *Wirts.* parent group; **~korn** *n* *Bot.* ergot; **~kuchen** *m* *Med.* placenta (*Pl.* placentae *od.* placentas); **~land** *n* mother country; **~leib** *m* womb

mütterlich I. *Adj.* **1.** (*der Mutter eigen*) maternal; (*von s-r/i-r etc. Mutter*) his (*od.* her *etc.*) mother's; *Erbteil*: from his (*od.* her *etc.*) mother; **2.** (*fürsorglich*) motherly; **II.** *Adv.* like a mother; **~ umsorgen** *auch* mother s.o.; **mütterlicherseits** *Adv.* on one's mother's side; **Mütterlichkeit** *f* motherliness; *Instinkt*: maternal instincts *Pl.*

Mutterliebe *f* motherly love

mutterlos I. *Adj.* motherless, without a mother; **II.** *Adv.* without a mother

Mutter|mal *n* birthmark; **~milch** *f* mother's milk; **mit ~ genährt** breast-fed; **etw. mit der ~ einsaugen** *fig.* imbibe s.th. with one's mother's milk, learn s.th. from the cradle; **~mörder** *m*, **~mörderin** *f* matricide; **~mund** *m* *Anat.* uterine orifice, *fachspr.* os uteri

Mutterschaftsvertretung *f* maternity cover

Mutternschlüssel *m* *Tech.* spanner, *Am.* wrench

Mutter|pass *m* ante-natal (*Am.* prenatal) progress record, maternity record; **~pflichten** *Pl.* duties as a mother; **~recht** *n* *Völkerkunde*: matrilineal succession, *weitS.* matriarchy; **~rolle** *f* **1.** role of a mother; **2.** *Theat., Film etc.*: part of a (*od.* the) mother; **~sau** *f* *Agr.* mother sow; **~schaf** *n* *Agr.* mother ewe

Mutterschaft *f* motherhood

Mutterschafts|geld *n* *nur Sg.* maternity benefit; **~urlaub** *m* maternity leave

Mutter|schiff *n* *Naut., Raumf.* mother ship; **~schoß** *m* *geh.* (mother's) womb

Mutterschutz *m* legal protection for expectant and nursing mothers; *etwa* maternity legislation; **~gesetz** *n* maternity law

Mutterschwein *n* *Agr.* mother sow

mutterseelenallein *Adj.* all alone, all on one's own, *umg.* on one's tod

Muttersöhnchen *n* mummy's (*Am.* mamma's) boy *od.* darling; (*Weichling*) sissy

Muttersprache *f* mother tongue, native language; **Muttersprachler** *m*; -*s*, -, **Muttersprachlerin** *f*; -, -*nen*; *Ling.* native speaker; **muttersprachlich** *Adj.* native language ...; *Unterricht etc.*: in one's native language

Mutterstelle *f*: **~ vertreten bei j-m** be like a (*od.* a second) mother to s.o.

Müttersterblichkeit *f* maternal (*od.* childbirth) mortality

Mutter|tag *m* Mother's Day; **~tier** *n* *Zool.* dam; **~witz** *m* nous; (*Schlagfertigkeit*) native wit

Mutti *f*; -, -*s*; *umg.* mum(my), *Am.* mom(my); *als Anrede*: Mum(my), *Am.* Mom(my)

Mutwille *m*; *nur Sg.*; (*absichtliche Bosheit*) wil(l)fulness; **etw. aus ~n tun** do s.th. from sheer devilment; **mutwillig I.** *Adj.* wil(l)ful; *Zerstörung etc.*: *auch* wanton; **II.** *Adv.*: **~ beschädigen** *auch* vandalize; **Mutwilligkeit** *f* wil(l)fulness; *von Zerstörung etc.*: wantonness, wanton nature (+ *Gen.* of)

Mütze *f* cap; *aus Wolle*: wool(l)y hat, *Am.* stocking cap; **eins auf die ~ kriegen** *umg.* get told off; **e-e ~ voll**

Schlaf *umg. fig.* a little nap; **Mützenschirm** *m* peak (of a [*od.* the] cap)

MV *Abk.* → **Megavolt**

MW *Abk.* (**Megawatt, Mittelwelle**) MW

MwSt., Mw.-St. *Abk.* (**Mehrwertsteuer**) VAT

Myanmar (*n*); -*s*; *Geog.* Myanmar; **Myanmare** *m*; -*n*, -*n* Burmese, Burman; **die ~n** the Burmese; **Myanmarin** *f*; -, -*nen* Burmese *od.* Burman (woman *od.* girl); **myanmarisch** *Adj.* Burmese, Burman

Mykene (*n*); -*s*; *Geog., hist.* Mycenae; **mykenisch** *Adj.* Mycen(a)ean

Mykologie *f*; -, *kein Pl.* mycology; **mykologisch** *Adj.* mycological

Mykose *f*; -, -*n*; *Med.* mycosis (*Pl.* mycoses)

Myom *n*; -*s*, -*e*; *Med.* myoma (*Pl.* myomas *od.* myomata)

Myopie *f*; -, *kein Pl.* (*Kurzsichtigkeit*) myopia

Myriade *f*; -, -*n*, *mst Pl.*; *geh.* myriad

Myrrhe *f*; -, -*n* myrrh

Myrte *f*; -, -*n*; *Bot.* myrtle

Myrten|kranz *m* (bride's) myrtle wreath; **~zweig** *m* myrtle branch

Mysterien *Pl.* in der Antike: mysteries; **~spiel** *n* *Lit.* mystery (*od.* miracle) play

mysteriös *Adj.* mysterious

Mysterium *n*; -*s*, *Mysterien*; *mst Reli.* mystery

Mystifikation *f*; -, -*en* mystification; **mystifizieren** *v/t.* make a mystery of

Mystik *f*; -, *kein Pl.* mysticism; **Mystiker** *m*; -*s*, -, **Mystikerin** *f*; -, -*nen* mystic; **mystisch** *Adj.* **1.** *Symbol, Lehre etc.*: mystic; (*die Mystik betreffend*) mystical; **2.** (*geheimnisvoll*) mysterious; **Mystizismus** *m*; -, *kein Pl.* mysticism; **mystizistisch** *Adj.* ... related to mysticism, tending toward(s) mysticism

Mythe *f*; -, -*n*; *altm.* myth; **Mythenbildung** *f* creation of myths, myth-making; **mythisch** *Adj.* mythical; (*legendär*) legendary; *Helden etc.*: of myth and legend

Mythologie *f*; -, -*n* mythology; **mythologisch** *Adj.* mythological; **mythologisieren** *v/t.* mythologize

Mythos *m*; -, *Mythen* **1.** (*auch Unwahrheit*) myth; **2.** (*Legende*) *auch Person*: legend; **zu Lebzeiten zum ~ werden** become a legend in one's own lifetime, become a living legend

Myxomatose *f*; -, -*n*; *Vet.* myxomatosis (*Pl.* myxomatoses)

Myzel *n*; -*s*, *Myzelien*; *Bio.* mycelium (*Pl.* mycelia)

N, n *n*; -, -, *umg. auch* -s N, n; **N wie in Nordpol** Buchstabieren: "n" for (*od.* as in) "November" (*Am. auch* "Nancy" *od.* "Nora")

na *Interj.* well!; *überrascht, verärgert:* hey!; **~, ~!** come on (now), *Sl.* oy!; **~ also!, ~ bitte!** *triumphierend:* see?, there you are, what did I tell you?; **~ ja** well(, what can one say?); *verlegen:* well(, you know); **~ gut!, ~ schön!** all right; **~ gut** *konzessiv:* fair enough; **~, so was!** fancy that, *umg.* what do you know; **~ und?** so (what)?; **~ warte!** *drohend:* just you wait!; **~ endlich!** about time too; **~, wie geht's?** how are things, then?; **~, denn mal los!** let's get going, then!; **~ und ob!** *umg.* you bet!; → **nanu**

Nabe *f*; -, -n hub

Nabel *m*; -s, - navel; **~ der Welt** *fig.* cent|re (*Am.* -er) of the universe; **~bruch** *m Med.* umbilical hernia

nabelfrei *Adj.:* **ein ~es T-Shirt** a crop top

Nabel|schau *f umg.* navel gazing; **~ betreiben** do some navel gazing; *längerfristig:* be all bound (*od.* wrapped) up with o.s.; **~schnur** *f* umbilical cord; **die ~ durchtrennen** cut the umbilical cord; **~strang** *m* umbilical cord

Naben|dynamo *m Etech.* hub dynamo; **~kappe** *f* hub cap; **~schaltung** *f beim Fahrrad:* hub gear

nach I. *Präp.* **1.** *räumlich:* to; (*bestimmt ~*) for, bound for; *Richtung: auch* toward(s); **~ außen** outward(s); **~ rechts** to the right; **~ unten** down; *im Haus:* downstairs; **~ oben** up; *im Haus:* upstairs; **~ England reisen** go to England; **~ England abreisen** leave for England; **der Zug ~ London** the train to London; *das Schiff fährt ~ Australien* is bound for (*od.* is going to) Australia; **~ Hause** home; *das Zimmer geht ~ hinten/vorn hinaus* the room faces the back/front; *der Balkon geht ~ Süden* the balcony faces south; *Balkon ~ Süden* south-facing balcony; *wir fahren ~ Norden* we're travel(l)ing north (*od.* northward[s]); *bei bestimmten Verben: die Blume richtet sich ~ der Sonne* the flower turns toward(s) the sun; *~ dem Arzt schicken* send for the doctor; *~ dem Messer greifen* grab for the knife; **2.** *zeitlich:* after; *fünf (Minuten) ~ eins* five (minutes) past (*Am. auch* after) one; *~ zehn Minuten* ten minutes later; *~ einer Stunde von jetzt an:* in an hour('s time); *~ Ankunft/Erhalt* on arrival (receipt); **3.** *Reihenfolge:* after; *einer ~ dem anderen* one by one, one after the other; *der Reihe ~* in turn; *der Reihe ~!* take (it in) turns!, one after the other!; *der Größe ~* by (*od.* according to) size; **4.** (*entsprechend*) according to; → *auch gemäß I;* **~ dem, was er sagte** *auch* going by what he said; **~ Ansicht** (+ *Gen.*) in (*od.* according to) the

opinion of; **~ meiner Ansicht** *od.* **meiner Ansicht ~** in my opinion; **~ Gewicht verkaufen** sell by weight; **~ Bedarf** as required; **s-e Uhr ~ dem Radio** *etc.* **stellen** set one's watch by the radio *etc.;* **wenn es ~ mir ginge** if I had my way; **dem Namen ~** by name; **s-m Namen/Akzent** *etc.* **~** judging *od.* going by his name/accent *etc.;* **Rehbraten ~ Art des Hauses** roast venison à la maison; **sie kommt ganz ~ der Mutter** she's just like her mother; **~ Musik tanzen** *etc.:* to music; **~ Noten** from music; **~ Vorlage zeichnen** draw from a pattern; **eine Geschichte ~ dem Leben** a story taken from real life; **es ist nicht ~ i-m Geschmack** it's not to her taste; **riechen/schmecken ~** smell (taste) of; **~ s-r Weise** in his usual way; **~ Shakespeare** after Shakespeare; **frei ~ Heine** freely adapted from Heine; **~ bestem Wissen** to the best of one's knowledge; **~ Stunden** *etc.* **gerechnet** in (terms of) hours *etc.;* → *Ermessen, Meinung etc.;* **5. ~ j-m fragen** ask for s.o.; **die Suche ~ dem Glück** *etc.* the pursuit of (*od.* search for) happiness *etc.;* **II.** *Adv.* after; *mir ~!* follow me!; **~ und ~** gradually, bit by bit, *Am. auch* little by little; **~ wie vor** still, as ever

nachäffen *v/t.* (*trennb., hat -ge-*) ape, mimic, take off; *verbal: auch* parrot; **Nachäfferei** *f*; -, -en aping, mimicking; *verbal: auch* parroting

nachahmen *v/t.* (*trennb. hat -ge-*) imitate, copy; (*zum Vorbild nehmen*) (try to) emulate; → *auch nachäffen;* **nachahmenswert** *Adj.* exemplary; **~es Beispiel** example worth following (*od.* trying to follow); **Nachahmer** *m*; -s, -, **Nachahmerin** *f*; -, -nen imitator; **~ finden** be imitated (*od.* copied, emulated); **Nachahmung** *f* **1.** *nur Sg.* imitation; **2.** (*Imitation*) imitation, copy

Nachahmungstäter *m*, **~in** *f* imitator; **Nachahmungstrieb** *m Psych., Verhaltensforschung:* imitative instinct; **nachahmungswürdig** *Adj.* worthy of imitation

nacharbeiten (*trennb., hat -ge-*) **I.** *v/t.* **1.** (*nachholen*) make up (for); **2.** (*nachbilden*) copy; *im Herstellungsprozess:* finish; (*ausbessern*) touch up; **II.** *v/i.* (*Arbeitszeit etc. nachholen*) make up for lost time, catch up (on one's working hours); (*länger arbeiten*) work late

Nachbar *m*; -n *od.* -s, -n neighbo(u)r (*auch fig.*); *im Nebenhaus: auch* next--door neighbo(u)r; *im Klassenzimmer etc.:* person (*od.* girl, boy *etc.*) sitting next to one; → *spitz I 4*

Nachbar|dorf *n* neighbo(u)ring village; **~garten** *m* neighbo(u)rs' (*od.* neighbo[u]r's, neighbo[u]ring) garden (*bes. Am.* yard), garden (*bes. Am.* yard) next door; **~gebiet** *n* **1.** neighbo(u)ring area; **2.** *fig.* related discipline;

~grundstück *n* neighbo(u)ring property, property next door; **~haus** *n* house next door; **im ~** next door

Nachbarin *f*; -, -nen → *Nachbar*

Nachbar|insel *f* neighbo(u)ring island; *Pl. auch* islands round about; **~land** *n* neighbo(u)ring country

nachbarlich I. *Adj.* **1.** (*gut~*) neighbo(u)rly; **2.** *Garten etc.:* next-door ...; *nachgestellt:* next door; **II.** *Adv.:* **~ verkehren mit** be on (good) neighbo(u)rly terms with

Nachbar|ort *m* nearby village (*od.* town, place); **~recht** *n Jur.* regulations restricting a person's influence to his or her own property and protecting the interests of his or her neighbo(u)rs

Nachbarschaft *f* **1.** *räumlich:* neighbo(u)rhood; (*Nachbarn*) neighbo(u)rs *Pl.;* (*Nähe*) vicinity; **2.** (*Verhältnis zwischen Nachbarn*): **sie pflegen (eine) gute ~** they try to be good neighbo(u)rs; **nachbarschaftlich** *Adj.* neighbo(u)rly; **Nachbarschaftshilfe** *f* **1.** neighbo(u)rly help; **2.** *Sozialwesen:* community aid

Nachbars|familie *f* family next door; **~frau** *f* lady next door; **~kind** *n* boy (*od.* girl) next door, *Pl.* children next door; **~leute** *Pl.* neighbo(u)rs, people next door

Nachbar|staat *m* neighbo(u)ring state; **~stadt** *f* neighbo(u)ring town; **~tisch** *m:* (**am**) **~** (at the) next table; **~volk** *n* neighbo(u)ring people *Sg.* (*od.* nation); **~wohnung** *f* neighbo(u)ring flat (*Am.* apartment), flat (*Am.* apartment) next door

Nachbau *m* copy, reproduction; **nachbauen** *v/t.* (*trennb., hat -ge-*) copy, reproduce

Nachbeben *n* aftershock

nachbehandeln *v/t.* (*trennb., hat*) **1.** *Med.* give s.o. *od.* s.th. follow-up treatment; *nach schwerem Eingriff: auch* give s.o. aftercare; **2.** *Tech. etc.* finish; (*ausbessern*) touch up; **Nachbehandlung** *f* **1.** *Med.* follow-up treatment; aftercare; **2.** *Tech. etc.* finishing work; touching-up

nachbekommen *v/t.* (*unreg., trennb., hat*) **1.** (*Essen*) get another helping (*od.* more helpings) of; **2.** (*Ersatzteile etc.*) get s.th. (later on), get hold of

nachberechnen *v/t.* (*trennb., hat*) recalculate

nachbereiten *v/t.* (*trennb., hat*); *Päd.* go over, revise; **Nachbereitung** *f* revision

nachbessern (*trennb., hat -ge-*) **I.** *v/t.* (*Haus*) do up; (*Farbe*) touch up; (*Schaden*) fix, repair; **II.** *v/i.* make repairs; *bei der Dachisolierung muss nachgebessert werden* the roof insulation needs repairing; **Nachbess(e)rung** *f von Schaden:* fixing, repairing; **die ~ der Farbe** touching up the paintwork; **Nachbesserungsklausel** *f Wirts.* clause that improves the terms of a contract

nachbestellen v/t. (trennb., hat) **1.** wiederholt: order some more of; Wirts. place a repeat order for; **2.** (nicht oder unvollständig Geliefertes) reorder; **Nachbestellung** f **1.** repeat order (+ Gen. for); **2.** reorder; → nachbestellen

nachbeten v/t. (trennb., hat -ge-); umg. pej. parrot; **Nachbeter** m, **Nachbeterin** f umg. pej. parrot

Nachbetrachtung f reflection

nachbezahlen (trennb., hat) **I.** v/t. pay for s.th. afterward(s) (od. later); (noch etwas) pay the rest; **II.** v/i. pay afterward(s) (od. later); **nachbezeichnet** Adj. Wirts. attr. following; nachgestellt: listed below

Nachbild n Opt. afterimage

nachbilden v/t. (trennb., hat -ge-) copy, reproduce; genau: replicate; **Nachbildung** f **1.** nur Sg.; Vorgang: copying, reproducing; exakt: replicating; **2.** Produkt: copy, reproduction; exakte: replica

nach|bleiben v/i. (unreg., trennb., ist -ge-) Dial. **1.** be left; **2.** (zurückbleiben) fall behind; **3.** → nachsitzen; ~blicken v/i. (trennb., hat -ge-): j-m ~ gaze after s.o., watch s.o. go etc.

Nachblüte f second flowering (auch fig.)

nachbluten v/i. (trennb., hat -ge-) start bleeding again; **Nachblutung** f Med. auch Pl. secondary bleeding

nachbohren v/i. (trennb. hat -ge-); umg. fig. probe, dig deeper; da muss ich mal ~ I'll have to do a bit of probing

Nachbörse f Fin., Wirts. after-hours market, kerb market; **nachbörslich** Adj.: ~er Handel after-hours market; die ~e Notierung the after-hours quotation

Nachbrenner m Flug. afterburner

nachbringen v/t. (unreg., trennb., hat -ge-) bring (od. take) s.th. later

nachchristlich Adj.: im ersten ~en Jahrhundert in the first century AD (od. A.D.)

nachdatieren v/t. (trennb., hat) antedate; **Nachdatierung** f antedating

nachdem Konj. **1.** zeitlich: after, when; ~ sie das gesagt hatte after she had said that, (after) having said that, after saying that; **2.** Dial. kausal: since, as, seeing as; **3.** je ~! it all depends; je ~, was er sagt depending on what he says

nachdenken v/i. (unreg., trennb., hat -ge-) think (über + Akk. about); ich werde darüber ~ I'll think about it, I'll think it over; denk mal nach think (hard); **Nachdenken** n thinking; (Überlegung) reflection; Zeit zum ~ brauchen need time to think (it over); nach einigem ~ after thinking about it, after giving it some thought

nachdenklich I. Adj. **1.** (gedankenvoll) pensive, thoughtful; (abwesend) lost in thought; ~es Gesicht thoughtful expression; j-n ~ machen od. stimmen set s.o. thinking; (stutzig machen) have s.o. wondering; er wurde ~ it had him thinking (stutzig: wondering); **2.** geh. thought-provoking; **II.** Adv.: ~ gestimmt pensive, thoughtful; **Nachdenklichkeit** f pensiveness; weitS. (Vorbehalt) reservations Pl., doubts Pl.

nachdichten v/t. (trennb., hat -ge-) (freely) adapt; **Nachdichtung** f (free) adaptation, free rendering

nachdrängen v/i. (trennb., hat -ge-) Menge etc.: push from behind; fig. build up

nachdrehen v/t. (trennb., hat -ge-) (Szene) reshoot

Nachdruck¹ m; nur Sg. (Betonung) stress, emphasis; ~ legen auf (+ Akk.) od. e-r Sache ~ verleihen stress, emphasize; mit ~ auf etw. hinweisen make a point of stressing s.th.; mit ~ für etw. eintreten press for s.th.

Nachdruck² m Druck. reprint; ~ verboten all rights reserved

nachdrucken v/t. (trennb., hat -ge-) reprint; wir müssen ~ we have to do a reprint

nachdrücklich I. Adj. emphatic; (beharrlich) insistent; (streng) firm; (ausdrücklich) explicit; ~e Warnung/Bitte urgent warning/plea; **II.** Adv. emphatically; etw. ~ empfehlen strongly recommend s.th.; etw. ~ dementieren strenuously deny; etw. ~ verlangen insist on s.th.; er riet ~ davon ab he strongly advised against it; **Nachdrücklichkeit** f emphasis; insistence; firmness; explicitness; urgency; → nachdrücklich

nachdunkeln v/i. (trennb., hat od. ist -ge-) darken, get darker

Nachdurst m umg. hum. (alcohol-induced) dehydration; ~ haben be dehydrated

nacheifern v/i. (trennb., hat -ge-): j-m ~ (strive to) emulate s.o., try to follow in s.o.'s footsteps; **nacheifernswert** Adj. präd. worth emulating

nacheilen v/i. (trennb., ist -ge-): j-m ~ hurry (od. run) after s.o.

nacheinander Adv. one after the other; zeitlich: auch in succession; drei Tage ~ three days running (od. in a row); kurz ~ in quick succession, at short intervals

nacheiszeitlich Adj. attr. post-glacial, post-Ice Age

nachempfinden v/t. (unreg., trennb., hat) **1.** (Gefühle etc.) understand; (Erlebnis etc.) imagine what s.th. is like; **2.** etw. ~ (+ Dat.) nachschaffend: model (od. base) s.th. on; e-r Sache nachempfunden sein auch be an adaptation of s.th.; **nachempfunden I.** P.P. → nachempfinden; **II.** Adj. Gefühl etc.: shared; Vergnügen, Erlebnis etc.: vicarious

Nachen m; -s, -; poet. boat; (Barke) barge; poet. bark, barque

nachentrichten v/t. (trennb., hat) pay later (zuzahlen: extra)

Nach|erbe m, ~erbin f Jur. reversionary heir, reversioner; ~erbschaft n Jur. inheritance by substitution

nacherleben v/t. (trennb., hat) relive

Nachernte f **1.** second harvest; **2.** (Nachlese) gleaning; konkret: gleanings Pl.

nacherzählen v/t. (trennb., hat) (wiedergeben) retell; Päd. give a summary of; (Film etc.) tell the story of; **Nacherzählung** f summary; retelling of a story (in one's own words); recall test

Nachf. Abk. → Nachfolger

Nachfahre m; -n, -n; geh. descendant

nachfahren (unreg., trennb.) **I.** v/i. (ist nachgefahren) follow on; j-m ~ follow s.o., im Auto etc.: auch drive after s.o.; **II.** v/t. (hat/ist) trace

nachfärben v/t. (trennb., hat -ge-) re-dye

nachfassen (trennb., hat -ge-) **I.** v/i. **1.** umg. (nachhaken) go into it; bei j-m ~ remind s.o. (wegen about); da muss ich mal ~ auch I'll have to (ring

[Am. call] up and) ask what's going on; **2.** umg. beim Essen: have (od. take) another helping; **3.** Sport, bes. Turnen: alter one's grip; (Ball erneut greifen) make a second attempt to grab the ball; **II.** v/t. umg. (Essen) have (od. take) another helping of, help o.s. to some more

nachfedern v/i. (trennb., hat -ge-) **1.** bes. Sport: in den Knien ~ bend one's knees on landing; **2.** (zurückfedern) spring back

Nachfeier f **1.** nach e-m Anlass: belated celebration; **2.** (zusätzliche Feier) additional celebration; **nachfeiern** v/t. (trennb., hat -ge-) celebrate s.th. later; auch catch up with the celebrations later

nachfinanzieren v/t. (trennb., hat) provide additional finance for; **Nachfinanzierung** f additional finance

Nachfolge f; nur Sg. succession; die ~ antreten succeed to the throne (od. title etc.); j-s ~ antreten succeed s.o.; in j-s ~ stehen geh. be successor to s.o.; ~kandidat m, ~kandidatin f successor candidate; ~konferenz f follow-up conference; ~modell n successor

nachfolgen v/i. (trennb., ist -ge-) (nachreisen etc.) follow on; j-m ~ follow s.o.; e-r Sache ~ follow (on from) s.th.; j-m im Amt ~ succeed s.o. in office; **nachfolgend I.** Part. Präs. → nachfolgen; **II.** Adj. subsequent; (jetzt ~) following; (sich ergebend) subsequent, ensuing, resulting; ~er Verkehr traffic coming from behind; die ~en Generationen later (zukünftig: auch future, coming) generations; im Nachfolgenden below

Nachfolge|organisation f successor organization; ~partei f successor party

Nachfolger m; -s, -, ~in f -, -nen successor

Nachfolge|regelung f regulations Pl. governing the succession; ~staat m Völkerrecht: successor state

nachfordern v/t. (trennb., hat -ge-) demand s.th. in addition; put in a claim for an extra ...; **Nachforderung** f additional demand (od. charge)

nachforschen v/i. (trennb., hat -ge-) investigate, inquire (od. look) into the matter; make inquiries (od. enquiries); **Nachforschung** f investigation, inquiry, enquiry; ~en anstellen od. betreiben → nachforschen

Nachfrage f **1.** (Erkundigung) inquiry, enquiry; danke der ~! mst hum., auch iro. kind of you to ask; **2.** Wirts. demand (nach for); starke/geringe ~ great/little demand; → Angebot 3; **3.** (Umfrage zum Wahlverhalten nach dem Wählen) exit poll; **nachfragen** (trennb., hat -ge-) **I.** v/i. **1.** bei j-m ~ ask s.o. (wegen about); bei e-m Amt etc. ~ ask at (wegen about), inquire at (about); **2.** einmal: ask again; mehrmals: ask repeatedly; **II.** v/t. Wirts. ask for

Nachfrage|rückgang m Wirts. drop (od. fall) in demand; ~schwäche f weak demand; ~schwankung f fluctuation in demand

Nachfrist f Jur. extension

nachfühlen v/t. (trennb., hat -ge-) understand; das kann ich dir ~ I know exactly how you (must) feel

nachfüllen vt/i. (trennb., hat -ge-) (etw. Leeres) refill; (etw. halb Leeres) top (Am. fill) up; darf ich (Ihnen) ~? can I top (Am. fill) you up again?; **Nachfüllpack** m Wirts. refill (pack)

Nachfürsorge *f schweiz. Med.* aftercare, follow-up treatment

Nachgang *m*: *im ~ bes. Amtsspr.* subsequently

nachgären *v/i.* (*reg. und unreg., trennb., hat od. ist -ge-*) ferment again; **Nachgärung** *f* secondary fermentation

nachgeben (*unreg., trennb., hat -ge-*) **I.** *v/i.* **1.** *Person*: give in (+ *Dat.* to), yield (to), relent; *j-m zu viel ~* be too soft with s.o.; **2.** *Material*: give; *Gemäuer etc.*: give way; *völlig*: collapse; **3.** *Wirts., Kurse, Preise*: drop; **II.** *v/t.*: *j-m* (*etw.*) *~ beim Essen*: give s.o. another helping (of s.th.); **III.** *v/t. fig.*: *einander nichts ~* (*ebenbürtig sein*) be equals, be just as good (*od.* bad *etc.*) as each other

nachgeboren *Adj.* **1.** posthumous; **2.** (*jünger*) younger; (*spät geboren*) late-born; **Nachgeborene** *m, f, -n, -n*; (*nach dem Tod des Vaters geborenes Kind*) posthumous child; (*Nachkömmling*) much younger child, *hum.* afterthought; *die ~n* future generations

Nachgebühr *f Post.* excess postage, (postal) surcharge

Nachgeburt *f Med.* afterbirth, placenta (*Pl.* placentae *od.* placentas); **nachgeburtlich** *Adj. Med.* postnatal, postpartum

nachgehen *v/i.* (*unreg., trennb., ist -ge-*) **1.** *j-m ~* follow (*od.* go after) s.o.; **2.** (*e-m Beruf*) pursue; (*Geschäften*) see to; (*s-n Neigungen*) indulge in; (*Vergnügen*) pursue; **3.** *fig.*: *j-m ~* (*im Gedächtnis haften*) linger in s.o.'s mind; (*verfolgen*) haunt s.o.; (*j-s Gewissen belasten*) prey on s.o.'s mind, *stärker*: weigh heavily on s.o.'s conscience; *die Sache geht ihm nach* he's haunted by it; *mir geht es ziemlich nach auch* I can't get it out of my mind, I can't stop thinking about it; **4.** (*e-m Vorfall etc.*) look into, follow s.th. up, investigate; **5.** *Uhr*: be slow; *jeden Tag zwei Minuten ~* lose two minutes a day

nach|gelassen I. *P.P.* → *nachlassen*; **II.** *Adj.* *Werk*: posthumous; **~gemacht I.** *P.P.* → *nachmachen*; **II.** *Adj.* (*gefälscht*) counterfeit; (*künstlich*) imitation ...; **~geordnet** *Adj.* subordinate

nachgerade *Adv.* **1.** (*praktisch*) virtually; (*fast*) almost; (*nichts anderes als*) absolutely; (*wirklich*) really; **2.** (*allmählich*) slowly, gradually

nachgeraten *v/i.* (*unreg., trennb., ist*): *j-m ~* take after s.o.

Nachgeschmack *m* aftertaste (*auch fig.*); *es hinterlässt e-n* (*unangenehmen*) *~ auch fig.* it leaves a bad taste in your mouth

nachgestellt I. *P.P.* → *nachstellen*; **II.** *Adj. Ling.* postpositive

nachgewiesenermaßen *Adv.* as has been prov|ed (*bes. Am.* -en) (*od.* shown); *er ist ~ ...* he has been prov|ed (*bes. Am.* -en) to be ...

nachgiebig *Adj.* **1.** (*weich*) soft; (*elastisch*) pliable, flexible; **2.** *Person*: compliant; (*weich*) soft; *Eltern etc.*: *auch* indulgent; **Nachgiebigkeit** *f* **1.** *e-r Sache*: flexibility, pliability; **2.** *e-r Person*: compliance; *von Eltern etc.*: *auch* indulgence

nachgießen *v/t.* (*unreg., trennb., hat -ge-*) (*Tee etc.*) pour (out) some more; *beim Kochen etc.*: add some more; *darf ich dir noch etwas Kaffee ~?* can I pour you some more coffee?, can I top you up again?

nachglühen *v/i.* (*trennb., hat -ge-*) continue to glow; **Nachglühen** *n*; *-s, kein Pl.* afterglow

nach|greifen *v/i.* (*unreg., trennb., hat -ge-*) *bes. Sport, Turnen*: alter one's grip; (*Ball erneut greifen*) make a second attempt to grab the ball; **~grübeln** *v/i.* (*trennb., hat -ge-*) brood (*über + Akk.* over); **~gucken** *v/i.* (*trennb., hat -ge-*) *umg.* → *nachsehen* I; **~haken** *v/i.* (*trennb., hat -ge-*) **1.** broach the subject again, go into it, do a bit of probing; *bei j-m ~* press s.o. (*in e-r Sache*: on); **2.** *beim Fußball*: tackle from behind

Nachhall *m* reverberation; *fig.* echo; **nachhallen** *v/i.* (*trennb., hat od. ist -ge-*) reverberate; *fig.* echo

nachhaltig I. *Adj.* **1.** lasting; *~er Geschmack* lingering aftertaste; *bei Wein*: long finish; **2.** *Öko., Energie, Rohstoffe*: sustainable; *e-e ~e Nutzung der natürlichen Ressourcen* a sustainable use of natural resources; **II.** *Adv.* **1.** (*lange Zeit*) for a long time; (*stark, tief*) strongly, deeply; *~ wirken* have a lasting (*od.* long-term) effect; *weitS. auch* make itself felt for a long time (*zukünftig*: to come); *j-n ~ beeindrucken auf Dauer*: leave a lasting impression on s.o.; (*sehr beeindrucken*) deeply impress s.o.; **2.** *Öko.* sustainably; *~ bewirtschaftete Naturflächen* sustainably managed expanses of natural landscape

Nachhaltigkeit *f Öko.* sustainability

nachhängen *v/i.* (*unreg., trennb, hat -ge-*) **1.** (*e-m Problem etc.*) dwell on; (*Träumen, Erinnerungen*) hang onto; **2.** (*nicht mitkommen*) lag behind; **3.** (*anhängen*): *j-m ~* stick to s.o.

nachhause *Adv.* *österr., schw.* (*nach Hause*) home; **Nachhauseweg** *m*: (*auf dem*) *~* (on the) way home

nachhelfen *v/i.* (*unreg., trennb., hat -ge-*) **1.** *auf Personen bezogen*: help (out); *j-m in etw. ~* help s.o. (out) with s.th., (*Nachhilfeunterricht geben*) *auch* coach s.o. in s.th., give s.o. private lessons in s.th.; *j-m od. j-s Gedächtnis ein wenig ~ umg. iro.* jog s.o.'s memory; **2.** *auf Sachen bezogen*: help things along; *mit zweifelhaften Mitteln*: use a trick or two; *den Dingen etwas ~* steer things in the right direction; *dem Glück ~* help fortune along the way, give fortune a helping hand

nachher *Adv.* **1.** afterward(s); (*später*) later (on); *bis ~!* see you later!; **2.** *umg.* (*womöglich*) perhaps

Nachhilfe *f* → *Nachhilfeunterricht*; **~lehrer** *m*, **~lehrerin** *f* coach, private tutor; **~schüler** *m*, **~schülerin** *f* private pupil; **~stunde** *f* private lesson; **~unterricht** *m* private lessons *Pl.*, coaching

Nachhinein: *im ~* afterward(s); (*rückblickend*) in retrospect, with hindsight; (*wenn es zu spät ist*) after the event

nachhinken *v/i.* (*trennb., ist -ge-*); *fig.* lag behind

Nachholbedarf *m Wirts. etc.* (unsatisfied) demand (*an + Dat.* for); *fig.* (unsatisfied) need (for); *großen ~ haben* have a lot of catching up to do, have to make up for lost time; **nachholen** *v/t.* (*trennb., hat -ge-*) **1.** fetch later; **2.** (*Versäumtes*) make up for; (*Schlaf, Lernstoff etc.*) catch up on; **Nachholspiel** *n Sport* rescheduled match (*od.* game)

Nachhut *f*; *-, -en* rearguard; *die ~ bilden auch fig.* bring up the rear

nachimpfen *v/t.* (*trennb., hat -ge-*) give s.o. a booster; **Nachimpfung** *f* booster, reinoculation

nach|jagen (*trennb.*) **I.** *v/i.* (*ist nachgejagt*) chase (after); run after; *fig.* (*dem Geld etc.*) chase after; **II.** *v/t.* (*hat*) (*j-m ein Telegramm etc.*) send after s.o.; **~jammern** *v/i.* (*trennb., hat -ge-*): *e-r Sache ~* mourn the loss of s.th., mourn after s.th.; **~karten** *v/i.* (*trennb., hat -ge-*); *umg.* reopen the subject; **~kaufen** *v/t.* (*trennb., hat -ge-*) *später*: buy afterwards; *zusätzlich*: buy in addition; (*Ersatzteile etc.*) buy replacements

Nachklang *m* **1.** echo (in one's ear); **2.** *fig. von Vergangenem*: reminiscence; (*Wirkung*) (after)effect

nachklingen *v/i.* (*unreg., trennb., ist -ge-*) echo; *auch fig. Worte*: linger, ring in one's ears; *lange ~ fig.* leave a deep impression (*in j-m* on s.o.), linger on (*in s.o.*['s mind])

Nachkomme *m*; *-n, -n* descendant; *ohne ~n sterben* die without issue *förm.*

nachkommen *v/i.* (*unreg., trennb., ist -ge-*) **1.** (*später kommen*) follow (on) later; **2.** (*folgen*) follow; **3.** (*Schritt halten*) keep up (+ *Dat.* with); **4.** (*e-m Wunsch, Befehl*) comply with; (*e-r Pflicht, e-m Versprechen*) fulfil(l), carry out; **5.** *Dial.*: *j-m ~* take after s.o.

Nachkommenschaft *f* descendants *Pl.*

Nachkömmling *m*; *-s, -e* **1.** → *Nachkomme*; **2.** (*Kind*) late arrival; *hum.* afterthought

Nachkontrolle *f* follow-up examination; **nachkontrollieren** *v/t.* (*trennb., hat*) check s.th. again (*od.* to make sure); *auch* do a double check

Nachkriegs|erscheinung *f* postwar phenomenon; **~generation** *f* postwar generation; **~jahr** *n* postwar year; *in den ersten ~en* in the first few years after the war; **~literatur** *f Lit.* postwar literature; **~zeit** *f* postwar era (*od.* years *Pl.*)

Nachkur *f Med.* period of convalescence (*following a health cure*)

nachladen *v/t./i.* (*unreg., trennb., hat -ge-*) reload; *Etech.* (*Akku*) recharge

Nachlass *m*; *-es, Nachlässe* **1.** (*Erbschaft*) estate; *literarischer ~* unpublished works; **2.** (*vom Preis*) discount (*auf + Akk.* on), reduction (on)

nachlassen (*unreg., trennb., hat -ge-*) **I.** *v/t.* **1.** (*lockern*) slacken; **2.** *etwas / 10 Dollar vom Preis ~* give a discount / a discount of $10; **3.** (*erlassen*): *j-m die Strafe ~* let s.o. off his (*od.* her) punishment; **4.** *Jägerspr.* (*Hund*) let loose; **5.** *Dial.* (*unterlassen*) stop; **II.** *v/i.* **1.** (*sich vermindern*) decrease, diminish; (*schwächer werden*) weaken; (*schlechter werden*) deteriorate; *Interesse*: flag; *Tempo*: slacken; *Wind*: drop; *Sturm, Regen*: let up; *Augen, Gesundheit etc.*: deteriorate, begin to fail; *Schmerz*: ease; *Wirkung*: wear off; *Fieber*: go down, abate *geh.*; *Person*: slack; *Leistung, Preise, Produktion etc.*: drop; *nicht ~!* no slacking!; *mein Gedächtnis lässt allmählich nach* my memory is (slowly) going; **2.** *Dial.* (*aufhören*) stop; **3.** *Jägerspr.* lay off; **Nachlassenschaft** *n geh.* estate; **Nachlasser** *m*; *-, -s*, **Nachlasserin** *f*; *-, -nen; Amtsspr.* person leaving an estate; (*Testator*) testator

Nachlass|gericht *n Jur.* probate court; **~gläubiger** *m*, **~gläubigerin** *f* creditor of the estate

nachlässig *Adj.* (*lässig*) careless, negligent; (*unordentlich*) slovenly, sloppy; (*gleichgültig*) indifferent; **nachlässigerweise** *Adv.* carelessly, negligently; in a slovenly (*od.* sloppy) way; indifferently; **Nachlässigkeit** *f* negligence, carelessness; slovenliness; → **nachlässig**

Nachlass|steuer *f* estate tax; **~verwalter** *m*, **~verwalterin** *f* executor

Nachlauf *m* **1.** *Chem.* tail; **2.** *Mot.* caster (angle); **nachlaufen** *v/i.* (*unreg., trennb., ist -ge-*) run after (+ *Dat. s.o. od. s.th.*); *umg.* (*e-m Mädchen*) chase (*od.* run, be) after; *fig.* (*dem Glück etc.*) chase after; **ich laufe ihm doch nicht nach!** *umg.* I'm not going to go running around after him!

nachleben *v/i.* (*trennb., hat -ge-*) (*e-m Vorbild etc.*) live up to, emulate; **Nachleben** *n* afterlife

nachlegen (*trennb., hat -ge-*) **I.** *v/t.*: *Kohle etc.*: **~** put some more coal *etc.* on; **II.** *v/i.* put some more coal (*od.* wood *etc.*) on (the fire); → *auch* **nachreichen** 2

Nachlese *f Agr.* gleaning; *konkret:* gleanings *Pl.*; *fig.* selection (of highlights), *literarische:* selection of previously unpublished works; **nachlesen** *v/t.* (*unreg., trennb., hat -ge-*) **1.** *Agr.* glean; **2.** *im Buch:* read (through); (*sich informieren*) read up on; (*nachschlagen*) check, look up

nachleuchten *v/i.* (*trennb., hat -ge-*) continue to glow; **Nachleuchten** *n*; *-s, kein Pl.* afterglow; *Phys.* luminescence

nachliefern *v/t.* (*trennb., hat -ge-*) send on (later), supply; **Nachlieferung** *f* later (*od.* additional) delivery

nachlösen *vt/i.* (*trennb., hat -ge-*) buy (a ticket) on the train *etc.* (*od.* at the other end)

nachm. *Abk.* → **nachmittags**

nachmachen *v/t.* (*trennb., hat -ge-*) **1.** copy (*j-m etw.* s.th. s.o. does); (*nachäffen*) imitate, mimic, *umg.* take off; (*fälschen*) forge; **das soll mir erst mal einer ~!** I'd like to see anyone do better; **so schnell macht ihm das keiner nach** he's hard to beat (when it comes to that); **2.** (*nachholen*) do (later); **~ müssen** still have to do

nachmalen *v/t.* (*trennb., hat -ge-*) **1.** copy; **2.** (*farblich verstärken*) paint over; **3.** *umg.:* **die Lippen/Augenbrauen ~** reapply one's lipstick / redraw one's eyebrows

nachmalig *Adj. altm.* later, subsequent

nachmessen *vt/i.* (*unreg., trennb., hat -ge-*) measure (again), check (the measurements of)

Nachmieter *m*, **~in** *f* new tenant; (*nächste[r] Mieter[in]*) next tenant; **sein ~** the person who took over his flat (*Am.* apartment); **ich muss e-n ~ suchen** I've got to find someone to take over the flat (*Am.* apartment)

Nachmittag *m* afternoon; **am ~** in the afternoon; **am späten ~** (in the) late afternoon; **heute ~** this afternoon; **nachmittägig** *Adj. attr.* afternoon; **nachmittäglich** *Adj.* afternoon ...; **nachmittags** *Adv.* in the afternoon(s), afternoons; **~ geschlossen** open mornings only

Nachmittags|kaffee *m* afternoon coffee; **~stunde** *f* hour of the afternoon; **zur frühen ~** in the early afternoon; **~unterricht** *m* afternoon lessons *Pl.*; **~vorstellung** *f* matinee

nachmustern *v/t.* (*trennb., hat -ge-*); *Mil.:* **j-n ~** give s.o. another medical examination; **Nachmusterung** *f Mil.*

further medical examination

Nachnahme *f*; *-, -n*; *Post., Wirts.* cash (*Am. auch* collect) on delivery (*Abk.* COD); **gegen** *od.* **per ~** COD, to be paid for on delivery; **per ~ schicken** send COD; **~gebühr** *f* COD charge; **~sendung** *f* COD delivery (*Wirts. auch* consignment)

Nachname *m* surname, last (*od.* family) name

nach|nehmen *v/t.* (*unreg., trennb., hat -ge-*) **1.** *sich* (*Dat.*) *etw.* **~** have (*od.* take) another helping of, have (*od.* take) some more; **2.** *Amtsspr.* charge *s.th.* COD; **~plappern** (*trennb., hat -ge-*) **I.** *v/t.* parrot, repeat; **II.** *v/i.* parrot

Nachporto *n Post.* excess postage, (postal) surcharge

nachprägen *v/t.* (*trennb., hat -ge-*) **1.** (*kopieren*) copy; *illegal: auch* forge, counterfeit; **2.** (*Münzen etc.*) mint more; **Nachprägung** *f* **1.** (*das Kopieren*) copying; forging; **2.** *Münze etc.:* copy; *illegal: auch* forgery, counterfeit

nachprüfbar *Adj.* verifiable; **Nachprüfbarkeit** *f* verifiability; **nachprüfen** *v/t.* (*trennb., hat -ge-*) **1.** check; (*untersuchen*) investigate; **2.** *Päd.* (*nochmals prüfen*) re-examine; (*später prüfen*) examine at a later date; **Nachprüfung** *f* **1.** check(ing); inspection; **2.** *Päd.* (*Wiederholungsprüfung*) re-examination; (*spätere Prüfung*) examination at a later date

nach|recherchieren (*trennb., hat*) *vt/i.* reinvestigate (*auch Fall, Thema etc.*); **~rechnen** *vt/i.* (*trennb., hat -ge-*) check

Nachrede *f*: **üble ~** malicious gossip; *Jur.* defamation (of character); *mündlich: auch* slander; **nachreden** *v/t.* (*trennb., hat -ge-*) repeat; *pej. gedankenlos etc.:* parrot, echo; **j-m etw. ~** say s.th. about s.o.; → *auch* **nachsagen**

Nachredner *m*, **~in** *f* follow-up (*od.* next) speaker

nachreichen *v/t.* (*trennb., hat -ge-*) **1.** (*Unterlagen etc.*) hand *s.th.* in (*od.* send *s.th.* on) later; **2.** *beim Essen:* serve some more

nachreifen *v/i.* (*trennb., ist -ge-*) carry on ripening

nach|reisen *v/i.* (*trennb., ist -ge-*) follow on (later), come on later; **j-m ~** join s.o. later; **~reiten** *v/i.* (*unreg., trennb., ist -ge-*) ride after (+ *Dat. s.o. od. s.th.*); **~rennen** *v/i.* (*unreg., trennb., ist -ge-*) → **nachlaufen**

Nachricht *f*; *-, -en* **1.** (*Meldung, Information*): (**e-e**) (a piece of) news *Sg.*; (*Botschaft, Mitteilung*) message; **die ~ vom Erdbeben** *etc.* (the) news of the earthquake *etc.*; **e-e gute/schlechte ~** good/bad news *Sg.*; **~ bekommen von** hear from; **die ~ bekommen, dass ...** be informed that ..., receive news of s.o. *od.* s.th. (+ *Ger.*); **e-e ~ hinterlassen** leave a message; **2.** *Pl.* (*Nachrichtensendung*) *Radio, TV:* news *Sg.*; **in den ~en** in (*TV* on) the news; **~en hören** listen to the news; **wir bringen** *od.* **Sie hören jetzt ~en** now here is the news

Nachrichten|agentur *f* news (*od.* press) agency, *Am. auch* wire service; **~austausch** *m* news exchange; **~beitrag** *m* news item

Nachrichtendienst *m* **1.** (*Geheimdienst*) intelligence service; **2.** *TV etc.* news service; **nachrichtendienstlich** *Adj. Mittel, Informationen, Aktivitä-*

ten: intelligence ...; *Karriere:* intelligence service ...

Nachrichten|magazin *n* news magazine; **~netz** *n* communications network; **~quelle** *f* news (*od.* information) source; **~redaktion** *f* newsroom; **~satellit** *m* communications satellite; **~sender** *m Radio, TV:* news station; *TV auch* news channel; **~sendung** *f* news broadcast (*od.* program[me]), *Am.* newscast; **~sperre** *f* news blackout; **e-e ~ verhängen** impose a ban on all news; **~sprecher** *m*, **~sprecherin** *f* newsreader, news presenter, *Am.* newscaster; **~studio** *n* news studio; **~technik** *f* communications engineering; **~übermittlung** *f* news transmission; **~wesen** *n*; *nur Sg.* communications *Pl.*; **~zentrale** *f* news cent|re (*Am.* -er)

nachrichtlich I. *Adj. attr.* news; **II.** *Adv.:* **das Schreiben geht ~ auch an Ihren Anwalt** *bes. Amtsspr.* your lawyer will also receive a copy of the letter

nachrücken *v/i.* (*trennb., ist -ge-*) **1.** move up (*auch fig.*); **2.** *Mil.* follow on; **3.** *Parl.:* **für j-n ~** take over s.o.'s seat in parliament; **Nachrücker** *m*; *-s, -*, **Nachrückerin** *f*;*-, -nen*; *Parl.* successor (to a *od.* the parliamentary seat)

Nachruf *m* obituary (**auf** + *Akk.* on); **nachrufen** (*unreg., trennb., hat -ge-*) **I.** *v/i.:* **j-m ~** call (*lauter:* shout) after s.o.; **II.** *v/t.:* **j-m etw. ~** call (*lauter:* shout) s.th. after s.o.

Nachruhm *m* posthumous fame; **nachrühmen** *v/t.* (*trennb., hat -ge-*): **ihm wird nachgerühmt, dass er ein guter Vermittler sei** he's said to be (*od.* credited with being, known as) a good mediator

nachrüsten (*trennb., hat -ge-*) **I.** *v/i.* *Mil.* stock up on arms, (try to) close the armaments gap; **II.** *v/t.* *Tech. etc.* retrofit; *weitS.* extend, expand; (*Computer etc.*) upgrade; **Nachrüstung** *f* stocking up on arms; retrofit; extending, expanding; upgrading; → **nachrüsten**; **Nachrüstungsbeschluss** *m hist.* decision to stock up on arms

nachsagen *v/t.* (*trennb., hat -ge-*) **1.** repeat; *pej. gedankenlos etc.:* parrot, echo; **2.** **j-m etw. ~** claim s.th. of s.o.; **j-m Schlechtes ~** speak badly (*od.* ill *förm.*) of s.o., cast a slur on s.o.; **j-m nur Gutes ~** not have a bad word to say about s.o.; **man sagt ihm nach, dass** he's said to (+ *Inf.*); **ihr wird Unehrlichkeit** *etc.* **nachgesagt** she's said to be dishonest *etc.*; **das lasse ich mir nicht ~!** I won't have that said of me; **ich lasse mir nichts ~** I won't have anyone speak badly of me

Nachsaison *f* low (*od.* off-peak) season

nachsalzen *vt/i.* (*unreg., trennb., hat -ge-*) add some more salt (to)

Nachsatz *m* **1.** additional (*od.* added) remark; *schriftlich: auch* postscript; **2.** *Ling.* final clause

nach|schauen *v/i.* (*trennb., hat -ge-*); *bes. südd., österr., schw.* → **nachsehen**; **~schenken** *vt/i.* (*trennb., hat -ge-*) pour some more (wine *etc.*) out; **darf ich** (**dir etwas Wein** *etc.*) **~?** can I pour you some more wine *etc.*?, can I top (*Am.* fill) you up again?; **~schicken** *v/t.* (*trennb., hat -ge-*) **1.** → **nachsenden**; **2.** *fig.* add; **~schieben** *v/t.* (*unreg., trennb., hat -ge-*) *umg.* add

Nachschlag *m* **1.** *beim Essen:* second helping; **2.** *Mus.* nachschlag

nachschlagen (*unreg., trennb., -ge-*) **I.** *v/t.* (*hat*) (*e-e Stelle, ein Wort*) look up; **II.** *v/i.* **1.** (*hat*) look *s.th.* (*od.* it) up; ~ *bei Shakespeare etc.* look *s.th.* (*od.* it) up in Shakespeare *etc.*; **2.** (*ist*): *j-m* ~ take after s.o.; **3.** (*hat*) *Sport, Fußball*: retaliate; **Nachschlagewerk** *n* reference book (*od.* work)

nachschleichen *v/i.* (*unreg., trennb., ist -ge-*): *j-m* ~ creep after s.o.; (*beschatten*) shadow s.o.

nachschleifen[1] *v/t.* (*unreg., trennb., hat -ge-*) *Tech.* regrind

nachschleifen[2] *v/t.* (*trennb., hat -ge-*) (*Schal etc.*) trail (along) behind one; (*schleppen*) drag (*od.* lug) (behind one); (*Bein*) drag

nachschleppen *v/t.* (*trennb., hat -ge-*) drag (*od.* lug) (behind one)

Nachschlüssel *m* duplicate key; (*Dietrich*) skeleton key

nach|schmecken *v/i.* (*trennb., hat -ge-*) have (*od.* leave) an aftertaste; **~schmeißen** *v/t.* (*unreg., trennb., hat -ge-*) *umg.* **1.** *j-m etw.* ~ throw s.th. after s.o.; **2.** *fig.*: *sie werden einem nachgeschmissen* they're ten a penny (*od.* dirt cheap); **~schminken** *v/t.* (*trennb., hat -ge-*): *j-n* ~ freshen up s.o.'s makeup; **~schneiden** *v/t.* (*unreg., trennb., hat -ge-*) recut; **~schnüffeln** *v/i.* (*trennb., hat -ge-*) snoop around; *j-m* ~ spy on s.o.; **~schreiben** *v/t.* (*unreg., trennb., hat -ge-*) *nach Diktat*: take down; (*abschreiben*) copy; *Päd.* (*Arbeit etc.*) do later; **~schreien** *v/t.* (*unreg., trennb. hat -ge-*): *j-m etw.* ~ shout s.th. after s.o.; **Nachschrift** *f* in Briefen: postscript (*Abk.* PS, P.S.)

Nachschub *m* **1.** *Mil.* supplies *Pl.*; (*Verstärkung*) reinforcements *Pl.*; **2.** *fig.* supply (**an** + *Dat.* of), supplies *Pl.* (of); **für** ~ **sorgen** keep the supplies coming (in); *an Arbeit*: make sure there's enough work to go (a)round; **~weg** *m* supply line

nachschulen *v/i.* (*trennb., hat -ge-*) do some further training; **Nachschulung** *f* **1.** further training; **2.** (*Kurs, Lehrgang*) further training course

Nachschuss *m* **1.** *Sport* shot on the rebound; **2.** *Wirts.* additional payment; **~pflicht** *f Wirts.* obligation to make additional payments; **~zahlung** *f Wirts.* additional payment

nachschwatzen *umg. pej.*, **nachschwätzen** *bes. südd. umg. pej. v/t.* (*trennb., hat -ge-*) parrot

nachschwingen *v/i.* (*unreg., trennb., hat -ge-*) **1.** *Saite etc.*: reverberate; **2.** *geh., fig. Gefühl*: linger

nachsehen (*unreg., trennb., hat -ge-*) **I.** *v/i.* **1.** (*nach etw. sehen*) go and see, (go and) have a look; *zur Sicherheit*: *auch* go and check (*od.* make sure); *da hätte ich als Erstes nachgesehen* that would have been the first place to look; **2.** *j-m* ~ gaze after s.o., follow s.o. with one's gaze; *beim Weggehen*: watch s.o. go; *e-m Auto etc.* ~ follow *s.th.* with one's gaze; *beim Wegfahren etc.*: watch *s.th.* leave (*od.* fly off *etc.*); **3.** → *nachschlagen* II 1; **II.** *v/t.* **1.** (*prüfen*) examine, inspect; (*kontrollieren*) check; (*Schulhefte*) correct; **2.** *j-m s-e Fehler etc.* ~ overlook (*od.* turn a blind eye to) s.o.'s mistakes *etc.*

Nachsehen *n*: *das* ~ *haben* lose out; (*nichts bekommen*) *auch* go away empty-handed; *ihm blieb* (*nur*) *das* ~ he was left empty-handed

Nachsende|anschrift *f* forwarding address; **~antrag** *m Post.* application to have mail forwarded; *Formular*: form for applying to have mail forwarded

nachsenden *v/t.* (*unreg., trennb., hat -ge-*) **1.** *bes. Post.* (*weiterleiten*) send on, forward; *bitte* ~! please forward; **2.** *später*: send on (later)

nachsetzen *v/i.* (*trennb., hat -ge-*): *j-m* ~ go (*od.* run) after s.o., chase (after) s.o., be after s.o., be at s.o.'s heels

Nachsicht *f* forbearance; (*Geduld, Toleranz*) patience, tolerance; (*Milde*) leniency; ~ *üben* be lenient; *mit* ~ *behandeln* show (some) leniency toward(s), make allowances for, not be too hard on; *da kenn ich keine* ~ I have no sympathy for that sort of thing; **nachsichtig** *Adj.* indulgent (*gegenüber* toward(s), with), forbearing *förm.*; (*geduldig, tolerant*) patient (with), tolerant (toward[s]); **Nachsichtigkeit** *f* forbearance; (*Geduld, Toleranz*) patience, tolerance; **nachsichtsvoll** *Adj.* → *nachsichtig*

Nachsilbe *f Ling.* suffix

nach|singen *v/t.* (*unreg., trennb., hat -ge-*) sing *s.th.* (*after hearing it first*); **~sinnen** *v/i.* (*unreg., trennb., hat -ge-*) *geh.* reflect (*über* on), muse (over, on), ponder (over, on); **~sitzen** *v/i.* (*unreg., trennb., hat -ge-*) *Schule*: be kept in, have detention; *j-n* ~ *lassen* give s.o. detention; ~ *müssen* be kept in, have detention

Nachsommer *m* late (*od.* Indian) summer

Nachsorge *f Med.* aftercare

Nach|spann *m*; -(*e*)*s*, -*e od.* Nachspänne *Film, TV*: credits *Pl.*; **~speise** *f* → *Nachtisch*; **~spiel** *n* **1.** *Theat.* epilog(ue); *Mus.* postlude; **2.** *fig.* sequel (*to*); *es hatte ein* ~ there was a sequel (to it); *die Sache wird noch ein* ~ *haben* the matter won't rest at that, there are bound to be consequences; *ein gerichtliches* ~ *haben* result in court proceedings; **3.** *sexuelles*: afterplay

nachspielen (*trennb., hat -ge-*) **I.** *v/t. Mus.* play; *j-m etw.* ~ play s.th. after s.o.; *auf gleiche Weise*: play s.th. like s.o.; *engS.* copy s.th. from s.o.; **II.** *v/i. Sport* play time; ~ *lassen* add time on for injuries

Nachspielzeit *f Sport, wegen Unterbrechungen*: stoppage time; *wegen Verletzungen*: injury time

nach|spionieren *v/i.* (*trennb., hat*) spy (*j-m* on s.o.); **~sprechen** (*unreg., trennb., hat -ge-*) **I.** *v/t.* repeat (*j-m etw.* what s.o. has just said); **II.** *v/i.*: *sprechen Sie mir nach* repeat after me; **~springen** *v/i.* (*unreg., trennb., ist -ge-*): *j-m* ~ jump after s.o.; **~spülen** (*trennb., hat -ge-*) **I.** *v/t.* **1.** rinse; **2.** *umg.*: *er spülte mit einem Bier nach* he washed it down with a beer; **II.** *v/i.* **1.** rinse; *im Abfluss*: run water down the sink *etc.*; **2.** *umg.* wash everything (*od.* it) down (*mit* with); **~spüren** *v/i.* (*trennb., hat -ge-*) **1.** *j-m* ~ (*folgen*) follow (*od.* shadow) s.o.; (*nachspionieren*) spy on s.o.; **2.** *e-m Problem, Verbrechen etc.*: look into, investigate; *e-m Geheimnis etc.*: try to get to the bottom of

nächst *Präp.* next to, close to; *fig. im Rang etc.*: after

nächst... **I.** *Adj. Reihenfolge, Zeit*: next; (*nächstgelegen*) nearest; (*am*) **~en Sonntag** next Sunday, *Brit. auch* Sunday next; *am* ~*en Tag* the next (*od.* following) day; *Fälligkeit*: *aus* ~*er Entfernung* at close range; *bei* ~*er od. bei der* ~*en Gelegenheit* as soon as I get

(*od.* he gets *etc.*) a chance, at the next best opportunity; *im* ~*en Augenblick* the next minute; *in den* ~*en Tagen* in the next few days; *in* ~*er Zeit* (some time) soon; ~*es Mal od. das* ~*e Mal od. beim* ~*en Mal* next time; *die* ~*en Verwandten* s.o.'s nearest relatives; **II.** *substantivisch*: *der, die, das Nächste* the next one (*od.* person, thing *etc.*); *was kommt als Nächstes?* what's next (on the agenda)?; *als Nächstes wird der Keller aufgeräumt* we *etc.* are going to tidy (*Am.* clean up) the cellar next; *der Nächste, bitte!* next, please!; *du bist als Nächster dran* it's your turn next, you're next; **III.** *Adv.*: *am* ~*en* nearest; *j-m am* ~*en stehen* be nearest to s.o.('s heart); *e-r Sache am* ~*en kommen* come closest to s.th.

nachstarren *v/i.* (*trennb., hat -ge-*): *j-m* ~ stare after s.o.

nächstbesser... *Adj.* next best

nächstbest... **I.** *Adj.* next best; (*irgendein*) *auch umg.* any old; *ins* ~*e Restaurant etc. gehen auch* go into the first restaurant *etc.* one happens to find (*od.* come across); *bei der* ~*en Gelegenheit* at the next opportunity, as soon as I *etc.* get a chance; **II.** *substantivisch*: *ich sprach den Nächstbesten an und fragte ...* I spoke to the first one I happened to find (*od.* came across) and asked ...

Nächste *m*; -*n*, -*n*; *geh.* (*Mitmensch*) fellow human being; *bibl.* neighbo(u)r; *jeder ist sich selbst der* ~ charity begins at home; *die Liebe zum* ~*n* love for one's neighbo(u)r; *du sollst deinen* ~*n lieben wie dich selbst bibl.* thou shalt love thy neighbo(u)r as thyself

nachstehen *v/i.* (*unreg., trennb., hat -ge-*): *keinem* ~ be second to none; *sie steht ihm in nichts nach* she can take him on any time; **nachstehend** **I.** *Part. Präs.* → *nachstehen*; **II.** *Adj.* following; *siehe* ~*e Beschreibung* see description below; *im Nachstehenden* below

nachsteigen *v/i.* (*unreg., trennb., ist -ge-*) **1.** *j-m* ~ climb (up) after s.o.; **2.** *umg.*: *e-m Mädchen etc.* ~ be (*od.* run) after a girl *etc.*

nachstellen **I.** *v/t.* **1.** *Tech.* (*justieren*) (re)adjust, reset; (*Uhr*) put (*Am.* turn) back; **2.** *Ling.* place after *s.th.*; *ein nachgestelltes Attribut* a postpositive attribute; **3.** (*Vorfall, Szene etc.*) reconstruct; **II.** *v/i.*: *j-m* ~ be after s.o., chase s.o.; *e-m Tier*: hunt; **Nachstellung** *f* **1.** *Tech.* (re)adjustment; **2.** *Ling.* postposition; **3.** *mst Pl.* (*Verfolgung*) persecution; (*Annäherungsversuche*) advances *Pl.*

Nächstenliebe *f* charity

nächstens *Adv.* soon, before long, shortly; (*das nächste Mal*) (the) next time; ~ *heiratet er sie noch! umg.* he'll be marrying her next (*od.* before we know it)

nächst|folgend *Adj.* following, next; **~gelegen** *Adj.* nearest; **~größer** *Adj.*: *das* ~*e Modell etc.* the next sized model *etc.* up; *Mary ist die Größte mit 1,58 m,* ~ *ist dann Sandra mit 1,47 m* Mary is the tallest at 1.58 m, next (tallest) is Sandra at 1.47 m; *der* (*od.* die, das) *Nächstgrößere* the next size up; **~höher** *Adj.* next ... up; **~jährig** *Adj.* next year's; **~liegend** *Adj.* nearest; *das Nächstliegende fig.* (*das Einleuchtendste*) the (most) obvious thing (to do *etc.*); *nach Priorität*: the next thing (to do *etc.*); **~möglich** *Adj.* next possible; *zeitlich*: *auch* earliest possible; **zum ~en Termin** at the earliest possible date, as soon as possible

nach|stoßen *v/i.* (*unreg., trennb., -ge-*) **1.** (*ist*); *bes. Mil.* move up from behind; **2.** (*hat*); *umg.* follow up; **~streben** *v/i.* (*trennb., hat -ge-*); *geh. e-r Sache*: strive after, aspire to; *e-m Vorbild*: emulate; **~strömen** *v/i.* (*trennb., ist -ge-*) **1.** *Wasser, Gas etc.*: come gushing (out) after; **2.** *fig. Menschen etc.*: follow in their hundreds (*od.* thousands); **~stürzen** *v/i.* (*trennb., ist -ge-*) **1.** *umg.* (*nachrennen*) rush after; **2.** *Steine, Erdmassen etc.*: *j-m* ~ plunge down after s.o.; **~suchen** *v/i.* (*trennb., hat -ge-*) **1.** have a (good) look, look and see; **2.** *geh.*: **um etw.** ~ apply for s.th.

Nachsynchronisation *f* TV, Film: post-dubbing, *umg.* post-sync; **nachsynchronisieren** *v/t.* (*trennb., hat*) (*Film*) post-dub, *umg.* post-sync

Nacht *f*; -, *Nächte* **1.** night; *diese* ~ tonight; *heute* ~ (*letzte* ~) last night; (*kommende* ~) tonight; *gestern* ~ last night; *in der* ~ *auf Montag* during Sunday night, Sunday during the night; *in der* ~ *vom 2. auf den 3. Mai* during the night of 2nd to 3rd May; *bei* ~ at night; *gute* ~*!* (*schlafe gut*) good night!; *wenn das stimmt - na dann, gute* ~*! umg.* if that's the case - well, that's that!; *im Schutze der* ~ under cover of darkness; *bis tief in die* ~ until (*od.* right into) the small hours (of the night); *in finsterer* ~ in the dead of night; *die ganze* ~ (*hindurch*) all night (long); *über* ~ overnight (*auch fig.*); *es wird* ~ it's getting dark; *zu(r)* ~ *essen südd., österr.* have one's evening meal; **2.** *in Wendungen*: *bei* ~ *und Nebel fig.* (*heimlich*) like a thief in the night; *hässlich wie die* ~ ugly as sin; *sich* (*Dat.*) *die* ~ *um die Ohren schlagen* stay up all night; → *mitten, schwarz* I 1

nachtaktiv *Adj. Zool.* nocturnal.

nachtanken (*trennb., hat -ge-*) **I.** *v/i.* fill up (the tank), get some more petrol (*Am.* gas); **II.** *v/t.*: **10 Liter** ~ put in another 10 lit|res (*Am.* -ers), put another 10 lit|res (*Am.* -ers) in the tank

Nacht|arbeit *f nur Sg.* night work, night shift(s *Pl.*); **~asyl** *n* night shelter; **~ausgabe** *f* late edition; **~bar** *f* → *Nachtlokal*; **~beleuchtung** *f* dimmed lights *Pl.* (*od.* lighting)

nachtblau *Adj.* midnight blue

nachtblind *Adj.* night blind; **Nachtblindheit** *f* night blindness

Nacht|creme *f Kosmetik*: night cream; **~dienst** *m* night duty (*od.* shift); ~ *haben Apotheke etc.*: be open all night; (*Schichtdienst haben*) be on night duty (*od.* shift)

Nachteil *m* disadvantage (*an* + *Dat.* of); (*Mangel*) *auch* drawback, shortcoming; *Sport, fig.* handicap; *die Sache hat nur einen* ~ there's just one disadvantage in it; *im* ~ *sein* be at a disadvantage (*j-m gegenüber* compared with s.o.); *von* ~ *sein* be disadvantageous, be a disadvantage; *zum* ~ *von* to the detriment of; *sich zu s-m* ~ *verändern* change for the worse; *e-r Sache zum* ~ *gereichen geh.* be to the detriment of s.th.; *dadurch entstehen uns nur* ~*e* it will only bring us disadvantages; *es soll nicht dein* ~ *sein* it won't be to your disadvantage, you

only stand to gain by it

nachteilig I. *Adj.* disadvantageous; (*schädlich*) detrimental; **~e Folgen** negative consequences; **II.** *Adv.*: ~ *beeinflussen od. sich* ~ *auswirken auf* have a detrimental (*od.* an adverse) effect on

Nachteinsatz *m Mil.* night mission, night(time) operation

nächtelang I. *Adj.*: **~e Gespräche** *etc.* night after night of discussion(s) *etc.*; **II.** *Adv.* for nights on end, night after night

nachten *v/i., unpers.*; *schw., poet.* grow dark

nächtens *Adv. geh.* at night

Nacht|essen *n südd., österr. schw.* → *Abendessen*; **~eule** *f umg. fig. hum.* night owl; **~express** *m Eisenb.* night (*od.* nighttime) express

Nacht|fahrt *f* nighttime journey, journey by night; *Pl.* mit dem Auto: driving at night, nighttime driving; **~fahrverbot** *n* ban on nighttime driving

Nachtfalter *m* **1.** *Zool.* moth; **2.** *umg. fig. hum.* (*Person*) night owl

Nachtflug *m* night flight; *Pl. auch* night flying *Sg.*; **~verbot** *n* ban on nighttime flying

Nachtfrost *m* night(time) frost; **strenger** ~ *Met.* severe overnight frost; **~gefahr** *f* possible nighttime frost

Nacht|gebet *n* evening prayer; *bes. für Kinder*: bedtime prayer; **~gespenst** *n* ghost; **~gewand** *n geh., auch hum.* nightdress; **~hemd** *n* nightdress, *umg.* nightie; (*für Männer*) nightshirt; **~himmel** *m nur Sg.* night sky, sky at night

Nachtigall *f*; -, -en; *Orn.* nightingale; ~, *ich* (*Dial.*: *ick*) *hör dir trapsen umg.* I get the picture (now); *engS.* so that's what he's *etc.* after(, is it?); **Nachtigallenschlag** *m* song of the nightingale

nächtigen *v/i.* spend the night; → *auch* **übernachten**; **Nächtigung** *f österr.* overnight stay

Nachtisch *m* dessert, *Brit. auch* sweet, pudding, *umg.* afters *Sg.*

Nacht|kasten *m*, **~kästchen** *n südd., österr.* bedside table, *Am.* nightstand; → *Nachttisch*; **~kerze** *f Bot.* evening primrose; **~klub** *m* night club; **~kühle** *f* cool of the night; **~lager** *n* place to sleep, place for the night; (*Bett*) bed; (*Biwak*) bivouac; **~leben** *n e-r Stadt etc.*: night life; *e-r Person*: *auch* nighttime activities *Pl.*

nächtlich *Adj.* nightly, nocturnal; **~e Ausgangssperre** dusk-to-dawn (*od.* nighttime) curfew; **~e Ruhestörung** nighttime disturbance(s *Pl.*); **~es Treiben** *e-r Person*: night life, nighttime (*iro.* nocturnal) activities *Pl.*; *e-r Stadt etc.*: bustling night life

Nacht|lokal *n* night club, *Am. auch* nightspot; **~luft** *f* night air

Nachtmahl *n österr., sonst geh.* evening meal; **nachtmahlen** *v/i.*; *nachtmahlt, nachtmahlte, hat genachtmahlt; österr.* have one's evening meal

Nacht|marsch *m Mil.* night march; **~mensch** *m* night owl *umg.*; **~mette** *f kirchl.* midnight mass; **~musik** *f Mus.* serenade; *Eine kleine* ~ A Little Serenade (*od.* Night Music), Eine Kleine Nachtmusik

nachtönen[1] *v/i.* (*trennb., hat -ge-*) echo, linger; → *auch* **nachklingen**

nachtönen[2] *v/t.* (*trennb., hat -ge-*) *farblich*: retint

Nacht|pfleger *m* night nurse; **~portier**

m night porter; **~programm** *n Radio etc.*: nighttime program(me)s *Pl.*; **~quartier** *n* place for the night

Nachtrag *m*; -(e)s, *Nachträge* supplement, addendum (*Pl.* addenda); *in e-r Rede, Diskussion etc.*: additional comment; (*Postskriptum*) postscript; (*Anhang*) appendix *ich hätte noch e-n* ~ *zu dem, was X sagte* may I add something to what X said

nachtragen *v/t.* (*unreg., trennb., hat -ge-*) **1.** *j-m etw.* ~ (*hinterhertragen*) carry s.th. behind s.o.; (*nachträglich bringen*) go after s.o. with s.th.; **2.** *fig.*: *j-m etw.* ~ hold s.th. against s.o., bear s.o. a grudge for s.th.; **3.** *schriftlich*: add (later); (*ergänzend bemerken*) add; *es bleibt noch nachzutragen, dass* ... it should be added that ...

nachtragend I. *Part. Präs.* → *nachtragen*; **II.** *Adj.* unforgiving, resentful

nachträglich I. *Adj.* (*ergänzend*) additional, supplementary; (*später*) later; (*verspätet*) belated; **II.** *Adv.* (*hinterher*) afterward(s); (*später*) later; ~ *herzliche Glückwünsche* belated best wishes

Nachtrags|... *im Subst.* additional, supplementary; **~haushalt** *m Pol.* supplementary budget

nachtrauern *v/i.* (*trennb., hat -ge-*) mourn (+ *Dat. s.o. od. s.th.*); *ihm wird keiner* ~ they *etc.* won't be sorry to see him go, *umg.* they'll *etc.* be glad to see the back of him

Nachtruhe *f* **1.** sleep; *j-s* ~ *stören* disturb s.o.'s sleep; **2.** nighttime peace; *die* ~ *einhalten* keep the peace at night

nachts *Adv.* at night, during the night, in the night; *um ein Uhr* ~ (at) one o'clock at night (*od.* in the morning); *dienstags* ~ (on) Tuesday nights

Nachtschattengewächs *n Bot.* solanum (*Pl.* Solanaceae)

Nachtschicht *f* night shift; ~ *haben* be on night shift

nachtschlafend *Adj.*: *zu* ~*er Zeit umg.* in the middle of the night

Nacht|schränkchen *n* → *Nachttisch*; **~schwärmer** *m* **1.** *Zool.* moth; **2.** *fig. hum.* (*Person*) night owl; **~schwester** *f* night nurse; **~seite** *f Astron.* nightside; *auch fig.* dark side

Nachtsichtigkeit *f Med.* scotopia, night vision

Nacht|speicherofen *m* (night) storage heater; **~strom** *m* off-peak electricity; **~stunde** *f*; *mst Pl.* hour of the night; *während der* ~*n* during the night

nachtsüber *Adv.* during (*od.* in) the night

Nacht|tarif *m* off-peak (*od.* cheap) rates *Pl.*; **~taxi** *n* night taxi (*for women*); **~tier** *n* nocturnal animal

Nachttisch *m* bedside table, *Am.* nightstand; **~lampe** *f* bedside lamp

Nacht|topf *m* chamber pot, *Brit. auch* jerry *umg.*; *für Kinder*: potty *umg.*; **~tresor** *m* night safe; **~übung** *f bes. Mil.* night(time) exercise

nachtun *v/t.* (*unreg., trennb., hat -ge-*) *umg.* → *nachmachen* 1

Nacht|-und-Nebel-Aktion *f* (dawn) swoop (*od.* raid), nighttime raid; **~vogel** *m* **1.** *Orn.* nocturnal bird; **2.** *umg. fig. hum.* (*Person*) night owl; **~vorstellung** *f* late-night show (*od.* performance); **~wache** *f* night watch (*auch Person*); *im Krankenhaus etc.*: night duty; **~wächter** *m* night watchman (*auch hist.*); *umg., pej.* twit, dope

nachtwandeln *v/i.* (*untr., hat od. ist genachtwandelt*) → *schlafwandeln*

Nachtwanderung *f* nighttime walk

Nachtwandler *m*; *-s*, *-*, **~in** *f*; *-*, *-nen* → **Schlafwandler**; **nachtwandlerisch** *Adj.* somnambulistic; → *auch* **schlafwandlerisch**

Nacht|zeit *f* night(time); **zur ~** at night; **~zeug** *n umg.* overnight things *Pl.*; **~zug** *m* (over)night train; **~zuschlag** *m für eigene Arbeit*: nighttime bonus; *für Dienstleistungen*: nighttime surcharge

nachuntersuchen *v/t.* (*trennb.*, *hat*) give *s.o.* a further checkup, do a further checkup on *s.o.*; **Nachuntersuchung** *f* follow-up check, further checkup

nachveranlagen *v/t.* (*trennb.*, *hat*) *Steuerwesen*: assess *s.o.* further; **Nachveranlagung** *f* supplementary assessment

nachverhandeln *v/i.* (*trennb.*, *hat*) negotiate further; **Nachverhandlung** *f* further negotiations *Pl.*

nachversichern *v/t.* (*trennb.*, *hat*) *in der Rentenversicherung*: pay in retrospective contributions; *von Sachwerten*: take out supplementary insurance on; **Nachversicherung** *f* payment of retrospective contributions; supplementary insurance

nachversteuern *v/t.* (*trennb.*, *hat*) *Steuerwesen*: pay supplementary tax on

nachvollziehbar *Adj.* understandable; **das ist für mich nicht ~** I can't understand it, it's beyond me; **nachvollziehen** *v/t.* (*unreg.*, *trennb. hat*) re-enact (in one's mind); (*verstehen*) understand; (*Tat etc.*) *auch* fathom; **ich kann das nicht ~** *auch* it's beyond me; → *auch* **nachvollziehbar**, **Nachvollzug** *m* understanding, fathoming

nachwachsen *v/i.* (*unreg.*, *trennb.*, *ist -ge-*) grow again; **nachwachsend** **I.** *Part. Präs.* → **nachwachsen**; **II.** *Adj.*: **die ~e Generation** the up-and-coming (*od.* rising, *bes. Am.* upcoming) generation; **~e Rohstoffe** renewable raw materials

Nach|wahl *f bes. Parl.* by-election; **~wehen** *Pl.* afterpains; *geh. fig.* painful consequences (*od.* aftermath *Sg.*)

nachweinen *v/i.* (*trennb.*, *hat -ge-*) cry over the loss of; **wir weinen ihm keine Träne nach** we don't shed any tears over him

Nachweis *m*; *-es*, *-e* proof (**für**, **über** + *Akk.* of), evidence (of, *Theorie etc.*: for); (*Zeugnis*) certificate; **der wissenschaftliche ~ für etw.** scientific proof (*od.* evidence) of s.th.; **den ~ führen**, **dass ...** prove that ..., furnish proof of s.th., provide evidence of s.th.

nachweisbar *Adj.* verifiable; *Chem.* detectable; (*offenkundig*) evident

nachweisen *v/t.* (*unreg.*, *trennb.*, *hat -ge-*) **1.** (*beweisen*) prove, show; **j-m etw. ~** prove that s.o. has done s.th.; **j-m e-n Irrtum ~** show that s.o. has made a mistake, point out a mistake to s.o.; **sie konnten ihr nichts ~** they couldn't prove anything (against her) (*od.* prove that she had done anything wrong); **Spuren e-s Giftes ~** detect traces of a poison; **2.** *Amtsspr.* (*vermitteln*) arrange; **nachweislich I.** *Adj.* demonstrable; **II.** *Adv.* demonstrably; **sie war ~ da** it has been proved (*od.* there is evidence) that she was there

Nachwelt *f*; *nur Sg.*: **die ~** posterity, future (*od.* later) generations; **für die ~ festhalten** record (*od.* preserve) for posterity

nach|werfen *v/t.* (*unreg.*, *trennb.*, *hat*

-ge-) **1.** **j-m etw. ~** throw s.th. after s.o.; **2.** *fig.* → **nachschmeißen** 2; **3.** *Telefon, Parkuhr etc.*: **noch e-e Münze ~** put in another coin, *Am. auch* feed the meter *etc.*; **~wiegen** (*unreg.*, *trennb.*, *hat -ge-*) **I.** *v/t.* check the weight of; **II.** *v/i.* check the weight; **~winken** *v/i.* (*trennb.*, *hat -ge-*): **j-m ~** wave after s.o.

nachwirken *v/i.* (*trennb.*, *hat -ge-*) **1.** **die Tabletten** etc. **wirken lange nach** it'll take a while before the effects of the tablets etc. wear off; **2.** **lange** (**auf j-n**) **~** *Erlebnis etc.*: leave a deep impression (on s.o.), have a lasting effect (on s.o.); **Nachwirkung** *f* aftereffect(s *Pl.*); (*Folgen*) consequences *Pl.*; *auch des Krieges*: aftermath

Nachwort *n* epilog(ue)

Nachwuchs *m* **1.** *the* young (*od.* up-and-coming, *bes. Am.* upcoming) generation; *beruflicher*: new blood; (*Rekruten*) recruits; *Wirts.* junior staff (*V. mst im Pl.*), trainees *Pl.*; **ärztlicher/wissenschaftlicher ~** *the* new generation (*umg.* breed) of doctors/academics, young doctors/academics, **2.** (*Kind[er]*) offspring (*V. im Sg. od. Pl.*); (*Neugeborenes*) new arrival, addition to the family; **sie erwarten ~** they're going to have a baby, there's a baby on the way; **~autor** *m*, **~autorin** *f* up-and-coming writer, promising young writer; **~bedarf** *m* need for recruits (*od.* young teachers *etc.*); **~förderung** *f* promotion of young talent; **~kraft** *f* junior worker (*od.* employee); **~mangel** *m* **1.** an *Arbeitskräften*: shortage of recruits; **2.** *bes. Sport*, an *Talenten*: dearth of young talent; **~sorgen** *Pl.*: **~ haben** have difficulty (in) finding recruits (*od.* young talent); **~spieler** *m*, **~spielerin** *f Sport* up-and-coming (young) player; **~talent** *n* promising young talent

nach|würzen *vt/i.* (*trennb.*, *hat -ge-*) season to taste; **~zahlen** *vt/i.* (*trennb.*, *hat -ge-*) pay extra (*od.* later); **~zählen** *vt/i.* (*trennb.*, *hat -ge-*) check; (*Wechselgeld*) count

Nachzahlung *f* additional (*od.* extra) payment

nachzeichnen *v/t.* (*trennb.*, *hat -ge-*) copy; (*pausen*) trace; *fig.* (*schildern*) portray

nachziehen (*unreg.*, *trennb.*, *-ge-*) **I.** *v/t.* (*hat*) **1.** drag (*od.* pull) behind one; (*Fuß*) drag; **2.** (*Strich*) trace; (*Augenbrauen*) pencil over; (*Lippenstift*) redo; **3.** (*Schraube*) tighten up; **II.** *v/i.* **1.** (*ist*) (*folgen*) follow; **er ist ihr nach Hamburg nachgezogen** he followed her to Hamburg; **2.** (*hat*) *Schach*: make the next move; **3.** (*hat*) *umg. fig.* follow suit

Nachzoll *m* supplementary duty

Nachzucht *f* **1.** *nur Sg.* (*erneute Aufzucht*) *von Tieren*: rebreeding; *von Pflanzen*: recultivation; **2.** (*Nachkommen*) offspring; **nachzüchten** *v/t.* (*trennb.*, *hat -ge-*) (*erneut züchten*) *von Tieren*: breed again; *von Pflanzen*: re-cultivate

Nachzug *m* **1.** *Eisenb.* relief train (*that follows a scheduled service*); **2.** *von Familienmitgliedern etc.*: **den ~ von Kindern ausländischer Arbeitnehmer erlauben** allow the children of foreign workers to join their families

Nachzügler *m*; *-s*, *-*, **~in** *f*; *-*, *-nen* **1.** in *e-r Gruppe*: straggler; (*Zuspätkommer*) latecomer; **2.** *umg.* (*Kind*) late arrival, *hum.* afterthought

Nachzugsaktien *Pl. Wirts.* deferred shares (*od.* stock *Sg.*)

Nachzugsverbot *n Jur.* law forbidding the families of one migrant (*worker*) to join him abroad

Nachzündung *f Tech.*, *Mot.* retarded ignition

Nackedei *m*; *-s*, *-s*; *umg.* nudie

Nacken *m*; *-s*, *-* nape (*od.* back) of the neck, neck; **den Kopf in den ~ werfen** throw back one's head; **den Hut in den ~ schieben** tilt one's hat back; **j-n im ~ haben** *fig.* have s.o. after one (*od.* hard on one's heels); *Druck ausübend*: have s.o. breathing down one's neck; **ihm sitzt die Angst im ~** *fig.* he's scared out of his wits (*od.* mind); → **Faust**, **Schalk**

nackend *Adj. altm.*, *noch hum.* naked

Nackenhaar *n* neck hair, hair on the back of one's neck

nackenlang *Adj.*: **~es Haar** hair reaching down over the back of one's neck

Nacken|rolle *f* bolster; **~schlag** *m* blow to the back of the neck; *fig.* blow, knock; (*Rückschlag*) setback; **e-n ~ erhalten** *fig.* take a knock, suffer a setback; **~schutz** *m* neck guard; **~starre** *f*, **~steifigkeit** *f Med.* stiff neck, stiffness of the neck; **~stütze** *f* headrest; *im Auto etc.*: *auch* head (*od.* neck) support; **~wirbel** *m Anat.* cervical vertebra

nackert, **nackicht**, **nackig** *Dial. auch umg. hum* → **nackt**

nackt *Adj.* naked; *auch Kunst*: nude; *Beine, Arme etc.*: bare; *fig. Wand, Baum etc.*: bare, naked; **~ und bloß** completely naked; **mit ~en Füßen** barefoot; **mit ~em Oberkörper** stripped to the waist; **sich ~ ausziehen** strip (naked); **~ baden** swim in the nude (*umg.* the raw), *Am. umg.* skinnydip; **j-n ~ malen** paint s.o. (in the) nude; **die ~e Armut** *fig.* naked poverty; **mit dem ~en Auge** *fig. hum.* with the (*od.* one's) naked eye; **auf dem ~en Boden** *fig.* on the cold hard ground; **mit dem ~en Leben davonkommen** escape with one's bare life; **~e Tatsachen** *fig.* (cold,) hard facts; *auch hum. euph.* bare facts; **die ~e Wahrheit** *fig.* the plain truth; **~e Angst stand ihm im Gesicht** sheer terror showed on his face; **mit ~en Worten** bluntly; → **Gewalt**

Nacktbaden *n*; *-s*, *kein Pl.* nude bathing, *Am. umg.* skinnydipping; **Nacktbadestrand** *m* nudist beach

Nackte *m*, *f*; *-n*, *-n* naked person; *auf Bild etc.*: nude

Nackt|foto *n* nude photograph; **~frosch** *m umg.*, *hum.* (*Kind*) nudie

Nacktheit *f* nakedness, nudity

Nacktmagazin *n umg.* nude (*umg.* girlie) magazine

Nacktsamer *m*; *-s*, *-*; *Bot.* gymnosperm; **nacktsamig** *Adj.* gymnospermous

Nackt|schnecke *f Zool.* slug; **~tänzer** *m*, **~tänzerin** *f* nude dancer; striptease artist, stripper; **~szene** *f Film*, *TV*: nude scene

Nadel *f*; *-*, *-n* **1.** needle (*auch*, *Tech.*, *Tannennadel etc.*); (*Steck-*, *Haar-*, *Hutnadel etc.*) pin (*auch Anstecknadel*, *kleine Brosche*); (*Brosche*) brooch, *Am.* pin; (*am Tonabnehmer*) stylus (*Pl. styli od. styluses*); **man hätte e-e ~ fallen hören können** you could have heard a pin drop; **e-e ~ im Heuhaufen** *fig.* a needle in a haystack; (**wie**) **auf ~n sitzen** *umg.* be on tenterhooks; **etw. mit heißer ~ nähen** *umg.* sew s.th.

N

in a hurry; *fig.* throw s.th. together in a hurry; **2.** (*Injektionsnadel*) needle; **an der ~ hängen** (*drogenabhängig sein*) *umg.* be on the needle, be a junkie *Sl.*; **~abweichung** *f* magnetic deviation; **~baum** *m Bot.* conifer, coniferous tree; **~brief** *m* packet of needles; **~drucker** *m Computer*: dot matrix printer; **~holz** *n* **1.** softwood; **2.** *mst Pl.* **Nadelhölzer** *Pl.* conifers; **~kissen** *n* pin-cushion; **~kopf** *m* pinhead; **~lager** *n Mot.* needle bearing
nadeln *v/i. Baum*: lose (*od.* shed) its needles
Nadel|öhr *n* eye of a (*od.* the) needle; *fig.* (*Engpass*) bottleneck; → **Kamel**; **~spitze** *f* needle point; **~stich** *m* **1.** pinprick (*auch fig.*); **2.** *Nähen*: stitch
Nadelstreifen *m*; *mst Pl.* **1.** *im Stoff*: pinstripe; **2.** *Anzug*: pinstripe suit; **~anzug** *m* pinstripe suit
Nadelwald *m Bot.* coniferous forest, *Pl. auch* woodland *Sg.*
Nadir *m*; *-s*, *kein Pl.*; *Astron.* nadir
Nagel *m*; *-s*, *Nägel Pl.* **1.** *Tech.* nail; (*Stift*) tack; **e-n ~ in die Wand schlagen** knock a nail into the wall; **ein ~ zu j-s Sarg** *umg. fig.* a nail in s.o.'s coffin; **etw. an den ~ hängen** *umg.* chuck s.th. in, give s.th. up; **den ~ auf den Kopf treffen** *umg. fig.* hit the nail on the head; **Nägel mit Köpfen machen** *umg. fig.* do a proper job of it (*od.* things), not do things by halves; **2.** (*Finger-, Zehennagel*) nail; **an den Nägeln kauen** bite (*od.* chew) one's nails; **es brennt mir unter den Nägeln** *umg. fig.* I'm itching to get it out of the way; **mir brennt die Zeit auf den Nägeln** *umg. fig.* I haven't got a minute to spare; **er gönnt ihr nicht das Schwarze unter dem ~** he begrudges her the air she breathes; **sich** (*Dat.*) **etw. unter den ~ reißen** *umg.* swipe (*od.* pinch) s.th., walk off with s.th.; (*Arbeit, Stelle etc.*) make sure one gets (hold of) s.th.; **3.** *Med.*; *in Knochen*: pin
Nagelbett *n Anat.* nail bed; **~entzündung** *f Med.* onychitis (*Pl.* onychitides)
Nagel|bohrer *m Tech.* gimlet; **~brett** *n* bed of nails; **~bürste** *f* nail brush; **~feile** *f* nail file; **~festiger** *m Kosmetik*: nail strengthener; **~haut** *f* cuticle
Nägelkauen *n*; *-s*, *kein Pl.* nailbiting
Nagellack *m* (finger)nail varnish (*Am.* polish); **~entferner** *m* (finger)nail varnish (*Am.* polish) remover
nageln *v/t.* nail (**an, auf** + *Akk.* to); (*zusammennageln*) nail together; *Med.* pin; **II.** *v/i. Sl. Motor.* knock
nagelneu *Adj. umg.* brand-new
Nagel|pflege *f* nail care; (*Maniküre*) manicure; **~probe** *f fig.* **1.** litmus test; **die ~ machen** do a litmus test (**mit** on); **2.** (*Prüfstein*) touchstone (**für** of); **~reiniger** *m* nail-cleaner; **~schere** *f*: (**e-e**) ~ (a pair of) nail scissors *Pl.*; **~schuh** *m* hobnail boot
Nagel|wurzel *f Anat.* nail root; **~zange** *f* **1.** (**e-e**) ~ (a pair of) nail clippers *Pl.*; **2.** *Tech.*: (**e-e**) ~ (a pair of) pincers *Pl.*
nagen *v/t/i.* gnaw; *knabbernd*: nibble (**an** + *Dat.* at); **~ an** (+ *Dat.*) *ätzend*: *auch Geol.* eat into, corrode; *fig.* gnaw at; **an e-m Knochen ~** gnaw at a bone; → **Hungertuch**; **II.** *v/refl.*: **sich durch etw. ~** gnaw through s.th.; *Säure*: eat through s.th.; **nagend I.** *Part. Präs.* → **nagen**; **II.** *Adj. Hunger*: gnawing; *Schmerz, Zweifel etc.*: nagging; **Nager**

m; *-s*, *-*, **Nagetier** *n Zool.* rodent; **Nagezahn** *m eines Nagers*: rodent incisor
nah I. *Adj.*; *näher*, *am nächsten* **1.** (*räumlich nicht weit*) *präd.* near, close; *attr.* nearby ...; *Naher Osten* Middle (*od.* Near) East; **2.** (*zeitlich bevorstehend*) forthcoming, *unmittelbar*: imminent; **in ~er Zukunft** in the near future; **3.** *fig. Verwandter, Freund, Beziehung etc.*: close; *i-e nächsten Verwandten* her closest relatives (*od.* immediate family); *sich sehr ~* be very close; **II.** *Adv.* **1.** *räumlich*: near, close; (*in der Nähe*) nearby; **~ an** (+ *Dat.*) *od.* **~ bei** *od.* **~** (+ *Dat.*) near (to), close to; *im ~e gelegenen Wald* in the nearby woods, in the woods nearby; *von ~em* from close up; *von od. aus ~ und fern* from far and near (*od.* wide); *komm mir nicht zu ~(e)!* *drohend*: (just) keep your distance; *weil ich erkältet bin etc.*: don't get too close to me; **2.** *fig.*: **~ verwandt** closely related; **3.** *j-m etw. ~e bringen* make s.th. accessible to s.o., help s.o. to appreciate (*od.* understand) s.th.; **4.** *j-m ~e gehen* affect s.o. deeply, have a deep effect on s.o.; **5.** *j-m ~e stehen* be close to s.o.; *e-e den Konservativen ~e stehende Zeitschrift* a conservatively orien(ta)ted magazine, a magazine with conservative leanings; *sie hat ihm damals näher gestanden* she was closer to him at that time; **6.** *j-m ~e kommen* get to know s.o.; *einander ~e / sehr ~e kommen* get to know each other / grow close, develop a close relationship; *~e kommen e-r Sache*: come close to, approach; **7.** *j-m etw. ~e legen* suggest s.th. to s.o.; *j-m ~e legen, etw. zu tun* urge s.o. to do s.th.; *es legt den Verdacht ~e, dass ...* it would seem to suggest that ...; *~e liegen* be obvious, stand to reason; *die Vermutung liegt ~e, dass ...* it would appear that ...; **8.** *j-m zu ~e treten* offend s.o., tread (*Am.* step) on s.o.'s toes; *ich war ~e daran zu kündigen* I very nearly handed in my notice, I was about to hand in my notice, I was (very) tempted to hand in my notice; *Verbindungen mit näher, nächst...* → **näher, nächst...**; **III.** *Präp. geh.* near, close to (*auch fig.*); **den Tränen ~** on the verge of tears, ready to burst into tears; **der Verzweiflung ~** on the verge of despair, getting desperate; **dem Tode ~** on the point of death, approaching death, close to death
...nah *im Adj.* **1.** *allg. im wörtl. Sinn*: near; *grenz~* near the border; **2.** *fig. auf j-n, etw. ausgerichtet, an j-m, etw. orientiert*: *kunden~* customer-orien(ta)ted; **3.** *fig. mit ähnlichen Zielen, ähnlich ausgerichtet, gestaltet etc.*: *gewerkschafts~* sympathetic to the unions; *jazz~* jazz-like
Nahangriff *m Mil.* close-range attack
Näharbeit *f* sewing, needlework; *eine ~* a piece of sewing (*od.* needlework)
Nah|aufnahme *f Fot.* close-up (shot); **~bereich** *m* **1.** (*unmittelbare Nachbarschaft*) neighbo(u)rhood, vicinity; (*Umgebung*) surroundings, environs *Pl.*; (*Vorstädte*) suburbs *Pl.*, suburban area(s *Pl.*); *weitS.* (*Region*) area, region; *der ~ von München* the Munich area; **2.** *Fot.* close-up range; **im ~** at close range; **~brille** *f*: (**e-e**) ~ (a pair of) reading glasses *Pl.*
nahe *Adj.* → **nah**
Nähe *f*; *-*, *kein Pl.* **1.** (*geringe räumliche*

Entfernung) nearness, proximity; (*Umgebung*) vicinity, neighbo(u)rhood; *in der ~* nearby; *in der ~ von* (*od.* + *Gen.*) near (to), quite close to; *der Park in der ~* the nearby park, the park nearby; *bei uns in der ~* near (to) where we live, not far from where we live; *hier in der ~* somewhere around here; *in der ~ bleiben* stay around; *in s-r ~* near (to) where he lives; *unmittelbar*: near (to) him; *aus der ~* close up, at close range; *aus der ~ betrachtet* seen at close range, on closer view; **2.** (*geringe zeitliche Entfernung*) closeness; *der Examenstermin ist in unmittelbare ~ gerückt* the day of the exam is imminent; → **greifbar, 3.** *enge Beziehung*: *menschliche ~* human contact; *j-s ~ suchen* seek s.o.'s company
...nähe *f im Subst.* → **...nah**; *e-e Wohnung in Zentrums~* a flat (*Am.* apartment) near the cent|re (*Am.* -er)
nahebei *Adv.* nearby, close by
nahe bringen → **nah** II 3
nahe gehen → **nah** II 4
Naheinstellung *f Fot.* close-up focus(-s)ing; *Aufnahme*: close-up
nahe kommen → **nah** II 6
nahe liegen → **nah** II 7
nahen I. *v/i.* approach; *zeitlich*: *auch* draw near; *Frühling etc.*: *auch* be on its way; **II.** *v/refl.* be approaching; (*bevorstehen*) be imminent; *sich j-m ~* approach s.o.
nähen I. *v/t.* sew; (*Kleid etc.*) make; (*Loch, Riss*) *auch* stitch; *Med.* stitch (up); *fachspr.* suture; **~ an** (+ *Akk.*) *od.* **auf** (+ *Akk.*) sew onto; *die Wunde muss genäht werden Med.* the wound needs stitching; *doppelt genäht hält besser umg. fig.* better safe than sorry; *bei nochmaliger Überprüfung*: *auch* just to make sure; **II.** *v/i.* sew; (*Näharbeiten machen*) do needlework; **Nähen** *n*; *-s*, *kein Pl.* sewing; (*Näharbeiten*) needlework; (*Schneidern*) dressmaking
nahend *Adj.* approaching; (*bevorstehend*) imminent; *Gefahr etc.*: *auch* impending
näher I. *Adj.* closer, nearer; *Weg*: shorter; (*genauer*) more detailed (*od.* precise), in greater detail; *die ~e Umgebung* the immediate vicinity; *bei ~er Betrachtung* on closer inspection; *fig.* on further consideration; → **nah, Nähere**; **II.** *Adv.* **1.** closer, nearer; *sich mit e-r Sache ~ befassen* go into a matter; (*etw.*) **~ beschreiben** be more precise (about s.th.); go into more detail (about s.th.); *j-m etw. ~ bringen* make s.th. (more) accessible to s.o., help s.o. to appreciate (*od.* understand) s.th. better; **2.** *j-n ~ kennen* know s.o. quite (*od.* fairly) well; *kennen Sie ihn ~?* how well do you know him?; **3.** **~ kommen** *od.* **treten** come closer; *treten Sie ~!* come in!, this way, please!, come closer; *j-m ~ kommen fig.* get closer to s.o.; *jetzt kommen wir der Sache (schon) ~! umg.* now we're getting there; *das kommt der Wahrheit schon ~* that's more like the truth; **4.** **~ liegen** (*wahrscheinlicher sein*) be more likely (*od.* obvious); (*vernünftiger sein*) be better, be more reasonable (*od.* sensible); *was liegt ~, als abzureisen* what could be more sensible than to leave; **~ liegend** (*wahrscheinlicher*) more likely (*od.* obvious); (*vernünftiger*) better, more reasonable (*od.* sensible); *das ~ Lie-*

gende *tun etc.* the (more) obvious thing (to do); *e-m Plan, Vorschlag etc.*; **5.** (*immer*) **~ rücken** *auch zeitlich*: get closer (and closer); → *auch* **nah**, **nächst**...

Nähere *n*; -, *kein Pl.* (further) details *Pl.*; *alles* **~ erfahren Sie später** you'll get all the details later; *nichts* **~s wissen** not know any details

Näherei *f*; -, *-en* 1. *nur Sg.*; *oft pej.* sewing; **2.** (*Näharbeiten*) needlework; (*Schneidern*) dressmaking; **3.** (*Betrieb*) sewing works

Naherholungsgebiet *n* greenbelt recreation area

Näherin *f*; -, *-nen* seamstress

näher| kommen, **~ liegen**, **~ liegend** → **näher** II

nähern I. *v/t.* bring near(er) (+ *Dat.* to); **II.** *v/refl.* approach (+ *Dat. s.o. od. s.th.*) (*auch zeitlich*); go (*od.* come) up (+ *Dat.* to); *e-r Frau etc.*: try to approach; *sich dem Ende* **~** draw to a close; *sich der platonischen Denkweise* **~** come close to the platonic way of thinking

näher| stehen, **~ treten** → **näher** II

Näherung *f Math.* approximation

näherungsweise *Adv.* approximately; **Näherungswert** *m Math.* approximate value

nahezu *Adv.* virtually, almost; **~ unmöglich** virtually (*od.* well-nigh) impossible; **~ 10 Tage** almost (*umg.* going on for) 10 days

Nähgarn *n* (sewing) cotton (*bes. Am.* thread)

Nahkampf *m Mil.* close combat, hand-to-hand fight(ing); *Flug.* dogfight(ing); *Boxen, Fechten*: infighting

Näh|kästchen *n*: *aus dem* **~ plaudern** *umg. hum.* tell tales out of school, give away secrets; **~kasten** *m* sewing box; **~korb** *m* work basket

nahm *Imperf.* → **nehmen**

Näh|maschine *f* sewing machine; **~maschinenöl** *n* sewing machine oil; **~nadel** *f* (sewing) needle

Nahost *ohne Art. Geog.*: *in* **~** in the Middle (*od.* Near) East

Nahost|... *im Subst.* Middle Eastern, Near Eastern; **~konflikt** *m*; *nur Sg.*; *Pol.* Middle East conflict

nahöstlich *Adj.* Middle Eastern, Near Eastern

Nähr|boden *m für Bakterien*: culture medium; *fig.* breeding ground (*für* of, for); **~brühe** *f für Bakterien*: nutrient fluid; **~creme** *f Kosmetik*: nutrient cream

nähren I. *v/t.* **1.** feed; *gut genährt aussehen umg. hum.* look well-fed; **2.** *geh.* (*ernähren*) support, maintain; **3.** *fig.* (*Hoffnung etc.*) nurture, (*Hass, Verdacht etc.*) *auch* fuel; **II.** *v/i.* be nourishing; **III.** *v/refl. geh.*: *sich von etw.* **~** live on s.th.; *Tier*: feed on s.th.

Nähr|flüssigkeit *f für Bakterien*: nutrient fluid; **~gebiet** *n Geog.* accumulation area

nahrhaft *Adj.* nutritious, nourishing

Nähr|lösung *f* **1.** *Med.* nutrient solution; **2.** *für Bakterien*: nutrient fluid; *in der Hydrokultur*: nutrient solution; **~mittel** *Pl.* cereal products; **~präparat** *n* nutrient (preparation), patent food; **~salz** *n* nutrient salt

Nährstoff *m mst Pl.* nutrient; **nährstoffarm** *Adj. präd. und nachgestellt*: low in nutrients; **Nährstoffgehalt** *m* nutrient content; **nährstoffreich** *Adj.* nutritious, *präd. und nachgestellt*: rich in nutrients

Nahrung *f* **1.** food; *flüssige* **~** liquids; **~ zu sich nehmen** eat, take food; → **verweigern** I; **2.** *fig.*: *geistige* **~** food for the mind; **~ geben** (+ *Dat.*) fuel; (*neue*) **~ erhalten** *od.* **finden** be fuel(l)ed, receive fresh impetus

Nahrungs|aufnahme *f* eating, food intake; *fachspr.* ingestion; → **verweigern** I; **~grundlage** *f* basic food; (*Grundnahrung*) staple diet; **~kette** *f Bio.* food chain; **~mangel** *m* food shortage; *e-r Person etc.*: lack of food

Nahrungsmittel *n*; *mst Pl.* food, foodstuff; **~allergie** *f Med.* food allergy; **~chemie** *f* food chemistry; **~chemiker** *m*, **~chemikerin** *f* food chemist; **~industrie** *f* food industry; **~vergiftung** *f Med.* food poisoning

Nahrungs|quelle *f* source of food; **~suche** *f* search for food; **~und-Genussmittelindustrie** *f* food, beverages and tobacco industry; **~verweigerung** *f* refusal to eat; *weitS.* hunger strike; **~zufuhr** *f* food intake; *fachspr.* ingestion

Nährwert *m* nutritional value; *e-n hohen* **~ haben** be highly nutritious; (*praktischer*) **~** *umg. fig.* practical value

Nähseide *f* sewing silk, *Am.* silk thread

Naht *f*; -, *Nähte* **1.** *beim Nähen*: seam; *aus allen od. sämtlichen Nähten platzen umg.* be bursting at the seams (*auch fig.*); **2.** *Tech.* seam, join; (*Schweißnaht*) *auch* weld; **3.** *Anat., Bot.* suture; *Med.* suture, stitches *Pl.*

nahtlos I. *Adj.* seamless; **~er Übergang** *fig.* smooth transition; **~e Bräune** all-over tan; **II.** *Adv.*: **~ ineinander übergehen** run on smoothly from one another, merge into one another; **~ braun** tanned all over

Nahtstelle *f* **1.** *Tech.* seam, join; (*Schweißnaht*) *auch* weld; **2.** *fig.* interface

Nähutensilien *Pl.* sewing things

Nahverkehr *m* local traffic; *Eisenb.* (*Vorortverkehr*) suburban services *Pl.*

Nahverkehrs|mittel *n* form of local transport(ation); **~zug** *m* commuter (*od.* local) train

nah verwandt → **nah** II 2

Nähzeug *n* sewing kit, sewing things *Pl.*

Nahziel *n* immediate target (*od.* objective), short-term target (*od.* objective)

naiv *Adj.* naive (*auch Kunst, Lit.*); *die Naive / den Naiven spielen umg.* act naive; **Naive** *f*; -, *-n*; *Theat.* the Ingénue; **Naivität** *f*; -, *kein Pl.* naivety, *bes. Am.* naiveté; **Naivling** *m*; *-s, -e*; *umg. pej.* simpleton

Name *m*; *-ns, -n* **1.** name; *mein* **~** *ist* ... my name is ...; *wie war doch gleich Ihr* **~**? what was your name again?; *mit* **~n** ... by the name of ..., called ...; *j-n mit* **~n anreden** call s.o. by his (*od.* her) name; *in der Diskussion fiel auch dein* **~** your name came up in the discussion too; *den* **~n** ... *tragen* go by the name of ..., be called ...; *Sache: auch* be known as ...; *s-n* **~n nennen** give one's name; *er hat dafür nur s-n* **~n hergegeben** he only lent his name to it; *j-n nach s-m* **~n fragen** ask s.o. his (*od.* her) name, ask s.o.'s name; (*nur*) *dem* **~n nach** in name only; *dem* **~n nach kennen** know s.o. *od. s.th.* by name; *dem* **~n nach könnte sie Koreanerin sein** judging by her name she could be Korean; *das Kind od. die Dinge beim rechten* **~n nennen**

call a spade a spade; *damit das Kind e-n* **~n hat** *umg.* just to give it a name, just to call it something; *die Rechnung etc. geht auf m-n* **~n** is on me; *es läuft unter s-m* **~n** it's in his name; *im* **~n von** ... in the name of ..., on behalf of ...; *im* **~n des Volkes** *Jur.* in the name of the people; *in Gottes* **~n!** *umg.* for heaven's sake!; → **Hase** 4, **Schall**; **2.** (*Ruf*) name, reputation; *als Bariton etc. hat er e-n guten* **~n** he has a good reputation as a baritone *etc.*; *e-n guten* **~n zu verlieren haben** have one's good name at stake; *sich* (*Dat.*) *e-n* **~n machen** make a name for o.s.

Namen|forschung *f* onomastics *Pl.* (*V. im Sg.*); **~geber** *m*, **~geberin** *f*: *der Dichter Platen war* **~ für unsere Schule** the poet Platen gave his name to our school; **~gebung** *f* naming; **~gedächtnis** *n* memory for names; **~kunde** *f* onomastics *Pl.* (*V. im Sg.*); **~liste** *f* list of names

namenlos I. *Adj.* **1.** anonymous, unnamed; *die Namenlosen Wirts. Sl.* no-name products (*od.* brands); **2.** *geh. fig.* (*unsäglich*) indescribable; **II.** *Adv. geh. fig.* (*unsäglich*) utterly, unspeakably

Namenregister *n* list of names

namens I. *Adv.* named, by the name of, called; **II.** *Präp.* (*im Namen von*) in the name of, on behalf of

Namens|aktie *f Wirts.* registered share; **~änderung** *f* change of name; **~gebung** *f* naming; **~nennung** *f* mentioning of a name (*od.* names); *des eigenen Namens*: mentioning of one's name; **~papier** *n Wirts.* registered security; **~patron** *m*, **~patronin** *f* saint after whom *s.o. is named*; **~recht** *n* right to a name; **~schild** *n* nameplate; *am Kleidungsstück*: badge, name tag; **~tag** *m* name day; **~träger** *m*, **~trägerin** *f* bearer of a (*od.* the) name; **~verwechslung** *f* mix-up over names; **~verzeichnis** *n* list of names; **~vetter** *m* namesake; **~wechsel** *m* name change, change of name; **~zeichen** *n* initials *Pl.*; **~zug** *m* signature

namentlich I. *Adj.* ... by name; **~e Aufführung** naming; **~e Liste** list of names; **~e Abstimmung** *Parl.* roll-call vote; **II.** *Adv.* **1.** (*beim Namen*) by name; → **erwähnen**; **2.** (*besonders*) especially, particularly, above all

Namen|weihe *f ehem. DDR*: non-religious naming ceremony in the former GDR which replaced the christening ceremony; **~wort** *n Ling.* noun

namhaft *Adj.* **1.** noted; (*berühmt*) renowned, famous; **2.** (*beträchtlich*) considerable, substantial; **3.** **~ machen** *bes. Amtsspr.* (*nennen*) name, (*identifizieren*) identify

Namibia (*n*); *-s; Geog.* Namibia; **Namibier** *m*; *-s, -e*, **Namibierin** *f*; -, *-nen* Namibian, *weiblich auch*: Namibian woman (*od.* girl *etc.*); **namibisch** *Adj.* Namibian

nämlich I. *Adv.* namely, that is (to say); *nachgestellt*: to be precise (*od.* exact); *er war* **~ krank** *begründend*: he was ill, you see; *es war ganz anders*, **~ so** ... it was quite different - in (actual) fact ...; **II.** *Adj.*; *nur attr.*; *altm.* the (very) same

Nämlichkeitsbescheinigung *f Zollwesen*: certificate of identity

Nandu *m*; *-s, -s*; *Orn.* rhea

nannte *Imperf.* → **nennen**

Nano|... *im Subst.* nano...; **~meter** *m*, *n* nanomet|re (*Am.* -er)

nanu *Interj.:* ~, *wo ist denn m-e Tasche?* *umg.* wait a minute, what have I done with my bag?; ~, *da hat ja einer aufgeräumt!* *umg.* well, well, (it looks as if) somebody's been tidying (*Am.* cleaning) up; ~, *was ist denn hier los?* *umg.* hey, what's all this about?

Napalm® *n*; *-s, kein Pl.* napalm; ~**bombe** *f* napalm bomb

Napf *m*; *(e)s, Näpfe* bowl; *sehr flach*: dish; ~**kuchen** *m* (tall) ring cake

Naphtha *n*; *-s, kein Pl. Petrochemie*: naphtha; **Naphthalin** *n*; *-s, kein Pl.*; *Chem.* naphthalene

napoleonisch *Adj.* Napoleonic

Nappaleder *n* nappa (leather)

Narbe *f*; *-, -n* **1.** scar; *es wird ohne ~ verheilen* it won't leave a scar; **2.** *Bot.* stigma (*Pl.* stigmas, *auch* stigmata); **3.** *Agr.* topsoil; **4.** *Gerberei*: grain; **narben** *v/t.* (*Leder*) grain

Narben|bildung *f Med.* scarring; ~**bruch** *m* post-operative (*od.* cicatricial) hernia; ~**gesicht** *n* scarred face; ~**leder** *n Gerberei*: grain (*od.* grained) leather

narbenlos *Adj.* unscarred, without a scar

narbig *Adj.* scarred

Narbung *f Leder*: graining

Narde *f*; *-, -n*; *Bot.* nard; **Nardenöl** *n* nard (*od.* spikenard) oil

Narkolepsie *f*; *-; -n*; *Med.* narcolepsy

Narkose *f*; *-, -n*; *Med., Mittel*: an(a)esthetic; *Zustand*: an(a)esthesia; *in ~* under an(a)esthetic; *in (der) ~ liegen* be under an(a)esthetic; *e-e ~ bekommen* be given an an(a)esthetic; *aus der ~ aufwachen* come round (*od.* to)

Narkose|arzt *m*, ~**ärztin** *f* anaesthetist, *Am.* anesthesiologist; ~**gewehr** *n* tranquil(l)izer gun; ~**maske** *f* an(a)esthetic mask; ~**mittel** *n* an(a)esthetic

Narkotikum *n*; *-s, Narkotika*; *Med.* an(a)esthetic; (*bes. Rauschgift*) narcotic; **narkotisch I.** *Adj.* an(a)esthetic, narcotic; **II.** *Adv.:* ~ *wirken* have an an(a)esthetic (*od.* narcotic) effect; **narkotisieren** *v/t.* an(a)esthetize; **Narkotismus** *m*; *-, kein Pl.* narcotism

Narr *m*; *-en, -en* **1.** *geh.* fool; *e-n ~en gefressen haben an* *umg. fig.* be wild (*od.* crazy) about; *j-n zum ~en halten* (*verspotten*) make a fool of s.o.; (*täuschen*) fool s.o.; *die ~en werden nicht alle Sprichw.* there's one born every minute; **2.** *hist.* jester, fool; **3.** (*Karnevalist*) carnival reveller

narrativ *Adj. Ling.* narrative

narren *v/t. geh.* (*verspotten*) make a fool of; (*täuschen*) fool

Narren|freiheit *f* fool's licen|ce (*Am.* -se); *bei ihr hat er ~* she lets him do what he likes; ~**hände** *Pl.:* ~ *beschmieren Tisch und Wände Sprichw.* people who write graffiti don't know any better; ~**haus** *n altm., noch fig.* madhouse; ~**kappe** *f* fool's cap; ~**kostüm** *n* jester's outfit; ~**streich** *m altm.* silly prank

Narretei *f*; *-, -en* → *Narrheit*

Narrheit *f auch Pl.* tomfoolery; (*Dummheit[en]*) folly

Närrin *f*; *-, -nen* → *Narr* 1, 3

närrisch *Adj.* **1.** (*verrückt*) mad, *umg.* crazy (*auf + Akk.* about); **2.** ~*es Treiben* carnival atmosphere

Narwal *m Zool.* narw(h)al

Narziss *m*; *- und -es, -e*; *geh.* Narcissus

Narzisse *f*; *-, -n*; *Bot.* narcissus (*Pl.* narcissi *od.* narcissuses); *gelbe ~* daffodil

Narzissmus *m*; *-, kein Pl.* narcissism; **Narzisst** *m*; *-en, -en*, **Narzisstin** *f*; *-, -nen* narcissist; **narzisstisch** *Adj.* narcissistic

NASA *f*; *-, kein Pl.*; *Raumf.* NASA (= National Aeronautics and Space Administration)

nasal *Adj.* nasal; **Nasal** *m*; *-s, -e*; *Ling.* nasal (sound); **nasalieren** *v/t.* nasalize; **Nasallaut** *m Ling.* nasal (sound)

naschen *vt/i.* nibble (between meals); *heimlich*: eat (*s.th. od.* things) on the sly; *gern ~* like to nibble (things); (*Süßes*) have a sweet tooth

Näschen *n* little nose; *ich hatte das richtige ~* (*habe richtig vermutet*) I was right; *ein ~ für etw. haben* (*ein Gespür für etw. haben*) have a nose for s.th.

Nascher *m*; *-s, -* nibbler, *Am.* nosher; → *auch Naschkatze*; **Nascherei** *f*; *-, -en* **1.** *nur Sg.* nibbling, *Am.* noshing; *heimlich*: eating on the sly; **2.** sweets (and chocolates) *Pl.*, *Am. auch* candy, nosherei *umg.*; **Nascherin** *f*; *-, -nen* → *Nascher*, **naschhaft** *Adj.:* ~ *sein* love to nibble things; (*gern Süßes essen*) have a sweet tooth

Nasch|katze *f* compulsive nibbler; *bei Süßem*: compulsive sweet-eater; *er ist e-e richtige ~ umg.* he's always nibbling things; *bei Süßem*: he's always eating sweet things; ~**sucht** *f*; *nur Sg.* addiction to nibbling; *bei Süßem*: addiction to sweet things

Nase¹ *f*; *-, -n* **1.** *Anat.* nose (*auch Naut., Flug. etc.*); (*Schnauze*) *auch* snout; *auf die ~ fallen auch. fig.* fall flat on one's face; *die ~ hoch tragen umg.* be stuck-up; *eins auf die ~ kriegen umg.* get a punch on the nose; *fig.* get a rap over (*Am.* on) the knuckles; *stärker: umg.* get it in the neck; → *bohren* III 2, *putzen* I, *rümpfen, zuhalten* I 1; **2.** (*Geruchssinn*) nose (*auch fig. Gespür*); *e-e gute ~ haben* have a keen sense of smell; *fig.* have good instincts; *e-e gute ~ für etw. haben fig.* have a good nose for s.th.; **3.** (*Felsvorsprung, Bergnase*) ledge; **4.** *umg.* (*Farbtropfen*) drip; **5.** *umg. fig. in Wendungen: pro ~ 10 Dollar* 10 dollars each (*od.* a head); *j-m etw. auf die ~ binden* tell s.o. all about s.th.; *j-n an der ~ herumführen* lead s.o. up the garden path; *j-m auf der ~ herumtanzen* play s.o. up; *j-m e-e lange ~ machen* thumb one's nose at s.o.; *triumphierend: auch* cock a snook at s.o.; *auf der ~ liegen* be laid up; *s-e ~ in alles (hinein)stecken* poke one's nose into everything; *die ~ vorn haben* be the winner(s); *j-n mit der ~ auf etw. stoßen* shove s.th. under s.o.'s nose; *es j-m unter die ~ reiben* rub s.o.'s nose in it, rub it in; *die ~ voll haben* be fed up (to the back teeth) (*von* with); *j-m etw. aus der ~ ziehen* worm (*od.* winkle) s.th. out of s.o.; *immer der ~ nach!* just follow your nose; *es liegt direkt vor d-r ~* it's right under (*od.* in front of) your nose; *der Bus fuhr uns vor der ~ weg* we missed the bus by seconds; *j-m die Tür vor der ~ zumachen od.* zuschlagen shut the door in s.o.'s face; *j-m etw. vor der ~ wegschnappen* snatch s.th. from right under s.o.'s nose; *fig. auch* beat s.o. to s.th.; *er sieht nicht weiter als s-e ~ (reicht)* he can't see beyond the end of his nose; *man kann es ihm an der ~ ansehen* it's written all over his face; *fass dich an d-e ei-*

gene ~! you can talk!; *es kann nicht immer nach d-r ~ gehen* you can't always have things your own way

Nase² *f*; *-, -n*; *Zool.* common nose

naselang *Adv.:* *alle ~ umg. zeitlich*: every few minutes; *weitS.* (*immer wieder*) over and over again; *räumlich*: every other step

näseln *v/i.* speak through one's nose (*od.* with a twang)

Nasen|affe *m Zool.* proboscis monkey; ~**atmung** *f* breathing through one's nose, nasal breathing; ~**bär** *m Zool.* coati(mondi *od.* -mundi)

Nasenbein *n Anat.* nosebone, nasal bone; ~**bruch** *m Med.* nasal fracture

Nasen|bluten *n*; *-s, kein Pl.* nosebleed(s *Pl.*); ~ *haben* have a nosebleed; ~**bohren** *n*; *-s, kein Pl.* poking one's nose; ~**flügel** *m Anat.* nostril; *weite ~* flared nostrils; ~**gang** *m Anat.* nasal passage; ~**gruß** *m Völkerkunde*: nose(-to-nose) greeting, nose-pressing; ~**haar** *n* nasal hair, *umg.* hairs *Pl.* in one's nose; ~**höhle** *f Anat.* nasal cavity; ~**korrektur** *f* rhinoplasty, *umg. a* nose job

nasenlang *Adv. umg.* → *naselang*

Nasen|länge *f*: *um e-e ~ fig.* by an inch; *j-m um e-e ~ voraus sein fig.* be just ahead of s.o.; ~**laut** *m Ling.* nasal (sound); ~**loch** *n* nostril; ~**nebenhöhle** *f Anat.* (para)nasal sinus; ~**plastik** *f* → *Nasenkorrektur*, ~-**Rachen-Raum** *m Med.* nasopharynx (*Pl.* nasopharynges *od.* nasopharynxes); ~**ring** *m* nose ring; ~**rücken** *m* bridge of the nose; ~**salbe** *f Pharm.* nose ointment; ~**sattel** *m Anat.* nasal saddle; ~**scheidewand** *f* nasal septum; ~**schleim** *m* nasal mucus; ~**schmuck** *m* nose jewellery (*Am.* jewelry); ~**sonde** *f* nasal probe; ~**spiegel** *m* **1.** *Med.* nasal speculum, rhinoscope; **2.** *Zool.* rhinarium; ~**spitze** *f* tip of the nose; *man sieht's ihm an der ~ an umg.* you can tell (by the look on his face); ~**spray** *m, n* nose (*od.* nasal) spray; ~**stüber** *m* **1.** *umg.* biff on (*bes. Am.* punch in) the nose; **2.** *Dial. fig.* (*Zurechtweisung*) rap over (*Am.* on) the knuckles *umg.*, dressing-down, *Brit. auch* wigging *umg.*; ~**tropfen** *Pl. Pharm.* nose drops; ~**wurzel** *f Anat.* base of the nose

Naserümpfen *n*; *-s, kein Pl.*; (*Missbilligung*) disapproval; (*Widerwille*) reluctance; (*Verachtung*) disdain; *kein Job zum ~* not a job to turn one's nose up at; **naserümpfend I.** *Adj.* (*missbilligend*) disapproving; (*unwillig*) reluctant; (*verächtlich*) disdainful; **II.** *Adv.* disapprovingly; reluctantly; disdainfully

naseweis *Adj. umg.* (*neunmalklug*) *attr.* smart-aleck, know-(it-)all; (*vorlaut, frech*) saucy, brassy; **Naseweis** *m*; *-es, -e*; *umg.* **1.** *Kind*: saucy (*od.* cheeky) little brat; **2.** (*Neunmalkluger*) smart aleck, know-(it-)all, wise guy, *Am. auch* smarty pants

nasführen *v/t.* (*untr., hat genasführt*) dupe, lead *s.o.* by the nose, have *s.o.* on *umg.*

Nashorn *n Zool.* rhinoceros, *umg.* rhino; ~**käfer** *n* rhinoceros beetle; ~**vogel** *m Orn.* hornbill

naslang *Adv. umg.* → *naselang*

nass *nasser und nässer, am nassesten und nässesten* **I.** *Adj.* wet (*auch Wetter etc.*); *triefend ~* dripping wet, soaking, drenched, wet through; ~ *machen* wet; *sich ~ machen* wet o.s.; *bes. Kind*:

auch wet his (*od.* her) pants; **j-n ~ machen** *Sport, umg. fig.* give s.o. a thrashing; **mach dich bloß nicht ~!** *umg.* (*hab dich nicht so!*) don't get your knickers in a twist!, keep your hair (*Am.* shirt) on!; **II.** *Adv.:* **~ geschwitzt** soaked in sweat, dripping with sweat; **sich ~ rasieren** wet-shave

Nass *n; -es, kein Pl.; lit.* **1.** water; **ins kühle ~ springen** take a plunge; **2. edles ~** precious liquid (*od.* drop); **3.** (*Regen*) wet

Nassauer *m; -s, -* **1.** *umg. pej.* sponger, scrounger; **2.** *umg. hum.* (*Regenschauer*) shower; (*Regenguss*) downpour; **nassauern I.** *v/i.* sponge (**bei** *j-m:* on), *umg.* scrounge (off); **II.** *v/t.* scrounge *s.th.* (**von** *j-m* off s.o.)

Nässe *f; -, kein Pl.* wet(ness); damp(ness), moisture; *100 km* **bei ~** *Zusatz bei Verkehrsschild:* in wet weather; **vor ~ schützen** keep dry (in a dry place); **~gefahr** *f Mot.* slippery roads *Pl.*

nässen I. *v/t.* **1.** *geh.* (*nass machen*) wet; **2.** *Dial.* (*anfeuchten*) moisten; **II.** *v/i. Wunde etc.:* weep

nässer *Komp. von* → **nass** wetter; **nässest...** *Sup. von* → **nass** wettest

Nassfäule *f* wet rot

nassforsch *Adj. altm. pej.* very forward; *umg.* cocky

nasskalt *Adj.* cold and damp; **~es Wetter** cold, damp weather

Nass|rasierer *m* **1.** wet shaver; **2.** (*Rasierapparat*) wet shaver; **~rasur** *f* wet shave; **~schleifen** *n; -s, kein Pl.; Tech.* wet grinding; **~schnee** *m* wet snow; **~zelle** *f* (prefabricated) bathroom unit

Nastuch *n südd., schw.* handkerchief, hankie *umg.*

Natel® *n; -s, -s; schw., Telek.* (*Handy*) mobile phone, *Am.* cellphone

Nation *f; -, -en* nation; **der Liebling der ~** *umg.* the nation's favo(u)rite

national I. *Adj.* national; **~e Gesinnung** nationalism; **~e Minderheit** ethnic minority; **II.** *Adv.* **~ gesinnt sein** be nationalistic; **das Problem der Massenarbeitslosigkeit in Europa kann nicht ~ gelöst werden** the problem of mass unemployment in Europe cannot be solved at national level

Nationalbank *f* national bank

nationalbewusst *Adj.* nationally conscious; **Nationalbewusstsein** *n* (feeling of) national identity

National|bibliothek *f* national library; **~charakter** *m* national character

Nationaldemokrat *m,* **~in** *f* National Democrat; **nationaldemokratisch** *Adj.* national democratic

Nationaldenkmal *n* national monument

Nationale *n; -s, -; österr., Amtsspr.* personal details; (*Fragebogen*) form asking for personal details

National|einkommen *n* national income; **~elf** *f Fußball:* national team (*od.* side); **Deutschlands ~** the German team; **~farben** *Pl.* national colo(u)rs; **~feiertag** *m* national (public) holiday; **~flagge** *f* national flag; **~galerie** *f* national gallery

National|garde *f* **1.** *hist.* National Guard; **2.** *in USA:* National Guard; **~gardist** *m* **1.** *hist.* National Guardsman; **2.** *in USA:* guardsman, National Guardsman

National|gefühl *n* national consciousness; (*Patriotismus*) patriotism; **~gericht** *n Gastr.* national dish; **~heiligtum** *n* national shrine; **~held** *m,* **~hel-**

din *f* national hero; **~hymne** *f* national anthem

nationalisieren *v/t.* **1.** (*verstaatlichen*) nationalize; **2.** (*einbürgern*) naturalize; **Nationalisierung** *f* nationalization; naturalization

Nationalismus *m; -, kein Pl.* nationalism; **Nationalist** *m; -en, -en,* **Nationalistin** *f; -, -nen* nationalist; **nationalistisch I.** *Adj.* nationalist ..., nationalistic; **II.** *Adv.* nationalistically

Nationalität *f; -, -en* **1.** nationality; **sie ist griechischer ~** she's of Greek nationality, she's Greek; **2.** (*Minderheit*) ethnic minority

Nationalitäten|frage *f* problem of ethnic minorities, ethnic issue (*od.* problem); **~konflikt** *m* ethnic conflict; **~staat** *m* multinational state

Nationalitäts|kennzeichen *f Verk., Flug., Segelsport:* nationality sticker; **~prinzip** *n; nur Sg.; Jur.* principle of nationality

National|kirche *f* national church; **~konvent** *m; nur Sg.; hist.* National Convention; **~literatur** *f Lit.* national literature; **~mannschaft** *f Sport* national team (*od.* side); **die englische ~** the English team; **sie spielt in der spanischen ~** she plays for Spain; **~museum** *n* national museum

nationalökonomisch *Adj.* economic

National|park *m* national park; **~rat** *m* **1.** *österr.* National Assembly; *schw.* National Council; **2.** (*Nationalratsmitglied*) *österr.* member of the National Assembly; *schw.* member of the National Council; **~rätin** *f österr., schw.* → **Nationalrat** 2

Nationalsozialismus *m hist.* National Socialism; **Nationalsozialist** *m,* **Nationalsozialistin** *f* National Socialist; **nationalsozialistisch** *Adj.* National Socialist

National|spieler *m,* **~spielerin** *f Sport* international (player); **~sport** *m* national sport; **~sprache** *f* national language

Nationalstaat *m* nation state; **nationalstaatlich** *Adj.* nation-state ...

National|stolz *m* national pride; **~straße** *f schw.* motorway, *Am.* freeway; **~theater** *n* national theat|re (*Am.* auch -er); **~tracht** *f* national costume; **~trainer** *m,* **~trainerin** *f Sport* manager of the national team; **Englands Nationaltrainer X** England('s) manager X; **~trikot** *n Sport* national strip (*Am.* jersey); **~versammlung** *f* National Assembly

nativ *Adj. Chem., Ling.* native

Nativismus *m; -, kein Pl. Psych., Völkerkunde:* nativism

Nativität *f; -, -en; Astrol.* horoscope

NATO, Nato *f; -, kein Pl.; Abk.:* **die ~** NATO, Nato (= North Atlantic Treaty Organization)

Nato|land *n; mst Pl.* NATO (*od.* Nato) country (*od.* member); **~mitglied(s)staat** *m* member of NATO (*od.* Nato), NATO (*od.* Nato) member; **~Osterweiterung** *f* NATO (*od.* Nato) eastern (*od.* eastward) expansion, NATO's (*od.* Nato's) expansion to the east

Natrium *n; -s, kein Pl.; Chem.* sodium; **~chlorid** *n* sodium chloride; **~hydroxid** *n* sodium hydroxide, caustic soda; **~karbonat** *n* sodium carbonate, (washing) soda; **~salz** *n* sodium salt; **~silikat** *n* sodium silicate; **~sulfat** *n* sodium sulphate

Natron *n; -s, kein Pl.; Chem.* sodium;

kohlensaures **~** sodium carbonate; **~lauge** *f* sodium hydroxide, caustic soda

Natter *f; -, -n; Zool.* adder, viper; **e-e ~ am Busen nähren** *geh. fig.* nurse a viper in one's bosom

Nattern|brut *f geh. pej. fig.* vipers' brood; **~hemd** *n Zool.* shed snake skin

Natur *f; -, -en* **1.** *nur Sg.; bes. abstrakt:* (*auch* **die ~**) nature; *in e-r bestimmten Gegend:* natural surroundings *Pl.; auf dem Land:* countryside; (*natürliche Umwelt*) natural environment; (*Mutter ~*) mother nature; **in der freien ~** out in the open; *Tiere:* in their natural habitat; **er liebt die ~** he's a real nature lover; *weitS.* he loves to be out in the open; **nach der ~ zeichnen** draw from nature; **zurück zur ~!** back to nature!; **2.** *nur Sg.; Eiche:* **~** natural oak; *Schnitzel* **~** *Gastr. escalope not cooked in breadcrumbs;* **von ~** (*aus*) by nature; **ich bin von ~ aus blond** I'm naturally blond; **3.** *mst Sg.* (*Wesensart, Eigentümlichkeit*) temperament, disposition; (*Charakter*) character; **e-e gesunde ~ haben** have a strong constitution; **j-m zur zweiten ~ werden** become second nature to s.o.; **es geht ihm wider die ~** it's not in (*od.* it's against) his nature (*zu* + *Inf.* to + *Inf.*); **die menschliche ~** human nature; **gegen die ~** unnatural; **die ~ verlangt ihr Recht** *hum.* wenn jemand auf die Toilette muss: nature calls; wenn jemand einschläft: there's no point in fighting it; **4.** *nur Sg.* (*Art, Beschaffenheit*) nature; **die Sache ist ernster ~** it's a serious matter; **es liegt in der ~ der Sache** it's in the nature of it (*od.* of things); **5.** (*Mensch*) type, sort; **sie ist e-e kämpferische ~** she's the aggressive type; **die beiden sind gegensätzliche ~en** they are different personalities

natura: *in ~* → *in natura*

Natural|abgaben *Pl.* contributions (*od.* payment *Sg.*) in kind; **~bezüge** *Pl.* remuneration *Sg.* in kind

Naturalien *Pl.* **1.** natural produce *Sg.;* **in ~ bezahlen** *etc.* pay *etc.* in kind; **2.** *naturwissenschaftliche:* natural history objects (*od.* specimens); **~sammlung** *f* natural history collection

naturalisieren *v/t.* naturalize; **Naturalisierung** *f* naturalization

Naturalismus *m; -, kein Pl.; Kunst, Lit.* naturalism; **Naturalist** *m; -en, -en,* **Naturalistin** *f; -, -nen* naturalist; **naturalistisch** *Adj.* naturalist(ic)

Natural|leistung *f* payment in kind; **~lohn** *m* wages *Pl.* in kind; **~wirtschaft** *f* barter economy

Natur|apostel *m umg. iro.* nature freak; **~arzt** *m,* **~ärztin** *f* naturopath; **~begabung** *f* **1.** natural gift; **2.** *Person:* natural

naturbelassen *Adj.* (*im Naturzustand*) natural, in its (*od.* their) natural state; (*unbehandelt*) untreated; *Landschaft:* unspoil|t (*Am.* -ed), left in its natural (*od.* original) state; **~e Lebensmittel** untreated (*od.* conservation) food; **Naturbelassenheit** *f* natural state

Natur|beobachtung *f* nature study, observation of nature; *von Tieren:* wildlife observation; **~beschreibung** *f* description of nature

naturblond *Adj.* naturally blond

Natur|bühne *f* open-air stage; **~bursche** *m* nature boy; **~darm** *f Fleischerei:* real intestine (*used as sausage skin*); **~denkmal** *n* natural monument

nature [na'tyːr] *indekl. Adj. nachgestellt; Gastr.* plain, au naturel; *Schnitzel etc.*: unbreaded

Naturell *n; -s, -e* temperament, disposition

Natur|ereignis *n,* **~erscheinung** *f* natural phenomenon; **~erzeugnis** *n* natural product

Naturfarbe *f (natürliche Farbe)* natural colo(u)r; *(Naturfarbstoff)* natural dye; **naturfarben** *Adj.* natural-colo(u)red

Natur|faser *f* natural fib|re *(Am. -er);* **~film** *m* nature film

Naturforscher *m,* **~in** *f* naturalist; **Naturforschung** *f* (natural) science

Naturfreund *m* nature lover; **Naturfreundin** *f* nature lover

Natur|gas *n* natural gas; **~gefühl** *n; nur Sg.; (Verbundenheit mit der Natur)* feeling for nature; *(Einstellung zur Natur)* attitude towards nature

natur|gegeben *Adj.* natural, decreed by nature; *Talent etc.*: a gift of nature; **~gemäß I.** *Adj. (natürlich)* natural; *(organisch)* organic; **II.** *Adv.* naturally; *(in der Natur der Sache liegend)* by definition

Naturgeschichte *f* natural history; **naturgeschichtlich** *Adj.* natural history ...

Naturgesetz *n* law of nature

naturgetreu I. *Adj.* true to nature; *wie in Wirklichkeit* realistic; **II.** *Adv.* realistically; **~** *darstellen* portray in a realistic way

Natur|gewalten *Pl.* elements; **~gottheit** *f Reli.* god of nature, natural deity; **~haar** *n* real hair; **~haushalt** *m* balance of nature, ecological balance

Naturheilkunde *f* naturopathy; **naturheilkundlich** *Adj.* naturopathic

Naturheilverfahren *n* naturopathic treatment; *Pl. auch* naturopathy *Sg.*

naturidentisch *Adj. Farbstoff etc.*: nature-identical

Naturist *m; -en, -en,* **~in** *f; -, -nen* naturist

Natur|katastrophe *f* natural disaster; **~kautschuk** *m* natural (india) rubber; **~kind** *n* child of nature; **~konstante** *f Phys.* (universal) constant; **~kosmetik** *f* natural makeup

Naturkost *f* health food(s *Pl.*); **~laden** *m* health food shop *(od. store)*

Natur|kraft *f* natural force; **~krause** *f* naturally frizzy hair, *umg.* natural frizz

Naturkunde *f; nur Sg.; altm.* (study of) natural history; *Päd.* nature study; **Naturkundler** *m; -s, -,* **Naturkundlerin** *f; -, -nen* naturalist; **naturkundlich** *Adj. attr.* natural history

Natur|landschaft *f (auch e-e ~)* unspoil|t *(Am. -ed) (od.* untouched, natural) countryside; **~lehrpfad** *m* nature trail

natürlich I. *Adj.* natural *(auch echt, angeboren, ungekünstelt etc.); (üblich)* normal; **~e** *Größe* actual *(od.* full) size; *die ~ste Sache der Welt* the most natural thing in the world; *e-s ~en Todes sterben* die a natural death; *das geht nicht mit ~en Dingen zu umg.* there's something fishy about it; **II.** *Adv.* naturally; *auch Interj.* of course; *sich ~ verhalten* act natural(ly); *ich könnte ~ ...* of course I could ..., I could always ...; *aber ~!* but of course!; **Natürlichkeit** *f* naturalness

Natur|locken *Pl.* natural curls; **~mensch** *m* child of nature, *iro.* nature boy

natur|nah(e) I. *Adj.* close to nature; *fig.* realistic, lifelike; **II.** *Adv.:* **~** *leben* live in close touch with nature; **~notwendig** *Adj.* necessary

Natur|park *m* nature reserve; **~perle** *f* natural pearl; **~phänomen** *n* natural phenomenon

Naturphilosophie *f* philosophy of nature; **naturphilosophisch** *Adj.* in terms of the philosophy of nature

Naturprodukt *n* natural product

Naturrecht *n; nur Sg.; Philos.* natural law; **naturrechtlich** *Adj.* in terms of natural law

Naturreichtümer *Pl.* natural resources

naturrein *Adj.* pure, unadulterated

Natur|reis *m* brown rice; **~religion** *f* nature religion; **~schauspiel** *n* spectacle of nature; **~schilderung** *f* description of nature; **~schönheit** *f; mst Pl.* beauty spot, area of natural beauty

Naturschutz *m* nature conservation; *unter ~ stehen* be protected (by law); *unter ~ stellen* protect by law; **Naturschützer** *m,* **Naturschützerin** *f* conservationist; **Naturschutzgebiet** *n* nature reserve, conservation area

Natur|seide *f* natural silk; **~stoff** *m* natural substance; **~talent** *n* **1.** natural talent; **2.** *(Person)* natural; **~ton** *m Mus.* natural note; **~trieb** *m geh.* natural instinct

naturtrüb *Adj. fachspr. Saft, Bier*: naturally cloudy

naturverbunden *Adj. (naturnah)* close to *(od.* in touch with) nature; *(naturliebend)* nature-loving ...; **~** *sein (naturnah leben)* live in close touch with nature; *(Naturfreund sein)* be a nature lover; **Naturverbundenheit** *f* close relationship to nature; love of nature

naturverträglich *Adj.* environmentally compatible

Naturvolk *n altm.* primitive people

naturwidrig *Adj.* unnatural

Naturwissenschaft *f* (natural) science; **Naturwissenschaftler** *m,* **Naturwissenschaftlerin** *f* scientist; **naturwissenschaftlich** *Adj.* scientific; **~es Fach** science subject

naturwüchsig *Adj.* natural

Natur|wunder *n* wonder of nature *(auch hum. Person);* **~zustand** *m* natural state

'nauf *Adv. südd.* → **hinauf**

'naus *Adv. südd.* → **hinaus**

Nautik *f; -, kein Pl.* navigation, nautical science; **Nautiker** *m; -s, -,* **Nautikerin** *f; -, -nen* navigator; **nautisch** *Adj.* nautical

Navigation *f; -, kein Pl.; Flug., Naut.* navigation

Navigations|fehler *m Flug., Naut.* navigational error; **~gerät** *n* navigation system; **~karte** *f* navigation chart; **~offizier** *m* navigator; **~raum** *m* chart room

Navigator *m; -s, -en,* **~in** *f; -, -nen Flug., Naut.* navigator; **navigatorisch** *Adj.* navigational; **navigieren** *vt/i.* navigate

Nazi *m; -s, -s; pej.* Nazi; **~herrschaft** *f hist. (auch die ~)* Nazi rule; **~regime** *n hist.* Nazi regime

Nazismus *m; -, kein Pl.; pej.* Nazism; **nazistisch** *Adj.* Nazi ...

Nazi|verbrechen *n hist.* Nazi crime *(od.* atrocity); **~vergangenheit** *f* Nazi past; **~zeit** *f* Nazi era, (period of) Nazi rule

NB *Abk. (notabene)* NB

n. Br. *Abk. (nördlicher Breite):* 45° n. *Br.* 45° N (latitude)

n. Chr. *Abk. (nach Christus)* A.D., AD (= anno Domini)

nd. *Abk. (niederdeutsch)* Low German

NDR *m; -, kein Pl.; Abk. (Norddeutscher Rundfunk)* North German Radio

ne *Adv. umg. (nicht [wahr])* bekräftigend: *die haben alle geschrien, ~, und dann ...* everyone shouted, didn't they; *fragend: du kennst ihn doch, ~?* you know him of course, don't you?

'ne *Abk. umg.* → **eine**

Neandertaler *m; -s, -* Anthropologie: *(auch der ~)* Neanderthal man

Neapel *(n); -s; Geog.* Naples; **Neapolitaner I.** *m; -s, -* **1.** Neapolitan; **2.** *österr. Gastr., Gebäck:* cream-filled wafer biscuit *(Am.* cookie); **II.** *indekl. Adj.* Neapolitan; **Neapolitanerin** *f; -, -nen* Neapolitan, Neapolitan woman *(od.* girl *etc.)*

Nearktis *f; -, kein Pl.; Geog., Zool.* Nearctic region

Nebbich *m; -s, -e Sl.* nobody

Nebel *m; -s, -* **1.** fog; *leichter*: mist; *(Dunst)* haze; *künstlicher*: smoke; *fig.* mist, veil, cloud; *bei (dichtem) ~* in (thick) fog; *fällt aus wegen ~! umg. fig.* it's off(, I'm afraid); **2.** *Astron.* nebula *(Pl.* nebulae *od.* nebulas); **~bank** *f* fog bank; **~bildung** *f* (formation *od.* buildup of) fog; **~boje** *f Naut.* fog buoy; **~decke** *f* fog cover, blanket of fog; **~düse** *f Tech.* fine spray attachment; **~feld** *n* fog bank; *kleineres*: patch of fog; **~fetzen** *Pl.* fog patches, patchy fog *Sg.*

nebelfeucht *Adj. Straße etc.*: wet with fog; *Wetter*: dank

Nebel|fleck *m Astron.* nebula *(Pl.* nebulae *od.* nebulas); **~glocke** *f* blanket of fog; **~granate** *f* smoke grenade

nebelgrau *Adj.* grey and misty

nebelhaft *Adj. fig.* hazy, dim, nebulous; *(vage)* fuzzy

Nebel|haufen *m Astron.* galactic cluster, cluster of galaxies; **~horn** *n Naut.* foghorn

nebelig *Adj.* → **neblig**

Nebel|kammer *f Phys.* cloud chamber; **~kerze** *f bes. Mil.* smoke candle; **~krähe** *f Zool.* hooded crow; **~leuchte** *f Mot.* fog lamp

nebeln I. *v/i.* **1.** *unpers. geh.* be foggy; *es nebelt* it's misty; *von dichterem Nebel*: it's foggy; **2.** become misty; **II.** *v/t. fachspr. (versprühen)* spray

Nebel|nässe *f* damp conditions caused by fog; **~nässen** *n; -s, kein Pl.* foggy drizzle; **~scheinwerfer** *m Mot.* fog lamp; **~schleier** *m geh., poet.* veil of mist *(od.* fog), haze; **~schlussleuchte** *f Mot.* rear fog lamp; **~schwaden** *Pl.* patchy fog *Sg.*, fog patches

nebelverhangen *Adj. präd. und nachgestellt*: shrouded in mist

Nebel|wald *m Geog.* cloud forest; **~wand** *f* fog bank; *Mil.* smoke screen; **~wetter** *n* foggy weather

neben *Präp.* **1.** *örtlich*: next to, beside; *die Polizeifahrzeuge fuhren ~ dem Konvoi her* the police vehicles drove alongside the convoy; *er saß dicht ~ ihr* he sat right beside her; *auf dem Parkplatz stand Auto ~ Auto* the car park *(Am.* parking lot) was packed with cars; *er duldet keinen Konkurrenten ~ sich fig.* he doesn't tolerate any close competition; **2.** *(verglichen mit)* compared with *(od.* to); **3.** *(außer)* apart *(bes. Am.* aside) from, besides; *(zusätzlich zu)* in addition to; *~ anderen Dingen* among(st) other things; *du sollst keine anderen Götter ~ mir haben bibl.* thou shalt have no other gods before me

Neben|abrede f Jur. collateral agreement; **~absicht** f secondary objective; (Hintergedanke) ulterior motive; **~akzent** m Ling. secondary stress; **~altar** m side altar

Nebenamt n 1. subsidiary office; 2. Telef. branch exchange; **nebenamtlich** I. Adj. Tätigkeit etc.: part-time …; II. Adv. e-e Stelle ausüben etc.: part--time, … on the side

nebenan Adv.: (**im Haus**) ~ next door; (**im Zimmer**) ~ auch in the next room; **bei uns** ~ next-door to us; **die Leute von** ~ the people next door

Neben|anschluss m Telef. extension; **~arbeit** f 1. job on the side, sideline; 2. **~en** less important (od. secondary) jobs; **~arm** m e-s Flusses: branch; **~ausgaben** Pl. extras; Wirts. incidental expenses; **~ausgang** m side exit; **~bau** m → **Nebengebäude**; **~bedeutung** f bes. Ling. connotation

nebenbei Adv. 1. (beiläufig) in passing; ~ **bemerkt** incidentally, by the way, apropos of nothing; 2. (nebenher) on the side; 3. (außerdem) nachgestellt: as well, besides

Nebenbemerkung f aside

Nebenberuf m sideline, job on the side; **sie ist im ~ Musiklehrerin** she teaches music as a sideline; **nebenberuflich** I. Adj.: **~e Arbeit** sideline, job on the side; II. Adv. as a sideline, on the side

Neben|beschäftigung f → **Nebenarbeit**, **Nebenberuf**; **~betrieb** m branch; (Fabrik) auch subsidiary plant

Nebenbuhler m, **~in** f rival (auch fig.)

Neben|darsteller m Theat. etc. supporting actor; Pl. supporting cast Sg. (auch V. im Pl.); **~dinge** Pl. trivialities; **~effekt** m side effect

nebeneinander Adv. next to each other; auch fig. side by side; zeitlich: at the same time, simultaneously; (gleichzeitig) concurrently; ~ bestehen coexist; ~ halten hold next to each other (od. side by side); ~ legen place (od. lay) next to each other (od. side by side); ~ liegen lie next to each other (od. side by side); ~ schalten Etech., Tech. (parallel schalten) connect in parallel; ~ sitzen sit next to each other (od. side by side); ~ stellen put (od. place) next to each other (od. side by side); vergleichend: compare

Nebeneinander n; -s, kein Pl.: **das ~ von Altem und Neuem** the juxtaposition of the old and the new; (friedliches) ~ Pol. (peaceful) coexistence

nebeneinanderher Adv. side by side

Neben|eingang m side entrance; **~einkommen** n extra income (on the side); **~einkünfte** Pl. additional earnings; **~einnahmen** Pl. extra income Sg.; **~erscheinung** f side effect; Med. secondary symptom; **~erwerb** m extra income; (Nebenberuf) job on the side

Nebenerwerbs|betrieb m part-time farming; **~landwirt** m, **~landwirtin** f part-time farmer

Neben|fach n 1. Päd., Univ. subsidiary (od. secondary) subject, umg. subsid, Am. minor (subject); 2. im Schrank etc.: side compartment; **~figur** f minor character; **~flügel** m side wing; **~fluss** m tributary; **~form** f variant; umg. **~frage** f side issue; **~frau** f hist., Völkerkunde: concubine; **~gebäude** n building next door, next(-door) building; (Anbau) outbuilding, annex(e); **~gebühren** Pl. extra charges; **~gedanke** m 1. second-

ary consideration; 2. (Hintergedanke) ulterior motive; **~gegenstand** m österr., Päd. → **Nebenfach** 1; **~geräusch** n 1. auch Pl. (background) noise; Radio: auch interference; Hi-Fi: background noise; 2. Med. secondary murmur; **~gericht** n side dish; **~gestein** n Geol. adjacent rock; **~gleis** n Eisenb. siding, Am. auch sidetrack; umg. fig. sideline; **~handlung** f subplot; **~haus** n house (od. building) next door, next house (od. building)

nebenher Adv. 1. (an der Seite) alongside, by my etc. side; 2. (gleichzeitig) at the same time; 3. verdienen etc.: on the side; **~fahren**, ~ **fahren** v/i. (unreg., trennb., ist -ge-) drive od. ride along beside s.o. (od. s.th.), drive (od. ride) alongside; **~laufen**, ~ **laufen** v/i. (unreg., trennb., ist -ge-) run (gehen: walk) along beside s.o. (od. s.th.)

nebenhin Adv. bemerken etc.: in passing, casually

Nebenhoden m Anat. epididymis (Pl. epididymides)

Nebenhöhle f Anat. sinus; **Nebenhöhlenentzündung** f Med. sinusitis

Neben|job m umg. → **Nebenarbeit**, **Nebenberuf**; **~klage** f Jur. incidental action; **~kläger** m, **~klägerin** f Jur. co-plaintiff; **~kosten** Pl. extra costs (od. expenses), extras; **~kriegsschauplatz** m secondary area of conflict; **~linie** f 1. Genealogie: collateral line; 2. Eisenb. branch line; **~mann** m person (sitting etc.) next to one, Am. seatmate

Nebenniere f Anat. adrenal gland

Nebennieren|hormon n Physiol. adrenaline; **~rinde** f Anat. adrenal cortex

nebenordnen v/t. (trennb., hat -ge-) Ling. coordinate; **Nebenordnung** f coordination

Neben|produkt n by-product (+ Gen. of); konkret: auch spin-off (from); **~raum** m 1. side room; (Abstellraum) storeroom; 2. (Raum nebenan) room next door, next room; **~rechte** Pl. Jur. subsidiary rights; **~rolle** f Theat. etc. minor part (fig. role); **~kleine** ~ bit part

Nebensache f minor consideration; **das ist** ~ that's not so important; **nebensächlich** Adj. (unwesentlich) unimportant, präd. auch not important; (nicht zur Sache gehörig) irrelevant; **Nebensächlichkeit** f (zweitrangiges Thema, Problem etc.) irrelevant matter, irrelevancy, side issue; (Belanglosigkeit) triviality

Neben|saison f low (od. off-peak od. off) season; **~satz** m Ling. subordinate clause; **~schaltung** f parallel connection; **~schilddrüse** f Anat. parathyroid (gland); **~schluss** m Etech. etc. parallel connection; **~spieler** m, **~spielerin** f Sport: **Keane und sein Nebenspieler Scholes** Keane and his fellow midfielder Scholes

nebenstehend Adj. und Adv. am Rande: in the margin; ~ (abgebildet) opposite

Neben|stelle f 1. (Filiale) branch; 2. Telef. extension; **~stellenanlage** f Telef. private branch exchange

Neben|straße f side street; auf dem Land: byroad; **~strecke** f 1. Eisenb. branch line; 2. (Entlastungsstraße) relief road; **~strömung** f job on the side, sideline; **~tisch** m: (am) ~ (at the) next table; **~titel** m subtitle; **~ton** m 1. Ling. secondary stress; 2. Pl. Mus. secondary notes; **~tür** f side door; **~veranstaltung** f side show; bei Fest-

spielen etc.: fringe event; **~verdienst** m extra earnings Pl. (od. income); **~weg** m side road; **~winkel** m Math. adjacent angle; **~wirkung** f side effect; Pl. fig. fallout Sg.; **~zimmer** n 1. next (od. adjoining) room, room next door; 2. im Lokal etc.: side room; hinten: room at the back; **~zweck** m secondary aim (od. objective)

neblig Adj. foggy, misty; **~trüb** misty and dull (od. overcast)

nebst Präp. altm. together (od. along) with; (einschließlich) including; **~bei** Adv. österr. → **nebenbei**; **~dem** Adv. schw. → **außerdem**

nebulös Adj. geh. fig. nebulous, hazy

Necessaire [nesɛ'sɛːɐ̯] n; -s, -s 1. (Reisenecessaire) toilet bag, Am. travel kit; 2. für die Maniküre: manicure set

necken v/t. tease (mit about); **sich od. einander** ~ tease each other (od. one another); → **lieben** I; **Neckerei** f; -, -en teasing

neckisch Adj. (schelmisch) playful; Bemerkung etc.: auch teasing; (kokett, kess) Kleidungsstück, Frisur etc.: coquettish; **was sind denn das für ~e Spielchen?** umg. hum. what sort of naughty games are these?

nee Adv. umg. nope, no; → auch **nein**

Neer f; -, -en; nordd. eddy; **~strömung** f nordd. back eddy current

Neffe m; -n, -n nephew

Negation f; -, -en negation

negativ I. Adj. negative (auch Phys., Math., Med., Etech., Fot.); **~e Auswirkungen haben** have an adverse effect (auf +Akk. on); **das Negative daran** the negative side of it (od. thing about it); **das ist nichts Negatives** there's nothing wrong with it; II. Adv. negatively; **etw. ~ beurteilen** see s.th. negatively, take a negative view of s.th.; **alles nur ~ sehen** auch always look on the negative side (of things); **du siehst das zu ~** you're being too pessimistic about it

Negativ n; -s, -e; Fot. negative

Negativ|beispiel n negative example; **~bilanz** f debit balance; **~bild** n negative; **~druck** m 1. reverse printing; 2. konkret: reverse print; **~film** m negative film; **~image** n negative image

Negativ|leistung f bad performance; **~liste** f 1. Med., Pharm. list of medicines that are not covered by statutory health insurance; 2. allg.: black list; **~schlagzeile** f, mst Pl. bad headline; **~werbung** f negative advertising

neger Adj. österr. umg. neg!: ~ **sein** be broke

Neger m; -s, - 1. neg! black; anthropologisch altm.: negro; (Schwarzafrikaner) black African; 2. TV Sl. idiot board; **Negerin** f; -, -nen; neg! black (woman od. girl); anthropologisch altm.: negro woman, negress; (Schwarzafrikanerin) black African woman (od. girl)

Neger|kuss m Gastr. chocolate-covered marshmallow; **~sklave** m, **~sklavin** f hist. negro slave

negieren v/t. (abstreiten) deny; (verneinen) negate; **Negierung** f denial; negation

Negligé [negli'ʒeː] n; -s, -s negligee

negrid Adj. Anthropologie: Negroid neg!

Négritude [negri'tyd] f; -, kein Pl. negritude

negroid Adj. Anthropologie: negroid; **Negroide** m, f; -n, -n Negroid neg!

Negus m; -, - und -se; hist. Negus

nehmen v/t.; *nimmt, nahm, hat genommen* **1.** (*[er]greifen, an sich bringen*) take; (*in Empfang* ～) receive; (*j-n einstellen*) take s.o.; (*kaufen*) take; *in die Hand / unter den Arm* ～ take in one's hand / put under one's arm; *etw. an sich* ～ take s.th.; *zu sich* ～ (*Person*) take s.o. in; *Gott hat sie zu sich genommen geh. euph.* God has called her home; *sich* (*Dat.*) *e-e Frau / e-n Mann* ～ (*heiraten*) *umg.* take a wife / a husband; *woher* ～ *und nicht stehlen? hum.* where (on earth) am I supposed to get hold of that (*od.* them *etc.*)?; *auf sich* ～ undertake, take upon o.s., (*Amt, Bürde*) assume, (*Verantwortung*) accept, take; *die Folgen auf sich* ～ bear the consequences; **2.** (*wegnehmen*) take; (*sich aneignen*) take away; (*rauben*) deprive of *hope, rights etc.*; *j-m die Angst etc.* ～ take away s.o.'s fear *etc.*; *j-m die Sicht* ～ block s.o.'s view; *das nimmt der Sache den od. jeden Reiz* that spoils it, that takes the fun out of it; *das lasse ich mir nicht* ～ I won't be done out of that; (*ich bin davon überzeugt*) nobody's going to talk me out of that; *er lässt es sich nicht* ～ *zu* (+ *Inf.*) he insists on (+ *Ger.*); **3.** (*essen*) have; *zu sich* ～ have; *ich habe den ganzen Tag noch nichts zu mir genommen* I haven't had anything to eat or drink all day; ～ *Sie noch Tee?* will you have some more tea?; *ich nehme Hühnchen mit Reis* I'll have chicken with rice; *einen* ～ *umg.* (*Schnaps*) have one; ～ *Sie doch noch einen* go on, have another one; **4.** *Medizin etc.*: take; *Drogen* ～ take drugs; → *Pille*; **5.** (*benutzen*) use; (*sich bedienen*) help o.s. to; (*Beförderungsmittel*) take; (*in Anspruch nehmen*) (*Anwalt etc.*) take, get (hold of); *man nehme Rezept*: take; **6.** (*bewältigen*) (*Hindernis*) take, clear; *Mot.* (*Kurve, Steigung*) take, negotiate; **7.** (*auffassen*): *wörtlich* ～ take literally; *nimm's nicht so tragisch umg.* don't take it to heart; **8.** (*sich vorstellen*): ～ *wir den Fall, dass* let's assume that, suppose that; ～ *wir e-n Dichter wie Shakespeare* let's take a poet such as Shakespeare; **9.** (*behandeln, umgehen mit*): *j-n zu* ～ *wissen* know how to handle s.o.; *er versteht es, die Kunden richtig zu* ～ he has a way with customers; *du musst ihn* ～, *wie er ist* you have to take him as he is; **10.** (*betrachten*): *du darfst das nicht wörtlich* ～ you shouldn't take it literally; *wie man's nimmt* it depends; **11.** *Sport* (*foulen*): *j-n hart* ～ commit a blatant foul on s.o.; **12.** *Mil.* take, capture; *nach langer Belagerung nahmen sie die Stadt* they took the city after a long siege; **13.** (*als Zahlung fordern*) charge, take

Nehmen n; -s, *kein Pl.*: *er ist hart im* ～ he can take a lot (of punishment); → *Geben* 1

Nehmer m; -s, -, ～*in* f; -, -*nen* taker; **Nehmerqualitäten** *Pl. Boxen*: ability *Sg.* to take punches

Nehrung f; -, -*en*; *Geog.* spit

Neid m; -(e)s, *kein Pl.* envy (*auf j-n*: of, *etw.*: at); (*Missgunst*) jealousy; *aus* (*purem*) ～ out of (sheer) envy; *grün od. gelb vor* ～ green with envy; *vor* ～ *vergehen od. erblassen* be eaten up (*od.* consumed) with envy; *das ist nur der* ～ *der Besitzlosen umg.* he's *etc.* just jealous because he *etc.* hasn't got one; → *blass* 1; **neiden** v/t.: *j-m etw.* ～ envy s.o. s.th.; **Neider** m; -s, -, Nei-

derin f; -, -*nen* envious person; *viele* ～ *haben* be the envy of many; **neiderfüllt I.** *Adj.* filled with envy, envious; **II.** *Adv.* (filled) with envy, enviously

Neid|hammel m *umg. pej.* envious (*od.* jealous) person; **neidisch** *Adj.* envious, jealous (*auf* + *Akk.* of); **neidlos** *Adj. und Adv.* without envy, ungrudging(ly *Adv.*); **neidvoll** *Adj. und Adv.* full of envy

Neige f; -, -*n* **1.** (*Abnahme*) decline; *zur* ～ *gehen* decline, wane; *Vorrat*: run low (*auch Wirts.*); *Tag, Leben etc.*: be drawing to an end; *bis zur* ～ *auskosten* savo(u)r to the last (*od.* the full); *bis zur bitteren* ～ to the bitter end; **2.** *im Glas etc.*: dregs *Pl.*

neigen I. v/t. bend, incline *förm.*; (*niederbeugen*) bow (down); (*kippen*) tilt, tip; **II.** v/refl. bend, lean; *Ebene*: slant; *Boden*: slope; (*sich verbeugen*) bow; → *zuneigen* I 1; **III.** v/i.: ～ *zu* fig. tend to (+ *Inf.*), have a tendency to (+ *Inf.*) (*od.* toward(s) [+ *Ger.*] *od.* s.th.); (*anfällig sein*) be susceptible to s.th., be prone to s.th. (*od.* + *Inf.*, + *Ger.*); *zu Unfällen* ～ be accident-prone; *er neigt zu Übertreibungen* he tends to exaggerate; *ich neige zu der Ansicht, dass* I'm inclined to think (that), I rather think (that); → *geneigt*

Neigung f **1.** inclination; (*geneigte Fläche*) slope, incline; *Straße*: gradient; *Math. etc.*; **2.** *fig.* (*Hang*) inclination (*zu* to, toward[s]), propensity (to, for); (*Vorliebe*) liking, penchant, predilection (for); *Wirts., Pol.* tendency, trend (toward[s]); (*Veranlagung*) disposition (for); *bes. zum Negativen*: proclivity (for); (*Zuneigung*) affection (for), love (of); *e-e* ～ *zur Philosophie etc. haben* have a philosophical *etc.* bent; *s-n* ～*en nachgeben* follow one's inclinations; *wenig* ～ *zeigen zu* (+ *Inf.*) (*keine Lust haben*) show little inclination to (+ *Inf.*); *er zeigt wenig* ～ *dazu* (*hat kein Talent*) he shows little talent in that direction

Neigetechnik f; *kein Pl.*; *Eisenb.* tilting technology; ～*zug* m tilting train

Neigungs|ehe f love match; ～*gruppe* f *bes. Päd.* club; ～ *Fußball* (school) football club; ～*winkel* m *Math.* angle of inclination (*od.* tilt)

nein *Adv.* **1.** no; ～ *sagen* say no; ～ *und abermals* ～! for the last time, no!; *aber* ～! *zusichernd*: of course not; *widersprechend*: no!; *geht er? -* ～ is he going? - no, he isn't; *haben Sie gerufen? -* ～ did you call? - no, I didn't; **2.** *Erstaunen, Überraschung ausdrückend*: ～, *ist das schön!* oh, how beautiful that is!; **3.** *eine vorangegangene Verneinung verstärkend*: ～, *das ist unmöglich* no, really that's impossible; **4.** *als Antwort Unglauben, Zweifel ausdrückend*: *jetzt will er sich auch noch eine Glatze schneiden lassen! -* ～! you don't say!, well - I never!; **5.** *bittend od. zweifelnd, nachgestellt*: *du gehst doch noch nicht,* ～? you're not going yet, are you?; **6.** *verstärkend*: *er schätzte,* ～, *er verehrte sie* he thought highly of her, no, he adored her

Nein n; -(s), -(s) no; (*Ablehnung*) refusal; *ein klares* ～ a straight no; *mit e-m* ～ *antworten* say no; (*ablehnen*) *auch* refuse

'nein *Adv. südd.* → *hinein*

Nein|sager m; -s, -, ～*sagerin* f; -, -*nen* obstructionist; ～*stimme* f *Parl.* no (*Pl.* noes), *Am.* nay

Nekrolog¹ m; -(e)s, -e obituary

Nekrolog² n; -(e)s, -e, **Nekrologium** n; -s, *Nekrologien*; *hist.* (*Verzeichnis*) obituary

Nekromantie f; -, *kein Pl.* necromancy

Nekrophilie f; -, *kein Pl.* necrophilia

Nekropole f; -, -*n Nekropolen*; *Archäol., hist.* necropolis

Nekrose f; -, -*n*; *Med.* necrosis (*Pl.* necroses)

nekrotisch *Adj. Med.* necrotic, dead

Nektar m; -s, -e **1.** *Bot. und Myth.* nectar; **2.** *Getränk*: fruit juice (*containing crushed fruit*)

Nektarine f; -, -*n*; *Bot.* nectarine

Nelke f; -, -*n*; *Bot.* **1.** (*Blume*) carnation; **2.** (*Gewürznelke*) clove

Nelken|gewächs n *Bot.* pinks *Pl.*; ～*öl* n clove oil; ～*pfeffer* m allspice, pimento; ～*wurz* f *Bot.* geum

Nematode m; -n, -n; *Zool.* nematode

Nemax m; -, *kein Pl.*; *Abk.* (*Neuer-Markt-Index*) Nemax

Nemesis f; -, *kein Pl.*; *geh.* nemesis (*Pl.* nemeses)

'nen *Abk. umg.* → *einen*

Nenn... *im Subst.* nominal; *Tech.* mst rated

nennbar *Adj.* nameable, *Am. auch* namable; (*nennenswert*) worth mentioning; *Summe*: appreciable

Nennbetrag m nominal amount (*od.* sum)

nennen; *nennt, nannte, hat genannt* **I.** v/t. name; (*benennen*) *auch* call, *förm.* designate; *spottend*: dub; *j-n nach j-m* ～ name (*od.* call) s.o. after s.o.; *j-n beim od. bei s-m Namen* ～ call s.o. by his (*od.* her) name; *j-n e-n Lügner* ～ call s.o. a liar; *Maria I., genannt „die Katholische"* Mary I, (otherwise) known as Mary the Catholic; *das nenne ich e-e Überraschung!* well, that really is a surprise!; *das nennst du e-n guten Wein?* is that what you call a good wine?; **1.** (*erwähnen*) mention; (*anführen*) quote; (*preisgeben*) reveal, give away; *kannst du mir den höchsten Berg der Welt* ～? can you name (*od.* what's) the highest mountain in the world?; *können Sie mir ein gutes Hotel* ～? can you give me the name of a good hotel?; **2.** (*benennen*) name; *morgen will das Parteipräsidium den Spitzenkandidaten* ～ the party executive committee wants to name the top candidate tomorrow; **II.** v/refl. be called; *wie nennt sich ...?* what's ... called?; *und das od. umg. so was nennt sich Lehrer* and he calls himself a teacher; *und das nennt sich Kultur* and that's supposed to be culture, and that goes by the name of culture, and they call it culture; → *Eigen, genannt, Name* 1

nennenswert *Adj.* worth mentioning; *Betrag etc.*: appreciable; *kein* ～*er Musiker etc.* no musician etc. to speak of; *keine* ～*e Leistung umg.* nothing to write home about; *nichts Nennenswertes* nothing worth mentioning

Nenner m; -s, -; *Math.* denominator; *auf e-n* (*gemeinsamen*) ～ *bringen fig.* bring down to a common denominator; *e-n gemeinsamen* ～ *finden* (*für*) *fig.* ein Vorhaben etc.: find some common ground on which to base (...)

Nenn|form f *Ling.* infinitive; ～*gebühr* f *Sport* entry fee (*to enter a competition*); ～*leistung* Tech. f rated power (*od.* output); ～*onkel* m *umg.* uncle in name only

nennt *Präs.* → *nennen*

Nenntante f *umg.* aunt in name only

Nennung *f* naming; (*Erwähnung*) mention; *Sport* entry; *bei der ~ ihres Namens* when her name was mentioned (*od.* called out)

Nenn|wert *m* Wirts. nominal (*od.* face) value; *zum/über/unter ~* at/above/below par

neo..., **Neo...** *im Subst. und Adj.* neo(-)..., Neo(-)...

Neodym *n*; *-s, kein Pl.*; *Chem.* neodymium

Neofaschismus *m* neo-fascism, neo-Fascism; **Neofaschist** *m*, **Neofaschistin** *f* neo-fascist, neo-Fascist; **neofaschistisch** *Adj.* neo-fascist, neo-Fascist

Neoklassizismus *m* neoclassicism; **Neoklassizist** *m*; *-en, -en*, **Neoklassizistin** *f*; *-, -nen* neoclassicist; **neoklassizistisch** *Adj.* neoclassical

Neo|kolonialismus *m* neocolonialism; **~liberalismus** *m* neoliberalism

Neolithikum *n*; *-s, kein Pl.* Neolithic period; **neolithisch** *Adj.* Neolithic

Neologismus *m*; *-, Neologismen*; *Ling.* neologism

Neon *n*; *-s, kein Pl.*; *Chem.* neon

Neonazi *m* neo-Nazi; **Neonazismus** *m* neo-Nazism; **Neonazist** *m*; *-en, -en*, **Neonazistin** *f*; *-, -nen* neo-Nazi; **neonazistisch** *Adj.* neo-Nazi

Neon|fisch *m* Zool. neon tetra; **~lampe** *f*, **~leuchte** *f* neon light (*od.* lamp); **~licht** *n* neon light; **~reklame** *f* neon sign; **~röhre** *f* neon tube; *Pl. auch* strip lighting *Sg.*

Neoplasma *n* Med. neoplasm

Neopren® *n*; *-s, kein Pl.* ncoprcnc®; **~anzug** *m* wet suit

Neorealismus *m* Literatur, Film: neorealism

Neozoikum *n*; *-s, kein Pl.*; *Geol.* Cenozoic; **neozoisch** *Adj.* Cenozoic

Nepal (*n*); *-s*; *Geog.* Nepal; **Nepalese** *m*; *-en, -en*, **Nepalesin** *f*; *-, -nen* Nepalese, Nepali, *weiblich auch*: Nepalese woman (*od.* girl); **nepalesisch** *Adj.* Nepali, Nepalese, Nepal ...; **Nepali** *n*; *-, kein Pl.* Ling. Nepali

Nephrit *m*; *-s, -e*; *Min.* nephrite

Nephritis *f*; *-, Nephritiden*; *Med.* nephritis (*Pl.* nephritides)

Nepotismus *m*; *-, kein Pl.* nepotism; **nepotistisch** *Adj.* nepotic, nepotistic

Nepp *m*; *-s, kein Pl.*; *umg. pej.* daylight (*Am.* highway) robbery, *a* rip-off; *es ist der reinste ~* it's a real rip-off

neppen. *v/t. umg. pej.* fleece, rip *s.o.* off; **Nepper** *m*; *-s, -*; *umg. pej.* rip-off artist

Nepplokal. *n umg. pej.* clip joint, rip-off place

Neptun *m*; *-s, kein Pl.*; *Astron., Myth.* Neptune; (*dem*) *~ opfern hum.* be seasick over the side of a ship

Neptunium *n*; *-s, kein Pl.*; *Chem.* neptunium

Nerv *m*; *-s, -en*; *Anat.* nerve; *Bot. auch* vein; *j-m auf die ~en fallen od. gehen umg.* get on *s.o.*'s nerves; *j-m den ~ töten od. rauben umg.* drive *s.o.* mad; *die ~en behalten* keep calm, *umg.* keep one's cool; *die ~en verlieren* lose one's nerve (*od.* head), *umg.* snap; *im Zorn*: lose one's temper (*umg.* one's cool); *an die ~en gehen umg.* be very upsetting; *er ist mit den ~en (völlig) fertig* his nerves are (absolutely) shot, he's a(n absolute) nervous wreck, *umg.* his nerves have been worn to a frazzle; *es kostet ~en* it's nerve-racking; *sie hat ~en wie Drahtseile* her nerves must be made of steel; *den ~*

haben zu (+ *Inf.*) *umg.* have the nerve to (+ *Inf.*); *der hat vielleicht ~en! umg.* he's got a (*Am.* a lot of) nerve (*od.* cheek); *d-e ~en möcht ich haben! umg.* I'd like to have some of your nerves; *dazu braucht's ganz schöne ~en! umg.* it takes a fair bit of nerve (to do that); *dazu hab ich keine ~en umg.* I don't have the nerve for that; *dieses Buch trifft den ~ der Zeit fig.* this book taps the pulse of the age

nerven *umg.* **I.** *v/t.: j-n ~* get on *s.o.*'s nerves; *der nervt mich vielleicht!* he doesn't half get (*Am.* he really gets) on my nerves; **II.** *v/i.: das nervt* it's annoying; *hör auf, du nervst* you're being annoying; → **genervt**

Nerven|anspannung *f* nervous tension; **~arzt** *m*, **~ärztin** *f* **1.** neurologist; **2.** *umg., altm.* psychiatrist

nervenaufreibend *Adj.* nerve-racking

Nerven|bahn *f* Anat., Physiol. nerve tract; **~belastung** *f* nervous strain

nervenberuhigend *Adj.*: *~ sein* calm the nerves

Nerven|bündel *n* **1.** *umg.* (*Person*) bag (*od.* bundle) of nerves; **2.** *Anat.* nerve fascicle; **~entzündung** *f* Med. neuritis (*Pl.* neuritides); **~faser** *f* Anat. nerve fib|re (*Am.* -er); **~gas** *n* nerve gas; **~gift** *n* nerve poison, neurotoxin; **~heilkunde** *f* neurology; **~kitzel** *m umg.* (*pej.* cheap) thrill(s *Pl.*); **~klinik** *f* psychiatric clinic; **~kostüm** *n umg. hum.* nerves *Pl.*; **~kraft** *f* strong nerves *Pl.*

nervenkrank *Adj.* Med. neuropathic; (*neurotisch*) neurotic; (*geisteskrank*) mentally ill; **Nervenkranke** *m, f* neuropath; neurotic (person); mentally ill person; **Nervenkrankheit** *f* nervous disease

Nerven|krieg *m* war of nerves; **~krise** *f* mental crisis; **~lähmung** *f* neuroparalysis (*Pl.* neuroparalyses); **~leiden** *n* nervous disease; **~mühle** *f umg.* (*Tätigkeit*) nerve-racking activity; (*Arbeitsplatz*) nerve-racking place to work; **~nahrung** *f*: *~ sein* be good for one's nerves; **~probe** *f* ordeal; **~reiz** *m* nervous impulse; **~sache** *f*: (*es ist reine*) *~* (it's all) a question of nerves; **~säge** *f umg.* pain (in the neck), *vulg.* pain in the arse (*Am.* ass); **~schmerz** *m auch Pl.* neuralgia; **~schock** *m* nervous shock

nervenschwach *Adj.*: *~ sein* have weak (*od.* bad) nerves; **Nervenschwäche** *f* weak nerves *Pl., Med.* neurasthenia

nervenstark *Adj.*: *~ sein* have strong nerves; **Nervenstärke** *f* strong nerves *Pl.*; **nervenstärkend** *Adj.*: *~es Mittel* tonic

Nerven|strang *m* Anat. (peripheral) nerve; **~system** *n* Anat., Physiol. nervous system; **~zelle** *f* Anat., Physiol. nerve cell, neuron, neurone; **~zentrum** *n* Anat., Physiol. nerve cent|re (*Am.* -er) (*auch fig.*)

nervenzerrüttend *Adj.* nerve-shattering; **Nervenzerrüttung** *f* shattered nerves *Pl.*

Nervenzusammenbruch *m*: (*e-n*) *~* (*erleiden*) (have a) nervous breakdown

nervig *Adj.* **1.** *Arm etc.*: sinewy; **2.** *umg. Angelegenheit, Person*: annoying, irritating

nervlich **I.** *Adj.* nervous; *~e Belastung* nervous strain, strain on the nerves; *sein ~er Zustand* (the state of) his nerves; **II.** *Adv.*: *~ bedingt* nervous;

sie ist ~ (*völlig*) *am Ende* her nerves are (absolutely) shot, she's a(n absolute) nervous wreck, *umg.* her nerves have been worn to a frazzle; *j-n ~ belasten Sache*: be a strain on *s.o.*'s nerves

nervös *Adj.* **1.** tense; (*unruhig*) fidgety, *umg.* twitchy; (*reizbar*) edgy, *umg.* uptight; (*aufgeregt*) on edge; (*ängstlich*) nervous; *e-n ~en Eindruck machen* seem nervous (*od.* on edge); *mach mich nicht ~!* don't make me nervous; *weitS.* (*geh mir nicht auf die Nerven!*) stop getting on my nerves; **2.** *Med., Bio.* nervous; **Nervosität** *f*, *-, kein Pl.* tenseness; edginess; nervousness; → **nervös**

nervtötend *Adj.* (*abstumpfend*) soul-destroying, mindless; *Lärm etc.*: nerve-racking

Nerz *m*; *-es, -e* **1.** *Zool.* mink; **2.** (*Mantel, Stola etc.*) mink (coat, stole *etc.*); **~farm** *f* mink farm; **~kragen** *m* mink collar; **~mantel** *m* mink (coat)

Nessel[1] *f*; *-, -n*; *Bot.* nettle; *sich in die ~n setzen umg. fig.* put one's foot in it

Nessel[2] *m*; *-s, -* *Stoff*: untreated cotton cloth

Nessel|ausschlag *m* nettle rash, hives *Sg.*; **~fieber** *n* nettle rash, hives *Sg.*; **~qualle** *f* Zool.: *blaue ~* cyanea lamarckii, blue jellyfish; *gelbe ~* cyanea capillata, lion's mane jellyfish; **~sucht** *f* nettle rash, hives *Sg.*; **~tier** *n* Zool. cnidarian

Nessessär *n*; *-s, -s* → **Necessaire**

Nest *n*; *-(e)s, -er* **1.** nest; *fig.* (*Heim*) *auch* home; *das eigene od. sein eigenes ~ beschmutzen* foul one's own nest; *da hat er sich aber ins gemachte ~ gesetzt umg.* he's done nicely for himself there, he's got everything laid on; **2.** *umg. hum.* (*Bett*) bed; *ins ~ gehen* turn in, hit the sack (*bes. Am.* hay); *ab ins ~!* off to bed!; **3.** *umg.* (*Kaff*) one-horse town; *pej.* (*elendes ~*) dump, hole; **4.** *umg.* (*Schlupfwinkel*) hideout; *das ~ leer finden* find the bird has flown; **~bau** *m*; *nur Sg.* nest-building; **~beschmutzer** *m*; *-s, -*, **~beschmutzerin** *f*; *-, -nen* *fig.* person guilty of fouling his (*od.* her) own nest; *er ist ein richtiger Nestbeschmutzer* he's always running his own family (*od.* company *etc.*) down; **~beschmutzung** *f* fouling one's own nest

nesteln **I.** *v/i.: ~ an* (+ *Dat.*) fumble (around) with; **II.** *v/t.* fasten

Nest|flüchter *m*; *-s, -*; *Zool.* precocial bird; **~häkchen** *n hum.* pet of the family; **~hocker** *m* **1.** *umg. fig.* stay-at-home; **2.** *Zool.* nidicolus; **~hockerin** *f*; *-, -nen*; *umg. fig.* stay-at-home

Nestling *m*; *-s, -e*; *Zool.* nestling

Nestor *m*; *-s, Nestoren*, **~in** *f*; *-, -nen* doyen

nestwarm *Adj.* warm from the nest; **Nestwärme** *f* fig. warmth and security (of the home)

Netikette, **Netiquette** *f*; *-, kein Pl. beim Chatten etc. im Internet*: netiquette

nett *Adj.* **1.** *allg., auch iro.* nice (*von j-m* of *s.o.*); (*niedlich, hübsch*) *auch* sweet, pretty, cute; (*freundlich*) kind, nice; *~, dass du kommst* (it's) nice of you to come; *sei so ~ und bring mir ein Bier* do me a favo(u)r and get me a beer, will you?; *sag doch mal etwas Nettes* go on, say something nice; **2.** *nur attr.*; *umg.* (*beträchtlich*) substantial; *e-n ~en Gewinn machen* make quite a profit; *er hat e-n ganz*

~en Bizeps he's got pretty big biceps; **ein ~es Sümmchen** a tidy sum, a pretty penny; **netterweise** *Adv.* very kindly; **könnten Sie mir ~ ...?** do you think you could possibly ... (for me)?; **Nettigkeit** *f* **1.** (*nette Art*) kindness; **2.** *mst Pl.*: **j-m ein paar ~en** (*ins Ohr*) **sagen** say a few nice words to s.o.

netto *Adv. Wirts.* net, clear

Netto|einkommen *n*, **~einkünfte** *Pl.* net income *Sg.*; **~einnahmen** *Pl.*, **~ertrag** *m* net proceeds *Pl.*; **~gehalt** *n* net salary; **mein ~ ist ... auch** I net ..., I take home ...; **~gewicht** *n* net weight; **~gewinn** *m* clear profit; **~kreditaufnahme** *f Verwaltungswesen*: net credit intake; **~lohn** *m* take-home pay; **~preis** *m* net price; **~umsatz** *m* net turnover (*od.* sales *Pl.*); **~verdienst** *m* net income

Netz *n*; *-es, -e* **1.** net (*auch Math. und fig.*); (*e-r Spinne*) web; **soziales ~** safety net (of social benefits); **den Ball ins ~ befördern** *Fußball*: put the ball into the net; **ans ~ gehen** *Tennis*: go up to the net; **j-m ins ~ gehen** *fig.* walk into s.o.'s trap; **s-e ~e auswerfen** *fig.* cast one's nets; **sich im ~ s-r Lügen verstricken** get caught up in a web of lies; **2.** (*Geflecht*) netting, mesh; (*Gepäcknetz*) rack; **3.** (*Verkehrs-, Verteilungssystem*) *Eisenb., Telef. etc.* network; (*Stromnetz*) mains *Pl.*; **ans ~ gehen** *Kraftwerk etc.*: go on stream; **vom ~ nehmen** (*Kraftwerk*) shut down

Netzanschluss *m Etech.* mains connection, *Am.* (electric) power supply; **~gerät** *n Etech.* mains (*Am.* electrical) appliance

netzartig *Adj.* net-shaped, *bes. fachspr.* reticular

Netz|aufschlag *m Sport, bes. Tennis*: let; **~auge** *f Zool.* compound eye; **~ausfall** *m Etech.* power failure; **~ball** *m Sport, beim Tennis, Tischtennis, Volleyball etc.*: net (ball); **~betreiber** *m*, **~betreiberin** *f* network operator

netzen *v/t.* **1.** wet, moisten; **2.** *Dial.* water

Netz|fehler *m Volleyball*: net (contact); **~flügler** *m*; *-s, -; Zool.* neuropteran (*Pl.* neuroptera)

netzförmig *Adj.* net-shaped, *bes. fachspr.* reticular

Netz|garn *n* netting yarn; **~gerät** *n Etech.* mains (*Am.* electrical) appliance; **~gewölbe** *n Archit.* net vault

Netzhaut *f Anat., des Auges*: retina (*Pl.* retinas *od.* retinae); **~ablösung** *f Med.* detached retina; **~entzündung** *f Med.* retinitis (*Pl.* retinitides)

Netz|hemd *n* string vest; **~karte** *f Eisenb. etc.* runaround ticket; **~magen** *m Zool.* reticulum (*Pl.* reticula); **~plan** *m Wirts.* network diagram; **~plantechnik** *f nur Sg.; Wirts.* network planning technique; **~roller** *m Sport, beim Tennis, Tischtennis, Volleyball etc.*: net cord; **~spannung** *f Etech.* mains (*Am.* supply) voltage; **~spiel** *n Tennis*: playing at the net; **~spieler** *m*, **~spielerin** *f Volleyball*: forward; **~stecker** *m Etech.* mains plug, power (*bes. Am.* electrical) outlet; **~strümpfe** *Pl.* fishnet stockings; **~teil** *n* power supply; *e-s Batteriegeräts*: mains (*Am.* AC) adapter; **~werk** *n* network

neu I. *Adj.*; *neuer, neu(e)ste* **1.** new; (*neuartig*) novel; (*kürzlich geschehen*) recent; (*im Entstehen begriffen*) rising; **ganz ~** brand-new; **das ist mir ~!** that's new(s) to me; **sie ist ~ in der Stadt / in diesem Beruf** she is new in town /

at this job; **noch wie ~** as good as new; **er ist nicht mehr ganz ~** *umg.* he's not as young as he was; **e-e ~e Seite beginnen** start a new page; **e-e ~e Flasche öffnen** open another bottle; **2.** (*neuzeitlich*) modern; **~ere Literatur** modern literature; **~ere Sprachen** modern languages; **~eren Datums** recent ...; **in ~erer Zeit** in recent times, of late; **~este Nachrichten** latest news *Sg.*; **die ~este Mode** the latest fashion(s *Pl.*); **3.** (*erneut, wieder*) renewed; **~er Anfang** fresh start; **ein ~es Leben beginnen** make a fresh start (in life); **~e Schwierigkeiten** more (*od.* renewed) difficulties; **4.** (*kürzlich geerntet*) *Kartoffeln etc.*: new; **~er Wein** new wine; **5.** (*sauber*) *Hemd etc.*: clean; **II.** *substantivisch*: **von ~em** afresh, anew; **von ~em anfangen** start anew (*od.* afresh); **seit ~estem** of late, since very recently, **seit ~estem kann man ...**: the latest thing is you can ...; → *auch* **Neue**[1],[2]; **III.** *Adv.* **1.** (*gerade erst*) **ich habe die Stelle ~ angetreten** I have just started the job; **~ hinzukommen** be new; **dies ist ~ hinzukommen** this has just been added; **dieses Modell ist ~ eingetroffen** this model has just come in; **~ entdeckt** newly discovered; **~ eröffnet** *ganz neu*: newly opened; **~ erschienene Bücher** recently published books, books that have just come out; **~ geschaffen** newly created; **die ~ Vermählten** the newlyweds; **2.** (*nochmals, wieder*) **~ anfangen** start anew (*od.* afresh); **~ auflegen** *Buch etc*: reprint; **~ beleben** revive; **~ einrichten** refurnish; **~ schreiben** rewrite; **~ tapezieren** repaper; **~ bearbeitet** new(ly revised); **~ eröffnet** (*wieder eröffnet*) reopened; **sich ~ einkleiden** get a new set of clothes; **sich ~ eindecken** get in fresh supplies

Neu|abschluss *m e-r Versicherung etc., erstmalig*: taking out a new insurance, etc.; *bei bestehendem Vertrag*: reissuing; **~anfang** *m* → **Neubeginn**; **~ankömmling** *m* newcomer; **~anschaffung** *f* **1.** recent purchase, new acquisition; *Pl. Bibliothek*: recent acquisitions; **schon wieder e-e ~!** something new again!; **2. die ~ von Möbeln** *etc.* buying new furniture *etc.*

neuapostolisch *Adj. kirchl.* New Apostolic; **die Neuapostolische Kirche** the New Apostolic Church

neuartig *Adj.* new, a new type of; **Neuartigkeit** *f* newness, novelty, novel aspect (+ *Gen.* of)

Neu|auflage *f* **1.** new edition; (*Neudruck*) reprint; **2.** *e-r Schallplatte*: reissue; **3.** *umg. fig.* repeat (performance); **~aufnahme** *f* **1.** *Person*: new admission; **die ~ von Wörtern in ein Wörterbuch**: the inclusion of neologisms (*od.* new words); **2.** *e-s Musikwerks etc.*: re-recording; **~ausgabe** *f* → **Neuauflage** 1

neubarock *Adj. Archit.* Neo-Baroque; **Neubarock** *m, n Stil*: Neo-Baroque

Neubau *m* **1.** (*Gebäude*) new building; **2.** *nur Sg.*; *Vorgang*: reconstruction; **~siedlung** *f* modern estate; **~strecke** *f Eisenb., als Neubau geplant*: railway (*Am.* rail) line due for (re)construction; *im Neubau befindlich*: railway (*Am.* rail) line undergoing (re)construction; **~wohnung** *f* modern flat (*Am.* apartment)

neu bearbeitet → *neu* III 2; **Neubearbeitung** *f* **1.** new (*od.* revised) version; *Buch etc.*: revised edition; *Theat.*

etc. adaptation; **2.** *Vorgang*: revision

Neu|beginn *m* fresh start, new beginning; **~belebung** *f* revival; **~besetzung** *f Theat.* recasting; *konkret*: new cast (*V. auch im Pl.*); **~bewertung** *f* reappraisal, reassessment, revaluation; **~bildung** *f* **1.** *Physiol.* regeneration; **2.** *fig.* new formation, reorganization; **3.** *Ling.* neologism; **~bürger** *m*, **~bürgerin** *f* new citizen

Neu-Delhi (*n*); *-s; Geog.* New Delhi

neudeutsch *Adj. mst pej.* trendy new German; **~ „Catering"** "catering" in modern German; **Neudeutsch** *n Ausdrucksweise*: modern German; **das ~e** modern German

Neudruck *m* reprint

Neue[1] *m, f; -n, -n* new man (*od.* woman *etc.*); (*Neuankömmling*) newcomer; **kennst du die ~ von Peter?** do you know Peter's new girlfriend?

Neue[2] *n; -n, kein Pl.*: **das ~ daran** what's new about it; **etw. ~s anfangen** start s.th. new; **der Reiz des ~n** the novelty value; **den Reiz des ~n verlieren** lose its novelty (*für* for), begin to pall (on); **aufs ~** afresh, anew; **auf ein ~s!** let's try again!; **das ~ste Mode** *etc.*: the latest thing; **weißt du schon das ~ste?** have you heard the latest (news) (*od.* the news?); **nichts ~s** nothing new; **das ist nichts ~s für mich** that's nothing new to me; **was gibt es ~s?** what's new?

Neu|einrichtung *f*: **die ~ einer Filiale** the opening of a new branch; **~einspielung** *f* new recording; **~einsteiger** *m*, **~einsteigerin** *f* newcomer (*bei* to); **~einstellung** *f* **1.** **die ~ von Arbeitskräften** the appointment of new members of staff; *Person*: new member of staff; **2.** *Tech. etc.* readjustment; **~einstudierung** *f Theat.* new production; **~entdeckung** *f* (new) discovery (*auch Person*); **~entwicklung** *f* (*konkret*: new) development

Neuer → **Neue**[1]

neuerdings *Adv.* recently, as of late; **~ gibt es ...** there have (*od.* has) recently been ..., the latest thing is there are (*od.* is) ...

Neuerer *m; -s, -*, **Neuerin** *f; -, -nen* innovator

neuerlich I. *Adj.* (*vor kurzem erfolgt*) recent; (*neu*) new; (*erneut*) *auch* repeated; (*weiter*) further; **ein ~er Versuch** *etc. auch* another attempt *etc.*; **II.** *Adv.* recently, of late, for a while now

neu eröffnet → *neu* III 1, 2

Neu|eröffnung *f* opening; *nach Renovierung etc.*: reopening; **~erscheinung** *f* new (*od.* recent) book (*od.* publication); *CD etc.*: new (*od.* recent) release

Neuerung *f* innovation; (*Änderung*) change; (*Besserung*) reform; **neuerungsfeindlich** *Adj.* hostile (*od.* opposed) to (any form of) innovation (*od.* reform); **Neuerungsgeist** *m; nur Sg.* spirit of innovation; **Neuerungssucht** *f; nur Sg.* mania for innovation (*od.* reform); **neuerungssüchtig** *Adj.* bent on innovation (*od.* reform); **~ sein** *auch* be a fanatical innovator (*od.* reformist)

Neu|erwerb *m*, **~erwerbung** *f* new acquisition; *Pl. Bibliothek etc.*: recent acquisitions; → *auch* **Neuanschaffung**

Neues → **Neue**[2]

Neu|fahrzeug *f* new vehicle; **~fassung** *f* revised version; **~festsetzung** *f* reassessment

Neufundland (n); -s; Geog. Newfoundland; **Neufundländer** m; -s, - **1.** Newfoundlander; **2.** Hund: Newfoundland (dog); **Neufundländerin** f; -, -nen Newfoundlander, woman (od. girl) from Newfoundland; **neufundländisch** Adj. Newfoundland

neugeboren Adj. newborn (auch fig.); **sich wie ~ fühlen** feel a different person; nach Krankheit: auch feel as good as new; **Neugeborene** n; -n, -n newborn (baby)

neu geschaffen → **neu** III 1

Neu|geschäft n; nur Sg.; Wirts. recent business; **~gestaltung** f **1.** Vorgang: redesigning, reshaping; organisatorisch: reorganization; restructuring; **2.** konkret: new design (od. structure)

Neugewürz n österr. allspice, pimento, pimiento

Neugier f; -, kein Pl., **Neugierde** f; -, kein Pl. curiosity, inquisitiveness; **aus** (reiner) **~** out of (sheer) curiosity; **neugierig** Adj. curious (**auf** + Akk. about); (vorwitzig) inquisitive, umg. nosy; **j-n ~ machen** arouse s.o.'s curiosity; **ich bin ~, ob ...** I wonder whether (od. if) ...; **da bin ich aber ~!** umg. iro. I can hardly wait!; **du bist aber ~!** umg. you're a real nosy parker; **sei nicht so ~!** umg. don't be so inquisitive (od. nosy)!; **viele Neugierige** lots of curious people

Neugliederung f reorganization, restructuring

Neugotik f Archit. Gothic Revival, neo-Gothic style (od. architecture); **neugotisch** Adj. neo-Gothic

neugriechisch Adj. modern Greek; **Neugriechisch** n Ling. modern Greek; **das ~e** modern Greek

Neu|gründung f **1.** new establishment; **2.** erneute: re-establishment; **3.** **~ e-s Vereins** etc. (recent) establishment of a new association etc.; **~gruppierung** f regrouping; bes. Pol. reshuffling

Neuguinea (n); -s; Geog. New Guinea

neuhebräisch Adj. modern Hebrew; **Neuhebräisch** n Ling. modern Hebrew; **das ~e** modern Hebrew

Neuheit f **1.** (Neusein) novelty; → auch **Neue²**; **2.** (Neuartiges) new development (od. idea etc.); **~en auf dem Modemarkt/Automarkt** the latest fashions / car models

neuhochdeutsch Adj. New High German; **Neuhochdeutsch** n Ling. New High German; **das ~e** New High German

Neuigkeit f **1.** (e-e) **~** (a piece of) news Sg.; **2.** Gegenstand: novelty

Neu|interpretation f new interpretation; **~inszenierung** f Theat. new production

Neujahr n New Year('s Day); **pros(i)t ~!** Happy New Year!

Neujahrs|abend m New Year's Eve; **~ansprache** f New Year speech; **~botschaft** f New Year message; **~empfang** m New Year reception; **~fest** n New Year's party; **~gruß** m; mst Pl. New Year greetings Pl., greetings Pl. for the new year; **~konzert** n New Year concert; **~morgen** m morning of New Year's Day; **~tag** m New Year's Day; **~wünsche** Pl. (best) wishes for the new year

Neukauf m Wirts. new purchase; **beim ~ eines Autos** when buying a new car

Neu|konstruktion f **1.** new construction; **2.** (Erneuerung) reconstruction; **~konzeption** f new conception; **~kunde** m, **~kundin** f Wirts. new customer

---

Neuland n virgin soil; fig. new territory (od. ground); **~ erschließen** auch fig. break new ground; **~ betreten/erobern** enter unknown / conquer new territory; **~gewinnung** f land reclamation

Neulatein n Ling. New Latin, Neo-Latin; **neulateinisch** Adj. New Latin, Neo-Latin

neulich Adv. the other day, recently; not so long ago; **~ abends** the other evening

Neuling m; -s, -e novice, beginner, Brit. auch tyro, Am. auch rookie; pej. greenhorn

neumodisch Adj. fashionable; pej. newfangled

Neumond m; nur Sg. new moon

neun Zahlw. nine; **alle ~e!** strike!; → **acht¹**

Neun f; -, -en Zahl: (number) nine; **ach, du grüne ~e!** umg. oh my goodness!; → **Acht¹** 1, 2, 4

Neunauge n Zool. lamprey

neunbändig Adj. nine-volume ..., in nine volumes

Neuneck n Math. nonagon

neuneinhalb Zahlw. nine and a half

Neuner m; -s, -; umg. nine

neunfach Adj. ninefold; **die ~e Menge** nine times the amount; **Neunfache** n; -n, kein Pl. nine times the amount

neunhundert Zahlw. nine hundred

neunjährig Adj. **1.** nine-year-old ...; **2.** (neun Jahre dauernd) nine-year ...; **Neunjährige** m,f; -n, -n nine-year-old; **neunjährlich** Adj. nine-yearly ...

neunköpfig Adj.: **~e Familie** etc. family etc. of nine

neunmal Adv. nine times; **neunmalig** Adj. präd. repeated nine times; Sieger: attr. nine-times ...; **nach ~er Aufforderung** at the ninth time of asking, after being asked nine times

neunmalklug Adj. umg. iro. smart-alecky; **Neunmalkluge** m, f; -n, -n; umg. know-(it-)all, smart aleck, Am. auch smarty pants

neunmonatig Adj. Kind: nine-month-old ...; Aufenthalt: nine-month ...; **neunmonatlich** Adj. nine-monthly ...

neunstellig Adj. Zahl: nine-digit ...

neunstöckig Adj. nine-stor(e)y ...

neunstündig Adj. nine-hour(-long) ...

neunt Adv.: **wir waren zu ~** there were nine of us; → **acht²**

neunt... Zahlw. ninth; → **acht...**

neuntägig Adj. **1.** nine-day(-long) ...; **2.** (neun Tage alt) nine-day-old ...

neuntausend Zahlw. nine thousand

Neunte m, f; -n, -n (the) ninth; → **Achte**

neunteilig Adj. nine-part ..., in nine parts

neuntel Bruchzahl ninth; → **achtel**; **Neuntel** n; -s, - ninth; → **Achtel**

neuntens Adv. ninth(ly), nine, in ninth place

Neunter → **Neunte**

Neuntöter m; -s, -; Orn. red-backed shrike

Neunundsechzig n; -, kein Pl.; Sl. sixty-nine

neunwöchentlich Adj. nine-weekly ...; **neunwöchig** Adj. **1.** nine-week ...; **2.** (neun Wochen alt) nine-week-old ...

neunzehn Zahlw. nineteen; **neunzehnhundert** Zahlw. nineteen hundred; **neunzehnt...** Zahlw. nineteenth; **Neunzehntel** n nineteenth (part)

19-Zöller m; -s, -; (Bildschirm) 19-inch monitor

---

neunzig Zahlw. ninety; → **achtzig**

Neunzig f; -, -en, mst Sg. Zahl: (number) ninety; → **Achtzig**

neunziger Adj.: **in den ~ Jahren** in the nineties; → **achtziger**

Neunziger¹ m; -s, - **1.** man in his nineties, förm. nonagenarian, ninetysomething umg.; **2.** Weinjahrgang: **ein ~ Châteauneuf-du-Pape** a 1990 Châteauneuf-du-Pape

Neunziger² Pl. → **Neunzigerjahre**

Neunzigerin f; -, -nen woman in her nineties, förm. nonagenarian, ninety-something umg.

Neunzigerjahre Pl.: **in den ~n** in the nineties

neunzigjährig Adj. Person: ninety-year-old ...; Zeitraum: ninety-year (--long) ...

neunzigst... Zahlw. ninetieth; → **achtzigst...**

Neu|ordnung f reform; **~organisation** f reorganization; **~orientierung** f reorientation

Neuphilologe m, **Neuphilologin** f student/teacher of modern languages and literature; **Neuphilologie** f modern languages and literature

Neu|prägung f recent coinage, neologism; **~preis** m Wirts. e-s Wagens etc.: price of car etc. when new, new price, price new; **~priester** m kath. recently ordained priest

Neuralgie f; -, -n; Med. neuralgia; **Neuralgiker** m; -s, -, **Neuralgikerin** f; -, -nen; Med. neuralgia sufferer, person suffering from neuralgia; **neuralgisch** Adj. neuralgic; **~er Punkt** fig e-r Person: sore spot (od. point), touchy subject; in e-m System etc.: critical spot; Pol. trouble spot

Neurasthenie f Med. neurasthenia; **Neurastheniker** m, **Neurasthenikerin** f neurasthenic; **neurasthenisch** Adj. neurasthenic

Neureg(e)lung f revision; organisatorische: reorganization

neureich Adj. pej. nouveau riche; **Neureiche** m, f pej. nouveau riche; **die ~n** the nouveaux riches

Neuritis f; -, Neuritiden; Med. neuritis (Pl. neuritides)

Neurochirurg m neurosurgeon; **Neurochirurgie** f neurosurgery; **Neurochirurgin** f neurosurgeon

Neurodermitis f; -, Neurodermitiden; Med. neurodermatitis (Pl. neurodermatitises od. neurodermatitides)

Neurologe m; -n, -n neurologist; **Neurologie** f; -, -n **1.** nur Sg. neurology; **2.** (Abteilung) neurological wing (od. section); **Neurologin** f; -, -nen neurologist; **neurologisch** Adj. neurological

Neuron n; -s, -e; Anat., Physiol. neurone, neuron; **neuronal** Adj. neuronal, neuronic

Neurose f; -, -n; Med., Psych. neurosis (Pl. neuroses); **Neurotiker** m; -s, -, **Neurotikerin** f; -, -nen; auch fig. neurotic; **neurotisch I.** Adj. neurotic; **II.** Adv. neurotically; **Neurotransmitter** m; -s, -; Med., Physiol. neurotransmitter

Neu|satz m; nur Sg.; Druck. new setting; **~schnee** m fresh snowfall; **~schöpfung** f **1.** new creation; **2.** Ling. neologism

Neuseeland (n); -s; Geog. New Zealand; **Neuseeländer** m; -s, -, **Neuseeländerin** f; -, -nen New Zealander, weiblich auch: woman (od. girl) from New Zealand; **neuseeländisch** Adj. New Zealand ..., from New Zealand

N

Neusilber n German (od. nickel) silver

Neusprachler m; -s, -, ~in f; -, -nen → **Neuphilologe** etc.; **neusprachlich** Adj.: ~er Unterricht etc. modern language teaching etc.; ~es Gymnasium grammar school with special emphasis on modern languages

Neustrukturierung f restructuring

neutestamentlich Adj. Theologie etc.: New Testament …

Neutöner m; -s, -, ~in f; -, -nen 1. mst iro. avant-garde musician; 2. Philosoph etc.: radical

neutral I. Adj. 1. neutral (auch Chem., Phys.); geschmacklich ~ sein have a neutral taste; 2. Ling. neuter; **II.** Adv.: sich ~ verhalten remain neutral; ~ reagieren Chem. react neutrally; **Neutrale** m, f; -n, -n; Pol. neutral

neutralisieren v/t. neutralize (auch fig.); Rennen: stop; **Neutralisierung** f neutralization; e-s Rennens: stopping

Neutralismus m; -, kein Pl.; Pol. neutralism; **neutralistisch** Adj. neutralist

Neutralität f; -, -en neutrality

Neutralitäts|abkommen n Pol. neutrality pact; ~erklärung f declaration of neutrality; ~politik f policy of neutrality; ~verletzung f violation of neutrality

Neutrino n; -s, -s Kernphysik: neutrino

Neutron n; -s, -en; Kernphysik: neutron

Neutronen|bombe f neutron bomb; ~strahlen Pl. neutron beams; ~waffe f neutron weapon; ~zahl f neutron count

Neutrum n; -s, Neutra und Neutren 1. Ling. neuter; Wort: auch neuter noun; 2. fig., mst pej. sexless person

Neu|verfilmung f remake; ~verhandlung f renegotiation

neuvermählt Adj. newly married (od. wed), newlywed …; als Neuvermählte grüßen … Kartengruß, Zeitungsanzeige: best wishes from the newlyweds …

Neu|verpflichtung f 1. (erneute Verpflichtung) re-engagement; bis zu 6 ~en im Jahr sind erlaubt it is permitted to engage six new people per year; 2. Person: new person; ~verschuldung f new indebtedness; new borrowings Pl.; ~verteilung f redistribution; ~wagen m new car; ~wahl f 1. election; die ~ des Vorsitzenden the election of a new chairman (od. chairperson); 2. Pol.: ~en (new) elections; ~ware f Wirts. new goods Pl. (bes. Am. merchandise Sg.)

Neuwert m Wirts. value as new; **neuwertig** Adj. as (good as) new; **Neuwertversicherung** f new for old insurance

Neuwort n Ling. new word, neologism

Neuzeit f; nur Sg. modern age; Geschichte etc. der ~ modern history etc.; **neuzeitlich** Adj. modern

Neu|züchtung f Pflanze: new variety; Tier: new breed; ~zugang m Sache Sport: Person: new acquisition; e-m Klub: new member; (neuer Student, Patient etc.) new admission; Pl. auch new intake Sg. of students etc., incoming students etc.; ~zulassung f Mot. registration of a new vehicle; Fahrzeug: newly registered vehicle; ~zustand m; nur Sg. mint condition

Newbie ['nju:bi] m; -, -s; Sl. newbie

Newcomer ['nju:kamɐ] m; -(s), -(s), ~in f; -, -nen newcomer

Newsgroup ['nju:zgru:p] f; -, -s im Internet: newsgroup (Diskussionsforum)

Newsletter ['nju:zlɛtɐ] m; -s, -s im Internet: newsletter

newtonsch Adj. Newtonian; das ~e Gravitationsgesetz Newton's law of gravity

n-fach Adj. Math.: die ~e Menge n-times the amount; **n-fache** n; -n, kein Pl. n-times the amount

nhd. Abk. → **neuhochdeutsch**

Niagarafälle Pl. Geog.: die ~ the Niagara Falls

nibbeln v/t. Tech. nibble; **Nibbler** m; -s, - nibbler

Nibelungen Pl. Myth. Nibelungs, Nibelungen; **Nibelungentreue** f; mst pej. undying (od. absolute, unquestioning) loyalty

nicht Adv. 1. not; er trinkt ~ allgemein: he doesn't drink; im Moment: he's not drinking; ich ging ~ I didn't go; ~ füttern! (please) do not feed; willst du oder ~? do you want to or not?; kommst du? – nein, ich komme ~ are you coming? - no, I'm not; ich ~ not me; der Apparat wollte ~ funktionieren wouldn't work; gar ~ not at all; das wollte ich doch gar ~ that's not what I wanted (at all), but I didn't want that; ~ doch! (lass das!) don't!, stop it!; (bitte) ~! (please) don't!; ~ einmal not even; alle lachten, nur sie ~ everyone laughed except for her; nur das ~! anything but that!; ~ dass ich wüsste not that I know of; ~, dass ich keine Lust hätte, ich darf ~ it's not that I don't want to, I'm not allowed to; ich glaube ~ I don't think so, ich kenne ihn auch ~ I don't know him either; sie sah es ~, und ich auch ~ and nor (od. neither) did I; du kennst ihn ~? - ich auch ~ nor do I; dann eben ~ don't, then; auch iro. nobody's forcing you; 2. umg., vor e-m Adj. mit negativer Bedeutung das Gegenteil ausdrückend: sie spielt ~ übel she plays quite well, Am. she doesn't play badly; das ist ~ ungeschickt gemacht that's quite cleverly done, Am. that's not half bad; 3. Verwunderung ausdrückend: was du ~ sagst! you don't say!; was es ~ alles gibt! well I never!; 4. zustimmende Antwort erwartend: kommst du ~ mit? you are coming, aren't you?; meinst du ~ auch? don't you think?; er ist krank, ~ wahr? he's ill, isn't he?; du tust es, ~ wahr? you 'will do it, won't you?; 5. vor Komp.: no, z.B. ~ besser no better; ~ mehr no longer, not … any more; ~ oft auch in…; ~ ratsam inadvisable; 7. oft auch non-…, Am. non…; ~ abtrennbar non--detachable; 8. oft auch un…; ~ gefärbt uncolo(u)red; 9. Verbindungen mit Partizip: ~ rostend Stahl: stainless; → **organisieren, rosten** etc.

Nichtachtung f disregard (+ Gen. of); j-n mit ~ strafen punish s.o. by ignoring him (od. her), Brit. auch send s.o. to Coventry

nichtadelig, nicht adelig Adj. common; **Nichtadelige** m, f commoner

nichtamtlich, nicht amtlich Adj. unofficial, non-official

Nicht|anerkennung f Pol. non-recognition; ~angriffspakt m non-aggression pact; ~beachtung f, ~befolgung f disregard (+ Gen. of), failure to comply (with), non-compliance (with); ~berufstätige m, f non-employed person; ~bestehen n 1. (Nichtvorhandensein) non-existence, absence; 2. e-r Prüfung: failure; das ~ der Prüfung failure of (od. in) the exam(ination), failing (to pass) the exam(ination); ~bezahlung f non-payment

nichtchristlich, nicht christlich Adj. non-Christian

Nichte f; -, -n niece

nichtehelich, nicht ehelich Adj. Kind: illegitimate

Nichteinbringungsfall m österr. Amtsspr.: im ~ in case of inability to pay

Nicht|einhaltung f Amtspr. non-compliance (+ Gen. with); ~einlösung f: bei ~ e-s Schecks: if not cashed; ~einmischung f non-intervention; ~eisenmetall n nonferrous metal; ~erfüllung f non-fulfil(l)ment, default; ~erscheinen n non-appearance, failure to attend; Jur. auch default

nichtexistent, nicht existent Adj. nonexistent

Nicht|fachmann m non-expert, layman; engS. non-professional; ~gebrauch m: bei ~ when not in use; ~gefallen n: bei ~ Wirts. if not satisfied; bei ~ Geld zurück satisfaction or money back; ~geschäftsfähige m, f; -n, -n; Jur. incompetent party; ~gewünschte n; -n, kein Pl.: ~s bitte streichen please delete anything you do not require

nichtig Adj. 1. geh. (belanglos) trivial; Freuden etc.: vain; 2. Jur. invalid; für ~ erklären declare null and void; null und ~ null and void; **Nichtigkeit** f 1. triviality; 2. (Leere) vanity; 3. Jur. nullity

Nichtigkeits|erklärung f annulment, nullification; ~klage f nullity action

Nichtinanspruchnahme f: bei ~ if not claimed

nichtkommunistisch, nicht kommunistisch Adj. non-Communist

nicht leitend → **leitend** II 2

Nichtleiter m Etech. non-conductor

Nichtmitglied n non-member; ~staat m non-member (od. non-aligned) state

Nichtnuklearstaat m non-nuclear state

nichtöffentlich, nicht öffentlich Adj. private; ~e Sitzung Jur. session in camera

nicht organisiert → **organisieren** III

Nichtraucher m 1. non-smoker; ich bin ~ I don't smoke; 2. kein Art. umg.: „~“ "Non-smoking"; ~abteil n non-smoking compartment, umg. non--smoker; ~lokal n non-smoking restaurant (od. bar etc.); ~zone f non-smoking area

nicht rostend → **rosten**

nichts unbest. Pron. 1. allein stehend: nothing; ich höre/sehe etc. ~ I can't hear/see etc. a thing; ~ als Ärger etc. nothing but trouble etc.; ~ ist schöner als there's nothing nicer than (+ Ger. od. to + Inf.); es geht ~ über (+Akk.) there's nothing like; gar ~ nothing at all; fast gar ~ hardly anything; für ~ und wieder ~ all for nothing; mir ~, dir ~ umg. just like that; weggehen etc.: auch without so much as a word (of goodbye, of explanation etc.); so viel wie ~ next to nothing; daraus ist ~ geworden nothing came of it; daraus wird ~ nothing will come of it; (es geht nicht) we'll have to forget about that(, I'm afraid); das geht dich ~ an it's none of your business; aus ~ wird ~ you can't make something out of nothing; von ~ kommt ~ you can't get something for nothing; das ist ~ für mich umg. that's not my thing; ~ zu danken! not at all, förm. don't mention it; es macht ~! it doesn't matter, never mind; ~ zu machen! umg. nothing doing; (*es kann nicht geändert werden*) it can't be helped; **~** *da!* *umg.* no way!; **er wird es zu ~ bringen** he'll never get anywhere (in life); **sich in ~ auflösen** *Projekt etc.*: go up in smoke, *auf rätselhafte Weise*: vanish into thin air; **ich komme zu ~** I never get time for anything, I never get (a)round to doing anything; **~ wie weg!** run!, *umg.* let's move!; **~ wie raus!** *umg.* let's get out of here quick!; **~ wie hin!** *umg.* what are we waiting for?; **2.** *mit Subst., Adj., Adv. od. Pron.*: **~ Neues** nothing new; **ich weiß ~ Genaues** I don't know any details; **sie hatte ~ Eiligeres zu tun als** (+ *Inf.*) she had nothing better to do than (+ *Inf.*); **~ weniger als** nothing less than; **~ weiter** *od. weiter* **~** nothing else; *zu diskutieren etc.*: *auch* nothing further; **~ dergleichen** no such thing, nothing of the kind; **~ anderes als** nothing but; **3.** *mit Part. Präs.*: **~ ahnend** unsuspecting; **~ sagend** *Musik, Film, Äußerung*: meaningless; *Gesicht*: expressionless; *Mensch*: insignificant

Nichts *n*; *-es*, *-e* **1.** *nur Sg.* nothing(ness); (*Leere*) void; **aus dem ~** from nowhere; **vor dem ~ stehen** be left with nothing; (*ganz von vorne anfangen müssen*) have to start from scratch; **2.** *nur Sg.*: **ein ~** (*Geringfügiges*) nothing; **sich um ein ~ streiten** fight over nothing (*od.* a triviality); **3.** *pej.* (*Person*) a nobody; **ein ~ sein** *auch* be totally insignificant

nichts ahnend → **nichts** 3

Nichtschwimmer *m* non-swimmer; **~becken** *n* beginners' pool; **Nichtschwimmerin** *f* non-swimmer

nichtsdestotrotz *umg., oft hum.*, **nichtsdestoweniger** *Adv.* nevertheless, nonetheless

Nichtsein *n* non-existence

Nichtsesshafte *m, f*; *-n, -n* person of no fixed abode, vagrant

Nichtskönner *m*, **~in** *f* incompetent (person), *umg.* washout, dead (*Am.* total) loss

Nichtsnutz *m*; *-es, -e*; *pej.* good-for-nothing; **nichtsnutzig** *Adj. pej.* useless, good-for-nothing; **Nichtsnutzigkeit** *f pej.* uselessness

nichts sagend → **nichts** 3

nichtstaatlich, **nicht staatlich** *Adj.* non-governmental; (*privat*) private

Nichtstuer *m*; *-s, -*, **~in** *f*; *-, -nen*; *pej.* idler, *umg.* loafer, layabout; **nichtstuerisch** *Adj.* idle; **Nichtstun** *n* idleness; **s-e Zeit etc. mit ~ verbringen** idle away one's time *etc.*

Nichtswisser *m*; *-s, -*, **~in** *f*; *-, -nen* ignoramus

nichtswürdig *Adj. geh.* base; (*verächtlich*) contemptible; **Nichtswürdigkeit** *f geh.* baseness; (*Verächtlichkeit*) contemptible nature (+ *Gen.* of), contemptibility

Nicht|tänzer *m*, **~tänzerin** *f* non-dancer; **~teilnahme** *f* non-participation; **~trinker** *m*, **~trinkerin** *f* teetotal(l)er; **~verbreitung** *f von Kernwaffen*: non-proliferation

Nichtverfolgerstaat *m* non-repressive country

Nicht|vorhandensein *n* absence; **~wähler** *m*, **~wählerin** *f* non-voter; **~weitergabe** *f* non-proliferation; **~wissen** *n* ignorance; **~zahlung** *f* non-payment (*von* of), default (on); **bei ~** in default of payment; **~zulassung** *f* non-admittance, non-admission; **~zustandekommen** *n* non-com-

pletion; **~zutreffende**, **nicht Zutreffende** *n*; *-n, kein Pl.*: **~s streichen!** delete where inapplicable

Nickel *n*; *-s, kein Pl.*; *Chem.* nickel; **~brille** *f*: (**e-e**) **~** (a pair of) steel-rimmed glasses *Pl.*, *umg.* granny glasses *Pl.*

nickelig *Adj. Dial.* nasty

Nickelmünze *f* nickel coin

nicken I. *v/i.* **1.** (*auch* **mit dem Kopf ~**) nod (one's head); *zum Gruß*: give a nod; *zustimmend* **~** nod in agreement; *beifällig* **~** nod approvingly, (one's) approval; **2.** *umg.* (*leicht schlafen*) doze, *umg.* be having forty winks; **II.** *v/t. Fußball Sl.*: **den Ball ins Tor ~** nod the ball into the goal; **Nicken** *n*; *-s, kein Pl.* nod(ding)

Nickerchen *n umg.* nap, snooze; **ein ~ machen** take a nap, have forty winks, get (*od.* have) a bit of shut-eye

Nickhaut *f Zool.* nictitating membrane

Nicki *m*; *-(s), -s*, **~pullover** *m* velour top

nicklig → **nickelig**

nie *Adv.* never; **fast ~** hardly ever; **~ wieder** never again; **noch ~** never (before); **man soll ~ „~" sagen** never say never (again); **~ und nimmer!** never in a lifetime!, never in my *etc.* life!

nieder I. *Adj.* **1.** low; *Wert, Rang*: inferior; *Dienststelle etc.*: lower; (*gemein*) common; *Gesinnung*: low, base, mean; **der ~e Adel** the gentry; **von ~er Geburt** of low(ly) birth, low-born; **2.** *Bio. etc.*: **~e Instinkte/Lebensformen** *etc.* lower *od.* primitive instincts/life forms *etc.*; **~e Entwicklungsstufe** early stage of evolution; **3.** *südd.* → **niedrig** I 1; **II.** *Adv.* low; (*herab*) down; **auf und ~** up and down; **~ mit den Verrätern!** down with the traitors!

Niederbayern (*n*); *-s; Geog.* Lower Bavaria; **niederbayrisch** *Adj.* Lower Bavarian

nieder|beugen (*trennb., hat -ge-*) *geh.* **I.** *v/t.* **1.** bend down; **2.** *fig.* weigh down; **II.** *v/refl.* bend down (**zu** to); **~brechen** (*unreg., trennb., -ge-*) *geh.* **I.** *v/t.* (*hat*) (*Mauer etc.*) knock down; **II.** *v/i.* (*ist*) collapse; **~brennen** (*unreg., trennb.*) **I.** *v/i.* (*ist niedergebrannt*) burn down (*od.* to the ground), be burn|t (*bes. Am. -ed*) down (*od.* to the ground); **II.** *v/t.* (*hat*) burn s.th. down (*od.* to the ground); **~bringen** *v/t.* (*unreg., trennb., hat -ge-*) *Bergb., Tech.* (*Schacht, Bohrung*) sink; **~brüllen** *v/t.* (*trennb., hat -ge-*) shout s.o. down; **~bügeln** *v/t.* (*trennb., hat -ge-*); *umg.* **1.** make mincemeat of *s.o.*; **2.** *Sport*: thrash, slaughter, clobber

niederdeutsch *Adj.* **1.** *Geog.* North German; **2.** *Ling.* Low German; **Niederdeutsch** *n Ling.* Low German; **das ~e** Low German

Niederdruck *m Tech.* low pressure

niederdrücken *v/t.* (*trennb., hat -ge-*) **1.** press down; (*Taste, Hebel*) depress; **2.** *geh., fig.* depress, weigh on *s.o.'s* mind

Niederdruckreifen *m Mot.* low pressure tyre (*Am.* tire)

Niedere *n*; *-n, kein Pl.*: **das ~** the baser instincts

nieder|fahren *v/i.* (*unreg., trennb., ist -ge-*); *geh.* descend; **~fallen** *v/i.* (*unreg., trennb., ist -ge-*); *geh.* fall down

Niederflur|bus *m Tech.* low floor bus; **~wagen** *m Straßenbahn*: low floor carriage (*Am.* streetcar)

niederfrequent *Adj. Etech., Phys.* low-frequency (*auch Ling., Wort*); **Nieder-**

frequenz *f* low frequency; (*Tonfrequenz*) audio frequency

Niedergang *m* **1.** *nur Sg.* decline; *e-r Weltmacht etc.*: *auch* decline and fall; *weitS.* collapse; **2.** *Naut.* companionway

niedergedrückt I. *P.P.* → **niederdrücken**; **II.** *Adj. fig.* dejected; **Niedergedrücktheit** *f* dejection, despondency

niedergehen *v/i.* (*unreg., trennb., ist -ge-*) **1.** *Lawine, Steinschlag etc.*: come down; *Regen etc.*: fall; *Gewitter*: break; *Vorhang etc.*: come down, drop; *Flug.* descend; (*landen*) touch down; **2.** *fig. Vorwürfe etc.*: rain down (**auf** + *Akk.* on)

niedergelassen I. *P.P.* → **niederlassen**; **II.** *Adj.*; *nur attr.*: **~er Arzt** registered doctor in private practice

niedergeschlagen I. *P.P.* → **niederschlagen**; **II.** *Adj. fig.* depressed, dejected, *umg.* down in the dumps; **Niedergeschlagenheit** *f* dejection, despondency, *umg.* the blues *Pl.*

nieder|hageln *v/i.* (*unreg., ist -ge-*) hail down (**auf** + *Akk.* on); *fig. Vorwürfe etc.*: rain down (on); **~halten** *v/t.* (*unreg., trennb., hat -ge-*) hold (*od.* keep) down; *fig.* (*unterdrücken*) suppress, oppress; **~hauen** *v/t.* (*unreg., trennb., hat -ge-*) cut down; **~holen** *v/t.* (*trennb., hat -ge-*) (*Flagge, Segel*) lower

nieder|kämpfen *v/t.* (*trennb., hat -ge-*) *auch fig.* fight down, overcome; **~kauern** *v/refl.* (*trennb., hat -ge-*) crouch (down); **~knallen** *v/t.* (*trennb., hat -ge-*); *umg.* put a bullet through *s.o.*; **~knien** (*trennb.*) **I.** *v/i.* (*ist -ge-*) kneel down; **II.** *v/refl.* (*hat*) kneel down; **~knüppeln** *v/t.* (*trennb., hat -ge-*) club *s.o.* down

niederkommen *v/i.* (*unreg., trennb., ist -ge-*); *altm.* give birth (to a child); *förm., lit.*: **~ mit** be delivered of; **Niederkunft** *f altm.* delivery, birth

Niederlage *f* **1.** *Mil. und fig.* defeat; *bes. Sport auch umg.* drubbing, thrashing; **e-e ~ erleiden** *od. umg.* **einstecken** be defeated, *förm.* suffer defeat (**gegen** at the hands of); **j-m e-e ~ beibringen** inflict a defeat on s.o., defeat *s.o.*; **e-e 0:1~** a 1-0 (= one-nil, *Am.* one to nothing) defeat; **2.** *Wirts.* (*Zweiggeschäft*) branch; (*Zwischenlage*) depot

Niederlande *Pl. Geog.*: **die ~** the Netherlands (*V. im Sg.*); **Niederländer** *m*; *-s, -* Dutchman; **Niederländerin** *f*; *-, -nen* Dutchwoman; Dutch girl; → *auch* **Niederländer**; **niederländisch** *Adj.* Dutch; *Regierung etc. auch*: Netherlands; **Niederländisch** *n*; *-en*; *Ling.* Dutch; **das ~e** Dutch

niederlassen (*unreg., trennb., hat -ge-*) **I.** *v/t.* let down, lower; **II.** *v/refl.* **1.** (*sich setzen*) sit down, take a seat; *Vogel*: settle, alight; **2.** (*e-n Wohnsitz nehmen*) take up residence; *langfristig*: settle; **3.** *sich als Anwalt etc.* **~** set s.o. up as a lawyer *etc.*; **Niederlassung** *f* **1.** (*das Niederlassen*) establishment (+ *Gen.* of); **2.** *Wirts.*, *gewerbliche*: place of business; (*Filiale*) branch office; *e-r Bank*: branch

Niederlassungs|freiheit *f*; *nur Sg.*; *Jur.* freedom of establishment; **~recht** *n*; *nur Sg.* right of establishment

niederlegen (*trennb., hat -ge-*) **I.** *v/t.* **1.** lay (*od.* put) down; **die Waffen ~** lay down one's weapons; **e-n Kranz ~** lay a wreath; **2.** *fig.* (*Amt*) resign from; **die Arbeit ~** (go on) strike, down tools, walk out; **3.** *Amtsspr., geh.: etw.* **schriftlich** ~ set down, put down in writing; **II.** *v/refl.* lie down; (*ins Bett gehen*) *auch* go to bed; **Niederlegung** *f:* ~ **des Amtes / der Königswürde** resignation from office / abdication from the throne

nieder|machen *v/t.* (*trennb., hat -ge-*); *umg.* **1.** massacre, slaughter; **2.** (*abkanzeln*) *umg.* give *s.o.* a roasting, bawl *s.o.* out; **~mähen** *v/t.* (*trennb., hat -ge-*) *fig.* mow down; **~metzeln** *v/t.* (*trennb., hat -ge-*) massacre, slaughter

Niederösterreich (*n*); *-s; Geog.* Lower Austria

nieder|prasseln *v/i.* (*trennb., ist -ge-*) **1.** pelt (*od.* lash) down; **2.** *fig. Beschimpfungen etc.*: rain down (*auf + Akk.* on); **~regnen** *v/i.* (*trennb., ist -ge-*) rain down; **~reißen** *v/t.* tear down (*auch fig. Schranken etc.*); (*Gebäude etc.*) pull down, demolish; **~ringen** *fig. v/t.* overpower

Niederrhein *m Geog.*: **der** ~ the Lower Rhine; **niederrheinisch** *Adj.* from the Lower Rhine

niederringen *v/t.* (*unreg., trennb., hat -ge-*) → **niederkämpfen**

Niedersachse *m man etc.* from Lower Saxony; **Niedersachsen** (*n*); *-s; Geog.* Lower Saxony; **Niedersächsin** *f* woman *etc.* from Lower Saxony; **niedersächsisch** *Adj.* from Lower Saxony

niederschießen (*unreg., trennb., -ge-*) **I.** *v/t.* (*hat*) shoot (*od.* gun) down; **II.** *v/i.* (*ist*) *vom Himmel*: shoot (*od.* swoop) down

Niederschlag *m* **1.** *Met.* rain(fall), *förm.* precipitation; **zeitweise Niederschläge, teils Regen, teils Schneeschauer** *im Wetterbericht:* occasional showers, some falling as snow; **radioaktiver** ~ nuclear fallout; **2.** *Chem.* precipitate; (*Bodensatz*) deposit, sediment; **3.** *Boxen:* knockdown; *bes. zehn:* knockout; **4.** *fig.:* **s-n ~ finden in** (*+Dat.*) (*s-n Ausdruck finden in*) find expression in; (*sich zeigen in*) show (itself) in, manifest itself in; (*sich widerspiegeln in*) be reflected in; **niederschlagen I.** *v/t.* (*unreg., trennb., hat -ge-*) **1.** (*j-n*) knock down; *Boxen: auch* floor; *bis zehn:* knock out; **2.** (*die Augen*) cast down; **3.** (*unterdrücken*) suppress; (*Aufstand*) put down, crush, quell; **4.** *Jur.* (*Verfahren*) quash; **II.** *v/refl.* **1.** *Chem.* precipitate, deposit; **2.** *fig.:* **sich ~ in** (*+ Dat.*) → **Niederschlag** 4; **niederschlagsarm** *Adj.:* **~es Gebiet** *etc.* low-precipitation area *etc.*; **niederschlagsfrei** *Adj.* dry

Niederschlagsmenge *f Met.* rainfall, precipitation

niederschlagsreich *Adj.:* **~es Gebiet** *etc.* high-precipitation area *etc.*

Niederschlagung *f* **1.** *e-s Aufstands etc.:* suppression, quelling; **2.** *Jur.* quashing

niederschmettern *v/t.* (*trennb., hat -ge-*) **1.** (*j-n*) floor; (*etw.*) dash to the ground; **2.** *fig.* crush, shatter; **niederschmetternd I.** *Part. Präs.* → **niederschmettern; II.** *Adj.* shattering, crushing

nieder|schreiben *v/t.* (*unreg., trennb., hat -ge-*) write (*od.* set) down, record; **~schreien** *v/t.* (*unreg., trennb., hat -ge-*) shout *s.o.* down

Niederschrift *f* **1.** (*Vorgang*) writing (*od.* setting) down (*+ Gen.* of), recording (of); **2.** (*Geschriebenes*) notes *Pl.*; (*Protokoll*) minutes *Pl.*

nieder|setzen (*trennb., hat -ge-*) **I.** *v/t.*

put (*od.* set) down; **II.** *v/refl.* sit down; **~sinken** *v/i.* (*unreg., trennb., ist -ge-*) sink (down); (*zusammenbrechen*) collapse; **~sitzen** *v/i.* (*unreg., trennb., ist -ge-*); *südd., österr., schw.* sit down

Niederspannung *f Etech.* low voltage

nieder|stechen *v/t.* (*unreg., trennb., hat -ge-*) stab (to death); **~stimmen** *v/t.* (*trennb., hat -ge-*) vote down; **~stoßen** (*unreg., trennb.*) **I.** *v/t.* (*hat niedergestoßen*); *geh.* knock down; **II.** *v/i.* (*ist*): ~ **auf** (*+ Akk.*) swoop down on; **~strecken** (*trennb., hat -ge-*); *geh.* **I.** *v/t.* floor, knock down; **II.** *v/refl.* (*sich hinlegen*) lie down; (*sich ausstrecken*) stretch out; **~stürzen** *v/i.* (*trennb., ist -ge-*); *geh.* **1.** fall down; *Pferd: auch* stumble; **2.** *Gesteinsmassen etc.*: come (crashing) down

niedertourig *Mot.* **I.** *Adj. Motor etc.*: low-rev; **II.** *Adv.:* ~ **fahren** run at low revs

Niedertracht *f*, *-, kein Pl.; geh.* **1.** (*Boshaftigkeit*) malice, spite; (*Verwerflichkeit*) vileness; **2.** (*boshafte Tat*) malicious (*od.* spiteful) act; (*verwerfliche Tat*) vile deed, *umg.* dirty trick; **niederträchtig** *Adj.* (*boshaft*) malicious, spiteful; (*verwerflich*) vile, low; *Motiv:* base; **Niederträchtigkeit** *f* **1.** *nur Sg.:* (*Boshaftigkeit*) malice, spite; (*Verwerflichkeit*) vileness; **2.** (*boshafte Tat*) malicious (*od.* spiteful) act; (*verwerfliche Tat*) vile deed, *umg.* dirty trick

nieder|trampeln *v/t.* (*trennb., hat -ge-*); *umg.* trample down (*lit.* underfoot); (*Menschen*) trample on; **~treten** *v/t.* (*unreg., trennb., hat -ge-*) tread down; (*Blumen*) tread (*bes. Am.* step) on, crush

Niederung *f* **1.** depression; *Pl.* low-lying areas; **2.** *fig.:* **die ~en des Lebens** the seamy side of life

Niederwald *m Forstwesen:* copse

niederwalzen *v/t.* (*trennb., hat -ge-*) **1.** flatten, mow down; **2.** *fig.* steamroller

niederwärts *Adv. geh.* downward(s)

niederwerfen (*unreg., trennb., hat -ge-*) **I.** *v/t.* **1.** throw (*od.* fling) down *od.* to the ground; *fig. von e-r Krankheit etc.* **niedergeworfen werden** be laid low; **2.** *fig.* (*Aufstand*) put down, crush, quell; **II.** *v/refl.:* **sich vor j-m ~** throw o.s. at *s.o.*'s feet; **Niederwerfung** *f e-s Aufstands:* quelling

Niederwild *n Jägerspr.* small game

niederzwingen *v/t.* (*unreg., trennb., hat -ge-*); *geh.* overpower, overcome; (*j-n*) *auch* bring to his (*od.* her) knees

niedlich *Adj.* **1.** sweet, cute; **das ist ja ~!** *umg. iro.* charming!; **2.** *Dial., mst iro.* tiny

Niednagel *m* hangnail

niedrig I. *Adj.* **1.** *an Höhe:* low; **~er Wasserstand** low water; **2.** *Preise, Gehälter etc.:* low; *Qualität:* inferior, low; **~er Gang** *Mot.* low gear; **3.** *von Stand:* low(ly), humble; **4.** *fig.* (*gemein*) low, mean, base; **~e Instinkte** base(r) instincts; **aus ~en Beweggründen handeln** act on base motives; **II.** *Adv.* **1.** *schweben, fliegen:* low; **2.** ~ **kalkulierte Preise** low prices; **wir setzten die monatlichen Raten ~ an** we fixed the monthly instal(l)ments at a low rate; **3.** (*gemein*) **ein ~ stehender Mensch** a lowly person

Niedrigenergiehaus *n* low-energy house

Niedrighaltung *f:* ~ **von Preisen** *etc.* keeping down prices *etc.*

Niedrigkeit *f* lowness; *der Preise, Kurse:* low level; *von Stand:* humbleness; *charakterliche:* baseness

Niedriglohn *m* low wage(s *Pl.*); **~gruppe** *f* low-wage bracket; **~land** *n* low-wage country

Niedrigpreis *m Wirts.* low price; **~land** *n* low-price (*od.* cheap) country

niedrigprozentig *Adj.* low percentage

niedrig stehend → **niedrig** II 3

Niedrigwasser *n* low tide (*od.* water)

niemals *Adv.* never; → *auch* **nie**

niemand *unbest. Pron.* nobody, no one; not … anybody; ~ **anders** nobody else; ~ **anders als** none other than; **sprich bloß mit ~(em) darüber** whatever you do don't tell anyone about it; **Niemand** *m;* *-(e)s, kein Pl.; pej.* (*unbedeutende Person*) a nobody

Niemandsland *n Mil. und fig.* no-man's-land

Niere *f;* *-, -n; Anat.* kidney; → **künstlich** I; **j-m an die ~n gehen** *umg. fig.* get to *s.o.*; (*j-n mitnehmen*) take it out of *s.o.*; → *auch* **Herz**[1] 8

Nierenbecken *n Anat.* renal pelvis; **~entzündung** *f Med.* pyelitis

Nierenentzündung *f Med.* kidney infection, *fachspr.* nephritis (*Pl.* nephritides)

nierenförmig *Adj.* kidney-shaped

Nierenkolik *f Med.* renal colic

nierenkrank *Adj.:* ~ **sein** have kidney trouble (*od.* a kidney disease); **Nierenkrankheit** *f*, **Nierenleiden** *n* kidney disease (*od.* trouble)

Nieren|schale *f Med.* kidney dish; **~spender** *m*, **~spenderin** *f* kidney donor

Nierenstein *m Med.* kidney stone; **~zertrümmerer** *m;* *-s, -* lithotripter

Nieren|tasche *f* belt bag, *umg.* bum bag, *Am.* fanny pack; **~tisch** *m* kidney-shaped table; **~transplantation** *f Med.* kidney transplant; **~tumor** *m Med.* renal (*od.* kidney) tumo(u)r; **~versagen** *n* kidney failure; **~wärmer** *m;* *-s, -* body belt

nieseln *v/i. unpers.* drizzle; **Nieselregen** *m* drizzle

niesen *v/i.* sneeze

Nies|pulver *n* sneezing powder; **~reiz** *m* urge to sneeze

Nießbrauch *m; nur Sg.; Jur.* usufruct; **Nießbraucher** *m;* *-s, -*, **Nießbraucherin** *f;* *-, -nen* usufructuary

Nießnutz *m;* *-es, kein Pl.* usufruct; **Nießnutzer** *m*, **Nießnutzerin** *f* usufructuary

Nieswurz *f;* *-, -en; Bot.* hellebore

Niet *m, n;* *-(e)s, -e; Tech.* → **Niete**[1]

Niete[1] *f;* *-, -n; Tech.* rivet; *für Kleidung:* stud

Niete[2] *f;* *-, -n;* (*Los*) blank; *umg. fig.* (*Reinfall*) flop, washout; *umg.* (*Person*) washout, dead (*Am.* total) loss

nieten *v/t.* rivet

Nieten|gürtel *m* studded belt; **~hose** *f:* (*e-e*) ~ (a pair of) jeans *Pl.* (with studs)

Niet|hammer *m Tech.* riveting hammer; **~kopf** *m* rivet head; **~presse** *f* riveting press

niet- und nagelfest *Adj.:* **alles, was nicht ~ war** *umg.* everything that wasn't nailed down

Nife *n;* *-, kein Pl. Geol.* nife

nigelnagelneu *Adj.; österr. und schw. umg.* brand-spanking new

Nigeria (*n*); *-s; Geog.* Nigeria; **Nigerianer** *m;* *-s, -*, **Nigerianerin** *f;* *-, -nen* Nigerian, *weiblich auch*: Nigerian woman (*od.* girl); **nigerianisch** *Adj.* Nigerian

Nigger *m*; *-s*, *-*; *pej.* nigger *neg!*
Nihilismus *m*; *-*, *kein Pl.* nihilism; **Nihilist** *m*; *-en*, *-en*, **Nihilistin** *f*; *-*, *-nen* nihilist; **nihilistisch** *Adj.* nihilistic
Nikkei-Index *m Fin.*, *Wirts.* Nikkei Index
Nikolaus[1] (*m*); *Nikolau s'*, *mit Art.*: *-*, *-e* Nicholas
Nikolaus[2] *m*; *-*, *-e und umg. hum. Nikoläuse* **1.** St. Nicholas; **2.** *nur Sg.* St. Nicholas' Day; **~abend** *m* St. Nicholas' Eve, Eve of St. Nicholas' (Day); **~tag** *m* St. Nicholas' Day
Nikolo *m*; *-s*, *-s*; *österr.* → **Nikolaus**[2]
Nikotin *n*; *-s*, *kein Pl.* nicotine; **nikotinarm** *Adj.* low in nicotine, low-nicotine …; **nikotinfrei** *Adj.* nicotine-free; **Nikotingehalt** *m* nicotine content; **nikotinhaltig** *Adj.*: **~ sein** contain nicotine; **Nikotinsäure** *f* niacin; **nikotinsüchtig** *Adj.* addicted to nicotine; **Nikotinvergiftung** *f* nicotine poisoning
Nil *m*; *-s*; *Geog.*: **der ~** the Nile; **~gans** *f Zool.* Egyptian goose; **~krokodil** *n Zool.* Nile crocodile
Nille *f*; *-*, *-n*; *vulg.* cock, dick
Nilpferd *n Zool.* hippopotamus (*Pl.* hippopotamuses *od.* hippopotami), *umg.* hippo
Nimbus *m*; *-*, *-se* **1.** *Kunst* nimbus (*Pl.* nimbuses *od.* nimbi), halo; **2.** *nur Sg.*; *fig.* aura (*Pl.* aurae *od.* auras); **von e-m geheimnisvollen ~ umgeben** surrounded by a (certain) mystique
nimmer *Adv.* **1.** *geh. altm.* never; **2.** *südd. österr.* never again → *auch* **nie**
Nimmerleinstag *m* → *Sankt-Nimmerleins-Tag*
nimmermehr *Adv.* **1.** *altm.* never; **2.** *südd., österr.* never again
nimmermüde *Adj. geh.* untiring, indefatigable
nimmersatt *Adj.*; *nur attr.*; *umg.* insatiable; **Nimmersatt** *m*; *- und -(e)s*, *-e*; *umg.* insatiable person
Nimmerwiedersehen *n*: **auf ~** *umg.*, *oft iro.* for good
nimmt *Präs.* → *nehmen*
Ninive (*n*); *-s*; *hist.* Nineveh
Niob *n*; *-s*, *kein Pl.*; *Chem.* niobium
Nippel *m*; *-s*, *-* **1.** *Tech.* fitting; *für Rohre*, (*Schmiernippel*) nipple; **2.** *vulg.* nipple
nippen *vt/i.* sip (**an** + *Dat.* at)
Nippes *Pl.* knick-knacks; *bes. pej.* bric-a-brac *Sg.*
Nippflut *f Met.*, *Naut.* neap tide
Nippsachen *Pl.* → *Nippes*
Nipptide *f Met.*, *Naut.* neap tide
nirgend *Adv. altm.* → *nirgends*; **~her** *Adv.* → *nirgendwoher*, **~hin** *Adv.* → *nirgendwohin*
nirgends *Adv.* nowhere, not … anywhere
nirgendwo *Adv.* nowhere, not … anywhere; **~her** *Adv.* from nowhere, not … from anywhere; **~hin** *Adv.* nowhere, not … anywhere
Nirwana *n*; *-(s)*, *kein Pl.* nirvana, Nirvana; **ins ~ eingehen** enter into nirvana (*od.* Nirvana); *fig. iro.* (*sterben*) go to meet one's Maker
Nische *f*; *-*, *-n* niche (*auch fig.*); *e-s Raums*: recess
Nisse *f*; *-*, *-n*; (*Lausei*) nit
nisten *v/i.* (build a) nest
Nist|höhle *f* nest(ing) hole; **~kasten** *m* nest(ing) box; **~platz** *m* nesting place; **~zeit** *f*: **zur ~** at nesting time, in the nesting season
Nitrat *n*; *-(e)s*, *-e*; *Chem.* nitrate; **~belastung** *f* nitrate pollution; **~gehalt** *m*

nitrate level (*im Boden*: *auch* levels *Pl.*)
Nitrid *n*; *-s*, *-e*; *Chem.* nitride
nitrieren *v/t.* **1.** *Chem.* nitrate; **2.** *v/t. Metall.* nitride; **nitriergehärtet** *Adj. Metall.* nitrided; **Nitrierstahl** *m* nitriding steel
nitrifizieren *v/t.* nitrify; **Nitrifizierung** *f* nitrification
Nitrit *n*; *-s*, *-e*; *Chem.* nitrite
Nitro|benzol *n Chem.* nitrobenzene; **~farbstoffe** *Pl.* nitro dyestuff *Sg.*
Nitrogenium *n*; *-s*, *kein Pl.*; *Chem.* nitrogen
Nitro|glyzerin *n Chem.* nitroglycerine; **~gruppe** *f* nitro group; **~lack** *m* nitrocellulose paint; **~phosphat** *n* nitrophosphate
Nitrosamin *n*; *-s*, *-e*; *Chem.* nitrosamine
nival *Adj. Met.* nival
Niveau [ni'vo:] *n*; *-s*, *-s* **1.** *auch von Preisen etc.*: level; **2.** (*Bildungsniveau etc.*) level, standard; **unter dem ~** not up to standard (*umg.* scratch); **~ haben** *Person*: have class (*od.* style), **ein hohes ~ haben** be of a high standard, be on a high level; **jemand von d-m ~** someone of your calib|re (*Am.* -er); **es ist unter s-m ~** it's not his level; *stärker*: it's beneath him (*iro. auch* his dignity)
niveau|frei *Adj. Verk.* on different levels; **~gleich** *Adj.* single-level
Niveaulinie *f Geog.* contour line
niveaulos *fig. Adj.* mediocre; *Person*: uncultured; **Niveaulosigkeit** *f* mediocrity; *e-r Person*: lack of culture (*od.* style)
Niveau|senkung *f* drop in level; **~unterschied** *m* difference in level (*fig. auch* standard); **~verlust** *fig. m* drop in standard
niveauvoll *Adj.* (*anspruchsvoll*) of a high standard; (*kultiviert*) cultivated; *Person*: *auch* cultured; *weitS.* sophisticated
nivellieren *v/t.* level
Nivellier|gerät *n* (telescope) level; **~latte** *f* level(l)ing rod
Nivellierung *f* level(l)ing
nix *unbest. Pron. umg.* → *nichts*
Nix *m*; *-es*, *-e*; *Myth.* water sprite, nix
Nixe *f*; *-*, *-n*; *Myth.* water nymph, nixie; *im Meer*: mermaid; *umg. fig. hum.* (*Badenixe*) bathing beauty
Nizza (*n*); *-s*; *Geog.* Nice
n. J. *Abk.* (**nächsten Jahres**) next year's, of next year
n. M. *Abk.* (**nächsten Monats**) next month's, of next month
NN *Abk.* → *Normalnull*
N. N. *Abk.* **1.** (**nomen nescio** *od.* **nominandum**) name unknown; **2.** → *Normalnull*
nobel *Adj.* **1.** *geh.* noble, high-minded; **2.** *umg.* (*großzügig*, *freigebig*) generous; **3.** *umg.* (*luxuriös*) classy, posh, *Am.* upmarket
Nobel|gegend *f umg.*, *mst iro.* posh (*Am.* upmarket) area (*od.* part of town); **~herberge** *f*, **~hotel** *n umg.*, *mst iro.* high-class (*umg.* posh, *Am.* upmarket) hotel
Nobelium *n*; *-s*, *kein Pl.*; *Chem.* nobelium
Nobel|karosse *f umg.*, *mst. iro* big flash(y) car; **~marke** *f umg.*, *mst iro.* posh (*Am.* classy) brand
Nobelpreis *m* Nobel Prize; **alternativer ~** Right Livelihood Award, Alternative Nobel Prize; **~träger** *m*, **~trägerin** *f* Nobel Prize winner, Nobel laureate

Nobel|restaurant *n umg.*, *mst iro.* top-class (*umg.* classy, posh) restaurant; **~viertel** *n umg.*, *mst iro.* posh (*Am.* upmarket) area
Noblesse [no'blɛs] *f*; *-*, *kein Pl.*; *geh. e-r Person*: high-mindedness, noble-mindedness
Nobody ['no:bɔdi] *m*; *-(s)*, *-s*; *mst pej.* nobody
noch I. *Adv.* **1.** still; **immer ~** *od.* **~ immer** still; **~ nicht** not yet; **~ ist es nicht zu spät** it's not too late yet; **~ nie** never (before); **~ lange nicht** *umg.* not by a long chalk (*Am.* shot); **wir sind ~ lange nicht fertig** *etc.* we're not nearly (*od.* nowhere near) ready *etc.*; **2.** *geringen zeitlichen Abstand ausdrückend*: **~ am selben Tag** that (very) same day; **~ gestern** only yesterday; **heute ~** (*bis heute*) to this day; **~ jetzt** even now; **sie war eben** *od.* **gerade ~ hier** she was here only a moment ago; **~ im 11. Jahrhundert** … as late as the 11th century …; **3.** *begrenzten zeitlichen Rahmen ausdrückend*: **der Brief muss heute ~** *od.* **~ heute zur Post®** *I etc.* have to get this letter to the post office by the end of today; **er starb ~ an der Unfallstelle** he died at the scene of the accident; **4.** (*nicht mehr als*): **er hat nur ~ 10 Dollar** he's only got 10 dollars left; **es sind** (*nur*) **~ 5 Kilometer bis zur Raststätte** it's (only) 5 more kilomet|res (*Am.* -ers) to the service station; **5.** (*ein weiteres Mal*, *zusätzlich*) more; **~** (*ein*)**mal** once more, one more time, again; *umg. bei Versprecher*: let's try that (one) again; **das ist ~ einmal gut gegangen** that was close (*od.* a close thing [*Am.* call]), *umg.* talk about lucky; **~ dazu** on top of that; **~ einer** one more, another one; **~ ein Stück** another (*od.* one more) piece; **~ ein Bier, bitte!** the same again, another beer, please; **~ zwei Kaffee, bitte!** two more coffees, please; **auch das ~!** that's all I *etc.* needed; **er hat Geld ~ und nöcher** *umg.* he's got piles (*od.* stacks) of money; **~ einmal so viel** as much again; **und ~ etwas** and another thing; **~ etwas?** anything else?; **was wollen Sie ~?** what more do you want?; (*und*) **was ~?** *umg.* (and) what else?; **wer kommt ~?** who else is coming?; **~ fünf Minuten** five minutes to go; *bittend*: five more minutes, another five minutes; → *fehlen* 1, 4, *gerade* II 2,3; **6.** (*möglicherweise*): **du kommst ~ zu spät!** you'll be late if you're not careful; **sie wird** (*schon*) **~ anrufen** she'll still call; **7.** (*zuvor*, *vorher*): **sie will erst ~ duschen** she just wants to have a shower first; **ich mache das ~ fertig** I'll just finish this; **8.** (*später*): **er wird ~ kommen** he will come; **vielleicht kann man das ~** (*ein*)**mal gebrauchen** perhaps it can be used again sometime; **9.** *beim Komparativ e-n höheren Grad ausdrückend*: **~ besser/mehr** even better/more; **~ schlauer als du** even smarter than you; *es klingt etc.* **nur ~ verdächtiger** even (*od.* all the) more suspicious; → *schön* I 6; **10.** *einräumend*: **jede ~ so kleine Spende zählt** every donation counts however small it is; **sei es ~ so klein** no matter how small it is, however small it may be; **mag sie auch ~ so sehr schimpfen** *od.* **wenn sie auch ~ so sehr schimpft** however (*od.* no matter how) much she grumbles; **11.** *verstärkend*: **das ist ~ Qualität** that's what I call quality; **da**

bekommt man ~ etwas für sein Geld at least there you get value for money (*Am. auch* something for your money); *da haben wir ja ~ Glück gehabt* we were lucky there; *der wird sich ~ wundern* he's in for a surprise; *man wird (doch) ~ fragen dürfen* I *etc.* was only asking; *das wirst du ~ bereuen drohend*: you're going to regret that; **12.** *fragend*: *da kannst du ~ lachen?* how can you find that funny?; *jetzt will er ~ baden?* he wants to go for a swim now?; *nach Vergessenem*: *wie heißt sie ~?* what's (*od.* what was) her name again?; **13.** (*weniger als*): *das kostet ~ keine 5 Dollar* it costs less than 5 dollars; *es dauert ~ keine 10 Minuten* it won't even take 10 minutes; *er kann ~ nicht einmal kochen* he can't even cook; **II.** *Konj.*: *sie hat keine Bekannten ~ Freunde in der Stadt geh.* she has no acquaintances or friends in the town; → **weder**

nochmalig *Adj.* renewed, second; **~e Untersuchung** re-examination; **nochmals** *Adv.* **1.** once more (*od.* again), again; **2.** (*wieder ...*) *auch* re...; **~ untersuchen** reinvestigate

Nöck *m*; -en, -en; *Myth.* water sprite

Nocken *m*; -s, -; *Tech.* cam; **~welle** *f* camshaft

Nockerl *n*; -s, -n; *bes. österr. Gastr.* dumpling; *Salzburger ~n* type of sweet whipped pudding eaten hot

Noir [nŏaːɐ̯] *n*; -s, *kein Pl.*; *beim Roulette*: black

NOK *n*; -(s), -s; *Abk.* (*Nationales Olympisches Komitee*) NOC

Noktambulismus *m*; -, *kein Pl.*; *Med.* noctambulism, somnabulism

nölen *v/i. bes. nordd. umg. pej.* **1.** (*trödeln*) dawdle, dilly-dally; **2.** (*maulen, mosern*) moan, bellyache

nolens volens *Adv.* like it or not, *förm.* willy-nilly

Nöler *m*; -s, -; *bes. nordd. umg. pej.* **1.** (*Trödler*) dawdler; **2.** (*Moserer*) moaner, bellyacher; **Nölerei** *f*; -, *kein Pl.*; *bes. nordd. umg.* **1.** (*Trödeln*) dawdling; **2.** (*Mosern*) moaning, bellyaching; **Nölerin** *f*; -, -nen → **Nöler**; **nölig** *Adj. bes. nordd. umg. pej.* slow, ponderous

Nomade *m*; -, -n nomad

Nomadendasein *n* → **Nomadenleben**; **nomadenhaft** *Adj.* nomadic

Nomaden|leben *n* nomadic life, life of a nomad (*od.* nomads); **~stamm** *m* nomadic tribe

Nomadentum *n* nomadism

Nomaden|volk *n* nomadic tribe (*od.* people); **~zelt** *n* nomad('s) tent

Nomadin *f*; -, -nen nomad, nomadic woman (*od.* girl *etc.*); **nomadisch** *Adj.* nomadic; **nomadisieren** *v/i.* lead a nomadic life

Nomen *n*; -s, - *und* Nomina; *Ling.* **1.** (*Substantiv*) noun; *~ proprium* proper noun; **2.** (*deklinierbares Wort*) declinable word

nomenklatorisch *Adj.* nomenclative, nomenclatorial; **Nomenklatur** *f*; -, -en nomenclature; **Nomenklatura** *f*; -, *kein Pl.* nomenklatura

nominal *Adj. Ling., Wirts.* nominal

Nominal|betrag *m* nominal sum; **~einkommen** *n* Wirts. nominal income

Nominal|form *f* Ling. nominal form; **~gruppe** *f* nominal group

nominalisieren *v/t. Ling.* nominalize; **Nominalisierung** *f* nominalization

Nominalismus *m*; -, *kein Pl.*; *Philos., Wirts.* nominalism; **Nominalist** *m*; -en,

-en; *Philos., Wirts.* nominalist

Nominallohn *m* Wirts. nominal (*od.* money) wages *Pl.*

Nominal|phrase *f* Ling. nominal phrase; **~satz** *m* nominal phrase; **~stil** *m* nominal style

Nominal|verzinsung *f* Wirts. nominal interest rate; **~wert** *m* nominal (*od.* face) value

Nominativ *m*; -s, -e; *Ling.* nominative (case); (*Wort im Nominativ*) nominative; **nominativisch** *Adj.* nominative

nominell *Adj.* nominal

nominieren *v/t.* nominate; **Nominierung** *f* nomination

Nomogramm *n* Math. nomogram, nomograph; **Nomographie** *f*; -, *kein Pl.* nomography

No-Name-Produkt ['noːneːm-] *n* Wirts. own-label (*Am.* house brand) product

Nonchalance [nõ̃ʃa'lãːs] *f*; -, *kein Pl.* nonchalance; **nonchalant** [nõ̃ʃa'lãː] *Adj.* nonchalant

None *f*; -, -n **1.** *Mus.* ninth; **2.** *kirchl.* (*Gebetsstunde*) nones *Pl.* (*auch V. im Sg.*)

Nonenakkord *m* Mus. ninth chord

nonfigurativ *Adj. Kunst* non-figurative

Non-Food-Abteilung [nɔn'fuːd-] *f* non-food section

Nonkonformismus *m*; -, *kein Pl.* nonconformism; **Nonkonformist** *m*, **Nonkonformistin** *f* nonconformist; **nonkonformistisch** *Adj.* nonconformist

Nonne *f*; -, -n **1.** nun; **2.** *Zool.* nun moth; **3.** *Archit.* concave tile; **nonnenhaft I.** *Adj.* nunlike; **II.** *Adv.*: *~ leben* live like a nun

Nonnen|haube *f* coif; **~kloster** *n* convent, *lit.* nunnery; **~orden** *m* order of nuns

Nonplusultra *n*; -, *kein Pl.*: *das ~* the ultimate, the last thing

Nonsens *m*; -(es), *kein Pl.* nonsense; **~dichtung** *f* nonsense verse (*od.* poem); *Pl.* nonsense poetry (*od.* verse) *Sg.*

nonstop *Adv.* nonstop

Nonstop|flug *m* nonstop flight; **~kino** *n* continuous performance cinema

nonverbal *Adj.* nonverbal

Noor *n*; -(e)s, -e; *nordd.* lagoon

Noppe *f*; -, -n *in Garn*: slub, burl; *auf Sohle, Gummimatte*: knobble; **noppen** *v/t.* (*Noppen auszupfen*) burl; *ein Garn ~* (*mit Noppen versehen*) add slubs to a thread; *eine Gummimatte ~* give a rubber mat a knobbly surface

Noppen|garn *n* slubbed yarn; **~gewebe** *n* slubbed material; **~glas** *n*; *nur Sg.* dimpled glass

noppig *Adj. Garn*: burled; *Sohle, Gummimatte*: knobbly

Nord *m* **1.** *ohne Art.*; *nur Nom. Sg.*; *Met., Naut.* north; *von od. aus ~* from the north; **2.** *ohne Art.*; *nur Nom. Sg.*; *nachgestellt*: *Duisburg ~* the north of Duisburg; *Eingang ~* (the) north entrance; **3.** -(e)s, -e; *Pl. selten*; *Naut., poet.* north wind, northerly

Nordafrika (*n*); *Geog.* North Africa; **Nordafrikaner** *m*, **Nordafrikanerin** *f* North African, *weiblich auch*: North African woman (*od.* girl); **nordafrikanisch** *Adj.* North African

Nordamerika (*n*); *Geog.* North America; **Nordamerikaner** *m*, **Nordamerikanerin** *f* North American; **nordamerikanisch** *Adj.* North American

Nordatlantikpakt *m*; *nur Sg.*; *Pol.* North Atlantic Treaty

norddeutsch *Adj.* North German; *im ~en Raum* in the north of Germany,

in Northern Germany; *die Norddeutsche Tiefebene Geog.* the North German lowlands *Pl.*; **Norddeutsche** *m, f* North German; **Norddeutschland** (*n*); *Geog.* North (*od.* Northern) Germany

Norden *m*; -s, *kein Pl.*; (*abgek.* **N**) north (*Abk.* N); (*nördlicher Landesteil*) North; *nach ~* north(wards), *Verkehr, Straße etc.*: northbound; *von od. aus dem ~* from the north; *im kalten ~* up in the cold north; *der hohe ~* the far north

Nordengland (*n*); *Geog.* Northern England; *in ~* in Northern England, in the north of England; **nordenglisch** *Adj.* northern (*od.* Northern) English

Nordeuropa (*n*); *Geog.* Northern Europe; **Nordeuropäer** *m*, **Nordeuropäerin** *f* North (*od.* Northern) European; **nordeuropäisch** *Adj.* North (*od.* Northern) European

Nord|fenster *n* north-facing window; **~flanke** *f* north side; *Met.* northern edge; **~flügel** *m* e-s Gebäudes: north wing

nordfriesisch *Adj.* North Fri(e)sian; *die Nordfriesischen Inseln Geog.* the North Fri(e)sian Islands; **Nordfriesland** (*n*); *Geog.* North Friesland

Nord|halbkugel *f*; *nur Sg.*; *Geog.* northern hemisphere; **~hang** *m* northern (*od.* north-facing) slope

Nordire *m* man (*od.* boy) from Northern Ireland, Ulsterman; **Nordirin** *f* woman (*od.* girl) from Northern Ireland; → **Nordire**; **nordirisch** *Adj.* Northern Irish

Nordirland (*n*); -s; *Geog.* Northern Ireland; **~konflikt** *m* Pol.: *der ~* the conflict in Northern Ireland, the Troubles

nordisch *Adj.* northern; (*skandinavisch*) Nordic; → **Kombination** 1

Nordist *m*; -en, -en scholar in Scandinavian studies; **Nordistik** *f* Scandinavian studies *Pl.*; **Nordistin** *f*; -, -nen scholar in Scandinavian studies; **nordistisch** *Adj. Veranstaltung, Lehrstuhl, Kolleg*: ... in Scandinavian studies; *Institut*: ... of Scandinavian studies

Nordkap *n*; *nur Sg.*; *Geog.* North Cape

Nordkorea (*n*); *Geog.* North Korea; **Nordkoreaner** *m*, **Nordkoreanerin** *f* North Korean, *weiblich auch*: North Korean woman (*od.* girl); **nordkoreanisch** *Adj.* North Korean

Nordküste *f* north coast; *an der ~* on the north coast

Nordländer *m*; -s, -, **~in** *f*; -, -nen Northerner; *Typ*: Nordic type; **nordländisch** *Adj. Klima etc.*: northern; *Typ*: *auch* Nordic

nördlich I. *Adj.* northern, north ...; *Wind*: northerly; *in ~er Richtung* north(wards); *Verkehr, Straße etc.*: northbound; *71° ~er Breite* 71 degrees north; **II.** *Adv.* (to the) north (*von* of); **III.** *Präp.* (+ *Gen.*) (to the) north of; **nördlichst...** *Adj.* northernmost

Nordlicht *n* **1.** northern lights *Pl.*, aurora borealis; **2.** *umg.* (*Person*) Northerner

Nordmannstanne *f* Bot. Nordmann fir

Nordnordost *m* **1.** *ohne Art.*; *nur Sg.* (*abgek.* **NNO**); *Met., Naut.* north-northeast (*Abk.* NNE); **2.** *Naut.* north--northeasterly (wind)

Nordnordwest *m* **1.** *ohne Art.*; *nur Sg.* (*abgek.* **NNW**); *Met., Naut.* north--northwest (*Abk.* NNW); **2.** *Naut.* north-northwesterly (wind)

Nordost *m* **1.** *ohne Art.*; *nur Sg.* (*abgek.* **NO**); *Met., Naut.* northeast (*Abk.* NE);

2. *Naut., poet.* northeaster, nor'easter; **Nordosten** *m* → *Nordost* 1; **nordöstlich I.** *Adj.* northeast(ern); *Wind*: northeasterly; *in ~er Richtung* northeastwards, towards the northeast; *Verkehr*: northeast bound; *Straße*: running in a northeasterly direction; **II.** *Adv.* (to the) northeast (*von* of); **III.** *Präp.* (+ *Gen.*) (to the) northeast of

Nord-Ostsee-Kanal *m*; *kein Pl.*; *Geog., Naut.* Kiel Canal

Nordostwind *m* northeast (*od.* northeasterly) wind

Nordpol *m Geog.* North Pole; *e-s Magneten* north pole

Nordpolar|gebiet *n* Arctic; **~kreis** *m* Arctic Circle; **~meer** *n*; *nur Sg.* Arctic Ocean

Nordpolexpedition *f* expedition to the North Pole

Nord|punkt *m Geog.* north point; **~rand** *m* north (*od.* northern) edge

Nordrhein-Westfalen (*n*); *-s*; *Geog.* North Rhine-Westphalia; **nordrhein--westfälisch** *Adj.* North Rhine-Westphalian

Nordsee *f Geog.*: *die ~* the North Sea; **~insel** *f* island in the North Sea; **~krabbe** *f Zool.* common (*od.* European brown) shrimp; **~küste** *f* North Sea coast

Nord|seite *f* north (*od.* northern) side; **~spitze** *f* northerly point; **~staaten** *Pl.*: *die ~ der USA*: the northern states; *hist. im Bürgerkrieg*: the North, the Union; **~stern** *m* pole star, North Star

Nord-Süd|-Dialog *m Pol.* North-South Dialog(ue); **~Gefälle** *n* north-south divide; **~Konflikt** *m* North-South conflict

nordsüdlich *Adj.* ... going from north to south; *Straße, Verbindung auch*: ... running from north to south; *~ verlaufen* run from north to south

Nordsüdrichtung *f*: *in ~ verlaufen* run from north to south

Nord|teil *m* north (*od.* northern) part; **~wand** *f e-s Berges*: north face

nordwärts *Adv.* north(wards)

Nordwest *m* **1.** *ohne Art.*; *nur Sg.* (*abgek.* NW); *Met., Naut.* northwest (*Abk.* NW); **2.** *Naut., poet.* northwester, nor'wester; **Nordwesten** *m* → *Nordwest* 1; **nordwestlich I.** *Adj.* northwest(ern); *Wind*: northwesterly; **II.** *Adv.* (to the) northwest; **III.** *Präp.* (+ *Gen.*) (to the) northwest of; **Nordwestwind** *m* northwest (*od.* northwesterly) wind

Nordwind *m* north wind

Nörgelei *f*; *-*, *-en*; *pej.* grumbling, moaning; *e-s Kindes*: niggling, *umg.* grizzling; **nörgelig** *Adj. attr.* grumbling, moaning; *Kind*: *attr.* niggling, *umg.* grizzling, *Am.* whining; **nörgeln** *v/i.* grumble, moan; *Kind*: niggle, *umg.* grizzle, *Am.* whine; **Nörgler** *m*; *-s*, *-*, **Nörglerin** *f*; *-*, *-nen* grumbler, moaner; **nörglerisch** *Adj. attr.* grumbling, moaning; *Kind*: *attr.* niggling, *umg.* grizzling, *Am.* whining; **nörglig** *Adj.* → *nörgelig*

Norm *f*; *-*, *-en* **1.** (*Richtschnur*) norm, standard; (*Regel*) *auch* rule; *als ~ gelten* be (considered) the norm; *sich an die ~en halten* stick to the norm; **2.** *Tech. etc.* standard specification; **3.** (*Leistungssoll*) norm, (production) quota

normal I. *Adj.* normal; (*konventionell*) conventional; (*gewöhnlich*) ordinary; *Abmessungen etc.*: standard ...; *das ist*

doch ganz ~ that's perfectly normal (*od.* natural); *es ist ~, dass es heiß wird* it's normal for it to get hot; *jeder ~e Mensch* any normal person, anyone in his right mind; *du bist wohl nicht mehr ~!* *umg.* have you gone out of your mind?; **II.** *Adv. umg.* **1.** (*normalerweise*) normally; **2.** *ich hab ganz ~ gefragt, aber er hat gleich losgebrüllt* I asked in a completely normal way but he immediately started shouting

Normal *n* (*mst ohne Art.*); *-s*, *kein Pl.*; *umg.* (*Normalbenzin*) regular

Normal|benzin *n* regular petrol (*Am.* gas); **~bürger** *m*, **~bürgerin** *f* the average citizen, *the* man (*weibl.* woman) in the street

Normale *f*; *-(n)*, *-n*; *Math.* normal

normalerweise *Adv.* normally, under normal circumstances; (*meistens*) usually

Normal|fall *m* normal case; *im ~* normally; **~form** *f bes. Sport* usual form; **~gewicht** *n* standard (*Person*: average) weight; **~größe** *f* normal (*od.* standard) size; **~höhe** *f fachspr. etwa* sea level; **~höhenpunkt** *m Vermessungswesen*: datum plane; **~horizont** *m Vermessungswesen*: datum surface, true level

normalisieren I. *v/t.* normalize; (*Körperfunktionen*) regulate; **II.** *v/refl.* return to normal; (*sich selbst regulieren*) regulate itself; **Normalisierung** *f* normalization; **Normalität** *f*; *-*, *kein Pl.* normality

Normal|maß *n* **1.** standard measurement; **2.** *fig.* standard, norm; **~null** *n*; *nur Sg. etwa* sea level; **~profil** *n* **1.** *Tech.* standard section; **2.** *Archit.* normal profile

Normalspur *f Eisenb.* standard ga(u)ge

Normal|temperatur *f* normal (*od.* standard) temperature; **~ton** *m Mus.* standard pitch; *Akustik*: reference tone; **~uhr** *f* (*Uhr mit maßgebender Zeitanzeige*) regulator; (*öffentliche Uhr*) public clock; **~verbrauch** *m* average (*od.* standard) consumption; **~verbraucher** *m*, **~verbraucherin** *f* average consumer; → *Otto*; **~wert** *m* standard value; **~zeit** *f* standard time; **~zustand** *m* normal conditions *Pl.*; *das ist der ~ umg. iro.* that's the way things are (around here)

Normandie *f*; *-*; *Geog.*: *die ~* Normandy; **Normanne** *m*; *-n*, *-n*, **Normannin** *f*; *-*, *-nen* Norman; **normannisch** *Adj.* Norman

normativ *Adj.* normative

Normblatt *n* standard specifications list

normen *v/t.* standardize

Normenausschuss *m* standards committee

Normenkontrolle *f Jur.* judicial review; **Normenkontrollklage** *f Jur.* action brought by federal or state government before constitutional court on questions of the constitutionality of a law, *Am.* constitutional law case

Norm|erfüllung *f* fulfil(l)ment of quotas; **~erhöhung** *f qualitativ*: raising of standards; *quantitativ*: raising of quotas

normgerecht *Adj. und Adv.* complying with standards

normieren *v/t.* standardize; **Normierung** *f*, **Normung** *f* standardization

Norne *f*; *-*, *-n*; *Myth.* Norn

Norwegen (*n*); *-s*; *Geog.* Norway; **Norweger** *m*; *-s*, *-*, **Norwegerin** *f*; *-*, *-nen* Norwegian, *weiblich auch*: Norwegian woman (*od.* girl)

Norweger|muster *n Handarbeit*: Norwegian pattern; **~pullover** *m* Norwegian pullover (*Am. auch* sweater)

norwegisch *Adj.* Norwegian; **Norwegisch** *n*; *-en*; *Ling.* Norwegian; *das ~e* Norwegian

Nostalgie *f*; *-*, *kein Pl.* nostalgia; **~welle** *f* wave of nostalgia

Nostalgiker *m*; *-s*, *-*, **~in** *f*; *-*, *-nen* nostalgic; **nostalgisch I.** *Adj.* nostalgic; **II.** *Adv.* nostalgically

Not *f*; *-*, *Nöte* **1.** *nur Sg.*; (*Mangel, Armut*) want, need, poverty; (*Notlage*) plight; (*Elend*) *auch* misery; *wirtschaftliche ~* economic plight; *~ leiden* suffer want (*od.* privation); *die ~ leidende Bevölkerung* the needy people; *in der Stunde der ~* at the hour of need; *in ~ geraten/sein* encounter hard times / be suffering want; *~ macht erfinderisch* necessity is the mother of invention; *in der ~ frisst der Teufel Fliegen umg.* any port in a storm, beggars can't be choosers; *~ kennt kein Gebot Sprichw.* necessity knows no law; **2.** (*Schwierigkeit*) difficulty, trouble; (*Bedrängnis*) distress; (*Gefahr*) danger; *in tausend Nöten sein* be in real trouble (*od.* a real mess); *in ~ sein* be in trouble; *in ~ geraten* run into difficulties; *in höchster ~* in dire straits; *Rettung in od. aus höchster ~* rescue from extreme difficulties; *in meiner etc. ~* in my etc. predicament; **3.** *nur Sg.* (*Mühe*): *s-e liebe ~ haben* have a hard time (of it), *ich hatte m-e liebe ~, wieder ans Ufer zu schwimmen* I had great difficulty in swimming back to the bank; **4.** *nur Sg.*; (*Notwendigkeit*) necessity; *ohne ~ solltest du das nicht tun* you shouldn't do that unless it's really necessary; *zur ~* if necessary, if need be; (*gerade noch*) at (*Am.* in) a pinch; *stärker*: if (the) worst comes to (the) worst; *wenn ~ am Mann ist* if need be; *stärker*: if (the) worst comes to (the) worst; *hier ist od. tut Hilfe ~ geh.* I etc. need help here; *aus der ~ e-e Tugend machen* make a virtue of necessity; *der ~ gehorchend geh.* bowing to necessity; → *knapp* I 5

notabene *Adv. altm.* **1.** (*wohlgemerkt*) mind you; **2.** (*übrigens*) by the way

Notanker *m auch fig.* sheet anchor

Notar *m*; *-s*, *-e* notary; **Notariat** *n*; *-(e)s*, *-e*; (*Amt*) notaryship; (*Kanzlei*) notary's office

notariell I. *Adj.* notarial, attested by (a) notary; **II.** *Adv.* by (a) notary; *~ beglaubigt* attested by (a) notary; **Notarin** *f*; *-*, *-nen* notary

Not|arzt *m*, **~ärztin** *f in der Notaufnahme etc.*: emergency doctor; *im Notdienst*: doctor on call

Notarztwagen *m* emergency ambulance

Notation *f*; *-*, *-en* (system of) notation

Notaufnahme *f* **1.** *im Krankenhaus*: emergency admission; *Stelle*: casualty (department); **2.** *von Flüchtlingen etc.*: provisional accommodation; **~lager** *n* (refugee) transit camp, reception cent|re (*Am.* -er)

Not|ausgabe *f e-r Zeitung*: skeleton edition; **~ausgang** *m* emergency exit; (*Feuertür*) fire exit (*od.* door); **~ausstieg** *m* escape hatch; **~behelf** *m* stopgap; **~beleuchtung** *f* emergency lighting; **~bett** *n* emergency bed; **~bremse** *f* emergency brake; *Eisenb. Brit.* communication cord; *die ~ ziehen* apply the emergency brake(s), pull the communication cord; *fig.* call a halt before it's too late; *Sport fig.* commit a professional foul; **~bremsung** *f* emergency stop; **~brücke** *f* temporary bridge; **~dienst** *m* standby duty; **~ haben** be on standby, *Arzt*: *auch* be on call; *Apotheke*: be open all night

Notdurft *f*: **s-e ~ verrichten** *geh.* relieve o.s.

notdürftig I. *Adj.* **1.** (*knapp*) scanty, meag|re (*Am.* -er); **2.** (*improvisiert*) makeshift; (*Not...*) emergency ...; (*provisorisch*) provisional, stopgap ...; **II.** *Adv.* **1.** **~ möbliert** etc. scantily furnished *etc.*; **2.** (*als Notbehelf*) as a makeshift (*od.* stopgap); (*irgendwie*) somehow or other; (*gerade eben*) just about; **~ reparieren** patch *s.th.* up (*temporarily*); **sich ~ durchschlagen** just about (manage to) scrape through

Note *f*; -, -n **1.** *Päd.* mark, *bes. Am.* grade; **2.** *Mus.* note; **ganze ~** semibreve, *Am.* whole note; **halbe ~** minim, *Am.* half note; **~n** *Koll.* music *Sg.*; *Blätter*: sheet music; **nach ~n singen** sing from music, *Am. auch* sight-sing; **er kennt** *od.* **kann keine ~n** he can't read music; **3.** *Pol.* memorandum (*Pl.* memoranda *od.* memorandums); **4.** (*Prägung*) touch, note; **e-e besondere ~ verleihen** add a special touch (+ *Dat.* to); **das ist s-e persönliche ~** that's his particular way of doing things, that's his (personal) trademark; **5.** *mst Pl.*; *Wirts.* → **Banknote**

Notebook ['no:tbʊk] *n*; -s, -s *Computer*: notebook

Noten|austausch *m Pol.* exchange of notes; **~bank** *f Fin.* central bank; **~blatt** *n* (sheet of) music; *Pl.* sheet music; **~durchschnitt** *m Päd.* average mark (*bes. Am.* grade); **~gebung** *f* → **Benotung**; **~heft** *n* music book; **~linien** *Pl. Mus.* lines; **~papier** *n* manuscript paper; **~presse** *f* money press; **~pult** *n* music stand; **~schlüssel** *m Mus.* clef; **~schrift** *f* musical notation; **~ständer** *m* music stand; **~system** *n* **1.** *Päd.* marking (*od.* grading) system; **2.** *Mus.* system of notation; **~wechsel** *m Pol.* exchange of notes; **~wert** *m Mus.* (time) value (of a note)

Notepad ['no:tpɛt] *n*; -s, -s *Computer*: notepad

Not|erbe *m Jur.* mandatory heir; **~erbin** *f* mandatory heiress

Notfall *m* emergency; **im** (**äußersten**) **~** in an (extreme) emergency, if (the) worst comes to (the) worst; **für den ~** just in case; **~ausweis** *m* emergency ID; **~medizin** *f nur Sg.* emergency medicine

notfalls *Adv.* (*wenn nötig*) if need be, if necessary; (*zur Not*) at (*Am.* in) a pinch

Notfrequenz *f Funk.* emergency frequency

notgedrungen I. *Adj.* (en)forced, involuntary; **II.** *Adv.* of necessity; **~ musste sie** she had no choice but to, she was forced to

Not|geld *n* emergency money; **~gemeinschaft** *f* **1.** emergency action group; **2.** companions *Pl.* in distress; **~groschen** *m* nest egg; (**sich** [*Dat.*]) **e-n ~ beiseite legen** save up (*Am.* put some money aside) for a rainy day; **~helfer** *m* helper in (time of) need; **die vierzehn ~** *kath.* the (fourteen) auxiliary saints; **~hilfe** *f Jur.* assistance in an emergency

notieren I. *v/t.* **1.** (*aufschreiben*) make

a note of, take down; *flüchtig*: jot down; **2.** *Wirts.* (*Kurse, Preise*) quote (*zu* at); **3.** *Sport* book; **4.** *Mus.* notate; **II.** *v/i. Wirts.* be quoted (*mit* at); ... **notierte um vier Punkte weniger** ... was four points down; **... notierten schwächer** ... were down; **Notierung** *f* **1.** *Mus.* notation; **2.** *Börse*: quotation

nötig I. *Adj.* **1.** (*erforderlich*) necessary; **ich habe nicht die ~e Geduld dafür** I don't have the patience needed for that; **für e-n Urlaub fehlt uns das ~e Kleingeld** we don't have enough money for a holiday; **mit dem ~en Respekt** with due respect; **brauchst du Hilfe? - danke, nicht ~!** no thank you, I'm fine; **2.** **wenn ~** if necessary, if need be; **wenn ~, bleibe ich länger** I'll stay longer if I need to; **3.** **es ist nicht** (**unbedingt**) **~, dass du kommst** there's no (real) need for you to come, you don't (really) need to (*od.* have to) come; **es ist wohl nicht ~, dass ich euch sage** I don't suppose there's any need for me to tell you (*od.* there's any need for you to be told); **das war doch wirklich nicht ~** *vorwurfsvoll*: did you *etc.* have to (do that)?; **das wäre aber wirklich nicht ~ gewesen** *anerkennend*: you really shouldn't have; **4.** **er hielt es nicht mal für ~ zu** (+ *Inf.*) he didn't even think (*od.* consider) it necessary to (+ *Inf.*); **das habe ich nicht ~** *iro.* I can do very well without that(, thank you); (**muss ich mir nicht bieten lassen**) I don't have to stand for that; **du hast es** (**gerade**) **~!** *iro.* you of all people!; **etw.** (**dringend**) **~ haben** (badly) need s.th., need s.th. (badly), be in (dire) need of s.th.; **II.** *Adv.*: **sie brauchen ganz ~ Hilfe** they are in really urgent need of help; **am ~sten brauchen wir warme Decken** we most urgently need warm blankets

Nötige *n*: **das ~** (**tun**) (do) whatever is necessary; **das ~ veranlassen** make the necessary arrangements; → **Nötigste**

nötigen *v/t.* (*drängen*) urge, press; (*zwingen*) force, compel; **er lässt sich nicht lange ~** *umg.* he doesn't need much coaxing (*od.* encouragement); **sich genötigt sehen zu** (+ *Inf.*) feel compelled to (+ *Inf.*)

nötigenfalls *Adv.* if need be, if necessary

Nötigste *n*; -n, *kein Pl.* the essentials; **nehmt nur das Nötigste mit** take only what you absolutely need (*od.* what you need most); **mit dem ~n ausstatten** equip with the bare essentials

Nötigung *f* **1.** *Jur.* constraint, duress; **2.** *geh.* constraint, coercion; **3.** urging; (*Zwang*) forcing, compelling

Notiz *f*; -, -en **1.** (*Vermerk*) note; **sich** (*Dat.*) **~en machen** make (*od.* take) notes (**über** + *Akk.* on); **2.** *in der Zeitung*: item; **3.** *Börse*: quotation; **4.** **~ nehmen von** take note of; **keine ~ nehmen von** ignore, take no notice of; **~block** *m* notepad, *bes. Am.* memo pad; **~buch** *n* notebook

Notizensammlung *f* collection of notes

Not|jahre *Pl.* years of hardship; **~lage** *f* predicament; (*Elend*) plight; *weitS.* (*schwierige Lage*) awkward (*od.* difficult) situation; **wirtschaftliche ~** economic plight; **~lager** *n* makeshift bed, *umg.* shakedown; → **Notunterkunft**

notlanden (*untr.*, *-ge-*) **I.** *v/i.* (*ist*) make a forced (*od.* emergency) landing, force-land; **II.** *v/t.* (*hat*): **sie musste**

das Flugzeug ~ she had to make an emergency landing; **Notlandung** *f* forced (*od.* emergency) landing

Not leidend → **Not** 1; **Notleidende, Not Leidende** *m, f* needy person; **die ~n** the needy

Not|leine *f* emergency cord; **~leiter** *f* fire escape; **~licht** *n* emergency lighting; **~lösung** *f* stopgap (solution *od.* measure); *provisorische*: provisional (*od.* temporary) solution; (*Ausweg*) expedient; **~lüge** *f* white lie; **~maßnahme** *f* emergency (*od.* stopgap) measure, expedient; **~nagel** *m umg.*, *pej. Person*: fill-in; **~operation** *f* emergency operation; *auch Pl. Koll.* emergency surgery; **~opfer** *n* emergency tax

notorisch I. *Adj.* compulsive, habitual, addictive; *Lügner, Spieler*: *auch* notorious; **~er Optimist** incorrigible optimist; **II.** *Adv.*: **er ist ~ pleite** he's habitually broke

Not|programm *n Pol.*, *Wirts.* emergency measures *Pl.*; **~proviant** *m* emergency rations *Pl.*; **~quartier** *n* → **Notunterkunft**

notreif *Adj. Agr.* prematurely ripe; **Notreife** *f* premature ripening

Notruf *m* **1.** *Telef.* emergency call; **2.** (*Nummer*) emergency number; **3.** *e-s Tieres*: alarm call; **~nummer** *f* emergency number; **~säule** *f* emergency telephone

Not|rutsche *f Flug.* emergency chute; **~schalter** *m Etech.* emergency switch

notschlachten *v/t.* (*untr.*, *hat -ge-*) destroy; **Notschlachtung** *f* forced slaughter

Not|schrei *m* **1.** *geh.* cry of distress; **2.** *e-s Tieres*: alarm call; **~signal** *n* distress signal; **~situation** *f* emergency (situation); → *auch* **Notlage**; **~sitz** *m* jump seat

Notstand *m* **1.** → **Notlage**; **2.** *Pol.* state of emergency; **den ~ ausrufen** declare a state of emergency

Notstands|gebiet *n* **1.** *wirtschaftlich*: depressed area; **2.** (*Katastrophengebiet*) disaster area; **~gesetze** *Pl. Jur.* emergency legislation *Sg.*, emergency powers act *Sg.*

Notstrom *m*; *nur Sg.*; *Etech.* emergency power; **~aggregat** *n* emergency generator

Nottaufe *f* baptism in extremis; **nottaufen** *v/t.* (*untr.*, *hat -ge-*): **ein Kind ~** baptize a child in extremis

Nottestament *n* emergency will

Not tun → **Not** 4

Not|unterkunft *f* provisional accommodation (*auch Pl.*); *für Obdachlose*: emergency shelter; **~verband** *m* emergency dressing; **~verkauf** *m* distress sale; **~verordnung** *f* emergency decree

notwassern (*untr.*, *-ge-*) **I.** *v/i.* (*ist*) make a crash-landing in the sea *od.* in a lake/river; **II.** *v/t.* (*hat*): **er hat das Flugzeug notgewassert** he crash-landed into the sea *od.* into a lake/river

Notwehr *f*; *nur Sg.*; *Jur.*: (**aus** *od.* **in**) **~** (in) self-defen|ce (*Am.* -se); **~handlung** *f* act of self-defen|ce (*Am.* -se)

notwendig I. *Adj.* necessary; (*dringlich*) urgent; (*wesentlich*) essential; (*unerlässlich*) indispensable; (*unausbleiblich, unausweichlich*) inevitable; **unbedingt ~** absolutely vital; → *auch* **Nötige, Nötigste**; **II.** *Adv.* (*dringend*) urgently; **~ brauchen** *auch* need badly, badly need; **notwendigerweise** *Adv.* necessarily, of necessity; (*als unaus-*

weichliche Folge) auch inevitably; **Notwendigkeit** *f* necessity; *Sache: auch* requirement; *(Dringlichkeit)* urgency

Notzeiten *Pl.* times *(od.* time *Sg.)* of need

Notzucht *f Jur. altm.* rape; **~ begehen an** (+ *Dat.)* commit rape on; **notzüchtigen** *v/t. (untr., hat ge-)* rape, commit rape on

Nougat ['nu:gat] *m, n; -s, -s →* **Nugat**

Nova *f; -, Novä; Astron.* nova *(Pl.* novae *od.* novas)

Novelle *f; -, -n* **1.** *Lit.* novella; **2.** *Parl.* amendment

novellieren *v/t. Parl.* amend; **Novellierung** *f* amendment

Novellist *m; -en, -en; Lit.* novella writer; **Novellistik** *f; -, kein Pl.* novella writing; **Novellistin** *f; -, -nen* novella writer; **novellistisch I.** *Adj.: das ~e Werk Thomas Manns* Thomas Mann's novellas; **II.** *Adv.: etw. ~ gestalten* write s.th. in the form of a novella

November *m; -(s), -, mst Sg.* November; → *April;* **novemberlich** *Adj.* November-like

November|nebel *m* November fog; **~revolution** *f hist.* November revolution

Novität *f; -, -en* novelty, something new; *Wirts.* new article, *umg.* newcomer to the market; *e-e ~ auf dem Buchmarkt* a (brand-)new publication, a book hot off the press *umg*

Novize *m; -n, -n; kath. und fig.* novice; **Noviziat** *n; -(e)s, -e; kath.* novitiate, noviciate *(auch Gebäude);* **Novizin** *f; -, -nen; kirchl. und fig.* novice

Novum *n; -s, Nova* novelty, something new

NPD *f; -, kein Pl.; Abk.* (**Nationaldemokratische Partei Deutschlands**) *German right-wing extremist party*

Nr. *Abk.* (**Nummer**) No., *Am. auch* #

NRW *Abk.* (**Nordrhein-Westfalen**) North Rhine-Westphalia

NS|... *im Subst.* Nazi; **~-Diktatur** *f* Nazi dictatorship; **~-Staat** *m* Nazi state; **~-Verbrechen** *n* Nazi crime *(od.* atrocity); **~-Verbrecher** *m,* **~-Verbrecherin** *f* Nazi (war) criminal; **~-Zeit** *f* Nazi era, (period of) Nazi rule

N.T. *Abk.* (**Neues Testament**) NT

n-t... *Zahlw. Math.* nth

nu *Adv.* → **nun** I 1

Nu *m: im ~ umg.* in no time, in a flash, before you knew it

Nuance ['nyã:sə] *f; -, -n* nuance, shade; *fig. (Spur)* trace, tinge, shade; *die ~n unterscheiden können* recognize the subtleties *(od.* subtle differences); **nuancenreich** *Adj.* rich in nuance, finely nuanced, full of nuances; **Nuancenreichtum** *m; nur Sg.* wealth of nuances; **nuancieren** [nyã'si:rən] **I.** *v/t.* nuance; **II.** *v/i.* be subtle; **nuanciert I.** *P.P.* → **nuancieren; II.** *Adj.* subtle; finely *(od.* subtly) distinguished; *Farben:* subtly graded

Nubien (*n); -s; Geog.* Nubia; **Nubier** *m; -s, -,* **Nubierin** *f; -, -nen* Nubian, *weiblich auch:* Nubian woman *(od.* girl); **nubisch** *Adj.* Nubian

Nubuk *n; -(s), kein Pl.,* **~leder** *n* nubuck

nüchtern I. *Adj.* **1.** *(Ggs. betrunken)* sober; *wieder ~ werden* sober up; *vollkommen ~ umg.* stone cold sober; **2.** *auf ~en Magen* on an empty stomach; *das war ein Schreck auf ~en Magen* that took me completely by surprise; *kommen Sie bitte ~ Med.* please

don't eat or drink anything before you come; **3.** *Einrichtung, Bau etc.:* functional, austere; *Kleidung etc.:* sober; *Wand:* cold, bare; **4.** *Einstellung, Urteil etc.:* sober; *weitS. (sachlich) Person, Einschätzung etc.:* rational, down-to-earth; *Tatsachen:* plain, bare; **II.** *Adv.* soberly; *weitS. (sachlich)* matter-of-factly; **~ denkend** realistic, sober(-minded); **Nüchternheit** *f* sobriety; austerity; coldness *etc.;* → **nüchtern**

Nuckel *m; -s, -; (Sauger)* teat, *Am.* nipple; *(Schnuller)* dummy, *Am.* pacifier; **nuckeln** *v/i. umg.: ~ an* (+ *Dat)* suck (at)

Nuckelpinne. *f umg.* phut-phut *(Am.* put-put) car

Nucken *Pl.,* **Nücken** *Pl. bes. nordd. umg.: er hat so s-e ~* he has his little moods; *der Motor hat s-e ~* the engine's rather temperamental

nuddeln *v/i. Dial.* **1.** suck (*an* +*Dat.* at); **2.** *(drehen)* twiddle (*an* + *Dat.* with); **3.** *Radio etc.:* drone (on)

Nudel *f; -, -n; Gastr.* noodle; *Pl. (~arten)* pasta *Sg.,* pastas; *ulkige ~ umg. fig.* funny character; **~brett** *n* board *(for rolling out pasta dough);* **~gericht** *n chinesisch:* noodle dish; *italienisch:* pasta dish; **~holz** *n* rolling pin

nudeln *v/t.* stuff, fatten; *wie genudelt sein umg.* be (absolutely) stuffed

Nudel|salat *m Gastr.* pasta salad; **~suppe** *f* noodle soup; **~walker** *m südd., österr.* rolling pin

Nudismus *m; -, kein Pl.* nudism; **Nudist** *m; -en, -en,* **Nudistin** *f; -, -nen* nudist

Nugat *m, n; -s, -s; Gastr.* nougat; **~füllung** *f* nougat filling

nuklear *Adj.* nuclear; **II.** *Adv.: ~ angetrieben* nuclear-powered; *~ bewaffnet* armed with nuclear weapons; **Nuklear...** *im Subst.* nuclear

Nuklear|kriminalität *f* nuclear crime; **~macht** *f* nuclear power; **~medizin** *f* nuclear medicine; **~sprengkopf** *m* nuclear warhead; **~stützpunkt** *m* nuclear base; **~unfall** *m* nuclear accident; **~waffe** *f* nuclear weapon

Nukleinsäure *f Biochemie:* nucleic acid

Nukleon *n; -s, -en; Phys.* nucleon

Nukleus *m; -, Nuklei; Anat., Bio., Ling.* nucleus *(Pl.* nuclei)

null I. *Zahlw.* **1.** nought, *Am. und fachspr.* zero; *Math. Brit.* nought; *~ Grad* zero degrees; *das Thermometer etc. steht auf/über/unter ~* is at/above/below zero; *~ Fehler* no *(Am.* zero) mistakes; *um ~ Uhr zehn* at ten past *(Am. auch* after) midnight, *förm.* at zero hours ten; *gleich ~ umg.* nil; *in der Stunde ~* at (the) zero hour; *bei ~ anfangen (od.* *form.* start from scratch); → *nichtig* 2; **2.** *in Dezimalzahlen:* O [əʊ]; *~ komma neun* (= *0,9*) O point nine (= *0.9);* *in ~ Komma nichts umg.* in next to no time; **3.** *in Telefonnummern:* O [əʊ], *Am. auch* zero; **4.** *Sport* nil, *Am.* nothing, zero; *Tennis:* love; *zwei zu ~* two-nil, *Am.* two to nothing; *zu ~ spielen Sport* not concede any goals; **II.** *indekl. Adj. umg.: ~ Ahnung haben* have no idea at all; *~ Bock auf etw. haben* not fancy s.th. at all

Null¹ *f; -, -en* **1.** *Ziffer:* nought, *Am.* zero; *Telef.* O [əʊ], *Am. auch* zero; *wie viel ~en hat ...?* how many noughts *(Am.* zeros) are there in ... *(od.* has ... got)?; **2.** *umg. pej. (Versager)* dead loss, complete washout

Null² *m, n; -(s), -s beim Skat:* null; *~ Hand* null from hand

nullachtfünfzehn *umg. pej.* **I.** *indekl. Adj.; nur präd.* nothing to write home about; **II.** *Adv.: im Laden wird man nur ~ bedient* the service in the shop is nothing to write home about; **Nullachtfünfzehn...** *im Subst.* run-of-the-mill..., nondescript...

Null-Bock|-Generation *f; nur Sg.* drop-out generation; **~-Haltung** *f; nur Sg.* couldn't-care-less attitude

Null|defizit *n* zero deficit, balanced budget; **~diät** *f* no-calorie *(od.* starvation) diet

nullen I. *v/i. umg. hum.* start one's second *etc.* decade; **II.** *v/t. Etech.* earth, *Am.* ground

Null|leiter *m Etech.* earth (wire), *Am.* ground (wire); **~linie** *f* zero; **~lösung** *f bes. Pol.* zero option; **~menge** *f Math.* null set; **~meridian** *m; nur Sg.* *Geog.* prime *(od.* zero) meridian; **~nummer** *f* **1.** *e-r Zeitung etc.:* pilot issue; **2.** *Sport Sl.* nil-nil draw

Null|punkt *m* zero; *(Gefrierpunkt) auch* freezing point; *fig.* rock bottom; *den ~ erreichen* drop to zero *(od.* freezing point), *fig. (auch auf dem ~ ankommen)* reach rock bottom; **~serie** *f Tech., Wirts.* pilot lot; **~stelle** *f Math.* zero; **~stellung** *f* zero setting; **~summenspiel** *n* zero-sum game *(auch fig.)*

nullt... *Zahlw.; Math.* zero

Null|tarif *m Eintritt:* free admission; *Beförderung:* free fares; *zum ~* free; **~wachstum** *n* zero growth

Numerale *n; -s, Numeralien und Numeralia; Ling.* numeral

Numeri *Pl. bibl.* Numbers

numerieren, Numerierung → **nummerieren, Nummerierung**

Numerik *f; -, kein Pl.; Tech.* numerical control

numerisch I. *Adj.* numerical; **II.** *Adv.: ~ gegliedert* divided up numerically

Numero *ohne Art. altm.: ~ drei* number three

Numerus *m; -, Numeri* **1.** *Ling.* number; **2.** *Math.* antilogarithm; **Numerus clausus** *m; -, kein Pl.; (abgek.* **NC**) *Univ.* limited *(od.* restricted) admission

Numismatik *f; -, kein Pl.* numismatics *Pl. (V. im Sg.*); **Numismatiker** *m; -s, -,* **Numismatikerin** *f; -, -nen* numismatist; **numismatisch** *Adj.* numismatic

Nummer *f; -, -n* **1.** *(Zahl)* number *(Abk.* No., *Am. auch* #, *Pl.* Nos.); *sie erreichen ihn unter der ~ ...* you can ring *(od.* call) him on ...; *laufende ~* serial number; *sie ist die ~ eins umg.* she's number one; *auf ~ Sicher gehen umg.* play it safe; *auf ~ Sicher sein* be doing time, be in the nick *(Am.* poky); → *Thema* 1; **2.** *e-r Zeitung etc.:* number, issue; **3.** *Wirts. (Größe)* size; *eine ~ od. ein paar ~n zu groß für j-n sein umg.* fig. be well out of s.o.'s league; **4.** *(Programm-, Zirkusnummer etc.)* number, routine, **5.** *umg. fig. (anonymer Mensch)* cipher; *(nur) e-e ~ sein* be (just) a number *(od.* statistic); **6.** *(Autokennzeichen)* registration, numberplate, *Am.* license plate; **7.** *umg. fig.: komische ~ Person:* funny character, *stärker:* weirdo; **8.** *vulg.* screw; *e-e ~ machen* have a screw

nummerieren *v/t.* number; **Nummerierung** *f* numbering

Nummern|konto *n* numbered (bank) account; **~scheibe** *f Telef.* dial;

~schild n Mot. number (Am. license) plate; am Haus etc.: number; **~skala** f graduated scale; **~tafel** f number; **~zeichen** n (#) number sign

nun I. Adv. 1. (jetzt) now; **von ~ an** from now on, förm. henceforth; (seitdem) from that time (onwards); **was ~?** what now (od. next)?; **was sagst du ~?** what do you say to that (then)?; **~ sag bloß …** umg. don't say …, you don't mean to say …; **~ erst sah er …** only then did he see …; 2. (also) zur Einleitung od. Fortsetzung der Rede: well; **~ denn!** aufmunternd: come on, then; **~ ja** zögernd: well(, you see); **~ gut!** all right; 3. fragend: **~?** well?; (wie geht's?) well, how are things?; **wenn er ~ …?** what if he …?; **kommst du ~ mit oder nicht?** so are you coming or not?; 4. (eben, halt): **so ist das ~** that's just the way it is; **da es ~ einmal so ist** since (od. being as) that's the way it is; **das mag ich ~ einmal nicht** I just don't like it; 5. verstärkend: **ist sie ~ verheiratet oder nicht?** so is she married or isn't she?; **das ist ~ wirklich nicht zu viel verlangt** that really isn't asking too much; **da hat man ~ ein Leben lang geschuftet** and to think that I etc. have slaved all my etc. life for that; → auch **jetzt**; II. Konj. altm.: **~ (da)** now that, since

nunmehr Adv. now; (von nun an) from now on; **es läuft ~ zwei Jahre lang** it's been going on for two years now

'nunter Adv. südd. → **hinunter**

Nuntiatur f; -, -en; kath. Amt, Amtssitz: nunciature; **Nuntius** m; -, Nuntien nuncio

nur I. Adv. 1. only; (nichts als) nothing but; (bloß) just; (einfach) simply; **wir waren ~ mehr fünf** Dial. there were only five of us left; **~ einmal** just once; **~ sie wusste es** etc. only she (od. she alone) knew etc., she was the only one to know etc.; **~ weil** just because; **nicht ~, sondern auch** not only, but also; **es ist ~, dass …** it's just that …; **~ gut, dass** it's a good thing that; **in ~ zwei Jahren** in just two (short) years, within two (short) years; **~ aus Bosheit** etc. out of sheer spite etc.; **warum fragst du? - ~ so** umg. I was just wondering; 2. (ausgenommen) except; **~, dass** except (that), apart from the fact that; 3. (irgend): **so viel ich ~ kann** as much as I possibly can; **es muss so schnell wie ~ möglich fertig werden** it's got to be finished in the quickest possible time; 4. auffordernd: **~ zu!** go on!, umg. what are you waiting for?; **~ nicht so schüchtern!** go on, don't be shy!; **~ keine Umstände!** please don't go to any trouble!; **verkaufe es ~ ja nicht** don't sell it whatever you do, just don't sell it; 5. dringender Wunsch: **wenn er ~ käme** if only he would come; **wäre ich ~ zu Hause geblieben!** if only I'd stayed at home; 6. nachdrücklich od. verwundert fragend: **wie kam er ~ hierher?** how on earth did he get here?; **was will er damit ~ sagen?** I wonder what he means (od. is driving at)?; **was habe ich ~ getan?** what (on earth) have I done?; **wie hat er es ~ geschafft?** how (on earth) did he manage that?; **was hat sie ~?** I wonder what's up (od. wrong) with her; 7. Steigerung ausdrückend: **das weißt du ~ zu gut** you know very (od. perfectly) well; **das ist ~ zu wahr** that's only too true; **das macht alles ~ noch schlimmer** that just makes it all

the worse; 8. umg.: **~ so** verstärkend: mst like mad; **der Wind hat ~ so gepfiffen** the wind was howling like mad; **es hat ~ so gescheppert** there was an almighty crash; II. Konj.: **~ habe ich vergessen …** only I forgot …; **ich komme gerne, ~ weiß ich nicht wann** I'd like to come but I just don't know when I can make it

Nurhausfrau f full-time housewife (Am. auch homemaker)

Nürnberg (n); -s; Geog. Nuremberg

Nürnberger[1] indekl. Adj. attr. Nuremberg

Nürnberger[2] m; -s, -, **~in** f; -, -nen inhabitant of Nuremberg; **ich bin Nürnberger** I'm (od. I come) from Nuremberg

nuscheln vt/i. umg. mumble; (etw.) **in den Bart ~** mumble od. mutter (s.th.) into one's beard

Nuss f; -, Nüsse 1. nut; **e-e harte ~** umg. fig. a hard nut to crack, a tough one; **du dumme ~!** umg. you twit!; **taube** (leere Nuss) hollow nut; umg. pej. (wertlose Sache) dead (Am. total) loss; Person: clod, numbskull; **j-m e-e auf die ~ geben** umg. bop s.o. on the head, auch etwa give s.o. a biff on the nose; 2. Gastr. eye (of) round; 3. Tech. socket; **~baum** m Bot. 1. walnut (tree); 2. Holz: walnut

nussbraun Adj. hazel(-colo[u]red)

nussig Adj. nutty

Nuss|knacker m nutcracker; umg. pej. (Mann) miserable sod (Am. wretch); **~kuchen** m nut cake; **~schale** f nutshell; fig. (kleines Boot) cockleshell; **~schokolade** f chocolate with nuts, nut chocolate; **~torte** f nut gateau (Am. torte)

Nüster f; -, -n; mst Pl. nostril

Nut f; -, -en; Tech. groove; **~ und Feder** Holz: tongue and groove, Metall. slot and key

Nute f; -, -n → **Nut**; **nuten** v/t. Tech. groove, channel; **Nuthobel** m Tech. grooving plane, plough

Nutria[1] f; -, -s; Zool. nutria, coypu

Nutria[2] m; -, -s Pelz: nutria, coypu

Nutsche f; -, -n; fachspr. (Filter) vacuum filter

Nutte f; -, -n; Sl. tart, Am. hooker; **nuttenhaft, nuttig** Adj. Sl. tarty

nutz Adj. südd., österr. → **nütze**

Nutzanwendung f practical use (od. benefit)

nutzbar Adj. usable; (nützlich) useful; (Gewinn bringend) productive; **~ machen** utilize; Wirts. auch exploit; (Naturkräfte etc.) harness; (ausnützen) take advantage of; **den Boden ~ machen** cultivate the land; **Nutzbarkeit** f usability; usefulness; **Nutzbarmachung** f utilization; Wirts. auch exploitation

nutzbringend I. Adj. profitable; II. Adv.: **~ anwenden** od. **verwenden** turn to good account, Am. make good on

nütze Adj.: **zu nichts ~ sein** be (completely) useless, umg. be a dead loss; **es war wenigstens zu etwas ~** at least it served some purpose; **wozu soll das ~ sein?** what's that supposed to achieve?

Nutzeffekt m Wirts. etc. efficiency; weitS. (Nutzen) (practical) use (od. value)

nutzen, nützen I. v/i. be of use, be useful (zu etw. for s.th.; j-m to s.o.); (vorteilhaft sein) be of advantage to, benefit (j-m to s.o.); **j-m ~ auch** bene-

fit s.o.; **das nützt (mir) nichts** that's no use (od. good) (to me); **das nützt wenig** that doesn't help much, that's not much help; **es nützt alles nichts, wir müssen gehen** we've got to go whether we like or not; **was nützt es, dass man spart?** what's the use (od. good) of saving?; **es nützt nichts zu heulen** it's no use crying; II. v/t. use, make use of; (Naturkräfte etc.) harness; (nutzbringend anwenden) put to good use; (ausnützen) take advantage of; **die Gelegenheit ~** take advantage of (od. seize) the opportunity; **du hast d-e Chance nicht genützt** you didn't take your chance

Nutzen m; -s, kein Pl. use; (Gewinn) profit, gain; (Vorteil) advantage; auch Jur. benefit; **praktischer ~** practical use (od. value); **von ~** useful, helpful; **zum ~ von** for the benefit of; **~ bringen** yield a profit; **~ ziehen aus** profit (od. benefit) from, capitalize on

Nutzen-Kosten-Analyse f Wirts. cost-benefit analysis

Nutzer m; -s, -, **~in** f; -, -nen 1. EDV user; 2. Amtsspr. user

Nutz|fahrzeug n utility (od. commercial) vehicle; **~fläche** f usable area (Wirts. floor space); Agr. agricultural acreage; **~garten** m kitchen garden; **~holz** n timber, Am. lumber; **~last** f bes. Mot. payload; **~leistung** f Tech. effective output (od. power)

nützlich Adj. useful; Rat, Person etc.: helpful; (dienlich) auch handy; **sich ~ machen** make o.s. useful; **es könnte dir ~ sein** it might be of some use to you; **sich als ~ erweisen** prove (to be) very useful; → **angenehm** I; **Nützlichkeit** f usefulness

Nützlichkeits|… im Subst. mst utilitarian; **~denken** n utilitarianism, utilitarian thinking; **~prinzip** n utility principle

Nützling m; -s, -e; Zool. beneficial animal

nutzlos Adj. useless; (vergeblich) auch futile; präd. auch no use; **alles Bitten war ~** all our etc. pleading was in vain; **Nutzlosigkeit** f uselessness; (Vergeblichkeit) futility

nutznießen v/i. (nutznießt, nutznießte, hat genutznießt); geh. benefit; **Nutznießer** m; -s, -, **Nutznießerin** f; -, -nen beneficiary; **die Nutznießer des neuen Gesetzes** those who (will) reap the benefits of the new law; **Nutznießung** f Jur. usufruct

Nutz|pflanze f useful plant; **~tier** n domestic animal; (Arbeitstier) working animal

Nutzung f use; utilization; des Bodens etc.: exploitation; (Anwendung) use, application

Nutzungs|dauer f Wirts. useful life; **~gebühr** f user fee; **~grad** m level of utilization; **~recht** n Jur. right of use

NVA f; -, kein Pl.; Abk. (**Nationale Volksarmee**) hist. National People's Army

NW Abk. (**Nordwest[en]**) NW

Nylon® n; -s, kein Pl. nylon; **~strümpfe** Pl. nylon stockings, nylons

Nymphchen n umg. (Kindfrau) nymphet; **Nymphe** f; -, -n; Myth. nymph; **nymphenhaft** Adj. nymphlike

nymphoman Adj. nymphomaniac, umg. nympho; **Nymphomanie** f; -, kein Pl. nymphomania; **Nymphomanin** f; -, -nen nymphomaniac, umg. nympho

O¹, o *n*; -, - *und umg.* -s O, o; *O wie Otto Buchstabieren:* "o" for (*od.* as in) "Oscar" (*Am. auch* "ocean")

O² *Abk.* (*Ost[en]*) E

o *Interj.* oh!; ~ *nein!* oh no!; (*aber nein*) *auch* goodness, no!

Ö, ö *n*; -, - *und umg.* -s o umlaut

Oase *f*; -, n oasis (*Pl.* oases); *fig. auch* haven

ob¹ *Konj.* **1.** *fragend od. zweifelnd:* whether, if; ~ *das gut geht?* will it be OK?; **2.** ~ ... (*oder nicht*) whether ... (or not); ~ *Frau,* ~ *Mann* it makes no difference whether it's a man or a woman; **3.** *als* ~ as if, as though; *so tun, als* ~ ... pretend that ...; *sie hat nur so getan, als* ~ *umg.* she was just pretending (*od.* putting it on); **4.** (*na*) *und* ~*!* *umg.* you bet!

ob² *Präp.* **1.** (+ *Gen.*) *altm.* (*wegen*) on account of; **2.** (+ *Dat.*) *altm., schw.* (*über*) above, over

OB¹ *m*; -(s), -s; *Abk.* (*Oberbürgermeister*) mayor

OB² *f*; -, -s; *Abk.* (*Oberbürgermeisterin*) mayor(ess)

o. B. *Abk.* (*ohne Befund*) negative

Obacht *f*; -, *kein Pl.*; *südd.* attention; ~*!* look (*od.* watch) out!, careful!; ~ *geben aufmerksam:* pay attention (*auf* + *Akk.* to), *vorsichtig:* be careful (with); *achtsam:* look (*od.* watch) out (for)

Obadja (*m*); -s, *mit Art.* -; *bibl.* Obadiah

Obdach *n*; -(e)s; *geh.* shelter

obdachlos *Adj.* homeless; *Tausende wurden* ~ thousands were left homeless; **Obdachlose** *m, f*; -n, -n homeless person; *die* ~*n* the homeless *Pl.*; *Asyl für* ~ shelter for the homeless

Obdachlosen|asyl *n* shelter for the homeless; ~*fürsorge* *f* care for the homeless; ~*heim* *n* shelter for the homeless

Obdachlosigkeit *f* homelessness

Obduktion *f*; -, -en; *Med., Jur.* postmortem, autopsy

Obduktions|befund *m* *Med.* postmortem findings *Pl.*, autopsy result; ~*bericht* *m* postmortem (*od.* autopsy) report; **Obduzent** *m*; -en, -en, **Obduzentin** *f*; -, -nen pathologist (*Am.* medical examiner) (*carrying out a postmortem*); **obduzieren** *v/t.* carry out a postmortem (*od.* an autopsy) on

O-Beine *Pl. umg.* bandy (*od.* bow) legs; **o-beinig, O-beinig** *Adj. umg.* bandy-legged, bow-legged

Obelisk *m*; -en, -en obelisk

oben *Adv.* **1.** at the top; (*obenauf*) on (the) top; ~*!* *als Aufschrift:* this side up!; ~ *links* at the top left; *im Bild:* in the top left-hand corner; ~ *am Tisch* at the head of the table; *da* ~ up there; *nach* ~ up(wards); *von* ~ from above; (*mit dem*) *Gesicht etc. nach* ~ face *etc.* up; *von* ~ *bis unten* from top to bottom; *Person:* from top to toe, from head to foot; ~ *ohne umg.* top-

less; *von* ~ *herab fig.* condescendingly; **2.** *im Text: siehe* ~ see above; ~ *erwähnt od. genannt* above(-mentioned); *nachgestellt:* mentioned above; ~ *stehend* above(-mentioned); *nachgestellt:* above; ~ *zitiert* quoted above; **3.** *im Haus:* upstairs; *nach* ~ upstairs; *von* ~ from upstairs; *der Lift fährt nach* ~ the lift (*Am.* elevator) is going up; *mit dem Lift nach* ~ *fahren* go up in the lift (*Am.* elevator); **4.** *umg.* (*im Norden*) up north; ~ *in den Highlands* up in the Highlands; **5.** *umg., in e-r Hierarchie od. Rangordnung:* at the top; *jetzt ist er ganz* ~ he's made it to the top now; *die da* ~ the top people, the powers that be; *das ist ein Befehl von ganz* ~ the order came from the very top; *ganz* ~ *stehen in e-r Tabelle etc.:* be in top spot; *in der Hitliste:* be at number one

oben|an *Adv.* at the top; ~ *stehen* be at the top; *in Rangordnung:* be in first place; *Frage:* have top priority; ~*auf* *Adv.* on (the) top; (*ganz*) ~ *sein umg. fig. wirtschaftlich etc.:* be on top; *stimmungsmäßig:* be on top of the world; *gesundheitlich:* be on (*Am.* in) top form; ~*drauf* *Adv.* on top; ~*drein* *Adv.* on top of everything, to top it all

oben| erwähnt, ~ **genannt** → *oben* 2

Obengenannte *n*; -n, *kein Pl.* above-mentioned matter

oben|herum *Adv.* around the top (*am Körper:* chest); ~*hin* *Adv.* superficially, perfunctorily

Oben-ohne|-Badeanzug *m* topless swimsuit; ~*-Bedienung* *f* topless waitress; ~*-Lokal* *n* topless bar

oben stehend → *oben* 2

Obenstehende *n*; -n, *kein Pl.*: *das* ~ the above

ober *Präp. österr.* above, over

Ober *m*; -s, -, **1.** waiter; (*Herr*) ~*!* waiter; **2.** *Spielkarte:* queen

ober...¹ *Adj.* upper; *in Rangfolge:* higher; *ganz oben:* top; *am* ~*en Ende* at the upper end; *am* ~*en Avon* on the upper (reaches of the) Avon; *der Obere See* Lake Superior; → *Obere, oberst...,* **zehntausend**

ober...² *im Adj. umg. Verstärkung ausdrückend:* mega, extra

Ober... *im Subst. umg. Verstärkung ausdrückend:* mega, top

Oberarm *m Anat.* upper arm; ~**knochen** *m* humerus (*Pl.* humeri)

Ober|arzt *m,* ~**ärztin** *f* consultant, *Am.* specialist; (*Vertreter[in] das Chefarztes*) assistant medical director; ~**aufsicht** *f*: *die* ~ *haben od. führen* have overall control (*über* + *Akk.* over), be in charge (of); ~**bau** *m* superstructure; ~**bauch** *m Anat.* upper abdomen

Oberbefehl *m*; *nur Sg.* supreme command (*über* + *Akk.* of); *den* ~ *haben* be commander-in-chief (*über* + *Akk.* of); **Oberbefehlshaber** *m,* **Oberbefehlshaberin** *f* supreme commander,

commander-in-chief, *umg.* supremo

Ober|begriff *m* **1.** generic term; **2.** (*Überschrift*) heading; ~**bekleidung** *f* outer garments *Pl.*; ~**bett** *n* quilt, *Brit. auch* duvet; ~**bewusstsein** *n Psych.* consciousness, conscious self; ~**bonze** *m umg.* big white chief, big shot; ~**bundesanwalt** *m,* ~**bundesanwältin** *f* chief public prosecutor; ~**bürgermeister** *m,* ~**bürgermeisterin** *f* (*abgek.* **OB**) mayor; ~**deck** *n Naut.,* e-s Busses upper deck

oberdeutsch *Adj. Ling.* Upper (*od.* Southern) German; **Oberdeutsch** *n Ling.* Upper (*od.* Southern) German; *das* ~**e** Upper (*od.* Southern) German

Obere *m*; -n, -n **1.** (high) authority; *die* ~*n* those in high places; **2.** e-s Klosters *etc.*: superior

oberfaul *Adj. umg.* very strange (indeed); (*anrüchig*) extremely fishy

Oberfeldwebel *m Mil.* staff sergeant; *Flug.* flight (*Am.* master) sergeant

Oberfläche *f* surface; *an der* ~ *auch fig.* on the surface; (*wieder*) *an die* ~ *steigen* (re)surface

Oberflächen|behandlung *f* surface treatment; ~**spannung** *f Phys.* surface tension; ~**struktur** *f auch Ling.* surface structure; ~**wasser** *n*; *nur Sg.* surface water

oberflächlich **I.** *Adj.* superficial; *Mensch: auch* shallow; (*flüchtig*) perfunctory, cursory; ~*e Bekanntschaft* casual (*od.* nodding) acquaintance; **II.** *Adv.* superficially; (*flüchtig*) perfunctorily, cursorily; ~ *betrachtet* on the surface; *ich kenne sie nur* ~ she's only a casual acquaintance, I don't know her very well; **Oberflächlichkeit** *f* superficiality; (*Seichtheit*) *auch* shallowness

Oberförster *m altm.* head forester (*bes. Am.* forest ranger)

obergärig *Adj.* top-fermented

Ober|gauner *m umg.* supercrook; ~**gefreite** *m, f Mil.* lance corporal, *Am.* private 1st class; *Flug.* leading aircraftman (*weiblich:* aircraftwoman), *Am.* airman (*weiblich:* airwoman) 3rd class; ~**gericht** *n schw. Jur.* higher (cantonal) court; ~**geschoss,** *österr.* ~**geschoß** *n* upper floor (*od.* stor[e]y); ~**gewalt** *f*: *die* ~ (*ausüben*) (have) supreme power; ~**grenze** *f* upper limit; *Wirts., Statistik etc.: auch* ceiling

oberhalb **I.** *Präp.* above; **II.** *Adv.* above

Ober|hand *f fig.*: *die* ~ *haben* have the upper hand; *die* ~ *gewinnen* get (*od.* gain) the upper hand (*über* + *Akk.* over); ~**haupt** *n* head; ~**haus** *n Parl.* Upper House; *in GB: auch* House of Lords; *in den USA: auch* Senate; ~**haut** *f Bio., Anat.* epidermis; ~**hemd** *n* shirt; ~**herrschaft** *f*; *nur Sg.* supremacy; ~**hirte** *m geh.* spiritual leader; ~**hitze** *f* top heat; (*nur*) *mit* ~ *backen* bake in the top oven; ~**hoheit** *f*;

nur Sg. supremacy; (*Souveränität*) sovereignty

Oberin *f*; -, *-nen* **1.** *kath.* Mother Superior; **2.** → *Oberschwester*

Ober|inspektor *m*, **~inspektorin** *f* chief inspector

oberirdisch I. *Adj.* surface ..., *präd. und nachgestellt*: above ground; **~e Leitung** *Etech.* overhead line; **II.** *Adv.* above ground

Oberitalien (*n*); *Geog.* Northern Italy; **oberitalienisch** *Adj.* North Italian

Ober|kante *f* upper (*od.* top) edge; **~kellner** *m* head waiter; **~kellnerin** *f* head waitress; **~kiefer** *m Anat.* upper jaw; **~klasse** *f* **1.** *Päd.* senior class; **2.** *gesellschaftlich*: upper class(es *Pl.*); **~kommandierende** *m*, *f*; *-n, -n* → *Oberbefehlshaber*, **~kommando** *n* **1.** *nur Sg.* → *Oberbefehl*; **2.** *Führungsstab*: command headquarters *Pl.* (*auch V. im Sg.*); **~körper** *m* upper part of the body; (*Brust*) chest; **mit nacktem ~** stripped to the waist; **~land** *n*; *nur Sg.* uplands *Pl.*; **Berner ~** *Geog.* Bernese Oberland; **~landesgericht** *n* (*abgek.* OLG) *Jur.* high court and court of appeal of a Land, higher regional court, *Am. etwa* district court; **~länge** *f Druck., e-s Buchstabens*: ascender

oberlastig *Adj. Naut.* top-heavy

Ober|lauf *m Geog. e-s Flusses*: upper reaches *Pl.*; **~leder** *n* uppers *Pl.*

Oberlehrer *m*, **~in** *f* **1.** *altm.* senior primary school teacher; **2.** *umg. pej.* schoolmasterly type; *Frau*: schoolmarm type; **oberlehrerhaft** *Adj. pej.* schoolmasterly; *Frau*: schoolmarmish

Oberleitung *f* **1.** (senior) management, overall control; **2.** *Etech.* overhead cable; **Oberleitungs(omni)bus** *m* trolley bus

Ober|leutnant *m Mil.* (*Am.* first) lieutenant; *Flug.* flying officer, *Am.* first lieutenant; **~licht** *n* **1.** skylight; *über e-r Tür*: fanlight; **2.** (*Licht von oben*) light from above; *Fot.* top lighting; **~liga** *f Sport* regional league

Oberlippe *f* upper lip; **Oberlippenbart** *m* moustache

Obermaterial *n*; **~ Leder** leather uppers *Pl.*

Oberösterreich (*n*); *Geog.* Upper Austria

Ober|priester *m*, **~priesterin** *f* high priest; **~prima** *f altm. last year of Gymnasium*; *in GB: etwa* Upper Sixth (form); *in den USA: etwa* senior grade, 12th grade; **~primaner** *m*, **~primanerin** *f altm. student in the last year of Gymnasium*; *in GB: etwa* Upper Sixth former; *in den USA: etwa* senior, 12th-grader; **~rabbiner** *m* chief rabbi; **~regierungsrat** *m*, **~regierungsrätin** *f etwa* senior civil servant

Oberrhein *m Geog.*: **der ~** the Upper Rhine; **oberrheinisch** *Adj.* from *bzw.* of the Upper Rhine; **die ~e Tiefebene** the Upper Rhine Valley

Obers *n*; -, *kein Pl.*; *österr.* cream

Oberschenkel *m Anat.* thigh; **~hals** *m* head of the femur; **~knochen** *m* femur, thigh bone

Oberschicht *f der Gesellschaft*: upper class(es *Pl.*)

oberschlächtig *Adj. Tech., Wasserrad*: overshot; **oberschlau I.** *Adj. umg.* too clever by half, *Am.* way too smart; **~er Typ** clever dick, *Am.* know-it-all; **II.** *Adv. reden*: as though one knows it all

Oberschlesien (*n*); *Geog. hist.* Upper Silesia

Ober|schule *f* → *Gymnasium*; **~schüler** *m*, **~schülerin** *f* → *Gymnasiast*; **~schulrat** *m*, **~schulrätin** *f* local education officer; **~schwester** *f* senior nursing officer, *Am.* head nurse; **~seite** *f* top (*od.* upper) surface

oberseits *Adv.* on the top, on its top surface

Ober|sekunda *f altm. seventh year of Gymnasium*; *in GB: etwa* Upper Fifth (form); *in den USA: etwa* 10th grade, sophomore year; **~seminar** *n Univ.* seminar for advanced students, *auch* postgraduate seminar

Oberst *m*; *-en und -s, -e*(*n*); *Mil.* colonel

oberst... *Adj.* uppermost, topmost; *Stufe, Stockwerk etc.*: top ...; *fig. Gericht, Behörde*: highest; **~e Klasse** *Päd.* top form (*Am.* class); **~e Aufsichtsbehörde** supervisory authority; **Oberster Gerichtshof** High (*Am.* Supreme) Court; **~es Gebot sein** be the first priority

Ober|staatsanwalt *m*, **~staatsanwältin** *f etwa* senior public prosecutor; **~stabsfeldwebel** *m Mil.* warrant officer 1st class (*Abk.* WOI), *Am.* warrant officer; *Flug.* warrant officer, *Am.* chief master sergeant; **~stadtdirektor** *m*, **~stadtdirektorin** *f* chief executive (of a town council)

Ober|steiger *m Bergb.* undermanager; **~stimme** *f Mus.* treble

Oberstleutnant *m Mil.* lieutenant colonel; *Flug. Brit.* wing commander

Ober|stoff *m* outer fabric; **~stübchen** *n*: **er ist nicht ganz richtig im ~** *umg. fig.* he's got a screw loose; **~studiendirektor** *m*, **~studiendirektorin** *f* head teacher, *Am.* principal (of a *Gymnasium* or vocational school); **~studienrat** *m*, **~studienrätin** *f* senior established secondary (*Am.* high) school teacher; **~stufe** *f Päd.* upper school, senior classes *Pl.*, *Am.* senior grades; **~teil** *m, n* upper part, top (*auch Kleidungsstück*); **~tertia** *f altm. fifth year of Gymnasium*; *in GB: etwa* Upper Fourth (form); *in den USA: etwa* 8th grade; **~ton** *m Mus.* harmonic, overtone; **~verwaltungsgericht** *n* higher administrative court; **~wasser** *n Schleuse*: upper water; *Mühle*: overshot water; **~ haben** *umg. fig.* have the upper hand; (*erfolgreich sein*) be riding high; **~ bekommen** get the upper hand; **~weite** *f* bust (measurement)

Obfrau *f* → *Obmännin*

obgleich *Konj.* (al)though

Obhut *f*; *nur Sg.*; *geh.* care; (*Schutz*) protection; *Jur.* custody; **in s-e ~ nehmen** take charge of; (*j-n*) *auch* take under one's wing

obig *Adj.*; *nur attr.*; *bes. Amtsspr.* above(-mentioned); **wie im Obigen erwähnt** as mentioned above

Objekt *n*; *-(e)s, -e* **1.** object (*auch Ling., Philos.*); **2.** *Wirts.* (*Vermögensgegenstand*) property; **3.** *Fot.* subject; **4.** *österr. Amtsspr.* building

objektiv *Adj.* objective; (*unparteiisch*) *auch* impartial, dispassionate *förm.*; *Urteil etc.*: *auch* unbias(s)ed; (*tatsächlich*) actual

Objektiv *n*; *-s, -e Mikroskop*: objective; *Fot.* lens; **~deckel** *m* lens cap; **~fassung** *f* lens mount

objektivieren *v/t.* objectivize; **Objektivierung** *f* objectivization

Objektivismus *m*; *-, kein Pl.*; *Philos.* objectivism; **objektivistisch I.** *Adj.* objectivistic; **II.** *Adv.* objectivistically

Objektivität *f*; *-, kein Pl.* objectivity

Objekt|kunst *f*; *nur Sg.* object art; **~satz** *m Ling.* object clause; **~schutz** *m* protection of property; **~sprache** *f Ling.* object language; **~tisch** *m e-s Mikroskops*: (specimen) stage; **~träger** *m des Mikroskops*: (specimen) slide

Oblate[1] *f*; -, *-n* wafer

Oblate[2] *m*; *-n, -n*; *kath.* oblate

Obleute *Pl.* → *Obmann*

obliegen *v/i.* (*unreg., untr., hat obgelegen und hat / österr. ist oblegen*): **j-m ~** *geh. als Pflicht*: be incumbent on s.o.; **Obliegenheit** *f geh.* obligation, duty

obligat *Adj.* **1.** obligatory; *iro.* (*unvermeidbar*) *auch* inevitable; **2.** *Mus.* obbligato; **mit ~er Violine** with violin obbligato

Obligation *f*; -, *-en*; *Wirts.* bond, debenture (bond); **Obligationenrecht** *n*; *nur Sg.*; *schw. Jur.* law of obligations

obligatorisch *Adj.* obligatory (*auch iro.*), compulsory

Obligatorium *n*; *-s, Obligatorien*; *schw.* obligation; (*Pflichtfach*) compulsory subject

Obligo *n*; *-s, -s*; *Wirts.* liability; **ohne ~** without recourse

Oblongtablette *f Pharm.* oblong tablet

Obmann *m*; *-(e)s, -männer od. -leute* **1.** (*Vorsitzender*) chairman, chair(person); **2.** (*Vertrauensmann*) representative; (*Sprecher*) spokesman, spokesperson; **Obmännin** *f*; -, *-nen* **1.** (*Vorsitzende*) chairwoman, chair(person); **2.** (*Vertrauensperson*) representative; (*Sprecherin*) spokeswoman, spokesperson

Oboe *f*; -, *-n*; *Mus.* oboe; **Oboist** *m*; *-en, -en*, **Oboistin** *f*; -, *-nen* oboist, oboe-player

Obolus *m*; -, *- und -se*: **s-n ~ entrichten** make one's little contribution, pay one's mite *altm.*

Obrigkeit *f*: **die ~** the authorities *Pl.*; *iro.* the powers *Pl.* that be; (*Regierung*) the government; **die weltliche und kirchliche ~** the temporal and spiritual authorities

Obrigkeits|denken *n* blind faith in (the infallibility of) authority; **obrigkeitsgläubig** *Adj.*: **~ sein** believe in the infallibility of authority

Obrigkeitsstaat *m* authoritarian state; **obrigkeitsstaatlich** *Adj.* ... of the authoritarian state

Obrist *m*; *-en, -en*; *Mil. altm.* colonel; **Obristenregime** *n pej.* military junta; **das ~** *hist.* the Colonels' regime

obschon *Konj. geh.* (al)though

Observanz *f*; -, *-en* **1.** *kath.* (*Befolgung*) observance; **2.** (*Ausrichtung*) leanings *Pl.*; (*Form, Prägung*) kind, type

Observation *f*; -, *-en polizeilich*: surveillance; *wissenschaftlich*: observation

Observatorium *n*; *-s, Observatorien*; *Astron.* observatory

observieren *v/t.* (*heimlich beobachten*) keep under surveillance; *wissenschaftlich*: observe; (*Patienten*) keep under observation

Obsession *f*; -, *-en*; *Psych.* obsession; **obsessiv** *Adj. Psych.* obsessive

Obsidian *m*; *-s, -e*; *Min.* obsidian

obsiegen *v/i.* (*untr., hat obsiegt und selten obgesiegt*); *geh. altm.* be victorious

obskur *Adj.* **1.** (*unklar, weithin unbekannt*) obscure; **2.** (*zweifelhaft*) dubious

Obskurantismus *m*; -, *kein Pl.* obscurantism

Obskurität f; -, kein Pl. **1.** obscurity; **2.** (Zweifelhaftigkeit) dubiousness, dubious nature (+ Gen. of)

obsolet Adj. obsolete

Obsorge f; nur Sg.; österr. Amtsspr. care (+ Gen. for)

Obst n; -(e)s, kein Pl. fruit; **~anbau** m; nur Sg., **~bau** m; nur Sg. fruit-growing

obstbaulich I. Adj.; nur attr. ... concerning fruit-growing; Nutzung: for fruit-growing; **II.** Adv. nutzen: for fruit-growing

Obst|baum m fruit tree; **~blüte** f Zeit: fruit blossom time; **~branntwein** m fruit brandy; **~ernte** f Vorgang: fruit harvest; Ergebnis: auch fruit crop; Zeit: fruit harvest(ing season); **~essig** m fruit vinegar

Obstetrik f; -, kein Pl.; Med. obstetrics Pl. (V. im Sg.)

Obst|garten m orchard; **~geist** m fachspr. fruit schnapps; **~händler** m, **~händlerin** f fruiterer, fruit seller

obstinat Adj. obstinate

Obstipation f; -, -en; Med. constipation

Obstkuchen m fruit flan (Am. pie)

Obstler m; -s, -; Dial. **1.** fruit schnapps; **2.** altm. → Obsthändler

Obst|messer n fruit knife; **~plantage** f fruit farm; mit Obstbäumen: fruit plantation, orchard

obstreich Adj. rich in fruit; Jahr: with a good fruit harvest

obstruieren v/t. bes. Parl. obstruct

Obstruktion f; -, -en; bes. Parl. obstruction; **~ betreiben** use obstructive tactics; mit Dauerreden: filibuster; **Obstruktionspolitik** f obstructionist policy; mit Dauerreden: filibustering; **obstruktiv** Adj. obstructive

Obst|saft m fruit juice; **~salat** m fruit salad; **~schale** f fruit bowl; **~sorte** f (kind of) fruit; **~tag** m fruit-only day; **~torte** f fruit flan (Am. pie); **~wasser** n fachspr. fruit schnapps; **~wein** m fruit wine

obszön Adj. obscene; umg. fig. Preise etc.: monstrous; **Obszönität** f; -, -en auch konkret: obscenity

Obus m; -ses, -se trolley bus

obwalten v/i. (untr., hat obgewaltet und obwaltet); geh. altm. prevail

obwohl Konj. (al)though

obzwar Konj. geh. (al)though

och Interj. umg. oh (dear)!

Ochlokratie f; -, -n ochlocracy, mob rule

Ochs m; -en, -en; südd., österr., schw., **Ochse** m; -n, -n **1.** ox (Pl. oxen); junger: bullock; **dastehen wie der ~ vorm Berg** od. **Scheunentor** umg. be at a complete loss (as to what to do); **den Ochsen hinter den Pflug spannen** fig. put the cart before the horse; **2.** umg. fig. (Idiot) oaf, ass

ochsen umg. **I.** v/i. cram, Brit. auch swot; **II.** v/t. bone up on, Brit. auch swot (od. mug) up on

Ochsen|auge n **1.** Archit. (Fenster) bull's-eye (window); **2.** Bot. ox-eye (daisy); **3.** Dial. Gastr. fried egg; **~brust** f Gastr. brisket of beef; **~fleisch** n beef; **~frosch** m Zool. bullfrog; **~gespann** n **1.** team of oxen; **2.** (Wagen) bullock cart; **~karren** m bullock cart; **~schlepp** m; -(e)s, -e; österr. Gastr. oxtail

Ochsenschwanz m oxtail; **~suppe** f Gastr. oxtail soup

Ochsen|tour f umg. hum. **1.** (Arbeit) hard slog; **2.** (mühsamer Aufstieg) slow (uphill) grind; fig. slow, hard road to the top; **~zunge** f Gastr. ox

tongue

Ochserei f; -, -en; umg. **1.** nur Sg. (constant) cramming (Brit. auch swotting); **2.** (Dummheit) stupid thing (to do)

Öchsle n; -s, -, **~grad** m degree Öchsle

Ocker m, n; -s, kein Pl. och|re (Am. -er); **ockerfarben**, **ockergelb** Adj. (yellow) och|re (Am. -er)

öd Adj. → öde

Ode f; -, -n; Lit. ode (**an** + Akk. to)

öde Adj. **1.** (verlassen, einsam) deserted, desolate; (unfruchtbar) barren; **2.** fig. (fade, eintönig) dull, tedious; (freudlos) bleak, dreary; **Öde** f; -, -n **1.** desolate area; unfruchtbar: barren waste; **2.** fig. dreariness; (Langeweile) tedium

Odem m; -s, kein Pl.; poet. breath

Ödem n; -s, -e; Med. (o)edema; **ödematös** Adj. (o)edematous

oder Konj. **1.** or; **~** (aber) otherwise, (or) else; drohend: or else!; **~** auch or rather; **~** so or something like that, or something along those lines; nach Zahlen: or so; **es kostet zehn Euro ~ so** auch it costs something in the region of (od. somewhere around) ten euros; **ich komme um 8 Uhr ~ so** I'll come (a)round about eight; → **entweder**, **2.** nachgestellt; fragend: **du bleibst doch, ~?** you 'are staying, aren't you?; **das liest sich gut, ~?** it's a good read, isn't it?

Odermennig m; -(e)s, -e; Bot. agrimony

Ödheit f **1.** desertedness, desolation; (Unfruchtbarkeit) barrenness; **2.** fig. (Eintönigkeit) dullness, tediousness; (Freudlosigkeit) dreariness

ödipal Adj. Psych. oedipal; **Ödipuskomplex** m; nur Sg.; Psych. Oedipus complex

Odium n; -s, kein Pl. odium

Ödland n; nur Sg.; Agr. wasteland

Odontologie f; -, kein Pl.; Med. odontology

Odyssee f; -, -n **1.** nur Sg.; (von Homer) **die ~** the Odyssey; **2.** fig. odyssey

Oeuvre ['ø:vrə] n; -, -s works Pl., oeuvre; **das beethovensche ~** Beethoven's works (od. oeuvre)

Öfchen n; -s, - small stove; elektrisches: small heater; zum Backen: small oven

Ofen m; -s, Öfen **1.** stove; elektrischer: heater; (Backofen) oven; zum Brennen, Rösten: kiln; (Hochofen) furnace; **hinterm ~ hocken** umg. fig. be a stay-at-home (Am. a home-body); **jetzt ist der ~ aus!** umg. that's it, that's the end, it's all over (for us etc.); → **Hund** 8; **2.** Dial. (Herd) cooker; **3.** heißer ~ Mot. Sl. (Motorrad) ton-up (Am. mean) machine; (schnelles Auto) muscle machine; **~bank** f bench by the stove

ofen|fertig Adj. Gastr. oven-ready; **~frisch** Adj. oven-fresh, hot from the oven

Ofen|heizung f stove heating, heating by means of stoves; **~kachel** f ceramic stove tile; **~klappe** f damper; Tür: stove door; **~lack** m stoving paint; **~loch** n firing (od. stoking) hole; Tür: stove door; **~platte** f hot plate; **~rohr** n stovepipe; **~röhre** f oven; **~schirm** m fire screen; **~setzer** m, **~setzerin** f stove fitter; **~trocknung** f Tech. etc. kiln-drying; **~tür** f stove door; des Backofens: oven door

off Adv. TV etc. out of vision (Abk. OOV), off(-screen); **Off** n; -, kein Pl.; **im ~** → **off**; **aus dem ~ sprechen** etc.

speak etc. off-screen (od. off-camera)

offen I. Adj. **1.** open; **~es Hemd** open-necked shirt; **bei ~em Fenster** with the window open; **mit ~em Mund dastehen** stand open-mouthed (od. gaping); **2.** (lose) Zucker etc.: loose; **~er Wein** wine by the glass; in e-r Karaffe: carafe wine; vom Fass: wine on tap; → **einrennen**, **Feuer** 1, **Licht** 1; **3.** Haare: loose; **mit ~en Haaren** with one's hair (hanging) loose; **4.** Arbeitsstelle: vacant; **~e Stellen** vacancies; **5.** (frei, unbehindert etc.): **~es Gelände** (wide) open country; **auf ~er See** on the open sea; **auf ~er Straße** in the middle of the street; **auf ~er Strecke** on the open road; Eisenb. between stations; **6.** (offenherzig, aufrichtig) open, sincere; (ehrlich) frank, candid; **~er Blick** open (od. honest) face; **ich will ganz ~ mit dir sein** I'll be quite frank with you; **7.** (aufgeschlossen) open(-minded); **~ für** (empfänglich) open to, receptive to; **8.** (deutlich erkennbar, nicht geheim) open; **~er Hass** undisguised hatred; **~e Kampfansage** open declaration of war; **~e Abstimmung** open vote; **~e Anspielung** broad allusion (auf + Akk. to); **~er Brief** open letter; **ein ~es Geheimnis** an open secret; **9.** (noch nicht bezahlt) unpaid; **dieser Posten ist noch ~** this item has still not been paid for; **10.** (noch nicht entschieden): **~e Fragen** open (od. unsettled) questions; **es ist noch alles ~** nothing has been decided yet, it's all up in the air still; **11.** Ling. open; **eine ~e Silbe** an open syllable; **II.** Adv. **1.** openly; **Wein ~ ausschenken** serve wine on tap; **2. sie trägt ihre Haare ~** she has her hair loose; **3.** (offenherzig, aufrichtig) openly, sincerely; (ohne Umschweife) frankly; **ich sage ~, was ich denke** I just say what I think; (j-m) **~ s-e Meinung sagen** speak one's mind (quite openly) (to s.o.), be perfectly open (od. frank) (with s.o.); **~ zur Schau stellen** display openly, make no secret of; **~ zugeben** auch admit (quite) frankly; **~ gestanden** to be frank, quite frankly; **~ auf der Hand liegen** be perfectly obvious; **4.** Ling.: **e-n Vokal / das o ~ aussprechen** pronounce a vowel in the open position / the o as an open vowel; **5.** mit Verben: **~ bleiben** stay open; Frage etc.: remain (od. be left) open (od. unsettled); **~ halten** (Tür etc.) hold open; (Geschäft etc., auch Augen) keep open; fig. (Termin, Auftrag etc.) keep open; (Ausweg, auch Entscheidung etc.) leave open; (Möglichkeit) leave (od. keep) open, reserve; **~ lassen** auch fig. leave open; **~ legen** fig. disclose; **~ liegen** zur Einsicht: be available for public scrutiny; **~ stehen** be (Tür: auch stand) open; Rechnung: be unpaid (od. outstanding), remain unsettled; **j-m ~ stehen** fig. be open to s.o.; **es steht ihm offen zu** (+ Inf.) he's free to (+ Inf.); **~ stehend** Tür etc.: open; Rechnung: outstanding, unsettled; **mit ~ stehendem Mund** open-mouthed

offenbar I. Adj. obvious, evident; (klar) clear, apparent (j-m to s.o.); Lüge, Absicht: obvious, blatant; **II.** Adv. (offensichtlich) obviously; (anscheinend) evidently, it seems ..., it would seem ...

offenbaren (offenbart, offenbarte, hat offenbart, altm. geoffenbart) **I.** v/t. (Geheimnis etc.) reveal, disclose; (zeigen) show (alle: + Dat. to); **II.** v/refl.

reveal o.s. (*als etw.* to be s.th.); *sich j-m ~* open one's heart to s.o.; **Offenbarung** *f* **1.** revelation; **2.** *nur Sg.*; *bibl.*: *die ~* (*des Johannes*) the Revelation of St (*od.* St.) John, the Book of Revelations; **Offenbarungseid** *m Jur.* oath of manifestation (*od.* disclosure); *den ~ leisten* swear an oath of manifestation (*od.* disclosure); *fig. Regierung etc.*: (come clean and) admit complete failure

offen| bleiben, ~ halten → **offen** II 5

Offenheit *f* openness, frankness; (*Ehrlichkeit*) sincerity

offenherzig *Adj.* **1.** open, frank, candid; (*aufrichtig*) sincere; **2.** *umg. fig. Kleid*: low-cut, ... with a plunging neckline; **Offenherzigkeit** *f* openness, frankness; (*Ehrlichkeit*) sincerity

offenkundig *Adj.* obvious, evident; (*deutlich*) clear, manifest *förm.*; *Lüge*: obvious, blatant; *~ werden* become apparent

offen lassen → **offen** II 5

offen legen → **offen** II 5; **Offenlegung** *f* disclosure

offen liegen → **offen** II 5

offensichtlich I. *Adj.* obvious; (*sichtbar*) visible; (*klar*) clear, plain; **II.** *Adv.* obviously; **Offensichtlichkeit** *f* obviousness

offensiv *Adj.* **1.** offensive; *Sport* attacking; **2.** *Wirts.* aggressive; **Offensive** *f*; *-, -n* offensive; *bes. Sport* attack, *Am.* 'offense; *fig.* (*Aktion*) campaign, *stärker*: war; *in die ~ gehen* go on the offensive (*od.* attack), launch an attack

Offensiv|krieg *m* offensive war(fare); *~spiel* *n Sport* attacking (*Am. mst* offensive) play (*konkret*: game); *~spieler* *m*, *~spielerin* *f* attacking player; *~stellung* *f* offensive position; *~taktik* *f* offensive tactics; *~waffe* *f* offensive weapon

offen stehen → **offen** II 5

öffentlich I. *Adj.* **1.** *allg.* public; *in ~er Sitzung* in open session; *es war ihr erster ~er Auftritt* it was her first public appearance; *das ~e Wohl* the public good; *die ~e Meinung* public opinion; *~es Recht* public law; *Missstände etc. ~ machen* bring abuses etc. to the public's attention; *~e Versteigerung* sale by public auction; *~e Toilette* public toilet (*Am.* rest room); *der Vortrag ist ~* the lecture is open to the public; → *Ärgernis, Interesse, Leben 6, Ordnung 2*; **2.** (*kommunal*) local authority ...; (*staatlich*) state ...; *~e Anleihen* government securities; *~e Schulen* state schools, *Am.* public schools; *~e Versorgungsbetriebe* public utilities; *~er Dienst* public sector; (*Beamtentum*) civil service; *ein Angestellter des ~en Dienstes* a public-sector employee; (*Beamte*) a civil servant; *die ~e Hand* the (state) authorities; *von der ~en Hand finanziert* state-funded, paid for out of public funds; *Müllbeseitigung ist e-e ~e Aufgabe* waste disposal is the responsibility of the local authority (*od.* is a public service); **II.** *Adv.* publicly, in public; *Jur.* in open session; *~ abstimmen* have an open vote; *~ bekannt machen* make public, announce publicly; *etw. ~ erklären* state s.th. in public; *Missstände ~ anprangern* launch a public attack on abuses

Öffentlichkeit *f* **1.** (*Bevölkerung*) public; *die breite ~* the general public, the public at large; *in aller ~* in public; (*ganz offen*) quite openly, in broad

daylight; *zum ersten Mal an od. vor die ~ treten* make one's first public appearance; *mit etw. an die ~ treten, etw. an die ~ bringen* bring s.th. to public attention (*od.* into the open); (*herausbringen*) come out with s.th.; *an die ~ dringen* leak out; *im Blickpunkt od. im Licht der ~ stehen* be in the limelight, be in the public eye; → *Ausschluss 2, Flucht¹ 2*; **2.** (*Öffentlichsein*) public nature (+ *Gen.* of); *~ der Rechtsprechung Jur.* administration of justice in open court

Öffentlichkeits|arbeit *f* public relations *Pl.* (work); *der Polizei etc.*: community relations *Pl.*; *~grundsatz* *m*; *nur Sg.*; *Jur.* principle of the public nature of court proceedings; *~referent* *m*, *~referentin* *f* public relations consultant; *umg.* spin doctor

öffentlichkeitsscheu *Adj.* publicity-shy; **Öffentlichkeitsscheu** *f* publicity-shyness

öffentlich-rechtlich *Adj.* under public law; *die Öffentlich-Rechtlichen* the public service broadcasting institutions

offerieren I. *v/t.* offer; *ein Sonderangebot ~* make a special offer; **II.** *v/i.*: *am günstigsten ~* make the best offer; **Offert** *n*; *-(e)s, -e*; *österr.*, **Offerte** *f*; *-, -n*; *Wirts.* offer; *bes. bei Ausschreibungen*: tender, bid

Office ['ɔfɪs] *n*; *-, -s*; *schw.* pantry

Offizial *m*; *-s, -e*; *kath.* vicar general

Offizial|delikt *n Jur.* offen|ce(*Am. -se*) for which proceedings are initiated by the public prosecutor; *~verteidiger* *m*, *~verteidigerin* *f Jur.* assigned counsel

offiziell I. *Adj.* official; (*förmlich*) auch formal; *Text*: accepted; *von ~er Seite ist bekannt gegeben worden* it has been officially announced; *plötzlich wurde er ganz ~* he suddenly adopted a very formal tone; **II.** *Adv.* officially; *~ bekannt geben, dass ...* make an official statement (to the effect) that ...;

Offizielle *m, f*; *-n, -n* official

Offizier *m*; *-s, -e* **1.** *Mil.* (commissioned) officer; *hoher ~* high-ranking officer; *~ vom Dienst* duty officer; **2.** *Schach*: piece other than a pawn; **Offizierin** *f*; *-, -nen* (female) officer

Offiziers|anwärter *m*, *~anwärterin* *f Mil.* officer cadet; *~kasino* *n* officers' mess; *~korps* *n* officer corps; *~laufbahn* *f* career as an officer, officer's career; *~messe* *f Naut.* wardroom; *~rang* *m* rank of an officer, officer's rank; *~schule* *f* officer candidate school (*Abk.* OCS)

offiziös *Adj.* semi-official

Offizium *n*; *-s, Offizien*; *kath.* **1.** *nur Sg.*: *das Heilige ~* *hist.* the highest authority in the Curia; **2.** (*Messe*) Divine Office; (*Stundengebet*) prayer said at the canonical hours

Off-Kommentar *m TV etc.* voice-over

offline ['ɔflaɪn] *Adv. EDV* offline; *~ gehen/arbeiten* go/work offline; **Offline-Betrieb** *m EDV* offline working

öffnen I. *v/t.* open; (*Mantel*) unbutton; (*Reißverschluss etc.*) undo; (*Fallschirm, Buch*) open; *er öffnete sich die Pulsadern* he slashed his wrists; *e-e Leiche ~* perform a postmortem; → *Auge 2*; **II.** *v/i.* open; *die Tür lässt sich nicht ~* the door won't open; *wir ~ erst um 10 Uhr* we don't open until ten; *niemand öffnete* nobody came to the door; → *geöffnet*; **III.** *v/refl.* **1.** open; *der Fallschirm öffnete sich nicht* the parachute failed to open; *die Erde öffnete sich* the earth opened

up; *nach Süden hin öffnet sich das Tal* the valley opens out to the south; **2.** *fig.*: *sich j-m ~* confide in s.o.; *sich j-s Vorstellungen ~* become receptive to (*od.* warm to) s.o.'s ideas; **3.** *fig.* (*sich erschließen*) neue Märkte, Möglichkeiten etc.: open up (*j-m* for s.o.);

Öffnen *n*; *-s, kein Pl.* opening; *vor dem ~ schütteln* shake before use;

Öffner *m*; *-s, -* opener; (*Türöffner*) door opener; **Öffnung** *f* opening (*nach* to) (*auch fig.*); (*Loch*) hole; (*Lücke*) gap; *Fot., Tech.* aperture; *bes. im Körper*: orifice *förm.*; *zum Rauchabzug etc.*: vent; *e-r Höhle*: mouth (+ *Gen.* of), entrance (to)

Öffnungszeiten *Pl.* opening (*Wirts.* business, *Bank*: banking) hours

Offroadfahrzeug *n* off-road vehicle

Offset|druck *m Druck.* offset (printing); *Produkt*: offset print; *~drucker* *m*, *~druckerin* *f* offset printer

Offshorebohrung ['ɔfʃɔːr-] *f Tech.* offshore drilling

Off|-Sprecher *m*, *~-Sprecherin* *f TV etc.* off-screen narrator (*od.* commentator); *~-Stimme* *f* off-screen voice, voice-over

o-förmig *Adj.* O-shaped, ring-shaped

oft *Adv.*; *öfter, am öftesten* often, frequently; *wie ~ muss ich dir noch sagen, dass ...* how often do I have to tell you (that) ...; *ziemlich ~* quite often, quite a lot; **öfter** *Adv.* **1.** more often; *je ~ ich sie sehe, desto mehr ...* the more I see of her, the more ...; **2.** (*wiederholt*) repeatedly; (*ziemlich oft*) quite often, quite a lot; (*ab und zu*) now and then; *schon ~* several times; *des Öfteren* quite often; (*wiederholt*) repeatedly; (*mehrmals*) several times; *öfters Adv. Dial.* → *öfter 2*

oftmalig *Adj.* (*häufig*) frequent; (*wiederholt*) repeated; **oftmals** *Adv.* often, frequently, many times; (*wiederholt*) repeatedly

o. g. *Abk.* (*oben genannt*) above-mentioned

ÖGB *m*; *-(s), kein Pl.*; *Abk.* (**Ö**sterrei-chischer **G**ewerkschafts**b**und) Austrian Trade (*Am.* Labor) Union Federation

oh *Interj.* oh; → *o*

oha *Interj. umg.* oho

Oheim *m*; *-s, -e*; *altm.* uncle

OHG *f*; *-, -s*; *Abk.* (**o**ffene **H**andelsgesellschaft) *Wirts.* general partnership

OH-Gruppe *f Chem.* hydroxyl group

oh, là, là *Interj.* gosh; *Verwunderung*: wow

Ohm *n*; *-(s), -*; *Phys.* ohm; **ohmsch** *Adj.* ohmic; *das ~e Gesetz* Ohm's law; **Ohmmeter** *n* ohmmeter; **Ohmzahl** *f* ohmage

ohne I. *Präp.* **1.** without; (*ausschließlich*) auch not counting, excluding; *ein Topf ~ Deckel* a pan without a lid; *wir sind momentan ~ Auto* we are without a car (*od.* haven't got a car) at the moment; *sie ging ~ Hut/Schuhe* she wasn't wearing a hat / any shoes; *wir sind fünf ~ die Kinder* we're five not counting (*od.* minus) the children; *~ mich!* (you can) count me out, I'm not having anything to do with it; *~ Zweifel* undoubtedly; *~ seine Schuld* through no fault of his (own); **2.** *~ weiteres* just like that; (*mühelos*) auch without any (great) effort; (*ohne Probleme*) without any problems (*od.* difficulty); *das machen wir ~ weiteres* we'll manage that easily; *das kannst du ~ weiteres akzeptieren* (*bedenken-*

los) you needn't worry (*od.* hesitate) about accepting that; **das geht nicht so ~ weiteres** that's not that simple; **3.** *umg. allein stehend*: **das ist gar nicht so ~** it's not bad, you know; (*ist schwieriger etc., als man denkt*) there's more to it than meets the eye, it's not that simple; **ich schlafe am liebsten ~** I prefer to swim in the nude; **du brauchst einen Ausweis, ~ lassen sie dich nicht rein** you need a pass, they won't let you in without (one); → **oben** 1; **II.** *Konj.*: ~ **dass**, ~ **zu** (+ *Inf.*) without (+ *Ger.*); ~ **dass ich ihn gesehen hatte** without (my) having seen him; ~ **auch nur zu lächeln** without so much as a smile

ohnedies *Adv.* → **ohnehin**
ohneeinander *Adv.* without one another
ohnegleichen *Adv.* unequal(l)ed, unparalleled; *pej. Sache*: unheard of; **e-e Katastrophe ~** a disaster without parallel, an unprecedented disaster
ohnehin *Adv.* anyhow, anyway; **sie ist ~ schon sehr reich** she is already very rich as it is
ohneweiters *Adv. österr.* (*ohne weiteres*) → **ohne** I 2
Ohnmacht *f*; -, -en **1.** *Med.* faint; *Anfall*: fainting fit; **aus der ~ erwachen** come (a)round, come to; **in ~ fallen** faint, pass out, lose consciousness; **ich bin fast in ~ gefallen** *umg. fig.* I nearly had a (fainting) fit; **2.** *nur Sg.* (*Machtlosigkeit*) helplessness, powerlessness, impotence (*gegenüber* in the face of); **ohnmächtig I.** *Adj.* **1.** *Med.* (*bewusstlos*) unconscious; ~ **werden** faint, pass out; **er ist ~** he's fainted (*od.* passed out); ~ **zusammenbrechen** collapse in a faint; **2.** (*machtlos*) (utterly) helpless, powerless, impotent (*gegenüber* in the face of); **II.** *Adv.* helplessly, impotently; **wir mussten ~ zusehen, wie** ... we had to look on, powerless (to help), as ...; **e-m Problem etc. ~ gegenüberstehen** be powerless in the face of a problem *etc.*; **Ohnmachtsanfall** *m* fainting fit
oho *Interj.* oho; *Widerspruch, Unwillen*: oh no; → **klein** I 8
Ohr *n*; -(e)s, -en **1.** *Anat.* ear (*auch fig. Gehör*); **gute/schlechte ~en haben** have good/poor hearing; **j-m etw. ins ~ flüstern** whisper s.th. into s.o.'s ear; **die ~en anlegen** *Hund, Pferd*: lay back its ears; **j-m eins hinter die ~en hauen** *umg.* give s.o. a clip (a)round the ears; → **taub** 1; **2.** *fig. in Wendungen*: **die ~en aufmachen** listen carefully; **die ~en spitzen** *od.* **lange ~en bekommen** prick up one's ears; **ganz ~ sein** be all ears; **ein ~ haben für** have an ear for; **ein feines ~ haben für** have a good ear for; **ein offenes ~ für j-n haben** be prepared to listen to s.o.; **ein offenes ~ finden** find a good listener; **ich habe es noch im ~** (*Musik etc.*) it's still going (a)round in my head; *stärker*: it's still ringing in my ears; **die Melodie geht leicht ins ~** it's a really catchy tune; **j-n übers ~ hauen** *umg.* rip s.o. off; **sich aufs ~ legen** *umg.* get some shuteye; **schreib dir das hinter die ~en!** *umg.* and don't you forget it!; **bis über beide ~en in Arbeit** *etc.* **stecken** *umg.* be up to one's ears in work *etc.*; **bis über beide ~en verliebt** *umg.* head over heels in love; **viel um die ~en haben** *umg.* have an awful lot on one's plate; **von e-m ~** (**bis**) **zum anderen grinsen** *umg.* grin from ear to ear; **mir**

klingen die ~en my ears are burning; **halt die ~en steif!** *umg.* keep your pecker (*Am.* chin) up!; **mir kam zu ~en, dass** I happened to hear that; **ich traute m-n ~en nicht** I couldn't believe my ears; **es ist nichts für fremde ~en** it's not for public consumption; **das ist nichts für zarte ~en** this is not for sensitive souls; **er hört nur mit halbem ~ hin** he's only half listening; **auf 'dem ~ ist er taub** he's deaf (*od.* he doesn't want to know) where that's concerned; **wasch dir mal die ~en!** *umg.* you should get your ears seen to; **zum einen ~ hinein, zum andern hinaus** in one ear, out the other; → **faustdick** I 2, **Nacht** 2, **schlackern**, **taub** 1, **trocken** I 4
Öhr *n*; -(e)s, -e eye
Ohren|arzt *m*, ~**ärztin** *f* ear specialist
ohrenbetäubend *Adj.* deafening, ear-splitting
Ohren|entzündung *f* inflammation of the ear, otitis (*Pl.* otitides); ~**heilkunde** *f* otology; ~**klappe** *f* earflap; ~**kneifer** *m* *Insekt*: earwig; ~**leiden** *n* ear complaint; ~**robbe** *f* *Zool.* eared seal; ~**sausen** *n*; -s, *kein Pl.* singing (*od.* ringing) in one's ear(s), tinnitus *fachspr.*; ~**schmalz** *n* ear wax; ~**schmaus** *m* treat for the ears; ~**schmerzen** *Pl.* earache *Sg.*; ~**schützer** *Pl.* earmuffs; ~**sessel** *m* wing chair; ~**spezialist** *m*, ~**spezialistin** *f* ear specialist; ~**zeuge** *m*, ~**zeugin** *f* earwitness
Ohrfeige *f* box (*od.* clip) round the ears; **ohrfeigen**; **ohrfeigt**, **ohrfeigte**, **hat geohrfeigt**; *v/t.*: **j-n ~** box s.o.'s ears; **ich könnte mich** (**selbst**) ~**!** *umg.* I could kick myself
Ohr|gehänge *n* pendant (*od.* drop) earrings *Pl.*; ~**geräusche** *Pl. Med.* tinnitus *Sg.*; ~**hörer** *m* earphone; ~**klipp** *m* ear-clip; ~**knopf** *m* tiny earphone; ~**läppchen** *n* earlobe; ~**marke** *f* *Tierzucht*: ear tag; ~**muschel** *f* **1.** *Anat.* (outer) ear; **2.** *e-s Kopfhörers*: earpiece
Ohropax® *n*; -, -(e) ear plug material
Ohr|ring *m* earring; ~**speicheldrüse** *f* *Anat.* parotid gland; ~**spülung** *f* *Med.* irrigation (*mit Spritze*: syringing) of the ear; ~**stecker** *m* (ear) stud; ~**trompete** *f* *Anat.* Eustachian tube; ~**wurm** *m* **1.** *Zool.* earwig; **2.** *umg. fig.* catchy tune
o. J. *Abk.* (**ohne Jahr**) n.d.
oje *umg.*, **ojemine** *altm. Interj.* oh dear
o. k., **O. K.** *Abk.* OK
Okapi *n*; -s, -s; *Zool.* okapi
Okarina *f*, -, -s *und* Okarinen; *Mus.* ocarina
okay [o'ke:] *Interj. umg.* OK, okay, okey-doke(y); **Okay** *n*; -(s), -s; *umg.* OK, okay
Okkasion *f*, -, -en; *Wirts.* bargain
Okkasionalismus *m*; -, *kein Pl.*; *Philos.* occasionalism
Okklusion *f*; -, -en occlusion
okklusiv *Adj. Med., Met.* occlusive
Okklusiv|pessar *n* *Med.* contraceptive pessary; ~**verband** *m* *Med.* occlusive dressing
okkult *Adj.* occult; **Okkulte** *n*; -n, *kein Pl.*: **das ~** the occult; **Okkultismus** *m*; -, *kein Pl.* occultism; **Okkultist** *m*; -en, -en, **Okkultistin** *f*; -, -nen occultist; **okkultistisch** *Adj.* occult ..., ... of the occult
Okkupant *m*; -en, -en, ~**in** *f*; -, -nen; *Mil.* occupier; **Okkupation** *f*; -, -en occupation; **Okkupationsmacht** *f* occu-

pying power; **okkupieren** *v/t.* occupy
Öko *m*; -s, -s; *umg. hum.* environmentalist
Öko|... *im Subst.*: eco(-); (*umweltfreundlich*) eco-friendly; *Agr.* organic; ~**anbau** *m*; *nur Sg.* eco-friendly (*od.* organic) cultivation
Öko|audit *n* *Wirts.* ecological audit; ~**bauer** *m*, ~**bäuerin** *f* organic farmer; ~**bewegung** *f* ecological movement; ~**bilanz** *f* ecological balance sheet; ~**katastrophe** *f* *umg.* ecological disaster, ecocide; ~**label** ['-le:bl] *n* *Wirts.* eco-label; ~**laden** *m* organic food and natural product shop (*Am.* store)
Öko|loge *m*; -n, -n ecologist; ~**logie** *f*; -, *kein Pl.* ecology; ~**login** *f*; -, -nen ecologist; **ökologisch** *Adj.* ecological; → **Gleichgewicht**
Ökonom *m*; -en, -en **1.** (*Wirtschaftswissenschaftler*) economist; (*Student*) *auch* economics student; **2.** (*Landwirt*) farmer; **Ökonomie** *f*; -, -n **1.** *nur Sg.* (*Wirtschaftlichkeit*) economy; **2.** (*Wirtschaftsstruktur*) economy; **3.** (*Wirtschaftswissenschaft*) economics *Pl.* (*V. im Sg.*); **Ökonomierat** *m*, **Ökonomierätin** *f* *österr.* (*title awarded to a*) *farmer of outstanding merit*; **ökonomisch I.** *Adj.* economic; (*sparsam*) economical; **II.** *Adv.* economically; ~ **umgehen mit** be economical with; **ökonomisieren** *v/t.* put on a sound economic basis; **Ökonomismus** *m*; -, *kein Pl.* economism
Ökopartei *f* eco(-)party, green party
Ökopax *m*; -, -e follower of the Ökopaxbewegung; ~**bewegung** *f* movement combining environmental and pacifist aims
Öko|siegel *n* *Öko.* eco-label; ~**sphäre** *f* ecosphere; ~**sponsoring** *n* *Wirts.* sponsoring of eco-friendly projects; ~**steuer** *f* *umg.* green tax; ~**system** *n* ecosystem
Ökotop *n*; -s, -e ecotope
Ökotrophologie *f* home economics *Pl.* (*V. im Sg.*)
Öko|wein *m* organic wine; ~**winzer** *m*, ~**winzerin** *f* eco(-)friendly vintner, organic wine grower
Oktaeder *n*; -s, -e; *Math.* octahedron (*Pl.* octahedra *od.* octahedrons); **oktaedrisch** *Adj.* octahedral
Oktagon *n*; -s, -e → **Oktogon**
Oktan *n*; -s, -e **1.** *Chem.* octane; **2.** *nur Sg.*; *Mot.* (*Oktanzahl*): **Super hat 95 ~** super is 95 octane
Oktanzahl *f* (*abgek. OZ*) *Mot.* octane rating (*od.* number)
Oktav¹ *n*; -s, *kein Pl.*; *Druck.* octavo
Oktav² *f*; -, -en **1.** *österr.* → **Oktave**; **2.** *kirchl.* octave
Oktave *f*; -, -n; *Mus.* octave
Oktavformat *n* *Druck.* octavo (format)
Oktett *n*; -(e)s, -e; *Mus.* octet
Oktober *m*; -(s), -, *mst Sg.* October; → **April**
Oktober|fest *n* *in München*: Munich October (Beer) Festival; *allg.*: October beer festival, *Am.* Oktoberfest; ~**revolution** *f*: **die ~** *hist.* the October Revolution
Oktogon *n*; -s, -e; *Math.* octagon (*auch Gebäudeform*)
oktroyieren [ɔktroa'ji:rən] *v/t. geh.*: **j-m etw. ~** impose s.th. on s.o.
Okular *n*; -s, -e; *Opt.* eyepiece
okulieren *v/t. Agr.* graft (a bud on); **Okuliermesser** *n* budding knife
Ökumene *f*; -, *kein Pl.*; *kirchl.* ecumenicalism, ecumenical movement; **ökumenisch** *Adj.* ecumenical; **Ökumeni-**

O

scher Rat der Kirchen World Council of Churches

Okzident *m*; *-s*, *kein Pl.*; *geh. altm.* Occident, West; **okzidental(isch)** *Adj.* occidental, western

ö. L. *Abk.* (*östlicher Länge*): **10°** ~ 10° east, 10° E

Öl *n*; *-(e)s*, *-e* oil; (*Erdöl*) *auch*: petroleum; ~ **exportierende Länder** oil-exporting countries; ~ **stoßen** strike oil; **mit** ~ **heizen** use oil for one's heating, have oil heating; **den Salat mit** ~ **anmachen** dress the salad with oil; **in** ~ **malen** paint in oils; ~ **ins Feuer gießen** *fig.* add fuel to the fire (*od.* flames); ~ **auf die Wogen gießen** *fig.* pour oil on troubled waters; **das geht mir runter wie** ~ *umg. fig.* that's music to my ears; ~**abscheider** *m*; *-s*, *-*; *Tech.* oil separator; ~**baum** *m Bot.* olive (tree); ~**berg** *m*; *nur Sg.*; *bibl.* Mount of Olives; ~**bild** *n* oil painting; ~**bohrung** *f* oil drilling

Oldie ['o:ldi] *m*; *-s*, *-s*; *umg.* **1.** *Schallplatte etc.*: oldie; **2.** *Person*: old-timer

Öldruck *m* **1.** *Kunst* oleograph; **2.** *Mot., Tech.* oil pressure; ~**anzeiger** *m* oil-pressure ga(u)ge; ~**bremse** *f Mot.* hydraulic brake

Oldtimer ['o:ldtaimɐ] *m*; *-s*, *-* **1.** *Mot.* vintage (*Brit. vor 1905*: veteran) car; **2.** *umg.* (*Person*) *umg.* old-timer

Oleander *m*; *-s*, *-*; *Bot.* oleander

Ölembargo *n* oil embargo

ölen *v/t.* oil; *Tech. auch* lubricate; (*einölen*) anoint; **wie geölt** *umg. fig.* like clockwork; → **Blitz** 1

Oleum *n*; *-s*, *Olea*; *Chem.* oleum

Öl|export *m* oil exports *Pl.*; ~**farbe** *f* oil-based paint; *Kunst* oil paint; **mit** ~**n malen** paint in oils; ~**feld** *n* oilfield; ~**feuerung** *f* oil firing; ~**film** *m* film of oil, oil film; ~**förderland** *n* oil-producing country; ~**fördermenge** *f* oil production (*od.* output); ~**förderung** *f* oil production; ~**frucht** *f Bot.* oleiferous fruit; ~**gemälde** *n* oil painting; ~**gesellschaft** *f* oil company; ~**gewinnung** *f* oil production; ~**götze** *m*: **wie ein** ~ *umg. pej.* like a stuffed dummy; ~**hafen** *m* oil tanker port

ölhaltig *Adj.* oily; *Bot.* oleaginous

Öl|handel *m* oil trade; ~**haut** *f Gewebe*: oilskin; ~**heizung** *f* oil-fired heating

ölig I. *Adj.* oily (*auch fig.*); *Wein*: rich; **II.** *Adv.* **1.** ~ **glänzen** have an oily sheen; **2.** *fig. pej.* in an oily manner; ~ **lächeln** smile an oily smile

Oligarch *m*; *-en*, *-en* oligarch; **Oligarchie** *f*; *-*, *-n* oligarchy; **oligarchisch** *Adj.* oligarchic

Oligopol *n*; *-s*, *-e*; *Wirts.* oligopoly; **oligopolistisch** *Adj.* oligopolistic

Oligozän *n*; *-s*, *kein Pl.*; *Geol.* Oligocene

Olim *ohne Art.*: **seit** ~**s Zeiten** *hum.* from (*od.* since) the year dot, *Am.* from (*od.* since) day one

Öl|import *m* oil imports *Pl.*; ~**industrie** *f* oil (*od.* petroleum) industry

oliv *indekl. Adj.* olive; **Oliv** *n*; *-s*, *-(s)* olive

Olive *f*; *-*, *-n*; *Bot.* olive; **Olivenbaum** *m* olive (tree)

olivenfarben *Adj.* olive(-colo[u]red)

Oliven|hain *m* olive grove; ~**öl** *n Gastr.* olive oil

oliv|farben *Adj.* olive(-colo[u]red); ~**grün** *Adj.* olive(-green)

Olivin *n*; *-s*, *-e*; *Min.* olivine

Öl|jacke *f* oilskin; ~**kanister** *m* oil tin (*Am.* canister); ~**kanne** *f* oil can; ~**ka-**

tastrophe *f* (*Tankerunglück*) disastrous oil spill; ~**konzern** *m* oil company; ~**krise** *f* oil crisis; ~**kuchen** *m* oilcake

oll *Adj. bes. nordd. umg.* old; **je** ~**er, je doller** the older they get, the crazier their ideas; → **Kamellen**

Öllampe *f* oil lamp

Olle *m, f*; *-n*, *-n*; *bes. nordd. umg.* **1.** *Mann*: old boy, *bes. Am.* old-timer; *Frau*: old dear, old girl; **2. der** ~ (*Vater, Ehemann*) the old man; (*Chef*) the boss; **die** ~ (*Mutter*) the old woman; (*Ehefrau*) *auch* the missus; **meine** ~**n** (*Eltern*) the parents, my people

Öl|leitung *f* oil pipe; **über weite Strecken**: oil pipeline; ~**malerei** *f* oil painting; ~**messstab** *m* dipstick; ~**mühle** *f* oil mill; ~**multi** *m* multinational oil corporation; ~**ofen** *m* oil heater (*od.* stove); ~**papier** *n* oil paper; ~**pest** *f* oil pollution; ~**pflanze** *f* oil-producing plant; ~**plattform** *f* oil rig (*od.* platform); ~**preis** *m* oil price; ~**quelle** *f* oil well; ~**raffinerie** *f* oil refinery; ~**rückstände** *Pl.* oil residues; ~**sardine** *f Gastr.* sardine in oil; ~**n** *Pl.* (tinned, *Am.* canned) sardines; *weitS.* tin (*od.* can) *Sg.* of sardines; ~**scheich** *m* oil sheik(h); ~**schicht** *f* layer of oil; *Film*: film of oil; (*Ölteppich*) oil slick; ~**schiefer** *m Geol.* oil shale; ~**schlamm** *m Mot.* (oil) sludge; ~**schwemme** *f* oil glut; ~**spur** *f* trail of oil

Ölstand *m Mot.* oil level; ~**anzeiger** *m* oil ga(u)ge, oil-level indicator

Öl|tank *m* oil tank; ~**tanker** *m* oil tanker

Öl|temperatur *f Mot.* oil temperature; ~**teppich** *m* oil slick; ~**unfall** *m* oil spill

Ölung *f* **1.** *Tech.* oiling, lubrication; **2.** *kirchl.* anointment; **die Letzte** ~ *kath.* the last rites, the anointment of the sick

Öl|verbrauch *m* oil consumption; ~**vorkommen** *n* oil field(s *Pl.*); (*Vorrat*) oil resources *Pl.*; ~**wanne** *f Mot.* sump, *Am.* oil pan; ~**wechsel** *m Mot.* oil change

Olymp *m*; *-s*, *kein Pl.* **1.** *Geog.* Mount Olympus; **der** ~ *Myth.* Olympus; **2.** *umg. hum. Theat.*: **der** ~ (*Galerie*) the gods; **auf dem** ~ in the gods

Olympia *n*, *mst. kein Art.*; *-s*, *kein Pl.* → **Olympiade** 1; ~**auswahl** *f* Olympic team

Olympiade *f*; *-*, *-n* **1.** (*Olympische Spiele*) Olympic Games *Pl.*, Olympics *Pl.*; **bei der letzten** ~ in the last Olympic Games; **2.** *hist.* (*Zeitraum*) olympiad

Olympia|dorf *n Sport* Olympic village; ~**dritte** *m, f* third-placed competitor in an Olympic event; ~**gelände** *n* Olympic complex (*od.* park); ~**gold** *n* Olympic gold; ~**jahr** *n* year of the Olympic Games, Olympic year; ~**mannschaft** *f* Olympic team; ~**medaille** *f* Olympic medal; ~**norm** *f* Olympic (qualification) standard; ~**qualifikation** *f* Olympic qualification

olympiareif *Adj.* ... of Olympic medal standard

Olympia|sieg *m* Olympic victory; ~**sieger** *m*, ~**siegerin** *f* Olympic champion (*od.* gold medal[l]ist); ~**stadion** *n* Olympic stadium; ~**teilnehmer** *m*, ~**teilnehmerin** *f* Olympic competitor

olympiaverdächtig *Adj. oft hum., iro.*: **das war e-e** ~**e Leistung** with that sort of performance they'll want you in the

Olympic team; *fig. hum.* you've really surpassed yourself there

Olympiazweite *m, f* second-placed competitor in an Olympic event; ~ **sein** come second in the Olympics

Olympionike *m*; *-n*, *-n*, **Olympionikin** *f*; *-*, *-nen* Olympic competitor (*Athlet*: athlete), Olympian; (*Sieger*) Olympic champion

olympisch *Adj. Sport* Olympic; **Olympische Spiele** → **Olympiade** 1; ~**es Gold** Olympic gold; ~**es Gold gewinnen** *auch* win an Olympic gold medal, win gold at the Olympics; **der** ~**e Gedanke** the Olympic ideal

Öl|zentralheizung *f* oil-fired central heating; ~**zeug** *n* oilskins *Pl.*; ~**zufuhr** *f* oil feed; ~**zweig** *m geh., lit.* olive branch

Oma *f*; *-*, *-s*; *umg.* **1.** (*Großmutter*) grandma, granny; **als Anrede, Eigenname**: Grandma, Granny; **2.** *oft pej.* (*ältere Frau*) old biddy

Ombuds|frau *f* **1.** *Parl.* (female) ombudsperson; **2.** (*Vertrauensfrau*) representative, spokeswoman; ~**mann** *m* **1.** *Parl.* ombudsman; **2.** (*Vertrauensmann*) representative, spokesman

Omega *n*; *-(s)*, *-s* omega

Omelett *n*; *-(e)s*, *-e und -s*, **Omelette** [ɔm'lɛt] *f*; *-*, *-n* omelette, *bes. Am.* omelet

Omen *n*; *-s*, *- und Omina* omen; **das ist ein gutes/schlechtes** ~ *auch* that augurs well/badly

Omi *f*; *-*, *-s*; *umg.* → **Oma** 1

Omikron *n*; *-(s)*, *-s* omicron

ominös *Adj.* ominous

Omnibus *m* bus; (*bes. Brit. Reisebus*) coach

Omnibus... *im Subst.* → **Bus**

omnipotent *Adj. geh.* omnipotent; **Omnipotenz** *f*; *nur Sg.* omnipotence

omnipräsent *Adj. geh.* omnipresent; **Omnipräsenz** *f* omnipresence

Omnium *n*; *-s*, *Omnien Radfahren*: cycle track race meeting

on *Adv. TV etc.* on screen; **On** *n*; *-*, *kein Pl.*: **im** ~ on screen; **im** ~ **sprechen** speak to camera

Onanie *f*; *-*, *kein Pl.* masturbation; **onanieren** *vt/i.* masturbate

Ondit [õ'di] *n*; *-(s)*, *-s* rumo(u)r; **e-m** ~ **zufolge ...** rumo(u)r has it that ...

ondulieren *v/t. altm.* crimp

Onkel *m*; *-s*, *- und umg. -s* **1.** uncle; ~ **Robert** Uncle Robert; **2.** *Kindersprache*: (*Mann*) nice man, gentleman; **der** ~ **Doktor** the (nice) doctor; **3.** *umg. fig.*: **der große** ~ one's big toe; **über den (großen)** ~ **gehen** walk pigeon-toed; **onkelhaft** *Adj.* avuncular

Onkologe *m*; *-n*, *-n*; *Med.* oncologist; **Onkologie** *f*; *-*, *kein Pl.* oncology; **Onkologin** *f*; *-*, *-nen* (female) oncologist; **onkologisch** *Adj.* oncological

online ['ɔnlain] *Adv. EDV* online; ~ **gehen** go online; **Onlinebetrieb** *m EDV* online working (*od.* operation)

Önologe *m*; *-n*, *-n* (o)enologist; **Önologie** *f*; *-*, *kein Pl.* (o)enology; **Önologin** *f*; *-*, *-nen* (female) (o)enologist; **önologisch** *Adj.* (o)enological

onomatopoetisch *Adj. Ling.* onomatopoeic; **Onomatopöie** *f*; *-*, *-n* onomatopoeia

Önorm *f*; *-*, *kein Pl.*; *Abk.* (**Österreichische Norm**) Austrian standard

On|-Sprecher *m*, ~**-Sprecherin** *f*; *TV etc.* onscreen announcer; **mit Kommentar**: onscreen commentator; ~**-Stimme** *f* voice on

Ontogenese *f Bio.* ontogenesis; **onto-**

genetisch *Adj.* ontogenetic

Ontologie *f; -, kein Pl.* ontology; **ontologisch** *Adj.* ontological

o. O. u. J. *Abk.* (**ohne Ort und Jahr**) n.p. n.d.

OP *m; -(s), -(s); Abk. → Operationssaal*

Opa *m; -s, -s; umg.* **1.** (*Großvater*) grandpa, grandad; *als Anrede, Eigenname*: Grandpa, Grandad; **~s Kino** *fig. hum.* the cinema (*Am.* movies *Pl.*) in the old days; **2.** *oft pej.* (*älterer Mann*) old fogey

opak *Adj. Glas*: opaque

Opal *m; -s, -e; Min.* opal

opaleszent *Adj. Opt.* opalescent; **Opaleszenz** *f; -, kein Pl.* opalescence

opalisieren *v/i.* opalesce; **opalisierend** *Adj.* opalescent

Op-Art *f; -, kein Pl.; Kunst* op art

OPEC *f; -, kein Pl.; Abk.* OPEC; **~Staat** *m* OPEC country (*od.* nation)

Openair [ˈoʊpnˈʔɛːɐ̯] *n; -s, -s* open-air festival; **~kino** *n* open-air cinema (*Am.* theater); (*Autokino*) drive-in cinema (*Am.* theater *od.* movie)

Openenddiskussion *f* open-ended discussion

Oper *f; -, -n; Mus.* (*auch die ~*) opera; *Gebäude*: opera house; *Ensemble*: opera (company); **komische ~** (German) light opera; **in die ~ gehen** go to the opera

operabel *Adj. Med., fachspr.* operable

Operand *m; -en, -en; EDV* operand

Operateur [opəraˈtøːɐ̯] *m; -s, -e, ~in f; -, -nen* **1.** *Med.* (operating) surgeon; **2.** *altm.* (*Filmvorführer*) projectionist; **Operation** *f; -, -en* **1.** *Med.* operation; **sich e-r ~ unterziehen** *auch* undergo surgery; **~ gelungen, Patient tot** *umg. fig.* it was a perfectly organized disaster (*umg.* cock-up); **2.** *Mil., Math., fachspr.* operation

operationalisieren *v/t. Päd. fachspr.* operationalize

Operations|basis *f bes. Mil.* base of operations; **~folgen** *Pl.* postoperative complications; **an den ~ sterben** *auch* die as a result of the operation; **~gebiet** *n Mil.* area of an operation; **~kosten** *Pl.* cost *Sg.* of an (*od.* the) operation; **~maske** *f* surgeon's mask; **~narbe** *f* scar from an (*od.* the) operation, *fachspr.* postoperative scar; **~pfleger** *m* (male) theatre nurse, *Am.* operating room nurse; **~saal** *m* (*abgek.* OP) *Med.* theatre (*Am.* room); **~schwester** *f* theatre nurse, *Am.* operating room nurse; **~team** *n* surgical team; **~tisch** *m* operating table

operativ I. *Adj.* **1.** *Med.* operative, surgical; **ein ~er Eingriff** an operation, a piece of surgery; **2.** *Mil.* operational, strategic; **3.** *Wirts.* operational; *Verluste: auch* operating; **das ~e Geschäft** the operational side of the business; **II.** *Adv.* **1.** *Med.:* **etw. ~ entfernen** operate to remove s.th., remove s.th. by (operative) surgery; **2.** *Wirts.* operationally; **sich ~ in den roten Zahlen befinden** be operating at a loss

Operator *m; -s, -en; Math., Ling., EDV* operator

Operette *f; -, -n; Mus.* operetta; **Operettenfilm** *m* film (version) of an operetta; **operettenhaft** *pej.* **I.** *Adj.* operetta(-)like; **II.** *Adv.* in the manner of an operetta

Operetten|melodie *f* tune from an operetta; *Pl.* tunes from operettas; **~musik** *f* operetta music; **~sänger** *m,*

~sängerin *f* operetta singer; **~staat** *m hum., mst pej.* (real-life) Ruritania; **~tenor** *m* operetta tenor

operieren I. *v/t. Med.:* **j-n ~** operate on s.o.; **am Magen operiert werden** have a stomach operation; **sich ~ lassen** have an operation; **II.** *v/i.* **1.** *bes. Mil.* operate; **2.** *fig.* (*vorgehen*) proceed; **vorsichtig ~** proceed with caution, handle matters carefully; **3.** *fig.* (*umgehen*): **~ mit** make use of

Opern|arie *f Mus.* operatic aria; **~ball** *m* opera ball; **~fan** *m* opera fan (*od.* buff); **~freund** *m,* **~freundin** *f* opera lover, keen opera-goer; **~führer** *m* opera guide; **~glas** *n:* (**ein**) **~** (a pair of) opera glasses *Pl.*

opernhaft I. *Adj.* operatic (*auch fig. pej.*); **II.** *Adv.* operatically

Opern|haus *n Mus.* opera house; **~komponist** *m,* **~komponistin** *f* operatic composer; **~konzert** *n* concert of operatic music; **~melodie** *f* tune from an opera; *Pl.* tunes from operas; **~musik** *f* operatic music; **~sänger** *m,* **~sängerin** *f* opera singer; **~text** *m* (opera) libretto

Opfer *n; -s, -* **1.** sacrifice (*auch fig.*); (*auch Opfergabe*) offering; **ein ~ bringen** make a sacrifice; **viele ~ an Zeit** *etc.* **bringen** invest a great deal of time *etc.* (**für** in); **keine ~ scheuen** consider no sacrifice too great, give one's all; **unter großen ~n** at great cost; **2.** (*der, die Geopferte od. Geschädigte*) victim (*auch fig. e-s Betrugs etc.*); (*e-s Unfalls etc.*) *auch* casualty; **zahlreiche ~ fordern** take a heavy toll on human life, cause heavy casualties, claim many victims; **e-r Sache zum ~ fallen** be the victim of s.th., fall victim to s.th.; **~altar** *m* sacrificial altar

opferbereit *Adj.* **1.** willing to make sacrifices; **2.** (*aufopfernd*) self-sacrificing; **Opferbereitschaft** *f* willingness to make sacrifices

Opfer|gabe *f* (sacrificial) offering; **~gang** *m* **1.** *geh. fig.* self-sacrifice; **2.** *kath.* offertory procession; **~lamm** *n* sacrificial lamb; *fig.* innocent victim; **wie ein ~** *umg.* like a lamb to the slaughter

opfern I. *v/t.* sacrifice; (*Tier, Früchte etc.*) *auch* offer up; **sein Leben ~** give (*od.* lay down) one's life; **II.** *v/i.* (make a) sacrifice; **III.** *v/refl.* sacrifice o.s. (**für** *od.* + *Dat.* for); **wer opfert sich und holt uns was zu trinken aus dem Keller?** *umg. hum.* who's volunteering to go and get us something to drink from the cellar?

Opfer|pfennig *m* small donation (*for the collection*); **~rolle** *f* role of victim; **~schale** *f hist., für Trankopfer:* patera; **~stätte** *f* sacrificial site; **~stock** *m* offertory box; **~tier** *n* sacrificial animal; **~tod** *m geh.* self-sacrifice

Opferung *f* sacrificing, sacrifice

Opferwille *m* willingness to make sacrifices

Ophthalmologe *m; -n, -n; Med.* ophthalmologist; **Ophthalmologie** *f; -, kein Pl.* ophthalmology; **Ophthalmologin** *f; -, -nen* (female) ophthalmologist; **ophthalmologisch** *Adj.* ophthalmological

Opi *m; -s, -s; Kinderspr. → Opa* 1

Opiat *n; -(e)s, -e* opiate

Opium *n; -s, kein Pl.* opium; **~ fürs Volk** *fig.* the opium of the people; **~anbau** *m* **1.** opium growing; **2.** *konkret:* opium plantation(s *Pl.*); **~handel** *m* opium trade (*od.* traffic); **~höhle** *f*

pej. opium den; **~pfeife** *f* opium pipe; **~schmuggel** *m* opium smuggling

Opiumsucht *f* opium addiction; **opiumsüchtig** *Adj.* addicted to opium; **Opiumsüchtige** *m, f* opium addict

Opossum *n; -s,-s ; Zool.* opossum

Opponent *m; -en, -en, ~in f; -, -nen* opponent; **opponieren** *v/i.* oppose, take the opposite view; **gegen etw. ~** oppose s.th.; (*sich wehren*) resist s.th.

opportun *Adj.* opportune, appropriate; **nicht ~** inopportune, inappropriate; **das wäre im Augenblick nicht ~** it's not the right moment (*od.* time) for it; **Opportunismus** *m; -, kein Pl.* opportunism; **Opportunist** *m; -en, -en,* **Opportunistin** *f; -, -nen* opportunist; **opportunistisch I.** *Adj.* opportunist, opportunistic; **II.** *Adv.* opportunistically

Opposition *f; -, -en; allg.* opposition (*auch Pol., Ling., Astron., Astrol.*); **~ betreiben** set up in opposition; **etw. aus bloßer ~ tun** do s.th. from sheer contrariness; **in ~ stehen zu** be opposed to; **Uranus steht in ~ zur Sonne** *Astron.* Uranus is in opposition to the sun; **oppositionell** *Adj.* opposition ...; *Kräfte:* of opposition; *Tendenz, Ansichten etc.:* opposing; **die Oppositionellen im Lande** the forces of opposition (*od.* dissent) in the country

Oppositions|bank *f Parl.* opposition bench; **auf der ~ sitzen** be in opposition; **~führer** *m,* **~führerin** *f* opposition leader, leader of the opposition; **~geist** *m; nur Sg.* spirit of opposition; **~partei** *f* opposition (party)

OP|-Pfleger *m → Operationspfleger;* **~-Schwester** *f → Operationsschwester*

Optant *m; -en, -en, ~in f; -, -nen* person choosing an option, optant *förm.*

Optativ *m; -s, -e; Ling.* optative

OP-Team *n* operating team

optieren I. *v/i.* **1.** *Pol.:* **für ein Land ~** opt for the nationality of a country; **2.** *Jur.:* **auf etw. ~** take an option on s.th.; **II.** *v/t. Jur.* take an option on

Optik *f; -, -en* **1.** *nur Sg.; Lehre:* optics *Pl.* (V. im *Sg.*); **2.** *Fot., e-r Kamera etc.:* optics *Pl.;* (*Objektiv*) lens; **3.** *nur Sg.; Wirts.* optical industry; **4.** *fig.* (*Einstellung, Standpunkt*) point of view; **das ist e-e Frage der ~** that depends on how you look at it; **5.** *umg. fig.* (*äußerer Eindruck, optische Wirkung*) visual impression; (*Image*) image; **das ist nur für die ~** that's just for show (*od.* appearances); **die ~ von etw. aufbessern** improve the appearance of s.th.; **Optiker** *m; -s, -,* **Optikerin** *f; -, -nen* optician

optimal I. *Adj.* best (possible), optimum ...; **das Zimmer ist ... auch** the room is ideal for ...; **II.** *Adv.:* **Möglichkeiten** *etc.* **~ ausnutzen** make the best possible use of possibilities *etc.;* **optimieren** *v/t.* optimize (*auch Math.*); **Optimierung** *f* optimization

Optimismus *m; -, kein Pl.* optimism; **vorsichtiger ~** cautious (*od.* guarded) optimism; **Optimist** *m; -en, -en,* **Optimistin** *f; -, -nen* optimist; **optimistisch I.** *Adj.* optimistic; **~e Börse** *Wirts.* bullish market; **II.** *Adv.* optimistically

Optimum *n; -s, Optima* optimum (*Pl.* optima *od.* optimums)

Option *f; -, -en* option (**auf** + *Akk.,* **für** on); *Jur. und Wirts. auch* (right of) first refusal; **optional** *Adj.* optional

Options|anleihe *f Wirts.* optional bond, bond cum warrant; **~geschäft** *n* **1.** *einzelnes*: option transaction; **2.** *nur Sg.* dealing in options; **~handel** *m* options trading; **~schein** *m* equity warrant

optisch I. *Adj.* optical; *Signal, Eindruck etc.*: visual; **aus ~en Gründen** for visual effect; **~e Täuschung** optical illusion; **II.** *Adv.*: **~ kaum wahrnehmbar** barely visible; **dadurch wirkt der Raum ~ größer** it makes the room look bigger

Optoelektronik *f* optoelectronics *Pl.* (*V. im Sg.*)

Optometrie *f*; *-, kein Pl.*; *Med.* optometry

opulent *Adj.* opulent, sumptuous; **Opulenz** *f*; *-, kein Pl.* opulence, sumptuousness

Opus *n*; *-, Opera* work, *mst hum.* opus; *Mus. mit Zahl*: opus

Orakel *n*; *-s, -* oracle (*auch fig.*); **in ~n reden** *fig.* speak in riddles; **orakelhaft** *Adj.* oracular; **orakeln** *v/i. umg.* make (mysterious) prophecies; **er orakelt gerne** he likes to play the oracle; **Orakelspruch** *m* oracle, oracular utterance

oral I. *Adj.* oral; **II.** *Adv.*: **~ verkehren** have oral intercourse; **Oralsex** *m* oral sex; **Oralverkehr** *m* oral intercourse

orange [o'rãːʒə] *indekl. Adj.* orange

Orange¹ *n*; *-, - Farbe*: orange

Orange² *f*; *-, -n*; *Bot., Frucht*: orange

Orangeade [orã'ʒaːdə] *f*; *-, -n* orangeade; **Orangeat** [orã'ʒaːt] *n*; *-s, -e*; *Gastr.* candied orange peel; **orangefarben** *Adj.* orange; **orangen** *Adj.* orange

Orangen|baum *m Bot.* orange tree; **~haut** *f Med.* orange skin; **~marmelade** *f Gastr.* (orange) marmalade; **~saft** *m* orange juice, *Am. umg. auch* OJ; **~schale** *f* orange peel; *Gastr. auch the* zest of an orange

Orangerie [orãʒə'riː] *f*; *-, -n*; *Archit.* orangery

orangerot *Adj.* orange-red

Orang-Utan *m*; *-s, -s*; *Zool.* orangutan(g)

Oranien (*n*); *-s*: **Wilhelm von ~** *hist.* William of Orange

Oranjefreistaat *m hist.*: **der ~** the Orange Free State

Oratorium *n*; *-s, Oratorien* **1.** *Mus.* oratorio; **2.** (*Betsaal*) oratory

Orbit *m*; *-s, -s*; *Raumf.* orbit

Orbital|bahn *f Raumf.* path of orbit; **~station** *Raumf.* orbiting space station

Orbiter *m*; *-s, -*; *Raumf.* orbiter

Orchester *n*; *-s, -*; *Mus.* **1.** orchestra; *Jazz etc.: auch* band; **2.** (**~graben**) orchestra (pit); **~begleitung** *f* orchestral accompaniment; **~fassung** *f* orchestral version; **~graben** *m* orchestra (pit); **~leiter** *m*, **~leiterin** *f* conductor; **~musik** *f* orchestral music; **~musiker** *m*, **~musikerin** *f* orchestral musician; **~probe** *f Theat.* orchestra rehearsal; **~sitz** *m Theat.* stall, *Am.* orchestra (seat); **~stück** *n* orchestral work (*od.* piece), piece for orchestra

orchestral *Adj.* orchestral

orchestrieren *v/t.* orchestrate; **Orchestrierung** *f* orchestration

Orchestrion *n*; *-s, Orchestrien*; *Mus.* orchestrion

Orchidee *f*; *-, -n*; *Bot.* orchid

Orden *m*; *-s, -* **1.** *kirchl. etc.* order; **2.** (*Auszeichnung*) decoration; *rund, aus Metall*: medal; **ordengeschmückt**

Adj. ... covered in medals, bemedal(l)ed; **Ordensband** *n* (decoration) ribbon

Ordens|bruder *m kirchl.* member of a monastic order, monk; **~frau** *f kirchl.* member of an order, nun; **~geistliche** *m* priest belonging to an order; **~geistlichkeit** *f* regular clergy *Pl.*; **~mann** *m* monk (of an order); **~priester** *m* priest belonging to an order; **~regel** *f* rule of a religious order; **~ritter** *m* knight of an order; **~schwester** *f* sister (of an order); **~tracht** *f kirchl.* habit (of a religious order)

Ordensverleihung *f* award of a decoration (*od.* medal)

ordentlich I. *Adj.* **1.** (*geordnet*) tidy, orderly; *Handschrift etc.*: neat,; **2.** (*ordnungsliebend*) tidy, orderly; **3.** (*geregelt*) *Leben etc.*: orderly; **4.** (*anständig*) respectable; **etwas Ordentliches lernen** learn a proper trade; **5.** (*planmäßig*) *Stellung etc.*: regular; **~e Kündigung** dismissal in due form; **~er Professor** *Univ.* (full) professor; → *Gericht¹* 1, *Mitglied*; **6.** *umg.* (*zufriedenstellend*) *Essen etc.*: decent; (*gehörig*) proper, decent; **e-e ~e Leistung** a really good job (*od.* piece of work); **e-n ~en Schluck nehmen** take a really good swig; **e-e ~e Tracht Prügel** a sound thrashing; **II.** *Adv.* **1.** tidily, neatly; **die Flaschen waren ~ aufgereiht** the bottles stood in a neat row; **räum dein Zimmer ~ auf** give your room a proper tidy (*Am.* a good cleanup); **2.** (*ganz gut*): (*ganz*) **~** pretty well; **er hat es ganz ~ gemacht** he made a decent (*od.* pretty good) job of it; **3.** *umg.* (*sehr*) really; **es hat ~ geschneit** the snow really came down; **j-n ~ verprügeln** give s.o. a sound thrashing

Order *f*; *-, -s und -n* **1.** *Mil., sonst altm.* order; **sich an s-e ~ halten** stick to one's orders; **auf ~ von** on the orders of; **2.** *Pl. -s*; *Wirts.* order; **an eigene ~** to my own order; **~eingang** *m Wirts.* receipt of an order; *Pl.* receipts of orders, incoming orders

ordern *vt/i.* order

Ordinale *n*; *-(s), Ordinalia*, **Ordinalzahl** *f Ling.* ordinal (number)

ordinär I. *Adj.* **1.** *mst pej.* (*vulgär*) vulgar; *im Aussehen*: tacky; *Witz, etc.*: dirty; **2.** *mst pej. Person, Aussehen etc.*: common; **3.** (*alltäglich, gewöhnlich*) ordinary, unremarkable; **4.** (*billig*) cheap, tawdry, *umg.* cheapo; **II.** *Adv.* in a vulgar way; **~ aussehen** look tacky; **ihr Lachen klingt ~** she has a vulgar laugh

Ordinariat *n*; *-(e)s, -e* **1.** *kirchl.* ordinariate, diocesan administration; **2.** *Univ.* chair; **Ordinarius** *m*; *-, Ordinarien* (full) professor

Ordinate *f*; *-, -n*; *Math.* ordinate; **Ordinatenachse** *f* axis of ordinates

Ordination *f*; *-, -en* **1.** *kirchl.* ordination; **2.** *Med.* (*Verordnung*) prescription; **3.** *österr. Med.* (*Arztpraxis, Sprechzimmer*) surgery; (*Sprechstunde*) consulting (*od.* surgery) hours *Pl.*, *Am.* office hours *Pl.*; **ordinieren** *v/t.* **1.** *kirchl.* ordain; **2.** *Med.* prescribe

ordnen I. *v/t.* (*sortieren*) sort (out), arrange; (*Gedanken*) sort out; (*Akten etc.*) organize, file; (*Blumen*) arrange; (*regeln*)(*Sache*) settle; (*Verkehr etc.*) regulate; (*sein Leben*) sort out; (*s-e Finanzen, Angelegenheiten*) put in order; **alphabetisch ~** arrange alphabeti-

cally (*od.* in alphabetical order); **nach Klassen ~** classify; → **geordnet**; **II.** *v/refl.*: **sich zu etw. ~** form into s.th.

Ordner *m*; *-s, -* **1.** (*Saal-, Festordner*) steward; *im Stadion, bei Umzügen, Autorennen etc.: auch* marshal; **2.** (*Hefter*) file; **3.** *EDV* (file) directory; **e-n ~ anlegen** compile a directory; **Ordnerin** *f*; *-, -nen* → *Ordner* 1

Ordnung *f* **1.** (*das Ordnen*) sorting, arrangement; *von Akten etc.*: organization; (*Regelung*) settlement; *von Verkehr*: regulation: *von Finanzen, Angelegenheiten*: putting in order; **2.** (*bestimmter Zustand*) order; **die öffentliche ~** law and order; **die göttliche ~** the divine order; **zur ~ rufen** call to order (*auch Parl.*); **3.** (*Ordentlichsein*) order, tidiness; **der ~ halber** for form's sake; **~ halten** keep things in order; **sehr auf ~ halten** be very keen on tidiness; **für ~ sorgen** maintain order; **~ schaffen** sort things out; *im Zimmer etc.*: tidy up; **~ muss sein!** you have to have order; **~ ist das halbe Leben** *Sprichw.* keeping things in order is half the battle; **4.** (*Gesundsein, Funktionieren*) order; **in ~ bringen** (*reparieren*) fix; (*erledigen*) settle, *umg.* fix; (*Problem etc.*) sort out; **in ~ sein** *umg.* be all right; **der Motor** *etc.* **ist nicht in ~** *umg.* there's something wrong with the engine *etc.*; **er ist nicht in ~** *umg.*, *gesundheitlich*: he's not well; **5.** *in Wertungen*: **sie ist in ~** there's nothing wrong with her, she's a nice person; **geht in ~!** *umg.* (that's) all right, *umg.* (that's) okay; **es ist alles in bester ~** everything's just fine; **das finde ich nicht in ~** *umg.* I don't think that's right; **6.** (*Vorschriften*) rules *Pl.*, regulations *Pl.*; **ein Verstoß gegen die geltende ~** an offence against current regulations; **7.** (*geordnete Lebensweise*) routine; **jedes Kind braucht seine ~** every child needs a routine; **8.** (*Rang*) order (*auch Bio.*); **... erster ~ ...** of the first order, *auch* first-class (*od.* -rate) ...; **Stern erster ~** *Astron.* star of the first magnitude; **9.** (*Anordnung*) arrangement, order; (*System*) *auch* system

Ordnungs|amt *n* (municipal) public order office; **~dienst** *m* duty as a steward (*bei Umzügen etc.*: marshal); (*Personen*) stewards, marshals; **~fimmel** *umg.* m obsession with tidiness (*od.* orderliness); **~geld** *n* → *Ordnungsstrafe*

ordnungs|gemäß I. *Adj.* proper, according to the rules; **II.** *Adv.* in due form; **~halber** *Adv.* as a matter of form

Ordnungs|hüter *m*, **~hüterin** *f mst iro.* custodian of the law; **~kräfte** *Pl.* law enforcement officers

Ordnungsliebe *f* love of order, (strong sense of) orderliness; **ordnungsliebend** *Adj.* orderly, tidy-minded

Ordnungsmacht *f* law enforcement agency; *im Ausland*: peacekeeper

ordnungsmäßig *Adj. und Adv.* **1.** (*nach e-m System*) in accordance with a certain (*od.* with the) system; **2.** *umg.* → *ordnungsgemäß*

Ordnungs|prinzip *n* system; **~ruf** *m bes. Parl.* call to order; **sich** (*Dat.*) **e-n ~ einhandeln** be called to order; **~strafe** *f* fine

ordnungswidrig I. *Adj.* against the regulations; *Parken etc.*: illegal; **II.** *Adv. parken etc.*: illegally; **sich ~**

verhalten infringe the regulations; **Ordnungswidrigkeit** *f* infringement of the regulations

Ordnungszahl *f* ordinal (number); *der Atome*: atomic number

Ordo(n)nanz *f*; -, -*en*; *Mil.* orderly; **~offizier** *m* orderly officer, aide-de-camp

Öre *n*; -*s*, - *od. f*; -, - *Währungseinheit*: öre

Oregano *m*; -, *kein Pl.*; *Bot.* oregano

ORF *m*; -(*s*), *kein Pl.*; *Abk.* (**Österreichischer Rundfunk**) Austrian Radio

Organ *n*; -*s*, -*e* **1.** *Anat.* organ; **2.** *umg.* (*Stimme*) voice; *die hat aber ein lautes ~!* she's got a voice like a foghorn; **3.** *fig.* (*Zeitung etc.*) organ; **4.** (*Amt, Stelle*) authority; *ausführendes ~ Pol.* executive body; **~bank** *f* organ bank

Organelle *f*; -, -*n*; *Bio.* organelle

Organ|einpflanzung *f Med.* implant (*of an od.* the organ); **~empfänger** *m*, **~empfängerin** *f* organ recipient; **~handel** *m* sale of (transplant) organs

Organigramm *n*; -*s*, -*e*; *Wirts.* organigram, organization chart

Organisation *f*; -, -*en* **1.** (*Zweckverband*) organization; *karitative ~en* charity organizations; **2.** *nur Sg.*; (*Organisieren*) organization; *die ~ des Parteitags lief reibungslos* organization-wise the party conference went without a hitch; **3.** (*Struktur*) organization

Organisations|form *f* form of organization; **~gabe** *f* organizational talent, talent for organization; **~grad** *m* *gewerkschaftlich*: level of (union) membership; **~plan** *m Wirts.* organizational plan; **~talent** *n* organizational talent, talent for organization; *sie ist ein wahres ~* she has a real talent for organization, she's really good at organizing

Organisator *m*; -*s*, -*en*, **~in** *f*; -, -*nen* organizer; **organisatorisch I.** *Adj.* organizational; **~e Probleme** organizational problems; **II.** *Adv.*: *~ begabt sein* have a talent for organization, be good at organizing

organisch *auch fig.* **I.** *Adj.* organic; **II.** *Adv.* organically

organisieren I. *v/t.* **1.** organize; (*Ausstellung*) *auch* mount; *das organisierte Verbrechen* organized crime; **2.** *umg.* (*beschaffen*) rustle up; **II.** *v/i.* organize things; *sie kann gut ~* she's good at organizing; **III.** *v/refl.* get together; (*gewerkschaftlich*) *organisierte/nicht organisierte Arbeitnehmer* unionized/non-union employees; → *auch* **gewerkschaftlich**

Organismus *m*; -, *Organismen* organism (*auch fig.*)

Organist *m*; -*en*, -*en*, **~in** *f*; -, -*nen* organist

Organizer ['ɔːɡənaɪzə] *m*; -*s*, - *Computer*: organizer

Organ|klage *f Jur.* suit brought by one federal institution against another *before the Federal Constitutional Court*; **~konserve** *f Med.* stored organ; **~mandat** *n österr., Amtsspr.* on-the-spot fine

Organogramm *n*; -*s*, -*e* **1.** *Psych.* diagram showing the assimilation of information by an organism; **2.** *Wirts.* organigram, organization chart

Organ|spende *f Med.* donation of an organ; **~spender** *m*, **~spenderin** *f* organ donor; **~transplantation** *f* organ transplant

Organverpflanzung *f Med.* organ transplant

Orgasmus *m*; -, *Orgasmen* orgasm; **orgastisch** *Adj.* orgasmic

Orgel *f*; -, -*n*; *Mus.* organ; **~bauer** *m*; -*s*, -, **~bauerin** *f*; -, -*nen* organ builder; **~konzert** *n* **1.** organ recital; **2.** (*Werk*) organ concerto; **~musik** *f* organ music

orgeln *v/i.* **1.** *Drehorgel*: grind (*od.* play) the barrel organ; **2.** *umg.* (*dröhnen*) roar; **3.** *vulg.* (*koitieren*) have a screw

Orgel|pfeife *f Mus.* organ pipe; *wie die ~n dastehen hum.* stand (in a row) in order of size; **~prospekt** *m* organ case; **~punkt** *m* pedal (*od.* organ) point; **~register** *n* organ stop; **~werk** *n* organ work

orgiastisch I. *Adj.* orgiastic; **II.** *Adv.* orgiastically; **Orgie** *f*; -, -*n* orgy (*auch fig.*); **~n feiern** have orgies

Orient *m*; -*s*, *kein Pl.*; *Geog.* **1.** Middle East and Central Asia; *der Vordere ~ Pol.* mst the Middle East; *hist.* the Levant; **2.** *altm.* Orient; **Orientale** *m*; -*n*, -*n*, **Orientalin** *f*; -, -*nen* person from the Middle East (or Central Asia); **orientalisch** *Adj.* (Middle) Eastern; **Orientalist** *m*; -*en*, -*en* (Middle Eastern) orientalist; **Orientalistik** *f*; -, *kein Pl.* Middle Eastern and oriental studies *Pl.*; **Orientalistin** *f*; -, -*nen* (Middle Eastern) orientalist; **orientalistisch** *Adj.* orientalist

orientieren I. *v/t.* **1.** (*informieren*) *j-n ~* inform s.o. (*über + Akk.* about), put s.o. in the picture (about), fill s.o. in (on); **2.** (*ausrichten*) orientate, *Am. auch* orient (*nach* towards); *nach links/rechts orientiert Pol.* oriented towards the left/right, with leftwing/rightwing orientation; **3.** *Dial.* (*hinlenken, -führen*): *j-n auf etw.* (*Akk.*) *~* point s.o. in the direction of s.th.; *alle Kräfte auf ein Ziel ~* direct (*od.* concentrate) all one's efforts on achieving an aim; **II.** *v/refl.* **1.** in e-r Stadt etc.: get (*od.* find) one's bearings (*an + Dat.* by); **2.** (*sich informieren*) inform o.s. (*über + Akk.* about, on); *gut orientiert* (*informiert*) well-informed, in the picture; **3.** *sich ~ an* (+ *Dat.*) (*sich ausrichten*) be orientated towards, be geared to; (*j-n als Leitbild nehmen*) model o.s. on; **4.** *Dial.* (*sich richten*): *sich auf etw.* (*Akk.*) *~* concentrate one's attention on s.th.

...orientiert *im Adj.*: *erfolgs~* orientated towards success, concentrating on success; *gewinn~* profit-oriented

Orientierung *f* **1.** orientation (*nach* towards) (*auch fig.*); *die ~ auf* (+ *Akk.*) the concentration (of attention) on; *die ~ verlieren auch fig.* lose one's bearings; **2.** (*Informieren*) informing; *zu Ihrer ~* for your information (*od.* guidance)

Orientierungs|daten *Pl. Wirts.* guideline data; **~hilfe** *f auch Pl.* guidance; *konkret*: guide; (*Einführung*) introduction; (*Orientierungspunkt*) landmark; (*Bezugspunkt*) reference point; *er gab mir e-e Karte als ~* he gave me a map to help me find my way; **~lauf** *m Sport* orienteering (race)

orientierungslos *Adj.* disoriented

Orientierungs|punkt *m* landmark; (*Bezugspunkt*) reference point; **~sinn** *m*; *nur Sg.* sense of direction, ability to find one's way; **~stufe** *f Päd.* two-year assessment stage after which pupils are allocated to appropriate secondary schools; **~zeichen** *n* landmark

Orientteppich *m* oriental carpet, *mst* Persian carpet

original I. *Adj.* original; (*echt*) genuine; **II.** *Adv. ~ verpackt* in the original packaging; *die Vase ist ~ 2. Dynastie* it is a genuine (*od.* authentic) Second Dynasty vase; *~ übertragen TV etc.*: transmit live

Original *n*; -*s*, -*e* **1.** (*Bild etc.*) original; (*Film*) original version; (*Schriftstück*) *auch* original copy; (*Tonband etc.*) master (copy); *im ~* in the original; *der Titel lautet im* (*englischen*) *~ ...* the original (English) title is ...; **2.** *umg.* (*Person*) (real) character

Original|abfüllung *f Wein*: estate-bottled wine; *Aufschrift*: estate-bottled; **~aufnahme** *f Tonband etc.*: original recording; *Foto*: original photograph; *Film etc.*: original copy; **~ausgabe** *f* first edition; **~dokument** *n* original document; **~fassung** *f* original version

originalgetreu I. *Adj.* faithful (to the original); **II.** *Adv.*: *~ nachbilden* copy faithfully (*od.* accurately)

Originalgröße *f* actual (*od.* original) size; *... in ~* actual-size ...; (*sehr groß*) full-size ...

Originalität *f*; -, *kein Pl.*; (*Echtheit*) genuineness, authenticity; (*Eigenständigkeit*) originality

Original|packung *f* original packaging; **~schauplatz** *m* actual site; *geschichtlich*: *auch* historical site; *an Originalschauplätzen gedreht Film etc.*: shot on location; **~text** *m* original (text); **~titel** *m* original title, title in the original language; **~ton** *m*; *nur Sg.* original sound; *Film*: live sound(track); *~ X* original sound of X; **~übertragung** *f TV etc.* live broadcast

originär *Adj.* original

originell I. *Adj.* **1.** original; (*neuartig*) novel; (*geistreich, witzig*) witty; *ein ~er Kopf sein* have an original (*od.* innovative) mind; **2.** *umg.* (*sonderbar, komisch*) strange, peculiar; **II.** *Adv.* originally; *das war ~ ausgedacht* that shows original (*od.* innovative) thinking

Orinoko *m*; -*s*; *Geog.*: *der ~* the Orinoco

Orion *m*; -*s*, *kein Pl.*; *Astron.* Orion

Orkan *m*; -(*e*)*s*, -*e* hurricane; **orkanartig** *Adj. Sturm*: almost hurricane-force ..., extremely violent; *Beifall*: thunderous; **~e Winde** force 11 gales; **Orkantief** *n Met.* hurricane-force depression (*od.* cyclone *od.* low); **Orkanstärke** *f*; *nur Sg.* hurricane force

Ornament *n*; -(*e*)*s*, -*e* ornament; (*Ornamentik*) *auch* ornamentation, decoration; *mit ~en* ornamented; **ornamental** *Adj. Kunst* ornamental, decorative; **Ornamentform** *f* ornamental form; **ornamentieren** *v/t.* ornament, decorate; **Ornamentik** *f*; -, *kein Pl.*; *Kunst* **1.** ornamentation; **2.** *e-r Kunstepoche etc.*: decorative art

Ornat *m*; -(*e*)*s*, -*e* robes *Pl.*, vestments *Pl.*; *in vollem ~ umg. hum.* in full fig

Ornithologe *m*; -*en*, -*en* ornithologist; *Laie*: bird-watcher; **Ornithologie** *f*; -, *kein Pl.* ornithology; *Hobby*: bird-watching; **Ornithologin** *f*; -, -*nen* → **Ornithologe**; **ornithologisch** *Adj.* ornithological

Orogenese *f*; -, -*n*; *Geol.* orogeny, orogenesis; **orogenetisch** *Adj.* orogenic

Ort¹ *m*; -(*e*)*s*, -*e* **1.** (*Platz, Stelle*) place; *der ~ der Handlung* the scene of the action; *ein ~ des Grauens* a place that inspires horror; *an ~ und Stelle* on the spot; *fig.* (*sofort*) *auch* there and then;

an ~ und Stelle gelangen reach one's destination; **es steht nicht an s-m ~** it's not where it belongs (*od.* should be); **am angegebenen ~** in the book already quoted, loc. cit.; **geometrischer ~** *Math.* locus (*Pl.* loci); **vor ~** (*an ~ und Stelle*) on the spot; (*am Arbeitsplatz*) on the job; **dies ist nicht der ~ für ...** *fig.* this is not the (time or) place for ...; **höheren ~(e)s** at a higher level; **2.** (*Ortschaft*) place; (*Dorf*) *auch* village; (*Stadt*) *auch* town

Ort² *n*; -(e)s, Örter; *Bergb.* coalface; **vor ~** at the face

Örtchen *n*; -s, -; *umg.*: **das (stille) ~** the loo, *Am.* the john

orten *v/t. Naut., Flug.* locate (*auch fig.*)

orthodox *Adj. Reli.* Orthodox; *fig.* orthodox; **die ~e Kirche** the Orthodox Church; → **griechisch-orthodox**; **Orthodoxie** *f*; -, *kein Pl.* orthodoxy

Orthographie *f*,, -n; *Ling.* orthography, spelling; **orthographisch I.** *Adj.* spelling ...; *fachspr.* orthographic(al); **II.** *Adv.*: **~ falsch/richtig** wrongly/correctly spelt

Orthopäde *m*; -en, -en; *Med.* orthop(a)edist; **Orthopädie** *f*; -, *kein Pl.* **1.** orthop(a)edics *Pl.*(*mst V. im Sg.*); **2.** *umg. Abteilung*: **auf der ~ liegen** be (a patient) in the orthop(a)edic department, be in an orthop(a)edic ward; **Orthopädin** *f*; -, *-nen* orthop(a)edist; **orthopädisch I.** *Adj.* orthop(a)edic; **II.** *Adv.* orthop(a)edically

Orthoptik *f Med.* orthoptics *Pl.* (*V. im Sg.*)

örtlich I. *Adj.* local; → **Betäubung** 1; **II.** *Adv.* locally; **das ist ~ verschieden** it varies from place to place; **Örtlichkeit** *f* **1.** locality, place; **die ~en kennen lernen** *od.* **sich mit den ~en vertraut machen** get to know (*od.* familiarize o.s. with) the area; **2.** *euph.* (*Toilette*) loo, *Am.* john

Orts|anfang *m*: **am ~ wohnen** live on the way into the village (*Stadt*: town); **~angabe** *f* place name (given in the address)

ortsansässig *Adj.* local; **ihre Familie ist schon lange ~** her family has been living locally (*im Dorf*: in the village, *in der Stadt*: in the town) for a long time; **Ortsansässige** *m*, *f*; -n, -n local resident; *im Dorf*: village resident; *in der Stadt*: resident of the town

Orts|ausgang *m* way out of the village (*Stadt*: town); **~begehung** *f* inspection of the locality (*Schauplatz*: scene); **~bereich** *m* local area; **im ~ Neuharlaching** in the Neuharlaching area; **~beschaffenheit** *f* topography; **~besichtigung** *f* **1.** *am Schauplatz*: inspection of (*od.* visit to) the scene; **2.** *e-r Ortschaft*: tour of the place; **~bestimmung** *f* **1.** (*Ortung*) position finding, location; **2.** *Ling.* adverbial qualification of place

ortsbeweglich *Adj. Tech. etc.* mobile

Ortsbild *n* appearance of the place; *e-r Stadt*: townscape

Ortschaft *f* place, locality; (*Dorf*) village; **geschlossene ~** built-up area

Orts|eingang *m* way into the village (*Stadt*: town); → *auch* **Ortsanfang**; **~empfang** *m Funk.* local reception; **~ende** *n*: **am ~ wohnen** live at the end of the village (*Stadt*: town)

orts|fest *Adj. Tech. etc.* stationary; **~fremd** *Adj.* non-local, outside ...; **~e Personen** people from outside the village (*Stadt*: town), strangers to the locality; **~gebunden** *Adj.* stationary; *In-*

dustrie: resources-bound; *Person*: tied to the locality

Orts|gespräch *n Telef.* local call; **~gruppe** *f* local branch; **~kenntnis** *f* local knowledge; **~kern** *m* cent|re (*Am.* -er) of the village (*Stadt*: town); **~krankenkasse** *f*: **Allgemeine ~** (*abgek.* AOK) *local branch of the national health insurance scheme*

ortskundig *Adj.*: **~ sein** know the place; (*sich auskennen*) know one's way around; **da müssen Sie einen Ortskundigen fragen** you must ask someone who knows the place

Orts|mitte *f* cent|re (*Am.* -er) of the village (*Stadt*: town); **~name** *m* place name; **~namenkunde** *f Ling.* research into place names; **~netz** *n Telef.* local exchange network; *Elektr.* local grid; **~netzkennzahl** *f Telef.* dialling code, *Am.* area code; **~polizei** *f* local police; **~präsident** *m*, **~präsidentin** *f schw.* chairperson of the town council; **~rand** *m* edge of the village (*Stadt*: town); **~schild** *n* place name sign, *Am.* city limit(s) marker; **~sender** *m* local radio station; **~sinn** *m*; *nur Sg.* sense of direction; **~tarif** *m Telef.*: (**zum**) **~** (at the) local rate; **~teil** *m* part of the town (*Dorf*: village)

ortsüblich *Adj.* customary local ...; → **Vergleichsmiete**

Ortsumgehung *f Verk.* bypass; (*Ringstraße*) ring road, *Am.* beltway

ortsungebunden *Adj. Person*: mobile; *weitS.* flexible; **~ sein** not be tied to a place

Orts|veränderung *f* → **Ortswechsel**; **~verein** *m* local association; **~verkehr** *m* local traffic; *Telef.* local telephone service; **~wechsel** *m* **1.** change of location; **2.** *fig.* change of scenery; **~zeit** *f* local time; **~zentrum** *n* → **Ortsmitte**; **~zulage** *f*, **~zuschlag** *m* weighting (allowance)

Ortung *f Naut., Flug.* position finding, location, locating; **Ortungsgerät** *n* position-finder

Oscar *m*; -s, -s *Film*: Oscar, Academy Award; **Oscarpreisträger** *m*, **Oscarpreisträgerin** *f* Oscar winner; **oscarverdächtig** *Adj. umg.* ... with a good chance of winning an Oscar; **~ sein** be an Oscar prospect; **Oscarverleihung** *f* Oscar award ceremony, *umg.* the Oscars

Öse *f*; -, -n eye; *Schuh*: eyelet

Oskar *m*: **er ist frech wie ~** *umg.* he's a cheeky devil

Osmane *m*; -n, -n, **Osmanin** *f*; -, *-nen*; *hist.* Ottoman; **osmanisch** *Adj.* Ottoman; **das Osmanische Reich** the Ottoman Empire

Osmium *n*; -s, *kein Pl.*; *Chem.* osmium

Osmose *f*; -, -n; *Bio., Chem.* osmosis; **osmotisch** *Adj.* osmotic

Ösophagus *m*; -, Ösophagi; *Anat.* (o)esophagus (*Pl.* [o]esophagi *od.* [o]esophaguses)

Ossi¹ *m*; -s, -s; *umg., oft pej.* East German type, Easterner

Ossi² *f*; -, -s; *umg., oft pej.* East German female, Easterner

Ost *m* **1.** *ohne Art.*; *nur Nom. Sg.*; *Met., Naut.* east; **von** *od.* **aus ~** from the east; **aus ~ und West** from East and West; *fig.* from all over the world; **2.** *ohne Art.*; *nur Nom. Sg.*; *nachgestellt*: **München ~** the east of Munich; **Eingang ~** the east entrance; **3.** -(e)s, -e; *Pl. selten*; *Naut., poet. Wind*: east wind, easterly; **4.** *ohne Art.*; *nur Nom. Sg.*; *nachgestellt*: **Aufbau ~** *hist., Pol.,*

Wirts. the rebuilding of the East German economy

Ostafrika (*n*); *Geog.* East Africa; **Ostafrikaner** *m*, **Ostafrikanerin** *f* East African; **ostafrikanisch** *Adj.* East African

Ost|agent *m*, **~agentin** *f* **1.** *hist.* Eastern Bloc agent (*od.* spy); **2.** *engS.* Russian (*od.* KGB) spy

Ostalgie *f*; -, *kein Pl.*; *umg.* nostalgia for the good old days of the GDR

ostasiatisch *Adj.* East Asian; **Ostasien** (*n*); *Geog.* East(ern) Asia

Ostblock *m*; *nur Sg.*; *hist.* Eastern Bloc; **~land** *n*, **~staat** *m hist.* Eastern Bloc country

ostdeutsch *Adj.* **1.** Eastern German; **im ~en Teil** in the eastern part of Germany, in Eastern Germany; **2.** *ehem. DDR*: East German; **Ostdeutsche** *m*, *f* **1.** Eastern German; **2.** *ehem. DDR*: East German; **Ostdeutschland** (*n*) **1.** *Geog.* Eastern Germany; **2.** *hist.* (*DDR*) East Germany

ostelbisch *Adj.* ... east of the Elbe

Osten *m*; -s, *kein Pl.* (*abgek.* O) east (*Abk.* E); (*östlicher Landesteil*) East; **nach ~** east(wards); *Verkehr, Straße etc.*: eastbound ...; **aus dem ~** from the east; **der ~ e-r Stadt**: the eastern part (*od.* districts *Pl.*); → **fern** I 1, **mittler...** 1, **nah** I 1

ostentativ *Adj.* (*unmissverständlich*) unmistakable, pointed; (*demonstrativ*) exaggerated, studied

Osteopathie *f*; -, -n; *Med.* osteopathy

Osteoporose *f*; -, -n; *Med.* osteoporosis (*Pl.* osteoporoses)

Osterbrauch *m Volkskunde*: Easter custom

Osterei *n* Easter egg; **Ostereiersuche** *f* Easter egg hunt

Oster|feiertag *m*: **am ersten/zweiten ~** on Easter Sunday/Monday; **über die ~e** over the Easter weekend; **~ferien** *Pl.* Easter holidays; **~fest** *n* Easter (holiday); **~feuer** *n* Easter eve bonfire; **~glocke** *f Bot.* daffodil; **~hase** *m* Easter bunny

Osterinsel *f Geog.*: **die ~** Easter Island

Oster|kerze *f kath.* paschal candle; **~lamm** *n* paschal lamb

österlich I. *Adj.* Easter ...; **es sieht sehr ~ aus** it looks (very much) like Easter; **II.** *Adv.*: **~ geschmückt** decorated for Easter, with Easter decorations

Ostermarsch *m* Easter march

Oster|montag *m* Easter Monday; **~morgen** *m* Easter (Sunday) morning

Ostern *n*; -, - Easter; **an** *od.* **zu ~** at Easter; **frohe** *od.* **fröhliche ~!** Happy Easter

Osternacht *f* Easter eve; *kirchliche Feier*: Easter eve service

Österreich (*n*); -s; *Geog.* Austria; **Österreicher** *m*; -s, -, **Österreicherin** *f*; -, -nen Austrian, *weiblich auch*: Austrian woman (*od.* girl); **österreichisch** *Adj.* Austrian; **österreichisch-ungarisch** *Adj. hist.* Austro--Hungarian; **Österreich-Ungarn** (*n*); -s; *hist.* Austria-Hungary

Oster|sonntag *m* Easter Sunday; **~spiel** *n Lit.* Easter play, passion play

Osterweiterung *f Pol.* eastward expansion

Oster|woche *f* Easter week; **~zeit** *f*; *nur Sg.* Eastertide

Osteuropa (*n*); *Geog.* Eastern Europe; **Osteuropäer** *m*, **Osteuropäerin** *f* East (*od.* Eastern) European; **osteuropäisch** *Adj.* East (*od.* Eastern) Eu-

O

ropean

Ost|flanke *f* eastern flank; *e-s Hoch-od. Tiefdruckgebietes*: eastern edge; **~flüchtling** *m hist.* refugee from the East (*aus der DDR*: from East Germany); **~flügel** *m e-s Gebäudes*: east wing

Ostfriese *m* East Frisian; **Ostfriesenwitz** *m* East Frisian joke, *etwa* Irish joke; **Ostfriesin** *f* East Frisian (woman *od.* girl); **ostfriesisch** *Adj.* East Frisian; *die Ostfriesischen Inseln* the East Frisian Islands; **Ostfriesland** (*n*); *Geog.* East Friesland

Ost|front *f hist.* eastern front; **~gebiet** *n* eastern area; *die deutschen ~e hist.* Germany's eastern territories; **~geld** *n*; *nur Sg.*; *hist. umg.* East German money

Ostgote *m*, **Ostgotin** *f hist.* Ostrogoth; **ostgotisch** *Adj.* Ostrogothic

Ost|jude *m*, **~jüdin** *f* East European Jew; **~kirche** *f* Eastern Orthodox Church; **~küste** *f* east coast; *an der ~* on the east coast

Ostler *m*; *-s, -*, **~in** *f*; *-, -nen*; *umg., oft pej.* East German type

östlich I. *Adj.* eastern, east …; *Wind, Richtung*: easterly; *Pol.* Eastern; *das ist sehr weit ~* that's a long way (to the) east; *15° ~er Länge* 15° east; **II.** *Adv.* (to the) east (*von* of); *weiter ~ liegen* be further east; **III.** *Präp.* (+ *Gen.*) east of; **östlichst…** *Adj.* easternmost

Ostmark¹ *f hist. Währung*: East German mark

Ostmark² *f*; *nur Sg.*; *hist.* **1.** *im Mittelalter*: East March; **2.** *Nazizeit*: Austria

Ostnordost *m* **1.** *ohne Art.*; *nur Sg.* (*abgek.* **ONO**); *Met., Naut.* east-north-heast (*Abk.* ENE); **2.** *Naut., Wind*: east-northeasterly

Ostpolitik *f Pol., hist.* ostpolitik

Ostpreußen (*n*); *Geog. hist.* East Prussia; **Ostpreuße** *m*, **Ostpreußin** *f* East Prussian; **ostpreußisch** *Adj.* East Prussian

Ostrand *m* eastern edge

Östrogen *n*; *-s, -e* (o)estrogen; **~spiegel** *m* (o)estrogen level

Ostrom (*n*); *hist.* the Eastern (Roman) Empire, the Byzantine Empire; **oströmisch** *Adj.*: *das Oströmische Reich* the Eastern (Roman) Empire, the Byzantine Empire

Ostsee *f Geog.*: *die ~* the Baltic; **~insel** *f* Baltic island; **~küste** *f* Baltic coast

Ost|seite *f* east side; **~spitze** *f* easternmost point; *e-s Sees*: eastern end

Ostsüdost *m* **1.** *ohne Art.*; *nur Sg.* (*abgek.* OSO); *Met., Naut.* east-southeast (*Abk.* ESE); **2.** *Naut. Wind*: east-southeasterly

Ost|teil *m* eastern part; **~wand** *f* east wall

ostwärts *Adv.* east(wards)

Ost-West|-Beziehungen *Pl. Pol.* East-West relations; **~Konflikt** *m*; *nur Sg.*; *hist.* East-West conflict

ostwestlich *Adj. und Adv.* east-west …, … from east to west

Ostwestrichtung *f*: *in ~ verlaufen* run from east to west

Ostwind *m* east wind

Ostzone *f*; *nur Sg.*; *altm.* **1.** Eastern (*od.* Soviet) zone; **2.** *hist., mst pej.* (*DDR*) East Germany

Oszillation *f*; *-, -en*; *Phys.* oscillation; **Oszillator** *m*; *-s, -en* oscillator; **oszillieren** *v/i.* oscillate

Oszillogramm *n*; *-s, -e*; *Phys., Med.* oscillogram

Oszillograph *m*; *-en, -en* oscillograph

Oszilloskop *n* oscilloscope, *umg.* scope

O-Ton *m umg.* original sound; → *auch* **Originalton**

Otoskop *n*; *-s, -e*; *Med.* otoscope

Otter¹ *f*; *-, -n*; *Zool.* viper, adder

Otter² *m*; *-s, -*; *Zool.* (*Fischotter*) otter

Otterngezücht *n geh., poet.* nest of vipers

Otto *m*; *-s, -s*; *umg.* **1.** *sehr groß*: whopper; **2.** *den flotten ~ haben* have the runs; **3.** *~ Normalverbraucher* your average (high-street) punter, Joe Bloggs, *Am.* Joe Blow

Ottomane¹ *f*; *-, -n*; *altm.* ottoman

Ottomane² *m*; *-n, -n*; *hist.* Ottoman

Ottomotor *m Mot.* Otto engine, four-stroke (internal combustion) engine

ÖTV *f*; *-, kein Pl.*; *Abk.* (**Gewerkschaft Öffentliche Dienste, Transport und Verkehr**) Public Service and Transport Union

out [aʊt] *Adv.* **1.** *umg.*: *~ sein Mode etc.*: be out; **2.** *österr. Sport*: *der Ball ist ~* the ball is out of play

Out [aʊt] *n*; *-(s), -(s)*; *österr. Sport*: *ins ~ gehen* go out of play

outen ['aʊtn] *umg.* **I.** *v/t.* out (*auch fig. hum.*); **II.** *v/refl.* come out

Outfit ['aʊtfɪt] *n*; *-(s), -s*; (*Kleidung, Ausstattung*) outfit

Outing ['aʊtɪŋ] outing; (*Selbstouting*) coming-out

Output ['aʊtpʊt] *m, n*; *-s, -s*; *Wirts., EDV* output

Outsourcing ['aʊtsɔːrsɪŋ] *n*; *-(s), kein Pl.*; *Wirts.* outsourcing

Ouvertüre [uver'tyːrə] *f*; *-, -n*; *Mus.* overture (*auch fig.*)

Ouzo ['uːzo] *m*; *-(s), -s*; (*Anisschnaps*) ouzo

oval *Adj.* oval; **Oval** *n*; *-s, -e* oval

Ovarium *n*; *-s, Ovarien*; *Anat., Bot.* ovary

Ovation *f*; *-, -en*; *geh.* ovation; *j-m ~en bereiten* give s.o. an ovation; *stehende ~en* standing ovations

OvD, O. v. D. *Abk.* (*Offizier vom Dienst*) *Mil.* duty officer

Overall ['oʊvərɔːl] *m*; *-s, -s* jump suit; (*Arbeitsoverall*) boiler suit, overalls *Pl., Am.* overall

Overhead|folie ['oːvɐhɛt-] *f* overhead transparency; **~projektor** *m* overhead projector

Overkill *n, m*; *-(s), kein Pl.*; *Mil.* overkill (*auch fig.*)

ÖVP *f*; *-, kein Pl.*; *Abk.* (**Österreichische Volkspartei**) Austrian People's Party

Ovulation *f*; *-, -en*; *Physiol.* ovulation; **Ovulationshemmer** *m Med., Pharm.* ovulation inhibitor

Oxalsäure *f Chem.* oxalic acid

Oxid *n*; *-(e)s, -e*; *Chem.* oxide; **Oxidation** *f*; *-, -en* oxidation; **Oxidationsmittel** *n* oxidizing agent, oxidant; **oxidieren I.** *v/i.* (*hat od. ist oxidiert*) oxidize; **II.** *v/t.* (*hat*) oxidize; **Oxidierung** *f* oxidization; **oxidisch** *Adj.* oxidized

Oxigen *n*; *-s, kein Pl.*, **Oxigenium** *n*; *-s, kein Pl.*; *Chem.* oxygen

Oxyd *etc.* → **Oxid** *etc.*

OZ *Abk.* (**Oktanzahl**) octane number (*od.* rating)

Ozean *m*; *-s, -e*; *Geog.* ocean; *der Atlantische ~* the Atlantic Ocean; *der Stille ~* the Pacific Ocean

Ozeandampfer *m* ocean liner

Ozeanien (*n*); *-s*; *Geog.* Oceania

ozeanisch *Adj.* **1.** oceanic; **2.** (*Ozeanien betreffend*) Oceanic

Ozeanographie *f*; *-, kein Pl.* oceanography; **ozeanographisch** *Adj.* oceanographic

Ozeanologe *m*; *-n, -n* oceanologist; **Ozeanologie** *f*; *-, kein Pl.* oceanology; **Ozeanologin** *f*; *-, -nen* (female) oceanologist; **ozeanologisch** *Adj.* oceanological

Ozean|riese *m* giant liner, leviathan (of the seas) *lit.*; **~überquerung** *f* ocean crossing

Ozelot *m*; *-s, -e und -s* **1.** *Zool.* ocelot; **2.** *Mantel*: ocelot (coat); *Stola*: ocelot stole

Ozon *m, n*; *-s, kein Pl.* **1.** *Chem., Phys.* ozone; *bodennahes ~* low-level ozone; **2.** *umg. hum.* fresh air; **Ozonabbau** *m* ozone depletion; **Ozongehalt** *m* ozone content; **ozonhaltig** *Adj.* ozoniferous; **ozonisieren** *v/t.* ozonize; **Ozonloch** *n* ozone hole, hole in the ozone layer; **Ozonosphäre** *f*; *nur Sg.*; *Met.* ozonosphere *fachspr.*, ozone layer; **ozonreich** *Adj.* high (*od.* rich) in ozone; **Ozonschicht** *f* ozone layer; **Ozontherapie** *f Med.* ozone therapy; **Ozonwerte** *Pl.* ozone levels

P, p *n*; -, - P, p; *P wie Paula* Buchstabieren: 'p' for (*od.* as in) 'Peter'

Paar *n*; -(*e*)*s*, -*e* **1.** *nach Zahlen, meist Dinge*: pair; *ein/zwei ~ Socken* a pair / two pairs of socks; *ein ~ Frankfurter* two frankfurters; *das sind zwei ~ Stiefel fig.* they are as different as chalk and cheese, this is a different kettle of fish; → *ungleich* I; **2.** (*Mann und Frau; Ehe-, Liebespaar*) couple; (*Tanzpaar*) *auch iro.* pair; *ein neu vermähltes ~* a newly married couple; *sie sind jetzt ein ~* they are man and wife now; *sie sind ein feines ~ iro.* they are a fine pair; **3.** *allg.* (*zwei Personen, Tiere etc.*) pair; *sich in ~en aufstellen* line up in pairs (*od.* by twos); *sie treten immer als ~ auf* you never see one of them without the other; *ein ~ Rebhühner/Fasanen* a brace of partridges/pheasants

paar *unbest. Pron.*: *ein ~* a few, some, a couple of *umg.*; *vor ein ~ Tagen* a couple of days ago, the other day; *alle ~ Minuten* every few minutes; *die ~ Euro wirst du wohl noch ausgeben können* surely you can afford that much; → *Zeile* 1

...paar *n, im Subst. allg.*: couple; *Eltern~* parents *Pl.*, mother and father; *Komiker~* comic duo; *Traum~* perfect couple, ideal couple

Paarbildung *f Phys.* pair production

paaren I. *v/refl.* **1.** *Zool.* mate; **2.** *fig.* (*sich vereinigen*) combine, be combined; *bei ihr paart sich Schnelligkeit mit Genauigkeit* she's fast and very accurate at the same time, she combines speed with accuracy; **II.** *v/t.* **1.** *Zool.* pair, mate; **2.** *fig.* (*Eigenschaften etc.*) combine, couple (*mit* with); **3.** *Sport* (*Mannschaften*) pair off, match (against each other)

Paarhufer *m*; -*s*, - cloven-hoofed animal

paarig *Adj.* in pairs, paired

Paar|lauf *m*, *~laufen n Sport* pair skating

paarmal *Adv.*: *ein ~* a few times, a couple of times *umg.*

Paarreim *m* rhyming couplets *Pl.*

Paarung *f* **1.** *Zool.* mating; **2.** *Sport* match, tie; **3.** *fig.* combination

Paarungs|trieb *m Zool.* mating urge; *~zeit f* mating season

paarweise *Adv.* in pairs, in twos

Pacht *f*; -, -*en* lease; (*~geld*) rent; *etw. in ~ haben* have s.th. on lease(hold); *etw. in ~ nehmen* take s.th. on lease, lease s.th.; *~dauer f* duration of a (*od.* the) lease

pachten I. *v/t.* (take on) lease; **II.** *fig.*: *er tut so, als hätte er die Weisheit für sich gepachtet* he acts as if he was the only person in the world with any brains

Pächter *m*; -*s*, -, *~in f*; -, -*nen* leaseholder; *eines Hofes usw.*: tenant

pachtfrei *Adj.* rent-free

Pacht|geld *n* rent; *~grundstück n* leasehold (property); *~hof m* (leasehold) farm; *~vertrag m* lease; *~zeit f* period of a (*od.* the) lease, term of lease; *~zins m* rent

Pack¹ *m*; -(*e*)*s*, -*e od.* Päcke; (*Bündel*) bundle; → *Sack* 1

Pack² *n*; -*s*, *kein Pl.; pej.* (*Gesindel*) rabble; *faules ~* lazy good-for-nothings; (*Männer*) lazy louts

...pack *m, im Subst. allg.* pack; *Dreier~* pack of three; *Sechser~* pack of six; *bes. bei Bier*: six-pack

Päckchen *n* parcel; *Postbezeichnung*: small packet; *~ Zigaretten* packet (*Am.*) of cigarettes

Packeis *n* pack ice

Packen *m*; -*s*, -; (*Haufen, Stapel, umg. Menge*) pile; (*Bündel*) bundle; *großer ~* (+ *Gen.*) *auch umg.* great wodge (*Am.* huge pile) of

packen I. *vt/i.* **1.** (*Koffer, Sachen etc.*) pack; (*Paket*) wrap up; *EDV* pack; *j-n ins Bett ~ fig.* pack s.o. off to bed; *ich muss noch ~* I still have to pack (my case), I've still got my packing to do; **2.** (*derb anfassen*) grab (hold of); **3.** *fig.* (*fesseln*) grip; *von Furcht etc. gepackt* gripped (*od.* seized) with fear *etc.*; *mich packt die Wut, wenn ich höre, dass ...* I get so angry when I hear that ..., it makes me so mad to hear that ...; *ihn hat's gepackt umg. Krankheit*: he's been laid low; *Liebe*: he's smitten; **4.** *umg. fig.* (*schaffen*) manage; *es ~* (*etw. erreichen, schaffen*) make it, do it; (*zurechtkommen*) manage, cope; **5.** *~ wir's! umg.* (*gehen wir!*) let's go, let's be on our way; **II.** *v/refl.* clear off, beat it

packend I. *Part. Präs.* → *packen*; **II.** *Adj.* gripping, exciting, riveting; **III.** *Adv.*: *es ist ~ erzählt* it's (*od.* it makes for) exciting reading

Packer *m*; -*s*, - **1.** packer; **2.** → *Möbelpacker*; **Packerei** *f*; -, -*en* **1.** packing department (*od.* office); **2.** *nur Sg.; umg.* (*das Packen*) packing; *ich hab diese ewige ~ satt* I'm fed up with this constant packing (and unpacking); **Packerin** *f*; -, -*nen* (female) packer

Pack|esel *m* (pack) mule; *fig.* packhorse; *~leinen n* sacking; *~material n* packing material; *~papier n* (brown) wrapping paper; *~pferd n* packhorse; *~sattel m* pack saddle; *~tasche f* pannier; *~tier n* pack animal

Packung *f* **1.** (*Schachtel*) packet, *Am.* package; *~ Tee* packet (*Am.* package) of tea; *~ Zigaretten* pack(et) of cigarettes; **2.** (*Verpackung*) package, parcel; (*Hülle*) wrapping; **3.** *Med., Kosmetik*: pack, compress; **4.** *Sport umg.* thrashing; *e-e ~ bekommen* get thrashed (*od.* slaughtered)

...packung *f, im Subst. allg.* pack; *Frischhalte~* vacuum (*od.* airtight) pack

Packungsbeilage *f* package insert, enclosed instructions *Pl.*; *zu Risiken und Nebenwirkungen lesen Sie die ~* read the enclosed leaflet for information on risks and side effects

Packzettel *m* packing slip

Pädagoge *m*; -*n*, -*n*, **Pädagogin** *f*; -, -*nen* **1.** (*Lehrer[in]*) teacher; **2.** (*Erziehungswissenschaftler[in]*) educationalist; (*Erzieher*) educator; **Pädagogik** *f* education(al theory), pedagogics (*V. im Sg.*), pedagogy; **pädagogisch I.** *Adj.* educational, pedagogical; *Pädagogische Hochschule* college of education, *Am.* teachers' college; *er hat keinerlei ~e Fähigkeiten* he has no idea how to teach; **II.** *Adv.*: *das ist ~ falsch* that's educationally wrong (*od.* not the way to teach)

Paddel *n*; -*s*, - paddle; **Paddelboot** *n* canoe; **paddeln** *v/i.* paddle

Päderast *m*; -*en*, -*en* pederast; **Päderastie** *f*; -, *kein Pl.* pederasty

Pädiatrie *f*; -, *kein Pl.; Med.* pediatrics (*V. im Sg.*)

paffen *vt/i. umg.* (*rauchen*) puff away (*s-e Pfeife etc.* at one's pipe *etc.*); *sie pafft nur* (*inhaliert nicht*) she just puffs at it, she doesn't inhale

Page *m*; -*n*, -*n* page; **Pagenfrisur** *f*, **Pagenkopf** *m* pageboy (hairstyle)

paginieren *v/t. Druck., EDV* paginate

Pagode *f*; -, -*n* pagoda

Paillette [pai'jɛtə] *f*; -, -*n* sequin; **paillettenbesetzt** *Adj.* sequined

Paket *n*; -(*e*)*s*, -*e* **1.** *Post. etc.* parcel, *Am. auch* package; (*Bündel*) bundle; **2.** (*große Packung*) large pack; **3.** *Pol.* package; **4.** *Wirts. Aktien*: parcel (of shares)

...paket *n, im Subst.* **1.** *allg. im wörtl. Sinn*: parcel (*Am. auch* package) of; **2.** *fig. zusammengehörige Anzahl*: *Gesetzes~* package of legislation

Paket|annahme *f* parcels counter; *~bombe f* parcel bomb; *~entgelt n* charge for sending a (*od.* the) parcel, parcel delivery charge; *Post.* parcel postage; *~karte f* (parcel) mailing form; *~post f* parcel post; *~schalter m* parcels counter; *~schnur f* parcel string, twine; *~sendung f* parcel, *Am.* package

Pakistani *m*; -(*s*), - *und f*; -, - Pakistani, *weiblich auch*: Pakistani woman (*od.* girl *etc.*); **pakistanisch** *Adj.* Pakistani

Pakt *m*; -(*e*)*s*, -*e* pact; (*Vereinbarung*) agreement; *e-n ~ schließen* make a pact (*od.* an agreement); **paktieren** *v/i. mst pej.* make a deal (*mit* with)

Palais [pa'lɛː] *n*; -, - palace

Paläolithikum *n*; -*s*, *kein Pl.* palaeolithic (*od. Am.* paleolithic) age; **paläolithisch** *Adj.* palaeolithic, *Am.* paleolithic

Paläologie *f*; -, *kein Pl.* palaeology, *Am.* paleology; **paläologisch** *Adj.* palaeological, *Am.* paleological

Paläontologe *m*; -*n*, -*n* palaeontologist, *Am.* paleontologist; **Paläontologie** *f*;

-, *kein Pl.* palaeontology, *Am.* paleontology; **Paläontologin** *f*; -, -*nen* (female) palaeontologist (*od. Am.* paleontologist); **paläontologisch** *Adj.* palaeontological, *Am.* paleontological

Palast *m*; -(*e*)*s*, *Paläste* palace; **palastartig** *Adj.* palatial

Palästina (*n*) *Geog.* Palestine

Palästinenser *m*; -*s*, - Palestinian; ~**in** *f*; -, -*nen* Palestinian woman (*od.* girl *etc.*); ~**lager** *n* Palestinian refugee camp; **palästinensisch** *Adj.* Palestinian

Palast|revolte *f*, ~**revolution** *f fig.* palace revolution (*od.* coup)

palatal *Adj. Med.*, *Ling.* palatal; **palatalisieren** *v/t. Ling.* palatalize

Palatschinke *f*; -, -*n*, *mst Pl.*; *österr.*, *Gastr.* rolled up pancake filled with jam, chocolate *etc.*

Palaver *n*; -*s*, -; *umg.*, *pej.* **1.** (*endloses Reden*) palaver, (big) discussion, *Am.* gabfest, chinwag; **2.** (*Getue*) fuss; **palavern** *v/i. umg.* yak, natter away, blather on

Palette *f*; -, -*n* **1.** *Kunst* palette; **2.** *fig.* (*breite*) ~ (wide) range; **bunte** ~ mixed bag; **die ganze** ~ the whole gamut (*od.* panoply); **3.** (*Laderost*) pallet

paletti: (**es ist**) **alles** ~ *umg.* everything's hunky-dory

Palisade *f*; -, *n* palisade; **Palisadenzaun** *m* stockade

Palisander *m*; -*s*, -, ~**holz** *n* rosewood

Palme I. *f*; -, -*n*; *Bot.* palm; **II.** *fig.*: **j-n auf die** ~ **bringen** *umg.* get s.o.'s goat; **auf die** ~ **gehen** *umg.* lose (*Sl.* blow) one's cool

Palmen|hain *m* palm grove; ~**strand** *m* palm(-lined) beach

Palm|kätzchen *n Bot.* catkin; ~**öl** *n* palm oil; ~**sonntag** *m kirchl.* Palm Sunday; ~**wedel** *m* palm frond

Pampa *f*; -, -*s*, *mst Pl.* pampas *Pl.*; *irgendwo in der* ~ *umg. fig.* out in the sticks; ~(**s**)**gras** *n* pampas grass

Pampe *f*; -, *n*; *pej.* mush; (*schweres Essen*) stodge

Pampelmuse *f*; -, -*n* grapefruit

Pampers® ['pɛmpɐs] *Pl. umg.* Pampers®

Pamphlet *n*; -(*e*)*s*, -*e*; (*Hetzschrift*) (political) pamphlet; *pej.* lampoon

pampig *Adj. umg.* **1.** stroppy, *Am.* touchy; (*stur*) bolshy, *Am.* pushy; **2.** *pej.* (*breiig*) mushy; (*schwer*) stodgy

pan..., **Pan...** *im Adj. und Subst.* pan(-)...

Panade *f*; -, -*n*; *Gastr.* batter

Panama (*n*) *Geog.* Panama; ~**kanal** *m* Panama Canal

Panamaer *m*; -*s*, -, ~**in** *f*; -, -*nen* Panamanian, *weiblich auch*: Panamanian woman (*od.* girl *etc.*); **panamaisch** *Adj.* Panamanian

panamerikanisch *Adj.* Pan-American; **Panamerikanismus** *m*; -, *kein Pl.* Pan-Americanism

Panda *m*; -*s*, -*s*, ~**bär** *m* panda

Pandora *f*; -; *Myth.*: **die Büchse der** ~ *auch fig.* Pandora's box

Paneel *n*; -*s*, -*e* panel(ing), wainscot

paneuropäisch *Adj.* Pan-European

Panflöte *f Mus.* panpipes *Pl.*

päng *Interj.* bang!, pow!

panieren *v/t. Gastr.* bread; **paniertes Schnitzel** schnitzel (*od.* cutlet *od.* escalope) in breadcrumbs; **Paniermehl** *n* breadcrumbs *Pl.*

Panik *f*; -, -*en* (*selten*) panic; (*Schrecken*) scare; (*panikartige Flucht*) stampede; *in* ~ *geraten* panic, start panicking; **keine** ~! don't panic

panikartig I. *Adj.*; panic ...; *Flucht*: panic-stricken; ~ *sein Handlung*: be undertaken in a state of panic; *Reaktion*: be one of panic; **II.** *Adv.* in (a) panic

Panik|mache *f* scaremongering, panic-mongering; scare tactics *Pl.*; ~**macher** *m* alarmist; ~**stimmung** *f*: *in* ~ *geraten* start panicking

panisch *Adj.* panic ...; *Flucht*, *Stimme*: panic-stricken; ~ *sein* be of panic proportions; *Reaktion*: be one of panic; ~**e Angst** (feeling of) sheer terror, (mortal) terror; ~**e Angst haben** be terrified (out of one's wits), be frightened out of one's mind

Pankreas *n*; -, *Pankreaten*; *Anat.* pancreas

Panne *f*; -, -*n* **1.** (*Störung*, *technische* ~) breakdown; *EDV* glitch; (*Reifenpanne*) puncture (*auch Fahrrad*), flat tyre (*Am.* tire), *bes. Am. auch* flat; **2.** *fig.* (*Missgeschick*) mishap; *bei Organisation*: hitch; *e-e kleine* ~ (*im Ablauf*) a slight hitch; *es kam zu mehreren peinlichen* ~*n* there were several embarrassing slip-ups

...panne *f*, *im Subst.*: *Versorgungs*~ breakdown in supplies

Pannendienst *m* breakdown (*Am. auch* emergency roadside) service

pannenfrei *Adj.* free from mishaps

Pannen|helfer *m* breakdown mechanic; ~**hilfe** *f* breakdown assistance; ~**kurs** *m* car maintenance course

pannensicher *Adj.* foolproof

Pannenstreifen *m umg. Verk.* (*Standspur*) hard shoulder, *Am.* shoulder

Panoptikum *n*; -*s*, *Panoptiken* waxworks *Pl.*

Panorama *n*; -*s*, *Panoramen* panorama; ~**bild** *n Fot.* panoramic photograph; ~**bus** *m* sightseeing bus (*od.* coach); ~**fenster** *n* panoramic (*od.* observation) window; *in der Wohnung*: picture window; ~**restaurant** *n* panoramic restaurant; (*Drehrestaurant*) revolving restaurant; ~**scheibe** *f Mot.* panoramic wind|screen (*Am.* -shield); ~**schwenk** *m Film*: pan(ned) shot; ~**straße** *f* scenic road; ~**weg** *m* scenic path

panschen I. *vt/i.* (*mit Wasser verdünnen*) water down; (*verfälschen*) adulterate; → **gepan(t)scht**; **II.** *v/i. im Wasser*: splash about (*Am.* around)

Pansen *m*; -*s*, - **1.** *Zool.* rumen; **2.** *umg. fig.* belly

Pan|theismus *m*; -, *kein Pl.* pantheism; ~**theist** *m*; -*en*, -*en*, ~**theistin** *f*; -, -*nen* pantheist; **pantheistisch** *Adj.* pantheist(ic)

Panther *m*; -*s*, - panther; **schwarzer** ~ black panther; **die Schwarzen** ~ *hist. Pol. USA*: the Black Panthers

Pantine *f*; -, -*n bes. nordd.* (*Holzschuh*) clog; *fig.* → **Latschen**, **Latsche**²

Pantoffel *m*; -*s*, -*n* slipper; *er steht unter dem* ~ *umg. fig.* he's a henpecked husband; ~**held** *m umg.* henpecked husband; ~**kino** *n umg.* box, tube; ~**tierchen** *n Zool.* slipper animalcule

Pantolette *f*; -, -*n* open-back shoe, mule

Pantomime¹ *f*; -, -*n*; (*stummes Spiel*) mime, dumb show

Panto|mime² *m*; -*n*, -*n*, ~**mimin** *f*; -*nen*; (*Künstler[in]*) mime (artist); **pantomimisch** *Adj.* mime ..., mimed, *präd.* in mime

pantschen *vt/i.* → **panschen**

Panzer *m*; -*s*, - **1.** *Mil.* (*Kampfwagen*) tank; (*Stahlhülle*) armo(u)r plating;

2. *hist.* (*Rüstung*) (suit of) armo(u)r; (*Kettenpanzer*) coat of mail; **3.** *fig.* wall *of silence etc.*; **4.** *Zool.* e-s *Käfers*, e-r *Schildkröte etc.*: shell, armo(u)r

Panzerabwehr *f Mil.* antitank defen|ce (*Am.* -se); ~**rakete** *f* antitank missile (*od.* rocket)

Panzer|division *f Mil.* armo(u)red division; ~**faust** *f Mil.* bazooka, antitank rocket launcher; ~**glas** *n* bulletproof glass; ~**grenadier** *m Mil.* armo(u)red infantry rifleman; ~**hemd** *n hist.* coat of mail; ~**jäger** *m Mil.* antitank gunner; ~**kanone** *f Mil.* tank gun; ~**kette** *f Mil.* (*Raupenkette*) tank track; ~**knacker** *m*; -*s*, -; *hum.* safebreaker; ~**kreuzer** *m Naut.*, *Mil.* armo(u)red cruiser, battle cruiser

panzern I. *v/t. auch Tech.* armo(u)r--plate; → **gepanzert**; **II.** *v/refl. hist.* (*Rüstung anlegen*) don one's armo(u)r; *fig.* shield o.s.; *im Voraus*: arm o.s.

Panzernashorn *n Zool.*: *Indisches* ~ Indian rhinoceros

Panzer|platte *f* armo(u)r-plate; ~**regiment** *n Mil.* armo(u)red regiment; ~**schiff** *n Naut.*, *Mil.* armo(u)r-plated vessel; ~**schrank** *m* safe; ~**spähwagen** *m Mil.* armo(u)red scout car; ~**truppen** *Pl. Mil.* armo(u)red troops, tank corps *Sg.*

Panzerung *f* **1.** (*Vorgang*) armo(u)ring; **2.** (*Schutz*) armo(u)r

Panzerwagen *m Mil.* tank

Papa *m*; -*s*, -*s* dad(dy), *Am. auch* pa(pa); *als Anrede*: Dad(dy), *Am. auch* Pa(pa)

Papagallo *m*; -(*s*), -*s od.* Papagalli beach romeo

Papagei *m*; -*s od.* -*en*, -*en Zool.* parrot (*auch fig.*); **papageienhaft** *Adj.* parrot(-)like

Papageien|krankheit *f Med.* psittacosis; ~**vogel** *m* (type of) parrot

Papeterie *f*; -, -*n*; *schw.*, *südd.* stationer('s)

Papier *n*; -*s*, -*e* **1.** *allg.* paper; (*Briefpapier*) *auch* stationery; *aus* ~ made of paper; *ein Stück/Blatt* ~ a piece/sheet of paper; ~ *verarbeitend Industrie etc.*: paper-processing; *zu* ~ *bringen* write down, commit to paper; *das steht nur auf dem* ~ it's pure theory; *die Ehe besteht nur auf dem* ~ it's a marriage on paper only; ~ *ist geduldig* you can (just) write down anything on paper, all sorts of rubbish end up on paper *umg.*; **2.** (*Dokument*) document; **Papiere** *Pl.* (*Urkunden*) papers, documents; (*Ausweispapiere*) (identity) papers; *Wirts.* (*Wertpapiere*) securities; *s-e* ~ *bekommen bei Entlassung*: get one's cards (*Am.* pink slip)

...papier *n*, *im Subst. allg.* paper; *Umwelt*~ recycled paper, paper with post-consumer content

Papier|abfälle *Pl.* waste paper *Sg.*; ~**block** *m* notepad; ~**brei** *m* pulp; ~**deutsch** *n* officialese

papierdünn *Adj.* wafer-thin

Papiereinzug *m von Drucker*, *Kopierer etc.*: paper feed

papieren *Adj.*; *nur attr.* paper ...; *präd.* made of paper; *fig. Stil*: prosy

Papier|fabrik *f* paper mill; ~**feile** *f* emery board; ~**fetzen** *m* scrap of paper; ~**flieger** *m* paper (aero)plane (*Am.* airplane); ~**form** *f Sport*: *von der* ~ *her* judging by his/her/their form on paper; ~**format** *n* size of paper, paper size; ~**geld** *n* paper money; (*Scheine*) notes *Pl.*, *Am.* bills *Pl.*; ~**geschäft** *n* stationer('s shop); **~gewicht** n 1. *im wörtl. Sinn*: weight of paper; **2.** *Sport* paperweight; **~handtuch** n paper towel; **~korb** m wastepaper basket, *Am. auch* waste basket; **~kram** m *umg.* paperwork; **~krieg** m red tape; **e-n ~ führen mit** be involved in an endless stream of correspondence with; **~mangel** m *im Drucker etc.*: lack of paper; **~manschette** f paper cuff; **~rand** m margin; **~schere** f: **(e-e) ~** (a pair of) paper scissors *Pl.*; **~schlange** f (paper) streamer; **~schnipsel** *Pl.* paper cuttings, shredded paper; **~serviette** f paper napkin; **~sorte** f type of paper; **~stau** m *im Kopierer etc.*: paper jam; **~taschentuch** n paper tissue (*umg.* hankie); **~tüte** f paper bag; **~verarbeitung** f paper processing; **~vorschub** m paper feed; **~waren** *Pl.* stationery *Sg.*; **~warenhandlung** f stationer('s shop, *Am.* store); **~windel** f paper nappy, *Am.* disposable diaper, Pampers®

papp *Interj. umg.*: **ich kann nicht mehr ~ sagen** I can't eat another thing

Papp m; -s, *kein Pl.* **1.** (*Brei*) pap, *pej.*, *auch umg.* goo; **2.** (*Klebstoff*) paste; **3.** → *Pappschnee*

Papp|band m hard paperback; **~becher** m paper cup; **~deckel** m (piece of) cardboard; *steifer*: (piece of) pasteboard

Pappe f; -, -n, *mst Sg.* cardboard; *dicker*: pasteboard, millboard; **aus ~** made of cardboard; **das ist nicht von ~** *umg., fig.* it's not to be sniffed at; **er ist nicht von ~** *umg., fig.* he's a force to be reckoned with

Pappel f; -, -n; *Bot.* poplar

päppeln *v/t. umg.* feed up; *fig.* coddle, pamper

pappen I. *v/t.* paste, stick (**an, auf** on); **II.** *v/i. Schnee etc.*: stick (**an +** *Dat.* to)

Pappendeckel m → *Pappdeckel*

Pappenheimer *Pl.*: **ich kenne meine ~** *umg.* I know who I'm dealing with

Pappenstiel m *umg.*: **für e-n ~** for a song; **das ist kein ~** it's not chicken-feed

papperlapapp *Interj.* rubbish!

pappig *Adj.* sticky; *Brei*: stodgy

Papp|kamerad m (cardboard) dummy, effigy; **~karton** m cardboard box, carton

Pappmaché [-ma'ʃeː] n papier mâché

Papp... *im Subst. fig.* cardboard ...

Papp|nase f false nose; *fig. umg.* (*Person*) cardboard cutout; **~schnee** m wet, compacted (*od.* heavy) snow; **~teller** m paper plate

Paprika m; -s, -(s) *od.* f; -, -(s) **1.** (*Gewürz*) paprika; **2.** (*Gemüse*) pepper; **~gemüse** n peperonata; **~schnitzel** n *Gastr.* escalope with paprika; **~schote** f pepper

Papst m; -es, *Päpste* pope; **e-e Audienz beim ~** an audience with the Pope; **...papst** m, *im Subst. fig.*: *Literatur~* literary pundit; *Jazz~* jazz buff (*od.* pundit)

Papst|audienz f audience with the Pope; **~krone** f (papal) tiara

Päpstin f; -, -nen; **die Päpstin Johanna** *Myth.* Pope Joan

päpstlich *Adj.* papal; *förm.* pontifical; **Päpstlicher Stuhl** Holy See; **~er als der Papst sein** be more Catholic than the Pope

Papst|tum n; -s, *kein Pl.* papacy; **~wahl** f papal elections *Pl.*, election of a new pope

Papyrus m; -, *Papyri* papyrus; **~hand-**schrift** f **1.** papyrus manuscript; **2.** → *Papyrusrolle*; **~rolle** f papyrus scroll; **~staude** f papyrus plant

Parabel f; -, -n **1.** *Lit.* parable; **2.** *Math.* parabola

Parabolantenne f satellite dish, dish aerial (*od.* antenna)

parabolisch *Adj.* parabolic

Parabolspiegel m parabolic reflector

Parade f; -, -n **1.** *Mil.* parade, review; (*Vorbeimarsch*) march-past; **die ~ abnehmen** take the salute; **2.** *Fechten, Boxen*: parry; *Fußball etc.*: (**glänzende**) **~** (brilliant) save; **j-m in die ~ fahren** *fig.* cut s.o. short; (*Pläne durchkreuzen*) throw a spanner (*Am.* monkey wrench) in(to) the works; **3.** *Reitsport*: halt; **~beispiel** n classic example

Paradeiser m; -s, -; *österr.* tomato

Parade|marsch m **1.** march-past; **2.** → *Paradeschritt*; **3.** *Mus.* military march; **~pferd** n showhorse; *fig.* showpiece; **~rolle** f: **das ist s-e ~** that's his party piece; **das ist für sie e-e ~** she was made (*od.* cut out) for the part; **~schritt** m drill step; (*Stechschritt*) goose-step; **~stück** n *fig.* showpiece

paradieren *v/i.* parade; **mit etw. ~** *fig.* show off with s.th.

Paradies n; -es, -e paradise; *bibl.* Garden of Eden; **das verlorene ~** paradise lost; **das ~ auf Erden** heaven on earth; **ich fühle mich wie im ~** (I feel as if) I; **...paradies** n, *im Subst.*: *Einkaufs~* paradise for shoppers, shoppers' paradise; *Vogel~* paradise for birds, bird sanctuary

paradiesisch I. *Adj.* heavenly; *lit.* paradisiacal; **II.** *Adv.*: **hier ist es ~ schön** it's like paradise (here)

Paradiesvogel m *Zool.* bird of paradise; *Astron.* Bird of Paradise, Apus; *fig.* (*auffälliger Mensch*) exotically dressed person, peacock

Paradigma n; -s, *Paradigmen od. Paradigmata fachspr.* paradigm; **Paradigmenwechsel** m *Pol.* paradigm shift

paradox *Adj.* paradoxical; **das Paradoxe daran** the paradoxical side of it; **paradoxerweise** *Adv.* paradoxically

Paraffin n; -s, -e paraffin, *Am.* kerosene

Paragraph m; -en, -en; *Jur.* section, article, paragraph; *im Vertrag*: clause; **nach ~ 6** according to Section (*od.* Clause *od.* Paragraph) 6

Paragraphen|dschungel m *umg.* (jungle of) red tape, maze of regulations; **~hengst** m *umg.* legal eagle; **~reiter** m *umg.* stickler for the rules; **~zeichen** n *Druck.* section mark, paragraph sign

Paraguay (n); -s; *Geog.* Paraguay

Paraguayer m; -s, -, **~in** f; -, -nen Paraguayan, *weiblich auch*: Paraguayan woman (*od.* girl *etc.*); **paraguayisch** *Adj.* Paraguayan

Parallaxe f; -, -n; *Phys.* parallax

parallel I. *Adj.* parallel (**mit** to, with); **II.** *Adv.* parallel; **~ (ver)laufen zu** run parallel to

Parallele f; -, -n parallel (line) (**zu** to) *fig.* parallel; **~n sehen zwischen** see parallels between

Parallelklasse f parallel class

Parallelogramm n; -s, -e parallelogram

Parallel|schwung m *Skifahren*: parallel turn; **~straße** f road (*od.* street) running parallel; **die nächste ~** the road parallel to this one; **~verschiebung** f *Math.* parallel translation

Paralyse f; -, -n paralysis; **paralysieren** *v/t.* paraly|se (*Am.* -ze); **Paralytiker** m; -s, -, **Paralytikerin** f; -, -nen, **paralytisch** *Adj.* paralytic

Parameter m; -s, - parameter

paramilitärisch *Adj.* paramilitary

Paranoia f; -, *kein Pl.*; *Psych.* paranoia; **paranoid** *Adj.* paranoid; **Paranoiker** m; -s, -, **Paranoikerin** f; -, -nen, **paranoisch** *Adj.* paranoiac

Paranuss f *Bot.* Brazil nut

paraphieren *v/t.* initial

Paraphrase f; -, -n, **paraphrasieren** *v/t.* paraphrase

Parapsycho|loge m parapsychologist; **~logie** f parapsychology; **~login** f (female) parapsychologist

Parasit m; -en, -en parasite (*auch fig.*); **parasitär** *Adj.* parasitic(al); **Parasitendasein** n parasitic existence, parasitism

parat *Adj.* ready; **immer ein Blatt Papier ~ haben** always have a piece of paper handy (*od.* at hand, at the ready); **er hat immer e-e Antwort/Ausrede ~** he's never at a loss for an answer/excuse

Paratyphus m *Med.* paratyphoid (fever)

Pärchen n **1.** couple; (*Zwillinge*) pair (of twins); **so ein nettes ~** what (*od.* such) a nice couple; **ein sauberes ~** *iro.* a fine pair; **2.** (*Tiere*) pair; **sind die beiden Chinchillas ein ~?** are the two chinchillas a male and female?

Parcours [par'kuːɐ] m; -, -; *Sport* course

Pardon I. n; -s, *kein Pl.*: **kein ~ kennen** be (absolutely) ruthless; **II.** *Interj.* (I'm) sorry, *Am. auch* excuse me

Parenthese f; -, -n parenthesis; **parenthetisch I.** *Adj.* parenthetical; **II.** *Adv.* (*nebenbei*) in parenthesis

par excellence [parɛksə'lãːs] *Adv.*; *immer nachgestellt*: **ein Kavalier ~** a cavalier par excellence (*od. Brit.* of the first water), a perfect gentleman

Parforce|jagd f coursing; *konkret*: course, hunt; **~ritt** m *fig.* (*Kraftakt*) feat

Parfüm [par'fyːm] n; -s, -s *od.* -e perfume; (*Wohlgeruch*) *auch* scent; **~duft** m perfume; *bestimmter*: scent

Parfümerie f; -, -n perfume shop (*Am.* store)

parfümieren I. *v/t.* perfume, scent; **II.** *v/refl.* put (some) perfume on; **sie parfümiert sich mit ...** she puts on ... (perfume); **parfümiert** *Adj.* scented

Parfüm|wolke f cloud of perfume; **~zerstäuber** m atomizer

pari *Adv.* **1.** *Wirts.* par; **auf** *od.* **al pari** at par; **2.** *auch Sport* (*gleich*): **die Chancen stehen pari** the odds are even

Paria m; -s, -s pariah

parieren *v/t.* **1.** *Fechten etc.*: parry (*auch fig. Frage etc.*); (*Ball*) save; **2.** (*Pferd*) pull up; **II.** *v/i.* **1.** *Fechten*: parry; **2.** (*gehorchen*) knuckle under; **willst du wohl ~?** will you please do as you're told!

Paris (n); *Geog.* Paris

Pariser I. m; -s, - **1.** Parisian; **2.** *umg.* (*Kondom*) rubber, French letter; **II.** *Adj.* Parisian, (of) Paris; **~in** f; -, -nen Parisian woman/girl, Parisienne

Parität f; -, -en parity (*auch Wirts.*); **paritätisch** *Adj.* equal, on equal terms; *nur attr.* parity ...; **~e Mitbestimmung** (worker) participation on equal terms

P

Park *m*; *-(e)s*, *-s* park; *von Schloss auch*: grounds *Pl.*

...park *m*, *im Subst.* **1.** (*Ort*) **Entsorgungs~** (nuclear) waste disposal site; **2.** (*firmeneigener Bestand*) **Geräte~** collection of equipment, plant

Parkanlage *f* park

Park|ausweis *m* parking ID (*od.* permit); **~bahn** *f Raumfahrt*: parking orbit

Parkbank *f*; *-*, *-bänke* park bench

Park|bucht *f* parking bay; *an der Straße*: lay-by, *Am.* pull-off; **~dauer** *f* parking period; **~deck** *n im Parkhaus*: parking level

parken *vt/i.* park; *Auto*: be parked (*auch* **geparkt sein**); **Parken verboten!** no parking

Parkerlaubnis *f* permission to park; (*Schein*) parking permit

Parkett *n*; *-(e)s*, *-e* **1.** (*Bodenbelag*) parquet (floor); **~** (*ver*)*legen* lay parquet; **2.** (*Tanzfläche*) dance floor; *ein Tänzchen aufs ~ legen hum.* trip the light fantastic; *sich auf dem ~ bewegen können fig.* be perfectly at ease in society, have plenty of savoir-faire; *auf dem diplomatischen ~* in diplomatic circles, in the diplomatic field; **3.** *Theat.* stalls *Pl.*, *Am.* orchestra; **4.** *Fin.* (*Börse*): *das ~* the floor (of the stock exchange); **~leger** *m*; *-s*, *-* parquet layer

Park|gebühr *f* parking fee; **~haus** *n* multi-storey car park, *Am.* multi-level parking lot

Parkinson'sche Krankheit, **parkinsonsche Krankheit** *f Med.*: *die ~* Parkinson's disease

Park|kralle *f* wheel clamp; **~leuchte** *f*, **~licht** *n* parking light; **~lücke** *f* parking space; **~möglichkeit** *f* place to park; **~möglichkeiten** *Pl.* room to park *Sg.*, parking spaces; **~platz** *m* **1.** *einzelner*: parking space; *e-n ~ suchen* look for a parking space (*od.* somewhere to park); **2.** *Anlage*: car park, *Am.* parking lot; **~scheibe** *f* parking disc (*Am.* permit); **~schein** *m* car park (*Am.* parking [lot]) ticket; **~scheinautomat** *m* car park (*Am.* parking) ticket machine; **~studium** *n* stopgap studies *Pl.*; **~sünder** *m*, **~sünderin** *f* parking offender (*od. Am.* scofflaw); **~uhr** *f* parking meter; **~verbot** *n*: *hier ist ~* there's no parking here; *im ~ stehen* be parked where there is no parking (*od.* in a no parking area, in a towaway zone); **~verbotsschild** *n* no-parking sign; **~vergehen** *n* parking offen|ce (*Am.* -se); **~zeit** *f* parking period

Parlament *n*; *-(e)s*, *-e Pol.* parliament; **Parlamentarier** *m*; *-s*, *-*, **Parlamentarierin** *f*; *-*, *-nen* member of parliament; *altgediente(r)*: parliamentarian; **parlamentarisch** *Adj.* parliamentary; **Parlamentarismus** *m*; *-*, *kein Pl.* parliamentarianism

Parlaments|auflösung *f* dissolving (*od.* dissolution) of parliament; **~ausschuss** *m* parliamentary committee; **~ferien** *Pl.* (parliamentary) recess *Sg.*; *in die ~ gehen* rise for the recess; **~gebäude** *n* parliament (building); *in London*: Houses *Pl.* of Parliament; **~mitglied** *n* member of parliament; *GB*: *auch* MP; **~präsident** *m* (parliamentary) president; *GB*: Speaker; **~sitzung** *f* sitting of parliament; **~wahlen** *Pl.* parliamentary elections; *GB*: general election *Sg.*

Parmesan *m*; *-(s)*, *kein Pl.*, **~käse** *m*

Gastr. Parmesan (cheese)

Parodie *f*; *-*, *-n* parody (*auf* + *Akk.* on), send-up (of) *umg.*; **parodieren** *v/t.* parody, do a take-off on (*od.* send-up of) *umg.*; **Parodist** *m*; *-en*, *-en*, **Parodistin** *f*; *-*, *-nen* parodist; **parodistisch** *Adj.* parodistic

Parodontose *f*; *-*, *-n*; *Med.* receding (*od.* shrinking) gums *Pl.*; *fachspr.* periodontosis

Parole *f*; *-*, *-n*; *Mil.* password; *fig.* watchword; *Pol. auch* slogan

Paroli *n*: *~ bieten* give as good as one gets; (*Einwände haben*) come up with objections

parsen *v/t. Gram.*, *EDV* parse

Part *m*; *-s*, *-s*; *Theat.*, *Mus.* part; (*Anteil*) share

Partei *f*; *-*, *-en* party (*auch Pol.*, *Jur.*); *Sport* side; *in Mietshaus*: tenant(s *Pl.*), household; *gegnerische ~* opponent(s *Pl.*); *Sport auch* other side, opposing team; *~ nehmen für j-n* side with s.o.; *gegen j-n ~ ergreifen* take sides against s.o.; *über den ~en stehen* remain impartial; *~ sein* be bias(s)ed, be prejudiced

Partei|apparat *m* party machine; **~ausschluss** *m* expulsion from a (*od.* the) party; **~austritt** *m* party defection; **~basis** *f* rank and file, grassroots (members) *Pl.*; **~bonze** *m* party bigwig; **~buch** *n* party card; **~chef** *m*, **~chefin** *f* party leader; **~chinesisch** *n umg.* party lingo; **~disziplin** *f* party discipline

Parteien|finanzierung *f Pol.* funding of political parties; **~gesetz** *n* political parties act; **~landschaft** *f* party scene, political constellation; **~staat** *m* party state

Partei|freund *m*, **~freundin** *f Pol.* fellow member (of the party), fellow travel(l)er *hum.*; **~funktionär** *m*, **~funktionärin** *f* party official; **~gänger** *m* party liner; **~genosse** *m*, **~genossin** *f* party member; **parteiintern I.** *Adj.* (inner-)party ..., *präd. auch* within the party; **~e Querelen** *f* party in-fighting; **II.** *Adv.* within the party

parteiisch *Adj.* bias(s)ed, prejudiced (*für* in favo[u]r of; *gegen* against); *sich ~ verhalten* show bias (*od.* prejudice)

Parteikasse *f Pol.* party funds *Pl.*

parteilich *Adj.* **1.** *Pol. Diskussion*, *Geschlossenheit etc.*: party ...; **2.** (*nicht neutral*) bias(s)ed, partial

Parteilinie *f Pol.* party line

parteilos *Adj.* independent, *attr. auch* non-party ...; **Parteilose** *m*, *f*; *-n*, *-n* independent

Parteimitglied *n Pol.* party member

Parteinahme *f*; *-*, *-n* siding (*für* with); *sich e-r ~ enthalten* not take sides, sit on the fence

Partei|politik *f Pol.* party politics *Pl.*; *konkret*: party policy (*od.* policies *Pl.*); **~politiker** *m*, **~politikerin** *f* party politician

parteipolitisch *Adj.* party political

Parteiprogramm *n* (party) manifesto (*od.* platform)

parteischädigend *Adj.* detrimental to party interests

Partei|schule *f* party cadre training institution; **~spende** *f* party (political) donation; **~spendenskandal** *m* party funding scandal; **~spitze** *f* party leadership (*od.* leaders *Pl.*); **~tag** *m* party conference (*Am.* convention)

parteiübergreifend *Adj.* cross-party

Partei|versammlung *f* party meeting

(*od.* rally); **~volk** *n* (party) rank and file; **~vorsitzende** *m*, *f* party leader; **~vorstand** *m* party executive; **~zentrale** *f* party headquarters (*V. auch im Sg.*); **~zugehörigkeit** *f* party affiliation; (*Mitgliedschaft*) party membership

Parterre [part'tɛrə] **I.** *n*; *-s*, *-s* ground floor, *Am. auch* first floor; *Theat.* rear stalls *Pl.*, *Am.* parquet; **II.** **parterre** *Adv.* on the ground (*Am. auch* first) floor; *Theat.* in the stalls (*Am.* parquet); **Parterrewohnung** *f* ground-floor flat, *Am.* ground- (*od.* first- -floor) apartment

Partial... *im Subst. mst* partial

Partie *f*; *-*, *-n* **1.** (*Teil*) part; *Med. auch* area, region; **2.** *Sport*, *Spiel*: game; *e-e ~ Schach* a game of chess; **3.** *Theat.*, *Mus.* part; **4.** *Wirts.* consignment, batch; **5.** *e-e gute ~* a good match; *e-e gute ~ machen* marry well; **6.** *mit von der ~ sein* be in on it

...partie *f*, *im Subst.*: *Land~* country excursion (*od.* outing)

partiell [par'tsiɛl] *Adj.* partial

Partikel[1] *n*; *-s*, *-* particle

Partikel[2] *f*; *-*, *-n*; *Gram.* particle

Partikularismus *m*; *-*, *kein Pl.* particularism

Partisan *m*; *-s od. -en*, *-en* partisan, guer(r)illa; **Partisanenkrieg** *m* guer(r)illa warfare; **Partisanin** *f*; *-*, *-nen* female partisan (*od.* guer(r)illa)

Partitur *f*; *-*, *-en*; *Mus.* score

Partizip *n*; *-s*, *Partizipien*; *Gram.* participle; **Partizipialsatz** *m Gram.* participial clause

partizipieren *v/i.* participate (*an* + *Dat.* in)

Partner *m*; *-s*, *-* partner; → **Gesprächspartner**; (*Ehemann*) *auch* husband; (*Freund*) *auch* boyfriend; *als j-s ~ spielen Sport* play as partner of s.o.; *Film etc.*: play opposite s.o.

...partner *m*, *im Subst.*: *Brief~* correspondent; *Schach~* chess partner; *Junior~* junior partner

Partner|beziehung *f* relationship (between two people); **~in** *f*; *-*, *-nen* partner; (*Ehefrau*) *auch* wife; (*Freundin*) *auch* girlfriend; **~look** *m* matching clothes *Pl.*

Partnerschaft *f* partnership; **partnerschaftlich** *Adj.* fair; *Verhältnis*: based on partnership; **~es Verhalten** cooperation; *auf ~er Basis* on a joint basis, on a basis of (mutual trust and) cooperation

Partner|stadt *f* twin town, *Am.* city in a cultural exchange agreement with another; *Frankfurt hat Birmingham als ~* Frankfurt is twinned with Birmingham; **~suche** *f* finding a (*od.* the right) partner, finding a mate *umg.*; **~tausch** *m* wife (*od.* partner) swapping; **~vermittlung** *f* dating agency; (*Eheinstitut*) marriage bureau; **~wahl** *f* choice of partner; **~wechsel** *m im Beruf*: change of partners; *im Privaten*: changing partners

partout [par'tuː] *Adv. umg.*: *er will ~ e-n Ferrari* he desperately wants a Ferrari, he just has to have a Ferrari; *sie wollte es ~ nicht machen* she absolutely refused to do it

Party *f*; *-*, *-s* party; *e-e ~ geben od. veranstalten* have (*od.* give) a party

...party *f*, *im Subst. allg.*: *Dinner~* dinner party; *Geburtstags~* birthday party

Party|keller *m* (basement) party room; **~löwe** *m umg.* party animal; **~muffel**

m umg. party pooper; **~service** *m* party (*od.* catering) service

Parzelle *f*; -, -*n* plot (of land), allotment, *bes. Am.* lot; **parzellieren** *v/t.* divide into lots, *Am. auch* plot; **Parzellierung** *f* division of land

Pascal *n*; -*s*, -; *Phys.* pascal

Pasch *m*; -(*e*)*s*, -*e od.* Päsche *beim Würfeln*: doublets; *beim Domino*: double; **e-n ~ würfeln** throw a double, throw doubles

...pasch *m*, *im Subst.*: **ein Vierer~/-Sechser~** a double four/six

Pascha *m*; -*s*, -*s* **1.** (*türkischer*) pasha; **2.** *hum.* pasha, lord and master, big boss; **er ist ein ausgesprochener ~** *fig.* he thinks he's Lord Muck, *Am.* he's a self-proclaimed aristocrat

paspelieren, paspeln *v/t.* (*Kleid, Kragen etc.*) pipe, trim with piping

Pass *m*; -*es*, Pässe **1.** (*Reisepass*) passport; **ein gefälschter/fälschungssicherer ~** a forged/forgery-proof passport; **e-n ~ ausstellen/verlängern/einziehen** issue/extend (*od.* renew) /confiscate a passport; **2.** *im Gebirge*: pass; **3.** *Sport* pass; **langer ~** long ball; **4.** *Sg.* (**~gang**) amble

...pass *m*, *im Subst.* **1.** *allg. im wörtl. Sinn*: passport; **Diplomaten~** diplomatic passport; **Spieler~** player's licence; **2.** *fig.*: **Gesundheits~** health certificate, certificate of health; **Zimmer~** *im Hotel*: room pass

passabel I. *Adj.* reasonable, passable; **er ist ein recht passabler Schachspieler** he's a reasonably good chess player; **II.** *Adv.* passably, reasonably well

Passage *f*; -, -*n* **1.** (*Durchgang*) passage(way); (*Einkaufspassage*) shopping arcade; **2.** *Mus., Text*: passage; *Film*: sequence, scene; **3.** (*Überfahrt*) crossing, passage; **4.** (*das Durchfahren*) passage

Passagier *m*; -*s*, -*e* passenger; **blinder ~** stowaway; **~aufkommen** *n* passenger traffic; **~dampfer** *m* passenger steamer, liner; **~gut** *n* luggage, *Am. auch* baggage; **~liste** *f* list of passengers

Passah *n*; -*s*, *kein Pl.* Passover; **~fest** *n* Passover; **~mahl** *n* Passover meal; (*jüdisch*) Seder

Passamt *n* passport office

Passant *m*; -*en*, -*en*, **~in** *f*; -, -*nen* passerby (*Pl.* passersby), *Pl. auch* people passing by; (*Fußgänger*) pedestrian

Passantrag *m* passport application form

Passat *m*; -(*e*)*s*, -*e*, **~wind** *m* trade wind

Pass|beamte *m*, **Passbeamtin** *f* passport officer; **~bestimmungen** *Pl.* passport regulations; **~bild** *n* passport photo(graph); **~bildautomat** *m* passport photo(graph) booth

Passe *f*; -, -*n am Kleid etc.*: yoke

passé [pa'se:] *Adj.* passé(e), out *umg.*; **das ist endgültig/längst ~** *umg.* that's died a death / that went out with the ark

passen I. *v/i.* **1.** (*die richtige Größe etc. haben*) fit (*j-m* s.o.; **auf etw.** s.th.); **es passt genau** it fits perfectly, it's a perfect fit; **2.** **~ zu** *j-m*: suit; *e-r Sache*: go with; (*farblich übereinstimmen mit*) match; **das passt zu ihm** *fig.* that's just like him, that's him all over; **3.** (*harmonieren, für j-n od. etw. geeignet sein*) fit; **sie ~ gut zueinander** they suit each other; **er passt nicht in diese Kreise** he doesn't fit (*od.* he's out of place) in these circles; **die Bemerkung passt hier nicht** that remark is out of

place here; **das hat gepasst** (*gesessen*) that hit home; **das passt mir gut** that suits me fine; **4.** (*genehm sein*) suit (+ *Dat.* s.o. *od.* s.th.), be suitable (*od.* convenient) (for s.o. *od.* s.th.); **morgen passt es ihm nicht** tomorrow doesn't suit him (*od.* is inconvenient for him); **das passt mir gut** that suits me fine; **nur wenn es ihnen** (**in den Kram**) **passt** only when they feel like it; **er / sein Gesicht passt mir nicht** I don't like him / the look on his face; **das könnte dir so ~!** you'd like that, wouldn't you?; **5.** *Kartenspiel*: pass; **ich passe!** pass; **da muss ich ~** *umg. fig.* you've got me there; **da musste er ~** *umg. fig.* he couldn't answer that one, that had him stumped; **6.** *Sport* pass; **II.** *v/t. Tech.* fit (**in** + *Akk.* into)

passend I. *Part. Präs.* → **passen**; **II.** *Adj.* suitable; *Zeit*: *auch* convenient (**für** to, for); *Bemerkung*: apt, fitting; *Wort*: right; *farblich*: matching; **~ zu der Hose etc.**: to go with, to match *the trousers etc.*; **ich halte es nicht für ~, dass er ...** I don't think it would be right (*od.* proper) for him to + *Inf.*; **hast du's ~?** have you got the right change?

Passepartout [paspar'tu:] *n* (*schw. m*); -*s*, -*s* **1.** mount; **2.** *schw.* (*Hauptschlüssel*) master-key

Pass|ersatz *m* replacement passport; **~fälscher** *m* passport forger

Passform *f Kleidung*: fit; **e-e gute ~ haben** be a good fit

Passfoto *n* → **Passbild**

Passgang *m* amble; **im ~ gehen** amble

Passgebühr *f* passport fee

Passhöhe *f* top of the pass, pass summit

passierbar *Adj.* passable; *Fluss, Kanal etc.*: negotiable

passieren I. *v/i.* (*sich ereignen*) happen; *j-m* **~** (*zustoßen*) happen to s.o.; **was ist passiert?** what's wrong?, what('s) happened?; **das kann jedem mal ~** that can happen to the best of us; **das kann auch nur dir ~** it's just like you, isn't it?; that could only happen to you; **das könnte mir nicht ~** that wouldn't happen to me; **das passiert mir nicht noch einmal** that won't happen (to me) again; **mir ist nichts passiert** I'm all right (*Am.* alright); **ist was passiert?** is everything all right (*Am.* alright)?, (is) anything wrong?; **es wird doch nichts passiert sein?** I hope there was no accident; **es ist nichts passiert** (*auch umg. sexuell*) nothing happened; **wenn mir mal was passiert** (*wenn ich sterbe*) *euph.* if something happens to me; **mir ist gerade was Merkwürdiges passiert** I just had a strange experience; **jetzt ist es passiert!** *umg.* that's done it (now); **... sonst passiert was!** *drohend*: ... or else!; **und was passiert nun?** and (what's going on) now?"; **II.** *v/t.* **1.** (*Ort, Stelle*) pass (by, through *etc.*); (*Brücke, Fluss*) cross; **2.** *Sport, Naut.* clear; **3.** (*Gemüse etc.*) strain, pass through a sieve

Passierschein *m* pass, permit

Passion *f*; -, -*en* **1.** passion; **Schach ist s-e ~** he's a passionate chess player, he's passionate about chess, chess is his passion; **2.** *kirchl., Mus., Kunst* Passion; **passioniert** *Adj.* (very) keen, enthusiastic; *stärker*: fanatical

Passions|blume *f Bot.* passion flower; **~spiel** *n* passion (*od.* Passion) play; **~woche** *f* Holy Week; **~zeit** *f kirchl.* Lent

passiv I. *Adj.* passive (*auch Gram., Sport, Med., Etech., Wirts.*); **~es Wahlrecht** eligibility; **~er Teilhaber** sleeping partner; **~e Handelsbilanz** adverse balance of trade; **II.** *Adv.*: **sich ~ verhalten** remain passive; *bes. Pol.* maintain a passive stance; **man kann nicht einfach ~ zusehen** you can't just sit back and watch (it all happen)

Passiv *n*; -*s*, *kein Pl.*; *Gram.* passive (voice)

Passiva *Pl. Wirts.* liabilities

passivisch *Adj. Gram.* passive; **etw. ~ ausdrücken** put something in the passive

Passivität *f*; -, *kein Pl.* passiveness, passivity (*auch Sport*); (*Tatenlosigkeit*) inaction; (*Teilnahmslosigkeit*) apathy; (*Trägheit*) inertia

Passiv|posten *m Wirts.* debit item; **~rauchen** *n* passive smoking; **~satz** *m Gram.* passive clause

Pass|kontrolle *f* passport control; **~stelle** *f* passport office; **~straße** *f* mountain pass

Passus *m*; -, - passage; **dieser ~ erlaubt/verbietet ...** this passage allows/forbids ...

Pass|verlängerung *f* extension (*od.* renewal) of a (*od.* one's) passport; **~zwang** *m* passport(s) required

Paste *f*; -, -*n*; *auch Gastr.* paste

Pastell *n*; -(*e*)*s*, -*e* pastel; **in ~ gemalt** painted in pastel colo(u)rs; **~farbe** *f* **1.** pastel; **2.** (*Farbton*) pastel colo(u)r (*od.* shade); **2farben** *Adj.* pastel(-colo[u]red); **~kreide** *f* pastel (chalk); **~malerei** *f* pastel (drawing); **~stift** *m* pastel (crayon); **~ton** *m* pastel shade; **~zeichnung** *f* pastel drawing

Pastete *f*; -, -*n Gastr.* pie; *feine*: pâté; (*Teighülle*) vol-au-vent case, pastry case

...pastete *f*, *im Subst.*, *Gastr.*: **Blätterteig~** puff pastry pie; **Geflügel~** chicken pie

...pastille *f*, *im Subst.*: **Husten~** cough sweet, *Am.* cough drop

Pasteten|bäcker *m*, **~bäckerin** *f* pastry-cook; **~form** *f* pastry case; **~füllung** *f* pie filling; **~teig** *m* pastry

pasteurisieren *v/t.* pasteurize

Pastille *f*; -, -*n* lozenge, pastille

Pastor *m*; -*s*, -*en* pastor, minister; *anglikanisch*: vicar; **pastoral** *Adj.* (*auch ländlich*) pastoral; **in ~em Ton** solemnly; **Pastorin** *f*; -, -*nen* pastor, minister; *anglikanisch*: vicar

Pate *m*; -*n*, -*n* **1.** (*Taufpate*) godfather (*auch fig. der Mafia*), *Pl.* godparents; **bei j-m ~ stehen** be s.o.'s godfather (*f* godmother); **~ stehen bei** *fig. Dichtung etc.*: be the inspiration for; *Idee etc.*: be behind; *Zufall*: play an important part in; **2.** *altm.* (*Patenkind*) godchild

Paten|kind *n* godchild; **~onkel** *m* godfather

Patenschaft *f* **1.** godparenthood; **2.** *finanzielle, auch e-s Kindes*: sponsorship; **e-e ~ übernehmen für ein Kind**: sponsor

Patensohn *m* godson

Patent *n*; -(*e*)*s*, -*e* **1.** patent (**auf** + *Akk.* for); **ein ~ anmelden/erteilen** apply for / issue a patent; **~ angemeldet** patent pending; **das ~ erlischt** the patent lapses (*od.* expires); **2.** *Mil.* commission; **sein ~ erwerben** get one's commission

patent *Adj. umg. Idee etc.*: clever; *stärker*: brilliant; **ein ~er Kerl** a good bloke, a great guy, (*auch Frau*) a good

sort
Patent|amt n patent office; **~anmeldung** f (patent) application
Patentante f godmother
Patent|anwalt m patent agent (Am. attorney); **~dauer** f life of a patent; **~erteilung** f issue of a patent; **2fähig** Adj. patentable
patentierbar Adj. patentable; **patentieren** v/t.; (**sich** Dat.) **etw. ~ lassen** take out a patent on s.th., have s.th. patented
Patent|inhaber m, **~inhaberin** f patentee, patent holder; **~lösung** f fig. magic formula, nostrum; **dafür gibt es keine ~** there's no ready-made solution for that
Patentochter f goddaughter
Patentrecht n (Gesetz) patent law; (Nutzungsrecht) patent right(s Pl.); **patentrechtlich** Adj. und Adv. under patent law; **~ geschützt** patented, protected (by patent)
Patent|rezept n → **Patentlösung; ~urkunde** f Jur. letters patent; **~verletzung** f patent infringement; **~verschluss** m swing stopper
Pater m; -s, - od. Patres; kirchl. father
Paternoster[1] n; -s, -; kirchl. the Lord's Prayer, paternoster
Paternoster[2] m; -s, -; (Aufzug) paternoster (lift, Am. elevator)
pathetisch Adj. lofty, emotional; pej. dramatic; **er redet so ~** he speaks so emotively
pathogen Adj. Med. pathogenic; **Pathogenese** f; -, -n Med. pathogenesis, pathogeny
Patho|loge m; -n, -n pathologist; **Pathologie** f; -, -n, mst Sg. 1. pathology; 2. (Abteilung) pathology department; **Pathologin** f; -, -nen pathologist; **pathologisch** Adj. pathological (auch fig.)
Pathos n; -, kein Pl. emotionalism; **falsches ~** bathos; **e-e Rede voller ~** a speech full of emotion
Patience f; -, -n (game of) patience, Am. (game of) solitaire
Patient m; -en, -en patient; **ich bin ~ bei Frau Dr. X** I'm a patient of Dr(.) X
Patientenbesuch m visit to a patient, doctor's visit
patientenfreundlich Adj. patient-friendly
Patienten|kartei f patients' file; **~überwachung** f monitoring of patients
Patientin f; -, -nen patient; → **Patient**
Patin f; -, -nen godmother
Patina f; -, kein Pl. patina (auch fig.); **~ ansetzen** gather (od. develop a) patina; fig. pej. wear thin; **patinieren** v/t. patinate
Patisserie f; -, -n; schw. patisserie, cake (Am. pastry) shop
Patriarch m; -en, -en patriarch (auch fig.); **patriarchalisch** Adj. patriarchal; **Patriarchat** n; -(e)s, -e (selten) patriarchy, patriarchal society
Patriot m; -en, -en, **~in** f; -, -nen patriot; **patriotisch I.** Adj. patriotic; **II.** Adv. patriotically; **Patriotismus** m; -, kein Pl. patriotism
Patrizier m; -s, - patrician; **patrizisch** Adj. patrician
Patron m; -s, -e patron; kirchl. patron saint; **übler ~** umg. pej. nasty customer, insolent fellow
Patronat n; -s, -e patronage
Patrone f; -, -n cartridge; Fot. auch cassette
...patrone f, im Subst.: **Ersatz~** replace-

ment cartridge; **Nachfüll~** refill (cartridge)
Patronen|füller m, **~füllhalter** m cartridge pen; **~gurt** m, **~gürtel** m cartridge belt; **~hülse** f cartridge case; **~tasche** f ammunition pouch
Patrouille [pa'trʊljə] f; -, -n patrol; **nächtliche ~n machen** do nighttime patrols
Patrouillen|boot n patrol boat; **~fahrt** f patrol; **~flug** m patrol flight; **~gang** m patrol
patrouillieren [patru'liːrən] v/i. patrol; (durch) **die Straßen / den Hafen ~** patrol the streets/harbo(u)r; **auf und ab ~** fig. pace up and down
patsch Interj. splat!; Schlag: smack!
Patsche f; -, -n 1. umg., Kinderspr. (Hand) hand, little paw; 2. umg. (Fliegenklatsche) fly-swat(ter); 3. schwierige Lage: (ganz schön) **in der ~ sitzen** umg. be in a real mess; **j-m aus der ~ helfen** get s.o. out of a tight spot, bale s.o. out
patschen v/i. Wasser: splash; (schlagen) smack
Patschen m; -s, -; österr. 1. (Hausschuh) slipper; 2. umg. (Reifenpanne) puncture, Am. flat
Patsch|hand f, **~händchen** n umg. (little) hand (od. mitt umg.)
patschnass Adj. soaked to the skin, soaking (wet), drenched
Patschuliöl n pa(t)chouli oil, patchoul(e)y oil
Patt n; -s, -s; Schach und Pol. fig.: stalemate; fig. auch deadlock
patt Adj. Schach: **~ sein** be a stalemate
Pattsituation f deadlock, stalemate, impasse
patzen v/i. umg. bungle, fluff (it), make a boob (Am. blunder); Mus. make a mistake; **Patzer** m; -s, -; umg. slip; stärker: (real) boob (Am. blunder)
patzig Adj. umg. snotty, Am. snippy; **werd bloß nicht ~** don't you get snotty (Am. snippy) with me
Pauke f; -, -n kettledrum, Pl. auch timpani; **mit ~n und Trompeten durchfallen** fig. fail miserably, make a real mess of it umg.; **auf die ~ hauen** umg. (feiern) have a real binge; (prahlen) blow one's horn
pauken I. v/i. 1. Mus. play the timpani (od. [kettle]drums); 2. umg. (lernen) cram, swot; 3. in schlagenden Verbindungen: (fechten) fence; **II.** v/t. umg. (Stoff) swot (od. bone, Am. auch cram) up on; **ich muss für morgen Vokabeln ~** I've got to bone up on vocabulary for tomorrow
Pauken|schlag m drumbeat; **mit e-m ~ beginnen/enden** fig. get off to a dramatic start / come to a dramatic end (od. finish); **~schläger** m timpanist, drummer; **~schlegel** m timpani (od. kettledrum) stick; auch drumstick; **~wirbel** m kettle-drum roll
Pauker m; -s, - 1. Mus. timpanist, drummer; 2. umg. (Lehrer) crammer, teacher; **unsere ~ waren gar nicht so übel** our teachers weren't bad at all; **Paukerei** f; -, kein Pl.; umg. cramming, swotting; **Paukstudio** n umg. crammer
Paukist m; -en, -en, **~in** f; -, -nen; Mus. timpanist
Pausbacken Pl. chubby cheeks; **pausbackig, pausbäckig** Adj. chubby(-cheeked)
pauschal I. Adj.; nur attr. 1. Summe: lump sum; Preis etc.: all-in ..., (all-)-

inclusive; **~e Erhöhung** across-the-board increase; 2. fig. (sehr allgemein) general; **e-e ~e Aussage/Verallgemeinerung** a sweeping statement/generalization; **II.** Adv. 1. **~ vergüten** pay a lump sum (od. flat rate) for; **j-m etw. ~ berechnen** charge s.o. a flat rate for s.th.; **es kostet ~ 3000 Euro** it's 3000 euros all in (od. [all-]inclusive); 2. **~ verurteilen** fig. condemn s.th. wholesale; **ich möchte es nicht ~ beurteilen** I wouldn't like to draw any general conclusions (od. make any general statements on the matter)
Pauschal|angebot n package deal; **~besteuerung** f Fin. → **Pauschalierung** 2; **~betrag** m inclusive price
Pauschale f; -, -n lump sum; im Hotel etc.: all-inclusive price; (Gebühr)
Pauschal|gebühr f flat rate; **~honorar** n flat-rate fee
pauschalieren v/t. 1. (Beträge) consolidate into a lump sum; 2. Fin. estimate
Pauschalierung f 1. (von Beträgen) consolidation into a lump sum; 2. Fin. (Steuer) taxation based on average figures, lump-sum taxation
pauschalisieren vt/i. generalize; (alles über e-n Kamm scheren) lump everything together, tar everything with the same brush umg.
Pauschal|preis m flat rate, estimated price; (Pauschalbetrag) inclusive price; **~reise** f package tour; **~summe** f lump sum; **~urlaub** m package holiday; **~urteil** n fig. sweeping statement, (broad) generalization; **~versicherung** f comprehensive insurance; **~wert** m overall value
Pausch|betrag m, **~summe** f lump sum
Pause[1] f; -, -n break; beim Reden etc.: pause; Schule: break, Am. recess; Theat., Sport interval; Am. und Film: intermission; Mus. rest; **kleine ~** short (od. quick, little) break; **es klingelt zur ~** the bell is ringing for break (Am. recess); **e-e ~ machen** od. **einlegen** take (od. have) a break; beim Reden: pause for a moment; **sie gönnt sich keine ~** she never lets up
Pause[2] f; -, -n 1. (Durchzeichnung) tracing; 2. (Lichtpause) copy; (Blaupause) blueprint; **pausen** v/t. 1. trace; 2. Tech. copy
...pause f, im Subst.: **Schul~** break, Am. recess; **Sitzungs~** adjournment; **Toiletten~** toilet break
Pausen|brot n breaktime snack; **~füller** m filler; **~halle** f break hall; **~hof** m schoolyard, playground
pausenlos Adj. uninterrupted, incessant, attr. auch nonstop ...; (unerbittlich) unrelenting
Pausen|pfiff m Sport half-time whistle; **~raum** m in Fabrik etc.: recreation room, break room, Am. employee lounge; **~stand** m Sport half-time score; **~taste** f pause button; **~zeichen** n Mus. rest; Radio: interval (od. station identification) signal
pausieren v/i. take a break; **~ müssen** Sport be out of action
Pauspapier n tracing paper
Pavian m; -s, -e baboon
Pavillon ['paviljɔŋ] m; -s, -s pavilion; (Messestand) (exhibition) stand
...pavillon m, im Subst.: **Garten~** summer house; **Ausstellungs~** exhibition hall (od. stand); **Konzert~** concert hall
Pazifik m Geog.: **der ~** the Pacific (Ocean)
pazifisch Adj. Pacific; **der Pazifische**

Ozean the Pacific

Pazifismus *m*; -, *kein Pl.* pacifism; **Pazifist** *m*; *-en*, *-en*, **Pazifistin** *f*; -, *-nen*, **pazifistisch** *Adj.* pacifist

PC *m*; *-s*, *-s*; (*Computer*) PC (= personal computer); **~-Benutzer** *m*, **~-Benutzerin** *f* PC user

Pech *n*; *-s*, *kein Pl.* **1.** (*Missgeschick etc.*) bad luck; **~ haben** be unlucky (**bei**, **mit** with); **~ gehabt!** bad (*umg.* tough) luck; **so ein ~!** *umg.* that's too bad; *auf sich selber bezogen*: just my luck; *er wird wirklich vom ~ verfolgt* his bad luck never lets up, he seems to have been born unlucky; *er hatte das ~, beide Mitarbeiter zu verlieren* he was unlucky enough (*od.* he had the bad luck) to lose both colleagues; **2.** (*Masse*) pitch; *wie ~ und Schwefel zusammenhalten umg. fig.* be (as) thick as thieves

Pechblende *f Min.* pitch blende

pechschwarz *Adj. Haare*: jet-black; *Nacht*: pitch-dark

Pech|stein *m* pitchstone; **~strähne** *f* run (*od.* streak) of bad luck; **e-e ~ haben** be down on one's luck, be going through an unlucky patch; **~vogel** *m* unlucky person

Pedal *n*; *-s*, *-e* **1.** pedal (*auch Mus.*); *in die ~e treten* pedal hard (*od.* away); (*so schnell man kann*) pedal for all one is worth; *tritt mal aufs ~!* step on it!; **2.** *Pl. umg.* (*Füße*) trotters

Pedant *m*; *-en*, *-en* pedant, stickler; **Pedanterie** *f*; -, *-n* (*selten*) pedantry, fussiness *umg.*; **Pedantin** *f*; -, *-nen* pedant, stickler; **pedantisch I.** *Adj.* pedantic, fussy; **II.** *Adv.* pedantically

Peddigrohr *n*; *-(e)s*, *kein Pl.* rattan

Pedell *m*; *-s*, *-e*; *altm. Univ.* porter; *Schule*: caretaker, *Am.* janitor

Pediküre *f*; -, *-n* **1.** (*Fußpflege*) pedicure; **2.** (*Fußpflegerin*) pedicurist; **pediküren** *v/t.* pedicure

Peeling ['pi:lɪŋ] *n*; *-s*, *-s*; (*auch Mittel*) facial (*od.* body) scrub

Peep-Show ['pi:pʃo:] *f*; -, *-s* peep show

Pegel *m*; *-s*, -; *Tech. und fig.* level; (*Wasserstandsmesser*) water gauge (*Am. auch* gage); **~anzeige** *f* level meter; **~regler** *m* level control; **~stand** *m* water level

Peilanlage *f* direction finder

peilen I. *v/t.* a) *Naut.*: *ein Schiff etc. ~* take a ship's *etc.* bearings, take (the) bearings, c) *fig.*: *die Lage ~ umg. fig.* see how the land lies; *Pol.* test the water; **II.** *v/i.* **1.** *Naut.* take (the) bearings, take one's bearings; **2.** *umg.* (*blicken*) peer, peep → *Daumen*

Peil|funk *m* radio direction finding; **~sender** *m* radio beacon

Peilung *f* location; *Radio, Flug.* direction finding; (*Resultat*) bearing(s *Pl.*)

Pein *f*; -, *kein Pl.*; *förm.*, *poet.* suffering; *stärker*: torment; *seelische ~* mental anguish; **peinigen** *v/t.* torment, torture; (*plagen*) harass, pester; **Peiniger** *m*; *-s*, -, **Peinigerin** *f*; -, *-nen* tormentor

peinlich I. *Adj.* **1.** (*unangenehm*) embarrassing; *Situation*: *auch* awkward; painful *umg.*; *es war mir sehr ~* (, *dass ich es vergessen hatte*) I was (*od.* felt) really embarrassed (at *od.* about having forgotten it); *es ist mir sehr ~, aber ich muss dich bitten, ...* I don't know how to put it, but I have to ask you, ...; **2.** (*sehr genau*) meticulous, painstaking; *in dem Haus herrschte ~e Ordnung* the house was

scrupulously tidy; **II.** *Adv.* **1.** *j-n ~ berühren* embarrass s.o.; **2.** *~ sauber* scrupulously clean; *~ genau* very (*od.* painfully) exact (*bei* about); *sie vermieden ~st, danach zu fragen* they took great care to avoid asking about it

Peinlichkeit *f* embarrassment; (*etw. Peinliches*) embarrassing remark (*od.* situation *etc.*)

Peitsche *f*; -, *-n* whip; *mit der ~ knallen* crack the whip; *e-m Pferd die ~ geben* whip a horse; **peitschen** *v/t.i.* whip; *auch fig. Regen etc.*: lash (*gegen* against); *Schüsse peitschten durch die Nacht* shots rang out through the night

Peitschen|hieb *m* lash (of the whip); **~knall** *m* crack of the whip; **~lampe** *f* street lamp (*od.* light); **~stiel** *m* whip handle

pejorativ *Adj.* (*Wort*) pejorative

Pekinese *m*; *-n*, *-n* (*Hund*) Pekin(g)ese

Peking (*n*); *-s* Beijing, Peking; **Pekinger** *m*; *-s*, -, **Pekingerin** *f*; -, *-nen* inhabitant of Beijing (*od.* Peking); **~mensch** *m*: *der ~* Peking man

Pektin *n*; *-s*, *-e Bio.* pectin

pekuniär *Adj. Wirts.* financial, pecuniary *geh.*

Pelargonie *f*; -, *-n Bot.* pelargonium (flower)

Pelerine *f*; -, *-n* cape

Pelikan *m*; *-s*, *-e Orn.* pelican

Pelle *f*; -, *-n* **1.** peel; *auch von Wurst*: skin; **2.** *umg. fig.*: *j-m auf die ~ rücken* crowd s.o.; *rück nicht so auf die ~* get off my back, will you

pellen I. *v/t.* peel (*auch Ei*); skin; **II.** *v/refl. Haut, Rücken etc.*: peel

Pellkartoffeln *Pl. Gastr.* potatoes boiled in their skins

Pelz *m*; *-es*, *-e* fur; *unbearbeitet*: skin, hide; (*~mantel*) fur (coat); *j-m auf den ~ rücken umg. fig.* (*zu nahe kommen*) come too close to s.o., crowd s.o.; (*bedrängen*) get on at s.o., pester s.o.

Pelzbesatz *m* fur trimming

Pelzfutter *n* fur lining; **pelzgefüttert** *Adj.* fur-lined

Pelz|handel *m* fur trade; **~händler** *m* furrier

pelzig *Adj.* furry; *Zunge*: furred; *Rettich*: stringy

Pelz|mantel *m* fur coat; **~mütze** *f* fur hat; **~robbe** *f Zool.* fur seal; **~tiere** *Pl.* fur-bearing animals, *Koll.* furs; **~tierjäger** *m* fur hunter; *mit Fallen*: (fur) trapper

Pendant [pã'dã:] *n*; *-s*, *-s* matching piece; *fig.* (*Ergänzung*) complement; (*Gegenstück*) counterpart (*auch Person*)

Pendel *n*; *-s*, - pendulum (*auch fig. und Esoterik*); **~bus** *m* shuttle bus; **~diplomatie** *f Pol.* shuttle diplomacy; **~flugzeug** *n* shuttle aircraft (*od.* plane); **~lampe** *f*, **~leuchte** *f* pendulum light

pendeln *v/i.* **1.** swing; *fachspr.* oscillate; *mit den Beinen ~* dangle one's legs; (*mit dem Oberkörper*) *~ Boxen*: weave; **2.** *Eisenb. etc.* shuttle; *Person*: commute; *zwischen X und Y ~ Bus etc.*: shuttle back and forth between X and Y; *Person*: commute from X to Y

Pendel|tür *f* swing door; **~uhr** *f* pendulum clock; **~verkehr** *m* **1.** shuttle service; **2.** → *Pendlerverkehr*; **~zug** *m* **1.** shuttle train; **2.** → *Pendlerzug*

Pendler *m*; *-s*, -, **~in** *f*; -, *-nen* commuter

Pendler|verkehr *m* (*Berufsverkehr*) commuter traffic; **~zug** *m* commuter

train

penetrant *Adj.* **1.** *Geruch*: penetrating, pungent; **2.** *umg. Person*: insistent, pushy; **Penetranz** *f*; -, *kein Pl.* **1.** *e-s Geruchs*: pungency; **2.** *umg.* (*Aufdringlichkeit*) pushiness, obtrusiveness

Penetration *f*; -, *-en* penetration; **penetrieren** *v/t.* penetrate

peng *Interj.* bang!

penibel *Adj.* meticulous; *pej.* fussy, per(s)nickety (*alle in* + *Dat.* about)

Penis *m*; -, *-se* penis; **~neid** *m Psych.* penis envy

Penizillin *n*; *-s*, *-e* penicillin; **~behandlung** *f* treatment with penicillin, penicillin therapy; **~spritze** *f* penicillin injection

Pennäler *m*; *-s*, -; *altm.*, *umg.* schoolboy; **pennälerhaft** *Adj.*: **~es Benehmen** schoolboy manners; **Pennälerin** *f*; -, *-nen*; *altm.*, *umg.* schoolgirl

Pennbruder *m umg.* → *Penner* 1; **Penne** *f*; -, *-n*; *umg.* school; **pennen** *v/i.* *umg.* **1.** (*schlafen*) kip, *Am.* snooze, have a kip (*Am.* snooze); **2.** (*nicht aufpassen*): *da hab ich wohl gepennt* I was daydreaming, **3.** *umg.* (*Sex haben*) sleep (*mit* with); **Penner** *m*; *-s*, -, **Pennerin** *f*; -, *-nen* pensioner, retiree **1.** (*Stadt-, Landstreicher[in]*) tramp, down-and-out, dosser; *Am.* hobo, bum; *Pl. auch* street people; **2.** (*verschlafener Mensch*) sleepyhead; (*unachtsamer Mensch*) dope

Pension *f*; -, *-en* **1.** *von Beamten*: (retirement) pension; *mst vom Arbeitgeber*: superannuation; *in ~ gehen* retire; *in ~ sein* be retired, live in retirement; **2.** (*Fremdenheim*) boarding house, pension; **Pensionär** *m*; *-s*, *-e*, **Pensionärin** *f*; -, *-nen* pensioner, retiree

Pensionat *n*; *-(e)s*, *-e* boarding school

pensionieren *v/t.* pension off; *sich ~ lassen* retire, go into retirement; *sich vorzeitig ~ lassen* take early retirement; **pensioniert** *Adj.* retired; **Pensionierung** *f* retirement; **Pensionist** *m*; *-en*, *-en*, **Pensionistin** *f*; -, *-nen*; *südd., österr., schw.* pensioner

Pensions|alter *n* retirement age; *im ~ sein* have reached retirement age; **~anspruch** *m* pension claim

pensionsberechtigt *Adj.* eligible for a pension

Pensions|fonds *m*, **~kasse** *f* pension (*od.* retirement) fund

pensionsreif *Adj.* due for retirement

Pensions|system *n* retirement plan, *Brit.* pension scheme

Pensum *n*; *-s*, *Pensen* (*selten*) (work) quota; *sein tägliches ~ schaffen umg.* do one's daily stint, put in one's time

...pensum *n*, *im Subst.*: *Durchschnitts~* average quota; *Jahres~* yearly quota; *Unterrichts~* curriculum

Pep *m*; -, *kein Pl.*; *umg.* zip; *die Show hat ~* the show has life; *ihm fehlt ein bisschen ~* he lacks a bit of get up and go

Peperoni *f*; -, *-(s) Bot.* chilli, *Am.* chili; *Gastr.* chillies *Pl.*, *Am.* chili(e)s *Pl.*; **~wurst** *f Gastr.* pep(p)eroni sausage

Pepita *m od. n*; *-s*, *-s* (*Muster*) shepherd's check (*od.* plaid)

peppig *Adj. umg.* peppy; **~e Klamotten** peppy gear

Peptid *n*; *-(e)s*, *-e* peptide

per *Präp. mit Akk.* **1.** (*mit, unter Verwendung von*) per, by; *~ Bahn* by train, by rail; *~ Anhalter od. Autostopp* hitchhiking; *~ Luftpost* (via) airmail; *~ Fax/E-Mail* by fax/e-mail; *~ pedes umg.* on foot, on shanks's pony, under one's own steam; **2.** *Amtsspr.* (*pro*): ~ **Kilo** per kilo; **3.** *Wirts.*: ~ **31.12.** by 31 December; ~ **annum** per year, per annum; → **du** 1

perdu [pɛrˈdyː] *Adj. umg.* lost

Perestroika *f*; -, *kein Pl.*; *Pol., hist.* perestroika

perfekt I. *Adj.* perfect; (*ideal*) ideal; *der Vertrag ist* ~ the contract is concluded (*od.* all settled); *e-e Sache* ~ *machen* settle (*od.* clinch) a deal *umg.*; *die Niederlage ist* ~ the defeat is total; ~ *im Kochen sein* be an expert cook; *e-e* ~*e Gastgeberin* the perfect hostess; *der* ~*e Wagen* the ultimate car; *in Spanisch ist er fast* ~ his Spanish is near-perfect, he speaks almost perfect Spanish; **II.** *Adv.*: *er spricht od. kann* ~ *Englisch* his (spoken) English is perfect, he speaks perfect English

Perfekt *n*; -*s*, -*e* (*selten*); *Gram.* perfect (tense)

Perfektion *f*; -, *kein Pl.* perfection; *mit* ~ to perfection; *etw. bis zur* ~ *treiben* do (*od.* practi|se, *Am.* -ce) s.th. to the point of perfection; **perfektionieren** *v/t.* perfect; **Perfektionismus** *m* perfectionism; **Perfektionist** *m*; -*en*, -*en*, **Perfektionistin** *f*; -, -*nen*, **perfektionistisch** *Adj.* perfectionist

perfid, perfide *Adj.* insidious; *lit.* perfidious

Perforation *f*; -, -*en* perforation; *im Schmalfilm etc.*: sprocket holes *Pl.*; **Perforationslinie** *f*: *an der* ~ *abreißen* tear along the perforation; **perforieren** *v/t.* perforate

Pergament *n*; -(*e*)*s*, -*e* parchment; *vom jungen Tier*: vellum; ~**handschrift** *f* parchment (manuscript); vellum manuscript; ~**papier** *n* greaseproof paper

Pergola *f*; -, *Pergolen* pergola, bower, arbour, *Am.* arbor

Periode *f*; -, -*n* **1.** period; *Etech.* cycle; **2.** (*Menstruation*) period; *m-e* ~ *ist ausgeblieben* I've missed my period; ...**periode** *f, im Subst.*: *Ruhe*~ quiet time; *Wachstums*~ period of growth; *Schönwetter*~ period of good weather

Periodensystem *n Chem.* periodic system

Periodikum *n*; -*s*, *Periodika* (*Zeitschrift*) periodical

periodisch I. *Adj.* periodic(al); ~*er Dezimalbruch Math.* recurring decimal; **II.** *Adv.*: ~ *auftretend* periodically recurring; **periodisieren** *v/t.* divide (up) into periods; **Periodisierung** *f* division into periods

peripher *Adj.* peripheral

Peripherie *f*; -, -*n* periphery; *e-r Stadt*: *auch* outskirts *Pl.*; *EDV* peripherals *Pl.*; ~**gerät** *n EDV* peripheral; *Pl.* peripheral equipment *Sg.*

Periskop *n*; -*s*, -*e* periscope

Peristaltik *f*; -, *kein Pl.*; *Med.* peristalsis

Perkussion *f*; -, -*en*; *auch Med.* percussion

perkutan *Adj. Med.* percutaneous

Perle *f*; -, -*n* **1.** pearl; *aus Glas, Holz etc.*: bead; *fig. von Schweiß*: bead, drop; ~*n vor die Säue* (*werfen*) *fig.* (cast) pearls before swine; **2.** *umg. Person*: gem, treasure; *Sache*: masterpiece

perlen *v/i.* **1.** *Getränk*: bubble, sparkle; *der Wein perlt etwas* the wine is sparkling; **2.** ~ *von* drip from; *der Schweiß perlte ihr auf der Stirn* her forehead was beaded with sweat

perlen|besetzt *Adj.*, ~**bestickt** *Adj.* set with pearls

Perlen|fischer *m*, ~**fischerin** *f* pearl fisher (*od.* diver)

perlengeschmückt *Adj.* decorated with pearls

Perlen|halsband *n* pearl choker; ~**kette** *f* pearl necklace; ~**schnur** *f* string of pearls; ~**stickerei** *f* beadwork; ~**taucher** *m*, ~**taucherin** *f* pearl diver (*od.* fisher); ~**zucht** *f* pearl cultivation

Perl|farben *Adj.* pearl-colo(u)red; ~**grau** *Adj.* pearl grey (*Am.* gray)

Perl|huhn *n Orn.* guinea fowl; ~**leinwand** *f* beaded screen; ~**muschel** *f Zool.* pearl oyster; ~**mutt** *n*; -*s*, *kein Pl.*, ~**mutter** *f od. n*; -, *kein Pl.* mother-of-pearl; *ein Griff etc. aus Perlmutt*(*er*) a mother-of-pearl handle *etc.*

Perlon® *n*; -, *kein Pl.* nylon; *altm.* perlon

Perl|schrift *f* pearl; ~**wein** *m* sparkling wine

perlweiß *Adj.* pearly white

Perlzwiebel *f Gastr.* pearl onion

permanent *Adj.* permanent; **Permanenz** *f*; -, *kein Pl.* permanence; *in* ~ constantly, continuously

Permanganat *n*; -*s*, -*e*; *Chem.* permanganate

permissiv *Adj.* permissive

perniziös *Adj. geh.* malignant

Perpendikel *n*; -*s*, - pendulum

perplex *Adj. umg.* (*überrascht*) amazed; (*verwirrt*) bewildered, nonplussed

Perron [pɛˈrõː] *m*; -*s*, -*s*; *schw.* platform

Persenning *f*; -, -*e*(*n*) *od.* -*s*; *bes. Naut.* tarpaulin

Perser *m*; -*s*, - **1.** Persian; **2.** (*Teppich*) Persian carpet; ~*in f*; -, -*nen* Persian; *weiblich auch*: Persian woman (*od.* girl *etc.*); ~**teppich** *m* Persian carpet

Persianer *m*; -*s*, -; (*Fell*) Persian lamb; (*Mantel*) Persian lamb (coat)

Persien (*n*); -*s Geogr.* Persia

Persiflage [pɛrziˈflaːʒə] *f*; -, -*n* satire (*auf* + *Akk.* on), pastiche (on), send-up (of), take-off (on) *umg.*; **persiflieren** *v/t.* satirize, burlesque, send up *umg.*

Persilschein *m umg., hum.* **1.** *hist.* denazification certificate; **2.** *fig.* clean bill of health

persisch I. *Adj.* Persian; **II. Persisch** *n*; -*en*; *Ling.* Persian; *das Persische* Persian, the Persian language

Person *f*; -, -*en* **1.** person; *einzelne auch*: individual; ~*en* people; *10 Euro pro* ~ 10 euros each (*od.* a head); *wir sind vier* ~*en* there are four of us; *e-e aus zehn* ~*en bestehende Gruppe* a group of ten; *für vier* ~*en Kochrezept*: serves four, makes four servings; *ich für m-e* ~ I for my part; as for me, I ...; *natürliche*/*juristische Person* natural/juristic person; *Angaben zur* ~ personal data; *j-n zur* ~ *vernehmen* question s.o. concerning his (*od.* her) identiy and particulars; *sich in der* ~ *irren* mistake s.o. for someone else; *so e-e freche* ~*!* *umg.* (such a) cheeky old so-and-so; *er ist die Geduld in* ~ he's the epitome of patience; **2.** *Theat.* character, person; *die* ~*en und ihre Darsteller* the characters and performers, the cast *Sg.*; *die* ~*en des Stücks* *fachspr.* dramatis personae; **3.** *Gram.*: *erste* ~ first person

Personal *n*; -*s*, *kein Pl.* staff *Sg.* (*mst V. im Pl.*), employees *Pl.*, personnel *Sg.* (*mst V. im Pl.*); (*Bedienstete*) staff, servants *Pl.*; *wir haben zu wenig* ~ we are short-staffed (*od.* understaffed)

...**personal** *n, im Subst.*: *Haus*~ servants; *Klinik*~, *Krankenhaus*~ hospital staff; *Reinigungs*~ cleaners *Pl.*, cleaning staff

Personal|abbau *m* cut(s *Pl.*) (*od.* cutback [*s Pl.*]) in staff, staff reduction(s *Pl.*), staff cuts *Pl.*, downsizing; ~**abteilung** *f* personnel department; ~**akte** *f* personal file; ~**aufwand** *m* personnel expenditure; ~**ausweis** *m* identity card, ID; ~**bedarf** *m* staff requirement(s *Pl.*); ~**beschaffung** *f* (personnel) recruitment; ~**büro** *n* personnel (*od.* human resources) department; ~**chef** *m*, ~**chefin** *f* personnel (*od.* human resources) manager

Personalcomputer [ˈpœːɐsənlkɔmˈpjuːtɐ] *m* (*abgek. PC*) personal computer

Personal|einsparung *f mst Pl.* personnel reduction (*od.* cutdown); ~**gesellschaft** *f Wirts.* unlimited company

Personalien *Pl.* particulars; *die od. j-s* ~ *aufnehmen* take down the (*od.* s.o.'s) particulars

personalintensiv *Adj.* labour-intensive, *Am.* labor-intensive

Personal|kosten *Pl.* payroll (*od.* personnel) costs; ~**mangel** *m* staff shortage, shortage of staff; *an* ~ *leiden* be understaffed; ~**planung** *f* staff planning; ~**politik** *f* personnel policy; ~**pronomen** *n Gram.* personal pronoun; ~**rat** *m öffentlicher Dienst*: staff council for civil servants; *Person*: representative on the staff council (for civil servants); ~**rätin** *f Person*: → **Personalrat**; ~**referent** *m*, ~**referentin** *f* personnel (*od.* human resources) consultant; ~**union** *f* **1.** *Pol.* personal union; **2.** *Wirts., Pol.* amalgamation (of functions *od.* posts *etc.*); *zwei Ämter in* ~ *ausüben* hold two offices; ~**versammlung** *f* staff meeting; ~**vertretung** *f* staff council for civil servants; ~**wechsel** *m* change in staff; (*Fluktuation*) staff turnover; ~**wesen** *n* personnel

Persönchen *n*: *ein winziges* ~ a tiny little person; *ein reizendes etc.* ~ a charming *etc.* little creature

personell I. *Adj.* personnel ..., human resources ...; **II.** *Adv.* with regard to personnel; ~ *unterbesetzt*/*überbesetzt* understaffed/overstaffed; ~ *bedingt sein* (*wegen zu wenig Personal*) be caused by understaffing; (*wegen Fehlern des Personals*) be due to staff problems

Personen|aufzug *m* lift, *Am.* elevator; ~**beförderung** *f* passenger transport; ~**beschreibung** *f* personal description

personenbezogen *Adj.*: ~*e Daten* personal data

Personen|fahndung *f* manhunt; ~**fähre** *f* passenger ferry

personengebunden *Adj. Genehmigung etc.*: non-transferable

Personen|gedächtnis *n* memory for (people and) faces; ~**kennziffer** *f* identity number, personal code; ~**kraftwagen** *m* (*abgek. Pkw*) (motor)-car, *Am. auch* auto(mobile); ~**kreis** *m* circle, group of people; ~**kult** *m* personality cult; ~**register** *n* index of names; ~**schaden** *m* personal injury; ~**stand** *m Jur.* marital status; ~**standsregister** *n* register of births, marriages, and deaths, *Am. etwa* bureau of vital statistics; ~**standsurkunde** *f* marriage certificate; ~**überprüfung** *f* identity check; ~**verkehr** *m* passenger traffic; ~**waage** *f*: (*e-e*) (a pair of) scales *Pl.*; *im Badezimmer*: *auch* (a

P

pair of) bathroom scales *Pl.*; **~wagen** *m* **1.** *Mot.* car, *Am.* automobile; **2.** *Eisenb.* passenger coach (*Am.* car); **~zug** *m* **1.** passenger train; **2.** (*Ggs. Schnellzug*) local train

Personifikation *f*; -, -*en* personification; **personifizieren** *v/t.* personify

persönlich I. *Adj.* personal; *auf Briefen: auch* private, confidential; **darf ich Ihnen e-e ~e Frage stellen?** can (*od.* may) I ask you something personal?; **Persönliches** *Zeitung:* personals; **II.** *Adv.* personally, in person; himself (*f* herself); **er wird ~ anwesend sein** he'll be personally present, he'll be there in person; **~ haften** be personally liable; **das ist nicht ~ gemeint** (please) don't take it personally; **das ist für dich ~** it's personal; *betont:* it's for you and you alone

Persönlichkeit *f* **1.** personality; **Laura ist schon e-e ~ über ein Kind:** Laura's a real little personality; → **gespalten**; **2.** (*bedeutende Person*) personality; **~ des öffentlichen Lebens** public figure

Persönlichkeits|entfaltung *f* personality development; **~recht** *n Jur.* personal (*od.* individual) right; **~spaltung** *f* split personality; **~wahl** *f Pol.* **1.** personality politics; **2. die Präsidentschaftswahl war e-e reine ~** the presidential election was focus(s)ed completely on the candidates' personalities

Perspektive *f*; -, *n* perspective (*auch fig.*); *fig.* (*Gesichtspunkt*) point of view, angle; (*Aussicht*) *auch* prospect(s *Pl.*); **hier stimmt die ~ nicht** he's *etc.* got the perspective wrong; **enge ~** *fig.* narrow view (*od.* perspective); **etw. aus der richtigen ~ sehen** see s.th. in perspective, get the right angle on s.th.

perspektivisch I. *Adj.; attr.* perspective ...; *Zeichnung etc.: präd.* in perspective; **II.** *Adv.:* **es stimmt ~ (nicht)** the perspective is right (wrong)

Peru (*n*); -*s*; *Geog.* Peru

Peruaner *m*; -*s*, -, **~in** *f*; -, -*nen* Peruvian, *weiblich auch:* Peruvian woman (*od.* girl *etc.*); **peruanisch** *Adj.* Peruvian

Perücke *f*; -, -*n* wig

pervers *Adj.* perverse (*auch fig.*), kinky *umg.*; **~es Hirn** twisted mind; **ein Perverser** a pervert; **Perversion** *f*; -, -*en* perversion; **pervertieren** *v/t.* pervert (**zu** to)

pesen *v/i. umg.* (*rasen*) belt, charge, zoom

Pessar *n*; -*s*, -*e* pessary (*od. Am. zur Empfängnisverhütung: auch* diaphragm, cap

Pessimismus *m*; -, *kein Pl.* pessimism; **Pessimist** *m*; -*en*, -*en*, **Pessimistin** *f*; -, -*nen* pessimist; **pessimistisch I.** *Adj.* pessimistic; **II.** *Adv.* pessimistically

Pest *f*; -, *kein Pl.* plague; **ich hasse es wie die ~** I can't stand it; **er hasst ihn wie die ~** he hates his guts, he hates him like the plague *umg.*; **das stinkt ja wie die ~** *umg.* it stinks something awful, what a stench; **~beule** *f* (plague) boil; **~gestank** *m* stench; **~hauch** *m fig.* miasma

Pestizid *n*; -*s*, -*e* pesticide

pestkrank *Adj.* **~ sein** have (caught) the plague; **Pestkranke** *m*, *f*; -*n*, -*n* plague victim, person with plague

Peter *m*; -*s*: **schwarzer ~** (*Spiel*) *etwa* black peter; **j-m den schwarzen ~ zuschieben** *fig.* pass the buck to s.o., leave someone holding the baby (*od.*

---

bag)

Peterle *n*; -(*s*); *südd.* (*Petersilie*) parsley

Petersilie *f*; -, -*n* parsley; **das hat ihm gründlich die ~ verhagelt** *umg. fig.* that really messed things up for him, that really threw a spanner (*Am.* monkey wrench) in(to) the works (for him)

Peterskirche *f*: **die ~ in Rom:** St Peter's (Basilica)

Peterwagen *m umg.* patrol car, *Am.* cherry top

PET-Flasche *f* (*Plastikflasche für Getränke*) PET bottle

Petition *f*; -, -*en* petition

Petitions|ausschuss *m* committee on petitions; **~recht** *n* right to petition

Petri Heil! *Interj.* (*Anglergruß*) Hail Peter! (*angler's greeting*), *etwa* good luck with the fishing

Petrochemie *f* petrochemistry; **petrochemisch** *Adj.* petrochemical

Petrol *n schw.*, **Petroleum** *n*; -*s*, *kein Pl.* paraffin, *Am.* kerosene

Petroleum|kocher *m* paraffin (*Am.* kerosene) stove; **~lampe** *f* paraffin (*Am.* kerosene) lamp

Petrus *m*; *Petri*; *bibl.* Peter; **an der Himmelspforte:** *mst* St(.) Peter; **Brief des ~** → **Petrusbrief**, **Petrusbrief** *m bibl.:* **der 1./2. ~** the 1st/2nd Epistle of St(.) Peter, Peter I/II

Petticoat ['petikoːt] *m*; -*s*, -*s* stiffened petticoat

Petting *n*; -(*s*), -*s* petting; **~ machen** indulge in petting

petto: **etw. in ~ haben** *umg.* have s.th. up one's sleeve

Petunie *f*; -, -*n*; *Bot.* petunia

Petze *f*; -, -*n*; *umg.* telltale, sneak; (**du**) **alte ~!** you sneaky so-and-so!, you little sneak!; **petzen** *vt/i. umg.* sneak, snitch; *wiederholt:* tell tales; **er hat's der Lehrerin gepetzt** he went and told the teacher about it; **Petzer** *m*; -*s*, -, **Petzerin** *f*; -, -*nen*; *umg.* telltale, sneak

peu à peu [pøaˈpøː] *Adv.* gradually, bit by bit, *Am. auch* little by little

Pfad *m*; -(*e*)*s*, -*e* path (*auch fig. und EDV*); **auf dem ~ der Tugend wandeln** *fig.* keep to the straight and narrow

Pfadfinder *m* boy scout; **er ist den ~n beigetreten** he joined the scouts; **~in** *f* girl guide, *Am.* girl scout; **~lager** *n* scout camp

Pfaffe *m*; -*n*, -*n*; *pej.* cleric; *umg. hum.* sky pilot, holy Joe, *Am. auch* holy roller

Pfahl *m*; -(*e*)*s*, *Pfähle* stake; (*Pfosten*) post; *Bauwesen:* pile; **j-m ein ~ im Fleisch sein** *fig.* be a thorn in s.o.'s flesh; **~bau** *m*; -(*e*)*s*, -*bauten* pile dwelling; *in frühen Kulturen:* lake dwelling; **~dorf** *n* pile-village

pfählen *v/t.* **1.** (*stützen*) prop up, support; (*Reben*) stake; **2.** *hist.* (*töten*) impale

Pfahl|muschel *f Zool.* common mussel; **~werk** *n* paling; *Mil.* palisade; **~wurzel** *f Bot.* tap root

Pfalz[1] *f*; -, -*en*; *hist.* (*Palast*) palace

Pfalz[2] *f*; -; *hist. Herrschaftsgebiet:* palatinate; *Geog.:* **die ~** the Palatinate, *umg.:* (*deutsches Bundesland*) Rhineland-Palatinate

Pfälzer I. *m*; -*s*, -; (*Einwohner*) Palatine; *auch* man from the Palatinate; **II.** *Adj.:* **~ Wein** wine from the Palatinate; **Pfälzerin** *f*; -, -*nen* Palatine (woman)

Pfalzgraf *m hist.* Count Palatine

pfälzisch *Adj.* Palatine, from the Palatinate

Pfand *n*; -(*e*)*s*, *Pfänder* **1.** *Wirts.* pledge; (*Bürgschaft*) security; **als ~ geben** pledge, pawn; **sein Wort als ~ geben** pledge one's word; **2.** *für Flaschen etc.:* deposit; **~ für etw. zahlen** pay a deposit on s.th.; **3.** *beim Pfänderspiel:* forfeit

pfändbar *Adj. Jur.* attachable, distrainable; **nicht ~ sein** be exempt from seizure under execution

Pfandbrief *m Wirts.* debenture bond, mortgage bond

pfänden *v/t. Jur.* (*etw.*) seize, distrain (upon); **j-n ~ lassen** levy a distress against s.o.

Pfänderspiel *n* (game of) forfeits *Pl.*

Pfand|flasche *f* deposit (*od.* returnable) bottle; **~geld** *n* deposit; **~haus** *n*, **~leihe** *f*; -, -*n* pawnshop; **~leiher** *m*; -*s*, -, **~leiherin** *f*; -, -*nen* pawnbroker; **~pflicht** *f* compulsory deposit *od.* compulsory deposits *Pl.* (on bottles, tins [*bes. Am.* cans *etc.*]); **~recht** *n* lien; **~schein** *m* pawn ticket

Pfändung *f Jur.* seizure (under execution) (+ *Gen.* of); *förm.* distraint (upon), distress

Pfändungs|befehl *m*, **~beschluss** *m Jur.* warrant of distress

Pfanne *f*; -, -*n* **1.** *Gastr.* (frying) pan, *Am. auch* skillet; **ich werd mir ein paar Eier in die ~ hauen** *umg.* I'm going to fry (up) a couple of eggs; **j-n in die ~ hauen** *umg. fig.* (*zurechtweisen, kritisieren*) give s.o. a (real) roasting, haul (*od.* rake) s.o. over the coals; (*bei anderen schlecht machen*) run s.o.down; **2.** (*Dachpfanne*) pantile; **3.** *Anat.* (*Gelenkpfanne*) socket; **4.** *Tech. Gießerei:* ladle; **5.** *etw. auf der ~ haben* *umg. fig.* have s.th. up one's sleeve

...pfanne *f*, *im Subst.* **1.** *allg. im wörtl. Sinn:* pan; **Teflon~®** Teflon® frying pan; **2.** (*Gericht*): **Gemüse~** pan-fried vegetables; **Nudel~** pasta bake; **Reis~** risotto

Pfannen|boden *m* bottom of a (*od.* the) frying pan; **~gericht** *n* fried dish

Pfannkuchen *m* pancake, *Am. auch* flapjack, hotcake; **Berliner ~** *etwa* doughnut; **aufgehen wie ein ~** *umg.* (*dick werden*) swell up like a balloon

Pfarr|amt *n* rectory, vicarage; **~bezirk** *m* parish

Pfarrei *f* parish; → **Pfarramt**, **Pfarrer** *m*; -*s*, -; *kath.* (parish) priest; *anglikanisch:* vicar, *Am.* rector; *nonkonformistisch od. Am.:* minister, preacher

Pfarrerin *f*; -, -*nen* woman priest; *anglikanisch auch:* woman vicar, *Am.* rector; *nonkonformistisch od. Am.:* (woman) minister, preacher

Pfarrerstochter *f* clergyman's daughter; *nonkonformistisch od. Am.:* minister's (*od. umg.* preacher's) daughter

Pfarrgemeinde *f* parish

Pfarr|haus *n* parsonage; *anglikanisch:* rectory, vicarage; **~helfer** *m*, **~helferin** *f* curate; **~kirche** *f* parish church

Pfau *m*; -(*e*)*s*, -*en* peacock; *Astron. der* **~** Pavo, the Peacock; **der ~ schlägt ein Rad** the peacock spreads its tail; **er ist ein eitler ~** *fig.* he is as vain as a peacock

Pfauen|auge *n* **1.** (*Schmetterling*) peacock butterfly; **2.** *in Pfauenfeder:* eye; *fachspr.* ocellus; **~feder** *f* peacock feather; **~henne** *f* peahen

Pfeffer *m*; -*s*, *kein Pl.* pepper; **~ und Salz** *fig.* (*Muster*) salt-and-pepper; **geh hin, wo der ~ wächst!** *umg.* get lost!, go jump in the lake!; **dem muss**

man ~ geben *umg. (od. vulg.* ~ *in den Arsch blasen*) he needs a real kick in the pants (*od. vulg.* in the arse, *Am.* ass); → *Hase* 4; ~gurke *f* gherkin
pfefferig *Adj.* peppery
Pfeffer|korn *n* peppercorn; ~kuchen *m etwa* gingerbread
Pfefferminz|aroma *n* peppermint flavo(u)ring; ~bonbon *m, n* peppermint
Pfefferminze *f; -, kein Pl.; Bot.* (pepper)mint
Pfefferminz|geschmack *m* peppermint taste (*od.* flavo(u)r); ~likör *m* crème de menthe, peppermint liqueur; ~tee *m* (pepper)mint tea
pfeffern *v/t.* **1.** pepper; *fig. (Rede etc.)* spice; **2.** *umg. (e-n Gegenstand werfen)* fling, chuck; *j-m e-e* ~ *umg.* give s.o. a clout ([a]round the ears); → *gepfeffert*
Pfeffer|steak *n* pepper steak, steak au poivre; ~streuer *m* pepper caster
pfeffrig *Adj.* peppery
Pfeife *f; -, -n* **1.** (*Trillerpfeife*) whistle; *Mus.* pipe; *Mil.* fife; *e-r Orgel:* (organ) pipe; *nach j-s* ~ *tanzen fig.* dance to s.o.'s tune; *alles tanzt nach s-r* ~ *fig.* he always plays first fiddle; **2.** (*Tabakspfeife*) pipe; *er raucht* ~ he smokes a pipe; **3.** *umg. (Versager)* dead loss; *du* ~! you are useless!
pfeifen *vt/i.; pfeift, pfiff, hat gepfiffen* **1.** (*Lied etc.*) whistle; *Polizist, Schiedsrichter etc.:* blow the whistle; *Wind, Geschoss:* whistle; *Theat.* (*aus~*) hiss, boo; *vor sich hin* ~ whistle to o.s.; ~*des Geräusch* whistling (sound); ~*der Atem* wheezing; **2.** *Sport* (*Fußballspiel etc. leiten*) (be) referee; (*Freistoß etc.*) give, award *a free kick etc.*; *er hat das Foul nicht gepfiffen* he didn't whistle for (*od.* call) the foul; **3.** *umg. fig.: ich pfeif drauf!* I don't give a damn; *ich pfeif auf die Meinung der Leute* I don't give a damn (*od.* I couldn't care less) what people think; *ich werd dir was* ~! you know what you can do; *dem werd ich was* ~! he can take a running jump (*od.* flying leap)
Pfeifen|besteck *n* pipe knife; ~kopf *m* **1.** pipe bowl; **2.** *umg. (Versager)* dead loss; ~raucher *m*, ~raucherin *f* pipe smoker; ~ständer *m* pipe rack; ~stiel *m* pipe stem; ~stopfer *m* tobacco tamper; ~tabak *m* pipe tobacco
Pfeifer *m; -s, -,* ~in *f; -, -nen* whistler; *Mus.* piper
Pfeif|konzert *n umg.* barrage of whistling and booing, hail of catcalls; ~ton *m* **1.** whistling sound; *bes. von Radio etc.:* high-pitched whine; **2.** *als Signal:* whistle; *bitte sprechen Sie nach dem* ~ *Anrufbeantworter:* please speak after the tone (*od.* bleep)
Pfeil *m; -(e)s, -e* arrow (*auch Richtungsweiser*); (*Wurfpfeil*) dart; *Astron. der* ~ the Arrow, Sagitta; *mit* ~ *und Bogen* with a bow and arrow; *wie ein* ~ *fig.* like a shot
Pfeiler *m; -s, -* pillar (*auch fig.*); *e-r Brücke:* pier; ~brücke *f* pier bridge
Pfeilflügel *m Flug.* swept-back wing
pfeilgerade I. *Adj.* (as) straight as an arrow; **II.** *Adv.* straight; *sitzen:* erect; *er kam* ~ *auf uns zu* he made a bee-line for us, he headed straight for us
Pfeil|gift *n* arrow poison; ~kraut *n Bot.* arrowhead; ~richtung *f: in* ~ in the direction of the arrow; 2schnell *Adj.* (as) quick as lightning; ~spitze *f* arrowhead; ~taste *f EDV* arrow key
Pfennig *m; -s, -e, hist., bei Summen: -*

pfennig; *50* ~ *rausbekommen* get 50 pfennigs change; *fig.: er hat keinen* ~ he hasn't (got) a penny to his name; *jeden* ~ *dreimal umdrehen* be very tight-fisted, count every penny; *s-n letzten* ~ *für etw. ausgeben* just manage to scrape together enough to buy s.th.; *das ist keinen* ~ *wert* it's not worth a bean (*Am.* dime); *ich würde keinen* ~ *für ihn geben* I wouldn't bet a penny on his chances; *wer den* ~ *nicht ehrt, ist des Talers nicht wert Sprichw. etwa* look after the pennies and the pounds (*Am.* dollars) will look after themselves; ~absatz *m* stiletto heel; ~artikel *m* cheap article; ~beträge *Pl.* tiny amounts; ~fuchser *m; -s, -; umg.* penny-pincher, skinflint; ~kraut *n Bot.* moneywort; ~stück *n hist.* one-pfennig piece (*od.* coin)
Pferch *m; -(e)s, -e* fold, pen; **pferchen** *v/t.* pen; *fig. auch* cram; *32 Schüler in e-n Raum* ~ cram (*od.* squeeze) 32 pupils (*Am.* students) into a room
Pferd *n; -es, -e* **1.** *Zool.* horse; *aufs* ~ *steigen* mount a horse; *vom* ~ *steigen* dismount; *zu* ~*e* on horseback; *Truppen etc.:* mounted; **2.** *Schach:* knight; **3.** *Turnen:* (vaulting) horse; **4.** *fig., in Wendungen: das* ~ *beim Schwanz aufzäumen* put the cart before the horse; *er arbeitet wie ein* ~ he works like a Trojan; *keine zehn* ~*e bringen mich dahin* wild horses couldn't drag me there; *mit ihr kann man* ~*e stehlen* she's a good sport; *er/sie ist unser bestes* ~ *im Stall* he's/she's the best person we've got; *ihm gehen leicht die* ~*e durch* he tends to fly off the handle; *mach nicht die* ~*e scheu! umg.* don't get worked up!, keep your shirt on!; *ich glaub, mich tritt ein* ~ *umg.* well blow me; → *auch Gaul, Ross*
Pferdchen *n* **1.** small horse; **2.** ~ *laufen haben Sl. Zuhältermilieu:* have a string of prostitutes (*Am. auch* hookers)
Pferde|äpfel *Pl. umg.* horse droppings, *Am.* road apples; ~bremse *f Zool.* horsefly; ~fleisch *n* horsemeat; ~freund *m*, ~freundin *f* horse-lover; ~fuhrwerk *n* horse and cart; ~fuß *m des Teufels:* cloven hoof; *fig.* drawback, snag; *die Sache hat e-n* ~ there's a snag (to it); ~futter *n* (horse's) feed, fodder; ~gebiss *n umg.* horsy teeth *Pl.; er lächelte mit s-m* ~ he gave a horsy grin; ~geschirr *n* horse's harness; ~gesicht *n umg.* horsy face; ~haar *n* horsehair; ~händler *m*, ~händlerin *f* horse dealer (*Am.* trader); ~knecht *m* groom; ~koppel *f* paddock; ~kuss *m umg. Sport* thigh knock; ~kutsche *f* horse-drawn carriage; ~länge *f* length; ~liebhaber *m*, ~liebhaberin *f* horse-lover; ~lotto *n etwa* sweepstakes *Pl.;* ~mist *m* horse dung, horse manure *Agr.;* ~narr *m*, ~närrin *f umg.* horse freak; ~natur *f: e-e* ~ *haben* (*od.* sein) have an iron constitution; ~pfleger *m*, ~pflegerin *f* groom; ~rasse *f* breed of horse; ~rennbahn *f* racecourse, racetrack; ~rennen *n* horse racing; *einzelnes:* horse race; ~rennsport *m: der* ~ horse racing, the turf; ~schlachter *m* horse butcher; ~schlitten *m* horse-drawn sleigh; ~schwanz *m* horse's tail; (*Frisur*) ponytail; ~sport *m* equestrian sports *Pl.;* ~stall *m* stable; ~stärke *f Tech.* horsepower (*abgek. HP*); ~steak *n* horsemeat steak; ~transporter *m*

horsebox; ~wagen *m* horse-drawn carriage; ~wette *f* horse-racing bet, bet on the horses; ~wirt *m*, ~wirtin *f* (*Beruf*) fully qualified groom; ~wurst *f* horsemeat sausage; ~zucht *f* horse breeding
pfetzen *v/t. südd. (kneifen)* pinch
Pfiff *m; -(e)s, -e* **1.** whistle; ~*e Theat. etc.* catcall(s), whistling *Sg.;* **2.** *nur Sg.; umg. (Stil)* style; *der Mantel hat* ~ that coat's got style; *der Sache den richtigen* ~ *geben* give it that extra something; **3.** *altm., umg. (Kniff): das ist ein Ding mit* ~ there's a trick to it
Pfifferling *m; -s, -e Bot.* chanterelle; *umg. fig.: keinen* ~ *wert* not worth a bean (*Am.* dime); *er schert sich keinen* ~ *drum umg.* he doesn't care two hoots about it
pfiffig *Adj.* smart; **Pfiffikus** *m, -, -se; umg.* crafty devil
Pfingsten *n; -, -* Whitsun; *kirchl. auch* Pentecost; *zu od. an* ~ at Whitsun, *Am.* on Pentecost Sunday
Pfingst|ferien *Pl.* Whitsun holidays (*od.* holiday *Sg.*), Whitsun break *Sg.;* ~montag *m* Whit Monday, *Am.* Monday after Pentecost; ~ochse *m umg.: rausgeputzt wie ein* ~ dressed up to the nines; ~rose *f Bot.* peony; ~sonntag *m* Whit Sunday; *kirchl. od. Am. auch* Pentecost
Pfirsich *m; -s, -e* peach; ~baum *m* peach tree; ~bowle *f* peach fruit cup; ~haut *f* peach (*od.* peaches and cream) complexion; ~kern *m* peach stone
Pflanze *f; -, -n* **1.** plant; ~n fressend herbivorous; **2.** *umg. (Person)* character
pflanzen I. *vt/i.* plant (*auch fig.*); *gepflanzt wird im Frühjahr* planting (out) is done in the spring; *in Töpfe* ~ pot; → *anpflanzen, aufpflanzen, einpflanzen;* **II.** *v/refl. umg.: sich aufs Sofa* ~ plonk (*Am.* plop) o.s. (down) on the sofa
Pflanzen|bau *m* cultivation of plants; (*Landwirtschaft*) agriculture; ~eiweiß *n* vegetable albumin (*od.* protein); ~extrakt *m* vegetable extract; ~farbstoff *m* vegetable dye; ~fresser *m* herbivore; ~gesellschaft *f Bot.* plant community; ~gift *n* **1.** vegetable poison; **2.** (*Herbizid*) herbicide; ~heilkunde *f* phytotherapy; ~kost *f* vegetable diet; ~krankheit *f* plant disease; ~kunde *f* botany; ~öl *n* vegetable oil; 2reich *Adj.* rich in plant life; ~reich *n* flora, vegetable kingdom; ~saft *m* sap; ~schädling *m* plant pest; ~schutz *m* plant protection; (*gegen Schädlinge*) pest control; ~schutzmittel *n* pesticide; ~welt *f* **1.** flora, vegetable kingdom; **2.** *e-s bestimmten Gebiets:* flora, plant life
Pflanzer *m; -s, -,* ~in *f; -, -nen* planter
Pflanzkartoffel *f Agr.* seed potato
pflanzlich *Adj.* vegetable ...; ~es Arzneimittel *plant remedy;* ~e Kost vegetarian food
Pflanzstock *m Agr.* dibble, dibber, digging stick
Pflanzung *f* **1.** (*das Pflanzen*) planting; **2.** (*Anlage*) plantation
Pflaster *n; -s, -* **1.** *Med.* (sticking) plaster, *Am.* adhesive tape; **2.** *e-r Straße:* road (surface), roadway; *teures* ~ *fig.* expensive spot (*Stadt:* place); *heißes* ~ dangerous place
Pflasterer *m*, **Pflästerer** *m; -s, -; südd., schw.* paver; (*Straßenarbeiter*) roadworker

P

Pflaster|maler *m* pavement (*Am.* sidewalk) artist; **~malerei** *f* **1.** pavement (*Am.* sidewalk) art; **2.** (*Bild*) pavement (*Am.* sidewalk) drawing; **~malerin** *f* (female) pavement (*Am.* sidewalk) artist

pflastern *v/t.* (*Straße*) surface, *Am.* pave; (*Bürgersteig*) pave, *Am.* lay (*sidewalks*)

Pflasterstein *m* paving stone

Pflaume *f*, -, -n **1.** *Frucht*: plum; gedörrte: prune; **2.** *umg. pej.* (*Versager*) twit, dead loss; *wenn j-d kneift*: chicken; **3.** *vulg.* cunt, pussy

Pflaumenbaum *m* *Bot.* plum tree

pflaumengroß *Adj.* plum-sized

Pflaumen|kern *m* plum stone; **~kuchen** *m* plum flan (*Am.* pie); **~schnaps** *m* plum brandy

pflaumenweich *Adj.* **1.** **~es Ei** soft-boiled egg; **2.** *er ist ~ umg.* he's a real softie

Pflege *f*; -, *kein Pl. allg.*: care (*auch der Haut, Zähne, e-s Kindes etc.*); *des Äußeren*: *auch* grooming; *e-s Kranken*: nursing care; *e-s Gartens*: tending; *der Künste, von Beziehungen*: cultivation; *Tech.* maintenance, service; *von Datenbanken etc.*: keeping up, updating; **ambulante ~** outpatient care; **häusliche ~** home nursing; *viel ~ brauchen* need a lot of care (*od.* attention); *ein Kind / e-n Hund in ~ nehmen* take a child/dog into one's care; *ein Kind* (*bei j-m*) *in ~ geben* put a child into (s.o.'s) care

...pflege *f, im Subst.*: **Auto~** car care; (*Wartung*) car maintenance; **Parkett~** care of parquet floors

pflegebedürftig *Adj.* in need of care; **Pflegebedürftigkeit** *f* need of care; **Grad der ~** amount of care needed

Pflege|beruf *m* nursing profession; **~dienst** *m* **1.** *für Kranke etc.*: nursing service; *ambulanter ~* outpatient care; **2.** *Tech.* servicing facility; *Mot.* car care (*od.* maintenance) service; **~eltern** *Pl.* foster parents; **~fall** *m* invalid; **~familie** *f* foster family; **~geld** *n* *für Behinderte etc.*: attendance (*od.* nursing) allowance; **~heim** *n* nursing home; **~kasse** *f* nursing insurance institution; **~kind** *n* foster child; **~kosten** *Pl.* nursing fees

pflegeleicht *Adj.* easy-care; *fig. Person*: easy to get along with

Pflege|mittel *n* shoe-care (*od.* skin-care *etc.*) product; **~mutter** *f* foster mother

pflegen I. *v/t.* **1.** (*pflegebedürftige Person*) look after, care for; (*Kind, Kranken*) *auch* nurse; (*Blumen, Garten*) tend; (*Kunst, Freundschaft*) cultivate; *j-n aufopfernd ~* sacrifice oneself to care for s.o.; *j-n gesund ~* nurse s.o. back to health; **2.** *etw. zu tun ~* be in the habit of doing s.th.; *sie pflegte zu sagen* she used to say, she would say; *solche Versuche ~ fehlzuschlagen* such attempts usually fail (*od.* tend to fail); **3.** *geh.* (*auch pflog, gepflogen*) (*Freundschaft, Interessen, Kunst*) foster, cultivate; *Umgang mit j-m ~* associate with s.o.; **II.** *v/refl.*: *sich ~* look after o.s.; *äußerlich*: take care of one's appearance

Pflegepauschale *f* all-inclusive payment for care needs

Pfleger *m*; -s, - **1.** → *Krankenpfleger*; **2.** *Jur.* curator, guardian; **~in** *f*; -, -nen **1.** nurse; **2.** *Jur.* curator, guardian

pflegerisch *Adj.*: **~e Berufe** caring (*od.* nursing) professions

Pflege|satz *m* (daily) charge for a hospital bed; **~sohn** *m* foster son; **~station** *f* nursing ward; **~stufe** *f* class of nursing care; **~ 1** *in der Pflegeversicherung*: first class nursing care; **~tochter** *f* foster daughter; **~vater** *m* foster father; **~vergütung** *f* nursing fee; **~versicherung** *f* nursing care insurance

pfleglich I. *Adj.* careful; **II.** *Adv.*: *etw./j-n ~ behandeln* take good care of s.th./s.o.

Pflegling *m*; -s, -e **1.** person/animal being looked after, charge; **2.** *Jur.* foster child

Pflegschaft *f* *für Kinder etc.*: guardianship; *für Vermögen*: trusteeship

Pflicht *f*; -, -en *duty*; *Sport* compulsory exercise(s *Pl.*); *s-e ~ tun* do one's duty; *s-e ~en verletzen* act contrary to (*od.* in breach of) one's duties; *es sich* (*Dat.*) *zur ~ machen zu* (+ *Inf.*) make it one's duty to (+ *Inf.*); *die ~ ruft* duty calls; *j-n in die ~ nehmen* take s.o. up on his (*od.* her) promise; *es ist ~* it's obligatory (*od.* compulsory); *es ist d-e* (*verdammte*) *~ und Schuldigkeit* it is your bounden duty; *die ehelichen ~en mst hum.* one's marital duties, one's duties as a husband (*od.* wife)

...pflicht *f, im Subst.*: **Aussage~** obligation to testify (*od.* give evidence); **Ausweis~** obligation to produce identification; **Fürsorge~** *Jur.* duty of care; **Wahl~** electoral duty

Pflicht|beitrag *m* compulsory contribution; **~besuch** *m* courtesy call

pflichtbewusst *Adj.* conscientious; **Pflichtbewusstsein** *n* sense of duty

Pflichteifer *m* devotion to duty, zeal; **pflichteifrig** *Adj.* zealous

Pflichtenkollision *f* **1.** conflicting duties *Pl.*; **2.** (*Loyalitätskonflikt*) conflict of loyalties

Pflicht|erfüllung *f* discharge of duties; **~fach** *n* *Päd.* compulsory subject; **~gefühl** *n* sense of duty

pflichtgemäß I. *Adj.* due, dutiful; **II.** *Adv.* duly, dutifully

...pflichtig *im Adj.*: **lohnsteuer~** subject to income tax

Pflicht|lauf *m*, **~laufen** *n* *Eiskunstlauf etc.*: compulsory figures *Pl.*; **~leistungen** *Pl.* standard insurance benefits; **~lektüre** *f* required reading (*auch hum.*); *für eine Prüfung*: set book(s *Pl.*), *Am.* required text(s *Pl.*); **~mensch** *m* very zealous person; **~mitgliedschaft** *f* compulsory membership

pflichtschuldig(st) *Adv.* dutifully

Pflichtteil *m, n* *Jur.* legal portion (*od.* share), *Am.* statutory share

Pflichtübung *f* *Sport* compulsory (*od.* set) exercise; *es war für ihn e-e reine ~ fig.* he did it purely out of a sense of duty

Pflichtunterricht *m* compulsory class(es *Pl.*)

pflichtvergessen *Adj.* neglectful, irresponsible; **Pflichtvergessenheit** *f* negligence in the performance of one's duty

Pflicht|verletzung *f* breach of duty; **~versäumnis** *n auch Jur.* neglect (*od.* dereliction) of duty; **~versicherung** *f* compulsory insurance; **~verteidiger** *m*, **~verteidigerin** *f* *Jur.* assigned counsel

pflichtwidrig I. *Adj.* disloyal, contrary to (one's) duty; **II.** *Adv.*: *sich ~ verhalten* go against one's duty; **Pflichtwidrigkeit** *f* breach of duty

Pflock *m*; -(e)s, *Pflöcke*; (*Zeltpflock*) peg; (*Pfahl*) post, stake

pflücken *v/t.* pick; **Pflücker** *m*; -s, -, **Pflückerin** *f*; -, -nen picker

Pflug *m*; -(e)s, *Pflüge* plough, *Am.* plow; **~bogen** *m* *Skisport*: plough, *Am.* plow

pflügen *v/t./i.* plough, *Am.* plow; **Pflüger** *m*; -s, - ploughman, *Am.* plowman

Pflugschar *f*; -, -en ploughshare, *Am.* plowshare

Pfortader *f* *Anat.* portal vein

Pforte *f*, -, -n **1.** (*Tor*) gate; (*Tür*) door; *e-r Klinik etc.*: entrance; *s-e ~n öffnen/schließen* open/close its doors; **2.** *fig.* gateway; *die ~n des Himmels / der Hölle fig.* the gates of heaven / of hell

Pförtner *m*; -s, - **1.** gatekeeper; (*Portier*) porter, *auch Am.* doorman; **2.** *Anat.* pylorus; **~haus** *n* gatekeeper's lodge, gatehouse; **~in** *f*; -, -nen (female) gatekeeper; (*weiblicher Portier*) (female) porter; **~loge** *f* reception; *am Toreingang*: gatekeeper's cabin, gate *umg.*

Pfosten *m*; -s, - post; *schmaler*: pole; (*Torpfosten*) (goal)post; **~schuss** *m* shot against the post; **~!** it's hit the post

Pfote *f*, -, -n **1.** paw; **2.** *umg.* (*Hand*) mitt, paw; **~n weg!** hands off!, get your dirty mitts (*od.* paws) off!; *er hat s-e ~n überall drin pej.* he has to be in on everything; *sich* (*Dat.*) *die ~n verbrennen fig.* burn one's fingers; **3.** *umg.* (*Handschrift*) scrawl

Pfropf *m*; -(e)s, -e plug (*auch Eiter- und Wattepfropf*); (*Blutpfropf*) (blood)clot, blockage; **Pfropfen** *m*; -s, - stopper; (*Korken*) cork; **pfropfen** *v/t.* **1.** (*zustöpseln*) plug, stop(per); (*Flasche*) stopper; *mit Korken*: cork; **2.** *Agr.* graft; **3.** (*hineinstopfen*) cram (*in* + *Akk.* into); → *gepfropft*

Pfründe *f*; -, -n; *kirchl.* prebend; (*Kirchenamt*) benefice; *fig.* sinecure

Pfuhl *m*; -(e)s, -e murky pool; *fig.* slough

pfui *Interj.* ugh! yuck!; *zum Hund od. Kind*: yuck!; (*lass das*) no!; *Sport etc.* boo!; *das ist ~ Kinderspr.* that's yucky; → *Teufel* 3

Pfund *n*; -(e)s, -e, *bei Summen*: - **1.** (*Gewicht*) pound (*abgek.* lb, *Pl.* lbs); *vier ~ Kartoffeln* four pounds of potatoes; *10 ~ zunehmen/abnehmen* put on / lose 10 pounds; *mehr ~e auf die Waage bringen* put on weight; **2.** (*Währung und Betrag*) pound; *10* (*englische*) *~* 10 pounds (sterling); *~ Sterling* pound sterling (*abgek.* £)

...pfünder *m, im Subst.*: pounder; *ein Viertel~* (*Hamburger*) a quarter-pounder

pfundig *Adj. südd., österr.* great

...pfündig *im Adj.*: *ein drei~es Hähnchen* a three-pound chicken

Pfund|münze *f* pound coin; **~note** *f* pound note

Pfundskerl *m umg.* great guy

pfundweise *Adv.* by the pound

Pfundzeichen *n* pound sign

Pfusch *m*; -(e)s, *kein Pl.* **1.** *umg.* botch-up, cock-up *Brit.*; *~ machen od. bauen* screw up, cock it up *Brit.*; *~ am Bau* botched building work; **2.** *österr.* (*Schwarzarbeit*) (undeclared) work done on the side; (*nach Feierabend*) moonlighting *umg.*; **~arbeit** *f umg.* bungling; (*Ergebnis*) botched job, botch-up

pfuschen *v/t./i.* **1.** *umg.* bungle; **2.** *österr.* (*schwarzarbeiten*) do (undeclared) jobs on the side; (*nach Feierabend*) moonlight *umg*.

Pfuscher *m*; *-s*, - **1.** *umg*. bungler; *im Beruf*: amateur; (*Gauner*) cowboy; (*Kurpfuscher*) quack; **2.** *österr*. (*Schwarzarbeiter*) *person who does* (*undeclared*) *jobs on the side*; (*nach Feierabend*) moonlighter *umg*.; **Pfuscherei** *f* → *Pfusch*; **Pfuscherin** *f*; -, *-nen*; *umg*. → *Pfuscher*

Pfütze *f*; -, *-n* puddle

...pfütze *f*, *im Subst*.: *Regen~* puddle of rainwater

phallisch *Adj*. phallic

Phallus *m*; -, *Phalli* phal\|lus, *Pl*. -li; **~symbol** *n* phallic symbol

Phänomen *n*; *-s*, *-e* phenome\|non, *Pl*. -na (*auch fig*.); *fig*. (*Person*) *auch* real phenomenon; (*Rätsel*) *auch* mystery; **phänomenal** *Adj*. phenomenal (*auch fig*.); **Phänomenologie** *f*; -, *kein Pl*. phenomenology

Phänotyp *m*, **~us** *m*; *-s bzw*. -, *Phänotypen* phenotype

Phantasie *etc*. → *Fantasie etc*.

Phantasmagorie *f*; -, *-n* **1.** (*Trugbild*) phantasm; **2.** *Theat. etc*. phantasmagoria

Phantom *n*; *-s*, *-e* phantom; **e-m ~ nachjagen** pursue an illusion; **~bild** *n* identikit® (*od*. photofit *od*. composite) picture; **~schmerzen** *Pl*. phantom pain *Sg*.

Pharao *m*; *-s*, *-nen*; *hist*. Pharaoh

Pharaonen\|grab *n* Pharaoh's (*od*. Pharaonic) tomb; **~reich** *n* **1.** Pharaonic kingdom (*Herrschaft*: reign); **2.** *das ~* Ancient Egypt

Pharisäer *m*; *-s*, - **1.** *hist*. Pharisee; **2.** *fig*. pharisee; *selbstgerechter auch*: self-righteous person; *heuchlerischer*: hypocrite; *intoleranter*: bigot; **3.** *fig*. (*Getränk*) coffee with rum and whipped cream; **pharisäerhaft** *Adj*. pharisaic(al); (*selbstgerecht*) *auch*: self-righteous, holier-than-thou; (*heuchlerisch*) hypocritical; (*intolerant*) bigoted

Pharma\|industrie *f* pharmaceutical(s) industry; **~keule** *f umg*. massive cocktail of medication

Pharmako\|loge *m*; *-n*, *-n* pharmacologist; **~logie** *f*; -, *kein Pl*. pharmacology; **~login** *f* (female) pharmacologist; **pharmakologisch** *Adj*. pharmacological

Pharma\|konzern *m* pharmaceutical(s) company; **~referent** *m*, **~referentin** *f* representative for a pharmaceutical(s) company; **~unternehmen** *n* pharmaceutical(s) company

Pharmazeut *m*; *-en*, *-en* pharmacist; **~in** *f*, -, *-nen* (female) pharmacist; **pharmazeutisch** *Adj*. pharmaceutical; **pharmazeutisch-technische Assistentin** *f* (*abgek*. **PTA**) pharmacist's assistant

Pharmazie *f*; -, *kein Pl*. pharmaceutics (*V. im Sg*.)

Phase *f*; -, *-n* phase (*auch Astron*., *Etech*.); *e-r Entwicklung*, *e-s Prozesses*: *auch* stage (*auch e-r Krankheit*); *in dieser ~* during this phase (*od*. stage), at this stage; *sich in e-r kritischen ~ befinden* be going through a critical phase (*od*. stage); *in die entscheidende od*. *umg*. *heiße ~ treten* enter the (*od*. its, their) critical phase (*od*. stage)

...phase *f*, *im Subst*.: *Erprobungs~* trial (*od*. testing) stage; *Schluss~* final phase (*od*. stage)

phasengleich *Adj*. in phase

Phasenmesser *m Etech*. phase meter

Phasenverschiebung *f Phys*. phase displacement; **phasenverschoben** *Adj*. out of phase

Phenol *n*; *-s*, *-e*; *Chem*. phenol

Pheromon *n*; *-s*, *-e*; *Bio*. pheromone

Philanthrop *m*; *-en*, *-en* philanthropist; **Philanthropie** *f*; -, *kein Pl*. philanthropy; **Philanthropin** *f*; -, *-nen* (female) philanthropist; **philanthropisch** *Adj*. philanthropic(al)

Philatelie *f*; -, *kein Pl*. philately; **Philatelist** *m*; *-en*, *-en*, **Philatelistin** *f*; -, *-nen* philatelist

Philharmonie *f*; -, *-n*; *Mus*. philharmonic orchestra; (*Konzertsaal*) philharmonic concert hall; **Philharmoniker** *Pl*.: *die Berliner etc*. ~ the Berlin *etc*. Philharmonic (Orchestra)

Philipperbrief *m bibl*.: *der ~* the (*od*. St[.] Paul's) Epistle to the Philippians, Philippians

Philippika *f*; -, *Philippiken*; *fig*. philippic, tirade

Philippinen *Pl. Geog*.: *die ~* the Philippines *Pl*., the Philippine Islands

Philippiner *m*; *-s*, -, **~in** *f*; -, *-nen* Filipino, *weiblich auch*: Filipino woman (*od*. girl *etc*.); **philippinisch** *Adj*. Philippine, *bes. Menschen*: *auch* Filipino

Philister *m*; *-s*, -, **philisterhaft** *Adj. fig. pej*. Philistine, philistine

Philologe *m*; *-n*, *-n* language and literature expert (*od*. teacher *od*. man *umg*.), *Am*. philologist; **Philologie** *f*; -, *-n* (study of) language and literature, *Am*. philology; **Philologin** *f*; -, *-nen* language and literature expert (*od*. teacher *od*. woman *umg*.), *Am*. (female) philologist; **philologisch** *Adj. attr*. language and literature ..., *Am*. philological

Philosoph *m*; *-en*, *-en* philosopher; **Philosophie** *f*; -, *-n* philosophy; **philosophieren** *v/i*. philosophize (*über* + *Akk*. on); **Philosophin** *f*; -, *-nen* (female) philosopher; **philosophisch** **I.** *Adj*. philosophical; *vom ~en Standpunkt* from a philosophical point of view, looking at it philosophically; **II.** *Adv*. philosophically; *~ argumentieren* argue in a philosophical manner (*od*. like a philosopher)

Phiole *f*; -, *-n* phial, vial

Phlegma *n*; *-s*, *kein Pl*.; (*Gemütsart*) lethargy, apathy; **Phlegmatiker** *m*, *-s*, -, **Phlegmatikerin** *f*; -, *-nen* apathetic type; **phlegmatisch** *Adj*. lethargic, apathetic

Phobie *f*; -, *-n* phobia; **Phobiker** *m*; *-s*, -, **Phobikerin** *f*; -, *-nen*, **phobisch** *Adj*. phobic

...phobie *f*, *im Subst*.: *allg*. ...phobia; *Anglo~* anglophobia

Phon *n*; *-s*, -; *Phys*. phon; *der Lärm betrug über 100 ~* the volume of noise was more than 100 phons

Phonem *n*; *-s*, *-e*; *Ling*. phoneme; **phonematisch 1.** *Adj*. phonemic; **2.** *Adv*.: *~ richtig* phonemically correct

Phonetik *f*; -, *kein Pl*. phonetics *Pl*. (*als Fach mit V. im Sg*.); **Phonetiker** *m*; *-s*, -, **Phonetikerin** *f -*, *-nen* phonetician; **phonetisch I.** *Adj*. phonetic; **II.** *Adv*. phonetically; *~ darstellen* transcribe

Phönix *m*; -: *wie* (*ein*) *~ aus der Asche steigen* rise (like a phoenix) from the ashes

Phönizier *m*; *-s*, -, **~in** *f*; -, *-nen* Phoenician, *weiblich auch*: Phoenician woman (*od*. girl *etc*.); **phönizisch** *Adj*. Phoenician

Phono\|eingang *m Tech*. phono input; **~kabel** *n* phono cable (*od*. cord)

Phono\|loge *m*; *-n*, *-n* phonologist; **~logie** *f*; -, *kein Pl*. phonology; **~login** *f*; -, *-nen* (female) phonologist

Phonotypistin *f*; -, *-nen* audiotypist

phon\|stark *Adj*. loud; *Wiedergabe*: high-volume; *Lautsprecher*: powerful; **Phonstärke** *f* volume (*od*. decibel) level; **Phonzahl** *f* number of phons (*od*. etwa decibels)

Phosphat *n*; *-(e)s*, *-e*; *Chem*. phosphate

phosphat\|frei *Adj*. phosphate-free; **~haltig** *Adj*. containing phosphates

Phosphor *m*; *-s*, *kein Pl*.; *Chem*. phosphorus; **~bombe** *f* incendiary bomb, firebomb

Phosphoreszenz *f*; -, *kein Pl*. phosphorescence; **phosphoreszieren** *v/i*. phosphoresce; **phosphoreszierend I.** *Part. Präs*. → *phosphoreszieren*; **II.** *Adj*. phosphorescent

phosphorhaltig *Adj*. phosphoric

Phosphorsäure *f Chem*. phosphoric acid

Photo... *siehe auch Foto...*

Photo\|biologie *f* photobiology; **~diode** *f* photodiode

photoelektrisch *Adj*. photoelectric, photovoltaic

Photoelement *n Etech*. photovoltaic cell

Photometrie *f*; -, *kein Pl*. photometry

Photon *n*; *-s*, *-en*; *Phys*. photon

Photosynthese *f*; -, *kein Pl*.; *Bio*. photosynthesis

Photovoltaik *f*; -, *kein Pl*.; *Etech*. photovoltaics *Pl*.; **~anlage** *f Etech*. photovoltaic array

Photozelle *f Etech*. photoelectric cell, electric eye

Phrase *f*; -, *-n* **1.** (*abgedroschene Redensart*) cliché, platitude; *bes. Pol*. catchphrase; *leere ~n* empty talk, claptrap *umg*.; *~n dreschen umg*. talk in clichés (*od*. platitudes); **2.** *Mus*., *Ling*. phrase

...phrase *f Ling*., *im Subst*.: *Nominal~* noun phrase

Phrasen\|drescher *m*; *-s*, -, **~drescherin** *f*; -, *-nen*; *umg*. phrasemonger; **~drescherei** *f -*, *-en*; *umg*. phrasemongering, hot air

phrasenhaft *Adj*. empty, meaningless

Phraseologie *f*; -, *-n* phraseology; **phraseologisch** *Adj*. phraseological

phrasieren *v/t. Mus*. phrase; **Phrasierung** *f Mus*. phrasing

pH-Wert *m Chem*. pH factor; **~-Bestimmung** *f* litmus test

Phylogenese *f*; -, *kein Pl*.; *Bio*. phylogenesis; **phylogenetisch** *Adj*. phylogenetic

Physik *f*; -, *kein Pl*. physics *Pl*. (*als Fach mit V. im Sg*.); **physikalisch** *Adj*. **1.** *Vorgang etc*.: physical; **2.** *die Physik betreffend*: *attr*. physics ...; *~es Gesetz* law of physics; *~e Einheiten* physical units; *~es Institut* institute (*od*. department) of physics; **3.** *Therapie etc*.: physical; **Physiker** *m*; *-s*, -, **Physikerin** *f*; -, *-nen* physicist

Physik\|lehrer *m*, **~lehrerin** *f* physics teacher; **~studium** *n* study of physics

Physikum *n*; *-s*, *Physika*; *Med*. preliminary medical examination

Physiognomie *f*; -, *-n* physiognomy

Physiologe *m*; *-n*, *-n* physiologist; **Physiologie** *f*; -, *kein Pl*. physiology; **Physiologin** *f*; -, *-nen* (female) physiologist; **physiologisch** *Adj*. physiological; *~e Kochsalzlösung* physiological saline solution

Physio\|therapeut *m*; *-en*, *-en*, **~thera-**

peutin f; -, -nen physiotherapist, physio umg.; **~therapie** f physiotherapy
Physis f; -, kein Pl. physical constitution; **physisch** Adj. physical
Pi n Math. pi; **die Zahl ~** the number represented by pi
Pianist m; -en, -en, **~in** f; -, -nen pianist
Piano n; -s, -s; Mus. altm., noch hum. piano; (Flügel) grand piano
Piaster m; -s, - Währung: piast|re, bes. Am. -er
picheln vt/i. umg. tipple, booze; **er hat anständig e-n gepichelt** he was knocking them back; **einen ~** wet one's whistle
Picke f; -, -n pick(axe), Am. pick(ax)
Pickel¹ m; -s, -; Med. spot, pimple; **e-n ~ ausdrücken** squeeze (out) a pimple
Pickel² m; -s, -; Tech. pick(axe), Am. pick(ax); (Eispickel) ice pick
Pickelgesicht n umg. **1.** spotty face; **2.** pej. (Person) spotty person, Am. zit face, pizza face; (Junge) pimply youth; Pl. auch spotty (od. pimply) teenagers, the acne brigade Sg.
Pickelhaube f spiked helmet
pickelig Adj. spotty, pimply
picken vt/i. **1.** peck; **etw. aus etw. ~** pick s.th. out of s.th.; **2.** österr. (kleben) stick
Pickerl n; -s, -n; österr. (Aufkleber) sticker; (Autobahnvignette) motorway (Am. tollway) pass (in the form of a windscreen [Am. windshield] sticker)
picklig Adj. → pickelig
Picknick n picnic; (ein) **~ machen** have (od. go for) a picnic
Picknick|koffer m picnic case; **~korb** m picnic basket (größer: hamper)
picobello umg. **I.** Adj. perfect, spot (Am. right) on umg.; **II.** Adv.: **~ sauber** etc. absolutely spotless etc.; **~ gekleidet** immaculately dressed; **er hat die Wohnung ~ aufgeräumt** he did a beautiful job of tidying the flat (Am. apartment)
Piefke m; -s, -s; umg. pej. **1.** (Wichtigtuer): **eingebildeter ~** conceited big-head; **2.** österr. (Deutscher) etwa Jerry umg., overbearing German
piek|fein umg. **I.** Adj. smart, posh, Am. snazzy; bes. Restaurant: auch swish, flashy; Kleidung etc.: (very) smart; **II.** Adv.: **sich ~ anziehen** put on one's Sunday best, put some smart gear on Sl.
piep Interj.: **~!** Vogel: cheep!; **er sagte nicht mal ~** umg. there wasn't a peep from him; **Piep** m umg. **1. du hast wohl 'n ~!** you must be crazy; **2. der wird keinen ~ mehr machen** (tot sein) we won't hear another peep out of him; → **Pieps**
piepe, piepegal Adj. umg.: **das ist mir ~** I don't care two hoots, I don't give a damn (od. Brit. a tinker's cuss)
piepen v/i. cheep, chirp; Mäuse: squeak; **bei dir piept's wohl** umg. you must be off your rocker; **es/er war zum Piepen** umg. it/he was a scream
Piepen Pl. umg. (Geld) dough Sg., dosh Brit. Sg., bread Sg.; **keine / e-e Menge ~** no readies / a pile (of dough), a load of dosh Brit., megabucks Am.
Piepmatz m; -es, Piepmätze; umg. birdie, Brit. auch dickybird
Pieps m; -es, -e; umg. **1.** peep, cheep; **er machte keinen ~** there wasn't a peep from him, he didn't utter a word; **ich will keinen ~ mehr hören!** I don't want (to hear) another peep out of you; **2.** auf Anrufbeantworter: → **Piep-**

ton
piepsen vt/i. **1.** umg. (mit Piepsstimme sagen, singen) squeak, pipe; **„Papi!"**, **piepste die Kleine** "Daddy!" squealed the little girl; **2.** Gerät: bleep; Maus etc.: squeak
Piepser m; -s, - **1.** → **Pieps** 1; **2.** (Funkrufempfänger) bleeper, Am. pager, beeper; **j-n über den ~ rufen** get s.o. on his bleeper (Am. pager)
piepsig Adj. Stimme: squeaky; **Piepsstimme** f squeaky voice
Piepton m bleep; **sprechen Sie nach dem ~!** speak after the tone
Pier m; -s, -e und f; -, -s; Naut. pier
piercen [pi:ɐsn] vt/i. pierce
piesacken v/t. umg. torment; mit Fragen etc.: pester; **die Klasse hat mich wieder ganz schön gepiesackt** the class really put me on the rack again
pieseln v/i. südd., schw., österr. umg. have a pee
Pietät f; -, kein Pl. reverence, piety; **pietätlos** Adj. irreverent; **pietätvoll** Adj. reverent
Pietismus m; -, kein Pl.; hist. Pietism; **Pietist** m; -en, -en, **Pietistin** f; -, -nen, **pietistisch** Adj. hist. Pietist
piezoelektrisch [pietsoʔeˈlɛktrɪʃ] Adj. Phys. piezoelectric; **Piezoelektrizität** [pietsoʔelɛktritsiˈtɛːt] f piezoelectricity
Pigment n; -(e)s, -e pigment; **~farbe** f pigment colo(u)r; **~fleck** m pigmentation mark, brown spot umg.; → **Altersfleck**
pigmentieren v/t., v/refl. pigment; **Pigmentierung** f pigmentation
Pigmentstörung f pigmentation disorder
Pik¹ m; -s, -e (Groll): **e-n ~ auf j-n haben** umg. have a grudge against s.o.
Pik² n; -s, -s; (Kartenfarbe) spades Pl.; (Einzelkarte) spade; im Subst. → **Herz...**
pikant Adj. **1.** Gastr. piquant (auch Wein), spicy; **2.** Witz etc.: racy, risqué; **~es Thema** delicate subject; **Pikanterie** f; -, -n **1.** piquancy; **2.** risqué remark (od. story etc.); **pikanterweise** Adv. piquantly
pikaresk Adj. Roman etc.: picaresque
Pike f; -, -n; hist. (Spieß) pike; **etw. von der ~ auf lernen** fig. learn s.th. from scratch (od. by starting at the bottom)
piken vt/i. umg. prick; **j-n mit etw. ~** stick s.th. into s.o.
pikiert Adj. put out, piqued, miffed umg.
Pikkolo m; -s, -s **1.** (Sekt) champagne miniature; **2.** (Kellner) trainee waiter; **~flöte** f piccolo
piksen vt/i. → **piken**
Piktogramm n; -s, -e pictograph; (Hinweisschild) symbol
Pilatus m; - → **Pontius**
Pilaw m; -s, kein Pl.; Gastr. pilau, pilaf(f)
Pilger m; -s, - pilgrim; **~fahrt** f pilgrimage; **~in** f; -,-nen (female) pilgrim; **pilgern** v/i. go on a pilgrimage; umg. fig. (gehen od. wandern) trek; **alles pilgerte ins Grüne** everyone made off into (Am. took off for) the countryside; **~schaft** f pilgrimage; **~stätte** f place of pilgrimage
Pille f; -, -n pill (auch Antibabypille), tablet; **die ~ nehmen** take (od. be on) the pill; **~ danach** morning-after pill; **e-e bittere ~** fig. a bitter pill (to swallow); **(j-m) die ~ ~ versüßen** fig. sugar the pill (for s.o.); **da helfen keine ~n** umg. it's hopeless

Pillen|dreher m **1.** Zool. scarab (beetle); **2.** hum. (Apotheker) pill-peddler; **~knick** m drop in the birthrate (due to the introduction of the pill), baby bust umg.
pillenmüde Adj. umg. tired of the pill, pill-weary
Pillen|pause f: **e-e ~ einlegen** go off (od. stop taking) the pill for a while; **~schlucker** m umg. pill-popper
Pilot m; -en, -en **1.** Flug. pilot; **2.** (Rennfahrer) racing (Am. racecar) driver
Pilotausgabe f pilot edition
Piloten|ausbildung f pilot's training; **~schein** m pilot's licen|ce (Am. -se)
Pilotfilm m pilot film
Pilotin f; -, -nen **1.** Flug. (female) pilot; **2.** (Rennfahrerin) (female) racing (Am. racecar) driver
Pilot|projekt n pilot project (od. scheme); **~studie** f pilot study; **~versuch** m pilot experiment
Pils n; -, -, **Pils(e)ner** n; -s, - Pils(e)ner (beer); **zwei Pils bitte!** two Pils(e)ners, please
Pilz m; -es, -e mst essbarer: mushroom; giftiger: toadstool, poisonous mushroom; fachspr., auch Med. fungus; → **Fußpilz, Hautpilz, Pilzkrankheit** etc.; **in die ~e gehen** go mushrooming (od. mushroom-picking); **wie ~e aus dem Boden schießen** fig. shoot up like mushrooms, mushroom
...pilz m, im Subst.: **Lamellen~** agaric, gill fungus; **Speise~** edible mushroom
Pilz|befall m attack by a fungus, fungal attack; **~beratung(sstelle)** f mushroom advisory cent|re (Am. -er)
pilzförmig Adj. mushroom-shaped, fungiform fachspr.
Pilz|gericht n Gastr. mushroom dish; **~kenner** m, **~kennerin** f mushroom expert; **~kopf** m, **~kopffrisur** f Beatle haircut; **~krankheit** f Med. fungal infection; fachspr. mycosis; **~kultur** f in Labor: culture of fungi; **~kunde** f mycology; **~rahmsuppe** f Gastr. cream of mushroom soup; **~sammler** m, **~sammlerin** f mushroom-gatherer; **~vergiftung** f mushroom poisoning
Piment m, n; -(e)s, -e; Gastr. allspice, pimento
Pimmel m; -s, -; Sl. willy, Am. dick, dong
pimpelig Adj. umg. (verweichlicht) namby-pamby; **er ist etwas ~** he's a bit of a sissy (od. baby)
pimpern vt/i. vulg. screw, Brit. auch bonk
Pimpf m; -(e)s, -e **1.** umg. squirt; **2.** hist., im Nationalsozialismus: pimpf (member of the Nazi Jungvolk)
Pinakothek f; -, -en picture (od. art) gallery
pingelig Adj. umg. fussy; attr. auch nit-picking; **sei nicht so ~!** don't be so pernickety (od. Am. persnickety); **da bin ich gar nicht ~** fig. I'm not particular (od. fussy) (about that)
Pingpong n; -s, kein Pl. ping-pong; → **Tischtennis** etc.
Pinguin m; -s, -e Zool. penguin
Pinie f; -, -n Bot. (stone) pine
Pinien|hain m pine grove; **~kern** m pine nut
pink Adj., **Pink** n; -s, -s Farbe: shocking pink
Pinke f; -, kein Pl.; umg., altm. cash, dough
Pinkel¹ m; -s, -; umg.: **feiner ~** toff, aristo; (Angeber) Lord Muck
Pinkel² f; -, -(n); nordd. Gastr. fatty, highly seasoned sausage containing ba-

con and groats

pinkeln *v/i. umg.* piddle, pee, tinkle; *subst. konstr.* have a piddle (*od.* pee *od.* tinkle); **~ gehen** go for a pee; *Mann: auch* take a leak *Sl.*; **ich muss mal ~** I need to pee

Pinkelpause *f umg. unterwegs*: loo (*Am.* pit) stop, stop for a pee

Pinne *f; -, -n; Naut.* tiller

pinnen *v/t. umg.* pin, stick (**an, auf +** *Akk.* on[to]); **Pinnwand** *f* pinboard

Pinscher *m; -s, -* pinscher; *umg., pej.* (*Person*) pipsqueak

Pinsel *m; -s, -* **1.** (paint)brush; **2.** *umg. pej.* (*Person*) twit; **eingebildeter ~** stuck-up prig; *stärker*: conceited ass

Pinselführung *f Kunst* brushwork

pinseln *vt/i.* paint (*auch Med.*)

Pinsel|stiel *m* (paint)brush handle; **~strich** *m* brushstroke

Pinte *f; -, -n; umg.* watering hole, *Brit. auch* boozer

Pinzette *f; -, -n:* (**e-e**) **~** (a pair of) tweezers *Pl.*

Pionier *m; -s, -e* **1.** pioneer; **2.** *Mil.* engineer; **3.** *hist. ehem. DDR*: **Junge ~e** Young Pioneers; **~arbeit** *f* pioneering work; **~geist** *m* pioneering spirit; **~in** *f; -, -nen* (female) pioneer; **~leistung** *f* pioneering venture (*od.* feat); **~truppe** *f Mil.* engineers *Pl.*; **~zeit** *f* early days *Pl.*, pioneering days *Pl.*

Pipapo *n; -s, kein Pl.; umg.*: **und das ganze ~** and all the rest (of it), and all that nonsense; **mit allem ~** *Auto etc.* with all the extras (*od.* trimmings), *Am. auch* with the whole nine yards

Pipeline ['paiplain] *f; -, -s* pipeline

Pipette *f; -, -n* pipette; **pipettieren** *v/i.* pipette

Pipi *n; -s, kein Pl.; umg.* wee-wee(s *Pl.*); **~ machen** do a wee(-wee); **ich muss mal ~** I need a wee

Pipifax *m umg., pej.* **1.** (*wertloses Zeug*) worthless trifles *Pl.*; **2.** (*Unsinn*) eyewash, *Am. auch* piddle, hooey

Piranha [pi'ranja] *m; -(s), -s; Zool.* piranha

Pirat *m; -en, -en* pirate

Piraten|ausgabe *f* pirate edition; **~flagge** *f* Jolly Roger; **~sender** *m* pirate radio station; *Pl. Koll. auch* pirate radio *Sg.*

Piraterie *f; -, -n* piracy

...piraterie *f, im Subst. fig.*: **Produkt~** product piracy; **Software~** software piracy

Piratin *f; -, -nen* female pirate

Pirogge *f; -, -n; Gastr.* pirogi, piroshki

Pirol *m; -s, -e; Orn.* oriole

Pirouette *f; -, -n* pirouette

Pirsch *f; -, kein Pl. Jagd*: deerstalking, *Am.* still hunt; **auf die ~ gehen** go deerstalking, *Am.* still-hunt; **pirschen** *v/i.* **1.** go deerstalking, stalk (the deer); **2.** (*schleichen*) (*auch sich ~*) creep (**an** + *Akk.* up to)

Pisse *f; -, kein Pl.; vulg.* piss; **pissen** *v/i. vulg.* piss; **~ gehen** go for a piss

Pissoir [pi'soaː] *n; -s, -e od. -s* (men's) urinal

Pistazie *f; -, -n* pistachio

Pistazienkern *m* (shelled) pistachio

Piste *f; -, -n* (*Rennstrecke*) (racing) track; *Skisport*: piste, ski run; *Flug.* runway; (*unbefestigte Straße*) track, dirt road

...piste *f, im Subst.*: **Start~** takeoff runway; **Beton~** (*Rennstrecke*) concrete track; *Flug.* concrete runway

Pisten|dienst *m* piste maintenance service; **~rowdy** *m umg.*, **~sau** *f umg.* ski hooligan (*Am. auch* hotdog), terror of

the slopes; **~wache** *f* ski patrol

Pistole *f; -, -n* pistol, gun; **auf j-n mit der ~ zielen** aim a pistol (*od.* gun) at s.o.; (**j-n**) **mit vorgehaltener ~** (**zwingen**) (force s.o.) at gunpoint; **j-m die ~ auf die Brust setzen** *fig.* hold a gun to s.o.'s head; **wie aus der ~ geschossen** like a shot

...pistole *f, im Subst.* **1.** *allg. im wörtl. Sinn*: pistol; *Sport~* sporting pistol; **2.** *Tech.*: *Lackier~* (paint) spraygun; *Löt~* soldering gun

Pistolen|griff *m* (pistol) butt; **~held** *m umg.* gunslinger; **~schuss** *m* pistol shot; **~tasche** *f* holster

pitschnass *Adj. umg.* wet through; *Person auch*: soaked to the skin

pittoresk *Adj.* picturesque

Pixel *n; -s, -; EDV* pixel

Pizza ['pitsa] *f; -, -s od. Pizzen* pizza; **~bäcker** *m*, **~bäckerin** *f* pizza cook; **~form** *f* pizza dish

Pizzeria [pitse'riːa] *f; -, -s od. Pizzerien* pizza house, pizzeria

PKW *m; -(s), -s; Abk.* (**Personenkraftwagen**) (private) car; **~-Fahrer** *m*, **~-Fahrerin** *f* car driver

Placebo *n; -s, -s* placebo; **~effekt** *m* placebo effect

placieren → **platzieren** *etc.*

placken *v/refl.* → **plagen** II; **Plackerei** *f; -, -en* drudgery, grind *umg.*

plädieren *v/i.* plead (**auf +** *Akk.*, **für** for) (*auch Jur.*); **auf Freispruch/lebenslänglich ~** plead for acquittal / a life sentence; **dafür ~, dass** ... argue that ...

Plädoyer [plɛdoa'jeː] *n; -s, -s* plea; *Jur.* (final) speech, summation; **ein** (**glänzendes**) **~ halten** *Jur.* make a (brilliant) final speech (*od.* summation, summing up)

Plafond [pla'fõː] *m; -s, -s* **1.** *südd., österr.* ceiling; **2.** *schw. Wirts.* ceiling, upper limit

Plage *f; -, -n*; (*Ärgernis*) (real) nuisance; (*Arbeit*) (real) grind *umg.*; *bibl.* plague; **es macht ihr das Leben zur ~** it makes life unbearable (*od.* a misery) for her; **es ist ihr zur ~ geworden** it's become a real problem for her

...plage *f, im Subst.*: **Kartoffelkäfer~** plague of Colorado (*Am.* potato) beetles

Plagegeist *m umg.* pest

plagen I. *v/t.* torment, plague *umg.*; *mit Bitten und Fragen*: pester, plague; *Sorgen etc.*: worry, bother, dog; **die Wespen ~ uns sehr** the wasps are a real pest; **was plagt dich?** what's eating you?; → **geplagt; II.** *v/refl.*: **sich ~** slave away (**mit** at); **er plagt sich mit s-n Zähnen / mit ständigem Kopfweh** his teeth are giving him a lot of trouble / his constant headaches are getting him down; **sie plagt sich mit ihren Schülern** her pupils (*Am.* students) give her a hard time

Plagiat *n; -(e)s, -e* plagiarism; **ein ~ begehen** plagiarize; **Plagiator** *m; -s, -en* plagiarist; **plagiieren** *vt/i.* plagiarize

Plaid [pleːt] *n, m; -s, -s*; (*Decke*) tartan (travel[l]ing) rug; (*Umhangtuch*) plaid

Plakat *n; -(e)s, -e* poster; *aus Pappe*: placard; **~e kleben** put up posters; **~e ankleben verboten** stick (*Am.* post) no bills

...plakat *n, im Subst.*: **Film~** film (*Am.* movie) poster; **Kunst~** art poster

Plakat-Aktion *f* poster campaign; **plakatieren** *v/t.* put up posters; **Plakatieren verboten** stick no bills, bill-posting prohibited; **II.** *v/t.* advertise

with posters; **plakativ** *Adj.* (*auffällig*) striking; *pej.* (*groß aufgemacht*) ostentatious; *stärker*: sensational; (*vordergründig*) simplistic

Plakat|kleber *m*, **~kleberin** *f* billposter, billsticker; **~maler** *m*, **~malerin** *f* poster artist (*od.* designer); **~säule** *f* advertising pillar (*Am.* kiosk); **~schrift** *f* block lettering, poster type; **~träger** *m* sandwich man; **~trägerin** *f* sandwich woman; **~wand** *f* hoarding, *bes. Am.* billboard

Plakette *f; -, -n*; (*Abzeichen*) badge; (*Aufkleber*) sticker; **e-e ~ tragen** wear a badge

plan I. *Adj.* level; **II.** *Adv.*: **~ liegen** lie flat (**auf +** *Dat.* on, against)

Plan¹ *m; -(e)s, Pläne* **1. a)** plan; (*Absicht*) *auch* intention; **e-n ~ fassen** devise a plan; **Pläne schmieden** make plans; *im neg. Sinn*: plot, scheme; **voller Pläne stecken** have all sorts of plans (*od.* ideas); **j-s Pläne durchkreuzen / zunichte machen** thwart/ruin (*od.* wreck) s.o.'s plans, **b)** (*Vorhaben*) project, scheme; **2.** (*Entwurf*) plan; (*Zeichnung*) *auch* draft, design; (*graphische Darstellung*) diagram; **3.** (*Karte*) map; (*Lage-, Stadtplan*) *auch* plan; **4.** (*Zeitplan etc.*) schedule, plan; **5.** *ehem. DDR*: (*Soll*) plan; **den ~ erfüllen** fulfil(l) the plan

Plan² *m*: **auf den ~ treten** turn up, come onto the scene; **auf den ~ rufen** call into action

...plan *m, im Subst.*: **Einsatz~** plan of action; **Veranstaltungs~** program(me) of events

Plane *f; -, -n* tarpaulin; *als Überdachung*: awning

...plane *f, im Subst.*: **Kunststoff~** plastic tarp(aulin); **Wagen~** car cover

planen *vt/i. allg.* plan; (*entwerfen*) *auch* design; *zeitlich*: plan ahead; *mit Geld*: budget; **lange im Voraus ~** plan well ahead; **ich habe nichts geplant** I've got nothing planned

Planer *m; -s, -*, **~in** *f; -, -nen* planner; *Wirts.* policy maker

Planerfüllung *f ehem. DDR*: fulfil(l)ment of quotas (*od.* targets)

planerisch I. *Adj.*; *nur attr.* planning ...; **II.** *Adv.* (*was die Planung betrifft*) from a planning perspective (*od.* point of view)

Planet *m; -en, -en* planet; **planetarisch** *Adj.* planetary; **Planetarium** *n; -s, Planetarien* planetarium

Planeten|bahn *f* orbit; **~system** *n* planetary system

planieren *v/t.* level; (*Gelände*) *auch* grade; **Planierraupe** *f* bulldozer

planimetrisch *Adj.* planimetric(al)

Planke *f; -, -n* plank, board

Plänkelei *f; -, -en*, **plänkeln** *v/i.* banter

Plankosten *Pl.* target cost *Sg.*

Plankton *n; -s, kein Pl.* plankton

planlos I. *Adj.* aimless, haphazard; **II.** *Adv.* aimlessly, haphazardly; **völlig ~ handeln** act without any plan, do s.th. willy-nilly; **Planlosigkeit** *f* haphazardness, haphazard nature (+ *Gen.* of)

planmäßig I. *Adj.* planned; *Flug. etc.* scheduled; (*systematisch*) systematic; **II.** *Adv.* as planned; *arbeiten etc.*: according to plan (*zeitlich*: schedule); *ankommen etc.*: on schedule; (*systematisch*) systematically

Planquadrat *n* grid square

Planschbecken *n* paddling pool; **planschen** *v/i.* splash (around); **Planscherei** *f; -, -en* splashing (around)

Plan|rückstand *m* backlog; **~soll** *n* target; **~spiel** *n* experimental game(s *Pl.*); *Mil.* map exercise; *Wirts.* planning (*od.* experimental) game; **~stelle** *f* (established *od.* permanent) post; *e-e freie ~ haben* have a vacancy

Plantage [plan'ta:ʒə] *f*; -, -*n* plantation ...**plantage** *f*, *im Subst.*: **Bananen~** banana plantation; **Erdbeer~** strawberry fields *Pl.*

Plantagen|arbeiter *m* plantation worker; **~besitzer** *m*, **~besitzerin** *f* planter, owner of a (*od.* the) plantation

plantschen *v/i.* → **planschen**

Planung *f* **1.** planning *etc.*; → **planen**; *zeitliche: auch* timing, scheduling; *in (der) ~ sein* be at the planning stage; *betriebliche ~* business (*od.* corporate) planning; **2.** → **Plan**[1] 2 ...**planung** *f*, *im Subst.*: **Wirtschafts~** economic planning

Planungs|abteilung *f* planning department; **~stadium** *n* planning stage; **~zeitraum** *m* planning period

planvoll I. *Adj.* systematic, methodical; **II.** *Adv.* systematically; **~ vorgehen** proceed methodically, be methodical

Planwagen *m* covered wagon

Plan|wirtschaft *f* planned economy; **~ziel** *n* target; **~ziffer** *f* target (figure)

Plappermaul *n* *umg.* chatterbox, blabbermouth; **plappern** *vt/i. umg.* babble (on); *er plappert nur Unsinn* he's just talking nonsense

Plaque [plak] *f*; -, -*s*; *Dent.* plaque

plärren *vt/i. umg.* (*weinen*) bawl; *Radio etc.*: blare

Pläsier *n*; -*s*, -*e*; *altm.* pleasure, delight; **Pläsierchen** *n*: *jedem Tierchen sein ~ hum.* each to his (*od.* her) own, everyone according to their own taste

Plasma *n*; -*s*, *Plasmen* plasma; **~bildschirm** *m* plasma display (*od.* screen); **~brenner** *m* plasma torch; **~konserve** *f* preserved (blood) plasma; **~physik** *f* plasma physics (*V. im Sg.*); **~spender** *m*, **~spenderin** *f* plasma donor

Plaste *f*; -, -*n*; *ostd.* plastic

Plastik[1] *f*; -, -*en* **1.** (*Kunst und Kunstwerk*) sculpture; **2.** *nur Sg.* (*Eigenschaft*) plasticity; **3.** *Med.* plastic surgery

Plastik[2] *n*; -*s*, *kein Pl.*; (*Kunststoff*) plastic; *aus ~* made of plastic; **~beutel** *m* plastic bag; *kleiner: auch* polythene bag; **~bombe** *f* plastic bomb; **~folie** *f* plastic film (*od.* sheeting); (*Küchenfolie*) kitchen film, *Am.* plastic wrap; (*Frischhaltefolie*) cling film, *Am.* plastic wrap; **~geld** *n*; *nur Sg.*; *hum.* plastic money; **~geschoss** *n* plastic bullet; **~sprengstoff** *m* plastic explosive(s *Pl.*); **~tüte** *f* plastic bag

Plastilin *n*; -*s*, *kein Pl.* etwa Plasticine®, *Am.* Play-Doh®

plastisch I. *Adj.* **1.** (*räumlich*) three-dimensional; **2.** *Beschreibung etc.*: graphic, vivid; **3.** *nur attr.*; *Kunst*: sculptural, plastic; *die ~en Arbeiten Dalis* Dali's three-dimensional works; **4.** *~e Chirurgie* plastic surgery; **5.** (*knetbar*) plastic, workable; *e-e ~e Masse* a workable mass; **II.** *Adv. etw. ~ schildern/darstellen* give a vivid description/portrayal of s.th.; *etw. ~ vor sich sehen* have a perfect mental picture of s.th.

Plastizität *f*; -, *kein Pl.* plasticity; *fig. einer Beschreibung*: vividness

Platane *f*; -, -*n* plane (*Am. auch* sycamore) (tree); **Platanenallee** *f* avenue of plane trees (*Am. auch* sycamores)

Plateau [pla'to:] *n*; -*s*, -*s* plateau;

~sohle *f* platform sole

Platin *n*; -*s*, *kein Pl.* platinum; **platinblond** *Adj.* platinum blonde

Platine *f*; -, -*n*; *Etech.* (circuit) board

Platinschmuck *m* platinum jewel(le)ry

Platitüde *f*; -, -*n*; *pej.* platitude; **~n von sich geben** talk in platitudes

platonisch *Adj.* Platonic; *Liebe, Beziehung etc.*: platonic

platsch *Interj.* splosh!, splash!; **platschen** *v/i.* splash; *ins Wasser ~* hit the water and make a splash (*od.* splashes)

plätschern *v/i. Regen*: patter (**gegen** against); *Wellen*: lap (against); *Brunnen*: splash; *Bach*: murmur, babble; *im Wasser*: splash about; *vor sich hin ~ umg. fig. Gespräch*: meander along

platt *Adj.* **1.** (*flach*) flat; (*eben*) level, even; *umg.* (*flachbrüstig*) flat-chested; *~ drücken etc.* flatten; *sich die Nase am Fenster ~ drücken* press one's nose flat against the window; *e-n Platten haben umg.* have a flat tyre (*Am.* tire), have a flat; **2.** *fig.* (*nichts sagend*) trite, uninspired; **3.** *Lüge etc.*: downright; *schärfer*: rotten; **4.** *umg. vor Staunen*: flabbergasted, floored; *da bin ich aber ~!* well I'll be blowed (*Am. auch* darned)!; **5.** *einen Betrieb ~ machen umg.* do for (*od.* kill off) a firm; *ich mach dich ~!* I'll get you!

Platt *n*; -(*s*), *kein Pl.*; *Ling.* → **Plattdeutsch**

Plättchen *n* small plate; *auch Anat.* lamina; *Tech., Bot.* lamella; (*Blutplättchen*) platelet

plattdeutsch *Adj.* Low German; **Plattdeutsch** *n*; -*en*, *kein Pl.*; *Ling.* Low German; *das ~e* Low German

Platte *f*; -, -*n* **1.** (*großer Teller*) dish; *kalte ~* cold cuts; **2.** *aus Glas, Metall etc.*: sheet; *aus Holz*: board; *aus Stein, Beton*: slab; (*Kachel*) tile; **3.** (*Tischplatte*) tabletop; *ausziehbar*: leaf; **4.** (*Herdplatte*) hotplate; **5.** (*Felsplatte*) ledge; **6.** (*Schallplatte*) record; *die ~ kenn ich schon umg. fig.* I've heard that one before; *der hat ganz schön was auf der ~ umg.* he's on the ball, he's really with it; **7.** *Computer*: hard disk; **8.** *umg.* (*Glatze*) bald pate; (*kahle Stelle*) bald patch; *e-e ~ haben/kriegen* be / be going bald

...**platte** *f*, *im Subst.* **1.** *aus best. Material*: **Stahl~** steel sheet; **2.** *für best. Zweck*: **Decken~** ceiling tile; *Tischtennis~* pingpong tabletop; **3.** *Gastr.*: **Gemüse~** (plate with a) selection of vegetables; **Schinken~** (plate with an) assortment of different types of ham

plätten *v/t.* iron, press; → **geplättet**

Platten|archiv *n* record library; **~aufnahme** *f* recording; **~bar** *f* (record) listening counter

Platten|bau *m* prefabricated building (made with concrete slabs); **~(bau)siedlung** *f* estate of prefabricated houses

Platten|cover ['platənkavɐ] *n* record sleeve; **~firma** *f* record company; **~geschäft** *n* record shop (*od. bes. Am.* store); **~industrie** *f* recording industry; **~laufwerk** *n* *Computer*: disk drive; **~sammlung** *f* record collection; **~spieler** *m* record player; *Hi-Fi*: turntable; **~ständer** *m* *mst* record rack; **~stapel** *m* *Computer*: disk pack

Plattentektonik *f* *Geol.* plate tectonics (*V. im Sg.*)

Platten|teller *m* turntable; **~wechsler** *m* record changer

Plattfisch *m* *Zool.* flatfish

Plattform *f* platform (*auch fig. Pol.*); *e-e gemeinsame ~ finden* share a common platform; *allg. auch*: find common ground

Plattfuß *m* flat foot; *umg. Mot.* flat tyre (*Am.* tire), flat

Plattheit *f* **1.** flatness; *geistige*: triteness; **2.** *pej.* (*Floskel*) trite remark, platitude

plattnasig *Adj.* flat-nosed

Plattwurm *m* flatworm

Platz *m*; -*es*, *Plätze* **1.** (*Raum*) room, space; *wir haben viel/wenig ~* we have plenty of / not much space; *~ machen* make room (*für* for); (*vorbeilassen, auch fig. den ~ räumen*) make way (for); *~ da!* move along, please!; *~ sparend* space-saving; *es ist kein ~ mehr* there's no room left; *es ist noch viel ~* there's plenty of room (left); *dafür finden wir noch ~* we'll fit (*od.* squeeze) that in somehow; *der Wagen bietet fünf Personen ~* the car has room for five (*od.* seats five); *das Stadion hat ~ für 30.000* the stadium holds 30,000; *wie viel ~ ist auf der Festplatte?* how much space is there on the hard disk?; *das hat in s-m Leben keinen ~* there's no room for that in his life; **2.** (*Sitzplatz, auch Flug. etc.*) seat, place; *Plätze reservieren lassen* reserve (*od.* book) seats; *~ nehmen* sit down; *bitte behalten Sie ~* please don't get up; *~! zum Hund*: down!; (*Sitz!*) sit!; *j-m s-n ~ anbieten* offer s.o. one's seat, give up one's seat for s.o.; *ist dieser ~ (noch) frei?* is this seat taken?; *dort hinten sind noch Plätze frei* there are still some seats at the back; *bis auf den letzten ~ gefüllt* filled to capacity; *es gibt keine festen Plätze* the seats are not numbered; **3.** (*Stelle, Standort*) place; *für Picknick, Urlaub etc.*: *auch* spot; *der Schlüssel hängt nicht an s-m ~* the key isn't where it should be; *Sport*: *auf die Plätze, fertig, los!* on your mark(s), get set, go!; *Brit. auch* ready, steady, go!; *er wich nicht vom ~* he didn't budge (*od.* move from the spot); *dein ~ ist bei d-r Firma* your place is with your company, your company is where you belong; *ein ~ an der Sonne auch fig.* a place in the sun; *fehl am ~(e) sein* be out of place; *beruflich etc.*: *auch* be a square peg in a round hole; *Bemerkung, Reaktion etc.*: be uncalled for; *hier ist Vorsicht am ~* we've got to be careful here, this calls for great care; **4.** (*Lücke*) space; *hier ist noch ein ~ (frei) für den Koffer* here's a (an empty) space for the case; *nach der Überschrift etwas ~ lassen* leave some space after the heading; **5.** (*Ort, Stadt*) place; *das beste Restaurant am ~e* the best restaurant in the place (*od.* in [the] town); **6.** (*Lage, auch Bau-, Zeltplatz etc.*) site; **7.** (*freier ~*) open space; (*öffentlicher ~*) square; *runder, in Namen*: Circus; **8.** (*Sportfeld*) field, pitch; *Tennis*: court; *Golf*: course; *der beste Mann auf dem ~* the best player on the field; *vom ~ stellen* send off; *auf eigenem/gegnerischem ~ spielen* play at home / away (from home); **9.** (*Studienplatz*) place (to study); *hast du schon e-n ~ gefunden?* have you been accepted anywhere?, have you got a place?; **10.** (*Stellung, Rang*) position; *Sport* place; *den ersten ~ belegen* take first place, come first; *auf ~ drei* in third place; *s-e Gegner auf die Plätze ver-*

weisen leave one's opponents trailing; *~ und Sieg Pferdewette*: each way bet
...platz *m, im Subst.* **1.** *Namen*: *Bahnhofs~* station square; **2.** *Sport etc.*: *Hockey~* hockey pitch (*Am.* field); *Reit~* riding ground; ˙**3.** (*Unterbringung*): *Heim~* place in a home; **4.** *Computer*: *Speicher~* memory
Platz|angebot *n* (amount of) space available; *~angst* *f umg.* claustrophobia; *Med.* agoraphobia; *~anweiser* *m*; *-s*, - usher; *~anweiserin* *f*, *-, -nen* usherette; *~bedarf* *m* space required
Plätzchen¹ *n* **1.** (little) place, spot; **2.** *ist hier noch ein ~ frei?* is there any room left for me?; *im Bus etc.*: is there a seat anywhere?; **3.** *sich* (*Dat.*) *ein ~ erobern fig.* carve out a niche for o.s.
Plätzchen² *n* (*Gebäck*) biscuit, *Am.* cookie
...plätzchen *n, im Subst.*: *Butter~* butter biscuit (*Am.* cookie); *Haferflocken~* oatcake; *Orangen~* orange thin
platzen *v/i.* **1.** burst (*auch Naht, Reifen*); *Hosennaht*: split; (*reißen*) crack, split; *Med.* rupture; *ihm ist e-e Ader geplatzt* he burst a blood vessel; *ins Zimmer ~* *umg. fig.* burst into the room; *vor Ungeduld, Neugier etc. ~* be bursting with; *ich platze (gleich)!* *umg.* (*bin so satt*) I'm full to bursting, I'm about to burst; *mir platzt die Blase!* *umg.* I'm dying to go to the loo (*Am.* john); → *Kragen, Naht* 1; **2.** *umg. fig. Plan etc.*: fall through; *Termin*: be cancelled; *Verlobung*: be broken off; *Drogenring etc.*: be smashed; *Wechsel, Scheck*: bounce; *~ lassen* (*Plan etc.*) upset, thwart, put an end to; (*Termin*) cancel; (*Theorie etc.*) explode; (*Freundschaft etc.*) break up; (*Drogenring etc.*) smash; (*Wechsel*) bounce
Platz|ersparnis *f* space saving; *aus Gründen der ~* for reasons of space; *~gründe* *Pl.*: *wir sind aus ~n umgezogen* we moved because we needed more space; *~halter* *m EDV, Ling.* placeholder; *~hirsch* *m umg. fig.* top dog
platzieren I. *v/t.* place (*auch Sport*); *im Restaurant*: seat, show *s.o.* to a table; **II.** *v/refl.*: *sich ~* position o.s.; *Sport* be placed (*als Dritter* third); *platziert I.* *P.P.* → *platzieren*; **II.** *Adj. Schuss*: well-placed
Platzierung *f Sport* placing; (*Platz*) place; *im Restaurant*: seating
Platz|karte *f Eisenb.* reservation (ticket); *~konzert* *n* promenade concert; *~mangel* *m* lack of space; *~miete* *f* **1.** rental charge, rent; *Tennis*: fee; **2.** *Theat.* subscription; *~ordner* *m*, *~ordnerin* *f Sport* steward; *~patrone* *f* blank cartridge; *~regen* *m* cloudburst, downpour; *~reservierung* *f* reservation; *~sperre* *f Sport* ban; *durch das Sportgericht*: ban on playing on one's home ground; *~verhältnisse* *Pl. Sport* state of the pitch (*Am.* field) *Sg.*; *~verweis* *m Sport* sending-off; *es gab im Ganzen vier ~e* four players were sent off altogether; *~vorteil* *m Sport* home advantage; *~wart* *m Sport* groundsman; *~wechsel* *m* **1.** change of places (*Sport* ends); **2.** *Wirts.* local bill; *~wunde* *f* cut; *Med.* laceration
Plauderei *f*; *-, -en* chat; **Plauderer** *m*; *-s*, -, **Plauderin** *f*; *-,-nen* conversationalist; *pej.* gossip; *er ist ein netter Plauderer* it's nice listening to him talk, he's a good conversationalist; **plaudern** *v/i.* (have a) chat; *fig.* (*etw. ver-*

raten) talk
Plauder|stündchen *n*, *~stunde* *f* (pleasant) chat; *~tasche* *f umg.* chatterbox; *~ton* *m* chatty tone, (light) conversational tone
Plausch *m*; *-(e)s*, *-e, mst Sg.*; *Dial.* chat, natter *umg.*; **plauschen** *v/i. Dial.* chat, (have a) natter (*od.* chinwag) *umg.*
plausibel *Adj.* plausible; *j-m etw. ~ machen* make s.th. clear to s.o.
Plauze *f* -, -*n*; *nordd., ostd., umg.* **1.** (*Lunge*) lung; *sich* (*Dat.*) *die ~ aus dem Leib schreien* burst one's lungs (shouting); *es auf der ~ haben* have a chesty cough, be chesty; **2.** (*Bauch*) belly; *sich* (*Dat.*) *die ~ voll schlagen* stuff o.s.
Play [ple:] *n*; -, *kein Pl.* play; *auf ~ drücken* press play (*od.* the play button)
Playback ['ple:bɛk] *n*; -, *kein Pl.* **1.** *TV etc.*: miming; (*Gesang*) *auch* singing to playback, *Am.* lip-sync(h); **2.** (*Verfahren*) double-tracking, multiple-tracking; *~verfahren* *n* → *Playback* 2
Play-off ['ple:ʔɔf] *n*; *-(s)*, *-s*; *Sport* play-off; *~Runde* *f Sport* play-off round, play-offs *Pl.*
Playtaste *f* play button
Plazenta *f*; -, *-s od.* *Plazenten*; *Anat., Bot.* placenta
Plazet *n*; *-s*, *-s* approval; *e-r Sache sein ~ geben* give one's approval for (*od.* blessing to) s.th.
plazieren → *platzieren*
Plebejer *m*; *-s*, -; *pej.* plebeian, pleb *umg.*; **plebejerhaft I.** *Adj.* → *plebejisch*; **II.** *Adv.*: *sich ~ benehmen* behave (*od.* act) like a pleb *umg.*; **plebejisch** *Adj.* plebeian, plebby *umg.*
Plebiszit *n*; *-(e)s*, *-e* plebiscite
Pleistozän *n*; *-s*, *kein Pl.*, **pleistozän** *Adj.* Pleistocene
Pleite *f*; -, -*n*; *umg.* **1.** *Wirts.* bankruptcy; *~ machen od.* ~ *gehen* go bankrupt, go bust; **2.** *fig.* failure, flop, washout; *das Konzert war e-e totale ~* the concert was a complete disaster
pleite *Adj. umg.* broke; *total ~* stony broke *Brit.*, stone-broke *Am.*; **Pleitegeier** *m*: *über vielen Firmen schwebt der ~* many firms are on the verge of bankruptcy (*od.* are about to go bust *umg.*)
Plektron, Plektrum *n*; *-s*, *Plektren od. Plektra*; *Mus.* plectrum, plucking device, *Am. auch* pick
plemplem *Adj. umg.* nuts; *du bist doch* (*vollkommen*) *~!* you're (completely) off your rocker (*od. Brit.* round the bend)
Plenar|debatte *f* debate of the full house; *~saal* *m* plenary assembly hall; *~sitzung* *f* plenary session
Plenum *n*; *-s*, *Plenen*; *Parl.* plenary assembly; *Jur.* full court; *bei Tagungen*: plenary session; *etw. im ~ diskutieren* discuss s.th. in plenary (session)
pleonastisch *Adj.* pleonastic(ally) *Adv.*)
Pleuelstange *f Tech.* connecting rod
Pleuritis *f*; -, *Pleuritiden*; *Med.* pleurisy
Plexiglas® *n*; *nur Sg. Brit.* perspex®, *Am.* Plexiglas®
Plissee *n*; *-s*, *-s* pleats *Pl.*; *~rock* *m* pleated skirt
plissieren *v/t.* pleat; **plissiert I.** *P.P.* → *plissieren*; **II.** *Adj.* pleated
PLO *f Pol.* PLO (= Palestine Liberation Organization); *~Führer* *m* PLO leader
Plombe *f*; -, -*n* **1.** *Tech.* (lead) seal; **2.** (*Zahnfüllung*) filling

...plombe *f*, *im Subst.* **1.** *Tech.* *Zoll~* customs seal; **2.** *Dent.* *Amalgam~* amalgam filling
plombieren *v/t.* **1.** *Tech.* seal, lead; *e-n LKW ~* put seals on a truck (*Brit. auch* lorry); **2.** (*Zahn*) fill
Plotter *m*; *-s*, -; *EDV* plotter
Plötze *f*; -, -*n*; *Zool.* roach
plötzlich I. *Adj.* sudden; → *Kindstod*; **II.** *Adv.* suddenly, all of a sudden; *~ war alles anders* from one minute (*od.* day) to the next everything had changed; *das kommt mir alles zu ~* it's all happening too fast (for my liking); *aber ein bisschen ~!* *umg.* (and) make it snappy!; **Plötzlichkeit** *f* suddenness
Pluderhosen *Pl.* harem pants, Turkish trousers; (*weite Hosen*) baggy trousers *umg. hum.*
Plumeau [ply'mo:] *n*; *-s*, *-s* featherbed
plump *Adj.* **1.** (*unförmig*) ungainly; (*unbeholfen*) clumsy, awkward; *fig. auch* heavy-handed; (*unfein*) crude; (*taktlos*) (very) direct, blunt; *e-e ~e Form* a clumsy (*od.* an ungainly) shape; **2.** *Lüge, Betrug etc.*: blatant, gross; *das war e-e ~e Ausrede* that was obviously just an excuse; *~e Anspielung* blatantly obvious reference; *e-e ~e Falle* a crude trap; *seine Bemerkungen sind mitunter sehr ~* he's very tactless at times; → *plumpvertraulich*, **Plumpheit** *f* ungainliness, clumsiness, crudeness; → *plump*
Plumps *umg.* **I.** *m*; *-es*, *-e* thud; *im Wasser*: plop; **II.** **plumps** *Interj.* bump!; *ins Wasser*: plop!; *plumps, da lag ich* with a bump I (slipped and) found myself lying there; **plumpsen** *v/i. umg.* (*fallen*) fall; *ins Wasser: auch* plop; **Plumpsklo** *n umg.* earth closet; *bes. Mil.* latrine
plumpvertraulich I. *Adj.* pally, chummy; **II.** *Adv.* in a pally way, as if we *etc.* were the best of pals
Plunder *m*; *kein Pl.*; *pej.* rubbish, junk
Plünderei *f*; -, *-en* → *Plünderung*, **Plünderer** *m*; *-s*, - looter, plunderer
Plundergebäck *n Gastr.* brioche-type (*od.* flaky) pastry
plündern *v/t./i.* (*Stadt*) loot, plunder, pillage; *umg.* (*Kühlschrank, Konto etc.*) raid; (*Obstbaum, Weihnachtsbaum*) strip (bare); (*Buch*) scavenge
Plunderstück *n Gastr.* puff pastry, brioche-type pastry
Plünderung *f* looting, plundering, pillaging
Plural *m*; *-s*, *-e, mst Sg.*; *Gram.* plural; *~bildung* *f* formation of the plural; *~endung* *f* plural ending
Pluralismus *m*; -, *kein Pl.* pluralism; **pluralistisch I.** *Adj.* pluralistic; **II.** *Adv.* pluralistically
Pluralität *f*; *-, -en der Meinungen etc.*: plurality
plus I. *Präp.* plus; *~/minus zwei Prozent* plus or minus two per cent (*bes. Am.* percent); *~/minus einen Tag* give or take a day; *~/minus Null abschneiden* break even; *~ zwei Prozent* plus or minus two per cent (*bes. Am.* percent); **II.** *Adv.* plus; *zwei Grad ~* plus two degrees, two degrees above zero; *die Note Zwei ~* *etwa* the mark beta plus, *Am.* B plus, B+; **III.** *Konj. Math.* plus; *zwölf ~ sieben ist* (*gleich*) *neunzehn* twelve plus seven is (*od.* equals) nineteen
Plus *n*; -, *kein Pl.* **1.** plus; (*Mehrbetrag, Gewinn*) profit; *im ~ sein* be in profit; *Konto*: be in credit; *bei Gleitzeitarbeit*:

ein ~ von 10 Stunden haben have 10 hours in hand, have banked 10 hours; **2.** (*Vorteil*) asset, advantage

Plüsch *m*, *-(e)s*, *kein Pl.* plush, fur fabric; **~augen** *Pl. umg.* dreamy eyes; **~bär** *m* furry teddy-bear; **~sessel** *m* plush armchair; **~tier** *n* soft (*od.* cuddly) toy, *Am.* stuffed animal

plusminus *Konj.*: **~ zwei Prozent** plus or minus two per cent (*bes. Am.* percent)

Plus|pol *m Etech.* positive pole; *einer Batterie*: positive terminal; **~punkt** *m* credit point; *fig.* advantage, plus (point)

Plusquamperfekt *n*; *-(e)s*, *-e*, *mst Sg.*; *Gram.* pluperfect (tense), past perfect

Plusseite *f Wirts. und fig.*: (**auf der**) **~** (on the) credit side

plustern *v/t. und v/refl.* → **aufplustern**

Pluszeichen *n Math.* plus (sign)

Plutokrat *m*; *-en*, *-en* plutocrat; **Plutokratie** *f*; *-*, *-n* plutocracy

Plutonium *n*; *-s*, *kein Pl.*; *Chem.* plutonium

Pneu [pnøː] *m*; *-s*, *-s*; *schw.* tyre, *Am.* tire

Pneumatik *f*, *-*, *-en*; *Phys.* pneumatics *Pl.* (*als Fach mit V. im Sg.*); **pneumatisch I.** *Adj.* pneumatic; **II.** *Adv.* pneumatically

Pneumonie *f*; *-*, *-n*, *mst Sg.*; *Med.* pneumonia

Po *m*; *-s*, *-s*; *umg.* → *Popo*; **~backe** *f umg.* buttock, cheek

Pöbel *m*; *-s*, *kein Pl.*; *pej.* (*Mob*) mob, rabble; (*Masse*) populace; **der ~** the masses, the hoi polloi; **Pöbelei** *f*; *-*, *-en* **1.** *auch Pl.* vulgar behavio(u)r; **2.** (*Bemerkung*) vulgar remark; **pöbelhaft** *Adj.* vulgar, uncouth

pochen *v/i.* knock; *leise*: tap; *Puls*: throb; *Herz*: beat, *stärker*: thump; **~ auf** (+*Akk.*) *fig.* (*bestehen auf*) insist on; (*prahlen mit*) make a big thing of

pochieren [pɔ'ʃiːrən] *v/t. Gastr.* poach

Pocke *f*; *-*, *-n*; *Med.* pock; **Pocken** *Pl.* smallpox *Sg.*

Pockenepidemie *f* smallpox epidemic

Pockennarbe *f* pockmark; **pockennarbig** *Adj.* pockmarked

Podest *n*; *-(e)s*, *-e* **1.** platform; *j-n auf ein ~ erheben fig.* put s.o. on a pedestal; *j-n von s-m ~ stoßen* knock s.o. off his (*od.* her) pedestal; **2.** (*Treppenabsatz*) half-landing

Podex *m*; *-(es)*, *-e*; *umg.*; (*Gesäß*) behind, *Am. auch* butt

Podium *n*; *-s*, *Podien* platform, rostrum; **Podiumsdiskussion** *f* panel (*od.* round-table) discussion

Poebene *f Geog.* Po basin, *etwa* Po valley

Poesie *f*; *-*, *kein Pl.* poetry (*auch fig.*); **~album** *n* autograph book

Poet *m*; *-en*, *-en* poet; **Poetik** *f*; *-*, *-en*, *mst Sg.* poetics (*V. im Sg.*), poetic theory; **Poetin** *f*; *-*, *-nen* poetess; **poetisch** *Adj.* poetic(al), lyrical; **~e Ader** poetic streak (*od.* vein); **~ werden** *umg.* wax lyrical

pofen *v/i.*; *umg.* (*schlafen*) snooze, *Brit. auch* kip

Pogrom *m*, *n*; *-s*, *-e* pogrom; **~stimmung** *f* feelings *Pl.* of racial hatred

Pointe ['poɛ̃ːtə] *f*; *-*, *-n e-r Geschichte*: point; *e-s Witzes*: punch line; **die ~ verderben** spoil the joke; **wo bleibt die ~?** so what was the point (of the story)?; **pointenreich** ['poɛ̃ːtnraiç] *Adj.* very witty; **pointiert** [poɛ̃'tiːrt] *Adj.* pointed

Pointillismus [poɛ̃ti'lɪsmʊs] *m Male-*

rei: pointillism

Pokal *m*; *-s*, *-e* cup, goblet; *Sport* cup; **~ der Landesmeister** European (Champions') Cup; *bis 1999*: **~ der Pokalsieger** European Cup Winners' Cup; **~endspiel** *n*, **~finale** *n* cup final; **~runde** *f* round (of the cup); **~spiel** *n* cup tie (*od.* match); **~verteidiger** *m* cup holder(s *Pl.*)

Pökel *m*; *-s*, *-* brine, pickle; **Pökelfleisch** *n* salt meat; *weitS.* cured (*Am. auch* jerked) meat; **pökeln** *v/t.* pickle

Poker *n*, *m*; *-s*, *kein Pl.* poker; **~gesicht** *n* poker face

pokern *v/i.* play poker; *fig.* gamble (**um** over); **sehr hoch ~** *fig.* gamble with high stakes

Pokerspiel *n* **1.** poker; **2.** game of poker

Pol *m*; *-s*, *-e* **1.** *Geog.* pole; **2.** *Etech.* pole; *einer Batterie*: terminal; **3. der ruhende ~** *fig.* the stabilizing element, the calming influence

Polacke *f*; *-n*, *-n*, **Polackin** *f*; *-*, *-nen*; *Sl.*, *pej.* Polack

polar *Adj.* polar (*auch Etech.*, *Math.*); *Met. auch* arctic; **~e Kälte** arctic cold; **Zustrom ~er Luftmassen** influx of polar air; **~e Kräfte** *fig.* diametrically opposed forces

Polar|eis *n* polar ice; **~expedition** *f* polar expedition; **~forscher** *m*, **~forscherin** *f* polar explorer; **~front** *f Met.* polar front; **~fuchs** *m Zool.* Arctic fox; **~gebiet** *n* polar region(s *Pl.*); **~grenze** *f* polar limit; **~himmel** *m* polar sky; **~hund** *m Zool.* husky

Polarisation *f*; *-*, *-en*; *Math.*, *Phys.* polarization (*auch fig.*); **Polarisationsfilter** *m*, *n* polarizing filter; **polarisieren I.** *v/t.* polarize; **II.** *v/refl.*: **sich ~** become (more and more) polarized; **Polarität** *f*; *-*, *kein Pl.* polarity (*auch fig.*)

Polar|kappe *f Geog.* polar (ice)cap; **~kreis** *m*: **nördlicher/südlicher ~** Arctic/Antarctic Circle; **~licht** *n* polar lights *Pl.*; **nördliches/südliches ~** northern/southern lights *Pl.*, *fachspr.* aurora borealis/australis; **~luft** *f* polar air (current); **~meer** *n*: **nördliches/südliches ~** Arctic/Antarctic Ocean

Polaroidkamera® [polaro'iːt-] *f* Polaroid ® (camera)

Polar|route *f* polar route; **über die ~ fliegen** take the polar route, fly over the North Pole; **~station** *f* polar research station; **~stern** *m* Pole Star; **~tag** *m* polar day; **~tief** *n* polar low; **~wolf** *m Zool.* Arctic wolf; **~zone** *f Geog.* frigid zone

Polderlandschaft *f* polder landscape

Pole *m*; *-n*, *-n* Pole

Polemik *f*; *-*, *-en* **1.** (*Schrift*) polemic (**gegen** against), attack (on, against); **2.** *nur Sg.* (*das Polemisieren*) polemics *Pl.*; (*Streit*) controversy, dispute; **Polemiker** *m*; *-s*, *-*, **Polemikerin** *f*; *-*, *-nen* polemicist; **polemisch** *Adj.* polemic(al); **polemisieren** *v/i.* polemicize (**gegen** against)

polen *v/t. Etech.* polarize; **falsch gepolt sein** *umg. fig.* have got it wrong, be on the wrong wavelength

Polen (*n*); *-s*; *Geog.* Poland

Polente *f*; *-*, *kein Pl.*; *umg. altm.*: **die ~** the cops *Pl.*, the fuzz *Pl. Sl.*

Polfilter *m*, *n Fot.* polarizing filter

Police [po'liːsə] *f*; *-*, *-n* (insurance) policy

Polier *m*; *-s*, *-e* foreman

polieren *v/t.* polish (*auch fig.*)

Polier|mittel *n* polish; **~tuch** *n* polish-

ing cloth

Poliklinik *f* outpatient clinic

Polin *f*; *-*, *-nen* Pole, Polish woman (*od.* girl)

Polio|impfung *f* polio vaccination; **~myelitis** *f*; *-*, *kein Pl.* poliomyelitis

Polit|büro *n* Politburo; **~drama** *n* political play

Politesse *f*; *-*, *-n* (woman) traffic warden, *Am. umg.* meter maid

Politik *f*; *-*, *-en*, *mst Sg.* politics *Pl.*; (*bestimmte Linie*) policy (**in Bezug auf**, **im Hinblick auf** on; **gegenüber** towards); (*Taktik*) tactics *Pl.*; (*Wissenschaft*) politics (*V. im Sg.*); **die internationale ~** international politics; **e-e ~ der Stärke** a policy of strength; **in die ~ gehen** go into politics; **über ~ sprechen** talk politics; → **machen** III 3

...politik *f*, *im Subst.*: **Abrüstungs~** disarmament policy

Politiker *m*; *-s*, *-*, **~in** *f*; *-*, *-nen* politician; *führende(r)*: statesman (*f* stateswoman); **Politikum** *n*; *-s*, *Politika* political issue; (*Ereignis*) political event

Politikverdrossenheit *f* boredom with politics

Politik|wissenschaft *f* political science; **~wissenschaftler** *m*, **~wissenschaftlerin** *f* political scientist

politisch I. *Adj.* political; *fig.* (*klug*) judicious, politic; **~er Beamter** civil servant implementing government policy; **~er Gefangener** political prisoner; **~e Polizei** state security police; **~e Wissenschaft(en)** political science(s); **II.** *Adv.* politically; **~ tätig** involved in politics, politically active; **~ interessiert** interested in politics, politically aware; **~ Verfolgte(r)** victim of political persecution; **Politische** *m*, *f*; *-n*, *-n* political prisoner

politisieren I. *v/i.* talk politics; **II.** *v/t.* politicize; (*j-n*) make s.o. politically aware

Polito|loge *m*, *-n*, *-n* political scientist; **~logie** *f*; *-*, *kein Pl.* political science; **~login** *f*; *-*, *-nen* (female) political scientist; **politologisch** *Adj.* political; *Forschung etc.*: in (the field of) political science

Polit|prominenz *f* political top brass, top politicians *Pl.*; **~satire** *f* political satire

Politur *f*; *-*, *-en* **1.** (*Mittel*) polish; **2.** (*Glanz*) polish, finish

Polizei *f*; *-*, *kein Pl.* police *Pl.*; (**~truppe**) police force; **die ~ kommt** the police are on their way; **bei der ~ sein** *beruflich*: be in the police force; (*auf der Wache*) be at the police station; **es mit der ~ zu tun kriegen** *umg.* get into trouble with the police; **j-m die ~ auf den Hals hetzen** *umg.* set the police on s.o.; **sich wöchentlich bei der ~ melden** report to the police every week

Polizei|aktion *f* police operation; **~apparat** *m* police force; **~arrest** *m* police custody; **~aufgebot** *n* police detachment; **starkes ~** large police presence; **~aufsicht** *f*: **unter ~ stehen/stellen** be/place under police surveillance; **~auto** *n* police (*Am. auch* patrol) car; **~beamte** *m* policeman, police officer, law enforcement officer; → *auch* **Polizist**; **~beamtin** *f* policewoman, police officer, law enforcement officer; → *auch* **Polizistin**

polizeibekannt *Adj. nur präd.* known to the police

Polizei|bericht *m* police report; **~boot** *n* police launch; **~chef** *m*, **~chefin** *f*

police chief, chief of police; → *auch*
Polizeipräsident; **⁓dienststelle** *f* police station, *Am. auch* precinct house;
⁓einsatz *m* police action (*od.* intervention); *unter starkem* ⁓ with the use of large numbers of police (*od.* a large police presence); **⁓film** *m* police drama; **⁓funk** *m* police radio; **⁓gewahrsam** *m*: *in* ⁓ *nehmen* take into police custody; **⁓gewalt** *f*: *die* ⁓ *haben* have police powers *Pl.*; *die Menge wurde mit* ⁓ *auseinander getrieben* the police dispersed the crowds by using force; **⁓gewerkschaft** *f* police trade union; **⁓griff** *m* arm-lock; *j-n im* ⁓ *abführen* frogmarch s.o. away; **⁓hund** *m* police dog, *Am. auch* K-9; **⁓knüppel** *m* truncheon, *Am.* billy club, blackjack; **⁓kommissar** *m*, **⁓kommissarin** *f* police superintendent; **⁓kontrolle** *f* police check; (*Kontrollpunkt*) police checkpoint; **⁓labor** *n* police (*od.* forensic) laboratory

polizeilich I. *Adj.* (of *od.* by the) police; *unter* ⁓*er Überwachung* under police surveillance; → *Führungszeugnis*; **II.** *Adv.*: *sich* ⁓ *anmelden/abmelden* register with the police (*od.* authorities) / inform the police (*od.* authorities) that one is moving; ⁓ *verboten* prohibited by law; *er wird* ⁓ *gesucht* the police are looking for (are after *umg.*) him

Polizei|marke *f* policeman's badge; **⁓meister** *m*, **⁓meisterin** *f* (junior) police officer; **⁓notruf** *m* emergency call (to the police); **⁓obermeister** *m*, **⁓obermeisterin** *f* senior police officer; **⁓posten** *m* police guard; **⁓präsident** *m*, **⁓präsidentin** *f* chief of police; *in GB*: *etwa* chief constable, *e-r Großstadt*: *mst* police commissioner; **⁓präsidium** *n* police headquarters *Pl. und Sg.*; **⁓protokoll** *n* police report; **⁓revier** *n* **1.** (*Bezirk*) (police) district, *Am.* (police) precinct; **2.** (*Dienststelle*) police station, *Am. auch* precinct house; **⁓schule** *f* police college; **⁓schüler** *m*, **⁓schülerin** *f* police cadet; *an einer Polizeischule*: police trainee; **⁓schutz** *m* police protection; **⁓spitzel** *m* (police) informer, stool pigeon *Sl.*, *Brit. Sl. auch* grass; **⁓staat** *m* police state; **⁓streife** *f* police patrol; (*Trupp*) *auch* police squad; (*einzelner Beamter*) police patrolman; **⁓stunde** *f* closing time; *um Mitternacht ist* ⁓ all restaurants and bars have to close at midnight; **⁓terror** *m* police terrorism (*od.* brutality); **⁓truppen** *Pl.* security forces; **⁓wache** *f* police station; **⁓waffe** *f* policeman's pistol; **⁓wagen** *m* police (*Am. auch* patrol) car; **⁓willkür** *f* arbitrary use of power by the police

Polizist *m*; *-en*, *-en* policeman, (police) constable; **Polizistin** *f*; *-*, *-nen* policewoman, ([woman] police) constable

Polizze *f*; *-*, *-n österr.* (insurance) policy

Polka *f*; *-*, *-s*; *Mus.* polka

Polkappe *f Geog.* polar cap

pollen ['po:ln] *vt/i. Informationstechnologie*: poll

Pollen *m*; *-s*, *-*; *Bot.* pollen; **⁓allergie** *f Med.* pollen allergy, allergic reaction to pollen; **⁓analyse** *f* pollen analysis; **⁓bericht** *m* (latest) pollen count; **⁓flug** *m* pollen dispersal; (*Menge*) pollen count; **⁓informationsdienst** *m* pollen count information service; **⁓korn** *n* grain of pollen; **⁓krankheit** *f Med.* pollinosis; **⁓sack** *m* pollen sac

Poller *m*; *-s*, *-*; *Naut.*, *Verk.* bollard

polnisch I. *Adj.* Polish; **II. Polnisch** *n*;

-en; *Ling.* Polish; *das Polnische* Polish

Polo *n*; *-s*, *kein Pl.* polo; **⁓hemd** *n* polo shirt; **⁓schläger** *m* mallet

Polstärke *f Etech.* pole strength

Polster *n*; *-s*, *- Sessel etc.*: upholstery; *Kleidung*: padding; *fig.* (*finanzielles* ⁓) reserves *Pl.*; *ein dickes/sicheres* ⁓ *fig.* a generous/safe cushion; → *Auftragspolster*, *Fettpolster*

...polster *n*, *im Subst.*: *Rücken⁓* back-pad

Polsterer *m*; *-s*, *-* upholsterer

Polster|garnitur *f*, **⁓gruppe** *f* upholstered (three-piece) suite; **Polsterin** *f*; *-*, *-nen* (female) upholsterer; **⁓möbel** *Pl.* **1.** upholstered furniture *Sg.*; **2.** → *Polstergarnitur*

polstern *v/t.* upholster; (*Kleidung*) pad; → *gepolstert*

Polster|pflanze *f Bot.* cushion plant, polster; **⁓sessel** *m* upholstered armchair, easy chair; **⁓stuhl** *m* upholstered chair; **⁓tür** *f* padded door

Polsterung *f* upholstery

Polterabend *m* eve-of-the-wedding party

polterig *Adj. umg.* rackety

poltern *v/i.* **1.** make a racket; (*fallen*) crash; (*sich polternd bewegen*) rumble (along); **⁓d umfallen** fall over (*od.* down) with a crash; *der LKW polterte durch die Straße* the lorry (*Am.* truck) rumbled down the street; **2.** *umg.* (*schimpfen*) rant and rave; **3.** *am Vorabend der Hochzeit*: have an eve-of-the-wedding party

Polwanderung *f Geog.* polar wandering

Polyamid® *n*; *-(e)s*, *-e*; *Chem.* polyamide

Polyäthylen *n*; *-s*, *-e*; *Chem.* polyethylene

polychrom *Adj.* polychrome; **Polychromie** *f*; *-*, *kein Pl. Kunst*: polychromy

Polyeder *n*; *-s*, *-*; *Math.* polyhedron

Polyester *m*; *-s*, *-*; *Chem.* polyester

polygam *Adj.* polygamous; **Polygamie** *f*; *-*, *kein Pl.*; (*Vielehe*) polygamy

polyglott *Adj.*, **Polyglotte** *m*, *f*; *-n*, *-n* polyglot

polymorph *Adj.* polymorphous, polymorphic

Polynesien (*n*); *-s*; *Geog.* Polynesia

Polynesier *m*; *-s*, *-*, **⁓in** *f*; *-*, *-nen* Polynesian, *weiblich auch*: Polynesian woman (*od.* girl); **polynesisch I.** *Adj.* Polynesian; **II. Polynesisch** *n*; *-en*; *Ling.* Polynesian; *das Polynesische* Polynesian, the Polynesian language

Polyp *m*; *-en* *-en* **1.** *Zool.* polyp; *altm.* (*Tintenfisch*) octopus; **2.** *Med.* polyp; *Pl.* (*Nasenpolypen*) adenoids; **3.** *umg. pej.* (*Polizist*) cop(per); *die* ⁓*en* the cops, the fuzz *Sl.*

polyphon *Adj. Mus.* polyphonic; **Polyphonie** *f*; *-*, *kein Pl.* polyphony

Polysa(c)charid *n*; *-(e)s*, *-e*; *Chem.* polysaccharide

Polysemie *f*; *-*, *kein Pl.* polysemy

polytechnisch *Adj.* polytechnic; ⁓*e Oberschule ehem. DDR*: *etwa* comprehensive school, *Am.* vocational high school

Polytheismus *m*; *-*, *kein Pl.* polytheism

Pomade *f*; *-*, *-n* pomade; **pomadig** *Adj.* **1.** *Haar*: slicked back (*od.* down); **2.** *fig.* (*schleimig*) smarmy; (*träge*) slow, sluggish

Pomeranze *f*; *-*, *-n*; *Bot.* bitter orange

Pommer *m*; *-s*, *-n*, **⁓in** *f*; *-*, *-nen* Pomer-

anian, *weiblich auch*: Pomeranian woman (*od.* girl); **Pommern** (*n*) *-s* Pomerania; **pommersch** *Adj.* Pomeranian

Pommes *Pl. umg.* chips, *Am.* (french) fries; *einmal* ⁓, *bitte* a bag (*od.* portion) of chips (*Am.* fries), please; **Pommes frites** [pɔm'frɪt] *Pl.* chips, *Am.* (french) fries; *auf der Speisekarte*: *auch* french-fried potatoes

Pomp *m*; *-(e)s*, *kein Pl.* pomp

Pompeji (*n*); *-s*; *Geog.* Pompeii

pompös *Adj.* pretentious; *Rede*: bombastic; *Empfang*, *Fest etc.*: extravagant, gorgeous

Pond *n*; *-s*, *-*; *Phys. altm.* gram-force

Pontifex *m*; *-*, *Pontifizes*; *hist.* pontiff; ⁓ *maximus* Pontifex maximus

Pontifikalamt *n kath.* Pontifical mass; **Pontifikat** *n*, *m*; *-(e)s*, *-e*; *kath.* papacy, pontificate

Pontius *m*: *von* ⁓ *zu Pilatus laufen* run (*od.* chase) from pillar to post

Ponton [pɔ̃'tɔ̃:] *m*; *-s*, *-s* pontoon

Pony¹ ['pɔni] *n*; *-s*, *-s* (*Pferd*) pony

Pony² ['pɔni] *m*; *-s*, *-s Haar*: fringe, *Am.* bangs *Pl.*; **⁓frisur** *f*: *e-e* ⁓ *tragen* have a fringe, *Am.* have bangs

Pool [pu:l] *m*; *-s*, *-s* **1.** (*Schwimmbecken*) (swimming) pool; **2.** *Fin.* pool

Poolbillard ['pu:lbɪljart] *n* pool, pocket billiards

Popanz *m*; *-es*, *-e* **1.** (*Schreckgespenst*) bogeyman; **2.** (*Marionette*) puppet

Pop-Art ['pɔpʔaːɐt] *f*; *-*, *kein Pl.* pop art

Pope *m*; *-n*, *-n* **1.** (Orthodox) priest; **2.** *pej.* cleric, holy Joe *umg.*, rev *Am. umg.*

Popel *m*; *-s*, *-*; *umg.* bog(e)y, bit of snot

popelig *Adj. umg.* (*dürftig*) miserable; (*knauserig*) stingy; *für* ⁓*e 10 Euro* for ten lousy euros

Popeline [pɔpə'li:n] *m*; *-s*, *-* poplin

popeln *v/i. umg.* (*auch*: *sich in der Nase* ⁓) pick one's nose

Pop|fan *m* pop fan; **⁓farbe** *f* loud colo(u)r; **⁓konzert** *n* pop concert; **⁓literatur** *f* pop literature; **⁓lyrik** *f* pop poetry; **⁓musik** *f* pop music

Popo *m*; *-s*, *-s*; *umg.* bottom, backside; *zum Kind*: bot(ty), *Am.* rear end, behind; **⁓scheitel** *m umg.* middle part(ing)

Popper *m*; *-s*, *-*; *umg. altm.* trendy, *Am.* preppy

poppig *Adj. Farben*, *Kleidung*: trendy; *Stil*, *Show*: colo(u)rful

Pop|sänger *m*, **⁓sängerin** *f* pop singer; **⁓star** *m* pop star; **⁓szene** *f* pop scene

populär *Adj.* popular; **popularisieren** *v/t.* popularize; **Popularität** *f*; *-*, *kein Pl.* popularity

populärwissenschaftlich *Adj.* popular(ized); *nur attr.* popular-science ...; ⁓*e Bücher* science books for the general public

Population *f*; *-*, *-en* population; **Populationsdichte** *f* population density

Populismus *m*; *-*, *kein Pl.* populism; **Populist** *m*; *-en*, *-en*, **Populistin** *f*; *-*, *-nen*, **populistisch** *Adj.* populist

Pop-up-Menü ['pɔpapmenyː] *in Computersoftware*: pop-up (menu)

Pore *f*; *-*, *-n* pore; *mir brach der Schweiß aus allen* ⁓*n vor Angst*: I broke out into a cold sweat; **porig** *Adj.* porous

Porno *m*; *-s*, *-s*; *umg.* porn; *sich* (*Dat.*) *e-n* ⁓ *reinziehen Sl.* watch a porn film (*od.* video *etc.*) *allg.*

...porno *m*, *im Subst.*: *Edel⁓* high-class

P

porn; *Gewalt*~ violent porn

Pornofilm *m* sex (*od.* porn) film, blue movie

Pornographie *f*; -, *kein Pl.* pornography; **pornographisch I.** *Adj.* pornographic; **II.** *Adv.* pornographically

Porno|heft *n* porn magazine; ~**kino** *n* blue (*od.* porn) movie theat|re (*Am.* -er)

porös *Adj.* porous; **Porosität** *f*; -, *kein Pl.* porosity

Porphyr *m*; -*s*, -*e*; *Min.* porphyry

Porree *m*; -*s*, -*s*; *Bot.* leek; *Gastr.* leeks *Pl.*

Portal *n*; -*s*, -*e* main entrance, portal

Portefeuille [pɔrtə'fœj] *n*; -*s*, -*s*; *Pol.* portfolio

Portemonnaie [pɔrtmɔ'neː] *n*; -*s*, -*s* (*Am.* change) purse; *ein dickes* ~ *haben umg. fig.* have wads (*od.* stacks) of money, be loaded, have deep pockets

Portier [pɔr'tjeː] *m*; -*s*, -*s* porter, doorman

portieren *v/t. schw., bes. Pol.* put up, nominate

Portion *f*; -, -*en* **1.** *bei Tisch:* helping, serving; *Tee, Kaffee:* pot; *e-e halbe* ~ half a portion; *e-e zweite* ~ a second helping; *e-e* ~ *Eis* one portion of ice-cream; *Kugel:* one scoop; **2.** *umg. fig. Mut etc.:* good deal, dose *of courage etc.*; *in kleinen* ~*en* in small doses; **3.** *umg. fig.: halbe* ~ half-pint, shrimp, titch; **portionieren** *v/t.* divide into portions; **Portionspackung** *f* one-serving size; **portionsweise** *Adv.* in portions

Porto *n*; -*s*, -*s od. Porti* postage (*für* on, for); ~ *zahlt Empfänger* postage to be paid by addressee

portofrei *Adj.* postage paid

Portokasse *f etwa* petty cash; *das zahlen die doch aus der* ~ *umg.* that's chickenfeed for them

portopflichtig *Adj.* subject to postage

Porträt [pɔr'trɛː] *n*; -*s*, -*s* portrait; ~**aufnahme** *f* portrait (photograph); ~**foto** *n* portrait (photograph)

porträtieren *v/t.* paint a portrait of; *fig.* portray

Porträt|maler [pɔr'trɛː-] *m*, ~**malerin** *f* portrait painter; ~**malerei** *f* portraiture; ~**skizze** *f* sketch for a portrait; ~**zeichnung** *f* sketched portrait

Portugal (*n*); -*s*; *Geog.* Portugal

Portugiese *m*; -*n*, -*n* Portuguese (*Pl.* Portuguese) (man *od.* boy); **Portugieser** *m*; -*s*, -; (*Rebsorte*) Portuguese vine; **Portugiesin** *f*; -, -*nen* Portuguese woman (*od.* girl *etc.*); **portugiesisch I.** *Adj.* Portuguese; **II. Portugiesisch** *n*; -*en*; *Ling.* Portuguese; *das Portugiesische* Portuguese, the Portuguese language

Portwein *m Gastr.* port

Porzellan *n*; -*s*, -*e* porcelain; (*auch Geschirr*) china; *chinesisches* ~ Chinese porcelain; *altes Meissener®* ~ Meissen ware; ~ *zerschlagen fig.* cause a lot of (unnecessary) trouble; ~**erde** *f* china clay, kaolin; ~**figur** *f* porcelain figure (*kleine:* figurine); ~**geschirr** *n* china; ~**laden** *m* china (*od.* porcelain) shop; → *Elefant*; ~**malerei** *f* painting on porcelain; ~**manufaktur** *f* **1.** (*Werkstatt*) china (*od.* porcelain) workshop; **2.** (*Herstellung*) china (*od.* porcelain) manufacture; ~**tasse** *f* china (*od.* porcelain) cup; ~**ware** *f* china(ware), porcelain

Posaune *f*; -, -*n* trombone; *fig.* trumpet; **posaunen I.** *v/i.* play the trom-

bone; **II.** *v/t. fig. pej.* trumpet; *etw. in die Gegend* ~ shout s.th. from the rooftops (*od.* hilltops), tell the whole world about s.th.

Posaunen|bläser *m*, ~**bläserin** *f* trombonist, trombone player

Posaunist *m*; -*en*, -*en*, ~**in** *f*; -, -*nen* trombonist

Pose *f*; -, -*n* pose; *e-e* ~ *einnehmen* take up a pose; *fig.* pose (*als* as); *sich in* ~ *werfen* put on one's best pose; *es ist alles nur* ~ it's all part of an (*od.* the, his *etc.*) act; **posieren** *v/i. pej.* pose

Position *f*; -, -*en* **1.** *allg.* position; (*Stellung, Rang*) *auch* standing, status; *Sport auch* place; (*Posten*) *auch* post; *gesellschaftliche* ~ social standing, position in society; *e-e leitende* ~ *haben* have a managerial position, have a position in management, have an executive position; *in führender/dritter* ~ *liegen Sport* be in first/third place (*od.* position); *s-e* ~ *durchgeben Naut., Flug.* relay one's position; *in* ~ *gehen Mil.* take up one's position; ~ *einnehmen! Film:* places, please!; ~ *beziehen* (*s-e Meinung sagen*) take a stand; **2.** *Wirts.* item; *die einzelnen* ~*en prüfen* check the individual items

positionieren *v/t.* position

Positions|anzeiger *m* position indicator; ~**bestimmung** *f Naut., Flug.* positioning; ~**leuchte** *f Mot.* side lamp; ~**lichter** *Pl. Flug., Naut.* navigation lights

positiv I. *Adj.* **1.** positive (*auch Phys., Math., Med., Etech., Fot.*); (*bejahend*) *auch* affirmative; (*konkret*) concrete; *e-e* ~*e Einstellung zum Leben/Beruf* a positive attitude to life / one's job; *das ist ja sehr* ~ that's excellent; ~*e Kritiken bekommen* get a good press (*od.* good write-ups); *das Positive daran* the good (*od.* positive) thing about it, the positive side of it; *er hat nur Positives über dich erzählt* he only had positive things to say about you; **2.** *Med.* positive; *ein* ~*er Befund* a positive result; *er ist* ~ *allg.:* he tested positive, he's positive; (*HIV*) he's (HIV) positive; **3.** *Jur., Philos.* positive; ~*es Recht* positive law; **II.** *Adv.* **1.** positively; *sich* ~ *auf etw. auswirken* have a positive effect on s.th.; *er hat sich* ~ *darüber geäußert* he was quite positive about it; *befürwortend:* *auch* he was in favo(u)r of it; *e-m Projekt etc.* ~ *gegenüberstehen* support (*od.* be in favo[u]r of) a project *etc.*; **2.** *umg.* (*sicher*): *weißt du das auch* ~? do you know that for certain (*od.* for sure)?

Positiv¹ *n*; -*s*, -*e*; *Fot.* positive

Positiv² *m*; -*s*, *kein Pl.*; *Gram.* positive

Positivismus *m*; -, *kein Pl.*; *Philos.* positivism; **Positivist** *m*; -*en*, -*en*, **Positivistin** *f*; -, -*nen* positivist; **positivistisch** *Adj.* positivist(ic)

Positivliste *f* **1.** *Med., Pharm.* list of *medicines that are covered by statutory health insurance*; **2.** *allg.:* list of recommended products, shops, procedures *etc.*

Positur *f*; -, -*en* pose; *sich in* ~ *setzen* strike a pose; *in* ~ *gehen Sport* take up one's stance

Posse *f*; -, -*n*; *Theat.* farce (*auch fig.*), burlesque

Possen *m*; -*s*, - **1.** *Pl.* (*Unsinn*) antics; ~ *reißen* act the clown, play the fool; **2.** *j-m e-n* ~ *spielen* play a trick on s.o.; **possenhaft** *Adj.* farcical; **Pos-**

senreißer *m*, **Possenreißerin** *f altm.* clown

Possessiv *n*; -*s*, -*e* possessive (form); **Possessivpronomen** *n* possessive pronoun

possierlich *Adj.* droll, comical, funny

Post® *f*; -, *kein Pl.*; *Post.* **1.** post, *bes. Am.* mail; *elektronische* ~ e-mail; *mit der* ~ by post, by mail; *mit getrennter* ~ under separate cover; *zur* ~ *geben*, *mit der* ~ *schicken* post, mail; *ist* ~ *für mich da?* are there any letters (*Am.* is there any mail *Am.*?); *ich lese gerade m-e* ~ I'm just reading (*od.* going through) my mail; *ich warte auf die* ~ I'm waiting for the postman (*Am.* mailman); *im Betrieb:* I'm waiting for the post (*Am.* mail) (to come); → *abgehen* I 1; **2.** (*Postamt*) post office; *Deutsche* ~ *AG* German Post Office plc (*Am.* inc.); *bei der* ~ *arbeiten* work for the post office; **3.** (~*dienst*) postal service

Post|abholer *m*; -*s*, - caller (for mail); ~**ablage** *f* correspondence file; ~**agentur** *f* sub-post office, *Am.* post-office substation

postalisch *Adj.* postal

Post|amt *n Post.* post office; ~**angestellte** *m*, *f* post office (*Am.* postal) employee; ~**anschrift** *f* postal (*Am.* mailing) address; ~**anweisung** *f* money (*od.* mailing) order; ~**ausgang** *m*; -*s*, *kein Pl.* outgoing mail; ~**auto** *n* post office (*Am.* mail) van; ~**bank** *f* postal savings bank; ~**beamte** *m*, ~**beamtin** *f* post office (*Am.* postal) clerk; ~**bote** *m* postman, postie *umg.*; *Am.* mailman, letter carrier; ~**botin** *f* postwoman, postie *umg.*; ~**bus** *m* post office bus

Post|dienst *m Post.* postal service; ~**eingang** *m* incoming mail

posten ['poːstn̩] *vt/i. Internet:* (*Nachricht, Message*) post

Posten *m*; -*s*, - **1.** *Mil.* (*Wache*) sentry, guard; ~ *stehen od. schieben* be on guard duty; **2.** *fig.*: *auf dem* ~ *sein umg.* be on the alert; *gesundheitlich:* be in good form (*od.* nick *umg.*); *wieder auf dem* ~ *sein* be back on one's feet (again), be fighting fit again; *nicht recht auf dem* ~ *sein* be a bit under the weather; → *verloren* II; **3.** *beruflicher:* post, position; **4.** *Wirts.* lot, batch; *e-r Rechnung:* item; (*Eintrag*) entry; *ein größerer* ~ *T-Shirts* a large batch of T-shirts

Postenjäger *m*, **Postenjägerin** *f* careerist, go-getter *umg.*

Poster ['poːstɐ] *n*; -*s*, - poster; ~**format** *n Fot.* poster-size

Postfach *n Post.* post office box, PO box

postfertig *Adj. Post.* ready for posting (*od.* mailing)

Post|gebühr *f Post.* postage; ~**geheimnis** *n* postal secrecy; ~**gepäck** *n Eisenb., Post.* mail freight; ~**gewerkschaft** *f* postal workers' union

Postgiro ['pɔstʒiːro] *n Post.* postal giro transfer; ~**amt** *n* postal giro office; *in GB:* Girobank; *in den USA:* postal check office; ~**konto** *n* (post office) giro account, *Am.* postal check account; ~**verkehr** *m* postal giro service (*od.* system)

posthum *Adj.* posthumous

postieren I. *v/t.* position, place; *Mil. auch* post; **II.** *v/refl.: sich* ~ position o.s.

Postille *f*; -, -*n* **1.** *Reli.:* devotional book; **2.** *pej.* sheet, *Am. auch* rag

Postillion ['pɔstɪljoːn] *m*; *-s*, *-e*; *hist.* stagecoach (*od.* mailcoach) driver
Posting ['poːstɪŋ] *n Internet*: posting
Postkarte *f* postcard; (*Ansichtskarte*) (picture) postcard
Postkarten|format *n*, **~größe** *f* postcard size; **in Postkartengröße** postcard-sized
Post|kasten *m* letterbox, postbox, *Am.* mailbox; **~kunde** *m*, **~kundin** *f* post office customer; **~kutsche** *f hist.* stagecoach
postlagernd *Adj. Post.* poste restante, *Am.* (in care of) general delivery
Postleitzahl *f Post.* postcode, *Am.* ZIP code
Postler *m*; *-s*, *-*, **~in** *f*; *-*, *-nen*; *umg.* post office worker
Post|mappe *f* correspondence folder (*od.* file); **~minister** *m*, **~ministerin** *f* postmaster general
postmodern *Adj.* postmodern; **Postmoderne** *f*: **die ~** Postmodernism
postoperativ *Adj. Med.* post-operative
Post|paket *n Post.* parcel, *Am. auch* package; **per ~** by parcel post; **~raub** *m* mail robbery, depredation of the mails *geh.*; **~sache** *f* post office mail; **~sack** *m* mailbag; **~schalter** *m* post office counter
Postscheck *m Post.* (post office) giro cheque, *Am.* postal check
Post|sendung *f* postal consignment; **~Shop** *m* post office shop; **~sparbuch** *n* post office (*Am.* postal) savings book
Postskript *n*; *-(e)s*, *-e*, **~um** *n*; *-s*, *Postskripta* postscript
Post|station *f hist.* posthouse; **~stelle** *f* **1.** *in Firma*: mail room; **2.** → **Postagentur**; **~stempel** *m* postmark; „**Datum des ~s**" date as per postmark
Postüberweisung *f Post.* postal (*od.* giro) transfer
Postulat *n*; *-(e)s*, *-e* **1.** (*Forderung*) imperative; **2.** *Philos.* postulate, thesis; **postulieren** *v/t.* postulate
postum *Adj.* posthumous
Post|verein *m* postal union; **~vertriebsstück** *n Post.* newspaper *etc.* to be delivered by the postal service; **~vollmacht** *f* postal proxy; **~wagen** *m Eisenb.* mail van, *Am.* mail car; **~weg** *m*: **auf dem ~** by post, by mail
postwendend *Adv.* by return (of post), by return mail; *umg. fig.* right away
Post|werbung *f Post.* direct mail (*od.* mail order) advertising; **~wertzeichen** *n* (postage) stamp; **~wurfsendung** *f* bulk mail consignment; *Pl. auch* bulk mail *Sg.*; **~zug** *m* mail train; **~zustellung** *f* postal delivery; **~zustellungsauftrag** *m* request for recorded delivery; **~zustellungsurkunde** *f* registered post (*Am.* mail) certificate
Pot *m*; *-s*, *kein Pl. bei Glücksspielen*: **den ~ gewinnen** win the pool (*od.* kitty)
Potemkinsche Dörfer [po'tɛmkiːnʃə-] *Pl. fig.* scam, façade; *engS.* Potemkin villages
potent *Adj.* **1.** *Physiol.* potent; **2.** (*mächtig*) powerful; (*einflussreich*) *auch* influential; (*zahlungskräftig*) solvent; (*tüchtig, fähig*) capable, able
Potentat *m*; *-en*, *-en* potentate
Potential → **Potenzial**
potentiell → **potenziell**
Potenz *f*; *-*, *-en* **1.** *Math.* power; **zweite ~** square; **dritte ~** cube; **acht in die zweite/dritte ~ erheben** eight squared/cubed; **acht in die vierte/fünfte** *etc.* **~ erheben** raise eight to the power of

four/five *etc.*; **2.** *nur Sg.*; *Physiol.* potency; **3.** *nur Sg.*; *fig.* ability; **~angst** *f* impotence-related anxiety
Potenzial *n*; *-s*, *-e* **1.** (*Möglichkeit[en]*) potential; **2.** *e-r Anlage etc.*: capacity; **3.** (*Anzahl Personen*) pool (**an** + *Dat.* of)
...potenzial *n*, *im Subst.*: *Energie~* potential energy, energy capacity; *Finanz~* financial potential (*od.* capacity); *Kräfte~* pool of forces, capacity to mobilize forces
potenziell *Adj.* potential
potenzieren *v/t.* **1.** *Math.* raise to a higher power, raise to the power; **2 mit 5 ~** raise 2 to the power (of) 5; **3 mit 2 ~ auch** square 3; **4 mit 3 ~ auch** cube 4; **2.** *fig.* (*auch v/refl.*: **sich ~**) multiply, intensify
Potenz|mittel *n* anti-impotence drug (*od.* remedy); **~schwäche** *f* impaired potency
potenzsteigernd *Adj.* potency (enhancing) *pills etc.*
Potenzstörung *f* virility problem, temporary impotence
Potpourri ['pɔtpuri] *n*; *-s*, *-s*; *Mus.* potpourri (*auch fig.*), medley
Pott *m*; *-(e)s*, *Pötte* **1.** *Dial.* (*Topf*) pot; *umg. Sport*: (*Pokal*) cup; **2.** *umg.* (*Nachttopf*) jerry, *Am.* bedpan; *für Kinder*: potty; **j-n auf den ~ setzen** *umg.* sit s.o. on the jerry (*Am.* pot); **3.** *umg.* (*Schiff*) tub; **4. wir müssen mit diesem Projekt/Vertrag zu ~e kommen** *umg.* we've got to get this project wound up / we've got to get this contract in the bag
Pottasche *f*; *nur Sg.* potash
potthässlich *Adj. umg. Stadt etc.*: plug-ugly, *Am.* butt-ugly; *Mensch*: as ugly as sin *nur präd.*
Pottwal *m Zool.* sperm whale
Poularde [pu'lardə] *f*; *-*, *-n*; *Gastr.* poulard
Poulet [pu'leː] *n*; *-s*, *-s*; *bes. schw.* young chicken, pullet
poussieren *umg. altm.* **I.** *v/i.* (*flirten*) flirt (**mit** with); **II.** *v/t.* (*umwerben*) curry favo(u)r with s.o.
Power ['pauə] *f*; *-*, *kein Pl.*; *umg.* power; **~ haben** be powerful; **~frau** [-frau] *f umg.* high-powered career woman;
powern ['pauɐn] *v/i. umg.* (*volle Leistung bringen*) (really) go for it; (*Produkt etc.*) push like anything
PR *Abk.* PR, public relations *Pl.*
Präambel *f*; *-*, *-n* preamble (**zu** to)
PR-Abteilung *f* PR (*od.* public relations) department
Pracht *f*; *-*, *kein Pl. von Gebäuden, Gewändern etc.*: splendour, *Am.* splendor; *von Farben*: richness; *kalte ~* cold splendo(u)r; **die ~ bei Hofe** courtly splendo(u)r; **es ist e-e ~** *umg.* it's brilliant; **es ist e-e ~, wie er Klavier spielt** it's a treat to hear him play the piano
...pracht *f*, *im Subst.*: *Blüten~* splendo(u)r of blossoms *mst kein Pl.*; *Feder~* magnificent display of feathers; *Locken~* (magnificent) head of curls
Pracht|ausgabe *f* deluxe edition; **~bau** *m* stately building; **~entfaltung** *f* display of splendo(u)r; **~exemplar** *n* (very) fine specimen, beauty *umg.*, humdinger *umg.*; *umg. Person*: cracker, humdinger
prächtig I. *Adj. optisch*: splendid, magnificent; *Bau*: *auch* stately; *Wetter*: glorious; *umg. Person*: great; (*großartig*) brilliant, great; **II.** *Adv. umg.*: **sich ~ unterhalten** have a great conversation; **sich ~ verstehen** get on (*Am.* along)

like a house on fire; **das hast du ~ gemacht!** good work (*od.* show)
Pracht|kerl *m umg.* humdinger, cracker; (*Baby*) bouncing baby; (*Hund*) beauty; **~mädchen** *n umg.* fine specimen of a girl, splendid girl, peach of a girl; **~saal** *m* stately hall; **~straße** *f* (splendid) boulevard; **~stück** *n* (very) fine specimen, beauty *umg.*
prachtvoll *Adj.* (*ausgezeichnet*) splendid; *Wetter*: *auch* glorious; (*sehr schön, großartig*) wonderful
Prachtwetter *n* splendid (*od.* glorious) weather
prädestinieren *v/t.* predestine; **prädestiniert zu** *od.* **für** (*vorherbestimmt*) predestined for; (*geeignet*) cut out for; **er ist für diese Rolle prädestiniert** he's made (*od.* cut out) for the part
Prädikat *n*; *-(e)s*, *-e*; *Gram.* predicate; (*Titel*) title; (*Wertung*) rating; (*Note*) mark, *Am.* grade; **der Film erhielt das ~ „wertvoll"** *etwa* the film was highly commended, the film was rated "commendable"; **Qualitätswein mit ~** → **Prädikatswein**; **prädikativ** *Adj. Gram.* predicative; **~ gebrauchen** use predicatively
Prädikats|examen *n* honours (*Am.* honors) degree; **~wein** *m* special quality wine, quality-tested wine (with special attributes)
prädisponiert *Adj.*: **~ für** predisposed toward(s)
Präfekt *m*; *-en*, *-en*; *auch hist.* prefect;
Präfektur *f*; *-*, *-en* prefecture
Präferenz *f*; *-*, *-en* preference (**für** for); **~liste** *f* list of preferences; *Personen*: short list
Präfix *n*; *-es*, *-e*; *Ling.* prefix
Prägedruck *m* relief print(ing); (*Hochprägung*) embossing; (*Tiefprägung*) tooling
prägen *v/t.* stamp; (*Geld*) mint; (*Leder, Metall etc.*) emboss; *fig.* (*Wort etc.*) coin; (*j-n, j-s Charakter*) form, mo(u)ld; (*Sache*) set the tone of, determine *s.th.*; **geprägt sein von** be marked by; *positiv*: *auch* be characterized by; **~der Einfluss** formative influence; **ein Tier ~ auf** (+ *Akk.*) *Psych.* condition an animal to; **Wälder und Seen ~ die Landschaft** woods and lakes lend the landscape its character (*od.* are the main features of this landscape); **er ist von s-r Umwelt geprägt** he's a product of his environment
Prägestempel *m für Münzen*: minting die; *Druck.* stamping die
Pragmatik *f*; *-*, *-en* **1.** *allg.* pragmatism; **2.** *Ling.* pragmatics (*V. im Sg.*); **3.** *österr. statute defining the grade structure of the civil service*; **Pragmatiker** *m*; *-s*, *-*, **Pragmatikerin** *f*; *-*, *-nen* pragmatist; **pragmatisch I.** *Adj.* pragmatic; **II.** *Adv.*: **~ denken/vorgehen** think/proceed pragmatically
pragmatisieren *v/t. österr.* appoint to the permanent staff
prägnant *Adj.* concise, to the point; *Stil*: pithy; **~es Beispiel** perfect (*od.* telling) example; **Prägnanz** *f*; *-*, *kein Pl.* conciseness, concision; *des Stils*: pithiness
Prägung *f* stamping, minting; embossing; *e-s Wortes etc.*: coinage; *fig.* stamp, character; *Psych.* disposition; → **prägen**; **Demokratie englischer ~** English-style democracy
...prägung *f*, *im Subst.*: *Erst/Nach~* first/succesive impression
Prägungsphase *f Psych.* formative

phase
Prähistorie f; -, kein Pl. prehistory;
Prähistoriker m, **Prähistorikerin** f
prehistorian; **prähistorisch** Adj. prehistoric
prahlen v/i. boast, brag (**mit** about);
(angeben) show off (**mit etw.** [with]
s.th.); **Prahler** m; -s, - boaster, braggart, show-off; **Prahlerei** f; -, -en;
(Prahlen) boasting, bragging; **Prahle-
rin** f; -, -nen boaster, braggart; **prahlerisch** Adj. boastful; (prunkend) showy
präjudizieren v/t. prejudice
präkolumbisch Adj. pre-Columbian
Praktik f; -, -en practice; Pl. auch methods; **unsaubere ~en** underhand methods; **praktikabel** Adj. practicable, feasible
Praktikant m; -en, -en trainee
Praktikantenstelle f trainee post
Praktikantin f; -, -nen trainee
Praktiker m; -s, -, **~in** f; -, -nen 1. practical person; 2. (Ggs. Theoretiker[in])
practitioner (of the trade); **ein alter
Praktiker** an old hand; 3. (Arzt, Ärztin) GP, Am. family practitioner
Praktikum n; -s, Praktika practical
training (period), traineeship; in der
Industrie: auch (industrial) placement,
Pl. auch industrial training Sg.
...praktikum n, im Subst.: **Auslands~**
work experience abroad; **Labor~**
placement (od. work experience) in a
laboratory; **Schul~** classroom experience
PR-Aktion f PR (od. public relations)
campaign
praktisch I. Adj. practical (auch ~ veranlagt); (bequem) handy (auch Gerät
etc.); (tatsächlich) actual; **~er Arzt** general practitioner, GP; **~e Ausbildung**
practical (od. on-the-job, hands-on)
training; **~es Beispiel** concrete example; **~er Versuch** Tech. field test; **im
~en Leben** in real life; **keinen ~en
Wert haben** be of no practical value;
II. Adv. practically; (so gut wie) auch
virtually, more or less; (in der Praxis)
in practice; **~ nie** very rarely, hardly
ever; **~ nichts** virtually (od. next to)
nothing; **... gibt es** od. **existiert ~ nicht
mehr** ... has all but disappeared
praktizieren I. v/t. carry out, put into
practice; (Methode) auch apply; (Reli-
gion etc.) practi|se (Am. -ce); **II.** v/i.
practi|se (Am. -ce); **als Arzt/Anwältin
~** practi|se (Am. -ce) medicine/law, be
a practi|sing (Am. -cing) doctor/law-
yer (Am. auch attorney); **er praktiziert
nicht mehr** he's no longer practi|sing
(Am. -cing)
Prälat m; -en, -en; kirchl. prelate
Praline f; -, -n chocolate; Pl. auch box
Sg. of chocolates; **e-e Schachtel Pralinen** a box of chocolates
prall I. Adj. 1. Ball, Luftballon: hard;
Segel: full; Früchte: firm; Tasche etc.:
bulging; Muskeln: taut; Arme, Schenkel: big strong; Brüste: firm, full, well-
-rounded; Backen: chubby; Euter: swollen; 2. Sonne: blazing; **II.** Adv.: **~ gefüllt** filled to bursting nur präd.; Brieftasche: bulging
prallen v/i. 1. **~ auf** (+ Akk.) od. **gegen**
(stoßen) bang into; stärker: crash into;
Person: bump into; stärker: run into;
mit dem Wagen: crash into; Ball: hit;
Wellen etc.: crash against; **mit dem
Kopf gegen etw. ~** hit one's head on
(od. against) s.th.; 2. Sonne: beat
down (**auf** + Akk. on)
Prallsack m Mot. airbag
prallvoll Adj. umg. full to bursting;

Saal etc.: auch umg. chock-a-block,
jampacked
Präludium n; -s, Präludien prelude
prämenstruell Adj. premenstrual; **~e
Beschwerden** premenstrual tension,
PMT
Prämie f; -, -n; (Preis) award, prize;
Wirts. (Versicherungsprämie etc.) premium; (Dividende, Leistungsprämie)
bonus (auch Sport)
...prämie f, im Subst.: **Bauspar~** building society premium, Am. savings and
loan association premium; **Abschuss~**
bounty; **Schlacht~** Agr. subsidy per
head of cattle slaughtered
prämien|begünstigt Adj. bonus-
-linked; **~es Sparen → Prämiensparen**;
~frei Adj. paid-up policy etc.
Prämiensparen n bonus savings
scheme (Am. plan)
prämi(i)eren v/t. award a prize to; **ein
prämi(i)erter Bulle/Film** a prize
(--winning) bull / an award-winning
film; **ein mehrfach prämi(i)erter Autor**
an author who has won many awards
(od. prizes); **Prämi(i)erung** f 1. awarding of a prize; 2. (Akt) presentation
(od. award od. prize-giving) ceremony;
3. (Preis) award, prize
Prämisse f; -, -n premise; **von falschen
~n ausgehen** start out on the wrong
premise, proceed from false premises
pränatal Adj. Med. prenatal, antenatal
prangen v/i. 1. **~ an** (+ Dat.) od. **auf** (+
Dat.) Bild, Name etc.: be emblazoned
on (od. across); **sein Gesicht prangte
an allen Reklamewänden** his face
stared out from all the hoardings
(Am. billboards); 2. lit. be resplendent
(**mit** with); (glänzen, leuchten) shine;
Diamanten etc.: sparkle, glitter; **~ mit
Sternen etc.:** be studded with; **an den
Bäumen prangten rote Blüten** the
trees were ablaze with red blossoms;
3. **~ mit** (zur Schau tragen) show off
with, parade
Pranger m; -s, -; hist. stocks Pl., pillory; **an den ~ stellen** fig. pillory
Pranke f; -, -n paw; umg. fig. (Hand)
(huge) paw; **Prankenhieb** m blow
(od. swipe) from a paw
Präparat n; -(e)s, -e 1. Pharm. etc.
preparation, compound; **ein rein
pflanzliches ~** a 100% vegetable (od.
plant-based) preparation; 2. für Mikroskopie: slide preparation; bes.
Anat. specimen
Präparator m; -s, -en, **~in** f; -, -nen
1. von Tieren: taxidermist; 2. (Sezierer)
dissector; 3. von Präparaten: prepara-
tor; in Labor: lab technician
präparieren I. v/t. 1. (vorbereiten) prepare (**auf** + Akk. for); 2. (sezieren)
dissect; 3. (konservieren) preserve;
II. v/refl.: **sich ~** prepare (**auf** + Akk.
for)
Präposition f; -, -en; Ling. preposition;
präpositional Adj. prepositional
präpotent Adj. österr. 1. altm. (übermächtig) prepotent; 2. österr. (arrogant) arrogant; (frech) impudent, impertinent; **Präpotenz** f; -, kein Pl.
1. altm. (Übermächtigkeit) prepotency;
2. österr. (Arroganz) arrogance;
(Frechheit) impudence, impertinence
Präraffaelit m; -en, -en Kunst Pre-
-Raphaelite
Prärie f; -, -n; Geog. prairie; **~hund** m
Zool. prairie dog; **~indianer** m Plains
Indian; **~landschaft** f plains landscape; **~wolf** m Zool. coyote
Präsens n; -, kein Pl.; Gram. present
(tense); **Verlaufsform des ~** present

continuous (form); **~form** f present
tense form
Präsent n; -(e)s, -e present, gift
präsent Adj. (anwesend, gegenwärtig)
present; (geistig ~) fully alert, with it
umg.; **hast du's noch ~?** (im Kopf)
can you remember?, is it still there?;
das Ganze ist mir noch ~ it's all still
fresh in my mind
präsentabel Adj. presentable
Präsentation f; -, -en presentation; **e-e
~ veranstalten** put on a presentation
Präsentator m; -s, -en, **Präsentatorin**
f; -, -nen; TV presenter; **präsentieren
I.** v/t. present; (vorstellen) present, introduce; **das Gewehr ~** Mil. present
arms; **j-m die Rechnung ~** fig. make
s.o. pay for (it); **II.** v/refl.: **sich ~** present o.s. (+ Dat. to)
Präsentier|griff m Mil. presentation of
arms; **~teller** m umg.: **auf dem ~ sitzen** be on show (for all to see)
Präsentkorb m (food) hamper
Präsenz f; -, kein Pl. presence; **~biblio-
thek** f reference library; **~diener** m
österr., Mil. recruit, conscript; **~dienst**
m 1. österr., Mil. national (Am. selective) service; 2. Amtsspr.: **~ haben** be
on duty; **~stärke** f Mil. effective
strength
Präser m; -s, -; umg. johnny (Sl.), rubber; **Präservativ** n; -s, -e condom
Präses m; -, Präsides 1. kath. chairman
of a (od. the) church assembly; 2. ev.
head of a (od. the) synod
Präsident m; -en, -en president; (Vorsitzender) auch chairman; des Parlaments: speaker; Jur. presiding judge;
Präsidentin f; -, -nen president; (Vorsitzende) auch chairwoman; → **Präsident**
Präsidentschaft f presidency; (Amtsperiode) auch term (of office)
Präsidentschafts|kandidat m, **~kan-
didatin** f presidential candidate;
~wahl f presidential election
präsidial Adj. Pol. presidential
Präsidial|demokratie f presidential
democracy; **~system** n presidential
democracy
präsidieren v/i. preside (**über** + Akk.
over); **Präsidium** n; -s, Präsidien
1. Amt: presidency, chair(manship);
2. (Führungsgremium e-s Vereins, e-r
Partei etc.) committee, board (of directors); 3. → **Polizeipräsidium** etc.
Präsidiums|sitzung f committee (od.
board) meeting; **~tagung** f conference
of the committee (od. board)
prasseln v/i. Regen, Hagel: patter (**auf**
+ Akk. on, Fenster: against); stärker:
beat down (on); aufs Fenster: beat
(against); Schüsse, auch fig. Fragen
etc.: rain down (on); Feuer: crackle
prassen v/i. umg. (in Luxus leben) live
it up, live the high life; (schlemmen)
feast; **mit s-m Geld ~** throw one's
money about (Am. around); **mit den
Vorräten ~** squander one's reserves;
Prasser m; -s, -; (Vielfraß) glutton;
(Verschwender) spendthrift; **Prasserei**
f; -, -en carousing; lavish lifestyle; high
life; **Prasserin** f; -, -nen -; (Vielfraß)
glutton; (Verschwenderin) spendthrift
Prätendent m; -en, -en, **~in** f; -, -nen
claimant (**auf** + Akk. to); (Thronanwärter) auch pretender (to)
prätentiös Adj. pretentious
Präteritum n; -s, Präterita; Gram. pret-
erite, past tense
Prävention f; -, -en prevention
präventiv Adj., **Präventiv...** im Subst.
preventive; Med. auch prophylactic

Präventiv|maßnahme f preventive measure; **~medizin** f preventive medicine; **~mittel** n Med. **1.** (*Prophylaxe*) prophylactic, preventive; **2.** (*Verhütungsmittel*) contraceptive; **~schlag** m Mil. preemptive strike

Praxis f, -, *Praxen* **1.** nur Sg. practice (*auch Handhabung*); (*Brauch*) auch usage; (*Erfahrung*) experience; **in der ~** in practice, in reality; **in die ~ umsetzen** put into practice; (*Plan*) put into effect; **nicht in die ~ umsetzbar** impracticable; **langjährige ~** long years of experience; **mir fehlt die ~** I haven't got the experience, I need more experience; **~ im Umgang mit Computern** hands-on experience with computers; **ein Beispiel aus der ~** a concrete (*od.* real-life) example, *auch* a case I have experienced myself; **2.** *e-s Arztes etc.*: practice; (*Raum*) auch consulting room; *Brit. Med. auch* surgery, *Am.* doctor's office; **e-e gut gehende ~** a thriving (*od.* flourishing) practice **...praxis** f, im Subst. **1.** (*Räume etc.*): *Landarzt~* country practice; **2.** (*Erfahrung*): *Berufs~* professional experience

praxisbezogen Adj. practically orient(at)ed; **~e Ausbildung** hands-on training; **Praxisbezug** m foundation in reality

praxis|fern Adj. theoretical, (purely) academic; **~fremd** Adj. *Studium etc.*: (highly) theoretical, academic; **~ sein** *Person*: have (had) no practical experience, have no idea of the practical demands of the job; **~gerecht** Adj. practical; **~nah** Adj. practical(ly orient(at)ed); realistic

Präzedenzfall m precedent; *Jur. auch* test case; **e-n ~ darstellen/schaffen** constitute/establish a precedent

präzise Adj. precise, exact; **präzisieren** v/t. specify; **können Sie es ~?** can you specify what you mean?, can you be more precise?; **Präzisierung** f specification; **Präzision** f, -, kein Pl. precision, accuracy

Präzisions|arbeit f Tech. und fig. precision work; **~instrument** n precision instrument; **~schütze** m (precision) marksman, sharpshooter; **~uhr** f precision watch (*Standuhr*: clock); **~waage** f precision scale(s Pl.)

predigen vt/i. preach (+ Dat. to, fig. at); (*j-m*) **immer wieder ~, dass ...** fig. constantly lecture (*od.* keep lecturing) to s.o. about ...; **j-m Vernunft ~** try to make s.o. see reason (*od.* sense)

Prediger m; -s, -, **~in** f; -, -nen preacher; **~seminar** n theological training college, seminary

Predigt f, -, -en sermon (*auch umg.* fig.); **e-e ~ halten** give (*od.* hold) a sermon (*über* + Akk. on); **j-m e-e ~ halten** give s.o. a lecture (*über* + Akk. on)

Preis m; -es, -e **1.** a) (*Kaufpreis*) price; (*Gebühr*) charge; (*Satz*) rate; (*Fahr-, Flugpreis*) fare; **die ~e erhöhen/senken** increase (*od.* raise) /lower prices; **zum ~ von ... kaufen** buy at a price (*od.* cost) of ...; **j-m e-n guten ~ machen** make s.o. a good offer; **unter ~ verkaufen** undersell; **weit unter ~ verkaufen** sell (at) cut-price; **zum halben ~ verkaufen** sell (at) half-price; **hoch im ~ stehen** fetch high prices; fig. be in demand; **~e vergleichen vor dem Kauf**: shop around; → **drücken** II 4, **stolz** I 3, b) fig., in Wendungen: **es hat alles s-n ~** there's a price to pay for everything; **jeder hat s-n ~** everyone

has their price; **um keinen ~** not for anything in the world; **2.** *im Wettbewerb*: prize (*auch* fig.); *Film etc.*: auch award; **der erste ~** first prize; **den zweiten ~ bekommen** get second prize, come second; **~ der Nationen** *Reitsport*: Prix des Nations; **3.** (*Belohnung*) reward; **e-n ~ auf j-s Kopf aussetzen** put a price on s.o.'s head; **4.** (*Lob*) praise **...preis** m, im Subst. **1.** (*Entgelt etc.*): *Eintritts~* admission charge; *Erster--Klasse-~* first-class fare; **2.** (*Auszeichnung*): *Hörspiel~* radio-play award (*od.* prize); *Kleinkunst~* cabaret award (*od.* prize)

Preis|absprache f price agreement; **~änderung** f change in price; **~en vorbehalten** (prices) subject to change (*od.* alteration); **~angabe** f quotation (of prices); **~angebot** n offer; *Wirts.* quotation; **~anstieg** m rise in prices; **~aufschlag** m markup; **~ausschreiben** n competition; **~auszeichnung** f price marking, price label(l)ing

preisbewusst I. Adj. price-conscious; **II.** Adv.: **~ einkaufen** shop around

Preis|bindung f price-fixing; *für Bücher*: retail price maintenance (*abgek.*: rpm), *in GB*: net book agreement; **~brecher** m price cutter; **~differenz** f difference in price(s); **~disziplin** f price restraint; **~druck** m pricing pressure; **~drücker** m price-cutter, undercutter, underseller; **~einbruch** m steep fall in prices

Preiselbeere f Bot. cranberry; **Preiselbeerkompott** n cranberry compote

Preisempfehlung f recommended price; **unverbindliche ~** recommended retail price (*abgek.*: r.r.p.)

preisen v/t. praise (*auch Gott*), extol; **~ als** *auch* hail as; → **glücklich** I 2

Preis|entwicklung f price trend; **~ermäßigung** f price reduction; **~frage** f **1.** prize question; *umg.* fig. (*heikle Frage*) sixty-four-thousand-dollar question; **2. es ist e-e ~** it's a question of price

Preisgabe f; nur Sg. e-s Geheimnisses etc.: revelation, unveiling; e-s Gebiets etc.: surrender; (*Verrat*) sellout **preisgeben** v/t. (*Geheimnis, Namen etc.*) give away, reveal (+ Dat. to); (*Heimat*) give up; (*Gebiet, Freiheit etc.*) surrender, give up; (*Prinzip, Ehre etc.*) sacrifice; (*sich Dat.*) **dem Gelächter etc.** expose (o.s.) to; **j-n dem Elend ~** abandon s.o. to poverty; **etw. dem Verfall ~** lct s.th. go to rack and ruin; (*hilflos*) **preisgegeben** (+ Dat.) at the mercy of

preisgebunden Adj. price-controlled **Preis|gefälle** n price gap; **~gefüge** n price structure

preisgekrönt Adj. prizewinning, *Film etc.*: auch award-winning

Preis|gericht n jury; **~gestaltung** f price formation; **~grenze** f price limit; **untere ~** bottom price **preisgünstig I.** Adj. → **preiswert**; **II.** Adv.: **er kauft immer sehr ~ ein** he always shops around for bargains (*od.* manages to find bargains); → **preiswert**

Preis|index m price index; **~kalkulation** f pricing; **~kampf** m price war; **~kategorie** f → **Preisklasse Preiskegeln** n Sport bowling (*od. Brit.* skittles) competition

Preis|klasse f price range; **~kontrolle** f price control

Preis|lage f price range; **in mittlerer ~**

medium-priced; **in der gleichen ~** umg. around the same price; **~lawine** f skyrocketing prices Pl.; **~-Leistungs-Verhältnis** n price-performance ratio; *umg.* value for money

preislich I. Adj. price; **~e Unterschiede** price differences, differences in price; **II.** Adv.: **es ist ~ günstig** it's a good price

Preis|liste f price list; **~-Lohn-Spirale** f prices and wages spiral; **~nachlass** m discount, markdown; **~niveau** n price level; **~notierung** f quotation; **~politik** f pricing policy; **~rätsel** n competition; **~richter** m, **~richterin** f judge; **~rückgang** m fall (*od.* drop) in prices; **~schießen** n shooting competition; **~schild** n price tag; **~schlager** m bargain offer; **~schwankungen** Pl. price fluctuations; **~senkung** f price cut; **~skala** f price range; **~spanne** f price margin; **~spirale** f price spiral, spiral of rising prices; **~stabilität** f stable prices, price stability, stability of prices; **~steigerung** f rise in prices; Pl. auch rising prices; **~stopp** m price freeze; **~sturz** m steep fall in prices; **~system** n price system, system of prices; **~träger** m, **~trägerin** f prizewinner; **~treiber** m profiteer, racketeer; **~überwachung** f price control; **~unterschied** m difference in price(s); **~verfall** m dramatic drop in prices, downward trend (*od.* movement) of prices; **~vergleich** m **1.** (*das Vergleichen*) comparing prices; **2.** in best. Fall: price comparison

Preis|verleihung f presentation (of prizes); **~verteilung** f distribution of prizes

Preisvorteil m saving

preiswert I. Adj. very reasonable; **II.** Adv.: **etw. ~ bekommen/anbieten** obtain/offer s.th. for a reasonable price; → **preisgünstig**

Preiszuschlag m surcharge

prekär Adj. Frage, Situation: awkward, tricky; stärker: really difficult; **~er Friede** uneasy peace

Prellbock m Eisenb. und fig. buffer **prellen** v/t. **1.** (*betrügen*) cheat, swindle, con (*um* out of) umg.; **die Zeche ~** leave without paying, do a bunk (*od.* runner) umg.; **2.** Med. bruise; **sich** (*Dat.*) **das Knie ~** bruise one's knee; **Prellschuss** m ricochet; **Prellung** f bruise; Med. contusion

Premier [prə'mie:] m; -s, -s; Pol. prime minister, premier

Premiere [prə'mie:rə] f; -, -n **1.** Theat. etc.: first (*od.* opening) night; (*Uraufführung*) premiere; **die Berliner ~ des neuen Films** the first Berlin showing of the new film; **der Autor konnte bei der ~ s-s Stückes nicht anwesend sein** the author couldn't be present at the first performance of his play; **2.** fig. hum. (*erstes Mal*) first time; **das ist seine ~ für Bayern München** this is his first appearance for Bayern Munich **...premiere** f, im Subst.: *Film~* film (*Am. auch* movie) premiere, first showing (of a film *od. Am.* movie); *Opern~* first night of an opera

Premieren|abend m Theat. etc.: first (*od.* opening) night; **~besucher** m, **~besucherin** f member of the first--night audience, first-nighter; **~fieber** n first-night nerves Pl.; **~kino** n first-run cinema (*Am.* movie theater); **~stimmung** f first-night atmosphere **Premierminister** [prə'mie:minɪstɐ] m,

~in f Pol. prime minister, premier
Presbyterianer m; -s, -, **~in** f; -, -nen;
presbyterianisch Adj. Reli. Presbyterian; **Presbyterianismus** m; -, kein Pl. Presbyterianism
preschen v/i. umg. Person, Fahrzeug: whiz(z), zoom; Pferd: gallop
pressant Adj. umg. urgent; **es ~ haben** be in a hurry
Presse f; -, -n **1.** nur Sg.; Zeitungswesen: press; **die ausländische ~** the foreign press, foreign newspapers and magazines; **es stand in der ~** it was in the papers; **sie wurde von der ~ überallhin verfolgt** the press (od. the papers) were at her heels wherever she went; **2.** a) Druck. (printing) press; **frisch aus der ~ kommen** come straight (od. hot) off the press, b) Tech. (Saftpresse) squeezer; (Knoblauchpresse) crusher
Presse|agentur f press agency; **~amt** n press office; **~archiv** n press archives Pl.; **~attaché** m press attaché; **~ausschnitt** m press (od. news) clipping, Am. auch cutting; **~ausweis** m press card; **~büro** n press agency; **~chef** m, **~chefin** f (chief) press officer; **~delikt** n press misdemeano(u)r; **~dienst** m news service; **~erklärung** f press release; **~feldzug** m → **~kampagne**; **~fotograf** m, **~fotografin** f press photographer; **~freiheit** f freedom of the press; **~gesetz** n press law; **~gespräch** n press interview; **~haus** n Verlag: newspaper publisher; **~jargon** m journalese; **~kabine** f Sport press box; **~kampagne** f press campaign; **~kommentar** m press commentary; **~konferenz** f press conference; **~konzern** m press (od. newspaper) group; **~korrespondent** m, **~korrespondentin** f newspaper correspondent; **~mappe** f press kit; **~meldung** f press report
pressen I. v/t. **1.** (Papier, Blumen etc.) press; (Stroh) bale; (Schallplatte) press; (Kunststoff) Brit. mould, Am. mold; (Wein) make; **2.** (Trauben, Oliven etc.) press; (Zitrone etc.) squeeze; **den Saft aus e-r Zitrone ~** squeeze (the juice out of) a lemon; **etw. aus j-m ~** fig. squeeze (od. force) s.th. out of s.o.; **3. ~ in** (+ Akk.) force (od. squeeze, stuff umg.) into; **an sich ~** hold tightly; (j-n) auch hug (tightly); **sich an die Wand ~** press o.s. against the wall; **sich flach an den Boden ~** lie absolutely flat on the ground; **j-m die Hand auf den Mund ~** clap one's hand over s.o.'s mouth; **Luft durch etw. ~** force air through s.th.; **4.** fig. (zwingen) force; **etw. in ein System ~** force s.th. into a system; **II.** v/i. bei der Geburt: push; Sänger etc.: force (the voice); → **gepresst**
Presse|notiz f news item; **~organ** n organ, mouthpiece; **~rat** m: **Deutscher ~** German Press Council; **~recht** n press law; **~referent** m, **~referentin** f press officer; **~schau** f press review; **~sprecher** m press spokesman (od. spokesperson); **~sprecherin** f press spokeswoman (od. spokesperson); **~stelle** f press office; für Öffentlichkeitsarbeit: public relations department; **~stimmen** Pl. press (od. newspaper) comments, extracts from the national (od. world) press; **die ~ sind sich einig** the newspapers agree; **~tribüne** f press stand; Parl. press gallery; **~verlautbarung** f press release; **~vertreter** m, **~vertreterin** f reporter; m

auch newspaper man; f auch newspaper woman; **~zar** m press baron, newspaper tycoon; **~zensur** f press censorship
Press|form f Tech., Glasherstellung: press (od. parison) mould (Am. mold); Maschinenbau: compression mould (Am. mold); **~glas** n pressed glass; **~hefe** f press yeast; **~holz** n compressed wood; **~holzplatte** f fibreboard, Am. fiberboard (od. hardboard)
pressieren v/i. umg. be urgent; **es pressiert mir** I'm in a hurry; **es pressiert allmählich** we're running out of time
Pression f; -, -en pressure; **(e-r Fülle von) ~en ausgesetzt sein** be under pressure (from all sides)
Presskopf m Gastr. brawn, Am. headcheese
Pressluft f compressed air; **~bohrer** m pneumatic drill; **~flasche** f compressed air cylinder; **~hammer** m pneumatic hammer, Am. jackhammer
Presssack m Gastr. → **Presskopf**
Pressspan m pressboard; **~platte** f pressboard sheet
Pressung f Schallplatte etc.: pressing; **erste ~** (von Olivenöl etc.) first pressing
...pressung f, im Subst.: **Kalt~** Metall. cold pressing; **Raub~** pirated pressing
Presswehen Pl. bei der Geburt: bearing-down with contractions, expulsive pains
Prestige [pres'ti:ʒǝ] n; -s, kein Pl. prestige; beruflliches, soziales: auch status; **an ~ verlieren/gewinnen** lose face / gain in prestige; **sein ~ wahren** save one's face; **~artikel** m prestige (od. vanity) item; **~denken** n status mentality; **~frage** f matter of prestige; **~gewinn** m gain in prestige; **ₒträchtig** Adj. prestigious, prestige ...
Pretiosen Pl. valuables
Preuße m; -n, -n Prussian; pej. (Norddeutscher) wretched North German; **so schnell schießen die ~n nicht** umg. fig. (immer langsam!) it's no good rushing it, you/we need to take your/ our time; (Vorsicht!) hold your horses, easy does it; **Preußen** (n); -s; hist. Prussia; **Preußentum** n; -s, kein Pl. Prussian character, Prussianness; **Preußin** f; -, -nen; hist. Prussian (woman od. girl); **preußisch** Adj. auch fig. Prussian; **Preußischblau** n Prussian blue
preziös Adj. Stil: stilted, affected; **Preziosen** Pl. valuables
prickeln v/i. **1.** Haut etc.: tingle; **2.** Sekt etc.: sparkle; **auf der Zunge ~** tickle one's tongue; **Prickeln** n; -s, kein Pl. **1.** in den Gliedern: tingling (od. prickling) (sensation), pins and needles Pl.; **2.** von Sekt: prickle; **3.** fig. (Reiz, Erregung) thrill; **prickelnd I.** Part. Präs. → **prickeln**; **II.** Adj. (spannend) exciting, stärker: thrilling; (sinnlich erregend) auch titillating; **es ist ein ~es Gefühl** fig. it gives you goose pimples (Am. auch goose bumps), it sends a shiver down your spine; **eine ~e Spannung** a tingle of excitement
Priel m; -(e)s, -e; Geog. narrow channel (in the North Sea mud flats), Am. tideway
Priem m; -(e)s, -e (Kautabak) quid, plug; **priemen** v/i. chew tobacco
Priester m; -s, -; Reli. priest; **zum ~ geweiht werden** be ordained (as) a priest; **Hoher ~** bibl. etc. High Priest

Priester|amt n priesthood, ministry; **~gewand** n priest's cassock; (liturgisches Gewand) vestment
Priesterin f; -, -nen priestess; **priesterlich** Adj. priestly
Priester|schaft f priesthood; **~seminar** n (Roman Catholic) seminary
Priestertum n; -s, kein Pl. priesthood
Priesterweihe f ordination; **die ~ empfangen** be ordained (as) a priest, take (holy) orders
Prim f; -, -en **1.** Mus. prime; **reine ~** perfect unison; **2.** kirchl. (Gebetsstunde) prime; (Stundengebet) prime (song); **3.** Fechten: prime
prima umg. **I.** Adj. super, great; **II.** Adv.: **das hast du ~ gemacht** well done, you've done a great job; **mir geht's ~** I'm fine, I'm feeling great; **sie hat ~ reagiert** her responses were right on (od. incredibly quick)
Prima f; -, Primen; Päd. **1.** altm. last two years of secondary school; Brit. etwa sixth form; Am. etwa grades 11 and 12; **2.** österr. first year (of secondary school)
Primaballerina f prima ballerina
Primadonna f; -, Primadonnen prima donna (auch fig.)
Prima-facie-Beweis ['pri:ma'fa:tsiǝ-] m Jur. prima facie evidence
Primaner m; -s, -, **~in** f; -, -nen **1.** altm.; student in the (second to) last year of Gymnasium; Brit. etwa sixth former; Am. etwa high school junior or senior; **2.** österr. first year (Gymnasium pupil)
primär I. Adj. primary; Frage, Problem: auch main; **im ~en Stadium** in the initial stage; e-r Krankheit: in the primary stage; **II.** Adv. primarily; **es geht uns ~ darum, dass die Firma überlebt** our main concern is that the company should survive
Primar|arzt m, **~ärztin** f österr. → **Chefarzt**
Primär|energie f primary energy; **~farbe** f primary colo(u)r
Primaria f; -, Primariae; österr. siehe **Chefärztin**; **Primarius** m; -, Primarii; österr. siehe **Chefarzt**
Primärliteratur f primary literature, literature proper
Primarschule f schw. primary school
Primärspannung f Etech. primary voltage
Primarstufe f Päd. primary stage (od. level)
Primärton m simple (od. primary) tone
Primas ['pri:mas] m **1.** -, -se od. Primaten; kirchl. primate; **2.** -, -se; (Geiger) (gipsy band) leader
Primat¹ m, n; -(e)s, -e primacy (**über** + Akk. over)
Primat² m; -en, -en; Zool. primate
Primel f; -, -n Bot. primula; (wilde) cowslip, primrose; **eingehen wie e-e ~** fig. umg. fade away completely, wilt away; lit. wither on the vine; Sport umg. get the worst of it, get a good drubbing
Primfaktor m Math. prime factor
primitiv I. Adj. primitive (auch Kunst); (einfach) basic; pej. (unwirksam) Werkzeug, Methode etc.: crude; **~e Bedürfnisse** basic needs; **die ~sten Kenntnisse** the most basic (od. rudimentary) knowledge, the absolute basics; **gegen die ~sten Regeln des Anstands verstoßen** Person: offend against the most elementary rules of behavio(u)r, have absolutely no sense of decency; **ein ~er Typ** umg. pej. a caveman, a peasant, a Neanderthal; **~e**

Ansichten uninformed views; *die Primitiven* *Pl.* (*Naturvölker*) the primitive peoples; **II.** *Adv.*: ~ *untergebracht sein* live in primitive (*od.* very basic) conditions; **Primitivität** *f; -, -en* **1.** *nur Sg.* primitiveness; (*Einfachheit*) basic nature; *pej. auch* crudeness; **2.** *Äußerung etc.*: crude idea; **Primitivling** *m; -s, -e; umg. pej.* peasant

Primus *m; -, -se od. Primi; altm.* best pupil, top boy; ~ *inter Pares* primus inter pares, first among equals

Primzahl *f Math.* prime number; ~**zerlegung** *f* prime factorization

Printmedien *Pl.* print media

Prinz *m; -en, -en* prince; *mein kleiner ~ Kind*: my little lad; **Prinzengarde** *f im Karneval*: King's Guard; **Prinzenpaar** *n* princely couple; *im Karneval*: Carnival King and Queen (*od.* prince and princess)

Prinzessin *f; -, -nen* princess

Prinzgemahl *m* prince consort

Prinzip *n; -s, -ien* **1.** principle; *aus ~* on principle; *im ~* basically, in principle; *oberstes ~* main (*od.* overriding) principle; *ein Mann mit ~ien* a man of principle; *sie hat es sich* (*Dat.*) *zum ~ gemacht zu* (+*Inf.*) she has made it a matter of (*od.* a point of) principle (+ *Ger.*); → *auch Grundsatz*; **2.** (*Gesetz*) principle, law; *es funktioniert nach dem ~* (+ *Gen.*) it works on the principle of

...prinzip *n, im Subst.*: *Arterhaltungs~* principle of the preservation of the species; *Lebens~* guiding principle; *Wirtschaftlichkeits~* efficiency rule

Prinzipal *m; -s, -e, ~in f; -, -nen; altm. Theat.* manager; *Wirts. eines Betriebs*: owner *allg.*

prinzipiell I. *Adj. Frage, Unterschied*: fundamental; **II.** *Adv.* (*im Prinzip*) basically, in principle; (*aus Prinzip*) on principle; *er macht das ~ nicht* he won't do it, as a matter of principle

Prinzipien|reiter *m umg.* stickler for principles; ~**reiterei** *f* moralizing, harping on (*od.* about) principles; ~**streit** *m* fight (*od.* battle) over principles (*od.* fundamental issues)

prinzipientreu *Adj.* true to one's principles; **Prinzipientreue** *f* adherence to one's principles

Prior *m; -s, -en kath.* prior; **Priorin** *f; -, -nen* prioress

Priorität *f; -, -en* priority (*über* + *Akk., vor* + *Dat.* over) (*auch Wirts. und Patentrecht*); ~*en setzen* establish priorities, take first things first; *du musst die richtigen ~en setzen* you've got to get your priorities right; *e-r Sache ~ geben od. einräumen* give priority to (*od.* prioritize) s.th.; **Prioritätenliste** *f* list of priorities

Prise *f; -, -n* **1.** *e-e ~ Salz/Tabak etc.* a pinch of salt/snuff *etc.*; **2.** *Naut.* prize

Prisma *n; -s, Prismen* prism; **prismatisch I.** *Adj.* prismatic; **II.** *Adv.* prismatically

prismenförmig *Adj.* prism-shaped, in the shape of a prism

Prismen|glas *n* prism(atic) binoculars *Pl.* (*od.* glass); ~**sucher** *m Fot.* pentaprism viewfinder

Pritsche *f; -, -n* **1.** (*Liege*) wooden bed, plank-bed; **2.** *Mot.* (*Ladefläche*) platform; **3.** *des Kaspers, im Karneval etc.*: slapstick; **Pritschenwagen** *m* pick-up truck, *Am.* pick-up

privat I. *Adj.* private; (*vertraulich*) *auch* confidential; (*persönlich*) *auch* personal; (*in Privatbesitz*) *auch* privately owned; *das ist m-e ~e Meinung* that's my personal opinion; *an ~* to private individuals; *etwas Privates* (*besprechen*) (talk about) something personal (*od.* a personal matter); *das Private kommt meist zu kurz* s.o.'s private affairs (*od.* life) gets neglected; *die ~e Wirtschaft* the private sector; *die Privaten umg.* commercial TV, private channnels; **II.** *Adv.* privately, in private; *j-n* (*nicht*) ~ *kennen* (not) know s.o. socially; *j-n ~ sprechen/besuchen* speak to s.o. privately (*od.* in private) / visit s.o. at home; *j-n ~ unterbringen* put s.o. up at a private place; *haben Sie ~ mit ihr zu tun?* do you have any private contact with her?; ~ *ist sie ganz anders* in private (*od.* at home) she's a different person; *ich bin ~ versichert* I am privately insured; *j-n ~ behandeln Med.* treat s.o. privately, give s.o. private treatment

Privat|abkommen *n,* private agreement; ~**adresse** *f* private (*od.* home) address; ~**angelegenheit** *f* private matter; ~**anschrift** *f* → *Privatadresse*; ~**audienz** *f* private audience; ~**ausgaben** *Pl.* personal expenses; ~**auto** *n* private car; ~**bahn** *f* privately owned railway (*Am.* railroad); ~**bank** *f* private bank; ~**besitz** *m* private property; *in ~* privately owned; *in ~ gelangen* pass into private hands; *das Bild etc. stammt aus ~* is from a private collection; ~**bett** *n Med., in Klinik*: pay bed; ~**brief** *m* personal letter; ~**detektiv** *m,* ~**detektivin** *f* private detective (*od.* investigator, *abgek.* PI); ~**dozent** *m,* ~**dozentin** *f Univ.* lecturer with the same qualification as a professor, but without holding post or title, *Am.* adjunct professor; ~**eigentum** *n* → *Privatbesitz*; ~**fernsehen** *n* **1.** commercial television (*od.* TV); **2.** (*Fernsehanstalt*) private (*od.* commercial) TV station; ~**finanzierung** *f* private financing (*od.* funding); ~**flugzeug** *n* private aircraft (*umg.* plane); ~**gebrauch** *m* private (*od.* personal) use; ~**gespräch** *n* private conversation; *Telef.* private call; *bitte keine ~e! umg. fig.* (*in der Schule etc.*) stop whispering!, let's all hear it!; (*mit dem Diensttelefon*) no private calls; ~**grundstück** *n*: *ein ~* private property; ~**hand** *f*: *aus ~* from a private collection; ~**haus** *n* private house

Privatier [priva'tie:] *m; -s, -s; altm.* person of independent means, person who lives on his private income

privatim [pri'va:tɪm] *Adv.* privately, in private; (*vertraulich*) confidentially

Privat|industrie *f* private sector industry; ~**initiative** *f* **1.** (private) initiative; ~ *zeigen* show some initiative; **2.** *Wirts.* private venture

privatisieren I. *v/t.* (*Ggs. verstaatlichen*) privatize; **II.** *v/i.* live on a (*od.* one's) private income; **Privatisierung** *f* privatization (+ *Gen.* of)

Privatissimum *n; -s, Privatissima; Univ.* etwa colloquium

Privatist *m; -en, -en, ~in f; -, -nen; österr.* pupil preparing privately for the Matura examination to qualify for university entrance

Privat|klage *f Jur.* private action; ~**klinik** *f Med.* private clinic (*od.* nursing home *od.* hospital); ~**konto** *n* personal account; ~**krankenkasse** *f* private health insurance organization; ~**krieg** *m* private feud; ~**leben** *n* private life; *sich ins ~ zurückziehen* retire from public life; *ich habe kaum noch ein ~*

I hardly have any time for myself; ~**lehrer** *m,* ~**lehrerin** *f* private tutor; ~**lektüre** *f* private reading; ~**liquidation** *f Med.* doctor's bill for private health treatment; ~**nummer** *f Telef.* private (*od.* home) number; ~**patient** *m,* ~**patientin** *f Med.* private patient; ~**person** *f* private individual; *es gehört e-r ~* it's privately owned; ~**praxis** *f Med.* private practice; ~**rechnung** *f* **1.** (separate) personal invoice; **2.** *Med.* → *Privatliquidation*

Privatrecht *n Jur.* private (*od.* civil) law; **privatrechtlich** *Adj.* under private law, *attr. auch* private(-law) ...

Privat|rente *f* private pension (scheme); ~**sache** *f* private matter; ~**sammlung** *f* private collection; ~**sekretär** *m,* ~**sekretärin** *f* private secretary; ~**sender** *m Radiosender*: commercial station; *TV* commercial channel; ~**sphäre** *f* private sphere; privacy; *Recht auf ~* privacy right; ~**station** *f Med.* private ward, first class ward; ~**stunden** *Pl.* private lessons (*od.* tuition *Sg.*); ~**unterkunft** *f* private accommodation(s *Pl.*); ~**unternehmen** *n* private firm; ~**unterricht** *m* → *Privatstunden*; ~**verbrauch** *m* personal consumption; ~**vergnügen** *n*: *das mache ich nicht zu m-m ~* I'm not doing it for my (personal) amusement; *was Sie hier machen, ist Ihr ~* what you do here is your (own) business; ~**vermögen** *n* personal assets *Pl.*; *großes*: personal fortune; ~**weg** *m* private road; *Fußweg*: private footpath; ~**wirtschaft** *f* private enterprise; ~**wohnung** *f* private flat (*Am.* apartment) (*od.* home); ~**zwecke** *Pl.*: *für ~* for private use

Privileg *n; -s, -ien* privilege; *ein ~ der Reichen* a rich man's prerogative; **privilegieren** *v/t.* grant s.o. a privilege; **privilegiert I.** *P.P.* → *privilegieren*; **II.** *Adj.* (very) privileged; *die Privilegierten Pl.* the privileged classes

pro I. *Präp.* (+ *Akk.*) **1.** for; ~ *und contra* (*den*) *Euro* for and against the euro; ~ *domo* for oneself, on one's own behalf; ~ *forma* pro forma, for form's sake, for the sake of form; **2.** (*je*) per; ~ *Jahr od. anno* per year, a year, per annum; ~ *Kopf* each, per head; *Einkommen ~ Kopf* per capita income; ~ *Stück* each, a piece; ~ *Stunde* an (*od.* per) hour; **II.** *Adv.*: *sind Sie ~ oder kontra* (*eingestellt*)? are you for or against (it)?

Pro *n; -s, kein Pl.*: ~ *und Kontra* the pros and cons *Pl.*

pro... *im Adj. und Adv. mst in politischem Kontext*: pro-; ~**europäisch** pro-European

Proband *m; -en, -en* **1.** *Psych., Med.* test subject, guinea pig *umg.*; **2.** *Jur.* offender on probation, probationer

probat *Adj.* tried and tested; *ein ~es Mittel gegen Erkältung etc.* an effective remedy (*od.* cure) for a cold *etc.*

Probe *f; -, -n* **1.** (*Erprobung*) test, trial; (*~durchlauf*) trial run, practice run; (*Überprüfung*) check; *zur ~* on a trial basis, to try *umg.*; *e-e ~ machen* do a test; *mit e-r Maschine, e-m Fahrzeug etc.*: do a trial run; *ein Auto etc. ~ fahren* give a car etc. a trial run, test-drive a car *etc.*; ~ *liegen/sitzen* view and try out a bed/chair; *etw. auf ~ nehmen od. kaufen Wirts.* buy s.th.on approval; *j-n auf ~ einstellen* employ s.o. on a trial basis; *Beamter auf ~* probationary civil servant; *Ehe auf ~ umg.* trial marriage; **2.** *Theat., Mus.*

P

etc. rehearsal; *Chor:* auch choir practice; (*Sprech-, Gesangsprobe*) audition; **~n** (*ab*)**halten** have rehearsals, rehearse *Theat.*; **~ singen** (sing for an) audition; **3.** (*Muster, Beispiel, Blutprobe etc.*) sample; *Kunst, Druck.* specimen; *iro.* (*Kostprobe*) taste; *e-e ~ s-s Könnens/Mutes etc. ablegen fig.* give a sample of what one can do / proof of one's bravery *etc.*; **4.** *Päd.* (*Prüfung*) test, exam; (*kurze*) quiz; *fig.:* **auf die ~ stellen** (put to the) test; **die ~ bestehen** stand (*od.* pass) the test; **5.** *Tech., Math.:* **die ~ machen** check; → **Exempel**

...probe *f, im Subst.* **1.** (*Muster etc.*): **Material~** sample; **Stuhl~** *Med.* stool sample; **2.** (*Test*): **Mikrophon~** microphone test; **3.** (*Üben*): **Orchester~** orchestral rehearsal

Probe|abstimmung *f* straw poll; **~abzug** *m Druck., Fot.* proof; **~alarm** *m* practice alarm, fire *etc.* drill; **~arbeit** *f* **1.** trial work; **2.** (*Beispiel*) specimen (piece); **3.** *Schule:* test piece; **~aufnahme** *f* **1.** *Film:* screen test; **~n machen** take a screen test; **2.** *Schallplatte etc.:* test recording; **~bohrung** *f* test drilling; **~ehe** *f* trial marriage; **~entnahme** *f* **1.** sampling; **2.** (*Probe*) sample; **~exemplar** *n* specimen copy, sample (copy)

Probe fahren → **Probe** 1

Probe|fahrt *f* test (*od.* trial) run; **~halbjahr** *n* probationary period (of six months); **~jahr** *n* probationary year; **~lauf** *m* test run

proben *vt/i.* rehearse; (*üben*) practi|se (*Am.* -ce); **den Ernstfall ~** have a dry run, practi|se (*Am.* -ce) for the real thing

Probenarbeit *f* rehearsals *Pl.*

Proben|material *n Med.* samples *Pl.*; **~nahme** *f; -, -n; Med.* taking samples, sampling

Probe|nummer *f* sample copy; **~packung** *f* sample pack; **~seite** *f* specimen page; **~sendung** *f* sample sent on approval; **~singen** *v/i.* → **Probe** 1; **~stück** *n* sample; **~turnen** *n* practice (*od.* warmup) exercises *Pl.*

probeweise *Adv.* on a trial basis; *eingestellt:* auch on probation; **~ etw. anders machen / etw. anderes benutzen** try doing s.th. differently / using s.th. different

Probe|wurf *m Sport, vor Wettkampf:* practice throw; **~zeit** *f* probationary (*od.* trial) period; **in der ~ sein** be on probation

probieren *vt/i.* **1.** (*versuchen*) try; (*aus~*) try out; *probier doch mal* try it (out), have a try (*od.* go); *probier es noch mal* try again, have another try (*od.* go); *es ~ mit* try s.th., s.o. (*od.* + *Ger.*), have a try at s.th. (*od.* + *Ger.*); *es bei j-m ~ umg.* try it on with s.o.; *Probieren geht über Studieren* the proof of the pudding is in the eating; **2.** (*kosten*) try, taste; *probier mal, ob* (*dir*) *das schmeckt* see if that tastes all right (*Am. umg.* alright), see if you like it; *kann ich mal ~?* can I have a taste?; **3.** (*anprobieren*) try on; *etw. wegen der Grösse ~* try s.th. on for size; **4.** *Theat.* (*proben*) rehearse

Probier|glas *n* **1.** *für Wein usw.:* tasting glass; **2.** → **Reagenzglas**; **~stube** *f* wine-tasting room

Problem *n; -s, -e* problem (*auch Math., Philos. etc.*); *ein kleines/großes/ schwieriges ~* a minor/major/difficult (*od.* thorny) problem; *das ~ ist od. be-*

steht darin, dass ... the problem is that ...; *~e haben, etw./j-n zu finden* have problems (*od.* difficulty *Sg.*) finding s.th./s.o.; *j-m ~e machen* cause s.o. problems; *~e wälzen* mull over problems; *es ist nicht ohne ~e* it's not without its (little) problems; *er muss immer ein ~ draus machen* he always has to make it into a problem (make a thing of it *umg.*); *kein ~!* no problem

...problem *n, im Subst.:* allg. problem; **Arbeitslosen~** unemployment problem, problem of the unemployed; **Rechts~** legal problem; **Zukunfts~** problem for the future; **Haar~** hair problem; **Orgasmus~** problem in achieving an orgasm

Problemanalytiker *m,* **~in** *f* problems analyst, *etwa* troubleshooter

Problematik *f; -, kein Pl.* problem(s *Pl.*); *die ~ der Arbeitslosigkeit* the problems of (*od.* surrounding) unemployment; *die ~ dieser Beziehung* the problematic nature of this relationship; **problematisch** *Adj.* problematic(al); (*fraglich*) questionable; **problematisieren** *v/t.* make a problem out of; *Päd.* formulate in problem form

Problem|bewusstsein *n* awareness of problems; **~fall** *m* problem (case), problematic case; **~haare** *Pl.* problem hair *Sg.*; **~kind** *n* problem child; **~komplex** *m* complex of problems; **~kreis** *m* range (*od.* complex) of problems

problem|los I. *Adj.* unproblematic(al), problem-free; **II.** *Adv.:* **~ ablaufen** go off without a hitch; *es ging ~* it all went smoothly (*od.* without a hitch); **~lösend** *Adj.* Denken, *Maßnahme:* problem-solving

Problemmüll *m* problem waste

problem|orientiert *Adj.* Ansatz *etc.:* problem-oriented; **~reich** *Adj.* (highly) problematic(al)

Problem|schüler *m,* **~schülerin** *f* problem pupil (*Am.* student)

Problem|stellung *f* **1.** presentation of a problem; **2.** problem; **~stück** *n Theat.* problem play

Procedere *n; -, -; geh.* procedure; *sich über das ~ einigen* agree on a modus operandi; *wie denkst du dir das weitere ~?* how do you think we should proceed from here on?

Produkt *n; -(e)s, -e* product (*auch Math.*); *Pl.* (*Naturprodukte*) produce *Sg.*; *ein ~ herstellen* manufacture a product; *er ist das ~ s-r Umwelt* he is the product of his background

Produktenbörse *f* commodity exchange

Produkt|fälscher *m* maker of counterfeit (*od.* fake) products; **~gestaltung** *f* product design; **~haftung** *f* product liability

Produktion *f; -, -en* **1.** production; *die ~ aufnehmen/einstellen* go into / cease production; **2.** *umg.,* Abteilung: shopfloor; *er arbeitete in der ~* he worked in production, he worked in a factory, he worked in the production line; **3.** (*Produkt*) production; **4.** *produzierte Menge auch:* output

...produktion *f, im Subst.:* **Massen~** mass production; **Tages~** daily production (*od.* output); **Fernseh~** television production; **Speichel~** saliva production

Produktions|abfall *m* drop in production; **~ablauf** *m* production process (*od.* sequence); **~anlage** *f* production

plant; **~ausfall** *m* loss of (*od.* in) production; **~ausstoß** *m* output; **~breite** *f* (horizontal) range of products; **~faktor** *m* factor influencing production; **~genossenschaft** *f* **1.** producers' co-operative; **2.** *landwirtschaftliche ~* (*abgek. LPG*) *hist. ehem. DDR:* agricultural (production) cooperative; **~güter** *Pl.* producer goods; **~kosten** *Pl.* production costs; **~leistung** *f* output capacity; **~leiter** *m,* **~leiterin** *f* production manager; **~mittel** *Pl.* production goods; *Marxismus:* means of production

produktionsreif *Adj.* ready for production

Produktions|rückgang *m* fall (*od.* drop) in production; **~stätte** *f* production plant; **~steigerung** *f quantitativ:* increase in production; *der Produktivität:* increased productivity; **~straße** *f* production line; **~technik** *f* production (*od.* manufacturing) technology; **~tiefe** *f* vertical range of products; **~verfahren** *n* production process; **~verhältnisse** *Pl. Marxismus:* productive relations, relations of production; **~weise** *f* production method; *Marxismus:* mode of production; **~zahlen** *Pl.* production figures; **~ziel** *n* production target; **~zuwachs** *m* increase (*od.* rise) in production; **~zweig** *m* branch of production (*od.* industry)

produktiv *Adj.* productive; **Produktivität** *f; -, kein Pl.* productivity

Produktivitäts|rente *f* productivity-related retirement pension; **~rückgang** *m* fall (*od.* drop) in productivity; **~steigerung** *f* increase (*od.* rise) in productivity

Produktiv|kraft *f* productive factor; **~kräfte** *Pl. Marxismus:* productive forces

Produkt|linie *f* product line; **~manager** *m,* **~managerin** *f* product manager; **~palette** *f* product range; **~piraterie** *f* product piracy

Produzent *m; -en, -en* producer (*auch Film, Schallplatten etc.*); manufacturer, maker; **Produzentenhaftung** *f* product (*od.* manufacturer's) liability; **Produzentin** *f; -, -nen* → **Produzent**

produzieren I. *v/t.* allg. produce; (*herstellen*) auch make; *Unsinn ~ umg.* churn out rubbish (*Am.* garbage); **II.** *v/refl. pej.* show off, make an exhibition of o.s.

Prof [prɔf] *m; -(s), -s; umg.* prof

profan *Adj.* **1.** profane, secular; **2.** (*alltäglich*) ordinary, *attr.* auch everyday …

Profanarchitektur *f* secular architecture

profanieren *v/t.* profane; *eine Kirche:* desecrate; (*säkularisieren*) secularize

Professionalismus *m* professionalism; **Professionalität** *f; -, kein Pl.* professionalism; *j-m die ~ absprechen* deny s.o.'s professional ability; **professionell I.** *Adj.* professional; **II.** *Adv.* professionally; *etw. ~ ausführen* make a professional job of s.th.; *ich schreibe jetzt ~* I'm writing professionally now, I'm now a professional writer; **Professionelle** *f; -n, -n; umg.* (*Prostituierte*) pro, *Am.* working girl

Professor *m; -s, -en* professor; *österr.* (*Gymnasiallehrer*) teacher at a Gymnasium; *ordentlicher ~* full professor; *zerstreuter ~ umg. hum.* absent-minded professor

...professor *m, im Subst.:* allg. professor *mit Fach:* professor of; **Architek-**

tur~ professor of architecture; **Fachhochschul~** polytechnic (*Am. auch* professional school) professor
professoral *Adj.*, **professorenhaft** *Adj.* professorial; *professorales Gehabe pej.* exaggeratedly professorial behavio(u)r; **Professorenschaft** *f* professoriate, professorial staff (of a university); **Professorentitel** *m* title of professor; **Professorin** *f*; *-, -nen* → *Professor*, **Professur** *f*; *-, -en* professorship, chair (*für* of); *e-e ~ haben/erhalten* have (*od.* hold) / be given a chair
Profi *m*; *-s, -s*; *umg.* pro; *da waren ~s am Werk* it looks like a professional job
Profi… *im Subst. (Sportler[in] etc.) mst* professional
…profi m, im Subst. **1.** *allg. (Sportler[in])* professional …; *Golf~* professional golfer, golf pro; *Rad~* professional (racing) cyclist; **2.** *fig.*: *Fernseh~* television pro; **3.** *mst Pl.*; *umg., in der Werbung (Experte)* expert; *Küchen~* kitchen maestro
Profi|boxer *m*, *~boxerin* *f* professional boxer; *~fußballer* *m*, *~fußballerin* *f* professional footballer (*bes. Am.* soccer player)
profihaft I. *Adj.* (highly) professional; **II.** *Adv.*: *sich ~ verhalten* behave in a thoroughly professional manner
Profikiller *m* professional (*od.* contract) killer
Profil *n*; *-s, -e* **1.** profile; *Tech. auch* section; *von Reifen, in der Sohle*: tread; *im ~* in profile; *der Reifen hat kaum noch ~* the tyre (*Am.* tire) has hardly any tread (*od.* is almost bald); **2.** *fig.* profile; *e-r Person*: personality; *ein unverwechselbares ~* a distinctive identity (*od.* image); *kein ~ haben Person*: have no personality; *Sache*: have no identity (*od.* profile); *die Partei etc. bemüht sich um ein klares ~* the party *etc.* is trying to acquire a distinctive identity (*od.* image)
Profilager *n*; *nur Sg.*; *Sport* the professionals *Pl.*
Profilansicht *f* profile
profilieren I. *v/t. Tech.* profile, shape; *weitS.* streamline; *fig.* give *s.th.* a clear profile; **II.** *v/refl. Politiker etc.*: distinguish o.s., make one's mark; **profiliert I.** *P.P.* → *profilieren*; **II.** *Adj. fig.* (*scharf umrissen*) clearly defined, clear-cut; *Persönlichkeit*: distinguished; *er ist ein ~er Politiker* he's made his mark as a politician; **Profilierung** *f*; *-, kein Pl.* profiling; *fig.* acquisition of a clear profile (*od.* identity)
Profiliga *f Sport* professional league
profillos *Adj.* lacking identity, characterless
Profil|neurose *f umg.* image neurosis; *er hat e-e ~ od. er leidet an e-r ~* he's obsessed with his image, he's always got to be in the limelight; *~reifen* *m* treaded tyre (*Am.* tire); *~sohle* *f* deep-tread sole; *~stahl* *m* sectional (*od.* structural) steel; *~tiefe* *f* tread depth; *~zeichnung* *f* drawing in profile
Profimannschaft *f Sport* professional team
profi|mäßig *Adv. umg.*: *er surft ~* he surfs professionally; *~reif Adj. umg.*: *das war ~* that was worthy of a professional; *e-e ~e Leistung* a performance up to professional standards
Profi|sportler *m*, *~sportlerin* *f* professional sportsperson, *m auch* profes-

sional sportsman; *f auch* professional sportswoman
Profit *m*; *-(e)s, -e* profit; → *Gewinn 2*
profitabel *Adj.* profitable; *stärker*: lucrative
Profit|denken *n* profit-orien(ta)ted mentality; *~geschäft* *n* profitable deal
Profitgier *f* greed for profit; **profitgierig** *Adj.* profit-greedy, money-grubbing
profitieren *v/i.* profit (*von, bei* from); *er kann dabei nur ~* he only stands to gain
Profit|jäger *m* profiteer; *2orientiert Adj.* profit-orient(at)ed; *~streben* *n* seeking for profit; *pej.* profit-mongering; *~sucht* *f* obsession with profit
pro forma → *pro I 1*
Proformarechnung *f Wirts.* pro forma invoice
profund *Adj.* profound
Progesteron *n*; *-s, kein Pl.*; *Med.* progesterone
Prognose *f*; *-, -n* prediction (*zu* regarding *od.* of); *Wirts. und Wetter*: forecast; *bes. Med.* prognosis; *düstere ~n* gloomy forecasts; *alle ihre ~n trafen ein* everything happened as she had predicted
Prognostik *f*; *-, kein Pl.*; *bes. Med.* art of prognosis; **Prognostiker** *m*; *-s, -*, **Prognostikerin** *f*; *-, -nen* prognosticator, *allg.* forecaster; **prognostisch** *Adj.* prognostic; **prognostizieren** *v/t.* forecast, predict; *altm. od. hum.* prognosticate
Programm *n*; *-s, -e* programme; *Am. und EDV* program; (*Zeitplan*) *auch* schedule; *Pol.* (political) program(me), agenda; *Tech. e-r Waschmaschine etc.*: program, cycle; *TV (Kanal)* channel; *Theat. etc. (Heft, Blatt)* program(me); *im ersten ~* on channel one; *nichts (Interessantes) im ~* (there's) nothing (interesting) on; *volles/umfangreiches ~* full/busy schedule; *s-e eigenen ~e schreiben EDV* write one's own programs; *mein ~ fürs Wochenende* my weekend schedule; *das steht nicht auf unserem ~ umg.* that's not on our list; *das passt mir überhaupt nicht ins ~ umg.* that doesn't suit me at all
…programm n, im Subst. **1.** *allg.* program(me); *Radio~* (schedule of) radio program(me)s *Pl.*; *Veranstaltungs~* program(me) of events; **2.** *EDV etc.*: *Zeichen~* graphics program; **3.** *Tech.* *Kurz~ Waschmaschine etc.*: short cycle; *Schleuder~* spin cycle
Programm|ablauf *m Tech., EDV* program(me) sequence; *~ablaufplan* *m EDV* flow chart
Programmatiker *m*; *-s, -*, *~in* *f*; *-, -nen* *bes. Pol.* program(me) planner; **programmatisch I.** *Adj.* programmatic; *~e Rede* keynote speech (*od.* address); **II.** *Adv.* programmatically
Programm|chef *m*, *~chefin* *f* head of program(me)s; *~datei* *f EDV* program (*od.* executable) file; *~dauer* *f* length of a (*od.* the) program(me); *~direktor* *m*, *~direktorin* *f TV* director of program(me)s; *2gemäß Adj. und Adv.* according to program(me) (*od.* schedule); *~gestaltung* *f* program(me) planning
programmgesteuert *Adj.* computer--controlled
Programm|heft *n* program(me); *~hinweis* *m TV*: *~e für heute Abend* details about tonight's program(me)s (*od.* viewing); *hier noch ein ~* a word about a program(me) coming up

shortly
programmierbar *Adj.* program(m)able;
programmieren *vt/i.* *EDV* program(me); **Programmierer** *m*; *-s, -*, **Programmiererin** *f*; *-, -nen* program(-m)er
Programmier|fehler *m* program(m)ing error; *~gerät* *n* program(m)er; *~sprache* *f* program(m)ing language
programmiert I. *P.P.* → *programmieren*; **II.** *Adj.* program(m)ed; *~er Unterricht* program(m)ed instruction; *auf Erfolg ~ sein fig.* be program(m)ed for success; *falsch ~ sein umg. fig.* be on the wrong wavelength; **Programmierung** *f* program(m)ing
Programm|kino *n* repertory cinema (*Am.* movie theater); *~musik* *f Mus.* program(me) music; *~platz* *m TV* program(me) slot; *~punkt* *m* item (on the agenda); *e-r Partei*: plank; *~speicher* *m EDV* program(m)able memory; *~taste* *f TV* channel selector (button); *Waschmaschine etc.*: cycle selector; *~übersicht* *f* program(me) summary; *~unterbrechung* *f* break in a (*od.* the) program(me); *~vorschau* *f* preview; *Film: auch* trailer; *~wahl* *f TV* channel selection; *Waschmaschine etc.*: cycle selection; *~wähler* *m TV* channel selector; *Waschmaschine etc.*: cycle selector; *~zeitschrift* *f* program (-me) guide, TV guide; *~zettel* *m* program(me) sheet; *Theat. auch* cast list
Progression *f*; *-, -en* progression; *in die ~ kommen steuerlich*: be taxed progressively; **progressiv** *Adj.*, **Progressive** *m, f*; *-n, -n* progressive
Prohibition *f*; *-, -en* prohibition
Projekt *n*; *-(e)s, -e* project; *~basis* *f*: *auf ~ arbeiten* be contracted for one project at a time; *~gruppe* *f* project team, task force; *~idee* *f* idea for a (*od.* the) project
projektieren *v/t.* project, plan; *projektierte Zahl* target figure
Projektil *n*; *-s, -e* projectile
Projektion *f*; *-, -en* projection (*auch Math., Psych.*)
Projektions|lampe *f* projector lamp; *~wand* *f* projection screen
Projektleiter *m*, *~in* *f* project manager
Projektor *m*; *-s, -en* projector
projektorientiert *Adj. Päd.* project--based
Projekt|studie *f* feasibility study; *~unterricht* *m* project-based teaching; *~woche* *f Päd.* week of project work
projizieren *v/t.* project (*auf + Akk.* onto) (*auch Psych.*)
Proklamation *f*; *-, -en* proclamation; **proklamieren** *v/t.* proclaim
Pro-Kopf-Einkommen *n* per capita income
Prokura *f*; *-, Prokuren*; *Wirts.* power of attorney; *~ erhalten* be granted power of attorney; **Prokurist** *m*; *-en, -en*, **Prokuristin** *f*; *-, -nen* authorized signatory
Prol *m*; *-s, -s*; *Sl. pej.* prole
Prolet *m*; *-en, -en*; *umg. pej.* **1.** (*Proletarier*) pleb, prole; **2.** (*grober Mensch*) peasant
Proletariat *n*; *-s, kein Pl.* proletariat; **Proletarier** *m*; *-s, -*, **Proletarierin** *f*; *-, -nen*, **proletarisch** *Adj.* proletarian
proletenhaft *Adj. pej.*, **prolig** *Adj. Sl. pej.* plebeian, plebby
Prolog *m*; *-(e)s, -e* prologue, *Am. auch* prolog
prolongieren *v/t. Wirts.* extend; *e-n Wechsel* renew
Promenade *f*; *-, -n* promenade

Promenaden|deck *n Naut.* promenade deck; **~konzert** *n* promenade concert; **~mischung** *f umg.* mongrel
promenieren *v/i.* promenade
Promi ['pro:mi] *m; -, -s; Abk. umg.* VIP; *bes. Film etc.*: celeb
Promille *n* (part) per thousand (*od.* mil); *umg.* blood alcohol; **er hatte 1,2 / zu viel ~** *umg.* he had 1.2 parts per thousand / too much alcohol in his blood; **~grenze** *f* (blood) alcohol limit; **~sünder** *m*, **~sünderin** *f* drink (*Am.* drunk) driver
prominent *Adj.* prominent; **~e Persönlichkeit** well-known personality; **Prominente** *m, f; -n, -n* public figure, VIP; *bes. Film etc.*: well-known personality, celebrity, celeb *umg.*
Prominenten|anwalt *m*, **~anwältin** *f* lawyer who acts for celebrities, star lawyer; **~arzt** *m*, **~ärztin** *f* doctor who treats celebrities; **~mannschaft** *f* celebrity team
Prominenz *f; -, kein Pl.* **1.** (*Personen*) VIPs *Pl.*, big names *Pl.*, top people *Pl. umg.*; (*Funktionäre etc.*) *auch* bigwigs *Pl. umg.*; **zur ~ gehören** be one of the leading figures; *auch* be one of the jet set; **2.** (*Prominentsein*) renown
Promiskuität *f; -, kein Pl.* promiscuity
promoten *v/t. Wirts., Sport* promote
Promotion¹ *f; -, -en; Univ.* doctorate, PhD; **an s-r ~ arbeiten** work on one's doctorate; **vor i-r ~** before obtaining her doctorate
Promotion² [pro'mouʃn] *f Wirt. Sport* promotion
Promotions|feier *f* degree ceremony; **~ordnung** *f Univ.* regulations *Pl.* governing conferring of doctorates; **~recht** *n Univ.* right to confer doctorates, *Am.* graduate accreditation
promovieren I. *v/i.* do a (*od.* one's) doctorate (*od.* PhD); **II.** *v/t.*: **j-n ~** award s.o. a doctorate (*od.* doctoral degree *od.* PhD)
prompt I. *Adj.* prompt, quick; **II.** *Adv. umg. iro.* of course, needless to say; **ich bin ~ drauf reingefallen** of course I fell for it straightaway; **Promptheit** *f* promptness
Pronomen *n; -s, - od. Pronomina*; *Ling.* pronoun; **pronominal** *Adj.*, **Pronominal...** *im Subst.* pronominal, pronoun ...
prononciert [pronõ'si:ɐt] **I.** *Adj.* pronounced; *Weigerung, Gegner etc.*: firm; *Anhänger*: firm, staunch; (*deutlich*) clear(-cut); **~e Aussprache** clear enunciation; **II.** *Adv.*: **sich ~ für/gegen etw. aussprechen** take a firm stand in support of / against s.th.
Propädeutik *f; -, -en* propaedeutics (*V. im Sg.*); **propädeutisch** *Adj.* propaedeutic
Propaganda *f; -, kein Pl.* propaganda; **~apparat** *m* propaganda machine; **~chef** *m*, **~chefin** *f* propaganda chief; **~feldzug** *m* propaganda campaign; *Wirts.* publicity (*od.* advertising) campaign; **~flut** *f* flood of propaganda; **~instrument** *n* instrument of propaganda, propaganda medium; **~krieg** *m* propaganda war(fare); **~lüge** *f* propagandist lie; **~manöver** *n* propaganda move; **~material** *n* propaganda material; **~rummel** *m umg.* ballyhoo, hype; **~ in den Medien** media hype; **~schrift** *f* propaganda leaflet; **~sendung** *f* propaganda broadcast; **~trommel** *f*: **die ~ rühren für** drum up some support for, beat the big drum for *umg.*
Propagandist *m; -en, -en*, **~in** *f; -,*

-nen, **propagandistisch** *Adj.* propagandist(ic)
propagieren *v/t.* (*Idee etc.*) propagate; (*Sache*) promote, push *umg.*; **etw. (in den Medien) lautstark ~** hype s.th.
Propan *n; -s, kein Pl.*, **~gas** *n Chem.* propane
Propeller *m; -s, -* propeller, prop *umg.*; **~antrieb** *m*: **Maschine mit ~** propeller aircraft; **~blatt** *n*, **~flügel** *m* propeller blade; **~maschine** *f* propeller aircraft
proper I. *Adj. umg.* neat, clean and tidy; **ein ~er junger Mann** a spruce young man; **II.** *Adv.*: **~ gekleidet** neatly dressed
Prophet *m; -en, -en* prophet; **der ~ Elias** the prophet Elijah; **der ~** (*Mohammed*) the Prophet; **ich bin doch kein ~** I can't read the stars; **dazu braucht man kein ~ zu sein** you don't need a crystal ball to foresee that; **der ~ gilt nichts im eigenen Lande** *bibl. auch fig.* a prophet is not without honour except in his own country; **Prophetengabe** *f* prophetic powers *Pl.*, powers *Pl.* (*od.* gift) of prophecy; **Prophetin** *f; -, -nen* prophetess; **prophetisch I.** *Adj.* prophetic; **~e Gabe → Prophetengabe**; **II.** *Adv.* prophetically
prophezeien *v/t.* (*verkünden*) prophesy; (*vorhersagen*) *auch* predict, forecast; **j-m Reichtum ~** predict that s.o. will become rich; **Prophezeiung** *f* prophecy; (*Vorhersage*) *auch* prediction, forecast; **die ~ hat sich erfüllt** the prophecy has been fulfilled (*od.* has come true)
prophylaktisch *Adj.* prophylactic, preventive; **Prophylaxe** *f; -, -n* prophylaxis; **zur ~ gegen** as a precaution against
Proportion *f; -, -en* proportion; **ihre ~en sind beachtlich** *umg., hum.* she's got a remarkable (*od.* an amazing) figure
proportional I. *Adj.* proportional; **umgekehrt ~** inversely proportional (**zu** to); **II.** *Adv.*: **~ verteilen** distribute proportionally
Proportionalschrift *f* proportional spacing
proportioniert *Adj.*: (**gut ~** well-)proportioned
Proporz *m; -es, -e* proportional representation (*also for the main civil service posts*); **~denken** *n* principle of proportional representation for all administrative posts; **~wahl** *f schw., österr.* (election by) proportional representation
proppe(n)voll *Adj. umg.* jam-packed, chock-a-block *nur präd.*, chock-full *nur präd.*; **der Bus war ~** the bus was chock-full of people
Propst *m; -es, Pröpste; kirchl.* provost; **Propstei** *f; -, -en* (provost's) parish; **Pröpstin** *f; -, -nen* (female) provost
Prorektor *m*, **~in** *f etwa* a) *Univ.* pro-vicechancellor, b) *e-r Schule*: deputy rector
Prosa *f; -, kein Pl.* **1.** prose; **in ~ verfassen** write in prose; **ein Stück/Bändchen ~** a piece / slim volume of prose; **2.** (*Gedicht*) prose poem; *Koll.* prose poetry; **3.** *geh., fig.* prosaicness, dullness; **~dichtung** *f* **1.** prosework, work of prose; *Koll.* prose writing; **2.** (*Gedicht*) prose poem; *Koll.* prose poetry
Prosaiker *m; -s, -*, **~in** *f; -, -nen* **1.** *fig.* sober (*od.* down-to-earth *od.* matter-of-fact) (sort of) person; **2.** *altm.* prose writer; **prosaisch I.** *Adj.* prosaic; *fig.* (*nüchtern*) down-to-earth, matter-of--

fact; (*alltäglich*) mundane; **ein recht ~er Stil** a very dull (*od.* unimaginative) style; **II.** *Adv.* prosaically; **Prosaist** *m; -en, -en*, **Prosaistin** *f; -, -nen*, **Prosaschriftsteller** *m*, **Prosaschriftstellerin** *f* prose writer
Prosa|text *m* prose text; *Pl. auch* prose writings; **~übersetzung** *f* prose translation
Proseminar *n Univ.* proseminar(y), (introductory) seminar
prosit I. *Interj.* → **prost**; **II. Prosit** *n; -s, -s*: **ein Prosit auf j-n ausbringen** toast s.o.
Prospekt *m; -(e)s, -e* **1.** brochure; (*Faltblatt*) *auch* leaflet; **2.** (*Ansicht*) prospect
...prospekt *m, im Subst.*: **Farb~** colo(u)r brochure
prost *Interj.* cheers!, your health!; **~ Neujahr!** happy New Year!; **na denn ~!** *umg. iro.* what a delightful prospect! *iro.*; → **Mahlzeit**
Prostata *f; -, kein Pl.*; *Anat.* prostate (gland); **~hypertrophie** *f Med.* prostatic hypertrophy; **~krebs** *m Med.* cancer of the prostate; **~operation** *f Med.* prostate operation; **~vergrößerung** *f Med.* enlargement of the prostate (gland), enlarged prostate
prostituieren *v/refl. fig. und altm.* im wörtl. Sinn: prostitute o.s.; **Prostituierte** *f; -n, -n* prostitute; **Prostitution** *f; -, kein Pl.* prostitution
Protagonist *m; -en, -en*, **~in** *f; -, -nen* protagonist; *fig.* (*Vorkämpfer[in]*) *auch* champion (+ *Gen.* of)
Protegé [prote'ʒe:] *m; -s, -s* protégé; *weibl. Person: auch* protégée; **protegieren** [prote'ʒi:rən] *v/t.* sponsor, promote
Protein *n; -s, -e* protein
protein|arm *Adj. nur präd.* low in protein, *attr.* low-protein; **~haltig** *Adj.* containing protein
proteinreich *Adj. nur präd.* high (*od.* rich) in protein, *attr.* high-protein ...
Protektion *f; -, -en* patronage, sponsorship; **Protektionismus** *m; -, kein Pl.* protectionism; **protektionistisch** *Adj.* protectionist; **Protektionswirtschaft** *f* favouritism, *Am.* favoritism
Protektor *m; -s, -en* protector; (*Gönner, Schirmherr*) patron; **Protektorat** *n; -(e)s, -e* protectorate; (*Schirmherrschaft*) patronage; **unter dem ~ von** under the auspices of
Protest *m; -(e)s, -e* protest; **aus ~ gegen** in (*od.* as a) protest against, in protest at; **aus ~ weggehen** leave in protest; **unter (lautem) ~ den Saal verlassen** walk out (in protest); **es hagelte ~e** there was a storm of protest; **e-n Wechsel zu ~ gehen lassen** *Wirts.* protest a bill; **~aktion** *f* (public) protest; protest campaign
Protestant *Reli. m; -en, -en*, **~in** *f; -, -nen*, Protestant; **protestantisch** *Adj.* Protestant; **Protestantismus** *m; -, kein Pl.* Protestantism
Protest|bewegung *f* protest movement; **~haltung** *f* rebellious attitude
protestieren *v/i.* protest (**gegen** against s.th., *Am. auch* s.th.); **ich protestiere!** I protest!; *Wirts., Fin.* protest, contest; **e-n Wechsel ~** protest a bill of exchange
Protest|kundgebung *f* protest rally, demonstration; **~lied** *n* protest song; **~note** *f Pol.* protest note; **~rufe** *Pl.* shouts of protest; **~schreiben** *n* (*Privatbrief*) letter of protest; **~sturm** *m* storm of protest, pub-

lic outcry; **~wähler** *m*, **~wählerin** *f* protest voter

Prothese *f*; -, *-n* **1.** artificial limb, prosthesis *fachspr.*; (*Beinprothese*) artificial leg; (*Armprothese*) artificial arm; **2.** (*Gebiss*) dentures *Pl.*

Prothesenträger *m*, **~in** *f* **1.** person with an artificial limb; **2.** denture-wearer

prothetisch *Adj.* prosthetic; **~e Behandlung** *Dent.* fitting of dentures

Protokoll *n*; -*s*, *-e* **1.** *von Sitzung*: minutes *Pl.*; *im Gericht, von Versuch etc.*: record; *im vollen Wortlaut*: transcript; (*das*) **~ führen** take (down) (*od.* keep) the minutes; **ins ~ aufnehmen** take down (in the minutes); *etw. zu ~ geben Jur.* give evidence of s.th., state s.th. in evidence; *etw. zu ~ nehmen* take s.th. down in evidence, put s.th. on record; **2.** (*diplomatisches*) protocol; *ein strenges ~* strict protocol; *das ~ einhalten* observe protocol; **3.** *Med. etc.*; *e-s Versuchs, e-r Operation etc.*: report, record; **4.** (*Strafmandat*) ticket; **5.** *EDV*: log

...protokoll *n*, *im Subst.* **1.** *Gerichts~* court record; *Sitzungs~* minutes *Pl.* of a (*od.* the) meeting; *Vernehmungs~* transcript of questioning, interview transcript; **2.** *Med. etc.*: *Versuchs~* record of an (*od.* the) experiment; *Verlaufs~* record

Protokollant *m*; *-en, -en*, **~in** *f*; -, *-nen* minute-taker, keeper of the minutes; *weitS.* secreatry; **protokollarisch I.** *Adj.* **1.** recorded; **~e Aussage** *Jur.* statement given in evidence; **2.** *Pol.* **~e Bestimmungen** rules of protocol; **II.** *Adv.*: **~ festhalten** take down (in the minutes), *Jur.* take down as evidence; **Protokollführer** *m*, **Protokollführerin** *f* minute-taker, keeper of the minutes; *Jur.* clerk of the court; *wer ist Protokollführer?* who's taking the minutes?

protokollieren *vt/i.* (*das Protokoll führen*) take the minutes; *Jur.* take the record; (*Äußerung etc.*) take down (in the minutes); (*Sitzung*) take the minutes of (*od.* at); *Jur.* take down (on record); (*Verhör*) record; (*Versuch etc.*) write a report on

Proton *n*; *-s*, *-en*; *Phys.* proton

Protoplasma *n*; *-s*, *kein Pl.*; *Bio.* protoplasm

Prototyp *m* **1.** *Tech. etc.* prototype; **2.** (*Inbegriff*): archetype; *der ~ e-s Kapitalisten etc.* the (*od.* your *umg.*) archetypal capitalist *etc.*; **prototypisch** *Adj.* archetypal

Protuberanz *f*; -, *-en*; *Astron.* prominence

Protz *m*; *-es*, *-e*; *umg.*, *pej.* show-off, swank

...protz *m*, *im Subst. umg., pej.*: *Potenz~* sexual potency show-off

Protzbau *m pej.* ostentatious (*od.* showy) building

protzen *v/i. umg.* swank; *mit etw. ~* show s.th. off; *er protzt gern mit s-m Geld/Wissen* he likes to flash his money around / let you know how knowledgeable he is; **Protzerei** *f*; -, *-en*; *umg.* swanking, showing off; **protzig** *umg.* **I.** *Adj.* *Geste*: ostentatious; *Sache*: *auch* showy, swanky; *Wagen*: flash(y); *e-e ~e Villa mit e-m ~en Pool* an ostentatious mansion with an ornate pool; **II.** *Adv.* ostentatiously

Provenienz *f*; -, *-en*; *geh.* origin, provenance; *Waren italienischer ~* goods of Italian origin; *unbekannter ~* of unknown origin

provenzalisch *Adj.* Provençal

Proviant *m*; *-s*, *-e* (*Pl. selten*) provisions *Pl.*, food; *Mil.* rations *Pl.*, food supply, supplies *Pl.*; **~kiste** *f* hamper; **~korb** *m* food basket

Provinz *f*; -, *en* **1.** province (*auch fig.*); **2.** (*Ggs. Hauptstadt*) the provinces *Pl.*; *das ist ja hier tiefste ~ pej.* what a backwater this is; *sie leben in der hintersten ~ umg.* they live at the back of beyond; **~blatt** *n* provincial newspaper, local rag *umg.*; **~hauptstadt** *f* provincial capital

provinziell *Adj.* provincial

Provinzler *m*; *-s*, -, **~in** *f*; -, *-nen*; *umg.* provincial; *pej.* country cousin, *Am. auch* hick

Provinz|nest *n umg.* provincial backwater, *bes. Am.* hick town, one-horse town; **~stadt** *f* provincial town; **~theater** *n* provincial theat|re (*Am. auch* -er)

Provision *f*; -, *-en*; *Wirts.* commission; *auf ~* on commission; **Provisionsbasis** *f*: *auf ~* on commission, on a commission basis

provisorisch I. *Adj.* provisional, temporary; (*behelfsmäßig*) *nur attr.* makeshift ...; **~e Lösung** stopgap solution; **~e Regierung** caretaker (*od.* provisional) government; **II.** *Adv.*: *etw. ~ reparieren* do a makeshift job on s.th., patch s.th. up for the time being

Provisorium *n*; *-s*, *Provisorien* provisional (*od.* temporary) arrangement, stopgap

provokant *Adj.* provocative; **Provokateur** [provoka'tøːɐ] *m*; *-s*, *-e*, **Provokateurin** *f*; -, *-nen* troublemaker, agent provocateur; **Provokation** *f*; -, *-en* provocation; **provokativ** *Adj.* provocative

provozieren *vt/i.* provoke; (*Tier*) torment; *er will nur ~* he's just trying to provoke (*od.* be provocative); *j-n dazu ~, etw. zu tun* provoke s.o. into doing s.th.; *sich nicht ~ lassen* not allow o.s. to be provoked; **provozierend I.** *Part. Präs. → provozieren*; **II.** *Adj.* provocative; **III.** *Adv.*: *j-n ~ ansehen/fragen* look at s.o. provocatively (*od.* challengingly) / ask s.o. provocative questions

Prozedere *n → Procedere*

Prozedur *f*; -, *-en* procedure, process; *das war vielleicht e-e ~! umg.* what a business (*od.* hassle *umg.*) (that was)!

Prozent *n*; -(*e*)*s*, *-e*, *bei Summen* - per cent, *bes. Am.* percent; **~e** percentage; (*Rabatt*) a discount; *zu fünf ~* at five per cent (*Am.* percent); *ich kann Ihnen zehn ~ geben* (*Rabatt*) I can knock off ten per cent (*Am.* percent)

...prozentig *im Adj.* ... per cent (*bes. Am.* percent); *e-e fünf~e Erhöhung* a five per cent (*Am.* percent) increase

Prozent|punkt *m* per cent, *bes. Am.* percent; *sie haben sich bei der Wahl um fünf ~e verbessert* they've gained another five per cent (*Am.* percent) of the vote; **~rechnung** *f* (calculation of) percentages *Pl.*; **~satz** *m* percentage

prozentual *Adj.* proportional; **~er Anteil** percentage

Prozentzeichen (%) per cent sign, *bes. Am.* percent sign

Prozess *m*; *-es*, *-e* **1.** (*Vorgang, Verfahren*) process; *→ Entwicklungsprozess, Lernprozess etc.*; **2.** *Jur.* (*Rechtsstreit*) lawsuit; (*Strafverfahren*) trial; *e-n ~ gewinnen/verlieren* win/lose a case; *gegen j-n e-n ~ anstrengen* bring an action against s.o., sue s.o.; *j-m den ~ machen* take s.o. to court; *mit j-m/etw. kurzen ~ machen fig.* make short work of s.o./s.th.

...prozess *m*, *im Subst.* **1.** *Jur. Sorgerechts~* custody case (*od.* suit); **2.** (*Vorgang*) *Alterungs~* ag(e)ing process; *Entstehungs~* genesis

prozess|fähig *Adj. Jur.* capable of suing or being sued; **~freudig** *Adj.* litigious; **~führend** *Adj.*: *die ~en Parteien* the litigants, the parties to the case

Prozess|führung *f Jur.* conduct of a (*od.* the) case; *allg.* litigation; **~gegner** *m*, **~gegnerin** *f* opposing party

prozessieren *v/i.* go to court; *gegen j-n ~* bring an action against s.o., take s.o. to court

Prozession *f*; -, *-en* procession

Prozesskosten *Pl. Jur.* legal costs; **~hilfe** *f* legal aid

Prozessor *m*; *-s*, *-en Computer*: processor

Prozess|ordnung *f Jur.* code of procedure; **~recht** *n* adjective (*od.* procedural) law; **~steuerung** *f EDV* process control; **£unfähig** *Adj.* incapable of suing or being sued; **~vollmacht** *f* power of attorney

prüde *Adj.* prudish; *ich bin (ja) nicht ~* I'm no prude; **Prüderie** *f*; -, *n* prudishness, prudery

Prüfautomat *m* (automatic) testing equipment

prüfen I. *vt/i.* **1.** *Päd.* test, give *s.o.* a test; *in Examen*: examine; *er prüft sehr streng* he's a tough examiner; *es wird schriftlich und mündlich geprüft* there will be a written and an oral test (*od.* exam); *j-s Russischkenntnisse ~* test s.o.'s knowledge of Russian; *staatlich geprüfter Dolmetscher/Skilehrer* state-certified interpreter / skiing instructor; **2.** (*feststellen*) check, test; **3.** (*erproben*) try (out), (put to the) test; **4.** *Tech.* (*abnehmen*) inspect; *Metall.* assay; (*untersuchen, genau betrachten*) examine, study; **5.** (*Vorfall, Beschwerde etc.*) investigate, look into; **6.** (*Vorschlag*) consider, have a close look at; *wir werden Ihr Angebot ~ in Geschäftsbrief*: we will study your offer; **7.** (*nach~, über~*) check; (*auf Richtigkeit*) *~* verify, check; *der Antrag wird geprüft* is under consideration; *etw. auf s-e Echtheit hin ~* check to see whether s.th. is genuine (*od.* authentic); **8.** *Wirts.* (*Bücher*) audit; *Jur.* (*Entscheidung*) review; **9.** *Sport* (*Torwart*) test; **10.** *geh.* (*psychisch belasten*) try; *er ist vom Leben schwer geprüft* he has had a raw deal from life; **II.** *v/refl.* do some soul-searching

prüfend I. *Part. Präs. → prüfen*; **II.** *Adj. Professor etc.*: examining; **~er Blick** searching look; **III.** *Adv.*: *j-n ~ ansehen* look searchingly at s.o., scrutinize s.o.; *etw. ~ anfassen* (take hold of and) feel s.th. all over

Prüfer *m*; *-s*, -, **~in** *f*; -, *-nen* **1.** *Päd.*, *Univ.* examiner; **2.** *Tech. etc.* tester; *zur Abnahme*: inspector; *Metall.* assayer; *Wirts.* auditor

Prüfgerät *n* testing apparatus

Prüfling *m*; *-s*, *-e* **1.** *Päd.* candidate; **2.** *Tech.* (test) specimen

Prüf|muster *n* specimen; **~stand** *m Tech.* test bench; *Mot. auch* test block; *auf dem ~ stehen fig.* be under close scrutiny, be on trial; **~stein** *m fig.* touchstone (*für* of); **~stück** *n* specimen; *kostenloses ~* (*Buch*) specimen

P

copy

Prüfung f **1.** Päd.: examination, exam; einzelne: auch test (auch fig.); für e-e ~ lernen study for an exam; durch e-e ~ fallen fail an exam; → ablegen II 3, abnehmen I 7, bestehen I 1, II 6; **2.** (Untersuchung) examination, investigation; sehr sorgfältige: scrutiny; (Nach-, Überprüfung) verification, check(ing); **3.** Tech. inspection; **4.** Wirts. audit; Jur. review; **5.** (Erprobung) trial, test; **6.** (psychische Belastung) trial, ordeal; Sport, schweres Spiel etc.: test, ordeal; sein Tod war e-e harte ~ für sie his death was a heavy cross for her to bear

...prüfung f, im Subst. **1.** Päd. etc.: Fachschulreife~ specialist college (Am. professional school) leaving examination; Führerschein~ driving test; **2.** Tech. etc.: Lebensmittel~ food inspection

Prüfungs\angst f exam nerves (od. jitters umg.) Pl.; ~arbeit f, ~aufgabe f exam(ination) question; ~ausschuss m Päd., Univ. board of examiners, examining board; bei Sachen: review board; ~bedingungen Pl. **1.** Päd. requirements for an examination candidate; **2.** Tech. test conditions; ~ergebnis n **1.** Päd. examination results Pl.; **2.** Tech. test result; ~fach n exam(ination) subject; ~fahrt f **1.** für Auto: test drive; **2.** für Fahrer: driving test; ~frage f exam(ination) question; ~kommission f → Prüfungsausschuss; ~note f exam(ination) mark (Am. grade); ~ordnung f exam(ination) regulations Pl.; ~teilnehmer m, ~teilnehmerin f exam(ination) participant, examinee; ~termin m **1.** exam(ination) date; **2.** Jur. meeting of creditors; ~verfahren n **1.** Päd. examination procedure; **2.** test(ing) method; ~zeugnis n certificate, diploma

Prüfverfahren n test(ing) method

Prügel[1] m; -s, -; (Knüppel) cudgel

Prügel[2] Pl. (auch Tracht ~) (good) hiding Sg.; für etw. ~ bekommen umg. fig. be hauled (od. raked) over the coals for s.th.; **Prügelei** f; -, -en brawl, scrap umg., free-for-all; **Prügelknabe** m scapegoat, fall guy umg.; **prügeln I.** v/t. mit Stock etc.: beat; **II.** v/refl.: sich (mit j-m) ~ (have a) fight (with s.o.); sich ~ um fight over; **Prügelstrafe** f corporal punishment

Prunk m; -(e)s, kein Pl. splendo(u)r, magnificence; e-s Festzugs etc.: pageantry; (Gepränge) pomp; ~bett n bed of state

prunken v/i. be resplendent; ~ mit flaunt s.th.; (prahlen mit) boast about

Prunkgemach n state apartment

prunk\liebend Adj.: der ~e Ludwig XIV. Louis XIV with his love of pomp (and splendo[u]r); ~los Adj. plain, unostentatious

Prunk\saal m (sumptuously decorated) hall of state; ~stück n showpiece

prunk\süchtig Adj. ostentatious; ~voll Adj. splendid, magnificent; (reich geschmückt) ornate

prusten v/i. vor Wut etc.: snort; vor Erschöpfung: pant, gasp for air; vor Lachen ~ burst out laughing, explode with laughter

PS[1] n im Brief: PS; → Postskript

PS[2] n; -, -; Mot. horsepower (Abk. hp); Bremsleistung: bhp; wie viel ~ hat der Wagen? - er hat 90 ~ how powerful is this car? - it has (an output of) 90 bhp

Psalm m; -s, -en; Reli. psalm; ein ~ Da-

vids a Psalm of David

Psalter m; -s, -; Reli. psalter

Pseudo... im Subst., **pseudo...** im Adj. pseudo-..., mock ...

Pseudo|demokrat m, ~demokratin f pseudo-democrat; ℒdemokratisch Adj. pseudo(-)democratic; ~krupp m Med. mild croup; ℒmodern Adj. pseudo(-)modern

Pseudonym n pseudonym; e-s Schriftstellers: auch pen name, nom de plume

Pseudowissenschaft f pseudo-science; **pseudowissenschaftlich** Adj. pseudo-scientific

PS-stark Adj. high-power(ed), powerful

pst Interj. **1.** (Ruhe!) ssh!; **2.** (he!) pst!

Psyche f; -, -n psyche; (Veranlagung) psychological makeup; (Geisteszustand) mental state; (Gemütszustand) state of mind; (Seele) soul; (Selbstgefühl) (human) ego

psychedelisch Adj. psychedelic

Psychiater m; -s, -, ~in f; -, -nen; Psych. psychiatrist; **Psychiatrie** f; -, -n **1.** nur Sg. psychiatry; **2.** (Abteilung) psychiatric ward; **psychiatrisch** Adj. psychiatric

psychisch I. Adj. psychological; stärker: mental; Druck, Reaktion etc.: emotional; ~e Belastung mental strain; **II.** Adv.: ~ bedingt psychological, all in the mind umg.; ~ belastet under mental strain; ~ krank mentally disturbed

Psychoanalyse f; -, kein Pl.; Psych. psychoanalysis; sich e-r ~ unterziehen undergo (od. submit to) psychoanalysis; **Psychoanalytiker** m, **Psychoanalytikerin** f psychoanalyst, analyst umg.; shrink Sl.; **psychoanalytisch I.** Adj. psychoanalytic(al); **II.** Adv.: ~ behandeln psychoanaly|se (Am. -ze)

psychogen Psych. **I.** Adj. psychogenic; **II.** Adv. psychogenically

Psycho|gramm n (personality) profile; ~krimi m psychological thriller; ~linguistik f Ling. psycholinguistics (V. im Sg.)

Psychologe m; -n, -n psychologist

...psychologe m, im Subst.: Diplom~ (university-)qualified psychologist; Gerichts~ court psychologist

Psychologie f; -, kein Pl. psychology; (psychologisches Verständnis) psychological insight

Psychologin f -, -nen (female) psychologist

...psychologin f, im Subst.: → ...psychologe

psychologisch I. Adj. psychological; **II.** Adv. psychologically, from a psychological point of view

psychologisieren v/t. psychologize

Psychomotorik f Psych. psychomotor functions Pl.

Psychopath m; -en, -en, ~in f; -, -nen psychopath; **psychopathisch** Adj. psychopathic

Psychopharmaka Pl. psychotropic (od. mood-altering) drugs

Psychose f; -, -n; Psych. psychosis (auch fig.)

...psychose f, im Subst.: Angst~ anxiety psychosis

Psychosomatik f; -, kein Pl.; Psych. psychosomatics (V. im Sg.); **psychosomatisch I.** Adj. psychosomatic; **II.** Adv. psychosomatically

Psychoterror m psychological blackmail

Psychotherapeut m, ~in f psy-

chotherapist; **psychotherapeutisch** Adj. psychotherapeutic; **Psychotherapie** f psychotherapy

Psychothriller m psychological thriller

Psychotiker m; -s, -, ~in f; -, -nen; Psych. psychotic; **psychotisch I.** Adj. psychotic; **II.** Adv. psychotically

Psychotonikum n; -s, Psychotonika; Pharm. stimulant

PTA f; -, -s; Abk. → pharmazeutisch--technische Assistentin

pubertär Adj. adolescent; ~e Probleme problems of puberty; ein Junge im ~en Alter a boy in puberty, a pubescent male fachspr.; es ist nur e-e ~e Erscheinung it's all part of puberty; **Pubertät** f; -, kein Pl. puberty; in die ~ kommen reach (the age of) puberty; **Pubertätsjahre** Pl. (age of) puberty Sg.; **Pubertätskrise** f puberty crisis; **pubertieren** v/i. be in (od. have reached) puberty

Publicity [pa'blısiti] f; -, kein Pl. publicity; e-s Ereignisses in den Medien auch: exposure; für ~ sorgen provide for publicity; **publicityscheu** [pa'blısiti-] Adj. nur attr. publicity-shunning

publik Adj. public; ~ machen publicize; die Sache ist längst ~ everybody knows about it; das darf auf keinen Fall ~ werden this mustn't get out whatever happens

Publikation f; -, -en **1.** publication; **2.** nur Sg. (das Veröffentlichen) publication

Publikations|rechte Pl. publication rights, rights of publication; ~verbot n ban on publication

Publikum n; -s, kein Pl. **1.** (Öffentlichkeit) the public; **2.** (Zuschauer etc.) audience; Radio: auch listeners Pl.; Sport spectators Pl., crowd; (Leser) readers Pl., readership; er ist beim ~ gut angekommen the audience loved him; die Bücher/Vorträge von X haben/finden ihr ~ X's books/lectures have/find their readership/audience; **3.** (Gäste) clientele; gemischtes ~ a mixed crowd

Publikums|erfolg m great success, hit; ~geschmack m popular taste; ~liebling m favo(u)rite; ~magnet m crowd-puller; ~resonanz f: viel/wenig ~ great/little popular appeal; ~verkehr m **1.** ~ haben be open (to the public); ~ von 9 bis 12 opening hours 9 to 12; **2.** ~ haben Angestellter: deal directly with the public (od. with customers); heute ist aber viel ~ there's a lot of coming and going today

publikumswirksam Adj. popular (with the public)

publizieren v/t. publish; **Publizist** m; -en, -en, **Publizistin** f; -, -nen journalist; **Publizistik** f journalism; **publizistisch** Adj. journalistic

Puck m; -s, -s; Sport, Eishockey: puck

Pudding m; -s, -s od. -e etwa blancmange, Am. pudding; (Mehlspeise) pudding; das sind doch keine Muskeln, das ist nur ~ umg. fig. that's not muscle, that's just flab; auf den ~ hauen umg. fig. run riot

...pudding m, im Subst., Gastr.: Rosinen~ etwa Brit. spotted dick, Am. suet pudding; Vanille~ vanilla pudding

Pudding|form f blancmange (Am. pudding) mo(u)ld; ~pulver n pudding mixture

Pudel m; -s, -. **1.** poodle; wie ein begossener ~ dastehen umg. look (quite) crestfallen; das also ist des ~s Kern fig. so that's what it's all about;

2. *umg.* (*Fehlwurf beim Kegeln*) miss; ~**mütze** *f* woolly hat, *Am.* stocking cap

pudel|nackt *Adj. umg.* stark naked, *Brit.* starkers; ~**nass** *Adj. umg.* soaking wet, drenched, soaked to the skin; ~**wohl** *Adj. umg.*: *sich ~ fühlen* feel great, feel on top of the world

Puder *m*; *-s*, - powder; ~**dose** *f* powder compact

pudern *v/t.* powder (*sich* one's face); *stark gepudert* heavily powdered

Puder|quaste *f* powder puff; ~**zucker** *m Gastr.* icing (*Am.* confectioner's *od.* powdered) sugar

puff *Interj.* bang!; *Dampflok:* chuff!

Puff[1] *n, m*; *-s*, *-s*; *umg.* (*Bordell*) brothel, knocking shop, *Am. auch* whorehouse; *in den ~ gehen* go to the brothel

Puff[2] *m*; *-(e)s*, *Püffe* **1.** *umg.* (*Stoß*) thump; *in die Rippen:* poke, dig (in the ribs); *vertraulicher:* nudge; *er kann schon e-n ~ vertragen fig.* he can take a knock (or two); **2.** (*Knall*) bang, pop

Puff[3] *m*; *-(e)s*, *-e od. -s* **1.** *für Wäsche:* linen basket; **2.** (*Hocker*) pouffe

Puffärmel *m* puffed sleeve

puffen I. *v/t. umg.* (*j-n*) thump; *vertraulich:* poke *s.o.* in the ribs, nudge; *in e-r Menge:* jostle; **II.** *v/i. Eisenb.* puff, chuff

Puffer *m*; *-s*, - **1.** *Eisenb., EDV und fig.:* buffer; **2.** (*Kartoffelpuffer*) potato fritter; ~**funktion** *f EDV* buffer function; ~**lösung** *f Chem.* buffer solution

puffern *v/t. EDV* buffer

Puffer|staat *m Pol.* buffer state; ~**zone** *f Pol.* buffer zone

Puffmais *m* popcorn; *süßer:* sweet popcorn, *Am.* caramel corn

Puffmutter *f umg.* madam

Puffreis *m* puffed rice

puh *Interj.* **1.** phew!; **2.** *bei Gestank:* poo!, pew!

pulen *vt/i. nordd. umg.*: *~ an* (+ *Dat.*) pick at; *~ in* (+ *Dat.*) poke around in; *Rosinen aus dem Kuchen ~* pick raisins out of the cake; *Krabben ~* peel prawns (*Am.* shrimp *Pl.*)

Pulk *m*; *-(e)s*, *-s od. -e* crowd; *auch Sport:* bunch; *von Fahrzeugen:* group, convoy; *beim Rennen:* pack; *Flug.* group

Pulle *f*; *-*, *-n*; *umg.* bottle; *ein Schluck aus der ~* a swig from the bottle; *volle ~ fahren fig.* drive flat out (*Am.* at full throttle); *die Anlage volle ~ aufdrehen* turn the stereo up full blast; *volle ~ schreien* scream at the top of one's voice

pullen *vt/i. Naut.* row

pullern *v/i. Dial. umg.* piddle, tinkle

Pulli *m*; *-s*, *-s*; *umg.* sweater, pullover, *Brit. auch* jumper

Pullman|limousine ['pʊlmanlimuziːnə] *f* limousine (with partition); (*lange*) stretch limo(usine); ~**wagen** *m Eisenb.* Pullman car

Pullover *m*; *-s*, - pullover, sweater, *Brit. auch* jumper

...pullover *m, im Subst.*: *Ringel~* (horizontally) striped pullover

Pullunder *m*; *-s*, - tank top, slipover

Puls *m*; *-es*, *kein Pl.*; *Med.* pulse; *hoher/niedriger ~* high/low pulse rate; *j-m den ~ fühlen* feel s.o.'s pulse; *fig.* sound s.o. out; *fig. am ~ der Zeit* on the ball, up to date; ~**ader** *f* artery; *sich* (*Dat.*) *die ~n öffnen od. aufschneiden* slash one's wrists; ~**frequenz** *f* pulse rate

pulsieren *v/i.* pulsate (*auch Blut*); *Schmerz:* throb; *fig.* pulsate; *~ mit fig.* throb (*od.* pulsate, vibrate) with; **pulsierend I.** *Part. Präs.* → *pulsieren*; **II.** *Adj. Großstadtleben etc.:* pulsating, vibrant

Puls|schlag *m* pulse; *einzelner:* pulse beat; (*Pulsfrequenz*) pulse rate; *fig.* vibrancy; ~**wärmer** *m*; *-s*, - wristlet; ~**zahl** *f* pulse rate

Pult *n*; *-(e)s*, *-e* desk; (*Rednerpult*) lectern; *sich ans od. hinters ~ setzen* take the platform; ~**dach** *n* lean-to (*od.* shed) roof

Pulver *n*; *-s*, - powder; (*Schießpulver*) (gun)powder; *umg. fig.* (*Geld*) cash, dough *Sl.*, bread *Sl.*; *zu ~ zerstoßen* pound to powder, pulverize; *er hat das ~ nicht erfunden umg. fig.* he's not very bright, he's not exactly an Einstein; *sein ~ verschossen haben* have shot one's bolt; *es/er ist keinen Schuss ~ wert* it's not worth a bean (*Am.* dime) / he's useless; ~**dampf** *m* gun smoke; ~**fass** *n* powder keg (*auch fig.*); *auf e-m ~ sitzen fig.* be sitting on top of a volcano

pulverförmig *Adj. attr.* powdered ..., *präd.* in powder form; **pulverig** *Adj.* powdery; **pulverisieren** *v/t.* pulverize

Pulverkaffee *m* instant coffee

pulvern *v/t. umg.*: *Millionen in die Luft ~ bei Feuerwerk:* blow away millions

Pulverschnee *m* powder (snow)

pulvrig *Adj.* powdery

Puma *m*; *-s*, *-s*; *Zool.* puma, *Am.* cougar

Pummel *m*; *-s*, -; *umg.*, **Pummelchen** *n umg.* roly-poly; **pummelig** *Adj. umg.* chubby, plump

Pump *m umg.*: *auf ~ kaufen* buy on tick (*Am.* credit); *ein Leben auf ~* living on credit

Pumpe *f*; *-*, *-n* pump; *umg.* (*Herz*) ticker; **pumpen** *vt/i.* **1.** pump (*in* + *Akk.* into); **2.** *umg.* (*leihen*) lend, *bes. Am.* loan; *sich* (*Dat.*) *etw. ~* borrow s.th. (*bei j-m* from *od. umg.* off *s.o.*); **3.** *umg.* do press-ups, *auch Am.* do push-ups

Pumpernickel *m*; *-s*, *kein Pl.*; *Gastr.* pumpernickel

Pumphose *f* baggy trousers *Pl.*

Pumps [pœmps] *m*; *-*, *-*; (*Schuh*) court shoe, *Am.* pump

Pump|spray ['pʊmpʃpreː] *m, n* pump-action spray; *für Parfüm auch:* atomizer; ~**station** *f* pumping station

Punching|ball ['pantʃɪŋbal] *m*, ~**birne** *f Boxen:* punchball

Punk [paŋk] *m*; *-s*, *-s* **1.** *nur Sg.* (*Bewegung, Musik*) punk; (*Musik*) *auch* punk rock; **2.** → *Punker*, **Punker** ['paŋkɐ] *m*; *-s*, -, **Punkerin** *f*; *-*, *-nen* punk; **Punkhaarschnitt** *m* punk hairstyle; **punkig** ['paŋkɪç] *Adj.* punky; **Punkrock** *m* punk rock

Punkt *m*; *-(e)s*, *-e* **1.** (*Fleck*) dot, spot (*auch am Kleid*); *der Grüne ~ Öko.* 'the Green Spot', a sign showing that the packaging so marked is recyclable; **2.** *Ling.* full stop, *Am.* period; *e-n ~ machen od. setzen* put a full stop (*Am.* period); *e-n ~ hinter etw. setzen fig.* bring s.th. to an end, settle s.th. (once and for all); *ohne ~ und Komma reden* talk nineteen to the dozen; *nun mach mal e-n ~! umg.* give it a break; **3.** *in E-Mail- und Internet-Adressen:* dot; **4.** (*Tüpfelchen*) dot; *Math.* point; *~e und Striche* dots and dashes; **5.** (*Stelle*) point, place, spot; **6.** (*Einzelheit*) item, point; (*Gesprächsthema*)

point, subject, topic; *in vielen ~en* in many respects; *dunkler ~ fig.* dark chapter, skeleton in the cupboard (*Am.* closet); *der springende ~* the point; *wunder ~* sore point; *~ für ~* point by point; **7.** (*Position*) point, position; *bis zu e-m gewissen ~* up to a point; **8.** *Sport etc.* point; *nach ~en siegen/verlieren Sport* win/lose on points; **9.** *mit Zeitangabe:* on the dot of, at the stroke of; *~ zehn Uhr* on the dot of (*od.* at the stroke of) ten o'clock, at ten o'clock on the dot; *bei Terminangabe:* ten o'clock sharp; → *neuralgisch, strittig, tot* 4

...punkt *m, im Subst.* **1.** (*Fleck, Stelle*): *Farb~* spot of colo(u)r; *Elfmeter~* penalty spot; **2.** (*Thema*): *Beratungs~* item under consideration; **3.** (*Bewertung*): *Zusatz~* additional point

Pünktchen *n* little spot (*od.* dot); *das ~ auf dem i fig.* the finishing touch, the icing on the cake

punkten *v/i. Sportler:* score, collect (*od.* pick up) points; *Kampfrichter:* award points

Punktevergabe *f* allocation of points

punktgleich *Adj.* level (on points); **Punktgleichheit** *f*: *bei ~ entscheidet die Tordifferenz* if teams are level on points, goal difference decides

punktieren *v/t.* **1.** *auch Mus.* dot; *punktierte Linie* dotted line; **2.** *Med.* puncture; **Punktiernadel** *f Med.* puncture needle; **Punktierung** *f* **1.** dotting; **2.** → *Punktion*; **Punktion** *f*; *-*, *-en*; *Med.* puncture

Punktlandung *f* precision landing

pünktlich I. *Adj.* punctual; *präd. Flug. etc. auch* on time; **II.** *Adv.* punctually, on time; **Pünktlichkeit** *f* punctuality

Punkt|richter *m*, ~**richterin** *f Sport* (points) judge

punktschweißen *vt/i. Tech.* spot-weld; **Punktschweißung** *f* spot-welding

Punkt|sieg *m Sport:* win on points; ~**sieger** *m*, ~**siegerin** *f* winner on points

Punktstrahler *m* (*Lampe*) spot(light)

Punktsystem *n Sport etc.:* points system

punktuell I. *Adj.* selective; **II.** *Adv.* selectively; (*Punkt für Punkt*) point by point; *~ Wirkung zeigen* have its effect in places (*od.* here and there)

punktum *Interj.* full stop; *und damit ~!* and that's that!

Punkt|wertung *f* **1.** points system; **2.** → *~zahl*; ~**zahl** *f* score

Punsch *m* punch

Punzarbeit *f Tech.* chasing; *von Leder:* tooling; **Punze** *f*; *-*, *-n* **1.** *Tech.* (*Werkzeug*) punch; **2.** (*Stempel für Edelmetall*) hallmark; **punzen** *v/t.* **1.** *Tech.* chase; *Leder:* tool; **2.** *auch:* **punzieren** (*Edelmetall stempeln*) hallmark

Pup [puːp] *m*; *-(e)s*, *-e*; *umg.* guff, fart *vulg.*; *e-n ~ lassen* let off, break wind, *Am.* cut a fart; **pupen** *v/i. umg.* fart, let off

Pupille *f*; *-*, *-n*; *Anat.* pupil

Pupillen|erweiterung *f* **1.** dilation of the pupil(s); **2.** (*Symptom*) dilated pupil(s); ~**verengung** *f* **1.** contraction of the pupil(s); **2.** (*Symptom*) contracted pupil(s)

Puppe *f*; *-*, *-n* **1.** doll; (*Marionette, auch fig.*) puppet, marionette; (*Kleiderpuppe*) dummy, mannequin; *bis in die ~n schlafen umg. fig.* sleep till all hours; *bis in die ~n feiern umg.* celebrate into the small (*Am.* wee) hours; *alle ~n tanzen lassen umg.* live it up, have a fling; **2.** (*umg. Mädchen*) bird, *Am.* doll; **e-e süße** ~ *umg. fig.* a sweetie; **3.** *Zool.* pupa, chrysalis; *des Seidenspinners*: cocoon

...puppe *f, im Subst.* **1.** (*Spielzeug*): **Porzellan**~ china doll; **2.** *Theat. etc.*: **Finger**~ finger puppet

Puppen|bett *n* doll's bed; ~**doktor** *m umg.* doll repairer; ~**geschirr** *n* doll's china set; ~**gesicht** *n* doll's face

puppenhaft *Adj.* doll-like

Puppen|haus *n* doll's house, *Am.* dollhouse; ~**kleidung** *f* doll's clothes *Pl.*; ~**küche** *f* doll's kitchen; ~**mutter** *f umg.* doll's child mother; ~**spiel** *n* puppet show; ~**spieler** *m*, ~**spielerin** *f* puppeteer; ~**theater** *n* **1.** puppet theat|re (*Am.* -er); **2.** (*Vorstellung*) puppet show; ~**wagen** *m* doll's pram, *Am.* doll carriage

puppig *Adj. umg.* **1.** (*niedlich*) cute; **2.** *Kinderspr.* (*einfach*) easy-peasy, *Am.* easy as pie

Pups *m*; *-es, -e*; *umg.* → *Pup*; **pupsen** ['puːpsn̩] *v/i. umg.* → *pupen*

pur *Adj.* pure; (*bloß*) *auch* sheer; **es war** ~**er Zufall** it was sheer (*od.* pure) coincidence; **aus** ~**er Neugier/Bosheit** from sheer curiosity / out of sheer malice; (**ein**) **Whisky** ~ (a) neat (*Am.* straight) whisk(e)y

Püree [pyˈreː] *n*; *-s, -s*; *Gastr.* puree, mash

...püree *n, im Subst.*: **Erbs(en)**~ pea puree, *Brit.* mushy peas *Pl.*; **Apfel**~ apple puree, *Am.* applesauce; **Kastanien**~ chestnut puree

pürieren *v/t. Gastr.* mash, puree; **Püriersieb** *n* (puree) strainer; **Pürierstab** *m* masher

purifizieren *v/t.* purify

Purin *n*; *-s, -e*; *Chem.* purine

Purismus *m*; *-, kein Pl.* purism; **Purist** *m*; *-en, -en*, **Puristin** *f*; *-, -nen* purist; **puristisch** *Adj.* purist(ic)

Puritaner *m*; *-s, -*, ~**in** *f*; *-, -nen* **1.** *hist.* Puritan; **2.** *fig.* puritan; **puritanisch I.** *Adj.* **1.** *hist.* Puritan; **2.** *fig.* puritanical; **II.** *Adv.* puritanically; ~ **leben / erzogen werden** live a life of puritanical severity / have a puritanical upbringing; **Puritanismus** *m*; *-, kein Pl.* **1.** *hist.* Puritanism; **2.** *fig.* puritanism

Purpur *m*, **purpurrot** *Adj. etwa* crimson; **Purpurschnecke** *f Zool.* purple shell (*od.* snail)

Purzel *m*; *-s, -*; *umg.* cute (little) fellow; **Purzelbaum** *m* forward roll, somersault; **purzeln** *v/i. umg. auch fig.* fall, tumble; **die Preise** ~ prices are tumbling

puschen, pushen ['puʃn̩] *v/t. Sl.* **1.** (*Drogen*) push; **2.** (*Ware etc. durch Werbung*) push; **den Tourismus** ~ promote tourism

Pusselarbeit *f umg.* fiddly (*od.* finicky) work (*od.* job); **Pusselei** *f*; *-, -en umg.* **1.** fiddling (*od.* tinkering) around; **2.** → *Pusselarbeit*; **pusselig** *Adj. umg. Person*: fussy; *Arbeit*: fiddly, finicky; **pusseln** *v/i. umg. im Haus, Garten*: potter (*Am.* putter) around; *am Radio etc.*: tinker (*od.* fiddle) around (**an** + *Dat.* with)

Puste *f*; *-, kein Pl.*; *umg.* puff, *Am.* breath; **ich hab keine** ~ **mehr** I'm puffed; → **ausgehen** 5; ~**blume** *f umg.* dandelion; ~**kuchen** *Interj. umg.* no way; (*leider nicht*) no such luck

Pustel *f*; *-, -n* pimple; *Med.* pustule

pusten *v/t/i. umg.* (*blasen*) blow; **erst** ~**!** *zum Kind beim Essen*: blow on it first; **es pustet ganz schön** it's blowing pretty hard; **er musste** ~ *Mot.* he was breathaly|sed (*Am.* -zed) (*od.* breath-tested); **ins Pusten kommen** start puffing and panting; **j-m das Gehirn aus dem Schädel** ~ blow s.o.'s brains out

putativ *Adj. Jur.* putative

Pute *f*; *-, -n*; *Zool.* turkey (hen); **dumme** ~ *umg. fig.* silly goose, stupid woman

Puten|braten *m Gastr.* roast turkey; ~**fleisch** *n* turkey (meat); ~**schinken** *m* smoked turkey; ~**schnitzel** *n* turkey escalope; ~**streifen** *Pl.* turkey goujons

Puter *m*; *-s, -* turkey (cock); **puterrot** *Adj.* (as) red as a lobster, scarlet; ~ **anlaufen** go scarlet in the face

put, put *Interj.* (*Lockruf für Hühner*) cluck, cluck; **Putput** *n*; *-s, -(s)*; *Kinderspr.* chick-chick

Putsch *m*; *-es, -e*; *Pol.* putsch, coup; **putschen** *v/i.* stage a coup; **Putschist** *m*; *-en, -en*, **Putschistin** *f*; *-, -nen* insurgent; **Putschversuch** *m* attempted coup, coup attempt

Pütt *m*; *-s, -e od. -s*; *Bergb. Dial.* mine, pit

Putte *f*; *-, -n Kunst*: putto

putten ['putn̩] *v/t/i. Golfspiel*: putt

Putz *m*; *-es, kein Pl.* **1.** *Archit.* plaster; *Etech.* **unter** ~ (*verlegt*) concealed; **auf den** ~ **hauen** *umg. fig.* (*viel Geld ausgeben*) have a fling; (*Krach schlagen*) kick up a row (*Am.* fuss); (*angeben*) show off; **2.** *umg.* (*Streit*): ~ **machen** start a row (*Am.* fight)

Putze *f*; *-, -n*; *umg.* (*Putzfrau*) cleaner, *Brit.* char

putzen I. *vt/i.* clean (*auch Gemüse*);

(*Schuhe*) *auch* polish, *Am.* shine; (*Silber*) clean; (*polieren*) polish; (*schmücken*) decorate; (*die Putzarbeit machen*) clean; do the cleaning; ~ **gehen** work as a cleaner; **sich** (*Dat.*) **die Nase** ~ blow (*od.* wipe) one's nose; **sich** (*Dat.*) **die Zähne** ~ brush one's teeth; **II.** *v/refl. Vogel*: preen itself (*od.* its feathers); *Katze etc.*: wash itself

Putzerei *f*; *-, -en* **1.** *umg.*: **die ewige** ~ the constant fag (*Am.* drudgery) of cleaning; **2.** *österr.* (*chemische Reinigung*) dry cleaners

Putz|fimmel *umg. m* cleaning mania (*od.* bug); ~**frau** *f* cleaner, cleaning lady; ~**hilfe** *f* (part-time) cleaner

putzig *Adj. umg.* comical, funny, droll; (*seltsam*) quaint

Putz|kolonne *f* cleaning crew (*od.* squad); ~**lappen** *m* cleaning rag; (*zum Blankreiben*) polishing rag; ~**mittel** *n* cleaner; (*Poliermittel*) polish

putzmunter *Adj. umg.* (*wach*) wide-awake; (*vergnügt*) perky, *Am.* chipper

Putz|teufel *m umg.* cleanliness freak; (*Manie*) **vom** ~ **besessen** bitten by the cleaning bug; ~**tuch** *n* cleaning rag; (*zum Polieren*) polishing cloth; ~**wolle** *f* cotton waste

puzzeln ['pazl̩n] *v/i.* do a jigsaw puzzle; **Puzzle** ['pazl] *n*; *-s, -s*, **Puzzlespiel** *n* jigsaw (puzzle); *fig.* (*kompliziertes Problem*) puzzle; **ein Puzzle mit 500 Teilen** a 500-piece jigsaw (puzzle)

Pygmäe *m*; *-n, -n* pygmy; **pygmäenhaft** *Adj.* pigmy(-)like; **Pygmäin** *f*; *-, -nen* pygmy woman (*od.* girl); **pygmäisch** *Adj.* pygmy attr.

Pyjama [pyˈdʒaːma] *m*; *-s, -s*: (**ein**) ~ (a pair of) pyjamas (*Am.* pajamas) *Pl.*; ~**hose** *f*: (**e-e**) ~ (a pair of) pyjama trousers (*Am.* pajama pants)

Pykniker *m*; *-s, -*, ~**in** *f*; *-, -nen* stocky type; **pyknisch** *Adj.* stocky

Pyramide *f*; *-, -n* pyramid (*auch Math. und fig.*); **pyramidenförmig** *Adj.* pyramid-shaped, in the shape of a pyramid; pyramidal; **Pyramidenstumpf** *m Math.* truncated pyramid

Pyrenäen *Pl.*: **die** ~ the Pyrenees; ~**halbinsel** *f* Iberian Peninsula

Pyromane *m*; *-n, -n* pyromaniac; **Pyromanie** *f*; *-, kein Pl.* pyromania; **Pyromanin** *f*; *-, -nen* (female) pyromaniac

Pyrotechnik *f* pyrotechnics (*V. im Sg.*)

Pyrrhussieg *m* Pyrrhic victory

pythagoreisch *Adj. Math.* Pythagorean; ~**er Lehrsatz** Pythagoras's theorem

Python *m*; *-, -s*, ~**schlange** *f Zool.* python

Q, q *n*; -, - *od. umg.* -s Q, q; *Q wie „Quelle"* Buchstabieren: "q" for (*od.* as in) "Queenie" (*Am.* "Queen")

qua *Präp. Amtsspr.* (*mittels*) by means of; (*geh.: kraft*) by virtue of; ~ *Erlass* (*vom …*) in accordance with the order (of …)

Quackelei *f*; -, *kein Pl.*; *Dial.* **1.** (*Geschwätz*) jabber(ing); **2.** (*Nörgelei*) grumbling, whining, *Brit.* whing(e)ing; *e-s Kindes:* whining, grizzling; **quackeln** *v/i. Dial.* **1.** (*schwatzen*) jabber (away); **2.** (*nörgeln*) grumble, whinge; *Kind:* whine, grizzle

Quacksalber *m*; -s, -; *pej.* quack, charlatan; **Quacksalberei** *f*; -, -en; *pej.* quackery; **quacksalberisch** *Adj. Methoden etc.: nur attr.* quack …; **quacksalbern** *v/i.* play the quack

Quaddel *f*; -, *-n*; *Med.* irritable patch, weal; (*Ausschlag*) *auch* rash

Quader *m*; -s, - **1.** (~*stein*) ashlar; **2.** *Math.* rectangular parallelepiped; ~*bau m* **1.** *nur Sg.*; *Bauweise:* ashlar construction (*od.* masonry); **2.** *Gebäude:* ashlar building; ~*stein m* ashlar

Quadrant *m*; -en, -en quadrant

Quadrat *n*; -(e)s, -e square; *zwei Meter im ~* two square met|res (*Am.* -ers), two met|res (*Am.* -ers) square; *ins ~ erheben* square; *fünf zum ~* five squared

Quadrat… *im Subst.* square …

quadratisch *Adj.* square; *Math.* quadratic

Quadrat|kilometer *m* square kilomet|re (*Am.* -er); ~*latschen Pl. umg.* **1.** (*Schuhe*) clodhoppers; **2.** (*Füße*) big trotters; ~*meter m* square met|re (*Am.* -er); ~*meterpreis m* price per square met|re (*Am.* -er); ~*schädel m umg.* square head, great block; *er ist ein* (*richtiger*) ~ he's so pigheaded

Quadratur *f*; -, -en; *Math.* quadrature; *etw. ist die ~ des Kreises fig.* s.th. is like trying to square the circle

Quadrat|wurzel *f* square root; *die ~ ziehen aus* work out the square root of; ~*zahl f* square number; ~*zentimeter m* square centimet|re (*Am.* -er)

quadrieren *v/t. Math.* square

Quadroaufnahme *f* quadraphonic (*umg.* quad) recording; **Quadrophonie** *f*; -, *kein Pl.*; *Mus.* quadraphonics (*V. im Sg.*); **quadrophon(isch)** *Adj.* quadraphonic; **Quadrosound** ['kvadrosaund] *m*; *nur Sg.* quadraphonic (*umg.* quad) sound

quak! *Interj. Frosch:* croak!; *Ente:* quack!

quaken *vt/i.* **1.** *Frosch:* croak; *Ente:* quack; **2.** *umg. Person:* yap, caw; *nörgelnd:* whine, *Brit.* whinge; *quak nicht wegen jeder Kleinigkeit!* don't whine (*od.* moan) about every little thing; **3.** *Plattenspieler, Radio:* yap, squawk

quäken *vt/i.* **1.** squawk; *tiefer:* croak; **2.** *Kind:* wail; *laut:* bawl

Quakente *f Kinderspr.* quack-quack

Quäker *m*; -s, -; *Reli.* Quaker; *die ~ Koll.* the Quakers, the Society of Friends; **Quäkerin** *f*; -, -nen (female) Quaker; **Quäkertum** *n*; -s, *kein Pl.* Quakerism

Qual *f*; -, -en torture, agony; *seelische: auch* (mental) anguish; *es ist e-e ~* it's torture, it's agony; *unter ~en* in great (*od.* terrible) pain; (*mit Schwierigkeiten*) with great difficulty; *zur ~ werden* become unbearable; *ihr Leben war e-e ~* life was unbearable for her; *j-m das Leben zur ~ machen* make s.o.'s life a misery; *sein Rheuma bereitet ihm große ~en* he's going through agony with his rheumatism; *die ~ der Ungewissheit* the agony of not knowing; *ein Tier von s-n ~en erlösen* put an animal out of its misery; *wir haben die ~ der Wahl* we're spoilt (*Am.* spoiled) for choice, we're in an agony of indecision

quälen I. *v/t.* torment (*auch fig.*); (*foltern*) *auch fig.* torture; *fig.* (*plagen*) harass, torment; *mit Bitten, Fragen etc.:* pester, plague; *ein Tier ~* maltreat (*allg.* be cruel to) an animal; *Hunger quälte ihn* he was tormented by hunger; *von Schmerzen gequält* racked with (*od.* tormented by) pain; *dieser Husten quält mich schon lange* this cough has been plaguing me for a long time; *Zweifel quälten ihn* he was torn by doubt; *quäl ihn nicht so!* stop tormenting him; *die Kinder quälten sie so lange, bis sie nachgab* the children went on pestering her until she gave in; *das Klavier ~ umg.* abuse the piano; → *gequält*; **II.** *v/refl.: sich ~ mit Gedanken:* torment o.s. with s.th. *od. nur Ger.*; *e-r Krankheit:* suffer greatly from (*od.* with) s.th.; (*sich abmühen*) struggle with s.th.; *sich durch den Schnee/Regen ~* battle one's way through the snow/rain; *sich durch ein Buch ~* plough (*Am.* trudge) (painfully) through a book; *sich ans Ziel ~ Sport* struggle to the finish; *sich umsonst ~* labo(u)r in vain; *sich zu Tode ~* worry o.s. to death

quälend I. *Part. Präs.* → *quälen*; **II.** *Adj. Schmerz:* excruciating; *Gedanke:* agonizing; *Hitze:* unbearable

Quälerei *f*; -, -en **1.** torment(ing), torture; (*Grausamkeit*) cruelty; *mit Bitten etc.:* pestering; **2.** (*umg. Anstrengung*) struggle; *es war e-e einzige ~* it was one long struggle; **quälerisch** *Adj.* agonizing; **Quälgeist** *m umg.* pest

Qualifikation *f*; -, -en **1.** qualification; *ihr fehlt / sie hat die nötige ~ dazu* she doesn't have / she has the necessary qualifications *Pl.* (for this); *Sport die ~ schaffen* manage to qualify; **2.** *Sport* (*Spiel, Runde*) qualifying game/round

Qualifikationsrunde *f Sport* qualifying round

qualifizieren I. *v/t.* **1.** (*die Qualifikation verleihen*) qualify (*zu* for; *als* as); **2.** (*einordnen*) classify; **II.** *v/refl.* **1.** *sich für etw. ~* get the necessary qualifications for s.th.; *sich als od. zum Techniker ~* qualify as an engineer; **2.** *Sport* qualify

qualifiziert I. *P.P.* → *qualifizieren*; **II.** *Adj.* qualified; *Fachmann etc.: auch* trained, competent; *Meinung etc.:* qualified, informed; *Diskussion etc.:* informed; **III.** *Adv.: sich ~ zu etw. äußern* give expert comment on s.th.

Qualifizierung *f* **1.** *auch Sport* qualification; **2.** (*Einordnung*) classification

Qualität *f*; -, -en quality; *Wirts. auch* (*Qualitätsstufe*) grade; *Leder etc. erster ~* first- (*od.* top-)grade leather etc.; *schlechte ~* poor quality (*od.* workmanship); *sie achtet auf / kauft nur ~* quality is important to her / she only buys quality (goods); *~ geht vor Quantität* quality before quantity; *er hat auch s-e ~en* he's got his good points

qualitativ I. *Adj. nur attr.* qualitative; **II.** *Adv.* in quality, with regard to quality; *ein ~ hochwertiges Material* a high-quality (*od.* high-grade) material; *die Kopien sind ~ schlecht* the copies are of poor quality

Qualitätsarbeit *f* high-quality workmanship

qualitätsbewusst I. *Adj.* quality-conscious; **II.** *Adv.: ~ einkaufen* shop for quality; **Qualitätsbewusstsein** *n* appreciation (*od.* awareness) of quality

Qualitäts|bezeichnung *f* quality grading; ~*erzeugnis n* (high-)quality product; ~*kontrolle f* quality control; ~*merkmal n* mark of quality

qualitätsmindernd *Adv.: sich ~ auswirken* have a devaluing effect (*auf + Akk.* on); **Qualitätsminderung** *f* reduction in quality

Qualitäts|norm *f* quality standard; ~*sicherung f* quality assurance; ~*steigerung f* improvement in quality; ~*stufe f* quality grade; ~*unterschied m* difference in quality; ~*ware f* quality goods *Pl.*; ~*wein m* quality wine (*meeting certain requirements and typical for a recognized wine area*); ~ *mit Prädikat etwa* premium quality wine (*made from grapes of a particular degree of ripeness*)

Qualle *f*; -,-*n*; *Zool.* jellyfish

Qualm *m*; -s, *kein Pl.* (thick) smoke; **qualmen I.** *v/i.* give off thick smoke; *es qualmt* there are clouds of smoke; *der Ofen / das Feuer qualmt* the stove/fire is giving off clouds of smoke; **II.** *vt/i. umg. Raucher:* smoke heavily; *e-e Zigarette etc. ~* puff away at a cigarette etc.; *sie qualmt wie ein Schlot* she smokes like a chimney; **Qualmerei** *f*; -, -en; *umg.* heavy smoking; *die ~ sein lassen* give up smoking; **qualmig** *Adj.* smoky; *Raum: auch* smoke-filled

qualvoll I. *Adj. Schmerzen:* excruciat-

Q

ing; *seelisch*: agonizing; *Ende, Tod*: extremely painful; **II.** *Adv.* **~ zugrunde gehen** die in agony (*od.* great pain)

Quant *n; -s, -en; Phys.* quantum

Quäntchen *n; -s, -, Pl. selten* tiny bit (of); **ein ~ Furcht/Ehre** a trace of fear/hono(u)r; **ein ~ Vernunft** a modicum of sense; **da ist kein ~ Wahrheit dran** there isn't a grain of truth in it; **es fehlte das ~ Glück** that little bit of luck was missing

Quanten|... *im Subst. Phys.* quantum; **~elektronik** *f Phys.* quantum electronics *V. im Sg.*; **~mechanik** *f Phys.* quantum mechanics (*V. im Sg.*); **~physik** *f* quantum physics (*V. im Sg.*); **~sprung** *m Phys., fig.* quantum leap; **~theorie** *f Phys.* quantum theory

quantifizierbar *Adj.* quantifiable; **quantifizieren** *v/t.* quantify; **Quantifizierung** *f* quantification

Quantität *f; -, -en* quantity; **~ ist nicht gleich Qualität** quantity is not to be confused with quality; → *Qualität*

quantitativ I. *Adj.* quantitative; **II.** *Adv.* quantitatively, in quantity

Quantum *n; -s, Quanten* quantity; (*Menge*) amount; (*Anteil*) quota; **das tägliche ~ Alkohol** *etc. umg.* one's daily dose of alcohol *etc.*; **ich hab mein ~ schon gehabt** *umg.* I've had my lot (*od.* share) for today

Quappe *f; -, -n; Zool.* **1.** (*Kaulquappe*) tadpole; **2.** (*Aalquappe*) burbot

Quarantäne *f; -, -n* quarantine; **unter ~ stehen** be in quarantine; **unter ~ stellen** place under (*od.* put in) quarantine; **~bestimmungen** *Pl.* quarantine regulations; **~station** *f* quarantine (*od.* isolation) ward

Quark¹ *m; -s, kein Pl.* **1.** quark, curd cheese, *Am. etwa* farmer's cheese; **2.** *umg.* → *Quatsch*

Quark² [kwɔːk] *n; -s, -s; Phys.* quark

Quark|füllung *f* quark filling; **~speise** *f* quark dessert; **~strudel** *m* quark-filled strudel; **~tasche** *f* quark turnover

Quart¹ *n; -s, -e, bei Mengen -;* (*Hohlmaß*) quart; *Druck.* quarto

Quart² *f; -, -en* **1.** *Mus.* fourth; **2.** *Fechten:* quart

Quarta *f; -, Quarten; Päd.* **1.** *altm.* third year (of grammar school); **2.** *österr.* fourth year (of grammar school)

Quartal *n; -s, -e* quarter (year), quarterly period

Quartals|... *im Subst.* quarterly; **~ende** *n* end of a (*od.* the) quarter; **sechs Wochen zum ~ kündigen** give notice six weeks before the end of the quarter; **~säufer** *m,* **~säuferin** *f umg.* periodic boozer

quartal(s)weise *Adj. und Adv.* quarterly

Quartaner *m; -s, -,* **~in** *f; -, -nen Päd.* **1.** *altm.* third-year (grammar school) pupil; **2.** *österr.* fourth-year (grammar school) pupil

Quartär *n; -s, kein Pl.; Geol.* Quaternary

Quartband *m* quarto volume

Quarte *f; -, -n; Mus.* fourth

Quartett *n; -(e)s, -e* **1.** *Mus.* quartet; *fig.* (*vier Personen*) quartet, foursome; **2.** (*Kartenspiel*) happy families (*V. im Sg.*), *Am.* go fish

Quartformat *n Druck.* quarto (format)

Quartier *n; -s, -e* **1.** accommodation, *bes. Am.* accommodations *Pl.*; **j-m ~ geben** put s.o. up; **2.** *Mil.* quarters *Pl.*; **~ beziehen** take up quarters; **bei j-m in ~ liegen** be billeted on s.o.; **3.** *österr., schw.* (*Stadtteil*) quarter, district

...quartier *n, im Subst.:* **Flüchtlings~** accommodation(s) for refugees; **Urlaubs~** holiday accommodation, *Am.* vacation lodgings

Quartier|meister *m Mil., altm.* quartermaster; **~suche** *f: auf ~ sein* be looking for accommodation (*od.* a place to live)

Quarz *m; -es, -e* quartz; *Etech.* (quartz) crystal, quartz

quarzgesteuert *Adj. Uhr:* quartz; *Oszillator, Sender etc.:* (quartz) crystal--controlled

Quarzglas *n* quartz glass

quarzhaltig *Adj.* containing quartz, quartziferous *fachspr.*

Quarzit *m; -s, -e* quartzite

Quarz|kristall *m* quartz crystal; **~sender** *m* (quartz) crystal-controlled transmitter; **~staublunge** *f Med.* silicosis; **~steuerung** *f* (quartz) crystal control; **~uhr** *f* quartz clock; (*Armbanduhr*) quartz watch; **~wecker** *m* quartz alarm clock

Quasar *m; -s, -e; Astron.* quasar

quasi I. *Adv.* more or less, virtually; (*gleichsam*) ... as it were; **II. quasi...** *im Adj., Quasi...* *im Subst.* quasi-...; (*fast*) semi-; **Quasisynonym** *n* quasi(-)synonym

Quasselbude *f umg.* talking shop

Quasselei *f; -, -en; umg.* **1.** yakking, jabbering; **2.** (*Blödsinn*) drivel, rubbish

Quassel|fritze *m; -n, -n; umg.,* **~kopf** *m umg.* windbag

quasseln *umg.* **1.** *v/i.* yak (away), witter on; *immerzu ~* never stop wittering (*od.* blathering) on; **2.** *v/t. dummes Zeug ~* spout a load of nonsense, blather on

Quasselstrippe *f umg.* **1.** (*Person*) windbag; (*mst Frau, Kind*) chatterbox; **2.** (*Telefon*) phone, *Brit.* blower

Quast *m; -(e)s, -e* **1.** *e-s Malers:* (wide) brush; **2.** → *Quaste*

Quaste *f; -, -n;* (*Troddel*) tassel; (*Puderquaste etc.*) powder *etc.* puff

Quastenflosser *m; -s, -; Zool.* crossopterygian

Quatsch *m; -(e)s, kein Pl.; umg.* **1.** (*unsinnige Äußerung*) rubbish, crap *Sl.*, rot *Brit. altm.*, *bes. Am.* garbage, trash; **so ein ~** what a lot (load *bes. Brit.*) of rubbish, *Am.* what a crock; **das ist doch ~** (*mit Soße*) that's utter nonsense; **red keinen ~!** don't talk rubbish *etc.*, stop talking rubbish *etc.*; (*das ist doch nicht wahr*) you're kidding; **2.** (*Handlungen*) **~ machen** (*Unsinn*) fool (*od.* mess) around; (*e-e Dummheit*) do something stupid; (*nur zum Spaß tun*) do something for a lark; **mach keinen ~!** (*Warnung vor Dummheit, Fehler etc.*) don't do anything stupid; **lass den ~!** stop it!, cut it out! *Sl.*

quatschen *umg.* **I.** *vt/i.* **1.** (*dumm reden*) blather, talk nonsense; (*plaudern*) natter; *pej.* blather; (*tratschen*) gossip; (*im Unterricht etc. schwatzen*) chatter; **2.** (*etw. verraten*) squeal, talk; **3.** (*äußern*) spout; **quatsch keinen Blödsinn!** don't talk rubbish (*od.* nonsense)!; **II.** *v/i. Boden, Schuhe:* squelch

quatschnass *Adj. umg.* sopping wet

Quatsch|kopf *m umg.* windbag; **~tüte** *f umg.* joker

Quecke *f; -, -n; Bot.* couch grass

Quecksilber *n Chem.* mercury, quicksilver *altm., noch fig.*; **~barometer** *n* mercury barometer; **~dampf** *m* mercury vapo(u)r

quecksilberfrei *Adj.* containing no mercury; **~ sein** contain no mercury

Quecksilbergehalt *m* mercury level; **quecksilberhaltig** *Adj.:* **~ sein** contain mercury

quecksilbern *Adj.* **1.** *Farbe etc.:* mercury; **2.** → *quecksilbrig*

Quecksilber|säule *f* mercury (column); **die ~ ist auf 30 Grad geklettert** the mercury has risen to 30 degrees; **~vergiftung** *f* mercury poisoning

quecksilbrig *Adj. Person:* live-wire, fidgety

Queen [kwiːn] *f; -, -s* **1.** **die ~** *in GB:* the Queen; **2.** *umg. fig.* diva; **3.** *Sl.* (*femininer Homosexueller*) dyke *neg!*

Quell *m; -s, kein Pl.; lit.* **~be** → *Quelle;* **~bewölkung** *f* cumulus clouds *Pl.*; **~code** *m EDV* source code

Quelle *f; -, -n* **1.** spring; *heiße/mineralhaltige ~* hot/mineral spring; **2.** *e-s Flusses:* source; **3.** (*Ursprung*) source; **aus sicherer ~** on good authority; **aus erster ~** firsthand; **du sitzt doch an der ~** you're right on the spot; **für Informationen:** *auch* you're right at the source; **e-e gute ~** (*Einkaufsmöglichkeit*) **für etw. haben** have a good source for s.th., know a good place to get s.th.; **die ~ des Lebens/Wissens** *lit.* the fountain of life / the fountain[head] of knowledge; **4.** *Lit.* (*Schriftquelle*) source; **mit ~n arbeiten** *im Unterricht:* use documentary material

quellen; *quillt, quoll, ist gequollen* **I.** *v/i.* **1.** (*hervordringen*) *auch fig.* pour; *Blut:* auch gush (**aus** out of *od.* from); **aus dem Boden ~** well up from under the ground; **über den Rand ~** well (*Dickflüssiges:* rise) over the edge; **die Augen quollen ihr** (*fast*) **aus dem Kopf** her eyes were (almost) popping out of her head; **2.** (*anschwellen*) swell; **~ lassen** (*Erbsen, Reis etc.*) leave to soak; **das Holz ist gequollen** the wood has swollen; **II.** *v/t.* **1.** (*einweichen*) soak; **2.** *Dial.* (*kochen*) (*Kartoffeln*) boil

Quellen|angabe *f Lit.* reference; **~angaben** *Pl. Koll.* list *Sg.* of sources, bibliography *Sg.*; **~forschung** *f* basic research; **~kritik** *f* verification of sources

Quellen|material *n Lit.* source material; **~nachweis** *m* **1.** reference; **2.** list of sources, bibliography

Quellensteuer *f Fin.* withholding tax

Quellen|studium *n Lit.* study of sources, basic research; **~verzeichnis** *n* list of sources, bibliography

Quellfluss *m Geog.* headstream

quellfrisch *Adj.* fresh from the spring; **Quellfrische** *f* freshness of spring water

Quellgebiet *n Geog., e-s Flusses:* headwaters *Pl.*

Quellprogramm *n EDV* source program

Quell|wasser *n* spring water; **~wolke** *f* cumulus (cloud)

Quengelei *f; -, -en; umg., Kind:* (*Weinen*) whining, *Brit.* grizzling; (*Drängen*) nagging; *von Erwachsenen:* whingeing, *Am.* harping; **quengelig** *Adj. umg. Kind:* whining; *Erwachsener:* whing(e)ing, *Am.* kvetching; **die Kinder werden ~** the children are getting fretful; **quengeln** *v/i. umg. Kind:* whine, *Brit.* grizzle; (*drängen*) nag; *Erwachsener:* whine, *Am.* harp, kvetch; **hör auf zu ~!** stop whining (*od.* nagging *od.* kvetching *od.* whingeing); **Quengler** *m; -s, -,* **Quenglerin** *f; -,*

-nen; *umg.* (*Kind*) whiner; (*Erwachsener*) whinger, *Am.* kvetcher

Quentchen → *Quäntchen*

quer *Adv.* crossways, crosswise; (*diagonal*) diagonally; (*rechtwinklig*) at right angles; **~ gestreift** horizontally striped; **~ über die Straße gehen** go straight across the road; (*schräg*) cross the road at an angle; **~ zu etw. stehen** be at right angles to s.th.; **~ gegenüber** diagonally opposite; **~ durch die Stadt laufen** *Straße*: run straight through the town; *Fußgänger*: walk all over town; **er lag ~ auf dem Bett** he was lying across the bed; **~ liegend** *Motor*: transverse, mounted crosswise; **~ übereinander legen** put cross|ways (*od.* –wise); **~ durch die Parteien** right across the parties, across party boundaries; **j-m ~ kommen** *umg.* (*behindern etc.*) get in s.o.'s way; **sich ~ legen** *umg.* (*Widerstand leisten*) be awkward, make difficulties; **~ schießen** *umg.* (*stören, behindern*) put a spanner in the works, *Am.* throw a (monkey) wrench into the works; → *kreuz*

Quer|achse *f* transverse (axis); **~balken** *m* crossbeam; *Tür*: lintel

querbeet *Adv. umg.* **1.** all over the place; (*querfeldein*) across country; **~ über die Felder laufen** run across the fields in any old direction; **2.** *fig.* at random, indiscriminately; **~ auswählen** pick *things* out at random; **~ alle Probleme erörtern** go through the whole gamut of problems

Querdenker *m*, **~in** *f* unconventional thinker

querdurch *Adv.* straight through

Quere *f*; -, *kein Pl.* **1.** width; **etw. der ~ nach messen** measure s.th.'s width; **2.** *fig.*: **j-m in die ~ kommen** (*hinderlich sein*) get in s.o.'s (*od.* the) way; (*zufällig begegnen*) run into s.o.

Quereinsteiger *m*, **~in** *f* newcomer from a different profession (*in + Dat.* to); **sie ist e-e ~in** she comes from a totally different profession, her new job is totally different from the work she did before; **bei uns gibt es viele ~** many of our employees (*Kollegen*: colleagues) have got a rather different professional (*od.* educational) background

Querelen *Pl.* quarrel(l)ing *Sg.*; (*kleinere Streitereien*) squabbling *Sg.*; **mit ~ enden** end in a quarrel

queren *v/t.* cross

Querfalte *f* cross pleat

querfeldein *Adv.* across country

Querfeldein|lauf *m* (*Sportart*) cross-country running; (*Wettbewerb*) cross-country race; **~rennen** *n Sport*, *mit Fahrrädern*: cyclo-cross

Quer|flöte *f Mus.* (transverse) flute; **~format** *n* horizontal format; **ein Foto im ~** a landscape photo

quer| gehen, **~ gestreift** *etc.* → *quer*

Querhaus *n Kirche*: transept

Querkopf *m umg.* awkward customer; **querköpfig** *Adj. umg.* awkward, perverse

Quer|lage *f Med.* transverse presentation; **~latte** *f Fußball*: crossbar; **~leiste** *f Tech.* cross-rib; **~linie** *f* diagonal line; **~pass** *m Fußball etc.*: cross-field (*od.* square) pass; **~pfeife** *f* fife; **~richtung** *f* transverse direction; **~ruder** *n Flug.* aileron; **~schiff** *n Kirche*: transept; **~schläger** *m* **1.** (*Geschoss*) ricochet; **2.** *umg.* obstructive type

Querschnitt *m* cross-section (*auch fig.* **durch** of); (*Zeichnung*) *auch* sectional

view; *fig. Oper etc.*: highlights *Pl.* (**durch** of); **ein ~ durch die Barockliteratur / europäische Geschichte** a selection (*od.* anthology) of baroque literature / highlights of European history

querschnittsgelähmt *Adj. Med.* paraplegic; paraly|sed (*Am.* -zed) from the waist (*od.* neck) down; **Querschnittslähmung** *f Med.* paraplegia

Quer|seite *f* short side; **~straße** *f* intersecting road, *Am.* cross road; *in der Stadt*: intersecting street; (*Abzweigung*) turning; **~streifen** *m* horizontal stripe; **~summe** *f* sum of the digits; **~tal** *n* transverse valley

Quertreiber *m umg. pej.* obstructive type; **Quertreiberei** *f*; -, -en obstructive (*stärker*: wrecking) tactics (*V. im Sg.*), sabotage attempts *Pl.*

Querulant *m*; -en, -en malcontent, grumbler, grouch *umg.*; **Querulantentum** *n*; -s, *kein Pl.* querulousness; **Querulantin** *f*; -, -nen → *Querulant*

Quer|verbindung *f konkret*: cross connection; *zwischen Orten*: direct connection; (*Straße*) link road; *zwischen Fachgebieten etc.*: link, connection; **~verweis** *m* cross-reference; **~wand** *f* partition

Quetsche[1] *f*, -, -n; *Dial.* (*Zwetsch[g]e*) damson plum

Quetsche[2] *f*, -, -n; *Dial.* (*Kartoffelpresse*) potato-crusher

Quetsche[3] *f*, -, -n; *Mus., umg.* (*Akkordeon*) squeeze-box

quetschen I. *v/t.* squeeze; (*zer~*) crush, squash; *Med.* bruise; **sich** (*Dat.*) **den Finger ~** pinch one's finger; **sich die Hand in der Tür ~** get one's hand caught in the door; **zu Tode gequetscht werden** be crushed to death; **Saft aus e-r Zitrone ~** squeeze a lemon; **II.** *v/refl. Med.* bruise o.s.; **sich in e-n Wagen etc. ~** squeeze (*od.* cram) into a car *etc.*; **sich durch die Menge ~** squeeze one's way through the crowd

Quetsch|falte *f* box pleat; **~kommode** *f umg.* (*Ziehharmonika*) squeeze-box

Quetschung *f*, **Quetschwunde** *f Med.* bruise; *fachspr.* contusion

Queue [kø:] *n*, *m*; -s, -s (billiard) cue

Quiche [kɪʃ] *f*; -, -s; *Gastr.* quiche; **~ Lorraine** quiche Lorraine

quick *Adj. nordd.* lively

quicklebendig *Adj. Kind*: (very) lively; *ältere Person*: sprightly

Quick|test *m Med.* quick test; **~wert** *m Med.* quick value

quiek(s)en *v/i.* squeak; *Ferkel*: squeal; **Quiekser** *m*; -s, -; *umg.* squeak; *von Ferkel*: squeal

quietschen *v/i.* squeak; *auch Person*: squeal; *Bremse*: squeal, screech; **sie quietschte vor Vergnügen** she squealed with delight; **mit ~den Reifen losfahren/bremsen** make a start / brake with squealing tyres (*Am.* tires); **Quietscher** *m*; -s, -; *umg.* squeak; *auch e-r Person*: squeal

quietsch|fidel *Adj. umg.* → *quietschvergnügt*; **~lebendig** *Adj. umg.* hyperactive; *bes. Kind*: full of beans *nur präd.*; (*sehr wach*) wide awake; **~vergnügt** *Adj. umg.* (very) chirpy, *Am.* chipper

quillt *Präs.* → *quellen*

Quint *f*; -, -en **1.** *Mus.* fifth; **2.** *Fechten*: quinte

Quinta *f*; -, *Quinten*; *Päd.* **1.** *altm.* second year (of grammar school); **2.** *österr.* fifth year (of grammar school); **Quintaner** *m*; -s, -, **Quintanerin** *f*; -,

-nen; *Päd.* **1.** *altm.* second-year (grammar school) pupil (*Am.* student); **2.** *österr.* fifth-year (grammar school) pupil (*Am.* student)

Quinte *f*; -, -n; *Mus.* fifth

Quintessenz *f* essence; (*wesentlicher Punkt*) essential point; **die ~ war ...** what it boiled (*od.* came) down to was ...

Quintett *n*; -s, -e quintet

Quirl *m*; -(e)s, -e **1.** blender (*with a star-shaped head*); **2.** *umg. fig.* (*Person*) live wire; **quirlen I.** *v/t.* (*Eier mit Zucker etc.*) blend with the quirl; **II.** *v/i. Wasser etc.*: swirl; **quirlig** *Adj. umg. Kind*: very lively; *Erwachsener*: bubbly; *Spieler, Temperament*: mercurial; **ein ~er Mittelstürmer** a very nimble cent|re (*Am.* -er) forward; **~es Treiben** hustle and bustle

quitt *Adj.*: *nur präd.*: **~ sein/werden mit j-m** be/get quits (*od.* even) with s.o. (*auch fig.*); **ich bin doch mit dir ~, oder?** I've squared up with you, haven't I?, we're quits (*od.* even) now, aren't we?

Quitte *f*; -, -n; *Bot.* quince; **quittegelb** *Adj. fig. Gesichtsfarbe*: sickly yellow; **~ aussehen** *umg. etwa* look (a bit) green about the gills

Quitten|baum *m Bot.* quince (tree); **~brot** *n* quince paste (*cut into slices or cubes*)

quittengelb *Adj.* quince-yellow

Quitten|käse *m österr.* → *Quittenbrot*; **~marmelade** *f* quince jam

quittieren *vt/i.* **1.** give (*od.* sign) a receipt for; **den Empfang der Ware ~** (*unterschreiben*) sign that one has received the goods, *Am.* sign for merchandise; *brieflich*: acknowledge receipt of the goods; **etw. mit e-m Lächeln etc.** answer (*od.* meet) s.th. with a smile *etc.*; **es wurde mit Beifall quittiert** it was greeted with applause; **2. den Dienst ~** *altm.* resign; *fig. Maschine etc.*: give up the ghost

Quittung *f* **1.** receipt; **e-e ~ ausstellen über** (+ *Akk.*) make a receipt out for; **gegen ~** on receipt; **2.** *fig.*: **das ist die ~ für d-n Leichtsinn** that's what you get for (*od.* that's what comes of) being so careless

Quittungs|block *m* receipt pad; **~formular** *n* receipt form (*od.* blank)

Quiz [kvɪs] *n*; -, -e, *mst Sg.* quiz; **~master** [-maːstɐ] *m*; -s, - question master, *Brit. auch* quizmaster; *TV* quiz-show host; *bei Sendung mit Spielen*: game-show host; **~sendung** *f* quiz show; *mit Spielen*: gameshow

quoll *Imperf.* → *quellen*

Quorum *n*; -s, *kein Pl.* quorum

Quote *f*; -, -n **1.** (*Verhältnismenge*) proportion, ratio; (*Rate*) rate; (*Anteil*) share; (*Gewinnquote*) dividend; **2.** *TV* (*Einschaltquote*) rating; **nach der ~ schielen** *umg.* have an eye on the ratings; **die Jagd auf die ~n** the battle of the ratings

Quoten|aktie *f Fin.* no-par-value stock; **~frau** *f umg.* token woman; **~jagd** *f m* *TV* battle of the ratings; **~könig** *m*, **~königin** *f TV* TV star with top ratings; **~regelung** *f* quota system

Quotient *m*; -en, -en; *Math.* quotient

quotieren *v/t.* **1.** *Börse*: quote; **2.** (*limitieren*) (*Importe, Einwanderungszahlen etc.*) fix quotas for; **Quotierung** *f* **1.** *Börse*: quotation; **2.** (*Limitierung*) fixing of quotas (**von** + *Gen.* for)

Q

R, r *n*; -, - *od. umg.* -s R, r; R wie „*Richard*" *Buchstabieren*: "r" for (*od.* as in) "Romeo"

Rabatt *m*; -(*e*)*s*, -*e*; *Wirts.* discount (*auf* + *Akk.* on); (*j-m*) ~ **gewähren** *od.* **einräumen** give (s.o.) a discount

...rabatt *m*, *im Subst.*: **Wiederverkäufer~** trade discount

Rabatte *f*; -, -*n*; (*Beet*) border

Rabattmarke *f altm. etwa* trading stamp

Rabatz *m*; -*es*, *kein Pl.*; *umg.* (*Krach*) row, ruckus, racket

Rabauke *m*; -*n*, -*n*; *umg.* hooligan

Rabbi *m*; -(*s*), -*s* rabbi; **Rabbinat** *n*; -(*e*)*s*, -*e* rabbinate; **Rabbiner** *m*; -*s*, - rabbi; **rabbinisch** *Adj.* rabbinical

Rabe *m*; -*n*, -*n*; *Orn.* raven; *ein weißer* ~ *fig.* a great rarity; *die klauen wie die ~n* they pinch anything they can get their hands on

Raben|aas *n pej.* cunning bastard; **~eltern** *Pl. fig. pej.* uncaring (*od.* cruel) parents; **~mutter** *f fig. pej.* uncaring (*od.* cruel) mother

rabenschwarz *Adj. Haare*: jet-black, raven; *Nacht*: pitch-black; *du bist ja ~!* (*schmutzig*) you're black as coal!; *~er Tag fig.* black day, bad-hair day *umg.*

Raben|vater *m pej.* uncaring (*od.* cruel) father; **~vogel** *m Orn.* member of the crow family

rabiat *Adj.* (*grob*) rough, brutal; (*rücksichtslos*) ruthless; (*rigoros*) drastic (*auch Maßnahmen*); *Ansichten*: radical; ~ *werden* go wild; (*gewalttätig*) get violent

Rabulist *m*; -*en*, -*en*; *pej.* sophist

Rache *f*; -, *kein Pl.* revenge; *lit.* vengeance; (*Heimzahlung*) *auch* retribution, retaliation; *Tag der ~* day of reckoning; ~ *nehmen* take revenge (*an* + *Dat.* on), avenge *s.th.*; *aus ~* in (*od.* out of) revenge; *auf ~ sinnen* plot (one's) revenge; *s-e ~ stillen od. befriedigen* satisfy one's desire (*lit.* thirst) for revenge; ~ *ist Blutwurst! umg.*, *hum.* just you wait!

Rachedurst *m geh.* thirst for revenge; **rachedurstig** *Adj. geh.* thirsting for revenge *nur präd.*, vengeful

Rache|engel *m* avenging angel; **~feldzug** *m* retaliation campaign; **~gefühl** *n* desire for revenge; (*Befriedigung*) vindictive feeling; **~gelüste** *Pl. geh.* craving *Sg.* for revenge

Rachen *m*; -*s*, - throat; *fachspr.* pharynx; *Tier*: mouth, jaws *Pl.*; *fig.* (*Abgrund*) abyss; *den Kopf in den ~ des Löwen stecken* put one's head in the lion's jaws; *j-m Geld in den ~ werfen* throw (ever more) money at s.o.; *j-m den ~ stopfen* give s.o. s.th. to keep him (*od.* her) quiet

rächen I. *v/t.* avenge; (*etw.*) *auch* take revenge for; *den Mord an s-r Tochter ~* avenge one's daughter's murder; **II.** *v/refl.* get one's revenge, get one's own back *umg.* (*an j-m* on s.o.); *es*

wird sich bitter ~, dass wir das tun we'll have to pay dearly for doing this; *s-e Essgewohnheiten rächten sich* his eating habits took their toll

Rachen|abstrich *m Med.* throat swab; **~blütler** *m*; -*s*, -; *Bot.* figwort, scrophularia; **~entzündung** *f Med.* pharyngitis; **~höhle** *f Physiol.* pharyngeal cavity; **~laut** *m* pharyngeal; **~mandel** *f Physiol.* the adenoids *Pl.*; *fachspr.* pharyngeal tonsil; **~putzer** *m umg.* rotgut

Rachepläne *Pl.*: ~ *schmieden* plot (one's) revenge

Rächer *m*; -*s*, -, **~in** *f*; -, -*nen* avenger

Racheschwur *m* oath of revenge; *e-n ~ tun* swear vengeance

Rachgier *f geh.* thirst for revenge; **rachgierig** *Adj. geh.* vengeful, out for revenge *nur präd.*

Rachitis *f Med.* rickets (*V. im Sg.*); **rachitisch** *Adj. Med.* rachitic *fachspr.*; *Kind auch*: with rickets

Rachsucht *f* thirst for revenge; **rachsüchtig** *Adj.* vengeful, out for revenge *nur präd.*

Racingreifen ['reːsɪŋ-] *m Mot.* racing tyre (*Am.* tire)

Racker *m*; -*s*, -; *umg.* (*Kind*) little rascal

rackern *v/i. umg.* slave (*od.* slog) away

Raclette ['raklɛt] *n*; -*s*, -*s und f*; -, -*s*; *Gastr.* raclette

Rad *n*; -(*e*)*s*, *Räder* **1.** wheel (*auch fig.*); *Essen auf Rädern* meals on wheels; *unter die Räder kommen* be run over; *fig.* go to the dogs; *das fünfte ~ am Wagen sein fig.* be the odd man out; *bei Paaren*: play gooseberry, *Am.* be the third wheel; *das ~ der Zeit / der Geschichte anhalten wollen fig. lit.* try to stop the march of time / the course of history; *aufs ~ geflochten werden hist.* be broken on the wheel; (*ein*) ~ *schlagen Pfau*: spread its tail; *Turnen*: turn (*od.* do) a cartwheel; **2.** (*Fahrrad*) bicycle, bike *umg.*; ~ *fahren* cycle, ride a bicycle (*od.* bike), bike *umg.*; *aufs/vom ~ steigen* get on (to) one's bicycle / get off (*od.* dismount) from one's bicycle; **3.** ~ *fahren umg.*, *fig. gegenüber Vorgesetzten*: suck up to the boss (while bullying those under you)

...rad *n*, *im Subst.* **1.** (*Fahrrad*) **Alu~** aluminium (*Am.* aluminum) bicycle; **Herren~** gent's (*Am.* men's) bicycle; **2.** *Tech.* **Ketten~** sprocket (wheel); **Scheiben~** disc (*Am.* disk) wheel

Rad|achse *f Tech.* axle; **~antrieb** *m* wheel drive

Radar *m, n*; -*s*, *kein Pl.* radar; *mit ~ ausgerüstet* equipped with radar, radar-equipped; **~anlage** *f* radar installation; **~antenne** *f* radar antenna (*Brit. auch* aerial); **~bild** *n* radar picture (*od.* image); **~bildschirm** *m* radar screen; **~falle** *f* (radar) speed trap; *in e-e ~ geraten* be caught in a speed

trap

radargelenkt *Adj.* radar-guided

Radar|gerät *n* radar unit; **~kontrolle** *f* radar speed check; **~netz** *n* radar network; **~peilung** *f* radar position finding; **~pistole** *f* radar gun; **~schirm** *m* radar screen

radarsicher *Adj.* radarproof

Radar|strahl *m* radar beam; **~überwachung** *f* radar monitoring; **~verfolgung** *f* radar tracking; **~wagen** *m* radar-equipped (police) car

Radau *m*; -*s*, *kein Pl.*; *umg.* row, ruckus, racket; ~ *machen* (*Lärm machen*) make a racket; (*Krach schlagen*) kick up a fuss (*od.* row); **~bruder** *m umg.* hooligan, rowdy

Radaufhängung *f Mot.* suspension

Radaumacher *m umg.* hooligan, rowdy

Radbruch *m* broken wheel

Rädchen *n* small (*od.* little) wheel; *ein ~ im Getriebe sein fig.* be a cog in the wheel (*od.* machine)

Raddampfer *m Naut.* paddle steamer

radebrechen I. *v/t*: *Englisch etc.* ~ speak broken English *etc.*; **II.** *v/i.* speak pidgin

radeln *umg.* **I.** *v/i.* cycle, bike; *morgens zur Schule ~* go to school by bike (*od.* bike it to school) in the mornings; **II. Radeln** *n*; -*s*, *kein Pl.* cycling

Rädelsführer *m*, **~in** *f* ringleader

Räder|fahrzeug *n* wheeled vehicle; **~getriebe** *n* gear transmission, gearing

rädern *hist. v/t.* break on the wheel; → *gerädert*; **Rädern** *n*; -*s*, *kein Pl.* breaking on the wheel

Räderwerk *n* mechanism, works *Pl.*; *Uhr*: *auch* clockwork; (*Getriebe*) gearing; *fig.* machinery; *ins ~ der Justiz geraten* get caught in the meshes of the law

radfahren → *Rad 2*

Rad|fahren *n*; -*s*, *kein Pl.* cycling; *er bringt ihr das ~ bei* he's teaching her to ride a bicycle; **~fahrer** *m*, **~fahrerin** *f* cyclist; *pej. fig.* toady, brown-nose, bootlicker; **~fahrweg** *m* → *Radweg*; **~felge** *f* wheel rim; **~gabel** *f* bicycle forks *Pl.*

Radi *m*; -*s*, -; *bayrisch*, *österr.* (white) radish, *Am.* daikon

radial I. *Adj.* radial; **II.** *Adv.*: ~ *angelegt* radially arranged, arranged in the shape of a star

Radialbohrmaschine *f* radial drill

Radiant *m*; -*en*, -*en* **1.** *Math.* radian; **2.** *Astron.* radiant

Radicchio [ra'dɪkjo] *m*; -(*s*), *kein Pl.*; *Gastr.* radicchio

radieren *vt/i.* **1.** rub out, erase; **2.** *Kunst*: etch

Radierer¹ *m*; -*s*, -; (*Radiergummi*) rubber, *bes. Am.* eraser

Radierer² *m*; -*s*, -; (*Künstler*) etcher

Radiererin *f*; -, -*nen*; (*Künstlerin*) etcher

Radier|gummi *m* rubber, *bes. Am.* eraser; **~kunst** *f* etching; **~messer** *n* erasing knife

Radierung *f* (*Bild*) etching

Radieschen *n* radish; *sich die ~ von unten ansehen umg.* be pushing up (the) daisies

radikal I. *Adj.* radical (*auch Pol.*); *Änderung, Maßnahmen etc.: auch* drastic; *der linke/rechte Flügel der Partei* the extreme left/right wing of the party; *e-e ~e Gesinnung haben* have a radical cast of mind; *ein ~er Verfechter der Todesstrafe* a fanatical advocate of the death penalty; *~e Mittel einsetzen* use drastic means; **II.** *Adv.* radically; *äußerst ~ denken* have extremely radical views; *~ reduzieren* reduce drastically; *~ mit der Vergangenheit brechen* make a clean (*od.* radical) break with the past

Radikal *n; -s, -e; Chem.* radical; *Math.* root; *Freie ~e Chem.* free radicals

Radikale *m, f; -n, -n; Pol.* radical, extremist; **Radikalenerlass** *m Pol.* ban on the employment of teachers and civil servants with radical political views

Radikalinski *m; -s, -s; pej.* (political) firebrand (*od.* extremist); (*Linker*) *auch umg.* lefty, pinko

radikalisieren I. *v/t.* make more radical, radicalize; **II.** *v/refl.* become increasingly radical (*od.* extreme); **Radikalisierung** *f* increasing radicalism; (*Radikalmachen*) radicalization

Radikalismus *m; -, Radikalismen* radicalism; **Radikalität** *f; -, kein Pl.* radical nature; *Maßnahmen:* drastic nature

Radikalkur *f Med.* drastic cure; *fig.* drastic measures *Pl.*

Radio *n, südd., schw., österr. auch m; -s, -s radio* (*Rundfunk*) radio, broadcasting; *~ hören* listen to the radio; *im ~* on the radio; *im ~ bringen od. übertragen* broadcast (on the radio); *~ Bremen* Radio Bremen; *siehe auch Rundfunk(...)*

radioaktiv I. *Adj.* radioactive; *schwach ~e Stoffe* low-level radioactive materials; *~er Niederschlag* (radioactive) fallout; *~e Strahlung* (radioactive) radiation; *~er Zerfall* radioactive decay; *~ machen* (radio)activate; **II.** *Adv.:* *~ strahlen* emit radioactivity; *~ verseucht* contaminated by radioactivity; **Radioaktivität** *f; nur Sg.* radioactivity

Radio|amateur *m*, **~amateurin** *f* radio ham; **~antenne** *f* radio aerial (*bes. Am.* antenna); **~apparat** *m → Radiogerät*, **~astronomie** *f* radio astronomy; **~chemie** *f* radiochemistry; **~durchsage** *f* special announcement (on the radio), *Am. auch* special bulletin; **~empfang** *m* radio reception; **~gerät** *n* radio (set); **~gramm** *n Med., Tech.* radiograph; **~graphie** *f Med., Tech.* radiography; **~hörer** *m*, **~hörerin** *f* (radio) listener; *Pl. auch* radio audience *Sg.*; **~karbonmethode** *f Chem.* radio carbon dating

Radiolarien *Pl. Zool.* radiolaria; **~schlamm** *m* radiolarian ooze

Radiologe *m; -n, -n; Med.* radiologist; **Radiologie** *f; -, kein Pl.* radiology; **Radiologin** *f; -, -nen* radiologist; **radiologisch** *Adj.* radiological

Radio|nachrichten *Pl.* radio news *Sg.*, news *Sg.* on the radio; **~programm** *n* radio schedule; **~quelle** *f Astron.* radio source; **~recorder** *m* radio-cassette recorder; **~röhre** *f Etech., altm.* radio valve (*Am.* tube); **~sender** *m* **1.** (*Station*) radio station; **2.** (*Gerät*)

radio transmitter; **~sendung** *f* (radio) program(me), (radio) broadcast; **~stern** *m Astron.* radio star; **~skop** *n* radio telescope; **~übertragung** *f* (radio) broadcast; **~wecker** *m* clock radio; **~wellen** *Pl.* radio waves; **~werbung** *f* radio advertising; *konkret:* radio advertisements (*od.* ads *umg.*) *Pl.*

Radium *n; -s, kein Pl.* radium; **~behandlung** *f*, **~therapie** *f* radium treatment

Radius *m; -, Radien; Math. und fig.* radius; *von Flugzeug, Schiff etc.:* (operating) range

Rad|kappe *f* hub cap; **~kasten** *m* wheel housing; **~kralle** *f* wheel clamp, *Am.* (Denver) boot; **~kranz** *m* (wheel) rim; **~kreuz** *n* wheel nut wrench (*od.* spider); **~lager** *n* wheel bearing

Radler *m; -s, -* **1.** *umg.* (*Radfahrer*) cyclist; **2.** *bes. südd.* (*Getränk*) shandy; **~halbe** *f* half-lit|re (*Am.* -er) of shandy; **~hose** *f* cycling shorts *Pl.*

Radlerin *f;-, -nen; umg.* cyclist

Radlermaß *f bes. südd.* large shandy

Rad|mutter *f* wheel nut; **~nabe** *f* (wheel) hub

Radon *n; -s, kein Pl.; Chem.* radon

Rad|rennbahn *f* cycling track; **~rennen** *n* cycle race; **~rennfahrer** *m*, **~rennfahrerin** *f* racing cyclist

...rädrig *in drei~es/sechs~es Fahrzeug* a three-/six-wheeled vehicle, a three-/six-wheeler

radschlagen *v/i. → Rad 1*

Rad|sport *m* cycling; **~sportler** *m*, **~sportlerin** *f* cyclist; **~stand** *m Mot.* wheelbase; **~tour** *f*, **~wanderung** *f* cycling tour; **~weg** *m* cycle track, cycleway

raffen *v/t.* **1.** (*an sich ~*) snatch, grab; **2.** (*Geld*) amass; **3.** (*Kleid*) gather up; *Nähen:* gather; **4.** (*Bericht etc.*) concentrate, condense; **5.** *umg.* (*kapieren*) get; *wann wirst du's endlich ~?* when will it finally penetrate your thick skull?

Raffgier *f* rapacity *förm.*; **raffgierig** *Adj.* grasping; *förm.* rapacious

Raffinade *f; -, -n* refined sugar; **Raffination** *f; -, -en* refining

Raffinement [rafinə'mã:] *n; -s, -s* finesse; *des Geschmacks etc.:* refinement

Raffinerie *f; -, -n* refinery

Raffinesse *f; -, -n* **1.** *kein Pl.* (*Schlauheit*) shrewdness, ingenuity; *des Geschmacks etc.:* refinement; **2.** (*Finesse*) refinement; *er versuchte es mit allen ~n* he tried all the tricks of the trade

raffinieren *v/t.* refine; **raffiniert I.** *P.P.* → *raffinieren*; **II.** *Adj.* refined; *Geschmack etc.:* sophisticated; (*geschickt*) clever, ingenious; (*schlau*) shrewd, crafty; *~!* very clever; *ein ~er Hund umg. fig.* a sly fox, a cunning bastard; **III.** *Adv.:* *sich ~ kleiden* dress stylishly (*od.* with sophistication); *ein ~ geschnittenes/geschlitztes Kleid* a cleverly cut/slit dress

Raffke *m; -s, -s; umg.* moneygrubber, shark

Raff|sucht *f* rapacity *förm.*; **~zahn** *m umg.* **1.** (*Zahn*) snaggletooth, *hum.* fang; **2.** *fig. pej.* shark

Rage ['ra:ʒə] *f; -, kein Pl.; umg.* rage, fury; *in ~ geraten* get furious, go wild

ragen *v/i.* tower, loom (*über + Akk.* above); *aus etw.:* rise (*aus* from); *horizontal:* project (*aus* from, out of); *in den Himmel ~* tower up (into the sky)

Raglan *m; -s, -s;* (*Mantel*) raglan (coat); **~mantel** *m* raglan coat

Ragout [ra'gu:] *n; -s, -s; Gastr.* ragout; **~fin** [-'fɛ̃] *n; -s, -s* gourmet ragout

...ragout *n, im Subst., Gastr.: Reh~* venison ragout

Rah, Rahe *f; -, Rahen; Naut.* yard

Rahm *m; -(e)s, kein Pl.* cream; *den ~ abschöpfen* skim off the cream, cream off the top of the milk; *fig.* skim (*od.* cream) off the best, take the pick of the bunch *umg., Am. auch* cherry-pick

Rahmen *m; -s, -* **1.** frame (*auch Tech., Mot.*); **2.** (*Rand*) edge, border; (*Grenzen*) limits *Pl.*; *im ~ e-s kurzen Artikels* within the limitations of a short article; *den ~ e-r Sache sprengen* go beyond the scope of *s.th.*; **3.** (*Gefüge*) framework, structure; *im ~ der geltenden Gesetze* within the framework of existing legislation; **4.** (*Bereich*) scope of a law etc.; *im ~ des Möglichen* within the realms of possibility; *im ~ der Ausstellung finden ... statt* the exhibition will include ...; *im ~ bleiben thematisch:* stick to what is relevant; *der Vorgaben:* keep within bounds; (*etw. nicht übertreiben*) not overdo it; *aus dem ~ fallen* (*ungewöhnlich sein*) be unusual, be out of the ordinary; (*sich schlecht benehmen*) step out of line; (*nicht passen*) be out of place; *Person: auch* be a square peg in a round hole; **5.** *fig.* (*Kulisse*) setting; *in engem/größerem ~* on a small/large scale; *e-e Feier in bescheidenem ~* a modest celebration (*od.* affair); *e-r Sache den richtigen ~ geben* do *s.th.* in style

...rahmen *m, im Subst. fig.: Entscheidungs~* decision-making context; *Finanz~* (prevailing) financial conditions *Pl.*; *Straf~* range of penalties; *Zeit~* time scale

rahmen *v/t.* (*Bild*) frame; (*Dia*) *auch* mount

Rahmen|abkommen *n Pol.* outline agreement; **~antenne** *f* frame (*od.* loop) aerial (*bes. Am.* antenna); **~bedingungen** *Pl.* **1.** general set-up *Sg.*; *günstige ~ für Investitionen* favo(u)rable context for investment; **2.** *e-s Vertrags:* general conditions; **~beschluss** *m* general enabling resolution; **~bestimmung** *f in Vertrag:* general provision; **~erzählung** *f in Roman etc.:* frame story; **~gesetz** *n Pol.* skeleton law (*providing guidelines for more specific legislation*); **~handlung** *f in Roman, Film etc.:* backstory, background story; **~plan** *m* outline plan; **~programm** *n* supporting program(me); *bei Festspielen: auch* fringe events *Pl.*; **~richtlinien** *Pl. Pol.* overall policy *Sg.*, general framework *Sg.* (for regulations); **~tarif** *m* agreed general working conditions *Pl.* (*as reflected in a collective agreement*); **~veranstaltung** *f* umbrella event; **~vertrag** *m* outline agreement

Rahm|geschnetzeltes *n; Gastr.* small thin pieces of meat in a cream sauce, *Am. etwa* stroganoff; **~joghurt** *m* full--fat cream yoghurt; **~käse** *m* full-fat cream cheese; **~schnitzel** *n* veal escalope with a cream sauce; **~soße** *f* cream sauce; **~spinat** *m* creamed spinach (*with sour cream*)

Rahmung *f* framing

Rahsegel *n Naut.* square sail

Rain *m* **1.** *Agr.* uncultivated strip, ba(u)lk; **2.** (*südd., schw. Abhang*)

slope; **~farn** *m Bot.* tansy
räkeln *v/refl.* → **rekeln**
Rakete *f; -, -n* rocket; *Mil. gelenkte:*
missile; *fig.* (*Sportler[in]*) ace; **e-e ~
abfeuern** launch a rocket (*Mil.* missile); **mit ~n beschießen** bombard with
missiles; **mit ~n bestücken** arm with
missiles; **mehrstufige ~** multistage
rocket
...rakete *f, im Subst.:* **Feuerwerks~**
(firework) rocket; **Luftabwehr~** anti-
-aircraft missile; **Silvester~** New Year
rocket
Raketen|abschussbasis *f* rocket
launching site; *Mil.* missile launching
site; **~abschussrampe** *f* (rocket)
launching pad; **~abwehr** *f* antiballistic
missile defen|ce (*Am.* -se); **~antrieb**
m rocket propulsion; **~aufschlag** *m*
umg. Tennis: explosive (*od.* lightning)
serve; **~basis** *f* missile launching site
raketenbestückt *Adj.* missile-carrying
Raketen|geschoss *n* missile;
~sprengkopf *m* missile warhead;
~start *m* lift-off, takeoff; **~startplatz**
m rocket (*Mil.* missile) launching site;
~stufe *f* (rocket) stage; **~stützpunkt**
m missile base; **~technik** *f* rocket
technology; **~triebwerk** *n* rocket engine; **~werfer** *m* rocket launcher;
~zeitalter *n* age of the rocket; **~zen-
trum** *n* rocket research cent|re (*Am.*
-er)
Rallye ['rɛli] *f; -, -s od. schw. n; -s, -s;*
Mot. rally; **e-e ~ fahren** compete in a
rally; **die ~ Monte Carlo** the Monte
Carlo Rally; **~fahrer** *m,* **~fahrerin** *f*
rally driver; **~sport** *m* rallying;
~Streifen *m* go-faster (*Am.* racing)
stripe
RAM *n; -s, -s Computer:* RAM, random
access memory
Rambo *m; -s, -s; umg.* hunk, Rambo
...-Rambo *m, im Subst.; umg.:* **Pisten~**
Rambo of the ski slopes, hunk on
skis; **Verkehrs~** Rambo behind the
wheel, roadhog
Ramm|bär *m Tech.* ram; **~bock** *m hist.*
battering ram
rammdösig *Adj. umg.* woozy
Ramme *f; -, -n; Tech.* ram(mer);
(*Pfahlramme*) pile-driver
rammeln *v/i.* **1.** *Zool.* mate; **2.** (*stoßen*)
jostle, shove; **3. an der Tür ~** *umg.* rattle at the door; **4.** *vulg.* (*koitieren*)
have a screw
rammen *v/t.* **1.** (*Auto, Schiff*) ram; **2. ~
in** (+ *Akk.*) (*Pfahl etc.*) ram (*od.*
drive) into; (*Messer etc.*) drive (*od.*
plunge) into
Rammklotz *m Tech.* ram
Rammler *m; -s, -;* (*männlicher Hase*)
buck
Rampe *f; -, -n schräg:* ramp; *waage-
recht:* (loading) platform; (*Startrampe*)
launching pad; *Theat.* apron, forestage;
vor die ~ treten come to the front of
the stage
Rampenlicht *n* footlights *Pl.;* **im ~ stehen** *im wörtl. Sinn:* stand in the footlights; *fig.* be in the limelight
ramponieren *v/t. umg.* (*Möbel, Auto
etc.*) knock *s.th.* about; (*Frisur etc.*)
spoil, mess up; **ramponiert** *umg.*
I. *P.P.* → **ramponieren; II.** *Adj.* **1.** *Sessel etc.:* battered (old) *armchair etc.;*
Haus, Lokal: run-down, seedy; **~ aussehen** be (*od.* look) the worse for
wear; **2.** *fig. Selbstbewusstsein:* dented;
Ruf, Image: tarnished
Ramsch[1] *m; -(e)s, kein Pl.; umg.* junk
Ramsch|laden *m* junk shop; **~verkauf**
m jumble (*Am.* rummage) sale; **~ware**

f cheap stuff
RAM-Speicher *m* RAM, random access memory
ran *Interj. umg.:* **~ an die Arbeit** *od.* **an
den Speck!** *umg.* let's get on with it
then!; *im V.* → **heran...;** → *auch* **rangehen, ranhalten, ranlassen, rannehmen** *etc.*
Rand *m; -(e)s, Ränder* **1.** edge; *e-s Tellers, e-r Brille etc.:* rim; *e-s Hutes:*
brim; (*Seitenrand*) margin; **Ränder unter den Augen** (dark) rings under the
eyes; **e-e Karte mit schwarzem ~** a
card with a black border; **ein ~ in der
Wanne** a tide-mark in the bath (*Am.*
ring in the bathtub); **etw. an den ~
schreiben** write s.th. in the margin;
am ~e der Stadt on the outskirts (of
the town); **am ~e des Abgrunds** on
the brink of the abyss; **2.** *fig.* verge;
am ~e der Gesellschaft on the fringe
(-s) of society; **am ~e der Legalität** just
inside the law; **an den ~** (*des Geschehens etc.*) **geraten** be marginalized;
am ~e erwähnen mention in passing;
das *od.* **so viel nur am ~e** I just mention that in passing; **am ~e behandeln**
(*Problem*) deal with *a problem* in
passing; **es interessiert mich nur am
~e** it's only of marginal interest to me;
er hat es nur am ~e miterlebt he
wasn't directly involved (*od.* affected
by it); **außer ~ und Band sein/geraten**
be going wild; *vor Freude etc.:* be beside o.s. / go wild (with joy); **zu ~e
kommen mit j-m/etw.** get on with s.o.
/ cope with s.th.; **3.** *umg.* (*Mund*) trap,
Brit. auch gob; **halt den ~!** *umg.* shut
up! shut your trap (*od.* face)
...rand *m, im Subst.* **1.** (*Teil*): **Außen~**
outer edge, outer rim, perimeter; **In-
nen~** inner edge; **Krater~** edge (*od.*
rim) of a (*od.* the) crater; **Orts~** outskirts *Pl.;* **Stoff~** selvedge; **2.** (*Streifen*)
Fett~ rim of fat; **Kalk~** ring of lime-
scale; **Schweiß~** ring left by perspiration, perspiration mark
Randale *f; -, kein Pl.; umg.:* **nach dem
Endspiel gab es ~** there were disturbances after the final; **randalieren** *v/i.*
go on the rampage, run riot; **~de Fans**
rampaging fans; (*Fußballfans*) football
hooligans; **Randalierer** *m; -s, -;* (*Rowdy*) hooligan, rowdy; *nach Alkoholkonsum:* lager lout *umg.*
Rand|beet *n* border; **~bemerkung** *f*
1. (*Notiz*) marginal note; **2.** (*Äußerung*) passing remark (*od.* comment);
~bevölkerung *f* fringe population;
~bezirk *m* outlying district
Rändelmutter *f Tech.* knurled nut
rändeln *v/t. Tech.* knurl
Rändelung *f* knurling; (*gerändelter
Rand*) knurled edge
Rand|erscheinung *f* secondary (*od.*
peripheral) phenomenon; (*Nebenwir-
kung*) spin-off (+ *Gen.* from); **~figur** *f*
marginal (*od.* peripheral) figure; *im
Roman etc.:* minor (*od.* peripheral)
character; **~gebiet** *n e-s Staates:* border region; *e-r Stadt:* outlying district;
Pl. outskirts; *fig.* peripheral (*od.*
fringe) area; (*Fach*) fringe subject; **~
der Physik** subsidiary area of physics;
~gruppe *f* soziale: fringe group; *radikale od. extremistische **~n** the extremist (*pej.* lunatic) fringe *Sg.*
...randig *im Adj.:* **breit~** broad-edged;
Hut: broad-brimmed; **schmal~** nar-
row-rimmed
Rand|lage *f* position on the outskirts;
~leiste *f* border; (*Gesims*) cornice
randlos *Adj. Brille:* rimless; *Foto:* bor-

derless; *Buchseite etc.:* without a margin
Rand|notiz *f* marginal note; **~problem**
n side issue; **~schärfe** *f Opt.* marginal
definition; **~siedlung** *f* housing estate
(*Am.* development) on the edge of a
town; **~staat** *m* border state; **~stein** *m*
kerbstone, *Am.* curbstone; **~steller** *m*
margin stop; **~stellung** *f:* **e-e ~ einnehmen** be on the fringes (of society);
~streifen *m* **1.** *Straße:* verge; *Autobahn:* hard shoulder, *Am.* shoulder;
2. *am Papier:* margin
randvoll *Adj. Glas:* full to the brim,
brimful; *Topf, Fass etc.:* full to the top;
Terminkalender etc.: packed; *umg.* (*betrunken*) pissed, plastered
Randzone *f* peripheral area
rang *Imperf.* → **ringen**
Rang *m; -(e)s, Ränge* **1.** rank; *Mil.*
(*Dienstgrad*) rank, *Am.* grade, rating
(*auch Naut.*); **ein Offizier von hohem
~** a high-ranking officer; **2.** *fig.* (*Stellung*) standing, status; **ein Mann von/
ohne ~ und Namen** a distinguished
(*od.* an eminent) person / a nobody;
alles, was ~ und Namen hat all the
big names, everybody who is anybody;
3. (*Güte*) quality; (*Bedeutung*) significance; **ein gesellschaftliches Ereignis
von hohem ~** a top-notch social occasion; **von europäischem ~** of European standing (*od.* ranking); **ersten ~es**
of the first rank (*od.* order); (*erstklassig*) first-class, first-rate; **ein Gitarrist
vom ~e Segovias** a guitarist of Sego-
via's stature; **j-m den ~ ablaufen** outdo
s.o., outstrip s.o.; **j-m den ~ streitig
machen** challenge s.o.; **4.** *Lotto, Toto:*
(dividend) class; **5.** *Sport* (*Platzierung*)
place; **6.** *in Kino, Theater etc.:* circle;
erster ~ *Theat.* dress circle, *Am. auch*
balcony; **zweiter ~** upper circle, *Am.
auch* second (*od.* upper) balcony; **dritter ~** gallery; **die Ränge** *Sport* the terraces; **vor leeren Rängen spielen** play
to an empty house (*Sport* before an
empty stadium)
...rang *m, im Subst.:* **Generals~** rank of
general
Rang|abzeichen *n* badge of rank; *Pl.*
insignia; **~älteste** *m, f; -n, -n* senior;
Mil. senior officer
Range *f; -, -n; umg. altm.* tearaway
rangehen *v/i.* (*unreg., trennb., ist -ge-*)
umg. **1. an etw. ~** go up to s.th.; **nicht
so nahe ~!** don't go so close!; **2.** *fig.*
(*Aufgabe etc.*) get stuck in (*Am.*
bogged down); **der geht aber ran!** *bei*
(*verbaler*) *Attacke:* he's really letting
fly.; *bei e-r Frau:* he's a fast worker
Rangelei *f; -, -en; umg.* scrapping; *fig.*
wrangling (**um** over); **rangeln** *v/i.*
umg. (*sich balgen*) scrap; **um etw. ~**
fig. wrangle over s.th.; (*Position etc.*)
tussle for s.th.
Rangfolge *f von Themen, Problemen
etc.:* order of precedence (*od.* priority); *in Tabelle etc.:* ranking
rang|gleich *Adj.* equal in rank; **~hoch**
Adj. senior, *auch Mil.* high-ranking;
~höchst *Adj.* most senior, *auch Mil.*
highest-ranking
Rangierbahnhof *m Eisenb.* marshal-
ling yard, *Am.* switchyard; **rangieren**
I. *vt/i. Eisenb.* shunt, *Am.* switch; *Mot.
etc.* manoeuvre, *Am.* maneuver;
II. *v/i.* (+ *Gen.* / + *Dat.*) rank above;
an erster Stelle ~ rank highest; **Rangierer** *m; -s, -; Eisenb.* shunter, *Am.*
switchman
Rangier|gleis *n* siding, *Am. auch*
switching track; **~lok** *f* shunting (*Am.*

switching) engine

Rang|liste f Sport etc. ranking list; Mil. Army (Naut. Navy, Flug. Air Force) List; ℠**mäßig** Adv. in rank; ⁓**ordnung** f von Themen, Problemen etc.: order of precedence (od. priority); in Hierarchie etc.: ranking; (Hackordnung, auch fig.) pecking order; ⁓**stufe** f rank; (Vorrang) priority

ranhalten v/refl. (unreg., trennb., hat -ge-) umg. **1.** (sich beeilen) get a move on; bei der Arbeit: get on with it; **2.** (nicht nachlassen) keep at it; **3.** (beim Essen zugreifen) dig in

rank Adj. Figur etc.: lithe, lissom; auch Birke: slender; ⁓ **und schlank** lithe and lissom

Ranke f; -, -n; Bot. tendril

Ränke Pl. altm. intrigues; ⁓ **schmieden** plot and scheme

ranken v/refl.: sich ⁓ climb up; **sich** ⁓ **um** twine (a)round; **um die Familie** ⁓ **sich viele Geschichten** fig. a lot of stories have grown up around the family

Rankengewächs n creeper

ran|klotzen v/i. (trennb., hat -ge-) umg.; (hart arbeiten) get stuck in, Am. get with it, go at it hammer and tongs; ⁓**kommen** v/i. (unreg., trennb., ist -ge-) umg. **an etw.** (+ Akk.) ⁓ reach s.th.; durch leichten Zugang: get at s.th.; (näher kommen) approach s.th.; → **herankommen**; ⁓**kriegen** v/t. (trennb., hat -ge-) umg.: **j-n** ⁓ **zur Arbeit**: make s.o. knuckle under; stärker: put s.o. through the mill; zur Mitarbeit: make s.o. pull his (od. her) weight; zur Verantwortung: get s.o. to take responsibility; (reinlegen) con s.o., take s.o. for a ride; ⁓**lassen** v/t. (unreg., trennb., hat -ge-) umg.: **j-n an etw.** ⁓ let s.o. get at s.th.; **sie lässt niemanden an sich ran** she won't let anyone (come) near her; **lass mich mal ran!** let me have a go (Am. try); ⁓**machen** v/refl. (trennb., hat -ge-) umg.: **sich an j-n** ⁓ make a pass at s.o.; **sich** ⁓ (beeilen) get a move on; ⁓**nehmen** v/t. (unreg., trennb., hat -ge-) umg. (Schüler) pick on; **der neue Biologielehrer nimmt uns ganz schön ran** the new biology teacher really gives us a hard time; **j-n** ⁓ put s.o. through his (od. her) paces; (zurechtweisen) let s.o. have it; ⁓**schmeißen** v/refl. (unreg., trennb., hat -ge-) umg.: **sich an j-n** ⁓ throw oneself at s.o.

Ranzen m; -s, -; (Schulmappe) satchel; → **Wanst**

ranzig Adj. rancid

rapid, rapide I. Adj. rapid; **II.** Adv. rapidly; ⁓ **ansteigen** rise rapidly, surge; ⁓ **sinken** sink fast, plummet; **mit der Wirtschaft geht es** ⁓ **bergab** the economy is rapidly going downhill (od. going downhill fast)

Rappe m; -n, -n black horse; **auf Schusters** ⁓ **unterwegs sein** umg. fig. go on Shanks's pony, hoof it

Rappel m; -s, kein Pl. umg.; (Fimmel) craze; **e-n** ⁓ **haben** have taken leave of one's senses; **sie kriegt wieder ihren** ⁓ she's in one of her crazy moods again

rappeldürr Adj. umg. thin as a rail

rappelig Adj. umg. crazy; **das macht e-n ja ganz** ⁓! this drives you (a)round the bend

rappeln umg. **I.** v/i. rattle; **bei ihm rappelt's wohl!** umg. he must be crazy (Brit. auch off his nut!); **II.** v/refl.: **sich aus dem Bett** ⁓ heave o.s. out of bed; **sich in die Höhe** ⁓ struggle up; fig.

---

struggle back onto one's feet

rappelvoll Adj. umg. jampacked, chock-a-block

Rappen m; -s, -, **Räppli** n; -s, - Schweiz: centime

Rapport m; -(e)s, -e **1.** (Bericht) report; **sich zum** ⁓ **melden bei** report to; **2.** Psych. rapport; **3.** fachspr., an Tapeten, Gardinen etc.: (pattern) repeat

Raps m; -es, -e; Bot. rape, Am. canola; (Samen) rapeseed; ⁓**öl** n rapeseed (Am. canola) oil

Rapunzel f; -, -n **1.** Bot. auch Pl. lamb's lettuce; **2.** (Märchenfigur) Rapunzel

rar Adj. rare; mst präd. scarce; **sich** ⁓ **machen** umg. make only rare appearances, not be seen around; **Rarität** f; -, -en rarity; (Kuriosität) curio; **gute Restaurants sind hier e-e** ⁓ good restaurants are few and far between here

Raritätenkabinett n curiosity cabinet

rasant Adj. **1.** umg. (schnell) Fahrer, Tempo etc.: very fast; Wagen auch hairy; Entwicklung, Fortschritt, Zunahme: rapid; stärker: lightning; Film, Handlung: fast-moving, action-packed; Spiel, Vortragsstil: dynamic; **in e-m** ⁓**en Tempo** at (a) terrific speed; **e-e** ⁓**e Kür** a breathtaking program(me); **2.** umg. (rassig) Frau, Kleid: smashing; **3.** (schnittig) racy; **ein** ⁓**er Sportwagen** a racy-looking sports car, a mean machine umg.; **4.** Ballistik: flat; **Rasanz** f; -, kein Pl. **1.** e-r Entwicklung: terrific speed; **2.** e-r Show, Darstellung: great verve, dynamism; **3.** Ballistik: flat trajectory

rasch I. Adj. quick; Handlung etc.: swift; Tempo: fast; **II.** Adv. quickly etc.; ⁓ **machen** be quick (mit etw. about s.th.); ⁓**!** hurry up!, quick!, make it snappy! umg.

rascheln I. v/i. rustle; **mit etw.** ⁓ make s.th. rustle; **II. Rascheln** n; -s, kein Pl. rustling, rustle

Raschheit f quickness, swiftness

rasen v/i. **1.** (ist) (sehr schnell fahren od. laufen) race (along), tear (along), speed (along); ⁓ **gegen** run into; Auto: auch crash into; **ich raste nach Hause** I dashed (od. rushed) home; **sein Puls/Herz rast** his pulse/heart is racing; **die Zeit rast** time is flying; **ein Bußgeld wegen Rasens** a fine for speeding; **2.** (hat) vor Zorn, im Fieber, Wahnsinn: rave; Sturm, See: rage; **vor Schmerz** ⁓ be delirious with pain; **vor Begeisterung** ⁓ be wild with enthusiasm

Rasen m; -s, -, mst Sg.; allg. grass; (Rasenfläche) lawn; auf ⁓ Sport on grass; ⁓ **betreten verboten!** keep off the grass; **er musste den** ⁓ **verlassen** Sport he was sent off; **der berühmte** ⁓ **Wembleys** Wembley's famous turf; **Spiele sollten auf dem grünen** ⁓ **entschieden werden** matches (od. games) should be decided on the field of play; **ihn deckt der kühle** ⁓ geh. he is five (Am. six) feet under

rasend I. Part. Präs. → **rasen**; **II.** Adj. **1.** ⁓**er Durst** raging thirst; ⁓**er Hunger** ravenous hunger; ⁓**e Schmerzen** searing (od. raging) pain; ⁓**e Kopfschmerzen** a splitting (od. raging) headache; ⁓**e Wut** violent rage; ⁓ **werden** go mad; **2.** Geschwindigkeit: nur attr. breakneck, terrific; **in** ⁓**er Fahrt** at breakneck speed; **III.** Adv. umg.: ⁓ **verliebt** madly in love, besotted; **er spielt** ⁓ **gern Backgammon** he loves backgammon, he's mad (od. wild)

---

about backgammon

Rasen|fläche f lawn; ⁓**heizung** f under-soil heating; ⁓**mäher** m lawnmower; ⁓**platz** m Tennis: grass court; ⁓**schere** f garden shears Pl.; ⁓**sport** m **1.** Koll. games played on grass; **2.** → **Rasensportart**; ⁓**sportart** f lawn game; Pl. Koll. lawn sports; ⁓**sprenger** m sprinkler; ⁓**stück** n patch of grass; ⁓**tennis** n lawn tennis

Raser m; -s, -; umg. Mot. speed maniac (od. merchant), Am. speedster, speed demon

Raserei f; -, kein Pl. **1.** (Wut) rage, fury; (Wahnsinn) frenzy, madness; **j-n zur** ⁓ **treiben** umg. drive s.o. (a)round the bend; **2.** umg. Mot. (reckless) speeding

Rasier|apparat m razor; ⁓**creme** f shaving cream

rasieren v/t. **1.** (auch sich ⁓) shave; **sich nass/trocken** ⁓ have a wet/dry shave; **sich** (Dat.) **den Bart / die Augenbrauen** ⁓ shave off one's beard/ eyebrows; **j-m den Kopf** ⁓ shave off all s.o.'s hair; **2.** umg. (Gebäude etc. zerstören) flatten, demolish; **3.** j-n ⁓ umg. (betrügen) pull a fast one on s.o.; **Rasierer** m umg. (electric) shaver

Rasier|klinge f razor blade; ⁓**messer** n (straight) razor; ⁓**pinsel** m shaving brush; ⁓**seife** f shaving soap; ⁓**sitz** m umg., hum., im Kino etc.: front row seat; ⁓**wasser** n vor der Rasur: pre-shave lotion; nach der Rasur: after-shave (lotion); ⁓**zeug** n shaving things Pl. (od. kit)

Räson [rɛˈzõː] f; -, kein Pl.: **j-n zur** ⁓ **bringen** talk some sense into s.o., bring s.o. round; **zur** ⁓ **kommen** see reason; **räsonieren** v/i. **1.** Dial. (nörgeln) moan; **2.** (weitschweifig reden) hold forth (über + Akk. on)

Raspel[1] f; -, -n; Tech. rasp; (Küchengerät) grater

Raspel[2] m; -s, -, mst Pl.; (Kokosraspel etc.) flake; → **Kokosraspel**, **Schokoladenraspel**

raspeln v/t. rasp; (schaben) grate; → **Süßholz**

rass, räss Adj. Dial. Käse etc.: strong, sharp; Gewürz, Gulasch etc.: hot; Alkohol: strong; Wind: biting; Witz: crude

Rasse f; -, -n **1.** race (auch fig.); Tierzucht: breed; **was für e-e** ⁓ (Hund etc.) **ist das?** what breed (of dog etc.) is that?; **e-e neue** ⁓ **züchten** create a new breed; **die menschliche** ⁓ the human race; **sie sind e-e** ⁓ **für sich** umg. pej. they're an odd (od. a strange) lot; **2.** umg. (Temperament) spirit; **die Frau / der Wagen hat** ⁓ umg. she's a woman of spirit / the car's a thoroughbred

Rasse|frau f umg. woman of spirit, hot-blooded woman; ⁓**hund** m pedigree (od. pure-bred) dog

Rassel f; -, -n rattle; ⁓**bande** f umg. noisy lot, bunch of rascals

rasseln v/i. **1.** rattle; Wecker: shrill; ⁓ **mit** rattle, (Schlüsseln) auch jangle; ⁓**des Geräusch** rattling (sound); **gegen e-e Mauer** ⁓ umg. crash against (Person, Auto: into) a wall; **2.** durch **e-e Prüfung** ⁓ umg. flunk an exam

Rassen|diskriminierung f racial discrimination; ⁓**fanatiker** m, ⁓**fanatikerin** f racist; ⁓**forscher** m, ⁓**forscherin** f hist. ethnologist; ⁓**forschung** f hist. ethnnology; ⁓**frage** f racial problem; ⁓**gesetze** Pl. hist., im Nationalsozialismus: racial laws; ⁓**hetze** f racial aggression; ⁓**ideologie** f racial theory (*od.* ideology); **~konflikt** *m* racial conflict; **~krawalle** *Pl.* race riots; **~kreuzung** *f von Tieren*: crossbreeding; (*Tier*) crossbreed; **~kunde** *f* racial anthropology; **~merkmal** *n* racial characteristic; **~mischung** *f Tiere*: crossbreeding; *Menschen*: interbreeding; **~politik** *f* racial policy; **~schande** *f hist.*, *im Nationalsozialismus*: *sexual relations with a non-Aryan*; **~schranke** *f* racial barrier; *für Farbige*: colo(u)r bar; **~trennung** *f* (racial) segregation; **~unruhen** *Pl.* race riots, racial unrest *Sg.*; **~vorurteil** *n* racial prejudice; **~wahn** *m* racial fanaticism

Rassepferd *n* thoroughbred (horse)
rasserein *Adj.* → **reinrassig**
Rasseweib *n umg.* woman of spirit, hot-blooded woman
rassig *Adj. Pferd etc.*: thoroughbred; (*temperamentvoll*) mettlesome; *Frau*: spirited, vivacious; *Wagen*: high-performance, sporty; *Zigeuner*, *Wein*: fiery; **sie ist e-e ~e Frau** she has spirit and style, she's a firecracker *umg.*; **ein ~er Typ** a hot-blooded type
rassisch I. *Adj.* racial; **II.** *Adv.* racially; **~ bedingt sein** have racial causes; **j-n ~ verfolgen** persecute s.o. because of his (*od.* her) race
Rassismus *m*; -, *kein Pl.* racism; **Rassist** *m*; -en, -en, **Rassistin** *f* -, -nen racist; **rassistisch I.** *Adj.* racist; **II.** *Adv.* in a racist manner; **sich ~ äußern** make racist remarks
Rast *f*; -, -en, *mst Sg.* rest; (*Pause*) *auch* break; **~ machen** (*anhalten*) make a stop; *beim Wandern*: have a rest
Rasta, **Rastafari** *m*; -s, -s, **Rastafarier** *m*; -s, - Rasta(farian)
Rasta|locken *Pl.* dreadlocks; **~musik** *f* Rastafarian music
rasten *v/i.* (take a) rest; **wer rastet, der rostet** once you stop you soon lose your ability, use it or lose it
Raster¹ *m*, *n*; -s, - **1.** *Fot.*, *Druck.* screen; **2.** *fig.* pattern, scheme; **das fällt aus dem ~ heraus** it doesn't fit into any pattern (*od.* scheme)
Raster² *n*; -s, -; *TV*, *Computer*: raster; **~fahndung** *f* computer search; **~mikroskop** *n* scanning electron microscope
rastern *v/t. Fot.* print in halftone; *TV* scan
Raster|punkt *m* halftone dot; *TV* picture element, pixel
Rasterung *f* scanning
Rast|haus *n* motorway (*Am.* highway) restaurant; *mit Übernachtung*: (motorway) motel; **~hof** *m* (motorway) motel
rastlos I. *Adj.* **1.** (*unermüdlich*) indefatigable, tireless; *Arbeit*: unceasing; **2.** (*unruhig*) restless; **II.** *Adv.*: **~ tätig sein** work nonstop, be on the go all the time *umg.*; **Rastlosigkeit** *f* **1.** (*Unermüdlichkeit*) tirelessness; **2.** (*Unruhe*) restlessness
Rast|platz *m* place for a rest; *Autobahn*: lay-by, *Am.* rest stop; **~stätte** *f* **1.** (*Gaststätte*) motorway (*Am.* highway) restaurant; **2.** (*Gelände*) (motorway, *Am.* Interstate) service area; *Schild*: Services *Pl.*
Rasur *f*; -, -en **1.** shave; **2.** (*Radieren*, *ausradierte Stelle*) erasure
Rat¹ *m*; -(e)s, *kein Pl.* advice; (*Empfehlung*) recommendation; (*Vorschlag*) suggestion; **ein ~** a piece of advice, some advice; **auf s-n ~ hin** on his advice (*od.* recommendation); **j-n um ~ fragen** ask s.o. for advice, ask s.o.'s advice; **~ suchende Personen** *od.* **~**

Suchende wenden sich bitte an (+ *Akk.*) those (*od.* anyone) seeking advice please consult; **j-s ~ befolgen** take (*od.* follow) s.o.'s advice; **nicht auf j-s ~ hören** ignore s.o.'s advice; **mit sich zu ~e gehen** think things over; **j-n zu ~e ziehen** consult s.o., seek s.o.'s advice; **~ schaffen** find ways and means; **~ wissen** know what to do; **keinen ~ mehr wissen** be at a loss as to what to do; **da ist guter ~ teuer** it's hard to say what to do; **j-m mit ~ und Tat zur Seite stehen** *od.* **beistehen** give s.o. one's advice and support; → *Zeit* 3
Rat² *m*; -(e)s, *Räte* **1.** (*Gremium*) council, board; **Europäischer ~** European Council; **in den ~ wählen** elect s.o. to the council; **im ~ sitzen** be on the council; **2.** (*Ratsmitglied*) council(l)or; → *Gemeinderat²*
...rat *m*, *im Subst.*: *Kirchen~* ecclesiastical council; (*Mitglied*) ecclesiastical council(l)or; *Kreis~* *etwa* district council; (*Mitglied*) district council(l)or; *Rundfunk~* Broadcasting Council
Rate *f*; -, -n **1.** *Wirts.* instal(l)ment; **auf ~n kaufen** buy by instal(l)ments; *Brit. auch* buy on hire purchase, *Am. auch* buy on the installment plan; **in ~n abzahlen** pay off in instal(l)ments; **2.** (*Quote*) rate; → *Wachstumsrate etc.*
...rate *f*, *im Subst.* **1.** *Wirts. Abzahlungs~* hire purchase instalment, *Am.* installment plan payment; *Darlehens~* loan payment; **2.** (*Quote*) *Abtreibungs~* abortion rate (*od.* figure)
Rätedemokratie *f* government by soviets
raten¹ *vt/i.*; *rät, riet, hat geraten*; (*beraten*) advise (**zu etw.** s.th.); **er riet (mir) zur Vorsicht** he advised me to be careful, he advised caution; **ich rate dir zu diesem Modell** I would advise you to take (*od.* I think you should take) this model; **das möchte ich dir geraten haben** *drohend*: just as well (for your sake), you'd better (not) *umg.*; → *auch geraten²*
raten² *vt/i.*; *rät, riet, hat geraten*; (*erraten*) guess; **~ Sie mal!** (have a) guess; **gut geraten!** good guess!; **falsch geraten!** wrong!; **dreimal darfst du ~** I'll give you three guesses; **das rätst du nie** you'll never guess; **das ist alles nur geraten** it's all guesswork
Raten|betrag *m* instal(l)ment (amount); **~kauf** *m* hire purchase, *Am.* installment plan purchase; **~käufer** *m*, **~käuferin** *f* hire purchase (*Am.* installment plan) buyer; **~kredit** *m* instal(l)ment credit; **~sparvertrag** *m* contract for saving by fixed instal(l)ments; **2weise** *Adv.* by instal(l)ments; **~zahlung** *f* payment by instal(l)ments; (*einzelne Zahlung*) instal(l)ment
Räterepublik *f Pol.* soviet republic
Rate|runde *f* round of a guessing game; **~spiel** *n* guessing game
Rat|geber *m* adviser, counsel(l)or; **ein guter/schlechter ~** *bes. fig.* a provider of good/bad advice; **2.** (*Buch etc.*) guide (**über** + *Akk.* to), self-help book (on), how-to book (on) *umg.*; **~geberin** *f* → *Ratgeber* 1
Rathaus *n* town (*bes. Am.* city) hall; **~fraktion** *f* party group on the town (*od.* city) council; **~partei** *f* party represented on the town (*od.* city) council; **~platz** *m* town hall square; **~saal** *m* town (*od.* city) hall council chamber; **~turm** *m* town hall tower

Ratifikation *f*; -, -en; *Pol.* ratification
Ratifikations|klausel *f Pol.* ratification clause; **~urkunde** *f* ratification document
ratifizieren *v/t. Pol.* ratify; **Ratifizierung** *f* ratification; **Ratifizierungs...** *im Subst. siehe Ratifikations...*
Rätin *f*; -, -nen → *Rat²* 2
Rating ['reːtɪŋ] *n*; -s, -s; *TV*, *Psych.*, *Soziol.* rating
Ratio *f*; -, *kein Pl.*: **die ~** reason; **mit der ~ entscheiden** make a reasoned (*od.* rational) decision
Ration *f*; -, -en ration; (*Anteil*) allowance, share; **j-s tägliche ~** *umg.* (*Alkohol etc.*) s.o.'s daily ration (*od.* dose); **eiserne ~** emergency (*od.* iron) rations; **j-n auf halbe ~ setzen** put s.o. on half rations
rational I. *Adj.* rational (*auch Math.*); **II.** *Adv.*: **~ denken/handeln** think/act rationally; **ein ~ denkender Typ** a rational person
rationalisieren *vt/i. Wirts.* rationalize, *bes. Am.* streamline; **Rationalisierung** *f* rationalization, *bes. Am.* streamlining; **Rationalisierungsmaßnahme** *f* efficiency measure
Rationalismus *m*; -, *kein Pl.*; *Philos.* rationalism
Rationalist *m*; -en, -en, **~in** *f*; -, -nen rationalist; **rationalistisch I.** *Adj.* rationalistic; **II.** *Adv.* in a rationalistic manner
rationell *Adj.* rational, reasonable; (*wirtschaftlich*, *produktiv*) efficient
rationieren *v/t.* ration; **Rationierung** *f* rationing
ratlos *Adj.* baffled; *präd. auch* at a loss; **~es Achselzucken** (a) despairing shrug; **Ratlosigkeit** *f* perplexity
rätoromanisch I. *Adj.* Rhaeto-Romanic; **II. Rätoromanisch** *n*; -en; *Ling.* Rhaeto-Romanic; **das Rätoromanische** the Rhaeto-Romanic language(s *Pl.*)
ratsam *Adj.* advisable; (*klug*) wise; **Ratsamkeit** *f* advisability
ratsch *Interj.* rip
Ratsch¹ *m*; -(e)s, -e; *umg.* ripping noise *allg.*
Ratsch² *m*; *indekl.*; *südd. österr. umg.* (*Schwätzchen*) natter, *Am.* chat; **e-n ~ machen** → *ratschen* 1
Ratsche *f*; -, -n **1.** (*Rassel*) rattle, clapper; **2.** *Tech.* (*Bohrratsche*) ratchet brace (*od.* drill), circle jack; (*Knarre*) ratchet (handle); *e-r Handbremse etc.*: ratchet; **3.** *umg. pej.* (*Schwätzerin*) gasbag; (*Klatschtante*) (old) gossip
ratschen *v/i. bes. südd. österr. schw.* **1.** (*hat*) *umg.* (*sich unterhalten*) have a natter (*od. Am.* chat); (*klatschen*) gossip; **2.** (*die Ratsche drehen*) swing a rattle (*od.* clapper)
Ratschlag *m* (piece of) advice
Rätsel *n*; -s, - riddle, puzzle (*auch fig.*); (*Geheimnis*) mystery; (*Wortspiel*) conundrum; (*Silbenrätsel*) charade; *geh.* enigma; **~ lösen** solve a riddle (*od.* mystery); **j-m ~ aufgeben** ask s.o. riddles; *fig.* puzzle s.o., *stärker*: baffle s.o.; **in ~n sprechen** *fig.* speak in riddles; **er ist mir ein ~** I can't make him out; **es ist mir ein ~** it's a (complete) mystery to me, it beats me *umg.*; **das ist des ~s Lösung!** that's the answer; **~ecke** *f* puzzle corner (*od.* section); **~frage** *f* puzzling question, riddle; (*Quizfrage*) question, quiz; **~freund** *m*, **~freundin** *f* keen (*Am.* avid) puzzler, puzzle enthusiast
rätselhaft *Adj.* puzzling; (*geheimnis-*

R

voll) mysterious; (*unergründlich*) enigmatic; *auf ~e Weise verschwinden etc.*: mysteriously

Rätsel|heft *n* puzzle book (*od.* magazine); **~lexikon** *n* treasury of puzzles

rätseln *v/i.* puzzle (*über* + *Akk.* over), speculate; *umg.* (*Rätsel lösen*) solve riddles (*od.* puzzles)

Rätselraten *n; -s, kein Pl.* guessing games *Pl.*; *fig.* speculation (*um* about, over, on)

Rats|herr *m* (town) council(l)or, alderman; **~sitzung** *f* council meeting

ratsuchend → *Rat*¹

Rats|versammlung *f* **1.** (*Gremium*) council, assembly; **2.** (*Sitzung*) council meeting; **~vorsitzende** *m, f; -n, -n* council chairperson; *männlich auch*: chairman; *weiblich auch*: chairwoman

Rattan *n; -s, -e* rattan; **~möbel** *Pl.* rattan (*od.* cane) furniture

Ratte *f; -, -n; Zool.* rat; *diese ~! fig. pej.* this dirty rat!; *die ~n verlassen das sinkende Schiff fig.* rats leave a sinking ship

Ratten|fänger *m* ratcatcher; *fig. pej.* pied piper; *der ~ von Hameln* the Pied Piper of Hamelin; **~nest** *n* rat's nest; *fig.* lair, den of thieves *etc.*; **~plage** *f* plague of rats; **~schwanz** *m* **1.** rat's tail; **2.** *umg.* (*Frisur*) pigtail; **3.** *ein* (*ganzer*) *~ von umg. fig.* a whole string of; **~schwänzchen** *n umg. hum. fig.* (*Frisur*) small pigtail

rattern *v/i.* **1.** (*hat*) rattle, clatter; *Maschinengewehr*: chatter; *Motor etc.*: roar; **2.** (*ist*): *durch die Straßen ~* clatter through the streets

Rattern *n; -s, kein Pl.*: *das ~ e-r Maschine / e-s MGs* the clatter of a machine / chatter of a machine gun; → *rattern*

Ratzefummel *m; -s, -; umg. Schülersprache*: rubber, *Am.* eraser

ratzekahl *Adv. umg.*: *alles ~ auffressen* polish off the lot; *e-n Baum ~ abfressen* strip a tree bare

ratzen *v/i. umg.* (*schlafen*) kip, *Am.* snooze

rau *Adj.* rough (*auch Haut, See, Wetter, Ton etc.*); *Wind*: raw; *Kälte*: biting, bitter; *Winter*: severe; *Klima*: harsh, raw; *Land, Gegend*: desolate; *Fell etc.*: rough, coarse; *Stimme*: harsh, grating; (*rauchig*) husky; (*heiser*) hoarse; *Leben*: tough, rough; (*streng*) harsh; (*grob*) coarse; *e-n ~en Hals haben* have a sore throat; *es herrscht ein ~er Ton* the general tone is harsh; *in Schule, Gefängnis*: there is a harsh regime (*od.* discipline); *~ aber herzlich umg.* bluff; *der ~e Norden* the frozen north; *in ~en Mengen umg.* ... galore, by the ton; *vorangestellt*: heaps of ...

Raub *m; -es, kein Pl.* **1.** robbery (*auch Jur.*); **2.** (*Entführung*) abduction; *der ~ der Sabinerinnen Kunst, Myth.* the rape of the Sabine women (*od.* the Sabines); **3.** (*Beute*) booty, loot; *auf ~ ausgehen Tier*: hunt its prey; *Dieb*: go out on the prowl; *ein ~ der Flammen werden fig.* be destroyed by fire, fall victim to the flames

...raub *m, im Subst.*: *Handtaschen~* bag-snatching; *Juwelen~* jewel(le)ry theft; *Kindes~* kidnapping (of a child)

Raubaufnahme *f von Musik etc.*: pirated (*od.* bootlegged) recording, bootleg *umg.*

Raubauz *m; -es, -e; umg.* rowdy

Raubbau *m* overexploitation (*an* + *Dat.* of), destructive (*od.* uncontrolled) exploitation (of); *~ an der*

Landschaft despoilation of the countryside; *~ am Baumbestand* overcutting; *mit s-r Gesundheit ~ treiben* ruin one's health by overdoing it

Raubein *n* rough diamond; **raubeinig** *Adj.* bluff

rauben *vt/i.* (*Geld etc.*) steal; (*Kind*) kidnap; *Fuchs etc.*: (*Hühner etc.*) make off with; *j-m etw. ~* steal s.th. from s.o.; *auch fig.* rob s.o. of s.th.; *j-m den Atem ~* take s.o.'s breath away; *j-m den Schlaf etc. ~* rob (*od.* deprive) s.o. of his (*od.* her) sleep *etc.*

Räuber *m; -s, -* robber; (*Straßenräuber*) highwayman; *unter die ~ gefallen sein umg.* be fleeced; **~bande** *f* band of thieves, burglary gang; **~geschichte** *f* **1.** story about robbers; **2.** *umg. fig.* (*Lügengeschichte*) cock-and-bull story; **~höhle** *f* den of robbers (*od.* thieves); *hier sieht's aus wie in e-r ~ umg.* this place is an absolute mess, it's like a pigsty in here

räuberisch *Adj. Tier*: predatory; *Person*: thieving; *Stämme etc.*: marauding; **~er Überfall** attack by robbers; *auf e-e Bank etc.*: raid; *durch e-n Stamm etc.*: predatory attack; **~e Erpressung** *Jur.* extortion by means of force; *in ~er Absicht Jur.* with intent to rob

räubern *v/i.* (*stehlen*) rob, steal; *im Kühlschrank etc. ~ umg. fig.* raid the fridge *etc.*

Räuber|pistole *f umg. fig.* cock-and-bull story; **~zivil** *n umg.*: *in ~ sein* wearing scruffy clothes; *komm ruhig in ~* come as you are, no need to dress up

Raub|fisch *m* predatory fish; **~fischerei** *f* poaching on another country's fishing grounds

Raubgier *f* rapacity; **raubgierig** *Adj.* rapacious

Raub|katze *f Zool.* predatory cat, feline predator; (*Großkatze*) big cat; **~kopie** *f* pirate copy, bootleg *umg.*; **~mord** *m* murder in the course of a robbery, robbery with murder, murder and robbery; **~mörder** *m* murderer and robber; **~mörderin** *f* murderess and robber; **~möwe** *f Orn.* skua; **~pressung** *f* pirate pressing, bootleg; **~ritter** *m hist.* robber baron

Raubtier *n Zool.* predator, beast of prey; **~fütterung** *f* feeding of wild beasts; *umg. fig. hum.* feeding of the hordes (of children); **~gehege** *n* predators' enclosure

Raub|überfall *m*: (*bewaffneter*) *~* (armed) robbery, holdup; *auf Person*: *auch* mugging; *auf Bank*: raid; **~vogel** *m Orn.* bird of prey; **~wild** *n Zool.* predators *Pl.* hunted as game; **~zug** *m* (*Überfall*) predatory attack, raid; (*Serie von Überfällen*) series of raids (*od.* forays); *auf ~ gehen* go raiding

Rauch *m; -(e)s, kein Pl.* smoke; (*Dunst, von Säuren etc.*) fumes *Pl.*; *dichter/ beißender ~* thick (*od.* dense) / acrid smoke; *Schinken etc. im ~* go to ham *etc.*; (*Fleisch*) *in den ~ hängen* smoke; *kein ~ ohne Feuer fig.* there's no smoke without fire, where there's smoke there's fire; *sich in ~ auflösen fig.* go up in smoke; *Pläne*: be wrecked (*od.* ruined); **~abzug** *m Heizkeller*: smoke outlet (*od.* extract); *Wohnzelt*: smoke outlet; **~bier** *n* smoked beer; **~bombe** *f* smoke bomb

rauchen I. *v/i.* (*Rauch abgeben*) smoke, give off smoke; *bes. Gase, Dämpfe*: fume; *es raucht* there's some smoke; *der Ofen/Schornstein raucht* the

stove/chimney is smoking; *mir rauchte der Kopf* my head started spinning; **II.** *vt/i.* (*Tabak*) smoke; *~ Sie?* do you smoke?; *Pfeife/Zigarre ~* smoke a pipe/cigar; *eine ~ umg.* have a smoke; *hast du was zu ~?* have you got a smoke?; *auf Lunge ~* inhale (when smoking); *passiv ~* smoke passively; *er raucht stark od. wie ein Schlot umg.* he's a heavy smoker, he smokes a lot (*od.* like a chimney); *Sie sollten weniger ~ / aufhören zu ~* you should smoke less / stop smoking

Rauchen *n; -s, kein Pl.* smoking; *~ verboten!* no smoking; *~ unerwünscht* smoking is discouraged; *das ~ aufgeben od. sich das ~ abgewöhnen* give up smoking; *~ gefährdet die Gesundheit* smoking is a danger to health

Rauchentwicklung *f* formation of smoke, smoke development

Raucher *m; -s, -* **1.** smoker; *ein starker ~ sein* be a heavy smoker; **2.** (*Abteil*) smoking compartment, smoker *umg.*; *ist hier ~?* is this a smoker?

Raucheraal *m Gastr.* smoked eel

Raucher|abteil *n* → *Raucher* 2; **~bein** *n Med.* smoker's leg; *fachspr.* claudication; **~besteck** *n* smoker's companion

Raucherei *f* food curing establishment, smokehouse

Räucher|fass *n* → *Rauchfass*; **~fisch** *m Gastr.* smoked fish; **~gefäß** *n* censer

Raucherhusten *m Med.* smoker's cough

Raucherin *f* → *Raucher* 1

Räucher|kammer *f Gastr.* smokehouse; **~kerze** *f* aromatic (*od.* scented) candle; *zur Desinfektion*: fumigating candle

Raucherkrebs *m Med.* smoker's (*od.* smoking-related) cancer

Räucherlachs *m Gastr.* smoked salmon

Raucherlunge *f Med.* smoker's lung

Räuchermännchen *n usually wooden figure containing an aromatic candle or joss* (*Am. incense*) *stick*

räuchern I. *v/t.* **1.** *Gastr.* (*Fleisch, Fisch etc.*) smoke, cure; *kalt/heiß ~* cure s.th. cold/hot; **2.** *desinfizierend*: fumigate; **II.** *v/i.* burn incense

Räucherofen *m Gastr.* curing oven

Raucherrisiko *n* risk taken by smokers

Räucher|schinken *m Gastr.* smoked ham; **~stäbchen** *n* joss (*Am. incense*) stick

Räucherung *f* **1.** *Gastr., von Fleisch, Fisch etc.*: smoking, curing; **2.** *desinfizierend*: fumigation

Räucherware *f Gastr.* smoked meat and fish products *Pl.*

Raucherzimmer *n* smoking room

Rauch|fahne *f* smoke trail; **~fang** *m* **1.** chimney hood; **2.** *österr.* (*Schornstein*) chimney

rauchfarben *Adj.* smoke-colo(u)red

Rauch|fass *n Reli. für Weihrauch*: censer; **~fleisch** *n Gastr.* smoked meat; (*Pökelfleisch*) salt meat, *Am. auch* jerky

rauchfrei *Adj.* **1.** (*rauchentwicklungsfrei*) smokeless; *~es Gebiet* smokeless zone; **2.** (*nicht für Raucher*): *~e Zone im Restaurant etc.*: no-smoking area (*od.* part)

Rauch|gas *n* flue (*od.* smoke) gas; **~gasfilter** *m od. n* electrostatic precipitator; **⚥geschwärzt** *Adj.* black with smoke; **~glas** *n* smoked glass

rauchig *Adj.* smoky *Stimme*: husky

Rauch|kanal *m* (chimney) flue; **~klap-**

pe f am Zelt: smoke flap; **~kringel** m smoke ring; **Ǝlos** Adj. smokeless; **~melder** m smoke detector; **~pilz** m mushroom cloud; **~quarz** m smoky quartz, cairngorm, smoke-stone; **~säule** f pillar of smoke; **~schwaden** Pl. billows of smoke; **~schwalbe** f Orn. (barn od. chimney) swallow; **~tabak** m smoking tobacco; **~tisch** m smoker's table; **~topas** m Min. smoky topaz; **~verbot** n ban on smoking; **hier herrscht ~** there's no smoking allowed here; **~vergiftung** f Med. smoke poisoning; **~verzehrer** m air freshener

Rauchwaren¹ Pl. tobacco products
Rauchwaren² Pl. (Pelze) furs
Rauch|werk n; nur Sg.; (Pelze) furs Pl.; **~wolke** f cloud of smoke; **~zeichen** n smoke signal
Räude f; -, -n; Vet. mange; **räudig** Adj. Vet. mangy; **du ~er Hund!** pej. you filthy scum!
rauen v/t. rough(en); (Tuch) tease, nap
rauf umg. Adv., **rauf...** im V. 1. → heraus...; 2. → hinauf...
Raufasertapete f woodchip paper
Raufbold m; -(e)s, -e ruffian
raufen I. v/t. pull (out); → Haar 1; **II.** v/i. und v/refl.: (sich ~) scuffle, brawl, tussle; **sie rauften sich um den Ball** they were fighting (od. scrapping) for the ball; **Rauferei** f; -, -en fight, brawl, scrap; **rauflustig** Adj. pugnacious; **~ sein** auch love to scrap
Raufutter n roughage
rauh → rau
Rauhaardackel m Zool. wire-haired dachshund; **rauhaarig** Adj. wire--haired
Rauheit f roughness; severity; harshness; coarseness etc.; → rau
Raum m; -(e)s, Räume 1. (Zimmer) room; 2. nur Sg.; (Platz) space, room; **viel ~ beanspruchen** take up a lot of space; **auf engstem ~ leben** live in cramped surroundings; **luftleerer ~** vacuum; 3. (Gegend, Gebiet) area; (Ausdehnung) expanse; **im ~ München** in the Munich area; **im süddeutschen ~** in southern Germany; 4. Phys., Philos. (auch Weltraum) space; **der offene** (od. leere) **~** the void; 5. nur Sg.; (Volumen) volume; (Fläche) area; 6. mst Sport (Platz auf Spielfeld) space; **freier ~** Sport open space; **den ~ decken** mark space; 7. nur Sg.; fig. (Spielraum) scope, room; **es nahm in der Diskussion e-n breiten ~ ein** it occupied a large part of the discussion; **~ geben** od. **gewähren** (e-m Gedanken) give way to; (e-r Hoffnung) entertain; (e-r Bitte) grant; **das Problem steht im ~** the problem demands an answer; **ich möchte die Frage einfach in den ~ stellen** I'd just like to throw up (od. pose) the question (for discussion)

...raum m, im Subst. 1. allg. (Zimmer) room; **Büro~** office; **Keller~** basement room; **Vor~** anteroom; 2. (Gebiet): **Wirtschafts~** industrial area
Raum|akustik f acoustics Pl. (of a od. the room); **~anzug** m spacesuit
Räumarbeiten Pl. → Räumungsarbeiten
Raum|aufteilung f division of space; **~ausnutzung** f use of space; **~ausstatter** m; -s, -, **~ausstatterin** f; -, -nen interior decorator; **~ausstattung** f (Vorgang) interior decoration; (Ergebnis) auch interior (of a room); **~bedarf** m required space, space required; **~bildverfahren** n Opt. stereoscopy; **~deckung** f Sport zone mark-ing

räumen I. v/t. 1. (fortschaffen) clear away, remove; **Minen ~** clear mines; **vom Meer auch:** sweep mines; **etw. in den Schrank ~** put s.th. away in the cupboard; **aus dem Weg ~** (etw.) clear (od. get) s.th. out of the way; fig. (Schwierigkeiten) get rid of, clear up; (Probleme) auch solve, remove; umg. fig. (j-n) eliminate allg.; 2. (Wohnung) move out of; formell: vacate; (Hotelzimmer) check out of; (Saal etc., auch Unfallstelle etc.) clear; (Schublade, Schreibtisch etc.) clear out; (Gebiet) evacuate, Mil. (aufgeben) auch leave; Mil. (Stellung) leave, retreat from; Wirts. (Lager) clear, sell off; **j-m den Platz ~** give s.o. one's seat; fig. make way for s.o.; **den Saal ~ lassen** Richter: have the court cleared; **s-e Stelle ~** leave one's position; **wir ~** (machen Räumungsverkauf) we are having a clearance; **II.** v/i. Dial. (aufräumen) clear up
Raumersparnis f saving of (od. in) space
Raum|fähre f Raumf. space shuttle; **~fahrer** m, **~fahrerin** f astronaut, männlich auch umg.: spaceman, weiblich auch umg.: spacewoman, bes. sowjetisch od. russisch: cosmonaut
Raumfahrt f Raumf. 1. space travel; 2. (Wissenschaft) astronautics (V. im Sg.); **~behörde** f space agency; **~geschichte** f history of space travel; **~medizin** f space medicine; **~pionier** m pioneer in space; **~programm** n space program(me); **~technik** f space technology; **~techniker** m, **~technikerin** f space engineer; **~zentrum** n space cent|re (Am. -er)
Raumfahrzeug n Raumf. spacecraft, spaceship
Räumfahrzeug n bulldozer; für Schnee: snowplough, Am. snowplow
Raum|flug m Raumf. space flight; **~forschung** f (aero)space research
Raum|gestalter m, **~gestalterin** f interior designer
raumgreifend Adj.: **~e Schritte** long strides
Raum|heizer m, **~heizgerät** n space heater; **~heizung** f space heating; **~inhalt** m volume, capacity
Raumkapsel f Raumf. space capsule
Raum|klang m stereophonic sound; **~klima** n room temperature and air quality, indoor climate
Räumkommando n detachment for clear-up operations
Raum|kunst f; nur Sg. (art of) interior design; **~kurve** f Math. skew curve
Raumlabor n space laboratory; (der Europäischen Weltraumbehörde) Spacelab
räumlich I. Adj. spatial, space ...; (dreidimensional) three-dimensional; **~e Enge** cramped conditions Pl.; **~e Wirkung** e-s Bildes: depth, three-dimensionality; **~es Sehen** three-dimensional vision; **~er Klang** stereophonic sound; **II.** Adv.: **~ sehen** see things three-dimensionally; **~ sehr beengt** cramped (for space)
Räumlichkeit f 1. mst Pl. (Raum) room; **die passenden ~en** suitable accommodation Sg. (Am. accommodations); 2. Malerei: depth, three-dimensionality
Raum|luftbelastung f indoor air pollution; **~mangel** m lack of space (od. room); restricted space; **~maß** n solid measure; **~meter** m, n cubic met|re

(Am. -er) measure (made of logs); konkret: cubic met|re (Am. -er); **~ordnung** f, **~ordnungsplan** m Pol. development plan; **~pfleger** m cleaner; **~pflegerin** f cleaning lady; **~planung** f Pol. development plan
Räumschaufel f (e-s Räumfahrzeugs) shovel
Raum|schiff n Raumf. spaceship; **~schutzanlage** f burglar/fire alarm system; **~sonde** f Raumf. space probe; **~station** f Raumf. space station (od. platform); **~strahlung** f Raumf. cosmic (od. space) radiation; **~teiler** m room divider, partition; **~temperatur** f room temperature; **~transporter** m Raumf. space shuttle
Räumtrupp m clearance gang (od. workers)
Räumung f 1. (Wegschaffen) removal; 2. (Leermachen) clearing; von Baugelände, Wald etc.: land clearing; bes. Wirts. clearance; **Ausverkauf wegen ~** clearance sale; 3. e-r Wohnung etc.: vacating; zwangsweise: eviction; 4. e-s Gebiets, auch Mil. evacuation
Räumungs|arbeiten Pl. clean-up operation(s); **~befehl** m eviction order; **~klage** f action for possession (Am. eviction); **~verkauf** m clearance sale
Raum|vorstellung f three-dimensional vision; **~-Zeit-Welt** f Phys. space-time continuum
Raunächte Pl. twelve nights of Christmas
raunen I. vt/i. whisper, murmur (beide auch fig.); **man raunte etwas von ...** there was some vague talk of ...; **II. Raunen** n; -s, kein Pl. whispering, murmur(ing)
Raupe f; -, -n 1. caterpillar; von Käferlarve: grub; 2. Tech. (Planierraupe) caterpillar-tracked (od. tracklaying) vehicle, caterpillar ®; (Raupenkette) caterpillar track
Raupen|befall m Agr. attack by caterpillars, infestation of caterpillars; **~fahrzeug** n Tech. caterpillar-tracked (od. tracklaying) vehicle; **~fraß** m Agr. caterpillar damage; **~kette** f Tech. caterpillar track; **~schlepper** m Tech. caterpillar (od. tracklaying) tractor
Raureif m white frost, hoarfrost
raus Adv. umg.: **~** (hier)! (get) out!, scram! Sl.; (hauen wir ab!) let's beat it!; **~ mit euch!** in den Garten etc.: (come on,) out you go; aus dem Auto etc.: (come on,) out you get (Am. come); **~ damit** od. **mit der Sprache!** (come on,) out with it!, spit it out!
raus... im V. 1. → heraus...; → auch rausschmeißen; 2. → hinaus...; → auch rausfeuern, rausfliegen
Rausch m; -es, Räusche intoxication, drunkenness; (von Drogen) high umg.; fig. delirious state; (auch Raserei) frenzy; (vor Glück etc.) rapture, exhilaration; **sich e-n ~ antrinken** get drunk; **s-n ~ ausschlafen** sleep it off; **im ~** under the influence (of alcohol); **im ~ der Geschwindigkeit** intoxicated (od. drunk) with speed; **im ~ der Begeisterung** carried away by one's enthusiasm, in a fit of enthusiasm; **im ~ der Leidenschaft** seized with (a burning) passion
Rauschabstand m Hi-Fi etc.: signal--to-noise ratio
rauscharm Adj. low-noise
Rauschebart m umg. hum. 1. flowing beard; 2. (bärtiger Mann) bearded wonder
rauschen v/i. 1. (hat) Wasser: rush;

Bach: murmur; *Brandung, Sturm*: roar; *Blätter, Seide etc.*: rustle; *Beifall*: ring, thunder; **es rauscht im Radio** there's (a lot of) interference (*od.* static) on the radio; **2.** (*ist*) *fig.* (*schwungvoll gehen*) sweep, sail; **sie rauschte beleidigt aus dem Zimmer** she swept out of the room in a huff; **Rauschen** *n*; *-s, nur Sg.*; *Phys.* (random *od.* background) noise; **rauschend I.** *Part. Präs.* → **rauschen; II.** *Adj.* **~er Beifall** rapturous applause; **~es Fest** lavish party (*od.* celebration); **e-e ~e Ballnacht** a glittering night at the ball

Rausch|faktor *m Hi-Fi etc.*: noise factor; **~filter** *n* noise filter (*od.* suppressor)

Rauschgift *n* narcotic, drug; *Koll.* narcotics *Pl.*, drugs *Pl.*; **~bekämpfung** *f* fight against drugs; **~dezernat** *n* narcotics (*od.* drug) squad; **~handel** *m* drug trafficking; **~händler** *m*, **~händlerin** *f* drug dealer

Rauschgiftsucht *f* drug addiction; **rauschgiftsüchtig** *Adj.* drug-addicted; *präd. auch* on drugs, addicted to drugs; **Rauschgiftsüchtige** *m, f*; *-n, -n* drug addict

Rauschgold *n* imitation gold foil

rauschhaft *Adj.* ecstatic

Rauschmittel *n* intoxicant; (*Rauschgift*) drug, narcotic

Rauschnarkose *f* short-term an(a)esthesia

Rauschsperre *f Hi-Fi etc.*: noise gate

Rauschunterdrückungssystem *n Hi-Fi etc.*: noise reduction system

Rauschzustand *m* intoxicated state, state of intoxication

rausekeln *v/t.* (*trennb., hat -ge-*) *umg.* freeze out

rausfeuern *v/t.* (*trennb., hat -ge-*) *umg.* (*entlassen*) fire, give *s.o.* the sack (*od.* boot)

rausfliegen *v/i.* (*unreg., trennb., ist -ge-*) *umg.* be kicked (*od.* booted, chucked, turfed) out; *aus e-r Stellung: auch* get the sack (*od.* boot)

raushalten (*unreg., trennb., hat -ge-*) *umg.* **I.** *v/refl.:* **sich aus etw. ~** keep out of s.th.; **sich da ~** keep out of it; **halt dich da raus!** *wohlmeinend*: don't get involved; *verärgert*: keep your nose out!; **II.** *v/t.* keep *s.o.* (*od. s.th.*) out of it; **~ aus etw.** keep *s.o.* (*od. s.th.*) out of s.th.

rauskriegen *v/t.* (*trennb., hat -ge-*) *umg.* → **herausbekommen**

räuspern *v/refl.* clear one's throat; **Räuspern** *n*; *-s, kein Pl.*: **ein lautes ~** a loud clearing of the throat

rausreißen *v/t.* (*unreg., trennb., hat -ge-*) *umg.* → **herausreißen**

rausschmeißen *v/t.* (*unreg., trennb., hat -ge-*) *umg.* throw out, chuck out; (*j-n*) *auch* kick out (*alle aus* of); (*entlassen*) *auch* fire *allg.*, give *s.o.* the boot; **Rausschmeißer** *m*; *-s, -*, **Rausschmeißerin** *f*; *-, -nen*; *umg.* bouncer *allg.*; **Rausschmiss** *m umg.* sacking, the boot

rausspringen *umg.* → **herausspringen**

Raute *f*; *-, -n* **1.** *Bot.* rue; **2.** *Math.* rhomb(us); *Her.* lozenge; (*Kartenfarbe*) diamond

rautenförmig *Adj.* diamond-shaped; **Rautenmuster** *n* diamond (knitting) pattern

Razzia *f*; *-, Razzien* (police) raid, police roundup, swoop *umg.*; **e-e ~ machen** make a raid (*auf + Akk.* on); **e-e ~ in** (+ *Dat.*) *od.* **auf** (+ *Akk.*) *veranstalten auch* raid, swoop on *umg.*

Re *n*; *-s, -s*; (*Skat*) redouble

Reagenz *n*; *-es, Reagenzien*; *Chem.* reagent; **~glas** *n* test tube; **~papier** *n* test paper

reagieren *v/i.* **1.** react (*auf + Akk.* to); *auch auf Behandlung etc.*: respond (to); **nicht ~ auf** (+ *Akk.*) (*nicht beachten*) ignore; **sie reagierte blitzschnell und verhinderte e-n Unfall** her reactions were lightning fast and prevented an accident; **ich bin gespannt, wie er darauf ~ wird** I wonder what he'll say (*od.* how he'll take it); **2.** *Chem.* react (**mit** with; **auf** + *Akk.* on)

Reaktion *f*; *-, -en* **1.** reaction (**auf** + *Akk.* to); *Med. auch* response (to), (*Reflex*) reflex; **wie** did she react (*od.* take it)?; **j-s gefühlsmäßige ~ auf etw.** s.o.'s gut reaction to s.th.; **2.** *Chem.* reaction (**mit** with; **auf** + *Akk.* on); **3.** *Pol.* reaction; **die Kräfte** *od.* **Vertreter der ~** reactionary forces, the forces of reaction

reaktionär *Adj.*, **Reaktionär** *m*; *-s, -e*, **Reaktionärin** *f*; *-, -nen*; *Pol.* reactionary

Reaktionsbehälter *m Chem. Tech.* autoclave

reaktionsfähig *Adj.* **1.** able to react, responsive; **2.** *Chem.* reactive; **Reaktionsfähigkeit** *f* **1.** reactions *Pl.*; **e-e gute ~ haben** have fast reactions; **2.** *Chem.* reactivity; *Tech.* (*e-s Sensors etc.*) responsivity

reaktionsfreudig *Adj. Chem.* reactive

Reaktionsgeschwindigkeit *f Chem.* reaction rate

reaktions|schnell *Adj.*: **~ sein** have fast reactions; **~träge** *Adj. Chem.* inert, weakly responsive

Reaktions|vermögen *n* → **Reaktionsfähigkeit; ~wärme** *m Chem.* heat of reaction; **~zeit** *f* reaction (*od.* response) time

reaktivieren *v/t.* (*Menschen*) recall, bring back (out of retirement) (*Schiff etc.*) recommission; *Med.* (*Glied*) rehabilitate; *Chem.* reactivate; **Reaktivierung** *f e-s Menschen*: recall; *e-s Schiffes etc.* recommissioning; *Med. e-s Gliedes*: rehabilitation; *Chem.* reactivation

Reaktor *m*; *-s, -en* reactor; → **anfahren** I 5, **herunterfahren** II 2, **hochfahren** II 3, **stilllegen** 1; **~gebäude** *n* reactor housing (*od.* dome), concrete sheet; **~gift** *n* toxin emanating from a nuclear reactor; **~kern** *m* reactor core; **~technik** *f* reactor technology; **~unfall** *m* reactor accident; **~unglück** *n* reactor disaster

real *Adj.* (*wirklich*) real; (*konkret*) concrete; (*realistisch*) realistic; *Wirts.* real; **~ existierender Sozialismus** *hist. iro.* real-life socialism

Real|einkommen *n* real income (*od.* earnings); **~gymnasium** *n altm.* secondary school emphasizing science subjects, maths and modern languages; *GB etwa* grammar school, *USA etwa* academic high school

Realien *Pl.* **1.** facts, realities; **2.** (*Sachkenntnisse*) expert knowledge *Sg.*

Realisation *f*; *-, kein Pl.* realization

realisierbar *Adj.* realizable; **der Plan ist nicht ~** the plan can't be put into practice; **realisieren I.** *v/t.* (*verwirklichen, begreifen*) realize; *Wirts. auch* convert into money; **II.** *v/refl.* materialize, be realized; **Realisierung** *f* realization; **Realismus** *m*; *-, kein Pl.* realism; **Sozialistischer ~** *Kunst, Lit.* so-

cialist realism; **Realist** *m*; *-en, -en*, **Realistin** *f*; *-, -nen* realist; **realistisch I.** *Adj.* realistic; **II.** *Adv.* realistically

Realität *f*; *-, -en* reality, *Pl.* (*Tatsachen*) *auch* facts; **in der ~** in real life; (*in Wirklichkeit*) in reality; **die ~ e-r Sache bezweifeln** doubt that s.th. really exists, doubt the reality of s.th.

realitäts|bezogen *Adj.* realistic; **~fern** *Adj.* unrealistic; *Person: auch* out of touch with reality; **~fremd** *Adj.* out of touch (with reality); **~nah** *Adj.* close to reality; *auch Person*: realistic

Realitäts|sinn *m* sense of reality; **~verlust** *m Psych.* derealization

Reality-TV [-ti:vi:] *n*; *-(s), kein Pl.* real-life television, *Am.* reality TV

Real|kapital *n Fin., Wirts.* physical assets *Pl.*, non-monetary capital; **~katalog** *m* subject catalogue; **~kredit** *m Fin.* real estate loan; **~last** *f* recurrent charge on real estate; **~lexikon** *n* (specialist) encyclop(a)edia; **~lohn** *m* real wage

Realo *m*; *-s, -s*; *Pol.* pragmatic Green

Realpolitik *f* realpolitik, political realism; **Realpolitiker** *m*, **Realpolitikerin** *f* political pragmatist; **realpolitisch** *Adj.* pragmatic, *präd.* realpolitik

Real|produkt *n Wirts.* real product; **~satire** *f* reality with the appearance of satire, realistic satire

Real|schulabschluss *m Päd. leaving certificate from a Realschule*; **~schule** *f secondary school leading to intermediate qualification*; *GB: etwa* middle school, *USA: etwa* middle (*od.* junior high) school; **~schüler** *m*, **~schülerin** *f* Realschule pupil

Real|steuer *f*; *mst Pl* (personal) property tax; **~union** *f Pol.* real union; **~wert** *m* real value

Realzeit *f EDV* real time; **~verarbeitung** *f* real-time processing

Reanimation *f Med.* reanimation; **reanimieren** *v/t.* reanimate

Reaumur ['rɛːomyːɐ] *n*; *nur Nom.*; (*abgek.* **R**) Réaumur; **80° R** 80°R; **~skala** *f* Réaumur scale

Reb|anlage *f* plantation of vines; **~berg** *m schw.* vineyard

Rebe *f*; *-, -n*; (*Weinranke*) vine tendril (*od.* shoot); (*Weinstock*) vine; *poet.* grape; **in den ~n arbeiten** work in the vineyards

Rebell *m*; *-en, -en* rebel (*auch fig.*); **Rebellen...** *im Subst.*: *Armee etc.* rebel; **rebellieren** *v/i.* rebel (*auch fig.*); **~de Studenten** rebellious students; **mein Magen rebelliert** my stomach is objecting (*od.* playing up); **Rebellin** *f*; *-, -nen* rebel; **Rebellion** *f*; *-, -en* rebellion; **rebellisch** *Adj.* rebellious (*auch fig.*); **~ werden** be up in arms; *Kinder*: start to play up; **j-n ~ machen** have s.o. up in arms

Rebensaft *m lit.* juice of the vine, wine

Rebfläche *f* area planted with vines

Rebhuhn ['reːphuːn] *n Orn.* partridge

Reb|land *n* land planted with vines; **~laus** *f Zool.* phylloxera; **~sorte** *f* type of grape; **~stock** *m* vine; **~terrasse** *f* vineyard terrace

Rebus *m*; *-, -se* rebus, picture puzzle

Rechaud [re'ʃoː] *m*; *n*; *-s, -s* warming plate; *Fondue*: burner, réchaud

Rechen I. *m*; *-s, -*; rake; **II. rechen** *vt/i.* rake (up); **Laub rechen** rake up leaves; **e-n Weg rechen** rake a path

Rechen|anlage *f* computer (system); **~art** *f* (type of) arithmetical operation; **~aufgabe** *f* sum; *schwierige*: arithmetical problem; **~buch** *n* arithmetic book; **~exempel** *n*: *ein einfaches ~* (a matter of) simple arithmetic; **~fehler** *m* mistake, miscalculation; **~genie** *n* mathematical genius; **~geschwindig-keit** *f Computer*: computing speed; **~kapazität** *f Computer*: computing capacity; **~künstler** *m*, **~künstlerin** *f* mathematical wizard; **~maschine** *f* calculator

Rechenschaft *f*: (*j-m*) *~ ablegen über* (*+ Akk.*) account (to s.o.) for; *j-m ~ schuldig sein od. schulden* be answerable (*od.* accountable) to s.o.; *zur ~ ziehen* call to account (*wegen* for *od.* over)

Rechenschafts|bericht *m* report, statement; **~pflicht** *f* obligation to account for one's actions; **⊋pflichtig** *Adj.* obliged to account for one's actions

Rechen|schieber *m Math., veraltet* slide rule; **~stift** *m fig.*: *den ~ ansetzen* do one's sums; **~technik** *f* **1.** *Math.* arithmetic technique; **2.** *EDV* computer technology; **~unterricht** *m* arithmetic teaching; (*Stunden*) arithmetic lessons; **~werk** *n Computer*: arithmetic unit; **~zeichen** *n* arithmetic sign; **~zentrum** *n* computer cent|re (*Am.* -er)

Recherche [re'ʃɛrʃə] *f*, -, -n investigation, inquiry; **recherchieren** [reʃɛr-'ʃiːrən] *vt/i.* investigate; *wissenschaftlich*: (do) research; (*Fall etc.*) investigate; (*Thema*) research, do research into

rechnen I. *v/i.* **1.** *Math.* calculate, make a calculation; *Päd. auch* do sums (*Am.* addition); *bei schwierigen Aufgaben*: do one's arithmetic; *richtig/falsch ~* calculate correctly /miscalculate; *gut/ nicht ~ können* be good / no good at figures; **2.** (*veranschlagen*) reckon, estimate; *grob gerechnet* at a rough estimate (*od.* guess); **3.** (*berechnen*) charge; *du kannst ja selbst ~!* work it out for yourself, *Am.* do the math; *von Montag an gerechnet* as from Monday; **4.** (*sparsam sein*) economize; *er kann nicht ~* (*mit Geld umgehen*) he doesn't know how to handle money; **5.** *~ auf* (*+ Akk.*) *od. mit* (*sich verlassen auf*) reckon (*od.* count *od.* rely) on; (*erwarten*) reckon with, expect; *ich rechne mit d-r Hilfe / d-m Verständnis* I'm counting on your help / I hope you'll understand; *mit mir brauchst du nicht zu ~!* count me out; *mit dir hatte ich* (*noch*) *gar nicht gerechnet* I hadn't expected you at all; *man muss mit allem / dem Schlimmsten ~* one must be prepared for anything / for the worst; *mit ihm wird man ~ müssen* he's one to look out for in the future; **6.** (*zählen*) count; *~ zu* count (*od.* rank) among; **II.** *v/t.* **1.** *Math.* calculate, work out; *e-e Aufgabe ~* work out a problem; *etw. schriftlich / im Kopf ~* work s.th. out on paper / in one's head; **2.** (*veranschlagen*) reckon (on), estimate; (*berücksichtigen*) take into account; *ich habe zwei Tassen Kaffee für jeden gerechnet* I've allowed for two cups of coffee each; *wir ~ für die Fahrt vier Stunden* we reckon on the journey will take (us) four hours (*od.* it'll take four hours to get there); *die Kinder nicht gerechnet* not counting the children; *alles in allem gerechnet* all in all; *j-n ~ zu* count (*od.* rank *od.* rate) s.o. among; **III.** *v/refl. umg.* bring in some money, pay off

Rechnen *n*; *-s*, *kein Pl.*; *Päd.* arithmetic

Rechner *m*; *-s*, - **1.** *er ist ein guter/ schlechter ~* he's good / no good at figures; **2.** (*Rechenmaschine*) calculator; (*Computer*) computer

rechner|gesteuert *Adj.* computer-controlled, computerized; **~gestützt** *Adj.* computer-aided

Rechnerin *f*; -, -nen → **Rechner** 1

rechnerisch I. *Adj.* mathematical, arithmetical; *~e Lösung* mathematical solution; **II.** *Adv.* mathematically, arithmetically; by way of calculation; *rein ~ gesehen* purely in terms of figures; *~ ist es zwar in Ordnung, aber...* it's OK as far as the figures go (*od.* the numbers look good) but ...

Rechnung *f*, -, *-en* **1.** (*Berechnung*) calculation; *richtige/falsche ~* correct calculation /miscalculation; *die ~ geht nicht auf* it doesn't work out; **2.** *für Waren, Dienstleistungen etc.*: bill; *Am., im Gasthaus*: check; *von Firma, Dienstleister auch*: invoice; *e-e ~ ausstellen* make out a bill (*od.* an invoice); *e-e ~ abschließen* close an account; *e-e fällige ~* a bill (*od.* an account) payable; *e-e ~ über 600 Euro* a bill (*od.* invoice) for 600 euros; *auf ~* on account (*od.* credit); *j-m etw. in ~ stellen* charge s.th. to s.o.'s account, charge (*od.* invoice) s.o. for s.th.; *laut ~* as per invoice; *e-e ~ begleichen* settle an account, pay a bill, clear an invoice; *e-e alte ~ zu begleichen haben* fig. have an account to settle (*mit* with); *etw. in ~ stellen od. e-r Sache ~ tragen* fig. take s.th. into account (*od.* consideration), make allowances for s.th.; *die ~, bitte!* can I have the bill (*Am.* check) please?; *das geht auf m-e ~* im Gasthaus: I'll see to that, it's on me umg.; *das geht auf s-e ~* fig. that's his doing; *die ~ ohne den Wirt machen* fig. get one's sums (*Am.* figures) wrong; *ich werde ihm die ~ präsentieren* fig. I'll make him pay for that; → *Strich* 1, *ausstellen* I 2

Rechnungs|abgrenzung *f Wirts.* deferral; **~amt** *n* audit office; **~betrag** *m* invoice total (*od.* amount); **~buch** *n* accounts book; **~einheit** *f* accounting unit; **~führer** *m*, **~führerin** *f* chief accountant; **~hof** *m*, **~jahr** *n* financial (*od.* fiscal) year; **~nummer** *f* invoice number; **~posten** *m* item, entry; **~prüfer** *m*, **~prüferin** *f* auditor; **~summe** *f* amount payable; **~wesen** *n* accountancy

recht¹ *Adj.* (*Ggs. link*) right; *~e Hand* right hand; *fig. auch* right-hand man; *~er Hand* (*rechts*) on the right; → **Rechte¹**

recht² **I. 1.** (*richtig*) right; *am ~en Ort* in the right place; *vom ~en Weg abkommen* lose one's way; *fig.* go off the rails, stray from the straight and narrow; *ich habe keinen ~en Appetit* I don't really feel like eating anything; *ganz ~!* quite right!, *Am.* absolutely!; *so ist's ~* that's right, that's the stuff umg.; *das ist nur ~ und billig* it's only fair (*od.* right and proper); *das ist alles ~ und schön, aber ...* that's all very well, but ...; *alles was ~ ist!* fair's fair; (*das geht zu weit*) you can go too far, there's a limit; *schon ~!* all right, *Am. umg.* alright; *was dem einen ~ ist, ist dem andern billig* what's sauce (*Am.* good) for the goose is sauce (*Am.* good) for the gander; **2.** (*passend, angebracht*) right, proper, suita-

ble; **3.** (*gesetzmäßig*) lawful, legitimate; **4.** (*wirklich*) true, real; *ein ~er Narr* a right (*Am.* complete) fool; **5.** (*gut*) good; **6.** *Pol.* right-wing, rightist; **7.** *Math.*: *~er Winkel* right angle; **8.** (*akzeptabel*) all right, *Am. umg.* alright; *mir ist's ~* I don't mind, it's all right (*Am. umg.* alright) with me, (it) suits me; *ihm ist jedes Mittel ~* he'll stop (stick umg.) at nothing; **9.** *subst.*: *nach dem Rechten sehen* make sure everything's all right (*Am. umg.* alright); *es war nichts Rechtes* it wasn't the real thing; *nichts Rechtes gelernt haben* have learnt (*Am.* learned) no proper trade; *aus ihm kann ja nichts Rechtes werden* he will never come to anything; *nichts Rechtes mit j-m/etw. anzufangen wissen* not know what to do with s.o./s.th.; → *Recht, richtig, Ding* 2, *Licht* 2, *schlecht* II 1; **II.** *Adv.* **1.** (*richtig*) properly; *~ daran tun zu* (*+ Inf.*) do right to (*+ Inf.*); *es geschieht ihr ~* it serves her right; *sie will es allen ~ machen* she wants to please everybody; *dir kann man auch nichts ~ machen* one can't do anything right for you, everything I do is wrong (for you); *ich weiß nicht ~* I'm not sure, I really don't know; *wenn ich es mir ~ überlege* when I think about it; *wenn ich Sie ~ verstehe* if I understand you right(ly); *ich seh wohl nicht ~!* I must be seeing things; *ich hör wohl nicht ~!* I can't believe what you're saying, say that again; (*das kann nicht dein Ernst sein*) you can't be serious; *du kommst mir gerade ~* just the person I want; *iro.* you're the last person I wanted (to see); **2.** (*sehr*) very; (*ziemlich*) rather, *bes. Am.* somewhat, pretty umg.; *~ geschickt* rather (*od.* very) clever, *Am. umg.* pretty smart; *~ gut* pretty good (*od.* well); *erst ~* all the more (so)

Recht *n*; *-(e)s, -e*; (*Gesetze*) law; (*Anspruch, Berechtigung*) right; (*Vollmacht, Befugnis*) authority; *bürgerliches/öffentliches ~* civil/public law; *~ und Ordnung* law and order; *nach geltendem ~* under existing law; *nach deutschem ~* under German law; *alle ~e vorbehalten* all rights reserved; *etw. mit vollem ~ tun* have every right to do s.th.; *von ~s wegen* by rights; *Jur.* by law; *~ sprechen* administer justice; *das ~ haben zu* (*+ Inf.*) have the right (*od.* be entitled) to (*+ Inf.*); *Bevollmächtigter*: be empowered to (*+ Inf.*); *~ haben* be right; *j-m ~ geben* concede (*widerwillig*: admit) that s.o. is right; *er hat* (*wieder*) *~ behalten* he was proved (to be) right (again); *im ~ sein, das ~ auf s-r Seite haben* be in the right; *das ~ auf Streik* the right to strike; *das ~ auf freie Meinungsäußerung* the right of free speech; *gleiches ~ für alle* equal rights for all; *auf s-m ~ bestehen* assert one's rights; (*wieder*) *zu s-m ~ kommen* come into one's own (again); *ich nehme mir das ~ zu* (*+ Inf.*) I take it upon myself to (*+ Inf.*); *mit welchem ~ tut er das?* what right has he got to do that?; *zu ~* rightly; *allein stehend*: rightly so; *zwischen ~ und Unrecht unterscheiden können* know right from wrong

...recht *n, im Subst.* **1.** (*Recht auf etwas*): *Anwesenheits~* right to be present; *Aufenthalts~* right of residence; **2.** *Rechtsnorm*: law

Rechte¹ *f*; -n, -n; *nur Sg.* (*Hand*) right hand; *Boxen*: right; *zur ~n* to (*od.* on)

the right

Rechte[2] *m, f; -n, -n* **1.** *Pol.* right-winger, rightist; *ein Sammelbecken der ~n* a den of right-wingers; **2.** *Pol. nur Sg. the* right; *e-r Partei*: right wing

Rechteck *n; -s, -e* rectangle; **rechteckig** *Adj.* rectangular

rechtens: *~ sein* be perfectly (*od.* quite) legal; *es war nicht ~, dass sie ihm kündigten* they weren't right (*od.* it wasn't right for them) to give him the sack

rechtfertigen I. *v/t.* justify; (*berechtigen*) *auch* warrant; *nicht zu ~(d)* unjustifiable, indefensible; *das rechtfertigt noch lange nicht so ein Benehmen* this is no kind of justification for such behavio(u)r; **II.** *v/refl.* vindicate (*od.* justify) o.s.; (*Rede und Antwort stehen*) give an account of o.s.; *sich wegen etw. ~ müssen* have to find some justification for s.th.; → *gerechtfertigt*

Rechtfertigung *f* justification; *zu m-r ~* in my defen|ce (*Am.* -se); *dafür gibt es keine ~* nothing can justify that **Rechtfertigungs|grund** *m* justification; *was lässt sich als ~ anführen?* what can be said in justification?; *~versuch* *m* attempt at justification **rechtgläubig** *Adj.* orthodox

Recht|haber *m; -s, -; pej.* opinionated person; (*Besserwisser*) know-all, *Am.* know-it-all; *~haberei f; -, kein Pl.; pej.* opinionated (*od.* know-all, *Am.* know-it-all) attitude; *~haberin f; -, -nen; pej.* → *Rechthaber*
rechthaberisch *Adj. pej.* opinionated, dogmatic; *ihre ~e Art* the way they always insist they're right (*od.* they know best)

rechtlich I. *Adj.* legal; (*rechtmäßig*) *auch* lawful, legitimate; *~e Grundlagen* legal grounds; **II.** *Adv.* legally *etc.*; *~ zulässig* permissible in law, lawful; *~ bindend* legally binding; *~ verpflichtet* bound by law; *er ist ~ verpflichtet zu* (+ *Inf.*) he is under a legal obligation to (+ *Inf.*)

rechtlos *Adj.* **1.** (*ohne Rechte*) *Person*: without rights; (*vogelfrei*) outlawed; *die ~e Stellung der Sklaven* the slaves' lack of rights; **2.** (*gesetzlos*) *Zustand*: lawless; **Rechtlosigkeit f 1.** *e-s Menschen*: lack of rights; **2.** (*Gesetzlosigkeit*) lawlessness

rechtmäßig *Adj.* lawful, legal; *Anspruch, Besitzer, Erbe*: legitimate, rightful; **Rechtmäßigkeit** *f* legality, legitimacy, lawfulness

rechts I. *Adv.* on the right(-hand side); (*nach ~*) (to the) right; *~ von* to the right of; *~ von ihm* on (*od.* to) his right; *~ oben/unten* top/bottom right, at the top/bottom on the right; *erste Querstraße ~* first turn(ing) on the right; *sich ~ halten, ~ fahren od. gehen* keep to the right; *~ überholen* overtake (*Am.* pass) on the right; *~ stehen Pol.* be on the right, be a right-winger; *~ stehend* right-wing; *~ wählen* vote for the right; **II.** *Präp.* (+ *Gen.*) on (*od.* to) the right of; *~ des Mains* on the right bank of the Main; *~ der Mitte Pol.* right of cent|re (*Am.* -er)

Rechts|abbieger *m Verk.* car *etc.* turning right, *Pl.* traffic *Sg.* turning right; *~abbiegespur f* right-hand turn(ing) (*od.* turn-off) lane
Rechtsabteilung *f* legal department
Rechtsabweichler *m, ~in f Pol.* right-wing deviationist

Rechts|angelegenheit *f Jur.* legal matter; *~anspruch m* legal claim (*auf + Akk.* on, to), (legal) right (to); *auf Eigentum an Land etc.*: title (to)
Rechts|anwalt *m, ~anwältin f Jur.* lawyer, *Brit. auch* solicitor; *plädierender: Brit.* barrister, *Am.* attorney; *sich e-n Rechtsanwalt nehmen* get oneself a lawyer (*Brit. auch* solicitor, *Am. auch* attorney); *~anwaltsbüro n* lawyer's (*Brit. auch* solicitor's, *Am. auch* attorney's) office; (*Firma*) law firm; *~anwaltschaft f the* bar
**Rechtsanwalts|gehilfin f Jur.* legal secretary; *~kammer f* law society; *in den USA*: Bar Association; *~kanzlei f* → *Rechtsanwaltsbüro*
**Rechts|auffassung f Jur.* conception (*od.* interpretation) of the law; *~ausschuss m Pol.* committee on legal affairs, judiciary committee
Rechtsaußen *m; -, -* **1.** *Fußball*: right wing, outside right; **2.** *Pol.* extreme right-winger
Rechts|behelf m (legal) remedy; *~beistand m* (*Rat*) legal advice; (*Person*) legal adviser and representative; *~belehrung f Jur.* **1.** instructions *Pl.* on rights of appeal; **2.** *der Geschworenen*: directions *Pl.*, *Am.* instruction (of the jury); **3.** *weitS.* legal information; *~berater m, ~beraterin f* legal adviser; *~beratung f* legal advice; *~beschwerde f* appeal; *~bewusstsein n* perversion of justice; *~bewusstsein n* sense of what is right (*od.* of right and wrong); *~brecher m, ~brecherin f* lawbreaker; *~bruch m* breach of law
rechtsbündig *Adj. Druck.* flush right, right-justified
rechtschaffen I. *Adj.* honest, upright; **II.** *Adv.* honestly; *~ leben* live an honest life; *sich ~ um etw. bemühen* make a genuine effort to achieve s.th.; *~ müde umg.* really tired; **Rechtschaffenheit** *f* uprightness, honesty; *formell*: probity
rechtschreiben I. *v/i. nur Inf.*: spell; **II. Rechtschreiben** *n* spelling; *im Rechtschreiben schwach sein* be bad at spelling (*od.* a bad speller)
Rechtschreib|fehler *m* spelling mistake; *~korrektur f* **1.** correction of spelling; **2.** → *Rechtschreibkorrekturprogramm*; *~korrekturprogramm n EDV* spellchecker; *~prüfung f EDV*: *automatische ~* automatic spellcheck; *~reform f* spelling (*od.* orthographic) reform; *~regel f* spelling rule; *~streit m* dispute over spelling
Rechtschreibung *f; nur Sg.* spelling, orthography; *in der ~ sicher sein* be confident about one's spelling; *die Regeln der ~ beherrschen* know the spelling rules
Rechtsdrall *m* right-hand twist; *e-s Wagens*: pull to the right; *fig. Pol.* rightist tendencies *Pl.*
rechtsdrehend *Adj. Chem.* dextrorotatory, dextrogyrate; **Rechtsdrehung** *f* turn to the right
Rechts|einwand *m Jur.* objection, demurrer *fachspr.*; *~empfinden n* sense of justice
rechtserheblich *Adj. Jur.* legally relevant
rechtsextrem *Adj. Pol.* extreme right-wing; **Rechtsextremismus** *m* right-wing extremism; **Rechtsextremist** *m*, **Rechtsextremistin** *f* right-wing extremist
rechts|fähig *Adj. Jur.*: *~ sein* have legal capacity *förm.*, be legally responsi-

ble; *~e Organisation* organization having legal capacity; **Rechtsfähigkeit** *f* legal capacity
Rechts|fall *m Jur.* (law) case; *~frage f* legal issue; point of law; *Ⴟfrei Adj. Jur.*: *~er Raum* unlegislated area; *~gefühl n* sense of justice; *~gelehrte m, f* legal scholar
rechtsgerichtet *Adj. Pol.* right-wing
**Rechts|geschäft n Jur.* legal transaction; *~geschichte f* history of law; *e-s Falles*: legal history
Rechtsgewinde *n Tech.* right-handed thread
Rechtsgrundlage *f* legal grounds *Pl*
rechtsgültig *Adj.* valid; *Vertrag etc.*: legally effective; → *rechtskräftig*
Rechts|gut n legally protected right; *~gutachten n* (legal) opinion, counsel's opinion
Rechtshänder *m; -s, -,* **Rechtshänderin** *f; -, -nen* right-hander; *er ist Rechtshänder* he's right-handed; **rechtshändig** *Adj.* right-handed; *Schlag etc.*: right-hand ...; **Rechtshändigkeit** *f* right-handedness
Rechtshandlung *f Jur.* legal act
rechtsherum *Adv.* clockwise; (*nach rechts*) (to the) right
Rechtshilfe *f Jur.* (*zwischen zwei Staaten*: mutual) assistance in law enforcement
Rechtskoalition *f Pol.* right-wing coalition
Rechtskraft *f; nur Sg. Jur.* legal force, validity; **rechtskräftig** *Adj.* legal(ly binding); *Urteil*: final; *~ werden* come into force, become effective; *er ist ~ verurteilt* final sentence has been passed on him
rechtskundig *Adj.* legally qualified
Rechtskurs *m* **1.** *Pol.* rightist policy (*schwächer*: tendencies *Pl.*); **2.** *beim Pferderennen*: right-handed course
Rechtskurve *f* right-hand bend; *e-e ~ machen Straße, Fahrzeug*: make a right turn, turn to the right
Rechtslage *f Jur.* legal position (*od.* situation)
rechtslastig *Adj.*: *~ sein* lean (*bes. Naut.* list) to the right; *fig. politisch*: lean towards the right, have rightist tendencies (*od.* leanings)
Rechtslehre *f Jur.* jurisprudence
Rechtslenker *m Mot.* right-hand drive vehicle
Rechtsmittel *n Jur.* legal remedy; *bes. bei höherer Instanz*: (right of) appeal; *~ einlegen* lodge an appeal; *~belehrung (des Klägers) f* instructions *Pl.* on (the defendant's) right(s) of appeal
Rechts|nachfolge *f Jur.* legal succession; *die ~ antreten* succeed to s.o.'s rights and obligations; *~nachfolger m, ~nachfolgerin f* legal successor; *~norm f* legal norm; *~ordnung f* legal system
rechtsorientiert *Adj. Pol.* rightist; *~ sein* have right-wing views; **Rechtsorientierung** *f* right-wing views *Pl.*; **Rechtspartei** *f* right-wing party, party of the right
Rechts|pflege *f Jur.* administration of justice; *~pfleger m, ~pflegerin f* judicial officer; *~philosophie f* philosophy of law
Rechtsprechung *f; nur Sg.; Jur.* **1.** *Koll.* administration of justice; **2.** *die ~* the judiciary
rechtsradikal *Adj. Pol. attr.* extreme right wing; *~ sein auch* be a right-wing extremist; **Rechtsradikale** *m, f; -n, -n* right-wing extremist; **Rechtsradika-**

R

lismus m right-wing extremism

Rechtsreform f Jur. legal reform

Rechtsregierung f Pol. right-wing government

rechtsrheinisch Geog. **I.** Adj. to the right of the Rhine; *das ~e Ufer* the right bank of the Rhine; **II.** Adv. to the right of the Rhine; (*am Ufer*) on the right bank of the Rhine; *~ gelegen* situated to the right (*od.* on the right bank) of the Rhine

Rechts|ruck m, **~rutsch** m Pol. swing to the right

Rechtssache f Jur. (legal) case

Rechtsschutz m Jur. legal protection

rechtsschutzversichert Adj. Jur. insured for legal costs; **Rechtsschutzversicherung** f legal costs insurance

Rechtsschwenk m Pol. swing to the right

rechtsseitig I. Adj. attr. right; *auch* präd. on the right(-hand side); (*Lähmung:* of the right side; **II.** Adv. befahren etc.:* on the right(-hand side); → *gelähmt*

Rechts|sicherheit f Jur. legal security; **~sprache** f legal language (*od.* terminology); **~spruch** m in Zivilsachen: judg(e)ment; in Strafsachen: sentence; von Geschworenen: verdict

Rechtsstaat m Pol. constitutional state; **rechtsstaatlich** Adj. constitutional; **Rechtsstaatlichkeit** f rule of law

Rechtsstandpunkt m Jur. legal point of view

rechts stehend Adj. → *rechts* I

Rechtsstellung f Jur. legal status (*od.* position)

Rechtssteuerung f Mot. right-hand drive

Rechts|streit m Jur. lawsuit, action, litigation; **~system** n judicial system; **~titel** m legal title

rechtsum Adv. Mil. to the right; *~ kehrt!* to the right, about turn!

rechtsungültig Adj. Jur. invalid; **Rechtsunsicherheit** f legal uncertainty; **rechtsunwirksam** Adj. (legally) ineffective

rechtsverbindlich Adj. legally binding (*für* [up]on); **Rechtsverbindlichkeit** f legally binding effect

Rechts|verdreher m umg. pettifogging lawyer, shyster umg.; **~verfahren** n legal procedure; (*Prozess*) (legal) action (*od.* proceedings Pl.); **~verhältnis** n legal relationship

Rechtsverkehr m Verk. right-hand traffic; *in Kanada ist ~* they drive on the right in Canada

Rechts|verletzung f Jur. infringement (of the law); **~verordnung** f statutory instrument; **~vertreter** m, **~vertreterin** f legal representative; (*Bevollmächtigte*) (authorized) agent; → *auch Rechtsanwalt*, **~vorschrift** f legal provision; **~weg** m legal process, course of law; *den ~ beschreiten* take legal action, go to court (*od.* law); *der ~ ist ausgeschlossen* there can be no recourse to litigation; *Wettbewerb:* the judges' decision is final

Rechtswendung f right turn; Pol. shift to the right

Rechtswesen n Jur. legal system

rechtswidrig Adj. Jur. illegal, unlawful, illicit; **Rechtswidrigkeit** f illegality, unlawfulness; (*Handlung*) illegal (*od.* unlawful) act

rechtswirksam Adj. → *rechtskräftig*; **Rechtswirksamkeit** f legal force (*od.* validity)

Rechtswissen|schaft f Jur. law, jurisprudence *förm.*; **~schaftler** m, **~schaftlerin** f jurist; **♀schaftlich** Adj. jurisprudential, juristic

rechtwink(e)lig I. Adj. right-angled; **II.** Adv.: *~ abzweigen* branch off at right angles

rechtzeitig I. Adj. (*zur rechten Zeit*) timely; (*pünktlich*) punctual; **II.** Adv. in time; (*pünktlich*) on time, punctually; (*früh genug*) in good time; *gerade noch ~* just in time; *ihr kommt gerade ~* you've come at just the right moment

Reck n; -(e)s, -e; Sport, Turnen: high (*od.* horizontal) bar; *am ~ turnen* exercise on the (high) bar

Recke m; -n, -n; lit. (*Krieger*) warrior

recken I. v/t. stretch; mit Geräten: rack; *den Hals nach etw. ~* crane one's neck to see s.th.; *den Arm in die Höhe ~* stretch one's arm upwards; **II.** v/refl.: *sich ~ und strecken* have a good stretch

Reck|stange f Sport high (*od.* horizontal) bar; **~turnen** n exercises Pl. on the (high) bar

Recorder [re'kɔrdɐ] m; -s, -; (tape, cassette *od.* video) recorder

recycelbar [riˈsaɪkəlbaːɐ] Adj. Öko. recyclable; **recyceln** [riˈsaɪkəln] v/t. recycle

Recycling [riˈsaɪklɪŋ] n; -s, kein Pl.; Öko. recycling; **~anlage** f recycling plant; **~papier** n recycled paper

Redakteur [redakˈtøːɐ] m; -s, -e, **~in** f; -, -nen editor; *verantwortlicher Redakteur* commissioning editor

...redakteur m, **~in** f, im Subst. ... editor

Redaktion f; -, -en **1.** (*Tätigkeit*) editing, editorial work; **~:** *Wolfgang W.* im Impressum etc.: edited by Wolfgang W.; **2.** (*Personal*) editorial staff (*mst V.* im Pl.*), editors Pl.; **3.** (*Büro*) editorial office (*od.* department); *in der ~* in the editorial department; *politische ~* politics department

...redaktion f, im Subst. **1.** (*Tätigkeit*) Schluss**~** final editing; **2.** (*Büro*) Anzeigen**~** advertising department; Bild**~** picture department; Kultur**~** cultural news department; **3.** (*Personal*) Zeitungs**~** editorial staff of a (*od.* the) newspaper

redaktionell I. Adj. editorial; **~er Teil** editorial section; **II.** Adv.: *~ bearbeiten* edit

Redaktions|konferenz f editorial meeting; **~leiter** m, **~leiterin** f head of the editorial department, managing editor; **~mitglied** n (editorial) staff member, sub-editor, Am. copy editor; **~räume** Pl. editorial offices; **~schluss** m copy deadline; *nach ~ eingegangen* stop-press (news); **~sitzung** f editorial meeting; **~statut** n working agreement between publishers and editors

Rede f; -, -n **1.** speech; (*Ansprache*) *auch* address; feierliche: oration; *die Freiheit der ~* the freedom of speecch; *die Kunst der ~* the art of rhetoric; *e-e ~ halten* make a speech; *keine langen ~n halten* come straight to the point, not beat about (*Am.* around) the bush; *j-m in die ~ fallen* interrupt s.o. (in mid-speech); (*große*) *~n schwingen* umg. talk big; *j-n mit leeren/schönen ~n hinhalten* put s.o. off with empty/fine words; *der langen ~ kurzer Sinn* to cut a long story short, in short, the long and the short of it;

2. (*Redeweise*) language, speech; *sich e-r sehr bildhaften ~ bedienen* make use of many metaphors; **3.** Ling. (*Sprechakt*) speech utterance; *die Unterscheidung von Sprache und ~* the distinction between language and speech; **4.** Gram. speech; *direkte/indirekte ~* Gram. direct/indirect (*od.* reported) speech; *erlebte ~* auch Lit. inner (*od.* interior) monologue; **5.** (*Gespräch*) talk; *die ~ bringen auf* (+ Akk.) bring s.th. up; *die ~ kam auf* (+ Akk.) the conversation turned to; *gerade war von dir die ~* we were just talking about you; *es ist die ~ von 100 Entlassungen* there is talk of 100 redundancies (*Am.* layoffs); *es war einmal die ~ davon, dass sie schließen* it was said at one time that they were closing down, there was talk at one time of their closing down; *es geht die ~, dass ...* rumo(u)r has it that ...; *davon kann keine ~ sein* (*das kommt nicht in Frage*) that's out of the question; (*darum geht es nicht*) that's not the point; *davon ist nicht die ~* that's not what I'm talking about; *davon war* (*gar*) *nicht die ~* that's not what it was all about; (*das kam nicht in Frage*) there was no question of that; *wovon ist die ~?* what are you (*od.* they) talking about?; *wovon ist eigentlich die ~?* what is this all about anyway?; (*das ist ja*) ~ umg. that's what I've been saying all along; *es ist nicht der ~ wert* it's hardly worth mentioning, it's nothing to speak of; *beim Danken:* don't mention it; (*j-m*) *~ und Antwort stehen* justify o.s. (to s.o.); *j-n zur ~ stellen* confront s.o.; (*vornehmen*) take s.o. to task (*wegen* for)

...rede f, im Subst.: Begrüßungs**~** welcome speech; Dankes**~** speech of thanks; Eröffnungs**~** inaugural (*od.* opening) speech (*od.* address)

Rede|duell n battle of words; **~figur** f figure of speech; **~fluss** m flow of words; *j-s ~ unterbrechen* interrupt s.o.'s flow; **~freiheit** f freedom of speech

redegewaltig Adj.: *~ sein* be a powerful speaker

redegewandt Adj. articulate, stärker: eloquent; bes. pej. glib; **Redegewandtheit** f eloquence, gift of speech

Redekunst f (art of) rhetoric

reden vt/i. **1.** (*sprechen*) speak (*mit* to, with); (*sich unterhalten*) talk (to, with); (*plaudern*) chat (to, with); *~ über* (+ Akk.) talk about; *stundenlang/ununterbrochen ~* talk for hours /incessantly; *sie redet zu laut/leise* she speaks too loudly/softly; *~ wir nicht mehr darüber* let's forget it; *man redet davon, dass ...* there is talk that ...; *darüber lässt sich ~* it's a possibility; *im Schlaf ~* talk in one's sleep; *er hat kein Wort geredet* he didn't say a word, he didn't open his mouth once; *rede doch* (*endlich*)! say something!; *mit sich selbst ~* talk to o.s.; *mit den Händen ~* gesticulate; *von ... gar nicht zu ~* not to mention ...; *da wir gerade davon ~* as we're on the subject; *er redet, wie er denkt* he says (exactly) what he thinks; *er redet anders, als er denkt* what he says and what he thinks are two different things; *du hast gut ~* it's all very well for you to talk, you can talk; *da redet man ja gegen e-e Wand* it's like talking to a brick wall; **2.** (*e-e Rede halten*) speak; *gut ~ können* be a good speaker; *er* *hört sich gern* ~ he likes the sound of his own voice; **3.** (*erörtern*) discuss; *über Politik* ~ talk politics; *über Gott und die Welt* ~ talk about everything under the sun; **4.** (*klatschen*) talk; *man redet über sie* people are talking about her; *im Büro wird viel geredet* there's a lot of gossip in the office; *er redet zu viel* he is a talker; **5.** ~ *mit* (*kommunizieren*) speak (*od.* talk) to; *sie* ~ *nicht miteinander* they're not speaking (*od.* talking) to each other, they're not on speaking terms; *mit sich* ~ *lassen* be willing to listen (*od.* discuss things); *bei Geschäft*: be open to offers; *sie lässt nicht mit sich* ~ she won't listen (to anyone); *so lasse ich nicht mit mir* ~ I won't be spoken to like that; *er weigert sich, mit uns zu* ~ he refuses to talk to us; *ich habe mit dir zu* ~ I'd like a word with you; *kannst du mal mit ihm* ~*?* can you have a word with him?; **6.** *pej.*: *er redet lauter Unsinn* he talks nothing but rubbish (*Am.* nonsense); *red keinen Quatsch!* *umg.* stop talking rubbish (*Am.* nonsense)!; *was redest du da?* what are you going on about?; **7.** *von sich* ~ *machen* (*bekannt werden*) get talked about; *er macht als Rennfahrer von sich* ~ he's made a name for himself as a racing driver (*Am.* racecar driver); *neulich hat er mit e-m Film von sich* ~ *gemacht* he recently got into the news with a film (*Am. auch* movie); **8.** *umg.* (*verraten*) talk; *irgendjemand hat geredet* someone has talked; **9.** *sich heiser* ~ talk oneself hoarse; *er redete sich in Zorn* he went on and on until he got really angry; → *auch sprechen*

Reden *n*; *-s*, *kein Pl.* talking; talk; *helser vom vielen* ~ hoarse from all this talking; *j-n zum* ~ *bringen* get s.o. to talk; *mit dem* ~ *tut er sich nicht schwer* he has no problems (*od.* inhibitions about) talking; *all mein* ~ *war umsonst* I might as well have been talking to a brick wall; ~ *ist Silber, Schweigen ist Gold Sprichw.* (speech is silvern,) silence is golden

Redensart *f* expression; *allgemeine* ~ common saying; *das ist nur so e-e* ~ it's just a figure of speech

Redenschreiber *m*, ~**in** *f* speechwriter

Rederei *f*, *-*, *-en*; *mst pej.* **1.** *nur Sg.* endless talk; *s-e ständige* ~ *ist unerträglich* his blathering (*od.* babbling) on is unbearable; **2.** (*Klatschgeschichte*) story; *all die* ~*en über* (+ *Akk.*) all the gossip (*od.* tittle-tattle) about; → *auch Gerede, Geschwätz*

Rede|schlacht *f* battle of words; ~**schwall** *m* torrent (*od.* flood) of words; ~**strom** *m* → *Redeschwall*; ~**talent** *n* **1.** talent as a speaker; **2.** (*Redner*) talented speaker; ~**übung** *f* speech-giving practice; ~**verbot** *n*: ~ *haben* be forbidden to speak; *j-m* ~ *erteilen* forbid s.o. to speak; ~**weise** *f* (manner of) speech, way of talking; ~**wendung** *f* figure of speech; (*idiomatische* ~) idiom, idiomatic expression; *feststehende* ~ set phrase; ~**zeit** *f* time allowed (*od.* allotted) for speakers; *die* ~ *überschreiten* speak over time

redigieren *vt/i.* edit

Rediskont *m*; *-s*, *-e*; *Fin.* rediscount; **rediskontieren** *vt/i. Fin.* rediscount

Redistribution *f*; *-*, *-en*; *Wirts.* redistribution of income

redlich I. *Adj.* honest; (*rechtschaffen*)

---

auch upright, square *umg.*; (*aufrichtig*) sincere, candid; **II.** *Adv.*: *sich* ~ *bemühen* do one's best, take great pains; ~ *teilen* divide fairly; *sich etw.* ~ *verdient haben* have really deserved s.th.; ~ *müde sein* be really tired; **Redlichkeit** *f* honesty, probity; uprightness; (*von Bürgern etc.*) worthiness; (*von Absichten etc.*) hono(u)rable nature, hono(u)rableness

Redner *m*; *-s*, *-* speaker; *ein guter/ schlechter* ~ a good/bad speaker; *kein großer* ~ *sein* not be much of a speaker; ~**bühne** *f* rostrum, dais; ~**gabe** *f* gift of oratory, gift of the gab *umg.*; **Rednerin** *f*; *-*, *-nen* → *Redner*, **rednerisch I.** *Adj.* rhetorical; **II.** *Adv.*: ~ *begabt sein* be a gifted speaker

Redner|liste *f* list of speakers; ~**podium** *n* podium; ~**pult** *n* lectern; ~**tribüne** *f* dais

Redoute [rɛˈduːtə] *f*; *-*, *-n* **1.** *hist. Mil.* redoubt; **2.** *österr. altm.* fancy-dress (*Am.* costume) ball; **3.** *altm.* grand hall

redselig *Adj.* talkative; loquacious *förm.*; garrulous *pej.*; **Redseligkeit** *f* talkativeness, loquacity *förm.*

Reduktion *f*; *-*, *-en* reduction (*auch Chem.*)

Reduktions|diät *f*, ~**kost** *f* slimming (*Am.* reducing) diet; ~**mittel** *n Chem.* reducing agent; ~**ofen** *m Chem.* smelting furnace

redundant *Adj.* redundant; **Redundanz** *f*; *-*, *kein Pl.* redundancy

Reduplikation *f*; *-*, *-en* reduplication

reduzieren I. *v/t. auch Chem., Math.* reduce (*auf* + *Akk.* to; *um* by); (*vermindern*) diminish; (*senken*) lower; (*Personal*) cut; *wir müssen unseren Ölverbrauch* ~ we must cut down on oil; **II.** *v/refl.* decrease (*auf* + *Akk.* to; *um* by); **Reduzierung** *f* reduction (*auf* + *Akk.* to; *um* by)

Reede *f*; *-*, *-n*; *Naut.* roadstead, roads *Pl.*; *auf* (*der*) ~ *liegen* be (lying) in the roads; **Reeder** *m*; *-s*, *-* shipowner; **Reederei** *f*; *-*, *-en* shipping company; **Reederin** *f*; *-*, *-nen* shipowner

reell I. *Adj.* **1.** *Person*: honest; *Firma*: solid, sound; *Gewinn*: solid; *Preis*: fair, realistic; ~*e Leistung* solid accomplishment; **2.** (*echt, wirklich*) real; ~*e Chance* real (*od.* genuine) chance; ~*e Zahl Math.* real number; **3.** *umg.* (*ordentlich*) *Portion etc.*: decent; *etw. Reelles* something worth having; (*etw. Sicheres*) something you can fall back on; **II.** *Adv.*: ~ *bedient werden* get decent service, *allg.* get one's money's worth

Reep *n nordd.* (*Tau*) rope

Reet *n*; *-s*, *kein Pl.*; *nordd.* reed(s *Pl.*); ~**dach** *n* roof thatched with reed; **reetgedeckt** *Adj.* thatched with reed

REFA|-Techniker *m*, ~**-Technikerin** *f Wirts.* time and motion study expert

Refektorium *n*; *-s*, *Refektorien*; *kirchl.*, *im Kloster*: refectory

Referat *n*; *-(e)s*, *-e* **1.** report (*auch mündlich*); (*Vortrag*) *auch* lecture, talk; *Päd., Univ.* (seminar) paper; *ein* ~ *halten Päd., Univ.* read (*od.* give, present) a paper; **2.** (*Dienststelle*) department, section; ~ *für Schulen und Sport* schools and sports department

Referatsleiter *m*, ~**in** *f* head of department (*od.* section), department (*od.* section) head

Referendar *m*; *-s*, *-e*; *im Staatsdienst* trainee; *Päd.* trainee teacher, *Am. auch* intern; *Jur.* junior lawyer (*od.* *Brit.* barrister), law (*od.* articled)

---

clerk; ~**ausbildung** *f*, **Referendariat** *n*; *-(e)s*, *-e* probationary training period; **Referendarin** *f*; *-*, *-nen* → *Referendar*, ~**zeit** *f* probationary (*od.* training) period, traineeship; *Päd.* teacher training; *Jur.* time under articles

Referendum *n*; *-s*, *Referenda od. Referenden*; *Pol.* referendum

Referent *m*; *-en*, *-en* **1.** (*Sprecher*) speaker; (*Berichterstatter*) *auch* reporter; *Jur., Parl.* referee; **2.** (*Sachbearbeiter*) adviser, consultant, expert; (*Referatsleiter*) head of a department (*od.* section); ~ *für Jugend und Sport* adviser for youth and sport; **3.** *Univ.* (*Gutachter*) examiner (of a doctoral thesis); **Referentenentwurf** *m Pol.* draft prepared by departmental advisers; **Referentin** *f*; *-*, *-nen* → *Referent*

Referenz *f*; *-*, *-en* reference; (*Person*) referee; *Pl.* (*Zeugnisse*) credentials; *darf ich Sie als* ~ *angeben?* may I use your name as a reference?, may I name you as a referee?

referieren *vt/i.* report (*über* + *Akk.* on); *in e-m Vortrag*: (give a) lecture (on); *bes. Univ.* give a paper (on); (*kurz*) *den Inhalt/Forschungsstand* ~ give a (brief) account of the content / status report on the research project

Reff¹ *n*; *-(e)s*, *-e* **1.** *Dial.* (*Tragekorb*) basket carried on the back, pannier; **2.** *umg., pej.* old hag

Reff² *n*; *-(e)s*, *-s*; *Naut.* reef; reefband; **reffen** *vt/i. Naut.* (*die Segel*) ~ reef sail

reflektieren *vt/i.* **1.** *Phys.* reflect; *dieses Glas reflektiert nicht* this glass is non-reflective; **2.** (*nachdenken*) reflect (*über* + *Akk.* [up]on); *etw. kritisch* ~ consider s.th. very carefully; **3.** *umg.*: ~ *auf* (+ *Akk.*) have one's eye on

Reflektor *m*; *-s*, *-en* reflector (*auch bei Scheinwerfer*), mirror; reflecting horizon

Reflex *m*; *-es*, *-e*; *Phys.* reflection; *Physiol., Psych.* reflex; *bedingter* ~ conditioned reflex; *unbedingter* ~ unconditioned reflex; *e-n* ~ *auslösen* produce a reflex; *gute* ~*e haben* have good reflexes; ~**bewegung** *f* reflex (action); ~**handlung** *f* reflex action

Reflexion *f*; *-*, *-en* **1.** *Phys.* reflection; **2.** (*Nachdenken*) reflection (*über* +*Akk.* [up]on); **Reflexionswinkel** *m Phys.* angle of reflection

reflexiv *Adj. Gram.* reflexive; **Reflexivpronomen** *n* reflexive (pronoun)

Reflex|zone *f Physiol.* reflexogenous zone; ~**zonenmassage** *f Med.* zone massage

Reform *f*; *-*, *-en* reform

Reformation *f*; *-*, *kein Pl.*; *Reli., hist.* Reformation

Reformations|fest *n*, ~**tag** *m kirchl.* Reformation Day; ~**zeit** *f hist.* age of the Reformation

Reformator *m*; *-s*, *-en*; *hist.* Reformer; **Reformatorin** *f*; *-*, *-nen* reformer, reformist

Reform|bedarf *m* need for reform; **reformbedürftig** *Adj.* in need of reform

Reform|bestrebungen *Pl.* reforming (*od.* reformatory) efforts; ~**bewegung** *f* reform movement

Reformer *m*; *-s*, *-*, ~**in** *f*; *-*, *-nen* reformer, reformist; **reformerisch** *Adj.* reformist

reformfreudig *Adj.* reform-minded; *stärker*: avid for reform

Reformhaus *n* health food shop (*Am.* store)

reformieren *v/t.* reform; **reformiert I.** *P.P.* → **reformieren**; **II.** *Adj. Kirche etc.*: Reformed; **Reformierte** *m, f; -n, -n; kirchl.* member of the Reformed Church

Reformismus *m; -, kein Pl.; Pol.* reformism; **reformistisch** *Adj.* reformist

Reform|kommunismus *m hist., Pol.* reform communism; **~kost** *f* health food(s *Pl.*); **~kurs** *m Pol.* reformist course; **auf ~ gehen** embark on a policy of reform; **~pädagogik** *f Päd. educational theory* favo(u)ring the promotion of the child's creativity; **~politik** *f Pol.* policy of reform, reformist policy; **~programm** *n* (*Maßnahmenbündel*) reform package; (*Konzept*) program (-me) of reform; **~stau** *m Pol.* reform logjam; (*Stillstand*) standstill on reforms; **~vorhaben** *n* proposed reforms *Pl.*; **~vorschlag** *m* proposal for reform; **~werk** *n* reforms *Pl.*

Refrain [rə'frɛ̃ː] *m; -s, -s; Mus.* refrain, chorus

Refraktion *f; -, -en; Opt.* refraction; **Refraktometer** *n; -s, -* refractometer

Refugium *n; -s, Refugien* sanctuary, (place of) refuge

Regal *n; -s, -e* **1.** (*an Wand etc.*) shelves *Pl.; Druck.* stand; **2.** *Mus.* (*Orgel*) regal; (*Orgelregister*) reed stop; **~brett** *n*, **~fach** *n* shelf; **~system** *n* shelving system; **~wand** *f* (*large*) wall unit; *nur Regale*: wall-to-wall shelving

Regatta *f; -, Regatten; Sport* regatta; (*einzelnes Rennen*) boat race

rege *Adj.* (*lebhaft*) lively; (*geschäftig*) busy; *Person: auch* active; (*munter*) alert; *Beteiligung etc.*: active; *Briefwechsel*: active; *Diskussion*: animated; *Geist*: active, alert; *Interesse*: lively, keen, active; *Phantasie*: vivid, fertile; **es herrschte ~r Verkehr** the roads were busy, traffic was heavy; **~ Nachfrage** brisk demand; **~ werden** stir; *Gefühle*: awaken, be stirred up; **er ist noch geistig ~** he's still very much with it (*od.* very much on the ball) *umg.*

Regel *f; -, -n* **1.** a) rule; (*Vorschrift auch*) regulation: (*Norm*) *auch* norm; (*Gewohnheit*) *auch* habit; **die ~n einhalten** observe (*od.* keep to) the rules; **gegen die ~(n) verstoßen** break the rules; **nach der ~** according to the rule; **in der ~** as a rule; **die ~ / schon fast die ~ sein** be the rule / almost always the case; **zur ~ werden** become a rule (*od.* habit); **sich etw. zur ~ machen** make it a rule to do s.th., make a habit of doing s.th.; → **Ausnahme**, b) **nach allen ~n der Kunst** (*gründlich, wie es sich gehört*) well and truly, good and proper; *besiegen*: in style; **man hat uns nach allen ~n der Kunst reingelegt** we were well and truly had; **2.** (*Menstruation*) period; *Koll.* periods *Pl.; **sie hat/bekommt ihre ~** she's got / is getting her period

Regel|anfrage *f Pol. query regarding the loyalty to the state of an applicant for a public service post*; **~arbeitszeit** *f* statutory working week

regelbar *Adj.* controllable, adjustable, *Am.* variable; **stufenlos ~** infinitely variable

Regel|blutung *f monthly period; Koll.* menstruation; **~buch** *n* rule book, book of rules; **~fall** *m* norm; **im ~ als a** rule; **~kreis** *m* control circuit; **~leistung** *f Sozialversicherung*: minimum social security benefit

regellos *Adj.* disorderly; (*unregelmäßig*) irregular, erratic; **es herrscht ein ~es Durcheinander** it's absolutely chaotic; **Regellosigkeit** *f* disorderliness; irregularity, erratic nature (+ *Gen.* of)

regelmäßig I. *Adj.* regular; *zeitlich: auch* periodical; (*geordnet*) regulated; **~er Gast** regular (guest); **~e Kirchgänger** (*Kunden, Besucher etc.*) *im jeweiligen Kontext*: regulars; **in ~en Abständen** at regular intervals; **II.** *Adv.* regularly; (*stets*) always, every time; **sie kommt ~ zu spät** she is always (*od.* forever) coming late, she keeps on coming late; **Regelmäßigkeit** *f* regularity; **in od. mit schöner ~** *iro.* with monotonous (*od.* persistent) regularity

regeln I. *v/t.* **1.** regulate; **den Verkehr ~** regulate (*od.* direct) the traffic; **2.** (*ordnen*) see to; (*erledigen*) settle; **es ist geregelt, wer wann was machen muss** there are rules laying down who should do what when; **ich regle alles** I put everything in order; **er wird das schon ~** he'll see to it (*od.* deal with it); **vor dem Urlaub gibt es noch einiges zu ~** there are still a few things to sort out before the holiday; **3.** *fachspr.* (*einstellen*) regulate, adjust; *auch* govern, control; **II.** *v/refl.* be regulated (*od.* governed) (*nach* by); **das wird sich schon (von selbst) ~** it'll sort itself out, it will come out right; → **geregelt**

Regelpult *n Tech.* control desk

regelrecht I. *Adj.* regular, proper; *umg.* (*ausgesprochen*) real, regular; *Katastrophe, Skandal*: absolute; **das ist ~er Betrug** this is simply fraud; **es war e-e ~e Unverschämtheit** it was downright (*od.* sheer) impertinence; **aus dem Streit wurde e-e ~e Schlägerei** the argument turned into a regular (*od.* an out-and-out) fight; **II.** *umg. Adv.*: **~ unmöglich etc.** absolutely impossible etc. allg.; **er ist ~ reingefallen** he really fell for it

Regel|satz *m Sozialhilfe*: basic (*od.* guideline) rate; **~schule** *f* standard school form; **~spur** *f Eisenb.* standard gauge; **~studienzeit** *f* (maximum) prescribed period of study; **~technik** *f* control engineering

Regelung *f* **1.** (*das Regeln*) regulation; **2.** (*Bestimmung*) arrangement, settlement; *im Gesetz, Vertrag*: provision; (*Richtlinie*) rule; **e-e einheitliche ~ finden** find an overall solution; **Regelungstechnik** *f* → **Regeltechnik**; **Regelungsvorschlag** *m* draft regulation

Regel|ventil *n Tech.* control valve; **~verstoß** *m Sport* → **Regelwidrigkeit**; **~werk** *n* complex of rules

regelwidrig I. *Adj.* irregular; *Sport* against the rules; **~es Spiel** foul play; **~er Einwurf** improperly executed throw-in; **II.** *Adv.*: **sich ~ verhalten** commit an infringement (*od.* offen|ce, *Am.* -se); **Regelwidrigkeit** *f* irregularity; *Sport* infringement, offen|ce (*Am.* -se); (*Foulspiel*) foul, unfair play

regen I. *v/refl.* stir, move; *Gefühl*: stir; **kein Lüftchen regte sich** there wasn't a breath of wind in the air; **bald regte sich erster Widerspruch** soon the first signs of opposition arose; → *auch* **rühren**; **II.** *v/t.* (*Finger etc.*) move; (*Blätter*) stir

Regen *m; -s, -, mst Sg.; Met.* rain; **leichter/starker ~** light/heavy rain; **bei strömendem ~** in pouring rain; **es sieht nach ~ aus** it looks like rain; **heute kriegen wir noch ~** we're in for

some rain today; **wir sind in den ~ gekommen** we got caught in the rain; **ein warmer ~** *fig.* a windfall; **j-n im ~ stehen lassen** *fig.* leave s.o. in the lurch; **vom ~ in die Traufe kommen** jump out of the frying pan into the fire; → **sauer** I 1

regenarm *Adj. Met., Geog.* dry; *fachspr., Gebiet*: low-precipitation ..., of low precipitation *präd.*, lacking (*od.* deficient) in rain

Regenbekleidung *f* rainwear

Regenbogen *m* rainbow; **~farben** *Pl.* colo(u)rs of the rainbow; **in allen ~ schillern** display all the colo(u)rs of the rainbow, be iridescent

regenbogenfarben, **regenbogenfarbig** *Adj.* rainbow-colo(u)red

Regenbogen|haut *f Anat.* iris; **~presse** *f umg.* trashy weeklies *Pl.*, trashy (*od.* pulp) magazines *Pl.*; **~trikot** *n Radsport*: rainbow jersey

Regendach *n* rain shelter, canopy; **regendicht** *Adj.* rainproof, waterproof

Regeneration *f; -, -en* regeneration; **regenerationsfähig** *Adj.* capable of regeneration, with regenerative powers; **Regenerationsfähigkeit** *f* regenerative ability (*od.* powers *Pl.*); **regenerieren I.** *vt/i.* regenerate; **s-e Kräfte ~** recover one's strength; **II.** *v/refl.* regenerate; (*sich erholen*) recover; **Regenerierung** *f* regeneration; **Regenerierungsfähigkeit** *f* regenerative ability (*od.* powers *Pl.*)

Regen|fälle *Pl.* rainfall *Sg.*, showers; **~front** *f* front carrying rain, storm front; **~gebiet** *n* area of rain

regenglatt *Adj.*: **auf ~er Straße** on a wet and slippery road

Regen|guss *m* heavy shower, downpour; **~haut** *f* plastic mac (*Am.* raincoat); **~kleidung** *f* rainwear; **~macher** *m* rainmaker; **~mantel** *m* raincoat, mac *Brit. umg.*; **~menge** *f* (amount of) rainfall; **~messer** *m* rain ga(u)ge

regennass *Adj.*: **auf ~er Straße** on a wet road

Regenpfeifer *m Orn.* plover

regenreich *Adj.* rainy, wet

Regen|rinne *f* gutter; **~rohr** *n* downpipe; **~schatten** *m Geog.* rain shadow; **~schauer** *m* (rain) shower; **~schirm** *m* umbrella; **ich bin gespannt wie ein ~** *umg.* I can't wait to find out (*od.* to hear what he says etc.) allg.; **~schreiber** *m Met.* rain gauge; **~schutz** *m* protection against the rain, weather protection

Regent *m; -en, -en* sovereign, ruler, monarch; *stellvertretender*: regent

Regentag *m* wet (*od.* rainy) day

Regentin *f; -, -nen* → **Regent**

Regen|tonne *f* water butt (*od.* barrel), *Am.* rain barrel; **~tropfen** *m* raindrop

Regentschaft *f eines Monarchen*: reign; *eines Regenten*: regency

Regen|umhang *m* rain cape, *Am.* poncho; **~wald** *m Geog.* rain forest; **tropischer ~** tropical rain forest; **~wasser** *n* rainwater, storm water; **~wetter** *n* wet (*od.* rainy) weather; **ein Gesicht machen wie 7 Tage ~** *umg.* make a face like a dying duck in a thunderstorm; **~wolke** *f* raincloud; **~wurm** *m* earthworm; **~zauber** *m* rain magic; **~zeit** *f* rainy season; **in den Tropen**: *auch* the rains *Pl.*

Reggae ['rɛgeː] *m; -(s), kein Pl.; Mus.* reggae

Regie [re'ʒiː] *f; -, kein Pl.; Theat., TV* production; *Film*: direction; (*Führung*) management; (*Verwaltung*) administration; **~ führen** *Theat.* produce; *Film:* direct (**bei etw.** s.th.); *fig. Sport (das Spiel bestimmen)* control the game; **unter der ~ von** directed by; **~:** ... *im Vorspann etc.:* Director: ...; **unter j-s ~** *Theat. etc.* produced by s.o.; *fig. (unter j-s Leitung)* under the management of s.o.; **Oscar für die beste ~** Oscar for best director; **etw. in eigener ~ machen** *fig.* do s.th. oneself (*od.* off one's own bat *Brit. umg.*)

Regie|anweisung *f Theat., TV* stage direction; **~assistent** *m*, **~assistentin** *f Film:* assistant director; *Theat.* assistant producer; **~assistenz** *f* work as an assistant director (*Theat.* assistant producer)

Regiebetrieb *m Wirts. publicly owned but independently run enterprise*

Regie|buch *n TV* director's (*Theat.* producer's) script; **~debut** [-deby:] *n Theat., TV: sein ~ geben* make one's debut as a director (*Theat.* producer); **~fehler** *m fig.* mistake, slip-up; **~pult** *n TV* control desk; **~raum** *m Funk.* (production) control room

regieren *vt/i.* govern (*auch Gram.*), rule; *Monarch etc.: auch* reign (over); **demokratisch regiert** democratically ruled (*od.* governed); **Königin Victoria regierte (Großbritannien) über 60 Jahre** Queen Victoria ruled (*od.* reigned) (over Great Britain) for more than 60 years; **der Regierende Bürgermeister von Berlin** the Governing Mayor of Berlin; **Terror und Korruption ~ das Land** terrorism and corruption reign in the country

Regierung *f Pol. (Kabinett)* government; (*Regierungszeit*) term of office; *e-s Königs etc.:* reign; **e-e demokratisch gewählte ~** a democratically elected government; **die ~ Bush** the Bush administration; **unter der ~ von Thatcher** *auch* under Thatcher; **an der ~** in power; **die ~ übernehmen** take power; *Kanzler etc.: auch* take office; *Monarch:* ascend the throne; **an die ~ kommen** come to power; *Kanzler etc.: auch* come into office; *Monarch:* come to (*od.* ascend) the throne; **an der ~ sein** be in power; *Kanzler etc.: auch* be in office; **die ~ stürzen** bring down the government; **e-e neue ~ bilden** form a new government

Regierungs|abkommen *n Pol.* agreement between governments, international agreement; **♀amtlich** *Adj.* official government ... *attr.;* **~anhänger** *m*, **~anhängerin** *f* government supporter; **~antritt** *m* coming into power, taking office; *e-s Monarchen:* accession to the throne; **bei s-m ~** when he came to power (*od.* took office); *Monarch:* when he ascended the throne; **~auftrag** *m* government order; **~bank** *f Parl.* government bench; **~beamte** *m, f* government official; **~bezirk** *m* primary administrative division of a *Land*, administrative district; *in GB: etwa* region; *in USA: etwa* county; **~bildung** *f* formation of a government; **sie erhielt den Auftrag zur ~** she was given the task of forming a government; **~bündnis** *n* coalition; **~chef** *m*, **~chefin** *f* head of government; **~delegation** *f* government delegation; **~direktor** *m*, **~direktorin** *f etwa* senior government official; **~ebene** *f: auf ~* at an intergovernmental level; **~erklärung** *f* government (*od.* policy) statement

regierungsfähig *Adj. Pol.* in a position to govern; **~e Mehrheit** working majority; **Regierungsfähigkeit** *f* capacity to govern

regierungsfeindlich *Pol.* **I.** *Adj.* oppositional, anti-government; **II.** *Adv.:* **sich ~ äußern** express anti-government sentiments

Regierungsform *f Pol.* (form of) government

regierungsfreundlich I. *Adj.* pro-government; **II.** *Adv.:* **sich ~ verhalten** *Presse etc.:* adopt a pro-government stance, support the government

Regierungs|gebäude *n* government building; **~geschäfte** *Pl.* government business *Sg.;* **die ~ führen** carry on government business; **~gewalt** *f* governmental power; **~koalition** *f* ruling coalition; **~kreise** *Pl.* government circles; **wie aus ~n verlautet** as is reported from government sources; **~krise** *f* government crisis; **~mannschaft** *f* government team; **~mitglied** *n* member of the government; **~neubildung** *f* formation of a new government; **es kommt zu e-r ~** there's going to be a change of government; **~partei** *f* ruling party; **~politik** *f* government policy; **~präsident** *m*, **~präsidentin** *f* chief administrative officer, chief executive (of an administrative district); **~rat** *m*, **~rätin** *f etwa* senior civil servant

Regierungsseite *f: von ~* from the government side

Regierungs|sitz *m* seat of government; **~sprecher** *m* government spokesperson (*männlich auch* spokesman); **~sprecherin** *f* government spokesperson (*od.* spokeswoman); **~system** *n* system of government

regierungstreu I. *Adj.* loyal to the government; **II.** *Adv.:* **sich ~ verhalten** remain loyal to the government

Regierungs|umbildung *f* cabinet reshuffle; **~verantwortung** *f: die ~ übernehmen** take over the responsibility of government, assume power; **~viertel** *n e-r Hauptstadt:* government quarter (*od.* district); **~vorlage** *f* government bill; **~wechsel** *m* change of government; **~zeit** *f* term of office; *e-es Monarchen:* reign

Regiestuhl *m TV* director's (*Theat.* producer's) chair

Regime [re'ʒi:m] *n; -s, -s od. -; Pol.* regime; *fig. (Leitung)* management; **~gegner** *m*, **~gegnerin** *f* opponent of the regime; **~kritik** *f* criticism of the regime; **~kritiker** *m*, **~kritikerin** *f* critic of the regime, dissident; **♀kritisch** *Adj.* critical of the regime, dissident

Regiment *n; -(e)s, -er od. -e* **1.** *Pl. -e;* (*Herrschaft*) government, rule; **das ~ führen** *fig.* be the boss, rule the roost; **sie führt das ~ im Haus** she wears the trousers (*Am.* pants); **ein strenges ~ führen** rule with a rod of iron; **2.** *Pl. -er; Mil.* regiment

Regiments|arzt *m*, **~ärztin** *f Mil.* regimental doctor; **~kommandeur** *m* regimental commander

Region *f; -, -en* region; *fig.:* **bestimmte ~en des Gehirns** certain areas of the brain; → **schweben** 1

...region *f, im Subst.* **1.** *Anat.* ... region; **2.** *Geog.* ... area

regional I. *Adj.* regional; **II.** *Adv.:* **~ begrenzt** restricted to a region (*od.* regions); **sich ~ unterscheiden** differ from region to region

Regional|ausgabe *f e-r Zeitung etc.:* regional issue (*od.* edition); **~bahn** *f Eisenb.* local railway (*Am.* railroad); **~express** *m Eisenb.* regional express; **~fernsehen** *n TV* regional (TV) programmes *Pl., Am.* local television; **~forschung** *f Pol.* regional studies *Pl.*

regionalisieren *v/t.* regionalize; **Regionalisierung** *f* regionalization

Regionalismus *m; -, Regionalismen; Pol.* regionalism

Regional|liga *f Sport* regional league; **~nachrichten** *Pl.* regional news *Sg., Am.* local news *Sg.;* **~presse** *f* local newspapers *Pl.;* **~programm** *n TV* regional programmes *Pl., Am.* local broadcasting; **~verkehr** *m Verk.* regional transport(ation); **~zug** *m Eisenb.* local train

Regisseur [reʒɪ'sø:ɐ] *m; -s, -e, ~in f; -, -nen; Theat., TV* producer; *Film:* director; **Regisseur im Mittelfeld** *Fußball:* playmaker in midfield

Register *n; -s, -* **1.** *im Buch:* index; → *auch Daumenregister;* **2.** (*Verzeichnis*) register (*auch EDV*), list; **3.** *Mus., e-r Orgel:* stop; **alle ~ ziehen** *fig.* pull out all the stops; **4.** *Druck.* register

Register|auszug *m* extract from a (*od.* the) register; **~band** *m* (bound) register; **~tonne** *f Naut. altm.* register ton

Registratur *f; -, -en* registry; *für Urkunden:* record office; (*Aktenschrank*) filing cabinet

Registrierballon *m Met.* weather balloon

registrieren *v/t.* register (*auch fig.*); *auch durch Apparate:* record; (*eintragen*) enter; **sich polizeilich ~ lassen** register with the police; **sie registrierte alles genau** *fig.* she was taking everything in, she didn't miss a thing; **es wurde von allen registriert** everyone noticed (it); **er hat es gar nicht registriert** it didn't even register with him

Registrierkasse *f* cash register

Registrierung *f* registration; (*Eintrag*) entry; *an Geräten:* reading(s *Pl.*)

Reglement [reglə'mã:] *n; -s, -s* regulations *Pl.*, rules *Pl.;* **gegen das ~ verstoßen** infringe the regulations; **reglementieren** *v/t.* regulate, regiment; **genau/streng reglementiert sein** be precisely/strictly regulated; **staatlich reglementierte Wirtschaft** state-controlled economy; **Reglementierung** *f* regimentation

Regler *m; -s, -; Tech.* regulator; *Etech.* control (knob)

reglos *Adj. und Adv.* motionless, still

regnen *v/i., unpers.* rain; *leicht:* drizzle; *heftig, in Strömen:* pour; **es fängt an / hört auf zu ~** it's beginning to rain / the rain is stopping; **es regnet stark** *od.* **in Strömen** it's pouring; **es regnete Kirschblüten** *fig.* it was raining cherry-blossoms; **es regnete Beschwerden** there was a flood of complaints, they were *etc.* inundated with complaints

Regner *m; -s, -* sprinkler

regnerisch I. *Adj.* rainy; **II.** *Adv.:* **der Tag begann ~** the day was wet to start with

Regress *m; -es, -e; Jur., Wirts.* redress, recourse; **j-n in ~ nehmen** have recourse against s.o.; **~anspruch** *m* claim of recourse; **~forderung** *f* recourse demand (*od.* claim)

Regression *f; -, -en* regression; **regressiv** *Adj.* regressive

Regresspflicht *f Jur., Wirts.* liability to recourse; **regresspflichtig** *Adj.* liable to recourse; **j-n ~ machen** render s.o. liable to recourse

regsam *Adj.* active, alert, lively

R

regulär I. *Adj.* regular; (*üblich*) usual, normal; (*gesetzlich*) legitimate; **II.** *Adv.*: ~ **verkaufen** *etc.* sell *etc.* at the normal (*od.* regular) price; **die Ware kostet ~** ... the normal (*od.* regular) price of this article is ...

Regularien *Pl.* standard items (on the agenda), usual business *Sg.*

regulativ I. *Adj.* regulative; **II. Regulativ** *n*; *-s, -e* regulative

Regulator *m*; *-s, -en* regulator; (*Pendeluhr*) adjustable pendulum clock

regulierbar *Adj.* adjustable; **regulieren I.** *v/t.* (*einstellen*) adjust, set; (*regeln*) regulate; (*Rechnung, Schaden*) settle; *Dent.*: **j-s Zähne ~ lassen** have s.o.'s teeth straightened; **II.** *v/refl.*: **sich** (**selbst**) ~ regulate itself; **Regulierung** *f* regulation; *Tech. auch* adjustment; *Wirts.* settlement

Regung *f* movement, motion; *Gefühl*: stirring; (*Anwandlung*) impulse; **e-r plötzlichen ~ folgend** on a sudden impulse; **keiner menschlichen ~ fähig** devoid of all human feeling; **den ~en des Herzens folgen** do what one's heart tells one, follow the dictates of one's heart; **er verspürte e-e menschliche ~ hum.** he had to answer a call of nature; **regungslos** *Adj. und Adv.* motionless, still

Reh *n*; *-(e)s, -e*; *Zool., allg.* (roe) deer; *Gastr.* venison; **ein scheues ~** a shy deer; *fig.* a timid person

Reha *f*; *-, -s*; *Abk.* **1.** → *Rehabilitation*; **2.** → *Rehaklinik*

Rehabilitand *m*; *-en, -en*, ~**in** *f*; *-, -nen* person undergoing rehabilitation; **Rehabilitation** *f*; *-, -en* rehabilitation (*auch Med. und sozial*), *Am. umg.* rehab

Rehabilitations|klinik *f* rehabilitation clinic; ~**zentrum** *n* rehabilitation cent|re (*Am.* -er)

rehabilitieren I. *v/t.* rehabilitate, *Am. umg.* rehab; **II.** *v/refl.*: **sich** (**voll**) ~ achieve (complete) rehabilitation; (*Ansehen wiederherstellen*) (completely) restore one's reputation; **Rehabilitierung** *f* → *Rehabilitation*

Reha|klinik *f Med.* rehabilitation clinic; ~**zentrum** *n* rehabilitation cent|re (*Am.* -er)

Reh|bock *m Zool.* roebuck; ~**braten** *m Gastr.* roast venison; 2**braun** *Adj.* light reddish brown; ~**geiß** *f Zool.* doe; ~**keule** *f Gastr.* leg of venison; ~**kitz** *n Zool.* fawn; ~**leder** *n* deerskin; ~**medaillon** *n Gastr.* medallion of venison; ~**rücken** *m Gastr.* saddle of venison; *fig.* (*Kuchen*) oblong cake with chocolate icing; ~**wild** *n Zool.* roe deer

Reibach *m*; *-s, kein Pl.*; *umg.*: **e-n großen ~ machen** make a big haul (*od.* killing); **den ~ teilen** divide the spoils *allg.*

Reibe *f*; *-, -n*; *Tech.* rasp; (*in der Küche*) grater

Reibeisen *n* **1.** *altm.* grater; **e-e Stimme wie ein ~** a grating (*od.* rasping) voice; **2.** *umg. pej.* (*Frau*) shrew

Reibekuchen *m Gastr.* potato pancake

Reibelaut *m Ling.* fricative

reiben; *reibt, rieb, hat gerieben* **I.** *vt/i.* rub; (*zerreiben*) grate; **etw. sauber/trocken ~** rub s.th. (until it is) clean/dry; **sich** (*Dat.*) **die Augen/Hände ~** rub one's eyes/hands; → *Nase*[1] 5; **II.** *v/refl. fig.*: **sich an j-m ~** not get on with s.o., quarrel with s.o., provoke s.o.; **sich aneinander ~** rub each other the wrong way

Reibereien *Pl.* (*Spannungen*) friction *Sg.*; (*Auseinandersetzungen*) brushes (*mit* with)

Reib|fläche *f* an Streichholzschachtel: striking surface; *e-r Reibe*: friction (*od.* scraping) surface; ~**käse** *m Gastr.* cheese for grating; (*gerieben*) grated cheese

Reibung *f* rubbing; *Tech.* friction (*auch fig.*)

Reibungs|elektrizität *f Phys.* frictional electricity; ~**fläche** *f fig.* cause (*od.* source) of friction

reibungslos I. *Adj.* smooth; **II.** *Adv.*: ~ **verlaufen** go off smoothly (*od.* without a hitch)

Reibungs|punkt *fig. m* cause (*od.* source) of friction; ~**verlust** *m* friction (-al) loss; ~**wärme** *f* frictional heat; ~**widerstand** *m* frictional resistance

reich I. *Adj.* rich (*auch Ernte, Farbe, Bodenschätze etc.*); (*wohlhabend*) *auch* wealthy, well-to-do; (*prächtig, üppig*) rich; *auch Mahl*: opulent; (*reichlich*) ample, abundant; *Leben*: full; *Phantasie*: rich, fertile; *Verzierungen*: rich, elaborate; ~ **an** (+ *Dat.*) rich in; ~**e Auswahl** wide selection; ... **in ~em Maße** in abundance, plenty of ...; ~ **an Erfahrungen sein** have experienced a lot (in one's life); **II.** *Adv.* richly; ~ **beschenkt** loaded with gifts; ~ **heiraten** marry (into) money; ~ **bebildert, ~ illustriert** lavishly illustrated; ~ **geschmückt** *Fassade, Innenraum etc.*: richly decorated

...reich *im Adj. mst* ...-rich; *präd. auch* rich in ...; **nährstoff~** nutrient-rich; *präd. auch* rich in nutrients

Reich *n*; *-(e)s, -e* empire (*auch fig.*); *lit.* realm (*auch fig.*); (*Königreich*) kingdom; **das Deutsche ~** *hist.* the (German) Reich; **das Dritte ~** *hist.* the Third Reich; **das ~ Gottes** *Reli.* the Kingdom of Heaven; **das ~ der Mitte** *hist.* (*China*) the Middle Kingdom; **das Weströmische/Oströmische ~** *hist.* the Western/Eastern (Roman) Empire; **das ~ der Natur** the natural world; **das ~ der Fantasie/Träume** the world of fantasy/dreams; **das ~ der Finsternis** the kingdom of darkness; **sein eigenes kleines ~ haben** *fig.* have one's own little kingdom (*od.* private world); → *Pflanzenreich, Tierreich*

Reiche *m, f*; *-n, -n*: **ein ~r** a rich man; **e-e ~** a rich woman; **die ~n** the rich *Pl.*

reichen I. *v/i.* **1.** a) (*sich räumlich erstrecken*) ~ **bis** reach (to); *hinauf*: reach (*od.* come) up to; *hinab*: reach (*od.* go) down to; **sie reicht ihm bis zur Schulter** she only comes up to his shoulder; **das Wasser reichte ihm bis zu den Schultern** the water was (*od.* came) up to his shoulders; **der Garten reicht bis zum Fluss** the garden stretches as far as (*od.* down to) the river; → *heranreichen, herankommen*, b) (*sich zeitlich erstrecken*) ~ **von ... bis** last (*od.* stretch) from ... till (*od.* until); **2.** a) (*ausreichen, genügen, langen*) be enough; **die Zeit wird nicht ~** there won't be enough time; **das Geld muss noch e-e Woche ~** the money has got to last another week; **das Gehalt reicht kaum zum Leben** the salary is barely enough to live on (*od.* to make ends meet), you can barely live off a salary like that; **es reicht für alle** there's enough to go (a)round (*od.* for everyone); **das Licht reicht nicht zum Lesen** there isn't enough light to read

by, you can't read in that light; **dazu reicht m-e Geduld nicht** I haven't got the patience for that (kind of thing); **das reicht!** that'll do; *rügend*: *auch* that's enough (of that)!; **mir reicht's!** *umg.* I've had enough; **jetzt reicht's mir aber!** *umg.* that's done it, that's it now, b) **mit etw. ~** *umg.* (*auskommen*) have enough of s.th. *allg.*; **mit dem Geld / der Zeit ~** have enough money/time; → *auch auskommen* 1, *ausreichen*; **II.** *v/t.* (*an-, darbieten*) offer; (*Essen*) serve; (*Abendmahl*) administer, give; (*geben*) hand, pass; **j-m etw. ~** hand (*od.* pass, give) s.o. s.th.; **reichst du mir bitte das Salz?** could you pass (me) the salt, please?; **nach dem Essen wurden Getränke gereicht** after the meal drinks were served; (*j-m*) **die Hand ~** hold out one's hand (to s.o.); **sich die Hände ~** shake hands

reichhaltig *Adj.* **1.** *Essen*: substantial; **2.** (*umfassend*) extensive; *Programm*: full; ~**e Informationen** a wealth of information; **Reichhaltigkeit** *f* extensiveness; *e-s Essens*: substantialness; *e-s Programms*: fullness; *von Informationen*: wealth

reichlich I. *Adj.* ample, plentiful; plenty of *time, food etc.*; *Bezahlung*: liberal, generous; **e-e ~e Stunde** a good hour; **II.** *Adv.* amply *etc.*; → I; *umg.* (*ziemlich*) pretty; ~ **versehen sein mit** have plenty of; **es dauert ~ zwei Tage** it will take a good two days; **du kommst ~ spät** *umg. iro.* you're a bit late(, aren't you?)

Reichs|acht *f hist* outlawry in the name of the Emperor; ~**adler** *m hist.* imperial eagle; ~**apfel** *m hist.* orb; ~**bahn** *f* **1.** *hist.* (German) national railway (*Am.* railroad); **2.** *ehem. DDR*: East German railway (*Am.* railroad); ~**deutsche** *m, f hist.* citizen of the (German) Reich; ~**gericht** *n hist.* supreme court of the (German) Reich; ~**gründung** *f hist.* foundation of the empire; *von 1871*: foundation of the German Reich; ~**hauptstadt** *f hist.* capital of the Reich, German capital; ~**insignien** *Pl. hist.* imperial insignia; ~**kanzlei** *f hist.* Chancellery of the Reich; ~**kanzler** *m hist.* Chancellor of the Reich; ~**kristallnacht** *f hist.* → *Kristallnacht*; ~**mark** *f hist.* reichsmark; ~**präsident** *m hist.* President of the Reich; ~**regierung** *f hist.* government of the (German) Reich; ~**stadt** *f hist.* free city (of the Holy Roman Empire); **freie ~** (imperial) free city; ~**tag** *m hist.* Reichstag; *im Mittelalter*: imperial diet; ~**verfassung** *f hist.* imperial constitution; ~**wehr** *f*; *nur Sg.*; *hist.* Army of the Reich, German Army, Reichswehr

Reichtum *m*; *-s, Reichtümer* riches *Pl.*, *auch fig.* wealth; *fig.* (*Fülle, Überfluss*) richness (*an* + *Dat.* in), abundance, affluence *förm.* (*an* + *Dat.* of); (*Vielfalt*) (great) variety; ~ **an Erfahrung(en)/Bodenschätzen** wealth of experience / richness in mineral resources

Reichweite *f* **1.** reach; *Mil., Funk., Flug. etc.*: range; (*Bereich, Aktionsradius*) radius (of action); **in/außer ~** within / out of reach (*Mil.* range); **immer in ~ haben** always have within reach (*od.* to hand); **noch nicht in ~ sein** *fig. Entscheidung etc.*: be not yet on the horizon; **2.** *Druck., e-r Buchauflage*: reprint period; **3.** *Wirts., e-s Werbemittels*: coverage

reif *Adj. Obst, Weichkäse etc.*: ripe; *Hartkäse, Wein: auch* mature; *Früchte, Wein, fig. Charakter, Wesensart*: mellow; *Mensch, Schönheit, Urteil, Plan*: mature; *Geschwür*: fully developed; **~ werden → reifen**; **körperlich/seelisch ~** physically/psychologically mature; **e-e ~e Frau** a mature woman; **~ für sein Alter sein** be mature for one's age; **noch nicht ~** (*genug*) **für** not yet ready (*od.* sufficiently experienced) for; **wenn die Zeit ~ ist** ... when the time is ripe ...; **ein Mann in ~eren Jahren** a man of mature age, a middle-aged man; **im ~en Alter von** at the ripe old age of; **~ sein für** (*Urlaub etc.*) be ready for; **~ fürs Irrenhaus** *umg.* fit for the loony bin; **~e Leistung** *umg. Sport etc.*: solid performance; *iro.* good show; **er ist ~** *umg.* he's in for it

Reif¹ *m; -(e)s, -e; lit.* (*Ring*) ring; (*Armreif*) bangle; (*Armband*) bracelet

Reif² *m; -(e)s, kein Pl.* white frost, hoarfrost

...reif *im Adj.* **1.** (*etw. verdienend*) **erholungs~** in need of a rest (*od.* recuperation); **2.** (*gut od. entwickelt genug*) **abfüll~** *Wein etc.*: ready for bottling; **ausführungs~** *Plan etc.*: ripe for execution; **fernseh~** *auch hum.* fit to be shown on television; **olympia~** good enough for the Olympics; **oscar~** deserving an Oscar

Reifbildung *f* formation of hoarfrost

Reife *f, -, kein Pl. von Obst, Käse etc.*: ripeness; *e-s Menschen, Plans, von Wein etc.*: maturity; **körperliche/geistige/seelische ~** physical/mental/psychological maturity; **mittlere ~** *Päd.; in USA*: intermediate high school certificate, *in GB: etwa* GCSEs *Pl.*; **dafür fehlt ihm** (*noch*) **die ~** he is not mature enough for that; **während der ~** (*beim Reifen*) *Obst etc.*: while ripening, during the ripening process; *Mensch*: during puberty

Reifegrad *m* degree of ripeness

reifen *v/i. Obst, Käse, etc.*: ripen; *Mensch, Plan, Wein etc.*: mature (**zu** into); *Med. Geschwür*: come to a head; **~ lassen** (*Käse*) leave to ripen; (*Wein etc.*) leave to mature; *fig.* (*Plan etc.*) develop; **in j-m ~** *Gedanke etc.*: start to form in s.o.'s mind; **zur Gewissheit ~** grow into certainty

Reifen *m; -s, -; Mot.* (*von Fahrrad*) tyre, *Am.* tire; (*Fass-, Kinder-, Zirkusreifen*) hoop; → **Reif¹**; **e-n ~ wechseln** *Mot.* change a tyre (*Am.* tire); **abgefahrene ~** worn tyres (*Am.* tires); **mit quietschenden ~** with tyres (*Am.* tires) squealing

Reifen|druck *m Mot.* tyre (*Am.* tire) pressure; **~panne** *f* flat tyre (*Am.* tire), puncture, flat *umg.*; **~profil** *n* (tyre, *Am.* tire) tread; **8 mm ~** 8 mm tread depth; **~schaden** *m* tyre (*Am.* tire) defect; **~wechsel** *m* tyre (*Am.* tire) change

Reife|prüfung *f Päd.* school leaving exam(s *Pl.*); → *auch* **Abitur**, **~zeit** *f* ripening period; *des Menschen*: adolescence; *weitS.* formative years *Pl.*; **~zeugnis** *n Päd.* school leaving certificate; *in GB: etwa* GCE A-levels *Pl.*, *in den USA*: high school diploma

Reifglätte *f Mot.* slippery frost

reiflich I. *Adj.* careful; **nach ~er Überlegung** after careful consideration; **II.** *Adv.* carefully; **das würde ich mir ~ überlegen** I'd be very careful about making any decisions on that

Reifrock *altm. m* crinoline

Reifung *f* ripening, maturing; *bes. Bio. und Med.* maturation

Reigen *m; -s, -* round dance; **den ~ eröffnen** open the dance; *auch fig.* lead off; **den ~ beschließen** *fig.* finish off; **ein bunter ~ von Melodien** *etc.* a medley of tunes *etc.*

Reihe *f, -, -n* **1.** row, line; (*Sitzreihe*) row; **wir saßen in der ersten ~** we had seats in the first row; (*sich*) **in e-r ~ aufstellen** line up, form a line; **in Reih und Glied stehen/aufstellen** be standing / stand (*od.* place) neatly in a row; **aus der ~ tanzen** *umg.* be different, have one's own way *allg.*; (*anstoßen*) step out of line; **2.** (*Anzahl, Folge*) series (*Sg.*); **sie hat e-e ~ von Büchern darüber geschrieben** she's written a series of books about it; **e-e ganze ~ von** a lot of, a whole string of *umg.*; **nach e-r ~ von Jahren** after a number of years; **3.** (*Aufeinanderfolge*) row, succession; **warten, bis man an die ~ kommt** wait (until it is) one's turn; **wer ist an der ~?** whose turn is it?; (*immer*) **der ~ nach** in turn, by turns, one after the other; **ich bin an der ~** it's my turn; **Sie sind nicht an der ~** it's not your turn; **ich kam außer der ~ dran** *beim Arzt etc.*: they took me before (it was) my turn; **erzähl der ~ nach!** tell it from the beginning, start at the beginning; **4.** (*Zeitschriften-, Buchreihe etc.*) series (*Sg.*); **die Sendung ist Teil e-r ~** the program(me) is part of a series; **5.** *fig., in Wendungen*: **aus den ~n der Abgeordneten etc.**: from the ranks of, from among; **e-n Verräter in den eigenen ~n haben** have a traitor in one's ranks; **die ~n lichten sich** *fig.* the ranks are thinning; (*wieder*) **in die ~ kommen** *umg.* get (back) on one's feet; **etw.** (*wieder*) **auf die ~ kriegen** *umg.* get s.th. sorted out; **6.** *Math.* (*Zahlenreihe*) progression, series (*Sg.*)

reihen I. *v/t.* line up; *beim Nähen*: tack; **Perlen auf e-e Schnur ~** string pearls (*od.* beads); **II.** *v/refl.*: **Fahrzeug reihte sich an Fahrzeug** there was an endless line of vehicles; **ein Problem reiht sich ans andere** one problem follows another

Reihen|endhaus *n* end-of-terrace house; **~fertigung** *f* series production; **~folge** *f* order, sequence; **alphabetische/zeitliche ~** alphabetical/chronological order; **der ~ nach** in order; **in umgekehrter ~** in reverse order; **~grab** *n* one in a row of graves; *Pl.* graves arranged in rows

Reihenhaus *n* terrace(d) house, *Am.* row house, townhouse; **~siedlung** *f* (terraced) housing estate, *Am.* row house (*od.* townhouse) development

Reihen|motor *m Mot.* in-line engine; **~schaltung** *f Etech.* series connection; **~untersuchung** *f Med.* mass screening

reihenweise *Adv.* in rows; *fig.* (*in großer Anzahl*) by the dozen *umg.*; (*hintereinander*) one after the other; **sie sind in der Hitze ~ umgekippt** they were dropping like flies in the heat

Reiher *m; -s, -; Orn.* heron; **kotzen wie ein ~** *Sl.* be as sick as a parrot (*Am.* dog)

Reiherhorst *m* heronry

reihern *v/i. Sl.* (*brechen*) puke, hurl

...reihig *im Adj.*: **zwei~/drei~** in two/three rows

reihum *Adv.* **1.** (*abwechselnd, der Reihe nach*) in turn; **wir fragten ~** we asked each in turn; **2.** (*rundherum*) (a)round; **~ gehen** be passed (a)round, go (a)round *umg.*; **etw. ~ gehen lassen** pass s.th. (a)round; **sie schaute ~** she looked around

Reim *m; -(e)s, -e;* (*auch Kinderreim, kurzes Gedicht*) rhyme; **männlicher/weiblicher ~** male/female rhyme; **kannst du dir darauf e-n ~ machen?** *fig.* can you make any sense (*od.* make heads or tails) of it?; **ich mache mir so m-n ~ darauf** I can put two and two together

reimen *vt/i. und v/refl.* (*sich*) **~** rhyme (**auf** +*Akk.*, **mit** with); **Werk und Berg ~ sich** Werk and Berg rhyme (with one another); **gut ~ können** be good at making up rhymes; **das reimt sich nicht** that doesn't rhyme; *fig.* that doesn't make sense (add up *umg.*);

Reimerei *f, -, -en; pej.* (piece of) doggerel; *Pl.* doggerel; making (bad) verses; (*Reimgeklingel*) jingling of rhymes

Reim|lexikon *n Lit.* rhyming dictionary; **²los** *Adj.* unrhymed; **~paar** *n* rhyming couplet

Reimport *m Wirts.* reimportation

Reim|schema *n Lit.* rhyme pattern (*od.* scheme); **~schmied** *m hum.* amateur poet, poetaster; **~wort** *n* rhyming word

rein¹ I. *Adj.* **1.** pure (*auch Chem., Bio., Ling., Seide, Wein, Alkohol und fig.*) (*sauber*) clean; (*klar*) *auch Gewissen*: clear; *Metall.* unalloyed; (*gereinigt*) purified; (*unverfälscht*) unadulterated (*auch fig.*); *Reli., Tier, Speise*: clean; *Gewinn*: net, clear; *Haut*: clear; *Blatt Papier*: clean, blank; **~e Baumwolle** pure (*od.* 100%) cotton; **~es Deutsch sprechen** speak a pure German; **ein ~es Gewissen** a clear (*od.* pure) conscience; → **Luft** 1, **Tisch** 4, **Wein** 1, **Weste**; → *auch* **reinwaschen**; **2.** a) *fig., umg. intensivierend, oft im Sup.*: (*bloß, nichts als*) utter, sheer, absolute; **das ist ~er Wahnsinn** that is sheer madness; **e-e ~e Frechheit** (a piece of) barefaced cheek (*Am.* nerve); **das ist ~e Theorie** that's only (*od.* simply) theory; **e-e ~e Formalität** a mere formality; **der ~e Hohn** pure (*od.* bitter) mockery; **ein ~er Zufall** a pure accident (*od.* coincidence); **~ste Freude** sheer (*od.* pure) joy; **er ist der ~ste Komiker** he's a real comedian; **die ~ste Komödie** a regular comedy, b) *fig. intensivierend*: (*ausschließlich, echt*) genuine, real; **die ~e Wahrheit** the plain truth; *Jur.* the truth, the whole truth, and nothing but the truth; **e-e ~e Arbeitergegend** a real working-class area; → **Vergnügen**; **II.** *Adv.* a) purely; **~ pflanzlich** purely vegetable; *nur attr.* pure (*od.* all) vegetable ...; *Essen*: strictly vegetarian; **~ pflanzliches Fett** pure vegetable fat; **~ leinen** pure linen; **~ seiden** pure silk; **~ silbern** pure silver; **~ wollen** all wool; **aus ~ naturwissenschaftlicher Sicht** from a strictly scientific point of view, b) *umg.* (*gänzlich*) absolutely; **~ gar nichts** absolutely nothing (nil *umg.*); **~ unmöglich** absolutely impossible; **~ zufällig** by pure accident (*od.* chance), purely by accident (*od.* chance); **aus ~ persönlichen Gründen** for purely personal reasons; **es geht schon ~ zeitlich nicht** there simply isn't (enough) time; **etw. ~ mechanisch tun** do s.th. just mechanically; **III.** *substantivisch*: **ins**

Reine bringen clear up, sort out; *mit j-m ins Reine kommen* get things straightened out with s.o.; *mit sich ins Reine kommen* straighten things out for o.s.; *etw. ins Reine schreiben* make a fair copy of s.th.

rein² *Adv. umg.* **1.** → *herein;* **2.** → *hinein*

rein... *im V.* **1.** → *auch herein...;* **2.** → *auch hinein...*

reinbeißen *v/i.* (*unreg., trennb., hat -ge-*) *umg.:* **in etw.** (*+ Akk.*) ~ bite into s.th.; *zum Reinbeißen aussehen* look scrumptious

Reineclaude [rɛːnəˈkloːdə] *f; -, -n; Bot.* greengage

Reinemachefrau *f* cleaning lady; **Reinemachen** *n; -s, kein Pl.* cleaning

reinerbig *Adj. Gnt.* homozygotous

Rein|erlös *m*, **~ertrag** *m* net proceeds *Pl.*, net (*od.* clear) profit

reineweg *Adv.* → *reinweg*

Reinfall *m umg.* flop, washout; (*Enttäuschung*) letdown; *die Party war ein glatter* ~ the party was a complete disaster; *hoffentlich erlebt ihr mit ihm / dem Auto keinen* ~ I hope (*od. umg.* hopefully) he / the car won't let you down; **reinfallen** *v/i.* (*unreg., trennb., ist -ge-*) *umg.:* (*drauf*) ~ fall for it; *wie konnte sie auf den* ~? how could she be taken in by him?; *mit dem Auto sind wir reingefallen* he took us for a ride / we were taken for a ride with that car; *ich fall' nicht noch mal rein* I won't be caught that way (*od.* fall into that trap) again

Reingeschmeckte *m, f; -n, -n; südd.* newcomer, new(ly arrived) resident

Rein|gewinn *m* net profit; ~ *(als)* ~ **erzielen** take ... in clear profit; **~haltung** *f: die* ~ *der Luft etc.* keeping the air *etc.* clean

reinhängen *v/refl.* (*trennb., hat -ge-*) *umg.* throw o.s. into it, give it all one's got; *sich zu sehr* ~ get too (much) involved, take it (*od.* s.th.) too seriously *allg.*

reinhauen (*trennb., hat -ge-*) *umg.* **I.** *v/i.* **1.** *beim Arbeiten:* get cracking, get stuck in, *Am. auch* set to it; *beim Essen:* dig in; **2.** *das haut voll rein!* that really knocks you for six (*Am.* for a loop); *der Urlaub hat ganz schön reingehauen* (*Geld gekostet*) the holiday (*Am.* vacation) made a big hole in our pockets; **II.** *v/t.* **1.** *sich* (*Dat.*) *etw.* ~ (*Essen*) polish off; (*Getränk*) knock back; **2.** *j-m e-e* ~ clobber s.o., thump s.o. (one)

Reinheit *f* purity, pureness, cleanness *etc.;* → *rein¹ I I*

Reinheits|gebot *n* (beer) purity requirement; **~grad** *m* purity standard, degree of purity

reinhören (*trennb., hat -ge-*) **I.** *v/i.* **in etw.** (*Akk.*) ~ listen to a snatch of s.th.; **II.** *v/refl.: sich in etw.* ~ get used to the sound of s.th.

reinigen *v/t.* **1.** *allg.:* clean; (*Gesichtshaut*) *auch* cleanse; (*waschen*) wash; (*Chem., Tech. Blut, Luft etc.*) purify, clarify; (*Gewässer etc.*) clean up; *sich* ~ *rituell:* perform one's ablutions; *sich selbst* ~ *Fluss etc.:* clean itself; *chemisch* ~ dry-clean; **2.** *fig., in Wendungen:* **~des Gewitter** argument that clears the air; *sich von e-m Verdacht* ~ clear o.s. of a suspicion

Reiniger *m; -s, -* **1.** *Mittel:* cleaning agent, cleaner; *für die Haut:* cleanser; **2.** *Beruf:* cleaner

...reiniger *m, im Subst.* ... cleaner

Reinigerin *f; -, -nen* cleaner

Reinigung *f* **1.** (*Tätigkeit*) cleaning *etc.;* (*Ritus*) ablutions *Pl.;* **2.** (*Firma*) (dry) cleaners (*V. im Sg.*); *chemische* ~ dry cleaning; *in der* ~ *Kleidung:* at the cleaners; *in die* ~ *bringen* take to the cleaners

Reinigungs|creme *f* cleansing cream; **~firma** *f für Textilien:* firm of dry cleaners, dry-cleaning company; *für Gebäude:* cleaning contractors *Pl.;* **~kraft** *f* **1.** (*Fäigkeit*) cleaning (*od.* cleansing) power (*od.* action); **2.** (*Person*) cleaner; **~milch** *f* cleansing milk; **~mittel** *n* cleaning agent, household cleaner; **~personal** *n* cleaning staff, cleaners *Pl.*

Reinkarnation *f; -, -en* reincarnation

reinkommen *v/i.* (*unreg., trennb., ist -ge-*) *umg.* **1.** *in e-n Film etc.* ~ manage to get into a film (*Am.* movie *etc.*); **2.** *sind Sie gut reingekommen?* *ins neue Jahr:* did you see the New Year in successfully?

reinkriegen *v/t.* (*trennb., hat -ge-*) *umg.* manage to get in

Reinkultur *f* pure culture; *Kitsch in* ~ *umg. fig.* pure unadulterated kitsch

reinlegen *v/t. umg.* → *hereinlegen*

reinlich *Adj.* clean; *als Eigenschaft:* cleanly; (*schmuck*) neat, tidy; **Reinlichkeit** *f* cleanliness; (*Ordentlichkeit*) neatness, tidiness; thoroughness; **reinlichkeitsliebend** *Adj.* with a love of cleanliness; **Reinlichkeitssinn** *m* sense of (the need for) cleanliness

Reinmachefrau *f* cleaning lady

reinrassig *Adj. Hund etc.:* pedigree, pure-bred; *Pferd:* thoroughbred; *Indianer etc.:* pure-blooded

rein|reißen *v/t.* (*unreg., trennb., hat -ge-*) *umg.* **1.** get s.o. into a real (*od.* right) mess; **2.** *finanziell:* set s.o. back (a fair bit) *allg.;* **~reiten** *v/t.* (*unreg., trennb., hat -ge-*) *umg. fig.* land s.o. in it; **~riechen** *v/i.* (*unreg., trennb., hat -ge-*) *umg.* → *reinschnuppern;* **~schlittern** *v/i. umg.: in etw.* ~ get o.s. involved in (*od.* with) s.th. *allg.*

Reinschiff *n; -s, kein Pl.; Naut.:* ~ *machen* clean the ship from stem to stern; *umg. fig.* have a general clear-out (*od.* spring-clean)

reinschnuppern *v/i.* (*trennb., hat -ge-*) *umg.: in etw.* ~ have a brief look at s.th.; (*Themenbereich etc.*) get a taste of s.th.

Rein|schrift *f* fair copy; **reinschriftlich** *Adj.* ~*e Fassung* fair copy

Reinverdienst *m* net earnings *Pl.*

reinvestieren *v/t. Wirts.* reinvest, plough (*Am.* plow) back; **Reinvestition** *f* reinvestment

reinwaschen *v/t. und v/refl.* (*unreg., trennb., hat -ge-*) *j-n/sich* ~ *fig.* whitewash s.o./o.s., clear s.o./o.s.; *sich von e-m Verdacht* ~ clear oneself of a suspicion

reinweg *Adv. umg.* absolutely, completely; *sie glaubt* ~ *alles* she believes absolutely everything; *es ist* ~ *zum Verrücktwerden* it simply drives you up the wall

reinwollen I. *Adj.* → *rein¹ II a;* **II.** *v/i.* → *hereinwollen*

rein|würgen *v/t.* (*unreg., trennb.*) *umg.* **1.** (*schlucken*) force down *allg.;* **2.** *j-m eins od. e.e* ~ let s.o. know about it; **~ziehen** *v/t.* (*unreg., trennb., hat -ge-*) *umg. fig.* **1.** *in etw. in etw.* (*mit*) ~ involve s.o. in s.th. *allg.;* **2.** *sich* (*Dat.*) *e-e* ~ (*Zigarette*) have a fag (*Am.* cig, smoke); *sich* (*Dat.*) *ein Video* ~ watch

a video *allg.*

Reis¹ *n; -es, -er; Bot.* twig

Reis² *m; -es, kein Pl.; Agr., Gastr.* rice; **~anbau** *m* growing (*od.* cultivation) of rice; **~auflauf** *m* baked rice pudding; **~branntwein** *m* rice spirit (*Am.* liquor); **~brei** *m* rice pudding

Reise *f; -, -n* trip; *längere: auch* journey; *Naut.* voyage; (*Überfahrt*) passage (*alle nach* + *Akk.* to); (*Rundreise*) tour (*in* + *Akk.* of); *e-e* ~ *machen* make (*od.* go on) a journey; *auf der* ~ on the journey; *auf der* ~ *nach ...* on the way to ...; *j-n/etw. mit auf die* ~ *nehmen* take s.o./s.th. with one (on the journey); *e-e* ~ *ans Meer / in die Berge* a trip to the sea / into the mountains; *wie war die Reise nach Ungarn?* how was your trip to Hungary?; *e-e* ~ *durch die USA* a tour (*od.* trip) of (*od.* through) the USA; *e-e* ~ *um die Welt* a voyage (*od.* trip) around the world; *die* ~*n des Marco Polo* the travels of Marco Polo; *gute* ~*!* have a pleasant journey!, have a good trip!; *viel auf* ~*n sein* do a lot of travel(l)ing; *wohin geht die* ~*?* where are you off to?; *fig.* what's on the agenda?; *e-e* ~ *in die Vergangenheit* a journey into the past; *persönliche:* a walk down memory lane; *e-e* ~ *in den Tod* a journey ending in death; *s-e letzte* ~ *antreten fig.* set off on one's last journey, go to meet one's Maker; *j-n auf die letzte* ~ *schicken fig.* give s.o. a good send-off *umg.; j-n auf die* ~ *schicken fig. Sport* (*Läufer, Fahrer*) send s.o. on his (*od.* her) way; (*Mitspieler durch Vorlage*) release s.o.(with a long pass)

Reise|abenteuer *n* travel adventure; (*Erzählung*) travel(l)er's tale; **~andenken** *n* souvenir; **~antritt** *m: vor/nach* ~ before/after setting off; **~apotheke** *f* first-aid kit; **~bedarf** *m* travel(l)ing requisites *Pl.;* **~begleiter** *m*, **~begleiterin** *f* **1.** travel(l)ing companion; **2.** → *Reiseleiter;* **~bekanntschaft** *f* travel(l)ing acquaintance; *sie ist e-e* ~ I met her on a (holiday, *Am.* vacation) trip; **~bericht** *m* account of a (*od.* the) journey; (*Buch, Film*) travelogue; **~beschränkungen** *Pl.* travel restrictions, restrictions on travel; **~beschreibung** *f* travelogue; (*Tagebuch*) travel diary; *im Prospekt:* travel plan; **~besteck** *n* traveller's set of cutlery, *Am.* portable utensils; **~büro** *n* travel agency (*od.* agent['s]); **~bürokauffrau** *f*, **~bürokaufmann** *m* qualified travel agent; **~bus** *m* coach, *Am.* bus; **~decke** *f* travel(l)ing rug; **~diplomatie** *f* shuttle diplomacy; **~erlaubnis** *f* permission to travel; *Amtsspr.* travel permit; **~erlebnis** *n* travel experience; *er erzählte von s-n* ~*sen* he spoke about his travels; **~erleichterungen** *Pl.* easing *Sg.* of travel restrictions; **²fertig** *Adj.* ready for departure; **~fieber** *n* holiday (*Am.* vacation) travel fever, excitement before a journey (*od.* trip), travel(l)ing spirits

Reiseführer¹ *m* (*Buch*) guide(book)

Reiseführer² *m*, **Reiseführerin** *f* (travel) guide, courier

Reise|gefährte *m*, **~gefährtin** *f* travel(l)ing companion; **~geld** *n* money for the journey; (*Fahrgeld*) (money for the) fare(s); **~genehmigung** *f* → *Reiseerlaubnis*

Reisegepäck *n* luggage, *bes. Am.* baggage; **~versicherung** *f* baggage insurance

Reise|geschwindigkeit f cruising speed; **~gesellschaft** f **1.** (tourist) party (od. group); **2.** (Veranstalter) tour operator; **~gewerbe** n itinerant trade; **~gruppe** f tourist party (od. group); **~journalismus** m travel journalism; **~kasse** f travel fund; **~koffer** m suitcase

Reisekosten Pl. travel expenses; **s-e ~ erstattet bekommen** be reimbursed for one's travel expenses; **~abrechnung** f travel expenses claim; **~erstattung** f reimbursement of travel expenses

Reise|krankenversicherung f foreign travel health(care) insurance; **~krankheit** f travel sickness; **~land** n tourist country (od. destination)

Reise|leiter m, **~leiterin** f courier, (travel) guide; **~leitung** f (Person[en]) courier(s), guide(s); (Tätigkeit) organization of the trip; allg. conducting tourist parties; **die ~ übernehmen** act as courier (od. guide); **die örtliche ~** the local tour management; **~lektüre** f something to read on the trip; für den Aufenthalt: holiday (Am. vacation) reading; **~limousine** f touring saloon (Am. sedan)

Reiselust f wanderlust, travel urge; **mich packt mal wieder die ~!** umg. I've been bitten by the travel bug (od. got itchy feet) again; **reiselustig** Adj.: **er ist sehr ~** he's a keen (Am. an avid) travel(l)er

reisemüde Adj. travel-weary

reisen v/i. travel (nach + Dat. to); (ab~) go, leave; **~ nach** auch go (on a trip) to; **ins Ausland ~** go abroad (Am. auch overseas); **durch den Südwesten ~** tour the southwest; **wir ~ am Sonntag** we leave on Sunday; **mit der Bahn / dem Flugzeug ~** travel by train/air; **Reisen** n; -s, kein Pl. travel(-l)ing; **sie war auf ~** she was travel(l)ing; → **bilden** II

Reisende m, f; -n, -n **1.** travel(l)er; (Fahrgast) passenger; **~ mit Kindern** passengers with children; **die Reisenden werden gebeten zu** (+ Inf.) passengers are requested to (+ Inf.); **2.** → **Handlungsreisende**

Reise|necessaire [-nesεsε:ɐ] m sponge (Am. toiletries) bag; **~pass** m passport; **~pläne** Pl. travel plans; **~ schmieden** plan a trip (od. trips); **~preis** m price of the trip; **~programm** n travel program(me); **~prospekt** m travel brochure; **~proviant** m food for the journey

Reiserei f; -, -en; umg. pej. constant (od. endless) travel(l)ing around; **ich hab' die ewige ~ satt** I'm fed up with constantly trailing around (from place to place)

Reisernte f rice harvest

Reise|route f route, itinerary; **~rücktrittskostenversicherung** f holiday (Am. vacation) cancel(l)ation insurance; **~ruf** m emergency radio message (to a driver); **~scheck** m traveller's cheque, Am. traveler's check; **~schilderung** f → **Reisebericht**; **~schreibmaschine** f portable typewriter; **~schriftsteller** m, **~schriftstellerin** f travel writer; **~spesen** Pl. travel(l)ing (od. travel) expenses; **~tagebuch** n travel diary (od. journal); **~tasche** f travel(l)ing bag, holdall, Am. carryall; **~unterlagen** Pl. travel documents; **~unternehmen** n travel firm; **~veranstalter** m, **~veranstalterin** f tour operator(s Pl.); **~verkehr** m holi-

day (od. tourist) traffic; **~verkehrskauffrau** f, **~verkehrskaufmann** m qualified travel agent; **~verpflegung** f → **Reiseproviant**; **~vorbereitungen** Pl. preparations for the trip; für den Urlaub: holiday preparations; **~wecker** m travel alarm (clock); **~welle** f surge of tourist (od. holiday) traffic; **~wetter** n **1.** (Urlaubswetter) holiday (Am. vacation) weather; **2.** (Wetter zum Reisen) (fine) weather for travel(l)ing; **~wetterbericht** m holiday (Am. vacation) weather report; **~zeit** f holiday (od. tourist, Am. vacation) season; **die beste ~** the best time to travel; **~ziel** n destination; **was ist Ihr ~?** where are you bound for?; **Spanien ist ein beliebtes ~** a lot of people go to Spain for their holiday(s) (Am. vacation); **~zug** m passenger train

Reis|feld n paddy (od. rice) field; **~gericht** n Gastr. rice dish

Reisig n; -s, kein Pl. brushwood; **~besen** m besom; **~bündel** n bundle of brushwood

Reis|korn n grain of rice, rice grain; **~mehl** n rice flour; **~papier** n rice paper; **~pflanze** f rice plant; **~rand** m Gastr.: **Frikassee im ~** fricassee in a ring of rice

Reißaus m umg.: **~ nehmen** take to one's heels allg., clear off

Reißbrett n drawing board; **~stift** m → **Reißzwecke**

Reis|schleim m Gastr. rice gruel (od. porridge); **~schnaps** m rice spirit (Am. liqueur)

reißen; reißt, riss, ist od. hat gerissen **I.** v/t. (hat) **1.** tear; (heraus~, ab~) pull; (Papier) tear, rip; (weg~) snatch; **e-e Seite aus e-m Buch ~** tear (od. rip) a page out of a book; **sich** (Dat.) **die Kleider vom Leibe ~** tear (od. rip) off one's clothes; **j-m etw. aus der Hand ~** snatch s.th. away from s.o. (od. out of s.o.'s hand); **der Sturm riss mir den Hut vom Kopf** the gale tore (od. whipped) the hat from my head; **2.** (in e-e Richtung zwingen) pull, drag; Fluten: sweep; **j-n zu Boden ~** drag s.o. to the ground; **das Lenkrad nach rechts ~** wrench the steering to the right; **der Fluss riss das Haus einfach mit sich** the river simply swept the house away; **zehn Skifahrer wurden von der Lawine mit in den Tod gerissen** the avalanche swept ten skiers to their deaths; **3.** (beschädigen) tear, rip; **sich** (Dat.) **ein Loch in die Hose ~** tear a hole in one's trousers (Am. pants); **4.** fig.: **aus dem Schlaf gerissen werden** be rudely awakened; **aus s-n Träumen gerissen werden** come down to earth with a bump umg.; **die Macht an sich ~** seize power; **die Führung an sich ~** Sport take the lead; weitS. take over, take command; **sie war hin und her gerissen** she couldn't make up her mind; (war begeistert) she was thrilled to bits (Am. pieces) umg.; **das reißt mich nicht gerade vom Hocker** umg. I can't say I'm thrilled, it's nothing to write home about; → **Witz** 1, **Zote** etc.; **5.** Raubtier: (töten) kill; **II.** vt/i. (hat) Sport a) Gewichtheben: lift in the snatch, b) Hochsprung, Pferdesport: knock off the bar; **er hat** (die 1,97 m) **dreimal gerissen** he failed three times (at 1.97 m); **III.** v/i. (a. ist) tear; Kette, Saite etc.: break; Lippen: chap; Nebel: lift suddenly; **der Film/Schnürsenkel ist gerissen** the film tore / the shoe-

lace broke; **da riss ihm die Geduld** his patience snapped (od. gave out [on him]); **2.** (hat) (zerren): **~ an** (+ Dat.) pull (od. tug) at; stärker,wütend: tear at; → **Strang** 1, **Strick** 1; **IV.** v/refl.: **sich ~ um** fig. fight (od. scramble) over, squabble) over; **sich um e-n Fußballer/Filmstar ~** try to outbid one another to get a footballer/ film star (Am. moviestar); **ich reiße mich nicht darum** I'm not that keen (Am. eager) (to have it); **ich reiße mich nicht darum, ihn kennenzulernen** I'm not exactly dying to get to know him

Reißen n; -s, kein Pl. **1.** tearing etc.; → **reißen**; **2.** (Gewichtheben) snatch; **3.** umg. (Rheuma) rheumatics Pl., Am. rheumatiz

reißend I. Part. Präs. → **reißen**; **II.** Adj. Fluss: torrential, in full spate präd.; Strömung: powerful; Schmerz: searing; Tier: rapacious; → **Absatz** 3

Reißer m; -s, -; umg. **1.** (Buch, Film etc.) thriller; **2.** (Ware) winner, money-spinner; **das Buch ist nicht gerade ein ~** the book isn't exactly a bestseller; **reißerisch I.** Adj. Schlagzeilen: sensational; Farben, Werbung: lurid; **II.** Adv.: **~ aufgemacht** in a lurid outfit

reißfest Adj. tearproof; **Reißfestigkeit** f **1.** resistance to tearing (od. breaking); **2.** Tech. tensile strength, tenacity

Reiß|leine f Fallschirm: rip cord; Ballon: rip(ping) line (od. cord), rip cord; **~nagel** m → **Reißzwecke**

Reis|stärke f Gastr. rice starch; **~stroh** n rice straw; **~suppe** f Gastr. rice soup

Reißverschluss m zip, Am. zipper; **mach den ~ an d-r Jacke zu/auf** zip up /unzip your jacket; **~system** n: **nach dem ~** Mot. using the alternate filtering-in system

Reiß|wolf m shredder; **~wolle** f reclaimed wool, shoddy; **~zahn** m fang; **~zeug** n set of drawing instruments; **~zwecke** f drawing pin, Am. thumbtack

Reiswein m rice wine; (japanischer ~) sake

Reit|anzug m riding habit; **~bahn** f riding arena

reiten; reitet, ritt, ist od. hat geritten **I.** v/i. (ist) ride (auf + Dat. on); **sie reitet gern** she likes (horse-)riding; **~ lernen** learn to ride; **gut/schlecht ~** be a good/bad rider; **im Galopp ~** (ride at a) gallop; **II.** v/t. (hat) ride; **ein Pferd/ Rennen ~** ride a horse / (in) a race; **ein Turnier ~** ride (od. compete) in a horse show; **sich wund ~** get saddle-sore; **über den Haufen ~** umg. ride s.o. down; **was hat dich eigentlich geritten, als du ...?** umg. what got into you when you...?; → **Teufel** 3

Reiten n; -s, kein Pl. (horse-)riding; **reitend I.** Part. Präs. → **reiten**; **II.** Adj. on horseback; **Reiter** m; -s, - **1.** rider, horseman; **ein guter/schlechter ~** a good/bad rider; → **blau** 2; **2.** Tech., Chem. rider; **spanische ~** barbed-wire barriers; **3.** auf Karteikarten: rider, tab; **Reiterei** f; -, -en **1.** Mil. cavalry; **2.** nur Sg.; umg. (das Reiten) (horse-)riding; **Reiterin** f; -, -nen rider, horsewoman; **reiterlich** Adj.: **~es Können** etc. riding ability etc.; **reiterlos I.** Adj. riderless; **II.** Adv. auch without a rider

Reiter|regiment n hist. cavalry regiment; **~standbild** n equestrian statue

Reit|gerte f riding crop; **~hose** f: (e-e)

R

~ (a pair of) (riding) breeches *Pl.*; **~lehrer** *m*, **~lehrerin** *f* riding instructor; **~peitsche** *f* riding whip; **~pferd** *n* saddle (*od.* riding) horse; **~sattel** *m* saddle; **~schule** *f* riding school; **~sitz** *m*: **im ~ auf etw. sitzen** sit astride s.th., straddle s.th.; **~sport** *m* (horse-)riding, equestrian sport(s *Pl.*); **~stall** *m* riding stable; **~stiefel** *m* riding boot

Reit|stunde *f* riding lesson; **~tier** *n* riding animal, mount; **~turnier** *n* horse show; **~ und Springturnier** *n* horse jumping show, show jumping event; **~unterricht** *m* riding lessons *Pl.*; **~weg** *m* bridle path (*od.* way)

Reiz *m*; *-es*, *-e* **1.** *Physiol.*, *Psych. und fig.* stimulus, *Pl.* stimuli; **e-n ~ auf etw. ausüben** act as a stimulus on s.th.; **zu vielen ~en ausgesetzt sein** have too many sources of stimulus, be exposed to too many stimuli; **2.** (*Wirkung, Anziehungskraft*) appeal, attraction; *e-r Landschaft etc.: auch* charm; **der ~ des Neuen** the novelty appeal; **der ~ des Verbotenen** the lure of forbidden fruit; **s-n ~ verlieren** lose its attraction, begin to pall (**für** on); **der ~ (an der Sache) liegt in** (+ *Dat.*) ... what is so fascinating about it is ...; **darin liegt gerade der ~** that's the whole fun of it; **s-e ~e spielen lassen** display one's charms; **sie spielt ihre weiblichen ~e aus** she brings her feminine charms into play; **j-s ~en erliegen** fall prey to s.o.'s charms

reizbar *Adj.* irritable, touchy, uptight *umg.*; (*jähzornig*) irascible; **er ist leicht ~** (*jähzornig*) he'll fly into a temper at the slightest thing; **Reizbarkeit** *f* irritability

reizen I. *v/t.* **1.** (*ärgern*) annoy, rile; (*provozieren*) provoke; **er ist nervös - reiz ihn nicht** he's on edge - don't irritate him; → **gereizt. 2.** *Med.* irritate; **3.** (*anregen*) (*Gefühle, Neugier etc.*) (a)rouse; (*Appetit*) stimulate, whet; (*Gaumen*) tickle; (*locken*) lure, tempt; **die Herausforderung reizt mich** the challenge really attracts (*od.* appeals to) me; **ihn reizt die Gefahr** danger has a great attraction for him, he likes to be where the danger is; **es reizte ihn, etwas ganz Neues zu machen** he was attracted by the idea of doing something completely different; **das kann mich (überhaupt) nicht ~** *umg.* that doesn't appeal to me in the slightest, it doesn't grab me (at all) *Sl.*; **4.** *Kartenspiel:* bid; **II.** *v/i.* **1.** *Med.* irritate the skin (*od.* eyes *etc.*), be an irritant; **2.** *Kartenspiel:* bid

reizend I. *Part. Präs.* → **reizen**; **II.** *Adj.* charming, delightful; **~es** (*kleines*) **Mädchen** enchanting (little) girl; **das ist ja ~ von Ihnen** how nice of you; **das ist ja ~!** how charming!; *iro.* charming(, I must say)!, this is a nice mess; **~e Aussichten!** *iro.* what a delightful prospect!

Reiz|gas *n* irritant gas; (*Tränengas*) tear gas; **~husten** *m Med.* dry cough

Reizker *m*; *-s*, *-*; *Bot.* lactarius, milk (*Am.* milky) cap

Reizklima *n* bracing climate

reizlos *Adj.* unattractive, lacking in charm; (*uninteressant*) uninteresting, boring; *Essen auch:* bland; **Reizlosigkeit** *f* unattractiveness, lack of charm; (*uninteressante Art*) uninteresting nature; *des Essens:* blandness

Reiz|mittel *n Med.* stimulant; **~schwelle** *f* stimulus threshold; **~stoff** *m* irritant; **~strom** *m Med.* current for

stimulation therapy; **~thema** *n* **1.** explosive topic, emotive issue; *Pol. auch* gut issue; **2.** *für einzelne:* touchy subject; **~therapie** *f Med.* stimulation therapy; **~überflutung** *f* stimulus satiation; *durch Medien:* media saturation

Reizung *f* irritation (*auch Med.*); (*Provokation*) provocation; (*Anregung*) stimulation

reizvoll *Adj.* charming, attractive; (*verlockend*) tempting; *Kontrast:* fascinating; **~e Aufgabe** interesting task

Reiz|wäsche *f* sexy underwear; **~wort** *n* emotive (*Psych. test*) word; **Geld war bei ihr ein ~** money was a touchy subject with her; **Atommüll ist zum ~ geworden** "nuclear waste" has become an emotive term

Rekapitulation *f*; *-*, *-en* recapitulation; **rekapitulieren** *vt/i.* recapitulate, sum up; **ich rekapituliere** to sum up (the main points again)

rekeln *v/refl.* (*sich strecken*) stretch; (*sich lümmeln*) sprawl, lounge around, loll (about); **sich in der Sonne ~** stretch out in in the sun

Reklamation *f*; *-*, *-en* complaint; *bes. Sport* protest

Reklame *f*; *-*, *-n*, *mst Sg.*; (*Werbung*) advertising; (*Anzeige*) advertisement, ad *umg.*, *Brit. auch* advert; *TV, Radio: auch* commercial; *Koll.* commercials *Pl.*; **~ machen für etw.** advertise s.th., promote s.th.; *umg.* plug s.th.; **keine gute ~ für etw. sein** *fig.* not be a very good advertisement for s.th.; → *auch* **Werbung 1**

Reklame... *im Subst. siehe auch* **Werbe...**

Reklame|bild *n* publicity picture; **~fläche** *f* area for advertising; (*Tafel*) billboard, *Brit. auch* hoarding; **~plakat** *n* advertising poster; *umgehängtes:* sandwich board (*od.* placard); **~schild** *n* advertising sign (*od.* [sign]board); **~tafel** *f* advertisement, billboard, *Brit. auch* hoarding

reklamieren *vt/i.* **1.** (*sich beschweren*) complain, make (*od.* lodge) a complaint; *bes. Sport* protest; (*beanstanden*) complain about; (*Gekauftes*) *auch* take back to the shop; (*Rechnung*) query; (*nicht Erhaltenes*) enquire (*od.* inquire) about; **~, dass ...** complain that ...; **~ gegen** *Sport* protest against; **2.** (*fordern*) claim; **Abseits/Elfmeter ~** appeal for an offside / a penalty; **e-e Idee** *etc.* **für sich ~** lay claim to an idea *etc.*, claim an idea *etc.* as one's own

rekonstruierbar *Adj.* reconstructible; **leicht/schwer ~** easy/difficult to reconstruct; **rekonstruieren** *v/t.* reconstruct; **Rekonstruktion** *f*; *-*, *-en* reconstruction

Rekonvaleszent *m*; *-en*, *-en*, **~in** *f*; *-*, *-nen* convalescent; **Rekonvaleszenz** *f*; *-*, *kein Pl.* convalescence

Rekord *m*; *-(e)s*, *-e* record; *weitS. auch* all-time high; **e-n ~ aufstellen/brechen** set up /break a record; **e-n ~ halten/ schlagen** hold/ beat a record; **alle ~e brechen** break all records; **der ~ liegt bei** the record is (*od.* stands at); **ein trauriger ~** *fig.* a lamentable record; **~besuch** *m* record attendance

Rekord... *im Subst.* record ...; **~flug** record-breaking flight; **~hoch** *Börse etc.*: record (*od.* all-time) high; **~tief** *Börse etc.*: record (*od.* all-time) low

Rekorder *m*; *-s*, *-* - recorder

Rekord|ergebnis *n* record result; **~ernte** *f* bumper crop; **~halter** *m*,

~halterin *f* record holder; **~inhaber** *m*, **~inhaberin** *f* record holder; **~internationale** *m*, *f Sport* sportsman (*od.* sportswoman) with the greatest number of international appearances for his/her country; **~jagd** *f*: **auf ~ gehen** go after a (*od.* the) record; **~laune** *f*: **in ~** in record-breaking mood; **~leistung** *f engS.* record-breaking performance; *weitS.* outstanding performance; **~marke** *f* record; **die ~ um 1 Zentimeter verbessern / um 1 Sekunde unterbieten** improve the record by 1 centimeter / by 1 second; **~meister** *m*, **~meisterin** *f* champion of champions; **~nationalspieler** *m*, **~nationalspielerin** *f* → **Rekordinternationale**

rekordverdächtig *Adj.* of seemingly record proportions; *Leistung:* that must be a record; **... ist ~** ... must be a record; **sie ist heute ~** today she can beat the record

Rekord|verlust *m Wirts.* record (--breaking) losses *Pl.*; **~versuch** *m* record attempt; **~zeit** *f* record time

Rekrut *m*; *-en*, *-en*; *Mil.* recruit (*auch fig.*)

Rekruten|ausbildung *f Mil.* training of recruits; **~gelöbnis** *n* recruit's oath of allegiance; **~zeit** *f* time (*od.* days *Pl.*) as a recruit

rekrutieren I. *v/t. Mil.* (*und Arbeitskräfte etc.*) recruit; **II.** *v/refl. fig.:* **sich ~ aus** be made up of; **Rekrutierung** *f* recruitment, recruiting; **Rekrutin** *f*; *-*, *-nen* (female) recruit

rektal I. *Adj. Med.* rectal; **II.** *Adv.*: **~ untersuchen / die Temperatur messen** examine s.th. / take s.o.'s temperature rectally

Rektion *f*; *-*, *-en*; *Gram.* government; (*Kasus*) case governed by a verb *etc.*

Rektor *m*; *-s*, *-en e-r Schule:* headmaster, *Am.* principal; *Univ.* vice-chancellor, *Am.* president; **Rektorat** *n*; *-(e)s*, *-e* **1.** (*Funktion*) headmastership; *Univ.* vice-chancellorship, *Am.* presidency; **2.** headmaster's (*Am.* principal's) office; *Univ.* vice-chancellor's (*Am.* president's) office; **Rektorin** *f*; *-*, *-nen* headmistress, *Am.* principal; *Univ.* vice-chancellor, *Am.* president

Rektoskop *n*; *-s*, *-e*; *Med.* proctoscope; **Rektoskopie** *f*; *-*, *-n*; *Med.* proctoscopy

Rektum *n*; *-s*, *Rekta*; *Anat.* rectum

rekursiv *Adj. Math.*, *Ling.* recursive

Relais [rə'lɛː] *n*; *-*, *-*; *Etech.* relay; **~schaltung** *f* relay circuit (*od.* connection); **~station** *f Funk.* relay station; **~steuerung** *f* control by relays, relay control

Relation *f*; *-*, *-en* relation(ship); *von Mengen:* proportion, ratio; **das steht in keiner ~ zu s-m Einkommen** it's out of all proportion to his income

relativ I. *Adj.* relative; **es ist alles ~** it's all relative; **II.** *Adv.* relatively, comparatively; **~ oft** relatively (*od.* fairly) often; **es verlief ~ gut** it went reasonably (*od.* relatively) well; **relativieren** *v/t.* **1.** put into perspective, see in perspective; **2.** (*einschränken*) qualify; **Relativierung** *f* **1.** putting s.th. into perspective; **2.** (*Einschränkung*) qualification

Relativität *f*; *-*, *-en*, *mst Sg.* relativity; **Relativitätstheorie** *f Phys.* theory of relativity

Relativ|pronomen *n Ling.*, *Gram.* relative pronoun; **~satz** *m* relative clause

Relaunch ['riːlɔntʃ] *m*, *n*; *-(e)s*, *-(e)s Wirts.* (*Neubeginn*) relaunch

Relaxans *n*; *-*, *Relaxanzien od.* Rela-

R

xantia; *Med.* relaxant

relaxen [ri'lɛksn] *v/i. umg.* take it easy, relax *allg.*

Relegation *f*; -, -en **1.** *bes. Univ.* expulsion; **2.** *Sport* → *Relegationsspiel*; **Relegationsspiel** *n Sport* relegation match; **relegieren** *v/t. bes. Univ.* expel

relevant *Adj.* relevant (*für* to), pertinent (to); **Relevanz** *f*; -, *kein Pl.* relevance (*für* to); **für etw. ~ sein** have (some) relevance to s.th.

Relief [re'lief] *n*; -s, -s relief; **~bild** *n* image in relief, relief; **~druck** *m* **1.** *Verfahren:* relief printing; **2.** *Ergebnis:* relief print; **~globus** *m* raised-relief globe; **~karte** *f* relief (*od.* embossed) map

Religion *f*; -, -en **1.** religion (*auch fig.*); (*Glaube*) faith; **2.** *nur Sg. Päd.* → *Religionsunterricht*

Religions|ausübung *f* religious practice; **freie ~** freedom of worship; **~bekenntnis** *n* confession; **~buch** *n* religious textbook; **~ersatz** *m* substitute religion; **~freiheit** *f* freedom of worship; **~gemeinschaft** *f* confession; *kleinere:* religious community; **~geschichte** *f* history of religion; **~krieg** *m* religious war; **~lehre** *f* religious education; **~lehrer** *m*, **~lehrerin** *f* religion instructor, *Brit.* RI (= religious instruction) teacher, RE (= religious education) teacher

religionslos *Adj.* without religion, *präd. auch* not religious

Religions|philosophie *f* philosophy of religion; **~stifter** *m*, **~stifterin** *f* founder of a (*od.* the) religion; **~streit** *m* religious dispute; *allg.* religious controversy; **~stunde** *f Brit.* RI lesson, RE lesson, *Am.* religion class; **~unterricht** *m Päd.* religious instruction (*Brit.* RI), religious education (*Brit.* RE); **~wissenschaft** *f* (comparative) theology; **~zugehörigkeit** *f* religious affiliation

religiös I. *Adj.* religious; (*fromm*) *auch* pious, devout; **~es Bekenntnis** religious confession, denomination; **~er Wahn** religious mania; **II.** *Adv.:* **~ leben** live in accordance with religious principles; **s-e Kinder ~ erziehen** give one's children a religious upbringing; **Religiosität** *f*; -, *kein Pl.* religiousness; (*Frömmigkeit*) piety

Relikt *n*; -(*e*)*s*, -e **1.** relic (+ *Gen.* of; *aus* from, of); (*Eigenschaft etc.*) *auch umg.* leftover (from); **2.** *Bio.* relict

Reling *f*; -, *kein Pl.*; *Naut.* railing

Reliquiar *n*; -s, -e reliquary; **Reliquie** *f*; -, -n relic

Reliquien|schrein *m* reliquary; **~verehrung** *f* worship of relics

Remake ['ri:me:k] *n*; -s, -s *Film:* remake

Remigrant *m*; -en, -en, **~in** *f*; -, -nen returning emigrant; *zurückgekehrt:* returned emigrant

remilitarisieren *v/t.* remilitarize, rearm; **Remilitarisierung** *f* remilitarization, rearmament

Reminiszenz *f*; -, en reminiscence (*an* + *Akk.* of); (*Erinnerungsstück*) memento (of)

remis [rə'mi:] *Adj. und Adv.:* **die Partie endete ~** the game ended in a draw; **~ spielen** draw, *Am. auch* tie; **Remis** *n*; -, *-* draw, *Am. auch* tie

Remittende *f*; -, -n return

Remmidemmi *n*; -s, *kein Pl.*; *umg.* wild celebration; **~ machen** (*Krach machen*) make a racket (*od.* a hell of a noise *Sl.*); (*feiern*) have a wild time of it

Remoulade [remu'la:də], **Remouladensoße** *f*; -, -n; *Gastr.* remoulade; *mit hart gekochtem Eigelb, Öl, Gurken und Kapern auch:* tartar sauce

Rempelei *f*; -, -en jostling; *Sport* pushing; **rempeln** *v/t. umg.* jostle, bump into, barge into *allg.*; *Sport* push, give *s.o.* a push, shove

REM-Phase *f* REM (*od.* rapid eye movement) phase

Rempler *m*; -s, *-* push, shove

Ren *n*; -s, -s; *Zool.* reindeer

Renaissance [rənɛ'sã:s] *f*; -, -n **1.** *nur Sg.*; *hist.* Renaissance; **2.** *fig.* renaissance, renascence, revival

Renaissance... *im Subst.* Kirche, Malerei, Möbel etc.: Renaissance ...

Rendezvous [rãde'vu:] *n*; -, *-* **1.** date, rendezvous; *heimliches ~ bes. iro.* tryst; **sich ein ~ geben** *fig.* Prominenz *etc.:* gather, come together; **2.** *Raumf.* docking; **~manöver** *n Raumf.* docking man|oeuvre (*Am.* -euver)

Rendite *f*; -, -n; *Wirts.* yield, profit, (rate of) return

Renegat *m*; -en, -en, **~in** *f*; -, -nen renegade

Reneklode [re:nə'klo:də] *f*; -, -n; *Bot.* greengage

renitent *Adj.* refractory; **Renitenz** *f*; -, *kein Pl.* refractoriness

Renn|auto *n* → *Rennwagen*; **~bahn** *f* *für Pferderennen:* racecourse, *Am.* race track; *Mot.* circuit, *Am.* speedway; *Laufsport:* track; **~boot** *n* powerboat

rennen; *rennt, rannte, ist od. hat gerannt* **I.** *v/i.* (*ist*) run; (*wett~*) race; (*rasen*) *auch* rush, tear, dash; **~ gegen** run against (*od.* into); **er rennt bei jeder Kleinigkeit zu s-r Mutter** *umg.* he goes running to his mother for every little thing; **er rennt zu jedem Popkonzert** *umg.* he goes to every pop concert that comes along, he can't miss any pop concert; **dauernd zum Arzt ~** be forever running to the doctor; **ins Verderben ~** *fig.* rush headlong into disaster; → *Wette*; **II.** *v/t.* (*hat*) **sich** (*Dat.*) (**an etw.** *Dat.*) **ein Loch in den Kopf ~** bang one's head (against something) and hurt it; **j-m ein Messer in den Bauch ~** *umg.* thrust a knife into s.o.'s stomach *allg.*; → *Haufen* 1

Rennen *n*; -s, *-* running; (*Wettrennen*) race; (*Rennveranstaltung*) race(s *Pl.*); **ein ~ fahren** drive in a race; **totes ~** dead heat; **aus dem ~ werfen** put *s.o.* out of the race; **das ~ machen** come in first; *fig.* come out on top; **j-n ins ~ schicken** *fig.* als Kandidaten *etc.:* send s.o. into the fray; **er liegt noch gut im ~** he's still well placed; *fig.* he's still going strong; *bei Bewerbung etc.:* he's still in the running; **das ~ ist gelaufen** *fig.* it's all over

Renner *m*; -s, *-* **1.** (*Pferd*) racehorse; **2.** *umg.* (*Erfolg*) hit; *Wirts.* winner; **das Buch wird ein ~** we're *etc.* onto a winner with that book; **1998 waren Handys der große ~** in 1998 mobile phones were the top sellers *allg.*

Rennerei *f*; -, -en; *umg.*, *oft pej.* running around

Renn|fahrer *m*, **~fahrerin** *f Mot.* racing driver, *Am.* racecar driver; *Fahrrad:* racing cyclist; *Motorrad:* racing motorcyclist; **~läufer** *m*, **~läuferin** *f Skisport:* ski racer; **~leitung** *f* race organization; (*Personen*) race organizers *Pl.*, race control; *bei Pferderennen:* *Brit.* stewards; **~lenker** *m* drop(ped) han-

dlebars Pl.; **~maschine** *f* racer; **~pferd** *n* racehorse; **~platz** *m* racecourse, *the* turf; **zum ~ gehen** go to the races; **~rad** *n* racing cycle, racer; **~reifen** *m* racing tyre (*Am.* tire); **~rodeln** *n* luge racing; **~rodler** *m*, **~rodlerin** *f* luge racer; **~schuhe** *Pl.* running shoes, spikes; **~sport** *m* racing; *mit Pferden auch:* the turf; **~stall** *m* racing stable; **~strecke** *f* race track, *Mot. auch* course; **~wagen** *m* racing car, *Am.* racecar; **~wette** *f* racing bet

Renommee [renɔ'me:] *n*; -s, -s, *mst Sg.* reputation; (*Ruhm*) fame, renown; **ein gutes ~ haben** have a good name (*od.* reputation); **an ~ einbüßen** suffer damage to one's reputation; **renommieren** *v/i.* boast (*mit* of)

Renommier|stück *n* showpiece; **~sucht** *f* desire to show off; **~universität** *f* prestigious university

renommiert I. *P.P.* → *renommieren*; **II.** *Adj.* famous, noted, renowned (*wegen* for); (highly) acclaimed; *Institut etc.:* auch prestigious; **e-e international ~e Klinik** a clinic with an international reputation

renovieren *vt/i.* renovate, refurbish, *Am. umg.* rehab; (*Innenraum*) redecorate; **Renovierung** *f* renovation; *Innenräume:* redecoration; *gründlich:* makeover

rentabel I. *Adj. Wirts.* profitable, viable; *weitS.* worthwhile; **II.** *Adv.:* **~ wirtschaften** operate at a profit, show a profit; **Rentabilität** *f*; -, *kein Pl.* profitability, viability

Rentabilitäts|grenze *f Wirts.* breakeven point; **~prüfung** *f* profitability audit; **~rechnung** *f* profitability evaluation; **~schwelle** *f* breakeven point

Rente *f*; -, -n **1.** (*Altersrente etc.*) pension, *Am. auch* retirement plan; **~ beziehen** draw a pension; **in ~ gehen** retire; **2.** (*Einkommen*) revenue; (*Jahresrente*) annuity; (*Zins*) interest; **3.** **~n** *Pl. Wirts.* → *Rentenpapiere*

Renten|alter *n*: **das ~** retirement age; **flexibles ~** flexible age of retirement; **~anpassung** *f* adjustment of pensions (to wages and prices); **~anspruch** *m* pension claim; **~basis** *f* annuity claim; **~beitrag** *m* (*monatliche Zahlung in die Rentenversicherung*) (monthly) contribution to the pension scheme (*Am.* retirement plan); **ständig steigende Rentenbeiträge** ever-increasing pension contributions; **~bemessungsgrundlage** *f* basis for the calculation of pensions, pension base

rentenberechtigt *Adj.* entitled to a pension; *Alter:* pensionable .

Renten|bescheid *m* pension notice; **~betrug** *m* pension fraud; **~eintrittsalter** *n* retirement age; *gesetzliches/tatsächliches ~* statutory/actual retirement age; **~empfänger** *m*, **~empfängerin** *f* pensioner; **~erhöhung** *f* pension increase; **~formel** *f* formula for the calculation of pensions; **~kasse** *f* (*Rentenversicherung*) (national) pension scheme, pension fund; **Milliardenloch in der ~** *fig.* pension fund announces (*od.* expects) multi-billion deficit; **~mark** *f hist.* rentenmark; **~markt** *m Wirts.* bond market; **~papiere** *Pl. Wirts.* fixed-interest bonds, fixed-income securities; **~politik** *f* pensions policy; **~reform** *f* pension(s) reform; **~system** *n* pensions system

rentenversichert *Adj.* covered by a pension scheme (*Am.* retirement plan); **Rentenversicherung** *f* (nation-

R

al) pension scheme, pension fund, *Am. etwa* Social Security; **Rentenversicherungsträger** *m* member of a pension scheme (*Am.* retirement plan)

Rentenwerte *Pl. Wirts.* fixed-interest securities

Rentier *n Zool.* reindeer; (*Karibu*) caribou

rentieren *v/refl.* → *lohnen* I

Rentierflechte *f Bot.* reindeer moss

Rentner *m; -s, -,* **~in** *f; -, -nen* (old age) pensioner, senior (citizen); **Rentnerstress** *m* retirement stress

reorganisieren *v/t.* reorganize

Rep *m; -s, -s od. pej. -se; Abk. umg.* → **Republikaner**

reparabel *Adj.* repairable; *nicht ~* beyond repair

Reparationen *Pl.,* **Reparationszahlung** *f* reparations (*Pl.*)

Reparatur *f; -, -en* repair(s *Pl.*); *in ~* in for repair, being repaired; *in od. zur ~ geben* take *s.th.* to be repaired

reparaturanfällig *Adj. Modell, Teil:* in need of frequent repair; *Teil:* susceptible to failure; *~ sein* need frequent repairs; **Reparaturanfälligkeit** *f* tendency to need frequent repairs; (*Rate*) failure rate

Reparatur|anleitung *f* repair manual; **~arbeiten** *Pl.* repairs, repair work *Sg.*

reparaturbedürftig *Adj.:* (*dringend*) *~* in need of (urgent) repair

Reparatur|kosten *Pl.* (cost *Sg.* of) repairs; **~schnelldienst** *m* fast repair service, while-you-wait repair service; **~set** *n* repair kit; **~werft** *f* repair yard; **~werkstatt** *f* workshop; *Mot.* garage

reparieren *v/t.* repair, mend, fix *umg.*; *den Fernseher ~ lassen* have the television repaired; *das ist nicht mehr zu ~* it can't be repaired, it's beyond repair

Repatriierung *f Pol.* **1.** (*Wiederverleihen der Staatsangehörigkeit*) restoration of citizenship; **2.** (*Heimführen*) repatriation

Repertoire [reper'toa:ɐ] *n; -s, -s* repertoire (*auch fig.*); **~stück** *n* repertory play

Repetent *m; -en, -en,* **~in** *f; -, -nen; Päd.* pupil who has to repeat a year, *Am.* repeater

repetieren I. *v/t.* (*Stoff*) revise; **II.** *v/i. Päd.* repeat a year

Repetier|gewehr *n* repeating rifle; **~uhr** *f* repeater, repeating watch

Repetition *f; -, -en* repetition; **Repetitor** *m; -s, -en,* **Repetitorin** *f; -, -nen* **1.** *Univ.* coach (for law students); **2.** *Mus.* répétiteur; **Repetitorium** *n; -s, Repetitorien;* (*Buch*) revision (*Am.* review) book; *Univ.* revision (*od.* cramming *umg.*) course (*od.* lesson)

Replik [re'pli:k] *f; -, -en* **1.** reply (*auch Jur.*), rejoinder; **2.** *Kunst:* (*Originalkopie*) replica; **Replikat** *n; -(e)s, -e* replica

Report *m; -(e)s, -e* report; *diskriminierender:* exposé; **Reportage** [repɔr'ta:ʒə] *f; -, -n;* (*Bericht*) report; (*Sport: Live-*) commentary (*über + Akk.* on); *die ~n über* (+ *Akk.*) ... *auch* (the) coverage of ...; **Reporter** *m; -s, -,* **Reporterin** *f; -, -nen* reporter

repräsentabel *Adj.* presentable; (*eindrucksvoll*) impressive; *stärker:* imposing

Repräsentant *m; -en, -en* representative; *e-r Theorie etc.:* exponent; **Repräsentantenhaus** *n USA: Parl.* House (of Representatives); **Reprä-**

---

sentantin *f; -, -nen* → **Repräsentant**; **Repräsentanz** *f; -, -en* **1.** *nur Sg.* representation; **2.** *Wirts.* agency; (*Filiale*) branch

Repräsentation *f; -, -en* (*Vertretung*) representation; (*Bewirtung von Gästen*) entertainment; *der ~ dienen* be for prestige purposes; *sehr auf ~ bedacht sein Firma:* be very concerned with its image

Repräsentations|aufwendung *f* entertainment expenses *Pl.;* **~bau** *m* prestige building; **~figur** *f* figurehead; **~pflichten** *Pl.* representational duties

repräsentativ *Adj.* **1.** *auch Pol.* representative (*für* of); *nicht ~ sein Ergebnis etc.:* not be representative (*od.* typical); **2.** (*imposant*) impressive, imposing; *attr. Auto etc.:* prestige ..., status ...

Repräsentativ|befragung *f* poll of a representative sample, repretative poll; **~erhebung** *f* controlled sampling; **~system** *n Pol.* representative government; **~umfrage** *f* → *Repräsentativbefragung*

repräsentieren I. *v/t.* represent; (*ein Aushängeschild sein für*) be a calling card for; *sie repräsentiert ihr Land sehr gut* she is a very good ambassador for her country; **II.** *v/i.* act in a representative capacity; (*Gäste bewirten*) entertain; *gut ~ können* be a good ambassador; *Gastgeberin:* be a good hostess

Repressalie *f; -, -n* reprisal; (*Vergeltung*) *auch* retaliation (*auch Pl.*); *~n ergreifen gegen* take reprisals on, retaliate against

Repression *f; -, -en* **1.** *Pol.* suppression, repression; **2.** *Psych.* repression; **repressionsfrei** *Adj.* free of suppression; **repressiv** *Adj.* repressive

Reprint ['ri:print] *m; -s, -s* reprint

Reprise *f; -, -n* **1.** *Theat.* revival; *Film:* rerun; *TV auch* repeat; *Schallplatte:* re-release, reissue; **2.** *Mus.* recapitulation

reprivatisieren *v/t.* reprivatize, denationalize; **Reprivatisierung** *f* reprivatization, denationalization

Repro *f; -, -s od. m; -s, -s; umg.* → *Reproduktion*

Reproduktion *f; -, -en; allg.* reproduction; **reproduzierbar** *Adj.* reproducible; **reproduzieren** *v/t. und v/refl.* reproduce

Repro|kamera *f* process camera; **~studio** *n* reprographic studio; **~technik** *f* reprographic (*od.* reproduction) technology; **~verfahren** *n* reproduction process; **~werkstatt** *f* reprographic studio

Reptil *n; -s, -ien; Zool.* reptile

Reptilienfonds *m Pol.* secret funds *Pl.*

Republik *f; -, -en* republic; *die ~ Österreich* the Republic of Austria

Republikaner *m; -s, -,* **~in** *f; -, -nen* **1.** (*Anhänger der Republik*) republican; **2.** *USA: Parl.* Republican; **3.** *BRD:* Republican; *die ~* the Republican Party; **republikanisch** *Adj.* **1.** (*für die Republik eintretend*) republican; **2.** *USA: Parl.* Republican

Republikflucht *f ehem. DDR:* illegal emigration from the GDR

Reputation *f; -, kein Pl.* reputation, standing

Requiem ['re:kviɛm] *n; -s, -s* requiem (mass)

requirieren *v/t.* requisition

Requisit *n; -s, -en* **1.** (*Teil*) requisite; **2.** *~en Theat.* (stage) properties, props

---

umg.; **Requisite** *f; -, -n; Theat.* **1.** property department; **2.** → *Requisitenkammer,* **Requisitenkammer** *f* property (*od.* props *umg.*) room; **Requisiteur** [rekvizi'tø:ɐ] *m; -s, -e* property man, *Am.* propman; **Requisiteurin** *f; -, -nen* property mistress, *Am.* propwoman, propgirl

Reseda *f; -, Reseden; Bot.* reseda

Resektion *f; -, -en; Med.* resection

Reservat *n; -(e)s, -e* **1.** *für Tiere, Pflanzen:* (nature) reserve; **2.** *der Indianer etc.:* reservation; **3.** (*Sonderrecht*) prerogative, preserve

Reserve *f; -, -n* **1.** (*Vorrat*) reserve supply, reserves *Pl.* (*an + Dat.* of); *stille ~n* hidden reserves; *in ~ halten* keep in reserve; **2.** *nur Sg.; Sport* reserves *Pl.,* reserve team; *Mil.* reserves *Pl.;* **3.** *nur Sg.;* (*Zurückhaltung*) reserve; *j-n aus der ~ locken* bring s.o. out of his (*od.* her) shell, draw s.o. out; **~bank** *f Sport* substitutes' bench; **~fonds** *m* reserve fund; **~kanister** *m* spare can; **~offizier** *m,* **~offizierin** *f Mil.* reserve officer; **~rad** *n* spare (wheel); **~reifen** *m* spare (tyre, *Am.* tire); **~spieler** *m,* **~spielerin** *f Sport* reserve, substitute; **~tank** *m* reserve tank; **~truppen** *Pl.* reserves

reservieren I. *vt.* (*auch ~ lassen*) reserve; (*vorbestellen*) *auch* book; **II.** *v/i.* make a reservation; *haben Sie reserviert? im Restaurant:* do you have a reservation?; **reserviert I.** *P.P.* → *reservieren;* **II.** *Adj.* reserved (*auch fig.* zurückhaltend); *sich ~ verhalten* keep one's distance; **Reserviertheit** *f* reserve; **Reservierung** *f* reservation

Reservist *m; -en, -en,* **~in** *f; -, -nen; Mil.* reservist; *fig. Sport* reserve, substitute

Reservoir [rezer'voa:ɐ] *n; -s, -e* reservoir (*auch fig.*) (*an + Dat.* of)

Residenz *f; -, -en* **1.** *allg.:* residence; **2.** (*Hauptstadt*) capital, royal seat; **~stadt** *f* capital, royal seat

residieren *v/i.* reside

Resignation *f; -, kein Pl.* resignation; **resignativ** *Adj.* resigned; **resignieren** *v/i.* give up; resign; **resigniert I.** *P.P.* → *resignieren;* **II.** *Adj.* resigned; **III.** *Adv.: ~ lächeln* give a resigned smile

resistent *Adj. Med.* resistant (*gegen* to); **Resistenz** *f; -, kein Pl.; Med.* resistance (*gegen* to)

resolut *Adj.* resolute, determined; *Persönlichkeit:* forceful; **Resolutheit** *f* resoluteness, determination; *von Persönlichkeit:* forcefulness

Resolution *f; -, -en* resolution

Resonanz *f; -, -en* resonance; *fig.* response; *auf (viel) ~ stoßen* evoke (considerable) interest; *der Plan fand keine ~* the plan didn't meet with any response; **~boden** *m* sounding board; **~kasten** *m,* **~körper** *m* sound box, resonating chamber (*od.* body), resonator; **~saite** *f* sympathetic string

Resopal® *n; -s, kein Pl.* melamine

resorbieren *v/t.* absorb; **Resorption** *f; -, -en* absorption

resozialisieren *v/t.* rehabilitate; **Resozialisierung** *f* rehabilitation

Respekt *m; -s, kein Pl.* respect (*vor + Dat.* for); *~ haben vor* (+ *Dat.*) respect; *großen ~ haben vor* (+ *Dat.*) have great respect for, hold *s.o.* in great respect; *stärker:* stand in awe of; *aus ~ gegenüber* out of respect for; *formell:* in deference to; *sich bei j-m ~ verschaffen* teach s.o. to respect one;

bei allem ~ with all due respect; **~!(, ~!)** umg. I'm impressed!, well done!, good for you!; → **einflößen; respektabel I.** Adj. respectable (auch weitS. beachtlich); **II.** Adv.: **sich ganz ~ schlagen** umg. become all respectable; **respekteinflößend, Respekt einflößend** Adj. impressive, stärker: awesome

respektieren v/t. respect

respektive Adv. (abgek. **resp.**) **1.** and … respectively; (und) and; **2.** (oder) or (alternatively); (either …) or (…, as the case may be); **3.** (oder vielmehr) or rather

respektlos Adj. disrespectful; **Respektlosigkeit** f **1.** Sg. disrespectfulness, lack of respect; **2.** (Handlung) disrespectful act; (Frechheit) (piece of) impertinence; (Äußerung) disrespectful remark

Respektsperson f figure of authority; (Vorgesetzter etc.) person in authority

respektvoll Adj. respectful

Ressentiment [rɛsãti'mãː] n; -s, -s nachtragend: ill feeling, hard feelings Pl., resentment; (Vorurteil) prejudice; **keinerlei ~s haben** harbo(u)r no ill feelings

Ressort [rɛ'soːɐ] n; -s, -s department; e-s Ministers: auch portfolio; (Zuständigkeit) province, area, preserve; **das fällt nicht in mein ~** that is not (within) my area; **~chef** m, **~chefin** f, **~leiter** m, **~leiterin** f head of department, department head; **~minister** m, **~ministerin** f departmental minister

Ressourcen [rɛ'sʊrsn̩] Pl. resources; (Geldmittel) auch funds

Rest m; -(e)s, -e **1.** allg.: rest; **der letzte ~** the last scrap; **der letzte ~ an Kraft** one's last ounce of strength; **das ist mein letzter ~ Zucker** that's my last scrap (od. the very last) of my sugar; **von den hundert Mark ist mir nur noch ein kleiner ~ übrig** there's very little left of the hundred marks; **sie können den ~ morgen bezahlen** you can pay the balance (od. amount remaining) tomorrow; **der ~ der Welt** the rest of the world; **wenn du e-n ~ von Anstand hättest** if you had the least bit of decency; **das gab ihm den ~** umg. fig. that finished him (off); **2.** Pl. (Restbestände) remainders; (Stoffreste) remnants; (Speisereste) leftovers; e-s Gebäudes, e-r Kultur etc.: remains; **heute gibt's ~e zu essen** today we've got leftovers; **ihre sterblichen ~e** her (mortal) remains; **3.** Math. remainder; Chem., Tech., Jur. residue; **10 lässt sich nicht durch 3 ohne ~ teilen** 3 does not go into 10 without a remainder; **20 geteilt durch 6 ist 3 ~ 2** 20 divided by 6 is 3 and two left over

Rest|alkohol m residual alcohol; **~auflage** f remaindered stock

Restaurant [rɛsto'rãː] n; -s, -s restaurant; **er isst oft im ~** he eats out a lot

Restauration f; -, -en **1.** Pol., Kunst: restoration; **2.** österr. restaurant; **Restaurationsarbeiten** Pl. restoration work Sg.; **Restaurationszeit** f hist. Restoration; **restaurativ** Adj. Pol. aimed at restoring the old order; **Restaurator** m; -s, -en, **Restauratorin** f; -, -nen restorer; **restaurieren** v/t. restore; **Restaurierung** f restoration

Rest|bestand m remaining stock; **~betrag** m balance, outstanding sum

Reste|essen n leftovers Pl.; **~verkauf** m remainder (od. remnant) sale; **~verwertung** f using up leftovers

Restforderung f residual claim

restituieren v/t. (Vermögen etc.) restore, make restitution of förm.

Restitution f; -, -en; förm. restitution

Restitutionsedikt n: **das ~** hist. the Edict of Restitution

Restlaufzeit f Fin. unexpired term, remaining life

restlich Adj. remaining; **der ~e Zucker/Abend** the rest of the sugar/evening

restlos I. Adj. complete, total; **II.** Adv. completely, totally, absolutely; **~ zufrieden** auch satisfied (od. perfectly) satisfied; **~ glücklich** perfectly happy; **~ erledigt** umg. done for; (erschöpft) absolutely whacked (Am. beat); **ich bin ~ bedient** umg. I've had enough, I've had about as much as I can take, that's the last straw; **etw. ~ aufessen** eat up every scrap of s.th.

Rest|posten m Wirts. remaining stock; von Büchern: remainder; Schildaufschrift: remnants; (Bücher) remaindered copies; **~programm** n remainder of the program(me); Sport remaining games Pl. (in a championship etc.)

Restriktion f; -, -en restriction; **j-m ~en auferlegen** place restrictions on s.o.; **Restriktionsmaßnahme** f restrictive measure; **restriktiv** Adj. restrictive; **~e Finanzpolitik** Pol. tight monetary policy

Rest|risiko n residual risk; **es bleibt ein ~** an element of risk remains; **~schuld** f Wirts. outstanding (od. remaining) debt; **~spannung** f Etech. residual voltage; **~strafe** f remaining sentence, the rest of the sentence; **~summe** f balance; **~süße** f Wein: 2 Gramm ~ 2 grams of residual sugar; **~urlaub** m holiday (Am. vacation) carried over, unused holiday (Am. vacation); formell: remaining holiday (Am. vacation) entitlement; **~wärme** f residual heat; **~wert** m residual value, value after depreciation; **~zahlung** f final payment (od. instal[l]ment), payment of the balance; **~zucker** m → **Restsüße**

Resultat n; -(e)s, -e result, outcome; Sport score; bei Rennen: results Pl.; **resultieren** v/i.: **~ aus** result from; **~ in etw.** result (od. end up) in s.th.

Resümee [rezy'meː] n; -s, -s summary, résumé; **ein kurzes ~ geben** give a brief résumé; **~ ziehen** sum up; **resümieren** vt/i. sum up, summarize, recapitulate

retardieren v/t. delay, retard; **~des Moment** Theat. retarding element; fig. delaying factor

Retorte f; -, -n retort; **aus der ~** Lebensmittel etc.: synthetic; Stadt: artificially created; Kind: → **Retortenbaby**

Retorten|baby n test-tube baby; **~stadt** f new town, artificially created city

retour [re'tuːɐ] Adv. bes. österr., schw. back; **einmal München (und) ~** one return to Munich, Am. a round-trip ticket to Munich

Retour|billet n schw. Verk. return (Am. round-trip) ticket; **~gang** m österr. Mot. reverse (gear); **~kutsche** f umg. tit for tat, riposte; **mit e-r ~ reagieren** give as good as one gets

retournieren [retur'niːrən] vt/i. Sport return the ball; (Waren) return

retrospektiv I. Adj. Sicht etc.: retrospective; **II.** Adv. betrachten etc.: retrospectively; **Retrospektive** f; -, -n **1. in der ~** in retrospect, looking back;

2. (Ausstellung) retrospective (exhibition) (+ Gen. of)

Retrovirus n retrovirus

retten I. v/t. save (auch fig.); aus dem Feuer etc.: auch rescue (**aus, vor** + Dat. from); (bergen) recover; bes. Naut. salvage (auch fig.), salve; **j-m das Leben ~** save s.o.'s life; **j-n vor dem Ertrinken ~** save s.o. from drowning; **die Situation / den Abend ~** fig. save the situation / rescue the evening; **bist du noch zu ~?** umg. have you gone completely mad?, have you lost your mind?; **er ist nicht mehr zu ~** umg. he's a lost cause, he's beyond help; **er rettete s-e Ehre** he vindicated his hono(u)r; **II.** v/i. Sport make a save; **den ~den Einfall haben** come up with the answer, save the day; **III.** v/refl. escape (**vor** + Dat. from); **sich ins Haus** etc. **~ können** manage to escape into the house etc.; **sich vor Arbeit** etc. **nicht mehr ~ können** be snowed under (od. inundated) with work etc.; **er konnte sich vor Angeboten nicht (mehr) ~** he was besieged with offers / swamped with work; **rette sich, wer kann!** iro. it's every man for himself

Retter m; -s, -, **~in** f; -, -nen rescuer, lit. deliverer, savio(u)r; bes. Reli. Saviour; **ein ~ in der Not** a friend in need; umg. iro. a knight in shining armo(u)r

Rettich m; -s, -e (large white) radish, mooli, Am. daikon

Rettung f; -, -en **1.** rescue (**aus** from); (Entkommen) escape; (Bergung) recovery; bes. Naut. salvaging; **das war s-e ~ / s-e letzte ~** that was his salvation / his last hope (of salvation), that's what saved him; **für ihn gab es keine ~** he was past help (od. beyond salvation); **du bist m-e ~** umg. fig. you're my salvation, you've saved me; **2.** österr. (Rettungsdienst) rescue (od. emergency) service; auch **Rettungswagen**

Rettungs|aktion f rescue operation (auch fig.); Wirts. auch rescue bid; **~anker** m sheet anchor (auch fig.); **~arzt** m, **~ärztin** f → **Notarzt, ~bombe** f rescue capsule (for a miner); **~boje** f lifebuoy; **~boot** n lifeboat; **~dienst** m rescue (od. emergency) service; **~fahrzeug** n rescue vehicle; **~fallschirm** m emergency parachute; **~flugzeug** n rescue aircraft; **~gerät** n rescue equipment; Bergb. rescue apparatus; **~hubschrauber** m rescue helicopter; **~insel** f (inflatable) life raft; **~kreuzer** m rescue vessel; **~leine** f lifeline

rettungslos I. Adj. hopeless; **II.** Adv. hopelessly (auch fig.), beyond all hope; **~ verloren** auch irretrievably lost; **~ verliebt** hopelessly in love (od. smitten); **e-e ~ verfahrene Situation** an irredeemably deadlocked situation

Rettungs|mannschaft f rescue team; Pl. auch relief workers; **~medaille** f life-saving medal; **~ring** m **1.** life belt (Am. auch preserver); **2.** umg. (dicker Bauch) spare tyre (Am. tire); **~schlauch** m rescue chute; **~schlitten** m rescue sledge (Am. sled), bloodwagon umg.; **~schuss** m: **finaler ~** fatal shot (fired by the police at a criminal to rescue a victim); **~schwimmen** n life saving; **~schwimmer** m, **~schwimmerin** f lifeguard; **~station** f first-aid post; **~system** n Raumf. escape system; **~versuch** m rescue attempt (od. bid); e-s Arztes: attempt to save s.o.'s life; **~wache** f rescue station (kleiner: post); **~wagen** m rescue (od. emergency) vehicle (od. car); (Krankenwagen) ambulance; **~wesen** n emergency services Pl.; **~weste** f life jacket (Am. auch vest)

Return [ri'tø:ɐn] m; -s, -s; Sport return

Retusche f;-, -n retouch; Pl. retouching, touching up; **retuschieren** v/t. retouch, touch up

Reue f; -, kein Pl. remorse (über + Akk. for); (Schmerz und Bedauern) penitence; bes. religiös: repentance (for); (Bedauern, Bedenken) compunction; (Zerknirschung) tiefe: contrition; **keine ~ empfinden** feel no remorse; **ohne die geringste ~** without the slightest compunction; **tätige ~** Jur. active remorse (with action to limit harm caused by one's crime)

reuen v/t. geh.: **es reut mich, ihn beleidigt zu haben** I regret having insulted him; **das Geld / die Zeit reut mich** I regret the money/time wasted; **reuevoll**, **reuig** Adj. repentant; **reumütig** I. Adj. repentant, contrite, präd. auch full of remorse; **~es Geständnis** remorseful confession; II. Adv.: **~ zurückkehren** return full of remorse

Reuse f; -, -n creel, fish basket

reüssieren v/i.; altm. be successful (**mit** with; **bei** in)

Revanche [re'vãːʃə] f; -, n revenge; **j-m ~ geben** give s.o. a chance to get even; **für etw. ~ nehmen** take (one's) revenge for s.th.; **~ fordern** issue a challenge to a return game (Sport auch match); **~foul** n retaliatory foul; **~kampf** m 1. Boxen etc.: return bout; 2. (Spiel) return match; **~krieg** m war of revenge; 2lüstern Adj. vengeful, präd. auch out for revenge; **~spiel** n return match

revanchieren [revã'ʃiːrən] v/refl. take revenge (**an** + Dat. on), get one's own back (on) umg.; als Dank: return the favo(u)r, pay s.o. back; **sich mit e-m bösen Foul am Gegner ~** retaliate with a vicious foul on (od. by viciously fouling) the other player; **sich mit e-m Blumenstrauß ~** show one's appreciation with a bunch of flowers

Revanchismus [revã'ʃɪsmʊs] m; kein Pl.; Pol., pej. revanchism; **Revanchist** m; -en, -en, **Revanchistin** f; -, -nen, **revanchistisch** Adj. revanchist

Reverenz f; -, -en reverence, respect, deference; **j-m s-e ~ erweisen** (ehren) show deference to s.o.; (besuchen) pay s.o. one's respects

Revers¹ [re'veːɐ] n, österr. m; -, -; (Aufschlag) lapel

Revers² [re'vɛrs] m; -(es), -(e) e-r Münze: reverse

Revers³ [re'vɛrs] m; -es, -e; (Schreiben) (written) declaration

reversibel Adj. reversible; **Reversibilität** f; -, kein Pl. reversibility

revidieren v/t. (korrigieren) revise; (überprüfen) check

Revier n; -s, -e; (bes. Polizeirevier) district, Am. precinct; (Runde) beat; (Wache) police station; (e-s Försters) district, range; Bergb. (coal)field; (Jagdrevier) hunting ground; (e-s Vogels etc.) territory; (e-s Kellners) tables Pl.; (Mil. Krankenrevier) sickbay, sick quarters; fig. preserve, domain; **sein ~ verteidigen** defend one's preserve; **~förster** m, **~försterin** f forest warden, forester, Am. auch forest ranger; **~wache** f police station

Revirement [revirə'mãː] n; -s, -s; Pol.

reshuffle

Revision f; -, -en 1. (Überprüfung) check, inspection; Wirts. audit; beim Zoll: examination; 2. Druck. checking corrected proofs; 3. (Änderung) revision, change; 4. Jur. appeal; **~ einlegen** lodge an appeal; **in (die) ~ gehen** proceed to appeal; → auch **Berufung** 1

Revisionismus m; -, kein Pl. revisionism

Revisions|antrag m Jur. notice of appeal; **~frist** f Jur. (statutory) period within which an appeal has to be lodged; **~gericht** n, **~instanz** f Jur. court of appeal; **~urteil** n Jur. appeal decision (od. verdict); **~verfahren** n appeal proceedings Pl.; **~verhandlung** f Jur. hearing of an appeal

Revisor m; -s, -en, **~in** f; -, -nen 1. Druck. reviser; 2. Wirts. auditor

Revolte f; -, -n revolt; **revoltieren** v/i. revolt; fig. Magen: protest, stärker: rebel

Revolution f; -, -en revolution; **die 1848er ~** the revolution of 1848; **die industrielle ~** the Industrial Revolution; **revolutionär** Adj., **Revolutionär** m; -s, -e, **Revolutionärin** f; -, -nen revolutionary (auch fig.); **revolutionieren** v/t. bes. fig. revolutionize; **Revolutionierung** f revolutionizing

Revolutions|führer m, **~führerin** f revolutionary leader; **~gericht** n revolutionary tribunal; **~rat** m revolutionary council; **~regierung** f revolutionary government; **~tribunal** n revolutionary tribunal

Revoluzzer m; -s, -, **~in** f; -, -nen; pej. would-be revolutionary, radical; **~ sein** act the revolutionary

Revolver m; -s, - revolver

Revolver|blatt n umg. pej. sensationalist rag; **~drehbank** f turret lathe; **~griff** m handgun butt; **~held** m gunslinger; **~kopf** m Tech. turret (head); **~kugel** f handgun bullet; **~lauf** m (revolver) barrel; **~mann** m gunman; **~schnauze** f umg. lippy person, Am. motormouth; **~schuss** m revolver shot, shot from a revolver; **~tasche** f holster (for a revolver); **~trommel** f drum magazine

Revue [re'vyː] f; -, -n 1. Theat. revue; 2. (Zeitschrift) review; **~ passieren lassen** fig. pass in review, unroll

Revue|film m film musical; **~girl** [-gøːɐl] n chorus girl; **~star** m musical star; **~tänzer** m, **~tänzerin** f chorus line dancer; **~theater** n revue theat|re (Am. auch -er); **~truppe** f revue company

Rezensent m; -en, -en, **~in** f; -, -nen critic, reviewer; **rezensieren** v/t. review, write a review on; **Rezension** f; -, -en review, write-up; **gute/schlechte ~en bekommen** auch get a good/bad press

Rezensions|exemplar n, **~stück** n review copy

Rezept n; -(e)s, -e 1. Med. prescription; **nur auf ~ erhältlich** available on prescription only, attr. prescription-only ...; **j-m ein ~ schreiben od. ausstellen** give s.o. a prescription; 2. (Kochrezept) recipe; 3. fig. cure, remedy (**gegen** for); **dafür gibt es kein allgemeines ~** fig. there's no general rule about that; **ein ~ für e-e glückliche Ehe** a recipe (od. formula) for a happy marriage; **~block** m prescription pad; **~formel** f formula for a prescribed medication

rezeptfrei I. Adj. attr. over-the-counter ..., non-prescription ...; **das Mittel ist**

~ this medication is available without a prescription; II. Adv.: **~ bekommen** get s.th. without a prescription (od. over the counter)

Rezeptgebühr f prescription charge

Rezeption f; -, -en 1. Hotel etc.: reception (desk); 2. nur Sg.; in der Literatur etc.: reception; **rezeptiv** I. Adj. Verhalten etc.: receptive, passive; II. Adv.: **sich rein ~ verhalten** be purely receptive (od. passive); **Rezeptivität** f; -, kein Pl. receptivity

Rezeptor m; -s, -en; Bio., Physiol. receptor

Rezeptpflicht f prescription requirement; **rezeptpflichtig** Adj. prescribable, available on prescription only; **~e Arzneimittel** prescription(-only) medications

Rezeptur f; -, -en; Pharm. making up of prescriptions, dispensing; (Raum) dispensary

Rezession f; -, -en; Wirts. recession; **Rezessionssphase** f period of recession

rezessiv Adj. Bio. recessive

Rezipient m; -en, -en, **~in** f; -, -nen; förm. recipient, receiver; Chem. und Phys. recipient; **rezipieren** v/t. (Ideen etc.) absorb, accept; (Buch etc.) receive

reziprok Adj. reciprocal; **Reziprozität** f; -, kein Pl. reciprocity

Rezitation f; -, -en recitation, recital; (öffentliche Lesung) reading; **Rezitativ** n; -s, -e; Mus. recitative; **Rezitator** m; -s, -en, **Rezitatorin** f; -, -nen reciter; **rezitieren** v/t. recite

R-Gespräch n Telef. reversed charges call, Am. auch collect call

Rhabarber m; -s, kein Pl.; auch fig. rhubarb; **~kompott** n stewed rhubarb; **~kuchen** m rhubarb flan (Am. pie)

Rhapsodie f; -, -n rhapsody; **rhapsodisch** Adj. rhapsodic

Rhein m; -s; Geog.: **der ~** the Rhine

Rheinarmee f: **die britische ~** the British Army of the Rhine (Abk. BAOR)

Rheinländer m; -s, -, **~in** f; -, -nen Rhinelander, weiblich auch: girl (od. woman) from the Rhineland; **rheinländisch** Adj. nur attr. Rhineland ..., ... from the Rhineland

Rheinland-Pfalz (n) Rhineland-Palatinate; **Rheinland-Pfälzer** m; -s, -, **Rheinland-Pfälzerin** f; -, -nen man (f woman) from the Rhineland-Palatinate; **~ sein** mst come from the Rhineland-Palatinate; **rheinland-pfälzisch** Adj. from the Rhineland-Palatinate; weitS. Rhenish

Rheinwein m Rhine wine; weitS. hock

Rhesus: **~ negativ/positiv** rhesus negative/positive; **~affe** m rhesus (monkey); **~faktor** m; nur Sg. rhesus factor

Rhetorik f; -, kein Pl. rhetoric; **über e-e glänzende ~ verfügen** have a brilliant oratorical style, be a brilliant speaker; **Rhetoriker** m; -s, -, **Rhetorikerin** f; -, -nen orator, rhetorician förm.; **ein ausgezeichneter Rhetoriker** a brilliant speaker; **Rhetorikkurs** m public speaking course; **Rhetorikseminar** n public speaking seminar; **rhetorisch** I. Adj. rhetorical; **~e Figur** rhetorical device; **~e Frage** rhetorical qustion; II. Adv.: **~ ist ~ sehr begabt** he has the gift of rhetoric; **j-m ~ überlegen sein** be a better speaker than s.o.

Rheuma n; -s, kein Pl. rheumatism, Brit. auch rheumatics Pl. umg.; **~ haben** suffer from rheumatism; **~decke** f thermal blanket (od. quilt); **~for-**

schung f rheumatic research, rheumatology; **~klinik** f rheumatic clinic; **~kranke** m, f rheumatic (sufferer); **~kur** f treatment for rheumatism; **~leiden** n (form of) rheumatism; **~mittel** n rheumatic medication; **~salbe** f rheumatic ointment

Rheumatiker m; -s, -, **~in** f; -, -nen rheumatic (sufferer); **rheumatisch** **I.** Adj. rheumatic, rheumaticky umg.; **II.** Adv. rheumatically; **Rheumatismus** m; -, Rheumatismen, mst Sg. → **Rheuma**

Rheumatologe m; -n, -n, **Rheumatologin** f; -, -nen rheumatologist; **Rheumawäsche** f thermal underwear

Rh-Faktor m; nur Sg. Med. Rh (od. rhesus) factor

Rhinozeros n; -ses, -se **1.** Zool. rhinoceros, rhino umg.; **2.** umg. (Dummkopf) dumbo, twit

Rh-negativ Adj. Med. Rh (od. rhesus) negative

Rhodium n; -s, kein Pl.; Chem. (abgek. Rh) rhodium

Rhododendron n, m; -s, Rhododendren; Bot. rhododendron

rhombisch Adj. rhombic; **Rhomboid** n; -(e)s, -e rhomboid; **Rhombus** m; -, Rhomben rhombus

Rhönrad n Turnen: aero wheels Pl.

Rh-positiv Adj. Med. Rh (od. rhesus) positive

Rhythmik f; -, kein Pl. (type of) rhythm; (Lehre) rhythmics (V. im Sg.); **Rhythmiker** m; -s, -, **Rhythmikerin** f; -, -nen rhythmist; **rhythmisch I.** Adj. rhythmic(al); **~e Gymnastik** rhythmic gymnastics (V. im Sg.); **ein gutes ~es Gefühl haben** have a good sense of rhythm; **II.** Adv.: **betonte Musik** music with a strong rhythm; **sich ~ bewegen** move rhythmically

Rhythmus m; -, Rhythmen rhythm; **im ~ klatschen** clap in time to the music, clap to the rhythm; **aus dem ~ kommen** lose the rhythm; Tänzer: get out of step; **~gitarre** f rhythm guitar; **~gruppe** f rhythm section; **~instrument** n rhythm instrument

Ribisel f; -, -(n); österr., Bot. → **Johannisbeere**; **~saft** m österr. redcurrant (Am. red currant) juice; **schwarzer ~** blackcurrant (Am. black currant) juice

Ribo|flavin n; -s, -e; Chem. riboflavin; **~nukleinsäure** f Chem. ribonucleic acid

Richt|antenne f directional aerial (bes. Am. antenna); **~baum** m tree used in a topping-out ceremony; **~block** m (executioner's) block

richten I. v/t. **1.** (lenken, wenden) direct, turn (auf + Akk. towards); (Gewehr, Kamera etc.) point (at); (Augen) turn (towards); (Aufmerksamkeit) direct, turn (to); (Brief, Frage etc.) address (an + Akk. to); (Kritik) direct, level (at); **e-e Frage an j-n / den Sprecher ~** put a question to s.o. / address a question to the speaker; **das war gegen dich gerichtet** that was aimed at (od. intended for, meant for) you; **alle Blicke richteten sich auf ...** (Akk.) all eyes turned to look at ... (od. in the direction of ...); **gerichtet auf** (+ Akk.) Mil., Rakete: targeted on; **2.** Dial. (zurechtmachen) (Bett) make; (Zimmer) tidy up; (Haare) do; (vorbereiten, zubereiten) get s.th. ready, prepare; (Tisch) lay the table; (ausbessern) repair, fix; (in Ordnung bringen) see to; **er wird's schon ~** umg. he'll fix

it; **3.** (einstellen) adjust; (Uhr) set (nach by); **4.** (geradebiegen) straighten, flatten; Med. (Knochenbruch etc.) set; (Bleche) level; **sich** (Dat.) **die Zähne ~ lassen** have one's teeth straightened; **5.** (urteilen) judge; Jur. auch pass sentence on; **II.** v/refl. **1. sich ~ nach** (Regeln, Wünschen) comply with; (abhängen von) depend on; (sich orientieren an) take one's cue from; (nach einem Vorbild) follow s.o.'s example; Sache: be model(l)ed after (od. on); **sich nach der Mode ~** follow the fashion; **sich nach den Vorschriften ~** observe the regulations; **nach der Uhr kannst du dich nicht ~** you can't go by that clock; **ich richte mich** (ganz) **nach Ihnen** whatever suits you best; **warum müssen sich alle nach ihr ~?** why does everybody have to fit in with her (od. what she wants)?; **2. sich ~ an** (+ Akk.) od. **gegen** be directed (od. aimed) at; **mein Verdacht richtet sich gegen ihn** I suspect him; **3. sich selbst ~** euph. take one's own life, III. v/i. judge (über j-n s.o.), pass judg(e)ment (on s.o.)

Richter m; -s, - judge; **Oberster ~** supreme judge; **Herr ~!** Anrede: Your Lordship, Am. Your Honor; **er ist ~ am Landgericht** he is a judge at the regional (Land) court; **zum ~ ernannt werden** be appointed (a) judge (od. called to the bench); **sich zum ~ machen** fig. set o.s. up in judg(e)ment; (das Buch der) **~ bibl.** (the Book of) Judges

Richter|amt n judicial office; **Richterin** f; -, -nen → **Richter**; **richterlich** Adj. judicial; **~recht** n judicial law; **~robe** f judge's gown (od. robe [s Pl.]); **~schaft** f judiciary

Richter-Skala f Richter scale; **das Erdbeben erreichte Stärke acht auf der ~** the earthquake registered eight on the Richter scale

Richter|spruch m (judge's) decision; (Strafe) sentence → **Urteil** 2; **~stuhl** m judge's seat; fig. judg(e)ment seat

Richt|fernrohr n sighting telescope; **~fest** n topping-out ceremony, builder's treat

Richtfunk m directional radio; **~antenne** f radio direction finder (od. RDF) aerial (bes. Am. antenna)

Richtgeschwindigkeit f recommended speed

richtig I. Adj. **1.** right; (fehlerfrei) auch correct; (wahr) true; **die ~e Antwort** the right answer; **~e Aussprache/ Übersetzung** correct pronunciation/ translation; **es war ~ von dir, dass du** you did right (od. it was right of you) to (+ Inf.); **das finde ich nicht ~** I don't think it's right; **so ist's ~!** umg. that's the idea; **2.** (echt, wirklich) real, genuine; (ordentlich) proper; **das ist nicht ihr ~er Name** that is not her real name; **ein ~er Engländer** a real (od. true) Englishman; **s-e ~e Mutter** his real (od. birth) mother; **er ist ein ~er Cowboy** he is a regular cowboy; **wir hatten keinen ~en Sommer** we didn't have any proper (od. decent) summer; **ein ~er Feigling/Idiot** umg. a proper coward/idiot; **3.** (angemessen) appropriate; **in e-m ~en Augenblick** at an appropriate moment; (geeignet) suitable; **das ist der ~e Mann!** he's just the man we etc. need; **4.** (gerecht) fair, right; → **Kopf** 2; **II.** Adv. **1.** properly, correctly; **geht d-e Uhr ~?** is your watch right?; **e-e ~ gehende Uhr** a

watch that gives the right time; **das Telefon** etc. **funktioniert nicht ~** the telephone isn't working properly; **nicht ~ aussprechen/schreiben** not pronounce/spell s.th. correctly; **du hörst gar nicht ~ zu** you're not listening (properly); **sehe ich das ~?** am I right?; **du kommst gerade ~!** you've come at just the right moment; iro. you're the last person I (od. we) need; **Sie sind der Chef? - ~!** umg. so you're the boss? - you've got it!; **ach ja, ~** yes, of course (od. you're right); **mal wieder ~ ausschlafen** have a really good sleep for once; **2.** (auf die ~e Weise) the right way; **mach es ~!** do it properly; **e-e Sache ~ anpacken** go about s.th. the right way; **3.** umg. (völlig) thoroughly, really; (wirklich) really; **noch nicht ~ gar** not properly cooked, not cooked right (Am. all the way) through; **nicht ~ heiß** not really hot; **ich fand ihn ~ nett** umg. I thought he was really nice; **sie tat mir ~ Leid** I was really sorry for her; **es tat ~ weh** it really hurt; **sie wurde ~ verlegen** she was really embarrassed; **da wurde ich erst ~ böse** then I really got angry; **4. ~ liegen** (tendenziell) be on the right track; (völlig recht haben) be absolutely right; **mit d-r Vermutung liegst du ~** you guessed right, your hunch was right; **bei mir liegen Sie ~** you've come to the right person; **er liegt immer ~** he always backs the right horse; **mit Pralinen liegst du** (bei ihr) **immer ~** you can't go wrong with chocolates (for her); **5. ~ stellen** put s.th. right, correct, rectify; auch set the record straight; **lassen Sie mich eines ~ stellen** let me just correct one point; **III.** substantivisch: **das Richtige** the right thing; **nichts Richtiges gelernt haben** have not learnt (Am. learned) any proper trade; **ich hab' den ganzen Tag noch nichts Richtiges gegessen** umg. I haven't had anything proper to eat all day; **er ist der Richtige** he's the right man; **sie ist nicht die Richtige für ihn** she's not right for him; **du bist mir der Richtige!** umg. you're a fine one; **ich hatte drei Richtige im Lotto** I got three numbers right (od. I matched three numbers) in the lottery; → **einzig** II

richtiggehend I. Adj. umg. regular, real; **ein ~er Tyrann** a thoroughgoing tyrant; **II.** Adv.: **~ böse** etc. really angry etc.; **das ist ja ~ großzügig** iro. aren't you overdoing the generosity?

Richtigkeit f correctness; (Fundiertheit) soundness; **die ~ e-r Sache überprüfen/bestätigen** check/confirm the correctness (od. accuracy) of s.th.; **es muss alles s-e ~ haben** everything has to be done properly

richtig liegen → **richtig** II 4; **richtig stellen** → **richtig** II 5

Richtigstellung f rectification, correction

Richt|kranz m, **~krone** f topping-out wreath

Richtlinie f guideline; **~n** auch (general) directions, instructions; **die ~n der Politik bestimmen** set the policy guidelines; **Richtlinienkompetenz** f bes. Pol. policy-making power(s Pl.)

Richt|mikrofon n directional microphone; **~platz** m hist. place of execution; **~preis** m recommended (od. guide) price; **~satz** m Wirts. standard rate; **~schnur** f fig. guiding principle; **~schwert** n executioner's sword;

~spruch m **1.** beim Richtfest: address at a topping-out ceremony; **2.** Jur. altm. judg(e)ment; **~strahler** m **1.** directional (od. beam) aerial (bes. Am. antenna); **2.** (Sender) beam transmitter

Richtung f; -, -en **1.** direction; (Weg) way; (Art, Hinsicht) line; (Kurs) course; **in die falsche/entgegengesetzte ~ gehen** od. **fahren** go in the wrong/opposite direction, go the wrong/opposite way; **aus allen ~en** from all directions, from all around (od. all over the place); **in ~ auf ...** (Akk.), **in ~ ...** in the direction of, towards; **in welcher ~ liegt ...?** which direction is ... from here?; **in südlicher ~ fahren**: in a southerly direction, south(wards); liegen: to the south; **in welche ~ gehen Sie?** which way (od. direction) are you going?; **er kommt aus dieser ~** he'll be coming from that direction; **die ~ stimmt** it's the right direction; fig. it's OK, you've got the right idea; **e-e andere ~ einschlagen** go in a different direction; fig. take a different course; **die ~ ändern** change course; **in e-e bestimmte ~ lenken** fig. be heading in a certain direction; **ein Schritt in die richtige ~** fig. a step in the right direction; **in dieser ~ bin ich total unbegabt** fig. I have no talents in that direction; **2.** fig. (Denkweise) line of thought; (Lehrmeinung) school of thought; in der Kunst: school; **3.** (Tendenz) trend, Pol. auch tendency; e-s Einzelnen: auch views Pl.; in e-r Partei: faction; **e-e bestimmte ~ vertreten** be representative of a certain trend

richtunggebend Adj. trend-setting; **~ sein für** point the way for

Richtungs|änderung f change of direction (od. course) (auch fig.); **~kämpfe** Pl. Pol. (fundamental) policy disputes

richtungs|los Adj. Existenz: aimless; **~ sein** be drifting; **Richtungslosigkeit** f lack of (a sense of) direction; e-r Existenz: aimlessness

Richtungs|pfeil m Mot. lane indication arrow; **~streit** m factional dispute; **~wahl** f Pol. election marking a change of course, landmark election; **~wechsel** m change in direction (od. of course)

richtung(s)weisend Adj. pointing the way; **~ sein** point the way ahead (od. to the future); **e-e ~e Entscheidung** a landmark decision

Richtwert m guide (od. approximate) value

Ricke f; -, -n; Zool. doe (of a roe deer)

rieb Imperf. → reiben

riechen; riecht, roch, hat gerochen; vt/i. smell (nach of); (wittern) scent; **~ an** (+ Dat.) smell at, sniff at; **gut/übel ~** smell good/bad; **süßlich/faulig ~** have a sickly sweet / foul (od. putrid) smell; **es riecht nach Gas** I can smell gas, there's a smell of gas; **die Luft riecht nach Schnee** I can smell snow in the air; **man riecht, dass er getrunken hat** you can tell by the smell that he's been drinking; **riech mal!** smell this!, have a sniff (od. whiff)! umg.; **ich rieche das Parfüm gern** I like the smell of that perfume; **ich kann Knoblauch nicht ~** I hate (the smell of) garlic; **~ nach Betrug** etc. fig. smack of corruption etc.; **ich kann ihn nicht ~** umg. fig. I can't stand him gespr.; **ich konnte es förmlich ~** fig. I could positively

smell it; **er hat es gerochen** umg. fig. he got wind of it; **sie hat sofort gerochen, dass etwas nicht stimmte** she immediately sensed that something was wrong; **das konnte ich doch nicht ~!** umg. fig. how was I to know? allg.; → **Braten, Lunte** 1, **Mund**

Riecher m; -s, -; umg. nose; **e-n guten ~ haben für** fig. have a (good) nose for; **ich hab' den richtigen ~ gehabt** I read the signs right

Riech|fläschchen n (bottle of) smelling salts Pl.; **~kolben** m umg. hum. hooter, Am. schnoz(zle); **~nerv** m olfactory nerve; **~organ** n **1.** olfactory organ; **2.** umg. (Nase) hooter, Am. schnoz(zle); **~salz** n smelling salts Pl.; **~stoff** m aromatic substance (od. essence od. oil), fragrance

Ried n; -(e)s, -e **1.** reeds Pl.; **2.** (Moor) marsh; → **Reet** etc.; **~gras** n sedge

rief Imperf. → **rufen**

Riege f; -, -n; Turnen und fig.: squad

Riegel m; -s, - (Verschluss) bolt; zum Einhaken: latch; Schokolade: row, Am. strip; Seife: bar, Am. cake; **den ~ vorlegen** put the bolt across, bolt the door etc.; **ein ~ Schokolade** a bar of chocolate; **e-r Sache e-n ~ vorschieben** fig. put a stop to s.th.; → **Schloss¹; riegeln** v/t. schw. bolt

Riemchensandale f strap sandal

Riemen¹ m; -s, -; Naut. oar; **sich in die ~ legen** lean into the oars; fig. put one's back into it

Riemen² m; -s, - mit Schnallen oder Löchern: strap; schmaler, langer: thong; Tech. (Treibriemen) (driving) belt; am Gewehr: sling; zum Schleifen: strop; (Schuhbändel) (leather) shoelace; (Hundeleine) (dog) lead; **den ~ enger schnallen** fig. tighten one's belt; **sich am ~ reißen** pull o.s. together; **~ahle** f drawing awl; **~antrieb** m Tech. belt drive; **mit ~** belt-driven; **~scheibe** f Tech. pulley

Riese m; -n, -n **1.** giant (auch fig.); **ein ~ von e-m Mann** etc. a giant of a man etc.; **ein ~ an Geist** fig. an intellectual giant; **2.** Sl. (fiktiver Tausendeuro-, Tausenddollarschein etc..): **für fünf ~n mach ich's** I'll do it for five grand

...riese m, im Subst., fig. mst ... giant; **Automobil~** huge car firm, motor (Am. automotive) industry giant; **Medien~** media giant

rieseln v/i. **1.** (ist gerieselt) Wasser, Sand etc.: trickle; Regen: drizzle; Schnee: fall softly; **ein Schauder rieselte ihr über den Rücken** a shiver ran down her spine; **2.** (hat) Quelle, Bach: babble

Riesen|... im Subst. giant ..., gigantic, mammoth ..., colossal; weitS. Anstrengung etc.: tremendous, superhuman ...; **~appetit** m umg. huge (od. tremendous, voracious) appetite; **~arbeit** f mammoth task; **~auswahl** f tremendous selection; **~baby** n **1.** huge baby; **2.** umg. fig. (Mann) (lumbering) hulk; (Hund) massive hound; **~blamage** f terrible disgrace; **das war e-e ~ für ihn** he made an absolute fool of himself; **~dummheit** f umg. mega boob (Am. auch boo-boo); **das war e-e ~** auch that was really stupid; **~durst** m umg.: **e-n ~ haben** have a terrific thirst; **~echse** f dinosaur; **~enttäuschung** f big (od. terrible) disappointment; **~erfolg** m huge success; Theat., Film: auch smash hit umg.; **~faultier** n ground sloth; **~fehler** m huge blunder, colossal error; **~felge** f Turnen: grand

circle; **~freude** f umg. great (od. tremendous) joy; **j-m e-e ~ machen** give s.o. tremendous pleasure, make s.o. blissfully happy; **~gewinn** m **1.** Wirts. huge profits Pl.; **2.** beim Spiel etc.: huge winnings Pl.

riesen|groß, ~haft Adj. → **riesig** I

Riesen|hunger m umg.: **e-n ~ haben** be ravenous; **~kaktus** m saguaro; **~känguruh** n **graues ~** great grey (Am. gray) kangaroo; **rotes ~** red kangaroo; **~konzern** m giant concern (od. company); **~krach** m umg. **1.** (Radau) racket; **2.** (Streit) huge row (Am. argument); **e-n ~ machen** hit the roof; **~kraft** f tremendous strength; **Riesenkräfte entwickeln** summon up incredible strength; **~krake** m giant squid; **~muschel** f giant clam; **~portion** f umg. giant portion; **e-e ~ Fleisch** a huge piece of meat; **~rad** n Ferris wheel; **~schildkröte** f giant turtle; **~schlange** f boa constrictor; **~schreck** m umg.: **e-n ~ kriegen** get a terrible fright; **~schritt** m giant stride (od. step); **sich mit ~en nähern** zeitlich: be approaching fast, be just around the corner; **~slalom** m giant slalom; **~spaß** m umg.: **e-n ~ haben** have a terrific time (od. tremendous fun); **~stern** m giant star; **~torlauf** m giant slalom; **~überraschung** f umg. terrific (od. tremendous) surprise; **~weib** n umg. **1.** huge woman, giantess; **2.** (tolle Frau) smasher, Am. knockout; **~welle** f Turnen: grand circle; **~wuchs** m gigantism; **~wut** f umg.: **e-e ~ (im Bauch) haben** be in a towering rage

riesig I. Adj. gigantic, enormous, huge (alle auch fig.); umg. (großartig) terrific; **das ist ja ~!** umg. auch that's tremendous!; **II.** Adv. umg. fig. (sehr) tremendously; **sich ~ freuen** be absolutely delighted, be over the moon Brit. umg.; **das amüsierte ihn ~** he was tickled pink; **sie war ~ nett** she was terribly nice; **es war ~ interessant** it was really interesting

Riesin f; -, -nen giantess

Riesling m; -s, -e riesling; **~-Silvaner** m; -s, - riesling-silvaner

riet Imperf. → **raten¹, raten²**

Riff n; -(e)s, -e reef; **auf ein ~ laufen** run onto a reef

Riffel f; -, -n **1.** (Vertiefung) groove; in e-er Säule: flute; (Erhöhung) rib; Pl. auch corrugations; **2.** (Kamm) ripple; **Riffelung** f corrugations Pl.; → **geriffelt**

Rigg n; -s, -s, **Riggung** f Naut. rigging

rigid(e) Adj. rigid

Rigipsplatte® f (type of) plasterboard, gypsum wallboard, Am. auch dry wall, Sheetrock®

rigoros I. Adj. rigorous; (streng) severe, austere; (unerbittlich) adamant, unrelenting; **da ist sie ganz ~** she's quite adamant (od. insistent) about that; **II.** Adv. etw. ~ ablehnen adamantly refuse s.th.; **~ durchgreifen** take rigorous action; **~ vorgehen gegen** take rigorous measures against; **Rigorosität** f; -, kein Pl. rigorousness; (Strenge) severity; (Unerbittlichkeit) unrelenting attitude

Rigorosum n; -s, Rigorosa; Univ. viva voce, viva umg., Am. (oral) defense

Rikscha f; -, -s ricksha(w)

Rille f; -, -n groove; **mit ~n versehen** grooved

rillenförmig Adj. groove-like

Rind n; -(e)s, -er **1.** (Kuh) cow; (Stier)

bull; **~er** cattle *Pl.*; **100 ~er** 100 (head of) cattle; **2.** *nur Sg.*; *(Fleisch)* beef; **Hackfleisch** *etc.* **vom ~** minced *(Am.* ground) beef

Rind... *im Subst. siehe auch* **Rinder...,** **Rinds...**

Rinde *f; -, -n von Baum:* bark; *(Brot-rinde)* crust; *von Käse:* rind; *Anat.* *(Gehirnrinde)* cortex; **ohne ~** → **rindenlos**

rindenlos *Adj. Baum:* barkless; *Brot:* crustless; *Käse:* rindless

Rinder|bandwurm *m Zool.* beef tapeworm; **~braten** *m Gastr.* joint of beef; *gebraten:* roast beef; **~bremse** *f Zool.* horsefly; **~brühe** *f Gastr.* beef stock; **~brust** *f Gastr.* brisket (of beef); **~filet** *n Gastr.* fillet of beef; **~gulasch** *n, m Gastr.* beef goulash; **~herde** *f* herd of cattle; **~herz** *n Gastr.* ox heart; **~leber** *f Gastr.* ox liver; **~lende** *f Gastr.* beef tenderloin; **~pest** *f Vet.* cattle plague, rinderpest; **~talg** *m* beef dripping *(Am. mst* drippings); **~wahn(sinn)** *m Vet.* mad cow disease; **~zucht** *f* cattle breeding *(od.* farming); **~zunge** *f Gastr.* ox tongue

Rindfleisch *n Gastr.* beef; **~brühe** *f Gastr.* beef tea

Rinds... *im Subst. siehe auch* **Rinder...**

Rinds|leder *n* cowhide; **~roulade** *f Gastr.* beef olive

Rindvieh *n umg.* → **Rindvieh 2**

Rindvieh *n* **1.** cattle *Pl.*; **2.** *Sl. (Idiot)* blockhead, stupid ass

Ring *m; -(e)s, -e* ring *(auch Chem., Bot., Tech., Boxen, Zirkus etc.);* *(Kreis)* circle; *Dichtung:* washer; *von Einmachglas:* rubber seal; *(Wurfring)* quoit, ring; *(Straße)* ring road, *Am.* beltway, orbital (road); *(Spionage-, Verbrecherring)* ring; *(Lesering)* book club; **~e Turnen:** rings; **e-n ~ anstecken** put on a ring, put a ring on one's finger; **e-n ~ im Ohr tragen** wear a ring in one's ear; **die ~e wechseln** exchange rings; **an den ~en turnen** exercise on the rings; **die olympischen ~e** the Olympic rings; **e-n ~ bilden** form a ring *(od.* circle); **Wurst im ~** sausage (in the form of a) ring; **~e unter den Augen** bags *(od.* [dark] rings) under one's eyes; **in den ~ steigen** climb into the ring; **~ frei!** *Boxen:* seconds out!

Ring|antenne *f* loop aerial *(Am.* antenna); **~arzt** *m,* **~ärztin** *f beim Boxen:* ringside doctor; **~bahn** *f* circular *(od.* belt) railway

Ringel *m; -s, -* little ring; *(Locke)* ringlet

Ringel|blume *f Bot.* marigold; **~muster** *n* (pattern with) horizontal stripes, hooped pattern

ringeln I. *v/t. (Haare, Schwanz)* curl; *um etw. herum:* coil, twine; **II.** *v/refl.* curl, coil o.s.; *schlängelnd:* wind, meander

Ringel|natter *f Zool.* grass snake; **~piez** *m; -(es), -e; umg.:* **~** (mit Anfassen) hop *allg.;* **~pullover** *m* horizontally striped *(od.* hooped) pullover; **~reihen** *m; -s, -* ring dance *(od.* a-ring-a-ring-o'-roses, *Am.* ring-around-the-rosey; **~schwanz** *m,* **~schwänzchen** *n* curly tail; **~spiel** *n österr.* roundabout, merry-go-round, *Am.* auch car(r)ousel; **~söckchen** *Pl.* hooped (ankle) socks; **~socken** *Pl.* hooped socks; **~taube** *f* wood pigeon

ringen; *ringt, rang, hat gerungen* **I.** *v/i.* **1.** *auch Sport* wrestle; **ich ringe aktiv seit zehn Jahren** I've been wrestling actively for ten years; **2.** *fig.:* **~ mit**

wrestle *(od.* grapple, vie) with; **mit sich ~** wrestle with o.s.; **mit dem Tod ~** wrestle with death, fight for one's life; **3. ~ um** struggle *(od.* fight, battle, vie) for; **um j-s Anerkennung** *etc.* **~** vie for s.o.'s recognition *etc.*; **4. nach Atem ~** gasp for breath; **nach Fassung ~** try to regain one's composure; **nach Worten ~** struggle for words; **II.** *v/t. geh.* wring; **verzweifelt die Hände ~** wring one's hands (in despair); **j-m etw. aus der Hand ~** wrench s.th. from s.o.'s hand; **III. Ringen** *n; -s, kein Pl.* wrestling; *(Catchen)* all-in *(Am.* freestyle *od.* championship) wrestling; *fig.* struggle (**um** for)

Ringer *m; -s, -, ~in f; -, -nen; Sport* wrestler; *(Catcher[in])* all-in *(Am.* freestyle) wrestler

Ring|fahndung *f* cordon search; **~finger** *m* ring finger

Ringform *f* shape of a ring; *(Kuchenform)* ring-shaped cake tin, tube tin, *Am.* Bundt pan; **ringförmig I.** *Adj.* ring-shaped; annular *fachspr.;* **II.** *Adv.:* **~ umschließen** encircle

Ring|graben *m* moat; **~haken** *m Bergsteigen:* ringed piton; **~kampf** *m Sport* **1. der ~** *(Sportart)* wrestling; **2.** *(einzelner Kampf)* wrestling match *(od.* bout); **~kämpfer** *m,* **~kämpferin** *f* → **Ringer; ~mauer** *f* ring wall; **~muskel** *m Anat.* sphincter (muscle); **~richter** *m,* **~richterin** *f Sport* referee

rings *Adv.* (all) around; **~ um** (all) around, all the way (a)round; **~ um die Kapelle sind Pappeln** the chapel is surrounded by poplars

Ringschlüssel *m* ring spanner, *Am.* box wrench

ringsherum *Adv.* **1.** all (a)round, all the way (a)round; **ein Teich mit e-m Zaun ~** a pond surrounded by a fence; **2.** *(überall)* on all sides, wherever you look(ed)

Ring|straße *f* ring road, *Am.* beltway, orbital (road); **~tausch** *m (mehrfacher Tausch)* three- *(od.* four- *etc.)* way exchange (of apartments *etc.)*; **~tennis** *n* quoits (V. *im Sg.),* deck tennis

ringsum, ringsumher *Adv.* → **ringsherum**

Ringvorlesung *f* series of lectures given by various speakers

Rinne *f; -, -n; (Fahr-, Bewässerungsrinne)* channel, groove; *(Dachrinne)* gutter; *(Ablaufrinne)* outlet, pipe; *(Meeresrinne)* trough

rinnen; *rinnt, rann, hat od. ist geronnen* *v/i.* **1.** *(ist)* run, flow; *Regen:* fall; **die Zeit rinnt (dahin)** time is slipping by *(od.* away); **das Geld rinnt mir (nur so) durch die Finger** money just slips through my fingers; **2.** *(hat) (undicht sein)* leak, drop, ooze; *Hahn:* run

Rinnsal *n; -(e)s, -e* rivulet; *von Blut, Schweiß, Farbe etc.:* trickle

Rinnstein *m* gutter; *fig.* → **Gosse 2**

Rippchen *n Gastr.* rib (of pork); *Pl.* spare ribs; → *auch* **Kasseler**

Rippe *f; -, -n; Anat., Bot., Tech., Flug., Archit., von Stoff:* rib; *Schokolade:* row, *Am.* strip; *(Kühl-, Heizrippe)* fin; *Mot. auch beim Kühler:* gill; **hohe ~** *Gastr.* rib roast; **er hat nichts auf den ~n** he's skin and bones; **ich kann es mir nicht aus den ~n schneiden** *umg.* I can't just produce it out of thin air; → **gerippt**

Rippelmarken *Pl.,* **Rippeln** *Pl. Geol.* ripple *(od.* rill) marks

Rippenbruch *m Med.* broken *(od.*

fractured) rib(s *Pl.*)

Rippenfell *n Anat.* pleura; **~entzündung** *f Med.* pleurisy

Rippen|heizkörper *m* ribbed (central heating) radiator; **~samt** *m* corduroy; **~speer** *m Gastr.:* **(Kasseler) ~** cured pork rib; **~stoß** *m* dig in the ribs, *heimlicher:* nudge; **~stück** *n Gastr.* rib cut

Rippli *n; -s, -; schw. Gastr.* → **Rippchen**

Rips *m; -es, -e; (Stoff)* rep(p)

Risiko *n; -s, Risiken* risk *(auch Wirts.);* **auf eigenes ~** at one's own risk; **ein ~ eingehen** take a risk *(od.* gamble); **~begrenzung** *f* risk limltation

risikobereit *Adj.* prepared to take risks; **Risikobereitschaft** *f* venturesomeness; *(Wagemut)* daring

Risikofaktor *m* risk factor

risiko|frei *Adj.* → **risikolos; ~freudig** *Adj.* venturesome

Risiko|geburt *f* birth likely to have complications, difficult birth; **~gruppe** *f* high-risk group; **~kapital** *n* risk *(od.* venture) capital; **~lebensversicherung** *f* short-term life insurance

risikolos *Adj.* safe, free of risk

Risiko|management *n Wirts., Börse:* risk management; **~mischung** *f Wirts.* risk spreading; **~patient** *m,* **~patientin** *f* high-risk patient; **~prämie** *f* risk premium

risikoreich *Adj. nur attr.* high-risk ..., hazardous; **~ sein** *auch* involve considerable risk

Risiko|schwangerschaft *f* high-risk *(od.* potential risk) pregnancy; **~versicherung** *f* term insurance; **~vorsorge** *f Wirts.* provision for risks; **~zuschlag** *m in Versicherung:* excess, loading

riskant *Adj.* risky, hazardous; *präd. auch* a risk

riskieren *v/t.* risk; **sein Geld ~ bei** risk one's money on; **s-e Stellung ~** risk losing one's job; **~, nass zu werden** run the risk of getting wet; **e-n Blick ~** risk a glance

Risotto *m, n; -(s), -s; Gastr.* risotto

Rispe *f; -, -n; Bot.* panicle; **Rispengras** *n* meadow grass

riss *Imperf.* → **reißen**

Riss *m; Risses, Risse in Stoff etc.:* tear, fissure, flaw; *(Spalt)* cleft, fissure split, chink; *in Gestein:* crevice; *(Gletscherriss)* crevasse; *(Sprung)* crack; *in der Haut:* chap; *fig.* rift, rupture; **innerhalb der Partei klafft ein ~** there's a (deep) rift within the party; **ihre Freundschaft hat e-n ~ bekommen** their friendship is showing signs of breaking up

rissig *Adj.* cracked, cracky; *Haut:* chapped; **~ werden** *Stoff etc.:* tear; *Mauer etc.:* develop cracks *(od.* a crack), crack; *Haut:* chap; *fig. Freundschaft etc.:* begin to break up

Risswunde *f Med.* gash, laceration *fachspr.*

Rist *m; -es, -e; Anat., des Fußes:* instep; *der Hand:* back of one's hand

ritt *Imperf.* → **reiten**

Ritt *m; -(e)s, -e* ride

Rittberger *m; -s, -; Sport:* **doppelter/dreifacher ~** double/triple loop

Ritter *m; -s, -* knight *(auch Ordensträger);* **zum ~ schlagen** knight; **ein ~ ohne Furcht und Tadel** a knight without fear and without reproach; *umg.* a knight in shining armo(u)r; **arme ~** *Gastr.* bread fritters

Ritter|burg *f* knight's castle; **~gut** *n hist.* manor; **~kreuz** *n Mil.* Knight's Cross

R

ritterlich *Adj.* knightly; *fig.* chivalrous, gallant; **Ritterlichkeit** *f* chivalry

Ritter|orden *m* order of knights; **~roman** *m* chivalrous romance (*od.* epic); **~rüstung** *f* suit of armo(u)r; **~saal** *m* great hall

Ritterschaft *f* 1. *the* knights *Pl.*; 2. (*Stand*) knighthood

Ritter|schlag *m* accolade; **den ~ empfangen** be knighted; **~sporn** *m Bot.* larkspur; **~stand** *m* knighthood; *in den ~ erheben* knight

Rittertum *n*; *-s, kein Pl.* knighthood, knightly lifestyle; *das ~* (*die Ritter*) the knights

Ritterzeit *f* age of chivalry

rittlings *Adv.*: **~ auf** (+ *Dat.*) astride (*od.* straddling) *s.th.*

Rittmeister *m Mil. hist.* (cavalry) captain

Ritual *n*; *-s, -e*; *auch fig.* ritual; **~handlung** *f* ritual (act)

ritualisieren *v/t.* ritualize, make into a ritual; **Ritualisierung** *f* ritualization

Ritualmord *m* ritual murder

rituell *Adj.* ritual

Ritus *m*; *-, Riten* rite

Ritz *m*; *-es, -e* scratch

Ritze *f*; *-, -n* crack; (*Zwischenraum*) gap

Ritzel *n*; *-s, -*; *Tech.* pinion

ritzen *v/t.* (*kratzen*) scratch; (*schneiden*) cut (*auch Glas*); (*schnitzen*) carve; *sich* (*Dat.*) *die Haut ~* scratch one's skin; → **geritzt**; **Ritzer** *m*; *-s, -*; *umg.* scratch

Rivale *m*; *-n, -n*, **Rivalin** *f*; *-, -nen* rival; **rivalisieren** *v/i.* compete, vie (*mit* with; *um* for); **~de Mächte** *etc.* rival powers *etc.*; **Rivalität** *f*; *-, -en* rivalry

Rizinusöl *n* castor oil

Roastbeef ['roːstbiːf] *n*; *-s, -s*; *Gastr.* (*Braten*) (joint of) roast beef; (*Aufschnitt*) (sliced) roast beef

Robbe *f*; *-, -n*; *Zool.* seal

robben *v/i.* crawl (on one's stomach)

Robben|fang *m* sealing; **~fänger** *m* sealer, seal hunter; **~fell** *n* sealskin; **~jagd** *f* seal hunting; **~schlag** *m* seal cull

Robe *f*; *-, -n*; (*Abendkleid*) evening dress; (*Talar*) robe(s *Pl.*)

Robinie *f*; *-, -n*; *Bot.* robinia, locust tree

Robinsonade *f*; *-, -n*; (*Abenteuer[roman]*) Robinson Crusoe-type adventure novel

roboten ['rɔbɔtn̩] *v/i. umg.* slave away

Roboter ['rɔbɔtɐ] *m*; *-s, -* robot (*auch fig.*); **~arm** *m* robotic arm

roboterhaft *Adj.* robot-like

Robotertechnik *f*, **Robotik** *f*; *-, kein Pl.* robotics (*V. im Sg.*)

robust *Adj.* robust; *Person: auch* sturdy; *Schuhe:* stout, sturdy; *Auto etc.:* rugged; **~es Nervenkostüm** strong nerves *Pl.*; **Robustheit** *f* robustness; stoutness, sturdiness

roch *Imperf.* → **riechen**

Rochade [rɔˈxaːdə] *f*; *-, -n Schach:* castling; *Sport* changing of positions; **rochieren** [rɔˈxiːrən] *v/i. Schach:* castle; *Sport* change positions

röcheln *v/i.* breathe noisily (*od.* stertorously *förm.*); *vor Anstrengung auch:* wheeze; *Sterbender:* give the death rattle

Rochen *m*; *-s, -*; *Zool.* ray

Rock¹ *m*; *-(e)s, Röcke* 1. *allg.:* skirt; (*Schottenrock*) kilt; **~ und Bluse** skirt and blouse; *die Röcke werden kürzer* hemlines are going up; *hinter jedem ~ her sein od. herlaufen umg.* chase af-

ter anything in a skirt; 2. *bes. Dial.* (*Jacke*) jacket, coat; *altm.* (*Uniform*) uniform; *der grüne ~ e-s Försters:* the green coat; *das Hemd ist mir näher als der ~ Sprichw.* charity begins at home; *des Königs ~ tragen* (*Soldat sein*) wear the king's coat

Rock² *m*; *-(s), kein Pl.*; *Mus.* rock; **~band** [-bɛnt] *f* rock band

Rocken *m*; *-s, -* distaff

rocken *v/i.* 1. play rock music; 2. dance to rock music

Rocker *m*; *-s, -* 1. rocker; 2. *umg.* (*Musiker*) rock musician, rocker; **~bande** *f* gang of rockers; **~braut** *f* rocker's moll

Rockfalte *f* skirt pleat

Rock|festival *n* rock festival; **~gruppe** *f* rock group (*od.* band)

rockig *Adj. Sl.* rock-like

Rockkonzert *n* rock concert

Rocklänge *f* skirt length

Rock|musik *f* rock music, rock; **~musiker** *m*, **~musikerin** *f* rock musician; **~oper** *f* rock opera; **~sänger** *m*, **~sängerin** *f* rock singer

Rock|saum *m* skirt hem; **~schoß** *m altm.* coattail; *er hängt an Mutters Rockschößen umg. fig.* he's tied to his mother's apron strings; *bes. Kleinkind:* he won't let his mother go anywhere without him

Rock|star *m* rock star; **~szene** *f* rock scene

Rockzipfel *m fig.* → **Rockschoß**

Rodel *m*; *-s, - od. f*; *-, -n*; *südd., österr.* toboggan, sledge; *Am.* sled, toboggan; (*Rennschlitten*) luge; *Ski und ~ gut* good snow conditions for skiing and tobogganing; **Rodelbahn** *f* toboggan run

rodeln *v/i.* toboggan, go sledging (*auch Am.* sledding, tobogganing); *Sportart:* luge

Rodeln *n*; *-s, kein Pl.* tobogganing; (*Sportart*) luge

Rodelschlitten *m* → **Rodel**

roden *vt/i.* (*Land*) clear; (*Bäume etc.*) root out; (*ernten*) lift; (*Kartoffeln*) *auch* dig up; (*Rüben*) *auch* pull up

Rodeo [roˈdeːo] *n*; *-s, -s* rodeo

Rodler *m*; *-s, -*, **~in** *f*; *-, -nen* tobogganist; *sportlich:* luger

Rodung *f* (*Vorgang*) clearing; (*Gebiet*) *auch* cleared woodland

Rogen *m*; *-s, kein Pl.*; *Zool.* roe, (fish) spawn, fish eggs *pl.*

Roggen *m*; *-s, kein Pl.*; *Bot.* rye; **~ähre** *f* eye of rye, spike (head) *fachspr.*; **~brot** *n Gastr.* rye bread; **~brötchen** *n Gastr.* rye bread roll; **~feld** *n Agr.* field of rye; **~mehl** *n Gastr.* rye flour; **~mischbrot** *n Gastr.* bread made from rye and wheat flour

roh *Adj.* 1. *Nahrungsmittel:* raw; → *Ei* 1; *das Fleisch ist innen noch ~* the meat is still uncooked inside; **~er Schinken** uncooked ham; **~e Klöße** dumplings made from grated raw potatoes; 2. (*unbehandelt*) *Diamant:* rough, *auch Stein:* uncut; *Häute:* untreated; (*primitiv verarbeitet*) crude; *Entwurf, Daten etc.:* rough; 3. (*derb, grob*) rough, coarse; **~e Sitten** uncouth manners; *ein ~er Kerl* a brute; *sie leidet unter s-r ~en Art* she suffers from his brutish behavio(u)r; *ein unglaublich ~es Verbrechen* an incredibly brutal (*od.* callous) crime; → *Gewalt* 1

Roh|bau *m Archit.* shell; *im ~ fertig* structurally complete; **~benzin** *n* petroleum; **~diamant** *m* rough (*od.* uncut) diamond

Roh|entwurf *m* rough draft; **~ertrag** *m* gross yield; **~erzeugnis** *n* raw product; **~faser** *f* raw fib|re (*Am.* -er); **~fassung** *f* rough draft; **~gewicht** *n* gross weight

Rohheit *f* 1. rawness; (*Grobheit*) roughness, coarseness; *ein Akt von erschreckender ~* an act of horrifying brutality; 2. (*rohe Handlung*) brutality, brutal act

Roh|kaffee *m* unroasted coffee; **~kautschuk** *m* raw rubber

Rohkost *f* raw fruit *Pl.* and vegetables; **Rohköstler** *m*; *-s, -*, **Rohköstlerin** *f*; *-, -nen* person who only eats raw fruit and vegetables

Rohling *m*; *-s, -e* 1. *pej.* brute, ruffian; 2. *Metall.* slug; *Gießerei:* blank; 3. (*CD-Rohling*) blank CD

Roh|material *n* raw material; **~metall** *n* crude metal; **~milch** *f* unpasteurized milk; **~milchkäse** *m* unpasteurized cheese

Rohöl *n* crude oil; **~preis** *m* price of crude (oil)

Rohprodukt *n* raw product

Rohr *n*; *-(e)s, -e* 1. *nur Sg.*; *Schilf:* reed; *Bambus etc.:* cane; *Möbel aus ~* cane furniture; *wie ein* (*schwankendes*) *~ im Wind fig.* like a reed in the wind; 2. *Tech.* pipe, tube, conduit; *bes. als Materialbezeichnung:* piping; (*Kanonenrohr*) barrel; *~e verlegen* lay pipes; *ein verstopftes/geplatztes ~* a blocked/burst pipe; *aus allen ~en schießen Schiff:* open up (*od.* blaze away) with all its guns; *fig. Mensch:* launch a full-blooded attack; *volles ~ fahren umg.* drive flat out (*Am.* at full speed); 3. (*Backrohr*) oven

Rohr|ammer *f Orn.* reed bunting; **~blatt** *n Mus.* reed; **~blattinstrument** *n* reed instrument; **~bruch** *m* burst pipe

Röhrchen *n Chem.* test tube; *für Tabletten:* tube; (*Trinkhalm*) straw; *ins ~ pusten* (*müssen*) *umg.* be breath-tested, be breathaly|sed (*Am.* -zed)

Rohrdommel *f*; *-, -*; *Orn.* bittern

Röhre *f*; *-, -n* 1. tube; *Leitung:* pipe; *Anat.* duct, canal; (*Luftröhre*) windpipe; (*Speiseröhre*) gullet; *Chem.* test tube; *kommunizierende ~n Phys.* communicating tubes; 2. *Etech.*, *TV* valve, *bes. Am.* tube; (*Leuchtröhre*) (neon) tube; *in die ~ gucken umg.* (*fernsehen*) gaze (*od.* goggle) at the box (*Am.* tube); *fig.* (*leer ausgehen*) be left high and dry; 3. (*Bratröhre*) oven; *e-n Braten etc. in die ~ schieben* shove a joint (*Am.* roast) etc. in the oven

röhren *v/i.* 1. *Hirsch:* bell; 2. *umg. Motorrad, Mensch etc.:* roar

Röhrenblütler *m*; *-s, -*; *Bot.* one of the tubiflorae; *die ~* the tubiflorae

Röhrenempfänger *m Funk.*, *hist.* valve receiver

röhrenförmig *Adj.* tubular

Röhren|hose *f umg.* drainpipe trousers *Pl.*; **~knochen** *m* long bone; **~leitung** *f* → **Rohrleitung**; **~pilz** *m Bot.* boletus; **~walzwerk** *n Tech.* tube (*od.* pipe) rolling mill; **~wurm** *m Zool.* tube worm

Rohr|flöte *f* reed pipe; **~geflecht** *n* canework

Röhricht *n*; *-s, -e*; *Bot.* reeds *Pl.*

Rohr|kolben *m Bot.* cattail, reed mace, bul(l)rush; **~krepierer** *m*; *-s, -*; *Mil.* barrel burst; *fig.* non-starter, *Brit. auch* damp squib, *Am. auch* dud; **~leitung** *f* pipe, piping, pipes *Pl.*; *für Kabel etc.:* conduit; (*Fernleitung*) pipe-

line; (*Versorgungsnetz*) mains *Pl.*
Röhrling *m*; *-s*, *-e*; *Bot.* boletus
Rohr\|möbel *Pl.* wicker furniture *Sg.*;
aus Bambusrohr. cane furniture; →
Stahlrohrmöbel; **~netz** *n* piping, network of pipes (*od.* tubes); **~post** *f*
pneumatic dispatch, air tube; **~sänger**
m Orn. reed warbler; **~schelle** *f* pipe
clip; **~schilf** *n Bot.* reed; **~spatz** *m*:
schimpfen wie ein ~ *umg.* rant and
rave; **~stock** *m* cane; **~stuhl** *m* wicker
chair; *aus Bambusrohr.* cane chair;
~zange *f* pipe wrench; gas pliers *Pl.*;
~zucker *m* cane sugar
Rohseide *f* raw silk; **rohseiden** *Adj.*
raw silk
Rohstoff *m* raw material
rohstoffarm *Adj.* lacking in raw materials
Rohstoff\|lieferant *m* raw materials
supplier; **~mangel** *m* shortage of raw
materials; **~quelle** *f* source of raw materials; **~preise** *Pl.* price *Sg.* of raw
materials
rohstoffreich *Adj.* rich in raw materials
Rohstoff\|reserve *f* reserve supply of
raw materials; **~verarbeitung** *f* processing of raw material
Roh\|tabak *m* raw tobacco; **~überset-
zung** *f* rough translation; **~wolle** *f*
raw wool; **~zucker** *m* raw (*od.* unrefined) sugar; **~zustand** *m* **1.** raw (*od.*
crude) state; **2.** *im* ~ *Pläne etc.*: in
draft form; *mein Artikel ist noch im* ~
I've only done a rough version of the
article (so far)
Rokoko *n*; *-(s)*, *kein Pl.*; *Kunst* rococo
Rokoko... *im Subst. Kirche, Malerei,
Möbel etc.*: rococo
Roll\|bahn *f zur Startbahn od. nach
Landung:* taxiway; (*Startbahn, Lande-
bahn*) runway; **~band** *n am Flughafen
etc.*: walkway; *für Gepäck*: conveyor
belt, carousel; **~bild** *n* scroll painting;
~braten *m* collared beef (*od.* pork
etc.)
Rolle[1] *f*; *-*, *-n* **1.** roll (*auch Geld-, Pa-
pier-, Tabakrolle etc.*); (*Draht-, Taurol-
le*) coil; (*Papyrusrolle*) roll, scroll; ~
Garn reel of cotton, *Am.* spool of
thread; **2.** (*Walze*) roller, cylinder; *an
Möbeln*: castor; *von Flaschenzug:* pulley; **3.** *Turnen*: roll; ~ *vorwärts/rück-
wärts* forward/backward roll; **4.** *fig.,
umg.*: *völlig von der* ~ *sein* have lost
one's grip on things; *Sport* have completely lost one's touch
Rolle[2] *f*; *-*, *-n*; *Theat. und fig.* role, part;
kleine ~ small (*od.* bit) part, minor
role; *führende* ~ lead; *s-e* ~ *lernen*
learn one's part (*od.* lines); *die* ~*n e-s
Stückes besetzen* cast a play; *ein
Stück mit verteilten* ~*n lesen* have a
play-reading; *die* ~ *ist ihr auf den Leib
geschrieben* the part could have been
written for her (*od.* suits her down to
the ground); *e-e* ~ *spielen fig.* play a
part (*od.* role) (*bei, in* + *Dat.* in); *e-e
große* ~ *spielen fig.* play an important
part (*od.* role); *Person, Firma: auch*
be a key player; *in e-r Firma etc.*: be
in an influential position; *e-e untergeordnete* ~ *spielen fig.* play a subsidiary role, be less important; *sich mit
der* ~ *des Zuschauers begnügen* be
content to be a mere spectator; *er
spielt gern e-e* ~ *pej.* he likes to be involved (in something); *er gefällt sich
in der* ~ *des ...* he likes playing the ...;
sich in der ~ *der Hausfrau etc.* (*nicht*)
wohlfühlen (not) feel at home in the
role of a housewife *etc.*; *Spiel mit ver-*

tauschten ~*n* reversal of roles; *das
spielt keine* ~ it doesn't matter, it
doesn't make any difference; *Geld
spielt keine* ~ money is no object; *aus
der* ~ *fallen* step out of line; *stärker:*
forget oneself
...rolle *f*, *im Subst.; fig.*: role of ...
rollen I. *v/i.* (*ist gerollt*) **1.** roll; *Mot.
auch* move; *Flug.* taxi; *See:* roll; *Donner:* rumble; **~des Material** *Eisenb.*
rolling stock; *Tränen rollten ihm über
die Wangen* tears rolled down his
cheeks; **2.** *fig.*: *die Sache rollt,*
we've set the ball rolling, we're on our
way; *stärker:* it's all systems go; *der
Rubel rollt umg.* the money's rolling
in; → *Kopf* 6; **II.** *v/t.* (*hat*) roll; *auf Rädern:* auch wheel; *sich* (*Dat.*) *e-e Zigarette* ~ roll (oneself) a cigarette; *etw.
zu e-r Kugel etc.* ~ roll s.th. into a ball
etc.; *etw. in Papier etc.* ~ roll s.th. up in
paper; *sich in s-e Decke* ~ roll (*od.*
wrap) oneself up in one's blanket; *die
Augen* ~ roll one's eyes; *das R* ~ roll
one's r's; *man kann sie* ~ *umg. fig.*
she's like a barrel, she's a real roly-poly; **III.** *v/refl.* (*hat*) roll; *Haar, Papier
etc.*: curl; *sich im Gras* ~ *Kinder:* roll
around in the grass
Rollen *n*; *-s*, *kein Pl.* rolling; *ins* ~ *kommen Lawine etc.*: start moving; *fig.* get
going, get under way; *die Sache ins* ~
bringen fig. set the ball rolling, get
things moving
Rollen\|antrieb *m Tech.* pulley drive;
~bild *n Soziol.* role model; **~beset-
zung** *f Theat.* **1.** casting; **2.** (*die Darsteller*) cast (*auch mit V. im Pl.*); **~er-
wartung** *f Soziol.* role expectation;
~fach *n Theat.* (type of) role; *ins* ~
gehen specialize in a certain type of
role; **~klischee** *n Soziol.* cliché role,
stereotype; **~konflikt** *m Soziol.* role
conflict, conflict of roles; **~lager** *n
Tech.* roller bearing; **~spiel** *n Psych.,
Päd. etc.* role play
rollenspezifisch I. *Adj.* role-specific;
II. *Adv.*: *sich* ~ *verhalten* behave in a
role-specific manner
Rollen\|studium *n Theat.* study of a
part; **~tausch** *m* role-swapping; *bei
gegensätzlichen Rollen:* reversal of
roles; **~verhalten** *n Soziol.* role beha-
vio(u)r; **~verständnis** *n* understanding of one's role; **~verteilung** *f* **1.** →
Rollenbesetzung, **2.** *fig.* the various
(*od.* respective) roles *Pl.*; *die traditionelle* ~ *zwischen Mann und Frau* the
traditional male and female roles
Roller *m*; *-s*, *-* **1.** *auch für Kinder:*
scooter; **2.** (*Brandungswelle*) (rolling)
breaker, roller; **3.** *zum Tünchen:* roller; **4.** (*Sprung*) western roll; **5.** *Fußball
etc.*: gentle ground shot; **6.** *Harzer* ~
Orn. Harz Mountain roller
Roller\|brett *n* skateboard; **~fahrer** *m,*
~fahrerin *f* scooter rider
Rollerskate [ˈrɔləskeːt] *n*; *-s* *-s* roller
skate
Roll\|feld *n Flug.* taxiway system; **~film**
m roll film; **~geld** *n* carriage (*od.*
freight *od.* shipping) charge (*for transportation of goods between customer
and freight depot*); **~gurt** *m* inertia
reel (*bes. Am.* automatic) seat belt;
~gut *n* rolling freight; **~hockey** *n
Sport* roller-skate hockey
Rolli *m*; *-s*, *-s*; *umg.* polo neck (*Am.*
turtleneck) (sweater)
rollieren *v/i.* (*abwechseln*) alternate;
~des System rotating system
Rollkommando *n* raiding party, heavy
squad, heavies *Pl. umg.*

Rollkragen *m* polo neck, *Am.* turtleneck; **~pulli** *m,* **~pullover** *m* polo-
-neck jumper, *Am.* turtleneck sweater;
Kurzform: polo neck, *Am.* turtleneck
Rollkunst\|lauf *m Sport* figure roller-
-skating; **~läufer** *m,* **~läuferin** *f* figure
roller skater
Roll\|kur *f Med.* treatment for gastric di-
sorders in which ingested medicine is
distributed by slowly rotating the body
Rollladen *m* (roller) shutter; (*Anlage*)
(roller) shutters *Pl.*; **~kasten** *m* (roller) shutter box
Rollmops *m Gastr.* rolled pickled herring, rollmop, *bes. Am.* rollmops
Rollo *n*; *-s*, *-s* (roller) blind, *Am. auch*
window shade
Roll\|schiene *f Rudern:* runner;
~schinken *m Gastr.* rolled ham;
~schrank *m* roll-front cabinet
Rollschuh *m* roller skate; ~ *laufen* roller-skate; **~bahn** *f* roller-skating rink;
~fahrer *m,* **~fahrerin** *f* roller skater;
~laufen *n* roller-skating; **~läufer** *m,*
~läuferin *f* roller skater
Roll\|sitz *m Rudern:* sliding seat; **~ski**
m training ski; **~splitt** *m* loose chippings *Pl.*; **~sprung** *m* western roll;
~steg *m* travolator, *Am.* moving walkway
Rollstuhl *m* wheelchair; **~fahren** *n
Sport* wheelchair racing; **~fahrer** *m,*
~fahrerin *f* wheelchair patient; *er ist
Rollstuhlfahrer* he's in (*od.* confined
to) a wheelchair
rollstuhlgerecht I. *Adj.* suitable for
wheelchairs, *Am. auch* handicapped
accessible; **II.** *Adv.*: ~ *bauen/einrich-
ten* build/arrange so as to be suitable
for wheelchairs, *Am.* make *s.th.* handicapped accessible
Rollstuhlsport *m* wheelchair athletics
(*od.* sport)
Roll\|tabak *m* roll tobacco; **~treppe** *f*
escalator
Rom[1] (*n*); *-s*; *Geog.* Rome; *im alten* ~
in ancient Rome; ~ *wurde auch nicht
an einem Tage erbaut fig.* Rome
wasn't built in a day; *viele Wege führen nach* ~ there's more than one way
(*od.* that isn't the only way) of doing
it; → *Zustand* 2
Rom[2] *m*; *-*, *-a* (European) gypsy, Romany, *Am. auch* Roma
ROM *n*; *-(s)*, *-(s)*; *EDV* ROM, read only memory
Roma *Pl.* → *Rom*[2]
Roman *m*; *-s*, *-e* novel, work of fiction;
das gibt es nur in ~*en* it's the stuff of
fiction (*od.* fairytales); *wie in e-m
schlechten* ~ like pulp fiction, *Am.
auch* like a dime novel; *erzähl doch
keine* ~*e! umg.* (*fasse dich kurz*) don't
give me the whole saga (*od.* spiel), cut
it short!, keep to the point, will you;
(*bleib bei der Wahrheit*) tell me another
Romanautor *m,* **~in** *f,* **Romancier**
[romãˈsieː] *m*; *-s*, *-s* novelist, novel
writer
Romane *m*; *-n*, *-n* speaker of a Romance language
Roman\|figur *f* character (in a novel);
~form *f* novel form; *in* ~ in the form
of a novel
romanhaft *Adj.* in the manner (*od.*
style) of a novel; (*nicht glaubhaft*) fanciful
Roman\|heft *n* cheap paperback novel;
~held *m* hero (of a *od.* the novel);
~heldin *f* heroine (of a *od.* the novel)
Romani *n*; *-(s)*; *Ling.* Romany
Romanik *f*; *-*, *kein Pl.*; *Kunst*: Roman-

R

esque (style); (*Epoche*) Romanesque period; **Romanin** *f; -, -nen* → *Romane*; **romanisch** *Adj. Ling. etc.* Romance *languages etc.*; *Volk, Land*: Latin; *Kunst*: Romanesque; **romanisieren** *v/t.* **1.** *hist.* romanize; **2.** (*Volk, Land etc.*) latinize; **3.** *Kunst* adapt to the Romanesque style; **Romanist** *m; -en, -en Ling.* student of Romance languages and literature, Romance scholar; **Romanistik** *f Ling.* (study of) Romance languages and literature, Romance studies *Pl.*; **Romanistin** *f; -, -nen* → *Romanist*; **romanistisch** *Adj. Ling.* Romance, ... of Romance languages and literature

Roman|literatur *f* fiction; **~schriftsteller** *m*, **~schriftstellerin** *f* novelist, novel writer

Romantik *f; -, kein Pl.* **1.** *Kunst etc.*: Romanticism, *the* Romantic movement; **2.** *fig.* romanticism (*auch Veranlagung*), romance; *die ~ e-s Sonnenuntergangs* the romantic nature of a sunset; *keinen Sinn für ~ haben* have no sense of romance; **Romantiker** *m; -s, -*, **Romantikerin** *f; -, -nen* Romantic; *fig.* romantic; **romantisch I.** *Adj.* romantic; *Kunst etc.*: Romantic; **II.** *Adv.*: *~ gelegen* romantically situated; *~ veranlagt sein* have a romantic nature; **romantisieren** *v/t.* romanticize; **Romantisierung** *f* romanticizing

Roman|trilogie *f* trilogy (of novels); **~verfilmung** *f* film (*Am. auch* movie) (version) of a novel

Romanze *f; -, -n; poet., Mus. und fig.* romance

Romanzyklus *m* cycle of novels

Römer *m; -s, -* **1.** *auch hist.* Roman; *die alten ~* the ancient Romans; **2.** (*Glas*) rummer; **~brief** *m bibl.*: *der ~* the (*od.* St Paul's) Epistle to the Romans, Romans (*V. im Sg.*)

Römerin *f; -, -nen* Roman (woman *od.* girl)

Römer|reich *n hist.*: Roman Empire; **~straße** *f* Roman road; **~topf®** *m Gastr.* oval earthenware pot, baking brick; **~zeit** *f hist.*: *die ~* Roman times *Pl.*, Ancient Rome

Romfahrt *f* journey to Rome; (*Pilgerfahrt*) pilgrimage to Rome

römisch *Adj.* Roman; **~-katholisch** *Adj.* Roman Catholic

Rommé ['rɔme] *n; -s, -s*; (*Kartenspiel*) rummy

Rondell [rɔ'dɛl] *n; -s, -e* **1.** *Bot.* round (*od.* circular) flowerbed; **2.** (*runder Platz*) circus, *Am.* plaza; *e-s Kreisverkehrs*: roundabout, *Am.* traffic circle, *Am. auch* rotary; **3.** *Archit.* (*runder Turm*) round tower; *kleiner*: turret

Rondo *n; -s, -s; Mus.* rondo

röntgen I. *v/t. Med.* x-ray, *auch* X-ray; **II. Röntgen** *n; -s, -* **1.** *Phys.* (*Einheit*) roentgen; **2.** *nur Sg.; Med.* (*das ~*) x-raying; *e-e Patientin zum Röntgen schicken* send a patient for (an) x-ray; **Röntgen|apparat** *m* x-ray machine; **~äquivalent** *n Phys.* roentgen equivalent man (*Abk.* rem); **~arzt** *m*, **~ärztin** *f Med.* radiologist; **~assistent** *m*, **~assistentin** *f* radiographer, x-ray technician; **~astronomie** *f Astron.* radio astronomy; **~aufnahme** *f Med.* x-ray; **~augen** *Pl. umg., fig.*: *~ haben* have x-ray eyes; **~behandlung** *f*, **~bestrahlung** *f* x-ray treatment, radiotherapy; **~bild** *n* x-ray; **~blick** *m umg., fig.* → *Röntgenaugen*; **~diagnostik** *f* radiodiagnosis; **~dosis** *f* x-ray dose; **~durchleuchtung** *f* radioscopy,

fluoroscopy; **~film** *m* x-ray film; **~gerät** *n* x-ray machine; **~kater** *m* x-ray sickness

Röntgenologe *m; -n, -n; Med.* radiologist; **Röntgenologie** *f; -, kein Pl.* radiology; **Röntgenologin** *f; -, -nen* radiologist; **röntgenologisch** *Adj.* radiological

Röntgen|röhre *f* x-ray tube; **~schirm** *m* x-ray screen; **~strahlen** *Pl.* x-rays; **~strahlung** *f* x-radiation; **~therapie** *f* x-ray treatment, radiotherapy; **~untersuchung** *f* x-ray (examination)

Ro-Ro-Schiff *n Verk.* roll-on roll-off ferry

Rosa *n; -s, umg. -s* pink; **rosa, rosafarben, rosarot** *Adj.* **1.** pink; *die Dinge durch e-e rosa(rote) Brille sehen* see the world through rose-colo(u)red (*od.* rose-tinted) spectacles (*Am.* glasses); **2.** *fig.* (*schwul*) gay; *die Rosa Liste Pol.* the (list of) Gay Rights candidates

Röschen *n* small rose; *vom Blumenkohl*: floweret

rosé [ro'ze:] *Adj.* pale pink

Rose *f; -, -n* **1.** *Bot.* rose; *er ist auch nicht auf ~n gebettet fig.* his life is no bed of roses; *keine ~ ohne Dornen* no rose without thorns; **2.** *Archit.* (*Fensterrose*) rose window; **3.** *Med.* erysipelas

Rosé¹ *n; -(s), -(s)* pale pink

Rosé² [ro'ze:] *m; -s, -s* rosé (wine)

Rosen|beet *n* bed of roses; **~blatt** *n* rose petal; **~blüte** *f* rose blossom; **~dorn** *m* (rose) thorn; **~duft** *m* scent of roses; **~garten** *m* rose garden; **~gewächs** *n Bot.* rose, rosaceous plant; **~holz** *n* rosewood; **~kohl** *m Gastr.* Brussels (*Brit. auch* Brussel) sprouts *Pl.*; **~kranz** *m kirchl.* rosary; *den ~ beten* say the rosary

Rosenmontag *m* Monday in Shrovetide, Shrove Monday; **Rosenmontagszug** *m* Rosenmontag (*od.* Shrovetide) carnival procession

Rosen|öl *n* attar of roses; **~paprika** *m Gastr.* hot paprika; **~quarz** *m Min.* rose quartz; (*Buschrose*) rose bush; **~stock** *m* rose tree; **~strauch** *m* rose bush; **~strauß** *m* bunch of roses; **~wasser** *n* rosewater; **~zucht** *f* rose-growing; **~züchter** *m*, **~züchterin** *f* rose-grower

Rosette *f; -, -n* rosette; (*Fenster*) rose window; *Tech.* rose

rosig *Adj.* rosy (*auch fig.*); *etw. in ~en Farben schildern* paint s.th. in rosy (*od.* bright) colo(u)rs, paint a rosy (*od.* bright) picture of s.th.; *es sieht nicht gerade ~ aus* things are looking pretty grim; *ihm geht's nicht gerade ~* he's not exactly having a wonderful time

Rosine *f; -, -n* raisin; (*Korinthe*) currant; *umg. fig.* gem; (*große*) *~n im Kopf haben umg. fig.* have big ideas; *sich die ~n herauspicken umg. fig.* take the pick of the bunch, pick out the plum jobs (*od.* sites *etc.*), *Am. auch* cherry-pick

Rosinen|bomber *m umg. hist.* supply plane (*during the Berlin airlift*); **~brot** *n Gastr.* currant bread; (*Laib*) currant loaf; **~kuchen** *m* currant cake

Rosmarin *m; -s, kein Pl.; Bot.* rosemary

Ross *n; Rosses, Rosse od. Rösser* horse, *lit.* steed; *hoch zu ~ hum.* on one's trusty steed; *sich (moralisch) aufs hohe ~ setzen fig.* get on one's (moral) high horse; *auf dem hohen ~*

sitzen be on one's high horse; *~ und Reiter nennen fig.* name names; **~äpfel** *Pl. Dial., hum.* horse droppings; *Am.* road apples; **~breiten** *Pl. Geog.* horse latitudes

Rösselsprung *m* **1.** *Schach*: knight's move; **2.** *type of crossword puzzle based on the knight's move*

Rosshaar *n* horsehair; **~matratze** *f* horsehair mattress

Ross|kastanie *f Bot.* horse chestnut; **~kur** *f umg.* drastic cure

Rosstäuscher *m; -s, -; umg.* con man; **~trick** *m umg.* confidence trick *förm.*, con, scam

Rost¹ *m; -(e)s, kein Pl.* rust (*auch fig., Bot.*); *~ ansetzen* (begin to) go rusty, get rusty (*auch fig.*); *von ~ zerfressen* rusted away

Rost² *m; -(e)s, -e*; (*Feuerrost*) grate; (*Gitterrost*) grille, grating; (*Bratrost*) grill; *Steak/Würstchen vom ~* grilled (*od.* barbecued) steak/sausages

rostbeständig *Adj.* rustproof

Rost|braten *m Gastr.* roast joint; **~bratwurst** *f* grilled sausage

rostbraun *Adj.* russet

Röstbrot *n Gastr.* toast

rosten *v/i.* rust; *auch fig.* get rusty; *nicht rostend* rustproof; *Stahl*: stainless

rösten *vt/i.* (*Fleisch*) roast, grill; (*Kaffee*) roast; (*Brot*) toast; (*Kartoffeln*) fry; *in der Sonne ~ hum.* roast in the sun; **Röster** *m; -s, -* toaster; **Rösterei** *f; -, -en für Kaffee etc.*: roast (*od.* roasting) house

Rostfarbe *f* anti-rust paint; (*Mennige*) red lead paint

rostfarben *Adj.* rust-colo(u)red, russet

Rost|fleck *m auf Kleidung*: rust stain; (*Roststelle*) spot of rust; **~fraß** *m* corrosion

rostfrei *Adj.* rustproof; *Stahl*: stainless

Rösti ['rø:sti] *Pl. bes. schw., Gastr.* shredded fried potatoes, rösti, *Am. etwa* hash browns

rostig *Adj.* rusty (*auch fig.*)

Röstkartoffeln *Pl. Gastr.* fried potatoes

Rost|krankheit *f Bot.* rust disease; **~laube** *f umg.* (*Auto*) rust heap, rust bucket; **~rot** *Adj.* rusty red, russet

Rostschutz *m* rust protection; **~farbe** *f* anti-rust paint; **~mittel** *n* anti-rust agent

Rost|stelle *f* patch (*kleine*: spot) of rust; **~umwandler** *m* rust converter

Röstzwiebeln *Pl. Gastr.* fried onions

rot I. *Adj.* **1.** red; *~e Rosen* red roses; *~es Haar haben auch* be a redhead; *~ vor Aufregung* red with excitement; *über beide Ohren ~ werden* blush intensely, turn crimson; *e-n ~en Kopf bekommen vor Anstrengung, Wut*: go red in the face; *vor Verlegenheit*: blush, go red; *er wird immer gleich ~* he blushes very easily; *auf j-n wie ein ~es Tuch wirken* be like a red rag to a bull for s.o.; *Person*: get s.o.'s blood up, get s.o.'s goat; *in den ~en Zahlen stehen* be in the red *umg.*; **2.** *in Eigennamen*: *Rotes Kreuz* Red Cross; *das Rote Meer* the Red Sea; *der Rote Platz (in Moskau)* Red Square (in Moscow); **3.** *Pol.* (*links*) red; *rote Socken pej.* recent term for former supporters of the East German regime, *etwa* lefties; **II. Adv.** **1.** *mit Verben und Partizipformen*: *~ anmalen* paint s.th. red; *lackierte Fingernägel* (-bright) red(-varnished) fingernails; *~ unterstreichen* underline s.th. in red;

die Blätter färben sich ~ the leaves are turning red; *sich* (*Dat.*) *die Haare* ~ *färben* dye one's hair red; ~ *gerändert* red-rimmed; ~ *gestreift* red--striped, … with red stripes; ~ *glühend* red-hot; ~ *unterlaufen Augen*: bloodshot, red; ~ *verweint Augen*: reddened from crying (*od.* with weeping); **2.** *Pol.* (*links*) red; ~ *angehaucht sein umg.* have left-wing leanings; → *auch* **blau**

Rot *n*; *-s, umg. -s* red; *Verkehrsampel*: red (light); *ein dunkles/helles/leuchtendes* ~ a dark/light/bright red; *bei* ~ at red; *bei* ~ *über die Ampel fahren* jump (shoot *umg.*) the lights; ~ *sehen Sport* be shown the red card; *e-m Spieler* ~ *zeigen* show a player the red card

Rotalgen *Pl. Bot.* red algae

Rotarier *m*; *-s, -* Rotarian; **rotarisch** *Adj.* Rotarian

Rotarmist *m*; *-en, -en,* ~*in f*; *-, -nen Mil., hist.* Red Army soldier

Rotation *f*; *-, -en* rotation

Rotations|achse *f* axis of rotation; ~**bewegung** *f* rotary motion; ~**druck** *m Druck.* rotary press printing; ~**kolbenmotor** *m* rotary piston engine; ~**maschine** *f Druck.* rotary press; ~**prinzip** *n Pol.* principle of rotating posts with set terms of office; *etwa* rota (*hum.* musical chairs) principle

Rotauge *n Zool.* roach

rot|äugig *Adj.* red-eyed; ~**backig,** ~**bäckig** *Adj.* red- (*od.* rosy-)cheeked

Rotbarsch *m Zool.* rosefish, ocean perch

rot|bärtig *Adj.* red-bearded; ~**blond** *Adj. Haare*: light red (dish blond), sandy; *Person*: sandy-haired; *Frau*: strawberry blond; ~ *sein Person*: have light red (*od.* sandy) hair; ~**braun** *Adj.* reddish brown, rufous; *Pferd*: chestnut, *nur attr.* sorrel …, bay …

Rotbuche *f Bot.* copper beech

Rotchina (*n*); *-s; hist. Pol.* Red China; **rotchinesisch** *Adj.* Red Chinese

Rote *m*, *f*; *-n, -n* **1.** *Pol.* Red, leftie *umg.*; **2.** *neg!* (*Indianer*) redskin *neg!*; **3.** (*Rothaarige*[*r*]) redhead

Röte *f*; *-, kein Pl.* redness, red; *am Himmel*: *auch* red glow; *im Gesicht*: redness, ruddyness; *bei Fieber, Verlegenheit etc.*: flush; *die* ~ *stieg ihm ins Gesicht* he colo(u)red up, he flushed (*Am.* blushed)

Rote-Armee-Fraktion *f*; *nur Sg.; hist.* (*abgek.* **RAF**) Red Army Faction

Rötel *m*; *-s, -* **1.** red chalk; **2.** (*Stift*) red chalk crayon

Röteln *Pl. Med.* German measles (*V. im Sg.*), rubella *Sg., fachspr.*

Rötelzeichnung *f* red chalk drawing

röten *geh.* **I.** *v/t.* redden; **II.** *v/refl.* turn red, redden; *Gesicht*: *auch* flush, *Am.* blush

Rot|färbung *f* red colo(u)ring; ~**filter** *m*, *n Fot.* red filter; ~**fuchs** *m* **1.** *Zool.* red fox; **2.** (*Pferd*) chestnut, sorrel, bay; **3.** *umg.* (*Person*) redhead, carrot-top; **4.** (*Pelz*) fox (fur); ~**glut** *f* red heat; ~**gold** *n* red gold

rotgrünblind *Adj.* (red-green) colo(u)r-blind

rothaarig *Adj.* red-haired

Rot|haarige *m*, *f*; *-n, -n* redhead; ~**haut** *f neg!* (*Indianer*) redskin *neg!*; ~**hirsch** *m Zool.* red deer

rotieren *v/i.* rotate (*auch Pol.*), revolve; *er ring an zu* ~ *umg.* he got into a flap; *ich bin am Rotieren umg.* I don't know whether I'm coming or going;

rotierend I. *Part. Präs.* → *rotieren*; **II.** *Adj.* rotating, revolving; ~**es System** *Pol., Wirts. etwa* rota (*Am.* rotation) system

Rot|käppchen *n*; *-s* (Little) Red Riding Hood; ~**kappe** *f Bot.* red boletus; ~**kehlchen** *n Orn.* robin (redbreast); ~**kohl** *m*, ~**kraut** *n Gastr.* red cabbage

Rotkreuz|flagge *f* Red Cross flag; ~**schwester** *f* Red Cross nurse

rot lackiert → *rot* **II 1**

Rotlauf *m*; *nur Sg.; Vet.* swine erysipelas

rötlich *Adj.* reddish; *Gesicht*: *auch* ruddy; ~**blond** *Adj.* reddish-blond

Rotlicht *n* red light (*auch Fot., Med.*); ~**bestrahlung** *f Med.* infrared rays *Pl.*; (*Behandlung*) infrared treatment; ~**lampe** *f* infrared lamp; ~**milieu** *n* milieu of the prostitute; ~**sünder** *m*, ~**sünderin** *f* red light offender; ~**viertel** *n* red-light district

Rotor *m*; *-s, -en* rotor; ~**blatt** *n* rotor blade

Rot|schwanz *m*, ~**schwänzchen** *n Orn.* redstart, redtail

rotsehen *v/i.* (*unreg., trennb., hat -ge-*) see red

Rotspecht *m Orn.* spotted woodpecker

Rot|stift *m* red pencil; (*Kugelschreiber etc.*) red pen; *mit* ~ *korrigieren* correct (*od.* do corrections) in red; *den* ~ *ansetzen fig.* make cuts (*bei* in), *Am. auch* blue-pencil; *dem* ~ *zum Opfer fallen Szene, Passage etc.*: fall victim to the censors, be cut; *Projekt, Gelder etc.*: be axed *umg.*, get the chop *umg.*; ~**tanne** *f Bot.* spruce

Rotte *f*; *-, -n; pej.* horde, mob, gang; *Mil.* pair; *von Wölfen*: pack; *von Wildschweinen*: herd; *von Arbeitern*: gang; **Rottenführer** *m* foreman

Rottweiler *m*; *-s, -; Zool.* Rottweiler

Rotunde *f*; *-, -n; Archit.* rotunda

Rötung *f* reddening

rotwangig *Adj.* red-cheeked, rosy--cheeked

Rotwein *m* red wine; ~**fleck** *m* (red) wine stain

Rot|welsch *n*; *-(s); Ling.* thieves' Latin; *das* ~*e* thieves' Latin; ~**wild** *n Zool.* red deer; ~**wurst** *f Gastr.* blood sausage, *etwa* black pudding

Rotz *m*; *-es, kein Pl.* **1.** *vulg.* (*Nasenschleim*) snot; ~ *und Wasser heulen umg.* bawl one's eyes out; *der ganze* ~ *pej.* the whole damn lot; **2.** *Vet.* glanders (*V. im Sg.*); ~**bengel** *m Sl. pej.* snotty (little) brat

rotzen *v/i. vulg.* sniff back one's snot; (*sich laut schnäuzen*) blow one's nose loudly *allg.*; (*spucken*) spit

Rotz|fahne *f vulg.* snotrag; ♀**frech** *Adj. umg.* snotty; ~**göre** *f Sl. pej.* snotty little madam

rotzig *Adj. vulg., auch Sl.* (*frech*) snotty *umg.*

Rotznase *f* **1.** *umg. e-s Kindes*: snotty nose; **2.** *Sl. pej.* snotty (*od.* snot--nosed) brat; *umg.* (*unerfahrener junger Mensch*) callow youth, greenhorn; **rotznäsig** *Adj. umg.* snotty; *fig. auch* bolshie, bolshy

Rotzunge *f Zool.* witch

Rouge [ruːʃ] *n*; *-s, -s* rouge; ~ *auftragen* put (some) rouge on

Roulade [ruˈlaːdə] *f*; *-, -n; Gastr. etwa* beef olive

Rouleau [ruˈloː] *n*; *-s, -s* (roller) blind, *Am. auch* (window) shade

Roulett [ruˈlɛt] *n*; *-(e)s, -e,* **Roulette** *n*; *-s, -s* roulette, roulette wheel; → *russisch*

Roulett(e)|kugel *f* roulette ball; ~**tisch** *m* roulette table

Route ['ruːtə] *f*; *-, -n* route; *die* ~ *über den Nordpol fliegen* fly (the route) via the North Pole; **Routenbeschreibung** *f* description of a (*od.* the) route; (*Wegbeschreibung*) directions *Pl.*; *bei e-r Rally*: route card

Routine [ruˈtiːnə] *f*; *-, kein Pl.* routine; (*Erfahrung, Übung*) practice, experience; *zur* ~ *werden* become (a matter of) routine; *ihr fehlt* (*beim Autofahren*) *noch die* ~ she doesn't have enough experience (of driving); ~**angelegenheit** *f* routine matter; ~**arbeit** *f* routine (work)

routinemäßig I. *Adj.* routine; ~*e Untersuchung* routine check-up; **II.** *Adv.* routinely, as a matter of routine

Routine|sache *f* **1.** routine affair (*od.* matter); **2.** *es ist* ~ it's a question of routine (*od.* practice); ~**untersuchung** *f* routine examination (*od.* check(-)up)

Routinier [rutiˈnjeː] *m*; *-s, -s* old hand

routiniert *Adj.* experienced, *attr. auch* seasoned …; (*gewandt*) skilled

Rowdy ['raudi] *m*; *-s, -s; pej.* lout, hooligan, hoodlum; **rowdyhaft 1.** *Adj.* loutish; **2.** *Adv.: sich* ~ *benehmen* behave like a hooligan (*od.* like hooligans); **Rowdytum** *n*; *-s, kein Pl.* hooliganism

Royalismus [roajaˈlɪsmʊs] *m*; *-, kein Pl.* royalism; **Royalist** [roajaˈlɪst] *m*; *-en, -en,* **Royalistin** *f*; *-, -nen,* **royalistisch** *Adj.* royalist

Rubbellos *n* scratch card

rubbeln *vt/i.* rub; *auf Los etc.*: scratch; (*trocken*~) rub *s.o.* down

Rübchen *n* small turnip; **Teltower** ~ *Gastr.* glazed turnip with bacon

Rübe *f*; *-, -n* **1.** (*weiße* ~) turnip; *rote* ~ beetroot; *gelbe* ~ carrot; **2.** *umg.* (*Kopf*) conk, pate, cabbage, noddle, noggin; *j-m eins über die* ~ *geben* conk *s.o.* (one); *eins auf die* ~ *kriegen* get bashed on the nut (*Am.* noggin); ~ *ab! Sl.* off with their heads!

Rubel *m*; *-s, -* rouble; *der* ~ *rollt!* the money's rolling in

Rüben|sirup *m* black treacle, *Am.* (blackstrap) molasses; ~**zucker** *m* beet sugar

rüber *Adv. umg.* **1.** → *herüber*, **2.** → *hinüber*

rüber… *im V.* **1.** → *auch herüber…*; **2.** → *auch hinüber…*

rüber|bringen *v/t.* (*unreg., trennb., hat -ge-*) *umg.* (*Botschaft, Gefühl etc.*) get across; *j-m s.th.* through (*j-m* to *s.o.*); ~**faxen** *v/t.* (*trennb., hat -ge-*) *umg.* fax *s.th.* through (*j-m* to *s.o.*); ~**kommen** *v/i.* (*unreg., trennb., ist -ge-*) *umg. Botschaft, Gefühl etc.*: come across; *ich hoffe, was ich wollte, ist rübergekommen* I hope it was clear what I wanted

Rubikon *m*; *-s: den* ~ *überschreiten* cross the Rubicon

Rubin *m*; *-s, -e* ruby; ♀**rot** *Adj.* ruby(-red)

Rubrik *f*; *-, -en* (*Spalte*) column; (*Kategorie*) category; *in e-r Handschrift*: rubric; *unter der* ~ … under the heading (*od.* category) (of); *unter die* ~ … *fallen* come under the heading …, belong in the … category; **rubrizieren** *v/t.* categorize

Rübsamen *m*; *-s, kein Pl.* oilseed rape, *Am.* canola

Ruch *m*; *-(e)s, Rüche* **1.** *selten, poet.* scent, odo(u)r; *der würzige* ~ *der Tannen* the spicy aroma of the pines;

R

2. *kein Pl.:* **im ~ der Korruption stehen** have the reputation of being corrupt; **in den ~ geraten, ein Betrüger zu sein** gain the reputation of (being) a swindler, become notorious as a swindler

ruchbar *Adj.:* **~ werden** become known; **als der Vorfall ~ wurde** *auch* when news of the incident got (a)round, when people found out about the incident

ruchlos *Adj.* wicked, contemptible; **Ruchlosigkeit** *f* profligacy; *(Handlung)* wicked act

ruck *Adv. umg.:* **~, zuck** in no time, in a flash

Ruck *m; -(e)s, -e* jerk; *im Zug etc.:* jolt *(auch fig.)*; **es gab e-n ~** there was a jerk *(od.* jolt); **~ nach links** *Pol.* swing to the left; **mit e-m ~** in one go; **sich** *(Dat.)* **e-n ~ geben** *fig.* pull o.s. together; **es ging ein ~ durch das Team** this made the team sit up (with a jolt), this gave the team a jolt

Rückansicht *f* rear view

Rückantwort *f* reply; **Postkarte mit ~** reply-paid *(Am.* business-reply) postcard; **~schein** *m* reply coupon

ruckartig I. *Adj.* jerky; **II.** *Adv.* with a jerk; *fig. (plötzlich)* suddenly

Rück|bank *f* *Mot.* rear seat (bench); **~besinnung** *f: die ~ auf* (+ *Akk.)* recalling, thinking back to, turning one's mind back to; **2bezüglich** *Adj. Ling.* reflexive; **~es Fürwort** reflexive pronoun; **~bildung** *f* *Med.* regression; *des Uterus nach der Geburt:* involution; *Bio.* degeneration; *Ling.* back formation; **~blende** *f* *Film:* flashback

Rückblick *m* review *(auf + Akk.* of); *(Bericht)* survey (of); **e-n ~ werfen auf** (+ *Akk.)* look back at; **im ~** in retrospect; **im ~ auf** (+ *Akk.)* looking back at, casting our eyes back on; **rückblickend I.** *Adj.* retrospective; **II.** *Adv.* in retrospect, looking back

Rückbuchung *f* *Fin.* reverse entry

rückdatieren *v/t.* *(untr., hat)* antedate

rucken I. *v/t.* jerk; **II.** *v/i.* (give a) jerk; *Zug etc.:* (give a) jolt

rücken I. *v/t. (hat gerückt)* move; *(schieben) auch* shift; *(weg~)* push (away); **II.** *v/i. (ist)* **1.** *an e-n bestimmten Ort:* move; **2.** *(Platz machen)* move; **ein Stückchen ~** move over (a bit); **näher ~** move closer, move up; *zeitlich:* approach, draw near; *bedrohlich:* loom up; **an j-s Stelle ~** take s.o.'s place; **er ist nicht von der Stelle gerückt** he didn't *(od.* wouldn't) budge; **das Ziel ist in weite Ferne gerückt** this goal has receded into the distant future; → **Blickfeld, greifbar** I 2, **Leib** 1, **Pelle** 2, **Pelz**

Rücken *m; -s, -* **1.** back *(auch Hand-, Stuhlrücken etc.)*; *(Bergrücken)* ridge, crest; *e-s Buchs:* spine; **auf dem ~ liegen** lie on one's back, lie supine; **j-m den ~ zuwenden** turn one's back on s.o.; **ein breiter/krummer ~** a broad/ hunched back; **~ an ~** back to back; **mit dem Wind im ~** with a following wind; **dabei lief es ihr (heiß und) kalt über den ~** it sent shivers down her spine; **der verlängerte ~** *hum.* the posterior *(od.* backside); **auf den ~ fallen** fall on one's back; **fig. umg. (überrascht)** be floored; **j-m in den ~ fallen** attack s.o. from behind; *fig.* stab s.o. in the back; **j-n im ~ haben** *Mil.* have s.o. in the rear; *fig.* have s.o. behind one *(od.* backing one up); **j-m den ~ decken** *fig.* back s.o. up; **j-m den ~**

stärken *fig.* give s.o. moral support; **sich den ~ freihalten** *auch fig.* cover o.s.; **hinter j-s ~** behind s.o.'s back; **j-m / e-r Sache den ~ kehren** turn one's back on s.o./s.th.; **e-n breiten ~ haben** *umg. fig.* have broad shoulders; **mit dem ~ zur Wand** *auch fig.* with one's back to the wall; **2.** *nur Sg.; Sport, umg. (Rückenschwimmen)* backstroke; **sie ist Favoritin über 200 Meter ~** she's favo(u)rite to win the 200 met|res *(Am.* -er) backstroke

Rücken|ausschnitt *m* back neckline; **~deckung** *f* *Mil.* rear cover; *fig.* backing, support; **~flosse** *f* dorsal *(od.* back) fin; **2frei** *Adj.* *Kleid:* low-backed; **~gymnastik** *f* back exercises *Pl.;* **~lage** *f: in ~* (lying) on one's back; **in ~ schwimmen** do the backstroke; **~lehne** *f* back(rest)

Rückenmark *n* *Anat.* spinal cord *(od.* marrow); **~erweichung** *f* *Med.* myelomalacia; **~punktion** *f* *Med.* lumbar *(od.* spinal) puncture; **~schwindsucht** *f* *Med.* tabes dorsalis; **~tumor** *m* *Med.* spinal tumor

Rücken|massage *f* back massage; **~muskulatur** *f* back muscles *Pl. (od.* musculature *Sg.);* **~nummer** *f* *Sport* number *(on the back of an athlete's shirt);* **der Läufer mit der ~ 4** the runner wearing number 4; **~panzer** *m* *Zool.* carapace; **~schmerzen** *Pl.* backache *Sg.,* back pains *(od.* pain *Sg.);* **~schule** *f* program(me) of back exercises; **~schwimmen** *n* backstroke; **~stärkung** *f* *fig.* backing, support; **~stück** *n* *Gastr.* chine; *vom Hammel, Wild:* saddle; **~training** *n* back exercises *Pl.*

Rückentwicklung *f* retrogression; *Med.* regression; *Bio.* degeneration

Rücken|verletzung *f* back injury; **~wind** *m* *Naut.* following wind; *Flug.* tail wind; *weitS.* wind blowing from behind; **~ haben** have the wind behind one; **~wirbel** *m* *Anat.* dorsal vertebra

Rück|erinnerung *f* reminiscence; **~eroberung** *f* reconquest; *Sport, des Titels etc.:* regaining, winning back

rückerstatten *v/t.* *(untr., hat)* refund, reimburse; **Rückerstattung** *f* refund(-ing), reimbursement, repayment; *Jur. (Rückgabe)* restitution

Rückfahr|karte *f* return ticket, *Am.* round-trip ticket; **~scheinwerfer** *m* reversing *(Am.* backup) light

Rückfahrt *f* return journey *(od.* trip); **auf der ~** *auch* on the way back

Rückfall *m* *Med.* relapse *(auch fig.);* *Jur.* repeat offen|ce *(Am.* -se); **e-n ~ haben** *Med.* have *(od.* suffer) a relapse; **rückfällig** *Adj.* *Jur.* *Sache:* revertible; *Verbrecher:* nur attr. reoffending ..., recidivist ...; **~ werden** *Jur.* reoffend; *fig.* backslide, have a relapse

Rückfälligkeit *f* *Jur.* recidivism

Rückfall|kriminalität *f* *Jur.* recidivism; **~quote** *f* *Jur.* reoffending rate; **~täter** *m,* **~täterin** *f* *Jur.* reoffending person, recidivist

Rück|fenster *n* *Mot.* rear window; **~flug** *m* return flight; **~fluss** *m* backflow, return flow; *Wirts.* reflux; **~forderung** *f* reclaim(ing)

Rückfrage *f* further inquiry *(od.* enquiry), query; **nach ~ bei unserem Abteilungsleiter ...** after checking with our head of department ...; **bei j-m ~ halten** → **rückfragen; rückfragen** *v/i. (untr., hat -ge-)* inquire; **bei j-m ~** check with s.o.

Rück|front *f* back, rear facade; **die Tür**

ist auf der ~ the door's at the back; **~führung** *f* **1.** *von Truppen:* return; **2.** *von Völkern:* repatriation, return; **3.** *Tech.* feedback; **~ von Abgasen** *Mot.* exhaust gas recirculation; **4.** *(Rückverfolgung)* tracing back *(auf + Akk.* to)

Rückgabe *f* return; *Fußball:* back pass; **~recht** *n* right of return; **etw. mit ~ bestellen** order s.th. on a sale or return basis; **~schalter** *m* return counter

Rückgang *m* decline, drop (+ *Gen.* in); *e-s Gletschers:* retreat; **rückgängig** *Adj.:* **~ machen** *(Auftrag etc.)* cancel; *(Vertrag) auch* annul, rescind; *(absagen) auch* call off

Rückgebäude *n* rear building

rückgewinnen *v/t.* *(unreg., untr., hat)* recover; *(Land)* reclaim; *(Rohstoffe)* recycle, recover; **Rückgewinnung** *f* recovery; *von Land:* reclamation; *von Rohstoffen:* recycling, recovery

Rückgliederung *f* reintegration

Rückgrat *n; -(e)s, -e; Anat.* spine, vertebral column; *auch fig.* backbone; **sich** *(Dat.)* **das ~ brechen** break one's back; **j-m das ~ brechen** *fig. (s-n Widerstand brechen)* break s.o.'s resistance; *(ruinieren)* ruin s.o.; **er hat kein ~** he's got no backbone, he's spineless *(od.* gutless *umg.);* **~ zeigen** show some guts *umg.;* **rückgratlos** *Adj.* spineless; **Rückgratverkrümmung** *f* *Med.* curvature of the spine

Rückgriff *m* **1.** **ein ~ auf ...** falling back on ..., reverting *(od.* going back) to ...; **der Stil stellt e-n ~ auf die Gotik dar** the style represents a return to the Gothic; **2.** *Jur.* → **Regress**

Rückhalt *m; nur Sg.* backing, support; **an j-m e-n festen ~ haben** receive firm support from s.o.; **ohne ~** → **rückhaltlos**

Rückhaltebecken *n* retention *(od.* holding *od.* high-water) reservoir

rückhaltlos I. *Adj. (bedenkenlos)* unreserved; *(offen)* (completely) frank; *Offenheit:* complete; *Vertrauen:* implicit; **II.** *Adv.* unreservedly, without reserve; *sprechen:* with complete frankness; **er sagte ~ s-e Meinung** he didn't pull any punches *umg.;* **j-m ~ vertrauen** trust s.o. implicitly; **Rückhaltlosigkeit** *f* unreserved nature; *(Offenheit)* complete frankness

Rückhand *f; nur Sg.* *Tennis etc.:* backhand; **e-n Ball (mit der) ~ spielen** play a ball backhand; **e-e schwache ~ haben** have a weak backhand

Rückkampf *m* **1.** → **Rückspiel; 2.** *Boxen etc.:* return fight *(od.* bout)

Rück|kauf *m* repurchase; **~kaufsrecht** *n* right of repurchase *(von Effekten:* redemption); **~kaufswert** *m* redemption value

Rückkehr *f* return *(auch fig.);* **bei m-r ~** on my return, when I get *(od.* got) back; **~ in den Beruf** return to one's former job; **Rückkehrer** *m; -s, -,* **Rückkehrerin** *f; -, -nen** homecomer; *in den Beruf:* person returning to his *(od.* her) former job; *(bes. Frauen nach Erziehungsurlaub)* returnee

Rück|kopplung *f* feedback *(auch fig.);* **~kunft** *f; -, kein Pl.; geh.* → **Rückkehr; ~lage** *f* **1.** *Wirts.* reserve(s *Pl.);* *(Ersparnisse)* savings *Pl.;* **2.** *Skisport:* backward lean

Rücklauf *m* **1.** *Videogerät etc.:* (fast) rewind; *Kamera:* rewind; **2.** *Tech.* return *(od.* back) stroke; *e-s Propellers:* slip; **3.** *e-s Gewässers:* reflux; **4.** *e-r Fragebogenaktion etc.:* number of returns; **rückläufig** *Adj.* declining, downward; *auch Astron., Bio., Med.* retrograde; **~e Tendenz** *Wirts.* downward trend; **die Zahlen sind ~** the figures show a downward trend; **Rücklauftaste** *f* rewind button

Rück|leuchte *f*, **~licht** *n* rear light, tail-light

rücklings *Adv.* backwards; (*von hinten*) from behind; (*auf dem Rücken*) on one's back; **~ auf dem Stuhl sitzen** sit on the chair facing backwards; **~ erschießen** shoot *s.o.* in the back

Rück|marsch *m* march back; (*Rückzug*) retreat; *hum.* **beim Spazieren**: walk back; **auf dem ~** on the march back; (*auf dem Rückzug*) during the retreat; **beim Spazieren**: on the walk (*od.* way) back; **~meldefrist** *f Univ.* term for re-registration; **~meldegebühr** *f Univ.* re-registration fee; **~meldung** *f* reporting back; *Univ.* re-registration; *Funk:* reply; *Etron.* feedback; **~nahme** *f* taking back; *e-r Behauptung etc.*: withdrawal; **~nahmeautomat** *m* machine for returnable bottles (*issuing a voucher for the amount due*); **~pass** *m Sport* back pass; **~porto** *n* return postage; **~prall** *m* rebound, resilience

Rückreise *f* return journey (*od.* trip); **auf der ~** *auch* on the way back; **~verkehr** *m* returning (*od.* homebound) traffic; **~welle** *f* surge of homebound traffic

Rückrollbremse *f* hill-holder

Rückruf *m* **1.** *Telef.* return call; **auf j-s ~ warten** wait for s.o. to call (*Brit. auch* ring) back; **2.** *Wirts.* → **Rückrufaktion**; **~aktion** *f Wirts.* recall

Rückrunde *f Sport* **1.** second half of the season; **2.** (*Rückspiel*) return match (*od.* leg)

Rucksack *m* rucksack, *Am.* backpack; **~tourismus** *m* backpacking; **~tourist** *m*, **~touristin** *f* backpacker

Rück|schau *f* review (**auf** +*Akk.* to); **etw. aus der ~ sehen** look back on s.th., view s.th. in retrospect; → *auch* **Rückblick**

Rückschlag *m* **1.** setback; *Med.* relapse; **e-n schweren ~ hinnehmen müssen** suffer a severe setback; **2.** *Sport* return; **3.** *e-s Gewehrs*: recoil; **4.** *e-r Flamme*: backfire, flashback

Rückschläger *m*, **~in** *f Tennis etc.*: returner of the ball, receiver

Rückschlagventil *n* non-return valve, check valve

Rück|schluss *m* inference (**aus** + *Akk.* from); **Rückschlüsse ziehen aus** draw conclusions from; **~schreiben** *n* reply

Rückschritt *m* step back, backward (*od.* retrograde) step; **rückschrittlich** *Adj.* reactionary

Rück|seite *f* back, rear; *e-s Blattes, e-r Münze etc.*: reverse; *e-s Stoffes*: wrong side; **siehe ~!** see overleaf; **~sendung** *f* return

Rücksicht *f*, -, -en **1.** *nur Sg.* consideration (**auf** + *Akk.* for); **aus** *od.* **mit ~ auf** (+*Akk.*) out of consideration for; **ohne ~ auf** (+ *Akk.*) regardless of; **ohne ~ auf Verluste** *umg.* regardless; **auf j-n ~ nehmen** show consideration for s.o.; **auf etw. ~ nehmen** make allowances for s.th., take s.th. into account; **keine ~ nehmen auf** (+ *Akk.*) *auch* pay no heed to; **keine ~ kennen** show no consideration (for others), *stärker*: be ruthless; (*alles wagen*) stop at nothing; **2.** *nur Pl.* (*Erwägungen*) consid-

erations; **aus familiären ~en** for family reasons

Rücksichtnahme *f*; -, *kein Pl.* consideration (**auf** + *Akk.* for)

rücksichtslos I. *Adj.* inconsiderate (**gegen** towards), thoughtless; *Autofahrer*: reckless; (*unbarmherzig*) ruthless; **ein ~er Karrierist** a ruthless careerist; **II.** *Adv.* inconsiderately *etc.*; **~ fahren** drive recklessly; **sich ~ vordrängen** push one's way to the front regardless of others; **~ vorgehen** *Regierung etc.*: take drastic action (*od.* measures) (**gegen** against); **Rücksichtslosigkeit** *f* thoughtlessness; (*Verantwortungslosigkeit*) recklessness; (*Schonungslosigkeit*) ruthlessness

rücksichtsvoll I. *Adj.* considerate (**gegenüber** + *Dat.* toward[s]), thoughtful; (*schonend*) gentle; **~es Verhalten** thoughtfulness; **II.** *Adv.*: **sich ~ verhalten** act considerately, show consideration; **j-n ~ behandeln** treat s.o. with consideration

Rück|siedler *m*, **~siedlerIn** *f* repatriate; **~sitz** *m* back seat; *Motorrad*: pillion; **~sog** *m von Feuer, Wasser*: backdraught, *Am.* backdraft; **~spiegel** *m Mot.* rear-view mirror; **~spiel** *n Sport* return match (*od.* leg); **~sprache** *f* consultation; **mit j-m ~ halten** *od.* **nehmen** confer with s.o., talk *s.th.* over with s.o.; **nach ~ mit j-m** after consulting (*od.* talking to) s.o.

Rückspulautomatik *f Fot., Video*: automatic (film) rewind; **rückspulen** *vt/i.* (*untr., hat -ge-*) *Tonband, Video etc.*: rewind; **Rückspultaste** *f* rewind key

Rückstand *m* **1.** (*Rest*) remains *Pl.*; *Chem.* residue; (*Bodensatz*) sediment; **Rückstände von Pestiziden im Fleisch** traces of pesticides remaining in the meat; **2.** *Wirts.*: **Rückstände** outstanding debts; **3.** (*Liefer-, Arbeitsrückstand*) backlog; **im ~ sein** be behind; **mit der Miete etc. im ~ sein** be in arrears (*Am.* be behind) with one's rent *etc.*; **4.** *Sport* deficit; **mit zwei Toren im ~ sein** *Fußball*: be two goals down

rückstandfrei I. *Adj.* free from deposits; *Verbrennung auch*: clean; **II.** *Adv.*: **~ verbrennen** burn without leaving deposits

rückständig *Adj.* **1.** out-of-date, antiquated, behind the times; (*unterentwickelt*) backward, underdeveloped; **2.** (*überfällig*) *Zahlung etc.* outstanding; **~e Miete/Steuern** rent/tax arrears; **Rückständigkeit** *f* backwardness

rückstandsfrei *Adj.* → **rückstandfrei**

Rückstau *m* **1.** *von Wasser*: backwater, backflow, backwash, afflux *fachspr.*; **2.** *Mot.* tailback, *Am.* line of traffic

Rückstellung *f* **1.** *Wirts.* transfer to reserve (*fund*); (*Summe*) reserve; **2.** *Etech., EDV* reset(ting); **3.** *vom Examen, Projekt etc.*: postponement (**um** + *Akk.* by)

Rückstoß *m Gewehr*: recoil; *Rakete*: reaction; **rückstoßfrei** *Adj.* recoilless

Rück|strahler *m* reflector; **~strom** *m*: **~ von Urlaubern** returning stream of holidaymakers (*Am.* vacationers); **~stufung** *f* downgrading; **~taste** *f Computer*: backspace (key); **~tausch** *m Fin.* return; **~ von Devisen** changing back foreign currency; **~transport** *m* return transport(ation)

Rücktritt *m* **1.** *vom Amt*: resignation; *vom Vertrag*: withdrawal (**vom** + *Dat.* from); **s-n ~ erklären** hand in one's resignation; **2.** *am Fahrrad*: → **Rück-**

trittbremse, **~bremse** *f* backpedal (*Am.* coaster) brake

Rücktritts|drohung *f* threat of resignation; **~erklärung** *f* announcement of (one's) resignation; **~forderung** *f* demand for his *etc.* resignation; **~gesuch** *n* offer of resignation; **sein ~ einreichen** tender one's resignation; **~recht** *n* right to rescind (**vom Vertrag** the contract)

rückübersetzen *v/t.* translate back; **Rückübersetzung** *f* back-translation

Rück|überweisung *f* repayment; **~umschlag** *m* reply-paid (*Am.* business reply) envelope; **adressierter und frankierter ~** stamped addressed envelope

rückvergüten *v/t.* (*untr., hat*) refund, reimburse; **Rückvergütung** *f* refund(ing), reimbursement

rückversichern (*untr., hat*) **I.** *v/t.* reinsure; **II.** *v/refl.* reinsure o.s.; *fig.* play safe; **Rückversicherung** *f* reinsurance

Rück|wand *f* back; *von Gebäuden*: back (*od.* rear) wall; **~wanderer** *m*, **~wanderin** *f* returning emigrant; **~wanderung** *f* remigration

rückwärtig *Adj.* rear, back

rückwärts *Adv.* **1.** backwards; **Salto ~** backward somersault; **Rolle ~** backward roll; **~ gehen** walk backwards; *fig.* be on the decline; **~ fahren** *Mot.* back (up), reverse; **~ aus der Garage fahren** back (the car) out of the garage; **~ einparken** back into a parking space; **ein Band etc. ~ laufen lassen** rewind (*od.* wind back) a tape *etc.*; **sich ~ wenden** *fig.* look back (to the past); **~ gewandt** *Haltung, Ideen*: backward-looking; **2.** *südd., österr.* (*hinten*) at the back; **von ~ kommen** come from behind (*od.* from the rear)

Rückwärts|bewegung *f* backward movement; *fig.* decline, falling off; **~drehung** *f* backward rotation; **~gang** *m Mot.* reverse gear; **im ~** in reverse (gear); **den ~ einlegen** get into reverse gear

Rückweg *m* way back (*od.* home); **den ~ antreten** head for home

ruckweise *Adv.* jerkily, in jerks

rückwirkend *Adj.* **I.** retrospective, *bes. Am.* retroactive; **II.** *Adv.*: **die Gehaltserhöhung gilt ~ ab April** the salary increase will be backdated (*Am. auch* retroactive) to April; **Rückwirkung** *f* **1.** repercussion; **2.** *Jur.*: **mit ~ vom** with retrospective (*Am.* retroactive) effect from

rückzahlbar *Adj.* repayable; *Effekten*: redeemable; **Rückzahlung** *f* repayment; *von Effekten*: redemption

Rückzieher *m*; -s, - **1.** *umg.* withdrawal *allg.*; *von e-er Behauptung*: climb-down; **e-n ~ machen** back out; *von e-er Behauptung*: climb down; **2.** *Fußball*: overhead kick

ruck, zuck *Adv. umg.* → **ruck**

Rückzug *m* retreat, withdrawal; **den ~ antreten** start to retreat; **Rückzugsgefecht** *n Mil. und fig.* rearguard action

Rucola *f*; -, *kein Pl. Salatpflanze*: rucola, garden (*Am.* salad) rocket

Rüde *m*; -n, -n; *Zool.* **1.** *Hund, Wolf etc.*: male (*dog, wolf etc.*); **2.** *Jägerspr.* hound, hunting dog

rüde I. *Adj.* coarse, uncouth; **~r Kerl** *umg. auch* lout, jerk, *Brit.* yob; **II.** *Adv.*: **sich ~ benehmen** behave like a lout (*Am.* jerk); *generell*: be uncouth

Rudel *n*; -s, - *von Hirschen etc.*: herd; *von Wölfen*: pack; *fig.* swarm, horde;

R

rudelweise *Adv. Hirsche etc.*: in herds; *Wölfe*: in packs; *fig.* in hordes
Ruder *n*; *-s, -* **1.** oar; (*Skull*) scull; (*Paddel*) paddle; **sich (kräftig) in die ~ legen** row strongly; *fig.* go hard at it; **2.** (*Steuerruder*) helm, wheel; (*Blatt*) rudder; *Flug.* (*Seitenruder*) rudder; **das ~ herumwerfen** *auch fig.* change course; **aus dem ~ laufen** *auch fig.* go off course; **am ~ sein** *fig. Pol.* be in power, be at the helm; **ans ~ kommen** come to power, take over the reins; **~blatt** *n* (oar) blade; (*Schiffsruder*) rudder blade; **~boot** *n* rowing boat
Ruderer *m*; *-s, -* rower; *Sport* oarsman
Ruder|gänger *m*; *-s, - Naut.* helmsman; **~haus** *n Naut.* wheelhouse
Ruderin *f*; *-, -nen* rower; *Sport* oarswoman
Ruderklub *m* rowing club
rudern I. *v/t.* (*hat gerudert*) row (*auch Boot, Rennen, j-n*); **II.** *v/i.* **1.** (*ist*) row (*nach* to); **2.** (*hat od. ist*) row (*gegen* against); **3.** (*hat*) *umg. fig., beim Laufen*: **mit den Armen ~** swing one's arms; *beim Schwimmen*: make vigorous strokes; *fig.* try to keep one's balance
Rudern *n*; *-s, kein Pl.* rowing
Ruder|regatta *f* (rowing) regatta; (*einzelnes Rennen*) boat race; **~schlag** *m* oarstroke; **~sport** *m* rowing
Rudiment *n*; *-(e)s, -e* **1.** (*Rest*) remnant; **2.** *Bio.* vestigial organ; **3.** *altm.*: **~e** (*Grundlagen*) rudiments; **rudimentär** *Adj.* rudimentary
Rudrer *m*; *-s, - → Ruderer*, **Rudrerin** *f*; *-, -nen → Ruderin*
Ruf *m*; *-(e)s, -e* **1.** shout; **anfeuernde ~e** shouts of encouragement; **2.** *von Vögeln etc., auch fig.*: call; **der ~ nach Freiheit** *fig.* the call for freedom; **dem ~ s-s Herzens folgen** follow the promptings *Pl.* of one's heart; **3.** *fig. bes. Univ.* (*Berufung*) offer of a professorship, call; **e-n ~ erhalten nach** be offered an appointment at; *Univ.* be offered a chair at; **4.** *fig.* reputation; **guter/schlechter ~** good/bad reputation; **von ~** of high repute, of (some) standing, of renown; **im ~ stehen, etw. zu sein** be reputed to be s.th.; **den ~ e-s Fachmannes etc. haben** be reputed to be an expert *etc.*; **sich** (*Dat.*) **e-n guten ~ erwerben** make a name for o.s.; **besser als sein ~ sein** be better than one's reputation, not be as black as one is painted; **j-n/etw. in e-n schlechten ~ bringen** give s.o./s.th. a bad name, bring s.o./s.th. into disrepute; **5.** *Telef.*: **~ 36345** Tel. 36345
rufen *v/t./i.*; *ruft, rief, hat gerufen* shout; *Vögel, auch fig.*: call; (*j-n*) call (*auch Arzt, Polizei etc.*); (*herbei~*) (*Taxi, Gepäckträger etc.*) call, hail; **~ nach** call for; **~ lassen** send for (*Arzt etc.*) *auch* call; **um Hilfe ~** cry (*od.* call) for help; **„Bravo"/ „Buh" ~** shout (*od.* cry) "bravo!" / shout "boo!"; **zum Essen/Gebet ~** call *people, etc.* to eat / call the faithful to prayer; **er heißt Martin, aber alle rufen ihn „Speedy"** his name is Martin, but everybody calls him "Speedy"; **die Pflicht ruft** duty calls; **die Arbeit ruft** I've got to get back to work, there's work waiting for me; **du kommst (mir) wie gerufen!** *umg.* you're just the person I need; **der Brief kam wie gerufen** *umg.* the letter came in handy; *→ Gedächtnis* 2, *Leben* 8
Rufen *n*; *-s, kein Pl.* shouting, calling, shouts *Pl.*, calls *Pl.*; **sie hat mein ~**

nicht gehört she didn't hear me calling
Rufer *m*; *-s, -*; *fig.*: **der ~ in der Wüste** a voice (crying) in the wilderness
Rüffel *m*; *-s, -*; *umg.* ticking off, dressing-down, *Brit. auch* wigging; **rüffeln** *v/t. umg.*: **j-n ~** tick s.o. off, give s.o. a dressing-down (*od.* wigging); *sehr laut*: bawl s.o. out
Ruf|mord *m* character assassination; *Jur.* defamation of character; **~mordkampagne** *f* smear campaign; **~name** *m* name by which one is called (*od.* known); **wie ist Ihr ~?** what name are you called by?; **~nummer** *f* telephone number; **~nummernspeicher** *m* telephone (number) memory; **~säule** *f* (*Notruf*) emergency (tele)phone; *für Taxi*: taxi (tele)phone
rufschädigend *Adj. Bemerkung etc.*: defamatory; **Rufschädigung** *f* defamation
Ruf|taste *f* call button; **~weite** *f*: **in ~** within call (*od.* earshot); **~zeichen** *n* call sign (*od.* signal); (*Klingelzeichen*) ring
Rugby ['rakbi] *n*; *-(s), kein Pl.* rugby; **~spiel** *n* rugby (football); *einzelnes*: rugby game (*od.* match)
Rüge *f*; *-, -n* rebuke, reprimand; (*Tadel*) reproach; *öffentliche*: censure; **e-e ~ erteilen → rügen**
rügen *v/t.* reprimand, rebuke, blame (*wegen* for); *scharf*: rap (*kritisieren*) criticize; *öffentlich*: censure, denounce; (*etw. ~*) find fault with
Ruhe *f*; *-, kein Pl.* **1.** (*Stille*) silence, peace (and quiet); **~!** (be) quiet!, silence!, order!; **~, bitte!** quiet, please; **gib doch endlich ~!** can't you be quiet?; (*auch: hör auf damit*) give over (*Am.* cut it out), will you; **es herrschte absolute ~** there wasn't a sound to be heard, *unter Zuhörern etc.*: there was dead silence; **~ vor dem Sturm** lull (*od.* calm) before the storm; **2.** (*Friede*) peace; **~ und Ordnung** law and order; **~ und (inneren) Frieden (wiederherstellen)** (restore) peace and tranquility; **3.** (*Entspannung, Erholung*) rest; **zur ~ kommen** *Pendel etc.*: come to rest; *Person*: settle down; **sie braucht (jetzt) ~** she needs rest (*Stille*: peace and quiet); **er gönnt mir keine ~** he doesn't give me a minute's rest, he keeps me going nonstop *umg.*; **sich zur ~ setzen** retire, go into retirement; **j-n zur letzten ~ betten** lay s.o. to rest; **ewige ~** eternal rest (*od.* peace); **jetzt hat die liebe Seele Ruh'** *umg.* peace and quiet at last; **4.** *innere*: *auch* peace of mind; (*Gelassenheit*) calm, composure, coolness; (*Geduld*) patience; (*Gemächlichkeit*) leisureliness; (**sie sagte mir) in aller ~** (she told me) (very) calmly; **überleg es dir in aller ~** take your time over (*od.* about) it; **~ bewahren** (*sich nicht aufregen*) keep one's composure (*od.* cool); (*still sein*) keep quiet; **sich nicht aus der ~ bringen lassen** keep one's composure, not get worked up; **nichts bringt ihn aus der ~** nothing upsets him; **er hat die ~ weg** *umg.* he's unflappable; (*trödelt*) he certainly takes his time; **immer mit der ~!** *umg.* (take it) easy!; *warnend*: easy does it!, keep your shirt on!; **er kann keine ~ finden** he just won't calm down; (*kann nicht schlafen*) he can't (get to) sleep; **sich zur ~ begeben** *form.* retire (to bed *od.* to rest); **angenehme ~!** sleep well; **er war die ~ selbst** he was as calm as could be, he

was as cool as a cucumber *umg.*; **~ haben vor** (+ *Dat.*) be unmolested by, be no longer bothered by; **5.** **lass mich in ~!** leave me alone; **lass mich damit in ~!** I don't want to hear about it, don't bother me about that; **er lässt mir keine ~** he does not give me any peace; **er lässt sie nicht in ~** he keeps pestering her; *Kind*: *auch* he gives her no peace; **es ließ ihm keine ~** he couldn't stop thinking about it, it haunted him, it preyed on his mind
Ruhebedürfnis *n* need for rest; **ruhebedürftig** *Adj.* in need of (a) rest
Ruhebett *n* couch, lounge, daybed
Ruhegehalt *n* (retiring) pension, retirement pay; **Ruhegehaltsempfänger** *m*, **Ruhegehaltsempfängerin** *f* pensioner
Ruhe|geld *n* (old age) pension; **~kissen** *n fig.*: **ein gutes Gewissen ist ein sanftes ~** a clear conscience allows one to sleep peacefully; **~lage** *f → Ruhestellung*
ruhelos *Adj.* restless; **Ruhelosigkeit** *f* restlessness
ruhen *v/i.* **1.** rest (*auch Toter*); *Arbeit, Verkehr etc.*: be at a standstill; **~ auf** (+ *Dat.*) *Blick, Last, Verantwortung etc.*: rest on; **ich wünsche, wohl zu ~** *förm.* have a good night's rest; **er ruhte (und rastete) nicht, bis ...** he didn't rest until ...; **~ lassen** (*Vergangenheit etc.*) forget (about); (*Problem, Angelegenheit etc.*) leave aside; (*Verfahren etc.*) suspend; **etw. ~ lassen** (*belassen*) let s.th. rest; **j-n nicht ~ lassen** *Gedanke etc.*: give s.o. no peace; **hier ruht hier** lies; **er ruhe in Frieden** may he rest in peace; **2.** *Verhandlungen, Verfahren*: have been suspended; **3.** *Jur. Vertrag, Forderung*: be in abeyance; **4.** *Vulkan*: be dormant
ruhend I. *Part. Präs. → ruhen*; **II.** *Adj. Kapital*: idle; *auch Vulkan*: dormant, quiescent; (*feststehend*) stationary; *Jur.* abeyant; **der ~e Verkehr** parked vehicles *Pl.*; **ein in sich selbst ~er Mensch** a well-balanced person
Ruhe|pause *f* rest; *kurze*: break, breather *umg.*; **~platz** *m* (*auch Grab*) resting place; **~raum** *m* rest (*Am.* break) room; **~sitz** *m* retirement home; **~stadium** *n Bio.* resting stage
Ruhe|stand *m* retirement; **im ~** (*abgek. i. R.*) retired (*abgek. ret.*); **in ~ gehen** *od.* **in den ~ treten** retire; **in den ~ versetzen** retire, pension off; **vorgezogener ~** early retirement; **~ständler** *m*, **~ständlerin** *f* retired person
Ruhe|stätte *f* place of rest; **letzte ~** *fig.* last (*od.* final) resting place; **~stellung** *f* **1.** *Tech. Maschine*: off position; **in ~** *Pendel etc.*: at rest; **2.** *Mil.*: **in ~** behind the lines, with the reserves; **~störer** *m weitS.* disturber of the peace; *engS.* noisy person; **~störung** *f* disturbance, noise; (*öffentliche*) **~** disturbance of the peace; **~tag** *m* closing day, day off; (*dienstfreier Tag*) day off; *Montag* **~** closed (on) Mondays; **~zustand** *m* state of rest; **im ~** (when) at rest
ruhig I. *Adj.* **1.** (*still*) quiet (*auch Farbe, Gegend etc., Wirts. Markt*); *präd.* (*auch bewegungslos*) still; **seid mal bitte e-n Moment ~!** please keep quiet just for a moment; **du bist ganz ~!** *drohend*: I don't want to hear another sound out of you; **in ~em Ton** in a calm (tone of) voice; **um sie ist es ~ geworden** *fig.* you don't hear anything about her any more; **2.** (*friedlich, ungestört*) quiet, peaceful, tranquil; (*ge-*

ruhsam) restful; *e-e ~e Kugel schieben umg.* be not exactly killing o.s.; *ich habe keine ~e Minute* I don't get a moment's (*od.* minute's) peace (*od.* rest); **3.** (*gelassen*) calm, composed, cool(-headed); (*leidenschaftslos*) even-tempered; (*beruhigt*) reassured; *Hand*: steady; *Nerven*: calm; *Gewissen*: clear; *~er Mensch* quiet person; *~ und gefasst* calm and collected; *~ werden* quiet(en) down; *~ bleiben* keep calm (*od.* one's temper); *sei ganz ~* (*unbesorgt*) there's no need to worry; *~! qui-et!*; (*dazu braucht man*) *e-e ~e Hand* (this needs) a steady hand; *~ Blut!* just keep calm, calm down; **4.** (*glatt, störungsfrei*) smooth; (*gemächlich*) leisurely (*auch Adv.*); *See*: calm; *Überfahrt*: smooth; **5.** *~ stellen Med.* (*Arm etc.*) immobilize; (*Patienten*) medikamentös: tranquil(l)ize; **II.** *Adv.* **1.** quietly *etc.*; *~ schlafen* sleep soundly; *~ wohnen* live in a quiet area; *~ verlaufen* be uneventful; (*reibungslos*) go off smoothly (*od.* without a hitch); *sich ~ verhalten* keep quiet, hold one's peace; *sie sahen ~ zu, wie er den Hund quälte* they just stood and watched him tormenting the dog; **2.** (*meinetwegen, getrost*) by all means; *du kannst ~ dableiben* by all means stay if you want, it's all right for you to stay; *das können Sie ~ tun* feel free (to do so); *du kannst mir ~ glauben* you can take my word for it; *du könntest mir ~ die Tür aufmachen* you might open the door for me

Ruhigstellung *f Med. e-s Gliedes*: immobilizing, immobilization; *e-s Patienten*: tranquil(l)izing

Ruhm *m*; *-(e)s, kein Pl.* fame; glory; *~ erlangen* win (*od.* achieve) fame, win renown; *zweifelhaften ~ erlangen* acquire a dubious reputation (*od.* notoriety); *er hat sich nicht gerade mit ~ bekleckert umg.* he didn't exactly cover himself in glory

ruhmbedeckt *Adj.* covered (*od.* bedecked) in glory; (*berühmt*) renowned

rühmen *v/t.* praise; *stärker*: extol, sing the praises of; *sich e-r Sache ~* boast s.th.; *er kann sich ~, e-r der weltbesten Stürmer zu sein* he can claim to be one of the best strikers in the world; **rühmenswert** *Adj.* praiseworthy, laudable, commendable, creditable

Ruhmes|blatt *n fig.* glorious chapter (*+ Gen.* in); *das war nicht gerade ein ~ für ihn umg.* he didn't exactly distinguish himself (with that) *allg.*; *~halle f* pantheon; *Am. Sport etc.* hall of fame; *~tat f* glorious deed

rühmlich *Adj.* praiseworthy, hono(u)rable, laudable; *e-e ~e Ausnahme* a notable exception; *kein ~es Ende nehmen* come to a bad end

ruhmlos *Adj.* inglorious

ruhmreich *Adj.* glorious; (*berühmt*) famous, renowned

Ruhmsucht *f* desire (*od.* thirst) for fame; **ruhmsüchtig** *Adj.* desiring fame

ruhmvoll *Adj.* → *ruhmreich*

Ruhr *f*; *-, kein Pl.; Med.* dysentery

Rühr|besen *m* whisk; *~eier Pl.* scrambled eggs

rühren I. *v/t.* **1.** (*um~*) stir; *Butter in die Soße ~* stir butter into the sauce; **2.** (*bewegen*) move; → *Finger* 2, *Trommel*, **3.** *fig. innerlich*: touch; (*ergreifen*) move; *das rührte ihn wenig* it left him cold, he was unmoved (by it); → *Don-*

ner, gerührt, rührend; **II.** *v/i.* **1.** (*um~*) stir; **2.** *~ an* (*+ Akk.*) touch; *fig.* (*erwähnen*) touch on; *an diesen Punkt darf man bei ihm nicht ~ fig.* you mustn't mention that to him, it's a sore point with him; *lass uns nicht an Vergangenes ~* let's not stir up the past; **3.** *~ von* come from, stem from; *das rührt daher, dass ...* that is due to the fact that ...; **III.** *v/refl.* **1.** (*sich bewegen*) stir, *auch Körperteil*: move; *er rührte sich nicht vom Fleck* he didn't budge; *ich konnte mich nicht mehr ~* I could no longer move; *rührt euch! Mil.* at ease!; **2.** *fig.* (*tätig werden*) do something; *nebenan rührt sich gar nichts* it's very quiet next door; *dreimal haben wir es schon beantragt, aber da rührt sich nichts* we have applied three times, but nothing ever happens; **3.** *fig.* (*sich bemerkbar machen*) Person: say something; Gefühl: stir; *wenn du was willst, musst du dich ~* if you want anything, you must say so (*od.* let me *etc.* know)

Rühren *n*; *-s, kein Pl.*: *ein menschliches ~ verspüren* be touched with pity; *hum.* (*s-e Notdurft verrichten müssen*) have to answer the call of nature

rührend I. *Part. Präs.* → *rühren*; **II.** *Adj.* touching, moving; (*liebevoll*) very kind; *ein ~er Anblick* a touching sight; *das ist ja ~!* that's really nice (*od.* sweet) of you; *iro.* that's really charming (I'm sure)!; *s-e Naivität hat etw. Rührendes* there's something touching (*od.* charming) about his naïvety, he's touchingly naïve; **III.** *Adv.* touchingly; *~ besorgt* touchingly concerned (*um* for)

Ruhrgebiet *n Geog.*: *das ~* the Ruhr

rührig *Adj.* active; (*unternehmungslustig*) *auch* enterprising, *Brit.* go-ahead *umg.*; *ein ~er Kopf* a nimble brain (*od.* mind *od.* wit); **Rührigkeit** *f* activeness, alertness; (*Unternehmungslust*) enterprise

Rühr|kuchen *m Gastr.* stirred cake; *~löffel m* stirring (*od.* mixing) spoon; *~maschine f* mixer; *in Bäckerei*: whipping unit

Rührmichnichtan *n*; *-, -; Bot.* touch-me-not

Ruhrpott *m*; *-(e)s; umg.* → *Ruhrgebiet*

Rührschüssel *f* mixing bowl

rührselig *Adj.* (over-)sentimental, maudlin; *~es Stück etc.* tearjerker *umg.*; **Rührseligkeit** *f* (excessive) sentimentality, maudlin nature

Rührstück *n Lit.* sentimental drama

Rührteig *m Gastr.* batter, cake mixture

Rührung *f* emotion; *vor ~ nicht sprechen können* be choked with emotion

Rührwerk *n* mixer; *Tech.* stirrer, stirring apparatus, agitator

Ruin *m*; *-s, kein Pl.* ruin; *e-s Menschen*: *auch* undoing; *vor dem ~ stehen* be on the verge (*od.* brink) of ruin; *du bist noch mein ~! umg.* you'll be the end of me!

Ruine *f*; *-, -n* ruin, ruins *Pl.*; *fig.* (*Person*) wreck

Ruinen|grundstück *n* ruined site; *nach Bombenanschlag*: bombed site; *~landschaft f* expanse of ruins (*od.* rubble)

ruinieren *v/t.* ruin (*sich* o.s.); (*die Wirtschaft*) *auch* wreck; **ruiniert I.** *P.P.* → *ruinieren*; **II.** *Adj.* ruined; **ruinös** *Adj.* ruinous

rülpsen *v/i. umg.* burp, belch; **Rülpser** *m*; *-s, -; umg.* burp, belch

rum *Adv. umg.* → *herum*

rum... im V. → *auch herum...*

Rum *m*; *-s, kein Pl.* rum; *Cola mit ~* Coke with rum, *Am.* rum and Coke

Rumäne *m*; *-n, -n* Romanian (*od.* Rumanian); **Rumänien** (*n*); *-s; Geog.* Romania (*od.* Rumania); **Rumänin** *f*; *-, -nen* Romanian (*od.* Rumanian) woman (*od.* girl *etc.*); **rumänisch I.** *Adj.* Romanian (*od.* Rumanian); **II. Rumänisch** *n*; *-(s); Ling.* Romanian (*od.* Rumanian); *das Rumänische* Romanian (*od.* Rumanian)

Rumba *f*; *-, -s; Mus.* rumba

rum|gammeln *v/i.* (*trennb., hat -ge-*) *umg.* loaf (*Am.* bum *Sl.*) around (*od.* about); *~hängen v/i.* (*unreg., trennb., hat -ge-*) *umg.*: *~ in* (*+ Dat.*) hang around in; *er hängt ständig mit diesen Typen rum* he keeps hanging around with this lot; *~kriegen v/t.* (*trennb., hat -ge-*) *umg. j-n ~* talk s.o. (a)round *allg.*; *sexuell*: get s.o.into bed; *die Zeit ~* manage to pass the time *allg.*

Rumkugel *f* (rum) truffle

rummachen *v/i.* (*trennb., hat -ge-*) *umg.*: *~ an* (*+ Dat.*) (*rumbasteln*) fiddle about with; *~ mit j-m* (*zusammmen sein*) *bes. Brit.* carry on with s.o.

Rummel *m*; *-s, kein Pl.; umg.* **1.** (*Geschäftigkeit*) (hustle and) bustle; (*Aufheben*) fuss *allg.*, to-do; (*Schau*) razz(a)matazz; *e-n großen ~ um etw. machen* make a big fuss (*od.* to-do) about s.th.; **2.** *bes. nordd.* (*Jahrmarkt*) *bes. Brit* (fun)fair, *Am.* (fun) fair, carnival; → *Rummelplatz*, *~platz m umg.* fairground; *großer od. als Dauereinrichtung*: amusement park; *auf den ~ gehen* go to the fair

rumoren *v/i.* make a noise; *auch emsig*: bang around; *Vulkan etc.* rumble; *es rumort in m-m Bauch/Kopf* my stomach's rumbling / my head's buzzing; *es rumorte im Volk* there was growing unrest among the people

Rumpelkammer *f* lumber room, *Am.* storeroom; *dein Zimmer ist ja die reinste ~ umg.* your room is nothing but a tip (*Am.* dump)

rumpeln *v/i.* rumble; (*Krach machen*) bang around

Rumpelstilzchen *n*; *-s* Rumpelstiltskin

Rumpf *m*; *-(e)s, Rümpfe; auch Anat.* trunk; *e-r Statue*: torso; *e-s Schiffes*: hull; *Flug.* fuselage, body; *~beuge f* bend from the hips; *~ seitwärts/vorwärts* trunk bending sideways/forwards

rümpfen *v/t.*: *die Nase ~* turn up one's nose (*über + Akk.* at)

Rumpf|fläche *f Geol.* peneplain, old plain; *~gebirge n* residual mountains *Pl.*, truncated upland; *~kabinett n* reduced (*od.* cut-down) cabinet; *~kreisen n*; *-s, kein Pl.* trunk rolling; *~programm n* truncated program(me)

Rumpsteak ['rʊmpsteːk] *n Gastr.* rump steak

rums *Interj.* bang!

rumsen *v/i. umg.* bang; *mit dem Kopf gegen die Tür ~* bang one's head against (*od.* on) the door; *da hat es gerumst fig.* (*e-n Unfall gegeben*) there was a crash

Rumtopf *m* fruits preserved in rum and sugar, *Am.* rumtopf

Run [ran] *m*; *-s, -s* run (*auf + Akk.* on)

rund I. *Adj.* round (*auch fig. Summe, Vokal, Zahl*); (*kreisrund*) *auch* circular; (*kugelförmig*) spherical; (*zylindrisch*) cylindrical; (*dicklich*) plump, podgy (*od.* pudgy), rotund *hum*; *Wangen*: round; (*abgerundet*) *Arbeit etc.*: well-rounded; *Wein*: mellow; *Feier*: perfect; *Bot. Blattform*: orbiculare, orbiculate; **ein ~es Dutzend** a round dozen, a dozen or so; **ein ~er Geburtstag** a birthday with a nought on (*Am.* with a zero), a big "O"; *Gespräche am ~en Tisch* roundtable talks; **II.** *Adv.* (*ungefähr*) about, around, roughly; **~ 30 Leute** 30 people or so; **~ um** (+ *Akk.*) (a)round; *der Motor läuft* **~** the engine's running smoothly; *ein Buch ~ um die Raumfahrt* a book all about (*od.* on every aspect of) space travel; → *rundgehen, rundheraus, rundweg*

Rund *n*; *-(e)s, kein Pl.* round; (*Kreis*) circle; **im weiten ~ der Arena** in the spacious circle of the arena

Rund|bau *m*; *Pl. -ten* rotunda, circular building; **~beet** *n* circular border; **~blick** *m* panorama, panoramic view

Rundbogen *m Archit.* round (*od.* Norman) arch; **~fenster** *n* window with a round (*od.* Norman) arch

Rund|brief *m* circular (letter); **~bürste** *f* curved brush

Runde *f*; *-, -n* **1.** (*Gesellschaft*) group, circle, crowd *umg.*; **e-e fröhliche ~** a happy circle; **einer fehlt in der ~** there's s.o. missing (from our group), we're not complete; **2.** (*Rundgang*) walk; *dienstlich*: round; *e-s Polizisten*: *auch* beat; **e-e ~ drehen** *umg. zu Fuß*: go for a walk (a)round the block; *mit dem Auto*: go for a spin; **e-e ~ fliegen** circle; **die ~ machen** *Flasche*: be passed (a)round; *Nachricht etc.*: go the rounds; *Arzt*: do one's rounds; **3.** *Sport, e-s Rennens*: lap; (*Durchgang*) round; *Boxen, Ringen etc.*: round; **die nächste ~ erreichen** get through to the next round; **4.** (**~ Bier etc.**) round; **e-e ~ schmeißen** *umg.* buy (*od.* stand) a round; **5.** (*gerade so*) **über die ~n kommen** *Boxen*: remain on one's feet; *fig.* (just about) make it; *finanziell*: *auch* make ends meet; *etw. über die ~n bringen* get s.th. over (and done) with; *j-m über die ~n helfen Geld etc.*: tide s.o. over

Rundeisen *n* round (bar); (*Werkzeug*) U-shaped ga(u)ge

runden I. *v/t.* round; **II.** *v/refl.* grow round; *fig.* (*Gestalt annehmen*) take shape; *das Bild rundet sich fig.* things are beginning to fall into place

Rundenrekord *m* lap record

Runderlass *m* circular (note)

runderneuern *v/t.* (*untr., hat*) *Mot.* (*Reifen*) retread, *Brit. auch* remould; *runderneuerter Reifen* retread, *Brit. auch* remould

Rund|fahrt *f* (sightseeing) tour, drive (a)round a (*oder* the) town *etc.*; *Sport* road rally; → *auch Rundreise*; **~feile** *f Tech.* round file; **~flug** *m* sightseeing flight; **~frage** *f* survey; **2fragen** *v/i.* (*trennb., hat -ge-*) ask around (*bei* among)

Rundfunk *m* broadcasting, radio; (*Gesellschaft*) broadcasting company; *im* **~** on the radio; *beim* **~** *sein* work in broadcasting (*od.* for radio); *im* **~** *übertragen* broadcast

Rundfunk|... *im Subst. siehe auch Funk..., Radio...*; **~anstalt** *f* broadcasting company; **~empfang** *m* radio reception; **~gerät** *n* radio (set); **~hörer** *m*, **~hörerin** *f* (radio) listener; *fig.* radio audience; **~kommentator** *m*, **~kommentatorin** *f* radio commentator

(on current affairs), radio journalist; **~programm** *n* radio program(me); (*Programmfolge*) radio program(me)s; (*Blatt etc.*) radio program(me) guide; **~reportage** *f* radio (*od.* broadcast) report (*Live*: commentary); **~reporter** *m*, **~reporterin** *f* radio reporter (*Live*: commentator); **~sender** *m* radio (*od.* broadcasting) station; (*Sendeanlage*) radio transmitter; **~sendung** *f* broadcast, (radio) program(me); **~sprecher** *m*, **~sprecherin** *f* (radio) announcer; **~station** *f* radio station; **~technik** *f* broadcasting technology; **~techniker** *m*, **~technikerin** *f* radio engineer; **~teilnehmer** *m* radio licen|ce (*Am.* -se) holder (*Am. auch* licensee); **~übertragung** *f* (radio) broadcast; **~werbung** *f* radio advertising (*od.* commercials *Pl.*)

Rundgang *m* **1.** round; (*Besichtigungsrundgang*) tour (*durch* of); **2.** (*Gebäudeteil*) gallery

rundgehen *v/i.* (*unreg., trennb., ist -ge-*) **1.** *Gerücht etc.*: go the rounds; *die Flasche ~ lassen* pass the bottle (a)round; **2.** *fig. heute geht's wieder rund! umg.* it's all go today; *im Bundestag ging's gestern wieder rund umg.* it was pretty lively in the Bundestag yesterday

Rundgesang *m* round, catch

rundheraus *Adv.* in plain terms, straight out, flatly, point-blank

rundherum *Adv.* **1.** round about, all (a)round; **2.** (*völlig*) absolutely; **~ nass werden** get completely soaked; **~ zufrieden** entirely satisfied

Rundholz *n* **1.** *Baum*: roundwood, round timber; *mst Pl. ungeschält*: uncleft wood; **2.** *Naut.* spar

rundköpfig *Nagel*: round-head(ed)

Rund|kornreis *m* round-grain rice; **~kurs** *m Sport* circuit

rundlich *Adj.* plump, chubby; **Rundlichkeit** *f* plumpness, chubbiness

Rund|magazin *n Fot. e-s Projektors*: rotary magazine; **~pfeiler** *m* round-shafted pillar; circular pier; **~reise** *f* tour (*durch* of); *e-e* **~ durch Asien** *auch* a tour of Asia; **~rücken** *m* hunchback, *Med.* kyphosis; **~ruf** *m* circular call; *Polizei*: call to all units; **~schädel** *m* brachycephalic skull *fachspr.*; **~schau** *f* **1.** (*Rundsicht*) panorama; **2.** *Funk., TV etc.*: review; **~schlag** *m* → *Rundumschlag*; **~schreiben** *n* circular (letter)

Rundsicht *f* → *Rundschau* 1; **~fenster** *n* wrap-round (*Am.* wraparound) window

Rund|strahler *m* omnidirectional aerial (*Am.* antenna); **~strecke** *f* circuit; **~stricknadel** *f* circular knitting needle; **~stück** *n nordd.* (oval) roll; **~tanz** *m* round dance

rundum *Adv.* all (a)round; *fig.* completely; **~ glücklich** *auch* perfectly happy

Rundum|erneuerung *f* general overhaul; **~schlag** *m* **1.** *Sport* roundhouse (blow); **2.** *fig.* sweeping attack (*gegen* on); *zum* **~ ausholen** lash out in all directions; **~sicht** *f* all-(a)round visibility

Rundung *f* curve (*auch hum. bei Frauen*)

Rund|wanderweg *m*, **~weg** *m* circular path (*od.* route) (for a walk)

rundweg *Adv.*: **~ leugnen** flatly deny; **~ ablehnen** refuse point-blank; **~ falsch** absolutely wrong

Rundzelt *n* bell tent

Rune *f*; *-, -n* rune

Runen|alphabet *n* runic alphabet; **~schrift** *f* runic characters *Pl.*, runes *Pl.*; **~stein** *m* rune stone

Runge *f* post, stake

Runkel *f*; *-, -n*; *österr., schw.*, **~rübe** *f Bot.* mangel-wurzel; (*Futterrübe*) beet

runter *Adv. umg.* **1.** → *herunter*, (*völlig*) *mit den Nerven ~ sein umg.* be a nervous wreck; *von Drogen ~ sein Sl.* be off drugs/heroin; **2.** → *hinunter*

runter... *im V.* → *auch herunter..., hinunter...*

runter|hauen *v/t.* (*trennb., hat -ge-*) *umg.* **1.** *j-m eine ~* give s.o. a clip (a)round the ears; *ich hau dir gleich eine runter!* you'll get a clip (a)round the ears if you're not careful; **2.** (*schnell wegarbeiten*) knock *s.th.* off; **~holen** *v/t.* (*trennb., hat -ge-*) **1.** get (*od.* fetch) *s.th.* down; **2.** *sich* (*Dat.*) *einen ~ vulg.* jerk off; **~lassen** *v/t.* (*unreg., trennb., hat -ge-*) *umg.*: *die Hosen ~* let one's trousers (*Am.* pants) down; *fig.* come clean; **~machen** *v/t.* (*trennb., hat -ge-*) *umg. fig.* (*j-n*) (*kritisieren*) run down, *stärker*: slate; (*zurechtweisen*) tear a strip off *s.o.*; **~rutschen** *v/t.* → *Buckel* 2

Runzel *f*; *-, -n* wrinkle; **~n haben** *Gesicht*: be wrinkled; **runz(e)lig** *Adj.* wrinkled; **runzeln** *v/t.* wrinkle; *die Stirn ~* knit one's brow, frown

Rüpel *m*; *-s, -*; *pej.* lout, yob; **Rüpelei** *f*; *-, -en*; *pej.* loutish behavio(u)r; (*Handlung*) (example of) loutishness; **rüpelhaft** *Adj. pej.* loutish, uncouth; **Rüpelhaftigkeit** *f* loutishness

rupfen *v/t.* (*aus~*) pull out; (*Huhn etc.*) pluck; *j-n ~ umg. fig.* take s.o. to the cleaners; (*betrügen*) fleece s.o.; → *Hühnchen*

Rupfen *m*; *-s, kein Pl.* burlap, *Brit. auch* hessian

Rupie ['ru:pi̯ə] *f*; *-, -n* rupee

ruppig *Adj. pej.* (*grob*) gruff, *Brit. auch* stroppy; **~ werden** turn nasty; **~es Spiel** rough (*od.* ill-tempered) game; *allg.* rough play; **Ruppigkeit** *f* gruffness, *Brit. auch* stroppiness *umg.*; *Sport* roughness

Ruprecht *m*; *-s*: *Knecht ~ helper to Santa Claus*

Rüsche *f*; *-, -n* frill

Rüschen|hemd *n* frill-fronted shirt; **~kleid** *n* frilled dress

Rush [raʃ] *m*; *-s, -s* **1.** *Sport* burst (of speed); **2.** *bes. Wirts.* burst of activity

Ruß *m*; *-es, -e* soot; *von Lampe*: lamp black; **rußbedeckt** *Adj.* covered in soot, sooty

Russe *m*; *-n, -n* Russian

Rüssel *m*; *-s, -*; (*Elefantenrüssel*) trunk; (*Schweinerüssel*) snout; (*Insektenrüssel*) proboscis; *umg.* (*Nase*) conk, hooter, *Am. auch* schnozzle; **2artig** *Adj.* trunk(-)like; **~bär** *m* coati; **~käfer** *m* weevil

rußen I. *v/i. Lampe*: smoke; **II.** *v/t.* blacken

Ruß|entwicklung *f* soot formation; **~filter** *m* soot filter; **~flocke** *f* speck of soot; **2geschwärzt** *Adj.* blackened with soot

rußig *Adj.* sooty

Russin *f*; *-, -nen* Russian (woman *od.* girl); **russisch** *Adj.* Russian; **~e Eier** egg mayonnaise; **~es Roulette** Russian roulette; **Russisch** *n*; *-(s); Ling.* Russian; *das ~e* Russian, the Russian language

Russischbrot *n* alphabet biscuits *Pl.* (*Am.* cookies)

russisch-orthodox *Adj. Reli.* Russian Orthodox

Russland (*n*); *-s*; *Geog.* Russia

Ruß|partikel *n*, *f* soot particle; **~schicht** *f* layer of soot

ruß|schwarz *Adj.* soot black, black as soot; **~verschmiert** *Adj.* smeared with soot

rüsten I. *v/i.* build up arms (*od.* one's arms stockpile); *zum Krieg* ~ arm for war; *um die Wette* ~ be competing in (*od.* be involved in) the arms race; *für den Kampf gerüstet* ready for the fray, ready to do battle; **II.** *v/refl.* prepare, get ready (*auch fig.*) (*zu, für* for); (*sich wappnen*) arm o.s.; *Mil.* arm (o.s.), build up arms (*od.* one's arms stockpile); **III.** *v/t. geh.* prepare

Rüster *f*; *-, -n*; *Bot.*, **~holz** *n* elm

rüstig *Adj.* sprightly; (*tätig*) active; *körperlich und geistig noch sehr* ~ still very active (*od.* alive) physically and mentally; **Rüstigkeit** *f* sprightliness

rustikal *Adj.* rustic, rural; **~e Möbel** rustic (*od.* country-style) furniture

Rüstung *f* **1.** *Mil.* (*Vorgang*) arming, armament; *konkret:* armaments *Pl.*; **2.** *hist.* (*Panzer*) armo(u)r

Rüstungs|auftrag *m* armaments contract; **~ausgaben** *Pl.* defen|ce (*Am.* -se) spending *Sg.*; **~begrenzung** *f*, **~beschränkung** *f* arms limitation; **~betrieb** *m* armament factory; **~elektronik** *f* defen|ce (*Am.* -se) electronics (*V. im Sg.*); **~etat** *m* defen|ce (*Am.* -se) budget; **~industrie** *f* armaments (*Am.* defense) industry; **~kontrolle** *f* arms control; **~konzern** *m* armaments group; **~politik** *f* arms policy; **~pro**

duktion *f* armaments production; **~stopp** *m* arms freeze; **~wettlauf** *m* arms race

Rüstzeug *n* **1.** (*Werkzeuge*) tools *Pl.*, equipment; **2.** *fig.* (*Fähigkeiten*) qualifications *Pl.*

Rute *f*; *-, -n* (willow) switch (*od.* stake); (*auch Zucht- od. Angelrute*) rod; *Zool.* penis; *hunt.* (*Schwanz*) tail; *bes. des Fuchses:* brush; → **Wünschelrute**

Ruten|bündel *n hist.* fasces; **~gänger** *m*; *-s, -,* **~gängerin** *f*; *-, -nen* diviner, dowser

Ruth *f*; *-*; *bibl.* Ruth; *das Buch* ~ (the Book of) Ruth

Rutsch *m*; *-(e)s, -e* slide; (*Erdrutsch*) landslide; *hum.* (*kurzer Ausflug*) little trip *allg.*; (*Spritztour*) jaunt; *in einem* ~ *umg.* in one go; *guten* ~ (*ins neue Jahr*)*!* Happy New Year!; **~bahn** *f* slide (*auch Eisbahn*), *Am.* chute; *fig.* (*glatte Straße*) skating rink; *die Straße ist die reinste* ~ the road is like a skating rink; **Rutsche** *f*; *-, -n* (*Schütte*) chute; (*Kinderrutsche*) slide

rutschen *v/i.* slide; (*aus~*) slip; *Mot.* skid; *Kupplung:* slip; *Hose, Rock:* be slipping; *in die Höhe* ~ *Rock:* ride up; *es ist mir aus der Hand gerutscht* it slipped (*od.* slid) out of my hand; *der Teppich rutscht* the carpet is slipping; *ins Rutschen kommen* start slipping; *Auto etc.:* go into a skid, start skidding; *auf den Knien* ~ slither (*od.* crawl) along on one's knees; *fig.* grovel (*vor j-n* to s.o.); *rutsch mal ein Stück umg.* can you move up a bit?; *schnell mal ins nächste Dorf* ~ *umg.* dash off to the next village *allg.*; *das*

Essen will nicht ~ *umg.* I just can't get this food down *allg.*; **Rutscherei** *f*; *-, kein Pl.*; *umg.*: *e-e einzige* ~ constant slipping and slithering (*Mot.* skidding all over the place) *allg.*

rutschfest *Adj. Stoff:* non-slip; *nur attr. Reifen:* non-skid; *Sohle:* non-slip; *e-n Teppich durch e-e Unterlage* ~ *machen* prevent a carpet from slipping by fitting an underlay; **Rutschfestigkeit** *f Stoff:* non-slip properties *Pl.*; *Reifen:* resistance to skidding, non-skid properties *Pl.*

Rutschgefahr *f*; *nur Sg.* danger (*od.* risk) of skidding; *Vorsicht,* ~*!* beware of slippery road

rutschig *Adj.* slippery

Rutschpartie *f umg.* (downhill) slide *allg.*; *die Fahrt war die reinste* ~ *fig.* the journey was completed in a succession of skids

Rüttelbeton *m* vibrated concrete

Rüttelei *f*; *-, kein Pl.*; *umg.*: *die Busfahrt war e-e einzige* ~ we were constantly shaken to pieces on the bus *allg.*

rütteln I. *v/t.* shake; (*Beton*) vibrate; *j-n an der Schulter* ~ shake s.o. by the shoulder; *j-n aus dem Schlaf* ~ shake s.o. to wake him (*od.* her) up; **II.** *v/i.* shake (*auch fig.*); *Wagen:* jolt; *Tech.* vibrate; *Flug.* buffet; *Greifvogel:* hover; *an der Tür* ~ shake the door; *mit Klappergeräusch:* rattle at the door; ~ *an* (+ *Dat.*) *fig.* shake; *daran ist nicht zu* ~ that's the way it is

Rüttelschwelle *f Verk.* rumble strip

Rüttler *m*; *-s, -* vibrator; *Druck.* jogger (for aligning the piles of sheets)

R

S, s *n*; -, - S, s; **S wie Samuel** *Buchstabieren*: "s" for (*od.* as in) "Sierra"

SA *f*; -, *kein Pl.*; *Abk.* (*Sturmabteilung*) *hist.* SA, (*Nazi*) stormtroops *Pl.* (*od.* stormtroopers *Pl.*)

Saal *m*; -(e)s, *Säle* hall; (*Konzertsaal*) *auch* auditorium; (*Unterrichtssaal*) classroom; (*Gerichtssaal*) courtroom; (*Ballsaal*) ballroom; **~miete** *f* hire (*Am.* rental) charge for a (*od.* the) hall; **~ordner** *m* steward; **~schlacht** *f* *bes. Am.* roughhouse, brawl *at a political meeting*; **~schutz** *m* stewards *Pl.*

Saarland *n*; -(e)s; *Geog.* Saarland

Saarländer *m*; -s, -, **~in** *f*; -, -nen Saarlander; *weiblich auch*: woman (*od.* girl *etc.*) from the Saarland; **saarländisch** *Adj.* Saarland ..., from the Saarland

Saat *f*; -, -en; *Agr.* **1.** *nur Sg.* (*Säen*) sowing; **2.** *nur Sg.* (*Saatgut*) seed(s *Pl.*); (*Same*) seed (*auch fig.*); **die ~ geht auf** the seed is coming up; *fig.* the results are beginning to show; **die ~ der Gewalt (geht auf)** the seeds of violence (are bearing fruit); **3.** (*Getreide*) crops *Pl.*; **~beet** *n* bed of seedlings

Saat|bett *n* *Agr.* seedbed; **~gut** *n* seed(s *Pl.*); *Getreide*: seed corn, *Am.* grain; **~kartoffel** *f* seed potato (*od.* tuber); **~korn** *n* seed (corn), *Am.* grain (for seed); **~krähe** *f* *Orn.* rook; **~zeit** *f* sowing time

Sabbat *m*; -s, -e; *Reli.* Sabbath; **am** *od.* **während des ~s** on the Sabbath; **~jahr** *n* sabbatical year

sabbeln *v/i. bes. nordd.* **1.** (*plappern*) jabber, blather (on); **2.** → **sabbern** 1

sabbern *v/i.* **1.** *Hund etc.*: dribble, *Am.* drool, slaver; *Baby*: dribble, *Am.* slobber; **er sabbert beim Sprechen** he slobbers when he speaks; **2.** *umg.* → **sabbeln** 1

Säbel *m*; -s, - sab|re (*Am.* -er); **mit dem ~ rasseln** *fig.* indulge in sab|re (*Am.* -er) rattling; **~beine** *umg., mst hum. Pl.* bandy (*od.* bow) legs *allg.*; **~fechten** *n* *Sport* sab|re (*Am.* -er) fencing; **~gerassel** *n* *fig.* sabre-rattling, *Am.* saberrattling; **~hieb** *m* sab|re (*Am.* -er) thrust

säbeln *v/t/i. umg.* hack (away at); **e-e Melone in Stücke ~** slice a melon into pieces

säbelrasselnd *Adj. pej.* sabre-rattling, *Am.* saber-rattling

Säbel|- und Degenfechten *n* (fencing with) sab|re (*Am.* -er) and épée; **~zahntiger** *m* sabre-toothed (*Am.* saber-toothed) tiger

Sabotage [zabo'ta:ʒə] *f*; -, *kein Pl.* sabotage; **~ begehen** carry out an act (*od.* acts) of sabotage; **Sabotageakt** *m* act of sabotage; **Saboteur** *m*; -s, -e, **-in** *f*; -, -nen saboteur; **sabotieren** *v/t/i.* sabotage; *fig. auch* torpedo; **Hacker können Flugzeuge ~** hackers can interfere with aircraft

Saccharin [zaxa'ri:n] *n*; -s, *kein Pl.* saccharin(e)

Sach|anlagen *Pl. Wirts.* tangible (*od.* fixed) assets, tangibles; **~antrag** *m* motion for debate

Sach|bearbeiter *m*, **~bearbeiterin** *f* *weitS.* clerical (*Am. auch* administrative) assistant; **~ für Export** *etc.* person who deals with exports *etc.*; **m-e Sachbearbeiterin beim Finanzamt** the person dealing with my affairs at the tax office (*Am.* at the IRS); **~bereich** *m* field, area; **~beschädigung** *f* *Jur.* damage to property, material damage

sachbezogen *Adj. Argumente, Angaben etc.*: pertinent

Sachbezüge *Pl.* payment *Sg.* (*od.* contributions) in kind

Sachbuch *n* non-fiction book (*od.* work); **~autor** *m*, **~autorin** *f* non-fiction writer; **~verlag** *m* non-fiction publisher(s *Pl.*)

Sachdebatte *f* *mst Pol.*, *über ein best. Thema*: debate on a particular topic

sachdienlich *Adj.* relevant, pertinent; (*nützlich*) helpful; **~e Hinweise bitte an ...** if you can help us in any way, please ring (*Am.* call) (*od.* write to) ...

Sachdiskussion *f* factual discussion

Sache *f*; -, -n **1.** (*Gegenstand*) thing; **~n** *umg. allg.* (*Kleidung etc.*) things; (*Habseligkeiten*) *auch* belongings; **häng deine ~n in den Schrank** hang up your things in the cupboard (*Am.* closet); *Gewalt gegen* **~n** *Jur.* (violent) damage to property; **warme ~n für den Winter** (*warme Kleidung*) warm things for the winter; **scharfe ~n** (*Schnaps etc.*) hard stuff *Sg.*; **2.** (*Angelegenheit*) affair; (*auch Vorfall*) matter, business; (*Problem, Frage*) matter; **das ist e-e ~ für sich** that's a completely different matter; *iro.* that's another story; **ich werde der ~ nachgehen** I'll look into the matter; **bei der ~ bleiben** keep to the point; **das gehört nicht zur ~** that's got nothing to do with it; **die ~ ist die, dass** the point is that; **in eigener ~ sprechen** speak on one's own behalf; **wie ist die ~ mit dem Auto ausgegangen?** how did that business with the car turn out?; **die ~ macht sich** *umg.* things are (*od.* it's) coming along fine; **das ist so e-e ~** it's not so easy; **e-e runde ~** a fine piece of work; **ich mag keine halben ~n** I don't like (any) half measures; **das ist e-e tolle/blöde ~** *umg.* that's fantastic / a stupid business; **ich habe die ganze ~ satt** I'm sick of the whole business; **die einfachste/natürlichste ~ der Welt** the simplest / most natural thing in the world; **das ist nicht jedermanns ~** that's not for everybody, that's not everybody's cup of tea; **j-m sagen, was ~ ist** *umg.* (*worauf es ankommt*) put s.o. in the picture *allg.*; (*die Meinung sagen*) tell s.o. what's what; **sie war ganz bei der ~** she was all attention (*od.* quite absorbed); **er**

war nicht (ganz) bei der ~ he had his mind on other things, he wasn't (quite) concentrating; **s-r ~ sicher sein** be sure of oneself; **sich s-r ~ sicher glauben** think o.s. sure of one's point; **zur ~ kommen** get to the point; (*handeln*) get down to business (brass tacks *umg.*); **zur ~!** can we get to the point?; **das tut nichts zur ~** that makes no difference; **das kommt der ~ schon näher** that's more like it; **das ist s-e ~** that's his business (*od.* affair); **das ist nicht m-e ~** that's got nothing to do with me; **mach keine ~n!** *umg. erstaunt*: you're kidding; *warnend*: no funny business; **~n gibt's(, die gibt's gar nicht)** *umg.* would you believe it *allg.*; **was machst du denn für ~n?** *umg.* what have you been up to then?; **du machst ~n!** *umg.* the things you get up to!; **3.** *Jur.* case; **in ~n A. gegen B.** *Jur.* in the matter of A versus B; **in ~n** *umg. fig.* with regard to, as to; **in ~n Umwelt** where the environment is concerned, in questions of the environment; **was tut sich in ~n Hausbau?** how are things on the housebuilding front?; **4.** (*Ziel, Anliegen*) cause; **für e-e gute/gerechte ~ kämpfen** fight for a good cause / for the cause of justice; **mit j-m gemeinsame ~ machen** make common cause with s.o.; **5.** (*Aufgabe*) job; **er versteht s-e ~** he knows his stuff; **sie hat ihre ~ gut gemacht** she did a good job; **es ist ~ des Gerichts zu entscheiden, ob ...** it is for the court to decide whether ...; **6. mit 100 ~n fahren** *Mot. umg.* do (*od.* drive) a hundred (miles an hour), *Brit. auch* do a ton

...sache *f, im Subst.* **1.** *Begründung*: **Einstellungs~** matter (*od.* question) of attitude; **2.** *Zuständigkeit*: **Frauen~** women's business; **Regierungs~** government matter

Sacheinlage *f Wirts.* non-cash investment (*od.* contribution)

...sachen *Pl., im Subst.*: **Baby~** baby things; **Schmink~** cosmetics; **Turn~** gym things (*od.* stuff *Sg.*)

Sachenrecht *n Jur.* law of property

Sachertorte *f* rich chocolate cake with apricot jam under the chocolate icing, Sachertorte

Sach|fahndung *f* search for lost or stolen property; **~frage** *f* factual issue

sachfremd I. *Adj.* irrelevant, extraneous; **e-e ~e Entscheidung** a decision made for unrelated reasons; **II.** *Adv.*: **~ argumentieren/entscheiden** put forward irrelevant arguments / decide on the basis of unrelated reasons

Sachgebiet *n* subject, field

sach|gemäß, **~gerecht I.** *Adj.* appropriate; (*fachmännisch*) proper; **II.** *Adv.*: **~ behandeln** treat with due (*od.* proper) care

Sach|katalog *m* subject catalog(ue); **~kenner** *m*, **~kennerin** *f* expert;

~**kenntnis** f expert knowledge

Sachkunde f **1.** expert knowledge; **2.** *Päd. Unterrichtsfach*: general knowledge; **sachkundig** *Adj. Urteil: attr.* expert …; *Person: auch* knowledgeable, well-informed; *sich* ~ *machen* inform o.s. (about the subject); **Sachkundige** m, f; -n, -n expert (on the subject)

Sach|lage f state of affairs, (present) situation, situation at present; *bei dieser* ~ under these circumstances, the situation being as it is; ~**leistung** f payment (*od.* contribution) in kind

sachlich I. *Adj. (objektiv)* objective; *(nüchtern)* matter-of-fact, down-to-earth; *(faktisch)* factual; *(zweckbetont)* functional; *Unterschied*: substantial, material; *ein* ~*es Design* a functional design; *mehrere* ~*e Fehler* several factual errors; ~*e Gründe* objective reasons; ~ *bleiben* keep to the facts; *(nicht persönlich werden)* remain objective; **II.** *Adv.:* ~ *falsch/richtig* factually wrong/correct; ~ *hat er Recht* his facts are right; ~ *argumentieren* argue objectively, use objective arguments; *an etw.* ~ *herangehen* approach s.th. objectively

sächlich *Adj. Ling.* neuter

Sachlichkeit f *(Objektivität)* objectivity; *(Nüchternheit)* matter-of-factness; *e-s Bauwerks etc.*: functionalism; *die Neue* ~ the New Realism

Sach|mangel m *Jur.* material defect; ~**register** n subject index; ~**schaden** m material damage, damage to property; *(Verlust)* loss of property

Sachse m; -n, -n; *auch hist.* Saxon; **sächseln** v/i. *umg.* **1.** speak in (*od.* the) Saxon dialect; **2.** have a Saxon accent; **Sachsen** (n); -s; *Geog.* Saxony; **Sächsin** f → *Sachse*; *auch* Saxon woman (*od.* girl); **sächsisch** *Adj.* Saxon; ~*er Genitiv Gram.* Saxon genitive; **Sächsisch** n; -en; *Ling.* Saxon; *das* ~*e* the Saxon dialect

Sachspende f donation in kind

sacht I. *Adj.* soft, gentle; **II.** *Adv.* softly, gently; *(behutsam)* cautiously; *(allmählich)* gradually; *(langsam)* slowly; *immer* ~*e!* *umg.* easy does it!

sachte *Adv.* → *sacht* II

Sachunterricht m *Brit.* personal and social education, *abgek.* P.S.E., *Am. etwa* health class

Sachverhalt m; -(e)s, -e facts *Pl.*, circumstances *Pl.*

Sachverstand m expertise; **Sachverständige** m, f; -n, -n expert; *Jur.* expert witness

Sachverständigen|gutachten n expert opinion; ~**rat** m board of experts

Sach|verzeichnis n index; ~**walter** m; -s, -; ~**walterin** f; -, -nen; *(Anwalt)* solicitor, counsel; *(Verwalter)* administrator; *(Treuhänder)* trustee; *(Vertreter)* agent, attorney; *fig.* advocate, champion (+ *Gen.* of); ~**wert** m real value; ~**e** tangible assets; ~**wissen** n *(Sachkenntnis)* expert knowledge; *(Faktenwissen)* factual knowledge; ~**wörterbuch** n encyclop(a)edia, dictionary (of art *etc.*); ~**zusammenhang** m factual connection; ~**zwang** m *mst Pl.* force of circumstance, situational constraint, practical necessity

Sack m; -(e)s, Säcke, *bei Summen*: - **1.** sack; *(Beutel)* bag; *Bot., Zool. auch* sac; *Dial. (Hosentasche)* (trouser, *Am.* pants) pocket; *ein/zehn* ~ *Kartoffeln* one sack / ten sacks of potatoes; *in* ~ *und Asche (gehen)* *fig.* (repent) in sackcloth and ashes; *ein* ~ *voll Geld* a pile of money; *mit* ~ *und Pack* (with) bag and baggage; *etw. im* ~ *haben umg.* have s.th. in the bag; *j-n in den* ~ *stecken umg.* knock spots off s.o.; **2.** *umg., pej.* sod, bugger, *Am.* bastard, jerk; *fauler* ~ *umg.* lazy bastard; *fetter* ~ *pej.* fatso; **3.** *vulg. (Hoden)* balls *Pl.*; *j-m auf den* ~ *gehen od. fallen Sl.* get on s.o.'s tits, get s.o.'s shirt out, *Am.* bug s.o., piss s.o. off; → *Katze* 1

sackartig *Adj.* sacklike

Sackbahnhof m *Eisenb.* terminus

Säckchen n small bag, sachet; *ein* ~ *Lavendel* a sachet of lavender

Säckel m; -s, -; *Dial.* **1.** moneybag; *tief in den* ~ *greifen fig.* dig deep into one's pockets; **2.** *umg. (Trottel)* oaf

sacken v/i. sink; *Boden etc.: auch* subside; *Person*: slump; *er sackte in die Knie* his knees gave way; → *absacken*

sackförmig *Adj.* sacklike, baggy

Sack|gasse f cul-de-sac, dead-end street; *fig.* dead end; *bes. Pol. etc.* impasse; *in e-e* ~ *geraten fig.* reach a dead end; *Gespräche*: reach deadlock; ~**hüpfen** n; -s, *kein Pl.* sack race; ~**karre** f, ~**karren** m sack barrow; ~**leinen** n sacking, burlap; ~**pfeife** f bagpipes *Pl.*

sackweise *Adv.* by the sackful

Sadismus m; -, *kein Pl.* sadism; **Sadist** m; -en, -en, **Sadistin** f; -, -nen sadist; **sadistisch I.** *Adj.* sadistic; **II.** *Adv.* sadistically

Sadomaso m; -, *kein Pl.*; *umg.* sadomasochist; **Sadomasochismus** m; -, *Sadomasochismen* **1.** *nur Sg.* sadomasochism; **2.** *(Handlung)* sadomasochistic act; **Sadomasochist** m; -en, en, **Sadomasochistin** f; -, -nen sadomasochist; **sadomasochistisch I.** *Adj.* sadomasochistic; **II.** *Adv.* sadomasochistically

säen v/t.i. sow (*auch fig.*); → *gesät*

Safari f; -, -s safari; *auf* ~ *gehen* go on safari; ~**look** [-luk] m safari look; ~**park** m wildlife reserve, safari park

Safe [ze:f] m; -s, -s safe; *(Banktresor) auch* safe-deposit box; *e-n* ~ *knacken umg.* crack (open) a safe

Safer Sex, Safersex ['ze:fɐ 'zɛks] m; -, *kein Pl.* safe sex; ~ *praktizieren* practi|se (*Am.* -ce) safe sex

Safeschlüssel m key to a (*od.* the) safe, safe key

Saffianleder n morocco leather

Safran m; -s, -e saffron; ♀**gelb** *Adj.* saffron yellow; ~**pulver** n saffron powder

Saft m; -(e)s, Säfte; *(Obst-, Fleisch-, Körpersaft)* juice; *von Bäumen etc.*: sap; *umg. (Strom etc.)* juice; *im vollen* ~ *stehen* Baum etc.: be full of sap; *im eigenen* ~ *schmoren* Gastr. braise (in its own juices); *j-n im eigenen* ~ *schmoren lassen umg. fig.* let s.o. stew in his (*od.* her) own juice; *ohne* ~ *und Kraft* → *saft- und kraftlos*

saftgrün *Adj.* sap (*od.* lush) green, verdant *lit.*; **Saftgrün** n sap (*od.* lush) green

saftig *Adj.* **1.** *Obst, Fleisch etc.*: juicy, succulent; *Wiese, Grün*: lush; **2.** *fig. Witz etc.*: spicy, saucy; *umg. Preise, Rechnung*: (a bit) steep; *das sind schon* ~*e Preise hier umg.* the prices are really steep here, they really slap it on here; *e-e* ~*e Geldstrafe* a stiff (*od.* hefty) fine; ~*e Niederlage umg.* crushing defeat; ~*e Ohrfeige umg.* hefty clout (a)round the ears

Saft|kur f juice diet; ~**laden** m *umg. pej.* dump

saftlos *Adj.* **1.** juiceless, dry; **2.** → *saft- und kraftlos*

Saft|presse f fruit press; *elektrisch*: juice extractor; *für Zitrusfrüchte*: lemon squeezer; ~**sack** m *Sl.* jerk; ~**tag** m day on a juice diet

saft- und kraftlos *Adj.* weak, insipid, lacklustre; *Rede: auch* wishy-washy *umg.*

Saga f; -, -s saga

Sage f; -, -n legend; *fig. (Gerücht)* rumo(u)r, myth; *der* ~ *nach* according to legend; *es geht die* ~ … the story goes …

Säge f; -, -n saw; ~**blatt** n saw blade; ~**bock** m sawhorse; ~**dach** n sawtooth roof; ~**fisch** m sawfish; ~**maschine** f machine saw; ~**mehl** n sawdust; ~**messer** n serrated knife; ~**mühle** f sawmill

sagen v/t. **1.** *allg. (äußern)* say; *j-m etw.* ~ say s.th. to s.o.; *(mitteilen)* tell s.o. s.th.; *sich (Dat.)* ~ say to oneself; *sag ihm, er soll kommen* tell him to come; *was sagst du dazu?* what do you say to that?; *da sag' ich nicht nein* I won't say no; *das sagt sich so leicht* (it's) easier said than done; *ich kann es nicht* ~ *(ich weiß es nicht)* I cannot say; *das kann ich dir* ~*! betont*: you can be sure of that; *(das kannst du mir glauben)* I can tell you, you can bank on that; *das kann man wohl od.* ~ you can say that again; *sag's frei heraus!* out with it!; *unter uns gesagt* between you and me; *du sagst es* you said it; *sag bloß, es regnet* don't say it's raining; *das kann jeder* ~ anyone can say that; *das sagst du so einfach* it's easy for you to say; *das kann man nicht so* ~ it's not as simple as that; *was ich noch* ~ *wollte sich erinnernd*: (oh yes,) I know what I was going to say, before I forget; *betonter*: there's something else (I wanted to say), and another thing; *wer sagt's denn betont*: what did I tell you; *ich hab's (dir) ja gleich gesagt!* I told you so; *(das ist) schwer zu* ~ it's hard to say; *es lässt sich nicht* ~, *ob/was* there's no telling whether/what; *das sagt man nicht* you shouldn't say things like that; *ich habe mir* ~ *lassen* I've been told; *man sagt, er sei im Ausland* they say he's abroad, he's supposed to be abroad; *was Sie nicht* ~*! umg.* you don't say!; *wem* ~ *Sie das? umg.* you're telling me!; *ich sag' mal* … I mean, …; *wie man so (schön) sagt* as the saying goes; ~ *wir zehn Stück* (let's) say ten (of them); *wer sagt das?* says who?, who says?; *(das) sagst du!* that's what you say, says you *umg.*; *ich wollte es nur gesagt haben* I just wanted to mention it; *wie gesagt bestätigend*: as I said; *aufgreifend*: as I was saying; *gesagt, getan!* no sooner said than done; **2.** *(anordnen)* *sag ihm, er soll hereinkommen* tell him to come in; *etwas/nichts zu* ~ *haben bei e-r Sache*: have a / have no say in; *bei ihr hat er nichts zu* ~ he has no say when she's around; *du hast mir nichts zu* ~ I won't have you telling me what to do; *er lässt sich nichts* ~ he won't be told, he won't listen to anyone; *das ließ er sich nicht zweimal* ~ he didn't need any further encouragement, he jumped at it *umg.*; *lass dir das gesagt sein* let that be a warning to you, put that in your pipe and smoke it *umg.*; **3.** *(bedeuten)* mean; *was willst du damit* ~*?* what are you getting at?; *sagt dir das etwas?* does that mean anything to you?, does that ring any bells? *umg.*; *wie sagt man ... auf Englisch?* what's the English for ...?, what's ... in English?, how do you say ... in English?; *das hat nichts zu ~* it doesn't mean anything; *das ist nicht gesagt* that's not necessarily so, not necessarily; *es od. damit ist nicht gesagt, dass* that doesn't mean (to say) that; *das sagt nichts über* (+*Akk.*) this is no comment on, this doesn't tell us anything about; **4.** (*nennen*) *in Berlin sagt man „Schrippen" statt „Brötchen"* in Berlin they say "Schrippen" instead of "Brötchen"; *sie sagt immer „Dicker" zu ihm* she always calls him "fatty"; → *Dank, Meinung, Wahrheit etc.*

Sagen *n*; *-s, kein Pl.*: *das ~ haben* have the final say (*od.* last word) (*bei, in* + *Dat.* in); *generell*: call the shots *umg.*

sägen *v/t./i.* saw; *umg. fig.* (*schnarchen*) saw wood

Sagengestalt *f* mythical (*od.* legendary) figure

sagenhaft I. *Adj.* **1.** *umg. fig.* (*unglaublich, auch negativ*) incredible; (*großartig*) fantastic, fabulous; *das ist ja ~!* that's incredible!; (*toll*) that's terrific!; **2.** *Gestalt etc.*: legendary, mythical; **II.** *Adv. umg.*: *~ teuer etc.* incredibly expensive *etc.*

Sagen|kreis *m* cycle of legends; *~schatz* *m* legends *Pl.*, folklore; *~tier* *n* mythical beast

sagenumwoben *Adj. nur attr.* legendary, epic; *nur präd.* shrouded in legend

Säge|späne *Pl.* wood shavings; *~werk* *n* sawmill; *~zahn* *m auch Etron.* sawtooth

Sago *m, n*; *-s, kein Pl.*; *Gastr.* sago; *~baum* *m Bot.* sago palm

sah *Imperf.* → *sehen*

Sahelzone *f*; *nur Sg.*; *Geog.* the Sahel

Sahne *f*; *-, kein Pl.* cream; (*Schlagsahne*) whipped cream; *süße/saure ~* sweet/sour cream; (*aller*)*erste ~ umg. fig.* first-rate, the tops; *~bonbon* *m, n* cream toffee, *Am.* taffy; *~eis* *n* ice cream; *~geschmack* *m*: *Pudding mit ~* creamy-flavo(u)red blancmange (*Am.* pudding); *~häubchen* *n* (small) cream topping; *umg. fig.* icing on the cake, crowning glory; *~joghurt* *m* cream yoghurt; *~kännchen* *n* cream jug, *Am.* creamer; *~käse* *m Gastr.* cream cheese; *~meerrettich* *m Gastr.* horseradish sauce; *~quark* *m Gastr.* cream (*od.* high-fat) quark, cream (*od.* high-fat) curd cheese; *~rolle* *f Gastr.* cream roll; *~schicht* *f* layer of cream; *~soße* *f Gastr.* cream sauce; *~stückchen* *n umg. fig.* real gem; *~torte* *f Gastr.* cream cake (*od.* gateau), *Am.* cream pie

sahnig *Adj.* creamy

Saibling *m*; *-s, -e*; *Zool.* char

Saison [zɛˈzõː] *f*; *-, -s*; *allg.* season; *außerhalb der ~* out of season, in the off-season; *~ haben umg. fig.* be greatly in demand

...saison *f, im Subst.*: *Pilz~* season for mushrooms; *Bundesliga~* (German) Bundesliga season

saisonabhängig *Adj.* seasonal

Saison|arbeit *f* seasonal work; *~arbeiter* *m*, *~arbeiterin* *f* seasonal worker; *~aufschlag* *m* seasonal charge (*od.* supplement); *~auftakt* *m*: *zum ~* to open (kick off *umg.*) the season, *weitS.* to get the season off to a good

start; *~ausverkauf* *m* end-of-season sale; *~bedarf* *m* seasonal consumption

saisonbedingt I. *Adj.* seasonal; **II.** *Adv.*: *~ einstellen/entlassen* take on / lay off workers on a seasonal basis

Saisonbeginn *m* beginning of the season

saisonbereinigt *Adj.* seasonally adjusted

Saison|beschäftigung *f* seasonal employment; *~betrieb* *m* **1.** (*Unternehmen*) seasonal business; **2.** (*Hochbetrieb*) peak-season activity; *~ende* *n* end of the season; *~eröffnung* *f* beginning of the season; *~geschäft* *n* seasonal business; *~schlussverkauf* *m* end-of-season sale; *~schwankungen* *Pl.* seasonal fluctuations (*od.* fluctuation *Sg.*); *~start* *m* beginning of the season; *~wanderung* *f* seasonal migration

Saite *f*; *-, -n* *von Gitarre, Tennisschläger etc.*: string; *andere ~n aufziehen umg. fig.* take a tougher line

Saiten|halter *m Mus.* *Geige*: tailpiece; *~instrument* *n* string(ed) instrument

...saitig *im Adj.*: *ein sechs~es Instrument* a six-stringed instrument

Säkasten *m Agr.* seed hopper

Sake *m*; *-, kein Pl.* *Gastr.* sake

Sakko *m, n*; *-s, -s*; (*sportlich*: sports) jacket

sakra *Interj. südd. umg.* damn!

sakral *Adj.* **1.** *kirchl.* religious; (*auch heilig*) sacred; **2.** *Anat.* sacral

Sakralbau *m*; *Pl. -ten*; *kirchl.* sacred building; *Pl. auch* sacred architecture *Sg.*

Sakrament I. *n*; *-(e)s, -e*; *kirchl.* sacrament; *heiliges ~* Blessed Sacrament; *die ~e austeilen* administer the sacraments; **II.** *Interj.*: *~* (*noch mal*)*!* *umg.* damn!; **sakramental** *Adj.* sacramental

Sakrileg *n*; *-(e)s, -e* sacrilege; *ein ~ begehen auch fig.* commit sacrilege

Sakristan *m*; *-s, -e*; *kath.* sacristan; **Sakristei** *f*; *-, -en* vestry, *Am. auch* sacristy

sakrosankt *Adj.* sacrosanct

säkular *Adj.* secular (*auch Astron.*); **Säkularisation** *f*; *-, -en* secularization; **säkularisieren** *v/t.* secularize; **Säkularisierung** *f* secularization

Salamander *m*; *-s, -*; *Zool.* salamander

Salami *f*; *-, -s*; *Gastr.* salami; *Mailänder ~* salami milanese; *~taktik* *f Pol.* salami tactics *Pl.*

Salär *n*; *-s, -e*; *bes. österr., schw.* salary

Salat *m*; *-(e)s, -e* **1.** *Gastr.* (*Gericht*) salad; *grüner/gemischter ~* green/mixed salad; *e-n ~ anmachen* put the dressing on a salad; **2.** *nur Sg.*; (*Kopfsalat etc.*) lettuce; *ein Kopf ~* a lettuce, *Am.* a head of lettuce; *da haben wir den ~! umg. fig.* now we're in a right (*Am.* real) mess

...salat *m, im Subst.* **1.** (*Speise*): *Meeresfrüchte~* seafood salad; **2.** (*Pflanze*): *Eisberg~* iceberg lettuce; **3.** *umg. fig.*: *Daten~* jumble (*od.* tangle) of data

Salat|bar *f* salad bar; *~beet* *n* lettuce bed; *~besteck* *n* salad servers (*Am.* tongs) *Pl.*; *~blatt* *n* lettuce leaf; *~dressing* *n* → *Salatsoße*; *~gabel* *f* salad fork; *~gurke* *f* cucumber; *~kartoffeln* *Pl.* potatoes (for potato salad); *~kopf* *m* (head of) lettuce; *~löffel* *m* salad spoon; *~majonäse* *f* (salad) mayonnaise; *~öl* *n* salad oil; *~platte* *f* salad dish; *Gastr.* (*Gericht*) salad; *~schleuder* *f* salad spinner; *~schüssel* *f* salad bowl; *~soße* *f* salad dress-

ing; *~staude* *f Dial.* → *Salatkopf*; *~teller* *m* salad plate; *Gastr.* (*Gericht*) mixed salad

Salbader *m*; *-s, -*; *pej., altm.* sanctimonious bore; **salbadern** *v/i. pej.* sound off, waffle on (sanctimoniously)

Salbe *f*; *-, -n* ointment; *bes. für Lippen*: salve, lip balm

Salbei *m*; *-s, kein Pl.*; *Bot.* sage; *~bonbon* *m, n* sage cough sweet (*Am.* drop); *~tee* *m* sage tea

salben *v/t. kirchl.* anoint; *j-n zum König ~* anoint s.o. king

Salben|dose *f* jar of ointment; *~verband* *m* dressing soaked in ointment

Salbung *f* anointing, *auch fig.* unction *geh.*; **salbungsvoll** *Adj. pej.* unctuous *geh.*

saldieren *v/t. Wirts.* balance, settle; *österr.* confirm payment

Saldo *m*; *-s, -s, Saldi od. Salden*; *Wirts.* balance; *der ~ beträgt ...* the balance is (*od.* amounts to) ...; *den ~ ausgleichen* clear the balance, balance the account; *per ~* on balance (*auch fig.*); *~übertrag* *m*, *~vortrag* *m* balance carried forward

Saline *f*; *-, -n* saltworks *Pl.* (*V. im Sg. od. Pl.*)

Salizylsäure *f Chem.* salicylic acid

Salm *m*; *-(e)s, -e*; *Zool.* salmon

Salmiak *m, n*; *-s, kein Pl.*; *Chem.* ammonium chloride; *~geist* *m; nur Sg.* ammonia solution, liquid ammonia; *~pastillen* *Pl.* ammoniac pastilles

Salmonellen *Pl. Med.* salmonellae; *~befall* *m* salmonella attack; *~verseucht* *Adj.* infected with salmonella; **Salmonellose** *f*; *-, -n*; *fachspr.* salmonellosis

Salomo, Salomon *m*; *-s od. Salomonis*; *bibl.* Solomon; *das Hohelied ~s* the Song of Solomon; *die Sprüche ~s* (the Book of) Proverbs; **salomonisch** *Adj.* Solomonic; *ein ~es Urteil fig.* a judg(e)ment of Solomon

Salon [zaˈlõː] *m*; *-s, -s* **1.** *altm.* drawing room, *Am.* parlor; *Naut.* saloon, lounge; (*Kosmetik-, Friseursalon etc.*) salon; **2.** (*Kunstausstellung*) art exhibition

...salon *m, im Subst.* (*Geschäft etc.*): *Herren~* gentlemen's hair salon; *Hut~* hat boutique

salon|fähig *Adj.* socially acceptable; *Kleidung etc.*: presentable; *Benehmen, Witz etc.*: respectable; *nicht ~* risqué, (a bit) near the knuckle *umg.*

Salon|kommunist *m*, *~kommunistin* *f umg.* parlo(u)r communist; *~löwe* *m* society lion; *~wagen* *m Eisenb.* Pullman (car)

salopp I. *Adj.* (*ungezwungen*) casual, laid-back; *Benehmen: auch* easygoing; *pej.* sloppy; *Ausdruck*: very colloquial; *stärker*: slangy; *er hat e-e allzu ~e Ausdrucksweise* his German (*od.* English etc.) is excessively slangy, he uses too much slang; **II.** *Adv.*: *sich ~ kleiden/benehmen* dress casually / behave in a laid-back manner; **Saloppheit** *f* **1.** casualness; *pej.* sloppiness; *Benehmen*: laid-back manner; *der Sprache*: slanginess; **2.** *Handlung*: casual act; *Ausdruck*: colloquialism; *stärker*: slangy expression

Salpeter *m*; *-s, kein Pl.*; *Chem.* saltpetre, nitre, *Am.* saltpeter, niter; **salpeterhaltig** *Adj.* nitrous, nitric; **Salpetersäure** *f* nitric acid; **salpetrig** *Adj.*: *~e Säure* nitrous acid

Salto *m*; *-s, -s od. geh. Salti* somersault; *e-n ~ machen od. drehen* turn (*od.*

do) a somersault; **Salto mortale** *m*; -, - *od. geh. Salti mortali Zirkus etc.*: salto mortale, death-defying leap

salü ['zaly] *Interj. bes. schw. zur Begrüßung*: hello!, hi!; *zum Abschied*: bye!, *Brit. auch* cheerio!

Salut *m*; -(*e*)*s*, *kein Pl.* salute; ~ **schießen** fire a salute; **salutieren** *v/i.* salute (**vor** *j-m* s.o.); **Salutschuss** *m* gun salute; **zehn Salutschüsse** a ten-gun salute

Salve *f*; -, -*n*; *Mil.* salvo; *aus Gewehren*: volley; *Artillerie*: round; (*Ehrensalve*) salute; *fig. von Applaus*: burst (of applause); *von Gelächter*: peal (of laughter); **e-e** ~ **abgeben** fire a salvo (*od.* volley *od.* round)

Salweide *f Bot.* sallow, goat willow

Salz *n*; -(*e*)*s*, -*e* **1.** *nur Sg.*; *auch fig.* salt; **etw. in** ~ **legen** salt s.th. down; **nicht das** ~ **zur Suppe haben** *fig.* live in dire poverty; **das** ~ **in der Suppe** *fig.* that extra something; ~ **auf** *od.* **in die Wunde streuen** *fig.* rub salt into the wound, rub it in *umg.*; **wie e-e Suppe ohne** ~ *fig.* like ham without eggs; **2.** *Chem.* salt; **die** ~**e der Salpetersäure** nitric acid salts; **kohlensaures** ~ carbonate; ~**ader** *f* vein of salt

salz|arm *Adj.*: ~**e Kost** low-salt diet; ~**artig** *Chem.* salinous, saline

Salz|bergwerk *n* salt mine; ~**brezel** *f* (salted) pretzel

Salzburger *Adj.*: ~ **Nockerln** *österr. Gastr.* Salzburg-style (sweet) soufflé *Sg.*

salzen *v/t.* salt; (*pökeln*) *auch* pickle; *fig.* salt, season; → **gesalzen**

Salz|fässchen *n* salt cellar, *Am.* salt shaker; ~**fleisch** *n Gastr.* salt meat

salzfrei *Adj.* salt-free; *Diät*: *auch* no-salt ...

Salz|gebäck *n Gastr.* savo(u)ry biscuits (*od.* snacks), *Am.* crackers *Pl.*; ~**gehalt** *m* salt content, saltiness; ~**gewinnung** *f* salt production; ~**glasur** *f Keramik*: salt glaze; ~**gurke** *f Gastr.* pickled gherkin, *Am.* pickle

salzhaltig *Adj.* saline; *Essen*: *auch* salty

Salzhering *m Gastr.* salted herring

salzig *Adj.* salty; *Wasser*: briny; *Boden*, *auch Med.*: saline

Salz|kartoffeln *Pl. Gastr.* boiled potatoes; ~**korn** *n* grain of salt; ~**lake** *f* (salt) brine; ~**lecke** *f für Kühe*, *Wild*: salt lick

salzlos *Adj.* salt-free, *attr. auch* no-salt ...

Salz|lösung *f* salt (*od.* saline) solution; ~**mandeln** *Pl.* salted almonds; ~**pfanne** *f Geol.* salt pan; ~**pflanze** *f* halophyte

salzreduziert *Adj. Kost*: reduced-salt ...

Salz|säule *f bibl.* pillar of salt; **zur** ~ **erstarren** *fig.* be (*od.* stand) rooted to the spot; ~**säure** *f Chem.* hydrochloric acid; ~**see** *m* salt lake; ~**stange** *f Gastr.* salt (*Am.* pretzel) stick; ~**stock** *m Geol.* salt dome; ~**straße** *f hist.* salt road; ~**streuer** *m* salt cellar, *Am.* salt shaker; ~**sumpf** *m* salt marsh; ~**teig** *m* salt dough; **Figuren aus** ~ figures in salt dough; ~**wasser** *n* salt water, sea water; *zum Kochen*: salted water; ~**wüste** *f* salt desert; *Geog.* salt flats *Pl.*

SA-Mann *m hist.* (Nazi) stormtrooper

Samariter *m*; -*s*, - **1.** (*barmherziger* ~ good) Samaritan; **2.** *schw.* → **Sanitäter**, ~**dienste** *Pl.*: *j-m* ~ **leisten** be a good Samaritan to s.o.

Sämaschine *f Agr.* seeder; (*Drillmaschine*) seed drill

Samba *f*; -, -*s od. m*; -*s*, -*s*; *Mus.* samba; ~ **tanzen** dance the samba

Sambesi *m*; -*s*; *Geog.* Zambezi

Sambia (*n*); -*s*; *Geog.* Zambia

Sambier *m*; -*s*, -, ~**in** *f* -, -*nen* Zambian, *weiblich auch*: Zambian woman (*od.* girl etc.)

Same *m*; -*ns*, -*n*, **Samen** *m*; -*s*, - **1.** seed; *Pl.* (*Saatgut*) seed(s); **2.** *nur Sg.*; *Physiol.* (*Sperma*) sperm, semen

Samen|anlage *f Bot.* ovule; ~**bank** *f* sperm bank; ~**erguss** *m* ejaculation; ~**faden** *m* spermatozoon *fachspr.*; ~**flüssigkeit** *f* semen; ~**händler** *m* seedsman; ~**handlung** *f* seed shop; ~**kapsel** *f* seed capsule; ~**korn** *n* seed (grain); ~**leiter** *m* sperm duct, vas deferens *fachspr.*; ~**spende** *f* sperm donation; ~**spender** *m* sperm donor; ~**strang** *m Physiol.* spermatic cord; ~**übertragung** *f* insemination; ~**zelle** *f* sperm(atozoon)

Sämereien *Pl.* seeds

sämig *Adj.* thick, creamy

Sämling *m*; -*s*, -*e* seedling

Sammel|aktion *f* fund-raising campaign (*od.* drive); *für Material*: collection; ~**album** *n* scrapbook; *für Fotos*: album; ~**anschluss** *m Telef.* private switchboard; *einzelner*: party line; ~**auftrag** *m* multiple transfer; ~**band** *m* anthology; ~**becken** *n* reservoir, tank; *Geog.* catchment (*Am. auch* watershed) area; *fig.* repository (+ *Gen.* of), rallying point (for), melting pot (for); ~**begriff** *m* generic term, collective name; *Ling.* collective noun; ~**bestellung** *f* collective order; ~**bezeichnung** *f* collective name; ~**büchse** *f* collecting box; ~**eifer** *m* collecting zeal, enthusiasm for collecting; ~**fahrschein** *m Eisenb.*, *für e-e Gruppe*: group ticket; (*Mehrfahrtenkarte*) multiple-ride ticket; ~**gut** *n Eisenb.* (general goods *Pl.* in) combined (*od.* mixed) consignment; ~**konto** *n* combined account; ~**lager** *n* assembly (*od.* transit) camp; ~**leidenschaft** *f* passion for collecting; ~**linse** *f Opt.* convex (*od.* converging) lens; *e-r zusammengesetzten Optik*: collecting lens; ~**mappe** *f* folder, file

sammeln I. *v/t.* **1.** (*Münzen*, *Spenden*, *Altpapier etc.*) collect; (*Holz*) gather; (*Beeren*, *Pilze etc.*) *auch* pick; (*Pflanzen*) botanize; (*Kräuter*) herborize; (*Wählerstimmen*) canvass for; **2.** (*versammeln*) gather; **versprengte Truppen** ~ rally scattered troops; **3.** (*Erfahrungen*, *Material etc.*) gather; (*Informationen*) collect, gather; **Kenntnisse** ~ store knowledge; **s-e Gedanken** ~ collect (*od.* gather) one's thoughts; → **gesammelt**; **II.** *v/refl.* **1.** (*sich ansammeln*) gather, accumulate, collect; *Opt.* focus; **2.** (*sich versammeln*) assemble, meet; **3.** (*sich konzentrieren*) collect (*od.* gather) one's thoughts; (*sich fassen*) compose o.s.; **III.** *v/i.* (*Geld sammeln*) collect money; *für j-n*: *auch* pass the hat (a)round

Sammeln *n*; -*s*, *kein Pl.* collecting; gathering; **das** ~ **von Nachrichten** news-gathering; **zum** ~ **blasen** *umg.* *fig.* call everyone together (ready for departure)

Sammel|name *m* collective name; ~**nummer** *f Telef.* communal (*od.* shared) number; ~**platz** *m*, ~**punkt** *m* **1.** meeting place; *bei Feuerausbruch etc.*: assembly point; **2.** *in Lager*: col-

lecting point; ~**stecker** *m* universal adapter (plug); ~**stelle** *f in Lager*: collecting point

Sammelsurium *n*; -*s*, *Sammelsurien*; *umg.* motley collection *allg.*, hotch-potch, *Am.* hodgepodge

Sammel|taxi *n* communal (*od.* shared) taxi; ~**transport** *m* mass transportation; *Wirts.* bulk shipment; ~**unterkunft** *f* communal accommodation; ~**trieb** *m* collecting urge (*od.* instinct); ~**verbot** *n für Pilze*, *Schnecken etc.*: ban on gathering (mushrooms, snails etc.); ~**visum** *n* group visa; ~**werk** *n* compilation; ~**wut** *f* collecting mania

Sammler *m*; -*s*, -, ~**in** *f*; -, -*nen* **1.** collector; *von Pilzen etc.*: picker, gatherer; **2.** *Jäger und* ~ hunter-gatherer; ~**börse** *f* collectors' fair; ~**fleiß** *m* dedication of a true collector; ~**markt** *m* collectors' bazaar; (*Zeitungsrubrik*) collector's items, collectibles; ~**objekt** *n*, ~**stück** *n* collector's item (*od.* piece), collectible; ~**wert** *m* collector's value

Sammlung *f* **1.** collection; *von Gedichten auch*: anthology; **anatomische/biologische** ~ anatomical/biological collection; **2.** *fig.* (*Fassung*, *Ruhe*) composure

...sammlung *f*, *im Subst.* **1.** (*Aktion*): **Altglas**~ collection of waste glass; **Kleider**~ old clothes collection; **2.** (*Gegenstände*): **Mineralien**~ collection of mineral samples

Samowar *m*; -*s*, -*e* samovar

Sample ['sa:mpl] *n*; -(*s*), -*s* (*Stichprobe*) sample; (*repräsentative Gruppe*) samplc (group)

Sampler ['sa:mplɐ] *m*; -*s*, -; *Mus.* (*Platte*) sampler

Samstag *m* Saturday; **langer** ~ Saturday-afternoon opening; → **Dienstag**

Samstagabend *m* Saturday evening; → **Dienstagabend**; ~**programm** *n TV* Saturday evening program(me)s *Pl.* (*od.* schedule)

Samstagmorgen *m* Saturday morning; → **Dienstagmorgen**

samstags *Adv.* on Saturdays; → **dienstags**

samt I. *Adv.*: ~ **und sonders** each and every one (*od.* the whole lot *umg.*) of them; **II.** *Präp.* together with, along with

Samt *m*; -(*e*)*s*, -*e*, *mst Sg.* velvet; *aus Baumwolle*: velveteen; **in** ~ **und Seide** (**gekleidet**) dressed in silks and satins; **samtartig** *Adj.* velvety

Samtband *n* velvet ribbon; *breiter*: velvet band

samtbraun *Adj.* velvety brown

samten *Adj.* **1.** (*aus Samt*) velvet; **2.** (*wie Samt*) *auch Stimme*, *Klang*: velvety

Samt|handschuh *m* velvet glove; *j-n* **mit** ~**en anfassen** *fig.* handle s.o. with kid gloves; ~**haut** *f* velvety skin; *Gesicht*: *auch* silken complexion

samtig *Adj.* velvety (*auch Wein*)

Samtkleid *n* velvet dress

sämtlich I. *Adj.* all; ~**e Anwesende(n)** all those present; **Goethes** ~**e Werke** Goethe's complete works, the complete works of Goethe; **II.** *Adv.* all; **er hat s-e Songs** ~ **selbst geschrieben** he wrote every one of his songs himself

Samtrock *m* velvet skirt

samtweich *Adj.* velvety-soft

Samuel *m*; -*s*; *bibl.* Samuel; **das 1. Buch** ~ the 1st Book of Samuel, Samuel I

Sanatorium *n*; -*s*, *Sanatorien* sanatori-

S

um, *bes. Am.* sanitarium

Sand *m; -(e)s, kein Pl.* sand; *auf ~ laufen Naut.* run aground; *auf ~ gebaut haben fig.* have built on sand (*od.* shaky foundations); *j-m ~ in die Augen streuen fig.* throw dust in s.o.'s eyes; *~ ins Getriebe streuen fig.* throw (*od.* put) a spanner (*Am.* monkey wrench) in the works; *etw. in den ~ setzen umg.* muff (up) (*od.* bungle) s.th.; *im ~e verlaufen* come to nothing (naught *lit.*); *Pläne etc.: auch* fizzle out *umg.*; *... wie ~ am Meer* countless ..., ... beyond number; → *Kopf* 6

Sandale *f; -, -n* sandal; **Sandalette** *f; -, -n* (high-heeled) sandal

Sand|bahn *f* dirt track; **~bahnrennen** *n Sport* dirt-track (*od.* speedway) racing (*einzelnes:* race); **~bank** *f* sandbank; **~berg** *m* sandy hill, sandhill; **~boden** *m* sandy soil (*od.* ground); **~burg** *f* sandcastle

Sand|dorn *m Bot.* sea buckthorn, sallow thorn; **~dornsaft** *m* buckthorn berry juice

Sanddüne *f* sand dune

Sandelholz *n* sandalwood

sandfarben *Adj.* sandy

Sand|floh *m Zool.* sand flea; **~grube** *f zur Sandgewinnung:* sand pit; *Sport Golf:* bunker, *bes. Am.* sand trap; **~haufen** *m* pile of sand

sandig *Adj.* full of sand, sandy

Sandinist *m; -en, -en,* **~in** *f; -, -nen; Pol., hist.* Sandinista; **sandinistisch** *Adj.* Sandinista

Sandkasten *m* sandpit, *Am.* sandbox; *Mil.* sandtable; **~spiel** *n Mil.* sandtable exercise

Sand|korn *n* grain of sand; **~kuchen** *m* **1.** Madeira cake; **2.** *im Sandkasten:* sand pie; **~mann** *m,* **~männchen** *n* sandman; **~papier** *n* sandpaper; *mit ~ abschmirgeln* (rub down with) sandpaper, sand down; **~platz** *m Tennis:* clay court; **~sack** *m* sandbag; *Boxen:* punching bag; **~schicht** *f* layer of sand; *Geol.* sand stratum

Sandstein *m* sandstone

Sandstrahl *m Tech.* sandblast; *mit ~ behandeln/reinigen* sandblast / clean by sandblasting; **sandstrahlen** *v/t.* (*untr., hat, ge-, fachspr. auch -ge-*) sandblast; **~gebläse** *n* sandblast unit

Sand|strand *m* sandy beach; **~sturm** *m* sandstorm

sandte *Imperf.* → *senden*

Sand|torte *f Gastr.* Madeira cake; **~uhr** *f* hourglass

Sandwich ['zɛntvɪtʃ] *n; -(e)s, -(e)s; Gastr.* sandwich; *überbackenes Schinken-Käse-~* toasted ham and cheese sandwich; **~bauweise** *f* sandwich construction; **~mann** *m Werbung:* sandwich man

Sandwüste *f* sand(y) desert

sanft I. *Adj. Berührung etc.:* soft, gentle; *Wesen, Augen:* gentle; *Farbe, Musik, Stimme etc.:* soft; *Regen, Brise:* gentle, light; *Druck etc.:* gentle; *Tod:* easy; *mit ~er Stimme* softly, gently, in a soft (*od.* gentle) voice; *mit ~er Gewalt* using gentle force; *~e Revolution* velvet revolution; *~e Geburt* natural childbirth; *sie ist ein ~es Wesen* she's a gentle soul; *es auf die ~e Tour versuchen* try a bit of soft soap; **II.** *Adv.: j-m etw. ~ beibringen* break s.th. to s.o. gently; *er geht nicht gerade ~ mit ihr um* he doesn't exactly treat her with kid gloves; *ihr behandelt ihn viel zu ~* you're much too soft with (*od.* easy on) him; *~ entschlafen*

pass away peacefully; *ruhe ~* rest in peace

Sänfte *f; -, -n* sedan (chair); **Sänftenträger** *m,* **Sänftenträgerin** *f* sedan-chair carrier

Sanftheit *f Berührung etc.:* softness, gentleness; *Wesen, Augen:* gentleness; *Farbe, Musik, Stimme etc.:* softness; *Regen, Brise:* gentleness, lightness; *Hügel etc.:* gentleness; *Druck, Gewalt etc.:* gentleness; *Tod:* ease

Sanftmut *f; -, kein Pl.* gentleness; (*Nachgiebigkeit*) meekness; **sanftmütig** *Adj.* gentle; (*nachgiebig*) meek

sang *Imperf.* → *singen*

Sang *m: mit ~ und Klang durchfallen umg.* fail miserably

Sänger¹ *m; -s, -; Orn.* songbird

Sänger² *m; -s, -,* **Sängerin** *f; -, -nen* singer; **Sängerknabe** *m* choirboy

sangesfreudig *Adj. altm., hum.* filled with a love of song; (*singend*) singing merrily

Sanguiniker *m; -s, -,* **~in** *f; -, -nen* sanguine person; **sanguinisch** *Adj.* sanguine

sang- und klanglos *Adv. umg.* (*unauffällig*) quietly, without ado; (*formlos*) unceremoniously; *~ untergehen Sport* be beaten out of sight

sanieren I. *v/t.* **1.** (*Stadtteil etc.*) redevelop, clean up; (*Haus*) refurbish, renovate; (*Umwelt, Fluss etc.*) rehabilitate; (*Zähne*) overhaul; **3.** *Wirts.* revitalize; (*Betrieb*) make profitable; *allg.* put back on its feet, rescue; **II.** *v/refl. Wirts.* (*Firma*) get back on its feet again; (*Person*) get out of the red *umg.*; *umg. fig.* (*sich bereichern*) line one's (own) pockets

Sanierung *f* **1.** *e-s Hauses:* refurbishment; *e-s Stadtteils:* redevelopment; *in Armengegenden:* slum clearance; **2.** *der Umwelt:* clean-up; *der Zähne:* overhaul; **3.** *Wirts.* revitalization; *e-s Betriebes:* restoration to profitability; *allg.* rescue

sanierungsbedürftig *Adj.* in need of rehabilitation (*Wohnung:* renovation); *Wirts.* in need of revitalization

Sanierungs|gebiet *n* redevelopment area; **~maßnahmen** *Pl.* **1.** redevelopment; *~ einleiten* begin redevelopment (work); **2.** *Wirts.* rescue packages (*od.* package *Sg.*); **~plan** *m,* **~programm** *n Wirts.* rescue package (*od.* scheme)

sanitär *Adj.* sanitary; *~e Anlagen* sanitary facilities; *die ~en Verhältnisse* sanitation *Sg.*

Sanitär|bereich *m* (field of) sanitation; **~geschäft** *n* sanitary goods store; **~technik** *f* sanitation technology

Sanitäter *m; -s, -,* **~in** *f; -, -nen* first-aider; *mit Sonderausbildung:* paramedic; *Mil.* medical orderly

Sanitäts|auto *n umg.* ambulance; **~dienst** *m Mil.* medical service; **~flugzeug** *n* air ambulance; **~kasten** *m* first-aid box (*bes. Am.* kit); **~korps** *n Mil.* medical corps; (*in GB:* Royal) Army Medical Corps; **~personal** *n* medical staff; **~raum** *m* first-aid room; **~soldat** *m Mil.* medical orderly; **~wache** *f Mil.* first-aid station; **~wagen** *m* ambulance; **~wesen** *n Mil.* medical service; **~zelt** *n* first-aid tent

sank *Imperf.* → *sinken*

Sank(r)a *m; -s, -s; Mil. umg.* (military) ambulance

Sankt *Adj.* (*abgek. St.*) Saint (*Abk.* St, *Am.* St.); *~ Nikolaus* St (*od.* St.) Nicholas; *als Weihnachtsmann:* Santa Claus; *~ Gallen* Sankt Gallen, St (*od.*

St.) Gall

Sanktion *f; -, -en* **1.** *geh.* (*Billigung*) sanction, (official) approval (*od.* permission); *Jur., kirchl.* (*Erteilung der Gesetzeskraft*) sanction, confirmation (*od.* ratification) *allg.*; **2.** *bes. Pol.* (*Zwangsmaßnahme*) sanction; *mit ~en drohen* threaten (to impose) sanctions; **sanktionieren** *v/t.* sanction; **Sanktionierung** *f* sanctioning

Sanktionsmaßnahmen *Pl. bes. Pol.* sanctions; *~ einleiten* apply sanctions

Sankt-Nimmerleins-Tag *m umg.: bis zum ~ warten etc.:* till the cows come home, till kingdom come *allg.*

sann *Imperf.* → *sinnen*

Sanskrit *n; -(e)s, kein Pl. Ling.* Sanskrit

Saphir *m; -s, -e* **1.** sapphire; **2.** *Hi-Fi:* (*Nadel*) (sapphire) stylus

sapphisch ['zapfɪʃ] *Adj.* Sapphic

Sarde *m; -n, -n* Sardinian

Sardelle *f; -, -n; Zool.* anchovy

Sardellenpaste *f Gastr.* anchovy paste

Sardin *f; -, -nen* Sardinian, Sardinian woman (*od.* girl)

Sardine *f; -, -n; Zool.* sardine, young pilchard; *dicht gedrängt wie die ~n* packed like sardines; **Sardinenbüchse** *f* sardine tin (*Am.* can); *wie in e-r ~* (packed) like sardines

Sardinien (*n*); *-s; Geog.* Sardinia

sardisch *Adj.,* **Sardisch** (*n*); *-en* Sardinian

sardonisch I. *Adj. Grinsen etc.:* sardonic; *~es Lachen Med.* sardonic (*od.* canine) laugh, risus sardonicus *fachspr.*; **II.** *Adv.* sardonically

Sarg *m; -(e)s, Särge* coffin, *Am. auch* casket; → *Nagel* 1; **~deckel** *m* coffin lid; **~nagel** *m* coffin nail; *umg. fig.* (*Zigarette*) cancer stick, coffin nail; **~tischler** *m,* **~tischlerin** *f* coffin (*Am. auch* casket-)maker; **~träger** *m,* **~trägerin** *f* pallbearer; **~tuch** *n* pall

Sari *m; -(s), -s* sari

Sarkasmus *m; -, Sarkasmen* **1.** *nur Sg.* sarcasm; **2.** (*Bemerkung*) sarcastic remark; **sarkastisch I.** *Adj.* sarcastic; **II.** *Adv.* sarcastically

Sarkom *n; -s, -e; Med.* sarcoma

Sarkophag *m; -(e)s, -e* sarcophagus

saß *Imperf.* → *sitzen*

Satan *m; -s bibl.* Satan; *fig.* satan, devil; **satanisch** *Adj.* satanic; **Satanismus** *m; -, kein Pl.* satanism

Satans|braten *m umg. hum.* (*freches Kind*) cheeky devil (*od.* rascal); (*üble Person*) blackguard *förm.*; **~messe** *f* black mass; **~pilz** *m Bot.* Satan's mushroom; **~weib** *n Sl. pej.* bitch, she-devil *allg.*

Satellit *m; -en, -en; Astron., Pol.* satellite; *über od. per ~* by (*od.* via) satellite

Satelliten|anlage *f* satellite TV installation; **~bahn** *f* satellite('s) orbit; **~bild** *n* satellite picture; **~empfänger** *m* satellite receiver; **~fernsehen** *n* satellite TV; **~foto** *n* satellite picture; **~funk** *m* satellite broadcasting (*od.* radio link); **~schüssel** *f* satellite dish; **~sender** *m* TV satellite (TV) station; **~staat** *m Pol.* satellite (state); **~stadt** *f* satellite town; **~technik** *f* satellite technology; **~übertragung** *f* satellite transmission; **~verbindung** *f* satellite link

Satin [za'tɛ̃:] *m; -s, kein Pl.* satin; *aus Baumwolle:* sateen; *Bettwäsche aus ~* satin sheets *Pl.*

Satire *f; -, -n* satire (*auf + Akk.* on);

Satirezeitschrift *f* satirical magazine;

Satiriker *m*; *-s*, *-*, **Satirikerin** *f*; *-*, *-nen* satirist; **satirisch** *Adj.* satirical

satt *Adj. und Adv.* **1.** (*gesättigt*) full; *sich ~ essen* eat one's fill; *sich an* (+ *Dat.*) *~ essen* fill o.s. with; *ich bin davon nicht ~ geworden* that wasn't enough for me; *bist du ~?* have you had enough (to eat)?; *es fällt ihm schwer, s-e Familie ~ zu bekommen* he finds it hard to feed his family; *das macht ~* that's very filling; **2.** *Farbton*: deep, rich; *Klang*: full; **3.** *fig.* (*selbstzufrieden*) complacent, smug; **4.** (*ansehnlich*) impressive; *umg.* (*großartig*) terrific; *es gab Kuchen ~* there was plenty of cake; *~e Preise* steep (*od.* hefty) prices; *er hat e-e ~e Million verdient* he earned a cool million; *e-e ~e Leistung* quite a feat, some feat, no mean feat; *etw./j-n gründlich ~ bekommen umg.* get sick and tired of s.th./s.o.; *ich hab die Sache so ~ umg.* I'm sick and tired of it, I'm fed up to the back teeth (*od.* up to here) with it; **6.** *er konnte sich nicht ~ daran sehen* he couldn't take his eyes off it; *ich habe mich daran ~ gesehen* I've seen enough (*od.* too much) of it, I've had my fill of that; *nicht ~ werden zu* (+ *Inf.*) never tire of (+ *Ger.*)

Sattel *m*; *-s*, *Sättel* **1.** (*Reit-*, *Fahrradsattel*, *auch Mot.*) saddle; *ohne ~ reiten* ride bareback; *aus dem ~ geworfen werden* be unseated (*od.* thrown off [one's horse]); *j-n in den ~ heben* hoist s.o. into the saddle; *fig.* give s.o. a leg up (*Am. auch* a boost); *j-n aus dem ~ heben* unseat s.o.; *fig.* oust s.o.; *fest im ~ sitzen auch fig.* be firmly in the saddle; *sich im ~ halten* have a good seat; *fig.* hold (firmly) onto the reins; **2.** (*Bergsattel*) saddle; **3.** (*Nasensattel*) bridge; **4.** *Schneiderei*: yoke

Sattel|dach *n* saddleback (roof); **~decke** *f* saddlecloth, *bes. Am.* saddle blanket

sattelfest *Adj. fig.*: *in etw. ~ sein* be well up in, know one's subject; *in Rechtschreibung absolut / nicht ganz ~ sein* have a firm grasp of / not be quite sure of one's spelling

Sattel|gurt *m* girth; **~knauf** *m*, **~knopf** *m* pommel

satteln *v/t.* saddle; *für etw. gesattelt sein fig.* be prepared for s.th.

Sattel|nase *f* saddlenose; **~pferd** *n* saddle horse; **~schlepper** *m Mot.* **1.** (*Sattelzug*) articulated lorry, artic *umg.*, *Am.* tractor-trailer, rig, semi *umg.*; **2.** (*Zugfahrzeug*) tractor; **~tasche** *f* saddlebag; **~zeug** *n* saddlery; **~zug** *m Mot.* articulated lorry, artic *umg.*, *Am.* tractor-trailer, rig, semi *umg.*

sattgrün *Adj.* deep green

Sattheit *f* **1.** *nach Mahlzeit*: ful(l)ness, replete (*od.* sated) feeling (*auch fig.*); **2.** *e-r Farbe*: richness; **3.** *pej.* (*Selbstzufriedenheit*) complacency, smugness

sättigen I. *v/t.* (*j-n*) feed, fill; (*Hunger*) satisfy (*auch fig.*); *Chem.*, *Wirts.* (*den Markt*) saturate; → *gesättigt*; **II.** *v/i. Nahrung*: be filling (*od.* satisfying); *Käsefondue sättigt schnell* cheese fondue soon fills you up (*od.* fills you up fast); **sättigend I.** *Part. Präs. → sättigen*; **II.** *Adj.* filling; **Sättigung** *f* **1.** (*Sattsein*) satiety *fachspr.*, repleteness; **2.** *Chem.*, *Wirts. und fig.* saturation

Sättigungs|gefühl *n* feeling of satiety (*od.* repleteness); **~grad** *m* degree of saturation; **~punkt** *m Chem.*, *Wirts.* *und fig.* saturation point

Sattler *m*; *-s*, *-* saddler; **Sattlerhandwerk** *n* saddler's craft; **Sattlerin** *f*; *-*, *-nen* (female) saddler; **Sattlerwerkstatt** *f* saddler's workshop, saddlery

sattsam *Adv.* more than enough; *es ist ~ bekannt* it's an only too well-known fact; *wir haben es ~ oft gehört* we've heard it all too often

saturieren *v/t.* saturate; **saturiert** *Adj. pej. Bürgertum*: smugly well-to-do, sated; **Saturiertheit** *f* smug affluence

Saturn [za'tʊrn] *m*; *-s*; *Astron.* Saturn

Satyr ['zaːtyr] *m*; *-s od.* *-n*, *-n*; *Myth.* satyr

Satz *m*; *-es*, *Sätze* **1.** sentence; *Ling. auch* clause; *e-n ~ bilden/umformen* form/recast a sentence; *mitten im ~ unterbrechen* break off in mid-sentence; *bitte e-n ~ dazu* please can we have a few words on that; **2.** *Philos.* (*Lehr-*, *Grundsatz*) principle, tenet; **3.** *Math.* theorem; *der ~ des Euklid* Euclid's theorem; **4.** *Druck.* (*das Setzen*) (type)setting; (*gesetzter Text*) composition; *computergestützter ~* computer typesetting (*od.* composition); *zweispaltiger ~* double-column page; *im ~ sein* be being set; *in den ~ gehen* go for setting; **5.** (*~ Briefmarken etc.*) set (of stamps etc.); (*Bausatz*) kit; *ein ~ Tische* a nest of tables; **6.** *Mus.* movement; **7.** *nur Sg.*; *Mus.* (*Kompositionsweise*) writing; (*Vertonung*) setting; **8.** *mst Sg.*; (*Bodensatz*) sediment, dregs *Pl.*; (*Kaffeesatz*) grounds *Pl.*; **9.** *Sport,Tennis etc.*: set; *mit 3:2 Sätzen gewinnen* win 3 sets to 2; *nach Sätzen führen* be ahead on sets; **10.** (*Preis*, *Tarif*) rate; *zum ~ von* at a rate of; **11.** (*Sprung*) leap, bound; *e-n ~ machen* (take a) leap; *er war in vier Sätzen oben* he was upstairs in four bounds

...satz *m*, *im Subst.* **1.** *Ling.*: *Attribut~* attributive clause; **2.** *Mus.*: *Anfangs~* first movement; **3.** *Wirts.*: *Beitrags~* rate of contribution; *Mindest~* minimum rate

Satz|akzent *m Ling.* sentence stress; **~analyse** *f Ling.* sentence analysis; **~anfang** *m Ling.* beginning of the sentence; **~anweisung** *f Druck.* printing (*od.* setting) instructions *Pl.*, markup *Sg.*; **~art** *f Ling.* type of clause; **~ausgleich** *m Tennis etc.*: level(l)ing of the set; **~aussage** *f Ling.* predicate; **~ball** *m Tennis etc.*: set point; **~bau** *m Ling.* sentence construction; **~befehl** *m Druck.* typographical command; **~ergänzung** *f Ling.* object; **~erweiterung** *f Ling.* continuation of the sentence; **~fehler** *m Druck.* misprint, printing error

satzfertig *Adj. Druck.* ready for setting; *~ machen* copy-edit

Satz|gefüge *n Ling.* complex sentence; **~gegenstand** *m Ling.* subject; **~gewinn** *m Tennis etc.*: winning of the set; *zum ~ aufschlagen* serve for the set; **~glied** *n Ling.* sentence component (*od.* part); **~herstellung** *f Druck.* setting

...sätzig *im Adj.*: *e-e drei~e Sinfonie* a three-movement symphony; *ein mehr~es Werk* a work in several movements

Satz|konstruktion *f* sentence construction; **~lehre** *f* syntax; **~melodie** *f* intonation

Satzrechner *m Druck.* (typesetting) computer; **satzreif** *Adj. Manuskript*: ready for setting

Satzreihe *f Ling.* compound sentence

Satz|spiegel *m Druck.* type area; **~teil** *m Ling.* part of a (*od.* the) sentence

Satzung *f* statutes *Pl.*; (*auch ~en*) *e-s Vereins etc.*: articles of association (*Am.* incorporation)

Satzungsänderung *f* amendment to the articles of association (*Am.* incorporation)

satzungsgemäß I. *Adj.* statutory; *nur präd.*, *bei e-r Gesellschaft*: in accordance with the articles of association (*Am.* incorporation); **II.** *Adv.* in accordance with the statutes; *e-r Gesellschaft*: in accordance with the articles of an association (*Am.* incorporation)

Satz|verbindung *f Ling.* compound sentence; **~verlust** *m Tennis etc.*: loss of a (*od.* the) set; **~vorlage** *f Druck.* script for setting, copy

satzweise *Adv.*: *~ vorgehen/korrigieren* proceed/correct sentence by sentence

Satz|zeichen *n Ling.* punctuation mark; *Pl. auch* punctuation *Sg.*; **~zusammenhang** *m* context

Sau *f*; *-*, *Säue od. Jägerspr. Sauen* **1.** sow; *Jägerspr.* (*Wildsau*) (wild) sow; **~en** (*Wildschweine*) wild boars; **2.** *pej.* swine; *gemeiner Kerl*: bastard; *Frau*: bitch; *dumme/fette ~* stupid/fat cow; **3.** *umg.*, *in Wendungen*: *unter aller ~* really lousy, the pits; *etw./j-n zur ~ machen* tear s.th./s.o. to pieces; *bluten wie e-e ~* bleed like a pig; *die ~ rauslassen* let one's hair down, let it all hang out; *keine ~ war da* not a soul was there *allg.*; *hier kennt sich doch keine ~ aus* how are you supposed to find anything in this place *allg.*; *wie e-e gesengte ~* like a lunatic; *fahren, rennen*: *auch* like the clappers, *Am.* like greased lightning; *es hat geregnet etc. wie d'~ Dial.* like crazy

sau~ *im Adj.*, *verstärkend*: **~gut** damn good; **~schlecht** really lousy, *Brit. auch* bloody awful

Sau|arbeit *f umg.* dirty work; (*schwere Arbeit*) hellish job; **~bande** *f*; *nur Sg.*; *umg.* bunch of good-for-nothings; **~bär** *m umg.* dirty pig; (*Kind*) piglet

sauber I. *Adj.* **1.** clean; *~ sein Kind*: be potty-trained; *Haustier*: be house-trained; *~ halten* (*Umwelt*, *Luft etc.*) keep clean; *~ machen* clean (up); (*e-m Baby die Windeln wechseln*) change; *in e-m Büro etc. ~ machen* do the cleaning in an office etc.; **2.** (*sorgfältig*, *ordentlich*) neat; *Arbeit*: *auch* decent; *Lösung*, *Plan etc.*: neat; (*anständig*) clean, decent; *Spielweise*: clean; (*fehlerfrei*) perfect; *Sport*, *Schlag etc.*: clean, accurate; *~ bleiben* keep one's nose clean *umg.*; *bleib ~! umg.* be good!, take care!; *die Sache ist nicht ganz ~* this business is not quite above board, it's a bit of a shady (*od.* dodgy) business; *der ist wohl nicht ganz ~ umg.* he's not quite all there; **3.** *~!* *umg. iro.* (that's really) great; *dein ~er Freund umg.* your wonderful friend; **II.** *Adv.* (*gewissenhaft*) conscientiously; (*ordentlich*) neatly; *das hast du ja ~ hingekriegt! umg. iro.* a fine job you made of that!

Sauberkeit *f* cleanliness, cleanness; (*Sorgfalt*, *Ordnung*) neatness; *fig. des Charakters*: integrity; **Sauberkeitsfimmel** *m* obsession with cleanliness (*od.* hygiene); (*Putzfimmel*) cleaning mania

säuberlich I. *Adj. nur attr.* neat; *Trennung etc.*: *auch* clear, clean; **II.** *Adv.*

neatly; **alles fein ~ ordnen** (*auf-, einräumen*) put everything into its right place; (*ordentlich machen*) make sure everything's neat and tidy; **wir müssen beide Aspekte ~ trennen** we must make a clear distinction between these two aspects

Saubermann *m iro.* Mr (*od.* Mr.) Clean

säubern *v/t.* **1.** clean; (*Wunde*) cleanse; (*frei machen*) clear (**von** of); **2.** *fig., auch Pol.* purge; **Säuberung** *f* **1.** cleaning; cleansing; clearing; **2.** → *Säuberungsaktion*

Säuberungs|aktion *f Pol.* purge; *Mil.* mopping-up operation; **~welle** *f Pol.* series (*od.* wave) of purges

saublöd *Adj. Sl.* → **saudoof**

Saubohne *f* broad (*bes. Am.* fava) bean

Sauce ['zɔːsə] *f; -, -n; Gastr.* → **Soße**; **~ hollandaise** hollandaise sauce; **Saucier** [zoˈsi̯eː] *m; -s, -s* sauce chef; **Sauciere** [zoˈsi̯eːrə] *f; -, -n* sauce boat, (*für Bratensaft*) gravy boat

Saudiaraber *m*, **~in** *f* Saudi (Arabian), *weiblich auch*: Saudi (Arabian) woman (*od.* girl); **Saudiarabien** (*n*); *-s*; *Geog.* Saudiarabia; **saudiarabisch**, **saudisch** *Adj.* Saudi (Arabian)

sau|doof, **~dumm** *Sl.* **I.** *Adj.*; *Person*: as thick as they come; *Sache*: really stupid (*od.* idiotic); **sie ist hübsch, aber ~** she's pretty but brainless; **das ist ja ~!** that's completely idiotic! *bei Geschehen/Tat*: what an utterly idiotic thing to happen (*od.* do); **II.** *Adv.*: **sich ~ anstellen/benehmen** pretend to be really stupid / behave like a complete idiot

sauen *v/i. umg.* **1.** (*Schmutz machen*) make a mess; **2.** (*obszön reden*) talk filth

sauer **I.** *Adj.* **1.** sour (*auch Boden, Geruch, Milch, Sahne*); *Chem.* acid; *Gurke*: pickled; → **Drops**; **saurer Regen** acid rain; **~ werden** turn sour; *Milch*: *auch* curdle; **2.** *umg. fig.* (*verärgert*) annoyed (**auf** + *Akk.* with, at) *allg.*, *stärker*: mad (at); **~ sein/werden** be/get cross; **ein saures Gesicht machen** pull a long face; **3.** **j-m das Leben ~ machen** *fig.*: make s.o.'s life a misery; **das ist ein saures Brot** it's a hard life; **es sich ~ werden lassen** put a lot into it; → **Apfel** 1, **Saures**; **II.** *Adv.* **1.** **~ einlegen** (*Heringe etc.*) pickle; **es stößt mir ~ auf Essen etc.**: it's giving me acid reflux, it keeps coming back *umg.*; **das wird ihm noch ~ aufstoßen** *fig.* that won't be the last he hears of it, he'll live to regret it; **~ reagieren** *Chem.* give an acid reaction; *fig.* get annoyed (*od.* mad) (**auf** + *Akk.* at); **2.** **~ sein Brot verdienen** have to work hard for one's money; **~ verdientes Geld** hard-earned money

Sauer|ampfer *m Bot.* sorrel; **~braten** *m Gastr.* sauerbraten; *marinated potroast*

Sauerei *f; -, -en; umg.* → **Schweinerei**

Sauer|kirsche *f Bot.* sour cherry; **~kohl** *m*, **~kraut** *n Gastr.* sauerkraut

Sauerländer *m*; *-s, -* man (*od.* boy) from the Sauerland; **~in** *f*; *-, -nen* woman (*od.* girl) from the Sauerland; **sauerländisch** *Adj. nur attr.* Sauerland …, from the Sauerland

säuerlich **I.** *Adj.* (slightly) sour (*auch fig.*); *bes. Chem.* acidulous; **~es Gesicht/Grinsen** rather sour face/grin; **II.** *Adv.* **~ riechen/schmecken** smell/ taste sourish (*Am.* slightly sour); **~ re-**

---

agieren/lächeln get rather annoyed / smile rather sourly

Sauermilch *f* sour milk

säuern *vt/i.* (make) sour; (*Teig*) leaven

Sauerrahm *m* sour cream

Sauerstoff *m Chem.* oxygen

sauerstoffarm *Adj.* low in oxygen; *Luft*: *auch* rarefied

Sauerstoff|armut *f* lack of oxygen; **~beatmung** *f Med.* oxygen treament; **~entzug** *m Chem.* deoxygenation; **~flasche** *f* oxygen cylinder; **~gehalt** *m* oxygen content; **~gerät** *n* oxygen apparatus; **♀haltig** *Adj.* oxygenous; **~mangel** *m* oxygen starvation; *Med. auch* anox(a)emia; **~maske** *f* oxygen mask; **♀reich** *Adj.* high in oxygen, oxygen-rich; **~therapie** *f Med.* oxygen therapy; **~versorgung** *f* oxygen supply; **~zelt** *n Med.* oxygen tent; **~zufuhr** *f* oxygen supply

Sauerteig *m Gastr.* sourdough (starter), leaven

Sauertopf *m umg.* sourpuss; **sauertöpfisch** *Adj. umg.* grumpy

Säuerung *f von Teig*: leavening

Sauf|bold *m*; *-(e)s, -e; umg.* boozer; **~bruder** *m umg.* **1.** → **Säufer**; **2.** boozing mate, *Am.* drinking buddy

saufen; **säuft, soff, hat gesoffen** *vt/i.* **1.** *umg.* booze; *allg.* drink; (*Nichtalkoholisches*) guzzle; **~ wie ein Loch** drink like a fish; **sich zu Tode ~** drink oneself to death; **2.** *Vieh etc.*: drink; **Säufer** *m*; *-s, -; umg.* boozer; *krankhaft*: dipso; **Sauferei** *f; -, -en; umg.* boozing; → *auch* **Saufgelage**; **Säuferin** *f; -, -nen* → **Säufer**

Säufer|leber *f umg.* hobnail liver; **~nase** *f umg.* drinker's nose; **~stimme** *f umg.* boozy voice

Sauf|gelage *n umg.* drinking bout, booze-up, soak, *Am.* binge, bender; **~kumpan** *m Sl.* boozing mate, *Am.* drinking buddy

Saufraß *m umg.* pigswill, muck

saufrech *Adj. umg.* damn cheeky

Sauftour *f Sl.* binge, *Brit. auch* pub crawl, *Am.* bar hop

Saugbagger *m Tech.* suction dredge(r)

saugemütlich *Adj. umg.* really cosy (*Am.* cozy)

saugen; **saugte od. sog, hat gesaugt od. gesogen** **I.** *v/i.* suck (**an etw.** [at] s.th.); *Baby*: *auch* suckle (at); **2.** (*saugte, hat gesaugt*) (*Staub saugen*) vacuum, *Brit. auch* hoover; *Person*: do the vacuuming (*Brit. auch* hoovering); **der neue Staubsauger saugt gut/schlecht** the new vacuum cleaner picks up the dirt well / doesn't pick up the dirt properly; **II.** *v/t.* **1.** suck; *Wurzeln etc.*: absorb (**aus** from), draw (out of); → **Finger** 2; **2.** (*Teppich*) vacuum, *Brit. auch* hoover; (*Dreck*) pick up; **III.** *v/refl.*: **sich voll Wasser etc. ~** soak up as much water etc. as it can

säugen *vt/i.* nurse, breastfeed

Sauger *m*; *-s, -* **1.** dummy, *Am.* pacifier; *an der Flasche*: teat, *Am.* nipple; **2.** *Tech.* suction apparatus; (*Saugheber*) siphon; **3.** → **Staubsauger**

Säugetier *n* mammal

saugfähig *Adj.* absorbent; **Saugfähigkeit** *f* absorptive capacity

Saug|flasche *f* feeding bottle; **~glocke** *f Tech.* suction cup; *Med. bei Entbindung*: vacuum extractor; **~heber** *m* siphon; **~kraft** *f* suction

Säugling *m*; *-s, -e* baby, infant *lit. od. fachspr.*

Säuglings|alter *n* infancy; **im ~** in infancy, at a very young age, in the first

---

few months; **~ernährung** *f* feeding of babies, infant feeding; **~nahrung** *f* baby food(s *Pl.*); **~pflege** *f* baby (*od.* infant *fachspr.*) care; **~schwester** *f* infant nurse; **~station** *f* neonatal care unit; **~sterblichkeit** *f* infant mortality

Saug|napf *m Zool.* sucker; **~pumpe** *f* suction pump; **~reflex** *m* sucking instinct

saugrob *Adj. umg.* bloody (*Am.* really *od.* incredibly) rude (*od.* rough)

Saug|rohr *n* suction pipe; **~rüssel** *m e-s Insekts*: proboscis; **~wirkung** *f* sucking action

Sau|hatz *f Jägerspr.* (wild) boar hunt; **~haufen** *m umg. pej.* bunch of ne'er--do-wells (*od.* wastrels); *ungepflegt*: scruffy lot; **~hitze** *f umg.* murderous (*od.* hellish) heat; **~hund** *m Sl.* bastard

Sauigel *m umg.* dirty swine; **sauigeln** *v/i. umg.* talk smut

säuisch **I.** *Adj.* **1.** *pej. Witz etc.*: obscene, filthy; → *auch* **saumäßig** I; **2.** *verstärkend*: hellish; **II.** *Adv. umg.* (*sehr*): **das tut ~ weh** it hurts like hell

saukalt *Adj. umg.* hellishly cold, *Am.* colder than hell; **Saukälte** *f umg.* hellish cold

Sau|kerl *m umg.* swine, bastard; **~klaue** *f umg.*: **e-e ~ haben** have dreadful handwriting; **~laden** *m umg.*: **ein ~ ist das hier!** this is a damn useless outfit!

Säule *f*, *-, -n* **1.** column; *auch von Rauch*: pillar; **e-e ~ der Gesellschaft/ Mannschaft** a pillar of society / a mainstay of the team; **2.** *Mot.* (*Zapfsäule*) pump

Säulen|diagramm *n Statistik*: bar chart; **♀förmig** *Adj.* pillar-shaped; **~fuß** *m Archit.* base of a (*od.* the) column; **~gang** *m Archit.* colonnade; **~halle** *f Archit.* columned hall; (*Vorbau*) portico; **~heilige** *m, f* stylite, pillar saint; **~kaktus** *m Bot.* candelabra cactus; **~kapitell** *n Archit.* capital (of a *od.* the pillar); **~ordnung** *f* order of columns; **~tempel** *m Archit.* colonnaded temple; **~umgang** *m Antike*: peristyle; **~vorbau** *m Archit.* portico

Saulus *m*; *-*; *bibl.* Saul; **vom ~ zum Paulus werden** *fig.* undergo a Pauline conversion

Saum *m*; *-(e)s, Säume* hem; (*Naht*) seam; (*Rand*) *auch fig.* border, edge

Saumagen *m*; *nur Sg.*; *Gastr.*: *Pfälzer ~* stuffed pig's stomach

saumäßig *umg.* **I.** *Adj. verstärkend*: damned; (*schlecht*) lousy; **er hatte ~es Pech** he had lousy (*od.* dreadful) luck, he was dreadfully unlucky; **II.** *Adv.* dreadfully; **sich ~ freuen** be as pleased as punch

säumen¹ *v/t.* (*Textilstück*) hem; *fig.* line; (*umgeben*) skirt; **Tausende säumten die Straßen** thousands lined the streets

säumen² *v/i. lit.* (*warten, zögern*) tarry

säumig *Adj. geh.* late, tardy; **~er Zahler** late payer, defaulter

Säumnis *n*; *-ses, -se od. f*; *-, -se*; *geh.* dilatoriness; (*Verzug*) delay; (*Nichterfüllung*) default; **~zuschlag** *m* extra charge (for late payment), late payment charge

Saum|pfad *m* mule track, bridle path; **~pferd** *n* packhorse

saumselig *Adj.* slow, sluggish; (*trödelnd*) dawdling; (*hinausschiebend*) dilatory *geh.*; (*nachlässig*) negligent; (*lässig*) slack

Saumtier *n* pack animal

Sauna f; -, -s od. Saunen sauna, Finnish bath; **in die ~ gehen** have (od. take) a sauna; **~besuch** m going to the sauna; **~besucher** m, **~besucherin** f sauna-goer, sauna-user; **~gänger** m, **~gängerin** f sauna-goer, sauna-user; **~ofen** m sauna stove

saunen, saunieren v/i. have (od. take) a sauna, sauna

Saupreuß(e) m südd. pej. blasted North German; ursprünglich in Bayern: etwa Prussian swine

Säure f; -, -n 1. nur Sg.; sourness; auch Med. im Magen: acidity; **der Wein hat viel/wenig ~** the wine has a high/low acidity; 2. Chem. acid; **~ liebende Pflanzen** acid-loving plants

säurearm Adj. low-acidity nur attrib.; low in acid nur präd.

Säure|attentäter m, **~attentäterin** f acid thrower; **~bad** n acid bath

säurebeständig Adj. acid-proof, acid-resistant

Säureblocker m; -s, -; Pharm. antacid

säure|fest Adj. acid-proof, acid-resistant; **~frei** Adj. non-acid

Säure|gehalt m, **~grad** m acidity, acid content

Sauregurkenzeit f umg. off season; Presse: silly season

säure|haltig Adj. acid, acidic; **~liebend** → Säure 2

Säuremantel m der Haut: acid layer

säurereduziert Adj. acid-reduced nur attrib.

Saures n: **gib ihm ~!** umg. let him have it!, sock it to him!

Saurier m; -s, -; Zool. dinosaur; saurian

...saurier m, im Subst.: **Flug~** pterosaur; **Raub~** predatory dinosaur

Saurierzeit f age of the dinosaur

Saus m: **in ~ und Braus leben** live on (od. off) the fat of the land

Sause f; -, -n; umg. (Zechtour) pub crawl, Am. bar-hopping; (Trinkgelage) booze-up, binge, bender; **e-e ~ machen in der Kneipe:** go on a pub crawl, Am. go bar-hopping; (ausgelassen feiern) have a booze-up

säuseln I. v/i. Blätter: rustle; Wind: murmur, whisper; **II.** v/t. Person: murmur

sausen v/i. 1. (hat gesaust) Wind: whistle; stärker: howl; **e-n ~ lassen** vulg. blow off, let off (a fart); 2. (ist) (sich schnell bewegen) rush, whizz, Am. whiz umg.; Geschoss etc.: whistle, whizz, Am. whiz umg.; **um die Ecke ~** tear (a)round the corner; 3. (ist) **durch e-e Prüfung ~** umg. fail allg. (od. bes. Am. flunk) an exam; 4. **~ lassen** umg. (Gelegenheit) pass up; (Vorhaben) give s.th. a miss, Am. pass on s.th.; (Person) drop; **lass den blöden Typ doch ~!** give the silly fool the brushoff, Am. blow the sucker off

Saustall m; nur Sg.; umg. pigsty, Am. auch pigpen; (Unordnung) absolute mess, a (bloody) shambles

sauteuer Adj. umg. dreadfully expensive

sautieren [zo'tiːrən] v/t. Gastr. sauté

Sauwetter n umg. lousy (Brit. auch bloody awful) weather

sauwohl Adv. umg.: **ich fühle mich ~** I feel really great

Sauwut f Sl.: **e-e ~ (im Bauch) haben** be absolutely fuming, be seething with rage, Am. be ballistic

Savanne f; -, -n; Geog. savanna(h)

...savanne f, im Subst.: **Feucht~** wet savanna(h)

Saxophon n; -s, -e; Mus. saxophone

...saxophon n, im Subst. Mus.: **Alt~** alto saxophone; **Tenor~** tenor saxophone

Saxophonist m; -en, -en, **~in** f; -, -nen, **Saxophonspieler** m, **Saxophonspielerin** f Mus. saxophonist, sax(ophone) player

S-Bahn f 1. suburban train; 2. (System) suburban railway (Am. rail service); **S-Bahnhof** m → **S-Bahn-Station**; **S-Bahn-Station** f suburban railway (Am. rail od. train) station; **S-Bahn-Zug** m suburban train

SB|-Laden m 1. self-service shop (Am. store); 2. → **SB-Markt**, **~-Markt** m (small) supermarket

s. Br. Abk. (südlicher Breite): **30° s. Br.** 30° S (latitude)

SB-Tankstelle f self-service petrol (Am. gas) station

Scampi ['skampi] Pl. Gastr. scampi

scannen ['skɛnən] v/t. Computer etc.: scan; **Scanner** ['skɛɐ] m; -s, - scanner; **Scanner-Kasse** f scanner till (Am. checkout)

Scene [siːn] f; -, -s; Sl. scene; **in der ~** among those in the know

sch Interj. ssh!, shush!

Schabe f; -, -n; Zool. cockroach, Am. auch roach; **Deutsche ~** German cockroach (Am. auch crotonbug)

Schabefleisch n Gastr. minced meat, Am. ground meat; Rindfleisch: hamburger

Schabeisen n scraper, shaver

schaben v/t./i. scrape (auch Tech.); auf Reibeisen: grate, rasp; (kratzen) scratch; (Felle) shave; **das Eis von der Scheibe ~** scrape the ice off the windscreen (Am. windshield)

Schaber m; -s, -; Mot. scraper

Schabernack m; -s, kein Pl. practical joke, prank(s Pl.); **~ treiben** play pranks, get up to nonsense

schäbig I. Adj. 1. (abgenutzt) shabby, tatty; (armselig) wretched, miserable; (verkommen) sleazy; **e-e ~e Ausrede** a shabby (od. poor) excuse; 2. (geizig) mean, stingy; (gemein) mean, rotten, nasty; (gering) Trinkgeld etc.: stingy, pathetic umg.; **sich richtig ~ vorkommen** feel really mean; **II.** Adv.: **~ gekleidet** shabbily dressed; **sich ausgesprochen ~ verhalten** behave in a really mean way; **Schäbigkeit** f shabbiness; des Verhaltens: meanness, nastiness

Schabkunst f nur Sg.; Kunst mezzotint

Schablone f; -, -n beim Malen: stencil; Tech. template; fig. beim Reden und Denken: cliché; beim Denken, Handeln: stereotype, set pattern; beim Arbeiten: auch fixed routine; **Buchstaben etc. mit e-r ~ auftragen** stencil lettering etc.; **j-n in e-e ~ pressen** fig. stereotype s.o.

Schablonendenken n thinking in clichés, stereotyped thinking

schablonen|haft, ~mäßig I. Adj. stereotyped; Bemerkung etc.: clichéd; (mechanisch) mechanical; nur attr. routine; **II.** Adv. ausgeführt etc.: mechanically, following a fixed routine; denken, reden: in clichés

schablonisieren v/t. fig. pej. stereotype

Schablonenzeichnung f stencil drawing

Schabracke f; -, -n 1. (Decke) saddlecloth, bes. Am. saddle blanket; 2. über Fenster: pelmet, Am. valance

Schabtechnik f Kunst mezzotint technique

Schach n; -s, kein Pl. 1. chess; 2. (Stellung) check; **~!** check!; **~ und matt!** checkmate!; **j-m ~ bieten** check s.o.; fig. make a stand against s.o.; **in ~ halten** hold in check (auch fig.); fig. mit der Pistole etc.: auch cover; (Kinder, Klasse) control; 3. → **Schachspiel**; **~aufgabe** f chess problem

Schachbrett n chessboard; **schachbrettartig I.** Adj. chequered, Am. checkered; **II.** Adv.: **~ angelegt** set out (od. arranged) like a chessboard

Schachbrettmuster n chequered (Am. checked od. checkerboard) pattern; **im ~** chequered, Am. checked

Schach|computer m chess computer; **~ecke** f in Zeitung: chess (problem) column

Schacher m; -s, kein Pl.; umg., pej. → **Schacherei**

Schächer m; -s, -; bibl. robber

Schacherei f; -, -en; pej. haggling, Am. hucksterism; bes. Pol. horse trading; **schachern** v/i. pej. haggle (um about, over); **~ mit** etw. trade, Am. huckster

Schach|figur f chessman, piece; fig. pawn; **~großmeister** m, **~großmeisterin** f chess grandmaster

schachmatt Adj. (check)mate; umg. fig. (erschöpft) dead beat, exhausted allg.; **~ setzen** auch fig. checkmate

Schach|meister m, **~meisterin** f chess champion; **~partie** f game of chess; **~programm** n Computer: chess software; **~spiel** n 1. (game of) chess; 2. (Brett und Figuren) chess set; **~spieler** m, **~spielerin** f chess player; **ein guter Schachspieler sein** auch be good at chess; fig. be a master tactician

Schacht m; -(e)s, Schächte shaft; Bergb. auch pit; e-s Industrieofens: stack; (Mannloch) manhole

...schacht m, im Subst.: **Lift~** lift (Am. elevator) shaft; **Bomben~** bomb bay

Schachtanlage f pit

Schachtel f; -, -n box (auch Streichholz-, Konfektschachtel etc.); aus Pappe: auch carton, cardboard box; (Schuhkarton) shoebox; für Hüte etc.: bandbox; (Zigarettenschachtel) packet, Am. pack; **alte ~** umg., pej. old bag

Schachtelhalm m Bot. horsetail

schachteln v/t. fit, nest; **eins ins andere ~** fit one thing into another

Schachtelsatz m convoluted (od. involved) sentence

schächten v/t./i. slaughter according to Jewish rites; **Schächter** m; -s, - kosher butcher

Schachtofen m Metall. shaft furnace

Schach|turnier n chess tournament; **~uhr** f chess clock; **~weltmeister** m, **~weltmeisterin** f world chess champion; **~weltmeisterschaft** f world chess championships Pl.; **~zug** m (chess) move; **geschickter ~** auch fig. clever move (od. gambit)

Schadbild n Öko. typical appearance of ecological damage

schade Adj. nur präd.: **(es ist sehr) ~** it's a (great od. real) pity, (it's) too bad; **wie ~** what a pity (od. shame); **es ist ~ drum** it's (such) a shame (od. waste); **~, dass du schon gehen musst** it's a) pity you have to go so soon; **dafür ist es/er zu ~** it's/he's too good for that; **es ist für ihn viel zu ~** it'd be wasted on him; **um das/den ist's nicht ~** it's no great loss; **es ist ~ um ihn** it's a (real) shame (with him); **dafür ist er sich zu ~** he thinks he's above that kind of thing; **er ist sich für nichts zu ~** he's not too proud for anything

Schade m → **Schaden**

Schädel m; -s, - skull (*auch umg. Hirn, Kopf*); → *auch* **Kopf, kahler ~** bald head; **e-n dicken ~ haben** *umg.* be stubborn (as a mule); **mir brummt der ~** my head is spinning (*vor Schmerz*: throbbing); *umg.*, **e-n Kater haben**: my head's going (a)round in circles; **j-m eins über den ~ geben** *umg.* hit s.o. over the head; → **einschlagen** I 2; **~(basis)bruch** m *Med.* fracture of the (base of the) skull; **~decke** f *Anat.* skullcap, calvaria *fachspr.*; **~form** f *Anat.* shape of the (*od.* a *od.* one's) skull; **~höhle** f *Anat.* cranial cavity; **~knochen** m *Anat.* cranial bone; **~lage** f *Med.* cephalic (*od.* head) presentation; **~messung** f *Med.* craniometry; **~verletzung** f *Med.* skull (*od.* head) injury

schaden v/i. (*j-m, e-r Sache*) damage, harm (*auch Ruf, Beziehung etc.*); (*schädlich sein für*) be harmful to; *bes. gesundheitlich, psychisch etc.*: have a harmful effect on; (*nachteilig sein*) *auch* be detrimental (*od.* harmful) to *förm.*; **das schadet der Gesundheit** it's bad for your health; **es schadet den Augen** this harms (*od.* is bad for) your eyes; **es schadet mehr, als dass es nützt** it does more harm than good; **es kann doch nicht(s) ~** there's no harm in it, is there?; it won't do any harm, will it?; **das schadet nichts** it doesn't do any harm; (*macht nichts*) it doesn't matter; **das schadet ihm gar nichts** (*geschieht ihm recht*) it serves him right; **es würde ihr (gar) nichts ~, wenn sie ...** it wouldn't do her any harm at all to (+ *Inf.*), it would do her good to (+ *Inf.*); **was schadet es schon, wenn ...** what does it matter if ...

Schaden m; -s, **Schäden** 1. damage (**an** + *Dat.* to); *bes. körperlich*: injury, harm; (*Gebrechen*) infirmity; (*Mangel*) defect; **j-m ~ zufügen** do s.o. harm; → *auch* **schaden**; **~ nehmen** be damaged; *Person, Gesundheit etc.*: suffer; **e-n am Knie haben** have a damaged knee; *bes. nach Unfall*: have a knee injury; **zu ~ kommen** be hurt (*od.* injured); **nicht zu ~ kommen** not come to any harm; 2. (*Beschädigung*) damage; **~ am Lack/Getriebe** damage to the paintwork/transmission; **es entstand (ein) ~ in Höhe von ...** damage amounting to ... was caused; **der Sturm richtete gewaltige Schäden an** the storm caused a tremendous amount of damage; 3. (*Verlust*) loss; *finanzieller ~* financial loss; **e-n ~ feststellen/festsetzen/regulieren** *Versicherung*: establish/assess/adjust a loss; 4. (*Nachteil*) disadvantage; **es soll dein ~ nicht sein** it won't be to your disadvantage; **wer den ~ hat, braucht für den Spott nicht zu sorgen** the laugh's always on the loser; **durch ~ wird man klug** once bitten twice shy

...schaden m, *im Subst.* 1. *gesundheitlich*: **Gelenk~** joint damage; **Haltungs~** harm to the posture; 2. (*Beschädigung, Verlust*): **Karosserie~** damage to the bodywork, body damage; **Manöver~** damage caused by (military) man|oeuvres (*Am.* -euvers)

Schadenberechnung f *Jur.* assessment of damages

Schadenersatz m compensation, in-

demnification; (*festgesetzte Geldsumme*) damages *Pl.*; **~ fordern/leisten** (*od.* **zahlen**) / **erhalten** claim/pay/recover damages; **auf ~ (ver)klagen** sue for damages; **~anspruch** m, **~forderung** f claim for damages; **~leistung** f compensation

Schaden|feststellung f determination of damage (*Verlust*: loss); **~freiheitsrabatt** m no-claim(s) bonus

Schadenfreude f malicious glee, gloating, schadenfreude; **schadenfroh I.** *Adj.* gloating; **~es Gelächter** malicious laughter, laughter at the expense of others; **II.** *Adv.* grinsen, bemerken: gloatingly, with malicious pleasure

Schaden|haftung f liability for damage; **~meldung** f claim; **~sachverständige** m, f claims adjuster

Schadens|aufnahme f recording of damage, damage report; **~begrenzung** f damage limitation; **~bilanz** f total damage (*od.* loss); **~ersatz** m → **Schadenersatz** etc.; **~fall** m case of damage (*od.* loss); *Versicherung*: claim; **~höhe** f amount of damages; **~klasse** f 1. *Autoversicherung*: insurance group; 2. *Öko.* degree of pollution; 3. *Sport (im Behindertensport)* degree of disablement; **~regulierung** f loss adjustment; **~summe** f amount of damages

Schadenversicherung f indemnity insurance

schadhaft *Adj.* (*fehlerhaft*) defective, faulty; (*beschädigt*) damaged; *Gebäude*: run-down, in disrepair; *Rohr, Leitung* (*leck*): leaking; *Zähne* (*faul*): decayed; **Schadhaftigkeit** f defective state; (*Beschädigtsein*) damaged state; *e-s Gebäudes*: state of disrepair

schädigen v/t. damage, (*Ruf, Ansehen, Funktion*) *auch* impair; (*j-n*) harm; **die Erbanlagen ~** harm the genes, do genetic damage; → *auch* **schaden**; **Schädigung** f damage (+ *Gen.* to), impairment (of), injury (to); **... führt zu schweren ~en der Leberfunktion** ... leads to seriously impaired functioning of the liver

schädlich *Adj.* harmful, injurious (+ *Dat. od. für* to); (*nachteilig*) detrimental (to); (*schlecht*) bad (for); *Stoffe, Gase etc.*: harmful, noxious; **~e Wirkung** harmful (*od.* detrimental *förm.*) effect; **es ist ~ für die Gesundheit** it's harmful to (*od.* bad for) your health, it's a health hazard; **Schädlichkeit** f harmfulness; (*Nachteiligkeit*) detrimental nature *förm.*

Schädling m; -s, -e pest; (*Pflanze*) *auch* harmful weed

...schädling m, *im Subst.*: **Garten~** garden pest; **Obst~** fruit pest

Schädlings|befall m attack by pests, (*pest*) infestation; **~bekämpfung** f pest control; **~bekämpfungsmittel** n pesticide

schadlos *Adj.*: **sich ~ halten an j-m/etw.** get compensation (*od.* recoup one's losses) from s.o. / be compensated with s.th.

Schadstoff m *Öko.* harmful (*od.* noxious) substance, pollutant; **Ausstoß chemischer ~e** emissions of chemical pollutants

schadstoffarm *Adj. Öko.* nur attr. low-emission; *auch Präd.* clean *umg.*

Schadstoff|ausstoß m *Öko.* pollutant (*od.* noxious) emission; **~bekämpfung** f pollution control

schadstoffbelastet *Adj. Öko.* polluted, pollutant-bearing (*od.* -laden);

Schadstoffbelastung f pollution level, pollutant burden

Schadstoffemission f *Öko.* pollutant (*od.* noxious) emission

schadstofffrei *Adj. Öko.* pollution-free, unpolluted

Schadstoff|konzentration f *Öko.* concentration of pollutants; **~normen** *Pl.*, **~richtlinien** *Pl.* emission standards; **~wert** m pollution level

Schadwirkung f harmful (*od.* injurious) effect

Schaf n; -(e)s, -e; *Zool.* sheep (*auch Pl.*); *umg. fig.* (*dummer Mensch*) twit; **ich ~!** fool that I am, I'm a fool; **schwarzes ~** *fig.* black sheep ([*in*] *der Familie* of the family)

...schaf n, *im Subst.*: **Haus~** domestic sheep; **Dickhorn~** bighorn (sheep)

Schafbock m *Zool.* ram

Schäfchen n 1. *Zool.* lamb; *umg. fig.* (*Dummerchen*) silly billy; **seine ~** *fig. mst hum.* (*Schützlinge*) his flock *Sg.*; **~ zählen** *fig.* count sheep; **sein(e) ~ ins Trockene bringen** *umg.* feather one's nest; 2. *Pl.* → **Schäfchenwolken**; **Schäfchenwolken** *Pl.* fleecy (*Brit. auch* cotton-wool) clouds

Schäfer m; -s, - shepherd; **~dichtung** f *Lit.* pastoral poetry; **~hund** m *Zool.* (*Hütehund*) sheepdog; **Deutscher ~** Alsatian, *bes. Am.* German shepherd (dog); **~hündin** f *Zool.* sheepdog bitch; **Deutsche ~** Alsatian bitch, *bes. Am.* German shepherd bitch

Schäferin f; -, -nen shepherdess

Schäferstündchen n (*lovers'*) tryst

Schaff n; -(e)s, -e; *südd., österr.* (*Gefäß*) tub

Schaffell n sheepskin

schaffen¹ v/t. schafft, schuf, hat geschaffen v/t. 1. (*Kunstwerk, Bedingungen, Arbeitsplätze etc.*) create (*auch erschaffen*); **sich** (*Dat.*) **Freunde/Feinde ~** make friends/enemies; **er ist zum Lehrer wie geschaffen** he's a born teacher, he's made to be a teacher; **er ist für den Posten wie geschaffen** he's perfect for the job; **im Anfang schuf Gott Himmel und Erde** *bibl.* in the beginning God created heaven and earth; 2. *Imperf. auch* schaffte; (*Ärger, Unruhe, Verdruss etc.*) cause; **j-m: ~** *auch* give s.o. s.th.; **Ordnung ~** sort things out; *bes. Pol.* establish (some sort of) order; **Linderung ~** bring relief; **Klarheit ~** clarify the situation; *bei falscher Anschuldigung*: set the record straight; **Platz für j-n ~** make room for s.o.

schaffen² **I.** v/t. 1. (*bewältigen*) manage; (*Schulaufgabe*) do; (*Prüfung*) pass; **viel ~** (manage to) get a lot done; **es ~** *umg.* make (*od.* do) it; **das wäre geschafft!** *Arbeit*: done it!, that's that!; *rechtzeitig*: made it!; **jetzt hast du's geschafft!** *iro.* (*etw. kaputt zu machen etc.*) now you've done it!; *etw. zeitlich*: **~** get s.th. done in time; *umg.*: **es nicht mehr hinaus ~** *um sich zu retten etc.*: not manage to get out any more; **er schafft es einfach nicht, pünktlich zu sein** he just can't bring himself to be punctual; **das hat noch keiner geschafft** nobody's managed that before; *anerkennend*: that was brilliant!; (*Überraschendes*) that's a new one!; *iro., Unfähigkeit*: that's unbeatable, that must be a record; **ihn schaffst du spielend** he's no match for you, you can beat him with your hands tied behind your back *umg.*; 2. (*hinbringen*) take; (*hinstellen, -legen* *etc.) auch* put; → **Hals** 3, **Weg** 2, **Welt** 2; **3. j-n ~** *umg. (erschöpfen)* take it out of s.o.; *nervlich:* get s.o. down; **4. ich habe damit nichts zu ~** I've got nothing to do with it, I wash my hands of it; **II.** *v/i.* **1.** *(tätig sein)* be active, work (hard); **2. sich zu ~ machen an** (+ *Dat.*) *e-r Sache:* busy o.s. with; *e-m Gerät etc.:* tinker about with; *unbefugt: auch* tamper with; **da macht sich j-d an Ihrem Auto zu ~** s.o. is doing something to your car; **was (zum Teufel) hast du hier zu ~?** *umg.* what (the hell) do you think you're doing here?; **ich weiß gar nicht, was ich hier zu ~ habe** I don't know what I'm doing here; **3. j-m (schwer) zu ~ machen** give s.o. a hard time; *gesundheitlich: auch* play s.o. up; **die Arbeitslosigkeit macht ihm ganz schön zu ~** unemployment has affected him deeply (*od.* is really getting him down); **III.** *vt/i. bes. Dial. (arbeiten)* work; **viel/nichts ~** do a lot of / not do any work

Schaffen *n*; *-s, kein Pl.* work(s *Pl.*); **frohes ~!** *etwa* good luck; *iro. etwa* don't work too hard

...schaffen *n, im Subst.:* **Kunst~** artistic work, (works of) art, objets d'art *geh. od. hum.;* **Film~** work(s) for the cinema, cinematic art

schaffend I. *Part. Präs.* → **schaffen¹, schaffen²; II.** *Adj.:* **der ~e Geist** the creative spirit (*od.* mind)

Schaffens|drang *m* creative urge; *(Arbeitslust)* (great) urge to be up and doing; **~kraft** *f* **1.** *(Kreativität)* creative power; **2.** *(Energie)* energy and drive; **~periode** *f* creative period; **~prozess** *m* creative process

Schaffer *m*; *-s, -* **1.** *bes. südd.* hard worker, slogger *umg.*; **2.** *Naut.* ship's cook; **Schafferei** *f*, *-, kein Pl.; bes. südd. umg.:* **diese endlose ~** this endless slogging away

Schaffleisch *n Gastr.* mutton

Schaffner *m*; *-s, -; Verk.* conductor, *im Zug: Brit. mst* guard; **Schaffnerin** *f*; *-, -nen* conductress

Schaffung *f* creation *etc.*; → **schaffen¹;** *(Gründung) auch* establishment

Schaf|garbe *f Bot.* yarrow; **~haltung** *f* keeping sheep, sheep management; **~herde** *f* flock of sheep; **~hirt** *m* shepherd; **~hirtin** *f* shepherdess; **~kopf** *m* **1.** *(Kartenspiel)* sheepshead; **2.** *umg.* → **Schafskopf; ~leder** *n* sheepskin

Schäflein *n* **1.** → **Schäfchen; 2.** *Pl. fig. e-s Pastors:* sheep, flock *Sg.*

Schafmilch *f* sheep's milk

Schafott *n*; *-(e)s, -e* scaffold

Schaf|pelz *m* → **Schafspelz, ~pferch** *m* sheepfold, sheepcote; **~schur** *f* sheepshearing

Schaf(s)käse *m* sheep's milk cheese

Schafs|kopf *m umg. fig.* blockhead, num(b)skull; **~milch** *f* sheep's milk; **~pelz** *m* sheepskin; **Wolf im ~** *fig.* wolf in sheep's clothing

Schafstall *m* sheep shed

Schaft *m*; *-(e)s, Schäfte* **1.** shaft; *e-s Gewehrs:* stock; *e-s Stiefels:* leg; *e-r Blume:* stalk; **2.** *bes. südd., schw. (Bord)* shelf; **~stiefel** *Pl.* high boots

Schaf|weide *f* sheep pasture; **~wolle** *f* sheep's wool; **~zucht** *f* sheep farming; **~züchter** *m*, **~züchterin** *f* sheep farmer

Schah *m*; *-s, -s; hist.* Shah

Schakal *m*; *-s, -e; Zool.* jackal

Schäkel *m*; *-s, -; Tech., Naut.* shackle

schäkern *v/i.* joke around; *(flirten)* flirt

schal I. *Adj. Getränk:* flat; *(abgestan-*

den) stale; *fig. (abgeschmackt)* stale; *(reizlos)* dull, boring; **~es Gefühl** empty feeling; **II.** *Adv.:* **~ schmecken** taste stale

Schal *m*; *-s, -s od. -e* **1.** scarf; **2.** *(Gardine)* curtain

Schälchen *n* (little *od.* small) bowl; *für Nachtisch etc.:* dessert bowl

Schale¹ *f*; *-, -n* **1.** *von Eiern, Nüssen, Muscheln:* shell; *von Früchten:* skin; *(Abgeschältes)* peel; *(Hülse)* husk; *Pl. (Kartoffelschalen)* peelings, *Am.* peels; *von Früchten:* parings, *Am.* peels; *Tech., am Bau:* shuttering; **Kartoffeln mit der ~ kochen/essen** cook/eat potatoes in their jackets (*Am. auch* skins); **er hat e-e raue ~** *fig.* he's a rough diamond (*Am.* diamond in the rough); **2.** *umg. fig. (gute Kleidung)* glad rags *Pl.;* **mst in ~** dressed up to the nines; **sich in ~ schmeißen** dress up, put on one's finery; **3.** *Jägerspr., vom Reh etc.: (Klaue)* hoof

Schale² *f*; *-, -n; (Gefäß)* bowl; *flache:* dish; *(Waagschale)* (scale)pan; **e-e ~ Tee** a cup of tea

schälen I. *v/t. (Obst, Kartoffeln etc.)* peel; *(Hülsenfrüchte)* shell; *(Tomate)* skin; *(Bäume)* bark; **II.** *v/refl. Bäume:* exfoliate; *Haut, Lackierung etc.:* peel (off); **ich schäle mich auf dem Rücken** my back is peeling

Schalenbau *m*, **~weise** *f Tech., bes. Flug.* monocoque (*od.* stressed-skin) construction; *Archit.* shell construction

schalen|förmig *Adj.* shell-shaped; **~los** *Adj.* without a shell; *Schnecke:* naked

Schalen|obst *n Bot.* nuts *Pl.;* indehiscent fruit *fachspr.;* **~sessel** *m* shell chair; **~sitz** *m Mot.* bucket seat; **~tier** *n Zool.* crustacean; **~e** *Pl. Gastr. etwa* shellfish; **~wild** *n Zool.* hoofed game

Schalholz *n*; *nur Sg.; Tech.* shutter(ing) (*od.* lining) boards *Pl.*

Schalk *m umg.:* **er hat den ~ im Nacken** he's always up to tricks; **ihm schaut der ~ aus den Augen** he's always got a (mischievous) twinkle in his eye; **schalkhaft I.** *Adj.* mischievous; **II.** *Adv.:* **~ lächeln** laugh mischievously; **Schalkhaftigkeit** *f* mischievousness

Schall *m*; *-(e)s, kein Pl.* sound; *von Glocken:* ringing, peal; *(Widerhall)* echo; **schneller als der ~** faster than (the speed of) sound; **Namen sind ~ und Rauch** what's in a name?

Schall|becher *m Mus.* bell; **~boden** *m Mus.* soundboard

schalldämmend *Adj.* → **schalldämpfend; Schalldämmung** *f* → **Schalldämpfung; schalldämpfend I.** *Adj.* sound-absorbing; **II.** *Adv.:* **~ wirken** act as a sound absorber; **Schalldämpfer** *m* sound absorber; *Mot.* silencer, *Am.* muffler; *an Schusswaffen:* silencer; *Mus.* → **Dämpfer** 2; **Schalldämpfung** *f* sound damping (*od.* absorption); *(Raum, Gebäude:* soundproofing, sound insulation

schalldicht *Adj.* soundproof (*auch v/t.* **~ machen**)

Schalldruck *m* sound pressure

schallen *v/i.* resound; *(laut klingen)* ring; *(dröhnen)* boom; **lautes Gelächter schallte durch den Saal** loud laughter filled the auditorium

schallend I. *Part. Präs.* → **schallen¹; II.** *Adj.* resounding; **~es Gelächter** loud laughter, peals *(spöttisch:* hoots, *Am.* rips) of laughter, guffaw; **~e Ohrfeige** resounding (*od.* good) box on

the ears; *fig.* slap in the face; **III.** *Adv.:* **~ lachen** roar with laughter

schallern *v/t. umg.:* **j-m e-e ~** clout (*od.* thump, clobber) s.o.; **e-e geschallert kriegen** get a clout (a)round the head

schallgedämpft *Adj. Waffe, Auspuff:* silenced

Schall|geschwindigkeit *f* speed of sound; **mit dreifacher ~** at three times the speed of sound; *fachspr.* Mach 3; **2isoliert** *Adj.* soundproof; **~leiter** *m Phys.* sound conductor; **~loch** *n Mus., in Instrumenten:* sound hole; *in Glockenturm:* belfry window; **~mauer** *f:* **(die) ~ (durchbrechen)** (break the) sound barrier; **~messung** *f Mil.* sound ranging; *Akustik:* sound level measurement

Schallplatte *f Mus.* record

Schallplatten|... *im Subst. siehe auch* **Platten...; ~archiv** *n* record archives *Pl.;* **~aufnahme** *f* (gramophone, *Am.* phonograph) recording; **~börse** *f* record collectors' mart; **~geschäft** *n* **1.** record shop *(bes. Am.* store); **2.** *Wirts.* record business; **~industrie** *f* recording industry; **~produktion** *f* **1.** recording; **2.** *(Verfahren)* record production, making records; **~ständer** *m* record rack; *im Geschäft: auch* (record) browser

schallschluckend *Adj.* sound-absorbing

Schallschutz *m* protection against noise

Schall|trichter *m am Lautsprecher:* cone; *Mus.* bell; **~wand** *f* baffle (board); **~welle** *f* sound wave

Schalmei *f*; *-, -en; Mus.* shawm

Schalotte *f*; *-, -n; Bot.* shallot

schalt *Imperf.* → **schelten**

Schaltanlage *f* switchgear

schaltbar *Adj. Etech.* switchable; *(steuerbar)* controllable; **leicht ~es Getriebe** easy gearchange (*Am.* gearshift)

Schalt|bild *n Etech.* circuit diagram; *Mot.* gearchange (*Am.* [gear]shift) pattern; **~brett** *n Etech.* switchboard, control panel; *Flug.* instrument panel; *Mot. auch* dashboard; **~element** *n Etech.* circuit element

schalten *vt/i.* **1.** *Tech., Etech.* switch *(auf* + *Akk.* to), turn; *mit e-m Hebel:* shift the lever(s); *(bedienen)* operate; *(steuern)* control; *(umschalten)* switch; *durch Kabelführung:* wire; *(Verbindung herstellen)* connect; **in Reihe ~** connect in series; **auf Grün** *etc.* **~** *Ampel:* turn *(od.* change to) green *etc.;* → **anschalten, ausschalten; 2.** *Mot., Fahrrad:* change *(Am.* shift) gear; *(Gang)* change, *(Am.* shift; *(anlassen)* start; *(Hebel)* shift; *(Kupplung)* engage; *(ausschalten)* disengage; **du musst mehr ~** you must change gear *(Am.* have to shift) more often; **3.** *TV, Radio:* **aufs nächste Programm ~** switch (*od.* change) over to the next program(me) *(TV* channel); **~ zu** *(Korrespondenten etc.)* switch *(od.* go) over to; **automatisch auf Stand-by ~** automatically switch to (*od.* go onto) standby; **4.** *umg. fig. (begreifen)* get the picture, catch on, click; **ich hab zu langsam od. spät geschaltet** I was too slow (on the uptake), I didn't react quick(ly) enough; **5.** *(handeln)* act; **frei ~ und walten können** be able to do as one likes (*od.* pleases); **6.** *(zusätzlich einfügen)* fit in; **e-e Anzeige ~** insert an advertisement

Schalter¹ *m*; *-s, -; Etech., Tech., Mot.* switch; *Etech. zum Ausschalten:* circuit breaker, cutout

Schalter² *m*; *-s, -* *Post®, Bank etc.*: counter; *Flughafen:* desk; *Eisenb.* ticket window; **~beamte** *m, f* counter clerk; man (*weiblich:* lady) at the counter; *Eisenb.* booking clerk, *Am.* ticket agent; **~dienst** *m* counter duty; **~halle** *f* (main) hall; **~öffnungszeit** *f* counter times *Pl.*; **~raum** *m* ticket office; **~schluss** *m* closing time; **~ ist um drei** banks close (*od.* the bank closes) at three; **~stunden** *Pl.* business hours; *e-r Bank:* banking hours

Schalt|getriebe *n* *Mot.* manual gearbox (*bes. Am.* transmission); **~hebel** *m* *Mot.* gear lever, *Am. auch* gearshift (lever); *Tech., Flug.* control lever; *Etech.* switch lever; **an den ~n der Macht sitzen** *fig.* hold the reins of power, be sitting at the controls

Schaltjahr *n* leap year

Schalt|kasten *m* *Etech. etc.* switchbox, control box (*od.* unit); **~knüppel** *m* *Mot.* gear lever, *Am. auch* gearshift (lever); **~kreis** *m* *Etech.* circuit; **~plan** *m* circuit diagram; **~pult** *n* control desk (*od.* panel), (control) console

Schalt|stelle *f* *Pol.* powerhouse; **~tafel** *f* → **Schaltbrett**

Schalttag *m* leap day

Schaltuhr *f* *Tech.* timer

Schaltung *f* 1. *Mot. als Bauteil:* gearchange (*Am.* gearshift) mechanism; *am Fahrrad:* change-speed mechanism, gears *Pl.*; *als Vorgang:* gear change, gearshift; 2. *Etech.* circuit; (*Schaltungsaufbau*) circuitry; (*Verbindung*) connection(s *Pl.*); (*Verdrahtung*) wiring; **integrierte ~** integrated circuit

Schaltzentrale *f* control cent|re (*Am.* -er); *fig.* nerve cent|re (*Am.* -er); *Pol.* powerhouse

Schalung *f* *Archit. für Betonierung:* shuttering

Schaluppe *f*; *-, -n*; *Naut.* sloop

Schalwild *n* *Zool.* hoofed game

Scham *f*; *-, kein Pl.* 1. shame; **keine ~ haben** have no (sense of) shame; **nur keine falsche ~!** no need to pretend you're shy; *beim Essen etc.:* no need to hold back; **vor ~ erröten** blush (*od.* go red) with shame; 2. *Anat.* genitals *Pl.*, private parts *Pl.*; *bes. Frau:* pudenda *Pl.*, *Anat.* vulva

Schamane *m*; *-n, -n* shaman; **Schamanismus** *m*; *-, kein Pl.* shamanism; **schamanistisch** *Adj.* shamanistic

Scham|behaarung *f* pubic hair; **~bein** *n* *Anat.* pubic bone

schämen *v/refl.* be (*od.* feel) ashamed (of o.s.); **sich wegen** *od.* **für etw. ~** be ashamed of (having done) s.th.; *du solltest dich (was) ~!* you ought to be ashamed of yourself; *schäm dich!, schämt euch!* shame on you!; *schämst du dich denn gar nicht?* have you no shame?; *er schämt sich nicht zu* (+ *Inf.*) he's not ashamed to (+ *Inf.*), he has no qualms about (+ *Ger.*)

Scham|frist *f* period of grace, grace period; **~gefühl** *n* sense of shame; *körperliches:* (sense of) modesty; *j-s ~ verletzen* offend s.o.'s sense of decency; **~gegend** *f* pubic region; **~grenze** *f* limit of decency; *hart an der ~* almost indecent; *Witz etc.:* close (*od.* near) to the bone; **~haare** *Pl.* pubic hair *Sg.*

schamhaft I. *Adj.* bashful; *Mädchen: auch* blushing; (*prüde*) prudish; II. *Adv.:* **~ erröten** blush modestly; **~**

den Blick senken *od.* **die Augen niederschlagen** look bashfully at the ground; **Schamhaftigkeit** *f* bashfulness; (*Prüderie*) prudishness

Scham|hügel *m* *Anat. der Frau:* mons veneris; *des Mannes:* mons pubis; **~lippen** *Pl. Anat.* labia, lips of the vulva

schamlos I. *Adj.* shameless; (*unsittlich*) indecent; *Beleidigung etc.:* brazen; *Lüge: auch* barefaced; *Kleidung:* immodest; II. *Adv.:* **er kann ~ lügen** he can lie shamelessly; **sich ~ kleiden** dress shamelessly; **Schamlosigkeit** *f* shamelessness; (*Unsittlichkeit*) indecency; *der Kleidung:* immodesty; (*Handlung*) shameless (*od.* indecent) act

Schamott¹ *m*; *-s, kein Pl.*; *umg.* junk

Schamott² *m*; *-s, kein Pl.*; *österr.*, **Schamotte** [ʃaˈmɔt] *f*; *-, kein Pl. Baumaterial:* fireclay

Schamotte|stein *m*, **~ziegel** *m* fire brick

Schampon *n*; *-s, -s*, **schamponieren** *v/t.* shampoo

Schampus *m*; *-, kein Pl.*; *umg.* champers, bubbly

schamrot *Adj.* red with shame (*od.* embarrassment), *Am.* red as a beet; **Schamröte** *f*: **die ~ stieg ihm ins Gesicht** he blushed with shame (*od.* embarrassment)

Schamteile *Pl.* genitals, private parts

schamvoll *Adj.* bashful

Schande *f*; *-, kein Pl.* disgrace; (*Unehre*) *auch* shame; (*öffentliches Ärgernis*) scandal; *j-m/etw. ~ machen* be a disgrace to s.o./s.th.; **bring shame on** s.o./s.th.; *er ist e-e ~ für s-e Familie / s-n Berufsstand* he is a disgrace (*od.* discredit) to his family/profession; *mach uns keine ~!* *umg.* try not to disgrace us (*od.* let us down); *zu m-r ~ muss ich gestehen* to my shame I have to admit, I'm ashamed to admit; *ach du ~!* *umg.* oh heck (*od.* hell)!

schänden *v/t.* 1. (*entweihen*) desecrate, defile; *ein Grab / e-e Leiche ~* desecrate a grave / violate a corpse; 2. (*Ansehen etc.*) disgrace, dishono(u)r, bring shame upon; 3. *altm.* (*sexuell missbrauchen*) violate, abuse; **Schänder** *m*; *-, -*, **Schänderin** *f*; *-, -nen* 1. (*Entweiher*) desecrator; 2. *des Ansehens etc.:* bringer of shame (*od.* dishono[u]r) (+ *Gen.* upon); 3. *altm. sexuell:* violator, rapist

Schandfleck *m* stain, blot; (*scheußlicher Anblick*) eyesore; (*Gebäude*) (architectural) eyesore, carbuncle; *ein ~ in der Landschaft* a blot on the landscape

schändlich I. *Adj.* shameful, disgraceful; (*schmachvoll*) ignominious; *Lüge etc.:* scandalous; *umg.* (*unerhört, sehr schlecht*) disgraceful; *in e-m ~en Zustand* in a disgraceful state; *ein ~er Lohn* a pittance (of a wage); II. *Adv.:* **~ lügen** come out with scandalous lies; *j-n ~ behandeln* treat s.o. disgracefully; **Schändlichkeit** *f* shamefulness, disgraceful nature; (*Tat*) disgraceful act

Schand|maul *n* 1. wicked (*od.* malicious) tongue; 2. (*Person*) wicked (*od.* malicious) gossip, slanderer; **~tat** *f* foul (*od.* contemptible) deed; *zu jeder ~ od. allen ~en bereit sein* *umg.* be good for a lark

Schändung *f* 1. (*Entweihung*) desecration, defilement (+ *Gen.* of); 2. *der Ehre etc.:* disgrace (+ *Gen.* to); 3. *altm. sexuelle:* abuse, violation (+ *Gen.* of)

Schank|betrieb *m* bar, *Brit. auch* public house; **~bier** *n* draught (*Am.* draft) beer

Schänke *f* → **Schenke**

Schanker *m*; *-s, -*; *Med.:* **harter/weicher ~** hard/soft chancre

Schank|erlaubnis *f* licence (to sell alcoholic drinks), *Am.* liquor license; **~raum** *m*, **~stube** *f* (public) bar; **~tisch** *m* bar; **~wirt** *m* barkeeper, *Brit. auch* publican

Schanze *f*; *-, -n* 1. *Sport* (*Sprungschanze*) ski jump; 2. *Mil.* entrenchment

Schanzen|rekord *m* *Sport* hill record; **~tisch** *m* *Skispringen:* take-off area

Schar *f*; *-, -en*; (*Menschenmenge*) (great) crowd, swarms *Pl.* (of people); *von Vögeln:* flock; *von Rebhühnern:* covey; *von Mädchen, Rehen, Lerchen:* bevy; *von Ameisen:* army; *von Engeln:* host; *in* (*hellen*) **~en** in droves; → **Pflugschar**

Schäre *f*; *-, -n*; *Geog.* skerry

scharen I. *v/t.:* **um sich ~** rally ([a]round one); *es gelang ihm, viele Gleichgesinnte um sich zu ~* he succeeded in gathering many like-minded people around him; II. *v/refl.* assemble, rally; **sich ~ um** crowd (a)round; (*j-n*) rally (a)round

scharenweise *Adv.* in droves *etc.*; → **Schar**, **die Schiffbrüchigen sind ~ ertrunken** of those shipwrecked a great number were drowned

scharf I. *Adj.* 1. *Messer etc.:* sharp (*auch fig.*); **~e Zunge** sharp tongue; 2. *Essen:* hot, spicy, highly seasoned; *Essig, Senf, Käse:* strong; *Geruch:* acrid, pungent; *Säure:* caustic; *Paprika, Pfeffer:* hot; *Alkohol:* strong; (*brennend*) sharp; *Waschmittel:* aggressive; **~e Saucen** picante sauces; **~e Sachen** *umg.* the hard stuff *Sg.*; *das ist vielleicht ein ~es Zeug* *umg.* it really burns your throat; 3. *Sinnesorgan etc.:* sharp; **~es Auge**, **~er Blick** sharp (*od.* keen) eye(s), keen eyesight; **~es Gehör** sharp ears, keen sense of hearing; **~er Verstand** keen (*od.* incisive) mind; 4. *Kritik, Zurechtweisung etc.:* harsh, severe; (*heftig*) hard; **~er Kritiker** severe critic; **~er Protest** fierce (*od.* sharp *od.* vehement) protest; **~er Widerstand** severe (*od.* stiff) opposition; *in ~em Ton* in a sharp tone; 5. (*durchdringend*) *Ton:* piercing, shrill; **~er Wind** biting (*od.* cutting) wind; *die Luft ist ~* there's a nip (*od.* bite) in the air; 6. (*hart, stark, aggressiv*) *Gegensatz:* stark; *ein ~er Gegner von ...* a sworn enemy of ...; **~e Konkurrenz** stiff competition; **~e Maßnahmen** strict (*od.* stringent) measures; *e-e ~e Satire über ...* a pungent satire on ...; *ein ~er Hund* an attack dog (*trained to attack intruders etc.*); *umg. fig.* hard taskmaster; *e-n Hund ~ machen* train a dog to attack people; *sie ist e-e ~e Prüferin* *umg.* she's a demanding (*od.* tough) examiner; 7. (*deutlich*) sharp, clear; **~e Gesichtszüge** sharp (*od.* clear-cut) features; *das Bild ist nicht ganz ~* the picture isn't quite sharp (*od.* is slightly blurred); *e-e schärfere Brille brauchen* need stronger spectacles; → *auch* **gestochen** III; 8. (*jäh, abrupt*) abrupt, sharp; **~e Kurve** sharp bend; **~e Kurven** *umg. fig.* a sensational figure *Sg.*; 9. (*schnell*) fast; **~er Ritt** hard ride; **~es Tempo** fast (*od.* sharp) pace; **~er Schuss** *Sport* powerful shot; 10. *umg.* (*versessen*) *auf j-n/etw.* **sein** be keen on (*Am.* eager about) s.o./s.th.; *stärker*: be wild about s.o./s.th.; ***ganz ~ darauf sein zu*** (+ *Inf.*) *umg.* be dead keen on (*Am.* wild about) (+ *Ger.*), be dead keen to (*Am.* dying to) (+ *Inf.*); **11.** *umg.* (*geil*) *bes. Brit.* randy, horny *Sl.*; **~ *wie Nachbars Lumpi*** as randy (*Am.* horny) as a dog on (*Am.* in) heat; ***~e Wäsche*** sexy underwear; ***j-n ~ machen*** turn s.o. on; **12.** *umg.* (*toll*) great, cool; ***das ist ja ~*** that's really (*Am.* real) cool; **13.** *Ling.* ***ein ~es „S"*** a German ß character; **14.** *Munition*: live; ***mit ~er Munition schießen*** shoot (*od.* fire) live bullets; **II.** *Adv.* **1.** sharply *etc.*; **~ *sehen/hören*** have sharp eyes/ears; **~ *geschnitten*** *Profil etc.*: clear-cut; **~ *anbraten*** (fry to) seal; **~ *bewachen*** keep a close guard (*fig.* watch, eye) on; **~ *aufpassen*** pay close attention, keep close watch; **~ *ins Auge fassen*** fix s.o. with one's eyes, *fig.* take a close look at s.o. (*od.* *s.th.*); **~ *durchgreifen*** take tough action (***bei*** against); **~ *ablehnen*** flatly reject; **~ *verurteilen/kritisieren*** severely condemn/criticize; **~ *formuliert*** sharply (*od.* strongly) worded; **~ *nachdenken*** think hard, have a good think; **~ *schießen*** shoot with live ammunition; ***in der Diskussion wurde ~ geschossen*** *fig.* there were some sharp exchanges during the discussion; **2. ~ *würzen*** season with hot spices; ***gerne ~ essen*** like highly seasoned (*od.* very spicy) food; **3.** (*genau*) sharply, accurately; **~ *einstellen*** *Fot.* focus (accurately); ***schärfer stellen*** *Bild*: make sharper; *Radio*: tune in better (*od.* more accurately); ***mit dieser Brille sehe ich nicht ~*** I can't see clearly with these spectacles (*Am.* glasses); **4.** (*mit Wucht*) **~ *bremsen*** brake hard, slam on the brakes; **~ *anfahren*** make a racing start; **5. ~ *rechts/links fahren*** *dicht am Straßenrand*: keep well in to the right/left, hug the right-hand/left-hand kerb (*Am.* curb); *unkontrolliert*: swerve (*od.* veer) to the right/left; (*abbiegen*) turn sharp right/left; **~ *an j-m vorbeifahren*** shave past s.o.; → ***schärfen***

Scharfblick *m*; *nur Sg.* perspicacity; **scharfblickend** *Adj.* sharp-sighted; *fig.* perspicacious

Schärfe *f*; -, *kein Pl.* **1.** sharpness *etc.*; → *scharf*, *der Sinne, des Verstands*: keenness, acuity; *e-s Arguments*: stridency; ***in aller ~*** in all strictness; ***e-r Kritik etc. ~ verleihen / die ~ nehmen*** make a criticism *etc.* harsh / rid a criticism *etc.* of its harsh tone; **2.** *von Essen*: spiciness, strong seasoning; *von Senf, Käse*: strength; *von Gewürz etc.*: hotness; **3.** *Opt.* definition, sharpness; ***e-m Bild mehr ~ geben*** make a picture sharper, sharpen a picture

Scharfeinstellung *f* focus(s)ing; (*Vorrichtung*) focus(s)ing control

schärfen I. *v/t.* sharpen (*auch fig.*); **II.** *v/refl.* *Blick etc.*: sharpen, become keener (*od.* more acute)

Schärfentiefe *f Fot.* depth of field (*od.* focus)

scharfkantig *Adj.* sharp-edged

scharf machen → *scharf* I 6, 11

Scharfmacher *m Pol. umg.* agitator, rabble-rouser, *Pl. Brit. auch* ginger group *Sg.*

Scharf|richter *m* executioner; **~schießen** *n Mil.* live shooting; **~schütze** *m* marksman; *Mil.* sniper; *fig. Fußball etc.*: sharpshooter

scharfsichtig *Adj.* sharp-sighted; *fig.*

perspicacious *förm.*

Scharfsinn *m*; *nur Sg.* astuteness, shrewdness; *bes. Pol., Wirts.* acumen; **scharfsinnig I.** *Adj.* astute, shrewd; *Analyse, Beobachtung etc.*: acute; *Bemerkung, Kritik etc.*: incisive; **II.** *Adv.*: **~ *beurteilen/bemerken*** make an astute (*od.* shrewd) judg(e)ment / remark shrewdly

scharfzüngig *Adj.* sharp-tongued; **Scharfzüngigkeit** *f* sharp tongue; (*Art*) sharp-tongued manner

Scharia [ʃaˈriːa] *f*; -, *kein Pl.*; *Reli.* sharia

Scharlach *m, n*; -s, *kein Pl.* **1.** (*Farbe*) scarlet; **2.** *nur m*; *Med.* scarlet fever; **scharlachrot** *Adj.* scarlet

Scharlatan *m*; -s, -e charlatan, fraud; (*Arzt*) charlatan, quack *umg.*; **Scharlatanerie** *f*; -, -n charlatanism; *ärztlich*: quackery; (*Handlung*) (piece of) charlatanism (*od.* *ärztlich*: quackery)

Scharmützel *n*; -s, -; *Mil. und fig.* skirmish

Scharnier *n*; -s, -e hinge; **~gelenk** *n* hinge joint

Schärpe *f*; -, -n sash

scharren *vt/i.* scrape (***mit den Füßen*** one's feet); scratch (*auch Huhn, Hund etc.*); *Pferd*: paw (at the ground); → *auch* **verscharren**

Scharte *f*; -, -n **1.** (*Kerbe*) notch, nick; → *Schießscharte, Hasenscharte*; ***e-e ~ auswetzen*** *fig.* make amends; **2.** *Bot.* saw wort; **schartig** *Adj.* nicked, jagged

scharwenzeln *v/i. umg.* bow and scrape *mst pej.*; ***um j-n ~*** dance attendance on s.o.

Schaschlik *n, m*; -s, -s, **~spieß** *m Gastr.* kebab

schassen *v/t. umg.* kick (*od.* boot) out

Schatten *m*; -s, - **1.** (*kühlender ~, Dunkel*) shade; ***sich in den ~ setzen*** sit in the shade; **~ *spenden*** give (plenty of) shade; **~ *spendend*** shady; ***im ~ stehen*** *auch fig.* be in the shade; ***in den ~ stellen*** put in(to) the shade; *fig. auch* outshine, eclipse, overshadow; (*Erwartungen*) exceed; ***ein ~ flog über sein Gesicht*** *fig.* his face darkened; **2.** (*Bild*) shadow; ***e-n ~ werfen*** cast a shadow (***auf*** + *Akk.* on) (*auch fig.*); ***die ~ werden länger/kürzer*** the shadows are lengthening / growing shorter; ***große Ereignisse werfen ihre ~ voraus*** *fig.* great events cast their shadows before; ***nicht der ~ e-s Verdachts*** not the slightest (cause for) suspicion; ***in j-s ~ stehen*** live in s.o.'s shadow, be eclipsed by s.o.; ***e-m ~ nachjagen*** chase butterflies (*Am.* rainbows); ***über s-n ~ springen*** overcome o.s.; ***man kann nicht über s-n eigenen ~ springen*** a leopard never changes (*od.* can't change) its spots; ***er ist nur noch ein ~ seiner selbst*** he's a (mere) shadow of his former self; **3.** (*Umriss, unklare Gestalt*) silhouette, (shadowy) shape; **4.** *Med. auf der Lunge etc.*: shadow (*auch unter den Augen*); **5.** (*ständiger Bewacher, Begleiter*) shadow; **6.** (*Geist*) shade; ***das Reich der ~*** *Myth.* the realm of the shades, Hades; ***die ~ der Vergangenheit*** the spect|res (*Am.* -ers) (*od.* ghosts *od.* shades) of the past; **7. *Mann, hast du 'nen ~?*** *Sl.* are you (a)round the bend (*od.* barking mad)?

Schatten|bild *n* shadowgraph; **~boxen** *n* shadow-boxing; **~dasein** *n*: ***ein ~ führen*** *od.* **fristen** live in the shadows

schattenhaft *Adj.* shadowy; **~e Vorstel-**

lung vague idea

Schattenkabinett *n Pol.* shadow cabinet

schattenlos *Adj.* without shade

Schatten|morelle *f Bot.* morello cherry; **~pflanze** *f Bot.* shade-loving plant; **~reich** *n Myth.* realm of the shades

schattenreich *Adj.* shady

Schatten|riss *m* silhouette; **~seite** *f* shady side; *fig.* (*Nachteil*) downside; ***die ~n des Fortschritts*** the negative aspects (*od.* downside) of progress; **~spender** *m* source of shade; **~spiel** *n* shadow play; **~wirtschaft** *f* underground (*od.* black) economy

schattieren *v/t.* shade; **Schattierung** *f* shading; (*Farbton*) shade, hue; *fig.* (*Nuance*) shade, nuance; ***Blau in allen ~en*** every possible shade of blue; ***aller ~en*** *fig.* of all shades (and colo[u]rs)

schattig *Adj.* shady; ***~e Wälder*** shadowy woods

Schatulle *f*; -, -n casket; (*Geldschatulle*) cash box; *altm.* (*Privatschatulle e-s Herrschers*) privy purse

Schatz *m*; -es, Schätze **1.** treasure; ***e-n ~ suchen*** search for treasure; **2.** *fig. Pl.* (*Kunstschätze, persönliche Schätze etc.*) treasures; (*Reichtümer*) riches; **3.** *fig.*: ***ein ~ an Erfahrungen etc.*** a wealth of experience *etc.*; ***Gesundheit ist ein wertvoller ~*** health is a precious possession; **4.** *umg. als Kosewort*: love, darling, sweetie, *Am.* honey, hon; ***du bist ein ~!*** you're an angel (*od.* a real dear)

...schatz *m, im Subst.* **1.** *allg. im wörtl. Sinn*: treasure; ***Piraten~*** pirates' treasure; **2.** *fig.*: ***Märchen~*** treasury (*od.* collection) of fairy tales; ***Sagen~*** collection of legends

Schatzamt *n* treasury

schätzbar *Adj.* assessable; ***schwer ~*** difficult to assess

Schatzbrief *m Fin.* treasury bill

Schätzchen *n umg.* → *Schatz* 4

schätzen *v/t.* **1.** (*in etwa berechnen*) estimate; ***ein Bild ~ lassen*** have a picture valued; ***etw. auf 1000 Euro ~*** estimate s.th. at 1000 euros; ***zu hoch ~*** overestimate; ***wie alt ~ Sie ihn?*** how old would you say he is?; ***schätz mal!*** (have a) guess!; ***grob geschätzt*** at a rough guess; **2.** *umg.* (*vermuten, annehmen*) reckon, *Am.* guess; ***ich schätze, es dauert noch drei Tage*** I reckon (*od.* I'd say) it's going to take another three days; ***ich schätze, er ist bei s-r Familie*** I imagine he's (*od.* he's probably) with his family; **3.** (*achten*) think highly of, hold s.o. in high regard (*od.* esteem); (*würdigen*) appreciate; ***ich schätze ihn sehr (als Kollegen)*** I value him greatly (as a colleague); ***ich weiß es zu ~*** I can appreciate it; (*j-s Hilfe etc.*) I really appreciate it; (*den Wert e-s Objekts etc.*) I know what it's worth; ***er weiß e-n guten Tropfen zu ~*** he really appreciates (*od.* enjoys) a good wine; ***j-n ~ lernen*** come (*od.* begin) to appreciate what s.o. is worth; → *glücklich* I 2, **geschätzt** II; **4.** *Wirts., Jur.* value, assess, appraise (*auf* + *Akk.* at)

schätzenswert *Adj.* commendable

Schätzer *m*; -s, -, **~in** *f*; -, -nen valuer; *Versicherung, Steuer*: assessor

Schatz|gräber *m*; -s, -, **~gräberin** *f*; -, -nen treasure hunter (*od.* seeker)

Schatzi *n*; -s, **Schatzilein** *n*; -s; *umg.* darling, sweetie(-pie), *Am.* honey, hon

Schatz|insel *f* treasure island; **~kammer** *f* treasury, treasure vault; **~kanz-**

S

ler *m in GB*: Chancellor of the Exchequer, *Am. etwa* Federal Reserve chairman; **~meister** *m*, **~meisterin** *f* treasurer; *Schule, Universität*: bursar

Schätzpreis *m* estimate, estimated price

Schatz|suche *f* treasure hunt(ing); *auf ~ gehen* go on a treasure hunt, go treasure hunting; **~sucher** *m*, **~sucherin** *f* treasure hunter (*od.* seeker); **~truhe** *f* treasure chest

Schätzung *f* **1.** estimate; *nach m-r ... according* to my reckoning ..., I reckon that ...; **2.** (*Würdigung*) appreciation; **3.** (*Hochachtung*) estimation, esteem; **4.** *Wirts., Jur.* valuation; *Versicherung, Steuer*: assessment

schätzungsweise *Adv.* roughly; (*ich schätze*) I reckon, I would guess, I think; *~ sieben Millionen Amerikaner* an estimated seven million Americans; *es werden ~ zehn Leute kommen* there should be about ten people coming; *wann wirst du es ~ fertig haben?* when do you think (*od.* reckon) you'll have it ready?

Schätzwert *m* estimated (*Steuer*: assessed) value

Schau *f; -, -en* **1.** *nur Sg.; TV* show; **2.** (*Ausstellung*) show, exhibition; *zur ~ stellen* (put on) display, exhibit; *fig.* (*Gefühle etc.*) display, parade; (*Wissen*) *auch* show off; *etw. zur ~ tragen* make a display of s.th.; **3.** *fig.* (*Effekt*) big show; *nur zur ~* only for show (*od.* effect); *e-e ~ abziehen umg.* put on a big show; *er macht auf ~ umg.* he's just a show-off; *j-m die ~ stehlen umg.* steal the show from s.o., upstage s.o.; **~bild** *n* (*Diagramm*) diagram; (*vereinfachende Darstellung*) sketch; **~bude** *f* (show) booth; **~bühne** *f* stage

Schauder *m; -s, -* **1.** shudder; *ein ~ überkam ihn* he was gripped by a sense of horror; *erregend* horrific; **2.** *vor Kälte*: shiver; *ein ~ lief ihm den Rücken hinunter* a shiver ran down his spine

schauderhaft I. *Adj.* horrible; dreadful (*auch fig. abscheulich*); *~e Schauspieler* dreadful (*starker*: appalling) actors; **II.** *Adv. umg.* dreadfully; *sie sind ~ eingerichtet* their furnishings are appalling; *sie singt/kocht ~* her singing/cooking is terrible

schaudern *v/i.* shudder (*vor +Dat.* at); *vor Kälte*: shiver *with cold*; *mich schaudert bei dem Gedanken* I shudder at the thought; *stärker*: the thought of it sends shivers down my spine; *uns schauderte beim Anblick der Opfer* we were horrified at the sight of the victims

Schaueffekt *m* visual effect

schauen I. *v/i.* → *auch sehen, gucken, blicken; bes. südd., österr., schw.* **1.** look (*auf + Akk.* at); *fig.* (*auf Pünktlichkeit etc.*) set great store by; *in die Zeitung / auf die Uhr ~* look at the paper / the clock; **2.** *böse etc.*: look; *was schaust du so?* what's up?, why are you looking like that?; *schau nicht so!* don't make such a face!; *die hat vielleicht geschaut!* you should have seen (the look on) her face; **3.** (*nachsehen*) have a look, look and see, go and see; *~ nach* check up on; (*Blumen etc.*) look after; (*Kindern etc.*) keep an eye on; *ich muss mal wieder nach Oma ~* I must go and see if granny's OK; **4.** *Dial.* (*zusehen*): *schau, dass ...* see (to it) that; *die soll ~, dass sie's selber macht* she

can get on with it herself; **5.** *schau (mal), ... umg.* erklärend: look ..., (you) see ...; **6.** *schau, schau! od. da schau her! Dial. umg.* well, what do you know!; **7.** *umg.*: *~ wir mal* (*warten wir es ab*) let's wait and see; **II.** *v/t.*: *Fernseh ~ Dial.* watch television

Schauer *m; -s, -* **1.** (*Regen etc., auch fig.*) shower; **2.** → *Schauder; schauerartig Adj.*: *~e Regenfälle* showers, showery spells

Schauergeschichte *f auch fig.* horror story; *fig. abschreckende: auch* scare story

schauerlich I. *Adj.* **1.** (*grausig*) horrific, ghastly; (*markerschütternd*) *auch* blood-curdling; **2.** (*umg. schlecht*) horrible, terrible; **II.** *Adv. umg. intensivierend*: terribly, dreadfully; *sie gibt wieder ~ an* she's being a terrible show-off again

Schauermann *m; Pl. Schauerleute Naut.* docker, *Am.* longshoreman

Schauermärchen *n* → *Schauergeschichte*

schauern *v/i.* → *schaudern*

Schauerroman *m Lit.* Gothic novel; *fig.* → *Schauergeschichte*

Schaufel *f; -, -n* **1.** shovel; *für Kinder*: spade; (*Kehrichtschaufel*) dustpan; **2.** (*Radschaufel*) paddle; *e-s Baggers*: scoop; *e-r Turbine*: vane; **3.** *am Geweih*: palm; **~bagger** *m* bucket excavator, *Am.* backhoe; **~blatt** *n* (shovel) blade

schaufelförmig *Adj.* shovel-like

schaufeln *vt/i.* shovel; (*Loch etc.*) dig; *Schnee ~* clear the snow away

Schaufelrad *n* paddle (wheel); *e-s Baggers*: bucket wheel; *e-r Turbine*: vane wheel; **~bagger** *m* bucket excavator, *Am.* backhoe; **~dampfer** *m Naut.* paddle(-wheel) steamer

Schaufenster *n* shop (*Am.* store) window; *fig.* showcase; *im ~ mst* in the window; *~ schmücken od. gestalten* window-dress; **~auslage** *f* window display; **~bummel** *m*: *e-n ~ machen* go window-shopping; **~dekorateur** *m*, **~dekorateurin** *f* windowdresser; **~dekoration** *f* window decorations *Pl.*; **~front** *f* shop front, *Am.* storefront; **~gestaltung** *f* window-dressing (design); **~puppe** *f* dummy, *bes. Am.* mannequin; **~scheibe** *f* shop (*Am.* store) window (pane)

Schau|fliegen *n* aerobatics *Pl.* (*V. im Sg.*); **~flug** *m* air display; **~geschäft** *n* show business, show biz *umg.*; **~kampf** *m Sport* exhibition fight; **~kasten** *m* showcase

Schaukel *f; -, -n* **1.** swing; **2.** (*Wippe*) seesaw; **~bewegung** *f* rocking motion

schaukelig *Adj.* **1.** *Überfahrt*: rough; *Flug, Autofahrt etc.*: *auch* bumpy; **2.** (*wacklig*) wobbly

schaukeln I. *v/i.* **1.** (*hat geschaukelt*) swing; *im Wind*: sway; *Wiege, Schiff*: rock; *an den Ringen ~* swing on the rings; *das Schiff zum Schaukeln bringen* make the boat pitch and roll, rock the boat; **2.** (*hat*) (*wippen*) seesaw; **3.** (*ist*) *umg.* stagger, sway; **II.** *v/t.* (*hat*) **1.** swing, (*wiegen*) rock; *die alte DC 3 schaukelte uns nach Panama* the old DC3 gave us a bumpy flight to Panama; **2.** *umg. fig.* (*zustande bringen*) wangle; *das werden wir schon ~ od. Papa wird das Kind schon ~* we'll manage (*od.* fix) that somehow, we'll swing it somehow, we'll see to that (, don't you worry)

Schaukel|pferd *n* rocking horse;

~stuhl *m* rocking chair

Schaulaufen *n Sport* exhibition skating

Schaulust *f* curiosity; *pej.* sensation-seeking; **schaulustig** *Adj.* curious; **Schaulustige** *m, f; -n, -n* onlooker; *pej.* gaper, gawker, sensation-seeker, *Am.* rubberneck *umg.*; *Pl. auch* crowds of onlookers

Schaum *m; -(e)s, Schäume, mst Sg.* foam (*auch Tech., Kunststoff*); (*Gischt*) spray; *auf Bier etc.*: froth, head; (*Geifer*) froth; (*Seifenschaum*) lather; *~ schlagen fig.* talk big; *er hatte ~ vor dem Mund* he was foaming (*od.* frothing) at the mouth; **~bad** *n* foam (*od.* bubble) bath; **~beton** *m* aerated concrete; **~bildung** *f* formation of foam, foaming; *von Seife etc.*: lathering; **~blase** *f* bubble

schäumen *v/i.* foam, froth; *Getränke*: bubble; *Bier*: foam; *Seife etc.*: lather; *Pferd*: foam at the mouth; *über den Rand ~* boil over; *vor Wut ~* fume with anger; **II.** *v/t. Tech.* (*Kunststoffe etc.*) foam

Schaum|festiger *m* mousse; **~gebäck** *n* meringue(s *Pl.*)

schaum|geboren *Adj. Myth.*: *die ~e Venus* foam-born Venus, Venus Aphrogeneia; **~gebremst** *Adj.*: *~e Waschmittel* low-sudsing detergents

Schaumgummi *m* foam rubber; **~kissen** *n* foam rubber cushion; **~matratze** *f* foam rubber mattress

schaumig *Adj.* frothy (*auch Bier*); *Seife*: lathery; *See*: foaming; *~ schlagen Gastr.* beat to a froth, beat until frothy

Schaum|kamm *m von Wellen*: white crest; **~kelle** *f* → *Schaumlöffel*; **~kraut** *n Bot.* cardamine; **~krone** *f von Wellen*: white crest, whitecap; *auf Bier*: head, froth; **~löffel** *m Gastr.* skimmer; **~löscher** *m*, **~löschgerät** *n* foam (fire) extinguisher

Schaumreiniger *m* foam cleaner

Schaumschläger *m umg. fig.* big mouth, gasbag; (*Angeber*) show-off; **Schaumschlägerei** *f; nur Sg.; umg. fig.* big talk, blather; (*Unsinn*) hot air; *alles nur ~* just a load of pretentious waffle

Schaumstoff *m Tech.* (plastic) foam, polyurethane (foam); **~auflage** *f*, **~matratze** *f* foam mattress

Schaum|teppich *m Flug.* foam carpet; **~wein** *m* sparkling wine

Schaupackung *f* dummy pack

Schauplatz *m e-s Unfalls, Verbrechens*: scene; (*Veranstaltungsort*) venue; *der ~ der Ereignisse ist ...* the events are set (*od.* take place) in; *direkt vom ~ des Geschehens* straight from the scene; *vom ~ abtreten fig. Pol.* leave the stage; *euph.* (*sterben*) pass away; → *Kriegsschauplatz*

Schau|programm *n Eiskunstlauf*: gala program(me); **~prozess** *m Jur.* show trial

schaurig I. *Adj.* spine-chilling; (*unheimlich*) eerie, creepy *umg.*; *umg.* (*grässlich*) awful, dreadful; *stärker*: appalling; *er spricht ein ~es Englisch* he speaks dreadful (*od.* appalling) English; *ein ~es Wahlergebnis* a disastrous election result; **II.** *Adv. umg.*: *~ schlecht* appallingly bad; **Schaurigkeit** *f* spine-chilling nature; (*Unheimlichkeit*) eeriness, creepiness *umg.*; *umg.* (*Grässlichkeit*) awfulness, dreadfulness; **schaurig-schön** *Adj. Anblick etc.*: wonderfully spine-chilling (*od.* eerie)

Schauspiel n **1.** Theat. play; drama; **2.** fig. spectacle, sight; **~direktor** m, **~direktorin** f impresario

Schauspieler m Theat., Film actor; fig. pej. play-actor; **~beruf** m acting career, career as an actor (od. actress); (die Schauspielerei) acting

Schauspielerei f Theat., Film acting; fig. play-acting; **Schauspielerin** f Theat., Film actress; fig. pej. play-actress; **schauspielerisch** Adj. Theat., Film acting; ihre **~en Leistungen** her achievement(s) as an actress; **schauspielern** v/i. (untr., hat -ge-) **1.** umg. (bes. als Laie) act; **2.** fig., bes. pej. play-act, put on an act

Schauspiel|haus n Theat. theat|re (Am. auch -er); **~kunst** f dramatic art; **~schule** f drama school; **~schüler** m, **~schülerin** f drama student; **~truppe** f company (of actors); **~unterricht** m drama lessons (od. classes) Pl.

Schau|steller m; -s, - (fairground) showman, Am. carny; auf Messen: exhibitor; **~stellerin** f; -, -nen show-woman

Schau|stück n showpiece, exhibit; (besonderes Beispiel) perfect example, specimen; Theat. lavish stage spectacle; **~tafel** f → **Schaubild**; **~turnen** n gymnastic display; **~vitrine** f showcase, display case

Scheck m; -s, -s; Wirts. cheque, Am. check (über + Akk. for); **~s beantragen** apply for a chequebook (Am. checkbook); → **ausstellen** I 2; **~betrug** m cheque fraud, Am. kiting (checks); **~betrüger** m, **~betrügerin** f cheque (Am. check) fraudster (bouncer umg.); **~buch** n chequebook, Am. checkbook

Schecke[1] m; -n, -n (Hengst) piebald (horse); (schwarz od.braun geschecktes männliches Rind) black (od. brown) and white bull (Pl. cattle)

Schecke[2] f; -, -n (Stute) piebald mare; (schwarz od. braun gescheckte Kuh) black (od. brown) and white cow

Scheck|fälscher m, **~fälscherin** f cheque (Am. check) forger; **~formular** n cheque (Am. check) form; **~heft** n chequebook, Am. checkbook

scheckig Adj. **1.** Pferd: piebald; mit kleineren Flecken: dappled; Hund, Kuh: with white patches; Haut: blotchy; umg. pej. (bunt) brightly patterned allg.; **2.** umg.: **sich ~ lachen** laugh oneself silly

Scheck|inhaber m, **~inhaberin** f bearer (of a cheque, Am. check); **~karte** f cheque (Am. banker's, Am. check) card; credit card; **~verkehr** m cheque (Am. check) transactions Pl.; **~vordruck** m cheque (Am. check) blank

scheel I. Adj. nur attr. Blick etc.: disapproving; (missgünstig) resentful; II. Adv.: j-n ~ ansehen look askance at s.o.

Scheffel m; -s, -; hist. bushel; **sein Licht unter den ~ stellen** fig. hide one's light under a bushel; **scheffeln** v/t. umg. (Geld) rake in; **die Millionen ~** they're raking in (od. netting) millions; **scheffelweise** Adv. umg. by the sackful

Scheibchen n Käse etc.: small (od. little) slice; → **Scheibe**; **scheibchenweise** Adv. fig. little by little, bit by bit

Scheibe f; -, -n **1.** allg. disc, Am. mst disk (auch umg. Schallplatte); (Schießscheibe) target; Eishockey: puck; Tech. disc (Am. disk), plate; (Blättchen) la-

mella; (Schleif-, Töpferscheibe) wheel; (Dichtungs-, Unterlegscheibe) washer, collar; **schwarze ~n** umg. (Schallplatten) vinyl records, LPs allg.; **manche Leute glauben heute noch, die Erde sei e-e ~** some people still think the earth is flat; **2.** Brot, Wurst etc.: slice; **in ~n schneiden** cut into slices; slice; **e-e ~ Mortadella** a slice of mortadella; **von ihm kannst du dir e-e ~ abschneiden** umg. fig. you could learn a thing or two from him allg., you could take a leaf out of his book; **3.** (Glasscheibe) pane, square; **die ~n putzen** clean the windows; → **einwerfen** I 2; → **Windschutzscheibe**; **4.** **~!** umg. euph. sugar!

Scheiben|bremse f Mot. disc (Am. auch disk) brake; **2förmig** Adj. disc-shaped, Am. disk-shaped; **~gardine** f net (Am. auch sheer) curtain; **~hantel** f Sport barbell; **~heizanlage** f demister, Am. defroster; **~honig** m **1.** comb honey, honey in the comb; **2.** umg. euph. Interj. → **Scheibenkleister**; **~kleister** Interj. umg. euph. Brit. (oh) sugar!; **~schießen** n target shooting (od. practi|ce); **~waschanlage** f, **~wascher** m; -s, - Mot. windscreen (Am. windshield) washer

scheibenweise Adv. in slices

Scheibenwischer m Mot. windscreen (Am. windshield) wiper; **~blatt** n Mot. windscreen (Am. windshield) wiper blade

Scheich m; -(e)s, -s od. -e sheik(h); umg. (Freund, Liebhaber) bloke, fella; **Scheichtum** n; -s, Scheichtümer sheik(h)dom

Scheide f; -, -n **1.** Anat. vagina; **2.** (Futteral) sheath (auch Bot.); e-s Schwerts: auch scabbard; **das Schwert aus der ~ ziehen** draw one's sword

scheiden; scheidet, schied, hat od. ist geschieden I. v/t. (hat) **1.** Jur. (Eheleute) divorce; (Ehe) dissolve; **sich ~ lassen** get a divorce, get divorced (von j-m from s.o.); **er lässt sich nicht von ihr ~** he won't give her a divorce; **ihre Ehe wurde 1999 geschieden** their marriage was dissolved (od. ended) in 1999; **bis dass der Tod uns scheidet** in Ehegelöbnis: till death us do part; **2.** (trennen) separate (auch Chem.), divide; II. v/i. (ist) (auseinander gehen) part; (abreisen) depart, leave; **aus dem Dienst ~** retire from service, resign; **aus dem Leben ~** depart this life, pass away; **freiwillig aus dem Leben ~** take one's own life; **Scheiden tut weh** parting is painful; III. v/refl. separate; **hier ~ sich die Geister** od. **Meinungen** fig. opinions are divided on that; → **geschieden**

Scheidenabstrich m Med. (vaginal) smear test

scheidend I. Part. Präs. → **scheiden**; II. Adj. Amtsträger: outgoing

Scheiden|krampf m Med. vaginal spasm; **~öffnung** f Anat. vaginal entrance, vulva

Scheide|wand f partition; fig. barrier; **~weg** m: **am ~ stehen** fig. be standing at the crossroads, be faced with a crucial decision

Scheidung f **1.** Jur. e-s Ehepaares: divorce; e-r Ehe: dissolution of a marriage; **die ~ einreichen** file for divorce; **in ~ leben** be getting a divorce; **2.** (Trennung) separation

Scheidungs|anwalt m, **~anwältin** f divorce lawyer; **~grund** m grounds Pl. for divorce; **~klage** f petition for di-

vorce; **~prozess** m divorce proceedings Pl. (od. suit); **~rate** f divorce rate; **~recht** n divorce legislation; **~termin** m court date (for the divorce settlement); **~urteil** n decree of divorce; **~vertrag** m separation (od. divorce) agreement

Schein[1] m; -(e)s, kein Pl.; (Licht) light; gedämpft: glow; (Lichtstrahl) ray of light; **im letzten ~ der untergehenden Sonne** in the last rays of the setting sun; **beim ~ e-r Kerze lesen** read by the light of a candle; → **auch Glanz** 1

Schein[2] m; -(e)s, -e **1.** (Zettel) slip; (Bescheinigung) certificate; **hier braucht man für alles e-n ~** here you need a piece of paper for everything; **2.** Univ. certificate (of attendance), bes. Am. credit; → **auch Seminarschein**; **3.** (Geldschein) (bank) note, Am. bill; **in kleinen/großen ~en** in small/large denominations

Schein[3] m; -s, kein Pl.; (Anschein) appearance(s); (Aussehen) air, look; **etw. (nur) zum ~ tun** (just) pretend to do s.th.; **den ~ wahren** keep up appearances; **dem ~ nach** (**zu urteilen**) to all appearances; **der ~ trügt** appearances are deceptive, you can't always go by appearances; **alles leerer ~** it's all empty preten|ce (Am. –se); → **auch Anschein**

...schein m, im Subst. **1.** (Licht): **Kerzen~** candlelight; **2.** (Dokument): **Abhol~** receipt (for collected goods); **Bezugs~** (ration) coupon; **Entlassungs~** certificate of discharge; **3.** (Geld): **Fünfeuro~** five-euro note (Am. bill); **Hundertdollar~** hundred dollar bill

Schein|... im Subst. oft apparent, mock, sham; auch Jur. fictitious; auch Med. pseudo; **~amateur** m, **~amateurin** f Sport shamateur; **~angriff** m feint; auch fig. mock attack (auf + Akk. on); **~argument** n specious (od. spurious) argument; **~asylant** m, **~asylantin** f bogus refugee; weitS. economic refugee (od. migrant)

scheinbar I. Adj. seeming; auch Widerspruch: apparent; (vorgeblich) false, fictitious; (wahrscheinlich) likely; **nur ~es Interesse** only feigned interest; **~er Grund** ostensible purpose; II. Adv. it seems ..., seemingly; on the face of it, on its face; → **auch anscheinend**; **er schaute ~ interessiert zu** he looked on with apparent interest

Schein|beschäftigung f bogus job; **~blüte** f **1.** der Wirtschaft: illusory boom; der Kultur: false flowering; **2.** Bot. composite flower; **~ehe** f sham marriage

scheinen[1]; scheint, schien, hat geschienen v/i. shine; (glänzen) gleam; **der Mond schien nicht** there was no moon

scheinen[2]; scheint, schien, hat geschienen v/i. (den Anschein haben) seem; äußerlich: appear; **er scheint interessiert (zu sein)** he seems (od. appears) to be interested; **es scheint mir** it seems to me, I have the impression; **er scheint nicht zu wollen** od. **mir scheint, er will nicht** he doesn't seem to want to; **es scheint nur so** it only seems (od. looks) like it (od. that way), that's only an illusion; **wie es scheint** as it seems; am Satzanfang: it seems, it would seem

Schein|firma f front (od. bogus) company; **~gefecht** n fig. mock fight; **~geschäft** n bogus transaction; **~grund** m apparent reason; (*Vorwand*) pretext

scheinheilig I. *Adj.* sanctimonious; (*heuchlerisch*) hypocritical; (*arglos tuend*) innocent; **~es Lächeln** false smile; **ihr ~es Getue** *umg. pej.* her innocent act; **II.** *Adv. fragen etc.*: innocently; **~ tun** *umg.* act (*od.* play) the innocent; **Scheinheiligkeit** *f* sanctimoniousness; (*Heuchelei*) hypocrisy; (*Unaufrichtigkeit*) insincerity

Schein|heirat *f* sham marriage; **~manöver** *n* dummy man|oeuvre (*Am.* -euver); **~problem** *n* apparent problem; **~schwangerschaft** *f* false pregnancy

scheinselbstständig *Adj. etwa* nominally self-employed; **Scheinselbstständigkeit** *f etwa* nominal self-employment

Scheintod *m* suspended animation, apparent death; **scheintot** *Adj.* in a state of suspended animation, seemingly dead; **er ist ja schon ~** (*ziemlich alt*) *umg.* he's got one foot in the grave; **Scheintote** *m, f* person in a state of suspended animation

Schein|vertrag *m* bogus contract; **~welt** *f* dream world; *EDV* virtual world (*od.* reality)

Scheinwerfer *m* floodlight; *Theat.* spotlight; (*Suchscheinwerfer*) searchlight; *Mot.* headlight, headlamp; **~kegel** *m* (fan-shaped) headlight beam; **~licht** *n* spotlight; *fig.* limelight; **im ~ der Öffentlichkeit stehen** *fig.* be very much in the public eye (*od.* in the limelight)

Scheinwiderstand *m Etech.* apparent resistance (*od.* impedance)

Scheiß *m*; *kein Gen., kein Pl.*; *umg.* crap; **das ist vielleicht ein ~** what a load of crap (*od.* bullshit)!; **mach keinen ~** don't do anything so damn stupid; → *auch* **Scheißdreck, Scheiße** 2

Scheiß..., scheiß... *im Subst. und Adj. umg.* damn(ed), blasted, *Brit. auch* bloody, *Am. auch* goddam; *vulg.* fucking; **Scheißdreck** *m umg.* → **Scheiß, Scheiße** 2

Scheiße *f*; -, *kein Pl.* **1.** *vulg.* (*Kot*) shit; **2.** *Sl. pej. fig.* (*Mist*) crap, bullshit; (*Schlamassel*) bloody (*Am.* goddam) mess; (*ärgerliche Situation*) bloody (*Am.* goddam) nuisance; (*verdammte*) ~*! od.* **so e-e ~!** bloody hell!, shit! *vulg.*, fuck! *vulg.*; **in der ~ sitzen** be in a godawful mess (*od.* in the shit); **~ bauen** make a balls-up, *Am.* screw up; **der Film ist ~** the film's (*Am.* movie's) crap; → *auch* **Scheiß**

scheißegal *Adj. Sl. nur präd.*: **das ist** (*mir*) ~**!** I don't give a damn!

scheißen *vt/i.*; *scheißt, schiss, hat geschissen*; *vulg.* shit, crap; (*vor Angst*) **in die Hosen ~** get the shits; **scheiß auf ... Sl.** to hell with ...; **denen werd ich was ~** *Sl.* they can damn well get lost

Scheißer *m*; -s, -; *vulg.* → **Scheißkerl**; **kleiner ~** little bugger; **Scheißerei** *f*; -, *kein Pl.*; *vulg.* (*Durchfall*): **die ~ haben** have the shits *Pl.*

scheißfreundlich *Adj. umg.* all friendly, as friendly as could be

Scheiß|haus *n vulg.* shithouse; **~kälte** *f umg.* godawful cold; **~kerl** *m vulg.* (bloody) bastard, turd, *Am.* son of a bitch, *Am.* motherfucker; **~kram** *m umg.* blasted stuff; **~laden** *m umg.* wretched (*od.* lousy) outfit; *stärker*: shitty dump; **ein ~ ist das hier** this place is real crap; *Arbeitsplatz*: what a bloody (*od.* fucking *vulg.*) place to

work in

scheiß|liberal *Adj. umg.* airy-fairy liberal; **~vornehm** *Adj. umg.* terribly posh

Scheißwetter *n umg.* godawful weather; (**so ein**) ~**!** what dreadful weather

Scheit *n*; -(e)s, -e: **~ Holz** piece of wood; *großes*: log

Scheitel *m*; -s, - *von Frisur*: parting; **e-n ~ ziehen** make a parting; → *auch* **scheiteln**; **vom ~ bis zur Sohle** from head (*od.* top) to toe; **vom Scheitel bis zur Sohle** (**ist er**) **ein Gentleman** every inch (he's) a gentleman; → **Scheitelpunkt**; **~käppchen** *n* skullcap

scheiteln *v/t.*: **das Haar ~** make a parting (*Am.* part); **sein Haar links/rechts / in der Mitte ~** part one's hair on the left / on the right / in the middle; → **gescheitelt**

Scheitelpunkt *m Math.* vertex, apex; *Astron.* zenith; *fig.* peak, apex; **auf dem ~ s-s Ruhms** *fig.* at the height (*od.* peak) of his fame

Scheiterhaufen *m für Leichenverbrennung*: funeral pyre; **auf dem ~ verbrannt werden** *hist.* be burnt at the stake

scheitern *v/i.* fail (**an** + *Dat.* because of), come to grief; *Pläne*: *auch* come to nothing, be thwarted (**an** + *Dat.* by); *Verhandlungen*: fail, break down; *Sport auch* be defeated (**an** + *Dat.* by); *Ehe*: break down, fail; **ein gescheiterter Versuch** an unsuccessful (*od.* a failed) attempt; **er ist** (**im Leben**) **gescheitert** he's one of life's failures; **daran ist er gescheitert** that was his undoing; **~ lassen** (*Vertrag*) sink; **an der Fünfprozenthürde scheitern** fail because of the five-per-cent clause; → **gescheitert**

Scheitern *n*; -s, *kein Pl.* failure, breakdown, defeat; → **scheitern**; **zum ~ bringen** frustrate, thwart; **zum ~ verurteilt** doomed to fail(ure)

Scheitholz *n* firewood

Schekel *m*; -s, - *israelische Währung*: shekel

Schelf *m, n*; -s, -e; *Geog.* (continental) shelf; **~meer** *n* shelf sea, offshore waters *Pl.*

Schellack ['ʃɛlak] *m*; -s, -e shellac; **mit ~ behandeln** shellac

Schelle *f*; -, -n **1.** (*Glöckchen*) bell; *Mus. Pl.* sleighbells; **2.** *Tech.* clamp, clip; **3.** *Dial.* clip round the ears; **4.** **~n** *Kartenspiel*: diamonds; **schellen** *v/i.* ring (the bell); **es hat geschellt** the doorbell (just) rang, somebody rang the bell

Schellen|baum *m Mus.* Turkish crescent, pavillon chinois; **~kappe** *f* fool's (*od.* jester's) cap (and bells)

Schellfisch *m Zool.* haddock

Schelm *m*; -(e)s, -e; *altm., hum.* rogue; (*bes. Kind*) rascal; **ein ~, der Böses dabei denkt** *Sprichw.* honi soit qui mal y pense, evil to him who evil thinks

Schelmen|roman *m* picaresque novel; **~streich** *m* practical joke, prank

schelmisch I. *Adj.* roguish; *Kind*: impish; **II.** *Adv.*: **~ lachen** laugh roguishly

Schelte *f*; -, *kein Pl.* telling-off, scolding; **die große ~** a real dressing-down, major carpeting *umg.*

...schelte *f, im Subst. mst Pol.*: **Gewerkschafts~** union bashing

schelten; *schilt, schalt, hat gescholten*; *geh. v/t./i.* scold, rebuke, reprimand (**wegen** for); **j-n e-n Taugenichts ~** call s.o. a good-for-nothing

Schema *n*; -s, -ta *od.* -s *od. Schemen*; (*System*) pattern, system; (*Entwurf*) scheme, plan; (*graphische Darstellung*) diagram; **nach e-m bestimmten ~ arbeiten** work according to a fixed (*od.* set) pattern (*od.* scheme); **er lässt sich in kein ~ pressen** *od.* **passt in kein ~** he doesn't fit into any pattern; **ein Aufsatz etc. nach ~ F** *umg. pej.* an unimaginative (*od.* a matter-of-fact) essay *etc.*

...schema *n, im Subst.* **1.** *Tech. mst* ...diagram; **Schalt~** wiring (*od.* circuit) diagram; **2.** *fig.*: **Denk~** thought pattern

schematisch I. *Adj.* **1.** *Zeichnung etc.*: schematic; **2.** *Arbeit etc.*: mechanical, routine ...; **II.** *Adv.* **1.** (*als Schema*) **~ darstellen** illustrate in (*od.* by means of) a diagram, draw a diagram of; **2.** *pej* (*routinemäßig*) **~ arbeiten** *etc.* work *etc.* according to a set routine; **schematisieren** *v/t.* schematize

Schemazeichnung *f* diagram

Schemel *m*; -s, - (foot)stool

...schemel *m, im Subst.*: **Melk~** milking stool

Schemen *m, n*; -s, - **1.** silhouette, shadowy outline; (*Schatten*) shadow; **man sah sie nur als ~** you could only make out their general shape, you could only see them in outline; **2.** (*Gespenst*) spect|re (*Am.* -er); **schemenhaft I.** *Adj.* shadowy (*geisterhaft*) ghostly; **II.** *Adv.*: **sich ~ abzeichnen gegen** be outlined (*od.* silhouetted) against

Schenke *f*; -, -n bar, *Brit. auch* pub; **auf dem Lande**: inn, tavern

Schenkel *m*; -s, - **1.** (*Oberschenkel*) thigh; (*Unterschenkel*) lower leg; *Gastr. von Frosch*: leg; *von Pute*: thigh; **sich auf die ~ schlagen** slap one's thighs; **2.** *Math. e-s Winkels*: side; *e-s Zirkels*: leg, *e-r Schere*: shank, handle; *Tech.* leg, flange; **~bruch** *m Med.* fractured thigh; **~hals** *m Anat.* neck of the femur; **~knochen** *m Anat.* femur, thighbone

schenken *v/t.* **1.** a) (*zum Geschenk machen*) give (as a present); *mst als Spende*: donate; **etw. geschenkt bekommen** get s.th. (as a present); **j-m etw. zum Geburtstag etc. ~** give s.o. s.th. for his (*od.* her) birthday *etc.*; **was soll ich ihm ~?** what should I give him?; **sie ~ sich nichts zu Weihnachten** they don't give each other Christmas presents, they don't exchange gifts at Christmas; **ich möchte nichts geschenkt haben** I don't want any presents; *fig. auch* I don't want any special treatment; **das möchte ich nicht geschenkt haben** I wouldn't take that as a gift, I wouldn't take it if you paid me for it, b) *fig. in Wendungen*: **sie hat ihm vier Kinder geschenkt** she provided him with (*od.* bore him) four children; **e-m Tier die Freiheit ~** set an animal free; **ihm ist nichts geschenkt worden** he's had to fight for everything he's got; **das ist ja** (**fast**) **geschenkt!** *umg.* it's a snip (*od.* giveaway), *Am.* it's a steal; **geschenkt!** *umg.* forget it!; **2. sich** (*Dat.*) **etw. ~** *umg. fig.* (*weglassen*) skip s.th., give s.th. a miss; **dein Mitleid kannst du dir ~** you can keep your sympathy, I don't need your sympathy; **er schenkt sich nichts** he doesn't make life easy for himself, he's hard on himself; **sie schenkten sich nichts** *Rivalen etc.*: they went at it hammer and tongs, they had a real go at each other; →

Aufmerksamkeit 1, *Gehör* 2, *Glaube* 1, *Leben* 1, *Vertrauen etc.*

Schenkung *f Jur.* gift; (*Spende*) donation (*an + Akk.* to); *e-e ~ machen* present a gift, make a donation

Schenkungs|steuer *f* capital transfer tax, gift tax; *~urkunde* *f* deed of gift (*od.* donation)

scheppern *v/i. umg.* rattle, clatter; *da hat's gescheppert umg., Autounfall:* there's been a bit of a smash there; *beim Erzählen:* then there was a crash; *jetzt hat's gescheppert Streit:* he's (*od.* she's) copped (*Am.* getting) it now

Scherbe *f; -, -n* **1.** shard, piece (of broken glass *etc.*); *Pl. auch* broken glass *Sg.* (*od.* pottery *etc. Sg.*); *in ~n schlagen* smash (to pieces); *in ~n gehen* get broken; *fig. Ehe etc.:* break up; *die ~n zusammenkehren* sweep up the shards (*od.* broken pieces); *fig.* pick up the pieces; *~n bringen Glück Sprichw.* break a thing, mend your luck; **2.** *Archäol.* potsherd

Scherben|gericht *n* ostracism; *~haufen* *m* pile of broken glass *etc.; fig. e-r Politik:* shattered remains *Pl.; mein Leben ist ein ~* my life is in ruins

Scherblatt *n* shaving blade

Schere *f; -, -n* **1.** (*e-e*) *~* (a pair of) scissors *Pl.;* (*Gartenschere*) shears *Pl.; der ~ zum Opfer fallen fig.* be cut out; *Projekt etc.:* get the chop; **2.** *Zool. e-s Krebses etc.:* claw, pincer; **3.** *Ringen, Turnen:* scissors *Pl.; Fußball:* scissors kick; **4.** *fig: die ~ zwischen Einnahmen und Ausgaben* the gap between income and expenditure

...schere *f, im Subst.* **1.** (*Werkzeug*): *Rosen~* secateurs *Pl.; Stoff~* dressmaker's scissors *Pl.; Schaf~* sheep shears; **2.** *fig.: Lohn~* wage differential

scheren[1] *schert, schor, hat geschoren v/t.* (*Schaf*) shear; (*Pudel*) clip; (*stutzen*) trim; (*Haare*) crop, cut; (*Hecke, Rasen*) cut; (*Strauch*) prune; *j-m den Kopf ~* shave s.o.'s head

scheren[2] *umg.* **I.** *v/t. das schert mich nicht* that doesn't worry me *allg.; was schert mich das?* what do I care?, so what?; **II.** *v/refl.* **1.** (*kümmern*) *sich nicht um etw. ~* not care about s.th.; (*nicht beachten*) (completely) ignore s.th.; *er schert sich e-n Dreck darum* he doesn't give a damn (about it); **2.** *sich ~* clear off, beat it; *scher dich zum Teufel!* go to hell!; *scher dich in dein Zimmer!* off to your room with you!

scherenartig *Adj.* scissors-like

Scheren|gitter *n Tech.* folding (*od.* concertina) grille; *~schleifer* *m,* *~schleiferin* *f* knife grinder; *~schnitt* *m Kunst* silhouette, cut-out; *~sprung* *m Turnen:* scissors jump; *~zaun* *m* diamond trellis fence

Schererei *f; -, -en, mst Pl.; umg. auch Pl.* trouble, hassle, *Brit.* aggro; *j-m viel ~en machen* give s.o. no end of trouble; *es gab wieder ~en* there were the usual hassles

Scherflein *n* mite; *sein ~ beisteuern* give one's little contribution; *fig.* do one's bit

Scherge *m; -n, -n* henchman

Scher|kopf *m* shaving head; *~maschine* *f* shearing machine; *~maus* *f Zool.* **1.** water vole; **2.** *österr., schw.* (*Maulwurf*) mole; *~messer* *n* shearing knife (*Klinge:* blade)

Scherung *f* **1.** *Tech.* shear; **2.** *Math.* shearing

Scherz *m; -es, -e* joke; *bes. mit Worten:* jest; *sich* (*Dat.*) *mit j-m e-n ~ erlauben* play a joke on s.o.; (*s-e*) *~e treiben mit* make fun of; *im ~ od. zum ~* for fun, as a joke, in joke (*od.* jest); *~ beiseite* joking apart (*od.* aside), (now) seriously; (*ganz*) *ohne ~ umg.* I'm not kidding, I kid you not *hum.; ich mache keine ~e drohend:* I'm not joking; *~artikel* *m* joke (article); *~bold* *m; -(e)s, -e; umg.* joker

scherzen *v/i.* **1.** joke, make jokes (*über +Akk.* about); *Sie ~! od. Sie belieben zu ~ hum.* you're joking, of course; *damit ist nicht zu ~* it's not to be taken lightly; *mir ist nicht nach Scherzen zumute* I'm not in a mood for joking; **2.** *mit j-m ~* (*schäkern*) fool about with s.o.

Scherzfrage *f* riddle, conundrum

scherzhaft *Adj.* jocular, facetious; (*humorvoll*) humorous; (*komisch*) funny

Scherzkeks *m umg.* joker

Scherzo ['skɛrtso] *n; -s, -s od. Scherzi; Mus.* scherzo

Scherzwort *n; Pl. -e* witticism, bon mot

scheu *Adj.* shy; (*ängstlich*) timid; (*schüchtern*) bashful; (*zurückhaltend*) reserved; (*spröde, zimperlich*) *Frau, Mädchen:* coy; *~ machen* startle, frighten; *~ werden Wild:* take fright; *Pferd:* shy (*durch* at)

Scheu *f; -, kein Pl.* shyness; timidity; reserve; (*Ehrfurcht*) awe; *die ~ vor etw. verlieren* no longer be in awe of s.th., lose one's inhibitions about s.th.

...scheu *im Adj.: hand~ Tier:* scared of hand movements

Scheuche *f; -, -n* scarecrow

scheuchen *v/t.* **1.** scare (off), frighten (away); (*wegjagen*) chase away; **2.** (*antreiben*) chase (after); *der wird dich* (*schon*) *~ umg.* he'll get you organized; *ich lasse mich nicht gern ~* I don't like being pushed

scheuen **I.** *v/i. Pferd etc.:* shy, take fright; *es scheute vor dem zweiten Hindernis* it refused at the second jump; **II.** *v/refl.: sich ~, etw. zu tun* be afraid of doing (*od.* to do) s.th.; (*zurückschrecken*) shy away (*od.* shrink) from doing s.th.; *sich nicht ~ zu* (+ *Inf.*) not be afraid to (+ *Inf.*); *pej.* dare to (+ *Inf.*), have the nerve to (+ *Inf.*) *umg.;* **III.** *v/t.* shun, avoid; (*fürchten*) shy away from; *keine Kosten/Mühen ~* spare no expense/pains

Scheuer *f; -, -n; Dial.* barn

Scheuer|bürste *f* scrub(bing) brush; *~lappen* *m* floor cloth; *~leiste* *f* **1.** skirting board, *Am.* base board; **2.** *Naut.* rubbing strake; *~mittel* *n* scouring agent, cleanser

scheuern **I.** *v/t.* **1.** scour, scrub; (*aufscheuern*) chafe; *sich* (*Dat.*) *die Zehen* (*wund*) *~* chafe (*od.* rub) one's toes until they are sore; **2.** *umg.: j-m eine ~* give s.o. a clout (a)round the ears; **II.** *v/i. Kragen etc.:* chafe; *am Hals ~* chafe at the neck

Scheuertuch *n* floor cloth

Scheuklappen *Pl.* blinkers (*auch fig.*), *Am.* blinders; *~ vor den Augen haben fig.* have blinkers on, wear blinkers, be blinkered; *~mentalität* *f* blinkered view (*od.* mentality)

Scheune *f; -, -n* barn

Scheunen|drescher *m umg.: essen wie ein ~* eat like a horse; *~tor* *n* barn door; → *Ochs*

Scheurebe *f* **1.** *nur Sg.;* (*Rebsorte*) Scheurebe grape; **2.** (*Wein*) Scheurebe

---

wine

Scheusal *n; -s, -e* monster (*auch fig. Person*); *umg.* (*bes. Kind*) horror, little beast

scheußlich **I.** *Adj.* horrible, dreadful (*beide auch umg. fig.*); *Aussehen: auch* hideous, ghastly; (*abstoßend*) *auch* revolting; *umg. Wetter etc.:* awful, rotten; *stärker:* atrocious; **II.** *Adv. umg.* (*furchtbar*) *bes. Brit.* dreadfully, terribly; *es tut ~ weh* it hurts like hell (*od.* something awful); *es schmeckt ~* it tastes awful (*od.* abominable *od.* ghastly); *sich ~ benehmen* behave abominably

Scheußlichkeit *f* **1.** (*Art*) horribleness, dreadfulness; *des Aussehens:* hideousness, ghastliness; *des Wetters:* awfulness, atrociousness; **2.** (*Tat*) dreadful deed; (*Greueltat*) atrocity; **3.** (*hässlicher Gegenstand*) hideous thing, monstrosity

Schi(...) *siehe* **Ski**(...)

Schicht *f; -, -en* **1.** layer; *Geol.* stratum (*Pl.* strata); *Bergb.* seam; *Farbe:* coat(ing), layer; *Öl:* film; *Fot.* emulsion; *e-e dicke ~ Staub* a thick layer of dust; **2.** *fig. Soziol.* class, *Pl. auch* social strata; *breite ~en der Bevölkerung* large sections; *die gebildete ~* the educated class; *aus allen ~en* from all levels of society; **3.** *Arbeitszeit:* shift; *~ haben, auf ~ sein* be on shift; *in der zweiten ~* on the second shift; *~ arbeiten* work shifts, do shift work

...schicht *f, im Subst.* **1.** (*Lage*): *Boden~* layer of soil; *Kultur~* cultural level; **2.** (*Masse*): *Dämm~, Isolier~* insulating layer, insulation; *Rost~* layer of rust; **3.** (*Klasse*): *Arbeiter~* working class

Schicht|arbeit *f* shift work; *~arbeiter* *m,* *~arbeiterin* *f* shift worker; *~betrieb* *m: im ~ arbeiten* work in shifts; *~dienst* *m* shift work

schichten *v/t.* pile up; (*Holz etc.*) *auch* stack

schichtenspezifisch *Adj.* *Soziol.* class-related, *nur attr.* class ...

Schicht|führer *m,* *~führerin* *f* shift manager; *~gestein* *n Geol.* sedimentary (*od.* stratified) rock; *~holz* *n* **1.** stacked wood; **2.** (*Sperrholz*) laminated wood; *~meister* *m,* *~meisterin* *f Bergb.* shift manager; *~technik* *f Etech.* substrate technology; *~stufe* *f Geol.* cuesta; *in Canyon:* river terrace

Schichtung *f* layered construction, arrangement in layers; *Geol., Soziol. und fig.* stratification

Schicht|unterricht *m* teaching in shifts; *~vulkan* *m Geol.* composite volcano; *~wechsel* *m* **1.** *Arbeit:* change of shift; *um sechs ist ~* we *etc.* change shifts at six; **2.** *Geol.* alternation of beds

schichtweise *Adv.* **1.** in layers, layer in layer; **2.** *bei der Arbeit:* in shifts

schick **I.** *Adj.* **1.** *Kleidung etc.:* (very) smart, stylish, chic; *sich ~ machen* smarten (*Am.* pretty) oneself up; *ein ~es rotes Kleid* a chic red dress; **2.** (*modisch, beliebt*) trendy, fashionable; *es gilt heute als ~ zu ...* it's considered trendy to ...; **II.** *Adv.: sich ~ anziehen* dress very smartly (*od.* stylishly); *~ ausgehen* go out in style

Schick *m; -(e)s, kein Pl.* stylishness; *von Benehmen etc.:* style; *Mode* chic; *das Kleid hat keinen ~* this dress has no style (to it); *sie hat ~* she's got style; *~ in die Sache bringen* put the final touch(es) to it

S

schicken I. *v/t.* send (**an** + *Akk.*, **nach, zu** to); **sich** (*Dat.*) *etw.* **~ lassen** have s.th. sent; **j-n ins Bett ~** send s.o. to bed; **j-n zum Bäcker ~** send s.o. to the baker's; **II.** *vt/i.*: (**j-n**) **nach j-m ~** send (s.o.) for s.o.; **III.** *v/refl.* **1. sich ~** *Dial.* (*beeilen*) hurry up; **schick dich!** *umg.* step on it!, get a move on!; **2. sich ~ für** (*geziemen*) be fitting for, befit *s.o. förm.*; **das schickt sich nicht** it's not done, it's not the done thing (**zu** + *Inf.* to + *Inf.*); **3. sich in etw ~** (*sich fügen*) resign o.s. to s.th.

Schickeria *f*; *-, kein Pl.*; *umg.* smart set, jet set

Schickimicki *m*; *-s, -s*; *umg.* trendy type; *Pl. auch* trendies, in-crowd

schicklich *Adj.* proper, fitting; (*geeignet*) suitable, convenient; *Zeit*: acceptable; *Benehmen*: seemly; → **schicken** III 2; **Schicklichkeit** *f* propriety, seemliness

Schicksal *n*; *-s, -e* fate; *dramatischer*: destiny, doom; (*Los*) *auch* lot; **das ~ herausfordern** tempt fate (*od.* providence); **es war sein ~ zu** (+ *Inf.*) he was destined to (+ *Inf.*); **j-n s-m überlassen** leave (*od.* abandon) s.o. to his (*od.* her fate); **das ~ wollte es, dass ...** fate would have it that ...; **das ~ hat es anders entschieden** fate had s.th. else in store; **sich in sein ~ fügen** submit (*od.* resign o.s.) to one's fate; **das ~ hat es gut mit ihm gemeint** fortune has favo(u)red (*od.* smiled on) her; (**das ist**) **~** *umg.* that's the luck of the draw; *dramatischer*: that's fate; (*das ist Pech*) *auch* that's hard luck; **~ spielen** *umg.* play (at being) God; → *auch* **Geschick¹**

schicksalhaft *Adj.* fateful

Schicksals|drama *n Lit.* fate tragedy; **~frage** *f* vital (*od.* fateful) question; **~fügung** *f* act of fate (*od.* providence); **~gefährte** *m*, **~gefährtin** *f* companion in distress, fellow sufferer; **~gemeinschaft** *f* companions *Pl.* in distress; **e-e ~ bilden** share a common destiny; **~genosse** *m*, **~genossin** *f* → **Schicksalsgefährte**; **~glaube** *m* fatalism; **~göttin** *f* goddess of fate; **die ~nen** *Myth.* the (three) Fates; **~schlag** *m* (tragic *od.* terrible) blow, stroke of fate; **Schicksalsschläge hinnehmen müssen** be buffeted by fate

schicksalsschwer *Adj.* fateful

Schicksals|tag *m* fateful day; **~tragödie** *f Lit., Theat.* fate drama (*od.* tragedy); **~wende** *f* change (*od.* reversal) of fortune; *sonderbare*: twist of fate

Schiebe|dach *n Mot.* sliding roof, sunroof; **~fenster** *n* sliding window; *nach oben verschiebbar*: sash window; **~leiter** *f* extension ladder

schieben; *schiebt, schob, hat geschoben* **I.** *vt/i.* **1.** push; *unsanft*: shove; (*Fahrrad, Karren etc.*) push, wheel; *in die Tasche, in den Mund etc.*: put; **wir mussten das Auto ~** we had to push the car (*od.* give the car a push); *in der Fußgängerzone müssen Radfahrer ~* cyclists must dismount in the pedestrian precinct (*Am.* zone); **den Riegel vor die Tür ~** bolt the door; **den Kuchen in den Ofen ~** put the cake in the oven; (**e-e Arbeit** *etc.*) **von einem Tag auf den anderen ~** put off (work *etc.*) from one day to the next; *ihn muss man immer erst ~ umg. fig.* he always needs a push (*stärker*: kick in the backside); → **Bank¹** 1, **Kugel** 2, **Wache** 1; **2.** (*sich drängeln*) push, *unsanft*: shove; **3.** *umg.* (*handeln*) **~ mit**

(*Waren*) traffic in; (*Drogen auch*) push; **Devisen ~** wheel and deal in currency; **4.** *fig.* (*beschuldigen*) **etw. auf j-n ~** (try to) blame s.o. for s.th.; → **Schuld** 1; **5. etw.** (*weit*) **von sich ~** deny all responsibility for s.th.; **II.** *v/refl.*: **sich nach vorn ~** push (one's way) to the front; *Sport, im Rennen*: move up (through the field); **sich nach oben ~** *Rock etc.*: slide (*od.* ride) up; *langsam*: work its way up; **Wolken schoben sich vor die Sonne** clouds covered (up) the sun

Schieber *m*; *-s, -* **1.** *Tech.* slide; (*Ventil*) slide valve; *an Rohrleitungen*: sluice (*od.* sliding) valve; *an Wasserbecken*: gate; *in e-m Motor*: sleeve; *am Ofen*: damper; (*Riegel*) bolt, bar; **2.** (*Essgerät für Kinder*) pusher; **3.** (*Geschäftemacher*) racketeer, (*Schwarzmarkthändler*) black marketeer; **4.** (*Tanz*) one-step; **5.** (*Bettpfanne*) bedpan; **6.** *Sport umg., Schimpfwort für Schiedsrichter*: fixer; **~!** it's a fix!

Schiebe|register *n EDV* shift register; **~regler** *m Radio etc.*: slide control

Schieberei *f*, *-, -en* **1.** pushing; (*Drängeln*) pushing (and shoving); **2.** (*illegale Geschäfte*) racketeering; (*Mauschelei*) wheeling and dealing; *auf dem schwarzen Markt*: black marketeering; *mit Drogen*: pushing

Schieber|geschäft *n* racket; *Pl. auch* racketeering *Sg.*; **~mütze** *f* peaked cap

Schiebe|tür *f* sliding door; **~wand** *f* sliding partition; **~wind** *m Flug.* tailwind; *Sport* following wind

Schiebkarre *f*, **Schiebkarren** *m* → **Schubkarre**

Schieblehre *f* cal(l)iper rule, cal(l)iper ga(u)ge

Schiebung *f fig.* manipulation, string-pulling; (*geheime Absprache*) *umg.* put-up job; *Sport auch umg.* fix; **die Zuschauer riefen „~"** the spectators shouted "It's rigged!"; **er ist nur durch ~ an den Job/Auftrag gekommen** he only got the job/commission by pulling strings

schied *Imperf.* → **scheiden**

Schiedsgericht *n Jur.* court of arbitration, arbitration tribunal; **internationales ~** international tribunal; *Sport etc.*: (panel of) judges; *beim Fechten*: jury; **schiedsgerichtlich I.** *Adj.* arbitral; **II.** *Adv.* by arbitration

Schiedsgerichts|barkeit *f Jur.* arbitral jurisdiction; **~hof** *m* court of arbitration; **Haager ~** Hague Tribunal

Schieds|kommission *f* court of arbitration, arbitration tribunal; **~mann** *m* arbitrator

Schiedsrichter *m* **1.** *Fußball, Handball, Rugby, Boxen, Eishockey, Basketball, Wasserball, Judo*: referee, ref *umg.*; *Tennis, Hockey, Baseball, Badminton, Cricket*: umpire; *Volleyball*: (*erster ~*) umpire; (*zweiter ~*) referee; *Pl. beim Fechten*: jury; **2.** *bei Wettbewerben*: judge; **3.** *Wirts., Jur.* arbitrator

Schiedsrichter|ball *m Sport* drop ball; **~beleidigung** *f* verbal abuse of a (*od.* the) referee (*Tennis etc.*: umpire); **~entscheidung** *f* referee's (*Tennis etc.*: umpire's) decision; *beim Wettbewerb*: judge's decision

Schiedsrichterin *f* → **Schiedsrichter**

Schiedsrichterkreis *m Eishockey*: cent|re (*Am.* -er) (*od.* face-off) circle

schiedsrichterlich I. *Adj. Befugnis*: arbitral; *Entscheidung etc.*: of the referee (*Tennis etc.*: umpire, *Jur.*: arbitrator) *präd.*; *allg.* refereeing (*Tennis etc.*: um-

piring, *Jur.*: arbitration) *nur attr.*; **~e Fehlentscheidung** wrong decision by the referee (*Tennis etc.*: umpire, *Jur.*: arbitrator); **II.** *Adv.*: **~ entscheiden** settle by arbitration

schiedsrichtern *v/i.* (*untr., hat*) arbitrate; *Sport mst* referee, ref *umg.*; *Tennis etc.*: umpire; → **Schiedsrichter**

Schieds|spruch *m Jur.* arbitration verdict; arbitral award; **e-n ~ fällen** make an award; **~stelle** *f* (independent) arbitration body; **~verfahren** *n* arbitration proceedings *Pl.*

schief I. *Adj.* **1.** crooked, not straight; (*nach e-r Seite hängend*) lop-sided, *Brit.* skew-whiff *umg.*; **~e Absätze** worn-down heels; **~e Schultern** sloping shoulders; **e-e ~e Linie** an oblique line; **der Schiefe Turm von Pisa** the Leaning Tower of Pisa; **~e Ebene** *Math., Phys.* inclined plane; **2.** *fig.* (*verdreht*) distorted; *Urteil*: warped; **~er Vergleich** lame comparison; **3. ~er Blick** *fig.* mistrustful look; **ein ~es Gesicht machen** pull a wry face; → **Bahn** 2, **Ebene** 2, **Licht** 3; **II.** *Adv.* **1.** crookedly; (*nach e-r Seite hängend*) lop-sidedly, *Brit.* skew-whiff *umg.*; **den Hut ~ aufsetzen** put on one's hat at an angle, tilt one's hat; **~ treten** (*Absätze*) wear down; **2.** *fig.* (*verzerrt*) **~ sehen** (*etw.*) misjudge; **~ darstellen** give a distorted account of; **3.** *umg. fig.* (*misstrauisch*) **~ ansehen** (*j-n*) look askance at; (*j-m misstrauen*) mistrust; **4.** **~ gehen** *od.* **~ laufen** *umg.* go wrong; **das wäre beinah ~ gegangen** that was a close shave; **es wird schon ~ gehen!** *hum.* it'll (*od.* you'll) be all right (*Am. umg.* alright); **5.** *umg.* (*falsch*) **~ gewickelt sein** be way out (*od.* way off target); **~ liegen** be barking up the wrong tree; **da liegst du total ~** you've got it all wrong, you're off the mark

Schiefer *m -s, -* **1.** (*Dachschiefer*) slate; *unbearbeitet*: shale, schist; **2.** *Dial.* (*Splitter*) splinter; **2̱blau** *Adj.* slate-blue; **~bruch** *m* slate quarry; **~dach** *n* slate roof; **2̱farben** *Adj.* slate-col-o(u)red; **~gebirge** *n* schist (*od.* slate) mountains

schieferig *Adj.* **1.** (*wie Schiefer*) slate-like, slaty; **2.** (*schieferfarben*) slate-col-o(u)red

Schiefer|platte *f* slate; **~tafel** *f* slate

schieflachen *v/refl.* (*trennb., hat -ge-*) *umg.*: kill o.s. (laughing), crease o.s.; **sich ~ über** (+ *Akk.*) laugh o.s. silly (*od.* one's head off) over

Schieflage *f fig.* tricky situation; *auch Geol.* inclined position, tilt; **in (e-e) gefährliche ~ geraten** get into serious difficulties

schiefwink(e)lig *Adj.* oblique-angled

Schielauge *n*: **ein ~ haben** squint, have a squint (in one eye); **~n machen** *nach umg. fig.* ogle at *allg.*; **schieläugig** *Adj.* squinting, squint-eyed; *nach innen*: cross-eyed

schielen *v/i.* **1.** squint, have a squint; *nach innen*: be cross-eyed; **auf e-m Auge ~** have a squint in one eye; **2.** *umg. über etw., um die Ecke*: peer; *durch das Schlüsselloch*: *auch* squint; **~ auf** (+*Akk.*) *od.* **nach** *heimlich*: squint at, sneak a glance at, have (*od.* take) a squint at; *begehrlich*: ogle (at) *pej.*; **~ nach** (*e-m Posten etc.*) hanker after, have one's eye on; **Schielen** *n*; *-s, kein Pl.* squint

schien *Imperf.* → **scheinen¹, scheinen²**

Schienbein *n Anat.* shin(bone), tibia

fachspr.; → *treten* II 1; **~schutz** *m*, **~schützer** *m Sport* shin guard (*od.* pad)

Schiene *f*; -, *-n* **1.** *Tech.* bar; (*Führungsschiene*) rail; *Med.* splint; *hist.* (*Teil der Rüstung*) splint; *am Schlitten*: metal face; **2.** *Eisenb.* **~n** rails, track; *aus den* **~n** *springen* be derailed, jump the rails; **3.** *fig.* track; *auf der politischen* **~** on the political trail (*od.* circuit)

...schiene *f, im Subst.* **1.** *Tech.*: *Eisenbahn~* (railway, *Am.* railroad) rail; *Gardinen~* curtain rail (*od.* rod); **2.** *fig.*: *Partei~* party trail; *Unterhaltungs~* entertainment circuit

schienen *v/t. Med.* put in a splint (*od.* in splints)

Schienen|bus *m* railcar; **~ersatzverkehr** *m Eisenb.* alternative transport(ation) (*when trains or trams are not running*) (*Am.* auch) rolling stock (*V. im Sg.*); **~fahrzeug** *n* rail vehicle; *Pl.*

schienen|gebunden *Adj.* railbound; **~gleich** *Adj.*: *Eisenb.* **~er Übergang** level (*Am.* grade) crossing

Schienen|nahverkehr *m Eisenb.* local (*od.* regional) rail transport(ation), suburban trains *Pl.*; **~netz** *n* railway (*Am.* railroad) network (*od.* system); **~strang** *m* track, railway (*Am.* railroad) line; **~strecke** *f* stretch (*od.* section) of track; **~verkehr** *m* rail traffic; **~weg** *m* railway (*Am.* railroad) line

schier[1] *Adv.* (*fast*) almost; (*geradezu*) virtually

schier[2] *Adj. nur attr.* **1.** (*rein*) pure; **~es Fleisch** perfect lean meat; **2.** *fig. Wahnsinn etc.*: sheer, complete; *der* **~e Neid** pure jealousy

Schierling *m*; *-s*, *-e*; *Bot.* hemlock; **Schierlingsbecher** *m* (cup of) hemlock; *den* **~** *trinken fig. lit.* drain the hemlock cup; *weitS.* poison o.s.

Schieß|anlage *f* indoor shooting range; **~ausbildung** *f* weapons training; *mit Gewehren*: rifle training; *mit Artillerie*: gunnery drill; **~baumwolle** *f* gun cotton; **~befehl** *m Mil.* order to fire (*od.* shoot)

Schießbude *f* shooting gallery; **Schießbudenfigur** *f* (shooting gallery) target; *er sieht aus wie e-e* **~** *umg. fig.* he looks as if he's run away from a circus

Schießeisen *n umg.* shooting iron

schießen; *schießt, schoss, hat bzw. ist geschossen* **I.** *v/i.* **1.** (*hat*) (*feuern*) shoot, fire; (*das Feuer eröffnen*) open fire; *auf* (+ *Akk.*) **~** shoot (*od.* fire) at; *gut* **~** *Person*: be a good shot; *Waffe*: shoot well; *scharf* **~** shoot with live ammunition; *stehen bleiben, oder ich schieße!* stop (right there), or I'll shoot; *gegen j-n* **~** *umg. fig.* have a go at s.o.; → *Pistole*; **2.** *bei Ballspielen*: shoot; *aufs Tor* **~** shoot at goal; *er schießt gut* he has a good shot on him; **3.** (*ist*) (*sausen*) shoot; *plötzlich schoss mir der Gedanke durch den Kopf* the thought suddenly occurred to me (*od.* flashed across my mind); **~** *aus Blut, Wasser*: shoot (*od.* gush) from (*od.* out of); *das Blut schoss ihr ins Gesicht* the blood rushed to her face; *er kam um die Ecke geschossen umg.* he shot (a)round the corner; *mit dem Auto*: *auch* he came zooming (a)round the corner; *in die Höhe* **~** *Pflanze, Kind etc.*: shoot up; → *Boden* 1, *Kraut* 1, *Pilz*, 4. **~** *lassen umg.* (*Pläne etc. aufgeben*) ditch, *Brit.* scupper; **5.** *Sl.* (*Rauschgift spritzen*) shoot (up),

mainline; **II.** *v/t.* (*hat*) **1.** shoot; (*Rakete, Kugel*) fire; *sich e-e Kugel durch den Kopf* **~** put a bullet through one's head; *j-n zum Krüppel* **~** shoot and maim s.o.; *e-n Satelliten in die Umlaufbahn* **~** launch a satellite into orbit; *j-m e-e* **~** *umg. fig.* sock s.o. one; **2.** *Fußball etc.*: (*Ball*) kick, shoot; *ein Tor* **~** score a goal; **III.** *v/refl.*: *sich mit j-m* **~** (*duellieren*) have a shoot-out with s.o.

Schießen *n*; *-s, kein Pl.*; (*Wettschießen*) shooting match; *es geht aus wie das Hornberger* **~** *umg.* it'll all come to nothing; *es/er ist zum* **~** *umg.* it's/he's a (real) scream

Schießerei *f*; -, *-en* **1.** gunfight, gun battle; *bes. persönliche od. mit der Polizei*: shoot-out; *durch Amokschützen*: random shooting; **2.** *umg.* (*unaufhörliches Schießen*) endless shooting *allg.*

Schieß|gewehr *n Kindersprache*: bang-bang gun; **~hund** *m umg.*: *aufpassen wie ein* **~** watch like a hawk; **~platz** *m Mil.* (shooting) range; **~prügel** *m umg.* shooter; **~pulver** *n* gunpowder; → *auch Pulver*, **~scharte** *f* embrasure, loophole; (*Zinne*) crenel; **~scheibe** *f* target; **~sport** *m* shooting; **~stand** *m* shooting range; **~übung** *f* target practice

schießwütig *Adj.* trigger-happy

Schiet *m*; *-s, kein Pl.*, **Schietkram** *m Dial. umg.* crap; (*so 'n*) **~!** what a load of crap!

Schifahren *n* → *Skilauf*

Schiff *n*; *-(e)s*, *-e* **1.** *Naut.* ship; *kleineres auch*: boat; *auf dem* **~** on board ship; *mit dem* **~** by ship; *klar* **~** *machen Naut.* clear the decks; *umg. fig.* clear the air; **~e Versenken** (*Spiel*) (game of) battleships; **2.** *Archit.* (*Mittelschiff*) nave; (*Seitenschiff*) aisle

schiffbar *Adj. Naut.* navigable; **~ machen** make navigable

Schiffbau *m Naut.* shipbuilding (industry); **Schiffbauer** *m*; *-s*, -, **Schiffbauerin** *f*; -, *-nen* shipbuilder

Schiffbau|ingenieur *m*, **~ingenieurin** *f* naval architect

Schiffbruch *m Naut.* shipwreck (*auch fig.*); **~ erleiden** *fig. Unternehmen*: founder; *Plan*: come to naught; **schiffbrüchig** *Adj.* shipwrecked; **Schiffbrüchige** *m, f*; *-n*, *-n* shipwrecked person; *auf e-r einsamen Insel*: *auch* castaway

Schiffchen *n* **1.** little boat; **2.** *Tech.* shuttle; **3.** *Mil.* (*Mütze*) forage cap

schiffen *v/i.* **1.** *vulg.* (*harnen*) have a slash, *Am.* take a piss; **2.** *unpers.*, *umg.* (*regnen*) *es schifft* it's tipping down; **3.** *altm.* (*mit e-m Schiff fahren*) ship, travel (*od.* go) by ship

Schiffer *m*; *-s*, -, **~in** *f*; -, *-nen*; *Naut.* sailor; (*Schiffsführer*) navigator; (*Handelsschiffskapitän*) skipper; (*Flussschiffer*) boatman; **~klavier** *n Mus.* accordion; **~knoten** *m Naut.* sailor's knot; **~mütze** *f Naut.* sailor's (peaked) cap

Schifffahrt *f*; *nur Sg. Naut.* navigation; shipping

Schifffahrts|amt *n Naut.* inland waterways authority; **~gesellschaft** *f* shipping company; **~linie** *f* shipping line; **~museum** *n* maritime museum; **~weg** *m* shipping route (*od.* lane); **~zeichen** *n* navigational sign

Schiffs|anlegestelle *f Naut.* ship's mooring; **~arzt** *m*, **~ärztin** *f* ship's doctor; **~ausflug** *m* boat trip; **~bauch** *m* ship's belly; **~besatzung** *f* (ship's) crew; **~brücke** *f* bridge

Schiffschaukel *f* swing boat, *Am. etwa* tilt-a-whirl

Schiffs|eigner *m*, **~eignerin** *f Naut.* shipowner; **~flagge** *f* ship's flag (*od.* colo[u]rs *Pl.*); *Mil.* ensign; **~führer** *m*, **~führerin** *f* boatman; (*Schiffskapitän*) master, skipper; **~hebewerk** *n* (canal) ship lift; **~junge** *m* cabin boy, deck hand; **~kapitän** *m* (ship's) captain, master; **~katastrophe** *f* disaster at sea; **~koch** *m* ship's cook; **~küche** *f* galley; **~ladung** *f* shipload; (*Fracht*) (ship's) cargo; **~laterne** *f* navigation light; **~makler** *m*, **~maklerin** *f* ship-broker; **~mannschaft** *f* (ship's) crew; **~modell** *n* model ship; **~offizier** *m* (ship's) officer; **~papiere** *Pl.* ship's papers; **~passage** *f* passage (on a ship); **~register** *n* register of shipping; **~reise** *f* sea voyage; (*Kreuzfahrt*) cruise; (*Überfahrt*) (sea) crossing; **~rumpf** *m* hull; **~schraube** *f* propeller, ship's screw; **~sirene** *f* ship's siren (*od.* foghorn); **~tagebuch** *n* ship's log; **~taufe** *f* naming of a (*od.* the) ship; **~unglück** *n* shipping accident; (*Zusammenstoß*) (ship) collision; **~verkehr** *m* shipping; **~werft** *f* shipyard, shipbuilding yard; **~zwieback** *m* ship's biscuit, *Am.* hardtack

Schiismus *m*; -, *kein Pl.*; *Reli.* Shiism, Shi'ism; **Schiit** *m*; *-en*, *-en* Shiite, Shi'ite; **Schiitin** *f*; -, *-nen*, **schiitisch** *Adj.* Shiite, Shi'ite

Schikane *f*; -, *-n* **1.** *auch Pl.* harassment; *etw. aus reiner* **~** *machen* do s.th. out of sheer petty spite (*Brit.* bloody-mindedness); **2.** *Rennsport*: chicane; **3.** *mit allen* **~n** (*ausgestattet*) *umg. fig.* with all the trimmings; *Küche, Haus*: with all mod cons, *Am.* with all the latest gadgets

schikanieren *v/t.* harass, *Brit.* mess s.o. about, *Am.* mess around with s.o; (*Schüler, Angestellten etc.*) pick on; *s-e Mitschüler* **~** bully the other pupils; **schikanös** *Adj. Maßnahme*: harassing, vexatious; *Mensch*: spiteful; *tyrannisierend*: bullying; *klein kariert*: pettifogging

Schild[1] *n*; *-(e)s*, *-er* **1.** (*Aushängeschild*) sign; (*Namensschild*) nameplate; (*Firmenschild*) fascia, *kleines*: nameplate; (*Warnschild*) sign; (*Wegweiser*) signpost; (*Verkehrsschild*) road sign; (*Straßenschild*) street sign; *auf dem* **~** *steht, dass ...* it says on the sign that ...; *sich nach den* **~ern richten** / *den* **~ern folgen** go by / follow the signs (*od.* signposts); *auf die* **~er achten** obey the signs; **2.** (*Etikett*) label; (*Anhänger*) tag

Schild[2] *m*; *-(e)s*, *-e* **1.** *Mil., hist.* shield; *etwas im* **~e führen** *fig.* be up to something *umg.*, be hatching something; *j-n auf den* **~ heben** *fig.* make s.o. one's leader (*Leitbild*): figurehead); **2.** *im Reaktor*: shield; **3.** *von Mütze*: peak

Schildbürger *m etwa* Gothamite, *Am.* local yokel; *weitS.* (*Dummkopf*) simpleton; **~streich** *m* piece of bungling, cock-up *umg.*

Schilddrüse *f Anat.* thyroid (gland)

Schilddrüsen|hormon *n* thyroxin(e); **~überfunktion** *f* hyperthyroidism *fachspr.*; overactive thyroid; **~unterfunktion** *f* hypothyrosis *fachspr.*; underactive thyroid

Schilder|brücke *f* gantry sign; **~haus** *n hist.* sentry box

schildern *v/t.* describe; (*erzählen*) *auch* relate *geh.*; (*skizzieren*) outline, sketch; (*charakterisieren*) portray; *etw. detailliert* ~ give a detailed account of s.th.; *in düsteren Farben* ~ paint a gloomy picture of; → *leuchtend* II 2; **Schilderung** *f* description; (*Erzählung*) account; *genaue* ~ *des Unfallhergangs* precise description of how the accident happened

Schilderwald *m* jungle (*od.* maze) of road signs

Schildknappe *m hist.* squire, shield--bearer

Schildknorpel *m Anat.* thyroid cartilage, Adam's apple

Schildkröte *f Zool., an Land lebend:* tortoise; *im Meer:* turtle; **Schildkrötensuppe** *f Gastr.* turtle soup; *falsche* ~ mock turtle soup

Schild|laus *f Zool.* scale insect; ~**mütze** *f* peaked cap; ~**patt** *n* tortoiseshell; ~**wache** *f altm. Mil.* sentry; (*Wachdienst*) sentry-go

Schilf *n; -(e)s, -e; Bot.* reed; *am Wasser:* reeds *Pl.; im* ~ among the reeds; ♀**bewachsen** *Adj.* reed-grown; ~**gras** *n Bot.* reed grass; ~**gürtel** *m* belt of reeds

schilfig *Adj.* reedy

Schilf|matte *f* rush mat; ~**rohr** *n* → **Schilf**

Schillerlocke *f* 1. (*Fisch*) (*rolled*) strip of smoked dogfish; 2. (*Gebäck*) cream horn

schillern *v/i.* shimmer; (*glänzen*) sparkle; *ins Rötliche* ~ have a reddish tinge; **schillernd I.** *Part. Präs.* → **schillern; II.** *Adj.* 1. iridescent, opalescent; *Stoffe:* shot; 2. *fig. Begriff etc.:* equivocal, ambiguous; *e-e Persönlichkeit negativ:* elusive character; *positiv:* colo(u)rful personality

Schilling *m; -s, -e, bei Summen -; hist.* schilling (*ehemalige österreichische Währung*)

schilpen *v/i.* chirp

schilt *Präs.* → **schelten**

Schimäre *f; -, -n; lit.* chimera; **schimärisch** *Adj.* chimeric(al)

Schimmel¹ *m; -s, -; Zool.* white horse

Schimmel² *m; -s, kein Pl.; Bot.* mo(u)ld; *bes. auf Papier, Leder etc.:* mildew; ~**bildung** *f* formation of mo(u)ld (*od.* mildew)

schimmelig I. *Adj. Lebensmittel:* mo(u)ldy; *Papier, Leder, Holz etc.:* mildewy; **II.** *Adv.: es riecht* ~ there's a mo(u)ldy (*od.* musty) smell; **schimmeln** *v/i.* go mo(u)ldy (*od.* mildewy); **Schimmelpilz** *m* mo(u)ld

Schimmer *m; -s, kein Pl.* 1. glimmer, gleam, shimmer (*auch von Stoff*); 2. *ein* ~ *Hoffnung fig.* a glimmer (*od.* flicker) of hope; *e-s Lächelns* flicker of a smile; *er hat keinen* (*blassen*) ~ *umg.* he hasn't got the foggiest (*od.* faintest), he hasn't got a clue, he doesn't know the first thing about *s.th.*

schimmern *v/i.* gleam, glimmer, shimmer; *Mondlicht etc.:* shine; *die Schrift schimmert durchs Papier* the writing shows through the paper

Schimpanse *m; -n, -n; Zool.* chimpanzee, chimp *umg.*

Schimpf *m; -(e)s, kein Pl.: mit* ~ *und Schande* ignominiously

Schimpfe *f; -, kein Pl.; umg.:* ~ *kriegen* get an earful

schimpfen I. *v/i.* scold, rail; ~ *über* (+ *Akk.*) complain (*od.* moan *umg.*) about; *stärker:* curse; *mit j-m* ~, *j-n* ~ tell s.o. off; *bitte nicht* ~*!* please don't shout at me; *du kriegst ganz arg geschimpft bes. Dial. umg.* you'll really

get it in the neck; *er schimpfte ihn e-n Lügner* he called him a liar; **II.** *v/refl. umg.: und so was schimpft sich Lehrer* and he calls himself a teacher *allg.*

Schimpferei *f; -, -en; umg.* (*dauerndes Meckern*) (constant) moaning (*stärker:* cursing); (*Zurechtweisen*) scolding; *des Eichelhähers etc.:* screeching; *der Affen:* screaming

Schimpfkanonade *f umg.* volley (*od.* stream, torrent) of abuse

schimpflich I. *Adj.* ignominious, shameful; (*demütigend*) *auch* humiliating; **II.** *Adv.:* ~ *behandeln* treat disgracefully; *entwürdigend:* humiliate

Schimpf|name *m* rude (*stärker:* nasty) name; *j-m* ~*n geben od. j-n mit* ~*n belegen* call s.o. names; ~**wort** *n* 1. *Pl.* abuse *Sg.;* 2. (*Fluch*) swearword; *Schimpfwörter gebrauchen* use bad language, swear

Schindanger *m altm.* knacker's yard

Schindel *f; -, -n* shingle; ~**dach** *n* shingle roof

schinden; *schindet, schindete, hat geschunden* **I.** *v/t.* 1. (*hart herannehmen*) drive hard; (*quälen*) maltreat, abuse; 2. *altm.* (*totes Tier*) flay, skin; 3. *umg.* (*Essen, Geld etc.*) scrounge; (*Zeilen*) pad (out); (*Arbeitszeit*) pile up; *Zeit* ~ play for time; *Eindruck* ~ try to impress; **II.** *v/refl.: sich* ~ (*und plagen*) slave away (*mit etw.* at s.th.); **Schinder** *m; -s, -* 1. slave driver; 2. *altm.* flayer, *Brit.* knacker; **Schinderei** *f; -, -en* exploitation, slavery; (*schwere Arbeit*) drudgery

Schindluder *n: mit j-m* ~ *treiben umg. fig.* treat s.o. like a slave, drive s.o. mercilessly (hard); *mit s-r Gesundheit* ~ *treiben* abuse (*od.* ruin) one's health *allg.*

Schindmähre *f umg.* nag

Schinken *m; -s, -* 1. *Gastr.* ham; *roher/ gekochter/geräucherter* ~ uncooked/ cooked/smoked ham; ~ *mit Ei* bacon (*od.* ham) and egg(s):; 2. *umg.* (*riesiges Gemälde*) huge (*od.* outsized) daub; (*dickes Buch*) fat tome; (*aufwendiger Film*) epic *allg.*

...schinken *m, im Subst.: Bären~* smoked bear meat; *Bauern~* farmhouse ham; *Hinter~* etwa gammon

Schinken|aufschnitt *m Gastr.* plate of cold ham; ~**brettchen** *n* wooden platter (*for eating cold meat etc.*); ~**brot** *n* ham sandwich; *offenes:* (piece of) bread with ham; ~**eier** *Pl.* ham and eggs; ~**fleckerln** *Pl. österr.* baked pasta and ham pieces; ~**nudeln** *Pl.* noodles with pieces of ham; ~**pastete** *f* ham pie; ~**platte** *f* plate of different ham types, *Am.* ham platter; ~**röllchen** *n* rolled stuffed slice of ham; ~**speck** *m Gastr. etwa* bacon; (*Fleischstück*) fat end; ~**wurst** *f* ham sausage

Schinto *m; -; Reli.* Shinto; **Schintoismus** *m; -, kein Pl.* Shintoism; **Schintoist** *m; -en, -en,* **Schintoistin** *f; -, -nen* Shintoist; **schintoistisch** *Adj.* Shintoist, Shinto ...

Schippe *f; -, -n* shovel; (*Spaten*) spade; *j-n auf die* ~ *nehmen umg. fig.* pull s.o.'s leg, have s.o. on; → *Tod* 2; **schippen** *v/t.* shovel; *e-e Grube* ~ dig a hole; *Schnee* ~ clear the snow away

schippern *v/i. umg.* cruise

Schiri *m; -s, -s; umg.* ref

Schirm *m; -(e)s, -e* 1. (*Regenschirm*) umbrella; (*Sonnenschirm*) parasol, sunshade; *den* ~ *aufspannen/schließen* put up / close one's umbrella

(*bzw.* sunshade); 2. *e-r Lampe:* shade; 3. *e-r Mütze:* peak; 4. (*Wand-, Fernseh-, Bildschirm*) screen; 5. (*Schutzvorrichtung*) shield, screen; 6. (*Fallschirm*) parachute; ~**bildaufnahme** *f* x-ray

schirmförmig *Adj.* umbrella-shaped

Schirm|herr *m* patron; ~**herrin** *f* patroness; ~**herrschaft** *f* patronage; *die* ~ *übernehmen* (agree to) become patron; ~**mütze** *f* peaked cap; ~**pilz** *m* parasol mushroom; ~**ständer** *m* umbrella stand

Schirokko *m; -s, -s; Met.* sirocco

Schisma *n; -s, Schismen od. Schismata; Reli.* schism; **Schismatiker** *m; -s, -,* **Schismatikerin** *f; -, -nen* schismatic, schismatist; **schismatisch** *Adj.* schismatic

Schispringen *n* → **Skispringen**

schiss *Imperf.* → **scheißen**

Schiss *m; Schisses, Schisse, mst Sg.* 1. *vulg.* shit; 2. *nur Sg.:* ~ *haben umg.* be scared stiff, have the shits *vulg.*

schizoid *Adj. Psych.* schizoid; **Schizoide** *m, f; -n, -n; Psych.* schizoid

schizophren *Adj.* 1. *Psych.* schizophrenic; 2. (*widersprüchlich*) completely contradictory; 3. (*absurd*) absurd, crazy *umg.*; **Schizophrene** *m, f; -n, -n; Psych.* schizophrenic; **Schizophrenie** *f; -, kein Pl.* 1. *Psych.* schizophrenia; 2. (*Widersinn*) contradictory nature

Schlabber|... *im Subst. Kleidung:* mst sloppy; ~**hosen** *Pl.* baggy trousers

schlabberig *Adj. umg.* 1. → **labb(e)rig** 1; 2. *Kleidung:* sloppy, baggy; *Stoff:* loose, limp

Schlabberlätzchen *n umg.* bib *allg.*

schlabbern *umg.* **I.** *vt/i. beim Essen:* slobber; (*[auf]schlürfen*) slurp; **II.** *v/i. Kleidung:* hang loosely; → **schlackern**

Schlacht *f; -, -en; auch fig.* battle (*bei* of; *fig. um* over, for); *j-m e-e* ~ *liefern auch fig.* do battle with s.o., battle against s.o.; *sich* (*Dat.*) *e-e erbitterte* ~ *liefern* engage in a fierce battle; *fig. Sport etc.:* fight fiercely

Schlachtbank *f* shambles *Pl.* (*mst V. im Sg.*); *j-n* (*wie ein Lamm*) *zur* ~ *führen fig.* lead s.o. (like a lamb) to the slaughter

schlachten *vt/i.* 1. kill; (*bes. größere Tiere*) slaughter; *unser Fleischer schlachtet noch selbst* our butcher still does his own slaughtering; 2. *fig.* (*metzeln*) massacre, slaughter; 3. *umg.* (*Schokoladenfigur etc.*) attack, (*verzehren*) devour *allg.*; → **Sparschwein**

Schlachtenbummler *m,* ~**in** *f Sport* away (*od.* travel[l]ing) supporter

Schlachter *m; -s, -; bes. nordd.* butcher

Schlächter *m; -s, -; auch fig.* butcher

Schlachterei *f; -, -en; bes. nordd.* butcher's (shop)

Schlächterei *f; -, -en* 1. butcher's shop; 2. *fig.* (*Blutbad*) massacre, slaughter, bloodbath

Schlachterin *f; -, -nen; bes. nordd.* (female) butcher

Schlacht|feld *n* battlefield; *hier sieht es aus wie auf e-m* ~ *fig.* this place looks as if a bomb had hit it (*od.* as if iit had been hit by a bomb); ~**fest** *n* 1. social gathering at which meat and sausages from freshly slaughtered pigs are served; 2. *Gastr. im Lokal:* serving of freshly slaughtered pig; ~**getümmel** *n* → **Schlachtgewühl**; ~**gewicht** *n von Tieren:* dressed weight; *nach dem Schlachten:* carcass weight; ~**gewühl** *n auch fig.* melee, *auch* melée; *mitten im* ~ *fig.* in the thick of it; *sich* ins ~ **werfen** enter (*od.* join) the fray; **~hof** *m* slaughterhouse, abattoir; **~messer** *n* butcher's knife; **~opfer** *n* (*Ritual*) sacrifice; (*Tier*) sacrificial animal; **~ordnung** *f* battle formation; **~plan** *m* plan of action (*auch fig.*); **~platte** *f Gastr.* → **Schlachtschüssel**

schlachtreif *Adj.* ready for slaughter(ing)

Schlacht|ross *n hist.* warhorse; **altes ~** *umg. fig.* old campaigner *allg.*; **~ruf** *m auch fig.* battle (*od.* war) cry; **~schiff** *n Mil.* battleship; **~schüssel** *f Gastr.* selection of boiled pork, pork sausages *etc.* from freshly slaughtered pigs with sauerkraut *etc.*; **~tag** *m* day for slaughtering; **Montag ist ~** slaughtering is done on Mondays; **~tier** *n* animal kept for meat; **das bald geschlachtet wird**: animal for slaughter

Schlachtung *f* slaughter(ing), kill(ing)

Schlachtvieh *n* animals *Pl.* kept for meat; **das bald geschlachtet wird**: animals *Pl.* for slaughter; (*Rinder*) beef cattle *Pl.*

Schlacke *f*; -, -*n* **1.** (*Asche*) clinker, cinders *Pl.*; *Metall.* slag, *auch fig.* dross; *Geol.* (volcanic) slag, scoria; **2.** *Pl.* (*Ballaststoffe*) roughage *Sg.*, fib|re (*Am.* -er) *Sg.*

Schlackendiät *f Gastr.* high-fib|re (*Am.* -er) diet

schlacken|frei 1. *nach Verbrennung*: non-clinkering, clinker-free, *attrib.* non-clinker; **2.** *Stoffwechsel*: free of waste (products); **~reich** *Adj. Gastr.* high-fib|re (*Am.* -er)

schlackern *v/i. umg.* wobble; *lose Kleidung etc.*: flap (*beide allg.*); **~de Knie** trembling knees; **ich habe nur noch mit den Ohren geschlackert** I couldn't believe my ears, I thought I was hearing things

Schlackwurst *f Gastr.* → **Zervelatwurst**

Schlaf *m*; -(e)s, kein *Pl.* sleep (*auch fig.*); *kurzer*: nap; **im ~** *auch fig.* in one's sleep; **e-n leichten/festen ~ haben** be a light/sound sleeper; **er findet keinen ~** he can't sleep, he can't get to sleep at night; **in tiefem ~ liegen** be fast asleep; **aus dem ~ gerissen werden** wake up with a start, be rudely awakened; **in den ~ singen/wiegen** lull/rock to sleep; **sich** (*Dat.*) **den ~ aus den Augen reiben** *od.* **wischen** rub the sleep from one's eyes; **j-n um den ~ bringen** give s.o. sleepless nights, rob s.o. of his (*od.* her) sleep; **vom ~ übermannt** overcome by sleep; **etw. im ~ beherrschen** be able to do s.th. in one's sleep (*od.* with one's eyes shut); **den Seinen gibt's der Herr im ~** *umg.* the lucky ones can rely on help from above, some people just get lucky, fortune favo(u)rs fools; → **Gerechte**

Schlafanzug *m*: (**ein**) ~ (a pair of) pyjamas (*Am.* pajamas) *Pl.*; **~hose** *f* pyjama (*Am.* pajama) trousers (*od.* bottoms) *Pl.*; **~jacke** *f* pyjama (*Am.* pajama) jacket (*od.* top)

Schlaf|augen *Pl.* **1.** *e-r Puppe*: sleeping eyes; **2.** *Mot. umg. e-s Autos*: pop-up headlights; **~bedürfnis** *n* sleep requirement

Schläfchen *n umg.* nap, snooze; (*Nickerchen*) catnap, forty winks

Schlafcouch *f* convertible sofa (*od.* settee), sofa bed

Schläfe *f*; -, -*n* temple; **graue ~n haben** be greying (*Am.* graying) at the temples

schlafen; *schläft, schlief, hat geschlafen v/i.* **1.** sleep, be asleep; **fest ~** be fast (*od.* sound) asleep; (*auch e-n festen Schlaf haben*) sleep like a log (*od.* top); **gut/schlecht ~** sleep well/badly, be a sound/poor sleeper; **~ gehen** *od.* **sich ~ legen** go to bed, turn in *umg.*; **j-n ~ legen** put s.o. to bed; **lange ~** have a (good,) long sleep; **sonntags länger ~** have a lie-in (*Am.* sleep late) on Sundays; **bis weit in den Tag hinein ~** sleep to all hours; **sich gesund ~** sleep o.s. back to health; **~ Sie darüber!** sleep on it; **es ließ ihn nicht ~** it gave him no peace, it wouldn't let him rest; → **Murmeltier. 2. bei j-m ~** (*übernachten*) sleep (*od.* spend the night) at s.o.'s place, stay overnight with s.o. (*od.* at s.o.'s place); **im Hotel ~** spend the night at a hotel; **in diesem Haus können sechs Personen ~** this house sleeps six; **auswärts ~** sleep away from home; **3.** *umg. fig.* (*unaufmerksam sein*) not pay attention *allg.*; **er schläft immer im Unterricht** he's always miles away (*od.* dreaming) during the lessons; **mit offenen Augen ~** (*sehr müde sein*) be dog-tired; (*träumen*) daydream; **schlaf nicht!** wake up!, *Brit.* wakey, wakey!; **nicht ~** (*sehr rege sein*) be on one's toes; **die Konkurrenz schläft nicht** our competitors are really with it; **die heimische Industrie hat mal wieder geschlafen** our own industry has been caught napping again; **4. ~ mit** (*Geschlechtsverkehr haben*) sleep with; **die beiden ~ miteinander** those two sleep together; **mit jedem ~** *pej.* sleep around

Schläfen|bein *n Anat.* temporal bone; **~gegend** *f* temporal region

Schlafengehen *n*: **vor dem ~** before one goes to bed, just before bedtime

Schlafenszeit *f* bedtime; **es ist ~** it's time for (*od.* to go to) bed

Schlafentzug *m* sleep deprivation

Schläfer[1] *m*; -*s*, -, **~in** *f*; -, -*nen* sleeper; **er ist ein unruhiger Schläfer** he's very restless in bed, he's a restless sleeper

Schläfer[2] *m*; -*s*, - (*potenzieller Terrorist*) sleeper (terrorist)

schlaff *Adj. Haut, Muskeln*: flabby; *Körper, Glieder, auch Händedruck*: limp, weak; *Seil*: slack; *Segel*: auch drooping; *Moral, Disziplin*: lax; *Party etc.*: lifeless, dead boring *umg.*; (*träge*) sluggish, lethargic; **~er Typ** *umg.* lethargic type, wimp

Schlaffheit *f* flabbiness; *des Körpers, Gliedes etc.*: limpness; *e-s Seiles, der Segel*: slackness; *der Moral, des Disziplins*: laxness; *e-r Party*: lifelessness; (*Trägheit*) sluggishness

Schlaffi *m*; -*s*, -*s*; *umg.* lethargic type; (*Schlappschwanz*) wimp; (*Langweiler*) tedious fellow, yawn

Schlaf|forschung *f* sleep research; **~gast** *m* overnight guest; **~gelegenheit** *f* place to sleep; **wir haben genügend ~en** we've got plenty of space for people to sleep; **~gewohnheiten** *Pl.* sleeping habits

Schlafittchen *n umg.*: **j-n beim ~ nehmen** collar s.o.; *fig.* take s.o. to task

Schlaf|koje *f* berth (*auch Eisenb., Flug.*); *für Matrosen*: bunk; **~krankheit** *f Med.* sleeping sickness; **~kur** *f Med.* sleep therapy; **~lied** *n* lullaby

schlaflos *Adj.* sleepless; **Schlaflosigkeit** *f* sleeplessness, *Med.* insomnia

Schlaf|mangel *m* lack of sleep; **~mittel** *n* sleep-inducing drug, hypnotic *fachspr.*; *als Tablette*: auch sleeping pill

(*od.* tablet); *umg. fig.* (*Person*) crashing bore; **das ist ja das reinste ~** *umg. fig.* it's enough to send you to sleep, talk about soporific; **~mohn** *m Bot.* opium poppy

Schlafmütze *f umg.* sleepyhead; (*unachtsamer od. träger Mensch*) dozy type; **aufstehen, du ~!** get up, you sleepyhead!; **schlafmützig** *Adj. umg.* dozy, dop(e)y

Schlaf|platz *m* space to sleep; **acht Schlafplätze** sleeping accommodation for eight; **~quartier** *n* sleeping quarters *Pl.*; **~raum** *m* dormitory

schläfrig *Adj.* sleepy (*auch Stimme, Augen*), drowsy

Schlaf|rock *m altm.* dressing gown; **Apfel im ~** *Gastr.* baked apple in pastry; **~saal** *m* dormitory

Schlafsack *m* sleeping bag; **~tourist** *m*, **~touristin** *f umg.* backpacker

Schlaf|sessel *m Flug. etc.* reclining seat; **~stadt** *f* dormitory town, *Am.* bedroom community; **~stätte** *f* place to sleep; **~stellung** *f* sleeping position; **s-e ~ einnehmen** settle into one's sleeping position; **~störungen** *Pl.* disturbed sleep *Sg.*; sleep disorders; **unter ~ leiden** *auch* have trouble sleeping

Schlafsucht *f* narcolepsy; **schlafsüchtig** *Adj.* narcoleptic

schläft *Präs.* → **schlafen**

Schlaf|tablette *f Pharm.* sleeping pill (*od.* tablet); **~tier** *n* soft (*od.* cuddly) toy; **~trunk** *m* sleeping draught; *umg.* (*Schnäpschen*) nightcap

schlaftrunken I. *Adj.* drowsy, *attr. auch* half-asleep …; *präd. auch* half asleep; (*noch nicht wach*) dop(e)y, still half asleep; **II.** *Adv.* drowsily; **j-n ~ ansehen** look at s.o. with bleary eyes;

Schlaf-Wach-Rhythmus *m* sleeping-waking cycle

Schlafwagen *m Eisenb.* sleeper, sleeping car; **~abteil** *n* sleeping compartment; **~schaffner** *m*, **~schaffnerin** *f* sleeping-car attendant

schlafwandeln *v/i.* (*untr., hat od. ist -ge-*) sleepwalk; **Schlafwandler** *m*; -*s*, -, **Schlafwandlerin** *f*; -, -*nen* sleepwalker, somnambulist; **schlafwandlerisch** *Adj.*: **mit ~er Sicherheit** as to the manner born, as if he'd *etc.* been doing it all his *etc.* life

Schlafzentrum *n Physiol.* sleep cent|re (*Am.* -er)

Schlafzimmer *n* bedroom; **sich ein neues ~ anschaffen** get a new bedroom suite; **~blick** *m* (*Augen*) bedroom (*od.* come-hither) eyes *Pl.*; (*Blick*) come-hither look; **~einrichtung** *f* bedroom furniture; (*Garnitur*) bedroom suite; **~geschichte** *f umg.* bedroom tale; **~schrank** *m* wardrobe, bedroom cupboard (*Am.* closet)

Schlag *m*; -(e)s, *Schläge* **1.** *mit der Faust*: blow, punch; *dumpfer*: thump; *mit der offenen Hand*: blow, whack *umg.*; *klatschender*: slap; *bes. bei Kindern*: smack; *leichter*: tap; *mit dem Stock*: whack; *mit der Peitsche*: lash of the whip; *fig.* (*Schicksalsschlag, Unglück*) blow; **Schläge bekommen** *auch fig.* get a (good) hiding (*od.* drubbing); **~ ins Gesicht** *auch fig.* slap in the face; **ein ~ unter die Gürtellinie** *auch fig.* a blow below the belt; **j-m e-n ~ versetzen** deal s.o. a blow; *fig. auch* hit s.o. hard; **zum entscheidenden ~ ausholen** *auch fig.* move in for the kill; **~ ins Wasser** *umg. fig.* (belly-)flop, washout; **~ ins Kontor** *umg.* nasty shock (*od.* surprise); **dann ging**

S

es ~ auf ~ then things started happening (fast); *auf einen od. mit einem ~* (*auf einmal*) in one go; (*plötzlich*) suddenly, from one moment to the next; *sie hat e-n ~* (*weg*) *umg.* she's got a screw loose; **2.** *Med. umg.* stroke; *kleiner ~* minor stroke; *e-n ~ bekommen* have a stroke; *sie waren wie vom ~ getroffen* they were thunderstruck; (*verblüfft sein*) they just stood gaping; *mich trifft der ~!* well I'll be blowed (*od. bes. Am.* damned)!; *ich dachte, mich trifft der ~* I didn't know what hit me; **3.** *Etech.* (electric) shock; (*Blitzschlag*) flash; *e-n tödlichen ~ bekommen* receive a fatal (electric) shock, be electrocuted; **4.** *Rudern, Schwimmen:* stroke; *Golf, Tennis etc.:* shot, stroke; **5.** (*Geräusch*) *dumpf:* thud; *e-r Glocke:* chime; *e-r Uhr: auch* stroke; (*Herz-, Puls-, Trommelschlag*) beat; *Donnern:* clap (of thunder); *der Nachtigall:* song; *~ sechs Uhr* on the stroke of six; **6.** *Mil.* (*Angriff*) strike; *der entscheidende ~* the decisive blow; **7.** *nur Sg.; fig.* (*Art*) sort; *auch Zool.:* stock, breed; *vom gleichen ~ sein* be made of the same stuff; *pej.* be tarred with the same brush; *Leute s-s ~es* men of his stamp (*od.* type); *vom alten ~* of the old school; *die Schotten sind ein eigener ~ umg.* the Scots are a strange lot; **8.** *umg.* (*Portion*) helping; **9.** *nur Sg.; österr.* (*Sahne*) whipped cream; → *Schlagobers*; **10.** *e-e Hose mit ~* (a pair of) flared trousers (*od.* flares); **11.** *Mot. etc.* (*Tür*) door; → *Hühnerschlag, Taubenschlag*

Schlag|abtausch *m; -(e)s, kein Pl.* **1.** *fig.* (hefty) exchange; *es kam zu e-m ~ zwischen ihnen* they clashed (*od.* crossed swords; *stärker:* came to blows) (*über + Akk.* over); **2.** *Boxen:* exchange of blows; *~ader f Anat.* artery; *~anfall m Med.* stroke; *e-n ~ bekommen* have a stroke

schlagartig I. *Adj.* sudden, abrupt; **II.** *Adv.* suddenly, all of a sudden, from one minute (*od.* day) to the next

Schlagball *m, ~spiel n Sport* rounders *Sg.*

schlagbar *Adj.* **1.** *Sport, Gegner etc.:* beatable; *er ist durchaus ~* it's perfectly possible to beat him; **2.** *Baum:* suitable for felling

Schlag|bass *m Mus.* plucked bass; *~baum m* barrier; *~bohrer m* hammer drill; *~bolzen m* striker, firing pin

Schlägel *m; -s, -* **1.** (*Holzhammer*) mallet; (*Hammer des Bergmanns*) miner's hammer; *~ und Eisen Bergb.* crossed hammers; **2.** *Mus.* (drum)stick

schlagen; *schlägt, schlug, hat bzw. ist geschlagen* **I.** *v/t.* (*hat*) **1.** hit; *wiederholt,* (*verprügeln*) beat; *mit der Faust:* hit, punch; *mit der offenen Hand:* hit, whack *umg.; klatschend:* slap; (*bes. Kinder*) smack; *mit dem Stock:* hit, beat; *mit der Peitsche:* whip; (*Eier, Sahne etc.*) beat; *j-n zu Boden ~* knock s.o. down, floor s.o.; (*k.o. ~*) knock s.o. out; *j-n blutig/krankenhausreif ~* hit s.o. until he (*od.* she) bleeds / needs hospital treatment; *stärker:* beat s.o. to a bleeding pulp / reduce s.o. to a hospital case; *an die Wand ~ mit Nägeln:* nail to the wall; *j-m etw. aus der Hand ~* knock s.th. out of s.o.'s hand; *j-m etw. um die Ohren ~* slap s.o. (a)round the ears with s.th.; *den Kopf ~ an* (+ *Akk.*) hit (*od.* bump, knock,

bang) one's head on (*od.* against); *e-e Notiz ans Brett ~* put a notice up on the board, pin a notice (up) onto the board; *Fußball etc.:* *den Ball zu ... ~* pass the ball to ...; *Erbsen etc. durch ein Sieb ~* pass through a sieve; *Nagel ~ in* (+ *Akk.*) hammer (*od.* drive) into; *ein Ei in die Pfanne ~* break an egg into the pan; *die Zähne ~ in* (+ *Akk.*) *Tier:* sink its teeth into; *die Augen zu Boden ~* cast one's eyes down; **2.** (*Bäume*) fell, cut down; **3.** (*Tür*) bang, slam; **4.** (*übertreffen*) beat; (*besiegen*) *auch* defeat, lick *umg.; wir haben sie 3:0 geschlagen* we beat them 3–0; *sich geschlagen geben* admit defeat, give up; **5.** *sich* (*Dat.*) *etw. aus dem Kopf od. Sinn ~* put s.th. out of one's mind, forget (about) s.th. *umg.;* **6.** *auf den Preis ~ Wirts.* add on to; **7.** *die Uhr schlug zehn* the clock struck ten; **8.** *in Papier ~* (*einwickeln*) wrap (up) in paper; *zur Seite ~* (*Decke etc.*) push aside; **9.** *Raubvogel etc.:* (*Beutetier*) kill; → *Alarm, Brücke 1, Flucht[1] 1, geschlagen, Kapital 2, Kreuz 1, Rad 1, Schaum, Waffe, Wurzel 1;* **II.** *v/i.* **1.** (*hat*) hit, strike; *Herz, Puls:* beat; *heftig:* throb; *Uhr:* strike; *Tür:* bang, slam; *Segel:* flap; *Rad:* run untrue, pull; *Pferd:* kick; *Nachtigall:* sing; *~ an* (+ *Akk.*) *od. gegen* hit; *mit etw. auf/gegen etw. ~* bang s.th. on/against s.th.; *gegen die Tür ~* hammer at the door; *j-m auf die Finger ~* rap s.o.'s knuckles; *nach j-m ~* hit out at; *um sich ~* lash out (in all directions), thrash about (*Am.* around); *mit den Flügeln ~ Vogel:* beat its wings; *sein Puls schlägt regelmäßig* his pulse is regular; **2.** (*hat od. ist*) *~ an* (+*Akk.*) *od. gegen Regen:* beat against; *Wellen:* beat (*od.* crash) against; **3.** (*ist*) *mit dem Kopf an od. gegen etw. ~* hit (*od.* bump, knock, bang) one's head against s.th.; *auf* (+ *Akk.*) *den Kreislauf etc. ~* affect; *die Arbeit etc. schlägt mir auf den Magen* is upsetting my stomach; **4.** (*ist*) *~ aus Flammen:* leap out of; *Rauch:* pour from (*od.* out of); *der Blitz schlug in den Baum* the lightning struck the tree; **5.** (*hat/ist*) (*nicht*) *in j-s Fach od. Ressort ~* (not) be part of s.o.'s job; **6.** (*ist*) *~ nach* (*arten nach*) take after; *sie schlägt ganz nach ihrer Mutter* she's just like her mother; **III.** *v/refl.* (*hat*) **1.** (*kämpfen*) (have a) fight (*mit* with); *sich mit j-m ~* fight it out with s.o.; (*duellieren*) fight a duel with s.o.; *sich ~ um* fight over; *sich gut ~ fig.* hold one's own, give a good account of o.s.; **2.** *sich auf j-s Seite ~* side with s.o.; *weitS.* (*übergehen*) go over to s.o.; *sich in die Büsche ~* slip away

schlagend I. *Part. Präs.* → *schlagen;* **II.** *Adj.* (*treffend*) apt; (*überzeugend*) convincing, very sound; *Gründe:* cogent; (*unwiderlegbar*) irrefutable; **2.** *~e Verbindung Univ.* duel(l)ing fraternity; **3.** *~e Wetter Bergb.* firedamp *Sg.;* **III.** *Adv.: etw. ~ beweisen/widerlegen* prove/refute s.th. conclusively

Schlager *m; -s, -* **1.** *Mus.* pop song; (*Erfolgsschlager*) hit (song *od.* tune); *der deutsche ~* the German hit song; **2.** *umg. Theat.* box-office hit; (*Verkaufsschlager*) winner, sales hit; (*Buch*) bestseller; (*tolle Sache*) hit, sensation

Schläger *m; -s, -* **1.** (*~typ*) thug; *er ist ein übler ~* he's always brawling; **2.** (*Gerät*) *Baseball etc.:* bat; *Tennis:*

racket, racquet; *Golf:* club; *Hockey:* stick; **3.** (*Schlagmann*) *Kricket:* batsman; *Baseball:* batter; **4.** *Boxen:* fighter; *im neg. Sinn:* bruiser; *er ist ein/kein harter ~* he packs / doesn't pack a hard punch

Schlägerei *f; -, -en* fight(ing), brawl, punch-up *umg.; allgemeine: auch* free-for-all; *e-e ~ anfangen* start a fight; *in e-e ~ geraten* get involved in a fight (*umg.* punch-up)

Schlager|festival *n* song contest; *~komponist m, ~komponistin f* popular music composer; *~musik f* popular music

Schlägermütze *f* peaked cap

Schlager|parade *f* hit parade; *~sänger m, ~sängerin f* pop singer; *~spiel n Sport* match (*Am. auch* game) of the day; *~star m etwa* pop star; *~text m* hit song lyrics *Pl.,* words *Pl.* of a (*od.* the) hit song; *~texter m, ~texterin f* writer of popular lyrics, pop lyricist

Schläger|truppe *f* gang of thugs; *~typ m* thug, bruiser *umg.,* bully boy *umg.*

Schlagerwettbewerb *m* song contest

schlagfertig *Adj.* quick-witted, quick off the mark *umg.; ~e Antwort* quick-witted retort (*od.* riposte), snappy answer; *das war ~!* that was a quick riposte!; **Schlagfertigkeit** *f* quick-wittedness, talent for quick repartee

schlagfest *Adj. Material:* impact-resistant

Schlag|frau *f Kricket:* batswoman; *Baseball:* (female) batter; *Rudern:* (female) stroke; *~gitarre f Mus.* electric guitar with soundbox, jazz guitar; *~holz n Sport* rounders bat, *Am. etwa* baseball bat; *~instrument n Mus.* percussion instrument; *Pl. auch* percussion *Sg.*

Schlagkraft *f; nur Sg. Boxen:* (power of) punch; *Mil.* fighting strength, strike power; *fig.* clout; *e-s Arguments:* force; **schlagkräftig** *Adj.* powerful; *Beweis:* → *schlagend II 1*

Schlaglicht *n Fot., Kunst:* highlight; *ein ~ werfen auf* (+ *Akk.*) *fig.* show up, spotlight; *positives:* highlight; **schlaglichtartig I.** *Adj.: ~e Erhellung e-s Problems:* spotlighting; **II.** *Adv.: ~ erhellen* spotlight

Schlag|loch *n* pothole; *~mann m Kricket:* batsman; *Baseball:* batter; *Rudern:* stroke; *~obers n österr., ~rahm m* → *Schlagsahne; ~ring m* knuckleduster, *Am.* brass knuckles *Pl.; ~sahne f* **1.** *geschlagene:* whipped cream; **2.** *flüssige, zum Schlagen:* whipping cream; *~schatten m* (intense) shadow; *~seite f; nur Sg.; Naut.* list; *~ haben Naut.* list; *umg. fig.* be a bit wonky (*Am.* shaky) on one's feet; *stärker:* be reeling drunkenly

schlagstark *Adj. Boxen:* hard-hitting

Schlagstock *m* baton, truncheon, *Am.* nightstick; *Mus.* drumstick; *Schlagstöcke einsetzen Polizei:* use (their) batons

schlägt *Präs.* → *schlagen*

Schlag|uhr *f* chiming clock; *~werk n e-r Uhr:* striking mechanism, strike

Schlagwetter *Pl. Bergb.* **1.** firedamp *Sg.;* **2.** (*Explosion*) firedamp explosion

Schlagwort *n* **1.** *Pl. -e;* catchword; (*Parole*) *auch* slogan; *das sind doch alles nur ~e pej.* they're nothing but empty slogans (*od.* catchphrases); **2.** *Pl. Schlagwörter;* (*Stichwort*) headword; *~katalog m* subject catalog(ue)

Schlagzahl *f Rudern:* number of

strokes, stroke rate

Schlagzeile f: (*große*) ~ (banner) head-line; ~*n machen* make (*od.* hit) the headlines; *das wird für ~n sorgen* that'll make good headline material (*od.* copy)

Schlagzeug n; -s, -e; *Mus.*, *in e-r Band*: drums *Pl.*; *im Orchester*: percussion (instruments *Pl.*); ~ *spielen* play (the) drums; *im Orchester*: play percussion; *und am* ~: *Phil Collins* with Phil Collins on drums; **Schlagzeuger** m; -s, -, **Schlagzeugerin** f; -, -nen; *Mus. in e-r Band*: drummer; *im Orchester*: percussionist

schlaksig *Adj.* lanky; (*ungeschickt*) gangling; *ein langer,* ~*er Typ umg.* a tall, gangling (*od.* lanky) fellow

Schlamassel m, n; -s, -, kein *Pl.*; *umg.* mess; (*Unordnung*) dog's breakfast, can of worms; *da haben wir den* ~*!* now we're in a real (*od.* right) mess

Schlamm m; -(e)s, -e *od.* Schlämme, *mst Sg.* mud; *schleimige Ablagerung von Öl, Abwasser etc.*: sludge; *sandiger Schlick*: silt; *arsenhaltige Schlämme* (types of) sludge containing arsenic

Schlamm|bad n *auch Med.* mudbath; ~**boden** m muddy soil; ~**flut** f river (*stillstehend*: sea) of mud

schlammig *Adj.* muddy

Schlämmkreide f whiting

Schlamm|lawine f mudslide; ~**massen** *Pl.* sea *Sg.* of mud; ~**packung** f *Med.* mudpack; ~**schlacht** f *umg.* **1.** *Pol. etc.* mudslinging; **2.** *Fußball*: mudbath

Schlampe f; -, -n; *umg. pej.* slut, slag *Sl.*

schlampen v/i. *umg.* (*unordentlich sein*) be slovenly, be sloppy; *bei der Arbeit*: do a slovenly (*od.* sloppy) job; *ständig*: be a slovenly worker; *bes. bei Schulaufgaben*: *auch* be careless; *die haben wieder einmal geschlampt* they made a mess of things (*stärker*: botched things up) again; **Schlamper** m; -s, -; *umg.* **1.** (*Person*) slovenly (*od.* messy) person (*bei der Arbeit*: worker); **2.** (*Mäppchen*) pencil case; **Schlamperei** f; -, -en; *umg. pej.* **1.** slovenliness, sloppiness; (*Nachlässigkeit*) carelessness; **2.** *konkret*: mess; (*Arbeit*) careless (*od.* slovenly, sloppy) work, slovenly (*od.* sloppy) job; **Schlamperin** f; -, -nen; *umg.* → **Schlamper**; **schlampert** *Adj.* südd., österr., → **schlampig**; **schlampig** *umg. pej.* **I.** *Adj.* slovenly, sloppy; *Arbeit*: *auch* slipshod; *äußerlich*: slovenly, frowzy; *Frau*: *auch* slatternly; **II.** *Adv.*: *schlampig rumlaufen/ arbeiten* run around in slovenly dress (*Am.* sloppy clothes) / do sloppy (*od.* slipshod) work; **Schlampigkeit** f *umg. pej.* slovenliness, sloppiness; ~**en** examples of slipshod work

schlang *Imperf.* → **schlingen¹, schlingen²**

Schlange f; -, -n **1.** *Zool.* snake; *bibl.* serpent; *Astron.* Serpent; (*falsche*) ~ *fig.* snake in the grass; **2.** *fig.* (*Menschenschlange*) queue, *bes. Am.* line; (*Autoschlange*) line (*Brit.* queue) (of cars); ~ *stehen, sich in e-e* ~ *stellen* queue (up), *bes. Am.* stand in line, line up (*alle* **um, nach** for)

schlängeln v/refl. *Weg*: wind; *Fluss*: *auch* meander; *zuckend, hin und her*: wriggle; *sich* ~ *durch* (*ein Loch etc.*) wriggle through; (*e-e Menge etc.*) weave (*od.* worm) one's way through

Schlangen|beschwörer m snake charmer; ~**biss** m snakebite; ~**ei** n

snake's egg; *fig.* source of disaster; ~**fraß** m *umg.* muck; ~**gift** n snake venom (*od.* poison); ♀**gleich** *Adv.* like a snake, sinuously; ~**grube** f snake pit (*auch fig.*); ~**gurke** f snake gourd (*od.* cucumber)

schlangenhaft *Adj.* snakelike, snaky

Schlangen|haut f snakeskin; ~**leder** n snakeskin; ~**linie** f wavy (wiggly *umg.*) line; *in* ~*n fahren* weave, zigzag (along the road); ~**mensch** m contortionist; ~**stern** m *Zool.* brittle (*od.* sand) star; ~**tanz** m **1.** *mit lebenden Schlangen*: dance with snakes; *der Indianer*: snake dance; **2.** *schlangenhaft*: snake dance

Schlangestehen n queueing (up), *bes. Am.* standing in line

schlank *Adj.* **1.** slim; *auf elegante Art*: slender; ~ *wie e-e Tanne* slim and willowy; ~ *werden* slim; (*abnehmen*) lose weight; *Obst etc.* *macht* ~ you don't (*od.* won't) put any weight on with fruit *etc.*; ~ *machende Kleidung etc.* clothes *etc.* that make one look slimmer; → **Linie** 5; **2.** *fig.*: ~*e Produktion / ~es Management* lean production/ management; **Schlankheit** f slimness, slenderness

Schlankheits|fimmel m *umg.* obsession with one's figure; ~**kost** f weight--reducing (*od.* dieting) foodstuff; ~**kur** f slimming (*Am.* reducing) program(me); *nur Diät*: slimming (*Am.* reducing) diet; *e-e* ~ *machen* go (*od.* be) on a slimming program(me) (*od.* diet), *Am. auch* be on a weight-loss program

Schlankmacher m slimming agent

schlank|weg *Adv. umg.* point-blank; *ich brachte es* ~ *nicht fertig* I simply couldn't do it; ~**wüchsig** *Adj.* tall and slim, willowy; *Baum*: tall and slender

schlapp I. *Adj.* **1.** (*erschöpft*) worn out; *nach e-r Krankheit*: run-down, washed-out *umg.*; (*ohne Schwung*) listless; (*geschwächt*) weak; *Körper, Glieder*: limp; **2.** *umg. pej.* feeble; ~*er Kerl* wimpish type; *das hat mich* ~*e 1000 Euro gekostet* (= *es war teuer*) it cost me a cool 1,000 euros; (= *es war billig*) it cost me a mere 1,000 euros; **3.** *Seil*: slack; ~*e Muskeln* flabby muscles; **II.** *Adv.*: *sich* ~ *fühlen* feel run--down (*od.* washed out); → *auch* **schlappmachen**

Schlappe f; -, -n; *umg.* setback; *e-e* (*empfindliche*) ~ *einstecken müssen* suffer a (severe) setback; *es setzte e-e 0:5-*~ *Sport* it was a 5-0 drubbing (*Am.* shutout)

schlappen *umg.* **I.** v/i. *Schuhe*: flap; *Person*: (*latschen*) shuffle along; **II.** v/t. (*schlürfen*) lap (up)

Schlappen m; -s, -; *umg.* (*Pantoffel*) slipper

Schlappheit f **1.** (*Erschöpfung*) exhaustion; *nach e-r Krankheit*: run--down state; *ohne Schwung*: listlessness; (*Schwäche*) weakness; *des Körpers, e-s Gliedes*: limpness; **2.** *umg. pej.* feebleness, wimpishness; **3.** *e-s Segels, e-s Muskels*: limpness

Schlapphut m slouch hat

schlappmachen v/i. (*trennb., hat -ge-*) *umg.* slow down; (*ein Tief erreichen*) hit a low; *körperlich*: wilt; (*aufgeben*) give up; (*zusammenbrechen*) flake out; *fig. Auto etc.*: give up the ghost; *in der Hitze* ~ will in (*od.* succumb to) the heat; *nicht* ~*! ermahnend*: no slacking!; *ermunternd*: come on, you can do it!; *die macht so schnell nicht schlapp* she won't give up that easily

Schlapp|ohr n **1.** floppy ear; **2.** *umg. fig.* → **Schlappschwanz**; ~**schwanz** m *umg. pej.* wimp, drip, dork

Schlaraffen|land n; *nur Sg.* (land of) Cockaigne; *fig. auch* land of milk and honey; *sich wie im* ~ *fühlen* have everything the heart could desire, be in the lap of luxury; ~**leben** n life of luxury, cushy (*od.* lush) life *umg.*

schlau I. *Adj.* (*klug*) clever, shrewd; (*listig*) crafty; *ein* ~*er Fuchs umg.* a crafty (*od.* sly) customer; *aus ihm werde ich nicht* ~ *umg.* I can't make him out; *daraus werde ich nicht* ~ *umg.* I can't make head or tail of it; *das war besonders* ~ *von dir iro.* that was particularly clever on your part; ~*es Buch umg.* reference book (*über + Akk.* on); *ein ganz Schlauer pej.* → **Schlauberger**; **II.** *Adv.*: *das hat er sich* ~ *ausgedacht!* that was good thinking on his part

Schlauberger m; -s, -; *umg., auch iro.* clever dick, smarty pants *Sg.*; *listig*: crafty type (*od.* customer)

Schlauch m; -(e)s, Schläuche **1.** (*Gartenschlauch*) hose, *Brit.* hosepipe; *von Fahrrad-, Autoreifen*: (inner) tube; *hist.* (*Weinschlauch etc.*) skin; *alter Wein in neuen Schläuchen fig.* old wine in new bottles; *auf dem* ~ *stehen umg. fig. momentan*: have a mental blank; (*ratlos sein*) be (completely) clueless; (*begriffsstutzig sein*) be slow on the uptake; **2.** *umg.* (*Strapaze*) hard slog; **3.** *das Zimmer ist ein* ~ *umg. fig.* the room's like a tunnel

Schlauchboot n rubber dinghy; (*Rettungsboot*) life raft, inflatable (boat); *großes*: (inflatable) raft; ~**fahren** n; -s, kein *Pl.* rafting; ~**fahrt** f rafting trip

schlauchen *umg.* vt/i. (*anstrengen, ermüden*) take it out of *s.o.*; *Mil.* put *s.o.* through it, give *s.o.* hell *Sl.*; → *geschlaucht*; *das schlaucht ganz schön* it really takes it out of you

schlauchlos *Adj. Mot.* tubeless

Schlauch|reifen m tube-type tyre (*Am.* tire); ~**trommel** f hose reel; ~**wagen** m hose cart (*od.* trolley)

Schläue f; -, kein *Pl.* cleverness, shrewdness; (*Listigkeit*) craftiness, cunning

schlauerweise *Adv.* cleverly (*auch iro.*); ~ *hat er nichts gesagt* he was wise (*bes. Am.* smart) enough not to say anything

Schlaufe f; -, -n loop

Schlaufuchs m *umg.* → **Schlauberger**

Schlauheit f → **Schläue**

Schlaukopf m *umg.*, **Schlaumeier** m; -s, -; *umg.* → **Schlauberger**

Schlawiner m; -s, -; *umg. hum.* rogue; (*Kind*) rascal

schlecht I. *Adj.* **1.** *allg.* bad (*Komp.* ~*er* worse, *Sup.* ~*est* worst); *Augen, Gesundheit, Gedächtnis, Qualität, Leistung etc.*: bad, poor; *nicht* ~*!* not bad!; ~*er Absatz Wirts.* poor sales; *ein* ~*es Geschäft* a bad deal; *wir hatten* (*nur*) ~*es Wetter* we had (nothing but) bad weather; *ich war ein* ~*er Schüler auch* I was no good at school (*od.* was a terrible student); *e-e* ~*e Nachricht* bad news *Sg.*; *zuerst die* ~*e Nachricht* first, the bad news; ~*e Zeiten* bad (*od.* hard) times; ~ *in etw. sein* be bad at *s.th.*; ~*er werden* get worse, deteriorate; **2.** (*böse*) bad; (*boshaft*) *auch* wicked; *sie hat e-n* ~*en Charakter* she has an evil disposition; *er ist abgrundtief* ~ he is rotten to the core; *ein* ~*er Freund* not a good friend, a treacherous friend; **3.** (*verdorben*) bad, off; (*schädlich*) bad; *Luft*: bad, stale; (*verschmutzt*) polluted; *Wasser*: polluted, contaminated; *Wein*: off; *die Milch ist* ~ has gone off (*Am.* bad), is off (*Am.* bad); **es muss weg, bevor's ~ wird** *umg.* we must get rid of it before it goes bad (*od.* off); **das feuchte Klima ist ~ für ihn** the damp climate is bad for him; **4.** (*unpassend*) bad; **im Moment ist es ~** just now is not a good time; **Freitagnachmittag ist ~** Friday afternoon is bad for me; **5.** *Gesundheit*: poor; **sein Zustand ist ~** he is in a bad way; **mir ist ~** I feel ill (*bes. Am.* sick); (*ich habe e-n Brechreiz*) I feel sick; **mir wird ~** (*ich muss brechen*) I'm going to be sick; **es kann einem ~ dabei werden** *umg.* it's enough to make you sick; → **Laune** 1, **Tag**[1] 4; **II.** *Adv.* **1.** *allg.* badly; **~ riechen/ schmecken** smell/taste bad; **er hört/ sieht ~** he can't hear/see very well; his hearing/eyesight is bad (*od.* poor); **ich verstehe dich ganz ~** I can hardly hear what you're saying; **~ aussehen** not look good; *gesundheitlich*: look ill; **~ dran sein** *umg.* be badly off; **es steht ~ um ihn** things aren't looking too good for him; *gesundheitlich*: he's in a bad way; **~ abschneiden** *bei Prüfung, Wettkampf etc.*: do badly; **~ besucht sein** *Lokal, Vorstellung etc.*: be poorly attended; **Sie wären ~ beraten zu** (+ *Inf.*) I wouldn't advise you to (+ *Inf.*), I would advise you against (+ *Ger.*); **~ gelaunt** grumpy, in a bad mood; **~ sitzend** *Anzug etc.*: badly-fitting; **~ und recht** after a fashion; **2. es geht ihm ~** he's having a bad (*od.* hard) time, things are going badly for him; *gesundheitlich*: he's not well (*stärker*: in a bad way); *finanziell*: he's in a bad way financially, he's pretty hard up *umg.*; **es ist mir noch nie so ~ gegangen** *gesundheitlich*: I've never been so ill; *finanziell, wirtschaftlich*: things have never been so bad (for me); **wenn das rauskommt, geht's euch aber ~** *umg.* if that gets out you'll be in for it; **3. ~ machen** *umg.* (*j-n*) run down, knock (*bei j-m* in front of s.o.); **4. ~ behandeln** treat badly, maltreat; **~ reden von** talk negatively about; (*schlecht machen*) run down, say nasty things about *umg.*; **ich bin auf ihn ~ zu sprechen** don't talk to me about him; **es bekam ihm ~** *Essen etc.*: it didn't agree with him; *fig.* it didn't do him any good; **er kann es sich ~ leisten zu** (+ *Inf.*) he can't really afford to (+ *Inf.*); **er hat nicht ~ gestaunt** *umg.* he wasn't half surprised; **heute geht es ~** (*passt nicht*) it's awkward (*od.* difficult) today; **ich kann ~ nein sagen** (*bin zu gutmütig*) I just can't say no, I find it hard to say no; (*in diesem Fall*) I can hardly (*od.* I can't very well) say no

Schlechte *n*; *-n*, *kein Pl.*: **sich zum ~n wenden** take a turn for the worse; **ich habe nie etwas ~s über sie gesagt** I never said a bad word (*od.* anything nasty) about her; **das ~ daran** the bad part about it, the negative side of it

schlechterdings *Adv. altm.* absolutely, simply

Schlechterstellung *f* worsening of one's position

schlechthin *Adv.* (*geradezu*) absolutely; (*an sich*) per se, as such; **der Renaissancemensch ~** the epitome of the Renaissance man, the classic Ren-

aissance man

Schlechtigkeit *f* (*Bosheit, Verworfenheit*) wickedness; (*Verderbtheit*) depravity; (*Niedrigkeit*) baseness; **ihr traue ich alle ~en der Welt zu** there's no form of depravity (*od.* wickedness) I would put past her

schlechtweg *Adv.* → **schlechthin**

Schlechtwetter *n*; *nur Sg.*; *Met.* bad weather; **~front** *f* bad weather front, storm front; **~gebiet** *n* area that experiences bad weather; **~geld** *n* bad weather allowance; **~periode** *f* spell of bad weather

schlecken *vt/i.* **1.** lick; (*auf~*) lap up; **ein Eis ~** lick an ice cream; **2.** → **naschen**; **Schleckerei** *f*; *-*, *-en* **1.** titbit, *Am.* tidbit; *umg.* (*Leckerbissen*) something to tickle one's tastebuds; (*Süßes*) something sweet; (*Bonbon*) sweet, *Am.* (piece of) candy; **2.** *nur Sg.* (*Naschen*) constant eating (of sweets, *Am. auch* candy etc.)

Schleckermaul *n*: **der ist aber ein ~** he's really got a sweet tooth; *pej. umg.* he's always gulping sweets

Schlegel *m*; *-s*, *-* **1.** *südd., österr. Gastr.* leg; **2.** → **Schlägel**

...schlegel *m*, *im Subst.*, *Gastr.*: **Hähnchen~** chicken leg; **Hasen~** leg of hare

Schlehdorn *m Bot.* blackthorn

Schlehe *f*; *-*, *-n*; *Bot.* (*Frucht*) sloe; (*Baum*) blackthorn

Schlehen|likör *m* sloe liqueur; **~schnaps** *m* sloe gin

Schlei *m*; *-(e)s*, *-e* → **Schleie**

Schleiche *f*; *-*, *-n*; *Zool.* (limbless) lizard of the Anguidae; (*Blindschleiche*) blindworm

schleichen; *schleicht*, *schlich*, *ist bzw. hat geschlichen* **I.** *v/i.* (*ist*) creep, sneak; *Dieb, Fuchs etc.*: prowl; *auf den Zehenspitzen*: tiptoe; *umg. erschöpft, langsam*: crawl (*auch Auto*); **ins Haus ~** sneak (*od.* slip, steal) into the house; **ums Haus ~** creep (*Dieb*: prowl) around the house; **II.** *v/refl.* (*hat*) creep, sneak; **er hat sich mit schlechtem Gewissen aus dem Haus geschlichen** he stole (*od.* slunk) out of the house with a bad conscience; **sich in j-s Vertrauen ~** *fig.* worm one's way into s.o.'s confidence

schleichend I. *Part. präs.* → **schleichen**; **II.** *Adj.* *Fieber, Krankheit*: lingering; (*tückisch*) insidious; (*chronisch*) chronic; **~er Tod** slow death; **~e Inflation** creeping inflation; **III.** *Adv.*: **die Krankheit verläuft oft ~** the disease is often very slow to develop

Schleicher *m*; *-s*, *-*; *umg.* **1.** *pej.* toady; **2.** *Mot.* crawler, *Am.* slowpoke; **Schleicherin** *f*; *-*, *-nen*; *pej.* → **Schleicher** 1; **schleicherisch** *Adj. pej.* toadying

Schleich|handel *m* illicit trade; **~katze** *f Zool.* viverrid; **~weg** *m* hidden (*od.* secret) path (*od.* route); *fig.* secret way (*od.* means); **auf ~en** *fig.* by devious ways and means; **~werbung** *f* surreptitious advertising, plugging *umg.*; **~ machen für** plug

Schleie *f*; *-*, *-n*; *Zool.* tench

Schleier *m*; *-s*, *-* veil; *im Islam*: yashmak; (*Nebel-*, *Dunstschleier*) veil of mist, haze; *Fot.* fog(ging); **den ~ nehmen** *kirchl.* take the veil; **alles wie durch e-n ~ sehen** see everything through a haze; **den ~** (*des Geheimnisses*) **lüften** *fig.* lift the veil of secrecy, unveil the secret; **den ~ des Vergessens über etw. breiten** draw a line under s.th., agree to forgive and forget

s.th.; **~eule** *f* barn owl; **~fahndung** *f* (police hunt by) spot checks *Pl.*

schleierhaft *Adj.* (*rätselhaft*) mysterious; (*unbegreiflich*) incomprehensible; **das ist mir** (*völlig*) **~** it's a (complete) mystery to me

Schleier|karpfen *m Zool.* tench; **~kraut** *n Bot.* baby's-breath, babies'-breath, gypsophila; **~tanz** *m* veil dance, dance of the veils; **~wolke** *f Met.* cirrostratus

Schleif|apparat *m* grinding (*für Messer*: sharpening) tool, grinder; **~band** *n* abrasive (*od.* polishing) belt

Schleife *f*; *-*, *-n im Haar*: ribbon; *an e-m Band*: bow; (*Kurve*) loop, horseshoe bend; *Flug.*, *auch Computer, Tonband etc.*: loop; **e-e ~ binden am Schuh**: tie a bow; **~n ziehen** *Flug.* circle (*über* + *Dat.* over, above)

schleifen[1] *vt/i.*; *schleift*, *schliff*, *hat geschliffen* **1.** (*schärfen*) sharpen; (*wetzen*) *auch* whet; *Tech.* (*glätten, abschmirgeln*) grind, abrade; *feiner*: smooth, polish (*auch fig.*); (*Edelsteine, Glas*) cut; **2.** *Mil. umg.* put through the mill; → **geschliffen**

schleifen[2] **I.** *v/t.* (*hat geschleift*) **1.** drag (along) (*auch fig.* *j-n*); (*Koffer etc.*) *auch* lug; **an den Haaren ~** drag by the hair; **j-n ins Konzert** *etc.* **~** *umg. fig.* drag s.o. along to a concert *etc.*; **2.** (*niederreißen*) pull down, demolish; **II.** *v/i.* (*hat od. ist*) *Schleppe etc.*: trail (*am Boden* along the ground); (*reiben*) rub (*an* +*Dat.* against); **das Rad schleift am Kotflügel** the wheel is rubbing against the (inside of the) wing (*Am.* fender); **die Füße ~ lassen** drag one's feet, shuffle (one's feet); **die Kupplung ~ lassen** *Mot.* slip the clutch; **er hat s-e Arbeit in letzter Zeit ~ lassen** he has let things slide recently (as far as work is concerned)

Schleifer *m*; *-s*, *-* **1.** *Tech.* grinder; (*Glasschleifer*) (glass) grinder (*od.* cutter); (*Edelsteinschleifer*) (gem) cutter; **2.** *Mus.* slide; **3.** *Mil. umg.* slave driver; **Schleiferei** *f*; *-*, *-en* **1.** *Tech.* grinding shop; **2.** *Mil. umg.* bull; (*Drillen*) square-bashing; **Schleiferin** *f*; *-*, *-nen* → **Schleifer** 1

Schleif|lack *m* matt lacquer; (*Ausführung*) eggshell finish; **~maschine** *f* grinding machine, grinder; **~mittel** *n* abrasive; **~papier** *n* sandpaper; **~rad** *n* grinding (*od.* polishing) wheel; **~riemen** *m* strop; **~ring** *m Etech.* slip ring; **~scheibe** *f* → **Schleifrad**; **~spur** *f* trail; **~stein** *m* whetstone; *drehbarer*: grindstone

Schleim *m*; *-(e)s*, *-e* **1.** slime; *Physiol.* mucus; *bes. der Atemwege*: phlegm; **2.** (*Suppe*) gruel; **~absonderung** *f* mucous secretion

Schleimbeutel *m Anat.* bursa; **~entzündung** *f Med.* bursitis; *am Knie*: *auch* housemaid's knee *umg.*

Schleimdrüse *f Anat.* mucous gland

schleimen *v/i.* **1.** *Physiol.* produce mucus; **2.** *umg. pej.* suck up (to people), toady to people; **Schleimer** *m*; *-s*, *-*, **Schleimerin** *f*; *-*, *-nen*; *umg. pej.* toady, bootlicker, brownnose

Schleimhaut *f Anat.* mucous membrane

schleimig *Adj.* slimy (*auch fig. pej.*); *Physiol.* mucous; (*zähflüssig*) viscous; **~er Typ** *umg. pej.* slimy type; (*Speichellecker*) bootlicker, brownnose

schleimlösend I. *Adj.* expectorant; **II.** *Adv.*: **~ wirken** have an expectorant effect

Schleim|scheißer *m vulg.* toady, bootlicker, brownnose; **~suppe** *f Gastr.* gruel

Schlemihl *m*; *-s, -e* **1.** (*Pechvogel*) unlucky devil, *Am.* schlemiel; **2.** (*umg. Gauner*) crafty customer

schlemmen *vt/i. Gastr.* gormandize; (*ein Schlemmermahl haben*) have a feast (blowout *Sl.*); (*etw. verzehren*) feast on, regale o.s. on; **wir haben mal wieder so richtig geschlemmt** we really gorged (*od.* stuffed) ourselves again (with glorious food), we really pigged out *umg.*; **Schlemmer** *m*; *-s, -*; (*Genüssling*) bon vivant; (*Feinschmecker*) gourmet

Schlemmerei *f*, *-, -en* gormandizing, feasting; **die Einladung war e-e einzige ~** I was (we were *etc.*) invited to one long round of feasting (*hum.* conspicuous consumption)

Schlemmerführer *m* guide to gourmet restaurants

schlemmerhaft *Adj.*: **~es Leben** life of gourmet feasting

Schlemmer|lokal *n Gastr.* gourmet restaurant; **~mahl** *n* (gourmet) feast, blowout *Sl.*; **~reise** *f* restaurant tour for gourmets; **~rezept** *n* rich recipe for gourmets

schlendern *v/i.* saunter, stroll; **wenn wir weiter so ~, kommen wir nie an** *umg.* if we walk this slowly, we'll never get there

Schlender|schritt *m*: **im ~ daherkommen** come sauntering (*od.* ambling, moseying *umg.*) along

Schlendrian *m*; *-(e)s, kein Pl.*; *umg. pej.* **1.** (*alter Trott*) humdrum routine, rut; **in den alten ~ zurückfallen** fall back into one's old ways (*od.* the old rut); **2.** (*Bummelei*) dawdling; (*Wurstelei*) muddling through

Schlenker *m*; *-s, -*; *umg.* **1.** *e-s Autos etc.*: swerve; **e-n ~ machen** swerve; **2.** *umg.* (*Abstecher*) detour; **3.** (*Abschweifung*) digression

schlenkern I. *vt/i.* swing; **II.** *v/i.*: **mit den Armen** *etc.* **~** swing one's arms *etc.*

schlenzen *v/t. Sport* scoop; *Fußball*: chip; **den Ball ins Tor ~** chip (*Am.* tip) the ball into the net; **Schlenzer** *m*; *-s, -*; *Sport* chip

Schlepp *m*: **in ~ nehmen** → **Schlepptau**; **~angel** *f* troll; **~anker** *m* sea anchor; **~bügel** *m am Skilift*: T-bar; **~dampfer** *m* steam tug

Schleppe *f*; *-, -n e-s Kleides*: train

schleppen I. *v/t.* **1.** (*ziehen*) drag (*auch fig. Person*); (*Koffer etc.*) *auch* lug, *Am. auch* schlep *umg.*; *Naut., Flug., Mot.* tow; **der Wagen musste in die Werkstatt geschleppt werden** the car had to be towed to the garage; **Kunden ~** *umg.* tout; **j-n in ein Konzert** *etc.* **~** *umg. fig.* drag s.o. along to a concert *etc.*; **2.** *umg.* (*tragen*) lug; **Umzugskartons nach oben ~** lug (*od.* cart) removers' (*Am.* packing) boxes upstairs; **nun schlepp ich den Brief schon tagelang durch die Gegend** *fig.* I've been carrying the letter around with me for days; **3.** *fig.* (*illegal befördern*) (*Flüchtlinge etc.*) smuggle; **II.** *v/refl.* **1.** *Person*: drag o.s. (along); (*mühsam gehen*) *auch* trudge, plod (along), *Am.* schlep; **der Dicke schleppte sich zur Tür** the fat guy moved ponderously towards (*Am.* schlepped toward) the door; **2.** *Sache*: drag on; **es schleppt sich seit Monaten** *etc.* it has been dragging on for months *etc.*; **3.** **sich ~ mit** *fig.* (*Kummer etc.*) be weighed

down by; (*e-r Erkältung*) be battling with

schleppend I. *Part. Präs.* → **schleppen**; **II.** *Adj.* (*träge, langsam*) sluggish, slow (*auch Wirts.*); (*mühsam*) labo(u)red; *Sprache*: slow, drawling; (*ermüdend*) tedious; **mit ~en Schritten gehen** shuffle along, drag one's feet; **III.** *Adv.*: **nur ~ vorangehen** *Arbeit, Gespräche etc.*: make very slow progress, inch along; **~ beginnen** get off to a slow start, be very slow to get off the ground

Schleppen|träger *m*, **~trägerin** *f* trainbearer

Schlepper *m*; *-s, -* **1.** tractor; *Naut.* tug; **2.** *umg.* (*Kundenwerber*) tout; **3.** (*Fluchthelfer*) helper of illegal immigrants; **~bande** *f* gang smuggling illegal immigrants

Schlepperei *f*; *-, -en*; *umg.* lugging (*Am. auch* schlepping) around

Schlepperorganisation *f* ring (*od.* syndicate) of touts

Schlepp|fahrzeug *n* towing vehicle; *zum Abschleppen*: recovery vehicle, *Am.* tow truck; **~kahn** *m* dumb barge, lighter; **~lift** *m* T-bar (lift), ski tow

Schleppnetz *n* dragnet; *bei der Hochseefischerei*: trawl (net); **~fahndung** *f* dragnet (hunt)

Schlepp|schiff *n* tug; **~seil** *n* towrope; **~start** *m Flug.* towed takeoff; **~tau** *n* towrope; **ins ~ nehmen** / **im ~ haben** *auch umg.* take/have in tow; **im ~ folgte ...** *fig.* in its (*od.* their) wake came ...; **~zug** *m Naut.* train of barges

Schlesien (*n*); *-s*; *Geog.* Silesia; **Schlesier** *m*; *-s, -*, **Schlesierin** *f*; *-, -nen* Silesian, *weiblich auch*: Silesian woman (*od.* girl); **Schlesier sein** be (a) Silesian, come from Silesia; **schlesisch I.** *Adj.* Silesian; **II. Schlesisch** *n*; *-en*; *Ling.* Silesian; **das Schlesische** Silesian

Schleswig-Holstein (*n*); *-s*; *Geog.* Schleswig-Holstein; **Schleswig-Holsteiner** *m*; *-s, -*, **Schleswig-Holsteinerin** *f*; *-, -nen* man (*f* woman *od.* girl *etc.*) from Schleswig-Holstein; **schleswig-holsteinisch** *Adj.* Schleswig-Holstein ..., from Schleswig-Holstein

Schleuder *f*; *-, -n* **1.** catapult, *Am.* slingshot; *ohne Gestell*: sling; **2.** *für Wäsche*: spin-drier; **3.** *Tech.* centrifuge; **4.** *für Honig etc.*: extractor, separator; **~beton** *m* spun concrete; **~brett** *n* springboard

Schleuderei *f*; *-, -en*; *umg.* (constant) skidding

Schleuder|gang *m e-r Waschmaschine*: spin; **~gefahr** *f* danger of skidding; **„~"** (*Verkehrszeichen*) Slippery Road; **~honig** *m* strained (*od.* extracted) honey; **~kurs** *m* **1.** *Mot.* skid-control course; **2.** *auf ~* *umg. fig.* careering out of control; **~maschine** *f* **1.** *Tech.* centrifuge; **2.** *für Honig etc.*: extractor, separator

schleudern I. *v/t.* (*hat geschleudert*) **1.** fling, hurl; (*wie*) *mit e-r Schleuder*: sling; **er wurde aus dem Fahrzeug geschleudert** he was thrown (*od.* flung) out of the car; **2.** *Tech. mit e-r Schleudermaschine*: centrifuge; **3.** (*Honig etc.*) strain, extract; **II.** *vt/i.* **1.** (*hat*) (*Wäsche*) spin-dry; *Maschine*: spin; **„nicht ~!"** *Waschanleitung*: do not spin; **2.** *v/i.* (*ist*) *Mot.* skid; **der Wagen ist auf od. gegen ein geparktes Fahrzeug geschleudert** the car skidded into a parked vehicle

Schleudern *n*; *-s, kein Pl.*: **ins ~ kommen** (go into a) skid, start skidding; *umg. fig.* start floundering; **bei solchen Aufgaben komme ich immer ins ~** I always get out of my depth with this sort of task; **j-n ins ~ bringen** *umg. fig.* throw s.o. (completely)

Schleuder|preis *m umg.* giveaway (*od.* rock-bottom) price; **~sitz** *m Flug.* ejector seat; *fig.* hot seat; **~trauma** *n Med.* whiplash; **~ware** *f umg.* goods *Pl.* at giveaway prices; *pej.* cheap stuff

schleunig I. *Adj. nur attr.* quick, prompt, speedy; (*hastig*) hasty; **II.** *Adv.* quickly, promptly; **schleunigst** *Adv.* at once, instantly; **aber ~!** at (*Am.* on) the double!; **~ das Weite suchen** disappear at (*Am.* on) the double

Schleuse *f*; *-, -n* sluice; *auch fig.* floodgate; *in Kanal*: lock (*auch Med., Raumf. etc.*); **der Himmel öffnete s-e ~n** *fig.* the heavens opened; **schleusen** *v/t.* **1.** (*Kanal*) lock; (*Schiff*) pass through a lock; **2.** *fig.* (*etw.*) channel; (*j-n*) steer, shepherd; (*Menschenmasse*) herd; **durch die Menge ~** steer *s.o.* through the crowd; **3.** *heimlich*: (*illegale Einwanderer etc.*) smuggle

Schleusen|kammer *f* lock chamber; **~tor** *n* sluice gate; *e-r Kanalschleuse*: lock gate; **~treppe** *f* flight of locks; **~wärter** *m*, **~wärterin** *f* lock keeper; *an Staudämmen etc.*: sluice keeper

Schleuser *m*; *-s, -*, **~in** *f*; *-, -nen* → **Schlepper** 3; **~bande** *f* → **Schlepperbande**

schlich *Imperf.* → **schleichen**

Schliche *Pl.* tricks; **j-m auf die ~ od. hinter j-s ~ kommen** find s.o. out, get wise to s.o.('s tricks)

schlicht I. *Adj.* **1.** (*einfach*) simple; (*ohne Schmuck*) plain; (*anspruchslos*) modest, unassuming, unpretentious; (*ungekünstelt*) artless, ingenuous; *Tatsache, Wahrheit*: plain; *Sprache, Stil, Worte*: unsophisticated, straightforward; **~e Eleganz** simple elegance; **~es Essen** plain food; (*Mahlzeit*) simple (*od.* frugal) meal; **~es Gemüt** simple (*od.* naive) mentality; (*Person*) simple soul; **~er Glaube** simple faith; **~e Menschen** simple (*od.* unsophisticated) people; **~es Wesen** simple nature; (*Person*) simple (*od.* unsophisticated) person; **in ~en Verhältnissen leben** be (*od.* live) in modest circumstances; **2.** **~ und ergreifend** *umg. fig.* not wonderful; **ich fand es ziemlich ~** *umg. pej.* I thought it was pretty basic; **II.** *Adv.*: **das ist ~ gelogen** that is simply untrue; **~ und einfach** *od.* **~ und ergreifend falsch/unsinnig** *umg.* absolutely (*od.* purely and simply) wrong / utter (*od.* pure, sheer, absolute) nonsense; **er hat, ~ gesagt, keine Ahnung** *umg.* to put it bluntly, he hasn't a clue

schlichten I. *vt/i.* (*Streit*) settle; *durch Schiedsspruch*: settle by arbitration; **zwischen zwei Parteien zu ~ versuchen** mediate between, try to smooth out the differences between; **II.** *v/t.* **1.** *fachspr.* (*glätten*) (*Holz, Metall*) smooth; (*Leder*) dress; **2.** *Dial.* (*schichten, stapeln*) pile up

Schlichter *m*; *-s, -*, **~in** *f*; *-, -nen* mediator, troubleshooter; *durch Schiedsspruch*: arbitrator; **~spruch** *m* (*Schiedsspruch*) arbitrator's award

Schlichtheit *f* plainness, simplicity *etc.*; → **schlicht** I 1

Schlichtung *f* arbitration, settlement

Schlichtungs|ausschuss *m* arbitration (*od.* conciliation) committee; **~stelle** *f* board (*od.* court) of arbitration; **~verfahren** *n* arbitration proceedings *Pl.*; **~versuch** *m* attempt at arbitration

schlichtweg *Adv.* absolutely, purely and simply

Schlick *m*; -(e)s, -e, *mst Sg.* silt; (*Schlamm*) mud; **~ablagerung** *f* deposition of silt, silting

schlickig *Adj.* muddy

schlief *Imperf.* → **schlafen**

Schliere *f*; -, -n **1.** *Tech.* streak, glass bubble; **2.** *auf e-r Glasscheibe*: streak

Schließanlage *f* set of dedicated locks

Schließe *f*; -, -n fastening, *Am.* fastener; *am Buch, Kleid, an der Handtasche etc.*: clasp

schließen; *schließt, schloss, hat geschlossen* **I.** *v/t.* **1.** a) (*zumachen*) close, shut; *sich* (*Dat.*) **das Kleid ~** do up one's dress; **die Augen ~** shut (*od.* close) one's eyes; *euph.* (*sterben*) close one's eyes for ever; → **Lücke**, b) (*einschließen etc.*) *mit Schlüssel*: lock; *mit Riegel*: bolt; **j-n in e-e Zelle ~** shut s.o. in a cell; **e-n Hund an die Kette ~** put a dog on the chain; **das Geld in die Schublade ~** lock the money away (*od.* up) in the drawer; → **Herz**[1] 8, c) (*Betrieb, Laden, Schule etc.*) close; *für immer od. langfristig*: *auch* shut (*od.* close) down; (*Stromkreis*) close, d) *fig.* (*Bündnis*) form, enter into; (*Vergleich*) reach, come to; → **Ehe, Freundschaft** 1, **Frieden** 1, **Vertrag** *etc.*, e) (*anschließen*): **etw. an etw. ~** *fig.* follow s.th. up with s.th.; **2.** (*beenden*) close, end, conclude; (*Brief, Rede*) *auch* wind up (**mit den Worten** by saying); (*Debatte, Versammlung*) close; **II.** *v/i.* **1.** a) (*zumachen*) shut, close; *Betrieb etc.*: close (*od.* shut) down; **tut mir Leid - wir ~ gleich** I am sorry - we are about to close, b) *Schloss, Schlüssel*: close, shut; **das Schloss schließt etwas schwer** the lock's a bit stiff; **das Fenster schließt schlecht** the window won't close properly; **Vorsicht, Türen ~ automatisch** Caution automatic doors; **2.** (*enden*) (come to a) close; *bei e-r Rede etc.* → I 2; **damit möchte ich ~** that is all I have to say; **~ mit Börse**; **3.** (*folgern*) conclude; **ich schließe daraus, dass** I conclude (*od.* take it) from this that; **von etw. auf etw. ~** infer (*od.* deduce) s.th. from s.th.; **von sich auf andere ~** judge others by o.s.; **auf etw. ~ lassen** suggest (*od.* point to) s.th.; **III.** *v/refl.* **1.** close, shut; *Wunde*: close (up); *Blüte*: close; **s-e Hände schlossen sich um i-n Hals** his hands closed around her throat; **2.** *an den Vortrag schloss sich ein Dokumentarfilm* the lecture was followed by a documentary; *an das Grundstück schließt sich ein Parkplatz* there is a car park (*Am.* parking lot) adjoining (*od.* next to) the site; → **Kreis** 1

Schließer[1] *m*; -s, -; (*Vorrichtung*) door--closer

Schließer[2] *m*; -s, -, **~in** *f*; -, -nen doorkeeper; *im Gefängnis*: jailer

Schließfach *n Bahnhof etc.*: (left-luggage) locker; *Post*®: post office box, PO box; *Bank*: safe deposit box; *in der Schule, im Zug etc.*: locker

schließlich *Adv.* **1.** finally, eventually, in the end; (*endlich*) at last; **~ und endlich** when all is said and done; **2.** (*immerhin*) after all; **~ bist du**

schon 18 you're 18 after all; I mean, you are 18 *umg.*

Schließmuskel *m Anat.* sphincter (muscle)

Schließung *f* **1.** closing, shutting; *e-s Betriebs etc.*: closure, shutdown, closing down; *e-r Debatte, Versammlung etc.*: closing; *Etech., des Stromkreises*: closing; *e-s Kontakts*: closure; **2.** *von Vertrag, Frieden etc.*: conclusion; *von Ehe*: solemnization; *von Bündnis*: formation

Schließzylinder *m* cylinder (*of a safety lock*)

schliff *Imperf.* → **schleifen**[1]

Schliff *m*; -(e)s, -e **1.** *nur Sg.*; *Tech.* (*Schleifen*) grinding; (*feiner*) polishing; (*Schärfen*) *auch* sharpening; *Edelstein, Glas*: cutting; **2.** *konkret*: grind; *feiner*: polish; *Messer etc.*: edge; *Edelstein, Glas*: cut; **3.** *nur Sg.*; *fig.* polish; **der letzte ~** the final touch; **e-r Sache den letzten ~ geben** put the finishing touch(es) to s.th.; **ihm fehlt noch der ~** he still has no social graces, he's still a bit rough and ready; **~fläche** *f Edelstein, Glas*: cut face; *Edelstein auch*: facet

schlimm *Adj.* **1.** *allg.* bad; **2.** *Person*: (*böse*) evil, wicked; (*unartig*) naughty; **3.** *Sache*: (*schwerwiegend*) bad, serious; (*sehr unangenehm*) bad; *stärker*: terrible; *Erkältung, Wunde etc.*: bad, nasty; **~er Finger/Hals** sore finger/throat; **~er Husten** bad (*od.* nasty) cough; **~e Folgen** *od.* **Auswirkungen** serious consequences; **das ist ja e-e ~e Sache** that's awful (*od.* terrible); **ist das denn so ~?** what's so bad about it?; **die letzte Zeit war ~** it's been tough going lately; **~e Zeiten** hard times; **es sieht ~ aus** it looks (pretty) bad; **das ist halb so ~!** it's not as bad as all that, it's nothing to get upset about; *verzeihend*: it doesn't matter, don't worry about it; **ist es ~, wenn ich nicht komme?** would it be awful (*od.* a nuisance) if I didn't come?; **4.** *Komp.* **~er** worse; *Sup.* **am ~sten** worst (of all); **etw. ~er machen** make s.th. worse; **~er werden** get worse, worsen; → **verschlimmern**; **es kommt noch ~er** there's worse to come; **es wird immer ~er** things are going from bad to worse; **um so ~er** so much the worse; **im ~sten Fall ...** at (the) worst ...; **5.** *Subst.* **das Schlimme/Schlimmste an der Sache ist** the awful/worst thing about it is; **ich sehe nichts Schlimmes darin** I don't see anything wrong in it; **es gibt Schlimmeres** things could be worse, worse things happen at sea; **das Schlimmste haben wir hinter uns** we've got over the worst; **wenn es zum Schlimmsten kommt, ...** if the worst comes to the worst

schlimmstenfalls *Adv.* at (the) worst; (*wenn es zum Schlimmsten kommt*) if worst comes to worst

Schlinge *f*; -, -n **1.** loop; *sich zusammenziehende*: noose; (*Armschlinge*) sling; (*Fangschlinge*) snare; *fig.* (*Falle*) snare, trap; **den Arm in der ~ tragen** have one's arm in a sling; **~n legen** set snares; **den Kopf aus der ~ ziehen** *fig.* wriggle out of it; **j-m die ~ um den Hals legen** place a noose around s.o.'s neck; *fig.* tighten the noose around s.o.'s neck; *bei e-r Fahndung*: close in on s.o.; **sich in s-r eigenen ~ fangen** *fig.* be hoist with one's own petard; **2.** *von Textilien*: loop; **3.** *Eiskunstlauf*

etc.: figure of eight, *Am.* figure eight; **...schlinge** *f*, *im Subst.*: **Draht~** wire snare; **Nylon~** nylon sling; **Henkers~** hangman's noose

Schlingel *m*; -s, -; *umg.* rascal, scallywag, *Am.* scalawag

schlingen[1]; *schlingt, schlang, hat geschlungen* **I.** *v/t.* (*binden*) tie; (*Schal etc.*) wrap (**um** around); **die Arme um j-s Hals ~** fling one's arms around s.o.'s neck; **II.** *v/refl.*: **sich um etw. ~** wind (*od.* twine, coil) (itself) around s.th.

schlingen[2] *vt/i.*; *schlingt, schlang, hat geschlungen*; (*etw.*) gulp (*od.* wolf) down, gobble *umg.*; (*hastig essen*) bolt one's food, gobble *umg.*; → **hinunterschlingen, verschlingen**

Schlinger|bewegung *f Naut.* rolling motion; **~kurs** *m fig.* wavering course; **auf ~** wavering (*od.* vacillating) from one possibility to another

schlingern *v/i. Schiff*: roll, lurch; *Person*: stagger, totter; *Mot., Anhänger*: lurch from side to side, weave

Schling|natter *f Zool.* smooth snake; **~pflanze** *f Bot.* climbing plant, creeper

Schlips *m*; -es, -e tie; **j-m auf den ~ treten** *umg. fig.* tread on s.o.'s toes; **sich auf den ~ getreten fühlen** *umg.* be miffed (*Am.* ticked off)

schlitteln *v/i. schw., österr.* → **rodeln**

Schlitten *m*; -s, - **1.** sledge, *Am.* sled; (*bes. Pferdeschlitten*) sleigh; (*Rodel*) toboggan, sledge, *Am.* sled; **~ fahren** go sledging (*Am.* sledding *od.* tobaganing); **mit j-m ~ fahren** *umg. fig.* haul (*od.* rake) s.o. over the coals; **2.** *umg.* (*Auto*) motor; **toller ~** fantastic (*Brit. auch* flash) car; **alter ~** old jalopy (*od.* beater), *Brit. auch* old banger; **3.** *Tech. e-r Schreibmaschine*: carriage; *Schiffbau*: cradle; **~bahn** *f* toboggan run; **~fahrt** *f* sleigh ride; **~hund** *m* sledge (*Am.* sled) dog; (*Eskimohund*) husky; **~kufe** *f* sledge (*Am.* sled) runner

Schlitterbahn *f* slide; **die Straße ist eine einzige ~** *umg. fig.* (*sehr glatt*) the road is like a skating rink

schlittern *v/i.* slide (**in** +*Akk.* into) (*auch fig.*); (*ausgleiten*) *auch* slip; *Auto*: skid; **ins Schlittern kommen** start to slip; *Auto*: (start to) skid, go into a skid

Schlittschuh *m Sport* ice skate; **~ laufen** *od.* **fahren** ice-skate, go ice skating; **~bahn** *f* ice rink; **~laufen** *n* ice skating; **~läufer** *m*, **~läuferin** *f* ice skater

Schlitz *m*; -es, -e **1.** slit (*auch im Kleid*); **2.** (*Hosenschlitz*) fly; **3.** (*Einwurfschlitz*) slot; **4.** *vulg.* (*Vagina*) cunt

...schlitz *m*, *im Subst.* **1.** (*Öffnung*): **Briefkasten~** letter slot; *weitS.* letterbox; **Seh~** observation slit; **2.** *im Kleid etc.*: **Rücken~** slit in the back

Schlitzauge *n neg!* (*auch pej. Person*) slit-eye; **schlitzäugig** *Adj. neg!* slit-eyed

schlitzen *v/t.* slit; → *auch* **aufschlitzen**

Schlitzohr *n umg. fig.* sly dog; (*Betrüger*) trickster; **er ist ein richtiges ~** he never misses a trick; **schlitzohrig** *umg.* **I.** *Adj.* crafty, wily, sly; **II.** *Adv.*: **ausgesprochen ~ zu Werke gehen** take a decidedly shifty approach; **Schlitzohrigkeit** *f umg.* craftiness, wiliness

Schlitz|schraube *f* slotted screw; **~verschluss** *m Fot.* focal-plane shutter

schlohweiß *Adj.* snow-white

schloss *Imperf.* → *schließen*

Schloss¹ *n*; *-es, Schlösser*; (*Türschloss, Gewehrschloss*) lock; (*Vorhängeschloss*) padlock; *an e-m Buch, e-r Handtasche etc.*: clasp; *das ~ aufbrechen* break (*od.* burst) the lock; *ins ~ fallen* slam shut; *j-n hinter ~ und Riegel bringen* put s.o. behind bars (in the clink *umg.*)

Schloss² *n*; *-es, Schlösser wie e-e Burg*: castle; (*Residenz, Palast*) palace; (*Herrenhaus*) mansion; *in Frankreich*: château; (*herrschaftliches Anwesen*) stately home; *das Heidelberger ~* Heidelberg Castle; *~ Schönbrunn* Schönbrunn Palace; *die Dornburger Schlösser* the stately homes (*od.* great houses) of Dornburg; *~anlage f* castle (*od.* palace) grounds *Pl.*; *2artig Adj.* palatial

Schlosser *m*; *-s, -* *für Schlösser*: locksmith; (*Metallarbeiter*) metalworker; (*Autoschlosser*) (car) mechanic; (*Maschinenschlosser*) mechanic, fitter; *~arbeiten Pl.* metalworking *Sg.*; *an Schlössern*: locksmithing *Sg.*; *Mot. etc.* mechanic's work *Sg.*

Schlosserei *f* 1. locksmith's *etc.* workshop; 2. (*Handwerk*) locksmith's *etc.* trade

Schlosserhandwerk *n* → *Schlosserei* 2

Schlosserin *f*; *-, -nen* → *Schlosser*

Schlosser|meister *m*, *~meisterin f* master locksmith *etc.*; → *Schlosser*, *~werkstatt f* → *Schlosserei* 1

Schloss|führung *f* guided tour of a (*od.* the) castle (*od.* palace); *~garten m* castle (*od.* palace) gardens *Pl.* (*od.* grounds *Pl.*); *~graben m* moat; *~herr m* lord of the castle; *~herrin f* lady of the castle; *~hof m* castle (*od.* palace) courtyard; *~hund m: heulen wie ein ~ umg.* howl one's eyes out; *~kapelle f* castle (*od.* palace) chapel; *oft* royal chapel; *~park m* castle (*od.* palace) grounds *Pl.*; *~ruine f* ruined castle, ruins *Pl.* of a (*od.* the) castle, castle ruins *Pl.*; *~theater n* palace theat|re (*Am. auch* -er); *~tor n* castle (*od.* palace) gate (*Einfahrt*: gateway); *~verwalter m*, *~verwalterin f* palace (*od.* castle) administrator; *~verwaltung f* palace (*od.* castle) administration; *~vogt m* castellan; *~wache f* palace guard

Schlot *m*; *-(e)s, -e* 1. chimney, smokestack; *e-s Vulkans*: chimney; *rauchen od. qualmen wie ein ~ umg.* smoke like a chimney; 2. *umg. pej.* (*Kerl*) slob

schlott(e)rig *Adj.* 1. (*wacklig, zitternd*) shaky, wobbly; *vor Schwäche*: shaky; *vor Alter*: doddery, *attr. auch* doddering; 2. *Kleidung*: baggy

schlottern *v/i.* 1. (*zittern*) shake, tremble; *vor Kälte*: shake, shiver (with cold); *vor Angst ~* tremble with fear; *mir schlotterten die Knie* my knees were shaking (*hum.* knocking); 2. *Kleidung etc.*: hang loose(ly), flap; **schlotternd I.** *Part. Präs.* → *schlottern*; **II.** *Adj.* 1. *mit ~en Knien* with shaking knees; 2. *~e Hosen* baggy trousers (*Am.* pants)

schlotzen *vt/i. südd. umg.* (*lutschen*) suck; *ein Viertele ~* sip a quarter lit|re (*Am.* -er) of wine

Schlucht *f*; *-, -en* ravine, gorge; *große*: canyon; *kleine*: gully

schluchzen I. *vt/i.* sob; *schluchz! umg.* sniff!; **II. Schluchzen** *n*; *-s, kein Pl.*

sobbing, sobs *Pl.*; **schluchzend I.** *Part. Präs.* → *schluchzen*; **II.** *Adj.*: *mit ~er Stimme* with a sob (in his *od.* her voice); *~e Geigen etc.* sighing violins *etc.*; **III.** *Adv.*: *sie warf sich ~ aufs Bett* she flung herself on the bed, sobbing; **Schluchzer** *m*; *-s, -* sob

Schluck *m*; *-(e)s, -e* gulp, mouthful; *kleiner*: sip; *umg. tüchtiger, von Schnaps etc.*: swig; *ein ~ Kaffee/Wein umg.* some (*od.* a drop of) coffee/wine; *in kleinen/großen ~en* in small sips / big gulps; *ich möchte e-n ~ zu trinken umg.* I'd like something to drink; *hast du mal 'nen ~? umg.* (*Alkohol*) have you anything (alcoholic) I could drink?

Schluckauf *m* hiccups *Pl.*; (*den od. e-n*) *~ haben* have (the) hiccups

Schluckbeschwerden *Pl.* difficulty *Sg.* in swallowing

Schlückchen *n umg.* sip, drop, (*Whisky*) *auch* wee dram; *trinkst du noch ein ~?* will you have another drop?; *bitte nur (noch) ein kleines ~!* just a little drop (for me); *ein ~ in Ehren kann niemand verwehren* nobody can say no to a good drop; **schlückchenweise** *Adv.*: *~ trinken* sip

schlucken I. *vt/i.* swallow; *nicht richtig ~ können* be unable to swallow properly; *einen ~ gehen umg.* go for a tipple; *da musste ich erst einmal ~* I had to swallow hard; *an etw. zu ~ haben fig.* have difficulty coming to terms with (*od.* swallowing) s.th.; **II.** *v/t.* 1. *umg. fig.* (*Betrieb etc.*) swallow up; (*Tadel etc.*) take, swallow; (*Schall, Licht etc.*) absorb; (*Geld*) swallow up; (*Benzin*) guzzle; *die Steuererhöhung werden wir ~ müssen* we will just have to absorb the tax increase; 2. *umg. fig.* (*glauben*) swallow, buy; *hat sie es geschluckt?* did she buy it?

Schlucker *m*; *-s, -*; *umg.*: *armer ~* poor devil (*od.* bastard *Sl.*)

Schluck|impfung *f Med.* oral vaccination; *~specht m umg.* (*Trinker*) boozer

schluckweise *Adv.* in sips, slowly

Schluderei *f*; *-, -en*; *umg.* sloppiness; **schlud(e)rig** *umg.* **I.** *Adj.* sloppy; *Arbeit*: *auch* slipshod; **II.** *Adv.*: *~ arbeiten* do slipshod (*od.* sloppy) work; *etw. ~ reparieren* do a botched repair on s.th.; **Schluderjan** *m*; *-s, -e*; *umg.* → *Schludrian* 1; **schludern** *v/i. umg.* do slipshod (*od.* sloppy) work; *bei der Berechnung ~* botch the calculation; → *auch schlampen*; **Schludrian** *m*; *-s, -e*; *umg.* 1. messy (*od.* chaotic) person; 2. *nur Sg.*: *hier ist der ~ eingerissen* things have got(ten) pretty chaotic in here; **Schludrigkeit** *f umg.* sloppiness

schlug *Imperf.* → *schlagen*

Schlummer *m*; *-s, kein Pl.* sleep; *lit.* slumber; → *auch Schläfchen*; *~lied n* lullaby

schlummern *v/i.* sleep; *lit.* slumber; *fig. auch* lie dormant; *in ihm ~ ungeahnte Talente* he has unsuspected latent (*od.* hidden) talents; **schlummernd I.** *Part. Präs.* → *schlummern*; **II.** *Adj. fig.* dormant; *auch Talent, Krankheit*: latent

Schlummer|rolle *f* bolster; *~stündchen n* nap; *~trunk m umg.* nightcap

Schlumpf *m*; *-(e)s, Schlümpfe* 1. (*Comicfigur*) smurf; 2. *umg. fig.* (*Zwerg*) dwarf, midget

Schlund *m*; *-(e)s, Schlünde* 1. *Anat.* (back of the) throat, *fachspr.* pharynx;

Zool. maw; 2. *fig. e-s Vulkans etc.*: (yawning) chasm; *der ~ der Hölle* the jaws of hell

Schlupf *m*; *-(e)s, Schlüpfe od. -e*, *mst Sg.*; *Tech.* slip

schlupfen *südd., österr., schw.*, **schlüpfen** *v/i.* 1. slip (*aus* out of); 2. *in den Mantel etc. schlüpfen* slip into one's coat *etc.*; *aus etw. schlüpfen* slip out of s.th., slip s.th. off; 3. *Vögel etc.*: hatch (out)

Schlüpfer *m*; *-s, -*; *altm.*: (*ein*) *~ für Männer, Kinder*: (a pair of) underpants (*Brit. auch* pants) *Pl.*; *für Frauen*: (a pair of) panties (*od. Brit. auch* knickers) *Pl.*

Schlupfloch *n* gap; (*Versteck*) hideout; *fig. im Gesetz etc.*: loophole

schlüpfrig *Adj.* 1. slippery (*auch fig.*); 2. (*anstößig*) *Witz etc.*: risqué, off-colo(u)r; **Schlüpfrigkeit** *f* 1. slipperiness; 2. (*Anstößigkeit*) risqué nature

Schlupf|wespe *f Zool.* ichneumon fly; *~winkel m* 1. hideout; (*Zufluchtsort*) refuge; *ruhig*: quiet corner; 2. *von Tieren*: hiding place; *~zeit f Zool.* hatching time

schlurfen *v/i.* (*schleppend gehen*) shuffle, drag one's feet

schlürfen *vt/i.* slurp; *vorsichtig, auch mit Genuss*: sip; *beim Essen/Trinken laut ~* slurp loudly while eating/drinking

Schluss *m*; *Schlusses, Schlüsse* 1. *nur Sg.* end; (*Abschluss*) conclusion; *Parl., e-r Debatte*: closing; *auf Antrag*: closure, *Am.* cloture; (*Geschäftsschluss*) closing time; (*Redaktionsschluss*) deadline; *~ für heute!* that's all for today; *~ damit!* stop it!, that'll do (now)!; *und damit ~!* and that's that, and that's the end of that; *am ~* at the end; (*letztendlich*) in the end; *irgendwann muss mal ~ sein* you've got to call a halt somewhere; *mit ihm ist ~ umg.* (*er muss sterben*) it's all over with him; (*er ist ruiniert*) he's done for; *zum ~* finally, to finish off; (*am Ende*) in the end; *kurz vor ~* shortly before closing time (*vor Dienstschluss*: before finishing work); *zum ~ kommen od. gelangen* come to a close; *zum ~ möchte ich noch sagen* in conclusion may I say; → *auch Ende*; 2. *~ machen* a) (*die Arbeit beenden*) finish work, knock off (for the day) *umg.*; *machen wir ~ für heute* let's call it a day, b) (*sich vom Partner trennen*) break it off; *sie hat mit ihm ~ gemacht* she's broken it off with him, she's given him the push, c) (*Selbstmord verüben*) put an end to it all, d) *~ machen mit* (*etw.*) stop; (*dem Rauchen etc.*) *auch* give up; (*j-m*) finish with; 3. *mst Sg.*; *e-s Buches, Films etc.*: ending; *dritter Teil und ~ am Freitag* third and final part on Friday; 4. (*hinterer Teil*) rear, back, end; 5. (*Folgerung*) conclusion; *e-n ~ ziehen* draw a conclusion, conclude (*aus* from); *zu dem ~ gelangen, dass ...* come to the conclusion that; → *voreilig* I, *Weisheit* 1; 6. *nur Sg.*; *Tech.* fit; *guten ~ haben* be a good fit; *Fenster, Tür auch*: close tightly; 7. *nur Sg.*; *Reiten*: *guten ~ haben* have a good grip (with the thighs) on the horse's flanks

Schluss|abstimmung *f* final vote; *~akkord m Mus.* final chord; *~akt m Theat.* final act (*auch fig.*), last act; *e-r Veranstaltung*: closing ceremony; *~akte f Pol.* final act; *~applaus m* applause at the end (of the performance); **~be-merkung** f final comment, concluding remark; **~bilanz** f Wirts. annual balance sheet; fig. **wenn ich die ~ ziehe** in the final analysis; **~bild** n Theat. final scene; **~dokument** n final document (od. statement); **~drittel** n Sport final period

Schlüssel m; -s, - 1. key (auch fig.); **der ~ steckt** the key is in the door; **die ~ der Stadt übergeben** hand over the keys of the town; **der ~ zum Erfolg** fig. the key to (od. secret of) success; 2. Mus. clef; 3. (Chiffrierschlüssel) key; Computer: key; **der ~ zu e-m genetischen Code** the key to a genetic code; 4. (Lösungsheft, -teil) key; 5. (Verteilungsschlüssel) ratio formula; **nach e-m anderen ~ verteilen** distribute according to a different scheme; 6. Tech. (Schraubenschlüssel) spanner, Am. wrench; verstellbarer: (adjustable) wrench, Am. auch crescent (od. monkey) wrench; **~anhänger** m key fob; **~bart** m bit, ward; **~begriff** m 1. key concept; 2. key term (od. word)

Schlüsselbein n Anat. collarbone; fachspr. clavicle; **~bruch** m Med. fractured (od. broken) collarbone

Schlüssel|blume f Bot. cowslip; (Primel) primrose; **~brett** n key rack; **~bund** m, n bunch of keys; **~dienst** m locksmith service; **wir mussten den ~ rufen** we had to call the locksmith; **~erlebnis** n crucial (od. formative) experience

schlüsselfertig Adj. ready for occupancy, ready to move into; bes. Wirts. turnkey …

Schlüssel|figur f key figure; Pol. etc. auch key player; **~funktion** f key function; **~gewalt** f R.C. power of the keys; Jur., der Ehefrau: wife's agency (in domestic matters); **~industrie** f key industry; **~kind** n umg. latchkey child; **~loch** n keyhole; **durchs ~ gucken** peep through the keyhole; **~position** f key position; **~qualifikation** f key qualification; **~reiz** m Psych. key stimulus; **~ring** m key ring; **~rolle** f key (od. crucial) role; **~roman** m Lit. roman-à-clef; **~satz** m 1. Tech. set of spanners (Am. wrenches); 2. (Aussage) key sentence; 3. Tennis etc.: crucial (od. deciding) set; **~spiel** n crucial game; **~stellung** f key position (auch Mil.); **~szene** f crucial scene; **~technologie** f key technology; **~übergabe** f completion; **feierliche ~** ceremonial handing over of the keys; **~wort** n 1. key word; 2. für Schloss: combination; für Text: code word; **~zahl** f key number

schlussendlich Adv. bes. schw. in conclusion, to conclude

Schlusserklärung f final statement

schlussfolgern vt/i. (untr., hat, ge-): **~ aus** conclude (od. infer) from; **~, dass …** conclude that …; **Schlussfolgerung** f conclusion, inference

Schlussformel f 1. Brief: complimentary close; 2. Vertrag: final clause

schlüssig I. Adj. 1. (folgerichtig) Argument: sound, logical; **~er Beweis** conclusive evidence; 2. **sich** (Dat.) **werden** make up one's mind (**über +** Akk. about), decide (about, on, as to); **sich** (Dat.) **~ sein** have decided, have made up one's mind; II. Adv.: **~ beweisen** prove conclusively; **Schlüssigkeit** f conclusiveness

Schluss|kapitel n final (od. last) chapter; **~kommuniqué** n final communi-

qué; **~kurs** m Börse: closing price, final quotation (+ Gen. for); Devisen: closing rate (for); **~läufer** m, **~läuferin** f Sport anchorman, f anchorwoman; **als Schlussläufer laufen** run the last leg; **~leuchte** f tail(-)light; **~licht** n tail(-)light; fig. Sport umg. tailender; (Mannschaft) bottom-of-the-table team, Am. cellar dweller; **das ~ bilden** umg. fig. bring up the rear; **~mann** m 1. → **Schlussläufer**, 2. umg. Fußball etc.: goalkeeper, goalie; **~notierungen** Pl. Börse: closing rates; **~pfiff** m Sport final whistle; **~phase** f final phase (od. stages Pl.); **~plädoyer** n summing up, final speech; **~pointe** f final point; **~punkt** m Ling. full stop, Am. period; **e-n ~ unter etw. setzen** fig. put an end to s.th. once and for all; **~rechnung** f 1. Wirts. final account; 2. Math. computation using the rule of three; **~redaktion** f final edit; **~resolution** f final resolution; **~runde** f final round, final(s Pl.); e-es Rennens: last lap; **~satz** m 1. concluding (od. closing) sentence; 2. Mus. last (od. final) movement; 3. Tennis etc.: final set; **~schein** m Wirts. contract note; **~sirene** f Eishockey etc.: final buzzer; **~sprung** m Turnen: (finishing) jump with legs together; **~spurt** m Sport final spurt; **~stein** m Archit. keystone; fig. culmination; **~strich** m final stroke; fig. **e-n ~ ziehen** consider the matter closed; **~szene** f final scene; **~tag** m Wirts. settlement day; **~teil** m final part; **~veranstaltung** f final event; **~verkauf** m (end-of-season) sale; **~wort** n closing words Pl.; (Schlussrede) closing speech; (Nachwort) epilogue; (Zusammenfassung) summary; **~zeichen** n Funk. end-of--message signal; **~zeiten** Pl. closing times; **~zeremonie** f auch Sport closing ceremony

Schmach f, -, kein Pl.; (Unehre) disgrace, shame; (Beleidigung) insult, affront; stärker: outrage; (Demütigung) humiliation; **etw. als ~ empfinden** find s.th. humiliating

schmachten v/i. 1. languish (**vor +** Dat. with); **vor Durst ~** be parched with thirst; **in der Hitze ~** wilt in the heat; 2. (sich sehnen) yearn, languish, pine (**nach** for); **j-n ~ lassen** keep s.o. on tenterhooks, let s.o. sweat it out umg.; **schmachtend** I. Part. Präs. → **schmachten**; II. Adj. hum. languishing, yearning; **~e Blicke** soulful looks

Schmachtfetzen m umg. weepie, tearjerker

schmächtig Adj. of slight build; (schwächlich) delicate, frail; **er ist klein und ~** he is small and slight (pej. weedy od. wispy); **Schmächtigkeit** f slightness (of build), pej. weediness (od. wispiness) (Schwächlichkeit) delicateness, frailty

Schmachtlocke f kiss-curl, Am. spit curl

schmachvoll I. Adj. shameful, ignominious; (demütigend) auch humiliating (auch Niederlage etc.); II. Adv.: **~ untergehen** suffer a humiliating defeat; → auch **schmählich**

Schmackes Pl. umg.: **mit ~** with great gusto

schmackhaft Adj. tasty; lit. savo(u)ry; **j-m etw. ~ machen** fig. make s.th. sound appealing to s.o., whet s.o.'s appetite for s.th.

Schmäh m; -s, -(s); österr. umg. 1. (Trick) con; (Unwahrheit) tall tale;

2. nur Sg. (Sprüche, Scherze) (amusing) patter

Schmähbrief m defamatory letter

schmähen förm. I. v/t. (beschimpfen) revile; (schlecht machen) disparage, run down umg., bad-mouth umg.; II. v/i. (lästern) blaspheme

schmählich I. Adj. → **schmachvoll** I; II. Adv. (ungeheuerlich) very badly; **j-n ~ im Stich lassen** leave s.o. disgracefully in the lurch, let s.o. down really badly

Schmäh|rede f 1. defamatory speech, diatribe; 2. **~n gegen j-n führen** heap abuse on s.o., revile s.o.; **~ruf** m shout of abuse; **~schrift** f diatribe; (Satire) lampoon

Schmähung f auch Pl. invective, vituperation; (Lästerung) blasphemy; (Verleumdung) calumny

schmal I. Adj. 1. narrow; (dünn) thin; Mensch, Buch: auch slim; Hüften, Hände: slim; Lippen: thin; Augen: narrow; Gesicht: narrow, thin; **~er Schnitt** slim fit; **er ist ~er geworden** he's lost weight; 2. (gering) meag|re (Am. -er); (ungenügend) poor; **~e Kost** meag|re (Am. -er) fare; II. Adv.: **~ geschnitten** Hose etc.: slim-fit

schmalbrüstig Adj. 1. narrow-chested; Möbelstück: narrow; 2. fig. Ansichten: narrow(-minded), hidebound; Film, Buch: lowbrow; Unternehmen: unambitious

schmälern v/t. (einschränken, verringern) curtail, reduce, diminish; (beeinträchtigen) impair (auch Rechte), detract from; (Verdienst etc.) belittle, do s.th. down; **Schmälerung** f curtailment, reduction; impairment; belittlement; → **schmälern**

Schmalfilm m (8mm or 16mm) cine--film (Am. movie film); **~kamera** f (8mm or 16mm) cine-camera (Am. movie camera)

Schmalhans m umg.: **bei uns ist ~ Küchenmeister** we're on short rations at home

schmal|hüftig Adj. slim-hipped; **~lippig** Adj. thin-lipped; **~schultrig** Adj. narrow-shouldered

Schmalseite f short side, narrow end

Schmalspur f; nur Sg.; Eisenb. narrow ga(u)ge

Schmalspur|… im Subst. 1. Eisenb. narrow-ga(u)ge …; 2. umg. fig. mst small-time …; **~akademiker** m, **~akademikerin** f umg. pej. graduate of a non-university institution (Am. of Podunk University); **~bahn** f Eisenb. narrow-ga(u)ge railway (Am. railroad)

schmalspurig I. Adj. nur attr. narrow--ga(u)ge …; II. Adv.: **dann geht die Linie ~ weiter** the line continues in narrow ga(u)ge; **er fährt sehr ~** Ski: his skis are always very close together

schmalwüchsig Adj. of slim build, very slim

Schmalz[1] n; -es, kein Pl. vom Schwein: lard; vom Braten: dripping; **~ auslassen** render down fat (od. dripping[s]); **~ in den Knochen haben** umg. have plenty of brawn; **das hat viel ~ gekostet** umg. that took a bit of muscle

Schmalz[2] m -es, kein Pl.; umg. (Sentimentalität) schmaltz; **ein Film mit viel ~** a very schmaltzy film

Schmalz|brot n Gastr. bread and dripping(s); **~gebäck** n, **~gebackenes** n deep-fried pastry

schmalzig Adj. umg. fig. schmaltzy, slushy-sentimental

Schmalzler m; -s, -; südd. (Schnupfta-

bak) snuff

Schmalztopf *m* pot of lard; *tief in den ~ greifen umg. fig.* lay on the sentiment with a trowel

Schmankerl *n; -s, -n; südd., österr.* **1.** (*Leckerbissen*) tasty titbit (*Am.* tidbit), delicacy; *fig.* (real) treat, something to savo(u)r; **2.** (*Gebäck*) cone-shaped sweet pastry

Schmant *m; -(e)s, kein Pl.; Gastr., Dial.* (sour) cream

schmarotzen *v/i.* **1.** *Zool., Bot.* be a parasite; *~ auf* (+ *Dat.*) live off, parasitize; **2.** *umg. fig. pej.* freeload, sponge; *grundsätzlich*: be a freeloader (*od.* sponger, scrounger; *bes. beim Staat*: parasite); *~ bei* sponge off (*od.* on), scrounge off (*od.* from); *bes. beim Staat*: live off

Schmarotzer *m; -s, -* **1.** *Zool., Bot.* parasite; **2.** *umg. fig. pej.* (*Person*) freeloader, scrounger, sponger; *bes. beim Staat*: freeloader; **schmarotzerhaft I.** *Adj.* **1.** *Zool., Bot.* parasitic; **2.** *umg. fig. pej. Mensch:* freeloading, sponging; **II.** *Adv.: ~ leben* live as a parasite; *umg. fig. pej. Mensch:* freeload; **Schmarotzerin** *f; -, -nen* → **Schmarotzer** 2; **schmarotzerisch** *Adj.* → **schmarotzerhaft, Schmarotzertum** *n; -s, kein Pl.* parasitism (*auch fig.*)

Schmarre *f; -, -n; umg.* (*Wunde*) cut; (*Narbe*) scar

Schmarren *m; -s, kein Pl.; österr., südd.* **1.** scrambled pancake; **2.** *umg. fig.* rubbish, crap, *bes. Am.* garbage; *so ein ~!* what a load of rubbish *etc.*; *das geht dich e-n ~ an* that's none of your (bloody) business

Schmatz *m; -es, Schmätze od. -e, mst Sg.; umg.* smacker; *liebe Grüße und e-n dicken ~ von deiner Rosi* love and a big kiss from your Rosi

schmatzen *v/i.* eat noisily; *schmatz nicht so!* close your mouth when you're eating; *er schmatzt furchtbar* he makes such a noise when he's eating; **schmatzend I.** *Part. Präs.* → **schmatzen**; **II.** *Adj.: ~es Geräusch* smacking sound; *~er Kuss* smacking great kiss *umg.*; **Schmatzer** *m; -s, -; umg.* → **Schmatz**

Schmauch *m; -(e)s, kein Pl.* dense smoke; **schmauchen** *vt/i. umg.* puff away (*s-e Pfeife etc.* at one's pipe *etc.*); **Schmauchspuren** *Pl.* traces of spent gunpowder (*after a shot*)

Schmaus *m; -es, kein Pl.; mst hum.* feast; *fig.* treat; *welch köstlicher ~!* what a delicious spread!; **schmausen** *umg.* **I.** *v/i.* feast; **II.** *v/t.* feast on, tuck into *umg.*

schmecken I. *v/t.* **1.** (*kosten*) taste, try; (*herauskosten*) (be able to) taste; *ich schmecke gar nichts* I can't taste a thing; *man schmeckt, dass der Fisch nicht frisch ist* you can tell from the taste that the fish isn't fresh; *schmeck mal!* have a taste; *lässt du mich mal (die Soße) ~?* can I have a taste (of the sauce)?; **2.** *Dial.* (*riechen*) smell; **II.** *v/i.* **1.** (*gut*) *~* taste good; *und dann e-n Schuss Kognak, sonst schmeckt's nicht* then give it a dash of brandy, otherwise it doesn't taste right; *ihm schmeckt es* he likes it; *umg.* (*er isst gern und viel*) he likes his food; *ich nehme nicht ab - mir schmeckt's zu gut umg.* I can't lose any weight, I enjoy my food too much; *mir hat's geschmeckt umg.* I enjoyed that; *das hat aber geschmeckt!* that was really delicious; *diese Torte*

schmeckt vielleicht toll! this cake is really scrumptious!; *Nudeln ~ mir immer umg.* give me noodles any time; *es schmeckt mir heute nicht so recht* I don't really have any appetite (*od.* feel like eating) today; *es sich ~ lassen umg.* tuck in; *lass es dir ~!* enjoy it!, tuck in!; *hat es Ihnen geschmeckt?* did you enjoy your meal?; *~ nach* taste of; *fig.* smack of; *es schmeckt wie selbstgebacken* it tastes homemade; *der Wein schmeckt nach Kork*(*en*) the wine is corked (*Am. auch* corky); *es schmeckt nach nichts* it doesn't taste of anything, it has no taste; *es schmeckt nach mehr umg. hum.* I hope there's more where that came from; **2.** *das schmeckt mir gar nicht auch* I don't like the sound (*od.* look) of that at all; *diese Kritik schmeckte ihr gar nicht* this criticism didn't go down at all well with her; **3.** *Dial.* (*riechen*) smell

Schmeichelei *f; -, -en; auch Pl. allg.* flattery; (*Bemerkung*) flattering remark, compliment; **schmeichelhaft** *Adj.* flattering (*auch fig.*)

Schmeichelkatze *f umg. fig.* little flatterer (*od.* cajoler)

schmeicheln *v/i.* (*j-m*) flatter; *lobend*: compliment; *zärtlich*: cajole; (*einwickeln*) butter up, soft-soap *umg.*; *das Foto ist aber geschmeichelt* it's a very flattering photo; *das schmeichelt s-r Eitelkeit* it flatters (*od.* tickles) his vanity; *ich fühle mich sehr geschmeichelt* I feel very flattered; *du brauchst* (*mir*) *gar nicht so zu ~* flattery will get you nowhere; *~de Musik* soft music

Schmeichler *m; -s, -, ~in f; -, -nen* flatterer; *du ~!* stop flattering me; **schmeichlerisch** *Adj.* flattering; *pej.* smooth-tongued; *Worte, Ton*: honeyed; (*anbiedernd*) ingratiating

schmeißen; *schmeißt, schmiss, hat geschmissen; umg.* **I.** *v/t.* **1.** throw, chuck; *heftiger*: fling, hurl; *j-n auf den Boden ~* hurl s.o. to the ground; *j-n von der Schule ~* kick s.o. out of the school; **2.** (*spendieren*) *e-e Runde ~* stand a round; *e-e Party (für j-n) ~* throw a party (for s.o.); **3.** *den Laden ~* run the show; *die Sache ~* manage (all right), swing it; *sie schmeißt schon den Haushalt* she knows how to run a household; **4.** (*aufgeben*) chuck (in); *das Studium / die Lehre ~* chuck in one's studies/apprenticeship; **5.** (*verderben*) mess up, muff; *die Vorstellung ~ Theat.* muff it; **II.** *v/i.*: *mit faulen Eiern* (*nach j-m*) *~* throw rotten eggs (at s.o.); *mit Geld um sich ~* throw one's money around; *mit Fremdwörtern um sich ~* spout (*od.* bandy) foreign words; **III.** *v/refl.*: *sich aufs Bett / in den Sessel ~* throw o.s. onto one's bed / drop into the armchair; *sich in den Mantel ~* get (*eilig*: dive) into one's coat, throw one's coat on; *sich auf j-n ~* fling o.s. on s.o.; *sich an j-n od. j-m an den Hals ~ fig.* throw o.s. at s.o.; → **Schale¹** 2

Schmeißfliege *f Zool.* bluebottle (fly)

Schmelz *m; -es, kein Pl.* **1.** enamel (*auch Zahnschmelz*); (*Glasur*) glaze; **2.** *fig. von Klang*: melodiousness, mellowness; *von Farbe*: lus|tre (*Am.* -ter)

schmelzbar *Adj.* meltable, fusible

Schmelze *f; -, -n* **1.** (*Schneeschmelze*) thaw(ing period); **2.** *Tech.* (*Vorgang*) smelting; (*geschmolzenes Material*) melt; (*flüssiges Metall*) molten metal; (*flüssiges Glas*) molten glass; (*flüssiges*

Gestein) liquid rock

schmelzen; *schmilzt, schmolz, hat bzw. ist geschmolzen* **I.** *v/i.* (*ist*) melt; *in Flüssigkeiten*: *auch* dissolve; (*flüssig werden*) *auch* liquefy; *fig.* (*weich werden*) melt; (*schwinden*) dwindle; *den Käse ~ lassen in Rezept*: melt the cheese; *die Begeisterung schmolz zusehends* the general enthusiasm faded visibly; **II.** *v/t.* (*hat*) melt; (*bes. Metalle*) smelt; (*flüssig machen*) liquefy; → **geschmolzen**

schmelzend I. *Part. Präs.* → **schmelzen**; **II.** *Adj.* melting; *Mus., Stimme*: mellow; *iro. Stimme, Ton*: dulcet; *Blick*: melting

Schmelzerei *f; -, -en* (iron) foundry

schmelzflüssig *Adj.* molten

Schmelz|hütte *f Tech.* (iron) foundry; *~käse m Gastr.* cheese spread; *in Scheiben*: cheese slices; *~ofen m Tech.* smelting furnace; *~punkt m Phys.* melting point; *~schweißen n Tech.* fusion welding; *~sicherung f Etech.* fusible cut-out; *~tiegel m* melting pot (*auch fig.*); *~wasser n* melted snow and ice; *Geol.* meltwater

Schmerbauch *m umg.* paunch, pot belly

Schmerz *m; -es, -en* **1.** pain; *anhaltend, dumpf*: *auch* ache; *~en haben* be in pain; *wo haben Sie ~en?* where does it hurt?; *unter unerträglichen ~en leiden* suffer unbearable pain; *ich habe keine ~en* I don't feel any pain; *vor ~ aufschreien* yell with pain; *ich im Kreuz haben* have a pain in one's back, have (a) backache; *j-m ein Mittel gegen die ~en verschreiben* prescribe s.o. a medication for the pain; *der ~ lässt nach* the pain is lessening; *hast du sonst noch ~en? umg. iro.* is that all?; *~ lass nach! umg., hum.* it can't be true!, that's all I needed!; **2.** *seelischer*: pain; (*Kummer*) *auch Pl.* grief, sorrow, heartache; (*j-m*) *~en verursachen* cause (s.o.) pain (*od.* distress); *tiefen ~ empfinden über* be deeply grieved over (*od.* about); *der ~ sitzt tief* the pain goes deep; *geteilter ~ ist halber ~ Sprichw.* a sorrow shared is a sorrow halved

Schmerzempfinden *n* sensation of pain; **schmerzempfindlich** *Adj.* sensitive to pain

schmerzen I. *v/i.* hurt; *Magen, Kopf*: ache; *Wunde*: be sore; *brennend*: smart; *mir ~ alle Glieder* all my limbs are aching; *e-e stark ~de Wunde* a very painful wound; *die Spritze schmerzt etwas/kaum* the injection hurts a little / hardly hurts at all; **II.** *v/t.* hurt (*auch fig.*); *es schmerzt mich auch fig.* it hurts (me); *es schmerzt mich, dass sie nie angerufen hat* it upsets me to think that she never rang up

Schmerzens|geld *n* compensation (*for injuries suffered*); *Jur.* compensatory damages *Pl.*; *~mann m Kunst* Man of Sorrows; *~mutter f Kunst* mater dolorosa, Our Lady of Sorrows; *~schrei m* cry (*lauter*: scream) of pain

schmerzerfüllt *Adj.* grief-stricken

Schmerzforschung *f Med.* pain research

schmerzfrei *Adj.* free of (*od.* from) pain; *Behandlung etc.*: painless

Schmerz|gefühl *n* (sensation of) pain; *~grenze f Physiol.* pain threshold; *die ~ ist erreicht/überschritten fig.* this is the limit / more than flesh and blood can stand

S

schmerzhaft *Adj.* painful; *fig. auch* distressing; **~e Stelle** sore place (*od.* area), tender spot

Schmerz|klinik *f Med.* pain clinic; **~kranke** *m, f* chronic pain sufferer

schmerzlich *fig.* **I.** *Adj.* painful; *Erinnerung, Verlust, Pflicht: auch* sad (*auch Lächeln*); **~e Gewissheit** painful awareness (*od.* certainty); **~es Verlangen** (bitter) yearning; **II.** *Adv.*: **j-n ~ vermissen** sorely miss s.o.; **j-n/etw. ~ in Erinnerung haben** remember s.o./s.th. with great sadness; **~ berührt** deeply saddened; **es hat mich ~ berührt** it made me very sad

schmerzlindernd *Adj.* pain-relieving, palliative (*auch* **~es Mittel**); *Salbe: auch* soothing; **Schmerzlinderung** *f* pain relief

schmerzlos **I.** *Adj.* painless; *das war aber kurz und* **~** *umg.* that was short and sweet; **II.** *Adv.*: **mach es kurz und ~** *umg.* get it over and done with

Schmerz|mittel *n Pharm.* painkiller, analgesic; **~punkt** *m Physiol.* pain trigger point; **~schwelle** *f Physiol., fig.* pain threshold

schmerzstillend **I.** *Adj.* painkilling, analgesic; **II.** *Adv.*: **es wirkt ~** it will kill the pain

Schmerz|tablette *f Pharm.* painkiller, analgesic; **~therapeut** *m*, **~therapeutin** *f Med.* pain therapist

schmerz|unempfindlich *Adj.* insensitive to pain; **~verzerrt** *Adj.* contorted with pain; **~voll** *Adj.* painful (*auch fig.*); → *auch* **schmerzlich**

Schmerzzentrum *n* pain cent|re (*Am.* -er)

Schmetterball *m Tennis etc.*: smash; *Volleyball:* spiked ball

Schmetterling *m; -s, -e; Zool.* butterfly (*auch Schwimmstil*)

Schmetterlings|blütler *m; -s, -; Bot.* one of the papilionaceae; **~kasten** *m* (glass) butterfly case; **~sammlung** *f* butterfly collection; **~schwimmen** *n*, **~stil** *m Sport* butterfly (stroke)

schmettern **I.** *v/t.* (*hat geschmettert*) **1.** smash (**in Stücke** to pieces); **~ gegen** hurl at; (*Schiff gegen Felsen etc.*) dash against; **2.** *Tennis:* smash; **mit der Vorhand/Rückhand ~** play a forehand/backhand smash; **3.** *umg.* (*ein Lied*) belt out; **II.** *v/i.* **1.** (*ist*) (*krachen*) crash; *Tür:* slam; *das Boot schmetterte auf den Felsen* the boat smashed against the rocks; **2.** (*hat*) *Tennis:* smash; *Volleyball:* spike; **3.** (*hat*) (*erklingen*) resound; *Stimme:* ring (out); *Vogel:* warble; *Trompete, Musik etc.:* blare (out)

Schmetterschlag *m* **1.** *Tennis etc.*: smash; **2.** *Volleyball:* spike

Schmied *m; -(e)s, -e* smith; (*Hufschmied*) blacksmith; *jeder ist s-s Glückes* **~** life is what you make it

Schmiede *f; -, -n* smithy; *in der Industrie auch:* forge; **~arbeit** *f* forging; (*Produkt*) wrought-iron work

Schmiedeeisen *n* malleable iron; *geschmiedet:* wrought iron; **schmiedeeisern** *Adj.* wrought-iron ...

Schmiede|hammer *m im Industriebetrieb:* forge hammer; *im Handwerk:* blacksmith's hammer; **~handwerk** *n* blacksmith's craft; **~kunst** *f* blacksmith's art

schmieden *vt/i.* forge (**zu** into); *fig.* *Komplott, Plan:* hatch; → **Eisen** 3, *Komplott*, *Plan*[1] 1 a, *Ränke*

Schmiede|ofen *m* forging furnace; **~presse** *f* forging press

Schmiedin *f; -, -nen* → *Schmied*

schmiegen **I.** *v/refl.*: **sich an j-n ~** cuddle up to s.o.; **sich in etw. ~** nestle into s.th.; **sich in e-e Decke ~** cuddle up inside a blanket; *das Kleid schmiegt sich an ihren Körper* the dress clings to (*od.* hugs) her figure; **II.** *v/t.*: **etw. in/an etw. ~** nestle s.th. in/against s.th.

schmiegsam *Adj.* pliant, flexible; *Leder etc.:* soft; (*geschmeidig*) supple; *Körper auch:* lithe; *fig.* (*anpassungsfähig*) adaptable

Schmier|block *m* scribbling pad; **~dienst** *m Tech.* lubrication service

Schmiere[1] *f; -, -n, mst Sg.* **1.** *Tech.* grease, lubricant; (*Schmutz*) muck; *klebriger:* goo *umg.*; **2.** *umg.* (*schlechtes Theater*) second-rate theat|re (*Am. auch* -er)

Schmiere[2] *f; -, kein Pl.* **1. ~ stehen** *umg.* keep a lookout; **2.** *Sl.* (*Polizei*) the fuzz

schmieren **I.** *v/t.* **1.** smear; *Tech., mit Fett:* grease; *mit Öl:* oil, lubricate; (*Brot*) butter; (*Butter etc.*) spread; *sich* (*Dat.*) *ein Brot ~* make o.s. a sandwich; *schmierst du mir ein Brot mit Käse?* can you make me a cheese sandwich (*od.* butter me a piece of bread with cheese on)?; *sich* (*Dat.*) *Creme ins Gesicht ~* rub cream into one's face; *wie geschmiert laufen fig.* run (*od.* go) like clockwork; **2.** (*schlecht schreiben*) scribble, scrawl; *pej.* (*malen od.* sprühen) (*Graffiti, Parolen*) daub; **3.** *j-m e-e ~ umg.* paste s.o. one; **4.** *j-n ~ umg.* (*bestechen*) grease s.o.'s palm; **II.** *v/i.* **1.** *Kugelschreiber etc.*: smudge; *Person:* (*schlecht schreiben*) scribble, scrawl; **2.** *Tech., Öl etc.*: lubricate

Schmieren|komödiant *m*, **~komödiantin** *f pej. altm.* ham (actor, *f* actress); *fig.* play-actor; **~komödie** *f pej.* primitive knockabout comedy; **~theater** *n pej.* second-rate theat|re (*Am. auch* -er)

Schmierer *m; -s, -.* **1.** *pej.* scribbler, scrawler; *von Parolen:* graffiti artist; (*Sprayer*) spray artist; **2.** *österr. Päd.* (*Spickzettel*) crib; **Schmiererei** *f; -, -en; pej.* **1.** smearing; (*Geschmiertes*) mess; (*nachlässige Handschrift*) scribble, scrawl; **2.** *an Wänden etc.*: daubing of graffiti; **~en** graffiti; **3.** (*wertloses od. anstößiges Geschreibsel*) scribbling; (*Skandaljournalismus*) muckraking; **Schmiererin** *f; -, -nen* → *Schmierer* 1

Schmier|fähigkeit *f* lubricity; **~fett** *n* (lubricating) grease; **~film** *m* film of lubricant; **~fink** *m umg.* (*Kind*) mucky pup, *Am.* grimy kid; (*Kritzler*) scrawler; (*Journalist*) muckraker

Schmiergeld *n* bribe money (*auch Pl.*), payoff; **~affäre** *f* case of bribery; **~zahlung** *f* bribe payment

schmierig **I.** *Adj.* **1.** (*fettig*) greasy; (*schmutzig*) grubby; *Küche etc.:* grimy; **2.** *pej.* (*unanständig*) smutty; (*ölig*) *Person:* oily, smarmy *umg.*; **II.** *Adv.*: **~ grinsen** *pej.* give an oily grin

Schmier|infektion *f Med.* smear infection; **~käse** *m Gastr.* cheese spread

Schmier|mittel *n Tech.* lubricant; **~nippel** *m* lubricating nipple; **~öl** *n* lubricating oil, lubricant; **~papier** *n* rough paper; **~pistole** *f* grease gun; **~seife** *f* soft soap; *grüne:* green soap; **~stoff** *m* lubricant

Schmierung *f Tech.* lubrication

Schmierzettel *m* scrap of paper, piece of rough paper

schmilzt *Präs.* → *schmelzen*

Schminke *f; -, kein Pl.* make(-)up (*auch Theat.*)

schminken **I.** *v/refl.* **1.** put one's (*od.* some) make(-)up on, put one's face on *umg. hum.*; **2.** *generell:* wear make(-)up; **sich stark ~** wear a lot of (*od.* wear heavy) make(-)up; **II.** *v/t.* **1.** make up; *sich* (*Dat.*) *die Lippen ~* put (some) lipstick on; *sich* (*Dat.*) *die Augen ~* put one's (*od.* some) eye make(-)up on; *generell:* wear eye make(-)up; **2.** *fig.* (*Bericht*) colo(u)r

Schmink|koffer *m* vanity case; **~täschchen** *n* make-up bag; **~tisch** *m* dressing table; **~topf** *m* make-up jar; **~utensilien** *Pl.* make-up accessories

Schmirgel *m; -s, kein Pl.* emery; **schmirgeln** *vt/i.* rub down; *mst mit Sandpapier:* sand

Schmirgel|papier *n* emery paper; (*Sandpapier*) sandpaper; **~scheibe** *f* sanding disc (*Am.* disk)

schmiss *Imperf.* → *schmeißen*

Schmiss *m; -es, -e* **1.** (*Hiebwunde*) gash; (*Narbe*) (duelling) scar; **2.** *nur Sg.; umg. fig.* (*Schwung*) verve, zip; **~ haben** *Person:* have plenty of zip; → *auch Schwung* 2; **schmissig** *Adj. umg.* zippy; *Musik:* sprightly, perky; *Marsch:* rousing

Schmock *m; -(e)s, Schmöcke od. -e od. -s; pej.* hack (writer)

Schmöker *m; -s, -; umg.*: **ein ~** a good read; („*Lesefutter*") something good to read; *dicker* **~** thick tome

schmökern *v/i. umg.* **1.** *im Buchladen, in Büchern:* browse; **~ in** (+ *Dat.*) (*Büchern*) browse through, dip into; (*e-m Buch*) browse (*od.* leaf) through; **2.** have one's nose in a book, be buried in a book (*od.* in books); *ab und zu schmökert er gern* he likes a good read now and again (*od.* then); *im Urlaub hab ich so richtig Zeit zum Schmökern* on holiday I have plenty of time to bury myself in a book

Schmollecke *f umg. fig.* → *Schmollwinkel*; **schmollen** *v/i.* sulk (*Schmollmund* *m umg.* pout (*auch e-n ~ machen*)); **Schmollwinkel** *m umg. fig.*: **sich in den ~ zurückziehen** go off in a huff

schmolz *Imperf.* → *schmelzen*

Schmonzes *m; -, kein Pl.; umg.* (*Geschwätz*) twaddle, tripe, bilge *altm.*

Schmorbraten *m Gastr.* pot roast

schmoren **I.** *v/t. Gastr.* braise, stew; **II.** *v/i. Gastr.* stew; *umg. fig. in der Hitze:* roast, bake; *j-n ~ lassen umg. fig.* let s.o. stew (in his *od.* her own juice), let s.o. sweat it out

Schmor|fleisch *n Gastr.* braising steak; **~gemüse** *n* vegetable casserole; **~pfanne** *f* stewpan; **~topf** *m* casserole

Schmu *m; -s, kein Pl.; umg.* (*Schwindel*) fiddle, scam, con; **~ machen** cheat, do a fiddle; *das ist doch* **~!** that's a fiddle (*od.* con)!

schmuck *Adj. altm., hum.* neat; *Person:* smart, spruce; *Mann: auch* dapper; (*hübsch*) pretty

Schmuck *m; -(e)s, kein Pl.* **1.** (*Schmuckstücke*) jewellery, *Am.* jewelry; **2.** (*Verzierung*) ornamentation, decoration; *konkret:* ornament

...schmuck *m, im Subst.* **1.** (*Schmucksachen*): *Gold***~** gold jewel(le)ry; **2.** (*Dekorationen*): *Altar***~** altar decoration; *Baum***~** (Christmas) tree decorations *Pl.*

schmücken **I.** *v/t.* decorate (*auch Christbaum*); (*verzieren*) *auch* adorn, deck out; (*verschönern*) embellish (*auch fig. Rede etc.*); *die Braut ~* adorn the bride with veil and wreath; **II.** *v/refl.* (*sich kleiden*) dress up; *sie schmückt sich gern* she likes wearing smart (*Am.* chic) clothes and jewel-(le)ry; → *Feder* 1

Schmuckkästchen *n* jewel(le)ry box; *fig.* gem; *das Haus ist ein ~ fig.* it's a gem of a house

schmucklos *Adj.* plain, unadorned; *Fassade etc.*: bare; (*schlicht*) simple; **Schmucklosigkeit** *f* plainness, lack of adornment; *von Fassade etc.*: bareness; (*Schlichtheit*) simplicity

Schmuck|nadel *f* brooch; **~sachen** *Pl.* jewellery *Sg.*, *bes. Am.* jewelry *Sg.*; *billige*: trinkets; **~stein** *m* jewel(le)ry stone, gemstone; **~stück** *n* piece of jewel(le)ry; *fig.* gem (*auch Person*), jewel; **~waren** *Pl.* jewellery *Sg.*, *bes. Am.* jewelry *Sg.*

Schmuddel *m*; *-s, kein Pl.*; *umg.* muck; **Schmuddelei** *f*; *-, -en*; *umg.* **1.** (*das Schmuddeln*) soiling; **2.** *nur Sg.* (*Zustand*) grubby state

schmuddelig *Adj. umg. pej.* grubby; (*schlampig*) slovenly; *ein ~es Hemd/ Lokal* a grubby shirt / trashy bar *etc.*

Schmuddel|kind *n umg.* grubby child; **~kram** *m umg.* smut; **~look** *m umg.* urchin look

schmuddeln *v/i. umg.* **1.** *Kleidung etc.*: get dirty (*od.* soiled); **2.** (*schmuddelig arbeiten etc.*) make a mess

Schmuddel|sex *m pej.* smutty sex; **~-TV** *n pej.* smut TV; **~wetter** *n umg.* lousy weather

Schmuggel *m*; *-s, kein Pl.* smuggling; *vom ~ leben* live on money made from smuggling; *~ treiben → schmuggeln*; **Schmuggelei** *f*; *-, -en* smuggling; **Schmuggelgut** *n* smuggled goods *Pl.*

schmuggeln *vt/i.* smuggle; *fig. auch* sneak; *Devisen ~* smuggle currency; *mit etw. ~* smuggle s.th.; *beim Schmuggeln erwischt werden* be caught smuggling; *ein Mädchen / e-n Jungen auf sein Zimmer ~* smuggle (*od.* sneak) a girl/boy into one's room

Schmuggelware *f* smuggled goods *Pl.*, contraband

Schmuggler *m*; *-s, -* smuggler; **~bande** *f* gang of smugglers

Schmugglerin *f*; *-, -nen* (female) smuggler

Schmuggler|organisation *f*, **~ring** *m* ring of smugglers; **~schiff** *n* smugglers' ship, ship carrying contraband

schmunzeln *v/i.* smile (to o.s.), grin

Schmus *m*; *-es, kein Pl.*; *umg.* waffle, nonsense; (*Getue*) fuss; *mach/red keinen ~!* don't make such a fuss / talk such waffle (*od.* nonsense)

Schmuse|decke *f umg.* cuddly blanket; **~katze** *f umg. fig.* cuddly type; (*Kind*) cuddly little thing; **~kurs** *m umg. fig.* friendly overtures *Pl.*; *auf ~ mit ... sein* be cosying (*Am.* cozying) up to ...

schmusen *v/i. umg.* **1.** cuddle (*mit j-m* s.o.); *Liebespaar*: kiss and cuddle, smooch; **2.** *pej.* (*schöntun*) soft-soap; **Schmuser** *m*; *-s, -*; *umg.* **1.** cuddly type; *mein Kater ist ein ganz großer ~* my cat loves to be fondled; **2.** *pej.* (*Schmeichler*) toady, fawner; **Schmuserei** *f*; *-, -en*; *umg.* **1.** cuddling; *von Liebespaar*: kissing and cuddling, smooching; **2.** *pej.* soft-soaping; **Schmuserin** *f*; *-, -nen → Schmuser*

Schmusetier *n* cuddly animal

Schmutz *m*; *-es, kein Pl.* **1.** dirt;

(*Schlamm auch*) mud; **2.** *fig.* filth, smut; *in den ~ ziehen fig.* drag through the mud; *j-n mit ~ bewerfen fig.* sling mud at s.o.

schmutzabweisend, Schmutz abweisend *Adj.* stain-resistant

Schmutz|blatt *n* **1.** *pej.* (*Zeitung*) filthy rag; **2.** *Druck.* half-title; **~bürste** *f* cleaning brush

schmutzen *v/i.* get dirty (*od.* soiled); *leicht ~ auch* soil easily

Schmutz|fänger *m* **1.** *am Auto*: mudflap; **2.** *in der Wohnung*: dust trap; **~fink** *m* **1.** *umg.* pig; (*Kind*) mucky pup, *Am.* grimy kind; **2.** *pej.* depraved type, lecher; *älter*: dirty old man; (*Journalist*) muckraker; **~fleck** *m* dirty mark; **~fracht** *f im Abwasser etc.*: dirt component

schmutzig *Adj.* dirty; *fig.* (*unanständig*) *auch* smutty; (*anrüchig*) dirty; **~es Weiß** *etc.* dirty white, off-white; *sich ~ machen* get (*o.s.*) dirty; *ich mach mir doch nicht die Hände ~ umg. fig. auch* I'm not getting involved in any dirty business; **~e Geschäfte** shady deals; **~e Phantasie** dirty mind; **~e Wäsche** **1.**; **~blau** *Adj.* dirty (*od.* greyish, *Am.* grayish) blue; **~ grau** *Adj.* dirty grey (*Am.* gray)

Schmutz|kampagne *f pej.* smear campaign; **~literatur** *f* pornography, smut; **~löser** *m* stain remover; **~schicht** *f* layer of dirt; **~spritzer** *m* splash of mud; **~titel** *m Druck.* half-title; **~wäsche** *f* dirty washing; **~wasser** *n* dirty water; (*Abwasser*) waste water, sewage; **~zulage** *f* bonus for dirty work

Schnabel *m*; *-s, Schnäbel* **1.** *Zool.* beak, bill; *e-r Schildkröte, e-s Kraken*: beak; *e-s Schnabeltiers*: bill; **2.** *umg.* (*Mund*) mouth, trap, *Brit. auch* gob; *halt den ~!* shut up!, shut your trap!; *sie spricht, wie ihr der ~ gewachsen ist* she doesn't mince her words; **3.** *e-r Kanne*: spout; *e-r Tasse*: lip; **4.** *hist.*, *e-s Schiffes*: prow

...schnabel *m*, *im Subst.*: *Gänse~* goose beak

schnabelförmig *Adj.* beak-shaped, beak(-)like

Schnabelhieb *m* peck

schnäbeln *v/i. Vögel*: bill; *umg. fig. Pärchen*: bill and coo

Schnabel|schuh *m hist.* shoe with a long pointed (*and often turned-up*) toe, crakow(e); **~tasse** *f* feeding cup; **~tier** *n Zool.* duckbilled platypus

schnabulieren I. *v/i. umg.* have a good munch, munch away; *gierig*: feed one's face, tuck in; **II.** *v/t.* munch; (*aufessen*) polish off

Schnack *m*; *-(e)s, -s*; *nordd.* **1.** (*Plauderei*) chat, natter; **'n kleinen ~ halten** have a little chat; **2.** (*Spruch*) phrase, saying; *witzig*: bon mot; **3.** *nur Sg. pej.* (*leeres Gerede*) empty (*od.* idle) chatter; (*Unsinn*) twaddle; *alles nur dummer ~* it's all just silly talk

schnackeln *v/i. bes. südd.* **1.** *mit den Fingern ~* snap one's fingers; **2.** *bei ihm hat's geschnackelt umg.* it finally clicked (with him); **3.** *umg.*: *es schnackelt* (*kracht*) there's a crash; *da hat's geschnackelt* there's been a row (*Am.* fight); (*e-n Unfall gegeben*) there's been a smash

schnacken *vt/i. nordd.* chat, natter; *kannst du Platt ~?* do you speak Low German?; *sie schnackt nur dummes Zeug* she just spouts inanities

Schnackerl *m od. n*; *-s, kein Pl. österr.* hiccup

Schnake *f*; *-, -n*; *Zool.* **1.** crane fly, *Brit. auch* daddy longlegs; **2.** (*Stechmücke*) mosquito, midge

Schnaken|plage *f* plague of mosquitoes; **~stich** *m* mosquito bite

Schnalle *f*; *-, -n* **1.** buckle, clasp; **2.** *südd., österr.* (*Klinke*) doorhandle; **3.** *blöde ~ umg. Dial.* stupid woman; **4.** *umg.* (*Prostituierte*) tart, *Am. auch* hooker; **schnallen** *v/t.* **1.** buckle; *mit Riemen etc.*: strap (*auf + Akk.* onto; *an + Akk.* to); *sich* (*Dat.*) *etw. um die Hüfte ~* strap s.th. round one's hips; *enger ~* tighten; *weiter ~* loosen; → *Gürtel* 1; **2.** *umg.* (*kapieren*) get; *hast du's endlich geschnallt?* has it finally clicked?; **Schnallenschuh** *m* buckled shoe; (*Skistiefel*) buckle boot

schnalzen *v/i.*: *mit den Fingern ~* snap one's fingers; *mit der Zunge ~* click one's tongue; *mit der Peitsche ~* crack one's (*od.* the) whip; **Schnalzer** *m*; *-s, -*; (*Zungenschnalzer*) click (*of the* tongue); (*Peitschenschnalzer*) crack (*of the whip*)

schnapp *Interj. beim Schließen*: snap, click; *e-r Schere*: snip; → *auch* **schnipp**

Schnäppchen *n umg.* bargain, giveaway, *Brit. auch* snip; **~börse** *f* bargain market; **~jäger** *m*, **~jägerin** *f umg.* bargain-hunter; **~paradies** *n* bargain-hunters' paradise

schnappen I. *v/t.* (*hat geschnappt*); *umg.* (*fangen, erwischen*) catch, nab; (*etw.*) grab; (*wegnehmen*) snatch; (*sich Dat.*) *etw. ~* (*an sich nehmen*) grab s.th.; *j-n am Arm ~* grab s.o.'s arm; *der Hund schnappte* (*sich Dat.*) *die Wurst* the dog snatched (*stahl*: nabbed, pinched) the sausage; *lasst euch ja nicht ~!* don't let yourselves be caught; *den werde ich mir ~! fig.* I'm going to nab him and tell him what's what; **II.** *v/i.* **1.** (*hat*) *nach etw. ~* snap (*od.* snatch, grab) at; *Hund*: snap at; *die Gans schnappte nach m-n Waden* the goose took a peck at my thighs; → *Luft* 1, 2; **2.** (*ist*) *ins Schloss ~* snap shut; *nach hinten/vorne ~* snap back/ forward; *nach oben ~* spring up (*od.* open)

Schnäpper *m*; *-s, -*; *Med. umg.* lancet

Schnapp|messer *n* (*Waffe*) flick knife, *Am.* switchblade; (*Klappmesser*) clasp knife; **~schloss** *n* spring lock; *an Ketten etc.*: spring catch; **~schuss** *m* snapshot (*auch fig.*), snap; *e-n ~ machen von* take a snap of; **~verschluss** *m* spring (*od.* snap) lock, spring catch

Schnaps *m*; *-es, Schnäpse umg.* spirit, *Am.* liquor; (*Klarer*) schnapps; (*allg. Spirituosen*) spirits *Pl.*, hard stuff, *Am. auch* hard liquor; *~ brennen* distil(l) spirit(s) (*klaren*: schnapps)

...schnaps *m, im Subst.*: *Obst~* fruit schnapps; *Birnen~* pear brandy; *Hefe~* yeast spirit (*Am.* liquor)

Schnaps|brenner *m* distiller; **~brennerei** *f* distillery; **~bruder** *m umg.* boozer, dipso; **~bude** *f umg.* boozer, lush

Schnäpschen *n umg.* snifter; *auf die Schnelle*: quickie

Schnaps|drossel *f umg.* boozer, dipso, lush; **~fahne** *f umg.*: *e-e ~ haben* reek of strong alcohol; **~flasche** *f* bottle of schnapps (*allg.* spirits); *leere*: schnapps (*allg.* spirits) bottle; **~glas** *n* shot glass; **~idee** *f umg.* hare-brained (*od.* crackpot) idea; **~leiche** *f umg. fig.* snoozing drunk; **~nase** *f umg.*

drinker's nose; **~zahl** f nice number (*comprising several of the same digit*)

schnarchen *v/i.* snore; **mit offenem Mund ~** snore with one's mouth open; **Schnarchen** n; *-s, kein Pl.* snoring; **sie wachte von s-m ~ auf** his snoring woke her up; **Schnarcher** m; *-s, -*, **Schnarcherin** f; *-, -nen* **1.** snorer; **ein starker Schnarcher** a bad snorer; **2.** umg. (*Ton*) snore

schnarren *vt/i.* rattle; *Klingel:* buzz; (*sprechen*) rasp; **mit ~der Stimme** in a rasping (*od.* gravelly, grating) voice

Schnatter|ente f **1.** *Zool.* gadwall.; **2.** umg. fig. chatterbox; **~gans** f, **~liese** f; *-, -n*; umg. chatterbox

schnattern *v/i.* **1.** *Gans:* cackle; *Ente:* quack; **2.** umg. fig. (*reden*) gabble (away), prattle; **sie schnatterten alle auf einmal** they were all jabbering away at the same time

schnauben; *schnaubt, schnaubte od. altm. schnob, hat geschnaubt od. altm. geschnoben; vt/i. Tier.* snort (*auch Person*); **sich** (*Dat.*) **die Nase ~** blow one's nose; **vor Wut** etc. **~** umg. snort with rage etc.

schnaufen *v/i.* breathe hard; *pfeifend:* wheeze; (*keuchen*) (puff and) pant; umg. (*atmen*) breathe; umg. Auto etc.: chug (along); **wir sind ganz schön ins Schnaufen gekommen** we were really puffing and panting (*Am.* huffing and puffing); **Schnaufer** m; *-s, -*; umg. breath; **den letzten ~ tun** snuff it, croak, breathe one's last

Schnauferl n umg. (*Oldtimer*) vintage (*bis 1904*: veteran) car

Schnauzbart m moustache, *Am.* mustache; **schnauzbärtig** *Adj.* moustachioed, *Am.* mustachioed

Schnauze f; *-, -n* **1.** *Tier.* snout; *Hund:* muzzle, nose; **2.** *Tech.* nozzle; **3.** umg. (*Mund*) mouth, trap, *Brit. auch* gob; **e-e freche ~ haben** umg. have a cheeky tongue (*Am.* fresh mouth); **halt die ~!** vulg. belt up!, shut your trap!; **du kriegst gleich eins auf die ~** vulg. you'll have my fist in your face if you're not careful; **die ~** (*gestrichen*) **voll haben** umg. be fed up to the back teeth (**von** with); **auf die ~ fallen** umg. auch fig. fall flat on one's face; **frei nach ~** umg. any old how; → auch *Maul*, *Mund*

schnauzen *vt/i.* umg. (*schimpfen*) snap; *laut:* bark

schnäuzen **I.** *v/t.:* **e-m Kind / sich die Nase ~** blow a child's / one's nose; **II.** *v/refl.:* **sich ~** blow one's nose

Schnauzer m; *-s, -* **1.** (*Hund*) schnauzer; **2.** umg. (*Schnurrbart*) moustache, *Am.* mustache

Schnecke f; *-, -n* **1.** *Zool.* snail; *ohne Haus:* slug; *Gastr.* snail: *auf der Speisekarte auch:* escargot; **er ist langsam wie e-e ~** he's such a slowcoach (*Am.* slowpoke); **j-n zur ~ machen** umg. come down on s.o. like a ton of bricks, have a real go at s.o.; **2.** mst *Pl.* (*Frisur*) earphone; **3.** *Verzierung, auch an Geige etc.:* scroll; *am Kapitell auch:* volute; **4.** (*Gebäck*) Chelsea bun, *Am. etwa* cinnamon roll; **5.** *Tech.* endless screw, worm; **6.** *Anat.* cochlea; **7.** *Archit.* (*Treppe*) spiral staircase; **8.** mst *Pl.; Jägerspr.* (*Hörner*) curling horn (of the mouflon)

Schnecken|antrieb m *Tech.* worm drive; **~bohrer** m *Tech.* single-twist drill; **~förderer** m *Tech.* screw (*od.* worm) conveyor

schneckenförmig *Adj.* spiral, winding

Schnecken|gang m **1. im ~** umg. at a snail's pace (*od.* crawl); **2.** *Anat.* cochlear canal; **~gehäuse** n (snail) shell; **~getriebe** n *Tech.* worm drive; **~haus** n (snail) shell; **sich in sein ~ zurückziehen** fig. go (*od.* withdraw) into one's shell; **~horn** n snail's horn; **~pfanne** f *Gastr.* escargotière; **~post** f umg. altm.: **mit der ~** at a snail's pace; hum. (*nicht per E-Mail*) by snail mail; **~rad** n *Tech.* worm gear; **~tempo** n umg.: **im ~** at a crawl, at a snail's pace

Schneckerl n österr. curl

Schnee m; *-s, nur Sg.* **1.** snow; **weiß wie ~** white as snow, snow-white; **der ~ bleibt liegen / nicht liegen** the snow lies / doesn't lie; **das ist doch ~ von gestern** umg. that's old hat; **im Jahre ~** österr. umg. in the year dot, *Am.* on day one; **2.** *Gastr.* beaten (*od.* whipped) egg whites *Pl.*; **3.** *Sl.* (*Kokain*) snow; **4.** *TV* snow

schneearm *Adj. Region, Winter:* with little snowfall

Schneeanzug m snow suit

Schneeball m snowball (*auch Bot.*); **~prinzip** n snowball effect; **~schlacht** f snowball fight; **~strauch** m *Bot.* snowball bush (*od.* tree); **~system** n *Wirts.* snowball (*od.* pyramid) sales system; **Gewinnspiel nach dem ~** pyramid profit scheme; **nach dem ~ zunehmen** snowball

schneebedeckt *Adj.* snow-covered, snowy; *Bergspitze: auch* snowcapped

Schneebesen m *Gastr.* whisk

schneeblind *Adj.* snow-blind; **Schneeblindheit** f snow blindness

Schnee|bob m bob(sleigh); **~brett** n windslab; **~brille** f: (**e-e**) **~** (a pair of) snow goggles *Pl.*; **~bruch** m *breaking of trees under the weight of the snow, snowbreak*; **~decke** f blanket of snow, snow covering; **geschlossene ~** unbroken covering of snow; **~eule** f *Orn.* snowy owl; **~fall** m snowfall; **~fang** m (roof) snow guard; **~fläche** f stretch of snow; **~flocke** f snowflake; **~fräse** f snowblower

schneefrei *Adj.* **1.** *Straße etc.:* free (*od.* clear) of snow; **~ machen** clear of snow; **2.** **~ haben** be off school because of the snow, *Am. auch* have a snow day

Schnee|gans f *Orn.* snow goose; **~gestöber** n kurz; snow flurry; *stark:* blizzard

schneeglatt *Adj.:* **~e Fahrbahnen** roads slippery with packed snow; **Schneeglätte** f slippery packed snow; *im Wetterbericht:* roads *Pl.* slippery with packed snow

Schnee|glöckchen n *Bot.* snowdrop; **~grenze** f snow line; **~hase** m *Zool.* snow hare; **~hemd** n *Mil.* white camouflage overall, snow shirt; **~höhe** f depth of snow; **~huhn** n *Orn.* ptarmigan; **~kanone** f snow cannon; **~ketten** *Pl.* snow chains; **~kettenpflicht** f obligation to fit snow chains, *Am. auch* chain law; **~könig** m umg.: **sich freuen wie ein ~** be tickled pink, be (as) pleased as punch; **~kristall** m snow crystal; **~landschaft** f snowy landscape; **~mann** m snowman; **e-n ~ bauen** make a snowman; **~matsch** m slush; **~mensch** m: **der ~** the Abominable Snowman; **~mobil** n snowmobile; **~pflug** m auch Skifahren: snowplough (*Am.* -plow); **~räumfahrzeug** n snowblower; **~raupe** f snowmobile for preparing ski runs, Sno-Cat®; **~regen** m sleet; **~schauer** m snow show-

er; **~schaufel** f snow shovel; **~schicht** f layer (*od.* covering) of snow; **~schippe** f → *Schneeschaufel*; **~schmelze** f thaw (of snow); **~schuh** m snowshoe

schneesicher *Adj.:* **~es Gebiet** etc. area etc. with snow guaranteed; **hier ist es bis in den Mai ~** you can be sure of having snow here until May

Schnee|sturm m snowstorm, blizzard; **~treiben** n driving snow; (*Schneegestöber*) (light) blizzard; **~verhältnisse** *Pl.* snow conditions; **~verwehung** f snowdrift; **~wechte** f snow cornice; **~wehe** f snowdrift

schneeweiß *Adj.* snow-white; *im Gesicht:* (as) white as a sheet

Schnee|weißchen n: **~ und Rosenrot** Snow-White and Rose-Red; **~wittchen** n: **~ und die sieben Zwerge** Snow White and the Seven Dwarfs

Schnee|wolke f snowcloud; **~zaun** m snow fence

Schneid m; *-(e)s od. südd., österr. f, -, kein Pl.*; umg. pluck, courage, guts *Pl.*; **es gehört ~ dazu** it takes guts (to do that); **j-m den ~ abkaufen** unnerve s.o.

Schneidbrenner m *Tech.* cutting torch

Schneide f; *-, -n* edge; *Tech.* cutting edge, blade; *fig.* → *Messer* 1; **~brett** n chopping (*od.* cutting) board; **~messer** n **1.** butcher's knife; **2.** *e-r Küchenmaschine:* cutter

schneiden; *schneidet, schnitt, hat geschnitten* **I.** *v/t.* **1.** cut (**aus** out of); (*Gras mähen*) auch mow; (*Braten*) carve; *Med.* cut; (*j-n*) operate on; **in Stücke ~** cut into pieces, cut up; **in** (*dünne*) **Scheiben ~** cut into (thin) slices, slice (thinly); *Gastr. auch* chop (finely); **in zwei Teile ~** cut in two; **2.** *fig.:* **hier ist e-e Luft zum Schneiden!** umg. it's really stuffy in here, *Brit. auch* there's a terrible fug in here; **3.** (*anschneiden*) (*Ball*) spin; *Billard:* put side on; *Fußball:* curve; **er schneidet jeden Ball** Tennis: he slices (*od.* puts spin on) every ball; **4.** **e-e Kurve ~** cut a corner; **j-n ~ beim Überholen:** cut in on s.o.; **5.** (*kreuzen*) **sich ~ Linien:** intersect; **6.** a) Funk. (*auf Tonband*) **~** tape, record, b) *TV* (*Film etc.*) edit; **7.** (*ignorieren*) **j-n ~** umg. fig. (*nicht grüßen*) cut s.o. dead; **sie wird von den Dorfbewohnern geschnitten** she is ostracized by the villagers; → *Gesicht[1]* 1, 2, *Grimasse*, *Haar* 1; **II.** *v/refl.* cut o.s.; → *Finger* 1; **da schneidet er sich aber** (*gewaltig*) umg. fig. he's very much mistaken there; **III.** *v/i.* **1.** *Wind:* cut right through one; *Med.* operate; **das Messer schneidet gut/schlecht** this knife cuts well / doesn't cut well; **gut ~** *Friseur:* be a good hairdresser (*od.* barber); **2.** (*Ball mit Effet spielen*) put spin (*Billard:* side) on the ball; **er schneidet immer** he always uses spin (*Billard:* side); → *geschnitten*, *schneidend*

schneidend **I.** *Part. Präs.* → *schneiden*; **II.** *Adj. Schmerz:* sharp; *Kälte, Wind etc.:* piercing, biting; *Hohn etc.:* caustic; *Stimme, Ton:* piercing, shrill

Schneider m; *-s, -* **1.** tailor; *für Damenmode:* dressmaker; **frieren wie ein ~** umg. be frozen stiff (*od.* to the bone); **2.** **aus dem ~ sein** umg. be out of the wood(s); *Skat:* have a little more than half the points; *Tischtennis:* have more than 11 points; **3.** umg. (*Gerät*) cutter; **4.** (*Insekt*) long-legged insect; (*Weberknecht*) crane fly, *Brit.*

auch daddy longlegs; **5.** *Jägerspr.* (*Hirsch*) runt

Schneideraum *m Film*: cutting room

Schneiderei *f*, -, -en **1.** *nur Sg.* (*Gewerbe*) tailoring, tailor's trade; *für Damen*: dressmaking, couture; *ihr hat die ~ immer Spaß gemacht* she has always enjoyed making clothes; **2.** tailor's (*od.* dressmaker's) shop

Schneiderhandwerk *n* tailoring; *Damenmode*: dressmaking, couture

Schneiderin *f*, -, -nen dressmaker; (*Herrenschneiderin*) (female) tailor

Schneider|kostüm *n* tailored (*od.* tailor-made) suit; **~kreide** *f* tailor's chalk; **~lehre** *f* apprenticeship as a tailor (*Damenmode*: dressmaker); **~meister** *m*, **~meisterin** *f* master tailor (*Damenmode*: dressmaker, couturier)

schneidern *vt/i.* do tailoring (*od.* dressmaking); *beruflich*: *auch* be a tailor (*od.* dressmaker); (*Kleidung*) make, tailor, sew; *sie schneidert sich alles selbst* she makes all her own clothes

Schneider|puppe *f* tailor's dummy, mannequin; **~sitz** *m*: *im ~* cross-legged; **~werkstatt** *f* tailor's (*Damenmode*: dressmaker's) workshop

Schneide|tisch *m* in *Film-, Tonstudio*: cutting (*od.* editing) table; **~werkzeug** *n* cutting tool; **~zahn** *m Anat.* incisor

schneidig I. *Adj.* (*zackig*) dynamic, snappy *umg.*; (*fesch*) dashing, snappy *umg.*; *Musik*: spirited, rousing; *in ~em Galopp* at a brisk gallop; **II.** *Adv.*: *~ angeritten kommen* ride up in a dashing manner; **Schneidigkeit** *f* dynamism, spirit; (*fesche Art*) dashing manner; *Musik*: rousing character; *des Spiels auch*: brio

schneien *vt/i.*, *unpers.* snow; *es schneit* it's snowing; *es schneite dicke Flocken / Konfetti* it was snowing big flakes / there was a shower of confetti; *ins Haus ~* *umg. fig.* blow in

Schneise *f*, -, -n *im Wald*: open strip; *Feuerschutz*: firebreak; *Flug.* (landing *od.* take-off) lane

schnell I. *Adj.* **1.** *mit hohem Tempo*: quick; *Auto, Läufer etc.*: fast; *Puls, Bewegung*: quick, rapid; *Bewegung, Fortschritt etc. auch*: swift; *ein Bußgeld für zu ~es Fahren* a fine for speeding; *~er werden* get faster; *Zug etc.*: pick up speed; *~e Bedienung* fast (*od.* quick, prompt) service; (*Person*) quick waiter (*od.* waitress); **2.** (*sofortig*) *Erwiderung, Maßnahme*: prompt, speedy; *in ~er Folge* in quick (*od.* rapid) succession; *auf ~stem Wege* as quickly as possible, by the quickest possible means; *e-e ~e Entscheidung treffen* make a quick decision; *das erfordert ~es Handeln* that calls for swift (*od.* immediate) action; **3.** *Wirts., Verkauf*: quick; *~er Umsatz* quick returns, fast turnover; **4.** (*rasch und flüchtig*) quick; **5.** (*geistig fix*) quick, fast; *er ist nicht gerade der Schnellste* iro. he's not exactly quick on the uptake; → *Brüter, Truppe* 2; **II.** *Adv.* quickly, fast; rapidly; promptly *etc.*; → I; *~ denken* do some quick thinking; *~ handeln* act fast (*od.* without delay); (*mach*) *~!* *umg.* hurry up!, get a move on!, step on it!; *das geht ~* it doesn't (*od.* won't) take long; *das geht nicht so ~* it can't be done that quickly, it takes time; *~er ging es nicht I etc.* couldn't do it any faster; *das geht mir zu ~* things are happening too fast for me (*od.* for my liking); (*ich komme nicht*

mit) I can't keep up; *ich gehe mal od. eben ~ zum Bäcker* I'm just going to pop round to the baker's (*Am.* zip out to the bakery); *ich muss ~ noch aufs Klo umg.* I must just pay a quick visit, *Am.* I have to visit the men's *etc.* room; *~ reich werden* get rich quick; *so ~ wie möglich* as quickly as possible; *er begreift ~* he's quick (on the uptake); *sie hat ~ und richtig reagiert* her reaction was really fast and right on; *er liest ~* he's a fast reader; *sein Atem ging ~* he was breathing fast; *wir wurden ~ bedient* the service was fast, we got served fast; *~ wirkend Medikament, Gift*: fast-acting; *das werden wir ganz ~ haben* we'll have that (done) in no time; *sie ist ~ verärgert/beleidigt* she is easily annoyed / she's quick to take offen|ce (*Am.* -se); *wie heißt er ~ noch?* *umg.* what's his name again?; → *nachmachen* 1

Schnellabschaltung *f Tech., von Kraftwerk etc.*: rapid closedown

Schnellbahn *f* suburban train, *Am.* rapid transit (train); → *S-Bahn*; **~strecke** *f* e-r *S-Bahn*: suburban (railway) (*Am.* rapid transit) line

Schnell|boot *n* **1.** *Sport* speedboat; **2.** *Mil.* high-speed (attack) craft, motor torpedo boat, *Am. auch* PT boat; **~dienst** *m* express service; **~durchgang** *m im ~ wiederholen* give a quick resumé of

Schnelle *f*, -, -n **1.** *nur Sg.* → *Schnelligkeit*; **2.** *umg. nur in auf die ~* quickly; (*eilig*) in a rush; (*kurzfristig*) at short notice; *etw. auf die ~ machen* do s.th. quickly; (*reparieren etc.*) *auch* make a quick job of s.th.; *oberflächlich*: do s.th. in a hurry, rush s.th.; **3.** → *Stromschnelle*

Schnelleingreiftruppe *f Mil.* rapid response (*od.* deployment) force

schnellen I. *v/i.* (*ist geschnellt*) shoot (up); *eine Forelle schnellte aus dem Wasser* a trout leapt out of the water; *in die Höhe ~* *fig. Kurse etc.*: shoot up, rocket; **II.** *v/t.* (*hat*) *mit den Fingern*: flick

Schnell|fahrer *m*, **~fahrerin** *f* fast driver

Schnellfeuer *n Mil.* rapid fire; **~gewehr** *n* automatic rifle

schnellfüßig *Adj.* nimble, light-footed, *lit.* fleet (of foot)

Schnell|gang *m Mot.* overdrive; *Tech.* rapid power traverse; *im ~ auch fig.* in overdrive; **~gaststätte** *f* fast-food restaurant; *mit Selbstbedienung auch*: cafeteria; (*Schnellimbiss*) snack bar

Schnellgericht¹ *n Gastr.* quick meal; (*Fertiggericht*) ready-to-serve meal, instant food *Sg.*; *Am., Mil.* MRE (= meal ready to eat)

Schnellgericht² *n Jur.* summary court

Schnellhefter *m* folder, ring binder

Schnelligkeit *f* quickness; *von Bewegung, Fortschritt, Entwicklung etc.*: *auch* swiftness, rapidity; *von Erwiderung, Maßnahme*: promptness; (*Tempo*) speed, pace; *Phys.* velocity; → *auch Geschwindigkeit*

Schnell|imbiss *m* snack bar; **~kochplatte** *f* high-speed ring (*Am.* hot plate); **~kochtopf** *m* pressure cooker; **~kurs** *m* crash course

Schnellläufer *m* **1.** *Astron.* high-velocity star; **2.** *Tech.* high-speed machine; **3.** *Sport altm.* (*Sprinter*) sprinter

schnelllebig *Adj. Insekt, Mode etc.*: short-lived; *in unserer ~en Zeit* in these fast-moving times; *der Compu-*

ter-Markt ist äußerst ~ the computer market is subject to extremely rapid change; **Schnelllebigkeit** *f* short-lived nature; (*schnelle Veränderung*) rapidity of change; (*Hektik*) hectic pace

Schnell|paket *n* express parcel (*Am.* package); **~reinigung** *f* express dry cleaning; **~restaurant** *n* → *Schnellgaststätte*; **~richter** *m*, **~richterin** *f* judge in summary proceedings; **~schuss** *m umg.* rush job; *das Buch war ein ~* the book was rushed out

schnellstens *Adv.* as quickly (*od.* soon) as possible (*Abk.* ASAP); *komm ~ nach Hause!* come home as fast as you can

schnellstmöglich I. *Adj.* fastest (*od.* quickest) possible; **II.** *Adv.* as quickly (*od.* fast) as possible (*Abk.* ASAP)

Schnell|straße *f Verk.* dual carriageway, *Am.* divided highway (*restricted to faster vehicles*); **~transporter** *m Mot.* express van; **~verband** *m Med.* first-aid dressing; **~verfahren** *n Jur.* summary proceedings *Pl.*; *Tech.* high-speed process; *im ~ umg. fig.* at high speed; *etw. im ~ lernen* do a crash course in s.th.; **~verkehr** *m Verk.* fast (--moving) traffic; **~vorlauf** *m Video etc.*: fast forward; **~zug** *m Eisenb.* fast train

Schnepfe *f*, -, -n **1.** *Orn.* snipe; **2.** *umg.* (*Prostituierte*) tart, *Am. auch* hooker; **3.** *pej., Schimpfwort für Mädchen od. Frau*: *blöde ~!* silly cow!

Schnepfen|jagd *f* snipe shooting; **~strich** *m* **1.** *Jägerspr.* mating flight of the snipe; **2.** *umg. fig.* (*Prostituiertenviertel*) red-light district; **~zug** *m* migration of the snipe

schnetzeln *v/t. Gastr.* shred; (*Fleisch*) cut into thin strips; → *Geschnetzelte*

schneuzen → *schnäuzen*

Schnickschnack *m*; -s, kein *Pl.*; *umg.* **1.** worthless trinkets (*od.* gewgaws) *Pl.*, knick-knacks *Pl.*; (*Äußerlichkeiten*) trappings *Pl.*, frills *Pl.*; *ohne ~* (*schlicht, zweckmäßig*) without any frills, no-frills …; **2.** (*Geschwätz*) waffle; (*Unsinn*) twaddle

schniefen I. *v/i. umg.* sniffle; **II.** *v/t. Sl.* (*Drogen*) sniff; **Schniefnase** *f umg.*: *e-e ~ haben* have a sniffy nose, have the sniffles

schniegeln I. *v/t. umg.* spruce up; (*Haar*) slick down; **II.** *v/refl.* spruce o.s. up (with exaggerated care); → *geschniegelt*

schnieke *Adj. Dial. umg.* **1.** (*schick*) snazzy; **2.** (*großartig*) great, fantastic

schnipp *Interj.* snip!; *~, schnapp!* snip, snip

Schnippchen *n umg.*: *j-m ein ~ schlagen* (manage to) outwit (*od.* get the better of) s.o.; (*s-n Verfolgern*) give s.o. the slip; *er hat dem Tod ein ~ geschlagen* he managed to cheat death

schnippeln *vt/i.* snip (*an + Dat.* at); *Gemüse ~* chop vegetables

schnippen I. *v/i.*: (*mit den Fingern*) *~* snap one's fingers; **II.** *v/t.* (*wegschnippen*) flick (*off od.* away *etc.*)

schnippisch I. *Adj. Bemerkung etc.*: cocky; *sie hat so e-e ~e Art* she has such a pert manner; **II.** *Adv. antworten, reagieren*: pertly

Schnipsel *m, n*; -s, - snippet; *von Papier*: *auch* scrap; **schnipseln** *vt/i. umg.* → *schnippeln*

schnipsen *vt/i. und v/i.* → *schnippen*

schnitt *Imperf.* → *schneiden*

Schnitt *m*; -(e)s, -e **1.** (*das Schneiden*) cutting; (*Mähen*) mowing; (*Ernten*) harvesting; **2.** *Film*: editing; (*Endversion*) final cut (*od.* edit); **3.** (*Einschnitt*) cut; (*Wunde*) cut; *große*: gash; *Med.* cut, incision; *Druck.* cut; **4.** (*Fasson, Form*) shape, cut; *e-r Wohnung*: layout, floorplan; *e-s Gesichts*: features *Pl.*; *e-s Kleides*: style; (*Frisur*) cut; **5.** (*~muster*) pattern; **6.** *Math.* intersection; *der goldene ~* the golden section; **7.** *umg.* (*Durchschnitt*) average; *im ~* on average; *im ~ betragen od. erreichen etc.* average; **8.** *Tech.* (*Zeichnung*) section(al view); → **Längsschnitt, Querschnitt; 9.** *umg.* (*Gewinn*) profit; *e-n guten ~ machen* make a healthy profit; **10.** *Bio., Med.* (*Präparat*) section

Schnitt|blumen *Pl.* cut flowers; **~bohnen** *Pl. Bot., Gastr.* green (*od.* string) beans, *Brit. auch* French beans; **~brot** *n* sliced (*od.* cut) bread; (*Laib*) sliced (*od.* cut) loaf

Schnittchen *n Gastr.* canapé, open sandwich

...schnittchen *n, im Subst.*: *Lachs~* salmon canapé

Schnitte *f*; *-, -n*; (*Scheibe*) slice; (*Brotscheibe*) slice of bread; (*belegtes Brot*) (open) sandwich

...schnitte *f, im Subst.* **1.** (*Scheibe*): *Graubrot~* slice of rye and wheat bread; **2.** (*belegtes Brot*): *Käse~* (slice of) bread and cheese; **3.** (*Kuchen etc.*): *Apfel~* apple slice

Schnitter *m*; *-s, -; altm.* reaper; *der ~ Tod lit.* the Grim Reaper; *~in f*; *-, -nen; altm.* reaper

schnittfest *Adj.* firm

Schnitt|fläche *f* **1.** *Math.* section; **2.** *von Käse, Spargel etc.*: cut end; *e-s Baumes etc.*: sawn surface; **~holz** *n* cut (*od.* sawn) timber

schnittig *Adj. bes. Auto*: sleek; (*sportlich*) racy; **Schnittigkeit** *f* sleekness; (*Sportlichkeit*) raciness

Schnitt|käse *m Gastr.* cheese suitable for slicing; (*aufgeschnittener Käse*) cheese slices *Pl.*; *halbfester ~* semi-hard cheese; **~lauch** *m Bot.* chives *Pl.*; *ein Bund ~* a bunch of chives; **~linie** *f Math.* (line of) intersection; *am Kreis*: secant; **~meister** *m*, **~meisterin** *f beim Film*: film editor; **~menge** *f Math.* intersection; **~muster** *n* (dressmaking) pattern; **~punkt** *m Math.* (point of) intersection

schnittreif *Adj. Agr., Getreide*: ready for harvesting

Schnitt|stärke *f bei Schneidemaschine*: slice thickness; **~stelle** *f Film etc.*: cut; *Computer*: interface; **~verletzung** *f Med.* cut; *große*: gash; **~winkel** *m Math.* angle of intersection; **~wunde** *f Med.* cut; *große*: gash

Schnitz *m*; *-es, -e; südd.* slice

Schnitz|altar *m* carved altar(piece); **~arbeit** *f* carving; **~bank** *f* carver's bench

Schnitzel *n*; *-s, -* **1.** *Gastr.* veal (*od.* pork etc.) escalope; *Wiener ~* (wiener)schnitzel; **2.** *auch m* (*Papierschnitzel*) bit, scrap (of paper); (*Holzschnitzel*) chip; *feiner*: shaving

...schnitzel *n, im Subst.*: *Hähnchen~* escalope of chicken

Schnitzel|fleisch *n* escalope meat; **~jagd** *f* paperchase

schnitzeln *v/t.* (*Gemüse etc.*) shred

schnitzen *v/t/i.* carve; *e-n Stock / e-e Flöte ~* carve a stick / carve out a whistle; *aus Elfenbein geschnitzt* carved in ivory; *er kann gut ~* he's a good carver; → *Holz* 2

Schnitzer *m*; *-s, -* **1.** *Künstler*: carver; **2.** *umg. fig.* blunder, boob; (*Bemerkung etc.*) gaffe, faux pas; *grober ~* real howler (*od.* boob); (*Fauxpas*) terrible gaffe

Schnitzerei *f*; *-, -en*; (*auch Objekt*) carving; **Schnitzerin** *f*; *-, -nen* carver

Schnitz|kunst *f* carving; **~messer** *n* woodcarving knife

schnob *Imperf.* → *schnauben*

schnodd(e)rig *Adj. umg. pej.* snotty; *bes. Junge*: cocky, brash; *bes. Mädchen*: pert; *er hat so e-e ~e Art* he has such a cocky manner; **Schnodd(e)rigkeit** *f umg. pej.* snottiness; *e-s Jungen auch*: cockiness, brashness; *e-s Mädchens auch*: pertness

schnöde *pej.* **I.** *Adj.* (*verächtlich*) contemptible, despicable; (*geringschätzig*) contemptuous; → *Mammon*; **II.** *Adv.*: *j-n ~ behandeln* treat s.o. with disdain (*od.* contempt)

Schnorchel *m*; *-s, -; Naut. und Tauchen*: snorkel; **schnorcheln** *v/i.* snorkel, go snorkel(l)ing

Schnörkel *m*; *-s, -* curlicue; *an Säulen, Möbeln etc.*: scroll; *beim Schreiben, auch stilistisch*: flourish; (*Krakel*) squiggle; *ein ~ als Unterschrift* a squiggle as a signature; *ohne ~* unfussy, clean; **schnörk(e)lig** *Adj. Schrift*: ornate; (*krakelig*) squiggly; *Stil*: flowery; *Baustil*: ornate, fussy; **schnörkellos** *Adj. Architektur, Design*: unfussy, clean; *Schrift*: plain; *Stil*: unfussy; *fig. Küche*: without any frills, plain; **Schnörkelschrift** *f* ornate writing

schnorren *v/t/i. umg.* scrounge (*bei* off, from), sponge (*bei* on, off); **Schnorrer** *m*; *-s, -*, **Schnorrerin** *f*; *-, -nen*; *umg.* scrounger, sponger

Schnösel *m umg. pej.* snotty (young) upstart (*od.* whippersnapper); *sich wie ein ~ aufführen* behave in an uppity manner; **schnöselig** *Adj. umg. pej.* snotty, cheeky

Schnuckelchen *n umg.*: *mein kleines ~* my little sweetie (*od.* pet); **schnuck(e)lig** *Adj. umg.* **1.** cute; (*nett*) nice; **2.** (*appetitlich*) appetizing; *etw. Schnuck(e)liges essen* eat s.th. delicious

Schnucki *n*; *-s, -s*, **Schnuckiputz** *m*; *-es, -e; umg.* sweetie pie

Schnüffelei *f*; *-, -en; umg.* **1.** (*Herumschnüffeln*) snooping; **2.** *von Klebstoff etc.*: sniffing (solvents), *mst* glue-sniffing

schnüffeln I. *v/i.* **1.** *Hund etc.*: sniff (*an + Dat.* at); *umg.* (*schniefen*) sniffle; **2.** *umg.* (*Klebstoff etc.*) sniff solvents; **3.** *umg. fig.* (*herumspionieren*) snoop around; *in j-s Akten ~* poke about in s.o.'s papers; **II.** *v/t. umg.* (*Klebstoff etc.*) sniff

Schnüffeln *n*; *-s, kein Pl.; umg.* **1.** (*Schnüffelei*) snooping; **2.** *von Klebstoff etc.*: glue-sniffing; *förm.* solvent abuse

Schnüffel|nase *f umg., pej. Person*: Nosy Parker; **~stoff** *m* (*Rauschgift*) solvent (*used for sniffing*)

Schnüffler *m*; *-s, -*, **~in** *f*; *-, -nen; umg.* **1.** snooper; (*Spion*) spy; **2.** *von Klebstoff etc.*: (solvent-, *mst* glue-)sniffer

Schnuller *m*; *-s, -* dummy, *Am.* pacifier; (*Sauger an Flasche*) teat, *Am.* nipple

Schnulze *f*; *-, -n; umg.* **1.** *Buch, Film etc.*: tearjerker; *auch Pl.* sobstuff, schmaltzy book (*od.* film etc.); **2.** *Schlager*: slushy (*od.* schmaltzy)

song; **Schnulzensänger** *m*, **Schnulzensängerin** *f umg.* crooner; **schnulzig** *Adj. umg.* soppy, schmaltzy

Schnupfen *m*; *-s, kein Pl.; Med.* (head) cold, *the* sniffles *umg.*; *sich e-n ~ holen* get a (head) cold

schnupfen *v/i.* **1.** (*Tabak*) take snuff; **2.** *bei laufender Nase*: sniff; **II.** *v/t.* (*Drogen*) snort; *Tabak ~* take snuff

Schnupfenmittel *n Med.* cold remedy

Schnupftabak *m* snuff

Schnupftuch *n Dial.* handkerchief

schnuppe *Adj. umg. präd.*: *das ist mir (völlig) ~* I couldn't care less (*od.* give a damn)

Schnupper|angebot *n umg.* trial offer; **~kurs** *m umg.* taster course

schnuppern *vt/i.* **1.** sniff (*an etw. [Dat.]* s.th.); *mal wieder Seeluft ~ fig.* be back by the sea, get a breath of sea air again; *Zirkusluft ~* breathe in the atmosphere of the circus; **2.** *umg. fig.* (*ausprobieren*) try things out

Schnupper|preis *m umg.* introductory price; **~tag** *m umg.* trial day; *Snowboard~* snowboard try-out day

Schnur *f*; *-, Schnüre* cord; (*Bindfaden*) (piece of) string; (*Angelschnur*) (fishing) line; *Etech.* flex, lead, *Am.* cord, cable; *von Telefon, Waschmaschine etc.*: cord; *Perlen auf e-e ~ ziehen* string pearls; *mit bunten Schnüren besetzt* decorated with colo(u)rful braiding *Sg.*

Schnur|band *n* → *Schnürsenkel*; **~boden** *m Theat.* the flies *Pl.*

Schnürchen *n umg. fig.*: *es klappte wie am ~* it went without a hitch (*od.* like clockwork); *bei ihm klappt es wie am ~* he's got it down to a fine art

schnüren I. *v/t.* (*hat geschnürt*) (*Schuhe*) lace (up); (*Paket*) tie up; *zu Bündeln ~* tie into bundles; *sich (Dat.) die Taille ~ altm.* lace one's waist (with a corset); → *Bündel* 1; **II.** *v/i.* **1.** (*hat*) *Verband etc.*: be too tight, *stärker*: stop the flow of blood; **2.** (*ist*) *Jägerspr., Fuchs etc.*: trot in a straight line; **III.** *v/refl.* (*hat*) *sich ins Fleisch etc. ~* cut into the flesh etc.

schnurgerade *umg.* **I.** *Adj. präd.* straight as a die, dead straight; **II.** *Adv.* dead straight; → *schnurstracks*

schnurlos *Adj.* cordless

Schnürl|regen *m österr.* persistent (heavy) rain; **~samt** *m österr.* corduroy

Schnurrbart *m* moustache, *Am.* mustache; **schnurrbärtig** *Adj.* ... with a moustache (*Am.* mustache), moustached, *Am.* mustached

Schnurre *f*; *-, -n* amusing story; (*Posse*) farce

schnurren *v/i.* **1.** (*hat geschnurrt*) *Katze, Stimme, Motor*: purr; (*summen*) hum; *Rad, Ventilator etc.*: whirr, *Am.* whir; *das Schnurren des Katers* the cat's purring (*od.* purrs *Pl.*); **2.** (*ist*) *umg. fig.* (*fahren, fliegen*) purr (along); *er ist mit s-m alten Moped in die Stadt geschnurrt* he buzzed (*leiser*: hummed) into town on his old moped

Schnurrhaare *Pl. Zool.* whiskers *Pl.*

Schnürriemen *m* strap; → *auch Schnürsenkel*

Schnür|schuh *m* lace-up (shoe); **~senkel** *m* shoelace; *für Stiefel*: bootlace, *bes. Am. auch* shoestring; **~stiefel** *m* lace-up boot

schnurstracks *Adv.* (*direkt*) straight; (*sofort*) immediately, straightaway; *~*

zugehen auf (+ *Akk.*) go (*od.* make) straight for, make a beeline for

schnurz, schnurzpiepegal *Adj. umg. präd.* → **schnuppe**

Schnute *f; -, -n; Dial. umg.* trap, *Brit. auch* gob; *e-e* ~ *machen od. ziehen* pull (*Am.* make) a face

Schoah *f; -, kein Pl.: die* ~ (*der Holocaust*) the Holocaust, the Shoah

schob *Imperf.* → **schieben**

Schober *m; -s, -* small hay barn; *südd., österr.* (*Heuhaufen*) haystack, rick

Schock[1] *m; -(e)s, -s; Med., auch fig.* shock; *e-n* ~ *haben* be in a state of shock; *unter* ~ *stehen* be suffering from shock; *e-n* (*schweren*) ~ *auslösen* trigger a (nasty) shock

Schock[2] *n; -(e)s, -e, bei Mengen -* **1.** *altm.: ein/zwei* ~ *Eier* five/ten dozen eggs; **2.** *umg.* (*Menge*) mass; *ein ganzes* ~ *Kinder* a whole crowd of children

schock|artig *Adj.* shock(-)like

Schockbehandlung *f Med.* shock treatment (*auch fig.*), (electro)shock therapy

schocken *vt/i. umg.* shock (*auch Med.*); *ich war / das hat mich schwer geschockt* I was very shocked / this gave me a nasty shock; **Schocker** *m; -s, -; umg.* (*Film, Roman etc.*) shocker, (spine-)chiller

Schockfarbe *f* garish colo(u)r; **schockfarben** *Adj.* garish

schock|frosten, ~**gefrieren** *v/t.* shock-freeze

schockieren *vt/i.* shock; **schockierend I.** *Part. Präs.* → **schockieren; II.** *Adj.* shocking; *stärker:* horrifying; (*beängstigend*) frightening; **schockiert I.** *P.P.* → **schockieren; II.** *Adj.* shocked; ~ *über* (+*Akk.*) shocked at

Schock|therapie *f Med.* shock treatment (*auch fig.*), (electro)shock therapy; ~**wirkung** *f* **1.** shock effect; **2.** *unter* ~ *stehen* be in a state of (*od.* suffering from) shock

Schofel *m; -s, -; umg.* **1.** (*Schund*) junk, trash; **2.** (*Schuft*) scoundrel; **schofel, schof(e)lig** *umg.* **I.** *Adj.* (*gemein*) mean, rotten, shabby; (*geizig*) mean, stingy; **II.** *Adv.: sich* ~ *verhalten* behave in a mean (*od.* rotten) way

Schöffe *m; -n, -n; Jur.* lay judge

Schöffen|gericht *n court in which decisions are rendered by lay judges;* **Schöffin** *f; -, -nen; Jur.* lay judge

Schoko *f; -, -s; umg.* chocolate

Schoko|eis *n umg.* chocolate ice cream; ~**guss** *m* chocolate icing (*Am. auch* frosting); ~**keks** *m* chocolate biscuit

Schokolade *f; -, -n* chocolate; *heiße* ~ hot chocolate; *e-e Tafel* ~ a bar of chocolate

...schokolade *f, im Subst.: Halbbitter*~ plain (*Am.* semisweet *od.* dark) chocolate

schokoladen *Adj. nur attr.* chocolate ...; ~**braun** *Adj.* chocolate (brown)

Schokoladen|creme *f* chocolate cream dessert; ~**eis** *n* chocolate ice cream

Schokoladenfarbe *f* chocolate (colo[u]r); **schokoladenfarben** *Adj.* chocolate(-colo[u]red)

Schokoladen|glasur *f,* ~**guss** *m* chocolate icing (*Am. auch* frosting); ~**herz** *n* chocolate heart; ~**keks** *m* chocolate biscuit, *Am.* chocolate (chip) cookie; ~**nikolaus** *m* chocolate Santa Claus; ~**osterhase** *m* chocolate Easter rabbit; ~**pudding** *m* chocolate blanc-

mange (*Am.* pudding); ~**raspel** *Pl.* grated chocolate *Pl.;* ~**riegel** *m* chocolate bar; ~**seite** *f umg. Profil:* best side; *des Lebens:* sunny side; *sich von s-r* ~ *zeigen* show one's best side; ~**tafel** *f* bar of chocolate; ~**torte** *f* chocolate gateau

Schokoriegel *m* chocolate (*Am. auch* candy) bar

Scholastik *f; -, kein Pl.; Philos.* scholasticism; **Scholastiker** *m; -s, -* scholastic; **scholastisch I.** *Adj.* scholastic; **II.** *Adv.* scholastically

scholl *Imperf.* → **schallen**

Scholle[1] *f; -, -n* **1.** (*Erdscholle*) clod (of earth); *auf heimatlicher* ~ *fig.* on one's native soil; **2.** (*Eisscholle*) (ice) floe; **3.** *Geol.* massif

Scholle[2] *f; -, -n; Zool. auch Pl.* plaice

Schollenfilet *n Gastr.* plaice fillet

Scholli *m umg.: mein lieber* ~*!* good heavens!, *Am. auch* oh boy!

Schöllkraut *n Bot.* celandine

schon *Adv.* **1.** *mit Zeitangaben:* already; ~ *damals* even then; ~ *früher* before; (*vor langer Zeit*) a long time ago; ~ *immer* always, all along; ~ *oft* often (enough); ~ *wieder* again; ~ *wieder!* not again!; ~ *nach fünf Minuten* after only five minutes; ~ *von Anfang an* right from the start, from the word go *umg.;* ~ *am nächsten Tag* the very next day; ~ *um 6 Uhr waren sie auf* they were already up at 6 o'clock; ~ *im 16. Jahrhundert* as early (*od.* as far back) as the 16th century; *das ist* ~ *lange her* that was long ago (*od.* way back); *wie lange sind Sie* ~ *hier?* how long have you been here?; **2.** (*bereits*) already; (~ *einmal, zuvor*) before; (*bis jetzt*) so far; *in Fragen:* yet; (*jemals*) ever; *ich habe* ~ *eins umg.* I've already got one; *hast du* ~ *einmal ...?* have you ever ...?; *sind Sie* ~ (*einmal*) *in Spanien gewesen?* have you ever been to Spain?; *ich war* ~ *ein paarmal dort* I've been there a couple of times; *wir kennen uns* ~ we've met, we do know one another; *ich habe ihn* ~ (*einmal*) *gesehen* I've seen him before somewhere; *danke, ich habe* ~ *zu trinken etc.:* no thanks, I'm fine; *da ist er ja* ~ *wieder* he's (*iro.* look who's) back again; *das kenne ich* ~ I know that, I've heard that before; *bei Entschuldigungen:* I've heard that one before; *ich habe* ~ *bessere Weine getrunken* I've tasted better wines in my time; *hast du* ~ *gehört?* have you heard?; *ist er* ~ *da?* has he come yet?, is he here yet?; (*früher als erwartet*) is he here already?; *werden Sie* ~ *bedient?* are you being served?; *ich bekomme* ~ it's OK, I'm being looked after; *warum willst du* ~ *gehen?* why are you leaving so early?; **3.** *zur Betonung* (*sogar, selbst*) even; ~ *ein Milligramm des Gifts kann tödlich sein* just (*od.* even) one milligram(me) of the poison can kill you; *ein Anruf hätte* ~ *genügt* (just) a phone call would have been enough; ~ *für 10 Euro* for only 10 euros; *Herrenhemden* ~ *ab 5 Euro* men's shirts from as little as 5 euros; *ich komme* (*ja*) ~*!* (I'm) coming!; *da sind wir* (*ja*) ~*!* here we are; *was gibt es denn* (*nun*) ~ *wieder?* what is it now (*od.* this time)?; *ich verstehe* ~ I see; **4.** (*allein*) ~ *s-e Stimme* just to hear his voice, his voice alone; ~ *der Name* the mere (mention of the *od.* his *etc.*) name, just to hear the (*od.* his *etc.*) name; ~ *der Anblick* just to

see it; ~ *der Gedanke* the very idea, the mere thought (of it); ~ *wegen* if only because of; *der Kinder etc.:* if only for the sake of; ~ *weil* if only because; **5.** *versichernd, verstärkend: sie wird's* ~ *schaffen* she'll make it all right; *beruhigend: auch* don't worry, she'll make it; *er kommt* ~ *noch* he'll come eventually; *die Zinsen steigen* ~ *noch* the interest rates are bound to go up; the interest rates will go up, you'll see; *ich mach's* ~ leave it to me; *das ist* ~ *möglich* that could be; *betonter:* that's quite possible; *das lässt sich* ~ *machen mit Vorbehalt:* we *etc.* might be able to do that, it's doable; (*es ist kein Problem*) that's no problem *umg.; wir können* ~ *mit ihm reden* (*sind bereit*) we don't mind talking to him; *ich kann mir* ~ *denken, was ...* I can (just) imagine what ...; *das war* ~ *Glückssache* that really was a stroke of luck; ~ *gut!* it's all right, never mind; (*das reicht*) that'll do; **6.** *umg. auffordernd, ermunternd: mach* ~*!* get a move on, will you?; *komm* ~*!* come on, then; *nun sag* ~*, wie's war* come on, tell us (*od.* me) what it was like; *gib's* ~ *zu!* come on, admit it!; **7.** *einräumend od. bedingend:* ~*, aber ...* yes, but ...; *ich verstehe/möchte* ~*, aber ...* I can see that / I'd like to, but ...; *ich kenne sie* ~*, aber ...* I do know her, but ...; *das ist* ~ *wahr, aber ...* that's (certainly) (*od.* may be) true, but ...; *wenn du* ~ (*mal*) *da bist* since you're here; **8.** (*ohnehin*) *es ist so* ~ *teuer genug* it's expensive enough as it is; *morgen* ~ *gar nicht* least of all tomorrow; **9.** *umg. rhetorisch: na wenn* ~*!* so what; *iro.* so?; *was macht das* ~*?* what does it matter?; *was heißt das* ~*?* so?, that doesn't mean a thing; *wer braucht/kauft sowas* ~*?* who on earth needs/buys something like that?; *was verstehst du* ~ *davon?* what do you know about it?; *wer könnte da* ~ *nein sagen?* who could possibly say no (to that)?; **10.** *umg. wenn* ~*, denn* ~ (*wenn man sich auf etw. einlässt*) in for a penny (*Am.* dime), in for a pound (*Am.* dollar); (*wenn man etw. unternimmt*) anything worth doing, is worth doing well

schön I. *Adj.* **1.** (*attraktiv*) nice; (*ausgesprochen* ~) beautiful; *Frau: auch* attractive; *Mann:* handsome, good-looking; *Kind:* lovely; *Tier:* beautiful; ~*e Schrift* nice handwriting; ~*e Stimme* attractive voice; *Singstimme:* beautiful voice; *e-e hinreißend* ~*e Frau* a stunningly beautiful woman; *sich* ~ *machen* dress up, make o.s. smart (*Am.* neat); (*sich schminken*) put one's make-up (*od.* face *umg.*) on; *sich für j-n* ~ *machen* try to look one's best for s.o.; **2.** *die* ~*en Künste* the fine arts; ~*e Literatur* belles-lettres *Pl.*, belletristic literature; **3.** (*gut*) good; (*nett*) nice; (*erlesen*) fine, choice; *ein* ~*er Erfolg* a great success; ~*es Wetter* good (*od.* fine) weather; ~*en Dank!* many thanks; *abweisend:* no thank you, thanks but no thanks *umg.; umg.* okay; *na* ~*!* (*also gut*) all right then; *zu* ~*, um wahr zu sein* too good to be true; *das ist alles* ~ *und gut, aber ...* that's all very well, but ...; *das Schöne daran* the great thing about it; → *anrichten* 2; *das Schönste kommt noch bes. iro.* you haven't heard the best part

yet, it gets better; **4.** (*angenehm*) nice, pleasant; **~er heißer Tee** *umg.* nice hot (cup of) tea; **ein paar ~e Stunden** a few pleasant (*stärker:* happy) hours; **es war sehr ~ auf dem Fest** it was great (*od.* very nice); **das war ein ~er Tag** that was a lovely day; **~en Tag noch!** *bes. Am.* have a nice day; **das ist ~ von ihm** that's (very) kind (*od.* nice) of him; **~er Tod** easy death; **~ wär's!** wouldn't that be nice; (*ist unwahrscheinlich*) what a hope!, that'll be the day!; **er macht nur ~e Worte** it's all fine words with him; **5.** *umg.* (*beträchtlich*) considerable; **ein ~es Stück** *od.* **e-e ~e Strecke laufen** walk quite a way (*od.* distance); **ein ~es Stück vorankommen** make a fair bit of progress; **ein ~es Stück Arbeit** a pretty big job; **e-e ~e Summe** a tidy sum; **ein ganz ~es Alter** a fine old age; **du hast mir e-n ~en Schreck eingejagt** you gave me quite a scare; **6.** *umg. iro.:* **das sind mir ~e Sachen** that's a fine kettle of fish; **du bist mir ein ~er Freund** a fine friend you are; **das wäre ja noch ~er!** that'd be the last straw, that's the last thing we want; → **Aussicht** 2, **Bescherung** 2; **7. e-s ~en Tages** one day; *zukünftig:* one of these days; **II.** *Adv.* **1.** nicely, beautifully *etc.*; → I; **2.** *umg.* (*sehr*) really, pretty; **~ warm** nice and warm; **der Kaffee ist ~ / ganz ~ heiß** the coffee is nice and hot / really hot; **sei ~ brav!** be a good boy (*od.* girl) now; **bleib ~ ruhig zum Kind:** you be quiet now; (*keine Aufregung*) just keep calm now; **es ist ganz ~ schwer** that's some weight; (*schwierig*) it's pretty difficult; **du hast mich ganz ~ erschreckt** you gave me quite a scare; **da wärst du ~ dumm** you'd be a right (*Am.* complete) fool; **3. du hast es ~!** lucky you!; **4.** *umg. iro.* **jetzt steh' ich ~ da** I look a right (*Am.* complete) fool now; **es kommt noch ~er** it gets even better, you haven't heard the best part yet; **5. wie man so ~ sagt** *umg.* as they say; **wie es so ~ heißt** *umg.* as the saying goes; → **schönmachen, schöntun**

Schonbezug *m* loose cover, *Am.* slipcover; *Mot.* seat cover

Schöndruck *m Druck.* printing of one side of the sheet, first printing

Schöne *f; -n, -n;* (*Frau*) beauty; *mst iro.* lovely lady; **die ~n der Nacht** the ladies of the night

schonen I. *v/t.* (*verschonen*) spare; (*pfleglich behandeln*) (*Sachen*) treat with care; (*j-n*) take good care of; (*Augen, Kräfte, Vorrat*) save; (*j-n nachsichtig behandeln*) be easy on; **j-s Gefühle ~** spare s.o.'s feelings; **ich wollte dich ~** I didn't want you to get upset; **um ihren kranken Mann zu ~** to make things easier for her sick husband; **der Gegner wurde nicht geschont** the opponent was given no quarter; **II.** *v/refl.* take it easy; **sie schont sich nicht** she doesn't spare herself

schönen *v/t.* **1.** (*Wein etc.*) clarify, fine; **2.** (*Farben*) brighten; **3.** (*Zahlen*) massage; (*Tatsachen*) dress up, put a spin on

schonend I. *Part. Präs.* → **schonen**; **II.** *Adj.* careful, gentle; (*rücksichtsvoll*) considerate; (*nachsichtig*) indulgent; *Waschmittel etc.:* mild; **III.** *Adv.:* **j-m etw. ~ beibringen** break s.th. to s.o. gently; **~ umgehen mit** look after, take care of; (*j-m*) handle with kid gloves;

nachsichtig: go easy on; **er behandelt sein Auto nicht gerade ~** he doesn't exactly treat his car gently

Schoner[1] *m; -s, -* cover; *auf Sofa, Lehnstuhl:* antimacassar; **~ an den Ärmeln tragen** wear sleeve-protectors

Schoner[2] *m; -s, -; Naut.* schooner

schönfärben *v/t.* (*trennb., hat -ge-*) *fig.* gloss over

Schönfärberei *f; nur Sg.* glossing over the facts

Schon|frist *f* (period of) grace; **~gang** *m* **1.** *Mot.* overdrive; **2.** (*Waschgang*) gentle wash, delicate cycle

Schöngeist *m* (a)esthete; **schöngeistig** *Adj.* (a)esthetic; **~e Literatur** belletristic literature, belles-lettres *Pl.*

Schönheit *f* beauty (*auch Frau*); **sie ist e-e richtige ~** she is a real beauty; **er/ sie ist (wirklich) keine ~** *umg.* he's no Adonis / she's no beauty; **~en der Natur:** beauty spots

Schönheits|begriff *m* concept of beauty; **~chirurg** *m*, **~chirurgin** *f* cosmetic surgeon; **~chirurgie** *f* cosmetic surgery; **~creme** *f* beauty cream; **~farm** *f* health farm; **~fehler** *m* blemish; *e-s Gegenstands:* (cosmetic) flaw; *fig.* flaw, snag; **die Sache hat nur e-n (kleinen) ~** *umg. fig.* it has just one (tiny) drawback (*od.* snag); **~fleck** *m* beauty spot; **~ideal** *n* ideal of beauty; **~königin** *f* beauty queen; **~konkurrenz** *f* beauty contest; **~korrektur** *f auch fig.* cosmetic change (*od.* improvement); **~operation** *f* cosmetic operation, cosmetic surgery; **~pflege** *f* beauty care; **~reparatur** *f* basic repair; *Mot.* touch-up job; **~salon** *m* → **Kosmetiksalon**; **~sinn** *m* sense of beauty, (a)esthetic sense (*od.* sensitivity); **~wettbewerb** *m* beauty contest

Schon|kaffee *m* mild coffee; **~klima** *n* temperate climate; **~kost** *f Med.* light diet (*od.* food)

Schönling *m; -s, -e; pej.* (young) Adonis; **sie geht mit so e-m ~** she's going around with one of those beautiful young men

schönmachen *v/i.* (*trennb., hat -ge-*) *Hund:* sit up (and beg)

schönreden (*trennb., hat -ge-*); *pej.* **I.** *v/i.* smooth-talk, *Am.* sweet-talk; **II.** *v/t.* (*Ergebnis etc.*) talk up

Schönredner *m*, **~in** *f pej.* smooth-talker, *Am.* sweet-talker

schönschreiben *v/i.* (*trennb., hat -ge-*) write neatly (*od.* in one's best handwriting)

Schönschreib|heft *n* writing book; *mit Vordruck:* copybook, *Am.* notebook; **~unterricht** *m* writing lessons *Pl.*

Schönschrift *f:* **etw. in ~ schreiben** write s.th. in neat (*od.* one's best) handwriting

Schöntuer *m; -s, -; pej.* flatterer; **Schöntuerei** *f; -, -en; pej.* flattery, soft soap *umg.*; **Schöntuerin** *f; -, -nen* flatterer; **schöntun** *v/i.* (*unreg., trennb., hat -ge-*) *umg.:* **j-m ~** flatter s.o.; (*sich einschmeicheln*) play (suck *umg.*) up to s.o.

Schonung *f* **1.** (*Pflege*) care; *e-r Sache: auch* careful treatment; (*Ruhephase nach Krankheit etc.*) rest, period of rest; (*Schutz*) protection; (*Nachsicht*) consideration, indulgence; (*Gnade*) mercy; **er braucht ~** he needs to be treated considerately; (*muss sich schonen*) he needs to take things easy; **zur ~ der Leser** so as not to offend (the) reader; **2.** (*Waldgebiet*) protected for-

est plantation; (*Jagdgehege*) reserve

schonungsbedürftig *Adj.* in need of rest (*od.* care)

schonungslos I. *Adj.* unsparing (*gegen* of); (*erbarmungslos*) merciless, pitiless; *weitS. auch* brutal; **II.** *Adv. vorgehen etc.:* mercilessly, pitilessly; **j-m etw. ~ sagen** tell s.o. s.th. bluntly; **Schonungslosigkeit** *f* mercilessness, ruthlessness; **mit derartiger ~** so unsparingly (*od.* ruthlessly); **schonungsvoll I.** *Adj.* considerate; (*milde*) gentle; **II.** *Adv. behandeln etc.:* considerately; (*milde*) gently

Schonwaschgang *m* → **Schongang** 2

Schönwetter *n umg. fig.:* **~ machen** smooth things over; **um ~ bitten** be as nice as pie; **~front** *f Met.* fine weather front; **~lage** *f* stable area of high pressure; **~wolke** *f* cumulus cloud

Schonzeit *f Jagd:* close season; **j-m e-e ~ einräumen** *fig.* allow s.o. a honeymoon period

Schopf *m; -(e)s, Schöpfe* **1.** (*Haarschopf*) shock (*od.* mop) (of hair); *von Vögeln:* tuft, crest; **j-n beim ~ packen** grab s.o. by the scruff of the neck; **die Gelegenheit beim ~ packen** *fig.* seize the opportunity, jump at the chance *umg.*; **ein Problem beim ~ packen** deal head-on with a problem; **2.** *schw., südd.* (*Schuppen, Scheune*) barn

Schöpf|brunnen *m* draw well; **~eimer** *m* bucket; *Tech. auch* scoop

schöpfen *v/t.* **1.** scoop; *mit e-m Löffel:* ladle; (*Wasser*) draw; *aus dem Boot:* bail (*od.* bale) (out); **2.** *geh.* (*gewinnen*) (*Kraft, Mut etc.*) draw, derive (*aus* from); **neue Kräfte ~** gain new strength; → **Atem, Verdacht, voll** I 7; **3.** *fachspr.* (*Papier*) dip; **4.** *geh.* (*erschaffen*) create

Schöpfer[1] *m; -s, -;* (*Schöpfkelle*) ladle

Schöpfer[2] *m; -s, -* creator; *nur Sg.* (*Gott*) the Creator; **der ~ von Onkel Dagobert** the creator of Uncle Scrooge; **Schöpfergeist** *m* creative genius; **Schöpferin** *f; -, -nen* creator

schöpferisch I. *Adj.* (*kreativ*) creative; (*produktiv*) productive; **e-e ~e Pause einlegen** have a break to get back into a creative frame of mind; *umg. hum. kurz:* pause for inspiration; **II.** *Adv.:* **~ veranlagt sein** be very creative, have a creative mind

Schöpferkraft *f* creative power

Schöpf|kelle *f*, **~löffel** *m* ladle; **~rad** *n* water wheel

Schöpfung *f* (*Geschaffenes*) creation; (*Kunstwerk etc.*) *auch* work; (*Erzeugnis*) *auch* product; (*die Welt*) the universe, creation; *nur Sg.; bibl.* the Creation; **die Herren der ~** *iro.* the lords of creation; → **Krone** 2

Schöpfungs|akt *m* creative act; **~geschichte** *f:* **die ~** the Creation story; **~tag** *m* day of the Creation

Schoppen *m; -s, -* **1.** (quarter- *od.* half-lit|re, *Am.* -er) glass of wine; **ein ~ Weißer/Roter** a glass of white/red wine; **2.** *bes. südd., schw.* (*Flasche fürs Baby*) bottle; **~wein** *m* wine by the glass

Schöps *m; -es, -e; Dial.* (*Hammel*) wether; (*Fleisch*) mutton

schor *Imperf.* → **scheren**[1]

Schorf *m; -(e)s, kein Pl.; Med.* scab (*auch Bot.*); **schorfig** *Adj.* scabby

Schorle *f; -, -(n) od. n; -s, -(s)* spritzer

...schorle *f, n, im Subst.:* **ein(e) Weißwein~ sauer** a dry white wine spritzer; **ein großes Apfelsaft~** a large apple juice and mineral water

Schornstein *m* chimney; (*Fabrik-schlot*) *auch* smoke stack; *Naut., Eisenb.* funnel; *etw. in den ~ schreiben umg.* say goodbye to s.th.; *der ~ muss rauchen umg.* the money has got to come from somewhere; **~feger** *m, -s, -, ~fegerin** *f; -, -nen* chimney sweep
Schose *f; -, -n* → *Chose*
schoss *Imperf.* → *schießen*
Schoß [ʃoːs] *m; -es, Schöße* **1.** lap; *auf j-s ~ sitzen* sit on s.o.'s lap (*weiter vorn*: knee); *komm auf m-n ~!* come (and) sit on my lap (*od.* knee); *die Hände in den ~ legen fig.* sit back and take things easy; (*Daumen drehen*) twiddle one's thumbs; *es ist ihm in den ~ gefallen fig.* it just fell into his lap; *ihm ist nichts in den ~ gefallen* he had to work for everything, he never had it easy; **2.** *geh.* (*Mutterleib*) womb; *ein Kind im ~ tragen geh.* be bearing a child; **3.** *fig. der Familie etc.*: bosom; *in den ~ der Familie/Kirche zurückkehren* return to the (family) fold / flock (of the church); (*sicher*) *wie in Abrahams ~ umg.* safe as houses, *Am.* safe as can be; **4.** *fig. an Kleidung*: (coat) tail; *mit wehenden Schößen* with coat tails flying
Schoßhund *m* lapdog
Schössling ['ʃœslɪŋ] *m; -s, -e; Bot.* (*Trieb*) shoot; (*Pflanze*) cutting
Schot *f; -, -en; Naut.* sheet
Schote *f; -, -n; Bot.* pod; (*Paprikaschote*) capsicum; **schotenförmig** *Adj.* pod-shaped
Schott *n; -(e)s, -en; Naut.* bulkhead; *~en dicht!* close bulkheads!; *nordd. fig.* close all windows and doors
Schotte *m; -n, -n* Scot, Scotsman; *die ~n* the Scots, the Scottish (people)
Schotten|karo *n,* **~muster** *n* tartan; **~mütze** *f* tam-o'-shanter, tammy *umg.*; **~rock** *m* **1.** *echter*: kilt; **2.** tartan (*od.* plaid) skirt; **~witz** *m* Scottish joke
Schotter *m; -s, kein Pl.; Tech.* gravel; *Straßenbau*: *auch* (road) metal; *Eisenb.* ballast; *Geol.* detritus; **Schotterdecke** *f* gravel surface; **schottern** *v/t.* gravel; *Straßenbau*: *auch* metal; *Eisenb.* ballast
Schotterstraße *f* gravel road
Schottin *f; -, -nen* Scotswoman, Scot
schottisch I. *Adj.* Scots, Scottish; **~er Whisky** Scotch (whisky); *die ~e Kirche* the Church of Scotland; *~e Schule Philos.* Scottish School; **II. Schottisch** *n; -en; Ling.* Scots; *das Schottische* Scots; **Schottland** (*n*); *-s; Geog.* Scotland
schraffieren *v/t.* hatch; *Kartographie*: hachure; **Schraffierung** *f* **1.** hatching; **2.** → *Schraffur*; **Schraffur** *f; -, en* *Kartographie*: hachures *Pl.*
schräg I. *Adj.* **1.** (*~ abfallend*) sloping (*auch Dach*), slanting (*auch Augen*); (*~ verlaufend*) diagonal; *Linie*: *auch* oblique; **~er Blick** sidelong glance; *fig.* disapproving look; **2.** *umg. fig.* oddball; *~e Ansichten* weird ideas; *~e Klamotten* way-out clothes; *~e Musik* off-beat music; *weitS.* (*Jazz*) hot jazz; *~er Vogel* shady-looking character; **II.** *Adv.* **1.** *schneiden, stellen etc.*: at an angle; *~ gestreift* diagonally striped; *~ stehende Augen* slanting eyes; *~ parken* park at an angle; *~ über die Straße gehen* cross the road at an angle; *j-n ~ ansehen* give s.o. a sidelong glance; *fig.* look askance at s.o.; *den Kopf ~ halten* have one's head tilted (*od.* cocked) to one side; **2.** *umg. fig.*

(*seltsam*) weirdly; *~ angezogen sein* be wearing way-out clothes
Schrägdach *n* pitched roof
Schräge *f; -, -n* slant; (*Gefälle*) slope, incline
Schräg|fahrt *f* *Skifahren*: traverse; **~heck** *n Mot.* fastback; **~lage** *f* slant; *Flug.* bank(ing); *Naut.* list; *Med., des Kindes*: oblique presentation; *fig.* → *Schieflage*; **~parken** *n* angle parking; **~schnitt** *m* **1.** *Math.* diagonal section; **2.** *Med.* oblique section; **3.** *Tech.* diagonal cut; **~schrift** *f* sloping (hand)writing; *Druck.* italics *Pl.*; **~spur** *f Video*: slant track; **~streifen** *m* diagonal stripe; **~strich** *m* slash, oblique; (*doppelter*) *umgekehrter ~* (double) backslash
Schramme *f; -, -n* scratch (*auch an Möbel, Auto etc.*)
Schrammelmusik *f österr., Mus.* music played especially in Viennese cafés by a quartet of violins, guitar and accordion
schrammen *v/t.* scratch, scrape; (*ein anderes Auto*) scratch, scrape (*against*); (*Haut*) *auch* graze; *sich* (*Dat.*) *die Knie blutig ~* scratch one's knees so that they bleed
Schrank *m; -(e)s, Schränke* **1.** cupboard, *bes. Am.* closet; (*Kleiderschrank, mst frei stehend*) wardrobe; (*Glasschrank*) cabinet; *e-n ~ aufbauen/abbauen* assemble/dismantle a cupboard; **2.** *umg.* (*großer Kerl*) great hulk; **~bett** *n* foldaway bed
Schränkchen *n* small cupboard, cabinet
Schranke *f; -, -n* **1.** barrier; *Eisenb. auch* gate; *Jur.* bar; *bis an die ~ vorfahren* drive up to the barrier; **2.** *mst Pl.*; *fig.* (*soziale ~, Handelsschranke etc.*) barrier; (*Grenze*) bounds *Pl.*, limits *Pl.*; *innerhalb der ~n des Gesetzes* within the bounds of the law; *e-r Sache ~n setzen* put a limit on; *e-r Sache sind* (*keine*) *~n gesetzt* there are (no) limits to; *in ~n halten* keep within bounds; *sich in ~n halten* restrain o.s.; *j-n in s-e ~n weisen* put s.o. in his (*od.* her) place, cut s.o. down to size; **3.** *Math.* bound; *obere/untere ~* upper/lower bound, majorant/minorant
Schrankelement *n* cupboard unit
Schranken *m; -s, -n österr.* → *Schranke*
schranken *v/t.* → *Schranke*; *(Bahnschranke)* level (*od. Am.* grade) crossing barrier (*od.* gate)
schrankenlos *Adj.* **1.** *fig.* boundless, unlimited; *negativ*: unbounded, unbridled; **2.** *Eisenb.* unguarded
Schrankenwärter *m,* **~in** *f Eisenb.* crossing keeper
Schrank|fach *n* compartment; **✶fertig** *Adj. Wäsche*: washed and ironed; **~koffer** *m* wardrobe trunk; **~raum** *m für Kleider*: wardrobe room, *Am. auch* closet (room); **~tür** *f* cupboard (*Am.* closet) door; *von Kleiderschrank*: wardrobe door; **~wand** *f* large wall unit, wall-to-wall cupboard (*Am.* closet); *e-e ~ aufbauen/abbauen* assemble/dismantle a wall unit
Schranze *f; -, -n; umg. pej.* toady, lackey
Schrapnell *n; -s, -e od. -s; Mil.* shrapnel shell
Schrat *m; -(e)s, -e;* (*Troll*) forest goblin; *umg. fig.* (*drolliger Kerl*) comical fellow
Schraubdeckel *m* screw top
Schraube *f; -, -n* **1.** screw; (*Schraubenbolzen*) bolt; *~ ohne Ende* endless screw; *fig.* vicious (*od.* never-ending)

spiral; *e-e ~ anziehen* tighten a screw; *die ~n anziehen fig.* put the screws on; *bei ihm ist e-e ~ locker umg.* he's got a screw loose; **2.** *Naut., Flug.* propeller; **3.** *Sport* twist; *beim Kunstspringen*: twist (*od.* spiral) dive; *Kunstfliegen*: vertical spin
schrauben I. *vt/i.* screw (*an + Akk.* onto); (*drehen*) twist, wind; *fester/loser ~* tighten/loosen the screw(s) of; *höher/niedriger ~* (*Bürostuhl etc.*) wind up/down, raise/lower; *niedriger ~ fig.* lower, scale down; *Preise/Erwartungen in die Höhe ~ fig.* make prices spiral / raise expectations; → *geschraubt*; **II.** *v/refl.*: *sich in die Höhe ~* spiral upward(s); *Auto*: wind its way up
Schrauben|bolzen *m* bolt; **~dreher** *m* screwdriver
schraubenförmig *Adj.* (cork)screw-shaped, spiral, helical
Schrauben|gang *m* screw thread; **~getriebe** *n* worm gear; **~gewinde** *n* screw thread; **~kopf** *m* screwhead; *e-s Schraubenbolzens*: bolthead; **~mutter** *f* nut; **~schlüssel** *m* spanner, *Am.* wrench; *verstellbarer*: (adjustable) wrench, *Am. auch* monkey (*od.* crescent) wrench; **~welle** *f* propeller shaft; **~winde** *f* screw jack; **~zieher** *m* screwdriver
Schraub|glas *n* screw-top jar; **~stock** *m* vice, *Am.* vise; **~verschluss** *m* screw cap (*od.* top); **~zwinge** *f* screw clamp
Schrebergarten *m etwa* allotment (garden); **~kolonie** *f* cluster of allotment gardens
Schreber|gärtner *m,* **~gärtnerin** *f etwa* allotment holder
Schreck *m; -(e)s, kein Pl.* fright; *er hat e-n ~ bekommen* he got a fright, it gave him a fright; (*es hat ihm Angst gemacht*) *auch* it gave him (*od.* he got) quite a scare; *krieg keinen ~* don't be scared; *umg.* (*stör dich nicht daran*) don't be too shocked; *vor ~ wie gelähmt sein* be scared stiff; *ein freudiger/süßer ~* a thrill of joy/delight; *~, lass nach! umg.* spare me!; → *einjagen, auch* Schrecken
Schrecke *f; -, -n; Zool.* → *Heuschrecke*
schrecken[1] *v/t.* **1.** frighten, scare; *stärker*: terrify; (*abschrecken*) put off; *das kann mich nicht ~* it doesn't worry me; *mich schreckt der lange Flug* the long flight puts me off, I'm scared of (*od.* worried about) the long flight; **2.** (*aufschrecken*) startle; **3.** *Jägerspr.*: *Wild ~* stop game in its tracks with a call
schrecken[2] *v/i.*; *schrickt, schreckte od. schrak, ist geschreckt* start; *aus dem Schlaf ~* wake up with a start
Schrecken *m; -s, -* **1.** *nur Sg.* (*große Angst*) terror; (*Entsetzen*) horror; (*Schreck*) fright; *~ erregend* frightening, *stärker*: terrifying; *in Angst und ~ versetzen* terrify; *der Fahrer kam mit dem ~ davon* the driver got away with no more than a fright; *zu m-m ~ hörte ich ...* to my horror I heard ..., I was horrified to hear ...; → *auch* Schreck; **2.** *mst Pl.*: *die ~ des Krieges etc.* the horrors of war *etc.*
Schreckensbild *n* horrifying sight (*od.* image)
schreckensbleich *Adj.* pale with fright, (as) white as a sheet
Schreckens|botschaft *f* terrible news *Sg.*; **~herrschaft** *f* reign of terror;

~meldung f terrible news Sg.; **~re-gime** n reign of terror; **~schrei** m scream of terror; **~szenario** n terrifying scenario; **~tat** f atrocity; **~vision** f terrifying vision; **~zeit** f time of horrors

schreckerfüllt Adj. terrified

Schreckgespenst n fig. (Sache) spect|re (Am. -er), nightmare; (Buhmann) bogeyman

schreckhaft Adj. easily scared, jumpy

Schrecklähmung f Med. paralytic shock

schrecklich I. Adj. awful, terrible, dreadful (alle auch umg. fig.); stärker: appalling; (Schrecken erregend) auch horrible; der Gestank war ~ the stench was awful (od. terrible, dreadful, appalling); sie haben e-n ~en Geschmack umg. they have awful (od. terrible, dreadful, appalling) taste; **II.** Adv. **1.** (entsetzlich) misshandeln, zurichten etc.: terribly, horribly; umg. (sehr schlecht) sich benehmen, stinken etc.: terribly, dreadfully, awfully; stärker: appallingly; sich ~ aufregen make a terrible (od. dreadful, awful, appalling) fuss; **2.** umg. fig. (ungemein) terribly, dreadfully, awfully; etw. ~ gern tun be terribly fond of doing s.th., really love doing s.th.; j-n ~ lieb haben be terribly (od. desperately) in love with s.o.; → auch furchtbar, **Schreck-lichkeit** f awfulness, terribleness, dreadfulness

Schrecknis n; -ses, -se; geh. horror

Schreck|reaktion f shock reaction; **~schraube** f umg., pej. zänkisch: virago; dem Aussehen nach: (hideous) fright

Schreckschuss m auch fig. warning shot; **~patrone** f blank cartridge; **~pistole** f blank (cartridge) pistol

Schrecksekunde f Mot. reaction time; weitS. moment of shock (od. terror); in der ersten ~ when the full horror first hits you

Schredder m; -s, -; Tech. shredder

Schrei m; -(e)s, -e freudiger, warnender etc.: shout, cry; brüllender: yell; durchdringender: scream; spitzer: shriek; (Brüller) e-r Menge: roar; kreischender, von Vögeln: screech(ing); (Ruf) call; die heiseren ~e der Möwen the harsh cries of the gulls; ~ der Entrüstung cry of indignation; fig. outcry; der ~ nach Rache the call (von vielen: clamo[u]r) for revenge; der letzte ~ umg. fig. the latest thing

...schrei m, im Subst.: Eulen~ owl's screech; Jubel~ jubilant cry (od. shout); Brunft~ bell

Schreib|arbeit f einzelne: writing task; Koll. auch Pl. paperwork; **~bedarf** m writing materials Pl., stationery; **~befehl** m EDV write command; **~block** m writing pad; **~büro** n typing pool; **~dienst** m typing service

Schreibe f; -, kein Pl.; umg. writing; (Stil) style; e-e flotte ~ haben have a fluent style

schreiben schreibt, schrieb, hat geschrieben **I.** vt/i. write (über + Akk. on, about); Tech., Instrument: record; j-m ~ write to s.o., Am. auch umg. write s.o.; (Bekannten) auch umg. drop s.o. a line; sich od. einander ~ write (to one another); formeller: correspond; schreib mal wieder! write again soon!; gut ~ Handschrift: have nice handwriting; Stil: be a good writer; sie schreibt für den „Spiegel" she writes articles for "Spiegel"; an etw. ~ be working on s.th.; mit Bleistift etc. ~ write in pencil etc.; mit der Maschine ~ type (up); auf Diskette ~ write to disk; wie schreibt er sich? how does he spell his name?; der Brief, in dem Sie uns ~, dass ... the letter in which you tell (od. inform) us that ...; wie die Zeitung schreibt according to the paper; wo steht geschrieben, dass ...? where does it say that ...?, where is it written that ...?; **II.** v/t. **1.** (verfassen) write; (Musikstück, Gedicht) auch compose; e-n Aufsatz etc. noch einmal ~ rewrite an essay etc.; (richtig) ~ (Wort) spell (right od. correctly); falsch ~ misspell; groß geschrieben werden fig. rank very high, be a high priority, be considered very important; (begehrt sein) be very much in demand; bei ihm wird Pünktlichkeit groß geschrieben auch he sets great store by punctuality; → großschreiben; Höflichkeit etc. wird bei ihr klein geschrieben politeness etc. is not one of her priorities; → kleinschreiben; getrennt ~ write in two words; → zusammenschreiben; wird das mit oder ohne „h" geschrieben? is that spelt (Am. spelled) with or without an 'h'?; ins Reine ~ make a fair copy of, write out neatly; s-n Namen unter etw. ~ unter Aufruf, Manifest etc.: put one's name to s.th.; (unterschreiben) sign s.th.; er kann kaum / nicht mal s-n Namen ~ umg. he can hardly write anything / can't even write his name; j-m Gedichte/Briefchen ~ write poems for s.o. / notes to s.o.; **2.** j-n arbeitsunfähig ~ certify s.o. as unfit for work; → krankschreiben, gesundschreiben; **3.** förm.: damals schrieb man das Jahr 1840 it was in the year 1840; **4.** Wirts. (Rechnung, Scheck) write out; make out (j-m to s.o.); j-m etw. auf die Rechnung ~ put s.th. on s.o.'s bill; → Kamin, Leib 1, Ohr 2, Zeile 1

Schreiben n; -s, - **1.** nur Sg. writing; **2.** (Brief) letter; kurzes: note; Ihr ~ vom ... your letter of the ...

Schreiber m; -s, - **1.** writer; der ~ dieses Briefes the writer (of this letter); förm. the undersigned; der ~ dieser Zeilen möchte ungenannt bleiben the person who wrote this wants to remain anonymous; **2.** altm. (Schriftführer) clerk; hist. scribe; **3.** Tech. recorder; (Stift) (recording) stylus; hast du mal 'nen ~? umg. have you got anything to write with?; **Schreiberei** f; -, -en; umg. (endless) writing; (Schreibarbeit) paperwork; pej. (Schmiererei) scribbling; **Schreiberin** f; -, -nen → Schreiber 1; **Schreiberling** m; -s, -e; pej. hack writer

schreibfaul Adj. umg. lazy about writing letters; **Schreibfaulheit** f umg. laziness about writing letters

Schreib|feder f pen; (Gänsefeder) quill; **~fehler** m spelling mistake; (Flüchtigkeitsfehler) slip of the pen; **~gerät** n writing implement; Tech. recording instrument, recorder

schreibgeschützt Adj. EDV write--protected

Schreib|heft n exercise book; **~kopf** m Computer: write head; **~kraft** f (shorthand) typist; Pl. auch clerical staff Sg. (V auch im Pl.); **~krampf** m writer's cramp

Schreib-Lesekopf m Computer: read--write head

Schreibmappe f writing case

Schreibmaschine f typewriter; mit der ~ schreiben type (up); mit der ~ geschrieben typewritten, typed, in typescript

Schreibmaschinen|papier n typing paper; **~schrift** f typewriter font; **~seite** f typed page

Schreib|material n, **~materialien** Pl. writing materials, stationery Sg.; **~messgerät** n registering apparatus; **~papier** n writing paper; **~pult** n (writing) desk; **~schrift** f handwriting; Druck. cursive script; **~schutz** m EDV write (od. file) protection; **~stift** m pen; **~stil** m style of writing, written style; **~stube** f Mil. orderly room; **~tafel** f **1.** hist. tablet; **2.** (Schiefertafel) slate

Schreibtisch m (writing) desk; **~garni-tur** f desk set; **~schublade** f desk drawer; **~stuhl** m desk chair; **~täter** m **1.** bei Verbrechen: desktop criminal; **2.** umg. hum., Beamter: desktop administrator

Schreibung f spelling; falsche ~ misspelling; nach der neuen ~ in the new spelling

Schreib|unterlage f pad for writing on; auf Schreibtisch: desk pad; **~ver-bot** n writing ban; ~ erhalten be forbidden to write

Schreibwaren Pl. writing materials, stationery Sg.; **~geschäft** n stationer's, stationery shop (Am. auch store); **~händler** m, **~händlerin** f stationer

Schreib|weise f spelling; (Stil) style; → auch Schreibung; **~wut** f obsession with writing, manic urge to write; vorübergehende: writing fit; **~zentrale** f typing pool; **~zeug** n writing things Pl.

schreien vt/i.; schreit, schrie, hat geschrien **1.** allg.: shout; gellend: yell; kreischend: scream, shriek; quietschend: squeal; (brüllen) roar (vor Lachen with laughter); kleines Kind: howl, stärker: scream; Affe, Eule, Möwe: screech; Hahn: crow; vor Schmerz ~ scream (od. howl) with pain; sich heiser ~ shout o.s. hoarse; sich (Dat.) die Kehle aus dem Hals ~ shout one's head off, yell until one is blue in the face; um Hilfe ~ shout for help; schrei nicht so, ich bin nicht taub no need to shout, I'm not deaf; er schreit immer gleich so he starts yelling at the slightest thing; **2.** ~ nach shout for; die jungen Vögel ~ nach Futter the young birds are clamo(u)ring for food; nach Rache ~ fig. call for revenge; das Gebäude schreit geradezu nach etwas Farbe the building is crying out for (od. desperately needs) a coat of paint; → Himmel 3

Schreien n; -s, kein Pl. shouting, shouts Pl.; es/er ist zum ~ umg. it's/he's a scream; **schreiend I.** Part. Präs. → schreien; **II.** Adj. Farben: garish, gaudy, loud; ~es Unrecht glaring (od. blatant) injustice; **III.** Adv.: die Kinder liefen ~ davon the children ran off shouting (vor Angst: screaming)

Schreier m; -s, - **1.** (Störer) noise-maker; **2.** (Querulant) moaner, whiner; (Unruhestifter) troublemaker; **Schreierei** f; -, -en; umg. (constant) yelling and screaming; fig. (Empörung) loud complaints Pl.; **Schreihals** m umg. loudmouth; (Krakeeler) brawler; (Baby) bawler; (Kind) noisy brat

Schreikrampf m screaming fit

Schrein m; -(e)s, -e e-r Reliquie: shrine; (Truhe) chest; (Sarg) coffin, Am. auch casket

Schreiner *m*; *-s*, - joiner, *bes. Am.* carpenter; **Schreinerei** *f*; *-*, *-en* joiner's (*od.* carpenter's) workshop; **Schreinerin** *f*; *-*, *-nen* joiner, *bes. Am.* carpenter; **Schreinermeister** *m*, **Schreinermeisterin** *f* master joiner (*bes. Am.* carpenter); **schreinern I.** *v/i.* do carpentry (*od.* woodworking); **II.** *v/t.* (*herstellen*) make

schreiten *v/i.*; *schreitet, schritt, ist geschritten* **1.** step (*zu* up to); *mit langen Schritten*: stride; *feierlich*: walk; *stolz*: stalk; *im Zimmer auf und ab ~* pace up and down the room; **2.** *fig.* (*beginnen*) *zu etw. ~* proceed to s.th.; *zum Äußersten ~* take drastic action; *zur Tat ~* set to work, get cracking *umg.*

schrickt *Präs.* → *schrecken²*

schrie *Imperf.* → *schreien*

schrieb *Imperf.* → *schreiben*

Schrieb *m*; *-s*, *-e*; *umg.* missive; *langer*: screed

Schrift *f*; *-*, *-en* **1.** (*Geschriebenes*) writing; (*Handschrift*) *auch* handwriting, hand; (*Zeichen*) characters *Pl.*, letters *Pl.*, script; *Druck.* script, typeface; → *auch Schreibschrift*; **in lateinischer ~** in Roman characters; *kyrillische ~* Cyrillic script; *hatten die Mayas e-e ~?* did the Mayas have a form of writing?; *e-e schöne/schlechte ~ haben* have nice/bad handwriting; **2.** (*Veröffentlichung*) publication; (*Abhandlung*) treatise; *kürzere*: paper; (*Werk*) work; (*Dokument*) document; *sämtliche ~en Kants* Kant's complete works; → *heilig* 1

...schrift *f*, *im Subst.* **1.** (*Zeichen*): *Gold~* gold letters *Pl.*; *Neon~* neon writing; **2.** (*Text*): *Beschwerde~* written objection; *Hetz~* inflammatory text

Schrift|art *f* type(face); *Computer*: font; *~bild* *n* typeface; *~deutsch* *n* written German; (*Hochdeutsch*) standard German

Schriftenreihe *f* series of texts (*wissenschaftliche*: papers)

Schrift|fälscher *m* (handwriting) forger; *~farbe* *f* colo(u)r of type; *~form* *f*; *nur Sg.*; *Jur.* written form; *in ~* in written form, in writing; *~führer* *m*, *~führerin* *f* secretary; *bei Versammlungen auch*: clerk; *~gelehrte* *m* *hist.* scribe; *~grad* *m* type size; *~gut* *n* writings *Pl.*; *das altgriechische ~* Ancient Greek literature; *~gutachten* *n* handwriting expert's opinion; *~leiter* *m*, *~leiterin* *f* *altm.* editor

schriftlich I. *Adj.* written, *nachgestellt*: in writing; *~e Prüfung* written exam(ination); *e-e/keine ~e Hausaufgabe* a piece of written homework / no written homework; **II.** *Adv.* in writing; in black and white; *j-n ~ prüfen* give s.o. a written test; *Fragen ~ beantworten* answer questions in writing; *j-n ~ verwarnen* send s.o. a written warning; *jetzt haben wir es ~* now we have it in black and white; *das kann ich dir ~ geben!* *umg.* I can guarantee you that, you can take it from me

Schrift|probe *f* handwriting specimen; *Druck.* type specimen; *~rolle* *f* scroll; *die ~n vom Toten Meer* the Dead Sea Scrolls; *~sachverständige* *m*, *f* handwriting expert; *~satz* *m* **1.** *Druck.* (*abgesetzter Text*) set type; *Vorgang, Verfahren*: typesetting; **2.** *Jur.* written statement; *~setzer* *m*, *~setzerin* *f*; *Druck.* typesetter, compositor; *~sprache* *f* written language; (*Hochsprache*) standard language

schriftsprachlich I. *Adj.* ... used in the written language; **II.** *Adv. ausdrücken etc.*: in the written language, in written style

Schriftsteller *m*; *-s*, - author, writer; *freier ~* freelance writer

...schriftsteller *m*, *im Subst.*: *Jugend~* author of books for the young; *Nachwuchs~* up-and-coming writer

Schriftstellerei *f*; *-*, *kein Pl.* writing; **Schriftstellerin** *f*; *-*, *-nen* author(ess), writer; **schriftstellerisch I.** *Adj.* literary; **II.** *Adv.* as a writer; **schriftstellern** *v/i.* be a writer, be an author; *nebenbei ~* write on the side

Schriftstellerverband *m* writers' union

Schrift|stück *n* paper, document; *~tafel* *f* *bibl.* tablet

Schrifttum *n*; *-s*, *kein Pl.* literature

Schrift|typ *m* *Druck.* typeface; *~verkehr* *m*, *~wechsel* *m* correspondence; *~zeichen* *n* character, letter; *~zug* *m* (*einzelner Strich*) stroke; (*Handschrift*) (hand)writing

schrill I. *Adj.* shrill; *auch fig.* strident; *ein ~er Typ* *umg.* a brash type; **II.** *Adv. lachen, reden*: shrilly; *~ angezogen* garishly dressed; **schrillen** *v/i.* shrill; **Schrillheit** *f* shrillness, *auch fig.* stridency

Schrippe *f*; *-*, *-n* *bes. in Berlin*: roll

schritt *Imperf.* → *schreiten*

Schritt *m*; *-(e)s*, *-e* **1.** step (*auch Tanzschritt*), pace (*auch als Maß*); *langer*: stride; *hörbarer*: (foot)step; *mit schnellen ~en* with quick steps, briskly; *e-n ~ zur Seite tun* step aside; *~ für ~* step by step; *fig. auch* little by little, gradually; *auf ~ und Tritt* (*überall*) at every turn; *j-m auf ~ und Tritt folgen* dog s.o.'s footsteps; *es sind nur ein paar ~e* it's not far; **2.** *fig.* (*Maßnahme*) step, move, *bes. Pl.* measures; *Politik der kleinen ~e* step-by-step policy; *rechtliche ~e erwägen/einleiten* consider/take legal action; *der erste ~ zur Besserung* the first step on the road to improvement; *den ersten ~ tun* take the first step; *vor j-d anderem*: make the first move; *den zweiten ~ vor dem ersten tun* put the cart before the horse; *den entscheidenden ~ tun* take the decisive step (*od.* the plunge); *wir sind keinen ~ weitergekommen* we haven't made the slightest progress (*od.* any headway at all); *e-n ~ zu weit gehen* overstep the mark; → *Selbsterkenntnis*; **3.** *nur Sg.* (*Gang*) step; *j-n am ~ erkennen* recognize s.o. by (the sound of) his *etc.* step; **4.** *nur Sg.* (*Tempo*) pace; *im ~* at a walking pace; *ein Pferd (im) ~ gehen lassen* make a horse go at a walk; *e-n schnellen ~ am Leib haben* *umg.* be a fast walker; *~ halten mit* keep up (*od.* keep pace) with; *fig. auch* keep abreast of; **5.** *mst Sg.*; *Hose, auch umg. Anat.*: crotch

Schritt|folge *f* sequence of steps; *~geschwindigkeit* *f* walking pace; *mit ~ fahren* go at walking pace (*od.* a crawl); *~länge* *f* *Hose*: inside leg, inseam

Schrittmacher *m* *Sport* pacemaker (*auch Med., fig.*); (*Motorradfahrer beim Radrennen*) pacer; *in der Mode*: *auch* trendsetter; *~funktion* *f*: *~ haben* serve as a pacemaker; *fig.* pave the way

Schritt|messer *m* pedometer; *~motor* *m* *EDV* stepper motor; *~tempo* *n* walking pace; *im ~ fahren* go at walking pace (*od.* a crawl), crawl (along); *„~"* auf Verkehrsschild: "dead slow"

schrittweise *fig.* **I.** *Adj.* gradual, step-by-step ...; **II.** *Adv.* step by step, gradually, by degrees, little by little; *~ einstellen* phase out (step by step)

Schritt|weite *f* (length of) stride; *~zähler* *m* pedometer

schroff I. *Adj.* **1.** (*steil, jäh*) steep, precipitous; **2.** *fig.* (*barsch*) gruff; (*kurz angebunden*) curt; *auch Verhalten*: brusque; (*unvermittelt*) abrupt; *~er Widerspruch* stark contradiction; *in ~em Gegensatz stehen zu* contrast sharply with; **II.** *Adv.* **1.** *abfallen, hochragen*: abruptly, precipitously; **2.** *fig.*: *~ zurückweisen* refuse curtly; *sich ~ abwenden* turn away abruptly; **Schroffheit** *f* **1.** *nur Sg.* steepness, precipitousness; **2.** *nur Sg.*; *fig.* curtness, abruptness; **3.** (*Bemerkung*) curt remark

schröpfen *v/t.* **1.** *Med.* cup; **2.** *umg. fig.* fleece, rip off; **3.** *Agr.* (*Obstbaum*) tap

Schrot *m, n*; *-(e)s*, *kein Pl.* **1.** (*Getreide*) coarse meal, whole grain; (*Malz*) crushed malt; **2.** *zum Schießen*: small shot, pellets *Pl.*, buckshot; *mit ~ schießen* shoot small shot; **3.** *von altem ~ und Korn* *fig.* of the old school; *ein Sizilianer von echtem ~ und Korn* a Sicilian born and bred, a true Sicilian; *~brot* *n* whole grain bread; *~büchse* *f* shotgun

schroten *v/t.* (*Getreide*) coarse-grind; (*Malz*) crush; bruise

Schrot|flinte *f* shotgun; *~korn* *n* coarse grain; *~kugel* *f* pellet; *~ladung* *f* round (*od.* charge) of shot; *~mühle* *f* coarse-grinding mill; *~patrone* *f* shot cartridge

Schrott *m*; *-(e)s*, *kein Pl.* **1.** scrap metal; *mit ~ handeln* deal in scrap (metal); *ein Auto zu ~ fahren* *umg.* smash up (*Brit. auch* write off, *Am.* total) a car; **2.** *umg.* (*kaputte Dinge, schlechter Qualität*) junk; **3.** *umg.* (*Blödsinn, schlechter Film etc.*) rubbish; *~auto* *n* scrap car; (*Unfallauto*) wrecked car, write-off, *Am.* total; *~handel* *m* scrap trade; *~händler* *m* scrap merchant; *~haufen* *m* scrap heap (*auch fig.*); *~platz* *m* scrapyard

schrottreif *Adj.* ready for the scrap heap; *~ fahren* *umg.* (*Auto*) write off, *Am.* total

Schrottwert *m* scrap value; *nur noch ~ haben* be only fit for scrap

schrubben *v/i.* scrub; **Schrubber** *m*; *-s*, - scrubbing brush

Schrulle *f*; *-*, *-n*; *umg.* **1.** quirk; (*Idee*) oddball (*Brit. auch* cranky) idea; **2.** *pej.* (*Frau*) old crone; **schrullenhaft, schrullig** *Adj.* *umg.* quirky, *Brit. auch* cranky; *sie wird immer schrulliger* she's becoming more and more of an oddball

schrumpelig *Adj.* (*runzelig*) wrinkled; (*eingeschrumpft und faltig*) shrivel(l)ed; **schrumpeln** *v/i.* → *schrumpfen*

schrumpfen *v/i.* shrink (*auch Tech., Med.*); (*schrumpeln*) shrivel; *fig.* (*abnehmen*) shrink, dwindle

Schrumpf|germane *m* *umg. hum.* pint-size Teuton; *~kopf* *m* shrunken head; *~leber* *f* *Med.* cirrhosis of the liver; *~niere* *f* *Med.* cirrhosis of the kidney

Schrumpfung *f* shrinking; *auch Med., Tech.* shrinkage, contraction; *Med.* atrophy; *fig.* reduction; *beabsichtigte*: *auch* scaling-down; **Schrumpfungsprozess** *m* *Wirts.* scaling-down process

Schrunde *f*; *-*, *-n* *Hautverletzung*:

crack, fissure; **schrundig** *Adj. Haut*: cracked, fissured

Schub *m*; *-(e)s, Schübe* **1.** *Phys., Tech.* (*Schiebekraft*) thrust (*auch e-s Triebwerks*); (*Querschub*) shear; **2.** (*Menge, Gruppe*) batch; *den nächsten ~ Besucher in die Ausstellung lassen* let the next batch of visitors into the exhibition; **3.** *Med.* phase; (*Anfall*) attack; *ein depressiver ~* a fit of depression; *in Schüben verlaufend* intermittent; **~düse** *f* thrust nozzle

Schuber *m*; *-s, -* slipcase; *im ~* in a slipcase

Schub|fach *n* drawer; **~karre** *f*, **~karren** *m* wheelbarrow; **~kasten** *m* drawer; **~kraft** *f* thrust; (*Querschub*) shear (-ing) force; **~lade** *f* drawer; *die Pläne blieben in der ~* *fig.* the plans remained in cold storage (*od.* on ice); *in e-e ~ stecken od. schieben* *fig.* pigeonhole; *in keine ~ passen* *fig.* not fit in any category

Schubladen|denken *n* *umg.* pigeonholing, stereotyped thinking; **~system** *n CD-Spieler*: front drawer loading

schubladisieren *v/t. schw. umg.* (*Pläne*) put into cold storage (*od.* on ice), shelve

Schubs *m*; *-es, -e*; *umg.* push, shove; *fig.* prod

Schubschiff *n* pusher, pushboat

schubsen *v/t. umg.* push, shove; *ihn muss man immer ein bisschen ~* *fig.* he always needs a bit of a prod; **Schubserei** *f*, *-, -en*; *umg.* pushing and shoving

schubweise *Adv.* in batches; (*nach und nach*) in bits and pieces *umg.*; *ankommen: auch umg.* in dribs and drabs; *~ verlaufen Krankheit*: proceed in phases

Schubwirkung *f* thrust effect

schüchtern I. *Adj.* shy; (*verschämt*) bashful; (*zaghaft*) timid; **~er Versuch** hesitant attempt; **II.** *Adv.* shyly; (*verschämt*) bashfully; (*zaghaft*) timidly; (**an**)**lächeln** give s.o. a shy smile; *und er, gar nicht ~, …* *umg.* and he, bold as brass, …; **Schüchternheit** *f* shyness; (*Verschämtheit*) bashfulness; (*Zaghaftigkeit*) timidity

schuckeln *v/i. umg.* **1.** (*hat geschuckelt*) rock, sway; **2.** (*ist*) rock (*stoßend*: jolt) and sway

schuf *Imperf.* → *schaffen*[1]

SCHUFA, Schufa *f*, *-, kein Pl.; Abk.* (*Schutzgemeinschaft für allgemeine Kreditsicherung*) organization collecting and providing information on creditworthiness, *Am. etwa* credit bureau

Schuft *m*; *-(e)s, -e; pej.* rogue, scoundrel; *dieser gemeine ~!* this lousy scumbag!, the rotten bastard *Sl.!*

schuften *v/i. umg.* slave (*od.* sweat) away, work one's butt off *Sl.*; **Schufterei** *f*, *-, -en; umg.* **1.** *nur Sg.* drudgery, hard graft; **2.** *der Umzug war vielleicht e-e ~!* the move was a really hard slog

schuftig *Adj. pej.* mean, despicable, rotten *umg.*

Schuh *m*; *-s, -e* shoe (*auch Tech.*); *j-m etw. in die ~ schieben umg. fig.* pin (the blame for) s.th. on s.o.; *wo drückt* (*dich*) *der ~?* *umg.* what's the trouble (*od.* problem)?; *umgekehrt wird ein ~ daraus!* *umg.* it's the exact opposite

...schuh *m*, *im Subst.*: *Baby~* baby shoe; *Braut~* bride's shoe; *Ganzleder~* all-leather shoe

Schuh|absatz *m* heel; **~anzieher** *m* shoehorn; **~band** *n* shoelace, *Am.*

auch shoestring; **~bürste** *f* shoe brush; **~creme** *f* shoe cream, shoe polish, *Am. auch* shoeshine; **~geschäft** *n* shoe shop (*Am.* store); **~größe** *f* shoe size; *fig.* → *Kragenweite*; *welche ~ haben Sie?* what's your shoe size? what size (*of*) shoe do you take (*od.* wear?); **~industrie** *f* footwear industry; **~karton** *m* shoebox; **~löffel** *m* shoehorn

Schuhmacher *m* shoemaker, cobbler; *Schuhe zum ~ bringen* take shoes to be repaired; **Schuhmacherei** *f*, *-, -en* **1.** *nur Sg.* shoemaking, shoemaker's trade; **2.** shoemaker's workshop; **Schuhmacherin** *f*, *-, -nen* shoemaker, cobbler

Schuhnummer *f* → *Schuhgröße*

schuhplatteln *v/i.* dance the Schuhplattler; **Schuhplattler** *m*; *-s, -* folk dance with rhythmic slapping of the shoe soles, knees and Lederhosen, performed in Upper Bavaria, the Tyrol and Carinthia

Schuh|putzer *m* **1.** shoe-cleaner, *bes. Am.* shoeshine boy, *altm.* bootblack; **2.** (*Gerät*) shoe-cleaner; **~putzerin** *f*, *-, -nen* shoe-cleaner, *Am.* shoeshine girl; **~putzzeug** *n* shoe-cleaning things *Pl.*; **~schrank** *m* shoe cabinet; **~sohle** *f* sole (of a *od.* the shoe); **~spitze** *f* toe of a (*od.* the) shoe; **~werk** *n* footwear, shoes *Pl.*, boots and shoes *Pl.*; *festes ~* a strong pair of shoes; **~wichse** *f* shoe polish

Schuko|steckdose® *f* earthed (*Am.* grounded) safety socket; **~stecker®** *m* earthed (*Am.* grounded) safety plug

Schul|abgänger *m*, **~abgängerin** *f* school-leaver, *Am. mit Abschluss*: high school graduate; *vorzeitig, ohne Abschluss*: high school dropout; **~abschluss** *m* school-leaving qualification, *Am. etwa* high school diploma; *welchen ~ strebt er an?* what qualification is he aiming for?; **~alter** *n* school age; **~amt** *n* education authority, *Am.* school board; **~amtsbezirk** *m* education authority area, *Am.* school district; **~anfang** *m* **1.** *nach den Ferien*: beginning of term; **2.** *morgens*: start of term; *ist um acht* school starts at eight; **3.** *für Schulanfänger*: first day at school; **~anfänger** *m*, **~anfängerin** *f* child starting school, school beginner; **~angebot** *n* choice of schools; **~angst** *f* fear of school; **~arbeit** *f* **1.** *auch Pl.* (*Hausaufgabe*) homework *Sg.*; *hast du noch ~en?* have you still got some homework to do?; **2.** *österr.* → *Klassenarbeit*; **~art** *f* type of school

Schularzt *m*, **Schulärztin** *f* school doctor; **schulärztlich** *Adj. Untersuchung etc.*: by the school doctor; **~es Attest** school doctor's certificate

Schul|atlas *m* school atlas; **~aufgabe** *f* **1.** → *Schularbeit*; **2.** *südd.* → *Klassenarbeit*; **~aufsatz** *m* school essay; **~aufsicht** *f* administration of schools; **~ausbildung** *f* school education; **~ausflug** *m* school outing, *Am.* field trip; **~ausschuss** *m* *etwa* board of governors, *Am.* school board; **~bank** *f* school desk; *die ~ drücken umg.* go to school; *noch mal die ~ drücken umg.* go back to school; **~beginn** *m* **1.** *nach den Ferien*: beginning of term; **2.** *morgens*: start of school; *~ ist um acht* school starts at eight; **~behörde** *f* education authority, *Am.* school board; **~beispiel** *n* classic (*od.* textbook) example (*für* of); **~besuch** *m* school attendance; **~betrieb** *m* running of a

(*od.* the) school; **~bezirk** *m* school catchment area, *Am.* school district; **~bildung** *f* school education; *höhere ~* secondary education; **~brot** *n* sandwich eaten during break (*Am.* recess); **~bub** *m Dial.* schoolboy

Schulbuch *n* schoolbook, textbook; **~autor** *m*, **~autorin** *f* schoolbook author; **~verlag** *m* educational publisher

Schul|bus *m* school bus; **~chor** *m* school choir; **~chronik** *f* record of school events

schuld *Adj.*: *~* (*an etw. Dat.*) *sein* be to blame (*od.* responsible) (for s.th.); *~ sind immer die anderen iro.* it's always someone else's fault

Schuld *f*, *-, nur bei 3.: -en, sonst kein Pl.* **1.** *nur Sg.* (*Verantwortung*) blame; *ihn trifft die ~* (*dafür*) he's responsible (*od.* to blame) (for it), it's his fault; *ich habe keine ~* I am not to blame, I am blameless; *ohne m-e ~* through no fault of mine (*od.* my own); *die ~ auf sich nehmen* take the blame, take responsibility; *die ~* (*an e-r Sache*) *auf j-n schieben*, *j-m die ~* (*an e-r Sache*) *zuschieben* pin the blame on s.o. (for s.th.); **2.** *nur Sg.* (*Schuldbewusstsein*) guilt; *moralische ~* moral guilt; *~ und Sühne* crime and punishment; *bibl.* sin and atonement; *schwere ~ auf sich laden* incur a heavy burden of guilt; *ich bin mir keiner ~ bewusst* I don't feel that I've done any wrong; **3.** *mst Pl.* (*Geldschuld*) debt (*auch fig.*); (*Verbindlichkeit*) liability; **~en haben**, *in ~en stecken* be in debt; **~en machen**, *in ~en geraten* get into debt; *formeller*: incur debts; *s-e ~en bezahlen* pay (*od.* settle) one's debts; *frei von ~en* free from (*od.* of) debt, debt-free; *Haus*: unencumbered, not mortgaged; *in j-s ~ sein od. stehen fig.* owe s.o. a debt of gratitude, be deeply indebted to s.o.

Schuld|bekenntnis *n* confession, admission of guilt; **~beweis** *m* proof (*od.* evidence) of (s.o.'s) guilt

schuldbewusst I. *Adj.* **1.** *Miene etc.*: guilty; **2.** *er war durchaus ~* he was well aware that he had done wrong (*od.* of his wrongdoing); **II.** *Adv. j-n ~ anschauen* look guiltily at s.o., give s.o. a guilty look; **Schuldbewusstsein** *n* sense of guilt

Schuldbuch *n Wirts.* debt register

Schuldeingeständnis *n* admission of guilt

schulden *v/t.: j-m etw. ~* owe s.o. s.th. (*auch fig. e-e Erklärung, das Leben etc.*); → *Dank*

Schulden|abbau *m* reduction of debt; **~abkommen** *n Pol.* debt agreement; **~beratung** *f* advisory service for debtors, *Am.* credit counseling; **~bereinigung** *f* settlement of debts; **~berg** *m umg.* mountain of debt; **~dienst** *m* debt servicing; **~erlass** *m* waiving of debts, debt relief

schuldenfrei *Adj.* free from (*od.* of) debt, debt-free; *Grundbesitz*: unencumbered, not mortgaged

Schulden|last *f* debt burden; *auf Grundbesitz*: encumbrance; **~machen** *n*; *-s, kein Pl.* getting into debt, *formeller*: incurring debts; **~macher** *m* (habitual) debtor; **~masse** *f Wirts.* (aggregate) liabilities *Pl.*; **~nachlass** *m* legacy of debt; **~politik** *f* debt management policy; **~rückzahlung** *f* debt repayment; **~stand** *m* debt repayment status; **~summe** *f* amount owed; **~tilgung** *f* settlement (*od.* discharge) of

S

debts
schuldfähig *Adj.* criminally liable; **Schuldfähigkeit** *f* criminal liability (*od.* responsibility)
Schul|dezernat *n* schools department; **~dezernent** *m*, **~dezernentin** *f* head of the schools department
Schuld|forderung *f* claim; **~frage** *f*: *die ~ klären* establish who is responsible (*od.* to blame); **~gefühl** *n auch Pl.* sense (*od.* feeling) of guilt, guilty feeling; (*schlechtes Gewissen*) guilty conscience; *s-e ~e ihr gegenüber* his sense of guilt where she is (*bzw.* was) concerned; **~geständnis** *n* → **Schuldbekenntnis**
schuldhaft I. *Adj.* culpable; *Verletzung etc.*: non-accidental; **II.** *Adv.* culpably; *etw. ~ versäumen/verursachen* be guilty of neglecting/causing s.th.
Schuldienst *m* teaching; *in den ~ treten* go into teaching; *im ~ sein* be a teacher; *aus dem ~ entlassen* dismiss from the teaching service
schuldig I. *Adj.* **1.** guilty (+ *Gen.* of); *j-n für ~ befinden Jur.* find s.o. guilty (*e-s Verbrechens* of a crime); *j-n ~ sprechen* pronounce s.o. guilty; *das Gericht erkannte auf ~* the court brought in a verdict of guilty; *sich ~ bekennen* plead guilty; *~ werden* (*Schuld auf sich laden*) incur guilt; **2.** (*verantwortlich*) responsible (*od.* to blame) (*an* + *Dat.* for); **3.** (*j-m*) *etw. ~ sein* owe (s.o.) s.th. *auch fig.*; *was bin ich (Ihnen) ~?* how much do I owe you?; *ich muss dir das Geld ~ bleiben* I'll have to owe you the money; *das bist du ihm ~* you owe it to him; *ich bin Ihnen Dank ~* I owe you a debt of gratitude; *den Beweis ist sie uns noch ~* she has yet to give us any proof; *das sind Sie Ihrer Stellung in der Firma ~* your position in the firm requires it of you; (*j-m*) *die Antwort ~ bleiben* give (s.o.) no answer; (*j-m*) *die Antwort nicht ~ bleiben* hit back (at s.o.); *sie blieb ihm nichts ~* she paid him back in his own coin; **4.** (*gebührend*) *j-m den ~en Respekt erweisen* show s.o. the respect due to him; **II.** *Adv.* guiltily; *~ geschieden* divorced as the guilty party; *ich fühle mich ~* I feel I'm to blame
Schuldige *m*, *f*; *-n*, *-n* culprit; *Jur.* guilty party, offender
Schuldiger *m*; *-s*, *-*; *bibl. nur im Vaterunser*: *wie wir vergeben unseren ~n* as we forgive those who trespass against us
Schuldigkeit *f* duty, obligation; → **Pflicht**
Schul|direktor *m*, **~direktorin** *f* → **Schulleiter**, **Schulleiterin**
Schuld|klage *f* action for debt; **~komplex** *m* guilt complex
schuldlos I. *Adj.* innocent (*an* + *Dat.* of), blameless; *präd. auch* without blame; **II.** *Adv.* innocently; *~ geschieden* divorced as the innocent party
Schuldner *m*; *-s*, *-*, **~in** *f*; *-*, *-nen* debtor
Schuldner|beratung *f* advisory service for debtors, *Am.* credit counseling; **~konto** *n* debtor's account; **~land** *n* debtor country (*od.* nation); **~verzug** *m Jur.* debtor's delay, delay in payment
Schuld|recht *n Jur.* law of obligations; **~schein** *m* promissory note, IOU (= I owe you); **~spruch** *m Jur.* verdict of guilty, conviction; **~übernahme** *f* assumption of debt

schuldunfähig *Adj.* not criminally liable; **Schuldunfähigkeit** *f* absence of criminal liability (*od.* responsibility)
Schuld|verhältnis *n Jur.* obligation; **~verschreibung** *f* debenture bond; **~zins** *m* debt interest; **~zuweisung** *f* apportioning of blame; *gegenseitige ~en* recriminations
Schule *f*; *-*, *-n* **1.** (*auch weitS.* Hochschule etc.) school; *höhere ~* secondary (*Am.* senior high) school; *auf od. in der ~* at school; *zur od. in die ~ gehen* go to school; *in welche ~ geht sie?* which school does she go to (*od.* is she at, *Am.* in)?; *noch zur ~ gehen* still be at school; *von der ~ fliegen umg.* be chucked (*Am.* kicked) out (of school); *aus der ~ kommen* come out of school; *nicht für die ~, sondern fürs Leben lernen wir* learning is for life and not for school; **2.** *fig.* (*auch wissenschaftliche, künstlerische Richtung*) school; *die Frankfurter ~* the Frankfurt School; *er ist bei s-m Onkel in die ~ gegangen* (*hat bei ihm sein Handwerk gelernt*) he learnt from (*od.* was trained by) his uncle; *durch e-e harte ~ gehen* learn the hard way; *~ machen* set a precedent; **3.** *nur Sg.*: *ein Kavalier der alten ~* a cavalier of the old school; **4.** *hohe ~ Reitsport*: manège, haute école; *die hohe ~ des Kochens* haute cuisine; → **schwänzen**
schulen *v/t.* train (*auch Auge, Gedächtnis*); *Pol. auch* indoctrinate; → **geschult**
Schul|englisch *n* school English; *dazu reicht mein ~ nicht* the English I learnt at school isn't good enough for that; **~entlassene** *m*, *f*; *-n*, *-n* school-leaver; *Am. mit Abschluss*: high school graduate; **~entwicklung** *f* school development
Schüler *m*; *-s*, *-* **1.** pupil, *Am.* student; (*Junge*) schoolboy; *älterer*, *Am. allg.* (school) student; *der beste ~ der Klasse* the best pupil (*Am.* student) in the class; *ein Treffen ehemaliger ~* a reunion of former pupils (*Am.* students) (*männlich*: old boys, *weiblich*: old girls); *ein ehemaliger ~ von mir* one of my old pupils (*Am.* students); **2.** (*Jünger*) disciple, follower (*auch Philos. etc.*); *e-s Malers etc.*: pupil; *ein Brecht-~* a Brecht disciple; *er ist ein Habermas-~* he was a student of Habermas
Schüler|arbeit *f* (piece of) a pupil's (*Am.* student's) work; **~austausch** *m* school exchange; *nicht schulgebunden*: student exchange; **~ausweis** *m* school pupil's (*od.* student's) identity card; **~band** [-bɛnt] *f* school band; **~beförderung** *f* transport(ation) for schoolchildren (*od.* school students); **~ermäßigung** *f* reduction for school pupils (*od.* students), *Am.* student discount; **~fahrkarte** *f* school pupil's (*od.* student's) ticket; **~hort** *m* day home for schoolchildren
Schülerin *f*; *-*, *-nen* → **Schüler**, *auch* schoolgirl; *er unterrichtet ~nen lieber als Schüler* he prefers teaching girls to boys
Schüler|jahrgang *m*: *mein ~* the pupils (*Am.* students) in my year at school; **~lotse** *m* (*pupil, Am. student acting as* a) school crossing patrol; **~mitverwaltung** *f* (*abgek.* **SMV**) school council; **~parlament** *n* interschool pupils' (*Am.* student) council
Schülerschaft *f*; *-*, *-en* pupils *Pl.*, *Am.* students *Pl.*

Schüler|sprache *f*; *nur Sg.* school slang; **~sprecher** *m*, **~sprecherin** *f* → **Schulsprecher**, **Schulsprecherin**; **~vertretung** *f* pupils' (*Am.* student) representation; **~zahl** *f* number of pupils (*Am.* students); *zurückgehende ~en* falling pupil numbers (*Am.* school enrollment); **~zeitung** *f* school magazine
Schul|fach *n* school subject; **~feier** *f* school function; **~ferien** *Pl.* (school) holidays, *Am.* school vacation *Sg.*; **~fernsehen** *n* school television; **~fest** *n* school function; *Party*: school party; **~flugzeug** *n* trainer (aircraft); **~form** *f* type of school; **~französisch** *n* school French; → *auch* **Schulenglisch**
schulfrei *Adj.*: *~er Tag* day off school, holiday; *morgen ist ~* there's no school tomorrow
Schul|freund *m*, **~freundin** *f* schoolfriend, friend from school, schoolmate; *in gleicher Klasse*: classmate; **~funk** *m* school broadcasts *Pl.*; **~gebäude** *n* school building; **~gebrauch** *m*: *für den ~* for school use; **~gelände** *n* school grounds *Pl.*, *Am.* campus; **~geld** *n* school fees *Pl.*; **~gesetz** *n* law governing the school system of a *Bundesland*; *etwa* education act; **~gottesdienst** *m* church service at school, school religious service; **~halbjahr** *n*: *1./2. ~* first/second half of the school year; **~heft** *n* exercise book, *Am.* (note)book; **~hof** *m* schoolyard, playground
schulintern I. *Adj.* internal (school) …; **II.** *Adv. regeln etc.*: within the school
schulisch I. *Adj. nur Attr.* school …, educational; *Probleme etc.*: at school; *~e Leistungen* performance *Sg.* at school, (standard of) schoolwork *Sg.*; **II.** *Adv.*: at school; *~ versagen* be a failure at school
Schuljahr *n* **1.** school year; **2.** (*Klasse*): *das 4./11. ~* the 4th/11th year
Schuljahresbeginn *m* beginning of the school year
Schul|junge *m* schoolboy; **~kamerad** *m*, **~kameradin** *f* schoolfriend, schoolmate; *in gleicher Klasse*: classmate; **~kenntnisse** *Pl.* knowledge *Sg.* gained at (*Am.* in) school (*in* + *Dat.* of); *~ in Französisch etc.* (-level) French etc.; **~kind** *n* schoolchild (*Pl.* schoolchildren), schoolkid *umg.*; **~klasse** *f* class, form; *Am.* class, grade; **~konferenz** *f* school meeting; (*Lehrerkonferenz*) staff (*Am.* faculty) meeting; **~küche** *f* school (teaching) kitchen; **~landheim** *n* schools field cent|re (*Am.* -er) in the country; **~lehrer** *m*, **~lehrerin** *f umg.* school teacher; **~leiter** *m* headmaster, head teacher, *Am.* principal; → *stellvertretend* I; **~leiterin** *f* headmistress, head teacher, *Am.* principal; → *stellvertretend* I; **~leitung** *f* school management; *Personen*: → **Schulleiter**, **Schulleiterin**; **~mädchen** *n* schoolgirl; **~mappe** *f* schoolbag
Schul|medizin *f* orthodox (school of) medicine; **~mediziner** *m*, **~medizinerin** *f* orthodox medical practitioner; **~meinung** *f*: *die ~* received opinion
Schulmeister *m umg.* (*Lehrer*) teacher of the old school; *pej.* schoolmasterly type; **schulmeisterlich** *Adj. pej.* schoolmasterly; **schulmeistern** *vt/i. pej.* (*untr.*, *hat*) lecture
Schul|musik *f* music in schools; **~musiker** *m*, **~musikerin** *f* school musi-

S

cian; **~orchester** *n* school orchestra; **~ordnung** *f* school regulations *Pl.*; **~pädagogik** *f* school pedagogy; **Seminar für ~** *etwa* teacher training college; **~partnerschaft** *f* school twinning

Schulpflicht *f* compulsory (school) education; **die ~ beginnt/endet mit ...** children have to go to school when they are ... / stay at school until they are ...; **schulpflichtig** *Adj. Attr.* ... of school age, school-age ...; **~ werden** reach school age

Schulpolitik *f* schools policy; *weitS.* educational policy; **schulpolitisch** *Adj.* related to schools (*od.* educational) policy; *Entscheidung:* affecting schools (*od.* educational) policy

Schul|praktikum *n* teaching practice; **~psychologe** *m*, **~psychologin** *f* educational psychologist; **~ranzen** *m* satchel; **~rat** *m*, **~rätin** *f* school inspector; **~raum** *m* classroom; **~recht** *n* legislation affecting schools; **~reform** *f* school reform

schulreif *Adj.* ready for school; **Schulreife** *f* readiness for school

Schul|sachen *Pl.* school things, things for school; **~schiff** *n Naut.* school (*od.* training) ship; **~schluss** *m* end of school; *vor den Ferien:* end of term; **wann habt ihr heute ~?** when does school finish today?, when do you get out of school today?; **~schwänzer** *m*, **~schwänzerin** *f umg.* truant; **~speisung** *f* school meals *Pl.*; **~sport** *m* school sport(s *Pl.*); **~sprecher** *m* pupils' representative, *etwa* head boy, *Am.* student representative; **~sprecherin** *f* pupils' representative, *etwa* head girl, *Am.* student representative; **~streik** *m* school strike; **~stress** *m* pressures *Pl.* of school life; **~stunde** *f* lesson, class, period; **~system** *n* school system; **~tag** *m* school day; **mein erster ~** my first day at school; **~tafel** *f* (black)board; *weiß:* (white)board; **~tasche** *f* schoolbag; (*Schultertasche*) satchel

Schulter *f*, -, -n; *Anat.* shoulder (*auch Tech.*, *Gastr.*); **~ an ~** shoulder to shoulder (*auch fig.*), *beim Rennen:* neck and neck; **mit den ~n zucken** shrug (one's shoulders); **j-m bis zur ~ reichen** come up to s.o.'s shoulder; **j-m auf die ~ klopfen** slap (*lobend:* pat) s.o. on the back; **j-n über die ~ ansehen** *fig.* look down one's nose at s.o.; → *kalt* I 3, *leicht* I 4

Schulter|blatt *n Anat.* shoulder blade; **~breite** *f* width of (the) shoulders

schulterfrei *Adj. Kleid:* off-the-shoulder; (*trägerlos*) strapless

Schultergelenk *n* shoulder joint

schulterhoch *Adj.* shoulder-high; **~ wachsen** grow to shoulder height; **Schulterhöhe** *f:* (**in**) **~** (at) shoulder height

Schulterklappe *f Mil.* epaulet(te)

schulterlang *Adj. Haare:* shoulder-length

schultern *v/t.* 1. (*Gewehr*) shoulder; (*Rucksack*) sling over one's shoulders; 2. *Ringen:* shoulder

Schulter|riemen *m* shoulder strap; **~schluss** *m* (*Solidarität*) closing of ranks (**zwischen** +*Dat.* between); *von Parteien, Verbündeten:* close alliance (**von** between); **sich im ~ befinden mit** be standing shoulder to shoulder with; **~sieg** *m Ringen:* win by fall; **~tasche** *f* shoulder bag; **~wurf** *m* shoulder throw; **~zucken** *n; -s, kein Pl.* shrug (of the shoulders)

Schultheiß *m; -en, -en; altm.* mayor

Schul|träger *m* authority responsible for the maintenance of a school; **~ ist ...** the school is maintained by ...; **~tüte** *f* cardboard cone filled with presents and sweets and given to children on their first day at school; **~typ** *m* type of school

Schulung *f* 1. training; *von Pferd auch:* schooling; (*Übung*) practi|ce (*Am.* -se); (*Erziehung*) education; *Pol. auch* instruction; 2. (*Lehrgang*) training course

Schulungs|kurs *m* training course; **~raum** *m* training (*od.* tutorial) room; **~zentrum** *n* training cent|re (*Am.* -er)

Schul|uniform *f* school uniform; **~unterricht** *m* school lessons *Pl.* (*od.* classes *Pl.*); **~versagen** *n* failure of a pupil (*Am.* student); **~versuch** *m* educational experiment; **~verwaltung** *f* school administration; **~wahl** *f* choice of school; **~wechsel** *m* change of school; **~weg** *m* way to school; (*Entfernung*) distance to school; **er hat e-n langen ~** he's got a long way to go to school; **~weisheit** *f* book learning; **~wesen** *n* school system; **~wissen** *n:* **mein ~** what I learnt (*Am.* learned) (*od.* they taught me) at school; **~wörterbuch** *n* school dictionary; **~zeit** *f* schooldays *Pl.*; **während m-r ~** in my schooldays, when I was at school; **~zentrum** *n* school complex; **~zeugnis** *n* (school) report, *Am.* report card

schummeln *umg.* I. *v/i.* cheat; **das ist geschummelt** that's cheating; **e-e Sechs wegen Schummelns bekommen** get a fail mark (*Am.* an F *od.* a failing grade) for cheating; II. *v/t. etw.* **~ in** (+ *Akk.*) (*ein Haus etc.*) smuggle into; (*e-e Tasche etc.*) slip into

schummerig *Adj.* dim, dimly lit; **mir wurde ~** (**vor Augen**) *umg.* everything went faint (in front of my eyes)

schummern I. *v/i., unpers. Dial.* get dark; II. *v/t. fachspr.* shade (with varying intensity)

Schummler *m; -s, -,* **~in** *f; -, -nen; umg.* cheat

Schund *m; -(e)s, kein Pl.* trash, rubbish; → *auch Schmutz,* **~heft** *n* trashy paperback; **~roman** *m* trashy novel

Schunkel|lied *n etwa* drinking song (*to which one can rock back and forth*); **~musik** *f* jolly (*od.* singalong) music

schunkeln *v/i.* rock, sway; *zur Musik:* sway to the music

schupfen *v/t südd., österr., schw.:* **j-n ~** give s.o. a little shove

Schupfen *m; -s, -; südd., österr.* (*Schuppen*) shed

Schupfer *m; -s, -; österr.* little shove

Schupo *m; -s, -s; umg. altm.* cop, *Brit. auch* copper, bobby

Schuppe *f; -, -n; Zool.* scale; *Pl.* (*Kopfschuppen*) dandruff *Sg.*, scurf *Sg.*; **es fiel mir wie ~n von den Augen** *fig.* my eyes were opened, the scales fell from my eyes *lit.*

schuppen I. *v/t.* (*Fisch*) scale; II. *v/i. Kopfhaut:* flake; III. *v/refl.* flake; *nach Sonnenbrand:* peel

Schuppen *m; -s, -.* 1. shed, *Am. auch* shack; *für Flugzeuge:* hangar; 2. *umg. pej.* (*Gebäude*) dump; (*Lokal etc.*) joint, dive; **riesiger ~** *umg.* huge place (*od.* pile); **hässlicher ~** real eyesore (of a building)

...schuppen *m, im Subst.:* **Boots~** boathouse; **Bretter~** wooden shed

Schuppen|bildung *f* dandruff; **~flechte** *f Med.* psoriasis

schuppenförmig *Adj.* scale-like, squamous *förm.*

Schuppen|panzer *m hist., Zool.* scale armo(u)r; **~tier** *n Zool.* pangolin, scaly anteater

schuppig I. *Adj.* scaly; *Haar:* dandruffy; II. *Adv.:* **sich ~ ablösen** flake

Schur *f, -, -en* 1. shearing; *e-r Hecke:* clipping; 2. (*Wolle*) fleece

schüren *v/t.* (*Feuer*) poke, rake; *fig.* stir up, *förm.* foment; **damit schürt man noch den Hass** this only serves to stir up more hatred (*od.* fan the flames of hatred)

schürfen I. *v/t.* 1. (*Haut*) scrape, graze; **sich** (*Dat.*) **das Knie ~** scrape (*od.* graze) one's knee; 2. (*Erz, Kohle*) mine opencast (*Am.* open-cut); II. *v/i. Bergb.* prospect (**nach** for), dig (for); **tiefer ~** *fig.* dig below the surface

Schürf|rechte *Pl.* opencast (*Am.* open-cut) mining rights; **~wunde** *f* graze, *Med.* abrasion

Schürhaken *m* (hooked) poker

schurigeln *v/t. umg.* → *piesacken*

Schurke *m; -n, -n; pej.* rogue; **dieser Schauspieler spielt meist den ~n** this actor usually plays the villain (*umg.* baddie, *Am.* bad guy); **Schurkenstaat** *m Pol. pej.* rogue state; **Schurkerei** *f; -, -en; pej.* villainous deed; **Schurkin** *f; -, -nen; pej.* rogue; **schurkisch** I. *Adj. pej.* despicable, villainous; II. *Adv. handeln etc.:* despicably

Schurwolle *f:* (**reine**) **~** (pure) virgin wool

Schurz *m; -es, -e* apron; (*Lendenschurz*) loincloth

Schürze *f; -, -n* apron; *für Frauen und Kinder: auch* pinafore, pinny *Brit. umg.*

...schürze *f, im Subst.:* **Dirndl~** apron of a dirndl dress

schürzen *v/t.* 1. (*Kleid*) gather up; **die Lippen ~** purse one's lips; 2. (*Knoten*) tie

Schürzen|band *n; Pl. Schürzenbänder* apron string; **~jäger** *m umg.* womanizer, philanderer; **~zipfel** *m:* **der Mutter am ~ hängen** *umg. fig.* be tied to one's mother's apron strings

Schuss *m; -es, Schüsse, bei Munition: Schuss* 1. shot (*auch Fot.*); *Fußball: auch* strike; (*Kugel*) bullet; (*Munition*) round; **ein ~ ins Schwarze** a bull's-eye (*auch fig.*); **er hatte noch drei ~** (*Munition*) he still had three shots (*od.* rounds) left; **er kam nicht zum ~** *Jäger, Fußballer, Fotograf etc.:* he couldn't get a shot in; *umg. fig.* he never got a chance; **der ~ ging ins Aus/Tor** the ball went into touch (*od.* out of play) / went in(to the goal); **er hat e-n guten ~** he has a good shot on him; **~ vor den Bug** *fig.* warning shot; **ein ~ in den Ofen** *umg. fig.* a complete flop, a dead loss; **der ~ ging nach hinten los** *umg. fig.* it was an own goal; **weit (ab) vom ~** *umg.* well out of harm's way; *wohnen etc.:* miles from anywhere; **e-n ~ haben** (*spinnen, verrückt sein*) have a screw loose; **die hat wohl 'nen ~** *umg.* she must be off her rocker; 3. **nur Sg.: ein ~ Wein** *etc.:* a dash of; *fig. Ironie etc.:* a touch of; **Orangensaft** *etc.* **mit ~** spiked orange juice *etc.*; 4. **nur Sg.:** *Skisport:* schuss (*auch im ~ fahren*); 5. *umg.* (*Drogeninjektion*) shot, fix *Sl.*; **sich e-n ~ setzen** *Drogen:* shoot up; **den goldenen ~ setzen** OD (o.s.); 6. *umg.:* **in ~ bringen** (*Wohnung, Garten etc.*) knock *s.th.* into shape; (*Auto, Uhr*

S

etc.) get *s.th.* working; (*Geschäft etc.*) get *s.th.* going again; (*Person*) get *s.o.* into shape (*od.* trim); **wieder in ~ kommen** *Garten, Person:* shape up again; *auch Auto:* get back into shape; **7.** *fig.:* **e-n ~ tun** (*wachsen*) shoot up; **8.** *Weberei:* weft, woof; **9.** *Bergb.* (*Bohrloch*) blast hole; (*Sprengung*) blast, charge; → **Pulver**

Schuss|bahn *f* **1.** line of fire; **2.** *Phys.* trajectory; **~bein** *n Fußball:* shooting foot

schussbereit *Adj.* ready to fire (*od.* shoot, *auch umg.* Fot.); *Waffe, umg. Kamera: auch* at the ready

Schussel *m;* -*s,* -; *umg.* dotty (*od.* batty) person; *zerstreuter: auch* scatterbrain, muddler; **ich ~!** I must be going dotty (*od.* batty, *Brit. auch* scatty)!

Schüssel *f;* -, -*n* **1.** bowl; *zum Servieren: auch* dish; **aus e-r ~ essen** *fig.* stick together; **vor leeren ~n sitzen** *umg. fig.* go hungry; → **Sprung** 6; **2.** *Med., für Bettlägerige:* bedpan; **3.** *TV, umg.* dish

schusselig *Adj. umg.* dotty, batty, *Brit. auch* scatty; (*zerstreut*) *auch* scatterbrained, muddle-headed; **schusseln** *umg. v/i.* **1.** (*hat geschusselt*) make careless mistakes (*bei* in); **2.** (*ist*) **aufgeregt durch die Gegend ~** dash about in a scatterbrained way

Schuss|faden *m Weberei:* weft, woof; **~fahrt** *f Skisport:* schuss; **~feld** *n* field of fire; **freies ~ haben** have a clear view of the target; *Sport:* have a clear shot at goal

schussfest *Adj.* bulletproof; *vor Granateinwirkung:* shellproof

Schussgelegenheit *f Sport* chance at a goal

schussgewaltig *Adj. Sport, Spieler:* with a powerful shot; *Mannschaft:* with considerable shooting power

Schuss|linie *f* line of fire; **in die ~ geraten** *auch fig.* come under fire (**von** from); **sich in die ~ begeben** *fig.* lay oneself open to a barrage of criticism; **~möglichkeit** *f Fußball:* scoring opportunity; **~position** *f* shooting position; **~richtung** *f* direction of fire

schuss|schwach *Adj. Sport* lacking shooting power; **~sicher** *Adj. Weste etc.:* bulletproof

schussstark *Adj. Sport* with considerable shooting power; **Schussstärke** *f Sport* shooting power

Schuss|verletzung *f* gunshot wound; **~waffe** *f* firearm; *Pl.* (*Handfeuerwaffen*) small arms; **~waffengebrauch** *m* use of a (*od.* the) gun; **~wechsel** *m* exchange of fire; *stärker:* gun battle; *fig.* heated exchange; **~weite** *f* range (of fire); **außer/in ~** out of/within range; **~wunde** *f* gunshot wound

Schuster *m;* -*s,* - shoemaker; *für Reparaturen:* shoe-repairer, cobbler; **~, bleib bei d-m Leisten!** *Sprichw.* don't meddle with things that don't concern you, the cobbler should stick to his last; → **Rappe, ~handwerk** *n* shoemaking

Schusterin *f;* -, -*nen* (female) shoemaker

Schuster|junge *m fig.* **1.** *bes. Berlin:* rye bread roll; **2.** *Druck.* orphan; **~lehrling** *m* shoemaker's apprentice

schustern *v/i.* **1.** mend shoes; **2.** *umg.* (*pfuschen*) bungle, botch it

Schuster|schemel *m* cobbler's stool; **~werkstatt** *f* shoemaker's (*für Reparaturen:* shoe repairer's) workshop

Schute *f;* -, -*n* **1.** *Naut.* barge, lighter; **2.** (*Hut*) poke bonnet

Schutt *m;* -(*e*)*s,* *kein Pl.* **1.** (*Abfall*) rubbish, *Am.* garbage; *Steine:* rubble; (*Trümmer*) *auch* debris, ruins *Pl.;* *Geol.* detritus; **~ abladen verboten!** no dumping, *Brit. auch* no tipping; **in ~ und Asche legen** raze to the ground; **2.** *umg. fig.* (*Untaugliches*) (a load of) rubbish (*od.* trash *od.* garbage); **~abladeplatz** *m* rubbish (*Am.* garbage) dump, *Brit. auch* tip; **~ablagerung** *f Geol.* detritus; **~berg** *m* mountain of rubbish (*Am.* garbage)

Schüttbeton *m* cast concrete

Schütte *f;* -, -*n* kitchen drawer for loose materials such as flour

Schüttel|becher *m* (cocktail) shaker; **~frost** *m* shivering fit, the shivers *Pl. umg.;* **~lähmung** *f Med.* Parkinson's disease

schütteln I. *vt/i.* shake; **vor dem Öffnen / vor Gebrauch gut ~!** shake well before opening / before use; **den Kopf** *od.* **mit dem Kopf ~** shake one's head; **j-m die Hand ~** shake s.o.'s hand, shake hands with s.o.; **vom Fieber geschüttelt werden** be shivering with fever; **da kann man nur den** (*od.* **mit dem**) **Kopf ~** *umg. fig.* one can only shake one's head in disbelief; → **Ärmel, Öffnen; II.** *v/refl.* shake, shudder (*vor Angst etc.:* with fear *etc.*); **sich vor Kälte ~** shiver with cold; **der nasse Hund schüttelte sich** the wet dog shook itself; **er schüttelte sich vor Lachen** *umg.* he shook with laughter

Schüttel|reim *m* spoonerism (*rhyming couplet with a humorous effect caused by swapping of initial consonants*); **~sieb** *n* vibrating screen

schütten I. *v/t.* (*gießen*) pour (*auch Tech.*); (*verschütten*) spill; (*Erde, Schutt etc.*) dump, tip; **auf e-n Haufen ~** heap up; **II.** *v/i., unpers. umg.:* **es schüttet** (*regnet*) it's pouring, *Brit. auch* it's bucketing (down)

schütter *Adj. Wachstum, Wald:* sparse; *Haar:* thinning; **mein Haar wird ~** my hair is getting thin, I'm going thin on top *umg.*

Schüttgut *n* bulk goods *Pl.*

Schutt|halde *f* **1.** *für Müll:* tip; **2.** *Geol.* scree, *bes. Am.* talus; **~haufen** *m* rubbish (*Am.* garbage) heap; *aus Steinen:* heap of rubble; **~kegel** *m Geol.* (conical) scree (*bes. Am.* talus); **~pflanze** *f* ruderal plant

Schutz *m;* -*es,* *kein Pl.* protection (**gegen, vor** + *Dat.* against, from); (*Geleit*) escort; (*Obdach, Zuflucht*) shelter, refuge; (*Obhut*) custody; (*Deckung*) cover; (*Erhaltung*) preservation, conservation; (*Wärmeschutz*) insulation; (*Sicherung*) safeguard; **den ~ des Gesetzes genießen** be protected by law; **~ suchen** seek protection; *vor dem Regen etc.:* look for (a) shelter; *fig.* seek refuge (**vor** + *Dat.* from; **bei** with); **sich ~ suchend an j-n wenden** turn to s.o. for protection; **ein ~ Suchender** a person seeking protection (*od.* shelter); **im ~ e des Deiches / der Dunkelheit** protected by the dyke / under cover of darkness; **j-n in ~ nehmen** protect s.o.; (*eintreten für*) come to s.o.'s defen[c]e (*Am.* -se), back s.o. up; **ich will niemanden in ~ nehmen** I don't want to take sides; **zum ~ gegen Erkältungen** *etc.* to ward off colds *etc.*, to build up one's resistance against colds *etc.;* **zum ~ gegen Strahlung** to protect (*od.* shield) against radiation

...schutz *m, im Subst.:* **Blick~** (protective) screen; **Frost~** frost protection;

Impf~ (protection through) inoculation (*od.* vaccination)

Schütz *n;* -*es,* -*e* **1.** *am Wehr etc.:* sluice gate; **2.** *Etech.* cutout

Schutz|anstrich *m* protective coat(ing); **~anzug** *m* protective clothing; **~bedürfnis** *n* need of protection; **schutzbedürftig** *Adj.* in need of protection

Schutz|befohlene *m, f;* -*n,* -*n Jur.* charge; **~behälter** *m* special container (for toxic waste *etc.*); **~behauptung** *f bes. Jur.* defensive lie; **~blech** *n* guard; *am Fahrrad, Oldtimer:* mudguard, *Am.* fender; **~brief** *m* **1.** *Mot.* accident and breakdown cover; **2.** *Pol., bes. hist.* safe conduct; **~brille** *f:* (**e-e**) **~** (a pair of) safety goggles *Pl.;* **~bündnis** *n* defensive alliance; **~dach** *n* protective roof, shelter; *kleines: mst* canopy; (*Markise*) awning

Schütze *m;* -*n,* -*n* **1.** marksman; *Sport, Mil. auch* rifleman; (*Bogenschütze*) archer; *Mil., als Dienstgrad:* private; **nach dem ~n wird noch gesucht** the hunt is still on for the gunman; **2.** *Fußball etc.:* scorer; **gefährlicher ~** dangerous striker; **3.** *nur Sg., Astrol.* Sagittarius; (**ein**) **~ sein** *Astrol.* be (a) Sagittarius (*od.* a Sagittarian)

schützen I. *v/t.* **1.** protect (**vor** + *Dat.* from); (*verteidigen*) defend (**gegen, vor** + *Dat.* against, from); (*sichern, bewahren*) guard (against); *gegen Wetter etc.:* shelter (from); (*decken*) cover; *weitS.* shield; (*abschirmen*) screen, shield; (*geleiten*) escort; (*erhalten*) preserve, conserve; (*Umwelt etc.*) *auch* protect; (*bewachen*) watch over; **bedrohte Arten müssen besser geschützt werden** endangered species must be better protected; **vor Hitze ~!** store away from heat; **vor Nässe ~!** keep dry, keep (*od.* store) in a dry place; **2.** *patentrechtlich* **~** patent, protect with a patent; *urheberrechtlich* **~** (protected by) copyright; **den Namen ~ lassen** register the name as a trademark; → **geschützt; II.** *v/refl.* protect o.s. (**gegen, vor** + *Dat.* from); **sich ~ vor** (+ *Dat.*) *auch* guard against

schützend I. *Part. Präs.* → **schützen; II.** *Adj.* protective; **III.** *Adv.:* **sich ~ vor j-n stellen** stand protectively in front of s.o.; *fig.* stand up for s.o.; **s-e Hand ~ über j-n halten** *fig.* take s.o. under one's wing

Schützen|fest *n* **1.** fair (with shooting competition); **der (letzte) Rest vom ~** *umg.* all that's left; **2.** *umg. Sport* goal spree; **~feuer** *n Mil.* rifle fire; (*selbstständiges Schießen*) independent fire

Schutzengel *m* guardian angel; **da hast du aber e-n ~ gehabt** *umg.* your guardian angel must have been watching over you

Schützen|graben *m Mil.* trench; **~heim** *n* rifle association's clubhouse, *Am.* gun (*od.* rifle) club; **~hilfe** *f umg. fig.* support, backing; **j-m ~ leisten** back s.o. up; **~kette** *f Mil.* staggered firing line; **~könig** *m,* **~königin** *f* **1.** champion marksman (*weiblich:* markswoman); **2.** *umg. Sport* top scorer; **~loch** *n* foxhole; **~panzer** *m* armo(u)red personnel carrier

schützenswert *Adj.* worth protecting, worthy of protection

Schützen|verein *m,* **~zunft** *f schw.* rifle association, *Am.* gun club

Schutz|farbe *f* **1.** protective paint; **2.** *Mil.* (*Tarnfarbe*) camouflage; **~färbung** *f Zool.* protective colo(u)ring, camouflage; **~film** *m* protective layer (*od.* coating); **~frist** *f* period of protection; *Patent*: life of a patent; *Urheberrecht*: term of copyright; **~funktion** *f* protective function; **~gebiet** *n* **1.** *Pol.* protectorate; **2.** → *Naturschutzgebiet*, **~gebühr** *f* **1.** token fee; **2.** → *Schutzgeld*; **~geleit** *n* escort

Schutzgeld *n* protection money; **~erpressung** *f* protection racketeering

Schutz|gewahrsam *m* protective custody; **~gitter** *n* **1.** (safety *od.* protective) grille; *Mot.* radiator grille; *vor dem Kamin*: fireguard; **2.** *Etech.* screen grid; (*Sicherheitsglas*) safety glass; **~haft** *f Pol.* preventive detention; **~handschuhe** *Pl.* protective gloves; **~heilige** *m, f* patron saint; **~helm** *m* (safety) helmet; *für Bauarbeiter etc.*: *auch* hard hat; **~herr** *m* (*Schirmherr*) patron; *Pol.* protector; **~herrin** *f* (*Schirmherrin*) patron(ess); *Pol.* protector, protectress; **~schaft** *f* protectorate; **~hülle** *f* (protective) cover; *für Ausweis*: holder; *e-s Buchs*: dust cover (*od.* jacket); **~hund** *m* guard dog; **~hütte** *f* shelter, refuge

schutzimpfen *v/t.* (*untr.*, *hat -ge-*) *Med.* inoculate, vaccinate; **Schutzimpfung** *f* inoculation, vaccination

Schützin *f*; -, *-nen* markswoman; (*Sportschützin*) riflewoman; → *Schütze* 2, 3

Schutz|kappe *f* protective cap; **~klausel** *f* protective clause; **~kleidung** *f* protective clothing; **~kontakt** *m Etech.* earthing (*Am.* grounding) contact; **~leiste** *f* protective strip

Schützling *m*; -s, -e charge, protégé; *weiblich*: protégée

schutzlos I. *Adj.* defenceless, *Am.* defenseless; *gegen Kälte, Regen etc.*: without protection (*od.* shelter); **II.** *Adv.*: *j-m ~ ausgeliefert sein* be entirely at s.o.'s mercy

Schutz|macht *f Pol.* protecting power; **~mann** *m*; *Pl.* Schutzleute; *altm.* policeman, *Brit.* constable; **~mantel** *m Tech.* protective casing; *e-s Reaktors*: radiation shield; **~marke** *f*: (*eingetragene*) ~ (registered) trademark; **~maske** *f* (protective) mask; **~maßnahme** *f* protective (*od.* safety) measure; (*Vorsichtsmaßnahme*) precaution(ary measure); **~mauer** *f* protective (*od.* screen) wall; *Mil.* defensive wall; **~mechanismus** *m* protective mechanism; **~mittel** *n* protective agent; *Med.* prophylactic; **~patron** *m*, **~patronin** *f* patron saint; **~polizei** *f* police *Pl.*, constabulary; **~polizist** *m* → *Schutzmann*; **~raum** *m* (*Luftschutzraum*) air-raid shelter; **~recht** *n Jur.* intellectual property right; **~schalter** *m Elektr.* circuit-breaker; **~schicht** *f* protective layer (*od.* coating); **~schild** *m* (protective) shield; *lebendiger od. menschlicher* ~ human shield; **~schirm** *m* (protective) screen, protective umbrella; **~stoff** *m Med.* antibody; (*Impfstoff*) vaccine; **~suchende** *m, f*; -n, -n → *Schutz*; **~umschlag** *m* dust cover, (dust) jacket; **~verband** *m* **1.** *Med.* protective bandage; **2.** *Verein*: protective association; **~vorkehrung** *f* safety device, guard; **~vorschrift** *f* safety regulation; **~wald** *m* barrier woodland; **~wirkung** *f* protective action

schutzwürdig *Adj.* worthy of protection; *Gebäude*: worthy of preservation; **Schutzwürdigkeit** *f*: *die Frage der ~ dieser Rechte* the question of whether these rights deserve protection

Schutz|zaun *m* protective fence; **~zoll** *m* protective duty

Schwa *n*; -(s), -(s); *Ling.* schwa (*Zeichen*: [ə])

schwabbelig *Adj.* umg. wobbly; *Körperteil*: flabby; **schwabbeln** *v/i.* umg. wobble

Schwabe *m*; -n, -n Swabian; **schwäbeln** *v/i.* **1.** speak in (*od.* the) Swabian dialect; **2.** have a Swabian accent; **Schwaben** (*n*); -s; *Geog.* Swabia; **Schwabenstreich** *m* folly, foolish act; **Schwäbin** *f*; -, *-nen* Swabian woman (*od.* girl); → *auch Schwabe*; **schwäbisch** *Adj.* Swabian; *die Schwäbische Alb Geog.* the Swabian Alb; **Schwäbisch** *n*; *-en*; *Ling.* Swabian (dialect); *das ~e* the Swabian dialect

schwach I. *Adj.* **1.** *allg.* weak; *Stimme*: weak, faint; *Hoffnung, Lächeln*: faint; *Motor*: low-powered; *Batterie*: low; *Puls*: weak, faint; *Ton, Geruch*: faint; *Licht*: dim; **~e Ähnlichkeit** slight resemblance; **~er Beifall** half-hearted applause; **~e Beteiligung** low (*od.* poor) turnout; **~e Erinnerung** faint (*od.* vague, dim) recollection; **~er Esser** poor eater; *das ~e Geschlecht* the weaker sex; *e-e ~e Stunde* a moment of weakness; **~er Trost** small consolation; **~er Versuch** feeble attempt; *e-n ~en Willen haben* be weak-willed; **~er Wind** slight (*od.* light) breeze; **2.** (*schlecht*) *Mannschaft etc., Schüler*: weak; *umg.* (*enttäuschend*) hopeless; *Gesundheit, Gedächtnis, Gehör*: poor; **~e Vorstellung** *Theat.* poor performance; *umg. fig.* (*schlechte Leistung*) poor show; *ein ~es Bild bieten* put up (*od.* on) a poor show; **~e Seite** → *Schwäche* 2; *e-s der schwächeren Stücke Brechts* one of Brecht's weaker plays; *ein Stützkurs für die Schwächeren* a support program(me) for weaker pupils; *sozial ~* socially disadvantaged; *die sozial Schwachen* the socially disadvantaged; **3.** (*nachgiebig*) soft; ~ *werden* weaken; *fig.* (*nachgeben*) *auch* relent; (*erliegen*) succumb; *er wurde ~ fig. auch* his resistance broke down; *bei dem Anblick wurde ich ~ umg.* I melted at the sight; *mach mich nicht ~! umg.* don't say things like that!; *nur nicht ~ werden! umg.* don't give in!; **4.** *schwächer werden* weaken (further), grow weaker; *Nachfrage*: fall off, decrease; *Sehkraft*: deteriorate; *Ton, Licht*: fade; *schulisch, künstlerisch*: → *abflauen* 1, 2, *nachlassen* II 1; **5.** *~ auf der Brust sein umg.* be out of pocket; **II.** *Adv.*: **1.** ~ *aktiv Phys., Substanz*: low-level; ~ *radioaktiv Phys.* ... emitting low-level radioactivity, low-level radioactive ...; ~ *besetzt Sport, Team*: weak; *Turnier*: with a poor entry; *Stadion etc.*: half empty; ~ *betont Ling., Silbe*: weakly stressed; ~ *begabt* not at all gifted; *Schüler*: low-ability; ~ *besucht sein* be poorly attended; ~ *motorisiert* low-powered; *sein Herz schlug nur noch* ~ he only had a faint heartbeat; ~ *dekliniertes Substantiv/Adjektiv* weak noun/adjective; **2.** (*schlecht*) ~ *spielen* play badly; ~ *entwickelt* poorly developed, underdeveloped

...schwach im Adj. **1.** *qualitätsmäßig*: *ausdrucks~* inarticulate, lacking expressive power; *inhalts~* with poor content; **2.** *leistungsmäßig*: *kondtions~* unfit, in poor shape; *lern~* with learning difficulties; **3.** *mit zu geringer Zahl*: *mitglieder~* with few members;

PS~ low-powered

schwach aktiv *etc.* → *schwach* II 1

Schwäche *f*; -, *-n* **1.** weakness; (*Gefühl*) (feeling of) faintness; (*Erschöpfung*) exhaustion; *von Ton, Licht*: faintness; *vor ~ nicht gehen können* be too weak to walk; **2.** (*schwache Seite*) weak point; *des Charakters*: *auch* weakness, failing, shortcoming; *menschliche ~n* human frailties; **3.** (*Vorliebe*) weakness (*für* for); (*Zuneigung zu*) soft spot (for); *e-e ~ für Süßigkeiten haben* have a weakness for sweets, have a sweet tooth; **4.** (*Leistungsschwäche*) weakness; (*schlechte Leistung*) shortcoming; **~n in Mathe** weaknesses (*od.* shortcomings) in math(s); *die ~n des Gegners* (*nicht*) *ausnützen* (not) take advantage of an opponent's weaknesses (*od.* shortcomings); **5.** (*Nachteil, Fehler*) weakness, shortcoming

...schwäche *f*, im Subst. **1.** *körperlich*: *Augen~* weak (*od.* poor) eyesight; *Kreislauf~* poor circulation; *Muskel~* muscular weakness (*fachspr.* asthenia); **2.** *leistungsmäßig*: *Tennis*: *Aufschlag~* weakness of serve; *Fußball*: *Abspiel~* weakness in passing, poor quality of passes; *Rechtschreib~* weakness in spelling, poor spelling

Schwäche|anfall *m*: *e-n ~ haben* suddenly feel faint; (*zusammenbrechen*) faint, collapse; **~gefühl** *n* faint feeling

schwächeln *v/i.* umg. weaken slightly; *der Dollar schwächelt* the dollar is showing signs of weakness

schwächen *vt/i.* weaken (*auch fig.*); (*Gesundheit*) undermine; (*Sehkraft etc.*) impair; (*vermindern*) (*Macht, Prestige, Einfluss etc.*) diminish; *Fieber/Fasten schwächt sehr* a fever / fasting makes you very weak; *stark geschwächt sein* be weakened considerably; *Gesundheit*: be seriously undermined; *Sehkraft etc.*: be seriously impaired; *Macht, Prestige, Einfluss etc.*: be greatly diminished; *die Krise hat die Wirtschaft stark geschwächt* the crisis seriously weakened the economy

Schwäche|phase *f* period of weakness; *Wirts.* bad period (+ *Gen.* for); *e-e ~ durchlaufen Sport etc.*: be going through a bad patch; **~zustand** *m Med.* weak condition, *förm.* (state of) debility; *Wirts.* weak state

Schwachheit *f* weakness (*auch fig.*); *bilde dir nur keine ~en ein! umg. fig.* don't go getting any false hopes, don't kid yourself

Schwachkopf *m* umg., pej. idiot, blockhead, twit

schwächlich *Adj.* weakly; (*zart, kränklich*) delicate, frail; *stärker*: sickly; *Wirts.* weak, frail

Schwächling *m*; -s, -e; pej. weakling (*auch fig.*)

Schwachpunkt *m* → *Schwachstelle*

schwachsichtig *Adj.* weak-sighted; **Schwachsichtigkeit** *f* weak-sightedness, amblyopia *fachspr.*

Schwachsinn *m*; nur Sg. **1.** umg. (*Blödsinn*) nonsense; *diesen ~ mach ich nicht länger mit* I'm not having anything more to do with this idiotic business; **2.** *Med.* feeble-mindedness; **schwachsinnig** *Adj.* **1.** umg. (*blödsinnig*) idiotic, inane; **2.** *Med.* mentally deficient, feeble-minded; **Schwachsinnige** *m, f*; -n, -n **1.** umg. moron, idiot; **2.** *Med.* imbecile

Schwachstelle *f* weak point (*od.* spot)

Schwachstrom *m* *Etech.* low-voltage current; **~technik** *f* communications technology

Schwächung *f* weakening; → *auch* **Abschwächung**

schwachwindig *Adj.* *Met.*: **morgen ~** light winds tomorrow

Schwaden *m*; *-s*, - cloud; *von Nebel*: *auch* patch; *giftige* **~** a toxic cloud *Sg.*

Schwadron *f*; -, *-en*; *Mil. hist.* squadron; **schwadronieren** *v/i.* *umg.* bluster, gas (*von* about)

Schwafelei *f*; -, *-en*; *umg.* twaddle, blether(ing); **Schwaf(e)ler** *m*; *-s*, -; *umg.* gasbag, waffler; **schwafeln** *umg.* **I.** *v/i.* waffle; **~ von** waffle (on) about, go on about; **II.** *v/t.*: *was schwafelt er da wieder?* what's he waffling (*od.* going) on about now?; **Schwaflerin** *f*; -, *-nen*; *umg.* waffler

Schwager *m*; *-s*, *Schwäger* brother-in-law; **Schwägerin** *f*; -, *-nen* sister-in-law

Schwalbe *f*; -, *-n*; *Orn.* swallow; *e-e* **~** *macht noch keinen Sommer Sprichw.* one swallow doesn't make a summer

Schwalbennest *n* swallow's nest; **Schwalbennestersuppe** *f* *Gastr.* bird's nest soup

Schwalbenschwanz *m* **1.** *Zool.* (*Schmetterling*) swallow-tail; **2.** *umg.* (*Frack*) swallow-tails *Pl.*, swallow-tailed coat

Schwall *m*; -(e)s, -e, *mst Sg. von Wasser etc.*: torrent; (*Bewegung*) surge (*auch von Luft, Gas*); *fig. von Worten*: flood; *von Schimpfwörtern*: volley, torrent; *von Fragen*: barrage; *von Musik etc.*: outburst

schwallen *v/i.* *Jugendspr. pej.* jabber away, blather on

schwamm *Imperf.* → **schwimmen**

Schwamm *m*; -(e)s, *Schwämme* **1.** *Zool. und weitS.* sponge; *mit e-m* **~** *abwaschen* sponge down; *sich wie ein* **~** *vollsaugen* soak up liquid like a sponge; **~** *drüber! umg. fig.* (let's) forget it; **2.** (*Hausschwamm*) dry rot; **3.** *südd., österr.* (*Pilz*) mushroom; *in die Schwämme gehen* go mushroom-picking

schwammartig *Adj.* sponge(-)like

Schwammerl *n*; *-s*, *-(n)*; *südd., österr.* mushroom

schwammig I. *Adj.* **1.** spongy; *Körper*: flabby; *Gesicht: auch* puffy; **2.** *fig. Begriff etc.*: woolly; **II.** *Adv. fig.*: **~** *formuliert* written in woolly language; **Schwammigkeit** *f* **1.** sponginess; *von Körper*: flabbiness; *von Gesicht*: puffiness; **2.** *fig. von Begriff etc.*: woolliness

Schwammtuch *n* sponge cloth

Schwan *m*; -(e)s, *Schwäne* **1.** *Orn.* swan; *mein lieber* **~***! umg.* überrascht: well, I'll be blowed (*Am.* darned)!; *verstärkend*: I (can) tell you; *vorwurfsvoll, zum Kind*: and I'm not joking; **2.** *nur Sg.*, *Astron.* *der* **~** Cygnus

schwand *Imperf.* → **schwinden**

schwanen *v/i.* *umg.*: *mir schwant od. es schwant mir, dass ...* something tells me that ..., I have a feeling that ...; *mir schwant nichts Gutes* I have a nasty feeling something's gone wrong (*od.* something awful is going to happen *etc.*)

Schwanen|gesang *m* *fig.* swansong; **~hals** *m* **1.** *Tech.* gooseneck; **2.** *fig. hum.* (*langer Hals*) swan neck

schwang *Imperf.* → **schwingen**

Schwang *m*: *im* **~**(*e*) *sein* (*in Mode sein*) be the fashion, be in (*od.* with

---

it) *umg.*

schwanger *Adj.* pregnant; *förm.* expectant; **~** *sein* *auch* be expecting; *im dritten Monat* **~** three months pregnant; *mit e-m Plan etc.* **~** *gehen* *umg.*, be hatching (out) a plan *etc.*

...schwanger *im Adj.*: *bedeutungs~* pregnant with meaning; *hoffnungs~* full of hope

Schwangere *f*; *-n*, *-n* pregnant woman, expectant mother

Schwangeren|beratung *f* antenatal (*Am.* prenatal) counsel(l)ing; **~fürsorge** *f* antenatal (*Am.* prenatal) care; **~gymnastik** *f* antenatal (*Am.* prenatal) exercises *Pl.*

schwängern *v/t.* **1.** make *s.o.* pregnant; **2.** *fig.* impregnate; *von Rauch geschwängert* thick with smoke

Schwangerschaft *f* pregnancy; *während der* **~** during pregnancy, while (one is) pregnant

Schwangerschafts|abbruch *m* abortion; **~beschwerden** *Pl.* pregnancy disorders; **~erbrechen** *n* morning sickness; **~gymnastik** *f* antenatal (*Am.* prenatal) exercises *Pl.*; **~konfliktberatung** *f* counsel(l)ing on pregnancy options; **~monat** *m* month of pregnancy; **~streifen** *Pl.* stretch marks, striae *fachspr.*; **~test** *m* pregnancy test; **~unterbrechung** *f* abortion; **~verhütung** *f* contraception; **~vorsorge** *f* antenatal (*Am.* prenatal) care; **~woche** *f* week of pregnancy; **~zeichen** *n* sign of pregnancy

Schwank *m*; -(e)s, *Schwänke* **1.** *Theat.* farce; **2.** *umg.* (amusing) story, anecdote; *Schwänke aus s-r Jugend* adventures of his youth

schwanken *v/i.* **1.** (*hat geschwankt*) sway; *Boden, Gelände: auch* shake, tremble; *Boot*: rock (from side to side); (*taumeln*) sway (from side to side), totter; *bes. Betrunkener: auch* stagger, reel; **2.** (*ist*) stagger, totter; *er schwankte über die Straße / aus dem Lokal* he tottered (*od.* staggered) across the street / out of the pub (*Am.* bar); **3.** (*hat*) *fig.* (*unentschlossen sein*) vacillate, waver, dither; (*sich ändern*) vary; *abwechselnd*: alternate; *Wirts., Kurse, Preise*: fluctuate; *Temperatur, Tech., Messwerte etc.*: fluctuate, vary; *ich schwanke noch fig.* I'm still undecided (*od.* dithering), I haven't made up my mind yet; *zwischen Hoffen und Bangen* **~** waver between hope and anxiety; *die Meinungen* **~** opinions vary; → *auch* **wanken**

Schwanken *n*; *-s*, *kein Pl.* **1.** swaying *etc.*; *ins* **~** *geraten Boot*: start to rock; *Boden*: start to sway (*od.* shake, tremble); *Person*: start to sway (*od.* totter), lose one's balance; **2.** *fig.* variation, fluctuation *etc.*; *ins* **~** *geraten Regierung etc.*: become insecure, begin to totter; *Hoffnung etc.*: be shaken, begin to waver

schwankend I. *Part. Präs.* → **schwanken**; **II.** *Adj.* **1.** swaying *etc.*; → **schwanken**; **2.** *fig.* (*unentschlossen*) undecided, irresolute, wavering; (*unbeständig*) unsteady, unstable (*auch Wirts.*); *Charakter*: unstable *personality*; **III.** *Adv.*: **~** *über die Straße gehen* totter (*od.* stagger) across the street

Schwankung *f* variation (+ *Gen.* in, of); (*Fluktuation*) fluctuation (in, of); (*Abweichung*) deviation; → *auch* **Konjunkturschwankungen, Temperaturschwankung etc.**; *seelische* **~en** emotional ups and downs

---

...schwankung *f*, *im Subst.*: *Blutdruck~* variation (*od.* fluctuation) in blood pressure; *Klima~* climatic variation

Schwankungsbreite *f* range of variation

Schwanz *m*; *-es*, *Schwänze* **1.** *Zool.* tail (*auch Flug. etc., auch Astron.*); *fig.* (*Schluss*) (tail) end; *mit dem* **~** *wedeln Hund*: wag its tail; *den* **~** *einziehen Hund*: put its tail between its legs; *umg. fig. Person*: come down a peg or two; *mit eingezogenem* **~** *abziehen Hund, umg. fig. Person*: slink off with its/one's tail between its/one's legs; *sich auf den* **~** *getreten fühlen umg. fig.* feel miffed (*od.* put out); **2.** *fig.* (*Reihe*) **~** *von Fragen etc.* string of questions *etc.*; *e-n ganzen* **~** *von Konsequenzen nach sich ziehen* have a whole host of consequences; **3.** *vulg.* (*Penis*) prick, cock, dick; **4.** *kein* **~** *umg.* (*niemand*) not a (bloody) soul

...schwanz *m*, *im Subst. Zool., auch fig.*: *Fisch~* fish tail; *Kuh~* cow's tail; *Drachen~* dragon's tail; *e-s Papierdrachens*: kite tail

Schwänzchen *n* **1.** little tail; **2.** *fig.* (*Haar*) pigtail; **3.** *umg.* (*Penis*) dick *Sl., Brit. auch* willy

schwänzeln *v/i.* *Hund*: wag its tail; *Person, beim Gehen*: mince (along); *um j-n* **~** *umg.* toady (*od.* suck up) to *s.o.*

schwänzen *v/t.* *umg.*: (*die Schule*) **~** play truant (*Am.* hookey), *Brit. auch* skive; *e-e Stunde* **~** skip a lesson (*Am.* class)

Schwanzende *n* *Zool.* tip of the tail; *Flug.* tail; *fig.* tail end

Schwänzer *m*; *-s*, -, **~in** *f*; -, *-nen*; *umg.* truant

Schwanz|feder *f* *Orn.* tail feather; **~flosse** *f* *Zool.* tail fin

schwanz|lastig *Adj.* *Flug.* tail-heavy; **~los** *Adj.* tailless

Schwanz|meise *f* *Orn.* long-tailed tit; **~spitze** *f* *Orn., Zool.* tip of the tail; **~stück** *n* tail piece (*auch vom Fisch*); *Rindfleisch*: rump

schwanzwedelnd *Adv.*: *der Hund kam* **~** *auf uns zu* the dog came up to us wagging its tail

schwapp *Interj.* splash; **schwappen** *v/i.* **1.** (*hat geschwappt*) slosh (around); **2.** (*ist*) (*überschwappen*) slop, spill (*auf + Akk.* onto); *die Aids-Welle ist nach Osteuropa geschwappt fig.* the AIDS epidemic has spread into Eastern Europe

Schwäre *f*; -, *-n* abscess, boil; **schwären** *v/i.* fester; (*eitern*) suppurate

Schwarm *m*; *-(e)s*, *Schwärme* **1.** *Insekten*: swarm; *Vögel*: flock; *auffliegender*: flush; *Fische*: shoal; *Personen*: crowd, swarm, herd *umg.*; *die Touristen kamen in Schwärmen umg.* the tourists came in hordes; **2.** *umg.* (*Angebeteter*) idol; *von jungen Mädchen*: heartthrob; *er war der* **~** *aller Schülerinnen* he was every schoolgirl's heartthrob (*od.* pin-up); **3.** (*sehnlicher Wunsch*) dream

schwärmen *v/i.* **1.** (*ist geschwärmt*) *Bienen, Menschen etc.*: swarm; **2.** (*hat*) *umg.* enthuse (*von* about), *stärker*: rave ([on] about); *träumerisch*: dream (of); *für etw.* **~** be mad (*od.* wild, crazy) about s.th.; *wir* **~** *immer noch von dem herrlichen Essen* we're still raving about the wonderful meal; *ins Schwärmen geraten* go into raptures

Schwärmer *m*; *-s*, - **1.** (*Träumer*) dreamer; (*Romantiker*) romantic; (*Be-*

geisterter) enthusiast; *stärker*: fanatic; *bes. Pol. etc.* zealot; **2.** *Zool.* (*Abendfalter*) hawkmoth; **3.** (*Feuerwerkskörper*) squib; **Schwärmerei** *f*; -, -en enthusiasm (**für** for); *stärker*: passion (for); (*Fanatismus*) fanaticism (for); *romantische*: romantic rapture; (*Vergötterung*) idolization, worship (of); **Schwärmerin** *f*; -, -nen → **Schwärmer** 1; **schwärmerisch I.** *Adj. Person*: enthusiastic, *stärker*: gushing; *Worte, Gefühle*: *auch* rapturous, effusive; (*verzückt*) enraptured; *Sekten etc.*: fanatical; **II.** *Adv.* enthusiastically, *stärker*: rapturously, with rapturous enthusiasm; **Schwarmgeist** *m*; *Pl.* -er zealot
Schwärmzeit *f Bienen etc.*: swarming time
Schwarte *f*; -, -n **1.** *von Speck*: rind; *gebratene*: crackling; *Jägerspr.* (*Haut*) skin; **arbeiten, dass die ~ kracht** *umg.* work like crazy; **2. dicke ~** *umg.* (*Buch*) fat tome; **3.** *Med.* pleural scar tissue; **Schwartenmagen** *m Gastr.* brawn, *Am.* headcheese
schwarz I. *Adj.* **1.** *allg.* black (*auch Kaffee, Tee, Hautfarbe*); (*sonnenverbrannt*) ... with a dark tan, dark brown; *umg.* (*schmutzig*) black, filthy; **~ wie die Nacht/Ebenholz** (as) black as night/ebony; **die ~en Amerikaner** the African Americans; **~ werden** (*schmutzig*) get black (*od.* filthy dirty); *Silber*: tarnish, go black; **mir wurde ~ vor Augen** everything went black; **~ von Menschen** Straße etc.: swarming with people; **2.** *feste Kombinationen*: **~e Blattern** *Med.* smallpox; **~es Brett** notice board, bulletin board; **der Schwarze Erdteil** the Dark Continent; **~es Gold** *fig.* black gold; **die ~e Kunst** (*Alchimie*) the black art; (*Druckkunst*) the art of printing; **~e Magie** Black Magic; **der ~e Mann** (*Afrikaner*) the black (man); *umg.* (*Schornsteinfeger*) the chimney sweep; *umg.* (*Kinderschreck*) the bogeyman; **das Schwarze Meer** *Geog.* the Black Sea; **der ~e Tod** *Med. hist.* the Black Death; **Schwarze Witwe** *Zool.* black widow; **3.** *fig.*: **~ auf weiß** in black and white, in cold print; **wieder ~e Zahlen schreiben** be in the black again; **da kann er warten, bis er ~ wird** *umg.* he can wait till he's blue in the face; **4.** (*düster*) black, gloomy; **~er Humor** black humo(u)r; *Theat.* black comedy; **~en Gedanken nachhängen** (*auf Rache sinnen*) be plotting revenge; (*schwermütig sein*) be sunk in gloom (and despondency); **5.** (*ungesetzlich*) illicit, illegal; **~e Kasse** *Pol.* slush fund; **die ~en Konten der Partei** the party's illegal accounts, the party's slush funds; **~e Liste** black list; **6.** *umg. Pol.* (*konservativ*) conservative, right-wing; *BRD*: Christian Democrat; *Reli.* (*katholisch*) Catholic; **7.** (*schlecht*) **~er Tag** black day; **der Schwarze Freitag** Black Friday; **8. ~es Loch** *Astron.* black hole; **9. ~er Peter** (*Spiel*) *etwa* old maid; **j-m den ~en Peter zuspielen** *umg. fig.* pass the buck to s.o.; **10.** *Kartenspiel*: **~ werden** not win a single trick; **→ Schaf** etc.; **II.** *Adv.* **1.** *geschrieben, gekleidet etc.*: in black; *färben, streichen*: black; **~ gerändert** *Umschlag etc.*: *mst attr.* black-edged; *Augen*: dark-rimmed; **~ gestreift** black-striped, with black stripes; **~ umrandet** with a black border; **s-n Kaffee/Tee ~ trinken** drink one's coffee black / one's tea without milk; **2.** (*illegal*) illegally, illi-

citly; **~ kaufen/verkaufen** buy/sell on the black market; **~ Schnaps brennen** distil(l) spirits (*Am.* liquor) illicitly; **etw. ~ machen lassen** (*in Schwarzarbeit*) have s.th. made by a moonlighter; → *auch* **schwarzfahren** etc.; **3.** *pessimistisch*: **~ malen** paint a gloomy picture (of), see the gloomy side (of); *grundsätzlich*: take a very pessimistic view (of); **~ sehen** be pessimistic (**für** about), take a dim view of things; *grundsätzlich*: always look on the dark side of things; **da sehe ich aber schwarz** I don't think there's much hope, things don't look too good; **4.** *umg.*: **sich ~ ärgern** be hopping mad; **ich hab mich ~ geärgert** (*über mich selbst*) I could have kicked myself; **5.** *Pol.*: **~ wählen** vote for the right-wing candidate *bzw.* party; *BRD*: vote Christian Democrat; *Österreich*: vote for the People's Party; → *auch* **blau, schwarz**
Schwarz *n*; -(es), *kein Pl.* black (*auch Farbe, Kleidung, beim Spiel*); **reines ~** pure black; **in ~ gehen** *od.* **~ tragen** be (dressed) in black, wear black; **ganz in ~ gekleidet sein** be dressed entirely in black; **aus ~ Weiß machen wollen** *fig.* try to twist things
Schwarzafrika *n* black Africa, sub-Saharan Africa; **Schwarzafrikaner** *m*, **Schwarzafrikanerin** *f* black African, *weiblich auch*: black African woman (*od.* girl); **schwarzafrikanisch** *Adj.* black African
Schwarzamerikaner *m*, **~in** *f* Afro-American, African American, *weiblich auch*: Afro-American (*od.* African American) woman (*od.* girl)
Schwarzarbeit *f*; *nur Sg.* illicit work, moonlighting *umg.*; **schwarzarbeiten** *v/i.* (*trennb., hat -ge-*) work on the side, moonlight *umg.*; **Schwarzarbeiter** *m*, **Schwarzarbeiterin** *f* illicit worker, moonlighter *umg.*
schwarzäugig *Adj.* black-eyed, dark-eyed
Schwarz|bär *m Zool.* black bear; **~bau** *m*: **bei dem Gartenhaus handelt es sich um e-n ~** the summer house was built without planning permission; **~beere** *f* bilberry, *bes. Am.* blueberry
schwarz|blau *Adj.* bluish black, blue-black; **~braun** *Adj.* brownish black
Schwarz|brenner *m* moonshiner *bes. Am. umg.*; **~brennerei** *f* illicit distilling; (*Anlage*) illicit (*umg.* moonshine) still
Schwarzbrot *n Gastr.* black bread
schwarzbunt *Adj. Vieh*: black and white; **Schwarzbunte** *f*; -n, -n Frisian (*Am.* Holstein) cow
Schwarze¹ *m, f*; -n, -n **1.** black, *weiblich auch*: black woman (*od.* girl); **2.** *umg.* (*Katholik[in]*) Catholic; (*Konservative[in]*) conservative, right-winger; *BRD*: Christian Democrat; **die ~n wählen** vote for a right-wing party (*BRD*: for the Christian Democrats, *Österreich*: for the People's Party); **3.** *umg.* (*Schwarzhaarige[r]*) black-haired type
Schwarze² *n*; -n, -n **1.** *nur Sg.*; *Zielscheibe*: bull's eye; **du hast ins ~ getroffen!** you've hit the nail on the head!, spot (*Am.* right) on!; **2.** **das kleine ~** (*Kleid*) that little black dress (*umg.* number); **3.** *nur Sg.*: **j-m nicht das ~ unter dem Nagel gönnen** *umg.* begrudge s.o. every little thing
Schwarze³ *m*; -n, -n; *bes. österr.* (*Kaffee*) black coffee

Schwärze *f*; -, *kein Pl.* **1.** blackness (*auch fig.*); (*Dunkelheit*) pitch darkness; **2.** (*Druckerschwärze*) printer's ink; (*Farbe*) black dye; **schwärzen** *v/t.* blacken (*auch fig.*), black; **geschwärzt von** black(ened) with
Schwarzenviertel *n* black neighbo(u)rhood
Schwarzerde *f Geol.* black earth
schwarzfahren *v/i.* (*unreg., trennb., ist -ge-*) **1.** *im Bus etc.*: travel without a ticket, ride without paying; *grundsätzlich*: be a fare dodger; (*das*) **Schwarzfahren kann teuer werden** fare-dodging can come expensive; **2.** *Mot.* drive without a licen|ce (*Am.* -se); **Schwarzfahrer** *m*, **Schwarzfahrerin** *f im Bus etc.*: fare dodger
Schwarz|geld *n* illicit earnings *Pl.*; **~geldaffäre** *f Pol.* illicit funds scandal
schwarz|grau *Adj.* greyish (*Am.* grayish) black; **~haarig** *Adj. attr.* black-haired
Schwarzhandel *m* black market; (*Tätigkeit*) black marketeering; **im ~** on the black market; **Schwarzhändler** *m*, **Schwarzhändlerin** *f* black marketeer; *mit Karten*: (ticket) tout, *Am.* scalper
schwarzhören *v/i.* listen (to the radio) without a licen|ce (*Am.* -se), be a radio-licen|ce (*Am.* -se) dodger (*Am.* scofflaw); **Schwarzhörer** *m*, **Schwarzhörerin** *f* radio-licen|ce (*Am.* -se) dodger (*Am.* scofflaw)
Schwarzkittel *m umg.* **1.** (*Wildschwein*) wild boar; **2.** *pej.* (*Geistlicher*) cleric; **3.** *Sport* referee, umpire
schwärzlich *Adj.* blackish
schwarz malen → **schwarz** II 3
Schwarzmaler *m umg.* pessimist; *stärker*: prophet of doom; **Schwarzmalerei** *f umg.* pessimism; (*Bild*) pessimistic view; (*Vorhersagen*) pessimistic (*od.* gloomy) forecasts *Pl.*; **Schwarzmalerin** *f umg.* → **Schwarzmaler**
Schwarzmarkt *m* black market; **~kurs** *m* black market exchange rate
Schwarz|pulver *n* black powder, gunpowder; **~rock** *m umg.* (*Geistlicher*) cleric
Schwarz-Rot-Gold *n* black, red and gold; **schwarzrotgold(en)** *Adj.* black, red and gold; **die schwarzrotgoldene Fahne** the black, red and gold flag, the German national flag
schwarzschlachten *vt/i.* (*trennb., hat -ge-*) *in Notzeiten*: slaughter (a pig etc.) illegally; **Schwarzschlachtung** *f* illegal slaughtering
schwarzsehen *v/i.* (*unreg., trennb., hat -ge-*) *TV* watch TV without a licen|ce (*Am.* -se), be a TV-licen|ce (*Am.* -se) dodger (*Am.* scofflaw); → **schwarz** II 3
Schwarzseher *m* **1.** pessimist, prophet of doom; **2.** *TV* TV-licen|ce (*Am.* -se) dodger (*Am.* scofflaw); **Schwarzseherei** *f*; -, -en, *mst Sg.*; *pej.* pessimism, gloomy views *Pl.*; **schwarzseherisch** *Adj.* pessimistic, *attr. auch* alarmist
schwarz umrandet *Adj.* → **schwarz** II 1
Schwarz|specht *m Orn.* black woodpecker; **~storch** *m Orn.* black stork; **~tee** *m* black tea
Schwarzwald *m*; -(e)s; *Geog.*: **der ~** the Black Forest
Schwarzwälder¹ *Adj.*: **~ Kirschtorte** Black Forest gateau (*Am.* cake)
Schwarzwälder² *m*, **~in** *f*; -, -nen inhabitant of the Black Forest
schwarzweiß I. *Adj. präd.* black and

white, *attr.* black-and-white (*Abk.* B&W, b&w) ...; **II.** *Adv.*: ~ **gestreift** with black and white stripes; ~ **fotografieren** take black-and-white photographs; ~ **malen** *fig.* depict (*od.* see) everything in (terms of) black and white

Schwarzweiß|aufnahme *f* black-and-white photograph; ~**film** *m* black-and-white film (*Am. auch* movie); ~**foto** *n* black-and-white photo (*od.* print); ~**fotografie** *f* **1.** *Verfahren:* black-and-white photography; **2.** (*Aufnahme*) black-and-white photograph; ~**malerei** *f*; *nur Sg.*, *fig.* seeing (*od.* depicting) everything in terms of black and white; *im Einzelfall:* black-and-white portrayal; ~**zeichnung** *f* black-and-white drawing

Schwarz|wild *n Koll.*; *Zool.* wild boar; ~**wurzel** *f Bot.* scorzonera, black salsify

Schwatz *m*; *-es*, *kein Pl.*, **Schwätzchen** *n umg.* chat, *Brit. auch* natter; *ein Schwätzchen halten* have a chat

schwatzen I. *v/i. umg.* (*plaudern*) chat, *Brit. auch* natter; (*inhaltlos reden*) blather on; *in der Schule:* talk (in class); (*klatschen*) gossip; (*ausplaudern*) talk, blab; *hört endlich auf zu ~!* stop chattering!; **II.** *v/t.* say; *dummes Zeug ~* talk a lot of nonsense (*od.* drivel)

Schwatzen *n*; *-s*, *kein Pl.*; *umg.* chatting; *inhaltloses:* blathering on; (*Klatschen*) gossiping; (*Ausplaudern*) talking, blabbing; *in der Schule:* **ein Eintrag wegen ~s** an entry in the register for talking in class

schwätzen *vt/i.* → **schwatzen**; **Schwätzer** *m*; *-s*, *-*; *umg.* prattler; *hochtrabend:* gasbag, windbag; (*Klatschtante*) gossip

Schwatzerei *f*; *-*, *-en*, **Schwätzerei** *f*; *-*, *-en*; *umg.* prattle, chatter; (*Klatsch*) gossip; *im Unterricht:* talking (in class); (*das Schwatzen*) *auch* chatting; (*Klatscherei*) gossiping; **Schwätzerin** *f*; *-*, *-nen*; *umg.* → **Schwätzer**

schwatzhaft *Adj.* talkative; *Stil, Dialoge:* chatty; **Schwatzhaftigkeit** *f* talkativeness; *von Stil, Dialog:* chattiness

Schwatz|maul *n*, ~**tante** *f umg.* prattler; (*bes. Kind*) chatterbox; (*Klatschtante*) gossip

Schwebe *f* **1.** *sich in der ~ halten* Vogel etc.: hover; *Ballon etc.:* float in the air; **2.** *fig. in der ~ sein* be undecided (*od.* in the balance); *Jur., Verfahren:* be pending; ~**bahn** *f* suspension railway; (*Seilbahn*) cable railway; ~**balken** *m Turnen:* (balance) beam

schweben *v/i.* **1.** (*hat*) *südd., österr., schw. ist geschwebt*) (*hängen*) be suspended, hang; *über e-r Stelle, Vogel etc.:* hover (*auch Ton*); *über dem Abgrund ~* hover above the abyss; *fig.* be faced with imminent disaster; *ihm war, als ob er schwebte* he felt as if he was walking on air; *über den Wolken ~, in höheren Regionen od. Sphären ~* *fig.* have one's head in the clouds; *in Illusionen ~* live in a world of fantasy; *noch im Raum ~* Ton: linger on; *j-m vor Augen ~* → **vorschweben**; *in Gefahr ~* be in danger; → **Lebensgefahr**. **2.** (*ist*) *durch die Luft:* float; *Vogel:* glide; (*hoch dahingleiten*) soar; (*gleiten*) glide (*über + Akk.* across); *die Tänzerin schwebte über die Bühne* the dancer floated (*od.* glided) across the stage; *zu Walzermusik schwebten wir durch den Saal* we

swept (*leichtfüßig:* glided) through the room to the music of a waltz; **3.** (*hat / südd., österr., schw. ist geschwebt*) *fig.* (*unentschieden sein*) be undecided; *in Ungewissheit ~* be (kept) in suspense; *zwischen Furcht und Hoffnung ~* hover between fear and hope; → *auch* **Schwebe**

schwebend I. *Part. Präs.* → **schweben**; **II.** *Adj.* floating, hovering *etc.*; → **schweben**; *Frage, Jur. Verfahren etc.:* pending; ~**en Schrittes daherkommen** come gliding along

Schwebezustand *m fig.* state of suspense; (*Zwischenstadium*) limbo

Schwebstoffe *Pl. Chem.* suspended matter *Sg.*

Schwede *m*; *-n*, *-n* Swede; ~ *sein* be Swedish; *hallo, alter ~ umg. fig.* hi there, old friend (*Am.* buddy); **Schweden** (*n*); *-s Geog.* Sweden

Schweden|platte *f Gastr.* dish of smorgasbord; ~**punsch** *m* Swedish (*od.* arrack) punch

Schwedin *f*; *-*, *-nen* Swede, Swedish woman (*od.* girl); **schwedisch I.** *Adj.* Swedish; *hinter ~en Gardinen umg. hum.* behind bars; **II. Schwedisch** *n*; *-en*; *Ling.* Swedish; *das Schwedische* Swedish

Schwefel *m*; *-s*, *kein Pl.*; *Chem.* sulphur, *Am.* sulfur

schwefelarm *Adj. attr.* low-sul|phur (*Am.* -fur)

Schwefel|bad *n* **1.** *Chem.* sul|phur (*Am.* -fur) bath; **2.** *Med.* (*Kurort*) (spa with) sul|phur (*Am.* -fur) springs *Pl.*; ~**dioxid** *n Chem.* sul|phur (*Am.* -fur) dioxide; ~**eisen** *n Chem.* iron (*od.* ferrous) sul|phide (*Am.* -fide)

schwefelfarben *Adj.* sul|phur (*Am.* -fur) yellow

Schwefelgehalt *m Chem.* sul|phur (*Am.* -fur) content

schwefel|gelb *Adj.* sul|phur (*Am.* -fur) yellow; ~**haltig** *Adj.* sul|phur(e)ous (*Am.* -fur(e)ous)

Schwefelkohlenstoff *m Chem.* carbon disul|phide (*Am.* -fide)

schwefeln *v/t. Chem.* sulphurate, *Am.* sulfurate; *auch Tech.* sulphurize, *Am.* sulfurize; (*ausräuchern*) fumigate with sul|phur (*Am.* -fur)

Schwefel|puder *n* sul|phur (*Am.* -fur) powder; ~**quelle** *f* sul|phur (*Am.* -fur) spring

schwefelsauer *Adj. Chem.* sulphuric, *Am.* sulfuric; *in bestimmten Verbindungen auch:* sul|phate (*Am.* -fate) of; *schwefelsaures Ammoniak* ammonium sul|phate (*Am.* -fate)

Schwefel|säure *f Chem.* sul|phuric (*Am.* -furic) acid; ~**wasserstoff** *m* hydrogen sul|phide (*Am.* -fide)

schweflig *Adj. Chem.* sulphurous, *Am.* sulfurous; ~**e Säure** sulphurous (*Am.* sulfurous) acid

Schweif *m*; *-(e)s*, *-e* tail (*auch Astron.*); *fig. von Anhängern etc.:* retinue, train; *vom Wein:* lingering aftertaste

schweifen I. *v/i.* wander, roam, rove; *den Blick / s-e Gedanken ~ lassen* let one's gaze/mind wander; **II.** *v/t. Tech.* curve

Schweige|geld *n* hush money; ~**marsch** *m* silent (protest) march; ~**minute** *f:* (*e-e*) ~ (a *od.* one) minute's silence, (a) one-minute silence (*zu Ehren + Gen.* in memory of; *einlegen* observe)

schweigen *v/i.*; *schweigt, schwieg, hat geschwiegen* **1.** (*still sein*) be (*od.* remain) silent; (*nicht antworten*) say

nothing, not say anything, not say a word; *... - ganz zu ~ von* ... - let alone, never mind, to say nothing of; **2.** (*zu etw. nichts sagen*) say nothing, remain silent; *zu etw. ~* make no comment on s.th.; ~ *über* (+ *Akk.*) keep silent about; *auf e-e Frage ~* make no reply (to a question), ignore a question; *zu j-s Vorwürfen ~* make no attempt to defend o.s. (against s.o.'s reproaches); *zu e-m Unrecht ~* not protest against an injustice; *ich habe lange zu od. über ...* (+ *Akk.*) *geschwiegen, aber jetzt ...* I have long remained silent (*od.* for a long time I have said nothing) about ..., but now ...; *schweig bloß davon!* don't mention that; *darüber schweigt das Gesetz* the law makes no mention of that; **3.** (*aufhören*) Lärm *etc.*: stop, cease; *seit heute ~ die Waffen* the ceasefire began today, *lit.* the guns fell silent today; **4.** (*für sich behalten*) keep one's mouth shut; *kannst du ~?* can you keep it to yourself (*od.* keep a secret)?; ~ *wie ein Grab* shut up like a clam

Schweigen *n*; *-s*, *kein Pl.* silence; ~ *bewahren* keep silent; *j-n zum ~ bringen* reduce s.o. to silence; *durch Drohungen, auch Mil.* silence s.o.; (*Kinder etc.*) make s.o. shut up; *sich* (*Dat.*) *j-s ~ erkaufen* bribe s.o. to say nothing; → **hüllen**, **Reden**

schweigend I. *Part. Präs.* → **schweigen**; **II.** *Adj.* silent; ~**e Mehrheit** *Pol.* silent majority; **III.** *Adv.*: in silence, without a word; *er ging ~ darüber hinweg* he made no mention of it, he ignored it

Schweigepflicht *f* (mandatory) professional secrecy; *die ärztliche ~* medical confidentiality; *der ~ unterliegen* be bound to observe confidentiality (*od.* professional secrecy)

Schweiger *m*; *-s*, *-* taciturn person, man of few words

schweigsam *Adj.* quiet; (*schweigend*) silent; (*wortkarg*) *auch* taciturn, uncommunicative; (*verschwiegen*) discreet; **Schweigsamkeit** *f* quietness; (*Schweigen*) silence; (*schweigsame Art*) taciturnity, uncommunicativeness; (*Verschwiegenheit*) discretion

Schwein *n*; *-(e)s*, *-e* **1.** *Zool.* pig, *bes. Am. auch* hog; (*Sau*) sow; (*Fleisch*) pork; *Cordon Bleu etc. vom ~ Gastr.* pork cordon bleu *etc.*; *wie ein ~ bluten umg.* bleed like a stuck pig; *er isst wie ein ~ pej.* he eats like a pig; **2.** *umg. pej.* (*schmutziger Kerl*) (filthy) pig; *umg. pej.* (*Lump*) swine, bastard *Sl.*; *kein ~ umg.* not a (blessed) soul; *das glaubt dir doch kein ~ umg.* you don't think anyone's going to buy that, do you?; *armes ~ umg.* poor wretch (*od.* bastard), *Brit. Sl. auch* poor sod; *faules ~ umg. pej.* lazy bastard, foul swine; **3.** ~ *haben umg.* be lucky (*od.* in luck); *da hast du aber ~ gehabt! umg.* talk about luck!

...schwein *n*, *im Subst.* **1.** *Zool.:* **Mutter~** mother sow; *Fluss~* river hog; *Nabel~* peccary, Mexican hog; **2.** *fig. pej.:* *Nazi~* Nazi bastard; *Kapitalisten~* capitalist pig

Schweinchen *n* little pig, piglet; *fig. umg.* (*Schmutzfink*) piggy, *Brit. auch* mucky pup

Schweine|arbeit *f umg.* dirty work; (*schwierige Arbeit*) beastly job; ~**bande** *f pej.* collection of bastards; ~**bauch** *m Gastr.* belly of pork; ~**bra-**

ten *m Gastr.* joint of pork; *gebraten*: roast pork; **~bucht** *f Geog.* Bay of Pigs; **~filet** *n Gastr.* fillet of pork; **~fleisch** *n Gastr.* pork; **~fraß** *m umg. fig. pej.* pigswill; **~futter** *n* pigfeed; *umg. fig. pej.* pigswill

Schweinegeld *n umg.*: **ein ~** heaps of money; **ein ~ verdienen** earn a packet (*Am.* bundle), rake it in

Schweine|hals *m* neck of pork; **~hirt** *m*, **~hirtin** *f altm.* swineherd

Schweinehund *m pej.* swine, bastard; **der innere ~** *umg.* one's baser instincts; **den inneren ~ überwinden** *umg.* get the better of one's alter ego

Schweine|keule *f Gastr.* leg of pork; **~koben** *m Agr.* pigsty, *Am.* pigpen; **~kotelett** *n Gastr.* pork chop; **~lende** *f Gastr.* pork tenderloin; **~mast** *f* pig fattening; **~mästerei** *f* pig-fattening unit; **~nacken** *m* blade shoulder of pork; **~pest** *f* swine fever, *Am.* hog cholera; **~pfote** *f* pig's trotter

Schweinepriester *m umg. pej.* bastard, *Am. auch* son of a bitch

Schweinerei *f, -, -en; umg.* **1.** (*Unordnung*) mess; (*Arbeit*) messy business; **das ist ja e-e ~ hier!** this place looks disgusting (*od.* like a pigsty, *Am. auch* pigpen); **2.** *fig.* (*Gemeinheit*) disgraceful business, scandal; **3.** (*Zote*) dirty joke; *stärker*: obscenity; *Pl.* smut *Sg.*; (*Verhalten*) *auch Pl.* obscenity, obscene behavio(u)r

Schweinerippchen *n Gastr.* spare rib (of pork)

Schweinerne *n; -n, kein Pl.; südd., österr.* roast pork

Schweine|rollbraten *m Gastr.* roast rolled pork; **~rücken** *m* saddle of pork; **~rüssel** *m* pig's snout; **~schinken** *m Gastr.* (pork) ham; **~schmalz** *n Gastr.* lard, *Brit. auch* dripping; **~schnitzel** *n Gastr.* pork escalope; **~schulter** *f Gastr.* shoulder of pork; **~seuche** *f* swine plague; **~speck** *m Gastr.* (pork) bacon; **~stall** *m* pigsty (*auch fig. pej.*), *Am. auch* pigpen; **dein Zimmer ist der reinste ~** *umg. pej.* your room is an appalling mess; **~steak** *n Gastr.* pork steak; **~zucht** *f* pig-breeding, *Am. auch* hog-raising; (*Betrieb*) pig-breeding unit; **~züchter** *m*, **~züchterin** *f* pig-breeder, *Am. auch* hog-raiser

Schweinigel *m; -s, -; umg.* **1.** (*Schmutzfink*) dirty pig, *Brit. auch* mucky pup; **2.** (*unanständiger Kerl*) dirty old man, dirty bugger *vulg. Sl.*; **Schweinigelei** *f, -, -en; umg.* **1.** dirty (*od.* smutty) remark (*Witz*: joke); *stärker*: obscenity; **2.** (*das Schweinigeln*) talking smut; (*Witzemachen*) telling dirty (*od.* smutty) jokes; **schweinigeln** *v/i.* (*untr., hat ge-*) *umg.* talk smut; (*Witze machen*) tell dirty (*od.* smutty) jokes

schweinisch *umg.* **I.** *Adj.* **1.** (*schmutzig*) filthy; **2.** *Witz etc.*: dirty, smutty; *Benehmen*: swinish, disgusting; **II.** *Adv.*: **sich ~ benehmen** behave disgustingly

Schweinkram *m umg.* → **Schweinerei** 1, 3

Schweins|... *im Subst. siehe auch* **Schweine...**; **~äuglein** *Pl. umg.* piggy eyes; **~füße** *Pl. Gastr.* pig's trotters; **~galopp** *m umg.*: **im ~** at (*Am.* on) the double, in double-quick time; **~haxe** *f Gastr.* knuckle of pork; **~kopf** *m* pig's head; **~kopfsülze** *f Gastr.* headcheese, brawn; **~leder** *n*, **²ledern** *Adj.* pigskin; **~ohr** *n* **1.** pig's ear; **2.** (*Gebäck*) Danish whirl (*Am.* pastry);

3. *Bot.* cantharellus

Schweiß *m; -es, kein Pl.* **1.** sweat; *formeller*: perspiration; **in ~ geraten** get into a sweat; **mir brach der ~ aus** I broke into a sweat; **ihm stand der ~ auf der Stirn** there were beads of sweat (*od.* the sweat stood out) on his brow; **in ~ gebadet** → **schweißgebadet**; **nach ~ riechen** smell (of sweat), have b.o. (*od.* BO, body odo[u]r); **es hat viel ~ gekostet** *fig.* it was hard work (a hard slog *umg.*, a real sweat *Sl.*); **im ~e s-s Angesichts** by the sweat of one's brow; **2.** *Jägerspr.* blood; **~absonderung** *f* perspiration

Schweißarbeiten *Pl. Tech.* welding operations

Schweiß|ausbruch *m*: **e-n ~ bekommen** break into a sweat; **~band** *n Sport* sweatband

schweißbedeckt *Adj. Gesicht*: sweaty, perspiring; *präd.* → **schweißgebadet**

Schweiß|brenner *m Tech.* welding torch; **~brille** *f*: (*e-e*) (a pair of) welding goggles *Pl.*

Schweißdrüse *f Physiol.* sweat gland

schweißen I. *v/t./i. Tech.* weld; **II.** *v/i. Jägerspr.* bleed; **Schweißer** *m; -s, -*, **Schweißerin** *f; -, -nen; Tech.* welder

Schweiß|fleck *m* sweat mark; **~füße** *Pl.* sweaty (*übel riechend*: smelly *umg.*) feet

schweißgebadet *Adj.* nur *präd.* bathed in sweat, dripping with sweat (*od.* perspiration)

Schweißgerät *n Tech.* welding apparatus

Schweiß|geruch *m* smell of sweat, body odo(u)r; **~hände** *Pl.* sweaty palms; **~hund** *m Jägerspr.* bloodhound

schweißig *Adj.* **1.** sweaty; **2.** *Jägerspr.*, *Tier*: bleeding; *Fährte*: bloody

Schweißnaht *f Tech.* weld(ed joint), (welding) seam

schweißnass *Adj. attr.* sweaty, *präd.* wet with (*stärker*: soaked in) sweat (*od.* perspiration)

Schweiß|perle *f* bead of perspiration; **~pore** *f* sweat pore

Schweiß|stelle *f* weld; **~technik** *f* welding technology

schweiß|treibend *Adj. Med.* sudorific, sweat-inducing; **~es Mittel** sudorific (agent); **~triefend** *Adj.* dripping with sweat (*od.* perspiration)

Schweißtropfen *m* bead of sweat (*od.* perspiration)

schweißüberströmt *Adj. Gesicht etc.*: streaming with sweat (*od.* perspiration)

Schweißung *f Tech.* welding; (*Ergebnis*) weld

Schweißverfahren *n Tech.* welding process

schweißverklebt *Adj.* sticky with sweat

Schweiz *f; -; Geog.* Switzerland; **aus/in der ~** from/in Switzerland; **in die ~** to Switzerland; **die deutsche/französische/italienische ~** German/French/Italian Switzerland

Schweizer I. *m; -s, -*; **1.** Swiss; **er ist ~** he is Swiss; **die ~** the Swiss (*Pl.*); **2.** *Agr.* (*Beruf*) dairyman; **3.** → **Schweizergardist**; **II.** *Adj.* Swiss; **~ Käse** Swiss cheese, *bes.* Emmental; **~ Messer** Swiss army knife

schweizerdeutsch *Adj.* Swiss German; **Schweizerdeutsch** *n; Ling.* Swiss German; **das ~e** Swiss German

Schweizer|garde *f* Swiss Guard; **~gardist** *m* Swiss Guard; **~haus** *n* traditional Swiss-style wooden house, chalet

Schweizerin *f, -, -nen* Swiss (woman *od.* girl)

schweizerisch *Adj.* Swiss

Schwelbrand *m* smo(u)ldering fire; **schwelen I.** *v/i.* smo(u)lder; *fig. auch* simmer; **in ihr schwelt der Hass** *geh.* hate smo(u)lders within her breast; **II.** *v/t. Tech.* carbonize at low temperature; (*Teer*) distil(l); **Schwelerei** *f, -, -en; Tech.* low temperature carbonization plant

schwelgen *v/i.* **1.** **~ in** (+ *Dat.*) revel in; *gröber*: wallow in; **der Film schwelgt nur so in Gefühlen** the film is a real emotional wallow; **in Farben** indulge in a riot of colo(u)r; **2.** (*essen und trinken*) indulge o.s., have a binge *umg.*; **Schwelgerei** *f; -, -en* (over)indulgence; (*Essen und Trinken*) *auch* feasting; **schwelgerisch I.** *Adj.* overindulgent, extravagant; (*sinnlich*) voluptuous; (*ausschweifend*) debauched; *Essen*: opulent, sumptuous; **II.** *Adv.*: **~ tafeln** enjoy a sumptuous meal; **~ erzählen** *etc.* tell stories *etc.* in an extravagant style

Schwelle *f; -, -n* **1.** *von Tür*: threshold (*auch Psych. und fig.*); *konkret*: step; **sie soll keinen Fuß mehr über m-e ~ setzen** *fig.* she'd better not darken my door again; **an der ~ e-r neuen Zeit** on the threshold of a new age; **an der ~ zum Erwachsensein stehen** be on the brink of adulthood; **an der ~ des Grabes** at death's door; **2.** *Eisenb.* sleeper, *bes. Am.* tie; **3.** *Geog.* swell

schwellen¹ (*schwillt, schwoll, ist geschwollen*) *v/i.* swell (*auch Lärm*); *Wasser*: auch rise; **das Flüsschen schwoll zu e-m reißenden Strom** the little river grew into a mighty torrent; → *auch* **anschwellen, geschwollen**

schwellen² *v/t.* **1.** swell; (*Segel*) fill out, billow; **die Brust ~** puff one's chest out; **mit stolzgeschwellter Brust** as proud as Punch, as proud as a peacock; **2.** *Dial.* (*kochen*) boil

Schwellen|angst *f Psych.* fear of entering unfamiliar places; *vor Unbekanntem*: etwa fear of the unknown; **~land** *n Pol.* newly industrialized country, NIC; **~preis** *m Wirts.* threshold price; **~wert** *m* threshold value

Schwellkörper *m Anat.* erectile tissue

Schwellung *f* swelling; (*Stelle*) *auch* swollen spot; **starke/abklingende ~** bad swelling / swelling that is going down

Schwemme *f; -, -n* **1.** watering place; **zur ~ führen** lead to the water; **2.** (*Bierlokal*) pub, *Am.* bar (*od.* tavern); (*Bierstube*) taproom; **3.** *Wirts.* (*Überangebot*) glut (**an** + *Dat.* of)

...schwemme *f, im Subst.* **1.** *von Ware*: **Obst~** glut of fruit; **2.** *fig.*: **Akademiker~** glut (*od.* excess) of university (*Am.* college) graduates

schwemmen *v/t.* wash (**an Land** ashore)

Schwemm|land *n* alluvial land (*od.* plain); **~stein** *m* alluvial gravel

Schwengel *m; -s, -* **1.** *e-r Glocke*: clapper, tongue; *e-r Pumpe*: handle; **2.** *vulg.* (*Penis*) cock, dick

Schwenk *m; -(e)s, -s* **1.** swing, swerve; **e-n ~ nach rechts/links machen** swing (*Mil.* wheel) to the right/left; *fig. politisch*: veer to the right/left; **2.** → **Schwenkaufnahme**; **~aufnahme** *f Film*: pan (shot) (**auf** +*Akk.* of); *vertikal*: tilt (shot)

Schwenkarm *m* swivel arm

schwenkbar *Adj. attr.* swivel ..., swivel(l)ing; *Kran etc.*: slewing, *Am.* slu-ing; **~ sein** be capable of swivel(l)ing

schwenken I. *v/t. (hat)* **1.** (*schwingen*) swing; (*Hut, Tuch etc.*) wave; (*Stock etc.*) brandish, flourish; **2.** *Tech.* swivel; (*Kran*) slew, *Am.* slue; **3.** (*Kamera*) pan; **4.** (*schütteln*) shake; *Gastr.* (*Kartoffeln etc.*) *in Butter etc.*: toss; **5.** (*ausspülen*) rinse; **II.** *v/i. (ist)* swing ([a]round); *Mil.* wheel (about, *Am.* around); *Kamera*: pan; **nach links/ rechts ~** *Auto*: swing to the left/right; *plötzlich*: swerve (to the) left/right; *fig. politisch*: veer to the right/left

Schwenker *m; -s, -* **1.** *für Kognak*: brandy balloon, *Am.* (brandy) snifter; **2.** *TV, Film*: cameraman's assistant

Schwenk|flügel *m Flug.* swing wing; **~kartoffeln** *Pl. Gastr.* potatoes tossed in butter; **~kran** *m Tech.* swivel (*od.* slewing) crane

Schwenkung *f* **1.** *Kran*: slewing, *Am.* sluing; *Mil.* wheel; *taktische*: wheeling man|oeuvre (*Am.* -euver); *der Filmkamera*: pan; *fig.* change of heart; *Pol.* change of alignment; **2.** (*völlige Umkehrung*) about-turn, volte-face

Schwenkvorrichtung *f* swivel mechanism

schwer I. *Adj.* **1.** *gewichtsmäßig*: heavy; **wie ~ bist du?** how much do you weigh?; **es ist zwei Pfund ~** it weighs (*od.* it's) two pounds; **ein drei Pfund ~er Braten** *etc.* a three-pound roast *etc.*; **2.** *fig., Angriff, Parfüm, Schritt, Unwetter, Verluste, Wein etc.*: heavy; (*gewichtig*) weighty; (*drückend*) oppressive; *Speise*: rich; (*schwer verdaulich*) heavy; *Zigarre, Duft*: strong; **~e Maschine** (*Motorrad*) powerful machine; **~er Boden** heavy soil, clay; **~es Gold** solid gold; **~es Wasser** *Chem.* heavy water; **~er Atem** labo(u)red breathing; **ich habe e-n ~en Kopf** my head's throbbing; **~en Herzens** reluctantly; (*traurig*) with a heavy heart; **3.** **~es Geld verdienen** *umg.* make big money, make a packet (*Am.* bundle); **~es Geld kosten** *umg.* cost serious money (*od.* a packet, *Am.* a bundle); **etliche Millionen ~ sein** be worth a few million; **4.** *Verbrechen*: serious, grave; (*schlimm*) bad; → *auch* **schlimm** 2; *verstärkend, Unfall, Wunde*: bad, serious; *Krankheit, Fehler, Irrtum*: serious; **~e Erkältung** bad (*od.* heavy) cold; **e-e ~e Gehirnerschütterung** severe concussion; **~er Schock** bad (*od.* severe, terrible) shock; **~e Körperverletzung** grievous bodily harm, *Brit. Abk.* GBH; **~er Diebstahl** aggravated theft; **~er Schlag** *fig.* heavy (*od.* hard) blow; **~er Junge** *umg.* hardened criminal, big-time crook; **5.** *Naut., Wetter*: stormy; **e-e ~e See** a heavy sea; **6.** (*schwierig*) hard, difficult, tough *umg.*; → *auch* **schwierig** I; *Musik*: difficult; *Buch*: heavy(-going); (*anstrengend*) hard, tough *umg.*; *Amt, Pflicht*: onerous; **~e Prüfung** severe test; **das Schwere daran** the difficult part about it; **~es Schicksal** hard lot; **~er Tag** (tough *umg.*) day; **er hatte e-e ~e Jugend** he had a hard time when he was young; **sie hat viel Schweres durchgemacht** she went through many hard times; → **Begriff** 1, **Blei** 1, **Geschütz** *etc.*; **II.** *Adv.* **1.** *bewaffnet etc.*: heavily *etc.*; **~ beladen** *Laster etc.*: heavily laden, with a heavy load (*Flug. etc.* cargo); *fig. Person, mit Sorgen etc.*: weighed down (**mit** with);

j-m ~ auf der Seele liegen prey on s.o.'s mind; **zu ~ gegessen haben** have eaten food that was too rich (*od.* heavy); **2.** (*schlimm*) badly; **es hat sie ~ getroffen** it hit her hard, it was a hard blow for her; **etw. ~ nehmen** take s.th. seriously; (*zu Herzen nehmen*) take s.th. to heart; **~ stürzen/verunglücken** have a bad (*od.* serious) fall/accident; **~ erkältet sein** have a bad (*od.* heavy) cold; **~ krank** seriously ill; **~ behindert** severely handicapped (*od.* disabled); **~ beschädigt** severely (*od.* badly) damaged; *Med.* severely disabled; **~ verletzt** seriously hurt (*od.* injured); **~ verwundet** seriously wounded; **~ betrunken** very drunk, drunk out of one's mind *umg.*; **~ enttäuscht** really (*od.* deeply) disappointed; **3.** (*hart*) **~ arbeiten** work hard; **~ verdient** hard-earned; **~ geprüft** sorely tried; **~ bestrafen** punish severely; **~ büßen** pay dearly; **4.** *umg.* (*sehr*) really; **~ aufpassen** watch like a hawk; **~ beleidigt** deeply offended; *bes. iro.* mortally wounded; **~ stolz sein auf** (+ *Akk.*) be very proud of; **das will ich ~ hoffen!** I should hope so!; *drohend*: you'd etc. better!; **er ist ~ in Ordnung** he's a really great guy; **~ reich sein** be loaded; **da hat er sich aber ~ getäuscht** he's very much mistaken there; **5.** (*nicht leicht*) **~ erziehbares Kind** difficult (*od.* problem) child; **~ erziehbar sein** have behavio(u)ral problems; **~ löslich** *Chem.* of low solubility, not easily soluble; (**sehr**) **~ verdaulich** indigestible, heavy; *fig. Buch etc.*: heavy(-going); **~ verkäuflich** difficult to sell; *attr. Wirts.* slow-selling ...; **~ verständlich** difficult (*od.* hard) to understand; (*entstellt*) *Nachricht etc.*: garbled; **~ verträglich** *Essen*: hard on the digestive system; *Medikament*: not easily tolerated; **das ist ~ zu beurteilen** it's difficult to say (*od.* judge); **~ zu sagen** difficult to say; **~ atmen/gehen** have difficulty breathing/walking; **~ hören** be hard of hearing; **auf dem Ohr hört sie ~** *umg. fig.* she doesn't want to know (when you mention that); **~ zu verstehen** difficult to understand, hard to grasp; **er ist ~ zu verstehen** *akustisch*: it's difficult to hear what he's saying; **sie sind nur ~ zu überzeugen** it's not easy to convince them; **keiner hat es so ~ wie wir** nobody has such a hard time of it as we do; **~ fallen** be difficult (+ *Dat.* for), not be easy (for); **es fällt ihm ~** *auch* he finds it hard; *seelisch*: it's hard on him; **Mathe ist mir immer ~ gefallen** I always found math(s) difficult; **es fällt ihr ~, sich zu bedanken** she finds it difficult to say thank you; **auch wenn's dir ~ fällt** whether you like it or not; **j-m etw. ~ machen** make s.th. difficult for s.o.; **j-m das Leben ~ machen** give s.o. a hard time; **sich mit etw. ~ tun** have a hard time with s.th.; *auch grundsätzlich*: find s.th. difficult; **er tut sich mit s-r Schwester ~** he doesn't get on (*Am.* along) with his sister; **~ wiegend** → **schwerwiegend**; → **Magen, schaffen**² II 3

...schwer *Adj., im Subst.* **1.** *im wörtl. Sinn*: **kilo~** weighing a kilogram (*od.* several kilos); **2.** *fig.*: **milliarden~** worth a billion (*od.* billions), billionaire ...

Schwerarbeit *f* (heavy) labo(u)r;
Schwerarbeiter *m*, **Schwerarbeiterin** *f* labo(u)rer

Schwerathlet *m* competitor in strength

events (*e.g. weightlifter, wrestler, shot-putter*); **Schwerathletik** *f* strength events *Pl.*; **Schwerathletin** *f* (female) competitor in strength events

Schwerbehinderte *m, f* disabled (*od.* severely handicapped) person

Schwerbehinderten|ausweis *m* disabled pass; **~fürsorge** *f* care of the disabled

Schwerbenzin *n* heavy petroleum

Schwerbeschädigte *m, f; -n, -n* disabled person

schwerblütig *Adj.* ponderous, stolid

Schwere *f; -, kein Pl.* **1.** weight; *Phys.* gravity; *von Bewegungen, Wein, Parfum, Speise etc.*: heaviness; **e-e bleierne ~ empfinden** feel a lead weight in one's limbs; **2.** (*Ernst*) seriousness, *auch e-s Verbrechens*: gravity; *e-r Strafe, e-s Unwetters etc.*: severity; (*Gewichtigkeit*) import, significance; **3.** (*Schwierigkeitsgrad*) difficulty

Schwerefeld *n Phys.* gravitational field

schwerelos I. *Adj.* weightless; **II.** *Adv.* weightlessly; **Schwerelosigkeit** *f* weightlessness

Schwerenöter *m; -s, -; umg. hum.* ladykiller; **alter ~!** you old charmer!

Schwererziehbare *m, f; -n, -n* difficult (*od.* problem) child

schwer fallen → **schwer** II 5

schwerfällig I. *Adj. Person*: ponderous, slow; (*unbeholfen, auch Bewegung*) awkward, clumsy; (*langsam, träge*) sluggish; *fig. Verfahren*: cumbersome; *Stil*: labo(u)red, stodgy *umg.*; *Buch*: *präd. auch* heavy going; **II.** *Adv.* **gehen, sich bewegen**: ponderously; (*unbeholfen*) awkwardly, clumsily; (*sprechen*): ponderously; **nur ~ vorankommen** make slow and labo(u)red progress; **Schwerfälligkeit** *f* ponderousness; (*Unbeholfenheit*) awkwardness, clumsiness; (*Trägheit*) sluggishness; *e-s Verfahrens*: cumbersomeness; *des Stils*: stodginess

schwer geprüft → **schwer** II 3

Schwergewicht *n* **1.** *nur Sg.*; *Sport* heavyweight; **Meister im ~** heavyweight champion; **es geht um die Weltmeisterschaft im ~** the world heavyweight championship is at stake; **2.** *nur Sg.*; *fig.* (main) emphasis; **das ~ lag auf** (+ *Dat.*) the emphasis was (*od.* fell) on, the focus of attention was on; **3.** *umg. fig.*: **er/sie ist ein ~** he's/she's no lightweight; *fig.* (*bedeutend*) he's/she's a heavyweight (*od.* big[-time] player); **schwergewichtig** *Adj. auch fig. Persönlichkeit*: heavyweight; **Schwergewichtler** *m; -s, -*, **Schwergewichtlerin** *f; -, -nen* heavyweight (*auch umg. schwere Person*)

Schwergewichts|boxer *m*, **~boxerin** *f* heavyweight boxer

schwerhörig *Adj.* hard of hearing; **bist du ~?** *umg.* are you deaf?; **sie ist auf dem Ohr ~** *umg. fig.* she doesn't want to know about that; **Schwerhörige** *m, f; -n, -n* person with hearing difficulties; **Schwerhörigkeit** *f* hardness of hearing, partial deafness

Schwer|industrie *f* heavy industry; **~kraft** *f Phys.* (force of) gravity

schwer krank → **schwer** II 2; **Schwerkranke** *m, f* seriously ill patient

Schwer|kriminelle *m, f* dangerous criminal, *Jur.* felon; **~laster** *m* heavy truck (*Brit. auch* lorry), *Brit. auch* HGV, juggernaut; **~lastverkehr** *m* heavy vehicle traffic

schwerlich *Adv.* hardly, scarcely

S

schwer löslich → *schwer* II 5
schwer machen → *schwer* II 5
Schwermetall n heavy metal; **schwermetallbelastet** Adj. polluted with heavy metal; **schwermetallhaltig** Adj. containing heavy metal
Schwermut f melancholy, gloom; *in tiefe ~ verfallen* sink into the depths of depression; **schwermütig** Adj. melancholy; *auch Gemälde etc.*: gloomy; **Schwermütigkeit** f melancholy, gloominess
schwer nehmen → *schwer* II 2
Schweröl n heavy oil
Schwerpunkt m 1. *Phys.* cent|re (*Am.* -er) of gravity; 2. *fig.* (*Hauptgebiet*) main area; (*Hauptgewicht*) main emphasis; *~e setzen* set priorities; → *auch Schwerpunktthema*
schwerpunktmäßig I. Adj. concentrating on certain main points; *~er Streik* pinpoint strike; **II.** Adv. *etw. ~ behandeln* highlight (*od.* concentrate on) s.th.; *gewisse Themen ~ behandeln/ prüfen* give certain subjects particular emphasis / examine certain subjects particularly thoroughly, concentrate on treating/examining certain subjects
Schwerpunkt|programm n priority program(me) (*od.* plan); *~streik* m selective (strike) action, pinpoint strike; *~thema* n main (discussion) topic; *in der Prüfung*: special subject
schwerreich Adj. *umg.* filthy rich, loaded *präd.*
Schwerst|abhängige m, f totally dependent (*engS.* addicted) person; *~arbeit* f very heavy labo(u)r; *~arbeiter* m, *~arbeiterin* f heavy labo(u)rer; *~behinderte* m, f severely disabled person; *~kranke* m, f critically ill patient; *~verwundete* m, f severely wounded person
Schwert n; -(e)s, -er 1. sword; *das ~ ziehen* draw one's sword; *durch das ~ richten* execute by the sword; *das ~ in die Scheide stecken* sheathe one's sword; *fig.* bury the hatchet; 2. *Segelboot*: centre|board (*Am.* center-)
Schwert|fechten n swordfighting; *~fisch* m *Zool.* swordfish
schwertförmig Adj. sword-shaped
Schwert|kampf m swordfight; *Sport* fencing bout with swords; → *Schwertfechten*; *~kämpfer* m, *~kämpferin* f swordfighter; *~lilie* f *Bot.* iris
Schwertransport m 1. heavy load; 2. → *Schwertransporter*; **Schwertransporter** m heavy truck (*Brit. auch* lorry), *bes. Amtsspr.* heavy goods (*Am.* heavyweight) vehicle
Schwert|schlucker m; -s, -, *~schluckerin* f; -, -nen sword swallower; *~spitze* f point of a sword, sword point; *~streich* m sword stroke
schwer tun → *schwer* II 5
Schwertwal m *Zool.* killer whale
Schwerverbrecher m, *~in* f dangerous criminal, *Jur.* felon
schwer| verdaulich → *schwer* II 5; *~ verdient* → *schwer* II 3; *~ verkäuflich* → *schwer* II 5
Schwerverkehr m heavy goods (*Am.* truck) traffic
schwer verletzt → *schwer* II 2
Schwerverletzte m, f serious casualty, seriously injured person
schwer| verständlich, *~ verträglich* → *schwer* II 5; *~ verwundet* → *schwer* II 2
Schwerverwundete m, f seriously wounded casualty
Schwerwasserreaktor m heavy water

reactor
schwerwiegend, **schwer wiegend** Adj. serious; *Vorwürfe*: *auch* grave; (*folgenschwer*) *Entscheidung etc.*: momentous
Schwester f; -, -n 1. sister (*auch fig.*); 2. (*Krankenschwester*) (hospital) nurse; 3. (*Ober-, Ordensschwester*) sister; *in Kloster*: nun; 4. *Wirts.* sister company; *ihre amerikanische ~* its American sister company; → *Schwesterfirma*; **Schwesterchen** n *umg.* little sister; *als Anrede*: sister dear, sis
Schwester|firma f, *~gesellschaft* f *Wirts.* affiliated company, sister company; *~herz* n *hum.* dear sister; *als Anrede*: sister dear, sis *umg.*
schwesterlich Adj. sisterly
Schwestern|helferin f nursing auxiliary (*Am.* assistant); *~liebe* f sisterly love; *~orden* m order of nuns, sisterhood; *~paar* n two sisters *Pl.*; *das ~ X* the X sisters
Schwesternschaft f nursing staff
Schwestern|schule f nursing college (*od.* school); *~schülerin* f student nurse; *~wohnheim* n nurses' hostel
Schwester|organisation f sister organization; *~partei* f sister party; *~schiff* n sister ship
Schwibbogen m *Archit.* flying buttress
schwieg *Imperf.* → *schweigen*
Schwieger|eltern *Pl.* parents-in-law; *~mutter* f mother-in-law, *Pl.* mothers--in-law; *~sohn* m son-in-law, *Pl.* sons--in-law; *~tochter* f daughter-in-law, *Pl.* daughters-in-law; *~vater* m father-in--law, *Pl.* fathers-in-law
Schwiele f; -, -n callus; (*Strieme*) weal; **schwielig** Adj. callous, horny
schwiem(e)lig Adj. *nordd. umg.* dizzy
schwierig I. Adj. difficult, *bes. präd.* *auch* hard; *Aufgabe, Job*: *auch* tough *umg.*; (*verwickelt*) complicated, intricate; (*unangenehm*) awkward; *Person*: difficult; *~er Fall* difficult case; (*Person*) *auch* problem case; *e-e zu ~e / nicht zu ~e Aufgabe* an excessively / a not too difficult task; *~e Lage* difficult (*od.* awkward) situation, predicament, fix *umg.*; *das macht alles noch ~er* that makes things even more difficult, that complicates matters even more; *in e-m ~en Alter sein* be at a difficult (*od.* an awkward) age; *das Schwierige daran* the difficult part of it; *das Schwierigste haben wir hinter uns* the most difficult part is behind us, the worst is over; **II.** Adv.: *sich ~ gestalten* *Verhandlungen etc.*: turn out to be difficult; *~ zu bedienen sein* *Maschine etc.*: be difficult to operate
Schwierigkeit f difficulty; (*Schwierigkeitsgrad*) level (of difficulty); *e-e Aufgabe mittlerer ~* a moderately difficult question; *e-e Kür mit vielen ~en* a (-free) program(me) with many difficulties; *~en haben, etw. zu tun* have difficulty (*od.* trouble) (in) doing s.th.; *j-m ~en machen od. bereiten* *Sache*: be a problem for s.o., cause s.o. problems; *Person*: make things difficult for s.o.; *sie haben wegen des Visums ~en gemacht* they made difficulties over the visa; *unnötige ~en machen* complicate matters unnecessarily; *das bereitete ihm keinerlei ~en* it was no trouble at all for him, he took it all in his stride; *auf ~en stoßen* run into difficulty (*od.* difficulties, problems); *in finanziellen ~en sein od. stecken* have financial problems; *mit j-m ~en haben* have problems with s.o.; *~en bekom-*

men get into trouble; (*Unannehmlichkeiten*) have trouble (*wegen* because of)
Schwierigkeits|grad m, *~stufe* f level (of difficulty)
schwillt *Präs.* → *schwellen*[1]
Schwimm|anzug m 1. *Sport* swimsuit; 2. *Mil.* wetsuit; *~bad* n swimming pool; (*Hallenbad*) *auch* indoor pool, *Brit. auch* swimming baths *Pl.*; *~bagger* m sand dredge(r); *~bahn* f lane; *~becken* n swimming pool; *~bewegung* f swimming action, stroke; *~blase* f e-s Fisches: air bladder; *~brille* f swimming goggles *Pl.*; *~dock* n floating dock
schwimmen; *schwimmt, schwamm, ist od. hat geschwommen* **I.** v/i. 1. (*mst ist*) swim; *~ gehen* go swimming, go for a swim; *sie schwimmt im Endlauf* she is swimming in the final; *auf dem Rücken ~* (*do*) backstroke; *über den Kanal ~* swim (across) the Channel; *e-e Fliege schwimmt in m-r Suppe* there's a fly (floating) in my soup; *alles schwamm vor s-n Augen* *fig.* everything started swimming in front of his eyes; 2. (*hat, südd., österr., schw. ist*) (*nicht untergehen*) float (*auch Holz, Leiche etc.*); *Schiff*: be afloat; *Papierschiffe ~ lassen* sail paper boats; *er schwimmt oben* *umg. fig.* he's got everything going for him; 3. (*ist*) *in s-m Blut ~* be lying in a pool of blood; *im Geld ~* be rolling in money; *im Glück ~* wallow in good fortune; 4. (*hat*) (*sehr nass sein*) be awash (*od.* flooded); *ihre Augen schwammen* (*in Tränen*) her eyes were filled with tears; 5. (*hat*) *umg.* (*unsicher sein*) be all at sea (*od.* floundering); **II.** v/t. (*ist od. hat*) swim (*auch e-e Strecke, e-n Rekord*); *Weltrekord ~* swim a world record time, make a world record in swimming; → *Strom* 3
Schwimmen n; -s, kein Pl. 1. swimming; *zum ~ gehen* go swimming; 2. *ins ~ kommen* *Schauspieler etc.*: start floundering; *Prüfling*: come unstuck; *Auto*: go into a skid
schwimmend I. Part. Präs. → *schwimmen*; **II.** Adj. 1. *Hotel, Restaurant, Garten, Parkett, Estrich etc.*: floating; 2. *in ~em Fett braten* fry in deep fat, deep-fry; **III.** Adv.: *~ e-n Fluss überqueren* swim across a river
Schwimmer m; -s, - 1. swimmer; 2. *Angeln, Tech., Flug., Mot.* float; *~becken* n swimmer's pool; **Schwimmerin** f; -, -nen swimmer; *~ventil* n float valve
schwimmfähig Adj. buoyant; *Fahrzeug*: amphibious
Schwimm|fahrzeug n amphibious vehicle; *~flosse* f fin; *Sport* flipper; *~flügel* Pl. water wings; *~fuß* m *Zool.* webbed foot; *~gürtel* m 1. (*cork*) swimming belt; 2. *umg.* (*Hüftspeck*) spare tyre (*Am.* tire); *~halle* f indoor (swimming) pool; *~haut* f von Wasservögeln: web; *~käfer* m *Zool.* diving beetle; *~kompass* m floating compass; *~kran* m floating crane; *~kurs* m swimming course (*od.* lessons *Pl.*); *~lehrer* m, *~lehrerin* f swimming instructor; *~meister* m, *~meisterin* f 1. (*Bademeister[in]*) swimming supervisor; 2. (*Wettbewerbssieger*) swimming champion; *~panzer* m *Mil.* amphibious tank; *~prüfung* f swimming test; *~reifen* m rubber ring; *~sport* m swimming; *~stil* m (*Technik*) swimming style; (*Butterfly etc.*) (swimming) stroke; *~unterricht* m swimming les-

sons *Pl.*; **~verein** *m* swimming club; **~vogel** *m* water bird; **~weste** *f* life jacket, life vest, *Am.* life preserver

Schwindel *m*; *-s, kein Pl.* **1.** dizziness; *Med.* vertigo; (*Schwindelanfall*) dizzy spell; *ihn überkam ein leichter/starker ~* he became slightly/very dizzy; *~ erregend* dizzy, giddy (*auch fig.*); *Zahlen, Preise*: astronomical; *sie balanciert in ~ erregender Höhe* she does her balancing act at a vertiginous (*od.* dizzy) height; **2.** *umg.* (*Betrug*) swindle; *Koll.* swindling; (*Lüge*) lie, fib; *dieses Schlankheitsmittel ist purer ~* this slimming agent (*Am.* diet formula) is a complete fraud (*od.* con); *auf e-n ~ hereinfallen* fall for a trick; *der ganze ~ ist aufgeflogen* the whole scam *Sl.* was exposed; *alles ~!* nothing but lies!; **3.** *der ganze ~ umg.* (*alles zusammen*) the whole caboodle; **~anfall** *m* dizzy spell

Schwindelei *f*; *-, -en*; *umg.* **1.** swindling; *von kleinen ~en leben* live off a series of little scams *Sl.*; **2.** (*das Lügen*) (constant) lying; *konkret*: lies *Pl.*

schwindelerregend, Schwindel erregend *Adj.* → **Schwindel** 1

Schwindelfirma *f* bogus company

schwindelfrei *Adj.: ~ sein* have no fear of heights, *bes. Brit. auch* have a good head for heights; *nicht ~* afraid of heights

Schwindelgefühl *n* dizzy feeling, dizziness

Schwindelgeschäft *n* bogus transaction

schwindelig *Adj.* → **schwindlig**

schwindeln I. *vt/i. umg.* (*lügen*) tell a fib (*od.* lie); *mehrmals*: tell fibs (*od.* lies), fib, lie; (*mogeln*) cheat; *das ist geschwindelt!* that's a lie!; **II.** *v/i.* (*schwindlig sein*) *mir od. mich schwindelt* I feel dizzy; *ihm schwindelte (der Kopf) bei dem Gedanken* his head reeled at the thought; **III.** *v/refl. umg.*: *sich durchs Examen ~* get through the exam by cheating; *sich durch alle Kontrollen/Instanzen ~* wangle (*od.* bluff) one's way through all the checkpoints/courts; **schwindelnd I.** *Part. Präs.* → **schwindeln**; **II.** *Adj.* (*Schwindel erregend*) dizzy; *in ~er Höhe* at a dizzy (*od.* vertiginous) height

Schwindelpreis *m* exorbitant (*umg.* jacked-up) price

schwinden; *schwindet, schwand, ist geschwunden*; *v/i. Einfluss, Macht*: dwindle, diminish; *Vorräte, Geld*: dwindle, run low; *Kräfte*: (begin to) fail (*od.* dwindle, seep away); *Farben, Schönheit, Hoffnung, Radiosender*: fade; *Interesse*: dwindle, drop off; *Misstrauen*: disappear; *Tech. fachspr., Werkstück*: shrink; *aus dem Gedächtnis ~* fade from one's memory; *mein Interesse schwand* I lost interest; *das Lächeln schwand aus s-m Gesicht* his face dropped; *ihm schwand der Mut* he lost courage, his courage failed him; *ihr schwanden die Sinne* she fainted (*od.* passed out); **Schwinden** *n*; *-s, kein Pl.* dwindling *etc.*; → **schwinden**; *das ~ der Hoffnung etc.* the fading of hope *etc.*; *im ~ begriffen* dwindling; *Macht etc.*: on the wane; **schwindend I.** *Part. Präs.* → **schwinden**; **II.** *Adj.* dwindling, diminishing

Schwindler *m*; *-s, -*, **~in** *f*; *-, -nen* swindler, cheat; (*Hochstapler[in]*) con artist *umg.*; (*Lügner[in]*) liar; **schwindlerisch** *Adj.* fraudulent

schwindlig I. *Adj. auch fig.* dizzy, gid-

dy; *mir wird od. ich werde ~* I feel dizzy; *mir wurde ~* I (suddenly) felt dizzy, I had a dizzy turn (*od.* spell); **II.** *Adv.*: *~ hoch hinaufsteigen* climb to a dizzy height

Schwindsucht *f Med. altm.* consumption; **schwindsüchtig** *Adj. altm.* consumptive; *umg. fig.* wasting away; **Schwindsüchtige** *m, f altm.* consumptive

Schwingachse *f Mot.* swing axle

Schwinge *f*; *-, -n* **1.** (*Flügel*) wing; *poet. auch* pinion; **2.** *Tech.* rocker arm

schwingen (*schwingt, schwang, ist od. hat geschwungen*) **I.** *v/t.* (*hat*) swing; *bes. drohend*: brandish, wield; (*Fahne, Tuch etc.*) wave; → **Rede** 1, **Tanzbein**; **II.** *v/refl.* (*hat*) swing o.s., jump (*auf + Akk.* onto); *sich über etw. ~* vault over s.th.; *sich von Ast zu Ast ~* swing from branch to branch; *sich in die Höhe ~* Adler etc.: soar (up) into the air; **III.** *v/i.* **1.** (*hat od. ist*) (*pendeln*) swing (*auch Turnen, Skisport etc.*); **2.** (*hat*) *Tech.* oscillate; *Saite etc.*: vibrate; *Ton etc.*: resonate; *zum Schwingen bringen* (*Saite*) make vibrate; (*Kristall*) cause to oscillate; → **geschwungen**

Schwingen *n*; *-s, kein Pl.*; *schw. Sport* Swiss-style wrestling

Schwinger *m*; *-s, -* Boxen: swing

Schwing|kreis *m Etech.* oscillating circuit; **~quarz** *m Tech.* piezoelectric crystal; **~schleifer** *m* orbital sander; **~tor** *n* up-and-over garage door; **~tür** *f* swing door

Schwingung *f Tech. und Akustik*: vibration; *auch Etech.* oscillation; *fig.* resonance; *etw. in ~en versetzen* set s.th. vibrating (*auch fig.*)

Schwingungsdämpfer *m* vibration damper

schwingungsfrei *Adj. nur präd.* free from vibration, *nur attr.* non-vibrating

Schwingungs|frequenz *f* oscillation frequency; **~weite** *f* amplitude; **~zahl** *f* oscillation frequency

schwipp *Interj.* splash!; **~, schwapp!** splish-splosh!

Schwipp|schwager *m umg.* husband's/wife's/brother's/sister's brother-in-law; **~schwägerin** *f umg.* husband's/wife's/brother's/sister's sister-in-law

Schwips *m*; *-es, -e*; *umg.*: *e-n ~ haben* be (a bit) tipsy (*od.* tiddly); *sich e-n ~ antrinken* get tipsy (*od.* tiddly)

schwirren *v/i.* **1.** (*ist geschwirrt*) whirr, *Am.* whir; *Pfeil etc.*: *auch umg.* (*sausen*) whiz(z); *Insekten*: buzz; *Schneeflocken*: whirl; *j-m durch den Kopf ~* *Zahlen, Gedanken*: spin round in s.o.'s head; *Fragen schwirrten durch den Saal* questions came flying from all directions (of the hall); *überall schwirrten Touristen* the place was swarming with tourists; **2.** (*hat*) *fig.*: *von Gerüchten etc. ~* be buzzing with rumo(u)rs *etc.*; *mir schwirrte der Kopf* my head was buzzing (*od.* spinning)

Schwitz|bad *n* steam bath; **~bläschen** *Pl.* heat blisters

Schwitze *f*; *-, -n*; *Gastr.* roux

schwitzen I. *v/i.* sweat; *formeller*: perspire; *Wände*: sweat; *Fenster*: steam up; *Käse etc.*: sweat; (*sich anstrengen*) *umg.* sweat away; *am ganzen Körper ~* be covered (*od.* soaked) in sweat; *sich ins Bett legen und richtig ~* go to bed and have a good sweat; *vor Angst etc. ~* sweat with fear *etc.*; *den lasse ich noch ein wenig ~ umg.* I'm going to let him sweat it out for a bit; **II.** *v/t.*

1. *Harz etc.~* sweat (out) resin *etc.*; *etw. nass ~* soak s.th. in sweat; *Blut (und Wasser) ~ fig.* sweat blood; **2.** *Mehl (in Butter) ~ Gastr.* sweat flour; **III.** *v/refl.*: *sich nass ~* be soaked in sweat, be dripping with sweat

Schwitzen *n*; *-s, kein Pl.* sweating, perspiration

schwitzig *Adj. umg.* sweaty

Schwitz|kasten *m Ringen*: headlock; **~kur** *f* sweating cure; **~packung** *f Med.* hot pack; **~wasser** *n* condensation

Schwof *m*; *-(e)s, -e*; *umg.* hop; *nach dem Abendessen ist ~* there'll be dancing after supper; **schwofen** *v/i. umg.* shake a leg; *wir haben bis drei Uhr geschwoft* we danced the night away until three

schwoll *Imperf.* → **schwellen**[1]

schwor *Imperf.* → **schwören**

schwören *vt/i.*; *schwört, schwor, hat geschworen* swear; *vor Gericht*: take the oath; (*Rache, Treue etc.*) swear, vow; *e-n Eid ~* take an oath; *auf die Bibel ~* swear on the Bible; *sich (Dat.) etw. ~* swear s.th. to o.s.; *sich (Dat.) ~, dass man* swear to (+ *Inf.*); *ich schwöre es (dir)* I'm prepared to swear it; *nachgestellt*: I swear; *er hat's mir geschworen* he gave me his oath on it; *~ auf (+ Akk.) fig.* (*vertrauen auf*) swear by; → **geschworen**

Schwuchtel *f*; *-, -n*; *pej.* (*Homosexueller*) queen *Sl.*

schwul *Adj. umg.* gay; *pej.* queer; *die ~e Sau vulg. pej.* the poncey pouf (*Am.* flaming queen)

schwül *Adj.* **1.** close, muggy, sultry; (*beklemmend*) oppressive, stifling; *~e Luft* close (*od.* oppressive) atmosphere; **2.** (*sinnlich*) *Duft, Traum, Fantasie*: sensuous; **Schwüle** *f*; *-, kein Pl.* **1.** sultriness; (*Hitze*) stifling heat; *der Stimmung*: oppressiveness; *in der ~ der Nacht* in the heat of the night; **2.** (*Sinnlichkeit*) sensuousness

Schwule *m*; *-n, -n*; *umg.* gay; *pej.* queer

Schwulen|bewegung *f* gay movement; **~ehe** *f* gay marriage; **2feindlich** *Adj.* anti-gay; **~hass** *m* homophobia; **~lokal** *n* gay bar; **~parade** *f* (gay) pride parade; **~politik** *f* gay politics; **~strich** *m* gay area; **~treff** *m umg.* gay meeting place (*od.* haunt); **~verfolgung** *f* persecution of gays

Schwulitäten *Pl. umg.* fix, scrape *Sg.*; *in ~ kommen* get into a fix

Schwulsein *n umg.* gay status

Schwulst *m*; *-es, kein Pl. Sprache*: bombast, fustian; *auch Kunst*: ornateness

schwulstig *Adj. Lippen*: thick, swollen

schwülstig *pej.* **I.** *Adj.* bombastic, pompous, inflated; *Kunststil*: ornate, florid; **II.** *Adv.* bombastically

schwumm(e)rig *Adj. umg.* **1.** → **schwindlig**; **2.** (*unbehaglich*) uneasy, apprehensive; *mir wird ganz ~, wenn ...* I get butterflies in my stomach when ...

Schwund *m*; *-(e)s, kein Pl. an Vorräten etc.*: dwindling; (*Verlust*) loss; *durch Schrumpfen, Eingehen*: shrinkage; *Radio*: fading; *Med.* atrophy; **~ausgleich** *m Radio*: anti-fading device, gain control

Schwung *m*; *-(e)s, Schwünge* **1.** (*Bewegung*) swing (*auch Turnen, Skisport*); *nach vorne*: jump, leap; (*Armbewegung, Pendelschwung*) sweep; (*ge-*

S

schwungene Linie) curve, sweep; **2.** *nur Sg.*; (*Geschwindigkeit*) speed; (*Kraft*) force; *fig.* (*Antrieb*) impetus; (*Energie, Elan*) energy, drive, punch; (*Schmiss*) verve; **~ holen zum Springen**: take a running jump; (*ausholen*) take a (big) swing; *die Tür mit e-m solchen ~ zuschlagen* slam the door with such force (*laut*: with such a bang); **j-n/etw. in ~ bringen** *fig.* get s.o./s.th. going; *das bringt dich wieder in ~* *umg. nach Krankheit etc.*: that'll get you back on your feet again; **~ in die Sache bringen** *umg.* liven things up; **etw. in ~ halten** *umg.* (*Betrieb, Kreislauf etc.*) keep s.th. going; (*Garten, Auto etc.*) keep s.th. up (*auch Fremdsprache etc.*), look after (*Am.* take care of) s.th., *Brit. auch* keep s.th. in good nick; (*richtig*) **in ~ kommen** *umg.* (really) get going; *Party, Diskussion etc.*: *auch* hot (*od.* heat) up; **in** (*vollem*) **~ sein** *umg.* be in full swing, be going great guns; *wenn er erst einmal in ~ ist* *umg.* once he gets going, once he gets into the swing of things; → *auch **Fahrt** 2*; **3.** *nur Sg. umg.* (*Menge, Anzahl*) batch, clutch; *von Leuten*: bunch; *von Platten, Heften etc.*: pile

Schwungfeder *f Orn.* flight (*od.* pinion) feather

schwunghaft I. *Adj. Handel*: brisk, flourishing; **II.** *Adv.*: *sich ~ entwickeln* grow rapidly; → *auch **schwungvoll***

Schwungkraft *f* **1.** *Phys.* centrifugal force; **2.** *fig.* energy, drive, punch

schwunglos *Adj.* lifeless; *Handel*: sluggish; *Aufführung*: lacklust|re (*Am.* -er)

Schwungrad *n Tech.* flywheel

schwungvoll I. *Adj.* (*energisch*) energetic, vigorous; *präd.* full of drive (*od.* go *umg.*); (*unternehmungslustig*) enterprising; (*lebhaft*) lively, spirited; *Rede*: punchy; *Stil*: racy; *Melodie*: lively; *Entwurf, Handschrift*: bold; *Linie*: sweeping; *Inszenierung*: lively, spirited; **~ sein** have plenty of go (*od.* pep) *umg.*; **II.** *Adv.* (*energisch*) energetically, with great vigo(u)r; (*lebhaft*) spiritedly, with great verve; *geschrieben*: racily; *Ravels „Bolero" muss man noch ~er spielen* Ravel's "Bolero" needs to be played with more brio (*od.* verve)

schwupp *Interj. umg.* (*im Handumdrehen*) (hey) presto!; *~!, fiel mir die Seife aus der Hand* and whoosh! the soap went flying; *~!, war er weg* before you knew it (*od.* in a flash) he was gone

schwuppdiwupp *Interj.* → *schwupp*

Schwur *m*; *-(e)s, Schwüre* oath; (*Gelübde*) vow; *e-n ~ leisten* take an oath; → *auch **Eid***

Schwurfinger *Pl.* thumb and two fingers raised in taking an oath

Schwurgericht *n Jur.* **1.** *in Deutschland*: *court made up of three professional and two lay judges*; **2.** *in USA und GB*: jury court; *altm.* (court of) assizes *Pl.*; **Schwurgerichtsverfahren** *n* **1.** *in Deutschland*: *legal proceedings before a court made up of three professional and two lay judges*; **2.** *in USA und GB*: process of trial by jury

Schwyzerdütsch *n*; *-(s)*; *schw.* → **Schweizerdeutsch**

Sciencefiction [ˈsaɪənsˈfɪkʃən] *f*; *-, kein Pl.* science fiction, sci-fi *umg.*; *~literatur* *f* science fiction (writing); *~Serie* *f* science fiction (*umg.* sci-fi)

series

Scientologe [saɪənˈloːgə] *m*; *-n, -n*, **Scientologin** [-ɪn] *f*; *-, -nen* Scientologist; **scientologisch** [-ɪʃ] *Adj.* Scientology …; **Scientology®** [saɪənˈtɔlədʒɪ] *f*; *-, kein Pl.* Scientology; *~ Kirche Deutschland* German Church of Scientology

Scotchterrier [ˈskɔtʃtɛriə] *m* Scotch terrier, scottie (dog) *umg.*

Screening [ˈskriːnɪŋ] *n*; *-(s), -s, ~Test* *m Med.* screening test

Scriptgirl [ˈskrɪptɡøːəl] *n*; *-s, -s* continuity girl

scrollen [ˈskroːlən] *vt/i. EDV* scroll

SDR *m*; *-, kein Pl.*; *Abk.* (**Süddeutscher Rundfunk**) South German Radio

SDS *m*; *-, kein Pl.*; *Abk.* (**Sozialistischer Deutscher Studentenbund**) German Socialist Union of Students

Sealskin [ˈziːlskɪn] *m, n*; *-s, -s* sealskin; (*Webpelz*) imitation sealskin

Séance [zeˈãːsə] *f*; *-, -n* séance

Seborrhö *f*; *-, -en*; *Med.* seborrh(o)ea, dandruff

sechs *Zahlw.* six; *~ Richtige im Lotto*: six matching numbers; → *auch **acht**¹*

Sechs *f*; *-, -en* **1.** *Zahl*: (number) six; *drei ~en würfeln* throw three sixes (*with the dice*); → *auch **Acht**¹ 1, 2, 4*; **2.** *Päd.* (*Note*): fail mark, *etwa* F; *in der Schweiz*: top mark, A; *e-e ~ schreiben etwa* get an F (*in der Schweiz*: an A); → *auch **Sechser***

sechsbändig I. *Adj. attr.* six-volume …, in six volumes; **II.** *Adv.*: *~ herausbringen etc.* publish *etc.* in six volumes

Sechseck *n* hexagon; **sechseckig** *Adj.* hexagonal

Sechser *m*; *-s, -*; *umg.* **1.** → *Sechs*; *drei ~ im Zeugnis haben* have a fail mark in three subjects in one's school report (*Am.* report card); **2.** *e-n ~ haben Lotto*: have (got) six matching numbers; **sechserlei** *Adj.* six kinds of; **Sechserpack** *m* six-pack

sechsfach *Adj.* sixfold; *die ~e Menge* six times the amount; *~er Sieger* six-time winner (*od.* champion)

sechshundert *Adj.* six hundred

sechsjährig *Adj. attr.* **1.** six-year-old …; **2.** (*sechs Jahre dauernd*) six-year …; **Sechsjährige** *m, f*; *-n, -n* six-year-old

Sechskampf *m Turnen*: competition with six events

Sechskant… *im Subst. Tech.* hexagon …; *~schraube* hexagon (*od.* hex *umg.*) bolt (*mit Ganzgewinde*: screw)

sechsköpfig *Adj.*: *~e Familie* family of six; *~es Ungeheuer* six-headed monster

Sechsling *m*; *-s, -e* sextuplet

sechsmal *Adv.* six times

sechsmonatig *Adj. attr.* **1.** *Baby*: six-month-old; **2.** six-month …; *nach e-m ~en Asienaufenthalt* after six months (*od.* a six-month stay) in Asia; **sechsmonatlich I.** *Adj. attr.* six-monthly …, half-yearly …; **II.** *Adv.* every six months

Sechspfünder *m umg.* six-pound baby *etc.*; (*Fisch*) six-pounder

sechs|schüssig *Adj. attr.* (*Waffe*) six-chambered; *der Colt Navy war ~* the Colt Navy was a six-shooter; *~seitig* *Adj.* six-sided, hexagonal; *Brief etc.*: six-page …; *~spurig* **I.** *Adj. attr.* six-lane …; **II.** *Adv.*: *e-e Straße ~ planen* design a road with six lanes; *~stellig* *Adj. attr. Zahl*: six-figure …; *~stöckig* *Adj. attr.* six-stor(e)y …; *~stündig*

Adj. attr. six-hour(-long) …

sechst *Adv.*: *zu ~* six of; *wir/sie waren zu ~* there were six of us/them

sechst… *Zahlw.* sixth; *~es Kapitel* chapter six; *am ~en April* on the sixth of April, on April the sixth; *6. April* 6th April, April 6(th)

Sechstagerennen *n* six-day race

sechstägig *Adj.* **1.** *attr.* six-day(-long) …; *das Seminar ist ~* the seminar lasts six days; **2.** *attr.* (*sechs Tage alt*) six-day-old …

sechstausend *Adj.* six thousand; **Sechstausender** *m* six-thousand met|re (*Am.* -er) (*etwa* twenty thousand foot) peak

Sechste *m, f*; *-n, -n* (the) sixth; *er war Sechster* he was (*od.* came) sixth; *Heinrich VI.* Henry VI (= Henry the Sixth)

sechsteilig *Adj. attr.* six-part …, *auch* präd. in six parts

Sechstel *n*; *-s, -* sixth

sechstens *Adv.* sixth(ly), six

sechswöchig *Adj. attr.* **1.** six-week …; **2.** (*sechs Wochen alt*) six-week-old …

Sechszylinder *m* **1.** (*Auto*) six-cylinder (car); **2.** → *Sechszylindermotor*, *~motor* *m* six-cylinder engine

sechzehn *Adj.* sixteen

Sechzehnmeterraum *m Fußball*: eighteen-yard area

sechzehnt… *Adj.* sixteenth; **Sechzehntel** *n*; *-s, -* sixteenth (part)

Sechzehntel|note *f Mus.* semiquaver, *Am.* sixteenth note

sechzig *Zahlw.* sixty; *Anfang/Mitte/Ende ~ sein* be in one's early/mid/late sixties; → *auch **achtzig***

Sechzig *f*; *-, -en, mst Sg. Zahl*: (number) sixty; → *auch **Achtzig***

sechziger *Adj.*: *in den ~ Jahren* in the sixties; *er ist in den Sechzigern* he's in his sixties

Sechziger¹ *m*; *-s, -*, *~in* *f*; *-, -nen* man/woman in his/her sixties; *förm.* sexagenarian; sixtysomething *umg.*

Sechziger² *Pl.*: *die wilden ~* *umg.* the swinging sixties

Sechzigerjahre *Pl.*: *in den ~n* in the sixties

sechzigjährig *Adj. attr. Person*: sixty-year-old …; *Zeitraum*: sixty-year …; *sein ~es Bestehen feiern* celebrate its sixtieth anniversary

sechzigst|… *Zahlw.* sixtieth; *er hat heute s-n Sechzigsten* he's sixty today, it's his sixtieth birthday today

secondhand [ˈsɛkəndˈhɛnd] *Adv.*: *etw. ~ kaufen/verkaufen* buy/sell s.th. secondhand

Secondhandladen [ˈsɛkəndˈhɛnd-] *m* secondhand (*od.* resale) shop (*Am. auch* store)

SED *f*; *-, kein Pl.*; *Abk.*; *hist.* (**Sozialistische Einheitspartei Deutschlands**) *ehem. DDR*: German Socialist Unity Party

Sedativum *n*; *-s, Sedativa*; *Pharm.* sedative; **sedieren** *vt/i. Med.* sedate

Sediment *n*; *-(e)s, -e* sediment; **sedimentär** *Adj.* sedimentary; **Sedimentgestein** *n* sedimentary rock

See¹ *f*; *-, nur in 2.*: *-n* **1.** *nur Sg.*; (*Meer, Naut. Seegang*) sea; *an der ~* by the sea(side); *an die ~ fahren* go to the seaside; *auf ~* at sea; *auf hoher ~* on the high seas; *in ~ gehen od. stechen* put to sea; *Segler*: *auch* set sail; *zur ~ fahren* be a sailor; *auf ~ bleiben* *fig. euph.* be lost at sea; *schwere ~ Naut.* heavy sea(s); → *offen I 5*; **2.** (*Pl. Seen*) *Naut.* (*Woge, Sturzwelle*) sea;

von e-r ~ über Bord gespült werden be washed overboard by a breaking sea (*od.* wave)

See² *m*; *-s, -n*; (*Binnensee*) lake; *am ~* by a (*od.* the) lake; *ein Haus am ~ auch* a lakeside house; *der Genfer ~* Lake Geneva

...see *m*, *im Subst.* **1.** *Geog.*: *Durchfluss~* lake with a through flow; **2.** *im Namen: Chiem~* (Lake) Chiemsee; *der Michigan~* Lake Michigan

See|aal *m* **1.** *Zool.* sea eel; *großer.* conger eel; **2.** *Gastr.* (*Dornhai*) dogfish; **~adler** *m Orn.* sea eagle; *europäischer. auch* ern(e); **~alpen** *Pl. Geog.* Maritime Alps; **~anemone** *f Zool.* sea anemone; **~bad** *n* seaside resort; **~bär** *m* **1.** *Zool.* fur seal; **2.** *umg. fig.*: *alter ~* seadog; **~beben** *n* seaquake; **~becken** *n Geog.* sea basin; **~bestattung** *f* burial at sea; **~blick** *m* view of the sea (*bzw.* lake); **~blockade** *f* naval blockade; **~bühne** *f* lake stage; **~elefant** *m Zool.* elephant seal; **~erfahrung** *f* experience of navigation

Seefahrer *m altm.* seafarer, sailor; **~nation** *f* seafaring nation (*od.* people)

Seefahrt *f* **1.** (*Schifffahrt*) seafaring, navigation; *die christliche ~* seafaring; *bei der christlichen ~ sein hum.* be a seafaring man; **2.** (*Seereise*) sea journey (*od.* voyage); (*Kreuzfahrt*) cruise

Seefahrts|amt *n* (regional) maritime navigation authority; **~schule** *f* nautical college

seefest *Adj.* **1.** *Schiff*: seaworthy; **2.** *~ / nicht ~ sein Person*: suffer / not suffer from seasickness, be a good/bad sailor

See|fisch *m* saltwater fish; **~fischerei** *f* (deep-)sea fishing; **~fracht** *f Wirts.* sea (*od.* ocean) freight (*od.* cargo); **~funk** *m* radio service to shipping, marine radio; **~gang** *m* sea; *leichter/schwerer ~* light/heavy sea (*od.* swell); **~gebiet** *n* waters *Pl.*; **~gefecht** *n* sea (*od.* naval) battle; **~gemälde** *n* seascape

seegestützt *Adj. Rakete*: sea-based

See|gras *n Bot.* eel grass; *zum Polstern*: sea grass; **~gurke** *f Zool.* sea cucumber; **~hafen** *m* seaport; **~handel** *m* maritime trade; **~hecht** *m Zool.* hake; **~herrschaft** *f* naval supremacy; **~höhe** *f* sea level

Seehund *m Zool.* seal; **~baby** *n* baby seal, seal pup; **~(s)fell** *n* sealskin

See|igel *m Zool.* sea urchin; **~jungfrau** *f* mermaid; **~kadett** *m*, **~kadettin** *f* naval cadet; **~karte** *f* nautical (*od.* sea) chart

seeklar *Adj.* ready to sail; *ein Boot ~ machen* prepare a boat for sea

Seeklima *n* maritime climate

seekrank *Adj.* seasick; *leicht ~ werden* be a bad sailor; **Seekrankheit** *f* seasickness

See|krieg *m* naval war; **~kuh** *f Zool.* sea cow, manatee; **~lachs** *m Zool.* coalfish, pollack; *Gastr.* rock salmon

Seele *f*; *-*, *-n* **1.** (*Gemüt*) *auch kirchl., Philos.* soul; (*psychische Verfassung*) state of mind, mental (*od.* emotional) state; (*Herz*) heart; *aus tiefster ~* with all one's heart; *danken*: from the bottom of one's heart; *er ist mit ganzer ~ dabei* he's in it heart and soul (*od.* one hundred percent); *er ist die ~ des Betriebs* he's the life and soul of the business; *j-m auf der ~ liegen od. lasten* weigh heavily on s.o.; *sich* (*Dat.*) *etw. von der ~ reden* get s.th. off one's chest; *sich* (*Dat.*) *die ~ aus dem Leib schreien* shout o.s. hoarse; *es tat ihm*

in der ~ weh it cut him to the quick; *du sprichst mir aus der ~* that's exactly how I feel (about it), my sentiments are exactly the same; *zwei ~n wohnen, ach, in m-r Brust lit. Faust*: two souls alas! are dwelling in my breast; *fig.* I'm torn between two alternatives; *nun hat die liebe ~ Ruh umg.* the poor soul has been put out of his/her misery; → *Herz¹* 8, *Leib* 1; **2.** *fig.* (*Mensch*) soul; *ein Dorf von gerade 100 ~n altm.* a village of just 100 souls; *e-e gute/treue ~* a good/faithful soul; *e-e ~ von Mensch od. von e-m Menschen* a really good soul; *zwei ~n und ein Gedanke* two minds and but a single thought; **3.** *e-r Waffe*: bore; *e-s Kabels*: core

Seelen|amt *n kirchl.* requiem; **~angst** *f* deep anxiety; **~arzt** *m*, **~ärztin** *f umg.* healer of minds; *weitS.* comforter; **~friede(n)** *m* peace of mind; **~größe** *f* magnanimity; **~heil** *n Reli.* salvation; *weitS. hum.* spiritual welfare; **~klempner** *m*, **~klempnerin** *f umg.* shrink, head-shrinker; **~lage** *f umg.* → *Seelenzustand;* **~landschaft** *f umg.* complete mindset; **~leben** *n* emotional life

seelenlos I. *Adj.* soulless; *Mensch*: *auch* unfeeling; *sein Spiel war ~* he played without any feeling; **II.** *Adv.*: *e-e Sonate ~ herunterspielen* reel off a sonata without any feeling (*od.* expression)

Seelen|massage *f umg.* (*Zuspruch*) pep talk; *e-e ~ brauchen* need bucking up; **~messe** *f* requiem; **~qual** *f* mental anguish

Seelenruhe *f* peace of mind; *weitS.* calmness, coolness; **seelenruhig** *Adv.* calmly; (*ungerührt*) *auch* coolly, without batting an eyelid

Seelen|stärke *f* strength of mind, fortitude; **~striptease** [-ʃtrɪptiːs] *m umg.* baring one's soul; **~tröster** *m umg.* (*Schnaps*) pick-me-up, bracer

seelenvergnügt I. *Adj. nur präd.* happy as a lark; **II.** *Adv.* quite happily

Seelenverkäufer *m umg.* **1.** (*altes Schiff*) leaky old tub; **2.** (*Mensch*) seller of souls

seelenverwandt *Adj.* congenial; *~ sein* be kindred spirits, be soulmates; **Seelenverwandtschaft** *f* spiritual kinship

Seelen|wanderung *f* transmigration of souls, metempsychosis; **~wärmer** *m*; *-s, -; umg.* **1.** (*Schnaps*) pick-me-up; **2.** (*Pulli etc.*) body warmer; **~zustand** *m* state of mind, mental state; *gefühlsmäßig*: emotional state

See|leute *Pl.* sailors, seamen; **~lilie** *f Zool.* sea lily

seelisch I. *Adj.* mental, psychological; (*Gemüts...*) spiritual, emotional; *~e Belastung* mental (*od.* emotional) strain; *~e Grausamkeit Jur.* mental cruelty; *~er Tiefpunkt* emotional low; *~e Verletzungen/Qualen* psychological damage *Sg.* (*od.* scars) / mental torture *Sg.*; (*nicht*) *die ~e Kraft zu etw. haben* (not) have the strength of mind to do s.th.; **II.** *Adv.*: *~ krank/gestört* mentally ill/disturbed; *es hat mich ~ sehr mitgenommen* it took a lot out of me emotionally, it left me emotionally drained; *~ bedingt* emotional, psychological

Seelöwe *m Zool.* sea lion

Seelsorge *f*; *nur Sg.* pastoral care; **Seelsorger** *m*; *-s, -*, **Seelsorgerin** *f*; *-, -nen* pastor, minister; **seelsorgerisch I.** *Adj.* pastoral; **II.** *Adv.*: *~ tätig sein*

be concerned with pastoral care, do pastoral work; *~ betreuen* cater for the spiritual needs of

See|luft *f* sea air; **~macht** *f* naval (*od.* maritime) power

Seemann *m*; *Pl. Seeleute* seaman, sailor; **seemännisch I.** *Adj. Ausdruck, Ausbildung*: nautical; *Erfahrung*: as a seaman; **II.** *Adv.*: *~ erfahren sein* have experience as a seaman, be an experienced seaman

Seemanns|amt *n* seamen's council; **~braut** *f* sailor's girl; **~gang** *m* sailor's walk (*od.* gait); **~garn** *n umg.*: *ein ~ spinnen* spin a yarn; *das ist doch ~!* that's a tall tale!; **~grab** *n* watery grave; **~heim** *n* sailors' home; **~lied** *n* (sea) shanty; **~sprache** *f* seaman's (*od.* nautical) language; (*Fachsprache*) nautical terminology

See|meile *f* nautical mile, sea mile; **~möwe** *f* seagull

Seen|kunde *f* limnology; **~landschaft** *f* lake district

Seenot *f*; *nur Sg.* distress (at sea); *Rettung aus ~* rescue at sea; **~(rettungs)dienst** *m* sea rescue service; **~(rettungs)flugzeug** *n* air-sea rescue aircraft; **~(rettungs)kreuzer** *m* sea rescue boat; **~ruf** *m* distress call (*at sea*); **~zeichen** *n* distress signal

Seenplatte *f* plain with many lakes; *die Finnische/Mecklenburger ~* the Finnish/Mecklenburg Lakeland

See|offizier *m* naval officer; **~otter** *m Zool.* sea otter; **~pferd(chen)** *n* seahorse; **~promenade** *f* seafront promenade; *am See*: lakeside promenade

Seeräuber *m* pirate; **Seeräuberei** *f*; *-*, *kein Pl.* piracy; **Seeräuberin** *f* (female) pirate; **Seeräuberschiff** *n* pirate ship

See|recht *n* maritime law; **~reederei** *f* shipping company; **~reise** *f* sea voyage; (*Kreuzfahrt*) cruise; **~rose** *f* **1.** *Bot.* water lily; **2.** *Zool.* sea anemony; **~sack** *m* (sailor's) kitbag; **~sand** *m* sea sand; **~schaden** *m* damage suffered at sea, average *fachspr.*; **~schiff** *n* seagoing (*für den Hochseebetrieb*: ocean-going) ship; **~schifffahrt** *f* sea shipping; (*Navigation*) marine navigation; **~schildkröte** *f* sea turtle; **~schlacht** *f* naval battle; **~schlange** *f* **1.** *Zool.* sea snake; **2.** *Myth.* sea serpent; **~schwalbe** *f* sea swallow, tern; **~seite** *f* seaward side; **~sieg** *m* naval victory; **~stern** *m Zool.* starfish; **~straße** *f* sea route, shipping lane; **~streitkräfte** *Pl.* naval forces; **~stück** *n Kunst*: seascape; **~stützpunkt** *m* naval base; **~tang** *m* seaweed; **~teufel** *m Zool.* angler, allmouth; *am Meeresgrund lebender*: monkfish; **~transport** *m* shipment by sea

seetüchtig *Adj.* seaworthy; *nicht ~* unseaworthy; **Seetüchtigkeit** *f* seaworthiness

See|ufer *n* lakeshore, lakeside; **~ungeheuer** *n Myth.* sea monster, monster from the deep; **²untüchtig** *Adj.* unseaworthy; **~verbindung** *f* sea route; **~versicherung** *f* marine insurance; **~vogel** *m* seabird

seewärts *Adv.* seaward(s)

Seewasser *n* sea water; (*Salzwasser*) salt water; **~aquarium** *n* sea water aquarium

Seeweg *m* sea route; *auf dem ~* by sea

Seewetter|bericht *m* shipping forecast; **~dienst** *m* meteorological service for shipping

See|wind *m* breeze off the sea, onshore wind; **~wolf** *m Zool.* wolf fish; *„Der ~"* *Roman von Jack London*: The Sea Wolf; **~zeichen** *n* navigation mark

Seezunge *f Zool.* sole; **Seezungenröllchen** *n Gastr.* fillets of sole rolled into paupiettes

Segel *n*; *-s*, *-* sail; *mit vollen ~* under full sail; *fig.* (at) full tilt; *die ~ hissen od. setzen* make sail; *unter ~ gehen* set sail; *die ~ streichen* strike sail; *fig. auch* give in, throw in the towel; → *Wind 2*

...segel *n*, *im Subst.*: *Ballon~* spinnaker; *Gaffel~* gaff sail

Segel|boot *n* sailing boat, *Am.* sailboat; *kleines*: sailing dinghy; (*Jacht*) yacht; **~fahrt** *f* sail(ing trip); **~fläche** *f* sail area

Segelfliegen *n* gliding; **Segelflieger** *m*, **Segelfliegerin** *f* glider (pilot); **Segelflug** *m* **1.** *einzelner*: glider flight; **2.** *nur Sg.*: (*Sport*) gliding

Segelflug|platz *m* gliding field; **~wetter** *n* (suitable) gliding weather; **~zeug** *n* glider

Segel|jacht *f* (sailing) yacht; **~karte** *f* chart; **♀klar** *Adj.* ready to sail; **~macher** *m*, **~macherin** *f* sailmaker

segeln I. *v/i.* **1.** (*ist gesegelt*) sail (*auch fig. Wolken*); *Flugzeug, Vogel*: glide; *Vogel, sehr hoch*: *auch* soar; **2.** (*ist od. hat*) (*~ gehen*) go sailing; *im Urlaub werden wir viel ~* we will do a lot of sailing on holiday (*Am.* vacation); **3.** (*ist*) *umg.*: *durchs Examen ~ umg.* flunk the exam; **II.** *v/t.* (*hat od. ist*) (*Boot etc., Rekord*) sail; (*Regatta*) sail in; *7 Knoten ~* sail at 7 knots; *e-n anderen Kurs ~ auch fig. Pol.* change course

Segeln *n*; *-s*, *kein Pl.* sailing

Segel|ohren *Pl. umg.* jug ears; **~partie** *f* sailing trip; **~regatta** *f* (sailing) regatta; **~schiff** *n* sailing ship (*od.* vessel); **~schule** *f* sailing school; **~sport** *m* sailing; **~törn** *m*; *-s*, *-s* (sailing) cruise; **~tour** *f* sailing tour, cruise

Segeltuch *n* canvas (*auch Wirts.*), sailcloth; **~plane** *f* canvas tarpaulin

Segelyacht *f* (sailing) yacht

Segen *m*, *-s*, *-* **1.** blessing; *kirchl. auch* benediction; *um Gottes ~ bitten* ask for God's blessing; *den ~ geben Priester*: give the benediction; *den ~ sprechen bei Tisch*: say grace; *heile, heile ~! Kinderspr.* there, there! make it better!; (*j-m*) *s-n ~ geben umg.* give (s.o.) one's blessing (*zu* on); **2.** (*Wohltat*) boon, godsend; *es ist ein ~, dass* what a blessing (that), thank God (that); *ein wahrer ~* a real blessing (*od.* godsend); *~ bringend* beneficial; *es ist kein reiner ~* it's a mixed blessing; *das bringt keinen ~* no good will come of it; *sich regen bringt ~ Sprichw. etwa* God helps those who help themselves; **3.** (*Ertrag*) (rich) yield; (*Fülle*) abundance; **4.** *nur Sg.; umg.*: *der ganze ~* the whole caboodle

...segen *m*, *im Subst.*: *Ernte~* (rich) harvest; *Kinder~* children

Segen bringend → *Segen 2*

segensreich *Adj.* beneficial; *Leben*: full of blessings

Segens|spruch *m* blessing, *kirchl. auch* benediction; **~wunsch** *m* blessing

Segler *m*; *-s*, *-* **1.** sailor; *e-r Jacht*: yachtsman; **2.** (*Segelschiff*) sailing vessel; **3.** (*Segelflugzeug*) glider; **4.** (*Vogel*) swift; **Seglerheim** *n* **1.** (*Vereinsheim*)

yacht club hostel; **2.** *früher*: old sailors' home; **Seglermütze** *f* yachtsman's cap; **Seglerin** *f*; *-*, *-nen* yachtswoman

Segment *n*; *-s*, *-e* segment; **segmentieren** *v/t.* segment; **Segmentierung** *f* segmentation

segnen *v/t.* **1.** bless; *Gott segne dich* God bless you; **2.** (*ausstatten*) bless, endow; *er ist nicht gerade mit Intelligenz/Schönheit gesegnet umg.* he is not exactly over-endowed with intelligence / blessed with great beauty; **3.** *fig.*: *das Zeitliche ~* depart this life; *ich segne den Tag, an dem diese Arbeit fertig ist umg.* I praise the day when this job is finished!; → *gesegnet*, **Segnung** *f* blessing, benediction; *~en der Zivilisation fig.* blessings of civilization; *das sind also die ~en des Fortschritts iro.* so this is what they call progress

Sehachse *f Med.* line of vision

sehbehindert *Adj.* partially sighted, visually handicapped (*Am. auch* challenged); *stark ~ sein* have severely impaired vision; **Sehbehinderte** *m*, *f* partially sighted person; *~ Pl.* the partially sighted *Pl.*; **Sehbehinderung** *f* impaired vision (*od.* sight)

sehen; *sieht*, *sah*, *hat gesehen* **I.** *v/i.* **1.** see; *gut/schlecht ~* have good/bad (*od.* poor) eyesight; *ich sehe nicht gut* I can't see very well; *sie sieht nur auf e-m Auge* she can only see with one eye, she only has sight in one eye; *sie konnte kaum aus den Augen ~* she could hardly keep her eyes open; *sehe ich richtig? umg.* I must be seeing things; **2.** (*hinsehen, blicken*) look; *auf s-e Uhr ~* look at one's watch; *sieh nur!, ~ Sie mal!* look!; *wenn ich recht gesehen habe* if I saw right, if my eyes weren't deceiving me; *wie ich sehe, ist er nicht hier* I see he's not here; *wie ich ~, ... as you can see, ...;* *siehe oben/unten* (*abgek. s.o./s.u.*) see above/below; **3.** *fig. ~ auf* (+*Akk.*) (*Wert legen auf*) set great store by, be (very) particular about; *~ nach* (*sorgen für*) look after; *wir müssen mal wieder nach Oma ~* we must look in on grandma again (to see that she's all right); *nach dem Essen ~* see to the dinner; *nach dem Braten ~* see how the joint is doing; *siehe da! umg.* lo and behold!; *sieh mal einer an! umg.* well, what do you know!; (*na,*) *siehst du! umg.* there you are; (*es ist geschehen, was ich voraussagte*) what did I tell you?, see?; *ich will ~, dass ich es dir besorge* I'll see if I can (*od.* I'll try to) get it for you; *man muss ~, wo man bleibt umg.* you have to look after number one; *sieh* (*zu*) *dass es erledigt wird* see (to it) that it gets done; *wir werden* (*schon*) *~* we'll (*od.* we shall) see, let's wait and see; **4.** (*einsehen, erkennen*) see, realize; *~ Sie, die Sache war so* you see, it was like this; *ich sehe schon, dass er keine Ahnung hat* I can see that he has no idea; *seht ihr denn nicht, dass ...?* can't you see that ...?; → *ähnlich* I, *klar* II 1; **II.** *v/t.* **1.** see; (*betrachten*) look at; *TV, Sport etc.*: watch; (*bemerken*) notice; *kann ich das mal ~?* can I have a look at that?; *ich sehe gerade die Tagesschau* I'm watching the news; *er sieht einfach alles* he doesn't miss a thing; *ich sehe überhaupt nichts* I can't see a thing; *ich sehe alles doppelt/verschwommen* I'm see-

ing everything double / everything's blurred; *flüchtig ~* catch a glimpse of; *zu ~ sein* (*hervorlugen*) show; (*ausgestellt sein*) be on show; *es war/gab nichts zu ~* you couldn't see a thing / there was nothing to see; *niemand war zu ~* there was nobody to be seen (*od.* in sight); **2.** *gern ~* like (to see); *er sieht es nicht gern, wenn sie ausgeht* he doesn't like her going out; *das sehe ich gar nicht gern* I hate to see that sort of thing; *sie kann ihn nicht mehr ~* (*leiden*) she can't stand (the sight of) him; **3.** (*erleben*) *er hat bessere Tage gesehen* he's seen better days; *das möchte ich* (*aber*) *~!* that'll be the day!; *das werden wir ja ~ umg.* we'll see; *skeptisch*: *auch* we'll see about that; *da sieht man es mal wieder umg.* it all goes to show; *hat man so etwas schon gesehen! umg.* did you ever see anything like it!; **4.** (*voraussehen*) *ich habe es kommen ~* I could see it coming; *ich sehe schon kommen, dass er kündigt* I can see him handing in his notice; **5.** *sich ~ lassen* put in an appearance; *umg.* (*ankommen, auftauchen*) turn up; *lass dich mal wieder ~! umg.* come and see me (*od.* us) again some time; *lass dich hier nie mehr ~!* don't you dare show your face here again!; *damit kannst du dich od. das kann sich ~ lassen umg.* that looks quite respectable; *weitS., bei Leistung etc.*: that's something to be proud of, that's a feather in your hat; **6.** (*treffen*) see; *sich od. einander ~* see each other; *wir ~ uns häufig* we see quite a lot of each other, we see each other quite often; *können wir uns nicht öfter ~?* can't we get together more often?; *wir ~ uns zum ersten Mal* we've never met before; **7.** *fig.* (*beurteilen, einschätzen*) see; *die Dinge ~, wie sie sind* see things for what they are; *ich sehe die Sache anders* I see it differently; *er sieht es schon richtig* he's got the picture, he's got it right; *du siehst es falsch* you've got it wrong; *wie ich die Sache sehe* as I see it; *das darf man nicht so eng ~ umg.* you mustn't take such a narrow view; *oder wie seh ich das? umg.* am I right?; *so gesehen* (looked at) in that light, from that point of view; *rechtlich etc. gesehen* from a legal etc. standpoint (*od.* point of view), legally etc.; *man muss beide Seiten ~* you have to see both aspects; **8.** *sich gezwungen ~ zu* (+ *Inf.*) find o.s. compelled to (+ *Inf.*); *ich sehe mich nicht imstande od. in der Lage zu* (+ *Inf.*) I don't see how I can possibly (+ *Inf.*)

Sehen *n*; *-s*, *kein Pl.* seeing; (*Sehkraft*) eyesight; (*nur*) *vom ~* (only) by sight; *die Leute kommen zum ~ und Gesehenwerden* these people come to see and be seen

sehenswert, **sehenswürdig** *Adj.* worth seeing; *Ort etc.*: *auch* worth a visit; (*lohnend*) worthwhile; *ein wirklich sehenswerter Film* a film (*Am. auch* movie) that's really worth seeing, a really worthwhile film (*Am. auch* movie); **Sehenswürdigkeit** *f* place of interest; (*Anziehungspunkt*) attraction; *~en e-r Stadt*: *auch* sights; *die ~en besichtigen* go sightseeing, see the sights

Seher *m*; *-s*, *-* **1.** seer, prophet; **2.** *Jägerspr.* eye; **Sehergabe** *f*; *nur Sg.* gift of prophecy, visionary powers *Pl.*; **Se-**

herin f; -, -nen seer, prophetess; **sehe-risch I.** Adj. prophetic, visionary; **II.** Adv. prophetically

Sehfehler m eye defect

sehgestört Adj.: ~ **sein** have defective sight

Seh|gewohnheiten Pl. TV viewing habits; **~hilfe** f seeing aid; **~kraft** f vision, (eye)sight; **nur noch die Hälfte der ~ besitzen** only have 50% vision; **~loch** n Anat. pupil

Sehne f; -, -n **1.** Anat. tendon, sinew; **2.** e-s Bogens: string; **3.** Math. chord

sehnen v/refl.: **sich ~ nach** long for; stärker: yearn for; schmachtend: pine for; **er sehnte sich danach zu** (+ Inf.) he was longing to (+ Inf.), he longed to (+ Inf.); **Sehnen** n; -s, kein Pl. → **Sehnsucht**

Sehnen|entzündung f tendonitis; **~riss** m torn tendon; **~scheidenent-zündung** f tendovaginitis; **~zerrung** f pulled tendon

Sehnerv m optic nerve

sehnig Adj. sinewy; Person: auch wiry; Fleisch: stringy

sehnlich I. Adj. nur attr. ardent, fervent; **sein ~ster Wunsch wäre ein Eigenheim** his greatest (od. most fervent) wish is to have a house of his own; **II.** Adv. ardently, fervently; **~(st) erwarten** await most eagerly

Sehnsucht f longing, yearning (**nach** for); **~ haben nach** long (od. yearn) for; **mit ~ erwarten** await with eager anticipation; **sehnsüchtig, sehn-suchtsvoll I.** Adj. longing, yearning; Blick, Stimme: auch wistful; **II.** Adv. longingly; **~ erwarten** await with eager anticipation

Seh|organ n visual organ, organ of sight; **~probe** f **1.** eye test; **2.** (Tafel) eye test chart; **~prüfung** f eye test

sehr Adv. **1.** vor Adj. und Adv.: very; (höchst) most, extremely; (~ etwa A; ~ viel vor Adj. und Adv.: very much, a great deal; vor Subst.: a great deal of; **~ gern** with great pleasure; **etw. ~ gern tun** like doing s.th. very much; **ich würde ~ gern mitkommen, aber ...** I'd really like to come (od. love to come), but ...; **noch e-e Tasse Kaffee? - ja, ~ gern** another cup of coffee? - yes please(, I'd love one); **ich bin ~ dafür/dagegen** I am very much in favo(u)r (of it) / against it; → **wohl²** 2; **2.** mit Verb: very much; **~ vermissen** auch miss badly (od. a lot); **so ~, dass** so much that; **wie ~ auch** however much, much as; **ich freue mich ~** I'm very glad (od. pleased); **sich ~ anstrengen** make a great effort; **schneit/regnet es ~?** is it snowing/raining heavily?; **danke ~!** thanks very much!, many thanks!; **bitte ~!** you're very welcome

Seh|rohr n Naut. periscope; **~schärfe** f keenness of vision; Med. visual acuity; **~schlitz** m **1.** in der Mütze etc.: eye slit; **2.** im Panzer: observation slit; **~schule** f sight training cent|re (Am. -er); **~schwäche** f bad eyesight; **~stö-rung** f sight defect; **~test** m eye test; **~vermögen** n vision, eyesight; **~weise** f (point of) view; künstlerisch: view of the world; **~weite** f visual range; **in/ außer ~** within/out of sight

seicht Adj. shallow (auch fig.); fig. Unterhaltung etc.: auch superficial; **e-e ~e Komödie** a trivial comedy; **Seichtheit** f shallowness (auch fig.); e-r Unterhaltung etc.: superficiality

seid Präs. → **sein¹**

Seide f; -, -n silk; **reine ~** pure silk

Seidel n; -s, -; (Bierkrug) beer mug, (beer) stein; österr. (0,35 Liter Bier) small glass of beer

Seidelbast m Bot. daphne

seiden Adj. (made of) silk; Glanz etc.: silky; **~e Unterwäsche** silk underwear; → **Faden¹** 3

seidenartig Adj. silk-like, silky

Seiden|atlas m silk satin; **~band** n silk ribbon; **~bluse** f silk blouse; **~faden** m silk thread; **~gewebe** n silk fabric; **~glanz** m silky (od. silken) sheen; **~kleid** n silk dress; **~malerei** f silk painting

seidenmatt Adj. Fot. etc.: semi-matt

Seidenpapier n tissue paper

Seidenraupe f silkworm; **Seidenrau-penzucht** f silkworm breeding, sericulture

Seiden|schal m silk scarf; **~spinner** m Zool. silk moth; **~spinnerei** f silk mill; **~stickerei** f silk embroidery; **~straße** f hist. Silk Road; **~strumpf** m silk stocking; **~tuch** n silk scarf

seidenweich Adj. (as) soft as silk, silky

seidig I. Adj. silky, silken; **II.** Adv.: ~ **glänzen** have a silky (od. silken) sheen; **sich ~ anfühlen** feel silky

Seife f; -, -n **1.** soap; **ein Stück ~** a bar of soap; **2.** Geol. alluvial deposit, Am. placer; **seifen** v/t. soap

Seifen|artikel Pl. → **Seifenwaren**; **~blase** f soap bubble; fig. bubble; **~n machen** blow bubbles; **wie e-e ~ zer-platzen** vanish into thin air; **dann platzte die ~** then the bubble burst; **~flocken** Pl. soap flakes

Seifenkiste f soapbox; **Seifenkisten-rennen** n soapbox derby

Seifen|lauge f soapsuds Pl.; **~oper** f TV soap opera; **~pulver** n soap powder; **~schale** f soap dish; **~schaum** m lather; **~spender** m soap dispenser; **~waren** Pl. (household soaps and) toiletries; **~wasser** n soapy water

seifig I. Adj. soapy; **II.** Adv.: **der Käse/ Cognac schmeckt ~** the cheese/brandy has a soapy taste

seihen v/t. strain

Seil n; -(e)s, -e rope; Mot. (Schleppseil) towrope; (Tau) cable; (Hochseil) tightrope; **am ~ gehen** Bergsteiger: be roped together; **auf dem ~ gehen/ba-lancieren** walk/balance on the tightrope; **auf dem ~ tanzen** fig. be walking a tightrope; **in den ~en hängen** Boxer, auch fig.: be on the ropes; **~akrobat** m, **~akrobatin** f tightrope (od. high wire) performer; **~bahn** f cable railway; (Standseilbahn) auch funicular railway; **~brücke** f rope bridge; **~hüp-fen** n; -s, kein Pl. skipping

Seilschaft f **1.** (Bergsteiger) rope team; **2.** fig. Pol. team, crew; **die alten ~en sind noch intakt** the old network (od. power structure) is still functioning

Seil|schwebebahn f → **Seilbahn**; **~springen** n → **Seilhüpfen**; **~tanz** m; nur Sg., **~tanzen** n tightrope walking; **~tänzer** m, **~tänzerin** f tightrope (od. high wire) performer; **~winde** f cable winch; **~ziehen** n tug-of-war (auch fig.); **~zug** m cable control

sein¹; ist, war, ist gewesen **I.** v/i. **1.** allg. be; **sind Sie es?** is that you?; **wer ist dort** od. **am Apparat?** who's speaking (od. calling)?; **ist da jemand?** is anybody there?; **ach, Sie sind es!** oh, it's you; **ich bin's** it's me; **wer ist das (überhaupt)?** who's that?; **2.** von Beruf, Nationalität, Herkunft, Religion

etc.: be; **was ist dein Vater eigentlich (von Beruf)?** what does your father actually do (for a living)?; **ich bin Klempner von Beruf** I'm a metalworker (umg. plumber) (by trade); **von Beruf bin ich eigentlich Lehrer, aber ich arbeite als Autor** I'm really a teacher (by profession), but I work as a writer; **er ist Buddhist** he's a Buddhist; **sind Sie Engländer** od. **Engländerin?** are you English?; **er ist aus Mexiko** he's (od. he comes) from Mexico; **er 'ist wer** umg. he's really somebody; **3.** (existieren) be (alive); **unser Vater ist nicht mehr** förm. our father is no longer alive; **ich denke, also bin ich** I think, therefore I am; **wenn du nicht gewesen wärst** if it hadn't been for you; **4.** vor Adj. etc., in best. Zustand, bei best. Tätigkeit: be; **er ist schon lange tot** he has been dead for a long time; **sei(d) nicht so laut!** don't be so noisy, stop making such a noise; **sei so gut und ...** do me a favo(u)r and ...; **würde you be so good as to ...?**; **wie teuer es auch (im-mer) ~ mag** however expensive it may be; **er ist beim Lesen** he's reading; **sie ist am Putzen** umg. she's doing the cleaning; **die Garage ist im Bau** the garage is being built; **sie ist jetzt 15 Jahre** she's 15 now; **es ist ein Jahr (her)**, **seit** it's a year since, it was a year ago that; **ich bin ja nicht so** umg. I'm not like that; **sei doch nicht so!** umg. don't be like that; **sei es, wie es sei** be that as it may; **wenn dem so sei** umg. if that's the case, in that case; **5.** (sich befinden, aufhalten) be; **es ist niemand zu Hause** there's nobody at home; **sie ist in Urlaub** she's on holiday; **warst du mal in London?** have you ever been to London?; **6.** qualita-tiv: **wie ist das Wetter bei euch?** how's the weather (od. what's the weather like) with you?; **wie ist er so als Chef?** what's he like as a boss?; **der Film / die Party war nichts** umg. the film (Am. auch movie) /party was a dead loss (Am. a washout); **7.** geeig-net, bestimmt: **Alkohol ist nichts für Kinder** alcohol isn't for children, children shouldn't touch alcohol; **das ist nichts für mich** that's not my cup of tea; (bin an Kauf etc. nicht interessiert) that's not for me; **8.** (scheinen): **mir ist, als kenne ich ihn schon** I have a feeling I know him; **es ist, als ob ...** it's as though ...; **9.** mit Dat. (sich füh-len): **mir ist kalt** I'm cold, I feel cold; **mir ist schlecht** I feel ill (bes. Am. sick); **mir ist nicht nach Arbeiten** umg. I don't feel like working, I'm not in the mood for work; **10.** verantwortlich, schuldig etc.: **wer war das?** (wer hat das getan?) who did that?; **ich war es** (habe es getan) it was me; **keiner will es gewesen sein** nobody will admit they did it, nobody's owning up; **du bist es!** beim Fangenspielen: you're it; **11.** mit zu (+ Inf.): **die Waren sind zu senden an ...** the goods are to be sent to ...; **das Spiel ist nicht mehr zu ge-winnen** the game can no longer be won, we can no longer win (the game); **er ist nicht mehr zu retten** he's past saving; umg. fig. he's a lost cause, he's beyond help; **es ist nun an dir zu** (+ Inf.) it's up to you to ... now; **12.** Math. etc.: **5 und 2 ist 7** five and two are (od. is, make[s]) seven; **x sei ...** let x be ...; **13.** mst unbest., oft in umg. Wendungen: **ist was?** umg. is anything (*od.* something) wrong?; *auch provozierend:* what's the problem?; *was ist mit dir? umg.* what's the matter (*od.* what's wrong) with you?; *so ist das nun mal umg.* that's the way it is; *wie ist es mit dir? umg.* what about you?; *mit dem Urlaub war nichts umg.* the holiday didn't work out, the holiday fell through; *Nachtisch ist heute nicht, Kinder umg.* there's no sweet (*Am.* dessert) for you today, children; *was nicht ist, kann ja noch werden umg.* there's plenty of time yet; *das war's umg.* that's it, that's the lot; *war das alles?* is that all (*od.* the lot)?; **14.** *mit Verben: etw. ~ lassen (nicht tun)* not do s.th.; (*aufhören*) stop doing s.th.; *lass es ~* stop it; (*rühr es nicht an*) leave it alone; (*kümmere dich nicht drum*) don't bother; *ich an d-r Stelle würde das ~ lassen* if I were you I wouldn't have anything to do with it; *am besten lassen wir es ganz ~* we'd better forget all about it; *muss das ~?* do you have to?; *was ~ muss, muss ~* whatever will be, will be; *kann od. mag ~ umg.* it's possible, it could be; *das kann nicht ~* that's impossible, it can't be; **15.** *im Konjunktiv: es sei denn(, dass)* unless; *sei es, dass ... oder dass ...* whether ... or ...; *wie wär's mit e-r Partie Schach?* how (*od.* what) about a game of chess?; *na, wie wär's mit uns beiden? umg.* how about the two of us getting together?; *und das wäre?* umg. and what might that be?; **II.** *Hilfsv.* have; *ich bin ihm schon begegnet* I've met him before; *die Sonne ist untergegangen* the sun has set (*od.* gone down); *er ist in Paris gesehen worden* he has been seen in Paris; *ich bin in Böhmen/1982 geboren* I was born in Bohemia / in 1982; *der neue Kanzler ist gewählt* the new Chancellor has been elected

sein² *I. Poss. Pron.* **1.** *adjektivisch:* his; *Mädchen:* her; *Sache:* its; *Tier: mst* its; *Haustier:* his; *Schiff, Staat: oft* her; *unbestimmt:* one's; *~ Glück machen* make one's fortune; *all ~ bisschen Geld* what little money he has (*od.* had); *Seine Majestät* His Majesty; *es kostet (gut) ~e tausend Dollar* it costs a good thousand dollars; **2.** *substantivisch:* his; *~er, ~e, ~(e)s, der (die, das) ~(ig)e od.* ²*(ig)e* his; *Mädchen:* hers; *jedem das Seine od. seine* to each his own; **II.** *pers. Pron.* (*Gen. von er und es*) of him; *Mädchen:* of her; *er war ~er nicht mehr mächtig* he had lost control of himself completely

Sein *n; -s, kein Pl.* being; (*Dasein*) *auch* existence; *~ und Schein* appearance and reality; *~ oder Nichtsein ...* to be or not to be ...; *es geht um ~ oder Nichtsein* it is a question of survival (*od.* a matter of life and death); *das ~ bestimmt das Bewusstsein* life determines consciousness

seinerseits *Adv.* as far as he's (*od.* he was; *Mädchen:* she's, she was) concerned; *Sache:* in its turn; *er hat dann ~ Anzeige erstattet* he for his part then notified the police

seinerzeit *Adv.* (*damals*) then, at that time; in those days; **seinerzeitig** *Adj. attr.: die ~en Verhältnisse* the conditions then prevailing

seinesgleichen *Pron.* (*ihm Gleichgestellte*) his equals *Pl.*; *unbestimmt:* one's equals *Pl.*; (*Gleichartige*) his kind *Pl.*, the likes *Pl.* of him *umg.*, his sort *Pl. umg.*; *unbestimmt:* one's own

kind *Pl.*; *bei e-r Sache:* its kind *Pl.*; *j-n wie ~ behandeln* treat s.o. as an (*od.* one's) equal; *er/es hat nicht ~* there is no one like him / nothing like it; *das sucht ~* it has no equal, that's unequal(l)ed (*od.* without equal)

seinetwegen *Adv.* **1.** (*ihm zuliebe*) for his sake; (*in s-r Sache*) on his behalf; **2.** (*von ihm aus*) as far as he is/was concerned; **3.** (*durch s-e Schuld etc.*) because of him; **seinetwillen** *Adv. auch um ~ förm.* for his sake

seinige → *sein¹* I 2

sein lassen → *sein¹* I 14

Seinslehre *f Philos.* ontology

Seismik *f; -, kein Pl.; Geol.* seismology; **seismisch** *Adj.* seismic

Seismogramm *n; -s, -e; Geol.* seismogram

Seismograph *m; -en, -en; Geol.* seismograph

Seismologe *m; -n, -n* seismologist; **Seismologie** *f Geol.* seismology; **Seismologin** *f; -, -nen* seismologist; **seismologisch** *Adj.* seismological

seit *I. Präp.; bei Zeitpunkt:* since; *bei Zeitraum:* for; *~ 2001* since 2001; *~ neun Uhr* since nine o'clock; *~ dem Mittelalter* since the Middle Ages; *~ damals, ~ der Zeit* → *seitdem* I; *~ einer Stunde* for an hour; *~ drei Wochen* for (the last) three weeks; *~ langem* for a long time; *~ Jahren* for years; *~ wann?* since when?; (*wie lange?*) how long (... for)?; *~ wann* (*wie lange*) *warten Sie schon?* how long have you been waiting?; *wir sind ~ zehn Jahren befreundet* we have been friends for ten years; *zum ersten Mal ~ Jahren* for the first time in years; **II.** *Konj.* since; *es ist ein Jahr her, ~ ...* it's (been) a year since ..., it was a year ago that ...; → *auch seitdem* II

seitdem *I. Adv.* since then, since that time; *nachgestellt:* since; **II.** *Konj.* since; *~ er umgezogen ist, ruft er nicht mehr an* since he moved he has stopped ringing up (*Am.* calling)

Seite *f; -, -n* **1.** side (*auch Sport, Math., e-r Schallplatte, Münze, e-s Blattes*); *auf der rechten/linken ~ fahren Mot.* drive on the right/left; *rechte/linke ~* right-hand/left-hand side; *e-s Stoffes:* right/wrong side; *hintere/vordere ~ e-s Hauses:* back/front; *er stand breitbeinig da, die Arme in die ~n gestemmt* with hands on hips, with arms akimbo; *e-e ~ Speck* a side of bacon; *die ~n wechseln Sport* change ends; *auch fig.* change sides; *an die od. zur ~ gehen* step aside; *zur ~ schieben auch fig.* push aside (*od.* out of the way); *an j-s ~* at (*od.* by) s.o.'s side, *sitting etc.* next to s.o.; *sich an j-s ~ sehen lassen* appear with s.o.; *~ an ~* side by side; *nach allen ~n* in all directions; *von allen ~n* from all around; *fig.* on all sides; *sich auf die ~ legen* lie (down) on one's side; *Schiff:* heel over on its side; *sie ist auf der rechten ~ gelähmt* she's paraly|sed (*Am.* -zed) on her right side; *auf die ~ schaffen, zur ~ legen* (*auch Geld*) put aside; *von der ~ ansehen* (*missgünstig*) look askance at; *j-m nicht von der ~ gehen* not leave s.o.'s side, *stärker:* stick to s.o. like a leech; *j-m zur ~ stehen* stand by s.o.; **2.** (*Buchseite etc.*) page; *ein Buch auf ~ 32 aufschlagen* open a book at page 32; *die ~n umblättern* thumb through the pages; *gelbe ~n Telef.* Yellow Pages; **3.** (*Eigenschaft,*

Charakterzug) side; *schwache/starke ~* weak spot / strong point; *sich von der besten ~ zeigen* show o.s. at one's best; *bewusst:* put one's best foot forward; *ganz neue ~n an j-m entdecken* discover new sides to s.o.'s character; *komm mir nicht von 'der ~* don't try that one on me; **4.** (*Aspekt*) side; *auf der einen ..., auf der anderen ~ ...* on the one hand ..., on the other hand ...; *von dieser ~ betrachtet* seen from that angle (*od.* standpoint, point of view), seen in that light; *e-r Sache die beste ~ abgewinnen* make the best (*od.* most) of s.th.; *e-r Sache e-e komische ~ abgewinnen* see the funny side of s.th.; *alles hat zwei ~n* there are two sides to everything; *auch die andere ~ sehen* see the other side (of the argument [*od.* problem]); **5.** (*Abstammung*) *von väterlicher/mütterlicher ~* on his (*od.* her, my, your, their) father's/mother's side; **6.** (*Partei, Instanz etc.*) side; *Jur. bei e-m Streit:* party; *j-n auf seine ~ bringen od. ziehen* win s.o. over to one's side; *auf welcher ~ stehst du?* whose side are you on?; *von offizieller ~* from official quarters; *von zuverlässiger ~ erfahren* learn from a reliable source; *von s-r ~ bestehen keine Bedenken* there are no objections on his part (*od.* as far as he is concerned); *auf ~* (+ *Gen.*) on the part of; *von ~* → *seitens*; **7.** *EDV, umg. im Internet:* site; *e-e ~ im Internet aufrufen* call up a site on the Net (*od.* Web), call up a web site

Seiten|-Airbag *m Mot.* lateral (*od.* side[-impact]) airbag; **~altar** *m* side altar; **~angabe** *f* page reference; **~ansicht** *f* **1.** side view; *Archit., Tech.* side elevation; **2.** *EDV* page view; **~arm** *m e-s Flusses:* side arm; **~aufprallschutz** *m Mot.* side impact protection system; **~aus** *n Sport* touch; *ins ~ gehen* go into touch; **~ausgang** *m* side exit; **~auslinie** *f Sport* touchline; **~blick** *m* sidelong glance; **~drucker** *m Computer:* page printer; **~eingang** *m* side entrance; **~einsteiger** *m*, **~einsteigerin** *f Pol. etc.* successful crossover politician (*od.* entertainer *etc.*); **~fenster** *n* side window; **~fläche** *f* lateral surface (*od.* face); **~flosse** *f Zool.* lateral fin; *Flug.* fin; **~flügel** *m* **1.** wing; **2.** *Altarbild:* side panel; **~format** *n* page format; **~formatierung** *f EDV* page formatting; **~gang** *m Eisenb.* corridor; **~gasse** *f* side street; *bes. im Armenviertel:* backstreet; *in e-r dunklen ~* in a dark backstreet; **~gebäude** *n* outhouse; (*Anbau*) (side) annex(e); **~gewehr** *n* bayonet; *mit aufgepflanztem ~* with fixed bayonet(s); **~halbierende** *f Math.* median; **~hieb** *m Fechten:* side cut; *fig.* sideswipe (*gegen, auf +Akk.* at); **~kante** *f* lateral edge; **~lage** *f* side (*od.* lateral) position; *in ~* on one's (*od.* its) side; **~lähmung** *f Med.* hemiplegia

seitenlang *I. Adj. Bericht etc.:* lengthy, ... going on for pages; *~e Beschwerden etc.* pages and pages of complaints *etc.*; **II.** *Adv.: etw. ~ beschreiben* fill pages describing s.th.

Seiten|länge *f* **1.** page length; **2.** *Math.* side length; **~layout** *n* page layout; **~lehne** *f* armrest; **~leitwerk** *n Flug.* tail fin (and rudder assembly); **~linie** *f* **1.** *e-r Familie:* collateral line; **2.** *Tennis:* sideline; *Fußball:* touchline; **~rand** *m* margin; **~ruder** *n Flug.* rudder

seitens *Präp.* + *Gen.* on the part of,

from; (von) by

Seiten|scheibe f Mot. side window; **~scheitel** m side parting (Am. part); **~schiff** n (side) aisle; **~schritt** m side step; **~schwimmen** n sidestroke; **~sprung** m fig. (extramarital) affair, Brit. auch bit on the side umg.; **~stechen** n stitch (in one's side); **~straße** f side street; bes. im Armenviertel: backstreet; **~streifen** m verge; der Autobahn: hard shoulder, Am. shoulder; **~ nicht befahrbar** soft verges (Am. shoulder); **~tal** n side valley; **~tasche** f side pocket; **~teil** n side; **~trakt** m side wing; **~tür** f side door (od. entrance); **~umbruch** m pagination, page makeup

seitenverkehrt I. Adj. the wrong way (a)round, backwards, back to front; **II.** Adv.: Dias ~ zeigen show slides the wrong way (a)round (od. backwards)

Seiten|vorschub m page feed; **~wagen** m sidecar; **~wahl** f Sport choice of ends; **~wand** f side wall; **~wechsel** m **1.** Sport change of ends; **2.** EDV page change; **~weg** m side path

seitenweise Adv. pages (and pages) of; **~ vorgehen** proceed a page at a time

Seitenwind m crosswind, side wind; **seitenwindempfindlich** Adj. Mot. sensitive to side winds

Seiten|zahl f page number; gesamte: number of pages; **~zählung** f EDV page count

seither Adv. since then (od. that time); nachgestellt: auch since; **seitherig** Adj. ... since then

...seitig I. im Adj. **1.** nur attr.; Manuskript etc.: drei~ three-page; mehr~ ... of several pages; **2.** auf genannter Seite: nord~ on the north side; rück~ on the back; **II.** im Adv.: ganz~ bedruckt etc.: over the full page

seitlich I. Adj. side ..., lateral; **~er Zusammenstoß** side-on (od. broadside) collision; siehe auch **Seiten...**; **II.** Adv. at the side; (zur Seite) to the side; **~ von** to the side of; **~ rammen** ram the side of; der Wagen prallte **~ gegen die Leitplanke** the car hit the crash barrier sideways on (Am. broadsided the crash barrier); **III.** Präp. + Gen. at (od. to) the side of

Seitpferd n Sport pommel horse

...seits im Adv. (ausgehend von) amtlicher~ officially; ärztlicher~ on the part of the doctors (od. medical profession)

seitwärts Adv. sideways; (zur Seite) to the side; (an der Seite) on the side

Sekante f; -, -n; Math. secant

Sekret n; -s, -e; Physiol. secretion

Sekretär m; -s, -e **1.** (male) secretary; (Assistent) assistant; **2.** (Schreibtisch) secretary, bureau; **3.** Zool. secretary (bird); **Sekretariat** n; -(e)s, -e (administrative) office; (Verwaltung) administration; **Sekretärin** f; -, -nen (female) secretary

Sekretion f; -, -en; Med., Geol. secretion

Sekt m; -(e)s, -e champagne-style sparkling wine; (Champagner) champagne; **~bar** f champagne bar

Sekte f; -, -n; oft pej. sect; extreme: cult

Sektempfang m champagne reception

Sekten|beauftragte m, f; -n, -n adviser on religious sects; **~führer** m, **~führerin** f leader of a (od. the) sect (od. cult); **~wesen** n sectarianism

Sekt|flasche f champagne bottle; **~frühstück** n champagne breakfast;

~glas n champagne glass

Sektierer m, **Sektiererin** f, **sektiererisch** Adj. sectarian; **Sektierertum** n; -s, kein Pl. sectarianism

Sektion f; -, -en **1.** (Abteilung) section, division, department; **2.** Med., e-s Tiers: dissection; (Obduktion) autopsy, postmortem

Sektions|befund m Med. postmortem findings Pl., results Pl. of a (od. the) postmortem; **~chef** m österr. head of department

Sekt|kelch m champagne glass; **~kellerei** f champagne cellars Pl.; **~korken** m champagne cork; **~kübel** m champagne bucket; **~laune** f umg.: sich in **~ zu etw. hinreißen lassen** be propelled into doing s.th. under the influence of champagne

Sektor m; -s, -en sector; fig. (Sachgebiet) auch area, field

...sektor m, im Subst. (Bereich): Energie~ energy sector

Sektorengrenze f hist. sector boundary

Sektschale f champagne glass (od. saucer)

Sekund f; -, -en → **Sekunde** 2

Sekunda f; -, Sekunden; Päd. **1.** altm. sixth and seventh year of grammar school; **2.** österr. second year (of grammar school); **Sekundaner** m; -s, -, **Sekundanerin** f; -, -nen; Päd. **1.** altm. pupil in the sixth or seventh year of grammar school; **2.** österr. second year (grammar school) pupil

Sekundant m; -en, -en beim Duell, Boxen, Schach: second

sekundär I. Adj. secondary; **als ~ einstufen** consider of secondary importance; **II.** Adv.: **~ in Betracht kommen** be a secondary consideration

Sekundär|... im Subst. mst secondary; **~infektion** f Med. secondary infection; **~literatur** f secondary literature

Sekundar|schule f schw. secondary school; **~stufe** f Päd. secondary school (Am. high school) level; **~ I** Brit. etwa lower and middle school, Am. etwa middle school, junior high (school); **~ II** Brit. etwa sixth form, Am. etwa senior high (school)

Sekundär|tugend f lesser virtue; **~vegetation** f Bio. secondary vegetation

Sekunde f; -, -n **1.** second (auch Math. und Mus.); **zehn Uhr auf die ~** ten o'clock on the dot; **mit e-r ~ Vorsprung** with a lead of a second; (eine) **~! umg.** just a second!; **2.** Mus. second; **große/kleine ~** major/minor second

...sekunde f, im Subst.: Hundertstel~ hundredth of a second

Sekunden|bruchteil m fraction of a second, split second; **~kleber** m superglue, instant glue

sekunden|genau Adj.: **~e Abrechnung** Telef. per-second billing; **~lang I.** Adj. attr. lasting (od. of) several seconds; **ein ~es Zögern** a few seconds' hesitation; **II.** Adv. for (several) seconds

Sekundenschlaf m am Steuer: momentary nodding off

sekundenschnell I. Adj. Reaktion, Entscheidung: split-second, lightning; Antwort: quick-fire; **II.** Adv.: **alles ging ~** it all happened in a matter of seconds (od. in a flash); **Sekundenschnelle** f: **in ~** in a matter of seconds

Sekundenzeiger m second hand

sekundieren v/i. second (j-m s.o.); Boxen, Schach: act as a second (j-m to s.o.); fig. support (s.o.), back (s.o.) up

sekündlich Adv. every (unbestimmt: any) second

Sekurit® n; -s, kein Pl. toughened (safety) glass

selbe Adj. same; **zur ~n Zeit** at the same time, simultaneously

selber Pron. umg. → **selbst** I 1

Selbermachen n; -s, kein Pl.; umg. do-it-yourself, DIY; **Möbel zum ~** furniture to make yourself; als Bausatz: self-assembly furniture; **Selbermacher** m umg. do-it-yourselfer, handyman, DIY man

selbige Pron. altm. od. hum. the (self)same; **in ~r Nacht** that same night

selbst I. Pron. **1.** ich **~** I myself; er **~** he himself; **mach es ~** Slogan: do it yourself; **sie möchte es ~ machen** she wants to do it herself (od. on her own); **das muss ich mir ~ ansehen** I'll have to see that for myself; **ich habe ihn nicht ~ gesprochen** I didn't talk to him myself (od. personally); **der Autor war ~ anwesend** the author was there in person (od. himself); **mit sich** (Dat.) **~ sprechen** talk to o.s.; **von ~** (eigenständig) of one's own accord; Sache: of its own accord, by itself; **~ ist der Mann** od. **die Frau!** there's nothing like doing it yourself; **er war die Höflichkeit ~** he was politeness personified (od. itself); **er ist die Ruhe ~** he's unflappable; **zu sich ~ kommen** collect one's thoughts, sort oneself out; **ich komme kaum mehr zu mir ~** vor Arbeit: I hardly get time to think, I hardly get a minute to myself; **wie geht's? - gut! und ~?** umg. how are you? - fine, and you?; **du bist ein Idiot! - ~ einer!** you're an idiot! - look who's talking! (od. it takes one to know one); **2.** von **~** by itself; (automatisch) automatically; **das versteht sich (doch) von ~** that goes without saying; **dann geht alles wie von ~** umg. then everything wil go like clockwork; **3.** mit P.P.: **~ erklärt**, **~ ernannt** attr. self-styled, self-proclaimed, förm. soi-disant; **~ erstellt** attr. Statistik, Datei etc.: self-compiled; **~ erworben** Eigentum: acquired with one's own money; **~ finanziert** Eigenheim etc.: paid for with one's own money, self-financed; **~ gebacken** Brot etc.: homemade; **~ gebastelt** homemade; **ist das ~ gebastelt?** did you make that yourself?; **~ gebaut** Haus etc.: built by the owner, self-built; **~ gebrannt** Schnaps: home-distilled; **~ gebraut** Bier: home-brewed; **~ gedrehte Zigarette** hand-rolled (od. roll-your--own) cigarette, Brit. auch roll-up; **~ gemacht** homemade; **~ genäht** Kleid etc.: self-made; **~ genutzt** Wohneigentum: owner-occupied; **~ gepflückt** Beeren etc.: picked o.s.; **~ geschneidert** homemade; **ist das ~ geschrieben?** did you write that yourself?; **~ gesteckte Grenzen** self-imposed limits; **~ gesteuert** Boot: self-drive; Tech. automatic; **~ gesteuertes Lernen** self-paced learning; **~ gestrickt** homemade; fig. Philosophie etc.: homespun; **ist das ~ gestrickt?** did you knit that yourself?; **~ gewählt** Isolation etc.: self-chosen; negativ: self-imposed; **~ gezogen** Gemüse etc.: homegrown; **~ verdient** Geld: made with one's own efforts; **mit ~ verdientem Geld** with one's hard-earned money; **~ verfasst** Aufsatz etc.: written o.s., of one's own composition; **II.** Adv. (sogar, auch) even; **~ wenn** even if

Selbst *n*; *-, kein Pl., geh.* self; **wieder sein altes ~ sein** be one's old self again; **das ~ aufgeben** surrender one's identity

Selbst|abholer *m person who collects goods, mail etc. himself/herself*; **Möbel für ~ zur Selbstmontage**: flatpack (*od.* self-assembly) furniture; **~achtung** *f* self-esteem, self-respect

selbständig *etc.* → **selbstständig**

Selbst|anklage *f* self-accusation, self-incrimination; **~ansteckung** *f Med.* autoinfection; **~anzeige** *f Jur.* self-denunciation; *steuerlich*: voluntary declaration; **~ erstatten** turn oneself in (to the police); *beim Finanzamt*: make a voluntary declaration; **~aufgabe** *f* surrender (*od.* erosion) of one's identity; **~auflösung** *f*: **vor der ~ stehen** be about to dissolve itself; **~ausbeutung** *f* self-exploitation; **~auslöser** *m Fot.* delayed action shutter release, self-timer

Selbstbedienung *f* self-service; **Restaurant mit ~** self-service restaurant, cafeteria; **ist hier ~?** is it self-service here?

Selbstbedienungs|laden *m* self-service shop (*Am.* store); (*Supermarkt*) (small) supermarket; **~mentalität** *f* self-service mentality; **~restaurant** *n* self-service restaurant, cafeteria

Selbst|befreiung *f* 1. *Jur.* (unaided) escape from custody; 2. *Psych.* self-liberation; **~befriedigung** *f* masturbation; **das ist reine ~** *fig.* it's pure self-gratification; **~befruchtung** *f Bot.* self-fertilization; **~behalt** *m*; *-(e)s, -e Versicherung*: excess; **~behauptung** *f* self-assertion, self-assertiveness; **~beherrschung** *f* self-control; **~bejahung** *f* (complete) self-satisfaction; **~bekenntnis** *n* confession; **~beköstigung** *f* self-catering; **~bemitleidung** *f* self-pity; **~beobachtung** *f* introspection, self-observation; **~beschränkung** *f* self-restraint; **~beschreibung** *f* self-portrayal; **~besinnung** *f* self-contemplation; **~bespiegelung** *f* narcissism; **~bestätigung** *f* boost to one's self-confidence; **das war für ihn e-e ~** that gave his self-confidence (*od.* ego) a boost; **Kinder brauchen ~** children need self-confidence; **~bestäubung** *f Bot.* self-pollination

selbstbestimmt *Adj.* self-determined, independent; **Selbstbestimmung** *f* self-determination; **Selbstbestimmungsrecht** *n* (right of) self-determination

Selbst|beteiligung *f Versicherung*: excess; **~betrug** *m* self-deception; **~beweihräucherung** *f pej.* self-adulation

selbstbewusst I. *Adj.* 1. (self-)confident, self-assured; 2. *Philos.* self-aware; **II.** *Adv.*: **~ auftreten** be self-confident (*od.* self-assured); **Selbstbewusstsein** *n* 1. self-confidence, self-assurance; 2. *Philos.* self-awareness

Selbstbezichtigung *f* self-accusation

selbstbezogen *Adj.* self-cent|red (*Am.* -ered), egocentric; **Selbstbezogenheit** *f* self-centredness (*Am.* -centeredness), obsession with oneself

Selbst|bild *n* self-image; **sein ~** the way he sees himself; **~bildnis** *n* self-portrait; **~biographie** *f* autobiography; **~bräunungscreme** *f Kosmetik*: self-tanning lotion (*od.* cream), *Am. auch* bronzer, bottle tan *umg.*; **~darsteller** *m*, **~darstellerin** *f*: **er ist ein**

genialer Selbstdarsteller he is brilliant when it comes to promoting his image; **~darstellung** *f* self-projection; (*Imagepflege*) image cultivation; **er nützt jede Chance zur ~** he takes every opportunity to promote his image; **~diagnose** *f Computer*: self-diagnosis; **~disziplin** *f* (self-)discipline; **~einschätzung** *f* self-assessment; (*Selbstbild*) self-image, image of oneself; **~entfaltung** *f* self-development; (*Selbstverwirklichung*) self-fulfil(l)ment; **~entfremdung** *f Philos.* alienation from self; **~entlader** *m fachspr.* (*LKW*) tipper truck, *Am.* dump truck; **~entzündung** *f* self-ignition, spontaneous combustion

Selbsterfahrung *f* self-awareness; **Selbsterfahrungsgruppe** *f* consciousness-raising (*od.* self-awareness) group

Selbsterhaltung *f* self-preservation; **Selbsterhaltungstrieb** *m* instinct for self-preservation

Selbst|erkenntnis *f* self-knowledge; **~ ist der erste Schritt zur Besserung** you can only improve if you first recognize your faults; **~erniedrigung** *f* self-abasement

Selbsterzeuger *m*, **~in** *f* producer of one's own food *etc.*, (largely) self-sufficient person

Selbstfahrer[1] *m* (*Rollstuhl*) self-propelled wheelchair

Sebstfahrer[2] *m*, **~in** *f Mot.*: **er ist Selbstfahrer** he drives himself, he doesn't have a chauffeur; **Autovermietung für Selbstfahrer** self-drive car hire (*Am.* rental)

Selbst|finanzierung *f* self-financing, financing with one's own funds; *im Betrieb*: internal generation of funds; **~findung** *f* self-discovery

Selbstgänger *m*; *-s, -; umg. fig.* 1. (*etwas, das problemlos von alleine funktioniert*): **Existenzgründungen in der Internet-Branche sind keine ~ mehr** Internet start-ups no longer generate automatic success without any hitches; **ich halte Bayern München nicht für e-n ~** I don't think Bayern München is hooked on success forever; **keine Unternehmensgemeinschaft ist ein ~** no merger runs that smoothly; **sind diese bevorzugten Industriestandorte nicht ~?** are these preferred industrial locations not self-perpetuating?; **ein ~ wird die neue Saison bestimmt nicht** we can't expect the new season to become a sweeping success (without a great deal of effort on our part); **Beach Volleyball ist kein ~ mehr** beach volleyball is no longer a popular game that easily attracts crowds; **für Sven als Legastheniker ist die Schule kein ~** Sven being dyslexic, going to school is no mean feat for him; 2. (*etwas Selbstverständliches*): **sein fünfter WM-Titel sei keinesfalls ein ~ gewesen** his fifth world title was by no means to be taken for granted; **glückliche Ehen sind heute nicht unbedingt ~** happy marriages aren't necessarily a matter of course nowadays; **es ist ein ~, dass die bestehenden Gesetze auch anzuwenden sind** it is self-evident that existing laws have to be applied; **erfolgreiche Öffentlichkeitsarbeit ist kein ~** successful PR work is by no means a self-fulfilling prophesy; **wir dachten, die Liebe wäre ein ~** we thought love would stay forever; 3. (*etwas, das sich notgedrungen*

ergeben muss): *O Mann, Puchheim*: **die spielten doch Kinderfußball. Das war doch ein ~** They were a walk-over; 4. (*etwas, das logischerweise zu erwarten ist*): **das zu erwartende Urteil wäre ein ~** the judgement would be the sort one would have expected; **Nein, das ist kein ~.** Ich glaube nicht, *dass jeder Athlet damit zufrieden ist, wenn eine bereits gefallene Entscheidung der Wettbewerbsleitung korrigiert wird.* No, I don't think this can be taken for granted; 5. (*etwas, das sich leicht erfolgreich vermarkten lässt*) surefire success; **ein ~ in Sachen Unterhaltung** an instant success in terms of entertainment; **unser neues Versicherungspaket ist konkurrenzlos - ein ~** our new insurance package is unrival(l)ed: sure seller; **wie die Soap „Big Brother“ zum ~ wurde** how the soap opera "Big Brother" became a regular feature on TV; **ein US-College-Radio-~** a piece of music very often played by US college radio stations; 6. (*etwas, das nicht viel Können abverlangt*): **das Gelände war für die Radsportler dennoch kein ~** nevertheless, the terrain wasn't that easy to tackle for the cyclists; **bei Hobby-Zauberkünstlern kommen oft ~ zum Einsatz** amateur magicians often use tricks that don't easily afford much skill and are nevertheless impressive; 7. (*ein Muss*): **diese Punk-Jazz-Nummer ist ein ~ für Musik-Freaks** (, *die romantische Akustiktitel ebenso lieben wie Punkgitarren*) this punkjazz piece is a must

Selbstgedrehte *f* hand-rolled (*od.* roll-your-own) cigarette, *Brit. auch* roll-up; **~ rauchen** roll one's own

selbstgefällig *Adj.* complacent, self-satisfied, smug; **Selbstgefälligkeit** *f* complacency, smugness

Selbstgefühl *n* → **Selbstwertgefühl**

selbstgenügsam *Adj.* contented, *präd. auch* satisfied with one's lot; (*bescheiden*) modest; **Selbstgenügsamkeit** *f* contentedness; (*Bescheidenheit*) modesty

selbstgerecht *Adj.* self-righteous, *attr. auch* Haltung *etc.*: holier-than-thou; **Selbstgerechtigkeit** *f* self-righteousness, self-righteous attitude

Selbstgespräch *n* monolog(ue); soliloquy; **~e führen** talk to o.s., soliloquize

selbsthaftend *Adj.* self-adhesive

Selbsthass *m* self-hate (*od.* -hatred)

selbstheilend *Adj.*: **~e Kräfte** self-healing powers; **Selbstheilungskraft** *f* self-healing power

selbstherrlich I. *Adj.* high-handed; (*überheblich*) overbearing, arrogant; **II.** *Adv.*: **~ handeln** behave high-handedly (*od.* arrogantly); **Selbstherrlichkeit** *f* high-handedness; (*Überheblichkeit*) arrogance

Selbsthilfe *f* self-help; **zur ~ schreiten** take matters into one's own hands; **Hilfe zur ~** helping people to help themselves; **~gruppe** *f* self-help group; **~verein** *m* self-help association

Selbst|induktion *f Etech.* self-induction; **~inszenierung** *f fig.* self-promotion, self-glorification

Selbstironie *f* self-irony, self-mockery; **selbstironisch** *Adj.* self-mocking

Selbstjustiz *f*: **~ üben** take the law into one's own hands

Selbstklebeetikett *n* self-adhesive label; **Selbstklebefolie** *f* self-adhesive film; **selbstklebend** *Adj.* (self-)adhe-

sive; *Umschlag*: self-seal ...
Selbstkontrolle *f* **1.** *engS. und Tech.* self-check(ing); *in der Schule etc.*: checking one's own work; *der Medien*: self-censorship, self-regulation; *Freiwillige* ~ *der Filmwirtschaft* (**FSK**) voluntary self-censorship by the film industry; **2.** (*Selbstbeherrschung*) self--control
Selbstkosten *Pl.* prime costs; **~preis** *m* cost price; *zum* ~ at cost (price)
Selbstkritik *f* self-criticism; ~ *üben* be self-critical; **selbstkritisch** *Adj.* self--critical
Selbst|ladepistole *f* self-loading pistol, automatic (pistol); **~läufer** *m umg. fig.* **1.** surefire success; **2.** → *Selbstgänger* 1 - 5, 7; **~laut** *m Ling.* vowel; **~lerner** *m* autodidact; *eine Software für* ~ (a) self-study (*od.* teach-yourself) software
selbstleuchtend *Adj.* luminous
Selbstlob *n* self-praise
selbstlos *Adj.* selfless, unselfish; **Selbstlosigkeit** *f* selflessness
Selbst|medikation *f* self-administered medication; **~mitleid** *n* self-pity; *in* ~ *verfallen* descend into self-pity
Selbstmord *m* suicide; ~ *begehen* commit suicide; *mit* ~ *drohen* threaten to commit suicide; ~ *auf Raten umg.* slow suicide; ~ *mit Messer und Gabel umg. fig.* killing oneself by overeating; **~absicht** *f* suicidal intentions *Pl.*; **~anschlag** *m* suicide attack
Selbstmörder *m*, **~in** *f* suicide (victim); *ich bin doch kein Selbstmörder! umg.* I'm not going to kill myself, I have no intention of committing suicide; **selbstmörderisch I.** *Adj. nur attr.* suicidal (*auch fig.*); **II.** *Adv.*: *sich* ~ *verhalten umg. fig.* behave in a suicidal manner; *er fährt geradezu* ~ *umg.* his driving is positively suicidal
Selbstmord|gedanken *Pl.* thoughts of suicide; *die* ~ *ließen ihn nicht los* the idea *Sg.* (*od.* thoughts) of suicide would not go away
selbstmordgefährdet *Adj.* suicidal; ~ *sein* have suicidal tendencies, be a potential suicide
Selbstmord|kandidat *m*, **~kandidatin** *f* potential suicide; **~kommando** *n* **1.** suicide mission; **2.** (*Personen*) suicide squad; **~rate** *f* suicide rate; **~versuch** *m* suicide attempt, attempted suicide; *e-n* ~ *machen* try (*od.* attempt) to commit suicide
Selbstporträt *n* self-portrait
selbstprüfend *Adj. EDV*: **~er Code** self-checking code
Selbstquälerei *f* self-torment, self-torture; **selbstquälerisch I.** *Adj.* self--tormenting; **II.** *Adv.*: *sich* ~ *den Kopf zermartern* rack one's brains in a torment
selbstredend *Adv. altm. od. hum.* naturally
Selbstreflexion *f* self-contemplation
selbstregelnd *Adj.* self-regulating
selbstreinigend *Adj. Grill etc.*: self--cleaning; **Selbstreinigungskraft** *f* self-cleaning power
Selbstschuss *m* spring gun; **~anlage** *f* automatic firing device
Selbstschutz *m* self-defen|ce (*Am.* -se)
selbstsicher I. *Adj.* self-confident, self-assured, sure of oneself; **II.** *Adv.*: ~ *auftreten* have a self-confident (*od.* self-assured) manner; **Selbstsicherheit** *f* self-confidence, self-assurance
selbstständig I. *Adj.* (*unabhängig*) in-

dependent; *wirtschaftlich*: self-supporting; *beruflich*, *Person*: independent, self-employed; *attr. Journalist*, *Architekt etc.*: freelance ...; *Staat*: autonomous; *an* ~*es Arbeiten gewöhnt* used to working on one's own; *sich* ~ *machen im Beruf*: start up one's own business; *Journalist etc.*: go freelance; *umg. fig.* (*verloren gehen*) disappear; *hum. Sache*: walk, grow legs; ~ *werden auch Pol.* become independent, *Land auch*: gain independence; **II.** *Adv.* independently (*ohne fremde Hilfe*) oneself, on one's own; ~ *denken* think for o.s.; ~ *arbeitender Drucker EDV* stand-alone printer; **Selbstständige** *m*, *f*; *-n*, *-n*; (*Geschäftsmann etc.*) self--employed person; (*Journalist etc.*) freelance(r); **Selbstständigkeit** *f* independence (*auch im Verhalten*), *Pol. auch* sovereignty, autonomy; *zur* ~ *erziehen* teach to be independent
Selbst|steuerung *f* automatic control; *Naut.* automatic steering; *Flug.* automatic pilot; **~studium** *n* self-study, private study; *im* ~ *aneignen etc.*: through self-study (*od.* private study)
Selbstsucht *f* selfishness, egotism; **selbstsüchtig** *Adj.* selfish, self-seeking, egotistic(al)
selbsttätig I. *Adj.* automatic; **II.** *Adv.* automatically
Selbst|täuschung *f* self-delusion; **~tor** *n Sport* own goal; **~tötung** *f* suicide
selbsttragend *Adj. Archit., Tech.* self--supporting; *Wirts.* self-sustaining; **~e** *Bauweise/Karosserie Mot.* unitary (*Am.* unitized) construction / monocoque (*Am.* unitized) bodywork
Selbst|überschätzung *f* conceitedness; *an* ~ *leiden umg.* have an exaggerated opinion of one's abilities; *weitS.* suffer from a swollen head; **~überwindung** *f* will power; *es kostete ihn viel* ~ it cost him a great effort of will; **~verachtung** *f* self-contempt
selbstverantwortlich I. *Adj.* independent, autonomous; **II.** *Adv.*: *etw.* ~ *leiten/entscheiden* be personally in charge of s.th. / responsible for a decision on s.th.; **Selbstverantwortung** *f*; *in* ~ *entscheiden etc.*: on one's own responsibility
Selbstverbrennung *f* self-immolation
selbstvergessen *Adj. und Adv.* lost in thought, oblivious to the world
Selbst|verlag *m*: *im* ~ self-published, published by the author; **~verleugnung** *f* self-denial
selbstverliebt *Adj.* in love with o.s., narcissistic; **Selbstverliebtheit** *f* self--love, narcissism
Selbst|vermarkter *m*, **~vermarkterin** *f* direct seller; **~vermarktung** *f* direct selling; **~vernichtung** *f* self-destruction
selbstverordnet *Adj.* self-prescribed; *Ruhepause etc.*: self-ordained
Selbst|verpfleger *m*, **~verpflegerin** *f* self-caterer, s.o. who cooks for him/ herself; **~verpflegung** *f* self-catering; **~verpflichtung** *f* self-commitment
Selbstverschulden *n* one's own fault; *es liegt* ~ / *kein* ~ *vor* there is some/no self-culpability in this case; **selbstverschuldet** *Adj.*: *der Unfall war* ~ he (*od.* she, they) caused the accident himself (*od.* herself, themselves)
Selbst|versorger *m*, **~versorgerin** *f*: *sie sind Selbstversorger* they're self--sufficient; *Appartements für* ~ self-catering flats, *Am.* apartments with cooking facilities; **~versorgung** *f* self-

-sufficiency; *im Urlaub*: self-catering
selbstverständlich I. *Adj.* (*natürlich*) (perfectly) natural; (*offensichtlich*) obvious; *das ist keineswegs* ~ that cannot be assumed; *etw. als* ~ *hinnehmen* take s.th. for granted; → *auch Selbstverständlichkeit*; **II.** *Adv.* of course, naturally; (*ohne Bedenken*) *etw. tun*: as a matter of course; *einschränkend* (*freilich*) of course; ~! (*natürlich!*, *sicher!*) of course!, *Am. auch* sure!; *wie* ~ *tat sie das für uns* she did this for us too, as though it were the most natural thing in the world
Selbstverständlichkeit *f*: *es ist doch e-e* ~, *dass* it goes without saying that, there's no question that, it's only natural that; *mit e-r* ~ with a naturalness (*od.* matter-of-factness); *das ist schließlich keine* ~*!* it's by no means a foregone conclusion; *er machte es mit e-r solchen* ~ he did it as if it was the most natural thing in the world; *sanitäre Anlagen sind dort keine* ~ you can't assume (*od.* take it for granted) that they have sanitation there; *ein 13. Monatsgehalt ist bei uns e-e* ~ in our firm (*od.* company) everybody gets an extra month's salary as a matter of course
Selbst|verständnis *n*: *j-s* ~ s.o.'s self--image, the image s.o. has of himself (*od.* herself); **~nationales** ~ national identity; **~verstümmelung** *f* self-mutilation; **~versuch** *m* self-experiment; *e-n* ~ *machen* experiment on oneself, use oneself as a guinea-pig; **~verteidigung** *f* self-defen|ce (*Am.* -se); **~vertrauen** *n* self-confidence, self-assurance
Selbstverwaltung *f* autonomy, self--government; **Selbstverwaltungsrecht** *n* right to autonomy
Selbst|verwirklichung *f* self-realization; *bes. Psych.* self-actualization; **~vorwurf** *m* self-reproach; *sich* (*Dat.*) *Selbstvorwürfe machen* reproach o.s.; **~wähler** *m Telef.* STD user, *Am.* direct dialing caller; **~wahrnehmung** *f* self-perception
Selbstwertgefühl *n* self-esteem; *ein übertriebenes* ~ *besitzen* have an exaggerated opinion of oneself
Selbst|zahler *m*, **~zahlerin** *f im Gesundheitswesen*: self-pay patient; **~zensur** *f* self-censorship; **~zerfleischung** *f* self-castigation
selbstzerstörerisch *Adj.* self-destructive
Selbstzeugnis *n* self-portrayal; *die Geschichte der Juden in* ~*sen* the self--history of the Jews, the/a history of the Jews as they saw themselves
selbstzufrieden *Adj. pej.* complacent, smug, self-satisfied; **Selbstzufriedenheit** *f pej.* complacency, smugness
Selbst|zweck *m* end in itself; *das ist reiner* ~ this is done purely for its own sake; **~zweifel** *m* self-doubt; ~ *bekommen* begin to have doubts about o.s.
selchen *v/t. österr., südd.* smoke; → *Geselche*; **Selchfleisch** *n* (*Geselchtes*) *österr.*, *südd.* smoked meat (*bes.* pork)
selektieren *v/t.* select; **Selektion** *f*; *-*, *-en* selection; **Selektionstheorie** *f Bio.* theory of natural selection; **selektiv I.** *Adj.* selective; **II.** *Adv.*: ~ *vorgehen* take a selective approach; **Selektivität** *f*; *-*, *kein Pl. Radio*: selectivity; **Selektorkanal** *m EDV* selector channel
Selen [ze'le:n] *n*; *-s*, *kein Pl.*; *Chem.*

S

selenium

Selfmademan ['sɛlfmeːdmən] *m*; -s, *Selfmademen* self-made man

selig I. *Adj.* **1.** *kirchl.* (*gesegnet, kath. selig gesprochen*) blessed; **~ preisen** bless; *fig.* (*verherrlichen*) glorify; **~ sprechen** *kath.* beatify; **2.** (*überglücklich*) overjoyed; *Gesichtsausdruck, Lächeln etc.*: blissful; *sie ist ganz ~ mit i-m neuen Auto* she is absolutely delighted (*umg.* thrilled to bits, *Am.* death) with her new car; **3.** *umg.* (*beschwipst*) tiddly; **4.** *nur attr.* (*verstorben*) late, deceased; *mein ~er Vater od. mein Vater ~ altm.* my late father; *Gott hab ihn ~* God rest his soul; → *glauben* I 1; **II.** *Adv.* **1.** **~ entschlafen** *geh. euph.* go to one's maker; **2.** *sich ~ in den Armen liegen* be wrapped in a blissful embrace; **~ lächeln** smile blissfully

Selige *m, f*; -n, -n; *kirchl.* blessed person; *die ~n* the Blessed; *die Gefilde der ~n* the Elysian fields; **Seligkeit** *f* **1.** *kirchl.* (state of) blessedness, beatitude; *ewige ~ auch* everlasting life; **2.** (*Glück*) perfect happiness, (sheer) bliss

Seligpreisung *f kirchl.* blessing; *die ~en bibl.* the Beatitudes

Seligsprechung *f kath.* beatification

Seller ['zɛlɐ] *m*; -s, - **1.** (*Produkt*) best-seller; **2.** (*Verkäufer[in]*) salesperson

...seller *m, im Subst.* **1.** (*Produkt*): *Top~* top seller; **2.** (*Verkäufer[in]*): *Top~* top salesperson

Sellerie *m*; -s, *f*; -, *kein Pl.* celeriac; (*Stangensellerie*) celery; **~knolle** *f* celeriac root; **~salat** *m* celeriac (root) salad; **~stange** *f* celery stalk; **~staude** *f* celery plant

selten I. *Adj.* rare; (*knapp, spärlich*) scarce; (*außergewöhnlich*) rare, exceptional; *ein ~er Gast* an infrequent visitor; *so etwas geht in den ~sten Fällen gut* such things very rarely turn out well; *etwas/nichts Seltenes* a/no rarity; *~er Vogel umg. fig.* odd character, queer fish; **II.** *Adv.* rarely, seldom; *höchst ~* extremely rarely, once in a blue moon; *es kommt ~ vor, dass er* he rarely ...; *der Wein ist so bekömmlich wie ~ einer* such a wholesome wine is only too rare; *ein ~ schönes Exemplar* an exceptionally beautiful specimen, a specimen of rare beauty; *e-e ~ dumme Frage umg.* a particularly stupid question; *~ so gelacht! umg.* I haven't laughed so much in a long time; **Seltenheit** *f* **1.** rarity, rareness; (*Knappheit*) scarcity; **2.** (*Sache*) rarity; *tödliche Unfälle sind leider keine ~* fatal accidents are unfortunately not uncommon; **Seltenheitswert** *m* rarity value; *ein Foto von od. mit ~* a photo showing a rare sight, a rare photo

Selters *f, n*; -, -, **~wasser** *n* mineral water, *Am. auch* seltzer

seltsam I. *Adj.* strange, odd, peculiar; *es ist schon ~* it's very strange; *mir ist ganz ~* I feel really strange; *mir ist etwas Seltsames passiert* a strange (*od.* odd, funny) thing happened to me; **II.** *Adv.* strangely; *j-n ~ ansehen* look at s.o. in a strange way, give s.o. a strange look; *ich war ~ berührt* it moved me in a strange way; **seltsamerweise** *Adv.* strangely (*od.* oddly) enough; **Seltsamkeit** *f* **1.** strangeness, oddness, peculiarity; **2.** (*Sache*) oddity

Semantik *f*; -, *kein Pl.* semantics *Pl.* (*als Fach V. im Sg.*); **Semantiker** *m*; -s, -, **Semantikerin** *f*; -, -nen semanti-

cist; **semantisch I.** *Adj.* semantic; **II.** *Adv.* semantically

Semester *n*; -s, - **1.** *Univ.* semester; *er ist im dritten ~* he's in his third semester; *ich habe acht ~ Jura studiert* I read (*Am.* studied) law for four years; *wie viel ~ musst du noch machen? umg.* how many semesters have you got to go?; *während des ~s* during term-time; *die höheren ~* the senior years; **2.** (*Student*) *die jüngeren ~* the first and second year students, *Am.* the underclassmen; *die älteren ~* the senior students, *Am. auch* the upper-classmen; *er ist schon ein älteres ~ hum. fig.* he's getting on (in years); **~arbeit** *f etwa* term paper; **~beginn** *m*: (*zu*) *~* (at the) beginning of the semester; **~ende** *n*: (*am*) *~* (at the) end of the semester; **~ferien** *Pl.* vacation *Sg., Brit. umg. auch* vac

...semestrig *im Adj. Studium etc.*: *vier~* four-semester, two-year; *mehr~* ... lasting several semesters

Semifinale *n* semifinal

Semikolon *n*; -s, -s semicolon

Seminar *n*; -s, -e **1.** *Univ., Fortbildung*: (*Lehrveranstaltung*) seminar; *ein ~ für Menschenführung* a seminar on human resource management; **2.** *Univ.* (*Institut*) department; *das englische od. anglistische ~* the English Department; **3.** *für Lehrerbildung*: teacher training college; **4.** (*Priesterseminar*) seminary; **~arbeit** *f Univ.* seminar paper

Seminarist *m*; -en, -en, **~in** *f*; -, -nen seminarist

Seminar|leiter *m*, **~leiterin** *f auch Fortbildung*: seminar leader; **~schein** *m* seminar attendance certificate; *e-n ~ machen umg.* complete a seminar; **~teilnehmer** *m*, **~teilnehmerin** *f* participant in a (*od.* the) seminar

Semiotik *f*; -, *kein Pl.* semiotics *Pl.* (*als Fach V. im Sg.*); **Semiotiker** *m*; -s, -, **Semiotikerin** *f*; -, -nen semiotician

semipermeabel *Adj.* semipermeable

Semit *m*; -en, -en, **Semitin** *f*; -, -nen Semite; **semitisch** *Adj. auch Ling.* Semitic; **~-hamitische Sprachen** Afro-Asiatic (*früher* Semito-Hamitic) languages; **Semitistik** *f*; -, *kein Pl.* Semitics (*als Fach V. im Sg.*)

Semmel *f*; -, -n *bes. österr., südd.* roll; *wie warme ~n weggehen umg.* be selling like hot cakes

...semmel *f, im Subst.*: *Butter~* buttered roll

semmelblond *Adj.* flaxen(-haired)

Semmel|brösel *Pl.* breadcrumbs; **~knödel** *m* bread dumpling; **~mehl** *n* breadcrumbs *Pl.*

sempern *v/i. österr. umg.* whine

Senat *m*; -s, -e **1.** *Pol., Univ.* senate; *in den USA*: Senate; *der Berliner/Hamburger ~* the Berlin/Hamburg Senate; **2.** *Jur.* panel of judges; *der Erste/Zweite ~ des Bundesverfassungsgerichts* the First/Second Instance of the Federal Constitutional Court; **Senator** *m*; -s, -en, **Senatorin** *f*; -, -nen senator; *in den USA*: Senator

Senats|beschluss *m* decree by the senate (*od.* Senate); **~mitglied** *n* member of the senate (*od.* Senate), senator, Senator; **~präsident** *m*, **~präsidentin** *f* chairman (*Frau*: chairwoman) of the senate; **~saal** *m* Senate chamber; **~sprecher** *m*, **~sprecherin** *f USA*: Senate Majority Leader, floor leader; **~wahlen** *Pl.* elections to the Senate

Sendbote *m fig.*: *~n des Frühlings etc.* harbingers of spring *lit.*

Sende|anlage *f* transmitter; **~anstalt** *f* broadcasting organization (*od.* station); **~antenne** *f* transmitting aerial (*Am.* antenna); **~beginn** *m*: *~ ist um ...* we are on the air from ..., transmission begins at ...; **~bereich** *m* transmission range (*od.* area), area served; **~betrieb** *m* (radio and television) broadcasting operations *Pl.*; **~erlaubnis** *f* permission to transmit; **~folge** *f* program(me) sequence, program(me)s *Pl.*; **~frequenz** *f* transmitting frequency; **~gebiet** *n* transmission range (*od.* area), area served; **~leistung** *f* transmitting power; **~mast** *m* transmitter mast, *Am.* broadcasting tower

senden; *sendet, sendete od. sandte, hat gesendet od. gesandt* **I.** *vt.* (*sendete, schw. auch sandte*) *Funk*: transmit; *Radio, TV: auch* broadcast; *in Stereo ~* broadcast in stereo; *wir ~ rund um die Uhr* we are on the air 24 hours a day; **II.** *v/t.* (*sandte*) (*schicken*) send (*nach j-m* for s.o.); (*übermitteln*) send, forward

Sende|pause *f* intermission, interval; *umg. fig.* silence; *jetzt hast du mal ~! umg.* put a sock in it, will you?, *Am.* shut your trap!; **~platz** *m* spot (*Am.* right) on the schedule

Sender *m*; -s, - *Funk, Radio*: transmitter; (*Faxgerät*) sending (*od.* transmitting) machine, sender; *Rundfunk*: radio station; *TV* television station

Sende|raum *m* studio; **~rechte** *Pl.* broadcasting rights; **~reihe** *f* series *Sg.* (of broadcasts)

Sender|netz *n* transmitter network; **~speicher** *m Radio*: station memory; **~suchlauf** *m* automatic tuning

Sende|saal *m* audience studio; **~schluss** *m* closedown; **~störung** *f* break in transmission; **~studio** *n* broadcasting studio; **~termin** *m* (scheduled) broadcasting time, time of transmission; **~turm** *m* radio (*TV* television) tower; **~zeit** *f* broadcasting time, time of transmission; *Koll.* air time; *die ~ überziehen* overrun; *zur besten ~* at prime time; **~zentrale** *f* broadcasting cent|re (*Am.* -er)

Sendung *f* **1.** (*Paket*) parcel, *bes. Am.* package; *Wirts.* consignment, *größer*: shipment; *e-e postlagernde ~* a poste restante (*Am.* general delivery) item; **2.** (*das Schicken*) sending; *von größeren Posten*: shipping; **3.** *Funk., TV*: (*das Senden*) transmission, broadcasting; *auf ~ sein* be on the air; *die neue Show wird am nächsten Sonntag auf ~ gehen* the new show will air next Sunday; **4.** (*Programm*) program(me); *Radio: auch* broadcast; **5.** (*Mission*) mission

Sendungsbewusstsein *n* sense of mission

Senegal (*n*); -(s); *Geog.* Senegal; **Senegalese** *m*, **Senegalesin** *f* Senegalese, *weiblich auch*: Senegalese woman (*od.* girl); **senegalesisch I.** *Adj.* Senegalese; **II. Senegalesisch** *n*; -en; *Ling.* Senegalese; *das Senegalesische* Senegalese

Senf *m*; -(e)s, -e, *mst Sg.* mustard (*auch Bot.*); *ein Glas / e-e Tube ~* a jar/tube of mustard; *scharfer/mittelscharfer/süßer ~* strong (*od.* hot) /medium-strength/mild mustard; *Dijon-~* Dijon mustard; *s-n ~ dazugeben umg. fig.* have one's say, *Am.* put in one's (own) two bits (*od.* cents)

senf|farben, **~farbig** *Adj.* mustard (yellow)

Senf|gas *n* mustard gas; **~glas** *n* mustard jar; **~gurke** *f* gherkin (*pickled with mustard seeds*); **~korn** *n* mustard seed; **~pulver** *n* mustard powder; **~soße** *f* mustard sauce; **~topf** *m* mustard pot; **~tube** *f* mustard tube

Senge *Pl. umg.:* **~ beziehen** get a thrashing

sengen I. *v/t.* singe; **~d und brennend** *altm. hist.* pillaging and burning; **II.** *v/i.* scorch

senil *Adj.* senile; **Senilität** *f; -, kein Pl.* senility

Senior *m; -s, -en* **1.** senior (*auch Sport*); **bei den ~en starten** compete in the senior class; **2.** (*in Familie, Mannschaft etc.*) oldest member; **3.** *Wirts.* senior partner; **mit dem ~ (der Firma) sprechen** speak to the old man; **4.** **~en** (*Rentner[innen]*) senior citizens, seniors *umg.*

senior *Adj.:* (**sen.**) senior (*Abk.* sen., Sr)

Senior|chef *m*, **~chefin** *f* partly retired owner of the firm (*whose son/daughter largely runs the business*)

Senioren|abend *m* senior citizens' evening; **~arbeit** *f* work with the elderly; **~beauftragte** *m, f* senior citizens' representative; **~beirat** *m* senior citizens' advisory committee; **~betreuung** *f* elder care, care of the elderly; **~fahrt** *f* senior citizens' trip

seniorengerecht *Adj.* (suitable) for the elderly; **~e Wohnungen** housing for the elderly

Senioren|gruppe *f* senior citizen's group; **~gymnastik** *f* exercises *Pl.* for the elderly; **~heim** *n* retirement home; **~klasse** *f Sport* senior class; **~mannschaft** *f* senior team; **~meister** *m*, **~meisterin** *f* senior champion (*Mannschaft*) senior champions; **~meisterschaft** *f* senior championship; **~pass** *m* senior citizen's (rail) pass; **~schnitzel** *n* small, tender portion of escalope *for the elderly*; **~schutzbund** *m* senior citizens' association; **~tagesstätte** *f* daycare cent|re (*Am.* -er) for the elderly; **~tanz** *m* (*Freizeitsport*) senior dance; (*Veranstaltung*) senior citizens' dance; **~teller** *m* dish for senior citizens; **~vertretung** *f* senior citizens' representatives *Pl.*; **~werkstatt** *f* senior citizens' workshop; **~wohnanlage** *f* housing development for the elderly; *betreut:* sheltered housing (*od.* assisted living) development; **~wohnheim** *n* retirement home; **~zentrum** *n* senior citizens' cent|re (*Am.* -er)

Seniorin *f; -, -nen* → **Senior**

Seniorität *f; -, kein Pl.* seniority; **Senioritätsprinzip** *n:* **nach dem ~** according to seniority

Senkblei *n* plumb line; *Naut.* plummet

Senke *f; -, -n; Geol.* depression, hollow

Senkel *m; -s, -* (*Schnürsenkel*) lace

senken I. *v/t.* **1.** (*sinken lassen*) lower (*auch Stimme, Fieber, Blutdruck*); (*Preise etc.*) lower, reduce, cut; (*Steuern*) reduce, cut; **die Augen ~** lower (*od.* cast) one's eyes (down); **den Kopf ~** bow one's head; **2.** *Tech.* sink (*auch Bergb., Brunnen*); **II.** *v/refl.* **1.** *Stimme:* be lowered; **2.** *Temperatur:* fall, drop; **3.** *Mauer:* sag; *Boden, Haus:* give way, subside; *Straße:* dip, fall off; *Wasserspiegel:* drop, fall; **ihr Busen hob und senkte sich** her bosom rose and fell

Senkfuß *m* fallen arches *Pl.*; **~einlage**

f arch support

Senkgrube *f* cesspit

senkrecht I. *Adj.* **1.** vertical; *bes. Math.* perpendicular; **halt dich ~!** *umg.* stay upright, don't fall over; **2.** *bes. schw. fig.* (*aufrecht, rechtschaffen*) upright; **II.** *Adv.* vertically; *Kreuzworträtsel:* down; **die Linien stehen ~ aufeinander** the lines are perpendicular (*od.* at right angles) to one another; (*fast*) **~ nach unten gehen** descend almost vertically; **~ in die Höhe steigen** climb vertically; *Rauch:* go straight up; **Senkrechte** *f; -n, -n* vertical; *Math.* perpendicular; → *auch* **Lot**

Senkrecht|start *m* vertical takeoff; **~starter** *m* **1.** *Flug.* vertical takeoff aircraft, jump jet *umg.*; **2.** *umg. fig.* whiz(z) kid, high flier; (*Buch etc.*) immediate success

Senkung *f* **1.** *Preise:* lowering (+ *Gen.* of), cut(s *Pl.*) (in); **2.** *Fundament:* setting; *Mauer, Decke:* sagging; *Boden, Haus:* subsidence; **3.** *Med.* (*Blutsenkung*) sedimentation

Senn *m; -s, -e; südd., österr., schw.* → **Senne[1]**

Senne[1] *m; -n, -n; südd., österr.* Alpine dairyman

Senne[2] *f; -, -n südd., österr.* Alpine pasture

Senner *m; -s, -; südd., österr.* Alpine herdsman and dairyman; **Sennerei** *f; -, -en; südd., österr., schw.* Alpine dairy farm; **Sennerin** *f; -, -nen; südd., österr.* Alpine herdswoman and dairymaid

Sennesblätter *Pl.* senna leaves

Sennhütte *f südd., österr.* mountain hut (*in an Alpine pasture*)

Sennin *f; -, -nen; südd., österr., schw.* → **Sennerin**

Sensation *f; -, -en* **1.** sensation; **e-e ~ verursachen** create a sensation, cause (*od.* create) (quite) a stir; **die Zuschauer wollen ~en sehen** the audience wants to see spectacular action (*od.* wants its thrills); **das ist schon e-e kleine ~** this is a bit of a sensation; **2.** *Med.* sensation; **sensationell I.** *Adj.* sensational; **II.** *Adv.:* **e-e ~ aufgemachte Story** a sensationalized story; **~ billig/erfolgreich** sensationally (*od.* amazingly) cheap/successful; **~ hoch gewinnen** win by a sensational margin

Sensations|blatt *n* sensational (news)paper; *Pl. auch* sensational (*od.* yellow) press *Sg.*; **~darsteller** *m* stuntman; **~darstellerin** *f* stuntwoman; **~gier** *f* craving for sensation; **~hascherei** *f* sensationalism

sensationshungrig *Adj.* sensation-seeking

Sensationsjournalismus *m* sensational journalism

Sensationslust *f* craving for sensation; **sensationslüstern** *Adj.* sensation-seeking

Sensations|mache *f pej.* sensationalism; **~meldung** *f* sensational news; (*Exklusivmeldung*) sensational scoop; **~presse** *f* sensational (*od.* yellow) press; **~prozess** *m* sensational trial; **~sucht** *f* obsessive craving for sensation

Sense *f; -, -n* scythe; **jetzt ist aber ~ (bei mir)!** *umg.* that's enough of that! (I've had enough)

Sensen|blatt *n* scythe blade; **~griff** *m* scythe handle, tang; **~mann** *m fig.* the Grim Reaper

sensibel *Adj.* sensitive (*auch Med.*);

(*überempfindlich*) hypersensitive; *Daten, Informationen: auch* delicate; **das ist ein höchst sensibler Bereich** this is an extremely sensitive (*od.* delicate) area; **Sensibelchen** *n umg.* sensitive soul; **sei nicht so ein ~!** don't be so sensitive (*leicht reizbar auch:* touchy, thin-skinned)!; **Sensibilisator** *m; -s, -en; Fot.* sensitizer; **sensibilisieren** *v/t.* sensitize (*auch Fot.*); **j-n für ... make s.o. sensitive to; **Sensibilität** *f* (*Feinfühligkeit*) sensitivity (*auch Med., Fot.*); (*Überempfindlichkeit*) hypersensitivity

sensitiv *Adj.* (hyper)sensitive; **Sensitivität** *f; -, kein Pl.* (hyper)sensitivity; **Sensitivitätstraining** *n Psych.* sensitivity training

Sensomotorik *f Psych.* sensorimotor functions *Pl.*

Sensor *m; -s, -en; Etech.* sensor; **Sensorbildschirm** *m Computer:* touch (-sensitive) screen; **sensorgesteuert** *Adj.* sensor-controlled; **Sensorik** *f; -, kein Pl.* **1.** sensory functions *Pl.*; **2.** *Tech.* sensor technology; **sensorisch I.** *Adj.* sensory; **II.** *Adv.* **1.** *Med.:* **~ gestört sein** have a sensory disability; **2.** *Tech., gesteuert etc.:* by sensors; **Sensorium** *n; -s, Sensorien; (Gespür*) sixth sense; **Sensortaste** *f* feather touch key, light action key (*Pl. auch* controls)

Sensualismus *m; -, kein Pl.* sensualism; **Sensualität** *f; -, kein Pl.; Med.* sensuality

Sentenz *f; -, -en* aphorism, saying; **sentenziös** *Adj.* sententious

sentimental *Adj.* sentimental; **Sentimentalität** *f; -, -en* sentimentality; **aus ~** for sentimental reasons

separat I. *Adj.* separate; **II.** *Adv.:* **~ wohnen** live apart, not live together; **~ aufbewahren/waschen** keep separate / wash separately

Separatismus *m; -, kein Pl; Pol.* separatism; **Separatist** *m; -en, -en*, **Separatistin** *f; -, -nen*, **separatistisch** *Adj.* separatist

Separator *m; -s, -en; Tech.* separator; **Separatorenfleisch** *n* separator meat, MRM (= *mechanically recovered meat*), reconstituted (*od.* processed) meat

Séparée [zepa'reː] *n; -s, -s* private side room

Sephardim *Pl.* Sephardim; **sephardisch** *Adj.* Sephardic

Sepia *f; -, Sepien* **1.** (*Farbstoff*) sepia; **2.** *Zool.* cuttlefish; **sepia** *Adj.* sepia; **sepiabraun** *Adj.* sepia (brown); **Sepiazeichnung** *f* sepia drawing

Sepp(e)l|hose *f* leather shorts *Pl.*, lederhosen *Pl.*; **~hut** *m traditional Bavarian hat*

Sepsis *f; -, Sepsen; Med.* sepsis

Sept *f; -, -en*, **Septe** *f; -, -n* → **Septim** 1

September *m; -s, -*; (*abgek.* **Sept.**) September; → **April**

Septett *n; -(e)s, -e, Mus.* septet

Septim *f; -, -en* **1.** *Mus.* seventh; **2.** *Fechten:* septime

Septime *f; -, n; Mus.* → **Septim** 1

septisch *Adj. Med.* septic

Sequenz *f; -, -en* sequence; *Kartenspiel:* run, set; *EDV* sequence

sequenziell *Adj. EDV* sequential

Serail [ze'raɪ] *n; -s, -s:* „**Die Entführung aus dem ~**" The Abduction from the Seraglio, *bekannt als* Il Seraglio

Serbe *m; -n, -n* Serb, Serbian; **Serbien** (*n*) *-s; Geog.* Serbia; **Serbin** *f; -, -nen* Serb, Serbian (woman *od.* girl); **ser-**

bisch *Adj.* Serbian
serbokroatisch I. *Adj. Ling.* Serbo-
-Croat (*od.* -Croatian);
II. Serbokroatisch *n; -en; Ling.* Serbo-Croat (*od.* -Croatian); *das Serbo-*
kroatische Serbo-Croat (*od.* -Croati-
an)
Serenade *f; -, -n; Mus.* serenade
Serie *f; -, -n* **1.** series *Sg.; Radio, TV:*
(*Fortsetzungsgeschichte*) serial; (*Satz*)
set; *Wirts.* line, range; *e-e 5-teilige* ~ a
five-part series; (*Fortsetzungsgeschich-*
te) a serial in five parts (*od.* instal(l)-
ments); **2.** *Wirts.:* *in* ~ *gehen* go into
series (*od.* full-scale) production; *in* ~
hergestellt werden be in full-scale
production
...serie *f, im Subst.* **1.** *Erfolgs~* series
of successes; **2.** *Radio, TV* (*Fortset-*
zungsgeschichte) *Krimi~* detective (*od.*
crime) serial
seriell I. *Adj.* serial (*auch EDV*); *~e*
Schnittstelle Etron. serial interface; *~e*
Herstellung mass production; **II.** *Adv.*
serially; *hergestellt:* in series
Serien|ausstattung *f* standard equip-
ment (*od.* fittings *Pl.*); *~bau m* series
production; *~betrieb m EDV* serial
operation; *~brief m* form (*EDV* mail-
-merge) letter; *~fahrzeug n* standard
vehicle; *~fertigung f* series production; *~held m TV* male lead (in a serial); *~heldin f TV* female lead (in a
serial); *~herstellung f* series production
serienmäßig I. *Adj.* standard; *die Air-*
bags etc. sind ~ the airbags *etc.* are
(fitted as) standard; *~e Herstellung*
mass production; **II.** *Adv.* (*genormt*)
as standard; *... hat Airbags etc.* ~ (*ein-*
gebaut) ... has airbags *etc.* (fitted) as
standard; ~ *herstellen* produce in series
Serien|modell *n* standard model;
~mörder m, ~mörderin f serial murderer; *~produktion f* assembly-line
production; *~nummer f* serial number
serienreif *Adj.* ready to go into (assembly-line) production; **Serienreife** *f*
readiness for (mass) production
Serien|schaltung *f Etech.* series con-
nection; *~täter m, ~täterin f* serial offender; *~unfall m* pile-up, *Am.* chain
accident; *~wagen m* standard car
serienweise *Adv.* **1.** *herstellen:* in series; *verkaufen:* in batches; **2.** *umg. fig.*
(*in großen Mengen*) wholesale
Serife *f; -, -n; Druck.* serif; **serifenlos**
Adj.: ~e Schrift sanserif typeface
seriös I. *Adj.* (*ernsthaft*) serious; (*an-*
ständig) respectable, responsible;
Wirts. auch reliable, trustworthy, *Fir-*
ma: auch reputable; *Kleidung:* respectable; *solche Werbung ist nicht* ~ that
sort of advertising is not to be taken
seriously; **II.** *Adv.: sich* ~ *verhalten*
behave in a trustworthy (*od.* responsible) manner; ~ *gekleidet* respectably
dressed; **Seriosität** *f; -, kein Pl.*
(*Ernsthaftigkeit*) seriousness; (*Anstän-*
digkeit) respectability; *bes. Wirts.*
probity, trustworthiness; → *seriös*
Sermon *m; -s, -e; pej.* lecture
Serologie *f; -, kein Pl.; Med.* serology;
serologisch I. *Adj.* serological;
II. *Adv. untersuchen etc.:* serologically;
seropositiv *Adj.* seropositive; *bei*
Aids: auch HIV-positive, HIV+; **se-**
rös *Adj. Med.* serous
Serpentin *m; -s, -e; Min.* serpentine
Serpentine *f; -, -n* **1.** (*Straßenkehre*)
hairpin bend; **2.** → *Serpentinenstra-*
ße; **Serpentinenstraße** *f* serpentine

(*od.* zigzag) mountain road
Serum *n; -s, Seren od. Sera* serum (*Pl.*
sera *od.* -s)
...serum *n, im Subst.: Immun~* immune
serum; *Anti~* antiserum; *Diphterie~*
diphtheria antitoxin
Serum|behandlung *f* serotherapy;
~krankheit f serum sickness
Server ['zɔːɐvɐ] *m; -s, -; EDV, Tennis:*
server
Service[1] [zɛr'viːs] *n; -(s), -;* (*Geschirr*)
dinner (*od.* tea, coffee) service
Service[2] ['zɔːɐvɪs] *m, n; -, -s, mst Sg.*
1. (*Bedienung*) service; *Tech.* (*Kun-*
dendienst) (after-sales) service; **2.** *Ten-*
nis: service, serve
Service|angebot *n* service provision;
~bereich m service sector
servicefreundlich *Adj.* easy to service
Service|leistung *f* service; *~stelle f*
service point; (*Abteilung*) service department; *~teil m* service part; *~tele-*
fon *n* service hotline
Servier|besteck *n* serving cutlery
(*Am.* utensils *Pl.*); *~brett n* tray
servieren I. *vt/i.* serve; *etw. zum Früh-*
stück ~ serve s.th. for breakfast; *Wein*
zum Essen ~ serve wine with a (*od.*
the) meal; *es ist serviert!* dinner is
served; *Lügen etc.* ~ *umg. fig.* give *s.o.*
lies *etc.; j-m den Ball (zum Torschuss)*
~ feed the ball to s.o. (for a shot at
goal); **II.** *v/i.* **1.** *Tennis:* serve; *stark/*
schwach ~ *allg.* have a powerful/poor
serve; *im besonderen Fall:* serve
powerfully/poorly; **2.** (*bedienen*) serve;
(*aufwarten*) auch wait (at table, *Am.*
on tables); *sie steht in der Küche,*
und ihr Mann serviert she's in the
kitchen while her husband serves the
food
Servieren *f; -, -nen* waitress
Servier|mädchen *n* waitress; *~tisch m*
serving table; *~tochter f schw.* waitress; *~wagen m* trolley
Serviette *f; -, -n* (table) napkin, *Brit.*
auch serviette
Servietten|knödel *m Gastr.* big dump-
ling cooked in a napkin and served in
slices; *~ring m* napkin ring, *Brit.* auch
serviette ring
servil *Adj. pej.* servile; **Servilität** *f; -,*
kein Pl. servility
Servo|bremse *f* power (*od.* servo)
brake; *~gerät n* servo unit; *~lenkung*
f power steering
Servus *Interj. bes. südd., österr. umg.*
1. (*grüß dich!*) hello!, hi!; **2.** (*tschüss!*)
see you!, *Am.* auch so long!
Sesam *m; -s, -s* sesame; (*Samen*) sesame seeds *Pl.;* ~ *öffne dich!* open sesame; *~brot n* sesame seed bread; *~kern*
m sesame seed; *~straße f TV* Sesame
Street
Sessel *m; -s, -* armchair, easy chair; *ös-*
terr. (*Stuhl*) chair; *an s-m* ~ *kleben*
umg. fig. cling to one's post (*od.* position); *das haut e-n vom* ~ / *nicht vom*
~ *umg. fig.* it blows your mind / it's
not exactly mind-blowing
...sessel *m, im Subst. allg.* ... chair;
Liege~ lounger; *Rohr~* wicker (*aus*
Bambusrohr: cane) (arm)chair; *Chef~*
executive chair
Sessel|bahn *f* chair lift; *~lehne f* chair
back; *~lift m* chair lift
sesshaft *Adj.* settled; (*ansässig*) resident; ~ *werden* settle (down); **Sess-**
haftigkeit *f* settled way of life
Session *f; -, -en; Parl.* session
Set *n, m; -s, -s* **1.** *auch TV, Film, EDV*
set; **2.** (*Platzdeckchen*) place mat
Setter *m; -s, -; Zool.* setter

setzen I. *v/t.* (*hat gesetzt*) **1.** *allg.* (*hin-*
tun) put; (*bes. Dinge*) auch place; (*j-n*)
auch sit; (*pflanzen*) plant; (*Mast*) put
up; (*stapeln*) (*Holz, Briketts*) pile up;
(*Denkmal*) erect, set up (*j-m* to s.o.);
(*Ofen*) put in, fix; (*Segel*) set; *beim*
Brettspiel: (*Figur*) move; *an Land* ~
put ashore; *j-n über den Fluss* ~ take
s.o. across the river; *an die Lippen* ~
raise to one's lips; *keinen Fuß mehr*
vor die Tür ~ never again set foot outside; *auf den Topf* ~ (*Kind*) put on the
potty; *e-n Wagen an die Mauer* ~ *umg.*
drive a car into a wall; *unter Wasser* ~
submerge; (*mit Wasser füllen*) flood;
2. (*Satzzeichen*) put (in); *s-e Unter-*
schrift ~ *unter* (+ *Akk.*) put one's signature to, sign; *etw. auf j-s Rechnung*
~ charge s.th. to s.o.'s account; **3.** *bei*
Wetten: bet, place (*auf* + *Akk.* on);
4. (*beauftragen*) *j-n an e-e Arbeit* ~ set
s.o. to work on a job; *daran werden*
wir unsere Computerfachleute ~ we'll
get our computer specialists onto that;
5. (*investieren*) *Arbeit, Geld* ~ *in* (+
Akk.) put into; *viel Arbeit/Zeit in etw.*
~ put a lot of work into s.th. / spend a
lot of time on s.th.; **6.** *Gerüchte in die*
Welt ~ spread rumo(u)rs; *ein Gedicht*
in Musik ~ set a poem to music;
7. (*festlegen*) *Frist, Grenze, Priorität,*
Ziel etc.: set; **8.** *Sport* (*j-n*) seed; *viele*
Gesetzte sind schon ausgeschieden
many seeded players (*od.* seeds) have
already gone out; **9.** *j-n über j-n* ~ *fig.*
(*höher einschätzen*) think more (highly) of s.o. than of s.o.; (*befördern*) promote s.o. above s.o.; → *Druck*[1] 4, *Er-*
staunen, Frist 2; → *auch gesetzt;*
10. *Druck.* set; **11.** *Jägerspr.* (*Junge*)
give birth to; **II.** *v/refl.* (*hat*) **1.** sit
down; *sich auf e-n Ast* ~ *Vogel:* land
(*od.* alight) on a branch; *sich zu j-m* ~
sit down beside s.o.; *darf ich mich zu*
Ihnen ~? may I join you?; *sich ans*
Fenster ~ sit down at (*od.* by, next to)
the window; *sich aufs Pferd* ~ mount
a horse; **2.** *sich vor j-n* ~ *Auto, Fahrer:*
cut in on (*od.* in front of) s.o.; *sich an*
die Arbeit ~ set to work; **3.** *fig.* (*sich*
senken) sink; *Bodensatz, Schaum,*
Staub: settle; *das muss sich erst* ~
umg. fig. (*Lernstoff etc.*) it has to sink
in; **III.** *v/i.* **1.** (*ist*) ~ *über* (+ *Akk.*)
jump over; → *übersetzen*[2] II; **2.** (*hat*)
bei Wetten: place one's bet; ~ *auf* (+
Akk.) bet on, back; *ich setze auf ihn!*
he's my man; **3.** (*hat*) *beim Brettspiel:*
move; **IV.** *v/impers. umg.: gleich setzt*
es was I can see trouble coming; *dro-*
hend: you just watch your step; *es hat*
mal wieder Prügel gesetzt we got
more smacks again
Setzer *m; -s, -; Druck.* compositor,
typesetter; **Setzerei** *f; -, -en* composing (*od.* case) room; **Setzerin** *f; -,*
-nen → *Setzer*
Setz|fehler *m* misprint, typographical
error; *~kasten m* **1.** *Druck.* typecase;
2. *Agr.* seedling box
Setzling *m; -s, -e* **1.** *Agr.* seedling;
2. *~e* (*Fische*) fry *Sg.*
Setzmaschine *f* typesetting machine
Seuche *f; -, -n* epidemic (*auch fig.*);
fig. pej. auch plague; *diese Handys*
sind e-e richtige ~! these mobile
phones have become a real plague
(*od.* scourge); **seuchenartig** *Adj. und*
Adv. epidemic; *Vermehrung etc.:* of
epidemic proportions; *sich* ~ *ausbrei-*
ten spread like the plague
Seuchen|bekämpfung *f* epidemic con-
trol; *~gebiet n* infested area; *~gefahr*

f danger of an epidemic; **~herd** *m* cent|re (*Am.* -er) of an (*od.* the) epidemic; **~schutz** *m* epidemic protection; **~überträger** *m* carrier of an epidemic

seufz *Interj. umg.* sniff!

seufzen *v/i.* sigh (**über** + *Akk.* at, over; **vor** +*Dat.* with); **seufzend I.** *Part. Präs.* → **seufzen**; **II.** *Adv.* with a sigh

Seufzer *m*; *-s*, - sigh; **e-n ~** (*der Erleichterung*) **ausstoßen** heave a sigh (of relief); **~brücke** *f* Bridge of Sighs

Sex [zɛks] *m*; *-(es)*, *kein Pl.* **1.** sex; **2. sie hat unheimlich viel / überhaupt keinen ~** she is extremely sexy / has no sex appeal; → **Safer Sex**; **~appeal** [-ʔəpiːl] *m*; *-s*, *kein Pl.* sex appeal

sexbesessen *Adj. pej.* obsessed with sex, sex-mad

Sex|bombe *f umg.* sex bomb, sexpot; **~club** *m* night club with sex for sale, sex joint *umg.*; **~film** *m* sex film, blue movie *umg.*; **~idol** *n* sex idol (*od.* symbol)

Sexismus *m*; -, *kein Pl.* sexism; **Sexist** *m*; *-en*, *-en*, **sexistisch** *Adj.* sexist

Sexmuffel *m umg.* sexless type

Sexologe *m*; *-n*, *-n* sexologist; **Sexologie** *f*; -, *kein Pl.* sexology, sex studies *Pl.*; **Sexologin** *f*; -, *-nen* sexologist

Sexorgie *f* orgy of sex

Sexperte *m*; *-n*, *-n*, **Sexpertin** *f*; -, *-nen*; *umg.* expert on sexual practices, sex hotshot

Sex|protz *m umg.* sexual athlete; **~puppe** *f* lifesize inflatable doll *for acting out sexual fantasies*; *umg. fig.* (*Frau*) sexpot, sex kitten; **~shop** *m* sex shop; **~symbol** *n fig.* sex symbol

Sext *f*; -, *-en* **1.** *Mus.* sixth; **große/kleine ~** major/minor sixth; **2.** *kirchl.* (*Gebetsstunde*) sext; **3.** *Fechten:* sixte

Sexta *f*; -, *Sexten*; *Päd.* **1.** *altm.* first year of grammar school; **2.** *österr.* sixth year (of grammar school); **Sextaner** *m*; *-s*, -; *Päd.* **1.** *altm.* first year grammar school pupil; **2.** *österr.* sixth-year (grammar school) pupil, *in GB etwa* sixth-former

Sextant *m*; *-en*, *-en* sextant

Sexte *f*; -, *-n* → **Sext** 1

Sextett *n*; *-(e)s*, *-e* sextet

Sextourismus *m umg.* sex tourism

Sexual|... *im Subst.* sexual, sex ...; **~atlas** *m* illustrated sex manual; **~aufklärung** *f* explaining the facts of life; *in der Schule:* sex education; **~beratung** *f* sexual counselling; **~delikt** *n* sex offen|ce (*Am.* -se); **~erziehung** *f* sex education; **~ethik** *f* sexual ethics *Pl.*; **~forschung** *f* sex(ual) research, sexology; **~hormon** *n* sex hormone

sexualisieren *v/t. Kinder:* make more sexually aware; *Atmosphäre:* make sexually charged

Sexualität *f*; -, *kein Pl.* sexuality

Sexual|kunde *f Päd.* sex education; **~leben** *n* sex life; **~moral** *f* sexual ethics *Pl.*; **~mord** *m* sex murder; **~neurose** *f* sex neurosis; **~objekt** *n* sex object; **~organ** *n* sex organ; **~pädagogik** *f* sex education; **~partner** *m*, **~partnerin** *f* sexual partner; **~praktiken** *Pl.* sexual practices; **~psychologie** *f* sexual psychology; **~strafrecht** *n* law governing sexual offences; **~straftäter** *m* sex offender; **~therapie** *f* sexual therapy; **~trieb** *m* sexual drive; **~verbrechen** *n* sex(ual) offence; **~verbrecher** *m* sex offender; **~verhalten** *n* sexual behavio(u)r; **~verkehr** *m* sexual intercourse; **~wissenschaft** *f* sexology; **~wissenschaftler** *m*, **~wissen-**

schaftlerin *f* sexologist

sexuell I. *Adj.* sexual; **~e Nötigung** sexual assault; **das Sexuelle ist mir nicht so wichtig** sex isn't that important to me; **II.** *Adv.:* **~ missbrauchen** abuse (sexually); **~ erregt** sexually aroused

Sex|versand *m* mail-order sex shop; **~welle** *f umg.* sex wave

sexy *Adj. umg. mst präd.* sexy

Seychellen [ze'ʃɛlən] *Pl.*; *Geog.:* **die ~** the Seychelles; **~nuss** *f Bot.* sea coconut

Sezession *f*; -, *-en* secession; **Wiener ~** *Kunst* Vienna Secession; **Sezessionist** *m*, *-en*, *-en*, **Sezessionistin** *f*; -, *-nen*, **sezessionistisch** *Adj.* secessionist, *Kunst* Secessionist

Sezessions|krieg *m hist.* war of secession; *in den USA:* (American) Civil War; **~stil** *m Kunst* Secessionist style

sezieren *v/t.* dissect; *fig. auch* analy|se (*Am.* -ze), take apart

Sezier|messer *n* scalpel; **~tisch** *m* dissecting table

SFB *m*; -, *kein Pl.*; *Abk.* (**Sender Freies Berlin**) Free Berlin Radio

s-förmig *Adj.* S-shaped

sfr. *m*; *-s*, -; *Abk.* (**Schweizer Franken**) Swiss francs *Pl.*

SGML *n*; -, *kein Pl.*; *Abk.* (**Standard Generalized Mark-up Language**) *EDV* SGML

Sgraffito *n*; *-s*, *-s und Sgraffiti*; *Kunst* sgraffito

Shag [ʃɛk] *m*; *-s*, *-s* shag (tobacco)

Shakehands ['ʃeːkʰɛnts] *n*; -, -; *allg.* shaking hands; *einzelnes:* handshake; **~ machen** *umg.* shake hands

Shaker ['ʃeːkɐ] *m*; *-s*, - **1.** (*Becher*) cocktail shaker; **2.** *Reli.* Shaker; **die ~** the Shakers

Shakespearebühne ['ʃeːkspiɐ-] *f Theat.* Shakespearean (*weitS.* Elizabethan) stage; **shakespearesch** ['ʃeːkspiɐʃ], **shakespearisch** ['ʃeːkspiːrɪʃ] *Adj. Drama, Stil:* Shakespearean

Shampoo ['ʃampu], **Shampoon** [ʃam'poːn] *n*; *-s*, *-s* shampoo

shampoonieren [ʃampo'niːrən] *v/t.* shampoo

Sherry ['ʃɛri] *m*; *-s*, *-s* sherry

Shetland|inseln ['ʃɛtlant-] *Pl.*; *Geog.:* **die ~** the Shetland Islands, the Shetlands; **~pony** *n* Shetland pony

Shift-Taste ['ʃɪft-] *f Computer:* shift key; **die ~ drücken** *auch* press shift

Shirt [ʃøːɐt] *m*; *-s*, *-s* T-shirt; (*Sporthemd*) sports shirt

Shit [ʃɪt] *m*, *auch n*; *-s*, *kein Pl. Sl.* (*Haschisch*) hash

Shogun ['ʃoːgun] *m*; *-s*, *-e*; *hist.* shogun, Shogun

Shootingstar ['ʃuːtɪŋstaɐ] *m* (*Person*) whizz-kid *umg.*; (*Schlager*) overnight chart-topper

Shopping ['ʃɔpɪŋ] *n*; *-s*, *kein Pl.* shopping

Shorts [ʃoːɐts] *Pl.* shorts; **Shorty** ['ʃoːɐti] *n*, *m*; *-s*, *-s* shorty pyjamas (*Am.* pajamas) *Pl.*

Show [ʃoː] *f*; -, *-s* → **Schau** 1; **~band** [-bɛnt] *f* show band; **~block** *m* entertainment section (*of a programme*); **~business** *n*; -, *kein Pl.* → **Showgeschäft**; **~einlage** *f umg. fig.:* **e-e ~ geben** put on an act; **~geschäft** *n* show business; **~master** *m* host, *Brit. auch* compere, *Am. auch* emcee, M.C.; **~programm** *n* show program(me); **~star** *m* star entertainer; **~view** [-vjuː] *n*; -, *kein Pl.*; *TV* Video Plus system

Shredder ['ʃrɛdɐ] *m*; *-s*, - shredder

Shrimps [ʃrɪmps] *Pl.*; *Gastr.* shrimps, *Am. auch* shrimp *Sg.*

Shuttle [ʃatl] *m*; *-s*, *-s*; *Raumf.*, *Verk.* shuttle; **~verkehr** *m* shuttle service

Siam (*n*); *-s*; *Geog.*, *hist.* Siam

Siamese *m*; *-n*, *-n*, **Siamesin** *f*; -, *-nen* Siamese, *weiblich auch:* Siamese woman (*od.* girl); **siamesisch** *Adj. hist.* Siamese; **~e Zwillinge** *Med.* Siamese twins

Siamkatze *f Zool.* Siamese cat

Sibirien (*n*); *-s*; *Geog.* Siberia; **Sibirier** *m*; *-s*, -, **Sibirierin** *f*; -, *-nen* Siberian, *weiblich auch:* Siberian woman (*od.* girl); **sibirisch** *Adj.* Siberian; **~e Kälte** *fig.* arctic temperatures

sibyllinisch I. *Adj.* sibylline, mysterious; **II.** *Adv.* **sich ~ ausdrücken** express oneself in veiled (*od.* mysterious) terms

sich *Pron.* **1.** oneself, yourself; *3. Person Sg.:* himself, herself, itself; *Pl.:* themselves; **2.** *nach Präp.:* *mst* him, her, it, *Pl.:* them; **das Haus an ~** the house itself; **an** (**und für**) **~** actually; (*genau genommen*) strictly speaking; (*wenn man sich das überlegt*) when you think about it; **das ist e-e Sache für ~** that's a separate matter; **sie haben kein Geld bei ~** (*Dat.*) with (*od.* on) them; **sie blickte um ~** she looked around (her); **hat er die Tür hinter ~** (*Dat.*) **zugemacht?** did he shut the door behind him?; **von ~** (*Dat.*) **aus** of one's own accord, off one's own bat *umg.*; **er lud sie zu ~** (*Dat.*) **ein** he invited them to his house; **etwas an ~** (*Dat.*) **haben** *fig.* have a special quality; **nicht ganz bei ~** (*Dat.*) **sein** be not qite with it; **wieder zu ~** (*Dat.*) **kommen** regain consciousness, come round; **dieser Wein/Fall hat es 'in ~** this wine/case is quite something; **3.** *mit refl. Verben:* oft unübersetzt; (*einander*) each other, one another; **wann habt ihr euch kennen gelernt?** when did you get to know one another?, when did you (two) meet?; **sie treffen ~ regelmäßig** they meet (up) regularly; **er kämpfte ~ durch die Menge** he fought his way through the crowd; **man muss ~ im Klaren darüber sein, dass** you've got to be aware of the fact that; **er putzte ~** (*Dat.*) **die Zähne und rasierte ~** he brushed his teeth and shaved; **~ freuen/wundern** be glad/astonished; **es stellt ~ die Frage, ob ...** the question arises whether ...; **~ selbst um etw. kümmern** look after s.th. o.s.; **jeder stellt ~ selbst vor** everyone introduces himself; → **auf I** 15, **für I** 2, 12, 13

Sichel *f*; -, *-n* sickle; **des Mondes:** crescent; **Hammer und ~** hammer and sickle; **sichelförmig** *Adj.* crescent-shaped; **sicheln** *vt/i.* cut with a sickle

Sichelzelle *f Med.* sickle cell

sicher I. *Adj.* **1.** (*gesichert, geschützt, geborgen*) safe (**vor** + *Dat.* from); (*gefahrlos*) safe (*auch Tech.*); (*fest*) firm, secure; *Einkommen, Existenz, Arbeitsplatz etc.:* secure; *Ort, Versteck etc.: mst* safe; **vor Neid ist keiner ~** none of us is above envy; **~ ist ~!** better safe than sorry; → **Geleit** 1; **2.** (*gewiss*) certain, sure; (*zuverlässig*) *Quelle etc.:* reliable, **~er Sieg** certain victory; **~e Methode** reliable (surefire *umg.*) method; **~es Zeichen** sure sign; **so viel ist ~:** this much is certain - ...; **die Stelle ist ihm ~** he's certain to get the job; → **Amen, Nummer** 1, **Quelle** 3; **3.** *Person:* (*überzeugt, wissend*) sure, certain; (*zu-*

versichtlich) confident; **e-r Sache ~ sein** be sure of s.th.; **er ist sich** (*Dat.*) **s-r Sache sehr ~** he's very sure (*kritisch*: a bit too sure) of himself; **bist du** (*dir*) **~? - ganz ~!** are you sure? - (I'm) positive; **du kannst ~ sein, dass** you can be sure (*od.* rest assured) that; **4.** (*geübt, fähig*) competent; (*zuverlässig*) reliable; (*selbstsicher*) confident, self-assured; *Instinkt, Urteil*: sure; **~es Auftreten** self-assurance; **~er Fahrer** confident (*Fahrt*: competent, reliable) driver; **~er Geschmack** reliable (*od.* sound) taste; **~e Hand** sure (*nicht zitternd*: steady) hand; **~er Schütze** sure shot; **II.** *Adv.* **1.** (*ohne Gefahr*) safely; **~ beherrschen** (*Wagen, Maschine etc.*) be in complete control of; **etw. ~ aufbewahren** keep s.th. safely (*od.* in a safe place); **nicht ~ auf den Beinen stehen** be a bit unsteady; **sich ~ fühlen** feel safe; *beim Autofahren, Skilaufen etc.*: feel confident; **~ wirkend** *Methode etc.*: reliable, surefire *umg.*; → *auch* **sichergehen, sicherstellen**; **2.** (*gewiss, bestimmt*) certainly; *auch Interj.*: (*aber*) **~!,** (*ganz*) **~!** certainly!, of course!; **sie freut sich ~ darüber** she's sure (*od.* bound) to be pleased, she'll certainly be pleased (about it); **das ist ~ gelogen** that's sure to be a lie; **du hast ~ recht** I'm sure you're right; → *auch* **sicherlich** I; **3. s-e Vokabeln ~ können** know one's vocabulary off pat, *Am.* have one's vocabulary down pat; **s-e Rolle ~ beherrschen** play one's part with complete assurance; **~ auftreten** have a self-assured (*od.* self-confident) manner, be very self-confident

...sicher *im Adj.* **1.** (**~ vor, gegen etw.**): **atombomben~** atomic bomb-proof; *lawinen~* safe (*od.* protected) from avalanches; **2.** (*gewandt, erfahren*) *stil~* with an assured (*od.* confident) style, stylistically assured; **geschmacks~** with sound taste

sichergehen *v/i.* (*unreg., trennb., ist -ge-*) be sure; (*sich vergewissern*) make sure; **um sicherzugehen** to be on the safe side, to make sure

Sicherheit *f* **1.** (*Sichersein, Schutz*) safety; *bes. Pol., Mil.* security; **öffentliche ~** public safety (*od.* security); **innere ~** *Pol.* internal security; **für j-s persönliche ~ garantieren** guarantee s.o.'s personal safety; **in ~ bringen** (*Person, Sache*) bring to safety; (*retten*) rescue; (*Sache*) *auch* get into a safe place; **sich in ~ bringen** escape from (*od.* get out of danger), reach safety; **sich durch e-n Sprung in ~ bringen** jump to safety; **in ~ sein** be safe (and sound); **sich/j-n in ~ wiegen** be lulled / lull s.o. into a false sense of security; **auf s-e ~ hin überprüfen** (*Gerät etc.*) do a safety check on; → **Arbeitsplatz; 2.** (*Gewissheit*) certainty; (*Zuverlässigkeit*) e-r *Quelle, Methode*: reliability; *von Geschmack, Urteil*: sureness, soundness; **mit ~** definitely; → *auch* **sicherlich; aber mit ~!** definitely! no doubt about it!; **etw. wird mit ~ eintreten** s.th. is bound to happen; **mit ziemlicher ~** almost certainly; **mit an ~ grenzender Wahrscheinlichkeit** very probably, if not certainly, **das kann man wohl mit ~ sagen** it would be safe to say that with certainty; **man kann mit ~ annehmen** one may safely assume; **3.** (**~ im Auftreten**, *Selbstsicherheit*) (self-)confidence, self-assurance; (*sicheres Können*) assured

(*od.* total) competence; **mit traumwandlerischer ~** with the sureness (*od.* sure instinct) of a sleepwalker; **er ist begabt, aber es fehlt ihm noch die ~** he is gifted but lacks assurance; **4.** (**~sleistung**, *Bürgschaft, Pfand*) security; *Wirts., durch Deckung*: cover; **was für e-n haben Sie?** what kind of security *Sg.* do you have?; **~ leisten** give security; **~** (*Kaution*) **stellen** *Jur.* stand bail

Sicherheits|... *im Subst.* körperlich und *Tech.* safety ...; *Pol., Mil., Wirts., Jur.* security ...; **~abstand** *m* safe distance; **den ~ einhalten** keep a safe distance (behind the vehicle in front); **~apparat** *m* security machine; **~aspekt** *m* security aspect; **~auflage** *f* security requirement; **~auto** *n* safety--conscious car; **~beamte** *m*, **~beamtin** *f*, **~beauftragte** *m*, *f* security officer; **~bedenken** *Pl.* security concerns; **~bedürfnis** *n* need for security; **~behälter** *m* containment dome (*of a reactor*); **~berater** *m*, **~beraterin** *f Pol.* (national) security adviser; **~bereich** *m* security sector; **~bestimmungen** *Pl.* safety regulations; *am Flughafen etc.*: security (control) *Sg.*, security regulations; **~bindung** *f Skisport:* safety binding; **~bügel** *m Mot.* roll bar; **~chef** *m*, **~chefin** *f* security chief; **~debatte** *f Pol.* debate on security; **~defizit** *n* security gap; (*Fehler*) lapse in safety provision; **~denken** *n* safety--conscious attitude; **~dienst** *m* security service; **~experte** *m*, **~expertin** *f* safety (*od.* security) expert; **~farbe** *f* high--visibility colo(u)r; **~film** *m* safety film; **~garantie** *f* guarantee of safety; **~gefühl** *n* feeling (*od.* sense) of security; **~glas** *n* safety glass; **~gründe** *Pl.: aus ~n* for reasons of safety, for safety's sake; **~gurt** *m* seat belt, *Mot. auch* safety belt

sicherheitshalber *Adv.* for safety('s sake), as a precaution; (*um sicherzugehen*) (just) to be on the safe side

Sicherheits|ingenieur *m*, **~ingenieurin** *f* safety expert; **~kategorie** *f* security category; **~kettchen** *n am Schmuck etc.*: safety chain; **~kette** *f* (safety) door chain; **~klausel** *f* escape clause; **~konferenz** *f* security conference; **~kontrolle** *f* security check; **~kopie** *f Computer:* backup (copy); **~kräfte** *Pl.* security forces; **~lage** *f* security situation; **~lampe** *f Bergb.* safety lamp; **~leistung** *f* security; *Jur.* bail; **~lücke** *f* security gap; **~mangel** *m → Sicherheitsdefizit;* **~maßnahme** *f* safety measure, precaution; *Pol.* security measure; **~nadel** *f* safety pin; **~niveau** *n* level of security; **~organe** *Pl.* instruments of security, security services; **~pakt** *m* security pact; **~personal** *n* security staff (*V. auch im Pl.*)

Sicherheitspolitik *f* security policy; **sicherheitspolitisch** *Adj.* relating to security policy

Sicherheits|polizei *f* security police *Pl.*; **~prüfung** *f* security examination; **~rat** *m:* **~** (*der Vereinten Nationen* United Nations) Security Council

sicherheitsrelevant *Adj.* relevant to security

Sicherheits|risiko *n Pol.* (*auch Person*) security risk; **~schleuse** *f* security door system; **~schloss** *n* safety (*od.* security) lock; **~sperre** *f* security barrier; **~standard** *m* standard of security; **~stufe** *f* level of security

Sicherheitstechnik *f* security technol-

ogy; *im Verkehrswesen etc.*: safety technology; **sicherheitstechnisch I.** *Adj.* relating to security (*od.* safety) technology; **II.** *Adv.*: **~ veraltet** etc. outmoded in its use of security (*od.* safety) technology

Sicherheits|trakt *m* high-security wing (*of a prison*); **~truppen** *Pl.* security forces; **~überprüfung** *f* security check; **~ventil** *n Tech.* safety valve; **~verstoß** *m* breach of security; (*Fehler*) security lapse; **~verwahrung** *f Jur.* preventive detention; **~vorkehrung** *f* safety precaution; *Pol. etc.* security measure; **unter strengen ~en** amid tight security; **~vorschriften** *Pl.* safety regulations

sicherlich I. *Adv.* surely; **er hat's ~ vergessen** he must have forgotten (it); (*ganz bestimmt*) he's bound to have forgotten (it), I bet he's forgotten (it) *umg.*; **sie kommt ~** I'm sure she'll come, she's sure to come; **II.** *Interj.*: **~!** of course, *bes. Am.* sure!; → *auch* **sicher** II 2

sichern I. *v/t.* **1.** (*gewährleisten*) safeguard (*vor + Dat., gegen* against); (*schützen*) *auch* protect (from); (*Arbeitsplätze, Existenz*) *auch* make secure; (*Bergsteiger, Tür*) secure; **2.** *EDV* (*Datei etc.*) save; **3.** (*verschaffen*) (*auch Polizei: Beweise, Spuren etc.*) secure; (*Karten etc.*) *auch* get hold of; **sich** (*Dat.*) **den Sieg / e-n Vorsprung ~** secure victory / a lead; **4.** (*Schusswaffe*) put the safety catch on; **~ gesichert; II.** *v/refl.*: **sich ~ vor + Dat.** (*oder gegen*) protect o.s. from, guard against,; **III.** *v/i.* Jägerspr. scent, test the wind

sicherstellen *v/t.* (*trennb., hat -ge-*) **1.** (*beschlagnahmen*) seize; (*Fahrzeug*) impound; (*in Gewahrsam nehmen*) put in safekeeping; **2.** (*garantieren*) guarantee; **~, dass** ensure that; **Sicherstellung** *f* **1.** seizure; **2.** (*Gewährleistung*) guarantee(ing)

Sicherung *f* **1.** *Etech.* fuse; *Tech.* (*Vorrichtung*) safety device; *Schusswaffe:* safety catch; **die ~ ist durchgebrannt** the fuse has blown; (**bei**) **ihm ist die ~ durchgebrannt** *umg. fig.* he blew a fuse; **2.** (*das Sichern*) safeguarding; (*Schützen*) protection; (*Verschaffen*) securing; *EDV* saving; → **sichern**

Sicherungs|datei *f EDV* backup file; **~hebel** *m Schusswaffe:* safety catch; **~kasten** *m Etech.* fuse box; **~kopie** *f EDV* backup copy; **~programm** *n* security system; *EDV* backup program; **~system** *n EDV* standby system; **~verwahrung** *f Jur.* preventive detention

sicher wirkend → sicher II 1

Sicht *f;* -, *kein Pl.* **1.** (*Sichtweite, -verhältnisse*) visibility; → *auch* **Sichtweite;** (*Aussicht*) view; **gute/schlechte ~** high/low *od.* poor visibility; **außer ~** out of sight; **in ~** (with)in view, in eyeshot; **in ~ kommen** come into view; **von hier hat man e-e weite ~** you can see for miles from here; **auf lange** *od.* **weite ~** *fig.* on a long-term basis; (*auf die Dauer*) in the long run; **auf kurze ~** in the short term; **es ist keine Besserung in ~** there's no prospect of improvement; **2.** (*Betrachtungsweise*) view, perspective; **aus s-r ~** from his point of view, as he sees it; **3.** *Wirts.:* **auf** *od.* **bei ~** at sight; (*zahlbar*) **sechzig Tage nach ~** (payable) at sixty days' sight (*od.* sixty days after sight)

sichtbar I. *Adj.* visible; (*freigelegt*) exposed; (*wahrnehmbar*) noticeable, perceptible; (*deutlich*) marked; (*offenbar, sichtlich*) obvious, evident, clear; **ohne ~en Erfolg** without any apparent (*od.* noticeable, appreciable) success; **ohne ~en Grund** for no apparent reason; **II.** *Adv.*: **es/er hat sich ~ gebessert** there's been / he's shown a noticeable (*od.* marked) improvement; **Sichtbarkeit** *f* visibility

Sicht|behinderung *f* poor visibility (**durch** due to); **~beton** *m* exposed concrete; **~blende** *f* screen; **~einlage** *f Bank*: sight deposit

sichten *v/t.* **1.** (*sehen*) sight; **2.** (*durchsehen*) look (*od.* go) through; *prüfend, sortierend*: sift through; (*ordnen*) sort (out)

Sicht|feld *n* field of view; **~fenster** *n* window; **~flug** *m Flug.* contact flight; **~grenze** *f* visibility limit; **~karte** *f* travel pass; (*Zeitkarte*) season ticket; **~kontakt** *m* eye contact

sichtlich I. *Adj.* visible; **II.** *Adv.* visibly; (*offensichtlich*) evidently

Sichtschutz *m* privacy fence (*od.* screen)

Sichtung *f* **1.** sighting; **2.** (*Überprüfung*) examination; (*Aussonderung*) sifting, sorting; **nach ~ der Unterlagen** after examining the documents

Sicht|verhältnisse *Pl.*: (**gute/schlechte**) ~ (good/poor) visibility *Sg.*; **~vermerk** *m* **1.** *im Pass*: visa; **2.** *Wirts.* endorsement; **~wechsel** *m Wirts.* bill payable on demand; **~weise** *f* view (of things); **~weite** *f* range of vision; **in ~** (with)in sight, within eyeshot; **außer ~** out of eyeshot

Sickergrube *f* soakaway, *Am.* dry well

sickern *v/i.* seep; (*tröpfeln*) trickle (**aus** out of; **in +** *Akk.* into); (*auch* **an die Öffentlichkeit**) ~ leak out; → *auch* **durchsickern, einsickern**

Sickerwasser *n* **1.** *von Deich etc.*: seeping water, seepage; **2.** (rain)water seeping into the ground; (*Grundwasser*) groundwater

Sideboard ['saidbo:ɐd] *n*; *-s, -s* sideboard

Siderit *m*; *-s, -e*; *Min.* siderite

sie *pers. Pron.* **1.** *3. Person f/Sg.*: she, *Akk.* her; *Sache*: it; **2.** *3. Person Pl.*: they, *Akk.* them; **3. Sie** *Anrede*: you (*auch Akk.*); **zu j-m Sie sagen** → **siezen; wir sind immer noch per Sie** we still call one another Sie; **Sie** *f*; *-, -s*; *umg.* **1. es ist e-e ~** *auch bei Tieren*: it's a she; **2.** *auf Badetüchern etc.*: hers

Sieb *n*; *-(e)s, -e* sieve; *für Flüssiges*: strainer; *für Gemüse*: colander; *für Sand etc.*: riddle, screen; *für Siebdruck*: screen; *für Öl, Benzin*: gauze filter; **ein Gedächtnis wie ein ~** *umg.* a memory like a sieve; **siebartig** *Adj.* sieve-like

Sieb|bein *n Anat.* ethmoid bone; **~druck** *m* silk-screen print (*Verfahren*: printing)

sieben[1] *v/t/i.* (pass through a) sieve; (*Gemüse etc.*) *auch* strain, sift; (*Sand etc.*) riddle, screen; *fig.* sift through; **da wird ganz schön gesiebt** *fig.* they have a tough screening procedure, they really pick and choose *umg.*; → **aussieben**

sieben[2] *Zahlw.* seven; → *auch* **acht**[1]

Sieben *f*; *-, -en und* - *Zahl*: (number) seven; → **Acht**[1] 1, 2, 4

sieben|armig *Adj.* seven-armed; **~er Leuchter** seven-branched candelabrum, *Reli.* menorah; **~bändig** *Adj. attr.* seven-volume ..., in seven volu-

---

mes

Siebenbürgen (*n*); *-s; Geog.* Transylvania; **Siebenbürger I.** *m*; *-s, -*, **Siebenbürgerin** *f*; *-, -nen* Transylvanian (German), *weiblich auch*: Transylvanian (German) woman (*od.* girl); (*Aussiedler[in]*) ethnic German from Transylvania; **II.** *Adj.*: **~ Sachse** Transylvanian German; **siebenbürgisch** *Adj.* Transylvanian

Siebeneck *n* heptagon; **siebeneckig** *Adj.* heptagonal

Siebener *m*; *-s, -*; *umg.* (*Bus etc.*) number seven; → **Sieben**

siebenfach *Adj.* sevenfold; **~e Menge** seven times the amount; **~er Sieger** seven-time winner (*od.* champion)

siebengescheit *Adj. umg.* smart-alecky

Siebengestirn *n Astron.*: **das ~** the Pleiades *Pl.*, the Seven Sisters *Pl.*

siebenhundert *Zahlw.* seven hundred

siebenjährig *Adj. attr.* **1.** seven-year-old ...; **2.** (*sieben Jahre dauernd*) seven-year ...; **der Siebenjährige Krieg** the Seven Years' War; **Siebenjährige** *m, f*; *-n, -n* seven-year-old

siebenköpfig *Adj. attr.* **1. ~e Familie** *etc.* family *etc.* of seven; **2. ~er Drache** seven-headed dragon

siebenmal *Adv.* seven times

Siebenmeilenstiefel *Pl. hum.* seven-league boots; **mit ~n** with giant strides

Siebenmeter *m Sport* penalty; **~linie** *f* penalty line

Siebenmonatskind *n Med.* seven-month baby

Sieben|pfünder *m*; *-s, -*; *umg.* seven-pound baby *etc.*; (*Fisch*) seven-pounder; **~sachen** *Pl. umg.* (all one's) things; **~schläfer** *m* **1.** *Zool.* (edible *od.* fat) dormouse; **Gemeiner ~** common dormouse; **2.** *nur Sg.*; 27th June (*the weather on this day being said to determine that of the next seven weeks*); *etwa* St (*od.* St.) Swithin's Day

sieben|seitig *Adj.* seven-sided, heptagonal; **~stellig** *Adj. attr. Zahl*: seven-figure ...; **~stöckig** *Adj. attr.* seven-stor(e)y ...; **~ sein** have seven storeys; **~stündig** *Adj. attr.* seven-hour(-long) ...

siebent *etc.* → **siebt** *etc.*; **Siebenter Himmel** *Islam*: seventh heaven; **im ~en Himmel** *umg. fig.* in seventh heaven, on cloud nine

siebentägig *Adj.* **1.** *attr.* seven-day (--long) ..., ... of a week; **~ sein** last seven days (*od.* a week); **2.** (*sieben Tage alt*) seven-day-old ..., week-old ...

siebentausend *Zahlw.* seven thousand; **Siebentausender** *m* seven-thousand met|re (*Am.* -er) (*etwa* twenty-three thousand foot) peak

siebenteilig *Adj. attr.* seven-part ...; *auch präd.* in seven parts

Sieb(en)tel *n*; *-s, -* seventh

sieb(en)tens *Adv.* seventh(ly), seven

Siebmaschine *f Tech.* screener, sifter

siebt *Adv.* seven of; **sie waren zu ~** there were seven of them; **wir gingen zu ~ hin** seven of us went

siebt... *Zahlw.* seventh; **~es Kapitel** chapter seven; **am ~en März** on the seventh of March, on March the seventh; **7. März** 7th March, March 7(th)

Siebte *m, f*; *-n, -n* (the) seventh; **er war ~r** he was (*od.* came) seventh; **Eduard VII.** Edward VII (= Edward the Seventh); **an jedem ~n** on every seventh day of the month

siebzehn *Zahlw.* seventeen; **Siebzehn und Vier** *Kartenspiel*: pontoon, *Am.*

---

blackjack; **siebzehnt** *Zahlw.* seventeenth; **Siebzehntel** *n* seventeenth (part)

17-Zöller *m*; *-s, -*; (*Bildschirm*) 17-inch monitor

siebzig *Zahlw.* seventy; **Anfang/Mitte/Ende ~ sein** be in one's early/mid/late seventies; → *auch* **achtzig**

Siebzig *f*; *-, -en, mst Sg. Zahl*: (number) seventy; → *auch* **Achtzig**

siebziger *Adj.*: **in den ~ Jahren** in the seventies; **sie ist in den Siebzigern** she's in her seventies

Siebziger *m*; *-s, -*, **~in** *f*; *-, -nen* man/woman in his/her seventies; *förm.* septuagenarian; seventysomething *umg.*

Siebzigerjahre *Pl.*: **in den ~n** in the seventies

siebzigjährig *Adj. attr. Person*: seventy-year-old ...; *Zeitraum*: seventy-year ...

siebzigst... *Zahlw.* seventieth; **sie hat heute ihren Siebzigsten** she's seventy today, it's her seventieth birthday today

siech *Adj. altm. od. fig. geh.* infirm, ailing; *fig. Industrie etc.*: ailing; → **dahinsiechend**; **Siechtum** *n*; *-s, kein Pl.*; *altm.* infirmity; *fig.* sickliness

siedeln *v/i.* settle; **das Bienenvolk hat gesiedelt** *fig.* the bees have colonized the hive

sieden; *siedete od. sott, hat gesiedet od. gesotten* **I.** *v/i.* (*siedete, hat gesiedet*) boil; (*simmern*) simmer; *fig. auch* seethe; **es siedete in ihr** she was seething (inside *od.* with rage, anger); **II.** *v/t.* (*mst sott, hat gesotten*) boil; *langsam*: simmer; **Seife ~** *altm.* obtain soap by boiling; → **gesotten, hart** II 1; **siedend I.** *Part. Präs.* → **sieden**; **II.** *Adj.* boiling; *fig. auch* seething; **in ~er Hitze** in sweltering heat; **III.** *Adv.*: **~ heiß** scalding (hot), boiling (*Essen*: piping) hot; **da fiel mir ~ heiß ein** *umg.* it suddenly struck me with horrible clarity, I suddenly remembered to my horror (*od.* with a shock)

Siede|punkt *m* boiling point (*auch fig.*); *fig. Pol. auch* flashpoint; **den ~ erreichen** *fig.* reach boiling point (*od.* a flashpoint); **~wasserreaktor** *m* boiling water reactor

Siedler *m*; *-s, -*, **~in** *f*; *-, -nen* settler

Siedlung *f* **1.** settlement; **2.** ([*Neu*]*Baugebiet*) (housing) development (*Brit. auch* estate)

Siedlungs|dichte *f* population density; **~form** *f* type of settlement; **~gebiet** *n* settlement (area); **~geschichte** *f* settlement history; **~gesellschaft** *f* housing association (*buying land for development*); **~haus** *n* house on a development, *Brit. auch* estate house; **~land** *n* land for development; **~politik** *f* settlement policies *Pl.*; **~raum** *m* settlement area; **~stopp** *m* cessation of development

Sieg *m*; *-es, -e* victory; *Sport etc.*: *auch* win; *fig. des Guten etc.*: triumph; **leichter ~** easy victory (*od.* win); **den ~ davontragen** be victorious, carry (*od.* win) the day *lit.*; **knapp den ~ verfehlen** be narrowly beaten; **auf ~ spielen** *Sport* play to win (*od.* for a win); **der Vernunft etc. zum ~ verhelfen** help common sense *etc.* to gain the upper hand; **~chance** *f* chance of victory (*od.* of winning)

Siegel *n*; *-s, -* seal (*auch fig.*); **ein ~ anbringen/aufbrechen** fix/break a seal; **ein Buch mit sieben ~n** *fig.* a closed book (**+** *Dat. od.* **für** to); **er hat es mir**

unter dem ~ der Verschwiegenheit erzählt he told me in the strictest confidence, he swore me to secrecy
Siegellack *m* sealing wax
siegeln *v/t.* seal (*auch Tech.*); → **versiegeln**; **Siegelring** *m* signet ring
siegen *v/i.* **1.** *im Wettkampf:* win; ~ **über** (+ *Akk.*) defeat, beat; **2.** *Mil. etc.* win; be victorious (**über** + *Akk.* over); *fig. Gerechtigkeit etc.:* triumph (over), carry the day *lit.*
Sieger *m; -s, -* **1.** *Sport etc.:* winner; *lit.* victor; (*Meister*) champion; **zweiter ~** runner-up; **knapper/überlegener ~** winner by a small/large margin; **als ~ hervorgehen aus** *auch fig.* emerge victorious from; **2.** *Mil. etc.* victor; (*Land*) *auch* victorious nation
...sieger *m, im Subst.* **1.** *Sport:* **K.-o.-Sieger** winner by a knockout; **2.** *im Vergleichswettbewerb etc.:* **Bundes.~** federal champion(s)
Siegerehrung *f Sport* presentation ceremony
Siegerin *f; -, -nen* → **Sieger**
Sieger|macht *f* victorious power; **die vier Siegermächte des 2. Weltkriegs:** the four victorious allies; **~mannschaft** *f Sport* winning team; **~podest** *n Sport* winners' rostrum; **~pokal** *m* (winner's) cup; **~pose** *f* victorious (*od.* triumphant) pose; **in ~** striking a triumphant pose; **~treppchen** *n:* **auf dem ~ stehen** stand on the winners' rostrum; **~typ** *m* determined competitor; **~urkunde** *f* winner's certificate
siegesbewusst I. *Adj.* confident of victory (*fig.* success); *fig. auch* confident; **II.** *Adv. auftreten, lächeln etc.:* confident of victory (*fig.* success); *fig. auch* confidently
Sieges|chance *f* chance of winning; **~feier** *f* victory celebration(s *Pl.*); **~freude** *f* joy of victory
siegesgewiss *Adj.* → **siegesbewusst**; **Siegesgewissheit** *f* confidence in one's victory (*fig.* success)
Sieges|göttin *f* goddess of victory; **die ~** Victory; **~kranz** *m* laurel wreath; **~parade** *f* winners' parade; **~preis** *m* winner's prize; **~rausch** *m* flush of victory; **~säule** *f* triumphal (*od.* victory) column; **~serie** *f Sport* series (*od.* run) of wins
siegessicher *Adj. und Adv.* → **siegesbewusst**
Sieges|taumel *m* euphoria of victory; **~tor** *n* **1.** *Archit.* triumphal arch; **2.** *Sport* winning goal; **~treffer** *m* winning goal; *Schießen:* winning shot; **~trophäe** *f* **1.** (winner's) trophy; **2.** (*Beute*) scalp, trophy
siegestrunken *Adj.* intoxicated (*od.* flushed) with victory, triumphant
Sieges|wille(n) *m* will to win (*fig.* succeed); **~zug** *m* triumphal procession; *fig.* triumphant progress; **in den 80er Jahren begann der ~ der CD** in the 80s the CD began its triumphant progress (*od.* began to sweep all before it)
sieglos *Adj.* unsuccessful; **~ bleiben** fail to win
Siegprämie *f* bonus for a win
siegreich I. *Adj.* **1.** *Sport etc.: attr.* winning ...; *auch fig.* successful, *lit.* victorious; **2.** *Feldzug etc.:* victorious, successful; *Heer: auch* triumphant; **II.** *Adv. ein Turnier etc.* **~ beenden** bring to a victorious conclusion, emerge as the winner of
siehste *Interj. umg.:* **~!** (*da haben wir's!*) there you are!; **~?** (*was hab ich*

gesagt?) what did I tell you!
sieht *Präs.* → **sehen**
Siel *m, n; -(e)s, -e* **1.** (*Deichschleuse*) sluice; *Wasserlauf:* sluiceway; **2.** (*Abwasserkanal*) sewer
Siele *f; -, -n; fig.:* **in den ~n sterben** die in harness
Siesta ['zi̯ɛsta] *f; -, -s und Siesten* siesta, afternoon nap; **~ halten** have a (*od.* one's) siesta, have an (*od.* one's) afternoon nap
siezen *v/t.* address *s.o.* as 'Sie', say 'Sie' to *s.o.*; **sich ~** say 'Sie' to one another, call one another 'Sie'
siffen *v/i. Sl. pej.* **1.** → **gammeln** 1; **2.** (*kleckern, Schmutz machen*) make a filthy mess; **siffig** *Adj. Sl. pej. Schuhe, Zimmer etc.:* filthy
Sigel *n; -s, -* short form, abbreviation; *fachspr.* grammalog(ue)
Sightseeing ['saɪtsiːɪŋ] *n; -(s), -s* sightseeing; **~ machen** go sightseeing; **~tour** *f* sightseeing tour
Signal *n; -s, -e* signal (*auch Eisenb.*); (*Zeichen*) sign; **das ~ steht auf „Halt"** the signal is at "stop"(*Eisenb.* "danger"); **~ geben** *Mot.* sound one's horn; **das ~ für Gefahr** the danger signal, the signal for danger; **das ~ zum Aufbruch** *fig.* the sign (for us *etc.*) to leave; **alle ~e stehen auf ...** *fig.* all the pointers are in favo(u)r of ...; **~e setzen** *fig.* point the way to the future
Signal|abschwächung *f Etech.* fading; **~anlage** *f* signal(l)ing installation, set of signals; **~brücke** *f Eisenb.* (signal) gantry
Signalement [zɪɡnalə'mãː] *n; -s, -s und schw. -e* **1.** *bes. schw.* (*Personenbeschreibung*) personal description; **2.** (*Pferdezucht*) characteristic features *Pl.*
Signal|fahne *f* signal flag; **~farbe** *f* striking colo(u)r; **~feuer** *n Naut.* signal light; **~funktion** *f* signalling function; **~gast** *m Naut.* signalman; **~glocke** *f* warning bell; **~horn** *n* **1.** *Mot.* horn; **2.** *Mil. altm.* bugle
signalisieren *v/t.* signal; *fig. etw.* **signalisiert etw.** s.th. indicates s.th., s.th. is a sign of s.th.
Signal|knopf *m* signal button; **~lampe** *f*, **~leuchte** *f* signal lamp; **~licht** *n* signal light; **~mast** *m* signal mast, semaphore; **~munition** *f* signal flares *Pl.*; **~pistole** *f* flare pistol
signalrot *Adj.* signal red
Signal|stärke *f Radio etc.:* signal strength; **~wirkung** *f* (effect of a) signal; **~ haben** act as a signal, point the way to the future
Signatarmacht *f* signatory (state *od.* power)
Signatur *f; -, -en* **1.** (*Namenszeichen*) initials *Pl.*; (*geh. Unterschrift, auch Mus.*) signature; **2.** *Druck.* signature (mark), *e-r Letter:* nick; **3.** *Bücherei:* shelfmark, *Am.* call number; **4.** *Landkarte:* conventional symbol
Signet [zɪn'jeː] *n; -s, -e und -s* (publisher's) imprint, publisher's mark
signieren *v/t.* sign, autograph; *mit Anfangsbuchstaben:* initial; **Signierstunde** *f* signing session; **signiert I.** *P. P.* → **signieren**; **II.** *Adj.* signed (by the author); **~es Exemplar** signed copy; **~e Autogrammkarte** celebrity *etc.* autograph
signifikant *Adj.* (highly) significant; *Merkmale etc.:* significant; **Signifikanz** *f; -, kein Pl.* significance; (*Auswirkungen*) implications *Pl.*
Signum *n; -s, Signa* **1.** (*Namenszeichen*)

initials *Pl.*; (*Monogramm*) monogram; **2.** (*Zeichen*) sign; (*Symbol*) symbol; **3.** *Med.* symptom
Sikh [ziːk] *m; -(s), -s* Sikh; **Sikhismus** *m; -, kein Pl.*, **Sikhreligion** *f* Sikhism
Silage [ziˈlaːʒə] *f; -, kein Pl.; Agr.* silage
Silbe *f; -, -n* syllable; **die ~n trennen** divide by syllables; **wie viele ~n schreiben Sie?** *Kurzschrift:* what is your shorthand speed?; **keine ~** not a word; **mit keiner ~ erwähnen** not breathe a word about; **ich verstehe keine ~** I can't understand a word, it's all Greek to me
Silben|betonung *f* syllabic stress; **~rätsel** *n* anagram (*using syllables*); **~trennung** *f* syllabification; *am Zeilenende:* (syllabic) word division (*od.* hyphenation); **~trenn(ungs)programm** *n Computer:* (syllabic) hyphenation program
Silber *n; -s, kein Pl.; Chem.* silver; (*Tafelsilber*) *auch* silverware; *fig.* (*Kleingeld*) change; **aus ~** (made of) silver; **sie holte ~** *umg. Sport* she got (the) silver; **einmal Gold und zweimal ~ für Russland** one gold and two silvers for Russia; **~anteil** *m* silver content; **~arbeit** *f* (*einzelne:* piece of) silverwork; **~becher** *m* silver goblet; **~bergbau** *m* silver mining; **~besteck** *n* silver (cutlery); **~blech** *n* silver sheet; **~blick** *m umg.* (slight) cast (*od.* squint); **~chlorid** *n Chem.* silver chloride; **~distel** *f Bot.* carline thistle; **~dollar** *m* silver dollar; **~draht** *m* silver wire; **~erz** *n* silver ore
silber|farben, **~farbig** *Adj.* silver(y)
Silber|fischchen *n Zool.* silverfish; **~folie** *f* silver foil; **~gehalt** *m* silver content; **~geld** *n* silver; **~geschirr** *n* silver(ware)
Silberglanz *m* **1.** silvery gleam; **2.** *Min.* argentite; **silberglänzend** *Adj.* with a silvery gleam
silbergrau *Adj.* silver(y)-grey (*Am.* -gray)
Silber|grube *f* silver mine; **~haar** *n* silvery hair
silber|haltig *Adj.* containing silver, *fachspr.* argentiferous; **~hell** *Adj. Ton, Stimme etc.:* silvery
Silber|hochzeit *f* silver wedding; **~legierung** *f* silver alloy
Silberling *m bibl.* piece of silver
Silber|locke *f* silvery lock (of hair); **~löffel** *m* silver spoon; **~löwe** *m Zool.* puma, *Am. auch* cougar, mountain lion
Silbermedaille *f* silver medal; **Silbermedaillengewinner** *m*, **Silbermedaillengewinnerin** *f* silver medal(l)ist
Silber|mine *f* silver mine; **~möwe** *f* silvery gull; **~münze** *f* silver coin
silbern I. *Adj. attr.* silver; *Stimme, Licht, Haar etc.:* silvery; **~e Hochzeit** silver wedding; **wenn man nicht gerade ~e Löffel klaut** *umg.* as long as you don't do anything stupid; → **Tablett**; **II.** *Adv.* like silver; **~ glänzen/klingen** have a silvery sheen (*od.* gleam) /sound
Silber|papier *n* silver paper; **~pappel** *f Bot.* white poplar; **~putzmittel** *n* silver polish; **~reif(en)** *m* silver bangle; **~reiher** *m Orn.* great white heron; **~ring** *m* silver ring; **~schmied** *m*, **~schmiedin** *f* silversmith; **~schmuck** *m* silver jewel(l)ery; **~schüssel** *f* silver dish; **~stift** *m* silverpoint instrument; (*Verfahren*) silverpoint; **~streif** *m fig.:* **ein ~ am Horizont** a ray of hope; **~strei-**

S

fen *m* silver strip; *fig.* → **Silberstreif**; **~teller** *m* silver plate; **~währung** *f* silver standard; **~waren** *Pl.* silver(ware) *Sg.*

silberweiß *Adj.* silvery white

Silberzwiebel *f* pearl onion

...silbig *im Adj.*: **fünf~** five-syllable ..., ... with five syllables; **viel~** polysyllabic

silbrig I. *Adj.* silvery; **II.** *Adv.* **~ schimmern/klingen** have a silvery gleam/sound

Silhouette *f*; -, -*n* silhouette, outline; *e-s Berges etc.*: *auch* contours *Pl.*; *e-r Stadt*: skyline; **sich als ~ abzeichnen gegen** be silhouetted (*od.* outlined) against

Silikat *n*; -(*e*)*s*, -*e*; *Chem.* silicate

Silikon *n*; -*s*, -*e*; *Chem.* silicone; **~busen** *m* silicone-enhanced breasts; **~dichtung** *f* silicone seal

silikonhaltig *Adj.* containing silicone

Silikon|implantat *n* silicone implant; **~kautschuk** *m* silicone rubber; **~-Opfer** *n* victim of silicone breast treatment

Silizium *n*; -*s*, *kein Pl.*; *Chem.* silicon; **~chip** *m*, **~platte** *f* silicon chip

Silo *m*, *n*; -*s*, -*s* silo; *umg. fig.* soulless high-rise block

...silo *m*, *im Subst.* **1.** *im wörtl. Sinn*: ... silo; **Futter~** feed silo; **2.** *umg. fig.*: **Hotel~** huge characterless hotel

Silofutter *n Agr.* silage

Silvaner *m*; -*s*, - *Rebsorte*, *Wein*: Silvaner

Silvester *m*, *n*; -*s*, - New Year's Eve; **zu** *od.* **an ~** on New Year's Eve; **~abend** *m* New Year's Eve; **~ball** *m* New Year's Eve ball; **~feier** *f* New Year's Eve party; **~nacht** *f* night of New Year's Eve

Simbabwe (*n*); -*s*; *Geog.* Zimbabwe; **simbabwisch** *Adj.* Zimbabwean

Simmerring® *m*; -(*e*)*s*, -*e*; *Tech.* shaft seal

simpel I. *Adj.* **1.** simple; (*schlicht*) *auch* plain; **das geht auf e-e ganz simple Idee zurück** it is based on a perfectly simple idea; **es fehlt an den ~sten Dingen** some of the most basic things are missing; **2.** *pej.* (*einfältig*) simple(--minded); **ein simples Gemüt haben** *umg. pej.* be simple-minded; **II.** *Adv.*: **1. etw. ganz ~ ausdrücken** express s.th. in really simple terms (*od.* in words of one syllable); **2.** *pej.*: **~ daherreden** talk away like a simpleton

Simpel *m*; -*s*, -; *umg. pej.* simpleton

Simplex *n*; -, -*e und Simplizia*; *Ling.* simplex

simplifizieren *v/t.* simplify

Simplizität *f*; -, *kein Pl.* simplicity

Sims *m*, *n*; -*es*, -*e* ledge; *Archit.* cornice; (*Kaminsims*) mantelpiece

Simsalabim *Interj.* abracadabra!

simsen *vt/i.* (*e-e SMS senden*): **j-m** (*etw.*) **~** text s.o. (s.th.)

Simulant *m*; -*en*, -*en*, **~in** *f*; -, -*nen* malingerer; **Simulation** *f*; -, -*en* simulation; **Simulator** *m*; -*s*, -*en*; *Tech.* simulator; **simulieren I.** *vt/i. pej.* sham, put it on *umg.*; (*sich krank stellen*) *auch* malinger; (*Krankheit*) sham, feign (illness); **II.** *v/t. Tech., Mil.* simulate

simultan I. *Adj. attr.* simultaneous; **II.** *Adv.*: **~ dolmetschen** do simultaneous interpreting; **~ gegen mehrere Gegner spielen** *Schach*: play several opponents simultaneously (*od.* at the same time)

Simultan|betrieb *m EDV* simultaneous operation; *weitS.* multi-tasking;

~dolmetschen *n*; -*s*, *kein Pl.* simultaneous interpreting; **~dolmetscher** *m*, **~dolmetscherin** *f* simultaneous interpreter; **~schach** *n* simultaneous chess; **~übertragung** *f Radio, TV*: simultaneous broadcast, simulcast; **~verarbeitung** *f EDV* multi-processing

sine tempore *Adv.* → **s.t.**

Sinfonie *f*; -, -*n*; *Mus.* symphony; **Sinfonieorchester** *n* symphony orchestra; **Sinfonietta** *f*; -, *Sinfonietten* sinfonietta; **Sinfoniker** *m*; -*s*, -, **Sinfonikerin** *f*; -, -*nen* (*Komponist*) symphonist; **2.** → **Symphoniker** 2; **sinfonisch I.** *Adj.* symphonic; **~e Dichtung** symphonic poem; **II.** *Adv.* symphonically

Singapur (*n*); -*s*; *Geog.* Singapore; **Singapurer** *m*; -*s*, -, **Singapurerin** *f*; -, -*nen* Singaporean, *weiblich auch*: Singaporean woman (*od.* girl); **singapurisch** *Adj.* Singaporean

singbar *Adj.* singable; **ein schwer ~er Part** a difficult part to sing

Singdrossel *f Orn.* song thrush

singen; *singt*, *sang*, *hat gesungen* **I.** *vt/i.* sing; (*Liturgie etc.*) chant; **richtig/falsch ~** sing in / out of tune; **er kann gut/nicht ~** he's a good singer / he can't sing; **~der Tonfall** lilting voice; **II.** *v/i.* **1.** *Stromleitungsdrähte etc.*: buzz, hum; **es singt mir im Ohr** my ears are ringing; **2.** *umg. fig.* (*die Polizei informieren*) squeal; **wenn Ede nicht gesungen hätte** *auch* if Ede hadn't spilled the beans; → **Blatt** 3, **Lied**, **Schlaf**

Singerei *f*; -, *kein Pl.*; *umg.*: **diese ewige ~** *pej.* this endless singing; **mit der ~ ganz gut verdienen** earn pretty well from one's singing

Singhalese *m*; -*n*, -*n*, **Singhalesin** *f*; -, -*nen* Sin(g)halese, *weiblich auch*: Sin(g)halese woman (*od.* girl); **singhalesisch I.** *Adj.* Sin(g)halese; **II. Singhalesisch** *n*; -*en*; *Ling.* Sin(g)halese; **das Singhalesische** Sin(g)halese

Singkreis *m* (small) choir

Single¹ [ˈzɪŋɡl̩] *m*; -(*s*), -*s Person*: single person; single man/ woman; *Pl.* singles; **ein ~ sein** be single, *Mann: auch* be a bachelor

Single² [ˈzɪŋɡl̩] *f*; -, -*s*; (*Schallplatte*) single

Single³ [ˈzɪŋɡl̩] *n*; -(*s*), -(*s*) *Tennis*: singles *Sg.*

Single|dasein *n* → **Singleleben**; **~haushalt** *m* single household; **~leben** *n* life as a single, singlehood; **~lokal** *n* singles bar

Singlesbar *f* singles bar

Singlewohnung *f* apartment (*Brit. auch* flat) for single occupation

Singsang *m*; -*s*, *kein Pl.* low, monotonous singing; **man hörte sn leisen ~** you could hear him quietly singing away to himself

Sing|spiel *n Mus.* musical play, *etwa* ballad opera; **~stimme** *f Mus.* singing voice

Singular *m*; -*s*, *kein Pl.*; *Ling.*: (**im**) **~** (in the) singular

singulär *Adj.* singular; (*einzigartig*) unique

Singularform *f* singular form

Singularität *f*; -, *kein Pl.* **1.** singularity; (*Einzigartigkeit*) uniqueness; **2.** *Met.* recurring weather pattern; **3.** *Math.* singular point, singularity

Singvogel *m Orn.* songbird

sinken; *sinkt*, *sank*, *ist gesunken* *v/i.* **1.** sink; *Schiff: auch* go down; *Boden*, *Erde*, *Hochwasser*: subside; *Nebel*: de-

scend, come down; **j-m in die Arme ~** fall into s.o.'s arms; **auf die Knie ~** drop to one's knees; **ins Bett ~** fall (*od.* collapse) into bed; **~ lassen** lower, drop (*auch Stimme*); **den Kopf ~ lassen** hang one's head; **2.** *Aktien, Kurs, Preise, Temperatur etc.*: fall, drop, go down; **der Verbrauch von Rindfleisch ist stark gesunken** beef consumption has fallen considerably; **3.** *fig.* *Ansehen, Einfluss*: diminish; *Hoffnung*: fade; **s-e Stimmung sank** his spirits sank; **in j-s Achtung ~** go down in s.o.'s opinion (*od.* esteem); **in der Gunst der Wähler ~** lose electoral support; → **Mut** 1, **Wert** 3; **sinkend I.** *Part. Präs.* → **sinken**; **II.** *Adj. Temperaturen, Preise etc.*: falling; **ein ~es Schiff** a sinking ship; **die ~e Sonne** the setting sun; **~es Glück** *fig.* flagging fortunes

Sink|flug *m* descent; *unbeabsichtigt*: loss of altitude; **im ~ sein** be coming down; *unbeabsichtigt*: be losing altitude; **~stoffe** *Pl.* deposits (*on a lake or river bed*)

Sinn *m*; -(*e*)*s*, -*e* **1.** (*Wahrnehmungssinn*) sense; **~e** (*sexuelle Begierde*) desires; (*Bewusstsein*) senses, consciousness *Sg.*; **im Rausch** *od.* **Taumel der ~e** in a sensual frenzy; **die fünf ~e** the five senses; **s-e fünf ~e beisammenhaben** have one's wits about one; **bist du von ~en?** have you taken leave of your senses?, are you out of your mind?; **2.** (*Denken, Gemüt*) mind; **im ~ haben** have in mind; **etw. im ~ behalten** keep (*od.* bear) s.th. in mind; **es kam mir in den ~** it occurred to me; **es will mir nicht aus dem ~** I can't get it out of my mind; **das will mir nicht in den ~** I just can't understand it; **aus den Augen, aus dem ~** out of sight, out of mind; **3.** (*Verständnis, Empfänglichkeit*) sense (**für** *od.* for), feeling (for); **mit j-m eines ~es sein** be of one mind with s.o., see eye to eye with s.o.; **~ haben für** (be able to) appreciate; **dafür habe ich keinen ~** it doesn't mean anything to me (do anything for me *umg.*), it's not really my thing (*Brit. auch* my cup of tea) *umg.*; **~ für Musik** an ear for music; **nur ~ für Geld haben** only be interested in money; **~ für das Schöne** an eye for beauty, a sense of beauty; **~ für das Ästhetische** an (a)esthetic sense, (a)esthetic sensitivity; **~ für Humor haben** have a sense of humo(u)r; **das ist so recht nach s-m ~** that's exactly what he likes; **mir steht der ~ nicht danach** I don't feel like it; **ganz in m-m ~** (*ist mir recht*) that suits me fine; (*hätte ich auch gemacht*) just as I would have done; **in diesem ~e** with this in mind, in this spirit; **beim Abschied**: on this note; **das ist nicht im ~e des Erfinders** *umg.* that wasn't the object of the exercise, that's not really what was intended; **4.** (*Bedeutung*) sense, meaning; (*Grundgedanke, eigentlicher ~*) (basic) idea; **der ~ des Lebens** the meaning of life; **im wahrsten ~e des Wortes** in the true sense of the word, (*buchstäblich*) literally; **im engeren/weiteren ~(e)** in the narrower/wider sense; **das gibt keinen ~** that doesn't make sense; **ich kann keinen ~ darin sehen zu** (+ *Inf.*) I don't see the point of (*od.* in) (+ *Ger.*); **5.** (*Zweck*) purpose; **~ und Zweck** the (whole) object *od.* purpose; **ohne ~ und Verstand** without rhyme or reason; **im ~e des**

Gesetzes etc.: for the purposes of, as defined by; **das hat keinen ~** (*ist zwecklos*) it's no use; **was hat es für e-n ~ zu** (+ *Inf.*) what's the point of (*od.* in) (+ *Ger.*); **das ist der ~ der Sache** that's the whole point; → **schlagen** I 5, **schwinden**

...sinn *m, im Subst.* **1.** (*Wahrnehmung*): **Gesichts~** (sense of) sight; **2.** (*Beziehung*): **Gerechtigkeits~** sense of justice; **Kunst~** appreciation of (*od.* feeling for) art; **3.** (*Bedeutung*): **Neben~** secondary meaning

Sinnbild *n* symbol (**für** of); (*Allegorie*) allegory (of); **sinnbildlich I.** *Adj.* symbolic; (*allegorisch*) allegorical; **II.** *Adv.* symbolically; (*allegorisch*) allegorically

sinnen *v/i.*; *sinnt, sann, hat gesonnen*; *förm.* reflect (**über** + *Akk.* [up]on), think (about); **~ auf** (+ *Akk.*) have thoughts of, plan; **auf Rache ~** plot revenge; **auf Flucht ~** be planning one's escape; *allg.* be thinking of (*od.* have thoughts of) escape; → **gesinnt**, **gesonnen**

Sinnen *n*; *-s, kein Pl.*; *förm.* reflection; **sein ~ und Trachten auf etw. richten** concentrate one's mind (and all one's efforts) on s.th.

sinnend I. *Part. Präs.* → **sinnen**; **II.** *Adj. förm.* pensive, thoughtful

Sinnenfreuden *Pl.* sensual enjoyment *Sg.*; **sinnenfreudig, sinnenfroh** *Adj.* sensuous

Sinnen|lust *f* sensual enjoyment, sensuality; **~mensch** *m* sensuous person

sinnentleert *Adj.* meaningless, hollow, *lit.* bereft of meaning

sinnentstellend I. *Adj.* misleading; **II.** *Adv.*: **etw. ~ wiedergeben** give a distorted (*od.* garbled) version of s.th.

Sinnenwelt *f the* material world

Sinnes|änderung *f* change of heart; **~art** *f* disposition; (*Denkart*) way of thinking; (*Einstellung*) (mental) attitude; **~eindruck** *m* sensation, sense impression; **~erfahrung** *f* sensory experience; (*Wahrnehmung*) sensory perception; **~nerv** *m* sensory nerve; **~organ** *n* sense organ; **~reiz** *m* sensory stimulus; **~störung** *f* sensory disorder; **~täuschung** *f* hallucination; **~wahrnehmung** *f* (*auch* **~en** *Pl.*) sensory perception; **~wandel** *m* change of heart; **~zellen** *Pl.* Anat., Zool. sensory cells

sinnfällig I. *Adj.* obvious; *Ausdruck*: clear, *stärker*: lucid; *Darstellung*: graphic; **~er Vergleich** apt comparison, good analogy; **II.** *Adv.*: **~ zum Ausdruck bringen** express s.th. clearly (*stärker*: lucidly); **Sinnfälligkeit** *f* obviousness; *des Ausdrucks*: clarity, *stärker*: lucidity; *e-r Darstellung*: graphic nature; *e-s Vergleichs*: aptness

Sinn|frage *f* question of the meaning (*od.* purpose) of life; **die ~ stellen** ask what is the meaning (*od.* purpose) of life; **~gebung** *f* interpretation; **~gehalt** *m* meaning; *im Wesentlichen*: gist

sinngemäß I. *Adj.* **1.** **~e Wiedergabe** *etc.* rough summary *etc.*; **2.** (*folgerichtig*) logical; **II.** *Adv.*: **~ schreibt er** the gist of what he writes is, basically what he writes is; **~ übersetzt** *etc.* roughly translated *etc.*

sinngetreu I. *Adj.* faithful; **II.** *Adv.* *wiedergeben, übersetzen*: faithfully

sinnieren *v/i.* muse, brood, ruminate (**über** + *Akk.* on)

sinnig *Adj. mst iro.* clever; (*passend*) appropriate; **sinnigerweise** *Adv.*

hum., oft iro. cleverly

Sinnkrise *f* crisis of doubt (in the meaning of life); (*Glaubenskrise*) crisis of faith

sinnlich I. *Adj.* **1.** *Erfahrung, Reiz, Eindruck*: sensory (*auch Philos.*); **2.** (*Ggs. geistig*) *Genuss, Freude etc.*: sensual; *Begierde, Verlangen auch* sexual; (*sinnenfreudig, die Sexualität ansprechend*) sensuous (*auch Tanz, Lippen etc.*); **~e Liebe** sensual (*od.* sexual) love; **ein ~er Mensch** a very sensual (*od.* physical) person; **e-e starke ~e Ausstrahlung haben** exude a powerful sensuality (*Sexualität*: sexuality); → *Wahrnehmung* 1; **II.** *Adv.*: **~ wahrnehmen** perceive with the senses; **j-n ~ erregen** arouse s.o. sensually; **Sinnlichkeit** *f* sensuality; *stärker*: voluptuousness; *von Lippen, Tanz etc.* sensuousness

sinnlos I. *Adj.* **1.** (*zwecklos*) pointless, senseless; *präd. auch* no use; **es ist ~ zu** (+ *Inf.*) it's no use (+ *Ger.*), there's no sense (*od.* point) in (+ *Ger.*); **das ist völlig ~** (*es ergibt keinen Sinn*) it doesn't make any sense at all; **2.** (*unsinnig*) senseless; (*bedeutungslos*) meaningless; **~e Gewalt** senseless (*od.* mindless) violence; **von ~er Wut erfüllt sein** be seized with a blind fury; **II.** *Adv.*: **sich ~ betrinken** get blind drunk, *Brit. auch* drink o.s. paralytic; **~ verprassen** *umg.* fritter away; **Sinnlosigkeit** *f* **1.** (*Zwecklosigkeit*) pointlessness, senselessness, futility; **2.** (*Unsinnigkeit*) senselessness; (*Bedeutungslosigkeit*) meaninglessness

sinnreich *Adj.* **1.** (*zweckmäßig, durchdacht*) ingenious, clever (*auch iro.*); **2.** (*tiefsinnig*) profound

Sinn|spruch *m* aphorism; (*Leitsatz*) maxim; **~suche** *f* search for meaning

sinn|verwandt *Adj.* synonymous; **~es Wort** synonym; **~verwirrend** *Adj.* bewildering

sinnvoll *Adj.* **1.** (*vernünftig*) sensible, *präd. auch* a good idea; (*klug*) wise; (*zweckdienlich*) practical, useful; **ökonomisch ~ sein** make good economic sense; **2.** (*e-n Sinn habend od. ergebend*) meaningful; **etw. Sinnvolles tun** do s.th. worthwhile (*od.* constructive); **sinnvollerweise** *Adv.* sensibly; **dafür nimmt man ~ ...** it's good to take ... for that

sinnwidrig *Adj.* nonsensical, absurd

Sinnzusammenhang *m* context

Sinologe *m*; *-n, -n* sinologist; **Sinologie** *f*, *-, kein Pl.* Chinese studies *Pl.*, sinology; **Sinologin** *f*; *-, -nen* sinologist

Sinter *m*; *-s, -*; *Geol.* sinter; **sintern** *vt/i. Tech.* sinter

Sintflut *f* flood (*auch fig.*); *bibl. the* Flood; **das ist ja die reinste ~!** *umg.* everything's completely flooded; **nach mir/uns die ~!** *umg.* who cares what happens when I'm / we're out of the way, I'm / we're all right and to hell with the consequences; **sintflutartig** *Adj.*: **~e Regenfälle** torrential rain *Sg.*

Sinti *Pl.* Sinti (gypsies); → *auch* **Roma**

Sinus *m*; *-, -(se)* **1.** *Math.* sine; **2.** *Anat.* sinus

Sinusitis *f*; *-, Sinusitiden*; *Med.* sinusitis

Sinus|kurve *f Math.* sine curve; **~leistung** *f* Hi-Fi: continuous undistorted output; **~schwingung** *f Phys.* harmonic (*od.* sinusoidal) oscillation

Siphon *m*; *-s, -s* **1.** *auch* **~flasche** (soda) siphon, *Am.* siphon (bottle); **2.** (*Ge-*

ruchsverschluss) (sanitary) trap

Sippe *f*; *-, -n*; (*Familie*) family; *umg.* clan; (*Stamm*) tribe; → **Sippschaft**

Sippenhaftung *f* liability of a family or tribe for (*political*) crimes or actions of one of its members

Sippschaft *f* **1.** *umg.* (*Familie*) clan, tribe; **2.** *pej.* (*Bande*) crowd; (*Gesindel*) riffraff, rabble

Sirene *f*; *-, -n* **1.** *Myth. und Tech.* siren; **2.** *Zool.* sirenian

Sirenen|geheul *n* wailing (of) sirens *Pl.*; **~gesang** *m* siren song

sirenenhaft *Adj. geh.* seductive; *Erscheinung: auch* siren(-)like

Sirius *m*; *-*; *Astron.* Sirius

sirren *v/i.* buzz

Sirup *m*; *-s, kein Pl.* treacle, *Am.* molasses *Sg.*; (*bes. Fruchtsirup*) syrup; **sirupartig** *Adj.* treacly, *Am.* syrupy

Sisal *m*; *-s, kein Pl.*; **~hanf** *m* sisal (hemp); **~teppich** *m* sisal mat

sistieren *v/t.* **1.** (*unterbrechen*) interrupt, break off; *Jur., Verfahren*: adjourn; **2.** *Jur.* (*festnehmen*) detain

Sisyphusarbeit *f* never-ending (*lit.* Sisyphean) task

Sit-in [zɪt'ʔɪn] *n*; *-s, -s*; (*Demonstration*) sit-in

Sitkom *f*; *-, -s*; *TV* sitcom

Sitte *f*; *-, -n* **1.** (*Brauch*) custom; **~n und Gebräuche** customs and traditions; **es ist ~, dass der Ehemann ...** it is the custom for the husband to (+ *Inf.*); **das ist bei uns nicht ~** we don't do that around here (*od.* in these parts); **die ~ verlangt, dass** tradition demands that; **2.** *mst Pl.* (*Ethik, Moral*) **gegen die (guten) ~n verstoßen** offend against common decency; **hier herrschen strenge ~n** there is a strict ethical (*od.* moral) code here; **lockere ~n** loose morals; **3.** *Pl.* (*Umgangsformen*) manners; **was sind denn das für ~n?** *umg.* what kind of behavio(u)r is that?, what a way to behave!; → **Land** 5; **4.** *umg.* (*Sittenpolizei*) vice squad

Sitten|apostel *m pej.* moralizer; **~bild** *n* **1.** **ein ~ der** (*damaligen*) *Zeit* a portrayal of the customs and morals of the time; **2.** *Kunst*: genre painting; **~dezernat** *n* vice squad; **~gemälde** *n* → **Sittenbild**; **~geschichte** *f* history of life and customs; **~gesetz** *n Philos.* law of ethics, moral law; **~kodex** *m* ethical (*od.* moral) code, mores *Pl.*; **~lehre** *f* ethics *Pl.* (*V. im Sg.*), moral philosophy

sittenlos *Adj.* immoral, dissolute; **Sittenlosigkeit** *f* immorality, (complete) lack of morals

Sitten|polizei *f* vice squad; **~prediger** *m pej.* moralizer

sittenstreng *Adj.* morally strict; (*asketisch*) austere; *weitS.* puritanical; **Sittenstrenge** *f* (*strenge Moral*) strict morality, high moral standards *Pl.*; (*Askese*) austerity; *weitS.* puritanism

Sitten|strolch *m pej.* (*sexual*) molester, sex offender; **~verfall** *m* moral decline; **~wächter** *m*, **~wächterin** *f pej.* guardian of moral standards

sittenwidrig I. *Adj. bes. Jur.* unethical; *Verhalten: auch* immoral; **II.** *Adv.*: **sich ~ verhalten** behave unethically (*gegen die Moral*: immorally); **Sittenwidrigkeit** *f Jur.* unethical nature

Sittich *m*; *-s, -e*; *Zool.* parakeet

sittlich I. *Adj.* moral; (*ethisch*) ethical; **ihm fehlt die ~e Reife** he is morally immature; **II.** *Adv. handeln etc.*: in accordance with moral principles; (*ethisch*) ethically; **~ hoch stehend**

with high moral standards; **Sittlich-keit** *f* morality; (*sittliches Empfinden*) morals *Pl.*

Sittlichkeits|delikt *n*, **~verbrechen** *n* sex crime, sex offen|ce (*Am.* -se); **~verbrecher** *m* sex offender

sittsam *altm. od. hum.* **I.** *Adj.* (*zurück-haltend*) demure; (*keusch*) chaste, modest; (*brav*) well-behaved; (*anstän-dig*) decent; **II.** *Adv.:* **sich fein ~ zu-rückhalten** *umg.* behave with good--mannered restraint; **Sittsamkeit** *f* de-mureness; (*Keuschheit*) chasteness, modesty; (*gute Sitten*) good manners *Pl.*; (*Anständigkeit*) decency

Situation *f;* -, -*en* situation; (*persönli-che, finanzielle ~ etc.*) *auch* position; → *auch* **Lage** 3; **situationsbedingt** *Adj. Verhalten:* situationally condi-tioned; *Enttäuschung:* arising from the situation; **Situationsbericht** *m* situa-tion report; **Situationskomik** *f* situa-tion comedy (*od.* humo[u]r)

situativ *Adj.* situational

situiert *Adj.:* **gut/besser ~ sein** well/better off, be affluent/more afflu-ent; **schlecht/schlechter ~ sein** be badly/worse off

Sitz *m;* -*es*, -*e* **1.** seat (*auch Parl., Ho-senboden*); **die Zuschauer von den ~en reißen** get the spectators wild with excitement; **das haut mich nicht vom ~** it doesn't do anything for me; **~ und Stimme haben** have a seat and a vote; **2.** (*Landsitz, Familiensitz etc.*) seat; (*Amtssitz*) residence; *e-r Instituti-on, Behörde:* seat; *e-r Organisation, e-s Unternehmens:* auch headquarters *Pl.* (*auch V. im Sg.*); (*Wohnsitz*) (place of) residence, *förm.* domicile; **der ~ der Firma ist** (**in**) **München** the firm's headquarters (*od.* main office) is in Munich; **3.** *Tech., auch Kleidung:* fit; **e-n guten ~ haben** *Kleidung:* fit well, sit well on *s.o.*; *Reitsport:* have a good seat, sit (the horse) well; **auf e-n ~** *umg. fig.* in one go

...sitz *m, im Subst.* **1.** *im wörtl. Sinn:* **Leder~** leather seat; **2.** *Pol. etc.* (*Funk-tion*): **Aufsichtsrats~** seat on the board; **3.** (*Gebäude, Ort*): **Amts~** offi-cial residence; **Land~** country seat

Sitz|bad *n* sitz bath; **~badewanne** *f* hip bath, sitz bath; **~bank** *f* bench; *ge-polstert:* seat; **~blockade** *f* sit-in, sit--down demonstration (*od.* demo *umg.*); **~ecke** *f* corner seating unit

sitzen *v/i.; sitzt, saß, hat od. bes. südd., österr., schw. ist gesessen* **1.** (*hat od. ist*) sit; **am Steuer / im Sattel ~** sit (*od.* be seated) at the (steering) wheel / in the saddle; **von morgens bis abends im Auto ~** spend the whole day sitting in the car; **sitz!** *zum Hund:* sit!; **bei j-m ~** sit beside (*od.* next to, with) s.o.; **~ Sie bequem?** are you comfortable?; **zu viel ~** spend too much time sitting (on one's backside *umg.*); **etw. im Sit-zen tun** do s.th. sitting down; **er sitzt auf s-m Geld** *umg. fig.* he's sitting on his money; **sag mal, sitzt du auf den Ohren?** *umg. fig.* are you deaf?, *Am. auch* have you got beans in your ears?; **2.** (*hat od. ist*) (*sein*) sit, be; **lieber zu Hause ~** prefer to sit (*od.* stay) at home; **beim Essen ~** be having one's dinner (*od.* lunch); **im Gefängnis ~** be in jail (clink *umg.*); → 5; **stundenlang vor dem Fernseher ~** spend hours (sit-ting) in front of the television, *stärker:* be glued to the television for hours *umg.*; **ich habe lange daran gesessen** I spent a lot of time on it; **über den**

Büchern **~** sit (poring) over one's books; **~ in** (+ *Dat.*) *Firma etc.:* have its headquarters in; **im Parlament ~** have a seat in Parliament, *Brit. auch* be an MP (*od.* a Member of Parlia-ment); **im Stadtrat ~** be on the (town *od.* city) council; **3.** (*hat od. ist*) *Klei-dung:* (*passen*) fit; (*richtig angezogen sein*) be on properly; **dein Hut sitzt schief** your hat's not on straight, your hat's crooked; **4.** (*hat*) *Modell:* sit (*j-m* for s.o.); **5.** (*hat*) *umg. im Gefängnis:* do time; **er saß sechs Monate wegen Diebstahl(s)** he did six months for theft; **er hat sein halbes Leben lang gesessen** he's spent half his life in jail; **6.** (*hat*) *umg.* (*treffen*) find the target; *bes. fig.* go (*od.* hit) home; **je-der Schuss/Schlag sitzt** every shot/ blow finds its target; **bei ihm sitzt je-der Handgriff** he knows exactly what he's doing; **jede Pointe hat gesessen** every punch line went home; **7.** (*hat od. ist*) *fig.* (*stecken*); **wo sitzt der Schmerz?** where does it hurt exactly?; **der Hass sitzt tief** the hatred runs *od.* goes deep; **mir sitzt der Schreck noch in den Gliedern** I'm still shaking with fright; **einen ~ haben** *umg.* have had one too many; **8.** (*hat*) *fig. gespr.* (*im Gedächtnis*) **~** have sunk in; **die Voka-beln ~ gut/schlecht** he *etc.* knows his *etc.* vocabulary off pat, *Am.* he's *etc.* got his *etc.* vocabulary down pat / his *etc.* vocabulary's shaky, he *etc.* needs to work on his *etc.* vocabulary; **9.** (*ist*) **~ bleiben** *auf Stuhl etc.:* remain (*od.* stay) seated; *umg. beim Tanz:* be left without a partner, be a wallflower; (*nicht geheiratet werden*) be left on the shelf; **bleiben Sie ~!** don't get up; (*im Theater etc.*) stay in your seat(s); **~ bleiben** *Päd.* have to repeat a year, *Brit. auch* stay down, *Am. auch* flunk *umg.;* **auf etw. ~ bleiben** be left with (*od.* stuck with) s.th.; **10.** (*hat*) **~ las-sen** *umg.* leave, desert, walk out on; (*Freund[in]*) leave, walk out on, jilt; (*versetzen*) stand *s.o.* up; (*im Stich las-sen*) let *s.o.* down, leave *s.o.* in the lurch; *e-n Vorwurf etc.* **nicht auf sich** (*Dat.*) **~ lassen** not stand for (*od.* take); **dass du so etwas auf dir ~ lässt!** I'm amazed that you would stand for that!; **11.** (*ist*) *schw.* (*sich set-zen*) sit down; → **Patsche** 3, **Tinte** *etc.*

sitzen bleiben → **~** 9

Sitzenbleiber *m;* -*s*, -, **~in** *f;* -, -*nen umg. pej.* pupil (*Am.* student) who has to repeat a year, *Am.* repeater, flunky

sitzend I. *Part. Präs.* → **sitzen; II.** *Adj.* **1.** **~e Lebensweise/Tätigkeit** sedentary lifestyle/occupation; **2.** **~e Figur** seated figure

sitzen lassen → **sitzen** 10

...sitzer *m, im Subst. Mot., Flug., (So-fa) etc.:* **Drei~** *etc.* three-seater *etc.*

Sitzerei *f;* -, *kein Pl.; umg.:* **ganz steif von der dauernden ~ sein** be stiff all over from the endless sitting around

Sitz|falte *f* in *Hose etc.:* crease from sitting; **~fläche** *f* seat (*auch umg. Ge-säß*); **~fleisch** *n umg.* ability to sit still; (*Ausdauer*) perseverance; stami-na; **er hat** (*aber*) **~** (*will nicht weg*) he doesn't seem to be in a hurry to leave; **er hat kein ~** he can't sit still; *bei der Arbeit:* he can't stick at (*Am.* to) any-thing; **~garnitur** *f* living-room (*dreitei-lig: auch* three-piece) suite; **~gelegen-heit** *f* seat, place to sit; *Pl.* seating *Sg.,* seats; **~gruppe** *f* → **Sitzgarnitur; ~hal-tung** *f* posture when seated, sitting

posture

...sitzig *im Adj. Mot., Flug., Sofa etc.:* **drei~** three-seater ...; **mehr~** ... seat-ing several people

Sitz|kissen *n* (seat) cushion; *auf dem Fußboden:* floor cushion; **~ordnung** *f* seating plan (*od.* arrangement); **~platz** *m* seat; *Pl. auch* seating; **Sitzplätze bieten für** have seating for, seat; **~polster** *n* seat cushion (*od.* squab); **~reihe** *f* row (of seats); **~schale** *f* mo(u)lded seat; **~stange** *f* perch; **~streik** *m* sit-in, sit-down strike

Sitzung *f* (*Konferenz*) meeting, confer-ence; *Parl. etc.* session, sitting; *Jur.* sit-ting, hearing; *beim Psychiater etc.:* ses-sion; *beim Arzt etc.:* appointment; *beim Maler etc.:* sitting; **auf** *od.* **bei, in e-r ~** at a meeting; **e-e lange ~** *umg. auf der Toilette:* a long session

...sitzung *f, im Subst.:* **Kommissions~** committee meeting; **Therapie~** therapy session

Sitzungs|geld *n* session fee; **~mara-thon** *n umg.* marathon session (*od.* meeting); **~pause** *f* break in the meet-ing (*od.* session); **~periode** *f Parl.* ses-sion; **~protokoll** *n* minutes *Pl.* (of the meeting); **~saal** *m* conference hall; *Parl.* chamber; **~zimmer** *n* conference room

Sitzverteilung *f Parl.* distribution of seats

Sixtinisch *Adj.:* **~e Kapelle** Sistine Chapel

Sizilianer *m;* -*s*, -, **~in** *f;* -, -*nen* Sicilian, *weiblich auch:* Sicilian woman (*od.* girl); **sizilianisch** *Adj.* Sicilian; **Sizili-en** (*n*); -*s; Geog.* Sicily

Skala *f;* -, *Skalen* scale (*auch Mus.*); *Thermometer: auch* range; *Radio, Ar-maturenbrett:* dial; (*Reihe*) range (*auch fig.*); **von e-r ~ ablesen** read off a scale; **die ganze ~** *fig.* the whole gam-ut (*od.* range)

...skala *f, im Subst.:* **Duft~** range of fra-grances; **Noten~** *Päd.* marking scale

Skalar *m;* -*s*, -*e; Math.* scalar

Skalen|beleuchtung *f* dial light (*od.* illumination); *Mot.* dash panel light; **~einteilung** *f* graduation; **~reiter** *m Radio:* station marker

Skalp *m;* -*s*, -*e* scalp

Skalpell *n;* -*s*, -*e; Med.* scalpel

skalpieren *v/t.* scalp; **Skalpjäger** *m* scalp hunter

Skandal *m;* -*s*, -*e* scandal (*um* sur-rounding); (*Schande*) *auch* disgrace; **es kam zu e-m ~** a scandal developed, there was a scandal; **~blatt** *n* scandal sheet; **~firma** *f* firm involved in a scandal; **~geschichte** *f* (piece of) scandal, scandalous story; **~nudel** *f umg.* magnet for scandal; **e-e ~ sein** always attract scandal, be constantly involved in scandal

skandalös *Adj.* scandalous; (*empö-rend*) *auch* shocking, disgraceful

Skandalpresse *f* scandalmongering press, yellow press

skandal|süchtig *Adj.* scandal-seeking; *Journalist:* scandalmongering; **~träch-tig** *Adj.* scandalous; **~umwittert** *Adj.* surrounded by scandal

skandieren *vt/i.* scan

Skandinavien (*n*); -*s; Geog.* Scandina-via; **Skandinavier** *m;* -*s*, -, **Skandina-vierin** *f;* -, -*nen* Scandinavian, *weiblich auch:* Scandinavian woman (*od.* girl); **skandinavisch** *Adj.* Scandinavian

Skarabäus *m;* -, *Skarabäen; Zool.* scar-ab

Skat *m;* -(*e*)*s*, -*e und* -*s* skat; **~abend** *m*

1. *regelmäßiger*: skat night; **2.** *ein* ~ an evening of skat; **~blatt** *n* pack (*Am.* deck) of skat cards; **~bruder** *m umg.* fellow skat player

Skateboard ['skeːtboːɐt] *n*, *-s*, *-s* skateboard; ~ *fahren* (ride a) skateboard; **Skateboardbahn** *f* skateboard rink; **Skateboarder** ['skeːtboːɐdɐ] *m*; *-s*, *-*, **Skateboarderin** *f*; *-*, *-nen* skateboarder

Skateboard|fahren *n* skateboarding; ~ *verboten!* no skateboards

skaten ['skeːtn̩] *v/i. umg.* (ride a) skateboard; **Skater** ['skeːtɐ] *m*; *-s*, *-*, **Skaterin** *f*; *-*, *-nen* skateboarder

Skatologie *f*; *-*, *kein Pl.* scatology; **skatologisch** *Adj.* scatological

Skat|partie *f* round (*od.* game) of skat; **~spieler** *m*, **~spielerin** *f* skat player

Skeleton ['skɛlətn] *m*; *-s*, *-s*; *Sport* skeleton (toboggan)

Skelett *n*; *-s*, *-e*; *Anat.* skeleton (*auch Bot.*, *Archit.*); *zum* ~ *abgemagert sein* be (just) skin and bones; **skelettieren** *v/t.* skeletonize; *e-e skelettierte Leiche* a corpse reduced to a skeleton

Skepsis *f*; *-*, *kein Pl.* scepticism, *Am.* skepticism; (*Zweifel*) doubt; *voller* ~ *sein* be very scep|tical (*Am.* skep-); *j-m od. e-r Sache mit* ~ *gegenüberstehen* be scep|tical (*Am.* skep-) about, have one's doubts about; **Skeptiker** *m*; *-s*, *-*, **Skeptikerin** *f*; *-*, *-nen* sceptic, *Am.* skeptic; **skeptisch I.** *Adj.* sceptical, *Am.* skeptical; *ich bin* ~, *ob* I am scep|tical (*Am.* skep-) whether; **II.** *Adv. klingen, schauen*: scep|tical (*Am.* skep-); *j-m/e-r Sache* ~ *gegenüberstehen* be scep|tical (*Am.* skep-) about s.o./s.th.; **Skeptizismus** *m*; *-*, *kein Pl.* scepticism, *Am.* skepticism

Sketch [skɛtʃ] *m*; *-es*, *-e und -es*; *Theat.* sketch, skit

Ski [ʃiː] *m*; *-s*, *- und -er* ski; ~ *laufen od. fahren* ski; (*Ski fahren gehen*) go skiing; *sehr gut* ~ *laufen od. fahren* ski very well, be a very good skier; → *Rodel*, **~akrobatik** *f* trick skiing; **~anorak** *m* ski jacket; **~anzug** *m* ski(ing) suit; **~ass** *n* skiing ace; **~ausrüstung** *f* skiing equipment (*od.* gear); **~bindung** *f* ski binding; *Pl. auch* ski fittings; **~bob** *m* skibob; **~brille** *f*: (*e-e*) ~ (a pair of) skiing goggles *Pl.*; **~club** *m* skiing club; **~fahren** *n* skiing; **~fahrer** *m*, **~fahrerin** *f* skier

Ski|fliegen *n* ski-flying; **~freizeit** *f* (school) skiing trip; **~gebiet** *n* skiing area; **~gymnastik** *f* skiing exercises *Pl.*; **~handschuh** *m* skiing glove; **~hang** *m* ski slope; **~haserl** *n*; *-s*, *-(n)*; *umg.* snow (*od.* ski) bunny; **~hose** *f*: (*e-e*) ~ (a pair of) ski pants *Pl.*; **~hütte** *f* ski hut (*Am.* lodge); **~kleidung** *f* skiwear; **~kurs** *m* skiing course; **~langlauf** *m* cross-country skiing; **~langläufer** *m*, **~langläuferin** *f* cross-country skier; **~lauf** *m*, **~laufen** *n* skiing; *zum Skilaufen fahren* go skiing; **~läufer** *m*, **~läuferin** *f* skier; **~lehrer** *m*, **~lehrerin** *f* skiing instructor; **~lift** *m* ski lift; **~marathon** *m* skiing marathon; **~mütze** *f* skiing hat (*od.* cap)

Skin [skɪn] *m*; *-s*, *-s*; *umg.* skin; **Skinhead** ['skɪnhɛt] *m*; *-s*, *-s* skinhead

Skink *m*; (*e*)*s*, *-e*; *Zool.* skink

Ski|paradies *n* skier's paradise; **~pass** *m* ski pass; **~piste** *f* ski run; **~pullover** *m* skiing pullover (*od.* sweater); **~rennen** *n* (*einzelnes Rennen*) ski race; (*Sport*) ski racing; **~rennläufer** *m*, **~rennläuferin** *f* ski racer; **~saison** *f* skiing season; **~schanze** *f* ski jump,

ski-jumping hill; **~schuh** *m* ski boot; **~schule** *f* skiing school; **~sport** *m* skiing; **~springen** *n* ski jumping; **~springer** *m*, **~springerin** *f* ski jumper; **~sprung** *m* ski jump; **~stiefel** *m* ski boot; **~stock** *m* ski pole; **~träger** *Pl. am Auto*: ski rack *Sg.*; **~unfall** *m* skiing accident; **~unterricht** *m* skiing instruction (*od.* lessons *Pl.*); **~urlaub** *m* skiing holiday (*Am.* vacation); **~verband** *m* skiing association; **~wachs** *n* ski wax; **~wandern** *n* ski-hiking; **~weltmeisterschaft** *f* skiing world championship; **~wochenende** *n* skiing weekend; **~zirkus** *m* **1.** (*Gebiet mit Skiliften*) network of skilifts; **2.** *umg.* (*internationale Wettkampfsaison*) ski racing circus

Skizze *f*; *-*, *-n* sketch (*auch literarisch*); (*Rohentwurf*) *auch* (rough) outline; *e-e* ~ *von etw. entwerfen* sketch s.th.

Skizzen|block *m* sketchpad; **~buch** *n* sketchbook

skizzenhaft I. *Adj.* sketchy, rough; **II.** *Adv. beschreiben*: in rough outline

Skizzenmappe *f* sketch portfolio

skizzieren *v/t.* sketch; *fig.* outline; *könnten Sie es kurz* ~? *fig.* could you give a brief outline (of it)?

Sklave *m*; *-n*, *-n* slave (*auch fig.*); **~n halten** keep slaves; *ein* ~ *s-r Gewohnheiten sein* be a slave to one's habits; *j-n zum* **~n machen** make s.o. one's slave

Sklavenarbeit *f* slave labo(u)r; *fig.* drudgery

Sklavenhalter *m* slaveholder

Sklaven|handel *m* slave trade; ~ *treiben* trade in slaves; **~händler** *m* slave trader; **~jagd** *f* slave hunting; **~markt** *m* slave market; **~treiber** *m*, **~treiberin** *f auch fig.* slavedriver

Sklaventum *n*; *-s*, *kein Pl.* slavery; **Sklaverei** *f*; *-*, *kein Pl.* slavery; *fig. auch* slavedriving; *es ist die reinste* ~ *fig.* it's sheer slavery (*od.* slave labo(u)r)

Sklavin *f*; *-*, *-nen* slave (*auch fig.*)

sklavisch I. *Adj. attr.* slavish; **II.** *Adv.*: *j-m* ~ *ergeben sein* be s.o.'s devoted slave; ~ *imitieren* imitate slavishly

Sklerose *f*; *-*, *-n*; *Med.*: (*multiple*) ~ (multiple) sclerosis (*Pl.* scleroses), *MS*; **sklerotisch** *Adj.* sclerotic

Skoliose *f*; *-*, *-n*; *Med.* scoliosis (*Pl.* scolioses)

skontieren *v/t. Wirts.* give a (cash) discount on; **Skonto** *m*, *n*; *-s*, *-s* cash discount; *geben Sie* ~? do you give a cash discount?

Skooter ['skuːtɐ] *m*; *-s*, *-* dodgem, bumper car

Skorbut *m*; *-(e)s*, *kein Pl.*; *Med.* scurvy; **skorbutisch** *Adj.* scorbutic

Skorpion *m*; *-s*, *-e* **1.** *Zool.* scorpion; **2.** (*Sternzeichen*) Scorpio; (*ein*) ~ *sein* be (a) Scorpio

Skript *n*; *-(e)s*, *-en und -s* **1.** *Film etc.*: script; **2.** *Univ.* lecture notes *Pl.*; **~girl** [-gøːɐl] *n*; *-s*, *-s* continuity girl

Skriptum *n*; *-s*, *Skripten*; *bes. österr. Univ.* lecture notes *Pl.*

Skrofulose *f*; *-*, *-n*; *Med.* scrofula

Skrotum *n*; *-s*, *Skrota*; *Anat.* scrotum (*Pl.* scrota *od.* -s)

Skrupel *m*; *-s*, *-* scruple; ~ *haben, etw. zu tun* have scruples about doing s.th.; *keine* ~ *kennen* have no scruples, be totally unscrupulous; *ohne jeden* ~ without the slightest scruple, completely unscrupulous

skrupellos I. *Adj.* unscrupulous; **II.** *Adv. ausbeuten, betrügen*: unscru-

pulously; *sie gehen absolut* ~ *vor* they are completely unscrupulous in their actions; **Skrupellosigkeit** *f* unscrupulousness

Skullboot *n Sport* scull; **skullen** *v/i.* scull; **Skuller** *m*; *-s*, *-*, **Skullerin** *f*; *-*, *-nen* sculler

Skulptur *f*; *-*, *-en* sculpture

Skulpturen|galerie *f Kunst* sculpture gallery; **~sammlung** *f* collection of sculptures; (*Museum*) sculpture collection (*od.* gallery)

Skunk *m*; *-s*, *-s und -e* **1.** *Zool.* skunk; **2.** *Pl. -s*; (*Pelz*) skunk

skurril *Adj.* (*seltsam*) bizarre, grotesque; (*absurd*) absurd; (*drollig*) comical; **Skurrilität** *f*; *-*, *-en* **1.** *nur Sg.* (*Seltsamkeit*) bizarreness, grotesqueness; (*Absurdität*) absurdity; (*Drolligkeit*) comical nature; **2.** (*Handlung etc.*) bizarre (*od.* grotesque) action; (*Absurdität*) absurdity

S-Kurve *f* double bend

Sky-Beamer ['skaibiːmɐ] *Lichttechnik*: skybeam

Slalom *m*; *-s*, *-s*; *Sport* slalom; ~ *fahren fig. Mot.* weave, zigzag; *beim Geschicklichkeitsfahren*: slalom; **~kurs** *m Sport* slalom course; *e-n* ~ *fahren fig.* drive a zigzag course; **~lauf** *m Sport* slalom; **~läufer** *m*, **~läuferin** *f* slalom skier (*od.* racer)

Slang [slɛŋ] *m*; *-s*, *-s* **1.** slang; **2.** *technischer etc.*: jargon; **~ausdruck** *m* slang expression

Slawe *m*; *-n*, *-n*, **Slawin** *f*; *-*, *-nen* Slav, *weiblich auch*: Slav woman (*od.* girl); **slawisch** *Adj.* Slav, Slavonic, *bes. Am.* Slavic; **Slawisch** *n*; *-en*; *Ling.* Slavonic, *bes. Am.* Slavic; *das* ~*e* Slavonic, *bes. Am.* Slavic; **Slawist** *m*; *-en*, *-en* Slavonicist, *bes. Am.* Slavicist; **Slawistik** *f*; *-*, *kein Pl.* Slavonic (*bes. Am.* Slavic) studies *Pl.*; **Slawistin** *f*; *-*, *-nen* Slavonicist, *bes. Am.* Slavicist; **slawistisch** *Adj.* related to Slavonic (*bes. Am.* Slavic) studies

Slingpumps ['slɪŋpœmps] *m* slingback (shoe)

Slip *m*; *-s*, *-s* **1.** (*Unterhose*): (*ein*) ~ (a pair of) briefs *Pl.*; (*Damenslip*) panties *Pl.*; **2.** *Tech.*, *e-s Propellers*: slip; **~einlage** *f* pantyliner

Slipper *m*; *-s*, *-* slip-on (shoe)

Slogan ['sloːgn] *m*; *-s*, *-s* slogan, catchphrase

Slowake *m*; *-n*, *-n* Slovak; **Slowakei** *f*; *-*; *Geog.* Slovakia; **Slowakin** *f*; *-*, *-nen* Slovak, Slovak woman (*od.* girl); **slowakisch** *Adj.* Slovak, Slovakian; **Slowakisch** *n*; *-en*; *Ling.* Slovak; *das* ~*e* Slovak

Slowene *m*; *-n*, *-n* Slovene; **Slowenien** (*n*); *-s*; *Geog.* Slovenia; **Slowenin** *f*; *-*, *-nen* Slovene, Slovene woman (*od.* girl); **slowenisch** *Adj.* Slovene; **Slowenisch** *n*; *-en*; *Ling.* Slovene; *das* ~*e* Slovene

Slum [slam] *m*; *-s*, *-s*, *mst Pl.* slum(s *Pl.*); *in amerikanischen Großstädten*: ghetto; **~bewohner** *m*, **~bewohnerin** *f* slum-dweller; **~siedlung** *f* slummy (*od.* down-at-heel) estate, *Am.* derelict (housing) project

Smalltalk ['smɔːltɔːk] *m*, *n*; *-s*, *-s* small talk; ~ *machen* make light conversation

S. M. *f*; *-*, *kein Pl.*; *Abk.* (*seine*[*r*] *Majestät*) HM

sm *f*; *-*, *-*; *Abk.* → *Seemeile*

Smaragd *m*; *-(e)s*, *-e* emerald; **~eidechse** *f Zool.* green lizard

smaragdgrün *Adj.* emerald (green)

smart *Adj.* **1.** *oft pej.* (*durchtrieben*) smart; **2.** (*schick*) smart

Smilie ☺ ['smaili] *m*; -(*s*), -*s*; *Computer* smiley(-face)

Smog [smɔk] *m*; -(*s*), *kein Pl.*; *Öko.* smog

Smogalarm *m Öko.* smog alert

Smoking ['smoːkɪŋ] *m*; -*s*, -*s* dinner jacket, *Am. auch* tuxedo; **~hemd** *n* dress shirt

SMS *f*; -, -; *Abk.* (**Short Message Service**) (*Kurznachricht auf dem Handy*) text message; **j-m e-e ~ schicken** text s.o.; **SMSen** ['zɪmzn̩] *vt/i.* (*Kurznachricht*) text s.o.; → **simsen**

Smutje ['smʊtjə] *m*; -*s*, -*s*; *Naut. umg.* ship's cook

SMV *f*; -, *kein Pl.*; *Abk.* (**Schülermitverwaltung** *od.* **-verantwortung**) school council

Snack [snɛk] *m*; -*s*, -*s*; *Gastr.* snack

Snob [snɔp] *m*; -*s*, -*s* snob; **Snobismus** *m*; -, *Snobismen* **1.** *nur Sg.* snobbishness, snobbery, snobbism; **2.** (*Handlung etc.*) piece of snobbery; (*Bemerkung*) snobbish remark; **snobistisch** *Adj.* snobbish

Snowboard ['snoːbɔːɐ̯t] *n*; -*s*, -*s* snowboard; **~ fahren** snowboard; **Snowboarden** *n*; -*s*, *kein Pl.* snowboarding; **Snowboarder** *m*; -*s*, -, **Snowboarderin** *f*; -, -*nen* snowboarder; **Snowboarding** *n* snowboarding

SO *Abk.* (**Südost[en]**) SO

s.o. *Abk.* (**siehe oben**) → **sehen** I 2

so I. *Adv.* **1.** (*in dieser Weise, so beschaffen*) like this (*od.* that); **~ ist es** *umg.* that's how it is; *bestätigend:* that's it, you've got it; **~ ist das Leben** that's life, such is life; **also, es ist ~:** you see, it's like him; **~ geht das nicht** *umg.* that's just not on; *eingreifend:* oh no you don't!; **das machst du gut ~** you're doing nicely, that's the way (to do it); **~ oder ~** one way or another; (*wie man's sieht*) whichever way you look at it; *verlierst du etc.: auch* whatever you do; **er meint es nicht ~** *umg.* he doesn't (really) mean it (to be taken) like that; **ich will mal nicht ~ sein** *umg.* I don't want to be difficult; **er hat ~ s-e Stimmungen** *umg.* he has his little moods; **~ tun, als ob** pretend; **tu doch nicht ~!** *umg.* stop putting it on (*od.* faking); **hab dich nicht ~!** *umg.* stop making such a fuss; **~ geht's, wenn du nicht hörst** that's what comes of not listening; **~ genannt** so-called (*auch bei Neuprägungen*); (*angeblich*) *auch* would-be; **~ sagt man** as they say; **~ steht es hier** that's what it says here; **..., ~ der Präsident ...**, according to the president; **...,** so the president maintains; **2.** *umg.:* **danke, es geht schon ~** it's all right, thanks; (*ich schaffe das schon*) I can manage, thanks; *warum fragst du? -* **nur ~** I just wondered; *einfach* **~** (*zum Spaß*) just for kicks; **ich habe auch ~ genug Arbeit** I've got enough work as it is; **3.** (*so sehr*) so much; **ich freue/schäme mich ~!** I'm so pleased/ashamed!; **was stinkt hier ~?** what's making this awful smell?, what stinks?; **sie hat ~ geschrien, dass ...** she screamed so much that ...; **4.** **~!** *umg.* right!; *abschließend:* **auch** that's that!; **~, nun mach/erzähl mal!** *umg.* come on, get on with it / spit it out!; **~? is** that right (*od.* so)?, really?; **~, ~! umg.** I see; *interessierter:* well, well!; **er ist hier - ~!** is he?; **er braucht Geld - ~!** *umg.* does he

(now)?; **ach ~!** oh(, I see)!; **5.** *vor Adv. und Adj.:* **~ kalt** *etc.* so cold *etc.*; *vergleichend:* **~ schlecht** *etc.* as bad *etc.*; **nicht ~ kalt** *etc.* not so cold *etc.*; *vergleichend: auch* not as cold *etc.*; **~ ... wie** *od.* **als** as ... as; **ich bin ~ wenig wie er daran interessiert** I'm no more interested in it than he is; **~ gut wie nichts** next to nothing; **e-e ~ große Menge** such a (large) quantity; **~ freundlich sein und** *od.* **zu** (+ *Inf.*) be so kind as to; **doppelt ~ viele** twice as many; **um ~ besser** so much the better, just as well; **um ~ mehr** all the more; **~ sehr, dass** so much (so) that, to such an extent that; **6.** *umg.:* **~ ein Tag** such a day, a day like this; *Ausruf:* what a day!; **~ ein Idiot!** what an idiot!; **~ ein Unsinn!** what nonsense!; **~ eins** one like this (*od.* that); **~ eine(r)** (*Ding*) one like this (*od.* that); (*Mensch*) someone like this (*od.* that); → *auch* **solch**; **7. ~ etwas** something like that; *bei Frage: auch* anything like that; *bei Verneinung:* anything like that; **~ etwas habe ich noch nie gesehen/gehört** I've never seen anything like it / I've never heard such a thing; (*na*) **~ was!** *umg.* really?, you don't say!; *zu sich selbst:* that's strange; *stärker:* would you believe it; **8. ~ viel** so much; **~ viel wie** as much as; **doppelt ~ viel** twice as much; **noch einmal ~ viel** as much again; **~ viel ist gewiss** *od.* **sicher** one thing is certain; **~ viel für heute** that's it for today; **~ viel wie e-e Zusage sein** be as good as an acceptance, amount to an acceptance; **9. ~ weit** so far; **es ist ~ weit ganz gut** it's OK as far as it goes; *bei e-m Vorgang:* so far so good; **es geht ihm ~ weit gut** he's (doing) quite well on the whole; **das ist ~ weit ja alles schön und gut, aber** *umg.* it's fine up to a point, but; **~ weit sein** (*Arbeit, Person*) be finished; (*bereit*) be ready; **endlich ist es ~ weit** it's ready (*od.* finished) at last; (*wir sind angekommen*) we've etc. finally made it; **es ist gleich ~ weit** we're etc. nearly there, any minute now; **10.** *umg.* (*ungefähr*) around, about; **~ in einer Stunde** in an hour or so, in about an hour; **~ alle acht Tage** every week or so; **~ um die 50** about fifty, fiftyish; **ich habe ~ das Gefühl, dass** I have a sort of feeling that, somehow I have the feeling that; **was treibst du ~?** what are you up to these days?; **was kostet es denn ~?** what sort of price were you thinking of (*od.* are they asking *etc.*)?; **wie findest du ihn denn ~?** what do you think of him then?; *er hieß Merkl oder* **~** or something like that, or something to that effect; **100 Euro oder ~** somewhere around 100 euros; **... und ~ ...** and so on; **II.** *Konj.* **1.** (*folglich, deshalb*) so; **und ~ kam es, dass ...** and so ..., that's how ...; **2.** (*wie sehr*) however; **~ schnell/viel du kannst** as fast/much as you can; **~ krank er auch ist** however ill he may be; **~ weit es reicht** as far as it goes; **~ dass** so that; **wie du mir, ~ ich dir** *umg.* tit for tat

sobald *Konj.:* **~** (*als*) as soon as; **~ er angekommen war** as soon as (the moment) he arrived; **~ es Ihnen möglich ist** as soon as you can; *Wirts.* at your earliest convenience

Söckchen *Pl.* ankle socks; *für Kinder:* (children's) socks

Socke *f*; -, -*n* sock; **sich auf die ~n machen** *umg.* make tracks, push off *Sl.*;

er war von den ~n *umg.* he nearly fell over backwards, he was flabbergasted

Sockel *m*; -*s*, - **1.** base (*auch Haus etc.*); *Säule, Statue etc.: auch* plinth, pedestal; **2.** *Etech.* socket; **3.** *Wirts.* → **Sockelbetrag, ~betrag** *m* basic allowance; **~rente** *f* basic pension

Socken *m*; -*s*, -; *südd., schw., österr.* → **Socke**; **~halter** *m* (sock) suspender, *Am.* garter

Soda *n*; -*s*, *kein Pl.* soda; *Chem. auch* sodium carbonate; → **Whisky**

sodann *Adv. altm.* then, *lit.* thereupon

sodass, so dass *Konj.* so that

Sodawasser *n* soda water

Sodbrennen *n* heartburn; **~ haben** have (got) heartburn; **starkes ~ haben** have a bad attack of heartburn

Sode *f*; -, -*n* piece of turf, sod

Sodom (*n*); -*s* Sodom

Sodomie *f*; -, *kein Pl.* bestiality; **Sodomit** *m*; -*en*, -*en* person committing bestiality

soeben *Adv.* just (now); (*in diesem Augenblick*) just, right now

Sofa *n*; -*s*, -*s* sofa, settee; **~ecke** *f* sofa corner; **~kissen** *n* sofa cushion; (*zusätzliches Zierkissen*) scatter cushion

sofern *Konj.* provided (that), as long as; **~ er nicht absagt** provided (*od.* as long as) he doesn't call it off, unless he calls it off

soff *Imperf.* → **saufen**

Soffitte *f*; -, -*n* **1.** *Theat.* border; **2.** *Glühlampe:* festoon (lamp) bulb

sofort *Adv.* straightaway, immediately, at once; (**ich komme**) **~!** just coming!; **ich bin ~ bei dir** I'll be with you right away, I'll be right with you; **er war ~ tot** he died instantly, it was (an) instant death; **das Kind fing ~ an zu schreien, als ich das Zimmer verließ** started screaming the moment (*od.* minute) I left the room *od.* as soon as I left the room; **lieferbar/zahlbar** spot delivery/payment; **... ab ~ durchgehend geöffnet** open 24 hours with immediate effect (*od.* from now on)

Sofort|ausstieg *m* immediate departure (**aus** from); **der ~ aus der Kernenergie** the immediate abandonment of nuclear energy; **~bildkamera** *f* instant camera; **~hilfe** *f* emergency relief

sofortig *Adj.* immediate; → **Wirkung**

Sofort|maßnahmen *Pl.* immediate steps; *für den Notfall:* emergency measures; **~programm** *n Pol.* crash program(me); **~zugriff** *m EDV* instant access

Softeis ['zɔft?aɪs] *n* soft ice

Softie ['zɔfti] *m*; -*s*, -*s* (real) softy

Software ['sɔftvɛːɐ̯] *f*; -, *kein Pl.* software; **~anbieter** *m* software provider; **~angebot** *n* range of software; **~entwicklung** *f* software development; *Pl.* software developments; **~hersteller** *m* software producer; **~paket** *n* software package; **~piraterie** *f* software piracy; **~programm** *n* program; **~schmiede** *f umg.* software house; **~technologie** *f* software engineering; **~unternehmen** *n* software firm (*od.* company)

Softwerker *m*; -*s*, -, **~in** *f*; -, -*nen* producer of software

sog *Imperf.* → **saugen**

sog. *Abk.* → **so genannt**

Sog *m*; -(*e*)*s*, *kein Pl.* suction; *Naut., Flug. auch* wake; (*Wirbel*) vortex (*Pl. auch* vortices); (*Unterströmung*) undertow; *fig.* vortex, maelstrom

sogar *Adv.* even; **sie war nicht nur im Endlauf, sie hat ~ den zweiten Platz**

erreicht she not only reached the final, she got no less than second place; **sehr gut, ~ ausgezeichnet** very good, excellent in fact

so genannt → **so** I 1

sogleich Adv. altm. → **sofort**

Sogwirkung f suction; fig. pull, magnetic attraction (**auf** + Akk. exerted on)

Sohle f, -, -n **1.** Fuß und Schuh: sole; **auf leisen ~n** fig. on tiptoe; (heimlich) stealthily; **e-e kesse ~ aufs Parkett legen** umg. be hot stuff on the dance floor, cut up a mean floor; **2.** (Tal-, Flusssohle) bottom; **3.** Bergb. floor; **sohlen** v/t. (re)sole

Sohn m; -(e)s, Söhne son; **ganz der ~ s-s Vaters** umg. a chip off the old block; **mein ~** gespr. Anrede: son; **der ~ Gottes** the Son of God; **der verlorene ~** bibl., fig. the prodigal son

...sohn m, im Subst.: **Adoptiv~** adopted son; **Königs~** king's son; **Wüsten~** son of the desert

Sohnemann m hum. son, sonny; **der ~** junior

soigniert [zoanˈjiːʀt] Adj. elegant; Erscheinung: auch soigné

Soiree [zoaˈreː] f, -, -n soiree, soirée

Soja f, -, kein Pl. soya, soy; **Sojabohne** f Bot., Gastr. soya bean, bes. Am. soybean; **Sojabohnenkeimlinge** Pl. soya bean (bes. Am. soybean) sprouts

Soja|brot n Gastr. soya (bes. Am. soybean) bread; **~milch** f soya (bes. Am. soy) milk; **~quark** m soya (bes. Am. soy) curd; **~soße** f soy(a) sauce; **~sprossen** Pl. soya bean (bes. Am. soybean) sprouts

Sokratiker m; -s, -, **sokratisch** Adj. Philos. Socratic

solang(e) Konj. as long as; (während) auch while; einschränkend: as (od. so) long as; **~ ich lebe** for the rest of my life; (bisher) all my life; **~ er nicht anruft, können wir nichts machen** we can't do anything until he rings up (Am. calls)

solar Adj. solar

Solar|anlage f solar power plant; **~antrieb** m solar drive; **~architektur** f architecture that exploits solar energy; **~batterie** f solar battery

solarbetrieben Adj. driven by solar power, solar-powered

Solar|energie f solar energy; **~fahrzeug** n solar-powered vehicle; **~farm** f solar farm; **~heizung** f solar heating

Solarium n; -s, Solarien solarium (Pl. -s od. solaria); (Sonnenbank) sunbed, sun bench

Solar|jahr n solar year; **~kollektor** m solar panel; **~kraftwerk** n solar energy plant, solar power station; **~mobil** n solar-powered vehicle; **~modul** n solar module

Solarplexus m; -, -; Physiol. solar plexus

Solar|strom m solar electricity; **~tankstelle** f solar electricity charging station (for electric cars); **~technik** f solar technology

solarthermisch Adj. solar energy ...

Solar|uhr f solar clock; **~wind** m solar winds (od. storms) Pl.

Solarzelle f solar cell; **Solarzellenbatterie** f solar battery

Solbad n **1.** (einzelnes Bad, Badehaus) brine bath; **2.** (Ort) saltwater spa

solch Pron. und Adj. such, that kind (od. sort) of, ... like that; **~ einer** someone (od. a person) like that; **~e Menschen** such people, people like that; **als ~er/~e/~es** as such; **ich hatte ~e Angst** I was so scared; **ich habe ~e Kopfschmerzen** I've got such a headache; **es gibt eben ~e und ~e** od. **sone und ~e** umg. it takes all kinds to make a world; **es gab ~e, die ..., und ~e, die ...** there were those who ... and those (od. others) who ...; → auch **so** I 6

solcherart I. Adj. such, that kind (od. sort) of, ... like that, ... of that kind (od. sort); **II.** Adv. (auf solche Art) in that (od. this) way; (durch solche Mittel) by such means; **solcherlei** Adj. such, that kind (od. sort) of, ... of that kind (od. sort); **solchermaßen** Adv. → **solcherart** II

Sold m; -(e)s, kein Pl.; Mil. pay; **in j-s ~ stehen** fig. be in s.o.'s pay (förm. employ); pej. be one of s.o.'s hirelings (od. lackeys)

Soldat m; -en, -en; Mil. soldier (auch Zool., Ameise etc.); allg. serviceman; **~ werden** join the army, join (od. sign) up; **gedienter ~** ex-serviceman, Am. veteran; **Der brave ~ Schwejk** The Good Soldier Schweik

Soldaten|beruf m Mil. military career (od. profession), army career; **~friedhof** m military (od. war) cemetery; **~grab** n war (od. soldier's) grave; **~leben** n army life, life in the army, a soldier's life; **~sprache** f soldiers'(od. army) slang; **~tod** m: **den ~ finden** förm. die in action (lit., hist. on the field of battle); **~uniform** f soldier's (od. military) uniform

Soldateska f; -, Soldatesken; Mil., pej. (rabble of) marauding troops Pl.

Soldatin f; -, -nen; Mil. (woman) soldier

soldatisch Adj. Mil. soldierly; (militärisch) military

Soldbuch n Mil. paybook

Söldner m; -s, -; Mil. mercenary, soldier of fortune; **~führer** m, **~führerin** f mercenaries' leader; **~heer** n army of mercenaries

Söldnerin f; -, -nen Mil. (woman) mercenary

Söldnertruppe f Mil. mercenary unit

Sole f; -, -n salt water, brine; **~bad** n brine bath

Solei n Gastr. pickled egg

solid Adj. → **solide**

Solidar|beitrag m contribution to a mutually supportive community; **~gemeinschaft** f mutually supportive community; **~haftung** f joint (and several) liability

solidarisch I. Adj. **1.** Front etc.: united; **e-e ~e Haltung zeigen** display solidarity; **sich ~ erklären mit** declare one's solidarity with; **2.** Jur. joint (and several); **II.** Adv. **1.** ~ handeln etc. act etc. in solidarity (mit with); **2.** Jur. jointly and severally; **solidarisieren** v/refl.: **sich ~ mit** demonstrate one's solidarity with; **wir müssen uns ~** we must stand together (od. close ranks, show a united front); **Solidarisierung** f demonstration of solidarity, closing of ranks; **Solidarität** f; -, kein Pl. solidarity

Solidaritäts|abgabe f solidarity payment; **~adresse** f (official) declaration of solidarity; **~beweis** m show of solidarity; **~bekundung** f declaration of solidarity; **~erklärung** f declaration of solidarity; **~fonds** m solidarity fund; **~gefühl** n feeling of solidarity; **~kundgebung** f solidarity rally (od. demonstration); **~streik** m sympathy strike, auch Pl. sympathetic action;

~schuldner m, **~schuldnerin** f joint debtor; **~veranstaltung** f solidarity meeting; **~zuschlag** m in Deutschland: solidarity supplement (added to income and corporation tax to help cover the costs of reunification)

Solidarpakt m agreement for a fair distribution of burdens between politicians, unions and employers

solide I. Adj. **1.** (stabil) Mauern, Material etc.: solid, robust, strong; Schuhe: sturdy, strong; **~ Möbel** (good,) solid (od. sturdy) furniture; **2.** (fundiert) Verhältnisse, Ausbildung, Kenntnisse: sound; Grundlage: firm, sound; **e-e ~ Arbeit** a sound piece of work; (Möbelstück etc.) auch a good, solid piece of workmanship; **e-e ~ Mahlzeit** a good square meal; **3.** (anständig, seriös) Person: auch sound, reputable; Firma: auch sound, reputable; Preise: reasonable; **~r Lebenswandel** solid, respectable lifestyle; **II.** Adv. **1.** (stabil) ~ gebaut well-built, solidly built; **2.** ganz ~ leben live a solid and respectable life; **Solidität** f; -, kein Pl. solidity (auch fig.); Wirts. soundness; (Achtbarkeit) respectability

Solist m; -en, -en, **1.** Mus. soloist; **2.** umg. fig. Sport player making a solo run; **Solistin** f; -, -nen → **Solist**; **solistisch** Adj. soloistic; (als Solist) as a soloist; Partie: solo ...

solitär Adj. Zool. solitary

Solitär m; -s, -e **1.** (Brillant) solitaire; **2.** nur Sg. (Spiel) solitaire

soll Präs. → **sollen**[1], **sollen**[2]

Soll n; -s, kein Pl.; Wirts. **1.** debit; (Liefersoll) (fixed) quota; **~ und Haben** debit and credit; **2.** (Produktionssoll) production quota; (Liefer-, Produktionsziel) target; **sein ~ erfüllt haben** umg. fig. have done one's bit (Am. part); **~bestand** m Wirts., an Werten etc.: calculated assets Pl.; an Vorräten: target inventory; **~bruchstelle** f Tech. predetermined breaking point

sollen[1] Modalv.; soll, sollte, hat sollen **1.** bei Aufgabe, Verpflichtungen etc.: be to, be supposed to; **er soll mich anrufen** he's to ring me up, tell him to ring me up; **ich soll erst abwaschen** I have to (od. I should) do the dishes first; **sie soll sich schonen** she's (supposed) to take it easy; **ich soll dir ausrichten, dass ...** I'm to tell you that ...; **ich soll dir schöne Grüße von ihm bestellen** he sends his regards, he asked me to give you his regards; **du solltest längst im Bett sein** you were supposed to be (od. should have been) in bed long ago; **er sollte Arzt werden** he was supposed to become a doctor, the idea was that he should (Am. auch would) become a doctor; **2.** in Fragen: **soll ich mitkommen?** shall I come too?, do you want me to come?; **3.** befehlend: **du sollst ihn in Ruhe lassen!** leave him alone!; **wie oft soll ich dir das noch sagen?** how many times do I have to tell you?; **du sollst nicht alles anfassen!** don't (od. you mustn't) touch everything!; **du sollst nicht töten** bibl. thou shalt not kill; **4.** bei Gedanken, Beabsichtigtem: **hier soll e-e Turnhalle gebaut werden** a gymnasium (od. gym umg.) is to be built here, there are plans to build a gymnasium (od. gym umg.) here; **er soll morgen ankommen** he's due (od. supposed) to arrive tomorrow; **das Buch soll Ihnen dabei helfen** the book is designed to help you with this; **m-e Kinder ~ es**

einmal besser haben I want my children to be better off (than I was); **5.** *bei unbestätigten Gerüchten etc.*: be supposed to, be said to; *sie soll sehr reich sein* she's supposed (*od.* said) to be very rich, they say she's very rich; **6.** *bei e-r bestimmten Vorstellung*: *was soll das sein?* what's that supposed to be?; *es sollte ein Geschenk werden* it was supposed (*od.* meant) to be a present; *soll das ein Witz sein?* *umg. ungehalten*: is this some sort of joke?; *wozu soll das gut sein?* *umg.* what's that in aid of?; **7.** *bei Anweisung, Drohung, Herausforderung etc.*: *er soll alles haben, was er will* he's to (*od.* he shall) have whatever he wants, let him have anything he wants; *das soll uns nicht stören* we won't let that bother us; *der soll nur kommen!* *umg.* just let him come!; *soll er es doch versuchen!* let him try!; *das sollst du mir büßen!* *umg.* I'll make you pay for that; *das soll mir mal einer nachmachen!* *umg.* I'd like to see anyone do better; **8.** (*Konjunktiv*) *bei Ratschlag, Vorwurf etc.*: should, ought to; *du solltest es mal sehen* you should (*od.* ought to) see it; *man hätte es ihm sagen ~* he ought to (*od.* should) have been told; *ich hätte es wissen ~* I should have known; *du solltest lieber nach Hause gehen* I think you'd better (*od.* you ought to) go home; *so sollte es sein* this is how it should (*od.* ought to) be; *so sollte das Wetter immer sein!* the weather should always be like this; *warum sollte ich (auch)?* why should I?, I don't see why I should; **9.** *bei Unentschlossenheit*: *was soll ich tun?* what shall (*od.* should) I do?; *verzweifelt*: *auch* what am I supposed to do?; *er wusste nicht, was er machen sollte* he didn't know what to do; *sie wussten nicht, ob sie lachen oder weinen sollten* they didn't know whether to laugh or cry; *was soll ich sagen?* what can I say?; *ratlos*: what am I (supposed) to say?; **10.** *bei e-r Möglichkeit*: *falls es irgendwelche Probleme geben sollte* if there should be (*od.* are) any problems; *sollte es nicht klappen, dann ...* if it all goes wrong, (then) ...; *man sollte annehmen* you would think; **11.** *bei Bestimmung, Schicksal*: be to; *sie sollte e-e berühmte Sängerin werden* she was (destined) to become a famous singer; *es hat nicht sein ~ od. umg. ~ sein* it wasn't meant to be; *ein Jahr sollte verstreichen, bis* it was to be another year before, a whole year was to pass before; *es sollte alles anders kommen* things were to turn out quite differently

sollen² *v/i.*; *soll, sollte, hat gesollt*; *umg.* **1.** (*irgendwohin müssen*) be (supposed) to go; *wo soll das hin?* where's it supposed to go?, where do you want me *etc.* to put it?; *du sollst sofort zum Chef* you are to go to (see) the boss right away; **2.** *was soll das?* (*was bedeutet das?*) what's all this about?; (*wozu soll es nützen?*) what's that for?; *verärgert*: what's the idea?, what are you playing at?, *Am. auch* what are you up to?; *was soll der Quatsch. Scheiß?* what's all this nonsense?; *was soll ich damit?* what am I supposed to do with it?; *soll er doch!* let him; (*es ist mir egal*) see if I care; *was soll's* so what; who cares

Söller *m*; *-s, -*; *Archit.* balcony
Soll|-ist-Vergleich *m Wirts.* target-performance comparison; **~seite** *f* debit side; **~stärke** *f Mil.* required (*od.* full) strength; **~wert** *m* rated (*od.* desired) value; *EDV, Regeltechnik*: set point; **~zinsen** *Pl.* debtor interest *Sg.*
Solo *n*; *-s, -s und Soli* **1.** *Mus. etc.* solo; *für Soli, Chor und Orchester* for soloists, chorus and orchestra; **2.** *umg. Fußball*: solo run (*od.* effort); **3.** *Kartenspiel*: solo
solo I. *Adj. umg.* alone; *ist er immer noch ~?* is he still unattached?; **II.** *Adv.* **1.** *Mus.* solo; *~ singen* sing a solo; **2.** *umg.* alone
Solo|auftritt *m Mus. etc.* solo performance; **~geiger** *m*, **~geigerin** *f* violin soloist; **~gesang** *m* (voice) solo; **~gitarre** *f* solo guitar; **~instrument** *n* solo instrument; **~karriere** *f* career as a soloist
Solomaschine *f Mot.* solo machine
Solo|part *m Mus.* solo (part); **~sänger** *m*, **~sängerin** *f* solo singer, soloist; **~spiel** *n Mus.* solo playing; **~stimme** *f* **1.** solo voice; **2.** (*Part*) solo part; **~stück** *n* solo (*auch Mus.*); **~tanz** *m* solo (dance); **~tänzer** *m*, **~tänzerin** *f* **1.** solo dancer; **2.** (*erste[r] Tänzer[in]*) principal dancer
Sol|quelle *f* salt water (*od.* brine) spring; **~salz** *n* brine salt
Solvens *n*; *-, Solvenzien und Solventia*; *Pharm.* solvent; **solvent** *Adj.* solvent; **Solvenz** *f*; *-, -en* solvency
Solwasser *n* salt water, brine
Somalia *n*; *-s*; *Geog.* Somalia
Somalier *m*; *-s, -*, **~in** *f*; *-, -nen* Somali, *weiblich auch*: Somali woman (*od.* girl); **Somaliland** *n hist.* Somaliland; **somalisch** *Adj.* Somali
somit *Adv.* thus, therefore, as a result; (*hiermit*) so
Sommer *m*; *-s, -* summer; *im ~* in (the) summer; *~ wie die. und Winter* all year round; → *Schwalbe*; **~abend** *m* summer evening; **~anfang** *m* beginning of summer; *laut Kalender*: first day of summer; **~deich** *m* (low) summer dike; **~fahrplan** *m* summer timetable (*Am.* schedule); **~fell** *n* summer coat; **~ferien** *Pl.* summer holidays (*bes. Am.* vacation *Sg.*); **~fest** *n* summer party; **~freizeit** *f* summer activity program(me); *im Ferienlager*: summer camp; **~frische** *f altm.* **1.** (*Ort*) countryside summer resort; **2.** (*Aufenthalt*) *nach X zur od.* *in die ~ fahren* go to X for a breath of fresh country air (in the summer); **~frischler** *m*; *-s, -*, **~gast** *m* summer visitor; **~gerste** *f* spring barley; **~getreide** *n* spring cereal; **~halbjahr** *n* summer months *Pl.*; *Päd. etwa* summer term (*Am. auch* semester, quarter); **~haus** *n* summer holiday (*Am.* vacation) house; **~hit** *m umg.* (*Mode*) hot summer fashion; (*Schlager*) summer hit; **~hitze** *f* summer heat, heat of summer; **~kleid** *n* **1.** summer dress; **2.** *Zool., von Tieren*: summer coat; *von Vögeln*: summer plumage; **~kleidung** *f* summer clothing; *Wirts.* summerwear; **~lager** *n* summer camp
sommerlich I. *Adj.* summery; *attr.* (*für den Sommer üblich*) summer ...; **II.** *Adv.*: *es wird ~ warm* it's getting warm and summery, the temperatures are reaching summer levels; *~ gekleidet* wearing summer clothes
Sommer|loch *n umg.* silly (*od.* dead) season; **~mode** *f* summer fashions *Pl.*;

~nacht *f* summer('s) night; **~nachtsfest** *n* summer night party; **~olympiade** *f Sport* Summer Olympics *Pl.*; **~pause** *f* summer break; *Pol.* summer recess; **~reifen** *m Mot.* normal tyre (*Am.* tire); **~residenz** *f* summer residence
sommers *Adv.* in summer; *~ wie winters* all year round
Sommer|sachen *Pl.* summer clothes; **~saison** *f* summer season; **~schlaf** *m Zool.* aestivation (*Am.* estivation); **~schlussverkauf** *m* summer sale(s); **~semester** *n Univ.* summer semester (*od.* term); **~sitz** *m* summer residence
Sommerski *m* glacier ski; **~gebiet** *n* summer skiing area
Sommersmog *m* summer smog; **~verordnung** *f* summer smog regulations *Pl.*
Sommer|sonnenwende *f* summer solstice; **~spiele** *Pl.*: *Olympische ~* Summer Olympics
Sommersprossen *Pl.* freckles; **sommersprossig** *Adj.* freckled
Sommer|tag *m* summer('s) day; **~theater** *n* **1.** summer theat|re (*Am.* -er); **2.** *umg. bes. Pol.* silly season; **~urlaub** *m* summer holiday (*Am.* vacation); **~weide** *f* summer pasture; **~weizen** *m* spring wheat; **~zeit** *f* **1.** summer(time); *während der ~* in summer(time); **2.** (*Uhrzeit*) daylight saving (*Am.* savings) time, *Brit. auch* summer time; *ab morgen gilt die ~* we switch to summer (*Am.* daylight savings) time tomorrow
somnambul *Adj.* somnambulistic; **Somnambule** *m, f*; *-n, -n* somnambulist
son, so 'n *Pron. umg.* (*so ein*) such a; *~e teure Hose* such an expensive pair of trousers (*Am.* pants); *so 'n langer Dünner* one of those tall thin types; *so 'n Mistwetter!* what miserable weather!; → *so* I 6, *solch*
Sonar *n*; *-s, -e*, **~gerät** *n Tech.* sonar
Sonate *f*; *-, -n*; *Mus.* sonata; **Sonatenform** *f* sonata form; **Sonatine** *f*; *-, -n* sonatina
Sonde *f*; *-, -n* **1.** *Med.* probe (*auch fig.*); *e-s Chirurgen*: sound; *zur Ernährung*: stomach tube; **2.** (*Radiosonde*) *Radar, Met.*: sonde; *Raumf.* probe; **3.** *Flug., Sicherheitskontrolle*: metal detector
...sonde *f*, *im Subst.*: *Blasen~* bladder sound; *Jupiter~* Jupiter probe
Sonder|... *im Subst.* special ...; **~abdruck** *m* offprint
Sonderabfall *m* hazardous waste; **~entsorgung** *f* hazardous waste disposal
Sonder|abgabe *f* special tax (*fachspr.* impost); **~abkommen** *n* special agreement; **~abschreibung** *f* special depreciation allowance; **~abteilung** *f* special department; **~aktion** *f* special campaign; *Wirts. auch* (special) promotion; **~anfertigung** *f* special version (*od.* model); (*Auto etc.*) *auch* (*Einzelanfertigung*) custom-made car *etc.*; **~angebot** *n* special offer; *etw. im ~ kaufen* get s.th. on special offer (*Am.* on sale); **~auftrag** *m* special mission; **~ausgabe** *f* **1.** *Buch*: special edition; **2.** *~n finanziell*: additional expenses; *steuerlich*: allowable expenses; **~ausschuss** *m* select committee; (*für Sonderaufgabe*) (special) task force (*od.* group); **~ausstattung** *f* special equipment; (*Extras*) (optional) extras *Pl.*; **~ausstellung** *f* special exhibition

sonderbar I. *Adj.* strange, odd; *er ist heute* ~ he's acting very strangely today; **II.** *Adv.:* ~ *aussehen* look strange; *es war* ~ *still* it was strangely quiet; **sonderbarerweise** *Adv.* strangely (*od.* oddly) enough
Sonder|beauftragte *m*, *f* special envoy; (*Bevollmächtigte*) plenipotentiary; **~bedeutung** *f* *e-s Wortes:* special (*od.* additional) meaning; **~befehl** *m* special order(s *Pl.*); **~behandlung** *f* special treatment (*auch fig.*); (*Bevorzugung*) *auch* preferential treatment; **~beilage** *f* (special) supplement; **~belastung** *f* special (*od.* extra) burden; **~bericht** *m* special report; **~berichterstatter** *m*, **~berichterstatterin** *f* special correspondent; **~bestimmung** *f* special provision (*od.* rule, condition); **~bevollmächtigte** *m*, *f* special representative (*od.* envoy); *Pol.* plenipotentiary; **~bewacher** *m*, **~bewacherin** *f* *Sport* special marker; **~botschafter** *m*, **~botschafterin** *f* *Pol.* special envoy; **~deponie** *f* special (*sehr gefährlich:* hazardous) waste storage facility; **~dezernat** *n* special police unit; **~druck** *m* offprint
Sondereinsatz *m* special action (*od.* operation); (*Auftrag*) special mission; **~kommando** *n* special mission unit; *größer:* task force
Sonder|erlaubnis *f* special permission; *konkret:* special permit; **~ermittler** *m*, **~ermittlerin** *f* special investigator; **~fahrt** *f* **1.** unscheduled (*od.* extra) run; **2.** (*Ausflug*) excursion; **~fall** *m* special case; (*Ausnahme*) exception; **~flug** *m* unscheduled (*od.* special) flight; **~fonds** *m* special fund; **~form** *f* special form; **~gebiet** *n* specialized area (*od.* field); **~genehmigung** *f* special permission; *konkret:* special permit; **~gericht** *n* special court; **~gesandte** *m*, *f* special envoy; **~gesetz** *n* special law
sondergleichen *Adv.* unparalleled; (*unerhört*) unheard of; *das ist e-e Frechheit* ~ I've never heard of such cheek
Sonder|gutachten *n* expert's opinion; **~heft** *n* special issue; **~interessen** *Pl.* special interests; **~kindergarten** *m* kindergarten for slow learners; **~klasse** *f* *Tanzsport etc.:* special class; *zur absoluten* ~ *gehören* *umg.* be absolutely top-flight; *der Auftritt etc. war* ~ *umg.* it was a top-drawer performance *etc.;* **~kommando** *n* special operations unit; **~kommission** *f* special commission; **~konjunktur** *f* *Wirts.* special trend (in economic activity); **~konzert** *n* special concert; **~konto** *n* special account; **~korrespondent** *m*, **~korrespondentin** *f* special correspondent; **~kosten** *Pl.* special (*od.* additional) costs; **~leistung** *f* special payment
sonderlich I. *Adj.* nur attr. particular; *kein ~es Vergnügen* not much fun; → *auch* **sonderbar; II.** *Adv.* particularly
Sonderling *m; -s, -e* eccentric, strange (*od.* odd) sort
Sonder|marke *f* special stamp; *Pl.* (*Satz* ~*n*) special issue *Sg.;* **~maschine** *f* *Flug.* unscheduled (*od.* special) flight; *in e-r* ~ *eintreffen* arrive on a special flight; **~meldung** *f* special announcement; **~mittel** *Pl.* special funds
Sondermüll *m* special waste; *sehr gefährlicher:* hazardous (*Giftmüll:* toxic) waste; **~abgabe** *f* delivery of hazardous waste; **~deponie** *f* hazardous waste dump; **~entsorgung** *f* hazard-

ous waste disposal; **~verbrennung** *f* hazardous waste incineration
sondern¹ *Konj.* but; *er fährt nicht,* ~ *er fliegt* he's not driving, he's flying, he's flying, not driving; *das ist kein Chinesisch,* ~ *Japanisch* that's not Chinese, that's (*od.* it's) Japanese; *nicht nur...,* ~ *auch...* not only..., but also...
sondern² *v/t.* separate (*von* from)
Sondernummer *f* special issue (*od.* edition)
Sonderpädagogik *f* *Päd.* remedial (*od.* special) education; **sonderpädagogisch** *Adj.* related to remedial (*od.* special) education
Sonder|parteitag *m* *Pol.* special party conference (*od. bes. Am.* convention); **~preis** *m* special (reduced) price; *T-Shirts zum* ~ *von* T-shirts on special offer (*Am.* on sale) at (*od.* for); **~prüfung** *f* *Fin.* special audit; **~recht** *n* special right; **~regelung** *f* special arrangement; **~rolle** *f* special role
sonders *Adv.* → *samt* I
Sonder|schicht *f* special (*od.* extra) shift; **~schule** *f* special school; **~schüler** *m*, **~schülerin** *f* pupil (*Am.* student) at a special school; **~schullehrer** *m*, **~schullehrerin** *f* teacher at a special school; **~schulpädagogik** *f* special school educational theory; **~sendung** *f* special broadcast; **~sitzung** *f* special session; **~sprache** *f* *Ling.* distinctive language (*of a certain social group*); **~status** *m* special status; **~stellung** *f* special position (*od.* status); **~stempel** *m* special postmark; **~tarif** *m* special (*od.* preferential) rate; **~topf** *m* *fig.* special kitty; **~urlaub** *m* special leave; *Mil. auch* emergency leave; *im Todesfall etc.:* compassionate leave; **~veranstaltung** *f* special event; **~verkauf** *m* special sale; **~vermögen** *n* *Jur.* special assets *Pl.;* **~verwaltungszone** *f* *Pol.:* ~ *Hongkong* the special administrative area of Hong Kong; **~vollmacht** *f* emergency powers *Pl.;* **~vorstellung** *f* special performance; **~weg** *m* special way; **~wunsch** *m* special request; **~zeichen** *n* special character, symbol; **~ziehung** *f* *Lotto etc.:* special drawing; **~ziehungsrechte** *Pl. Wirts.* special drawing rights; **~zubehör** *n* (optional) extras *Pl.;* **~zug** *m* special train; *für Ausflüge:* excursion train; **~zulage** *f* special bonus
sondieren *vt/i.* **1.** (*erkunden*) sound out; *die Lage* ~ see how the land lies; **2.** *Med.* probe; **3.** *Naut.* sound; **Sondierung** *f* **1.** sounding out; **~en** exploratory talks; **2.** *Med.* probe; **3.** *Naut.* sounding; **Sondierungsgespräch** *n* *auch Pl.* exploratory talks *Pl.*
Sonett *n; -(e)s, -e* sonnet
Song *m; -s, -s* **1.** *Popmusik:* song; **2.** (*Chanson*) chanson; **~schreiber** *m*, **~schreiberin** *f* songwriter; **~text** *m* (song) lyrics *Pl.*
Sonnabend *m* Saturday; (*am*) ~ on Saturday; **sonnabends** *Adv.* on Saturday(s); *siehe auch* **Samstag...**
Sonne *f; -, -n* **1.** *nur Sg.* sun; (*Sonnenlicht*) sun(light); (*Sonnenschein*) sun(shine); *an der* ~ in the sun; *ich gehe raus an die* ~ I'm going out into the sun(shine) (*od.* to get some sun[shine]); *hier ist* ~ the sun is shining here; *geh mir aus der* ~ get out of the sun; *keine* ~ *vertragen* be unable to take the sun; *von der* ~ *beschienen* sunlit; *die* ~ *lacht* the sun is shining brightly; **2.** *Astron.* sun; → *Platz* 3;

sonnen *v/refl.* sun oneself, bask in the sun; *sich* ~ *in* (+ *Dat.*) *fig.* bask (*od.* revel) in
Sonnen|aktivität *f* solar activity; **~anbeter** *m*, **~anbeterin** *f* sun worshipper
sonnenarm *Adj.* lacking in sunshine; *es ist e-e* ~*e Gegend* it's an area where there is little sunshine
Sonnen|aufgang *m* sunrise; *bei* ~ at sunrise, when the sun comes up; **~bad** *n: ein* ~ *nehmen* sunbathe, (go and) lie in the sun; **~baden** *n* sunbathing; **~bahn** *f* sun's path (*od.* orbit); *scheinbare* ~ *Astron.* ecliptic; **~bank** *f* sunbed, sun bench
sonnenbeheizt *Adj.* solar-heated
Sonnen|bestrahlung *f* (exposure to) sunlight; **~blende** *f* **1.** *Fot.* lens hood; **2.** *Mot.* (sun) visor; **~blocker** *m; -s, -* sunblock
Sonnenblume *f* sunflower; **Sonnenblumenkern** *m* sunflower seed; **Sonnenblumenöl** *n* sunflower oil
Sonnen|brand *m* sunburn; *sich* (*Dat.*) *e-n* ~ *holen* get sun|burnt (*Am. auch* -burned); **~bräune** *f* (sun)tan; **~brille** *f:* (*e-e*) ~ (a pair of) sunglasses *Pl.;* **~creme** *f* sun cream; **~dach** *n* **1.** (*Markise*) sun canopy, awning; **2.** *Mot.* sunroof, sliding roof; **~deck** *n* *Naut.* sun deck
sonnendurchflutet *Adj.* flooded with sunshine
Sonnen|einstrahlung *f* solar radiation; **~energie** *f* solar energy; **~ferne** *f* *Astron.* aphelion; **~finsternis** *f* eclipse of the sun, solar eclipse; **~fleck** *m* sunspot
sonnengebräunt *Adj.* (sun)tanned, bronzed
Sonnengeflecht *n* *Anat.* solar plexus
sonnen|gereift *Adj.* sun-ripened; **~getrocknet** *Adj.* sun-dried
Sonnen|glut *f* blazing heat (of the sun); **~gott** *m* sun god; **~göttin** *f* sun goddess
sonnenhungrig *Adj.* hungry for the sun; *attr. Touristen etc.:* sun-seeking ...; **Sonnenhungrige** *m, f; -n, -n* sun-seeker; **Sonnenhut** *m* sunhat; **Sonnenjahr** *n* solar year
sonnenklar *Adj. umg. präd.* (as) clear as daylight; **~er Beweis** crystal-clear evidence
Sonnen|kollektor *m* solar panel; **~könig** *m* *hist.: der* ~ the Sun King, le Roi Soleil; **~kraftwerk** *n* solar power station; **~kult** *m* sun cult; *umg. fig.* sun worship; **~licht** *n:* (*bei*) ~ (in) sunlight; **~liege** *f* sunbed, sun bench
sonnenlos *Adj. attr.* sunless
Sonnen|milch *f* suntan lotion; **~nähe** *f* *Astron.* perihelion; **~ofen** *m* solar furnace; **~öl** *n* suntan oil; **~paddel** *n* *Raumf.* solar paddle; **~protuberanzen** *Pl.* solar prominences
sonnenreich *Adj.* (very) sunny; *es ist e-e* ~*e Gegend* it's an area where there is plenty of sunshine
Sonnen|rollo *n* sun blind; **~scheibe** *f* sun's disc (*Am.* disk)
Sonnenschein *m* *nur Sg.* sunshine; *bei strahlendem* ~ in brilliant sunshine; **~dauer** *f* hours *Pl.* of sunshine
Sonnenschirm *m* sunshade; *für Damen:* parasol
Sonnenschutz *m* protection (against sunburn); **~creme** *f* suntan cream; **~faktor** *m* (sunburn) protection factor; **~mittel** *n* sunscreen; *flüssig:* suntan lotion; (*Creme*) suntan cream
Sonnensegel *n* **1.** (*Plane*) awning; **2.** *Raumf.* solar sail

Sonnenseite f sunny side; **sonnenseitig I.** Adj. attr. on the sunny side; **II.** Adv.: ~ (gelegen) on the sunny side
sonnensicher Adj. with guaranteed sunshine
Sonnen|stand m position of the sun; **~stich** m sunstroke; **e-n ~ haben/bekommen** have/get sunstroke; **e-n ~ haben** umg. fig. have a touch of the sun; **~strahl** m ray of sunshine, sunbeam; **~strahlung** f solar radiation; **~studio** n solarium, tanning salon; **~system** n solar system; **~tag** m **1.** sunny day; **der Juni hatte 20 ~e** there were 20 days of sunshine in June; **2.** Astron. solar day; **mittlerer/wahrer ~** mean/true solar day; **~tau** m Bot. sundew; **~tempel** m temple of the sun; **~tierchen** n heliozoan
sonnenüberflutet Adj. attr. sun-drenched
Sonnen|uhr f sundial; **~untergang** m: **(bei) ~** (at) sunset (Am. auch sundown)
sonnenverbrannt Adj. Mensch: sunburnt; Erde etc.: scorched
Sonnen|wärme f warmth of the sun; **~warte** f solar observatory; **~wende** f solstice; **~wind** m Phys. solar wind; **~zeit** f Astron. solar time; **~zelle** f solar cell
sonnig Adj. sunny (auch fig. Lächeln etc.); fig. Aussichten etc.: bright, rosy; → **Gemüt** 1
Sonntag m Sunday; **(am) ~** on Sunday; **Weißer ~** Low Sunday; **Sonntagabend** etc. → **Dienstagabend** etc.; **sonntäglich I.** Adj. attr. Sunday ...; **nach dem ~en Kirchgang** after going to church on Sunday,; **II.** Adv.: **~ gekleidet** dressed in one's Sunday best; **sonntags** Adv. on Sunday(s)
Sonntags|anzug m one's Sunday best, one's best suit; **~arbeit** f Sunday work(ing); **~ausflug** m Sunday trip (im Auto: drive); **~ausflügler** m, **~ausflüglerin** f Sunday tripper; **~ausgabe** f Sunday edition; **~beilage** f Sunday supplement; **~blatt** n Sunday (news)paper; **~braten** m Sunday roast; **~dienst** m: **~ haben** have to work on Sunday(s); Apotheke: be open on Sunday(s); **~fahrer** m, **~fahrerin** f pej. Sunday driver; **~fahrverbot** n Sunday driving ban; **~gesicht** n: **von j-m nur das ~ kennen** only know s.o. from his (od. her) good side; **~gottesdienst** m Sunday service; **~kind** n: **er ist ein ~** he was born on a Sunday; (Glückskind) he was born under a lucky star; **~kleid** n one's Sunday best; **~kleidung** f Sunday (Am. auch Sunday-go-to-meeting umg.) clothes; **~messe** f Sunday mass; **~redner** m, **~rednerin** f grandiloquent speaker; **~ruhe** f Sunday peace; **die ~ einhalten/stören** respect/disturb s.o.'s Sunday peace and quiet; **~schule** f Sunday school; **~spaziergang** m Sunday walk; **~staat** m umg. one's glad rags Pl.; **~zeitung** f Sunday paper
Sonn- und Feiertage Pl. Sundays and public holidays; **sonn- und feiertags** Adv. on Sundays and public holidays
Sonnwend|feier f midsummer festival (od. celebrations Pl.); **~feuer** n midsummer festival bonfire
Sonnyboy ['zɔnibɔy] m, -s, -s; umg. blue-eyed boy
Sonographie f; -, -n; Med. sonography
sonor Adj. sonorous
sonst Adv. **1.** (andernfalls) auch drohend: otherwise, or else, or; **iss das**

auf, **~ setzt es was!** you'd better eat that up, or else!; **~ wüsste ich es** but for that I would know; **2.** (außerdem, im Übrigen) otherwise, apart from that (od. him etc.); (davon abgesehen) other than that; **~ ist er ganz nett** otherwise he's quite nice; **wer ~?** who else?; **wie ~?** how else?; **was denn ~?** iro. what do (od. did) you think?; **3. ~ jemand** (umg. wer) somebody (od. someone) else; in Fragen: anybody else; (irgendeiner) (just) anybody, anyone; **da könnte ja ~ jemand kommen** absolutely anyone could come along; **4. ~ was** something else; (irgendetwas) anything; (wünschen Sie) ~ noch (et)was? anything else?; **nimm e-n Stock oder ~ was** take a stick or something; **du kannst ~ was machen** you can do whatever you like; **er kann mir ~ was geben** I don't care what he gives me; **~ nichts** nothing else; **wenn es ~ nichts ist** if that's all (it is); **5. ~ wie** some other way; **mach es so oder ~ wie** do it whichever way you like; **6. ~ wo** somewhere else; **er könnte ~ wo sein** he could be anywhere; **wir könnten schon ~ wo sein!** we could be miles away by now; **~ nirgends** nowhere else; **~ wohin** somewhere else; **das kannst du dir ~ wohin stecken!** you can stuff it!; **7.** (für gewöhnlich) usually; (zu e-r anderen Zeit) some other time; (früher) previously; **~ kam immer ihr Bruder** her brother always used to come; **sag was - du weißt doch ~ immer alles** umg. iro. say something - you usually know it all; **wie ~** as usual; **~ einmal** some other day; **besser als ~** better than usual; **dieses ~ so ausgezeichnete Wörterbuch** this otherwise excellent dictionary
sonstig Adj. other; **~e Kenntnisse** Lebenslauf etc.: further skills; **das ~e Essen** the rest of the food; **alles Sonstige erfährst du dort** everything else you will be told there; **Sonstiges** als Überschrift: Miscellaneous; Tagesordnung etc.: Other (business od. expenses etc.)
sonst jemand → **sonst** 3
sonst was → **sonst** 4
sonst wer → **sonst** 3
sonst wie → **sonst** 5
sonst wo → **sonst** 6
sonst wohin → **sonst** 6
sooft Konj. whenever, every time; **Sie wollen** as often as you like; **~ ich es ihm auch sage, er hört einfach nicht** I can tell him as often as I like, he never listens
Soor m; -(e)s, -e, **~pilz** m Med. thrush
Sophismus m; -, Sophismen; Philos. sophism; **Sophist** m; -en, -en; Philos. sophist; pej. auch quibbler; **Sophisterei** f; -, -en; pej. sophistry; (Haarspalterei) quibbling, splitting (of) hairs; **Sophistin** f; -, -nen; Philos. sophist; pej. auch quibbler; **sophistisch** Adj. Philos., pej. sophistic; pej. (haarspalterisch) hairsplitting
Sopran m; -s, -e; Mus. **1.** nur Sg. (Stimmlage, Partie) soprano; (Knabensopran) treble; **den ~ singen** sing the soprano (od. treble) part; **2.** nur Sg. (Stimme im Chor) soprano section, sopranos Pl.; (Knabenstimmen) treble section, trebles Pl.; **3.** (Person, Stimme) soprano; (Knabensopran) treble; **lyrischer/dramatischer/schlanker ~** lyric/dramatic/light soprano; **~blockflöte** f descant (Am. soprano) record-

er
Sopranist m; -en, -en; Mus. treble, boy soprano; **~in** f; -, -nen; Mus. soprano
Sopran|saxophon n Mus. soprano saxophone; **~schlüssel** m Mus. treble clef; **~stimme** f **1.** soprano voice; **2.** (Partie) soprano part; für Knaben: treble part
Sorbe m; -n, -n, **Sorbin** f; -, -nen Sorb, Am. auch Wend, weiblich auch: Sorb (Am. auch Wend) woman (od. girl)
Sorbinsäure f Chem. sorbic acid
sorbisch Adj., **Sorbisch** n Ling. Sorbian, Am. auch Lusatian, Wendish
Sorbit m; -s, kein Pl.; Chem. sorbitol
Sorge f; -, -n **1.** (Besorgnis) worry, concern (um over, about); (Angst) fear(s Pl.) (for, about); **~n** worries, problems; **Kummer und ~n** worries and problems; **finanzielle ~n** financial worries, money problems; **j-m ~n machen** (beunruhigen) worry s.o.; (Probleme bereiten) cause s.o. trouble; **sich** (Dat.) **~n machen** be worried (um about); **ich hab mir schon ~n gemacht** I was beginning to get worried; **vor ~n graue Haare bekommen** go grey (Am. gray) with worry; **er ist frei von ~n** he hasn't got any problems; **'die ~ sind wir (wenigstens) los** that's one problem less; **ich komm aus den ~n nicht heraus** it's just one problem (od. thing) after another; **das ist m-e geringste ~** that's the least of my worries; **s-e ~n in Alkohol ertränken** drown one's sorrows; **keine ~!** umg. don't (you) worry; **d-e ~n möchte ich haben!** iro. if that's all you've got to worry about; **kleine Kinder - kleine ~n, große Kinder - große ~n** Sprichw. the bigger children get, the bigger the worries; **2.** (Mühe, Fürsorge, auch Jur.) care (für for); **~ tragen für** see to, take care of; **dafür ~ tragen, dass** see to it that, make sure (that); **lass das m-e ~ sein** leave that to me; → **auch sorgen** II
sorgen I. v/i.: **~ für** (pflegen, betreuen) look after, bes. Am. take care of; (etw. beschaffen) provide; (Sorge tragen für) take care of, see to; (sicherstellen) ensure; **für sich selbst ~** fend for o.s.; **dafür werde ich ~** I'll see to that, I'll make sure of that; **für ihn ist gesorgt** he's provided for (od. taken care of); **für Stimmung ist gesorgt** we've (od. they've etc.) made sure that everybody will have a good time (Brit. auch that things will go with a swing); **für Speis und Trank** od. **Speisen und Getränke ist gesorgt** we've (od. they've etc.) made sure that that there's plenty to eat and drink; **II.** v/refl. be worried, worry (um, wegen about); **sorg dich nicht!** don't worry!
...sorgen Pl., im Subst.: **Existenz~** worries about how to make a living, livelihood worries; **Kleider~** clothes problems
Sorgen|brecher m umg. problem solver, cure for all ills; **~falten** Pl. worry lines
sorgenfrei I. Adj. free from care (od. worry), carefree; **II.** Adv.: **~ leben** lead a carefree existence
Sorgenkind n problem child; fig. one's biggest worry, problem number one
sorgenlos Adj. und Adv. → **sorgenfrei**
Sorgentelefon n helpline
sorgenvoll I. Adj. full of worries; **~e Miene** worried look; **II.** Adv. anxiously, worriedly; **~ in die Zukunft blicken** view the future with (great) concern

S

Sorge|pflicht f parental responsibility; **~recht** n Jur. custody (*für* of); *j-m das ~ für j-n entziehen* withdraw custody of s.o. from s.o.

Sorgfalt f; -, *kein Pl.* care; (*Gewissenhaftigkeit*) *auch* scrupulousness, conscientiousness; (*Gründlichkeit*) thoroughness; *große ~ verwenden auf* (+ *Akk.*) take great pains over; *mehr ~ auf etw. verwenden* take more care over s.th.; *die nötige ~ walten lassen* take the necessary care; **sorgfältig I.** *Adj.* careful; (*gewissenhaft*) conscientious; (*gründlich*) thorough; **II.** *Adv.* carefully, with care; (*gewissenhaft*) conscientiously; (*gründlich*) thoroughly; **Sorgfältigkeit** f carefulness; (*Gewissenhaftigkeit*) conscientiousness; (*Gründlichkeit*) thoroughness; **Sorgfaltspflicht** f duty of care (*to a child*); *die ~ verletzen* neglect one's duty to provide for one's children

sorglich *Adj. altm.* → **sorgsam, sorgfältig**

sorglos I. *Adj.* **1.** (*sorgenfrei*) carefree, free from care (*od.* worry); (*unbekümmert*) nonchalant, *stärker*: happy-go--lucky; **~e Einstellung** carefree (*od.* nonchalant) attitude; **2.** (*unachtsam*) careless; (*gedankenlos*) thoughtless; **~er Umgang mit Wertgegenständen** careless treatment of valuables; **II.** *Adv.* **1.** free from care (*od.* worry); *~ in den Tag hineinleben* live for the day; **2.** (*unachtsam*) carelessly; *erschreckend ~ mit der Umwelt umgehen* be terribly thoughtless about the environment; *er geht mit s-n Sachen sehr ~ um* he doesn't care how he treats his things; **Sorglosigkeit** f **1.** freedom from care; (*Haltung*) carefree attitude, nonchalance; **2.** (*Unachtsamkeit*) carelessness

sorgsam I. *Adj.* careful; (*fürsorglich*) solicitous; **II.** *Adv. auch* with great care; **Sorgsamkeit** f carefulness

Sorte f; -, -n **1.** (*Art*) sort, kind; *Obst: auch* variety; *Speiseeis etc.*: flavo(u)r; (*Marke*) brand; *Wirts.* (*Qualität*) quality, grade; *beste od. erste ~* finest (*od.* prime) quality, top grade; *e-e ganz teure/billige ~ Zigarren* a very expensive/cheap type of cigar; *milde ~* (*Kaffee*) mild blend; *das ist e-e komische ~* (*Mensch*) *umg.* they're a strange bunch (*od.* lot); **2.** *Fin.*: **~n** (*Devisen*) foreign currency (*od.* exchange) *Sg.*

...sorte f, *im Subst.* (*Art*): *Apfel~* variety of apple; *Getreide~* (type of) grain; *Käse~* (type of) cheese

Sorten|geschäft n, **~handel** m *Fin.* foreign currency dealing; **~kurs** m exchange rate (*for notes and coins*); **~produktion** f *Wirts.* continuous batch production

sorten|rein I. *Adj.* unmixed; *Wein:* single varietal, unblended; *Abfallstoffe etc.*: of one type; **II.** *Adv. keltern:* using only (grapes of) one variety; *Abfälle trennen:* according to type; **~typisch** *Adj.* characteristic; *Wein:* typical of this varietal

Sortier|anlage f sorting system; **~band** n conveyor belt

sortieren v/t. sort (**nach** according to); (*ordnen*) arrange; *nach Qualität:* grade; *alphabetisch ~* put into alphabetical order, alphabetize; *Sortieren nach Nummern / von Daten EDV* numerical/data sorting; *ich muss erst m-e Gedanken ~ umg.* I've got to straighten things out in my mind first; **Sortierer** m; -s, -; *auch Tech.* sorter;

Sortiererin f; -, -nen sorter

Sortier|folge f *EDV* sort sequence; **~maschine** f sorter, sorting machine; **~programm** n sort program

sortiert I. *P.P.* → **sortieren**; **II.** *Adj.* **1.** *Lager, Geschäft: gut ~* well-stocked (*in* + *Dat.* with); **2.** (*ausgewählt*) select, fine; **3.** (*gemischt*): *Schrauben, ~* (selection of) assorted screws; **Sortierung** f **1.** (*Vorgang*) sorting; (*Auswahl*) selection, assortment; *feinste ~* selection of finest quality goods; **2.** *EDV* sort

Sortiment n; -(e)s, -e **1.** *Wirts.* range (*an* + *Dat.* of); *ein breites/reichhaltiges ~ anbieten* offer a wide (*od.* extensive) range; **2.** (*Buchhandel*) retail book trade (*Am.* business)

Sortimenter m; -s, -, **Sortimentsbuchhändler** m retail bookseller

SOS n; -, *kein Pl.* SOS; (*ein*) *~ funken* send an SOS

sosehr *Konj.*: *~* (*auch*) however much, no matter how much; *~ er sich bemüht* however hard he tries, he can try as hard as he likes

Sosein n *Philos.* essence

SOS-Kinderdorf n SOS Children's Village (*for* [*mainly refugee*] *orphans, structured around family units*)

soso *umg.* **I.** *Adv.* (*mittelprächtig*) so--so; **II.** *Interj. überrascht, amüsiert, iro.* well, well!; *gleichgültig:* I see; *vorwurfsvoll:* I see

SOS-Ruf m SOS (call *od.* message)

Soße f; -, -n **1.** *Gastr.* sauce; (*Bratensaft, -soße*) gravy; (*Salatsoße*) dressing; **2.** *umg.* (*Brühe*) goo

soßen v/t. (*Tabak*) treat with a sauce

Soßen|löffel m sauce (*od.* gravy) spoon; **~pulver** n sauce mix; *für Bratensaft:* gravy powder (*od.* mix); **~schüssel** f sauceboat; *für Bratensaft:* gravy boat

SOS-Signal n SOS signal

sott *Imperf.* → **sieden**

Sottise [zɔ'tiːzə] f; -, -n; *pej.* silly thing; (*Bemerkung*) *auch* silly remark

Soufflé [zu'fleː] n; -s, -s; *Gastr.* soufflé

Souffleur [zu'fløːɐ̯] m; -s, -e prompter; **Souffleurkasten** m prompt box; **Souffleuse** [zu'fløːzə] f; -, -n prompter

soufflieren [zu'fliːrən] **I.** v/t.: *j-m etw. ~* prompt s.o. with s.th.; *fig.* whisper s.th. to s.o., tell s.o. s.th. under one's breath; **II.** v/i. *Theat.* prompt; be (*od.* work as) a prompter

Sound m; -s, -s *Jazz etc.*: sound

Soundkarte f *Computer:* sound card

soundso *umg.* **I.** *Adv.: ~ viel* so and so much; *~ viele* so and so many; *~ oft* every so often; (*sehr oft*) time and again; **II.** *Adj.: nach Paragraph ~* according to paragraph such and such; *Herr Soundso* Mr (*od.* Mr.) So-and-so

soundsovielte *Adj. umg.* **1.** *am ~n März* on March the such and such; **2.** (*x-te*) umpteenth; *zum ~n Mal* for the umpteenth time

Soundtrack ['zaʊnttrɛk] m; -s, -s sound track

Souper [zu'peː] n; -s, -s; *geh.* (formal) dinner; **soupieren** [zu'piːrən] v/i. *geh.* dine, have dinner

Soutane [zu'taːnə] f; -, -n; *kirchl.* cassock

Souterrain [zutɛ'rɛ̃ː] n; -s, -s basement; **~wohnung** f basement flat, *Am.* basement (*od.* garden) apartment

Souvenir [zuvə'niːɐ̯] n; -s, -s souvenir; *umg. fig. auch* reminder; **~laden** m souvenir shop; **~stand** m souvenir stall

souverän [zuvə'rɛːn] **I.** *Adj.* **1.** (*überlegen*) supreme; *Sieg:* commanding, overwhelming; (*die Lage beherrschend*) in complete control (of the situation); (*nicht aus der Ruhe zu bringen*) unflappable; *~e Beherrschung e-s Gebiets:* commanding knowledge; *~es Lächeln* superior smile; *~! umg.* that was classy; **2.** *Pol.* sovereign; *~ werden* achieve sovereignty; **II.** *Adv.* with the greatest of ease; (*gelassen*) unperturbed; (*großartig*) in superior style; *~ gewinnen* win commandingly (*od.* convincingly); *ein Gebiet / die Lage ~ beherrschen* have a commanding knowledge of a subject / complete control of the situation

Souverän m; -s, -e sovereign; **Souveränität** f; -, *kein Pl.* **1.** *Pol.* sovereignty; **2.** (*Überlegenheit*) supremacy; *e-s Sieges etc.*: commanding nature; (*Sicherheit*) authority, self-confidence; **Souveränitätserklärung** f declaration of sovereignty

soviel *Konj.*: *~ ich weiß* as far as I know; *~ ich gehört habe* from what I've heard

so viel → **so** I 8

soweit *Konj.* as far as; *~ das Auge reicht* as far as the eye can see; *~ er beteiligt ist* insofar (*od.* in so far) as he's involved

so weit → **so** I 9

sowenig *Konj.*: *~ auch* however little, little as

so wenig → **so** I 5

sowie *Konj.* **1.** (*neben*) as well as, and, plus; *sie schreibt Zeitungs- und Zeitschriftenartikel ~ Reiseführer* she writes newspaper and magazine articles as well as travel guides; **2.** (*sobald*): *~ sie eintrifft etc.* as soon as (*od.* the moment *od.* the minute) she gets here *etc.*; *vergangenheitsbezogen: auch* just as she arrived

sowieso *Adv. umg.* anyway, anyhow, in any case; *ich hätte es ~ getan / nicht getan* I would/wouldn't have done it anyway; (*das*) *~!* that goes without saying, absolutely; *Herr Sowieso* Mr (*od.* Mr.) So-and-so

Sowjet m; -s, -s; *hist.* Soviet; *Oberster ~* Supreme Soviet; **~bürger** m, **~bürgerin** f Soviet citizen

sowjetisch *Adj.* Soviet

Sowjet|regierung f *hist.* Soviet government; **~republik** f *hist.* Soviet Republic; *Union der Sozialistischen ~en hist.* Union of Soviet Socialist Republics; **°russisch** *Adj.* Soviet(-Russian); **~union** f *hist.* Soviet Union; **~zeit** f Soviet period; *in/aus der ~* in/from the Soviet period; *zu ~en* in Soviet days

sowohl *Konj.*: *~ ... als auch* both ... and; ... as well as ...

Sozi m; -s, -s; *pej.* Socialist

Sozia f; -, -s **1.** *Wirts.* (female) partner; **2.** *oft hum.* (*Beifahrerin*) (female) pillion passenger

sozial I. *Adj.* social; (*sozial eingestellt*) socially minded; *der Mensch ist ein ~es Wesen* man is a social animal; *~e Ausgaben* social (*Am.* welfare) spending; *~e Einrichtungen* public services; *~e Sicherheit* social security; *~e Gegensätze* class differences; *die ~e Frage* the social question; *~er Wandel* social change; *~e Stellung* social rank, (social) status; *~er Wohnungsbau* low--rent housing (*for the socially disadvantaged*), *Brit. etwa* council housing, *Am. etwa* public housing; *~e Indikati-*

on social factor (*in abortions etc.*); **freiwilliges ~es Jahr** year of voluntary social service; **e-n ~en Beruf haben** be in a caring profession; → **Marktwirtschaft, Netz** 1; **II.** *Adv.*: **~ denken** be socially minded; **~ schwach** socially underprivileged; **~ benachteiligt/begünstigt** socially disadvantaged/advantaged

Sozial|abbau *m* cuts *Pl.* in social services; **~abgaben** *Pl.* social security contributions; **~amt** *n* social security office; **~arbeit** *f* social work; **~arbeiter** *m*, **~arbeiterin** *f* social worker; **~ausgaben** *Pl.* social expenditure *Sg.*; **~ausschuss** *m* (*e-s Parlaments etc.*) social services committee; **~bau** *m* home for the socially deprived; **~behörde** *f* social security office; **~beitrag** *m* social security contribution; **~bereich** *m* social (*Am.* benefit) sector; **~beruf** *m* social services profession; **in e-m ~ arbeiten** do social work; **~bindung** *f* social obligation; **~darwinismus** *m* social Darwinism

Sozial|demokrat *m* *Pol.* social democrat; **~demokratie** *f* social democracy; **~demokratin** *f* social democrat; **2demokratisch** *Adj.* social democratic

Sozial|dezernat *n* social services department; **~dezernent** *m*, **~dezernentin** *f* member of the social services department

Sozial|dienst *m* social service; **~dumping** [-dampɪŋ] *n pej.* wage cost-cutting (*e.g. by employing foreign workers as subcontractors*); **~einrichtung** *f* social service; **~enzyklika** *f kirchl.* social encyclical; **~etat** *m Pol.* social services budget; **~ethik** *f* social ethics *Sg.*; **~experte** *m*, **~expertin** *f* social affairs expert; **~fall** *m* welfare case; **~forscher** *m*, **~forscherin** *f* social researcher; **~forschung** *f* social research; **~fürsorge** *f* 1. *hist.* in der DDR (*Sozialarbeit*) social work; 2. *altm.* (*Sozialhilfe*) social security benefit; **~gericht** *n* social security tribunal; **~gerichtsbarkeit** *f* jurisdiction in social security matters

Sozialgeschichte *f hist.* social history; **sozialgeschichtlich** *Adj.* social history ...; *Abhandlung usw.*: ... on social history

Sozialgesetz *n* social security law; **~buch** *n* social security statute book

Sozialhaushalt *m* social security budget

Sozialhilfe *f* social security benefit; (*Geldleistungen*) *auch Brit.* income support, *Am.* welfare (payments) *Pl.*; **~bezieher** *m*, **~bezieherin** *f* recipient of benefits (*od.* income support, *Am.* welfare, public assistance); **~empfänger** *m*, **~empfängerin** *f*: **~ sein** be on social security (*od.* income support, *Am.* welfare *od.* public assistance); **~gesetz** *n* law governing social security benefits; **~kosten** *Pl.* social security benefit costs; **~leistung** *f* (social security) benefit payment; **~satz** *m* 1. rate of (social security) benefit; 2. (*Einkommengrenze*) income level qualifying for income support (*Am.* welfare *od.* public assistance)

Sozialhygiene *f* public hygiene

Sozialisation *f*; -, *kein Pl.*; *Psych.* socialization; **sozialisieren** *v/t.* 1. *Wirts.* nationalize; 2. *Psych.* socialize; **Sozialisierung** *f* 1. *Wirts.* nationalization; 2. *Psych.* socialization

Sozialismus *m*; -, *kein Pl.*; *Pol.* socialism; **demokratischer ~** democratic so-

cialism; → **real; Sozialist** *m*; -en, -en, **Sozialistin** *f*; -, -nen socialist; **sozialistisch** *Adj.* socialist; **die Sozialistische Internationale** the Socialist International; **~er Realismus** socialist realism

Sozial|kasse *f* social security benefits office; **~klausel** *f* protective clause for the socially disadvantaged; **~kosten** *Pl.* social expenditure *Sg.*

Sozialkritik *f* social criticism; **sozialkritisch** *Adj.* sociocritical

Sozialkunde *f* social studies *Pl.*; **~lehrer** *m*, **~lehrerin** *f* social studies teacher

Sozial|lasten *Pl.* social expenditure *Sg.*; **~lehre** *f kirchl.* code of social ethics; **~leistungen** *Pl.* social benefits; *zusätzliche, vom Arbeitgeber.* fringe benefits; **~lohn** *m* social wage; **~medizin** *f* social medicine; **~miete** *f* low rent for the socially disadvantaged; **~mieter** *m*, **~mieterin** *f* socially disadvantaged tenant (*paying a low rent*), *Am. etwa* public housing tenant; **~minister** *m*, **~ministerin** *f* Minister of Social Security, *Am. etwa* Health and Human Services Secretary; **~ministerium** *n* Ministry of Social Security, *Am. etwa* Health and Human Services Department; **~neid** *m* class envy; **~ökologie** *f* social ecology; **~ökonomie** *f* social economics *Pl.* (*V. im Sg.*); **~ordnung** *f* social order

Sozialpädagoge *m* social education worker; **Sozialpädagogik** *f* social education; **Sozialpädagogin** *f* social education worker; **sozialpädagogisch** *Adj.* social education ..., ... relating to social education

Sozial|pakt *m* agreement on social measures (*between government, unions and employers*); **~partner** *Pl.* employers and employees, *the* two sides of industry; **~partnerschaft** *f* social partnership; **~plan** *m* social plan (*for alleviating hardship in a redundancy* [*Am. layoff*] *situation*)

Sozialpolitik *f* social policy (*od.* policies *Pl.*); **Sozialpolitiker** *m*, **Sozialpolitikerin** *f* social policy expert; **sozialpolitisch** *Adj.* sociopolitical, social

Sozial|prestige *n* social prestige (*od.* standing); **~produkt** *n* gross national product; **~psychiatrie** *f* social psychiatry; **~psychologe** *m* social psychologist; **~recht** *n* social legislation; **~referat** *n* social work department; **~reform** *f* social reform; **~rente** *f* social security pension; **~rentner** *m*, **~rentnerin** *f* pensioner with a social security pension; **~ressort** *n* social work department; **~revolutionär** *m*, **~revolutionärin** *f* social revolutionary

Sozialstaat *m* welfare state; **sozialstaatlich** *Adj.* relating to the welfare state

Sozial|station *f* public health and advice cent|re (*Am.* -er); **~struktur** *f* social structure; **~system** *n* social system; **~therapie** *f* social therapy; **~union** *f* unified social welfare system; **~verhalten** *n Päd., Psych.* social behavio(u)r

Sozialversicherung *f* social insurance, *Brit.* National Insurance, *Am.* Social Security

Sozialversicherungs|ausweis *m* social insurance (*Brit.* National Insurance, *Am.* Social Security) card; **~beitrag** *m* social insurance (*Brit.* National Insurance, *Am.* Social Security) contribution

sozialversicherungspflichtig *Adj.* liable for social insurance (*Brit.* National Insurance, *Am.* Social Security)

Sozialversicherungs|system *n* social insurance (*Brit.* National Insurance, *Am.* Social Security) system; **~träger** *m*, **~trägerin** *f* social insurance (*Brit.* National Insurance, *Am.* Social Security) provider

sozialverträglich *Adj.* socially acceptable; **Sozialverträglichkeit** *f* socially acceptable nature

Sozialwesen *n* social services *Pl.*

Sozialwirt *m*, **~in** *f* social economist; **Sozialwirtschaft** *f* social economics *Pl.* (*V. im Sg.*); **sozialwirtschaftlich** *Adj.* socioeconomic

Sozialwissenschaften *Pl.* social sciences; **Sozialwissenschaftler** *m*, **Sozialwissenschaftlerin** *f* social scientist

Sozial|wohnung *f* low-rent apartment (*for the socially disadvantaged*), *Brit. etwa* council flat, *Am. etwa* public housing apartment; **~zentrum** *n* social cent|re (*Am.* -er); **~zulage** *f* supplementary benefit (*zum Lohn:* allowance)

Sozietät *f*; -, -en 1. *Wirts.* joint practice; 2. *Soziol.* (branch of) society, social group

Soziogramm *n*; -s, -e sociogram

Soziokultur *f* socioculture; **soziokulturell** *Adj.* sociocultural

Soziolekt *m*; -(e)s, -e; *Ling.* sociolect

Soziolinguistik *f Ling.* sociolinguistics *Pl.* (*V. im Sg.*); **soziolinguistisch** *Adj.* sociolinguistic

Soziologe *m*; -n, -n sociologist; **Soziologie** *f*; -, *kein Pl.* sociology; **Soziologin** *f*; -, -nen sociologist; **soziologisch** *Adj.* sociological

sozioökonomisch *Adj.* socioeconomic

Sozius *m*; -, -se *od.* Sozii *od. bes. Anwälte etc.* Sozien 1. *Pl. mst* Sozii, *bes. Anwälte etc.* Sozien; *Wirts.* partner; 2. (*Beifahrersitz*) pillion (seat); 3. (*Beifahrer*) pillion rider; 4. *Pl.* -se; *umg.* (*Kumpel*) buddy, *bes. Brit.* mate; **~fahrer** *m*, **~fahrerin** *f* pillion rider; **~sitz** *m* pillion seat; **auf dem ~ mitfahren** ride (on the) pillion

sozusagen *Adv.* as it were, so to speak; **er ist ~** ... *auch* you might say he's ... (*od.* call him ...)

Spachtel *m*; -s, -, *südd. auch f*; -, -n 1. spatula; *für Kitt, Masse etc.*: putty knife; *für Mörtel*: trowel; *zum Abkratzen*: scraper; *des Kunstmalers*: palette knife; 2. (*Masse*) filler; **~kitt** *m* mastic; (*Masse*) filler; **~masse** *f* filler

spachteln I. *v/t. Tech.* (*glätten*) level out; (*Fugen, Lackschäden*) fill; (*auftragen*) apply with a spatula (*od.* putty knife); **die Farben ~** apply the paint with a palette knife; **II.** *v/i. umg.* (*tüchtig essen*) tuck in

Spagat¹ *m*, *n*; -(e)s, -e 1. *Turnen etc.*: the splits *Pl.*; **~ machen** do the splits; **in den ~ gehen/springen** go/jump into the splits position; 2. *fig.*: **der ~ zwischen ... und ...** the balancing act between ... and ...

Spagat² *m*; -(e)s, -e; *südd.* (*Schnur*) string

Spaghetti¹ [ʃpaˈgɛti] *Pl. Gastr.* spaghetti *Sg.*; **schwarze ~** sepia spaghetti

Spaghetti² *m*; -(s), -s; *pej. Sl.* (*Italiener*) wop *neg!*, *Brit. auch* Eyetie *neg!*, *Am. auch* Dago *neg!*

Spaghetti|-Eis *n* spaghetti ice cream; **~fresser** *m*; -s, -; *neg!* wop *neg!*, *Brit. auch* Eyetie *neg!*, *Am. auch* Dago *neg!*; **~gericht** *n* spaghetti dish; **~soße** *f* spaghetti sauce; **~topf** *m* spaghetti pan; **~träger** *m am Kleid etc.*: spaghetti strap; **~zange** *f* spaghetti tongs *Pl.*

spähen *v/i.* peer; *bes. durch Loch etc.*: peep; *Mil.* reconnoit|re (*Am.* -er), make a reconnaissance; **~ nach** look out for, keep an eye out for *umg.*; **Späher** *m*; *-s, -*, **Späherin** *f*; *-, -nen* scout (*auch Sport*); *bes. Mil.* (*Ausguckposten*) lookout; *fig.* spy

Spähtrupp *m Mil.* reconnaissance (*od.* scouting) party *od.* patrol

Spalier [ʃpaˈliːɐ] *n*; *-s, -e* **1.** *Agr.* trellis; *für Obst*: espalier *fachspr.*; **2.** *fig.* (*Reihe*) double line, rows *Pl.*; (*Ehrenspalier*) guard of hono(u)r, hono(u)r guard; **~ stehen** *od.* **ein ~ bilden** *Mil.* form an hono(u)r guard; *Zuschauer*: line the route; **~obst** *n Agr.* wall (*fachspr.* espalier) fruit

Spalt *m*; *-(e)s, -e* crack; (*Lücke*) gap; (*Schlitz*) slit; **die Tür e-n ~ offen lassen** leave the door slightly ajar (*od.* open a crack); → *auch* **Spalte** 1, 2

spaltbar *Adj. Phys.* fissile, fissionable

spaltbreit *Adj.* narrow; **Spaltbreit** *m*; *-, kein Pl.*: **e-n ~ öffnen** open a crack (*od.* slightly)

Spalte *f*; *-, -n* **1.** → **Spalt**; **2.** *Geol.* fissure, cleft; *große*: crevice; (*Gletscherspalte*) crevasse; **3.** *Druck., der Zeitung etc.*: column; **nach ~n bezahlt werden** be paid by the column; **4.** *vulg.* (*Vagina*) hole

spalten; *hat gespalten od. gespaltet* **I.** *v/t.* split (*auch Atom*); (*Holz*) mit *Beil*: chop; *Chem.* (*zersetzen*) decompose; *fig.* split (up), divide; **in zwei Teile ~** split in two; **diese Frage hat die Nation gespalten** this issue has divided the nation; → *auch* **Haar** 3; **II.** *v/refl.* split; *fig.* split (up), *passiv*: *auch* be divided (up) (**in** + *Akk.* into); → **gespalten**

Spalten|abstand *m Druck.* space between columns; **~breite** *f* column width

spaltenweise *Adv. Druck. setzen etc.*: in columns; *bezahlen etc.*: by the column

Spaltfuß *m Med.* cleft foot

...spaltig *im Adj.*: **drei~** three-column ..., of three columns

Spalt|leder *n* skiver; **~material** *n Phys.* fissile material; **~öffnung** *f Bot.* stoma; *Pl.* stomata; **~pilz** *m* **1.** *Biol., Med.* bacterium; **2.** *fig.* (spirit of) discord; **~produkt** *n Phys.* fission product

Spaltung *f* splitting; *Chem.* separation; *e-r Verbindung*: decomposition; *des Atoms*: splitting, fission; *fig.* split (*auch e-r Partei*); *der Meinungen, e-s Landes*: division; *bes. kirchl.* schism; **~ des Bewusstseins** *Psych.* dissociation of consciousness

Spamming [ˈspɛmɪŋ] *n*; *-s, kein Pl. Internet*: spamming (*Versenden unwichtiger od. belangloser Nachrichten, von Werbung etc. an Foren, Newsgroups od. als E-Mail*)

Span *m*; *-(e)s, Späne, mst Pl.*: **Späne** shavings; (*Metallspäne*) filings; **wo gehobelt wird, fallen Späne** *Sprichw.* you can't make an omelette without breaking eggs; **spanabhebend** *Adj.*: **~e Werkzeuge** cutting tools; **~e Bearbeitung** metal cutting; **spanen** *v/t.* cut, machine; **~de Bearbeitung** machining; **~de Werkzeuge** cutting tools; **spänen** *v/t.* (*Parkett etc.*) rub down with steel wool

Spanferkel *n Zool.* suckling pig

Spange *f*; *-, -n* clasp; (*Schnalle*) buckle; (*Haarspange*) hair slide, *Am.* barrette; (*Armspange*) bangle, bracelet; (*Zahnspange*) brace; (*Schuhriemen*) strap; **Spangenschuh** *m* strap shoe

Spanien (*n*); *-s; Geog.* Spain; **Spanier** *m*; *-s, -*, **Spanierin** *f*; *-, -nen* Spaniard, *weiblich auch*: Spanish woman (*od.* girl)

spanisch *Adj.* Spanish; **~e Wand** folding screen; **~er Reiter** *Mil.* barbed wire barrier; **das kommt mir ~ vor** *umg. fig.* that strikes me as odd (*verdächtig*: fishy); **Spanisch** *n*; *-en*; *Ling.* Spanish; **das ~e** Spanish

spanlos *Adj.*: **~e Bearbeitung** *od.* **Formung** (non-cutting) metalworking, metal forming

spann *Imperf.* → **spinnen**

Spann *m*; *-(e)s, -e*; *Anat.* instep

Spann|beton *m* pre-stressed concrete; **~betttuch** *n* fitted (*Am. auch* contour) sheet; **~breite** *f* → **Spannweite**

Spanne *f*; *-, -n* **1.** *zeitlich*: **e-e kurze ~** a short space of time; **e-e ~ von fünf Tagen** a five-day period; **2.** (*Gewinn*) margin, *Am. auch* spread; **3.** (*Längenmaß*) span

spannen I. *v/t.* **1.** stretch; (*straff ~*) tighten; (*Muskeln*) flex, tense; (*Bogen*) draw; *Tech.* (*Werkstück*) clamp; (*Feder*) tighten, tension; (*Gewehr, Kamera*) cock; *fig.* (*Nerven*) strain; **Leinwand auf e-n Rahmen ~** stretch a canvas over a frame; **e-n Bogen Papier in die Schreibmaschine ~** put a sheet of paper in(to) the typewriter; **neue Saiten auf e-e Gitarre ~** restring a guitar; **e-n Tennisschläger ~** put a tennis racket in a press; **s-e Erwartungen zu hoch ~** *fig.* pitch one's expectations too high; **2.** (*befestigen*) (*Wäscheleine*) put up; **vor den Wagen ~** (*Pferde*) harness to the carriage; **3.** *fachspr.*: **die Tragflächen des Flugzeugs ~ 18 Meter** the aircraft has a wingspan of 18 met|res (*Am.* -ers); **4.** *umg.* (*merken*) get wise to; → **Folter** 2, **gespannt**; **II.** *v/refl.* stretch (**über** + *Akk.* across, over); *Muskel*: flex; *Haut*: be taut (*od.* tight); **sich über e-n Fluss ~** span a river; **III.** *v/i.* **1.** *Rock, Schuhe*: be (too) tight; *Haut*: be taut (*od.* tight); **2. ~ auf** (+ *Akk.*) *fig.* (*erwarten*) be anxiously waiting for; (*beobachten*) follow closely, have one's eyes fixed on

spannend I. *Part. Präs.* → **spannen**; **II.** *Adj.* exciting; *Buch, Film etc.*: *auch* full of suspense; (*fesselnd*) gripping; *umg.* (*interessant*) fascinating; **der Wahlkampf war bis zum Schluss ~** the election was a cliffhanger (right to the end); **mach's nicht so ~!** *umg.* don't keep us on tenterhooks (*od.* in suspense), (come on,) get on with it; **III.** *Adv.*: **er schreibt ~** he writes in a gripping style; (*Sachbücher*) *auch* he knows how to hold your interest; **das Buch ist ~ geschrieben** it's a gripping (*od.* an exciting) book; **der Film ist unheimlich ~ gemacht** *umg.* the film is packed full of suspense

Spanner¹ *m*; *-s, -*; (*Schuhspanner*) shoe tree; *für Hosen, Tennisschläger etc.*: press

Spanner² *m umg. pej.* (*Voyeur*) peeping Tom; **hau ab, du ~!** beat it, you nosy bastard!

...spänner *m*; *-s, -, im Subst.*: **Zwei~** carriage and pair; **Sechs~** six-in-hand

Spanngardine *f* net curtain

...spännig *im Adj. Kutsche etc.*: **zwei~** drawn by two horses; **sechs~** drawn by six horses

Spann|kraft *f*; *nur Sg.* elasticity; *Phys.* tension; *fig.* energy, vigo(u)r; **~laken** *n* fitted (*Am. auch* contour) sheet; **~rahmen** *m Tech.* tenter (frame); **~säge** *f* frame saw

Spannung *f* **1.** *Tech., mechanische*: tension; *elastische*: stress; *verformende*: strain; (*Druck, Gasspannung*) pressure; *Archit., im Material*: stress; **2.** *Etech.* voltage; **unter ~** live; **Jens steht ständig unter ~** *fig.* (*ist sehr aktiv*) Jens is a real live wire; (*ist sehr angespannt*) Jens is always very tense (*im Stress*: under constant strain); **3.** *fig.* excitement, tension; *nervliche*: tension, tenseness; *durch Ungewissheit*: suspense; (*Erwartung*) eager expectation; **mit od. voll ~ erwarten etc.**: with bated breath; **voller ~** → **spannend**; **es kam keine ~ auf** there was no tension (*od.* excitement); **die ~ stieg ins Unerträgliche** the tension (*od.* suspense) became unbearable; **die ~ ließ nach** the tension was relieved; **4.** *mst Pl.* (*Zwistigkeit, Unstimmigkeit*) tension *Sg.*; **es herrschen ~en in ihrer Ehe** their marriage is under some strain at the moment; **ein Abbau der ~en** a reduction of tension

Spannungs|abfall *m Etech.* voltage drop; **~bogen** *m* build-up of tension; **~fall** *m Pol.*: **im ~** where there is tension; **~feld** *n* **1.** *fig.* field of tension (*od.* conflict), flash point; **2.** *Etech.* electric field; **~gebiet** *n* → **Spannungsherd**

spannungsgeladen *Adj. Atmosphäre etc.*: ... charged with tension, (extremely) tense; *Roman, Film etc.*: full of suspense (*od.* excitement), (very) exciting, gripping

Spannungs|herd *m Pol.* area of tension (*od.* conflict), trouble spot, hot spot *umg.*; **~kopfschmerzen** *Pl.*: **~ haben** have a tension headache *Sg.*

spannungslos *Adj. Verhältnis etc.*: free from tension

Spannungs|moment *n* suspense factor; **~prüfer** *m Etech.* continuity tester; **~regler** *m Etech.* voltage regulator

spannungsreich *Adj.* **1.** *Roman, Film etc.*: full of suspense (*od.* excitement), (very) exciting, gripping; **2.** *Beziehung*: tense, strained

Spannungs|verhältnis *n* tense (*od.* strained) relationship (*Pol. auch* relations *Pl.*); **~wähler** *m Etech.* voltage selector; **~zustand** *m* state of tension

Spann|vorrichtung *f Tech.* tensioner; **~weite** *f* (*Flügelspannweite*) (wing)span; *Archit.* span; *fig.* scope, range

Spanplatte *f* chipboard

Spant *n*; *-(e)s, -en, mst Pl.* **1.** *Naut.* frame, rib; **2.** *auch m*; *Flug.* frame, former

Spar|aktion *f* economy drive; **~appell** *m* appeal to make savings; **~auflage** *f* requirement to make savings, mandatory spending reduction; **~auto** *n* economy car; **~brief** *m* savings certificate, *Am.* savings bond; **~buch** *n* passbook, *Brit. auch* savings book; **~büchse** *f* money box; **~budget** *n* austerity budget; **~dose** *f* money box; **~eckzins** *m Wirts.* basic savings rate; **~einlagen** *Pl.* savings deposits

sparen I. *v/t.* (*Geld, Kosten, Kräfte, Mühe, Platz, Zeit*) save; **ich habe eini-**

ges gespart I've managed to save (up) a bit; (**viel Geld**) **an Heizkosten ~** save (a lot) on heating bills; **das spart uns e-e Menge Zeit und Geld** this will save us a whole lot of time and money; **das hättest du dir ~ können** you could have saved (*od.* spared) yourself the trouble (*od.* effort); *iro.* you needn't have bothered; **spar dir d-e Worte!** save your breath; **spar dir d-e Ratschläge!** I can do without your advice, you can keep your advice; **~ Sie sich solche Bemerkungen** (you should) keep such remarks to yourself; **II.** *v/i.* save; (*sich einschränken*) cut down (on expenses), economize; **für** *od.* **auf etw. ~** save up for s.th.; **am falschen Ende ~** make false economies; **~ an** (+ *Dat.*) *od.* **mit** save on; (*wenig verwenden*) be sparing with; *knauserig*: stint on, be stingy with; **nicht ~ mit** be lavish (*od.* generous) with; **man hatte an nichts gespart** no expense had been spared

Sparen *n*; *-s*, kein *Pl. auf Sparkonto etc.*: saving; *bei Ausgaben*: economizing; **Sparer** *m*; *-s*, -, **Sparerin** *f*; -, *-nen* saver

Sparflamme *f*; *nur Sg.* low flame; (*Zündflamme*) pilot light; **auf ~ kochen** *umg. fig.* make economies, cut down (on spending)

Sparförderungsmaßnahmen *Pl.* savings incentive scheme *Sg.*

Spargang *m Mot.* overdrive; **e-n ~ einlegen** *fig.* cut down on expenses

Spargel *m*; *-s*, -, *schw.*, *südd. auch -n*; *Bot.* asparagus; **Schwetzinger ~** white asparagus from Schwetzingen; **~ stechen/schälen** cut/peel asparagus; **e-e Portion ~** a serving of asparagus; **~cremesuppe** *f Gastr.* cream of asparagus (soup)

Spargeld *n mst Pl.* savings

Spargel|essen *n Gastr.*, *Mahlzeit*: meal of asparagus; **~gegend** *f* asparagus-growing area; **~gemüse** *n Gastr.* asparagus; **~gericht** *n Gastr.* asparagus dish; **~messer** *n* asparagus knife; **~saison** *f* asparagus season; **~salat** *m Gastr.* asparagus salad; **~spitzen** *Pl.* asparagus tips; **~stange** *f* asparagus stalk; **~stecher** *m*, **~stecherin** *f* asparagus harvester; **~suppe** *f Gastr.* asparagus soup; **~zeit** *f* asparagus season

Spar|groschen *m* nest egg; **~guthaben** *n* savings account (balance); **~haushalt** *m Pol.* austerity budget; **~kasse** *f Wirts.* savings bank

Sparkassen|buch *n* → *Sparbuch*; **~direktor** *m*, **~direktorin** *f* savings bank manager; **~filiale** *f* savings bank branch; **~verband** *m* association of savings banks

Spar|kommissar *m*, **~kommissarin** *f* (budget) controller (*Am. auch* comptroller); **~konto** *n* savings account; **~konzept** *n* savings plan; **~kurs** *m* economy drive

spärlich I. *Adj.* (*wenig*) scanty, meag|re (*Am. -er*); *Lob, Kenntnisse*: scant, scanty; (*dünn gesät*) sparse; (*dürftig, schlecht*) poor; *Wirts. Nachfrage*: low, slack; *Haarwuchs*: thin; *Kleidung*: scanty, skimpy; **~er Beifall** a trickle of applause; **~e Reste** (a few) scraps; **die Reaktionen waren ~** there was little response; **II.** *Adv.*: **~ bekleidet** scantily (*od.* skimpily) dressed, scantily clad; **~ beleuchtet** poorly (*od.* badly) lit; **~ besucht** poorly attended; **~ bevölkert** sparsely (*od.* thinly) populated; **Spärlichkeit** *f* scantiness; *der Kleidung*:

auch skimpiness; *des Wuchses*: sparseness, *der Haare*: *auch* thinness; *der Nachfrage*: slackness

Spar|liste *f* list of economies; **~maßnahmen** *Pl.* economy (*od.* austerity) measures; **~modell** *n* savings plan; **~motor** *m* economy engine; **~packung** *f* economy size (*od.* pack); **~paket** *n Pol.* austerity (*od.* cuts) package; **ein ~ schnüren** put together a package of cuts; **~pfennig** *m* nest egg; **~pläne** *Pl.* cost-cutting plans; **~politik** *f* policy of austerity; **~potential** *n* potential for savings; **~prämie** *f* savings premium; **~preis** *m* (special) low price; **~programm** *n* **1.** *Pol.* cuts (*od.* austerity) program(me); **2.** *Waschmaschine*: economy cycle; **~quote** *f* savings-income ratio

Sparren *m*; *-s*, - rafter; **e-n ~ locker haben** *umg. fig.* have a screw loose (somewhere)

sparren *v/i. Boxen*: spar; **Sparring** *n*; *-s*, *-s* sparring

Sparrings|partner *m*, **~partnerin** *f* sparring partner

Sparrunde *f Pol.* round of talks on possible economies

sparsam I. *Adj.* economical; *Person*: *auch* thrifty; *Einrichtung, Möblierung*: scanty; **~ im Verbrauch** economical; **er ist sehr ~** *mst* he's (very) careful with his money; **sind die Schotten wirklich so ~?** are the Scots really so stingy?; **~en Gebrauch von etw. machen** use s.th. sparingly, make sparing use of s.th.; **~er Beifall** *umg. fig.* meag|re (*Am. -er*) applause; **II.** *Adv.* auftragen, verbrauchen etc.: sparingly; **~ umgehen mit** go easy on, be sparing with; *mit s-n Kräften*: save; **~(er) wirtschaften** economize (more), practise great(er) economy; **~ leben** live economically (*od.* frugally); **~ möbliert** scantily furnished

Sparsamkeit *f* economy (*auch e-s Wagens etc.*); *e-r Person auch*: thrift(iness); *strengste*: austerity; (*Einfachheit*) frugality; *der Möblierung*: scantiness; **Sparsamkeitsgrund** *m*: **aus Sparsamkeitsgründen** for reasons of economy, in order to economize

Spar|schwein *n* piggy bank; **das ~ schlachten** (**müssen**) *umg.* (have to) rob the piggy bank; **~strumpf** *m* money sock

Spartakusbund *m Pol. hist.* Spartacus League

Spartaner *m*; *-s*, -, **~in** *f*; -, *-nen* Spartan; *weiblich auch* Spartan woman (*od.* girl); **spartanisch I.** *Adj.* **1.** *hist.* Spartan; **2.** *fig.* spartan; **II.** *Adv.*: **~ leben** lead a spartan life; **sehr ~ eingerichtet** very austerely furnished

Spartarif *m bei Strom, Gas etc.*: economy rate; *Telef.* reduced rate

Sparte *f*; -, *-n* **1.** branch; *der Wissenschaft*: *auch* field; *e-s Konzerns*: division; **e-e wichtige ~ der Wirtschaft** an important sector of industry; **2.** (*Zeitungsrubrik*) section; (*Spalte*) column; **Spartenkanal** *m TV* special interest channel

Spar|tipp *m* economy tip; **~vertrag** *m* savings agreement; **~volumen** *n* targeted savings figure; **~ziel** *n Pol.* savings target; **~zins** *m* interest on savings; **~zulage** *f* (tax-free) savings bonus; **~zwang** *m* obligation to make savings (*od.* cuts)

spasmisch, **spasmodisch** *Med.* **I.** *Adj.* spasmodic; **II.** *Adv.* spasmodically

spasmolytisch *Adj. Med.* spasmolytic, anti-spasmodic

Spaß *m*; *-es*, *Späße* **1.** (*Scherz*) joke; (*Streich*) prank; **lass die Späße, ja?** *umg.* stop this fooling around; **2.** *nur Sg.*; (*Vergnügen*) fun; **~ an etw haben** enjoy s.th.; **~ machen** *Sache*: be (great) fun; **es macht ihm** (**großen**) **~** he (really) enjoys it, he gets a (big) kick out of it *umg.*; **wenn's dir ~ macht** if you'd like to; *sarkastisch*: if that's your idea of fun; **es macht keinen ~** it's no fun; **es macht mir keinen ~ mehr** I'm fed up with it, I don't enjoy it any more; **sich** (*Dat.*) **e-n ~ daraus machen, etw. zu tun** take great delight in doing s.th.; **er denkt nur an s-n ~** he's only interested in having a good time; **da ist uns der ~ vergangen** it (really) spoilt (*Am.* spoiled) things (for us), it put a damper on things (for us); **viel ~!** have fun, enjoy yourself (*od.* yourselves); **aus** *od.* **zum ~** for fun; **nur** (**so**) **zum ~** *umg.* just for the fun of it, just for kicks *umg.*; **du machst mir vielleicht ~!** *iro.* I like that!, that's not funny!; **3.** *umg.* (*Sache*) **was kostet der** (**ganze**) **~?** *umg.* how much is all that going to set me back?; **ein teurer ~** *umg. fig.* an expensive business; **4.** *nur Sg.*; *Ggs. Ernst.*: **~ machen** *Person*: be joking, **sie versteht keinen ~** she can't take a joke; *weitS.* (*mit ihr ist nicht zu spaßen*) she won't stand for any nonsense; **da verstehe ich keinen ~** I take such things seriously; **in Geldsachen versteht er keinen ~** when it comes to money, he doesn't mess about (*Am.* around); (*ist er peinlich genau*) he counts every penny; **~ beiseite!** (*jetzt aber im Ernst!*) seriously, though (*od.* now); (*kein Scherz!*) joking aside; **da hört der ~ auf** that's beyond a joke, *Am.* that's not funny anymore; **aus ~ wurde Ernst** what had started in fun became deadly earnest; **das ist kein ~** it's no joke

Späßchen *n* little joke; **ich habe mir ein ~ erlaubt** I was just having a little joke (*od.* a bit of fun)

spaßen *v/i.* joke; **damit ist nicht zu ~** it's no joke (*od.* joking matter); **mit ihm ist nicht zu ~** he won't stand for any nonsense; *bei Gesprochenem*: you've got to watch what you say when he's around; **ich spaße nicht!** I'm not joking, I mean it

spaßeshalber *Adv.* (just) for the fun of it

spaßig *Adj.* funny

Spaß|macher *m*, **~macherin** *f* comedian; *im Zirkus*: clown; **~verderber** *m*, **~verderberin** *f* spoilsport; (*j-d, der nicht mitmacht*) *auch umg.* wet blanket; **~vogel** *m* comedian

Spastiker *m*; *-s*, -, **~in** *f*; -, *-nen*; *Med.* spastic; **spastisch I.** *Adj.* spastic; *umg. fig. pej.* loony; **II.** *Adv.* spastically; **~ gelähmt** spastic

spät I. *Adj.* late; **es ist/wird ~** it's late / getting late; **wie ~ ist es** *od.* **haben wir** *umg.*? what time is it?; **so ~ ist es schon?** is it really that late?, is that the time?; **dafür ist es nie zu ~** it's never too late (for that); **gestern Abend wurde es ~** it went on (*od.* I was *etc.* up) till late last night; **heute Abend wird's wieder ~** it's going to be late again tonight; (*ich komme spät von der Arbeit*) *auch* I'll be home (*od.* back) late again tonight; **am ~en Nachmittag** in the late afternoon, late

S

in the afternoon; *bis in die ~en Nacht-stunden* till late at night; *ein ~er Rembrandt* a late (work by) Rembrandt; *der ~e Goethe* the late(r) Goethe, Goethe in his later works; *ein ~es Mädchen umg.* an old maid; → *auch später* I; **II.** *Adv.* late; *bes. fig. (zu später Stunde)* at a late hour; *(spät im Leben)* late (on) in life; *zu ~ kommen* be late *(zu* for); *er kam fünf Minuten zu ~* he was five minutes late; *~ in der Nacht* late at night; *von früh bis ~* from morning till night; *~ aufstehen* get up late, *(gewöhnlich)* be a late riser; *~ dran sein umg.* be (running) late; → *auch später* II

spätabends *Adv.* late at night

Spät|antike *f: die ~* late antiquity; **~aussiedler** *m,* **~aussiedlerin** *f person of German origin emigrating from Eastern Europe after 1945*

Spätbarock *n, m,* **spätbarock** *Adj.* late Baroque

Spät|burgunder *m (Rebsorte)* Pinot noir; **~dienst** *m:* ~ *(haben* be on) late shift

Spatel *m; -s, -* spatula

Spaten *m; -s, -* spade; **~blatt** *n* spade blade; **~stich** *m* cut of the spade; *den ersten ~ tun beim Baubeginn:* cut the first sod, *Am.* break ground

Spätentwickler *m; -s, -,* **~in** *f; -, -nen* late developer

später I. *Adj.* later *(als* than); *attr. (zukünftig) auch* future; *attr. (nachfolgend)* subsequent, ... to come; *je ~ der Abend, desto schöner/lieber die Gäste hum.* latecomers are all the more welcome; **II.** *Adv.* later; *(späterhin)* later on; *früher oder ~* sooner or later; *e-n Zug ~ fahren* take the next train; *~ wirst du vielleicht anders darüber denken* some day *(od.* when you're older) you might see it differently; *an ~ denken* think of the future; *jetzt, ein Jahr ~* a year later; *bis ~!* see you later

späterhin *Adv.* later on

spätestens *Adv.* at the latest *(nachgestellt);* not later than; *du kriegst sie ~ am Freitag* you'll have them by Friday at the latest; *~ da wurde mir klar, dass ...* it was then (if not before) that I realized ...

Spät|folgen *Pl.* delayed after-effects; **~geburt** *f* retarded *(od.* post-term) birth

Spätgotik *f Archit.* late Gothic (style); *hist.* late Gothic period; **spätgotisch** *Adj.* late Gothic

Spät|heimkehrer *m* late-returning prisoner of war, late returnee (from a prisoner-of-war camp); **~herbst** *m* late autumn *(Am.* fall); **~kartoffel** *f* late (crop) potato; **~latein** *n* Late Latin

Spätlese *f* **1.** *(Wein)* spätlese, late vintage wine; **2.** *(Ernte)* late vintage *(od.* harvest)

Spätling *m; -s, -e* **1.** late fruit; **2.** *(spät geborenes Kind)* latecomer, afterthought *hum.; umg. fig. (Werk)* late work

Spätmittelalter *n* late Middle Ages *Pl.*

Spätnachmittag *m* late afternoon; *am ~* in the late afternoon, late in the afternoon; **spätnachmittags** *Adv.* in the late afternoon, late in the afternoon

Spät|nachrichten *Pl.* late(-night) news *Sg.;* **~obst** *n* late fruit; **~phase** *f* late phase; **~programm** *n* Radio, TV: late-night program(me); **~schäden** *Pl.* delayed side effects; *Med.* late sequelae;

~schicht *f* late shift; *~ haben* be on late shift; **~sommer** *m* late summer; **~stadium** *n* late stage; **~vorstellung** *f* late-night performance; **~werk** *n* **1.** *Koll.* late(r) work; **2.** *(einzelnes)* late work; **~winter** *m* late winter

Spatz *m; -en und -es, -en* **1.** *Orn.* sparrow; *essen wie ein ~ fig.* pick at one's food; *grundsätzlich:* be a poor eater; *mit Kanonen auf ~en schießen* use a steamroller to crack a nut; *das pfeifen die ~en von den od. allen Dächern* it's all over town, everyone knows about it; *lieber den ~ in der Hand als die Taube auf dem Dach* a bird in the hand is worth two in the bush; **2.** *umg. (Kosewort)* darling; *bes. Kind: auch* sweetie; **Spatzenhirn** *n umg.* birdbrain, peabrain

Spätzle *Pl.; Gastr.* type of short, flat noodles; spaetzle; **~brett** *n* spaetzle board; **~presse** *f* spaetzle press

Spät|zünder *m umg.* **1.** *~ sein* be slow on the uptake, be a bit slow-witted; **2.** → *Spätentwickler;* **~zündung** *f Mot.* retarded ignition; *~ haben umg. fig.* be slow on the uptake

spazieren *v/i.* walk (around), stroll; *~ gehen* go for a walk *(od.* stroll); *er geht gern im Wald ~* he likes to walk *(od.* go for walks) in *od.* through the woods; *wir waren im Wald ~* we went for a walk in *(od.* through) the woods; *~ fahren* go for a ride *(od.* run, *umg.* spin) (in the car); *j-n ~ fahren* take s.o. for a ride *(od.* run, *umg.* spin) (in the car); *j-n ~ führen* take s.o. (out) for a walk; *den Hund ~ führen auch* walk the dog

spazieren gehen *etc.* → *spazieren*

Spazierengehen *n* walking, walks *Pl.*

Spazier|fahrt *f* drive, run, spin *umg.; e-e kurze ~ machen* go for a short drive *(od.* run, *umg.* spin); **~gang** *m* **1.** walk, stroll; *e-n ~ machen* go for a walk *(od.* stroll); *machst du mit uns e-n ~?* are you going to come for a walk with us?; **2.** *umg. fig. (etw. sehr Einfaches)* doddle; *das Spiel / die Prüfung war ein ~* the game was a walkover / the exam was a doddle *(Am.* cinch); **~gänger** *m; -s, -,* **~gängerin** *f; -, -nen* walker, stroller; **~stock** *m* (walking) stick, cane; **~weg** *m* (foot)path, walk

SPD *f; -, kein Pl.; Abk. (Sozialdemokratische Partei Deutschlands)* SPD; **~Mitglied** *n* SPD member; **~nah** *Adj.* sympathetic to the SPD

Specht *m; -(e)s, -e* woodpecker; *nicht schlecht, Herr ~ umg. fig.* well done, that man!

...specht *m, im Subst.:* **Grau~** grey-headed woodpecker; **Schwarz~** black woodpecker

Special ['spɛʃl] *n; -s, -s; TV etc. (Sondersendung)* special; *(Personality-Show)* star's own show

Speck *m; -(e)s, kein Pl.* **1.** *(Schweinespeck)* bacon fat; *(durchwachsener etc.)* bacon; *durchwachsener/fetter ~* streaky bacon / bacon fat; *~ auslassen* render down bacon fat; *ran an den ~! umg. fig.* let's get stuck in *(Am.* let's get going) (, then); *mit ~ fängt man Mäuse* you have to use a sprat to catch a mackerel; → *Made;* **2.** *umg. (Fettpolster)* flab; *~ ansetzen* put it on, put on the flab; *der ~ muss weg* you, I *etc.* must get rid of the flab; **~bauch** *m umg.* pot-belly; **~gürtel** *m fig. um e-e Stadt:* (ring of) suburban sprawl

speckig *Adj.* **1.** *(schmierig)* greasy; **2.** *(dick, fett)* fat

Speck|käfer *m Zool.* larder *(od.* bacon) beetle; **~mantel** *m Gastr.: im ~* wrapped in bacon; **~nacken** *m umg.* fat neck; **~scheibe** *f* bacon rasher *(Am.* slice); **~schwarte** *f* bacon rind; *geröstete ~* crackling; **~seite** *f* side of bacon, flitch; **~stein** *m Min.* soapstone, steatite; **~streifen** *m* lardon, lardoon; **~würfel** *m etwa* diced pancetta

Spediteur [ʃpedi'tøːr] *m; -s, -e* haul|ier *(Am. -er),* haulage contractor; *auch per Schiff:* carrier, shipper; *(Möbelspediteur)* furniture remover, *Am.* moving company; *(Vermittler)* forwarding *(bes. Naut.* shipping) agent; **Spedition** *f; -, -en* **1.** *(Tätigkeit)* haulage; *(Senden)* forwarding; *bes. Naut.* shipping; *von Möbeln:* furniture removal; **2.** *(Firma)* haulage company; *(Vermittlung)* forwarding *(bes. Naut.* shipping) agency; *(Möbelspedition)* removal firm, *Am.* moving company

Speditions|firma *f* → *Spedition* 2; **~geschäft** *n Wirts.: das ~* the haulage (and shipping) business; **~kauffrau** *f,* **~kaufmann** *m* forwarding *(bes. Naut.* shipping) agent; **~unternehmen** *n* → *Spedition* 2

Speed [spiːd] *n; -s, -s; Sl.* speed

Speer *m; -(e)s, -e* spear; *Sport* javelin; **~fisch** *m* marlin; **~schaft** *m* shaft of a *(od.* the) spear *(Sport* javelin); **~schleuder** *f* spear catapult; **~spitze** *f* tip of a *(od.* the) spear; *auch fig.* spearhead; **~werfen** *n Sport* (throwing the) javelin; **~werfer** *m,* **~werferin** *f* javelin thrower; **~wurf** *m* **1.** *(Disziplin)* (throwing the) javelin; *die Goldmedaille im ~* the gold medal in the javelin; **2.** *(einzelner)* javelin throw

Speiche *f; -, -n* **1.** spoke; *dem Schicksal in die ~n greifen* try to change the course of fate; **2.** *Anat.* radius

Speichel *m; -s, kein Pl.* saliva, spittle, spit *umg.;* **~bildung** *f* salivation; **~drüse** *f* salivary gland; **~fluss** *m* flow of saliva, salivation; *übermäßiger ~* hypersalivation

Speichellecker *m; -s, -; pej.* toady, bootlicker; **Speichelleckerei** *f pej.* toadying, sucking-up

speicheln *v/i.* salivate

Speichelprobe *f* saliva sample

speichenlos *Adj.* spokeless, without spokes; **Speichenrad** *n* spoke wheel; *mit Drahtspeichen:* wire wheel

Speicher *m; -s, -* **1.** *(Lagerhaus)* warehouse; **2.** *(Kornspeicher)* granary, silo, *bes. Am.* (grain) elevator; **3.** *(Dachboden)* loft; *(Dachkammer)* attic; **4.** *im Computer:* memory; **~adresse** *f EDV* storage address; **~bank** *f EDV* memory bank; **2bar** *Adj. EDV* storable, savable; **~batterie** *f Etech.* accumulator, storage battery; **~becken** *n für Trinkwasser etc.:* reservoir; **~bedarf** *m EDV* memory requirement; **~chip** *m EDV* memory chip; **~dichte** *f EDV* bit density; **~element** *n EDV* storage element, memory cell; **~erweiterung** *f EDV* memory expansion; **~funktion** *f EDV* memory function; **~kapazität** *f von Lager, Akku etc.:* storage capacity; *EDV* memory capacity; **~kraftwerk** *n* storage power station; **~medium** *n EDV* storage medium

speichern *v/t.* store *(auch Etech.); EDV (abspeichern) auch* save *(auf + Akk.* onto); *Wirts.* stockpile; *(Wissen etc.) auch* accumulate

Speicher|ofen *m* storage heater; **~platz** *m EDV* storage (*od.* memory) location; **~schutz** *m EDV* memory protection; **~überlauf** *m EDV* memory overflow
Speicherung *f* storage, storing; *EDV auch* saving
Speicher|verwaltung *f EDV* memory management; **~zelle** *f EDV* memory cell; **~zugriff** *m EDV* memory access
speien *vt/i. speit, spie, hat gespie(e)n* **1.** spit; *fig.* spew, belch; (*Wasser*) spout; *Feuer ~* spew (*od.* belch) out flames; *Vulkan*: spew fire; **2.** (*sich erbrechen*) vomit, be sick
Speis¹ *m; -es, kein Pl.; Dial.* (*Mörtel*) mortar
Speis² *f; -, -en* **1.** *mst hum.: vielen Dank für ~ und Trank* many thanks for wining and dining us (*od.* me); **2.** *österr. → Speisekammer*
Speise *f; -, -n* **1.** *auch Pl.* food; (*Gericht*) dish; *warme und kalte ~n* hot and cold dishes; *~n und Getränke* (*nicht*) *inbegriffen* (not) including food and drink; **2.** *bes. nordd.* (*Pudding*) pudding, sweet; **~apfel** *m* eating apple, eater; **~brei** *m Med.* chyme; **~eis** *n* ice cream; **~fett** *n* edible (*od.* cooking) fat; **~gaststätte** *f* restaurant; **~kammer** *f* pantry, larder; **~karte** *f* menu; **~kartoffel** *f* edible potato; **~lokal** *n* restaurant
speisen I. *vt/i.* eat, *förm., bes. abends:* dine, *zu Mittag ~* (have) lunch; *zu Abend ~* have dinner, dine; *dort kann man exklusiv ~* you can eat really well there, they serve top-class food there; *wir haben sehr gut gespeist* we had an excellent meal; *Hummer / die feinsten Dinge ~* dine on lobster / the finest delicacies; **II.** *v/t. Tech., Etech., förm.* (*verpflegen*) feed
Speisen|aufzug *m* service lift (*Am.* elevator), dumb waiter; **~folge** *f* order of courses; **~zubereitung** *f* food preparation
Speise|öl *n* cooking oil; *für Salate:* salad oil; **~pilz** *m* edible mushroom; **~plan** *m* this week's *etc.* menu; **~raum** *m* dining room; **~reste** *Pl.* leftovers; *zwischen den Zähnen:* food particles; **~röhre** *f Anat.* (o)esophagus, gullet *umg.;* **~saal** *m* dining hall; *im Hotel:* dining room; *Univ., im Kloster etc.: auch* refectory; **~salz** *n* table salt; **~schrank** *m* food cupboard; **~stärke** *f* cornflour, *Am.* cornstarch; **~wagen** *m Eisenb.* dining (*od.* restaurant) car, *bes. Am.* diner; **~wasser** *n Tech.* feed water; **~zettel** *m* menu; **~zimmer** *n* dining room
Speisung *f* **1.** *förm.* feeding; **2.** *Etech.* supply
speiübel *Adj.: mir ist ~* I think I'm going to throw up (*Brit. auch* be sick); *da wird e-m ~, wenn man das hört fig.* it makes you sick (*stärker:* it turns your stomach) when you hear that kind of thing
Spektakel¹ *m; -s, -, mst Sg.; umg.* **1.** (*Lärm*) din, racket; *e-n ~ machen* make a terrible racket; **2.** (*Zank*) rumpus; **3.** (*Umstände*) palaver, fuss; *so ein ~!* what a palaver!, what a fuss!
Spektakel² *n; -s, -* spectacle (*Medienspektakel*) media event; *der Sonnenuntergang war ein großartiges ~* the sunset was really a sight to see (*od.* really spectacular)
spektakulär *Adj.* spectacular
Spektral|analyse *f* spectrum analysis; **~apparat** *m Opt.* spectroscopic instru-

ment; **~bereich** *m* spectral range; **~farbe** *f* colo(u)r of the spectrum
Spektrograph *m; -en, -en* spectrograph
Spektrometer *n; -s, -* spectrometer
Spektroskop *n; -s, -e* spectroscope
Spektrum *n; -s, Spektren* spectrum (*Pl.* spectra) (*auch fig.*); *fig.* (*Palette*) range
Spekulant *m; -en, -en* speculator; **Spekulantentum** *n; -s, kein Pl.* speculating (activities *Pl.*); **Spekulantin** *f; -, -nen* speculator
Spekulation *f; -, -en* **1.** (*Vermutung[en]*) speculation; *~en anstellen* speculate; **2.** *Philos.* speculation; **3.** *Wirts.* speculation; *die ~ mit Aktien* speculating with shares, *Am.* stock market speculation
Spekulations|geschäft *n* speculative transaction (*od.* deal); **~gewinne** *Pl.* speculative gains; **~objekt** *n* object of speculation; **~verluste** *Pl.* speculative losses; **~welle** *f* wave of speculation
Spekulatius *m; -, -* thin, mildly gingery Christmas biscuit (*Am.* cookie) in the shape of a traditional figure, *Am. etwa* gingerbread man
spekulativ I. *Adj.* speculative; **II.** *Adv.* speculatively, by means of speculation
spekulieren *v/i.* speculate (*über +* Akk. on); *Wirts.* speculate (*in +* Dat. in), play the stock market; *~ auf* (+ Akk.) *Wirts.* speculate on; *umg.* (*haben wollen*) pin one's hopes on; *→ Baisse, Hausse*
Spekulum *n; -s, Spekula; Med.* speculum (*Pl.* specula)
Spelunke *f umg. pej.* (low) dive
Spelze *f; -, -n* husk; *von Grasblüte:* glume
spendabel *Adj. umg.* (very) generous
Spende *f; -, -n* donation; (*Beitrag*) contribution; *bitte e-e kleine ~!* please can you give (*od.* spare) a small amount?; *es kamen zwei Millionen an ~n zusammen* two million marks (in donations) were raised
...spende *f, im Subst.: Kleider~* donation of clothes; *Medikamenten~* donation of medicines
spenden I. *vt/i.* give (*od.* donate) money, make a donation (*für* to, in aid of); (*Geld etc.*) give, donate; *großzügig ~* give generously; *bei uns wird viel gespendet* people give a lot of money to charity in this country; **II.** *v/t.* **1.** (*Licht etc.*) give, provide; (*Wärme*) give out; **2.** (*Blut, Organ*) give, donate; **3.** (*Lob*) give; *lit.* bestow (+ *Dat.* on); *Trost ~* offer (some) consolation; **4.** (*Sakramente*) administer; *→ Beifall*
Spenden|affäre *f Pol.* donations fraud; **~aktion** *f* fund-raising (*od.* charity) drive; **~aufkommen** *n* money raised from donations; **~aufruf** *m* appeal for funds; **~bereitschaft** *f* readiness to donate money; **~bescheinigung** *f* receipt for a donation to charity
spendenfreudig *Adj.* keen (*Am.* eager) to donate money; **Spendenfreudigkeit** *f* keenness (*Am.* eagerness) to donate money
Spenden|geld *n* money donated; **~kampagne** *f* fund-raising campaign; **~konto** *n* donations account; **~quittung** *f* receipt for a donation; **~sammlung** *f* fund-raising collection
Spender *m; -s, -* **1.** (*Person*) donor; *auf den edlen ~! umg.* here's to the generous provider!; **2.** (*Behälter, Automat*) dispenser
...spender *m, im Subst.* **1.** (*Gerät*):

Handtuch~ towel dispenser; *Feuchtigkeits~* moisturizer; **2.** *fig.: Kraft~* provider (*od.* source) of strength; *Vitamin~* source of vitamins
Spender|ausweis *m* donor card; **~blut** *n* donated blood; **~herz** *n* donor heart
Spenderin *f; -, -nen → Spender* 1
Spender|niere *f* donor kidney; **~organ** *n* donor organ
spendieren *v/t. umg.: j-m etw. ~* treat s.o. to s.th.; *j-m ein Bier ~* stand (*od.* buy) s.o. a beer; *ich spendier den Wein für eine Feier:* I'll provide the wine, the wine's on me; **spendierfreudig** *Adj.* generous; **Spendierhosen** *Pl. umg.: die ~ anhaben* be in a generous mood
Spengler *m; -s, -; bes. südd., österr., schw.* metal worker; *umg.* (*Installateur*) plumber; (*Gasinstallateur*) gas (*Am.* pipe) fitter; (*Heizungsinstallateur*) heating engineer; (*Autospengler*) panel-beater *Am.* bodywork man; **Spenglerei** *f; -, -en bes. südd., österr., schw.* **1.** *nur Sg.* (*Gewerbe*) metal working; *umg.* plumbing; (*Gasinstallation*) gas fitting; (*Heizungsinstallation*) heating installations *Pl.*; (*Autospenglerei*) panel-beating, *Am.* bodywork; **2.** (*Betrieb*) (firm of) metal workers (*umg.* plumbers); (*Gasinstallateure*) (firm of) gas (*Am.* pipe) fitters; (*Heizungsinstallateure*) (firm of) heating engineers; (*Autospengler Pl.*) (firm of) panel-beaters, *Am.* body shop; **Spenglerin** *f; -, -nen → Spengler*
Spenzer *m; -s, -* **1.** (*Jacke*) short, tight-fitting jacket; **2.** (*Hemd*) short-sleeved undergarment
Sperber *m; -s, -; Orn.* sparrowhawk
Sperenzchen, Sperenzien *Pl. umg.: ~ machen* be awkward, make trouble; (*Umstände machen*) make a fuss
Sperling *m; -s, -e; Orn.* sparrow
Sperma *n; -s, Spermen und Spermata; Physiol.* sperm; **Spermatozoon** *n; -s, Spermatozoen* spermatozoon (*Pl.* spermatozoa); **Spermium** *n; -s, Spermien* sperm cell
sperrangelweit *Adv. umg.: ~ offen* wide open; *den Mund ~ aufmachen* (*gaffen*) gape; *das Tor zu etw. ~ öffnen fig.* make s.th. easily accessible to all
Sperrbezirk *m* restricted area; *für bestimmte Personen: auch* no-go area
Sperre *f; -, -n* **1.** (*Schranke*) barrier; (*Straßensperre*) road block; (*Barrikade*) barricade; *e-e ~ durchbrechen* break through a barrier (*od.* barricade); **2.** *Tech.* lock, locking device; **3.** (*Maßnahme*) ban; *Wirts., Naut. auch* embargo; (*Blockade*) blockade; *Sport* suspension; *e-e ~ über etw. verhängen Wirts.* impose a ban (*od.* an embargo) on s.th.; *e-e ~* (*von drei Monaten*) *über j-n verhängen Sport* impose a (three-month) suspension on s.o., suspend s.o. (for three months); *e-e ~ aufheben Wirts.* lift an embargo; *Sport* cancel a suspension; *→ Ausgangssperre, Nachrichtensperre;* **4.** *fig. umg.: e-e ~ haben* (*geistig weggetreten sein*) have a mental block (*od.* a complete blank)
...sperre *f, im Subst.: Export~* export embargo (*od.* ban); *Urlaubs~ Mil.* cancel(l)ation of leave; *Zahlungs~* block on payments
sperren I. *v/t.* **1.** (*Straße*) block; *amtlich:* close (*für den Verkehr* to traffic); *durch Absperrmannschaften:* cordon off; (*Brücke, Hafen etc.*) close;

2. (*schließen*) shut, close; *mit Schloss*: lock; (*verriegeln*) bolt; *Tech.* lock; *EDV* block; 3. (*einsperren*) lock up; *in e-e Einzelzelle ~* put in solitary confinement; 4. *Druck.* space (out); 5. (*Warenverkehr*) put an embargo on; (*Gas, Telefon, Strom etc.*) cut off; (*Löhne, Zahlungen*) stop, freeze; (*Konto*) block; (*Scheck*) stop, cancel; (*Kreditkarte*) cancel; *fig.* (*verbieten*) ban, prohibit; *Sport* (*j-n*) *durch Spielod. Startverbot*: suspend, disqualify; *er wird für das nächste Spiel gesperrt* he is banned for the next game; → *gesperrt*; 6. *Sport* block; *unfair*: obstruct; *Sperren ohne Ball* obstruction off the ball; **II.** *v/refl. fig.* ba(u)lk (*gegen etw.* at s.th.), resist (s.th.); **III.** *v/i. bes. südd., österr.* (*klemmen*) jam

Sperr|feuer *n Mil.* barrage; *ins ~ der Kritik geraten fig.* come under fire; **~frist** *f* waiting period; **~gebiet** *n* restricted area; *für bestimmte Personen: auch* no-go area; *militärisches ~* prohibited area (for military operations); **~gepäck** *n* bulky luggage; **~gürtel** *m* (police) cordon; *Pol.* cordon sanitaire; **~gut** *n* bulky goods *Pl.* (*Am.* freight *Sg.*)

Sperrholz *n* plywood; **~platte** *f* piece (*od.* sheet) of plywood

sperrig *Adj.* bulky; (*unhandlich*) unwieldy

Sperr|klausel *f* restrictive clause; **~konto** *n* blocked (*Am.* frozen) account; **~mauer** *f* dam wall; **~minorität** *f* blocking minority

Sperrmüll *m* bulky rubbish (*od.* refuse, *Am.* garbage); *etw. auf den ~ stellen* throw s.th. away with the large refuse (*Am.* garbage) items; *den Stuhl habe ich aus dem ~* I got this chair when somebody threw it out; **~abfuhr** *f* bulky refuse (*Am.* garbage) pickup

Sperr|schrift *f* spaced writing; **~sitz** *m Theat.* seat in the front stalls; *im Zirkus*: front seat; *im Kino*: seat at the back; **~stunde** *f* 1. (*Ausgehverbot*) curfew; 2. → *Polizeistunde*; **~taste** *f* locking button

Sperrung *f* 1. blocking (*auch Verkehr, Konto, Radar*); *e-r Straße, Brücke etc. amtlich*: closing (off); 2. *Tech.* locking; *EDV* blocking; 3. → *Sperre 3*

Sperr|ventil *n* stop valve; (*Hahn*) stopcock; **~vermerk** *m Wirts.* non-negotiability clause; (*Anmerkung*) note restricting access; **~vorrichtung** *f Tech.* locking device, catch; **~zeit** *f* 1. (*von Lokal*) closing time; 2. (*Zeit ohne Arbeitslosengeld*) exclusion period (from unemployment benefit); **~zone** *f* → *Sperrgebiet*

Spesen *Pl. Wirts.* expenses; *auf ~* on expenses; *s-e ~ erstattet bekommen* be reimbursed for one's expenses; **~abrechnung** *f* calculation of expenses; **~erstattung** *f* reimbursement for expenses; **2frei** *Adj.* free of charge; **~konto** *n* expense account; **~quittung** *f* receipt for expenses; **~rechnung** *f* statement of expenses; **~ritter** *pej. m* expense-account big spender

Spezereien *Pl. altm.* (*Gewürze*) spices; *österr.* (*Delikatessen*) exotic delicacies

Spezi¹ *m; -s, -(s); Dial.* pal, *Am.* buddy

Spezi² *n; -s, -* cola and lemonade mix

spezial *Adj. altm.* → *speziell*

Spezial|anfertigung *f* made-to-order item, specially made item; **~ausbildung** *f* special(ized) training; **~ausführung** *f* special model (*od.* version, design); *Mot. auch* limited edition;

~effekt *m mst Pl.* special effect; **~einheit** *f* special unit, special task force; **~fach** *n* special subject; **~fahrzeug** *n* special-purpose vehicle; **~fall** *m* special case; **~firma** *f* specialist firm; **~gebiet** *n* special field (*od.* area), speciality, *Am.* specialty; **~gerät** *n* special device; **~geschäft** *n* specialist shop (*Am.* store), specialist(s *Pl.*)

spezialisieren *v/refl.: sich auf etw. ~* specialize in s.th.; *man sollte sich nicht zu früh ~* one shouldn't specialize too young; **spezialisiert I.** *P.P.* → *spezialisieren*; **II.** *Adj.* specialized; *sie sind ~ auf* (+ *Akk.*) they specialize in, their speciality (*Am.* specialty) is; **Spezialisierung** *f* specialization

Spezialist *m; -en, -en; auch Med.* specialist; *~ sein in* (+ *Akk.*) specialize in; *ich bin* (*kein*) *~ auf dem Gebiet* I'm (not) a specialist in that field; **Spezialistin** *f; -, -nen* → *Spezialist*

Spezialität *f; -, -en* speciality, *Am.* specialty

Spezialitäten|geschäft *n* delicatessen shop; **~restaurant** *n* restaurant serving local *od.* national specialities (*Am.* specialties)

Spezial|kamera *f* special-purpose camera; **~kenntnisse** *Pl.* specialized knowledge; **~kleidung** *f* special clothing; **~klinik** *f* specialist clinic; **~lager** *n* 1. *Pol., hist.* (*KZ*) concentration camp; *UdSSR:* Gulag camp; 2. *Wirts.* special warehouse; 3. *Tech.* special bearing; **~preis** *m* 1. (*Auszeichnung*) special prize; 2. *Wirts.* special price; **~slalom** *m Sport* separate slalom (*not part of the combined event*); **~training** *n Sport* special training; **~wissen** *n* special(ized) knowledge

speziell I. *Adj.* special; (*individuell*) specific, particular; *in diesem ~en Fall* in this particular case; *dieses Gebiet ist schon sehr ~* this is a highly specialized field; *mein ganz ~er Freund iro.* a very particular friend of mine; *auf dein ~es Wohl umg.* (to) your very good health!; **II.** *Adv.* specially; *in e-m besonderen Fall*: specifically; *~ angefertigt* specially made, made-to-order, *bes. Am.* custom-made

Spezies *f; -, -* 1. *Bio.* species; *fig. pej.* breed; *ein ~ seltsame ~* (*von Mensch*) *umg.* a strange breed (*od.* type of person); 2. *Math.* fundamental operation of arithmetic; 3. *Jur.* specific object as a subject of debt

Spezifikation *f; -, -en* specification

Spezifikum *n; -s, Spezifika* 1. (*Besonderheit*) specific feature; 2. *Med.* specific

spezifisch I. *Adj.* specific (*auch Med.*); *~es Gewicht* specific weight (*Phys.* gravity); *~ sein für* be specific (*od.* peculiar) to; **II.** *Adv.* specifically

...spezifisch *im Adj.: gattungs~* specific (*od.* peculiar) to the type, type-specific; *system~* system-specific

spezifizieren *v/t.* specify; *im Einzelnen*: give details of; **Spezifizierung** *f* specification

Sphäre *f; -, -n* sphere (*auch fig.*); → *schweben 1*; **sphärisch** *Adj.* spherical; *~e Musik* music of the spheres

Sphinx *f; -, -e und Sphingen* sphinx (*auch fig.*); *das Rätsel der ~ Myth.* the riddle of the Sphinx; *wie e-e ~ lächeln* give a sphinxlike smile; *sie ist e-e ~ fig.* she is sphinxlike (*od.* inscrutable)

Spickbraten *m* larded roast

spicken *v/t.* 1. *Gastr.* lard; *fig.* (*Rede etc.*) interlard; *e-n Vortrag mit witzi-*gen *Bemerkungen ~* intersperse a lecture with witty remarks; → *gespickt*; 2. *umg.* (*bestechen*) *j-n ~* grease s.o.'s palm; **II.** *vt/i. umg.* (*abschreiben*) crib

Spick|nadel *f* larding pin; **~zettel** *m umg.* crib, *Am. auch* pony, cheat sheet; *fig.* (*Notizzettel*) (sheet of) notes *Pl.*

spie *Imperf.* → *speien*

Spiegel *m; -s, -* 1. mirror (*auch fig.*); *Med.* (*Spekulum*) speculum; *j-m e-n ~ vorhalten fig.* hold a mirror up to s.o.; *die Ereignisse der Woche im ~ der Presse* the week's events as seen by the press; 2. (*Stand e-r Flüssigkeit, auch des Blutzuckers etc.*) level; 3. *Jägerspr., bei Reh etc.*: escutcheon; *bei Ente etc.*: speculum; → *Satzspiegel*

...spiegel *m, im Subst.* (*Menge*): *Glukose~* (blood) glucose level

Spiegelbild *n* mirror image; *fig.* mirror, reflection; *sie ist das ~ ihrer Mutter* she's the spitting image of her mother

spiegelbildlich I. *Adj. attr.* mirror-image ...; **II.** *Adv.: etw. ~ drucken* print s.th. in mirror image

spiegelblank *Adj.* shiny, gleaming; *weitS. umg.* (*sauber*) squeaky clean; *~ putzen* polish s.th. until it shines

Spiegelei *n Gastr.* fried egg, *Am.* fried egg sunny-side up

Spiegelfechterei *f fig.* shadow-boxing; (*Vortäuschung*) bluff, eyewash

spiegelfrei *Adj.* non-glare, anti-dazzle

Spiegelglas *n* mirror glass

spiegelglatt *Adj. Meer etc.*: glassy, (as) smooth as glass; *Straße*: like glass; *Parkett etc.*: (as) slippery as ice

Spiegel|kabinett *n* hall of (distorting) mirrors; **~karpfen** *m* mirror carp

spiegeln I. *v/i.* (*glitzern*) glitter, shine; (*reflektieren*) reflect the light; *stärker*: (*blenden*) dazzle, glare; *m-e Brille spiegelt so* I get so much dazzle (*Am.* glare) with my glasses; **II.** *v/t.* 1. reflect (*auch fig.*); 2. *Med.* (*Magen, Kehlkopf etc.*) examine with a speculum; **III.** *v/refl.* be reflected; *fig. auch* be mirrored

Spiegelreflexkamera *f:* (*einäugige ~* single-lens) reflex camera

Spiegel|saal *m* hall of mirrors; **~schrank** *m* mirror wardrobe; **~schrift** *f* mirror writing; *Druck.* reflected face; **~teleskop** *n* reflecting telescope; **~tisch** *m* dressing table, *Am.* vanity (table)

Spiegelung *f* 1. reflection (*Luftspiegelung*) mirage; 2. *Med.* endoscopy

spiegelverkehrt I. *Adj.* back-to-front, *Am.* backward; **II.** *Adv. abbilden*: in mirror image

Spiegelwand *f* wall of mirrors

Spiel *n; -(e)s, -e* 1. *nur Sg.* (*das Spielen*) play(ing); *für Geld*: gambling; *dem ~ verfallen sein* be an inveterate gambler; 2. (*Gesellschaftsspiel, Ballspiel, Glücksspiel, Brettspiel, Partie*) game; (*bes. Mannschaftssport*) match; *~, Satz und Sieg Tennis*: game, set and match; *im ~ sein Ball*: be in play; *fig.* be involved (*bei* in); *ins ~ bringen Sport* (*j-n*) bring s.o. on; *fig.* (*etw*) bring s.th. into play; (*j-n*) get s.o. involved; *aus dem ~ nehmen Sport* take s.o. off; *das ~ machen Fußball etc.*: control (*od.* dominate) the game; *machen Sie Ihr ~! Roulette*: faites vos jeux; *wie steht das ~? Sport* what's the score?; *leichtes ~ haben* have an easy win; *fig.* have an easy job of it; *das ~ ist aus* the game's over; *fig.* the game's up; **3.** (*Schauspiel*) play; **4.** (*Spielweise*) *Theat.*, *Mus.* playing, performance; *Sport* play; *gefährliches ~ Fußball*: dangerous play; **5.** *mst Sg.*; *fig.*: *~ der Farben etc.* play of colo(u)rs *etc.*; *ein ~ des Zufalls* one of fortune's little tricks; *das ~ des Schicksals* the vagaries *Pl.* of fortune; *ein seltsames ~ der Natur* a freak of nature; *ein ~ mit dem Feuer* playing with fire; *ein ~ mit der Liebe* trifling with love; *ein ~ mit Worten* a play on words; **6.** *Koll.* (*Brett, Figuren etc.*) set, game; *ein ~ Karten* a pack (*od.* deck) of cards; *ein ~ aufstellen* lay out a game; **7.** *fig.*: *freies ~ haben* have the field to o.s.; *j-s ~ durchschauen* see through s.o.'s (little) game; *freies ~ der Kräfte* free interplay of forces; *auf dem ~ stehen* be at stake; *aufs ~ setzen* (put at) risk; *j-n/etw. aus dem ~ lassen* leave s.o./s.th. out of it; *ein doppeltes ~ mit j-m treiben* double-cross s.o.; *es war e-e gehörige Portion Glück im ~* there was a fair bit of luck involved; *die Hand im ~ haben* have a finger in the pie; **8.** *Tech.* play; *erwünschtes*: clearance; *zulässiges*: allowance; *die Lenkung/Bremse hat zu viel ~* there is too much play in the steering / the brake needs taking up (*od.* adjusting); → *auch* **abgekartet** II, **Miene**, **olympisch** *etc.*

Spiel|abbruch *m Sport* abandonment of the game (*od.* of play); **~abschnitt** *m* period (of play); (*Halbzeit*) half; **~alter** *n Psych.* playing age; **~anzug** *m* playsuit; **~art** *f Bio. und fig.* variety; *Pop in all s-n ~en* pop music of every description; **~aufbau** *m Sport* build-up (of an attack), series of moves; **~ausfall** *m Sport* cancel(l)ation of the game (*od.* match); **~ausgang** *m Sport* result; **~automat** *m* gaming (*od.* amusement) machine; *mit Geldgewinn*: *auch* fruit (*Am.* slot) machine, one-armed bandit; **~ball** *m* ball; *Tennis*: game point; *Billard*: cue ball; *fig.* plaything; *ein ~ der Wellen sein* be at the mercy of the waves; **~bank** *f* (gambling) casino

spielbar *Adj.* playable

Spiel|beginn *m* start of play, *Fußball*: kick-off; **~bein** *n* free leg

spiel|berechtigt *Adj. Sport* eligible (to play); **~bereit** *Adj.* ready to play; *Spieler*: *auch* match-ready

Spielbericht *m Sport* match (*Am. auch* game) report

spielbestimmend *Adj. Sport* dominating play; *die ~e Mannschaft* the dominant team

Spiel|betrieb *m Sport the* matches *bzw.* games; **~brett** *n* **1.** *Brettspiele*: (game) board; **2.** *Basketball*: backboard

Spielchen *n umg.* little game; *lass die ~, ja?* *fig.* (*keine Tricks!*) stop those little games of yours, none of your little games

Spiel|dauer *f Kassette etc.*: playing time; → *Spielzeit*; **~dose** *f* musical box, *Am.* music box; **~ecke** *f für Kinder im Kaufhaus etc.*: play corner

Spiele|computer *m* game computer; **~konsole** *f* games console

spielen *v/t./i.* **1.** *allg.* play (*auch Schach, Karten etc.*); *Klavier ~* play the piano; *Trumpf ~* play a trump; *Verstecken ~* play hide-and-seek; *falsch ~ Mus.* play a wrong note (*od.* the wrong note[s]); *den Kindern beim Spielen zuschauen* watch the children (at) play; *zum*

Spielen rauskommen come out to play; *mit dem Bleistift ~* fiddle (*od.* play) around with one's pencil; *mit Worten ~* play (around) with words; *das Radio spielt den ganzen Tag umg.* the radio is on all day; **2.** *bei e-m Glücksspiel*: gamble (*um* for); *Lotto ~* go in for (*od.* play) the lottery; *falsch ~* cheat; *aus Leidenschaft ~* have a passion for gambling; *hoch ~* play for high stakes; *sich um sein Vermögen ~* gamble away one's fortune; *mit s-m Leben ~ fig.* gamble with one's life, put one's life at risk; **3.** *Sport*: *gut/schlecht ~* play well/badly; *unentschieden ~ gegen* draw (*Am. auch* tie) with; **3:0** *~* win 3-0; *zu Null ~ Fußball etc.*: keep a clean sheet; *Tennis etc.*: win the game to love; *A spielte gegen B* A played (against) B; *den Ball hoch/flach ~* play the ball in the air / along the ground; (*den Ball*) *mit Effet ~* make the ball swerve; *Billard*: put side on the ball; *Libero ~* play as a sweeper; *bei od. für Ajax ~* play for Ajax; *sich an die Spitze ~* work one's (*Mannschaft*: their) way to the top (of the table); **4.** *Theat.* (*aufführen*) play, perform; (*Film*) show; *~ in +Dat. Szene, Stück*: be set in; *Programm, Film*: be on at; *~ an (+ Dat.) Stück*: be on at; *Schauspieler*: be (engaged) at; *was wird heute Abend gespielt?* what's on tonight?; *wann ~ Sie wieder „Hamlet"?* when are you performing (*umg.* doing) Hamlet again?; *was wird hier gespielt? umg.* what's going on here?; **5.** (*Rolle*) play, act; *den Hamlet / die Hauptrolle ~* play Hamlet / the lead; *gut/schlecht ~* act well/badly, give a good/bad performance; *den Gastgeber ~ umg. fig.* play the host; *den Beleidigten ~ umg.* act (all) offended; *den Kranken ~ umg.* pretend to be ill; *die feine Dame ~ umg.* act genteel, put on airs; *der Chef / mein Computer / das Wetter spielt verrückt umg. fig.* the boss is being impossible / my computer is playing up / the weather's gone crazy; → *gespielt*; **6.** *fig.*: *mit j-m ~* play around with s.o., mess s.o. about; *mit dem Gedanken ~, etw. zu tun* toy with the idea of doing s.th.; *mit dem Feuer ~* play with fire; *ein falsches Spiel ~* play false; **7.** *fig.*: *~ lassen* bring into play; *die Muskeln ~ lassen* flex one's muscles; *s-e Beziehungen ~ lassen* pull a few strings; *s-n Charme ~ lassen* use one's charms; *Mann*: *auch* turn on the charm; **8.** *in allen Farben ~* sparkle in all colo(u)rs, iridesce; *ins Rötliche ~* have a reddish tinge; → *Geige*, *krank*, *Rolle*[2], *Theater* 2, 4, *Wand etc.*

spielend I. *Part. Präs.* → *spielen*; **II.** *Adv.*: *~* (*leicht*) easily, effortlessly; *er ist ~ damit fertig geworden* he took it all in his stride, it was dead (*Am.* really) easy for him; *das schaffst du ~ umg.* you can do that in your sleep; *~ gewinnen* win hands down

Spielende *n*: *gegen ~* toward(s) the end of the game (*od.* match); *zehn Minuten vor ~* ten minutes from time (*od.* before the end of play)

spielentscheidend *Adj. Sport, Treffer etc.*: deciding; *letztlich ~ war ...* in the end what decided the game was ...

Spieler *m*; *-s, -* player; (*Glücksspieler*) gambler

Spielerei *f*; *-, -en* **1.** (*Herumspielen*) playing (*od.* messing, fooling) about (*od.* around); *Schluss mit der ~!* stop

messing (*od.* fooling) about; **2.** (*Zeitvertreib*) hobby; *es ist für sie eher e-e ~* it's more of a hobby for her, she just does it for the fun of it; **3.** (*Leichtigkeit*) child's play; **4.** *umg.* (*Gerät*) technische *etc.*: gadget; (*Spielzeug*) toy; *das ist doch reine ~! umg. pej.* it's pure gimmickry

Spielerin *f*; *-, -nen* → *Spieler*

spielerisch I. *Adj. attr.* **1.** *Sport Können etc.*: playing ...; *Theat.* acting ...; *~e Überlegenheit* greater playing (*Theat.* acting) ability; **2.** (*verspielt*) playful; *mit ~er Leichtigkeit* with the greatest of ease; **II.** *Adv.* **1.** *Sport* as regards playing ability; *sie sind ~ ausgezeichnet/überlegen* they are excellent players / the better players; **2.** (*wie im Spiel*): *~ nach etw. schnappen* grab playfully at s.th.; *etw. ~ erlernen* learn s.th. with the greatest of ease

Spielernatur *f* born gambler

Spieler|stamm *m Sport* squad; **~Trainer** *m Sport* player-manager; **~vermittler** *m Sport* player's agent; **~wechsel** *m Sport* substitution

Spielfarbe *f Karten*: suit

Spielfeld *n* field, pitch; *Tennis*: court; **~hälfte** *f* half (of the field; *Tennis*: of the court); **~rand** *m* touchline

Spiel|fest *n für Kinder*: party with organized games, game(s) party; **~figur** *f* piece

Spielfilm *m* feature (film); **~handlung** *f* (feature) film (*Am.* movie) plot

Spielfläche *f Theat.* stage floor; *Sport* pitch, playing area, *Am.* field

spielfrei *Adj.* **1.** *Theat.*: *Montag ist ~* there's no performance on Monday; **2.** *Sport*: *das Wochenende ist ~* there are no matches this weekend

spielfreudig *Adj.* enthusiastic (about playing)

Spiel|führer *m*, **~führerin** *f* (team) captain; **~gefährte** *m*, **~gefährtin** *f* playmate; **~geld** *n* **1.** (*Einsatz*) stake; **2.** (*Spielmarken*) counters, chips *Pl.*; **3.** *unechtes Geld in bestimmten Spielen*: toy (*od.* play) money; **~gemeinschaft** *f bei Lotto, Toto etc.*: syndicate; **~geschehen** *n Sport* (run of) play, action; **~gestalter** *m*, **~gestalterin** *f Sport* playmaker; **~gruppe** *f* playgroup; **~hälfte** *f Sport* half (of the match *od.* game); **~halle** *f* amusement arcade; **~handlung** *f* plot; **~hölle** *f* gambling den; **~höschen** *n* rompers *Pl.*; **~kamerad** *m*, **~kameradin** *f* playmate; **~karte** *f* playing card; **~kasino** *n* (gambling) casino; **~kiste** *f* toy chest; **~klasse** *f Sport* division; **~kleidung** *f Sport* kit, *Am.* uniform; *bes. Fußball*: *auch* strip, *Am.* uniform; **~kreis** *m* (amateur) theat|re (*Am. auch* -er) group; (*Musiker*) music group; **~laune** *f*: *in glänzender ~ bes. Sport* in brilliant form; **~leidenschaft** *f* passion for gambling; **~leiter** *m*, **~leiterin** *f* **1.** *Theat.*, TV producer, director; **2.** TV gameshow host; (*Quizmaster*) quiz master; **3.** *Sport* organizer; **~macher** *m*, **~macherin** *f Sport* playmaker; **~mann** *m Pl. Spielleute* **1.** *hist.* minstrel; **2.** *im Spielmannszug*: bandsman

Spielmannszug *m* marching (drum and fife) band

Spiel|marke *f* counter, chip; **~minute** *f* minute (of play); **~oper** *f* (German) light opera, Spieloper *fachspr.*; **~ort** *m* venue

Spielothek *f*; *-, -en* games library

Spiel|pause f **1.** Sport (half-time) interval; **2.** Sport (Sommerpause etc.) break; **~plan** m Theat. etc. program(me); e-r Repertoirebühne: repertory; TV schedule; **auf dem ~ sein** be included in the program(me) (TV schedule); **~platz** m playground; **~praxis** f: **viel ~ haben** have had plenty of match practice; **~programm** n EDV games program; **~ratte** f (board) games freak; **~raum** m elbow room, room to move; beim Parken etc.: room for manoeuvre (Am. maneuver); Tech. clearance; fig. bei Auslegung etc.: scope, latitude; zeitlich: time; (Flexibilität) leeway; Wirts. (Spanne) margin; **~regel** f rule; **~n** fig. rules of the game); **sich an die ~n halten** stick to the rules; auch fig. play the game; **~runde** f round; **~sachen** Pl. auch fig. toys; **~salon** m amusement arcade; **~schuld** f gambling debt; **~stand** m score; **beim ~ von ...** with the score at ..., when the score was ...

spielstark Adj. high-performing ...; **Spielstärke** f high performance

Spiel|stätte f play area; **~straße** f play street

Spielsucht f nur Sg. gambling addiction, compulsive gambling; **spielsüchtig** Adj. addicted to gambling

Spiel|system n **1.** Glücksspiel: gambling system; **2.** Sport system of play; **~szene** f **1.** Sport sporting scene; **2.** TV etc.: game scene; **~tag** m Sport day (of league matches); **der 6. ~ der Bundesliga** the sixth day of the Bundesliga matches (od. of the Bundesliga season); **~teufel** m: **vom ~ besessen sein** be a compulsive gambler; **~therapie** f Psych. play therapy; **~tisch** m games table; für Kartenspiele: card table; bei Glücksspielen: gaming table; **~trieb** m play instinct; **~uhr** f musical clock; **~unterbrechung** f stoppage; **~verbot** n Sport suspension; **~ haben** have been suspended; **~verderber** m; -s, -, **~verderberin** f; -, -nen spoilsport; **~vereinigung** f (abgek. SV, SpVgg) Sport, in Namen: Sports Club; **~verlängerung** f extra time, Am. overtime; **~verlauf** m Sport play; **den ganzen ~ auf den Kopf stellen** be completely against the run of play

Spielwaren Pl. toys; **~abteilung** f toy department; Schild: toys (and games); **~geschäft** n toy shop (Am. store); **~industrie** f toy industry; **~messe** f toy (trade) fair

Spiel|weise f style of play(ing); **aggressive ~** aggressive play; **~werk** n Tech. musical box (Am. music box) mechanism; **~wiese** f grass play area; umg. fig. playground; **~witz** m Sport imagination; **~zeit** f **1.** Sport playing time; **nach e-r ~ von 31 Minuten** 31 minutes into the game; **2.** (Spielsaison) season; Film: (Laufzeit) run; (Länge) duration; **der Film hat e-e ~ von zwei Stunden** the film lasts two hours (od. is two hours long)

Spielzeug n einzelnes: toy (auch fig.); Koll. toys Pl.

Spielzeug|auto n toy car; **~eisenbahn** f toy train(s Pl.), train set; **~pistole** f toy pistol

Spiel|zimmer n **1.** games room; **2.** für Kinder: playroom; **~zug** m Sport move

Spiere f; -, -n; Naut. spar, boom

Spieß m; -es, -e **1.** (Bratspieß) spit; (Fleischspieß) skewer; hist. (Speer) spear; **Ochs am ~** spit-roasted ox; **den**

~ umdrehen fig. turn the tables (**gegen** on); **schreien wie am ~** scream blue (Am. bloody) murder; **2.** Mil. Sl. (Hauptfeldwebel) etwa sarge; **3.** Jägerspr. spike; → **braten** I; **~braten** m spit roast

Spießbürger m, **~in** f pej. (narrow-minded) petty bourgeois; **spießbürgerlich** Adj. pej. (narrow-minded) petty bourgeois; **Spießbürgertum** n; -s, kein Pl.; pej. **1.** (narrow-minded) petty bourgeois conformism; **2.** (die Spießbürger) petty bourgeois society

spießen v/t. spear, lance; **~ in** (+ Akk.) stick into; stärker: thrust into; **etw. auf die Gabel ~** skewer s.th. with one's fork

Spießer m; -s, - **1.** umg. pej. → **Spießbürger**, **2.** Jägerspr. spike buck; **Spießerin** f; -, -nen; umg. pej. → **Spießbürger**; **~tum** n; -s, kein Pl.; umg. pej. → **Spießbürgertum**

Spieß|geselle m hum. (Kumpan) mate, Am. buddy; bes. pej. crony; **~hirsch** m Zool. spike buck

spießig umg. pej. **I.** Adj. → **spießbürgerlich**; **~e Klamotten** unstylish (Brit. gespr. auch naff) middle-class gear Sg.; **e-e Kleinstadt** a stuffy petty bourgeois small town; **II.** Adv. gekleidet, eingerichtet: in stuffily conventional petty bourgeois style; **Spießigkeit** f umg. pej. stuffy petty bourgeois attitude

Spießruten Pl.: **~ laufen** hist., fig. run the gauntlet

Spikes [ʃpaiks] Pl. **1.** Sport spikes; **2.** Mot. studs; (Reifen) studded tyres (Am. tires); **~reifen** Pl. studded tyres (Am. tires)

spillerig Adj. bes. nordd. spindly; Mensch: skinny

Spin [spɪn] m; -s, -s **1.** Phys. spin; **2.** Sport spin; Billard: side

spinal Adj. spinal; **~e Kinderlähmung** polio(myelitis)

Spinat m; -(e)s, kein Pl.; Bot. spinach; **junger ~** baby spinach

Spinatwachtel f umg. pej. old crone

Spind m, n; -(e)s, -e locker

Spindel f; -, -n **1.** spindle (auch Bio., Bot.); Archit. newel (post); **2.** (Hydrometer) hydrometer; **spindeldürr** Adj. umg. (as) thin as a rake (Am. rail); Arme etc.: spindly, skinny

Spinett n; -(e)s, -e; Mus. spinet

Spinnaker m; -s, -; Naut. spinnaker

Spinndrüse f Zool. silk gland; der Spinne: spinneret

Spinne f; -, -n **1.** Zool. spider; **pfui ~!** umg. fig. yuck!, how yucky!; **2.** für Wäsche: rotary clothes line; **spinnefeind** Adj. umg.: **er ist ihr ~** he can't stand (the sight of) her, he hates her guts

spinnen; spinnt, spann, hat gesponnen **I.** vt/i. **1.** spin; **die Spinne spinnt ihr Netz** the spider spins its web; **ein Netz von Intrigen ~** fig. weave a web of intrigue; **ein Garn ~** umg. fig. spin a yarn; **2.** umg. **es ist alles gesponnen** he's (od. she's) made it all up, it's a load of rubbish (Am. it's a crock); **II.** v/i. umg. (verrückt sein) be mad (od. nuts, crazy, off one's rocker); (Unsinn reden) talk rubbish; **du spinnst wohl!** you must be crazy (od. off your rocker)!; **spinn ich?** am I imagining things?; **ich glaub, ich spinne** ärgerlich: I don't believe it!, it can't be!; **er fängt an zu ~** he's (slowly) going mad (od. [a]round the bend), he's losing his marbles

Spinnen|faden m spider's thread; **~netz** n spider('s) web; (Spinnwebe) cobweb; **~tier** n Zool. arachnid

Spinner m; -s, - **1.** Beruf: spinner; **2.** umg. (Verrückter) crackpot, bes. Am. screwball; **was hat dieser ~ dir wieder erzählt?** what did that nutcase tell you this time?; **3.** Zool. silkworm moth; **Spinnerei** f; -, -en **1.** nur Sg. spinning; **2.** (Fabrik) spinning mill; **3.** umg. fig. crazy (od. crackpot) idea; modische: fad, craze; (Unsinn) nonsense

Spinnerin f; -, -nen **1.** Beruf: spinner; **2.** umg. (Verrückte) madwoman

spinnert Adj. Dial. umg. mad, crazy

Spinn|rad n spinning wheel; **~stube** f hist. spinning room; **~webe** f cobweb

spintisieren v/i. pej. get crackpot ideas (**über** + Akk. about); **Spintisierer** m; -s, -, **Spintisiererin** f; -, -nen; pej. crackpot

Spion m; -s, -e **1.** spy; **2.** an der Tür: spyhole, peephole

Spionage f; -, kein Pl. spying, espionage; **~ treiben** (act as a) spy; **~abwehr** f counter-espionage, counter-intelligence; **~affäre** f espionage affair; **~dienst** m intelligence (Brit. auch secret) service; **~film** m spy film (od. thriller); **~flug** m reconnaissance flight, spying mission; **~flugzeug** n spy plane, umg. spy in the sky; **~netz** n spy network; **~organisation** f spy(ing) organization; **~prozess** m espionage trial; **~ring** m spy ring; **~satellit** m spy satellite, spy in the sky umg.; **~schiff** n spy ship; **~tätigkeit** f spying activities Pl.; **~verdacht** m: **unter ~ stehen** be suspected of being a spy (od. of having spied for s.o.)

spionieren v/i. spy; fig. snoop around; **~ für** (act as a) spy for, be spying for; → **ausspionieren**

Spionin f; -, -nen (female) spy

Spiral|block m (note)book with a spiral binding; **~bohrer** m Tech. twist drill

Spirale f; -, -n **1.** spiral; Math. helix; **2.** aus Draht: coil; **3.** Med. (Pessar) coil, IUD; **4.** Wirts. (Preisspirale etc.) spiral

Spiralfeder f coil spring

spiralförmig Adj. spiral(-shaped), helical

Spiral|kabel n coiled cord; **~nebel** m Astron. spiral nebula

Spiritismus m; -, kein Pl. spiritualism, spiritism; **Spiritist** m; -en, -en spiritualist; **spiritistisch** Adj. spiritualist

Spiritual ['spɪrɪtjuəl] n, m; -s, -s; Mus. spiritual

spirituell Adj. spiritual

Spirituosen Pl. spirits, Am. liquor Sg.; **~werbung** f spirits (Am. alcohol) advertising

Spiritus m; -, kein Pl. spirit; **~kocher** m spirit stove; **~lampe** f spirit lamp

Spiritus Rector m; -, -; geh. prime mover

Spital n; -s, Spitäler; österr., schw. hospital

spitz I. Adj. **1.** pointed; Bleistift etc.: sharp; Math., Winkel: acute; **mit ~em Ausschnitt** with a V-neck, V-necked; **etw. mit ~en Fingern anfassen** pick s.th. up with a look of disgust; **2.** fig. (abgezehrt) pinched, peaky; **3.** fig. (bissig) Rede etc.: pointed; Person: sarcastic; Zunge: sharp; **~e Bemerkung** barbed (od. cutting) remark; **4.** umg. fig.: **~ sein auf** (+ Akk.) have the hots for; **er ist ~ wie Nachbars Lumpi** he's a randy old goat; **II.** *Adv.* **1.** **~ zusammenlaufen** taper to a point; **2.** (*bissig*) *sagen, bemerken*: sharply; → *auch* **spitzbekommen, spitzkriegen**

Spitz¹ *m*; *-es, -e*; *Zool.* Pomeranian, spitz

Spitz² *umg.*: **~ auf Knopf stehen** be touch and go

Spitzbart *m* **1.** goatee (beard); **2.** *umg.* (*Mann*) man with a goatee (beard); **spitzbärtig** *Adj.* with a goatee (beard)

Spitzbauch *m* paunch; *umg.* beer belly

spitzbekommen *v/t.* (*unreg., trennb., hat*) *umg.* cotton on to, get wise to (*dass* the fact that)

Spitzbogen *m* pointed (*od.* lancet) arch; **~fenster** *n* lancet window

Spitzbube *m*, **Spitzbübin** *f*; *-, -nen*; *altm. pej.* scoundrel; *umg.* (*Kind*) rascal; **spitzbübisch** *Adj.* impish, mischievous

Spitzdach *n* pointed roof

Spitze¹ *f*; *-, -n* **1.** point; (*Gipfel*) peak, top, summit; (*Baumspitze*) top; (*spitzes Ende*) *auch e-s Fingers*: tip; (*Kinnspitze, Haarspitze*) end; (*Schuhspitze*) toe; *e-r Feder*: point; (*Turmspitze*) spire; *e-r Insel*: tip; **die ~ des Eisbergs** *auch fig.* the tip of the iceberg; **2.** (*Zigarettenspitze*) (cigarette) holder; (*Pfeifenspitze*) mouthpiece; (*Zigarrenspitze*) end, *Am.* butt; **3.** *e-s Zuges*: front; *e-r Kolonne*: head; *Mil.* (*Angriffsspitze*) (spear)head; *Sport* (*Führung*) lead; *Fußball*: (*Stürmer*) striker; **an der ~ des Staates/Konzerns** *etc.* at the head of the state/company *etc.*; **an die ~ kommen** *Sport* take over the lead; *Pol.* take over the reins of power; **an der ~ der Entwicklung** *etc.* **stehen** be in the vanguard of progress *etc.*; **an der ~ liegen** *Sport* be in the lead; *der Tabelle*: be at the top; **sich an die ~ setzen** take the lead; *der Tabelle*: go to the top; **4.** (*Höchstwert*) peak, high; (*Höchstgeschwindigkeit*) top (*od.* maximum) speed; **s-e erreichen** *zahlenmäßig etc.*: peak, reach its peak; **etw. auf die ~ treiben** carry s.th. too far; **der Wagen fährt 200 ~** *umg.* the car does 125 (mph); **5.** (*Spitzenposition*) top position; (*Leitung e-s Unternehmens etc.*) management; *e-r Partei*: leadership; **~n der Partei** *etc.*: top brass *umg.*; **die ~n der Gesellschaft** the leading figures (lights *umg.*) of society; **6.** *umg.* (*großartig*) brilliant, super; **das war** (**einsame**) **~** it was (absolutely) brilliant (*stärker*: sensational); **sie ist absolute ~** she's the tops; → *auch* **spitze**; **7.** (*bissige Bemerkung*) barb, sideswipe (*gegen* at); **8.** *fig.*: **j-m die ~ bieten** stand up to s.o.; **j-s Worten die ~ nehmen** take the sting out of s.o.'s words

Spitze² *f*; *-, -n*; (*Gewebe*) lace; **Brüsseler ~n** Brussels lace *Sg.*

spitze *umg.* **I.** *Adj. und Interj.* great, super, magic; **II.** *Adv.*: **~ aussehen** look super (*stärker*: sensational, stunning); **sie hat ~ gespielt** she played sensationally (*od.* fantastically); **das hast du ~ gemacht** you did that brilliantly

...spitze *f, im Subst.* **1.** *wörtl.*: **Nadel~** point of a needle; **2.** (*Leitung*) **Konzern~** management of a combine; **Fraktions~** leadership of a/the parliamentary party; **3.** (*Höchstwert*) **Bedarfs~** peak in demand; **Temperatur~** maximum temperature

Spitzel *m*; *-s, -*; *pej.* informer; (*Polizei-*

spitzel) *Brit. auch* grass *umg., Am. auch* stool pigeon *umg.*; *im Betrieb*: company spy; (*Schnüffler*) snooper; **Spitzeldienst** *m mst Pl.* activity as an informer; **~e leisten** act as an informer; **spitzeln** *v/i. pej.* spy; (*herumschnüffeln*) snoop around

spitzen I. *v/t.* (*Bleistift*) sharpen; **den Mund ~** purse one's lips; **die Ohren ~** prick up one's ears (*auch weitS. hellhörig werden*); **II.** *v/i. und v/refl. umg.*: (**sich**) **auf etw. ~** have one's eye on s.th.; (*begierig erwarten*) look forward eagerly to s.th.

Spitzen|... *im Subst. oft* top ...; *beruflich*: leading, top-ranking ...; *qualitätsmäßig*: top-quality ..., first-rate (*od.* -class) ...; *leistungsmäßig*: peak ...; *auf höchster Ebene*: top-level; (*hervorragend*) outstanding; **~amt** *n* senior (*od.* high) office; **~angebot** *n* top-of-the-range (*Am.* -line) item; **~bedarf** *m* peak demand; **~beamter** *m*, **~beamtin** *f* top-ranking official; **~belastung** *f* peak load

Spitzen|bluse *f* lace blouse; **~deckchen** *n* lace doily

Spitzen|einkommen *n* top income; **~ergebnis** *n* outstanding result; **~erzeugnis** *n* top-quality product; **~fahrer** *m*, **~fahrerin** *f Sport* top (*od.* leading) driver; **~feld** *n Sport* leading group; **~funktionär** *m*, **~funktionärin** *f* top-ranking official; **~gehalt** *n* top salary; **~geschwindigkeit** *f* top speed; **~gespräch** *n* top-level talks *Pl.*; *Pol.* (*Gipfel*) summit (meeting); **~gruppe** *f* **1.** top bracket; **2.** *Sport* leading group; **in die ~ aufrücken** *Sport* move up to join the leaders

Spitzenhöschen *n* lace panties *Pl.*

Spitzen|jahr *n* outstanding year; **~jahrgang** *m* (*Wein etc.*) top-quality (*od.* outstanding) vintage; **~kampf** *m Boxen*: big fight; **~kandidat** *m*, **~kandidatin** *f* leading (*od.* number one) candidate, front-runner; **~klasse** *f* top class (*od.* flight); **ein Cognac** *etc.* **der ~** a top-quality (*od.* top-drawer, ultrafine) cognac *etc.*; **ein Läufer der ~** a runner of the top flight

Spitzen|klöppelei *f* lacemaking; **~klöpplerin** *f* lacemaker

Spitzen|kraft *f* outstanding worker; (*Manager*) top-level executive; **~lage** *f* top location; **~last** *f Elektr.* peak load; **~leistung** *f* outstanding (*od.* top-class) performance; *in der Wissenschaft etc.*: outstanding achievement; *Tech., Maschine, Fabrik*: peak output; *Auto*: peak performance; *Etech.* peak power; **~lohn** *m* top wage(s *Pl.*); **~mannschaft** *f* top team; **~marke** *f* top (*od.* leading) brand; **~modell** *n* top-of-the-range (*Am.* -line) model; **~politiker** *m*, **~politikerin** *f* leading (*od.* top-ranking, front-rank) politician; **~position** *f* top position; *Sport* place at the top of the table; **~preis** *m* top price; (*auch niedriger Preis*) best (possible) price; **~produkt** *n* top-quality (*od.* high-end) product; **~qualität** *f* top (*od.* prime) quality; **~reiter** *m Sport und fig.* front runner; (*Auto etc.*) best-seller, market leader, number one; (*Film etc.*) number one (at the box office); *der Hitparade*: number one hit; **~spiel** *n* big match; **~spieler** *m*, **~spielerin** *f* top(-ranking) player; **~sportler** *m* top(-ranking) sportsman; **~sportlerin** *f* top(-ranking) sportswoman; **~steuersatz** *m* maximum tax rate; **~tanz** *m* dance on points, *Am.*

toe dance

Spitzentaschentuch *n* lace(-edged) handkerchief

Spitzen|technik *f*, **~technologie** *f* high-end (*od.* state of the art) technology; **~verdiener** *m*, **~verdienerin** *f* top earner; **~vertreter** *m*, **~vertreterin** *f der Wirtschaft etc.*: leading representative; **~wagen** *m* top-of-the-range car, flagship model; *emotional*: superb car; **~wein** *m* top-quality (*od.* top-rated) wine; **~wert** *m* peak value; **~e an der Börse**: leaders; **~wetter** *n umg.* brilliant weather; **~zeit** *f* **1.** *Sport* best (*od.* record) time; **2.** *Verkehr etc.*: peak period

Spitzer *m*; *-s, -* (pencil) sharpener

spitzfindig *Adj.* (*kleinlich*) pedantic, nitpicking *umg.*; *attr.* (*haarspalterisch*) hair-splitting ...; **Spitzfindigkeit** *f* pedantry; (*Haarspalterei*) hair-splitting

Spitz|giebel *m* pointed gable; **~hacke** *f* pickaxe, *Am.* pickax

spitzig *Adj. altm.* **1.** pointed; **2.** → *spitz* I 3

Spitz|kehre *f* **1.** hairpin bend (*od.* turn); **2.** *Skisport*: kick turn; **~kohl** *m* Chinese leaf cabbage, *Am. auch* napa cabbage

spitzkriegen *v/t.* (*trennb., hat -ge-*) *umg.* cotton on to, tumble to (*dass* the fact that)

Spitz|marke *f Druck.* (side) head; **~maus** *f* **1.** *Zool.* shrew; **2.** *umg.* (*Person*) weasel-face; **~name** *m* nickname; **~wegerich** *m Bot.* ribwort

spitz|wink(e)lig I. *Adj. Math.* acute; **II.** *Adv.*: **~ zusammenlaufen** come together at an acute angle; **~züngig** *Adj.* sharp-tongued

Spleen [ʃpliːn] *m*; *-s, -s*; *umg.* (*Idee*) cranky idea; (*Gewohnheit*) strange habit, eccentricity; **spleenig** [ˈʃpliːnɪç] *Adj. umg.* cranky; **~er Typ** crank, weirdo

spleißen *v/t.*; *spleißt, spliss, hat gesplissen*; *Naut.* splice

Splint *m*; *-(e)s, -e* **1.** *Tech.* cotter pin; **2.** *nurSg.*; (*Holz*) sapwood

spliss *Imperf.* → *spleißen*

Spliss *m*; *-, kein Pl.*; (*Haarschädigung*) split ends *Pl.*

Splitt *m*; *-s, kein Pl.* (loose) chippings *Pl.*; *zum Streuen*: grit; *im Betongemisch*: aggregate

splitten *v/t. bes. Wirts.* (*auch Wahlstimmen*) split

Splitter *m*; *-s, -* splinter; (*Bruchstück, auch Granatsplitter*) fragment; **sich** (*Dat.*) **e-n ~ einreißen** get a splinter under one's skin; **~bombe** *f* fragmentation bomb; **~bruch** *m Med.* chip fracture

splitterfasernackt *Adj. umg.* stark (*Am. auch* buck) naked, starkers *Brit. Sl.*

Splittergruppe *f Pol.* splinter (*od.* breakaway) group

splitterig *Adj.* splintery

splittern *v/t./i.* splinter; *Glas*: shatter

splitternackt *Adj. umg.* stark naked

Splitterpartei *f Pol.* splinter party

Splitting *n*; *-s, -s* **1.** *Wirts., von Aktien etc.*: splitting; **2.** *Pol.* distribution of first and second votes among the parties; **3.** *Steuer*: spouses' tax-sharing scheme

SPÖ *f*; *-, kein Pl.*; *Abk.* (**Sozialistische Partei Österreichs**) Austrian Socialist Party

Spoiler [ˈʃpɔylɐ] *m*; *-s, -*; *Mot.* spoiler

Spökenkieker *m*; *-s, -*; *nordd.* **1.** (*Hellseher*) clairvoyant; **2.** *umg.* (*Spintisie-*

rer) crackpot

sponsern *v/t.* sponsor

Sponsion *f*; -, *-en*; *österr.* (*Verleihung des Magistertitels*) conferment of the MA degree

Sponsor *m*; -*s*, *-en*, ~**in** *f*; -, *-nen* sponsor

Sponsoren|geld *n* sponsorship (money); ~**suche** *f* looking for sponsors

Sponsoring ['ʃpɔnzɔrɪŋ] *n*; -*s*, *kein Pl.* sponsorship; **Sponsorvertrag** *m* sponsorship agreement (*od.* contract)

spontan I. *Adj.* spontaneous; **II.** *Adv.* spontaneously; *entscheiden*: on the spur of the moment

Spontan(e)ität *f*; -, *kein Pl.* spontaneity

Spontan|heilung *f* spontaneous recovery (*e-r Wunde*: healing); ~**kauf** *m* impulse purchase; *Pl.* impulse buying *Sg.*; ~**urlaub** *m* impulse holiday

Sponti *m*; -*s*, -*s*; *Pol. umg.* member of a leftist group rejecting dogma

sporadisch I. *Adj.* sporadic; **II.** *Adv.* sporadically; (*hin und wieder*) *auch* every once in a while

Spore *f*; -, -*n*; *Bot., Med.* spore

Sporen *Pl.* → *Spore, Sporn*

Sporen|pflanze *f* cryptogam; ~**tierchen** *n Zool.* **1.** *Pl.* (*Stamm*) sporozoa; **2.** (*Einzeltierchen*) sporozoon

Sporn *m*; -(*e*)*s*, *Sporen bzw. Sporne* **1.** (*Pl. Sporen*) spur (*auch Zool. und fig.*); *e-m Pferd die Sporen geben* give a horse a touch of the spurs; *sich* (*Dat.*) *s-e* (*ersten*) *Sporen verdienen fig.* win one's spurs; **2.** *Flug.* (*Pl. Sporne*) tail skid; ~**spornen** *v/t.* spur

Sport *m*; -(*e*)*s*, *kein Pl.* **1.** *allg.* sport, *bes. Am.* sports *Sg. od. Pl.* (*auch fig.*); (*Sportart*) sport; *die Welt des ~s* the world of sport(s); *viel ~ treiben* do (*od.* go in for) a lot of sport(s); **2.** *in der Schule*: physical education (*abgek.* **PE**); **3.** *fig.* (*Steckenpferd*) hobby; *etw zum ~ machen* do s.th. as a hobby (*zum Spaß*: for fun); *ein teurer ~* an expensive pastime; *sich* (*Dat.*) *e-n ~ daraus machen, etw zu tun umg.* delight in doing s.th.

...sport *m*, *im Subst.*: *Ball~ allg.* ball games *Pl.*; *Sportart*: ball game; *Freizeit~* recreational sport (*bes. Am.* sports *Pl.*); *Wettkampf~* competitive sport (*bes. Am.* sports *Pl.*)

Sport|abzeichen *n* sports (achievement) badge; ~**amt** *n e-r Stadt*: sports and leisure department; ~**angler** *m*, ~**anglerin** *f* angler; ~**anlage** *f* sports complex; ~**anzug** *m* (*Freizeitanzug*) casual suit; ~**art** *f* sport

Sportartikel *Pl.* sports (*Am.* sporting) equipment *Sg.* (*od.* goods); ~**hersteller** *m* sports (*Am.* sporting) goods manufacturer

Sport|arzt *m*, ~**ärztin** *f* sports physician; ~**ausrüstung** *f* sports equipment

sportbegeistert *Adj.* keen (*stärker*: mad) on sport(s); **Sportbegeisterte** *m*, *f* sports fan

Sport|beilage *f* sports section (*od.* pages *Pl.*); ~**bekleidung** *f* sportswear

Sportbericht *m* sports report (*od.* news); ~**erstatter** *m*, ~**erstatterin** *f* sports correspondent

Sport|betrieb *m* sports activities *Pl.*; ~**boot** *n* leisure boat; ~**bund** *m* sports federation; ~**club** *m* sports club; ~**dezernat** *n* (council) sports and leisure department; ~**direktor** *m*, ~**direktorin** *f* sports director; ~**dress** *m* sportswear

sporteln *v/i. umg.* do a bit of sport(s), dabble in sport(s)

Sport|ereignis *n* sports event; ~**fan** *m* sports fan; ~**fechten** *n* fencing; ~**feld** *n* sports ground; ~**fest** *n* sports meeting; *in der Schule etc.*: sports day, *Brit. auch* school sports *Pl.*; ~**fischen** *n* angling; ~**fischer** *m*, ~**fischerin** *f* angler; ~**flieger** *m*, ~**fliegerin** *f* amateur pilot; ~**flugzeug** *n* sports plane, light (two-seater) aircraft; ~**freund** *m*, ~**freundin** *f* **1.** sports fan; **2.** *Sporttreibende*: (keen) sportsman (*f* sportswoman), athlete; **3.** (*Partner[in]*) sporting companion; ~**funktionär** *m*, ~**funktionärin** *f* sports official; ~**geist** *m* sportsmanship, sense of fairness; *keinen ~ haben* be very unsporting; ~**gelände** *n* sports ground; ~**gerät** *n* piece of sports apparatus; *Koll., auch Pl.* sports apparatus *Sg.*; ~**gericht** *n* sports tribunal; ~**geschäft** *n* sports shop (*Am.* store); ~**gewehr** *n* sporting gun; ~**halle** *f* sports hall; (*Turnhalle*) gymnasium, gym *umg.*; ~**hemd** *n* sports (*Am.* sport) shirt; ~**hilfe** *f*: *Deutsche ~* sporting association seeking sponsors and distributing financial support; ~**hochschule** *f* college of physical education; ~**hotel** *n* sporting hotel; ~**internat** *n* special sports boarding school; ~**invalide** *m*, *f* sports invalid

sportiv *Adj.* sporty

Sport|jacke *f* sports (*Am.* sport) jacket; ~**journalist** *m*, ~**journalistin** *f* sports journalist, sportswriter; ~**kamerad** *m*, ~**kameradin** *f* sporting companion; ~**kegler** *m*, ~**keglerin** *f* competitive bowler; ~**kleidung** *f* sportswear; ~**kommentator** *m*, ~**kommentatorin** *f* sports commentator; ~**kurs** *m* sports training course; ~**lehrer** *m*, ~**lehrerin** *f* sports instructor; *in der Schule*: PE (= physical education) teacher; ~**leiter** *m*, ~**leiterin** *f* sports director

Sportler *m*; -*s*, - sportsman, athlete; *~ des Jahres* Sports Personality of the Year; ~**ehrung** *f* reception to hono(u)r sportspeople (*od.* athletes); ~**heim** *n* club house; ~**herz** *n Med.* athlete's heart

Sportlerin *f*; -, *-nen* sportswoman, (woman) athlete

sportlich I. *Adj.* **1.** *im Charakter, auch Frau, Auto*: sporty; *bes. Mann, auch Aussehen*: athletic; *Kleidung*: casual (*flott*) sporty; *Frisur*: short but smart; *~ sein Person*: go in for sport(s), be keen on sport (*Am.* eager about sports); *in ~em Tempo* at a brisk pace; **2.** (*fair*) sporting, sportsmanlike; *~es Verhalten* sporting behavio(u)r; **3.** (*im Zusammenhang mit Sport*) sporting ...; *~e Leistungen* sporting performances; **II.** *Adv.* **1.** (*rasant*) sportily; *gekleidet auch* casually; *~ fahren Mot.* drive fast; **2.** (*fair*) *sich verhalten*: sportingly, in a sportsmanlike manner; **3.** *sich ~ betätigen* go in for sport(s); *~ begabt sein* have a talent for sport(s); ~**elegant** *Adj.* casually elegant, smart but casual

Sportlichkeit *f* **1.** (*sportlicher Charakter*) *e-s Menschen, Autos etc.*: sportiness; **2.** (*Fairness*) sporting (*od.* sportsmanlike) behavio(u)r, fair play; **3.** (*Begabung, Können*) sporting talent (*od.* ability)

Sportmaschine *f Flug.* → *Sportflugzeug*

Sportmedizin *f* sports medicine; **Sportmediziner** *m*, **Sportmedizinerin** *f* practitioner of sports medicine; **sportmedizinisch** *Adj. Institut, Frage*

etc.: ... of sports medicine; *Forschung*: ... into sports medicine; *Abhandlung*: ... concerning sports medicine

Sport|meldung *f* sports item; ~**motor** *m* sports engine; ~**nachrichten** *Pl.* sports news *Sg.*; ~**platz** *m* sports ground; (*ohne Gebäude*) sports field; *e-r Schule auch* playing field

Sportpolitik *f* sports policy; **sportpolitisch** *Adj.* relating to sports policy

Sport|programm *n TV* **1.** (*Sendung*) sports program(me); **2.** (*Kanal*) sports channel; ~**rad** *n* sports bike; ~**redakteur** *m*, ~**redakteurin** *f* sports editor; ~**redaktion** *f* sports desk; ~**reportage** *f* (*Bericht*) sports report; *Funk., TV, bes. live*: running commentary (on a game *etc.*); (*das Berichten*) sports reporting; ~**reporter** *m*, ~**reporterin** *f* sports reporter; ~**schau** *f TV* sports review; ~**schuh** *m* **1.** *Sport* sports shoe; **2.** casual shoe; ~**schütze** *m*, ~**schützin** *f* (sporting) marksman; ~**seite** *f* sports page; ~**sender** *m* sports channel; ~**sendung** *f* sports program(me), sportscast

Sports|freund *m umg.* **1.** (*Kumpel*) mate, *Am.* buddy; **2.** → *Sportfreund*; ~**kanone** *f umg.* (sporting) ace; ~**mann** *m Pl. mst Sportsleute* sportsman

Sport|stadion *n* sports stadium; ~**stätte** *f* sporting venue, *Am.* sports arena; ~**student** *m*, ~**studentin** *f* sport(s) student; ~**stunde** *f* sports (*Schule*: PE) lesson; ~**tasche** *f* sports (*od.* gym) bag; ~**tauchen** *n* skin diving; *mit Atemgerät*: scuba diving; ~**taucher** *m*, ~**taucherin** *f* skin diver; *mit Atemgerät*: scuba diver; ~**teil** *m e-r Zeitung*: sports section; ~**unfall** *m* sports accident; ~**unterricht** *m* sports lesson(s *Pl.*); *Schule*: physical education (*abgek.* **PE**); ~**veranstaltung** *f* sporting (*od.* sports) event; *mit mehreren Rennen o.ä.*: sports meeting; ~**verein** *m* sports club; ~**verletzung** *f* sports injury; ~**waffe** *f Schießsport*: sporting gun (*Pistole*: pistol); *Fechten*: fencing weapon; ~**wagen** *m* **1.** *Mot.* sports car; **2.** (*Kinderwagen*) pushchair, *Am.* stroller; ~**wissenschaft** *f* sports science; ~**zeitung** *f* sports magazine; ~**zentrum** *n* sports cent|re (*Am.* -er); ~**zeug** *n* sports gear (*od.* kit)

Spot [spɔt] *m*; -*s*, -*s* **1.** (*Werbespot*) commercial; **2.** (*Scheinwerfer*) spotlight, spot

Spotlight ['spɔtlait] *n*; -*s*, -*s* spotlight, spot

Spotmarkt ['spɔtmarkt] *m Wirts.* spot market

Spott *m*; -(*e*)*s*, *kein Pl.* mockery, ridicule; *in der Schule etc., auch gutmütiger*: teasing; *verächtlicher*: scorn; *zum ~* (*der Leute*) *werden* become a (general) laughing stock; *j-n mit Hohn und ~ überschütten* heap scorn on s.o.; *s-n ~ mit j-m treiben* make fun of s.o.; → *Schaden* 4

spottbillig *Adj. umg.* dirt cheap

Spottdrossel *f Orn.* mockingbird

Spöttelei *f*, -, *-en* mockery; (*Bemerkung*) gibe, jibe; **spötteln** *v/i.* mock, gibe (*über +Akk.* at)

spotten *v/i.* mock, laugh, *höhnisch*: scoff (*über +Akk.* at); *über j-n* (*sich lustig machen*) make fun of s.o.; *jeder Beschreibung ~* defy (*od.* beggar) description

Spötter *m*; -*s*, - mocker; *alter ~! umg.* you're forever poking fun (*höhnisch*: scoffing); **Spötterei** *f* → *Spott*; **Spöt-**

terin f; -, -nen → *Spötter*

Spott|figur f joke figure, butt of ridicule; **~gedicht** n satirical poem; **~geld** n umg. laughable sum (od. price), pittance; **für ein ~** auch dirt cheap, for next to nothing

spöttisch I. *Adj.* mocking; (höhnisch) derisive; (verächtlich) scornful; **II.** *Adv.* grinsen, anschauen: mockingly; **etw. ~ abtun** dismiss s.th. scornfully

Spott|lied n satirical song; **~name** m (nasty) nickname; **~preis** m umg. ridiculous(ly low) price, giveaway price; **zu e-m ~** dirt cheap, for next to nothing; **~vogel** m 1. Orn. mockingbird; 2. umg. fig. mocker, scoffer

sprach *Imperf.* → *sprechen*

Sprach|atlas m linguistic atlas; **~ausgabe** f EDV speech (od. voice) output; **~barriere** f language barrier

sprachbegabt *Adj.* linguistically gifted (od. talented), präd. auch good at languages; **Sprachbegabung** f gift (od. talent) for languages, linguistic talent

Sprachbeherrschung f command of a (od. the) language

sprachbehindert *Adj.*: **~ sein** have a speech defect

Sprach|beratung f language advisory service; **~computer** m 1. computer with a voice synthesizer; 2. (Wörterbuch) electronic pocket dictionary; **~didaktik** f language-teaching method

Sprache f, -, -n 1. allg., e-s Volkes etc.: language, bes. lit. tongue; **alte ~n** ancient languages; **e-e ~ beherrschen** be able to speak a language; **in deutscher ~** in German; **Publikationen** etc. **in deutscher ~** German-language publications etc.; **die ~ der Musik** fig. the language of music; **e-e andere ~ sprechen** fig. (Gegensätzliches bezeugen) tell a different story; **e-e deutliche ~ sprechen** fig. Sache: speak for itself (od. themselves); 2. (Sprechfähigkeit) speech; (Ausdrucksweise) language, speech, way of speaking; bes. e-r Gruppe: ... talk; **die ~ verlieren durch Schock** etc.: be unable to speak, lose one's speech; **hast du die ~ verloren?** have you lost your tongue?; (he)**raus mit der ~!** umg. (come on,) out with it!; **mir blieb die ~ weg** I was speechless; **zur ~ bringen** bring up, raise; **zur ~ kommen** come up; 3. (Aussprache) articulation, diction; **der ~ nach kommt er aus Berlin** judging by the way he speaks, he comes from Berlin; → **beherrschen** I 3, **herausrücken** II, **verschlagen¹** 3

Sprach|ebene f speech level, register; **~eingabe** f EDV speech (od. voice) input; **~empfinden** n feeling for (the) language

Sprachen|gewirr n babel; **~schule** f language school; **~studium** n language studies Pl.

Sprach|erkennung f EDV speech (od. voice) recognition; **~erwerb** m language acquisition

...spracherwerb m, im Subst.: **Erst~** first language acquisition

Sprach|fähigkeit f capacity for verbal communication; **~familie** f family of languages; **die germanische ~** the Germanic (family of) languages; **~fehler** m Med. speech impediment (od. defect); **~forscher** m, **~forscherin** f linguistic researcher; **~forschung** f linguistic research (od. studies Pl.); **~führer** m phrasebook; **~gebiet** n speech area; **deutsches ~** (a) German-speak-

ing area; **~gebrauch** m usage; **~gefühl** n feeling for (the) language; **~gemisch** n linguistic mix, mixture of languages; **~genie** n linguistic genius; **~geschichte** f 1. history of language, language history; e-r bestimmten Sprache: history of the language; 2. (Teilgebiet) historical linguistics Pl. (V. im Sg.); **~gesetz** n linguistic law

sprach|gesteuert *Adj.* voice-activated; **~gestört** *Adj.* Med. aphasic; **~ sein** mst have a speech disorder (od. impediment)

Sprachgewalt f eloquence, power of utterance lit.; **sprachgewaltig** *Adj.* eloquent; Dichtung, Redner: auch powerful

sprachgewandt *Adj.* articulate; in Fremdsprachen: proficient in languages; **~ sein** auch have a way with words

Sprach|grenze f language (od. linguistic) boundary; **~gut** n linguistic heritage; **~heilschule** f school of speech therapy

...sprachig im Adj. 1. in e-r gewissen Sprache: ...-language ...; e-e gewisse Sprache sprechend: ...-speaking; **deutsch~e Publikationen** German-language publications; **französisch~e Führer** French-speaking guides; 2. wie viele Sprachen deckend bzw. sprechend: -lingual; **ein ein~es/mehr~es Wörterbuch** a monolingual/multilingual dictionary

Sprach|insel f linguistic enclave (od. island); **~kenntnisse** Pl. knowledge Sg. of languages; e-r best. Sprache: knowledge Sg. of a (od. the) language; **englische ~** knowledge (od. command) of English; **gute englische ~ erwünscht** good command of English desirable; **~kompetenz** f linguistic ability (od. competence); **~kultur** f linguistic sophistication (od. standards Pl.)

sprachkundig *Adj.* good at languages

Sprach|kunst f literary artistry; **~künstler** m, **~künstlerin** f wordsmith; **~kurs** m language course; **~labor** n language laboratory (lab umg.); **~lehre** f grammar; (Buch) grammar (book); **~lehrer** m, **~lehrerin** f language teacher; **~lenkung** f language manipulation, manipulation of a (od. the) language

sprachlich I. *Adj.* attr. language ..., linguistic; (grammatisch) grammatical; (stilistisch) stylistic; **~er Fehler** grammatical error; **~e Kommunikation** verbal communication, communicating through language; **II.** *Adv.* linguistically; (grammatisch) grammatically; (stilistisch) stylistically; wertend: from a language point of view; **der Aufsatz ist ~ schwach** the essay is badly written (od. stylistically bad); **~ richtig/falsch** grammatically correct/incorrect

sprachlos *Adj.* speechless (vor + Dat. with); **da war er ~** it left him speechless; **Sprachlosigkeit** f speechlessness

Sprach|melodie f speech melody, intonation; **~minderheit** f linguistic minority; **~niveau** n level of language; **~norm** f Regeln: linguistic norm(s Pl.); Sprachgebrauch: prescribed usage; **~pflege** f maintaining linguistic standards; (Purismus) (pursuit of) linguistic purism; **~philosophie** f philosophy of language; **~probleme** Pl. language (od. linguistic) problems; **~prüfung** f language examination; **~psychologie** f psychology of language;

~raum m → *Sprachgebiet*; **~reform** f language (od. linguistic) reform(s Pl.), reforming a (od. the) language; **~regel** f grammatical rule; **~regelung** f Pol. official version; **nach offizieller ~ heißt es ...** the official version is ...; **~reise** f language study trip; **~rohr** n wörtlich: megaphone; fig. mouthpiece; (Zeitschrift etc.) organ; **~schatz** m vocabulary; **~schnitzer** m umg. (linguistic) howler; stilistischer: solecism; (Wortverwechslung) malapropism

Sprachschöpfer m, **~in** f linguistic innovator; **sprachschöpferisch** *Adj.* linguistically innovative (od. creative); **Sprachschöpfung** f linguistic innovation

Sprach|schranke f language barrier; **~schule** f language school; **~schwierigkeiten** Pl. language difficulties, difficulty Sg. with a (od. the) language; **~störung** f speech impediment; **~studium** n language studies Pl.; **nach abgeschlossenem ~** Univ. after completing a language degree (course); **~talent** n 1. gift (od. talent) for languages; 2. (Person) gifted linguist; **~unterricht** m language teaching; **englischer ~** English lessons; **~verarbeitung** f EDV speech (od. voice) processing; **~verhalten** n speech behavio(u)r; **~vermögen** n faculty of speech

Sprachwissenschaft f linguistics Sg.; **vergleichende ~en** comparative linguistics; **Sprachwissenschaftler** m, **Sprachwissenschaftlerin** f linguist; **sprachwissenschaftlich I.** *Adj.* linguistic; **II.** *Adv.* linguistically

Sprach|witz m linguistic joke; **~zentrum** n Anat. speech centre|re (Am. -er)

sprang *Imperf.* → *springen*

Spray [ʃpreː] m, n; -s, -s spray; **~dose** f spray can

sprayen ['ʃpreːən] vt/i. spray; **Sprayer** ['ʃpreːɐ] m; -s, -, **Sprayerin** f; -, -nen spray artist

Sprech|akt m Ling. speech act; **~anlage** f intercom; an der Haustür: entryphone; **~blase** f (speech) balloon; **~chor** m 1. chorus; **im ~ rufen** chant; 2. (Text) chorus, chant, chanted slogan; 3. (Demonstranten) chorus of demonstrators

sprechen; spricht, sprach, hat gesprochen **I.** v/i. 1. speak (mit to, with; zu to; über + Akk., von mst about); (reden, sich unterhalten) talk; **im Fernsehen ~** speak on television; **~ lernen** learn to talk; **er spricht nicht viel** he doesn't say much; **er soll möglichst wenig ~** he should talk as little as possible; **sie ~ nicht miteinander** they're not talking (od. speaking) to each other, they're not on speaking terms; **über Politik/Geschäfte ~** talk politics/business; **sprich mal mit ihm darüber** have a word with him about it; **mit sich selbst ~** talk to oneself; **von etwas anderem ~** talk about something else, change the subject; **schlecht über j-n ~** speak ill of s.o.; **wir kamen auf Indien zu ~** the subject of India came up; **unter uns gesprochen** between you and me; **ich spreche aus Erfahrung** I speak from experience; **allgemein gesprochen** generally speaking; **da wir gerade von ... ~** talking of ...; **jeder spricht davon** everybody's talking about it, it's the talk of the town; **sprich!** umg. spit it out!; **sie ist nicht gut auf ihn zu ~** she hasn't a single good word for him, he's in her bad books; **2.** (*e-e Rede halten*) speak, give a speech (*Vortrag*: talk) (*über + Akk.* on); **vor e-r großen Zuhörerzahl** ~ speak in front of (*od.* to) a large audience; **er kann** (**nicht**) **gut frei** ~ he's (not) good at speaking off the cuff; **3.**; **4.** ~ **für** als *Vertreter*: speak for (*od.* on behalf of); *vermittelnd*: put in a good word for; *befürwortend*: plead for, argue in favo(u)r of; ~ **gegen** (*e-e Sache*) argue (*stärker*: speak out) against; **das spricht für ihn** that says something for him, that's one thing in his favo(u)r; **das spricht für s-e Unschuld** that would seem to indicate he's innocent; **vieles spricht dafür** there's much to be said for it; **vieles spricht dafür/dagegen, dass ...** it seems very likely/unlikely that ...; **alles spricht dafür, dass sie es war** all the evidence points to her (as the guilty party); **vieles spricht dagegen** there are many reasons for not doing it (*od.* why one shouldn't); **was spricht dafür?** give me one good reason why we should (do it *etc.*); **5.** *fig.*: **aus s-n Worten spricht der Neid** you can tell he's jealous by the way he speaks; *stärker*: there's jealousy in his every word; **aus ihren Augen sprach die Verzweiflung** her eyes were filled with despair, her eyes spoke volumes of despair; → **Anzeichen, Band¹** 2, **Recht, schuldig** I 1; **II.** *v/t.* (*sagen*) say; (*e-e Sprache*) speak; (*ein Gebet, Wort*) say; (*Gedicht*) recite; (*Nachrichten*) read; **s-e ersten Worte** ~ *Baby*: say its first few words; **etw. auf Tonband** ~ record s.th. on tape; **sie spricht ausgezeichnet Englisch** she speaks English very well, she speaks excellent English; **das Urteil** ~ pronounce judg(e)ment; **die Kosten, sprich Anschaffung und Versicherung, ...** the costs, i.e. (*od.* that is to say) purchase and insurance, ...; **2.** (*aussprechen*) pronounce; **3.** (*konsultieren*) speak to, see; **kann ich Sie kurz** ~? can I have a (quick) word with you?; **für ihn bin ich nicht zu** ~ I'm not in for him, if he calls I'm not here; **ich bin heute für niemanden zu** ~ I'm not available (*od.* in) for anybody today, I'm not here today - no matter who calls; **wir** ~ **uns noch!** *drohend*: you haven't heard the last of this

Sprechen *n*; *-s, kein Pl.* speaking, talking; **j-n zum** ~ **bringen** get s.o. to talk; (*zwingen*) make s.o. talk; **das** ~ **fällt ihm schwer** he finds it difficult to speak (*wegen Hemmungen etc.*: talk)

sprechend I. *Part. Präs.* → **sprechen**; **II.** *Adj. Augen, Gesten*: (very) expressive, eloquent; (*überzeugend*) convincing; ~**e Puppe** talking doll; ~**es Beispiel** graphic illustration

Sprecher *m*; *-s, -* **1.** (*Redner*) speaker (*auch e-r Sache etc.*); (*Ansager*) announcer; (*Nachrichtensprecher*) newsreader, *bes. Am.* newscaster *od.* anchor; (*Erzähler*) narrator; (*Wortführer, Vertreter*) spokesman, spokesperson (+ *Gen.* for); *Parl.* Speaker; **zum** ~ **e-r Gruppe/Sache werden** become the spokesman (*od.* spokesperson) for a group/cause, speak out in favo(u)r of a group/cause; **2.** *Sl.* (*Besuchszeit im Gefängnis*) visiting time; **Sprecherin** *f*; *-, -nen* (*Rednerin*) speaker; (*Ansagerin*) announcer; (*Nachrichtensprecherin*) newsreader, *bes. Am.* newscaster, *bes. Am.* anchor; (*Erzählerin*) narra-

tor; (*Wortführerin, Vertreterin*) spokeswoman, spokesperson (+ *Gen.* for); *Parl.* Speaker

Sprecherziehung *f* speech training, elocution

sprechfaul *Adj.* **1.** taciturn; *pej.* too lazy to open one's mouth; **2.** ~ **sein** *Kind*: be a late (*od.* lazy) talker

Sprechfunk *m* **1.** radiotelephony (*abgek.* R/T); **über** ~ **in Verbindung stehen mit** be in radio contact with; **2.** → **Sprechfunkgerät**; ~**gerät** *n* radiotelephone; *tragbar*: walkie-talkie

Sprech|gerät *n* → **Sprechanlage**; ~**gesang** *m* sprechgesang; ~**melodie** *f* *Ling.* speech melody, intonation; ~**muschel** *f* mouthpiece; ~**organ** *n* *Anat.* speech organ; ~**pause** *f* pause (*while speaking*); ~**probe** *f* *bei Lautsprecheranlage*: sound check; ~**puppe** *f* talking doll; ~**rhythmus** *m* *Ling.* speech rhythm; ~**rolle** *f* *Theat.* speaking part; ~**schulung** *f* speech training, elocution; ~**silbe** *f* *Ling.* phonetic syllable; ~**stimme** *f* (speaking) voice

Sprechstunde *f* *des Arztes*: consulting (*od.* surgery) hours *Pl.*, *Am.* office hours *Pl.*; *e-s Lehrers, Professors, Bürgermeisters etc.*: consultation hours, *Am.* office hours; **wann hat er** ~? *Med.* when are his surgery (*Am.* office) hours?; *Brit. auch* when does he have surgery?; *Lehrer etc.*: when is he available (for consultation)?, when can one see him?; **ich soll zu ihr in die** ~ she wants to see me (personally); *Med. auch* she wants me to come to the surgery (*Am.* office); **Sprechstundenhilfe** *f* doctor's assistant; *nur beim Empfang*: (doctor's) receptionist

Sprech|tag *m* public consultation day; ~**taste** *f* talk button (*od.* key); ~**theater** *n* theat|re (*Am. auch* -er) of the spoken word, straight theat|re (*Am. auch* -er); ~**übung** *f* speech (*od.* elocution) exercise; ~**unterricht** *m* elocution lessons *Pl.*; ~**verbindung** *f* *Funk.* voice connection; ~**weise** *f* way of speaking; ~**werkzeuge** *Pl.* speech organs, organs of speech; ~**zeit** *f* **1.** *im Gefängnis etc.*: visiting time; **2.** *am Telefon*: call time; **3.** → **Sprechstunde**; ~**zimmer** *n* consulting room, surgery, *Am. auch* (doctor's *etc.*) office; *für Eltern*: (teacher's) consultation room

Spreißel *m*; *-s, -* **1.** *bes. südd.* (*Splitter*) splinter; **2.** *bes. österr.* (*Holzstück*) stick; (*Span*) wood shaving; *zum Anheizen*: (piece of) kindling

spreizen I. *v/t.* **1.** spread; (*Beine*) *auch* straddle; (*Finger*) splay (out); **2.** *Funk.* spread; **II.** *v/refl.* (*sich zieren*) play hard to get; (*sich aufblähen*) give o.s. airs; → **gespreizt**

Spreiz|fuß *m* *Med.* splayfoot; ~**hose** *f* T-splint

Spreng|arbeiten *Pl.* blasting operations; ~**bombe** *f* high-explosive (*Abk.* HE) bomb, demolition bomb

Sprengel *m*; *-s, -* *e-s Pfarrers*: parish; *e-s Bischofs*: diocese

sprengen I. *vt/i.* (*hat gesprengt*) **1.** (*auf*~) burst open; (*Tür*) *auch* force; (*Fesseln, Griff etc.*) burst, break; *mit Dynamit etc.*: blast; (*in die Luft* ~) blow up; **im Steinbruch wird gesprengt** they are blasting in the quarry; **das Eis hat die Flasche gesprengt** the ice has caused the bottle to burst; **2.** (*Versammlung*) break up; (*Menschenmenge*) disperse; (*Spielbank*) break; → **Rahmen** 2; **3.** (*bespritzen*)

sprinkle, spray; (*Pflanzen*) water; **II.** *v/i.* (*ist gesprengt*); *geh.* gallop, ride hard

Sprenger *m*; *-s, -*; (*Rasensprenger*) sprinkler

Spreng|gelatine *f* blasting gelatin(e), nitrogelatin(e), *Am. auch* gelatin dynamite, gelignite; ~**kapsel** *f* detonator; ~**kommando** *n* demolition squad; *zur Bombenentschärfung*: bomb disposal unit; ~**kopf** *m* warhead; ~**körper** *m* explosive (device); ~**kraft** *f* explosive force; ~**ladung** *f* explosive charge; ~**meister** *m*, ~**meisterin** *f* blaster; ~**satz** *m* explosive charge

Sprengstoff *m* explosive; *fig.* dynamite; ~**anschlag** *m*, ~**attentat** *n* bomb attack; **auf unsere Botschaft wurde gestern ein Sprengstoffanschlag verübt** a bomb attack was made yesterday on our embassy; ~**experte** *m*, ~**expertin** *f* explosives expert; ~**paket** *n* parcel bomb; ~**täter** *m* bomber

Sprengtrupp *m* → **Sprengkommando**

Sprengung *f* **1.** *mit Sprengstoff*: blasting; *in die Luft*: blowing up; *von Tür*: bursting (*od.* forcing) open; *von Fesseln*: bursting, breaking; **2.** *e-r Versammlung*: breaking-up, dispersal; **3.** (*Bespritzen*) sprinkling, spraying; *von Pflanzen*: watering

Spreng|wagen *m* sprinkler truck, street sprinkler; ~**wirkung** *f* explosive effect

Sprenkel *m*; *-s, -* spot, speck(le); **sprenkeln** *v/t.* spot, speck(le); → **gesprenkelt**

Spreu *f*; *-, kein Pl.* chaff; **die** ~ **vom Weizen trennen** *auch fig.* separate the wheat from the chaff

spricht *Präs.* → **sprechen**

Sprichwort *n*; *-(e)s, Sprichwörter* proverb, (proverbial) saying; **wie das** ~ **sagt** as the saying goes; **sprichwörtlich** *Adj.* proverbial (*auch fig.*); ~**e Redensart** proverbial saying; **sein Geiz ist schon** ~ *auch* he's got a real reputation for being mean; **das war die** ~**e Katze im Sack** it was (a case of) the proverbial pig in a poke

sprießen *v/i.*; *sprießt, spross, ist gesprossen* shoot (up), come up; (*keimen*) germinate, sprout; *fig. Liebe etc.*: awaken, burgeon *lit.*; **ihm sprießt der Bart** his beard is beginning to grow

Spriet *n*; *-(e)s, -e*; *Naut.* sprit

Spring|bock *m* *Zool.* springbok; ~**brunnen** *m* fountain

springen; *springt, sprang, ist od. hat gesprungen* **I.** *v/i.* (*ist*) **1.** jump (*auch Reitsport, Skisport etc.*); *weit*: leap; *hüpfend*: hop, skip; *Raubtier, beim Fang*: pounce; *Stabhochsprung*: vault; *Schwimmsport*: dive; *Brettspiel*: jump; *vom Pferd* ~ jump (*od.* leap) off one's horse; **zur Seite** ~ jump out of the way; **j-m an den Hals** ~ go for s.o. (*od.* s.o.'s throat); **2.** *Ball etc.*: bounce; **aus den Gleisen** ~ jump the rails; **die Ampel sprang auf Gelb** the traffic light(s) suddenly changed to amber (*Am.* yellow); **3.** *Wasser, Blut*: spurt; **4.** *bes. südd. umg.* (*rennen*) run, dash; **spring mal geschwind zum Bäcker!** could you dash (*Brit. auch* nip) down to the baker's (*Am.* bakery)?; **5.** (*eilfertig zu Diensten sein*) jump to one's feet; **andere für sich** ~ **lassen** get other people to wait on one (*od.* run one's errands); **sie braucht nur zu winken, dann springt er schon** she only has to bend her little finger and he jumps to attention; **6.** (*für j-n einspringen*) act as stand-in; ***ich musste ~, weil er im Urlaub ist*** I had to stand in (*od.* take over) because he's on holiday (*Am.* vacation); **7.** (*zer~*) crack; *Saite*: break; ***in tausend Stücke ~*** be smashed to smithereens; ***die Tasse ist gesprungen*** the cup is cracked; **8.** (*Gedankensprünge machen*) jump (about *od.* around); **9.** *umg. fig.*: **~ lassen** (*Geld*) fork out, cough up; ***etwas ~ lassen*** be generous; ***etw. für j-n ~ lassen*** treat s.o. to s.th.; **II.** *v/t.* (*hat od. ist*) (*Weite*) jump; ***e-n Rekord ~*** make a record jump; ***e-n Salto ~*** do (*od.* turn) a somersault; → ***Auge*** 2, ***gesprungen***, ***Klinge***, ***Punkt*** 6

Springen *n*; *-s*, *kein Pl.* jumping; (*Stabhochsprung*) pole-vaulting; *Schwimmsport*: diving; (*Fallschirmspringen*) (parachute) jumping

Springer *m*; *-s*, *-* **1.** *Sport* jumper; *Schwimmsport*: diver; (*Fallschirmspringer*) parachutist; **2.** *Schach*: knight; **3.** *in e-r Firma*: stand-in; **Springerin** *f*; *-*, *-nen* → **Springer** 1,3

Springerstiefel *m* parachutist's boot

Spring|flut *f* spring tide; **~form** *f* (*Kuchenform*) springform; **~insfeld** *m* harum-scarum; **~kraut** *n Bot.* touch-me-not

springlebendig *Adj. umg. präd.* full of beans; *im Alter*: very sprightly

Spring|maus *f* jerboa; **~messer** *n* flick knife, *Am.* switchblade; **~reiten** *n* show jumping; **~reiter** *m*, **~reiterin** *f* show jumper; **~rollo** *n* roller blind, *Am. auch* window shade; **~seil** *n* skipping rope; **~tide** *f* spring tide; **~turnier** *n* show-jumping event

Sprinkler *m*; *-s*, *-* sprinkler; **~anlage** *f* sprinkler system

Sprint *m*; *-s*, *-s*, **sprinten** *v/i. Sport* sprint, *Am. mst* dash; **Sprinter** *m*; *-s*, *-*, **Sprinterin** *f*; *-*, *-nen* sprinter

Sprint|staffel *f Sport* sprint relay team; **~strecke** *f* sprint distance

Sprit *m*; *-s*, *kein Pl.* **1.** *umg.* (*Benzin*) juice, *bes. Am.* gas; **~ tanken** fill up with petrol (*Am.* gas); **2.** *umg.* (*Schnaps*) shorts *Pl.*; **3.** *fachspr.* (*Äthylalkohol*) ethyl alcohol, ethanol; **~preis** *m umg.* price of petrol (*Am.* gas); **~verbrauch** *m* petrol (*Am.* gas) consumption

Spritz|apparat *m* spray(er); (*Spritzpistole*) spray gun; **~besteck** *n Med.* (set of) instruments *Pl.* for giving injections; *für Drogen*: needles *Pl.*; **~beton** *m* gun(ned) concrete; **~beutel** *m* piping bag; **~bild** *n* **1.** *Kunst* spray painting; **2.** *Tech.*, *von Spritzpistole*: spray pattern; **~düse** *f* spray nozzle

Spritze *f*; *-*, *-n* **1.** (*Handspritze*) syringe (*auch Med.*); *Med.* (*Einspritzung*) injection, shot *umg.*, *Brit. auch* jab *umg.*; ***e-e ~ bekommen*** get (*od.* have, be given) an injection (*od.* a shot *umg.*); ***sich*** (*Dat.*) ***e-e ~ setzen*** shoot up *Sl.*; ***an der ~ hängen*** *Sl.* be on the needle; **2.** (*Feuerspritze*) hose; **3.** *umg.* (*Maschinenpistole*) sub(-)machine gun; **4.** *umg. fig.* (*Geld*) shot in the arm, cash injection

...spritze *f*, *im Subst.* **1.** *Med.*: ***Betäubungs~*** an(a)esthetic injection; **2.** (*Gerät*): ***Blumen~*** flower spray; ***Garnier~*** piping syringe (*for cake decoration*)

spritzen I. *v/t.* (*hat gespritzt*) **1.** (*e-e Flüssigkeit*) squirt; (*größere Menge*) spray (*auch Parfüm, Pflanzenschutzmittel, Farbe*); **nass ~** spray (with water); *ungewollt: auch* make wet; ***sich*** (*Dat.*) ***etw. aufs Hemd ~*** spatter (*od.*

splash, spray) s.th. on one's shirt, spatter *etc.* one's shirt with s.th.; ***Sahne / j-s Namen auf e-e Torte ~*** pipe cream / s.o.'s name on a cake; **2.** (*sprengen*) spray, sprinkle (***mit*** with); (*Garten, Pflanzen mit Wasser*) water; **3.** *Med.* (*Mittel*) inject; (*Person*) *auch* give *s.o.* an injection (*od.* shot *umg.*); (*Rauschgift*) *Sl.* shoot (up), mainline; **sich ~** give o.s. an injection, inject o.s.; ***sich lassen*** go for (*od.* have, get) an injection (*od.* shot *umg.*); **4.** (*Getränk*) mix with (soda) water; → **gespritzt**, **Gespritzte**; **5.** (*lackieren*) (*Auto etc.*) spray; **6.** *Tech.* (*Metall*) die-cast; (*Plastik*) inject; **II.** *v/i.* **1.** (*hat*) *Wasser etc.*: splash, spray; *Blut*: spurt; *stärker*: gush; *heißes Fett*: spray; ***Achtung, es spritzt!*** watch out, it's spraying (*od.* splashing) all over the place; **2.** (*ist*) ***auf etw. ~*** splash onto s.th.; **3.** (*hat*) *Med.* give (*s.o.*) an injection (*od.* shot *umg.*); *umg.* (*Rauschgift ~*) *Sl.* shoot up, mainline; ***er ist zuckerkrank und muss täglich ~*** he's (a) diabetic and has to have a daily injection (*od.* shot *umg.*); **4.** (*ist*) *umg.* (*eilen*) zoom, *Brit. auch* nip (***nach, zu*** [a]round to)

Spritzen|automat *m* machine providing sterile needles for drug addicts; **~tausch** *m* needle-sharing; **~wagen** *m* fire engine, *Am.* fire truck

Spritzer *m*; *-s*, *-* **1.** splash, drop; (*Schuss*) dash; ***ein paar ~ Spülmittel*** a couple of squirts of washing-up (*Am.* dishwashing) liquid; **2.** *Parfüm etc.*: spray; **3.** *von Schmutz etc.*: splash; ***voller ~ sein*** be spattered; (*Farbspritzer*) be spattered with paint

Spritz|fahrt *f* → **Spritztour**, **~flasche** *f* spray bottle; **~gebäck** *n Gastr.* shortbread biscuits (*Am.* cookies) *Pl.* (*in fancy shapes*); **~gerät** *n* spray(er); (*Spritzpistole*) spray gun; **~guss** *m* *Tech.*, *Metall*: die-casting; *Kunststoff*: injection mo(u)lding

spritzig *Adj.* **1.** *Wein*: crisp, tangy; **2.** (*schwungvoll*) *Dialog, Theaterstück etc.*: sparkling, scintillating, zippy *umg.*; (*witzig*) witty; **3.** *Sport, Spiel*: zippy *umg.*; *Stürmer, Kreisläufer etc.*: sharp; **4.** *Auto*: zippy *umg.*, *Brit. umg. auch* nippy; **Spritzigkeit** *f* **1.** *von Wein*: crispness, tanginess; **2.** (*Schwung*) sparkle, zip *umg.*; (*Witzigkeit*) wittiness; **3.** *Sport* liveliness; **4.** *e-s Autos*: liveliness, zip *umg.*

Spritz|kuchen *m Gastr.* cruller; **~lack** *m* spray paint; **~mittel** *n* spray; **~pistole** *f* spray gun; **~tour** *f umg.*: (*e-e*) **~** (**machen**) (go for a) spin (*od.* jaunt [through the countryside])

spröde *Adj.* **1.** brittle (*auch Fingernägel, Haare*); *Haut*: rough, chapped; *Stimme*: harsh, grating; **2.** (*abweisend*) aloof, stand-offish; *Mädchen*: demure; ***~r Charme*** diffident charm; ***sie ist e-e ~ Schönheit*** she has an austere beauty; **Sprödheit** *f* **1.** brittleness; *von Haut*: roughness; *von Stimme*: harshness; **2.** *von Mensch*: aloofness; *e-s Mädchens*: demureness

spross *Imperf.* → **sprießen**

Spross *m*; *-es*, *-e od. -en* **1.** *Bot.* shoot; **2.** *nur Sg.*; *geh.* (*Nachkomme*) offspring, *lit.* scion; ***der letzte ~ des Geschlechts*** the last of the line; ***das ist unser jüngster ~*** *hum.* he's our youngest; (*Kleinkind*) he's the latest addition

Sprosse *f*; *-*, *-n* **1.** *e-r Leiter*: rung (*auch fig.*); *am Fenster*: glazing bar, *Am.* muntin, sash bar; **2.** *des Geweihs*:

tine

sprossen *Imperf.* → **sprießen**

Sprossen *Pl. Gastr.* beansprouts, *Am. auch* sprouts

Sprossen|fenster *n* window with glazing bars (*Am.* muntins); **~kohl** *m* österr. Brussels sprouts *Pl.*; **~leiter** *f* ladder; **~wand** *f Turnen*: wall bars *Pl.*

Sprössling *m*; *-s*, *-e*; *umg.* offspring, *Brit. hum. auch* (*Kleinkind*) sprog; (*Sohn*) *auch* junior; → *auch* **Spross** 2

Sprotte *f*; *-*, *-n*; *Zool.* sprat

Spruch *m*; *-(e)s*, *Sprüche* **1.** saying; (*Lehrspruch*) dictum; (*Weisheit*) *auch* aphorism, maxim; (*Sinnspruch*) epigram; (*Bibelstelle*) *auch* quotation; (*Wahlspruch, Losung*) slogan; (**große**) ***Sprüche machen*, *klopfen** *umg.* talk big, shoot one's mouth off; (***das sind*) *alles Sprüche!*** *umg.* it's all talk, it's just hot air; **2.** (*Schiedsspruch*) ruling; *Jur.* (*Urteil*) judg(e)ment; *in Strafsachen*: sentence; *der Geschworenen*: verdict; → **Salomo**

...spruch *m*, *im Subst.*: ***Grab~*** epitaph, gravestone inscription; ***Kalender~*** calendar motto

Spruch|band *n Pl. -bänder* banner; *Archit.* banderole; **~dichtung** *f Lit.* (medieval) aphoristic poetry

Sprüche|klopfer *m*, **~macher** *m* *umg.* big talker

Sprüchlein *n umg.*: ***sein ~ hersagen*** say one's little piece (*od.* party piece), rattle off the usual spiel

spruchreif *Adj.*: ***die Sache ist noch nicht ~*** it's not official (*od.* for general consumption) yet

Spruchweisheit *f* wise aphorism

Sprudel *m*; *-s*, *-*; (*auch saurer ~*) (sparkling) mineral water; *gesüßt*: fizzy (*Am.* carbonated) (soft) drink; ***süßer ~ mit Zitronengeschmack*** (sweet) lemonade

sprudeln *v/i.* **1.** (*hat gesprudelt*) *Quelle etc.*: bubble; (*kochen*) bubble (away); *Getränk*: fizz, be fizzy; ***~ vor*** *fig. Begeisterung etc.* bubble (over) with; **2.** (*ist*) *Wasser, aus der Erde etc.*: bubble up (***aus*** out of, from); *stärker*: gush (out of); ***aus der Flasche ~*** fizz (*stärker*: spurt) out of the bottle; **sprudelnd I.** *Part. Präs.* → **sprudeln**; **II.** *Adj. Quelle*: bubbling; *Getränk*: sparkling, fizzy; *fig.* effervescent; ***ein ~es Temperament*** a bubbly (*od.* an exuberant, ebullient) temperament; **III.** *Adv.*: ***heißes Wasser*** water on a rolling boil

Sprühdose *f* spray can, aerosol (can)

sprühen I. *v/t.* (*hat gesprüht*) spray; (*besprengen*) sprinkle; **II.** *v/i.* **1.** (*hat*) spray; *fig. Augen*: flash (***vor + Dat.*** with); ***vor Ideen ~*** *fig.* be bubbling over with ideas; ***vor Temperament ~*** be a live wire *umg.*; *bes. Sport* be a bundle of energy; ***von Geist ~*** sparkle with wit; **2.** (*hat*) ***es sprüht*** (*nieselt*) it's drizzling; **3.** (*ist*) *Funken*: fly; **sprühend I.** *Part. Präs.* → **sprühen**; **II.** *Adj.* **1.** **~e** *Gischt* spray, foam; **2.** *Laune, Temperament*: bubbly, sparkling; *Witz etc.*: sparkling

Sprüh|flasche *f* spray bottle; **~nebel** *m* (Scotch) mist; **~regen** *m* fine drizzle

Sprung *m*; *-(e)s*, *Sprünge* **1.** jump (*auch Sport und EDV*); (*großer ~*) *auch* leap; *Turnen, über Pferd, Stabhochsprung*: vault; *Schwimmsport*: dive; ***zum ~ ansetzen*** prepare to jump, gather oneself for a jump; ***ein weiter ~*** a long (*od.* big) jump; **2.** *umg.* (*kurze*

Entfernung) **es ist nur ein ~ bis dorthin** it's only a stone's throw from here, it's just down the road (*od.* [a]round the corner); **bedingter ~** *EDV* conditional branch (*od.* jump); **3.** *fig.*: **~ ins Ungewisse** *od.* **kalte Wasser** leap in the dark; **ein großer ~ nach vorn sein** *Entwurf etc.*: be a great advance (**gegenüber** on); **e-n ~ machen** take a leap; **den ~ wagen** take the plunge; **damit kann er keine großen Sprünge machen** he won't be able to do much on that; **4.** *fig.*: **auf dem ~ sein, etw. zu tun** be about to do s.th., be on the point of doing s.th.; **auf e-n ~ vorbeikommen** *umg.* drop in (**bei** on), pop [a]round (and see *s.o.*); **sie ist immer auf dem ~** *umg.* she's always on the go (*od.* hop); **5.** *umg. fig.*: **j-m auf die Sprünge kommen** find s.o. out, get wise to s.o.('s tricks *od.* game); **j-m auf die Sprünge helfen** help s.o. along; *beruflich etc.: auch* give s.o. a leg up (*Am.* a boost); **j-s Gedächtnis auf die Sprünge helfen** jog s.o.'s memory; **6.** (*Riss*) crack; (*Materialfehler, auch im Edelstein*) flaw; **e-n ~ haben** be cracked (*od.* flawed); **e-n ~ in der Schüssel haben** *umg. fig.* not be quite all there

...sprung *m, im Subst.* **1.** *im wörtl. Sinn:* **Start~** *Schwimmsport:* opening dive; **Todes~** death leap; **Sechsmeter~** six-met|re (*Am.* -er) jump; **2.** *fig.:* **Entwicklungs~** leap forward in development; **Leistungs~** sudden big increase in performance

Sprung|becken *n* diving pool; **~bein** *n* **1.** *Anat.* ankle-bone; **2.** *Sport* takeoff leg

sprungbereit *Adj. und Adv.* ready to jump; *umg. zum Weggehen:* all set to go

Sprung|brett *n* **1.** *Turnen, Schwimmsport:* springboard; *Schwimmsport: mst* diving board; **2.** *fig.* springboard (**für** for); (*Ausgangspunkt*) starting point; **~deckel** *m* spring lid; *e-r Uhr:* watch cap

Sprungfeder *f* (coil) spring; **~matratze** *f* spring mattress

Sprung|gelenk *n* ankle joint; *Pferd etc.:* hock; **~grube** *f Sport* pit

sprunghaft I. *Adj.* **1.** *Mensch:* erratic; *Wirts.* erratic, spasmodic; *Denken:* disjointed; **2.** (*abrupt*) sudden; (*rapide*) rapid; **~er Anstieg** sharp rise (*od.* increase), jump (**der Preise** *etc.* in prices *etc.*); **II.** *Adv. steigen etc.:* by leaps and bounds; → *auch* **sprungweise**; **Sprunghaftigkeit** *f* **1.** erratic nature; *des Denkens:* disjointedness; **2.** (*Abruptheit*) suddenness; (*Rapidheit*) rapidity

Sprung|kraft *f Sport* takeoff power; **~pferd** *n Turnen:* vaulting horse; **~schanze** *f Sport* ski jump, ski jumping hill; **~seil** *n* skipping (*Am.* jump) rope; **~stab** *m Sport* vaulting pole; **~technik** *f Sport* jumping technique; *Schwimmsport:* diving technique; **~tuch** *n Feuerwehr:* jumping (*od.* safety) sheet; **~turm** *m Sport* diving platform

sprungweise *Adv.* in jumps; *fig.* by leaps and bounds; (*unregelmäßig*) in (*od.* by) fits and starts

Sprungweite *f Sport* jumping distance

SPS *f;* -, *kein Pl.;* *Abk.* (**Sozialdemokratische Partei der Schweiz**) Swiss Social Democratic Party

Spucke *f;* -, *kein Pl.;* *umg.* spittle, spit; **da blieb mir die ~ weg** I just gulped,

my jaw dropped

spucken I. *v/t.* spit (out); (*Blut etc.*) spit, cough up; *Vulkan:* (*Lava*) spew (out); (*Feuer*) belch; **große Töne ~** *umg. fig.* talk big, shoot one's mouth off; **II.** *v/i.* **1.** spit; **~ nach** spit at; **j-m ins Gesicht ~** spit in s.o.'s face; **in die Hände ~** *fig.* roll up one's sleeves; **j-m in die Suppe ~** *umg. fig.* put a spoke in s.o.'s wheel; **2.** *umg.* (*sich erbrechen*) throw up, *Brit. auch* be sick; **ich muss ~** I'm going to be sick; **3.** *umg. Motor:* splutter; → **Gift** 2

Spuck|napf *m* spittoon, *Am. auch* cuspidor; **~tüte** *f* sick bag

Spuk *m;* -(e)s, *kein Pl.* **1.** (*gespenstisches Treiben*) haunting, ghostly happenings *Pl.;* **nächtlicher ~** things that go bump in the night; **2.** (*Geistererscheinung*) apparition, spect|re (*Am.* -er); **3.** *fig.* (*schreckliches Geschehen*) nightmare; **es erschien wie ein ~** it all seemed like a bad dream; **dem ganzen ~ ein Ende machen** put an end to the whole ghastly business

spuken *v/i. unpers.* **1.** **es spukt** (**in dem Haus** *etc.*) the house *etc.* is haunted; **durch das Schloss** *etc.* **~** haunt (*od.* walk) the castle *etc.;* **2.** *fig.:* **die Idee spukt bei ihm im Kopf** he's obsessed with the idea; **der Gedanke spukt noch immer in den Köpfen** people still believe in it, the idea still hasn't been laid to rest; **bei dir spukt's wohl!** *umg.* you must be off your rocker

Spuk|erscheinung *f* apparition; **~geschichte** *f* ghost story

spukhaft *Adj.* ghostly; *Ort, Atmosphäre:* eerie

Spukschloss *n* haunted castle

Spül|automat *m* dishwasher; **~becken** *n* sink; *beim Zahnarzt:* basin; **~bürste** *f* washing-up (*Am.* dishwashing) brush

Spule *f;* -, *-n* **1.** spool, reel; *der Nähmaschine etc.:* bobbin; **2.** *Etech.* coil

Spüle *f;* -, *-n* **1.** sink unit; **2.** *umg.* (*Spülmaschine*) dishwasher

spulen *v/t.* spool, reel (**auf** +Akk. onto)

spülen I. *v/t./i.* rinse; (*Toilette*) flush; *Med.* (*Wunde, Hohlorgan*) *auch* irrigate; (*Scheide*) douche; *Tech.* (*Motor etc.*) flush; (*Geschirr*) **~** wash (*od.* do) the dishes, *Brit. auch* wash up, do the washing up; **die Waschmaschine spült gerade** the washing machine is on rinse at the moment; **bitte** (**gut**) **~!** *beim Zahnarzt:* have a (good) rinse, rinse out (well); **II.** *v/t.:* **an Land ~** wash ashore, wash up; **III.** *v/i. Toilette:* flush; *mit Kette: auch* pull the chain

Spulen(tonband)gerät *n* open-reel (*Am.* reel-to-reel) tape recorder

Spüler *m;* -s, -, **~in** *f;* -, -nen (*Person*) dishwasher, *Brit. auch* washer-up (-upper *umg.*)

Spülgang *m* rinse (cycle)

Spül|kasten *m* cistern; **~klosett** *n* water closet; (*Geschirr*) **~lappen** *m* dishcloth, *Brit. auch* washing-up cloth

Spülmaschine *f* dishwasher; **spülmaschinenfest** *Adj.* dishwasher-safe

Spül|mittel *n* washing-up liquid, *Am.* dishwashing detergent (*od.* liquid); **~programm** *n Waschmaschine:* rinse cycle; *Spülmaschine:* wash program(me); **~schüssel** *f* washing-up (*Am.* dishwashing) basin; **~tuch** *n* dishcloth

Spülung *f* **1.** rinse (*auch Mundspülung*); *Med., e-r Wunde, e-s Hohlorgans:* irrigation; (*Haarspülmittel*) conditioner; *der Scheide:* douche; *Tech.,*

Mot. flushing; *Toilette:* flush; **2.** (*Spülkasten*) cistern, *Am. auch* tank

Spülwasser *n* rinsing water; *für Geschirr:* washing-up (*Am.* dishwashing) water; *schmutziges:* dishwater (*auch fig. pej.*)

Spulwurm *m* roundworm

Spund *m;* -(e)s, *Spünde und* -e **1.** *Pl. Spünde; e-s Fasses:* bung; *Tischlerei:* tongue; **2.** *Pl.* -e; *umg.:* **junger ~** (young) whippersnapper; **~hahn** *m* (wooden) tap; **~loch** *n* bunghole; **~wand** *f* sheet pile wall

Spur *f;* -, -en **1.** *im Sand, Schnee etc.:* track(s *Pl.*); (*Schneckenspur, Blutspur, Leuchtspur, Fährte*) trail; *Jagd: auch* scent; (*Bremsspur*) skidmark; **e-e ~ aufnehmen** pick up a trail; **keine ~ hinterlassen** leave no trace; *Verbrecher:* leave no clues (*od.* evidence); **vom Täter fehlt jede ~** there are no clues as to who did it; **immer noch keine ~ von der Vermissten** there is still no trace (*od.* sign) of the missing woman (*od.* girl); **die ~ führt nach ...** the trail leads (*od.* takes us) to ...; **j-m auf die ~ kommen** get onto s.o.'s trail (*od.* track); **e-r Sache auf die ~ kommen** get onto s.th.; (*finden*) track s.th. down; **auf der falschen ~ sein** be on the wrong track; **j-n auf die richtige ~ bringen** put s.o. on the right track; **auf j-s ~ wandeln** follow in s.o.'s tracks; **2.** (*Fahrspur*) lane; (*Schienen*) track(s *Pl.*); (*e-r Loipe*) track; **linke/rechte ~** *Mot.* left-hand/right-hand lane; **die ~ halten** keep in lane; **die ~ wechseln** switch lanes; **in der ~ sein / aus der ~ gehen** *Langlauf:* be in / leave the track(s); **3.** (*Spurweite*) *Eisenb.* ga(u)ge; *Mot.* track; **4.** *des Tonbands, EDV:* track; **5.** (*Fahrtlinie*) **~ halten** stay on (*od.* keep to) its line; **aus der ~ geraten/ausbrechen** swerve off course; **6.** (*Rest, kleine Menge*) trace; *Gastr.* touch; **e-e ~ zu stark/süß** a touch (*od.* shade) too strong/sweet; **nicht die leiseste ~ e-s Zweifels/Verdachts haben** have not the slightest shadow of a doubt/suspicion; **keine ~ von Anständigkeit** *etc.* not a scrap of decency *etc.;* **keine ~!** *umg.* not at all!, no way!; **7.** (*Anzeichen*) trace, sign; *Pl.* (*Überreste*) remains; **~en des Krieges** traces left behind by the war, scars (*od.* marks) of war; **~en des Alters** signs of old age; *s-e* **~en hinterlassen** *Trauma etc.:* leave its marks; → **heiß** I 1

...spur *f, im Subst.* **1.** **Fuchs~** fox's scent; **Reifen~** tyre mark, *Am.* tire track; **Öl~** trail of oil; **2.** **Langlauf~** cross-country ski track; **3.** **Mittel~** cent|re (*Am.* -er) lane

spürbar I. *Adj.* noticeable, perceptible; (*deutlich*) marked, distinct; (*beträchtlich*) considerable; (*greifbar*) tangible; **~ werden** *auch* make itself felt; **es gab e-e ~e Erleichterung** you could feel (*od.* sense) the relief; **II.** *Adv.* noticeably; (*beträchtlich*) considerably

Spurbreite *f* → **Spurweite**

spuren I. *v/t./i. Skisport:* lay a track; **e-e Loipe ~** lay a track to mark a trail; **alle Loipen sind gespurt** all the trails have tracks; **II.** *v/i. umg.* (*sich fügen*) toe the line

spüren *v/t.* **1.** *bes. körperlich:* feel; **ich hab nichts gespürt** *bei e-r Spritze etc.:* I didn't feel a thing; **jetzt spüre ich den Wein** I'm beginning to feel the effect(s) of the wine, the wine's beginning to take effect; **ich spüre mein Al-**

ter I can tell I'm getting old, old age is creeping up on me *umg.*; *ich spüre sämtliche Knochen* I feel as if every single bone in my body is aching; *ich spür's wieder im Rücken* od. *spür wieder m-n Rücken umg.* my back's playing (me) up again; **2.** (*empfinden*) feel; *intuitiv: auch* sense; (*merken*) notice; *ich spürte Scham* I felt a sense of shame; *etw. zu ~ bekommen* find out what s.th. is like; (*j-s Zorn etc.*) get a taste of s.th.; *ich habe ihn m-e Enttäuschung schon ~ lassen* I made no attempt to hide my disappointment from him; *du wirst es noch zu ~ bekommen* (*die Folgen d-s Handelns*) it'll all come back on you; *ich hab's am eigenen Leib gespürt* I went through it all myself, I experienced it (at) firsthand; *es war deutlich zu ~* it was obvious; *von Hass etc. war nichts zu ~* there was no sign (*od.* trace) of hatred *etc.*

Spuren|element *n* trace element; **~sicherung** *f* **1.** securing of evidence; **2.** (*Abteilung*) forensic squad; **~suche** *f* search for clues (*od.* evidence)

Spürhund *m* **1.** tracker dog, sniffer dog; **2.** *fig.* (*Schnüffler*) sleuth

spurlos *Adv.* without (leaving a) trace; *~ verschwinden* vanish into thin air, disappear without trace; *es ist nicht ~ an ihm vorübergegangen* it's left its mark (on him)

Spür|nase *f umg.* **1.** (good) nose (*auch fig.*); **2.** (*Person*) snooper; **~panzer** *m Mil.* NBC (= *nuclear, biological and chemical*) reconnaissance system

Spurrillen *Pl. Verk.* ruts *in the road surface caused by heavy traffic*

Spürsinn *m; nur Sg.* **1.** *e-s Tiers:* sense of smell; **2.** *fig.* nose, instinct

Spurt *m; -(e)s, -s; Sport* sprint, spurt, (quick) burst; *e-n ~ einlegen* put on a spurt; **spurten** *v/i.* **1.** sprint; *die letzten 50 Meter ~* put on a spurt for the last 50 met|res (*Am.* -ers), do a 50 met|re (*Am.* -er) sprint finish; **2.** *umg.* (*schnell laufen*) sprint; *ich bin ganz schön gespurtet* I really had to step on it, you should have seen me run; **spurtschnell** *Adj. Läufer:* capable of a strong spurt; *Auto:* with good acceleration, very lively; **spurtstark** *Adj.* → *spurtschnell*

Spur|wechsel *m Mot.* changing lanes; **~weite** *f Eisenb.* ga(u)ge; *Mot. e-s Autos:* track

sputen *v/refl. altm. od. hum.* make haste

Squash [skvɔʃ] *n; -, kein Pl.* squash; **~center** *n* squash cent|re (*Am.* -er), squash courts *Pl.*; **~halle** *f* squash courts *Pl.*; **~schläger** *m* squash racket; **~spiel** *n* game of squash; **~spieler** *m,* **~spielerin** *f* squash player

SR *m; -s, kein Pl.; Abk.* (*Saarländischer Rundfunk*) Saarland Radio

SRG *f; -, kein Pl. Abk.* (*Schweizerische Radio- und Fernsehgesellschaft*) Swiss Radio and Television Company

Sri Lanka (*n*); *-s; Geog.* Sri Lanka; **Srilanker** *m; -s, -,* **Srilankerin** *f; -, -nen* Sri Lankan, *weiblich auch:* Sri Lankan woman (*od.* girl); **srilankisch** *Adj.* Sri Lankan

SS¹ *Abk.* → *Sommersemester*

SS² *f; -, kein Pl. Abk. hist.* SS, *elite corps of the Nazi party;* **~-Mann** *m* (*Pl.* SS-Männer) member of the SS

SSO *m; -(e)s, kein Pl. Abk.* (*Südsüdost*) SSE

SSV *Abk.* → *Sommerschlussverkauf*

SSW *m; -(e)s, kein Pl.; Abk.* (*Südsüdwest*) SSW

st [st] *Interj.* pst!; (*Ruhe!*) ssh!

St. *Abk.* **1.** *n* → *Stück;* **2.** *m undekl.* (*Sankt*) St, *Am.* St.

s.t. *Abk.* (*sine tempore*): *18 Uhr ~* 6 pm sharp; → *auch c.t.*

Staat¹ *m; -(e)s, -en* **1.** state; (*Land, Nation*) *auch* country, nation; *~ im ~* state within a state; *von ~s wegen* by government decree; *beim ~ arbeiten* be employed by the government, be a civil servant; *die Vereinigten ~en* the United States; *die zwei deutschen ~en hist.* the two Germanies; **2.** *Zool., der Ameisen, Bienen:* colony

Staat² *m; -(e)s, kein Pl.*; (*Pracht*) pomp, splendo(u)r; (*beste Kleidung*) finery; *großen ~ machen bei Empfängen etc.*: roll out the red carpet; *bei Kleidung:* dress up in one's best, put on all one's finery; *damit kannst du keinen ~ machen umg.* that's nothing to write home about

...staat *m, in Subst.: Feudal~* feudal state; *Unrechts~* state without justice

Staaten|bund *m Pol.* confederacy, confederation (of states); **~bündnis** *n* alliance (of states); **~gemeinschaft** *f* community of states

staatenlos *Adj.* stateless; **Staatenlose** *m, f; -n, -n* stateless person; **Staatenlosigkeit** *f* statelessness

staatlich I. *Adj. attr.* state...; *Maßnahmen, Vorschriften, Subventionen etc.*: government ...; (*staatseigen*) *Industrie etc.*: nationalized, state-owned; *Unternehmen:* public; **~e Mittel** government funds, public money; **II.** *Adv.:* **~ anerkannt** officially recognized (*od.* approved); **~ gefördert** state-sponsored; **~ gelenkt** *od.* **geleitet** state-control(l)ed, state-run; **~ geprüft** (*abgek. staatl. gepr.*) state-certified; **staatlicherseits** *Adv.* on the part of the state

Staats|affäre *f* affair of state; *e-e ~ aus etw. machen umg. fig.* make a big thing (*od.* affair) (*Am.* a federal case) (out) of s.th.; **~akt** *m* **1.** act of state; **2.** (*Feier*) state occasion (*od.* ceremony); **~aktion** *f* → *Staatsaffäre;* **~amt** *n* office of state, public office; **~angehörige** *m, f* citizen, national; *britischer ~r auch* a British subject; **~angehörigkeit** *f*: (*doppelte ~* dual) nationality, citizenship; *er hat die französische ~* he has French nationality (*od.* citizenship); **~angelegenheit** *f* affair of state; **~anleihe** *f* government loan; (*Wertpapier*) government bond (*Pl. auch* securities, stocks)

Staatsanwalt *m,* **Staatsanwältin** *f Jur.* public prosecutor, *Am. mst* district attorney (*Abk.* D.A.); **staatsanwaltlich** *Adj.* public prosecutor's ..., *Am.* district attorney's ...; **Staatsanwaltschaft** *f* **1.** public prosecutor's office, *Am. mst* district attorney's office; **2.** (*Anwälte*) (body of) public prosecutors *Pl.*

Staats|apparat *m* state machinery; **~archiv** *n* state archives *Pl.*; *in GB:* Public Record Office; *in USA:* National Archives, (*in den einzelnen Staaten*) Bureau of Vital Statistics; **~ausgaben** *Pl.* public expenditure *Sg.*, government spending *Sg.*; **~bahn** *f* state railway (*Am.* railroad); **~bank** *f* state (*od.* national) bank; **~bankett** *n* state (*od.* official) banquet; **~bankrott** *m* national bankruptcy; **~beamte** *m,* **~beamtin** *f* civil servant; **~begräbnis**

n state funeral; **~besitz** *m* state property; *als Recht:* state ownership; *in ~* state-owned; **~besuch** *m* state visit; **~betrieb** *m* state-owned enterprise; **~bibliothek** *f* national (*od.* state) library; **~bürger** *m,* **~bürgerin** *f* citizen

Staatsbürger|kunde *f* civics *Pl.* (*V. im Sg.*); civic studies *Pl.*; **~rechte** *Pl.* civil rights

Staatsbürgerschaft *f* → *Staatsangehörigkeit*

Staats|bürgschaft *f* government guarantee (*on a loan*); **~chef** *m,* **~chefin** *f* head of state; **~diener** *m,* **~dienerin** *f* civil servant; *hum.* servant of the state; **~dienst** *m* civil (*od.* public) service; *im ~ sein* be a civil servant

staatseigen *Adj.* state-owned; **Staatseigentum** *n* government (*od.* state) property; *als Recht:* public (*od.* state) ownership

Staats|einnahmen *Pl.* public revenue *Sg.*; **~empfang** *m* official reception; **~examen** *n* state examination(s *Pl.*); *sein ~ machen auch* take one's degree; **~farben** *Pl.* national colo(u)rs

Staatsfeind *m* public enemy; **staatsfeindlich** *Adj.* subversive, anti(-)state; **~e Aktivitäten** activities against the state

Staats|finanzen *Pl.* public finances; **~flagge** *f* national flag; **~form** *f* state type (*od.* system); **~gast** *m* (official) guest of the state; **~gebiet** *n* state territory; *sich auf britischem ~ befinden* be on British territory

staatsgefährdend *Adj.* endangering state security, subversive

Staats|gefangene *m, f* prisoner of state, political prisoner; **~gefängnis** *n* state prison; **~geheimnis** *n* state secret; *das ist kein ~ umg. fig.* that's top secret / no great secret; **~gelder** *Pl.* public funds; **~geschäfte** *Pl.* affairs of state; *die ~ führen* conduct the affairs of state, govern the country

Staatsgewalt *f Pol.* **1.** *abstrakt:* state authority; **2.** *Organ:* executive body of the state; *gesetzgebende ~* legislature; *vollziehende ~* executive; *richterliche ~* judiciary

Staats|grenze *f* state frontier (*od.* border); **~gründung** *f* founding of a (*od.* the) state; **~gut** *n* state-owned estate; **~haftung** *f* state (*od.* government) liability; **~haushalt** *m* (national) budget; **~hoheit** *f* sovereignty; **~interesse** *n* interests *Pl.* of the state, public interest; **~kanzlei** *f* state chancellery; **~karosse** *f* state carriage; **~kasse** *f* (public) treasury, public purse; *in GB:* the Exchequer; *in den USA:* the (Federal) Treasury; **~kirche** *f* established (*od.* state) church; **~kosten** *Pl.: auf ~* at (the) public expense; **~lehre** *f* political science; **~macht** *f* state power

Staatsmann *m* statesman; **staatsmännisch I.** *Adj.* statesmanlike; **II.** *Adv. denken, handeln:* in a statesmanlike manner

Staats|minister *m,* **~ministerin** *f* secretary of state, *Am. etwa* secretary of the interior; **~ministerium** *n* ministry, *Am.* department; **~mittel** *Pl.* public funds; **~monopol** *n* state monopoly; **~oberhaupt** *n* head of state; (*Monarch*) sovereign; **~oper** *f* State Opera; **~orchester** *n* State Orchestra; **~ordnung** *f* state system; **~organ** *n* instrument of state; **~papiere** *Pl.* → *Staatsanleihe;* **~partei** *f* (sole) ruling party

staatspolitisch *Adj. attr.* national political ...; **~e Angelegenheiten** matters of state

Staats|polizei f state police; **~präsident** m (state) president; **~prüfung** f state examination(s Pl.); *für Regierungsbeamte:* civil service examination(s Pl.); **~quote** f Pol., Wirts. public sector share in GNP; **~räson** f: *(aus Gründen der)* ~ (for) reasons Pl. of state; **~rat** m **1.** council of state; *in GB:* Privy Council; *schw.* cantonal government; *ehem. DDR:* State Council; **2.,** *auch* **~rätin** f *(Person)* council(-l)or of state; *in GB:* Privy Councillor; *schw.* cantonal government council(-l)or; **~ratsvorsitzende** m, f *ehem. DDR:* Chairman of the State Council; *schw.* president of a (od. the) cantonal government

Staatsrecht n nur Sg.; Pol., Jur. constitutional law; *(öffentliches Recht)* public law; **Staatsrechtler** m, **Staatsrechtlerin** f constitutional law expert; **staatsrechtlich** Adj. und Adv. under (od. relating to) constitutional law, constitutional; *(öffentlich-rechtlich)* under (od. relating to) public law

Staats|regierung f state (od. national) government; **~religion** f state religion; **~säckel** n hum. *(Staatshaushalt)* state coffers Pl.; **~schauspieler** m, **~schauspielerin** f *actor/actress recognized by the state for outstanding ability;* **~schulden** Pl. national (od. public) debt Sg.; **~schützer** m umg. member of the state security service; Pl. auch state security service; **~sekretär** m, **~sekretärin** f etwa Brit. permanent secretary, Am. undersecretary; *parlamentarischer* ~ parliamentary secretary

Staatssicherheit f national (od. state) security; *Ministerium für* ~ ehem. DDR: Ministry of State Security; **Staatssicherheitsdienst** m *(auch hist. DDR)* state security service

Staats|sprache f official (state) language; **~streich** m coup (d'état); **~theater** n state theat|re *(Am.* -er)

staatstragend Adj. representing the state; *Theater, Partei:* establishment ...

Staats|trauer f national mourning; **~trauertag** m national day of mourning; **~unternehmen** n state (od. public) enterprise; **~verbrechen** n political crime; **~verdrossenheit** f disillusionment with politics, political apathy; **~verfassung** f (national) constitution; **~vermögen** n national assets Pl.; **~verschuldung** f national (od. public) debt; **~vertrag** m international treaty; *der Österreichische* ~ the Austrian State Treaty; **~wesen** n state, förm. body politic; **~wissenschaft** f political science; **~wohl** n public welfare; **~zuschuss** m government subsidy (od. grant)

Stab m; -(e)s, **Stäbe 1.** *(Stock)* stick; *(Stange)* rod; *(Gitterstab)* bar; *(Wanderstab)* staff; *(Hirtenstab)* crook; *(Bischofsstab)* crosier, crozier; *(Zauberstab)* wand; *(Staffel-, Dirigenten-, Marschallstab)* baton; *Stabhochsprung:* pole; *den* ~ *führen* Mus. conduct; *den* ~ *über j-n brechen* fig. condemn s.o. (outright); **2.** *(Mitarbeiter)* staff Sg. *(mst V. im Pl.);* *(Krisenstab etc.)* team, squad umg.; **3.** Mil. *(Offiziere)* staff officers Pl.; *(Hauptquartier)* headquarters *(V. im Sg. od. Pl.);* **~antenne** f rod aerial *(Am. auch* antenna)

Stäbchen n **1.** Dim. von Stab; **2.** *(Essstäbchen)* chopstick; **3.** Mikado: jack-

straw; **4.** der Retina: rod; **5.** *(Bazillus)* (rod-shaped) bacillus, rod; **6.** umg. *(Zigarette)* ciggy, smoke

stabförmig Adj. rod-shaped

Stabheuschrecke f Zool. stick insect

Stabhoch|springer m, **~springerin** f Sport pole vaulter; **~sprung** m pole vaulting

stabil I. Adj. **1.** stable *(auch Pol., Wirts. Preise, Währung etc.); (gleich bleibend)* steady; *ihr Kreislauf ist* ~ her circulation has stabilized; **2.** *(fest, robust)* solid, sturdy; *Körperbau:* sturdy, robust; *Konstitution:* strong, robust; *e-e* **~e** *Gesundheit haben* enjoy sound *(stärker:* robust) health; **II.** Adv.: ~ **gebaut** solidly built, solid

Stabilisator m; -s, -en stabilizer; Mot. anti-roll bar, Am. stabilizer bar; **stabilisieren** v/t. und v/refl. stabilize; **Stabilisierung** f stabilization

Stabilisierungs|flosse f Flug., Naut. stabilizer; **~maßnahmen** Pl. stabilization measures; *Wirts.* moves to stabilize the economy *(Pol.* the political situation etc.)

Stabilität f **1.** stability; **2.** der Bauart etc.: solidity, sturdiness; der Konstitution, Gesundheit: soundness, *stärker:* robustness

Stabilitätsfaktor m stabilizing factor

stabilitätsorientiert Adj. based on (od. aimed at) stability

Stabilitäts|pakt m Wirts. stability pact; **~politik** f Pol., Wirts. policy of stability

Stab|kirche f stave church; **~lampe** f (electric) torch, Am. flashlight; **~magnet** n bar magnet; **~reim** m Lit. stave rhyme *(a form of alliteration)*

Stabs|arzt m, **~ärztin** f Mil., Med. medical corps captain, medical officer; **~chef** m Mil. chief of staff; **~feldwebel** m Mil. Brit. warrant officer class II *(Abk.* WO II), Am. master sergeant; **~offizier** m Mil. field *(beim Stab:* staff) officer; **~stelle** f Mil. staff headquarters *(V. im Sg. od. Pl.),* command cent|re *(Am.* -er); fig. in Ministerium, Konzern etc.: nerve cent|re *(Am.* -er)

Stabübergabe f Sport baton change

stach Imperf. → **stechen**

Stachel m; -s, -; Bot. prickle, *(Dorn)* thorn; Zool. spine, *e-s Stachelschweins:* auch quill; *e-s Insekts:* sting; *(Metallspitze)* auch am Cello etc.: spike; *am Sporn:* point; *am Stacheldraht:* barb; fig. *(Schmerzendes)* sting, *(Ansporn)* spur; *j-m ein* ~ *im Fleische sein* be a thorn in s.o.'s flesh *(od.* side); *der* ~ *des Ehrgeizes trieb sie an* she was goaded *(od.* spurred on) by ambition; *e-r Sache den* ~ *nehmen* take the sting out of s.th.; *wider den* ~ *löcken* kick against the pricks

Stachelbeere f gooseberry

Stachelbeerstrauch m Bot. gooseberry bush

Stacheldraht m barbed wire; *hinter* ~ *sitzen* be behind barbed wire; *als Kriegsgefangene(r):* be a prisoner of war; **~verhau** m barbed wire entanglement; **~zaun** m barbed wire fence

Stachel|halsband n spiked collar; **~häuter** m; -s, -; Zool. echinoderm

stachelig Adj. prickly *(auch Bot., fig. Mensch); (borstig)* Bart, Kinn: auch bristly; Zool. spiny; fig. *(boshaft)* Reden etc.: barbed

stacheln I. v/t. *(antreiben)* spur on; *(aufreizen)* goad; **II.** v/i. umg. fig. Bart etc.: be prickly

Stachel|rochen m Zool. stingray; **~schwein** n Zool. porcupine

stachlig Adj. → **stachelig**

Stack [stæk] m; -s, -s; EDV stack

stad Adj. südd., österr. quiet; *sei* ~*!* be quiet!

Stadel m; -s, -, österr. auch -n; Dial. barn

Stadion n; -s, Stadien; Sport stadium; **~besucher** m, **~besucherin** f spectator (in a *[od.* the] stadium); **~sprecher** m, **~sprecherin** f stadium announcer

Stadium n; -s, Stadien stage, phase; *in diesem* ~ in *(od.* during) this phase, at *(od.* during) this stage; *Krebs etc. im frühen/letzten* ~ cancer at an early stage / in its final *(od.* terminal) stage; → **vorgerückt** II

...stadium n, im Subst.: Vorbereitungs**~** preparatory stage *(od.* phase)

Stadt f; -, **Städte 1.** town, Am. amtlich: city; *(Großstadt)* city; *in der* ~ in town; *in e-r bestimmten:* in the town; *in die* ~ *gehen* go into town, Am. auch go downtown; *die* ~ *Köln* the city of Cologne, *die Ewige* ~ the Eternal City; *die Goldene* ~ the Golden City (of Prague); **2.** *(Gemeinde)* municipality; *(Stadtverwaltung)* town council; *e-r Großstadt:* city council; *bei der* ~ *arbeiten* work for the (city) council *(bei Großstadt:* auch corporation); *die* ~ *Köln (Stadtverwaltung)* (the) Cologne City Council

Stadt|ansicht f view of the town *(Großstadt:* city); **~anzeiger** m: Kölner ~ Cologne Advertiser; **~archiv** n municipal archives Pl.

stadtauswärts Adv. out of town

Stadt|auto n town car; **~autobahn** f urban motorway *(Am.* expressway); **~bad** n municipal (swimming) baths Pl. *(Am.* pool Sg.); **~bahn** f metropolitan railway, Am. rapid transit, Am. light rail; **~bauamt** n municipal planning and building control office; **~baumeister** m, **~baumeisterin** f municipal architect; **~baurat** m, **~baurätin** f head of the municipal planning and building control office; **~behörde** n municipal authority

stadtbekannt Adj. known all over town; *ein* **~es** *Original* a well-known local character

Stadt|besichtigung f town *(Großstadt:* city) sightseeing tour; **~bevölkerung** f **1.** urban population; **2.** bestimmte: town's *(od.* city's) inhabitants Pl.; **~bewohner** m, **~bewohnerin** f town *(Großstadt:* city) dweller, urbanite; **~bezirk** m municipal district; *in London und New York:* borough; *in anderen Städten:* ward, district; **~bibliothek** f municipal library, Am. mst public library; **~bild** n townscape; *e-r Großstadt:* cityscape; *das* ~ *hat sich stark verändert* the (appearance of the) town *(od.* city) has changed a lot; **~bücherei** f municipal (lending) library, Am. mst public library; **~bummel** m: *(e-n)* ~ *(machen* go for a) stroll through the town

Städtchen n small town

Stadt|chronik f town *(Großstadt:* city) history; **~direktor** m, **~direktorin** f town clerk, Am. city manager

Städtebau m urban development; *(Planung)* town *(Am.* city) planning; **~förderung** f promotion of urban development

städtebaulich I. Adj. attr. town *(Am. auch* city) planning ...; **~e Planung**

town (*Am. auch* city) planning; ~**e** *Sünden* town (*Am. auch* city) planning disasters; **II.** *Adv.* from a town (*Am. auch* city) planning perspective

Städte|bund *m hist.* league of cities (*od.* towns); ~**führer** *m* city guide

stadt|eigen *Adj. attr.* municipal; ~**einwärts** *Adv.* into town

Stadtentwicklung *f* urban development

Städte|partnerschaft *f auch Pl.* (town) twinning; *zwischen München und Edinburgh besteht e-e* ~ Munich and Edinburgh are twinned; ~**planung** *f* town (*Am. auch* city) planning

Städter *m; -s, -,* ~**in** *f; -, -nen* town (*Großstadt:* city) dweller, urbanite; *vom Standpunkt des Landbewohners:* townie *umg.*

Städte|tag *m* conference of municipal authorities; ~**verbindungen** *Pl. Eisenb.* (*Fahrplan*) inter-city services; ~**vergleich** *m* comparison between cities; *im* ~ *hat München die niedrigste Arbeitslosenrate* (when compared with others,) Munich is the city with the lowest unemployment figures

Stadt|fahrt *f* town trip; *im Auto: auch* drive in (*od.* around) town; *im Taxi:* ride within city limits; *das Auto ist für* ~*en gut geeignet* this car is ideal for town driving (*od.* getting around town); ~**fest** *n* town festival; ~**flitzer** *m Mot. umg.* zippy little town car; ~**flucht** *f* exodus from the cities, flight to the country; *die* ~ *hat zugenommen* more and more people are leaving the cities (and moving to the country)

Stadtführer[1] *m* (*Buch*) town (*e-r Großstadt:* city) guide

Stadtführer[2] *m,* ~**in** *f* town (*in Großstadt:* city) guide

Stadt|führung *f* guided tour of the town (*Großstadt:* city); ~**garten** *m* municipal gardens *Pl.*; ~**gärtnerei** *f* town nursery; ~**gas** *n* town (*Am.* municipal) gas; ~**gebiet** *n* municipal area; ~**gemeinde** *n* municipality; ~**geschichte** *f* town (*e-r Großstadt:* city) history; *die Freiburger* ~ the history of Freiburg; ~**gespräch** *n* **1.** *Telef.* local call; **2.** ~ *sein fig.* be the talk of the town; ~**graben** *m* town moat; ~**grenze** *f* town (*e-r Großstadt:* city) boundary, *bes. Am.* city limits *Pl.*; ~**gründer** *m,* ~**gründerin** *f* city founder; ~**gründung** *f* founding of a (*od.* the) city; ~**guerilla** *m* urban guer(r)illa; ~**halle** *f* municipal hall; ~**haus** *n* town house; ~**indianer** *m* urban hippie; ~**innere** *n* town (*e-r Großstadt:* city) cent|re (*Am.* -er), *Am. auch* downtown (area)

städtisch I. *Adj.* urban, *attr. auch* town ..., city ...; *bes. verwaltungsmäßig:* municipal; (*groß~*) metropolitan; *Teile Berlins wirken eher ländlich als* ~ parts of Berlin are more like the country than the city; **II.** *Adv.:* ~ *verwaltet* municipally run (*od.* control[l]ed)

Stadt|jubiläum *n* anniversary of the founding of the town (*Großstadt:* city); ~**kämmerer** *m,* ~**kämmerin** *f* (*e-r Großstadt:* city) treasurer; ~**kasse** *f* town (*e-r Großstadt:* city) treasurer's office; ~**kern** *m* town (*e-r Großstadt:* city) cent|re (*Am.* -er), heart of the town, *Am. auch* downtown area; ~**kind** *n* **1.** town (*e-r Großstadt:* city) child; **2.** → *Städter,* ~**klatsch** *m* town gossip; ~**klima** *n* urban climate; ~**kreis** *m* urban district; ~ *Freiburg* administrative district of Freiburg; ~**kultur** *f*

1. *nur Sg.* town's (*e-r Großstadt:* city's) cultural life; **2.** *hist.* city civilization; ~**landschaft** *f* urban landscape, townscape; *e-r Großstadt:* cityscape; ~**lauf** *m Sport* street race; ~**leben** *n* urban (*od.* city) life; ~**luft** *f* city air; ~**magazin** *n* city events guide; ~**mauer** *f* town (*od.* city) wall; ~**meisterschaften** *Pl.* city championships; ~**mensch** *m* town person, townie *umg.*; ~**mitte** *f* town (*e-r Großstadt:* city) cent|re (*Am.* -er), *Am. auch* downtown area; ~**möbel** *Pl.* (*Fahrradständer, Sperrpfosten, Bänke etc.*) street furniture *Sg.*; ~**musikant** *m* town musician; *die Bremer* ~**en** the town band of Bremen

stadtnah I. *Adj.* close to the town (*zu Großstadt:* the city); **II.** *Adv.:* ~ *gelegen* (situated) close to the town (*zu Großstadt:* the city); **Stadtnähe** *f: in* ~ (*gelegen*) (located) close to the town (*zu Großstadt:* the city)

Stadt|oberhaupt *n* municipal leader; (*Bürgermeister[in]*) mayor; ~**park** *m* municipal (*od.* city) park; ~**parlament** *n Pol.* city council; ~**plan** *m* town (*e-r Großstadt:* city) plan, street map; ~**planer** *m,* ~**planerin** *f* town (*Am. auch* city) planner; ~**planung** *f* town (*Am.* city) planning; ~**quartier** *n* district; *weitS.* part of the town (*e-r Großstadt:* city)

Stadtrand *m* outskirts *Pl.* of the town (*od. der Großstadt:* the city); *am* ~ on the outskirts of the town (*od.* the city); ~**siedlung** *f* suburban estate (*od.* development)

Stadt|rat *m Pol.* **1.** (*Gremium*) town (*e-r Großstadt:* city) council; **2.,** *auch* ~**rätin** *f* town (*e-r Großstadt:* city) council(l)or; ~**ratsfraktion** *f* governing party (in the council); ~**recht** *n hist.* rights and privileges *Pl.* of a town; *das* ~ *erhalten* receive its (*bzw.* the) town charter; ~**regierung** *f* town (*e-r Großstadt:* city) administration; ~**region** *f* conurbation

Stadt|reinigung *f* **1.** town (*e-r Großstadt:* city) cleaning; **2.** (*Betrieb*) town (*e-r Großstadt:* city) cleansing department; ~**rundfahrt** *f* city (*in e-r kleineren Stadt:* town) sightseeing tour; *e-e* ~ *in Straßburg machen* go on a sightseeing tour of Strasbourg; ~**rundgang** *m* guided walking tour of the town (*Großstadt:* city); ~**sanierung** *f* urban redevelopment (*weitS.* renewal); *in Elendsvierteln:* slum clearance; ~**schreiber** *m,* ~**schreiberin** *f* **1.** *hist.* town clerk; **2.** (*Schriftsteller[in]*) resident writer (*appointed to write about a town*); ~**sparkasse** *f* municipal savings bank; ~**staat** *m* city state

Stadtstreicher *m* city vagrant; *pej.* tramp; *Pl. auch* street people; **Stadtstreicherei** *f* urban vagrancy; **Stadtstreicherin** *f* bag lady; → *auch Stadtstreicher*

Stadtteil *m* district; *weitS.* part of the town (*e-r Großstadt:* city); ~**fest** *n* local (district) festival; (*Jahrmarkt*) local fair

Stadt|theater *n* municipal theat|re (*Am. auch* -er); ~**tor** *n* town (*od.* city) gate; ~**väter** *Pl. fig.* city fathers; ~**umfahrung** *f Mot.* (city) bypass; ~**verkehr** *m* urban (*od.* city) traffic; ~**verwaltung** *f* municipal authorities *Pl.*; ~**viertel** *n* district, *weitS.* part of the town (*e-r Großstadt:* city); ~**wagen** *m* town car; ~**wald** *m* municipally owned woods *Pl.*, city forest; ~**wappen** *n*

town's (*od.* city's) coat of arms; ~**werke** *Pl.* municipal utilities; (*Abteilung*) municipal department *Sg.* of works; ~**wohnung** *f* town (*in der Großstadt:* city) apartment (*Brit. auch* flat); ~**zeitung** *f* town (*e-r Großstadt:* city) newspaper; ~**zentrum** *n* → *Stadtmitte*

Stafette *f; -, -n* relay (of messengers)

Staffage [ʃtaˈfaːʒə] *f; -, kein Pl.* **1.** *mst pej.:* (**nur**) ~ a façade, a (big) sham; **2.** *Kunst:* staffage

Staffel *f; -, -n* **1.** *Sport* (~*lauf*) relay (race); **2.** *Sport* (*Mannschaft*) team, squad; *für den* ~*lauf:* relay team; **3.** *Mil., Flug.* etwa squadron

Staffel|beteiligung *f Wirts.* graduated participation (*in a cooperative*); ~**bruch** *m Geol.* step fault

Staffelei *f; -, -en Kunst:* easel

Staffel|lauf *m* relay race; ~**läufer** *m,* ~**läuferin** *f* relay runner (*Skifahrer:* skier); ~**miete** *f* graduated rent

staffeln *v/t.* **1.** (*Steuern, Löhne etc.*) grade, graduate (*nach* according to); **2.** (*schräg abgestuft anordnen*) arrange in a stagger; *fig. Arbeitszeit etc.:* stagger; → *gestaffelt*

Staffelpreise *Pl.* graduated (*od.* sliding-scale) prices

Staffel|schwimmen *n Sport* relay swimming; ~**stab** *m* baton

Staffeltarif *m Wirts.* graduated tariff

Staffelung *f* **1.** *Flug., Sport etc.:* staggering; **2.** *Wirts., von Steuern, Zinsen etc.:* auch graduation; *nach Einkommen:* progressive rates *Pl.*; (*Lohngefälle*) pay differential(s *Pl.*)

Staffelwettbewerb *m Sport* relay (race)

Staffelzinsen *Pl. Wirts.* graduated interest *Sg.*

staffieren *v/t.* → *ausstaffieren*

Stagflation *f; -, -en; Wirts.* stagflation

Stagnation *f; -, -en, mst Sg.* stagnation; **stagnieren** *v/i.* stagnate; **stagnierend I.** *Part. Präs.* → *stagnieren;* **II.** *Adj.* stagnant

Stagsegel *n Naut.* staysail

stahl *Imperf.* → *stehlen*

Stahl *m; -s, kein Pl.* steel; *aus* ~ made of steel; *die* ~ *verarbeitende Industrie* the steel(-processing) industry; *Nerven aus* ~ *fig.* nerves of stecl; ~**arbeiter** *m,* ~**arbeiterin** *f* steelworker; ~**band** *n* (*Material*) steel strip; (*Fertigprodukt*) steel band; ~**bau** *m; Pl. -bauten* **1.** (*Gebäude*) steel-frame building; **2.** *kein Pl.* (*Bautechnik*) steel(-girder) construction; ~**beton** *m* reinforced concrete, ferro-concrete; ~**betonbau** *m; Pl. -bauten* **1.** (*Gebäude*): reinforced concrete building; **2.** *kein Pl.* (*Bautechnik, Branche*) reinforced concrete construction

stahlblau *Adj.* steel-blue

Stahl|blech *n* sheet steel; (*Stück*) steel sheet; ~**branche** *f* steel industry; ~**brille** *f:* (*e-e*) ~ (a pair of) steel- (*Am. auch* wire-)rimmed glasses *Pl.*; ~**bürste** *f* wire brush; ~**draht** *m* steel wire

stählen *v/t.* (*abhärten*) steel (*sich* o.s.); *s-n Körper* ~ toughen (*od.* harden) one's body

stählern *Adj. attr.* steel ..., made of steel; *fig.* steely (*auch Blick*); *Griff, Herz, Muskeln:* of steel; *ein* ~*er Wille* an iron will

Stahl|erzeugung *f* steel production; ~**feder** *f* **1.** steel spring; **2.** (*Schreibfeder*) steel nib; ~**flasche** *f* steel cylinder; ~**gerüst** *n* (*Baugerüst*) steel scaffolding; (*Skelett*) girder frame

S

stahlgrau *Adj.* steel-grey (*Am.* -gray)

Stahlgürtelreifen *m Mot.* steel-braced radial (tyre, *Am.* tire)

stahlhart *Adj.* (as) hard as steel; → *auch* **stählern**

Stahl|helm *m* steel helmet; **~hütte** *f* steelworks *mst Sg.*; **~industrie** *f* steel industry; **~kammer** *f* strongroom; **~kocher** *m*, **~kocherin** *f* steelworker; **~konstruktion** *f* → *Stahlbau*; **~kugel** *f* steel ball; **~mantelgeschoss** *n* steel jacketed bullet; **~platte** *f* steel plate; **~produktion** *f* steel production

Stahlrohr *n* steel tube; **~möbel** *Pl.* tubular steel furniture *Sg.*

Stahl|ross *n hum.* (*Fahrrad*) bike; **~saite** *f Mus.* steel (*od.* metal) string; **~schrank** *m* steel cabinet; **~seil** *n* steel cable; **~stich** *m* steel engraving; **~stift** *m* steel pin; **~träger** *m* steel girder; **~trosse** *f* steel cable

Stahl verarbeitend *Adj.* → *Stahl*

Stahl|waren *Pl.* steel goods; **~werk** *n* steelworks *mst Sg.*, steel mill

stak *Imperf.* → *stecken* II

staken *vt/i. nordd.* punt; **Staken** *m*; *-s, -; nordd.* punt pole

Staket *n*; *-(e)s, -e*, **Staketenzaun** *m* picket fence

stakkato *Adj. und Adv.*, **Stakkato** *n*; *-s, -s und Stakkati; Mus.* staccato

staksen *v/i. umg.* stalk, strut; **staksig** *umg.* **I.** *Adj.* spindly-legged; (*ungelenk*) gawky; (*unsicher*) teetering; **II.** *Adv. gehen, sich bewegen*: as though on stilts, gawkily

Stalagmit *m*; *-s und -en, -e(n); Geol.* stalagmite

Stalaktit *m*; *-s und -en, -e(n); Geol.* stalactite

Stalinismus *m*; *-, kein Pl.; Pol. hist.* Stalinism; **Stalinist** *m*; *-en, -en*, **Stalinistin** *f*; *-, -nen* Stalinist; **stalinistisch** **I.** *Adj.* Stalinist; **II.** *Adv. geführt, erzogen etc.*: according to Stalinist principles

Stalinorgel *f Mil. hist.* multiple rocket launcher

Stall *m*; *-(e)s, Ställe* **1.** (*Pferdestall*) stable; (*Kuhstall*) cowshed, *Am. auch* barn; (*Schweinestall*) sty, *Am. auch* pen; *fig.* (*Rennstall*) stable; *Motorrennen*: team; *umg. fig.* (*Zimmer*) hole; **den ~ ausmisten** muck out the stable; *fig.* have a good clearout; **aus e-m guten ~** *umg. fig.* (*Familie*) from a good stable; **ein ganzer ~ voll** *umg. fig.* a whole horde of; → *Pferd* 4; **2.** *umg.* (*Hosenschlitz*) flies *Pl.*, fly

Stallbursche *m* stable lad (*od.* boy)

Ställchen *n* (*Laufgitter*) playpen

Stall|dünger *m* (farmyard) manure; **~gebäude** *n* stable building; (*Kuhstall*) cowshed; **~geruch** *m fig.: der richtige ~** the right pedigree (*od.* breeding); **~hase** *m* rabbit; **~knecht** *m* stable lad (*od.* boy); *für Kühe*: cowhand, cowboy; **~magd** *f* stable maid; *für Kühe*: cowgirl; **~meister** *m* head groom; **~mist** *m* (farmyard) manure

Stallungen *Pl.* stabling *Sg.*, stables

Stall|wache *f*: *fig.*: **~ halten** hold the fort; **~wächter** *m fig.* caretaker

Stamm *m*; *-(e)s, Stämme* **1.** *Bot.* trunk; **2.** *bei Naturvölkern*: tribe; (*Geschlecht*) stock, lineage; (*Familie*) family, line; **vom ~e Nimm sein** *hum.* be out for what one can get in life; **3.** *Bio.* phylum; *Bakterien*: strain; *Vieh*: breed; **4.** *Ling., e-s Wortes*: root, stem; **5.** (*fester Bestand*) (*Mitarbeiter etc.*) permanent staff (*V. im Sg. od. Pl.*); (*Kundschaft*) regular customers

Pl.; Sport regular players *Pl.*; **zum ~ gehören** be one of the regulars; *Sport* have a regular place in the team; *Angestellte(r)*: be a permanent member of (the) staff; **~aktie** *f Wirts.* ordinary (*Am.* common) share; *Am. auch* common stock *Sg.*; **~baum** *m* family tree; *Zool.* pedigree; *Bio.* phylogenetic tree; **~belegschaft** *f* permanent workforce; **~betrieb** *m* parent company; **~buch** *n* e-r *Familie*: family register; **j-m etw. ins ~ schreiben** *fig.* make s.o. take s.th. to heart; **~datei** *f EDV* master file; **~daten** *Pl. EDV* master data; **~einlage** *f Wirts.* original investment, partner's capital share

stammeln *vt/i.* stammer; *Med. auch* stutter

Stammeltern *Pl.* progenitors

stammen *v/i.*: **~ von** *od.* **aus** come from; *zeitlich*: date from, go back to; **diese Gläser ~ noch von der Großmutter** these glasses used to be my grandmother's; **die Formulierung/Zeichnung stammt von ihm** that's his wording/drawing; **das stammt nicht von mir!** *iro.* I had nothing to do with that; **ich weiß, von wem das stammt** *umg.* I know who was responsible for that (*od.* who that was)

Stammes|bewusstsein *n* (feeling of) tribal identity; **~entwicklung** *f Bio.* phylogenesis; **~fehde** *f* tribal feud; **~führer** *m*, **~fürst** *m* (tribal) chieftain

Stammesgeschichte *f Bio.* phylogenesis; **stammesgeschichtlich** *Adj. Bio.* phylogen(et)ic

Stammes|häuptling *m* (tribal) chieftain; **~kunde** *f* ethnology; **~sitte** *f* tribal custom (*od.* tradition); **~zugehörigkeit** *f* membership of a tribe, tribal identity

Stamm|form *f* **1.** *Ling.* principal form; **die ~en von „geben"** the principal parts (*od.* tenses) of "geben"; **2.** *Bio.* base form; **~gast** *m* habitué (*in + Dat.*, **bei** of), regular (at) *umg.*; **~gericht** *n* set dish (*for regular customers*); **~geschäft** *n* original (*od.* parent) store; **~halter** *m umg.* son and heir; **~haus** *n Wirts.* (*Gebäude*) original company building; (*Zentrale*) company headquarters *Pl.*, head office; (*Gesellschaft*) parent company; **~hirn** *n Anat.* brainstem; **~holz** *n* trunk wood

stämmig *Adj.* stocky, thickset; *Beine*: sturdy

Stamm|kapital *n Wirts.* (authorized) share capital, *Am.* common stock capital; **~kneipe** *f umg.* regular watering hole, favo(u)rite bar (*Brit.* pub); **~kunde** *m*, **~kundin** *f* regular customer; **~kundschaft** *f* regulars *Pl.*, regular customers *Pl.*; **~land** *n* ancestral homeland; **~lokal** *n umg.* favo(u)rite haunt; → *Stammkneipe*; **~mannschaft** *f* regular team, starting team; **~mutter** *f* progenitrix *förm.*

Stamm|personal *n* permanent staff (*mst V. im Pl.*); (*Mindestzahl*) skeleton staff (*mst V. im Pl.*); **~platz** *m*: **j-s ~** s.o.'s usual seat; **~ in e-r Mannschaft etc.** regular place in a team *etc.*; **~publikum** *n Theat. etc.* regular audience; *auch umg. im Lokal*: regulars *Pl.*, regular customers *Pl.*; **~silbe** *f Ling.* root syllable; **~sitz** *m* **1.** (*Familiensitz*) ancestral seat; **2.** *Wirts.* (company) headquarters *Pl.*, head office; **~spieler** *m*, **~spielerin** *f* regular (player); **~tafel** *f* genealogical (*od.* ancestral) table

Stammtisch *m* regulars' (reserved) table; (*Personen*) group of regulars; **montags habe ich ~** on Mondays I meet my friends down at the pub (*Am.* local *od.* bar); **~bruder** *m umg.* regular drinking companion (*od.* mate); **~parole** *f pej.* bar(-)room cliché; **~politik** *f pej.* bar(-)room politics *Pl.*; **~runde** *f* group of regulars

Stammvater *m* progenitor

stammverwandt *Adj.* **1.** kindred, related; **2.** *Ling.* with a common derivation, cognate

Stamm|vokal *m* root vowel; **~wähler** *m*, **~wählerin** *f* loyal voter; **~wählerschaft** *f* party faithful; **~wort** *n Ling.* etymon *fachspr.*; **~würze** *f* original wort; **Starkbier hat 18% ~** strong ale has an original gravity of 18%; **~zelle** *f Gnt.* stem cell; **embryonale ~** embryonic stem cell

Stamperl *n*; *-s, -n; bayr., österr.* (small) schnapps glass; **ein ~ trinken** etwa have a snifter

stampfen **I.** *v/i.* **1.** (*hat*) (*schwer auftreten*) stamp; **mit dem Fuß ~** stamp one's foot; **2.** (*hat*) (*klopfend arbeiten*) pound, thump; **3.** (*ist*) (*stampfend gehen*) tramp, stomp; **durch die Gegend ~** *umg.* tramp (*od.* stomp) along; **4.** (*hat*) *Naut.* pitch; **II.** *v/t.* (*hat*) *Tech.* (*feststampfen*) tamp, ram (down); (*Erde, Lehm etc.*) stamp (down); (*Kartoffeln*) mash; (*Trauben*) crush; *im Mörser*: pound, crush; **aus dem Boden ~** *fig.* produce s.th. out of thin air

Stampfen *n*; *-s, kein Pl.* **1.** *Naut.* pitching; **2.** (*Geräusch e-r Maschine etc.*) pounding, thumping; **Stampfer** *m*; *-s, -* **1.** *Tech.* tamper; **2.** (*Kartoffelstampfer*) masher; **3.** *umg.* (*Bein*) stump; **Stampfkartoffeln** *Pl. Gastr.* mashed potatoes

stand *Imperf.* → *stehen*

Stand *m*; *-(e)s, Stände* **1.** *nur Sg.* (*aufrechtes Stehen*) standing position; (*Halt*) footing, foothold; **aus dem ~** from a standing position; *fig.* (*ohne zu überlegen*) off the top of one's head *umg.*; **Sprung/Start aus dem ~** standing jump/start; **im ~** when standing still; *Mot.* while stationary; *Turnen*: **nach dem Abgang (vom Reck) im sicheren ~ landen** make a secure landing from the horizontal bar; **keinen (festen) ~ haben** *Person*: have no firm foothold; **bei j-m e-n schweren ~ haben** have a hard time of it with s.o.; **2.** *nur Sg.* (*Zustand*) state; (*Beschaffenheit*) condition; (*Lage*) situation, position; (*Niveau*) level, standard; *e-s Wettkampfes*: score; **der ~ der Dinge** the present state of affairs, the way things are; **nach dem (jetzigen) ~ der Dinge** as matters stand (at the moment); **neuester ~** *od.* **auf dem neuesten ~** (*der Technik*) sein *Gerät etc.*: be state-of-the-art; *Patentwesen*: **der ~ der Technik** the prior art; **den höchsten ~ erreichen** reach its (*od.* one's) peak (*od.* highest level); **etw. auf den neuesten ~ bringen** update s.th., bring s.th. up to date; **auf dem ~ von 1950** as it was (*od.* they were) in 1950; **~: 01.07.2002** as at 01/07/2002, *Am.* **~:** 07-01-2002; **in den (heiligen) ~ der Ehe treten** enter the (holy) state of matrimony; → *außerstande, imstande, instand, zustande*; **3.** *Sport* (*Spielstand*) score; **beim ~ von 2:1** with the score at 2-1; **4.** (*Wasserstand*) level; *Astron.* position; *Wirts., von Kursen, Preisen, des Marktes*: level; (*Kilometerstand*) etwa mileage; **auf dem Ta-**

cho: speedometer reading; (*Zähler-stand*) reading; (*Kontostand*) balance; **5.** (*soziale Stellung*) social status (*od.* position, standing); (*Klasse*) class; (*Rechts-, Familienstand*) status; (*Beruf*) profession; **der geistliche ~** the clergy; **die höheren Stände** the upper classes; **der dritte ~** *hist.* the third estate; **über s-m ~ heiraten** marry above one's station; **6.** (*Verkaufsstand*) stall; *bes. für Zeitungen*: kiosk; (*Messestand*) stand; **e-e Pizza am ~ essen** eat a pizza at a stand-up stall (*od.* kiosk, *Am.* auch concession stand)

...stand *m, im Subst.* **1.** (*Ergebnis*): **Zwischen~** interim position; *Sport* latest score; **2.** (*Verkaufstisch*): **Bratwurst~** hot dog stall (*Am.* stand); **3.** (*Position, Wert*): **Benzin~** petrol (*Am.* gas) level; **Hygrometer~** hygrometer reading; **4.** (*Schicht*): **Kleinbürger~** lower middle class, petty bourgeoisie; **Offiziers~** officer class

Standard *m; -s, -s* standard; (*Niveau*) *auch* level; **auf hohem/niedrigem ~** of a high/low standard; **~abweichung** *f* standard deviation; **~ausführung** *f* standard type (*od.* model, design); **~ausrüstung** *f* standard equipment (*Sport* gear); **~aussprache** *f* standard pronunciation; *in GB*: *auch* received pronunciation; **~brief** *m Post.* standard (*Am.* regular) (size of) letter; **~format** *n Post. etc.*: standard (*Am.* regular) format

standardisieren *v/t.* standardize; **Standardisierung** *f* standardization

Standard|klasse *f Flug.* tourist class, *Am.* coach (*od.* economy) (class); **~kosten** *Pl. Wirts.* standard cost *Sg.*; **~modell** *n* standard model; **~preis** *m* standard price; **~programm** *n* standard program(me); **~repertoire** *n* standard repertoire; **~schrift** *f EDV* standard font; **~sendung** *f Post.* standard postal item; **~situation** *f Sport* set piece; **~software** *f* standard software; **~sprache** *f* standard language; **~tanz** *m* standard dance; **~werk** *n* standard work; **~werte** *Pl. Wirts.* (*Aktien*) leaders; **~zeit** *f* standard time

Standarte *f; -, -n* standard; *kleine*: guidon; **Standartenträger** *m* standard bearer

Stand|bein *n* standing leg; *Sport* support leg; *Basketball*: pivot leg; *Fechten*: rear leg; **das ~ unserer Wirtschaft** *fig.* the pillar of our economy; **ein ~ im Ausland haben** *fig. Firma*: have a foothold abroad; **~bild** *n* **1.** (*Foto*) still; *Film, Video*: still frame; **2.** (*Statue*) statue

Stand-by [ʃtɛntˈbaɪ] *n; -(s), -s* **1.** *Flug.* standby; **2.** *Etron.* standby (mode); **3. ~ haben** *Arzt etc.*: be on standby; **~-Flug** *m* standby flight; **~-Modus** *m* standby mode; **~-Tarif** *m* standby fare

Ständchen *n* serenade; **j-m ein ~ bringen** serenade s.o.

Ständeordnung *f hist.* estates system

Stander *m; -s, -* pennant

Ständer *m; -s, -* **1.** stand; (*Gestell*) *auch* rack; *Archit.* (*senkrechter Balken*) upright; → **Bücherständer** *etc.*; **2.** *vulg.* (*Erektion*) hard-on

Ständerat *m schw.* **1.** *nur Sg.* upper chamber (*with cantonal representatives*); **2.** (*Person*) member of the upper chamber (*representing a canton*)

Ständerpilz *m Bot.* basidiomycete

Standesamt *n* registry office, *Am.* bureau of vital statistics; **standesamt-**

lich I. *Adj.*: **~e Trauung** civil wedding, *Brit. mst* registry office wedding; **II.** *Adv.*: **~ heiraten** get married in a civil (wedding) ceremony, *Brit. mst* get married at a registry office

Standes|beamte *m*, **~beamtin** *f* registrar

standesbewusst *Adj.* class-conscious

Standesdünkel *m* class snobbery, snobbishness

standesgemäß *Adj. und Adv.* in keeping with one's station; **(nicht) ~ heiraten** (not) marry as befits one's social status

Standes|organisation *f* professional organization; **~register** *n* register of births, marriages and deaths (*Am.* burials); **~schranken** *Pl.* class (*od.* social) barriers

Ständestaat *m hist.* corporative state

Standesunterschied *m* class distinction, difference in class

standfest *Adj.* steady; *bes. Tech.* stable; **~e Abwehr** *Sport* strong defen|ce (*Am.* -se); **nicht mehr ganz ~** *umg. fig.* a bit tiddly (*Am.* tipsy); → *auch* **standhaft**; **Standfestigkeit** *f* steadiness; *bes. Tech.* stability; *fig.* (*gegenüber Alkohol*) ability to take one's drink; → *auch* **Standhaftigkeit**

Stand|fläche *f* **1.** *auf der etw. steht*: support surface; **2.** (*Platz für Möbel etc.*) (floor) space; **~foto** *n* still; **~fuß-ball** *m umg.*: **~ spielen** play at a walking pace; **~gas** *n Mot.* idling mixture; **~gebühr** *f* → **Standgeld** 1; **~geld** *n* **1.** stall fee; *bei e-r Messe*: demurrage; **2.** *Eisenb.* demurrage; **~gericht** *n Mil.* drumhead court martial

standhaft I. *Adj.* steadfast; (*unerschütterlich*) firm, unwavering, *Vertreter, Anhänger etc.*: *auch* staunch; (*entschlossen*) resolute; (*beharrlich*) persevering; **II.** *Adv.*: **~ ablehnen** firmly (*od.* steadfastly) refuse; **etw. ~ verteidigen** defend s.th. staunchly; **Standhaftigkeit** *f* steadfastness; (*Unerschütterlichkeit*) firmness; *e-s Vertreters, Anhängers etc.*: staunchness; (*Entschlossenheit*) resoluteness, resolution; (*Beharrlichkeit*) perseverance

standhalten *v/i.* (*unreg., trennb., hat -ge-*) *Person*: hold one's ground (*od.* own), stand firm; *Deich etc.*: hold out (+ *Dat.* against); (*e-m Angriff, Stoß etc.*) withstand; (*e-r Kritik etc.*) stand up to; **j-s Blick ~** resist s.o.'s gaze; **sie konnte ihren neugierigen Blicken nicht ~** their inquisitive stares were too much for her; **e-r Überprüfung nicht ~** not bear close scrutiny; → **Vergleich** 1

ständig I. *Adj. Adresse, Personal etc.*: permanent; (*fortwährend*) constant, continual; (*laufend*) continuous; (*regelmäßig*) steady; *Einkommen*: fixed, regular; *Regel, Praxis*: established; **~er Ausschuss** standing committee; **~er Begleiter** constant companion; **~er Beirat** permanent council; **~er Korrespondent** resident correspondent; *in* **~er Sorge leben** live in a state of constant worry; *in* **~er Verbindung stehen mit** be in constant contact with; **dein ~es Gejammer geht mir auf die Nerven** your constant (*od.* endless) moaning gets on my nerves; **II.** *Adv.* permanently; constantly, forever; **etw. ~ sagen/tun** keep saying/doing s.th.; **er meckert ~ über das Essen** *umg.* he's always (*od.* forever) complaining about the food, he keeps (*od.* never stops) complaining about the food

Standl *n; -s, -; österr.* stall

Stand|leitung *f Telef.* dedicated line; **~licht** *n Mot.* parking lights *Pl.*; *vorne*: sidelights *Pl.*; **mit ~ fahren** drive on sidelights; **~miete** *f* stall rent

Standort *m* **1.** position (*auch Naut. etc.*), location; *e-r Industrie etc.*: site; (*Ort*) place; *Mil.* (*Garnison*) garrison, *Am.* post; **den ~ bestimmen von** locate; **~ Deutschland** Germany as an industrial base; **2.** *nur Sg.; fig.* position; (*Einstellung*) attitude, standpoint; **j-s politischer ~** s.o.'s political stance

Standort|bedingung *f* condition regarding location; **~bestimmung** *f* location; *Radar*: fixing; *fig.* definition of one's position; **e-e ~ machen** *fig.* define one's position, take a clear stand; **~debatte** *f* debate on industrial locations; **~entscheidung** *f*: **~ für X** decision to use X as the location; **~faktor** *m* location factor

standortgerecht *Adj.* suitable for the site (*od.* location)

Standort|katalog *m* shelf catalog(ue); **~kommandant** *m Mil.* garrison (*Am.* post) commander; **~sicherung** *f* investment incentives *Pl. provided by government to attract business to an area*; **~suche** *f* search for a location; **~vorteil** *m Wirts.* locational advantage; **~wahl** *f* choice of site (*od.* location); **~wechsel** *m* change of location, relocation

Stand|pauke *f umg.* lecture, dressing-down, telling-off; **j-m e-e ~ halten** give s.o. a good dressing-down (*od.* telling-off); **~photo** *n* → **Standfoto**; **~platz** *m* stand; *für Taxis: Brit. auch* rank, *Am.* cab (*od.* taxi) stand

Standpunkt *m* point of view, standpoint, stance; **den ~ vertreten** *od.* **auf dem ~ stehen** *od.* **sich auf den ~ stellen, dass** take the view (*od.* line) that; **von s-m ~ aus** from his point of view; **vom medizinischen ~ (aus)** from a medical standpoint (*od.* point of view); **s-n ~ vertreten dürfen** be able to put one's point of view; **das ist doch kein ~!** what sort of attitude is that!

Standquartier *n* base

Standrecht *n Mil.* martial law; **standrechtlich** *Adj. und Adv.* under martial law; **die Meuterer wurden ~ erschossen** the mutineers were summarily executed (under martial law)

Standseilbahn *f* funicular (railway)

standsicher *Adj.* steady; *Konstruktion*: stable

Stand|spur *f*, **~streifen** *m Verk.* hard shoulder, *Am.* shoulder; **~uhr** *f* grandfather clock; **~ventilator** *m* floor-standing fan; **~vermögen** *n* → **Stehvermögen**; **~vogel** *m Zool.* sedentary bird; **~waage** *f Turnen*: horizontal balance

Stange *f; -, -n* **1.** pole; *kleinere*: rod; (*Kleiderstange*) rail; (*Pfosten*) post; (*Vogelstange*) perch; *Ballett etc.*: bar; **von der ~** *Kleidung*: *attr.* off-the-peg ..., *präd.* off the peg; **2.** *Zimt, Lakritze etc.*: stick; **e-e ~ Zigaretten** a carton of cigarettes; **3.** *fig., in Wendungen*: **bei der ~ bleiben** *umg.* stick it out (to the end), hang in there; **j-n bei der ~ halten** *umg.* keep s.o. at it, keep s.o.'s nose to the grindstone; **j-m die ~ halten** *umg.* back s.o. up, stand (*od.* stick) up for s.o.; **e-e ~ Geld** *umg.* a tidy sum, a packet, *Am.* a bundle; **4.** *Jägerspr.* side branch (of the antlers); **5.** *vulg.* (*Penis*) hard-on

...stange f, im Subst. **1.** im wörtl. Sinn: **Bambus~** bamboo rod; **Messing~** brass rod; massiv: brass bar; **2.** der Form nach: **Baguette~** baguette; **Laugen~** salt (Am. pretzel) stick; **Sellerie~** stick of celery

Stängel m; -s, -: Bot. stalk, stem; **ich bin fast vom ~ gefallen** umg. you could have knocked me down with a feather, I nearly fell over backwards; **fall nicht vom ~!** umg. take a deep breath, are you sitting down?

Stangen|bohne f Bot. runner (od. string) bean; **~glas** n tall thin glass; **~sellerie** m, f Bot. celery; **~spargel** m Bot. asparagus spears Pl.; **~weißbrot** n Gastr. French stick, baguette

Stanitzel n; -s, -: österr. (spitze Tüte) (pointed) bag; (Speiseeistüte) cone

stank Imperf. → **stinken**

Stänkerer m; -s, -: umg. (Querulant) grouser; gegen j-n: stirrer, Am. rabble-rouser; (Lästerer) spiteful type; **stänkern** v/i. umg. (nörgeln) grouse; (Streit schüren) stir up (od. make) trouble; **gegen j-n ~** go on (Am. mouth off) about s.o.

Stanniol n; -s, kein Pl., **~papier** n tin foil; (Silberpapier) silver paper

Stanze f; -, -n **1.** Tech. (Lochstanze) punch; (Maschine) punching machine; (Prägestempel) stamp; **2.** Lit. (Strophe) ottava rima, eight-line stanza; **stanzen** v/t. Tech. punch; (prägen) stamp

Stapel m; -s, - **1.** pile; hoher, ordentlicher: stack; EDV batch; **zu e-m ~ schichten** pile up, make a pile of; **ein ~ Bücher** a pile (od. stack) of books; **ein ~ Wäsche** a pile of laundry; **2.** Naut. stocks Pl.; **auf ~ legen** Naut. lay down; **vom ~ laufen** be launched; **vom ~ lassen** launch; umg. fig. pej. (äußern) come out with, trot out; (Angriff, Kampagne) launch; (Witz) crack; (Rede) make; **3.** Tech. (Faserlänge) staple; **~anlage** f am Kopierer: stacking attachment

stapelbar Adj. stackable; Stühle etc.: stacking

Stapel|box f stacking box; **~datei** f EDV batch file; **~glas** n stacking glass; **~holz** n chopped wood (for stacking); **~kasten** m stacking crate; **~lauf** m launching

stapeln I. v/t. stack, pile up; **II.** v/refl. pile up

Stapel|speicher m EDV push-down store; **~verarbeitung** f EDV batch processing; **~waren** Pl. staple commodities

stapelweise Adv. in piles; **bei ihm liegen die Computerhefte ~ herum** he's got piles (od. stacks umg.) of computer magazines lying around (at home)

Stapfen Pl. footprints; **stapfen** v/i. trudge

Staphylokokkeninfektion f Med. staphylococcal infection; **Staphylokokkus** m; -, Staphylokokken; Med. staphylococcus (Pl. staphylococci)

Stapler m; -s, - **1.** stacking machine; **2.** → **Gabelstapler**

Star¹ m; -s, -e; Orn. starling

Star² [ʃtaːɐ̯] m, -s, -s Film etc.: star

Star³ m; -(e)s, kein Pl.; Med.: grauer ~ cataract(s Pl.); grüner ~ glaucoma; **am ~ operiert werden** have one's cataracts removed; **j-m den ~ stechen** umg. fig. remove the scales from s.o.'s eyes, open s.o.'s eyes

...star m, im Subst.: **Bühnen~** stage star, star of the stage; **Sprint~** star sprinter

Star|allüren Pl. pej. airs (and graces) (of a star); **~ annehmen/zeigen** put on the airs of a star / behave like a prima donna; **~anwalt** m, **~anwältin** f star (od. top) lawyer (Am. auch attorney, Am. auch rainmaker Sl.; **~architekt** m, **~architektin** f big-name (od. top) architect; **~aufgebot** n collection of stars; **~autor** m, **~autorin** f star (od. best-selling) author

starb Imperf. → **sterben**

Starbesetzung f star cast

Starbrille f Med. spectacles Pl. with cataract lenses

Star|dirigent m, **~dirigentin** f Mus. star conductor

Star|gast m star guest; **~journalist** m, **~journalistin** f star (od. top) journalist

stark I. Adj. **1.** allg. strong (auch Ähnlichkeit, Argument, Band, Brille, Eindruck, Gefühl, Geruch, Geschmack, Getränk, Gift, Glaube, Licht, Nerven, Parfüm, Vorteil, Wille etc.); Gegner, Kandidat, Motor, Organisation, Stellung: auch powerful; (kräftig) Mensch: strong; Sache: auch robust, sturdy; (mächtig) powerful; **das ~e Geschlecht** umg. the stronger sex; **~es Mittel** Med. strong (od. potent) medication; **~e Seite** fig. strong point, strength, forte; **sich ~ machen für** stand up for; **den ~en Mann markieren** umg. try to act tough; **Politik der ~en Hand** heavy-handed policy, strongarm tactics Pl.; **~e Truppenverbände** strong (od. large) troop units; **e-e 200 Mann ~e Kompanie** a company of 200 men, a 200-strong company; **sie waren 200 Mann ~** they were 200 men strong; **etwas Starkes trinken** umg. drink some hard stuff; **2.** (beleibt) stout; (dick) Wand etc.: thick; **er ist stärker geworden** he's put on weight; **für die stärkere Frau** od. Figur euph. for the fuller figure; **das Buch ist 600 Seiten ~** the book is 600 pages long; **5 mm ~er Karton** cardboard 5 mm thick; **3.** (intensiv) intense; (heftig) violent; Erkältung, Raucher, Regen, Trinker, Verkehr etc.: heavy; Frost, Schmerzen, Anfall etc.: severe; **e-n ~en Haarwuchs haben** (dichtes Haar) have thick hair; (schnell wachsend) have a luxuriant growth of hair; **~er Beifall** loud applause; **~e Nachfrage** great (od. heavy) demand; **~e Schmerzen haben** be in severe pain; **~e Übertreibung** gross exaggeration; **ein Film der ~en Gefühle** a film of intense emotions, an intensely emotional film; **4.** umg. iro. (schlimm) bad; **das ist (wirklich) ~!, das ist ein ~es Stück!** that's (really) a bit much (od. a bit thick)!; **5.** (gut) good; umg. (großartig) great; **Roths stärkster Roman** Roth's best (od. strongest) novel; **e-e ~e Leistung** a fine performance; **~ in der Abwehr** Sport strong in defen|ce (Am. -se); **echt ~** Sl. real cool; **7.** Ling., Verb etc.: strong; → **Blutung, Polizeiaufgebot, Stück 8, Verdacht** etc.; **II. Adv. 1.** (sehr) strongly; **~ befahren** (Straße etc.) busy; **~ behaart** very hairy; **~ benachteiligt** severely handicapped; **~ beschäftigt** very busy; **~ betont** strongly stressed; **~ erkältet sein** have a bad cold; **~ gewürzt** highly seasoned; **~ übertrieben** grossly exaggerated; **~ ansteigen** rise sharply; **sich ~ verändern** change radically; **~ bluten** bleed heavily (od. profusely); **~ regnen** rain heavily, pour; **~ riechen** have a strong smell; **~ rauchen** Person: be a heavy smoker; **~ wirken** have a strong effect; **~ wirkend** Mittel etc.. powerful; **j-n ~ im Verdacht haben** have strong suspicions about s.o.; **2.** (gut) well; **sie hat ~ gespielt** Sport she played really well (stärker: brilliantly); umg. Mus. her playing (Theat. her acting) was great; **unheimlich ~ aussehen/singen** umg. look really great (od. fantastic) / sing incredibly well

...stark im Adj. **1.** (kräftig) **nerven~** with strong nerves; **saug~** with powerful suction; **2.** (zahlenmäßig stark) **mitglieder~** with a large number of members; **3.** (gut) **gedächtnis~** with a good memory; **kopfball~** good at heading the ball

Starkbier n strong (od. high-alcohol) beer; in GB: strong ale, Am. malt liquor

Stärke¹ f; -, -n **1.** nur Sg. strength (auch körperliche Kraft); (Macht, Tech., Leistung) power; e-r Brille: strength; e-s Fernglases: power; (zahlenmäßige ~) strength, size; **Politik der ~** power politics; **2.** (Maß) thickness; Tech., auch von Metall: ga(u)ge; (Durchmesser) diameter; **3.** Chem. strength, concentration; Med. auch potency; **das Mittel gibt es in drei ~n** the agent (Med. medication) is available in three strengths; **4.** mst Sg.; (Intensität) intensity; (Heftigkeit) violence; von Erkältung, Regen, Verkehr etc.: heaviness; von Frost, Schmerzen, Anfall etc.: severity; **5.** fig. (starke Seite) strong point, strength, forte; **j-n mit s-n ~n und Schwächen lieben** love s.o. for both their strengths and their weaknesses; **es gehört nicht zu s-n ~n** it's not one of his strong points (od. strengths); → **Richter-Skala**

Stärke² f; -, -n; mst Sg.; (Speise-, Wäschestärke) starch

...stärke f, im Subst. **1.** (Kraft): **Konzentrations~** intensity (od. degree) of concentration; **Nerven~** strength of nerve; **2.** (Intensität): **Beben~** strength of an (od. the) earthquake; **Druck~** intensity of pressure; **3.** (Substanz): **Kartoffel~** potato starch

Stärkegehalt m starch content; **stärkehaltig** Adj. starchy; **~ sein** auch contain starch; **Stärkemehl** n cornflour, Am. cornstarch

stärken I. v/t. **1.** strengthen (auch fig.); (Gesundheit) build up; (Mut, Selbstsicherheit) boost, build up; (Macht) increase; **j-m den Rücken ~** back s.o. up; **2.** (Wäsche) starch; **II.** v/refl. lit. fortify o.s.; (etw. essen) have a bite to eat; (etw. trinken) have a drink

stärkend I. Part. Präs. → **stärken**; **II. Adj.: ~es Mittel** tonic, restorative

Stärke|verhältnis n Pol. Parl. strength (od. state) of the parties; **~zucker** m glucose

Star|kritiker m, **~kritikerin** f star (od. top) critic

Starkstrom m Etech. high-voltage (od. heavy) current; **~kabel** n high-voltage (od. power) cable; **~leitung** f power line; **~technik** f electrical engineering (not including telecommunications), heavy current engineering; **~techniker** m, **~technikerin** f electrical engineer (not concerned with telecommunications)

Starkult m star cult

Stärkung f strengthening; (Erfrischung) refreshment; umg. (Schnaps

etc.) bracer; *e-e ~ zu sich nehmen* have something to fortify o.s.; **Stär-kungsmittel** *n Med.* tonic, restorative
stark wirkend → *stark* II 1
Star|mannequin *n*, **~model** *n* star model, supermodel; **~parade** *f* star gala

starr I. *Adj.* **1.** rigid; (*steif*) stiff; (*bewegungslos*) motionless; (*~ angebracht*) fixed; **~er Blick/Gesichtsausdruck** fixed (*od.* rigid) stare/expression; *~ vor Entsetzen* paraly|sed (*Am.* -zed) (*od.* transfixed) with horror; *~ vor Staunen* dumbfounded; *~ vor Kälte* stiff with cold; *~ stehen bleiben* stand transfixed, stop dead in one's tracks; **2.** *Prinzipien etc.*: rigid, firm; *Haltung*: rigid; (*unnachgiebig*) inflexible, unbending, unyielding; **~es Budget** *Wirts.* fixed budget; **II.** *Adv.* rigidly; *~ ansehen* stare fixedly at; *~ an etw. festhalten* adhere rigidly (*od.* stubbornly) to s.th.
Starrachse *f Mot.* rigid axle
Starre *f*; -, *kein Pl.* stiffness, rigidity
starren[1] *v/i.* stare (*auf + Akk.* at); *vor sich hin ~ od. ins Leere ~* stare into space
starren[2] *v/i.*: *~ vor* (+ *Dat.*) *od. von* (*voll sein von*) bristle with; *vor Schmutz ~* be thick with dirt
Starrflügler *m Flug.* fixed-wing aircraft
Starrheit *f* rigidity; (*Steifheit*) stiffness; (*Bewegungslosigkeit*) motionlessness; *fig.* (*Unnachgiebigkeit*) inflexibility
Starrkopf *m* pigheaded (*od.* obstinate) person; **starrköpfig** *Adj.* pigheaded, obstinate
Starrkrampf *m Med.* tetanus
Starrsinn *m* pigheadedness, obstinacy; **starrsinnig** *Adj.* pigheaded, obstinate
Starrummel *m pej.* celebrity hype
Start *m*; -s, -s **1.** *Sport, Mot., fig.* start; *Sport* (*Startlinie*) start, starting line; *~ und Ziel* start and finish (line); *am ~ Sport* at the start, on the starting line; *vom ~ weg* from the start; *e-n guten/ schlechten ~ erwischen Sport und fig.* get off to (*od.* make) a good/bad start; *über ~ gehen EDV* click the start icon, click on start; *~ frei für ... fig.* all clear for (the launching of) ...; *der ~ ins Berufsleben* one's first experience of (*od.* introduction to) working life; *der ~ des Projekts wird verschoben* the launch of the project is being postponed; **2.** *Flug.* take-off; *Rakete*: launching, lift-off; *zum ~ freigeben Flug.* clear for take-off
Start|adresse *f EDV* start address; **~auflage** *f e-s Buches*: initial print run; **~automatik** *f Mot.* automatic choke; **~bahn** *f Flug.* (take-off) runway; **~bedingung** *f Sport* requirement for entry
start|berechtigt *Adj. Sport* eligible (to enter); **~bereit** *Adj.* ready to start; *Flug.* ready for take-off; *umg. fig.* ready to go
Start|bit *n EDV* start bit; **~block** *m Sport, Schwimmen*: starting block
starten I. *v/i.* (*ist gestartet*) **1.** *Sport, Mot. etc.* start; *zu früh ~ Sport* jump the start; *bei Kälte startet der Wagen schlecht* the car is difficult to start in cold weather; **2.** *Sport* (*teilnehmen*) compete, take part (*bei* in); *~ für* (*Italien, e-n Verein etc.*) compete (*beim Rennen*: race, *Läufer*: run) for; **3.** *Flug.* take off; **4.** (*aufbrechen*) leave; *zu e-r Expedition / zum Mond ~* set off on an expedition / for the moon; *können wir ~?* *umg.* (*losgehen*, -*fahren*) can we

get going now?; **II.** *v/t.* start; *umg. fig.* (*Unternehmen, Aktion etc.*) *auch* launch; *der Wagen lässt sich nicht ~* the car won't start; *im nächsten Monat ~ wir e-e große Werbekampagne* next month we are launching a big advertising campaign
Starter *m*; -s, -; *Mot. und Sport* starter; **Starterin** *f*; -, *-nen*; *Sport* starter; **Starterklappe** *f Mot.* choke (flap)
Start|erlaubnis *f* **1.** *Flug.* (take-off) clearance; **2.** *Sport* permission to take part; **~fenster** *n Raumf.* launch window; **~flagge** *f* starter's flag; **~geld** *n Sport* **1.** (*Gebühr*) entry fee; **2.** (*Honorar*) starting money; **~geschwindigkeit** *f Flug.* take-off speed
Starthilfe *f* **1.** *Flug.* assisted take-off (*auch Abflug mit ~*); **2.** *Wirts.* initial aid, start-up cash *umg.*; **3.** *j-m ~ geben Mot.* help s.o. get started; *mit Starthilfekabel*: give s.o. a jump start; *fig.* give s.o. a start (in life); **~kabel** *n Mot.* jump leads *Pl.*, *Am.* jumper (cables) *Pl.*, booster cables *Pl.*
Startkapital *n Wirts.* start-up capital
startklar *Adj. Flug.* ready for take-off; *Sport, umg.* (*reisebereit*) ready to start, ready for the off (*Am.* whistle)
Start|kommando *n Sport* starting signal; **~läufer** *m*, **~läuferin** *f* first leg runner; **~leiste** *f EDV* start bar; **~linie** *f Sport* starting line; **~loch** *n* starting hole; *langsam aus den Startlöchern kommen* get off to a slow start; *schon in den Startlöchern sitzen umg. fig.* be ready for the off (*Am.* whistle); *vor Kampf, Wahl etc.*: ready for the fray; **~nummer** *f* (competitor's) number; **~pistole** *f* starting pistol; **~platz** *m* **1.** start; *Autorennen*: *auch* starting grid; **2.** *Raumf.* launch site; **~position** *f* starting position; *Autorennen*: grid position; **~punkt** *m* starting point; **~rampe** *f Raumf.* launch(ing) pad; **~schuss** *m Sport* starting (gun) signal; *den ~ geben* fire the starter's gun; *fig.* give the go-ahead (*od.* green light) (*zu, für* for); **~schwierigkeiten** *Pl. Flug.* difficulties during take-off; *Sport* difficulties at the start; *fig.* teething troubles; **~seite** *f EDV* startup page *of a website*; **~signal** *n Sport* starting signal; *Flug.* take-off signal; *umg. fig.* go-ahead, green light; **~sprung** *m Schwimmsport*: racing start, dive (at the start); **~strecke** *f Flug.* take-off run; **~termin** *m Raumf.* launch schedule; *fig. für Projekt etc.*: start date; **~ und Landebahn** *f Flug.* runway; **~verbot** *n* **1.** *Sport* suspension; *zwei Jahre ~ haben* be suspended for two years; **2.** *Flug.* grounding; *e-m Flugzeug ~ erteilen* ground an aircraft; **~zeichen** *n* → *Startsignal*
Stasi *f*; - *od. m*; -s, *kein Pl.*; *hist. DDR. umg.* Stasi, secret police *Pl.*; **~-Akte** *f* Stasi file; **~-Mitarbeiter** *m*, **~-Mitarbeiterin** *f*: (*ehemalige[r] ~* former) member of the Stasi; **~-Spitzel** *m* Stasi informer
Statement ['ste:tmənt] *n*; -s, -s statement; *ein ~ abgeben* give a statement (*über + Akk.* on), make a (*od.* an official) statement (on)
Statik *f*; -, *kein Pl.* **1.** *Phys., Etech., Archit.* statics *Pl.* (*als Fach V. im Sg.*); *die ~ e-r Brücke berechnen* calculate the static equilibrium of a bridge; **2.** *fig.* inertia; **Statiker** *m*; -s, -, **Statikerin** *f*; -, *-nen*; *Archit.* structural engineer, stress analyst
Station *f*; -, *-en* **1.** *Eisenb.* station;

(*Haltestelle, Aufenthaltsort*) stop; **2.** (*Aufenthalt*) stopover; *~ machen in* stop over in (*od.* at); **3.** *Radio, Met. etc.*: station; **4.** *e-r Klinik*: ward; *der Arzt ist auf ~* the doctor is doing his rounds; **5.** *fig.* (*Stadium*) *e-r Entwicklung, Ausbildung etc.*: stage; **6.** *bibl. des Kreuzwegs*: station (of the Cross)
stationär I. *Adj.* **1.** stationary (*auch Tech.*); (*gleich bleibend*) steady, constant; **2.** *Med. attr.* in-patient ...; **~e Aufnahme** admission as an in-patient; **~e Behandlung** in-patient treatment; *die Behandlung ist ~* the treatment is in hospital; **II.** *Adv.*: *~ aufnehmen* admit as an in-patient; *~ behandelter Patient* in-patient; *~ behandeln* treat in hospital (*Am.* a hospital)
stationieren *v/t. Mil.* station; **Stationierung** *f* stationing
Stations|arzt *m*, **~ärztin** *f* ward doctor; **~pfleger** *m* ward nurse; **~schwester** *f* ward sister; **~taste** *f am Radio*: preset tuning button; **~vorsteher** *m*, **~vorsteherin** *f Eisenb.* stationmaster
statisch I. *Adj.* **1.** *Phys.* static; *Gesetze*: of statics; *Archit.* structural; **~e Berechnung** structural analysis; *aus ~en Gründen* for structural reasons; **~e Organe** *Anat.* organs of equilibrium; **~er Speicher** *EDV* static memory; **2.** *Elektr.* static; **3.** *fig.* static, inert; *die ~e Hierarchie der Firma* the firm's rigid (*od.* inflexible) hierarchy; *~e und dynamische Verben* static and dynamic verbs; **II.** *Adv.* **1.** *Phys.* statically; *Archit.* structurally; **2.** *Elektr.* statically; *sich ~ aufladen* (*Oberfläche, Haare etc.*) become charged with static (electricity)
Statist *m*; -en, -en; *Theat., Film*: extra; *auch fig.* bit player; *zu ~en degradiert werden fig.* be reduced to playing minor roles; **Statistenrolle** *f* walk-on part; *auch fig.* bit part, minor role
Statistik *f*; -, *-en* **1.** *Koll.* statistics *Pl.*; *e-e ~* a set of statistics; (*Erhebung*) a statistical survey; *die ~ zeigt* (the) statistics show, according to the statistics; *e-e ~ aufstellen* compile (a set of) statistics (*über + Akk.* on), make a statistical survey (of); **2.** *nur Sg.*; (*Fach*) statistics *Sg.*; **Statistiker** *m*; -s, -, **Statistikerin** *f*; -, *-nen* statistician, statistical expert
Statistin *f*; -, *-nen*; *Theat., Film*: → *Statist*
statistisch I. *Adj.* statistical; *~e Erhebung* statistical survey; *~es Jahrbuch* annual abstract of statistics; *Statistisches Bundesamt* Federal Office of Statistics; **II.** *Adv.*: *~ gesehen* according to the statistics, statistically; *~ belegen* demonstrate by means of statistics
Stativ *n*; -s, -e tripod; **~aufnahme** *f* tripod shot; **~kamera** *f* stand camera; **~wagen** *m* tripod dolly
statt[1] **I.** *Präp.* (+ *Gen., umg. auch + Dat.*) instead of; → *stattdessen*; **II.** *Konj.*: *~ zu + Inf.* instead of ...ing; *~ hier zu sitzen, ~ dass wir hier sitzen* instead of sitting here
statt[2] *Präp.*: *an j-s ~* in s.o.'s place; *an Kindes ~ annehmen* adopt
Statt *f*; -, *kein Pl.*; *altm.* (*Ort*) place; *fig.* (*Stelle*) stead
stattdessen *Adv.* instead (of this); *aber ~* instead of which
Stätte *f*; -, *-n* place; (*Schauplatz*) scene; *bes. hist., Archäol.* site; *historische ~* historic site; *e-e geweihte ~* a consecrated site, consecrated ground; *~ des*

S

Friedens haven of peace; *e-e ~ des Grauens* a place of horror; *~n der Erinnerung/Jugend* places of the past / of one's youth

stattfinden *v/i.* (*unreg., trennb., hat -ge-*) take place, be; (*sich ereignen*) happen; (*abgehalten werden*) be held; *es wird bei Regen im Saal ~* it will take place in the hall if it's raining; *unter Ausschluss der Öffentlichkeit ~ Sitzung:* not be open to the public; *bes. Jur.* be held in camera; *die Sitzung findet am Freitag statt* the meeting is (*od.* will be) on Friday, *formeller:* the meeting will be held (*od.* take place) on Friday

stattgeben *v/i.* (*unreg., trennb., hat -ge-*) *Amtsspr.* (*e-r Bitte etc.*) grant

statthaft *Adj. Amtsspr. präd.* admissible, permissible; (*gesetzlich ~*) legal; *nicht ~* not admissible; *Rauchen etc.:* not permitted

Statthalter *m; -s, -; hist.* governor

stattlich *Adj.* **1.** (*groß, prachtvoll*) magnificent; (*würdevoll*) stately; (*eindrucksvoll*) imposing, impressive; (*kräftig gebaut*) *attr.* well-built ..., *präd.* well built; *Bursche:* strapping; *e-e ~e Erscheinung* a commanding (*od.* imposing) figure; **2.** (*beträchtlich*) considerable; *Summe:* auch handsome; *Familie:* large; *~e 100 000 Euro* a cool 100, 000 euros; **Stattlichkeit** *f* (*Größe, Pracht*) magnificence, grandeur; (*Würde*) stateliness; (*eindrucksvolle Art*) impressiveness; *von Mensch:* imposing presence (*Körperbau:* build)

Statue *f; -, -n* statue; **statuenhaft** *Adj.* statue(-)like, statuesque

Statuette *f; -, -n* statuette

statuieren *v/t.:* *ein Exempel ~* set an (*od.* a warning) example; *an j-m ein Exempel ~* make an example of s.o.

Statur *f; -, kein Pl.* build; *auch fig.* stature; *von kräftiger ~ sein* be powerfully built; *von ~ eher klein* (a bit) on the short side; *sie ist zierlich von ~* she is slightly (*od.* daintily) built

Status *m; -, kein Pl.* **1.** (*gesellschaftlicher etc., auch Rechtsstellung*) status; **2.** (*Lage*) state, status; **3.** *EDV* status; *~ Nascendi m; --, kein Pl.; Chem.* nascent state; *~ quo m; - -, kein Pl.* status quo; *den ~ aufrechterhalten* maintain the status quo; *~symbol n* status symbol; *~verlust m* loss of status; *~zeile f EDV* status line

Statut *n; -(e)s, -en* **1.** statute, regulation; *~en aufstellen* draw up statutes; **2.** *Pl.; e-r Handelsgesellschaft:* articles of association; **statutarisch** *Adj.* statutory; **Statutenänderung** *f* amendment of statutes

statuten|gemäß *Adj.* in accordance with the statutes; *~widrig Adj.* contrary to the statutes

Stau *m; -(e)s, -s und -e* **1.** *Pl. -s; Mot.* traffic jam; (*Rückstau*) tailback, *Am.* backup; *im ~ stehen od. stecken* be stuck (*od.* caught up) in a traffic jam; *ein ~ von fünf Kilometern Länge* a five-kilomet|re (*Am.* -er) tailback (*Am.* backup); *es kommt zu ~s* tailbacks (*Am.* backups) are forming; *regelmäßig:* tailbacks (*Am.* backups) form; **2.** *mst Sg.;* (*Ansammlung*) accumulation, build-up; *es kam zu e-m ~ des Baches/Blutes* the stream became blocked / the bloodstream became congested; → *auch Stauung*

Staub *m; -(e)s, kein Pl.* dust; (*Pulver*) powder; *Bot.* pollen; *von e-r Schicht ~ bedeckt* covered with a layer of dust;

(*im Schlafzimmer*) *~ saugen* vacuum (*Brit. auch* hoover) (the bedroom); *~ wischen* dust, do the dusting; *den ~ wischen von* dust (down); *zu ~ zerfallen* crumble into dust; *sich vor j-m in den ~ werfen fig. etw.* erbittend: throw o.s. at s.o.'s feet; *unterwürfig:* grovel before s.o. (*od.* at s.o.'s feet); *sich aus dem ~ machen umg.* clear off, make a (quick) getaway; → *aufwirbeln* I

staubbedeckt *Adj.* dust-covered, covered in dust; *stärker:* thick with dust

Staub|beutel *m* **1.** *Bot.* anther; **2.** *im Staubsauger:* dust bag; *~blatt n Bot.* stamen

Stäubchen *n* speck of dust

staubdicht *Adj.* dustproof

Staubecken *n* reservoir

stauben *v/i.* make a lot of dust; *es staubt* there's a lot of dust; *pass auf, sonst staubt's! umg.* watch it, or there'll be trouble

stäuben **I.** *v/t.:* *Mehl etc. über etw. ~* dust s.th. with flour *etc.;* **II.** *v/i.* **1.** *Wasser, Schnee:* spray; **2.** *Blüten:* pollinate

Stau|berater *m,* *~beraterin f* traffic congestion adviser

Staub|explosion *f* dust explosion; *~faden m Bot.* filament; *~fahne f* dust devil

Staub|fänger *m umg.* dust trap; *~filter m* dust filter; *~flocke f* piece of fluff, *Am. auch* dust bunny *umg.*

staubfrei *Adj.* dust-free, *präd. auch* free of dust

Staubgefäß *n Bot.* stamen

staubig *Adj.* dusty

Staub|korn *n* dust particle, speck of dust; *~lappen m* duster; *~lawine f* powder (snow) avalanche

Stäubling *m Bot.* puffball

Staub|lunge *f Med.* pneumoconiosis (*Pl.* pneumoconioses); *durch Quarzstaub hervorgerufen:* silicosis (*Pl.* silicoses); *~partikel n* dust particle

staubsaugen, Staub saugen *vt/i.* vacuum, *Brit. auch* hoover; **Staubsauger** *m* vacuum cleaner, *Brit. auch* hoover; *elektronischer ~ fig.* (*Abhörsystem*) bugging system

Staub|schicht *f* layer of dust; *~teilchen n* dust particle

staubtrocken *Adj.* **1.** *Lack:* etwa touch-dry; **2.** *umg.* dry as dust

Staub|tuch *n* duster; *~wedel m* feather duster; *~wolke f* cloud of dust; *~zucker m* icing (*Am.* confectioner's *od.* powdered) sugar

stauchen *v/t.* **1.** ram, thrust; *mit dem Fuß:* stub; (*verbiegen*) bend; **2.** (*Sack Getreide etc.*) shake down; **3.** *Tech.* (*Werkstück*) compress, upset *fachspr.;* (*Bolzenköpfe*) head, clinch; **4.** *Med.* → *verstauchen;* **5.** *fig.* → *zusammenstauchen*

Staudamm *m* dam

Staude *f; -, -n; Bot.* **1.** (perennial) herbaceous plant; **2.** *bes. südd.* (*Strauch*) shrub; **staudenartig** *Adj.* herbaceous

Staudensellerie *m, f Bot.* celery (stalks *Pl.*)

stauen **I.** *v/t.* **1.** (*Wasser, Fluss*) dam (up); (*Blut*) stop (*od.* stem) the flow of; **2.** *Naut.* (*Güter etc.*) stow (away); **II.** *v/refl.* **1.** (*zum Stillstand kommen*) *Wasser:* be held back (and accumulate), back up; *Blut:* become congested; **2.** (*sich ansammeln*) pile up, accumulate; *Menschen:* gather; *Verkehr:* back up, be(come) congested; *fig. Wut etc.:* build up; *die Leute stauten sich am Eingang* people were crowding the entrance; *die Autos stauten sich vor*

dem Tor there was a long line of cars (*od.* the cars backed up) in front of the gate

Stauende *n Mot.* end of the tailback (*Am.* backup)

Stauer *m; -s, -; Naut.* stevedore

Stau|gefahr *f* risk of tailbacks (*Am.* backups); *~länge f* length of a (*od.* the) tailback (*Am.* backup); *~mauer f* dam; *~meldung f* traffic report

staunen **I.** *v/i.* be amazed (*über + Akk.* at); *bewundernd:* marvel (at); *wir haben nur noch gestaunt umg.* we were simply amazed, we just gaped; *da staunst du, was? umg.* I thought that would surprise you; (*über mich*) *auch* you didn't think I could, did you?; *man höre und staune umg.* I don't believe it!, that's incredible!; → *Laie;* **II.** *v/t. umg.* → *Bauklotz*

Staunen *n; -s, kein Pl.* astonishment, amazement; (*Bewunderung*) awe; *in ~ versetzen* amaze, astonish; **staunenerregend, Staunen erregend** *Adj.* astonishing; **staunenswert** *Adj.* astonishing, amazing

Staupe *f; -, -n; Vet.* distemper

Stau|raum *m* **1.** *Naut.* (*Platz*) stowage (space); **2.** *für Wasser:* dam water basin; *~see m* reservoir; *~stufe f* barrage (as one of a series)

Stauung *f* **1.** (*Ansammlung*) build-up; *Med. und Verkehr allg.:* auch *Pl.* congestion; *von Menschen:* crowd, press; *e-e ~ des Verkehrs* a traffic jam; **2.** (*das Stauen*) *von Fluss, Wasser:* damming; *von Blut:* stemming the flow

Stau|warnung *f* warning of traffic congestion; *~wasser n* backwater

Steak [ste:k] *n; -s, -s; Gastr.* steak; *wie möchten Sie Ihr ~?* how would you like your steak (done)?; *~ Tatar* steak tartare

...steak *n, im Subst.* **1.** *nach Tier:* **Rinder~** beef steak; **Hirschkalb~** young venison steak; **Lachs~** salmon steak; **2.** *nach Schnitt:* **Hüft~** fillet steak; **Kalbsrücken~** veal loin steak; **Zwischenrippen~** cutlet; **3.** *nach Zubereitung:* **Minuten~** minute steak

Steak|fleisch *n* steak; *~haus n* steakhouse; *~teller m* **1.** *Teller:* steak plate; **2.** *Gericht:* steak dish (with vegetables and salad etc.)

Stearin *n; -s, -e; Chem.* stearin; *~säure f Chem.* stearic acid

Steatit *m; -s, -e; Min.* steatite

Stech|apfel *m Bot.* thorn apple; *~beitel m, ~eisen n* chisel

stechen; *sticht, stach, hat gestochen* **I.** *vt/i.* **1.** *Nadel, Dorn etc.:* prick; *Wespe etc.:* sting; *Mücke:* bite; *mit e-m Messer:* stab; *Wolle:* prick, be prickly; *Sonne:* burn; *mit dem Messer nach j-m ~* stab at (*od.* attack) s.o. with a knife; *sich* (*Dat.*) *in den Daumen ~* prick one's thumb; *mich hat etw. gestochen* s.th. has stung (*od.* bitten) me; *in die/der Nase ~ fig. Geruch:* sting one's nose; *j-m in die Augen ~* strike s.o., catch s.o.'s eye; **2.** *Kartenspiel:* take a trick; *mit e-r Trumpfkarte:* trump, play a trump; *mit dem König den Buben ~* take (*od.* trump) the jack with the king; **3.** (*die Kontrolluhr*) *~* clock in (*od.* on); *beim Weggehen:* clock out (*od.* off); → *See¹* 1; **II.** *v/t.* **1.** (*Torf, Rasen, Spargel*) cut; **2.** (*Schwein*) stick; **3.** (*Aale*) spear; **4.** *in Kupfer:* cut, engrave (*in + Akk.* into); → *gestochen, Hafer,* **III.** *v/i.* **1.** *Sport etc.:* have a play(-)off; *Pferde-*

sport: jump off; **2.** (*schmerzen*): **mein Herz sticht** I've got a sharp (*od.* pricking) pain in my heart; **IV.** *v/refl.* prick o.s. (**an** + *Dat.* on; **mit** with); **V.** *v/i.*, *unpers.*: **es sticht mir** *od.* **mich im Rücken / in der Seite** I've got a sharp (*wiederholt*: stabbing) pain in my back/side; **bei Seitenstechen**: I've got a stitch

Stechen *n*; *-s, kein Pl.* **1.** sharp (*wiederholt*: stabbing) pain; (*Seitenstechen*) stitch; **2.** *Sport etc.*: play-off, *Am.* playoff; *Pferdesport*: jump-off

stechend I. *Part. Präs.* → **stechen**; **II.** *Adj. Blick*: piercing; *Geruch*: pungent; *Schmerz*: sharp; *wiederholt*: stabbing; **III.** *Adv.*: **~ riechen** give off a pungent smell; **j-n ~ ansehen** give s.o. a piercing glance

Stecher *m*; *-s, -* **1.** (*Graveur*) engraver; **2.** *am Gewehr*: hair trigger; **3.** *vulg.* (*Liebhaber*) sexual partner

Stech|fliege *f Zool.* stable fly; (*Bremse*) horsefly; **~ginster** *m Bot.* gorse; **~kahn** *m* punt; **~karte** *f* clocking-in card, *Am.* timecard; **~mücke** *f Zool.* mosquito; **~paddel** *n Kanusport*: single-bladed paddle; **~palme** *f Bot.* holly; **~rüssel** *m Zool.* proboscis (*Pl.* proboscises *od.* proboscides *od.* proboscises); **~schritt** *m* goosestep; **im ~ marschieren** goosestep; **~uhr** *f* time clock; **~zirkel** *m* dividers *Pl.*

steckbar *Adj. Verbindung etc.*: plug-in; **~e Baugruppe/Einheit** plug-in assembly/unit

Steckbrief *m* (*Plakat*) "wanted" poster; (*Beschreibung*) description of the wanted person; *fig.* profile (+ *Gen.* of); *über Sache*: fact file (on); **steckbrieflich** *Adv.*: **~ gesucht werden** be wanted (for questioning *etc.*)

Steckbuchse *f Etron.* socket; *Computer*: port

Steckdose *f Etech.* (wall) socket, power point, *bes. Am.* outlet; **Steckdosenschutz** *m* socket cover, *Am.* outlet plate

stecken; *steckt, steckte od. stak, hat od. ist gesteckt* **I.** *v/t.* (*hat*) **1.** *irgendwohin*: put, stick *umg.*; *heimlich*: slip; (*Blumen*) arrange; *mit Nadeln*: pin; (*Saum*) tack; **die Hände in die Hosentaschen ~** stick one's hands in one's trouser (*Am.* pant) pockets; **sich** (*Dat.*) **heimlich etw. in die Tasche** *etc.* **~** slip s.th. secretively into one's pocket *etc.*; **den Kopf aus dem Fenster ~** stick one's head out of (*Am. auch* out) the window; **sich** (*Dat.*) **die Haare zu e-m Knoten ~** put one's hair up in a knot; **sich** (*Dat.*) **e-e Blume ins Haar ~** put (*od.* stick *umg.*) a flower in one's hair; **2.** *umg.* (*bringen*) put, stick; **j-n ins Gefängnis/Bett ~** put s.o. in prison / to bed; **j-n in e-e Anstalt ~** stick s.o. in an institution; **ich weiß nicht, wohin ich ihn ~ soll** *fig.* I can't place him; **3.** *Geld, Zeit etc.* **~ in** + *Akk.* put into, invest in; **4.** *umg.* (*verraten*) tell; **wer hat ihm das gesteckt?** who told him (that)?, who passed that on to him?; **es j-m tüchtig ~** *umg.* tell s.o. what's what; **5.** *Agr.* (*Erbsen, Kartoffeln etc.*) plant; **6.** *umg.* (*aufgeben*) give up, chuck in; **ich glaub, ich steck's!** I think I'll give up (*od.* chuck it in); → *hineinstecken*, *Brand* 1, *Nase*[1] 1, *Tasche* 2, *Ziel* 4; **II.** *v/i.* (*Imperf. altm. auch stak, hat, südd., österr., schw. auch ist gesteckt*) **1.** (*sich befinden*) be; (*festsitzen*) be stuck; *Kugel, Splitter etc.*: be lodged (*od.* embedded) in; **der**

Schlüssel steckt the key's in the door; **~ bleiben** get stuck; *umg. fig.* *Vortragen*: *auch* dry up, come unstuck; *Theat. auch* forget one's lines; *Verhandlungen*: come to a standstill, reach deadlock; **mitten im Satz ~ bleiben** *fig.* break off in mid-sentence; **das Projekt ist in den Anfangsstadien ~ geblieben** the project didn't get beyond the early stages; **den Schlüssel ~ lassen** leave the key in the door; **lass das Messer ~!** leave your knife where it is; → *Anfang* 3, *Decke* 2, *gesteckt*, *Hals* 3, *Haut* 4; **2.** *umg. fig.* (*sein*) be; **voller Fehler ~** *Brief etc.*: be full of mistakes; **mitten in den Prüfungen ~** be in the middle of (*od.* in the throes of) (taking) one's exams; **er steckt immer zu Hause** he's stuck at home all the time, he never goes out; **wo steckst du denn (so lange)?** where have you been (all this time)?, where did you get to (all this time)?; **wo steckt er bloß immer?** where does he keep disappearing to (*od.* hiding himself)?; **da steckt 'er dahinter** he's at the bottom of it, he's behind it (all); **darin steckt viel Arbeit** a lot of work has gone into it; **in dem Geschäft steckt e-e Menge Geld** (*es wurde viel investiert*) a lot of money has gone into that business; (*man kann viel verdienen*) there's a packet (*Am.* bundle) of money to be made out of that business; **zeigen, was in einem steckt** show what one is made of; **in ihm steckt etwas** he's got what it takes, he'll go far (*od.* a long way)

Stecken *m*; *-s, -* stick; → *Dreck* 2

stecken| bleiben → **stecken** II 1; **~ lassen** → **stecken** II 1

Steckenpferd *n* (*Spielzeug, fig. Lieblingsthema*) hobbyhorse; (*Liebhaberei*) favo(u)rite pastime

Stecker *m*; *-s, -*; *Etech.* plug; **Steckerleiste** *f Etech.* multiple extension socket, *Am.* outlet strip

Steck|karte *f EDV* expansion card (*od.* board); **~kontakt** *m Etech.* plug

Steckling *m*; *-s, -e*; *Bot.* cutting

Steckmodul *n Tech.* plug-in module

Stecknadel *f* pin; **wie e-e ~ (im Heuhaufen) suchen** *fig.* hunt high and low for; **da sucht man e-e ~ im Heuhaufen** it's like looking for a needle in a haystack; **~kissen** *n* pincushion

Stecknadelkopf *m* pinhead; **stecknadelkopfgroß** *Adj.* nachgestellt: the size of (*od.* no bigger than) a pinhead

Steck|platz *m EDV* slot; **~rübe** *f Bot.* turnip; **~schach** *n* pocket (*od.* miniature) chess set; **~schloss** *n* lock security pin; **~schlüssel** *m Tech.* socket wrench (*Brit. auch* spanner); **~schuh** *m Fot.* accessory shoe; **~schuss** *m* gunshot wound with lodged bullet; **~tuch** *n* breast-pocket handkerchief; **~verbinder** *m Tech.* plug-in connector; **~verbindung** *f Tech.* plug-in connection; **~zwiebel** *f Bot.* bulb for planting

Steg *m*; *-(e)s, -e* **1.** (*Brücke*) footbridge; (*Brett*) plank; *an Maschinen*: catwalk; *Naut.* jetty, landing stage; (*Laufsteg*) gangplank; **2.** *der Brille*: bridge; *an der Hose*: stirrup; **3.** *Mus.* bridge; **4.** *Tech.* crosspiece, bar; **5.** *Druck.* gutter; **~hose** *f* stirrup pants

Stegreif *m*: **aus dem ~** off the cuff; **aus dem ~ spielen** *od.* **dichten** *etc.* improvise, extemporize; **~dichter** *m*, **~dichterin** *f* extempore poet; **~komödie** *f* improvised comedy; **~rede** *f* impromp-

tu (*od.* off-the-cuff) speech

Stehaufmännchen *n* **1.** (*Spielzeug*) roly-poly, tumbler; **2.** *fig.* resilient person; **er ist ein richtiges ~** he keeps bouncing back

Steh|ausschank *m*, **~bierhalle** *f* stand-up bar; **~bild** *n Film*: still; **~bündchen** *n* stand-up collar; **~empfang** *m* stand-up reception

stehen; *steht, stand, hat, südd., österr., schw. auch ist gestanden* **I.** *v/i.* **1.** (*aufrecht sein*) *Person, Ding*: stand; **der Kleine kann schon ~** he can stand up (*od.* stand on his own) already; **ich kann vor Müdigkeit kaum noch ~** I'm so tired I can hardly stand up; **plötzlich stand er vor mir** suddenly he was standing there in front of me; **j-n (einfach) ~ lassen** (just) leave s.o. standing there; **vor Dreck ~** *umg.* be stiff with dirt; **das Hotel soll Ende Mai ~** the hotel is supposed to be standing (*od.* complete) by the end of May; **2.** (*sich befinden*) be; **wo ~ die Gläser?** where are the glasses?; **der Wein steht kalt** the wine has been chilled; **die Pflanze steht zu dunkel** that plant needs more light; **der Keller steht voll Wasser** the cellar's flooded (*od.* full of water); **3.** (*stillstehen*) stand still; *Uhr etc.*: have stopped; **der Verkehr stand** the traffic was at (*od.* had come to) a standstill; **die Luft steht draußen**: it's very still (*schwül*: close); **drinnen**: the air is thick in here; **~ bleiben** *Person, beim Vortragen etc.*: stop (short); *Uhr*: stop; *Maschine*: *auch* come to a standstill (*auch fig.*); *Motor*: *auch* stall; *Herz*: stop beating; *Zeit*: stand still; **halt, ~ bleiben (oder ich schieße)!** stop (or I'll shoot)!; **nicht ~ bleiben!** move along, please!, keep moving!; **wo waren wir ~ geblieben?** *fig.* where were we?; *im Buch etc.*: *auch* where did we get to?; **mir ist das Herz fast ~ geblieben** my heart missed a beat; **das Kind ist in der Entwicklung ~ geblieben** the child is (a bit) backward; **4.** **~ bleiben** (*vergessen werden*) be left behind; **~ lassen** (*zurücklassen, auch vergessen*) leave behind; (*Essen*) not touch, leave (untouched); **ihr könnt das Geschirr ruhig ~ lassen** you can just leave the dishes; **alles ~ und liegen lassen** drop everything; **man sollte sein Auto auch mal ~ lassen** you should occasionally leave your car at home; **5.** **~ in** (+ *Dat.*) (*geschrieben sein*) be (written) in; **im Brief steht** the letter says; **hier steht, (dass)** it says here (that); **wo steht das (geschrieben)?** where does it say that?; *fig. bei Verbot etc.*: since when is that a crime?, says who? *umg.*; **hier muss ein Komma ~** there should be a comma here; **nach diesem Verb steht der Konjunktiv** that verb takes (*od.* requires) the subjunctive; **auf e-r Liste ~** be on a list; **~ lassen** (*nicht streichen*) leave (in); (*übersehen, Fehler*) overlook, miss; **~ bleiben** (*nicht verändert werden*) stay, be left; **bitte ~ lassen!** (*Tafelanschrieb etc.*) please leave, please don't rub out; **das kann so nicht ~ bleiben** (*Text, Behauptung, Formulierung etc.*) you can't leave it like that; **soll das so ~ bleiben?** is it supposed to stay like that?; **6.** *umg.* (*feststehen*) be fixed, be finalized; **die Mannschaft / der Plan steht** the team/plan has been finalized; **der Termin steht** the date is fixed; **7.** *mit Wert-, Zahlenangabe etc.*: **~ auf** (+ *Dat.*) *Ska-*

la etc.: show, be at; *Aktien etc.*: be at; *der Zeiger steht auf null* the needle is at (*od.* on) zero; *das Thermometer steht auf 10 Grad* the thermometer shows (*od.* is pointing to) 10 degrees; *wie steht der Dollar?* how high is the dollar?, what's the dollar worth?; *der Dollar steht bei ...* the dollar stands at (*od.* is worth) ...; *höher denn je ~ Währung, Aktienkurs etc.*: have reached an all-time high; *zu ~ kommen auf* (*kosten*) cost, come to; **8.** *mit Strafe od. Belohnung*: *auf Diebstahl steht e-e Freiheitsstrafe* theft is punishable by imprisonment; *auf die Ergreifung des Täters ~ 10.000 Euro Belohnung* there's a reward of 10,000 euros for the capture of the person who did it; **9.** *wo steht er politisch?* what are his political leanings?; *er steht* (*politisch*) *links* (politically) he's on the left; **10.** *umg.*: *auf j-n/etw. ~* like (*od.* fancy) s.o./s.th.; *er steht auf modernen Jazz* he's into modern jazz; *sie steht auf große, dunkle Typen* she goes for the tall dark type; *da steh ich nicht drauf* it doesn't turn me on; **11.** *fig.*: *~ für* stand for; *stellvertretend*: represent; *der Name steht für Qualität* the name stands (*od.* is a byword) for quality; **12.** *fig. hinter j-m ~* be behind s.o.; *voll hinter j-m ~* be backing s.o. all the way (*od.* up to the hilt); *gut/ schlecht mit j-m ~* get on / not get on (very well) with s.o.; *über/unter j-m ~* be above/below s.o.; *er steht über solchen Dingen* he's above that kind of thing; **13.** *fig.*: *zu j-m/etw. ~* stand by s.o./s.th.; *wie stehst du dazu?* what do you think (about it)?, what are your feelings (on the matter)?; **14.** *unter Alkohol ~* be under the influence of alcohol, have been drinking; *vor großen Schwierigkeiten ~* face great difficulties; *vor dem Ruin ~* be on the brink of ruin; *er steht vor s-r Abschlussprüfung* he's got his final exams coming up; **15.** *fig.*: *wie ~ die Dinge?* how are things?; *die Sache steht gut* things are looking good; *das Ganze steht und fällt mit ...* the whole thing stands or falls on ...; *die Chancen ~ fifty-fifty* the odds are even; → *Aufsicht* 1, *Debatte, Einfluss, Sinn* 3; **16.** (*kleiden*) *j-m ~* suit s.o.; *der Hut etc. steht dir gut* that hat *etc.* (really) suits you; **17.** *sich* (*Dat.*) *e-n Bart ~ lassen* grow a beard; **18.** *umg. Penis*: be erect; *er stand ihm Sl. Penis*: he had a hard-on; **II.** *v/t.*: *e-n Sprung ~ Eiskunstlauf, Turnen*: land a jump; *kann er diese Weite ~?* can he make this distance (without falling)?; → *Mann* 5, *Modell* 2, *Pate* 1, *Posten* 1; **III.** *v/refl.*: *sich gut/schlecht mit j-m ~* get on / not get on (well) with s.o.; *er steht sich gut* he's not doing badly; **IV.** *v/i. unpers.* **1.** *wie steht es um ...?* (*etw., j-n*) how is/are ... (getting on)?; *wie steht es um s-e Doktorarbeit?* what's the position with his doctorate?; *es steht gut/schlecht um ihn* things are going well/badly for him, he's doing well/badly; *Aussichten*: things are looking good/bad for him; *mit i-r Gesundheit steht es schlecht* she's in a bad way (healthwise); *na,* (*wie geht's,*) *wie steht's?* *umg.* and how are we?; *wie steht's mit e-m Bier?* *umg.* how about a beer?; (*und*) *wie stehts es mit dir?* *umg.* how about you?; **2.** *Sport*: *es steht 2:1* the score is 2-1 (*für* to); *wie* (*viel*) *steht es?*

what's the score?; **3.** *es steht zu befürchten, dass* it is to be feared that; *es steht nicht bei mir zu* (+ *Inf.*) it's not for me to (+ *Inf.*), it's not up to me to (+ *Inf.*)

Stehen *n; -s, kein Pl.* **1.** *etw. im ~ tun* do s.th. while standing (up); *er macht alles im ~* he does everything standing up; *vom vielen ~ bekommt sie Rückenschmerzen* she gets back pain from all this standing (*od.* because she has to stand so much); **2.** *zum ~ bringen* bring to a stop (*od.* standstill); (*Blutung* etc.) stop; *zum ~ kommen* come to a halt (*od.* standstill)

stehen bleiben → *stehen* I 3, 4, 5

stehend I. *Part. Präs.* → *stehen*; **II.** *Adj.* **1.** standing (*auch Start*); *Wasser*: *auch* stagnant; (*aufrecht*) upright; *~en Fußes* on the spot, straightaway; **2.** (*stillstehend*) stationary; *~es Bild TV, EDV* still (frame); **3.** (*ständig*) permanent; *~er Ausdruck* standing (*od.* stock) phrase; **III.** *Adv.* (*im Stehen*) standing (up); *~ k.o.* out on one's feet

stehen lassen → *stehen* I 1, 4, 5, 17

Steher *m; -s, -* **1.** (*Pferd*) (good) stayer; **2.** (*Radfahrer*) motor-paced rider; *~rennen* *n* motor-paced (long-distance) race

Steh|geiger *m*, *~geigerin* *f* (café) violinist; *~imbiss* *m* stand-up snack bar; *~kneipe* *f* stand-up bar; *~kragen* *m* stand-up collar; *~lampe* *f* standard lamp, *Am.* floor lamp, torchiere; *~leiter* *f* stepladder

stehlen *stiehlt, stahl, hat gestohlen* **I.** *vt/i.* **1.** steal (*j-m etw.* s.th. from s.o.); *Brit. umg.* nick; (*plagiieren*) *auch umg.* lift (*aus, von* from); *sie haben ihm sein ganzes Geld gestohlen* they stole all his money (from him), they robbed him of all his money; *ich glaube, sie stiehlt* I think she steals (things); **2.** *fig., in Wendungen*: *j-m die Zeit ~ fig.* waste s.o.'s time; *er hat mir e-n ganzen Tag gestohlen* he wasted a whole day of my time; *j-m den Schlaf / die Ruhe ~* rob (*od.* deprive) s.o. of his (*od.* her) sleep / peace and quiet; *woher nehmen und nicht ~?* *umg.* where on earth can one get hold of such a thing (short of stealing it)?; → *gestohlen*; **II.** *v/refl.*: *sich aus dem Haus* etc. *~* steal (*od.* sneak) out of the house *etc.*

Steh|platz *m*: *e-n ~ bekommen* *im Bus*: have to stand; *Theat.* etc.: get a standing ticket; (*nur noch*) *Stehplätze* standing room (only), *abgek.* SRO; *~pult* *n* standing desk; *~tribünen* *Pl.* terraces; *~vermögen* *n* stamina; (*Durchhaltevermögen*) perseverance, staying power

Steiermark *f; -; Geog.* Styria; *in der ~* in Styria

steif I. *Adj.* **1.** stiff (*auch Körperteil, Eischnee etc.*); *bes. Phys.* (*starr*) rigid; (*fest*) *auch* firm; *Penis*: hard; *~er Hals* stiff neck; *~ vor Kälte* stiff with cold; *~er Hut* homburg (hat); *~ wie ein Brett* (as) stiff as a board; *~ werden* go stiff; *Person*: get stiff; *Penis*: get hard; *Muskeln und fig.*: stiffen; *ich bin* (*vom vielen Sitzen*) *ganz ~ geworden* I'm really stiff (from all this sitting around); *~ schlagen* beat until stiff; *halt die Ohren steif!* chin up!; **2.** *fig.* stiff; *Bewegung*: *auch* wooden (*auch Lächeln, Interpretation*); (*förmlich*) *auch* formal; *~e Haltung* stiff (*od.* rigid) posture; *Deutsche gelten oft als ~* Germans

are often thought to be stiff and formal; **3.** (*stark*) *~e Brise* stiff breeze; *~er Grog* strong hot grog; **II.** *Adv.* **1.** stiffly; *~ gefroren* *auch fig.* frozen stiff; **2.** *fig.* stiffly; (*förmlich*) *auch* formally; *dort geht es mir zu ~ zu* it's too stiff and formal there for my liking; **3.** *~ und fest behaupten, dass* insist that, swear that; *~ und fest glauben, dass* firmly believe that

steifbeinig I. *Adj.* stiff-legged; **II.** *Adv.* with stiff legs

Steife *f; -, kein Pl.* stiffness; **steifen** *v/t.* (*Wäsche*) stiffen; (*Mauer*) brace

Steifftier® *n* Steiff soft toy (*Am.* stuffed animal)

Steifheit *f* stiffness; *fig., von Bewegungen, Interpretation*: *auch* woodenness; (*Förmlichkeit*) *auch* formality; → *steif* I

Steig *m; -(e)s, -e* steep path

Steigbügel *m* stirrup (*auch Anat.*); *~halter* *m Pol. pej.* henchman, stooge *umg.*; *j-s ~ sein* give s.o. a leg up (*Am.* a boost); (*an die Macht helfen*) help bring s.o. to power

Steige *f; -, -n* **1.** *für Obst etc.*: crate; **2.** *bes. südd., österr.* (*Straße*) steep road

Steigeisen *n* climbing iron; *Bergsteigen*: *auch* crampon

steigen *steigt, stieg, ist gestiegen* **I.** *v/i.* **1.** *hinauf*: climb; *in die Luft*: *auch* rise; *Flug.* climb (*auf + Akk.* to); *Ballon*: *auch* ascend; *Nebel*: lift; *Wasserspiegel*: rise; *Sonne*: rise, come up; *auf e-n Berg etc. ~* climb (up) a mountain *etc.*; *in den Keller / die Schlucht ~* climb (*od.* go) down into the cellar/ravine; *aufs Pferd ~* mount (*od.* get on) one's horse; *vom Pferd ~* dismount (from one's horse), get off one's horse; *vom Fahrrad ~* get off (*od.* dismount from) one's bicycle; *aus dem Wasser ~* come out of the water; *in die / aus der Wanne ~* climb (*od.* get) into / out of the bath; *ins / aus dem Bett ~* *umg.* get into / out of bed; *zu j-m ins Bett ~* *umg.* get into bed with s.o.; *auf den Thron ~* ascend the throne; *e-n Drachen/Ballon ~ lassen* fly a kite / send up a balloon; *~ aus* → *auch aussteigen* 1; *~ in* (+ *Akk.*) → *auch einsteigen* 1; **2.** (*treten*) step; *auf die Bremse ~* slam the brakes on, step on the brakes; *in die Hose ~* get (*od.* step) into one's trousers (*Am.* pants); **3.** *das Blut stieg ihr ins Gesicht* the blood rushed to her face; *Tränen stiegen ihr in die Augen* tears welled up in her eyes; *etw. steigt j-m in die Nase* s.th. gets up (*od.* into) s.o.'s nose; **4.** (*höher werden*) *auch Spannung*: rise; *Fieber, Temperatur, Thermometer*: *auch* go up; (*zunehmen*) go up, increase; (*bedrohlich*: escalate; *Wirts., Preise, Kurse etc.*: rise (*bis zu* to), go up; *die Stimmung stieg merklich* the general mood improved noticeably, everyone's spirits rose markedly; *die Ansprüche/Aussichten sind gestiegen* demands have grown / prospects have improved; **5.** *Pferd*: (*sich aufbäumen*) rear; **6.** *umg.* (*stattfinden*): *heute Abend steigt eine Fete* there's a party (on) tonight, there's going to be a party tonight; *der Coup steigt am Freitag* the coup will happen on Friday; → *Achtung* 1, *Dach* 3, *Kopf* 2, *Wert* 3; **II.** *v/t.*: *Treppen ~* climb stairs

steigend I. *Part. Präs.* → *steigen*; **II.** *Adj.* (*zunehmend*) rising, increasing; (*wachsend*) growing; *Interesse, Po-*

pularität, Schulden, Wichtigkeit etc.: *auch* mounting; **~e Reihe** *Math.* ascending series; **~e Tendenz** *Börse*: upward tendency; **30 000, Tendenz: ~** *Statistik*: 30,000 and rising

Steiger *m*; *-s, -*; *Bergb.* pit foreman

steigerbar *Adj. Ling.* capable of forming a comparative (and superlative)

Steigerer *m*; *-s, -* bidder

Steigerin *f*; *-, -nen* **1.** *Bergb.* pit forewoman; **2.** *bei Auktion*: bidder

steigern I. *v/t.* **1.** increase; (*Spannung, Wirkung*) *auch* heighten, intensify; (*Wert*)*auch* put up, enhance; (*verbessern*) improve, enhance; (*verschlimmern*) exacerbate; (*Produktion, Tempo*) increase, step up; **2.** *Ling.* compare; **Adjektive steigert man auf „-er, -est" oder „more, most"** the comparative and superlative of adjectives are formed with "-er" and "-est" or "more" and "most"; **II.** *v/refl.* increase; (*wachsen*) *auch* grow; *Preise*: rise, go up, increase; *Spannung*: rise; *auch Erregung*: mount; (*sich verbessern*) improve (one's performance); **im Finale konnte sie sich nochmals ~** in the final she succeeded in finding that extra something (*Tennis etc.*: in raising her game); → *auch* **hineinsteigern**; **III.** *v/i. auf e-r Auktion*: bid; (*erhöhen*) raise the amount (*auf + Akk.* to)

Steigerung *f* **1.** increase; *von Spannung, Wirkung*: *auch* heightening, intensification; *von Wert*: *auch* enhancement; (*Verbesserung*) improvement; (*Verschlimmerung*) exacerbation; **2.** *Ling.* comparison; (*Form*) comparative *bzw.* superlative

steigerungsfähig *Adj.* **1.** capable of being increased (*od.* of improvement); **die Produktion ist ~** production can be increased (*od.* improved); **2.** *Ling.* → *steigerbar*

Steigerungs|form *f Ling.* comparative or superlative form; **~stufe** *f Ling.*: **erste/zweite ~** middle/highest degree of comparison, comparative/superlative (form); **~rate** *f* rate of increase

Steig|fähigkeit *f Mot.* hill-climbing ability; **~flug** *m* climb; **~geschwindigkeit** *f* climbing speed, rate of climb; **~höhe** *f* altitude; **~leistung** *f Mot.* hill-climbing performance; **~leitung** *f* riser; **~riemen** *m* stirrup leather; **~rohr** *n* riser (pipe *od.* duct)

Steigung *f Eisenb., Straße*: gradient; (*Hang*) uphill stretch, hill; **die Straße hat e-e ~ von 20%** the road has a gradient of 1 in 5 (*Am.* has a 20% grade); **an der ~ runterschalten** change down on the uphill stretch; **Steigungswinkel** *m* angle of gradient (*Flug.* climb)

steil I. *Adj.* **1.** steep; (*abschüssig*) precipitous; **~er Abfall** steep (*od.* sharp, *stärker*: sheer) drop; **~e Abfahrt** *Ski*: steep piste (*od.* downhill course); **~er Aufstieg** steep ascent; *fig.* (*auch* **~e Karriere**) meteoric rise; **2.** *Sport, Pass, Zuspiel*: deep; **3.** *altm. Jugendspr.* fabulous, super; **~er Zahn** stunning wench; **II.** *Adv.* **1.** steeply; **~ ansteigen** rise steeply; *fig. auch* rise sharply, soar; **~ abfallen** slope down (*od.* fall away) steeply; *fig.* drop sharply, plummet; **es geht ~ nach unten** *Pfad etc.*: it leads steeply down; **~ aufsteigen** *Flug.* climb steeply; **~ aufragend** soaring; **2.** *Sport*: **den Ball ~ spielen** play the ball deep (*od.* long)

Steil|abfahrt *f Ski*: steep piste (*od.* downhill course); **~flug** *m Flug.* verti-

cal flight; **~hang** *m* steep slope, escarpment

Steilheit *f* steepness; *Phys., von Röhren*: slope

Steil|kurve *f* steeply banked corner (*Am.* turn); **~küste** *f* steep coast, (line of) cliffs *Pl.*; **~pass** *m Fußball*: long ball, through pass; **~ufer** *n* steep bank, cliffs *Pl.*; **~vorlage** *f Sport* long ball (*od.* through pass) downfield

Steilwand *f* (steep) rock face; **~fahrer** *m*, **~fahrerin** *f* wall-of-death rider; **~zelt** *n* frame tent

Stein *m*; *-(e)s, -e* **1.** stone, *Am. auch* rock; *kleiner, glatter*: pebble; (*Ziegel*) brick; (*Felsen*) rock; (*Edelstein*) (precious) stone, gem; (*Grab-, Denkmalstein*) stone; *in Obst*: stone, kernel; *Med.* stone; **es blieb kein ~ auf dem andern** there wasn't a stone left standing; **~ des Anstoßes** *fig.* bone of contention; **der ~ der Weisen** the philosopher's stone; **den ~ ins Rollen bringen** *fig.* set the ball rolling; **den ersten ~ werfen** *fig.* cast the first stone; **j-m ~e in den Weg legen** *fig.* place obstacles in s.o.'s path; **mir fällt ein ~ vom Herzen** that's (*od.* that takes) a load off my mind; **dass es e-n ~ erweichen könnte** so as to soften the hardest of hearts (*od.* a heart of stone); → *Tropfen*; **2.** *nur Sg.*; (*Substanz*) stone; (*Felsen*) rock; **hart wie ~** rock-hard; **ein Herz aus ~** *fig.* a heart of stone; **~ und Bein schwören** *umg.* swear by all that is holy; **es friert ~ und Bein** *umg.* it's freezing really hard, it's cold enough to freeze the balls off a brass monkey, *Am.* it's colder than a welldigger's ass in January; **3.** *Brettspiel*: piece; **bei j-m e-n ~ im Brett haben** be in s.o.'s good books *umg.*, be well in with s.o. *umg.*; **4.** *Dial.* (*Bierkrug*) stein, stone tankard

Steinadler *m* golden eagle

steinalt *Adj.* ancient; **~ werden** live to a great age

Stein|axt *f hist.* stone axe; **~bau** *m -s, -ten* stone building; **~beißer** *m*; *-s, -*; *Zool.* groundling; **~block** *m* block of stone; (*Fels*) boulder; **~bock** *m* **1.** *Zool.* ibex; **2.** (*Sternzeichen*) Capricorn; (*ein*) **~ sein** be (a) Capricorn; **~boden** *m* **1.** rocky ground; **2.** *innen*: stone floor; **~bohrer** *m.* masonry drill; *für Gestein*: rock drill; **~brech** *m*; *-(e)s, -e*; *Bot.* saxifrage; **~brecher** *m* **1.** (*Maschine*) rock crusher; **2.** (*Person*) quarryman; **~brocken** *m* lump of stone; **~bruch** *m* quarry; **als ~ benutzen** *fig.* use as a source; **~butt** *m* turbot; **~druck** *m* **1.** *nur Sg.* lithography; **2.** (*Graphik*) lithograph; **~eiche** *f* holm oak

steinern *Adj. attr.* stone …; *fig.* stony; **~es Herz** *fig.* heart of stone; **~e Miene** stony expression

Steinerweichen *fig. n*: **zum ~** heart-rending(ly)

Steinewerfer *m* stone-thrower

Stein|fliege *f Zool.* stone fly; **~fliese** *f* flagstone; **~fraß** *m* stone erosion; **~frucht** *f* stone fruit, drupe; **~fußboden** *m* stone floor; **~garten** *m* rockery, rock garden

Steingut *n nur Sg.* stoneware; **~geschirr** *n* stoneware (crockery)

Steinhagel *m* hail of stones

steinhart *Adj.* rock-hard

Stein|haufen *m* pile of stones; **~haus** *n* stone house

steinig *Adj.* stony; **ein langer, ~er Weg** *fig.* a long and difficult path

steinigen *v/t.* stone to death; **die ~ mich, wenn ich das tue** *umg. fig.* they'll crucify me if I do that; **Steinigung** *f* stoning

Steinkauz *m Orn.* little owlet

Steinkohle *f* hard coal; **Steinkohlen...** *im Subst. siehe auch* **Kohlen...**

Steinkohlen|bergwerk *n Bergb.* coal mine, colliery; **~einheit** *f* (*abgek.* **SKE**) thermal unit for coal; **~revier** *n* coal-mining area, coalfield

Stein|krug *m* stoneware jug (*Am.* pitcher); (*Trinkgefäß*) stoneware mug, stein; **~lawine** *f* rock avalanche; **~leiden** *n Med.* (*Gallensteine*) gallstones *Pl.*; (*Nierensteine*) kidney stones *Pl.*; (*Blasensteine*) bladder stones *Pl.*; **~marder** *m Zool.* stone (*od.* beech) marten; **~metz** *m*; *-en, -en*, **~metzin** *f*; *-, -nen* stonemason; **~obst** *n* stone fruit, drupe

Steinpilz *m Bot.* cep, boletus; **~kremsuppe** *f Gastr.* cream of cep mushroom soup

Stein|platte *f* stone slab; (*Fliese*) flagstone; **~quader** *m* ashlar

steinreich *Adj. umg.* loaded, stinking rich, *präd. auch* rolling (in it)

Steinsalz *n* rock salt

Steinschlag *m* rockfall; *auf Schild*: falling rocks *Pl.*; **~gefahr** *f*: **Achtung! ~!** Danger - Falling rocks

Stein|schleuder *f* sling; *mit Gestell*: catapult, *Am.* slingshot; **~schlossgewehr** *n hist.* flintlock rifle; **~tafel** *f* stone tablet; **~topf** *m* stoneware pot; **~wall** *m* stone rampart; **~wild** *n Zool.* ibex; **~wolle** *f* rock wool; **~wurf** *m* throwing of a stone (*od.* of stones); **nur e-n ~ entfernt** *fig.* only a stone's throw away; **~wüste** *f* stone desert

Steinzeit *f* Stone Age

steinzeitlich *Adj. attr.* Stone Age …; *umg. fig.* antediluvian

Steinzeit|mensch *m*: **der ~** (*auch* **die ~en**) Stone Age man; **~methoden** *Pl. umg. fig.* antediluvian methods

Steinzeug *n* stoneware

Steirer *m*; *-s, -*, **~in** *f*; *-, -nen* Styrian (*weiblich auch*: Styrian woman (*od.* girl)); **steirisch** *Adj.* Styrian

Steiß *m*; *-es, -e* **1.** *Anat.* (*Steißbein*) coccyx (*Pl.* coccyges *od.* coccyxes); (*Gesäß*) buttocks *Pl.*; **2.** *Jägerspr.* (*Schwanz*) rudimentary tail; **~bein** *n Anat.* coccyx (*Pl.* coccyges *od.* coccyxes); **~geburt** *f Med.* breech delivery; **~lage** *f Med.* breech presentation

Stele *f*; *-, -n*; *Archäol.* stele

Stellage [ʃtɛˈlaːʒə] *f*; *-, -n* **1.** (*Gestell*) stand, rack; **2.** *Wirts., Börse*: put and call (*abgek.* **pac**)

stellar *Adj. Astron.* stellar

Stelldichein *n*; *-(s), -(s)*; *altm.* rendezvous, *lit. und iro.* tryst; *Sport* meet; **sich ein ~ geben** arrange to meet, get together

Stelle *f*; *-, -n* **1.** (*Ort*) place; (*Punkt*) point; (*Standort*) position; **an anderer ~** somewhere else, elsewhere; *fig.* at some other point; **an dieser ~** here; *fig.* at this point; **an genau dieser ~** at this exact (*od.* very) spot; **auf der ~ treten** *fig.* mark time; **nicht von der ~ kommen** *fig.* not make any progress, not get anywhere; *Verhandlungen*: *auch* be deadlocked; **sich nicht von der ~ rühren** not move (*od.* budge); **zur ~ sein** be on the spot (*od.* there); **er ist immer zur ~** he's always there when you need him; **sich zur ~ melden** report (*bei j-m* to s.o.); **auf der ~** there and then, straightaway, immediately; **er war auf der ~ tot** he died immediately; **2.** (*Fleck*) spot; *abgenutzte, schmutzige etc.: auch* patch; **undichte ~** leak; **wunde ~** sore; (*Schnitt*) cut; **entzündete ~** inflammation; **empfindliche ~** tender (*od.* sore) spot, *fig.* sensitive (*od.* sore) spot; **schwache od. verwundbare ~** *fig.* weak (*od.* vulnerable) spot; → *auch* **Rotstelle** *etc.*; **3.** *Wirts.* (*Arbeitsstelle*) job; *formeller:* position, post; **freie ~** (job) vacancy; **e-e ~ ausschreiben/besetzen** advertise/occupy (*od.* fill) a position (*od.* post); **e-e ~ sperren** leave a position vacant (for a time); **die ~ wechseln** change jobs; → *auch* **Stellung** 2; **4.** *in Rangordnung etc.:* place; **an erster ~** first(ly); **an erster ~ stehen** come first; *Sache: auch* be top priority; **an erster ~ der Tagesordnung stehen** be at the top of the agenda; **an erster ~ möchte ich ...** first and foremost I'd like to ...; **5. an ~ von** (*od.* + *Gen.*) in place of, instead of; *bes. Jur.* in lieu of; (**ich**) **an deiner ~** if I were you; **ich möchte nicht an s-r ~ sein** I wouldn't like to be in his shoes; **an die ~ treten von** take the place of; *Person:* take over from; *ersatzweise:* replace, stand in for; *Gesetz etc.:* supersede; **6.** *im Buch etc.:* place; *längere, auch Mus.:* passage; **7.** *Math.* figure, digit; (*Dezimalstelle*) (decimal) place; *EDV* position; **bis auf drei ~n nach dem Komma** up to three decimal places; **8.** (*Behörde*) authority; (*Dienststelle*) office; **e-e staatliche/ kirchliche ~** a government/church office; → **zuständig** 1

...stelle *f, im Subst.* **1.** (*Ort*): **die Fund~ von etw.** the place where s.th was found; **2.** (*Arbeitsstelle*): **Pfarr~** post as parish priest (*evangelisch:* pastor); **Dreiviertel~** three-quarter-time job; **3.** (*Institution*): **Beschwerde~** complaints cent|re (*Am.* -er)

stellen I. *v/t.* **1.** *etw. irgendwohin ~* put (*od.* place, *aufrecht:* stand) s.th. somewhere; **kalt ~** chill; **warm ~** *Kaltes:* heat; *Warmes:* keep warm; **etw. über etw. ~** *fig.* place s.th. above s.th. else, value s.th. more highly than s.th. else; **j-n über j-n ~** promote s.o. above s.o. else; (*einschätzen*) think more highly of s.o. (than s.o. else); **j-n/etw. in den Mittelpunkt ~** focus (attention) on s.o./s.th., make s.o./s.th. the cent|re (*Am.* -er) of attention; **vor e-e Entscheidung gestellt werden** be faced (*od.* confronted) with a decision; **2.** (*einstellen*) set (**auf** + *Akk.* to, at); (*regulieren*) regulate, adjust; **leiser od. niedriger ~** turn down; **lauter od. höher ~** turn up; **den Wecker auf sechs ~** set the alarm for six; **3.** (*in die Enge treiben*) corner; (*fangen*) catch; (*Wild*) hunt down; **4.** (*bereitstellen*) provide (**j-m etw.** s.o. with s.th.); (*auch Truppen*) supply; (*beisteuern*) contribute; *Jur.* (*Zeugen*) produce, come up with *umg.*; **Dienstwagen wird gestellt** a company car is provided; **5.** (*anordnen*) arrange; **II.** *v/refl.* **1.** *sich irgendwohin ~* go and stand somewhere; *bes. Sport, Mil.* position o.s. (*od.* take up position) somewhere; **2. sich der Polizei etc. ~** give o.s. up (*bes. Mil.* surrender) to the police *etc.*; **sich e-m Gegner etc. ~** take on an opponent *etc.*; **sich e-r Herausforderung ~** take up (*od.* meet) a challenge; **sich der Kritik** *etc.* **~** face up to criticism *etc.*; **die Probleme, die sich uns ~** the problems we are up against (*od.* we face); **4.** (*sich*

verhalten) **wie stellt er sich dazu?** what is his attitude (to it)?, what does he think of it?; **sich gegen j-n/etw. ~** oppose s.o./s.th.; **sich gut mit j-m ~** *neu:* get into s.o.'s good books, get in with s.o. *umg.*; *anhaltend:* keep on the right side of s.o., stay in s.o.'s good books, keep in with s.o. *umg.*; **sich hinter j-n ~** back s.o. up; **sich (schützend) vor j-n ~** shield s.o.; **5.** (*simulieren*): **sich krank ~** pretend to be ill (*Am.* sick); *förm.* feign illness; **stell dich nicht so dumm!** stop pretending to be stupid; (*Unwissen/Verständnislosigkeit vortäuschend*) stop pretending you don't know/understand; **sich schlafend ~** pretend to be asleep, play possum *umg.*; **sich tot ~** pretend to be dead; → **Abrede** 1, **Aussicht** 2, **Antrag** 1, **Bedingung** 1, **Bein** 1, **Diagnose**, **Dienst** 1, **Falle** 1, **Forderung** 1, **Frage** 1, 3, **gestellt**, **Kopf** 1, **Rechnung** 2, **taub** 1, **Wahl** 2, **Weiche**[2]; → *auch* **bereitstellen, gleichstellen, richtig stellen** *etc.*

Stellen|abbau *m Wirts.* reduction in staff, staff reductions *Pl.*; **~angebot** *n* job offer (*od.* opening); **~e Überschrift:** vacancies, situations vacant; **~anzeige** *f*, **~ausschreibung** *f* job advertisement; **~beschreibung** *f* job description (*od.* specification); **~besetzung** *f* filling of a (*od.* the) post; **~bewerber** *m*, **~bewerberin** *f* job applicant; applicant for a (*od.* the) job; **~einsparung** *f* cutting of a (*od.* the) job; *Pl.* job cuts; **~gesuch** *n* **1.** (*Inserat*) situation wanted advertisement; **„~e" Überschrift:** "Situations Wanted"; **2.** (*Bewerbung*) job application; **~knappheit** *f* shortage of jobs; **~kürzung** *f* job cuts *Pl.*

stellenlos *Adj.* unemployed, jobless; **Stellenlose** *m*, *f*; *-n*, *-n* unemployed person

Stellen|markt *m Wirts.* job market; **~plan** *m* staffing schedule

Stellen|streichungen *Pl.* job cuts; **~suche** *f* job-hunting; **auf ~ sein** be looking for a job; **~suchende** *m*, *f*; *-n*, *-n* job seeker; **~vermittlung** *f* employment agency; **~wechsel** *m* change of job

stellenweise *Adv.* here and there, in places; **~ Regen** rain in places; **das Buch ist ~ interessant** the book has some interesting parts

Stellenwert *m* **1.** *Math.* place value; **2.** *fig.* rating, (relative) importance; **e-n hohen ~ haben** *als Einstufung:* rate highly; (*allgemein wichtig sein*) play an important role

Stellfläche *f* space (for placing items); *für Autos:* parking space

...stellig *im Adj. allg.* ...-figure, ...-digit; **zwei~e Zahl** two-figure (*od.* -digit) number

Stell|hebel *m Tech.* adjusting lever; **~macher** *m*, **~macherin** *f* cartwright

Stellplatz *m* parking space; *für Zelt etc.:* site, place

Stell|rad *n* regulator; **~schraube** *f Tech.* adjusting screw

Stellung *f* **1.** (*Position, auch des Körpers*) position; *EDV* status; **~ zu** position in relation to; **e-e kauernde** *etc.* **~ einnehmen** take up a crouching *etc.* position; **2.** (*berufliche ~*) post, position; **e-e ~ als Assistent haben** have an assistant's post, work as an assistant; **3.** (*Rang*) position, status; (*Ansehen*) standing; **soziale ~** social status (*od.* class); (*Ansehen*) position in soci-

ety, social standing (*od.* status); **4.** *Mil.* position; (*Frontlinie*) front line(s *Pl.*); **e-s Geschützes:** emplacement; **e-e ~ beziehen** move into position; **die ~ halten** hold the position; **in ~ bringen** bring into position; (*Geschütz*) emplace; **5.** (*Einstellung*) position, stance; **~ beziehen** take a stand; **zu etw. ~ nehmen** take a stand on s.th.; (*sich äußern*) *auch* give one's view on s.th.; **~ nehmen für** come out in favo(u)r of, back (up); **~ nehmen gegen** oppose, come out against

...stellung *f, im Subst.* **1.** *körperliche:* **Fehl~** wrong position; **Lippen~** position of the lips; **2.** *Tech. etc.:* **Schalter~** switch position

Stellungnahme *f*; *-*, *-n*; (*Meinung, Gutachten*) opinion (**zu** on); (*Erklärung*) comment, statement (on); **e-e ~ abgeben** make a statement (**zu, über** + *Akk.* on), comment (on); **um j-s ~ bitten** ask for s.o.'s opinion, ask s.o. for his (*od.* her) comments

Stellungs|befehl *m Mil.* call-up papers *Pl.*, *Am.* draft card; **~fehler** *m Sport* positional error; **~krieg** *m Mil.* static (*od.* position) warfare; (*Grabenkrieg*) trench warfare

stellungslos *Adj.* → **stellenlos**

Stellungs|spiel *n Sport* positional play; **~suche** *f* → **Stellensuche**; **~suchende** *m*, *f*; *-en*, *-en* job seeker; **~wechsel** *m* change of position; *Arbeit: auch* change of job

stellvertretend I. *Adj.* amtlich, vorübergehend: acting (**für** for); *von Amts wegen:* deputy ...; **~e(r) Geschäftsführer(in)** deputy (*od.* assistant) manager; **~er Vorsitzender** vice chairman; *vorübergehend:* acting chairman; **~e Vorsitzende** vice chairwoman; *vorübergehend:* acting chairwoman; *neutral:* vice chair(person); *vorübergehend:* acting chair(person); **~er Schulleiter** deputy headmaster, *Am.* assistant principal; **~e Schulleiterin** deputy headmistress, *Am.* assistant principal; *neutral:* deputy head, *Am.* assistant principal; **II.** *Adv.:* **~ für** (*im Namen von*) on behalf of; (*anstelle von*) deputizing (*od.* standing in) for

Stellvertreter *m*, **~in** *f* representative, delegate; *amtlich:* deputy; *des Schulleiters:* deputy head, *Am.* assistant principal; (*Ersatzperson*) substitute; (*e-s Arztes*) locum, *Am.* substitute doctor; (*Bevollmächtigte[r]*) proxy; **er kommt als ~ des Ministers** he is deputizing for the minister; → **Vertreter**

Stellvertreterkrieg *m* proxy war

Stellvertretung *f* **1.** *für e-e Firma etc.:* representation; (*Person*) representative; *e-s Amtsträgers:* deputizing; (*Person*) deputy; **j-s ~ übernehmen** deputize for s.o.; **2.** *als Ersatz:* substitution; **3.** *Wirts.* (*Betrieb*) agency; **in ~** on behalf of; *Wirts., Jur. bei Unterschriften:* per proxy, p.p.; → **Vertretung**

Stell|wand *f* partition; **~werk** *n Eisenb.* signal box, *Am.* switch tower

Stelze *f*; *-*, *-n* **1.** stilt; **~n** *umg. fig.* (*Beine*) spindly (*od.* matchstick) legs; **auf ~n gehen** walk on stilts; **wie auf ~n gehen** *umg.* walk stiffly (as if on stilts); **2.** *Zool.* wagtail; **3.** *österr. Gastr.* knuckle of pork; **stelzen** *v/i.* strut, stalk (along); → **gestelzt**

Stelz|fuß *m* wooden leg; (*auch fig. Person*) *umg.* peg leg; **~vogel** *m Zool.* wader, wading bird

Stemm|bogen *m Sport, Skisport:* stem turn; **~eisen** *n* crowbar; (*Meißel*) chisel

stemmen I. v/t. **1.** (drücken) press; (hochwuchten) heave up; (Gewicht heben) lift over one's head, snatch; (sie hatte) **die Arme in die Seiten gestemmt** (she stood with) arms akimbo; **die Arme in die Seiten ~** place one's hands on one's hips; **2.** Tech. (Löcher) chisel (out); **3.** einen ~ umg. (Bier etc.) hoist one; **4.** umg. (stehlen) make off with; **II.** v/refl.: **sich gegen etw. ~** press (od. brace o.s.) against s.th.; fig. resist s.th.; **er stemmt sich dagegen** fig. auch he's digging in his heels, Brit. umg. auch he's dead set against it; **sich in die Höhe ~** haul oneself to one's feet; **III.** v/i. Skisport: stem

Stemmen n; -s, kein Pl.; Sport, beim Gewichtheben: snatch, Am. auch clean and jerk

Stemm|meißel m mor|tice (Am. -tise) chisel; **~schwung** m Skisport: stem turn

Stempel m; -s, - **1.** aus Gummi: (rubber) stamp; (Prägestempel, Stanze) die, punch; **2.** (~abdruck) stamp; (Siegel) seal; (Poststempel) postmark; auf Edelmetall: hallmark; Wirts., auf Fleischwaren, Vieh: brand; **mit e-m ~ versehen** stamp; **den ~ vom 15. tragen** be postmarked the 15th; **ein ~ im Pass** a stamp in one's passport; **e-r Sache s-n ~ aufdrücken** fig. leave one's mark (od. imprint) on s.th.; **3.** Bot. pistil; **4.** Bergb. pit prop

Stempel|aufdruck m → **Stempel** 2; **~farbe** f stamping ink; **~geld** n umg. altm. dole (money), Am. welfare (check); **~glanz** m newly minted gleam; (Zustand) mint condition; **~kissen** n ink (od. stamp) pad

stempeln I. v/t. stamp; (entwerten) (Briefmarke) cancel; (Brief) postmark; (Edelmetalle) hallmark; **die Marke ist (nicht) gestempelt** the stamp is (un)used; **zu etw. ~** fig. mark as s.th.; (brandmarken) brand (as) s.th.; **II.** v/i.: **bei Arbeitsantritt/Arbeitsende ~** clock in/out od. off; **~ gehen** umg. be on the dole (Am. on welfare)

Stempel|ständer m stamp rack; **~uhr** f time clock

Stenge f; -, -n; Naut. topmast

Stengel → **Stängel**

Steno f; -, kein Pl.; umg. shorthand; **~block** m shorthand pad

Stenogramm n; -s, -e shorthand notes Pl.

Stenograph m; -en, -en stenographer; **Stenographie** f; -, kein Pl. shorthand, stenography förm.; **stenographieren** I. v/i. write shorthand; II. v/t. write (mitschreibend: take down) in shorthand; **Stenographin** f; -, -nen stenographer; **stenographisch** I. Adj. shorthand; II. Adv. (in) shorthand

Steno|kurs m shorthand course; **~typistin** f; -, -nen shorthand typist

Stentorstimme f lit. stentorian voice

Stenz m; -es, -e; umg. **1.** fop; **2.** (Zuhälter) pimp

Stepp [ʃtep] n; -s, -s **1.** beim Dreisprung: step; **2.** (tanz) tap dance

Stepp|anorak m quilted anorak (Am. parka); **~decke** f quilt, duvet; Am. quilt, comforter

Steppe f; -, -n steppe; → auch **Pampa**, **Prärie**, **Savanne**, **Tundra**

steppen¹ v/t. backstitch; Tech. quilt

steppen² v/i. (tanzen) tap-dance; **sie kann ausgezeichnet ~** she's a very good tap-dancer

Steppen|bewohner m, **~bewohnerin** f

inhabitant of the steppe; **die ~ Asiens** the Asian steppe peoples; **~fuchs** m Zool. corsac; **~gras** n steppe grass; **~vegetation** f steppe vegetation; **~wolf** m Zool. coyote, prairie wolf

Steppjacke f quilted jacket

Steppke m; -(s), -s; nordd. umg. young nipper

Stepp|naht f backstitch seam; **~stich** m backstitch

Stepp|tanz m tap dancing; **~tänzer** m, **~tänzerin** f tap-dancer

Ster m; -s, -e und -s, bei Mengen -; (Raummaß) stere

Sterbe|begleiter m, **~begleiterin** f support worker with terminal patients; **~begleitung** f terminal patient support; **~bett** n: (auf dem) ~ (on one's) deathbed; **~fall** m death; **im ~** Jur. in the event of death (od. decease); **~geläut** n death knell; **~geld** n payment on death (covering funeral expenses); **~glocke** f funeral bell; **~helfer** m, **~helferin** f assistant in euthanasia; **~hilfe** f **1.** (Euthanasie) euthanasia; (Tötung auf Verlangen) mercy killing, assisted suicide; **aktive/passive ~** active/passive euthanasia; **~ leisten** carry out euthanasia; **2.** pflegerische: terminal care; **3.** → **Sterbegeld**; **~kasse** f funeral expenses insurance scheme, Am. prepaid funeral; **~klinik** f hospice

sterben stirbt, starb, ist gestorben I. v/i. die (auch fig.); (dahinscheiden) pass away (od. on); Jur. decease; umg. fig. Projekt etc.: die a death; **e-s natürlichen Todes ~** die a natural death; **an e-r Krankheit/Wunde ~** die of an illness / from a wound; **~ für** die for, give one's life for; **vor Scham/Neugier** etc. **~** fig. die of shame/curiosity etc.; **wir sind vor Langeweile fast gestorben** umg. auch we were bored to death (od. tears), we were bored out of our minds; **davon stirbst du nicht gleich!** umg. it won't kill you; **der ist für mich gestorben** umg. he doesn't exist as far as I'm concerned; **die Sache ist gestorben** umg. it's all over and done with; **„Gestorben!"** Film, TV, Einstellung: that's it!; **und wenn sie nicht gestorben sind, dann leben sie noch heute** and they all lived happily ever after; **II.** v/t.: **den Heldentod ~** die a hero's death; Mil. die in action; **tausend Tode sterben** die a thousand deaths

Sterben n; -s, kein Pl. dying, death; **im ~ liegen** be dying, be at death's door lit.; **zum ~ langweilig** umg. deadly dull, dull as death; **zum ~ müde** umg. ready to drop, dog-tired; **zum Leben zu wenig, zum ~ zu viel** barely enough to keep body and soul together

...sterben n im Subst. **1.** im wörtl. Sinn: Flüchtlings**~** mortality among refugees; Ulmen**~** Dutch elm disease; **2.** fig.: Bauern**~** decline in farming; Kino**~** disappearance of cinemas (Am. movie theaters)

sterbend I. Part. Präs. → **sterben**; **II.** Adj. dying; fig. auch moribund; **III.** Adv. dying; **noch ~ hat er sie verflucht** even as he died he cursed her (name); **Sterbende** m, f; -en, -en dying person (od. man, f woman), **die ~n** auch the dying Pl.

Sterbens|angst f mortal terror; **e-e ~ haben vor** (+ Dat.) auch be terrified of (od. by); **j-m e-e ~ einjagen** put the fear of death into s.o.

sterbens|elend Adv.: **sich ~ fühlen** feel ghastly, feel like death (warmed

over) umg.; **~krank** Adj. **1.** (todkrank) terminally ill; **2. sich ~ fühlen** feel like death warmed over umg.; **~langweilig** Adj. deadly dull; **~müde** Adj. geh. ready to drop, dog-tired umg.

Sterbens|seele f: **keine ~** not a (living) soul; **~wort** n, **~wörtchen** n umg.: **kein ~** not a single word; **kein ~ sagen** not breathe a word

Sterbe|rate f mortality rate; **~sakramente** Pl. last rites; **~stunde** f hour of death; **~tafel** f Statistik: mortality chart; **~urkunde** f death certificate; **~ziffer** f mortality rate; **~zimmer** n: **Beethovens ~** room in which Beethoven died

sterblich I. Adj. mortal; **die ~en Überreste** od. **die ~e Hülle** one's mortal remains; **II.** Adv. (sehr) terribly; **~ verliebt** umg. really smitten; **Sterbliche** m, f; -n, -n mortal; **wir gewöhnlichen ~n** we lesser mortals; **Sterblichkeit** f mortality

Sterblichkeits|rate f, **~ziffer** f mortality rate

Stereo n; -s, kein Pl. stereo; **in ~ aufnehmen/senden** record/broadcast in stereo

stereo I. Adj. **1.** stereo; **2.** Fot. stereoscopic; **II.** Adv. empfangen etc.: in stereo

Stereo|... im Subst. stereo; **~anlage** f stereo system, stereo; **~aufnahme** f stereo recording; **~bild** n stereoscopic picture; **~empfang** m stereo reception; **~fotografie** f stereoscopic photography; **~gerät** n stereo unit, piece of stereo equipment

Stereo|kamera f stereoscopic camera; **~lautsprecher** m stereo loudspeaker

Stereometrie f; -, kein Pl.; Math. stereometry

Stereomikroskop n stereoscopic microscope

stereophon I. Adj. stereophonic; **II.** Adv. stereophonically; **Stereophonie** f; -, kein Pl. stereophony

Stereoskopie f; -, kein Pl. stereoscopy

Stereo|ton m stereo sound; **~turm** m (stereo) equipment tower

stereotyp I. Adj. **1.** Druck. attr. stereotype ...; **2.** fig. stereotyped; **~e Antwort** stock reply, stereotyped answer; **~e Redewendung** hackneyed phrase; **~es Lächeln** mechanical smile; **II. Stereotyp** n; -s, -e; Psych. stereotype

Stereotypie f; -, -n **1.** nur Sg.; Druck. stereotype printing; **2.** Druck. stereotype; **3.** nur Sg.; Med. stereotypy

steril Adj. auch fig. sterile; **~ machen** sterilize; **~e Atmosphäre** fig. auch barren atmosphere; **Sterilisation** f; -, -en sterilization; **Sterilisator** m; -s, -en sterilizer; **Sterilisierbox** f für Babyflaschen: sterilizing unit; **sterilisieren** v/t. sterilize; (Katze) auch spay; **Sterilisierung** f sterilization; **Sterilität** f sterility (auch fig.)

Sterling ['ʃtɛrlɪŋ] m; -s, -e sterling; **Pfund ~** pound sterling; **~silber** n sterling silver

Stern¹ m; -(e)s, -e **1.** star (auch fig.); **mit ~en besät** starry, star-studded; **der ~ der Weisen** the Star of Bethlehem; **aufgehender ~** auch fig. rising star; **es geht ein neuer ~ auf** fig. there's a new star on the horizon; **unter fremden ~en** lit. under foreign skies; **ein/mein guter ~** a/my lucky star; **nach den ~en greifen** reach for the stars; **sie ist unter e-m glücklichen/unglücklichen ~**

geboren she was born under a lucky / an unlucky star; *unter e-m glücklichen/unglücklichen* ~ *stehen* have fortune on one's side / be ill-fated; *das steht noch in den* ~*en (geschrieben)* that's in the lap of the gods; *was sagen die* ~*e?* what's in the stars?; *die* ~*e lügen nicht* the stars can't lie; *sein* ~ *ist im Sinken* his star is on the wane, he's had his day; ~*e sehen* umg. see stars; **2.** (*Form, Symbol*) star; *fünf-/sechszackiger* ~ five-/six-pointed star; *eine Eins mit* ~ etwa alpha (*Am.* A) plus; *ein Restaurant mit drei* ~*en* a three-star restaurant; **3.** *bei Pferden:* blaze; **4.** *bei Wild:* iris

Stern² m; -s, -e; Naut. stern

Sternanis m star aniseed

stern|bedeckt, ~**besät** Adj. starry, star-studded

Stern|bild n constellation; *des Tierkreises:* sign of the zodiac; *das* ~ *des Großen Bären* the constellation of Ursa Major (*od.* the Great Bear, *Am.* auch the Big Dipper); → **Sternzeichen**

Sternchen n **1.** little star; **2.** umg. Film etc.: starlet; **3.** Druck. asterisk

Stern|deuter m; -s, -, ~**deuterin** f; -, -nen astrologer; ~**deutung** f astrology

...sternelokal n, im Subst.: *Zwei.../Drei...* two-/three-star restaurant

Sternen|banner n der USA: *das* ~ the star-spangled banner, the Stars and Stripes (*V. im Sg.*); ~**himmel** m **1.** night sky; **2.** sternbedeckt: starry sky

sternenklar Adj. → **sternklar**

Sternen|licht n, ~**schein** m starlight, light of the stars; ~**zelt** n poet. starry firmament

Sternfahrt f Mot. car rally (*with different starting points*)

sternförmig Adj. star-shaped; Bot. auch stellate; (*strahlig*, auch Tech.) radial

Stern|frucht f Bot. carambola, Am. auch star fruit; ~**globus** m celestial globe; ~**gucker** m; -s, -, ~**guckerin** f; -, -nen; umg. stargazer

sternhagelvoll Adj. umg. paralytic, pissed as a newt Sl., Am. three sheets to the wind Sl.

Sternhaufen m Astron. star cluster

sternhell Adj. starlit

Stern|jahr n sidereal year; ~**karte** f celestial chart; ~**katalog** m Astron. star catalog(ue)

sternklar Adj. starlit, attr. auch starry; ~*er Himmel* auch clear night sky; *in* ~*er Nacht* on a clear starlit night

Sternkunde f astronomy

sternlos Adj. starless

Stern|marsch m *demonstration march in which marchers converge from different directions on a central point*; ~**motor** m radial engine; ~**schnuppe** f shooting star; ~**singen** n carol singing at Epiphany; ~**singer** m Dial. carol singer at Epiphany; ~**stunde** f (*Höhepunkt*) great moment; (*Wendepunkt*) turning point; *e-e* ~ *der Menschheit* a defining moment in the history of mankind (*od.* civilization); ~**system** n Astron. galaxy; ~**tag** m Astron. sidereal day; ~**warte** f observatory; ~**wolke** f Astron. star cloud; ~**zeichen** n star sign, sign of the zodiac; *welches* ~ *haben Sie?* what's your star sign?, which sign of the zodiac are you?; *er ist im* ~ *des Skorpions geboren* he was born under (the sign of) Scorpio; ~**zeit** f Astron. sidereal time

Steroid n; -(e)s, -e steroid; **Steroidhormon** n steroid hormone

Sterz m; -es, -e **1.** Zool. tail; **2.** (*Pflugsterz*) tail; **3.** südd., österr. Gastr. flat cake made with maize flour (*Am.* cornmeal), polenta, semolina, etc.

stet Adj. → **stetig, Tropfen**

Stethoskop n; -s, -e; Med. stethoscope

stetig Adj. **1.** (*beständig*) continuous, constant; **2.** (*gleichmäßig*) steady; **Stetigkeit** f **1.** (*Beständigkeit*) continuous (*od.* constant) nature; **2.** (*Gleichmäßigkeit*) steadiness; **3.** Math. continuity

stets Adv. (*immer*) always; (*jedesmal*) every time; (*ständig*) constantly, continually; ~ *steigend* constantly (*od.* ever-) increasing

Steuer¹ n; -s, -; Mot. (steering) wheel; Naut. helm; Flug. controls Pl.; (*Seitensteuer*) rudder; *am* ~ *sitzen* be seated at the wheel (Naut. helm, Flug. controls); *das* ~ *herumreißen* wrench the wheel (Naut. helm) hard over; *das* ~ *übernehmen* take over at the wheel (Naut., fig. at the helm); Flug. take over (at) the controls; *das* ~ *fest in der Hand haben* fig. be firmly in control; *das* ~ *herumwerfen* fig. alter course (radically)

Steuer² f; -, -n tax (*auf* + Dat. on); *kommunale:* local tax; *in GB:* council tax; *auf Gütern:* duty; *direkte/indirekte* ~*n* direct/indirect taxes (*od.* taxation); *von der* ~ *absetzen* set against tax; → **erheben** I 5

Steuer|abkommen n tax agreement; ~**abzug** m tax deduction; ~**abzugsverfahren** n tax deduction at source

Steueraggregat n Tech. control unit; Raumf. steering gear

Steuer|angelegenheit f tax affair (*od.* matter); ~**anreiz** m tax incentive; ~**anwalt** m, ~**anwältin** f tax lawyer

Steuer|art f tax category; ~**aufkommen** n tax revenue, tax yield; ~**aufsicht** f tax office's supervisory function; ~**ausfall** m tax deficit, loss in taxes; ~**ausgleich** m tax equalization

steuerbar¹ Adj. Tech. controllable

steuerbar² Adj. Amtsspr. taxable

Steuerbefehl m EDV control command

Steuerbefreiung f tax exemption

steuerbegünstigt Adj. benefiting from tax concessions; *Spenden etc.:* tax-deductible; *Sparen:* tax-linked

Steuer|behörde f tax authorities Pl.; ~**belastung** f tax burden; ~**bemessung** f tax assessment (*od.* calculation); ~**bemessungsgrundlage** f basis of tax assessment, tax base; ~**berater** m, ~**beraterin** f tax adviser; ~**beratung** f tax counsel(l)ing; ~**bescheid** m tax assessment; ~**betrug** m tax evasion; ~**bevollmächtigte** m, f tax consultant; ~**bilanz** f tax balance sheet

Steuerblock m EDV control block

Steuerbord n; nur Sg.; Naut. starboard; *nach* ~ to starboard; **steuerbord(s)** Adv. Naut. to starboard

Steuerbus m Etron. control bus

Steuer|delikt n tax offence (*Am.* violation); ~**ehrlichkeit** f honesty in tax matters

Steuereinheit f **1.** Wirts. taxable item; **2.** Etron. control unit

Steuer|einnahmen Pl. → **Steueraufkommen**; ~**entlastung** f tax relief; ~**erhebung** f collection of taxes; ~**erhöhung** f tax increase; ~**erklärung** f tax return; ~**erlass** m tax exemption; ~**erleichterung** f tax relief; ~**ermäßigung** f tax allowance; ~**ersparnis** f

tax saving; ~**erstattung** f tax refund; ~**fachgehilfe** m, ~**fachgehilfin** f assistant tax adviser; ~**fahnder** m, ~**fahnderin** f tax investigator (*Am.* auditor); ~**fahndung** f (bureau for the) investigation of tax offences, *Am.* tax audit bureau; ~**festsetzung** f tax assessment; ~**flucht** f tax evasion (by absconding or placing money in offshore accounts); ~**flüchtling** m tax fugitive

Steuerfrau f Rudern: woman at the helm

steuerfrei Adj. tax-free, tax-exempt; *Waren:* duty-free

Steuer|freibetrag m tax-free allowance; ~**freiheit** f tax exemption; ~**geheimnis** n confidentiality of tax returns and other information supplied; ~**gelder** Pl. taxpayers' money Sg., taxes

Steuergerät n Tech. control device, controller; Stereo: receiver

Steuer|gerechtigkeit f fiscal justice; ~**gesetzgebung** f fiscal (*od.* tax) legislation

Steuergitter n Etron. control grid

Steuer|groschen m umg. taxpayers' money; ~**haftung** f Jur. tax liability; ~**harmonisierung** f harmonization of taxes

Steuerhebel m control lever

Steuer|hinterziehung f tax evasion; ~**hoheit** f tax sovereignty; ~**karte** f: (*Lohnsteuerkarte* wage) tax card

Steuerkette f Mot. timing chain

Steuerklasse f tax bracket

Steuerknüppel m Flug. control stick, umg. joystick

Steuerlast f tax burden

steuerlich I. Adj. attr. tax ...; *Vorteil, Nachteil, Wohnsitz etc.:* auch fiscal; *aus* ~*en Gründen* for tax reasons (*od.* purposes); II. Adv.: ~ (*gesehen*) from a tax point of view; ~ *absetzbar* od. *abzugsfähig* tax-deductible; ~ *günstig* with tax advantages (*od.* low tax liability); ~ *veranlagen* assess for taxation

steuerlos I. Adj. rudderless, out of control; II. Adv.: ~ *in die Tiefe trudeln* plunge helplessly out of control

Steuermann m **1.** Naut. altm. helmsman; (*Dienstgrad*) mate; **2.** Rudern: cox; *Zweier mit/ohne* ~ coxed/coxless pair; **3.** Etron. controller; **Steuermannspatent** n Naut. mate's certificate

Steuermarke f **1.** revenue stamp; **2.** (*Hundemarke*) dog licence disc, Am. dog tag

Steuer|mehreinnahmen Pl. revenue surplus; ~**mindereinnahmen** Pl. revenue shortfall

steuermindernd I. Adj. tax-reducing; II. Adv.: *sich* ~ *auswirken* have the effect of reducing tax

Steuer|mittel Pl. tax revenues, ~**moral** f (general) attitude to paying tax

steuern I. v/t. (*hat gesteuert*) **1.** Naut. steer, navigate; *als Lotse:* pilot; Mot. steer; Flug. navigate, pilot; **2.** Tech., Computer: control; fig. (*leiten*) control, run; (*lenken*) steer, guide; ~*d eingreifen in* (+ Akk.) fig. intervene in; II. v/i. **1.** (*hat*) Naut. be at the helm; Mot. be at the wheel; **2.** (*ist*) Schiff: head (*nach Süden* southward); ~ *nach* be bound for; *heimwärts* ~ fig. head homewards (*od.* for home); *wohin steuert Europa?* which direction (*od.* where) is Europe headed?; *in sein Unglück* ~ fig. head for disaster

Steuer|nachlass m im Voraus: tax allowance; *im Nachhinein*: tax rebate; **~nachzahlung** *f* additional tax payment; **~oase** *f* tax haven (*od*. shelter); **~paradies** *n* tax haven (*od*. shelter); **~pflicht** *f* tax liability

steuerpflichtig *Adj*. taxable; *Ware*: dutiable; **Steuerpflichtige** *m, f; -n, -n* taxpayer

Steuerpolitik *f* fiscal (*od*. tax) policy; **steuerpolitisch I.** *Adj*. relating to fiscal (*od*. tax) policy; *Maßnahmen*: fiscal; **II.** *Adv.*: **~** (*gesehen*) seen in the context of fiscal policy

Steuerprogramm *n EDV* control program

Steuer|progression *f* progressive taxation; **~prüfer** *m*, **~prüferin** *f* tax auditor; **~prüfung** *f* tax audit

Steuer|pult *n Etech*. control desk; *Computer*: control panel, console; **~rad** *n Mot.* (steering) wheel; *Naut.* wheel, helm; *Flug.* (*Steuerknüppel*) control stick

Steuerrecht *n* tax law(s *Pl.*), *Jur. auch* fiscal law; *Fachanwalt für* **~** tax lawyer; **steuerrechtlich I.** *Adj. attr.* tax law ...; (*gemäß dem Steuerrecht*) according to the tax laws; **II.** *Adv.* where tax law is concerned

Steuer|reform *f* tax reform(s *Pl.*); **~rückzahlung** *f* tax rebate

Steuerruder *n Naut.* helm; *unter Wasser*: rudder; *Flug.* control surface

Steuer|sache *f* tax matter (*od.* affair); **~satz** *m* tax rate

Steuersäule *f Mot.* steering column

Steuer|schätzung *f* tax estimate; **~schlupfloch** *n* tax loophole; **~schraube** *f*: *die* **~** *anziehen*/*überdrehen* bleed the taxpayer / bleed the taxpayer white (*Am.* dry); **~schuld** *f* tax(es *Pl.*) due, tax liability; *Bilanz*: tax accrued; *e-e* **~** (*in Höhe*) *von 5000 Euro* a tax liability (*überfällig*: tax arrears) of 5,000 euros; **~schuldner** *m*, **~schuldnerin** *f* taxpayer; **~senkung** *f* tax cut (*od*. reduction); **~stundung** *f* tax deferral; **~system** *n* **1.** *Wirts.* tax system; **2.** *Tech.* control system; **~tabelle** *f* tax scale

Steuerung *f* **1.** (*Tätigkeit*) steering; *Flug.* piloting; *Tech., Etech., allg. und fig.* control; *der* **~** *bedürfen fig.* need guidance; **2.** (*Vorrichtung*) control system; *Mot.* (*Lenkung*) steering; *Flug.* controls *Pl.*

Steuerungs|instrument *n* control device; **~konsole** *f EDV* control console; **~mechanismus** *m* control mechanism; **~schaltung** *f Etron.* control circuit; **~system** *n* control system; **~taste** *f EDV* control key; **~** *und Regeltechnik* *f* control engineering

Steuer|veranlagung *f* tax assessment; **~ventil** *n* control valve; **~vergehen** *n* tax offence (*Am.* violation); **~vergünstigung** *f* tax break (*od*. concession); *Pl. auch* tax relief *Sg.*; **~vermeidung** *f* tax avoidance; **~vorteil** *m* tax benefit (*od*. break); **~werk** *n EDV* control unit; **~wesen** *n nur Sg.* taxation system; **~zahler** *m*, **~zahlerin** *f* taxpayer; *Bund der Steuerzahler* Taxpayers' Federation; *alles auf Kosten des Steuerzahlers* all paid for by the taxpayer; **~zahlung** *f* tax payment; **~zeichen** *n* **1.** *EDV* control character; **2.** *Wirts.* revenue stamp

Steven *m; -s, -; Naut.* (*Vorsteven*) stem; (*Achtersteven*) sternpost

Steward ['stjuːɐt] *m; -s, -s* steward; *Flug. auch* flight attendant; **Stewardess** ['stjuːɐdɛs] *f; -, -en* stewardess;

Flug. auch flight attendant

stibitzen *v/t. umg.* pinch, snitch, *Brit. auch* nick

Stich *m; -(e)s, -e* **1.** (*Nadelstich etc.*) prick; (*Wespen-, Bienenstich*) sting; (*Mückenstich*) bite; (*Messerstich*) stab; **2.** (*Wunde*) stab wound; **3.** *Fechten*: hit; **4.** *mit dem Spaten*: cut; **5.** (*Schmerz*) stabbing pain; **~e haben** *in der Seite* have a stitch; *es gab mir* **e-n** **~** *fig.* it really hurt; **6.** *Nähen*: stitch; *er musste mit fünf* **~en** *genäht werden* he had to have five stitches; **7.** (*Kupferstich etc.*) engraving; **8.** *ein* **~** *ins Blaue* a tinge of blue; *im Foto*: a blue cast; **9.** *Kartenspiel*: trick; *e-n* **~** *machen* make (*Am.* take) a trick; *keinen* **~** *bekommen* *Fußball etc.*: not get a look in; *in e-r Diskussion*: make no mark; **10.** *im* **~** *lassen* let down, fail; (*nicht helfen*) leave in the lurch; (*verlassen*) abandon, desert; (*Familie, Freundin etc.*) *auch* walk out on; **11.** *e-n* **~** *haben umg.* Milch *etc.*: be (slightly) off; *umg. Person*: be a bit touched; *du hast wohl* **e-n** **~**! *umg.* have you gone mad (*od.* off your rocker)?; **12.** **~** *halten* Argument *etc.*: hold water

Stich|bahn *f Eisenb.* branch line; **~blatt** *n von Schwert, Degen etc.*: guard

Stichel *m; -s, -* graver, burin

Stichelei *f; -, -en* gibe(s *Pl.*), dig(s *Pl.*), barbed remark(s *Pl.*); **sticheln I.** *v/i.* *fig.* make barbed remarks; *ständig gegen j-n* be constantly making barbed remarks about s.o., constantly have one's knife into s.o.; **II.** *vt/i.* (*nähen, sticken*) stitch

stichfest *Adj.* → *hieb- und stichfest*

Stichflamme *f* jet of flame; *Tech.* (fine) jet

Stichfrage *f* tie-breaking question

stichhaltig I. *Adj.* valid, sound; *Beweis*: conclusive; *seine Theorie ist nicht* **~** his theory doesn't hold water; **II.** *Adv.*: *etw* **~** *begründen* provide valid reasons for s.th.; **Stichhaltigkeit** *f* validity, soundness; *von Beweis*: conclusiveness

Stich|kampf *m Sport* play(-)off; **~kanal** *m* **1.** *Naut.* linking canal; **2.** *bei Stichwunde*: puncture channel, (course of the) entry wound

Stichling *m; -s, -e; Zool.* stickleback

Stichprobe *f* **1.** spot check; *Rechnungsprüfung*: sample audit; *e-e* **~** *machen* do (*od.* carry out) a spot check; **2.** *von Waren*: random sample; *e-e* **~** *machen* take a random sample; **3.** *Statistik*: sampling; **stichprobenartig** *Adj.* random; **Stichprobenprüfung** *f* examination of random samples

Stich|punkt *m* (*Schlüsselbegriff für Vortrag etc.*) key word (*od.* point); *Pl. als Gedächtnisstütze*: notes; *sich* (*Dat.*) *ein paar* **~e** *machen* jot down a few notes; *für den Vortrag habe ich mir folgende* **~e** *notiert* I've noted down the following key points for the lecture; **~säge** *f* compass (*od.* keyhole) saw; **~straße** *f* cul-de-sac

sticht *Präs.* → *stechen*

Stichtag *m* cutoff date; (*letzter Termin*) deadline

Stich|verletzung *f* stab wound, knife wound; **~waffe** *f* thrust weapon; **~wahl** *f Pol.* runoff

Stichwort *n* **1.** *Pl. Stichwörter; im Wörterbuch etc.*: headword; (*Eintrag*) entry; *im Register etc.*: word, entry; **2.** *Pl. Stichworte; Theat. und fig.* cue;

(*Schlüsselwort*) key word; *j-m das* **~** *für s-n Auftritt geben* give s.o. the cue for his (*od.* her) entrance; *sich* (*Dat.*) *ein paar* **~e** *aufschreiben* jot down a few notes; *in* **~en** *festhalten* make a few notes on; **stichwortartig I.** *Adj.* in note form; **II.** *Adv.* in note form; *ich habe es* **~** *notiert auch* I've jotted down a few notes; **~** *zusammenfassen* sum up the key points of

Stichwort|katalog *m* subject catalog(ue); **~register** *n*, **~verzeichnis** *n* index

Stichwunde *f* stab wound

Stickarbeit *f* embroidery

sticken *vt/i.* embroider; *ein Monogramm auf etw.* **~** embroider a monogram on s.th.

Sticker¹ ['stɪkɐ] *m; -s, -*; (*Aufkleber*) sticker

Sticker² *m; -s, -* embroiderer; **Stickerei** *f; -, -en* **1.** *nur Sg.* embroidery; **2.** *konkret*: piece of embroidery; **Stickerin** *f; -, -nen* embroiderer

Stickgarn *n* embroidery thread

stickig *Adj. Raum*: stuffy; *Luft*: stale; *Außenluft*: sticky, muggy

Stick|maschine *f* embroidery machine; **~muster** *n* embroidery pattern; **~nadel** *f* embroidery needle

Stickoxid *n*, **Stickoxyd** *n Chem.* nitrogen oxide

Stickrahmen *m* tambour (frame)

Stickstoff *m; nur Sg.*; (*abgek.* N) *Chem.* nitrogen; **~flüssiger** **~** liquid nitrogen; **~dünger** *m* nitrogenous fertilizer

stickstoff|frei *Adj.* nitrogen-free; **~haltig** *Adj.* nitrogenous

Stickstoff|oxid *n*, **~oxyd** *n Chem.* nitrogen oxide; **~verbindung** *f* nitrogen compound

stieben *v/i.; stiebt, stob od. stiebte, ist gestoben od. gestiebt* fly (about) (*auch Funken*); *Flüssigkeit*: spray; *die Funken stoben nur so* the sparks flew; *in alle Richtungen* **~** (*laufen, fliegen*) scatter in all directions

Stiefbruder *m* stepbrother

Stiefel *m; -s, -* **1.** boot; *mit* **~n** *treten* trample underfoot; *das sind zwei Paar* **~** *fig.* they're two completely different things, they're as different as chalk and cheese; *j-m die* **~** *lecken fig. pej.* lick s.o.'s boots; *das haut mich aus den* **~n** *umg.* well blow me down; *das hat ihn aus den* **~n** *gehauen umg.* he nearly fell over backwards; **2.** (*Bierglas*) glass beer boot *holding 2 lit\|res* (*Am. -ers*); *er kann e-n* **~** *vertragen* he can take his drink, he can hold his liquor; **3.** *s-n alten* **~** *weitermachen umg.* carry on in the same old way, be stuck in a rut *pej.*; *e-n* **~** *zusammenreden*/*zusammenspielen umg.* talk/play a load of rubbish; *was redest du da für e-n* **~** *zusammen? umg.* what on earth are you going on about?

Stiefelabsatz *m* heel of a (*od.* the) boot

Stiefelette *f; -, -n* ankle boot; *für Frauen: auch* bootee

Stiefelknecht *m* bootjack

stiefeln *v/i. umg.* foot it, hoof it; → *gestiefelt*

Stiefel|schaft *m* boot leg; **~spitze** *f* tip (*od.* toe) of a (*od.* the) boot

Stiefeltern *Pl.* stepparents

Stief|geschwister *Pl.* stepbrother(s) and stepsister(s), step-siblings; **~kind** *n* stepchild (*auch fig.*); **~mutter** *f* stepmother (*auch fig.*)

Stiefmütterchen *n Bot.* pansy

stiefmütterlich I. *Adj. Behandlung*

etc.: shabby; **II.** *Adv.*: ~ **behandeln** (*Pflanzen, Tier, Sache*) neglect; **sie sind ~ behandelt worden** they have been treated like poor relations

Stief|schwester *f* stepsister; **~sohn** *m* stepson; **~tochter** *f* stepdaughter; **~vater** *m* stepfather

stieg *Imperf.* → **steigen**

Stiege *f; -, -n* **1.** (steep) narrow wooden stairs *Pl.*; **2.** *südd., österr.* (*Treppe*) staircase, stairs *Pl.*

Stieglitz *m; -es, -e; Zool.* goldfinch

stiehlt *Präs.* → **stehlen**

Stiel *m; -(e)s, -e* **1.** (*Griff*) handle; (*Besenstiel*) broomstick; *an Pfeife, Glas:* stem; **Eis am ~** ice lolly, *Am.* Popsicle ®; **2.** *Bot.* stalk; → **Stumpf**

Stiel|auge *n Zool.* stalk eye; *mit machen umg.* goggle, gawk; **er hat aber ~n gemacht!** *umg.* his eyes were on stalks; *vor Staunen:* his eyes nearly popped out of his head; **~eiche** *f Bot.* English oak; **~glas** *n* stemmed glass

...stielig *im Adj.*: **kurz~e/lang~e Rosen** short-/long-stemmed roses

Stielkamm *m* tail comb

stier *Adj.* **1.** **~er Blick** glassy (*od.* vacant) stare; **2.** *umg.* (*pleite*) broke, *Brit. auch* skint

Stier *m; -(e)s, -e* **1.** *Zool.* bull; **junger ~** bullock; **brüllen wie ein ~** *fig.* bellow (at the top of one's voice); **den ~ bei den Hörnern packen** *fig.* take the bull by the horns; **2.** *nur Sg.; Astrol.* (*Sternzeichen*) Taurus; **3.** *Astrol.* (*ein*) **~ sein** be a(n) Taurus, be a Taurean

stieren *v/i.* stare, gape (**auf** +*Akk.* at); **vor sich hin ~** stare into space

Stierkalb *n* bull calf

Stierkampf *m* bullfight; **~arena** *f* bullring

Stier|kämpfer *m*, **~kämpferin** *f* bullfighter

Stiernacken *m* bull neck; **stiernackig** *Adj.* bullnecked

Stiesel *m; -s, -; umg.* boor, lout; **stieselig** *Adj. umg.* boorish, loutish

stieß *Imperf.* → **stoßen**

Stift¹ *m; -(e)s, -e* **1.** *Tech.* pin; (*Holzstift*) *auch* peg; **2.** (*Bleistift*) pencil; (*Buntstift*) crayon; *mit Tinte schreibend:* pen; (*Filzstift*) felt pen; (*Kugelschreiber*) ballpoint, *Brit. auch* biro®; *EDV* (light) pen; **hast du irgendeinen ~?** have you got something to write with?, have you got a pen (of some sort)?; **3.** *umg.* (*Lehrling*) (young) apprentice; **4.** *umg.* (*Knirps*) (young) nipper

Stift² *n; -(e)s, -e* **1.** religious foundation (*od.* institution); (*Kloster*) monastery; *für Nonnen:* convent; **2.** (*Altersheim*) old people's home

Stiftcomputer *m* *für handschriftliche Eingabe:* light pen computer

stiften *v/t.* **1.** (*Geld etc.*) donate; (*Schule etc.*) found; (*spendieren*) provide, supply; **2.** (*verursachen*) cause; **Chaos ~** create (*od.* cause) havoc; **Frieden ~** make peace; **Unfrieden ~** cause (*od.* make) trouble, sow discord *lit.*; **Unheil ~** cause disaster; → *auch* **anstiften**; **3.** **~ gehen** *umg.* make off, make o.s. scarce

Stiftenkopf *m umg.* crew cut

Stifter *m; -s, -* founder; (*Schenker*) donor, *Am. auch* sponsor, *hist. auch* benefactor; **~figur** *f hist. Kunst.* representation of a benefactor (*e-s Gründers:* founder); **Stifterin** *f; -, -nen* → **Stifter**

Stifts|dame *f hist.* canoness; **~herr** *m hist.* canon; **~hütte** *f Reli.* Tabernacle; **~kirche** *f* collegiate church

Stiftung *f* **1.** (*Schenkung*) endowment, donation; **2.** (*Institution*) foundation

Stiftungs|fest *n* Founder's Day; **~rat** *m* foundation's management council; **~urkunde** *f* deed of foundation; **~vermögen** *n* sum endowed, endowment fund

Stiftzahn *m* pivot tooth (*od.* crown)

Stigma *n; -s, Stigmen und Stigmata* **1.** *kath.* stigma (*Pl.* stigmata); **2.** *fig.* stigma (*Pl.* stigmas); **Stigmatisation** *f; -, -en* stigmatization; **stigmatisieren** *v/t.* stigmatize, brand (**als** as); **stigmatisiert I.** *P.P.* → **stigmatisieren**; **II.** *Adj.* branded (**als** as); *auch kath.* stigmatized; **Stigmatisierte** *m, f; -n, -n* **1.** *kath.* stigmatic; **2.** *fig.* stigmatized person; **Stigmatisierung** *f* stigmatization

Stil *m; -(e)s, -e* **1.** *allg.* style; **e-e Kirche im spätgotischen ~** a church in late Gothic style, a late Gothic church; **im ~ der 50er Jahre** in the style (*od.* manner) of the 50s; **e-n guten/schlechten** *etc.* **~ fahren/schwimmen** have a good/ bad *etc.* driving/swimming style; **2.** *nur Sg.* style; **ein Kavalier alten ~s** a gentleman of the old school; **im großen ~** in (grand) style; (*in großem Ausmaß*) on a grand scale; **Betrügereien großen ~s** large-scale (*od.* wholesale) fraud; **~ haben** have style; **das ist nicht mein ~** that's not my style, that's not the way I like to do things; **das ist schlechter ~** that's bad form; **in dem ~ ging die Diskussion weiter** the discussion continued along those lines (*od.* in that vein); **~analyse** *f* stylistic analysis

stilbildend *Adj.*: **für j-n ~ wirken** have a formative influence on s.o.'s style

Stil|blüte *f* stylistic blunder; **~bruch** *m* (sudden) break in style, stylistic incongruity; **das wäre ein ~** *fig.* that would be out of style (*od.* incongruous); **~ebene** *f* stylistic register, level of style

stilecht I. *Adj.* true to style; (*historisch* ~) in period; **II.** *adv.* in authentic (*historisch* ~ in period) style

Stil|element *n* stylistic element; **~empfinden** *n* sense of style, stylistic sensitivity; **~epoche** *f* stylistic period

Stilett *n; -s, -e* stiletto

Stil|fehler *m* stylistic lapse (*od.* fault); **~figur** *f* stylistic figure; **~gefühl** *n* sense of style, stylistic sensitivity

stilgerecht *Adj.* in proper (*od.* appropriate) style; (*geziemend*) *auch* appropriate, in keeping

stilisieren *v/t.* stylize; **stilisiert I.** *Part. Präs.* → **stilisieren**; **II.** *Adj.* stylized

Stilist *m; -en, -en* stylist (*auch Sport*); **Stilistik** *f; -, kein Pl.* **1.** stylistics *Pl.* (*V. im Sg.*); **2.** (*Handbuch*) style manual; **Stilistin** *f; -, -nen* stylist; **stilistisch I.** *Adj.* stylistic; **in ~er Hinsicht** stylistically, from a stylistic point of view; **II.** *Adv.* stylistically; **~ gut** (*geschrieben*) written in (a) good style

Stilkunde *f* → **Stilistik**

still *Adj.* **1.** (*ruhig*) quiet (*auch zurückhaltend*); (*lautlos, wortlos*) *auch* silent; (*friedlich*) peaceful; **sei ~!** (be) quiet!; **warum bist du so ~?** why are you so silent? why don't you say anything?; **zu den Stillen in der Klasse gehören** be one of the quiet ones in the class; **~ werden** become (*od.* go) quiet; **plötzlich wurde es ganz ~** suddenly everything went quiet (*od.* there was silence); **~ bleiben** keep quiet; **~es Gebet** silent prayer; **2.** *fig.* quiet; (*heimlich*) secret; **um ihn ist es ~ geworden**

fig. you don't hear anything about him these days; **in e-r ~en Stunde** in a quiet moment; **in ~em Einverständnis** by tacit agreement; **~e Übereinkunft** *Wirts.* tacit understanding; **~es Glück** quiet bliss; **~er Verehrer** secret admirer; **~er Vorwurf** silent reproach; **~e Reserven** hidden reserves; **~er Teilhaber** *Wirts.* sleeping (*Am.* silent) partner; **im Stillen** (*innerlich*) inwardly; (*heimlich*) secretly; **im Stillen fluchte ich** I was cursing to myself (*od.* inside, under my breath); **~e Jahreszeit** *Wirts.* dead season; **~es Örtchen** *umg.* smallest room, *Am.* john; **3.** (*regungslos*) still, motionless; **~ bleiben** keep still; **bleib doch mal ~!** keep still, will you; **sitzt endlich still!** do sit still!; **4.** *Luft, See, Gefühle:* calm; **~ werden** *Wind etc.*: calm down; **der Stille Ozean** the Pacific (Ocean); **~e Wasser sind tief** *Sprichw.* still waters run deep; **er ist ein ~es Wasser** he's a dark horse; → **Kämmerlein**

Stillarbeit *f nur Sg.; Päd.* silent work

Still-BH *m* nursing bra

still bleiben → **still** 1

Stille *f; -, kein Pl.* silence; (*plötzliches Verstummen*) *auch* hush; (*Ruhe*) quiet, *auch des Meeres:* calm; **in aller ~** quietly; (*unbemerkt*) unnoticed; (*heimlich*) *auch* secretly, without a word to anyone, on the quiet *umg.*; **die Beerdigung findet in aller ~ statt** it's a very quiet funeral; **die ~ der Nacht** the silence of night; **in der ~ der Nacht** in the still(ness) of the night; **es herrschte gefräßige ~** *umg. hum.* everybody was too busy eating to say anything

Stilleben → **Stillleben**

Stillehre *f* **1.** stylistics *Pl.* (*V. im Sg.*); **2.** (*Handbuch*) style manual

stillen I. *vt/i.* (*Säugling*) breastfeed, nurse; **II.** *v/t.* **1.** (*Blut*) stop, sta(u)nch, **e-e starke Blutung ~** *Med.* arrest a h(a)emorrhage; **2.** (*Durst*) quench; (*Hunger*) satisfy; *fig.* (*Neugier, Bedürfnisse etc.*) satisfy; (*Lust, Verlangen*) *auch* satiate; **nachdem der erste Hunger gestillt ist** when the edge has been taken off your hunger; **3.** (*Schmerz*) ease

Stillen *n; -s, kein Pl.* breastfeeding; **stillend I.** *Part. Präs.* → **stillen**; **II.** *Adj.*: **~e Mütter** nursing mothers

stillgelegt I. *P.P.* → **stilllegen**; **II.** *Adj. Bergwerk:* disused

Stillhalteabkommen *n* standstill agreement, moratorium; **stillhalten** *v/i.* (*unreg., trennb., hat -ge-*) keep still; *fig.* (*nicht reagieren*) keep quiet; **Stillhalten** *n; -s, kein Pl.* standstill; (*Verzicht*) moratorium; (*Schweigen*) silence

Stillleben *n; -s, - Kunst.* still life

stilllegen *v/t.* (*getr. ll-l*) (*trennb., hat -ge-*) **1.** (*Betrieb, Reaktor*) shut down; (*Fahrzeug*) lay up; (*Maschine etc.*) put out of operation; (*Schiff*) put out of commission; (*Verkehr etc.*) stop; **2.** *Med.* immobilize; **Stilllegung** *f* shutdown, closure; stoppage

stillliegen *v/i.* (*getr. ll-l*) (*unreg., trennb., hat und südd., österr., schw. ist -ge-*) lie dormant, lie idle; *Betrieb:* *auch* be shut down; *Verkehr, Handel etc.*: be at a standstill

stillos I. *Adj.* **1.** (in) bad style (*od.* taste); **2.** *Zimmer etc.*: **~ sein** have no (sense of) style; **II.** *Adv.* in bad style; **e-n Stilbruch aufweisend:** out of style; **Stillosigkeit** *f* lack of style

Stillschweigen *n* silence (*auch Jur.*); ~

bewahren maintain strict silence (**über** + *Akk.* on); **j-m ~ auferlegen** swear s.o. to silence; **stillschweigend I.** *Adj.* silent; **~es Übereinkommen** tacit agreement; **~e Duldung** tacit consent (+ *Gen.* to), (silent) acquiescence (in); *Jur.* (*Einverständnis*) connivance (in); **II.** *Adv.* silently, in silence, without a word; *fig.* tacitly; **etw. ~ übergehen** pass s.th. over in silence; **~ dulden** tacitly consent to, (silently) acquiesce in

stillsitzen *v/i.* (*unreg., trennb., hat und südd., österr., schw. ist -ge-*): **sie kann nicht ~** *fig.* (*ohne Arbeit sein*) she can't sit still, she's always got to be on the go; → *auch* **still** 3

Stillstand *m; nur Sg.* standstill; *von Produktion*: stoppage; *in der Entwicklung*: stagnation (*auch Wirts.*); *von Verhandlungen*: deadlock, breakdown; **~ des Herzens** cardiac arrest; **zum ~ bringen** stop (*auch Blutung, Infektion etc.*); (*Fahrzeug*) *auch* bring to a halt (*od.* standstill); (*Kämpfe etc.*) put an end (*od.* a stop) to, end; **zum ~ kommen** stop (*auch Blutung etc.*), *auch fig.* come to a halt (*od.* standstill); *Kämpfe etc.*: come to a stop (*od.* an end), end; *Verhandlungen*: come to a standstill, reach deadlock; **stillstehen** *v/i.* (*unreg., trennb., hat und südd., österr., schw. ist -ge-*) **1.** *Verkehr, Wirtschaft etc.*: be at a standstill; *Maschine*: be (*od.* stand) idle; **die Zeit scheint stillzustehen** time seems to be standing still; **2.** (*stehen bleiben*) *Maschine*: stop (*working*); *Motor*: stop; *Herz*: stop (*beating*); **mein Herz stand still** *fig.* my heart stopped (*od.* stood still); **3.** *Mil.* stand to attention; **stillgestanden!** attention!

stillvergnügt I. *Adj.* inwardly content; *Lächeln*: serene:; **II.** *Adv.*: **~ lächeln** smile serenely

Stillzeit *f* lactation (*od.* nursing) period **Stil|merkmal** *n* stylistic feature; **~mittel** *n* stylistic device; **~möbel** *Pl.* **1.** *nachgemachte*: reproduction furniture *Sg.*; **2.** *echte*: period furniture *Sg.*; **~note** *f* *Sport* style mark; **~richtung** *f* style **stilsicher I.** *Adj.* stylistically assured; **II.** *Adv.* in an assured style; **Stilsicherheit** *f* stylistic assurance

Stilübung *f* stylistic exercise, exercise in style

stilvoll I. *Adj.* stylish; **II.** *Adv.* stylishly; **~ eingerichtet** *auch* furnished in style

Stilwörterbuch *n* dictionary of (correct) usage, style manual

Stimm|abgabe *f* voting, vote; **~anteil** *m* share of the vote; **~aufwand** *m* vocal effort; **mit großem ~** at the top of one's voice; **~band** *n* vocal cord

stimmberechtigt *Adj.* eligible to vote; **nicht ~** *attr.* non-voting ..., *präd.* unable to vote, without a vote; **Stimmberechtigte** *m, f; -n, -n* person entitled to vote

Stimm|bezirk *m* constituency; **~bildung** *f* voice production; **~bruch** *m* breaking of the voice; **er ist im ~** his voice is breaking; **~bürger** *m schw.* voter, elector

Stimme *f; -, -n* **1.** voice (*auch Singstimme und fig.*); **mit lauter/bebender ~** in a loud/trembling voice; **gut bei ~ sein** be in good voice; **die ~ verlieren** lose one's voice; **mit verstellter ~** in a disguised voice; **e-e innere ~** an inner voice; **der ~ des Herzens/Gewissens folgen** obey the dictates of one's heart/conscience; **2.** *Mus.* (*Stimmlage*)

---

voice; (*Partie*) (voice) part; (*Instrumentalstimme*) part; **3.** (*Meinung*) voice, opinion; (*Sprecher*) speaker, voice; **die ~ des Volkes** the voice of the people; **die ~ der Öffentlichkeit** public opinion; **es gibt ~n, die ...** there are those who ...; **es mehren sich die ~n, dass** more and more people are of the opinion that; **4.** *Wahl*: vote; **e-e ~ haben** have a vote; **s-e ~ abgeben** cast one's vote, vote; **j-m s-e ~ geben** vote for s.o., give s.o. one's vote; **sich der ~ enthalten** abstain (from voting); → **abgeben** I 9, **entscheidend** II

stimmen I. *v/t.* **1.** (*Instrument*) tune (**nach** to); **höher/tiefer ~** tune up/down; **die Instrumente ~** *Orchester, momentan*: be tuning up; **2. j-n glücklich ~** make s.o. happy; **j-n traurig ~** sadden s.o., make s.o. sad; **j-n heiter ~** put s.o. in a cheerful (*od.* good) mood; **j-n optimistisch ~** give s.o. cause for optimism; → **günstig** I, **nachdenklich** I 1; **II.** *v/i.* **1.** (*richtig sein*) be right, be correct; (*wahr sein*) be true; **stimmts?** am I right, is(n't) that right?; (*das*) **stimmt** (*ganz genau*) that's (absolutely) right; **das stimmt ja hinten und vorne nicht!** *umg.* (*ist gelogen*) it's a pack of lies; *Rechnung etc.*: it's all up the creek; **stimmt so!** keep the change, that's all right; **da stimmt etwas nicht** there's something wrong here; (*es ist verdächtig*) there's something fishy going on (here); **bei dem Auto stimmt einfach alles** everything is right about this car, with this car everything is just as it should be; **die Bezahlung stimmt** *umg.* the pay is fine; **der Preis muss ~** *umg.* the price must be right; **Hauptsache, die Kasse stimmt!** *umg.* the main thing is to have the cash (you need); **2. ~ für** vote for (*od.* in favo[u]r of); **~ gegen** vote against; **mit Ja ~** vote for (*od.* in favo[u]r); **mit Nein ~** vote against

Stimmen|anteil *m* share of the vote; **~auszählung** *f* (vote) count; **~einbuße** *f* → **Stimmenverlust**, **~fang** *m pej.* vote catching; **auf ~ gehen** set out to catch votes; **~gewinn** *m* gain (*od.* increase) in votes; **~gewirr** *n* babble of voices; **~gleichheit** *f* tied vote, tie; **bei ~** in the event of a tie; **~mehrheit** *f* majority of votes; **einfache ~** simple majority

Stimmenthaltung *f* abstention; **~ üben** abstain (from voting)

Stimmen|verhältnis *n* proportion of votes; **~verlust** *m* loss of votes; **~e erleiden** lose votes; **~werbung** *f* canvassing; **~zuwachs** *m* gain (*od.* increase) in votes

Stimmer *m; -s, -, ~in* *f; -, -nen; Mus.* tuner

Stimm|führung *f Mus.* vocal line; **~gabel** *f Mus.* tuning fork

stimmgewaltig I. *Adj.* powerful- (*od.* strong-)voiced; **~ sein** have a powerful voice; **II.** *Adv.* in a powerful (*od.* strong) voice

stimmhaft I. *Adj. Ling.* voiced; **II.** *Adv.*: **das S etc. ~ sprechen** voice the s *etc.*; **Stimmhaftigkeit** *f* voiced nature

stimmig *Adj. Argumentation, Schema etc.*: coherent, consistent; *Interpretation, Aufführung etc.*: *auch* well-rounded; *Welt*: ordered, harmonious; **in sich ~ sein** be coherent (*od.* consistent), form an intrinsic whole

...stimmig *im Adj.* **1.** *Mus.*: **vier-/fünf~** *etc.* four-/five-part *etc.*; **2.** *Protest etc.*:

---

tausend~ from a thousand voices

Stimmigkeit *f* coherence, consistency

Stimmlage *f Mus.* (*Bereich*) register; (*Tonhöhe*) pitch

stimmlich I. *Adj.* vocal; **in guter** *etc.* **~er Verfassung** in good voice; **II.** *Adv.* vocally; **~ in Form** in good voice

stimmlos I. *Adj. Ling.* voiceless, unvoiced; **II.** *Adv.*: **das S etc. ~ sprechen** not voice the s *etc.*; **Stimmlosigkeit** *f* unvoiced nature

Stimm|organ *n Anat.* vocal organ; **~recht** *n* (right to) vote; *bes. für Parlamentswahlen*: franchise; **allgemeines ~** universal suffrage; **das ~ ausüben** exercise one's right to vote

Stimm|ritze *f Anat.* glottis; **~ritzenlaut** *Phon.* glottal stop

Stimm|schlüssel *m Mus.* tuning hammer (*od.* key); **~umfang** *m* vocal range

Stimmung *f* **1.** (*Gemütsverfassung*) mood; **in guter ~** in good spirits, cheerful; (*gut gelaunt*) in a good mood; **in schlechter ~** in low spirits, depressed; (*schlecht gelaunt*) in a bad mood; (*nicht*) **in der ~ sein, etw. zu tun** (not) feel like doing s.th., (not) be in the mood for doing s.th. (*od.* to do s.th.); **~en unterworfen sein** be subject to swings (*od.* changes) of mood (*Am. auch* mood swings), be moody; **2.** (*Atmosphäre, Gesamteindruck*) atmosphere; **3.** *nur Sg.*; *von Arbeitern, Truppen etc.*: morale; *der Öffentlichkeit*: public sentiment (*od.* opinion), *the* public mood; *Wirts. Börse*: tone; **die ~ in der Belegschaft ist schlecht** morale among the staff is at a low ebb; **deutschfeindliche ~** anti--German sentiment (*od.* feeling); **feindselige ~** (feeling of) animosity; **~ machen für/gegen** drum up enthusiasm for / whip up hostile feelings against; **4.** *nur Sg.*; (*Ausgelassenheit*) high spirits *Pl.*; **für ~ sorgen** liven things up (a bit); *auf e-r Feier*: *auch* put some life into the party; **in ~ kommen** get going; *Feier etc.*: *auch* liven up; **die ~ verderben** put a damper on things; → **gedrückt** II

Stimmungs|barometer *n der öffentlichen Meinung*: barometer of public mood; **das ~ steht auf null** the general mood is at rock bottom, everyone's in the doldrums; **das ~ steigt** *umg.* the general mood is on the up; **~bild** *n* **1.** (*Gemälde*) atmospheric (*od.* mood) painting; **2.** (*Beschreibung*) atmospheric description; **~kanone** *f umg.*: **er ist e-e richtige ~** he's always the life and soul of the party; **~lage** *f* prevailing mood; **~mache** *f pej.* (cheap) propaganda (*trying to manipulate public opinion*); **gegen j-n**: smear campaign; **~musik** *f* cheerful light music; *zum Mitsingen*: singalong music; **~umschwung** *m* (complete) change of mood; *psych.* mood swing; *Pol.* U-turn; *Wirts., Börse*: change in mood (*od.* tone)

stimmungsvoll I. *Adj.* atmospheric, full of atmosphere; *Gedicht*: evocative; **II.** *Adv.* evocatively; *vortragen, spielen*: with great feeling

Stimmungs|wandel *m,* **~wechsel** *m* → **Stimmungsumschwung**

Stimm|verhalten *n* voting habits *Pl.*; **~vieh** *n pej.* inertia voters *Pl.*, voting fodder *umg.*; **~wechsel** *m* → **Stimmbruch**; **~zettel** *m* ballot paper

Stimulans *n; -, Stimulanzien; Med.* stimulant; *fig. auch* stimulus (*Pl.* sti-

S

muli); **Stimulanz** *f*; -, *-en* stimulus (*Pl.* stimuli); *fig. auch* shot in the arm, fillip; **Stimulation** *f*; -, *-en* stimulation; **stimulieren** *v/t.* stimulate; *j-n* (*zu etw.*) ~ spur s.o. on (to s.th.); **Stimulierung** *f* stimulation; **Stimulus** *m*; -, *Stimuli* stimulus (*Pl.* stimuli)

stinkbesoffen *Adj. umg.* plastered, (completely) sloshed, *Brit. auch* pissed as a newt

Stink|bombe *f* stink bomb; **~drüse** *f Zool.* stink gland

Stinkefinger *m umg.* (*Geste*) single-finger salute (*indicating contempt*); (*j-m*) **den ~ zeigen** give (*Am. auch* flip) (s.o.) the bird

stinken *v/i.*; *stinkt, stank, hat gestunken* **1.** stink (*nach* of), reek (of); *aus dem Mund ~* have bad (*od.* foul) breath; *nach Schweiß/Knoblauch ~* reek of sweat/garlic; *es stinkt nach Gas* it smells of gas; *der Fisch stinkt schon* the fish already reeks (*Brit. umg.* has a pong); *wie ein Bock od. die Pest ~* smell to high heaven; *was stinkt denn hier so?* what's making that awful smell?; → *bestialisch* II; **2.** *umg. fig.*: *vor Geld ~* stink of money, be stinking rich; *vor Faulheit ~* be bone idle; **3.** *umg. fig.*: *etwas stinkt an der Sache* there's something fishy about it; *das/er stinkt mir* I'm sick of it/him; *mir stinkt's!* I'm fed up to the back teeth (*Am.* up to here); *was mir am meisten stinkt* what really bugs (*od.* gets to, *Brit. auch* narks) me; **stinkend I.** *Part. Präs.* → *stinken*; **II.** *Adj.* smelly, *stärker:* stinking; (*faulig*) putrid

Stinker *m*; -s, -; *umg.* **1.** *pej.* (*Auto, Zigarre etc.*) stinking thing, stinker; (*j-d*) smelly type; **2.** *fig.* (*Person*) *kleiner ~* little scumbag; *reaktionärer ~ pej.* reactionary arsehole (*Am.* asshole)

stink|fein *Adj. umg.* bone idle; **~fein** *Adj. umg.* la-di-da, hoity-toity, *Brit. auch* dead posh

stinkig *Adj. umg.* **1.** *pej. Zigarre, Unterhose etc.*: smelly, *stärker:* stinking; **2.** *fig.*: ~ *sein* (*missgelaunt*) be in a foul mood

Stinkkäse *m* smelly (*Brit. auch* pongy) cheese

stinklangweilig *Adj. umg.* deadly boring; ~ *sein auch* be a crashing bore; *es war ~ auch* we were bored out of our minds

Stink|laune *f umg.*: *e-e ~ haben* be in a stinker of a mood, be in a foul mood; **~morchel** *f Bot.* stinkhorn

stink|normal *Adj. umg.* dead (*Am.* totally) normal; **~reich** *Adj. umg.* stinking rich; **~sauer** *Adj. umg.* fuming; ~ *sein auf j-n* be really mad at s.o.

Stink|stiefel *m umg. pej.* surly bastard; **~tier** *n Zool.* skunk; *umg. pej.* (*Person*) nasty piece of work, arsehole, *Am.* asshole

stinkvornehm *umg.* **I.** *Adj. Lokal etc.*: really classy (*Brit. auch* swish); *Leute:* ever so superior; **II.** *Adv.*: *sie tun immer so ~* they always pretend to be ever so superior

Stink|wut *f umg.*: *e-e ~ haben* be (absolutely) fuming (*od.* livid), *e-e ~ auf j-n haben* be really mad at s.o.

Stint *m*; *-(e)s, -e*; *Zool.* smelt

Stipendiat *m*; *-en, -en*, **~in** *f*; -, *-nen* recipient of a grant, grantee; *wegen Begabung:* scholarship holder, ...*-scholar*

Stipendium *n*; *-s, Stipendien* grant; *für Begabte:* scholarship; *Am. allg.* scholarship

Stippe *f*; -, *-n*; *bes. nordd.* (*Soße*) thick gravy; **stippen** *v/t. bes. nordd.*: *etw. in etw. Akk.* ~ dunk s.th. in s.th.

Stippvisite *f umg.* flying visit (*nach* to); *e-r Stadt: auch* quick tour (of); *bei j-m e-e ~ machen* drop in (briefly) on s.o., pop (a)round to see s.o.

stirbt *Präs.* → *sterben*

Stirn *f*; -, *-en, mst Sg.* forehead, *lit.* brow; *hohe/niedrige/fliehende ~* high/low/sloping forehead; *die ~ runzeln* wrinkle one's brow; *missbilligend:* frown (*über + Akk.* on; *fig.*); *die ~ haben, etw. zu tun pej.* have the cheek (*od.* nerve, brass *umg.*) to do s.th.; *j-m/e-r Sache die ~ bieten* defy s.o./s.th.; *es steht ihm auf der ~ geschrieben* it's written all over his face; **~band** *n* headband, sweatband; **~bein** *n Anat.* frontal bone; **~falte** *f* wrinkle on one's forehead; **~glatze** *f* receding hairline; **~haar** *n* front hair; **~höhle** *f Anat.* (frontal) sinus

Stirnhöhlen|entzündung *f Med.* (frontal) sinusitis; **~vereiterung** *f* suppurative (frontal) sinusitis

Stirn|locke *f* forelock, curl on one's forehead; **~rad** *n Tech.* spur gear

Stirnrunzeln *n* frown(ing); **stirnrunzelnd** *Adv.* frowningly, with a frown

Stirn|seite *f* front (side *od.* end); **~spiegel** *m Med.* forehead mirror; **~wand** *f* front (*od.* end) wall

stob *Imperf.* → *stieben*

stöbern *v/i.* **1.** *in Schubladen etc.*: rummage around (*nach* for); *in den Akten ~* rummage through (*od.* delve into) the files; *in Zeitschriften/Büchern ~* thumb (*od.* leaf) through magazines/books; *in Büchern nach Hinweisen ~* hunt for references in books; **2.** *Jägerspr. Hund:* hunt about (*Am.* around) (*nach* for); **3.** *Dial.* (*sauber machen*) get the place shipshape

stochastisch *Adj.* stochastic; *Komponente, Prozess:* random

Stocherkahn *m südd.* punt; **stochern** *v/i.* **1.** ~ (*in + Dat.*) poke (about in); *im Feuer ~* poke the fire; *in den Zähnen ~* pick one's teeth; *in s-m Essen ~* pick at one's food; **2.** (*Kahn fahren*) punt; *Stochern gehen* go punting; **Stochern** *n*; *-s, kein Pl.* poking

Stock[1] *m*; *-(e)s, Stöcke* **1.** *abgeschnittener Ast:* stick (*auch Spazierstock, Hockeyschläger*); (*Skistock*) *auch* pole; (*Schlagstock*) cudgel; *von Polizei:* truncheon, *Am. auch* nightstick, billy (club); (*Rohrstock*) cane; (*Billardstock*) cue; (*Taktstock*) baton; *mit dem ~ drohen* threaten with the cane; *am ~ gehen* walk with a stick; *umg. fig.* be on one's last legs; *finanziell: auch* be down to nothing; *hoher ~ Eishockey:* high-sticking; **2.** *Bot.* (*Weinstock*) vine; (*Blumenstock*) (flowering) pot plant; **3.** (*Baumstumpf, Wurzelstock*) stock; *über ~ und Stein* up hill and down dale; **4.** (*Gebirgsstock*) massif; **5.** (*Bienenstock*) hive; → *Opferstock etc.*

Stock[2] *m*; *-(e)s, -*; (*Stockwerk*) floor, stor(e)y; *im ersten ~ wohnen* live on the first (*Am.* second) floor; *vier ~ hoch* four storeys (*Am.* stories) high

stock|besoffen, **~betrunken** *Adj. umg.* plastered, (completely) sloshed *Sl.*, *Brit. auch* pissed as a newt *Sl.*

Stockbetten *Pl.* bunk beds

stock|blind *Adj. umg. präd.* blind as a bat; **~dumm** *Adj. umg. präd.* (as) thick as two short planks (*Am.* as a board); **~dunkel**, **~duster** *Adj. umg. präd.* pitch dark

Stöckelabsatz *m* high heel; (*Pfennigabsatz*) stiletto heel; **stöckeln** *v/i* (*ist*) *umg.* totter (on high heels); **Stöckelschuhe** *Pl.* high-heeled shoes; *mit Pfennigabsätzen:* stilettos

stocken *v/i.* **1.** (*hat gestockt*) *im Sprechen, Gehen etc.*: falter; (*zögern*) hesitate; *Gespräch:* falter, flag; *Wirts., Geschäfte:* flag, slacken; (*plötzlich aufhören*) stop short; *Fahrt:* be interrupted; *Motor:* cut out; *Verhandlungen etc.*: break down, come to a standstill; *Verkehr:* be held up; *immer wieder:* be subject to hold-ups, proceed in fits and starts; *ihm stockte das Herz fig.* his heart missed a beat; *ihm stockte der Atem* he caught his breath; *ihr stockte das Blut in den Adern* her blood froze; **2.** (*hat*) *Med., Blut:* clot, coagulate; **3.** (*hat od. ist*) *südd., österr., schw.; Milch:* curdle; **4.** (*stockig werden*) *Papier etc.*: get mildew spots

Stocken *n*; *-s, kein Pl.*: *ins ~ geraten Sprecher:* (begin to) falter; *Verhandlungen:* break down, come to a standstill; *Geschäfte etc.*: begin to fall off (*od.* slacken); *Motor:* start to miss (*od.* cut out)

stockend I. *Part. Präs.* → *stocken*; **II.** *Adj. Stimme, Gespräch, Herzschlag etc.*: faltering; *Gang:* halting; *mit ~er Stimme* in a faltering voice; *~er Atem* short, sharp breaths; *~e Schritte* halting (*od.* faltering) steps; *~er Verkehr* stop-go (*od.* slow-moving) traffic; *~e Verhandlungen* slow-moving (*od.* faltering) talks; **III.** *Adv.* haltingly; *leise und ~ sprechen* speak in a soft, faltering voice; *wir kommen nur ~ voran* we progress in fits and starts

Stockente *f Orn.* mallard

Stockerl *n österr.* **1.** (*Hocker*) stool; **2.** *Sport* (*Siegerpodest*) winners' rostrum (*Am.* platform)

Stockfehler *m Hockey, Eishockey:* stick penalty

stockfinster *Adj. umg.* pitch dark; *es herrschte ~e Nacht* the night was black as pitch

Stockfisch *m* dried cod; *umg. fig.* (*Mensch*) boring old coot

Stockfleck *m* spot (*größer:* patch) of mildew; **stockfleckig** *Adj.* mildewy

stockheiser *Adj. umg. präd.* terribly hoarse; *ich bin ~ auch* I have hardly any voice left

Stockhieb *m* blow (*seitwärts:* swipe) with a stick; *mit dem Rohrstock:* stroke of the cane

stockig *Adj.* mildewy

...stöckig *im Adj. attr.* ...*-stor(e)y*, ...*-storeyed* (*Am.* -storied)

stockkonservativ *Adj. umg.* ultra-conservative

Stocknagel *m* walking-stick badge (*collected by hikers and mountaineers*)

stock|nüchtern *Adj. umg. präd.* stone-cold sober; **~sauer** *Adj. umg. präd.* absolutely livid, fuming

Stock|schirm *m* walking-stick umbrella; **~schlag** *m* blow with a stick (*Schlagstock:* truncheon); *mit Rohrstock:* stroke of a cane; **~schnupfen** *m Med.* heavy cold, *fachspr.* chronic rhinitis; **~schwämmchen** *n Bot.* little cluster fungus

stock|solide *Adj. umg.* (*stabil*) really solid (*od.* strong); (*fundiert*) very sound; (*anständig*) thoroughly respectable; **~steif** *Adj. umg.* (as) stiff as a board; *fig.* (*formell*) stiff and unbending; *ein ~er Jurist* a stiff and starchy lawyer; **~taub** *Adj. umg.* as deaf as a post, stone-deaf

Stockung *f* **1.** (*Verzögerung, auch im Verkehr*) holdup, delay; (*Zögern, auch im Sprechen*) hesitation; **~en im Verkehr etc.**: auch congestion; **ohne ~en verlaufen** go without a hitch; **2.** (*Stillstand*) standstill; *in Verhandlungen*: auch deadlock; *Med.* stasis; *des Bluts*: coagulation

Stockwerk *n* floor, stor(e)y; *Geol.* stratum; **im ersten ~** on the first (*Am.* second) floor; **im oberen ~** upstairs

Stockzahn *m süüd., österr., schw.* molar

Stoff *m*; *-(e)s, -e* **1.** (*Textil*) material, fabric; (*Tuch*) cloth; **~ für ein Kleid kaufen** buy material for a dress; **2.** (*Substanz*) substance; **pflanzliche/synthetische ~e** vegetable matter *Sg.* / synthetic materials; **leicht entflammbare ~e** inflammable substances (*od.* materials); **3.** (*Thema*) subject matter; *in der Schule*: auch material; (*Thema*) topic; (*Gesprächsstoff*) topic(s *Pl.*) (for discussion); **zu e-m Roman etc.**: material (**zu, für** for); **zu vermittelnder/beherrschender ~** material to be passed on / taken in; **~ zum Nachdenken** food for thought; **der ~ wurde mehrfach verfilmt** this subject has been filmed several times; **4.** *nur Sg. umg.* (*Alkohol, Rauschgift*) stuff; **sich** (*Dat.*) **~ besorgen** get o.s. some dope

...stoff *m, im Subst.* **1.** (*Material, Substanz*): **Heiz~** heating material; **Ersatz~** substitute; **Geruchs~** aromatic substance; **2.** (*Textil*): **Frottee~** towel(l)ing, terrycloth; **Gardinen~** curtain material; **Leinen~** linen (material); **3.** *fig.* (*Thema etc.*): **Diskussions~** topic(s) for discussion; **Film~** material for a film; **Roman~** material for a novel

Stoff|bahn *f* length of material; **~ballen** *m* bale of cloth; **~druck** *m* textile printing

Stoffel *m*; *-s, -; umg.* boor; **stoff(e)lig** *umg. Adj.* boorish, uncouth

Stoff|farbe *f* (fabric) dye; **~fetzen** *m* scrap of material (*od.* cloth); **~fülle** *f bes. Päd.* wealth of material; **~gebiet** *n Päd.* subject area; **~hose** *f* cloth trousers (*Am.* pants); **~kreislauf** *m Öko.* circular flow of materials

stofflich I. *Adj.* Fülle etc.: of material (*e-s Buches*: auch of subject matter); **1.** (*materiell*) material; **II.** *Adv.*: **~** (*gesehen*) as regards the subject matter

Stoff|muster *n* **1.** pattern; **2.** (*Warenprobe*) sample; **~puppe** *f* rag doll; **~rest** *m* remnant; *kleiner*: scrap of material; **~sammlung** *f zu e-m Buch etc.*: collection of material; **~serviette** *f* cloth (table) napkin; **~tier** *n* soft toy (animal), *Am.* stuffed animal

Stoffwechsel *m* metabolism

Stoffwechsel... *im Subst.* metabolic ...; **~krankheit** *f* metabolic disease; **~produkt** *n* product of metabolism

stöhnen *v/i.* **1.** groan (**vor** + *Dat.* with); **vor Lust ~** moan with pleasure; **alle ~ unter der Hitze** everyone is groaning because of the heat; **„Wasser!", stöhnte er** "Water!", he moaned; **2.** (*sich beklagen*) moan, complain (**über** +*Akk.* about); **Stöhnen** *n*; *-s, kein Pl.* groaning; (*Klagen*) moaning, complaining; → **stöhnen**; (**ein**) **leises ~** soft moaning

Stoiker *m*; *-s, -*, **~in** *f*; *-, -nen* Stoic (philosopher); *fig.* stoic; **stoisch I.** *Adj.* Stoic; *fig.* stoic(al); **mit ~er Ruhe** *fig.* with stoic calm; **II.** *Adv.* stoically; **Stoizismus** *m*; *-, kein Pl.* Stoi-

---

cism; *fig.* stoicism

Stola *f*; *-, Stolen* **1.** *Mode*: stole, *bes. Am.* auch wrap; **2.** *kirchl.* stole

Stolle *f*; *-, -n* (*Weihnachtsstolle*) stollen (cake)

Stollen *m*; *-s, -* **1.** *Bergb.* gallery; **2.** (*Weihnachtsstollen*) stollen (cake); **3.** *am Schuh*: stud

Stolperdraht *m auch fig.* trip wire

stolpern *v/i.* trip (up); *auch fig.* stumble; **~ durch etc.** stumble through etc.; **~ über** (+ *Akk.*) trip over, trip up on; *fig.* (*e-e schwierige Stelle etc.*) stumble over; (*zufällig entdecken*) stumble across; (*alte Bekannte etc.*) bump into; (*e-e Affäre etc.*) come to grief over; **über s-e eigenen Füße ~** trip over one's own feet; **über jede Kleinigkeit ~** (*Anstoß nehmen*) take exception to every little thing; **ins Stolpern geraten** trip (up), lose one's footing; *fig.* come a cropper *umg.*

Stolperstein *m fig.* stumbling block (**auf dem Weg zu** on the way to)

stolz I. *Adj.* **1.** proud (**auf** + *Akk.* of); **darauf kannst du ~ sein** that's something to be proud of; **ganz ~ hat er s-n neuen Pass vorgezeigt** he proudly produced his new passport; **~ wie ein Pfau/Spanier** (as) proud as a peacock; **2.** *pej.* (*hochmütig*) proud; **warum so ~?** don't you know me any more?; **er war zu ~, uns zu grüßen** he was too full of himself to acknowledge our presence; **3.** *fig.* (*imposant*) impressive; *Gebäude*: proud, imposing; **e-e ~e Summe** a handsome (*umg.* tidy) sum; **ein ~er Preis** a hefty (*od.* steep) price; **II.** *Adv.* proudly; **~ in die Runde blicken** look proudly (a)round the assembled company

Stolz *m*; *-es, kein Pl.* pride (**auf** + *Akk.* in); **voller ~ sprechen über etc.**: full of pride, proudly; **s-n ~ daransetzen, etw. zu tun** make it a point of hono(u)r to do s.th.; **das lässt sein ~ nicht zu** he's too proud to do that; **etw. aus falschem Stolz ausschlagen** refuse s.th. from a false sense of pride; **sie hat keinen ~** she has no (sense of) pride; **er hat eben auch s-n ~** he does have his pride; **sie ist der ~ i-r Eltern** her parents are very proud of her; **der Ferrari ist sein ganzer ~** the Ferrari is his pride and joy

stolzgeschwellt I. *Adj.* swollen (*od.* bursting) with pride; **mit ~er Brust** with one's chest puffed out; **II.** *Adv.*: **~ trat er ins Zimmer** he strutted proudly into the room

stolzieren *v/i. pej.* strut, swagger

Stomatitis *f*; *-, Stomatitiden*; *Med.* stomatitis

stop *Interj. auf Schildern*: stop; → **stopp**

Stop-and-go-Verkehr ['stɔp ɛnt 'goː-] *m Verk.* stop-go (*Am.* stop-and-go) traffic

Stopfei *n* darning egg

stopfen I. *v/t/i.* (*Strümpfe etc.*) darn, mend; **Oma stopft beim Fernsehen** Granny does her darning while watching TV; **II.** *v/t.* **1.** (*hineinstopfen*) stuff (**in** + *Akk.* into); (*füllen*) (*Kissen etc.*) stuff; (*Pfeife, Wurst*) fill; **sich** (*Dat.*) **das Hemd in die Hose ~** tuck one's shirt into one's trousers; **sich** (*Dat.*) **Süßigkeiten in den Mund ~** stuff sweets into one's mouth; **j-m den Mund ~** *fig.* silence s.o., shut s.o. up *umg.*; → **gestopft**; (*ausfüllen, zumachen*) (*Lücke*) fill; (*Loch*) auch plug; **3.** (*mästen*) stuff, fatten; **III.** *v/i.* **1.** (*sät-*

---

tigen) be filling; **Reis stopft** auch rice fills you up; **2.** (*verstopfen*) cause constipation; **das stopft** auch that gives you constipation

Stopfen[1] *n*; *-s, kein Pl.* **1.** *von Socken etc.*: darning; **2.** *Gastr.* stuffing

Stopfen[2] *m*; *-s, -* stopper; (*Korken*) cork

Stopf|garn *n* darning cotton; **~leber** *f Gastr.* oversize liver (of a fattened goose); **~nadel** *f* darning needle; **~pilz** *m* pin cushion; **~wolle** *f* darning wool

Stopp *m*; *-s, -s* **1.** stop; *Wirts.* (*Verbot*) ban (**für** on); (*Preis-, Lohnstopp*) freeze; **e-n kurzen ~ einlegen** make a short stop; **2.** *Tennis etc.*: drop shot

stopp *Interj.* stop!; **~** (*mal*), **...** (*Moment*) just a moment, *Brit. umg.* auch hang about

Stoppball *m Tennis etc.*: drop shot

Stoppel|acker *m* stubble field; **~bart** *m* stubbly beard; **~feld** *n* stubble field; **~haar** *n* bristle haircut

stoppelig *Adj.* stubbly

Stoppeln *Pl.* (*Getreide, Bart*) stubble *Sg.*

stoppen *v/t/i.* **1.** stop; **die Produktion ~** halt (*od.* stop) production; **er war nicht mehr zu ~** there was no stopping him; **den Ball ~** stop the ball; **2.** *mit der Stoppuhr*: time, do the timing; **ich habe 6,4 Sekunden gestoppt** I timed it at 6.4 seconds, I made the time 6.4 seconds; **Stopper** *m*; *-s, -* **1.** (*Zeitnehmer*) timekeeper; **2.** (*Türstopper*) doorstop(per); **3.** *Fußball*: cent|re (*Am.* -er) half

Stopp|licht *n Mot.* brake light; **~schild** *n* stop sign; **~signal** *n* stop signal, signal to stop; **~straße** *f* road with a stop sign, *Am.* stop street; **~taste** *f* stop button; **~uhr** *f* stopwatch

Stöpsel *m*; *-s, -* **1.** stopper; *im Waschbecken*: plug; *Etech.* (*Stecker*) plug; **2.** *umg. fig.* (*kleiner Kerl*) midget; **stöpseln** *v/t.* plug (*auch Etech.*)

Stör *m*; *-s, -e*; *Zool.* sturgeon

Störaktion *f* disruptive action

störanfällig *Adj.* Gerät: fault-prone, liable to break down; (*empfindlich*) very sensitive; *auch Auto*: temperamental; *Radio*: interference-prone, susceptible to interference; *fig. Wirtschaft etc.*: susceptible, sensitive; **Störanfälligkeit** *f* (*Empfindlichkeit*) sensitivity; *bei Fehlfunktion*: tendency to develop faults, tendency to break down; *Radio*: susceptibility to interference; *fig.* susceptibility, sensitivity

Storch *m*; *-(e)s, Störche*; *Orn.* stork; **wie der ~ im Salat** *umg. fig.* stiff-leggedly; **da brat mir einer e-n ~!** *umg.* well I'll be blowed (*Am.* darned)!; **~beine** *Pl. umg.* spindly (*od.* matchstick) legs

Storchen|gang *m umg.* stalking gait, stalk; **e-n ~ haben** walk like a stork; **~nest** *n* stork's nest

Störchin *f*; *-, -nen* female stork; **Störchlein** *n* baby stork

Storchschnabel *m* **1.** stork's bill; **2.** *Tech.* pantograph; **3.** *Bot.* cranesbill

Stördienst *m* fault-clearing service; *Telef.* auch the engineers *Pl.*

Store [ʃtoːɐ̯] *m*; *-s, -s* net curtain

stören I. *v/t/i.* **1.** disturb; (*unterbrechen*) auch interrupt; (*dazwischenkommen*) get in the way, interfere; (*ablenken*) distract; (*im Weg sein*) be in the way; *Gebäude etc.*: spoil the view; (*unangenehm sein*) be awkward; (*lästig sein*) be a nuisance; (*belästigen*) bother (*auch j-m missfallen, j-m etw. ausma-*

chen); (*Harmonie etc. zerstören*) spoil; (*beeinträchtigen*) impair; (*behindern*) obstruct; **störe ich?** am I disturbing you?; **darf ich Sie kurz ~?** could I bother you for a minute?; **lassen Sie sich nicht ~!** don't let me disturb you; **er lässt sich durch nichts ~** he doesn't let anything bother him, he's completely unflappable; **du störst nur** you're (just) in the way; **„(bitte) nicht ~!"** (please) do not disturb; **stört es Sie, wenn ich rauche?** do you mind if I smoke?, would it bother you if I smoked?; **das stört mich nicht** I don't mind (that), it doesn't bother me; **was stört dich daran?** what is it you don't like about it?; **das (Gesamt)Bild ~** spoil the effect; **j-s Pläne ~** upset s.o.'s plans; **2.** (*Unruhe stiften*) (*e-e Versammlung, den Unterricht*) disrupt; *in der Schule*: cause a disturbance (*od.* trouble); be disruptive; **die beiden ~ dauernd (den Unterricht)** those two constantly interrupt (the lesson); **wer stört, fliegt raus!** any troublemakers must leave the room; **3.** (*Radioempfang*) interfere with; (*auch Sender*) jam; → **gestört**; **II.** *v/refl.*: **sich an etw. ~** be bothered by s.th.; (*Anstoß nehmen*) take exception to s.th.; **ich störe mich nicht daran** it doesn't bother me

Stören *n*; *-s*, *kein Pl.* *bes. bewusstes*: disruption; (*Unterbrechen*) interruption; **würdet ihr bitte das dauernde ~ lassen?** would you please stop interrupting?; → **Störung** 1, 3

störend I. *Part. Präs.* → **stören**; **II.** *Adj.* disturbing; (*ablenkend*) distracting; (*lästig*) irritating, annoying; (*dazwischentretend*) interfering; (*unterbrechend*) disruptive; **etw als ~ empfinden** find s.th. irritating; **III.** *Adv.*: ~ **wirken** be (*od.* get) in the way; (*lästig*) be a nuisance; (*unterbrechend*) have a disruptive effect (**auf** + *Akk.* on)

Störenfried *m*; *-(e)s*, *-e* troublemaker; *umg. fig.* (*ungeladener Besucher*) intruder, interloper

Störer *m*; *-s*, *-* troublemaker, disruptive element

Stör|faktor *m* (source of) disturbance, disruptive element;, *lästig*: nuisance (element); **~fall** *m* (nuclear power station) malfunction (*Panne*: breakdown); **der ~ von Harrisburg** the Three Mile Island nuclear accident; **~feuer** *n* *Mil.* harassing fire; **~frequenz** *f* jamming frequency; **~geräusch** *n* *Radio*: *auch Pl.* background noise; *durch Sender*: interference; *atmosphärisches*: atmospherics *Pl.*; *elektrostatisches*: static; *beabsichtigtes*: jamming; **~manöver** *n* *auch Pl.* disruptive action

stornieren *v/t.* *Wirts.* (*Auftrag*) cancel; **e-e Buchung ~** reverse an entry; **Stornierung** *f* *e-s Auftrags*: cancellation, *Am.* cancelation; *e-r Buchung*: reversal

Storno *m*, *n*; *-s*, *Storni* → **Stornierung**; **~gebühr** *f* *Wirts.* cancel(l)ation fee

störrisch *Adj.* (*halsstarrig*) stubborn, obstinate; (*unlenksam*) unmanageable, refractory; *Pferd*: restive

Störsender *m* jamming station, jammer

störsicher *Adj.* protected from interference, interference-free; **Störsignal** *n* interference signal

Störung *f* **1.** (*Störendes*) disturbance; (*Unterbrechung*) interruption; (*Einmischung*) interference; (*Behinderung*) obstruction; *des Unterrichts*, *e-r Versammlung*: disruption, interruption; **entschuldigen Sie die ~!** sorry to disturb (*od.* bother) you; **es gab wiederholte ~en durch Randalierer** hooligans caused repeated disturbances; **2.** *Tech.* fault, defect; *EDV auch* malfunction; *TV* fault; (*Betriebsstörung*) failure, breakdown; **wir bitten die ~ zu entschuldigen** *TV*, *Ansage*: we apologize for the fault / (*Ausfall*) breakdown in transmission; **ohne ~ verlaufen** go off smoothly; **3.** *Radio*, *durch Sender*: *auch Pl.* interference; *absichtliche*: jamming; **atmosphärische ~en** atmospherics; *umg. fig.* (*geladene Atmosphäre*) charged atmosphere; *im Verhältnis*: tensions *Pl.*, *bes. Brit. auch* ructions *Pl.*; **4.** *Med.* disorder; *stärker*: malfunction; **5.** *Met.* disturbance

störungsanfällig *Adj.* → **störanfällig**

Störungs|anzeige *f* fault indicator; **~dienst** *m* fault-clearing service; *Telef.* *auch* the engineers *Pl.*

störungsfrei *Adj.* **1.** undisturbed; *Ablauf*: smooth; **2.** *Radio*: interference-free; *Tech.* trouble-free

störungssicher *Adj.* **~es System** *EDV* fault-protected system

Störungs|stelle *f* → **Störungsdienst**; **~suche** *f* fault location; *bes. Etron.* fault-finding; (*auch Beseitigung*) trouble-shooting

Story ['sto:ri] *f*; *-*, *-s* story; **e-e gute ~ für die Titelseite** a good front-page story; **erzähl keine ~s** *umg.* don't tell tall stories

Stoß *m*; *-es*, *Stöße* **1.** push; (*Mil. Vorstoß*) *auch Fechten*: thrust; *mit Messer etc.* stab; *mit der Faust*: punch; *mit dem Fuß*: kick; *mit dem Kopf, den Hörnern*: butt; *mit e-m Stock etc.*: poke; *in die Rippen*: dig (in the ribs), nudge; *Schwimmen, Rudern*: stroke; *Kugelstoßen*: put; *Billard*: stroke; **j-n versetzen** give s.o. a push; *fig.* shake s.o. (up); **s-m Herzen e-n ~ geben** *fig.* make an effort, force o.s.; **2.** (*Aufprall*) impact; (*Schock*) shock; (*Erdstoß*) tremor, shock; (*Ruck*) jolt, jerk; (*Explosions-, Wind-, Trompetenstoß*) blast; **3.** *Med.* (*Vitaminstoß etc.*) massive dose; (*Stapel*) pile; *Holz*: *auch* stack; *Briefe*: batch; **5.** *Tech.* joint; **6.** *Bergb.* stope, face

stoßartig I. *Adj.* intermittent (*auch Tech., Etech.*); (*ruckartig*) jerky; **II.** *Adv.* intermittently; (*ruckartig*) jerkily

Stoß|band *n* *an Hose*: edging tape; **~behandlung** *f* *Med.* massive-dose treatment; **~betrieb** *m* **1.** *Verkehr*: rush hour; *Geschäft etc.*: peak period (*od.* hours *Pl.*); **2.** *Etron.* (period of) peak demand, peak time; **~dämpfer** *m* *Mot., Flug.* shock absorber

Stößel *m*; *-s*, *-* *im Mörser*: pestle; *Mot., in Pumpe, Ventilstössel*: tappet

stoßempfindlich *Adj.* sensitive to shock; **nicht ~** *Uhr*: shockproof

stoßen; **stößt, stieß, hat od. ist gestoßen** **I.** *v/t.* (*hat*) push; (*e-e Waffe*) thrust; *mit der Faust*: punch; *mit dem Fuß*: kick; (*puffen*) nudge, jostle; *mit e-m Stock etc.*: poke; (*rammen*) ram; (*treiben*) drive; *Sport* (*Kugel*) put; *im Mörser*: pound; *vulg.* (*Frau*) fuck, bang; **j-n in die Rippen ~** nudge s.o., give s.o. a dig in the ribs; **j-n vor e-n Zug ~** push s.o. in front of a train; **j-n mit dem Kopf ~** butt s.o. in the head; **j-m das Messer in die Brust ~** plunge a knife into s.o.'s chest; **von** sich ~ push away; *fig.* disown; **s-e Zehen ~ an** (+ *Dat.*) stub one's toes on (*od.* against); **aus dem Verein ~** expel from the club; → **Bescheid** 3, **Kopf** 6, **Nase**[1] 5; **II.** *v/refl.* (*hat*) (*sich wehtun*) knock o.s., hurt o.s.; **sich ~ an** (+*Dat.*) knock (*od.* run, bump) against; *fig.* take offen|ce (*Am.* -se) at, take exception to; **an der Unordnung darfst du dich nicht ~** just ignore the mess, you mustn't mind the mess; **III.** *v/i.* **1.** (*hat*) *Bock etc.*: butt; **mit dem Kopf ~** *auch Boxen*: butt; **2.** (*ist*) **~ an** (+*Akk.*) *od.* **gegen** bump into, knock (o.s.) against; **~ an** (+*Akk.*) *fig.* (*grenzen an*) border on, *förm.* abut on; **ich bin bei dem Marathon an meine (eigenen) Grenzen gestoßen** I was touching my limits (of endurance) in the marathon; **mit dem Kopf gegen die Tür ~** bump (*od.* knock) one's head against *od.* on the door *etc.*; **~ auf** (+ *Akk.*) *fig.* (*Erdöl*) strike; *Straße etc.*: lead onto, hit *umg.*; (*zufällig begegnen*) (happen to) meet, come across, run (*od.* bump) into; (*entdecken*) come across, stumble on; (*Ablehnung, Widerstand etc.*) meet with; **zu j-m, e-r Partei etc. ~** join (up with); **auf s-e Beute ~** *Greifvogel*: swoop down on its prey; → **Horn**[1] 2

stoßfest *Adj.* shockproof, shock-resistant; **Stoßfestigkeit** *f* shock resistance

Stoß|gebet *n* quick prayer; **ein ~ zum Himmel senden** say a quick prayer; **~geschäft** *n* peak-period business; **~kante** *f* *e-r Hose*: bottom edge; **~kraft** *f* *Tech.* impact; *weitS.* impetus, drive, force; *e-r Idee, des Intellekts etc.*: thrust; **~prüfung** *f* *Tech.* impact test; **~richtung** *f* *Mil. und fig.* thrust; **~seufzer** *m* deep (*od.* loud) sigh

stoßsicher *Adj.* shockproof

Stoßstange *f* *Mot.* bumper

stößt *Präs.* → **stoßen**

Stoß|therapie *f* *Med.* massive-dose treatment; **~trupp** *m* *Mil.* assault party, (unit of) shock troops; **~verkehr** *m* rush-hour traffic; **~waffe** *f* thrust weapon

stoßweise I. *Adj.* intermittent, sporadic; **II.** *Adv.* **1.** intermittently, sporadically; *atmen, sich bewegen*: in fits and starts; (*ruckartig*) jerkily; **2.** *in Stapeln*: in piles

Stoß|welle *f* *auch Med.* shock wave; **~zahn** *m* tusk; **~zeit** *f* peak period; *Verkehr*: rush hour

Stotterei *f*; *-*, *-en*; *pej.* (constant) stammering; **Stotterer** *m*; *-s*, *-*, **Stotterin** *f*; *-*, *-nen* stammerer; **stottern I.** *v/i.* stammer, stutter; *krankhaft*: *auch* have a stammer; *Mot.* splutter; **er stottert stark/leicht** he has a pronounced/light stammer; **II.** *v/t.* stammer, stutter; **e-e Antwort ~** stammer out a reply

Stottern *n*; *-s*, *kein Pl.* stutter(ing), stammer(ing); **ins ~ kommen** begin to stammer (*od.* stutter); **auf ~ kaufen** *umg.* buy on the never-never (*Am.* on the installment plan)

Stövchen *n* (coffeepot, *für Teekanne*: teapot) warmer, hotplate

stracks *Adv.* → **schnurstracks**

Stradivari *f*; *-*, *-(s)*, **Stradivarigeige** *f* Stradivarius, Strad *umg.*

Straf|akte *f* *Jur.* case record (*od.* file); **~aktion** *f* punitive action; **~androhung** *f* threat of punishment; **unter ~** under penalty; **~anstalt** *f* penal institution, prison, *Am. auch* penitentiary; **~antrag** *m* *Jur.* **1.** **~ stellen** bring an action, start legal proceedings; **2.** *des*

Staatsanwalts: demand for a stated penalty; *e-n* ~ *stellen* demand a stated penalty; ~**anzeige** *f Jur.* charge; ~ *erstatten gegen* bring a charge against; ~**arbeit** *f Schule*: extra (home)work, *Brit. auch* imposition; *e-e* ~ *bekommen* be given extra (home)work; ~**arrest** *m Mil.* detention; ~**aufschub** *m* reprieve; ~**aussetzung** *f Jur.* suspension of (*od.* suspended) sentence (*zur Bewährung* on probation)

Strafbank *f Sport* penalty bench; *Eishockey, Rugby*: penalty box, sin bin *umg.*; *zwei Minuten auf die* ~ *müssen* be sent off for two minutes, get a two- -minute penalty

strafbar *Adj.* punishable, *stärker*: criminal; ~*e Handlung* punishable offen|ce (*Am.* -se); ~ *sein* be a punishable offen|ce (*Am.* -se); *sich* ~ *machen* commit a punishable offen|ce (*Am.* -se), make o.s. liable to prosecution; **Strafbarkeit** *f* punishable nature

Straf|befehl *m Jur.* order of summary punishment; ~**bestimmung** *f* penal provision (*od.* clause)

strafbewehrt *Adj. Jur.*: *dieses Gesetz ist* ~ infringement of this law carries a penalty

Strafe *f*; -, -*n* punishment; *Jur. auch* penalty; (*Freiheitsstrafe*) sentence; (*Geldstrafe*) fine; *Sport* penalty; *lit.* (*Vergeltung*) retribution; *bei* ~ *von* on pain (*od.* penalty) of; *zur* ~ as a punishment; *unter* ~ *stehen* be a punishable offen|ce (*Am.* -se); *etw. unter* ~ *stellen* make s.th. a punishable offen|ce (*Am.* -se); *darauf stehen hohe* ~*n* this carries heavy penalties; ~ *zahlen* pay a fine; *das ist die* ~ (*dafür, dass du mir nicht gehorcht hast*) that's what you get (for disobeying me); ~ *muss sein* there's nothing like a bit of discipline; *die* ~ *folgt auf dem Fuß* punishment (*lit.* retribution) is swift; *es ist e-e* ~ (*für mich*) *zu* (+ *Inf.*) *fig.* it's a punishment (for me) to (+ *Inf.*); → *abbüßen, antreten* II 1

Strafecke *f Sport, Hockey*: penalty corner

strafen *v/t.* punish; *bes. Sport: auch fig.* penalize; *mit e-m Bußgeld*: fine; *mit dieser Familie ist er gestraft genug umg.* to have a family like that is punishment enough; → *Lüge, Verachtung*; **strafend** *I. Part. Präs.* → *strafen*; *II. Adj.* punitive; (*rächend*) avenging; *Blick*: reproachful, censorious; ~*e Worte* words of reproach; *III. Adv. ansehen etc.*: reproachfully

Straf|entlassene *m, f*; -*n*, -*n* discharged prisoner; ~**erlass** *m* remission (of sentence); *bedingter* ~ conditional pardon

straferschwerend *Adj.* → *strafverschärfend*

Strafexpedition *f* punitive campaign

straff *I. Adj.* (*eng, gespannt*) tight (*auch Kontrolle, Planung*); *Seil, Sehne, Muskel*: taut; *Haut*: smooth, taut; *Stil*: concise, economical, elegant; *Inhalt e-s Buchs etc.*: rigorous; *Disziplin*: strict, rigid; ~*er Busen* firm breasts *Pl.*; ~*e Haltung* straight posture; ~*e Handlung* tight (*od.* taut) plot; ~*e Unternehmensleitung* firm management; *II. Adv.* tightly; ~ *anliegen Bluse etc.*: fit tightly, be close-fitting; *Haare*: be combed flat; *zusammengebunden*: be pulled back tightly; ~ *anziehen* (*Schraube etc.*) tighten; (*Seil etc.*) *auch* pull tight; *die Zügel* ~*er anziehen fig.* draw the reins tighter; ~ *organisiert*

tightly organized; ~ *führen* keep a tight rein on

straffällig *Adj. Jur.* liable to prosecution; (*schuldig*) guilty of a crime; ~ *werden* offend, commit an offen|ce (*Am.* -se); ~*er Jugendlicher* young offender; **Straffällige** *m, f*; -*n*, -*n* offender; **Straffälligkeit** *f* liability to prosecution

straffen *I. v/t.* tighten; (*Seil etc.*) tauten, pull taut; (*Handlung etc.*) tighten up, tauten; (*Organisation*) streamline, tighten up; *sich* (*Dat.*) *die Gesichtshaut / den Busen* ~ *lassen* have a facelift / have one's breasts lifted; *der Aufsatz müsste noch etwas gestrafft werden* the essay still needs a little tightening up; *II. v/refl.* tighten; *Person*: straighten up, draw o.s. up; **Straffheit** *f* tightness; *von Seil, Sehne, Muskel*: tautness; *von Haut*: smoothness; *von Busen*: firmness; *von Stil*: conciseness

straffrei *Jur. I. Adj.* exempt from punishment; *II. Adv. auch* with impunity; → *ausgehen* 8; **Straffreiheit** *f* impunity; (*Immunität*) immunity (from criminal prosecution)

Straffung *f* tightening; *von Seil etc.*: tautening; *von Handlung etc.*: tightening up; *von Organisation*: streamlining; ~ *der Gesichtshaut* facelift

Straf|gefangene *m, f* prisoner, convict; ~**gericht** *n* **1.** *Jur.* criminal court; *Mil., Wirts.* tribunal; **2.** *fig.* punishment, chastisement; *das göttliche* ~ Divine Judg(e)ment; ~**gerichtsbarkeit** *f Jur.* penal jurisdiction; ~**gesetz** *n Jur.* penal law; ~**gesetzbuch** *n Jur.* penal code; ~**gesetzgebung** *f Jur.* penal legislation; ~**justiz** *f Jur.* criminal justice; ~**kammer** *f Jur.* criminal division; ~**kompanie** *f Mil.* punishment battalion; ~**lager** *n* penal (*od.* punishment) camp

sträflich *I. Adj.* **1.** criminal, punishable; ~*e Vernachlässigung* criminal neglect; **2.** *fig.* (*tadelnswert*) reprehensible; (*unverzeihlich*) inexcusable, unpardonable; *II. Adv.* (*unerhört*) terribly; *j-n* ~ *vernachlässigen* neglect s.o. criminally, be guilty of criminal neglect towards s.o.

Sträfling *m*; -*s*, -*e* prisoner, convict

Sträflings|anzug *m* convict's suit; ~**kleidung** *f* prison clothing; ~**kolonie** *f* penal colony

straflos *Adj.* → *straffrei*; **Straflosigkeit** *f* → *Straffreiheit*

Straf|mandat *n Verk.* ticket (*for parking, speeding, etc.*); ~**maß** *n Jur.* (length of) sentence; *Geldstrafe*: amount of the fine; *das* ~ *festsetzen* fix the sentence / *Geldstrafe*: amount of the fine; ~**maßnahmen** *Pl.* punitive measures; ~ *ergreifen* take punitive action; *Wirts.* apply (*od.* impose) sanctions

strafmildernd *Jur. I. Adj.*: ~*e Umstände* mitigating (*od.* extenuating) circumstances; *II. Adv.*: ~ *wirken* be considered in mitigation; **Strafmilderung** *f* mitigation of sentence, commutation

Strafminute *f Sport*: *er erhielt zwei* ~*n Eishockey etc.*: he got a two-minute penalty, he was sent off for two minutes

strafmündig *Adj.* of criminally responsible age; **Strafmündigkeit** *f* age of criminal responsibility

Straf|porto *n umg.* excess postage, surcharge; *3 Euro* ~ *zahlen* pay 3 euros excess postage; ~**predigt** *f umg.* lec-

ture; *j-m e-e* ~ *halten* give s.o. a lecture

Strafprozess *m Jur.* (criminal) trial, criminal case; ~**ordnung** *f* code of criminal procedure

Straf|punkt *m Sport* penalty point; ~**rahmen** *m Jur.* range of penalties (*Gefängnisstrafen*: sentences); ~**raum** *m Sport* penalty area; ~**raumgrenze** *f* eighteen-yard line

Strafrecht *n Jur.* criminal law; **Strafrechtler** *m*; -*s*, -, **Strafrechtlerin** *f*; -, -*nen* criminal law specialist; **strafrechtlich** *I. Adj.* penal, criminal; *Fragen, Probleme*: ... of criminal law; ~*e Verfolgung* criminal prosecution; *II. Adv.*: ~ *verfolgen* prosecute (under criminal law)

Strafrechtsreform *f* criminal law reform

Straf|register *n* criminal records *Pl.*; *e-s Täters*: criminal record; *umg. fig.* list of sins (*od.* transgressions); ~**richter** *m*, ~**richterin** *f* criminal judge; ~**runde** *f Sport, Biathlon*: penalty lap; ~**sache** *f Jur.* criminal case (*od.* matter); ~**senat** *m Jur.* decision-making body of the senior Land court and the Federal Supreme Court; ~**stoß** *m Fußball*: penalty kick; *e-n* ~ *verhängen* give a penalty; → *verwandeln* I 2

Straftat *f Jur.* (criminal) offen|ce (*Am.* -se); *schwere*: crime; **Straftatbestand** *m* statutory offen|ce (*Am.* -se); **Straftäter** *m*, **Straftäterin** *f* offender

Straf|tilgung *f Jur.* deletion (*od.* clearing) of a criminal record; ~**umwandlung** *f* commutation (of a sentence); ~**verbüßung** *f* serving (of) a sentence; ~**vereitelung** *f* prevention of the execution of a sentence; ~**verfahren** *n* criminal procedure (*konkret*: proceedings *Pl.*); → *auch Strafprozess*; ~**verfolgung** *f* (criminal) prosecution

strafverschärfend *I. Adj.* aggravating; *II. Adv.*: *sich* ~ *auswirken* have an aggravating effect; **Strafverschärfung** *f* increase of penalty

strafversetzen *v/t.* (*untr., hat*) transfer s.o. for disciplinary reasons; **Strafversetzung** *f* transfer for disciplinary reasons

Straf|verteidiger *m*, ~**verteidigerin** *f Jur.* counsel for the defen|ce (*Am.* -se); ~**vollstreckung** *f* execution of a sentence; *im Gefängnis*: imprisonment

Strafvollzug *m Jur.* execution of a (prison) sentence; *weitS.* imprisonment; *offener*: day release; **Strafvollzugsanstalt** *f Jur.* penal institution, *Am. auch* penitentiary

straf|weise *Adv.* for disciplinary reasons; ~**würdig** *Adj.* punishable

Straf|wurf *m Sport* penalty throw; ~**zeit** *f Sport* time penalty; ~**zettel** *m Verk.* ticket; *wegen Falschparkens*: parking ticket; ~**zumessung** *f Jur.* fixing of the sentence

Strahl *m*; -(*e*)*s*, -*en*; *auch Phys. und fig.* ray; (*Lichtstrahl, gebündelter* ~) beam; (*Sonnenstrahl*) ray (of sunlight), (sun)beam; *durchdringender*: shaft of (sun)light; *von Blitz, Feuer*: flash; (*Wasserstrahl*) jet (*auch Tech.*); *langer*: stream; *kosmische* ~*en* cosmic radiation *Sg.* (*od.* rays); ~*en aussenden* emit radiation *Sg.*; *vor schädlichen* ~*en schützen* protect from harmful radiation *Sg.*; ~**antrieb** *m Flug.* jet propulsion

Strahlemann *m umg.* smiley; *da kommt der* ~ *auch* here comes the man with the big smile

strahlen I. v/i. **1.** Phys. emit rays, radiate; radioaktiv: emit radiation; **2.** (glänzen) shine; (funkeln) sparkle (auch Augen); fig. Gesicht, Person: beam; Augen, Gesicht, plötzlich: light up; **über das ganze Gesicht** od. umg. **beide Backen** ~ be all smiles, be beaming all over one's face; ~ (**vor Freude/ Glück**) be radiant (with joy/happiness); **da strahlte er** he beamed (at this); **II.** v/t. (ausstrahlen) auch fig. radiate

Strahlen|behandlung f radiotherapy, ray treatment; ~**belastung** f exposure to radiation (od. radioactivity); (Grad der ~) radioactivity level; **natürliche ~** natural (background) radiation; ~**biologie** f radiobiology; ~**brechung** f refraction; ~**bündel** n, ~**büschel** n pencil of rays, beam

strahlend I. Part. Präs. → strahlen; **II.** Adj. **1.** Phys. radiating; (radioaktiv) radioactive; **2.** ~**er Sonnenschein** bright (od. brilliant) sunshine; ~**es Wetter** glorious weather; **3.** ~**e Augen** bright (od. shining) eyes; ~**es Gesicht** beaming face (od. expression); ~**es Lächeln** beaming smile; ~**e Schönheit** radiant beauty; **III.** Adv. **1.** ~ **vor Freude** beaming with joy; **j-n** ~ **anlächeln** beam at s.o.; **2.** ~ **weiß** gleaming white; Zähne: pearly white; ~ **blaue Augen** shining blue eyes; ~ **helles Licht** brilliant light; ~ **schönes Wetter** glorious weather

Strahlendosis f radiation dose

strahlenförmig I. Adj. radial; **II.** Adv. angeordnet: radially; **sich ~ ausbreiten** radiate outwards

Strahlenforschung f radiology

strahlengeschädigt Adj. damaged by radiation: Person: suffering from radiation damage

Strahlen|kater m Med. umg. mild radiation sickness; ~**krankheit** f radiation sickness; ~**kranz** m halo, nimbus; Kunst glory; ~**messgerät** n radiation meter, actinometer; ~**pilz** m Bio. ray fungus; ~**quelle** f radiation source; ~**schaden** m, ~**schädigung** f radiation damage

Strahlenschutz m radiation protection; (Vorrichtung) radiation screen (od. shield); ~**verordnung** f statute governing radiation protection

strahlensicher Adj. radiation-proof

Strahlen|therapie f radiotherapy; ~**tierchen** n radiolarian; ~**tod** m death by radiation; ~**überwachung** f monitoring of radiation (levels)

strahlenverseucht Adj. contaminated (by radiation)

Strahlenwolke f radioactive cloud

Strahler m; -s, - **1.** (Gerät) radiator; **2.** (Licht) spotlight; **3.** (Heizstrahler) radiant heater; **4.** Phys. (Substanz) radiation source; (Reflektor) reflector; **schwarzer** ~ non-reflecting surface

strahlig Adj. radial

Strahl|kraft f radiation intensity; geh. fig. (Ausstrahlung) charisma; ~**rohr** n für Schlauch: (adjustable jet) spray head; ~**ruder** n Tech. rocket steering paddle; ~**triebwerk** n jet engine

Strahlung f radiation; **radioaktive ~** radioactivity

strahlungsarm Adj. EDV, Bildschirm: attr. low-radiation …

Strahlungs|belastung f pollution by radiation; ~**energie** f radiation energy; ~**gürtel** m Phys. (Van Allen) radiation belt; ~**intensität** f radiant flux density, intensity of radiation; ~**messer** m ra-

diation meter; ~**wärme** f radiant heat

Strähnchen Pl. in der Frisur: highlights

Strähne f; -, -n **1.** (Haar) strand; **blonde/graue** ~ blonde/grey (Am. gray) streak; **2.** → **Glückssträhne, Pechsträhne; strähnig** Adj. Haar: straggly

stramm I. Adj. **1.** (straff, fest sitzend) tight; Seil: auch taut; **2.** ~**e Haltung** straight (od. erect) posture; ~**e Disziplin** strict discipline; ~**es Tempo** brisk pace; **3.** umg. (überzeugt) Katholik, Marxist etc.: staunch, strict; **4.** (kräftig) robust; auch Beine: sturdy; ~**er Junge** strapping youth; ~**e Waden** sturdy (od. powerful) thighs; **5.** umg. (betrunken) tight; **6.** ~**er Max** Gastr. ham and fried egg on bread; **II.** Adv. **1.** anziehen etc.: tight(ly); ~ **sitzen** Schuhe etc.: fit tightly; **2.** umg. (zügig) ~ **gehen** walk briskly; **3.** umg. (streng) katholisch, marxistisch: staunchly, strictly; ~ **konservativ sein** be a true-blue conservative; **Strammheit** f **1.** (Straffheit) tightness; **2.** (gerade Haltung) straightness, erectness; (Strenge) strictness; **3.** (kräftige Art) robustness, sturdiness

stramm|stehen v/i. Mil. stand to attention; ~**ziehen** v/t. pull s.th. tight; **j-m die Hosen** ~ umg. fig. give s.o. a good hiding

Strampel|anzug m romper suit, playsuit; ~**höschen** n, ~**hose** f rompers Pl.

strampeln I. vt/i. (hat gestrampelt) **1.** kick; wild: thrash about; sich wehrend: struggle; **2.** umg. (sich plagen) slog away; **man muss schon ganz schön** ~ it's a real sweat (od. slog); **II.** vt/i. (ist) umg. (Rad fahren) pedal (away); **wir sind gestern 30 km gestrampelt** we pedal(l)ed 19 miles yesterday, yesterday we did 19 miles on our bikes

Strampelsack m (baby's) sleeping bag; **Strampler** m; -s, - romper suit

Strand m; -(e)s, Strände; (auch Badestrand) beach; (Meeresufer) (sea)shore; **am** ~ on the beach (od. shore); **an den** ~ **gehen** go (down) to the beach; **auf** ~ **laufen** Naut. run aground; ~**anzug** m beach suit; ~**bad** n bathing (Am. swimming) beach; ~**burg** f beach shelter (with walls of sand); (Sandburg) sandcastle; ~**café** n seafront café; ~**distel** f Bot. sea holly

stranden v/i. run aground; fig. (scheitern) fail

Strand|gut n nur Sg. flotsam and jetsam (auch fig. Menschen); ~**hafer** m Bot. marram grass; ~**haubitze** f: **voll wie e-e** ~ umg. (as) drunk as a lord, plastered; ~**hotel** n seafront hotel; ~**kleidung** f beachwear; ~**korb** m (wicker) beach chair; ~**läufer** m Zool. sandpiper; ~**nelke** f Bot. sea lavender; ~**promenade** f (seafront) promenade; ~**see** m Geog. lagoon; ~**segeln** n sand-yachting

Strandung f running aground; auf e-m Strand: beaching

Strandwache f lifeguard(s Pl.)

Strang m; -(e)s, Stränge **1.** cord (auch Anat.); (Seil) rope; (Garn) skein, hank; fig. der Handlung: strand; **wenn wir alle an einem** ~ **ziehen** fig. if we all get together, if we join forces; **über die Stränge schlagen** umg. fig. kick over the traces; **wenn alle Stränge reißen** umg. fig. if (the) worst comes to (the) worst, if all else fails; **2.** Tod durch den ~ death by hanging; **j-n zum Tod durch den** ~ **verurteilen** sen-

tence s.o. to be hanged; **3.** (Schienen) track

Strangulation f; -, -en strangulation; **strangulieren** v/t. **1.** ([er]würgen) strangle; **2.** Med. strangulate; **Strangulierung** f **1.** ([Er]Würgen) strangling, strangulation; **2.** Med. strangulation

Strapaze f; -, -n; auch Pl. strain; **es ist mit** ~**n verbunden** there's a lot of hard work involved; **die** ~**n des Alltags** the pressures (and worries) of day-to-day living; **es ist e-e** ~ auch it's hard work, it's tough going umg.; **sich von den** ~**n der Arbeit erholen** recover from the stress and strain of work; **er war den** ~**n nicht gewachsen** he couldn't take (od. stand up to) the strain

strapazieren v/t. strain, be a strain on, be hard on (auch Augen, Beziehung, Nerven); (j-n) auch take it out of umg.; (ermüden) exhaust, wear out; (Geduld, Hirn) tax, (Geduld) auch test, try; (Haut, Haare) be hard (od. rough) on; (schlecht behandeln) ill-treat, treat badly; (Kleidung etc.) be hard on; (Ausdruck etc.) overwork, overuse, stärker. flog to death; **strapaziert werden** auch umg.; Person: take a beating, have a rough time of it; Auto, Gerät: auch see some hard use; **strapazierfähig** Adj. **1.** Kleidung: hardwearing; Stoff, Teppich, Schuhe etc.: auch tough; **der Mantel ist sehr** ~ auch the coat will take a lot of wear and tear (od. hard use); **2.** Nerven: tough; **strapaziert I.** P.P. → strapazieren; **II.** Adj. Kleidung, Teppich etc.: worn; Person, Beziehung etc.: strained; Nerven: auch frayed; Haut, Haar: ill-treated; Hirn: overtaxed; **strapaziös** Adj. strenuous, tough umg.; nervlich: taxing, trying

Straps m; -es, -e suspender, Am. garter; (Hüftgürtel) suspender belt, Am. garterbelt

Strass [ʃtras] m; Strasses, kein Pl. paste; (~schmuck) paste jewellery (Am. jewelry)

straßauf, straßab Adv. up and down the street

Straßburg (n); -s; Geog. Strasbourg

Straße f; -, -n **1.** (Fahrbahn und ~ als Verbindungsweg, Betonung auf den Verkehr) road; (~ in der Stadt mit Bürgersteig und angrenzenden Gebäuden, Betonung auf das Straßenleben) street; **die** ~ **zum Bahnhof** the road (leading) to the station (Am. train station); in der Stadt: the street leading (up) to the station (Am. train station); **e-e laute** ~ viel Verkehr: a noisy road; viel menschliches Treiben: a noisy street; **auf der** ~ in (bes. Am. on) the street; (auf der Fahrbahn) on the road; **auf der** ~ **spielen** play in the street; **auf die** ~ **laufen** aus e-m Haus: run out into the street; auf die Fahrbahn: run into to the road; **das Postamt ist in der nächsten** ~ the post office is in (Am. on) the next street; **das Zimmer geht zur** ~ the room faces the street (od. road); **an der** ~ at the roadside; **Verkauf über die** ~ → Straßenverkauf; **2.** fig., in Wendungen: **auf offener** ~ in broad daylight; **auf die** ~ **gehen** (demonstrieren) take to the streets (für in support of); **j-n auf die** ~ **setzen** throw (od. turn) s.o. out (onto the street); **auf der** ~ **liegen** od. **sitzen** Arbeitsloser: be jobless; Obdachloser: be on the streets, have no roof over one's head; **dort liegt das Geld auf der** ~ the streets are paved with gold there; *der Mann auf der* ~ the man in (*Am.* on) the street, *Brit. auch umg. altm.* the man on the Clapham omnibus; *Jugendliche von der* ~ *holen* rescue juveniles from a life on the streets; *der Druck der* ~ pressure from the mass of the people (*od.* population); **3.** *nur Sg.*: *die ganze* ~ (*Bewohner*) the whole street, everyone in (*Am.* on) the street; **4.** *Geog.* (*Meeresenge*) strait(s *Pl.*); *die* ~ *von Dover* the Straits of Dover; *die* ~ *von Gibraltar mst* the Straits of Gibraltar; *die* ~ *von Hormuz* the Strait of Hormuz

Straßen|anzug *m* lounge (*Am.* business) suit; ~**arbeiten** *Pl.* roadworks, *Am.* roadwork *Sg.*; ~**arbeiter** *m*, ~**arbeiterin** *f* roadworker

Straßenbahn *f* tram, *Am.* streetcar, trolley; ~ *fahren* go in a tram (*Am.* streetcar, trolley)

Straßenbahner *m; -s, -,* ~**in** *f; -, -nen umg.* (*Fahrer[in]*) tram driver, *Am.* motorman; (*Schaffner[in]*) tram (*Am.* streetcar) conductor

Straßenbahn|fahrer *m,* ~**fahrerin** *f* **1.** tram driver, *Am.* motorman; **2.** (*Fahrgast*) tram (*Am.* streetcar) passenger; ~**gleis** *n* tramline, *Am.* streetcar track; ~**haltestelle** *f* tram (*Am.* streetcar) stop; ~**linie** *f* tram route, *Am.* streetcar line; ~**schaffner** *m,* ~**schaffnerin** *f* tram (*Am.* streetcar) conductor; ~**schiene** *f* tramline, *Am.* streetcar track; ~**wagen** *m* tramcar, *Am.* streetcar

Straßen|bau *m* road construction; ~**bauamt** *n* Highways Department; ~**belag** *m* road surface; ~**beleuchtung** *f* street lighting; ~**benutzungsgebühr** *f* road toll; ~**bild** *n* street scene; *Obdachlose gehören immer mehr zum* ~ vagrants are increasingly seen in the streets; ~**böschung** *f* road embankment; ~**breite** *f* road width; ~**café** *n* pavement (*Am.* sidewalk) café; ~**decke** *f* road surface; ~**dorf** *n* street village; ~**ecke** *f* street corner; *an der* ~ on (*od.* at) the street corner *od.* corner of the street; *sie wohnt zwei* ~*n weiter* she lives two blocks (further) up; ~**fahrzeug** *n* road vehicle; ~**feger** *m; -s, -,* **1.** *auch* ~**fegerin** *f; -, -nen* street sweeper (*bes. Am.* cleaner); **2.** *TV* program(me) (*Reihe:* series) that everybody watches; ~**fest** *n* street party; ~**führung** *f* line of a (*od.* the) road; ~**glätte** *f* slippery road (*Pl.*); *bei* ~ when the roads are slippery (*vereist:* icy); ~**graben** *m* (roadside) ditch; ~**handel** *m* street trading; ~**händler** *m,* ~**händlerin** *f* street trader, *Am.* hawker; ~**junge** *m* street urchin; ~**kampf** *m* street fight(ing); *Pl.* street fighting *Sg.,* fighting *Sg.* in the street(s); ~**karte** *f* road map; ~**kehrer** *m; -s, -,* ~**kehrerin** *f; -, -nen,* street sweeper (*bes. Am.* cleaner); ~**kind** *n* street urchin, child of the streets; ~**kontrolle** *f* (road) checkpoint; ~**köter** *m umg.* stray dog; ~**kreuzer** *m umg.* big flashy car, *Am. auch* pimpmobile *Sl.*; ~**kreuzung** *f* crossroads *Sg.,* intersection; ~**kriminalität** *f* street crime; ~**künstler** *m,* ~**künstlerin** *f* street artist; ~**lage** *f e-s Autos:* roadholding; *e-e gute* ~ *haben* have good roadholding, hold the road well; ~**lärm** *m* street noise, noise from the street; ~**laterne** *f* street lamp; ~**mädchen** *n* streetwalker, prostitute; ~**markierung** *f* road marking; ~**meisterei** *f*

highways (maintenance) department; ~**musikant** *m,* ~**musikantin** *f* street musician, busker; ~**name** *m* street name; ~**netz** *n* road network; ~**pflaster** *n* road surface (*Am.* pavement); ~**rand** *m:* (*am*) ~ (at the) roadside; ~**raub** *m* mugging, street robbery; *hist.* highway robbery; ~**räuber** *m* mugger; *hist.* highwayman; ~**reinigung** *f* street cleaning; ~**rennen** *n* road race; ~**sammlung** *f* street collection; ~**schäden** *Pl.* damage *Sg.* to the road surface (*Am.* pavement); ~**!** (*Schildaufschrift*) road damage; ~**schild** *n* street sign; ~**schlacht** *f* street battle (*od.* riot); *auch Pl.* rioting *Sg.* in the street(s); ~**schlucht** *f* canyon between high buildings; ~**schuhe** *Pl.* walking shoes; ~**seite** *f linke etc.*: side of the road (*od.* street); ~**sperre** *f* road block; ~**sperrung** *f* road (*od.* street) closure; ~**strich** *m* **1.** streetwalking; **2.** (*Gegend*) red-light district; ~**theater** *n* street theat|re (*Am. auch* -er); ~**tunnel** *m* road tunnel; ~**überführung** *f* flyover, *Am.* overpass (*od.* viaduct); ~**unterführung** *f* underpass; ~**verhältnisse** *Pl.* road conditions; ~**verkauf** *m* **1.** street trading; **2.** *Gastr.* take-away (*Am.* carryout) food (*od.* snacks *Pl. etc.*), *Am. auch* food *etc.* to go; (*Stelle*) takeaway, *Am.* carryout; ~**verkäufer** *m,* ~**verkäuferin** *f* street vendor; ~**verkehr** *m* (road) traffic

Straßenverkehrs|ordnung *f* (*abgek.* StVO*) road traffic regulations *Pl., in* GB: Highway Code, *in* USA: rules of the road *umg.*; ~**recht** *n* road traffic regulations *Pl.*

Straßen|verzeichnis *n* index of street names; ~**wacht** *f* road patrol; ~**walze** *f* road roller, (*Dampfwalze*) steamroller; ~**zoll** *m* road toll; ~**zug** *m* street (lined with houses); (*Häuserblock*) block; ~**zustand** *m* road conditions *Pl.*

Stratege *m; -n, -n* strategist; **Strategie** *f; -, -n* strategy; **Strategin** *f; -, -nen* strategist; **strategisch I.** *Adj.* strategic; **II.** *Adv.* strategically

Stratosphäre *f; -, kein Pl.* stratosphere; **stratosphärisch** *Adj.* stratospherical

Stratus *m; -, Strati,* **Stratuswolke** *f Met.* stratus cloud

sträuben *I. v/refl.* **1.** *Haare:* stand on end; *wie Borsten:* bristle; **2.** *fig.* (*sich widersetzen, wehren*) refuse, kick up a fuss *umg.*; *körperlich:* kick and struggle; *sich* ~ *gegen* resist, fight; *körperlich:* struggle against; *sich* ~, *etw. zu tun* refuse to do s.th.; *er sträubte sich dagegen, es zu machen auch* he just wouldn't do it; *alles in mir sträubt sich, es zu tun* every fibre (*Am.* fiber) in my being is against doing it, I can't bring myself to do it; → *Haar* 3; **II.** *v/t.* (*Federn*) ruffle (up)

Strauch *m; -(e)s, Sträuche* shrub, bush; ~**dieb** *m: du siehst aus wie ein* ~! *umg.* you look like a tramp

straucheln *v/i.* **1.** *auch fig.* stumble (*auch Pferd*), lose one's footing; **2.** *fig.* (*auf die schiefe Bahn geraten*) stray off the straight and narrow; **3.** (*scheitern*) fail; *an etw.* ~ come to grief over s.th., *Brit. umg. auch* come a cropper with s.th.

Strauchtomate *f* tomato on the vine

Strauß¹ *m; -es, -e; Orn.* ostrich

Strauß² *m; -es, Sträuße* bunch; (*Blumenstrauß*) bunch of flowers; *bes. zu e-m Anlass*: bouquet; *kleiner, bunter*: *auch* spray; *ein* ~ *Nelken* a bunch of

carnations

Strauß³ *m; -es, Sträuße; altm.* fight, struggle; (*Streit*) quarrel; *e-n* ~ *mit j-m ausfechten* (have a) fight with s.o., fight it out with s.o.; (*etw. ausdiskutieren*) have it out with s.o. *umg.*

Strauß|ei *n* ostrich egg; ~**farm** *f* ostrich farm; ~**feder** *f* ostrich feather

Strauß(en)wirtschaft *f bes. südd.* winegrower's house with a bunch of greenery over the door as a sign that (the new) wine can be drunk on the premises

strawanzen *v/i. österr.* roam about

Streamer ['striːmɐ] *m; -s, -;* *EDV* (tape) streamer; ~**laufwerk** *n EDV* streaming tape drive

Strebe *f; -, -n,* ~**balken** *m Archit.* brace, strut; ~**bogen** *m* flying buttress

streben *v/i.* **1.** (*hat gestrebt*) strive (*nach* for); ~ *nach auch* pursue, *förm.* aspire to; (*bes. Geld*) *auch* run after *umg.*; *danach* ~, *etw. zu tun* strive (*od.* aspire) to do s.th.; **2.** (*hat*) *umg.* (*ein[e] Streber[in] sein*) *Schule:* be a swot (*Am.* grind); **3.** (*ist*) ~ *nach* (*sich irgendwohin bewegen*) move towards (*od.* in the direction of) (*angezogen werden*) be drawn to(wards); *in die Höhe* ~ soar upwards

Streben *n; -s, kein Pl.* striving (*nach* for), aspiration (to + *Inf.*); (*Tendenz*) tendency (to, toward[s]); *das* ~ *nach Glück* the pursuit of (*od.* search for) happiness; *sein ganzes* ~ *ging in Richtung ...* all his energies and aspirations were directed toward(s) (doing) s.th.

Strebepfeiler *m* buttress

Streber *m; -s, -; pej. Schule:* swot, *Am.* grind; *im Beruf:* pushy type; *er ist ein* ~ *beruflich auch* he's overambitious (*od.* very pushy); **Streberei** *f; -, kein Pl.; pej.* overambition, pushiness; **streberhaft** *Adj. pej.* overambitious, pushy; **Streberin** *f; -, -nen; pej.* → **Streber, Strebernatur** *f* → **Streber, Strebertum** *n; -s, kein Pl.; pej. Schule:* swotting, *Am.* grinding; *im Beruf:* overambitiousness, pushiness

strebsam I. *Adj.* assiduous, diligent; (*eifrig*) ambitious; *Schüler:* keen, *Am.* eager; **II.** *Adv.* assiduously, diligently; **Strebsamkeit** *f* assiduous striving (for success)

Streckbett *n* orthop(a)edic bed

Strecke *f; -, -n* **1.** stretch (*auch Teilstrecke*); (*Wegstrecke, Flugstrecke*) route; *Sport, fig. in ein Rennen:* course; *Math.* line; *EDV* link path; *Telef.* line; *Eisenb.* section (of line); *die* ~ *München–Köln* (*Route*) the Munich–Cologne route; *Verk.* the road (*Eisenb.* line, section) from Munich to Cologne; (*Reise*) the journey from Munich to Cologne; *auf freier* ~ *Eisenb.* between stations; *umg.* in the middle of nowhere; (*auf der Straße*) on the open road; *die Straße ist auf e-r* ~ *von 5 km gesperrt* a 5 km stretch of the road is closed; *auf der* ~ *bleiben fig.* im Konkurrenzkampf: fall by the wayside; *Sport auch* drop out (of the race); *die guten Vorsätze blieben auf der* ~ good intentions fell by the wayside; **2.** (*Entfernung*) *auch Sport* distance; *e-n Teil der* ~ *zu Fuß gehen* walk part of the way; *es ist e-e ganze* ~ (*bis dorthin*) it's quite a long distance (*od.* way, stretch); *über weite* ~*n auch fig.* for long stretches; *das Buch ist über lange* ~*n langweilig* the book has long boring sections (*lit.* has its longueurs); **3.** *Bergb.* roadway, gallery; **4.** *Jagd:* bag; *zur ~ bringen* (*Tier*) kill, shoot down, bag; *fig.* (*Verbrecher etc.*) hunt down, catch; *weitS.* (*Gegner*) lay low

...strecke *f, im Subst.* **1.** (*Weg*): *Autobahn~* stretch of motorway; *Gleis~* stretch (*od.* section) of track; **2.** *Sport, für Rennen:* course; *Abfahrts~* downhill course; *Hindernis~* obstacle course; *Reitsport, Hindernislauf:* steeplechase course

strecken I. *v/t.* **1.** stretch; *s-e Beine/ Glieder ~* stretch one's legs/limbs; *die Hand/den Finger ~* put (stick *umg.*) one's hand/finger up, *Am. mst* raise one's hand; *den Kopf aus dem Fenster ~* stick one's head out of the window; *das gebrochene Bein ~ Med.* straighten the broken leg; → *gestreckt, vier,* **2.** (*Suppe etc.*) stretch; (*rationieren, auch Geld, Vorräte etc.*) make last, eke out (*verdünnen*) thin, dilute; (*Vortrag etc.*) stretch, drag out; **3.** *die Waffen ~* lay down arms, surrender; *fig. auch* give in; *j-n zu Boden ~* floor s.o., lay s.o. low; **4.** *Jägerspr.* (*erlegen*) kill; **II.** *v/refl.* **1.** stretch (o.s.); *bei Müdigkeit:* have a stretch; *sich ins Gras ~* stretch out on the grass; *der Torwart musste sich ganz schön ~* the goalkeeper had to be at full stretch; → *Decke* 2, *recken* II; **2.** *etw. streckt sich in die Länge* s.th. goes on longer than expected, s.th. drags on *pej.*

Strecken|abschnitt *m bes. Eisenb.* section; *Sport; bei Rallye, Radrennen:* stage; *~arbeiter m, ~arbeiterin f Eisenb.* platelayer, *Am.* tracklayer; *~flug m Segelfliegen:* long distance gliding; *~führung f* routing; *e-r Rennstrecke:* course; *~länge f* distance; *~netz n Eisenb.* rail network; *Flug.* (flying) routes *Pl.*; *~posten m Sport* (*Kontrollstelle*) checkpoint, control; (*Verpflegungsposten*) supply station; *~rekord m Sport* course (*Leichtathletik:* track) record; *~stilllegung f Eisenb.* line closure; *~tauchen n Sport* distance diving; *~wärter m, ~wärterin f* linesman, *Am.* trackwalker

streckenweise *Adv.* in places; (*teilweise*) in parts; (*zeitweise*) from time to time

Streck|mittel *n* filler, diluting element; *~muskel m Anat.* extensor (muscle); *~sitz m Turnen:* seated position with legs stretched out

Streckung *f* **1.** stretching; **2.** *beim Wachstum:* fast-growth period

Streckverband *m Med.* traction bandage; *ein Bein etc. im ~* a leg *etc.* in high traction

Streetball ['striːtbɔːl] *m; -s, kein Pl.* streetball

Streetwork ['striːtvøːɐk] *f; -, kein Pl.* outreach social work; **Streetworker** ['striːtvøːɐkə] *m; -s, -,* **Streetworkerin** *f; -, -nen* outreach social worker

Streich *m, -(e)s, -e* **1.** (*lustiger ~*) prank, trick, (practical) joke; *Till Eulenspiegels lustige ~e* Till Eulenspiegel's merry pranks; *dummer ~* silly (*od.* childish) prank; *j-m e-n ~ spielen* play a (nasty) trick on s.o.; *das Wetter hat uns e-n ~ gespielt* the weather played a nasty trick on us; *mein Gedächtnis hat mir e-n ~ gespielt* my memory played me up (*Am.* played a trick on me); **2.** *lit. mit der Faust, dem Schwert:* blow; *mit der flachen Hand:* slap; *mit dem Stock:* stroke; *auf einen*

~ at one blow; *fig.* in one go, in one fell swoop

Streicheleinheit *f mst Pl.* **1.** stroke, *Pl. auch* stroking *Sg.*; **2.** *umg. fig.* (*Lob*) pat on the back; (*Liebe*) some love and affection, *hum.* care and attention; *jeder braucht s-e ~en* everyone needs a pat on the back (*Liebe:* a bit of love and affection) once in a while

streicheln *vt/i.* stroke; (*liebkosen*) *auch* fondle; *j-m übers Haar ~* stroke s.o.'s hair; *der Hund lässt sich nicht ~* the dog won't let you stroke him; **Streichelzoo** *m* petting zoo

streichen; *streicht, strich, hat od. ist gestrichen* **I.** *v/t.* (*hat*) **1.** *mit Farbe:* paint; (*Butter etc., auch Brot*) spread; *Salbe ~ auf* (+ *Akk.*) put ointment on, rub ointment (gently) on, *förm.* apply ointment to; *die Farbe lässt sich gut ~* the paint goes on well; *sich* (*Dat.*) *ein Brot ~* butter o.s. a piece of bread; *etw. durch ein Sieb ~* strain s.th.; → *frisch* II 1; **2.** (*mit der Hand ~*) stroke; (*weg~*) brush away *etc.*; *sich* (*Dat.*) *den Bart ~* stroke one's beard; (*sich* [*Dat.*]) *das Haar aus der Stirn ~* brush the hair out of one's face (*od.* eyes); **3.** (*aus~*) cross out, delete; (*Passage, Programmpunkt etc.*) cut (out); (*Auftrag etc.*) cancel; (*Gelder*) cut, axe; (*Stelle*) freeze, axe; (*Strafe, Schulden*) waive; *von der Liste ~* cross off the list; *j-m das Taschengeld ~* stop s.o.'s pocket money (*od.* allowance); *den Urlaub haben wir vorerst gestrichen* we've had to give up the holiday (*Am.* vacation); *etw. aus dem Gedächtnis ~* wipe s.th. out of one's memory; → *Nichtzutreffende;* **4.** (*Flagge, Segel*) strike, haul down; **II.** *v/i.* **1.** (*ist*) *~ über* (+ *Akk.*) (*gleiten über*) glide over, (*das Wasser*) skim across; *Wind:* waft across, *stärker:* sweep across; *j-m um die Beine ~ Katze:* rub against s.o.'s legs; **2.** (*hat*) *j-m über das Haar ~* stroke s.o.'s hair; → *auch streicheln;* **3.** (*ist*) *~ durch* (*wandern durch*) roam, wander; *ums Haus ~* prowl (*od.* stalk) around the house; *die Katze streicht um den Vogelkäfig* the cat is prowling (a)round the birdcage; → *gestrichen,* → *auch streifen* II

Streicher *m; -s, -, ~in f; -, -nen; Mus.* string player; *die ~* the strings, the string section

streichfähig *Adj.: ~ sein* spread easily; **Streichfähigkeit** *f* spreading property

streichfertig *Adj. Farbe:* ready for application

Streichholz *n* match; *mst gebrauchtes, zum Basteln etc.:* matchstick; *~heftchen n* book of matches, *bes. Am.* matchbook; *~kopf m* match head; *~schachtel f* matchbox

Streich|instrument *n Mus.* string(ed) instrument; *~käse m* cheese spread; *~musik f* music for strings; *~orchester n* string orchestra; *~quartett n* string quartet; *~quintett n* string quintet; *~trio n* string trio

Streichung *f* cancellation, *Am.* cancelation; *im Text:* deletion; *von Geldern:* cut(s *Pl.*); (*Vorgang*) cutting, axing; *die ~ von Stellen* job cuts *Pl.*; (*Vorgang*) the axing of (*od.* cutting down on) jobs

Streichwurst *f* sausage spread

Streif *m; -(e)s, -e geh.* → *Streifen*

Streifband *n* (postal) wrapper

Streife *f; -(e)s, -n* patrol (*auch Mannschaft, auch Mil.*); *~ gehen* go on patrol; *auf ~ sein Polizist:* be on one's beat

streifen I. *v/t.* (*hat gestreift*) **1.** (*berühren*) touch, brush against; *Auto:* scrape against; *Kugel:* graze; *fig.* (*Thema*) touch (up)on; *die Kugel hat ihn am Kopf gestreift* the bullet grazed the side (*od.* top) of his head; *mit dem Blick ~* glance at; **2.** (*abstreifen*) slip off; *den Ring vom Finger ~* slip (*od.* take) the ring off (one's finger); *ein T-Shirt über den Kopf ~* slip a T-shirt on (over one's head), slip into a T-shirt; *e-e Wollmütze über den Kopf ~* slip a woolly hat (*Am.* stocking cap) over one's head; *die Blätter vom Stiel ~* strip the leaves off the stalk; *den Teig von den Fingern ~* wipe the dough off one's fingers; **II.** *v/i.* (*ist*) (*wandern*) (*auch ~ durch*) wander, roam

Streifen *m; -s, -* **1.** stripe (*auch an Kleidung, Uniform etc.*); *dünner, unregelmäßiger:* streak; (*Linie*) line; *ein heller ~ am Horizont* a streak of light on the horizon; **2.** (*kurzes, schmales Stück*) strip; (*Gelände*) strip (of land); *Mil.* sector; (*Papier*) strip; (*Klebe-, Loch-streifen*) tape; (*Film*) strip; *weitS.* film; *in ~ schneiden* cut into strips; *e-n ~ drehen* make a film

Streifen|beamte *m, ~beamtin f* policeman/policewoman on patrol duty; *~dienst m* patrol duty; *~gang m* (patrol) round

Streifenmuster *n* striped pattern

Streifen|polizist *m, ~polizistin f* policeman/policewoman on patrol duty

Streifenwagen *m* (police) patrol car; *Am. auch* squad car, cruiser

streifig *Adj.* streaky

Streif|licht *n* ray of light; *Fot.* glancing light; *e-s Autos:* passing headlights *Pl.*; *fig.* sidelight; *interessante ~er werfen auf fig.* give some interesting sidelights on; *~schuss m* grazing shot; (*Wunde*) (bullet) graze; *e-n ~ bekommen* be grazed (by a bullet); *~zug m* **1.** foray (*in* + *Akk., durch* into); *Streifzüge durch die Gegend machen* make a few forays into the surrounding area; **2.** *fig.: literarischer ~* literary excursion; *ein ~ durch die Geschichte des Films* an exploration of the history of filmmaking

Streik *m; -(e)s, -s; allg.* strike; *kurzfristige Arbeitsniederlegung:* (work) stoppage, walkout; *wilder ~* unofficial (*od.* wildcat) strike; *e-n ~ ausrufen* call a strike; *in den ~ treten* go on strike; *sich im ~ befinden* be on strike; *mit* (*e-m*) *~ drohen* threaten to go on strike

streikanfällig *Adj.* strike-prone

Streik|aufruf *m* strike call, call for a strike, call to strike; *~brecher m; -s, -, ~brecherin f; -, -nen* strikebreaker, blackleg, scab *umg.*; *~drohung f* threat of a strike, strike threat

streiken *v/i.* **1.** strike, go (*od.* be) on strike; *überall im Lande wird gestreikt* there are strikes (*od.* workers are on strike) all over the country; **2.** *umg. fig.* (*nicht mitmachen*) refuse to cooperate; *Auto:* refuse to start; *Gerät, Motor etc.:* be on the blink; *Magen:* protest; *ich streike!* I'm not doing it, I refuse; (*ich gebe auf*) I'm opting out; *der Computer streikt mal wieder* the computer's on the blink (*od.* has given up) again; **Streikende** *m, f; -n, -n* striker

Streik|front *f* strike front; *~geld n* strike pay; *~kasse f* strike fund; *~leitung f* strike committee; *~lokal n* strikers' meeting place; **~posten** m picket; **~ stehen** picket; **~recht** n right to strike; **~tag** m day of the strike; **~verbot** n ban on striking; **~welle** f wave (*od.* series) of strikes

Streit m, -(e)s, kein Pl. argument, quarrel (*über* + *Akk.*, *um* about, over); *unter Wissenschaftlern, Politikern etc.*: dispute; (*Gezänk*) squabble; (*Streiterei*) wrangling; *lärmender*: row, *Am.* blow-up; *handgreiflicher*: brawl, fight; **~ haben/anfangen** have/start an argument (*od.* quarrel); *ehelicher* ~ *heftiger*: marital row (*Am.* squabble); **mit den Nachbarn ~ haben** have a dispute (*od.* be in dispute) with one's neighbo(u)rs; **er sucht immer ~** he is always picking quarrels *Pl.*; **in ~ geraten mit** get into an argument with; *handgreiflich*: come to blows with; **mit j-m im ~ liegen** be engaged in a quarrel with s.o., be at loggerheads with s.o.; **e-n ~ schlichten** settle a dispute; **miteinander im ~ liegen** fig. *Gefühle*: conflict (*od.* be in conflict) with one another; **suchst du ~?** umg. are you looking for trouble?; → *auch* **streiten**; → **Zaun**

Streitaxt f battleax(e); **die ~ begraben** fig. bury the hatchet

streitbar *Adj.* quarrelsome; (*kämpferisch*) pugnacious; (*kriegerisch*) belligerent; **Streitbarkeit** f quarrelsomeness; (*kämpferische Art*) pugnacity; (*kriegerische Art*) belligerence

streiten v/i. *und* v/refl.; *streitet, stritt, hat gestritten* **1.** (*auch miteinander od.* **sich ~**) argue, quarrel, have an argument (*über* +*Akk.* about, over); *heftig*: have a row; *handgreiflich*: fight, have a fight; (*aufeinander prallen*) clash, come to blows; **sich darüber ~, ob** have an argument over (*od.* as to) whether; **sie ~ sich dauernd** they fight like cats and dogs; **hört auf zu ~!** stop squabbling!; **ich möchte mich nicht ~** I don't want to argue; **2.** (*diskutieren*) argue (*über* +*Akk.* about, over); **darüber lässt sich ~** that's arguable (*od.* debatable), *Brit. auch* that's a moot point; **3.** *lit.* (*kämpfen*) fight (**für/gegen** for/against)

Streiter m; -s, -; *lit.* fighter (**für/gegen** for/against); **~ für die Freiheit** *etc. auch* champion of freedom *etc.*; **Streiterei** f; -, -en arguing, quarrel(l)ing; *heftig*: rowing, *Am.* fighting; *handgreiflich*: fighting; **Streiterin** f; -, -nen; *lit.* → **Streiter**

Streit|fall m dispute, conflict; *Jur.* case; **im ~** in case of dispute; **~frage** f (*Kontroverse*) dispute, controversy (**über** +*Akk.* over; **ob** over whether); (*strittiger Punkt*) disputed (*od.* controversial) issue (**ob** of whether); **~gegenstand** m subject of the argument (*od.* dispute), bone of contention; *bei Diskussion: auch* point at issue; *Jur.* matter in dispute; **~gespräch** n debate, *förm.* disputation; **~hahn** m, **~hammel** m umg. quarrelsome type; **ein ~ sein** *auch* always be picking a quarrel

streitig *Adj. Jur.* litigious; (*umstritten*) contested, *präd.* in dispute, at issue; **j-m etw. ~ machen** dispute s.o.'s right to s.th.; → **Rang** 3, **strittig**

Streitigkeiten *Pl.* quarrel(l)ing *Sg.*, disputes; → *auch* **Streit**; **die ~ beilegen** settle one's differences

Streitkräfte *Pl. Mil.* armed forces; **feindliche ~** enemy forces

Streitkultur f culture of debate; **politische ~** culture of political debate; **e-e ~ entwickeln** find civilized ways of dis-

---

cussing *our etc.* problems

Streitlust f belligerence, aggressive nature; **streitlustig I.** *Adj.* belligerent, aggressive; **II.** *Adv. ansehen etc.*: belligerently

Streit|macht f **1.** military force; **2.** → **Streitkräfte**; **~objekt** n → **Streitgegenstand**; **~punkt** m *zur Debatte stehend*: point at issue; (*Zankapfel*) bone of contention; **~sache** f dispute; *Jur.* (*Prozess*) lawsuit; **~schrift** f polemical writing, pamphlet

Streitsucht f *nur Sg.* quarrelsomeness; (*Kampflust*) belligerence; **streitsüchtig** *Adj.* quarrelsome, argumentative; (*kampflustig*) belligerent

Streit|wagen m *hist.* (war) chariot; **~wert** m *Jur.* value in dispute, amount involved

streng I. *Adj.* **1.** (*hart, unerbittlich*) severe (*auch Blick, Kritik, Maßnahme, Strafe, Richter, Winter etc.*); (*unnachsichtig*) stern (*auch Blick, Gesicht*); (*hart*) *auch* harsh, hard; (*unnachgiebig*) rigid; *Lebensführung, Charakter, Stil*: austere; *Frisur, Kleid*: severe; **~e Worte** harsh words; **2.** *Person, Diät, Disziplin, Erziehung, Vorschrift etc.*: strict; *Anforderungen, Prüfung*: rigorous; *Maßnahme, Regel*: strict, stringent; **~ sein zu** *od.* **mit j-m** be strict with (*od.* hard on) s.o.; **er ist ~, aber gerecht** he is strict but fair; **~er Aufbau** *e-s Dramas etc.*: tight structure; **~ste Diskretion** absolute discretion; **~er Katholik** strict Catholic; **~e Sitten** strict morals; **~es Stillschweigen** strict secrecy; **~e Trennung** strict division (*od.* separation); → **Regiment** 1; **3.** *Geschmack, Geruch*: acrid, pungent; **II.** *Adv.* **1.** severely; **~ geschnitten** *Gesicht*: with severe features; *Kleid, Frisur*: severely styled; **j-n ~ ansehen** give s.o. a severe look; **~ durchgreifen** take stringent (*od.* rigorous) measures; **~ erziehen** bring up strictly; **2.** (*genau*) strictly; **~ genommen** strictly speaking; **~ befolgen, sich ~ an etw. halten** adhere strictly to; **~ geheim** top secret; **~ vertraulich** in strict confidence; *auch amtlich*: strictly confidential; **~ Diät leben** follow a strict diet; **~(stens) verboten** strictly forbidden (*od.* prohibited); **~ katholisch sein** be a strict Catholic; **j-n ~ bewachen** keep s.o. under close watch (*od.* surveillance); **~ unterscheiden zwischen** make a clear (--cut) distinction between; → **Vorschrift**

Strenge f; -, kein Pl. **1.** (*Härte, Unerbittlichkeit*) severity, harshness; *von Gesicht etc.*: sternness; **mit unnachsichtiger ~** with unrelenting severity; **klassische ~** *e-s Bauwerks, von Zügen*: classical austerity; **2.** *von Person, Vorschrift etc.*: strictness; *von Maßnahmen*: stringency, rigo(u)r; **3.** *von Geruch*: pungency

streng genommen → **streng** II 2

strenggläubig *Adj.* (very) strict; **~er Katholik** *etc.* strict (*od.* orthodox) Catholic *etc.*

streng nehmen → **streng** II 2

strengstens *Adv.* → **streng** II 2

Streptokokke f; -, -n, **Streptokokkus** m; -, Streptokokken; *Biol.* streptococcus (*Pl.* streptococci)

Streptomyzin n; -s, kein Pl.; *Med., Pharm.* streptomycin

Stress m; -es, kein Pl. **1.** (*Anspannung*) stress; *schwer od. voll* **im ~ sein** umg. be under (a lot of) stress (*od.* pressure); **bloß kein ~!** umg. just take

---

it easy; **2.** umg. (*Ärger*) **~ mit den Eltern haben** have a lot of hassle with one's parents; **mach keinen ~, Mann!** don't hassle me; **~bewältigung** f stress management, coping with stress

stressen umg. **I.** v/t. put under stress, give a hard time; **die Arbeit stresst mich zur Zeit** *auch* my work's really stressful (*od.* getting to me) at the moment umg.; **ich bin gestresst** I'm under a lot of pressure (*od.* stärker: stress); **er ist zurzeit ziemlich gestresst** *auch* he's got an awful lot on his plate at the moment umg.; **II.** v/i. be stressful; **weißt du, dass du stresst?** umg. do you know that you're a strain (*od.* hard work)?;

Stressfaktor m stress factor; **Stressforschung** f stress research

stress|frei *Adj.* stress-free; **~geplagt** *Adj. attr.* stressed out umg.

stressig *Adj.* umg. stressful

Stressor m; -s, -en stress factor; **Stresssituation** f stressful situation

Stretch [strɛtʃ] m; -(e)s, -es stretch fabric; **~hose** f stretch trousers (*Am.* pants) *Pl.*

Stretching ['strɛtʃɪŋ] n; -s, kein Pl. stretching (exercises *Pl.*)

Stretchlimousine f stretch limousine, stretch limo umg.

Streu f; -, kein Pl. straw (*as litter*)

Streu|besitz m *Wirts.* widespread shareholding; **~blumen** *Pl.* (*Muster*) scattered flowers (*as a pattern*); **~büchse** f → **Streudose**; **~dienst** m *im Winter*: (road-)gritting service, *Am.* (road) maintenance crew; **kein ~!** *Schild*: untreated road; **~dose** f shaker; *für Salz*: salt cellar (*Am.* shaker); *für Pfeffer*: pepper pot (*Am.* shaker); *für Mehl*: dredger

streuen I. v/t. (*Sand etc.*) scatter; (*Mist*) spread; (*Blumen*) strew, scatter; (*Samen*) sow; (*Salz, Zucker etc.*) sprinkle; (*Straße*) grit; *mit Salz*: salt; *Phys.* scatter; *fig.* (*Gelder*) distribute; *wahllos*: scatter, hand out indiscriminately; **II.** v/i. *Mil., Geschoss, Gewehr, Phys., Strahlen etc.*: scatter

Streuer m; -s, - shaker

Streu|fahrzeug n salt truck, salt (*od.* sand) spreader, *Brit. mst* gritting lorry; **~feuer** n *Mil.* scattered fire; (*Flächenfeuer*) area fire; (*Seitenfeuer*) sweeping fire; **~gut** n (road) grit; **~licht** n *Phys., Fot.* scattered light

streunen v/i. **1.** (*hat gestreunt*) roam about, stray; **~der Hund** stray dog; **2.** (*ist*) **durch die Straßen ~** roam (*od.* wander) the streets; **Streuner** m; -s, -; **Streunerin** f; -, -nen tramp, vagrant

Streu|pflicht f (householders') duty to grit pavements and paths; **~salz** n (thawing) salt; *für Straßen*: road salt; **~sand** m (road) sand, grit

Streusel m, n; -s, -; *Gastr.* crumble topping (*made of butter, sugar and flour*); **~kuchen** m cake with crumble topping; **aussehen wie ein ~** umg. fig. be covered in pimples

Streuung f scattering (*auch Mil. etc.*); (*Verteilung*) dissemination; (*Abweichung*) deviation; *Mil., auch Statistik etc.*: dispersion, spread; *Phys.* scatter(ing), dispersion

Streuzucker m *grob*: granulated sugar; *fein*: caster sugar

strich *Imperf.* → **streichen**

Strich m; -(e)s, -e **1.** (*Linie*) line; (*Gedanken-, Morsestrich*) dash; (*Binde-, Trennungsstrich*) hyphen; (*Schrägstrich*) slash, slant; *auf Skala*: mark;

am Kompass: point; (*Pinselstrich*) stroke (of the brush); *Mus.* (*Bogenstrich*) stroke; *mit wenigen ~en* with a few strokes; *fig.* in brief outlines; *e-n ~ durch etw. machen* cross s.th. out; *j-m e-n ~ durch die Rechnung machen fig.* wreck s.o.'s plans; *e-n* (*dicken*) *~ unter etw. machen od. ziehen* make a clean break with s.th., put s.th. behind one; *keinen ~ tun od. machen umg.* not do a stroke of work; *ein ~ in der Landschaft sein umg.* be as thin as a rake (*Am.* rail; *unter dem ~* all in all, at the end of the day; **2.** *Kunst* (*Pinselführung*) brush strokes *Pl.* (*od.* technique); *Mus.* (*Bogenführung*) bowing (technique); **3.** *nur Sg.*; *von Haar, Fell*: lie; *von Teppich*: pile; *von Samt*: nap; *mit dem/gegen den ~ bürsten* brush the right/wrong way; *das ging mir gegen den ~ umg.* it went against the grain; *nach ~ und Faden umg.* good and proper; **4.** (*Landstrich*) region, *schmaler*: strip (of land); **5.** *nur Sg. umg.* (*Bordellviertel*) red-light district; *umg.* (*Prostitution*) prostitution; *auf den ~ gehen umg. Prostituierte*: walk the streets, *Brit. auch* go on the game; *j-n auf den ~ schicken* make s.o. walk the streets

Strich|ätzung *f Druck.* line block (*od.* plate)

Strichcode *m* bar code; *~leser m* bar code scanner

stricheln *vt/i.* sketch *s.th.* in; (*schraffieren*) hatch; → *gestrichelt*

Stricher *m*; *-s, -*, **Strichjunge** *m pej.* rent boy, *Am.* hustler

Strich|kode *m* bar code; *~liste f* check list; *e-e ~ führen auch fig.* keep a careful record *od.* account (*über + Akk.* of); *~mädchen n pej.* streetwalker; *Brit. auch* tart *umg.*, *Am. auch* hooker *umg.*; *~männchen n* matchstick man; *~punkt m* semicolon; *~vogel m Zool.* flocking bird

strichweise *Adv.* in parts; *~ Regen* scattered showers

Strichzeichnung *f* line drawing

Strick *m*; *-(e)s, -e* **1.** (piece of) rope; *dünner: auch* cord; → *Strang* 1; *j-m aus etw. e-n ~ drehen* (*wollen*) *fig.* use s.th. against s.o.; *wenn alle ~e reißen* if (the) worst comes to (the) worst; *den od.* (*sich* [*Dat.*]) *e-n ~ nehmen umg.* hang o.s.; **2.** *umg. fig.*: *fauler ~* lazy so-and-so

Strick|arbeit *f* knitting; *~bündchen n* knitted welt

stricken *vt/i.* knit; *zwei links, zwei rechts ~* purl two, knit two; **Stricker** *m*; *-s, -*, **Strickerin** *f*; *-, -nen* knitter; **Strickerei** *f* **1.** *nur Sg.* knitting; **2.** (*Fabrik*) knitting mill

Strick|garn *n* knitting yarn; *~jacke f* cardigan; *~kleid n* knit(ted) dress

Strickleiter *f* rope ladder

Strick|maschine *f* knitting machine; *~mode f* knitwear fashion; *~muster n* knitting pattern; *immer nach dem gleichen ~ fig.* always following the same old formula; *~mütze f* knitted/ woollen (*Am.* stocking) cap; *~nadel f* knitting needle; *~waren Pl.* knitwear *Sg.*; *~weste f* knit(ted) waistcoat (*Am.* vest; *mit Ärmeln*: cardigan; *~zeug n* knitting; (*Zubehör*) knitting things *Pl.*

Striegel *m*; *-s, -* curry-comb; **striegeln** *v/t.* (*Pferd*) groom; (*bürsten*) brush; → *gestriegelt*

Striemen *m, -s, -* weal

striezen *v/t. Dial. umg.* (*quälen*) harass

strikt I. *Adj.* strict; *das ~e Gegenteil*

the exact opposite; **II.** *Adv.* strictly; *~ befolgen* adhere strictly (*od.* rigidly) to; (*es*) *~ ablehnen, etw. zu tun* flatly refuse to do s.th.; → *auch streng*

String [ʃtrɪŋ] *m*; *-s, -s* tanga, G-string

stringent *Adj.* compelling; **Stringenz** *f*; *-, kein Pl.* compelling nature

Stringtanga *m*; *-s, -s* G-string, string tanga, thong

Strip [ʃtrɪp] *m*; *-s, -s* **1.** → *Striptease*; **2.** (*Streifen*) strip

Strippe *f*; *-, -n*; *umg.* cord, string; *j-n an der ~ haben* have s.o. on the phone; (*dauernd*) *an der ~ hängen* be (constantly) on the phone

strippen *v/i. umg.* strip; *als Nummer*: perform a striptease, do a strip; *als Beruf*: be a stripper

Strippenzieher *m*; *-s, -*; *Telef. umg.* cable-layer; *fig.* (*Macher, Drahtzieher*) wire-puller, mastermind (behind the scenes)

Stripper [ʃtrɪpɐ] *m*; *-s, -*, *~in f*; *-, -nen; umg.* stripper

Striptease [ʃtrɪptiːs] *m*; *-, kein Pl.* striptease; *~lokal n* striptease club, strip joint *umg.*; *~nummer f* striptease act; *~tänzer m, ~tänzerin f* striptease artist, exotic dancer, stripper

stritt *Imperf.* → *streiten*

strittig *Adj.* → *auch streitig*; contentious; *~er Punkt* point at issue; *weitS. auch* moot point; *das ist durchaus ~* that is debatable

Strizzi [ʃtrɪtsi] *m*; *-s, -s*; *bes. südd., schw., österr.* **1.** (*Strolch*) rascal; **2.** (*Zuhälter*) pimp

Stroboskop *n*; *-s, -e* stroboscope; **Stroboskoplicht** *n* strobe light

Stroganoff [ʃtroːganɔf] *n*; *-s, -s; Gastr.* (*auch Filet ~*) beef stroganoff

Stroh *n*; *-(e)s, kein Pl.* straw; *auf Dach*: thatch; *ein Dach mit ~ decken* thatch a roof with straw; *wie ~ schmecken umg.* taste like cardboard, have no taste (at all); *~ im Kopf haben umg.* be as thick as two short planks (*Am.* as a board), have sawdust between one's ears; *leeres ~ dreschen umg. fig.* flog a dead horse; (*belangloses Zeug reden*) talk a lot of hot air; *~ballen m* bale of straw

strohblond *Adj. Haar*: flaxen; *Mensch*: flaxen-haired

Stroh|blume *f* **1.** immortelle; **2.** (*Helychrisum*) strawflower; *~dach n* thatched roof

stroh|dumm *Adj. umg.* as thick as two short planks (*Am.* as a board); *~farben, ~farbig Adj.* straw-colo(u)red

Strohfeuer *n* straw fire; *ein* (*kurzes*) *~ fig.* a flash in the pan

stroh|gedeckt *Adj.* thatched; *~gelb Adj.* straw-colo(u)red

Stroh|halm *m* (*auch Trinkhalm*) straw; *die Bäume wie ~e knicken* bend the trees double (like straws); *nach e-m ~ greifen, sich an e-n ~ klammern fig.* clutch at straws; *~hut m* straw hat

strohig I. *Adj. Haar*: like straw; *Orangen, Zwieback*: dry and tasteless; **II.** *Adv.*: *~ schmecken* taste like cardboard

Stroh|kopf *m umg.* blockhead, thicko; *~lager n* straw mattress, palliasse *altm.*; *~mann m* **1.** straw doll; (*Vogelscheuche*) scarecrow; **2.** *fig.* front man; *~matte f* straw mat; *~puppe f* straw doll; *~sack m* straw mattress, palliasse *altm.*; *ach du heiliger ~! umg.* good grief!, I'll be blowed (*Am.* darned)!

strohtrocken *Adj.* (as) dry as a bone, bone-dry

Stroh|witwe *f hum.* grass widow; *~witwer m hum.* grass widower

Strolch *m*; *-(e)s, -e* **1.** *pej.* (*Gauner*) ruffian; **2.** *umg.* (*Kind*) rascal, scamp; **strolchen** *v/i.* roam idly about; *~ durch* roam aimlessly through; **Strolchenfahrt** *f schw.* joyride

Strom *m*; *-(e)s, Ströme* **1.** (*Fluss*) (large) river; *fig.* → *Strom 4*; **2.** (*Luft, Lava, auch fig. Blut, Tränen, Menschen, Verkehr etc.*) stream; *stärker*: torrent; *endloser ~ von Menschen, Verkehr etc.*: endless stream; *in Strömen fließen Sekt etc.*: flow like water; *es gießt in Strömen* it's pouring; **3.** (*Strömung*) current (*auch fig.*); *mit dem/gegen den ~ schwimmen* swim with/against the current (*fig.* tide); *fig. auch* go with/ against the flow; **4.** *Etech.* (electric) current; *weitS.* (*Elektrizität*) electricity; (*Stromzufuhr*) *auch* power (supply), electricity supply; *der ~ fiel aus* there was a power failure; *der ~ wird abgeschaltet* the electricity is (being cut) off, we are having a power cut; *~ führendes Kabel* live wire (*größer*: cable); *~ sparend* power-saving; *unter ~ stehen* (*Kabel etc.*) be live; *dauernd unter ~ stehen fig.* (*Perso*) be constantly on the go

...strom *m, im Subst.*: *Atom~* nuclear electricity; *Batterie~* battery current; *Netz~* mains (*Am.* supply) current

stromab *Adv.* → *stromabwärts*

Strom|abnehmer *m Etech.* **1.** (*Gerät*) (current) collector; **2.** (*Verbraucher*) electricity consumer; *~abnehmerin f* → *Stromabnehmer 2*; *~abschaltung f* (*Vorgang*) cutting off of power; *konkret*: power cut

stromabwärts *Adv.* downstream, downriver, down the river

Strom|anbieter *m* electricity supplier; *~anschluss m* connection to the mains (*Am.* power supply), mains (*Am.* grid) connection

stromauf(wärts) *Adv.* upstream, upriver, up the river

Strom|ausfall *m* power failure; *~bedarf m* demand for electricity

strömen *v/i.* stream; *Fluss*: flow (powerfully); *Regen*: pour; (*herausströmen*) pour, gush (*auch Blut*); *fig. Menschen*: stream, pour (*aus* out of; *in + Akk.* into); *das Publikum strömt* the public comes in droves; **strömend I.** *Part. Präs.* → *strömen*; **II.** *Adj.*: *bei ~em Regen* in (the) pouring rain

Stromer *m*; *-s, -*, *~in f*; *-, -nen; umg.* vagrant, tramp, *Am.* hobo; *fig.* (*Herumtreiber*[*in*]) roamer, vagabond; **stromern** *v/i. umg.* roam about; *~ durch* roam (through)

Strom|erzeuger *m* (electricity) generator; *~erzeugung f* electricity (*od.* power) generation; *~ führend* → *Strom 4*; *~kabel n* electric (*od.* power) cable; *~kosten Pl.* electricity (*od.* power) costs; *~kreis m Etech.* circuit; *~leitung f* power line; *~lieferant m f* electricity supplier

Stromlinie *f Phys.* streamline; **Stromlinienform** *f* streamlined shape, streamlining; **stromlinienförmig I.** *Adj.* streamlined; **II.** *Adv.*: *~ gestalten* streamline

Strom|markt *m* electricity supply market; *~netz n* (electricity) mains (*Am.* grid), power supply; *~preis m* electricity price; *~produktion f* electricity production (*od.* generation); *~quelle f Etech.* power source; *~rechnung f*

electricity bill; **~schiene** f 1. Eisenb. conductor rail; 2. Etech. (Sammelschiene) bus bar; **~schlag** m electric shock; **~schnelle** f mst Pl. rapid; **~spannung** f Etech. voltage

stromsparend, Strom sparend → **Strom** 4

Strom|speicher m storage battery; **~sperre** f Etech. power cut; **~stärke** f Etech. current (strength); in Ampere gemessen: amperage; **~stoß** m Etech. impulse; schädlicher: electric shock; **~tarif** m tariff of electricity charges; einzelner: electricity rate

Strömung f 1. Fluss, Meer: current; von Luft: auch airstream; Phys. flow, flux; kalte/warme ~ im Meer cold/warm sea (od. ocean) current; 2. fig. current, trend; (Bewegung) movement

Strömungslehre f Phys. bei Flüssigkeiten: hydrodynamics (V. im Sg.); bei Luft, Gasen: aerodynamics (V. im Sg.)

Strom|verbrauch m electricity (od. power) consumption; **~verbraucher** m, **~verbraucherin** f electricity consumer; **~versorger** m electricity supplier; **~versorgung** f power (od. electricity) supply; **~wandler** m (current) transformer; **~wirtschaft** f electricity generating industry; **~zähler** m electricity meter

Strontium n; -s, kein Pl.; (abgek. Sr) Chem. strontium

Strophe f; -, -n verse; von Gedicht: auch stanza; von Ode: auch strophe

...strophig im Adj.: ein drei~/mehr~es Gedicht a poem with three/several verses

strotzen v/i.: ~ von od. vor (+ Dat.) be full of; vor Fehlern ~ auch be bristling (od. riddled) with mistakes; vor Gesundheit etc. ~ be brimming (od. bursting) with health etc.; vor Dreck ~ be caked with dirt; vor Geld ~ be rolling in money

strubbelig Adj. umg. Haare: tousled; Fell auch: dishevel(l)ed; **Strubbelkopf** m umg. tousled hair, shock of hair; (Person) shock-head

Strudel m; -s, - 1. whirlpool; großer: maelstrom; fig. auch vortex; vom ~ der Ereignisse mitgerissen werden be caught up in the whirl of events; sich in den ~ des Karnevals stürzen plunge into the carnival bedlam; 2. Gastr. strudel; **strudeln** v/i. eddy, swirl

Struktur f; -, -en 1. structure; e-r Organisation: auch set-up; soziale ~en social structures (od. patterns); etw. in s-r ~ verändern make structural alterations to s.th.; 2. e-s Gewebes: texture

Strukturalismus m; -, kein Pl. structuralism; **strukturalistisch** Adj. structuralist

Struktur|analyse f structural analysis; **~änderung** f structural alteration (od. change)

strukturbedingt Adj. structural

Strukturelement n structural element, part of the structure

strukturell 1. Adj. structural; 2. Adv. structurally; ~ schwach Land, Gebiet: with a weak infrastructure, underdeveloped

Struktur|formel f Chem. structural formula; **~gewebe** n textured fabric

strukturieren v/t. 1. structure; e-e Firma neu ~ restructure a firm; 2. (Stoff etc.) texture; **strukturiert** I. P.P. → **strukturieren**; II. Adj.: gut ~er Aufsatz well-structured (od. organized) essay; **Strukturierung** f structuring

Struktur|krise f structural crisis; **~politik** f structural policy; **~reform** f structural reform

strukturschwach Adj. ... with a weak infrastructure; **~es Gebiet** auch underdeveloped area; **~es Land** developing country; **Strukturschwäche** f weakness of infrastructure

Struktur|tapete f textured wallpaper; **~wandel** m structural change, change in structure

Strumpf m; -(e)s, Strümpfe; (Damenstrumpf) stocking; (Kniestrumpf, Socke) sock; ein Paar Strümpfe a pair of stockings/socks; in Strümpfen herumlaufen run around in one's stocking(ed) feet / socks; sein Geld im ~ haben fig. keep one's money under the mattress; **~band** n garter

Strumpfhalter m suspender, Am. garter; **~gürtel** m suspender belt, Am. garter belt

Strumpf|hose f tights Pl., Am. pantyhose Pl.; e-e ~ a pair of tights, Am. a pantyhose; **~maske** f stocking mask; **~waren** Pl. hosiery Sg.

Strunk m; -(e)s, Strünke stalk; e-s Baums: (Stamm) trunk; (Stumpf) stump

struppig Adj. Haare: tousled, unkempt; Fell: tangled; Hund: shaggy; Bart: bristly; **Struppigkeit** f tousled (od. unkempt) state; von Fell: tangled state; von Hund: shagginess; von Bart: bristliness

Struwwelpeter m; -s; (Figur) der ~ Shock-headed Peter

Strychnin [ʃtryçˈniːn] n; -s, kein Pl.; Chem. strychnine

Stubben m; -s, -; nordd. tree stump

Stube f; -, -n 1. (living) room; gute ~ front room; (nur immer) rein in die gute ~! umg. come on in!; 2. Mil. barrack room

Stuben|älteste m, f Mil. room leader; **~appell** m Mil. room roll-call; **~arrest** m: ~ haben umg. Kind: have to stay in, be grounded umg.; **~fliege** f (common) housefly; **~hocker** m pej. stay-at-home; **~kamerad** m, **~kameradin** f Mil. roommate

stubenrein Adj. 1. Tier: house-trained; 2. umg. fig.: nicht ganz ~ Witz: risqué, slightly off colo(u)r, Brit. auch a bit near the bone

Stubenwagen m bassinet

Stuck m; -(e)s, kein Pl. stucco; in ~ gearbeitet Decke: decorated with stucco

Stück n; -(e)s, -e, bei Mengen - 1. allg. piece; (Teil) auch bit; e-s Wegs: stretch; Brot: slice; Zucker: lump; ~ Papier piece of paper; zum Schmieren: auch scrap of paper; ~ Seife bar (Rest: piece) of soap; ein hübsches ~ Geld umg. a tidy (little) sum; ~ für ~ bit by bit, little by little; in ~e gehen break into pieces; in ~e schlagen smash to bits; in ~e reißen tear to pieces; ein ~ deutscher Geschichte a piece (od. chapter) of German history; ein gutes ~ größer/kleiner etc. quite a bit bigger/smaller etc.; ein hartes ~ Arbeit a difficult job; in vielen ~en fig. in many respects (od. ways); große ~e halten auf think highly of, (anhimmeln) think the world of; sich (Dat.) große ~e einbilden have a very high opinion of oneself; aus freien ~en of one's own free will, off one's own bat umg.; 2. zusammenhängendes Ganzes, Einzelexemplar, zur Bezeichnung von Mengen: piece; drei Mark das ~ three marks each (od. apiece); ich nehme zwei ~

I'll take two (of them); aus 'einem ~ geschnitten cut from one piece; Käse am ~ kaufen buy cheese by the piece (od. unsliced); von diesem Buch wurden 10 000 ~ verkauft 10,000 copies of the book were sold; ~ Land piece (od. plot) of land, kleines: patch; zehn ~ Vieh ten head of cattle; alles in e-m Stück all in one piece; 3. (Entfernung) j-n ein (kurzes) ~ begleiten walk a short way with s.o.; ein gutes ~ (Weges) quite a way (od. distance); ein gutes ~ weiterkommen auch fig. make a fair bit (od. quite a lot) of headway; 4. (Exemplar) specimen; ein seltenes ~ a rare specimen; mein bestes ~ umg. my most prized possession; (auch Person) my pride and joy; 5. Mus. piece (of music); auf e-r CD etc.: piece; moderne Musik: mst track; 6. Theat. play; 7. umg. fig.: (Person) freches ~ cheeky so-and-so; dummes/faules ~ dimwit / lazy so-and-so, lazybones; 8. umg. (Tat) das ist doch ein starkes ~! that's pretty rich, that's a bit thick; da hast du dir aber ein ~ geleistet! you've really gone and done it (this time)!

Stückarbeit f piecework

Stuckarbeiten Pl. stucco (work)

Stuckateur m; -s, -e, **~in** f; -, -nen plasterer; **Stuckatur** f; -, -en stucco (work)

Stückchen n small piece (od. bit); emotionaler: little piece (od. bit); j-n ein ~ begleiten walk a short way with s.o.; → **rücken** II 2

Stuckdecke f stucco(ed) ceiling

stückeln I. v/t. 1. Nähen: (zusammensetzen) patch (od. piece) together; 2. (Aktien) denominate; II. v/i.: ~ müssen beim Nähen etc.: have to patch (od. use patches); bei Summe: have to make up the amount with smaller denominations; **Stückelung** f 1. (das Stückeln) patching; 2. von Aktien: denomination

stücken v/t. (zusammensetzen) patch (od. piece) together

Stücke|schreiber m, **~schreiberin** f playwright, dramatist

Stück|gut n Wirts. 1. piece goods Pl.; 2. (Paket) parcel(s Pl.); **~kosten** Pl. unit cost Sg. (od. costs); **~liste** f parts list; **~lohn** m piece rate

Stuckmarmor m imitation marble (consisting of painted plaster)

Stückpreis m unit price

stückweise Adv. little by little, bit by bit; Wirts. by the piece

Stück|werk n pej. patchwork; (Halbheiten) half measures Pl.; ~ sein/bleiben be scrappy (od. patchy) / be no more than half measures; **~zahl** f number of pieces; **~zinsen** Pl. Wirts. accrued interest Sg. (on shares); (zusätzliche Zinsen) additional interest Sg.

Student m; -en, -en student; ~ der Biologie biology student, student of biology

Studenten|austausch m student exchange; **~ausweis** m student card; **~bewegung** f student movement; **~blume** f Bot. French marigold; **~bude** f umg. (student's) digs Pl.; **~futter** n Gastr. assortment of nuts and raisins, Am. trail mix; **~gemeinde** f Protestant (od. Catholic etc.) student community; **~heim** n students hostel, hall of residence, Am. dormitory; **~lied** n student song; **~parlament** n student parliament; **~pfarrer** m, **~pfarrerin** f student (*od.* college) chaplain; **~pro-test** *m* student protest; **~rat** *m* students' council; **~revolte** *f* student revolt

Studentenschaft *f* student body, students *Pl.*

Studenten|unruhen *Pl.* student unrest *Sg.*; **~verbindung** *f* student association; (*Korporation*) (student) fraternity; **~vertreter** *m*, **~vertreterin** *f* student representative; **~vertretung** *f* student parliament; **~werk** *n* student administration (and social welfare organization); **~wohnheim** *n* → *Studentenheim*, **~zeit** *f* student days *Pl.*, *Am.* auch college days *Pl.*

Studentin *f*; -, -nen → *Student*

studentisch *Adj. attr.* student ...; **~e Verbindung** student fraternity

Studis *Pl. umg.* (*Studenten*) students

Studie *f*; -, -n study (*auch Malerei, Fot.*); (*Entwurf*) sketch; (*Umfrage*) survey

Studien|abbrecher *m*; -s, -, **~abbrecherin** *f*; -, -nen university (*od.* college) dropout; **~abschluss** *m* final examinations *Pl.*, finals *Pl.*; degree; *die Universität ohne ~ verlassen* leave university (*Am.* college) without a degree, drop out of university (*Am.* college); *welchen ~ haben Sie?* what sort of degree have you got?; **~anfänger** *m*, **~anfängerin** *f* university entrant, first-year (student), *Brit. auch* fresher, *Am.* freshman; **~aufenthalt** *m* study visit; *nach e-m zweijährigen ~ in X* after spending two years studying in X; **~ausgabe** *f* student's edition; **~beratung** *f* course guidance; (*Stelle*) course guidance (*od.* academic advisory) service; **~bewerber** *m*, **~bewerberin** *f* university (*od.* college) applicant; **~buch** *n* course attendance record; **~dauer** *f* → *Studienzeit* 2; **~direktor** *m*, **~direktorin** *f* director of studies (*empowered to act as deputy head* [*Am. vice-principal*]); **~fach** *n* subject (of study); **~fahrt** *f* study trip; **~freund** *m*, **~freundin** *f* friend from university (*od.* college); **~gang** *m* university course (of study); (*Lehrplan*) syllabus; **~gebühren** *Pl.* tuition fees, *Am.* tuition *Sg.*

studienhalber *Adv.* for study purposes

Studien|jahr *n* academic year; **~kolleg** *n Univ.* introductory course (for foreign students); **~kollege** *m*, **~kollegin** *f* fellow student; **~kreis** *m* study group; **~objekt** *n* object of study; **~ort** *m* place of study; **~platz** *m* university (*od.* college) place, *Am.* admission (as a student in college *etc.*); **~rat** *m*, **~rätin** *f* (established) graduate secondary school teacher, *Am.* qualified high school teacher; **~referendar** *m*, **~referendarin** *f etwa* student secondary (*Am.* high) school teacher, *Am. auch* intern; **~reform** *f* university course reform; **~reise** *f* study trip, educational tour; **~seminar** *n* teacher training college

Studienzeit *f* 1. → *Studentenzeit*; 2. (*Dauer des Studiums*) length of a university course, period of study; *die ~ für Mathematik* the length of a mathematics course; **~begrenzung** *f Univ.* limitation of the period of study; **~verkürzung** *f Univ.* shortening of the period of study

studieren I. *vt/i.* **1.** study; (*e-e Hochschule besuchen*) go to university (*Am. auch* college); *mit Angabe des Studienfachs: Brit. auch* read; *er stu-*

diert Jura he's studying (*Brit. auch* reading) law, he's a law student; *sie studiert im 3. Semester Medizin* she's in her third semester reading (*Am.* studying) medicine (*od.* her third semester of medical school); *studiert haben* have had a university (*Am.* college) education; *sie hat studiert* auch she's a graduate, she's been to university (*Am. auch* college); *wo hast du studiert?* where did you go to university (*Am. auch* college)?, which university (*Am. auch* college) did you go to?; **II.** *v/t.* (*durchlesen, prüfen*) study; *intensiv: auch* scrutinize; *die Speisekarte ~ umg.* study (*od.* scrutinize) the menu; *die Landessitten ~* make a study of the national customs; **Studierende** *m, f*; -n,-n student

studiert I. *P.P.* → *studieren*; **II.** *Adj.* university (*Am.* college) educated; *~er Biologe* biology graduate; **Studierte** *m, f*; -n, -n; *umg.* university (*Am.* college) graduate

Studio *n*; -s, -s studio; (*Film, TV, Funk., Komplex*) *auch* studios *Pl.*; **~aufnahme** *f* studio recording; **~bühne** *f* studio (*oft* experimental) theat|re (*Am. auch* -er); **~gast** *m Funk. etc.*: studio guest; **~musiker** *m*, **~musikerin** *f* studio musician; **~qualität** *f Mus. etc.*: studio quality

Studiosus *m*; -, *Studiosi*; *umg. hum.* student

Studiotechnik *f Mus. etc.*: studio technology

Studium *n*; -s, *Studien* **1.** *nur Sg.*; *Univ., Studiengang:* course of study; *mit Diplom:* university course (*ending with the State Examination*); *in GB, USA etc.*: degree course; *während m-s ~s* when I was at university (*Am. auch* college); *sich* (*Dat.*) *sein ~ verdienen* work one's way through university (*Am. auch* college); *ein ~ aufnehmen* start at university (*Am. auch* college); *das ~ der Geschichte* the study of history; (*Studiengang*) the history course; *sein ~ abschließen* complete one's university course, take one's finals; **2.** (*Erforschung, Beobachtung*) study; *als Hobby betreibe ich Studien zur Ahnenforschung* genealogical studies are my hobby, I study genealogy as a hobby; *ich war gerade beim ~ des Fernsehprogramms, als ...* I was just looking to see what was on television when ...

Studium generale *n*; - -, *kein Pl.* inter-faculty lecture courses on general subjects

Stufe *f*; -, -n **1.** *e-r Treppe, Trittleiter:* step; *e-r Leiter:* rung (*auch fig.*); *Geol.* stage; *im Gelände:* terrace; *zwei ~n auf einmal nehmen* take two steps at a time; **2.** *e-r Rakete etc.*: stage; *e-r Schaltung: auch* step; **3.** (*Stadium*) stage; (*Rang*) rank, grade; (*Niveau*) level, standard; *auf gleicher ~ mit* on a level (*od.* par) with; *auf eine ~ stellen* place on a level (*od.* par) with, equate with; *sich mit j-m auf eine ~ stellen auch* see oneself as s.o.'s equal; *die höchste ~ des Erfolgs* the pinnacle of success; *die nächste ~ s-r Karriere* the next stage (*od.* step) in his career; *verschiedene ~n der Entwicklung* different stages of development; **4.** (*Tonstufe*) interval; *e-r Tonleiter:* step; **5.** (*Farbstufe*) shade; → *auch Oberstufe, Unterstufe etc.*

stufen *v/t.* **1.** step; (*Gelände*) *auch* terrace; **2.** *fig.* (*staffeln*) grade, graduate

stufenartig *Adj. und Adv.* → *stufenförmig*

Stufen|barren *m Turnen:* asymmetrical (*Am.* uneven) bars *Pl.*; **~dach** *n* stepped roof; **~folge** *f fig.* graduation, sequence of stages

stufenförmig I. *Adj.* stepped; *fig.* graded, graduated; **II.** *Adv.* in steps; *fig. auch* in stages

Stufen|heck *n Mot.* notchback; **~landschaft** *f* terraced landscape; **~leiter** *f* step ladder; *fig.* ladder; *gesellschaftliche ~* social ladder

stufenlos I. *Adj. Tech., Schaltung etc.*: infinitely variable; *Dimmer:* continuously variable; *~es Verändern der Größe* continuous size adjustment; **II.** *Adv.* continuously; *~ verstellbar* continuously adjustable

Stufen|plan *m* step-by-step plan; **~pyramide** *f* step(ped) pyramid; **~schnitt** *m* layered hairstyle (*od.* haircut); **~tarifvertrag** *m* graded wage agreement

stufenweise I. *Adj.* gradual, progressive; **II.** *Adv.* step by step, by degrees; *in Abschnitten:* in stages, gradually

stufig I. *Adj. Haarschnitt:* layered; **II.** *Adv.*: *Haare ~ schneiden* layer hair

Stuhl *m*; -(e)s, *Stühle* **1.** chair; *der elektrische ~* the electric chair; **2.** *fig.*: *j-m den ~ vor die Tür setzen* turn s.o. out; (*entlassen*) fire s.o., give s.o. the sack (*Am.* boot) *umg.*; *sich zwischen zwei Stühle setzen* fall between two stools; *zwischen zwei Stühlen sitzen* have fallen between two stools; *mich hat es fast vom ~ gehauen umg.* I nearly fell over backwards; *das reißt od.* haut *niemand vom ~ umg.* nobody's going to get excited about that; *an j-s Sägen umg.* try to topple s.o.; *an s-m ~ kleben umg.* cling to one's post; **3.** *kath.*: *der Heilige ~* the Holy See; **4.** *Med.* (*Kot*) stool(s *Pl.*); → *Stuhlgang*

Stuhl|aufsatz *m für Kinder:* booster seat; **~bein** *n* chairleg, leg of a (*od.* the) chair; **~drang** *m Med.* urge to empty one's bowels; **~gang** *m Med.* bowel movement; *~ haben* have a bowel movement; *harten/weichen ~ haben* have hard/soft stools; **~kissen** *n* chair cushion; **~lehne** *f* back of a (*od.* the) chair, chair back; **~reihe** *f* row of chairs; **~untersuchung** *f Med.* stool examination; **~verhaltung** *f Med.* obstipation; **~verstopfung** *f Med.* constipation

Stuka *m*; -s, -s; *Abk.* → *Sturzkampfflugzeug*

Stukkateur *etc.* → *Stuckateur etc.*

Stulle *f*; -, -n; *nordd.* slice of bread (and butter); *belegte:* (open) sandwich

Stulpe *f*; -, -n *am Stiefel:* bucket top; (*Manschette*) (turned-up) cuff

stülpen *v/t.* (*um*) turn *s.th.* upside down; (*Ärmel etc.*) turn up; *nach außen ~* turn inside out; *auf od. über etw. ~* put *s.th.* on (*od.* over) s.th.

Stulpenstiefel *m* bucket top boot

Stülpnase *f* turned-up nose

stumm I. *Adj.* **1.** dumb; (*still*) silent; *Ling.* silent, mute; *fig.* silent; *Gruß, Klage: auch* wordless; *von Geburt an ~ sein* be dumb from birth; *~ vor* (+ *Dat.*) *fig. Erstaunen etc.*: speechless with, *stärker:* struck dumb with; *~e Rolle* non-speaking part; *~er Zeuge* silent witness; *~er Vorwurf* silent (*od.* wordless) reproach; *~ wie ein Fisch sein* shut up like a clam; *j-n ~ machen umg. fig.* silence s.o.; **2.** *Med.*: *~e Infektion* symptomless infection; → *Die-*

ner 3; **II.** *Adv.* silently; **~ *dasitzen*** sit there without saying a word; *sich* **~ *ansehen*** look at one another in silence; **Stumme** *m, f; -n, -n* mute
Stummel *m; -s, -; (Zahn etc.)* stump; *e-r Zigarre etc.:* butt, stub; *e-s Bleistifts, e-r Kerze:* stub; **~schwanz** *m* stumpy *(Am.* stubby) tail; *(gestutzter Schwanz)* bobtail
Stummfilm *m* silent film *(Am.* movie); **~zeit** *f* silent film *(Am.* movie) era
Stummheit *f* dumbness; *(Schweigsamkeit)* silence
Stumpen *m; -s, -* **1.** *(Zigarre)* short, stumpy *(Am.* stubby) cigar; **2.** *Dial. (Stumpf)* (tree) stump
Stümper *m; -s, -; pej.* bungler; *bei manueller Arbeit:* botcher; ***hier waren ~ am Werk*** *Reparatur etc.:* this has been botched; **Stümperei** *f, -, -en; umg. pej.* bungling, incompetence; *bei manueller Arbeit, Reparatur:* botching; *e-e ~* a piece of bungling *(od.* incompetence); *(e-e schlechte Arbeit)* a botched job, a botch; **stümperhaft** *pej.* **I.** *Adj.* bungling, incompetent; *(laienhaft)* amateurish; ***~e Arbeit*** (a) botched job, (a) botch; **II.** *Adv.:* **~ ausgeführt sein** be an incompetent *(laienhaft:* amateurish) piece of work; **stümpern** *v/i. pej.* bungle (one's work); *bei Reparatur etc.:* do a botched job
stumpf **I.** *Adj.* **1.** *Bleistift, Messer etc.:* blunt; **~ *werden*** go blunt; **2.** *Math., Winkel:* obtuse; *Kegel:* truncated; **3.** *Reim:* masculine; **4.** *(glanzlos) auch Haar:* dull; **5.** *(stumpfsinnig)* dull; *(teilnahmslos)* stolid, apathetic; *Sinne:* dulled; **~er *Blick*** blank *(od.* vacant) look; **~ *gegenüber* ...** insensitive to; **II.** *Adv.:* **~ *vor sich hin starren*** stare blankly into space
Stumpf *m; -(e)s, Stümpfe* stump; *etw.* **mit ~ und Stiel ausrotten** eradicate s.th. root and branch
Stumpfheit *f* **1.** *e-s Messers etc.:* bluntness; **2.** *(Glanzlosigkeit)* dullness; **3.** *von Mensch:* apathy; *der Sinne:* dullness
Stumpfsinn *m; nur Sg. von Mensch:* dullness, apathy; *e-r Tätigkeit:* tedium, monotony; ***diese Arbeit ist doch (der reine) ~!*** *umg.* this job is sheer (mindless) tedium; **stumpfsinnig** **I.** *Adj.* dull; *(teilnahmslos)* stolid, apathetic; *Arbeit etc.:* tedious, mindless, soul-destroying; ***dabei wird man ja ~!*** *umg.* this makes you into a mindless moron; **II.** *Adv.:* **~ *vor sich hin starren*** stare blankly *(od.* vacantly) into space
stumpfwink(e)lig *Adj.* obtuse(-angled)
Stündchen *n umg.:* **auf ein ~ rüberkommen** *etc.* come over *etc.* for an hour or so; → **Stündlein**
Stunde *f; -, -n* **1.** hour; ***alle zwei ~n*** every two hours, every other hour; ***immer zur vollen ~*** every hour on the hour; *e-e Rede etc.* **von drei ~n** *(Dauer)* a three-hour speech *etc.;* ***e-e knappe/volle ~*** barely an hour/a full hour; **von ~ zu ~** with every hour (that passes *od.* passed); **~ *um* ~** *verging* the hours passed by; **50 Meilen in der ~** *Mot.* 50 miles an *(od.* per) hour; *für Korrekturlesen zahlen wir 20 Euro die* **~** for proofreading we pay 20 euros an hour; → **halb** I 2, **geschlagen** II 3; **2.** *(Unterricht)* lesson; *in der Schule: auch* period; ***~n geben*** give lessons; ***~n nehmen bei*** have lessons with; **was habt ihr in der ersten ~?** what do you have in the first period?, what's your

first lesson?; **3.** *fig. geh.* hour, moment; *(Zeitpunkt) auch* time; ***schöne ~n mit j-m verbringen*** spend happy hours with s.o., have a wonderful time with s.o.; *j-s schwerste ~* s.o.'s darkest hour; **bis zur ~** as yet, up till now; **zu *später/früher* ~** at a late/an early hour; **die blaue ~** *poet.* the twilight hour; **zur gewohnten ~** at the accustomed *(od.* usual) hour; **zu jeder ~** at any time; **zur ~** at the moment; *die Gespräche dauern zur ~ noch an* the talks are still in progress; *s-e ~n sind gezählt fig.* his days are numbered; *s-e letzte* **~ *hat geschlagen*** his last hour has come; *s-e (große) ~ ist gekommen* his (great) moment has come; *die ~ der Entscheidung ist gekommen* the moment *(od.* time) of decision has come; *die ~ der Rache ist gekommen* the hour of reckoning has come; *die ~ des Abschieds ist gekommen* it is time to part *(od.* say goodbye); *die ~ der Wahrheit* the moment of truth; *die ~ null* (the time of) starting over from scratch; *in e-r schwachen ~* in a moment of weakness; *ein Mann der ersten ~* a pioneer; *in e-r stillen ~* in a quiet moment (of reflection); *die Gunst der ~ nutzen* strike while the iron is hot; *er wusste, was die ~ geschlagen hatte* he knew what the score was, he had seen the writing on the wall; → **vorgerückt**
stunden *v/t. Wirts.: etw.* **~** defer payment for s.th., *Jur.* grant respite for s.th.; *(j-m)* **die Zahlung ~** extend the period of payment (for s.o.)
Stunden|ausfall *m Päd.* cancel(l)ed classes *Pl.;* **~buch** *n Kunst hist.* book of hours; **~gebet** *n kirchl.* prayer said at the canonical hours; **~geschwindigkeit** *f* (average) speed per hour; **~hotel** *n* hotel letting rooms by the hour to couples; **~kilometer** *Pl.; umg.* kilomet|res *(Am.* -ers) per hour *(Abk.* kph); **~kreis** *m Astron.* hour circle
stundenlang **I.** *Adj. attr.* hours of, hour after hour of; *nachgestellt:* lasting (for) hours; **nach ~er Suche** after searching for hours; **II.** *Adv.* for hours (and hours), for hours on end
Stunden|lohn *m* hourly wage; **~plan** *m* timetable, *Am.* schedule; **~satz** *m (Bezahlung)* hourly rate; **~schlag** *m* striking of the hour; **~takt** *m: der Bus etc. verkehrt im* **~** every hour
stundenweise **I.** *Adj. attr. Vertretung, Bezahlung etc.:* hourly, *nachgestellt:* by the hour; **II.** *Adv.* by the hour
...-Stunden-Woche *f, im Subst.:* **30~** 30-hour (work) week
Stunden|zahl *f* number of hours (worked), workload; *e-s Lehrers: auch* teaching load; **~zeiger** *m* hour hand
Stündlein *n: sein letztes ~ hat geschlagen umg.* his last hour has come
stündlich **I.** *Adj. attr.* hourly; **Abfahrt ist ~** there are departures every hour, it is an hourly service; **II.** *Adv.* **1.** every hour, hourly; **2.** *(zu jeder Zeit)* any time (now); **er kann ~ ankommen** he could be here any time (now)
Stundung *f Wirts.* deferment (of payment)
Stunk *m; -s, kein Pl.; umg.* row, stink, *Am. auch* dust-up; **~ *machen*** kick up a row *(od.* stink, *Am.* fuss); **es wird ~ geben** there'll be trouble *(stärker:* a real stink); **mit j-m ~ haben** have a lot of hassle with s.o.
Stunt [stant] *m; -s, -s* stunt; *e-n* **~ ausführen** do a stunt; **~frau** *f* stunt wom-

an; **~man** ['-mɛn] *m; -s, Stuntmen* stunt man; **~woman** ['-vʊmən] *f; -, Stuntwomen* stunt woman
stupend *Adj.* stupendous, amazing
stupid(e) *Adj. pej.* **1.** *(geistlos)* moronic, brainless; **2.**; **3.** *(geisttötend)* mindless, soul-destroying; **Stupidität** *f; -, kein Pl.; pej.* **1.** *(Geistlosigkeit)* brainlessness; **2.** *e-r Tätigkeit:* mindlessness
Stups *m; -es, -e; umg.* nudge; *fig. (Anstoß)* prod; *j-m e-n* **~ geben** give s.o. a nudge *(fig.* prod); **stupsen** *v/t. umg.* nudge
Stupsnase *f* snub nose; **stupsnasig** *Adj.* snub-nosed
stur *mst pej.* **I.** *Adj. (starrsinnig)* stubborn, obstinate; *stärker:* pigheaded; *(unnachgiebig) auch* unyielding, unwavering; *(verbissen)* dogged; *(stumpf)* stolid, dour; *(geisttötend)* mindless; *ein* **~er *Bock*** *umg.* a pigheaded type; ***da rin bin ich ganz ~*** I must insist on that, I won't budge on that; ***bleib einfach ~!*** just dig in your heels, don't budge an inch; **II.** *Adv.:* **~ *nach Vorschrift*** strictly according to the letter (of the law); **~ *bei s-r Meinung bleiben*** stick doggedly to one's opinion; ***immer ~ geradeaus laufen*** *umg.* keep going straight on; **Sturheit** *f* stubbornness, obstinacy; *stärker:* pigheadedness; *(Verbissenheit)* doggedness; *(Stumpfheit)* stolidity, dourness; *(geisttötende Art)* mindlessness
Sturm *m; -(e)s, Stürme* **1.** storm; *(starker Wind)* gale; *lit.* tempest; *das Barometer steht auf ~* the barometer is pointing to 'storm'; *fig.* there's trouble brewing; **~ *läuten*** ring the alarm bell; *fig. (klingeln)* lean on the bell; *e-n* **~ *der Entrüstung auslösen*** cause a huge (public) outcry; **~ *des Protests*** storm of protest; *ein* **~ *im Wasserglas*** a storm in a teacup, *Am.* a tempest in a teapot; **2.** **~ *und Drang*** *Lit.* Sturm und Drang, Storm and Stress; → **Sturm--und-Drang-Zeit**; **3.** *Mil. (Angriff, auch fig.)* attack, assault; **~ *auf Waren/e-e Bank*** *Wirts.* rush for goods *(Am.* merchandise) /run on a bank; **~ *laufen gegen*** be up in arms against; *etw. / fig.* *j-n im* **~ erobern** take s.th. by storm / sweep s.o. off his *(od.* her) feet; **4.** *nur Sg.; Sport (Stürmerreihe)* forward line, forwards *Pl.;* **im ~ spielen** play in a forward position *(od.* up front); *e-n starken/schwachen* **~ *haben*** have a strong/weak attack; **~abteilung** *f hist.* SA, (Nazi) stormtroops *Pl. od.* stormtroopers *Pl.;* **~angriff** *m Mil.* assault; **~bö** *f* squall; **~bock** *m hist.* battering ram; **~boot** *n Mil.* assault boat
stürmen **I.** *v/t. (hat gestürmt) Mil.* storm *(auch weitS.* die Bühne etc.); *fig. (Geschäft, Kasse)* besiege; *(e-e Bank)* make a run on; **II.** *v/i.* **1.** *(hat) Mil. und Fußball etc.:* attack; *(als Stürmer spielen)* play in a forward position *(od.* up front); **2.** *(hat) Wind:* rage; **3.** *(ist) fig.* wütend, irgendwohin: storm; *(rennen)* charge, rush; *die Kinder stürmten aus der Schule* the children came charging out of the school; **III.** *v/impers. (hat):* **es stürmt** there's a gale blowing; *letzte Nacht hat es furchtbar gestürmt* there was a terrible gale last night
Stürmer *m; -s, -* **1.** *Fußball etc.:* striker, forward; **2.** **~ *und Dränger*** *Lit.* Sturm und Drang *(od.* Storm and Stress) writer; *fig.* hot-headed fanatic
Stürmerfoul *n Sport* offensive foul

S

Stürmerin f; -, -nen Fußball etc.: striker, forward

Sturmflut f storm tide

sturmfrei Adj. umg.: **heute abend hab ich ~e Bude** I've got the run of the place tonight, the coast is clear tonight

Sturmgepäck n Mil. combat pack

sturmgepeitscht Adj. attr. See, Wellen: storm-tossed; Bäume: bending before the storm

Sturmglocke f alarm bell, tocsin

stürmisch I. Adj. **1.** Wetter: stormy; **~e See** stormy (od. rough) seas Pl.; **~e Überfahrt** rough crossing; **2.** fig. Liebe: tempestuous, passionate; Affäre: auch stormy; Liebhaber: passionate; Debatte: stormy; Beifall: tumultuous; (frenetisch) frenzied; Protest, Reaktion: vehement, violent; Entwicklung etc.: meteoric; **~e Begrüßung** rapturous welcome; lautstark: tumultuous welcome; **~er Jubel** wild rejoicing; **~e Umarmung** passionate embrace; **e-e ~e Zeit** turbulent times Pl.; **II.** Adv.: **~ verlaufen** Debatte etc.: follow a stormy course; Entwicklung: proceed at a whirlwind pace; **~ protestieren** protest vehemently (od. violently); **etw. ~ fordern** clamo(u)r for s.th.; **man applaudierte ~** there was tumultuous applause; **~ begrüßt werden** be given a rapturous (od. tumultuous) welcome; **nicht so ~!** easy does it!, hold your horses!

Sturm|laterne f storm lantern, hurricane lamp; **~leiter** f **1.** hist. scaling ladder; **2.** Naut. rope ladder; **~möwe** f Zool. seagull; **~nacht** f **1.** (stürmische Nacht) stormy night; **2.** (Nacht des Sturms) night of the storm

sturmreif Mil. **I.** Adj. ready to be stormed; **II.** Adv.: **~ schießen** subject to a softening-up barrage

Sturm|reihe f Sport forward line, attack; **~schaden** m storm damage; **~schritt** m: **im ~** at (Am. on) the double

sturmschwach Sport **I.** Adj. weak up front, weak in attack (Am. offense); **II.** Adv.: **~ spielen** show weakness in attack, play without any effective attack (Am. offense)

Sturm|segel n storm sail; **~spitze** f Sport spearhead (of the attack)

sturmstark Sport **I.** Adj. strong up front, strong in attack; **II.** Adv.: **~ spielen** show strength in attack, attack strongly

Sturm|tief n deep depression, cyclone; **~-und-Drang-Zeit** f Lit. Sturm und Drang (od. Storm and Stress) period; **zu m-r ~** fig. hum. in my days of youthful exuberance; **~vogel** m Zool. (stormy) petrel; **~warnung** f gale warning; **~warnungszeichen** n storm signal; (Kegel) storm cone

Sturz¹ m; -es, Stürze **1.** (sudden) fall; ins Wasser, in die Tiefe: plunge; **~ vom Fahrrad / aus dem Fenster** fall off a (od. the) bicycle / out of the window; **e-n ~ bauen** od. **drehen** umg. have a fall; **mit Motorrad:** have an accident; **es kam zu mehreren schweren Stürzen** Sport there were several serious falls (od. crashes); **2.** Wirts., der Kurse, Preise: sharp drop, stärker: slump; der Börse: crash; **~ der Temperatur** etc. (sharp) drop in temperature etc.; **3.** e-r Regierung: (down)fall, e-s Politikers etc.: downfall; durch Gewalt: overthrow

Sturz² m; -es, Stürze **1.** Tech., Rad: camber; **2.** Archit., Fenster, Tür: lintel

Sturzbach m torrent (auch fig.)

sturz|besoffen, **~betrunken** Adj. umg. (completely) sloshed, plastered

Sturz|bomber m Mil. dive bomber; **~bügel** m Mot. crash bar, roll bar

stürzen **I.** v/i. (ist gestürzt) **1.** fall; in die Tiefe: plunge, plummet; ins Wasser: dive, plunge; **schwer ~** have a bad (od. heavy) fall; (bewusstlos) **zu Boden ~** fall to the ground (unconscious), collapse; **vom Fahrrad ~** fall off one's bicycle; **aus dem Fenster ~** fall out of the window; **ins Meer ~** Flugzeug: plunge (od. dive) into the sea; **2.** Wirts., Kurse, Preise: fall (od. drop) sharply, tumble; Temperatur: drop sharply, plunge; **3.** Pol., Regierung etc.: fall; Minister: be removed from office; **der Minister stürzte über diesen Skandal** auch this scandal brought about (od. led to) the minister's downfall; **4.** Gelände: drop; **in die Tiefe ~** Abhang etc.: drop sheer, plunge down; **die Felsen ~ dort 100 Meter in die Tiefe** the cliffs have a sheer drop of 100 met|res (Am. -ers) at that point; **5.** (rennen) rush, dash; **ins Zimmer ~** auch burst into the room; **j-m in die Arme ~** fall (od. fling o.s.) into s.o.'s arms; **II.** v/t. (hat) **1.** (stoßen) throw; **j-n/etw. aus dem Fenster/von der Brücke ~** throw so./s.th. out of the window/from (od. off) the bridge; **j-n ins Elend etc. ~** plunge s.o. into misery etc.; → Verderben; **2.** (umkippen) turn s.th. upside down; (Pudding etc.) turn out of the mo(u)ld (od. tin); **Nicht ~!** Kistenaufschrift: this side up; **3.** (Regierung etc.) bring down, bring about the downfall of; stärker: overthrow; **III.** v/refl. (hat) **1.** **sich ins Wasser ~** plunge into the water; **sich aus dem Fenster ~** plunge (od. fling o.s.) out of the window; **sich in Unkosten ~** go to great expense, spare no expense; **sich in die Arbeit ~** throw o.s. into (od. immerse o.s. in) one's work; **sich ins Nachtleben ~** umg. abandon o.s. to the pleasures of nightlife; → Verderben etc.; **2.** **sich ~ auf** (+ Akk.) (j-n) rush to(wards); aggressiv: rush at; (herfallen über) auch Raubkatze: pounce on; Raubvogel: swoop down on; umg. fig. (ein Buffet etc.) fall upon, attack; **sich aufeinander ~** fall upon each other; **sich auf die Süßigkeiten ~** umg. pounce on (od. attack) the sweets; **sich auf die Geschenke ~** umg. fall upon the presents

Sturz|flug m nosedive; fig. crash; **~flut** f torrent (of water); vom Meer: tidal wave; (Regen) torrential downpour; fig. torrent; **~geburt** f Med. precipitate delivery; **~helm** m crash helmet; **~kampfflugzeug** n (abgek. Stuka) dive bomber; **~see** f breaker

Stuss m; -es, kein Pl.; umg. garbage, trash, bes. Brit. rubbish; **so ein ~!** what a lot (Brit. auch load) of garbage; **red keinen ~!** stop talking such garbage (bes. Brit. auch rubbish)

Stute f; -, -n mare

Stuten m; -s, -; nordd., Gastr. fruit loaf

Stuten|fohlen n filly; **~milch** f mare's milk

Stutz m; -es, -e und Stütze; schw. (Hang) steep slope

Stütz m; -es, -e Turnen: support

Stützbalken m supporting beam, brace

Stütze f; -, -n **1.** support, prop; **2.** fig. support, (Rückendeckung) auch backing; (Person) mainstay; **sie war mir e-e große ~** she gave me a lot of support; **3.** umg. (Arbeitslosenhilfe) unemployment benefit, Brit. auch dole (money)

stutzen¹ v/t. (beschneiden) cut; (Bart, Haar) trim; (Baum) prune, lop; (Hecke) clip, trim; (Flügel) clip; (Ohren) crop; (Schwanz) dock

stutzen² v/i. (plötzlich innehalten) stop short; (verwundert sein) be taken aback, stärker: catch one's breath; (zögern) hesitate; (zweimal hingucken müssen) do a double take umg.

Stutzen m; -s, - **1.** short rifle, carbine; **2.** Tech. (Rohrverbindung) connecting piece; Mot., zum Einfüllen: filler neck; **3.** (Fußballstrumpf) football sock; (Wadenstrumpf) knee sock

stützen **I.** v/t. **1.** support; (abstützen) auch prop up; Archit. shore up; **s-e Ellenbogen ~ auf** (+Akk.) prop (od. rest) one's elbows on; **j-n beim Gehen ~** support s.o. as they walk; **sie ging auf e-n Stock gestützt** she walked leaning (od. supporting herself) on a stick; **2.** fig. support, back (up); Wirts. (Kurse, Währung) support; **etw. ~ auf** (+Akk.) base s.th. on; **II.** v/refl.: **sich ~ auf** (+Akk.) rest on; Person: lean on; fig. Argument, Urteil etc.: be based on, rest on; (auf e-e Quelle) auch draw upon; **sich beim Gehen auf etw./j-n ~** walk leaning (od. supporting o.s.) on s.th./s.o.

Stutzer m; -s, -; altm. pej. dandy; **stutzerhaft** Adj. altm. pej. dandyish

Stutzflügel m (Klavier) baby grand

Stützgewebe n Anat. supporting tissue

stutzig Adj.: **~ werden** be taken aback; (verwirrt) be puzzled; **j-n ~ machen** perplex (od. puzzle) s.o.; (nachdenklich stimmen) have s.o. wondering; (Verdacht erregen bei) arouse s.o.'s suspicion

Stütz|korsett n support corset; **~kurs** m Päd. supplementary course (for weak pupils), Am. remedial course; **~mauer** f retaining wall; **~pfeiler** m supporting pillar, buttress; **~punkt** m **1.** Mil. (military) base; **2.** Tech. fulcrum; **~rad** n supporting wheel; am Kinderfahrrad: stabilizer; **~sprung** m Turnen: supported jump; **~strumpf** m support stocking

Stützung f support; (Unterstützung) auch backing

Stützungskäufe Pl. Wirts. support buying Sg.

Stützverband m Med. support bandage

StVO f; -, kein Pl.; Abk. → Straßenverkehrsordnung

stylen ['stailən] **I.** v/t. design; (Haare) style; **II.** v/refl. umg. give o.s. a makeover; → gestylt; **Styling** ['stailiŋ] n; -s, kein Pl. design, styling

Styropor® n; -s, kein Pl. expanded polystyrene, Am. styrofoam®; **~kleber** m polystyrene adhesive

s.u. Abk. (siehe unten) see below

Suaheli¹ [zʊaˈheːli] n; -(s), kein Pl.; Ling. Swahili

Suaheli² m; -(s), -(s) und f; -, -(s) (Person) Swahili

subalpin Adj. Geog. subalpine

subaltern Adj. **1.** Stellung etc.: subordinate; **2.** pej. Verhalten etc.: (unterwürfig) servile, obsequious; (untertänig) subservient; **Subalterne** m, f; -n, -n **1.** subordinate; bes. Mil. subaltern; **2.** pej. toady

Subjekt n; -(e)s, -e **1.** Ling., Philos. subject; **2.** pej. (Person) individual, character; **übles** ~ *umg.* nasty piece of work

subjektiv I. *Adj.* subjective; *Jur.* → **Tatbestand**; **II.** *Adv.* subjectively; **zu** ~ **urteilen** be too subjective in one's judg(e)ment; **Subjektivismus** *m*; -, *kein Pl.*; *Philos.* subjectivism; **Subjektivität** *f*; -, *kein Pl.* subjectivity

Sub|kategorie *f* subcategory; **~kontinent** *m* subcontinent

Subkultur *f* subculture; **subkulturell** *Adj.* subcultural

subkutan *Adj. Med.* subcutaneous

sublim *Adj. Unterschied, Ironie etc.*: subtle; (*erhaben*) *Gedanke etc.*: sublime; **Sublimation** *f*; -, -en; *Chem.* sublimation; **sublimieren** *v/t.* sublimate; **Sublimierung** *f* sublimation

Subordination *f*; -, -en subordination; **subordinieren** *v/t. und v/refl.* subordinate

subpolar *Adj.* subpolar

subsidiär *Adj.* **1.** (*unterstützend*) supplementary; **2.** (*behelfsmäßig*) provisional; **Subsidiarität** *f*; -, *kein Pl. Pol.* subsidiarity; **Subsidiaritätsprinzip** *n Pol.* subsidiarity principle

Subskribent *m*; -en, -en, **~in** *f*; -, -nen subscriber; **subskribieren I.** *v/t.* subscribe to; **II.** *v/i.*: ~ **auf** (+ *Akk.*) subscribe to; **Subskription** *f*; -, -en subscription; **Subskriptionspreis** *m* subscription price

Subspezies *f Bio.* subspecies

substantiell *Adj.* substantial

Substantiv *n*; -s, -e; *Ling.* noun; **substantivieren** *v/t.* nominalize; **substantiviert I.** *Part. Präs.* → **substantivieren**; **II.** *Adj.*: **~es Adjektiv** nominalized adjective; **substantivisch I.** *Adj.* nominal; **II.** *Adv.* nominally, as a noun

Substanz *f*; -, -en **1.** (*Stoff*) substance; **2.** *Wirts.* capital, assets *Pl.*; **von der** ~ **leben** live on one's capital; **die** ~ **angreifen** draw on one's reserves, spend down one's capital; **3.** *fig.* (*Wesen*) substance; (*Kern*) core; **das geht an die** ~ *umg.* it really takes it out of you; **substanzlos** *Adj.* insubstantial, lacking in substance; **Substanzverlust** *m* loss of substance; *Wirts.* loss of (capital) assets (*od.* reserves), asset erosion

substituieren *v/t.* substitute (**A durch B** B for A)

Substitut[1] *m*; -en, -en; *Wirts.* assistant manager

Substitut[2] *n*; -(e)s, -e; (*Ersatz*) substitute

Substitutin *f*; -, -nen; *Wirts.* assistant manager(ess)

Substitution *f*; -, -en substitution

Substitutionstherapie *f Med.* substitution therapy

Substrat *n*; -(e)s, -e substratum (*Pl.* substrata); *Biol., Chem.* substrate

subsumieren *v/t.* subsume (**unter** + *Dat.* under)

Subsystem *n* subsystem

subtil I. *Adj.* subtle; **II.** *Adv.* subtly; **Subtilität** *f*; -, -en **1.** *nur Sg.; Eigenschaft*: subtlety, subtle nature; **2.** *konkret*: subtlety

Subtrahend *m*; -en, -en; *Math.* subtrahend; **subtrahieren** *v/t.* subtract; **Subtraktion** *f*; -, -en subtraction

Subtropen *Pl.; Geog.* subtropics; **subtropisch** *Adj.* subtropical

Sub|unternehmen *n Wirts.* subcontracting firm, subcontractor; **~unternehmer** *m*, **~unternehmerin** *f* subcontractor

Subvention *f*; -, -en; *Wirts.* subsidy;

subventionieren *v/t.* subsidize; **subventioniert I.** *P.P.* → **subventionieren**; **II.** *Adj.* subsidized; **staatlich** ~ state-subsidized, state-aided; **Subventionierung** *f* subsidization

Subventions|abbau *m Wirts., Pol.* cutback on subsidies; **~betrug** *m* subsidy fraud

Subversion *f*; -, -en; *Pol.* subversion; **subversiv** *Adj.* subversive

Such|aktion *f* search; **polizeiliche** ~ police search (*od.* hunt); → **Suche**; **~anzeige** *f* **1.** (*Vermisstenanzeige*) missing person bulletin; **2.** *Zeitung*: wanted advertisement, *umg.* want ad; **~automatik** *f Etron.* automatic search; **~befehl** *m EDV* search command; **~begriff** *m EDV* search word; **~dienst** *m* tracing service

Suche *f*; -, *kein Pl.* search (*auch EDV*) (*nach* for); *nach e-m Verbrecher*: search hunt (for); *fig. nach Glück etc.*: search (for), quest (for), pursuit (of); **auf der** ~ **nach** in search of; **auf der** ~ **nach Glück** *etc. auch* in quest of happiness *etc.*; **auf der** ~ **sein nach** be looking (*od.* on the lookout) for, be searching for; **sich auf die** ~ **machen** start looking (*nach* for); **die** ~ **ergebnislos abbrechen** abandon the search having found nothing

suchen I. *v/t.* **1.** look for; *intensiver*: search for; (*Frieden, Rat, Trost, Zuflucht etc.*) seek *mst förm.*; (*Vermisste etc.*) try to trace; (*Verbrecher*) hunt (for), try to track down; **du wirst gesucht** they're looking for you, you're wanted *umg.*; **er wird wegen Diebstahls gesucht** he is wanted for robbery; *in Anzeigen*: **Zimmer/Mechaniker gesucht** room/mechanic wanted; **Pilze** ~ look for mushrooms, go mushrooming; **Hilfe** ~ seek help; **Abenteuer** ~ seek adventure; **e-e neue Stelle** ~ look for (*od.* try to find) a new job; **Streit mit j-m** ~ be trying to pick a quarrel with s.o.; **das Weite** ~ take to one's heels; ~ **Sie jemand?** are you looking for someone (*od.* anyone in particular)?; ~ **Sie etwas Bestimmtes?** are you looking for a particular thing (*od.* anything particular)?; **was** ~ **Sie hier?** what are you doing here?; **was suchst du hier?** *auch umg.* what are you after?; **Sie haben hier nichts zu** ~ you have no business here; **das hat hier nichts zu** ~ that has no place here; **die beiden haben sich gesucht und gefunden** those two were made for each other (*od.* are a perfect couple); **sich** (*Dat.*) **e-n Weg durch die Menge** ~ pick one's way through the crowd; **2.** *förm.* (*versuchen*) seek; **j-n zu verstehen** ~ seek (*od.* try) to understand s.o.; **seinesgleichen** ~; **II.** *v/i.* look; *intensiver*: search (**nach** for); **nach Worten** ~ try to find the right words; (*sprachlos sein*) be at a loss for words; **da kannst du lange** ~ you'll never find that; **in allen Taschen/Schränken** ~ search (through) *od.* go through all one's pockets/all the cupboards (*Am.* closets)

Sucher *m*; -s, -; *Fot.* viewfinder

Sucherei *f*; -, -en; *umg.* (constant) searching

Sucherkamera *f* viewfinder camera

Such|funktion *f EDV* search function; **~hund** *m* tracker (*od.* sniffer) dog, blood hound *umg.*

Suchlauf *m Radio, Video etc.*: scanning, search mode (*od.* function); **~au-**

tomatik *f* automatic search; **~taste** *f* cue/review (*od.* scan) button

Such|liste *f* list of missing persons; *der Polizei*: list of wanted persons, wanted list; **~mannschaft** *f* search party; **~maschine** *f EDV* search engine; **~maske** *f EDV* search panel; **~meldung** *f* missing person bulletin (*od.* police message); **~scheinwerfer** *m* searchlight

Sucht *f*; -, *Süchte nach Rauschgift, Alkohol etc.*: addiction (*nach* to); (*übertriebenes Verlangen*) craving (for); (*Manie*) mania (for); **das ist bei ihm zur** ~ **geworden** *Alkohol etc.*: he's become addicted to it; (*zur Manie*) it's become an obsession with him

...sucht *f, im Subst.* **1.** *Med.* addiction; **Betäubungsmittel~** narcotic addiction, addiction to narcotics; **Kokain~** cocaine addiction; **Nikotin~** nicotine addiction; **2.** (*Manie*): **Fernseh~** addiction to (*od.* obsession with) television, TV mania; **Nasch~** addiction to sweet things

Sucht|beratung *f* addiction counsel(l)ing; (*Stelle*) addiction counsel(l)ing cent|re (*Am.* -er); **~gefahr** *f* danger of addiction; **~gefährdete** *m, f*; -n, -n person in danger of addiction, potential addict; **~gift** *n* addictive drug

süchtig *Adj.* **1.** addicted; ~ **werden** become addicted (*nach* to), get hooked (on) *umg.*; ~ **machen** *Droge etc.*: be addictive (*auch fig.*); **2.** ~ **sein nach** (*gierig*) have a craving for, lust after; **er ist** ~ **danach** *auch* it's like a drug for him

...süchtig *im Adj.* **1.** *Med.* addicted to ...; **2.** *fig.*: **fernseh~** addicted to (*od.* obsessed with) television; **nasch~** addicted to sweet things

Süchtige *m, f*; -n, -n addict, junkie *Sl.*

Suchtklinik *f* detoxification (*od.* detox *umg.*) cent|re (*Am.* -er)

suchtkrank *Adj.* addicted; **Suchtkranke** *m, f Med.* addict

Sucht|mittel *n* addictive drug (*od.* substance); **~prävention** *f* prevention of addiction

Suchtrupp *m* search party

Sucht|therapie *f* addiction therapy; **~verhalten** *n* addictive behavio(u)r

Suchwort *n EDV* search word

Sud *m*; -(e)s, -e **1.** *von Gemüse*: cooking water; *von Fleisch und Fisch*: stock; **den Braten aus dem** ~ **nehmen** take the roast out of its juices; **2.** *Chem.* extract, *fachspr.* decoction; **3.** *beim Brauen*: mash

Süd *m* **1.** *ohne Art.*; *nur Nom. Sg.*; *Met., Naut.* south; **von** *od.* **aus** ~ from the south; **2.** *ohne Art.*; *nur Nom. Sg.*; *nachgestellt*: **München** ~ the south of Munich; **Eingang** ~ (the) south entrance; **3.** -(e)s, -e; *Pl. selten*; *Naut., poet.* south wind, southerly

Südafrika (*n*); -s; *Geog.* South Africa

Südafrikaner *m*, **~in** *f* South African, *weiblich auch*: South African woman (*od.* girl) **südafrikanisch** *Adj.* South African

Südamerika (*n*); -s; *Geog.* South America

Südamerikaner *m*, **~in** *f* South American, *weiblich auch*: South American woman (*od.* girl); **südamerikanisch** *Adj.* South American

Sudan *m*; -s; *Geog.*: **der** ~ the Sudan

Sudanese *m*; -n, -n, **Sudanesin** *f*; -, -nen Sudanese, *weiblich auch*: Sudanese woman (*od.* girl); **sudanesisch** *Adj.* Sudanese

Südatlantik *m Geog.* South Atlantic

süddeutsch *Adj.* South German; *im ~en Raum* in the south of Germany, in Southern Germany; **Süddeutsche** *m, f* South German, *weiblich auch:* South German woman (*od.* girl); **Süddeutschland** (*n*) *Geog.* South Germany

Sudelei *f; -, -en; umg. pej.* (*Gepantsche, Schmutz*) mess; **sudeln** *umg. pej.* **I.** *v/i.* (*manschen*) make a mess; **II.** *v/t.* (*kritzeln*) scribble, scrawl

Süden *m; -s, kein Pl.* the south; (*südlicher Landesteil*) South; *von ~* from the south; *nach ~* south(wards); *Verkehr, Fahrbahn etc.:* southbound; *Straße:* to the south, going south; *Balkon nach ~* south-facing balcony; *im ~ Londons/Englands* in South London / the South of England; *im sonnigen ~* in the sunny south; *im Mittelmeerraum:* by the Mediterranean; *im tiefen ~* in the far south; *USA:* in the Deep South, in Dixie(land)

Südengland (*n*) *Geog.* Southern England, the South of England; **südenglisch** *Adj.* southern (*od.* Southern) English

sudetendeutsch *Adj.* Sudeten German; **Sudetendeutsche** *m, f* Sudeten German, *weiblich auch:* Sudeten German woman (*od.* girl); **Sudetenland** *n* Sudetenland

Südeuropa (*n*); *-s; Geog.* Southern Europe

Südeuropäer *m, ~in* f South (*od.* Southern) European, *weiblich auch:* South (*od.* Southern) European woman (*od.* girl); **südeuropäisch** *Adj.* South (*od.* Southern) European

Süd|fenster *n* south-facing window, window facing south; **~flanke** *f* south flank; *e-s Gebirges:* southern escarpment

Südfrankreich (*n*) *Geog.* Southern France, the South of France; **Südfranzose** *m* man from the South of France; **Südfranzösin** *f* woman (*od.* girl) from the South of France; **südfranzösisch** *Adj.* Southern French; *Ort etc.:* in the South of France; *Klima etc.:* of the South of France; *Person, Produkt:* from the South of France

Süd|früchte *Pl.* tropical (*od.* southern) fruits; **~halbkugel** *f Geog.* southern hemisphere; **~hälfte** *f* southern half; **~hang** *m* southern (*od.* south-facing) slope

Sudhaus *n* mashhouse

Süditalien (*n*) *Geog.* Southern Italy, the South of Italy; **Süditaliener** *m* man from the South of Italy; **Süditalienerin** *f* woman (*od.* girl) from the South of Italy; **süditalienisch** *Adj.* Southern Italian; *Ort etc.:* in the South of Italy; *Klima etc.:* of the South of Italy; *Person, Produkt:* from the South of Italy

Südkorea (*n*) *Geog.* South Korea

Südkoreaner *m, ~in* f South Korean, *weiblich auch:* South Korean woman (*od.* girl); **südkoreanisch** *Adj.* South Korean

Süd|kurve *f Sport* south end (*of a football ground*); **~küste** *f* south coast; **~lage** *f* southern aspect

Südländer *m, ~in* f Mediterranean type; **südländisch** *Adj. Klima etc.:* Mediterranean; *Typ: auch* Latin (*auch Temperament*)

südlich **I.** *Adj. attr.* southern, south ...; *Wind:* southerly; *in ~er Richtung* south(wards); *Verkehr, Fahrbahn etc.:*

southbound; *Verkehr auch, Straße:* going south; *das ist sehr weit ~* that's a long way (to the) south; **II.** *Adv.* (to the) south (*von* of); (*weiter*) *~ fahren* go (further) south; (*weiter*) *~ liegen* be (further) to the south; **III.** *Präp.* (+ *Gen.*) (to the) south of; **südlichste** *Adj.* southernmost

Südlicht *n* southern lights *Pl.*, aurora australis

Südost *m; -, kein Pl.* **1.** *ohne Art.* southeast; **2.** *Naut.* (*Wind*) southeasterly

südostasiatisch *Adj.* Southeast Asian; **Südostasien** (*n*) *Geog.* Southeast Asia

Südosten *m* (*abgek.* **SO**) southeast (*Abk.* SE); *der Wind weht aus ~* the wind is from the southeast; *im ~ Englands* in the Southeast of England, in Southeast England

Südosteuropa (*n*) *Geog.* Southeast Europe

Südosteuropäer *m, ~in* f Southeast European, *weiblich auch:* Southeast European woman (*od.* girl); **südosteuropäisch** *Adj.* Southeast European

südöstlich **I.** *Adj. attr.* southeast(ern); *Wind:* southeasterly; **II.** *Adv.* (to the) southeast; **III.** *Präp.* (+ *Gen.*) (to the) southeast of

Südpazifik *m Geog.* the South Pacific

Südpol *m Geog.* South Pole

Südpolar|gebiet *n* Antarctic; **~meer** *n* Antarctic Ocean

Südrand *m* southern edge; *e-r Schlucht:* south rim

Südsee *f Geog.: die ~* the South Seas *Pl.*, the (South) Pacific; **~insel** *f* South Sea (*od.* Pacific) island; **~insulaner** *m, ~insulanerin* f South Sea (*od.* Pacific) islander

Süd|seite *f* south (*od.* southern) side; **~spitze** *f e-r Insel:* southern tip

Südstaaten *Pl.: die ~ der USA:* the Southern States, the South; **Südstaatler** *m; -s, - 1., auch* **Südstaatlerin** *f; -, -nen in den USA:* Southerner; **2.** *hist.* Confederate

Südsüdost *m; -, kein Pl.* **1.** *ohne Art.* south-southeast; **2.** *Naut.* (*Wind*) south-southeasterly; **Südsüdosten** *m* south-southeast; **Südsüdwest** *m; -, kein Pl.* **1.** *ohne Art.* south-southwest; **2.** *Naut.* (*Wind*) south-southwesterly; **Südsüdwesten** *m* south-southwest

Südteil *m* southern part

Südtirol (*n*) *Geog.* South Tyrol; *italienisches Gebiet:* Alto Adige

Südtiroler¹ *m*, **Südtirolerin** *f* South Tyrolean, *weiblich auch:* South Tyrolean woman (*od.* girl)

Südtiroler², **südtirolerisch** *Adj.* South Tyrolean

Südufer *n* south bank

südwärts *Adv.* south(wards)

Südwest *m; -, kein Pl.* **1.** *ohne Art.* southwest; **2.** *Naut.* (*Wind*) southwesterly; **Südwesten** *m* (*abgek.* **SW**) southwest (*Abk.* SW); **Südwester** *m; -s, -;* (*Hut*) sou'wester; **südwestlich** **I.** *Adj.* southwest(ern); *Wind:* southwesterly; **II.** *Adv.* (to the) southwest; **III.** *Präp.* (+ *Gen.*) (to the) southwest of

Südwest|rundfunk *m* (*abgek.* **SWR**) Southwest German Radio; **~wind** *m* southwest wind, southwesterly (wind)

Südwind *m* south wind, southerly (wind)

Sues|kanal *m Geog.: der ~* the Suez Canal; **~krise** *f hist.* Suez crisis

Suff *m; -(e)s, kein Pl.; umg.* alcohol;

(*Trinken*) boozing; *sich dem ~ ergeben* take to (*od.* hit) the bottle; *dem ~ verfallen sein* be on the bottle; *er hat es im ~ gesagt* he said that when under the influence, he'd had a few when he said that

süffeln *vt/i. umg.* tipple; *Spätlese ~* quaff (*genüsslich:* savo[u]r) a Spätlese

süffig *Adj. Wein:* palatable; *dieser Wein ist sehr ~ auch* this wine goes down well

süffisant *pej.* **I.** *Adj.* smug, complacent; **II.** *Adv. lächeln, bemerken:* smugly, complacently; **Süffisanz** *f; -, kein Pl.* smugness, complacency

Suffix *n; -es, -e; Ling.* suffix

Suffragette [zufra'gɛtə] *f; -, -n; hist.* suffragette

suggerieren *v/t.* suggest; *j-m etw. ~* put s.th. into s.o.'s mind; *j-m ~, dass ...* talk s.o. into thinking (*od.* believing) that ...

Suggestion *f; -, -en* suggestion

suggestiv *Adj.* suggestive; **Suggestivfrage** *f* leading question

Suhle *f; -, -n* muddy pool; **suhlen** *v/refl.* wallow (*auch fig.*)

Sühne *f; -, kein Pl.* expiation, atonement; (*Buße*) penance; *~ leisten für* do penance for; **sühnen** *geh.* **I.** *v/t.* expiate, atone for; *e-e Schuld mit dem Tod ~* pay the ultimate penalty for one's guilt; **II.** *v/i.: für etw. ~* atone for s.th.

Sühne|opfer *n* expiatory sacrifice; **~versuch** *m Jur.* attempt at reconciliation

Suite ['sviːtə] *f; -, -n* **1.** (*Zimmerflucht*) suite (of rooms); **2.** *Mus.* suite

Suizid *m; -(e)s, -e, förm.* suicide; **suizidgefährdet** *Adj.* close to suicide; *~ sein auch* have suicidal tendencies, be a potential suicide; **Suizidversuch** *m* suicide attempt

Sujet [zy'ʒeː] *n; -s, -s Kunst:* subject

Sukkade *f; -,-n* candied peel

Sukkulente *f; -, -n; Bot.* succulent

Sukzession *f; -, -en* succession

sukzessiv *Adj.* gradual; *~e Veränderung auch* step-by-step change; **sukzessive** *Adv.* little by little, step by step

Sulfat *n; -(e)s, -e; Chem.* sulphate, *Am.* sulfate

Sulfid *n; -(e)s, -e; Chem.* sulphide, *Am.* sulfide

Sulfit *n; -s, -e; Chem.* sulphite, *Am.* sulfite

Sulfonamid *n; -(e)s, -e; Pharm.* sulphonamide, *Am.* sulfonamide; *Pl. auch* sulpha (*Am.* sulfa) drugs

Sulky ['zʊlki] *n; -s, -s Pferdesport:* sulky

Sultan *m; -s, -e* sultan; **Sultanat** *n; -(e)s, -e* sultanate; **Sultanin** *f; -, -nen* sultana

Sultanine *f; -, -n; Gastr.* (*Rosine*) sultana

Sülze *f; -, -n; Gastr.* (*Speise*) diced meat (*od.* brawn) in aspic, *Am.* headcheese; (*Aspik*) aspic

sülzen *v/i. umg. pej.* blether (*Am.* blather) on; *bes. um etw. zu erreichen:* give a long-winded spiel

sulzig *Adj. Schnee:* slushy

Sulzschnee *m* slush

Sumerer *m; -s, -; hist.* Sumerian; **sumerisch** **I.** *Adj.* Sumerian; **II. Sumerisch** *n; -(s); Ling. hist.* Sumerian; *das Sumerische* Sumerian

summarisch **I.** *Adj.* summary (*auch Jur.*); **II.** *Adv.* summarily; *~ zusammenfassen* summarize

S

summa summarum *Adv. kosten etc.*: in total; (*alles in allem gesehen*) all in all, when everything is taken into account; *der Umzug hat ~ 11 500 Euro gekostet* the removal (*Am.* moving) costs came to a grand total of 11,500 euros

Sümmchen *n umg.*: *ein hübsches ~* a tidy little sum

Summe *f; -, -n* sum; (*Gesamtsumme*) *auch* (sum) total; (*Betrag*) amount; *fig. des Wissens etc.*: sum total; *e-e schöne ~* a handsome sum; *die ~ s-r Tätigkeit ziehen fig.* sum up what one has achieved

summen I. *vt/i. Insekt etc.*: buzz; *weicher*: hum; *eintönig*: drone; *vor sich hin ~* hum away to oneself; *e-e Melodie ~* hum a tune; **II. Summen** *n, -s, kein Pl.* buzz(ing); *weicher*: hum(ming); (*Geräusch*) buzzing (*od.* humming) noise

Summer *m; -s, -; Etech.* buzzer

summieren I. *v/t.* add up; **II.** *v/refl.* add (*od.* mount) up (*auf + Akk, zu* to); *es summiert sich* it all adds up

Summton *m* buzz, buzzing signal; *Telef.* dialling (*Am.* dial) tone

Sumo *n; -, kein Pl., ~ringen n Sport* sumo wrestling; *~ringer m* sumo wrestler

Sumpf *m; -(e)s, Sümpfe* **1.** marsh; *weitläufiger, bes.* (*sub*)*tropisch*: swamp; (*kleineres Gebiet*) bog; **2.** *fig.* quagmire; *ein ~ der Korruption* a morass of corruption; *~biber m Zool.* (*Nutria*) coypu; *~blüte f umg. fig. pej.* evil excrescence; *~dotterblume f* marsh marigold

sumpfen *v/i. umg.* live it up until a late hour, carouse the night away

Sumpf|fieber *n Med.* marsh fever, malaria; *~gas n* marsh gas; *~gebiet n* marsh(land); *bes.* (*sub*)*tropisch*: swamp; *~huhn n* **1.** *Orn.* crake; **2.** *umg. hum.* boozer

sumpfig *Adj.* marshy; *bes.* (*sub*)*tropisch*: swampy

Sumpf|land *n* marsh(land); *bes.* (*sub*)*tropisch*: swamp; *~otter m Zool.* (*Nerz*) mink; *~pflanze f Bot.* marsh plant; *~schildkröte f Zool.* mud turtle; *~vogel m Orn.* wader; *~zypresse f Bot.* swamp (*od.* bald) cypress

Sums *m; -es, kein Pl.; umg.* fuss, *Brit. auch* carry-on; *mach nicht so e-n ~* don't make such a fuss

Sund *m; -(e)s, -e; Geog.* sound, strait

Sünde *f; -, -n* sin; *e-e ~ begehen* commit a sin, sin; *s-e ~n beichten* confess one's sins; *j-m s-e ~n vergeben* forgive s.o. his (*od.* her) sins; *für s-e ~n büßen* atone for one's sins; *die ~n der Städteplaner* the misdeeds of the town planners; *das ist doch keine ~* it's not a crime

Sünden|babel *n* sink (*Stätte*: den) of iniquity, hotbed of vice; *~bekenntnis n* confession of one's sins; *~bock m* scapegoat, fall guy *umg.*; *j-n zum ~ machen* use s.o. as a scapegoat; *~fall m: der ~* the Fall (of Man); *~register n umg.* catalog(ue) of transgressions (*od.* misdeeds)

Sünder *m; -s, -* sinner; *armer ~* poor wretch; *du alter ~!* umg. you old devil!; **Sünderin** *f, -, -nen* sinner

sündhaft I. *Adj.* sinful, wicked; *ein ~er Preis umg. fig.* a shocking (*stärker*: outrageous) price; **II.** *Adv.*: *~ teuer umg. fig.* shockingly (*stärker*: outrageously) expensive; **Sündhaftigkeit** *f* sinfulness

sündig *Adj.* sinful; (*schuldig*) guilty; *~ werden an* (+ *Dat.*) sin against; *die ~ste Meile der Welt* the world's most notorious vice strip

sündigen *v/i.* **1.** sin (*gegen* against); *an j-m ~* sin against (*od.* wrong) s.o.; **2.** *fig. auf e-m Gebiet*: commit a sin; **3.** *umg.* (*zu viel essen etc.*) (over)indulge; *Weihnachten haben wir wieder zu viel gesündigt* we overindulged (*od.* overdid it) again at Christmas

super *umg.* **I.** *indekl. Adj. und Interj.* super, great; *e-e ~ Schau* a brilliant (*od.* fantastic) show; **II.** *Adv.* fantastically; *sie hat ~ gespielt* she played fantastically well; *er war ~ gut drauf* (*war gut gelaunt*) he was in a fantastic mood; (*bot eine fantastische Leistung*) he did fantastically well; *wir haben uns ~ erholt* we feel tons better

Super *n; -s, kein Pl.* **1.** *verbleit*: four--star (petrol), *Am.* premium (gas); **2.** *~ bleifrei* super unleaded

Superbenzin *n* **1.** *verbleit*: four-star (petrol), *Am.* premium (gas); **2.** *bleifreies ~* super unleaded

superbillig *Adj. umg.* ultra-cheap, fantastically cheap

Super|cup *m Sport* Cup Winners' Cup; *~ding n umg.* (real) humdinger

superfein *Adj. umg.* **1.** *Güter*: top-quality; *Qualität*: top; **2.** *Menschen*: terribly superior

Superfrau *f umg.* superwoman

Super|-G ['zu:pɐdʒi:] *m; -(s), -(s) Skisport*: super-G; *~-GAU m* worst-case scenario nuclear accident

supergeil *Adj. umg.* (*toll*) supercool, dead wicked

supergescheit *Adj. umg.* incredibly clever; *iro.* (*allzu gescheit*) too clever by half; **Supergescheite** *m, f; -n, -n; umg.* superbrain; *iro.* know-all, *Am.* know-it-all

Superheld *m umg.* superhero

Superintendent *m; -en, -en, ~in f; -, -nen; ev.* dean

superklug *Adj. umg. iro.* too clever by half

Superlativ *m Ling., fig.* superlative; *ein Land der ~e* a country of superlatives (*od.* with the best of everything); **superlativisch** *Adj. Ling., fig.* superlative

superleicht *Adj.* **1.** *umg.* (*einfach*) dead (*Am.* too) easy; *~ sein auch* be a cinch; **2.** *im Gewicht*: ultra-light(-weight); **Superleichtgewicht** *n Sport* super-lightweight

Super|macht *f Pol.* superpower; *~mann m umg.* superman

Supermarkt *m* supermarket; *großer*: *auch* superstore

Super|minister *m, ~ministerin f* superminister (*who took on two or more different portfolios*)

supermodern *Adj.* ultramodern

Super|nova *f; -, Supernovä; Astron.* supernova (*Pl.* supernovae *od.* supernovas); *~phosphat n Chem.* superphosphate; *~preis m umg.* fantastic (*od.* incredible) price; *~sache f umg.* fantastic thing

super|schick *Adj. umg.* ultra hip, *Brit. auch* dead chic; *~schnell umg.* **I.** *Adj.* incredibly fast, *präd. auch* like greased lightning; **II.** *Adv.* quick as a flash, in no time; *~schwer Adj. umg.* ultraheavy, extra heavy

Superschwergewicht *n Sport* superheavyweight; **Superschwergewichtler** *m Sport* superheavyweight

Super|sparpreis *m umg.* supersaver; *~star m* superstar; *~tanker m* supertanker; *~weib n umg.* fantastic looker; *~zeichen n EDV* supersign

Süppchen *n: sein eigenes ~ kochen umg. fig.* do one's own thing

Suppe *f; -, -n; Gastr.* soup; *klare ~* clear soup; *die ~ auslöffeln müssen umg. fig.* have to face the consequences (of one's actions); *j-m/sich* (*Dat.*) *e-e schöne ~ einbrocken umg.* get s.o./o.s. into a nice mess; *j-m die ~ versalzen umg. fig.* spoil s.o.'s (*od.* all the) fun; (*Pläne durchkreuzen*) throw a spanner (*Am.* wrench) in the works

Suppen|einlage *f Gastr.* noodles, dumplings, rice etc. added to clear soup; *~extrakt m* soup concentrate; *~fleisch n* meat for making soup; *~gemüse n* vegetables for making soup; *~grün n; -(s), kein Pl.* bunch of herbs and vegetables for flavo(u)ring soup; *~huhn n* boiling fowl; *~kasper m; -s; umg.* soup-hater; *~kelle f* soup ladle; *~knochen m* soup bone; *~küche f* soup kitchen; *~löffel m* soup spoon; *~nudeln Pl.* noodles for soup; *~schildkröte f* green turtle; *~schüssel f* soup tureen; *~tasse f* soup cup; *~teller m* soup plate; *~terrine f* (soup) tureen; *~würfel m* stock cube

Supplement *n; -(e)s, -e* supplement; **supplementär** *Adj.* supplementary

Supplement|band *m* supplement(ary volume)

Suppositorium *n; -s, Suppositorien; Pharm.* suppository

Supraleiter *m Etech.* superconductor

supranational *Adj.* supranational

Supremat *m, n; -(e)s, -e,* **Suprematie** *f; -,* supremacy

Sure *f; -, -n; Reli.* sura(h)

Surfboard ['zɐːɐfboːɐt] *n; -s, -s,* **Surfbrett** ['zɐːɐfbrɛt] *n Sport Wellenreiten*: surfboard; *Windsurfen*: sailboard, windsurfer

surfen ['zɐːɐfn] **I.** *v/i.* **1.** surf; *im Internet ~ umg. fig.* surf the internet; **2.** *Sport* windsurf; **II.** *v/t; -s, kein Pl.* **1.** surfing; **2.** *Sport* windsurfing; **Surfer** *m; -s, -,* **Surferin** *f; -, -nen* **1.** surfer (*auch im Internet*); **2.** windsurfer

Surrealismus *m; -, kein Pl.; Kunst* surrealism; **Surrealist** *m; -en, -en,* **Surrealistin** *f; -, -nen* surrealist; **surrealistisch I.** *Adj.* surrealistic, *attr. auch* surrealist …; **II.** *Adv.* surrealistically

surren *v/i.* **1.** (*hat gesurrt*) *Kamera, Motor etc.*: whirr, *Am.* whir; *leiser*: hum; *Insekt*: buzz; **2.** (*ist*): *e-e Fliege surrte durch die Luft* a fly buzzed through the air

Surrogat *n; -(e)s, -e; fachspr.* substitute, surrogate

suspekt *Adj.* suspect, suspicious; (*fragwürdig*) *auch* dubious; *er ist mir ~* I'm not so sure about him

suspendieren *v/t.* suspend; *vom Dienst/Training ~* suspend from his (*od.* her) post/from training; **Suspendierung** *f* suspension; **Suspension** *f; -, -en; auch Chem.* suspension; **suspensiv** *Adj.*: *~es Veto* power of delay

Suspensorium *n; -s, Suspensorien* **1.** *Med.* suspensory bandage, sling; **2.** *Sport* jockstrap, athletic support; *Ballspiele*: box

süß I. *Adj.* **1.** sweet (*auch umg. goldig*); *Klang*: *auch* melodious; *~es Ding umg.* sweet (*bes. Am. auch* cute) little thing; *gern ~e Sachen essen* have a sweet tooth; *etwas Süßes zum Nach-*

tisch something sweet for dessert; **ach, wie ~!** oh, how sweet (*Kind etc.*: *auch* cute)!; **2.** (*übertrieben freundlich*): **~es Lächeln** sugary smile; **~e Reden** honeyed words; **II.** *Adv.* sweetly; **~ schmecken/duften** have a sweet taste/scent

Süße[1] *f*; -, *kein Pl.* sweetness

Süße[2] *m, f*; -*n*, -*n*; *umg.* sweetie, sweetheart; **hallo, ihr ~n!** hi there, girls (*bzw.* boys)!

süßen *vt/i.* sweeten; (*zuckern*) *auch* add sugar to; *Kaffee etc.*: put sugar in; **ich süße mit Honig** I use honey as a sweetener

Süßholz *n* liquorice, *bes. Am.* licorice; **~ raspeln** *umg. fig.* turn on the charm

Süßigkeiten *Pl.* sweets, *Am.* candy *Sg.*

Süß|kartoffel *f Bot.* sweet potato, *Am. auch* yam; **~kirsche** *f Bot.* sweet cherry

süßlich I. *Adj.* **1.** (*leicht süß*) sweetish; *pej.* (*unangenehm*) sickly sweet; **leicht ~** on the sweet side; **2.** *fig.* (*kitschig*) sickly (sweet); (*sentimental*) mawkish; *Miene, Stimme etc.*: *auch* ever so sweet *umg.*; *Lächeln*: sugary; **II.** *Adv.* **1.** *riechen, schmecken*: sickly sweet; **2.** *fig.* **~ lächeln** give a sugary smile; **Süßlichkeit** *f* **1.** slight sweetness; *pej. unangenehm*: sickly sweetness; **2.** *fig.* (*kitschige Art*) sickliness, (*Sentimentalität*) mawkishness; *e-s Lächelns*: sugariness

Süßmost *m Gastr.* unfermented fruit juice

Süßrahmbutter *f Gastr.* creamery butter

süßsauer I. *Adj.* **1.** *Gastr.* sweet and sour; **2.** *Lächeln*: forced; **II.** *Adv.*: **~ eingelegte Gurken** pickled gherkins, *Am.* (cucumber) pickles

Süß|speise *f Gastr.* sweet, dessert; **~stoff** *m Gastr.* sweetener; **~waren** *Pl.* confectionery *Sg., Am.* candy *Sg.*

Süßwasser *n* fresh water; **Süßwasser...** *im Subst.* freshwater ...; **~fisch** *m Zool.* freshwater fish; **~polyp** *m Zool.* hydra

Süßwein *m* dessert wine

SV *m*; -; *Abk.* (**Sportverein**) SC

svw. *Abk.* (**so viel wie**) → **so** I 8

SW *Abk.* (**Südwest[en]**) SW

Swasiland (*n*); -*s* Swaziland

Sweatshirt ['svɛtʃøːɐ̯t] *n*; -*s*, -*s* sweatshirt

Swimmingpool ['svɪmɪŋpuːl] *m*; -*s*, -*s* swimming pool

Swing [svɪŋ] *m*; -(*s*), -*s*; *Mus.* **1.** *nur Sg.* (*Jazzrichtung*) swing; **2.** (*Tanz*) swing; **~ tanzen** swing; **3.** *nur Sg.*; *Wirts.* swing; **swingen** ['svɪŋən] *v/i.* **1.** *Mus., Stück*: have a swing to it; *Spieler*: swing it; **2.** *Sl.* (*Gruppensex betreiben*) swing; **Swinger** ['svɪŋɐ] *m*; -*s*, - **1.** (*Mantel*) swing coat; **2.** *Sl.* (*auch* **Swingerin**; *f*; -, -*nen*) (*Person*) swinger; **Swinging** ['svɪŋɪŋ] *n*; -*s*, *kein Pl.*; *Sl.* (*Gruppensex*) swinging

SWR *Abk.* → **Südwestrundfunk**

syllabisch I. *Adj.* syllabic; **II.** *Adv.* syllabically

Syllogismus *m*; -, *Syllogismen* syllogism; **syllogistisch I.** *Adj.* syllogistic; **II.** *Adv.* syllogistically

Symbiose *f*; -, -*n* symbiosis (*Pl.* symbioses); **symbiotisch I.** *Adj.* symbiotic; **II.** *Adv.* symbiotically

Symbol *n*; -*s*, -*e* symbol (**für** of *od. Gen.*); (*Zeichen*) *auch* sign; *EDV* symbol; (*Merkmal*) badge; **~charakter** *m* symbolic character (*od.* meaning); **~figur** *f* symbolic figure (**für** for *od.*

Gen.), symbol (of); **~gehalt** *m* symbolic content

symbolhaft I. *Adj.* symbolic (**für** of); **II.** *Adv.* symbolically; **Symbolhaftigkeit** *f* symbolic nature; **Symbolik** *f*; -, *kein Pl.* symbolism; **symbolisch I.** *Adj.* symbolic (**für** of); **~er Beitrag** token contribution; **II.** *Adv.* symbolically; **~ darstellen** be a symbol of, symbolize; **~ zu verstehen** to be taken symbolically; **symbolisieren** *v/t.* symbolize; **Symbolismus** *m Kunst* Symbolism

Symbol|kraft *f* symbolic power; **~leiste** *f EDV* toolbar; **~sprache** *f auch EDV* symbolic language

symbolträchtig *Adj.* highly (*od.* deeply) symbolic, steeped in symbolism; **Symbolträchtigkeit** *f* highly symbolic nature, deep symbolism

Symbolwert *m* symbolic value (*od.* significance)

Symmetrie *f*; -, -*n* symmetry (*auch fig.*); **~achse** *f Math.* axis of symmetry, symmetric axis; **~ebene** *f Math.* plane of symmetry

symmetrisch I. *Adj.* symmetrical; *Math. auch* symmetric; **II.** *Adv.* symmetrically

Sympathie *f*; -, -*n*; (*Zuneigung*) liking; (*Anteilnahme*) sympathy; (*Unterstützung*) support; **bei aller ~** much as I like him (*od.* her, them *etc.*); **große ~n genießen bei** be very popular among, be well-liked among; **der Plan hat m-e volle ~** the plan has my full support (*od.* backing); **~bekundung** *f* demonstration of sympathy; **~kundgebung** *f* demonstration of support; **~streik** *m* sympathy (*od.* sympathetic) strike; **~träger** *m*, **~trägerin** *f* sympathetic figure; *beliebt*: popular figure; **~welle** *f* wave of sympathy

Sympathikus *m*; -, *kein Pl.*; *Physiol.* sympathetic nervous system; (*einzelner Nerv*) sympathetic nerve

Sympathisant *m*; -*en*, -*en* sympathizer; **Sympathisantentum** *n*; -*s*, *kein Pl.* group of sympathizers; **Sympathisantin** *f*; -, -*nen* (female) sympathizer

sympathisch *Adj.* **1.** lik(e)able, congenial, (very) pleasant, personable, (very) nice *umg.*; *Stimme, Art, Lächeln etc.*: pleasant, engaging, nice *umg.*; **er ist mir ~** I think he's nice, I like him; **er ist mir überhaupt nicht ~** I don't like him at all; **2.** *Physiol.* sympathetic

sympathisieren *v/i.*: **~ mit** sympathize with; **mit den Kommunisten** *etc.* **~** *auch* be a communist *etc.* sympathizer

Symphonie(...) *siehe* **Sinfonie(...)**; **Symphoniker** *m*; -*s*, - **1.** → **Sinfoniker** 1; **2.** (*Orchestermitglied*) member of a symphony orchestra; **die Wiener ~** the Vienna Symphony Orchestra; **symphonisch** *Adj.* → **sinfonisch**

Symposion *n*; -*s*, *Symposien*, **Symposium** *n*; -*s*, *Symposien* symposium (*Pl.* symposia *od.* symposiums)

Symptom *n*; -*s*, -*e*; *auch fig.* symptom (**für** of); **~e von etw. zeigen** *auch* show signs of s.th.; **Symptomatik** *f*; -, *kein Pl.* **1.** *e-r Krankheit*: symptoms *Pl.*; **2.** (*Fach*) symptomatology; **symptomatisch I.** *Adj. auch fig.* symptomatic (**für** of); **II.** *Adv.* symptomatically

Synagoge *f*; -, -*n* synagogue

Synapse *f*; -, -*n*; *Physiol.* synapse

Synästhesie *f*; -, -*n*; *Med., Psych., Lit.* syn(a)esthesia

synchron I. *Adj.* synchronous; *Ling. etc.* synchronic; **II.** *Adv.*: **~ laufen** *od.*

geschaltet sein be synchronized; **Bild und Ton laufen nicht ~** picture and sound are out of sync *umg.*

Synchron|fassung *f* (*Film*) dubbed version; **~getriebe** *n Mot.* synchromesh gearbox (*bes. Am.* transmission)

Synchronie *f*; -, *kein Pl.*; *Ling.* synchrony

Synchronisation *f*; -, -*en* synchronization; *Film*: dubbing; **synchronisieren** *v/t.* synchronize; (*Film*) dub; **synchronisch** *Adj. Ling. etc.*: synchronic; **synchronisiert I.** *P.P.* → **synchronisieren**; **II.** *Adj.* synchronized; *Mot., Getriebe*: synchromesh; *Film, in e-r Fremdsprache*: dubbed; **~e Fassung** dubbed version; **der Film ist ~** the film has been dubbed; **deutsch** *etc.* **~** dubbed in German *etc.*, with a German *etc.* soundtrack

Synchron|schwimmen *n Sport* synchronized swimming; **~sprecher** *m* dubbing actor; **~sprecherin** *f* dubbing actress; **~stimme** *f* **1.** dubbing voice; **2.** *im fertigen Film*: dubbed voice

Syndikat *n*; -(*e*)*s*, -*e* syndicate; **zu e-m ~ zusammenschließen** form a syndicate, syndicate

Syndikus *m*; -, -*se und Syndizi*; *Jur.* company lawyer (*od.* legal adviser), *Am.* corporation counsel

Syndrom *n*; -*s*, -*e*; *Med. und weitS.* syndrome

synergetisch *Adj.* synergetic; **Synergie** *f*; -, *kein Pl.* synergy; **Synergieeffekt** *m* synergetic effect

Synkope *f*; -, -*n*; *Ling.* syncope; *Mus.* syncopation; **synkopieren** *v/t. Mus., Ling.* syncopate; **synkopisch** *Adj. Mus.* syncopated; *Ling.* syncopal

Synkretismus *m*; -, *kein Pl.* syncretism; **synkretistisch** *Adj.* syncretic

Synodale *m, f*; -*n*, -*n* synod member; **Synode** *f*; -, -*n* synod

synonym *Adj.* synonymous (**zu** with); **Synonym** *n*; -*s*, -*e und Synonyma*; *Ling.* synonym; **Synonymik** *f*; -, -*en* **1.** *nur Sg.* (*Fachgebiet*) synonymics *Pl.* (*V. im Sg.*); **2.** (*Buch*) dictionary of synonyms; thesaurus; **Synonymwörterbuch** *n* dictionary of synonyms; (*Thesaurus*) thesaurus

Synopse *f*; -, -*n*, **Synopsis** *f*; -, *Synopsen* overall view; (*Abriss e-r Handlung*) synopsis (*Pl.* synopses); **Synoptiker** *m*; -*s*, - Synoptist; **synoptisch I.** *Adj.* synoptic; **die ~en Evangelien** the Synoptic Gospels; **II.** *Adv.* synoptically

Syntagma *n*; -*s*, *Syntagmen und Syntagmata*; *Ling.* syntagm; **syntagmatisch I.** *Adj.* syntagmatic; **II.** *Adv.* syntagmatically

syntaktisch *Ling.* **I.** *Adj. attr.* syntactic(al); **II.** *Adv.* syntactically

Syntax *f*; -, *kein Pl.*; *Ling.* syntax; **~fehler** *m* error of syntax, syntactical error

Synthese *f*; -, -*n* synthesis (*Pl.* syntheses)

Synthesizer ['zʏntəsaizɐ] *m*; -*s*, - synthesizer

Synthetik (*n*); -*s*, *kein Pl.* synthetic (fib|re [*Am.* -er]), man-made fib|re (*Am.* -er); **das ist alles ~** it's all synthetic(s); **synthetisch I.** *Adj.* synthetic; **II.** *Adv.*: **~ herstellen** produce synthetically; **synthetisieren** *v/t. Chem.* synthetize

Syphilis *f*; -, *kein Pl. Med.* syphilis; **syphiliskrank** *Adj. attr.* syphilitic; **syphilitisch** *Adj.* syphilitic

Syrien (*n*); -*s* *Geog.* Syria; **Syrer** *m*;

-s, -, **Syrerin** *f*; *-, -nen* Syrian, *weiblich auch*: Syrian woman (*od.* girl *etc.*); **syrisch** *Adj.* Syrian
System *n*; *-s, -e* system; (*Methode*) *auch* method; *der Eisenbahn etc.*: system, network; *mit ~ arbeiten* work systematically (*od.* methodically); *dahinter steckt ~* there's method in (*od.* to) it; *in ein ~ bringen* systematize; *ein ~ spielen Lotto*: use a system; *allg.* gamble (*Roulette etc.*: play) with a system; **~absturz** *m EDV* system crash; **~analyse** *f* systems analysis; **~analytiker** *m*, **~analytikerin** *f* systems analyst
Systematik *f*; *-, -en* **1.** (*Aufbau*) system, method; **2.** (*Lehre*) systematics *Pl.* (*V. im Sg.*); **Systematiker** *m*; *-s, -*, **Systematikerin** *f*; *-, -nen* systematist; *weitS.* systematic person; **systematisch I.** *Adj.* systematic, methodical; **II.** *Adv.* systematically; **systematisieren** *v/t.* systematize
Systembauweise *f* system building
systembedingt I. *Adj.* system-related; **II.** *Adv.* in a system-related manner
System|datei *f EDV* system file; **~fehler** *m EDV* system error
systemimmanent *Adj.* inherent in a (*od.* the) system
systemisch *Adj. Bio.* systemic
systemkonform I. *Adj.* (politically) conformist; **II.** *Adv.*: *sich ~ verhalten* conform (to the political system)
Systemkritik *f* criticism of the system; **Systemkritiker** *m*, **Systemkritikerin** *f* dissident; **systemkritisch** *Adj. attr.* dissident …
systemlos I. *Adj.* unsystematic, unmethodical; **II.** *Adv.* vorgehen *etc.*: without any system
System|software *f EDV* system software; **~steuerung** *f EDV* system control; **~theorie** *f* systems theory; **~veränderung** *f* change in the system; **~vergleich** *m* comparison of systems; **~wechsel** *m* change of system; **~wette** *f Lotto etc.*: gamble according to a system; **~zwang** *m* imposed conformism
Systole *f*; *-, -n*; *Med.* systole; **systolisch** *Adj. Med. Blutdruck*: systolic
Szenario *n*; *-s, -s*, **Szenarium** *n*; *-s, Szenarien* scenario
Szene *f*; *-, -n* **1.** scene (*auch Theat.*, *auch Anblick, Schauplatz*); *in ~ setzen Theat., fig.* stage; *sich in ~ setzen fig.* draw attention to o.s., put o.s. into the limelight; *die ~ betreten* come on the scene; **2.** (*Streit*) scene; (*j-m*) *e-e ~ machen* make a scene (for s.o.'s benefit); **3.** *politische, literarische etc.*: scene; *die ~ umg.* alternative society

...szene *f*, *im Subst.* **1.** *Theat., Film*: scene; **Massen~** crowd scene; **Schluss~** final scene; **2.** (*Bereich*) *mst* scene; **Drogen~** drugs scene; **Musik~** music scene (*od.* world)
Szene|gänger *m umg.* hipster, *member of a fashionable subculture*; **~kneipe** *f umg.* hip joint, *bar fashionable with a certain clique*
Szenen|applaus *m* spontaneous applause; **~bild** *n* (stage) set, stage setting; **~folge** *f* sequence of scenes; **~wechsel** *m* scene change; *fig.* change of scene
Szenerie *f*; *-, -n* **1.** (*Bühnendekoration*) scenery; **2.** (*Schauplatz*) setting; **3.** (*Landschaft*) scenery
Szenetreff *m umg.* meeting place for members of a fashionable clique
szenisch I. *Adj.* scenic; **~e Darstellung** staging, (stage) presentation; **II.** *Adv.* scenically; **~ darstellen** stage, put on stage
Szepter *n*; *-s, -* scept|re (*Am.* -er)
Szintigramm *n*; *-s, -e*; *Med.* scintigram; **Szintigraphie** *f*; *-, kein Pl.*; *Med.* scintigraphy
Szylla *f*: *zwischen ~ und Charybdis* between Scylla and Charybdis, between the devil and the deep blue sea

T, t *n*; -, - T, t; *T wie Theodor* Buchstabieren: "t" for (*od.* as in) "Tango"

Tabak *m*; -*s*, -*e* tobacco; ~ **schnupfen** snuff, take snuff; **~anbau** *m* tobacco growing (*od.* cultivation *od.* farming); **~blatt** *n* tobacco leaf; **~ernte** *f* **1.** (*das Ernten*) tobacco harvest(ing); **2.** (*Ertrag*) tobacco crop; **~fabrik** *f zur Verarbeitung*: tobacco processing plant; (*Zigarettenfabrik*) cigarette factory; **~geschäft** *n* tobacconist's, *Am.* cigar store, smoke shop; **~händler** *m*, **~händlerin** *f* tobacconist; **~industrie** *f* tobacco industry; **~laden** *m* tobacconist's, *Am.* cigar store, smoke shop; **~mischung** *f* blend of tobacco; **~monopol** *n* tobacco monopoly; **~pflanze** *f* tobacco plant; **~plantage** *f* tobacco plantation; **~qualm** *m* tobacco smoke

Tabaks|beutel *m* tobacco pouch; **~dose** *f* tobacco tin; *für Schnupftabak*: snuffbox; **~pfeife** *f* pipe

Tabak|steuer *f* tobacco duty; **~waren** *Pl.* tobacco products, cigarettes and tobacco; *Geschäftsschild*: tobacconist, *Am.* tobacco; **~werbung** *f* cigarette (*für Pfeifentabak*: tobacco) advertising (*od.* advertisements *Pl.*)

Tabatiere [taba'tie:rə] *f*; -, -*n* **1.** *bes. österr.* (*Tabaksdose*) tobacco tin; **2.** *bes. österr.* (*Zigarettenetui*) cigarette case; **3.** *altm. für Schnupftabaksdose*: snuffbox

tabellarisch *Adj.* tabular, tabulated; **~er Lebenslauf** curriculum vitae (*od.* CV, *Am.* résumé) (set out) in tabular form; **tabellarisieren** *v/t.* tabulate

Tabelle *f*; -, -*n* table; *graphische*: chart; *Sport und fig.*: league table; **ganz oben/unten in der ~** *Sport* at the top/bottom of the table; **die ~ anführen** be league leaders, be at the top of the (league) table, head the (league) table

Tabellen|ende *n*: (**am ~** at the) bottom of the league (*od.* table), *Am. umg.* (be) cellar-dwelling; **~erste** *m*, *f* league leaders Pl.; **Tabellenerster sein** *auch* be (at the) top of the table (*od.* league)

Tabellenform *f*: **in ~** (set out) in tabular form, tabulated

Tabellen|führer *m*, **~führerin** *f Sport* → *Tabellenerste*; **~führung** *f* league leadership, position at the top of the table; **die ~ abgeben/zurückerobern** give up / regain the lead (of the table)

Tabellenkalkulation *f EDV* spreadsheet calculation

Tabellen|letzte *m*, *f* bottom team, *Am.* cellar-dwellers Pl.; **~r sein** *auch* be at the bottom of the table (*od.* league), *Am.* be cellar-dwellers; **~platz** *m Sport* position in the table (*od.* league)

Tabellen|rang *m Sport* → **~platz**; **~spitze** *f Sport* top position in the (league) table; (**an der** ~ at the) top of the league (*od.* table); **~stand** *m Sport* (league) rankings Pl.

tabellieren *v/t.* tabulate

Tabernakel *m*, *n*; -*s*, - **1.** *kath.* tabernacle; **2.** *Archit.* baldachin, canopy

Tableau [ta'blo:] *n*; -*s*, -*s* **1.** *Theat.* tableau (vivant); **2.** *österr.* (*Mieterverzeichnis im Hausflur*) residents' list

Tablett *n*; -(*e*)*s*, -*s und* -*e* tray; **j-m etw. auf e-m silbernen ~ servieren** *umg. fig.* hand s.o. s.th. on a plate (*Am.* a silver platter); **das kommt nicht aufs ~** *umg.* that's out of the question.

Tablette *f*; -, -*n* tablet, pill; **tablettenabhängig** *Adj. präd. od. nachgestellt*: dependent on (*od.* addicted to) pills; ~ **sein** *auch* be a pill-popper *umg.*; **Tablettenform** *f*: **in ~** in tablets, in tablet form; **Tablettenröhrchen** *n* pill tube; **Tablettensucht** *f* addiction to pills; **tablettensüchtig** *Adj. präd. od. nachgestellt*: addicted to pills; ~ **sein** *auch* be a pill-popper *umg.*; **Tablettensüchtige** *m*, *f* pill addict, pill-popper

tabu *Adj.* taboo; ~ **sein** *auch* be a no-no *umg.*; **das Thema ist für sie ~** it's a taboo subject (*od.* topic) with her, she simply won't talk about it

Tabu *n*; -*s*, -*s* taboo; **ein ~ brechen** break a taboo; **~bruch** *m* breach of taboo, breaking the taboo

tabufrei *Adj.*: **~e Gesellschaft** permissive (*od.* anything-goes *umg.*) society; **tabuieren**, **tabuisieren** *v/t.* (put under) taboo; **Tabuisierung** *f* tabooing

Tabula rasa *f*; - -, *kein Pl.* **1.** *Philos.* tabula rasa; **2.** ~ **machen** make a clean sweep

Tabulator *m*; -*s*, -*en* tabulator; **~taste** *f* *Computer.* tab key

Tabu|schranke *f* taboo (barrier); **~thema** *n* taboo subject (*od.* topic); **~verletzung** *f* breaking (*od.* infringement) of a taboo; **~wort** *n* taboo word (*od.* term); **~zone** *f* taboo zone, no-go area

Tacheles: ~ **reden** *umg.* be frank, talk turkey (*mit* with)

Tacho *m*; -*s*, -*s*; *umg.*, **Tachometer** *m*, *n*; -*s*, -; *Mot.* speedometer

Tachometer|nadel *f Mot.* speedometer needle; **~stand** *m* mileage, odometer reading, number of kilomet|res (*Am.* -ers) (*od.* miles) on the clock; **beim ~ von 10.000 km** at 10,000 km (*od.* 6,000 miles), after clocking up 10,000 km (*od.* 6,000 miles)

Tachykardie *f*; -, -*n*; *Med.* tachycardia

Tacker *m*; -*s*, - tacker; **tackern** *v/t.* staple

Tadel *m*; -*s*, - **1.** (*Rüge*) reprimand, rebuke *geh.*; (*Vorwurf*) reproach; (*Kritik*) criticism; **j-m e-n ~ erteilen** reprimand s.o.; **ihn trifft kein ~** he's not (*od.* in no way) to blame; **über jeden ~ erhaben** *lit.* beyond (*od.* above) reproach; **2.** *geh.* (*Makel*) blemish, fault, flaw; **ein Ritter ohne Furcht und ~** a knight without fear or reproach; **tadellos I.** *Adj.* (*makellos*) flawless, perfect; (*ausgezeichnet, auch umg. fig.*) perfect; **das ist doch ~** *auch* there's nothing wrong with it, it's fine; **II.** *Adv. sich benehmen etc.*: perfectly, irreproachably; *umg. laufen, hinkriegen*: fine, perfectly (OK); **tadeln** *v/t.* (*rügen*) (*Person*) reprimand, rebuke *geh.*, reprove *geh.*, censure *geh*; (*Verhalten, Arbeit*) criticize, find fault with, find unsatisfactory; *stärker*: condemn; (*schelten*) scold, give *s.o.* a telling off, berate *geh.*; (*missbilligen*) disapprove of; **tadelnd I.** *Part. Präs.* → *tadeln*; **II.** *Adj.* (*vorwurfsvoll*) reproachful; (*missbilligend*) disapproving, censorious *geh.*; **III.** *Adv. anblicken etc.*: reproachfully *etc.*; **tadelnswert** *Adj.* reprehensible, inappropriate

Tadschike *m*; -*n*, -*n*, **Tadschikin** *f*; -, -*nen* Tajik; *weiblich auch*: Tajik woman (*od.* girl); **tadschikisch** *Adj.* Tajik; **Tadschikistan** (*n*); -*s*; *Geog.* Tajikistan

Tadsch Mahal *n*; -*s*, *kein Pl.* Taj Mahal

Taekwondo *n*; -, *kein Pl.* tae kwon do

Tafel *f*; -, -*n* **1.** (*Schultafel*) (*weiße*) (white)board; (*für Kreide*) (black)board, *Am. auch* chalkboard; (*Schiefertafel*) slate; *hist.* (*Schreibtafel*) tablet; **an die ~ schreiben** write (up) on the (black- *altm.*) board; **die ~ putzen** clean the board, wipe the board clean; **2.** (*Anschlagbrett*) notice (*Am.* bulletin) board; *mit Grafiken*: display board; (*Schild*) notice, sign(board); (*Platte, auch Bildtafel*) plate; *aus Stein*: slab, tablet; *aus Holz*: panel, board; (*Gedenktafel*) plaque; (*Blech*) sheet, plate; **e-e ~ mit den Wanderwegen** *etc.* a board (*od.* notice) showing the trails *etc.*; **3.** (*Schalttafel*) control panel, console, switchboard; **4.** (*Tabelle*) **5.** *Schokolade*: bar; **6.** *lit.* (*Esstisch*) (dinner) table; *bei Festessen*: festive table (*od.* board); *bei formellen Essen*: banqueting table; **7.** (*Mittagessen*) lunch(eon); (*Abendessen*) dinner; **j-n zur ~ bitten** announce (*od.* inform *s.o.*) that lunch(eon) (*bzw.* dinner) is served; *informell*: tell s.o. lunch (*bzw.* dinner *etc.*) is ready; **die ~ aufheben** rise (from table, *Am.* the table); **8.** *Geol.* plateau, table; → *Anzeigetafel etc.*

Tafel|apfel *m* eating (*od.* dessert) apple; **~berg** *m Geol.* table (*od.* flat-topped) mountain, mesa; (*Eisberg*) tabular (ice)berg; **der ~** *Geog.*, *von Kapstadt*: Table Mountain; **~bild** *n* **1.** panel painting; **2.** *Schule*: what is (*od.* was) on the board; **~dienst** *m*; *nur Sg.*: **wer hat ~?** who's the blackboard monitor?

tafelfertig I. *Adj.* ready to serve; **II.** *Adv.*: ~ **zubereitet** ready to serve

Tafel|freuden *Pl. lit.* gastronomic (*od.* culinary) delights, delights of the table; **~geschäft** *n Wirts.* over-the-counter transaction(s *Pl.*); **~geschirr** *n* (best *od.* good) china; *Satz*: *auch* dinner service; **~glas** *n*; *nur Sg.* (*ungeschliffenes Glas*) sheet glass; (*Spiegelglas*) plate glass; **~kreide** *f* (blackboard) chalk; **~land** *n Geol.* tableland, plateau; **~lappen** *m* (blackboard, *Am. auch* chalkboard) cloth (*od.* duster); **~malerei** *f* panel painting; **~musik** *f Gattung:* domestic (*od.* table) music; *von Telemann:* Tafelmusik

tafeln *v/i. förm.* dine; *umg. hum.* (*schmausen*) feast, banquet

täfeln *v/t.* panel; (*Wand*) *auch* wainscot

Tafel|obst *n* dessert fruit; **~öl** *n* salad oil; **~runde** *f* (company at) (the) table; *König Artus und die* **~** King Arthur and the Knights of the Round Table; **~salz** *n* table salt; **~silber** *n* silver cutlery, *Am.* silverware, silver service; **~spitz** *m*; *-es, -e*; *österr., südd.*; *Gastr.* boiled fillet of beef haunch

Täfelung *f* panel(l)ing; *am unteren Wandteil: auch* wainscoting

Tafel|wasser *n* (bottled) mineral water, table water; **~wein** *m* **1.** *Gütebezeichnung:* vin ordinaire, mass-produced wine; **2.** (*Tischwein*) table wine

Taft *m*; *-(e)s, -e* taffeta; **~kleid** *n* taffeta dress (*od.* gown)

Tag¹ *m*; *-(e)s, -e* **1.** *Ggs. zu Nacht:* day(-time); *am od.* **bei ~e** during the day, in the daytime, by day; (*bei Tageslicht*) in daylight; *es wird* **~** it's getting light; *früh am* **~e** early in the day; **~** *und Nacht* day and night; *es ist ein Unterschied wie* **~** *und Nacht* there's (absolutely) no comparison, it's as different as day and night; **2.** *Teil der Woche:* day; *dreimal am* **~** three times a day; *am nächsten* **~** (on) the next day; *am* **~** *zuvor* the day before; *an jenem* **~** on that (particular) day; *e-s* **~es** one day; *zukünftig: auch* some day; *welcher* **~** *ist heute?* what day is it today?; *ein* **~** *wie jeder andere* a perfectly ordinary day, a day like any other; *den ganzen* **~** all day (long), throughout the day; *den lieben langen* **~** *umg.* the livelong day; **~** *für* **~**, *um* **~** day after day; *er wird* **~** *für* **~** *besser* he's getting better every day (*od.* from day to day, day by day); *von* **~** *zu* **~** from day to day; *von e-m* **~** *auf den andern* from one day to the next, overnight; *jeden zweiten* **~** every other day; *dieser* **~e** (*neulich*) the other day; (*zurzeit*) these days; *auf od.* **für ein paar ~e** for a couple of (*od.* a few) days; *auf den* **~** (*genau*) to the day; *bis auf den heutigen* **~** to this day; *sich* (*Dat.*) *ein paar schöne* **~e** *machen* take a break (*od.* go off and enjoy o.s.) for a couple of (*od.* a few) days; *freier* **~** day off; **~** *der Arbeit* Labo(u)r Day; **~** *der Deutschen Einheit* Day of German Unity; *der* **~** *des Herrn förm.* the Lord's day (*od.* Day). **3.** *als Gruß:* **guten ~!** *od.* **~!** *umg. morgens:* (good) morning; *nachmittags:* good afternoon, hello *umg.*, *bes. Am. auch* hi, howdy *umg.*; *bei Vorstellung:* how d'you do *förm.*, hello; **~** *auch! umg.* (oh,) hi!; (*bei j-m*) **guten ~** *sagen* pop in and say hello (to s.o.); (*e-n*) **schönen ~** *noch!* have a nice day, all the best; **4.** *fig.:* **an den** **~** **bringen/kommen** bring/come to light; **an den** **~** **legen** display, show, exhibit; *er hat bessere* **~e** *gesehen* he's seen better times (*od.* days); *auf m-e alten* **~e** *umg.* at my (great) age; *s-e* **~e** *sind gezählt* his days are numbered; *in den* **~** *hinein leben* live from day to day, (just) take things as they come; *er hat s-n* **guten/schlechten** **~** he's in a

good/bad mood today; *heute hab ich keinen guten* **~** it's not my day today, I seem to be having an off day (today), I'm having one of those days *umg.*; *das dauert ewig und drei* **~e** *umg.* it's taking an age (and a half), it's taking years; *es ist noch nicht aller* **~e** *Abend* it's early days yet; *morgen ist auch noch ein* **~** let it go (*od.* let that do) for today, tomorrow's another day; **5.** **~e** *umg.* (*Regel*) period; *sie hat ihre* **~e** she's got her period, it's that (*od.* the) time of the month (for her); *wann kriegst du d-e* **~e?** when's your period due?; **6.** *unter* **~e** *Bergb.* underground; *über* **~e** above ground, (on the) surface; → *Abend* 1, **acht¹**, *helllicht*, *jüngst...*, *Tür* 1, *vierzehn*, *zutage* etc.

Tag² [tɛk] *n*; *-s, -s*; *EDV* tag

tagaktiv *Adj. Zool.* diurnal

tagaus *Adv.:* **~**, *tagein* day in, day out, day after day

Tagblindheit *f* day blindness

Tage|bau *m Bergb., Verfahren:* opencast mining, *Am.* strip mining; *Anlage:* opencast mine, *Am.* strip mine; **~blatt** *n* daily (paper)

Tagebuch *n* **1.** diary; *Lit.* chronicle(s *Pl.*), journal, annals *Pl.*; **~** *führen* (*über +Akk.*) keep a record (*od.* diary) (of); **2.** *Wirts.* daybook; **~eintrag** *m* diary entry

Tage|dieb *m altm. pej.* idler, loafer, good-for-nothing; **~geld** *n* **1.** (*Spesen*) daily (subsistence) allowance; **2.** *bei Krankheit:* daily rate, payment per day; **3.** *mst* **~er** *Pl. Parl.* (*Diäten*) allowance *Sg.*

tagein *Adv.* → **tagaus**

tagelang I. *Adj.* lasting for days; *fig.* endless; **II.** *Adv.* for days (and days), for days at a time, for days on end

Tagelohn *m* daily wage; *im* **~** *arbeiten* work by the day; **Tagelöhner** *m*; *-s, -*, **Tagelöhnerin** *f*; *-, -nen* day labo(u)rer

tagen *v/i.* **1.** (*e-e Tagung abhalten*) have a meeting (*od.* conference), sit (in conference); *Jur., Parl.* be in session; *bis in den Morgen* **~** *umg. fig.* have an all-night conference, make a night of it; **2.** *es fängt an zu* **~** *lit.* day (*od.* dawn) is breaking, day is dawning

Tagereise *f* day's journey

Tagesablauf *m* day; *gewöhnlicher* **~** daily (*od.* day-to-day) routine

tagesaktuell *Adj.* highly topical

Tages|anbruch *m* daybreak, dawn, first light; *bei* **~** at daybreak, at dawn, at first light, at the first light of day *geh.*; **~arbeit** *f* **1.** (*Arbeit e-s Tages*) a day's work, whole-day job; **2.** (*tägliche Arbeit*) daily work (*od.* tasks *Pl.*); **~ausflug** *m* day trip, (day) excursion; **~bedarf** *m* daily requirement(s *Pl.*); **~befehl** *m* order of the day; **~bericht** *m* daily report (*od.* bulletin); **~betreuung** *f* day care, *Am. auch* daycare; **~creme** *f* day cream; **~decke** *f* bedspread, counterpane; **~einnahmen** *Pl.* day's takings *Pl.*; **~ereignisse** *Pl.* events of the day, *weitS. auch* current affairs; *TV etc. the* day's *od.* today's news *Sg.* (and current affairs); **~etappe** *f* daily (*od.* day's) stage; **~fahrt** *f* day trip, (day) excursion; **~form** *f Sport etc.:* form on the day

Tages|gericht *n Gastr.* dish of the day; **~geschäft** *n allg.* routine (*od.* day-to-day) business; (*Einzeltransaktion*) day order; **~geschehen** *n* → Tagesereignisse; **~gespräch** *n* topic number one, *the* topic of the moment, *the* talk

of the town *umg.*; **~hälfte** *f* half of the day; **~heim** *n allg.* day care centre, *Am.* daycare center; *für Kleinkinder:* day nursery; **~höchsttemperaturen** *Pl.* maximum temperatures (by day), day maxima; *an e-m bestimmten Tag:* highest temperatures (of the day); **~karte** *f* **1.** (*Fahr- od. Eintrittskarte*) day ticket (*od.* pass); **2.** *Gastr.* menu for the day; today's menu; **~kasse** *f* **1.** *Theat. etc.* box office; **2.** (*Einnahmen*) day's takings *Pl.*; **~kind** *n* day-care child; **~klinik** *f* outpatients' clinic; *im Krankenhaus: auch* outpatients' department; **~kurs** *m* **1.** *Fin., Devisen:* (today's *od.* the current) exchange rate; *Effekten:* market (*od.* current) price; **2.** *Päd.* day-release course; **~leistung** *f* daily output

Tageslicht *n* daylight; *bei* **~** in (the) daylight; (*vor Dunkelheit*) before dark, while it is (*od.* was etc.) still light; *das* **~** *scheuen* shun the daylight (*od.* light of day); *fig. auch* have s.th. to hide; *ans* **~** *kommen fig.* come to light, become known; *ans* **~** *bringen allg.* bring to light, reveal; (*Verbrechen etc.*) expose, bring out into the open; **~aufnahme** *f* daylight shot (*od.* exposure); **~projektor** *m* overhead projector, OHP

Tages|lohn *m* (*Geldsumme*) day's pay; (*Lohnsatz*) daily wage, pay per day; **~marsch** *m* day's march (*auch Strecke*); *drei Tagesmärsche von hier* three days' march from here; **~menü** *n Gastr.* today's (*od.* the day's) special, menu (*od.* set meal) of the day; **~mutter** *f* childminder, *Am.* babysitter, daycare worker

Tagesordnung *f* (*abgek.* **TO**) (*the* day's) agenda; (*ganz oben*) *auf der* **~** *stehen* be (high) on the agenda; *zur* **~** *übergehen* proceed to the order of the day *förm.*; *umg.* (*anfangen*) get down to business, get started; (*wie gewohnt weitermachen*) get on with things again, get back to normal; *an der* **~** *sein fig.* be nothing unusual; *das ist hier an der* **~** *auch* it (*od.* that) happens all the time around here, that's par for the course; **Tagesordnungspunkt** *m* (*abgek.* **TOP**) item on the agenda, agenda item, agendum *geh.*

Tagespensum *n* daily quota (*od.* stint *umg.*)

Tagespflege *f* day care, *Am. auch* daycare; **~mutter** *f* childminder, *Am.* babysitter, daycare worker; **~stelle** *f* day care centre, *Am.* daycare center

Tagespolitik *f* day-to-day politics *Pl.*, current (*od.* public) affairs *Pl.*; **tagespolitisch** *Adj.* current political

Tages|preis *m* current (market) price, ruling price; **~presse** *f* daily press, dailies *Pl.*; **~produktion** *f* daily production (*od.* output), output per day; **~programm** *n* day's programme (*Am.* program), schedule for the day; *Parl.* order of the day; **~ration** *f* daily ration(s *Pl.*); **~raum** *m* dayroom; **~reise** *f* (*Ausflug*) day trip, (day) excursion; *e-e* **~** / *zwei* **~n** (*von hier*) a day's / two days' journey, *Am.* a day / two days' (travel) (from here); **~rückfahrkarte** *f* day return (ticket); **~satz** *m* **1.** (*Lohn etc.*) daily rate; **2.** (*Verpflegungssatz*) daily ration(s *Pl.*); **3.** *Jur.* income-related per diem unit (*of fine*); *j-n zu 10 Tagessätzen in Höhe von ... verurteilen etwa* impose a ten-unit fine at the rate of ... on s.o.; **~schau** *f TV* television news *Sg*; **~sieger** *m*, **~siegerin** *f* day's winner (*od.* victor), victor for the day; *bei Etappenrennen*: stage winner; **~stätte** *f* day-care centre, *Am.* daycare center; **~suppe** *f Gastr.* soup of the day, soup du jour; **~temperatur** *f* day(time) temperature; **~tour** *f* day trip, (day) excursion; **~umsatz** *m Wirts.* **1.** (*Durchschnittswert*) daily turnover; **2.** (*aktueller*) *the* day's turnover; **~verlauf** *m* course of the day; **~zeit** *f* time (of day), hour *geh.*; *um diese ~* at this time of day (*od.* hour *geh.*); *zu jeder ~* (at) any time of day; *zu jeder Tages- und Nachtzeit* (at) any time (of the) day or night; **~zeitung** *f* daily (newspaper)

Tagetes *f*, -, -; *Bot.* tagetes, marigold

tageweise *Adv.* (*nur kurzfristig*) on a day-to-day basis; (*an manchen Tagen*) on certain days

Tagewerk *n*; *nur Sg.*; *geh.* day's work; *sein ~ verrichtet haben* have done one's work for the day

Tagfalter *m Zool.* butterfly

taggen ['tɛgn] *vt/i.* *EDV* tag

taghell I. *Adj.* **1.** *durch Tageslicht*: daylight, *präd.* broad daylight; **2.** *wie am Tag*: (as) light (*od.* bright) as day; **II.** *Adv.*: *~ erleuchtet* lit up (*od.* illuminated) as bright as day, brilliantly lit

täglich I. *Adj.* daily; (*Alltags...*) everyday; *sein ~ Brot verdienen umg.* hum earn a (*od.* one's) living *allg.*; *so wichtig wie das ~e Brot* as necessary as the air we breathe; *~es Geld Wirts.* call (*od.* demand) money; **II.** *Adv.* every day, daily, once a day; *Wirts. auch* per day, per diem; *zweimal ~* twice a day; *sie arbeitet ~ drei Stunden* she works three hours a day, she does three hours (*od.* hours' *geh.*) work a day, she goes to work for three hours a (*od.* every) day; *der Zug verkehrt ~ außer Sonntag* the train runs every day except Sunday

tags *Adv.*: *~ darauf* (on) the following (*od.* next) day, the day after (that *umg.*); *~ zuvor* the day before (that *umg.*), the previous day, on the preceding day *geh.*, a day earlier

Tagschicht *f* day shift; *~ haben* be on day shift

tagsüber *Adv.* (*während des Tages*) during the day; (*den ganzen Tag*) all day (long)

tagtäglich I. *Adv.* every (single) day; day in, day out, every day without fail; **II.** *Adj.* daily, day-to-day, everyday, quotidian *geh.*

Tagtraum *m* daydream; **Tagträumer** *m* daydreamer; **Tagträumerei** *f* daydreaming; **Tagträumerin** *f* daydreamer

Tagundnacht|betrieb *m* 24-hour (*od.* round-the-clock) (*Am.* 24/7) service (*im Einzelhandel*: *auch* opening); **~gleiche** *f* equinox

Tagung *f* conference, *bes. Am. auch* convention

Tagungs|bericht *m* (conference) proceedings *Pl.*; **~hotel** *n für Tagungen geeignet*: hotel with conference facilities; *konkret*: conference hotel; **~ort** *m* (conference) venue; **~raum** *m* conference room; *großer*: *auch* conference hall, auditorium; **~stätte** *f* conference venue (*Am. auch* location); **~teilnehmer** *m*, **~teilnehmerin** *f* (conference) participant; *Pl. auch* those attending the conference

Tagwerk *n*; *nur Sg.* *südd.*, *österr.* → *Tagewerk*

Taifun *m*; *-s*, *-e* typhoon

Taiga *f*; *-*, *kein Pl.*; *Geog.* taiga

Taille ['taljə] *f*, *-*, *-n* **1.** *Körperteil, auch entsprechender Teil e-s Kleidungsstücks*: waist; *auf ~ gearbeitet* close-fitting at the waist; **2.** *altm.* (*Mieder*) bodice; **3.** *hist.* (*Steuer*) tallage; **tailliert** [tal'ji:ɐt] *Adj.* waisted; *Hemd*: tapered

Taiwan (*n*); *-s*; *Geog.* Taiwan; **Taiwanese** *m*; *-n*, *-n*, **Taiwanesin** *f*; *-*, *-nen* Taiwanese, *weiblich auch*: Taiwanese woman (*od.* girl); **taiwanesisch** *Adj.* Taiwanese

Takelage [takə'la:ʒə] *f*; *-*, *-n*; *Naut.* (masts and) rigging; **Takelung** *f Naut.* **1.** (*Auftakeln*) rigging; **2.** (*Takelage*) rigging; (*Art der Takelage*) rig

Takt[1] *m*; *-(e)s*, *-e* **1.** *Mus.* (*rhythmische Gliederung*) time, rhythm; *den ~ schlagen* beat time; *den ~ halten, im ~ bleiben* keep time; *den ~ angeben* give the time (*od.* beat); *fig.* call the tune, set the pace; *aus dem ~ kommen* lose the beat; *fig.* be put off one's stroke; *j-n aus dem ~ bringen fig.* put s.o. off his (*od.* her) stroke; *stärker*: throw *umg.* (*od.* disconcert) s.o.; **2.** *Mus.* (*Takteinheit*) bar; *ein paar ~e* a few (*od.* a couple of) bars; *fig.* (*Worte*) a few words, something *Sg.*; **3.** *Lit., Verslehre*: beat, (metrical) stress; **4.** (*Bewegungsrhythmus*) rhythm; *beim Rudern*: *auch* stroke; **5.** *Mot.* stroke; **6.** *Etron.* (processor) speed

Takt[2] *m*; *-(e)s*, *kein Pl.*; (*Feingefühl*) tact(fulness), sensitivity, delicacy; *wenig/keinen ~ haben* have not much / no tact, be not a particularly tactful / be a totally tactless person *etc.*; *mit großem ~ behandeln* treat (*od.* handle *od.* deal with) s.o. (*od. s.th.*) very tactfully (*od.* diplomatically *od.* sensitively); → *taktlos, taktvoll*

Taktart *f Mus.* time

takten *v/t.* *Tech.*, *EDV* clock; *ein mit 1200 MHz getakteter Prozessor* a processor rated at 1200 MHz

Takt|frequenz *f Computer*: clock frequency (*od.* rate); **~gefühl** *n* tact(fulness); → *Takt*[2]

taktieren *v/i.* manoeuvre, *Am.* maneuver; *geschickt ~ allg.* play it cleverly, play clever *umg.*, make the right moves; *generell*: be a good (*od.* skilled *od.* adroit *etc.*) tactician, be a smart operator (*Am. auch* cookie) *umg.*

Taktik *f*; *-*, *-en* tactics *Pl.* (*auch V. im Sg.*); *eine verfehlte ~* bad tactics, an inappropriate course of action; **Taktiker** *m*; *-s*, *-*, **Taktikerin** *f*; *-*, *-nen* tactician; → *taktieren*

taktisch I. *Adj.* tactical (*auch fig.*); **II.** *Adv.*: *~ vorgehen* use tactics (*od.* one's head *umg.*), make a considered approach; *das war ~ geschickt* that was a clever (*od.* smart *umg.*) move, that was good tactics

taktlos *Adj.* tactless, indiscreet, thoughtless; *er ist ein ~er Mensch auch* he has no sense of tact; **Taktlosigkeit** *f* (*taktlose Art*) tactlessness, thoughtlessness, lack of tact (*od.* discretion); (*taktlose Handlung etc.*) failure (*od.* breach) of tact, indiscretion; *das war e-e ~* that was a tactless thing to say (*od.* do)

Takt|stock *m Mus.* baton; **~strich** *Mus. m* bar-line; **~verkehr** *m Verk.* fixed-interval service(*s Pl.*)

taktvoll I. *Adj.* tactful, diplomatic, discreet; **II.** *Adv.* *sich verhalten etc.*: tact-

fully, diplomatically, discreetly; *~ über etw. hinweggehen* tactfully ignore s.th.; (*nicht erwähnen*) *auch* tactfully refrain from mentioning s.th

Taktwechsel *m Mus.* change of time, time change

Tal *n*; *-(e)s*, *Täler* valley (*in Schottland*: glen); *über Berg und ~* up hill and down dale; *im Herbst werden die Herden zu ~(e) getrieben* in autumn they drive the animals down to the valley(s) (*od.* down off the mountain); *sich in e-m ~ befinden fig. Wirtschaft etc.*: be in (*od.* have reached) a trough ...**tal** *im Subst.* **1.** *Geog.*: **Kerb~** V-shaped valley; **Kasten~** canyon, gorge; **2.** *bes. Wirts., Pol. fig.*: **Beschäftigungs~** period of high unemployment; **Konjunktur~** cyclical trough, low point in the economic cycle

talab(wärts) *Adv.* down the valley

Talar *m*; *-s*, *-e*; *Jur.* robe, gown; *kirchl.* cassock; *Univ.* gown

talauf(wärts) *Adv.* up the valley

Tal|boden *m* valley floor (*od.* bottom); **~enge** *f* gorge

Talent *n*; *-s*, *-e* **1.** (*Begabung*) talent, gift; *musikalisches ~* musical talent, a gift for music; *kein ~ haben* lack talent; *viel/wenig ~ haben* be highly talented / not very talented; **2.** (*Person*) talented person; *~e Pl.* talent *Sg. umg.*; *sie ist sein echtes ~* she's got real talent (*od.* a gift), she's brilliant *umg.*; *ein viel versprechendes ~* a highly promising new talent, a (young) artist *etc.* of great promise (*od.* with real potential); *neue ~e suchen* look for fresh talent, talent-spot *umg.*, *Am.* scout; **3.** *hist.* (*Münze*) talent

talentiert *Adj.* talented, gifted

Talent|probe *f Sänger etc.*: audition, trial; (*Werk*) sample, trial piece; **~schmiede** *f Institution*: talent school; *umg.* hotbed of talent; **~suche** *f* search (*od.* hunt) for (new) talent; **~sucher** *m*, **~sucherin** *f* talent scout; *Sport* scout

Taler *m*; *-s*, *-*; *hist.* t(h)aler

Talfahrt *f* descent; *Mot. und Ski*: *auch* downhill run; *fig.* decline, slide; *Wirts. auch* downward trend; *e-r Währung*: *auch* (downward) slide

Talg *m*; *-(e)s*, *kein Pl.* *roher*: suet; *ausgelassener*: tallow; *Physiol.* sebum; **Talgdrüse** *f Anat.* sebaceous gland; **talgig** *Adj.* greasy, fatty

Talisman *m*; *-s*, *-e*; (*Stein etc.*) lucky charm, talisman *geh.*; (*Maskottchen*) mascot, lucky doll *etc.*

Talje *f*; *-*, *-n*; *Naut.* block and tackle

Talk[1] *m*; *-(e)s*, *kein Pl.* (*Talkum*) talcum (powder), talc; (*Mineral*) talc

Talk[2] [to:k] *m*; *-s*, *-s*; *umg.* (*Plauderei*) (small) talk, chitchat; *TV* chat; **talken** ['to:kn] *v/i.* *umg.* *TV* talk, chat

Talkessel *m Geog.* (deep *od.* enclosed) valley

Talkmaster ['to:kma:stɐ] *m*; *-s*, *-*, **~in** *f*; *-*, *-nen* chat-show (*Am.* talk-show) host; **Talk-Show** ['to:kʃo:] *f* chat (*Am.* talk) show

Talkum *n -s*, *kein Pl.*, **~puder** *n* talcum powder

Talmi *n*; *-s*, *kein Pl.* pinchbeck; *fig. auch* cheap imitation(*s Pl.*); **~gold** *n* pinchbeck

Talmud *m*; *-s*, *kein Pl.* Talmud; **talmudisch** *Adj.* Talmudic

Talmulde *f Geog.* (shallow) valley, basin

Talon [ta'lõ:] *m*; *-s*, *-s* **1.** *Wirts.* talon, certificate of renewal, renewal coupon; **2.** (*Kontrollabschnitt*) counterfoil, control slip, stub; **3.** *Spiele:* pick-up pile, *Am.* stack, undealt cards *Pl.* (*bzw.* counters *etc.*); **4.** *Mus.* frog

Tal|ski *m* downhill (*od.* lower) ski; **~sohle** *f Geog.* valley bottom (*od.* floor), bottom of a (*od.* the) valley; *fig. Wirts.* trough; **die ~ erreichen** *fig.* bottom out; **~sperre** *f* (reservoir and) dam; **~station** *f Bergbahn:* valley station, lower terminal; *Schlepplift etc.:* bottom end

talwärts *Adv.* downhill, down toward(s) (*od.* into) the valley; (*flussabwärts*) downstream; → *auch* **talab(wärts**)

Tamagotchi® [tama'gɔtʃi] *n; -(s), -s* tamago(t)chi

Tamarinde *f; -, -n; Bot.* tamarind

Tamariske *f; -, -n; Bot.* tamarisk

Tambour *m;-s, -e* **1.** (*Trommler*) drummer; **2.** *Archit.* tambour; **~major** *m* drum major

Tamburin *n; -s, -e; Mus.* tambourine

Tamile *m; -n, -n,* **Tamilin** *f; -, -nen* Tamil, *weiblich auch:* Tamil woman (*od.* girl); **tamilisch** *Adj.* Tamil; **Tamilisch** *n; -(s); Ling.* Tamil; **das ~e** Tamil, the Tamil language

Tampon *m; -s, -s* **1.** *Med. etc.* tampon; *für Wunde: auch* swab, plug; **2.** *Kunst* canvas, dabber; **tamponieren** *v/t.* plug, tampon

Tamtam *n; -s, -s* **1.** (*Gong*) tom-tom, tam-tam; **2.** *kein Pl.; umg.* (*Trara*) fuss, to-do, carry-on; (*Lärm*) noise; (*Reklame*) ballyhoo, hype; **mit großem ~ feiern** *etc.*: with much ballyhoo; **viel ~ machen um** make a (great) fuss of

Tand *m; -s, kein Pl.;* (*Kinkerlitzchen*) trinkets *Pl.,* gewgaws *Pl., Am. auch* geegaws *Pl.;* (*wertloser Kram*) (cheap) rubbish (*od.* trash), gimcrack stuff

Tändelei *f; -, -en; allg.* dilly-dallying, playing around, messing about *umg.*; (*Liebelei*) flirting; **tändeln** *v/i. allg.* play around, mess about *umg.*; (*flirten*) flirt

Tandem *n; -s, -s* (*Fahrrad*) tandem; *Tech. auch* tandem arrangement (*od.* set-up); *fig.* twosome, duo, pair; **~ fahren** ride (*bei Pferdewagen:* drive) a tandem

Tandler *m; -s, -, ~in* *f; -, -nen; bes. österr. umg.* **1.** (*Trödler[in]*) used goods trader, secondhand dealer; **2.** (*langsamer Mensch*) slow|coach (*Am.* -poke), slow mover

Tang *m; -s, kein Pl.; Bot.* seaweed, kelp

Tanga|höschen *n,* **~slip** *m* tanga, G-string

Tangens *m; -, -; Math.* tan(gent); **Tangente** *f; -, -n; Math.* tangent; (*Straße*) expressway, bypass, ring road; **tangential** *Adj.* tangential; **tangieren** *v/t.* **1.** (*berühren, betreffen*) affect, concern; (*am Rande betreffen*) relate (indirectly) to, have bearing on; **das tangiert mich nicht** that has nothing to do with me, that's no concern of mine, that's not my province; **etw. nur ~** be peripheral to s.th.; **2.** (*erwähnen etc.*) touch on, allude (in passing) to; **3.** *Math.* be tangent to

Tango *m; -s, -s; Mus.* tango; **~ tanzen** (do the) tango; **~tänzer** *m,* **~tänzerin** *f* tango dancer

Tank *m, -s, -s* **1.** tank, container; **2.** *altm. Mil.* tank; **~deckel** *m Mot.* fuel (*od.* filler) cap

tanken I. *v/i. Mot.* get petrol (*od.* diesel, *Am.* gas *etc.*), put petrol (*Am.* gas) *etc.* in; *bes. Lkw:* refuel; *voll:* fill (*od.* tank) up; *Flug.* refuel; **wir müs-**

sen ~ *auch* we need (*od.* we've got to get) petrol *etc.*; **ich habe voll getankt** I('ve) filled her (*od.* it) up; **II.** *v/t.* **1.** *Mot.* put (*petrol etc.*) in, fill up with; *Flug., Naut.* take on; **wir ~ immer Super bleifrei** we use unleaded four star petrol (*Am.* premium [grade] gas); **2.** **frische Luft ~** *umg. fig.* get some (*od.* a lungful of) fresh air; **Kraft ~** *fig.* build up one's strength; **er hat zu viel getankt** *umg. fig.* he's had too much, he's tanked (*Am.* loaded)

Tanker *m; -s, -; Naut.* (oil) tanker; **~flotte** *f* tanker fleet; **~unfall** *m* tanker accident (*geringfügig:* mishap), accident (*od.* mishap) involving a tanker; **~unglück** *n* tanker disaster, major accident involving a tanker

Tank|fahrzeug *n* tanker; **~flugzeug** *n* tanker (aircraft); **~füllung** *f* tankful; **mit e-r ~ komme ich bis München** I can get to Munich on a tankful; **~inhalt** *m* (*Rauminhalt*) tank volume; (*Menge an Treibstoff etc. im Tank*) tank contents *Pl.*; **~lager** *n* (fuel) storage depot; **~laster** *m,* **~lastzug** *m* tanker; **~löschfahrzeug** *n* fire tender (*Am.* truck); **~säule** *f* petrol (*Am.* gas) pump; **~schiff** *n Naut.* tanker

Tankstelle *f* filling (*od.* petrol) station, *Am.* filling (*od.* gas) station; *an Autobahnen:* service station; *Koll. Brit. auch* forecourts *Pl.*

Tankstellen|netz *n* filling station (*od.* retail fuel distribution) network; **~pächter** *m,* **~pächterin** *f* filling-station leaseholder (*od.* tenant, *Am.* franchisee); **~überfall** *m* service station holdup, raid on a service station

Tank|uhr *f* fuel gauge; **~verschluss** *m Mot.* fuel (*od.* filller) cap; **~wagen** *m* tanker; **~wart** *m* petrol pump (*Am.* gas station) attendant

Tanne *f; -, -n; Bot.* **1.** *Baum:* fir (tree); **schlank wie e-e ~** slender and willowy; **2.** *nur Sg., Holz:* fir; *in Möbeln:* pine, whitewood; **e-e Schrankwand aus ~** a wall unit in pine, a pine wall unit

Tannen|baum *m* **1.** *Bot.* fir (tree); **2.** (*Weihnachtsbaum*) Christmas tree; **~grün** *n* sprigs *Pl.* of fir, fir branches *Pl.*; **~häher** *m Orn.* nutcracker; **~holz** *n* fir (wood); **~honig** *m* fir honey; **~meise** *f Orn.* coal tit; **~nadel** *f* fir needle; **~wald** *m* fir wood; **~zapfen** *m* fir cone; **~zweig** *m* fir branch, sprig of fir

Tannin *n; -s, -e* tannin

Tansania (*n*) *-s; Geog.* Tanzania; **Tansanier** *m; -s, -,* **Tansanierin** *f; -, -nen* Tanzanian, *weiblich auch:* Tanzanian woman (*od.* girl); **tansanisch** *Adj.* Tanzanian

Tantal *n, -s, kein Pl.;* (*abgek.* **Ta**) *Chem.* tantalum

Tantalusqualen *Pl.:* **wir haben ~ gelitten** it was torture (*od.* so tantalizing) for us

Tante *f; -, -n* aunt, auntie *umg.; umg., oft pej.* (*Frau*) woman; *ältere: auch* old duck, old bag *Sl. pej.;* **~ Lindy** Aunt(ie) Lindy; **sag der ~ guten Tag!** *Kinderspr.* say hello to the (nice) lady; **komische ~** *umg.* funny old bird

Tante-Emma-Laden *m umg.* (small) corner shop, *Am.* mom-and-pop grocery *etc.* store

tantenhaft *Adj.* schoolmarmish, old-maidish, fussy, (over-)solicitous

Tantieme [tãˈtjɛːmə] *f; -, -n* **1.** share in profits; **2.** *mst Pl.* (*Autorentantiemen etc.*) royalties

Tanz *m; -es, Tänze* **1.** *z. B. Walzer:*

dance; **j-n zum ~ auffordern** ask s.o. for a dance; **darf ich um den nächsten ~ bitten?** may I have the next dance?; **2.** *nur Sg.* (*Veranstaltung*) dance; **zum ~ gehen** go to a dance; **hier ist jeden Abend ~** they have dancing every night here; **~ bis in die frühen Morgen** all-night dance (*od.* dancing); **der ~ um das Goldene Kalb** *fig.* worshipping (*od.* worship of) the golden calf, worship of Mammon; **ein ~ auf dem Vulkan** *fig. etwa* fiddling on the deck of the Titanic; **3.** *nur Sg.;* (*Tanzkunst*) dancing, dance *fachspr.;* **4.** *nur Sg.; umg. fig.* (*Aufheben*) song and dance; *umg.* (*Prozedur*) rigmarole; **e-n ~ aufführen** *umg. fig.* make a song and dance (*od.* a great to-do) (**wegen** about), make an (*od.* a big) issue; **~abend** *m* **1.** dance, evening's dancing; **2.** (*Aufführung*) dance show, evening of dance; **~bar** *f* bar with dancing (*od.* with a dance band)

Tanz|bär *m* dancing (*od.* performing) bear; **~bein** *n:* **das ~ schwingen** *umg.* shake a leg, trip the light fantastic; **~boden** *m* **1.** (*Fläche*) dance floor; **2.** (*Saal*) dance hall; **~café** *n* café with dancing (*od.* dance music)

Tänzchen *n umg.* → *Tanz* 1, 4; **ein ~ wagen** venture to dance, try a step or two

Tanz|club *m* dance (*od.* dancing) club; **~einlage** *f* dance interlude, interlude featuring dancers

tänzeln *v/i. Pferd, nervös:* sidle about; *übermütig:* prance; *Boxer:* bob and weave; **sie tänzelte ins Zimmer** *fröhlich:* she came skipping (*kokett, geziert:* minced [her way]; *selbstgefällig:* pranced) into the room

tanzen *vt/i.* dance (*auch fig. Blätter etc.*); **es wurde viel getanzt** there was plenty (*od.* lots) of dancing; **nach dem Essen wird getanzt** there's dancing afterward[s] (*od.* after dinner); **es darf getanzt werden** it's time to take your partners (for the first dance); **e-n Walzer/Cha-Cha-Cha ~** dance (*od.* do) a waltz / the cha-cha; **sich in Ekstase ~** dance till one feels ecstatic; **auf dem Seil ~** walk the (*fig.:* a) tightrope; **auf den Wellen ~** *fig. Schiff:* rock on the waves, lift (briskly) to the sea; *kleines Boot:* bob (up and down) (*od.* dance) on the waves; **die Wörter tanzten ihm vor den Augen** the words were jerking about (*od.* swimming) before his eyes; → *Derwisch, Pfeife* 1, *Tango etc.*

Tänzer *m; -s, -,* **~in** *f; -, -nen* dancer; *im Ballett:* ballet dancer, *weiblich auch* ballerina; **ein guter/schlechter Tänzer sein** be / not be a good dancer; **tänzerisch I.** *Adj. Bewegung:* dance-like, dancing; **~e Begabung** dancing talent, talent as a dancer (*od.* as dancers); **~e Ausbildung** dance (*od.* ballet) training; **~e Darbietungen** dance (*od.* ballet) performances; **e-e große ~e Leistung** a magnificent piece of dancing; **II.** *Adv.:* **~ begabt** talented as a dancer; **~ hervorragend** technically superb (as dance *bzw.* as a dancer *od.* as dancers)

Tanz|fläche *f* dance floor; **~kapelle** *f* dance band; **~kreis** *m* group of friends who go dancing; **~kurs** *m* dancing course (*od.* lessons *Pl.*); **~lehrer** *m,* **~lehrerin** *f* dancing instructor (*od.* teacher); **~lokal** *n* café with dancing, (small) dance hall; **~mariechen** *n Karneval:* dancing girl; (*Vortänzerin*) lead dancer; **~maske** *f* (ritual) dance mask; **~musik** *f* dance music; **~orchester** *n* dance band; **~paar** *n* couple (dancing); **~parkett** *n* dance-floor; **~partner** *m*, **~partnerin** *f* (dancing) partner; **~saal** *m* dance hall; **~schritt** *m* (dance) step; **~schuh** *m* **1.** *für Gesellschaftstanz*: dancing shoe; *Herrenschuh*: *auch* dancing pump; **2.** ballet shoe; **~schule** *f* dance school, school of dance; **~schüler** *m*, **~schülerin** *f* dancing pupil, student of dance, *Am.* dance student; **~sport** *m* competition dancing; **~stunde** *f* dancing class (*od.* lesson); *zur ~ gehen* go to a dancing class, take dancing lessons; *aktuell*: go to one's dancing class (*od.* lesson); **~tee** *m* tea dance, thé dansant *förm.*; **~theater** *n* dance theat|re (*Am. auch* -er); **~turnier** *n* dancing contest (*od.* competition); **~unterricht** *m* dancing class(es *Pl.*) (*od.* lessons *Pl.*); **~veranstaltung** *f* dance

Taoismus *m*; -, *kein Pl.*; *Philos.* Taoism; **taoistisch** *Adj.* Taoist

Tapedeck ['te:pdɛk] *n* tape deck

Tapet *n*: *etw. aufs ~ bringen* raise s.th., bring s.th. up (for discussion); *aufs ~ kommen* be brought up, come up

Tapete *f*; -, -*n* wallpaper; *die ~n wechseln umg. fig.* have a change of scene, seek fresh pastures *geh.*; (*umziehen*) *auch* move (away); *beruflich*: change jobs, move to a new job

Tapeten|bahn *f* strip of wallpaper; **~kleister** *m* wallpaper paste; **~muster** *n* wallpaper pattern (*od.* design); **~rolle** *f* roll of wallpaper; **~wechsel** *m fig.* change of scene

Tapezierarbeiten *Pl.* wallpapering *Sg.*; *österr.* (*Polstern*) upholstering *Sg.*; **tapezieren** *v/t./i.* (*Wände*) wallpaper, decorate; *österr.* (*Möbel*) upholster; *neu ~* redecorate; **Tapezierer** *m*; -*s*, -, **Tapeziererin** *f*; -, -*nen von Wänden*: decorator, paper-hanger; *österr.* (*Polsterer*) upholsterer

Tapeziertisch *m* pasting table

tapfer I. *Adj.* **1.** *bei Gefahren, Schwierigkeiten*: brave; *Kämpfer*: *auch* valiant *geh.*; *bes. Kind, Unterlegene(r)*: *auch* plucky; **2.** *bei Schmerzen, seelischen Regungen*: brave, plucky, stoical *geh.*; **II.** *Adv.* bravely, valiantly *geh.*, pluckily, stoically *geh.*; *sich ~ schlagen Mil., Sport auch* fight like a hero (*od.* heroes); *fig.* put up a good fight; *sie hat es ~ ertragen* she put on a brave front, she took it on the chin; *die Schmerzen ~ ertragen* bear (*od.* endure) the pain bravely, cope bravely with (*od.* refuse to give in to) the pain; **Tapferkeit** *f* (*Mut*) bravery, courage, pluck; *bes. im Kampf*: valo(u)r *geh.*, gallantry *geh.*; (*Fassung*) courage, stoicism, pluck, grit *umg.*; **Tapferkeitsmedaille** *f* medal for bravery

Tapioka *f*; -, *kein Pl.*; *Gastr.* tapioca

Tapir *m*; -*s*, -*e*; *Zool.* tapir

Tapisserie *f*; -, -*n* **1.** (*Wandteppich*) tapestry, wall-hanging; **2.** (*Stickerei*) (piece of) embroidery

tapp *Interj.*: *~, ~! (Geräusch von Schritten)* pad pad pad, flap flap

tappen *v/i.* **1.** (*gehen*) pad (*od.* step) (hesitantly); *durchs Zimmer etc. ~* make (feel) one's way through the room *etc.*; *in e-e Falle ~* walk (right) into a trap; **2.** *Schritte*: sound, be audible; **3.** *altm.* (*tasten*) grope (about *od.* [a]round) (*nach* for); *im Dunkeln ~ fig.* grope in the dark

täppisch *Adj. umg. Bewegungen*: clumsy, ungainly; *bei Personen auch* awkward; *Benehmen*: clumsy, inept, gauche; *Person*: clumsy(-looking), awkward-looking; *junger Mensch*: *auch* gawky

tapsen *v/i.* → *tappen* 1, 2; **tapsig** *umg.* **I.** *Adj.* clumsy, shambling; *~ wie ein Bär* like a lumbering bear; **II.** *Adv.*: *gehen, sich bewegen*: clumsily

Tara *f*; -, *Taren*; *Wirts.* **1.** (*Gewicht der Verpackung*) tare; **2.** (*Verpackung*) packing (material)

Tarantel *f*; -, -*n*; *Zool.* tarantula; *wie von der ~ gestochen* sprang *er auf* as if something (*od.* a snake) had bitten him, as if he'd been stung

tarieren *v/t.* **1.** *Wirts.* tare; **2.** (*Waage*) counterbalance

Tarif *m*; -*s*, -*e*; *Wirts.* **1.** (*Preis*) charge, (fixed) price, standard rate; *bei Verkehrsmitteln*: fare; **2.** (*Preisverzeichnis*) tariff, scale of charges; *bei Verkehrsmitteln*: fares *Pl.*, fares scale; **3.** (*Lohn*) pay scale; (*Gehalt*) salary scale; *nach/unter/über ~ bezahlen* pay at/below/above the standard rate; *über ~ auch* above scale

Tarif|abschluss *m Wirts.* pay (*od.* wage) settlement, collective wage agreement; **~änderung** *f Gebühren*: change in the rate, new (*od.* revised) scale of charges; *Fahrpreise*: fares revision, revised fares *Pl.*; **~auseinandersetzung** *f* pay (*od.* wage) dispute; **~autonomie** *f* (right of) free collective bargaining; **~bereich** *m* rate band

Tarif|dschungel *m Telef.* plethora of different (phone) charges; **~erhöhung** *f* **1.** *Gebühren*: increase in rates (*od.* charges); *Fahrpreise*: fare[s] increase (*od.* rise, *Am.* hike); **2.** *Lohn*: increase in pay rates, (across-the-board) pay increase (*od.* rise, *Am.* raise); **~gebiet** *n Verk., U-Bahn etc.*: (fares) zone

Tarif|gehalt *n* standard salary; **~gespräch** *n Wirts.* pay (*od.* wage) talks *Pl.* (*od.* negotiations *Pl.*); **~gruppe** *f* salary (*od.* wage) bracket, salary grade; **~hoheit** *f* (right of) free collective bargaining; **~kommission** *f e-s Tarifpartners*: wage (*od.* pay) bargaining committee; *beider Tarifpartner*: joint negotiating committee (on pay), wages commission; **~konflikt** *m* pay (*od.* wage) dispute

tariflich I. *Adj. attr. Gebühren, Zoll*: tariff ...; *Lohn*: standard ..., agreed ...; **II.** *Adv. Gebühren, Zoll*: according to the tariff; *Lohn*: according to scale, by agreement

Tarif|lohn *m Wirts.* standard wage(s *Pl.*) (*od.* rate of pay); **~partei** *f*, **~partner** *m* party to a wage agreement, side in wage (*od.* collective) bargaining; *Pl. auch* union(s) and management, social partners

Tarifpolitik *f Wirts., Zoll*: tariff policy; *Lohn*: pay (*od.* wages) policy; **tarifpolitisch** *Adj. nachgestellt*: related to tariff (*bzw.* pay) policy

Tarifrecht *n Wirts., Jur.* collective bargaining law; **tarifrechtlich** *Adj.* ... of collective bargaining law

Tarif|runde *f Wirts.* pay round; **~satz** *m bei Gebühren*: tariff rate; *Lohn*: (standard) wage rate (*od.* rate of pay); **~streit** *m Wirts., Zoll*: tariff issue (*od.* dispute); *Lohn*: pay (*od.* wage) dispute; **~system** *n Wirts., Zoll, Gebühren*: tariff(s) system; *Löhne*: collective pay agreements system; *Verk.* fares system; **~verbund** *m Verk.* fare association, fares area; **~vereinbarung** *f* →

Tarifabschluss; **~verhandlungen** *Pl. Wirts.* wage (*od.* pay) negotiations

Tarifvertrag *m Wirts.* wage (*od.* collective) agreement, wage settlement; **tarifvertraglich** *Adj.*: *~e Regelungen* regulations concerning collective agreements; **Tarifvertragspartei** *f* party to the (*od.* a) wage agreement, contracting party

Tarifzone *f Verk.* fare zone

Tarn|anstrich *m Mil.* camouflage paint (*od.* markings *Pl.*); **~anzug** *m* camouflage suit (*od.* fatigues *Pl.*), camouflage

tarnen I. *v/t. bes. Mil.* camouflage; (*Identität, Gefühle etc.*) disguise; *die Radarfalle war geschickt getarnt* the radar trap was well disguised; *als Punker getarnte Drogenfahnder* drugs investigators made up (*od.* disguised) as punks; **II.** *v/refl.*: *sich tarnen als* disguise o.s. as, get o.s. (*Am.* dress) up *umg.* to look like

Tarnfarbe *f Zool.* camouflage; *Mil.* camouflage (paint)

Tarnkappe *f Myth.* cap of invisibility, magic hood; **Tarnkappenbomber** *m Mil.* stealth bomber

Tarn|name *m* code name, cover name; **~netz** *n Mil.* camouflage netting; **~organisation** *f* cover (*od.* front) organization

Tarnung *f* camouflage (*auch fig. und EDV-Virus*), disguise, cover

Tarock *m, n*; -*s*, -*s* taroc, tarok

Tarot [ta'ro:] *n, m*; -*s*, -*s* tarot

Tartanbahn *f Sport* tartan track

Tasche *f*; -, -*n* **1.** *zum Tragen*: (*Einkaufs-, Reisetasche etc.*) bag; (*Reisetasche*) *auch* grip, holdall; (*Handtasche*) (hand)bag, *Am. auch* purse; *für Kamera, Handy etc.*: case; **2.** *in Kleidung etc.*: pocket; *in die ~ stecken* put in one's pocket; *zum Behalten*: pocket (*auch fig.*); *die Hände in die ~n stecken* put one's hands in one's pockets; *etw. aus der ~ ziehen* take (*od.* produce) s.th. from one's pocket; *j-m etw. aus der ~ ziehen fig.* trick (*od.* diddle *umg.*) s.o. out of s.th.; *j-n in die ~ stecken umg. fig.* be head and shoulders above s.o.; *er steckt s-e Mitschüler in die ~ auch* his classmates are no match for him (*od.* are not in the same league); *er steckt die Hände in die ~n fig.* he doesn't lift a finger, he doesn't do a stroke of work; *j-m auf der ~ liegen* live off s.o.; *in die eigene ~ arbeiten od. wirtschaften* line one's (own) pockets; *etw. aus eigener ~ bezahlen* pay for s.th. out of one's own pocket; *tief in die ~ greifen müssen* have to dig deep into one's pockets (*od.* break the piggy-bank); *sich (Dat.) in die eigene ~ lügen* fool (*od.* kid) o.s.; **3.** (*Fach*) *im Rucksack etc.*: pocket, compartment; **4.** *Gastr.* pastry case; *e-e ~ schneiden in ein Fleischstück zum Füllen*: cut a pouch in *a piece of meat for stuffing*; **5.** *Vet.* vulva

Taschen|ausgabe *f* pocket edition; **~billard** *n umg.* pocket billiards *Pl.* (*V. im Sg.*)

Taschenbuch *n* **1.** (*broschiertes Buch*) paperback; **2.** (*Notizbuch*) notebook; **~ausgabe** *f* paperback edition (*od.* version); **~reihe** *f* paperback series

Taschen|computer *m* palmtop (*od.* handheld) computer; **~dieb** *m*, **~diebin** *f* pickpocket, sneak-thief; **~diebstahl** *m* pickpocketing; **~fahrplan** *m* pocket (*od.* handy) timetable; **~format** *n* pocket (*od.* handy) size; *im ~* pocket-size(d); *ein Casanova im* ~ *umg. hum.* a wannabe (*od.* little) Casanova; **~geld** *n* pocket money, *Am.* allowance; **~inhalt** *m* **1.** contents *Pl.* of the (*od.* a *etc.*) bag, bag's contents *Pl.*; **2.** pocket contents *Pl.*; **~kalender** *m* (pocket) diary, *Am.* datebook; **~kamm** *m* (small) comb, pocket comb; **~kontrolle** *f* pocket check (*od.* search); *bei Gepäck:* bag search; **~krebs** *m Zool.* edible (*od.* common) crab; **~lampe** *f* (pocket) torch, *Am.* flashlight; **~messer** *n* penknife, *Am.* pocketknife; **~rechner** *m* (pocket) calculator; **~schirm** *m* compact (*od.* telescopic) umbrella; **~spiegel** *m* handbag mirror

Taschenspieler *m* conjurer, *Am.* magician; **~trick** *m fig.* piece of juggling; *bes. Pl. auch* sleight of hand *Sg.*

Taschen|tuch *n* handkerchief, hank|ie (*od.* -y) *umg.*; **~uhr** *f* pocket (*od.* fob) watch; **~wörterbuch** *n* pocket(-sized) dictionary

Tässchen *n Dim. von Tasse: noch ein* ~*?* have (*od.* like) a drop more?

Tasse *f*; -, -n cup; *bei Mengenangabe:* cup(ful); *e-e* ~ *Tee etc.* a cup of tea *etc.*; *er hat nicht alle* ~*n im Schrank umg. fig.* he's not all there, he's got a screw loose (somewhere), he's (mildly) gaga; → *trüb(e)* I 6

tassenfertig *Adj. Suppe, Getränk:* instant, made in the cup; **Tassenrand** *m* rim (*od.* lip) (of the cup); *am* ~ *ist Lippenstift* there's lipstick (*od.* a lipstick mark) on the cup

Tastatur *f*; -, -en keyboard, keys *Pl.*; **~eingabe** *f EDV* keyboard input, key strokes *Pl.*, keying-in

tastbar *Adj. bes. Med.* palpable

Taste *f*; -, -n; *Klavier etc., EDV* key; *Tech.* (Drucktaste) *auch* pushbutton; *e-e* ~ *betätigen od. drücken* press (*od.* hit) a key; *mächtig in die* ~*n hauen umg.* thump the keys, bash out the tunes

Tastempfindung *f* feel, tactile sensation

tasten I. *v/i. vorsichtig:* feel; *energischer:* grope; *ungeschickt:* fumble (*nach* for); *nach dem Lichtschalter / s-r Brieftasche* ~ feel (*od.* grope) for the light-switch / one's wallet; *der Blinde tastete mit e-m Stock* the blind man felt (a)round (*od.* his way) with a stick; **II.** *v/refl.* (*sich s-n Weg suchen*) feel (*od.* grope) one's way; **III.** *v/t.* **1.** feel, run one's fingers over; *Med.* palpate; **2.** (*eingeben*) enter, key in; *e-n Funkspruch* ~ key (*od.* type *od.* tap) in a radio message; **tastend I.** *Part. Präs.* → *tasten;* **II.** *Adj.* groping, uncertain; **~e Schritte** hesitant (*od.* uncertain) steps; *fig.* tentative moves (*od.* steps); **III.** *Adv.* (*mit den Fingern*) by feel (*od.* touch), with the fingers; (*zögernd, unsicher*) uncertainly, hesitantly, gropingly; *etw.* ~ *wahrnehmen* identify (*od.* recognize) s.th. by feel (*od.* touch *od.* its shape); *sich* ~ *durch den dunklen Flur bewegen* feel (*od.* grope) one's way along the (pitch-)dark corridor

Tasten|anschlag *m* **1.** *Tech.* touch; **2.** (*Niederdrücken e-r Taste*) keystroke; **~druck** *m* press(ing) of a key (*od.* button); *auf* ~ at the touch of a button; **~feld** *n* keypad; **~instrument** *n* keyboard instrument; **~kombination** *f EDV* key combination; **~reihe** *f* row of keys (*od.* buttons); **~telefon** *n* pushbutton telephone

Taster *m*; -s, - **1.** *Zool.* feeler, antenna;

2. *Tech.* (*Fühler*) scanner, sensor, probe; **3.** (*Werkzeug zum Messen*) (pair of) cal(l)ipers *Pl.*

Tast|haar *n* tactile hair; **~organ** *n* tactile organ, organ of touch; **~sinn** *m* sense of touch

tat *Imperf.* → *tun*

Tat *f*; -, -en **1.** (*das Tun, Handeln*) action; *durch* ~*en* in action, through (one's) actions, in practice; *Mann der* ~ man of action, doer; **2.** (*etw., was j-d tut*) act(ion), deed *geh.*; (*Straftat*) offen|ce (*Am.* -se); (*Verbrechen*) crime, felony; *schlimme:* (evil *od.* wicked) deed; ~ *der Verzweiflung* act of desperation; *grausame* ~ act of cruelty, cruel (*od.* callous) thing to do; *e-e* ~ *gestehen/leugnen* admit (*od.* confess to) / deny an offen|ce (*Am.* -se) (*od.* having done *s.th.*); *zu s-n* ~*en stehen* stand by one's actions (*od.* what one has done); *e-e gute* ~ *vollbringen* do a good deed; *den Worten* ~*en folgen lassen* suit the action to the word, be as good as one's word, take action; *auf frischer* ~ *ertappen* catch *s.o.* red-handed (*od.* in the act); *in der* ~ indeed; *er hat es in der* ~ *gemacht* (and) he actually did it, (and) he did (in fact) do it; → *Rat¹, schreiten* 2, *umsetzen* I 2

Tatar¹ *m*; -*en*, -*en* Ta(r)tar

Tatar² *n*; -*s, kein Pl.; Gastr.* **1.** (*Fleisch*) raw minced (*Am.* ground) beef, *Am. auch* raw hamburger; **2.** *zubereitet:* steak tartare; **~beefsteak** *n Gastr.* steak tartare; **~brötchen** *n Gastr.* steak tartare in a bun

Tatarin *f*; -, -*nen* Ta(r)tar, Ta(r)tar woman (*od.* girl); **tatarisch** *Adj.* Ta(r)tar

tätärätä *Interj.* tantantara!, di-di-di-da!

Tat|bestand *m* (*Sachlage*) state of affairs; (*Gegebenheiten*) facts *Pl.*, circumstances *Pl.*, (whole) truth of the matter; *Jur.* facts *Pl.* of the case; ~ *des Betrugs / des § 218* offen|ce (*Am.* -se) of fraud / under § 218; *objektiver/ subjektiver* ~ actus rea / mens rea, objective/subjective elements *Pl.* of the offen|ce (*Am.* -se); **~beteiligte** *m, f Jur.* culprit; **~beteiligung** *f* complicity, involvement; **~einheit** *f; nur Sg.: in* ~ *mit Jur.* in coincidence with

Tatendrang *m* energy, zest for action, get-up-and-go quality; *voller* ~ *sein umg.* be raring to go

Tatendurst *m* zest (*od.* thirst) for action; **tatendurstig** *Adj.* thirsting for action, champing (*od.* chafing) at the bit

tatenlos I. *Adj.* inactive, idle; **II.** *Adv.* inactively, idly; ~ *zusehen* stand by, sit back and watch; **Tatenlosigkeit** *f* passivity, failure to act

Täter *m*; -*s*, - culprit (*auch hum.*), perpetrator (*auch hum.*); *Jur.* offender; *wer war der* ~*?* who did it?, who was responsible (*od.* the culprit)?, who was the guilty party? *hum.*; *die Jagd nach dem* ~ the hunt for the killer *etc.* (*od.* the person responsible); *als* ~ *verdächtig sein* be a suspect; **Täterbeschreibung** *f* description of the wanted man *etc.*; **Täterin** *f*; -, -*nen* (female) culprit, perpetrator (*auch hum.*), woman (*od.* girl) who did it; *Jur.* (female) offender; **Täterkreis** *m* persons *Pl.* (*od.* those *Pl.*) suspected of having been involved; **Täter-Opfer- -Beziehung** *f Psych.* offender-victim relationship, Stockholm syndrome; **Täterprofil** *n* profile of the (*od.* an) of-

fender (*od.* the killer *etc.*), criminal profile; **Täterschaft** *f Jur.* **1.** (*Tätersein*) guilt, involvement, committing (*od.* commission) of an offen|ce (*Am.* -se); **2.** (*die Täter*) culprits *Pl.*, persons responsible

Tathergang *m* sequence of events, *bei Verbrechen auch* particulars *Pl.* of the crime

tätig *Adj.* **1.** (*beruflich arbeitend*) employed, working; ~ *sein als* work (*od.* be employed) as, (*fungieren*) act as; ~ *sein bei e-r Firma* work for; *in e-m Institut etc.* ~ *sein* work at an institute *etc.*; **2.** (*sich betätigend*) busy, (hard) at work, working (hard); *Vulkan:* active; ~ *werden* act, take action, intervene; **3.** (*geschäftig, rührig*) busy, hard-working, industrious, energetic; **4.** (*wirksam, tatkräftig*) active, effective, practical; ~*e Reue zeigen bes. Jur.* show one's remorse through one's actions

tätigen *v/t. Wirts.* (*Geschäfte etc.*) effect, transact; (*Investitionen*) place; (*Anruf*) make, put through; *Geschäfte* ~ *auch* do business; *e-n Abschluss* ~ conclude a deal; *e-n Einkauf* ~ make a purchase, negotiate an acquisition

Tätigkeit *f* **1.** (*das Sichbeschäftigen mit etw.*) activity; (*Funktion, Aufgabe*) activity, function, task, job; *das gehört zu den* ~*en e-r Hausfrau* that's one of a housewife's jobs (*od.* the things a housewife has to do); **2.** *berufliche:* occupation, job, (*Beruf*) *auch* profession; *sie nimmt i-e* ~ *als Lehrerin wieder auf* she's going (*bzw.* coming) back to teaching; *wir bieten e-e interessante* ~ *im Verlagswesen* we offer varied and interesting work in publishing (*od.* in a publishing environment); **3.** *des Herzens, e-r Maschine:* action; *e-s Vulkans:* activity

...tätigkeit *f, im Subst.* **1.** (*Arbeit*) *Forschungs*~ research (activity *od.* work); *Verwaltungs*~ administration, administrative duties *Pl.*; *Agenten*~ espionage, spying activities *Pl.*; **2.** (*Aktivität*) *Aufklärungs*~ *der Öffentlichkeit:* information campaign; *Mil.* reconnaissance (operations *Pl. od.* activity); *Kampf*~ military operations *Pl.*, fighting, action

Tätigkeits|bereich *m* field of activity, sphere (of activities), province; **~bericht** *m* progress report; **~beschreibung** *f* job description; **~feld** *n* → **~bereich**; **~merkmal** *n* job feature, feature of the job

Tatkraft *f; nur Sg.* (*Energie*) energy, vigo(u)r, dynamism, drive; (*Unternehmungsgeist*) enterprise, resourcefulness; **tatkräftig I.** *Adj.* dynamic, energetic, active, resourceful; ~*er Mensch auch* doer, achiever, can-do type *umg.*; **II.** *Adv. unterstützen etc.:* energetically, vigorously, effectively

tätlich I. *Adj.* violent; ~ *werden* become violent, use physical violence; *miteinander: auch* come to blows; **II.** *Adv.: j-n* ~ *angreifen* assault (*od.* physically attack) s.o.; **Tätlichkeit** *f* (physical) violence; *es kam zu* ~*en* fighting (*od.* a fight) broke out, there was violence

Tat|mensch *m* man of action, doer; **~motiv** *n* motive (for the crime)

Tatort *m* scene of the crime

tätowieren *v/t.* tattoo; *sich* ~ *lassen* get (*od.* have) o.s. tattoocd; **Tätowierer** *m*; -*s*, -, **Tätowiererin** *f*; -, -*nen* tattooist; **Tätowierstudio** *n* tattoo studio (*Am.* parlor); **tätowiert I.** *P.P.* → *täto-*

T

wieren; **II.** *Adj.* tattooed; **Tätowierung** *f* **1.** (*Bild*) tattoo; **2.** *nur Sg.* (*das Tätowieren*) tattooing

Tatsache *f*; -, -n fact; **den ~n ins Auge sehen** face the facts, be realistic; **j-n vor vollendete ~n stellen** present (*od.* confront) s.o. with a fait accompli; (**vollendete**) **~n schaffen** create a fait accompli, pre-empt the issue; **es beruht auf ~n** it's founded (*od.* based) on fact; **~ ist, dass** the fact (of the matter) is that; → **Boden** 6, **nackt**

Tatsachen|behauptung *f* allegation; **~bericht** *m* true story (*od.* account), factual account, report; *TV, Film etc.*: *auch* documentary; **~entscheidung** *f* *Sport* referee's decision; **~roman** *m* documentary novel; *Pl. Koll. auch* faction *Sg.*

tatsächlich I. *Adj.* real, actual, true; **II.** *adv.* really, ...; **~?** really?, do you (*od.* is it *etc.*) really?; **es regnet ~** it (really) 'is raining; **es hat ~ geklappt** it actually worked, it 'did work; **~ aber** but in reality, the fact is (however) that

tätscheln *v/t.* (*leicht schlagen*) pat; (*streicheln*) stroke

Tattergreis *m* *umg.* doddery old man, old dodderer; **Tatterich** *m*; -s, *kein Pl.*; *umg.*: **den ~ haben** have the shakes (*od.* trembles); **tatt(e)rig** *Adj. umg.* (*alt und unsicher*) doddery; (*zittrig*) shaky, trembly; *bei Aufregung*: trembling

Tatumstand *m* relevant circumstance (*od.* fact); **Tatumstände** *Pl.* circumstances (*od.* facts) of the case

tatütata *Interj.* nee-naw, nee-naw

Tatverdacht *m* suspicion (of a criminal act); **unter** (**dringendem**) **~ stehen** be under suspicion, be a prime suspect; *mit Ergänzung*: be (strongly) suspected (*zu* + *Inf.* of + *Ger.*); **tatverdächtig** *Adj.* under suspicion, suspected; **Tatverdächtige** *m, f* suspect

Tat|waffe *f* weapon (involved *od.* used); *bei Mord*: *auch* murder weapon; **~werkzeug** *n* implement (*od.* object) used (in the crime)

Tatze *f*; -, -n paw (*auch umg. Hand*)

Tat|zeit *f* time at which the crime (*od.* offen|ce [*Am.* -se] *od.* incident *etc.*) took place; **während der ~** at the time of the crime, while the crime was being carried out, at the relevant (*od.* operative) time; **~zeitpunkt** *m* moment (*od.* point) at which the crime was carried out, moment (*od.* point) at which the offen|ce (*Am.* –se) (*od.* incident) took place

Tat|zeuge *m*, **~zeugin** *f* witness to (*od.* of) the crime; *Augenzeuge auch* eye witness

Tau¹ *m*; -s, *kein Pl.* dew

Tau² *n*; -(e)s, -e; (*Strick*) rope; *Naut. auch* hawser, line

taub *Adj.* **1.** *Person*: (*gehörlos*) deaf (*fig.* **gegen**, **für** to); (*stocktaub*) stone deaf; (*schwerhörig*) hard of hearing; **er ist auf dem linken Ohr ~** he's deaf in his left ear; *fig.* he only hears what he wants to hear; **~ werden** go deaf, lose one's hearing; **sich ~ stellen** pretend not to hear, play deaf; **auf ~e Ohren stoßen** *fig.* fall on deaf ears; **~en Ohren predigen** talk to the winds, waste one's breath; **auf 'dem Ohr bin ich ~** *umg.* don't bother asking about that, I'm not budging on that one; **2.** *Glieder*: numb; **ein ~es Gefühl** a (feeling of) numbness, a numb (*od.* dead) feeling; **~ werden** go numb, lose its (*od.* their) feeling; **3.** (*leer, wertlos*) Ähre,

Nuss: empty; *Ei*: infertile; **~e Nuss** *fig.* dead loss, washout, non-starter, dud; **4. ~es Gestein** *Bergb.* attle, gangue, matrix

Täubchen *n* *Dim. von Taube*; *Gastr.* young (wood)pigeon; *Kosewort*: (my) pet, (my) darling

Taube¹ *m, f*; -n, -n deaf person; *Pl. mst* the hard of hearing, the deaf, deaf people

Taube² *f*; -, -n; *Orn.* pigeon; *Rhet., kirchl.* dove; *Pol.* (*Ggs. Falke*) dove; *Astron.* Columba, the Dove; **gebratene ~** *Gastr.* roast (wood)pigeon

Taubendreck *m* pigeon droppings *Pl.*

Taubenei *n* pigeon's egg; **taubeneigroß** *Adj.* (about) the size of a pigeon's egg, pigeon-egg-sized

taubengrau *Adj.* dove-grey (*Am.* -gray)

Tauben|schlag *m* dovecot(e); **hier geht's zu wie in e-m ~** *umg. fig.* it's like Piccadilly Circus (*Am.* Grand Central Station) (a)round here, this place is (getting) like Euston (*Am.* Grand Central) Station; **~schwanz** *m* *Zool.* humming bird moth; **~zucht** *f* pigeon-breeding (*od.* -fancying); **~züchter** *m*, **~züchterin** *f* pigeon breeder (*od.* fancier)

Tauber *m*; -s, -, **Täuber** *m*; -s, -, **Täuberich** *m*; -s, -e cock pigeon

Taubheit *f* *Gehör*: deafness; *der Glieder etc.*: numbness; **Taubheitsgefühl** *n* numb feeling, numbness

Täubling *m*; -s, -e *Pilz*: russula

Taubnessel *f* *Bot.* deadnettle

taubstumm *Adj.* deaf and dumb; **Taubstumme** *m, f* deaf mute, deaf and dumb person

Taubstummensprache *f* deaf-and-dumb language

Tauch|bad *n* *für Silber etc.*: dipping-trough (*od.* bath); *Med.* plunge bath; **~boot** *n* submersible (boat); **~club** *m* diving club

tauchen I. *v/i.* **1.** (*hat od. ist getaucht*) dive (**nach** for); **2.** (*ist*) (*untertauchen*) submerge; *U-Boot*: *auch* dive; *bes. kurz od. teilweise*: dip; **die Sonne tauchte unter den Horizont** the sun dipped (*od.* sank) beneath (*od.* below) the horizon; **3.** (*hat od. ist*) (*unter Wasser schwimmen*) *ohne Gerät*: (skin-)dive; *mit Gerät*: (scuba-)dive; **er kann zwei Minuten ~** he can stay under (water) for two minutes; **4.** (*ist*) (*in etw. hinein~*) sink, disappear, merge, fade (**in** + *Akk.* into); **ins Dunkel ~** fade into (*od.* disappear in[to]) the darkness; **5.** (*ist*) (*auf~*) emerge, appear, come up (**aus** out of *od.* from); *Schwimmer etc., schnell*: *auch* bob up; **e-e Insel tauchte aus dem Meer** an island emerged (*od.* detached itself) from the surrounding sea; **II.** *v/t.* (*hat*) dip (**in** + *Akk.* in[to]); *länger*: immerse (*od.* bathe) (in); (*Person*) *mit Gewalt*: duck; *länger*: hold under; **die Landschaft wurde in goldenes Licht getaucht** the countryside was bathed in (a) golden light (*od.* radiance)

Tauchen *n*; -s, *kein Pl.* diving; *mit Gerät*: (scuba-)diving; *Tiefsee*: (deep-sea) diving

Taucher *m*; -s, - diver (*auch Tier*); **~anzug** *m* *Tiefsee*: diver's suit; *Sport etc.*: wetsuit; **~ausrüstung** *f* diving equipment (*od.* kit *od.* gear); **~brille** *f*: (**e-e**) ~ (a pair of) diving (*od.* diver's) goggles *Pl.*; **~glocke** *f* diving bell; **~helm** *m* diver's helmet

Taucherin *f*; -, -nen (woman *od.* girl) diver, female diver

Taucher|krankheit *f* the bends *Pl.* (*auch V. im Sg.*), nitrogen narcosis *fachspr.*; **~maske** *f* diving (*od.* diver's) mask

Tauch|fahrt *f* dive, underwater voyage (*od.* sortie); **~gang** *m* dive; **~gerät** *n* (scuba-)diving equipment (*od.* gear)

tauchklar *Adj. U-Boot*: ready to submerge, clear to dive

Tauch|kugel *f* bathysphere; **~kurs** *m* diving course; **~schule** *f* diving school

Tauchsieder *m*; -s, - immersion heater

Tauch|sport *m* *ohne Gerät*: skin diving; *mit Gerät*: scuba diving; **~station** *f* *U-Boot*: diving station; **auf ~ gehen** dive, submerge; *umg. fig.* fade from the scene, go into hiding, quietly vanish

tauen I. *v/i.* **1.** (*ist getaut*) Eis, Schnee: thaw, melt; **der Schnee ist von den Dächern getaut** the snow (has) melted off the roofs; **2.** *unpers.* (*hat*) **es taut** it's thawing; **II.** *v/t.* (*hat*): **die Sonne hat den Schnee getaut** the snow (has) melted away (*od.* thawed) in the sunshine, the sun (has) melted the snow

Taufbecken *n* (baptismal) font

Taufe *f*; -, -n **1.** *kirchl.* baptism; *e-s Kindes*: *auch* christening; **die ~ empfangen** be baptized (*od.* christened); **2.** *fig., e-s Schiffes*: naming (ceremony); *e-n Verein etc.* **aus der ~ heben** start up a club *etc.*; **ein Projekt aus der ~ heben** launch a project; **taufen** *v/t.* **1.** *kirchl.* baptize, christen (*auch fig.*); **sich ~ lassen** get (o.s.) baptized; **j-n auf den Namen Anna ~** baptize s.o. as (*od.* christen s.o.) Anna; **2.** (*nennen*) call, name *geh.*; **ich taufe dich auf den Namen ...** *bei Schiffstaufe*: I name this ship ...; **Täufer** *m*; -s, -; *kirchl.* **1.** → **Johannes¹**; **2.** *Pl.* the Baptists

Tauf|feier *f* *kirchl.* christening (ceremony), baptism; **~kirche** *f* baptist(e)ry; **~kleid** *n* christening dress (*od.* robe), chrisom

Tauffliege *f* *Zool.* fruit fly

Täufling *m*; -s, -e child (*od.* person) to be baptized

Tauf|name *m* Christian (*Am. und bei Nichtchristen auch* given) name; **~pate** *m* godfather; *Pl.* godparents; **~patin** *f* godmother; **~register** *n* *kirchl.* baptismal register

taufrisch *Adj.* **1.** (*feucht vom Tau*) dewy; **2.** (*ganz frisch*) fresh (*auch fig*); *Person*: *auch* bright-eyed and bushy-tailed; **ein Strauß ~er Rosen** a bunch of fresh-picked roses; **sie ist auch nicht mehr ganz ~** *umg.* she's no spring chicken, she's past her prime

Tauf|schein *m* baptismal certificate; **~stein** *m* (baptismal) font

taugen *v/i.* **1.** (*wert sein*) **nichts ~** be no good (*od.* useless); **es taugt wenig** it isn't (*od.* it's not) much good; **taugt es etwas?** is it any good?; **es taugt alles nichts** *umg.* (*nutzt nichts*) it's no use, it's (all) a waste of time, we're (*od.* they're *etc.*) not getting anywhere; **er taugt nichts** *charakterlich*: he's not reliable, he's no good; **2.** (*geeignet sein*) be suitable (*od.* appropriate *geh.*); **sie taugt nicht zu dieser** *od.* **für diese Arbeit** she's not suited to (*od.* the right person for) this kind of work; **er taugt nicht zum Redner** he's not cut out for public speaking; *schärfer*: he's a hopeless (public) speaker; **3.** *österr.*: **wenn's dir nicht taugt** (*gefällt*) if it (*od.* that) doesn't suit you, if

you don't like it
Taugenichts *m*; *-es*, *-e* good-for-nothing
tauglich *Adj.* suitable, appropriate *geh.* (*für*, *zu* for); *Person: auch* qualified, competent, fit; *Mil.* fit (for service); *für voll/bedingt ~ erklären Mil.* pass *s.o.* fit / partially fit
...tauglich *im Adj.*: **hochsee~** *attr.* ocean-going, ...with ocean-going capability; **winter~** *attr.* all- (*od.* four-) season ..., winter ...; ... for winter use; **zucht~** *attr.* breeding(-quality) ...; ... of breeding quality
Tauglichkeit *f* suitability; *Mil.* fitness
Taumel *m*; *-s*, *kein Pl.* **1.** (*Schwindel*) (fit *od.* feeling of) dizziness (*od.* giddiness); *fig.* whirl; **2.** (*Rausch*) frenzy, rapture; *wie im ~* as if possessed; *im ~ der Begeisterung* carried away with enthusiasm; *im ~ der Sinne* in a sensual frenzy; **taumelig I.** *Adj.* **1.** (*schwindlig*) dizzy, giddy; (*benommen*) dazed; *ganz ~ vor Glück* giddy (*od.* delirious) with happiness; **2.** (*taumelnd*) *Person:* reeling, staggering, lurching; **II.** *Adv. gehen etc.*: unsteadily; **taumeln** *v/i.* **1.** (*hat od. ist getaumelt*) reel, stagger, sway; *ins Taumeln geraten Flugzeug*: go into a spin; **2.** (*ist*) *ins Bett*: collapse, fall; *nach vorn etc.*: lurch, stagger
Taupunkt *m Phys.* dewpoint
Taurus *m*; *-*, *kein Pl.*; *Geog.*: *der ~* the Taurus Mountains *Pl.* (*od.* range)
Tausch *m*; *-(e)s*, *kein Pl.* exchange, swap *umg.*; *im ~ für od. gegen* in exchange (*od. umg.* as a swap) for; *e-n guten/schlechten ~ machen* make (*od.* get) a good/bad deal; **~börse** *f* barter exchange; *Ort:* bartering cent|re (*Am.* -er)
tauschen *v/t/i.* exchange (*auch fig. Blicke, Worte, Schläge*); swap *umg.* (*auch fig. Schläge*); *die Plätze ~* change (*od. umg.* swap) places; *die Spieler tauschten die Trikots* the players exchanged shirts; *wollen wir ~?* shall we swap?, (would you) like to swap?; *tausche Fahrrad gegen Kinderbett* bicycle offered in exchange for cot; *sie hat mit e-r Kollegin getauscht* she did a swap with a colleague, she got a colleague to stand in for her; *die Partner ~* swap partners; *ich möchte nicht mit ihm ~* I wouldn't like to be in his shoes (*od.* place); *ich möchte mit keinem ~* I wouldn't (want to) swap with anyone
täuschen I. *v/t.* **1.** (*hereinlegen*) deceive, trick, fool *umg.*, con *umg.*, hoodwink *umg.*; *er hat uns ganz bewusst getäuscht* he deliberately deceived us; *sich ~ lassen* be deceived, be taken in, (let o.s.) be fooled (*von* by); *wenn mich nicht alles täuscht* unless I'm (*od.* if I'm not) much mistaken; **2.** (*irreführen*) mislead, lead astray; **3.** *Augen, Gedächtnis*: deceive; *wenn mein Gedächtnis mich nicht täuscht* if my memory serves me correctly, if I remember correctly (*od.* rightly *umg.*); **II.** *v/i.* **1.** (*irreführen*) be deceptive; *Sport:* feint; *Rugby:* sell a (*od.* the) dummy; **3.** *Schüler, bei Klassenarbeit etc.*: cheat, use dishonest methods *förm.*; *der Raum wirkt sehr groß - das täuscht* at first sight the room is huge - but it's not (actually) as big as it looks; **III.** *v/refl.* be (*od.* get it *umg.*) wrong, be mistaken; *oder täusche ich mich?* or am I wrong?, or have I got it wrong? *umg.*; *sich in j-m ~* be completely wrong about s.o.; *da*

täuscht er sich aber! he's very much mistaken there (*od.* about that), well, he's got another think (*Am.* thing) coming (on that one)!; *täusche dich bloß nicht!* make no mistake (about it)
täuschend I. *Part. Präs. →* **täuschen**; **II.** *Adj.* deceptive; **~e Ähnlichkeit** striking resemblance (*mit* to); **III.** *Adv.*: *j-m/e-r Sache ~ ähnlich sein* look exactly like s.o./s.th.; *er sieht s-m Bruder ~ ähnlich auch* he's the spit and image *od.* (*od.* spitting image *umg.*) of his brother, he and his brother are as (a)like as two peas in a pod; *es wirkt ~ echt* it could be real (*od.* genuine), it would fool anyone
Täuscher *m*; *-s*, *~in* *f*; *-*, *-nen pej.* deceiver, fraud, cheat, swindler, con merchant *umg.*
Tausch|geschäft *n* exchange (deal), swap *umg.*; **~handel** *m* **1.** *konkret:* exchange (deal), swap *umg.*; **2.** *allg.* barter(ing); *~ treiben* barter
tauschieren *v/t.* damascene, inlay; **Tauschierung** *f* damascene (work)
Tauschobjekt *n* object of exchange (*od.* barter), goods *Pl.* for barter
Täuschung *f* **1.** (*das Täuschen*) (practice of *förm.*) deception, deceit, fraud; *arglistige ~* wil(l)ful deceit; **2.** (*Sichtäuschen, Getäuschtsein*) self-deception, (self-)delusion; (*Irrtum*) mistake, illusion, false impression; *stärker:* delusion; (*Trugschluss*) fallacy; *optische ~* optical illusion; *sie gaben sich hinsichtlich ... keiner ~ hin* they were under no illusion(s) about (*od.* as to) ...
Täuschungs|absicht *f* intent(ion) to deceive; **~manöver** *n Mil.* feint; *fig.* diversion; **~versuch** *m* attempt to deceive (*Jur. auch* defraud); *Schule:* (attempted) cheating, attempt to cheat
Tausch|wert *m* exchange (*od.* barter) value; **~wirtschaft** *f* barter economy
tausend *Zahlw.* a (*od.* one) thousand; (*zahllose*) thousands of; *~ Euro* a (*od.* one) thousand euros; *~ und abertausend* thousands and thousands (*mit Substantiv* of); *ich muss noch ~ Dinge erledigen* I've still got a thousand things to do; *~ Dank!* thanks ever so much; *~ Küsse* thousand kisses
Tausend *n*; *-s*, *-e und -* thousand; *zu ~en* by the thousand; *in die ~e gehen* run into thousands
Tausender *m*; *-s*, *-* **1.** (*Zahl*) thousand; **2.** *umg.* (*Geldschein*) thousand-pound (*od.* dollar etc.) note (*Am.* bill)
tausenderlei *Adj.* **1.** (*von verschiedener Art*) a thousand different (kinds of), myriad; **2.** (*sehr viele*) countless, innumerable, a thousand, thousands of
tausendfach I. *Adj.* thousandfold; *in ~er Ausführung* a thousand copies (of ...); *das Tausendfache* a thousand times as much; **II.** *Adv.* a thousand times
Tausendfüß(l)er *m*; *-s*, *- Zool.* centipede; *seltener:* millipede
Tausendjahrfeier *f* millenary, millennium, thousandth anniversary
tausendjährig *Adj. attr.* thousand-year-old ..., a thousand years old, of a thousand years; *~es Jubiläum* millenary, millennial (*od.* thousand-year) jubilee; *das ~e Reich hist.* the Thousand-Year Reich; *bibl.* the Millennium
tausendmal *Adv.* a thousand times; *ich bitte ~ um Verzeihung geh. od. iro.* I am most dreadfully sorry
Tausendmarkschein *m hist.* thousand-mark note (*Am.* bill)

Tausendsas(s)a *m*; *-s*, *-(s)*; *umg.* amazing guy, real whizz-kid, boy wonder *iro.*
tausendst... *Zahlw.* thousandth; *→ acht...*; **Tausendste** *m*, *f*; *-n*, *-n* thousandth; **tausendstel** *Zahlw.* thousandth; *vier ~ Sekunden* four milliseconds, one two-hundred-and-fiftieth of a second; **Tausendstel** *n*; *-s*, *-* thousandth (part), one-thousandth
Tausendstelsekunde *f* millisecond, thousandth of a second
tausendundein *Adj.*: *ein Märchen aus Tausendundeine(r) Nacht* one of the Tales of (*od.* a tale from) the Arabian Nights
Tautologie *f*; *-*, *-n* tautology; **tautologisch** *Adj.* tautologous, tautological
Tautropfen *m* dewdrop
Tauwerk *n*; *nur Sg.* **1.** (*Tau als Material*) rope; **2.** *e-s Schiffes:* rigging
Tauwetter *n* thaw (*auch fig. Pol.*)
Tauziehen *n*; *-s*, *kein Pl.* tug-of-war (*um* for) (*auch fig.*)
Taverne *f*; *-*, *-n griechische, italienische:* taverna
Taxameter *m*, *n*; *-s*, *-* taximeter
Taxator *m*; *-s*, *-en*, *~in* *f*; *-*, *-nen* valuer, assessor
Taxe *f*; *-*, *-n* **1.** (*festgesetzter Preis*) rate; (*Gebühr*) fee; (*Steuer*) tax; **2.** (*Schätzung*) estimate, valuation; **3.** *umg. →* **Taxi**
Taxi *n*, *schw. m*; *-s*, *-s* taxi, cab; *Fahrzeugtyp:* taxicab; *~!* taxi!; *mit dem ~ fahren* go by taxi (*od.* cab), take a taxi (*od.* cab); *~ fahren beruflich:* be a taxi-driver (*Am. auch* cabby *umg.*), drive a taxi (for a living); *ein ~ rufen telefonisch:* call (*od.* phone for) a taxi, call a cab; *auf der Straße:* hail a taxi (*od.* cab)
taxieren *v/t.* **1.** (*schätzen*) estimate; *Wirts., Jur.* value, assess; **2.** *umg.* (*prüfend betrachten*) size up, look critically at, cast an eye over; **3.** *geh.* (*einschätzen*) (*Situation etc.*) read, size up, diagnose; **Taxierung** *f* estimate, valuation, assessment
Taxi|fahren *n*; *-s*, *kein Pl. beruflich:* taxi- (*od.* cab-)driving, driving a taxi *etc.*; **~fahrer** *m*, **~fahrerin** *f* taxi (*od.* cab) driver; *in Großstadt: auch* cabby *umg.*; **~fahrt** *f* taxi trip, journey (*od.* trip) by taxi; *kurze: auch* taxi ride, ride in a taxi; **~stand** *m* taxi rank, *bes. Am.* taxi stand, cabstand; **~unternehmen** *n* taxi firm (*Am.* company); **~zentrale** *f* taxi control cent|re (*Am.* -er)
Taxonomie *f*; *-*, *kein Pl.*; *Bio., Päd. etc.*: taxonomy
Tax|preis *m* assessed price; **~wert** *m* assessed (*od.* estimated) value
Tb, Tbc *f*; *-*, *kein Pl.*; *Abk.* (**Tuberkulose**) *Med.* TB, tuberculosis; **Tb(c)-Kranke** *m*, *f* TB (*od.* tuberculosis) patient; *Pl. oft auch* TB cases
Teak [ti:k] *n*; *-s*, *kein Pl.* teak; **~holz** *n*; *nur Sg.* teak; *Tisch aus ~* teak table
Team [ti:m] *n*; *-s*, *-s* team; *im ~ arbeiten* work in a team; **~arbeit** *f* teamwork; *etw. in ~ machen* do s.th. as a team; **~chef** *m*, **~chefin** *f* team manager
Team|gefährte *m*, **~gefährtin** *f* team(-)mate, fellow team member; **~geist** *m* team spirit; **~work** ['-wø:ɐ̯k] *n*; *-s*, *kein Pl. →* **Teamarbeit**
Technetium *n*; *-s*, *kein Pl.*; (*abgek.* **Tc**) *Chem.* technetium
Technik *f*; *-*, *-en* **1.** *nur Sg.* (*Technologie*) technology; *angewandte: mst* engineering, applied technology; *Studien-*

T

fach: engineering; *die moderne ~* modern (*od.* today's) technology; *von ~ verstehe ich gar nichts* I don't know the first thing about technical matters, I'm hopeless with anything technical (*od.* when it comes to technical things); → *Stand* 2; **2.** (*Methode, Verfahren*) technique (*auch Kunst, Sport etc.*), method, procedure, routine; *hoch entwickelte ~en* advanced techniques; **3.** *nur Sg.*; *Sport, Kunst* (*Können*) technique, technical ability, mastery; *er verfügt über e-e hervorragende ~* he has superb technique (*od.* prodigious technical ability); **4.** *nur Sg.* (*technische Ausrüstung*) technology, technical resources *Pl.* (*od.* equipment); *e-e Firma mit modernster ~* a company using state-of-the-art technology; **5.** *nur Sg.* (*technische Beschaffenheit e-r Maschine etc.*) mechanics *Pl.*, operation; **6.** *nur Sg.* (*Abteilung*) technical department, engineering side *umg.*; *jemanden von der ~ rufen* send for one of the technical people

...technik *f, im Subst.: mst* ... technology, ...engineering, ... technique(s *Pl.*); → *Technik*; *Arbeits~* (*Wissensbereich*) industrial engineering; (*Verfahren*) work(ing) technique; *Schweiß~* welding engineering (*od.* technology); *Wurf~ Sport* throwing technique

Techniker *m; -s, -, ~in f; -, -nen* **1.** (*Fachkraft*) (technical) specialist, engineer; (*Wissenschaftler[in]*) technologist; *bes. technische Unterstützung:* technician; **2.** (*Spezialist, auch Sportler*) technician

Technikum *n; -s, Technika* college (*od.* institute) of (advanced) technology

technisch I. *Adj.* **1.** *Tech., Abteilung, Verfahren etc.: attr.* engineering ...; (*wissenschaftlich*) technological; *allg.:* technical; *~e Anlagen* technical facilities (*od.* installations); *im Krankenhaus etc.: auch* technology; *Technische Hochschule* college (*od.* institute) of technology; *Technische Universität* technological university, (university-level) institute of advanced technology (*od.* science and technology), *Am. auch* polytechnic institute; *~es Leiter* technical director; *~es Personal* technical staff; *~er Kundendienst* customer engineering *fachspr.*, (after-sales) technical support (*od.* back-up *umg.*); *~er Zeichner /~e Zeichnerin* technical (*od.* engineering) draughtsman/draughtswoman; *~e Zeichnung* technical drawing; *~e Schwierigkeiten* technical problems (*od.* difficulties); *aus (verfahrens)~en Gründen* on technical grounds, for technical reasons; *Technischer Überwachungs-Verein* → *TÜV*; **2.** (*bes. betriebs~, auch Kunst, Sport etc.*) technical; *~er K.o.* technical knockout, TKO; **3.** *fig.* (*sachlich, rein formal, theoretisch*) technical; **II.** *Adv.: ~ begabt/interessiert* with an aptitude for things technical / technical(ly)-minded; *~ ausgereift* technologically mature (*od.* sophisticated); *e-e ~ schwierige Kür* a (-free) program(me) of great technical difficulty, a technically demanding (-free) program(me)

...technisch *im Adj.:* of ..., ...-related, ...-specific; *druck~* printing ..., technical; *fertigungs~* production ..., manufacturing ..., ... of production (engineering); *steuer~* tax ..., revenue ..., ... of taxation

technisieren *v/t.* mechanize; **techni-**

siert I. *P.P.* → *technisieren*; **II.** *Adj. Fertigungsmethoden etc.:* mechanical, mechanized; **Technisierung** *f* mechanization

Techno ['tɛçno] *m, n; -(s), kein Pl.; Mus.* techno

Technokrat *m; -en, -en* technocrat; **Technokratie** *f; -, kein Pl.* technocracy; **Technokratin** *f; -, -nen* technocrat; **technokratisch** *Adj.* technocrat(ic)

Technologe *m; -n, -n* technologist

Technologie *f; -, -n* technology; *~park m* technology (*od.* science) park; *~transfer m* technology transfer; *~werte Pl. Börse:* tech stocks; *~zentrum n* technology cent|re (*Am.* -er) (*od.* complex *od.* park)

Technologin *f; -, -nen* (woman *od.* female) technologist; **technologisch** *Adj.* technological

Technomusik ['tɛçno-] *f Mus.* techno (music)

Techtelmechtel *n; -s, -; umg.* carrying-on, flirtation, affair; *ein ~ mit j-m haben* be carrying on (*od.* doing a line, *Am.* fooling around) with s.o.

Teckel *m; -s, -; Zool.* (*Dackel*) dachshund

Teddy *m; -s, -s, ~bär m* teddy bear; *~futter n* fleece lining

Tee *m; -s, Sorten -s* **1.** tea; (*e-n*) *~ machen od. kochen* make some tea, make a pot (*od.* cup) of tea; *~ trinken* have a cup of tea; *schwarzer/grüner ~* black/green tea; *zwei ~ mit Zitrone* two teas with lemon; *abwarten und ~ trinken! umg. fig.* (let's [*od.* you'll just have to]) wait and see; *e-n im ~ haben umg. fig.* have had one too many, be (a bit) squiffy (*Am.* tipsy); **2.** *nur Sg.* (*Teenachmittag*) (afternoon) tea; *er kommt zum ~* he's coming to (*od.* for) tea

Tee|beutel *m* teabag; *~blatt n* tealeaf; *~dose f* tea caddy (*od.* tin); *~Ei n* infuser, tea ball; *~gebäck n* biscuits *Pl., Am.* cookies *Pl.*; *~glas n* tea glass; *~haus n japanisches:* teahouse; (*Geschäft*) (specialist) tea merchant; *~kanne f* teapot; *~kessel m* kettle; *~küche f* (tea) kitchen; *~licht n* tea warmer (candle), tea light

Teelöffel *m* teaspoon; *zwei (gestrichene) ~ voll* two (level) teaspoons(ful) (*od.* teaspoonfuls); *ein ~ Zucker* a (*od.* one) teaspoonful of sugar; **teelöffelweise** *Adv.* a teaspoonful at a time

Teemischung *f* blend of tea, tea blend

Teenager ['tiːneːdʒɐ] *m; -s, -* teenager; *Soziol.* adolescent

Teenager... *im Subst.* teenage ..., adolescent ...

Teenie ['tiːni] *m; -s, -s; umg.* teenybopper, young teenager; **Teens** ['tiːnz] *Pl. umg.* teens, teenagers, teenage set *Sg.*; **Teeny** ['tiːni] *m; -s, Teenies; umg.* → *Teenie*

Tee|pause *f* tea break; *~plantage f* tea plantation

Teer *m; -(e)s, kein Pl.* tar; *~decke f* tarred (road) surface, *Am. auch* pavement

teeren *v/t.* tar; *~ und federn* tar and feather

Teerfarbstoff *m* aniline dye

Teerose *f* tea rose

Teer|pappe *f* bituminous roofing felt, tar paper; *~seife f* coal-tar soap; *~straße f* tarred road

Tee|service *n* teaset, tea service; *~sieb n* tea strainer; *~sorte f* type of tea:; *~strauch* tea plant; *~tasse f* teacup; *~trinker m, ~trinkerin f: ich bin ~* I

drink tea, I'm a tea-drinker; *~wasser n: das ~ aufsetzen* put on the water (*in GB:* kettle) for (some) tea; *~wurst f Gastr.* smooth-textured sausage for spreading on bread etc.; *~zeremonie f* tea ceremony

Teflon® *n; -s, kein Pl.* Teflon, teflon; **teflonbeschichtet** *Adj.* Teflon-coated; **Teflonpfanne** *f* Teflon(-coated) frying pan

Teich *m; -(e)s, -e* pond; *e-n ~ anlegen* create a (garden) pool (*od.* pond), put in a pond *umg.*; *der große ~ fig.* (*der Atlantik*) the water, the (herring) pond *umg.*; *über den großen ~ fahren* cross the water (*od.* pond); *~huhn n Orn.* moorhen; *~muschel f Zool.* swan mussel; *~rose f Bot.* water lily; *~wirtschaft f* fish-farming

Teig *m; -(e)s, Sorten -e* dough; (*Teigmasse, Eierteig*) batter; *den ~ kneten/gehen lassen* knead the dough / leave the dough to rise; **teigig** *Adj.* doughy, pasty (*beide auch fig.*); *Kuchen etc.:* (*nicht gar*) not cooked, still wet

Teig|rädchen *n* pastry-cutting wheel; *~schüssel f* mixing bowl; *~tasche f Gastr.* pastry case; *~waren Pl.* pasta *Sg.*, pastas

Teil¹ *m; -(e)s, -e* **1.** part (*auch e-s Buches etc.*); *ein ~ davon* part (*od.* some) of it; *der größte ~* (+ *Gen.*) most of, the greater part of *geh.*; *bes. Menschen: auch* the majority of, most; *nur ein kleiner ~ stimmte dafür* only a minority were (*od.* was) in favo(u)r; *der arbeitende ~ der Bevölkerung* the working population; *im ersten ~ des Films am Anfang:* early on in the film; *bei Mehrteiler:* in part one of the film; *zu gleichen ~en* equally; *in zwei ~e zerbrechen* break in two; *aus allen ~en der Welt* from all over the world; *zum ~* partly, in part; *zum größten ~* largely, for the most part; *ich habe die Arbeit zum größten ~ fertig* I've more or less finished the work; *der Film war zum ~ sehr spannend* the film was very exciting in parts, there were some very exciting bits (*bes. Am.* parts) in the film; *wir sind zum ~ gefahren, zum ~ gelaufen* we drove part of the way and walked the rest; **2.** (*Partei*) side; *Jur.* party; *für beide ~e vorteilhaft* of advantage to both sides, mutually beneficial (*od.* advantageous)

Teil² *m, n; -(e)s, -e;* (*Anteil*) share, portion *geh.*; *sein ~ beitragen* do one's part (*Brit. auch* bit); *ich für mein(en) ~ ...* I for my part ..., as for me, I ...; *ich habe mir so mein ~ gedacht* I didn't (want to) say anything(, but I thought my thoughts); *er hat sein(en) ~ weg* he got his share; *fig.* he got what was coming to him; *dazu gehört ein gut ~ Frechheit* you've got to be pretty cheeky to do that (kind of thing), you need plenty of cheek (*od.* a certain amount of gall) if you're going to do that sort of thing

Teil³ *n; -(e)s, -e* **1.** (*Bestandteil, auch Tech.*) part, component, element; *das defekte ~ muss ausgetauscht werden* the faulty part needs to (*od.* must) be replaced; **2.** (*Stück*) piece; *ein Service mit 24 ~en* a 24-piece set (*od.* service); (*Kleidungsstück*) piece, (separate) item; *nur drei ~e zur Anprobe mitnehmen Schild vor Anprobekabine:* no more than three items to be taken for trying on; **3.** *umg.* (*Ding*) thing; (*Gerät*) gadget; *wo hast du dieses geile ~ gekauft?* where did you get that (*od.*

this), it's wild!; *das ~ macht es nicht mehr* this useless thing has given up the ghost

Teil‖abriss *m* partial demolition; **~abschnitt** *m* (*Strecke*) section; (*Bauabschnitt*) stage; **~abzug** *m Mil.* partial withdrawal; **~ansicht** *f* partial view; **~aspekt** *m* part, aspect; *das ist nur ein ~ des Problems* it's only part (*od.* one aspect *od.* one dimension) of the problem; **~autonomie** *f Pol.* partial (*od.* limited) autonomy

teilbar *Adj.* divisible; **Teilbarkeit** *f* divisibility

Teil‖bereich *m* section, sector, subdivision; **~betrag** *m* partial amount, component (sum), tranche; *bei Zahlung*: part payment; (*Rate*) instal(l)ment

Teilchen *n* **1.** particle (*auch Phys.*); **2.** *Dial.* (*Gebäck*) pastry, cake; **~beschleuniger** *m Phys.* particle accelerator; **~strahlung** *f Phys.* particulate radiation

teilen I. *v/t.* **1.** divide (*in* + *Akk.* into); (*auf~*) *auch* split (up); (*aus~, ver~*) share out, distribute, apportion *geh.*, divide up; *35 durch 7 ~* divide 35 by 7; *zwölf geteilt durch drei ist (gleich) vier* twelve divided by three is (*od.* equals) four; *etw. in gleiche Teile ~* divide s.th. (up) into equal parts; *in Grade ~* (*Messinstrument*) calibrate, graduate; **2.** (*j-s Ansicht, Bett, Gefühle, Schicksal etc.*) share; *ich teile d-e Meinung (nicht)* I (can't) agree with you (*über* + *Akk.* on, about); (*sich* [*Dat.*]) *etw.* (*mit j-m*) *~* share s.th. (with s.o.), split s.th. (with s.o.); *je zur Hälfte*: go halves on s.th. (with s.o.), split s.th. fifty-fifty (with s.o.); → *geteilt*; **II.** *v/refl.* **1.** divide; *Partei etc.*: *auch* split; *Zelle*: divide; *Menschen*: split up, separate; *Straße*: fork; *Vorhang*: open, part; **2.** *sich in etw. ~* share (*od.* split) s.th.; *von zweien*: *auch* go halves (on s.th.); *sich in die Kosten ~* share expenses; **III.** *v/i.* share; *er teilt nicht gern* he doesn't like sharing

Teiler *m; -s, -;* *Math.* factor, divisor; *der größte gemeinsame ~* the highest common factor

Teil‖erfolg *m* partial (*od.* qualified) success; **~ergebnis** *n Wahlen etc.*: first (*od.* interim) results *Pl.*; *Math. etc.* subtotal; **~gebiet** *n* (subsidiary) branch; **~genehmigung** *f* partial (planning) permission, partial building permit; **~geständnis** *n Jur.* partial confession (*od.* admission of guilt)

teilhaben *v/i.* (*unreg., trennb., hat -ge-*) participate, be involved, have a share (*od.* an interest) (*an* + *Dat.* in); *an Freude etc.*: share (in); **Teilhabe** *f; -, kein Pl.* participation, involvement, interest (*an* + *Dat.* in); **Teilhaber** *m; -s, -,* **Teilhaberin** *f; -, -nen; Wirts.* partner, associate, shareholder; *stiller ~* sleeping (*Am.* silent) partner

teilhaftig *Adj. lit.*: *e-r Sache ~ werden* be blessed with s.th., have s.th. bestowed on one

...teilig *im Adj.*: *zwei~* ... in two parts; *Anzug*: two-piece ...

Teilinvalidität *f* partial disablement

Teilkasko *f; -, kein Pl.; umg.* partial coverage insurance; **teilkaskoversichern** *v/t.* (*trennb., hat*) take out partial insurance cover; **Teilkaskoversicherung** *f Mot.* partial coverage insurance

Teil‖lieferung *f* part delivery (*od.* consignment); **~lösung** *f* partial solution; **~menge** *f Math.* subset

teilmöbliert *Adj.* partly (*od.* part-)furnished

Teilnahme *f; -, kein Pl.* **1.** (*aktives Teilnehmen*) participation, involvement (*an* + *Dat.* in) (*auch Jur.*), complicity *pej.*; *an e-r Versammlung*: attendance (at); *die ~ ist freiwillig* attendance (is) optional (*od.* voluntary); **2.** *fig.* (*Interesse*) interest (*an* + *Dat.* in); (*Mitgefühl*) sympathy (with), concern (for), *stärker*: compassion (for); (*Beileidsbezeugung*) condolences *Pl.* (on); *j-m s-e herzliche Teilnahme aussprechen* express one's (deepest *förm.*) sympathy to s.o., offer s.o. one's condolences *förm.*

teilnahmeberechtigt *Adj.* eligible; **Teilnahmeberechtigung** *f allg.* eligibility; *konkret*: qualification

Teilnahme‖gebühr *f* entry (*od.* participation) fee; **~voraussetzung** *f* Eignung etc.: entry requirement(s *Pl.*), prerequisite(s *Pl.*) for entry; (*Bedingung*) condition of entry

teilnahmslos I. *Adj.* (*apathisch*) apathetic; (*gleichgültig*) indifferent, uninterested; **II.** *Adv.* apathetically *etc.*; *sie saß vollkommen ~ da* she just sat there(, completely uninvolved), she (just) sat there like part of the furniture *umg.*; **Teilnahmslosigkeit** *f* apathy; (*Gleichgültigkeit*) indifference

teilnahmsvoll I. *Adj.* sympathetic, concerned; **II.** *Adv.* sympathetically, in a concerned way

teilnehmen *v/i.* (*unreg., trennb., hat -ge-*) **1.** *aktiv*: take part (*an* + *Dat.* in), participate (in), be involved (in); (*anwesend sein*) be present (at), attend (*s.th.*); *er nahm am Zweiten Weltkrieg teil* he fought (*od.* was) in the Second World War (*bes. Am.* in World War II); **2.** *fig. geistig*: take an interest (*an* + *Dat.* in); *mitfühlend*: sympathize (with); *mit 96 nimmt er noch an allem teil* he's 96 but (he's) still very alert (*od.* he still takes an interest in everything going on)

Teilnehmer *m; -s, -* **1.** *aktiver*: participant; *Pl. auch* those involved; *Sport*: competitor, entrant; (*Anwesender*) member of the group (*od.* audience etc.); *die ~* (*Anwesenden*) those present, the group (*od.* audience etc.) (*V. auch im Pl.*); *~ an der Schlussrunde Sport* finalist; **2.** *Telef.* subscriber; *der ~ meldet sich nicht Telef.* there's no reply (from that number); → *Rundfunkteilnehmer etc.*; **~feld** *n Sport* (field of) competitors *Pl.*, participants *Pl.*, entry; **~gebühr** *f* entry (*od.* participation) fee

Teilnehmerin *f; -, -nen* → **Teilnehmer**

Teilnehmer‖kennung *f EDV* tag; **~kreis** *m* (all) participants *Pl.*, (all) those *Pl.* involved (*od.* attending); **~land** *n* participating country, country participating; **~liste** *f* list of participants (*Sport auch* entrants); **~staat** *m* participating country, country participating; **~zahl** *f* *aktive Teilnehmer*: number of participants (*Sport auch* entrants); *Anwesende*: attendance (figure)

Teil‖prothese *f Dent.* (partial) denture; **~punkte** *Pl. Math.* division sign *Sg.* (*od.* colon *Sg.*); **~rückzug** *m* partial retreat (*od.* withdrawal *euph.*)

teils *Adv.* partly, in part; *es war ~ sehr langweilig* some of it was (*od.* some parts of it were) extremely boring; *~ ..., ~ ...* part(ly) ..., part(ly) ...; *~, ~ umg.* (*wechselnd, leidlich*) so-so,

mixed; *Gesundheit*: *auch* up and down; *hat es dir gefallen? - ~, ~* it was okay, it wasn't too bad; *~ bewölkt, ~ heiter* (variable cloudy and) sunny periods; *sie kamen ~ zu Fuß, ~ mit dem Fahrrad* some came on foot, some (*od.* others) on bicycles

Teil‖schuldverschreibung *f Wirts.* fractional (*od.* partial) debenture (bond); **~sieg** *m* partial (*od.* qualified) victory; **~sperrung** *f Verk.* partial closure; **~staat** *m* constituent state; **~strecke** *f Eisenb.* section; *Bus etc.*: (fare) stage; (*Etappe*) stage; *Sport* stage, leg; **~strich** *m Tech.* graduation (*od.* calibration) mark; **~stück** *n* (*Bruchstück*) fragment; (*Abschnitt*) section

Teilung *f* division (*auch Bio., Math.*); *Pol., von Gewalten*: separation; *e-s Landes*: partition; (*Verteilung*) distribution; *in Anteilen*: sharing, allocation; *e-r Straße*: division

Teilungs‖artikel *m Gram.* partitive article; **~klage** *f Jur.* action for partition (of assets); **~masse** *f Jur.* (bankrupt's) estate, available assets *Pl.*; **~zeichen** *n Math.* division sign

teilweise I. *Adv.* partially, partly, in part(s); (*in einigen Fällen*) in some cases; (*stellenweise*) in (some) places; **II.** *Adj. attr.* partial

Teilzahlung *f* part payment; (*Rate*) instal(l)ment; (*Ratenzahlung*) payment by instal(l)ments; *auf ~ kaufen* buy on instal(l)ments (*od.* credit *od.* Brit. auch hire purchase)

Teilzahlungs‖bank *f* finance house, credit institution; **~geschäft** *n* (*Gewerbe*) hire purchase business, credit selling; (*Transaktion*) hire purchase (*od.* credit) transaction (*od.* deal); **~kauf** *m* hire purchase, buying on credit; **~kredit** *m* hire purchase credit, *Am.* installment credit; (*Darlehen*) hire purchase loan, *Am.* deferred payment loan

Teilzeit *f; nur Sg.* part-time; *~ arbeiten* work (*od.* be employed) part-time; *das Recht auf ~* the right to work part-time; **~arbeit** *f* part-time work (*od.* employment); **~arbeitsplatz** *m* part-time job (*od.* post)

teilzeitbeschäftigt *Adj.* employed (*od.* working) part-time

Teilzeit‖beschäftigte *m, f* part-time employee (*od.* worker), part-timer *umg.*; **~beschäftigung** *f* part-time employment (*od.* work); **~kraft** *f* part--time employee (*od.* worker); *Fabrikarbeit, Landwirtschaft*: *auch* part-time hand

Tein [te'iːn] *n; -s, kein Pl.* theine

Teint [tɛ̃ː] *m, -s, -s* (*Hauttönung*) *Gesicht*: complexion, colo(u)ring; *Körper*: skincolo(u)r; (*Beschaffenheit der Gesichtshaut*) skin, complexion; *sie hat e-n unreinen ~* she's got bad skin (*od.* a pimply complexion)

T-Eisen *n* T-iron, T-beam

Tektonik *f; -, kein Pl.* **1.** *Geol., Archit.* tectonics *Pl.* (*V. auch im Sg.*); **2.** *Lit.* architecture, (artistic) structure, (overall) design; **tektonisch** *Adj.* tectonic, structural; **~e Verschiebungen** *Geol.* tectonic (*od.* plate) movements

Tele *n; -(s), -(s); Fot. umg.* telephoto (lens)

Tele‖arbeit *f* teleworking; **~arbeiter** *m*, **~arbeiterin** teleworker; **~arbeitsplatz** *m* home-based job, post (*Am.* job) working from home

Telebrief *m Post.* teletex® (*Am.* telex)

letter, fax; **per** ~ by fax

Telefax *n*; -, -*e*; *Telek.* **1.** (*Mitteilung*) fax; **2.** (*Gerät*) fax (*od.* facsimile *geh.*) machine; → **Fax**; **telefaxen** *vt/i.* mst nur im *Inf.* fax; → **faxen**

Telefon *n*; -*s*, -*e* telephone, phone; **am** ~ (*telefoniert*) on the phone; (*auf e-n Anruf wartend*) (waiting) by (*od.* at) the (tele)phone; **ans** ~ **gehen** (*ins Nebenzimmer etc.*: go to) answer the phone; **gehst du mal ans** ~**?** can you take that (call)?, can you answer (*od.* get *umg.*) the phone?; **ans** ~ **rufen** call *s.o.* to the (tele)phone; **du wirst am** ~ **gewünscht** you're wanted on the (tele)phone; **(kein)** ~ **haben** (not) be on the phone, *bes. Am.* (not) have a phone; **sich** (*Dat.*) ~ **legen lassen** get the phone in; **am** ~ **hängen** *umg.* yammer on the telephone

Telefon|aktion *f* telephone campaign; ~**anlage** *f* (tele)phone system; ~**anruf** *m* (tele)phone call; ~**ansage** *f* telephone information service; *konkret* (*Nachricht*) recorded message; ~**anschluss** *m* telephone connection (*od.* line); *als Nebenanschluss*: extension (line); ~ **haben** be on the phone, *bes. Am.* have a phone; ~**apparat** *m* (tele)phone

Telefonat *n*; -(*e*)*s*, -*e* → **Telefongespräch**

Telefon|auskunft *f* *Telef.* directory enquiries *Pl., Am.* information; ~**banking** *n* telephone banking; ~**buch** *n* telephone directory, phone book; ~**dienst** *m* telephone service; ~**gebühr** *f* (tele)phone charge; ~**gespräch** *n* (*Gespräch*) (tele)phone conversation; **ein** ~ **führen** make a (tele)phone call; → **Telefonat**; ~**häuschen** *n* telephone box (*od.* kiosk), (public) call-box, payphone; ~**hörer** *m* (telephone) receiver

Telefonie *f*; -, *kein Pl.; Telef.* telephony, telephonic communication

telefonieren *v/i.* (tele)phone, ring (*od.* call) up, call; **mit j-m** ~ *auch* talk to *s.o.* on (*od.* over) the (tele)phone; **nach Amerika** etc. ~ *umg.* phone to (*od.* call) the U.S. *etc.*; **er telefoniert ständig** he's on the phone all day, he's never off the phone; **darf ich mal** ~**?** may I use the phone (for a moment) (please)?

telefonisch I. *Adj.* (tele)phone ..., telephonic; ~**e Mitteilung** telephone message; ~**e Beratung** *ärztliche etc.* telephone consultation; ~**e Zeitansage** speaking clock, *Am.* prerecorded time message; **II.** *Adv.* by (tele)phone, on (*od.* over) the (tele)phone; *fachspr.* telephonically; ~ **nicht erreichbar zu Hause**: not on the phone; *verreist etc.*: not reachable (*od.* contactable) by phone; **sich** ~ **entschuldigen** ring (*od.* phone) to apologize

Telefonist *m*; -*en*, -*en*, ~**in** *f*; -, -*nen* (telephone) operator, telephonist

Telefonitis *f*; -, *kein Pl.; umg.:* **die** ~ **haben** be never off the phone, be addicted to the phone

Telefon|kabel *n* (tele)phone cord (*Brit.* auch lead); ~**karte** *f* phonecard; ~**kosten** *Pl. Firma:* telephone costs; *Einzelperson:* (tele)phone expenses; ~**kunde** *m*, ~**kundin** *f* (tele)phone subscriber, phone customer; ~**leitung** *f* telephone line; ~**marketing** *n* telephone selling, *Am.* telemarketing; ~**netz** *n* telephone network; ~**nummer** *f* (tele)phone number; ~**rechnung** *f* (tele)phone bill; ~**schnur** *f* (tele)phone cord (*Brit.*

auch lead); ~**seelsorge** *f etwa* help line, crisis line; *in GB: auch the* Samaritans *Pl.*; ~**sex** *m* telephone sex, phone sex, sex line(s *Pl.*); ~**terror** *m* telephone harassment; ~**überwachung** *f* (tele)phone tapping, listening in *umg.*; ~**umfrage** *f* (tele)phone survey; ~**verbindung** *f* telephone connection; ~**verkehr** *m* telephone use, communication by phone; ~**vermittlung** *f* switchboard; ~**verzeichnis** *n* telephone list; ~**zelle** *f* (tele)phone box, call box, *Am.* (tele)phone booth; ~**zentrale** *f im Betrieb:* switchboard, operator

Telefotografie *f* **1.** *nur Sg.* telephotography; **2.** (*Bild*) telephoto shot

telegen *Adj. TV* telegenic

Telegraf *m*; -*en*, -*en* telegraph

Telegrafen|amt *n* telegraph office; ~**leitung** *f* telegraph line; ~**mast** *m*, ~**stange** *f* telegraph pole

Telegrafie *f*; -, *kein Pl.* telegraphy; **drahtlose** ~ radiotelegraphy; **telegrafieren** *vt/i.* telegraph, wire; (*kabeln*) cable; **telegrafisch I.** *Adj.* telegraphic; ~**e Überweisung** telegraphic (*od.* cable) transfer; **II.** *Adv.* telegraphically, by telegraph, by wire; *gekabelt:* by cable; **Telegrafist** *m*; -*en*, -*en*, **Telegrafistin** *f*; -, -*nen* telegraphist, telegrapher

Telegramm *n*; -*s*, -*e* telegram; *ins Ausland: auch* cable(gram); ~**adresse** *f* telegraphic address; ~**formular** *n* telegram form (*Am.* blank); ~**stil** *m* telegram style, telegraphese; **im** ~ in telegraphese

Telegraph(...) *siehe* **Telegraf(...)**

Telekinese *f*; -, *kein Pl.* telekinesis; **telekinetisch I.** *Adj.* telekinetic; **II.** *Adv.* telekinetically

Telekolleg *n*; -*s*, *kein Pl.; in GB: etwa* the Open University; *Am. etwa* correspondence school with televised lessons

Telekom *f*; -, *kein Pl.: Deutsche* ~ Deutsche Telekom, (*the*) German telecommunications corporation

Telekommunikation *f* telecommunications *Pl.* (*auch V. im Sg.*)

Telekommunikations|industrie *f* telecom(munications) industry; ~**konzern** *m* (tele)communications group; ~**unternehmen** *n* telecommunications firm (*od.* company), *Am. auch* telco *umg.*

Telemark *m*; -*s*, -*s Skisport:* telemark (turn)

Telematik *f*; -, *kein Pl.* telematics *Pl.* (*V. auch im Sg.*)

Tele|medizin *f* telemedicine; ~**objektiv** *n* telephoto lens

Teleologie *f*; -, *kein Pl.* teleology; **teleologisch** *Adj.* teleological

Telepath *m*; -*en*, -*en* telepathist; **Telepathie** *f*; -, *kein Pl.* telepathy; **Telepathin** *f*; -, -*nen* (female) telepathist; **telepathisch I.** *Adj.* telepathic; **II.** *Adv.* telepathically

Telephon(...) *siehe* **Telefon(...)**

Teleprompter® *m*; -*s*, -; *TV* autocue, *Am.* teleprompter®

Teleshopping *n*; -, *kein Pl.* teleshopping

Teleskop *n*; -*s*, -*e* telescope; ~**antenne** *f* telescopic aerial (*od.* antenna); ~**auge** *n Zool.* telescope eye

teleskopisch I. *Adj.* telescopic; **II.** *Adv.* telescopically

Tele|spiel *n TV* game; ~**text** *m*; *nur Sg.; TV* teletext

Telex *n*; -, -*e* **1.** *nur Sg.* (*System*) telex

(system); **2.** (*Mitteilung*) telex; **3.** (*Gerät*) telex machine; **telexen** *v/t.* telex (**an** + *Akk.* to)

Teller *m*; -*s*, - **1.** plate; **flacher/tiefer** ~ shallow (*od.* flat) / deep plate; *bei größeren: auch* dinner/soup plate; **zwei** (**voll**) **Suppe** two plate(ful)s of soup; **sich** (*Dat.*) **etw. auf den** ~ **tun** help o.s. to s.th., put s.th. on one's plate; **2.** (*Plattenteller*) turntable; **3.** *am Skistock:* basket; **4.** *Jägerspr.* ear; ~**brett** *n* plate shelf; ~**eisen** *n* spring trap (*od.* snare); ~**fleisch** *n bes. österr. Gastr.* boiled beef (*od.* pork) (pieces); ~**gericht** *n Gastr.* simple meal (served on one plate); ~**mine** *f Mil.* anti-tank mine; ~**rand** *m* rim (of the plate); **nicht über den** ~ **gucken können** *umg. fig.* not be able to see beyond the end of one's nose; ~**wärmer** *m* plate warmer; ~**wäscher** *m*, ~**wäscherin** *f* dishwasher

Tellur *n*; -*s*, *kein Pl.*; (*abgek.* **Te**) *Chem.* tellurium

Tempel *m*; -*s*, - temple; ~**anlage** *f* temple building(s *Pl.*), temple and precinct(s); ~**bau** *m*; *Pl.* -*ten* **1.** (*Gebäude*) temple (building); **2.** *nur Sg.* (*das Bauen*) temple-building, construction of the (*od.* a *etc.*) temple; ~**herr** *m hist.* (Knight) Templar; ~**orden** *m hist.* → **Templerorden**; ~**ritter** *m* **1.** *hist.* (Knight) Templar; **2.** (*Freimaurer*) Knight Templar; ~**tanz** *m* temple (*od.* sacred) dance; ~**tänzerin** *f* temple dancer

Tempera *f*; -, -*s*, ~**farbe** *f* tempera, distemper *altm.*; ~**malerei** *f* tempera (painting), (painting in) distemper *altm.*

Temperament *n*; -(*e*)*s*, -*e* **1.** (*Wesensart*) temperament, disposition, character, nature; **hitziges** ~ hot temper; **ruhiges** ~ quiet disposition (*od.* nature); **er hat ein ruhiges** ~ *auch* he's very quiet by nature; **2.** *nur Sg.* (*Lebhaftigkeit*) vivacity, liveliness; (*Schwung*) verve, spirit; **er hat** ~ (*ist lebhaft*) he's very lively; (*hat Schwung*) he's got lots of spirit, he's a very go-ahead type; (*ist leicht erregbar*) he's got a short fuse (*od.* a fiery temperament *geh.*), he tends to get worked up easily; **er hat kein** ~ there's no life in him, he's got no real spark; **ihr** ~ **ist mit ihr durchgegangen** she got carried away, she got the bit between her teeth; **temperamentlos** *Adj.* spiritless; **Temperamentssache** *f: das ist* ~ it's a matter of temperament, *auch* he *etc.* can't help it, he's *etc.* (just) like that, that's the way he *etc.* is; **temperamentvoll** *Adj.* (*lebhaft*) very lively, vivacious; (*feurig*) fiery, spirited; (*ungestüm*) impetuous, hasty; *Auto:* zippy

Temperatur *n*; -(*e*)*s*, -*e* temperature; **bei e-r** ~ **von 8 Grad** at (a temperature of) 8 degrees; **bei** ~**en um ...** at temperatures around; ~**en bis zu ...** temperatures (of) up to; (*Tiefstwerte*) temperatures as low as; (**erhöhte**) ~ **haben** *Med.* have (*od.* be running) a temperature; *j-s* ~ **messen** take s.o.'s temperature; ~**anstieg** *m* rise in temperature(s); ~**ausgleich** *m* temperature balance (*od.* equalization); ~**fühler** *m Tech.* temperature sensor; ~**kurve** *f* temperature curve (*od.* graph); ~**messung** *f* temperature reading; ~**regler** *m* thermostat; ~**rückgang** *m* drop (*od.* fall) in temperature(s); ~**schwankung** *f* variation (*od.* change) in temperature; *Pl. auch* variable (*od.* fluctuating) temperatures; **~sturz** *m* sudden (*od.* sharp) drop (*od.* fall) in temperature; **~unterschied** *m* difference in temperature

temperieren *v/t.* temper (*auch Mus.*); **gut temperiert sein** have the right temperature

Templerorden *m hist.* Order of the Templar(s) (*od.* Knights Templar)

Tempi *Pl.* → **Tempo²**

Tempo¹ *n*; -*s*, -*s*, *mst Sg.* **1.** (*Geschwindigkeit*) speed, rate; **in rasendem ~** at breakneck speed; **in langsamem ~** at a slow pace, sedately; **das ~ angeben** set the pace; **aufs ~ drücken** *umg.* speed things up, step up the pace; **der hat vielleicht ein ~ drauf!** *umg.* he's doing some speed!, he's fairly moving!; **~!** *umg.* step on it!; **2.** *Fechten:* period; (*Schlag*) stop cut; (*Stoß*) stop thrust

Tempo² *n*; -*s*, *Tempi*; *Mus.* tempo (*Pl.* tempi); **aus dem ~ fallen** fail to keep time

Tempo®³ *n*; -*s*, -*s*; *umg.* (*Papiertaschentuch*) tissue, *umg.* Kleenex®

Tempo|begrenzung *f* speed limit (*od.* restriction); **~-30-Zone** *f* 20 m.p.h. zone (*od.* area); **~limit** *n* speed limit; **~macher** *m*, **~macherin** *f Sport* pacemaker, pacesetter

Tempomat *m*; -*en*, -*en*; *Mot.* cruise control

temporal *Adj. Ling.* temporal, of time; **~es Adverb** adverb of time; **Temporalsatz** *m* temporal clause, adverbial clause of time

temporär *Adj.* temporary; **~e Datei** *EDV* temp(orary) file

temporeich *Adj.* quickfire, fast-moving

Tempo|sünder *m*, **~sünderin** *f* speeding motorist, motorist who breaks the speed limit; **~taschentuch** *n umg.* tissue, *umg.* Kleenex®; **~wechsel** *m* change of tempo

Tempus *n*; -, *Tempora*; *Ling.* tense

Tendenz *f*; -, -*en* **1.** (*Entwicklung*) tendency (**zu** toward[s]); (*Entwicklungstrend*) trend, tendency; *Wirts.*, *Börse:* trend, sentiment; *pej. Pol.* slant; **steigende/fallende ~** *Wirts.* upward/downward trend, buoyant/depressed sentiment; **~ steigend/fallend** *Wirts.* prices *etc.* rising/falling; *fig.* outlook bright/deteriorating; *bei Person:* prospects bright/poor; **2.** (*Hang, Neigung*) tendency (**zu** to), inclination (to), disposition (to); **die ~ haben, etw. zu tun** have a tendency (*od.* tend *od.* be inclined) to do s.th.; **3.** (*einseitige Darstellungsweise*) *mst pej.* slant, bias, spin *umg.*, tendentiousness *geh.*; **~betrieb** *m Jur., Wirts.* proselytizing body (*od.* organization)

tendenziell I. *Adj.:* **es gibt e-e ~e Besserung** there are signs of improvement, the general trend is for the better, on balance things are getting better; **II.** *Adv.:* **~ unterscheiden sich die Parteiprogramme nicht** the broad tendency (*od.* outline) of the party manifestos (*Am. auch* platforms) is the same, the differences between the party manifestos (*Am. auch* platforms) are of detail rather than of substance; **tendenziös** *Adj.* tendentious, bias(s)ed, slanted

Tendenz|literatur *f Lit.* tendentious literature; **~wende** *f* change of direction, new trend (*od.* direction)

Tender *m*; -*s*, - **1.** *Eisenb.* tender; **2.** *Naut.* tender, supplies ship, victual(-l)er

tendieren *v/i.* tend (**nach, zu** to, to-

ward[s]); **dazu ~ zu** (+ *Inf.*) tend (*od.* incline) to (+ *Inf.*) (*od.* toward[s] + *Ger.*), be apt (*od.* inclined) to (+ *Inf.*); **nach rechts/links ~** *Pol.* have right-wing/left-wing tendencies *od.* leanings, be right-wing (*od.* rightist) / left-wing (*od.* leftist) in one's sympathies; **nach oben/unten ~** *Wirts.* show an upward / a downward trend, be buoyant / drift lower

Teneriffa (*n*); -*s*; *Geog.* Tenerif(f)e

Tenne *f*; -, -*n* threshing floor

Tennis *n*; -, *kein Pl.*; *Sport* tennis; **~anlage** *f* tennis courts *Pl.*; **~arm** *m Med.* tennis elbow; **~ball** *m* tennis ball; **~club** *m* tennis club; **~crack** ['-krɛk] *m umg.* tennis star, top tennis player; **~dress** *m* tennis kit (*Am.* outfit) (*od.* clothes *Pl.*); *Wirts.* tenniswear; **~halle** *f* covered court; **~kleidung** *f* tennis kit (*Am.* outfit) (*od.* whites *Pl.*); *im Geschäft:* tenniswear; **~maschine** *f* ball machine; **~match** *n* tennis match; **~meisterschaft** *f* tennis championship (*od.* tournament); **~partner** *m*, **~partnerin** *f* tennis (*od.* doubles) partner; **~platz** *m* tennis court; **~schläger** *m* tennis racket (*od.* racquet *geh.*); **~schuhe** *Pl.* tennis shoes; **~spiel** *n* **1.** *mst. Pl.* (*Sportart*) (the game of) tennis; **2.** *nur Sg.* (*das Spielen*) (playing) tennis; **3.** (*Partie*) game of tennis; **~spieler** *m*, **~spielerin** *f* tennis player; **~sport** *m* tennis (as a sport), the game of tennis; **~stunde** *f* tennis lesson; **~turnier** *n* tennis tournament; **~wand** *f* practice wall

Tenno *m*; -*s*, -*s* Tenno

'Tenor¹ *m*; -*s*, *kein Pl.* **1.** (*allgemeine Tendenz, Einstellung*) tenor, drift; (*wesentlicher Inhalt*) essence, substance, gist; **den gleichen ~ haben** be to the same tenor (*od.* mode), be to the same effect; **2.** *Jur.* (*Wortlaut*) (actual) wording

Te'nor² *m*; -*s*, *Tenöre*; *Mus.* **1.** tenor (voice *od.* part); **er singt ~** he sings tenor, he's a tenor; **2.** *Person:* tenor (singer *od.* player); **3.** *nur Sg.* (*Tenöre im Chor*) the tenors *Pl.*

Tenor|saxophon *n* tenor sax(ophone); **~schlüssel** *m Mus.* tenor clef; **~stimme** *f* tenor (voice)

Tenside *Pl. Chem.* surfactants

Tentakel *m*, *n*; -*s*, - **1.** *Zool.* tentacle; **2.** *Bot.* tentacle, hair

Teppich *m*; -*s*, -*e* carpet, *Am. auch* rug; **den roten ~ ausrollen** roll out the red carpet (*auch fig.*); *fig. auch* give *s.o.* the red carpet treatment; **fliegender ~** magic carpet; **etw. unter den ~ kehren** *fig.* sweep s.th. under the carpet (*Am. auch* rug); **auf dem ~ bleiben** be reasonable (*od.* realistic); **~boden** *m* fitted carpet, wall-to-wall carpeting; **~bürste** *f* carpet brush; **~fliesen** *Pl.* carpet tiles; **~händler** *m*, **~händlerin** *f* carpet dealer, *Am. auch* rug merchant; *Einzelhandel: auch* carpet retailer (*Am. auch* merchant); **~kehrer** *m* carpet-sweeper; **~kehrmaschine** *f* mechanical carpet-sweeper; **~klopfer** *m* carpet beater; **~knüpfer** *m*; -*s*, -, **~knüpferin** *f*; -, -*nen* carpet-maker; **~schaum** *m* carpet foam; **~stab** *m* auf Treppenstufen: stair-rod; **~stange** *f* carpet-beating stand

Terbium *n*; -*s*, *kein Pl.*; (*abgek.* **Tb**) *Chem.* terbium

Term *m*; -*s*, -*e*; *Math.*, *Phys.* term

Termln *m*; -*s*, -*e* **1.** (*vereinbarte Zusammenkunft, auch beim Arzt etc.*) appointment (**bei** with); (*vereinbarter*

Tag) date; (*Stunde*) time; **ein ~ beim Arzt** *auch* an appointment at the doctor's; **e-n ~ festsetzen** fix (*od.* agree on) a date; **sich** (*Dat.*) **e-n ~ geben lassen** get an appointment; **viele ~e haben** have a busy schedule, have a lot of appointments (to keep) (*od.* things on *umg. od.* engagements *förm.*); **e-n ~ vereinbaren/absagen** make/cancel an appointment; **e-n ~ vereinbaren** *auch* agree a date (*od.* time); **der ~ steht noch nicht fest** the date (*od.* time) has still to be fixed (*od.* decided); **2.** (*Abgabetermin, Fristablauf*) deadline, last date, latest time; **e-n ~ einhalten** meet a deadline; **3.** *Jur.* (*Verhandlung*) hearing

Terminabsprache *f* **1.** *Frist:* negotiation of a (*od.* the) deadline; **2.** *Zeitpunkt:* agreeing (of *od.* on) a date (*od.* time)

Terminal ['tɐːɐmɪn|] *m*, *n*; -*s*, -*s* **1.** *Flug.*, *auch Fracht:* terminal; **2.** *nur n*; *Computer:* terminal

Termin|arbeit *f* scheduled work, work to a fixed schedule; **~börse** *f Wirts.* futures exchange, forward market; **~druck** *m* time (*od.* deadline) pressure; **unter ~ stehen** *spezifisch:* be under pressure to meet a deadline; *allg.* have a (very) tight schedule; **~einlagen** *Pl. Wirts.* term (*od.* time) deposits

termin|gebunden *Adj. Person:* committed (*od.* tied) to a deadline; *Arbeit etc.:* fixed-completion (*od.* -delivery) ..., ... to a deadline (*od.* timetable); **~gemäß**, **~gerecht I.** *Adj. Fertigstellung etc.:* punctual, ... on time (*od.* schedule), ... to deadline; **II.** *Adv.* on schedule, on time, within the deadline

Termin|geschäft *n Wirts. allg.* futures (*od.* options) trading; (*Einzeltransaktion*) forward deal; **~kalender** *m* appointments book, diary; *Jur.* cause list, *Am.* docket; **e-n vollen ~ haben** have a busy (*stärker:* packed) schedule (*od.* a full diary)

terminieren *v/t.* **1.** (*befristen*) limit, set a time-limit for; **2.** (*festlegen*) schedule, fix (*od.* name *od.* set) a date for; **Terminierung** *f* (*Befristung*) limiting, limitation; (*Festlegung*) scheduling, fixing

Terminkontrakt *m* futures contract

terminlich I. *Adj. Festlegung etc.:* scheduling ..., timing ..., ... of scheduling (*od.* timing); **~e Schwierigkeiten haben** *engS.* have difficulty meeting a (*od.* the) deadline; *weitS.* (*zu viele Verpflichtungen haben*) have a very tight schedule; **aus ~en Gründen** owing to (*od.* because of) prior commitments; **II.** *Adv. festlegen etc.:* as regards date (*od.* time); **~ hinkommen** make a (*od.* the) deadline, make it (*od.* get there) in time; **ich schaffe es ~ nicht** I can't manage (*od.* do) it timewise, I can't fit it in

Terminmarkt *m Wirts.* futures (*od.* forward) market

Terminologie *f*; -, -*n* terminology; **terminologisch** *Adj.* terminological

Termin|plan *m* (*Kalender*) (time) schedule, appointments list; (*Programm*) program(me), agenda; **~planer** *m* (*Kalender*) personal organizer, Filofax®; **~planung** *f* scheduling, setting up a time schedule; **~schwierigkeiten** *Pl.:* **in ~ sein** *engS.* have difficulty meeting a (*od.* the) deadline; *weitS.* (*zu viele Verpflichtungen haben*) have a very tight schedule

Terminus *m*; -, *Termini* term; **Terminus technicus** *m*; - -, *Termini technici* technical term
Terminverschiebung *f* postponement
Termite *f*; -, -*n*; *Zool.* termite
Termiten|hügel *m* termites' nest; **~staat** *m* termite colony
Terpene *Pl. Chem.* terpenes
Terpentin *n*; -*s*, -*e* turpentine; **~öl** *n* turps *umg.*, oil of turpentine
Terrain [tɛˈrɛ̃ː] *n*; -*s*, -*s* **1.** *bes. Mil.* (*Gelände*) terrain, ground, country; *fig.* lie (*Am.* lay) of the land; *sich auf bekanntem ~ befinden fig.* be on familiar ground (*od.* territory); *das ~ vorbereiten fig.* do the groundwork; *das ~ sondieren umg. fig.* see how the land lies, reconnoit|re (*Am.* -er); **2.** (*Grundstück*) plot (of land), *Am. auch* lot; (*Bauplatz*) building site (*Am. auch* lot); **3.** *Geog.* earth surface, surface features *Pl.*, landforms *Pl.*
Terrakotta *f*; -, *Terrakotten* **1.** *nur Sg.* terracotta; **2.** (*Gegenstand*) terracotta object (*od.* vase *od.* figure *etc.*)
Terrarium *n*; -*s*, *Terrarien* terrarium
Terrasse *f*; -, -*n* terrace (*auch Geol.*)
terrassenförmig I. *Adj.* terraced, ... in terraces; **II.** *Adv.*: *~ anlegen* terrace, lay *s.th.* out in terraces
Terrassen|garten *m* terraced garden; **~haus** *n* stepped building, terrace; **~tür** *f* patio door
Terrazzo [tɛˈratso] *m*; -(*s*), *Terrazzi* terrazzo
terrestrisch *Adj.* terrestrial
Terrier *m*; -*s*, -; *Zool.* terrier
Terrine *f*; -, -*n* tureen
territorial *Adj.* territorial
Territorial|gewässer *Pl.* territorial waters; **~heer** *n* territorial army; **~hoheit** *f* territorial sovereignty
Territorialitätsprinzip *n Jur.* principle of territoriality, jus soli
Territorialstaat *m* territorial state
Territorium *n*; -*s*, *Territorien* territory
Terror *m*; -*s*, *kein Pl.* **1.** (*Terrorismus*) terrorism, act(s *Pl.*) of terror, terror; *das ist der reinste ~ umg.* that's terror tactics, that's pure blackmail; **2.** (*Terrorherrschaft*) rule by terror, State terror, reign of terror *hist. und fig.*; **3.** (*große Angst*) (blind) terror; **4.** *umg.* (*Streit*) quarrel(l)ing, fighting (state of) strife; *bei denen zu Hause ist immer ~* at home they are always fighting (*od.* at each other's throats); **5.** *umg.* (*Ärger*) fuss, uproar, stink; **~machen** go wild (*od.* spare *od.* ballistic); *mach keinen ~!* there's no need to make (*od.* kick up) such a fuss, (please) don't go over the top like that!, *Am. auch* keep your shirt on!; **~akt** *m* act of terrorism; **~aktion** *f* (*Anschlag*) terrorist attack; (*geplante Folge von Anschlägen*) terrorist campaign; **~anschlag** *m* terrorist attack (*od.* outrage *pej.*); **~bande** *f* group (*od.* gang) of terrorists; **~bekämpfung** *f* counter-terrorism, *the* fight against terrorism; **~herrschaft** *f* reign of terror
terrorisieren *v/t.* terrorize; **Terrorisierung** *f* terrorization, use of terror(ist) tactics
Terrorismus *m*; -, *kein Pl.* terrorism; **Terrorismusbekämpfung** *f* counter-terrorism, *the* fight against terrorism
Terrorist *m*; -*en*, -*en* terrorist
Terroristen|gruppe *f* terrorist group (*od.* cell); **~prozess** *m* terrorist trial
Terroristin *f*; -, -*nen* (female) terrorist
terroristisch *Adj.* terrorist; **~e Gewalt-**

tat act of terrorism; **~e Vereinigung** terrorist organization
Terror|kommando *n* terrorist command group (*od.* high command); **~methoden** *Pl.* terrorist methods (*od.* tactics), terror *Sg.*; **~organisation** *f* terrorist organization; **~regime** *n* terrorist regime; **~szene** *f* terrorist scene; **~welle** *f* wave of terrorism, series of terrorist outrages
Tertia *f*; -, *Tertien Päd. altm.* third and fourth year in a German secondary school; *österr.* third year in an Austrian Gymnasium; **Tertianer** *m*; -*s*, -, **Tertianerin** *f*; -, -*nen Päd. altm.* member of the Tertia; *österr.* third-year (secondary-school) pupil
tertiär *Adj.* **1.** tertiary; **~er Bereich** *Päd.* → *Tertiärbereich*; **2.** *Geol.* Tertiary; **3.** *Chem.* tertiary; **4.** (*drittrangig*) third-rate
Tertiär *n*; -*s*, *kein Pl.*; *Geol.* Tertiary (period); **~bereich** *m Päd.* tertiary level (of education), higher (and further) education
Terz *f*; -, -*en* **1.** *Mus.* third; *große/kleine ~* major/minor third; **2.** *kirchl.* (*Gebetsstunde*) terce; **3.** *Fechten:* tierce
Terzett *n*; -(*e*)*s*, -*e*; *Mus.* trio, terzetto
Terzine *f*; -, -*n*; *mst Pl.*; *Lit.* terza rima *Sg.*
Tesafilm® *m*; *nur Sg.* sellotape®, *bes. Am.* scotch tape®
Tessin *n*; -*s*; *Geog.* Ticino; **Tessiner** *m*; -*s*, -, **Tessinerin** *f*; -, -*nen* inhabitant of (*od.* person from) Ticino, *weiblich auch:* Ticinese woman (*od.* girl); **tessinisch** *Adj.* Ticinese
Test *m*; -*s*, -*s und* -*e* test; *bes. Wirts.* trial; *Päd.* test; (*schriftliche Wiederholung*) written test; *kurzer: auch* quiz
Testament *n*; -(*e*)*s*, -*e* **1.** will; *Jur.* last will and testament; *sein ~ machen* make one's (*od.* a) will; *j-n im ~ bedenken* remember (*od.* include) s.o. in one's will; *ein ~ anfechten* contest (*od.* dispute) a will; *j-s politisches ~ fig.* s.o.'s political legacy; *da kannst du gleich dein ~ machen! umg. fig.* you're for the high jump and no mistake!, *Am.* your name is mud!; **2.** *bibl.:* *Altes/Neues ~* Old/New Testament; **testamentarisch I.** *Adj.* testamentary; **II.** *Adv.* by will; *~ verfügen* dispose by will, lay down (*od.* provide) in one's will
Testaments|eröffnung *f* opening (*od.* reading) of a (*od.* the) will; **~vollstrecker** *m*, **~vollstreckerin** *f* executor, *weiblich auch:* executrix; (*Nachlassverwalter[in]*) administrator; **~vollstreckung** *f* execution of a (*od.* the) will
Testat *n*; -(*e*)*s*, -*e*; *Univ.* certificate, attestation
Test|aufgabe *f* test question (*od.* assignment); **~batterie** *f Psych.* test battery (*od.* series), set of tests; **~betrieb** *m Computer:* test mode; **~bild** *n TV* test card (*Am.* pattern); **~bohrung** *f* trial drilling
testen *v/t.* test; *~ auf* (+ *Akk.*) test for; *j-n auf s-e Reaktionsfähigkeit etc. ~* test s.o.'s reactions *etc.*; **Tester** *m*; -*s*, - tester, person conducting a (*od.* the) test
Testergebnis *n* result(s *Pl.*) of a (*od.* the) test
Testerin *f*; -, -*nen* (female) tester, woman (*od.* girl) conducting a (*od.* the) test
Test|fahrer *m*, **~fahrerin** *f* test driver; **~fahrt** *f* test drive; **~fall** *m* test case; **~flug** *m* test flight; **~frage** *f* test ques-

tion; **~gelände** *n* testing ground, research (*od.* experimental) facility
testieren I. *v/i.* make a will; **II.** *v/t.* (*bescheinigen*) certify, attest; **testierfähig** *Adj. Jur.* capable of making a will; **Testierfähigkeit** *f Jur.* capacity (*od.* fitness) to make a will, testamentary capacity
Testikel *m*; -*s*, -; *Anat.* testicle
Test|lauf *m allg.* trial (run); *Wirts.* pre-launch trial; **~methode** *f* test(ing) method(ology)
Testosteron *n*; -*s*, *kein Pl.*; *Med.* testosterone
Test|person *f* test subject; **~phase** *f* test(ing) stage, trial (*od.* experimental) period; **~pilot** *m*, **~pilotin** *f* test pilot; **~reihe** *f* series of tests, test series; **~serie** *f* **1.** → *Testreihe*; **2.** (*getestete Serie*) experimental (*od.* development) series; **~spiel** *n Sport* trial game (*od.* match)
Teststopp *m* test ban, ban on (nuclear) tests *od.* testing; **~abkommen** *n Pol.* test ban treaty
Test|strecke *f* test track; **~streifen** *m Med.* test strip; **~verfahren** *n* **1.** (*Methode*) test(ing) method(s *Pl.*) (*od.* methodology); **2.** (*Verwendung von Tests*) use of tests (*od.* testing); **~wahl** *f umg. Pol.* etwa straw poll; **~zweck** *m*: *zu ~en* for experimental purposes (only), as a trial
Tetanus *m*; -, *kein Pl.*; *Med.* tetanus; **~(schutz)impfung** *f* tetanus vaccination; **~serum** *n* anti-tetanus serum; **~spritze** *f* tetanus injection (jab, *Am.* shot *umg.*)
Tete-a-Tete [teta'tɛːt] *n*; -, -*s*; *bes. hum.* (*Schäferstündchen*) tryst; (*Privatgespräch*) tete-a-tete
Tetraeder *n*; -*s*, -; *Math.* tetrahedron
Tetralogie *f*; -, -*n*; *Lit.* tetralogy
teuer I. *Adj.* **1.** (*kostspielig*) expensive, *bes. Brit. auch* dear; *etw. für teures Geld kaufen* pay a lot of (*vorwurfsvoll:* auch pay good) money for s.th.; *wie ~ ist es?* how much is it?, what does it cost?; *Fleisch ist teurer geworden* meat prices have (*od.* meat has) gone up, meat has got(ten) more expensive; *es ist ganz schön ~ umg.* it's not exactly cheap, it's a lot of money; → *Pflaster*, *Spaß* **3**; **2.** *fig. altm. od. iro.* (*lieb*) dear (*j-m* to s.o.); *j-m lieb und ~ sein* be (very) dear to s.o.; *wertvoller Besitz etc.:* be s.o.'s pride and joy; *Kleinkind etc.:* be the apple of s.o.'s eye; *teurer Freund* good friend; *Anrede:* my good fellow (*od.* man); *m-e Teuerste* my beloved; **II.** *Adv.* dear(ly); *etw. zu ~ kaufen* pay too much (*od.* over the odds) for s.th.; *das kam ihn ~ zu stehen* it cost him a fortune; *fig.* he had to pay dearly for it; *sein Leben so ~ wie möglich verkaufen* sell one's life as dearly as possible, fight to the death; → *bezahlen* I 3, *erkaufen*
Teuerung *f* rise in prices; *allg.* price rises (*od.* increases) *Pl.*, price inflation
Teuerungs|ausgleich *m* adjustment for inflation; **~rate** *f* (*Inflation*) inflation rate, rate of inflation; **~welle** *f* wave of price increases; **~zulage** *f*, **~zuschlag** *m* cost-of-living allowance (*od.* bonus)
Teufel *m*; -*s*, - **1.** *nur Sg.*: *der ~* the Devil (*od.* devil), Satan, Old Nick *umg.*; *vom ~ besessen sein* be possessed by the devil; *den ~ austreiben* exorcize the devil; *bei j-m:* exorcize s.o.; *der ~ soll dich holen! umg.* (oh,)

to hell with you!; **2.** (*Dämon*) devil, demon, imp; *fig.* (*böser Mensch*) devil (incarnate *geh.*); **kleiner ~** little devil; **armer ~** poor devil (*od.* blighter *umg. od.* sod *Sl.*); **3.** *umg.* in *Wendungen:* **~** (**auch**)**!** blimey!, bloody hell! *Sl., Am.* holy Toledo!; **pfui ~!** angeekelt: yuck!, ugh!; *entrüstet:* that's disgusting!; **scher dich ~!** go to hell!; **j-n zum ~ jagen** send s.o. packing, kick s.o. out; **j-n zum ~ wünschen** wish s.o. in hell; **wer/wo/was zum ~?** who/where/ what the devil (the hell *Sl.*)?; **der ~** God knows; **zum ~ sein** *Geld etc.:* have gone (*od.* be) down the drain; *Motor etc.:* have had it (*od.* its chips), be phut (*Am.* kaput); **wie der ~** *od.* **auf ~ komm raus** *arbeiten etc.:* like the devil, like crazy; *rennen etc.:* like crazy (hell *Sl.*); **in ~s Küche kommen** get (o.s.) into a right (hell of a *Sl.*) mess, be up shit creek *Sl.*; **wenn sie das sieht** *etc.,* **dann ist der ~ los** there'll be merry hell (*Am.* be hell to pay), she'll hit the roof (*Am.* go ballistic); **dort ist der ~ los** there's all hell (let) loose (*od.* it's bloody chaos) (over) there; **vor Feiertagen ist bei uns der ~ los** (*sehr viel Betrieb*) things are always frantic here just before a break; **bist du des ~s?** have you gone mad?; **den ~ werd ich tun** I'll be damned (*od.* blowed, *Am.* darned) if I do, like hell I will *Sl.*; **er schert sich den ~ drum** he doesn't give a damn (about that); **der ~ steckt im Detail** the devil's in the details, it's the little things that always cause the problems; **den ~ an die Wand malen** tempt fate; **ihn reitet der ~** the devil's got into him; **da hat der ~ s-e Hand im Spiel** the whole thing's jinxed; **es müsste schon mit dem ~ zugehen, wenn es nicht klappen sollte** you'd have to be hellishly unlucky for it not to work out; **das hieße, den ~ mit dem Beelzebub austreiben** that would be out of the frying pan into the fire; **wenn man vom ~ spricht**(, **dann ist er nicht weit**) speak (*od.* talk) of the devil (and he's sure to appear); **etw. fürchten wie der ~ das Weihwasser** dread s.th., be terrified (*od.* petrified) of s.th.; **hinter etw. her sein wie der ~ hinter der armen Seele** not rest till one gets one's hands on s.th.
Teufelei *f;* -, -en; *umg.* piece of devil(-t)ry, devilish trick
Teufelin *f;* -, -nen; *fig.* **1.** *umg.* (*temperamentvolle Frau*) live wire, bit of a devil; (*Unruhestifterin*) firebrand, harridan; **2.** *pej.* (*bösartige Frau*) she-devil, devil in human form
Teufels|austreibung *f* exorcism; *bibl.* casting out of devils (*od.* unclean spirits); **~braten** *m altm. umg.* **1.** *hum.* (*Schlingel*) rogue, rascal, rapscallion, madcap; **2.** (*boshafter Mensch*) (real) bad lot; **~kerl** *m umg.* daredevil, devil (*od.* hell) of a guy; **~kreis** *m nur Sg.; fig.* vicious circle; **~kralle** *f Bot.* rampion, phyteuma; **~kult** *m* (cult of) devil-worship, satanic cult; **~messe** *f* Black Mass; **~weib** *n umg.* **1.** *bewundernd:* live wire, bit of a devil; **2.** *pej.* she-devil; **~werk** *n altm.* (the) devil's handiwork; *Gegenstand: auch* instrument of the devil; **~zeug** *n umg.* infernal (*od.* hellish *od.* appalling) stuff
teuflisch I. *Adj.* **1.** diabolical, of the devil; **2.** (*bösartig, grausam*) devilish, diabolical, fiendish, evil; **~es Lächeln** fiendish grin, evil leer; **3.** *umg. verstärkend:* hellish, massive, terrific; **II.** *Adv.*

---

devilishly, diabolically, fiendishly; **~ kalt** *etc. umg.* hellish(ly) (*od.* fiendishly) cold *etc.,* cold *etc.* as hell *Sl.*
Teutone *m;* -*n,* -*n,* **Teutonin** *f;* -, -*nen* Teuton; **teutonisch** *Adj. auch fig.* Teutonic
Text *m;* -(e)s, -e **1.** text (*auch Druck.*); (*Wortlaut*) (actual) wording, words *Pl.* used; *fig.* plot, thread; **e-e Nachricht mit dem ~ ...** a message saying ...; **der ~ lautet wörtlich: ...** the actual wording is, the words used are: ..., what the text actually says is: ...; **den ~ e-r Rede drucken** print (*od.* reproduce) a speech in full (*od.* the full text of a speech); **e-n ~ erfassen** *bes. EDV* put a text on disk (*od.* on computer), capture a text; **j-n aus dem ~ bringen** *fig.* put s.o. off (his *od.* her stroke); **weiter im ~!** *umg.* go on!, keep going!; **2.** (*Auszug*) passage (of text), extract; *Ling.* text; *e-s Schauspielers:* lines *Pl.,* part; **s-n ~ lernen** learn one's part (*od.* lines); **3.** *Mus., e-s Liedes:* words *Pl.,* lyrics; *Oper:* libretto; **4.** (*Unterschrift zu einer Abbildung*) caption
Text|analyse *f Ling., Päd.* text(ual) analysis, analysis of texts (*od.* a text); **~aufgabe** *f* **1.** *Math.* problem; **2.** *zum Textverständnis:* comprehension test, text (comprehension) assignment; **~ausgabe** *f* (scholarly) edition (of a [*od.* the] text); **~baustein** *m* text module; *EDV* (piece of) autotext; **~buch** *n Oper:* libretto; *Musical:* book; **~dichter** *m,* **~dichterin** *f Lied:* songwriter, lyricist; *Oper:* librettist; **~eingabe** *f Handy etc.:* (short) text message input
texten *vt/i.* (*Lied etc.*) write the words (for); *Mus.* write (the) lyrics (for); *Werbung:* copywrite, write (the) copy (for); **Texter** *m;* -*s,* -, *Hörspiel etc.:* script writer; *Werbung:* copywriter; (*Schlagertexter*) songwriter, lyricist
Texterfassung *f bes. EDV* putting a text on disk (*od.* on computer); *mit Scanner: auch* scanning in (of) a text
Texterin *f;* -, -*nen* → **Texter**
Text|fassung *f* version of a (*od.* the) text; **~gestaltung** *f EDV* text formatting (and layout)
textil *Adj.* textile; **~es Werken** *Schule:* fabrics and design
Textil|arbeiter *m,* **~arbeiterin** *f* textile worker; **~betrieb** *m* textile firm (*od.* business); **~branche** *f* textiles sector, textiles *Pl.;* **~bremse** *f Sport, umg.* shirt-grabbing; **~chemie** *f* textile chemistry; **~fabrik** *f* textile factory (*od.* plant)
textilfrei *umg.* **I.** *Adj.* nude, *präd. auch* starkers, *Am.* stark naked; **~er Strand** nudist beach; **II.** *Adv. baden etc.:* (in the) nude; **~ baden** *auch* skinny-dip
Textilien *Pl.* textiles
Textil|industrie *f* textile industry; **~strand** *m umg.* covered-up beach, beach where costumes (*Am.* swimwear) must be worn
textilverarbeitend *Adj.* textile-manufacturing
Textilwaren *Pl.* textiles
Textkritik *f; nur Sg.* textual criticism; **textkritisch** *Adj.* critical, of (textual) criticism
textlich I. *Adj. attr. Gestaltung etc.:* text(ual), of the text; **II.** *Adv. gesehen etc.:* as (*od.* in terms of) text, as regards (the) text; **etw. ~ verändern** make textual changes (*od.* a textual change) to s.th., alter (*od.* modify) the wording (*od.* text) of s.th.

Text|marker *m* marker pen, highlighter; **~passage** *f* passage (in a *od.* the text); **~programm** *n EDV* word processing program, word processor; **~sammlung** *f Päd. etc.:* anthology (of texts), text collection; **~sorte** *f Ling., Päd.* text type; **~stelle** *f* passage (in a *od.* the text); **~teil** *m* main body (of a *od.* the work), continuous text section
Textur *f;* -, -*en* **1.** *e-s Stücks etc.:* (detailed) structure; **2.** *Geol., Chem., Tech.* texture, structure
Textverarbeitung *f EDV* word processing
Textverarbeitungs|programm *n* word processing program; **~system** *n* **1.** word processing system; **2.** word processor
Text|vergleich *m* comparison of texts, text(ual) comparison; **~vorlage** *f* original text (*od.* document)
T-förmig *Adj.* T-shaped, ... in the form of a T
TH *f;* -, -*s; Abk.* (**Technische Hochschule**) → **technisch** I 1
Thailand (*n*) -*s; Geog.* Thailand; **Thailänder** *m;* -*s,* -, **Thailänderin** *f;* -, -*nen* Thai, *weiblich auch:* Thai woman (*od.* girl); **thailändisch** *Adj.* Thai; **Thailändisch** *n;* -(*s*); *Ling.* Thai; **das ~e** the Thai language
Thallium *n;* -*s, kein Pl.;* (*abgek.* **Tl**) *Chemie* thallium
Theater *n;* -*s,* -. **1.** (*Gebäude*) theat|re (*Am. auch* -er); **2.** *nur Sg.;* (*Institution*) (the) theat|re (*Am. auch* -er); (*die Bühne*) the stage; **beim ~ sein** have a theat|re (*Am. auch* -er) job, *mst* be an actor (*od.* actress), act for a living; **zum ~ gehen** go on the stage; **sie will zum ~** (**gehen**) *auch* she wants to be(come) an actress, she wants to act; **ich habe als Student viel ~ gespielt** in my university days (*od.* when I was a student) I did a lot of acting (*od.* I was very into theat|re [*Am. auch* -er]); **ins ~ gehen** go to the theat|re (*Am. auch* -er); **das antike/epische/ absurde ~** ancient theat|re / epic theat|re / theat|re of the absurd (*Am. auch* -er); **wann fängt das ~ an?** (*Vorstellung*) when does the performance begin?; **3.** *nur Sg.;* (*Publikum*) audience; **das ganze ~ lachte** the audience roared with laughter; **4.** *nur Sg.; umg. fig. pej.* (*Verstellung*) play-acting, histrionics *Pl. geh.;* **~ spielen** put on an act; *bes. Sport* play-act; **das ist alles nur ~** (*gespielt*) that's just put on, that's all play-acting; **5.** *nur Sg.; umg. fig. pej.* (*Aufregung, Ärger*) fuss, to-do, excitement, bother, trouble, carry-on; (*j-m*) **ein ~ wegen etw. machen** kick up a fuss (with s.o.) about s.th.; **mach kein ~!** don't make such a fuss!; **es ist immer das gleiche ~** it's always the same old carry-on (*Am.* spiel); **das war (vielleicht) ein ~** (*Aufregung*) that was a bit of a flap (if I ever saw one); (*Aufwand*) that was a (right) carry-on (*Am.* a huge foofaraw)
Theater|abend *m Theat.* evening at the theat|re, theat|re visit (*Am. auch* -er); **~abonnement** *n* theat|re (*Am. auch* -er) subscription (*od.* season ticket); **~agent** *m,* **~agentin** *f* theatrical agent; **~agentur** *f* theatrical agency; **~aufführung** *f* play, theatrical performance *geh.;* **~besuch** *m* theat|re visit, visit to the (*od.* a) theat|rc (*Am. auch* -er); **~besucher** *m,* **~besucherin** *f* theatregoer, *Am. auch* theatergoer; **~bühne** *f* stage; **~donner** *m* stage

(*od.* artificial) thunder; **alles nur ~!** *fig.* they're *etc.* just making a lot of noise, it's pure hype *fig.*, it's all just sound and fury *geh.*; **~ensemble** *n* theat|re (*Am. auch* -er) ensemble; **~ferien** *Pl.* theat|er (*Am. auch* -er) holidays *Pl.* (*od.* close season); **~festival** *n* drama festival; **~gänger** *m*; *-s*, *-*, **~gängerin** *f*; *-*, *-nen* theatregoer, *Am. auch* theatergoer; **wir sind begeisterte ~** we love going to the theat|re, *Am. auch* -er; **~geschichte** *f* history of the theat|re (*Am. auch* -er); **~ schreiben** *fig.* make theatrical history; **~karte** *f* theat|re (*Am. auch* -er) ticket; **~kasse** *f* (theat|re, *Am. auch* -er) box office; **~kritik** *f* **1.** *nur Sg. Koll.* drama criticism, theat|re (*Am. auch* -er) reviews *Pl.*; **2.** (*Rezension*) theat|re (*Am. auch* -er) (*od.* play) review; **~kritiker** *m*, **~kritikerin** *f* drama critic; **~leitung** *f* theat|re (*Am. auch* -er) management (team); **~leute** *Pl.* (professional) theat|re (*Am. auch* -er) people; **~probe** *f* (play) rehearsal; **~produktion** *f* dramatic (*od.* theatrical) production; **~programm** *n* **1.** (*Spielpläne*) theat|re's (*Am. auch* -er's) program(me) (-of forthcoming events); **2.** (*Heft*) theat|re (*Am. auch* -er) program(me) (book); **~publikum** *n* theat|re (*Am. auch* -er) audience; **~regisseur** *m*, **~regisseurin** *f* theat|re (*Am. auch* -er) director; **~saal** *m* auditorium, theat|re (*Am. auch* -er); **~skandal** *m* scandal in the theatrical world; **~stück** *n* (stage) play, drama; **~vorstellung** *f* (stage) performance; **~werkstatt** *f* **1.** (*technische Unterstützung*) theat|re (*Am. auch* -er) workshop; **2.** *fig.* (*Bühne*) drama workshop; **~wissenschaft** *f allg.* theory of drama; *Studienfach*: theat|re (*Am. auch* -er) studies *Pl.*; **~wissenschaftler** *m*, **~wissenschaftlerin** *f* drama expert, expert on dramatic theory (and practice)

Theatralik *f*; *-*, *kein Pl.*; *pej.* histrionics *Pl.*, self-dramatization; **theatralisch I.** *Adj.* theatrical (*auch fig. pej.*), histrionic *fig. pej.*; **sein ~es Gehabe** his histrionics *Pl.*, his (love of) strutting and posing; **II.** *Adv. pej. herumstelzen, ankündigen etc.*: theatrically, affectedly

Theismus *m*; *-*, *kein Pl.* theism; **theistisch** *Adj.* theistic

Theke *f*; *-*, *-n in Lokal*: bar; (*Ladentisch*) counter; **an der ~ stehen** stand at the bar (*od.* counter); **unter der ~** *fig.* under the counter

Thema *n*; *-s*, *Themen und altm. Themata* **1.** *e-s Buchs etc.*: subject, topic; *e-s literarischen Werkes*: *auch* theme; **ein aktuelles ~** a topical (*od.* current) issue; **5 Themen zur Wahl stellen** give a choice of 5 topics, give 5 topics to choose from; **zum ~ kommen** get (*od.* come) to the point; **beim ~ bleiben** stick (*od.* keep) to the point (*od.* one's theme); **vom ~ abkommen** fail to keep to the point, lose sight of the topic; **das ~ wechseln** change the subject; **das ~ verfehlen beim Aufsatz:** go completely off the subject, not answer the question; **~ verfehlt** irrelevant; **~ Nummer eins** the number one topic; (*Sex*) everybody's favo(u)rite topic; **das ist ein heikles/leidiges ~** that's a delicate subject / an unpleasant topic; **das ist für mich kein ~ mehr** I don't want to hear another word about it; **kein ~!** *umg.* (*kein Problem*) no problem!; **2.** *Mus.* theme; **ein ~ variieren**

compose (*spielen* play) variations on a theme; **3.** *Ling.* theme

Thematik *f*, *-*, *-en, mst Sg.* **1.** *gedanklich*: subject (matter), (inter-related) themes *Pl.*, topics *Pl.*; **2.** *Mus.* thematic invention; **thematisch I.** *Adj.* **1.** *allg.* thematic; **nach ~en Gesichtspunkten geordnet** arranged by (*od.* according to) subject; **2.** *Mus.* thematic; **~es Verzeichnis** thematic catalog(ue); **II.** *Adv.* thematically; **~ ist der Aufsatz interessant** the subject matter of the essay is interesting, the essay is on an interesting subject (*od.* topic); **thematisieren** *v/t.*: **etw. ~** make s.th. a subject of discussion (*od.* the theme of a book *etc.*), explore problems (*od.* the issue *etc.*) of s.th.; **Thematisierung** *f* discussion, examination, exploration

Thema|verfehlung *f*: **wegen ~ e-e 6 bekommen** get an F for deviating from the subject; **~wechsel** *m* change of subject (*od.* topic); **~:** ... switching (*od.* moving on) to another subject *od.* topic now ...

Themen|abend *m TV etc.*: theme evening; **~bereich** *m* subject area; **~katalog** *m* list of topics (*od.* subjects); **~komplex** *m* complex of themes, inter-related themes *Pl.*; **~kreis** *m* subject area; **~park** *m* theme park; **~schwerpunkt** *m* (broad) main theme, underlying (general) theme; **~stellung** *f* formulation (of the topic), angle (*od.* perspective) on the topic; **~vielfalt** *f e-s Romans etc.*: multiplicity of themes, thematic complexity; *bei Gesprächen etc.*: host of topics; **~wahl** *f* choice (*od.* selection) of topics (*od.* a topic)

Themse *f*; *-*; *Geog.*: **die ~** the Thames

Theokratie *f*; *-*, *-n* theocracy

Theologe *m*; *-n*, *-n* theologian

Theologie *f*, *-*, *-n*, *mst Sg.* theology; **~professor** *m*, **~professorin** *f* professor of theology (*od.* divinity); **~student** *m*, **~studentin** *f* theology (*od.* divinity) student, theologue *umg.*; **~studium** *n* theology (*od.* divinity) studies *Pl.*, (degree) course in theology

Theologin *f*; *-*, *-nen* (female) theologian; **theologisch** *Adj.* theological

Theorem *n*; *-s*, *-e* theorem

Theoretiker *m*; *-s*, *-*, **~in** *f*; *-*, *-nen* **1.** (*Wissenschaftler*) theoretician; **2.** *pej.* theorist; **er ist reiner ~** he has a very theoretical approach to things; **theoretisch I.** *Adj.* theoretical; *pej.* academic; **~er Unterricht** theory instruction (*od.* teaching); **II.** *Adv.* theoretically, in theory; **~ hat er Recht** *auch* he's right in theory; **nehmen wir rein ~ an ...** let's assume for the sake of argument ...; **theoretisieren** *v/i.* theorize, conjecture

Theorie *f*; *-*, *-n* **1.** theory (+ *Gen.* of, *über* + *Akk.*, *zu* on, about); **e-e ~ aufstellen** put forward (*od.* propound *geh.*) a theory; **... - so die ~ ...** - or so the theory goes, or that's the theory anyway; **2.** *nur Sg.*; *Ggs. Praxis*: theory, the theoretical side; (*Unterricht*) (teaching of *od.* instruction in) theory; **in der ~** in theory; **das ist reine ~** that's all (*od.* pure) theory; **das ist graue ~** it sounds all right in theory; **die ~ in die Praxis umsetzen** apply the theory, put the theory into practice

Theoriegebäude *n* (*Gefüge*) theoretical edifice; (*Konstrukt*) theoretical construct

Therapeut *m*; *-en*, *-en* therapist; **Therapeutik** *f*; *-*, *kein Pl.* therapeutics *Pl.* (*V. im Sg.*); **Therapeutikum** *n*; *-s*, *Therapeutika* therapeutic (agent); **Therapeutin** *f*; *-*, *-nen* (female) therapist; **therapeutisch I.** *Adj.* therapeutic; **II.** *Adv.* therapeutically

Therapie *f*; *-*, *-n*; *Med.*, *Psych.* therapy, treatment; **e-e ~ machen** undergo (*od.* have) therapy, undergo (*od.* have) a (course of) treatment; **e-r ~ unterziehen** treat, give *s.o.* therapy; **e-e ~ abbrechen** stop (*od.* suspend) a course of therapy; **~einrichtung** *f* treatment facilities *Pl.*; **~erfolg** *m* success with a therapy; **~platz** *m* place on the treatment list; **e-n ~ bekommen** be accepted (*od.* taken on) as a patient

therapieren *v/t. Med.*, *Psych.* treat, give *s.o.* (a course of) treatment, give *s.o.* therapy

Thermal|bad *n* **1.** (*Kurort*) spa with hot springs, thermal spa; **2.** (*Behandlung*) thermal bath; **3.** (*Schwimmbad*) thermal baths *Pl.*; **~quelle** *f* thermal (*od.* hot) spring; **~schwimmbad** *n* thermal baths *Pl.*

Therme *f*; *-*, *-n* **1.** thermal (*od.* hot) spring; *Pl. auch* (ancient) Roman baths; **2.** *Tech.* (gas) water heater, *Brit. auch* geyser

Thermik *f*; *-*, *kein Pl.*; *Met.* thermal activity, thermals *Pl.*; **thermisch** *Adj.* thermal

Thermo|chemie *f* thermochemistry; **~drucker** *m* thermal printer

Thermodynamik *f* thermodynamics *Pl.* (*V. im Sg.*); **thermodynamisch** *Adj.* thermodynamic

thermoelektrisch *Adj.* thermoelectric

Thermohose *f*: (*e-e*) (a pair of) thermal trousers (*Am.* pants) *Pl.*

Thermometer *n*; *-s*, *-* thermometer; **~stand** *m engS.* thermometer reading; *weitS.* temperature

thermonuklear *Adj.* thermonuclear

Thermopanefenster® [tɛrmo'peɪn-] *f* double- (*od.* triple-)glazed window, sealed window unit

Thermopapier *n* thermal paper

Thermoplaste *Pl. Chem.* thermoplastics; **thermoplastisch** *Adj.* thermoplastic

Thermos|flasche® *f* thermos (*od.* vacuum) flask (*Am.* bottle); **~kanne**® *f* (*Kaffeekanne*) thermal coffee pot; → *auch* **Thermosflasche**

Thermostat *m*; *-s und -en*, *-e(n)* thermostat

Thermowäsche *f* thermal underwear (*od.* underclothing)

Thesaurus *m*; *-*, *Thesauren und Thesauri* **1.** (*thematisch geordnetes Wörterbuch*) thesaurus (*Pl.* thesauri *od.* thesauruses); **2.** *hist.* (*Schatzhaus*) treasury

These *f*; *-*, *-n* thesis (*Pl.* theses), hypothesis (*Pl.* hypotheses); (*Theorie*) theory; **Luthers 95 ~n** Luther's 95 theses (*od.* propositions); **Thesenpapier** *n Univ. etc.*: (academic *od.* research) paper; *Zusammenfassung*: synopsis (of a lecture)

Thessalonicher *m*; *-s*, *-*; *hist.* Thessalonian; **Brief an die ~** → **Thessalonicherbrief**, **~brief** *m bibl.*: **der 1./2. ~** the (*od.* St [*od.* St.] Paul's) 1st/2nd Epistle (*od.* Letter) to the Thessalonians, Thessalonians I/II

Thing *n*; *-(e)s*, *-e*; *hist.* thing; **~platz** *m*, **~stätte** *f hist.* thingstead

Thomas *m*; *-*; *fig.*: **ungläubiger ~** doubting Thomas

Thomasverfahren *n nur Sg.; Metall.* Thomas-Gilchrist (*od.* basic Bessemer) process

Thon *m; -s, -s und -e; schw. Zool.* tuna, tunny

Thora *f; -, kein Pl.* Torah; **~rolle** *f* Torah scroll; **~schrein** *m* ark of the Law

Thorax *m; -es, -e; Anat.* thorax

Thriller ['θrɪlɐ] *m; -s, -* thriller

Thrombose *f; -, -n; Med.* thrombosis (*Pl.* thromboses); **~strümpfe** *Pl. Med.* anti-thrombotic stockings

thrombotisch *Adj. Med.* thrombotic

Thron *m; -(e)s, -e* throne (*auch fig.*); **den ~ besteigen** ascend (*od.* accede to) the throne; **auf den ~ verzichten** renounce (one's right *od.* claim to) the throne; **j-m auf den ~ folgen** succeed s.o. on the throne; **vom ~ stoßen** *auch fig.* dethrone, oust (from the throne; **sein ~ wackelt** *umg., auch fig.* his throne looks insecure; **auf dem ~ sitzen** *fig., hum.* be on the throne; **~anwärter** *m,* **~anwärterin** *f* (*Thronfolger*) heir apparent; *bei Streitfällen:* claimant to the throne; **~besteigung** *f* accession to the throne

thronen *v/i. Person:* be enthroned (*auch fig.*); *fig. Sache* (*Burg etc.*): stand proud(ly), dominate the scene *etc.; darüber thront ...* it is crowned by...; **auf s-m Sessel ~** *umg.* be enthroned in one's armchair

Thron|erbe *m,* **~erbin** *f* heir to the throne; **~folge** *f; nur Sg.* succession; **~folger** *m,* **~folgerin** *f* successor to the throne; **~räuber** *m* usurper (of the throne); **~rede** *f* speech from the throne; *in GB:* Queen's (*od.* King's) Speech; **~saal** *m* throne room

Thuja *f; -, Thujen; Bot.* thuja, arbor vitae

Thunfisch *m Zool.* tuna (fish), tunny

Thüringen (*n*) *-s; Geog.* Thuringia, Thüringen; **Thüringer I.** *m; -s, -;* Thuringian; **~ sein** be (a) Thuringian, come from Thuringia; **II.** *f; -, -; Gastr.* (*Wurst*) Thuringian sausage; **III.** *Adj.* Thuringian; **~ Wald** Thuringian Forest; **~ Rostbratwurst** *Gastr.* Thuringian sausage; **Thüringerin** *f; -, -nen* Thuringian (woman *od.* girl); **thüringisch** *Adj.* Thuringian, from Thuringia

Thusnelda *f; -, -s; umg., neg.!* bird, chick; **kommt deine ~ auch mit?** is that bird (*Am.* chick) of yours coming (along) too?

Thymian *m; -s, kein Pl.; Bot.* thyme

Thymusdrüse *f* thymus (gland)

Tiara *f; -, Tiaren ; kirchl., hist.* tiara

Tibet (*n*) *-s; Geog.* Tibet; **Tibet(an)er** *m; -s, -,* **Tibet(an)erin** *f; -, -nen* Tibetan, *weiblich auch:* Tibetan woman (*od.* girl); **tibet(an)isch** *Adj.* Tibetan; **Tibetisch** *n; -en; Ling.* Tibetan; **das ~e** the Tibetan language

Tic *m; -s, -s* → **Tick**[1]

Tick[1] *m; -s, -s; Med.* tic

Tick[2] *m; -s, -s; umg.* **1.** (*Schrulle*) (strange) quirk (*od.* foible); **e-n ~ haben** be a bit mad, be rather strange, have strange ways; **2.** (*Nuance*) shade, touch, tinge; **e-n ~ schneller/besser** a shade (*od.* marginally) faster/better

ticken I. *v/i.* **1.** *Uhr etc.:* tick; **2.** *umg.:* **er tickt nicht richtig** *od.* **bei ihm tickt's nicht richtig** he's not (quite) all there, he's got a screw loose somewhere; **Frauen ~ etwas anders** women's thought-processes are rather different, women react rather differently; **II.** *v/t. Sl.* twig, *Am.* catch on; **Ticker** *m; -s, -; Sl.* (stock) ticker, telex

Ticket *n; -s, -s* ticket

ticktack *Interj.* tick-tock; **~ machen** *Kindersp.* go tick-tock

Ticktack *f; -, -s; Kindersp.* (*Uhr*) tick-tock

Tide *f; -, -n* tide

Tidenhub *m* tidal range

tief I. *Adj.* **1.** *allg.* deep; **60 cm ~** *Schrank etc.:* 60 cm deep; **ein 3 m ~es Becken** a 3-met|re (*Am.* -er) (deep) pool, a pool 3 m deep; **e-e 10 cm ~e Wunde** a wound 10 cm deep; **~er Fall** *Bergwand etc.:* long fall; *fig.* great fall; **~er Teller** soup plate; **~er Ausschnitt** *Kleidungsstück:* deep décolleté (*od.* cleavage); **~er Boden** *Gartenboden etc.:* deep soil; *aufgeweicht:* muddy (*od.* soft) ground; *Fußball etc.:* heavy (*od.* muddy) pitch; **es liegt ~er Schnee** there's deep snow (on the ground); **stille Wasser sind ~** *Sprichw.* still waters run deep; **2.** *fig. Gedanke, Erkenntnis, Wissen etc.:* profound, deep; **3.** *oft fig.* (*niedrig*) low (*auch Ton*); *Stimme:* deep; **den ~sten Stand erreicht haben** *Sonne:* have reached its lowest point; *Kurs, Beziehungen etc.:* have reached an all-time low; **4.** *Farbton:* deep, dark; **~e Schatten** dark shadows, *unter den Augen:* auch dark rings; **5.** *intensivierend:* deep; **aus ~stem Herzen** from the bottom of one's heart, from the depths of one's being *geh.;* **im ~sten Innern** in one's heart of hearts, deep down (inside); **im ~sten Winter** in the depths (*od.* dead) of winter; **im ~sten Afrika** in darkest Africa, in the (dark) heart of Africa; **im ~en Süden der USA** in the Deep South (*od.* deep south); **in ~er Trauer** in deep mourning; **II.** *Adv.* **1.** deep(ly), deep (*od.* far) down, down low; **zwei Stockwerke ~er** two floors down; **~ fallen** fall a long way (*od.* from a great height); *fig.* sink low (*stärker:* to the depths); **er ist ~ gesunken** he's really come down in the world; **~er kann er nicht mehr sinken** he can't sink any lower, he has hit rock-bottom; **~ ausgeschnitten** deeply décolleté, (very) low-cut, with a plunging neckline; **~ atmen** *länger:* breathe deeply; *einmal:* take a deep breath (*auch fig.*); **sich ~ bücken** bend (*od.* get *umg.*) down low (*od.* right down); **j-m ~ in die Augen sehen** look deep into s.o.'s eyes; **~ in Gedanken** deep in thought; **in e-r Sache ~ drinstecken** *umg.* be in it up to one's neck, be right in there; **das geht bei ihr nicht sehr ~** (*beeindruckt nicht*) that doesn't cut much ice with (*od.* much of an impression on) her; (*verletzt nicht*) that doesn't bother her (too much), she doesn't mind that (too much); **~ im Süden** far (*od.* to the) south, in the far south; **bis ~ in die Nacht** deep (*od.* far) into the night, till the (wee *hum.*) small hours; **bis ~ in den Herbst hinein** till late (in the) autumn (*Am.* fall), till well on in the autumn (*Am.* fall); **~ blickend** (very) perceptive; **das lässt ~ blicken** that's very revealing, that says a lot about *s.th.;* **~ gehend** *Wunde etc.:* deep; *fig.* (*gründlich*) thorough; (*intensiv*) intensive; **~ greifend** far-reaching, radical; **~ schürfend** probing, penetrating; *Gespräch:* profound, searching, deeply serious; **~ sitzend** *fig. Probleme etc:* deep-seated; **~ verschneit** snowbound, ... deep in snow; **2.** (*niedrig*) low; (*unten*) deep, deep (*od.* right) down; **die Sonne**

steht ~ the sun is low; **~ liegen** *Ort etc.:* be low-lying; **~ fliegen** fly low, fly at low altitude(s); **~ gelegen** low(er)--lying; **~er gelegt** *Mot.* lowered-suspension ...; **~er gestellt** *EDV Text:* subscript; **~ liegend** *Gebiet etc.:* low(-lying); *Augen:* deep-set, *auch Tech.* sunken; *fig.* deep(-seated); **zu ~ singen** sing flat; **~ stehend** *in Rangordnung:* low-ranking, inferior, lowly; *Sonne:* low; **moralisch ~ stehend** morally corrupt; **3.** *intensivierend:* (*sehr, stark*) **~ beleidigt** deeply offended, mortally insulted, black affronted *Dial.;* **~ betrübt** *durch etw.:* deeply saddened (*od.* grieved); (*traurig*) deeply unhappy; **~ bewegt** deeply (*od.* very) moved, deeply touched; **~ empfunden** deep--felt, deeply felt, heartfelt, from the heart; **~ erschüttert** *Person:* deeply (*od.* profoundly) affected (*od.* moved); *Vertrauen etc.:* badly shaken; **~ gekränkt** *etc.* **sein** be deeply hurt *etc.*

Tief *n; -s, -s* **1.** *Met.* low (*auch fig.*), depression, trough, low-pressure area, cyclone *fachspr.;* **gerade ein ~ haben** *fig.* be having (*od.* going through) a low (*od.* a bad patch), be rather down at the moment; **2.** *Naut.* (navigable) channel

Tiefausläufer *m Met.* front (associated with an area of low pressure)

Tiefbau *m; nur Sg.* **1.** (*Teilgebiet des Bauwesens*) civil engineering *excluding erection of buildings,* structural engineering; *engS.* underground engineering; → *auch* **Hochbau**; **2.** (*Bergbau unter Tage*) deep mining; **~amt** *n* planning authority

tief| beleidigt, ~ betrübt → tief II 3

Tiefbettscanner *m EDV* deepbed scanner

tief bewegt → *tief* II 3

tiefblau *Adj.* deep blue

tief blickend → *tief* II 1

Tiefbohrung *f Bergb.* (*Bohren*) deep boring; (*Bohrloch*) deep bore

tiefbraun *Adj.* deep brown

Tiefbrunnen *m* deep well

Tiefdruck *m Met.* low pressure; **~gebiet** *n* → **Tief** 1; **~rinne** *f Met.* trough (of low pressure)

Tiefe *f; -, -n* **1.** *allg.* depth; (*Abgrund*) abyss, depths *Pl.; unterseeisch:* auch deep, trench; **e-e ~ von 90 m haben** be 90 m deep; **in e-r ~ von ...** at a depth of ...; **in großer ~** at great depth(s); **in die ~ blicken/stürzen** look down / plummet (down) into the depths; **die ~n des Meeres** the depths of the sea; **die ~n aussteuern** *Musikanlage etc.:* adjust the bass; **das Leben mit s-n Höhen und ~n** life with its ups and downs (*od.* high points and low points); **die verborgenen ~n der menschlichen Seele** (the) hidden depths (*od.* mysterious recesses) of human personality (*od.* the human heart); **2.** *nur Sg.; lit.* (*Meer*) the deep, the ocean; **auf ~ gehen** *U-Boot:* dive; **3.** *nur Sg.; e-r Stimme, e-s Tones:* deepness; *e-s Tones: auch* low pitch, lowness; *von Gefühlen etc.:* depth, intensity; (*Tiefgründigkeit*) deepness, profundity; **die ~ i-s Schmerzes** the violence (*od.* intensity) of her (*od.* their) grief; **aus der ~ m-s Herzens** from the bottom of my heart, with all my heart

Tiefebene *f Geog.* lowlands *Pl.,* low-lying country; **die Norddeutsche/Oberrheinische ~** the North German Plain / the Upper Rhine Valley

tief empfunden → *tief* II 3
Tiefen|bestrahlung *f Med.* deep therapy; **~interview** *n* in-depth interview; **~messung** *f* depth sounding
Tiefenpsychologe *m Psych.* depth psychologist; **Tiefenpsychologie** *f* depth psychology; **Tiefenpsychologin** *f* (female) depth psychologist; **tiefenpsychologisch** *Adj.* of (*od.* involving) depth psychology
Tiefen|rausch *m* rapture of the deep; **~regler** *m* bass control; **~ruder** *n Naut.* diving plane (and/or forward vertical rudder); **~schärfe** *f Fot.* depth of field (*od.* focus); **~sehen** *n Med.* three-dimensional (*od.* perspective) vision; **~struktur** *f Ling.* deep structure
tiefenwirksam *Adj. Pharm.* deep-acting; **Tiefenwirkung** *f e-r Massage etc.*: deep action; *Bild, Foto*: three-dimensionality, (sense of) depth
tiefer gelegt, ~ gestellt → *tief* II 2
tiefernst *Adj.* deadly serious
tief erschüttert → *tief* II 3
Tief|flieger *m* low-flying aircraft; **geistiger ~** *umg. fig.* lowbrow; **~flug** *m* low-level flight; *Pl. auch* low(-level) flying *Sg.*; **im ~** at low altitude
Tiefgang *m; nur Sg.; Naut.* draught, *Am.* draft; *fig.* depth; **geringen/großen ~ haben** *Naut.* have a shallow/ deep draught (*Am.* draft); **keinen geistigen ~ haben** be an intellectual lightweight
Tiefgarage *f* underground car park (*od.* carpark, *Am.* parking garage)
tief gehend → *tief* II 1
tiefgefrieren *v/t.* (*unreg., untr., hat -ge-*) deep-freeze; **tiefgefroren I.** *P.P.* → *tiefgefrieren*; **II.** *Adj.* deep-frozen
tiefgekühlt I. *P.P.* → *tiefkühlen*; **II.** *Adj. allg.* (deep-)frozen; *Getränk*: chilled, ice-cold
tief gelegen → *tief* II 2
Tiefgeschoss *n* basement
tief greifend → *tief* II 1
tiefgründig *Adj.* **1.** *Betrachtungen etc.*: deep, profound; **2.** *Agr. Boden*: deep
tiefkühlen *vt/i.* (*untr., hat -ge-*) deep-freeze
Tiefkühl|fach *n* freezing compartment; **~kette** *f* frozen food chain, cold chain; **~kost** *f* frozen foods *Pl.*; **~schrank** *m* (upright) freezer, deep-freeze; **~truhe** *f* deep-freeze, (chest) freezer
Tieflader *m; -s, -; Mot.* low loader, low-loader vehicle
Tiefland *n* lowland(s *Pl.*)
tief liegend → *tief* II 2
Tief|punkt *m* low (point); **e-n absoluten ~ erreicht haben** have reached an all-time low (*od.* its *od.* their nadir *geh.*); *Stimmung*: have hit rock bottom; **e-n seelischen ~ haben** be very depressed, be feeling utterly wretched, be having (*od.* going through) a real low
tief|religiös *Adj.* deeply religious, devout; **~rot** *Adj.* deep red
Tiefschlaf *m* deep sleep; **sich im ~ befinden** be in a deep sleep, be fast asleep; **~phase** *f* slow-wave (*od.* S) sleep period
Tiefschlag *m Boxen*: low punch, hit below the belt (*auch fig.*)
Tiefschnee *m* deep powder, deep (powder) snow; **~fahren** *n Skisport*: off-piste (*od.* deep powder) skiing
tief schürfend → *tief* II 1
tiefschwarz *Adj.* deep black, jet-black, inky black, pitch-black; *Pol., umg.* ultra-conservative, reactionary
Tiefsee *f Geog.* deep sea; **~bergbau** *m*

deep-sea (*od.* undersea) mining; **~forschung** *f* (*Erforschung*) deep-sea exploration; (*Wissenschaft*) deep-sea research; **~graben** *m* deep-sea (*od.* deep ocean) trench; **~tauchen** *n* deep-sea diving
Tiefsinn *m; nur Sg.;* (*Gehalt*) deep(er) (*od.* profound) meaning; (*Hintergründigkeit*) profundity; (*Nachdenklichkeit*) thoughtfulness, reflectiveness, pensiveness; (*Schwermut*) melancholy, pensiveness; **tiefsinnig** *Adj.* (*hintergründig*) profound, deep; (*nachdenklich*) meditative, thoughtful, pensive; (*schwermütig*) melancholy, pensive
tief sitzend → *tief* II 1
Tiefstand *m* low, lowest level; **absoluter ~** all-time low; → *auch Tiefpunkt*
Tiefstapelei *f; -, -en* **1.** (*Untertreibung*) understatement; **2.** *nur Sg.; in eigener Sache*: modesty, self-effacement; **tiefstapeln** *v/i.* (*trennb., hat -ge-*) understate the case (*od.* things), play things down; *in eigener Sache*: be very modest (*od.* self-effacing), gloss over one's own role, be over-modest; **Tiefstapler** *m; -s, -,* **Tiefstaplerin** *f; -, -nen: ein ~ sein* like to understate things; *in eigener Sache*: be a very modest (*od.* self-effacing) person
Tiefstart *m Sport* crouch start
tief stehend → *tief* II 2
Tiefst|kurs *m* lowest rate; **~preise** *Pl.* rock-bottom prices
Tiefstrahler *m* floodlight
Tiefst|temperatur *f* minimum (*od.* lowest) temperature; **~wert** *m* **1.** lowest value (*od.* reading); **2.** → *Tiefsttemperatur*
Tieftauchen *n* deep diving
Tieftemperaturphysik *f Phys.* low temperature (*od.* cryo-)physics *Pl.* (*V. im Sg.*)
Tieftöner *m; -s, - Lautsprecher*: woofer
tieftraurig *Adj.* desperately sad (*od.* unhappy)
tief verschneit → *tief* II 1
Tiegel *m; -s, -* **1.** (*Kochtopf*) saucepan, stewpan; (*Schmelztiegel*) crucible; *für Creme etc.*: dish; **2.** *Druck.* platen
Tier *n; -(e)s, -e* animal; *großes, wildes*: *auch* beast; (*Haustier*) domestic animal, pet (animal); *fig.* (*Mensch*) brute; *stärker*: animal; **der König der ~e** *fig.* (*Löwe*) the King of (the) Beasts; **hohes** *od.* **großes ~** *umg. fig.* bigwig, big shot, big noise, high-up; **sich wie ein ~ benehmen** behave like a wild beast, show savagery; **~art** *f* animal species
Tierarzt *m,* **Tierärztin** *f Vet.* vet, veterinary surgeon, *Am.* veterinarian; **tierärztlich I.** *Adj.* veterinary; **II.** *Adv. kontrollieren etc.*: scientifically (*od.* professionally *od.* officially) (by a vet)
Tier|asyl *n* → *Tierheim*; **~bestand** *m* animal population, (the) number of animals; **~buch** *n* book about (*od.* on) animals; *Erzählung: auch* animal story; **~fabel** *f Lit.* animal fable; **~film** *m* film about animals; **~freund** *m,* **~freundin** *f* animal lover; **~friedhof** *m* pet cemetery; **~futter** *n* **1.** *allg.* animal food; *für frei lebende Tiere*: animal fodder; **2.** *Wirts., bei Massentierhaltung*: animal feed; **3.** *für Haustiere*: pet food(s *Pl.*); **~garten** *m* (small) zoo; **~gehege** *n* (animal) enclosure; **~geographie** *f Zool., Geog., Öko.* zoogeography, animal distribution; **~geschichte** *f* animal story, story about (*od.* involving) animals
Tier|halter *m,* **~halterin** *f* **1.** (*Liebhaber*) pet owner; **2.** *Agr.* (*Züchter*) live-

stock breeder; **3.** *Jur.* keeper (of the animal[s]); **~haltung** *f* **1.** (*Liebhaberei*) keeping a pet (*od.* of pets); **2.** *Agr.* (*Zucht*) livestock breeding, stock-breeding; *Jur.* keeping of livestock
Tier|handlung *f* pet shop; **~heim** *n* animal refuge (*od.* shelter)
tierisch I. *Adj. attr.* **1.** *von e-m Tier*: *attr.* animal ...; *fig. Gefühl etc.*: primitive; **~e Fette** animal fats; **~e Instinkte** animal instincts; **2.** *pej.* brutish, animal-like, mindless; (*roh, grausam*) brutal, savage; **~e Grausamkeit** savage (*od.* bestial) cruelty; **3.** *fig.* (*ungeheuer*) terrific, terrible, incredible; **e-e ~e Angst** (blind) panic, (an) irrational fear; **~e Schmerzen** *umg.* terrible pain *Sg.* (*od.* pains); **~er Ernst** deadly seriousness; **4.** *Jugendspr.* (*toll*) great, fab, fantastic; **II.** *Adv. umg. fig.*: **~ ernst** deadly serious, *präd. auch* too deadly serious; **~ schwer** *Gewicht*: bloody *Sl.* heavy, incredibly heavy; (*schwierig*) bloody *Sl.* difficult (*od.* hard); **~ schuften müssen** have to work one's butt off, (have to) sweat blood; **sich ~ freuen** be over the moon
Tierklinik *f* veterinary clinic, animal hospital
Tierkörperbeseitigungsanstalt *f* carcass disposal cent|re (*Am.* -er) (*od.* plant)
Tierkreis *m Astron.* zodiac; **~zeichen** *n* sign of the zodiac
Tierkunde *f* zoology, animal biology
tierlieb *Adj.* fond of animals; **~ sein** *auch* like (*stärker*: love) animals; **Tierliebe** *f* love of animals
Tier|markt *m Zeitungsrubrik*: Pets (and Livestock); **~medizin** *f* veterinary medicine; **~mehl** *n aus Tierabfällen, Tierfutter*: meat and bone meal, animal meal; *Düngemittel*: animal product fertilizer; **~park** *m* zoo, zoo(logical) park; **~pension** *f Hunde*: boarding kennels *Pl.* (*Am. auch* kennel *Sg.*); *Katzen*: (boarding) cattery; *allg.* boarding establishment for pets; **~pfleger** *m,* **~pflegerin** *f* keeper; **~plastik** *f* animal figure (*od.* sculpture); *bes. aus Holz: auch* carved animal; **~präparator** *m,* **~präparatorin** *f* taxidermist; **~psychologie** *f* animal psychology; **~quäler** *m* animal abuser, person guilty of maltreating (*od.* cruelty to) animals; **~quälerei** *f* cruelty to (*od.* mistreatment of) animals *od.* pets; *umg. fig.* cruelty to animals; **~quälerin** *f* → *Tierquäler*; **~reich** *n* animal kingdom; **~schau** *f* menagerie; **~schutz** *m allg.* protection of animals; *für wild lebende Tiere*: animal conservation
Tierschützer *m; -s, -,* **~in** *f; -, -nen für Nutz- und Haustiere*: animal welfarist; *für wild lebende Tiere*: wildlife conservationist
Tierschutz|gebiet *n* wildlife (*od.* game) reserve; **~gesetz** *n* animal welfare legislation, law(s) protecting animals; **~verein** *m* society for the prevention of cruelty to animals
Tier|sendung *f TV* animal program(me), program(me) about animals; **~staat** *m Zool.* animal colony; **~stimmenimitator** *m,* **~stimmenimitatorin** *f* animal (call) mimic; **~transport** *m* transportation of animals (*od.* livestock); **~transporter** *m* animal (*od.* livestock) transporter; *für Rinder*: *Brit. auch* cattle lorry
Tierversuch *m* animal experiment, experiment on (*od.* involving) animals;

Tierversuchsgegner *m* anti-vivisectionist, animal rights campaigner (*od.* activist)

Tier|verwertung *f* animal waste processing; **~wanderung** *f* Zool. animal migration; **~welt** *f* fauna, animal life, animals *Pl.*; **~zucht** *f allg.* breeding of animals; *Nutztiere:* livestock breeding

Tiger *m*; *-s, -*; *Zool.* tiger; **~auge** *n* Min. tiger's eye; **~färbung** *f* tiger stripes *Pl.*, tiger striping; **~fell** *n* tiger skin; **~fisch** *m Zool.* tiger fish, tigerfish; **~hai** *m Zool.* tiger shark

Tigerin *f*; *-, -nen*; *Zool.* tigress

Tiger|katze *f Zool.* tiger cat; **~lilie** *f Bot.* tiger lily

tigern *v/i. umg.:* **durch die Straßen ~ weit, lange:** traipse (*od.* trog *od.* schlep) through the streets; *ziellos:* mooch around town; → **getigert**

Tiger|python *f Zool.* Indian python; **~staat** *m Wirts.* tiger economy

Tilde *f*; *-, -n* tilde, swung dash

tilgbar *Adj. Wirts.* redeemable, repayable; **tilgen** *v/t.* **1.** (*streichen*) delete; *auch Druck.*, *EDV* strike out, cancel; (*löschen*) erase (*auch EDV*), expunge *geh.*; (*vernichten*) destroy, eradicate; **2.** *Wirts.* (*Schuld*) pay off, repay; (*Anleihe*) redeem; **3.** *fig.* (*sühnen*) expiate, pay for, purge; (*Erinnerung*) blot out, purge; **e-e Schmach ~** expunge (*aggressiv:* avenge) a humiliation; (*Besseres leisten*) redeem o.s. (after a disgrace)

Tilgung *f* **1.** *Druck. etc.* erasure, deletion; (*Vernichtung*) eradication; **2.** *Wirts.* redemption, repayment, amortization; **ein Baudarlehen mit 1%iger ~** a 1% monthly repayment mortgage; **3.** *fig.* (*Sühne*) expiation; → **tilgen**

Tilgungs|anleihe *f Wirts.* redemption (*od.* amortization) loan; **~fonds** *m* redemption (*od.* amortization *od.* sinking) fund; **~rate** *f* (*Zahlungsbasis*) redemption rate; (*Betrag*) redemption instal(l)ment; **~zeichen** *n Druck. etc.:* deletion sign; **~zeitraum** *m Wirts.* redemption (*od.* repayment *od.* amortization) period

Timbre ['tɛ̃:brə] *n*; *-s, -s* timbre

timen [taimən] *v/t.* time; **gut/schlecht getimt** well/badly timed; **gut getimt** *attr. auch* well-timed

Timer ['taimɐ] *m*; *-s, -* timer

Timesharing ['taimʃɛːrɪŋ] *n*; *-s, -s bei Ferienwohnungen etc.:* time sharing

Timing ['taimɪŋ] *n*; *-s, -s* timing

Timotheus *m*; *-*; *bibl.* Timothy; **Brief an ~** → **Timotheusbrief**, **~brief** *m bibl.:* **der 1./2. ~** the (*od.* St 1st *od.* St.) Paul's) 1st/2nd Epistle (*od.* Letter) to Timothy, Timothy I/II

tingeln *v/i. umg.* **1.** (*hat getingelt*) *Theat.* do small-time acting, act in repertory up and down the country, dabble in amateur acting; *Sänger, Musiker etc.:* perform in various places, do gigs where one can get them; **2.** (*ist*): **durch Kneipen/Süddeutschland ~** tour (*od.* do the rounds of) the pubs (*Am.* clubs) / tour (*od.* travel around in) South Germany; **Tingeltangel** *m*; *-s, -*; *altm. umg.* **1.** (*Lokal*) music-hall, pub (*od.* cafe) with music; **2.** (*Musik, Unterhaltung*) variety (shows *Pl.*)

Tinktur *f*; *-, -en* tincture

Tinnef *m*; *-s, kein Pl.*; *umg. pej.* (*Plunder*) rubbish, trash, junk, worthless stuff; (*Unsinn*) rubbish, nonsense, tripe, *Am.* garbage

Tinte *f*; *-, -n* ink; **mit ~ schreiben** write

in ink, use ink; **in der ~ sitzen** *umg. fig.* be up the creek (*od.* in the soup); **klar wie dicke ~** *umg.* blindingly obvious; **tintenblau** *Adj.* deep (*od.* dark) blue

Tinten|fass *n* inkpot, inkwell; **~fisch** *m Zool.* cuttlefish; (*Kalmar*) squid; (*Krake*) octopus; **~fleck** *m auf Papier etc.* ink blot, blot of ink; *auf Kleidung etc.:* ink stain; **~killer** *m* correction pen; **~klecks** *m* ink blot (*od.* stain); **~patrone** *f* ink cartridge

Tintenstrahldrucker *m EDV* ink-jet printer

Tintentod *m umg.* correction pen

Tintling *m*; *-s, -e*; *Bot.* ink cap

Tipi *n*; *-s, -s* (*Indianerzelt*) tepee

Tipp *m*; *-s, -s* **1.** *Sport und fig.:* tip; (*Wink*) hint; (*Fingerzeig*) pointer, lead; *an die Polizei:* tip-off; **ein heißer ~** a hot tip; **j-m e-n ~ geben** (*Rat*) give s.o. a tip (*od.* piece of advice); (*warnen*) tip s.o. off *umg.*, give s.o. a tip-off *umg.*; **2.** (*Wette*) bet, forecast, selection

Tippelbruder *m umg.* tramp, knight of the road(s) *hum.*, *Am.* hobo; **tippeln** *v/i. umg.* **1.** walk, hoof it, use Shanks's mare (*od.* pony); **2.** *als Landstreicher:* tramp; **3.** *Kleinkind:* toddle

tippen I. *v/i.* **1.** (*berühren*) **~ an** (+ *Akk.*) (*leicht berühren*) tap (lightly), touch; **kurz auf die Bremse ~** dab the brakes, apply a touch of brake; **im Gespräch an etw. ~** *fig.* touch on (*od.* refer obliquely to *geh.*) s.th. (in conversation); **2.** *umg. Lotto:* do (*Am.* play) the lottery; *Toto:* do the (football) pools; **3.** *umg.* (*raten*) guess; **ich tippe auf ihn** I reckon it's (*od.* it'll be) him; **ich tippe (darauf), dass ...** I reckon (that) ..., I bet ...; **II.** *vt/i. umg.* (*Maschine schreiben*) (*Brief etc.*) type; **e-n Brief ~** type (up) a letter; (*gut*) **~ können** be a good typist

Tipp-Ex® *n*; *-, kein Pl.* Tipp-Ex®, *Am.* whiteout

Tippfehler *m* typing error, typo *umg.*

Tipp|gemeinschaft *f* betting (*od.* lotto) pool; **~schein** *m Toto:* (football) pools coupon; *Lotto:* lottery ticket

Tippse *f*; *-n -n*; *umg., neg!* typist

tipp, tapp *Interj.* pitter-patter

tipptopp *umg.* **I.** *Adj.* (*ausgezeichnet*) first class, first-rate, spot on ...; **II.** *Adv.:* **~ sauber** spick and span, spotless, immaculate; **~ gekleidet** immaculately (*od.* flawlessly) dressed (*od.* turned out); **das hat sie ~ hingekriegt** she managed that superbly, she made a superb job of it

Tippzettel *m Toto:* (football) pools coupon; *Lotto:* lottery ticket

Tirade *f*; *-, -n* **1.** *pej.* (*langatmige Rede*) tirade, harangue; **sich in langen ~n ergehen** harangue one's hearers at length, indulge in lengthy tirades; **2.** → **Hetztirade** *etc.*; **3.** *Mus.* run

Tiramisu [tirami'zu:] *n*; *-s, -s*; *Gastr.* tiramisu

Tirol (*n*); *-s*; *Geog.* Tyrol; **Tiroler I.** *m*; *-s, -*; Tyrolean, Tyrolese; **~ sein** be (a) Tyrolean, come from (the) Tyrol; **II.** *Adj.* Tyrolean, Tyrolese; **Tirolerin** *f*; *-, -nen* Tyrolean woman (*od.* girl); → **Tiroler**; **tirolerisch** *Adj.* Tyrolean, Tyrolese

Tisch *m*; *-(e)s, -e* **1.** table; **am ~ sitzen** sit (*od.* be seated) at the table (*Familie etc.: auch* (a)round the table); **sich an den ~ setzen** sit down (*od.* take one's seat *geh.*) at the table; **vom ~ aufstehen** get up (from the table),

stand up; *bei Mahlzeiten: auch* leave the table; → **abräumen** II 1, **decken** II 1; **2.** *Koll.* (*Leute*): **der ganze ~ konnte mithören** the whole table (*od.* everyone at the table) could hear (*od.* was listening); **3.** *nur Sg.*; *fig.* (*Essen*): **bei ~** at table *geh.*, at lunch *etc.*; **bei ~ sitzen** be having lunch *etc.*, be eating; **zu ~ gehen** go for (*od.* to) lunch *etc.*; **darf ich zu ~ bitten?** shall we sit down at the table?; **wenn das Essen aufgetragen ist:** lunch (*od.* dinner) is served (*od.* ready), let's have something to eat now; **essen, was auf den ~ kommt** eat what one is given, eat whatever is put before one; **getrennt von ~ und Bett** separated; **zum ~ des Herrn treten** *kirchl.* come to the Lord's table, take communion; **4.** *fig.* in Wendungen: **bar auf den ~** cash down; **mit etw. reinen ~ machen** get s.th. sorted out properly (*od.* once and for all); **etw. fällt unter den ~** s.th. falls flat (*od.* by the wayside), s.th. is passed over (*od.* ignored), s.th. is not taken up (*od.* pursued); **e-e Angelegenheit unter den ~ fallen lassen** (quietly) drop a matter; (*nicht beachten*) (choose to) ignore a matter; **j-n unter den ~ trinken** *umg.* drink s.o. under the table; **j-n über den ~ ziehen** *umg.* fleece (*od.* rook) s.o., take s.o. to the cleaners; **vom ~ wischen** *od.* **fegen** sweep (*od.* brush) aside; **die Sache muss vom ~** has got to be settled; **Streitende an einen ~ bringen** bring the parties *etc.* face to face, get the parties *etc.* to agree to talks; **Entscheidung am grünen ~** bureaucratic decision; *Sport* decision at administrative level (*od.* by the sport's ruling body); (**über**) **etw.** (*Akk.*) **am grünen ~ entscheiden** decide on s.th. from a bureaucratic ivory tower; → **hauen** II 1

Tisch|bein *n* table leg; **~besen** *m* crumb brush; **~computer** *m* desktop computer; **~dame** *f* dinner partner; **~decke** *f* tablecloth; **~ende** *n*: **am oberen/unteren ~** at the head/foot of the table

tischfertig *Adj. Speise:* ready-to-serve

Tisch|feuerzeug *n* table lighter; **~fußball** *m* table football; **~gebet** *n* grace; **das ~ sprechen** say grace; **~gespräch** *n auch Pl.* table talk; **~grill** *m* table barbecue (*od.* grill); **~herr** *m* dinner partner; **~kante** *f* edge of a (*od.* the) table; **~karte** *f* place card; **~kopierer** *m* desktop (photo)copier; **~lampe** *f* table lamp

Tischleindeckdich *n* im Märchen: magic (*od.* wishing) table; *umg.* cushy set-up, gravy train, free lunch for life

Tischler *m*; *-s, -* carpenter, joiner; (*Kunsttischler*) cabinet(-)maker; **Tischlerarbeit** *f* carpentry, joinery, woodworking; **Tischlerei** *f*; *-, -en* **1.** *nur Sg.* (*Handwerk*) carpentry, joinery, woodworking; **2.** (*Werkstatt*) carpenter's (*od.* joiner's) workshop, joinery business; **Tischlerin** *f*; *-, -nen* woman (*od.* girl) carpenter (*od.* joiner); **Tischlermeister** *m*, **~meisterin** *f* master carpenter; **tischlern I.** *v/i.* do carpentry; **er tischlert gern** he enjoys carpentry, he likes woodworking (*od.* working with wood); **II.** *v/t.* (*Möbel*) make; **Tischlerplatte** *f* blockboard

Tisch|manieren *Pl.* table manners (*od.* etiquette *Sg.*); **~nachbar** *m*, **~nachbarin** *f* neighbo(u)r; **mein(e) Tischnachbar(in)** the person (*od.* man, woman) sitting next to me (at dinner *etc.*);

~ordnung *f* seating plan (*od.* arrangements *Pl.*); **~platte** *f* table(-)top, table surface, table; **~rechner** *m* (*Rechenmaschine*) desk(top) calculator; (*Computer*) desktop computer; **~rede** *f* after-dinner speech; *mit Trinkspruch: auch* toast; **~reihe** *f* row of tables; **~schmuck** *m* table decoration(s *Pl.*); **~schublade** *f* table drawer; **~telefon** *n Büro:* desk (tele)phone; *Nachtlokal:* phone on the table, table phone

Tischtennis *n Sport* table tennis, ping-pong *umg.*; **~ball** *m* table-tennis (ping-pong *umg.*) ball; **~netz** *n* table-tennis net; **~platte** *f* table-tennis board (*od.* table); **~schläger** *m* table-tennis bat (*Am.* paddle); **~spieler** *m*, **~spielerin** *f* table-tennis player

Tisch|tuch *n* tablecloth; **~vorlage** *f für Seminar etc.:* handout; *für Ausschusssitzung etc.:* tabled paper(s *Pl.*); **~wäsche** *f* table linen; **~wein** *m Gastr.* table wine; **~zeit** *f* **1.** (*Essenszeit*) mealtime; **2.** (*Mittagspause*) lunch hour (*od.* break)

Titan¹ *m; -en, -en; Myth.* Titan; *fig.* titan, giant, titanic figure

Titan² *n; -s, kein Pl.; Chem.* (*abgek.* **Ti**) titanium

Titane *m; -n, -n → Titan¹*

titanenhaft *Adj.*, **titanisch** *Adj.* titanic

Titel *m; -s, -* **1.** *e-s Buches etc.:* title; (*Überschrift*) title, heading, header; *das Buch trägt den ~* the title of the book is; *mit dem ~* entitled; **2.** *Verlagswesen* a) *bestimmtes Buch:* title, b) (*Titelseite*) title page; **3.** (*Rang, Amt etc.*) title, designation; *Sport: mst* title; *j-m e-n ~ verleihen* confer a title on s.o.; *j-n mit s-m ~ anreden* address s.o. by his (*od.* her) title; *der ~ e-s Weltmeisters* the world title; *den ~ gewinnen/verlieren Sport* win/lose the title; **4.** *Wirts., bei Kosten:* head (*od.* category) (of expenditure); *der größte ~ im Etat* the biggest item in the budget; **5.** *Jur.* (*Abschnitt*) section, *Am. auch* title

Titel|anwärter *m*, **~anwärterin** *f*, **~aspirant** *m*, **~aspirantin** *f* title contender, (potential) challenger for the title; **~bild** *n e-s Buches:* frontispiece; *e-r Zeitschrift:* cover picture (*od.* illustration, photo), (front) cover; **~blatt** *n* title page

Titelei *f; -, -en; Druck.* prelims *Pl.*, front matter

Titel|figur *f* eponymous hero; **~geschichte** *f* lead (*od.* cover) story; **~gewinn** *m Sport* winning (of) the title, championship victory; **~held** *m* (eponymous) hero; **~heldin** *f* (eponymous) heroine; **~kampf** *m Sport* title match (*Boxen: auch* fight, bout); **~melodie** *f* theme (*od.* signature) tune; **~musik** *f* theme music; **~rolle** *f Theat. etc.:* title role; **~schutz** *m Jur.* copyright; **~seite** *f* title page; *e-r Zeitschrift: auch* (front) cover; **~song** *m* title song; **~story** *f* cover story; **~träger** *m*, **~trägerin** *f Sport* titleholder; **~verteidiger** *m*, **~verteidigerin** *f* titleholder, defending champion; **~zeile** *f Buch, Artikel:* title (line); *Zeitungsbericht:* headline

Titten *Pl. vulg.* tits, knockers, boobs, headlights; *an die ~ fassen* go for her tits

Titularbischof *m kath etwa* suffragan bishop

titulieren *v/t.* address; *j-n als od. mit„I-diot“ ~* call s.o. (*od.* describe s.o. as) an idiot

Titus *m; -; bibl.* Titus; *Brief an ~ → Titusbrief*, **~brief** *m bibl.: der ~* the (*od.* St [*od.* St.] Paul's) Epistle (*od.* Letter) to Titus, Titus

tja *Interj.* well

TNT *n; -, kein Pl.; Abk.* (**Trinitrotuluol**) TNT

Toast [toːst] *m; -(e)s, -s* **1.** (*Röstbrot*) toast; (*Scheibe*) slice (*od.* piece) of toast; **~ Hawai(i)** *Gastr.* toast Hawaii (*light hot dish consisting of ham, pineapple and melted cheese on toast*); **2.** (*Trinkspruch*) toast; *auf j-n e-n ~ ausbringen* propose a toast to s.o., propose s.o.'s health; **Toastbrot** *n allg.* bread for toasting; (*Scheibe*) slice (*od.* piece) of toast; **toasten** ['toːstn̩] **I.** *v/t.* (*Brot*) toast; **II.** *v/i.* (*Trinkspruch ausbringen*) drink a toast (*auf + Akk.* to); **Toaster** ['toːstɐ] *m; -s, -;* (*Gerät*) toaster

Tobak *m umg. fig.: das ist starker ~!* that's strong stuff!, that's a bit thick (*od.* much)!

Tobel *m, schw. n; -s, -; südd., schw., österr.* gorge, ravine, gully

toben *v/i.* **1.** (*hat getobt*) *Person:* rave, be (*od.* go) raving mad, go berserk; *vor Empörung, Begeisterung etc.:* go (*od.* be) wild (*od.* mad) (*vor + Dat.* with); *Kind:* romp, let off steam; *Sturm, Gewitter, See etc., auch Schlacht:* rage; *die ~de See* the raging (*od.* storm-lashed) sea, the sea (*od.* ocean *geh.*) in turmoil; **2.** (*ist*): *durchs Haus / durch die Straßen ~* storm through the house/streets; *ausgelassen:* career (*od.* charge) (a)round the house / through the streets

Tobsucht *f; nur Sg.* uncontrolled rage, (a) frenzy of rage; *die ~ kriegen umg. fig.* go berserk (*od.* ballistic), throw a tantrum; **tobsüchtig** *Adj.* raving (mad); **Tobsuchtsanfall** *m* paroxysm of fury (*od.* rage); *Kind: auch* tantrum; *e-n ~ bekommen* throw a tantrum, fly into a (violent) rage

Tochter *f; -, Töchter* **1.** *leibliche:* daughter; *die ~ des Hauses* the daughter of the house; *sie ist ganz die ~ ihres Vaters* she is very much her father's daughter, she takes very much after her father; *höhere Töchter altm. od. hum.* (well-bred) young ladies, young ladies of good class (*od.* background); **2.** *Wirts., Sl.* (*Tochterunternehmen*) subsidiary; **3.** *schw. altm* (*Angestellte*) girl, female (*od.* woman) employee

Tochter|firma *f Wirts.* subsidiary (company); *unter 50%:* affiliated company, affiliate; **~geschwulst** *f Med.* secondary tumo(u)r; **~gesellschaft** *f → Tochterfirma*; **~zelle** *f Bio.* daughter cell

Tod *m; -es, -e, mst Sg.* **1.** death; *bes. fig.* demise; *fig.* decease, death; *durch Ersticken/Verhungern* death by suffocation / from starvation; *zu ~e kommen* die, perish *lit.*, be killed, lose one's life; *zum ~e führen allg.* cause (*s.o.'s*) death; *Krankheit etc.:* be fatal; *Schlag etc.: auch* be mortal *geh.*; *e-s natürlichen ~es sterben* die a natural death; *zu ~e stürzen* fall to one's death; *e-n leichten ~ haben* (just) slip peacefully away; *dem ~(e) geweiht sein Soldaten etc.:* be doomed (to die); *Schwerkranke:* be dying (*od.* approaching death), be doomed *lit.*; *der Arzt konnte nur noch den ~ feststellen* by the time the doctor arrived he (*od.* she) was dead; *zum ~e verurteilen* sentence to death; *j-n zum ~ durch den Strang verurteilen* sentence s.o. to death by hanging (*od.* to the noose *lit.*); *zu ~e prügeln/quälen* beat (*od.* batter) /torture *s.o.* to death; *j-n in den ~ treiben* drive s.o. to his (*od.* her) death; *über den ~ hinaus* beyond the grave; **2.** *nur Sg.: der ~ als Gestalt:* death, Death *lit.*; *dem ~ ins Auge sehen* come face to face with death; *mit dem ~(e) ringen* be fighting for life, be at death's door; *Wettlauf mit dem ~* race with (*od.* against) death; *dem ~ von der Schippe springen* escape from the jaws of death, cheat death; *aussehen wie der (leibhaftige) ~* look like death (warmed up [*Am.* over] *umg.*); *der schwarze/weiße ~* the Black Death / the white death; *umsonst ist der ~ Sprichw.* nothing in life is free - except death; **3.** *fig.: sich (Dat.) den ~ holen* (*sich erkälten*) catch one's death (of cold); *sich zu ~e arbeiten* work o.s. to death; *das wäre der ~ der Demokratie* that would be the end (*od.* death) of democracy; *Misstrauen ist der ~ jeder Beziehung* mistrust is poison to a relationship; *tausend ~e sterben vor Angst, Sorge etc.:* die a thousand deaths; *j-n zu ~e erschrecken/langweilen* scare (*od.* frighten) / bore s.o. to death; *ich bin zu ~e erschrocken* I got the shock (*od.* fright) of my life; *sich zu ~e schämen* nearly die of shame (*od.* embarrassment), be (utterly) mortified; *ich kann ihn auf den ~ nicht leiden* I can't stand (*stärker:* I hate) the sight of him, I (utterly) detest (*od.* loathe) him; *das kann ich auf den ~ nicht leiden* I hate it like poison; → *Leben* 1

tod|bringend *Adj. Krankheit:* deadly, fatal, mortal *geh.*; *Gift etc.:* lethal, deadly; **~elend** *Adj. umg.: mir ist ~* I feel terrible (*od.* really rotten), I think I'm going to die *hum.*; **~ernst I.** *Adj.* deadly (dead *umg.*) serious; *es ist mir ~ (damit)* I am totally serious (*stärker:* in deadly earnest) (about this); **II.** *Adv.* in (deadly) earnest; *es ~ meinen* be in deadly earnest, really mean it

Todes|ahnung *f* premonition of death; **~angst** *f* fear of death; *fig.* mortal fear; *Todesängste ausstehen* be scared to death, be frightened (*od.* scared) out of one's mind (*od.* wits); **~anzeige** *f* death announcement; **~art** *f* way to die, manner of *s.o.'s* death; **~drohung** *f* death threat; **~engel** *m Reli.* angel of death (*auch fig.*); **~erklärung** *f Jur.* (official) declaration that *s.o.* is dead; *Schriftstück:* death certificate; **~fahrt** *f* fatal journey (*od.* trip *od.* run *etc.*); *die ~ des ICE* the ICE's fatal (*od.* last) journey; **~fall** *m* death; (*Tod e-s Angehörigen*) *auch* bereavement; *im ~* in the event of (*the insured's etc.*) death, on death; **~falle** *f* death-trap; *der Tunnel wurde zur ~* the tunnel was (*od.* became) a death-trap; **~flug** *m* fatal flight; **~folge** *f Jur.: schwere Körperverletzung mit ~* grievous bodily harm resulting in death; **~gefahr** *f* mortal (*od.* deadly) danger; *sich in ~ begeben* risk one's life, put one's life at risk, risk death; **~jahr** *n* year of *s.o.'s* death, year in which *s.o.* died; **~kampf** *m* death throes *Pl.*, death agony; *langer/kurzer ~* slow/quick death; *langer ~ auch* long (*od.* slow) agony; **~kandidat** *m*, **~kandidatin** *f* **1.** doomed man (*od.* woman); *Med.* terminally ill patient; **2.** (*verurteilte Person*) condemned man (*od.* woman); **~kommando** *n* death squad; **~lager** *n* death camp

Todesmut *m* (the) highest personal courage, true heroism, *bes. Mil.* great gallantry; **todesmutig I.** *Adj.* heroic, fearless, unflinching, intrepid *mst iro.*; **II.** *Adv.*: **sich ~ den Angreifern entgegenwerfen** charge the attacking forces with self-sacrificing bravery

Todes|nachricht *f* news of *s.o.*'s death; **~opfer** *n* death, fatality, life lost, person (*Pl. auch* people) killed; **Zahl der ~** death toll, number (of people) killed (*od.* dead); **der Unfall forderte zwei ~** two people were killed in the accident, the accident claimed (*od.* cost) two lives; **~qualen** *Pl.* final (*od.* death) agony *Sg.*; **~ ausstehen** *fig.* go through absolute agony; **~schuss** *m* fatal shot; **e-n ~ abgeben** *gezielt*: shoot to kill; **~schütze** *m*, **~schützin** *f* person who fired (*od.* discharged) the fatal shot(s); **~schwadron** *f* death squad; **~sehnsucht** *f* longing (*od.* yearning) for death; **~spirale** *f Sport* death spiral; **~stoß** *m* death blow (*auch fig.*), *mst fig. auch* coup de grace *geh.*; **den ~ versetzen** deliver the death-blow (+ *Dat.* to); **~strafe** *f* capital punishment, death penalty; *Urteil*: death penalty (*od.* sentence); **bei ~** on penalty of death; **~streifen** *m*: **der ~ an der deutsch-deutschen Grenze** *hist.* the "death strip" along (*od.* on) the German-German border; **~stunde** *f* hour (*od.* moment) of death; **~tag** *m* day (*weitS.* anniversary) of *s.o.*'s death, day *s.o.* died *auch weitS.*; **~trieb** *m Psych.* death wish; **~umstand** *m* circumstance attending a death; *Pl.* circumstances of a (*od.* the *od. s.o.*'s) death; **~ursache** *f* cause of death; **~urteil** *n* (*Spruch*) death sentence (*auch fig.*); (*Urkunde*) death warrant (*auch fig.*); **das ~ vollstrecken** carry out the death sentence; **~verachtung** *f* defiance of death, fearlessness (*od.* unconcern) in the face of death; **mit ~** fearlessly, with utter fearlessness, disregarding the danger; *umg. fig.* in a fit of recklessness (*od.* bravado)

Todes|zeit *f* time of death; **~zelle** *f* death cell; *Pl. auch* death row *Sg.*

Todfeind *m*, **Todfeindin** *f hasserfüllt*: bitter (*od.* implacable) enemy (*od.* foe *geh.*), mortal enemy; *gefährlich*: deadly enemy (*od.* foe); **Todfeindschaft** *f* bitter (*od.* implacable) hatred, deadly enmity

tod|geweiht *Adj.* doomed; **~krank** *Adj. Präd.* desperately (*od.* critically) ill; (*unheilbar krank*) *auch* terminally (*od.* mortally *geh.*) ill, dying; **~langweilig** *Adj. umg.* deadly, deadly boring (*od.* dull), dead boring *umg.*

tödlich I. *Adj.* (*den Tod herbeiführend*) fatal; (*potenziell*) lethal, deadly; *umg.* (*unerträglich*) deadly; **~er Unfall** fatal accident; **~e Dosis/Waffe** lethal dose / weapon (*od.* deadly) weapon; **~es Gift** deadly (*od.* lethal) poison; **mit ~em Ausgang** with fatal results; **~e Gefahr** danger to life, deadly danger; *lit.* mortal danger (*od.* peril); **mit ~er Sicherheit** with deadly accuracy; **II.** *Adv.*: **~ verunglücken** be killed in an accident, have a fatal accident; **~ wirken** have fatal results, cause death; **~ verlaufen** end in death, be fatal; **sich ~ langweilen** *umg. fig.* be bored

to death (*od.* out of one's mind); **~ beleidigt** *umg.* mortally offended (*od.* affronted)

tod|müde *umg.* **I.** *Adj.* ready to drop, dog-tired, shattered, exhausted; **II.** *Adv.*: **~ ins Bett sinken** sink wearily (*od.* collapse) into bed; **~schick** *umg.* **I.** *Adj.* really (*od.* dead) smart; **II.** *Adv.*: **~ kleiden** dress trendily (*od.* smartly), always have the latest clothes

todsicher *umg.* **I.** *Adj.* dead sure (*od.* certain); *Methode etc.*: absolutely reliable, guaranteed, sure-fire *oft iro.*; *Urteil, Ziel*: unerring; *Geschäft*: dead safe; *Gewinn*: guaranteed; **~e Sache** dead certainty, (dead) cert; **II.** *Adv.* (*zweifellos*) definitely, for sure; **er kommt ~** auch there's no way he won't come, he'll come all right

Todsünde *f* deadly (*od.* mortal) sin; **es wäre e-e ~ zu** (+ *Inf.*) it would be a sin (*od.* unforgivable *od.* unpardonable) (for *s.o.*) to (+ *Inf.*)

tod|traurig *Adj.* terribly (*od.* desperately) unhappy; *Gesicht etc.*: *auch* terribly sad; **~unglücklich** *Adj.* terribly (*od.* desperately) unhappy

Töff *n*, *m*; *-s*, *-s*; *schw.* motorbike, motorcycle

Töfftöff *n*; *-s*, *-s*; *Kindersp.* beep-beep (car)

Tofu *m*; *-(s)*, *kein Pl.*; *Gastr.* tofu

Toga *f*; *-*, *Togen*; *hist.* toga

Tohuwabohu *n*; *-(s)*, *-s* complete (*od.* total *od.* utter) chaos, bedlam

Toilette *f*; *-*, *-n* **1.** (*WC*) toilet, lavatory, *Brit. auch* loo *umg.*, *Am. mst* bathroom, john *umg.*; *öffentliche*: public lavatory (*od.* convenience *od.* toilets *Pl.*), *Am.* restroom; **→ Toilettenhäuschen**; **auf der ~ sein** be (gone) in the toilet *etc.*; **auf die ~ müssen** have (*od.* need) to go to the toilet *etc.*, need the toilet *etc. Kinderspr. und umg.*; *etw.* **die ~ runterspülen** flush s.th. down the toilet; **2.** (*Toilettenbecken*) toilet (bowl), lavatory (pan *od.* bowl); **3.** *altm.*: **~ machen** (*sich ankleiden etc.*) be completing one's toilet (*od.* getting ready); **4.** *altm.* (*Kleidung*) dress; **in großer ~** in full evening dress, dressed for a splendid occasion

Toiletten|anlage *f* toilet facilities *Pl.*; *Amtsspr. auch* sanitary facilities *Pl.* (*od.* arrangements *Pl.*); **~artikel** *m* toilet article; *Pl. mst* toiletries; **~becken** *n* → **Toilette** 2; **~deckel** *m* toilet lid; **~fenster** *n* toilet (*od.* lavatory, *Am.* bathroom) window; **~frau** *f* lavatory attendant; **~häuschen** *n* (outside) toilet; *ohne Wasserspülung*: privy, *Am. auch* outhouse; *mobiles*: portaloo, *Am.* port-a-potty; **~mann** *m* lavatory attendant; **~papier** *n* toilet (*od.* loo *Brit. umg. od.* lavatory) paper, *Am. auch* bathroom tissue *euph.*; **~seife** *f* toilet soap; **~sitz** *m* toilet (*od.* lavatory) seat; **~spülung** *f* toilet (*od.* lavatory) flush (mechanism); **die ~ betätigen** flush the toilet *etc.*, pull the chain *umg. altm.*; **~tasche** *f* toilet bag (*Am.* kit), washbag; **~tisch** *m* dressing (*Am.* vanity) table; **~tür** *f* toilet *etc.* (*Am.* bathroom) door; **~wagen** *m* mobile toilet (unit)

toi-toi-toi *Interj. umg.* touch wood; (*viel Glück!*) good luck!, *Brit. auch* best of British!

Tokaier *m*; *-s*, *-*, **~wein** *m* Tokay

Tokio *etc.* → **Tokyo** *etc.*

Tokyo (*n*); *-s*; *Geog.* Tokyo; **Tokyoter** *m*; *-s*, *-*, **Tokyoterin** *f*; *-*, *-nen* Tokyoite,

citizen of Tokyo, *weiblich auch*: Tokyo woman (*od.* girl)

Töle *f*; *-*, *-n*; *umg. pej.* (*Hund*) cur, mutt, dog

tolerabel *Adj.* tolerable, acceptable, *präd. auch* all right *umg.*

tolerant *Adj.* tolerant (**gegen** toward[s], about, of), broadminded (about), easygoing

Toleranz *f*; *-*, *-en* **1.** *nur Sg.* tolerance (**gegen** toward[s], of); **~ üben** exercise tolerance; **2.** *Med.* tolerance (**gegen** of); **3.** *Tech.*, *von Messgeräten*: tolerance (limit); **maximale/enge ~en** *Tech.* maximum / very limited tolerances; **~bereich** *m* range of tolerance; **~dosis** *f* tolerated dose; **~grenze** *f* margin of tolerance, tolerance limit; **~schwelle** *f* tolerance threshold

tolerierbar *Adj.* tolerable, acceptable, endurable; **tolerieren** *v/t.* (*dulden*) tolerate, put up with, turn a blind eye to; *Tech.* allow (*od.* permit) a tolerance of; **Tolerierung** *f* toleration, acceptance

toll I. *Adj.* **1.** (*unglaublich*) incredible, amazing, extraordinary; **es war e-e ~e Sache** *od.* **ein ~es Ding** it was incredible (*od.* amazing), it was an amazing business; **das ist ja e-e ~e Geschichte** that's the most amazing (*od.* an incredible) story; *unwahr*: that's a tall story; **2.** *umg.* (*großartig*) great, fantastic, brilliant, really cool (*alle auch iro.*); **es war nicht so ~** it wasn't that great (*od.* wasn't so hot); **ein ~er Kerl** *männlich*: a great guy (*od.* bloke, *Am.* dude); *weiblich*: a great girl (*od.* lass *Brit.*); *allg.* a great character; **das Tollste war die Musik** what was really great was the music, the best thing of all was the music; **3.** (*wild*) mad, wild, crazy; **ein ~es Treiben** crazy (*od.* mad) goings-on; *im Karneval*: crazy happenings; **die** (**drei**) **~en Tage** (*Karneval*) the Three Crazy Days (*last 3 days of Carnival*); **4.** (*schlimm*) awful, terrible, dreadful, intolerable; **5.** *altm.* (*geistesgestört*) insane, mad; **II.** *Adv.* **1.** *umg.* (*großartig*) *spielen etc.*: brilliantly, superbly; **es hat uns ganz ~ gefallen** we loved it, we thought it was fantastic (*od.* absolutely brilliant); **von hier oben sieht man ganz ~** you get a fantastic (*od.* terrific) view (from) up here; **das hast du ja ~ hingekriegt** *iro.* (-and) a fine job you('ve) made of that!; **2.** (*wild, verrückt*) **wie ~** like mad, like crazy, like hell; **es kommt noch ~er** (wait,) it gets better, you haven't heard it all, there's more to come; **er treibt es zu ~** he carries things (*od.* he goes) too far, he overdoes it; **3.** (*schlimm*) badly, dreadfully, awfully, in a big way; **es regnete ganz ~** it was pouring (with) rain, it was raining cats and dogs *umg.*, *Brit. umg. auch* it was pissing down *Sl.*

tolldreist *Adj.* (*mutig*) *präd.* (as) bold as brass; (*verwegen*) audacious; *Lüge etc.*: brazen

Tolle *f*; *-*, *-n*; *umg.* quiff, *Am.* coif

tollen *v/i.* **1.** (*hat getollt*) *Kinder*: romp (around); *stärker*: play rough games, let off steam; **2.** (*ist*) **durch das Haus** *etc.* **~** romp (*od.* charge *od.* gallop) around the house *etc.*

Tollhaus *n*: **hier geht's zu wie im ~!** it's like a madhouse around (*od.* in) here

Tollheit *f*; *-*, *-en* **1.** *nur Sg.* (*Zustand*, *auch Unsinnigkeit*) madness, lunacy; **2.** (*Handlung*) idiocy, crazy move; *Pl. auch* lunatic (*od.* crazy) behavio(u)r

Tollität f; -, -en; hum.: *s-e/ihre* ~ His/Her Royal Craziness

Tollkirsche f Bot. deadly nightshade, belladonna

tollkühn Adj. daredevil ..., (highly) daring, audacious; *Handlung: auch* very risky; pej. reckless, foolhardy; **Tollkühnheit** f **1.** (*das Tollkühnsein*) audacity, recklessness pej., foolhardiness pej.; e-r Person: auch daring, nerve; **2.** (*tollkühne Handlung*) reckless pej. (od. foolhardy pej. od. daring) act (od. thing to do), act of daring, escapade

Tollpatsch m; -(e)s, -e; umg. clumsy oaf, clown; **tollpatschig** umg. **I.** Adj. oafish, blundering ..., gawky; **II.** Adv. sich bewegen etc.: clumsily, gawkily; *sich ~ anstellen* behave like an oaf (od. cluelessly)

Tollwut f Med. rabies; ~**gefahr** f rabies danger, risk of (catching) rabies

tollwütig Adj. rabid; *wie e-n ~en Hund erschießen* shoot s.o. (down) like a mad dog

Tölpel m; -s, - **1.** umg. pej. dolt, oaf, clown, (clumsy) idiot; **2.** Orn. gannet, booby; als Gattung: member of the Sulidae; **tölpelhaft** Adj. umg. pej. doltish, oafish; **Tölpelhaftigkeit** f umg. pej. oafishness, idiotic behavio(u)r

Tomahawk ['tɔmahaːk] m; -s, -s tomahawk

Tomate f; -, -n; Bot. tomato; *rot werden wie e-e ~* go (od. turn) as red as a beetroot (Am. beet)

Tomaten|ketchup m, n tomato ketchup (od. sauce); ~**mark** n tomato purée (Am. paste); ~**saft** m tomato juice; ~**salat** m tomato salad; ~**scheibe** f tomato slice, slice of tomato; ~**soße** f tomato sauce; ~**staude** f tomato plant; ~**suppe** f tomato soup

Tombola f; -, -s und Tombolen tombola, raffle

Tomogramm n; -(e)s, -e; Med. tomogram, CT scan, CAT scan; **Tomograph** m; -en, -en; Med. tomograph; **Tomographie** f; -, -n; Med. tomography

Ton¹ m; -(e)s, Töne **1.** (*Geräusch*) sound; (heller, dunkler ~) auch tone; *er hat keinen ~ gesagt od. von sich gegeben* he didn't say (od. utter) a word; *keinen ~ herausbringen* (heiser sein etc.) have lost one's voice; (gehemmt sein etc.) not open one's mouth, not utter a word; *keinen ~ mehr!* not another word!; **2.** Mus., einzelner: note, Am. auch tone; (Tonhöhe) pitch, note; (Klang) tone, sound, ring; *ganzer/halber ~* whole tone / semitone; *den ~ angeben* give the note; **3.** fig. in Wendungen: *den ~ angeben* (befehlen) call the tune; (die Atmosphäre bestimmen) set the tone; *in den höchsten Tönen loben* umg. sing the praises of, praise s.o. to the skies oft iro.; *große Töne spucken* umg. talk big, brag; *hast du Töne?* umg. would you believe it?, did you ever hear the like (of that)?; **4.** nur Sg.; TV, Film: sound; *Bild und ~ sind ausgefallen* the sound and the picture have both gone; → auch anschlagen I 3; **5.** (Betonung, auch fig.) accent, stress, emphasis; **6.** nur Sg.; (Sprechweise) tone; *ich verbitte mir diesen ~* I will not be spoken to like that (od. in that tone); (bitte) *nicht in diesem ~!* (please) don't take that tone with me!; *der ~ macht die Musik* it's not what

you say but how you say it; *den richtigen ~ treffen* strike the right note, find the right approach, pitch it (just) right; *e-n anderen/schärferen ~ anschlagen* take a different / more aggressive tone (od. approach); **7.** nur Sg.: *der gute ~* good taste; *zum guten ~ gehören* be (a matter of) good taste (od. good form altm. od. iro.); **8.** (Farbton) tone; (Nuance) auch shade; *~ in ~ Kleidung:* in matching shades; *e-n ~ zu hell* etc. a bit (od. slightly) (too) light etc., a little on the light etc. side

Ton² m; -s, -e, mst Sg.; Geol. clay; *in ~ modellieren* model in (od. with) clay

Tonabnehmer m cartridge, pickup; ~**system** n pick-up system

tonal Adj. tonal; **Tonalität** f; -, kein Pl. tonality

tonangebend Adj. allg. leading; Mode: trend-setting; *~ sein* auch set the tone (bei of)

Ton|arm m pickup (arm), tonearm; ~**art** f Mus.; fig. tone; *e-e andere ~ anschlagen* fig. change one's tune (od. approach), strike a different note; ~**aufnahme** f, ~**aufzeichnung** f (sound) recording; ~**ausfall** m TV loss of sound; kurzer: (sound) dropout

Tonband n; Pl. -bänder (recording) tape; *auf ~ aufnehmen* (record on) tape, record; ~**aufnahme** f tape recording; ~**gerät** n tape recorder; ~**protokoll** n taped record

Ton|bildschau f slide show with soundtrack; ~**blende** f tone and volume control(s Pl.)

Tonboden m clay(ey) soil

Ton|dichtung f Mus. (Werk) symphonic (od. tone) poem; (Gattung) program(me) music; ~**dokument** n sound document, historic recording

tönen¹ v/i. (schallen) sound, ring; (widerhallen) resound; umg. fig. (Reden schwingen) hold forth;„*Ich bin der Größte!*", tönte er "I am the greatest!" he bragged (od. prated)

tönen² v/t. (färben) tint; (Haare) auch colo(u)r; dunkler: tone; *sich* (Dat.) *das Haar blond ~ lassen* have one's hair bleached

Toner m; -s, -; Druck. toner

Tonerde f argillaceous (od. clayey) earth; Chem. alumina; *essigsaure ~* (basic) alumin(i)um acetate

Tonerkassette f Druck. toner cartridge

tönern Adj. Gegenstand: clay ..., präd. od. nachgestellt: made of (od. from) clay; Klang: hollow; *~e Füße* feet of clay; *auf ~en Füßen stehen* fig. rest (od. be) on shaky foundations

Ton|fall m **1.** Ling. intonation; *mit schwäbischem ~* with (od. in) a Swabian accent; **2.** (Ton): *in e-m arroganten ~* in an arrogant tone; ~**film** m sound film; ~**folge** f sequence of notes; weitS. melody; ~**frequenz** f audio frequency

Ton|gefäß n earthenware vessel (od. bowl etc.); ~**geschirr** n pottery, earthenware

Tongeschlecht n Mus. mode, scale

tonhaltig Adj. clayey, argillaceous

Tonhöhe f Phys., Mus. pitch

Tonika f; -, Toniken; Mus. **1.** e-r Tonleiter: keynote, home (od. tonic) note; **2.** (e-s Musikstücks) home (od. tonic) key; **3.** (Dreiklang auf der 1. Stufe) key (od. tonic) chord

Tonikum n; -s, Tonika; Med. tonic

Ton|ingenieur m, ~**ingenieurin** f sound engineer; ~**kabine** f Film:

sound booth; ~**kamera** f Film: sound camera; ~**konserve** f sound recording; umg. auch Pl. canned music; ~**kopf** m von Tonbandgerät: recording (od. audio) head; von Plattenspieler: cartridge, pickup

Tonkrug m earthenware (od. stoneware) pitcher (od. jug)

Ton|kunst f nur Sg.; geh. (the art of) music, music as an art; ~**künstler** m, ~**künstlerin** f **1.** (Virtuose) musician; **2.** (Komponist) composer

Ton|lage f Mus. pitch; ~**leiter** f scale

tonlos Adj. soundless; fig. Stimme: flat, toneless

Ton|malerei f Mus. tone painting, pictorialism (in music); ~**meister** m, ~**meisterin** f sound mixer (od. engineer)

Tonnage [tɔ'naːʒə] f; -, -n; Naut. tonnage

Tonne f; -, -n **1.** barrel; für Wein, Whisky etc.: auch cask; (Öltonne) Menge: barrel; (Behälter) drum; (Regentonne) butt, Am. rain barrel; (Mülleimer) dustbin, Am. trashcan; *sie ist e-e richtige ~* umg., pej. she's a right fatso (od. a two-ton Tessie); **2.** (Gewichtseinheit) (metric) ton, tonne; (BRT) (gross registered) ton; *e-e fünf ~n schwere Maschine* an engine weighing five tons, a five-ton engine; **3.** Naut. (Seezeichen) buoy, marker

Tonnen|dach n Archit. barrel roof; ~**gewölbe** n Archit. barrel vault

tonnen|schwer Adj. attr. enormously heavy, nachgestellt: weighing tons; ~**weise** Adv. by the ton(ne), in lots of a ton(ne); (in großen Mengen) by the ton

...tonner m; -s, - im Subst. (LKW): *Drei~/Fünf~* three-/five-tonner

Ton|pfeife f clay pipe; ~**plastik** f pottery (od. earthenware) figure

Ton|qualität f sound quality; ~**quelle** f sound source; ~**regler** m tone control; ~**satz** m Mus. **1.** (mehrstimmige Komposition) polyphonic work; **2.** (Harmonielehre und Kontrapunkt) harmony and counterpoint; ~**satzlehre** f Mus. (theory of) harmony and counterpoint

Ton|schicht f clay layer, layer of clay; ~**schiefer** m slate

Ton|schnitt m sound editing; ~**schöpfung** f Mus. (musical) composition; ~**signal** n sound (od. audible) signal

Tonsillektomie f; -, -n; Med. tonsillectomy; **Tonsillitis** f; -, Tonsillitiden; Med. tonsillitis

Ton|spur f Film: sound track; ~**störung** f auch Pl. sound interference; ~**studio** n recording (od. sound) studio; *im ~* auch at the recording studios; ~**stufe** f Mus. pitch

Tonsur f; -, -en tonsure; umg. fig. auch monk's patch

Tonsystem n Mus. tonal system, tonality

Tontafel f clay tablet

Tontaube f clay pigeon; **Tontaubenschießen** n clay pigeon shooting, trapshooting

Ton|technik f sound (od. audio) engineering; ~**techniker** m, ~**technikerin** f sound engineer; ~**träger** m sound storage medium, sound carrier; ~**umfang** m **1.** Mus. range; **2.** Akustik: (human) hearing (od. auditory) range

Tönung f **1.** tone (auch Fot.), shade (beide auch fig.); **2.** nur Sg.; (das Tönen) toning, shading; **3.** (Mittel) toner; **Tönungsmittel** n fürs Haar: rinse, colo(u)r(ing)

Tonus *m*; -, *Toni* **1.** *Med.* tone, tonicity; **2.** *Mus.* whole tone

Tonwaren *Pl.* pottery *Sg.*, earthenware *Sg.*

Ton|wert *m* *Fot.* tonal range (*od.* value); **~wiedergabe** *f* sound reproduction

Tonziegel *m* (*Baustein*) clay brick; (*Dachziegel*) (clay) tile

Tool [tu:l] *n*; -*s*, -*s*; *EDV* tool

TOP *m*; -, *kein Pl.*; *Abk.* → *Tagesordnungspunkt*

top *Adj.* *umg.* first-rate, first-class, top--notch; **s-e Kenntnisse sind ~** he's a real expert; **die Lage ist ~** it's an ideal situation; *von Haus, Grundstück etc.*: it's an ideal location

Top *n*; -*s*, -*s*; (*Oberteil, Bluse*) top

topaktuell *Adj.* highly topical, right up to the minute, red-hot *umg.*

Topangebot *n* **1.** (*sehr günstiges*) really good offer; **2.** (*höchstes*) highest offer (*od.* bid)

Topas *m*; -(*es*), -*e* topaz

Topathlet *m*, **~in** *f* top athlete

Topf *m*; -(*e*)*s*, *Töpfe* **1.** *allg.* pot; (*Kochtopf*) *auch* saucepan, stewpan; (*Blumentopf*) flowerpot; *zur Aufbewahrung von Essbarem*: *mst* jar; *für Milch etc.*: jug; *großer*: *auch* pitcher; **ein ~ (voll) Suppe** (*Kochtopf*) a pot (*od.* saucepan) of soup; (*Schüssel*) a bowl (*großer*: *auch* tureen) of soup; **e-n ~ Kartoffeln aufsetzen** put some potatoes on to boil; **ein ~ Schmalz** a jar of lard (*od.* dripping); **alles in einen ~ werfen** *umg.* *fig.* lump everything (*od.* everyone *od.* them all) with the same brush; **j-m in die Töpfe gucken** *umg.* *fig.* poke one's nose (*od.* pry) into s.o.'s affairs; **2.** *umg.* (*Nachttopf*) potty); **auf den ~ müssen** *Kinderspr.* need one's potty; *umg.* (*auf die Toilette*) need the bog (*Am.* the john) (*od.* toilet); → *auch* **Töpfchen**

Topfavorit *m*, **~in** *f* absolute (*od.* most *umg.*) favo(u)rite

Topfblume *f* potted flower, flower in a pot

Töpfchen *n* **1.** small pot; **2.** *umg.* *für Kinder*: potty; (*Nachttopf*) (chamber-)pot, jerry; **aufs ~ gehen** *Kinderspr.* go on (*od.* do) the potty; → *auch* **Topf** 2

Topfdeckel *m* *Kochtopf*: saucepan lid; *Behälter*: lid of the pot (*od.* jar *etc.*)

Topfen *m*; -*s*, *kein Pl.*; *südd.*, *österr.* quark; **~strudel** *m* *südd.*, *österr.* cheese (*od.* quark) strudel

Töpfer *m*; -*s*, - potter; **Töpferei** *f*; -, -*en* **1.** *nur Sg.* (*Handwerk*) pottery; **2.** (*Werkstatt*) potter's workshop; **Töpferhandwerk** *n* (*the craft of*) pottery, pottery as a craft; **Töpferin** *f*; -, -*nen* (*woman od.* female) potter; **Töpferkurs** *m* pottery class(es *Pl.*); **töpfern** *vt/i.* do (*od.* make) pottery; (*e-n Töpferkurs besuchen*) go to pottery classes; (*Krug etc.*) make; **sie töpfert gern** she is a keen (*amateur*) potter, she enjoys making pottery

Töpfer|scheibe *f* potter's wheel; **~ware** *f* pottery, earthenware; **~werkstatt** *f* potter's workshop, pottery

Topf|gucker *m*; -*s*, -; *umg.* pot-lid lifter; (*neugieriger Mensch*) nosy parker, busybody; **~handschuh** *m* oven glove (*od.* mitt)

topfit *Adj.* *umg.* *nur präd.* in top form, at the top of one's form, in peak condition

Topf|kratzer *m* pan-scrubber; **~lappen** *m* oven cloth

Topform *f* *umg.*: **in ~ sein** be in top form

Topfpflanze *f* pot(ted) plant

Toplader *m*; -*s*, - top loader

Topleistung *f* *umg.* top (*od.* outstanding) performance

Topmanagement *n* top management; (*die Manager*) chief executives *Pl.*; **Topmanager** *m*, **Topmanagerin** *f* top executive

Topmodell *n* top model

topmodisch *Adj.* dead (*od.* ultra-)fashionable, *präd.* last word *od.* cri

Topographie *f*; -, -*n* topography; **topographisch** *Adj.* topographical

Topologie *f*; -, *kein Pl.* topology; **topologisch** *Adj.* topological

Topos *m*; -, *Topoi*; *Lit.* topos (*Pl.* topoi)

topp *Interj.* done!, agreed!; **~, die Wette gilt!** you're on!, it's a bet!

Topp *m*; -*s*, -*e*(*n*) *und* -*s*; *Naut.* masthead, mast-top; **über die ~en geflaggt** dressed overall; **~segel** *n* topsail

Topspiel *n* *Sport* top game, big match

Topspin ['tɔpspɪn] *m*; -*s*, -*s*; *Tennis etc.*: (*Drehung*) topspin; (*Schlag*) topspin stroke

Top|star *m* top star; **~zustand** *m*: **in ~** in excellent condition, A1, as new

Tor¹ *n*; -(*e*)*s*, -*e* **1.** gate (*auch Stadttor und fig.*); (*Öffnung, Einfahrt*) gateway (*auch fig.*); (*Torbogen*) archway; (*Garagentor etc.*) door; **vor dem ~en der Stadt** at (*od.* outside) the city gate(s); **das Brandenburger ~** the Brandenburg Gate; **das ~ zur Welt** *fig.* the gateway to the world; **2.** *Sport*: (*Ziel, Treffer*) goal; **im ~ stehen** be in goal; **vor dem ~** in the goalmouth, (right) in front of (the) goal; **ein ~ schießen** score (a goal); **ein ~ geben** *Schiedsrichter*: allow a goal; (*immer*) **noch kein ~** still no score, no score yet; **ein Spiel auf ein ~** one-way traffic; **~! Ruf**: goal!; **3.** *Skisport etc.*: gate

Tor² *m*; -*en*, -*en*; *altm.* (*Narr*) fool

Tor|aus *n* *Sport*: **ins ~ gehen** *Ball*: go behind for a goalkick (*bzw.* corner); **~ausbeute** *f* *Sport*, *umg.* *Fußball etc.*: **geringe ~** small tally of goals; **~bau** *m* *Pl.* -*ten*; *Archit.* gatehouse; **~bogen** *m* *Archit.* archway, (arched) gateway

Tor|chance *f* *Sport* chance (to score), scoring chance (*od.* opportunity), opening; **e-e (klare) ~ herausspielen** create an (a clear) opening; **e-e ~ nutzen/vergeben** take/waste a scoring opportunity; **~differenz** *f* goal difference

Toreador *m*; -*s* *und* -*en*, -*e*(*n*) toreador

Tor|einfahrt *f* entrance gate, entrance gateway; **~erfolg** *m* *Sport* goal; **zu e-m ~ kommen** (manage to) score a goal

Torero *m*; -*s*, -*s* torero

Toresschluss *m*: **kurz vor ~** at the last minute (*od.* the eleventh hour), in the nick of time *umg.*

Torf *m*; -(*e*)*s*, *kein Pl.* peat; **~ stechen** cut peat; **~ballen** *m* bale of peat; **~boden** *m* peaty soil; **~gewinnung** *f* harvesting (*od.* cutting) of peat

torfig *Adj.* peaty

Torf|moor *n* peat bog; **~moos** *n* *Bot.* sphagnum (*od.* peat) moss; **~mull** *m* peatdust

Torfrau *f* *Sport* (woman) goalkeeper (*od.* goalie *umg.*)

Torf|stecher *m*, **~stecherin** *f* peat cutter; **~stich** *m* (*Stechen*) peat cutting; (*Stelle*) peat-cutting site

torgefährlich *Adj.* *Sport*, *Spieler*: dangerous, potent; **Torgefährlichkeit** *f* goal-scoring potential

Torgelegenheit *f* → *Torchance*

Torheit *f*; -, -*en*; *geh.* **1.** *nur Sg.*; (*mangelnde Klugheit*) foolishness, stupidity; **2.** *Handlung*: foolish act, folly, stupid thing to do; **e-e ~ begehen** do something foolish (*od.* silly *od.* stupid), commit a folly

Torhüter *m*, **~in** *f* *Sport* goalkeeper, goalie *umg.*

töricht *Adj.* foolish, silly, naive *geh.*; **törichterweise** *Adv.* foolishly, stupidly, naively *geh.*

Tor|instinkt *m* *Sport* goal instinct, ability to sense an opening; **~jäger** *m*, **~jägerin** *f* prolific scorer, goal-getter; **~jubel** *m* jubilation at (*od.* over) the (*od.* a) goal

torkelig *Adj.* *umg.* unsteady, swaying; *stärker*: staggering, reeling; **torkeln** *v/i.* **1.** (*hat getorkelt*) stagger, reel, lurch; **2.** (*ist*): **aus der Kneipe / ins Bett ~** stagger out of the pub / slump into bed

Tor|latte *f* *Sport* crossbar; **~lauf** *m* slalom; **~linie** *f* goal line

torlos *Sport* **I.** *Adj.* *attr.* goalless; **II.** *Adv.*: **die Begegnung endete ~** the match ended nil-all (*Am.* 0-0)

Tor|mann *m* goalkeeper, goalie *umg.*; **~möglichkeit** *f* → *Torchance*

Törn *m*; -*s*, -*s*; *Naut.* **1.** (*Fahrt*) cruise (*od.* trip); **2.** (*Turnus*) spell, turn; (*Wachtörn*) watch; **3.** (*Schlinge*) kink; **4.** (*Rauschzustand*) trip

Tornado *m*; -*s*, -*s* **1.** *Met.* tornado; **2.** (*Boot*) Tornado (class boat)

Tornähe *f* *Sport*: **in ~** *Sport* near the goal

Tornister *m*; -*s*, -; *Mil.* kit bag, (field) pack; (*Schulranzen*) *etwa* satchel, schoolbag

torpedieren *v/t.* *Naut. und fig.* torpedo; **Torpedierung** *f* torpedoing

Torpedo *m*; -*s*, -*s*; *Naut.* torpedo; **~boot** *n* torpedo boat; **~schacht** *m* torpedo bay

Tor|pfosten *m* gatepost, doorpost; *Sport* goalpost; **an den ~ gehen** *Ball*: hit (*od.* strike) the post; **~raum** *m* *Sport* goalmouth

torreich *Adj.* *Sport* high-scoring ...; **~e Begegnung** high-scoring encounter (*od.* match)

Torschlusspanik *f* *umg.* last-minute panic; *e-s od. e-r Unverheirateten*: fear of being left on the shelf, fear of missing the boat

Torschuss *m* *Sport* shot at goal

Torschütze *m* *Sport* (goal) scorer; **Torschützenkönig** *m* *Sport* top scorer; **Torschützin** *f* *Sport* (goal) scorer

Torsion *f*; -, -*en*; *Phys.*, *Tech.* torsion, twist; *Math.* torsion

Torsionsfestigkeit *f* torsional strength

Torso *m*; -*s*, -*s* *und Torsi* torso (*Pl.* torsos, *Am. auch* torsi) (*auch fig.*)

Torsteher *m*, **~in** *f* *Sport* goalkeeper, goalie *umg.*

Tort *m*; -(*e*)*s*, *kein Pl.*; *altm.*: **j-m e-n ~ antun** wrong (*od.* injure) s.o., do s.o. an injury

Törtchen *n* tartlet, small tart

Torte *f*; -, -*n*; *Gastr.* gateau, layer cake, torte; (*Obsttorte*) fruit tart (*od.* flan)

Tortellini *Pl.* *Gastr.* tortellini

Torten|boden *m* flan base; **~diagramm** *n* *Statistik*: pie chart; **~guss** *m* glaze; **~heber** *m* cake knife (*od.* server); **~platte** *f* cake plate (*od.* platter); **~schlacht** *f* custard-pie battle; **~spritze** *f* icing nozzle, piping bag

Tortur *f*; -, -*en* ordeal, torture; **das war e-e ~** *auch umg.* it was hell

T

Torturm *m* gate tower

Tor|verhältnis *n Sport* goal difference; **~wart** *m Sport* goalkeeper, goalie *umg.*

tosen *v/i.* **1.** (*hat getost*) roar, rage; **2.** (*ist*): *der Sturm toste über die Küste* the storm roared in from the sea; **tosend I.** *Part. Präs.* → *tosen*; **II.** *Adj.*: *~er Beifall* thunderous applause

Toskana *f; -*; *Geog.* Tuscany; **toskanisch** *Adj.* Tuscan, of (*od.* from) Tuscany

tot *Adj.* **1.** a) (*nicht mehr lebend*) dead (*auch Baum*); *bes. Jur.* deceased; *klinisch ~* clinically dead; *~ umfallen* drop dead; *für ~ erklären* declare dead; *er war sofort od. auf der Stelle ~* he died instantly; *~ geboren attr.* stillborn; *fig. Versuch etc.*: abortive; *mehr ~ als lebendig* more dead than alive, b) *fig.*: *halb ~ vor Angst* half-dead with fear, petrified (with fear); *er ist ein ~er Mann* he's a dead man (a goner *umg.*), he's had it *umg.*; *den ~en Mann machen umg.* float (horizontally and face down) (on the water), *Am.* do the dead-man's float; *ich bin einfach ~ umg.* I'm dead (*od.* finished); *sich ~ stellen* play dead (possum *umg.*); *~ und begraben umg.* all over and finished (*od.* forgotten), (all) over and done with, dead and buried, past and gone *umg.*, ancient history; **2.** (*leblos, auch unbewohnt etc.*) lifeless, dead (*beide auch fig.*); *Vulkan*: extinct, dead, defunct *geh.*; (*öde*) desolate; (*verlassen*) deserted, empty; *Farben, Augen*: dull, lifeless; *das Tote Meer Geog.* the Dead Sea; **3.** *Tech., Etech., Wirts. Konto, Sprache*: *auch* defunct *geh.*; **4.** *fig., in Wendungen*: *~es Rennen auch fig.* dead heat; *~er Punkt Tech.* dead cent|re (*Am.* -er); *fig.* deadlock, (*Müdigkeit*) low point; *den ~en Punkt überwinden bei Verhandlungen etc.*: find a way forward, break the deadlock; *Mensch*: get one's second wind, pick o.s. up; *~er Winkel Autofahren etc.*: blind spot; *Mil.* dead angle; (*Gelände*) dead ground; → *Gleis* 1, *Hose* 2

total I. *Adj. attr.* total, complete; *~er Krieg* total (*od.* all-out) war; *~es Chaos* utter (*od.* complete) chaos; *~er Reinfall umg.* washout, (total) fiasco; **II.** *Adv.* totally, completely; *~ verrückt umg.* raving (*od.* stark staring) mad, completely bonkers; *~ besoffen umg.* paralytic, pissed (*Am.* soused) out of one's mind *Sl.*; *~ gut umg.* brilliant; *du machst es ~ falsch umg.* you're doing it all wrong; *das hab ich ~ vergessen umg.* I forgot all about that (*od.* it), I completely forgot (about) it

Total|ansicht *f* general view; **~ausfall** *m* **1.** *der Stromversorgung*: complete blackout (*od.* supply failure); *e-r Maschine etc.*: (major) breakdown; *der Triebwerke*: failure, loss; **2.** *umg.* (*Person*) *bes. Sport* dead loss; **~ausverkauf** *m* clearance sale; *bei Geschäftsaufgabe*: *auch* closing-down (*Am. auch* going-out-of-business) sale

Totale *f; -, -n Film*: full shot

Totalerhebung *f* (*Volkszählung*) universal (*od.* full) census

Totalisator *m; -s, -en* **1.** *Sport* tote, totalizator; **2.** *Met.* rain gauge

totalitär I. *Adj.* totalitarian; **II.** *Adv. regieren etc.*: rule by totalitarian methods; **Totalitarismus** *m; -, kein Pl.* totalitarianism

Totalität *f; -, -en, mst Sg.* totality

Total|operation *f Med.* total removal (of an organ); *der Gebärmutter*: hysterectomy; **~schaden** *m* total loss; *Mot.* write-off; **~verweigerer** *m* conscientious objector to both military service and civilian alternative

tot|arbeiten *v/refl.* (*trennb., hat -ge-*) *umg.* work o.s. to death; **~ärgern** *v/refl.* (*trennb., hat -ge-*) *umg.* be (*od.* get) really annoyed (*stärker*: angry *od.* mad); *ich hab mich totgeärgert* (*über mich selbst*) I could have kicked myself; *stärker*: I was furious with myself

Tote *m, f; -n, -n* dead person, dead man (*weiblich*: woman *od.* girl) (*Leiche*) (dead) body, corpse; *Mil.* casualty; *die ~n* the dead; *Reli.* the departed; *bei dem Unfall gab es fünf ~* five people were killed in the accident; *e-n ~n bestatten* bury (*od.* inter *geh.*) someone; *wie ein ~r schlafen umg.* sleep like a log; *stärker*: sleep the sleep of the dead (*od.* truly exhausted); *das weckt ~ auf umg.* that (noise *etc.*) would raise (*od.* wake[n]) the dead

Totem *n; -s, -s* totem; **Totemfigur** *f* totem (figure); **Totemismus** *m; -, kein Pl.* totemism; **Totempfahl** *m* totem pole

töten I. *vt/i.* kill; *fig. auch* destroy; *du sollst nicht ~ bibl.* thou shalt not kill; → *Nerv*; **II.** *v/refl.* kill o.s., commit suicide, take one's (own) life, die by one's own hand *geh.*

Toten|bahre *f* bier; **~bett** *n* deathbed; *auf dem ~* on one's deathbed

totenblass *Adj.* deathly pale, (as) white as a sheet; **Totenblässe** *f* pallor of death; *fig.* deathly pallor

totenbleich *Adj.* deathly pale, (as) white as a sheet

Toten|ehrung *f* commemoration (*od.* hono[u]ring) of the dead; **~feier** *f* remembrance ceremony; **~flecke** *Pl.* postmortem (*od.* cadaveric) lividity *Sg.*; **~glocke** *f* (death) knell, mourning bell; **~gräber** *m* **1.** *Friedhof*: gravedigger; **2.** *Zool.* burying beetle; **~hemd** *n* shroud; **~klage** *f* **1.** *der Verwandten etc.*: lament for (*od.* lamentation of) the dead; *Lit., Dial. auch* keening; **2.** (*Musik*) dirge, lament; **3.** *Literatur*: dirge, lament, threnody

Totenkopf *m* **1.** death's head (*auch Symbol*), skull; (*Giftzeichen etc., Piratenflagge*) skull and crossbones; **2.** *Zool.* death's-head hawkmoth; **~äffchen** *n Zool.* squirrel monkey

Toten|kult *m* cult of the dead; **~maske** *f* death mask; **~messe** *f kath.* requiem (mass); **~reich** *n* realm of the dead, underworld; *griechische Mythologie*: *auch* Hades; **~ruhe** *f* (*Tod*) rest (*od.* peace) in death; *Störung der ~* desecration (*stärker*: violation) of a grave (*od.* of graves); **~schädel** *m* skull; **~schein** *m* death certificate; **~sonntag** *m* last Sunday before Advent commemorating the dead; **~stadt** *f* necropolis; **~starre** *f* rigor mortis

totenstill *Adj.* (as) silent as the grave; **Totenstille** *f* dead silence, deathly hush *lit.*; *es herrschte ~* not a sound was to be heard, the silence was absolute

Toten|tanz *m Kunst*: dance of death, danse macabre; **~trompete** *f Bot.* horn of plenty; **~wache** *f* deathwatch, vigil, *bes. in keltischen Ländern*: wake

totfahren *v/t.* (*unreg., trennb., hat -ge-*) run over and kill

tot geboren → *tot* 1 a; **Totgeburt** *f*

(*Geburt*) stillbirth; (*Kind*) stillborn child

totgeglaubt *Adj.* presumed dead; *sein ~er Onkel* his uncle who was presumed dead (*od.* who[m] everyone believed to be dead), his uncle, the one they (all) thought was dead

Totgesagte *m, f; -n, -n* the one (they had) declared dead; *fig. the* one they had written off; **~ leben länger** *Sprichw. etwa* there's no tonic like reading your own obituary

tot|kriegen *v/t.* (*trennb., hat -ge-*) *umg.*: *er ist nicht totzukriegen* he just goes on for ever, there's simply no stopping him; **~lachen** *v/refl.* (*trennb., hat -ge-*) *umg.* (nearly) die laughing, kill o.s. (laughing); *es ist zum Totlachen* it's a scream (*od.* a real hoot); **~laufen** *v/refl.* (*unreg., trennb., hat -ge-*) *umg. fig.* peter (*od.* fizzle) out, play itself out, tail off (and stop); **~machen** (*trennb., hat -ge-*) *umg.* **I.** *v/t.* kill; *fig.* (*Konkurrenz*) eliminate, get rid of; **II.** *v/refl.* sacrifice (*od.* kill) o.s., run o.s. into the ground

Toto *n; -s, kein Pl.* **1.** (*Totalisator*) tote; **2.** (*Fußballtoto*) (football) pools *Pl.*; *~ spielen* do the pools; *im ~ gewinnen* win (on) the pools; **~schein** *m*, **~zettel** *m* pools (*od.* football pool) coupon

tot|reden *v/t.* (*trennb., hat -ge-*) *umg.*: *j-n ~* talk s.o. into the ground, wear s.o. down; **~reiten** *v/t.* (*unreg., trennb., hat -ge-*) *umg.* (*Thema*) flog to death; **~sagen** *v/t.* (*trennb., hat -ge-*): *j-n ~* say (*behaupten*: maintain; *melden*: report) that s.o. is dead; **~schießen** *v/t.* (*unreg., trennb., hat -ge-*) *umg.* shoot s.o. dead

Totschlag *m; nur Sg.; Jur.* manslaughter, (culpable) homicide, second-degree murder

totschlagen *v/t.* (*unreg., trennb., hat -ge-*) kill; *mit Schlägen*: beat (*od.* batter, *mit Knüppel*: *auch* cudgel) to death; *fig.* (*übertreffen*) beat hollow (*od.* out of sight), knock for six, outclass, put in the shade; *Zeit ~ umg. fig.* kill time; *den Tag ~ umg.* get through the day (somehow), put time in; *er lässt sich lieber ~, als ... umg.* he'd die rather (*od.* rather die) than ...; *du kannst mich ~, aber ... umg. fig.* hono[u]r bright, for the life of me, strike me dead *Sl.*

Totschläger *m; -s, -* **1.** *Person*: killer *pej.*; *person who commits a homicide* (*usually manslaughter*); **2.** (*Schlagstock*) cosh, club, life preserver *altm.*, *Am.* blackjack

tot|schweigen *v/t.* (*unreg., trennb., hat -ge-*) hush up, keep quiet (*od.* under wraps); *etw. ~ auch* pretend s.th. never happened; **~stechen** *v/t.* (*unreg., trennb., hat -ge-*) *umg.* stab s.o. to death

tot stellen → *tot* 1

tot|trampeln *v/t.* (*trennb., hat -ge-*) *Tier*: trample s.o. to death; *Person(en)*: stamp s.o. to death; **~treten** *v/t.* (*unreg., trennb., hat -ge-*) kick s.o. to death

Tötung *f* killing; *Jur.* homicide; *fahrlässige ~ Jur.* involuntary homicide; *~ auf Verlangen Jur.* mercy killing, killing on demand

Tötungs|absicht *f Jur.* intent(ion) to kill; **~delikt** *n Jur.* crime of causing death; **~versuch** *m* murder attempt, attempted murder

Totzeit *f EDV* downtime

Touch [tatʃ] *m; -s, -s; umg.* (*Fluidum*)

(indefinable) quality, character, feel; **e-r Sache e-n besonderen ~ geben** lend s.th. a certain je ne sais quoi

touchieren [tu'ʃiːrən] v/t. bes. Sport touch, brush; (Fahrzeug) bump; Med. (austasten) palpate; (abätzen) cauterize

Touch|bildschirm ['tatʃ-] m; -s, -e, **Touchscreen** ['tatʃskriːn] m; -s, -s; EDV touchscreen; **~pad** ['tatʃpɛd] n; -s, -s; EDV touchpad

Toupet [tu'peː] n; -s, -s (Haarteil) toupet, toupee, hairpiece, rug Sl.

toupieren [tu'peː] v/t. back-comb

Tour [tuːɐ] f; -, -en **1.** (Rundgang, -fahrt) tour (**durch** of, around), circuit (of); (Ausflug) excursion, trip; zu Fuß: walk, ramble, hike; (Strecke) stretch; **auf ~ gehen** (verreisen) go off on a trip; (auf Tournee) go (off) on tour; **auf ~ sein** (unterwegs sein) be on the road; **2.** Tech. (Umdrehung) revolution, turn; **mit 4000 ~en pro Minute laufen** Mot. run at 4000 rpm (od. revolutions per minute); **auf ~en bringen** Mot. rev (up), open up; fig. (in Schwung bringen) get s.o. (od. s.th.) going (od. moving od. up to speed); (wütend machen) get s.o. worked up (od. hot under the collar), really irk (od. rile) s.o.; **auf ~en kommen** Mot. pick up, rev up, open up; umg. fig. (in Schwung geraten) get into one's swing (od. stride), get going (od. moving); (wütend werden) get mad (od. worked up); **auf vollen ~en laufen** be going full blast (od. full out), be on full power; umg. fig Arbeit, Produktion, Party etc.: be in full swing; **in einer ~** umg. (ununterbrochen) incessantly, non-stop; **3.** umg. (Trick) ploy, dodge, trick; **komm mir bloß nicht auf diese ~!** don't try that one on me; **j-m die ~ vermasseln** queer s.o.'s pitch, Am. spoil s.o.'s chances of success; → **krumm** 3, **link, sanft** I

touren ['tuːrən] v/i. umg. (auf Tournee sein) be on tour, be touring; (auf Tournee gehen) go on (a) tour

Touren|karte f tourist map; **~rad** n touring bicycle; **~ski** m touring ski; **~skifahren** n ski touring, off-piste (Am. off-trail) skiing; **~wagen** m touring car, gran turismo (car), tourer; **~zähler** m rev(olution) counter

Touri m; -(s), -s, mst Pl.; umg. (Tourist) tourie

Tourismus m; -, kein Pl. tourism

...tourismus m, im Subst. **1.** allg. im wörtl. Sinn: ... tourism; **Alpen~** tourism in the Alps; **Auslands~** foreign travel, travel abroad; **Öko~** ecotourism, environmentally-compatible tourism, green tourism; **2.** zweckgebunden: ... tourism; **Bildungs~** allg., auch Einzelkunden: cultural tourism; Schulgruppen etc.: educational travel, travel for educational purposes; **Einkaufs~** shopping trips Pl. abroad, international shopping trips Pl.; **Kongress~** international conference hopping, conference tourism; **Kultur~** cultural tourism, travel for cultural purposes; **3.** fig. oft pej. Auslagern e-r Aktivität in andere Länder etc.: **Abtreibungs~** abortion abroad, having an abortion in another country; **Müll~** export(ing) of problem waste; **4.** fig. oft pej.: **Katastrophen~** disaster sightseeing, ghoul tourism pej.

Tourismus|börse f travel fair, tourist industry convention (od. fair); **~industrie** f tourist trade (od. industry)

Tourist m; -en, -en tourist

Touristen|attraktion f tourist attraction; **~bus** m tour bus, tour(ing) coach; **~gruppe** f group (od. bunch) of tourists; (Reisegruppe) tour group; **~hotel** n tourist (od. budget) hotel; **~klasse** f Flug. economy class; **~menü** n tourist menu; **~ort** m (tourist) resort, popular holiday (Am. vacation) cent|re (Am. -er); **~rummel** m umg. etwa hordes Pl. of tourists; saisonbedingt: auch tourist invasion (**in** +Dat. of); **~strom** m stream (stärker: flood) of tourists; **abseits vom ~** off the tourist (od. beaten) track

Touristik f; -, kein Pl. (travel and) tourism; **~börse** f → **Tourismusbörse**; **~unternehmen** n travel firm (od. company, Am. agency), tour operator

Touristin f; -, -nen (woman od. girl od. female) tourist; **touristisch I.** Adj. attr. tourist ..., auch präd. tourism-related; **II.** Adv.: **ein Gebiet** etc. **~ erschließen** develop (od. open up) a region etc. for tourism (od. as a tourist destination)

Tournedos [tʊrnə'doː] n; -, -; Gastr. tournedos

Tournee f; -, -n tour; **auf ~ gehen/sein** go/be on tour; **~theater** n touring company

Tower ['taʊɐ] m; -(s), -; Flug. control tower; **~gehäuse** n Computer: tower system

Toxikologie f; -, kein Pl. toxicology; **toxikologisch** Adj. toxicological; **Toxin** n; -s, -e; Med., Bio. toxin; **toxisch** Adj. toxic

Trab m; -s, kein Pl. **1.** Gangart bei Pferden: trot; **in ~ fallen** settle into a trot; **im ~** at a (od. the) trot; **2.** fig., umg.: **j-n auf ~ bringen** get s.o. moving (od. up to speed); **j-n in ~ halten** keep s.o. on his (od. her) toes (od. on the go); **immer auf ~ sein** always be on the go

Trabant m; -en, -en; Astron. satellite; **Trabantenstadt** f (Satellitenstadt) satellite town; (Wohnstadt) outlying residential area, distant suburb

traben v/i. **1.** (hat od. ist getrabt) (im Trab laufen, reiten) trot; **2.** (ist) auch umg., fig. Mensch: walk (briskly), trot (along), go on foot; **er trabte zur Schule** he trotted along (od. hurried) to school

Traber m; -s, - Pferd: trotter; **~bahn** f trotting circuit (od. course); **~krankheit** f Vet. scrapie

Trabi, Trabbi m; -(s), -s; umg. Trab(b)i (small GDR.-produced car now enjoying a degree of cult status)

Trab|reiten n trotting; **~rennbahn** f trotting course; **~rennen** n (Sport) trotting; (Veranstaltung) trotting race; **~rennfahrer** m, **~rennfahrerin** f trotting competitor

Trachee f; -, -n **1.** Zool. trachea; **2.** Bot. trachea, wood vessel

Tracht f; -, -en **1.** (Kleidung) dress; (Landestracht) traditional (od. national) costume; (Schwesterntracht etc.) uniform; **sie kamen in Schwarzwälder ~** they came in traditional Black Forest costume(s); **2.** nur Sg. → **Prügel²**

trachten v/i.: **~ nach** geh. strive for (od. after); (danach) **~ zu** (+ Inf.) endeavo(u)r (od. strive) to (+ Inf.), do one's best to (+ Inf.); **j-m nach dem Leben ~** be out to kill s.o., be after s.o.'s life (head umg.); **Trachten** n; -s, kein Pl.; geh. pursuit (nach of), striving (after, for), endeavo(u)r(s Pl.); → **Sinnen**

Trachten|anzug m: (**im**) **~** (in) tradi-

tional costume; **~gruppe** f dancers etc. Pl. in traditional costume(s); **~jacke** f traditional jacket (od. jerkin); **~kapelle** f traditional band, band in traditional costume; **~kostüm** n traditional costume; **~look** m ethnic (od. traditional costume) look; **~mode** f traditional fashion (od. style); **~verein** m society for traditional costumes

trächtig Adj. pregnant (auch fig. **von, mit** with)

...trächtig im Adj.: **erfolgs~** rising, coming, promising, ... with (od. of) (great) potential; **fehler~** Person: fallible, error-prone; Arbeitsgebiet: tricky, präd. full of pitfalls, high-risk ..., dicey umg.

Trächtigkeit f e-s Säugetiers: gestation (period); fig. (Gewichtigkeit) weightiness, implicit (od. latent) significance

Trackball ['trɛkbɔːl] m; -s, -s; EDV trackball

tradieren v/t. hand down, pass on; **tradiert I.** Part. Präs. → **tradieren**; **II.** Adj.: **~e Rollen** traditional roles

Tradition f; -, -en tradition; **nach alter ~** by (old-established) tradition; **zur ~ werden** become a tradition, become established (od. traditional); **Traditionalismus** m; -, kein Pl. traditionalism, adherence to traditional values; **Traditionalist** m; -en, -en, **Traditionalistin** f; -, -nen traditionalist; **traditionalistisch** Adj. traditionalist; **traditionell** Adj. traditional

Traditionsbetrieb m traditional (od. long-established) business

traditionsbewusst I. Adj. (der Tradition verhaftet) traditional(ly)-minded; (Tradition aktiv bewahrend) tradition-conscious; **~ sein** have a sense of tradition; **II.** Adv. in a tradition-conscious way; **Traditionsbewusstsein** n sense of tradition

traditions|gebunden Adj. Person: traditional(ly)-minded; Denken, Kunst etc.: traditionalist, ... on traditional lines, hidebound pej.; **~gemäß** Adv. in keeping (od. line) with tradition

Traditionspflege f keeping up (od. upholding od. maintaining) (of) tradition(s)

traditionsreich Adj. steeped in tradition, historic

Traditionsverein m Sport long-established club

traf Imperf. → **treffen**

Trafik [tra'fɪk] f; -, -en; österr. tobacconist's, Am. smoke shop; **Trafikant** m; -en, -en, **Trafikantin** f; -, -nen; österr. tobacconist

Trafo m; -s, -s; Etech. transformer; **~häuschen** n transformer (substation); **~station** f transformer substation

Tragbahre f stretcher

tragbar Adj. **1.** Fernseher etc.: portable; Filmkamera etc.: hand-held; Computer: laptop; **2.** Kleidung: fit for wear, wearable, respectable; **3.** fig. (annehmbar) acceptable; (zumutbar) tolerable; (finanziell) **nicht mehr ~** beyond one's means, unaffordable

Trage f; -, -n **1.** (Tragbahre) stretcher; primitive: litter; **2.** zum Lastentragen: pack frame, rigid framework (for loads); **3.** auf Baustelle etc.: handbarrow

träge Adj. (langsam) sluggish (auch weitS. und Wirts.), slow-moving; Mensch: auch lethargic, listless, indolent; (schläfrig) drowsy, sleepy; (leblos, auch Phys.) inert; **geistig ~** pej. mentally slow (*od.* sluggish), dull; **~ Masse** *Phys.* inertial mass

Trage|eigenschaften *Pl. von Textilien*: wearing characteristics, durability *Sg.*; **~griff** *m* handle; **~gurt** *m* (carrying-)sling, harness; **~korb** *m* (carrying-)basket; *für Babys*: Moses (basket); *für Gartenarbeit*: trug

tragen; *trägt*, *trug*, *hat getragen* **I.** *v/t.* **1.** (*halten*) carry, have; (*mitnehmen*) take; (*stützen*) support; *etw. bei sich ~* have (*od.* carry) s.th. on (*od.* with) one; *den Arm in e-r Schlinge ~* have (*od.* wear) one's arm in a sling; *den Kopf hoch ~* hold one's head high (*od.* erect); *nichts Schweres ~ dürfen* not be allowed to carry weights (*od.* lift anything heavy); *so schnell ihn s-e Füße trugen* as fast as his feet would carry him; *sich von den Wellen ~ lassen* float on the waves; *die Brücke trägt maximal 10 t* the bridge has a maximum (permitted) load of 10 tons; **2.** (*am Körper ~, auch Brille*) wear, have on; (*Schmuck*) *mst* wear; (*Pistole, Schwert etc.*) *in der Hand*: hold; *an der Hüfte*: wear; *e-n Bart etc.* **~** have (*od.* wear *od.* sport *iro.*) a beard *etc.*; *man trägt die Röcke wieder kürzer* short skirts are in again, skirts are (being worn) shorter again; *das kannst du gut ~* it really suits you, that's nice on you; *die Haare lang/kurz ~* wear (*od.* have) one's hair long/short; *das Recht, Waffen zu ~* the right to bear arms *förm.* (*od.* to carry a firearm [*od.* gun]); **3.** (*Früchte, fig. Namen, Verlust etc.*) bear, take on, meet, be responsible for; (*Folgen, Verantwortung*) bear, take, accept, (*Folgen*) *auch* live with; *die Aufschrift / den Titel ~* bear (*od.* carry) the heading / carry the title; *den Schaden ~* pay (*od.* stump up *umg.*) for the damage; **4.** *fig.* (*ertragen*) bear, endure; *wie trägt sie es?* how's she taking it?, how's she bearing up?; → *Herz*[1] 8, *Rechnung* 2, *Trauer* 2, *Zins* 1; → *getragen*; **II.** *v/i.* **1.** (*hervorbringen*) *Baum*: bear fruit; *Zool.* be pregnant; *bes. Nutztiere*: *auch* be in calf/foal/pig/lamb *etc.*; *zum Tragen kommen fig.* take effect, bring results, bear fruit(s); **2.** (*reichen*) *Stimme*: carry; *das Gewehr trägt nicht so weit* the weapon doesn't have the range; **3.** (*schleppen*) carry weights (*od.* things); *nicht schwer ~ dürfen* not be allowed to carry weights (*od.* lift anything heavy); *schwer ~ an etw.* (+ *Dat.*) have a hard time carrying (*od.* coping with) s.th.; *schwer zu ~ haben* be loaded down, be heavily burdened, be carrying a considerable load; *fig.* be weighed down (*od.* burdened) (*an* + *Dat.* by), have a hard time (of it) coping (*an* + *Dat.* with); **4.** *Eis etc.*: hold; **III.** *v/refl.* **1.** *sich gut ~ Stoff*: wear (well), be hardwearing; **2.** *Geschäft etc.*: pay (its way); *die Einrichtung trägt sich (nicht) selbst* the facility is (not) self-financing, the facility pays (does not pay) its own way; **3.** *fig.*: *sich mit der Absicht od. dem Gedanken ~, etw. zu tun* be thinking of (*od.* about) doing s.th., be considering (*od.* contemplating) doing s.th.

tragend I. *Part. Präs.* → *tragen*; **II.** *Adj. Wand*: load-bearing; *Idee*: central, main; *Rolle*: *auch* leading, principal; *Stimme e-s Sängers etc.*: powerful; *im Gespräch etc.*: carrying, penetrating; *sich selbst ~* self-financing, self-funding

Träger *m*; *-s*, - **1.** *von Lasten*: carrier, bearer; (*Gepäckträger*) porter; *e-r Tragbahre*: stretcher-bearer; **2.** *von Kleidungsstücken, Brille etc.*: wearer; **3.** *fig. e-s Namens, Titels*: bearer (*Sport* holder); *e-r Idee*: upholder, champion; (*Institution*) responsible authority, body responsible for *s.th.*; (*Treuhänder*) (body of) trustees *Pl.*; (*Förderer*) sponsor(s *Pl.*), sponsoring body *od.* company; → *Bauträger*, *Flugzeugträger*, *Preisträger etc.*; **4.** *an Kleidung*: (shoulder) strap; → *Hosenträger*, **5.** *Tech.* support, bracket; *Archit.* supporting beam; (*Eisenlängsträger*) girder; **6.** *ein ~ Bier* a crate (*Am.* case) of beer

Träger|frequenz *f Flug., Etron.* carrier frequency; **~gesellschaft** *f Wirts.* sponsoring company

Trägerin *f*; *-*, *-nen* → *Träger* 1-3

Träger|kleid *n* pinafore dress, *Am.* jumper; **~kolonne** *f* line of porters (*od.* bearers *altm.*)

trägerlos *Adj. Kleidungsstück*: strapless

Träger|rakete *f Raumf.* launch vehicle; **~rock** *m* **1.** skirt with straps; **2.** → *Trägerkleid*

Trägerschaft *f* sponsorship, trusteeship; **Trägerverein** *m* board of trustees

Trage|tasche *f* **1.** carrier bag; **2.** *für Babys*: carrycot, *Am.* (portable) bassinet; **~tuch** *n für Babys*: sling; **~tüte** *f* carrier bag

tragfähig *Adj.* **1.** load-bearing, strong, *präd. od. nachgestellt*: capable of taking a load; **2.** *fig.* (*fundiert*) sound, viable; (*stabil*) firm, stable; *Kompromiss*: (mutually) acceptable, worthwhile; **~e Mehrheit** working (*od.* useful) majority; **Tragfähigkeit** *f* **1.** load (--carrying) capacity, bearing strength; *Brücke*: safe load; *Kran, Flug.*: lifting capacity; *Naut.* tonnage; *Boot*: buoyancy; **2.** *fig.* soundness, viability; stability; acceptability; → *tragfähig* 2

Tragfläche *f Flug.* wing, aerofoil; *Naut.* hydrofoil; **Tragflächenboot** *n* hydrofoil

Tragflügel *m Flug.* wing, aerofoil; *Naut.* hydrofoil; **~boot** *n* hydrofoil

Trägheit *f* (*Langsamkeit*) sluggishness; (*Lustlosigkeit*) lethargy, listlessness; (*Schläfrigkeit*) drowsiness; *Phys.* inertia (*auch fig.*); *Chem.* inactivity; → *träge*

Trägheits|gesetz *n* law of inertia; **~moment** *n* moment of inertia; **~navigation** *f Flug. etc.*: inertial navigation (system)

Tragik *f*; *-*, *kein Pl. e-r Situation etc.*: tragedy; (*tragisches Element*) tragic element (*od.* aspect *od.* quality); *die ~ daran auch* the tragic thing about it

Tragikomik *f*; *-*, *kein Pl.* tragicomedy; (*tragikomisches Element*) tragicomic element (*od.* aspect); **tragikomisch I.** *Adj.* tragicomic; **II.** *Adv.* tragicomically; **Tragikomödie** *f* tragicomedy

tragisch I. *Adj.* tragic; *das Tragische daran* the tragic thing about it; *das ist nicht weiter ~ umg.* it's not the end of the world, it's not such a big deal; **II.** *Adv.* tragically; *nimm's nicht so ~!* don't take it to heart, it's not the end of the world

Trag|kraft *f* → *Tragfähigkeit* 1; **~last** *f* load, burden; (*Tragkraft*) (load) capacity; **~lufthalle** *f* air-supported (*od.* inflatable) building

Tragöde *m*; *-n, -n*; *Theat.* tragic actor, actor of tragic roles

Tragödie *f*; *-*, *-n*; *Lit.* tragedy (*auch fig.*); (*Ereignis*) *auch* tragic event; *mach nicht gleich e-e ~ draus umg.* there's no need to make a full-scale drama out of it, try not to get too het up about it; *das ist doch keine ~ umg. fig.* that's not the end of the world; **Tragödiendichter** *m*, **Tragödiendichterin** *f* tragedian, tragic writer (*od.* dramatist)

Tragödin *f*; *-*, *-nen*; *Theat.* tragic actress, tragédienne

Trag|pfeiler *m* (load-carrying) pillar; *e-r Brücke*: support; **~riemen** *m* (carrying-)strap; *am Gewehr*: sling; **~rolle** *f Tech.* conveyor roller; **~seil** *n Tech.* support cable (*od.* rope); **~sessel** *m* sedan chair

trägt *Präs.* → *tragen*

Trag|tasche *f* carrier bag; **~weite** *f* **1.** *fig.* (*Bedeutung*) significance, implications *Pl.*; *von großer ~ fig.* significant, of great import (*od.* consequence); *von großer ~ sein auch* have far-reaching implications (*od.* consequences *od.* repercussions); **2.** *Mil.* (*Schussweite*) range, carry; **3.** *Naut.* (*Sicht*) visibility; **~werk** *n* **1.** *Flug.* wing assembly (*od.* unit); **2.** *Tech.* supporting structure, load-bearing element

Trailer ['treːlɐ] *m*; *-s*, - **1.** (*Vorfilm*) trailer; (*Filmstreifenende*) leader; **2.** *Mot.* (lorry) trailer (unit)

Trainer ['trɛːnɐ] *m*; *-s*, -; *Sport* trainer, coach; *Fußball*: manager; **Trainerbank** *f* (trainer's) bench; **Trainerin** *f*; *-*, *-nen* → *Trainer*

Trainerschein *m Sport* trainer's certificate (*od.* licence); *s-n Trainerschein machen* qualify (professionally) as a trainer

trainieren [trɛ'niːrən] **I.** *v/i.* train, be in (*od.* undergo) training (*für, auf* + *Akk.* for); *fleißig ~* train hard; **II.** *v/t.* (*j-n*) coach (*auf* + *Akk.* for); *Hochsprung etc. ~* practi|se (*Am.* -ce) (*od.* train for) the (*od.* one's) high jump *etc.*; *das Gedächtnis etc. ~ fig.* train one's memory *etc.*

Training ['trɛːnɪŋ] *n*; *-s*, *kein Pl.*; *Sport* training, practice (*auch Motorsport*); *Motorsport* (*Qualifikation*) qualifying; *zum ~ gehen* go to (*od.* attend) training (*od.* practice *od.* a training session); *nicht zum ~ kommen* miss training (*od.* practice *od.* a training session); *ein hartes/zweistündiges ~ absolvieren* complete a hard (*od.* rigorous) / two-hour training session; *Schnellster im ~ sein Motorsport*: be fastest (*od.* quickest) in practice (*Formel 1*: qualifying); → *autogen*

Trainings|anzug *m Sport* tracksuit; **~einheit** *f* training unit; **~gelände** *n Ballspiele*: training facility, practice ground; *Leichtathletik*: training facility, practice track; *Motorsport*: practice circuit (*od.* facility); **~hose** *f* (*e-e*) **~** (a pair of) tracksuit bottoms *Pl.* (*od.* trousers, *Am.* pants *Pl.*); **~jacke** *f* tracksuit top; **~lager** *n* training camp; **~lauf** *m* training run; *fig.* (*Test*) trial (*od.* dry) run, rehearsal; **~methode** *f* training method(s *Pl.*); **~möglichkeit** *f* **1.** (*Gelegenheit*) chance to train (*od.* practi|se [*Am.* -ce]); (*Anlage etc.*) training (*Motorsport*: practice) facilities *Pl.*; **2.** (*mögliche Übung*) possible training technique, training idea; **~programm** *n* training (*od.* practice) program(me) *od.* schedule; **~rück-stand** *m* lack of match fitness; **~schnellste** *m,f; -n, -n Motorsport:* fastest (*od.* quickest) in practice (*Formel 1:* qualifying); **~zeit** *f* (*gefahrene, gelaufene Zeit*) time in practice; **~zentrum** *n* training cent|re (*Am.* -er) (*od.* facility), coaching facility

Trakt *m; -(e)s, -e* **1.** (*Gebäudeteil*) part, section; (*Flügel*) wing; **2.** *Anat.* tract; **3.** (*Teilstrecke*) section

Traktat *n; -(e)s, -e; altm.*; (*Abhandlung*) treatise; *kirchl.* tract

traktieren *v/t.* (*belästigen*) pester, importune; (*misshandeln*) maltreat; **mit Schlägen ~** beat up, administer a beating to; **j-n mit Vorwürfen ~** *umg.* keep going on at s.o., bombard s.o. with complaints

Traktor *m; -s, -en* tractor; **~ fahren** drive a tractor

trallala *Interj.* tra-la-la; **Trallala** *n; -(s), kein Pl.; umg.:* **das ganze ~** (*Brimborium*) all the (*od.* the whole) rigmarole

trällern *vt/i.* warble, trill; (*ein Lied*) **vor sich hin ~** trill away (*od.* a song) to o.s.

Tram *f; -, -s, schw. n; -s, -s; Verk., Dial.,* **~bahn** *f südd., schw., österr.* tram, *Am.* streetcar; **mit der** *od. schweiz.* **dem**) **Tram** by (*od.* on the) tram, *Am.* by streetcar

Traminer *m; -s, -* **1.** (*Wein*) Traminer; **2.** *nur Sg.* (*Rebsorte*) Traminer grape

Trampel *m, n; -s, -; umg.* (clumsy) oaf; *schärfer:* boor; **das ist ein ~!** what a plonker (*Am.* klutz)!; **trampeln** *vt/i.* **1.** (*hat getrampelt*) trample; **auf der Stelle:** *auch* stamp; **Beifall ~** stamp one's applause, stamp in approval; **zu Tode ~** trample to death; **2.** (*ist*) **über den jungen Rasen ~** trample over the newly-seeded grass

Trampel|pfad *m* beaten path; **~tier** *n* **1.** *Zool.* Bactrian camel; **2.** *umg.* clumsy oaf; **pass auf, du ~!** look out, clumsy!; *schärfer:* look out, you clumsy idiot!

trampen ['trɛmpn̩] *v/i.* hitchhike, hitch (it) *umg.*; **Tramper** ['trɛmpɐ] *m; -s, -,* **Tramperin** *f; -, -nen* hitchhiker

Trampolin *n; -s, -e* trampoline; **~springen** *n* trampolining

Trampschiff ['trɛmp-] *n Naut.* tramp (steamer)

Tramway ['tramvai] *f -, -s; österr.* tram, *Am.* streetcar

Tran *m -(e)s, kein Pl. von Walen:* train oil; *von Fischen:* fish oil; **im ~** *umg.* dop(e)y, not with it; (*abwesend*) in a dream (*od.* dwam *Dial.*)

Trance ['trãːs] *f; -, -n* trance; **in ~ fallen** go into a trance; **in ~ versetzen** put into a trance; **tranceartig** *Adj.* trance--like; **Trancezustand** *m* (state of) trance

Tranche ['trãːʃə] *f; -, -n* **1.** *Gastr.* (thick) slice; **2.** *Wirts.* tranche, instal(l)ment

Tranchierbesteck [trã'ʃiːɐ̯-] *n:* (**ein**) **~** (a pair of) carvers *Pl.*, carving knife and fork; **tranchieren** [trã'ʃiːrən] *vt/i.* carve, cut; **Tranchiermesser** *n* carving knife

Träne *f; -, -n* **1.** tear; **den ~n nahe** nearly in tears, near to tears, on the verge (*od.* brink) of tears; **mit den ~n kämpfen** fight back the tears, do one's best not to cry; **in ~n ausbrechen** burst into tears; **in ~n aufgelöst sein** be in floods of tears; **~n vergießen** shed tears; **bittere ~n weinen** weep (*od.* shed) bitter tears; **unter ~n** in tears,

weeping; **unter ~n erzählte er uns alles** he was in tears (*od.* he wept) as he told us everything; **~n in den Augen haben** have tears in one's eyes; **j-n zu ~n rühren** move s.o. to tears; **keine ~ wert** not worth shedding (any) tears over (*od.* getting upset about); **j-m/e-r Sache keine ~ nachweinen** be glad to see the back of s.o./s.th.; **wir haben ~n gelacht** we laughed till we cried; **mir kommen die ~n** *umg. iro.* my heart bleeds for you *etc.*, you *etc.* bring tears to my eyes; → **aufgelöst** II 2, **nachweinen** *etc.*; **2.** *umg. pej.* (*Schlafmütze, Flasche*) wally, nerd

tränen *v/i.* water; **mir ~ die Augen** my eyes are watering; **Tränen** *n; -s, kein Pl.; Med.* weeping, tearing

tränenblind *Adj.* blinded with tears

Tränendrüse *f Anat.* lacrimal gland; **auf die ~n drücken** *umg. fig.* go for the heart-strings

tränen|erstickt *Adj.:* **mit ~er Stimme** in a choked voice, in a voice choked with tears; **~feucht** *Adj. Augen:* bright with tears, tearful; *Gesicht:* wet with tears, tear-stained; *Brief etc.:* tear--stained; *Kopfkissen etc.:* damp

Tränen|flüssigkeit *f* tears *Pl.*; **~flut** *f geh.* flood of tears

Tränengas *n* tear gas; **~granate** *f* tear--gas grenade; **~pistole** *f,* **~revolver** *m* tear-gas pistol

Tränenkanal *m Anat.* tear duct

tränen|nass *Adj.* wet with tears, tear--stained; **~reich** *Adj.* tearful

Tränen|sack *m Anat.* lacrimal sac; **Tränensäcke haben** have bags under the (*od.* one's) eyes; **~schleier** *m* blur of tears; **~tier** *n umg. fig.* **1.** (*Heulsuse*) *bes. Kind:* crybaby; *Erwachsene(r):* weepy type; **2.** (*Flasche*) wally, nerd

tränenüberströmt I. *Adj.* streaming (*od.* wet) with tears, **ihr ~es Gesicht** her face with the tears pouring down it; **II.** *Adv.* in (floods of) tears

tranig *Adj.* **1.** *Geschmack etc.:* fishy, like fish oil; **2.** *umg. fig.* (*langsam*) (dead) slow, dull, boring

trank *Imperf.* → **trinken**

Trank *m; -(e)s, Tränke, mst Sg.; geh.* drink; → **Speis²** 1

Tränke *f; -, -n am Fluss etc.:* watering place; (*Becken*) drinking (*od.* cattle) trough; **tränken** *v/t.* **1.** (*Vieh, Pflanze*) water; **2.** (*durch~*) soak; **ein mit Öl getränkter Wattebausch** a cotton (wool) swab soaked in oil

Transaktion *f; -, -en* transaction

transalpin(isch) *Adj.* transalpine

Transatlantik... *im Subst.,* **transatlantisch** *Adj.* transatlantic

Transe *f; -, -n; umg.* (*Transvestit*) trannie, *Am.* TV

Transfer *m; -s, -s; Wirts., Flug., Sport, Psych.* transfer

Transferenz *f; -, -en; Ling.* transference

transferieren *v/t.* transfer (**an** + *Akk.*, **auf** + *Akk.* to)

Transfer|leistung *f Päd.* transfer effect; *Wirts.* transfer; **~liste** *f Sport* transfer list; **~straße** *f Tech.* automated production (*od.* assembly) line; **~summe** *f Sport* transfer fee

Transfiguration *f; -, -en* transfiguration

Transformation *f; -, -en* transformation

Transformationsgrammatik *f Ling.* transformational grammar

Transformator *m; -s, -en; Etech.* transformer; *siehe auch* **Trafo...**

transformieren *v/t. auch Etech., Math., Psych.* transform

Transfusion *f; -, -en; Med.* transfusion

Transistor *m; -s, -en; Etech.* transistor; **~gerät** *n* transistor radio, tranny *umg.*

transistor(is)ieren *v/t. Etech.* transistorize; **transistor(is)iert I.** *P.P.* → *transistor(is)ieren;* **II.** *Adj.* transistorized, solid-state

Transistor|radio *n Etech.* transistor radio; **~zündung** *f* electronic ignition, transistorized ignition (system)

Transit *m; -s,-e* transit; **~abkommen** *n* transit convention; **~güter** *Pl. Wirts.* transit goods; **~halle** *f* transit lounge; **~handel** *m* transit trade

transitiv *Adj. Ling.* transitive

Transit|lager *n* transit camp; **~passagier** *m* transit passenger; **~e nach ...** transit passengers bound for (*od.* continuing their flight to) ...; **~reisende** *m, f* → *Transitpassagier,* **~strecke** *f* transit road (*od.* route); **~verkehr** *m* transit traffic (*Wirts.* auch trade); **~visum** *n* transit visa

Transkaukasien (*n*) *Geog.* Transcaucasia

transkribieren *vt/i.* transcribe; **Transkription** *f; -, -en* transcription; *in Lautschrift:* phonetic transcription

Transmission *f; -, -en; Tech.* transmission; **Transmissionsriemen** *m Tech.* transmission belt

trans|national *Adj.* transnational, international; **~ozeanisch** *Adj.* transoceanic

transparent *Adj.* transparent (*auch fig.*); **~ machen** *fig.* make (*od.* render *geh.*) transparent (*od.* accessible); **Transparent** *n; -(e)s, -e* **1.** *für Overhead-Projektor etc.:* transparency; **2.** *bei Demonstrationen:* banner; **Transparentpapier** *n* tracing paper; **Transparenz** *f; -, kein Pl.* transparency

Transpiration *f; -, kein Pl.; Physiol.* perspiration; *Bot.* transpiration; **transpirieren** *v/i. Person:* perspire; *Pflanze:* transpire

Transplantat *n; -(e)s, -e; Med.* transplant, transplanted organ; *noch zu transplantierendes:* organ for transplant; **Transplantation** *f; -, -en* transplant (operation); *von Haut:* graft; (*das Transplantieren*) transplantation, *Haut:* grafting; **die ~ von Organen** organ transplant(s *Pl.*)

Transplantationsmedizin *f Med.* transplant(ation) medicine

transplantieren *v/t. Med.* (*Organ*) transplant; (*Haut*) graft; *Bot.* graft; **j-m e-e fremde Niere ~** give s.o. a kidney transplant

Transponder *m; -s, -; Etron.* transponder

transponieren *v/t.* transpose (*auch Mus.*)

Transport *m; -(e)s, -e* **1.** (*Beförderung*) transport(ation), conveyance; *von Gütern:* auch freight, haulage; **während des ~s** in transit, en route; **ein ~ des Kranken ist nicht möglich** the patient cannot be moved; **2.** (*Waren etc.*) (freight) consignment; **ein ~ mit Hilfsgütern** an aid consignment; **ein ~ Flüchtlinge/Soldaten** a cargo of refugees / a troop transport; **3.** (*Filmtransport*) winding (mechanism); **transportabel** *Adj.* (*mobil*) transportable; (*tragbar*) portable

Transport|arbeiter *m,* **~arbeiterin** *f* transport(ation) worker; **~automatik** *f Fot.* automatic winding, automatic (film) advance; **~band** *n* conveyor belt; **~behälter** *m* (freight) container; **~box** *f für kleine Tiere:* pet-carrier

Transporter *m* → *Transportfahrzeug, Transportflugzeug, Transportschiff*

Transporteur *m*; *-s, -e* **1.** *Spedition*: carrier, haulage firm (*od.* contractor), haulier, *Am.* hauler; **2.** *an Nähmaschine*: shuttle

transportfähig *Adj. allg.* transportable; *Kranke, Tiere*: fit for transportation

Transport|fahrzeug *n* transporter; **~firma** *f* haulage company (*od.* contractors *Pl.*), *Am.* (common) carrier; **~flugzeug** *n* **1.** *allg.* transport (*od.* cargo) aircraft; **2.** *Mil. auch* troop transport; **~gefährdung** *f Jur.* causing a hazard to (*road, air etc.*) traffic (*Naut.* to navigation); **~hebel** *m Fot.* film advance lever; **~hubschrauber** *m* cargo (*od.* transport) helicopter

transportieren I. *v/t.* (*befördern*) transport; (*tragen*) carry; (*Kranke etc.*) take; *an e-n anderen Ort: auch* move, transfer; (*Film*) wind on, advance; *fig.* (*vermitteln*) (*Meinung etc.*) convey, communicate; **II.** *v/i. Kamera*: wind on, advance; *die Kamera hat nicht transportiert* the wind-on mechanism didn't work

Transport|kosten *Pl.* transport(ation) charges; *Wirts.* forwarding charges; *Naut.* freight (charges); **~maschine** *f Flug.* transport (aircraft), cargo aircraft, freighter; **~mittel** *n* form of transport, (means of) transport(ation); **~netz** *n* transport(ation) network; *zum Gütertransport: auch* freight network; **~schaden** *m* damage in transit; **~schiff** *n* freighter, cargo vessel; *Mil.* troopship; **~unternehmen** *n* haulage company (*od.* contractors *Pl.*), *Am.* (common) carrier; **~unternehmer** *m*, **~unternehmerin** *f* haulier, haulage contractor; **~versicherung** *f* transport (*od.* transit) insurance; **~walze** *f Tech.* transport (*od.* conveyor) roller; **~wesen** *n* transportation, traffic and transport

Transrapid® *m* (*Magnetschwebebahn*) Transrapid maglev train

Transsexualismus *m*; *-, kein Pl.*, **Transsexualität** *f* transsexualism; **transsexuell** *Adj.*, **Transsexuelle** *m, f*; *-n, -n* transsexual

transsibirisch *Adj.*: **Transsibirische Eisenbahn** Trans-Siberian Railway

Transsilvanien (*n*); *-s; Geog. hist.* Transylvania

Transsubstantiation *f*; *-, -en; kath.* transubstantiation

Transuran *n Chemie* transuranic element

Transuse *f*; *-, -n; umg.* slowcoach, *Am.* slowpoke

Transvestismus *m*; *-, kein Pl.* transvestism; **Transvestit** *m*; *-en, -en* transvestite

transzendent, **transzendental** *Adj.* transcendental; **Transzendentalphilosophie** *f* transcendental philosophy; **Transzendenz** *f*; *-, kein Pl.; allg.* transcendence; *als Eigenschaft Gottes*: transcendent nature; *Bereich*: realm beyond (empirical experience)

Trantüte *f umg.* slow mover

Trapez *n*; *-es, -e; Math.* trapezium, *Am.* trapezoid; *Turnen*: trapeze; *am ~ turnen* do a trapeze act; **~akt** *m* trapeze act

trapezförmig *Adj.* trapezium-shaped (*Am.* trapezoid-shaped)

Trapez|künstler *m*, **~künstlerin** *f* trapeze artist

Trapezoid *n*; *-(e)s, -e; Math.* trapezoid, *Am.* trapezium

trapp *Interj.* clatter, clack; *von Hufen: auch* clop

Trappe *f*; *-, -n; Orn.* bustard

trappeln *v/i.* **1.** (*hat getrappelt*) *Pferd etc.*: clatter, go clip-clop; **2.** (*ist*) *Kind etc.*: patter

Trapper *m*; *-s, -* trapper

Trappist *m*; *-en, -en; kath.* Trappist (monk)

Trappisten|käse *m Gastr.* Trappist cheese; **~orden** *m kath.* Trappist order

Trappistin *f*; *-, -nen* Trappist (nun)

trapsen *v/i. umg.* clump, clomp; → *Nachtigall*

trara *Interj.* tantantara, dididida; **Trara** *n*; *-s, kein Pl.* **1.** (*Hornsignal*) fanfare; **2.** *umg.* fuss, to-do, carry-on, hullabaloo; *viel ~ machen* make a big (*od.* great) fuss *od.* to-do (*um* about); *ohne viel ~* without much fuss (*od.* fanfare), without a lot of carry-on (*Am.* rigmarole)

Trasse *f*; *-, -n; Tech.* **1.** (*Linienführung*) line, (projected) route (*od.* path); **2.** (*Bahn-, Straßendamm*) embankment; (*Bahnkörper*) (railway, *Am.* railroad) line, permanent way

Trassenführung *f* → *Trasse* 1

trassieren *v/t.* **1.** *Tech.* mark (out) the line of; **2.** *Wirts.* draw (a bill of exchange)

trat *Imperf.* → *treten*

Tratsch *m*; *-(e)s, kein Pl.; umg.* gossip; **Tratsche** *f*; *-, -n; umg.* (old) gossip; **tratschen** *v/i. umg.* (pass on) gossip; *er tratscht viel zu viel* he's a terrible (*od.* an old) gossip; **Tratscherei** *f*; *-, -en; umg.* gossip(ing), tittle-tattle

Trattoria *f*; *-, Trattorien* trattoria

Traualtar *m* altar; *vor den ~ treten geh.* exchange vows (in church); *j-n zum ~ führen altm.* lead s.o. to the altar

Traube *f*; *-, -n* **1.** (*Weintrauben am Stiel*) bunch of grapes; (*Beere*) grape; *~n lesen/keltern* harvest/press grapes; *die ~n hängen (j-m) zu hoch fig.* it's sour grapes; **2.** *fig.* cluster; *Blütenstand*: flower cluster; *von Beeren*: bunch (*od.* cluster) of berries; *e-e von Menschen* a group (*od.* knot *od.* small crowd) of people

Trauben|hyazinthe *f Bot.* grape hyacinth; **~kur** *f* grape (diet) cure; **~lese** *f* grape harvest; **~most** *m* grape must; **~saft** *m* grape juice; **~sorte** *f* (variety of) grape, grape variety; **~wickler** *m Zool.* vine leafroller; **~zucker** *m* glucose, dextrose

trauen¹ I. *v/i.* (*j-m od. e-r Sache*) trust; *ich traute m-n Ohren/Augen nicht* I couldn't believe my ears/eyes; *ich trau' der Sache nicht* I'm not quite easy in my mind, *Am.* something about this bothers me; *stärker*: I don't like the look of it; → *Frieden* 4, *Weg* 2; **II.** *v/t.*: *sich etw. ~* (*wagen*) have the courage to do s.th., dare (to) do s.th.; *er traut sich was!* the nerve!; **III.** *v/refl.*: *sich ~, etw. zu tun* dare (to) do s.th.; *ich trau' mich nicht nach Hause* I daren't (*Am.* I don't dare to) go home, I'm scared to go home; *sich (nicht) aus dem Haus ~* be frightened to leave the house, not venture out of the house; *er traut sich nicht ins Wasser* he's scared of the water (*od.* to go in); *ich möchte schon, aber ich trau' mich nicht* I'd like (*stärker*: love) to, but I daren't (*Am.* don't dare); *auch* I'd like (*stärker*: love) to, but I haven't got the nerve; *du traust dich ja doch nicht!* you wouldn't dare!, you don't

have the nerve!

trauen² *v/t.* **1.** *sich ~ lassen* get married, marry; *sich kirchlich/standesamtlich ~ lassen* get married in church / at a registry office (*Am. etwa* in a civil ceremony *od.* by a justice of the peace); **2.** (*die Zeremonie durchführen*) marry

Trauer *f*; *-, kein Pl.* **1.** sorrow, (deep) sadness, grief (*um, wegen* over, at); *um e-n Toten*: grief (over, for), mourning (for), (*das Trauern*) *auch* grieving (over, for); (*Trauerzeit*) mourning (period); *in tiefer ~* in deep mourning; *tiefe ~ empfinden* feel deep sadness (*über* + *Akk.* at), grieve deeply (over), be deeply grieved *förm.* (at); **2.** (*Trauerkleidung*) mourning clothes *Pl.*; *~ tragen od. in ~ sein* wear (*od.* be dressed in) mourning; *e-e Dame in ~* a lady in mourning

Trauer|anzeige *f* death announcement; **~arbeit** *f Psych.* process of grieving; *~ leisten* come to terms with one's bereavement (through mourning); **~beflaggung** *f*: *es wurde ~ angeordnet* flags were ordered to be flown at half-mast; **~brief** *m* black-edged letter, death announcement; **~fall** *m* death, bereavement; *e-n ~ in der Familie haben* have (*od.* suffer *geh.*) a bereavement, have a death in the family; **~feier** *f* funeral service; **~feierlichkeiten** *Pl.* funeral *Sg.* (and interment), obsequies *hist., förm.*; **~flor** *m* (black) crepe; **~gäste** *Pl.* mourners; **~geleit** *n* (funeral) cortege; **~gemeinde** *f* funeral congregation, those *Pl.* attending the funeral service; „*Liebe ~*" "Dear friends"; **~gottesdienst** *m* funeral service; **~haus** *n* home of the deceased, house of mourning *lit.*; „*An das ~ Müller" Brief*: "The Müller Family"; *mit Blumen etc.*: "To the Müller family (in your time of loss *od.* with our deepest sympathy"); **~jahr** *n* year of mourning; **~karte** *f* black-edged card, death announcement; **~kleidung** *f* mourning clothes *Pl.*; *e-r Witwe: auch* (widow's) weeds *Pl. altm.*; *~ tragen* wear (*od.* be dressed in) mourning; *Witwe: auch* be wearing *od.* be in (widow's) weeds; **~kloß** *m umg.* wet blanket, depressing person, *Am. auch* downer; **~mantel** *m Zool.* Camberwell Beauty, *Am.* mourning cloak; **~marsch** *m* funeral march; **~miene** *f umg.* long face, doleful expression; *e-e ~ aufsetzen* pull a long face, assume (*od.* put on) a doleful expression; **~musik** *f* funeral music

trauern *v/i. um eine(n) Tote(n)*: mourn (*um* for); *weitS.* grieve (for, over); *äußerlich*: be in mourning; *die ~den Hinterbliebenen* the bereaved (relatives); *weitS.* those left to mourn (*s.o.'s* passing)

Trauer|rand *m* black edge(s *Pl.*), black edging (*od.* border); *mit ~* black-edged (*od.* -bordered); *Trauerränder umg. hum.* black (*od.* grimy) fingernails; **~rede** *f* funeral oration, eulogy; **~schleier** *m* black veil; **~spiel** *n* tragedy; *fig.* sorry affair (*od.* mess); *es ist schon ein ~ fig. auch* it's enough to make you weep; **~weide** *f Bot.* weeping willow; **~zeit** *f* time (*von vorgeschriebener Länge*: period) of mourning; **~zug** *m* funeral procession, (funeral) cortege *förm.*

Traufe *f*; *-, -n* eaves *Pl.*; (*Traufrinne*) gutter, *in Schottland*: rone; → *Regen*

träufeln I. *v/t.* let *s.th.* trickle (*in +*

Akk. into, onto), trickle (into, onto); (*Ohrentropfen etc.*) put (into); *Gastr.* drizzle (over, onto); **II.** *v/i.* drip, trickle, dribble

traulich I. *Adj. altm.* (*heimelig*) homely, friendly, cosy, *Am.* homey, cozy; (*vertraulich*) co|sy (*Am.* -zy), intimate, close; **in ~er Runde** in an intimate circle, among intimates; **II.** *Adv. zusammensitzen etc.*: at ease together; **Traulichkeit** *f* (*Heimeligkeit*) homeliness, cosiness, *Am.* homeyness, coziness; (*Vertraulichkeit*) intimacy, closeness

Traum *m; -(e)s, Träume* dream (*auch fig. Ideal, umg. etw. sehr Schönes*); **böser ~** bad dream; **im ~** in a (*od.* one's) dream; **j-m im ~ erscheinen** appear to s.o. in a dream; **e-n ~ deuten** interpret a dream; **es war wie ein ~** *engS.* it was like a dream; (*wunderschön*) it was unbelievably beautiful; **im ~ nicht daran denken** not dream of it, not contemplate it; **das fällt mir nicht im ~ ein** I wouldn't (even) dream of (doing *etc.*) it, it (*od.* that) would never have occurred to me; **die Frau** *etc.* **m-r Träume** the woman *etc.* of my dreams; **das ist mein ~** that's my dream (*od.* what I dream of); **aus der ~!** *umg.* so much for that, that's the end of that(, I suppose); **aus der ~ vom Urlaub** *umg. auch* that's put paid to my holiday (prospects), *Am.* that does in my (hopes of a) vacation; **es ist ein ~ von (e-m) Auto** *etc. umg.* the car's *etc.* a dream, it's a dream (of a) car *etc.*; **Träume sind Schäume** what's in a dream?

Trauma *n; -s, Traumata und Traumen; Med., Psych.* trauma (*Pl.* traumas *od.* traumata); **traumatisch I.** *Adj.* traumatic; **II.** *Adv.*: **~ bedingt** traumatic in origin, of traumatic origin; **traumatisiert** *Adj.* traumatized; **Traumatologie** *f; -, kein Pl.* traumatology

Traum|beruf *m umg.* dream job; **~bild** *n engS.* dream vision; (*Wunschbild*) dream, ideal; **~deutung** *f* interpretation of dreams, dream interpretation

träumen *v/i.* **1.** (*etw. Bestimmtes im Traum erleben*) *im Schlaf*: dream (**von** of, about); *wachend*: (day)dream; **mir träumte** *lit.* I dreamt (*od.* dreamed); **schlecht ~** have a bad dream; **hast du was geträumt?** did you have any dreams?; **ich habe was ganz Furchtbares geträumt** I had a terrible dream (*od.* a [terrible] nightmare); **das hätte ich mir nie ~ lassen** *fig.* I never dreamed it was possible (*od.* could happen); **2.** (*s-e Gedanken schweifen lassen, unaufmerksam sein*) dream; **du träumst wohl!** *umg.* (*wach auf!*) wakey, wakey!; (*das ist nicht dein Ernst*) you must be joking; **Träumer** *m; -s, -* (day)dreamer; **Träumerei** *f; -, -en* (day)dreaming; (*Traum*) daydream; (*auch Mus.*) reverie

Traumergebnis *n* dream result, outcome too good to be true

Träumerin *f; -, -nen* (day)dreamer; **träumerisch I.** *Adj.* (*verträumt*) dreamy; (*sehnsüchtig*) wistful; **~er Mensch** dreamer, dreamy person; **II.** *Adv.* (*geistesabwesend*) *anblicken etc.*: dreamily; *sehnsüchtig*: wistfully, longingly

Traum|fabrik *f* dream factory; **~frau** *f umg.* the woman of one's dreams

traumhaft *umg.* **I.** *Adj.* **1.** (*wie in e-m Traum*) dreamlike; **2.** (*wunderschön*) (absolutely) wonderful; *Wetter*: perfect, unbelievable; **II.** *Adv.*: **~ schön**

absolutely beautiful, fabulous, out of this world; **~ sicher** uncannily assured; **sie hat ~ gespielt** she played exquisitely, her performance (*od.* playing) was sheer magic

Traum|haus *n umg.* dream home (*od.* house); **~hochzeit** *f umg.* fairytale wedding; **~land** *n* dreamland; **~mann** *m umg.* the man of one's dreams; **~paar** *n umg.* perfect couple; *Pol., Sport etc.*: dream ticket; **~reise** *f umg.* dream holiday (*od.* trip); **~schiff** *n umg.* fabulous cruise ship, floating palace *auch iro.*; **~strand** *m* fabulous (*od.* heavenly) beach; **die kilometerlangen Traumstrände der Algarve** the Algarve's miles of flawless beaches; **~tänzer** *m*, **~tänzerin** *f umg. fig.* dreamer

traumverloren *Adj.* lost in (one's) dreams, away with the fairies *umg.*, rapt *geh.*

traumwandlerisch I. *Adj.*: **mit ~er Sicherheit** with uncanny instinct (*od.* assurance); **II.** *Adv.*: **~ sicher** with uncanny instinct (*od.* assurance)

Traumwelt *f e-r Einzelperson*: dream (*od.* fantasy) world; *weitS.* (*phantastische Welt*) world of fantasy

traurig *Adj.* **1.** (*betrübt*) sad (**über** + *Akk.* about), unhappy (about, at); **~ darüber, dass** sad that; **~ stimmen** sadden, depress, make *s.o.* (feel) sad; **mach kein so ~es Gesicht** don't look so sad; **2.** (*beklagenswert*) sad, sorry, pitiable; **~er Anblick** sad (*od.* sorry) sight, sorry (*od.* dismal) spectacle; **~e Pflicht** sad duty; **~er Rest** sad remains *Pl.*; **~er Zustand** sorry state, lamentable condition; → *Bilanz* 2; **ein ~es Ende nehmen** come to an unhappy (*od.* a sad) end; (**das ist**) **~ aber wahr** it's the sad truth, unfortunately that's the way it is; **es ist ~ genug, dass** *pej.* it's bad (*od.* deplorable) enough that; **e-e ~e Figur machen** cut a sorry (*od.* poor) figure; (**e-e**) **~e Berühmtheit erlangen** achieve (*od.* acquire *od.* gain) (regrettable) notoriety; **Traurigkeit** *f* (*Traurigsein*) sadness, unhappiness, depression; (*trauriges Ereignis*) sad thing (*od.* event); **kein Kind von ~ sein** *umg.* be (always) full of the joys

Trau|ring *m* wedding ring; **~schein** *m* marriage certificate; **Ehe ohne ~** *umg. fig.* living together, common-law marriage, cohabitation

traut *Adj.* homely, *Am.* homey; *iro.* cosy (*Am.* cozy) (little); **~es Heim, Glück allein** home sweet home; **im ~en Kreis der Familie** in the bosom of one's family, in the family circle (*auch iro.*)

Traute *f; -, kein Pl.; umg.* nerve, guts (*Pl., V. mst im Sg.*), bottle; **keine ~ haben** lack (*od.* not have) (the) nerve *etc.*

Trauung *f* (*Akt des Trauens*) marriage ceremony; (*Hochzeit*) wedding

Trau|zeuge *m*, **~zeugin** *f* witness to a (*od.* the) marriage

Travellerscheck ['trɛvələ-] *m* traveller's cheque, *Am.* traveler's check

traversieren *v/i.* **1.** *Reiten*: move in traverse, sidestep; **2.** *Fechten*: traverse; **3.** *Bergsteigen, Skisport*: traverse

Travestie *f; -, -n* **1.** *Lit.* travesty; **2.** (*Inhalt der ~show*) drag; **~show** *f* drag show

Trawler ['trɔːlɐ] *m; -s, -; Naut.* trawler

Treck *m; -s, -s;* (*beschwerliche Reise*) trek; ([*Wagen-*]*Zug*) (wagon) train; *von Siedlern, Flüchtlingen: auch* column

Trecker *m; -s, -* tractor

Treff¹ *m; -s, -s; umg.* **1.** (*Treffen*) get-together, date, meeting; **e-n ~ vereinbaren** arrange to meet (up) (somewhere); **2.** → *Treffpunkt*

Treff² *n; -s, -s Karten*: club(s *Pl.*)

treffen; *trifft, traf, hat od. ist getroffen* **I.** *vt/i.* (*hat*) **1.** *Schlag, Geschoss, Schütze*: hit, strike; *nicht ~ auch* miss; **die Kugel traf ihn an der Schulter** the bullet struck (*od.* hit) his shoulder (*od.* him in the shoulder); **tödlich getroffen** mortally (*od.* fatally) wounded; → *Blitz, getroffen¹*; **2.** *fig.* (*finden, erkennen, erraten*) get, find, hit; (*Stimmung etc.*) catch, capture; (**du hast's**) **getroffen!** *umg. fig.* you've got it!, spot-on!, *Am.* bull's-eye!, bingo!; **es gut ~** be (*od.* strike) lucky (**mit** with); **die richtige Wahl ~** make the right choice; **damit hast du s-n Geschmack genau getroffen** that's exactly the sort of thing (*od.* the style *etc.*) he likes; **du hast genau das Richtige getroffen** (*Geschenk etc.*) *auch* you got it exactly right, you couldn't have picked a better present *etc.*; **da hast du ihn gut getroffen** *auf Foto etc.*: that's a good picture of him, you (have) caught him well; **wen trifft es heute mit dem Abwasch?** *umg.* whose turn is it to wash up (*Am.* do the dishes) today, who's on the washing-up (*Am.* the dishes) today?; **3.** (*j-m begegnen*) meet; *zufällig auch* run into; **sich ~** meet (up); **4.** *fig.* (*kränken*) wound, hurt, get at; **du hast ihn zutiefst getroffen** you (have) hurt him deeply; **damit hast du ihn wirklich getroffen** you hit him where it really hurt (with that one); **damit kannst du mich nicht ~** you can't get at me with that, that line doesn't bother me; **ihr Tod hat ihn schwer getroffen** her (*od.* their) death affected him deeply; **5.** (*betreffen*) concern; *nachteilig*: affect (adversely); *empfindlich*: hit *s.o.* (*od. s.th.*) hard, be of great concern to; **der Vorwurf trifft mich nicht** I don't feel (I'm) responsible, I can't be reproached (*od.* blamed) for that, that was not my fault; → *Schuld* 1; **6.** *als Funktionsverb*: (*Anordnungen etc.*) *mst* make; (*Vereinbarung etc.*) *auch* reach, come to; → *Anstalt* 2, *Auswahl* 1, *Entscheidung, Ton¹* 5, *Vorkehrung etc.*; **II.** *v/i.* (*ist*): **~ auf** (+ *Akk.*) (*Widerstand etc.*) meet with, encounter, run into; (*zufällig finden*) come across *s.th.*, stumble on *s.o. od. s.th.*; (*Öl etc.*) strike, hit *umg.*; (*als Gegner bekommen*) come up against, meet; **III.** *v/refl.* (*hat*) **1. sich mit j-m ~** meet (up with) s.o.; **sie ~ sich heimlich** they are meeting secretly; **2. das trifft sich gut/schlecht** that suits me *etc.* (*od.* works in) fine / that's (rather) awkward, that doesn't fit in at all; **es trifft sich gut, dass ...** it's handy that ..., it's lucky (that) ...

Treffen *n; -s, -* **1.** (*Zusammentreffen*) meeting; *gesellschaftliches*: get-together, gathering; *e-r Familie, ehemaligen Klasse etc.*: reunion; *regelmäßige ~ vereinbaren* arrange (*od.* set up) regular meetings *etc.*; *Argumente etc.* **ins ~ führen** *geh. fig.* put forward, advance, bring to bear; **2.** (*Wettkampf*) *Sport* meet(ing), contest, event; (*Aufeinandertreffen*) encounter; (*Spiel*) match, *bes. Am.* game

treffend I. *Part. Präs.* → *treffen*; **II.** *Adj.* (*passend*) apt, appropriate, well-judged; **~er Vergleich** good (*od.*

T

apt *od.* well-chosen) comparison; **III.** *Adv.*: **du hast ihn ~ beschrieben** that's a good description (of him), you've got him to a T *umg.*, that just about sums him up *umg.*; **~ ausgedrückt!** well said!, Hear, hear!

Treffer *m*; *-s,* - hit (*auch Fechten, Boxen*); (*Volltreffer*) direct hit; *Fußball*: goal; *fig.* (*Glücksstreffer*) lucky strike; (*Gewinnlos*) winner; **~ erzielen** score (hits, *Fußball*: goals); **jeder Schuss ein ~** every (*od.* each) shot on target; **e-n/mehrere ~ erhalten** *Mil. Schiff etc.*: receive (*od.* take *od.* suffer *geh.*) a (direct) hit / several (direct) hits, be hit once / a number of times; **e-n ~ anzeigen** *Sport etc.*: signal a hit; **~anzeige** *f Sport* score (*od.* hit) indicator; **~quote** *f* score (*od.* hit) ratio

treffgenau *Adj. Waffe*: accurate

trefflich *altm., noch hum. od. iro.* **I.** *Adj. Person*: als *Mensch*: fine, outstanding, admirable, excellent; *im Ausüben e-r Tätigkeit*: outstanding, excellent, first-rate; *Wein etc.*: (*erlesen*) fine, excellent, superb, exquisite; **II.** *Adv.*: **sich ~ auf etw. verstehen** be expert in (*od.* an expert on) s.th.

Treffpunkt *m* **1.** meeting place, place to meet; *im Flughafen*: rendezvous point; *EDV* meeting point; **2.** *Math.* (point of) intersection

treffsicher I. *Adj. Schütze*: accurate, (dead) reliable, first-class, *Terrorist etc.*: *auch* deadly; *Sport, Torjäger*: dangerous; *fig. Urteil*: unerring, (wholly) reliable, sound; *Ausdrucksweise*: precise, well-judged; **er hat ein ~es Urteilsvermögen** he's got good (*od.* sound) judg(e)ment, his judg(e)ment (*od.* assessment) is usually spot-on (*Am.* right on the money) *umg.*; **II.** *Adv. mit e-r Waffe umgehen etc.*: accurately, effectively, with unerring aim; *fig. ausdrücken, darstellen*: precisely, elegantly; **Treffsicherheit** *f als Schütze etc.*: accuracy, effectiveness, reliability; *fig. des Urteils etc.*: soundness, reliability; *der Ausdrucksweise*: precision, elegance

Treib|achse *f Tech.* driving axle; **~eis** *n* drift ice, ice floes *Pl.*

treiben; *treibt, trieb, hat od. ist getrieben* **I.** *v/t.* (*hat*) **1.** drive (*auch Vieh, Wild, Räder, Ball, Etron., Nagel, fig.* an-, *austreiben*); *Strömung*: carry, sweep, wash; *Wellen*: wash, sweep; *Wind*: blow, sweep, drive; *Luft*: carry; (*Person*) (*antreiben*) *auch* impel, motivate; (*austreiben*) *auch* expel; **etw. ans Ufer ~** wash (*od.* drive) s.th. ashore; **e-n Tunnel in den Fels ~** cut a tunnel into the rock; **in die Höhe ~** (*Preise*) force up (*od.* higher); **zur Verzweiflung ~** drive (*od.* reduce) *s.o.* to despair; **j-n in den Wahnsinn ~** drive s.o. mad *umg.*, cause s.o. to lose his (*od.* her) reason; **j-n zur Eile ~** hurry s.o., urge s.o. to hurry (*od.* be quick), urge s.o. on; → **Tod** 1; **2.** (*Blätter etc.*) sprout; (*Pflanzen*) force; (*Urin*) produce; **es treibt einem den Schweiß auf die Stirn** it gets you sweating; **3.** (*Metall*) chase, work; → **getrieben**; **4.** (*betreiben*) do, engage in (*auch Sport*); (*Handel, Gewerbe etc.*) engage in, be engaged in, carry on; *Jur.* (*Ehebruch, Unzucht etc.*) commit; **was treibst du da?** what are you up to (*od.* doing)?; **was treibst du denn so?** what are you doing with yourself (*od.* what are you up to) these days?; **treibt es nicht zu toll!** don't overdo it!, don't

go mad!; **es mit j-m ~** *umg.* have (*od.* be having) it off (*Am.* be doing it) with s.o.; **es übel mit j-m ~** (severely) maltreat s.o.; (*Kinder, Pfleglinge etc.*:) abuse s.o.; → **Aufwand** 2, **Enge** 4, **Spitze¹** 4, **Unfug** 1; **II.** *v/i.* **1.** (*ist*) *im Wasser*: float; *von Wind und Strömung bewegt*: drift, be carried; *Schnee, Rauch*: drift, be carried; **sich ~ lassen** drift (*auch fig.*); **aufs offene Meer / an Land ~** drift (*od.* be carried) out to sea / be washed ashore (*od.* up on the shore [*od.* coast]); **2.** (*hat*) (*keimen*) sprout; *Med.* (*Urin ~*) be (*od.* act as) a diuretic; (*gären*) ferment, work; **das bayrische Bier treibt ganz schön** *umg.* Bavarian beer goes right through you; → **Kraft** 2; **3.** (*hat*) (*drängen*) **er treibt immer** he's always breathing down your neck, he's always pushing you

Treiben *n*; *-s, kein Pl.*; (*Tun*) activity, activities *Pl. auch pej.*, practices *Pl. mst pej.*; (*Vorgänge*) *auch* goings-on *Pl.* (*mst pej.*); (*Machenschaften*) intriguing, intrigues *Pl.*, machinations *Pl. pej. od. hum.*; (*geschäftiges ~*) bustle, bustling activity; **buntes ~** *auch* hustle and bustle; **geschäftiges ~** a buzz (*od.* flurry) of activity; **sich ins närrische ~ stürzen** descend to a carnival atmosphere; **wir beobachten sein ~ schon lange** we have been keeping an eye on him (*od.* his activities) for quite some time; **dem/j-s ~ ein Ende setzen** put a stop to the(se) practices / s.o.'s activities

Treiber *m*; *-s,* - **1.** (*Viehtreiber*) drover; *Jagd*: beater; **2.** *umg.* (*Antreiber*) slave-driver; **3.** *EDV* driver

Treib|gas *n* fuel gas; *in Spraydosen*: propellant; **~gut** *n* floating refuse, flotsam; *angeschwemmtes und fig.*: flotsam and jetsam

Treibhaus *n* hothouse, greenhouse; **wie im ~** like an oven; **~effekt** *m* greenhouse effect; **~gas** *n* greenhouse gas; **~luft** *f mst pej.* sultry (*od.* hot and humid) air (*od.* atmosphere); **~pflanze** *f* hothouse plant

Treib|holz *n* driftwood; **~jagd** *f* drive, shoot (with beaters), battue; *fig.* roundup; *Pol.* witch-hunt; **~ladung** *f* propellant; **~mine** *f Mil.* drift mine; **~mittel** *n* **1.** *Tech., Chem.* propellant; **2.** *Gastr.* raising agent; **~netz** *n* drift net; **~rad** *n* driving wheel; **~riemen** *m* drive (*od.* transmission) belt; **~sand** *m* quicksand; **~satz** *m Tech.* propellant (mixture)

Treibstoff *m Mot. und Flug.* fuel, *bes. Am.* gas; *bes. Rakete*: propellant; → *auch* **Kraftstoff, Benzin**; **~tank** *m* fuel (*Am.* gas) tank; **~verbrauch** *m* fuel consumption

treideln *vt/i.* haul, tow

Trekking *n*; *-s, kein Pl.* **1.** (*Tätigkeit*) trekking; **2.** *konkret*: trek, trekking tour; **~rad** *n* hybrid bike

Trema *n*; *-s, -s und Tremata*; *Ling.* di(-a)eresis (*Pl.* di[a]ereses); *Med.* gap between central incisors

Tremolo *n*; *-s, -s*; *Mus.* tremolo

Tremor *m*; *-s, -es*; *Med.* tremor

Trenchcoat ['trɛntʃkoːt] *m*; *-s, -s* trench coat

Trend *m*; *-s, -s* trend (**zu** toward[s]); **der ~ geht hin zu …** the trend is to(-ward[s]) …; **voll im ~ liegen** *umg.* be right in (*od.* the height of) fashion; **~forschung** *f* trend research, focus group sampling; **~meldung** *f auch Pl.* early indications *Pl.* (*od.* returns *Pl.*);

vor Wahlen etc.: predictions *Pl.*; *bei Umfrage*: exit poll; **~scout** *m*; *-s, -s* forecaster; **~setter** ['-zɛtɐ] *m*; *-s, -,* **~setterin** *f*; *-, -nen*; *umg.* trendsetter; **~wende** *f* turn of the tide, reversal of trend, change of (*od.* in) direction

trendy ['trɛndi] *indekl. Adj.*; *umg.* trendy

trennbar *Adj. allg., auch Ling.* separable; (*abtrennbar*) detachable, removable

Trenndiät *f* → **Trennkost**

trennen I. *v/t.* **1.** (*ab-, loslösen*) detach (**von, aus** from), remove (from); (*abschneiden, auch fig.*) cut off (from), sever (from); (*herausschneiden*) cut out (of, from); (*Glied etc.*) sever; *operativ*: amputate, take off; (*auftrennen*) (*Jacke etc.*) unpick; **das Futter aus der Jacke ~** remove the lining from (*od.* take the lining out of) the jacket; **den Kopf vom Rumpf ~** sever the head from the body, cut the head off; **2.** (*etw. Zusammengesetztes in s-e Bestandteile zerlegen*) separate, break down (*auch Tech., Chem., Müll etc.*); (*sortieren*) sort, categorize, split up, break down, break up, divide, reduce (*auch Müll, Material etc.*); (*Verbindung e-s Stoffes mit e-m anderen auflösen*) separate; (*Erz vom Gestein*) separate out, extract; (*zerteilen, zersägen*) cut up, saw up; **3.** (*räumlich auseinander bringen, ihr Verhältnis lösen*) separate, divide, (*Familie*) *auch* split up, break up; (*Rassen etc., Geschlechter*) segregate; (*Boxer*) separate; (*absondern*) isolate, separate out, keep separate; **er versuchte die Kämpfenden zu ~** he tried to break up the fight (*od.* to separate the combatants *geh.*); **durch den Krieg getrennt werden** *Familie etc.*: be split up by the war; *Landesteile etc.*: be divided (*od.* partitioned) as a result of the war; **4.** (*unterscheiden, auseinander halten*) (*Begriffe*) distinguish (between), demarcate *geh.*; **das Private vom Beruflichen ~** keep one's private life and one's job separate; **5.** (*zwischen Personen etc. e-e Kluft bilden*) separate, divide; **die beiden trennt zu viel** they (*od.* the two of them) don't have enough in common, they are incompatible in too many ways; **uns ~ Welten** we're worlds apart; **6.** (*e-e Grenze darstellen*) demarcate, mark a boundary between, divide; (*zwischen zwei Bereichen liegen*) be (*od.* lie *etc.*) between, separate (**von** from); **nur noch ein paar Tage ~ uns von Weihnachten** we've only got a few days to go till Christmas, (there are) only a few days between us and Christmas now; **7.** (*teilen*) divide; (*Wort, nach Silben*) divide (up), hyphenate, break; **8.** *Telef.* cut off, disconnect; **wir sind getrennt worden** we were cut off; → **getrennt, Tisch** 3; **II.** *v/i.*: **~ zwischen** distinguish between; **III.** *v/refl.* **1.** (*auseinander gehen*) part company, go one's separate ways; (*sich verabschieden*) say goodbye; **die Mannschaften trennten sich unentschieden** the teams had to settle for a draw, the match ended in a draw; **hier ~ sich unsere Wege** *bes. fig.* this is where we go our separate ways; **2.** (*e-e Gemeinschaft, Partnerschaft etc. aufgeben*) split up (**von** with), end one's association (with), agree to part; *Ehepartner*: separate, split up; **sie hat sich von i-m Mann getrennt** she and her husband have split up, she's left her husband; **3. sich ~ von** (*e-r Sache*) part with, let go; (*e-r Idee etc.*) give up, get away from, abandon; **von dem Gedanken wirst du dich ~ müssen** *auch* you'll (just) have to rethink that (*od.* forget the idea); **ich konnte mich von dem Auto / von dem Anblick nicht ~** I couldn't bear (*od.* bring myself) to part with the car / /I couldn't take my eyes off it; **er kann sich von nichts ~** he just can't let go, he has to hold on to everything

Trenn|kost *f* food combining, harmonious (*od.* compatible) eating; *nach dem Erfinder: the* Hay diet; **~linie** *f* dividing (*od.* demarcation) line; **~programm** *n EDV zur Silbentrennung:* hyphenation program

trennscharf *Adj.:* **~ sein** *Radio:* have good selectivity; **Trennschärfe** *f Radio etc.:* selectivity

Trenn|scheibe *f* **1.** (glass) partition; **2.** *Tech.* circular cutter, cutting wheel; **~strich** *m* hyphen

Trennung *f* separation (*auch Tech., Chem.*); (*Absonderung, Rassentrennung*) segregation; (*Teilung*) division; (*Silbentrennung*) syllabi(fi)cation; *am Zeilenende:* → *auch* **trennen**; **~ von Tisch und Bett** judicial (*od.* legal) separation; **in ~ leben** be separated; **seit ihrer ~** since they (got) separated, since they split up *umg.*

Trennungs|angst *f* separation anxiety; **~entschädigung** *f* separation allowance; **~geld** *n* separation allowance; **~linie** *f* dividing line; **~regeln** *Pl.* hyphenation rules; **~schmerz** *m nur Sg.* pain of parting, sense of loss (at the [*od.* a] separation), trauma of separation *geh.*; **~schock** *m Psych.* shock of separation; **~strich** *m* hyphen; **e-n ~ ziehen zwischen** *fig.* draw a clear dividing line between, make a clear distinction between; **~zeichen** *n* hyphen

Trennwand *f* partition, dividing wall; *leichte: auch* divider

Trense *f,* -, -n (*Mundstück*) (snaffle) bit; (*Trensenzaum*) snaffle

treppab *Adv.* downstairs, down the stairs (*od.* steps); → **treppauf**

treppauf *Adv.* upstairs, up the stairs (*od.* steps); **~, treppab** up and down the stairs; **~ komme ich manchmal ins Schwitzen** going up (the) stairs sometimes makes me break out in a sweat

Treppchen *n Dim.* → **Treppe**; **sie verpasste nur knapp e-n Platz auf dem ~** she only just missed (*od.* lost out on *umg.*) a place on the victory podium

Treppe *f,* -, -n **1.** *im Haus:* (*eine*) ~ (a flight of) stairs *Pl.,* staircase, *Am. auch* stairway; *vor dem Haus etc.:* (*e-e*) ~ (a flight of) steps *Pl.;* **zwei ~n hoch** on the second (*Am.* third) floor, two stor|eys (*Am.* -ies) (*od.* floors) up; **die ~ hinauf/hinunter** up/down the stairs; **er kann kaum die ~n steigen** he can hardly climb (up) the stairs, he can barely manage (to get up) the stairs; **die ~ hinauffallen** *umg. fig.* shoot up the ladder; **2.** (*einzelne Stufe*) stair, (*Steinstufe*) step

Treppen|absatz *m* (half-)landing; **~aufgang** *m* stairwell, access stairs *Pl.;* **~geländer** *n* ban(n)isters *Pl.;* **das ~ runterrutschen** slide down the ba(n)nisters; **~haus** *n* stairwell, staircase, stairs *Pl.; am Eingang:* hallway; **im ~** *auf der Treppe:* in the hallway; *unten:* in the hallway; **~lift** *m für Behinderte:* stair lift; **~schritt** *m Skisport:* sidestep(ping); **~steigen** *n* climbing

(*od.* going up) (the) stairs; **~stufe** *f* step; *im Haus:* stair; **~witz** *m:* **ein ~ der Weltgeschichte** one of history's ironies

Tresen *m,* -s, -; (*Schanktisch*) bar; (*Ladentisch*) counter

Tresor *m,* -s, -e; (*Panzerschrank*) safe; (*Stahlkammer*) strongroom, vault; **~fach** *n* safe deposit box; **~knacker** *m umg.* safe-breaker, cracksman; **~raum** *m* strongroom; **~schlüssel** *m* **1.** key to a (*od.* the) safe; **2.** strongroom key

Trespe *f,* -, -n; *Bot.* brome(grass)

Tresse *f,* -, -n braid; *Mil.* stripe; *Pl. Koll. auch* scrambled egg *Sg.(Am.* eggs *Pl.*) *umg.*

Trester *m,* -s, - **1.** *mst Pl.;* (*Apfelrückstände*) pomace *Sg.; von Trauben:* marc *Sg.;* **2.** (*Schnaps*) grappa, marc; **~schnaps** *m* grappa, marc

Tret|auto *n* pedal car; **~boot** *n* pedal boat, pedalo; **~eimer** *m* pedal bin

treten; *tritt, trat, getreten* **I.** *v/i.* (*ist*) **1.** (*sich mit e-m Schritt od. Schritten in e-e bestimmte Richtung bewegen*) step, walk, go, move; **zur Seite ~** step (*od.* move) aside (*od.* to one side); **j-m in den Weg ~** step into s.o.'s path; (*den Weg versperren*) block s.o.'s path; **zu j-m ~** *bes. mit e-m Anliegen:* walk (*od.* go) up to s.o.; (*sich zu j-m gesellen*) join s.o.; **in ein Zimmer ~** go into (*od.* walk into *od.* enter; *kommen:* come into) a room; **ans Fenster ~** go (over) to the window; **über die Schwelle ~** cross the threshold; **~ Sie näher!** step this way!; **sie war auf s-e Seite getreten** *fig.* she had chosen (*od.* joined) his side; **2.** *Sachen:* (*sich [scheinbar] bewegen*) go, come, pass; **die Sonne trat hinter die Wolken** the sun disappeared behind the clouds; *auch* the sun went in *umg.;* **die Tränen traten ihm in die Augen** tears came to (*od.* welled up in) his eyes; **der Schweiß trat ihr auf die Stirn** (beads of) sweat formed (*od.* stood out) on her forehead (*od.* face); **über die Ufer ~** *Fluss:* overflow (its banks), flood; **3.** (*unabsichtlich den Fuß auf, in etw. setzen*) stand, step, tread (**auf/in** + *Akk.* on/in); **j-m auf den Fuß ~** tread (*Am.* step) on s.o.'s toes (*od.* foot); **du bist** (*auch* **hast**) **in etw. getreten** you've put your foot (*od.* you've trodden *geh.*) in s.th.; **4.** (*absichtlich den Fuß auf, in etw. setzen*) tread, step, place one's foot (*od.* feet) (**auf/in** + *Akk.* on/in); (*stampfen*) stamp; (*trampeln*) trample; **auf etw. ~** tread (*bes. Am.* step) on s.th.; **man wusste nicht, wohin man ~ sollte** you didn't know where to put your feet (*od.* where to step); **von e-m Fuß auf den andern ~** hop from one leg (*od.* foot) to the other; **II.** *v/t.* **1.** (*hat*) (*j-m, e-r Sache e-n Fußtritt versetzen*) kick, give *s.o.* (*od.* s.th.) a kick; **nach j-m ~** (take a) kick (*od.* kick out) at s.o.; **j-m gegen das Schienbein ~** kick s.o. in the shin(s); **~ gegen** *unabsichtlich:* accidentally kick (against), walk into; *absichtlich:* kick; *fig.* (*j-n drängen*) prod, put pressure on (*stärker:* kick); **man muss ihn immer ~** *umg. fig.* you have to keep prodding him; (*j-n schikanieren*) (*auch* **mit Füßen ~**) bully, trample on; **2.** (*hat*) (*durch e-n Tritt, Tritte bewirken*) kick; **e-e Ecke / e-n Elfmeter ~** take a corner (*od.* kick) / a penalty; **e-n Pfad durch den Schnee ~** kick (*od.* stamp out) a path through (*od.* in) the

snow; **sich** (*Dat.*) **den Schmutz von den Schuhen ~** kick (*od.* stamp) the muck off one's boots; **3.** (*hat*) (*durch Fußdruck betätigen, bewirken*) press down (with the foot), depress; *Radfahrer:* pedal; **die Kupplung/Pedale ~** depress the clutch (pedal) / work the pedals (*Fahrrad:* pedal, push on the pedals); **aufs Gas ~** put one's foot down *umg.,* step on it (*od.* on the gas) *umg.,* put the pedal to the metal *umg.;* **auf die Bremse ~** brake, apply the brakes; *Vollbremsung:* stand on the brakes *umg.;* **4.** (*durch Darauftreten an e-e bestimmte Stelle gelangen lassen*) get, run, tread; **sich** (*Dat.*) **e-n Dorn in den Fuß ~** get a thorn in (*od.* run a thorn into) one's foot; **5.** *Agr.* (*begatten*) tread, mount; → **nah** II 8, **näher** II 3; → **Dienst** 3, **Hühnerauge**, **Kraft** 6, **Schlips**, **Stelle** 1, **zutage** 2

Treter[1] *m,* -s, -, **~in** *f,* -, -nen; *Sport, umg.* dirty player

Treter[2] *Pl. umg.* (*Schuhe*) (well-worn) shoes

Tret|lager *n am Fahrrad:* pedal(-crank) bearing; **~mine** *f Mil.* anti-personnel mine; **~mühle** *f* treadmill (*auch fig.*); **~roller** *m* (type of child's) scooter

treu I. *Adj.* (*beständig, anhänglich*) faithful (+ *Dat.* to); (*treu gesinnt*) loyal (to); (*ergeben*) devoted (to); *Kunde etc.:* loyal, long-standing; *Blick:* innocent, guileless, trusting; **~er Freund** loyal (*od.* faithful *od.* true) friend; **~e Augen** *e-r Person:* honest eyes; *e-s Hundes:* (big,) faithful (*od.* trusting) eyes; **nicht ~ sein** *Partner:* be unfaithful; **j-m ~ bleiben** be faithful to s.o.; **e-e ~e Seele** *umg.* a good (*od.* decent) soul; **sich** (*Dat.*) **/ s-n Grundsätzen ~ bleiben** remain true to o.s. / one's principles; **s-m Entschluss ~ bleiben** stick to (*od.* by) one's decision; **sich** (*Dat.*) **immer selbst ~ geblieben sein** have always been one's own person, have always stuck to one's principles; **der Erfolg ist ihm ~ geblieben** success did not desert him, he enjoyed continued success; **zu ~en Händen übergeben** hand *s.o.* (*od.* s.th.) over for safekeeping, leave *s.o.* (*od.* s.th.) in good hands; **für ~e Dienste** for loyal (*od.* faithful) service; **II.** *Adv.* faithfully *etc.;* **j-m ~ ergeben sein** be (utterly) devoted to s.o.; **~ sorgend** devoted; **~ und brav** *umg.* faithfully; **er hat s-r Firma ~ gedient** he served his company well (*od.* wholeheartedly)

Treu *f:* **auf ~ und Glauben** in good faith, on trust

...treu *im Adj.* **1.** *im wörtl. Sinn:* **moskau~** loyal (*od.* sympathetic) to Moscow, in the Moscow camp; **NATO-~** loyal (*od.* sympathetic) to NATO; **2.** (*getreu*) *form:* **~** warp-resistant; **text~** faithful (to the text), accurate

treu|deutsch *Adj. umg.* typically German, Teutonic *iro. pej.;* **~doof** *umg.* **I.** *Adj.* naive, artless, gullible; **II.** *Adv.:* **j-n ~ ansehen** gaze trustingly at s.o. (like a spaniel)

Treue *f,* -, *kein Pl.;* (*Anhänglichkeit*) loyalty, faithfulness; *eheliche:* faithfulness, fidelity; (*Genauigkeit, Nähe zum Original*) faithfulness; **j-m ewige ~ schwören** swear (*od.* vow) eternal fidelity to s.o.; **es mit der ~ nicht so genau nehmen** *umg.* not be overly concerned with the niceties of faithfulness; **j-m/einander die ~ halten** keep faith with s.o. / one another; **~bekenntnis** *n* pledge (*od.* oath) of loyal-

T

ty; **~bruch** *m* breach of faith; **~eid** *m* oath of allegiance (*od.* fealty); **~ge-löbnis** *n* pledge (*od.* oath) of loyalty; **~pflicht** *f*; *nur Sg.*; *Jur.* (duty of) allegiance; **~prämie** *f* loyalty bonus; **~punkt** *m zur Anrechnung für Kundenkarte etc.*: reward point; **~rabatt** *m* loyalty discount

treu ergeben → treu II

Treue|schwur *m n* pledge (*od.* oath) of loyalty; **~versprechen** *n* promise (*od.* affirmation) of loyalty

Treuhand *f*; *nur Sg.*; *Jur.* trust; *hist.* → *Treuhandanstalt*, **~anstalt** *f hist. transitional privatization agency 1990 - 94 after the reunification of Germany*

Treuhänder *m*; *-s, -*, **~in** *f*; *-, -nen* trustee; **treuhänderisch I.** *Adj.* fiduciary; **II.** *Adv.* in trust; **~ verwalten** hold in trust

Treuhand|gebiet *n* trust territory; **~gesellschaft** *f* trust(ee) company; **~konto** *n* trust (*od.* fiduciary) account

Treuhandschaft *f* trusteeship

treuherzig I. *Adj.* (*arglos*) guileless, innocent, straightforward; (*naiv*) ingenuous, naive; (*gutgläubig*) trusting; **~er Blick/Typ** trusting gaze / honest (*od.* straightforward) type (*od.* person); **II.** *Adv.* anschauen *etc.*: trustingly, guilelessly; **Treuherzigkeit** *f* guilelessness, innocence, honesty; naivety, ingenuousness; → *treuherzig*

treulos I. *Adj.* disloyal (**gegen** to); **~er Ehemann** unfaithful husband; **II.** *Adv.*: **~ gegen j-n handeln** be disloyal to s.o., betray s.o.'s trust; **Treulosigkeit** *f* disloyalty; *e-s Ehepartners etc.*: unfaithfulness

treu sorgend → treu II

Trevira® *n*; *-(s)*, *kein Pl.* Trevira®

Triade *f*; *-, -n* **1.** *Reli., Lit., Math.* triad; *Reli. und fig. auch* trinity; **2.** (*Verbrecherorganisation*) triad

Triage [tri'a:ʒə] *f*; *-, -n*; *Med.* triage

Triangel *m, n*; *-s, -* **1.** *Mus.* triangle; **2.** *umg.* (*Riss in Kleidung*) three-cornered tear

Trias *f*; *-, kein Pl.*; *Geol.* Triassic (rocks *Pl.*), Trias; *allg. geh.* triad, trinity

Triathlet *m*; *-en, -en*, **~in** *f*; *-, -nen*; *Sport* triathlete; **Triathlon** *n*; *-s, -s* triathlon

Tribun *m*; *-s und -en, -e(n)* tribune

Tribunal *n*; *-s, -e* tribunal

Tribüne *f*; *-, -n* **1.** *für Zuschauer* (*in e-m Stadion etc.*): stand; **vor vollen/ leeren ~n spielen** play to a capacity crowd / to empty stands; **2.** *für Prominenz bei e-r Parade etc.*: reviewing stand (*od.* platform); *für Redner*: platform, rostrum

Tribünen|platz *m für Zuschauer*: seat in the stand, stand seat; **~reihe** *f* row in the stand

Tribut *m*; *-(e)s, -e*; *hist.* (*Abgabe*) tribute, contribution; *fig.* (*Opfer*) toll; *e-r Sache s-n ~ zollen fig.* pay tribute to; **e-n hohen ~ an Menschenleben fordern** take a heavy toll on human lives, be achieved at a high cost in human life; **tributpflichtig** *Adj. hist.* tributary (*j-m* to s.o.)

Trichine *f*; *-, -n*; *Zool.* trichina; **Trichinenschau** *f Vet.* trichinization check; **trichinös** *Adj. Vet.* trichinous, trichinotic; **Trichinose** *f*; *-, -n*; *Vet.* trichinosis, trichiniasis

Trichter *m*; *-s, - zum Abfüllen*: funnel; (*Bomben-, Vulkantrichter*) crater; **auf den** (*richtigen*) **~ kommen** *umg.* get it, get the hang, twig, *Am. auch* catch on; *bei Handhabung e-s Geräts etc.*: auch

get the knack; **auf den** (*richtigen*) **~ bringen** *umg.* put (*od.* get) it across to, get s.o. on the right (*od.* same) wavelength, show s.o. the knack; **trichterförmig** *Adj.* funnel-shaped

Trichter|grammophon *n hist.* horn gramophone; **~mündung** *f Geog.* estuary

Trick *m*; *-s, -s* **1.** (*Täuschungsmanöver*) trick; *weitS. auch* ploy, ruse, gambit; *Film*: special effect; **mit e-m ~ den Gegner täuschen** *Sport* outwit the opposition (*od.* opponent) (with a feint); *Rugby*: sell a dummy; **auf e-n** (*üblen*) **~ hereinfallen** be the victim of (*od.* taken in by) a (mean) trick; **2.** (*Kniff*) trick, (special) technique, (special) way of doing something; *auf intuitives Erfassen bezogen*: knack; **das ist der ganze ~ dabei** *umg.* that's all there is to it; **den ~ heraushaben** *umg.* have got the knack (*od.* hang) of it; **3.** *Artistik*: trick, act, routine; *gefährlicher od. verblüffender*: feat; **~aufnahme** *f Film, Fot.* trick shot; *Fot. Pl.* trick photography *Sg.*; *Tonband*: trick recording; **~betrug** *m* deception, trick; **~betrüger** *m*, **~betrügerin** *f* confidence trickster, swindler, *männlich auch* conman; **~dieb** *m*, **~diebin** *f* confidence thief; **~diebstahl** *m allg.* theft involving deception (*od.* fraud); *Einzelfall*: swindle

Trickfilm *m* animated cartoon (film); **~zeichner** *m*, **~zeichnerin** *f* cartoonist, animator

Trick|kiste *f box* (*fig.* bag) of tricks; (**tief**) **in die ~ greifen** *fig.* use all one's wiles (*od.* guile)

trickreich I. *Adj.* artful, subtle, tricky, (tactically) clever; **II.** *Adv.* spielen *etc.*: deceptively, cleverly

tricksen *umg.* **I.** *v/i. Sport* feint, swerve; *allg.* play (it) clever, finesse, cheat *pej.*; **II.** *v/t.*: **das werden wir schon ~** we'll manage (*od.* work) (*durch Mogeln*) wangle *od.* fix) it somehow; **Trickser** *m*; *-s, -*, **Trickserin** *f*, *-, -nen*; *umg.* tricky operator (*od.* customer), trickster *umg.*; *Sport auch* deceptive (*od.* inventive) player; **Trickserei** *f*; *-, -en*; *umg.*, *oft pej.* (*Raffinesse*) artfulness, guile, subtlety; (*Mogeln*) cheating, tricks *Pl.*, dodges *Pl.*

Trickski¹ *m Sport* hotdog(ging) (*od.* freestyle) ski

Trickski² *n*; *-, kein Pl.*, **~laufen** *n* freestyle skiing, hot-dogging *umg.*

trieb *Imperf.* → *treiben*

Trieb *m*; *-(e)s, -e* **1.** *Bot.* young shoot; **2.** (*treibende Kraft*) driving force; (*Antrieb*) impulse; **3.** (*Drang*) urge, need, compulsion, *weitS. auch* instinct; *Psych.* drive; *Pl. auch* instinctual nature *Sg.* *Koll.*; (*Verlangen*) desire; (*Geschlechtstrieb*) sex drive; **tierischer/ mütterlicher ~** animal/maternal instinct; **s-e ~e befriedigen/beherrschen** indulge (*od.* gratify *pej.*) / restrain one's natural instincts (*od.* impulses); **4.** *Tech.* drive; **~feder** *f* mainspring; *fig.* driving force (+ *Gen.* behind), main motive (for, behind)

triebhaft I. *Adj. Handlung, Verhalten*: instinctive, compulsive; (*sexuell*) *auch* sexually motivated (*od.* driven); *Person*: impulse-driven; **~er Mensch** *auch* someone dominated by his (*od.* her) instinctual needs; **II.** *Adv.* handeln *etc.*: compulsively; *engS.* from a sexual motive; **Triebhaftigkeit** *f* animal instincts *Pl.*; *engS.* sexuality

Trieb|handlung *f* compulsive (*engS.*

sexually motivated) act; **~kraft** *f* **1.** propelling (*od.* motive) power; *fig.* driving force, (*Person*) *auch* powerhouse (+ *Gen.* behind); **2.** *von Hefe etc.*: potency; *Bot. von Saatgut*: vigo(u)r, germinative power; **~leben** *n* instinctual life (*od.* nature); *engS.* sex life, sexuality, sexual needs *Pl.*; **~täter** *m*, **~verbrecher** *m* sex offender; **~wagen** *m Eisenb.* railcar, diesel unit; (*Straßenbahn*) tramcar, *Am.* streetcar; *bei einfachem ~ mit Anhänger*: front (part); (*Obus*) trolley-bus

Triebwerk *n Flug. etc.* engine; **~schaden** *m* engine fault

Triefauge *n* watery eye; **triefäugig** *Adj.* watery-eyed, rheumy-eyed

triefen *v/i.*; *triefte und troff, hat od. ist getrieft* **1.** (*ist*) (*in Tropfen fallen*) drip; **2.** (*ist*) (*in kleinen Rinnsälen fließen*) trickle; *Speichel*: *auch* dribble; **3.** (*hat*) (*so nass sein, dass Flüssigkeit herunterfließt, austritt*) be dripping (*od.* soaking) (wet); *Auge, Nase*: run; **~ vor** (+ *Dat.*) be dripping with; *fig.* ooze, exude *geh.*; **von/vor Nässe ~** be dripping (*od.* soaking) (wet); **vor Spott ~** *fig.* *Worte etc.*: bristle (*od.* be heavy) with irony (*od.* sarcasm); *Person*: be full of mockery; **~d nass** dripping (*od.* soaking) wet; **Triefnase** *f umg.* runny (*od.* snotty *pej.*) nose; **triefnass** *Adj. umg.* dripping (*od.* soaking) wet; **~e Haare** dripping wet hair *Sg.*; **du bist ja ~!** (but) you're soaking!

Triennale *f*; *-, -n* triennial celebration (*od.* festival)

triezen *v/t. umg. allg.* tease, torment; (*j-n dazu auswählen*) pick on; *mit Bitten etc.*: plague

trifft *Präs.* → *treffen*

Triforium *n*; *-s, Triforien*; *Archit.* triforium (*Pl.* triforia)

Trift *f*; *-, -en* **1.** *Dial.* (*Weide*) (poor) pastureland, grazing, sheepwalks *Pl.*; **2.** *Dial.* (*Weg*) grassy track, cattle track; **3.** → *Drift*

triftig *Adj.* (*begründet*) sound; (*schwerwiegend*) weighty; (*zwingend*) cogent, compelling; (*überzeugend*) convincing; **~er Grund** good (*od.* sufficient *od.* strong) reason

Trigonometrie *f*; *-, kein Pl.*; *Math.* trigonometry; **trigonometrisch** *Adj.* trigonometric(al)

Trikolore *f*; *-, -n* tricolo(u)r; **die** (**französische**) **~** the (French) Tricolo(u)r

Trikot¹ [tri'ko:] *n*; *-s, -s* **1.** (*Sporthemd*) shirt, jersey; *Leichtathletik*: singlet; **das gelbe ~** *Radsport*: the (leader's) yellow jersey; **die ~s tauschen nach dem Spiel**: swap (*od.* exchange) strips (*od.* shirts); **2.** *Ballett*: leotard

Trikot² [tri'ko:] *m*; *-s, -s*; (*Stoff*) tricot, single knit fabric; **Trikotagen** [triko-'ta:ʒn] *Pl.* knitwear *Sg.*, knitted goods

Trikotwerbung *f* shirt advertising

Triller *m*; *-s, -*; *Mus.* trill; **trillern** *vt/i.* (*singen*) trill; *Vogel*: warble; *Schiedsrichter*: whistle; **ein Lied ~** trill a song (*od.* tune); *Vogel*: sing; **Trillerpfeife** *f* (signal[l]ing) whistle

Trilliarde *f*; *-, -n a* thousand trillion, *Am.* sextillion, 10 to the 21st power

Trillion *f*; *-, -en* trillion, *Am.* quintillion, 10 to the 18th power

Trilobit *m*; *-en, -en*; *Zool.* trilobite

Trilogie *f*; *-, -n* trilogy

Trimester *n*; *-s, -* term (within a three-term year)

Trimm-dich-Pfad *m* fitness (*od.* keep-fit) trail

trimmen I. *v/t.* **1.** (*stutzen, Naut., Flug.*)

trim; *umg.* (*Auto etc.*) soup up, tweak; *auf alt* ~ do *s.th.* up (*od.* doctor *s.th.*) to look old, give *s.th.* an old (*od.* antique) look; **2.** (*trainieren*) train, get *s.o.* into shape; *für e-e Prüfung etc.*: prepare, train up, drill, coach; *auf Ordnung etc.* ~ train *s.o.* to be tidy *etc.*; → *getrimmt*; **II.** *v/refl.* keep fit; *sich auf jugendlich* ~ try to look younger than one is, go for a young look, dress mutton up as lamb; → *getrimmt*

Trimm|pfad *m* fitness (*od.* keep-fit) trail; **~trab** *m* (*Tätigkeit*) jogging; *einzelner Lauf*: jog

Trinität *f*; -, *kein Pl.*; *Reli.* trinity, the Trinity; **Trinitatis** *n*; -, *kein Pl.*; *kirchl.* Trinity Sunday

trinkbar *Adj.* (*genießbar*) drinkable, potable *fachspr.*; *umg.* (*leidlich*) (quite) drinkable; *etwas Trinkbares* something to drink

trinken *v/t./i.*; *trinkt, trank, hat getrunken* drink (*auch übermäßig Alkohol*); *ein Bier* ~ have a beer; *e-n Tee* ~ have a cup (*od.* glass) of tea; *was* ~ *Sie?* what would you like to drink?; (*bes. Alkohol*) *auch* what'll you have?, what are you drinking?, what's your poison? *altm. umg. hum.*; ~ *auf* (+ *Akk.*) (*j-n od. etw.*) drink to; *ich möchte nur etw.* ~ (nothing to eat, thank you,) I'd just like *s.th.* to drink (*od.* a drink); *darauf müssen wir* (*einen*) ~ *umg.* we'll have to drink to that, that calls for a drink; *ich brauche was zu* ~ *umg.* I need a drink, give me a drink; *gern einen* ~ *umg.* be fond of (*od.* partial to) a drop, like one's drink (*od.* one's beer *etc.*); *er trinkt keinen Tropfen* he doesn't touch drink (*od.* a drop *od.* it); *einen umg. od. etwas* ~ *gehen* go for a drink (*Bier: auch* beer *od.* pint); ~ *wir noch was umg.* let's have another drink (*od.* one); *der Wein lässt sich* ~ *umg.* this wine isn't (too) bad; *positiv anerkennend: auch* this is a decent wine; → *Wohl*

Trinker *m*; -s, -; (*Alkoholiker*) alcoholic, heavy drinker

Trinkerei *f*; -, -en; *umg. Alkohol*: drink(ing); *er kann die* ~ *nicht lassen* he (just) won't give up the booze, he can't get off the bottle

Trinkerheilanstalt *f* (alcohol) detox(ification) cent|re (*Am.* -er)

Trinkerin *f*; -, -nen (female) alcoholic, woman (*od.* girl) who drinks heavily

trinkfertig *Adj.* ready-to-drink ..., *präd.* ready to drink

trinkfest *Adj.*: ~ *sein* hold one's drink (liquor *umg.*) well, be able to take a lot; **Trinkfestigkeit** *f* ability to hold one's drink (liquor *umg.*)

trinkfreudig *Adj.*: ~ *sein* like (*od.* be fond of) one's drink

Trink|gefäß *n* **1.** *Archäologie etc.*: drinking vessel; **2.** *allg.* something to drink out of; (*Tasse*) cup; (*Glas*) glass; **~gelage** *n* drinking session, piss-up *umg.*, bender *Sl.*; **~geld** *n* tip; *fig. pej.* pittance, *Am. auch* chump change; *j-m ein* ~ *geben auch* tip *s.o.*; *was gibt man hier für* (*ein*) ~*?* how much do you tip here?, what sort of tip do you give here?; **~halle** *f im Kurort*: pump room; (*Kiosk*) refreshment kiosk; **~halm** *m* (drinking) straw; **~kur** *f* mineral cure; **~lied** *n* drinking song; **~schale** *f* (drinking) bowl, (shallow) cup; **~spruch** *m* toast; *e-n* ~ *auf j-n ausbringen Sprecher*: propose (*Anwesende*: drink) a toast to *s.o.*

Trinkwasser *n* drinking water; *kein* ~ *Schild: auch* not for drinking; **~aufbereitungsanlage** *f* water purification plant; **~gewinnung** *f* production of drinking water; **~leitung** *f* water main; *weitS.* water supply; **~qualität** *f* (drinking) water quality; **~reservoir** *n* water authority reservoir; **~versorgung** *f* drinking water provision (*od.* supply), supply of drinking water

Trio *n*; -s, -s trio (*auch umg. fig.*)

Triode *f*; -, -n; *Etron.* triode

Triole *f*; -, -n; *Mus.* triplet

Trip *m*; -s, -s **1.** (*Reise*) trip; **2.** *umg.* (*Drogenrausch*) trip; (*Dosis*) fix; *auf e-m* ~ *sein* be on a trip; **3.** *umg.* (*Phase*) trip, thing, fad, craze; *auf dem esoterischen/ökologischen* ~ *sein* be into mysticism / the environment

...trip *im Subst. umg.* trip, thing, fad, craze; *Esoterik*~ mysticism thing; *Öko*~ green thing, anti-pollution trip; *sie ist seit einiger Zeit auf dem Spar*~ she's been on an economy drive for some time now, she's been having a "save money" phase

trippeln *v/i. geziert, auf hohen Absätzen etc.*: mince (along); *Kind*: toddle (along); **Trippelschritt** *m* short (*od.* little step); *Kind: Pl. auch* toddle *Sg.*, toddling steps

Tripper *m*; -s, -; *Med.* gonorrh(o)ea, *the clap umg.*; *e-n* ~ *haben umg.* have (a dose of) the clap

Triptychon *n*; -s, *Triptychen und Triptycha* triptych

trist *Adj. Leben etc.*: dreary, joyless, empty; *Aussichten, Witterung*: dismal, depressing, gloomy; *Farbe*: drab, dull, gloomy, depressing; *Gegend*: dreary; (*verlassen*) lonely; **Tristesse** [tris'tɛs] *f*; -, -n, *mst Sg.* dreariness, sadness, gloom, melancholy

Tritium *n*; -s, *kein Pl.*; (*abgek.* **T**) tritium

tritt *Präs.* → *treten*

Tritt *m*; -(e)s, -e **1.** (*Aufsetzen e-s Fußes*) step; *hörbar*: footstep; (*Art und Weise, wie j-d s-e Füße setzt*) step, walk, gait; *e-n leichten* ~ *haben* have a light step; *e-n schweren* ~ *haben* have a heavy tread, walk heavily, stomp around *umg. hum.*; **2.** (*Gehen od. Marschieren im gleichen Rhythmus*) step, pace; *aus dem* ~ *geraten* fall out of step, break step; *aus dem* ~ *geraten sein fig.* be having a hard time, be going through a bad patch; *Sport etc.*: have lost one's rhythm; *wieder* ~ *fassen* fall in(to) step; *fig.* get back on an even keel; *Sport etc.*: recover one's form; **3.** (*Fußtritt*) kick; *j-m e-n* ~ *versetzen* give *s.o.* a kick; *j-m e-n* ~ *geben umg. fig.* give *s.o.* the push, chuck *s.o.* out; **4.** (*Stufe*) step (*auch beim Eisklettern etc.*); *in Felswand etc.*: foothold; (*waagerechte Fläche e-r Treppe*) tread (*senkrechte*: riser); *Kutsche*: step; **5.** (*Gestell mit Stufen*) stepladder; (*set of*) steps *Pl.*; **6.** *Tech.* (*Fußhebel*) treadle, pedal; **7.** *Jägerspr.* (*Spur*) (hoof)print; (*Fuß*) foot; → *auch Trittbrett*

Trittbrett *n Mot.* step, *ältere Autos*: running-board; **~fahrer** *m umg. pej.* freeloader

trittfest *Adj. Leiter etc.*: safe; *Teppichboden*: hard-wearing, durable, resistant

Tritt|leiter *f* stepladder; **~schalldämmung** *f* footstep silencing (measures *Pl.*)

Triumph *m*; -(e)s, -e triumph; *im* ~ in triumph, triumphantly; **~e feiern** *fig.*

be very successful, be on a roll *umg.*; *stärker*: revel (*od.* exult) in one's success; **triumphal I.** *Adj.* triumphant (*präd. auch* a triumph); **II.** *Adv. empfangen, feiern etc.*: ecstatically, with acclaim

Triumph|bogen *m* triumphal arch; *in Paris*: Arc de Triomphe; **~gefühl** *n* sense (*od.* feeling) of triumph, triumph, exultation

triumphieren *v/i.* (*Triumphgefühl empfinden*) triumph; *schadenfroh*: gloat *pej.*; (*siegen*) triumph (*über* + *Akk.* over); *am Ende triumphierte die Gerechtigkeit* justice triumphed in the end, in the end justice was served; **triumphierend I.** *Adj.* triumphant; **II.** *Adv.* lächeln, sagen *etc.*: triumphantly; (*schadenfroh*) gloatingly *pej.*

Triumph|säule *f* triumphal column; **~wagen** *m hist.* triumphal chariot; **~zug** *m* triumphal procession; *e-n* ~ *antreten durch fig.* set out to conquer

Triumvirat *n*; -(e)s, -e; *hist.* triumvirate

trivial *Adj.* trivial, shallow; *Bemerkung*: *auch* trite, banal; (*alltäglich*) commonplace, everyday, ordinary, trivial, banal *geh.*

Trivialität *f*; -, -en **1.** *nur Sg.*; (*Plattheit*) *Eigenschaft*: triviality, shallowness, triteness; (*Gewöhnlichkeit*) ordinariness, banality; **2.** *Äußerung, Gesprächsthema etc.*: triviality, banality; *Pl. auch* trivia *Pl.*, trifles *Pl.*; (*alltägliche Erscheinung*) ordinary (*od.* commonplace) thing, commonplace

Trivial|literatur *f* light fiction; **~roman** *pej. m* light (*od.* popular) novel, trashy novel *pej.*

Trizeps *m*; -(es), -e; *Anat.* triceps

trochäisch *Adj.* trochaic; **Trochäus** *m*; -, *Trochäen* trochee, trochaic foot

trocken I. *Adj.* **1.** dry (*auch Brot, Husten, Kuh, fig. Bemerkung, Humor, Person, Wein*); *Land*: *auch* arid; *Holz*: (well-)seasoned; *~e Kälte* crisp cold; *~ werden* dry (out); *im Trockenen* somewhere dry, in a dry place; *bei Regen: auch* under shelter; **2.** (*langweilig*) dry, dull, boring; **3.** *Akustik*: dry; *Knall*: dry, sharp; *~er Knall auch* crack; *e-e ~e Rechte ans Kinn des Gegners* a crisp right(hander) to (*od.* on) his opponent's jaw; *ein ~er Schuss aus 15 Metern Fußball*: a 15-yard (*od.* -met|re, *Am.* -er) drive; **4.** *fig., in Wendungen*: *da blieb kein Auge* ~ *umg. vor Lachen*: we (*od.* they) couldn't stop laughing, we (*od.* they) were falling about (*Am.* were doubled over *od.* rolling in the aisles); *vor Rührung*: there wasn't a dry eye in the place *auch iro.*, we *etc.* all had tears in our eyes; ~ *sein umg.* (*keinen Alkohol mehr trinken*) be on the wagon; *ich sitze* (*völlig*) *auf dem Trockenen umg. fig.* (*ohne Geld*) I'm stony (*Am.* stone) broke (*od.* completely on the rocks); (*ohne Getränk*) I'm staring into an empty glass, I'm parched; (*ohne Information*) I don't know (*od.* have no idea) what's going on, I'm all at sea; (*ich weiß nicht weiter*) I'm stuck (*od.* stymied); *noch nicht* ~ *hinter den Ohren* still wet behind the ears; → *Kehle* 1, *Schäfchen etc.*; **II.** *Adv.*: ~ *nach Hause kommen* get home before the rain really starts (*od.* without getting wet); *sich* ~ *rasieren* dry-shave, use an electric shaver (*od.* razor); ~ *aufbewahren* keep in a dry place; ~ *bemerken, dass ... fig.* remark (*od.* observe) drily that ...

Trocken|automat *m* tumble drier (*od.* dryer); **~batterie** *f* dry cell battery

Trockenbeerenauslese *f* Trockenbeerenauslese; *choice wine made from grapes left to dry on the vine*

Trocken|blume *f* dried flower; **~boden** *m* drying-loft, airing-space; **~dock** *n* *Naut.* dry dock; *ein Schiff ins ~ bringen* bring a ship into dry dock, dry-dock a ship; **~ei** *n* egg powder, dehydrated egg(s *Pl.*); **~eis** *n* dry ice; **~element** *n* *Etech.* dry cell; **~fäule** *f* *Bot.* dry rot, heartrot; *Archit.* dry rot; **~futter** *n* dry feed, provender; **~gebiet** *n* dry zone; **~gemüse** *n* dried (*od.* dehydrated) vegetables *Pl.*; **~gestell** *n* *allg.*, *auch für Geschirr:* drying rack; *für Wäsche:* clothes horse (*od.* drier); **~gewicht** *n* dry weight; **~gürtel** *m* *Geog.* dry belt (*od.* zone); **~haube** *f* hood drier; **~hefe** *f* dried yeast

Trockenheit *f* dryness (*auch fig.*); *Geog.* aridity; (*Dürre*) drought

Trocken|klosett *n* chemical toilet; **~kurs** *m* dry-ski *etc.* course; *umg. fig.* dry run

trockenlegen *v/t.* **1.** (*Land, Bergb., Schacht*) drain; *umg. fig.* (*j-n*) dry (*s.o.*) out, get (*s.o.*) dried out; **2.** (*Säugling*): *ein Baby ~* change a baby's nappy (*Am.* diaper); *das Baby ~ auch* change the baby *umg.*; **Trockenlegung** *f* draining

Trocken|masse *f* dry matter; *30% Fett in der ~* fat content 30% dry weight; **~milch** *f* dried (*od.* powdered) milk, milk powder; **~obst** *n* dried fruit; **~periode** *f* dry spell; (*Dürre*) drought; **~presse** *f* *Fot.* dry press; **~rasen** *m* *Geog.* arid grassland; **~rasierer** *m* **1.** (*Apparat*) (electric) shaver, electric razor; **2.** (*Mann*) dry shaver; *ich bin ~* I use an electric shaver (*od.* razor); **~rasur** *f* dry shave (*od.* shaving); **~raum** *m* drying-room

trocken|reiben *v/t.* (*unreg., trennb., hat -ge-*) rub (*od.* towel) dry; **~reinigen** *v/t.* (*untr., hat -ge-*) dry-clean

Trocken|reinigung *f* dry-cleaning; **~savanne** *f* *Geog.* arid savanna(h)

Trockenschleuder *f* spin-drier; **trockenschleudern** *v/t.* (*untr., hat -ge-*) spin-dry

Trocken|shampoo *n* dry shampoo; **~spiritus** *m* fuel tablet(s *Pl.*); **~ständer** *m* *für Wäsche:* clothes horse; *für Geschirr:* drying rack; **~starre** *f* *Zool.* drought torpor, dry weather diapause; **~substanz** *f* → **Trockenmasse**; **~übung** *f* dry ski *etc.* exercise; *umg. fig.* dry run; **~wald** *m* *Geog.* dry (*od.* xerophytic *fachspr.*) forest; **~wäsche** *f* dry washing

trockenwischen *v/t.* (*trennb., hat -ge-*) wipe *s.th.* dry

Trocken|zeit *f* dry season; **~zelle** *f* dry cell

trocknen I. *v/t.* (*hat getrocknet*) dry; *die Wäsche im Keller ~* dry (*od.* air) the washing (down) in the basement; *sich (Dat.) die Tränen ~* wipe one's tears away, dry one's eyes (*od.* tears); *sich von der Sonne ~ lassen* dry off in the sun; *an der Luft getrocknet Gastr.* air-dried; **II.** *v/i.* (*ist*) dry; *die Wäsche trocknet auf der Leine* the washing is hanging out to dry (*od.* is on the line); *langsam/schnell ~* take a long time to dry / dry quickly; *die Teller werden schon von alleine ~* just leave the plates to dry; *die Wäsche zum Trocknen aufhängen* hang up the washing, hang the washing up to dry;

Trockner *m; -s, -* drier

Troddel *f; -, -n* tassel; **~blume** *f* *Bot.* snowbell

Trödel *m; -s, kein Pl.* junk; *pej. auch* rubbish

Trödelei *f; -, -en; umg.* dawdling

Trödel|laden *m* junk shop; **~markt** *m* flea market

trödeln *v/i. umg.* dawdle; *trödel nicht so!* don't dawdle!, (do) get a move on!

Trödler *m; -s, -, ~in** *f; -, -nen* **1.** junk dealer, junkshop owner; **2.** *umg.* dawdler, slowcoach; *Am.* slowpoke

troff *Imperf.* → **triefen**

trog *Imperf.* → **trügen**

Trog *m; -(e)s, Tröge zum Füttern etc.:* trough; (*Bottich*) vat; *für Wäsche:* tub; *Geol.* glacial trough; *Met.* trough (of low pressure)

Troglodyt *m; -en, -en* troglodyte

Troika ['trɔyka] *f; -, -s* troika (*auch Pol.*)

Troja (*n*); *-s; hist.* Troy; **Trojaner** *m; -en, -en*, **Trojanerin** *f; -, -nen; hist.* Trojan, *weiblich auch:* Trojan woman; **trojanisch** *Adj.* **1.** *hist.* Trojan; *der Trojanische Krieg* the Trojan War; *das Trojanische Pferd* the Trojan Horse; **2.** *fig. Trojanisches Pferd auch EDV* Trojan horse

Troll *m; -(e)s, -e* troll; **~blume** *f* *Bot.* globeflower

trollen *v/refl. umg. gemächlich:* stroll (*od.* amble) off (*od.* away), toddle off; *beschämt:* shuffle off, retreat, withdraw, make o.s. scarce; *troll dich!* push off!, buzz off!, clear out!

Trollinger *m; -s, -* **1.** *nur Sg.* (*Rebsorte*) Trollinger (grape); **2.** (*Wein*) Trollinger (wine), wine from the Trollinger grape

Trommel *f; -, -n* drum (*auch Tech., für Kabel etc.*); *Tech. auch* cylinder, barrel; *für etw. die ~ rühren fig.* beat (*od.* bang) the (big) drum for *s.th.*, plug *s.th. umg.*; **~bremse** *f* *Tech.* drum brake

Trommelei *f; -, -en; umg.* (constant) drumming, drum noise

Trommel|fell *n* **1.** *Anat.* eardrum; *ihm ist das ~ geplatzt* he has burst an eardrum; *da platzt e-m ja das ~ umg. fig.* it would deafen you, it's deafening; **2.** *Mus.* drumskin, *bes. Am.* drumhead; **~feuer** *n* *Mil.* barrage (*auch fig. von Fragen etc.*)

trommeln *vt/i.* drum; *Regen:* beat, *sehr stark:* drum; (*schlagen*) hammer (*auf + Akk.* at, on), bang (on); (*Rhythmus, Marsch etc.*) drum, beat, tap (out); *Jägerspr., Hase bei Revierverteidigung:* box; *bei Gefahr:* thump; *mit den Fingern ~* drum one's fingers

Trommel|revolver *m* revolver; **~schlag** *m* drumbeat, beat of the (*od.* a) drum; **~stock** *m* drumstick; **~waschmaschine** *f* drum washing machine; **~wirbel** *m* drum roll; *gedämpfter:* ruffle, muffled drum roll

Trommler *m; -s, -, ~in** *f; -, -nen* drummer

Trompete *f; -, -n* trumpet; *altm. für Signale etc.: auch* bugle; *Anat. altm.* Eustachian tube; → *Pauke*; **trompeten I.** *v/i.* play the trumpet; *Elefant:* trumpet; *umg.* (*sich schnäuzen*) honk one's nose loudly, blow one's nose resoundingly; **II.** *v/t.* (*Musikstück*) play *s.th.* on the trumpet; *umg. fig.* (*verkünden*) trumpet abroad, broadcast; *sie muss natürlich alles gleich durch die Gegend ~!* *umg. fig.* and of course she

then has to go and tell everyone (*od.* the world) all about it!

Trompeten|baum *m* *Bot.* trumpet tree, common catalpa; **~signal** *n* trumpet (*od.* bugle) call; **~solo** *n* trumpet solo; **~stoß** *m* blast on the trumpet, trumpet blast

Trompeter *m; -s, -, ~in** *f; -, -nen* trumpeter, trumpet player; *Mil. altm. auch* bugler

Tropen *Pl.* tropics; **~anzug** *m* tropical suit; **~fieber** *n* tropical fever; **~helm** *m* pith helmet, sun helmet; **~holz** *n* tropical timber, timber from tropical climates; **~institut** *n* institute for tropical diseases; **~klima** *n* tropical climate; **~koller** *m* tropical frenzy; **~krankheit** *f* tropical disease; **~medizin** *f* tropical medicine; **~pflanze** *f* tropical plant

tropentauglich *Adj.* fit for the tropics, *attr. auch* tropical; **Tropentauglichkeit** *f* usefulness in the tropics

Tropenwald *m* *Geog.* tropical forest

Tropf[1] *m; -(e)s, Tröpfe; umg. altm.* simpleton; *armer ~* poor wretch (*od.* soul)

Tropf[2] *m; -(e)s, -e; Med.* drip, *Am.* I.V.; *am ~ hängen* be on a drip (*Am.* an I.V.); *e-n ~ anlegen* put up a drip (*Am.* an I.V.); *viele Theater hängen am ~ von Sponsoren* a lot of theat|res (*Am. auch* -ers) are on permanent life support from their sponsors

Tröpfchen *n* droplet, small drop; **~infektion** *f* *Med.* droplet infection; **~modell** *n* *Phys.* droplet model

tröpfchenweise *Adv.* **1.** (*sickernd, langsam*) in drops, drop by drop; *umg. fig.* in dribs and drabs; *das Wasser kommt nur ~ durch* is only dripping (*od.* seeping) through; **2.** *Medizin einnehmen etc.:* in (the form of) drops

tröpfeln I. *v/i.* **1.** (*ist getröpfelt*) *Flüssigkeit:* (*herabrinnen*) trickle, dribble (*auf + Akk.* onto; *in + Akk.* into; *an + Dat.* hinunter down); *in einzelnen Tropfen:* drip; **2.** (*hat*) *Wasserhahn:* dribble, drip; → 1; *es tröpfelt* (*regnet leicht*) it's spitting; **II.** *v/t.* (*hat*) dribble *s.th.*, let *s.th.* drip (*auf + Akk.* onto; *in + Akk.* into); (*Ohrentropfen etc.*) put in; *Gastr.* drizzle (over)

tropfen *vt/i.* (*hat od. ist getropft*) → **tröpfeln**; **II.** *v/i.* **1.** (*hat*) *Kerze:* drip, gutter; *Wasserhahn:* drip; **2.** (*ist*) *Schweiß, Nässe von Bäumen etc.:* drip (*auf + Akk.* onto; *in + Akk.* into)

Tropfen *m; -s, -* drop (*auch fig.*); *von Schweiß etc.:* bead; *Pl. Med.* drops; *es regnet in dicken ~* big raindrops are falling; *es ist noch kein ~ Regen gefallen* so far not a drop of rain has fallen; *ihm stand der Schweiß in dicken ~ auf der Stirn* he had big beads of sweat on his forehead; *edler ~ fig.* fine (*od.* high-class) wine *etc.*, (drop of the) good stuff, classy tipple *hum.*; *er hat seitdem keinen ~* (*Alkohol*) *getrunken* he hasn't touched a drop since (then); *wir haben keinen ~ Milch im Haus* we haven't (got) a drop of milk in the house; *ein ~ auf den heißen Stein* a drop in the ocean; *steter ~ höhlt den Stein Sprichw.* little strokes fell big oaks, many a mickle makes a muckle; **~fänger** *m an Kanne:* dripcatcher

Tropfenform *f* *Tech.* (tear)drop shape; **tropfenförmig** *Adj.* drop-shaped

tropfenweise *Adv.* → **tröpfchenweise**

Tropf|flasche *f* dropper bottle; **~infusion** *f* *Med.* intravenous drip

tropfnass *Adj. umg.* dripping wet; →

auch **triefnass**
Tropfstein *m hängender*: stalactite; *stehender*: stalagmite; **~höhle** *f* stalactite cave, (limestone) cave with stalactites and stalagmites
Trophäe *f*; -, *-n* trophy; **Trophäenschrank** *m für Preise*: display cabinet
tropisch *Adj.* tropical
Troposphäre *f*; -, *kein Pl.*; *Met.* troposphere
Tross *m*; *-es, -e* **1.** *Mil. altm.* baggage train; **2.** (*Gefolge*) retinue, (camp-)followers *Pl.*, hangers-on *Pl.*; **3.** (*Zug von Demonstranten etc.*) line, body of people
Trosse *f*; -, *-n* hawser
Trost *m*; *-(e)s, kein Pl.* consolation, comfort; **schwacher ~** scant (*od.* small) consolation, cold comfort; **mein einziger ~** my one (*od.* only) consolation; **zum ~** as a (*od.* by way of) consolation; **ein ~, dass ...** at least ..., it's a help that...; **zum ~ kann ich dir sagen ...** if it's any consolation (to you) ...; **~ suchen bei** *j-m*: look for (some) consolation (*od.* a shoulder to cry on *umg.*); **~ suchen in** (+ *Dat.*) (*od.* **bei**) *e-r Sache*: seek comfort (*od.* consolation) in; **~ zusprechen** → **trösten**; **du bist wohl nicht (recht) bei ~!** *umg. fig.* have you gone mad?, you're not serious?; → **finden** I
trösten I. *v/t.* console, comfort; (*aufmuntern*) cheer up; **das tröstet mich** that makes me feel better; **II.** *v/refl.* console o.s.; **sich mit e-m Glas Wein** *etc.*: ~ *auch* comfort o.s. with; **sich mit dem Gedanken ~, dass** draw comfort from the fact that; **tröste dich, ihm geht's noch schlimmer** if it's any consolation ...; **sich mit j-m ~** *nach enttäuschter Liebe*: turn to s.o. on the rebound; **tröstend I.** *Part. Präs.*: → **trösten**; **II.** *Adj.* comforting, consoling; **~e Worte** *auch* words of comfort; **Tröster** *m*; -, - comforter, consoler; *bibl.* comforter; **Trösterin** *f*; -, *-nen* comforter, consoler; **tröstlich** *Adj.* comforting, consoling; (*aufmunternd*) cheering; **der Gedanke hat etwas Tröstliches für mich** I find some comfort in the thought
trostlos *Adj. Situation etc.*: hopeless, depressing; (*jämmerlich*) pathetic; *Aussichten, Wetter etc.*: bleak; (*freudlos*) cheerless; *Person*: miserable, *stärker*: desperate; (*untröstlich*) unconsolable; **~e ~e Gegend** a dreary place; **Trostlosigkeit** *f e-r Situation*: hopelessness; *e-r Person*: wretchedness
Trost|pflaster *n umg.* consolation; **~preis** *m* consolation prize
trostreich *Adj.* consoling, comforting
Tröstung *f* consolation, comfort; **versehen mit den ~en der Kirche** *kirchl.* having received the last rites, fully shriven
Trott *m*; *-(e)s, kein Pl.* **1.** trot; **im ~ gehen** *Pferd*: **2.** *fig.* **täglicher ~** (everyday) routine; **der alte ~** the same old rut; **in den alten ~ zurückfallen** fall back into one's old ways
Trottel *m*; *-s, -*; *umg.* dope; **alter ~** old fool; **ich ~!** what an idiot I am!; **trottelig I.** *Adj. umg.* dop(e)y; (*vergesslich*) absent-minded; (*senil*) senile; **II.** *Adv.*: **sich ~ anstellen** act stupidly
trotten *v/i.* trot (along)
Trotteur [trɔ'tøːɐ] *m*; *-s, -s* casual (shoe)
Trottinett *n*; *-s, -e*; *schw.* (*Roller*) scooter
Trottoir [trɔ'toaːɐ] *n*; *-s, -s und -e*; *bes.*

südd., schw., österr. pavement, *Am.* sidewalk
trotz *Präp.* in spite of, despite; **~ allem** in spite of everything; **~ alledem** for all that; **~ s-r Vorsicht** in spite of (*od.* despite) the care he took, however careful he was; **~ all s-r Bemühungen** *auch* for all his efforts
Trotz *m*; *-es, kein Pl.* defiance; (*Störrigkeit*) stubbornness, obstinacy, pigheadedness; **aus ~** just to be stubborn; (*aus Boshaftigkeit*) out of spite; **j-m zum ~** to spite s.o.; **ihrer Warnung zum ~** in defiance of (*od.* flouting) her warning; **~alter** *n*: (**im**) ~ (at a) defiant (*od.* difficult) age
trotzdem I. *Adv.* (but) still, all the same, nevertheless; *am Satzanfang*: *auch* even so; **sie hat es ~ getan** she still did it, she did it all the same (*od.* nevertheless, she just went ahead and did it; **II.** *Konj. umg.* although, even though, despite the fact that
trotzen *v/i.* (*j-m, e-r Sache*) defy, brave; (*Widerstand leisten*) resist; (*störrisch sein*) be stubborn; **e-r Gefahr** *etc.* ~ brave a danger *etc.*
trotzig I. *Adj.* defiant; (*eigensinnig*) stubborn, pigheaded; **ein ~es Gesicht machen** pull a stubborn face; **II.** *Adv.*: **~ schweigen** remain defiantly silent
Trotzkismus *m*; -, *kein Pl.*; *Pol.* Trotskyism; **Trotzkist** *m*; *-en, -en*, **Trotzkistin** *f*; -, *-nen*; *Pol.* Trotskyist, Trotskyite; **trotzkistisch** *Adj.* Trotskyist, Trotskyite
Trotzkopf *m umg.* stubborn old so--and-so; **trotzköpfig** *Adj. umg.* stubborn
Trotz|phase *f* stubborn (*od.* defiant) phase, difficult age; **~reaktion** *f* act of defiance
Troubadour ['truːbaduːɐ] *m*; *-s, -e und -s*; *Lit.* troubadour; *fig.* (*Chansonnier*) singer
Trouble ['trabḷ] *m*; *-s, kein Pl.*; *umg.* trouble; **~ machen** cause trouble
trüb(e) I. *Adj.* **1.** *Flüssigkeit*: cloudy; *Teich etc.*: murky; **im Trüben fischen** *fig.* fish in troubled waters; **2.** *Spiegel*: clouded, cloudy; **trüb werden** *Augenlinsen*: become cloudy; **3.** (*glanzlos, unklar*) dull (*auch Farben*); **4.** *Licht*: dim; **in e-m trüben Licht erscheinen** *fig.* appear in a bad light; **5.** *Tag, Wetter*: dull, dreary, dismal; **heute ist es trüb** today will be dull and cloudy; **6.** *Gedanken, Stimmung etc.*: dismal, gloomy; **es sieht ganz schön trübe aus** *umg. fig.* things are looking rather (*bes. Am.* pretty) bleak; **trübe Tasse** *umg.* wet blanket; **II.** *Adv.*: **trüb blicken** *fig.* look gloomily; **Trübe** *f*; -, *kein Pl. e-r Flüssigkeit, e-s Spiegels*: cloudiness; (*Glanzlosigkeit*) dullness; *des Lichtes*: dimness; *e-s Tages, des Wetters*: dullness, dreariness; *e-s Gedankens, e-r Stimmung*: gloominess
Trubel *m*; *-s, kein Pl.* bustle; *auch von Ereignissen*: tumult; (*Rummel*) hurly--burly; (*Gewirr*) chaos; *umg.* (*Zirkus*) fuss; **sich in den ~ stürzen** throw o.s. into the fray; **dem** (*vorweihnachtlichen*) ~ **entgehen** escape the (pre--Christmas) rush; **aus dem ~ nicht herauskommen** (*keine Ruhe finden*) not get any peace
trüben I. *v/t.* **1.** (*Flüssigkeit*) cloud; *mit Sand etc.*: *auch* muddy; (*glanzlos, unklar machen*) dull; **2.** (*Silber, Spiegel etc.*) tarnish; **3.** (*Sicht, Sinn*) blur; **4.** (*Freude etc.*) spoil, mar; (*Stimmung*) spoil, dampen; (*Verstand*) dull,

cloud; (*Bewusstsein*) cloud; (*Beziehungen*) cloud, cast a shadow over; **seitdem ist unser Verhältnis getrübt** since then our relationship has become strained; → **Wässerchen**; **II.** *v/refl. Flüssigkeit*: become (*od.* go) cloudy; (*glanzlos werden*) become (*od.* go) dull; *Blick*: become blurred; *Beziehungen*: cool off (slightly), become (slightly) strained; **der Himmel trübt sich** the sky is getting overcast
Trübsal *f*; -, *kein Pl.*; (*Elend*) misery; (*Not*) distress; (*Leid*) grief, sorrow; **~ blasen** *umg.* mope; **trübselig I.** *Adj.* gloomy; (*elend*) wretched, miserable; (*öde*) dreary, bleak; **II.** *Adv.* dasitzen, vor sich hin schauen etc.: gloomily
Trübsinn *m*; *nur Sg.* melancholy, gloom, mood of dejection; **in ~ verfallen** fall into melancholy; **trübsinnig I.** *Adj.* melancholic, gloomy, dejected; **II.** *Adv.* dasitzen etc.: gloomily, dejectedly
Trübung *f* **1.** clouding; blurring *etc.*; *Med., der Linse etc.*: opacity; **2.** *nur Sg.*; (*Zustand*) cloudiness; dullness *etc.*; → **trüben**
trudeln *v/i.* **1.** (*ist getrudelt*) *Flug.* spin; **2.** (*ist*): **durch die Stadt** *etc.* ~ *umg.* mosey around town *etc.*
Trudeln *n*; *-s, kein Pl.*: **ins ~ kommen** get (*od.* go) into a tailspin
Trüffel *f*; -, *-n, umg. mst m*; *-s, -*; *Bot. und Konfekt*: truffle; **Pastete mit ~n** *Gastr.* truffle pâté; **~konfekt** *n* (chocolate) truffle
trüffeln *v/t. Gastr.* flavo(u)r with truffles; **getrüffelte Gänseleber** goose liver with truffles
Trüffelschwein *n* truffle pig
trug *Imperf.* → **tragen**
Trug *m*; *-(e)s, kein Pl.* **1.** *der Sinne*: delusion; **2.** *altm.* deceit, fraud; → **Lug**; **~bild** *n* hallucination; (*falsche Hoffnung*) delusion
trügen *vt/i.*: *trügt, trog, hat getrogen* deceive; (*trügerisch sein*) be deceptive; (*irreführen*) be misleading; **wenn mich mein Gedächtnis nicht trügt** if my memory serves me right, if I remember rightly; **wenn mich nicht alles trügt** unless I'm very much mistaken; → **Schein³**; **trügerisch** *Adj.* deceptive; (*irreführend*) misleading; *Person*: deceitful; *Schluss*: misguided, wrong; *Argument*: fallacious; *Hoffnung*: vain, illusory; *Eis, Wetter*: treacherous; **ein ~es Spiel spielen** *geh.* play a treacherous game
Trugschluss *m* fallacy; (*unlogische Folgerung*) non sequitur; **e-m ~ unterliegen** be labo(u)ring under a misapprehension
Truhe *f*; -, *-n* chest
Trumm *n*; *-(e)s, Trümmer; umg.* (*großer, schwerer Gegenstand*) whopper; **ein ~ von e-m Buch** a great tome of a book; **ein ~ von e-m Kerl** a man mountain, a giant of a man; **so ein ~** (*von e-m Schnitzel etc.*) such a whopper (of an escalope *etc.*)
Trümmer *Pl.* **1.** ruins; (*Schutt*) rubble *Sg.*, debris *Sg.*; **in ~ legen** (*Gebäude, Stadt etc.*) raze (to the ground); **in ~n liegen** be (lying) in ruins; **unter den ~n begraben sein** be (*od.* lie) buried in the rubble; **vor den ~n s-r Existenz stehen** *fig.* contemplate the ruins of one's existence; **2.** (*Stücke*) fragments; **in ~ gehen** shatter; **in ~ schlagen** smash to pieces; **3.** (*Überreste*) remnants, remains; **4.** *Flug.* wreck(age) *Sg.*; **unter den ~n** *Flug.* among the

wreckage

Trümmer|feld n field of rubble; **~fraktur** f Med. comminuted (od. multiple) fracture; **~frau** f hist. woman who helped to clear away debris in Germany after World War II; **~landschaft** f scene of destruction

Trumpf m; -(e)s, Trümpfe trump (card); **was ist ~?** what's trump(s)?; **alle Trümpfe in der Hand haben** have (fig. hold) all the trumps; **e-n ~ ausspielen** play a trump; fig. play one's trump card; **s-e Trümpfe ausspielen** fig. play all one's trump cards; **j-m die Trümpfe aus der Hand nehmen** fig. steal s.o.'s thunder; **gute Laune war ~** being in good spirits was what mattered

Trumpfass n ace of trumps

trumpfen vt/i. trump, play a trump (card)

Trumpf|farbe f trumps Pl.; **~karte** f trump (card)

Trunk m; -(e)s, Trünke, mst Sg. 1. (Getränk) drink; 2. (Alkoholismus) drink(ing); **sich dem ~ ergeben** take to drink (od. the bottle umg.); **dem ~ verfallen sein** have taken to drink; iro. have succumbed to the demon drink; (Alkoholiker sein) be a drinker, be on the bottle umg.; **trunken** Adj. geh. 1. fig.: **~ vor Freude/Glück** etc. drunk with joy/happiness; 2. (betrunken) präd. drunk (von with); geh. intoxicated, inebriated; **Trunkenbold** m; -(e)s, -e pej. drunkard; **Trunkenheit** f 1. drunkenness; geh. intoxication, inebriation; **~ am Steuer** Jur. drink-driving, bes. Am. drunk(en) driving; **im Zustand völliger ~** in a state of complete intoxication; 2. fig. geh. intoxication

Trunkenheits|delikt n drinking (od. alcohol) offen|ce (Am. -se); **~fahrt** f: **wegen e-r ~ verhaftet werden** etc. for drink- (Am. drunk[en]) driving

Trunksucht f; nur Sg. alcoholism, dipsomania; **trunksüchtig** Adj.: **~ sein** be an alcoholic; **Trunksüchtige** m, f; -n, -n alcoholic

Trupp m; -s, -s troop (auch von Tieren); Mil. detachment, Polizei: auch squad; **ein ~ Bauarbeiter** a group of builders

Truppe f; -, -n 1. Mil. troops Pl.; (Einheit) unit; Pl. Mil. troops, forces; 2. nur Sg.; Mil. (kämpfende ~) troops Pl., forces Pl., army; **Dienst bei der ~** military service; **die Moral/Schlagkraft der ~** the morale of the troops / strike power of the forces; (unerlaubte) Entfernung von der ~ absence without leave; **von der schnellen ~ sein** umg. fig. be a fast worker; 3. Theat. company, troupe; Sport team

Truppen|abbau m Mil. reduction in forces; **~abzug** m troop withdrawal, withdrawal (od. pull-out) of troops; **~aufmarsch** m deployment of troops; (Massierung) buildup of troops; **~betreuung** f troop welfare; **~bewegungen** Pl. troop movement Sg.; **~einheit** f unit; **~gattung** f branch (of the service); **~kontingent** n contingent of troops; **~konzentration** f massing of troops; **~parade** f military parade; **~schau** f military review; **~stärke** f troop (od. military) strength, number of troops; **~teil** m unit; **~transport** m troop transportation; **~transporter** m Naut. troopship; Flug. troop carrier; **~übung** f field exercise, manoeuvre, Am. maneuver; **~übungsplatz** m military training area; **~verband** m unit, formation; mit besonderem Auftrag:

task force; **~verband(s)platz** m (field) dressing station; **~verpflegung** f army rations Pl., army provisions Pl.

Trust [trast] m; -s, -s; Wirts. trust

Truthahn m Orn. turkey (cock); **~fleisch** n turkey; **~keule** f turkey leg (od. drumstick); **~schnitzel** n turkey escalope (Am. auch schnitzel)

Trut|henne f Orn. turkey; **~huhn** n 1. Orn. turkey; 2. turkey hen

Trutzburg f hist. castle constructed for the siege of an enemy castle

Tsatsiki m; -s, -s; Gastr. tzatziki

Tschad m; -s; Geog. Chad; **Tschader** m; -s, -, **Tschaderin** f; -, -nen Chadian, weiblich auch: Chadian woman (od. girl etc.); **tschadisch** Adj. Chadian

Tschador m; -s, -s; (Schleier) chador

Tschako m; -s, -s; hist. shako

tschau Interj. umg. ciao, see you

Tscheche m; -n, -n Czech; **Tschechei** f; -; neg!; after 1918 unofficial term for the regions of Bohemia and Moravia etwa Czechoslovakia; **Tschechien** (n); -s; Geog. Czech Republic, Czechia; **Tschechin** f; -, -nen Czech, Czech woman (od. girl etc.); **tschechisch** Adj. Czech; **die Tschechische Republik** the Czech Republic; **Tschechisch** n; -en; Ling. Czech; **das ~e** Czech

Tschechoslowakei f; -; hist. Geog. Czechoslovakia; **tschechoslowakisch** Adj. hist. Czechoslovak, Czechoslovakian

Tschetnik m; -s, -s; Pol. Chetnik

Tschetschenien (n); -s; Geog. Chechnya; **tschetschenisch** Adj. Chechen

tschüs Interj. umg. bye, see you

Tsetsefliege f Zool. tsetse fly

T-Shirt [ti:ʃɔːt] n; -s, -s T-shirt, tee-shirt

TSV m; -s, -s; Abk. (Turn- und Sportverein) bes. in Namen: **~ Ulm** etwa Ulm Sports Club

T-Träger m Tech. T-beam, T-girder

TU f; -, -s; Abk. (Technische Universität) → technisch I 1; **~ Berlin** Berlin Technical University

Tuba f; -, Tuben 1. Mus. tuba; 2. Anat. → Tube 2

Tube f; -, -n 1. tube; **e-e ~ Zahnpasta** a tube of toothpaste; **auf die ~ drücken** umg. fig. step on it; 2. Anat. Eustachian tube; (Eileiter) Fallopian tube

Tuberkel m; -s, -; Med. tubercle; **~bakterien** Pl. Med. tubercle bacilli

Tuberkulin n; -s, -e; Med. tuberculin; **~test** m Med. tuberculin test

tuberkulös Adj. Med. tubercular

Tuberkulose f; -, -n; Med. tuberculosis; **offene/geschlossene ~** tuberculosis disease/infection; siehe auch Tb(c)...; **tuberkulosefrei** Adj. tuberculosis-free; **Tuberkulosekranke** m, f TB (od. tuberculosis) patient (od. case)

Tuch n; -(e)s, Tücher und -e 1. Pl. Tücher cloth; (Hals-, Kopftuch) scarf; (Laken etc.) sheet; (Handtuch) towel; **das rote ~ Stierkampf**: the red cape; **das ist ein rotes ~ für ihn** it's like a red rag to a bull (for him); **in trockenen Tüchern sein** fig., Geschäft, Vertrag etc.: be wrapped up; be signed, sealed and delivered; 2. Pl. Tuche; (Stoff) cloth; (Segeltuch) canvas

Tuch|fabrik f cloth factory; **~fühlung** f close contact; **auf ~** shoulder to shoulder; **~ haben mit** fig. be in close contact with, be rubbing shoulders with; **~handel** m cloth trade; **~macher** m, **~macherin** f clothworker; **~mantel** m fabric coat

tüchtig I. Adj. 1. (fähig) capable, able, competent; (fleißig) hard-working; (leistungsfähig) efficient; **~er Arbeiter** auch good worker; **~ in** (+ Dat.) good at (+ Ger.); (sehr) **~ im Beruf sein** be (very) good at one's job; 2. (ausgezeichnet) excellent; 3. umg. (groß, stark) good; (anständig) decent; **e-e ~e Tracht Prügel** a good hiding; **ein ~er Schrecken** a real fright; **ein ~er Esser** a good (od. big) eater; **e-n ~en Appetit haben** be really hungry; **II.** Adv. umg.: **~ schneien** snow hard; **~ arbeiten** work hard; **~ zulangen** tuck in, dig in; **~ essen** od. **trinken** put away a fair (od. decent) amount; **sich ~ ärgern** be (od. get) really annoyed; **Tüchtigkeit** f ability, competence; efficiency; (Fleiß) diligence

Tücke f; -, -n 1. (Boshaftigkeit) spite, maliciousness, malice; (Hinterlist) deceit; stärker: insidiousness; **er ist voller ~** (Arglist) you've got to watch him; → **List**; 2. (heimtückische Handlung) wile; Pl. auch trickery Sg.; 3. (verborgener Defekt) hidden weakness; (Gefahr) hidden danger; **es hat so s-e ~n** umg. it's not as easy as it looks; Gerät etc.: it's a bit tricky (to handle); **die ~ des Objekts** umg. the perverse nature of inanimate objects

tuckern v/i. 1. (hat getuckert) Motor etc.: put-put; 2. (ist) (fahren) chug (along)

tückisch Adj. malicious, spiteful; (heimtückisch) insidious (auch Krankheit, Gefahr etc.); (gefährlich) dangerous, treacherous

tüdelig Adj. bes. nordd. umg. doddery

Tuff m; -s, -e; Geol. tuff; **~stein** m 1. tufa; 2. nur Sg. (Tuff) tuff

Tüftelarbeit f, **Tüftelei** f; -, -en; umg. 1. nur Sg. fiddly work; 2. a fiddly job (od. business); (auch Denkarbeit) tricky work, a tricky business (od. problem); **tüftelig** Adj. umg. 1. fiddly; auch Denkarbeit: tricky; 2. Person: (genau) very exact; (pedantisch) fussy; **tüfteln** v/i.: **an etw.** (Dat.) **~** fiddle about with, tinker with; (e-r Denkaufgabe) try to work (od. puzzle) out, stärker: rack one's brains over; **Tüftler** m; -s, -, **Tüftlerin** f; -, -nen; umg. tinkerer; **er ist ein Tüftler** auch he likes to fiddle around with things

Tugend f; -, -en 1. (Moral) virtue; **auf dem Pfad der ~ wandeln** geh. keep to the straight and narrow; 2. (Eigenschaft) virtue; **m-e ~en und m-e Fehler** my strengths and my weaknesses; → Not 4; **Tugendbold** m; -(e)s, -e; iro. paragon of virtue; **tugendhaft** Adj. oft iro. virtuous; **Tugendhaftigkeit** f oft iro. virtuousness; **Tugendwächter** m, **Tugendwächterin** f iro. moral watchdog

Tukan m; -s, -e; Orn. toucan

Tüll m; -s, fachspr. -e tulle; für Gardinen: net

Tülle f; -, -n; Dial. an Teekanne etc.: spout; Tech. socket

Tüllgardinen Pl. net (od. lace od. sheer) curtains

Tulpe f; -, -n 1. Bot. tulip; 2. (Glas) tulip(-shaped) glass

Tulpen|beet n bed of tulips; **~zwiebel** f tulip bulb

tummeln v/refl. 1. romp around; im Wasser: jump (od. splash) around od. about; 2. Dial. (sich beeilen) hurry up; **wir müssen uns ~** we have to get a move on; **Tummelplatz** m playground; fig. stomping ground (auch Zool.); **~**

für Extremisten etc. auch hotbed of extremism *etc.*

Tümmler *m*; *-s, -* **1.** *Orn.* tumbler; **2.** *Zool.* (*Delphin*) porpoise

Tumor *m*; *-s, -en und umg. -e*; *Med.* tumo(u)r; **~zellen** *Pl. Med.* tumo(u)r (*od.* cancer) cells

Tümpel *m*; *-s, -* pond; *kleiner*: puddle

Tumult *m*; *-(e)s, -e* tumult, *stärker*: riot; *lärmend*: commotion, uproar; *für ~ sorgen* cause a riot; *im ~ untergehen Worte etc.*: be drowned out by the uproar; *es kam zu schweren ~en* there was heavy rioting; **tumultartig** *Adj.* riotous; **~e Ausschreitungen** near-rioting; **~e Szenen** scenes of uproar (*stärker*: rioting); *im Parlament etc.*: tumultuous scenes

tun; *tut, tat, hat getan* **I.** *v/t.* **1.** do; *was tust du da?* what are you doing?; *tu endlich was!* come on, do something!; *etw. ~ gegen* do s.th. about *s.th.*; *Dienst ~* serve; *s-e Arbeit ~* do one's job; *Wunder ~* work miracles; *was ist zu ~?* what is there to be done?, what's on the agenda? *umg.*: *was noch zu ~ bleibt, ...* what remains to be done ...; *man tut, was man kann umg.* you do what you can; *was tut man nicht alles* the things I do for them *etc.*; *viel/nichts zu ~ haben* have lots/nothing to do; *ich hab' noch zu ~* I'm busy, I've still got a few things to do; *ich hab' sowieso in der Stadt zu ~* I'm going to be in town anyway, I've got other things to do in town; *er hat mit sich selbst genug zu ~* he's got enough on his plate as it is; *darunter tu ich's nicht umg.* I'll not do it for less; *damit ist es nicht getan* that's not all there is to it, there's more to it than that; *das tut man nicht!* you don't do things like that, that (just) isn't done; *er kann ~ und lassen, was er will* he can do whatever he likes; *tu, was du nicht lassen kannst umg.* well, I can't stop you; well, if you (really) must; *das tut nichts zur Sache* that's got nothing to do with it; *(das) tut nichts umg.* (it) doesn't matter; *es ~ euph.* (*Geschlechtsverkehr haben*) do it; → *auch machen*; **2.** *statt Verb in nominalen Ausdrücken*: *e-e Äußerung ~* make a remark; *e-n Sprung ~* jump; *s-e Wirkung ~* have its effect; *auf einmal tat es e-n furchtbaren Knall* suddenly there was a terrible bang; **3.** *umg.* (*hin~*) put; *Salz in die Suppe ~* add salt to the soup; *tut alles wieder dahin, wo es hingehört!* put everything back where it belongs!; *j-n in ein Heim etc. ~* put s.o. in a home *etc.*; **4.** (*wehtun, verletzen*): *j-m etwas ~* do something to s.o., hurt s.o.; *ich tu dir nichts* I won't hurt you; *was hat er dir getan?* what did he do (to you)?; *ich habe ihm nichts getan* I didn't do anything (to him), I didn't touch him; *er wird dir schon nichts ~! umg.* he won't bite you; *hast du dir was getan?* did you hurt yourself?, are you all right?; *der Hund tut nichts* the dog doesn't bite; **5.** *umg.*: *ein Messer tut's auch* a knife will do; *der Anzug tut's noch ein paar Jahre* there's a few more years' wear in that suit; *das Radio tut's nicht (mehr richtig)* the radio doesn't work (properly anymore); **6.** *fig.*: *was hat das damit zu ~?* what's that got to do with it?; *das hat damit nichts zu ~* that's (got) nothing to do with it; *es zu ~ haben mit* be dealing with, find o.s. up against; *es mit dem*

Herzen zu ~ haben umg. have a problem with one's heart; *sonst kriegst du es mit mir zu ~ umg.* or else you'll be in trouble with me; *ich will damit / mit ihm nichts (mehr) zu ~ haben* I don't want to have anything to do with it/him (anymore); *und was habe ich damit zu ~?* and where do I come in(to it)?; → *getan, Leid* 2; **II.** *v/i.* **1.** *so ~, als ob* pretend to (+ *Inf.*) (*od.* that ...); *er tut nur so* he's only pretending, he's putting it on; *tu doch nicht so! umg.* stop pretending, who are you trying to kid; (*übertreib nicht!*) stop exaggerating, stop making such a fuss; *höflich etc. ~* act polite *etc.*; **2.** *du tätest gut daran, jetzt zu gehen* it might be a good idea if you went now; *er tut gut daran, den Mund zu halten* he would do well to keep his mouth shut; → *gut* II 1; **3.** *unpers. umg.*: *es tut sich was* things are happening; (*es rührt sich was*) I can hear stirrings; *es tut sich (überhaupt) nichts* there's nothing happening (at all)

Tun *n*; *-s, kein Pl.*; (*auch ~ und Lassen*) activities *Pl.*, movements *Pl.*, action(s *Pl.*); (*Verhalten*) behavio(u)r; *die Folgen s-s ~s* the consequences of his actions

Tünche *f*; *-, -n* **1.** whitewash; **2.** *nur Sg.*; *fig.*: *es ist nur ~* it's just a veneer, it's just for show; **tünchen** *v/t.* whitewash

Tundra *f*; *-, Tundren*; *Geog.* tundra

tunen ['tjuːnən] *v/t. Mot.* tune (up); **Tuner** ['tjuːnɐ] *m*; *-s, -*; *Etron.* tuner

Tunesien (*n*); *-s*; *Geog.* Tunisia; **Tunesier** *m*, **Tunesierin** *f*; *-, -nen* Tunisian, *weiblich auch*: Tunisian woman (*od.* girl *etc.*); **tunesisch** *Adj.* Tunisian

Tunichtgut *m*; *-(e)s, -e*; *altm. umg.* good-for-nothing

Tunika *f*; *-, Tuniken*; *hist.* tunic; (*Kleid*) tunic

Tuning ['tjuːnɪŋ] *n*; *-s, kein Pl.*; *Mot.* tuning

Tunke *f*; *-, -n*; *Gastr.* sauce; (*Bratensoße*) gravy; **tunken** *v/t. Dial.* dip

tunlichst *Adv.* (*möglichst*) if at all possible, as far as possible; (*unbedingt*) at all costs; *er sollte Fette ~ vermeiden* he is urged to avoid all fats; *das wirst du ~ bleiben lassen umg.* you won't do anything of the sort

Tunnel *m*; *-s, -* tunnel; **~bau** *m nur Sg.* tunnel construction; *Arbeiten*: work on a (*od.* the) tunnel; **~brand** *m* tunnel fire, fire in a (*od.* the) tunnel; **~katastrophe** *f* tunnel disaster; **~röhre** *f* tunnel pipe; **~schacht** *m* tunnel shaft

Tunte *f*; *-, -n*; *pej.* **1.** (*Frau*) woman, female; **2.** (*Homosexueller*) fairy, pansy; **Tuntenball** *m umg.* drag queens' ball; **tuntenhaft, tuntig** *Adj. pej.* **1.** womanly; **2.** (*wie ein Homosexueller*) camp

Tüpfelchen *n* dot; *das ~ auf dem i fig.* the icing on the cake; *im neg. Sinn*: the last straw

tüpfeln *v/t.* dot, spot; → *getüpfelt*

tupfen I. *v/t.* **1.** (*mit Tupfen versehen*) dot; *siehe auch getupft, getüpfelt*; **2.** (*Wunde etc.*) dab; *Creme etc. ~ auf* (+ *Akk.*) dab on; *sich* (*Dat.*) *den Schweiß vom Gesicht ~* mop the sweat off one's face; **II.** *v/i.*: *j-m auf die Schulter etc. ~* tap s.o. on the shoulder *etc.*

Tupfen *m*; *-s, -* dot, *größer*: spot

Tupfer *m*; *-s, -* **1.** *Med.* swab; **2.** (*Tüpfel*) dot, *größer*: spot; *die Feier bekommt*

dadurch e-n farbigen ~ fig. it gives the party a bit of colo(u)r

Tür *f*; *-, -en* **1.** door; *in der ~* in the door(way); *vor der ~* at the door; *~ an ~ wohnen* live next door to each other; *er wohnt e-e ~ weiter* he lives next door (*od.* in the next house, flat, apartment *etc.*); *von ~ zu ~ gehen* go from door to door; *an die ~ gehen* answer the door; *kannst du mal an die ~ gehen? auch* can you get the door?; *da ist die ~! umg.* you know the way out; *mach die ~ von außen zu! umg.* don't forget to shut the door behind you; *ich komme überhaupt nicht vor die ~* I'm stuck in the house (*od.* flat *etc.*) all day long, I never get out; *ich bin gerade zur ~ rein* I just got in this minute; *j-m die ~ vor der Nase zuschlagen auch fig.* shut the door in s.o.'s face; *Tag der offenen ~* open day (*Am.* house); **2.** *fig.*: *Weihnachten steht vor der ~* Christmas is just around the corner; *e-r Sache ~ und Tor öffnen* give free reign to; *die ~ für Verhandlungen offen halten* keep an open door for negotiations; *mit der ~ ins Haus fallen umg.* blurt it out; *j-n vor die ~ setzen umg.* turn (*od.* throw) s.o. out; *zwischen ~ und Angel umg.* in a hurry, (just) as he was (they were *etc.*) leaving; *du kriegst die ~ nicht zu! umg.* goodness me!, well I never!; → *einrennen, verschlossen* II 1, *weisen* I 1

Türangel *f* (door) hinge

Turban *m*; *-s, -e* turban

Turbine *f*; *-, -n*; *Tech.* turbine

Turbinen|antrieb *m Tech.* turbine propulsion; **~flugzeug** *n* turbojet (aircraft); **~haus** *n* turbine house; **~triebwerk** *n* jet turbine engine

Turbo *m*; *-s, -s*; *Mot.* **1.** (*Turbolader*) turbocharger; **2.** (*Auto*) turbo; **~diesel** *m* turbo diesel; **~generator** *m* turbo-generator; **~lader** *m*; *-s, -* turbocharger; **~motor** *m* turboengine

Turbo-Prop-Flugzeug *n Flug.* turboprop (aircraft)

turbulent I. *Adj.* turbulent, hectic; **II.** *Adv.*: *es ging ~ zu* things got quite hectic (*od.* heated); **Turbulenz** *f*; *-, -en*; *auch Pl.* turbulence (*auch Phys.*)

Türdrücker *m* **1.** door opener; **2.** (*Klinke*) door handle

...türer *m*; *-s, -*; *im Subst.*; *Mot.*: *Zwei-/Vier~* two-/four-door

Turf *m*; *-s, kein Pl.*; (*Pferderennbahn*) turf

Tür|falle *f schw.* door handle; **~flügel** *m* (lefthand/righthand) door (*in a pair of doors*); **~füllung** *f* door panel; **~griff** *m* door handle; **~heber** *m metal device that automatically lifts a door slightly on opening*

...türig *im Adj.*: *zwei~es/vier~es Modell* two-/four-door model

Türke *m*; *-n, -n* **1.** Turk; *er ist ~ auch* he is Turkish; **2.** *umg. neg.!*: *e-n ~n bauen* pretend, fake; *die Szene war ein ~* the scene was faked; **3.** *umg.* Turkish restaurant; *zum ~n gehen* go to a Turkish place; **Türkei** *f*; *-*; *Geog.* Turkey; *in/aus der ~* in/from Turkey; **türken** *v/t. umg. neg.!* (*Papiere etc.*) fake; (*Zahlen etc.*) fiddle

Türken|koffer *m umg. neg!* (*Plastiktüte*) plastic bag; **~taube** *f Orn.* collared dove

Turkey ['tøːɐki] *m*; *-s, -s*; *Sl.*: *auf ~ sein/kommen* be in / go into cold turkey

Türkin *f*; *-, -nen* Turk(ish woman *od.*

girl); **sie ist** ~ *auch* she is Turkish

Türkis *m*; *-es*, *-e*; *Min.* turquoise; **türkis** *indekl. Adj.* turquoise; **türkisblau**, **türkisfarben**, **türkisfarbig** *Adj.* turquoise

türkisch *Adj.* Turkish; ~*er Honig* nougat; ~*es Bad* Turkish bath; **Türkisch** *n*; *-(s)*; *Ling.* Turkish; *das* ~*e* Turkish

türkischsprachig *Adj.* (*in türkischer Sprache*) Turkish, Turkish-language; (*Türkisch sprechend*) Turkish-speaking

Tür|klingel *f* doorbell; ~**klinke** *f* door handle; ~**klopfer** *m* knocker

Turkmene *m*; *-n*, *-n* Turkmen (*Pl.* Turkmen[s]), Turkoman (*Pl.* Turkomans); **Turkmenien** (*n*); *-s*; *Geog.* Turkmenistan; **Turkmenin** *f*; *-*, *-nen* Turkmenian woman (*od.* girl *etc.*); **turkmenisch** *Adj.* Turkmenian; **Turkmenistan** (*n*); *-s*; *Geog.* Turkmenistan

Türknauf *m* doorknob

Turk|sprache *f Ling.* Turkic language; ~**volk** *n* Turkic people

Turm *m*; *-(e)s*, *Türme* tower (*auch fig.*); (*Kirchturm*) *auch* steeple; (*Sprungturm*) diving tower; *Schach*: castle, rook

Turmalin *m*; *-s*, *-e*; *Min.* tourmaline

Turmbau *m*: *der* ~ *zu Babel bibl.* (the building of) the Tower of Babel

Türmchen *n* turret

türmen I. *v/t.* pile (up); **II.** *v/refl.* pile up; *auf s-m Schreibtisch* ~ *sich die Akten umg.* the files are piled up on his desk; **III.** *v/i. umg.* (*ausreißen*) bolt, scarper, do a bunk

Türmer *m*; *-s*, *-*, ~**in** *f*; *-*, *-nen*; *bes. hist.* tower keeper

Turm|falke *m Orn.* kestrel; ~**haube** *f Archit.* cupola

turmhoch I. *Adj.* huge, towering; **II.** *Adv.*: *j-m* ~ *überlegen sein fig.* be head and shoulders above s.o.

Turm|spitze *f* spire; ~**springen** *n* high diving; ~**uhr** *f* tower clock, clock (*in a tower*); *in Kirchturm*: church clock; ~**zimmer** *n* tower room

Turn|anzug *m* gym (*od.* PE) outfit; ~**beutel** *m* gym (*od.* PE) bag

turnen I. *vt/i.* (*hat geturnt*) do gymnastics (*auch am Gerät*); *in der Schule*: *auch* do PE (= physical education), do gym; *e-e Übung am Barren etc.* ~ do (*od.* perform) an exercise on the parallel bars *etc.*; **II.** *v/i.* (*ist*) *umg.*: *über die Mauer / durch die Bäume* ~ clamber over the wall / bound through the trees

Turnen *n*; *-s*, *kein Pl.* gymnastics *Pl.* (*V. im Sg.*); *in der Schule*: PE (= physical education), gym

Turner *m*; *-s*, *-* gymnast

Turnerei *f*; *-*, *kein Pl.*; *umg.* (*Turnen*) gymnastics *Pl.* (*V. im Sg.*); (*waghalsige Kletterei*) acrobatics *Pl.*

Turnerin *f*; *-*, *-nen* gymnast

turnerisch I. *Adj. Können, Übung etc.*: gymnastic; **II.** *Adv. begabt etc.*: gymnastically; *ihre Übung war* ~ *hervorragend* her exercise was an excellent piece of gynmastics

Turn|fest *n engS.* gymnastics festival; *weitS.* keep-fit (*Am.* fitness) festival; *e-r Schule*: sports day; ~**gerät** *n* (piece of) gymnastics apparatus; ~**halle** *f* gymnasium, gym; ~**hemd** *n* gym shirt (*od.* top); ~**hose** *f*: (*e-e*) ~ (a pair of) gym shorts *Pl.*

Turnier *n*; *-s*, *-e* **1.** tournament; **2.** *hist.* (jousting) tournament; ~**mannschaft** *f*: *e-e gute* ~ a team that performs particularly well in tournaments; ~**pferd** *n* show horse; ~**platz** *m* tournament

venue; ~**reiter** *m*, ~**reiterin** *f* show jumper; ~**sieg** *m* tournament win; ~**sieger** *m*, ~**siegerin** *f* winner of a (*od.* the) tournament; ~**tanz** *m* **1.** *nur Sg.* ballroom dancing; **2.** (*zugelassener Tanz*) ballroom dance (*permitted in competition*); ~**tänzer** *m*, ~**tänzerin** *f* ballroom dancer; ~**teilnehmer** *m*, ~**teilnehmerin** *f* participant in a (*od.* the) tournament

Turnlehrer *m*, ~**in** *f* gym instructor (*od.* teacher); *in der Schule*: PE (= physical education) teacher

Turnschuh *m* trainer, *Am.* sneaker; *ich bin fit wie ein* ~ *umg.* (*sehr fit*) I'm incredibly fit; ~**generation** *f nur Sg.*; *umg.* 80s youth

Turn|stunde *f* gym lesson, PE (= physical education) lesson; ~**übung** *f* (gymnastic) exercise; ~ **und Sportverein** *m* (*abgek. TSV*) sports club; ~**unterricht** *m* PE (= physical education) lesson(s *Pl.*)

Turnus *m*; *-*, *-se* rota, *Am.* roster; *im* ~ → *turnusmäßig* II; *im* ~ *von drei Wochen* every three weeks; **turnusmäßig I.** *Adj.* rotational; *im* ~*en Wechsel* in rotation; **II.** *Adv.* in rotation, by turns; *Personal* ~ *auswechseln* rotate

Turn|vater *m*: ~ *Jahn hist.* Friedrich Jahn, the "father of gynmastics"; ~**verein** *m* (*abgek. TV*) gymnastics club; ~**zeug** *n umg.* gym kit, gym things *Pl.*

Tür|öffner *m* door opener; ~**pfosten** *m* doorpost; ~**rahmen** *m* doorframe; ~**schild** *n* doorplate; ~**schloss** *n* lock; ~**schwelle** *f* threshold; ~**spalt** *m* crack (of a *od.* the door); ~**steher** *m vor Bar etc.*: bouncer; ~**stock** *m südd.*, *österr.* doorframe; ~**sturz** *m Pl. -e und -stürze*; *Archit.* lintel

turteln *v/i. umg.* bill and coo

Turteltaube *f* turtledove; *umg. fig. Pl.* lovey-doveys

Tusch *m*; *-(e)s*, *-e* flourish; *e-n kräftigen* ~ *spielen* play a great fanfare

Tusche *f*; *-*, *-n* Indian ink; (*Wasserfarbe*) watercolo(u)r

Tuschelei *f*; *-*, *-en*; *oft pej.* whispering (behind *s.o.'s* back); **tuscheln** *vt/i.* whisper (behind *s.o.'s* back); *über die beiden wird getuschelt* people are whispering about them (behind their backs)

tuschen *vt/i.* draw in Indian ink; *mit Farben*: paint in watercolo(u)rs; *sich* (*Dat.*) *die Wimpern* ~ put some (*od.* one's) mascara on

Tusch|kasten *m* paintbox; ~**malerei** *f japanische etc.*: ink painting; ~**zeichnung** *f* India(n) ink drawing

Tussi *f*; *-*, *-s*; *Sl.* **1.** *pej.* bird, chick, girlie; *geile* ~ (*begierig auf Sex*) tart, slapper, *Am.* nympho; (*attraktiv*) tasty bird; **2.** (*Freundin*) bird, *Am.* squeeze

tut [tuːt] *Interj. Kinderspr.* beep-beep!, toot-toot!

Tüte *f*; *-*, *-n* **1.** (paper) bag; (*Plastiktüte*) plastic bag; (*Spucktüte*) sick bag; ~*n kleben umg.* (*im Gefängnis sitzen*) be behind bars, be doing time; *kommt nicht in die* ~*! umg.* no way; *angeben wie e-e* ~ *voll Mücken umg.* blow one's own trumpet; **2.** (*Eiswaffel*) (ice-cream) cone; **3.** *umg.*: *in die* ~ *blasen müssen* be breathalyzed, *Am.* get a breath test; **4.**; **5.** *umg. mst pej.* (*Person*): *du* ~*!* you sod (*Am.* jerk)!

tuten *v/i.* toot, honk, blow one's horn; *der Dampfer tutete dreimal* the steamer sounded its horn three times; → *Ahnung* 2

Tutor *m*; *-s*, *-en*, ~**in** *f*; *-*, *-nen*; *Univ. etc.*: (*Leiter von Tutorien*) tutor; (*Betreuer von Studienanfängern*) tutor, older student in a student hall who helps introduce new students to college life;

Tutorium *n*; *-s*, *Tutorien*; *Univ. etc.*: tutorial (*held by a graduate student*)

TÜV [tʏf] *m*; *-s*, *kein Pl.* (**Technischer Überwachungs-Verein**) safety standards authority; *ich muss zum* ~ *umg. etwa* my MOT's due, *Am.* my car's up for an inspection; (*nicht*) *durch den* ~ *kommen etwa* get through (fail) one's MOT (*Am.* safety inspection); *ein Auto durch/über den* ~ *bringen* get a car through its MOT (*Am.* safety inspection); *etw. vom* ~ *abnehmen lassen* (*Aufzug etc.*) have s.th. approved by the safety standards authority; **TÜV-geprüft** *Adj.* safety-tested; **TÜV-Plakette** *f* disc displayed on number plate showing the vehicle has passed its MOT (*Am.* safety inspection)

TV[1] *m*; *-s*, *kein Pl.*; *Abk.* → **Turnverein**

TV[2] *n*; *-*, *kein Pl.*; *Abk.* (**Television**) TV; **TV-Gerät** *n* TV set

Tweed [tviːt] *m*; *-s*, *-s und -e*; (*Stoff*) tweed

Twen *m*; *-(s)*, *-s*; *altm.* person in his (*od.* her) twenties, twenty-something *umg.*

Twill *m*; *-s*, *-s und -e*; (*Stoff*) twill

Twist[1] *m*; *-(e)s*, *-e*; (*Garn*) twist

Twist[2] *m*; *-s*, *-s* **1.** (*Tanz*) twist; ~ *tanzen* → *twisten*; **2.** *nur Sg.*; *Tennis etc.*: (*Drall*) spin; *ein mit* ~ *geschlagener Ball* a ball hit with spin; **3.** *Turnen*: (*Schraube*) twist; **twisten** *v/i.* (*Twist tanzen*) twist, do (*od.* dance) the twist

Tympanon *n*; *-s*, *Tympana* **1.** *Archit.* tympanum (*Pl.* tympanums *od.* tympana); **2.** *Mus.* tympan

Typ *m*; *-s*, *umg. auch* *-en*, *-en* **1.** type; *Tech. auch* model; *ein Kampfflugzeug vom* ~ *F117* an F117 fighter plane; **2.** (*Art Mensch*) type; *ein ruhiger etc.* ~ *auch* a quiet *etc.* sort of person; *ein dufter/kaputter* ~ *umg.* a smashing (*Am.* great) person / a wreck; *er ist nicht der richtige* ~ he's not the right sort of person (for the job *etc.*); *er/sie ist nicht mein* ~ he's/she's not my type; *dein* ~ *wird verlangt umg.* you're wanted; *dein* ~ *ist hier nicht gefragt umg.* we don't want your sort ([a]round) here; **3.** *umg.* (*Mann*) guy, bloke, *Am.* dude; (*Freund*) bloke, *Am.* guy; *was will der* ~*?* what does that guy want?; *solche* ~*en können mir gestohlen bleiben* guys like that can get lost

Type *f*; *-*, *-n* **1.** *Druck. und Schreibmaschine*: type; **2.** *umg.* (*Kauz*) character; *e-e komische* ~ a strange character; → *auch Typ* 2, 3

Typen|bezeichnung *f Tech.* type designation; ~**lehre** *f bes. Psych.* typology

Typenrad *n* daisy wheel; ~**schreibmaschine** *f* daisy-wheel typewriter

Typen|satz *m Druck.* typesetting; ~**schild** *n Tech.* identification plate

Typhus *m*; *-*, *kein Pl.*; *Med.* typhoid; ~**epidemie** *f* typhoid epidemic; ~**erkrankung** *f* typhoid; ~**kranke** *m*, *f* typhoid patient (*od.* case)

typisch I. *Adj.* typical (*für* of); *ein* ~*es Beispiel auch* a classic example; ~*e Symptome* classic symptoms; *das ist wieder mal* ~ *umg.* that's just typical(, isn't it); **II.** *Adv.*: ~ *englisch!* that's typically English, that's the English for you *umg.*; *das ist* ~ *Bernd umg.* that's just like Bernd, that's Bernd all over; **~ Mann/Frau!** *umg.* typical male/female!, that's just typical of a man/woman; **typischerweise** *Adv.* typically

typisieren *v/t.* typify; *Tech.* standardize; **Typisierung** *f* typification; *Tech.* standardization

Typographie *f*; -, -*n*; *Druck.* **1.** *nur Sg.* typography; **2.** (*Gestaltung*) typography; **typographisch I.** *Adj.* typographic(al); **II.** *Adv.* typographically

Typologie *f*; -, -*n* typology; **typologisch** *Adj.* typological

Typus *m*; -, *Typen* type; → **Typ** 1, 2

Tyrann *m*; -*en*, -*en* tyrant (*auch fig.*), despot; **m-e Tochter ist ein kleiner ~** *umg.* my daughter is a little tyrant; **Tyrannei** *f*; -, *kein Pl.* tyranny, despotism; **von der ~ befreien** free from tyranny; **Tyrannenherrschaft** *f* tyranny, despotic rule; **Tyrannenmord** *m* ty-

rannicide; **tyrannisch** *Adj.* tyrannical, despotic; (*herrschsüchtig*) domineering; **tyrannisieren** *v/t.* tyrannize, oppress; *fig.* tyrannize, bully *s.o.*

Tyrannosaurus *m*; -, *Tyrannosaurier*; *Zool.* tyrannosaurus; **Tyrannosaurus Rex** *m*; - -, *kein Pl.* tyrannosaurus rex, T rex *umg.*

Tyrrhenisch *Adj. Geog.*: **das ~e Meer** the Tyrrhenian Sea

U, u *n*; -, - *und umg.* -*s* U, u; *U wie Ul-rich Buchstabieren*: "u" for (*od.* as in) "Uniform"

Ü, ü *n*; -, - *und umg.* -*s* u umlaut, ue

u.a. *Abk.* I. (*und andere[s]*) and others, *Sachen*: and other things; II. (*unter anderem od. anderen*) among other things, *Personen*: among others

u. A. w. g., U. A. w. g. *Abk.* (*um Antwort wird gebeten*) RSVP, R.S.V.P.

U-Bahn *f* underground; *in London*: *auch* the tube; *Am.* subway; *in Washington etc.*: metro; (*Zug*) underground train; *in London*: *auch.* tube train; *Am.* subway train; *mit der ~ fahren* go by (*od.* take) the underground *etc.*; ~-Haltestelle *f* underground (*in London*: *auch* tube, *Am.* subway) stop

U-Bahnhof *m* underground (*in London*: *auch* tube, *Am.* subway) station

U-Bahn|-Netz *n* underground (*Am.* subway) system; ~-Schacht *m* underground (*Am.* subway) shaft; ~-Station *f* underground station; *in London*: *auch* tube station; *Am.* subway station; ~-Wagen *m* underground carriage; *Am.* subway car

übel I. *Adj.* 1. (*schlimm*) *Ruf etc.*: bad; (*scheußlich*) horrible, nasty; (*gemein*) *Kerl, Trick etc.*: nasty; (*moralisch verwerflich*) unsavo(u)ry; *üble Geschäfte* shady dealings; *er ist kein übler Kerl umg.* he's all right; *übles Schimpfwort* horrible swearword; → *Nachrede*; 2. (*unangenehm*) unpleasant; (*gemein*) nasty; *ich bin in e-e üble Sache hineingeschlittert* I stumbled into a nasty situation; *nicht ~ umg.* not bad; *kein übler Gedanke umg.* not a bad idea; 3. (*stinkend*) foul (*auch umg. Wetter*); *Geruch, Geschmack auch*: awful; 4. *mir ist ~* I feel sick; *dabei kann einem ~ werden* it's enough to make you sick; II. *Adv.* 1. (*schlecht, unangenehm*) badly; *~ riechen* smell (awful), stink; *~ riechend* foul smelling; *Atem*: foul; *das riecht/schmeckt gar nicht ~* it doesn't smell/taste at all bad; 2. *fig.* (*schlecht, schlimm*) badly; *j-n auf ~ste Weise beschimpfen* insult s.o. in a very unpleasant way; *es ging ~ aus* it turned out badly; *~ dran sein umg.* be in a bad way; *~ gelaunt längere Zeit*: bad-tempered, grumpy *umg.*; *vorübergehend*: *auch* in a bad (*stärker*: foul) mood; *~ gesinnt* ill-disposed (+ *Dat.* toward[s]); *das klingt nicht ~ umg.* that's not a bad idea; *ich hätte nicht ~ Lust ihn anzuzeigen etc. umg.* I have a good mind to report *etc.* him; 3. (*negativ, nachteilig*) badly; *etw. ~ nehmen* take *s.th.* amiss, take offen|ce (*Am.* -se) at; *j-m etw. ~ nehmen längerfristig*: hold *s.th.* against s.o.; *du nimmst es mir doch nicht ~, oder?* you're not offended, are you?; *j-m ~ wollen* be ill-disposed toward(s) s.o.; (*j-m schaden wollen*) be out to harm s.o., have it in for s.o. *umg.*; → *mitspielen* I 5,

vermerken 2, *wohl*[1] 2, *zurichten* 2

Übel *n*; -*s*, - evil; (*Missstand*) *the* trouble; (*Leiden*) complaint; *die ~ des Kapitalismus etc.* the evils of capitalism *etc.*; *ein schlimmes ~ Drogenmissbrauch etc.* a scourge; *notwendiges ~* necessary evil; *das kleinere ~* the lesser of the two evils; *die Wurzel allen ~s* the root of all evil; *das ~ an der Wurzel packen* tackle the root of the problem; *der Grund od. die Ursache des ganzen ~s* the root cause of all the trouble; *von ~* no good; *zu allem ~* to top it all; *erlöse uns von dem ~* deliver us from evil; → *doppelt* I

übel| gelaunt, ~ gesinnt → übel II 2

Übelkeit *f* feeling of sickness, sick feeling, nausea; *e-e plötzliche ~ verspüren* suddenly feel sick (*od.* nauseous)

übellaunig *Adj.* (*übel gelaunt*) → übel II 2; Übellaunigkeit *f* bad-temperedness, grumpiness *umg.*

übel nehmen → übel II 3

übel riechend → übel II 1

Übeltat *f iro.* misdeed; Übeltäter *m*, Übeltäterin *f* malefactor; (*Verbrecher*) *auch* perpetrator (of the crime); *iro.* miscreant

übel wollen → übel II 3

üben *vt/i. Mus., Sport etc.*: practi|se (*Am.* -ce); *Mil.* drill; (*schulen*) train; *Geige etc.* ~ practi|se (*Am.* -ce) the violin *etc.*; *fleißig* ~ practi|se (*Am.* -ce) hard; (*sich in*) *Geduld* ~ exercise (a bit of) patience; *du musst dich in Geduld ~ auch* you'll just have to be patient; *Rache* ~ take revenge; → *Kritik* 1, *Nachsicht etc.*

über I. *Präp.* 1. *räumlich*: over, above; (*höher als*) *auch* higher than; (*~ … hinaus*) beyond; *sie wohnt ~ uns* she lives (on the floor) above us; *~ der Stadt tobte ein Gewitter* a storm was raging over the town; *~ uns nichts als blauer Himmel* nothing above us but blue sky; *er stand bis ~ die Knöchel im Schlamm* the mud came up past his ankles; *j-m stehen fig.* (*überlegen sein*) be above s.o. (*auch beruflich*); *~ den Dingen stehen fig.* be above such things; 2. (*quer ~*) across; *~ die Straße gehen* cross the street; *~ den Fluss schwimmen* swim across the river; *j-m über das Haar streichen* stroke s.o.'s hair; *Tränen liefen ihr ~ die Wangen* tears ran down her cheeks; 3. (*in Richtung*) via, through; *~ München nach Rom* to Rome via Munich; *geht der Zug ~ Frankfurt?* does the train go through (*od.* via) Frankfurt?; 4. *bei e-r Tätigkeit etc.*: over; *~ den Büchern sitzen* sit over one's books; *~ der Arbeit / s-r Lektüre einschlafen* fall asleep over one's work / while reading; 5. *~ m-e Kräfte* beyond my strength; *das geht ~ m-n Verstand* it's beyond me, it's above my head; *das geht ihm ~ alles* it means more than anything to him; *es geht nichts ~ …*

there's nothing like …; 6. (*mehr als*) over, more than; *amtlich*: exceeding; *Temperaturen ~ null* above freezing (*od.* zero); *~ 30 Grad* over 30 degrees; *er ist ~ 70 Jahre alt* past (*od.* over) seventy; *man muss ~ 18 (Jahre) sein* you must be over 18; 7. (+ *Akk.*) (*wegen*) over, about; *~ j-n lachen* laugh at / make fun of s.o.; *sich ~ etw. Sorgen machen* worry about s.th.; 8. (+ *Akk.*) (*in Höhe von*): *e-e Rechnung ~ 400 Euro* a bill for 400 euros; 9. (*während*) during, while; *~ Nacht* overnight; *~ das Wochenende* over the weekend; *~ einige Jahre verteilt* spread over several years; *~ kurz oder lang* sooner or later; *~ all dem Gerede habe ich die Kinder ganz vergessen* with all this chatting I completely forgot about the children; 10. (+ *Akk.*) *Thema; nachdenken, sprechen etc.*: about; *Abhandlung, Werk, Vortrag*: on; *~ Geschäfte / den Beruf / Politik reden* talk business/shop/politics; 11. *verstärkend*: *Fehler ~ Fehler* one mistake after the other; *Ärger ~ Ärger* no end of trouble; *er hat Schulden ~ Schulden* he's up to his ears in debt; II. *Adv.*: *~ und ~ all over; die ganze Zeit ~* all along; *den ganzen Tag etc. ~* throughout the day *etc.*; *etw. ~ sein* have had enough of s.th., be sick and tired of s.th.; → *übrig, überhaben etc.*

über…, Über… *im Adj., Subst. etc. mst* over…, hyper…

überall *Adv.* everywhere; *örtlich begrenzt*: *auch* all over the place *umg.*; *~ in der Stadt / an der Wand etc.* all over town / the wall *etc.*; *~ wo* wherever; *er ist ~ tätowiert* he is covered in tattoos; *sie ist ~ beliebt* everyone loves her, she is loved by everybody; *er muss sich ~ einmischen! umg.* he has to interfere in everything; ~her *Adv.*: *von ~* from all around, from all over the place *umg.*; *weitS.* from all four corners of the earth; *Kritik etc.*: from all sides; ~hin *Adv.* everywhere, in all directions, all over the place *umg.*; *weitS.* to the four corners of the earth

überaltert *Adj. Ehrbegriffe etc.*: outmoded; *Bevölkerung*: containing too high a percentage of older people; *~ sein Betrieb etc.*: have a high (*od.* too high a) percentage of old people; *der Betrieb ist technisch total ~* the company is using technology that is completely obsolete; Überalterung *f* ag(e)ing; (*Zustand*) *e-s Betriebs etc.*: high percentage of old people; *in technischer Hinsicht*: obsoleteness

Überangebot *n Wirts.* oversupply, glut (*an + Dat.* of); (*Überschuss*) surplus (of); *ein ~ an* (+ *Dat.*) *weitS.* (far) too many (*od.* much) …; *es herrscht ein ~ an …* there are far too many …, there is far too much …; *bei dem ~ weiß man nicht, was man nehmen soll*: with so many things to choose from

überängstlich I. *Adj.* overanxious; *er ist ~ auch* he's always worried (that) something's going to go wrong; **II.** *Adv. reagieren etc.:* overanxiously; **Überängstlichkeit** *f* overanxiousness, hyperanxiety

überanstrengen (*untr.*, *hat*) **I.** *v/t.* overexert, strain; **II.** *v/refl.* overexert o.s., overdo things *umg.*; **Überanstrengung** *f* overexertion, strain

überantworten *v/t.* (*untr.*, *hat*) hand over (+ *Dat.* to); *j-m ~ auch* commit *s.th. od. s.o.* into s.o.'s hands; **Überantwortung** *f* handing over; committal

überarbeiten (*untr.*, *hat*) **I.** *v/t.* rework, go over *s.th.* (again); (*Buch etc.*) revise; *EDV* revise; **II.** *v/refl.* overwork, overdo things *umg.*; **überarbeitet I.** *P.P.* → *überarbeiten*; **II.** *Adj.* **1.** *Person:* overworked; *sie ist ~ auch* she's been doing too much (*od.* overdoing things *umg.*); **2.** *Buch etc.:* revised; **Überarbeitung** *f* **1.** reworking; *e-s Buchs etc.:* revision; **2.** (*Überanstrengung*) overwork; *weitS.* exhaustion

überaus *Adv.* exceedingly, extremely

überbacken¹ *v/t.* (*unreg.*, *untr.*, *hat*) brown; *mit Käse ~* bake with a cheese topping

überbacken² **I.** *P.P.* → *überbacken¹*; **II.** *Adj. Gastr.* au gratin *nachgestellt*

Überbau *m Philos.*, *Archit.* superstructure; **überbauen** *v/t.* (*untr.*, *hat*) build over

überbeanspruchen *v/t.* (*untr.*, *hat*) **1.** (*Person*) overexert, put too great a strain on; (*Augen etc.*) *auch* strain; (*Fantasie etc.*) tax; **2.** *Tech.* overstress; *durch Last:* overload; **Überbeanspruchung** *f* **1.** overexertion, strain; **2.** *Tech.* overstressing; *durch Last:* overloading

Über|begriff *m* umbrella term; **~bein** *n Med.* exostosis (*Pl.* exostoses); (*Knoten*) node

überbekommen *v/t.* (*unreg.*, *trennb.*, *hat*); *umg.* get sick and tired of; *er hat's ~ auch* he's had enough (of it)

überbelasten *v/t.* (*untr.*, *hat*) overload; **Überbelastung** *f* overload(ing)

überbelegen *v/t.* (*untr.*, *hat*) (*Hotel*, *Heim*, *Krankenzimmer etc.*) overcrowd; **überbelegt I.** *P.P.* → *überbelegen*; **II.** *Adj. Hotel*, *Heim*, *Krankenzimmer etc.:* overcrowded; *Kurs:* oversubscribed; **Überbelegung** *f* overcrowding

überbelichtet *Adj.* overexposed; **Überbelichtung** *f* overexposure

Überbeschäftigung *f* overemployment

überbesetzt *Adj.* overstaffed; **Überbesetzung** *f* overmanning, overstaffing

überbetonen *v/t.* (*untr.*, *hat*) overemphasize, overplay; **Überbetonung** *f* overemphasis (+ *Gen.* on)

überbetrieblich *Adj.* extra-company, extra-plant; *in größerem Rahmen:* industry-wide

überbevölkert *Adj.* overpopulated; **Überbevölkerung** *f* overpopulation

überbewerten *v/t.* (*untr.*, *hat*) overrate; **Überbewertung** *f* overrating

überbezahlt *Adj. Person*, *Stelle:* overpaid; *mit 40.000 Euro ist der Wagen klar ~* the car is obviously too expensive (*od.* clearly overpriced) at 40,000 euros

überbietbar *Adj.: nicht od. kaum ~* unsurpassable, the height of …; **überbieten** *v/t.* (*unreg.*, *untr.*, *hat*) outbid; (*Rekord*) break (*um* by); *fig.* outdo;

sich gegenseitig ~ fig. vie with one another (*an* +*Dat.* in); *kaum zu ~* unsurpassed; *e-e kaum zu ~de Frechheit* the height of insolence

Überbiss *m*; *-es*, *-e* overbite

überblättern *v/t.* (*untr.*, *hat*) (*flüchtig durchblättern*) leaf through; (*beim Lesen auslassen*) skip over (*od.* past)

Überbleibsel *n*; *-s*, *-*; *umg.* remnant, *Pl. auch* remains; *e-r Mahlzeit:* leftovers *Pl.*; *fig.* remnant (*aus e-r Zeit:* of, from), holdover (from)

überblenden *v/t.* (*trennb.*, *hat* *-ge*) (cross-)fade, fade over; *~ auf* (+ *Akk.*) *od. zu* fade to, go (*od.* pass) over to

Überblick *m* view; *fig.* overall view, *bes. Am.* overview (*alle auf*, *über +Akk.* of); (*Abriss*) survey; (*Zusammenfassung*) summary, synopsis (*Pl.* synopses); *e-n ~ über etw.* (*Akk.*) *gewinnen fig.* get the general idea of s.th.; *den ~ behalten* keep track; *den ~ verlieren* lose track of things; *den ~ über etw.* (*Akk.*) *verlieren* lose track of s.th.; *ich habe keinen ~ mehr auch* I don't know what's going on any more; *ihm fehlt der ~* he doesn't have an overall picture (*od.* perspective), he lacks an overview; **überblicken** *v/t.* (*untr.*, *hat*) **1.** overlook, have a view of; **2.** *fig.* grasp; → *auch überschauen*; *die Lage ~* have things under control

überborden *v/i.* (*untr.*, *ist*) **1.** *Freude*, *Erregung etc.:* be excessive; *~der Verkehr* excessive amount of traffic; **2.** *bes. schw.:* *der Fluss ist überbordet* the river has burst its banks

überbraten *v/t.* (*unreg.*, *trennb.*, *hat* *-ge*-); *umg.:* *j-m eins ~* give s.o. a wallop

überbreit *Adj. Reifen etc.:* extra wide; **Überbreite** *f* excess width

überbringen *v/t.* (*unreg.*, *untr.*, *hat*) deliver (*j-m etw.* s.th. to s.o.); **Überbringer** *m*; *-s*, *-*; **Überbringerin** *f*; *-*, *-nen* bearer; **Überbringung** *f* delivery

überbrückbar *Adj.* bridgeable; **überbrücken** *v/t.* (*untr.*, *hat*) **1.** *fig.* (*Lücke etc.*) bridge; (*Zeit*) *auch* fill in; (*Gegensätze*) reconcile; *e-e Zeit der Arbeitslosigkeit etc. ~* tide o.s. over during a period of unemployment *etc.*; **2.** *altm.* (*Fluss*, *Schlucht etc.*) bridge, span; **3.** *Etech.* bypass, shunt; **Überbrückung** *f* **1.** *fig.* bridging; *von Gegensätzen:* reconciliation; *hier - als ~ gebe ich dir 200 Euro* here, I'll give you 200 euros to tide you over; **2.** *altm.*, *von Fluss*, *Schlucht etc.:* bridging; **3.** *Etech.* bypass, shunting; (*Überbrückungsdraht*) jumper (wire)

Überbrückungs|geld *n* interim allowance; *~hilfe* *f* temporary (financial) assistance; *~kredit* *m* bridging loan; *~maßnahme* *f* stopgap measure; *~widerstand* *m Etech.* shunt resistor

überbuchen *vt/i.* (*untr.*, *hat*) overbook; **überbucht I.** *P.P.* → *überbuchen*; **II.** *Adj.* overbooked; **Überbuchung** *f* overbooking

überdachen *v/t.* (*untr.*, *hat*) roof over, build a roof over; (*Weg*, *Platz etc.*) cover over; **überdacht I.** *P.P.* → *überdachen*; **II.** *Adj.* covered; **Überdachung** *f* **1.** (*das Überdachen*) roofing over; **2.** (*Dach*) roof

überdauern *v/t.* (*untr.*, *hat*) outlast; (*Krieg etc.*) survive; *die Zeit ~* stand the test of time; *s-e Werke haben ihn überdauert* his works lived on after his death

Überdecke *f* cover; **überdecken** *v/t.* (*untr.*, *hat*) **1.** cover (up); **2.** (*Geruch*,

Geschmack) mask, conceal; (*verhüllen*) obscure; (*Geräusch*) drown out; *der Muskatgeschmack überdeckt alles* you can't taste anything else for the nutmeg

überdehnen *v/t.* (*untr.*, *hat*) overstretch; (*Muskel*) stretch, pull; *einige Szenen wirken überdehnt fig.* some scenes feel to be too long; **Überdehnung** *f* overstretching; *e-s Muskels:* pulling, straining, *konkret:* strain

überdenken *v/t.* (*unreg.*, *untr.*, *hat*) think *s.th.* over; *neu ~* reassess; *etw. noch einmal ~* think s.th. over once more (*od.* again)

überdeutlich I. *Adj.* unmistakable, all too clear; **II.** *Adv.* all too clearly, loud and clear *umg.*; *dabei hab ich's ihm ~ gesagt* although I spelled it out to him (in words of one syllable)

überdies *Adv.* besides, moreover

überdimensional *Adj.* outsize(d), *Am. umg. auch* jumbo; *weitS.* huge; larger--than-life …, *präd.* larger than life; **überdimensioniert** *Adj.* oversized, *Am. umg. auch* jumbo

überdosieren *vt/i.* (*untr.*, *hat*) overdose; *etw. ~ auch* go over the dose (on s.th.); **Überdosis** *f* overdose; *an e-r ~ Heroin sterben* OD on heroin *umg.*

überdrehen *v/t.* (*untr.*, *hat*) (*Uhr*) overwind; (*Motor*) overrev; (*Gewinde*) strip; (*Film*) overcrank; *Sport* (*Sprung*) overrotate; **überdreht I.** *P.P.* → *überdrehen*; **II.** *Adj. umg. fig.* **1.** *Person:* wound up, overexcited; **2.** *Ideen etc.:* eccentric, off-beat

Überdruck *m*; *-(e)s*, *Überdrücke*; *Phys.*, *Tech.* overpressure; *ein Reifen mit ~* an overinflated tyre; *~ventil* *n* pressure relief (*od.* safety) valve

Überdruss *m*; *-es*, *kein Pl.* weariness; (*Übersättigung*) surfeit; *bis zum ~* ad nauseam; *ich musste es mir bis zum ~ anhören umg.* I had to listen to it till it was coming out of my ears; **überdrüssig** *Adj.: e-r Sache ~ sein/ werden* be/get tired (*od.* weary) of s.th.; *e-r Sache ~ werden auch* weary of s.th.; *ich bin der Sache ~ auch* I feel jaded; *sie ist m-r ~ geworden* she's grown tired of me

überdurchschnittlich I. *Adj.* attr. above-average …, higher-than-average …; *präd.* above (*od.* higher than) average; *weitS.* (*~ gut*) outstanding; **II.** *Adv.* (*auch ~ gut*) outstandingly (well); (*mehr/besser als der Durchschnitt*) more/better than average; *~ verdienen* have a higher-than-average income; *~ bezahlt werden* be paid better than the average

überdüngen *v/t.* (*untr.*, *hat*) (*Boden*) overfertilize; **Überdüngung** *f* overfertilization

übereck *Adv. stehen etc.:* diagonally, at an angle

Übereifer *m* overkeenness, overzealousness; **übereifrig** *Adj.* overkeen, overzealous

übereignen *v/t.* (*untr.*, *hat*): *j-m etw. ~* make s.th. over to s.o.; **Übereignung** *f Jur.* transference (*an* + *Akk.* to)

übereilen (*untr.*, *hat*) **I.** *v/t.* rush; *die Sache ~* rush things; *nichts ~* not rush things; *e-n Entschluss ~* make a rash/ hasty decision, rush a decision; **II.** *v/refl.* rush things; **übereilt I.** *P.P.* → *übereilen*; **II.** *Adj.* rash, (over)hasty, precipitate

übereinander *Adv.* **1.** *liegen*, *stapeln*, *stellen:* on top of each other (*od.* one

U

another), one on top of the other; ~ **legen** put (*od.* lay) on top of each other (*od.* one another), stack; ~ **schichten** stack on top of each other (*od.* one another); **die Beine ~ schlagen** cross one's legs; **2.** *sprechen etc.*: about one another

übereinkommen *v/i.* (*unreg., trennb., ist -ge-*) agree; **wir sind (mit ihnen) übereingekommen, dass ...** we have agreed (with them) that ...; **man ist übereingekommen, dass ...** it has been agreed that ...; **Übereinkommen** *n; -s, -*, **Übereinkunft** *f; -, Übereinkünfte* agreement, understanding, arrangement; (*Vergleich*) settlement; **e-e Übereinkunft treffen** (mit *j-m*) come to) an agreement, strike a deal

übereinstimmen *v/i.* (*trennb., hat -ge-*) *Angaben, Zahlen etc.*: tally, correspond, agree, concur; *Farben, Muster etc.*: match, go together; *Ling.* agree; **mit *j-m* ~** agree with s.o. (**über** + **Akk.**, **in** +*Dat.* on); **übereinstimmend I.** *Part. Präs.* → **übereinstimmen**; **II.** *Adj.* corresponding; *Meinung, Bericht etc.*: concurring; (*einstimmig*) unanimous; *Farben*: matching; **III.** *Adv. erklären etc.*: unanimously; ~ **mit** in accordance (*od.* conformity *geh.*, agreement) with; **es wurde ~ berichtet, dass ...** reports agreed that ...; **es wurde ~ festgestellt, dass ...** everybody agreed that ..., there was unanimous agreement that ...; **Übereinstimmung** *f* (*Einigkeit, Einklang*) agreement, unison; (*Entsprechung*) correspondence, concurrence; (*Harmonie*) harmony, accord; ~ **erzielen** come to (*od.* reach) an agreement; **in ~ bringen** make things tally, get things to tally, square things (up) *umg.*; **in ~ mit *j-m* handeln** act in unison with s.o.; **in ~ stehen** → **übereinstimmen**; **in ~ mit** in agreement (*od.* accordance, conformity *geh.*) with, in keeping (*od.* line) with; **es besteht (keine) ~ zwischen X und Y** X and Y (don't) agree *od.* tally, X and Y are(n't) in agreement

überempfindlich *Adj.* hypersensitive, oversensitive (**gegen** to); *Med.* (*allergisch*) hypersensitive; **Überempfindlichkeit** *f* hypersensitivity, oversensitivity; *Med.* (*Allergie*) hypersensitivity

übererfüllen *v/t.* (*untr., hat*) (*Norm, Soll*) exceed, overfulfil(l)

Überernährung *f* overfeeding

über'essen *v/refl.* (*unreg., untr., hat*) (*bei e-r Mahlzeit zu viel essen*) overeat; **sich überessen haben** *auch* have had too much (**an** + *Dat.* of)

über'fahren¹ *v/t.* (*unreg., untr., hat*) **1.** (*Person, Hund etc.*) run over, knock down; **2.** (*Signal*) drive through (*Linie etc.*) cross, pass; **die Ampel ~** go through a red light, shoot (*Am.* run) the lights *umg.*; **3.** *fig.* (*j-n*) steamroller *s.o.* (into it)

'überfahren² (*unreg., trennb. -ge-*) **I.** *v/i.* (*ist*) cross (over); **II.** *v/t.* (*hat*) take (*od.* ferry) across; **Überfahrt** *f* crossing

Überfall *m; -(e)s, Überfälle* attack (**auf** + *Akk.* on); *auf der Straße*: *auch* mugging; *aus dem Hinterhalt*: ambush (attack) (on); (*Raubüberfall*) raid (on); *mit Waffendrohung*: hold-up; *gewalttätiger*: assault (on); *auf ein Dorf etc.*: raid (on) (*auch Flug.*); *auf ein Land*: invasion (of); *umg. fig.* (*Besuch*) descent (on), invasion (of s.o.'s house etc.); **dies ist ein ~!** this is a stick-up!

umg.; **e-n ~ auf *j-n* planen** *umg. fig.* plan to descend on s.o.; **überfallartig** *Adj. umg.* attacking

überfallen *v/t.* (*unreg., untr., hat*) attack; *auf der Straße*: *auch* mug; *aus dem Hinterhalt*: waylay, ambush; (*Bank etc.*) raid; *mit Waffendrohung*: hold up; *gewalttätig*: assault; (*Dorf etc.*) raid; (*Land*) invade; *umg. fig.* (*besuchen*) descend on; (*unterwegs ~*) waylay; **von Müdigkeit etc. ~ werden** be overcome by tiredness *etc.*; **plötzlich wurde ich von Müdigkeit ~** *auch* suddenly a feeling of tiredness came over me (*od.* hit me); **entschuldigen Sie, dass ich Sie einfach so überfalle** sorry for just dropping in on you like this; ***j-n* mit e-r Frage/Aufgabe etc. ~** spring a question/job *etc.* on s.o.

überfällig *Adj.* overdue; **längst ~** long overdue; **seit drei Tagen od. drei Tage ~ sein** be three days overdue; **dass du sie entlassen hast, war längst ~** her dismissal was long overdue, you should have dismissed her a long time ago

Überfallkommando *n* riot squad

überfeinert *Adj.* overrefined

überfischen *v/t.* (*untr., hat*) overfish; **Überfischung** *f* overfishing

überfliegen *v/t.* (*unreg., untr., hat*) **1.** fly over; *tief*: buzz *umg.*; **2.** *fig.* (*lesen*) glance over, skim (through); *e-e Liste etc.* **mit den Augen ~** *auch* run one's eyes over (*od.* down) a list *etc.*; **3.** *Lächeln etc.*: flit across *s.o.'s* face

'Überflieger *m umg.* high-flier

überfließen *v/i.* (*unreg., trennb., ist -ge-*) overflow (*auch fig.* **von** with); **aus etw. ~** flow over the top of s.th.

Überflug *m Flug.* overflight; ***j-m den ~ verbieten** refuse to allow s.o. to fly over one's land

überflügeln *v/t.* (*untr., hat*) *fig.* surpass, outstrip; **Überflügelung** *f* surpassing, outstripping

Überfluss *m; nur Sg.* abundance; (*Überschuss*) surplus; (*Überangebot*) glut (**alle: an** + *Dat.* of); **im ~ leben** live affluently; **~ haben an** (+ *Dat.*), *etw.* **im ~ haben** have plenty of; *Gegend, Gewässer etc.*: *auch* abound in; *Papier etc.* **im ~ vorhanden** there's plenty of paper *etc.* (available); **zu allem ~** as if that wasn't enough, to top it all *umg.*; **~gesellschaft** *f* affluent society

überflüssig *Adj.* superfluous; (*unnötig*) *auch* unnecessary; (*unerwünscht*) undesired, superfluous; *Bemerkung etc.*: superfluous, uncalled-for; *Arbeitskräfte*: spare, superfluous; **~ machen** render superfluous *etc.*; **~ zu sagen, dass** needless to say, ...; **sich ~ vorkommen** *umg.* feel superfluous; (*stören*) feel in the way; **du bist hier ~** *umg.* (*du störst*) you're in the way here; *stärker*: beat it!, get lost!; **überflüssigerweise** *Adv.* unnecessarily; (*grundlos*) for no real (*od.* good) reason; **Überflüssigkeit** *f* superfluousness

überfluten *v/t.* (*untr., hat*) *auch fig.* flood, inundate; **überflutet I.** *P.P.* → **überfluten**; **II.** *Adj.* *Straße etc.* flooded; **Überflutung** *f* flooding; *fig.* inundation

überfordern *v/t.* (*untr., hat*) *Person*: expect (*od.* demand) too much of *s.o.*; *Sache*: be too much for *s.o.* (to handle), be more than *s.o.* can cope with; (*Körper*) overtax, strain; **damit überfordert er die Schüler** that's demand-

ing too much of his pupils; **überfordert I.** *P.P.* → **überfordern**; **II.** *Adj.*: **er ist ~** he can't cope, he's taken on too much; **damit ist er ~** it's too much for him, it's expecting too much of him; **ich fühle mich ~** I don't think I can cope (with it) *od.* manage (it); **Überforderung** *f*: **es ist e-e ~** it's (expecting) too much (**für** of)

überformen *v/t.* (*untr., hat*) superimpose; **überformt I.** *P.P.* → **überformen**; **II.** *Adj.*: **glazial ~** *Geog.* glacially formed (*od.* shaped)

überfrachten *v/t.* (*untr., hat*) *auch fig.* overload; **überfrachtet I.** *P.P.* → **überfrachten**; **II.** *Adj.* *fig.* overloaded, weighed down (**mit** with); **Überfrachtung** *f* overloading

überfragt *Adj.*: **da bin ich ~** I'm afraid I can't answer that (one) for you, you've got me there *umg.*; **sich ~ fühlen** feel out of one's depth

überfremden *v/t.* (*untr., hat*) *pej.* infiltrate with foreign influences; **überfremdet werden** become infiltrated by foreign influences; **Überfremdung** *f* *pej.* foreign infiltration (*Wirts.* control)

überfressen *v/refl.* (*unreg., untr., hat*) *umg.* overeat; **sich ~ an** (+ *Dat.*) eat too much (*od.* many) of s.th.

überfrieren *v/i.* (*unreg., untr., ist*) freeze over

'überführen¹ *v/t.* (*trennb., hat -ge-*) **1. in den gasförmigen etc. Zustand ~** convert into a gaseous *etc.* state; **2.** → **überführen²** 1

über'führen² *v/t.* (*untr., hat*) **1.** (*befördern*) take, transfer; (*auch Tote*) transport; *Flug.* *auch* fly; *Mot.* (*Neuwagen etc.*) transport; **2.** *Jur.* (*als schuldig erweisen*) find guilty (+ *Gen.* of), convict (of); **3.** (*Straße, Fluss etc.*) span; **Überführung** *f* **1.** transportation; **2.** *Jur.* conviction; **3.** *Straße*: flyover, overpass; *Eisenb.* viaduct; **Überführungskosten** *Pl. Mot.* transportation costs

Überfülle *f* overabundance, profusion (**von** of); **überfüllen** *v/t.* (*untr., hat*) (*Raum etc.*) overcrowd; (*Tank, Flasche etc.*) overfill; **nicht ~!** *Tech.* do not overload; (*Tank*) do not overfill; **überfüllt I.** *P.P.* → **überfüllen**; **II.** *Adj.* (*over*)crowded; *Raum, Bus etc.*: *auch präd.* crammed full, (*jam*)packed *umg.*; *Kurs etc.*: oversubscribed; **~e Straßen** *etc.* congested roads *etc.*; **~e Vorlesungen** crowded lecture halls; **~er Luftraum** congested airspace, crowded air lanes; **Überfüllung** *f* overcrowding; *EDV* congestion; **wegen ~ geschlossen** full up

Überfunktion *f Med.* hyperactivity; **wegen ~ der Schilddrüse** *etc.* because of a hyperactive thyroid *etc.*

überfüttern *v/t.* (*untr., hat*) overfeed; *fig. mit Daten, Fakten etc.*: overwhelm; **Überfütterung** *f* overfeeding; *fig.* overwhelming

Übergabe *f; -, -n* **1.** *von Schlüssel, Wohnung etc.*: handing-over (*auch e-s Amtes etc.*); *Mil.* surrender; (*Eröffnung e-s Gebäudes etc.*) opening; **2.** *Telek.* transfer

Übergang *m* **1.** (*Übergangsstelle*) crossing (point); (*Brücke*) footbridge; *Eisenb.* level (*Am.* grade) crossing; **2.** (*das Überqueren*) crossing; **3.** *fig.* (*Wechsel, Überleitung*) transition; (*Abstufung*) shading; **~ vom Wachen zum Schlafen / vom Studium zum Beruf** transition from wakefulness to sleep / from studying to working; **ohne (jeden) ~** without (any) transition; *farb-*

lich etc.: without (any) shading; **4.** *nur Sg.*; (*Übergangszeit*) transitional period; (*vorläufiger Zustand*) transitional state; (*Zwischenlösung*) temporary solution, stopgap; (*nur*) *für den ~* (*für e-e Übergangszeit*) (just) for the transitional period; *ich habe die Wohnung nur für den ~* (*als Notbehelf*) the flat (*Am.* apartment) is only a stopgap

Übergangs|bestimmungen *Pl.* provisional regulations; **~erscheinung** *f* transitional phenomenon (*od.* aspect); **~geld** *n* interim payment (*od.* allowance); **~heim** *n* halfway house; **~kabinett** *n* provisional cabinet; **~lager** *n* transit camp

übergangslos I. *Adj. nachgestellt*: without transition; **II.** *Adv.* without transition, directly; *sich ~ aneinander reihen* run on from one another (*od.* without a break)

Übergangs|lösung *f* interim solution, temporary arrangement; **~mantel** *m* coat for spring and autumn; **~phase** *f* transitional phase; **~regelung** *f* temporary arrangement; **~regierung** *f* caretaker (*od.* transitional, interim) government; **~stadium** *n* transitional stage

übergangsweise *Adv.* for the transitional period

Übergangszeit *f* transitional period

Übergardine *f* curtain

übergeben (*unreg., untr., hat*) **I.** *v/t.* hand over; *feierlich*: present; *Mil. etc.* surrender; *EDV* (*Daten*) transfer; *j-m etw. ~* hand s.th. over to s.o.; *feierlich*: present s.o. with s.th.; (*anvertrauen*) entrust s.o. with s.th.; *e-e Sache dem Gericht ~* take a matter to court; *dem Verkehr ~* open to traffic; **II.** *v/refl.* (*erbrechen*) vomit, be sick, *bes. Am.* throw up; *ich musste mich auf der Überfahrt zweimal ~* I was sick (*Am.* I threw up) twice during the crossing

'übergehen¹ *v/i.* (*unreg., trennb., ist -ge-*) **1.** go (*od.* pass) over (*zu* to); *~ auf* (*+ Akk.*) *auf e-n Nachfolger, Stellvertreter*: pass to, devolve upon *geh.*; **2.** *~ in* (*+ Akk.*) pass into; *sich wandelnd*: turn into; *Farbe, Ton, Stimmung etc.*: blend (*od.* merge) into; *der Regen wird in Schnee ~* the rain will turn to snow; *ineinander ~ Farben*: blend; *in j-s Besitz ~* pass into s.o.'s possession (*od.* hands); *in andere Hände ~* change hands; **3.** *~ zu zum nächsten Punkt etc.*: pass on to, move on to, proceed to *förm.*; *zum Feind, zu e-r anderen Partei*: go over to, defect to; **4.** *die Augen gingen ihm über umg. vor Staunen*: his eyes nearly popped out of his head

über'gehen² *v/t.* (*unreg., untr., hat*) (*hinweggehen über*) pass s.th. over (*mit Stillschweigen* in silence); (*missachten*) disregard; (*nicht beachten, ignorieren*) ignore; (*auslassen*) leave out, omit, skip *umg.*; (*nicht berücksichtigen*) pass s.o. over, leave s.o. out; *sich übergangen fühlen* feel snubbed (*od.* left out)

über|genau *Adj.* overscrupulous; *umg. pej.* (*kleinlich*) picky; **~genug** *Adv.* more than enough; **~geordnet I.** *P.P.* → *überordnen*; **II.** *Adj. Amt etc.*: higher; (*vorrangig*) of overriding importance; *e-r Sache ~ sein* have priority over s.th.; *dieses Projekt ist von ~er Bedeutung* this project is of overriding importance

Übergepäck *n Flug.* excess baggage; *15 Kilo ~ haben* have 15 kilos of excess baggage

übergeschnappt *Adj. umg.* cracked, crazy

Übergewicht *n; nur Sg.* **1.** overweight; *von Briefen etc.*: excess weight; (*zehn Kilo*) *~ haben Person*: be (ten kilos) overweight; *Gepäck etc.*: be (ten kilos) over the limit; **2.** *fig.* preponderance (*an + Dat.* of); *Pol. etc.* supremacy; (*Vorherrschen*) predominance; *das ~ haben* predominate; (*vorherrschen*) be predominant; *... haben das ~ auch* there is a preponderance of ...; *das ~ gewinnen* gain the upper hand, come out on top; **3.** (*das*) *~ bekommen* lose one's balance, topple over; **übergewichtig** *Adj.* overweight

über'gießen¹ *v/t.* (*unreg., untr., hat*) pour water *etc.* over; douse (*mit* with); (*Braten*) baste; *sich mit Benzin etc. ~* douse o.s. in (*od.* with) petrol (*Am.* gasoline *etc.*)

'übergießen² *v/t.* (*unreg., trennb., hat -ge-*) (*verschütten*) spill

überglücklich *Adj. präd.* overjoyed, over the moon *umg.*

übergreifen *v/i.* (*unreg., trennb., hat -ge-*) **1.** *~ auf* (*+ Akk.*) *Feuer, Epidemie, Panik etc.*: spread to; *Kämpfe: auch* spill over into; **2.** *Turnen, Tasteninstrument*: cross one's hands over; **übergreifend I.** *P.P.* → *übergreifen*; **II.** *Adj.* (*allgemein*) general; (*umfassend*) comprehensive; (*allumfassend*) global

Übergriff *m* encroachment, infringement (*auf + Akk.* on); *auf Territorium*: incursion (into); *es kam zu ~en durch die Polizei etc.* attacks were carried out by the police *etc.*

übergroß *Adj.* outsize(d), oversized; **Übergröße** *f Kleidung*: outsize; *Hemden etc. in ~n* outsize shirts *etc.*

überhaben *v/t.* (*unreg., trennb., hat -ge-*) *umg.* **1.** (*Mantel etc.*) have on; **2.** (*übrig haben*) have left (over); **3.** *fig.* (*satt haben*) be sick and tired of, be fed up with

überhand|nehmen *quantitativ*: increase uncontrollably; (*außer Kontrolle geraten*) get out of hand (*od.* control); *Unkraut, Verbrechen: auch* become rampant; **Überhandnehmen** *n; -s, kein Pl.* uncontrolled spread

Überhang *m* overhang; *Archit. auch* projection; (*Zweige*) overhanging branches *Pl.*; *fig.* (*Überschuss*) surplus, excess

überhängen (*unreg., trennb., hat -ge-*) **I.** *v/i.* overhang; *Archit.* project; **II.** *v/t.* hang s.th. over; (*Mantel*) throw over one's shoulders; *sich* (*Dat.*) *e-n Mantel ~* put (*od.* throw) a coat (a)round one's shoulders; *sich* (*Dat.*) *die Tasche ~* hang one's bag over one's shoulder

Überhangmandat *n Pol.* extra parliamentary seat awarded to a party in addition to those gained in vote based on proportional representation

überhastet I. *Adj.* hasty; **II.** *Adv. ohne nachzudenken*: hastily; (*zu schnell*) too quickly; *etw. ~ tun* do s.th. hastily (*od.* too quickly)

überhäufen *v/t.* (*untr., hat*): *j-n ~ mit* inundate (*od.* swamp) s.o. with; *mit Ehren, Vorwürfen etc.*: heap *hono(u)rs/reproaches etc.* on s.o.; *mit Geschenken*: shower s.o. with

überhaupt *Adv.* (*insgesamt*) generally, on the whole, altogether; (*eigentlich*) actually; *in Fragen*: *oft* anyway; (*überdies, außerdem*) besides; *~ nicht* not at all; (*niemals*) never; *~ nichts* nothing

(at all); *~ kein ... no ... at all, no ...* of any sort; *sie hat ja ~ keine Kenntnisse* she doesn't know anything at all; *du hast ja ~ keine Ahnung* you have absolutely no idea; *wenn ~* if at all; *du hättest es ~ nicht tun sollen* you shouldn't have done it in the first place; *gibt es ~ e-e Möglichkeit?* is there any chance at all?; *dürfen die das ~?* are they actually allowed to do that?; *kennst du ihn ~?* do you know him at all?; *was wollen Sie ~?* what do you want anyway?; *wer/wo etc. ist er ~?* who/where *etc.* is he anyway?; *wissen Sie ~, wen Sie vor sich haben?* do you have any idea who you're talking to?; *hast du ~ schon was gegessen?* have you actually had anything to eat yet?; *er ist ~ sehr begabt* of course, he 'is very talented (altogether); *das hätte ich ~ gern gewusst* I would have particularly liked to have known that; *und ~, ... umg.* (and) besides ...; *und ~! umg.* so there!

überheblich *Adj.* overbearing, arrogant; **Überheblichkeit** *f* arrogance

überheizen *v/t.* (*untr., hat*) overheat; *ein total überheiztes Zimmer* a completely overheated room

überhitzen *v/t.* (*untr., hat*) overheat (*auch fig., Wirts.*); *Tech.* superheat; **überhitzt I.** *P.P.* → *überhitzen*; **II.** *Adj. Motor*: overheated; *Person*: hot (and sticky); *Gesicht*: red, flushed; *das ist s-e ~e Fantasie* it's just his imagination running wild; **Überhitzung** *f* overheating; *Tech.* superheating

überhöhen *v/t.* (*untr., hat*) (*Straßenkurve etc.*) bank; **überhöht I.** *P.P.* → *überhöhen*; **II.** *Adj.* **1.** *Kurve*: banked; **2.** *Preise etc.*: excessive (*auch Geschwindigkeit*), exorbitant, ridiculous *umg.*; *mit ~er Geschwindigkeit fahren* go over (*od.* break) the speed limit

über'holen¹ *v/t.* (*untr., hat*) **1.** (*vorbeigehen, -fahren an*) pass, overtake; *fig.* overtake, *stärker*: outstrip; *man darf nur links ~* you are only allowed to overtake (*Am.* pass) on the left; *sie hat ihn längst überholt fig. auch* she's left him trailing; **2.** *Tech.* overhaul, recondition

'überholen² (*trennb., hat -ge-*) **I.** *v/t.* **1.** ferry *s.o.* over; *hol über!* ferry!; **2.** *Naut.*: *das Segel ~* gybe, *Am.* jibe; **II.** *v/i. Naut., Schiff*: keel over

Überhol|manöver *n Mot.* overtaking manoeuvre (*Am.* maneuver); **~spur** *f* passing lane

überholt I. *P.P.* → *überholen¹*; **II.** *Adj.* (*veraltet*) (out)dated, outmoded; *bes. Ideen: auch* antiquated; *das ist doch längst ~! umg.* that went out of date ages ago!

Überholung *f Tech.* overhaul, reconditioning; **überholungsbedürftig** *Adj. präd.* in need of an overhaul

Überhol|verbot *n* "No Overtaking" (rule *od.* sign); *hier herrscht ~* overtaking is not permitted here; **~versuch** *m* attempt to overtake (*od.* at overtaking); **~vorgang** *m*: *vor/nach dem ~* before/after overtaking; *während des ~s* when (*od.* while) overtaking

überhören *v/t.* (*untr., hat*) not hear; (*Worte*) miss, not catch; *absichtlich*: ignore; *das will ich überhört haben! umg.* I'll pretend I didn't hear that!; *so etwas überhört sie einfach umg.* she just ignores that sort of thing

Über-Ich *n Psych.* superego

überindividuell *Adj.* superindividual

überinterpretieren *v/t.* (*untr.*, *hat*) overinterpret

überirdisch **I.** *Adj.* supernatural; (*himmlisch*) celestial, heavenly; **von ~er Schönheit** *fig.* of divine beauty; (*einfach*) **~!** *umg.* simply divine!; **II.** *Adv.* schön etc.: (*himmlisch*) divinely; (*übernatürlich*) ethereally

überkandidelt *Adj. umg.* slightly eccentric (*od.* off-beam)

Überkapazitäten *Pl. bes. Wirts.* overcapacity *Sg.*

überkippen *v/i.* (*trennb.*, *ist -ge-*) **1.** → **umkippen** II; **2.** *Stimme:* crack

überkleben *v/t.* (*untr.*, *hat*) stick s.th. over s.th.; **die Plakate mit etw. ~** stick s.th. over the posters; **der Name etc. ist überklebt** something has been stuck over the name *etc.*

überklettern *v/t.* (*untr.*, *hat*) (*Zaun etc.*) climb over

überkochen *v/i.* (*trennb.*, *ist -ge-*) boil over (*auch fig.*)

über'kommen¹ **I.** *v/t.* (*unreg.*, *untr.*, *hat*): *Furcht etc.* **überkam ihn** he was overcome by fear *etc.*; **II.** *v/i.* (*unreg.*, *untr. ist*): **diese Sitte ist uns ~** this custom has been handed down (*od.* has come down) to us

überkommen² **I.** *P.P.* → **überkommen¹**; **II.** *Adj.* traditional; (*veraltet*) antiquated, obsolete; **das sind ~e Moralvorstellungen** those are old-fashioned ideas about morality

überkompensieren (*untr.*, *hat*) **I.** *v/t.* overcompensate for; **II.** *v/i.* overcompensate

überkonfessionell *Adj.* interdenominational

Überkopfball *m Tennis etc.:* smash

überkreuzen *v/refl.* (*untr.*, *hat*) coincide; *negativ:* clash

überkriegen *v/t.* (*trennb.*, *hat -ge-*); *umg.* get fed up with, tire of

überkritisch *Adj.* overcritical, overly critical

überkronen *v/t.* (*untr.*, *hat*); *Dent.* (*Zahn*) crown

überkrustet *Adj.* covered (*mit* in); *Gastr.* with a topping of cheese and breadcrumbs; **die Schuhe waren mit Dreck ~** *auch* the shoes were caked with mud

überladen¹ *v/t.* (*untr.*, *hat*) **1.** (*Fahrzeug etc.*) overload; **2.** *Etron.* overload; (*Batterie*) overcharge; **3.** *mit Arbeit:* load down; **4.** *fig.* (*übermäßig verzieren etc.*) clutter

überladen² **I.** *P.P.* → **überladen¹**; **II.** *Adj.* **1.** *Fahrzeug etc.:* overloaded; **2.** *Etron.* overloaded; (*Batterie*) overcharged; **3.** *fig. Stil:* overladen, florid; (*übermäßig verziert etc.*) cluttered

überlagern (*untr.*, *hat*) **I.** *v/t.* overlay (*auch Etron.*); *teilweise:* overlap; *Geol.* overlie; *Radio:* heterodyne; (*Sender*) jam; **überlagert von** *fig. neuen Problemen etc.:* superimposed by, *stärker:* displaced by; **II.** *v/refl.* overlap; **Überlagerung** *f* overlapping; *Etron.* interference; *Radio:* heterodyning

Überland|bus *m* long-distance coach, *Am.* interstate bus; **~fahrt** *f Mot.* cross-country trip; **~leitung** *f Etech.* power line; **~leitungsmast** *m Etech.* grid (*Am.* high-tension line) pylon

überlang *Adj.* overlong; **~e Spieldauer** extended play; **Überlänge** *f:* **~ haben** be overlong; **ein Film mit ~** an unusually long film (*bes. Am.* movie)

überlappen *v/t.* und *v/refl.* (*untr.*, *hat*); *Tech.* overlap (*auch fig.*); **Überlappung** *f* (*das Überlappen*) overlapping;

(*überlappte Stelle*) overlap; *EDV* (*das Überlappen*) overlapping; (*überlappte Stelle*) overlap

überlassen *v/t.* (*unreg.*, *untr.*, *hat*): **j-m etw. ~** let s.o. have s.th., leave s.th. to s.o.; (*anheimstellen*) leave s.th. to s.o.; **j-m ein Kind/Tier ~** (*in Obhut geben*) leave a child/animal in s.o.'s care; *etw.* **dem Schicksal/Zufall** *etc.* **~** leave s.th. to fate/chance *etc.*; **es j-m / dem Zufall** *etc.* **~ zu** (+ *Inf.*) leave it to s.o. / to chance *etc.* to (+ *Inf.*); **j-n sich selbst ~** leave s.o. to fend for himself (*od.* herself); **j-n s-m Schicksal ~** leave s.o. to his (*od.* her) fate; **sich selbst ~ sein** be left to one's own devices; **~ Sie das mir** leave that to me; **das überlasse ich dir** that's up to you, I'll leave that to you; **es bleibt ihm ~, was er tun will** it's up to him what he wants to do; **Überlassung** *f* handing over; (*Benutzung*) use

überlasten *v/t.* (*untr.*, *hat*) **1.** overload (*auch Etech.*, *Tech.*, *Hardware*); **2.** *fig.* strain (*auch Herz etc.*), put too great a strain on; **überlastet** **I.** *P.P.* → **überlasten**; **II.** *Adj.* **1.** overloaded (*auch Etech.*, *Tech.*); **2.** *fig.* under strain; *durch Arbeit:* overworked; **Überlastung** *f* **1.** overloading (*auch Etech.*, *Tech.*, *Hardware*, *Netzwerk*); **2.** *fig.* strain; **Überlastungsanzeige** *f EDV* overload indicator

Überlauf *m* overflow (*auch EDV*)

'überlaufen¹ *v/i.* (*unreg.*, *trennb.*, *ist -ge-*) **1.** run over; *Kochendes:* boil over; **das Fass zum Überlaufen bringen** *fig.* be the last straw; **2.** *Mil.* desert; *zum Feind:* go over, defect (**zu** to)

über'laufen² *v/t.* (*unreg.*, *untr.*, *hat*) **1.** *Touristen etc.:* overrun; *Sport* (*Markierung etc.*) overshoot; (*Hürden*) jump; **von Vertretern ~ werden** be overrun with representatives; **er überlief die gesamte Abwehr** *Sport* he beat (*od.* outran) the entire defen|ce (*Am.* -se); **2.** *fig.:* **es überlief mich** (*heiß und*) **kalt** it sent a shiver down my spine, I went hot and cold

überlaufen³ **I.** *P.P.* → **überlaufen²**; **II.** *Adj. Gegend etc.:* overcrowded (*von* with); *Arzt etc.:* overrun with patients *etc.*; **touristisch total ~** completely overrun with tourists

Überläufer *m*, **~in** *f Mil.* deserter; *Pol.* auch defector, turncoat, traitor, renegade

Überlauf|rohr *n* overflow pipe; **~ventil** *n* overflow valve

überleben (*untr.*, *hat*) **I.** *vt/i.* survive (*auch weitS.* überstehen); **das überlebe ich nicht** *umg. auch* that'll be the death of me; **du wirst es ~!** *umg.* it won't kill you, you'll survive; **II.** *v/refl. altm.* become dated; **Überleben** *n nur Sg.* survival; **ums ~ kämpfen** fight for survival; **Überlebende** *m*, *f* survivor

Überlebenschance *f* chance(s *Pl.*) of survival

überlebensfähig *Adj. präd. und nachgestellt:* capable of surviving; **Überlebensfähigkeit** *f* survivability

Überlebensfrage *f* question of survival; **bei dieser Wahl stellt sich für die Partei die ~** this election will determine the survival of the party

überlebensgroß *Adj. attr.* larger-than-life ..., *präd.* larger than life; **Überlebensgröße** *f: in ~* ... larger-than-life; *präd.* larger than life

Überlebens|kampf *m* fight (*od.* struggle) for survival; **~künstler** *m* survi-

vor; **~strategie** *f* survival strategy; **~training** *n* survival training

überlebenswichtig *Adj. präd. und nachgestellt:* important for survival

Überlebenswille *m* will to survive

überlebt **I.** *P.P.* → **überleben**; **II.** *Adj. Vorstellungen etc.:* outmoded, old-fashioned

über'legen¹ *vt/i.* (*untr.*, *hat*) (*nachdenken*) think (about *s.th.*), consider, ponder *geh.* (*s.th.*); **sich** (+ *Dat.*) *etw.* **~** think about *s.th.*, think *s.th.* over; **überleg mal!** just think about it!; **~, ob/wie** *etc.* consider whether/how *etc.*; *etw.* **noch einmal ~** reconsider s.th.; **es sich wieder od. anders ~** change one's mind; **wenn ich es mir recht überlege** when I think about it; **sich etw. genau ~** think carefully about s.th.; **ich habe mir etw. überlegt** (*habe e-n Plan*) I've thought of s.th.; **das würde ich mir zweimal ~** I'd think twice about that (*od.* before doing that); (*lange*) **hin und her ~** *umg.* deliberate (for ages); **ohne zu ~** without thinking; (*sofort*) like a shot *umg.*; **ohne lange zu ~** without thinking twice; **ich würde nicht lange ~** I wouldn't waste too much time thinking about it; **ich hätte nicht lange überlegt** I wouldn't have given it a second thought

'überlegen² *v/t.* (*trennb.*, *hat -ge-*) lay s.th. over s.o. od. s.th., cover s.o. od. s.th. with s.th.; **ein Kind ~** *umg.* put a child over one's knee

über'legen³ **I.** *Adj.* **1.** superior (+ *Dat.* to; *an* +*Dat.* in); *Sport Sieg:* convincing; **in Mathe ist sie mir ~** she's better than me at math(s); **j-m weit ~ sein** be more than a match for s.o., be head and shoulders above s.o.; **haushoch ~ sein** *Sport* be vastly superior; → **zahlenmäßig** II; **2.** *Benehmen, Lächeln:* superior; *Benehmen:* auch supercilious; **~e Miene** superior air; **II.** *Adv.* **1.** (*in ~er Manier*) in superior style; (*überzeugend*) convincingly; *siegen:* auch in style; **2.** (*überheblich*) in a superior manner, in a supercilious way

Überlegenheit *f; nur Sg.* superiority; **Überlegenheitsgefühl** *n* sense of superiority

überlegenswert *Adj. präd. und nachgestellt:* worth considering

überlegt **I.** *P.P.* → **überlegen¹**; **II.** *Adj. Entschluss etc.:* considered; *attr.* (*durchdacht*) well-thought-out ..., well-planned ..., *präd.* well thought out, well planned; (*umsichtig*) circumspect; **III.** *Adv. handeln etc.:* with careful consideration; **Überlegtheit** *f; nur Sg.* (*Umsicht*) circumspection

Überlegung *f* **1.** *nur Sg.*; (*das Überlegen*) consideration, reflection; (*Erwägung*) consideration; **bei näherer ~** on closer reflection; **bei nüchterner ~** looking at it in a more sober light; **ohne ~** (*gedankenlos*) without thinking; (*schnell*) without thinking twice; **nach reiflicher ~** after due consideration; **2.** (*Gesichtspunkt*) point (of view); **aus dieser ~ heraus** for this reason; **~en anstellen** consider; *etw.* **in s-e ~en einbeziehen** take s.th. into consideration; **mehrere ~en sprechen dafür/dagegen** on consideration, several factors speak in favo(u)r of / against it

überleiten *v/i.* (*trennb.*, *hat -ge-*) lead (**zu** to); *Regelungen:* change (**zu** to); *Sendung, Thema:* link (**zu** to); **Überleitung** *f* transition; *von Regelungen:* changing; *von Sendung, Thema:* linking

überlesen *v/t.* (*unreg., untr., hat*) **1.** (*überfliegen*) run (*od.* skim) through; **2.** (*übersehen*) overlook

überliefern *v/t.* (*untr., hat*) *der Nachwelt*: hand down (+ *Dat.* to), pass on (to); *aus dieser Zeit ist nichts überliefert* no records of (*od.* from) this period have survived; *es ist* (*schriftlich*) *überliefert* there are (written) records testifying to it; *es ist überliefert, dass dokumentarisch*: records indicate that; *durch Sagen etc.*: tradition has it that; **überliefert I.** *P.P.* → *überliefern*; **II.** *Adj.* (*herkömmlich*) traditional; *~es Wissen* knowledge that has been handed down (through the ages); **Überlieferung** *f* **1.** *nur Sg.*; (*das Überliefern*) handing down (*an* + *Akk.* to), passing on (to); *von Texten*: transmission; **2.** (*Tradition*) tradition; (*Quellen, Zeugnisse*) records *Pl.*; *~en* (*Schriften*) writings, texts; *mündliche ~* oral tradition

überlisten *v/t.* (*untr., hat*) outwit, outsmart *I*

überm *Präp. + Art. umg. über dem*; → *über* I

Übermacht *f nur Sg.* superiority, superior strength; *in der ~ sein* be in a superior position, have the upper hand; *gegen e-e ~ ankämpfen* fight against a superior force; **übermächtig** *Adj.* **1.** *Feind etc.*: superior (in strength); **2.** *Gefühl etc.*: overpowering; *~ werden Wunsch, Gier etc.*: become overpowering

übermalen *v/t.* (*untr., hat*) paint over; *die Fresken wurden weiß übermalt* the frescoes were painted over with white paint; **Übermalung** *f* **1.** (*das Übermalen*) painting over; **2.** (*Farbschicht*) overpainted layer

übermannen *v/t.* (*untr., hat*) overcome; *weitS.* (*überwältigen*) overwhelm; *vom Schlaf etc. übermannt* overcome by sleep etc.

übermannshoch *Adj. präd. und nachgestellt*: taller than a man

Übermaß *n*; *nur Sg.* excess (*an* +*Dat.* of); *pej.* overkill (of); *Tech.* oversize; *ein ~ an Fleisch etc. produzieren* produce an excessive amount of meat etc.; *im ~ tun* do *s.th.* to excess; *im ~ haben* have more than enough of *s.th.*; *... ist im ~ vorhanden* there's an overabundance of ...; **übermäßig I.** *Adj.* excessive; (*unmäßig*) *auch* immoderate; (*übertrieben*) exaggerated; (*überreichlich*) overabundant; *sie sollte auf ~en Alkoholkonsum etc. verzichten* she shouldn't drink inordinate amounts of alcohol *etc.*; **II.** *Adv.* excessively, overly ..., too much; *arbeiten, trainieren etc.*: *auch* too hard; *großzügig etc.*: *auch* to a fault *nachgestellt*; *~ betonen* overemphasize, emphasize unduly; *nicht ~ begeistert etc. umg.* not overly enthusiastic *etc.*; *du hast dich ja nicht gerade ~ angestrengt als Tadel*: you didn't exactly strain yourself

Übermensch *m* superman; *in den Schriften von Nietzsche*: *auch* Übermensch; **übermenschlich** *Adj.* superhuman; *Übermenschliches leisten* perform a superhuman feat (*od.* superhuman feats *Pl.*)

übermitteln *v/t.* (*untr., hat*) transmit, convey (+ *Dat.* to); (*weiterleiten*) pass *s.th.* on (+ *Dat.* to); *j-m etw. telefonisch / per Post® etc. ~* (*Nachricht, Glückwünsche etc.*) send s.o. sth. by phone/post (*Am.* mail *etc.*); **Übermitt-**

lung *f* transmission

übermorgen *Adv.* the day after tomorrow; *wir treffen uns ~ früh/Früh* we're meeting the day after tomorrow in the morning

übermüdet *Adj.* overtired; **Übermüdung** *f* overtiredness; *vor ~ einschlafen* fall asleep from exhaustion

Übermut *m* (*Ausgelassenheit*) high spirits *Pl.*; (*Mutwille*) wantonness; (*Dreistigkeit*) cockiness; *aus od. vor* (*lauter*) *~* out of (pure) high spirits; *~ tut selten gut Sprichw.* it will all end in tears, there will be tears before bedtime; **übermütig I.** *Adj.* high-spirited, *präd. auch* in high spirits; (*mutwillig*) wanton; (*dreist*) cocky; *die Kinder waren ganz ~* the children were full of high spirits; **II.** *Adv. herumtollen etc.*: in high spirits

übernächst... *Adj.* the next but one, *the* second (one); *~e Woche* the week after next

übernachten *v/i.* (*untr., hat*) spend the night (*bei j-m* at s.o.'s place), stay overnight (at s.o.'s place); *im Freien ~ auch* sleep in the open (*od.* under the stars); *zu Hause / nicht zu Hause ~* spend the night at home / away from home; *wollt ihr bei uns ~? heute*: do you want to spend (*od.* stay) the night at our place?; *mehrere Tage*: do you want to stay at our place?; *in der Ferienwohnung können sechs Personen ~* the holiday flat (*Am.* vacation apartment) sleeps six

übernächtig(t) *Adj.* tired (from lack of sleep); *aussehen*: bleary-eyed

Übernachtung *f* overnight stay; *~ mit Frühstück* bed and breakfast; *vier ~en* (*mit Frühstück*) four nights (with breakfast); *Teilnahme mit/ohne ~* attendance including/excluding overnight accommodation

Übernachtungs|gast *m* overnight guest; *~möglichkeit f auch Pl.* overnight accommodation, place to stay (for the night) *umg.*

Übernahme *f*, -, -n **1.** taking over; *bes. der Macht, Wirts., e-r Firma*: takeover; *feindliche ~ Wirts.* hostile takeover; **2.** *nur Sg.*; *der Verantwortung, e-s Amts*: assumption; *sich zur ~ der Kosten bereit erklären* declare oneself willing to meet the costs; **3.** *von Methoden, Begriffen etc., auch Ling.*: adoption; *wörtliche ~n* literal borrowings; **4.** *Etron., EDV* entry (*od.* transfer) key; *~angebot n Wirts. etc.*: takeover bid

übernational *Adj.* supranational

übernatürlich *Adj.* supernatural

übernehmen (*unreg., untr., hat*) **I.** *v/t.* **1.** take over (*auch Macht, Führung, Amt, Wirts., Firma*); (*Staffelstab*) receive; *e-e neue Klasse ~ als Lehrer*: take over a new class; **2.** (*sich kümmern um, erledigen*) take care of; (*Arbeit etc.*) take on; (*Kosten*) meet, agree to pay; (*die Getränke ~ wir* we're buying the drinks; *e-e Stunde* (*von j-m*) *~ als Lehrer*: take over a class (from s.o.); *er übernahm es zu* (+ *Inf.*) he undertook to (+ *Inf.*), he took it upon himself to (+ *Inf.*); *das übernehme ich umg.* I'll take care of that; **3.** *Jur.* (*Fall, Verteidigung etc.*) take on; (*Pflicht*) accept; **4.** *Naut.* (*Ladung, Passagiere*) take on board; (*Arbeitskräfte nach Firmenübernahme*) keep on, continue to employ; **5.** (*Verfahrensweise, Begriffe etc.*) adopt; (*Wörter*) borrow, take; *Etron., EDV* transfer;

(*Daten etc.*) import, accept; *e-e Sendung von der BBC ~ TV* show a BBC program(me); *Ideen etc. einfach ~ pej.* lift; → *Bürgschaft, Steuer¹, Verantwortung* 1; **II.** *v/i.* take over (*von j-m*: from); *jetzt ~ Sie!* now you take over!; **III.** *v/refl.* (*es übertreiben*) overdo it (*od.* things); *mit Arbeit etc.*: take on too much, bite off more than one can chew *umg.*; (*sich überschätzen*) overestimate one's capabilities, overplay one's hand; *finanziell*: overreach o.s.; *beim Essen*: overeat; *sich kräftemäßig ~* overexert o.s.; *sich bei der Arbeit / beim Sport etc. ~* do too much work/ sport *etc.*; *mit dem Hauskauf haben sie sich übernommen* they overreached themselves in buying the house; *übernimm dich nur nicht! iro.* don't overdo it!; **Übernehmer** *m*; *-s*, -; *Wirts.* purchaser, purchasing company; *der ~ der Kosten / des Falls* the person taking over the costs/case

übernervös *Adj.* very edgy; *~ sein* be very on edge, *umg. auch* be a bundle of nerves

überordnen *v/t.* (*untr., hat -ge-*): *j-n j-m / e-r Sache ~* set s.o. above s.o./s.th.; *etw. j-m / e-r Sache ~ auch* give priority to s.th. over s.o./s.th.; → *übergeordnet*

überparteilich *Adj. Zeitung*: non-partisan, independent; *~e Entscheidung etc.*: all-party decision *etc.*; **Überparteilichkeit** *f von Zeitung*: independence; *die ~ ist äußerst wichtig Parl. etc.* it is extremely important that this is an all--party decision

überpinseln *v/t.* (*untr., hat*) *umg.* paint over

Überproduktion *f* overproduction

überproportional I. *Adj.* disproportionate (*zu* to); **II.** *Adv.*: *~ vertreten* overrepresented

überprüfbar *Adj.* checkable; (*Behauptung etc.*) verifiable; **überprüfen** *v/t.* (*untr., hat*) **1.** (*untersuchen*) check, examine; *genau*: scrutinize; (*j-n*) *politisch etc.*: screen, vet; (*nachprüfen*) check; *auf Echtheit, Wahrheit*: verify; *auf Brauchbarkeit*: test; *j-n als Polizist etc.*: check s.o. out; *j-s Personalien ~* check s.o.'s particulars; *etw. auf s-e Funktionsfähigkeit* (*hin*) *~* check s.th. to see if it is in working order; *j-n auf s-e Stasi-Mitarbeit* (*hin*) *~* screen s.o. for Stasi collaboration; *bei dringendem Verdacht*: investigate s.o.'s collaboration with the Stasi; **2.** (*Standpunkt etc., noch einmal überdenken*) reconsider, review; (*Urteil, auch Jur.*) revise; **Überprüfung** *f* examination, scrutiny; check; verification; test; reconsideration; revision; → *überprüfen*; **Überprüfungsverfahren** *n* **1.** *Pol.* vetting process; **2.** *Tech.* inspection process

überqualifiziert *Adj.* overqualified

überquellen *v/i.* (*unreg., trennb., ist -ge-*) *auch fig.* overflow, brim over (*von* with); *die Augen quollen ihm über* his eyes overflowed with tears

überqueren *v/t.* (*untr., hat*) cross; **Überquerung** *f* crossing

überragen *v/t.* (*untr., hat*) **1.** tower above; (*j-n*) *auch* be taller than; **2.** *fig.* outclass, outshine (*an* + *Dat.* in); **überragend I.** *Part. Präs.* → *überragen*; **II.** *Adj. fig.* outstanding, brilliant; *durch s-e ~e Persönlichkeit* through sheer force of personality

überraschen *v/t/i.* (*untr., hat*) surprise; *Unvorhergesehenes, Unwetter etc.*: catch *s.o.* out, *Am.* trip *s.o.* up, catch

U

s.o. by surprise; (*überrumpeln*) take s.o. by surprise; *j-n bei etw.* ~ (*ertappen*) catch s.o. doing s.th.; *der Einbrecher wurde von e-m Nachbarn überrascht* the burglar was surprised by a neighbo(u)r; *im Schlaf überrascht werden* be caught sleeping; *der Torwart wurde von dem Schuss überrascht* the shot caught the goalkeeper unawares; *vom Regen überrascht werden* be caught in the rain; *es überrascht, dass ...* it's surprising that ...; *lassen wir uns* ~ *umg.* let's wait and see

überraschend I. *Part. Präs.* → *überraschen*; **II.** *Adj.* surprising; (*unerwartet*) unexpected, sudden; *das Überraschende daran* the surprising thing about it; **III.** *Adv.* surprisingly; ~ **kommen** come as a surprise (*für* to); **überraschenderweise** *Adv.* surprisingly

überrascht I. *P.P.* → *überraschen*; **II.** *Adj.* surprised (*von* by, at); *sich* ~ / *nicht* ~ *zeigen* show a certain surprise / show no surprise; **III.** *Adv.* with (*od.* in) surprise

Überraschung *f* surprise; *als Geschenk etc.*: *auch* treat; *e-e* (*kleine*) ~ (*kleines Geschenk etc.*) a little something; *als* ~ *zum Geburtstag* as a birthday treat; *j-m e-e* ~ *bereiten* surprise s.o., give s.o. a surprise; *für* (*e-e*) ~ *sorgen* cause a surprise; *zu j-s* ~ to s.o.'s surprise; *vor lauter* ~ in pure amazement; *e-e böse* ~ a nasty surprise; *so e-e* ~! what a surprise!

Überraschungs|angriff *m* surprise attack; ~**coup** *m* surprise coup; ~**effekt** *m* surprise effect; ~**erfolg** *m* unexpected success, surprise success (*od.* hit); ~**gast** *m auch TV etc.*: surprise guest; ~**moment** *n* element of surprise; ~**sieg** *m* unexpected (*od.* surprise) victory (*od.* win); ~**sieger** *m*, ~**siegerin** *f* surprise winner

überreagieren *v/i.* (*untr., hat*) overreact; **Überreaktion** *f* overreaction (*auf* + *Akk.* to)

überreden *v/t.* (*untr., hat*) persuade (*zu* to), talk (*into* bring) s.o. (a)round; *j-n zu etw.* ~ talk s.o. into (doing) s.th.; **Überredung** *f* persuasion

Überredungs|gabe *f* persuasiveness; ~**kunst** *f* **1.** art of persuasion; **2.** *auch Pl.* powers *Pl.* of persuasion

überregional I. *Adj.* supraregional; *Zeitung*: national; *Sendung, Kampagne etc.*: nationwide; **II.** *Adv.* nationally; ~ *bekannt werden* become well-known throughout the country

überreich I. *Adj.* overabundant; (*üppig*) lavish; *ein* ~*es Angebot an* a profusion of; ~ *sein an* (+ *Dat.*) have more than enough of; *Sache: auch* abound in; *in* ~*em Maß* overabundantly; (*üppig*) lavishly; (*übermäßig*) overly ...; **II.** *Adv.* overabundantly; (*üppig*) lavishly; (*übermäßig*) overly ...; *j-n* ~ *beschenken* lavish presents on s.o., shower s.o. with presents

überreichen *v/t.* (*untr., hat*) hand s.th. (over); *feierlich*: present s.th. (*j-m* to s.o.)

überreichlich I. *Adj.* overabundant, ample; **II.** *Adv.* amply; → *auch überreich*

Überreichung *f* presentation

Überreichweite *f e-s Senders*: overshoot

überreif *Adj.* overripe; **Überreife** *f* overripeness

überreißen *v/t.* (*unreg., untr., hat*); Ten-

nis *etc.* (*Ball*) lob

überreizen (*untr., hat*) **I.** *v/t.* **1.** (*Haut etc.*) irritate; (*Augen, Nerven*) strain; **2.** (*auf- od. anregen*) overexcite; **II.** *v/i. und v/refl.*: (**sich**) ~ *Kartenspiel*: overcall; **überreizt I.** *P.P.* → *überreizen*; **II.** *Adj.* overwrought; (*reizbar*) irritable; (*nervös*) on edge; **Überreiztheit** *f*; *nur Sg.* overwrought state; (*Reizbarkeit*) irritability; (*Nervosität*) edginess; **Überreizung** *f* (*das Überreizen*) *von Haut etc.*: irritation; *von Augen, Nerven*: straining; (*das Aufregen*) overexcitement; (*die Überreiztheit*) → *Überreiztheit*

überrennen *v/t.* (*unreg., trennb., hat*) knock down; *bes. Mil.* overrun; *fig.* bulldoze; *sich nicht* ~ *lassen* not let oneself be bulldozed

überrepräsentiert *Adj.* overrepresented

Überrest *m mst Pl.* remains *Pl.*; *Pl. e-r Kultur etc.*: relics; → *sterblich* I

überrieseln *v/t.* (*untr., hat*); *geh. Flüssigkeit*: trickle down; (*Feld etc.*) irrigate; *es überrieselte mich heiß und kalt fig.* it sent hot and cold shivers down my spine

überrissen I. *P.P.* → *überreißen*; **II.** *Adj. Tennis etc.*: *ein* ~*er Ball* a lob

Überrollbügel *m Mot.* roll bar

überrollen *v/t.* (*untr., hat*); *Mil.* overrun; *Zug etc.*: run over; *fig.* steamroller

überrumpeln *v/t.* (*untr., hat*) catch s.o. unawares (*od.* by surprise), throw *s.o.* off (his *od.* her) guard; *sich* ~ *lassen* be caught napping; *j-n mit e-r Frage* ~ surprise s.o. with a question; *lass dich von ihm bloß nicht* ~ just don't let him catch you unawares; **Überrump(e)lung** *f* surprise attack

überrunden *v/t.* (*untr., hat*); *Sport* lap; *fig.* outstrip; **Überrundung** *f Sport* lapping; *fig.* outstripping

übers *Präp.* + *Art.*; *umg.* **über das**; → *Knie* 1, *Ohr* 2

übersät *Adj.*: ~ *mit* strewn (*od.* littered, dotted) with, covered in; *Narben*: pitted with

übersättigen *v/t.* (*untr., hat*) oversaturate; *Wirts.* (*Markt*) *auch* glut; *Chem.* supersaturate; **übersättigt I.** *P.P.* → *übersättigen*; **II.** *Adj. Wirts., Markt*: glutted; *Chem.* supersaturated; **2.** *fig.* sated; **Übersättigung** *f* surfeit; *Wirts.* glut(ting); *Chem.* supersaturation

übersäuern *v/t.* (*untr., hat*) overacidify (*auch Med., Agr.*); **Übersäuerung** *f* hyperacidity (*auch Med.*); *Agr., des Bodens*: overacidity, sourness

Überschall *m* ultrasound; ~**flugzeug** *n Flug.* supersonic aircraft; ~**geschwindigkeit** *f* supersonic speed; *mit* ~ *fliegen* travel faster than the speed of sound; ~**knall** *m* sonic boom

überschatten *v/t.* (*untr., hat*) overshadow; *fig.* cast a cloud over; **überschattet von** *fig.* clouded by

überschätzen (*untr., hat*) **I.** *v/t.* overestimate; (*Können etc.*) overrate; *ein totál überschätzter Roman etc.*: a completely overrated novel *etc.*; **II.** *v/refl.* have too high an opinion of o.s.; *er überschätzt sich auch* he's not as good (*od.* clever) as he thinks; *er hat sich mal wieder völlig überschätzt* he has completely overestimated himself again; **Überschätzung** *f* overestimation; (*Überbewertung*) overrating

überschaubar *Adj.* clear; (*leicht verständlich*) *auch* easy to grasp; (*kontrollierbar*) manageable; *Folgen, Risi-*

ko *etc.*: calculable; *in der* ~*en Zukunft* in the foreseeable future; ~ *bleiben Menge, Größe etc.*: keep within reasonable (*od.* manageable) limits, *Entwicklung, Situation etc.*: not get out of hand; *kaum* ~ *sein Folgen etc.*: be virtually incalculable; **Überschaubarkeit** *f*; *nur Sg.* clarity; comprehensibility; manageability; → *überschaubar*; **überschauen** *v/t.* (*untr., hat*); *wörtl.* (*Bucht etc.*) look out over; (*verstehen*) have a good idea of; (*im Griff haben*) have under control; (*Entwicklung etc.*) keep track of; (*Folgen, Risiko etc.*) be able to calculate

überschäumen *v/i.* (*trennb., ist -ge-*) froth over; *fig.* bubble over (*vor* + *Dat.* with); *vor Wut*: fume; **überschäumend I.** *Part. Präs.* → *überschäumen*; **II.** *Adj. fig.* ebullient, exuberant; ~*e Freude* unbridled joy; *sie hat ein* ~*es Temperament* she is vivacious (*od.* bubbly); *von* ~*er Fröhlichkeit* with exuberant happiness

überschlafen *v/t.* (*untr., hat*) sleep on *s.th.*; *er wird den Vorschlag erst mal* ~ he is going to sleep on the suggestion first of all; *das muss ich erst mal* ~ I'll have to sleep on it first

Überschlag *m* **1.** *Turnen*: somersault; (*Handstand mit* ~) handspring; *Flug.* loop; *e-n* ~ *machen* do (*od.* turn) a somersault (*od.* handspring); *Flug.* loop the loop; **2.** *beim Rechnen*: (rough) estimate; **3.** *Etech.* flashover

über'schlagen¹ (*unreg., untr., hat*) **I.** *v/t.* **1.** (*überblättern*) skip, miss; **2.** (*schätzen*) calculate roughly, give a rough estimate of; **II.** *v/refl.* **1.** *Person*: go head over heels; *Auto etc.*: overturn; *Flug.* loop the loop; *beim Landen*: nose over; **2.** *Stimme*: crack; **3.** *fig.*: *die Ereignisse überschlugen sich* things started happening very fast; **4.** *sich vor Hilfsbereitschaft etc.* (*fast*) ~ *umg. fig.* (almost) trip over o.s. in an attempt to help *etc.*

'überschlagen² (*unreg., trennb., -ge-*) **I.** *v/t.* (*hat übergeschlagen*): *die Beine* ~ cross one's legs; **II.** *v/i.* (*ist*) **1.** *Funke*: spark (*od.* jump) over; **2.** *fig.*: ~ *in* (+ *Akk.*) turn into

überschlagen³ I. *P.P.* → *überschlagen¹*; **II.** *Adj.* (*lauwarm*) lukewarm, tepid

überschlägig *Adj. Kosten etc.*: estimated

überschnappen *v/i.* (*trennb., ist -ge-*) **1.** *umg.* (*verrückt werden*) go crazy, crack up, go mad; *sag mal, bist du jetzt völlig übergeschnappt?* hey, have you completely lost your mind?; → *auch übergeschnappt*; **2.** *Stimme*: crack

überschneiden *v/refl.* (*unreg., untr., hat*) **1.** overlap; *zwei Linien*: intersect; **2.** *fig. zeitlich*: coincide; *teilweise*: overlap; (*sich überkreuzen, einander in die Quere geraten*) clash; *die beiden Sendungen* ~ *sich* the two program(me)s clash; **Überschneidung** *f* **1.** overlapping; intersection; **2.** *fig.* coincidence; clash(ing)

Überschreibemodus *m EDV* overwrite mode

überschreiben *v/t.* (*unreg., untr., hat*) **1.** (*Aufsatz etc.*) head; **2.** (*übertragen*) transfer; (*Besitz*) *auch* make s.th. over (+ *Dat.* to); (*Rechte*) sign over (to); **3.** *EDV* overwrite; **Überschreibung** *f* **1.** *bes. Jur.* transference; **2.** *EDV, von Zeilen etc.*: overwriting

überschreien *v/t.* (*Redner etc.*) shout

down
überschreiten *v/t.* (*unreg., untr., hat*)
1. cross; *Überschreiten der Gleise verboten* passengers must not cross the tracks; **2.** *fig.* (*Maß, Grenze*) exceed, overstep; (*Gesetz*) violate, infringe; (*Geschwindigkeit*) exceed; (*Summe*) go over, top; *die Milliardengrenze ~* top the billion (*Brit. auch* the one thousand million) mark; *die zulässige Geschwindigkeit um ... km/h ~* exceed the speed limit by ... km/h; *er hat die Siebzig bereits überschritten* he's already over (*od.* past) seventy; → *Grenze* 2; **Überschreitung** *f* **1.** crossing (+ *Gen.* of); **2.** *fig.* overstepping *etc.*; *Jur.* violation, infringement, contravention *geh.*; *~ der zulässigen Geschwindigkeit* exceeding (*od.* breaking) the speed limit
Überschrift *f* heading, title; (*Schlagzeile*) headline
Überschuhe *Pl.* overshoes, galoshes, *Am. auch* rubbers
überschuldet *Adj.* heavily indebted; *Land:* debt-heavy; *~ sein auch* have heavy debts, be heavily (*od.* deeply) in debt; **Überschuldung** *f* debt overload, heavy debts *Pl.*
Überschuss *m* surplus (*an + Dat.* of); (*Gewinn*) profit; *ein ~ an Waren/Energie etc. auch* surplus goods/energy *etc.*; **überschüssig** *Adj.* surplus, excess
über'schütten[1] *v/t.* (*untr., hat*): *mit etw. ~* throw s.th. over (*od.* at) *s.th. od. s.o.,* (*Flüssigkeit*) spill s.th. (all) over *s.th. od. s.o.;* *mit Geschenken, Ehren etc. ~ fig.* shower *s.o.* with, heap ... on *s.o.*
'überschütten[2] *v/t.* (*untr., hat -ge-*); *umg.:* *j-m etw. ~* throw s.th. over s.o; (*Flüssigkeit*) spill s.th. over s.o.; *s-n Kaffee ~* spill one's coffee
Überschwang *m;-(e)s, kein Pl.* exuberance; *im ~ der Gefühle* carried away by one's feelings; *im ~ der Begeisterung* in a wave of enthusiasm
überschwänglich **I.** *Adj.* effusive, gushing; **II.** *Adv.* effusively, gushingly; *sich ~ bedanken etc.* express one's thanks *etc.* effusively; *e-n Erfolg ~ feiern* celebrate a success wildly; **Überschwänglichkeit** *f* effusiveness
überschwappen *v/i.* (*trennb., ist -ge-*) *Flüssigkeit:* slop over (the edge); *Gefäß:* slop (over)
überschwemmen *v/t.* (*untr., hat*) flood, *fig. auch* inundate; *Wirts.* (*den Markt*) flood, glut; **überschwemmt** **I.** *P.P.* → *überschwemmen;* **II.** *Adj.* flooded; *fig. Markt:* glutted; *~ mit Aufträgen, Besuchern etc.:* swamped with; **Überschwemmung** *f* flooding; (*Hochwasser*) flood; *im Bad e-e ~ anrichten umg. fig.* flood the bathroom (*by splashing*)
Überschwemmungs|gebiet *n* flood area; *~katastrophe* *f* flood disaster
überschwenglich → *überschwänglich;* **Überschwenglichkeit** *f* → *Überschwänglichkeit*
Übersee *ohne Art.: in/nach ~* overseas; *von ~* from overseas; *~hafen* *m* international port; *~handel* *m* overseas trade (*bes. Am.* commerce)
überseeisch *Adj. attr.* overseas ...
übersehbar *Adj. Gelände etc.:* open; *fig. Folgen, Risiko:* calculable; *Schaden etc.:* assessable; *Lage etc.:* clear; → *auch überschaubar*
über'sehen[1] *v/t.* (*unreg., untr., hat*)
1. → *überblicken;* **2.** (*erfassen*) grasp;

(*abschätzen*) assess; → *auch überschauen;* **3.** (*nicht bemerken*) overlook, miss; (*nicht beachten*) ignore; (*Mangel etc.*) absichtlich: turn a blind eye to; *von j-m ~ werden* escape s.o.'s notice; *bewusst ~* deliberately ignore; *ein Problem etc. ist nicht mehr zu ~* can no longer be ignored
'übersehen[2] *v/t.* (*unreg., trennb., hat -ge-*); *umg.:* *sich (Dat.) etw. ~* grow tired of s.th.; *das Kleid hab ich mir übergesehen* I've grown tired of the dress
übersenden *v/t.* (*unreg., untr., hat*) send (*j-m etw.* s.o. s.th., s.th. to s.o.); *anbei ~ wir Ihnen ...* please find enclosed...; **Übersendung** *f* sending
übersetzbar *Adj.* translatable; *schwer/kaum ~* hard / virtually impossible to translate; **Übersetzbarkeit** *f; nur Sg.* translatability
über'setzen[1] *vt/i.* (*untr., hat*) **1.** translate (*in + Akk.* into; *aus* from); (*etw.*) *schriftlich ~* produce a written translation (of s.th.); *falsch ~* translate wrong(ly), mistranslate; *das lässt sich nicht/schwer ~* it's impossible/difficult to translate; *etw. in Musik/Bilder ~* translate s.th. into music/pictures; **2.** *Tech.* transmit
'übersetzen[2] (*trennb., -ge-*) **I.** *v/t.* (*hat*) ferry *s.o. od. s.th.* across (*od.* over); **II.** *v/i.* (*hat od. ist*) ferry across the river *etc.*
Übersetzer *m; -s, -, ~in* *f; -, -nen* translator; *EDV* compiler
übersetzt **I.** *P.P.* → *übersetzen*[1]; **II.** *Adj.* **1.** *Tech.: richtig ~ sein* have the correct transmission; *~es Programm* *EDV* compiled program; **2.** *bes. schw.* (*übertrieben hoch*) *Preis, Geschwindigkeit etc.:* excessive
Übersetzung *f* **1.** translation (*aus* from; *in + Akk.* into); (*Version*) version; *EDV* translation; *wir schreiben morgen e-e ~* (*Klassenarbeit*) we're going to do a translation tomorrow; **2.** *Tech.* (*Übersetzungsverhältnis*) (gear) ratio, gearing; *große od. hohe / kleine ~* high/low ratio
Übersetzungs|arbeit *f* translation work (*einzelne:* job); *~büro* *n* translation agency; *~fehler* *m* translation error (*od.* mistake); mistranslation; *~programm* *n* *EDV* translation program; *~verhältnis* *n* *Tech.* transmission ratio; *von Getrieben:* gear ratio
Übersicht *f nur Sg.* **1.** (*Überblick*) overall view, *bes. Am.* overview; *e-e ~ bekommen* obtain a general idea (*über +Akk.* of); *sich e-e ~ verschaffen* brief o.s. (*über +Akk.* on), find out what's going on *umg.;* *die ~ verlieren* lose track of things; *ihm fehlt die ~* he doesn't know what is going on *umg.;* **2.** (*Zusammenfassung*) survey; (*Tabelle*) table, chart; *e-e ~ über etw. geben* give an outline of s.th.
übersichtlich **I.** *Adj.* **1.** *Gelände etc.:* open; *Kurve:* clear; *die Kreuzung ist ~* the crossing (*Am.* intersection) permits a clear view; **2.** *fig.* (*klar dargestellt*) clear(ly arranged); *in der Fassung:* lucid; **II.** *Adv.: ~ dargestellt etc.* clearly represented *etc.;* **Übersichtlichkeit** *f; nur Sg.;* (*klare Darstellung*) clarity; (*Anlage*) clear arrangement (*od.* layout)
Übersichts|karte *f* general map; *~plan* *m* general plan; *~tabelle* *f* (synoptic) chart; *~tafel* *f* general overview board
übersiedeln *v/i.* (*trennb., ist -ge-*) move (*nach* to); **Übersiedler** *m,* **Übersied-**

-lerin *f* **1.** migrant; **2.** *hist.* East German migrant (*to the Federal Republic of Germany*); **Übersiedlung** *f* move (*nach* to); (*Auswanderung*) migration
übersinnlich *Adj.* **1.** *Kräfte etc.:* extrasensory, psychic, supernormal; *~e Wahrnehmung* extrasensory perception, ESP; **2.** (*übernatürlich*) supernatural
überspannen *v/t.* (*untr., hat*) **1.** (*Fluss etc.*) span; *Archit.* vault; (*bespannen*) cover; **2.** (*zu stark spannen*) overstretch; *Tech.* strain; (*Saite*) pull too tight; **3.** *fig.* (*Forderungen*) carry too far; → *Bogen* 3; **überspannt** **I.** *P.P.* → *überspannen;* **II.** *Adj.* **1.** (*affektiert*) unnatural, affected; (*exaltiert*) highly-strung; (*hysterisch*) hysterical; (*exzentrisch*) eccentric; **2.** (*übertrieben, überspitzt*) exaggerated, over the top, OTT *umg.;* **Überspanntheit** *f* **1.** unnaturalness, affectedness, affectation; highly-strung nature; hysteria; **2.** exaggeratedness; → *überspannt*
Überspannung *f Etech.* excess voltage; **Überspannungsschutz** *m Etech.* overvoltage (*Am.* surge) protection
überspezialisiert *Adj.* overspecialized; **Überspezialisierung** *f* overspecialization
überspielen *v/t.* (*untr., hat*) **1.** (*nicht merken lassen*) cover *s.th.* up; *etw. geschickt ~* do a good job of covering s.th. up; *j-n* (*ausschalten*) eliminate s.o. (*by cunning means*); **2.** (*Aufnahme*) record (*auf + Akk.* onto); (*auch Daten*) transfer (to); **3.** *Sport* outplay; **Überspielung** *f* (*Aufnahme*) (re)recording
überspitzt **I.** *Adj. Formulierung etc.:* oversubtle; (*übertrieben*) exaggerated; **II.** *Adv.* in an oversubtle way; (*übertrieben*) in an exaggerated way; *~ ausdrücken* exaggerate
über'springen[1] *v/t.* (*unreg., untr., hat*) **1.** jump (*over*), clear; **2.** *fig.* (*übergehen*) skip; *e-e Klasse etc. ~* skip a class *etc.*
'überspringen[2] *v/i.* (*unreg., trennb., hat -ge-*) leap over (*od.* across); *Etech.* flash; *durch ~de Funken in Brand geraten* be set on fire by flying sparks; *~ von ... zu fig. im Gespräch etc.:* flit from ... to; *s-e Fröhlichkeit sprang auf alle über* everybody was infected by his cheerfulness; *fig.* → *auch Funke* 1
übersprudeln *v/i.* (*trennb., ist -ge-*) bubble over (*fig. vor + Dat.* with); **übersprudelnd** **I.** *Part. Präs.* → *übersprudeln;* **II.** *Adj. Laune:* bubbly; *Temperament:* frothy
über'sprühen[1] *v/t.* (*untr., hat*) spray; *etw. mit etw. ~* spray s.th. with s.th., spray s.th. onto s.th.
'übersprühen[2] *v/i.* (*trennb., ist -ge-*): *~ vor (+ Dat.*) bubble over with
Übersprunghandlung *f Verhaltensforschung:* sparking-over (*od.* substitute) activity
überspülen *v/t.* (*untr., hat*) wash over
überstaatlich *Adj.* supranational
überstechen *v/t.* (*unreg., untr., hat*) *bei Kartenspielen:* beat
über'stehen[1] *v/t.* (*unreg., untr., hat*) (*Krankheit, Not etc.*) get over, recover from; (*Katastrophe etc., auch lebend überstehen*) survive, come out of *s.th.* alive; (*Strapaze*) survive *umg.;* (*Sturm, Krise*) weather, ride out; *das Schlimmste überstanden haben Kranker:* be out of danger; *umg. fig.* be over the worst; *etw. überstanden ha-*

ben *umg.* have got s.th. over (and done) with; **das wäre überstanden!** *umg.* that's that (over and done with), that's that out of the way; **sie hat es überstanden** *euph.* (*ist tot*) she's at rest now

'überstehen² *v/i.* (*unreg., trennb., hat, südd., schw., österr. ist -ge-*) jut out, project

übersteigen *v/t.* (*unreg., untr., hat*) **1.** cross, climb over; **2.** *fig.* go beyond, exceed (*auch Erwartungen, Verständnis etc.*); *Wirts. auch* top

übersteigert *Adj.* exaggerated; *Psych., Geltungsbedürfnis etc.: auch* hypertrophied; **~e Erwartungen** high expectations

überstellen *v/t.* (*untr., hat*); *Amtsspr.* hand over; **Überstellung** *f* handing over

übersteuern (*untr., hat*) **I.** *v/t.* (*Verstärker*) overdrive; (*Tonband*) saturate; (*Mikrofon*) overload; **II.** *v/i. Mot.* oversteer; **Übersteuerung** *f Etron.* overdriving; saturating; overloading → **übersteuern**

überstimmen *v/t.* (*untr., hat*) outvote; (*Veto*) override; *Antrag:* vote down

überstrahlen *v/t.* (*untr., hat*) **1.** *Licht:* light up, flood; **2.** *fig.* outshine, eclipse

überstrapazieren *v/t.* (*untr., hat*) **1.** wear out; (*Nerven etc.*) *auch* strain; **2.** *fig.* (*Begriff etc.*) flog to death; (*Geduld*) overtax; (*Gastfreundschaft*) overstrain; **Überstrapazierung** *f fig.* wearing out; straining; flogging to death; overtaxing; overstraining → **überstrapazieren**

überstrecken *v/t.* (*untr., hat*) overstretch

überstreichen *v/t.* (*unreg., untr., hat*) **1.** coat (over); *mit Farbe:* paint over; **2.** *noch einmal:* recoat, repaint; **3.** *Etech.* (*Messbereich*) scan

überstreifen *v/t.* (*trennb., hat -ge-*) slip s.th. over; *sich* (*Dat.*) **~** (*Kondom etc.*) slip s.th. on

über'strömen¹ *v/t.* (*untr., hat*) flood; → **überströmt**

'überströmen² *v/i.* (*trennb., ist -ge-*) **1.** overflow, run over; **2.** *fig.* overflow (*vor + Dat.* with); *auf andere:* spread (*auf + Akk.* to); **überströmend I.** *Part. Präs.* → **überströmen²**; **II.** *Adj. Gefühlsäußerung etc.:* overflowing, exuberant; *zu sehr:* effusive, gushing

überströmt I. *P.P.* → **überströmen¹**; **II.** *Adj.:* **~ von** (*überflutet von*) flooded with; *auch fig.* inundated with; *von Schweiß etc.:* pouring with; *von Licht:* flooded with; **sein Gesicht war von Tränen ~** the tears were streaming down his face

überstülpen *v/t.* (*trennb., hat -ge-*) (*sich* [*Dat.*]) *etw.* **~** put s.th. on; (*Hut etc.*) *auch* pop s.th. on one's head; **warum wollt ihr anderen Menschen euren Glauben ~?** *fig.* why do you want to impose your belief on other people?

Überstunde *f* hour of overtime; *Pl.* overtime *Sg.*; **~n machen** work (*od.* do) overtime; **zwei ~n abfeiern** use up two hours of overtime; **Überstundenzuschlag** *m* overtime premium (*od.* bonus)

überstürzen (*untr., hat*) **I.** *v/t.* rush; **man soll nichts ~** one should never rush into things; **II.** *v/refl. Person:* rush things; **die Ereignisse überstürzten sich** things started happening very fast; **überstürzt I.** *P.P.* → **überstür-**

zen; **II.** *Adj.* hasty; *bes. Entschluss:* rash; *Flucht:* hurried; **III.** *Adv.:* **~ handeln** act hastily

übertariflich I. *Adj.:* **~e Bezahlung** salary in excess of the agreed scale; **II.** *Adv.:* **~ bezahlt werden** receive a salary in excess of the agreed scale

überteuert I. *Adj.* overpriced; **II.** *Adv. anbieten etc.:* at an exorbitant price

Übertitel *m, -s, -* in *Opernaufführungen etc.:* surtitle

übertölpeln *v/t.* (*untr., hat*) dupe, take in; **ich hab mich total ~ lassen** I was completely taken in

übertönen *v/t.* (*untr., hat*) drown (out); **der Chor übertönte die Solistin** the choir drowned out the soloist; **sie versuchte die laute Klasse zu ~** she tried to shout over the noisy class

Übertopf *m* cachepot, ornamental flowerpot holder

Übertrag *m; -(e)s, Überträge; Wirts.* amount carried over; *Math.* amount carried over (*od.* forward)

übertragbar *Adj.* **1.** transferable (*auf + Akk.* to); **nicht ~** non-transferable; *Wirts.* non-negotiable; **2.** *Med.* infectious, catching; **~e Krankheit** *durch Berührung:* contagious disease; **Übertragbarkeit** *f; nur Sg.* **1.** transferability; **2.** *Med.* infectiousness; *durch Berührung:* contagiousness

übertragen¹ (*unreg., untr., hat*) **I.** *v/t.* **1.** transfer (*auf + Akk.* to); *ins Heft etc.:* copy out (*in + Akk.* into); **2.** *Tech., Phys., Etech.* transmit; *Funk., TV auch* broadcast; *EDV* transfer; translate; *im Fernsehen ~ auch* televise; *live ~* broadcast live; **3.** (*Besitz*) make over (*auf + Akk. j-n:* to), transfer (to); (*Grundeigentum*) convey (to); (*Amt, Titel*) confer ([up]on); (*Vollmachten*) delegate (to); **Rechte etc. auf j-n ~** vest s.o. with rights *etc.*; *etw. auf j-s Namen ~* register s.th. in s.o.'s name; **4.** *j-m die Ausführung etc. von etw. ~* charge (*od.* entrust) s.o. with; *j-m* (*mehr*) *Verantwortung ~* give s.o. (more) responsibility; **5.** (*übersetzen*) translate; *ins Englische etc. ~* translate into (*od.* render in[to]) English *etc.*; *in Verse/Prosa ~* put into verse/prose; **6.** (*Stenogramm*) transcribe; *Mus., in andere Tonart:* change (*od.* put) into a different key; **7.** (*anwenden*) apply; **8.** (*Stimmung etc., auch Krankheit*) communicate (*auf + Akk.* to); **Malaria wird durch Insekten ~** malaria is transmitted by insects; **9.** *Med.* (*Blut etc.*) transfuse; *Organ:* transplant; *plastische Chirurgie:* transplant, graft; **10.** *Med.* (*Baby*) carry post-term; **II.** *v/refl. Stimmung, Panik etc.:* spread (*auf + Akk.* to); *Krankheit: auch* be transmitted (to), be passed on (to); **i-e Fröhlichkeit übertrug sich auf uns alle** we were all infected by her cheerfulness

übertragen² **I.** *P.P.* → **übertragen¹**; **II.** *Adj.* **1.** *Bedeutung etc.:* figurative; **im ~en Sinn** in the figurative sense; **2.** *Med.:* **~es Kind** post-term infant

Überträger *m; -s, -; Med.* carrier

Übertragung *f* **1.** (*alle auf + Akk.* to) transfer (*auch Wirts.*); *von Rechten etc.:* assignment; (*Delegierung*) delegation; *e-s Amtes:* conferment; *von Grundeigentum:* conveyance; **2.** *Radio, TV* broadcast, transmission; *Tech., Phys.* transmission; *EDV* transfer, transmission; **3.** *e-r Krankheit:* transmission; (*Ansteckung*) infection; **4.** *Med., von Blut:* transfusion; *von*

Organ, Gewebe etc.: transplant; *Vorgang:* transplanting; **5.** (*Übersetzung*) translation (**ins Deutsche** *etc.* into German *etc.*), rendering (in[to]); **6.** (*von Kurzschrift, auch vom Tonband*) transcription; *Ergebnis:* transcript; (*Anwendung*) application

Übertragungs|art *f Telek., EDV etc.* transmission mode; **~fehler** *m Telek., EDV* transmission error; **~geschwindigkeit** *f Telek., EDV* transmission speed; **~rate** *f Telek.* transmission rate; **~rechte** *Pl. TV etc.* broadcasting rights; **~wagen** *m Radio, TV* outside broadcast (*od.* OB) van (*od.* unit), *Am.* television truck

übertreffen *v/t.* (*unreg., untr., hat*) (*Person*) excel (**sich selbst** o.s.), outstrip; (*auch Sache*) surpass, beat (*alle:* **an** + *Dat.*, **in** + *Dat.* in); (*Befürchtungen, Hoffnungen etc.*) go beyond, surpass, exceed; **alle Erwartungen ~** exceed all expectations; **nur noch übertroffen werden von ...** be second only to ...; **nicht zu ~ sein** be unbeatable; **mit dem Menü hat Heidi sich selbst übertroffen** Heidi has surpassed herself with this set menu

übertreiben *v/t/i.* exaggerate; (*Tätigkeit*) overdo (*zu weit gehen mit*) *auch* carry s.th. too far; (*übertrieben darstellen*) exaggerate, overstate; **es ~** *umg.* take things too far (*od.* to extremes), go over the top; **stark ~** grossly exaggerate, lay it on thick *umg.*; **sie übertreibt** (**es**) **mit der** *od.* **i-r Sparsamkeit** she takes her economizing too far; **übertreib nicht so!** *umg.* stop exaggerating; **das Buch ist toll - sie hat wirklich nicht übertrieben** she really wasn't exaggerating; **man kann's auch ~** *umg.* you can take things too far; → **übertrieben**; **Übertreibung** *f* exaggeration, overstatement; **man kann ohne ~ sagen, ...** it's no exaggeration to say

'übertreten¹ *v/i.* (*unreg., trennb., ist od. hat -ge-*) **1.** (*ist*) pass, step over; *in e-e andere Schule etc.:* move (to); **2.** (*ist, hat*); *Sport* step out of bounds (*od.* over the line); *Weitsprung:* overstep the board; **ungültiger Versuch wegen Übertretens** no-jump due to overstepping; **3.** (*ist*); *Fluss:* overflow (its banks); **4.** (*ist*); *Pol. etc.* go over (*zu* to); *kirchl.* convert (to)

über'treten² *v/t.* (*untr., hat*) (*Gesetz etc.*) violate, infringe; **Übertretung** *f Jur.* violation, infringement (+ *Gen.* of); *absolut: auch* offen|ce (*Am.* -se)

übertrieben I. *P.P.* → **übertreiben**; **II.** *Adj.* exaggerated; *bes. Verhalten etc.: auch* over-the-top *umg.*, OTT *umg.*; (*unmäßig*) *Preis, Forderungen etc.:* excessive; *Ansichten:* extreme; *leicht ~* slightly exaggerated; **etw. in ~em Maße tun** overdo s.th., go to extremes with s.th.; **20 % Trinkgeld? - das ist nun wirklich ~** that's really excessive, that's way too much *umg.*; **III.** *Adv.* exaggeratedly; (*unmäßig*) excessively; *großzügig/liberal etc.:* to a fault *nachgestellt*; **~ ängstlich** overanxious; **~ reagieren** overreact; **~ freundlich** *pej.* overfriendly

Übertritt *m* **1.** *Pol.* defection (*zu* to); *kirchl.* conversion (to); **2.** *Schule:* move, change; **der ~ ins Gymnasium** *etc.* transferring to the grammar school *etc.*; **Übertrittszeugnis** *n Schule:* report with the average mark (*Am.* grade) required to enter a school of a higher academic standard

übertrumpfen *v/t.* (*untr., hat*) trump;

fig. auch outdo, go one better than; ***sich gegenseitig mit etw. zu ~ versuchen*** try to outdo one another with s.th.

übertünchen *v/t.* (*untr.*, *hat*) whitewash; *fig. auch* gloss over

überübermorgen *Adv.* in three days' time

Übervater *m* grand old man

überversichern *v/t.* (*untr.*, *hat*) overinsure; ***sich ~*** overinsure o.s.; **überversichert I.** *P.P.* → *überversichern*; **II.** *Adj. Person:* overinsured

Überversorgung *f* oversupply (***mit*** of)

übervölkert *Adj.* overpopulated; **Übervölkerung** *f*; *nur Sg.* overpopulation

übervoll *Adj. Gefäß etc.*: too full, full to overflowing (***von*** with); *Raum etc.*: *auch* overcrowded (with)

übervorsichtig *Adj.* overcautious

übervorteilen *v/t.* (*untr.*, *hat*) cheat, do *umg.*; **Übervorteilung** *f* cheating

überwachen *v/t.* (*untr.*, *hat*); (*beaufsichtigen*) supervise; *polizeilich:* keep under surveillance; *Med.*, *wissenschaftlich:* observe; *TV*, *Funk.* monitor; *EDV* monitor; ***die Tankstelle wird mit Videokameras überwacht*** (video) surveillance cameras are used to monitor the petrol (*Am.* gas) station

überwachsen¹ *v/t.* (*untr.*, *hat*) grow all over, cover

überwachsen² I. *P.P.* → *überwachsen¹*; **II.** *Adj.* overgrown (***mit*** with)

Überwachung *f* supervision; *polizeilich:* surveillance, policing; *Med. etc.*: observation; *TV*, *Funk.*, *EDV* monitoring

Überwachungs|anlage *f im Geschäft etc.*: closed-circuit television; **~kamera** *f* (video) surveillance (*od.* security) camera; **~staat** *m pej.* Big Brother state; **~system** *n* surveillance (*od.* monitoring) system; **~zentrale** *f* control cent|re (*Am.* -er)

überwältigen *v/t.* (*untr.*, *hat*) **1.** overpower; **2.** *fig. Gefühle etc.*: overcome; ***überwältigt werden von e-m Anblick*** *etc.*: be overwhelmed by; ***vom Schlaf*** *etc.*: be overcome with; **überwältigend I.** *Part. Präs.* → *überwältigen*; **II.** *Adj. Anblick, Eindrücke etc.*: overwhelming (*auch Pol.*, *Mehrheit*); *Schönheit: auch* breathtaking; ***nicht*** (***gerade***) ***~*** *umg. iro.* nothing to write home about, no great shakes; **Überwältigung** *f* overpowering (+ *Gen.* of); *stärker:* defeat

überwechseln *v/i.* (*trennb.*, *ist* -ge-) **1.** **~ auf** (+ *Akk.*) *auf ein anderes Thema, e-e andere Schule etc.*: switch to; **auf die andere Seite ~** *Pol.* go over to the other side; **2.** *Wild, Person etc.*: cross over (**auf** + *Akk.* **zu** to); **zur anderen Straßenseite ~** cross the road; **auf e-e andere Spur ~** *Mot.* change (*od.* switch) lanes

überweisen *v/t.* (*unreg.*, *untr.*, *hat*) **1.** (*Geld*) transfer (**auf ein Konto:** to); *per Post®:* remit (+ *Dat.* to); **j-m Geld ~** transfer money to s.o.'s account; **2.** (*Patienten*) refer (+ *Dat. od.* **an** + *Akk.* to); **Überweisung** *f* **1.** *von Geld:* transfer; *per Post:* remittance; **2.** *e-s Patienten:* referral; (*Schein*) letter of referral; **j-m e-e ~ schreiben** write s.o. a letter of referral

Überweisungs|auftrag *m* remittance order; **~formular** *n* transfer form; **~schein** *m Med.* letter of referral, referral slip

überweit *Adj.* too large (*od.* big); *Mode:* outsize, *Am. auch* extended size;

Wirts. extra large; **Überweite** *f* extra large size

'überwerfen¹ *v/t.* (*unreg.*, *trennb.*, *hat* -ge-); (*Kleidungsstück*) slip on; *eilig:* throw on

über'werfen² *v/refl.* (*unreg.*, *untr.*, *hat*): ***sich mit j-m ~*** fall out with s.o.; ***er hat sich mit s-r Schwester/Familie völlig überworfen*** he has fallen out completely (*od.* had a complete falling out) with his sister/family

überwiegen *vt/i.* (*unreg.*, *untr.*, *hat*) *zahlenmäßig:* predominate; (*vorherrschen*) *auch* be predominant; ***Zustimmung überwog*** there was a consensus, most people *etc.* were in agreement; ***die Neugier überwog s-e Angst*** his curiosity outweighed his fear; **überwiegend I.** *Part. Präs.* → *überwiegen*; **II.** *Adj.* predominant; (*vorherrschend*) prevailing; ***der ~e Teil von Personen, Stimmen etc.*: the majority; *von Dingen:* the greater part, the bulk; ***die ~e Mehrheit*** the vast majority; ***zum ~en Teil*** → III; **III.** *Adv.* predominantly; *weitS.* (*hauptsächlich*) mainly, chiefly, (*zum größten Teil*) for the most part; **~ trocken** *Met.* mainly (*od.* mostly) dry

überwindbar *Adj.* surmountable; **überwinden** (*unreg.*, *untr.*, *hat*) **I.** *v/t.* (*Ängste, Schwächen etc.*) overcome; (*Krise, Krankheit etc.*) get over; *lit.* (*besiegen*) conquer (*auch fig. Ängste etc.*); (*Standpunkt etc.*) get away from, outgrow; (*Entwicklungsstadium etc.*) get past; **ein Hindernis ~** clear a hurdle; **große Entfernungen zu Fuß ~** cover great distances on foot; **den Krebs / den Hunger in der Welt ~ wollen** want to beat cancer / eradicate hunger from the world; → *auch überwunden*; **II.** *v/refl.*: ***sich*** (***selbst***) ***~*** overcome one's inhibitions; (*sich zwingen*) force o.s.; **sich dazu ~ zu** (+ *Inf.*) bring (*od.* get) o.s. to (+ *Inf.*); **ich musste mich ~, (um) zu** (+ *Inf.*) I had to force myself to (+ *Inf.*), I really had to make an effort to (+ *Inf.*); **sich zu e-r Arbeit ~ müssen** force o.s. to do a job; **Überwindung** *f* **1.** (*Niederlage*) defeat; (*Sieg*) conquest; **2.** (*Anstrengung*) (conscious *od.* concerted) effort; (*Selbstüberwindung*) will power; **es kostete mich ~ / einige** *od.* **viel ~** I had to force myself / it took a real effort of will

überwintern (*untr.*, *hat*) **I.** *v/i.* **1.** (*den Winter verbringen*) spend the winter (**in** + *Dat.* in, at); **2.** (*den Winter überstehen*) overwinter; *engS.* (*Winterschlaf halten*) hibernate; **II.** *v/t.* (*Pflanzen etc.*) overwinter; **Überwinterung** *f* overwintering

überwölben *v/t.* (*untr.*, *hat*) vault; *Dach etc.*: *auch* form a vault over

überwuchern *v/t.* (*untr.*, *hat*) overgrow; **Überwucherung** *f* overgrowth

überwunden I. *P.P.* → *überwinden*; **II.** *Adj.*: **ein ~er Standpunkt** an opinion (that) one has outgrown; **ein ~es Vorurteil** *etc.* a prejudice *etc.* (that) one has overcome; **der Rassismus** *etc.* **in diesem Land ist noch lange nicht ~** there is still a long way to go before the fight against racism *etc.* in this country has been won; **die Tuberkulose galt schon als ~** the fight against tuberculosis was already considered (to have been) won

Überwurf *m* **1.** wrap, shawl; **2.** *Ringen:* sit-back

Überzahl *f*; *nur Sg.*: **in der ~ sein** be in

---

the majority; *weitS.* (*überwiegen*) predominate; *Gegner:* be superior in number; *Sport etc.*: have a numerical advantage; ***die Mädchen sind in der ~ auch*** the girls outnumber the boys

überzählig *Adj. attr.* (*überschüssig*) surplus ...; (*übrig*) spare ...; ***drei Leute waren ~*** there were three people too many

überzeichnen *v/t.* (*untr.*, *hat*) **1.** *Wirts.* oversubscribe; **2.** (*übertrieben darstellen*) overdraw; **überzeichnet I.** *P.P.* → *überzeichnen*; **II.** *Adj.* **1.** *Wirts.* oversubscribed; **2.** (*übertrieben dargestellt*) overdrawn; **Überzeichnung** *f* **1.** *Wirts.* oversubscription; **2.** overdrawing; *weitS.* caricature

Überzeit *f schw.* (*Überstunden*) overtime

überzeugen (*untr.*, *hat*) **I.** *v/t.* convince (***von*** of); **j-n ~, dass** *auch* persuade s.o. that; **j-n zu ~ suchen** reason with s.o.; **er lässt sich nicht ~** he won't be persuaded; **II.** *v/i. durch Leistung:* be convincing; ***das Team überzeugte in jeder Hinsicht*** the team gave a convincing performance in every respect; **III.** *v/refl.* satisfy o.s. (***von*** as to); go and see (*od.* find out) for o.s.; ***~ Sie sich selbst!*** go and see for yourself; **sich von der Wahrheit e-r Aussage ~** verify (*umg.* check out) a statement; ***davon muss ich mich selbst ~*** I'll have to see that for myself

überzeugend I. *Part. Präs.* → *überzeugen*; **II.** *Adj.* convincing (*auch Leistung etc.*); *Argument, Beweis: auch* conclusive; *auch Sieg:* telling; **~ sein** *od. wirken* *Argument etc.*: *auch* carry conviction; **nicht ~ sein** *od. wirken* *auch* lack conviction; **III.** *Adv.* (*be*)*siegen etc.*: convincingly

überzeugt I. *P.P.* → *überzeugen*; **II.** *Adj.* convinced (***von*** of), positive (about); *Sozialist, Christ etc.*: convinced; **fest von e-r Sache ~ sein** be thoroughly convinced of s.th.; **von sich selbst** (**sehr**) **~ sein** have a (very) high opinion of o.s.; **ich bin noch nicht** (**ganz**) **~** *auch* I'm not (completely) persuaded yet

Überzeugung *f* conviction; (*fester Glaube*) firm belief; *politische etc.*: convictions *Pl.*; **gemeinsame ~** shared belief; **gegen s-e ~ handeln** go against one's convictions; **der ~ sein, dass ...** be convinced that ...; *weitS.* (*der Meinung sein*) be of the opinion that ...; **der festen ~ sein, dass ...** be firmly (*od.* absolutely) convinced that ...; **zu der ~ gelangen, dass ...** come to the conclusion that, come to believe that ...; **wenn Sie wirklich der ~ sind** if that's what you really believe; **zu s-r ~ stehen** have the courage of one's convictions

Überzeugungs|arbeit *f* **1.** (*Überreden*) effort at persuasion; ***es war einiges an ~ zu leisten*** there was a lot of persuading (*od.* convincing) to do; **2.** *Pol. altm.* pro-Communist agitation; **~kraft** *f* powers *Pl.* of persuasion; *e-s Arguments etc.*: persuasiveness, logic; **~täter** *m*: ***er ist ein ~*** he committed the crime out of moral (*od.* religious, political) conviction; *umg. fig.* (*handelt aus Überzeugung*) he acts on conviction; **politischer ~** politically-motivated offender, political criminal

über'ziehen¹ (*unreg.*, *untr.*, *hat*) **I.** *v/t.* **1.** (*bedecken, einhüllen*) cover; (*Kissen etc.*) put a cover on; (*Kopfkissen*) put a pillowslip (*bes. Am.* pillowcase) on;

U

Gastr. coat; **das Bett ~** make up the bed; **das Bett frisch ~** change the sheets (on the bed), change the bed linens, put clean sheets on (the bed); **neu ~** (*Polstermöbel*) reupholster; **2.** (*übertreiben*) overdo, exaggerate; **s-e Kritik ~** overdo (*od.* go overboard with) one's criticism; **II.** *v/refl. Himmel:* become overcast; **es überzieht sich** it's clouding over; **III.** *vt/i.* **1.** *Wirts.* overdraw (one's account *od.* credit); (*Konto, Kredit*) overdraw; **2.** *zeitlich:* go over the time limit (**um** by), break the deadline; *terminlich:* fail to meet the deadline; (*Redezeit, Sendezeit etc.*) overrun (**um** by); **etw. ~** *auch* go on longer than allowed

'überziehen² *v/t.* (*unreg., trennb., hat -ge-*) put on, slip over; **sich** (*Dat.*) **etw. Warmes ~** put on s.th. warm; **j-m eins ~ umg.** land s.o. one; **Überzieher** *m; -s, -* **1.** *umg.* (*Kondom*) rubber; **2.** *altm.* (*Mantel*) overcoat

Überziehung *f Wirts., von Konto, Kredit:* overdraft

Überziehungs|kredit *m Wirts.* overdraft facility; **~zins** *m* overdraft interest rate

überzogen I. *P.P.* → **überziehen¹**; **II.** *Adj.* **1.** *Gastr. etc.* coated; **2.** *Wirts., Konto:* overdrawn; **3.** (*übertrieben*) exaggerated; **total ~** *umg.* over the top, OTT

überzüchtet *Adj. Bio.* overbred; *Tech. etc. und fig.* oversophisticated

überzuckern *v/t.* (*untr., hat*) sugar over

Überzug *m* **1.** (*Kissenhülle*) pillowcase, pillowslip; **2.** (*dünne Schicht*) coat; *aus Schokolade etc.:* coating

ubiquitär *Adj. Bio.* ubiquitous

üblich *Adj.* usual, customary; (*herkömmlich*) conventional; (*normal*) normal, *bes. Tech.* standard; **der Bus kam mit der ~en Verspätung an** the bus arrived late as usual; **wie ~** as usual; **es ist bei uns (so) ~, dass ...** it's a custom with us that ...; **das ist allgemein ~** that's quite normal (*od.* common) (**bei** for), that's the norm; **das ist bei ihr so ~** that's quite usual for her; *pej.* that's her usual way of doing things; **Übliche** *n; -n, kein Pl.:* **das ~** the usual thing; **das ~?** *in der Bar etc.:* the usual?; **üblicherweise** *Adv.* usually, normally

U-Boot *n Mil., Naut.* submarine; *umg. fig.* (*Spitzel*) mole; **~Besatzung** *f* submarine crew; **~Kommandant** *m* submarine commander; **~Krieg** *m* submarine war(fare); **~Stützpunkt** *m* submarine base

übrig *Adj.* **1.** (*als Rest verbleibend*) remaining; **das ~e ..., die ~en ...** the rest of the ...; (*verbleibende[n]*) *auch* the remaining ...; **~ bleiben** *od.* **sein** be left (over); **~ behalten** *od.* **haben** have s.th. left; **~ lassen** leave (*j-m etw.* s.o. s.th); **es blieb mir nichts anderes ~** (**als es zu tun**) I had no choice (but to do it); **was blieb mir anderes ~?** what (else) could I do?; **... lässt viel/wenig/ nichts zu wünschen ~ ...** leaves a lot / little / nothing to be desired; **~ haben** have s.th. to spare; **keine Zeit ~ haben** have no time to spare; **hätten Sie vielleicht ein paar Minuten/Mark für mich ~?** I wonder if you could spare me a couple of minutes/marks?; **3.** *fig.:* **etw. ~ haben für** have a soft spot for; **nichts ~ haben für** not care much for; **für Mauscheleien habe ich gar nichts ~** I've no time for

wheeling and dealing; **4.** *subst.:* **die Übrigen** the rest (of them); **das Übrige** the rest (of it); **alles Übrige, alle Übrigen** all the rest; **im Übrigen** (*ansonsten*) (as) for the rest; → **übrigens**; **ein Übriges tun** do one more thing; **Sie können ein Übriges tun und Anzeige erstatten** you could do one last thing and file a report

übrig bleiben → **übrig** 1

übrigens *Adv.* (*nebenbei bemerkt*) by the way, incidentally; (*außerdem*) besides; **~, was ich noch sagen wollte, ... auch** oh yes (*od.* yeah *umg.*), what I was going to say was, ...; **das schmeckt ~ sehr gut** it actually tastes very good, it 'does taste very good; **das war ~ eben mein Chef** that was my boss, by the way

übrig haben → **übrig** 2, 3

übrig lassen → **übrig** 1

Übung *f* **1.** *nur Sg.;* (*das Üben od. Geübtsein*) practice; **aus der ~ sein/kommen** be/get out of practice; **in ~ sein** be in (good) form; **in (der) ~ bleiben** stay in practice; → **Meister** 2; **2.** (*einzelne, Übungsaufgabe*) exercise (*auch Mus., Turnen etc.*); **e-e ~ am Reck turnen** do (*od.* perform) an exercise on the horizontal bar; **3.** *Univ. etc.:* seminar; **4.** *der Feuerwehr etc.:* drill, exercise; **5.** *Reli.:* **geistliche ~en** spiritual exercises

Übungs|arbeit *f* mock test; **~aufgabe** *f* exercise; **~buch** *n* **1.** book of exercises; **2.** *zu e-m Lehrbuch:* workbook; **~flug** *m* practice run; **~gelände** *n* training ground

übungshalber *Adv.* (just) for practice, to keep a hand in

Übungs|hang *m Skisport:* nursery (*od.* beginners') slope, *Am.* bunny run; **~heft** *n* exercise book; **~leiter** *m*, **~leiterin** *f im Turnverein etc.:* trainer, coach; *hum.* (*Trainer[in]*) coach; **~munition** *f* blank ammunition; **~platz** *m Mil.* training area; *Sport* training ground; **~raum** *m für Musiker etc.:* practice room; **~sache** *f:* **das ist reine ~!** it's all a matter of practi|ce (*Am. auch* -se) *od.* training

UdSSR *f; -;* *Abk. hist.* (**Union der Sozialistischen Sowjetrepubliken**) USSR (= Union of Soviet Socialist Republics)

UEFA|-Cup *m*, **~-Pokal** *m* UEFA (= Union of European Football Associations) cup

U-Eisen *n; -s, -; Tech.* U-iron

Ufer *n; -s, -;* (*Meeresufer*) shore; (*Seeufer*) shores *Pl.;* (*Flussufer*) bank; **ans ~** ashore; **am ~** on the shore; *e-s Sees:* on the edge of the lake; *e-s Flusses:* on the banks of the river; **über die ~ treten** overflow (its banks); **das sichere ~ erreichen** reach dry land; *fig.* reach terra firma; **zu neuen ~n aufbrechen** *fig.* head in a new direction; **vom andern ~ ~** *umg.* (*homosexuell*) gay; *pej.* queer; **~befestigung** *f auch Pl.* bank reinforcement; **~böschung** *f*, **~damm** *m* embankment

uferlos *Adj. fig.* boundless; *Debatte etc.:* endless; *Pläne:* extravagant, wild; **ins Uferlose führen** be endless, go on and on; **das führt ins Uferlose** *auch* where does it (all) end?

Ufer|promenade *f* esplanade; *am Meer:* promenade; *am Fluss:* riverside path; *am See:* lakeside path; **~straße** *f am Meer:* coast road; *am Fluss:* riverside road; *am See:* lakeside road; **~streifen** *m* bank; **~weg** *m am Meer:*

shore (*od.* coastal) path; *am Fluss:* riverside path; *am See:* lakeside path; **~zone** *f* shore area

uff *Interj. umg.;* (*ist das schwer!*) phew, oof; *überrascht:* ooh

Ufo *n; -(s), -s; Abk.* UFO, unidentified flying object; *engS.* flying saucer *umg.;* **Ufologe** *m; -n, -n*, **Ufologin** *f; -, -nen* ufologist

u-förmig *Adj.* U-shaped

Uganda (*n*); *-s; Geog.* Uganda; **Ugander** *m; -s, -*, **Uganderin** *f; -, -nen* Ugandan, *weiblich auch:* Ugandan woman (*od.* girl *etc.*); **ugandisch** *Adj.* Ugandan

uh *Interj. umg.* ugh

U-Haft *f* → **Untersuchungshaft**

Uhr *f; -, -en* **1.** clock; (*Armband-, Taschenuhr*) watch; **nach m-r ~ ist es vier** it's four o'clock by (*od.* according to) my watch; **2.** *nur Sg.; Uhrzeit:* **um vier ~** at four o'clock; **um wie viel ~?** (at) what time?; **wie viel ~ ist es?** what time is it?, what's the time?; **wie viel ~ haben Sie?** what time do you make it (*Am.* have you got?)?; **wie viel ~ ungefähr?** approximately (*od.* round about) what time?; **3.** *fig.:* **rund um die ~** (a)round the clock; **rund um die ~ geöffnet** open 24 hours (*bes. Am.* 24/7), open night and day; **ein Rennen gegen die ~** a race against the clock (*od.* against time); **wissen, was die ~ geschlagen hat** know how things stand; **dort gehen die ~en anders** they do things differently there; → **ablaufen** I 5, **inner...**, **schlagen** I 7

Uhr(arm)band *n* watch|strap (*Am.* -band)

Uhren|geschäft *n* watchmaker's (*od.* clockmaker's) shop; **~industrie** *f* clock and watch industry

Uhr|feder *f* watch spring; **~glas** *n* watch glass; **~kette** *f* watch chain; **~macher** *m*, **~macherin** *f* watchmaker, clockmaker, horologist *altm. und geh.;* **~werk** *n* watch (*od.* clock) mechanism, works *Pl.;* **wie ein ~** mechanical(ly); **mit der Regelmäßigkeit e-s ~s** regular as clockwork

Uhrzeiger *m* (clock *od.* watch) hand; **~sinn** *m:* **im ~** clockwise; **entgegen dem ~** anti-clockwise, *Am.* counterclockwise, *schottisch:* widdershins

Uhrzeit *f* time; **um welche ~ ...?** at what time?; **haben Sie die genaue ~?** do you have the exact time?; → *auch* **Uhr** 2

Uhu *m; -s, -s; Orn.* eagle owl

ui *Interj.* wow

Ukas *m; -ses, -se; hist.* ukase; *umg.* edict

Ukraine [ukra'i:nə] *f; -; Geog.* Ukraine; **Ukrainer** *m; -s, -*, **Ukrainerin** *f; -, -nen* Ukrainian; *weiblich auch:* Ukrainian woman (*od.* girl *etc.*); **ukrainisch** *Adj.* Ukrainian; **Ukrainisch** *n; -en; Ling.* Ukrainian; **das ~e** Ukrainian

Ukulele *f; -, -n* ukulele, uke

UKW *ohne Art. Abk.* (**Ultrakurzwelle**) *Phys.* USW (= ultrashort wave); *Radio etc.:* VHF (= very high frequency); **auf ~ senden/empfangen** *etc.* on VHF; **~-Bereich** *m* VHF range; **~-Sender** *m* VHF station

Ulan *m; -en, -en; Mil. hist.* uhlan, ulan

Ulk *m; -(e)s, kein Pl.* joke; **aus ~** *umg.* for a laugh, as a joke; **e-n ~ machen** play (*od.* clown) around; → *auch* **Spaß**, **ulken** *v/i.* clown (*od.* play) around; **mit Worten:** joke; **ulkig** *Adj. umg.* funny (*auch seltsam*); **Ulknudel** *f umg.;* (*bes. Komikerin*) joker

Ulme *f*; -, -*n*; *Bot.* elm; **Ulmensterben** *n* Dutch elm disease

ultimativ I. *Adj.*: ~*e Forderung* ultimatum (*Pl.* ultimatums *od.* ultimata); ~*en Charakter haben* take the form of an ultimatum; **II.** *Adv.* in the form of an ultimatum; **Ultimatum** *n*; -*s*, *Ultimaten* ultimatum (*Pl.* ultimatums *od.* ultimata); *j-m ein* ~ *stellen* give s.o. an ultimatum; *das* ~ *läuft heute ab* today is the deadline for the ultimatum

Ultimo *m*; -*s*, -*s*; *Wirts.* last (trading) day of the month; *bis* ~ until the last day of the month; (*spätestens*) by the last day of the month; *fig.* until the last minute

Ultra *m*; -*s*, -*s*; *Pol.* extremist

ultrahocherhitzt *Adj. attr. Milch*: long-life ...

Ultra|kurzwelle *f Phys.* ultra-short wave; *Radio etc.*: very high frequency (*Abk.* VHF); *siehe auch* **UKW**...; ~**leichtflugzeug** *n* microlight plane

ultramarin *Adj.*, **Ultramarin** *n*; -*s*, *kein Pl.* ultramarine

ultra|modern *Adj.* ultramodern; ~**rechts** *Adj. attr.* extreme right-wing

Ultraschall *m Phys.* ultrasound; *mit* ~ *untersuchen* examine by using ultrasound; ~**bild** *n* ultrasound image; ~**diagnostik** *f* ultrasound diagnostics *Pl.* (*V. im Sg.*); ~**gerät** *n* ultrasound scanner; ~**ortung** *f*, ~**peilung** *f* ultrasonic sounding; ~**untersuchung** *f* ultrasound scan, sonogram; ~**welle** *f* ultrasonic wave

ultraviolett *Adj.* ultraviolet; ~*e Strahlung* ultraviolet radiation; **Ultraviolett** *n* ultraviolet

um I. *Präp.* (+ *Akk.*) **1.** *räumlich*: round, *Am.* around; **2.** *zeitlich, ungefähr*: about, around; *genau*: at; *so* ~ *halb fünf umg.* at around (*od.* about) half past four; **3.** *Maß*: ~ ... *steigen, kürzen etc.*: by; ~ *die Häfte größer etc.*: by half; **4.** (*für*) for; ~ *5 Euro etc. österr.* for five euros; *Schritt* ~ *Schritt* step by step; **5.** (*in Bezug auf*) about; *kämpfen, bitten etc.*: for; → *drehen* IV 1, 3, 4, *handeln*[1] I 4; **6.** ~ *j-s/e-r Sache willen* for the sake of; → *ums etc.*; **II.** *Konj.*: ~ *zu* (+ *Inf.*) (in order) to (+ *Inf.*); ~ *ehrlich zu sein* to be honest; *zu krank,* ~ *zu arbeiten* too ill to work; **III.** *Adv.* **1.** (*etwa*) about, around; **2.** (*vorüber*): ~ *sein* be over; *die Zeit ist* ~ *bei Prüfung, Quiz etc.*: time's up; **3.** ~ *und* ~ (*ganz und gar*) completely

umadressieren *v/t.* (*trennb., hat*) redirect

umändern *v/t.* (*trennb., hat* -*ge*) change, alter; **Umänderung** *f* change, alteration

umarbeiten *v/t.* (*trennb., hat* -*ge*); (*ändern*) change, modify; (*Kleid etc.*) remodel; (*Buch etc.*) revise, adapt; (*Schriftstück*) rewrite, recast; *für den Film etc.*: adapt; *e-n Ring etc.* ~ *lassen* have a ring *etc.* altered

umarmen *v/t.* (*untr., hat*) embrace; *fest*: hug (*beide auch sich* ~); *sie umarmten und küssten sich* they embraced (*od.* hugged) and kissed; **Umarmung** *f* embrace; *feste*: hug

Umbau *m Pl.* -*ten e-s Hauses*: renovation, *Am. auch* rehab; *zu etw. Neuem*: conversion; (*Umänderung*) alteration(s *Pl.*); (*umgebauter Teil*) altered section; *fig.* reorganization; *wegen* ~ *geschlossen* closed for renovation; *der* ~ *der Feuerwache zum Kulturzentrum* the conversion of the fire station into a cultural cent|re (*Am.* -*er*); ~**arbeiten**

Pl. renovation work *Sg.*; *zu etw. Neuem*: conversion work *Sg.*; *zu e-r Umänderung*: alteration work *Sg.*

'umbauen[1] (*trennb., hat* -*ge*) **I.** *vt/i.* **1.** renovate, *Am. auch* rehab; *zu etw. Neuem*: convert; (*umändern*) alter; ~ *in* (+ *Akk.*) *od.* *zu auch* turn into; *wir bauen um Schild etc.*: alterations in progress; **2.** *fig.* reorganize; **II.** *v/i. Theat., Film*: change the setting

um'bauen[2] *v/t.* (*untr., hat*) build around, surround; *umbauter Raum* enclosed space

Umbaukosten *Pl.* renovation (*od.* conversion *od.* alteration) costs → *Umbau*

umbehalten *v/t.* (*unreg., trennb., hat*) keep *s.th.* on

umbenennen *v/t.* (*unreg., trennb., hat*) rename, rechristen (*in* + *Akk.* [as] *s.th.*); **Umbenennung** *f* renaming

umbesetzen *vt/i.* (*trennb., hat*) *Theat.* recast; *Pol.* reshuffle; **Umbesetzung** *f Theat.* recasting; *Pol.* reshuffle

umbetten *v/t.* (*trennb., hat* -*ge*) **1.** (*Kranken etc.*) move to another bed; (*Leiche*) rebury; **2.** (*Fluss*) rechannel; **Umbettung** *f* **1.** *e-r Leiche*: reburial; **2.** *e-s Flusses*: rechannel(l)ing

umbiegen (*unreg., trennb.*, -*ge*) **I.** *v/t.* (*hat*) bend; *nach unten*: turn down; *nach oben*: turn up; **II.** *v/i.* (*ist*) *Mot.* turn (a)round, turn back (again)

umbilden *v/t.* (*trennb., hat* -*ge*) reshape, remodel; (*neu organisieren*) reorganize; (*Regierung etc.*) reshuffle; **Umbildung** *f* reshaping, remodel(l)ing; reorganization; *Pol.* reshuffle

umbinden *v/t.* (*unreg., trennb., hat* -*ge*) tie (a)round; (*Schürze, Krawatte etc.*) put on

umblasen *v/t.* (*unreg., trennb, hat* -*ge*) blow down (*od.* over); *umg. fig.* blow away

umblättern (*trennb., hat* -*ge*) **I.** *v/i.* turn (over) the page; **II.** *v/t.*: *die Seite* ~ turn over the page

umblicken *v/refl.* (*trennb., hat* -*ge*) → *umsehen*

Umbra *f*, -, *kein Pl. Farbe*: umber

'umbrechen[1] (*unreg., trennb.*, -*ge*) **I.** *v/t.* (*hat*); (*Baum etc.*) break down; *Agr.* (*Boden*) break up; **II.** *v/i.* (*ist*) break

um'brechen[2] *v/t.* (*unreg., untr., hat*); *Druck.* make up

umbringen (*unreg., trennb., hat* -*ge*) **I.** *v/t.* kill, murder; **II.** *v/refl.* kill o.s., commit suicide; *du wirst dich noch* ~! *umg. fig.* you'll kill yourself if you're not careful; *das bringt mich noch um! umg.* that'll be the death of me; *sich* (*fast*) ~ *umg.* bend over backwards

Umbruch *m* **1.** (*Wandel*) (great) upheaval, deep-rooted change; *sich in e-m* ~ *befinden* be going through a time of upheaval; **2.** *mst Sg.*; *Druck., EDV* make-up; **3.** *Agr.* ploughing, *Am.* plowing; ~**phase** *f* period of upheaval

Umbruch(s)zeit *f* time of upheaval

umbuchen *vt/i.* (*trennb., hat* -*ge*) **1.** *Wirts.* transfer (*auf* + *Akk.* to); **2.** *Flug.* change one's booking (*Am.* reservation); (*Flug, Termin etc.*) change; *j-n auf e-n anderen Flug etc.*: transfer s.o. (on)to another flight *etc.*; **Umbuchung** *f* **1.** *Wirts.* transfer (*auf* + *Akk.* to); **2.** *e-s Flugs*: change in booking (*Am.* reservation); **Umbuchungsgebühr** *f* alteration fee

umdenken *v/i.* (*unreg., trennb., hat* -*ge*) change one's ideas (*od.* approach); ~ *müssen* have to do some

rethinking; *in od.* *bei etw.* ~ change one's ideas about *s.th.*; **Umdenken** *n* shift in thinking, rethink; *dabei ist* ~ *angesagt* this calls for a rethink; **Umdenk(ungs)prozess** *m* rethinking process

umdeuten *v/t.* (*trennb., hat* -*ge*) give a new interpretation to; **Umdeutung** *f* reinterpretation, new interpretation

umdichten *v/t.* (*trennb., hat* -*ge*) rework; *fig.* (*verfälschen*) falsify

umdirigieren *v/t.* (*trennb., hat* -*ge*) redirect

umdisponieren (*trennb., hat*) *v/i.* change one's arrangements (*od.* plans)

umdrängen *v/t.* (*untr., hat*) throng around, crowd

umdrehen (*trennb.*, -*ge*) **I.** *v/t.* (*hat*) turn ([a]round); *fig.* (*Spion etc.*) turn; *j-m den Arm* ~ twist s.o.'s arm; *die Taschen* ~ *auch umg. fig.* turn out one's pockets; → *Magen, Mark*[3], *Mund, Pfennig, Spieß* 1; **II.** *v/i.* (*hat, ist*) turn (a)round, turn back (again); **III.** *v/refl.* (*hat*) turn (a)round; *sich* ~ *nach* turn (a)round to look at; *sich auf dem Absatz* ~ *fig.* turn on one's heel, turn tail; → *drehen* IV; **Umdrehung** *f* turn (*auch Tech., der Schraube etc.*); *Tech., Phys.* revolution, rotation; ~*en pro Minute* (*abgek.* *U/min*) revolutions per minute (*abgek.* rpm)

Umdrehungs|geschwindigkeit *f* speed of rotation; ~**zahl** *f* speed, number of revolutions per minute *etc.*

umeinander *Adv. räumlich*: (a)round each other; *sich kümmern etc.*: about each other

umerziehen *v/t.* (*unreg., trennb., hat*) re-educate; **Umerziehung** *f* re-education; **Umerziehungslager** *n* re-education camp

um'fahren[1] *v/t.* (*unreg., untr., hat*) drive (*Naut.* sail) (a)round; (*Kap*) *auch* round; (*vermeiden*) bypass; *den Stau etc. großräumig* ~ steer well clear of the traffic jam *etc.*

'umfahren[2] *v/t.* (*unreg., trennb., hat* -*ge*) run down, run over; (*auch etw.*) knock down

Umfahrung *f* **1.** *e-s Ortes etc.*: driving (*Naut.* sailing) (a)round; (*das Vermeiden*) bypassing of *s.th.*; *die* ~ *des Kaps* the rounding of the cape; **2.** *bes. schw., österr.* (*Umgehungsstraße*) bypass

Umfall *m umg. pej.* about-turn, about-face

umfallen *v/i.* (*unreg., trennb., ist* -*ge*) **1.** fall (down *od.* over); (*ohnmächtig werden*) faint; (*zusammenbrechen*) collapse; *zum Umfallen müde* ready to drop; → *tot* 1 a; **2.** *umg. pej.* (*nachgeben*) give in; (*aufgeben*) yield, capitulate; *der Zeuge ist umgefallen* the witness has given in; **Umfaller** *m*; -*s*, -; *umg. pej.* weathercock

Umfang *m*; -(*e*)*s*, *Umfänge* **1.** *e-s Kreises etc.*: circumference (*auch Math.*); **2.** *e-r Person, e-s Baums etc.*: girth; *s-e Oberarme haben e-n* ~ *von 40 cm* his upper arms measure 40cm in circumference; **3.** *e-s Geländes etc.*: area; (*Ausdehnung*) extent; **4.** *fig.* extent (*auch e-s Schadens etc.*), size (*auch wissenschaftlicher Arbeiten*); (*Reichweite, Bereich*) range; *e-s Projkts etc.*: scope; *e-e Stimme von drei Oktaven* ~ a voice with a range of three octaves; *e-n ungeahnten* ~ *annehmen* Problem *etc.*: take on unexpected proportions; *in vollem* ~(*e*) fully; *in großem* ~(*e*) on a large scale, large-scale ...

umfangen v/t. (unreg., untr., hat); (umarmen) embrace; fig. surround; **Dunkelheit/Stille umfing sie** darkness/silence enveloped her; **umfänglich** Adj. **1.** Absperrungen, Vorbereitungen: extensive; Sammlung, Briefwechsel etc.: extensive; **2.** umg., hum. Person: voluminous

umfangreich I. Adj. **1.** Recherchen, Wissen etc.: extensive; ~es **Werk** substantial work, hefty tome umg.; **2.** (geräumig) spacious; **3.** Singstimme: **seine Stimme ist äußerst** ~ his voice has an enormous range; **4.** umg. (dick) voluminous; **II.** Adv. dokumentieren, darstellen etc.: extensively

Umfangsberechnung f calculation of the size (od. circumference od. area); → **Umfang**; e-s geplanten Buches etc.: estimated size

umfärben v/t. (trennb., hat -ge-) dye a different colo(u)r

umfassen v/t. (untr., hat) **1.** (umsäumen) enclose, surround; Mil. encircle; **2.** (umarmen, umschlingen) embrace, put one's arms (a)round; (mit der Hand) grip; **3.** fig. (in sich schließen) contain, comprise; (bestehen aus) consist of; zeitlich: cover; **umfassend I.** Part. Präs. → **umfassen**; **II.** Adj. comprehensive, extensive; (vollständig) complete, full; (durchgreifend) sweeping, drastic; ~es **Geständnis** full confession; **III.** Adv. informieren etc.: comprehensively; (vollständig) completely, fully; (durchgreifend) drastically; **Umfassung** f (Einfassung, Einfriedung) enclosure

Umfeld n; nur Sg.; (Umgebung) environment, milieu; (Gebiet) sphere; **das soziale** ~ **des Angeklagten** the social environment of the accused; **aus dem rechtsextremistischen** ~ from the circles Pl. of the far-right

um'fliegen¹ v/t. (unreg., untr., hat) fly (a)round s.th.

'umfliegen² v/i. (unreg., trennb., ist -ge-); umg. fall over

umfließen v/t. (unreg., untr., hat) flow (a)round s.th.

umflort Adj. **1.** Blick, Stimme: veiled; **2.** Bild etc.: präd. und nachgestellt: surrounded by flowers

umformatieren v/t. (trennb., hat) EDV reformat; **Umformatierung** f reformatting

umformen v/t. (trennb., hat -ge-) reshape; (Konstruktion etc.) redesign; Etech. transform, convert; Ling. (Satz etc.) convert; **direkte in indirekte Rede** ~ convert direct speech into reported speech; **die Technik hat den Menschen umgeformt** technology has transformed humankind; **Umformer** m; -s, -; Etech. converter, transformer

umformulieren v/t. (trennb., hat) reword, rephrase; **nur leicht umformuliert wiedergeben** reword slightly; **Umformulierung** f rewording, rephrasing

Umformung f reshaping; conversion; transformation; → **umformen**

Umfrage f inquiry; öffentliche: (public) opinion poll, survey (**über** + Akk. on); **die** ~ **hat ergeben, dass ...** the results of the survey show that ...; ~**werte** Pl. (opinion) poll results

umfrieden v/t. (untr., hat) enclose, fence off, put a fence up (a)round; **mit e-r Mauer** ~ enclose with a wall; **Umfriedung** f enclosure, fence

umfüllen v/t. (trennb., hat -ge-) pour (od. put) into another container (od. jug etc.); (Wein) decant; **Wein aus**

Fässern in Flaschen ~ pour wine from barrels into bottles

umfunktionieren v/t. (trennb., hat) convert (**zu** into); **e-e Vorlesung in e-e Demo** ~ turn a lecture into a demo; **Umfunktionierung** f conversion (**zu** into)

Umgang m **1.** nur Sg.; (soziale Kontakte) contact, relations Pl.; (Bekanntenkreis) company, acquaintances Pl., (circle of) friends Pl.; ~ **haben** od. **pflegen mit** associate with; **guten/ schlechten** ~ **haben** keep good/bad company; **sie ist kein** ~ **für dich** she's not your type, she's not the sort of person you ought to be hanging around with pej. umg.; **2.** nur Sg.; (Beschäftigung): **der** ~ **mit Kindern/Kunden** etc. dealing with children/customers etc.; **der ständige** ~ **mit Büchern/ Tieren** etc. having a lot to do with books/animals etc.; **im** ~ **mit** (in) dealing with; **geschickt sein im** ~ **mit Kindern** have a way with children; **den** ~ **mit Wörterbüchern** etc. **lernen** learn how to use (od. handle) dictionaries etc.; **3.** Archit. gallery; **4.** kirchl. procession

umgänglich Adj. affable, amiable, Präd. auch easy to get along with; **Umgänglichkeit** f; nur Sg. affability, amiability

Umgangs|formen Pl. manners; (Verhalten) behavio(u)r Sg. in public; **j-s** ~ auch the way Sg. s.o. treats other people; **er hat keine** ~ he doesn't know how to behave (toward[s] other people); **gute** ~ **besitzen** have good manners; ~**recht** n Jur. right of access

Umgangssprache f colloquial language; (saloppe Sprache, Slang) slang; **die englische** ~ colloquial English etc.; (**die**) ~ **ist dort überall Englisch** English is used everywhere there as the language of communication; **umgangssprachlich I.** Adj. colloquial; **II.** Adv. colloquially; **sehr/zu** ~ **geschrieben** etc. written etc. in a very colloquial style / in too colloquial a style

Umgangston m: **es herrscht ein guter/ rüder** ~ there's a good atmosphere, they get along well with each other / they are rude to one another; **die haben e-n** ~**!** just listen to the way they talk to each other; **er fand nicht den richtigen** ~ he couldn't find the right level of communication

umgarnen v/t. (untr., hat) ensnare

umgeben v/t. (unreg., untr., hat) surround (**sich** o.s.; **mit** with); **mit Mauern / e-m Zaun** ~ wall/fence in

Umgebung f **1.** e-r Stadt etc.: surroundings Pl., environs Pl.; **in der** ~ (+ Gen.) od. **von** in the vicinity of; e-r Stadt etc.: on the outskirts of; (um ... herum) (a)round; **2.** (Nachbarschaft) neighbo(u)rhood; j-s: environment (auch Milieu), weitS. auch vicinity; **gibt es** (**hier**) **in der** ~ **ein Hotel?** is there a hotel around here (od. in the vicinity)?; **e-e bekannte/fremde** ~ familiar/unfamiliar surroundings; **sich an e-e neue** ~ **gewöhnen/anpassen** get used to / adapt to new surroundings; **3.** e-r hoch gestellten Persönlichkeit etc.: entourage; **die Menschen s-r nächsten** ~ the people he is closest to; **4.** Phon. environment

Umgebungs|bedingungen Pl. environmental conditions; ~**temperatur** f ambient temperature

Umgegend f, -, -en; umg. surrounding

area

'umgehen¹ v/i. (unreg., trennb., ist -ge-) **1.** go (a)round; (die Runde machen) Gerücht etc.: circulate, go the rounds umg.; Gespenst: walk; **an** od. **in e-m Ort** ~ haunt a place; **2.** ~ **mit** (etw., j-m) manuell und fig.: handle; (behandeln) treat; (fertig werden mit) manage, deal with; (Maschine, Apparat etc., bedienen) use, work; (**gut**) ~ **können mit** know how to handle etc.; (geschickt sein im Umgang mit) have a way with, be good with; **er kann nicht mit Geld** ~ he's no good with money; **ich weiß gar nicht, wie ich damit** ~ **soll** I don't know what to do with it; fig. (mit e-m Problem) I don't know how to handle (od. deal with) it; → **schonend** III, **sparsam** II

um'gehen² v/t. (unreg., untr., hat) **1.** go (a)round; (Stadt, Verkehr etc., auch Etech.) bypass; **2.** fig. (vermeiden) avoid; (auch Gesetz etc.) evade; geschickt: elude, sidestep, get (a)round umg.; **es lässt sich nicht** ~ there's no getting around it; **es lässt sich nicht** ~, **dass er ...** there's no way he can avoid (od. get [a]round) (+ Ger.)

umgehend I. Part. Präs. → **umgehen¹**; **II.** Adj. immediate; **ich bitte um** ~**e Antwort/Zusendung** etc. please reply / send it etc. promptly; **III.** Adv. immediately

Umgehung f bypassing; (Straße) bypass; fig. avoidance, auch Jur. evasion; **unter** ~ **des Dienstwegs** by circumventing the proper channels; **Umgehungsstraße** f bypass; (Ringstraße) ring road, Am. beltway

umgekehrt I. P.P. → **umkehren**; **II.** Adj. Reihenfolge etc.: reverse, inverted; (entgegengesetzt) opposite, contrary; **es ist genau** ~**!** (no,) it's exactly the other way (a)round; **in** ~**er Reihenfolge** in reverse order; **III.** Adv. the other way (a)round; (dagegen ...) on the other hand, conversely; **was er will, will sie nicht und** ~ and vice versa; **es kam genau** ~ the opposite happened

umgestalten v/t. (trennb., hat) reshape; Tech. etc. auch redesign; (neu ordnen) auch rearrange; **Umgestaltung** f reshaping; redesigning; rearrangement

umgestülpt I. P.P. → **umstülpen**; **II.** Adj. von innen nach außen: attr. inside-out ..., präd. inside out; von oben nach unten: attr. upside-down ..., präd. upside down; Behälter: upturned

umgestürzt I. P.P. → **umstürzen**; **II.** Adj. fallen; Lastwagen etc.: overturned

umgewöhnen v/refl. (trennb., hat -ge-) readapt

umgießen v/t. (unreg., trennb., hat -ge-) **1.** → **umfüllen**; **2.** Metall. refound, recast; **3.** umg. (verschütten) spill

umgraben vt/i. (unreg., trennb., hat -ge-); (Garten) dig over; (Boden) break up; **erst** ~, **dann säen** dig (Am. turn) over the soil before sowing

um'greifen¹ v/t. (unreg., untr., hat) **1.** (umschließen) surround; **2.** fig. comprise; **3.** mit den Händen: grasp; mit den Armen: put (od. get) one's arms (a)round

'umgreifen² v/i. (unreg., trennb., hat -ge-) change one's grip

umgrenzen v/t. (untr., hat) **1.** (umschließen) surround, enclose, encircle; **2.** fig. define; **Umgrenzung** f **1.** enclosure; **2.** fig. e-s Begriffs etc.: definition

umgruppieren v/t. (trennb., hat) regroup; (*Unternehmen*) reshuffle; **Umgruppierung** *f* regrouping; reshuffling; → *umgruppieren*

umgucken *v/refl.* (*trennb.*, *hat -ge-*); *umg.* → *umsehen*; **der wird sich (noch) ~!** *fig.* he's in for a surprise!

umhaben *v/t.* (*unreg.*, *trennb.*, *hat -ge-*); *umg.* have on

umhacken *v/t.* (*trennb.*, *hat -ge-*); (*Baum etc.*) chop (*od.* cut) down; (*Unkraut etc.*) cut down

Umhang *m*; *-(e)s*, *Umhänge* cape

umhängen *v/t.* (*trennb.*, *hat -ge-*) **1.** (*Schal etc.*) put on; (*Gewehr*) sling over one's shoulder; (*beide auch sich* [*Dat.*] *~*); *sich* (*Dat.*) *e-e Decke etc. ~* drape a blanket *etc.* around one's shoulders; **2.** (*Bild etc.*) rehang, hang somewhere else

Umhängetasche *f* shoulder bag

umhauen *v/t.* (*trennb.*, *hat -ge-*) **1.** (*fällen*) fell, cut down; *umg.* (*Angreifer etc.*) knock down; **2.** *umg. fig.* bowl over, floor; *Starkbier etc.*: knock *s.o.* out; *es haut mich fast umgehauen Nachricht etc.*: I was floored; *ihn haut so schnell nichts um* he's not so easily floored

umher *Adv.* (a)round, about; → *auch herum...*; *~blicken* *v/i.* (*trennb.*, *hat -ge-*) look around; *~gehen* *v/i.* (*unreg.*, *trennb.*, *ist -ge-*) walk around (*od.* about); *~irren* *v/i.* (*trennb.*, *ist -ge-*) wander around *od.* about (lost, like a lost soul); *in e-m Ort ~* wander around a place; *~laufen* *v/i.* (*unreg.*, *trennb.*, *ist -ge-*) (*rennen*) run around (*od.* about); (*gehen*) walk around (*od.* about); *~schweifen* *v/i.* (*trennb.*, *ist -ge-*) roam (*od.* wander) around (*od.* about); *~streifen* *v/i.* (*trennb.*, *ist -ge-*) wander around (*od.* about); *~treiben* (*unreg.*, *trennb.*, *-ge-*) **I.** *v/t.* (*hat*) drive around (*od.* about); **II.** *v/i.* (*ist*) drift around (*od.* about); **III.** *v/refl.* (*hat*) hang around (*od.* about); *~ziehen* *v/i.* (*trennb.*, *ist -ge-*) move around

umhinkönnen *v/i.* (*unreg.*, *trennb.*, *hat -ge-*) *ich kann nicht umhin, es zu tun* I can't help doing it; (*kann es nicht vermeiden*) I can't avoid doing it

umhören *v/refl.* (*trennb.*, *hat -ge-*) keep one's ears open, ask around; *sich nach e-r Stelle ~* ask around about a job

umhüllen *v/t.* (*untr.*, *hat*) wrap up (*mit* in), cover (in, with); **umhüllt I.** *P.P.* → *umhüllen*; **II.** *Adj. von Dunkelheit etc.*: enveloped, shrouded (*von* in); **Umhüllung** *f* wrapping

umjubeln *v/t.* (*untr.*, *hat*) cheer; **umjubelt I.** *P.P.* → *umjubeln*; **II.** *Adj.* **1.** celebrated; *von der Menge ~ auch* cheered by the crowd; **2.** *fig.* extremely popular (*von* with); *allgemein ~ werden* enjoy popular acclaim, be widely acclaimed

umkämpfen *v/t.* (*untr.*, *hat*); *Mil.* fight for; (*Gebiet etc.*, *auch fig. Privileg etc.*) dispute; *fig.* (*Sieg etc.*) contest, dispute; → *heiß* II 2

Umkehr *f*; *-*, *kein Pl.* **1.** turning back, return; *j-n zur ~ zwingen* force s.o. to turn back; **2.** *fig.* (*Änderung*) (complete) change; *Pol.* about-face, about-turn, volte-face; (*Reue*) repentance

umkehrbar *Adj.* reversible; *nicht ~* non-reversible

umkehren (*trennb.*, *-ge-*) **I.** *v/i.* (*ist*) turn back; (*den gleichen Weg zurückgehen*) retrace one's steps; *auf halbem Weg / kurz vor dem Ziel ~* turn back halfway / just before reaching one's

goal; *jetzt können wir nicht mehr ~* *fig.* there's no going back now; **II.** *v/t.* (*hat*) turn *s.th.* (a)round; (*das Unterste zuoberst kehren*) turn *s.th.* upside down; (*Tasche etc.*, *umstülpen*) turn *s.th.* (inside) out; *Tech.*, *Etech.*, *fig.* (*Reihenfolge*, *Verfahren etc.*) reverse; *Math.*, *EDV* invert; **III.** *v/refl.* (*hat*) turn (a)round; (*auf den Kopf stellen*) turn on its head; *fig.* reverse; *die Situation kehrte sich um* there was a sudden reverse in the situation; *die Verhältnisse kehrten sich um* the tables turned; → *auch umdrehen*

Umkehr|film *m* *Fot.* reversal film; *~funktion* *f* *Math.* inverse function; *~schluss* *m* *Jur.* argumentum e contrario

Umkehrung *f* *e-r Reihenfolge*: reversal; *von Werten*, *Hierarchien etc.*: inversion; *in der Logik*: conversion

umkippen (*trennb.*, *-ge-*) **I.** *v/t.* (*hat*) tip over; (*umstoßen*) knock over; **II.** *v/i.* (*ist*) **1.** tip over; (*umfallen*) fall over; **2.** *umg.* (*ohnmächtig werden*) faint, keel over; **3.** (*ins Gegenteil umschlagen*) switch (completely); *Stimme*: crack; *umg. gesinnungsmäßig etc.*: give in; *die Stimmung im Saal kippte um* the atmosphere in the room changed; *die Enttäuschung kippte um in Gewalt* disappointment turned into violence; **4.** *Gewässer*: die; *Wein etc.*: go off; → *auch umfallen*

umklammern *v/t.* (*untr.*, *hat*) **1.** clutch onto, hold tight onto; *mit den Fingern*: clutch, grip; (*in der Hand halten*) clasp; *mit den Armen/Beinen ~* wrap one's arms/legs (a)round; *der Ertrinkende umklammerte s-n Retter* the drowning man held tight onto his rescuer; **2.** (*einzwängen*) squeeze in; (*einschließen*) close in on; (*einkreisen*) encircle, surround on all sides; **Umklammerung** *f* **1.** (*tödliche*) *~* (deadly) embrace; *sich aus der ~ lösen* free o.s. from the embrace; **2.** *Boxen*: clinch

umklappbar *Adj.* collapsible, *attr. auch* folding ...; *der Rücksitz ist nach vorn ~ Mot.* the back seat folds down; **umklappen** *v/t.* turn down, fold (back)

Umkleide *f*; *-*, *-n*; *umg.* changing (*Am. auch* dressing) room; **Umkleidekabine** *f* (changing) cubicle; **umkleiden** *v/refl.* (*trennb.*, *hat -ge-*) change (one's clothes), put some other clothes on; **Umkleideraum** *m* *in Geschäft*: changing room; *Theat.* dressing room; *Sport auch* changing (*od.* locker) room

umknicken (*trennb.*, *-ge-*) **I.** *v/t.* (*hat*) **1.** bend (over); *Bäume etc. wie Streichhölzer ~* snap trees *etc.* in half like matchsticks; **2.** (*Papier*) fold (down); **II.** *v/i.* (*ist*) **1.** *Baum etc.*: bend; (*brechen*) snap; *die Blumen sind umgeknickt* the flowers have been bent over; **2.** (*auch mit dem Fuß ~*) twist one's ankle

umkommen *v/i.* (*unreg.*, *trennb.*, *ist -ge-*) **1.** die, be killed, perish *geh.*; *wir sind vor Hitze/Langeweile etc. fast umgekommen umg. fig.* we nearly died of heat/boredom *etc.*; **2.** *fig. Lebensmittel*: go off (*Am.* bad); *man soll nichts ~ lassen* one shouldn't let anything go to waste

Umkreis *m*; *nur Sg.* **1.** (*Umgebung*) vicinity; *im ~ von drei Meilen etc.* within a radius of three miles *etc.*, for three miles *etc.* around; **2.** *fig. e-r Person*: circle(*s Pl.*) surrounding *s.o.*; *ihr engster ~* those closest to her; *im ~ des Kanzlers* those close to the chancellor;

3. *Math.* circumcircle

umkreisen *v/t.* (*untr.*, *hat*) circle ([a]round); *Planet etc.*: revolve (a)round (*auch fig. Gedanken etc.*), orbit; *Satellit*, *Raumschiff*: orbit; **Umkreisung** *f* circling; *Raumf.* orbiting

umkrempeln *v/t.* (*trennb.*, *hat -ge-*) **1.** (*aufschlagen*) roll up; (*umstülpen*) turn *s.th.* inside out; **2.** (*Wohnung etc.*) turn *s.th.* upside down (*od.* on its head); **3.** (*Pläne etc.*) change completely; *umg.* (*j-n*) change; *j-n ~ in* (+ *Akk.*) turn s.o. into; *j-n völlig ~ umg.* make a new person (*od.* somebody new) out of s.o.; *den ganzen Laden ~ umg.* change the whole shop (*Am. auch* store) completely

umkurven *v/t.* (*untr.*, *hat*) (*Platz*, *Rennstrecke etc.*) curve around; (*Hindernis*) swerve around; (*überholen*) swerve around

umladen *vt/i.* (*unreg.*, *trennb.*, *hat -ge-*) reload (*auf*, *in* + *Akk.* onto); (*Frachter etc.*) reload

Umlage *f* (*umgelegter Betrag*) share of the cost; *die ~ betrug ...* each person had to pay ...; *e-e ~ machen* split the cost

um'lagern[1] *v/t.* (*untr.*, *hat*) surround; (*belagern*, *auch fig.*) besiege, belagern *geh.*; *umlagert von Reportern usw.*: surrounded by

'umlagern[2] *v/t.* (*trennb.*, *hat -ge-*) move, transfer (*in* + *Akk.* [in]to; *nach* to), put in another place; *der Patient muss alle zwei Stunden umgelagert werden* the patient must be turned every two hours

Umlageverfahren *n* assessment system

Umland *n*; *nur Sg.* environs *Pl.*, hinterland, surrounding countryside; *im Freiburger ~* in the area surrounding Freiburg

Umlauf *m* **1.** *nur Sg.*; *Phys.*, *Tech.* rotation, revolution; **2.** *Astron.*, *Raumf.* (*Umkreisung*) orbit; *Springreiten*: round; *die Erde braucht für einen ~ um die Sonne ein Jahr* the earth takes a year to revolve around the sun; **3.** *nur Sg.*; *des Geldes*: circulation; *in ~ bringen od. setzen* put in circulation, circulate, issue; (*Kapital*) float; (*Gerücht*) start; *ein Gerücht in ~ setzen auch* get a rumo(u)r going; *im ~ sein* be in circulation; *Gerücht: auch* be going (a)round; **4.** (*Rundschreiben*) circular (letter); *als Überschrift*: please circulate; **5.** *Med.* (*Entzündung*) whitlow; *~bahn* *f* orbit; *auf s-e ~ bringen* put into orbit

'umlaufen[1] *v/i.* (*unreg.*, *trennb.*, *-ge-*) **I.** *v/i.* (*ist*) *Tech. etc.* revolve, rotate; *Blut*, *Geld*, *Bericht*, *Gerücht*: circulate; **II.** *v/t.* (*hat*) *umg.* (*j-n*) knock over

um'laufen[2] *v/t.* (*untr.*, *hat*) run (*od.* move) around; (*Platz*, *Rennstrecke etc.*) run around

umlaufend I. *Part. Präs.* → *umlaufen*[1], *umlaufen*[2]; **II.** *Adj.* Balkon *etc.*: surrounding

Umlauf|geschwindigkeit *f* orbiting speed; *~kapital* *n* current liabilities *Pl.*; *~rendite* *f* *Wirts.* flat yield; *~vermögen* *n* current assets *Pl.*; *~zeit* *f* period (of revolution *etc.*); *Satellit*: orbital period

Umlaut *m* *Ling.* umlaut, (vowel) mutation; (*Laut*) umlaut, mutated vowel; *a~* a-umlaut

umlegen (*trennb.*, *hat -ge-*) **I.** *v/t.* **1.** *nach unten od. seitlich*: turn (*od.* lay) down; *an e-e andere Stelle*: move (*auch Kranken*), transfer; *Telef.* transfer; **2.** (*Kragen, Tuch etc.*) put on (*auch* **sich** [*Dat.*] **~**); **3.** (*Saum*) tuck; **4.** *Tech.* (*Hebel*) turn; (*Schalter etc.*) throw; (*Autositz*) fold down; **5.** (*Mast*) bring down; (*Baum*) fell; **6.** *fig.* (*Kosten*) divide (*auf + Akk.* among); **7.** *fig.* (*Termin*) change, shift (*auf + Akk.* to); **8.** *umg.* (*töten*) bump off; (*niederschlagen*) floor, knock down; **9.** *vulg.* (*Mädchen*) lay *Sl.*; **II.** *v/refl.* **1.** *Getreide etc.*: be flattened; *Boot etc.*: capsize; **Umlegung** *f* **1.** *von Grundstücken etc.*: distribution; *e-s Kranken etc.*: moving; **2.** *von Kosten*: division; **3.** *e-s Termins etc.*: changing

umleiten *v/t.* (*trennb., hat -ge-*) **1.** *Verk.* (*Verkehr*) divert, *Am. auch* detour; **2.** (*Wasserlauf etc.*) divert; **3.** (*Transport, Nachschub etc.*) reroute; **4.** *Telef.* (*Gespräch*) redirect; *EDV* (*Daten*) *auch* reroute

Umleitung *f* **1.** *Verk.* diversion; rerouting; (*Umleitungsstrecke*) diversion, detour; *auf Schildern*: diversion, *Am.* detour; **~ auf die Gegenfahrbahn** contraflow, *Am.* opposite-bound traffic; **2.** *e-s Wasserlaufs*: diversion; **3.** *von Transport, Nachschub etc.*: rerouting; **4.** *Telef., EDV* redirecting, rerouting

Umleitungs|**schild** *n Verk.* diversion (*Am.* detour) sign; **~strecke** *f* diversion, detour

umlenken *v/t.* (*trennb., hat -ge-*) **1.** *ein Auto etc.* **~** turn a car *etc.* (a)round; **2.** *fig.* (*Kräfte etc.*) redirect, rechannel; (*Absichten, Trend etc.*) lead in another direction; *Phys.* deflect; → *auch* **umleiten**

umlernen *v/i.* (*trennb., hat -ge-*) *beruflich*: retrain; **~ müssen** *fig.* have to change one's ideas

umliegend *Adj. attr.* surrounding, neighbo(u)ring, *nachgestellt*: in the vicinity, round about; **die ~e Gegend** the neighbo(u)rhood; (*Umgebung*) the surrounding area

Umluft *f* circulating air; **~betrieb** *m*: **Backofen mit ~** fan-assisted (*Am.* convection) oven; **~herd** *m* cooker (*Am.* stove) with a fan-assisted (*Am.* convection) oven

ummähen *v/t.* (*trennb., hat -ge-*) *Sport, umg.* bring down

ummanteln *v/t.* (*untr., hat*); *Tech.* coat, sheathe (*mit* in); **Ummantelung** *f* coat, sheath

ummauern *v/t.* (*untr., hat*) wall in, build a wall (a)round

ummelden *v/t. und v/refl.* (*trennb., hat -ge-*): **j-n/sich ~** register s.o.'s/one's change of address; **ein Auto ~** change the address under which a car is registered

ummodeln *v/t.* (*trennb., hat -ge-*) remodel, reshape; (*Person, Methode etc.*) change; **die müssen natürlich gleich wieder alles ~** *umg.* of course they have to immediately go and change everything again

ummünzen *v/t.* (*trennb., hat -ge-*); *fig.* turn (*in + Akk.* into); **e-e Niederlage in e-n Sieg ~** make a defeat look like a victory

umnachtet *Adj.* (*auch geistig ~*) mentally deranged; **Umnachtung** *f* (*auch geistige ~*) mental derangement

umnähen *v/t.* (*untr., hat*) stitch

umnebelt *Adj. fig. Blick, Sinne*: befuddled; *Augen*: misty

umnieten *v/t.* (*trennb., hat -ge-*); *umg.* blow away

umnummerieren *v/t.* (*trennb., hat*) renumber

Umnutzung *f* conversion

umordnen *v/t.* (*trennb., hat -ge-*) rearrange; *in der Reihenfolge*: change (*od.* rearrange) the order of

umorganisieren *v/t.* (*trennb., hat*) reorganize

umorientieren *v/refl.* (*untr., hat*) reorient(ate); **Umorientierung** *f* reorientation

umpacken *v/t.* (*trennb., hat -ge-*) repack

'umpflanzen[1] *v/t.* (*trennb., hat -ge-*) replant; (*Zimmerpflanze*) repot

um'pflanzen[2] *v/t.* (*untr., hat*) put plants around, surround with plants; **mit Bäumen ~** plant trees around

umpflügen *v/t.* (*trennb., hat -ge-*) plough (*Am.* plow) up

umpolen *v/t.* (*trennb., hat -ge-*) **1.** *Etech.* reverse (the polarity of); **2.** *umg. fig.* change

umprogrammieren *v/t.* (*trennb., hat*); *EDV* reprogram; *fig.* (*j-n*) reprogram(me); **Umprogrammierung** *f* reprogramming

umquartieren *v/t.* (*trennb., hat*) reaccommodate; *umg.* (*Kranken*) move

umrahmen *v/t.* (*untr., hat*) **1.** frame; **2.** *fig. Sache*: serve as a setting for; *musikalisch ~ Orchester etc.*: provide the music for; **Umrahmung** *f* **1.** framing; *konkret*: frame; **2.** *fig.* setting, framework; **musikalische ~** musical framework

umranden *v/t.* (*untr., hat*) border; **umrandet I.** *P.P.* → **umranden**; **II.** *Adj.* bordered, edged (*von* with); **schwarz ~** edged in black; **schwarz/rot ~e Augen** black-/red-rimmed eyes; **rot ~e Augen haben** have red rims around one's eyes; **Umrandung** *f* border, edge

umranken *v/t.* (*untr., hat*) twine (itself) (a)round; **umrankt I.** *P.P.* → **umranken**; **II.** *Adj.*: **~ von** entwined with; *Pflanzen etc.*: *auch* covered in; **von Efeu ~** ivy-covered; **von Legenden ~** *fig.* surrounded by legend

umrändert *Adj.* → **umrandet** II

umräumen *v/t./i.* (*trennb., hat -ge-*) **1.** move (to another place); **2.** (*Zimmer etc.*) rearrange; **ich räume seit Tagen um** I've been rearranging things for days

umrechnen *v/t.* (*trennb., hat -ge-*) convert (*in + Akk.* into); **in Dollar umgerechnet** in (terms of) dollars; **Umrechnung** *f* conversion (*in + Akk.* into)

Umrechnungs|**formel** *f für Celsius/ Fahrenheit etc.*: conversion formula; **~kurs** *m Wirts.* exchange rate, rate of exchange; **~tabelle** *f* conversion table

'umreißen[1] *v/t.* (*unreg., trennb., hat -ge-*) pull down; (*umstoßen*) knock down

um'reißen[2] *v/t.* (*unreg., untr., hat*) outline; **etw. kurz ~** outline s.th. briefly; → **umrissen**

umrennen *v/t.* (*unreg., trennb., hat -ge-*) run (*od.* knock) down

umringen *v/t.* (*untr., hat*) form (*od.* make) a circle around; *Menge, begeistert*: throng (a)round; (*umgeben*) surround (*auch fig.*)

Umriss *m* outline (*auch fig.*), contours *Pl.*; **in kräftigen/groben ~en** in bold/ rough outline; **in ~en schildern** outline; **feste ~e bekommen** begin to take shape

umrissen I. *P.P.* → **umreißen**[2]; **II.** *Adj.*: **scharf ~** sharply outlined; **fest ~e Vorstellungen** clearly-defined ideas

Umriss|**linie** *f* outline; (*Kontur*) contour line; **~zeichnung** *f* outline drawing

umrühren *v/t./i.* (*trennb., hat -ge-*) stir; **unter ständigem Umrühren kochen** *etc.* boil *etc.* while stirring continuously

umrunden *v/t.* (*untr., hat*) walk (*od.* go, drive *etc.*) (a)round; **Umrundung** *f*: **nach der ~ des Kaps** after sailing (a)round the cape

umrüsten (*trennb., hat -ge-*) **I.** *v/t. Tech.* adapt (*auf + Akk.* to); *Mil.* re-equip (with); **die Räder auf andere Felgen ~** change the rims on the wheels; **II.** *v/i.*: **~ auf** (*+ Akk.*) convert to; **Umrüstung** *f Tech.* adaptation (*auf + Akk.* to); *Mil.* re-equipping (with); *weitS.* conversion (to)

ums *Präp. + Art.*; *Kurzf. von* **um das**; → **Leben** 1, 8, **verrecken** 1

umsatteln (*trennb., hat -ge-*) **I.** *v/i. fig. im Beruf*: change jobs; *im Studium*: change one's subject, change subjects; **~ auf** (*+ Akk.*) switch to; **II.** *v/t.* (*Pferd*) resaddle

Umsatz *m Wirts.* turnover; (*Absatz*) *auch* sales *Pl.*; (*Einnahmen*) returns *Pl.*; *Fin., e-s Kontos*: account transactions *Pl.*; **e-n großen ~ an ... machen** *od.* **haben** have a large turnover of ...; **~ machen** make money; **~anstieg** *m* increase in turnover; **~beteiligung** *f* Gewinn: commission; *Arbeitsverhältnis*: working on a commission basis; **mit** *od.* **auf ~ beschäftigt sein** *etc.* be employed *etc.* on a commission basis; **~einbruch** *m* drop in turnover; **~einbuße** *f* drop in turnover; **~entwicklung** *f* sales trend; **~erwartung** *f* estimated sales *Pl.*; **~minus** *n* drop (*Am. auch* downturn) in sales; **~plus** *n* increase (*Am. auch* upturn) in sales; **~rückgang** *m* drop in sales; **~sprung** *m* jump in sales

umsatzstark *Adj. attr.* hot-selling

Umsatz|**steigerung** *f* sales increase; **~steuer** *f* turnover tax; **~zahl** *f* sales figure; **~ziel** *n* sales target; **~zuwachs** *m* growth in sales

umsäumen *v/t.* (*untr., hat*) hem; *fig.* surround; (*Straßen etc.*) line

umschalten (*trennb., hat -ge-*) **I.** *v/t.* switch (over) (*auf + Akk.* to); **II.** *v/i.* **1.** switch over (*auf + Akk., nach* to); *Ampel*: change (*auf + Akk.* to); **auf Grün** *etc.* **~** *Ampel*: *auch* turn green *etc.*; **das will ich nicht sehen - schalt um!** TV I don't want to watch that – turn it over (*Am.* change the channel)!; **zur Fortsetzung des Programms schalten wir um nach ...** we're going over to ... where this program(me) will continue; **2.** *umg. fig.* (*sich einstellen*) adjust (*auf + Akk.* to); **nach dem Urlaub wieder ~** adjust back after one's holiday (*Am.* vacation); **Umschalter** *m* **1.** *Etech.* commutator; **2.** *Schreibmaschine etc.*: shift key

Umschalt|**hebel** *m* reversing lever; **~taste** *f Computer etc.*: shift key

Umschaltung *f* switching (over); *von Ampel*: changing; (*Sich-einstellen*) adjustment; *groß-klein*: shifting

Umschau *f*; *nur Sg.* **1.** **~ halten** (have a) look around (*nach* for); **2.** *Zeitung etc.*: review; *TV etwa* news; **umschauen** *v/refl.* (*trennb., hat -ge-*) → **umsehen**

umschichten *v/t.* (*trennb., hat -ge-*) rearrange; *fig. auch* regroup, reshuffle; **Umschichtung** *f* regrouping; **gesellschaftliche ~** shift in social structure

umschiffen *v/t.* (*untr., hat*) sail (a)round; (*die Erde*) *auch* circumnavigate; (*Kap*) sail (a)round, round; *geschickt alle Schwierigkeiten ~ fig.* skilfully avoid any difficulties; **Umschiffung** *f* sailing (a)round; circumnavigation; rounding; → *umschiffen*

Umschlag *m* **1.** (*Briefumschlag*) envelope; (*Hülle*) cover; *e-s Buches: auch* (dust) jacket; *am Ärmel*: cuff; *an der Hose*: turn-up, *Am.* cuff; *Med.* compress; **2.** *Wirts., von Waren*: handling; *e-s Hafens*: goods *Pl.* handled; **3.** *fig. des Wetters, der Stimmung etc.*: change; → *Umschwung*

Umschlagbahnhof *m Eisenb.* rail loading station

umschlagen (*unreg., trennb., -ge-*) **I.** *v/i.* (*ist*) **1.** (*umkippen*) overturn; *Boot etc.: auch* capsize; **2.** (*sich ändern*) turn, suddenly change, change (abruptly) (*alle: in + Akk.* into); *Wind*: veer ([a]round); *Stimme*: crack; *Wein etc.*: go off; **II.** *v/t.* (*hat*) **1.** ([*um*]*wenden, Blatt etc.*) turn (over); (*Saum, Ärmel*) turn up; (*Kragen*) turn down; **2.** (*umstoßen*) knock over (*od.* down); (*Baum etc., fällen*) cut down; **3.** (*Tuch etc., umlegen*) (*auch sich* [*Dat.*] *~*) put on, wrap (a)round one's neck (*od.* shoulders); **4.** *Wirts.* (*Waren*) handle; *engS.* (*umladen*) transfer, tran(s)ship

Umschlag|hafen *m Naut.* port of tran(s)shipment; *~platz m* trading cent|re (*Am.* -er); *Naut.* place of tran(s)shipment

umschließen *v/t.* (*unreg., untr., hat*) surround, enclose; *mit Händen*: clasp; *mit Armen*: embrace, wrap one's arms (a)round; *fig.* (*umfassen*) encompass, embrace

umschlingen *v/t.* (*unreg., untr., hat*); (*umarmen*) embrace; *Pflanze*: twine itself (a)round; → *umschlungen*; **umschlingen I.** *P.P.* → *umschlingen*; **II.** *Adj.*: *vom Meer etc. ~* surrounded by the sea (*od.* by water); **III.** *Adv.*: *sie gingen eng ~* they walked along with their arms wrapped tightly (a)round one another; *sich fest ~ halten* be clasped in a firm embrace

umschmeicheln *v/t.* (*untr., hat*) sweet-talk; (*Mädchen*) *auch* woo

umschmeißen *v/t.* (*unreg., trennb., hat -ge-*); *umg.* → *umwerfen*

umschnallen *v/t.* (*trennb., hat -ge-*) buckle on; (*Gürtel*) put on

um'schreiben¹ *v/t.* (*unreg., untr., hat*) **1.** circumscribe (*auch Math.*), paraphrase; express *s.th.* in different terms; (*nicht direkt ansprechen*) skirt around; *es gibt keine direkte Übersetzung - man muss es ~* there's no direct translation - you've got to use a paraphrase; **2.** (*definieren*) define; (*zusammenfassen*) sum up

'umschreiben² *v/t.* (*unreg., trennb., hat -ge-*) **1.** (*nochmals schreiben*) rewrite; (*abschreiben, übertragen, transkribieren*) transcribe; **2.** (*Besitz*) transfer, make over (*auf + Akk.* to)

Umschreibung *f mit Worten*: circumscription, paraphrase; (*Beschreibung*) definition; → *um'schreiben¹*

Umschrift *f Ling.* transcription; *phonetische*: phonetic transcription

umschulden (*trennb., hat -ge-*) **I.** *v/t. Wirts.* (*Anleihe etc.*) convert; (*Firma etc.*) change the terms of debt of; **II.** *v/i.* (*sich anders, vor allem günstiger, verschulden*) reschedule; **Umschuldung** *f* debt conversion (*od.* rescheduling)

umschulen *vt/i.* (*trennb., hat -ge-*); (*Kind*) move to another school; *beruflich*: retrain (*zu od. als* as); *ich habe auf Altenpfleger umgeschult* I've retrained (*od.* undergone retraining) as a geriatric nurse; **Umschüler** *m*, **Umschülerin** *f* person undergoing retraining; **Umschulung** *f e-s Kindes*: transfer to another school; *berufliche*: retraining

Umschulungs|kurs *m* retraining course (*od.* program[me]); *~maßnahme f* retraining measure

umschütten *v/t.* (*trennb., hat -ge-*) **1.** → *umgießen* 1; **2.** (*umstoßen*) spill, knock over

umschwärmen *v/t.* (*untr., hat*) **1.** swarm (a)round; **2.** *fig.* (*j-n*) idolize; *von Teenagern umschwärmt werden* be a teen idol; **umschwärmt I.** *P.P.* → *umschwärmen*; **II.** *Adj. fig.* idolized; *bes. Frau*: greatly admired; *~ sein von vielen Leuten etc.*: be surrounded by; *von Verehrern etc.*: be in great demand with

Umschweife *Pl.*: *ohne (lange) ~* without further ado; (*ohne viel Zeit zu verlieren*) without wasting any (more) time; (*ohne viele Umstände*) without much fuss; (*geradeheraus*) *sagen*: straight out; *keine langen ~ machen* get (*od.* come) straight to the point; *sie haben sich ohne lange ~ entschieden* they didn't waste any time deciding; *etw. ohne ~ sagen auch* come straight out with s.th.; *etw. ohne ~ tun auch* get straight down to s.th.

umschwenken *v/i.* (*trennb., hat -ge-*) wheel (a)round; *fig. und Met.* veer (a)round; *Pol.* do an about-face (*od.* about-turn, *Am.* a U-turn), do a volte-face

umschwirren *v/t.* (*untr., hat*) buzz around; *Motten umschwirrten die Lampe* moths were whirring around the lamp

Umschwung *m* **1.** (sudden) change (+ *Gen.* in, of); *bes. Pol.* swing (*auch Stimmungsumschwung*); (*Umwälzung*) upheaval; *~ der Meinung etc. auch* reversal of opinion *etc.*; **2.** *Turnen*: circle

umsegeln *v/t.* (*untr., hat*) sail (a)round; (*Welt*) *auch* circumnavigate; (*Kap*) sail (a)round, round; **Umseg(e)lung** *f* sailing (a)round; circumnavigation; rounding; → *umsegeln*

umsehen *v/refl.* (*unreg., trennb., hat -ge-*) **1.** (*zurückblicken*) look (*od.* glance) back *od.* (a)round; **2.** (*herumschauen*) look (a)round; *fig. suchend*: look (a)round; *nach* (*nach* for), be on the lookout (for); *sich an e-m Ort etc. ~* have a look (a)round a place *etc.*; *du wirst dich noch ~! umg. fig.* you're in for a surprise (or two)

um sein → *um* III 2

umseitig I. *Adv.* overleaf; *bei Foto etc.*: on the reverse (*od.* back); **II.** *Adj. Text etc., nachgestellt*: overleaf

umsetzbar *Adj. Idee, Plan*: practicable; *nicht ~* impossible to implement

umsetzen (*trennb., hat -ge-*) **I.** *v/t.* **1.** (*Schüler, Gegenstand etc.*) move (*in, auf +Akk.* to); *Agr.* transplant; *Tech.* change over; *Eisenb.* rearrange; *Turnen* (*Hände*) twist; **2.** (*umwandeln*) convert (*in + Akk.* into); *Phys., Chem. etc. auch* transform (into); (*Pläne etc.*) implement; *in die Tat ~* put into action; *er hat gute Ideen etc., aber er kann sie nicht ~* but he can't translate them into action; → *Praxis* 1; **3.** *Wirts.* (*Ware*) sell; (*Geld[wert]*) turn over;

sein Geld ~ umg. spend one's money (*in + Akk.* on); **II.** *v/refl.* **1.** *Schüler etc.*: sit somewhere else; **2.** (*sich umwandeln*) be converted; (*in + Akk.* into)

Umsetzer *m*; *-s, -*; *Etron.* converter; *EDV* converter; **Umsetzung** *f* (*Umwandlung*) conversion (*in + Akk.* into); *wir haben gute Ideen, aber es mangelt noch an der ~* we have some good ideas but we still haven't put them into practice

Umsichgreifen *n*; *-s, kein Pl.* (*Ausbreitung*) (rapid) spread; *von Ideen, Sekten etc.*: proliferation

Umsicht *f*; *nur Sg.* circumspection; *große ~ zeigen* demonstrate great prudence; *mit ~ zu Werke gehen* prudently set to work; **umsichtig I.** *Adj.* circumspect; *sich ~ zeigen* show prudence, show o.s to be prudent; **II.** *Adv. handeln, vorgehen*: prudently

umsiedeln (*trennb., -ge-*) **I.** *v/t.* (*hat*) resettle; **II.** *v/i.* (*ist*) move (to another place); **Umsiedler** *m*, **Umsiedlerin** *f* resettler; **Umsiedlung** *f* resettlement; (*Übersiedeln*) move (*nach* to)

umso *Konj.*: *je ... ~ ...* the...the...; *je schneller du es erledigen kannst, ~ besser* the faster you can do it, the better; *~ besser!* so much the better!; *~ schlimmer!* so much the worse!; *~ mehr* all the more, (so much) the more (*als* as; *weil* because); *~ weniger* (all) the less; *je länger ich darüber nachdenke, ~ weniger gefällt mir die Sache* the less I like it

umsonst *Adv.* **1.** (*unentgeltlich*) for nothing, free (of charge); *etw. ~ bekommen* get s.th. for free; *nichts ist ~* nothing comes for free; → *Tod* 2; **2.** (*vergebens*) for nothing; *es war ~* it was a waste of time, it was all for nothing; *wir versuchten zu helfen, aber es war ~* we tried to help but it was in vain; *ich habe euch nicht ~ gewarnt etc.* (*aus gutem Grund*) not without (good) reason did I warn you *etc.*; *das hast du nicht ~ getan! drohend*: you'll pay for that!

umsorgen *v/t.* (*untr., hat*) look after (*Am.* take care of) *s.o.*

um'spannen¹ *v/t.* (*untr., hat*) **1.** reach round; *mit der Hand*: clasp; **2.** *fig.* cover; *bes. zeitlich*: span

'umspannen² *v/t.* (*trennb., hat -ge-*) **1.** *Etech.* transform; **2.** (*Pferde etc.*) change; **Umspannwerk** *n Etech.* transformer (station)

umspielen *v/t.* (*untr., hat*) **1.** *Fußball etc.*: dribble (a)round; **2.** *fig. Wellen etc.*: lap (a)round; *Lächeln*: play around (*od.* about) 4

umspringen *v/i.* (*unreg., trennb., ist -ge-*) **1.** *Wind*: veer; **2.** *Ampel*: change (*auf + Akk.* to); **3.** *Skisport*: jump-turn; *Turnen* (*sich im Sprung drehen*) perform a jump-turn; *am Gerät*: perform a release move; **4.** (*behandeln*) treat; (*Sache*) *auch* handle; *so kannst du mit mir nicht ~* you can't treat me like that

umspulen *vt/i.* (*trennb., hat -ge-*) rewind

umspülen *v/t.* (*untr., hat*) *Gewässer*: wash (*sanft*: lap) around

Umstand *m* **1.** (*Tatsache*) fact; (*Einzelheit*) detail; **Umstände** (*Lage*) circumstances, conditions, state of affairs; *äußere Umstände* external circumstances; *mildernde Umstände Jur.* mitigating circumstances; *nähere Umstände* (further) particulars; *unter*

Umständen (*möglicherweise*) possibly, perhaps; (*notfalls*) if need be; *unter allen Umständen* whatever happens, *förm.* at all events; *unter keinen Umständen* under no circumstances, on no account (*od.* condition); *unter diesen Umständen* under the circumstances, as matters stand; *es geht ihm den Umständen entsprechend* (*gut*) he's as well as can be expected given the circumstances; *in anderen Umständen euph. altm.* in the family way; **2.** *mst Pl.*: *Umstände* (*unnötiger Aufwand*) fuss; (*Mühe*) trouble; *so ein ~ wegen ...* what a lot of fuss over ...; *viel Umstände machen Person*: make a lot of fuss (*wegen* about); *Sache*: cause a lot of trouble, be a lot of trouble; *machen Sie* (*sich*) *keine Umstände!* don't go to any trouble; *wenn es Ihnen keine Umstände macht* if it's no trouble (to you); *nicht viel Umstände machen mit* make short work of; **umständehalber** *Adv.* owing to circumstances; *... ~ zu verkaufen* forced (*od.* compulsory) sale: ...
umständlich I. *Adj.* (*verwickelt*) complicated; (*langatmig*) longwinded; (*pedantisch*) pedantic; (*ungeschickt*) awkward; (*unnötig ~*) fussy; *das ist viel zu ~* that's far too much trouble, that's much too complicated; *~e Methode auch* roundabout way of doing s.th. (*od.* it); *er hat so e-e ~e Art* he has such a roundabout (*od.* fiddly) way of doing things; *sei doch nicht so ~!* *umg.* don't make such a palaver (*Am.* a big deal)!; **II.** *Adv.* awkwardly; fussily, pedantically *etc.*; → I; *etw. ~ erzählen* narrate at great length, give a longwinded account of; *~er geht's wohl nicht? iro.* couldn't you think of a more complicated way of doing it?; *warum einfach, wenn's auch ~ geht iro.* why make things easy when you can make them difficult?; **Umständlichkeit** *f; nur Sg.* complicated nature; longwindedness; pedantry; fussiness; *in aller ~ erzählen etc.*: at great length, in all its tortured detail
Umstands|bestimmung *f Ling.* adverbial phrase; *~ des Ortes / der Zeit / des Grundes* adverbial of place/time/reason; *~kleid* *n* maternity dress; *~krämer* *m umg. pej.* pain, fusspot; *~mode* *f* maternity wear; *~wort* *n Ling.* adverb
umstehen *v/t.* (*unreg., untr., hat*) stand (a)round; *die Wiese war von Bäumen umstanden* the meadow was surrounded by trees
umstehend I. *Part. Präs.* → **umstehen**; **II.** *Adj. Seite*: next; *Text, nachgestellt*: overleaf; *die Umstehenden* the bystanders; *bitte auch Umstehendes beachten!* please turn over, pto; **III.** *Adv.* overleaf
Umsteige|bahnhof *m* interchange (station); *~möglichkeit f*: *hier haben Sie eine ~ in die Linie 2* you can change here for Line 2; *~ nach X Durchsage*: change for X
umsteigen *v/i.* (*unreg., trennb., ist -ge-*) **1.** change (*in +Akk.* [on]to; *nach* for); *bei Verkehrsmitteln*: change trains (*od.* buses *etc.*); **2.** *umg. fig.* switch (*auf + Akk.* to), change over (to); **3.** *Skisport*: perform a step turn; **Umsteiger** *m; -s, -*, **Umsteigerin** *f -, -nen*; *umg.* **1.** *fig. person changing his or her job*; **2.** *Flug.* connecting (*od.* transfer) passenger
umstellbar *Adj.* **1.** *Sitz, Hebel*: adjustable; **2.** *Einstellung*: adaptable

um'stellen¹ *v/t.* (*untr., hat*) surround; *das Gebäude ist umstellt* the building is surrounded
'umstellen² (*trennb., hat -ge-*) **I.** *vt/i.* **1.** *räumlich*: move ([a]round); (*einzelnen Gegenstand*) *auch* move to (*od.* put in) a different place; (*umordnen, Zimmer, Gegenstände etc.*) *auch fig.* rearrange, change (a)round; (*Reihenfolge*) rearrange; *fig.* (*umgruppieren*) regroup; **2.** (*Uhr, Apparat etc.*) adjust; *auf Sommerzeit ~* set to summer (*Am.* daylight saving) time; *von Stereo auf Mono etc. ~* switch from stereo to mono *etc.*; **3.** *fig.* switch, change over, convert (*von ... auf + Akk.* from ... to); *seit dem Unfall musste sie ihr Leben völlig ~* since the accident she has had to rearrange her life completely; *auf Computer/Container ~ auch* computerize/containerize; → *auch* II 2; **II.** *v/refl.* **1.** (*sich umgewöhnen*) adapt (o.s.), adjust (o.s.) (*auf + Akk.* to), *Person*; *absolut*: *auch* get used to the change (*od.* to it *umg.*); *in s-r Einstellung*: *auch* change one's attitude (toward[s]); *sich auf die neuen Verhältnisse etc. ~* adapt to the new conditions; **2.** *sich ~ auf* (+ *Akk.*) change (*bes. Tech.* switch) over to; *sich ~ von ... auf ...* (+ *Akk.*) (*e-e andere Methode, Energiequelle, Lebensweise etc.*) change (*bes. Tech.* switch) over from ... to ...; **Umstellung** *f* rearrangement; regrouping; adjustment; switch, changeover *etc.*; → **'umstellen²**
Umstieg *m; -(e)s, kein Pl.; fig. Vorgang*: changing, switching (*von* from; *auf + Akk.* to); (*Wechsel*) switch, changeover
umstimmen *v/t.* (*trennb., hat -ge-*) **1.** *Mus.* retune, tune to another pitch; *~ auf* (+*Akk.*) tune to; **2.** *fig.*: *j-n ~* bring s.o. (a)round (*auf + Akk.* to), change s.o.'s mind, persuade s.o. otherwise; *sie ließ sich nicht ~* she wouldn't change her mind; **3.** *Med.* (*Organ*) change
umstoßen *v/t.* (*unreg., trennb., hat -ge-*) **1.** knock down (*od.* over); **2.** *fig.* (*Urteil, Entscheidung*) overrule; (*Plan etc.*) upset; (*Testament*) change; → **un-umstößlich**
umstricken *v/t.* (*untr., hat*) *fig.* ensnare
umstritten *Adj.* disputed; *Sport etc.*: contested; *~e Frage etc.* controversial (*od.* contentious, *Am. auch* hot-button *umg.*) issue *etc.*; *als Künstler ist er* (*eher*) *~* he is (rather) controversial as an artist; *das Spätwerk des Autors ist äußerst ~* the author's late work is the subject of great controversy
umstrukturieren *v/t.* (*trennb., hat*) restructure; **Umstrukturierung** *f* restructuring
umstülpen *v/t.* (*trennb., hat -ge-*) *von innen nach außen*: turn *s.th.* inside out; *von oben nach unten*: turn *s.th.* upside down; *fig.* (*System, Leben etc.*) turn *s.th.* upside down; → **umgestülpt**
Umsturz *m* coup; *~ der Regierung etc.* overthrow of the government *etc.*
umstürzen (*trennb., -ge-*) **I.** *v/t.* (*hat*) **1.** knock over; **2.** *Pol.* overthrow, topple; **II.** *v/i.* (*ist*); *Gegenstand*: fall down (*od.* over); *Baum bei e-m Sturm*: be blown over; → **umgestürzt**; **Umstürzler** *m; -s, -* revolutionary, subversive; **umstürzlerisch** *Adj.* subversive
Umsturz|pläne *Pl.* plans to overthrow the government *etc.*; *~versuch* *m* attempted coup (*od.* overthrow of the government *etc.*)

umtata *Interj. und Adv.* oompah
umtaufen *v/t.* (*trennb., hat -ge-*) **1.** *umg. fig.* (*umbenennen*) rename, rechristen (*auf +Akk.* as); **2.** *Reli.* rebaptize
Umtausch *m* exchange; *reduzierte Ware ist vom ~ ausgeschlossen* reduced articles cannot be exchanged; *bei ~ Gutschein oder Geld zurück* returned goods can be exchanged for a credit note (*Am.* for store credit) or a cash refund; **umtauschbar** *Adj.* exchangeable; **umtauschen** *v/t.* (*trennb., hat -ge-*) exchange (*gegen* for); (*Ware*) *auch* take back to the shop (*Am.* store); *sie haben es ohne weiteres umgetauscht auch* they gave me another one straightaway
Umtausch|aktion *f* swap transaction; *~kurs* *m Fin.* exchange rate; *~recht* *n* right to exchange goods
umtopfen *v/t.* (*trennb., hat -ge-*) repot
umtreiben *v/t.* (*unreg., trennb., hat -ge-*): *etw. treibt j-n um* s.th. gives s.o. no rest, s.th. haunts s.o.
Umtrieb *m; -(e)s, -e* **1.** *Pl.* machinations, intrigues; (*staatsfeindliche*) *~e* (subversive) activities; **2.** *Agr. length of useful life of a perennial crop or animal stock*; **3.** *Pl. schw.* (*Umstände*) (*unnötiger Aufwand*) fuss; (*Mühe*) trouble; **umtriebig** *Adj.* busy, bustling
Umtrunk *m; mst Sg.* drink; *anschließend lade ich zu e-m kleinen ~* I'd like to invite you for a little drink afterwards
umtun *v/refl.* (*unreg., trennb., hat -ge-*); *umg.* (*aktiv werden*) get to work on s.th.; (*aktiv sein*) be working on s.th.; *sich in e-m Laden etc. ~* look around a shop (*bes. Am.* store *etc.*); *sich ~ nach* (*suchen*) look (around) for
U-Musik *f* light (*od.* popular) music
Umverpackung *f* secondary packaging
umverteilen *v/t.* (*trennb., hat*) redistribute; **Umverteilung** *f* redistribution
Umwälzanlage *f* circulating pump
umwälzen *v/t.* (*trennb., hat -ge-*) **1.** roll over; *Tech.* circulate; **2.** *fig.* revolutionize; **umwälzend I.** *Part. Präs.* → **umwälzen**; **II.** *Adj. Erfindung etc.*: revolutionary
Umwälzpumpe *f Tech.* circulating pump
Umwälzung *f* **1.** *Tech.* circulation; **2.** *fig. Pol. etc.* revolution, upheaval
umwandeln *v/t.* (*trennb., hat -ge-*) change, transform (*in + Akk., zu* into); *Phys., Etech.* transform, convert (*auch EDV*); *Jur.* (*Strafe*) commute (into); *er ist wie umgewandelt* he's a completely different person, he's a changed man; **Umwandler** *m; -s, -*; *Etech.* converter, transducer, modifier; **Umwandlung** *f* change; transformation (*in + Akk., zu* into); *Wirts., Etech., EDV* conversion; *Jur.* commutation
umwechseln *v/t.* (*trennb., hat -ge-*); (*Geld*) change (*in + Akk.* into); *Dollar in Euro etc. ~ auch* exchange dollars for euros *etc.*; **Umwechslung** *f* exchange (*von ... in + Akk.* of ... for, *Geld*: *auch* of ... into)
Umweg *m* detour; *e-n ~ machen* take the long way (a)round, make a detour; *kleiner ~* little (*od.* slight) detour; *auf ~en fig.* indirectly, in a roundabout way; *negativ*: by devious means; *ohne ~e* straight, directly
'umwehen¹ *v/t.* (*trennb., hat -ge-*) blow down (*od.* over)
um'wehen² *v/t.* (*untr., hat*) *Brise etc.*:

waft around

Umwelt f; nur Sg. **1.** Öko. (natural) environment; **unsere ~** auch the world in which we live, the world around us; **2.** (Umgebung) milieu, background; konkret: surroundings Pl.; **er fühlte sich von s-r ~ missverstanden** he felt misunderstood by the people around him

Umwelt|... im Subst.; bes. Öko. mst environmental; **~abgabe** f Öko. environmental levy; **~aktivist** m, **~aktivistin** f environmental activist; **~amt** n environment agency; **~aspekt** m environmental consideration; **~auflage** f environmental requirement; **~ausschuss** m environmental committee; **~beauftragte** m, f environmental officer

umweltbedingt Adj. Öko. environmental, nachgestellt: due to environmental factors

Umwelt|bedingungen Pl. environmental factors; **~behörde** f environmental authority

umweltbelastend Adj. Öko. polluting ..., harmful to the environment; **Umweltbelastung** f auch Pl. (environmental) pollution

Umwelt|berater m, **~beraterin** f Öko. environmental advis|er (od. -or); **~bericht** m environmental report; **~bewegung** f environmental (od. Green) movement

umweltbewusst Adj. Öko. environment-conscious, environmentally aware; **Umweltbewusstsein** n environmental awareness

Umwelt|bilanz f Öko. environmental balance sheet; **~bundesamt** n federal environment agency; **~dezernat** n environment department; **~dezernent** m, **~dezernentin** f head of the environment department; **~einflüsse** Pl. environmental influences; **~engel** m Zeichen: symbol denoting environmentally-friendly products in Germany; **~entlastung** f environmental relief; **~experte** m, **~expertin** f environmental expert, expert on the environment; **~faktor** m environmental factor

umweltfeindlich Adj. Öko. harmful to the environment; Politik etc.: attr. anti-environment ..., präd. und nachgestellt: hostile to the environment

umweltfreundlich Adj. Öko. environment-friendly, environmentally friendly, eco-friendly; **Umweltfreundlichkeit** f eco-friendliness

Umweltgefährdung f Öko. endangering of the environment

umwelt|gerecht Adj. Öko. environmentally compatible; **~geschädigt** Adj.: **~ sein** have been damaged (od. affected) by pollution

Umwelt|gesetz n Öko. environmental law; **~gift** n pollutant; **~gipfel** m Pol. environment summit; **~initiative** f environmental initiative; **~karte** f good-value season ticket for use on public transport(ation); **~katastrophe** f environmental disaster; **~kommissar** m, **~kommissarin** f der EU: environment commissioner; der Polizei: police inspector charged with investigating environmental crimes; **~konferenz** f environment conference; **~kriminalität** f environmental crime, crimes Pl. against the environment; **~minister** m, **~ministerin** f environment minister, minister of the environment; in GB: Environment Secretary, Secretary of State for the Environment; in den USA: director (od. head) of the Envi-

ronmental Protection Agency; **~ministerium** n ministry of the environment, environment ministry; in GB: Department of the Environment; in den USA: Environmental Protection Agency, EPA; **~organisation** f environmental organisation

umweltorientiert Adj. Öko. environment(ally) conscious

Umweltpapier n recycled paper

Umweltpolitik f Öko. environmental policy; **umweltpolitisch** Adj. ecopolitical

Umwelt|problem n Öko. environmental problem; **~problematik** f environmental issues Pl.; **~programm** n der UNO: environmental program(me); **~rat** m: **Deutscher ~** body of experts providing advice to the German government on environmental matters; **Europäischer ~** council of European environment ministers; **~referent** m, **~referentin** f environmental expert; **~ressort** n environment department; **~schäden** Pl. damage Sg. to the environment

umwelt|schädigend Adj., **~schädlich** Adj. Öko. harmful to the environment

Umweltschadstoff m Öko. pollutant

umweltschonend Öko. **I.** Adj. environment-friendly; environmentally friendly, eco-friendly; **II.** Adv. in an environmentally-friendly etc. manner

Umweltschutz m Öko. environmental protection, conservation, pollution control

Umweltschutz|... im Subst. → auch **Umwelt...**; **~bestimmung** f environmental protection regulation

Umweltschützer m, **~in** f environmentalist, conservationist

Umweltschutz|organisation f Öko. environmental (od. conservation) organization; **~papier** n recycled paper

Umwelt|skandal m Öko. environmental (od. ecological) scandal; **~sünder** m (environmental) polluter; **~technik** f environmental (od. green) technology; **~ticket** n good-value season ticket for use on public transport(ation); **~tipp** m environmental tip; **~tourismus** m ecotourism; **~verschmutzung** f (environmental) pollution

umweltverträglich Adj. Öko. environment-friendly, environmentally compatible; **Umweltverträglichkeit** f environmental compatibility; **Umweltverträglichkeitsprüfung** f Öko. environmental impact assessment, ecotest

Umwelt|vorsorge f Öko. care for the environment; **Abteilung ~** environment (od. environmental planning) department; **~zeichen** n symbol denoting environmentally friendly products in Germany; **~zerstörung** f destruction of the environment, ecotage; völlige: auch ecocide

umwenden ([unreg.], trennb., hat -ge-) **I.** v/t. turn (over); (Auto etc.) turn (a)round; **II.** v/refl. turn (a)round; **III.** v/i. Auto etc.: turn (a)round

umwerben v/t. (unreg., untr., hat) court, woo; **Kunden mit Rabatten etc. ~** use discounts to woo (od. draw) customers; → **umworben**

umwerfen (unreg., trennb., hat -ge-) v/t. **1.** knock down; (Glas etc.) knock over; **2. sich etw. ~** throw s.th. on (od. over one's shoulders); **3.** fig. (Plan etc.) upset; **etw. wirft j-n um** umg. (bringt ihn aus der Fassung) s.th. bowls s.o. over, s.th. throws s.o.; **ein Glas wird dich nicht gleich ~** one glass won't knock

you out; **ihn wirft so leicht nichts um** umg. he's not so easily thrown; **umwerfend** umg. **I.** Adj. Erlebnis etc.: amazing; (einfach) ~ (absolutely) staggering; **von ~er Komik** hilariously funny; **du siehst ~ aus!** you look stunning!; **II.** Adv.: **~ komisch** hilarious; **~ komisch sein** auch be a scream umg.

umwerten v/t. (trennb., hat -ge-) re-evaluate; **e-e Idee** etc. ~ give new meaning to an idea etc.

umwickeln v/t. (untr., hat); (einwickeln) wrap up (mit in); Med. bandage (with); **etw. mit Draht** etc. ~ wind some wire etc. (a)round s.th.; **etw. mit e-r Schnur** etc. ~ tie some string etc. (a)round s.th.

umwidmen v/t. (trennb., hat -ge-) etw. **~ in** (+ Akk.) redesignate s.th. as; **Umwidmung** f redesignation

umwittert Adj.: **von Geheimnissen ~** shrouded in mystery

umwölken (untr., hat) **I.** v/refl. **1.** lit. Himmel: cloud over, become overcast; **2.** fig. Gesicht etc.: cloud over, darken; **II.** v/t. fig. (Gesicht etc.) cloud, darken

umworben I. P.P. → **umwerben**; **II.** Adj. (much) sought-after; **der von mehreren Vereinen ~e Spieler** the player (whom od. that) several clubs have been wanting to sign

umwühlen v/t. (trennb., hat -ge-) churn up

umzäunen v/t. (untr., hat) fence in, enclose; **Umzäunung** f enclosure, fence, fencing

'umziehen¹ (unreg., trennb., -ge-) **I.** v/refl. (hat) change (one's clothes), put on some other clothes; **II.** v/t. (hat); (j-n) change s.o.'s clothes; **III.** v/i. (ist); (die Wohnung wechseln) move (house od. flats), Am. move, relocate; **in ein anderes Klassenzimmer** etc. ~ move to another classroom etc.

um'ziehen² v/t. (unreg., untr., hat): **von Stacheldraht umzogen** surrounded by barbed wire

umzingeln v/t. (untr., hat) surround, encircle; **Umzingelung** f encirclement

Umzug m **1.** parade; feierlicher: procession; **2.** (Wohnungswechsel) move; Am. und von Firmen: auch relocation; **ihnen blieb nur der ~ ins Ausland** the only option left open to them was to move abroad (Am. auch overseas)

Umzugs|firma f removal firm, Am. mover, van line; **~karton** m packing case; **~kosten** Pl. cost Sg. of moving; beim Umzug e-r Firma: relocation (od. moving) expenses; **~pauschale** f relocation package; **~termin** m (Tag) removal (Am. moving) date; (äußerster Termin) removal (Am. moving) deadline

UN Pl.; Abk.: **die ~** Pol. the UN Sg.

unabänderlich Adj. unalterable, irrevocable; **sich ins Unabänderliche fügen** resign o.s. to the inevitable; **Unabänderlichkeit** f unalterability, irrevocable nature (+ Gen. of), irrevocability

unabdingbar Adj. (unverzichtbar) indispensable; Rechte: inalienable

unabhängig I. Adj. independent (von of); **~ von** (ohne Rücksicht auf) irrespective of; **~ davon, ob ...** regardless of whether ...; **II.** Adv. independently; **das geschieht ~ von / davon, ob ...** that will happen irrespective of / of whether ...; **Unabhängige** m, f; -en, -en; Pol. independent; **Unabhängigkeit** f nur Sg. independence

Unabhängigkeits|bestrebungen Pl. drive for independence; **~bewegung** f independence movement; **~erklärung** *f* declaration of independence; **~kampf** *m* fight for independence; **~krieg** *m* war of independence; **~tag** *m in den USA*: Independence Day, *the* Fourth of July

unabkömmlich *Adj.* indispensable; (*momentan* **~**) busy; *sie ist im Moment* **~** *auch* she can't get away at the moment

unablässig I. *Adj.* incessant, unremitting; *Anstrengungen*: unrelenting; **II.** *Adv. reden etc.*: incessantly

unabsehbar *Adj.* unforeseeable; *Verlust etc.*: incalculable; (*endlos*) endless; *zeitlich*: *auch* interminable; *auf* **~e** *Zeit* for an indefinite period of time; *im Negativsatz*: for the foreseeable future

unabsichtlich I. *Adj.* unintentional; **II.** *Adv. kränken etc.*: unintentionally; *wie* **~** *berühren* touch seemingly unintentionally

unabwendbar *Adj.* inevitable, unavoidable; **~es** *Ereignis Jur.* inevitable incident; **Unabwendbarkeit** *f; nur Sg.* inevitability, unavoidable nature (+ *Gen.* of), unavoidability

unachtsam I. *Adj.* inattentive; (*nachlässig*) careless, negligent; *nur attr.* (*unbedacht*) inadvertent ...; **II.** *Adv. behandeln etc.*: carelessly, negligently; **Unachtsamkeit** *f* inattentiveness; carelessness, negligence; inadvertence; → *unachtsam*

unähnlich *Adj.* dissimilar (+ *Dat.* to); **~** *sein* (+ *Dat.*) *auch* be unlike *s.o. od. s.th.*; *j-m od. e-r Sache nicht* **~** *sehen* look like (*od.* resemble) s.o. *od.* s.th.; **Unähnlichkeit** *f; nur Sg.* dissimilarity (*mit* to)

unakzeptabel *Adj.* unacceptable

unanfechtbar *Adj.* incontestable; *Urteil*: final; **Unanfechtbarkeit** *f; nur Sg.* incontestability

unangebracht *Adj.* inappropriate, *präd. auch* out of place; *Bemerkung*: *auch* out of turn; *etw. für* **~** *halten* consider s.th. inappropriate

unangefochten I. *Adj* (*unbestritten*) undisputed; *Meister, Machthaber etc.*: *auch* unchallenged; (*unbehindert*) unhindered; **II.** *Adv.*: *wir passierten* **~** *die Grenze* we crossed the border without being challenged

unangekündigt *Adj. Klassenarbeit*: unannounced; *Besuch*: unexpected; *die Durchführung von* **~en** *Dopingkontrollen* the carrying-out of random drugs tests

unangemeldet I. *Adj.* unannounced; *Besuch*: unexpected; *Patient*: *nachgestellt*: without an appointment; **II.** *Adv.* **1.** unannounced; (*unvermittelt*) without any warning; **~** *zum Arzt gehen* go to the doctor without making an appointment, just walk in to the doctor('s); *entschuldigen Sie, dass ich* **~** *komme* forgive me for not letting you know I was coming, I'm sorry for turning up unannounced; **2.** (*nicht polizeilich gemeldet*): **~** *in ... wohnen* live in ... without being registered (with the police)

unangemessen I. *Adj.* (*unmäßig*) immoderate; (*zu hoch*) *auch* unreasonable, out of proportion (+ *Dat.* to); (*unpassend*) unsuitable, inappropriate; (*unzulänglich*) inadequate; **II.** *Adv.*: **~** *hoch Preis etc.*: disproportionately high; **~** (*scharf*) *reagieren* react unreasonably (sharply); **Unangemessenheit** *f; nur Sg.* immoderacy; unreasonableness; inappropriateness; inadequa-

cy; → *unangemessen*

unangenehm I. *Adj.* unpleasant, disagreeable; *engS.* (*böse, widerlich*) nasty; (*misslich, peinlich*) awkward; **~e** *Fragen stellen* ask awkward questions; *das Unangenehme daran ist ...* the unpleasant thing about it is ...; *er kann recht* **~** *werden* he can get quite nasty (at times); *..., sonst werde ich* **~** or else I'll start to turn nasty; *ihm ist es* **~**, *mit ihr reden zu müssen* he hates having to talk to her; *es ist mir furchtbar* **~** I hate it, I find it terribly unpleasant (*od.* embarrassing); **II.** *Adv.* **~** *kalt etc.*: unpleasantly (*od.* disagreeably) cold *etc.*; **~** *überrascht werden* have an unpleasant (*od.* a nasty) surprise; **~** *auffallen* (*e-n schlechten Eindruck machen*) make a bad impression; (*sich schlecht benehmen*) make a nuisance of o.s.; *j-m* **~** *auffallen* annoy s.o.; *j-n* **~** *berühren* give s.o. an awkward feeling; *sich* **~** *bemerkbar machen Sache*: be (quite) unpleasant

unangepasst *Adj. Verhalten etc.*: nonconformist; *völlig* **~** *sein* be a total nonconformist; **Unangepasstheit** *f; nur Sg.* nonconformism; *Benehmen*: nonconformist behavio(u)r

unangetastet *Adj.* untouched; **~** *bleiben Recht, Prinzip etc.*: remain intact; *das Gesetz lässt die Pressefreiheit* **~** the law leaves the freedom of the press untouched

unangreifbar *Adj.* unassailable; *Urteil*: non-appealable; *fig.* invulnerable, unassailable

unannehmbar *Adj.* unacceptable; **Unannehmbarkeit** *f; nur Sg.* unacceptability

Unannehmlichkeit *f; mst Pl.* trouble *Sg.*; *j-m* **~en** *bereiten* cause s.o. trouble; **~en** *bekommen* run into difficulties

unansehnlich *Adj.* unsightly; *Person*: *auch* plain, *Am. auch* homely; **Unansehnlichkeit** *f* unsightliness; plainness, homeliness

unanständig *Adj.* indecent, (*obszön*) obscene; *Witz*: rude; *Sprache*: *auch* foul; **~es** *Wort auch* four-letter word; **Unanständigkeit** *f* indecency; (*Obszönität*) obscenity

unantastbar *Adj.* unimpeachable; *Rechte*: inviolable; *die Würde des Menschen ist* **~** human dignity is sacrosanct; **Unantastbarkeit** *f; nur Sg.* unimpeachability; *von Rechten*: inviolability

unanwendbar *Adj.* inapplicable

unappetitlich I. *Adj.* unappetizing; *auch fig.* unsavo(u)ry, off-putting; *die ganze Affäre ist* **~** *fig.* the whole business is disgusting; **II.** *Adv.* *aussehen, riechen etc.*: unappetizing, disgusting; **Unappetitlichkeit** *f* unsavo(u)riness

Unart *f* bad habit; *e-s Kindes*: naughtiness; *dieses dauernde Spucken ist e-e widerliche* **~** this constant spitting is a disgusting habit; **unartig** *Adj.* naughty

unartikuliert *Adj.* **1.** inarticulate; **2.** (*nicht ausgesprochen*) unarticulated; **~** *bleiben* be left unexpressed

unästhetisch *Adj.* un(a)esthetic; *weitS.* unpleasant, off-putting; (*hässlich*) ugly; *Boxen etc.* *finde ich* **~** I find boxing *etc.* revolting

unattraktiv I. *Adj.* unattractive; **II.** *Adv.* unattractively; *auf mich wirkt er* **~** I don't find him attractive

unaufdringlich *Adj.* unobtrusive; **Unaufdringlichkeit** *f* unobtrusiveness

unauffällig I. *Adj.* inconspicuous, discreet; (*unaufdringlich*) unobtrusive; **II.** *Adv.* inconspicuously, discreetly, unobtrusively; *sich kleiden etc.*: unobtrusively; **~** *beobachten* observe discreetly; *sich* **~** *verhalten* keep one's head down, keep a low profile; **~** *verschwinden* disappear without anyone noticing, slip away unnoticed; **Unauffälligkeit** *f; nur Sg.* inconspicuousness, discreetness, unobtrusiveness

unauffindbar *Adj. präd.* not to be found; *gesuchte Person*: *auch* untraceable; **~** *bleiben* remain nowhere to be found

unaufgefordert I. *Adj.* unasked-for, unbidden; *Wirts.* unsolicited; **II.** *Adv.* of one's own accord, without being asked

unaufgeklärt *Adj. Verbrechen etc.*: unsolved; *weitS.* unexplained

unaufgeregt *Adj.* unexcited, calm

unaufgeschlossen *Adj.* (*engstirnig*) narrow-minded; **~** *sein auch* have a closed mind; **~** *sein gegenüber* be closed to; (*nichts anfangen können mit*) *auch* have no appreciation of

unaufhaltsam I. *Adj.* unstoppable; (*unerbittlich*) inexorable; **II.** *Adv. näher rücken, weitergehen etc.*: inexorably; **Unaufhaltsamkeit** *f; nur Sg.* inexorability

unaufhörlich I. *Adj.* incessant, continuous; (*endlos*) endless; **II.** *Adv.* incessantly, continuously; *regnen etc.*: *auch* without stopping; *es regnete* **~** *auch* it just kept on raining

unauflösbar *Adj. Vertrag*: indissoluble; *auch Math., Chem.* insoluble; *Widerspruch*: irreconcilable; **~es** *Ganzes* indivisible whole; **Unauflösbarkeit** *f; nur Sg.* indissolubility; insolubility; irreconcilability; → *unauflösbar*, **unauflöslich** *Adj.* → *unauflösbar*, **Unauflöslichkeit** *f* → *Unauflösbarkeit*

unaufmerksam I. *Adj.* inattentive; (*gedankenlos*) thoughtless, (*nachlässig*) careless; **II.** *Adv.*: *sich gegenüber j-m* **~** *verhalten* be very inattentive to s.o.; **Unaufmerksamkeit** *f; nur Sg.* inattentiveness; thoughtlessness; carelessness; → *unaufmerksam*

unaufrichtig *Adj.* insincere, dishonest; **Unaufrichtigkeit** *f* insincerity, dishonesty

unaufschiebbar *Adj.* urgent; *ein* **~er** *Termin* an urgent (*od.* pressing) deadline; *es ist* **~** it has to be dealt with straightaway (*bes. Am.* right now), it cannot be put off (*od.* postponed); **Unaufschiebbarkeit** *f; nur Sg.* urgency, pressing nature

unausbleiblich *Adj.* inevitable; *das war* **~** *auch* that was bound to happen

unausdenkbar *Adj.* unimaginable, unthinkable

unausführbar *Adj.* impracticable, unfeasible; **Unausführbarkeit** *f* impracticability, unfeasibility

unausgefüllt *Adj.* **1.** *Formular etc.*: blank; **2.** *fig. Person*: unfulfilled; *Tag, Leben*: empty; (*innerlich*) **~** *sein* be unfulfilled

unausgeglichen *Adj.* unbalanced; *Wesen*: unstable; **Unausgeglichenheit** *f* imbalance; *des Wesens*: instability

unausgegoren *Adj. bes. pej.*; (*undurchdacht*) not thought through (to the end); (*unfertig*) unfinished; (*unreif*) immature; **~** *sein auch* need time to mature; *das ist alles noch völlig* **~** it's all still completely half-baked

unausgeschlafen *Adj.* tired; (*über-*

nächtigt) lacking in sleep, not well rested; **du bist noch ~** you haven't had enough sleep; **~ aussehen** look as if one has not had enough sleep, not look well rested

unausgesprochen *Adj.* unspoken, silent

unausgetragen *Adj.* **1. ein ~er Konflikt** a conflict that never came to pass; **2. ~es Kind** premature baby

unauslöschlich I. *Adj. Eindruck etc.*: indelible; *Hass etc.*: inextinguishable, ineradicable; **II.** *Adv.*: **~ eingeprägt** engraved on *s.o.'s* mind

unausrottbar *Adj. fig. Vorurteil etc.*: ineradicable

unaussprechlich I. *Adj.* inexpressible, ineffable; *(unsagbar)* unspeakable; *(unbeschreiblich)* indescribable; **II.** *Adv. (unsagbar)* unspeakably; *(unbeschreiblich)* indescribably, *nachgestellt*: beyond description

unausstehlich *Adj. (unerträglich)* unbearable, intolerable; *(widerlich)* detestable; **er war wieder ~ (zu mir)** he was unbearable (toward[s] me) again; **es ist mir ~** I detest it; **es ist mir ~, es zu tun** I detest having to do it

unausweichlich I. *Adj.* inevitable, unavoidable, inescapable; **II.** *Adv. auf j-n zukommen etc.*: inevitably, unavoidably; **Unausweichlichkeit** *f; nur Sg.* inevitability

unbändig I. *Adj. (ungezügelt)* unrestrained; *Hass, Zorn etc.*: *auch* unbridled; *Kraft etc.*: boundless, unbridled; *(wild)* wild; *Durst, Freude etc.*: enormous; tremendous; **~es Kind** *etc.* unruly child *etc.*; **II.** *Adv. lachen*: unrestrainedly; **sich ~ freuen** be enormously pleased; **~ herumtoben** *etc.* romp around *etc.* boisterously

unbar I. *Adj. Zahlung etc.*: cashless; *Transaktion*: non-cash; **II.** *Adv.*: **~ bezahlen** make a cashless payment

unbarmherzig I. *Adj. (erbarmungslos)* merciless, pitiless, relentless; **II.** *Adv. bestrafen*: mercilessly; **die Uhr lief ~** *fig.* time was passing relentlessly by; **Umbarmherzigkeit** *f; nur Sg.* mercilessness, (complete) lack of mercy *(od.* pity*)*

unbeabsichtigt *Adj.* unintentional; *attr. (ungewollt)* inadvertent ...

unbeachtet *Adj.* unnoticed; *Drohung etc.*: unheeded; **~ lassen** ignore

unbeachtlich *Adj.*: **nicht ~** not insignificant

unbeanstandet I. *Adj. Ware*: unobjected; *Entscheidung etc.*: unopposed, uncontested; **~ lassen** let *s.th.* pass; **II.** *Adv.* without any objection; **der Wagen konnte ~ passieren** the car was allowed through without being stopped

unbeantwortbar *Adj.* unanswerable; **unbeantwortet** *Adj.* unanswered; **e-n Brief** *etc.* **~ lassen** leave a letter *etc.* unanswered

unbearbeitet *Adj. Fassung etc.*: original, *präd. und nachgestellt*: in its original state; *Tech. etc.* unworked; *(unbehandelt)* untreated; **eine ~e Akte** a file that has not been dealt with; **etw. ~ liegen lassen / weitergeben** leave s.th. lying / pass s.th. on without dealing with it

unbeaufsichtigt I. *Adj.* unsupervised; **II.** *Adv.*: **~ spielen lassen** *etc.* let play *etc.* unsupervised

unbebaut *Adj.* **1.** *Gelände*: undeveloped; **~es Grundstück** empty site, vacant lot; **2.** *Agr.* untilled, idle, fallow

unbedacht I. *Adj.* thoughtless; *Handlung etc.*: unconsidered, ill-considered; **II.** *Adv. handeln etc.*: thoughtlessly

unbedarft *umg.* **I.** *Adj.* naive, simple; *(uneingeweiht)* uninitiated; *(unerfahren)* inexperienced; **völlig ~ sein** be thoroughly naive; **II.** *Adv. lächeln etc.*: naively; **Unbedarftheit** *f; nur Sg.* naivety; inexperience

unbedenklich I. *Adj. (sicher, risikolos)* safe; *(unschädlich)* harmless; *j-s Zustand ist ~* gives no cause for concern; **II.** *Adv. (bedenkenlos)* safely; *(ohne zu zögern)* without hesitation; **etw. ~ tun können** be able to do s.th. without hesitation; *(j-m)* **~ zustimmen können** be able to agree (with s.o.) without reservation; **Unbedenklichkeit** *f* safeness; harmlessness; → *unbedenklich*

Unbedenklichkeits|erklärung *f* official declaration that a substance etc. is harmless; **~bescheinigung** *f Jur. Fin.* certificate awarded by the tax office in cases where land ownership is being transferred proving that an individual has paid all his or her taxes

unbedeutend I. *Adj.* insignificant; *(geringfügig) auch* negligible; **II.** *Adv.* *(geringfügig)* slightly

unbedingt I. *Adj.* **1.** unconditional *(auch schw., österr. Jur., Strafe)*; *(völlig)* absolute; *Gehorsam, Vertrauen*: implicit; **2.** *Physiol., Reflex*: unconditional; **3.** *EDV* unconditional; **II.** *Adv.* **1.** *(absolut, unter allen Umständen)* absolutely; *(wirklich)* really, absolutely; *(um jeden Preis)* at all costs, whatever happens; **ich muss ihn ~ sprechen** I absolutely have to speak with him, I really must speak with him; **den Film muss man ~ gesehen haben** the film's an absolute must, *Am.* the movie is a must-see; **du musst ~ kommen** *etc.* you've got to come *etc.*; **sie will ~ heiraten / ein Ferrari** she is determined to get married / have a Ferrari; **muss es denn ~ ein ... sein?** does it absolutely have to be a ...?; **nicht ~** not necessarily; **2.** *schw., österr. Jur. verurteilen*: without probation; **Unbedingtheit** *f; nur Sg.* absoluteness

unbeeindruckt I. *Adj.*: **~ (bleiben)** (remain) unimpressed; **er war ~** it made no impression on him; **II.** *Adv.*: **er machte ~ weiter** he went on undeterred

unbeeinflussbar *Adj. Person*: unswayable, resolute; *Dynamik*: inalterable; **unbeeinflusst** *Adj.* uninfluenced, unswayed; *(neutral)* unbias(s)ed

unbeeinträchtigt *Adj.* unimpaired; *(nicht tangiert)* unaffected *(durch* by*)*

unbefahrbar *Adj.* impassable; *Gewässer*: unnavigable

unbefangen I. *Adj.* **1.** *(unparteiisch)* impartial; *auch Jur.* unbias(s)ed; **2.** *(nicht verlegen)* uninhibited; *(natürlich)* natural, free; **II.** *Adv.* **1.** *(unvoreingenommen)* without prejudice *(od.* bias*)*; *(unparteiisch)* impartially; **2.** *(ohne Verlegenheit)* without any inhibitions, free from inhibition(s of any sort); *(natürlich, frei)* naturally, freely; **Unbefangenheit** *f* **1.** *(Unparteilichkeit)* impartiality; **2.** *(Natürlichkeit)* naturalness, lack of inhibition

unbefestigt *Adj. Straße*: unsurfaced; **~e Straße** *auch* dirt track *(Am.* road*)*

unbefleckt *Adj. fig.* unsullied; **die Unbefleckte Empfängnis** *kirchl.* the Immaculate Conception

unbefriedigend *Adj.* unsatisfactory;

unbefriedigt *Adj.* dissatisfied; *sexuell*: unsatisfied

unbefristet I. *Adj.* unlimited; **II.** *Adv.* for an unlimited *(od.* indefinite*)* period, indefinitely

unbefruchtet *Adj.* unfertilized

unbefugt *Adj.* unauthorized; **Unbefugte** *m, f, -n, -n* unauthorized person; **Zutritt für ~ verboten** no unauthorized entry

unbegabt *Adj.* untalented; **sportlich/ künstlerisch ~ sein** have no sporting/ artistic talent; **technisch ~ sein** have no technical flair; **Unbegabtheit** *f; nur Sg.* lack of talent

unbegehbar *Adj.* impassable; *Eis, Dach etc.*: *präd.* unsafe to walk on

unbegleitet I. *Adj.* unaccompanied; **II.** *Adv.*: **nachts ~ durch den Park gehen** walk alone through the park at night

unbeglichen *Adj.*: **~e Rechnung** *etc.* unpaid bill, unsettled account

unbegreiflich *Adj.* incomprehensible (+ *Dat.* to); *(unerklärlich)* inexplicable (to); **es ist mir völlig ~** I just can't understand it, it beats me *umg.*; **es ist mir völlig ~, wie** *od.* **dass ...**: I just can't understand why *(od.* how*)* ..., it's beyond me how ..., it beats me how ... *umg.*; **unbegreiflicherweise** *Adv.* inexplicably

unbegrenzt I. *Adj.* unlimited; *lit. (grenzenlos)* boundless; *Aufenthaltserlaubnis*: indefinite, permanent; **zeitlich ~** unlimited, with no time limit; **auf ~e Dauer** indefinite; **das Land der ~en Möglichkeiten** the land of limitless opportunity; **II.** *Adv. gültig, haltbar etc.*: indefinitely; **er kann ~ sein Konto überziehen** he has an unlimited overdraft on his account; **Unbegrenztheit** *f* limitlessness; *(Grenzenlosigkeit)* boundlessness; **~ der Vorräte** *etc.* unlimited supplies *etc.*

unbegründet *Adj.* unfounded; *Anklage*: *auch* baseless; *Antrag*: invalid; **dein Verdacht** *etc.* **ist ~** *auch* there's no cause for your suspicion *etc.*; **e-e Klage als ~ abweisen** *Jur.* dismiss a complaint on lack of grounds; **e-n Antrag als ~ zurückweisen** reject an application because it fails to meet the required criteria

unbehaart *Adj.* hairless

Unbehagen *n* **1.** (feeling of) unease; **das ~ an der Politik** *etc.* **wächst** the feeling of discontent with politics *etc.* is growing; **2.** *körperliches*: discomfort; *(Übelkeit)* queasiness; **unbehaglich** *Adj.* uncomfortable; *fig. Gefühl etc.*: *auch* uneasy; **sich ~ fühlen** *fig.* feel uneasy, be ill at ease; **Unbehaglichkeit** *f* uncomfortableness, discomfort; *fig. auch* uneasiness, feeling of unease

unbehandelt *Adj. Obst etc.*: untreated; *Wunde, Krankheit*: untreated; **die Schale ist ~** the peel has not been treated with chemicals

unbehaust *Adj. geh.* homeless

unbehelligt I. *Adj.* undisturbed; *(ungehindert)* unhindered; **von j-m ~ bleiben** be left alone by s.o.; **hier bist du von den Fans ~** the fans won't disturb you here; **II.** *Adv.*: **j-n ~ durchlassen** let s.o. through *(od.* pass*)* without questioning; **~ nachts nach Hause gehen** walk home at night without being molested

unbeherrscht I. *Adj. Person*: lacking in self-control; *Äußerung, Reaktion etc.*: uncontrolled; **~ sein** have no self-control; **II.** *Adv. handeln etc.*: without

self-control; *losbrüllen etc.*: without restraint; *essen etc.: auch* greedily; **Unbeherrschtheit** *f* lack of self-control
unbehindert I. *Adj.* unhindered, unimpeded; *Sicht*: clear; **II.** *Adv. passieren etc.*: unhindered; *völlig ~ zum Schuss kommen Sport* get a clear shot at (the) goal
unbeholfen I. *Adj.* **1.** *Bewegung etc.*: clumsy, awkward; *er ist ~ im Ausdruck* he is not very good at expressing himself; **2.** *(hilflos)* helpless; *pej.* hopeless; **II.** *Adv. sich bewegen etc.*: clumsily, awkwardly; *sich ~ ausdrücken* express oneself clumsily; **Unbeholfenheit** *f; nur Sg.* **1.** clumsiness, awkwardness; **2.** *(Hilflosigkeit)* helplessness
unbeirrbar I. *Adj.* unswerving, single-minded; **II.** *Adv.*: *~ s-e Ziele verfolgen* pursue one's aims single-mindedly; **Unbeirrbarkeit** *f; nur Sg.* unswervingness, single-mindedness; **unbeirrt I.** *Adj. Kämpfer etc.*: single-minded; **II.** *Adv. handeln, kämpfen etc.*: single-mindedly; *~ weitermachen* carry on regardless; *~ festhalten an e-m Glauben etc.*: persist in
unbekannt *Adj.* unknown (*+ Dat.* to); *(nicht vertraut)* unfamiliar (to); *~e Größe auch fig.* unknown quantity; *das war mir ~* I didn't know that, I wasn't aware of that; *es ist mir nicht ~, dass* I'm quite aware that; *ich bin hier ~* I'm a stranger here; *Ort und Zeit sind noch ~* a time and place have yet to be decided; *gegen Unbekannt Jur.* versus a person (*od.* persons) unknown
Unbekannte[1] *f; -n, -n; Math.: die ~ auch fig.* the unknown; *Gleichung mit zwei ~n* equation with two unknowns, binomial equation
Unbekannte[2] *m, f; -n, -n* unknown (*od.* unidentified) person (*od.* man, woman); *(Fremde[r])* stranger; *sie wurde von ~n entführt* she was kidnapped by persons unknown; *Verabredung mit e-r ~n* blind date; *der große ~ mst iro.* the mystery man
unbekannterweise *Adv.*: *grüßen Sie sie ~ von mir* please give her my regards, even though we haven't met yet
unbekleidet I. *Adj.* undressed, with nothing on; *er wurde mit e-r ~en Schönen erwischt* he was caught with a beautiful naked woman; **II.** *Adv. herumlaufen etc.*: with nothing on
unbekümmert I. *Adj.* unconcerned, nonchalant; *(sorglos)* carefree; *~e Einstellung auch* cavalier approach; **II.** *Adv. lachen, in den Tag hinein leben etc.*: in a carefree way; *das können Sie ~ tun* you don't have to worry about doing that; **Unbekümmertheit** *f; nur Sg.* unconcern, lack of concern, nonchalance; carefree attitude (*od.* approach, manner)
unbelastet I. *Adj.* **1.** *(ohne Last)* unloaded, unladen, with nothing on (*od.* in) it; *Bein, Ski etc.*: unweighted; *Tech., Maschine etc.*: running idle; *Bauteil*: unstressed; **2.** *finanziell, Haus, Grundstück etc.*: unencumbered; **3.** *fig. (frei)* free (*von* from); *engS. (frei von Sorgen etc.)* free from (*od.* without [any]) worries, carefree; *~ von Vorurteilen/Skrupeln etc.*: without prejudice/scruple *etc.*; **4.** *(makellos) Vergangenheit etc.*: clean, unblemished; *~ sein Person*: have a clean record, not have blotted one's copybook, *Am.* not have any black marks against one; **5.** *Öko., Luft, Wasser, Boden etc*: un-

polluted; *Lebensmittel*: uncontaminated; **II.** *Adv.* **1.** *(sorgenfrei)* without worries; *~ durchs Leben gehen* lead an untroubled life; **2.** *(ohne Vorurteile)* without prejudice (*od.* preconceptions), impartially
unbelebt *Adj.* **1.** *Materie, Natur*: inanimate; **2.** *Straße etc.*: unfrequented; *Gegend etc.*: deserted; *Stadt, Lokal etc.*: dead
unbeleckt *Adj. umg.* clueless; *von der Kultur ~* untouched by civilization
unbelehrbar *Adj. (stur)* incorrigible; *(eingefleischt)* inveterate; *Faschist, Kommunist, Rassist etc.*: dyed-in-the-wool, unreconstructed, die-hard; *diese Fanatiker sind ~* these fanatics will never learn (*od.* change); *die Unbelehrbaren* the die-hards, the hard-core fanatics, people who will never change (their ways); *Straftäter*: the inveterate offenders; **Unbelehrbarkeit** *f; nur Sg.* incorrigibility; *mit der Tat haben sie mal wieder i-e ~ bewiesen* what they have done shows yet again that they simply never learn (*od.* change)
unbeleuchtet *Adj. Straße etc.*: unlit; *Fahrzeug*: without lights
unbelichtet *Adj. Fot.* unexposed
unbeliebt *Adj.* unpopular (*bei* with); *er ist sehr ~ auch* not many people like him; *sich (mit etw. bei j-m) ~ machen* make o.s. unpopular (with s.o.); *er ist bei den Schülern gar nicht so ~* the students actually quite like him (*Am.* actually like him a lot), he is by no means so unpopular with the students; **Unbeliebtheit** *f* unpopularity
unbemannt *Adj.* **1.** unmanned; *Flug*. pilotless; **2.** *umg. hum. (ohne Mann)* without a man; *(unverheiratet)* husbandless
unbemerkbar *Adj.* imperceptible; **unbemerkt** *Adj. und Adv.* unnoticed, unseen; *~ bleiben* go unnoticed; *sie gelangten völlig ~ in den Tresorraum* they managed to make their way into the vault completely unnoticed
unbemittelt *Adj.* penniless, without means *nachgestellt*
unbenommen *Adj.*: *es bleibt Ihnen ~ zu* (*+ Inf.*) you are at liberty to (*+ Inf.*); *dieses Privileg bleibt Ihnen ~* this is your undisputed right (*od.* prerogative)
unbenutzbar *Adj.* unusable; *pej.* useless; **unbenutzt** *Adj.* **1.** unused (*auch EDV*); *es ist ~ auch* nobody's used it; **2.** *(sauber) Besteck*: clean; **3.** *(unbewohnt)* unoccupied, vacant
unbeobachtet *Adj.* unobserved; *in e-m ~en Moment* when nobody's looking; *wenn man sich ganz ~ fühlt* when you feel you are completely alone
unbequem *Adj.* **1.** uncomfortable; **2.** *(umständlich, unpassend)* inconvenient; *(lästig)* irksome; *er ist ihnen ~ geworden* he has become a nuisance (*od.* embarrassment) to them; **3.** *Frage etc.*: awkward, embarrassing; **Unbequemlichkeit** *f* **1.** *nur Sg.* uncomfortableness, discomfort; **2.** *mst Pl.*: *~en (Unannehmlichkeiten)* inconvenience *Sg.*, stärker: trouble *Sg.*; **3.** *nur Sg.*: *e-r Frage etc.*: awkwardness, embarrassing nature (*+ Gen.* of)
unberechenbar *Adj.* incalculable; *auch Person*: unpredictable; **Unberechenbarkeit** *f* unpredictability
unberechtigt *Adj. (unbefugt)* unauthorized; *(ungerechtfertigt)* unjustified; *(grundlos)* unfounded; *(unerlaubt)* forbidden; **unberechtigterweise** *Adv.*

(unbefugt) without authorization; *(ungerechtfertigt)* unjustifiably, without justification; *(grundlos)* without good reason; *(unerlaubt)* without permission
unberücksichtigt *Adj.* unconsidered, not taken into account; *~ lassen* discount, disregard, make no allowance for; *~ bleiben* not be taken into account, be disregarded
Unberührbare *m, f, -n, -n* untouchable
unberührt I. *Adj.* untouched; *Natur*: unspoil|t (*Am.* -ed), pristine; *Boden, Schnee*: virgin; *ein Stückchen ~e Natur* a piece of unspoil|t (*Am.* -ed) countryside; *~es Mädchen* virgin; *~ lassen* (*Essen etc.*) leave untouched; *es ließ sie ~ fig.* it left her cold; **II.** *Adv.*: *~ in die Ehe gehen* be a virgin when one marries
unbeschadet *Präp. (ungeachtet)* irrespective of, notwithstanding (*+ Gen. s.th.*)
unbeschädigt *Adj.* undamaged; *(intakt)* intact
unbeschäftigt *Adj.* idle; *(arbeitslos)* unemployed
unbescheiden *Adj.* immodest; *(zu anspruchsvoll)* extravagant
unbescholten *Adj.* respectable; *~ sein Jur.* have a clean record; **Unbescholtenheit** *f; nur Sg.* good reputation (*od.* name); *Jur.* clean record
unbeschrankt *Adj.*: *~er Bahnübergang* open crossing; *Schild*: Crossing No Gates
unbeschränkt I. *Adj.* unrestricted, full; *auch Macht, Jur., Eigentum*: absolute; **II.** *Adv.* without restrictions; *~ viel(e) ...* unlimited (amounts *od.* numbers of) ...
unbeschreiblich I. *Adj.* indescribable; *es ist ~ auch* I (just) can't describe it; **II.** *Adv.* indescribably, ... beyond description
unbeschrieben *Adj. Papier*: blank; *EDV* empty; *ein ~es Blatt sein fig. (unbekannt)* be an unknown quantity; *(unerfahren)* be inexperienced; *er ist kein ~es Blatt umg. fig. (hat schon einiges auf dem Kerbholz)* he hasn't kept clear of trouble
unbeschwert I. *Adj.* carefree; *Art: auch* lighthearted; *~ von* free from, unencumbered by; **II.** *Adv.*: *~ leben können* be able to live free from worry; *~ in Urlaub fahren* go off on holiday (*Am.* vacation) without a care in the world; **Unbeschwertheit** *f; nur Sg.* carefree nature; lightheartedness
unbesehen *Adv. (ohne es zu sehen)* without seeing (*od.* having seen) it, sight unseen; *(bedenkenlos)* safely; *(ohne zu zögern)* without hesitation; *(ohne weiteres)* just like that, without thinking twice; *das glaube ich ~* I don't doubt it in the least
unbesetzt *Adj. Stelle*: vacant; *Platz etc.: auch* unoccupied (*beide auch EDV*), free; *Rolle*: uncast
unbesiedelt *Adj. Gebiet*: unsettled
unbesiegbar *Adj.* invincible; **Unbesiegbarkeit** *f* invincibility; **unbesiegt I.** *Adj.* undefeated; *Spieler, Mannschaft: auch* unbeaten; **II.** *Adv. ins Endspiel kommen etc.*: undefeated, unbeaten
unbesonnen *Adj. (unüberlegt) Handlung etc.*: thoughtless; *(übereilt) Entscheidung etc.*: rash; *weitS. Person: auch* impulsive; **Unbesonnenheit** *f* **1.** *nur Sg.* thoughtlessness; rashness; impulsiveness; **2.** *Handlung*: thought-

less (*od.* rash *od.* impulsive) act
unbesorgt I. *Adj. nur präd.* unconcerned (**wegen** about); **seien Sie ~** don't worry; **II.** *Adv.* (*getrost*) safely
unbespielbar *Adj. Rasen, Platz*: unplayable
unbespielt *Adj. Cassette etc.*: blank, empty
unbeständig *Adj.* unsteady, unstable; *Wetter*: changeable, unsettled; *Wirts., Markt*: unsettled; **Unbeständigkeit** *f* instability; *des Wetters*: changeableness; *Wirts.* unsettledness
unbestätigt *Adj.* unconfirmed
unbestechlich *Adj.* **1.** incorruptible; **2.** *fig. Urteil etc.*: unerring; **Unbestechlichkeit** *f* incorruptibility, integrity
unbestimmbar *Adj.* indefinable; (*vage*) vague, indeterminate; *Pflanze etc.*: unclassifiable; **e-e Frau ~en Alters** a woman of uncertain age; **unbestimmt I.** *Adj.* **1.** *Gefühl, Vorstellung etc.*: vague; **2.** (*ungewiss*) uncertain; *Zeitraum, Ling., Artikel etc.*: indefinite; *Math. Ergebnis, Gleichung*: indeterminate; *Integral*: indefinite; **auf ~e Zeit** indefinitely; **etw. ~ lassen** leave s.th. open; **II.** *Adv. gehalten, formuliert etc.*: vaguely; **Unbestimmtheit** *f* **1.** vagueness; **2.** (*Ungewissheit*) uncertainty
unbestraft *Adj.* unpunished; → **straffrei**
unbestreitbar I. *Adj.* indisputable, unquestionable; **II.** *Adv.* indisputably, unquestionably; **unbestritten I.** *Adj.* undisputed, uncontested; **II.** *Adv.* indisputably, without doubt
unbeteiligt I. *Adj.* **1.** (*teilnahmslos*) indifferent, unconcerned; **er schien seltsam ~** he seemed strangely unconcerned; **2.** *an e-r Tat etc.*: uninvolved; **an e-r Sache ~ sein** not be involved in s.th.; *Wirts.* have no interest in s.th.; **ein Unbeteiligter** an onlooker, a bystander; (*Außenseiter*) an outsider; (*Unschuldiger*) an innocent party; **völlig ~e Personen** people who have nothing at all to do with *s.th.*; **bei e-m Angriff, Unfall etc.**: completely innocent people; **II.** *Adv.* dabeistehen etc.: without being (*od.* getting) involved
unbetont *Adj. Phon., Silbe etc.*: unstressed
unbeträchtlich *Adj.* insignificant, negligible; **nicht ~** quite considerable, not inconsiderable
unbeugsam *Adj. fig. Wille, Person, Haltung etc.*: unbending; *weitS.* (*nicht kompromissbereit*) uncompromising; (*dickköpfig, stur*) stubborn, inflexible; **~er Wille** iron will; **Unbeugsamkeit** *f; nur Sg.* unbending (*od.* uncompromising) attitude; *des Willens, der Haltung etc.*: unbendingness
unbewacht *Adj.* unguarded (*auch fig.*); *Bahnübergang, Parkplatz*: unmonitored
unbewaffnet *Adj. und Adv.* unarmed
unbewältigt *Adj. Problem*: unresolved; *Erlebnis*: that one (*od.* s.o.) has not (yet) come to terms with; **die ~e Vergangenheit** the past with which people are still coming (*od.* trying to come) to terms
unbeweglich *Adj.* immobile; (*bewegungslos*) motionless; *fig.* rigid; **~e Sachen** immovables; (*geistig*) **~ sein** be inflexible; → **Gut** 1; **Unbeweglichkeit** *f* immobility; motionlessness; *fig.* rigidness, rigidity
unbewegt *Adj. Gesicht*: expressionless; (*unbeeindruckt, ohne Gefühle*) un-

moved; **mit ~er Miene** with a fixed expression; **er blieb völlig ~** he remained completely unmoved
unbeweibt *Adj. umg. hum.* without a woman; (*unverheiratet*) wifeless
unbeweisbar *Adj.* unprovable; **es ist ~ auch** it can't be proved; **unbewiesen** *Adj. attr.* unproven, *präd.* not proved
unbewohnbar *Adj.* uninhabitable; **Unbewohnbarkeit** *f* uninhabitability; **unbewohnt** *Adj.* uninhabited; *Gebäude*: *auch* unoccupied, vacant
unbewusst I. *Adj.* unconscious (+ *Gen.* of); (*unwillkürlich, instinktiv*) involuntary, instinctive, mechanical; **II.** *Adv.* unconsciously; (*unabsichtlich*) unwittingly; **er hat falsch ausgesagt, bewusst oder ~** wittingly or unwittingly; **Unbewusste** *n; -n, kein Pl.*; *Psych.*: **das ~** the unconscious (mind)
unbezahlbar *Adj.* unaffordable, far too expensive, beyond one's (*od.* anyone's) reach; *Preis etc.*: prohibitive; *fig.* invaluable, priceless; *umg.* (*unersetzlich*) worth its weight in gold; *umg. Humor*: priceless; **unbezahlt** *Adj.* unpaid (*auch Urlaub*)
unbezähmbar *Adj. fig.* uncontrollable; *Hunger, Durst, Neugier*: insatiable
unbezweifelbar *Adj.* unquestionable
unbezwingbar *Adj.* invincible; *Festung etc.*: impregnable; *Gefühl*: uncontrollable
Unbilden *Pl. geh.* rigo(u)rs; **die ~ der Witterung** the inclemency *Sg.* of the weather
Unbill *f; -, kein Pl.*; *lit., altm.*; *des Krieges etc.*: the evils *Pl.* (+ *Gen.* of); *des Alltags etc.*: the rigo(u)rs
unbillig *Adj. geh.* unreasonable, unfair; **~e Härte** undue hardship
unblutig I. *Adj.* bloodless; *Med.* non-operative; **II.** *Adv.* without bloodshed
unbotmäßig *Adj. lit., hum.* insubordinate; *weitS.* rebellious, refractory; **Unbotmäßigkeit** *f* insubordination
unbrauchbar *Adj.* useless, of no use (to s.o.); (*ungeeignet*) unsuitable; *Tech.* unserviceable; *Material*: *attr. auch* waste ...; *Plan etc.*: impracticable, unworkable; **für Hausarbeit etc. völlig ~ sein** *Person*: be useless when it comes to housework *etc.*; **~ machen** *Tech.* put out of action, make unserviceable; **Unbrauchbarkeit** *f* uselessness; *Tech.* unserviceability; *von Plänen etc.*: impracticability
unbürokratisch I. *Adj.* unbureaucratic; **II.** *Adv.* unbureaucratically, without a lot of red tape
unchristlich I. *Adj.* unchristian; **zu e-r ~en Zeit anrufen** *etc. umg. fig.* phone up at some ungodly hour; **II.** *Adv. handeln etc.*: in an unchristian way
und *Konj.* **1.** and; **drei ~ drei ist** (*gleich*) **sechs** three and three is (*od.* are) six; **um die ~ die Zeit** at such and such a time; **... sagte er ~ lächelte ...** he said, smiling; **er ist imstande ~ macht es** he's quite capable of doing it; **2.** *mst in wörtlicher Rede*: **~?** well?; **na ~?** *umg.* so (what)?; **~ ob!** *umg.* you bet!, Am. auch and how!; **~ tschüs!** *umg. iro.* (*lass mich in Ruhe!*) bye-bye, get lost; **~ so weiter(, ~ so fort)** and so on (and so forth); **~ ~ ~** etc. etc. etc.; **er will es nicht - ~ ich auch nicht** neither (*od.* nor) do I, me neither *umg.*; **ich ~ Tennis spielen?** *iro.* me, play tennis?; **du ~ fleißig?** *iro.* you, hardworking?; **~ wenn** (*auch*) even if; **~ wenn du mich zehnmal fragst** however (*od.* no matter how)

many times you ask me; **sei so gut ~ hilf mir** please be so kind as to help me; **3.** *verstärkend*: **er fragte ~ fragte** he (just) kept on asking; **wir überlegten ~ überlegten** we racked our brains; **der Regen wollte ~ wollte nicht aufhören** the rain just wouldn't stop; **der Lärm wurde stärker ~ stärker** the noise got louder and louder; **aus dem ~ dem Grunde** for this and that reason; → **so** I 10, II 1, **wie** I 3
Undank *m* ingratitude, ungratefulness; **~ ernten** get no (*od.* very little) thanks for *s.th.*; **~ ist der Welt Lohn** *Sprichw.* don't expect any gratitude; **undankbar** *Adj.* ungrateful; *Aufgabe etc.*: thankless; **Undankbarkeit** *f* ingratitude, ungratefulness
undatiert *Adj.* undated
undefinierbar I. *Adj.* indefinable; **II.** *Adv. umg.*: **~ schmecken** *etc.* taste funny
undeklinierbar *Adj.* indeclinable
undemokratisch I. *Adj.* undemocratic; **II.** *Adv.* undemocratically
undenkbar *Adj.* unthinkable
undenklich *Adj.*: **seit ~en Zeiten** from (*od.* since) time immemorial, ever since I can remember; *weitS.* for ages
Undercoveragent [ande'kavɐ-] *m*, **~in** *f* undercover agent
Underdog ['andɐdɔg] *m*; *-s, -s* underdog
undeutlich I. *Adj.* indistinct, not clear; (*unbestimmt*) *auch* Äußerung, Eindruck: vague; *Schrift*: illegible; *Aussprache*: unclear; *stärker* unintelligible; **II.** *Adv.* schreiben, sich ausdrücken *etc.*: unclearly; (*ungenau*) vaguely; **~ zu erkennen sein** be difficult to make out; **Undeutlichkeit** *f* indistinctness; vagueness; illegibility
undeutsch *Adj. oft pej.* un-German
undicht *Adj.* leaking; *Deckel etc.*: not tight; (*wasserdurchlässig*) not waterproof, not watertight; (*luftdurchlässig*) not airtight; (*porös*) porous; **~ sein** *auch* be leaking; **~e Stelle** *auch fig. Pol.* leak
undifferenziert I. *Adj.* (*grob vereinfacht*) (too) simple, simplistic; (*feinere Unterschiede nicht berücksichtigend*) undiscriminating, indiscriminate; (*pauschal*) wholesale; *Urteil, Behauptung etc.*: sweeping; **II.** *Adv.* simplistically; indiscriminately; wholesale; → I; **~ urteilen** make a sweeping judg(e)ment; **Undifferenziertheit** *f* simplistic nature (*e-r Person*: attitude, way of thinking); lack of discrimination
Unding *n nur Sg.* absurdity; **es wäre ein ~ zu** (+ *Inf.*) *auch* it would be absurd to (+ *Inf.*); **das ist doch wirklich ein ~** that really is absurd (*od.* ridiculous)
undiplomatisch I. *Adj.* undiplomatic, tactless; **II.** *Adv.* undiplomatically
undiszipliniert *Adj.* undisciplined
undogmatisch I. *Adj.* undogmatic; **II.** *Adv.* undogmatically; **ein Problem ~ angehen** approach a problem without recourse to dogma
undramatisch I. *Adj.* **1.** *Stil etc.*: undramatic; **2.** *fig. Verlauf etc.*: uneventful, unexciting, tame; **II.** *Adv.* undramatically; uneventfully; **die Aussprache verlief völlig ~** the discussion was entirely uneventful (*od.* was a completely tame affair)
unduldsam *Adj.* intolerant; **Unduldsamkeit** *f* intolerance
undurchdringlich *Adj.* **1.** impenetrable; **2.** *Miene*: inscrutable; **Undurchdring-**

lichkeit *f; nur Sg.* **1.** impenetrability; **2.** *der Miene*: inscrutability

undurchführbar *Adj.* impracticable, unworkable; **Undurchführbarkeit** *f* impracticability

undurchlässig *Adj.* impervious, impermeable (*beide*: **für** to); **Undurchlässigkeit** *f* imperviousness, impermeability

undurchschaubar *Adj. Person, Absichten, Lächeln etc.*: inscrutable; *weitS.* (*geheimnisvoll*) mysterious, arcane; (*obskur*) obscure; **Undurchschaubarkeit** *f* inscrutability; mysteriousness, mysterious nature (+ *Gen.* of)

undurchsichtig *Adj.* opaque; *fig. Person*: impenetrable; (*obskur, dubios*) *Machenschaften, Pläne etc.*: obscure; **Undurchsichtigkeit** *f* opacity; *fig.* impenetrability; obscurity

Und-Zeichen *n* (*Zeichen* &) ampersand

uneben *Adj.* uneven; *Weg etc.*: *auch* rough, bumpy; **nicht ~** *umg. fig.* not bad; **Unebenheit** *f* **1.** *nur Sg.* unevenness; bumpiness; **2.** (*unebene Stelle*) unevenness, uneven spot, bump *umg.*

unecht *Adj.* **1.** not genuine; (*gefälscht*) counterfeit, fake; (*nachgemacht*) imitation ..., artificial; *Farbe*: fading, not fast; *Math.* improper; **2.** *fig. Gefühle*: not genuine, false, insincere; *Lächeln*: *auch* artificial; → *auch* **falsch**

unedel *Adj. attr. Metalle*: base ...

uneffektiv *Adj.* ineffective

unehelich I. *Adj. Kind*: illegitimate; *Mutter*: unmarried; **II.** *Adv.*: **~ geboren** illegitimate

Unehre *f; nur Sg.* dishono(u)r; **j-m ~ machen** dishono(u)r s.o., bring dishono(u)r (*od.* disgrace) on s.o.; **unehrenhaft I.** *Adj.* dishono(u)rable; **II.** *Adv.*: **~ entlassen werden** *Mil.* be dishono(u)rably discharged

unehrlich I. *Adj.* dishonest; (*falsch*) insincere; **auf ~e Weise** by dishonest means, dishonestly; **II.** *Adv. sich verhalten etc.*: dishonestly; **Unehrlichkeit** *f* dishonesty; (*Unaufrichtigkeit*) insincerity

uneidlich *Adj. Jur.*: **~e Falschaussage** false statement made while not under oath

uneigennützig I. *Adj.* unselfish; **II.** *Adv. handeln, helfen etc.*: unselfishly; **Uneigennützigkeit** *f* unselfishness

uneigentlich I. *Adj. Math., Zahl, Integral*: improper; **II.** *Adv. umg.* (*tatsächlich*) actually; (*in Wahrheit*) if I'm etc. honest

uneinbringlich *Adj. Wirts.*: **~e Forderungen** bad debts

uneingeschränkt *Adj. attr.* unrestricted, unlimited; *Vertrauen*: absolute; *Lob etc.*: unqualified, unreserved; *Unterstützung, Maßnahme*: all-out ...

uneingestanden *Adj.* unacknowledged

uneingeweiht *Adj.* uninitiated; **für Uneingeweihte** for the uninitiated

uneinheitlich *Adj.* non-uniform, inconsistent; (*verschieden*) varied; (*unterschiedlich*) varying; *Wirts., Kurse, Preise*: irregular; **Uneinheitlichkeit** *f* lack of uniformity, inconsistency; varied nature (+ *Gen.* of); *Wirts.* irregularity

uneinholbar I. *Adj. Vorsprung etc.*: unassailable; **II.** *Adv.*: **~ an der Spitze liegen** *etc.* have an unassailable lead, lead by too wide a margin to be caught (*od.* overtaken)

uneinig *Adj. mst präd.* divided, disunit-

ed; (**sich**) **~ sein** be in disagreement, be at issue (**über** + *Akk.* about, on); (*zerstritten*) be at variance; **mit sich selbst ~ sein** be at odds with o.s., be conflicted; **ich bin mit mir selbst noch ~** I'm still undecided; **Uneinigkeit** *f* dividedness; disagreement; *stärker*: dissension

uneinnehmbar *Adj.* impregnable

uneins *Adj. nur präd.*: **~ sein** → **uneinig**

uneinsichtig *Adj.* stubborn; **sie ist so ~** *auch* she just won't listen to reason, you can't reason with her; **Uneinsichtigkeit** *f* stubbornness, refusal to listen to reason

unempfänglich *Adj.* unreceptive, impervious, insensible (*alle*: **für** to); **Unempfänglichkeit** *f* unreceptiveness, imperviousness, insensibility (*alle*: **für** to)

unempfindlich *Adj.* insensitive (**gegen, für** to); (*abgehärtet*) inured (to); *fig.* (*gleichgültig*) indifferent (to); *Teppichboden, Tischdecke etc.*: hardwearing and stain-resistant; **~ gegen Nässe** *etc.* **sein** be unaffected by damp *etc.*; **Unempfindlichkeit** *f; nur Sg.* insensitivity (**gegen, für** to), lack of sensitivity (towards); indifference (to[wards]); *e-s Teppichs etc.*: durability

unendlich I. *Adj. Phys., Math., Mus.* infinite (*auch fig.* Geduld, Sorgfalt, Vergnügen *etc.*); **~e Zahl** *Math.* infinite quantity; **das Unendliche** infinity (*auch Math.*); **~er Kreislauf** recurring spiral; **auf ~ einstellen** *Fot.* focus at infinity; (**bis**) **ins Unendliche** on and on and on, endlessly, ad infinitum; **das geht ins Unendliche** it's never-ending; **II.** *Adv.* infinitely; *fig.* (*sehr*) exceedingly, incredibly *umg.*; *traurig, glücklich etc.*: tremendously; **sich ~ freuen** *etc.* be pleased *etc.* no end *umg.*; **~ klein** infinitesimal; **~ lang** endless; **~ lange warten** *umg.* wait for absolute (-ly) ages; **~ viel(e)** *Zahl*: an infinite number (of); *Menge*: an infinite amount (of); **~ viel(e) Sorgen** *etc.* no end of trouble *etc.*

Unendlichkeit *f* **1.** **die ~** infinity; **2.** *der Weite etc.*: endlessness, infinity; *des Weltalls*: boundlessness; **3.** *umg.*: **e-e ~ warten** wait for ages (*od.* for an age and a half); **es kam mir wie e-e ~ vor** it seemed like an eternity to me

unentbehrlich *Adj.* indispensable (+ *Dat. od.* **für** to); **sich für ~ halten** consider o.s. to be indispensable; **sich ~ machen** make o.s. indispensable; **Unentbehrlichkeit** *f* indispensability

unentdeckt *Adj.* undiscovered; **die Tat blieb lange ~** the crime remained (*od.* went) for a long time undiscovered

unentgeltlich *Adj. und Adv.* free (of charge)

unentrinnbar *Adj.* inescapable, ineluctable; **das Schicksal** *etc.* **ist ~** *auch* there's no escaping fate *etc.*

unentschieden I. *Adj.* undecided (*auch Person*); *Frage*: open, unsettled; **~es Spiel** tie; **~es Rennen** dead heat, tie; **II.** *Adv.*: **~ spielen** draw; **~ enden** end in a draw (*od.* tie); **es steht ~** the scores are level, *Am.* the score is even; **es stand bis kurz vor dem Schlusspfiff ~** the scores were level (*Am.* the score was even) until shortly before the final whistle; **die Mannschaften haben sich** (**1:1**) **getrennt** the game ended in a 1-1 [= one all] draw

Unentschieden *n; -s, -; Sport* draw, tie; **auf ~ spielen** play for a draw; **ein ~ er-**

zielen *Mannschaft*: manage a draw; **Unentschiedenheit** *f* undecidedness

unentschlossen *Adj.* undecided, irresolute; **~ sein** *auch* waver, hesitate, vacillate; **ich bin noch ~, ob ich es kaufen soll oder nicht** I'm still undecided (*od.* I still can't decide) whether to buy it or not; **Unentschlossenheit** *f* vacillation, hesitation; (*Eigenschaft*) indecision

unentschuldbar *Adj.* inexcusable, unpardonable; **unentschuldigt I.** *Adj.*: **~es Fehlen** unexcused absence; **II.** *Adv.*: **~ fehlen** be absent without an excuse

unentwegt I. *Adv.* (*unermüdlich*) tirelessly; (*zielstrebig*) unswervingly; (*unterbrochen*) incessantly; **er redete ~** *auch* he wouldn't stop talking; **j-n ~ ansehen** keep one's eyes fixed on s.o.; **II.** *Adj. nur attr. Arbeit etc*: ceaseless, constant; *Person*: indefatigable, tireless; **ein ~er Kämpfer für** a tireless (steadfast *lit.*) campaigner for; **e-e Hand voll Unentwegte** a few diehards; *positiver*: a few stalwarts

unentwirrbar *Adj.* inextricable

unentzifferbar *Adj.* indecipherable

unerbittlich I. *Adj.* relentless (*auch Kampf*); *Hass, Opposition etc.*: unrelenting; (*erbarmungslos*) merciless; *Schicksal*: inexorable; **mit ~er Härte** with ruthless severity, mercilessly; **II.** *Adv. durchgreifen etc*: ruthlessly; **Unerbittlichkeit** *f; nur Sg.* relentlessness; unrelenting nature (+ *Gen.* of); mercilessness; inexorability; → **unerbittlich**

unerfahren *Adj.* inexperienced (**in** + *Dat.* in), new (to); **Unerfahrenheit** *f* inexperience, lack of experience

unerfindlich *Adj.* inexplicable; **aus ~en Gründen** for some obscure reason; **es ist mir** (**völlig**) **~** it's a (complete) mystery to me

unerforschlich *Adj. fig.* unfathomable; **nach Gottes ~em Ratschluss** in accordance with God's unfathomable decree; **unerforscht** *Adj.* unexplored, uncharted (*auch fig.*); **~es Gebiet** *auch fig.* uncharted territory

unerfreulich *Adj.* unpleasant; (*ärgerlich*) annoying; **so was Unerfreuliches!** *auch* what a nuisance; **ich habe e-e ~e Mitteilung zu machen** I've got some unpleasant news for you, I'm afraid; **das ist alles höchst ~** all this is extremely unpleasant

unerfüllbar *Adj.* unrealizable; **unerfüllt** *Adj.* unfulfilled

unergiebig *Adj.* (*keinen Nutzen bringend, auch fig.*) unproductive; (*unrentabel*) unprofitable; *Informationsquellen etc.*: unhelpful; (*nicht der Mühe wert*) not worth one's while; **es war ~** *auch* it didn't get us *etc.* any further; **das Thema ist ~** *auch* the subject leads nowhere; **Unergiebigkeit** *f* unproductiveness; unprofitability; dead-end nature *umg.* (+ *Gen.* of); → **unergiebig**

unergründlich *Adj.* unfathomable; *fig.* inscrutable

unerheblich *Adj.* (*unbedeutend*) insignificant, unimportant; (*gering*) slight; (*irrelevant*) irrelevant

unerhört I. *Adj.* **1.** (*empörend*) outrageous, scandalous; **~!** what a cheek!, *Am.* what nerve!; **2.** *umg.* (*sehr viel etc.*) tremendous, incredible; **sie hatte ~es Glück** she was incredibly lucky; **3.** (*noch nie dagewesen*) unheard-of, unprecedented; **4.** (*nicht erhört*) *Gebet* *etc.*: unanswered; *Liebe, Liebhaber*: unrequited; **II.** *Adv.*: *fleißig, schwierig, spannend etc.* incredibly; *leiden etc.*: terribly; **~** (*viel*) *arbeiten* work incredibly hard; *sich* **~** *benehmen* behave outrageously

unerkannt I. *Adj.* unrecognized, unidentified; **~** *bleiben* remain unrecognized (*bzw.* unidentified); **II.** *Adv.*: **~** *entkommen* escape unrecognized (*od.* without being recognized)

unerklärbar, unerklärlich *Adj.* inexplicable; *es ist* **~** *auch* it's a (real) mystery

unerklärt *Adj. attr.* **1.** *Krieg, Liebe*: undeclared; **2.** *Erscheinung*: unexplained

unerlässlich *Adj.* essential, imperative

unerlaubt I. *Adj. attr.* unauthorized, *präd.* prohibited, not allowed (*od.* permitted); (*ungesetzlich*) illegal, illicit; **~***e Handlung* unlawful act; *Jur.* tort; **~***es Betreten* trespassing; **~***es Fernbleiben* unauthorized absence; *von der Schule*: truancy; **~***e Entfernung von der Truppe* *Mil.* absence without leave; **~***er Zugriff EDV* unauthorized access; → *Eingriff* 1; **II.** *Adv.* without permission (*od.* authorization); *dem Unterricht* **~** *fernbleiben* play truant (*Am.* hooky *umg.*), skip classes; **unerlaubterweise** *Adv.* without permission

unerledigt *Adj.* **1.** *allg.* not (yet) dealt with; (*unfertig*) unfinished; *Problem etc.*: unsettled; *vieles ist* **~** *geblieben* a great many things have still to be dealt with; **2.** *Wirts.* outstanding; *Rechnung*: unpaid; *ein Ordner mit der Aufschrift* „**~**" a file marked "pending"

unermesslich I. *Adj.* immeasurable, immense, vast; **~***e Weite* boundless spaces; *bis ins Unermessliche* on and on and on, endlessly, ad infinitum; **II.** *Adv. reich, groß etc.*: phenomenally; **Unermesslichkeit** *f; nur Sg.* immeasurableness; *auch des Weltalls etc.*: immensity, vastness

unermüdlich I. *Adj. Person*: tireless, indefatigable; *Bemühen*: *auch* unremitting, ceaseless; *er ist* **~** *bei s-r Arbeit* he works tirelessly; **II.** *Adv. schaffen, üben etc.*: tirelessly; *sich* **~** *einsetzen auch Sport*: be totally committed, give 110 per cent

unernst *Adj.* not serious, frivolous; **Unernst** *m* lack of seriousness, frivolity

unerprobt *Adj.* untested

unerquicklich *Adj.* unpleasant, unedifying

unerreichbar I. *Adj.* **1.** inaccessible; *auch fig.* out of (*s.o.'s*) reach, beyond *s.o.'s* reach; *fig. auch* unattainable; **2.** *telefonisch etc.*: *er war* **~** we etc. couldn't get hold of him; **II.** *Adv.*: *Medikamente für Kinder* **~** *aufbewahren* keep medicines out of the reach of children; *sie sind für uns* **~** *im Urlaub* they're away on holiday (*Am.* vacation) and we can't reach them; **unerreicht** *Adj. fig.* unequal(l)ed, unrival(l)ed, second to none; **~***e Leistung* record performance; *der Rekord ist* **~** *geblieben* the record has never been equal(l)ed

unersättlich *Adj.* insatiable (*auch fig.*), voracious; *darin ist er* **~** he can't get enough of it; **Unersättlichkeit** *f; nur Sg.* insatiability, insatiable appetite (*beide auch fig.*), voracity

unerschlossen *Adj. Gelände etc.*: undeveloped; *Wirts. Quellen, Märkte*: *auch* untapped

unerschöpflich *Adj.* inexhaustible

unerschrocken I. *Adj.* intrepid, undaunted; **II.** *Adv.*: **~** *für etw. eintreten* courageously take up the cause for s.th.; **Unerschrockenheit** *f; nur Sg.* intrepidity, intrepid nature (+ *Gen.* of)

unerschütterlich I. *Adj.* unshak(e)able; *Person*: *auch* unflappable; (*unerschrocken*) intrepid; *s-e Ruhe ist* **~** he's imperturbable; **II.** *Adv. konservativ etc.*: staunchly; **~** *an etw. festhalten* cling steadfastly to s.th.

unerschwinglich *Adj.* (far) too expensive, unaffordable, beyond one's (*od.* anyone's) means; *Preis, Steuer etc.*: prohibitive

unersetzlich *Adj.* irreplaceable; *Verlust*: *auch* irrecoverable; *auch Schaden*: irreparable; *er hält sich für* **~** he thinks there's nobody who could take his place

unersprießlich *Adj.* **1.** unprofitable; *Bemühen*: fruitless; **2.** (*unerfreulich*) unpleasant

unerträglich I. *Adj.* unbearable, intolerable; *förm.* insufferable (*alle auch fig. Person*); *er ist heute wieder* **~** he's being insufferable again today; *es ist* (*mir*) **~**, *das mit ansehen zu müssen* I can't bear to have to watch it; **II.** *Adv. heiß, laut, schmerzen etc.*: unbearably

unerwähnt *Adj.* unmentioned; **~** *lassen auch* fail to mention, make no mention of, pass s.th. over (in silence); *ich möchte nicht* **~** *lassen, dass ...* it would be remiss of me not to mention that ...

unerwartet I. *Adj.* unexpected; (*unvorhergesehen*) unforeseen; **~***er Besuch/Angriff etc.* surprise visitors/attack etc.; **~***er Gewinn Wirts.* windfall profit; *dann geschah etw. völlig Unerwartetes* then something completely unexpected happened, then something happened that took us etc. all by surprise; **II.** *Adv.* unexpectedly; *es kam völlig* **~** *auch* it took us all (*od.* everyone) by surprise; *er starb plötzlich und* **~** he died suddenly and unexpectedly

unerwidert *Adj. Brief etc.*: unanswered; *Liebe*: unrequited; *der Brief blieb* **~** the letter was left unanswered

unerwünscht *Adj.* undesirable, unwelcome; *Kind*: unwanted; *du bist hier* **~** you're not welcome around here; *ich glaub, ich bin hier* **~** I know when I'm not welcome; *Rauchen*: **~** thank you for not smoking; *Hunde etc.* **~** no dogs *etc.* please

UNESCO *f; -, kein Pl.; Pol., Abk.*: *die* **~** UNESCO

unfähig *Adj.* **1.** (*außerstande*): **~**, *etw. zu tun* unable to do s.th., incapable of doing s.th.; **2.** (*untauglich*) incompetent; **~** *zu e-m Amt etc.*: unqualified for; *als Schulleiter ist er total* **~** as a headmaster (*Am.* principal) he's totally useless; **Unfähigkeit** *f; nur Sg.* **1.** inability (*zu* + *Inf.* to + *Inf.*); **2.** (*Untauglichkeit*) incompetence; *j-m* **~** *vorwerfen/bescheinigen* accuse s.o. of incompetence / certify s.o. (as) incompetent

unfair *Adj.* unfair; *das war* **~** *auch* that wasn't fair; **Unfairness** *f* unfairness

Unfall *m* accident; *leichter/schwerer/tödlicher* **~** slight/serious/fatal accident; *e-n* **~** *bauen umg.* cause an accident; *bei* **~** *bitte ich zu verständigen*: *...* in case of accident please inform *...*; *bei e-m* **~** *ums Leben kommen / verletzt werden* be killed / hurt (*od.*

injured) in an accident; **~***arzt m*, **~***ärztin* *f* casualty doctor, *Am.* emergency (room) physician; **~***aufnahme* *f durch die Polizei*: taking down details of the (*od.* an) accident; **~***beteiligte m, f* person involved in the (*od.* an) accident; **~***bilanz* *f* accident figures (*od.* statistics); **~***chirurgie* *f* casualty (*Am.* emergency) surgery, *Am. auch* trauma surgery; (*Abteilung*) casualty ward, *Am.* emergency room, ER; **~***fahrer m*, **~***fahrerin* *f* driver responsible for an (*od.* the) accident; **~***fahrzeug n* vehicle involved in the (*od.* an) accident; **~***flucht etc.* → *Fahrerflucht etc.*; **~***folgen Pl.* consequences of an (*od.* the) accident; *an den* **~** *sterben* die as a result of the accident

unfallfrei I. *Adj.* accident-free; **II.** *Adv.* without an (*od.* a single) accident; *ich fahre seit 30 Jahren* **~** I've been driving for 30 years and have never had an accident

Unfall|gefahr *f* danger (*od.* risk) of an accident (*od.* of accidents), hazard; *es besteht erhöhte* **~** there is an increased risk of an accident (*od.* of accidents) (happening); **~***gegner m* person involved in an accident who claims damages or compensation or against whom such a claim is made; **~***geschädigte m, f* accident victim, casualty; **~***geschehen n* course of events leading up to and during an (*od.* the) accident; **~***häufigkeit* *f* frequency of accidents; **~***hergang m* course of events leading up to and during an (*od.* the) accident; **~***hilfe* *f* **1.** *nur Sg.* first aid at the scene of an (*od.* the) accident; **2.** (*Station*) first-aid station; *im Krankenhaus*: casualty (department), *Am.* emergency room; **~***klinik f*, **~***krankenhaus n* hospital with a casualty department (*Am.* an emergency room *od.* a shock-trauma unit); **~***medizin* *f* accident and emergency medicine; **~***opfer n* accident victim; **~***ort m* scene of an (*od.* the) accident; **~***quote f*, **~***rate f* accident rate; **~***rente* *f* accident benefit; **~***rettungsdienst m* accident emergency service; **~***risiko n* accident risk; **~***schaden m* damage caused by an (*od.* the) accident; **~***schutz m bes. am Arbeitsplatz*: accident prevention; *Versicherung*: accident cover; **~***schwerpunkt m* accident black spot; **~***serie* *f* series of accidents; **~***skizze* *f* diagram (*od.* sketch) of how the accident happened; **~***station* *f* first-aid station; *im Krankenhaus*: casualty (department), *Am.* emergency room; **~***statistik* *f* accident statistics; **~***stelle* *f* scene of the accident; **~***tod m* accidental death, death in an accident; *förm.* death by misadventure; **~***tote m, f* accident victim; *Zahl der* **~***n* number of people killed in (road) accidents, road deaths

unfallträchtig *Adj. Stelle*: hazardous; *Tätigkeit etc.*: hazardous, risky

Unfall|ursache *f* cause of an (*od.* the) accident; **~***verhütung* *f* accident prevention; **~***verletzte m, f* accident victim, casualty; **~***verletzung* *f* accident injury; **~***versicherung* *f* accident insurance; **~***verursacher m*, **~***verursacherin* *f* person responsible for an (*od.* the) accident; **~***wagen m* **1.** (*Rettungsfahrzeug*) ambulance; **2.** (*beschädigter Wagen*) car damaged in an (*od.* the) accident; **~***zeit* *f* time at which an (*od.* the) accident took place; **~***zeuge m* witness of (*od.* to) an (*od.* the) accident; **~ziffer** f number of accidents

unfassbar Adj. (unergründlich) unfathomable; (unbegreiflich) incomprehensible; (unvorstellbar) incredible; **das ist für mich ~** I just can't believe it

unfehlbar I. Adj. (nie irrend) infallible (auch kath.); (zuverlässig) unerring; **mit ~em Instinkt** with an unerring instinct; **II.** Adv. (bestimmt) for certain; (unweigerlich) inevitably; **Unfehlbarkeit** f infallibility; **Unfehlbarkeitsdogma** n kath. doctrine of papal infallibility

unfein I. Adj. Bemerkung etc.: indelicate; Benehmen: ungentlemanly, unladylike, präd. auch bad form, not nice; (grob) crude, crass; **etw. auf ~e Art ausdrücken** express s.th. rather crudely; **als ~ gelten** be considered bad form; **II.** Adv.: **sich ~ benehmen/ausdrücken** show a lack of good manners in the way one behaves / expresses oneself

unfern Präp.: **~ des Marktes** od. **vom Markt** etc. not far from the market-place

unfertig Adj. unfinished, incomplete; Wirts. Produkte: auch semifinished; fig. Mensch: (unreif) immature

Unflat m; -(e)s, kein Pl. dirt, filth; **~ auf j-n schütten** fig. hurl abuse at s.o.; **unflätig I.** Adj. dirty, stärker: obscene; **II.** Adv. schimpfen etc.: obscenely; **Unflätigkeit** f obscenity

unflexibel Adj. inflexible

unflektiert Adj. Gram. uninflected

unflott Adj. umg.: **nicht ~** not bad at all; Kleidung etc.: natty

unfolgsam Adj. disobedient; **Unfolgsamkeit** f disobedience

unformatiert Adj. EDV unformatted

unförmig I. Adj. (missgestaltet) misshapen; (massig, sperrig) bulky; (aufgebläht) bloated; (extrem fettleibig) obese; **II.** Adv.: **~ dick** bloated; Mensch: auch obese; **der Fuß ist ~ angeschwollen** the foot has swollen out of shape; **Unförmigkeit** f; nur Sg. deformity, misshapenness; (Massigkeit) bulkiness; (Dicke) bloatedness; (Fettleibigkeit) obesity

unfrankiert I. Adj. unstamped; **II.** Adv. auch without a stamp

unfrei I. Adj. **1.** Volk etc.: präd. not free, attr. subject …; weitS. unliberated; **2.** (eingeschränkt) restricted; auch Psych., Person: inhibited; **3.** Post., Paket etc.: unfranked; **II.** Adv. **1.** **~ geboren** etc. born (as) a serf (od. slave); **2.** Post.: **~ senden** send unfranked; **Unfreiheit** f; nur Sg. servitude, bondage; **in ~ geboren** born (as) a serf (od. slave)

unfreiwillig I. Adj. involuntary; (gezwungen) compulsory; (unabsichtlich) unintentional; **~e Komik** unintentional humo(u)r; **ein ~es Bad nehmen** umg. take a ducking; **II.** Adv. involuntarily; unintentionally; (gegen s-n Willen) against one's will; **etw. ~ tun** auch be forced to do s.th.

unfreundlich I. Adj. unfriendly (auch Wetter, Klima, Atmosphäre etc.); (ungefällig) unobliging; Klima, Zimmer etc.: cheerless; **in ~em Ton** in an unfriendly tone; **II.** Adv. behandeln, antworten etc.: in an unfriendly way; **Unfreundlichkeit** f unfriendliness; weitS. (Unhöflichkeit) rudeness

Unfriede m; -ns, kein Pl., **Unfrieden** m; -s, kein Pl. discord; **in Unfrieden leben mit** live in disharmony with; **sie haben**

sich in Unfrieden getrennt they parted on fighting terms

unfrisiert Adj. **1.** Haar, Person: unkempt; **2.** fig. Bericht etc.: undoctored; **3.** Mot. not souped up

unfruchtbar Adj. **1.** Erde: infertile, barren; (steril) sterile; **die ~en Tage der Frau** a woman's infertile period; **2.** fig. Gespräch etc.: fruitless; Arbeit: unproductive; **auf ~en Boden fallen** fall on stony ground, **bei j-m auf ~en Boden fallen** be lost on s.o.; **Unfruchtbarkeit** f **1.** infertility, barrenness; sterility; **2.** fig. fruitlessness; → **unfruchtbar**

Unfug m; -(e)s, kein Pl. **1.** mischief; **~ machen** od. **treiben** get (od. be) up to mischief (od. no good); **~ treiben mit** fool around with; **grober ~** Jur. public nuisance; **lass den ~!** stop messing around!; **mach keinen ~!** no mischief!, behave yourself!; **2.** (Unsinn) nonsense; **das ist doch alles ~!** it's all a load of nonsense

unfühlbar Adj. imperceptible

Ungar m; -n, -n, **~in** f; -, -nen Hungarian, weiblich auch: Hungarian woman (od. girl etc.); **ungarisch** Adj. Hungarian; **Ungarisch** n; -en; Ling. Hungarian; **das ~e** Hungarian; **Ungarn** (n); -s; Geog. Hungary

ungastlich Adj. inhospitable; **Ungastlichkeit** f inhospitableness, inhospitable nature (+ Gen. of)

ungeachtet Präp. regardless of, irrespective of, notwithstanding (+ Gen. s.th.); (trotz) despite

ungeahndet I. Adj. unpunished; **II.** Adv. auch with impunity

ungeahnt Adj. undreamt-of; (unerwartet) unexpected; **sie entwickelte ~e Kräfte** she found unsuspected reserves of strength, she found strength she never knew she had

ungebändigt Adj. Kraft, Gewalt etc.: unrestrained

ungebärdig Adj. unruly

ungebeten I. Adj. Gast: uninvited; **II.** Adv.: **~ kommen** come unasked, come without being asked (od. invited)

ungebildet Adj. uneducated; **Ungebildetheit** f lack of education

ungeboren Adj. unborn; **die Ungeborenen** the unborn

ungebräuchlich Adj. unusual; **es ist ein ~es Wort** etc. it's not a very common word etc.

ungebraucht Adj. unused; (sauber) Handtuch etc.: clean

ungebremst I. Adj. Wucht etc.: unrestrained; **~er Optimismus** fig. unbridled optimism; **II.** Adv. fahren, auftreffen etc.: without braking; (at) full speed (auch fig.); **~ weitergehen** continue unabated; **der PC-Markt wächst ~** the market for PCs just keeps on growing

ungebrochen Adj. **1.** Wille, Glaube etc.: unbroken; Kraft etc.: unfailing; **2.** Lichtstrahl: unrefracted; Linie: solid; Farben: undiluted

ungebührlich I. Adj. (ungehörig) improper, unseemly; (unangemessen) undue; **II.** Adv. (mehr als recht ist) unduly; **sich ~ benehmen** misbehave, step out of line

ungebunden Adj. **1.** Buch: unbound, in sheets; **2.** (nicht geschnürt) undone, unfastened; **in ~en Schuhen herumlaufen** go around with one's shoelaces undone; **3.** Person: unattached; beruflich: freelance; politisch: independent; **ein ~es Leben führen** live a life with

no strings; **frei und ~** footloose and fancy-free umg.; **4.** Lit.: **~e Rede** prose; **5.** Gastr., Suppe etc.: unthickened; **6.** Mus. (nicht legato) detached

ungedämpft Adj. Mus., Phys. undamped; Schlag, Aufprall: uncushioned; → **ungebremst**

ungedeckt Adj. **1.** Scheck etc.: uncovered; **2.** (ohne Schutz) unprotected, exposed; Sport, Spieler: unmarked; Boxen: unguarded; Schach, Turm etc.: unprotected; **3.** Dach: open, uncovered, without slates etc.; **der Tisch ist noch ~** the table hasn't been laid (Am. set) yet

ungedruckt Adj. Text etc.: unprinted

Ungeduld f impatience; **mit ~** impatiently; **voller ~** terribly impatiently; **s-e ~ wuchs** he was getting more and more impatient; **ungeduldig** Adj. impatient

ungeeignet Adj. unsuited (**zu** for), unsuitable (for); Person: auch unqualified (for); **ein ~er Moment** an inopportune (od. the wrong) moment; **sie ist denkbar ~** she couldn't be less suited

ungefähr I. Adv. (etwa) about, approximately, around; (mehr oder weniger) more or less; **~ wann** od. **wann ~?** approximately when, when approximately?; **~ um elf** around eleven; **wo ~?** whereabouts?, roughly where?; **~ dort, wo die Post® ist** about where the post office is; **~ wie …** more or less like …, much like …; **wie viel wird es ~ kosten?** roughly how much will it cost?; **so ~** something like that umg.; **wenn ich ~ wüsste, was er will** if I had some idea of what he wants; **so hat es sich ~ zugetragen** that's roughly how it happened; **das heißt ~** it means roughly; **was ~ kommt in der Prüfung dran?** what sort of thing is likely to come up in the exam?; **~ wie …** more or less like …, much like …; **nicht von ~** not without reason, not for nothing; (wie) **von ~** (as if) by chance; **II.** Adj. (annähernd) approximate; (grob) Schätzung etc.: rough

ungefährdet I. Adj. safe; (gesichert) assured; **s-e Zwei in Mathe ist ~** he's sure of getting a B in math(s); **mein Arbeitsplatz ist ~** my job is not at risk (od. is secure); **II.** Adv. without danger, out of harm's way

ungefährlich Adj. harmless, not dangerous, safe; Mittel etc.: harmless, innocuous; **diese Gegend ist völlig ~** this area is completely safe; **es ist nicht ganz ~** it's a bit risky, there's a slight risk involved; **Ungefährlichkeit** f e-s Tiers etc.: harmlessness; e-s Unternehmens: safeness

ungefällig Adj. unobliging; **Ungefälligkeit** f unobligingness

ungefärbt Adj. **1.** undyed, not dyed; Seide: raw; **2.** fig. Bericht etc.: unbias(s)ed; Wahrheit: unvarnished

ungefestigt Adj. Charakter etc.: unmo(u)lded, (still) developing od. maturing

ungefiltert Adj. Tech., Wasser etc.: unfiltered; fig. Tatsachen etc.: unpredigested

ungeformt Adj. unformed, unshaped; (ohne Form) shapeless

ungefragt I. Adj. unasked; **II.** Adv. auch without being asked; **er mischt sich ständig ~ ein** he's always interfering where he's not wanted

ungefrühstückt Adj. umg., hum. on an empty stomach, without any breakfast

ungefügig Adj. refractory

ungehalten I. *Adj.* (*unwillig*) annoyed (*über* + *Akk.* at), *stärker*: indignant (at); **II.** *Adv. reagieren etc.*: with annoyance; *stärker*: indignantly; **Ungehaltenheit** *f; nur Sg.* annoyance; indignation

ungeheizt *Adj.* unheated

ungehemmt I. *Adj.* uninhibited; (*ungehindert*) unchecked; **II.** *Adv.* freely, without restraint; unchecked

ungeheuchelt *Adj.* unfeigned, sincere

ungeheuer I. *Adj.* enormous, immense; *umg.* (*toll*) tremendous, terrific; *Schmerzen, Krach etc.*: dreadful, incredible *umg.*; **ungeheurer Fehler** colossal mistake; *ins Ungeheure steigen etc.* reach monstrous proportions; **II.** *Adv.* (*sehr*) enormously *etc.*; → I; *sich ~ freuen* be incredibly pleased, be over the moon *umg.* (*über* + *Akk.* about); *es ist ~ wichtig* it's of the utmost importance, it's tremendously important; *er kommt sich ~ klug vor* he thinks he's terribly clever

Ungeheuer *n; -s,* - monster (*auch fig.*)

ungeheuerlich *Adj.* monstrous; (*empörend*) outrageous; **Ungeheuerlichkeit** *f* **1.** *nur Sg.* enormity, monstrousness; **2.** *konkret*: atrocity; *diese Anschuldigung ist e-e ~* this accusation is monstrous

ungehindert I. *Adj.* unhindered; (*unkontrolliert*) unchecked; **II.** *Adv.* *die Grenze passieren etc.*: unhindered

ungehobelt *Adj.* **1.** *Tech.* not planed; **2.** *fig.* uncouth; (*schwerfällig*) clumsy; *~er Kerl pej.* boorish type

ungehörig I. *Adj.* (*unschicklich*) improper, unseemly; (*frech*) impertinent; **II.** *Adv.*: *sich ~ benehmen etc.* behave improperly (*od.* in an unseemly fashion); **Ungehörigkeit** *f* impropriety; (*Frechheit*) impertinence; *es ist* (*einfach*) *e-e ~ zu* (+ *Inf.*) it's (sheer) bad manners to (+ *Inf.*)

ungehorsam *Adj.* disobedient (*gegenüber* to); **Ungehorsam** *m* disobedience

ungehört *Adj. und Adv.* unheard; *~ verhallen Rufe*: go unheard; *fig. Bitte etc.*: *auch* fall on deaf ears

Ungeist *m* evil spirit, demon

ungekämmt *Adj. und Adv.* uncombed

ungeklärt I. *Adj.* **1.** unsettled, (still) open; *Problem*: unsolved; *aus noch ~en Gründen* for reasons as yet unexplained; **2.** *~e Abwässer* untreated (*od.* raw) sewage *Sg.*; **II.** *Adv.*: *die Abwässer fließen ~ ins Meer* untreated sewage is flowing into the sea

ungekocht *Adj.* uncooked, raw; *Wasser etc.*: unboiled

ungekrönt *Adj.* uncrowned (*auch fig.*)

ungekündigt *Adj.*: *in ~er Stellung* not under notice (to leave)

ungekünstelt I. *Adj.* unaffected, natural; **II.** *Adv. sich benehmen, sprechen etc.*: naturally, without affectation

ungekürzt I. *Adj. Buch*: unabridged; *Film*: uncut; *~e Fassung Film*: long version; **II.** *Adv.*: *e-n Film ~ zeigen* show a film uncut; *e-e Rede etc. ~ abdrucken* print the full text of a speech

ungeladen *Adj.* **1.** *Gast*: uninvited; **2.** *Feuerwaffe*: unloaded; **3.** *Akku, Batterie*: empty, *bes. Am.* dead

ungelegen *Adj.* inconvenient; *Zeitpunkt*: *auch* inopportune; *das kommt mir sehr ~* that doesn't suit me at all; *zeitlich*: *auch* that's come at an awkward time (for me); *komme ich ~?* am I disturbing you?; **Ungelegenheiten** *Pl.*: *j-m ~ machen* put s.o. out, incon-

venience s.o.

ungelehrig *Adj.* unteachable

ungelenk I. *Adj.* clumsy, awkward; (*steif*) stiff; **II.** *Adv.* clumsily; **ungelenkig** *Adj.* stiff

ungelernt *Adj. Arbeit(er)*: unskilled

ungelesen *Adj. Buch etc.*: unread

ungeliebt *Adj.* unloved; *den ~en Beruf aufgeben* give up the job one dislikes (*od. stärker* detests); *den ~en Mann verlassen* leave the husband one does not love

ungelogen *Adv. umg.*: *ich habe ~ 20 Seiten geschafft* I honestly did (*od.* no kidding, I managed) 20 pages; *~, so war es!* honest, that's the way it was

ungelöst *Adj. Fall etc.*: unsolved

Ungemach *n; -(e)s, kein Pl.; altm.* adversity, hardship

ungemacht *Adj. Bett*: unmade

ungemahlen *Adj. Kaffee etc.*: unground

ungemein I. *Adj.* enormous, great; **II.** *Adv.* (*sehr*) tremendously, extremely; *~ viel(e)* a tremendous (*od.* an enormous) amount *od.* number (of); *sich ~ freuen* be tremendously glad, be very very pleased

ungemindert *Adj.* undiminished

ungemütlich *Adj.* uncomfortable (*auch fig. Lage, Gefühl etc.*); *Zimmer etc.*: cheerless; *~ werden umg. fig. Person, Lage etc.*: get (*od.* turn) nasty; *sonst werde ich ~ umg. fig.* otherwise I might turn nasty; *es wird langsam ~ umg. fig.* things are turning a bit nasty; **Ungemütlichkeit** *f; nur Sg.* uncomfortableness; *e-s Zimmers etc.*: cheerlessness; *~ der Atmosphäre etc.* uncomfortable atmosphere *etc.*

ungenannt *Adj.* unnamed; *Person*: *auch* anonymous, nameless; *der Spender möchte ~ bleiben* the donor wishes to remain anonymous

ungenau I. *Adj.* (*nicht exakt*) inexact; (*unpräzise*) imprecise; (*nicht richtig*) inaccurate; (*undeutlich*) vague; **II.** *Adv.* inaccurately, imprecisely; vaguely; *er arbeitet mir zu ~* his work is not accurate enough for my liking; *du hast ~ gemessen* you didn't measure accurately; **Ungenauigkeit** *f* **1.** *nur Sg.* inexactness; imprecision; inaccuracy; vagueness; → *ungenau*; **2.** (*Fehler*) inaccuracy; *ihr sind einige ~en unterlaufen* she got a few things slightly wrong

ungenehmigt I. *Adj. Baumaßnahme, Abschuss etc.*: unauthorized; **II.** *Adv. bauen, aufstellen etc.*: without authorization

ungeniert I. *Adj.* uninhibited; **II.** *Adv.* uninhibitedly; (*frei heraus*) openly; *gähnen, sich kratzen etc.*: unconcernedly, without qualms; *völlig ~* (*selbstsicher*) with such aplomb; *sich ~ vor allen ausziehen* undress in front of everybody without embarrassment; *sich ~ hinwegsetzen über* (+ *Akk.*) blithely ignore; *greifen Sie ~ zu!* feel free to help yourself

ungenießbar *Adj.* **1.** *Speisen, Pilz*: inedible; *Getränke*: undrinkable; **2.** *umg. fig. Person*: unbearable, *präd. auch* hard to take; *Buch etc.*: impossible (to read *etc.*); *sie ist mal wieder ~* she's in a foul mood again today

ungenormt *Adj.* non-standard

Ungenügen *n; -s, kein Pl.* inadequacy; **ungenügend** *Adj.* insufficient, *präd. auch* not enough; (*nicht zufrieden stellend*) inadequate; *Leistung, Note*: un-

satisfactory; *in der Schule etc.*: fail, F

ungenutzt, ungenützt *Adj.* unused; *Rohstoffe etc.*: unexploited; *Kapital*: dead; *EDV, Kapazität, Zeit*: spare; *Raum*: free; *e-e Gelegenheit ~ lassen* let an opportunity slip, pass up an opportunity

ungeordnet *Adj.* unsorted, not yet sorted out; (*unordentlich*) disordered, disorderly

ungepflastert *Adj.* unpaved

ungepflegt *Adj. Garten etc.*: neglected; *Person*: untidy, *stärker*: scruffy; *~ wirken Person*: look scruffy; **Ungepflegtheit** *f; nur Sg.* neglected state; *e-r Person*: untidiness, *stärker*: scruffiness

ungeplant *Adj.* unplanned (*auch umg. Kind*)

ungeprüft *Adj. und Adv.* unchecked

ungerade *Adj.* uneven, not straight; *EDV, Math. Zahl, Funktion etc.*: odd

ungeraten *Adj. Kind*: *attr.* wayward; (*ungezogen*) ill-mannered; *sein Sohn ist ~ weitS auch* his son has turned out badly

ungerechnet *Präp. und Adj.* not counting …

ungerecht I. *Adj.* unjust (*gegen* toward[s]), unfair (to[ward(s)]); **II.** *Adv. behandeln, beurteilen etc.*: unjustly, unfairly; **ungerechterweise** *Adv.* unjustly

ungerechtfertigt I. *Adj.* unjustified, unwarranted; *~e Bereicherung Jur.* unjust enrichment; **II.** *Adv. verdächtigen etc.*: unjustly

Ungerechtigkeit *f* **1.** *nur Sg.* injustice (*gegen* to); **2.** (*Zustand, Handlung*) injustice; *soziale ~en* social injustice(s); *j-s ~en nicht länger hinnehmen* no longer put up with s.o.'s unjust treatment

ungeregelt *Adj.* **1.** unregulated; (*regellos*) irregular (*auch Leben, Einkommen*); (*unordentlich*) disorderly; **2.** *Mot., Katalysator*: open-loop

ungereimt *Adj.* unrhymed; *fig.* (*unstimmig*) inconsistent; *stärker*: absurd; *~es Zeug reden* talk (a lot of) nonsense; **Ungereimtheit** *f* inconsistency; *~en auch* contradictions; *es ist voller ~en auch* it's completely incongruous

ungern *Adv.* unwillingly, grudgingly; (*widerwillig*) reluctantly; *er tut es (äuBerst*) *~ auch* he doesn't like doing it (at all); *machst du's also? - ~* I'm not keen (*Am.* eager) (, but I suppose I'll have to); *etw. nicht ~ tun* be not unwilling to do s.th.

ungerührt *Adj. fig.* unmoved (*von* by), impassive; *Miene*: indifferent; *~ bleiben* remain unmoved

ungesagt *Adj.* unsaid

ungesalzen *Adj.* unsalted

ungesättigt *Adj. Chem.* unsaturated; *mehrfach ~* polyunsaturated; *mehrfach ~e Fettsäuren auch* polyunsaturates

ungesäuert *Adj. Brot*: unleavened

ungeschält *Adj. Obst*: unpeeled; *Reis*: unpolished

ungeschehen *Adj.*: *~ machen* undo; *das kann man nicht ~ machen* it can't be undone

Ungeschick *n,* **Ungeschicklichkeit** *f* ineptitude; *körperliche(s)*: *auch* clumsiness; **ungeschickt I.** *Adj.* clumsy (*auch Formulierung etc.*), hamfisted; *Verhalten etc.*: inept; (*undiplomatisch*) undiplomatic, tactless; *~er Mensch auch* s.o. who is all fingers and thumbs, *Am.* klutz; **II.** *Adv.*: *sich ~ anstellen* be clumsy; *sich ~ ausdrü-*

U

cken express o.s. clumsily (*od.* in a clumsy fashion)

ungeschlacht *Adj.* **1.** *Körper:* ungainly; *Hände etc.:* massive; *ein ~er Kerl* a great hulking brute; **2.** (*ungeschickt*) clumsy, awkward; **3.** (*grob*) uncouth, rough

ungeschlagen *Adj.* undefeated, unbeaten; *seit Jahren ~ sein* not have been beaten for years

ungeschliffen *Adj.* **1.** unpolished; *Edelstein:* uncut, rough; **2.** *fig. Person, Stil etc.:* unpolished; *stärker, Person:* uncouth

ungeschmälert *Adj.* undiminished

ungeschminkt **I.** *Adj.* **1.** without makeup; *sie ist ~ auch* she isn't made up, she's not wearing makeup; **2.** *fig.* unvarnished, unadorned; *j-m die ~e Wahrheit sagen* tell s.o. the truth straight out; *die ~en Tatsachen* the bare facts; **II.** *Adv.* **1.** without makeup; **2.** *fig.: j-m ~ die Wahrheit sagen* tell s.o. the truth straight out

ungeschönt *Adj. Darstellung etc.:* unprettified

ungeschoren *Adj.* **1.** unshorn; **2.** *fig.:* ~ *davonkommen od. bleiben* get off lightly (*ungestraft:* scot-free); *j-n ~ lassen* leave s.o. in peace; (*verschonen*) spare s.o.

ungeschrieben *Adj.:* ~*es Gesetz* unwritten law

ungeschult *Adj.* untrained (*auch Ohr etc.*)

ungeschützt **I.** *Adj.* unprotected; *gegen Sonne etc.:* exposed; ~*er Sex* unprotected (*od.* unsafe) sex; **II.** *Adv.* without protection; ~ *Verkehr haben* have sex without a condom

ungesehen *Adj. und Adv.* unseen, unnoticed, without anybody noticing

ungesellig *Adj.* unsociable; *Zool., Tier:* non-gregarious

ungesetzlich *Adj.* illegal, unlawful, illicit; *für ~ erklären* declare illegal (*od.* unlawful), outlaw; **Ungesetzlichkeit** *f* illegality, unlawfulness

ungesichert **I.** *Adj.* **1.** *Waffe:* with the safety catch off; *Fahrzeug, Unfall-, Baustelle etc.:* unsecured; *Bergsteiger:* climbing without belays; *Artist etc.:* working without a safety net (*bzw.* rope); **2.** *Beweis, Meldung:* unsubstantiated; **3.** *Fin., Darlehen etc.:* unsecured; **4.** *EDV Netzwerk, Verbindung:* insecure; **II.** *Adv. klettern etc.:* without belays; *auf dem Seil gehen, am Trapez turnen etc.:* without a safety net

ungesittet **I.** *Adj.* uncivilized; (*unmanierlich*) bad-mannered; **II.** *Adv.: sich ~ benehmen etc.* misbehave, behave *etc.* in an uncivilized fashion

ungestalt *Adj.* **1.** *altm.* misshapen; **2.** (*formlos*) shapeless

ungestempelt *Adj. Post.* unstamped

ungestillt *Adj.* **1.** *Neugier, Sehnsucht etc.:* unsatisfied; **2.** *Hunger:* unappeased, unsatisfied; *Durst:* unquenched

ungestört **I.** *Adj.* undisturbed; *Ablauf, Vorgang etc.:* uninterrupted; *Ort etc.:* peaceful; *hier sind wir ~* here we can be undisturbed, nobody will disturb us here; **II.** *Adv. arbeiten etc.:* undisturbed, in peace; *ablaufen etc.:* smoothly, without interruptions; ~ *ein Nickerchen machen* have a peaceful nap; *die Einbrecher konnten ~ die Wohnung ausräumen* the thieves were able to clear out the flat (*Am.* apartment) without being disturbed

ungestraft **I.** *Adj.* unpunished; **II.** *Adv.*

unpunished, with impunity; ~ *davonkommen* go unpunished

ungestüm **I.** *Adj.* impetuous; (*heftig, schnell*) vehement, tempestuous; *Umarmung:* passionate; *Begrüßung:* enthusiastic; **II.** *Adv.* impetuously; *stärker:* with wild abandon; *umarmen:* passionately; ~ *von s-m Hund begrüßt werden* be greeted enthusiastically by one's dog; **Ungestüm** *n; -s, kein Pl.* impetuosity; (*Heftigkeit*) vehemence; *mit od. in jugendlichem ~* with youthful impetuosity

ungesühnt *Adj.* unexpiated

ungesund **I.** *Adj.* unhealthy; *fig. auch* unwholesome; *Rauchen ist ~ auch* smoking is bad for you (*od.* your health); ~ *aussehen* look unwell; *e-n ~en Ehrgeiz haben* be too ambitious for one's own good; **II.** *Adv.: sich ~ ernähren* eat unhealthily, have an unhealthy diet

ungesüßt *Adj.* unsweetened

ungetan *Adj.: etw. ~ lassen* leave s.th. undone

ungeteilt *Adj.* **1.** undivided, whole; **2.** *fig. Aufmerksamkeit etc.:* undivided; *Zustimmung:* unanimous

ungetrübt *Adj.* **1.** unclouded, clear; **2.** *fig.* perfect, unspoil|t (*Am.* -ed), pristine; *Freude:* unalloyed; *ihr Glück blieb nicht lange ~* their happiness was too perfect to last long

Ungetüm *n; -s, -e* monster (*auch fig.*); *ein ~ von e-m Hut etc.* a monstrosity of a hat *etc.*

ungeübt *Adj.* unpracti|sed (*Am.* -ced); *Person:* präd. auch out of practice; ~ *sein in* (+ *Dat.*) not have had much practice in; **Ungeübtheit** *f; nur Sg.* lack of practice

ungewandt *Adj.* clumsy; *auch Verhalten:* inept

ungewaschen *Adj. und Adv.* unwashed

ungewiss *Adj.* uncertain; (*unentschieden*) undecided; *es ist noch ~, ob/wie etc.* it's still uncertain (as to) whether/how *etc.*; *j-n im Ungewissen lassen* not to let s.o. know, keep s.o. guessing; *im Ungewissen sein/bleiben über* (+ *Akk.*) be/remain uncertain (*od.* unsure, *od.* in the dark) about; *Sprung ins Ungewisse* leap in the dark; *e-e Fahrt ins Ungewisse* a journey into the unknown; **Ungewissheit** *f* uncertainty

ungewöhnlich **I.** *Adj.* unusual, (*bemerkenswert*) exceptional, remarkable; *das ist durchaus nichts Ungewöhnliches* it's nothing at all unusual; **II.** *Adv.* unusually, uncommonly; ~ *viel Blut verlieren* lose an exceptional amount of blood; ~ *wenig Verkehr* far less traffic than usual

ungewohnt **I.** *Adj. Umgebung etc.:* strange; (*neu*) new (*für* to); (*unüblich*) unusual; *das ist für mich ganz ~ auch* I'm not used to it at all; **II.** *Adv.* unusually; *sie war ~ freundlich zu mir* she was much more friendly toward(s) me than she usually is

ungewollt **I.** *Adj.* unintentional; *Wirkung etc.:* unintended; (*unwillkürlich*) involuntary; *Schwangerschaft:* unwanted; **II.** *Adv. kränken etc.:* unintentionally, without meaning to; ~ *verraten* give away unintentionally; *durch unbesonnene Äußerung:* let slip by accident; ~ *schwanger werden* get pregnant by accident

ungewürzt *Adj. und Adv.* unseasoned

ungezählt *Adj.* **1.** (*zahllos*) countless,

innumerable; ~*e Male* countless times; **2.** (*nicht gezählt*) uncounted

ungezähmt *Adj.* **1.** untamed, wild; **2.** *fig. Leidenschaft:* unbridled

Ungeziefer *n; -s, kein Pl.* vermin (*auch fig. pej.*); ~*befall* *m* infestation; ~*bekämpfung* *f* vermin control; ~*vernichtung* *f* disinfestation

ungezielt *Adj. Schuss:* random

ungeziert **I.** *Adj.* unaffected; **II.** *Adv. reden etc.:* unaffectedly

ungezogen *Adj.* naughty; (*frech*) cheeky, *bes. Am.* smart; **Ungezogenheit** *f* naughtiness; (*Frechheit*) cheekiness, cheek

ungezuckert *Adj.* sugar-free; *Weinbau:* (*nicht angereichert*) unfortified

ungezügelt *Adj. fig. Gefühle etc.:* unbridled; ~*es Temperament* volatile temper

ungezwungen **I.** *Adj.* unconstrained, casual; **II.** *Adv.* casually, without constraint; *lachen etc.:* unrestrainedly; *es geht völlig ~ zu* it's all very casual (*od.* free and easy), everybody just does their own thing; **Ungezwungenheit** *f; nur Sg.;* (*Zwanglosigkeit*) lack of constraint; *e-r Veranstaltung etc.: auch* casual atmosphere; (*Ungeniertheit, Natürlichkeit*) naturalness

Unglaube *m* disbelief; *kirchl.* lack of faith, unbelief; **unglaubhaft** *Adj.* implausible, unconvincing; *weitS.* unrealistic; → *unglaubwürdig*; **ungläubig** **I.** *Adj.* incredulous (*auch Blick, Lächeln etc.*), *auch kirchl.* unbelieving; ~*er Thomas* bibl. doubting Thomas (*auch umg. fig.*); **II.** *Adv.* incredulously; *j-n ansehen etc.:* in disbelief; ~ *lächeln/schauen etc. auch* give an incredulous smile/look *etc.*; **unglaublich** **I.** *Adj.* incredible (*auch gewaltig*), unbelievable; (*unerhört*) incredible, outrageous; ~*, was der sich erlaubt* he takes the most incredible liberties; ~*es Glück haben* have incredible luck; **II.** *Adv. umg.* incredibly, unbelievably; ~ *lange warten müssen* have to wait an incredibly long time; **unglaubwürdig** **I.** *Adj. Aussage, Sache:* implausible; *Person:* unreliable, untrustworthy; *Politiker etc.:* not credible; ~*er Zeuge* unreliable witness; *sich ~ machen* lose credibility; **II.** *Adv.:* ~ *klingen* sound implausible; **Unglaubwürdigkeit** *f; nur Sg.* implausibility; unreliability, untrustworthiness; lack of credibility

ungleich **I.** *Adj.* (*unähnlich*) dissimilar; *Chancen, Kampf etc.:* unequal; *Math.* unequal; ~*e Gegner* ill-matched opponents; *von ~er Länge* of varying length *etc.*; *zwei ~e Schuhe etc.* two odd (*od.* mismatched) shoes *etc.*, two shoes *etc.* that aren't a pair; *die beiden sind ein ~es Paar* they make an odd couple, those two; those two are not well suited; *x ~ 10 Math.* x is not equal to 10; **II.** *Adv.* **1.** *behandeln etc.:* not equally; ~ *lang/stark etc.* different in length/strength *etc.*; ~ *verteilt Mittel, Chancen etc.:* unequally divided; **2.** *vor Komparativ:* (*weitaus*): ~ *besser* far (*od.* much) better; *stärker:* incomparably better; ~ *schwieriger* more difficult; *stärker:* incomparably more difficult; **III.** *Präp.* (+ *Dat.*) unlike; **Ungleichbehandlung** *f* discrimination

ungleichförmig *Adj.* variable; (*unsymmetrisch*) asymmetrical

Ungleichgewicht *n* (state of) imbalance

Ungleichheit *f* dissimilarity; *der Chan-*

cen etc.: inequality
ungleichmäßig I. *Adj.* irregular (*auch Atem, Puls, Herzschlag etc.*); *Entwicklung etc.*: unsteady; *Verteilung*: uneven; *Handschrift*: erratic; **II.** *Adv. verteilt etc.*: unequally, unevenly; *atmen etc.*: irregularly; → *auch* **ungleich**; **Ungleichmäßigkeit** *f* irregularity; unsteadiness; unevenness; erratic nature (+ *Gen.* of)
Ungleichung *f Math.* inequation
Ungleich-Zeichen *n Math.* unequals sign
Unglück *n*; *-(e)s, -e, mst Unglücksfälle* **1.** (*Unfall*) accident; (*Zug-, Flugzeugunglück etc., Katastrophe*) disaster; (*Missgeschick*) mishap; **schweres ~** serious accident, *weitS.* disaster; **ein ~ ereignete sich in …** an accident happened in …; **in … kam es zu e-m schweren ~** there was a serious accident in …; **das ist kein ~!** *umg. fig.* (*nicht so schlimm*) it's not a disaster; **2.** *nur Sg.* misfortune; (*Pech*) bad luck; **das bringt ~** it's bad luck; **es ist kein ~, dass** it's no bad thing that; **in sein ~ rennen** rush headlong into disaster; **j-n ins ~ stürzen** bring disaster (up)on s.o.; **das ~ magisch anziehen** seem to attract disaster, be very accident-prone; **zu allem ~** to crown it all; **ein ~ kommt selten allein** *Sprichw.* it never rains but it pours, when it rains it pours; → *auch* **Glück** 1, **Unheil**; **3.** *nur Sg.* (*Elend*) distress, misery
unglücklich I. *Adj.* **1.** (*traurig*) unhappy, sad; **ein ~es Gesicht machen** pull a long face; **e-n ~en Eindruck machen** look (*bzw.* seem) very unhappy; **2.** (*ungünstig, widrig*) unfortunate; *attr. Wahl, Zufall, Formulierung etc.*: *auch* unhappy …; (*ungeschickt*) *Bewegung etc.*: awkward, clumsy; (*vom Pech verfolgt*) unlucky; **ein ~es Ende nehmen** come to an unfortunate end; **e-e ~e Hand haben** be unlucky (*mit, bei* with, when it comes to); **e-e ~e Hand haben mit** *Geschäftspartnern etc.*: not be very good at dealing with; **e-e ~e Figur abgeben** *umg.* cut a sorry figure; **der Unglückliche ist ertrunken** the poor man drowned; **3.** *Liebe*: unrequited; **II.** *Adv.* **1.** (*traurig*) sadly, unhappily; **2.** (*schlecht, ungünstig*): ~ **enden** *od.* **ausgehen** end unhappily, come to an unhappy end; *stärker*: turn out badly, end in disaster; **es ist ~ gelaufen** it went badly; ~ **verlieren** lose through bad luck; ~ **stürzen** fall awkwardly, have a bad fall; ~ **ausrutschen** slip awkwardly; **3.** *sich ausdrücken etc.*: in an unfortunate manner; (*ungeschickt*) awkwardly; **4.** ~ **verliebt sein** be crossed in love; ~ **verheiratet sein** be unhappily married; **unglücklicherweise** *Adv.* unfortunately
Unglücks|bote *m* bringer of bad tidings; **~botschaft** *f* bad news *Sg.*
unglückselig *Adj.* unfortunate; (*beklagenswert*) lamentable; (*verhängnisvoll*) ill-fated; *Liebende*: star-crossed
Unglücks|fahrer *m*, **~fahrerin** *f* driver responsible for the accident; **~fall** *m* misfortune; (*Unfall*) accident; **~maschine** *f* crashed plane *od.* aircraft; **~nachricht** *f* piece of bad news; (*Nachricht vom Unglück*) news of the accident (*od.* disaster); **~ort** *m* scene of the accident; **~rabe** *m* unlucky person; **er ist ein ~** *auch* some people are just born unlucky; **~serie** *f* spate (*od.* series) of accidents; **~stelle** *f* scene of the accident; **~tag** *m* fateful (*od.*

black) day; **~ursache** *f* cause of an (*od.* the) accident; **~wurm** *m umg. fig.* → **Unglücksrabe**
Ungnade *f nur Sg.; oft iro.* disfavo(u)r; **in ~ fallen** fall from favo(u)r; **in ~ fallen bei** fall out of favo(u)r with; **in ~ sein** be in the doghouse (**bei** with); **ungnädig I.** *Adj.* ungracious, unkind; (*übellaunig*) grumpy *umg.*; (*verärgert*) cross; **II.** *Adv.*: ~ **aufnehmen** take *s.th.* in (*od.* with) bad grace
ungrammatisch *Adj. Ling.* ungrammatical
ungültig *Adj.* invalid; (*null und nichtig*) null and void; *Gesetz*: inoperative; *Münze etc.*: not legal tender; *Tor etc.*: disallowed; *Pol., Stimme*: spoil|t (*Am.* -ed); **für ~ erklären** declare null and void, annul (*auch Ehe*); (*Tor*) disallow; ~ **werden** *Pass etc.*: expire; ~ **machen** cancel; **Ungültigkeit** *f*; *nur Sg.* invalidity; *e-s Vertrags etc.*: *auch* nullity (*auch EDV*)
Ungunst *f*; *-, kein Pl.*; (*Unwillen*) disfavo(u)r, ill will; **die ~ des Wetters / der Stunde** *fig.* the inclemency of the weather / inauspiciousness of the hour; **Ungunsten** *Pl.*: **zu j-s ~** to s.o.'s disadvantage; **das spricht zu s-n ~** that tells against him
ungünstig I. *Adj. Bedingungen etc.*: unfavo(u)rable; *Termin etc.*: inconvenient; *Zeitpunkt*: *auch* inopportune; *Foto, Frisur etc.*: unflattering; (*unglücklich*) unfortunate; **bei ~em Wetter** if the weather is bad; **II.** *Adv.*: **du stehst hier ~** you haven't picked a very good place to stand; **die Chancen stehen ~** the odds are not in our favo(u)r; ~ **angezogen sein** wear s.th. that does nothing for one (*od.* that does not show one off to best advantage)
ungut *Adj.* bad; *Gefühl*: funny; **ich hatte ein ~es Gefühl dabei** I had a funny feeling about it; **nichts für ~!** no offen|ce (*Am.* -se) meant, no hard feelings
unhaltbar I. *Adj.* **1.** *Argument, Theorie etc.*: untenable; *Zustände*: intolerable; **2.** *Sport, Schuss*: unstoppable; **das Tor war nicht ~** the shot should have been saved; **3.** *Mil., Festung, Linie etc.*: indefensible; **II.** *Adv. Sport*: ~ **ins lange Eck schießen** shoot into the far corner giving the keeper no chance; **Unhaltbarkeit** *f*; *nur Sg. e-s Arguments etc.*: untenable nature (+ *Gen.* of); *von Zuständen etc.*: intolerability
unhandlich *Adj.* unwieldy; **Unhandlichkeit** *f*; *nur Sg.* unwieldiness
unharmonisch *Adj. Mus. und fig.* discordant, unharmonious; *fig. Farben*: *attr.* clashing
Unheil *n*; *-s, kein Pl.* disaster; (*Schaden*) harm; ~ **anrichten** wreak havoc; ~ **über das Land bringen** bring disaster on the country; **das ~ kommen sehen** foresee disaster; ~ **bringend** fatal, baneful; ~ **verkündend** ominous, fateful
unheilbar I. *Adj.* incurable; *Krebs, Patient*: terminal; *fig.* irreparable; **II.** *Adv.*: ~ **krank sein** be suffering from an incurable disease, be incurably ill; ~ **zerrüttet** *Jur., Ehe*: irretrievably broken down; **Unheilbarkeit** *f*; *nur Sg.* incurability
unheilvoll *Adj.* disastrous, baneful; *Stimmung, Blick*: sinister
unheimlich I. *Adj.* **1.** uncanny, eerie, weird (*alle auch fig.*); **ein ~es Gefühl beschlich sie** an eerie feeling crept over her; **uns wurde ~** we got an eerie

(*od.* weird) feeling; **unser Nachbar ist mir ~** our neighbo(u)r gives me the creeps; **~e Geschichten von Stephen King** spine-chilling stories by Stephen King; **das Unheimliche im Werk Edgar Allan Poes** the uncanny in the works of Edgar Allan Poe; **2.** *umg. fig.* (*ungeheuer*) terrific, fantastic; *Schmerzen, Respekt etc.*: incredible; **ich hatte e-e ~e Angst** I was incredibly scared; **~en Hunger haben** be incredibly hungry; **II.** *Adv.* **1.** **mir war ~ zumute** I had a weird feeling; ~ **klingen** *etc.* sound weird; **2.** *umg.* incredibly; ~ **viel**(**e**) a terrific amount (of); **sich ~ freuen** be incredibly pleased, be over the moon; **es macht ~ viel Spaß** it's great fun; ~ **lange warten müssen** have to wait an incredibly long time
unhistorisch *Adj.* unhistoric
unhöflich I. *Adj.* impolite; *stärker*: rude (**zu j-m** to s.o.); **~er Kerl** *umg.* ill-mannered oaf; **ich wollte nicht ~ sein** I didn't mean to be rude; **II.** *Adv. abweisen, antworten etc.*: rudely; **Unhöflichkeit I.** *f*; *nur Sg.* impoliteness, *stärker*: rudeness; **2.** (*Bemerkung etc.*) rude remark
Unhold *m*; *-(e)s, -e* monster
unhörbar *Adj.* inaudible
unhygienisch I. *Adj.* unhygienic; **II.** *Adv.* unhygienically
uni [ˈyni] *Adj. Farbton*: plain; *Material, Stoff*: self-colo(u)red, solid-colo(u)red; **das Kostüm ist ~** the suit is in a plain material; **e-e ~ Krawatte** a plain tie; **e-e Hose in ~-beige** a pair of trousers (*Am.* pants *od.* slacks) in plain beige
Uni *f*; *-, -s*; *umg.* uni, *Am.* school, college; **auf der ~** at uni, *Am.* in school; **frisch von der ~** just down from uni, *Am.* just home *etc.* from school; **~ball** *m* uni (*Am.* college) ball; **~bibliothek** *f* uni (*Am.* school) library
UNICEF *f*; *-, kein Pl.*; *Abk.*: (*die*) ~ UNICEF; **~-Botschafter** *m*, **~-Botschafterin** *f* UNICEF ambassador
unidiomatisch *Adj. Ling.* unidiomatic
uniert *Adj. kirchl.*: ~ **Kirchen** Uniate Churches
unifarben [ˈyni-] *Adj.* plain, self-colo(u)red
Uniform *f*; *-, -en* uniform; ~ **tragen** wear uniform; **in ~ kommen** come in uniform; **uniform** *Adj.* uniform
Uniformhemd *n* uniform shirt
uniformiert I. *Adj.* **1.** uniformed, in uniform; **2.** (*einheitlich*) uniform; **II.** *Adv. erscheinen etc.*: in uniform; **Uniformierte** *m, f*; *-n, -n* person in uniform; **Uniformiertheit** *f*; *nur Sg.* uniformity; **Uniformität** *f*; *-, kein Pl.* uniformity
Uniform|träger *m*, **~trägerin** *f* person in uniform; **~zwang** *m* requirement to wear uniform
Unikat *n*; *-(e)s, -e* **1.** *Kunstwerk etc.*: unique example; **2.** *Bot. etc.* unique specimen
Uniklinik *f Med.* university hospital
Unikum *n*; *-s, Unika und -s* **1.** *Pl. Unika* unique specimen (*od.* example) (*auch iro.* **an** [+ *Dat.*] **von** of), one-off, *Am.* one-of-a-kind; **2.** *Pl. -s*; *umg.* (*Person*) original, real character, one-off, *Am.* one-of-a-kind
unilateral *Adj.* unilateral
Unimog® *m*; *-(s), -s*; *Mot.* Unimog
uninformiert *Adj.* uninformed
unintelligent *Adj.* unintelligent
uninteressant *Adj.* uninteresting, not interesting; (*belanglos*) of no interest (**für** to); (*irrelevant*) irrelevant (to);

U

(*nicht lohnend*, *nicht attraktiv*) unattractive (for); **preislich ~** unattractively priced; **nicht ~** not uninteresting **uninteressiert** *Adj.* uninterested (**an** [+ *Dat.*] in); **Uninteressiertheit** *f*; *nur Sg.* lack of interest
Union *f*; -, *-en* **1.** union; **2.** (*Europäische ~*) EU; **3.** *BRD*: (*CDU-CSU*) the CDU and CSU
Unions|abgeordnete *m*, *f*; *Pol.* Bundestag member for the CDU or CSU; **~fraktion** *f* *Pol.* CDU and CSU parliamentary coalition group; **~politiker** *m*, **~politikerin** *f* *BRD*: politician from the CDU or CSU
Unisexmode *f* unisex fashions *Pl.* (*od.* look)
unisono *Adv. Mus.* in unison; *fig. auch* unanimously
Unitarier *m*; *-s*, -; *Reli.* Unitarian; **unitarisch** *Adj.* **1.** *Pol.* unitarian; **2.** *Reli.* Unitarian
universal *Adj.* universal; *Goethes Wissen war ~* Goethe's knowledge was all-embracing
Universal|... *im Subst.*; *Tech.* multipurpose ...; **~bildung** *f* all-embracing education; *Wissen*: comprehensive knowledge; **~erbe** *m*, **~erbin** *f* sole heir; **~genie** *n* universal genius; *umg.* (*Alleskönner*) all-rounder
Universalität *f*; -, *kein Pl.* universality
Universalmittel *n* *Med. und fig.* panacea, cure-all
universell I. *Adj.* universal; *Gerät etc.*: all-purpose ...; **II.** *Adv.* universally; **~ verwendbar** all-purpose; **~ begabt** multi-talented
universitär *Adj.* university ...
Universität *f*; -, *-en*; *Univ.* university; *USA, nur für den ersten Grad*: *auch* college; *die Freie ~ Berlin* the Free University of Berlin; *die ~ besuchen* go to university (*Am. auch* college); *an der ~* at university, *Am. auch* in college; *auf welcher ~ ist er?* which university does he go to?; *an der Freiburger ~ studieren/lehren* study/teach at the University of Freiburg (*od.* at Freiburg University); → *technisch* I 1
Universitäts|abschluss *m* *Univ.* university degree; **~angehörige** *m*, *f* member of a (*od.* the) university; **~angestellte** *m*, *f* university employee; **~ausbildung** *f* university education; **~bibliothek** *f* university library; **~gebäude** *n* university building; **~gelände** *n* university grounds *Pl.*, campus; **~institut** *n* university(-related) institute; **~klinik** *f* **~klinikum** *n* university hospital; **~laufbahn** *f* university (*od.* academic) career; *die ~ einschlagen* begin a university (*od.* an academic) career; **~lehrer** *m*, **~lehrerin** *f* university teacher; **~professor** *m*, **~professorin** *f* university professor; **~stadt** *f* university (*Am.* college) town; **~studium** *n* **1.** *abgeschlossenes*: university degree; **2.** studies *Pl.* at university; *das Abitur berechtigt zu e-m ~* (*passing*) the Abitur entitles one to study at a university
Universum *n*; *-s*, *kein Pl.* universe (*auch fig.*)
unkalkulierbar *Adj.* incalculable
unkameradschaftlich I. *Adj.* unfriendly, uncomradely; **II.** *Adv.*: *sich ~ verhalten* be unfriendly, behave in an unfriendly way
Unke *f*; -, *-n* **1.** *Zool.* fire-bellied toad; **2.** *umg. fig.* (*Unheilverkünder*) Jeremiah, prophet of doom; **unken** *vt/i. umg.* predict the worst, prophesy doom; *~,*

dass ... gloomily predict that ...; *„das geht sicher schief"*, *unkte er* "it's bound to go wrong", he prophesied gloomily
unkenntlich *Adj.* unrecognizable; *Schrift*: indecipherable; *~ machen* (*entstellen*) disfigure; (*verzerren*) distort; (*Schrift etc.*) deface; (*verkleiden*) disguise; *die Personen auf dem Foto ~ machen* make the people in the photo unrecognizable; **Unkenntlichkeit** *f*: *bis zur ~* beyond recognition; *bis zur ~ entstellt auch* completely disfigured
Unkenntnis *f*; -, *kein Pl.* ignorance; *in ~* (+ *Gen.*) unaware of, not knowing (about) *s.th.*; *j-n in ~ lassen* keep s.o. in ignorance (*über* + *Akk.* of, about), keep s.o. in the dark (*über* + *Akk.* about); *~ schützt vor Strafe nicht* ignorance of the law is no excuse
Unkenruf *m* **1.** *fig.* gloomy prediction, prophecy of doom; *allen ~en zum Trotz auch* despite all predictions to the contrary; **2.** *Zool.* croak of the fire-bellied toad
unklar I. *Adj.* **1.** unclear, not clear; (*undeutlich*) indistinct; *fig.* vague, obscure; (*ungewiss*) uncertain; *Gedanken, Vorstellung*: *auch* woolly *umg.*, fuzzy *umg.*; *mir ist* (*völlig*) *~, wie/wo etc.* I've (absolutely) no idea how/where *etc.*; *mir ist noch ~, ...* I'm still unclear (as to) ...; *im Unklaren sein/lassen über* (+ *Akk.*) be/leave *s.o.* in the dark about; *ich bin mir noch im Unklaren* I'm still not clear (*od.* sure, *od.* certain); **2.** *Naut.*, *Boot etc.*: not ready, not clear; **II.** *Adv.* sich ausdrücken *etc.*: unclearly; *sehen, erkennen*: dimly; *~ zu erkennen sein* be hard to make out; **Unklarheit** *f* lack of clarity; vagueness, obscurity; uncertainty; → *unklar, es herrscht ~ darüber, ob* it's not clear whether; *darüber herrscht absolute ~* it's completely unclear (as yet); *weitS.* it's a complete mystery
unklug *Adj.* unwise, imprudent; **Unklugheit** *f* **1.** *nur Sg.* imprudence; **2.** *konkret*: imprudent thing to do
unkollegial I. *Adj.* unhelpful, uncooperative, lacking team spirit; **II.** *Adv.*: *sich ~ verhalten* be unhelpful *etc.*, behave in an unhelpful *etc.* way
unkommentiert *Adj. Ausgabe etc.*: without a commentary
unkompliziert *Adj.* uncomplicated (*auch Mensch*), simple; **Unkompliziertheit** *f* *nur Sg.* uncomplicatedness, uncomplicated nature (+ *Gen.* of)
unkontrollierbar *Adj.* **1.** (*nicht zu* [*über*]*prüfen*) impossible to check; **2.** (*nicht zu beherrschen*) uncontrollable; **unkontrolliert I.** *Adj.* uncontrolled; **II.** *Adv.* uncontrolled, uncontrollably
unkonventionell I. *Adj.* unconventional; **II.** *Adv. eingerichtet etc.*: in an unconventional way; *in unserer Firma geht es ~ zu* we do things in an unconventional way in our company
unkonzentriert I. *Adj. Person, Handlungsweise etc.*: lacking in concentration; *Arbeit, Handlung etc.*: done without concentration; *er ist ~* he lacks concentration; *vorübergehend*: he isn't concentrating, he hasn't got his mind on the job; **II.** *Adv. arbeiten, fahren etc.*: without concentrating (on what one is doing); **Unkonzentriertheit** *f*; *nur Sg.* lack of concentration
unkoordiniert *Adj. Bewegungen, Planung etc.*: uncoordinated
unkorrekt I. *Adj.* incorrect; *Verhalten*:

auch improper; **II.** *Adv.* sich verhalten, behandeln *etc.*: incorrectly, improperly; **Unkorrektheit** *f* **1.** *nur Sg.* incorrectness; **2.** *Handlung, Äußerung etc.*: impropriety, improper act (*bzw.* remark *etc.*); **finanzielle ~en** financial improprieties
Unkosten *Pl.* costs, expenses, expense *Sg.*; *mit erheblichen ~ verbunden* involving considerable expense; *sich an den ~ beteiligen* share in the cost(s); → *stürzen* III 1; **~beitrag** *m* contribution (toward[s] expenses); *gegen e-n ~ von ...* in return for a contribution (toward[s] expenses) of; **~beteiligung** *f* share in the cost(s); *gegen ~* in return for taking a share in the cost(s)
Unkraut *n* weed(s *Pl.*); *~ jäten* weed (the garden), do some weeding; *~ vergeht nicht fig.* ill weeds grow apace; **~bekämpfung** *f* weed control; **~vertilgungsmittel** *n* weedkiller, herbicide
unkritisch I. *Adj.* uncritical; **II.** *Adv. übernehmen etc.*: uncritically
unkultiviert I. *Adj.* uncultivated; *Person*: uncultured; **II.** *Adv. sich benehmen etc.*: in an uncultured way; **Unkultiviertheit** *f* (complete) lack of culture, unculturedness
unkündbar *Adj. Stellung*: permanent; *Vertrag*: irrevocable; *Wirts., Anleihe etc.*: irredeemable; *in ~er Stellung* in a permanent post; *sie ist ~ auch* she can't be sacked (*Am.* fired) *umg.*; **Unkündbarkeit** *f*; *nur Sg.* permanence; irrevocability; irredeemability; → *unkündbar*
unkundig *Adj.* (*unwissend*) ignorant (+ *Gen.* of); (*uneingeweiht*) uninitiated; *e-r Sache ~ sein* have no knowledge of s.th.; *des Lesens ~* unable to read; *ein Leitfaden für Unkundige hum.* a beginner's guide
unlängst *Adv.* recently, not so long ago
unlauter *Adj.* dishonest, dubious, shady *umg.*; **~er Wettbewerb** *Wirts.* unfair competition
unleidlich *Adj.* **1.** (*unerträglich*) unbearable, intolerable; **2.** (*übellaunig*) bad-tempered; *auch vorübergehend*: grumpy *umg.*; *in e-r ~en Stimmung sein* be in a foul mood
unlesbar *Adj.* unreadable; **unleserlich I.** *Adj.* illegible; **II.** *Adv. schreiben*: illegibly; *fast ~ klein* so small as to be almost illegible, nearly too small to read; **Unleserlichkeit** *f*; *nur Sg.* illegibility
unleugbar *Adj.* undeniable
unlieb *Adj.*: *es war ihr nicht ~* it suited her fine
unliebenswürdig *Adj.* unkind, unobliging
unliebsam *Adj.* disagreeable, unpleasant; *Besuch, Gast*: unwelcome
unlin(i)iert *Adj.* unruled
Unlogik *f* illogicality; **unlogisch** *Adj.* illogical
unlösbar I. *Adj.* **1.** *Problem etc.*: insoluble; *ein ~es Problem auch* a problem that can't be solved; **2.** (*untrennbar*) inseparable; *Teil*: integral; *Ehe*: indissoluble; **II.** *Adv. verbunden, Klebeteile etc.*: inseparably, permanently; *~ verflochten od. verbunden fig.* inextricably linked; **Unlösbarkeit** *f*; *nur Sg.* **1.** insolubility; **2.** inseparability; indissolubility; → *unlösbar*
unlöslich *Adj. Chem.* insoluble
Unlust *f* *nur Sg.*; (*Apathie*) listlessness; (*Widerwille*) reluctance; *~ verspüren* feel reluctance; *mit ~ s-e Arbeit tun*

do one's work reluctantly; **~gefühl** *n* (great) reluctance; (*Abneigung*) aversion (*gegenüber* to); **unlustig** *Adj.* (*Unlust empfindend*) reluctant, disinclined, unenthusiastic

unmanierlich I. *Adj.* ill-mannered; **II.** *Adv.* in an ill-mannered way

unmännlich *Adj.* unmanly; (*weibisch*) effeminate; **feige und ~** cowardly and effeminate

Unmasse *f umg.* → **Unmenge**

unmaßgeblich I. *Adj.* irrelevant; (*unbedeutend*) insignificant; *weitS.* of no consequence; *Meinung, Person etc.*: unauthoritative; **nach m-r ~en Meinung** in my humble opinion; **II.** *Adv.*: **~ an etw. beteiligt sein** play an insignificant part in s.th.

unmäßig I. *Adj.* immoderate, excessive; *bes. im Trinken*: intemperate; **~ in s-n Forderungen sein** make excessive demands; **~en Hunger haben** be extraordinarily hungry; **II.** *Adv. trinken, essen etc.*: excessively, to excess; *stolz etc.*: inordinately; **~ dick** excessively fat; **Unmäßigkeit** *f; nur Sg.* immoderation, extravagance; excess(es *Pl.*); *bes. im Trinken*: intemperance

Unmenge *f* vast amount (*Anzahl*: *auch* number) (*von, an* + *Dat.* of)

Unmensch *m* monster, brute; **sei kein ~!** *hum.* have a heart; **man ist ja** (*schließlich*) **kein ~** *umg.* I'm not a monster; **unmenschlich I.** *Adj.* inhuman, cruel; *umg.* (*sehr groß*) tremendous; *Hitze, Kälte*: unbearable; **~es Leid** unbearable suffering; (*schier*) **Unmenschliches leisten** perform superhuman feats; **II.** *Adv. behandeln, quälen etc.*: inhumanly, cruelly; **~** (*viel*) **zu tun haben** *umg.* have a terrific amount (*od.* masses of things) to do, be rushed off one's feet; **Unmenschlichkeit** *f* **1.** *nur Sg.* inhumanity, cruelty; **2.** *konkret*: act of inhumanity (*od.* cruelty), inhumane (*od.* cruel) act

unmerklich I. *Adj.* imperceptible; **e-e fast ~e Änderung** *auch* a subtle change; **II.** *Adv.*: **nahezu ~ vor sich gehen** proceed almost imperceptibly

unmessbar *Adj.* unmeasurable

unmethodisch *Adj.* unmethodical

UN-Mission *f* UN mission

unmissverständlich I. *Adj.* unmistakable; *Antwort etc.*: unequivocal; **die Formulierung ist ~** the wording is unambiguous; **das war ~** there was no mistaking what it meant; *iro.* (*ich verstehe schon*) I can take a hint; **II.** *Adv.* unmistakably; (*deutlich*) plainly; **j-m ~ sagen, dass** make it perfectly clear (*od.* bring it home) to s.o. that, tell s.o. in no uncertain terms that; **~ zu verstehen geben, dass** make it perfectly clear that, make no bones about the fact that

unmittelbar I. *Adj. nur attr.; Nähe, Eindrücke etc.*: immediate; *Folgen etc.*: *auch* direct; *Gefahr, Aufgabe etc.*: immediate, imminent; **in ~er Nähe** (+ *Gen. od.* **von**) in the immediate vicinity of, right next to; **II.** *Adv. örtlich*: right, directly; *zeitlich*: straight, immediately, directly; **~ vor** (+ *Dat.*) right in front of; *zeitlich*: just before; **~ bevorstehend** imminent; **~ darauf** immediately afterwards, straight (*Am.* right) after; **~ erleben** experience (at) first hand; **Unmittelbarkeit** *f; nur Sg.* immediacy; directness

unmöbliert *Adj. und Adv.* unfurnished

unmodern I. *Adj.* dated; (*altmodisch*) old-fashioned; **~ werden** go out of fashion, become dated; **schnell ~ werden** *auch* date quickly; **II.** *Adv. sich kleiden, einrichten etc.*: in an old-fashioned way; **~ kurz etc.** unfashionably short *etc.*; **das ist ~ gedacht** that's not how people think nowadays

unmöglich I. *Adj.* impossible (*auch umg. fig. Mensch etc.*); *umg. fig. Kleid, Benehmen etc.*: *auch* dreadful; (*das ist*) **~** (*es geht nicht*) (that's) impossible, no way *umg.*; (*nicht tragbar*) it's too much, it won't do, it's not on *umg.*; **das war ~ von ihm** it was disgraceful (*od.* dreadful) of him; **zu e-r ~en Stunde** at an ungodly hour; **Unmögliches verlangen** ask the impossible; **sich ~ machen** *fig.* (*sein Ansehen verlieren*) compromise o.s.; *stärker*: put o.s. beyond the pale; (*sich lächerlich machen*) make a fool of o.s.; **j-n ~ machen** (*blamieren*) bring discredit on s.o.; (*lächerlich machen*) make s.o. look a fool; **II.** *Adv.* not possibly; *sich benehmen etc.*: abysmally; **er behandelt sie ~** he treats her disgracefully; **wir können ~ zulassen, dass** we can't possibly allow s.o./s.th. to; **er kleidet sich ~** he wears the most dreadful clothes; **das geht ~** that's impossible (*od.* out of the question); **Unmöglichkeit** *f* impossibility (**zu** + *Inf.* of + *Ger.*); **das ist ein Ding der ~** *umg.* that's quite impossible, *Am.* that's a nonstarter

Unmoral *f* immorality; **unmoralisch** *Adj.* immoral; **das ist doch nichts Unmoralisches** *umg.* there's nothing immoral about it

unmotiviert I. *Adj.* unmotivated; *Handlung etc.*: unprompted; *Ling., Lit.* non-transparent; **II.** *Adv.* for no (apparent) reason, just like that *umg.*

unmündig *Adj.* **1.** *attr.* under-age, *präd.* under age, not of age; **2.** *fig. politisch etc.*: immature; **Unmündigkeit** *f; nur Sg.* **1.** *Jur.* minority; **2.** *fig.* (mental) immaturity

unmusikalisch *Adj.* unmusical; **ich bin völlig ~** *auch* I'm not at all musical

unmusisch *Adj.* unartistic

Unmut *m* (*Missfallen*) displeasure; (*Ärger*) annoyance (**über** + *Akk.* at); **s-m ~ Luft machen** give vent to one's displeasure *geh.*; **Unmutsäußerung** *f* expression of annoyance, angry remark

unnachahmlich *Adj.* inimitable; **Unnachahmlichkeit** *f; nur Sg.* inimitability, inimitableness

unnachgiebig *Adj.* unyielding, intransigent, inflexible; (*kompromisslos*) uncompromising; *bes. Pol. attr.* hardline; **~e Haltung** hardline stance (*od.* posture); **Unnachgiebigkeit** *f* unyieldingness, intransigence, inflexibility; uncompromising attitude (*od.* stance); *Pol.* hardline approach (*od.* stance)

unnachsichtig I. *Adj.* strict, severe; **II.** *Adv. bestrafen etc.*: severely; **Unnachsichtigkeit** *f; nur Sg.* strictness, severity

unnahbar *Adj.* unapproachable; *pej.* aloof, stand-offish; **~ wirken** seem unapproachable; **Unnahbarkeit** *f; nur Sg.* unapproachability; aloofness

unnatürlich I. *Adj.* unnatural (*auch fig.*); (*geziert*) affected; **II.** *Adv. sich benehmen etc.*: unnaturally; (*geziert*) affectedly; *lachen, sprechen etc.*: affectedly; **mit ~ hoher etc. Stimme** in an unnaturally high *etc.* voice; **Unnatürlichkeit** *f* unnaturalness; affectation

unnormal I. *Adj.* not normal, *stärker*: abnormal; **II.** *Adv.* abnormally

unnötig I. *Adj.* unnecessary; (*überflüssig*) superfluous; *Aufwand, Mühe etc.*: needless, unnecessary; (**es ist**) **~ zu sagen, dass** it goes without saying that; **II.** *Adv.*: **sich ~ in Gefahr bringen** *etc.* put o.s. in danger *etc.* unnecessarily; **unnötigerweise** *Adv.* unnecessarily, needlessly

unnütz *Adj.* useless; (*sinnlos*) *auch* pointless; (*unnötig*) unnecessary; **~es Gerede** idle talk; **~es Zeug** *umg.* useless stuff

UNO *f, -, kein Pl.; Abk., Pol.*: **die ~** the UN; **~-Botschafter** *m,* **~-Botschafterin** *f* ambassador to the UN

unökonomisch *Adj.* uneconomical

UNO-Mitglied *n Pol.* member of the United Nations, UN member

unordentlich I. *Adj.* disorderly; *Zimmer etc., auch Person*: untidy; **II.** *Adv. arbeiten, Hefte, Bücher führen*: in a disorderly way; **Unordentlichkeit** *f* disorderliness; untidiness, *bes. Am.* messiness; **Unordnung** *f* disorder(liness), *a* mess; **in ~** in disorder, in a mess, in (complete) disarray; **in ~ bringen** mess up; **dort herrscht e-e furchtbare ~** the place is (in) a terrible mess

unorganisch *Adj.* inorganic

unorganisiert *Adj.* disorganized; *Arbeitnehmer*: not organized

unorthodox I. *Adj.* unorthodox; **II.** *Adv. vorgehen etc.*: in an unorthodox way

UNO|-Soldat *m Pol.* UN soldier; **~-Truppen** *Pl.* UN troops; **~-Vollversammlung** *f* UN (*od.* United Nations) assembly

unpädagogisch I. *Adj.*: **~** (**sein**) (go) against educational principles; **~e Vorgehensweise** method that is educationally unsound; **II.** *Adv.*: **sich ~ verhalten** behave in a way that is inappropriate for a teacher

unparfümiert *Adj.* non-scented, fragrance-free, aroma-free

unparteiisch I. *Adj.* impartial, unbias(s)ed, disinterested; (*gerecht*) even-handed; **ein ~er Dritter** a neutral third party; **ein Unparteiischer soll entscheiden** a neutral person should decide; **II.** *Adv. urteilen etc.*: impartially; **Unparteiische** *m, f, -n, -n; Sport* referee

unparteilich *Adj.* **1.** *Pol.* non-party, *Am.* nonpartisan; **2.** (*unparteisch*) impartial, unbias(s)ed; **Unparteilichkeit** *f; nur Sg.* impartiality

unpassend *Adj.* unsuitable; (*unangebracht*) inappropriate, out of place; (*unschicklich*) improper; (*zur Unzeit*) untimely; **im ~sten Augenblick** at the most inconvenient (*od.* inopportune) moment; **~er geht's nicht** *umg.* it coundn't be less suitable

unpassierbar *Adj. Straße, Brücke etc.*: impassable

unpässlich *Adj.* indisposed, unwell, out of sorts; **Unpässlichkeit** *f* indisposition

unpathetisch *Adj.* unemotional

Unperson *f* unperson, non-person; **j-n zur ~ erklären** designate s.o. as an non(-)person; **unpersönlich I.** *Adj.* impersonal (*auch Gram.*); **II.** *Adv.* impersonally; **dort geht es sehr ~ zu** the way they do things there is too impersonal

unpfändbar *Adj.* unseizable

unplatziert I. *Adj. Sport* random; **II.** *Adv.*: **~ schießen** *etc.* shoot *etc.* at random

unplugged ['anplakt] *Adj. Mus.* un-

plugged
unpolitisch *Adj.* unpolitical
unpopulär *Adj.* unpopular; **Unpopularität** *f* unpopularity
unpraktikabel *Adj.* impracticable; **unpraktisch** *Adj.* impractical (*auch Mensch*); **unpraktizierbar** *Adj.* unworkable
unprätentiös *Adj. geh.* unpretentious
unpräzis(e) *Adj.* imprecise
unproblematisch I. *Adj.* unproblematic; II. *Adv.* unproblematically
unproduktiv I. *Adj.* unproductive; *Wirts.* non-productive; II. *Adv. arbeiten etc.:* unproductively
unprofessionell *Adj.* unprofessional
unproportioniert *Adj.* disproportionate, *präd.* out of proportion
unpünktlich I. *Adj.* 1. *Person:* late; *generell:* unpunctual; *er ist ~ generell:* auch he's never on time; 2. *Zug etc.:* late; *der Zug etc. ist ~ auch* the train etc. isn't (running) on time; II. *Adv. kommen etc.:* late; **Unpünktlichkeit** *f gewohnheitsmäßige:* unpunctuality, lack of punctuality; *aktuelle:* being (*od.* arriving *etc.*) late; *diese ~!* they *etc.* never turn up on time, they're *etc.* never on time
unqualifiziert *Adj.* unqualified; *Bemerkung:* inept
unrasiert I. *Adj.* unshaven; *~ und fern der Heimat hum.* living out of a suitcase; II. *Adv.: ~ ins Büro gehen etc.* go into the office *etc.* unshaven (*od.* without shaving)
Unrast *f nur Sg.* restlessness
Unrat *m; -(e)s, kein Pl.* rubbish, *Am.* garbage; *~ wittern fig.* smell a rat
unrationell *Adj.* inefficient
unrealistisch I. *Adj.* unrealistic, II. *Adv.* unrealistically
unrecht *Adj.* (*falsch, auch nicht gut*) wrong; (*ungelegen*) inopportune; *j-m ~ tun* do s.o. an injustice, do s.o. wrong; *~ haben → Unrecht*; *nichts Unrechtes tun* do nothing wrong; **Unrecht** *n nur Sg.* wrong; (*Ungerechtigkeit*) injustice; *j-m ein ~ tun od. zufügen* do s.o. an injustice, do s.o. wrong; *im ~ sein* (*od. ~ haben*) be (in the) wrong; (*sich irren*) auch be mistaken; *sich ins ~ setzen* put o.s. in the wrong; *er hat nicht so ganz ~* there's something in what he says; *j-m ~ geben* disagree with s.o.; *fig. Tatsache, Folgen etc.:* prove s.o. wrong; *ihm ist ~ geschehen* he has been wronged; *zu ~* wrongfully, wrongly, unjustly
unrechtmäßig I. *Adj.* wrongful, unlawful; II. *Adv. sich aneignen etc.:* wrongfully, unlawfully; **Unrechtmäßigkeit** *f* wrongfulness, unlawfulness
Unrechts|bewusstsein *n* consciousness of doing wrong; *~regime n* tyrannical regime; *~staat m etwa* police state, *a state that is the opposite of a Rechtsstaat*
unredlich I. *Adj.* dishonest, *attr. auch* underhand; II. *Adv. handeln etc.:* dishonestly; **Unredlichkeit** *f* dishonesty
unreell *Adj.* (*unseriös, dubios*) dubious; (*unlauter*) unfair; (*unredlich*) dishonest
unreflektiert *Adj.* unreflected
unregelmäßig I. *Adj.* irregular (*auch Puls, Verb etc.*); *weitS.* (*sprunghaft, erratisch*) erratic; (*holperig, uneben*) *auch Schrift:* uneven; *Math., Figur:* irregular; II. *Adv. atmen, schlagen, steigern etc.:* irregularly; *schreiben etc.:* unevenly; *zahlen, abrechnen:* at irregular intervals; (*sprunghaft*) erratically;

Unregelmäßigkeit *f* irregularity (*auch konkret Verstoß, Betrügerei etc.*)
unregierbar *Adj.* ungovernable; **Unregierbarkeit** *f* ungovernability
unreif *Adj.* unripe; *Früchte:* auch green; *fig.* immature; *~er Bursche* callow youth; **Unreife** *f* immaturity
unrein *Adj.* impure (*auch fig. Gedanken etc.*); *Wäsche:* dirty; *Luft, Wasser:* dirty, polluted; *Haut:* bad, blemished; *Ton:* impure; *ins Unreine schreiben* make a rough copy of; *ins Unreine sprechen umg.* say off the record; **Unreinheit** *f* impurity (*auch konkret*); dirtiness; pollution, polluted state; → *unrein*
unrentabel *Adj. Wirts.* unprofitable
UN-Resolution *f* UN resolution
unrettbar I. *Adj.* irrecoverable; II. *Adv.: ~ verloren* irretrievably lost; *Person:* beyond help; *Land etc., wirtschaftlich:* beyond recovery
unrichtig *Adj.* incorrect, wrong; *Annahme, Eindruck:* auch erroneous; **Unrichtigkeit** *f* incorrectness
Unruh *f; -, -en e-r Uhr:* balance spring
Unruhe *f; -, -n* 1. *nur Sg.;* (*Unrast, Nervosität*) restlessness (*auch Zappelei*); (*Besorgnis*) uneasiness, anxiety; *von e-r nervösen ~ ergriffen* a prey to nervous anxiety; *in ~ versetzen* worry; *stärker:* alarm; *~ stiften* cause a disturbance; 2. *nur Sg.;* (*Lärm*) noise; 3. (*Tumult*) commotion; *~n Pol.* unrest *Sg.,* disturbances; *~herd m* trouble spot; *~stifter m, ~stifterin f* troublemaker
unruhig I. *Adj.* restless; (*unregelmäßig*) *Puls, Atmung etc.:* irregular, uneven; *Schlaf:* broken, fitful; *Muster etc.:* restless; *fig.* uneasy (*wegen* about); (*besorgt*) anxious, worried; (*laut*) noisy; *Zeiten:* troubled; *~ werden* (*besorgt*) get worried; *~e See* rough (*od.* choppy) seas; II. *Adv. herumgehen, um sich blicken etc.:* restlessly; (*besorgt*) anxiously; *schlafen:* fitfully; *der Motor läuft ~* the engine isn't running smoothly
unrühmlich *Adj.* inglorious; *ein ~es Ende nehmen* come to an inglorious end
unrund *Adv. Tech.: ~ laufen* run untrue
uns 1. *pers. Pron.* (*Dat. + Akk. von wir*) (to) us; *ein Freund von ~* a friend of ours; *ein Gruß von ~* (*beiden*) regards from (both of) us; *bei ~* (*zu Hause*) at home; at our house (*od.* place); (*in der Firma etc.*) in our company *etc.*; (*in Deutschland etc.*) at home, in our country; *das gehört ~* that belongs to us; 2. *refl. Pron.* (to) ourselves; *wir haben ~ gefreut/geschämt etc.* we were glad/ashamed; *wir kaufen/leisten ~ ...* we're buying (ourselves) / treating ourselves to ...; *unter ~ gesagt* between you and me; *wir blickten hinter ~* we looked behind us, we looked back; 3. *reziprokes Pron.* (*einander*) each other; *wir sehen ~ nie* we never see each other
unsachgemäß I. *Adj. Behandlung etc.:* improper, inexpert; II. *Adv. behandeln, umgehen mit etc.:* improperly, inexpertly
unsachlich I. *Adj.* unobjective, subjective; (*nicht relevant*) irrelevant; *wir wollen nicht ~ werden* let's try and stick to the facts; II. *Adv. diskutieren etc.:* in an unobjective way; **Unsachlichkeit** *f* lack of objectivity
unsagbar, unsäglich I. *Adj.* unspeaka-

ble, unutterable, inexpressible; II. *Adv.* unspeakably *etc.*; *nachgestellt:* beyond words
unsanft I. *Adj.* (*grob*) rough; (*hart*) hard; (*böse, unangenehm*) bad, (*auch unvermittelt, unfreundlich*) rude, (*~es Erwachen* rude awakening; II. *Adv.: ~ aus dem Schlaf gerissen werden* be rudely awakened
unsauber I. *Adj.* 1. (*schmutzig*) dirty (*auch Arbeit*); (*unordentlich*) messy, careless, sloppy; *fig. Mus.* impure; (*falsch*) off-key; 2. (*unlauter*) unfair, *attr. auch* underhand; *Geschäft, Methode:* auch dubious, shady *umg.*; *Sport* dirty, unfair; II. *Adv.* 1. *arbeiten etc.:* carelessly, sloppily; *Mus. spielen, singen:* off key; 2. *Sport, spielen, boxen etc.:* dirty, unfairly; **Unsauberkeit** *f* 1. (*Schmutzigkeit*) dirtiness; (*Unordentlichkeit*) messiness, carelessness, sloppiness; *Mus.* inaccuracy; 2. *Handlung:* dirty trick; *Sport* foul
unschädlich *Adj.* harmless; *~ machen* render harmless; *umg.* (*j-n*) put s.o. out of action; **Unschädlichkeit** *f* harmlessness
unscharf I. *Adj.* blunt; *Bild:* blurred, fuzzy, unsharp, out of focus; *Formulierung:* hazy, fuzzy, vague; II. *Adv. ich sehe alles ~* everything looks blurred (*od.* blurry) to me; *~ eingestellt Radio etc.* not tuned (in) properly; *Fernrohr etc.:* out of focus
Unschärfe *f Opt., Fot.* 1. *nur Sg.* lack of definition; 2. (*unscharfe Stelle*) blur; *~bereich m Opt., Fot.* blurred area, blur; *~relation f Phys.* uncertainty relation
unschätzbar *Adj.* invaluable; *Wert, Bedeutung etc.:* inestimable
unscheinbar *Adj.* insignificant; (*unauffällig*) inconspicuous; *Person:* unprepossessing, nondescript; **Unscheinbarkeit** *f; nur Sg.* insignificance; inconspicuousness; unprepossessing nature (+ *Gen.* of)
unschicklich I. *Adj.* improper, unseemly; (*unanständig*) indecent; II. *Adv. sich benehmen etc.:* in an unseemly fashion; **Unschicklichkeit** *f* 1. *nur Sg.* impropriety, unseemliness; indecency; 2. *Handlung etc.:* inappropriateness
unschlagbar I. *Adj.* unbeatable (*in + Dat.* at, when it comes to); (*unübertroffen*) unrival(l)ed; *Argument, Beweis etc.:* irrefutable; II. *Adv. schnell, schlagfertig etc.:* supremely
unschlüssig I. *Adj.* undecided; (*zögernd*) hesitant, wavering; (*nicht schlüssig*) inconclusive; *ich bin mir ~* I haven't made up my mind yet (*über + Akk.* about); II. *Adv. in die Verhandlung gehen etc.:* without having made up one's mind; *~ stehen bleiben* come to a stop, unable to make up one's mind; **Unschlüssigkeit** *f; nur Sg.* undecidedness
unschön I. *Adj.* unlovely, unsightly; (*unfair*) unfair, unkind, not nice; (*unerfreulich*) unpleasant; *~er Anblick* eyesore; *~e Tätlichkeit Sport* ugly foul; II. *Adv.* in a not very nice way; *klingen etc.:* not (very) nice
Unschuld *f nur Sg.* 1. innocence; (*Reinheit*) purity (*of heart od.* mind); *s-e ~ beteuern* protest (*od.* maintain) one's innocence; *in aller ~* quite innocently; *ich wasche m-e Hände in ~* I wash my hands of it; *~ vom Lande umg.* country cousin; 2. (*Jungfräulichkeit*) virginity; *s-e ~ verlieren* lose

one's viginity (*fig.* innocence); *j-m die ~ nehmen* take s.o.'s virginity; **unschuldig I.** *Adj.* **1.** innocent (*an* + *Dat.* of); *an e-m Unglück etc.*: not responsible (for); (*harmlos*) harmless; *sich für ~ erklären Jur.* plead not guilty; *es traf vor allem ~e Frauen und Kinder* it was mainly innocent women and children who suffered; **2.** *altm.* (*jungfräulich*) untouched, *attr. auch* virgin *attr.*; *sie ist noch ~* she is still a virgin; **II.** *Adv.* innocently; *dreinblicken, gucken*: innocent; *er wurde ~ bestraft* he was punished although he was innocent; *~ geschieden altm.* divorced and judged the innocent party in the case; *du brauchst gar nicht so ~ zu tun umg.* don't try and play the innocent with me

Unschulds|beteuerungen *Pl.* protestations of innocence; *~beweis m* proof of *s.o.'s* innocence; *~engel m*, *~lamm n iro.* innocent little angel; *~miene f* air of innocence

unschuldsvoll I. *Adj.* innocent; *~er Blick auch* look of innocence; **II.** *Adv.* innocently

unschwer *Adv.* without difficulty

unselbstständig *Adj.* dependent (on others); (*unbeholfen, hilflos*) helpless; *er ist so ~ auch* he can't do anything on his own; *Einkommen aus ~er Arbeit* wage and salary incomes *Pl.*; **Unselbstständigkeit** *f* dependence (on others); helplessness

unselig *Adj. mst attr. Vorfall, Leidenschaft etc.*: unfortunate; *stärker*: disastrous

unsensibel *Adj.* insensitive

unsentimental *Adj.* unsentimental

unser I. *Poss. Pron.* **1.** *adjektivisch*: our; *e-r ~er Freunde* a friend of ours; *Vater ~ bibl.* Our Father; **2.** *substantivisch*: ours; *~er, ~e, ~(e)s, unsrer, unsre, unsres, der/die/das ~e od. uns(e)rige* ours; **II.** *pers. Pron.* (*Gen. von wir*) of us; *~ aller Wunsch* the wish of all of us

unsereiner, unsereins *unbest. Pron. umg.* people like us, the likes of us, our sort

unsererseits *Adv.* for our part, as far as we are concerned; *~ bestehen keine Bedenken etc.* there are no misgivings on our part, we have no misgivings

unseresgleichen *unbest. Pron.* people like us

unser(e)twegen *Adv.* for our sake, on our account; (*wegen uns*) because of us

uns(e)rige *Poss. Pron.* → *unser* I 2

unseriös *Adj. pej. Geschäft etc.*: dubious; *Zeitung*: popular; *Schrift, Wissenschaftler etc.*: not to be taken seriously, lightweight; (*unzuverlässig*) untrustworthy; *~er Typ umg.* slippery character; *es ist e-e ~e Schrift etc.* it's not a serious piece of writing *etc.*; *das ist keineswegs ~* this is perfectly above board

unsicher I. *Adj.* **1.** (*gefährdet*) insecure; (*gefährlich*) unsafe; *Gegend, Straße etc.*: dangerous; *die Arbeitsplätze werden immer ~er* jobs are getting more and more insecure; *die Gegend ~ machen* terrorize the neighbo(u)rhood; *umg. fig.* (*ausgehen, sich amüsieren*) paint the town red; **2.** (*ungewiss, auch unzuverlässig*) uncertain; (*ohne Gewissheit*) unsure, uncertain; (*sich*) *sein, ob/wann etc.* not be sure (as to) whether/when *etc.*; **3.** (*unstet*) un-

steady (*auch Hand, Beine*); *Person*: (*ohne Selbstsicherheit*) insecure, unsure of o.s., *stärker*: lacking in self--confidence; *~ auf den Beinen* shaky, wobbly; *~er Autofahrer etc.* driver who lacks assurance (*od.* is unsure of himself), unreliable driver; *~ im Rechnen etc.* shaky on arithmetic *etc.*; *j-n ~ machen* make s.o. unsure of himself (*od.* herself), *stärker*: rattle s.o.; **II.** *Adv. Auto fahren etc.*: unreliably; *nach i-m Sturz geht sie noch sehr ~* she's still very shaky (*od.* unsteady) on her feet after her fall; *sich ~ fühlen* feel insecure; **Unsicherheit** *f* insecurity; unsteadiness; uncertainty; → *unsicher*; *tiefe ~ e-r Person*: deep sense of insecurity; **Unsicherheitsfaktor** *m* element of uncertainty

unsichtbar *Adj.* invisible (*für* to); *sich ~ machen im Märchen etc.*: make o.s. invisible; *umg. fig.* (*verschwinden*) make o.s. scarce, disappear; **Unsichtbarkeit** *f* invisibility

unsinkbar *Adj.* unsinkable

Unsinn *m nur Sg.* nonsense; *~ machen* fool around; (*e-n Fehler machen*) mess up, *Brit. auch* cock up *Sl.*, *Am. auch* foul (*od.* screw) up; *~ reden/verzapfen umg.* talk a lot of nonsense/rot *Sl.*; *~!* *umg.* nonsense!, *Brit. auch* rubbish!, *Am. auch* garbage!; *echt? - mach keinen ~! umg. ungläubig*: really? - you're kidding!; (*machen Sie*) *keinen ~!* *warnend, drohend bei Festnahme, Überfall etc.*: don't try any funny business; *mach ja keinen ~! zu jm.* behave yourself, no nonsense!; → *auch Quatsch*; **unsinnig I.** *Adj.* (*sinnlos, dumm*) silly; *stärker*: ridiculous, absurd; *Preise, Forderungen etc.*: ridiculous; *Hitze etc.*: incredible, terrible, dreadful; **II.** *Adv.* **1.** *sich wie ~ gebärden* behave insanely (*od.* like a madman); **2.** *umg.* (*übermäßig*) terribly, incredibly

unsinnlich *Adj.* non-sensual

Unsitte *f* bad habit; (*Missstand*) nuisance

unsittlich I. *Adj.* immoral, indecent; *~er Antrag* improper suggestion; **II.** *Adv. berühren*: immorally, indecently; *sich j-m ~ nähern* make indecent advances to s.o.; **Unsittlichkeit** *f* **1.** *nur Sg.* immorality, indecency; **2.** *Handlung etc.*: immoral (*od.* indecent) act

unsolidarisch I. *Adj.* showing a lack of solidarity; **II.** *Adv.* in a way that does not show solidarity; *sich gegenüber j-m ~ verhalten* show a lack of solidarity with s.o., not keep faith with s.o.

unsolid(e) I. *Adj.* **1.** *Person, Lebensweise*: loose-living, disreputable; (*ausschweifend*) dissolute, dissipated; *Firma etc.*: dubious; **2.** *Bau etc.*: unstable, unsolid; *Arbeit*: shoddy, careless; **II.** *Adv.* **1.** *leben*: dissolutely; **2.** *~ gearbeitet etc.* shoddily made *etc.*

unsortiert *Adj.* unsorted

unsozial *Adj.* unsocial; *Verhalten*: anti-social

unspektakulär *Adj.* unspectacular

unspezifisch *Adj.* unspecific, non-specific

unsportlich I. *Adj.* **1.** unathletic; **2.** (*unfair*) unsporting, unsportsmanlike; **II.** *Adv. sich verhalten etc.*: unsportingly; **Unsportlichkeit** *f* **1.** *nur Sg.* unsportingness, unsportsmanlike conduct; **2.** *Handlung*: unsporting act

unstabil *Adj.* unstable

unstatthaft *Adj.* inadmissible, not allowed; (*verboten*) illicit

unsterblich I. *Adj.* immortal (*auch Künstler etc.*); *Liebe*: undying; *mit diesem Buch hat sie sich ~ gemacht* this book immortalized her; **II.** *Adv.* **1.** immortally; **2.** *umg.* (*sehr*) awfully, dreadfully; *sich ~ blamieren* make an absolute fool of o.s.; *~ verliebt* hopelessly in love (*in* + *Akk.* with), smitten; **Unsterbliche** *m, f; -n, -n* immortal; **Unsterblichkeit** *f* immortality; *in die ~ eingehen* be immortalized

Unstern *m nur Sg.* unlucky star; *etw. steht unter e-m ~* s.th. is ill-fated

unstet I. *Adj.* (*wechselhaft, unbeständig*) changeable, unstable; (*ruhelos*) restless; *Leben*: *auch* unsettled; *Blick*: shifty; *ein ~es Leben führen* lead an unsettled life; **II.** *Adv.* (*ruhelos*) restlessly

unstillbar *Adj.* **1.** *Hunger*: insatiable; *Durst*: unquenchable; **2.** *fig. Sehnsucht etc.*: insatiable

Unstimmigkeit *f* **1.** *nur Sg.* discrepancy, inconsistency; **2.** *~en bei der Abrechnung etc.* discrepancies in the accounting *etc.*; **3.** (*Meinungsverschiedenheit*) *auch Pl.* disagreement; *stärker*: friction; *es kam zu ~en* there was a difference of opinion; *stärker*: there was a dispute

unstreitig I. *Adj.* undeniable, indisputable; **II.** *Adv. feststehen etc.*: indisputably

unstrukturiert *Adj.* unstructured

Unsumme *f auch Pl.* enormous sum; *der Neubau wird ~n kosten od. verschlingen* the cost of the new building will be astronomical

unsymmetrisch *Adj.* asymmetrical

Unsympath *m; -en, -en; umg. pej.* unsympathetic (*od.* unpleasant) person; *in Filmen etc.*: unsympathetic character, villain; **unsympathisch** *Adj.* unpleasant, unappealing; *abstoßend*: off--putting; *er/es ist mir ~* I don't like him/it; *~ aussehen* put one (*od.* s.o.) off; *der Gedanke ist mir höchst ~* I find the idea totally unappealing; *e-e gar nicht ~e Vorstellung* an idea that is not without its attractions

unsystematisch *Adj.* unsystematic(al)

untadelig I. *Adj.* **1.** *Benehmen etc.*: flawless, irreproachable, beyond reproach; **2.** *Material, Leistung*: flawless; *Kleidung*: immaculate; **II.** *Adv. sich benehmen etc.*: irreproachably; *gekleidet*: immaculately

untalentiert *Adj.* untalented

Untat *f* atrocity, outrage, evil deed

untätig I. *Adj.* inactive; *Vulkan*: *auch* dormant; (*müßig, träge*) idle; **II.** *Adv.*: *~ herumsitzen* sit around doing nothing (twiddling one's thumbs *umg.*); *~ zusehen müssen* have to stand idly by; **Untätigkeit** *f; nur Sg.* inactivity; idleness

untauglich *Adj.* (*nicht zu gebrauchen*) unsuitable; *engS.* (*unfähig*) incompetent, incapable; *Mil.* unfit (for service); *~ für auch* not suited to; **Untauglichkeit** *f* unsuitability; incompetence; *Mil.* unfitness

unteilbar *Adj.* indivisible; **Unteilbarkeit** *f* indivisibility

unten *Adv.* **1.** (down) below; *im Hause*: downstairs; *umg.* (*im Süden*) down south; *nach ~* down(wards); *im Hause*: downstairs; *~ am See* down by the lake; *da ~* down there; *ganz ~* right (down) at the bottom; *weiter ~* further down; *von ~* from below; *von oben*

bis ~ from top to bottom (*Person: auch* toe); **siehe ~** see below; **siehe S.7 ~** see p.7 bottom; **mit dem Gesicht nach ~** face down; **rechts ~** at the bottom right; **sich ~ waschen** *euph.* wash one's lower parts; **er ist bei mir ~ durch** *umg.* I'm through with him; **~ erwähnt** *od.* **genannt** undermentioned; *nachgestellt:* mentioned below; **~ stehend** *in Text:* following, below (*beide nachgestellt*); **bitte ~ Stehendes beachten** please see below; **2.** *gesellschaftlich etc.:* at the bottom; **er steht ganz ~ (in der Hierarchie)** he's right at the bottom (of the hierarchy *od.* totem pole *umg.*); **sich von ~ hochdienen** work one's way up (the ladder); *Mil.* rise from the ranks

unten|drunter *Adv.* *umg.* underneath; **~durch** *Adv.* *umg.* through; **bei uns ist sie ~** we're through with her, we're (*od.* we've) finished (*od.* done) with her; **~(he)rum** *Adv.* *umg.* down below

unter **I.** *Präp.* (+ *Dat. od. Akk.*) **1.** under, below; (*bes. direkt ~*) under, below; **~ ... hervor** from under ...; **~ 21 (Jahren)** under 21 (years of age); **~ zehn Euro** under (*od.* less than) ten euros; **~ s-r Regierung** under (*od.* during) his reign; **~ sich** (*Dat.*) **haben** (*Angestellte, Abteilung etc.*) be in charge of; **„Land ~“** "flood"; **2.** (*zwischen*) among; **einer ~ vielen** one of many; **nicht einer ~ hundert** not one in a hundred; **~ anderem** (*abgek. u.a.*) among other things; **(sich) mischen ~** (+ *Akk.*) mix with; **3. ~ Beifall** amid applause; **~ Tränen** in tears, tearfully; **~ großem Gelächter** amid gales of laughter; **4. ~ der Woche** during the week; **~ Mittag/Tags** around midday / during the day; **5. ~ diesem Gesichtspunkt** from this point of view; **was versteht man ~ ...?** what is meant by ...?; → **Kritik** 1, **Würde** 1, **uns** 2; **II.** *Adj.* → **untere**

Unter *m*; *-s*, *-* *Spielkarte:* jack, knave *altm.*

Unter|abschnitt *m* subsection; **~abteilung** *f* subdivision; **~arm** *m* forearm; **~ausschuss** *m* subcommittee; **~bau** *m*; *Pl.* *-bauten* **1.** *Tech.* substructure (*auch Eisenb.*); (*Fundament*) foundation; **2.** *nur Sg.*; *fig.* foundation, base; *bes. wirtschaftlich:* infrastructure; **~bauch** *m* *Anat.* lower abdomen

unterbauen *v/t.* (*untr., hat*) **1.** *Tech.* support (from below); (*unterlegen*) underlay; **2.** *fig.* (*Theorie etc.*) underpin, shore up

Unterbegriff *m* *Philos.* subconcept

Unterbekleidung *f* underclothes *Pl.*

unterbelegt *Adj.* *Hotel, Klinik etc.:* not full, not filled to capacity; *weitS.* half-empty; *Kurs etc.:* undersubscribed

unterbelichtet *Adj.* *Fot.* underexposed; **geistig ~** *umg.* *fig.* a bit dim, not exactly bright *iro.*

unterbeschäftigt *Adj.* *Wirts.* underemployed; **Unterbeschäftigung** *f* underemployment

unterbesetzt *Adj.* understaffed, short-staffed

Unterbett *n* underblanket

unterbevölkert *Adj.* underpopulated

unterbewerten *v/t.* (*untr., hat*) undervalue; (*unterschätzen*) underrate; **Unterbewertung** *f* undervaluation; underrating

unterbewusst *Adj.* *Psych.* subconscious; **das Unterbewusste** the subconscious; **Unterbewusstsein** *n* subconscious; **im ~** subconsciously

unterbezahlt *Adj.* underpaid; **Unterbe-**

zahlung *f* underpayment

Unterbezirk *m* subdistrict

unterbieten *v/t.* (*unreg., untr., hat*) underbid; *Wirts.* (*Preis*) undercut; (*Konkurrenz*) undersell; (*Rekord*) beat; **es ist kaum mehr zu ~** *umg.* *fig.* it can hardly get any worse (than that); **an Niveau kaum zu ~** as low (*od.* bad) as you can get

unterbinden *v/t.* (*unreg., untr., hat*) put a stop to; (*verhindern*) prevent; **Unterbindung** *f* stopping, ending; prevention

unterbleiben *v/i.* (*unreg., untr., ist*) (*nicht getan werden*) not be done (*od.* undertaken); (*nicht geschehen*) not take place; **es hat zu ~** (*muss aufhören*) it must stop; (*darf nicht geschehen*) it mustn't be done, it mustn't happen

Unterboden *m* **1.** *Geog.* subsoil; **2.** *Mot.* underside; **~schutz** *m* *Mot.* underseal, *Am.* undercoat; **~wäsche** *f* *Mot.* undercar wash

unterbrechen *vt/i.* (*unreg., untr., hat*) interrupt; (*j-n beim Sprechen*) *auch* cut *s.o.* short; *Telef.* cut off; (*Spiel*) hold up; (*Schwangerschaft*) terminate; *Jur.* (*Strafverhandlung*) adjourn; *Etech.* interrupt; (*auflockern*) (*Muster, Programm etc.*) break up; **die Fahrt** *od.* **Reise ~** break one's journey; **darf ich mal kurz ~?** may I interrupt for a moment?; **der Bahnverkehr zwischen Basel und Freiburg ist unterbrochen** the rail (*od.* train) service between Basel and Freiburg has been suspended; **die Ebene wird von tiefen Schluchten unterbrochen** deep gorges break the level expanse of the plain

Unterbrecher *m*; *-s*, *-*; *Etech.* interrupter, contact breaker; **~kontakt** *m* *Etech.* make-and-break contact

Unterbrechung *f* interruption; (*auch Pause*) break; (*Vertagung*) adjournment etc.; → **unterbrechen**; **ohne ~** without stopping, nonstop; **mit ~en** (*periodisch*) intermittently

unterbreiten *v/t.* (*untr., hat*) (*Angebot etc.*) submit (+ *Dat.* to); (*Vorschlag*) *auch* put forward; **Unterbreitung** *f* submission (+ *Gen.* of)

unterbringen *v/t.* (*unreg., trennb., hat -ge-*); (*beherbergen*) accommodate, put *s.o.* up; *in e-r Firma etc.:* get *s.o.* a job (*in* + *Dat.*, *bei* with); (*lagern*) store; (*Gepäck etc.*) put; *bei Platzmangel:* get (*in* + *Dat.* into); (*Interessenten finden für*) have *s.th.* accepted (*bei* by); *umg.* *fig.* (*geistig einordnen*) place; **j-n ~** *in e-m Krankenhaus, Heim etc.:* put *s.o.* into; *in e-r Schule etc.:* put *s.o.* in, get *s.o.* into; **gut untergebracht sein** *im Urlaub etc.:* have a nice place to stay; **wie sind Sie untergebracht?** what sort of place are you staying in?; **in dem Asyl etc. kann man 100 Leute ~** the home etc. accommodates a hundred (people); **die Akten sind im Keller untergebracht** the files are kept in the cellar; **den Nachtisch bring ich auch noch unter** *umg.* I think I could manage the dessert as well

Unterbringung *f* (*Unterkunft*) accommodation, lodging; (*Vorgang*) housing; **~ von Dingen:** finding a place for, putting *s.th.* away

Unterbringungsmöglichkeit *f* *auch Pl.:* accommodation

Unterbruch *m*; *-(e)s*, *Unterbrüche*; *schw.* interruption

unterbuttern *v/t.* (*trennb., hat -ge-*) *umg.:* **lass dich nicht ~** (*unterdrücken*)

don't let them etc. walk all over you; (*nicht zur Geltung kommen*) make sure you get noticed; **in so e-r Riesenfirma wird man leicht untergebuttert** when you work for a firm as big as that, your talents can easily go unnoticed

Unterdeck *n* *Naut.* lower deck

unterderhand → **Hand**[1] 3

unterdessen *Adv.* (*inzwischen*) in the meantime, meanwhile

Unterdruck *m*; *-(e)s*, *Unterdrücke* **1.** *Phys.* subpressure; **2.** *nur Sg.*; *Med.* low blood pressure

unterdrücken *v/t.* (*untr., hat*); (*Gefühl etc., auch Opposition, Freiheit, Aufstand, Informationen etc.*) suppress; (*Fluch, Lachen, Seufzer etc.*) *auch* stifle; (*Volk etc.*) oppress; (*Ehefrau etc.*) keep *s.o.* under one's thumb; *EDV* (*Zeilen etc.*) suppress; **die Unterdrückten** the oppressed; **Unterdrücker** *m*; *-s*, *-*, **Unterdrückerin** *f*; *-*, *-nen* suppressor, oppressor

Unterdruckkammer *f* decompression chamber

Unterdrückung *f* suppression, oppression

unterdurchschnittlich **I.** *Adj.* *attr.* below-average, *präd. und nachgestellt:* below average; **II.** *Adv.* **begabt etc.** less than averagely; **verdienen etc.:** less than the average

untere *Adj.* *Ende, Grenze, Klasse, Seite etc.:* lower; **am ~n Flusslauf** in the lower reaches (of the river); → **unterst...**

untereinander *Adv.* **1.** one below the other; **die Zahlen stehen genau ~** the figures are exactly aligned one beneath the other; **2.** (*gegenseitig*) one another; (*miteinander*) among themselves, yourselves etc.; **sich ~ helfen** help one another

Untereinheit *f* subunit

unterentwickelt *Adj.* underdeveloped; *Kind, Land, Wirtschaft:* *auch* backward; *Psych.* subnormal; **geistig und körperlich ~** mentally and physically underdeveloped; **Unterentwicklung** *f* underdevelopment

unterernährt *Adj.* undernourished, malnutrition; **Unterernährung** *f* malnutrition

Unterfamilie *f* *Zool.* subfamily

unterfangen (*unreg., untr., hat*) **I.** *v/refl.* *altm.:* **sich ~ zu** (+ *Inf.*) dare (to) (+ *Inf.*), venture to (+ *Inf.*); **II.** *v/t.* *Archit.* underpin

Unterfangen *n*; *-s*, *-*; *mst Sg.* venture, undertaking

unterfassen *v/t.* (*trennb., hat -ge-*): **j-n ~** take *s.o.*'s arm; **untergefasst gehen** walk arm in arm

unterfliegen *v/t.* (*unreg., untr., hat*); (*Radar etc.*) fly underneath (*od.* below)

unterfordern *v/t.* (*untr., hat*) make too few demands on, not stretch *s.o.* enough; *im Unterricht:* *auch* ask too little of; **in dieser Stufe ist er unterfordert** this level is too easy for him; **sich unterfordert fühlen** feel one is not being stretched (*od.* challenged); **Unterforderung** *f* making too few demands

Unterführung *f* (*für Fußgänger etc.*) subway, *bes. Am.* (*pedestrian*) underpass; *für den Verkehr:* underpass

Unterfunktion *f* *Med.* hypofunction, insufficiency

Untergang *m* **1.** *der Sonne etc.:* setting; **2.** *Naut.* sinking; **3.** *nur Sg.*; *fig.* allmählicher: decline; totaler: downfall;

e-s *Reichs etc.*: fall; *e-r Kultur etc.*: extinction; (*Ruin*) *auch iro.* ruin; *das ist noch sein* ~ *auch umg. fig.* that'll be the ruin of him yet; *dem* ~ *geweiht sein* be doomed; → *Weltuntergang*; **Untergangsstimmung** *f* doomsday atmosphere

untergärig *Adj.* bottom-fermented; *Hefe*: bottom-fermenting

Untergattung *f Bio.* subgenus (*Pl.* subgenera)

untergeben *Adj.*: *j-m* ~ *sein* be subordinate to s.o.; **Untergebene** *m, f; -n, -n* subordinate, inferior, *pej.* underling

untergegangen I. *P.P.* → *untergehen*; **II.** *Adj.* **1.** *Schiff etc.*: sunken; **2.** *Sonne etc.*: set; **3.** *Reich, Kultur etc.*: vanished

untergehakt I. *P.P.* → *unterhaken*; **II.** *Adv.*: ~ *gehen* go arm in arm

untergehen *v/i.* (*unreg., trennb., ist -ge-*) **1.** *Sonne etc.*: set; **2.** *Naut.* go down (*od.* under), sink; *er ging unter und ertrank* he went under (and drowned); **3.** *fig.* decline; *Reich etc.*: fall; *Kultur, Volk*: die out; *Person*: perish; *Welt*: end; *davon geht die Welt nicht unter! umg.* it's not the end of the world(, you know); **4.** (*nicht mehr zu unterscheiden sein*) be lost (*in* + *Dat.* in); *stärker*: be swallowed up (by); *Worte*: *auch* be drowned out (*im Lärm* by the noise); *alles Weitere ging im Jubel unter* the rest was drowned in the general rejoicing; → *untergegangen*

untergeordnet *Adj.* subordinate (+ *Dat.* to); *fig. auch* ancillary (to); *Bedeutung*: secondary, *auch Rolle*: minor; *Ling.* subordinate; *das/er spielt e-e* ~*e Rolle* it/he plays a minor role

Unter|geschoss *n* basement; *zweites/drittes* ~ sub-basement/sub-sub-basement; ~**gestell** *n* **1.** support; *Mot.* underframe; **2.** *umg. fig.* (*Beine*) pins *Pl.*; (*Unterkörper*) undercarriage

Untergewicht *n* underweight; (*5 Kilo*) ~ *haben* be (5 kilos) underweight; **untergewichtig** *Adj.*: ~ *sein* be underweight

untergliedern *v/t.* (*untr., hat*) subdivide (*in* +*Akk.* into); **Untergliederung** *f* subdivision

unter'graben[1] *v/t.* (*unreg., untr., hat*) **1.** undermine, hollow out; **2.** *fig.* (*Gesundheit, Stellung etc.*) undermine; (*Vertrauen etc.*) *auch* erode

'untergraben[2] *v/t.* (*unreg., trennb., hat*) (*Dünger etc.*) dig in

Untergrabung *f fig. des Vertrauens etc.*: undermining

Untergrenze *f* lower limit

Untergriff *m Sport* **1.** *Ringen*: body lock; **2.** *Turnen*: reverse grip

Untergrund *m* **1.** subsoil; (*Fundament*) foundation; *beim Streichen*: ground(ing), undercoat; (*Hintergrund*) background; **2.** *nur Sg.; Pol., Kunst etc.*: underground; *in den* ~ *gehen Pol.* go underground; ~**bahn** *f* underground; *in London: auch* the tube; *Am.* subway; ~**bewegung** *f* underground movement; ~**film** *m* underground film

untergründig *Adj. fig.* under the surface, hidden

Untergrund|kämpfer *m*, ~**kämpferin** *f* resistance fighter, guer(r)illa; ~**literatur** *f* underground literature; ~**musik** *f* underground music; ~**organisation** *f Pol.* underground organization

Untergruppe *f* subgroup

unterhaken *v/t.* (*trennb., hat*): *j-n* ~ take s.o.'s arm; *sich* ~ link arms; → *untergehakt*

unterhalb I. *Präp.* below, under (+ *Gen. od. von s.th.*); **II.** *Adv.* underneath

Unterhalt *m; -(e)s, kein Pl.* **1.** support, maintenance; **2.** (*Lebensunterhalt*) livelihood, living; *für j-s/s-n* ~ *aufkommen* support s.o./o.s.; *s-n* ~ (*selbst*) *verdienen* earn one's (own) living (*durch* by); ~ *zahlen Jur.* pay maintenance (*Am.* alimony; *Anspruch auf* ~ *haben* have a claim for maintenance (*Am.* alimony); *auf* ~ *verklagen* sue for maintenance (*Am.* alimony)

'unterhalten[1] *v/t.* (*unreg., trennb., hat -ge-*) *umg.* hold s.th. underneath

unter'halten[2] (*unreg., untr., hat*) **I.** *v/t.* **1.** (*Institution etc.*) maintain; (*Geschäft etc.*) keep up, keep s.th. going; (*Familie etc.*) support; (*Briefwechsel, Beziehungen*) keep up; (*Konto*) keep, have; *das Feuer* ~ keep the fire burning; **2.** (*j-n*) (*j-m die Zeit vertreiben*) entertain; (*belustigen*) *auch* amuse; *das Publikum mit Musik* ~ entertain the audience by playing some music; **II.** *v/refl.* **1.** talk (*mit j-m über etw. [Akk.]* to s.o. about s.th.); *sich ungestört* ~ have a quiet chat; **2.** (*sich vergnügen*) enjoy o.s., have a good time; **unterhaltend I.** *Part. Präs.* → *unterhalten*[2]; **II.** *Adj.* → *unterhaltsam*; **Unterhalter** *m; -s, -ein guter* ~ *sein* be very entertaining (*od.* amusing; (*interessanter Gesprächspartner*) be a good conversationalist; **unterhaltsam** *Adj.* entertaining; (*lustig*) *auch* amusing

Unterhalts|anspruch *m* maintenance claim; ~**beihilfe** *f* maintenance grant; ~**beitrag** *m* contribution to maintenance

unterhaltsberechtigt *Adj.* entitled to maintenance; **Unterhaltsberechtigte** *m, f; -n, -n* person entitled to maintenance (*Am.* alimony)

Unterhalts|geld *n* maintenance, *Am.* alimony; ~**klage** *f* maintenance action, *Am.* alimony suit; ~**kosten** *Pl.* maintenance (*Am.* alimony) costs

Unterhaltspflicht *f* obligation to pay maintenance (*Am.* alimony); **unterhaltspflichtig** *Adj.* obliged to pay maintenance (*Am.* alimony); **Unterhaltspflichtige** *m, f; -n, -n* person obliged to pay maintenance (*Am.* alimony)

Unterhaltszahlung *f* maintenance (*Am.* alimony) payment

Unterhaltung *f* **1.** *nur Sg.* (*Vergnügen*) entertainment; (*Zerstreuung*) diversion; *zu j-s* ~ for s.o.'s entertainment (*od.* amusement); *seichte* ~ *pej.* mindless entertainment; **2.** (*Gespräch*) conversation, talk, chat; **3.** (*Pflege*) upkeep, maintenance; ~ *diplomatischer Beziehungen* maintenance of diplomatic relations

Unterhaltungs|angebot *n* program(me) of entertainment, the entertainment(s) on offer; ~**branche** *f* entertainment industry; ~**elektronik** *f* home entertainment products *Pl.*, video and audio equipment; ~**film** *m* film made as light entertainment; ~**industrie** *f* entertainment industry; ~**kosten** *Pl.* maintenance (*Am.* alimony) costs; ~**künstler** *m*, ~**künstlerin** *f* entertainer; ~**literatur** *f* light reading (*od.* fiction); ~**musik** *f* light (*od.* popular) music; ~**programm** *n*, ~**sendung** *f* (light) entertainment program(me); ~**wert** *m* entertainment value

unterhandeln *v/i.* (*untr., hat*) negotiate; **Unterhändler** *m*, **Unterhändlerin** *f*

negotiator; **Unterhandlung** *f* negotiations *Pl.*, talks *Pl.*

Unterhaus *n Pol.* **1.** lower house; **2.** *nur Sg.; in GB*: House of Commons; *in den USA*: House of Representatives; ~**abgeordnete** *m, f* member of the lower house, *Brit. etwa* MP, *Am.* congress|man (*od.* -woman), representative; ~**wahl** *f* elections *Pl.* for the lower house; *in GB*: general election; *in US*: congressional election

Unterhemd *n* vest, *Am.* undershirt

unterhöhlen *v/t.* (*untr., hat*) **1.** hollow out; **2.** *fig.* undermine, erode; **Unterhöhlung** *f* **1.** *nur Sg.* hollowing out; **2.** *fig.* undermining, erosion

Unterholz *n; nur Sg.* undergrowth

Unterhose *f*: (*e-e*) ~ (a pair of) underpants *Pl.*; (*Damenslip*) pants *Pl.*, panties *Pl.*; (*e-e*) *lange* ~ (a pair of) longjohns

unterirdisch I. *Adj.* subterranean, underground (*beide auch fig.*); **II.** *Adv.* *verlegen, verlaufen etc.*: underground

unterjochen *v/t.* (*untr., hat*) subjugate; **Unterjochung** *f* subjugation

unterjubeln *v/t.* (*trennb., hat -ge-*); *umg.*: *j-m etw.* ~ (*zuschieben*) pin s.th. on s.o.; (*andrehen*) palm (*od.* fob) s.th. off on s.o.

unterkellern *v/t.* (*untr., hat*) build a cellar (*od.* basement) under; **unterkellert I.** *P.P.* → *unterkellern*; **II.** *Adj. attr. Haus etc.*: with a cellar (*od.* basement); (*voll*) ~ *sein* have a cellar (*od.* basement) (under the whole house); *nicht* ~ *sein* have no cellar (*od.* basement)

Unterkiefer *m Anat.* lower jaw; *Knochen*: mandible; *sein* ~ *fiel herunter umg.* his jaw dropped

Unterklasse *f* **1.** *Bio.* subclass; **2.** *Soziol.* underclass

Unterkleid *n* (full-length) slip

unterkommen *v/i.* (*unreg., trennb., ist -ge-*) find a place (*in* + *Dat.* in); *engS.* (*Unterkunft finden*) find accommodation (in); (*Arbeit finden*) find a job (*bei* with); ~ *bei e-r Firma*: *auch* be taken on (*Am.* be hired) by; *so etwas ist mir noch nicht untergekommen umg.* I've never come across anything like it (*od.* the likes of it) before; **Unterkommen** *n; -s, -, mst Sg.* → *Unterkunft*

Unterkörper *m* lower part of the body

unterkriechen *v/i.* (*unreg., trennb., ist -ge-*) (*Schutz suchen*) find shelter; (*sich verstecken*) hide (away)

unterkriegen *v/t.* (*trennb., hat -ge-*); *umg. nervlich etc.*: get s.o. down; (*bezwingen*) make s.o. knuckle under; *sich nicht* ~ *lassen* not let it get one down; *lass dich nicht* ~*!* don't let it get you down

unterkühlen (*untr., hat*) **I.** *v/t.* undercool; *Tech. auch* supercool; **II.** *v/refl. Med.* get hypothermia; **unterkühlt** *Adj.* undercooled; *Person*: suffering from exposure (*od.* hypothermia); *fig. Beziehungen etc.*: very cool, *stärker*: frosty; (*Wesens-)Art, Stil etc.*: cool, subdued; **Unterkühlung** *f Med.* exposure; *auch im Haus etc.*: hypothermia; *Tech.* undercooling, supercooling; *an* ~ *sterben* die of exposure

Unterkunft *f; -, Unterkünfte* accommodation, lodging; *Mil.* quarters *Pl.*, billet; ~ *und Verpflegung* board and lodging; *j-m* ~ *gewähren* accommodate s.o., put s.o. up; **Unterkunftsverzeichnis** *f* list of places to stay

Unterlage *f; -, -n* **1.** padding; *Tech.*

base, support; **2.** *für Kleinkinder*: waterproof sheet; **3.** *zum Schreiben*: something to write on; (*Schreibtischunterlage*) desk pad; **4.** *fig. finanziell etc.*: basis; **5.** *e-e gute ~ umg. für den Alkohol*: some blotting paper, a good lining for your stomach; **6.** *~n (Akten)* (supporting) documents, records, material *Sg.*; **7.** *Agr. (Wildling)* stock
...unterlagen *Pl. im Subst.*: **Arbeits~** work documents (*od.* papers); **Prüfungs~** exam papers; **Versicherungs~** insurance documents
Unterlagscheibe *f Tech.* washer
Unterland *n; nur Sg.* lowland
Unterlass *m*: **ohne ~** (*unaufhörlich*) incessantly; (*ununterbrochen*) without a letup
unterlassen *v/t. (unreg., untr., hat)* **1.** (*bleiben lassen*) refrain from (+ *Ger.*); (*aufhören mit*) stop (+ *Ger.*); (*Bemerkung*) leave unsaid, (*auch Witz*) drop; **unterlass diese Bemerkungen, bitte** we can do without your comments, thank you *iro.*; **2.** *es ~ zu* (+ *Inf.*) omit (*od.* fail) to (+ *Inf.*); *schuldhaft*: neglect to (+ *Inf.*); **~e Hilfeleistung** *Jur.* failure to give assistance; **Unterlassung** *f* omission; neglect; **auf ~ klagen** *Jur.* apply for an injunction
Unterlassungs|klage *f Jur.* action to obtain an injunction; **~sünde** *f mst iro.* sin of omission
Unterlauf *m -(e)s Flusses etc.*: lower course
unterlaufen¹ (*unreg., untr.*) **I.** *v/t. (hat unterlaufen*); (*Hindernis etc., auch fig.*) avoid, dodge *umg.*; *Sport (Gegner)* charge *s.o.* who is leaping for the ball; **den Ball ~** *Tennis etc.*: misjudge a high ball; **II.** *v/i. (ist)*; *Fehler etc.: (auch j-m ~)* creep in; **mir ist ein Fehler ~** I've made a mistake
unterlaufen² **I.** *P.P.* → **unterlaufen¹**; **II.** *Adj.*: **mit Blut ~** *Auge*: bloodshot; **die Stelle ist bläulich** *etc.* **~** there's a bluish *etc.* discolo(u)ration in that area
Unterleder *n* sole leather
'unterlegen¹ *v/t. (trennb., hat -ge-)* lay (*od.* put) under
unter'legen² *v/t. (untr., hat)* **1.** underlay, line, back (*mit* with); **2.** **mit Musik ~** add music to
unter'legen³ *Adj.*: **j-m ~ sein** be inferior to s.o., not be up to s.o.; **zahlenmäßig ~ sein** be outnumbered, be inferior in numbers; **die ~e Partei** *etc.* the losing party *etc.*; **Unterlegene** *m, f; -n, -n* loser, *umg.* underdog; **Unterlegenheit** *f* inferiority (*gegenüber* to)
Unterleib *m; mst Sg.* abdomen, belly; *bei Frauen: auch* womb area; **e-n Tritt in den ~ kriegen** get a kick in the belly; **Beschwerden im ~ bei Frauen**: gyn(a)ecological problems
Unterleibchen *n südd., schw., österr.* vest, *Am.* undershirt
Unterleibs|geschichte *f euph.* gyn(a)ecological problem; **~krebs** *m Med.* abdominal cancer; *bei Frauen: auch* cancer of the womb; **~operation** *f Med.* gyn(a)ecological operation; **~schmerzen** *Pl.* abdominal pains; (*Menstruationsschmerzen*) period pains
unterliegen *v/i. (unreg., untr., ist)* **1.** be defeated *od.* beaten (+ *Dat.* by); *Sport auch* lose (to); *e-r Versuchung, Krankheit etc.*: succumb (to); **e-r Täuschung ~** be deceived, be duped; **2.** *Gesetzen, Bestimmungen etc.*: be subject to; *Ge-*

bühren etc.: be liable to; *Prinzip, Regel, Trend etc.*: depend on, be governed by; **Schwankungen ~** be subject to fluctuation, fluctuate, vary; **es unterliegt keinem Zweifel, dass** there is no doubt that
Unterlippe *f* lower lip
unterm *Präp. mit Art. umg.* = **unter dem**
untermalen *v/t. (untr., hat)* **1.** (*grundieren*) prime; **2.** *fig. (e-n Hintergrund geben)* provide a background for; (*Farbe geben*) lend some colo(u)r to; **~ mit** (*begleiten mit*) accompany with; (*beleben mit*) liven up with; (*unterstreichen mit*) underscore with; **etw. musikalisch ~** provide a musical accompaniment for s.th.; **etw. mit Gesten ~** reinforce s.th. with gestures; **Untermalung** *f* **1.** (*Hintergrund*) background; (*Begleitung*) accompaniment; **2.** *Kunst*: priming coat
untermauern *v/t. (untr., hat)* underpin, shore up; *fig. (Theorie etc.) auch* substantiate, corroborate; **Untermauerung** *f Tech.* underpinning; *fig. auch* back-up, support
Untermenge *f Math.* subset
untermengen *v/t. (trennb., hat -ge-)* mix in, add; **~ unter** *od.* **in** (+ *Akk.*) mix into, add to
Untermensch *m* **1.** *pej.* psychopath; **2.** *pej. Nazideutsch*: subhuman
Untermenü *n EDV* submenu
Untermiete *f nur Sg.* subtenancy; **in** *od.* **zur ~ wohnen** live in lodgings, *Am.* rent a room; **j-n in** *od.* **zur ~ nehmen** sublet to s.o.; **in e-r Privatwohnung**: take s.o. as a lodger; **Untermieter** *m*, **Untermieterin** *f* subtenant, lodger
unterminieren *v/t. (untr., hat) auch fig.* undermine; **Unterminierung** *f* undermining
untermischen *v/t. (trennb., hat -ge-)* mix in **to unter** + *Akk.*, **in** + *Akk.*), add (to)
untern *Präp. mit Art. umg.* = **unter den**
unternehmen *v/t. (unreg., untr., hat)* do; (*durchführen*) undertake; **e-n Ausflug ~** go on (*od.* make) a trip; **lasst uns heute etwas ~** let's do something today; **sie ~ viel zusammen** they do a lot together; **e-n Versuch ~** make (*od.* launch) an attempt; **er unternahm nichts** he did nothing; **dagegen muss man etwas ~** something has got to be done about it; **so geht es nicht weiter - wir müssen etwas ~** it can't go on like this, we've got to do something
Unternehmen *n; -s, -* **1.** *Wirts.* (*Betrieb*) firm, (*business*) enterprise, business, concern, company; **privates/ staatliches ~** private (*od.* privately owned) / state-owned (*od.* -run) concern; **ein ~ gründen** set up a business; **2.** (*Vorhaben*) enterprise, undertaking; (*Projekt*) project; *Mil.* operation; **ein gewagtes ~** a bold (*bzw.* risky) undertaking; **bei dem ~ kamen vier Menschen ums Leben** four people were killed during the operation
Unternehmens|... *siehe auch* **Firmen...**; **~berater** *m*, **~beraterin** *f Wirts.* management consultant; **~beratung** *f* management consultancy; **~bewertung** *f Wirts.* due diligence (analysis, report, process *etc.*); **~form** *f* (*od.* type) of enterprise; **~gründung** *f* founding of a business (*od.* firm); **~gruppe** *f* group; **~leitung** *f* management; **~politik** *f* business policy; *e-r Firma etc.*: company policy; **~spitze** *f Wirts.* top management; **~sprecher** *m*,

~sprecherin *f* company spokes|man (*bzw.* -woman, *bes. Am.* -person); **~standort** *m* business location, location of a (*od.* the) business (*od.* company *etc.*); **~struktur** *f* structure of an (*od.* the) enterprise
unternehmensweit *Adj.*: **~es Netzwerk** *EDV* corporate network
Unternehmer *m; -s, -; Wirts.* entrepreneur, (big *umg.*) businessman; (*Eigentümer e-r Firma*) owner; (*Arbeitgeber*) employer; (*Industrieller*) industrialist; **die ~ Koll.** the business community *Sg.*; **Arbeiter und ~** workers and bosses
unternehmerfreundlich *Adj.* business-friendly
Unternehmergeist *m nur Sg.* spirit of enterprise, entrepreneurial spirit, entrepreneurialism
Unternehmerin *f; -, -nen; Wirts.* entrepreneur, businesswoman; (*Eigentümerin e-r Firma*) owner; (*Arbeitgeberin*) employer; (*Industrielle*) industrialist
unternehmerisch *Wirts.* **I.** *Adj.* entrepreneurial, enterprise ...; **~e Leistung** (great) business achievement; **~es Risiko** business risk; **II.** *Adv.* **denken** *etc.*: entrepreneurially
Unternehmer|seite *f* the employers' side; **auf** *od.* **von der ~** from the employers' side; **~tum** *n; -s, kein Pl.*; *Wirts.* **1.** entrepreneurship; **2.** (*die Unternehmer*) the business community, the employers *Pl.*; **freies ~** free enterprise; **~verband** *m* employers' association
Unternehmung *f* **1.** (*Ausflug etc.*) activity; **keine Zeit für ~en** no time to do things; **2.** *Wirts.* → **Unternehmen**
Unternehmungs|geist *m nur Sg.* (spirit of) enterprise, initiative, get-up-and-go *umg.*; **~lust** *f nur Sg.* (spirit of) enterprise, initiative, get-up-and-go *umg.*; **voller ~** with lots of initiative (*od.* get-up-and-go *umg.*)
unternehmungslustig *Adj.* enterprising; (*aktiv*) active; (*verwegen*) adventurous; **sich ~ fühlen** (*od.* **~ sein**) feel *od.* be in the mood to do something; (*abenteuerlustig*) feel *od.* be adventurous; **du wirkst so ~** you come across as so dynamic
Unteroffizier *m* (*abgek.* **Uffz.**) *Mil.* non-commissioned officer, NCO; *Dienstgrad*: sergeant; *Flug.* corporal, *Am.* airman 1st class; **~ vom Dienst** (*abgek.* **UvD**) duty NCO
unterordnen (*trennb., hat -ge-*) **I.** *v/refl.* submit (+ *Dat.* to); **er kann sich nicht ~** he can't take orders; **II.** *v/t.* subordinate (+ *Dat.* to); → **untergeordnet**; **unterordnend I.** *Part. Präs.* → **unterordnen**; **II.** *Adj. Gram., Konjunktion*: subordinating; **Unterordnung** *f* **1.** subordination; **2.** *Bio.* suborder
Unterorganisation *f* subsidiary organization
Unterpfand *n lit.* pledge
unterpflügen *v/t. (trennb., hat -ge-)* plough (*Am.* plow) s.th. under (*auch fig.*)
Unterprima *f Päd., altm.* eighth form (*Am.* grade) *in a German secondary school, Brit. etwa* Lower Sixth, *Am. etwa* high-school junior or senior year
unterprivilegiert *Adj.* underprivileged; **die Unterprivilegierten** the underprivileged (*Pl.*)
Unterpunkt *m* **1.** subordinate point; **2.** *unter e-m Buchstaben*: dot underneath

Unterprogramm *n EDV* subroutine
unterqueren *v/t.* (*untr., hat*) pass underneath
Unterredung *f* talk; *mit j-m e-e ~ führen* have talks (*od.* a talk) with s.o.
unterrepräsentiert *Adj.* under-represented
Unterricht *m*; *-(e)s, kein Pl.*; *Päd.* instruction, teaching; (*Stunden*) lessons *Pl.*; *Schule: auch* classes *Pl.*; *~ geben* teach, give lessons; *Schule: auch* hold classes; *~ nehmen* have lessons (*in + Dat.* in); *der ~ in Deutsch/Informatik etc.* German/IT lessons (*od.* classes); *der ~ beginnt/endet um* classes *Pl.* begin/end at; *morgen fällt der ~ aus* there will be no class (*od.* lessons) tomorrow; *in e-m bestimmten Fach:* there will be no class (*od.* lesson) tomorrow; *es fällt zu viel ~ aus* too much teaching time is being lost; *am ~ teilnehmen* take part in classes (*od.* lessons); *den ~ stören* be a nuisance in class; *dem ~ fernbleiben* stay away from class (*od.* lessons); *den ~ schwänzen umg.* play truant; *j-s ~ übernehmen* take over s.o.'s class; *guter/schlechter ~* good/bad teaching
unterrichten (*untr., hat*) **I.** *vt/i.* **1.** teach, be a teacher; (*Stunden geben*) give lessons; *j-n in etw.* (*Dat.*) *~* teach s.o. how to do s.th.; *in e-r Technik etc.:* give s.o. instruction in s.th.; *sie unterrichtet an e-r Gesamtschule* she teaches in a comprehensive school; *ich unterrichte Sport und Englisch* I teach PE and English; *sechs Stunden die Woche ~* teach six classes a week; *die 11. Klasse in Physik ~* teach physics to class 11; **2.** (*informieren*) inform (*von, über + Akk.* of); *j-n laufend ~* keep s.o. informed (*od.* posted); *falsch ~* misinform; **II.** *v/refl.: sich ~ über* (+ *Akk.*) inform o.s. about; acquaint o.s. with; *unterrichtet sein* be (well-)informed (*über + Akk.* about)
Unterrichts|angebot *n Päd.* subjects taught; *~ausfall* *m* cancel(l)ation of a class (*bzw.* of classes); *es gibt zu viele Unterrichtsausfälle* too many classes are being cancel(l)ed; *~beginn* *m* starting time for school (*bzw.* classes); *~ ist um 8.00* school starts at 8.00 (*Am.* 8:00); *~betrieb* *m* classes *Pl.*, lessons *Pl.*; *es herrscht ganz normaler ~* classes are being held entirely as normal; *~einheit* *f* teaching unit; *~erfahrung* *f* teaching (*od.* classroom) experience; *~fach* *n* (teaching) subject; *~film* *m* educational film; *~form* *f* form of teaching; *neue ~en* new forms of teaching
unterrichtsfrei *Adj.*: *~e Stunde* free period; *~er Tag* day off school; *morgen haben wir ~* there are no classes (*od.* lessons) tomorrow
Unterrichts|gegenstand *m Päd.* subject, topic; *~material* *n* teaching materials *Pl.*; *~methode* *f* teaching method; *~mittel* *Pl.* teaching aids; *~raum* *m* classroom; *~schluss* *m* end of school (*bzw.* classes); *~sprache* *f* language of instruction; *~ ist Englisch auch* classes are conducted in English; *~stoff* *m* subject matter, topic *for a class*; *~stunde* *f* lesson; *Schule: auch* class, period; *fünf ~n in Geschichte* five periods of history; *~vertretung* *f* cover(ing) (for a teacher who is absent); *~vorbereitung* *f* teaching preparation; *schriftliche ~* written preparation (for a class); *~zeit* *f* teaching time; *~ziel* *n* teaching objective; *das ~*

erreichen/verfehlen achieve / fail to achieve one's objective in one's teaching; *~zwecke Pl.: zu ~n* for teaching purposes
Unterrichtung *f* (*Unterweisung*) instruction; (*Informierung*) informing
Unterrock *m* slip
unterrühren *v/t.* (*trennb., hat -ge-*) stir in
unters *Präp. mit Art. umg.* = *unter das*
untersagen *v/t.* (*untr., hat*) *amtlich:* prohibit; *gesetzlich:* outlaw; *j-m ~, etw. zu tun* order s.o. not to do s.th., forbid s.o. to do s.th.; *amtlich:* prohibit s.o. from doing s.th.; *j-m das Autofahren etc. ~* ban s.o. from driving *etc.*; *er hat es mir untersagt auch* he won't let me (do it); *das Betreten des Raumes ist strengstens untersagt* it is strictly forbidden to enter the room; **Untersagung** *f* prohibition
Untersatz *m* mat; *für Gläser:* coaster; *für Blumentöpfe:* saucer; *fahrbarer ~ umg.* wheels
Unterschallgeschwindigkeit *f* subsonic speed
unterschätzen *v/t.* (*untr., hat*) underestimate, (*Fähigkeiten etc.*) *auch* underrate; **Unterschätzung** *f* underestimation; underrating
unterscheidbar *Adj.* distinguishable
unterscheiden (*unreg., untr., hat*) **I.** *vt/i.* distinguish (*zwischen + Dat.* between), make a distinction (between); (*erkennen*) *aus e-r Menge, aus der Ferne etc.:* distinguish, make out; *etw. ~ von ... auch* tell s.th. from ...; *sie sind kaum zu ~* you can hardly tell the difference; *Zwillinge etc.:* you can hardly tell them apart; *zwischen A und B ~ können* be able to distinguish (*od.* to tell the difference) between A and B; *das unterscheidet ihn von ...* that sets him apart from ...; **II.** *v/refl.* differ (*von* from); *sich ~ dadurch, dass* differ in (+ *Ger.*); *wie od. worin unterscheidet sich A von B?* what's the difference between A and B?, in what way(s) are A and B different (*-od.* do A and B differ)?; *A und B ~ sich nicht* there's no difference between A and B; **unterscheidend I.** *Part. Präs.* → *unterscheiden*; **II.** *Adj.* distinctive, characteristic; *Math.* differentiating; **Unterscheidung** *f* differentiation; (*Unterschied*) difference, distinction
Unterscheidungs|merkmal *n* distinguishing (*od.* distinctive) feature *od.* mark; *~vermögen* *n* powers *Pl.* of discernment (*od.* distinction)
Unterschenkel *m Anat.* lower leg
Unterschicht *f* **1.** *Geol.* substratum; **2.** *Soziol.* lower class(es *Pl.*)
'unterschieben¹ *v/t.* (*unreg., trennb., hat -ge-*) **1.** push *s.th.* under(neath) (+ *Dat. s.th., s.o.*); **2.** *fig.: j-m etw. ~* (*in böser Absicht zuschieben*) foist s.th. (off) on s.o.; (*unterstellen*) (falsely) attribute s.th. to s.o., (wrongly) accuse s.o. of (doing) s.th.; *j-m ein Kind ~* father a child on s.o., claim that s.o. is the father of a child; *man wollte ihr die Schuld an dem Fehler ~* they tried to blame the mistake on her
unter'schieben² *v/t.* (*unreg., untr., hat*): *j-m etw. ~* (*in böser Absicht zuschieben*) foist s.th. (off) on s.o.; (*unterstellen*) (falsely) attribute s.th. to s.o., (wrongly) accuse s.o. of (doing) s.th.; **Unterschiebung** *f* (wrongful) accusation
Unterschied *m*; *-(e)s, -e* difference, dis-

tinction; *e-n ~ machen* make a distinction, distinguish; (*auch unterschiedlich behandeln*) discriminate (*zwischen + Dat.* between); *ein feiner ~* a fine (*od.* subtle) distinction, a subtle difference; *ich sehe keinen ~* I can't see any (*od.* the) difference; *zum ~ von* unlike *s.th. od. s.o.*, as distinct from, in contrast to; *ohne ~* indiscriminately; (*ausnahmslos*) without exception; *das ist ein großer ~* that makes a big difference; *der ~ besteht darin, dass* the difference lies in the fact that; *das macht e-n/keinen ~* that makes a/no difference; *der kleine ~ umg. hum.* the difference between the sexes; (*Penis*) willy; *es lebe der kleine ~ umg. hum.* vive la différence; → *Tag¹* 1
unterschiedlich I. *Adj.* different; (*voneinander abweichend*) varying, varied; *~ sein* (*nicht einheitlich*) vary; *mit ~em Erfolg* with varying degrees of success; **II.** *Adv.* (*verschieden, anders*) differently; *~ groß/gut/hell etc.* varying in size/quality/ brightness *etc.*, of varying size/quality/brightness *etc.*; *~ groß/gut sein auch* vary in size/quality; *~ reagieren* vary in their *etc.* reactions, have varying reactions; *es wurde ganz ~ aufgenommen* reactions (to it) varied greatly; *wir beurteilen das ziemlich ~* our views on that differ considerably; *~ behandeln* treat differently; *engS.* (*benachteiligen*) discriminate against; **Unterschiedlichkeit** *f* (*Unterschied*) difference (+ *Gen.* between); (*Uneinheitlichkeit*) variableness, varying nature (+ *Gen.* of); **unterschiedslos I.** *Adj.* indiscriminate; **II.** *Adv.* indiscriminately; (*ausnahmslos*) *auch* without exception
'unterschlagen¹ *v/t.* (*unreg., trennb., hat -ge-*) (*Beine*) cross; (*Bettlaken*) tuck in
unter'schlagen² *v/t.* (*unreg., untr., hat*); (*Geld*) embezzle; (*Brief*) intercept; (*Beweisstück, Testament*) suppress; *fig.* (*verheimlichen*) hold back, keep quiet about, suppress; *den Rest unterschlug sie ihm* she kept the rest from him; **Unterschlagung** *f* embezzlement; *fig.* suppression
Unterschlupf *m*; *-(e)s, -e*; *mst Sg.*; (*Schlupfwinkel*) hiding place, hideout *umg.*; (*Obdach*) shelter, refuge; *weitS.* somewhere to go; **unterschlüpfen** *v/i.* (*trennb., ist -ge-*) *umg.* take shelter; (*sich verstecken*) hide (away); *~ in* (+ *Dat.*) (*unterkommen*) find a place in
unterschreiben *vt/i.* (*unreg., untr., hat*) sign; *fig.* subscribe to; *mit vollem Namen ~* sign one's full name
unterschreiten *v/t.* (*unreg., untr., hat*) remain under, fall short of; *auch Temperatur:* fall below; **Unterschreitung** *f* remaining below, falling short
Unterschrift *f* signature; *seine ~ unter einen Vertrag etc. setzen* put one's signature to a contract *etc.*, sign one's name on (*od.* under) a contract *etc.*; *zur ~ vorlegen* present for signature; *~en sammeln* collect signatures (for a petition); *es trägt s-e ~* it has his signature on it, it bears his signature; *fig.* it bears his stamp, his smell is all over it *umg. pej.*
Unterschriften|aktion *f* petition; *e-e ~ durchführen* get up a petition; *~liste* *f* list of signatures; *~mappe* *f* signature folder; *~sammlung* *f* → *Unterschriftenaktion*
unterschriftsberechtigt *Adj.* authorized to sign

Unterschrifts|fälschung f forging of a signature (od. signatures); **~probe** f specimen signature

unterschriftsreif Adj. ready for signature

unterschwellig Adj. underlying; Psych. subliminal, sub-threshold

Unterseeboot n Naut. submarine; siehe auch **U-Boot(...)**

unterseeisch Adj. submarine

Unterseite f underside, bottom

Untersekunda f Päd., altm. sixth year in a German secondary school

unter'setzen[1] v/t. (untr., hat); Tech. reduce; Etech. step down; (durchsetzen, mischen) mix s.th. with s.th.

'untersetzen[2] v/t. (trennb., hat -ge-) put (od. place) under(neath); **Untersetzer** m; -s, - für Gläser etc.: coaster; für Blumentöpfe: saucer

untersetzt I. P.P. → **untersetzen**[1]; II. Adj. Person: stocky, thickset

Unterspannung f Etech. undervoltage

unterspülen v/t. (untr., hat); (Häuser etc.) wash away the foundations of; (Ufer etc.) hollow out; **Unterspülung** f washing away the foundations; des Ufers etc.: hollowing out

unterst... Adj. lowest, bottom; das Unterste zuoberst kehren turn everything upside down

Unterstaatssekretär m Pol. undersecretary of state

Unterstadt f lower part of a (bzw. the) town

Unterstand m shelter; Mil. auch dugout

unter'stehen[1] (unreg., untr., hat) I. v/i.: j-m od. j-s Aufsicht ~ be under s.o., be answerable to s.o.; Wirts. und amtlich: auch report to s.o.; **e-m Gesetz** ~ be subject to a law; **e-r Behörde** etc. ~ come under an authority etc.; II. v/refl. dare; **sich** ~ **zu** (+ Inf.) dare (to) (+ Inf.), have the audacity (od. nerve, cheek) to (+ Inf.); ~ **Sie sich!** don't you dare!; **was** ~ **Sie sich?** how dare you?

'unterstehen[2] v/i. (unreg., trennb., ist -ge-) shelter, take shelter

'unterstellen[1] (trennb., hat -ge-) I. v/t. 1. unter etw.: put (od. place) under(neath); 2. (unterbringen) put (in + Dat. in[to]); (dalassen) leave (**bei j-m** at s.o.'s place); (lagern) store (**bei** at); II. v/refl. zum Schutz: shelter, take shelter (**vor** + Dat. from)

unter'stellen[2] v/t. (untr., hat) 1. negativ: j-m ~, dass ... allege (od. imply, insinuate) that s.o. ...; **j-m etw.** ~ Handlung: allege that s.o. has done (zeitneutral: is capable of doing) s.th.; (unlautere Motive etc.) allege (od. imply) that s.o. has s.th.; **j-m böse Absichten** ~ impute bad intentions to s.o.; 2. (vorläufig annehmen) suppose, assume; ~ **wir einmal** let's assume (for the sake of argument); **wenn man dies unterstellt** granting that this is (od. was) so; 3. j-m etw./j-n ~ put s.o. in charge of s.th./s.o.; **j-m unterstellt werden** be placed under s.o.('s command Mil.); **Unterstellung** f 1. (Behauptung) allegation, insinuation; **e-e böswillige** ~ a malicious insinuation; 2. (das Unterstellen) being placed under, subordination (to)

unterstreichen v/t. (unreg., untr., hat) underline, underscore; fig. (betonen) auch emphasize; **die Fehler rot** ~ underline the mistakes in red; **Unterstreichung** f underlining, underscoring; fig. auch emphasizing; **Unter-**

strich m Tastaturzeichen, in E-Mail-Adressen: underscore, underline

Unterströmung f undercurrent (auch fig.); Geol. underflow

Unterstufe f Päd. lower (Am. grade) school, junior (Am. lower) grades Pl.

unterstützen v/t. (untr., hat) support; (Kandidaten etc.) auch back up; (helfen) auch finanziell: assist, aid (**bei** in); (fördern) auch promote; (Wirtschaft etc.) support, bolster; (Antrag, Plan, Projekt etc.) support, give s.th. one's backing; **mit Rat und Tat** ~ give advice and support to, support s.o. in both word and deed geh.; **den Heilungsprozess** ~ assist the healing process; **Unterstützer** m; -s, -, **Unterstützerin** f; -, -nen supporter, backer; **Unterstützung** f support; backing; (Hilfe) auch finanzielle: assistance, aid; finanzielle staatliche: subsidy, (government) aid od. grant; **zur** ~ (+ Gen.) in support of; ~ **beziehen** be on social security; **ein Mittel zur** ~ **der Abwehrkräfte** a drug that reinforces the body's defen|ces (Am. -ses)

unterstützungs|bedürftig Adj. needy; **~berechtigt** Adj. entitled to relief

Untersuch m; -s, -e; schw. examination, inquiry, investigation

untersuchen v/t. (untr., hat) examine (auch Med.); (inspizieren) inspect; (e-n Fall etc.) inquire (od. look) into, investigate (alle auch Jur. und wissenschaftlich); Chem. und weitS. analy|se (Am. -ze); (testen) test (**auf** + Akk. for); **auf Schadstoffe/Fingerabdrücke** etc. **hin** test s.th. for harmful substances / check (od. examine) s.th. for fingerprints; **auf** od. **nach Waffen** etc. ~ search (od. for weapons etc.; **s-e Zähne** etc. **gründlich** ~ **lassen** have one's teeth etc. thoroughly examined (od. checked), have a thorough examination (od. checkup) done on one's teeth etc.

Untersuchung f examination; Med. auch checkup; e-s Sachverhalts: inquiry (+ Gen. into), investigation (of) (beide auch Jur.); (Durchsuchung von Gepäck etc.) search; (Probe) test; Chem. und weitS. analysis (Pl. analyses) (of); (Studie) study (of); ~ (Forschung) research; **amtliche** ~ public inquiry; ~ **e-s Stoffes** etc. **auf etw.** (Akk.) **hin** analysis of a substance etc. for s.th.; ~ **von Blut/Urin** etc. **auf** (+ Akk.) blood/urine etc. test for ...

Untersuchungs|ausschuss m investigating committee; **~beamte** m, f investigating official; **~befund** m Med. results Pl. of the test, (test) findings Pl.; **~behörde** f investigating authority; **~bericht** m inquiry report; **~ergebnis** n result of an (bzw. the) investigation; **~gefangene** m, f prisoner on remand (Am. awaiting trial); **~gefängnis** n remand prison, Am. jail, detention center; **~haft** f (abgek. U-Haft) custody, detention (pending trial), Am. pretrial detention; **in** ~ **sein** od. **sitzen** be on remand (Am. in custody awaiting trial); **in** ~ **nehmen** commit s.o. for trial; **~häftling** m prisoner on remand (Am. awaiting trial); **~kommission** f board (od. committee) of inquiry; **~methode** f method of inquiry (od. investigation); **~richter** m, **~richterin** f examining magistrate; **~stuhl** m Med. gyn(a)ecological chair; **~verfahren** n 1. Jur. investigative procedure; 2. Med. etc. procedure for examining; **~zimmer** n in einer Arztpra-

xis: surgery, Am. doctor's office

Untertagebau m Bergb. underground mining

untertags Adv. schw., österr. during the day, in the daytime

Untertan m; -s und -en, -en subject; **Menschen zu** ~**en erziehen** educate people to be underlings; **untertan** Adj. präd. subject (+ Dat. to); **j-n** ~ **machen** subject s.o. (+ Dat. to); **sich die Natur** ~ **machen** subjugate nature (to o.s.); **untertänig** pej. I. Adj. subservient; **Euer** ~**ster Diener** altm. od. hum. your most obedient servant; II. Adv.: **j-n** ~(**st**) **bitten** mst hum. humbly beg s.o.; **Untertanengeist** m nur Sg.; pej. slave spirit; (Untertänigkeit) subservience; **Untertänigkeit** f pej. subservience; **Untertanin** f; -, -nen subject

untertariflich Adj. und Adv.; Wirts. under the agreed rate; ~ **bezahlt werden** be paid less than the agreed rate

Untertasse f saucer; → **fliegend** II

untertauchen (trennb.) I. v/i. (ist -ge-) 1. dive; U-Boot: submerge; (Ertrinkender) go under; 2. fig. disappear; Verbrecher etc.: go underground, go into hiding; II. v/t. (hat -ge-); (j-n) duck; (Gegenstand) submerge, immerse

Unterteil n lower part, bottom (auch von Bikini etc.), base

unterteilen v/t. (untr., hat); (aufteilen) divide (up) (**in** +Akk. into); (gliedern) subdivide (into); **der Schrank ist in viele Fächer unterteilt** the cupboard is divided up into many compartments; **Unterteilung** f division (**in** + Akk. into); (Gliederung) subdivision (into)

Untertertia f Päd., altm. fourth year in a German secondary school

Untertitel m subtitle; Film: auch caption; **Original(fassung) mit deutschen** ~**n** original version with German subtitles; **untertiteln** v/t. (untr., hat) subtitle, give subtitles to

Unterton m undertone (auch fig.); **e-n ironischen** ~ **haben** have an ironical undertone

untertourig Mot. I. Adj. attr. ... at low revs; II. Adv. at low revs

untertreiben vt/i. (unreg., untr., hat) understate, play down; **er untertreibt gern** he's fond of understatement; **das ist untertrieben** that's an understatement; **Untertreibung** f understatement

untertunneln v/t. (untr., hat) tunnel under (od. through); **untertunnelt sein/werden** have a tunnel made (od. dug, od. driven) under (od. through) it; **die Frankfurter Innenstadt wird untertunnelt** a tunnel is being built (od. dug, od. driven) under Frankfurt city centre (Am. under downtown Frankfurt); **Untertunnelung** f 1. (Tunnel) tunnel; 2. Vorgang: tunnel(l)ing under

untervermieten vt/i. (untr., hat) sublet; **wir dürfen nicht** ~ we're not allowed to sublet; **Untervermieter** m, **Untervermieterin** f subletter; **Untervermietung** f subletting

unterversichern v/t. (untr., hat) underinsure; **unterversichert** I. P.P. → **unterversichern**; II. Adj. underinsured; **Unterversicherung** f underinsurance

unterversorgt Adj. undersupplied; **Unterversorgung** f undersupply(ing)

Unterverzeichnis n EDV subdirectory

unterwandern v/t. (untr., hat); Pol. infiltrate; **Unterwanderung** f infiltration

Unterwäsche f 1. nur Sg. underwear;

für Damen: *auch* lingerie, undies *umg.*; **in ~** in one's underwear; **sich bis auf die ~ ausziehen** strip to one's underwear; **2.** *umg. Mot.* undercar wash

Unterwasser|aufnahme *f* underwater photograph; *bei Filmen*: underwater shot; **~forscher** *m*, **~forscherin** *f* (deep-sea) oceanographer; **~fotografie** *f nur Sg.* underwater photography; **~jagd** *f* subaqua (*od.* underwater) fishing; **~kamera** *f* underwater camera; **~massage** *f* underwater massage; **~station** *f* undersea research station (*od.* laboratory); **~welt** *f* submarine world

unterwegs *Adv.* on the (*od.* one's *od.* its) way; (*auf dem Weg, beim Transport etc.*) *auch* en route; *beruflich etc.*: away; *im Auto*: *auch* on the road; (*außer Haus*) out (and about); **ich war gestern den ganzen Tag ~** I was out and about (*gehetzt*: I was rushing around from one place to another) all day yesterday; **der Brief** *etc.* **ist ~** the letter is on its way; **~ ist mir etw. eingefallen** I had an idea on the way (here *od.* there); **von ~ anrufen** phone (*bes. Am.* call) up while one is away; **bei ihr ist was Kleines** *etc.* **~** *umg. euph.* she's expecting

unterweisen *v/t.* (*unreg., untr., hat*) instruct (**in** + *Dat.* in); **Unterweisung** *f* instruction

Unterwelt *f* underworld (*auch fig.*)

unterwerfen (*unreg., untr., hat*) **I.** *v/t.* (*Volk, Land etc.*) subject (**s-r Herrschaft** to one's rule), subdue, subjugate; **II.** *v/refl.* submit (+ *Dat.* to); **Unterwerfung** *f* subjection, subjugation; submission; → **unterwerfen**; **unterworfen I.** *P.P.* → **unterwerfen**; **II.** *Adj.*: **e-r Sache ~ sein** be subject to s.th.; **Launen ~ sein** *auch* be moody; **Änderungen ~ sein** be subject to alteration *Sg.*

unterwürfig *pej.* **I.** *Adj.* subservient, obsequious; **II.** *Adv.* lächeln, sich verhalten *etc.*: obsequiously; **Unterwürfigkeit** *f* subservience, obsequiousness

Unterzahl *f nur Sg.*: **in ~** *Sport etc.*: with a player (*bzw.* with players) off the field (*bzw.* the ice), with a player (*bzw.* X players) short; *Fußball*: with only ten *etc.* men

unterzeichnen *vt/i.* (*untr., hat*) sign; **Unterzeichner** *m*, **Unterzeichnerin** *f* the undersigned; *e-s Vertrags*: signatory; **Unterzeichnerstaat** *m* signatory state; **Unterzeichnete** *m, f* the undersigned; **Unterzeichnung** *f* signing

Unterzentrum *n* subcent|re (*Am.* -er)

Unterzeug *n umg.* underthings *Pl.*

'unterziehen¹ *v/t.* (*unreg., trennb., hat -ge-*) **1.** (*Kleider*) put on underneath; **2.** *Gastr.* (*Eigelb, Creme etc.*) fold in; **3.** *Archit.* (*Träger etc.*) put in (underneath)

unter'ziehen² (*unreg., untr., hat*) **I.** *v/refl.*: **sich etw.** (*Dat.*) **~** *e-r Operation etc.*: undergo, have; *e-r Prüfung*: take; *e-m Training, e-r Arbeit etc.*: do; **sich der Mühe ~ zu** (+ *Inf.*) take the trouble to (+ *Inf.*); **II.** *v/t. e-r Kontrolle, e-m Verhör etc.*: put through, submit to; **e-r Prüfung ~** *auch* test, examine; **e-m Verhör ~** *auch* interrogate

Unterzucker *m*, **Unterzuckerung** *f Med.* hypoglyc(a)emia

Untiefe *f* (*seichte Stelle*) shallow, shoal; *lit.* (*große Tiefe*) abyss

Untier *n* monster (*auch fig.*)

Untote *m, f* one of the undead; (*Zom-*

bie) zombie; (*Vampir*) vampire; **die ~n** the undead

untragbar *Adj.* intolerable; *Kosten, Preise*: prohibitive; **für s-e Partei** *etc.* **~ werden** become a liability to one's party *etc.*

untrainiert *Adj.* untrained

untrennbar I. *Adj.* inseparable; **II.** *Adv.*: **~ verbunden** inseparably bound up (**mit** with); **Untrennbarkeit** *f* inseparability

untreu *Adj.* unfaithful, disloyal (+ *Dat.* to); **~ werden** (+ *Dat.*) be unfaithful to; *fig.* break faith with; (*s-n Grundsätzen, e-r Politik etc.*) abandon, give up; **sich** (*Dat.*) **selbst ~ werden** be untrue to oneself; **Untreue** *f* **1.** unfaithfulness, disloyalty; *bes. eheliche*: infidelity (*alle*: **gegenüber** to[ward(s)]); **2.** *Jur.* embezzlement

untrinkbar *Adj.* undrinkable

untröstlich *Adj.* inconsolable, disconsolate; *weitS. auch* deeply sorry; **ich bin ~!** *über m-n Fehler etc.*: how can I ever forgive myself

untrüglich *Adj. Anzeichen, Symptom etc.*: unmistakable; *stärker: attr.* sure; **~es Gefühl für etw.** unerring instinct for s.th.

untüchtig *Adj.* incapable, incompetent

Untugend *f* bad habit; (*Laster*) vice

untypisch *Adj.* atypical (**für** of), out of character (for)

unübel *Adj. umg.*: **gar nicht so ~** not so bad, not bad at all

unüberbietbar *Adj.* unparalleled, hard to beat *umg.*

unüberbrückbar *Adj. fig. Kluft etc.*: unbridgeable; *Gegensätze*: irreconcilable, insurmountable

unüberhörbar I. *Adj.* distinct, *präd. auch* loud and clear; **es war ~** *auch* you couldn't miss it; **II.** *Adv.* distinctly

unüberlegt I. *Adj.* ill-considered; (*übereilt*) rash; **etw. Unüberlegtes tun** do s.th. rash; **II.** *Adv.* handeln *etc.*: without thinking (*od.* considering); **Unüberlegtheit** *f* rashness; *konkret*: rash act (*od.* action)

unüberschaubar *Adj.* → **unübersehbar** 1, 2, **unübersichtlich**

unübersehbar *Adj.* **1.** immense, vast; **2.** *Folgen etc.*: incalculable; **3.** *attr. Fehler etc.*: glaring

unübersichtlich *Adj.* **1.** *Gelände etc.*: broken; **~e Kurve** blind corner; **die Kreuzung** *etc.* **ist ~** it's difficult (*od.* impossible) to see (the traffic) at that crossing *etc.*; **2.** *fig.* (*unklar*) unclear; (*verworren*) confusing; **Unübersichtlichkeit** *f* **1.** *e-s Geländes etc.*: brokenness; **2.** (*Unklarheit*) confusingness, confusion

unübertrefflich I. *Adj.* unsurpassable, matchless; **II.** *Adv.* gut, witzig *etc.*: supremely; *noch stärker*: superlatively; **unübertroffen** *Adj.* unsurpassed, unmatched

unüberwindbar, **unüberwindlich** *Adj.* invincible; *Schwierigkeit, Gegensätze etc.*: insurmountable, insuperable

unüblich *Adj.* unusual, not usual; **es ist ~ zu** (+ *Inf.*) *auch* you don't usually, it's not usual to

unumgänglich *Adj.* unavoidable; (*unausweichlich*) inevitable; (*notwendig*) indispensable; *auch zu tun etc.*: absolutely essential, imperative; **Unumgänglichkeit** *f* unavoidability, inevitability; (*unbedingte Notwendigkeit*) indispensability, indispensable nature (+ *Gen.* of)

unumkehrbar *Adj.* irreversible

unumschränkt I. *Adj.* unlimited; *Pol. Macht etc.*: absolute; **II.** *Adv.* herrschen *etc.*: with absolute power

unumstößlich *Adj. Tatsache etc.*: irrefutable, incontrovertible; *Entscheidung etc.*: irrevocable

unumstritten *Adj.* undisputed

unumwunden I. *Adj.* (*ehrlich*) frank; *Bekenntnis, Anerkennung etc.*: open; **II.** *Adv.* (*direkt, offen*) point-blank, straight out; **~ zugeben** admit frankly (*od.* openly)

ununterbrochen I. *Adj.* uninterrupted; *Linie, Reihe etc.*: *auch* unbroken; (*ständig*) continuous; (*unaufhörlich*) incessant; **in ~er Reihenfolge** in an unbroken series; **II.** *Adv.* uninterruptedly; continuously; incessantly; **er hat ~ geschrien** *etc. auch* he wouldn't stop screaming *etc.*; **sie redet ~** she never stops talking; **~ im Einsatz sein** be continuously on duty

unveränderbar *Adj.* unchangeable, unalterable; **unveränderlich** *Adj.* unchanging; *auch Ling.* invariable; (*beständig*) constant, stable; *EDV Daten*: permanent; **Unveränderlichkeit** *f* unchangingness; stability; **unverändert I.** *Adj.* unchanged, *präd. auch* (just) as it was; **ihr Zustand ist seit Tagen ~** her condition has not changed (*od.* has remained unchanged, *od.* has remained the same) for several days; **II.** *Adv.*: **~ schlecht** *etc.* as bad *etc.* as ever

unverantwortlich *Adj.* irresponsible; **Unverantwortlichkeit** *f* **1.** irresponsibility (*auch Handlung*); **2.** *schw., österr. Parl.* unaccountability

unverarbeitet *Adj.* **1.** *Tech.* unfinished, unprocessed; **2.** *fig.* undigested

unveräußerlich *Adj. Recht etc.*: inalienable

unverbesserlich *Adj.* incorrigible, inveterate …, hopeless *umg.*; **~er Trinker** *etc.* hardened drinker *etc.*; **er ist eben ~** *umg.* he's just a hopeless case; **Unverbesserlichkeit** *f* incorrigibility

unverbildet *Adj.* unspoil|t (*Am.* -ed), uncorrupted

unverbindlich I. *Adj.* **1.** *Angebot etc.*: non-binding, without obligation; *Auskunft etc.*: without guarantee (as to correctness); *Stellungnahme etc.*: non-committal; **2.** *Person*: (very) non-committal; (*reserviert*) detached; (*kurz angebunden*) curt; **II.** *Adv. Wirts.* without obligation; *sich äußern etc.*: in a non-committal way; *Auskunft geben etc.*: without guarantee; **Unverbindlichkeit** *f* **1.** *Wirts.* freedom from obligation; **2.** *e-r Person*: non-committal (*od.* detached) manner; curtness

unverbleit *Adj.* unleaded, lead-free

unverblümt I. *Adj. Meinung etc.*: undisguised; *Art*: outspoken, blunt, forthright; **II.** *Adv.* bluntly, openly; **j-m ~ die Meinung sagen** tell s.o. bluntly what one thinks, not mince one's words, not pull any punches; **Unverblümtheit** *f; nur Sg.* bluntness (**s-r Redeweise** with which he speaks)

unverbraucht *Adj.* unused; *Lebenskraft*: unspent; (*frisch*) fresh; *Mensch*: full of energy; *auch Geist etc.*: full of vigo(u)r; **du schaffst das schon, denn: du bist noch jung und ~** you're still young and full of energy

unverbrüchlich *Adj. Loyalität, Treue etc.*: unswerving, steadfast

unverbürgt *Adj.* unconfirmed

unverdächtig I. *Adj.* **1.** unsuspicious; **2.** (*nicht unter Verdacht*) unsuspected,

U

not under suspicion; **II.** *Adv. sich be-nehmen etc.*: in such a way as not to arouse suspicion

unverdaulich *Adj.* indigestible (*auch fig.*); **unverdaut** *Adj.* undigested (*auch fig.*)

unverderblich *Adj. Ware*: non-perishable

unverdient *Adj.* undeserved; **unver-dientermaßen**, **unverdienterweise** *Adv.* undeservedly

unverdorben *Adj.* unspoilt, *fig. auch* uncorrupted; **Unverdorbenheit** *f* unspoilt quality *od.* nature (+ *Gen.* of)

unverdrossen I. *Adj.* untiring, indefatigable, unflagging; **II.** *Adv.* untiringly, indefatigably, unflaggingly; *~ weiter-machen (unverzagt)* continue undaunted; **Unverdrossenheit** *f* indefatigability

unverdünnt I. *Adj.* undiluted; *Whisky etc.*: neat, *auch Am.* straight (up); **II.** *Adv. verwenden etc.*: neat; *Alkohol ~ trinken* drink alcohol neat, (*Am.* straight [up])

unvereinbar *Adj.* incompatible; *Gegen-sätze*: irreconcilable; **Unvereinbarkeit** *f* incompatibility; *von Gegensätzen*: irreconcilability, irreconcilable nature (+ *Gen.* of)

unverfälscht *Adj.* unadulterated, pure; *fig. auch* genuine; *~es Schwäbisch sprechen* speak pure Swabian; **Unver-fälschtheit** *f* unadulterated quality (+ *Gen.* of), pureness; genuineness; → *unverfälscht*

unverfänglich *Adj.* harmless, innocuous; **Unverfänglichkeit** *f* harmlessness, innocuousness

unverfroren *Adj.* unabashed, *stärker*: shameless, brazen; **Unverfrorenheit** *f* brazenness; *auch konkret*: insolence

unvergänglich *Adj.* immortal; *Erinne-rung, Ruhm*: undying, everlasting, unfading; *Rock 'n' Roll ist ~* rock 'n' roll is here to stay (*od.* will never die); **Unvergänglichkeit** *f* immortality; everlastingness; → *unvergänglich*

unvergessen *Adj.* unforgotten; *es/er wird uns ~ bleiben* we shall never forget it/him; **unvergesslich** *Adj.* unforgettable; *das wird mir ~ bleiben* I shall never forget it

unvergleichlich I. *Adj.* incomparable; (*unübertroffen*) *auch* unrival(l)ed; **II.** *Adv. schön etc.*: incomparably; *~ viel besser etc.* much much better *etc.*, ever so much better *etc.*

unverhältnismäßig *Adv.* disproportionately; (*unmäßig*) excessively, unreasonably; *~ kalt etc.* exceedingly cold *etc.*; **Unverhältnismäßigkeit** *f* disproportionateness; *~ der Mittel* disproportionateness of the means

unverheiratet *Adj.* unmarried, single; *m-e ~e Tante* my maiden aunt

unverhofft I. *Adj.* (*unerwartet*) unexpected; *~ kommt oft Sprichw.* life is full of surprises; **II.** *Adv.* unexpectedly; *es kam ganz ~ auch* I just wasn't expecting it

unverhohlen I. *Adj.* undisguised, open; **II.** *Adv.* openly; *etw. ~ zeigen auch* make no secret of s.th.

unverhüllt I. *Adj.* unveiled; (*bloß*) bare; *fig.* undisguised; **II.** *Adv. sich zeigen etc.*: unveiled; (*nackt*) naked; *fig.* (*offen*) openly, undisguisedly

unverkäuflich *Adj.* **1.** not for sale; *~es Muster* free sample; *Aufschrift*: sample not for sale; **2.** (*nicht absetzbar*) unsal(e)able

unverkennbar I. *Adj.* unmistakable; *es*

ist ~, dass it's quite obvious that; **II.** *Adv.* unmistakably; *es ist ~ s-e Handschrift* there's no mistaking his handwriting, it's his handwriting all right; *das ist ~ ein Picasso* it's definitely a Picasso

unverkrampft I. *Adj. Art, Spiel etc.*: relaxed, unconstrained; **II.** *Adv. sich be-nehmen etc.*: in a relaxed way; *ich sehe das völlig ~ umg.* I'm quite relaxed about it

unverlangt I. *Adj.* unsolicited, not asked for; **II.** *Adv.: ~ eingesandt Ma-nuskript etc.*: unsolicited; *~ gelieferte Ware* unsolicited goods

unverlässlich *Adj.* unreliable

unverletzlich *Adj.* inviolable; **Unver-letzlichkeit** *f* inviolability; **unverletzt** *Adj.* unhurt, safe (and sound); *Siegel etc.*: unbroken

unvermeidbar *Adj.* unavoidable; **un-vermeidlich I.** *Adj.* inevitable (*auch umg. fig. nicht wegzudenken, obligato-risch*); (*unvermeidbar*) unavoidable; (*zwangsläufig*) inevitable (*auch iro.*); *sich ins Unvermeidliche fügen* bow to the inevitable; **II.** *Adv.* inevitably; unavoidably; (*in jedem Fall*) *auch* without fail; **Unvermeidlichkeit** *f* inevitability; unavoidability

unvermindert *Adj. und Adv.* undiminished

unvermischt *Adj. und Adv.* unmixed, unblended

unvermittelt I. *Adj.* abrupt, sudden; **II.** *Adv.*: (*völlig*) *~* (quite) suddenly *od.* abruptly; *geschehen etc.*: *auch* without (any) warning; *es kam so ~* there was absolutely no warning

Unvermögen *n nur Sg.* inability, incapacity; *es war reines ~* it was sheer incompetence

unvermögend *Adj.* (*arm*) impecunious, without means; *nicht ~* fairly well-off

unvermutet I. *Adj.* unexpected; **II.** *Adv.* unexpectedly

Unvernunft *f* unreasonableness; (*Tor-heit*) folly, stupidity; **unvernünftig I.** *Adj.* unreasonable; (*töricht*) foolish; *etw. Unvernünftiges tun* do s.th. stupid; **II.** *Adv. leben, fahren etc.*: dangerously, irresponsibly, in a way that is not good for one; *~ viel trinken / lan-ge aufbleiben etc.* drink an excessive amount / stay up unreasonably late

unveröffentlicht *Adj.* unpublished

unverpackt *Adj.* (*lose*) unpacked, unpackaged; (*nicht eingewickelt*) unwrapped

unverputzt *Adj.* unplastered

unverrichtet *Adj.* → *Ding* 2

unverrückbar I. *Adj.* unshak(e)able; **II.** *Adv.: ~ feststehen* be incontrovertible; *Entschluss*: be absolutely final

unverschämt I. *Adj.* impertinent, insolent, impudent; *attr. Lüge*: barefaced, *Am. auch* bald-faced; *umg. Preis, For-derung*: outrageous; (*ein*) *~es Glück haben umg.* be damned lucky; *~ wer-den* get (*od.* be) impertinent; *weitS.* go too far; *jetzt wird er ~ in s-n Forde-rungen etc.*: now he's gone too far; **II.** *Adv. lügen*: shamelessly; *umg. teuer etc.*: outrageously; *er sieht ~ gut aus umg.* he's disgustingly (*od.* damned) good-looking; *~ braun sein* be disgustingly tanned; **Unverschämtheit** *f* impertinence, insolence, impudence; *die ~ haben zu* (+ *Inf.*) have the nerve (*od.* cheek) to (+ *Inf.*); *das ist e-e ~!* it's outrageous!; *noch e-e solche ~ und er fliegt raus umg.* one more

crack (*bzw. Handlung*: clever trick) like that and he'll be out on his ear!

unverschlossen *Adj.* **1.** (*unabgeschlos-sen*) unlocked; **2.** *Brief*: unsealed

unverschlüsselt *Adj. und Adv. Daten*: uncoded; *TV* free to air, *Am.* without blackouts

unverschuldet I. *Adj.: ein ~er Unfall* an accident for which one is not responsible; *in e-e ~e Notlage geraten* get into difficulties that are not of one's own making; **II.** *Adv.* through no fault of one's own

unversehens *Adv.* unexpectedly, all of a sudden, suddenly

unversehrt *Adj.* unhurt, unscathed; *Sa-che*: intact; **Unversehrtheit** *f e-r Per-son*: being unhurt (*od.* uninjured); *e-s Siegels etc.*: intactness; *von Daten*: integrity; *das Recht auf körperliche ~ / ~ der Wohnung* the right to freedom from bodily harm / the inviolability of one's home

unversöhnlich I. *Adj.* irreconcilable (*auch Gegensätze*); **II.** *Adv.: sich ~ ge-genüberstehen* be irreconcilable; **Un-versöhnlichkeit** *f* irreconcilability

unversorgt *Adj. finanziell*: unprovided for; *Menschen, Jugendliche*: who have not been provided for (*od.* taken care of); *Bewerber*: who have not found a job; *Gebiet, Gegend*: that is not covered (by a supply service *bzw.* not connected to a network), *Am.* unimproved, not hooked up *to municipal water, sewer, etc.*

Unverstand *m* (*Unwissenheit*) ignorance; (*Dummheit*) foolishness; **unver-standen** *Adj.* (*missverstanden*) misunderstood; (*nicht verstanden*) not understood; *sich* (*von j-m*) *~ fühlen* feel misunderstood (by s.o.); **unverstän-dig** *Adj.* (*unwissend*) ignorant; *Kind*: too young to know; (*dumm*) stupid, foolish

unverständlich *Adj.* (*undeutlich*) unintelligible; (*nicht nachvollziehbar*) incomprehensible (*auch Verhalten etc.*); *Grund*: obscure; *das ist mir völlig ~* (*ich kann es nicht nachvollziehen*) I just can't understand it; (*es ist mir zu hoch*) it's beyond me (completely); (*ich kann nichts damit anfangen*) I can't make head or tail (*Am.* heads or tails) of it; **Unverständlichkeit** *f* unintelligibility; incomprehensibility; → *unverständlich*

Unverständnis *n* lack of understanding; *für Kunst etc.*: lack of appreciation; *auf ~ stoßen* find no sympathy

unversteuert *Adj.* untaxed

unversucht *Adj.: nichts ~ lassen* try everything (*um zu* + *Inf.* to + *Inf.*), leave no stone unturned (in one's attempt to + *Inf.*)

unverträglich I. *Adj.* **1.** *Speise*: indigestible; **2.** (*zänkisch*) quarrelsome, cantankerous, *Am. auch* ornery; **3.** (*unver-einbar*) incompatible (*auch Med. und EDV*); **Unverträglichkeit** *f* **1.** *von Speise*: indigestibility; **2.** *von Person*: quarrelsomeness, cantankerousness, *Am. auch* orneriness; **3.** *Unvereinbar-keit*: incompatibility (*auch Med. und EDV*)

unverwandt I. *Adj. Blick*: fixed; **II.** *Adv.* fixedly; *j-n ~ ansehen* fix one's gaze on s.o.; *er sah sie ~ an auch* he couldn't take his eyes off her

unverwechselbar *Adj.* unmistakable

unverwertbar *Adj.* unusable

unverwundbar *Adj.* invulnerable; **Un-verwundbarkeit** *f* invulnerability

unverwüstlich *Adj.* indestructible (*auch fig. Person etc.*); *fig. Humor etc.*: inexhaustible; **sie ist ~** *fig. auch* she keeps bouncing back, you can't get her down; **Unverwüstlichkeit** *f* indestructibility; inexhaustibility; → *unverwüstlich*

unverzagt *Adj. und Adv.* undaunted

unverzeihlich *Adj.* inexcusable, unforgivable; **es ist ~** *auch* there's no excuse for it

unverzichtbar *Adj.* indispensable, (absolutely) essential; *Recht*: inalienable; **Unverzichtbarkeit** *f* indispensability; *e-s Rechts*: inalienability

unverzinslich *Adj.* non-interest-bearing; *Darlehen*: interest-free

unverzollt **I.** *Adj.* uncleared; *Aufschrift*: duty unpaid; **II.** *Adv. einführen etc.*: without paying duty

unverzüglich **I.** *Adj.* immediate, prompt; **II.** *Adv.* immediately, straightaway, without delay

unvollendet *Adj.* unfinished; **die Unvollendete** *Mus.* the (*od. Schubert's*) Unfinished (Symphony)

unvollkommen **I.** *Adj.* imperfect; **II.** *Adv.*: **nur ~ beherrschen** have only an imperfect grasp of; **Unvollkommenheit** *f* imperfection (*auch konkret*)

unvollständig **I.** *Adj.* incomplete; **II.** *Adv. ausfüllen, entleeren etc.*: not completely, not fully, only partially; **Unvollständigkeit** *f* incompleteness

unvorbereitet **I.** *Adj.* unprepared; *Rede*: impromptu; **II.** *Adv.*: **~ reden** ad-lib; **~ in e-e Prüfung gehen** take (*od. do*) an exam without any preparation; **es traf ihn ~** it came as a complete surprise (*od. shock*) to him, it caught him unawares

unvoreingenommen **I.** *Adj.* (*ohne Vorurteile*) unbias(s)ed, unprejudiced; (*objektiv*) objective; **II.** *Adv. begegnen, beurteilen etc.*: without preconceptions; (*objektiv*) objectively; **Unvoreingenommenheit** *f* impartiality, lack of (*od.* freedom from) prejudice; (*Objektivität*) objectivity

unvorhergesehen **I.** *Adj.* (*vorher nicht abzusehen*) unforeseen; (*unerwartet*) unexpected; **II.** *Adv.* unexpectedly; **~ Besuch bekommen** have unexpected visitors (*od.* an unexpected visitor); **unvorhersehbar** *Adj.* unforeseeable

unvorschriftsmäßig **I.** *Adj.* improper; *Verhalten etc.*: *auch* contrary to the regulations; **II.** *Adv. parken etc.*: improperly

unvorsichtig **I.** *Adj.* careless; (*unklug*) imprudent; (*übereilt*) rash; **er war so ~, sein Auto offen zu lassen** he was careless enough to leave his car open; **II.** *Adv.* careless; (*unklug*) imprudently; (*übereilt*) rashly; **unvorsichtigerweise** *Adv.* carelessly; **er hat es ~ liegen lassen** *auch* he was careless enough to leave it behind; **Unvorsichtigkeit** *f* carelessness; imprudence; rashness; → *unvorsichtig*

unvorstellbar **I.** *Adj.* inconceivable, unimaginable, unthinkable; (*unglaublich*) incredible; *Angst, Schmerzen etc.*: incredible, terrible; **es ist mir ~, dass** ... it's inconceivable to me that ...; **falls das Unvorstellbare eintritt** in case the unthinkable happens; **II.** *Adv. groß, schön etc.*: unimaginably; **~ leiden müssen** have to suffer terribly

unvorteilhaft **I.** *Adj.* 1. *Kleid, Frisur etc.*: unbecoming, unflattering; **für j-n ~ sein** not suit s.o.; **~ aussehen** look

unattractive; 2. *wirtschaftlich*: unprofitable; **~es Geschäft** bad deal; **II.** *Adv.* 1. **sich ~ kleiden** wear the wrong clothes (for one's figure *etc.*); 2. **sich ~ auswirken** prove disadvantageous (**für** for); **sich für j-n ~ auswirken** *auch* prove to be to s.o.'s disadvantage

unwägbar *Adj.* imponderable; (*nicht kalkulierbar*) incalculable; **Unwägbarkeit** *f* imponderability (*auch konkret*); incalculability

unwahr *Adj.* untrue, false; **was er sagt, ist ~** *auch* he's not telling the truth; **Unwahrheit** *f* untruthfulness; *konkret*: untruth, falsehood; **er sagt die ~** he's not telling the truth

unwahrscheinlich **I.** *Adj.* unlikely, improbable; *umg. fig.* incredible; **du hattest ~es Glück** you had incredible luck; **es ist (höchst) ~, dass** ... it's highly unlikely that ...; **II.** *Adv. umg.*: **~ gut etc.** incredibly good *etc.*; **Unwahrscheinlichkeit** *f* unlikelihood, improbability

unwandelbar *Adj.* unchanging, constant; *Liebe etc.*: steadfast

unwegsam *Adj. Gebirge, Urwald etc.*: virtually impassable; **~es Gelände etc.** difficult (*od.* rough) terrain; **Unwegsamkeit** *f* roughness; impassability

unweiblich *Adj.* unfeminine

unweigerlich **I.** *Adj.* inevitable; **II.** *Adv.* without fail, inevitably; **es führte ~ zu e-r Zinserhöhung** it led to an inevitable rise in interest rates; **diese Frage musste ~ kommen** it was inevitable that this question would come up

unweit *Präp.*: **~ unseres Hotels etc.** not far from our hotel *etc.*

unwert *Adj.* 1. *geh.* → *unwürdig*; 2. **~es Leben** *Nazideutsch*: worthless life; **Unwert** *m*; -(e)s, *kein Pl.*; *geh.* worthlessness; **Wert und ~ der Schulbildung etc.** the merits and demerits of school education

Unwesen *n* dreadful state of affairs; **sein ~ treiben** be up to no good, be on the rampage; **sein ~ treiben in** (+ *Dat.*) wreak havoc in, terrorize

unwesentlich **I.** *Adj.* inessential (**für** to); *weitS.* (*nebensächlich*) marginal (to); (*unwichtig*) unimportant (for, to), insignificant (to); (*irrelevant*) irrelevant, immaterial (to); (*kaum bemerkbar*) negligible; **II.** *Adv.* (*wenig*) slightly, marginally; (*kaum*) negligibly; **nur ~ jünger als sie** just slightly younger than her (*od.* she *geh.*)

Unwetter *n* (thunder)storm; **es gibt ein ~** there's a storm brewing; **ein ~ brach los** a storm broke; **ein verheerendes ~** a devastating storm

unwichtig *Adj.* not important, insignificant; (*irrelevant*) irrelevant; **Geld ist dabei völlig ~** money is completely irrelevant (*od.* is simply not an issue) in this instance; **Unwichtigkeit** *f* 1. unimportance, insignificance; irrelevance; 2. *konkret*: triviality, unimportant matter

unwiderlegbar *Adj.* irrefutable, incontrovertible

unwiderruflich **I.** *Adj.* irrevocable (*auch Wirts.*); **II.** *Adv.* irrevocably; (*ganz bestimmt*) definitely, positively; **es steht ~ fest, dass** it's absolutely definite (*od.* certain) that; **Unwiderruflichkeit** *f* irrevocability

unwidersprochen *Adj.*: **~ bleiben** stand uncontradicted; **etw. ~ hinnehmen** take s.th. without contradiction (*od.* without a word of protest), swal-

low s.th. whole *umg.*

unwiderstehlich *Adj.* irresistible; (*bezwingend*) compelling; **~es Verlangen nach Schokolade etc.** irresistible (*od.* overpowering) urge to eat chocolate *etc.*, overpowering desire for chocolate *etc.*; **sich für ~ halten** consider o.s. to be irresistible; **Unwiderstehlichkeit** *f* irresistibility

unwiederbringlich **I.** *Adj.* irretrievable; **II.** *Adv.*: **~ dahin** irretrievably lost, lost (*od.* gone) forever

Unwille, Unwillen *m* displeasure, stärker: anger; **j-s Unwillen erregen** arouse s.o.'s displeasure (*od. stärker*: ire); **s-m Unwillen Luft machen** give vent to one's displeasure; **unwillentlich** **I.** *Adv.* unintentionally; **II.** *Adj.* unintentional; **unwillig** **I.** *Adj.* (*ungehalten*) indignant (**über** + *Akk.* at); (*widerstrebend*) unwilling, reluctant; **II.** *Adv.* (*ungehalten*) indignantly; (*widerstrebend*) unwillingly, reluctantly; **Unwilligkeit** *f* indignation; (*Widerwilligkeit*) unwillingness, reluctance

unwillkommen *Adj.* unwelcome; **nicht ~ sein** not be unwelcome

unwillkürlich **I.** *Adj. Bewegung, Gedanke etc.*: involuntary; (*instinktiv*) instinctive; (*mechanisch*) automatic; **II.** *Adv.* involuntarily; instinctively; automatically; **~ musste ich an ihn denken etc.** I couldn't help thinking of him *etc.*

unwirklich *Adj.* unreal

unwirksam *Adj.* ineffective; *Jur.* (*nicht in Kraft*) inoperative; (*null and nichtig*) null and void; **Unwirksamkeit** *f* ineffectiveness; *Jur.* inoperativeness

unwirsch **I.** *Adj.* gruff, brusque; **II.** *Adv. antworten etc.*: gruffly, brusquely; **j-n ~ abfertigen** give s.o. short shrift

unwirtlich *Adj.* inhospitable

unwirtschaftlich *Adj.* uneconomical; (*unrentabel*) unviable; (*unrationell*) inefficient; **Unwirtschaftlichkeit** *f* uneconomicalness; inefficiency; unviability

Unwissen *n* → *Unwissenheit*; **unwissend** *Adj.* ignorant; *Kind*: too young to know; **sich ~ stellen** pretend ignorance; **Unwissenheit** *f*: (**aus**) **~** (out of) ignorance; **~ schützt vor Strafe nicht** *Sprichw.* ignorance (of the law) is no excuse

unwissenschaftlich **I.** *Adj. Methode, Zeitalter etc.*: unscientific; *Ansatz, Argumentation etc.*: unscholarly; **II.** *Adv. vorgehen etc.*: unscientifically; in an unscholarly way

unwissentlich **I.** *Adv.* unknowingly, *lit.* unwittingly; **II.** *Adj.* unknowing, unwitting

unwohl *Adj.* 1. unwell; **mir ist ~** I don't feel well; 2. (*unbehaglich*) uneasy; **dabei wird mir ganz ~** it gives me a very uneasy feeling; **Unwohlsein** *n* indisposition; (*Übelkeit*) feeling of sickness, nausea

unwohnlich *Adj.* (*ungemütlich*) uncomfortable; (*nicht anheimelnd*) un|homely (*Am.* -homey), cheerless

Unwort *n* ghastly neologism, non-word

Unwucht *f*; -, -en; *Tech.* imbalance

unwürdig *Adj.* unworthy (+ *Gen.* of); (*würdelos*) undignified; (*schändlich*) disgraceful; (*entwürdigend*) degrading; **das ist seiner ~** that is beneath him

Unzahl *f*; *nur Sg.*: **e-e ~ von** a host of, an enormous number of, innumerable, no end of *umg.*; **unzählbar** *Adj. Ling.* uncountable; → *unzählig*; **unzählig**

U

I. *Adj. nur attr.* innumerable, countless, numberless; *~e Menschen etc. auch* scores of people *etc.*; *~e Mal*(e) any number of (*od.* countless) times, umpteen times *umg.*, times without number *geh.*; *Unzählige wurden verhaftet* scores (*mehr:* hundreds) of people were arrested; **II.** *Adv.:* **~ viele** countless

unzähmbar *Adj.* untam(e)able; *fig.* indomitable

Unze *f; -, -n* ounce (*Abk.* oz.); *e-e ~ Gold* an ounce of gold

Unzeit *f: zur ~* at an inopportune time; **unzeitgemäß** *Adj.* (*altmodisch*) old--fashioned, dated, behind the times; (*unpassend*) unseasonable (*auch Witterung*), inopportune

unzensiert *Adj.* uncensored

unzerbrechlich *Adj.* unbreakable; **Unzerbrechlichkeit** *f* unbreakability

unzerkaut I. *Adj.* unchewed; **II.** *Adv.:* **~ herunterschlucken** swallow *s.th.* without chewing it

unzerreißbar *Adj.* untearable, non--tear(ing)

unzerstörbar *Adj.* indestructible; **Unzerstörbarkeit** *f* indestructibility

unzertrennlich *Adj.* inseparable; **Unzertrennliche** *Pl. Zool.* lovebirds; **Unzertrennlichkeit** *f* inseparability

unziemlich *Adj. altm.* unseemly

unzivilisiert *Adj.* uncivilized; **Unzivilisiertheit** *f* uncivilized nature (*od.* state), lack of civilization

Unzucht *f; nur Sg.; Jur.* sexual offen|ce (*Am.* -se), (act of) indecency; *~ treiben* fornicate; *~ mit Minderjährigen* sexual relations with minors; *gewerbsmäßige ~* prostitution; **unzüchtig** *Adj.* lewd, lascivious; *Geste, Handlung, Film etc.:* obscene; **Unzüchtigkeit** *f* indecency; obscenity

unzufrieden *Adj.* dissatisfied, *bes. dauernd:* discontented; **Unzufriedenheit** *f* dissatisfaction, discontent, discontentment

unzugänglich I. *Adj.* inaccessible (*auch Tech.*), unapproachable; *~ für fig.* impervious to, deaf to; **II.** *Adv.:* **Arzneimittel für Kinder ~ aufbewahren** keep medicines out of the reach of children; **Unzugänglichkeit** *f* inaccessibility, unapproachability; *fig.* imperviousness (*für* to)

unzukömmlich *Adj.* **1.** *österr.* (*unzulänglich*) inadequate; **2.** *bes. österr.; Begünstigung etc.:* unjustified; **3.** *schw.* (*unzuträglich*) unhealthy; **Unzukömmlichkeiten** *Pl. schw., österr.* (*Unstimmigkeiten*) discrepancies; (*Unzulänglichkeiten*) inadequacies; shortcomings

unzulänglich I. *Adj.* inadequate; (*mangelhaft, ungenügend*) deficient, insufficient; **II.** *Adv.* inadequately; **Unzulänglichkeit** *f* inadequacy; deficiency; (*Schwäche*) shortcoming, failing

unzulässig *Adj.* inadmissible; *Geschwindigkeit etc.:* above the legal limit, excessive; *Jur., Beeinflussung:* undue; *EDV* invalid; **unzulässigerweise** *Adv.* inadmissibly; **Unzulässigkeit** *f* inadmissibility

unzumutbar *Adj.* unreasonable, too much to expect (*od.* ask [for]); (*unannehmbar*) unacceptable; *das ist für ihn ~* you can't expect him to put up with (*od.* accept, do *etc.*) that

unzurechnungsfähig *Adj. Jur.* non compos mentis, of unsound mind, *Am. auch* incompetent; *für ~ erklären* declare to be of unsound mind; **Unzu-**

rechnungsfähigkeit *f* diminished responsibility, *Am.* incompetence

unzureichend I. *Adj.* insufficient, inadequate; **II.** *Adv. versorgen etc.:* insufficiently, inadequately

unzusammenhängend I. *Adj.* disconnected, disjointed; *Rede etc.:* incoherent; **II.** *Adv. reden etc.:* disjointedly, incoherently

unzuständig *Adj.* not responsible (*für* for); *~ sein Jur.* have no jurisdiction (*für* over); *sich für ~ erklären* declare that *s.th.* is outside one's jurisdiction (*od.* competence)

unzustellbar *Adj. Post:* undelivered; *falls ~, bitte zurück an Absender* if undelivered, please return to sender

unzuträglich *Adj.* detrimental (+ *Dat.* to); **Unzuträglichkeit** *f* detrimental nature *od.* effect(s *Pl.*) (+ *Gen.* of)

unzutreffend *Adj.* incorrect; (*unbegründet*) unfounded; (*nicht anwendbar*) inapplicable; *Unzutreffendes bitte streichen!* delete where inapplicable

unzuverlässig *Adj.* unreliable; (*nicht vertrauenswürdig*) untrustworthy; **Unzuverlässigkeit** *f* unreliability; untrustworthiness

unzweckmäßig *Adj.* (*unangebracht*) inexpedient; (*ungeeignet*) unsuitable; **Unzweckmäßigkeit** *f* inexpediency; unsuitability

unzweideutig I. *Adj.* unequivocal, unambiguous; (*eindeutig*) explicit, plain, clear; **II.** *Adv.:* **~ zu verstehen geben, dass** make it quite clear (*od.* plain) that; **Unzweideutigkeit** *f* unambiguousness; explicitness

unzweifelhaft I. *Adj.* unquestionable, indubitable; **II.** *Adv.* doubtless, without (a) doubt, undoubtedly

Update ['apde:t] *n; -s, -s; EDV* update

Upgrade ['apgre:t] *n; -s, -s; EDV* upgrade

üppig I. *Adj.* **1.** *Vegetation, Pflanzenwuchs, Haar etc.:* luxuriant; *Wiese, Laub, auch fig. Leben:* lush; **2.** *Mahlzeit etc.:* sumptuous, opulent; *Speise, Nahrung:* rich; **3.** *Figur, Formen etc.:* full; (*sinnlich*) voluptuous; *Blondine:* busty; *Busen:* ample; **4.** *umg.* (*reichlich*) *Trinkgeld, Portion etc.:* generous, *attr. auch* big fat; *e-e* (*ziemlich*) *~e Angelegenheit umg. Fest etc.:* a really plush do; *nicht gerade ~ umg.* not overwhelming(ly much); *j-m ein ~es Gehalt zahlen umg.* pay *s.o.* a fat (*od.* huge) salary; **II.** *Adv. wachsen etc.:* luxuriantly; *~ speisen* have a sumptuous meal; *~ essen* eat rich foods; *j-n ~ beschenken* shower *s.o.* with presents; *~ leben* live a life of luxury, live off the fat of the land, live the life of Riley, *Am. auch* live high on the hog; (*zu viel essen und trinken*) not stint *o.s.; nicht gerade ~ bezahlen/verdienen umg.* not pay/earn an enormous amount; **Üppigkeit** *f; nur Sg.* luxuriance; thick growth; lushness; sumptuousness, opulence; richness; voluptuousness; → *üppig*

Ur... *im Subst.* **1.** (*ursprünglich*) original ...; *primeval ...;* (*erst*) first; *Urfassung* original version; *Urgestalt* original form; *Urozean* primeval ocean; **2.** *Phys.* standard; *Urmeter* standard met|re (*Am.* -er)

ur... *im Adj.* (*sehr*) extremely

Urabstimmung *f* strike ballot, secret ballot (on strike action)

Urahn(e) *m,* **Urahne** *f* (earliest) ancestor; *Pl. auch* forefathers

Ural *m; -s; Geog., Fluss:* Ural; *Gebirge:*

Urals *Pl.*

uralt *Adj.* ancient, (as) old as the hills *umg.; umg. Witz, Trick:* hoary (*od.* creaky) old, *präd.* as old as the hills; *Problem:* age-old; *seit ~en Zeiten* from (*od.* since) time immemorial; *aus ~en Zeiten* from long, long ago, from way back when *umg.*

Uran *n; -s, kein Pl.; Chem.* uranium; *~abbau m* uranium mining; *~anreicherung f* uranium enrichment; *~anreicherungsanlage f* uranium enrichment plant; *~aufbereitung f* uranium processing; *~bergbau m* uranium mining; *~erz n* uranium ore

Urangst *f Psych.* primordial fear

uranhaltig *Adj.* uranium-bearing

Uranus *m; -, kein Pl.; Astron.* Uranus

Uranvorkommen *n* uranium deposit

uraufführen *v/t.* (*untr., hat -ge-*) première; *die Oper / der Film wurde 1924 uraufgeführt* the opera was first performed / the film (*bes. Am.* movie) was first shown in 1924; **Uraufführung** *f* first performance; *auch Film:* première

Urausgabe *f* first (*od.* original) edition

urban *Adj.* urbane; **urbanisieren** *v/t.* urbanize; **Urbanisierung** *f* urbanization; **Urbanität** *f; -, kein Pl.* urbanity, urbaneness

urbar *Adj.:* **~ machen** cultivate; (*Urwald etc.*) clear; (*Wüste etc.*) reclaim; **Urbarmachung** *f* cultivation; clearing; reclamation; → *urbar*

Urbedeutung *f* original meaning

Urbeginn *m* very first beginnings *Pl.; von ~ an* from the very beginning

Urbevölkerung *f* (ab)original population (*od.* inhabitants *Pl.*); → *Ureinwohner*

Urbild *n* **1.** model, prototype; *das ~ von Shakepeares Romeo* the model for Shakespeare's Romeo; **2.** (*Inbegriff*) type, embodiment

urchig *Adj. schw.* → *urig*

Urchristentum *n: das ~* early Christianity; **urchristlich** *Adj.* early Christian

urdeutsch *Adj. präd.* German to the core, as German as you can get *umg.; e-e ~e Sitte etc.* a good old-fashioned German custom

ureigen *Adj.: ~es Interesse* vested interest; *in Ihrem ~sten Interesse* in your own best interest(s); *das ist m-e ~ste Angelegenheit* that's my business and nobody else's

Ureinwohner *Pl.* (ab)original inhabitants (*od.* population *Sg.*); *die ~ Australiens* the Australian aborigines; *die amerikanischen ~* the original inhabitants of America, the Native Americans

Ureltern *Pl.* ancestors

Urenkel *m* great-grandson; **Urenkelin** *f* great-granddaughter

Urethan *n; -s, -e; Chem.* urethane

Urfassung *f* original version

Urform *f* archetype

urgemütlich *Adj.* really cosy (*Am.* cozy)

urgermanisch *Adj.* Teutonic; *Ling.* Proto-Germanic

Urgeschichte *f: die ~* prehistory; **urgeschichtlich** *Adj.* prehistoric

Urgestein *n* **1.** primary rocks *Pl.;* **2.** *fig.: politisches etc. ~* a politician *etc.* born and bred

Urgewalt *f* elemental force

urgieren *vt/i. österr. Amtsspr.* **1.** (*dringend nachsuchen*) request *s.th.;* **2.** (*um schnelle[re] Erledigung bitten*) ask for *s.th.* to be done (more) quickly, ask for a speedy decision

Urgroß|eltern *Pl.* great-grandparents; **~mutter** *f* great-grandmother; **~vater** *m* great-grandfather

Urgrund *m* origin, (original) source

Urheber *m*; *-s, -,* **~in** *f*; *-, -nen* author; (*Schöpfer[in]*) creator; **geistiger ~** spiritual father; **Urheberrecht** *n* copyright (*für, von* on); (*Gesetz*) copyright law; **urheberrechtlich I.** *Adj. attr.* copyright ...; **II.** *Adv.:* **~ geschützt** (protected by) copyright; **Urheberschaft** *f; nur Sg.* authorship; **Urheberschutz** *m* copyright protection

Urheimat *f* original home(land)

urig *Adj.* **1.** (*bodenständig*) *Mensch, Bauer etc.*: rooted in the local soil, indigenous; (*derb, kernig*) earthy; (*rustikal*) rustic; (*ungekünstelt*) unsophisticated; (*ungeschliffen*) unrefined; *ein ~er Typ umg.* a true son of the soil, a native son; (*Original*) an original; **2.** *Essen*: local, regional; **3.** *Lokal etc.*: traditional; (*folkloristisch*) ethnic; → *auch* **urwüchsig**

Urin *m*; *-s, kein Pl.* urine; *ich spür's im ~ umg. fig.* I can feel it in my bones; **Urinal** *n*; *-s, -e* **1.** (*Bettflasche*) urinal, bedpan; **2.** (*Becken*) urinal; **urinieren** *v/i.* urinate; **Urinprobe** *f* urine specimen

Urinstinkt *m* primeval instinct

Urinuntersuchung *f* urine test, urinalysis (*Pl.* urinalyses)

Urkanton *m schw. hist.* original canton

Urknall *m* big bang, Big Bang

urkomisch *Adj.* hilarious

Urkraft *f* elemental force

Urkunde *f*; *-, -n* document; (*Eigentumsurkunde*) deed; (*Siegerurkunde*) certificate, diploma; *e-e ~ ausstellen/fälschen* issue/forge a document

urkundenecht *Adj. Tinte* indelible

Urkunden|fälscher *m*, **~fälscherin** *f* document forger; **~fälschung** *f* forgery of documents; *wegen ~ bestraft werden etc.*: for forging documents

urkundlich I. *Adj.* documentary; (*verbürgt*) authentic; **II.** *Adv.* authentically; **~ belegt** documented; **~ erwähnt werden** be mentioned in a document; *der Bau wird erstmals im 9. Jahrhundert ~ erwähnt* the first documentary evidence of the building goes back to the 9th century

Urlandschaft *f* primeval landscape

Urlaub *m*; *-(e)s, -e* **1.** (*Ferien*) holidays *Pl., bes. Am.* vacation; *auf od. im ~* on holiday, *bes. Am.* on vacation; *in ~ gehen od. fahren* go on holiday (*bes. Am.* vacation); *ein zweiwöchiger etc. ~* a two-week *etc.* holiday (*bes. Am.* vacation); *im ~ an die See etc. fahren* go on holiday (*bes. Am.* vacation) to the seaside (*Am.* the ocean *od.* beach *etc.*); *~ in Florida machen* go on holiday (*bes. Am.* vacation) to Florida; *ein verregneter ~* a holiday (*bes. Am.* vacation) spoil|t (*Am.* -ed) by rain; *den ~ abbrechen* break off (*Am.* cut short) one's holiday (*bes. Am.* vacation); *schönen ~!* have a good holiday (*bes. Am.* a nice vacation)!; *~ machen von der Familie, dem Alltag etc.*: take a holiday (*bes. Am.* vacation) from; **2.** (*arbeitsfreie Zeit*) holiday; *Mil.* leave; *unbezahlter ~* unpaid holiday, unpaid leave; *~ bis zum Wecken Mil.* night leave; *~ beantragen* ask for time off; *keinen ~ bekommen* get no holiday(s) (*bes. Am.* vacation); *~ eintragen* put down one's holiday (*Am.* va-

cation dates); *~ haben* be on (*Am.* have a) holiday; *noch ~ haben* (*Resturlaub*) still have some holiday (*Am.* vacation time) left; *wir machen ~ vom ... bis zum ... Schild, Anzeige etc.*: we are on holiday (*Am.* vacation) from ... to ...; *sich* (*Dat.*) *~ / e-n Tag ~ nehmen* take time / take a day off; *in ~ schicken* send off on holiday (*bes. Am.* vacation), send on leave; *vom ~ zurück in Anzeige etc.*: returned from holiday, *Am.* back from vacation

urlauben *v/i. umg.* holiday, *bes. Am.* vacation

Urlauber *m*; *-s, -,* **~in** *f*; *-, -nen* holidaymaker, *Am.* vacationer; *Mil.* person on leave; **~strom** *m* stream of holidaymakers (*Am.* vacationers)

Urlaubs|... *im Subst. → auch* **Ferien...**; **~adresse** *f*, **~anschrift** *f* holiday (*bes. Am.* vacation) address; **~anspruch** *m* holiday (*Am.* vacation) entitlement; **~antrag** *m* request for time off (*od.* leave); **~bekanntschaft** *f* holiday (*bes. Am.* vacation) acquaintance; **~domizil** *n* holiday (*bes. Am.* vacation) accommodation; **~flirt** *m* holiday flirtation, *Am.* vacation dalliance; **~foto** *n* holiday (*bes. Am.* vacation) snap; **~gast** *m* holiday (*bes. Am.* vacation) guest; **~gebiet** *n* holiday (*bes. Am.* resort) area; **~geld** *n* holiday (*bes. Am.* vacation) pay; *erspartes*: money for one's holiday (*bes. Am.* vacation); **~kasse** *f umg.* money (saved up) for a holiday (*bes. Am.* vacation); *leere ~* no money (saved up) for a holiday (*bes. Am.* vacation); **~land** *n* holiday (*bes. Am.* vacation) country; *mein liebstes ~* my favo(u)rite country for a holiday (*Am.* vacation); **~liste** *f* list of holidays *Pl.*; **~ort** *m* holiday (*bes. Am.* vacation) resort; **~paradies** *n* holiday(makers') (*Am.* vacation) paradise; **~pläne** *Pl.* holiday (*bes. Am.* vacation) plans; **~planung** *f* holiday (*bes. Am.* vacation) planning

urlaubsreif *Adj. mst präd.* in (desperate) need of a holiday (*bes. Am.* vacation)

Urlaubs|reise *f* holiday (*Am.* vacation) trip; **~saison** *f* holiday (*bes. Am.* vacation) season; **~sperre** *f* **1.** ban on taking leave (*bzw.* taking time off); *es besteht ~* nobody is being allowed to take time off; *Mil.* all leave has been cancel(l)ed; **2.** *österr.* (*Betriebsurlaub*) holiday (*Am.* vacation) closure; **~stimmung** *f* holiday (*bes. Am.* vacation) mood; *in ~ sein* be in holiday (*bes. Am.* vacation) mood; **~tag** *m* (a day's) holiday (*bes. Am.* vacation); *zwei etc. ~e nehmen vom Anspruch*: take two days off; **~vertretung** *f* **1.** (*Person*) holiday (*Am.* vacation) replacement; *für j-n ~ machen* stand in for s.o. while he (*od.* she) is on holiday (*Am.* vacation); *X ist m-e ~* X will be standing in for me when I'm on holiday (*Am.* vacation); **2.** (*Planung*) holiday stand-in scheme, *Am.* vacation replacement plan; **~woche** *f*: *erste etc. ~* first *etc.* week of one's holiday (*bes. Am.* vacation); *herrliche ~n im Schwarzwald etc.* happy holidays in the Black Forest; **~zeit** *f* holiday (*bes. Am.* vacation) season *od.* period; *die beste ~* the best time for a holiday (*bes. Am.* vacation); **~ziel** *n* vacation spot; (*auch Land*) tourist destination

Urmeer *n* primeval sea

Urmensch *m*: *der ~* primitive man

Urmutter *f* first mother

Urne *f*; *-, -n* urn; (*Wahlurne*) *auch* ballot box

Urnen|beisetzung *f* urn burial; **~feld** *n hist.* urnfield; **~gang** *m* polling, polls *Pl.*; *80% beteiligten sich am ~* there was an 80% turnout at the polls; **~grab** *n* urn grave; **~halle** *f* columbarium (*Pl.* columbaria)

Urologe *m*; *-en, -en; Med.* urologist; **Urologie** *f*; *-, kein Pl.* urology; **Urologin** *f*; *-, -nen* urologist; **urologisch I.** *Adj.* urological; **II.** *Adv. untersuchen etc.*: urologically

Uroma *f umg.* great-grandma; **Uropa** *m umg.* great-granddad (*od.* -grandpa)

urplötzlich I. *Adj.* sudden, totally unexpected; **II.** *Adv.* all of a sudden, completely out of the blue

Urprodukt *n* primary product; **Urproduktion** *f Wirts.* primary production

Urquell *m mst Sg.; lit.* primary source

Ursache *f* cause (+ *Gen. od. für* of); (*Grund*) reason (for); (*Anlass*) occasion (for); *aus bisher ungeklärter ~* for reasons that have yet to be explained; *nach den ~n forschen* search for the causes; do research into the causes; *ich habe (alle) ~ zu* (+ *Inf.*) I have (every) reason to (+ *Inf.*); *er hat keine ~ zu* (+ *Inf.*) there's no reason why he should ...; *~ und Wirkung* cause and effect; *kleine ~, große Wirkung* great oaks from little acorns grow; *keine ~!* not at all, *förm.* don't mention it; *Antwort auf Entschuldigung*: that's all right; **Ursachenforschung** *f Philos.* (a)etiology; *wir müssen ~ betreiben* (*nach den Ursachen forschen*) we need to do some research into the causes of this; **ursächlich I.** *Adj.* causal; *sie stehen in ~em Zusammenhang* they are causally connected; *für etw. ~ sein* be the cause of s.th.; **II.** *Adv.* causally

Urschlamm *m*, **Urschleim** *m* primeval sludge

Urschrei *m Psych.* primal scream

Urschrift *f* original (text *od.* copy)

Ursprache *f* **1.** (*Originalsprache*) original language; *in der ~* in the original (language); **2.** (*Grundsprache*) protolanguage

Ursprung *m* **1.** origin(s *Pl.*); *weitS.* (*Anfang*) beginnings *Pl.*; *s-n ~ haben in* (*Dat.*) originate in (*od.* from), stem from, have one's (*od.* its) origin(s) in; *griechischen ~s* of Greek origin (*Person*: *auch* extraction); *Wirts.* made in Greece; *Wort*: be of Greek origin, go back to Greek, be originally Greek; **2.** *Math.* origin; **ursprünglich I.** *Adj.* **1.** original; (*anfänglich*) initial; *die ~e Begeisterung etc. auch* the enthusiasm *etc.* that was there at the beginning (*od.* to start with); **2.** (*natürlich, unverfälscht*) natural, unspoil|t (*Am.* -ed), pristine; *~es Gebiet* wilderness area; **II.** *Adv.* originally, at the beginning, to start (off) with; (*zuerst*) at first; *~ wollte ich Medizin studieren, aber dann ...* at first I wanted to study medicine, but then ...; **Ursprünglichkeit** *f; nur Sg.* naturalness; unspoil|t (*Am.* -ed) quality (*od.* state) (+ *Gen. of*)

Ursprungs|bezeichnung *f Wirts.*: *kontrollierte ~* certified indication of (country of) origin; *Wein*: appellation contrôlée; **~gebiet** *n* area of origin; **~land** *n Wirts.* country of origin; **~zeugnis** *n Wirts.* certificate of origin

Urständ *f umg.*: *fröhliche ~ feiern* rise from the ashes; *pej.* rear its ugly head

U

again

Urstoff m primary matter; *Chem.* element

Urstromtal n *Geol.* glacial valley

Ursulinen *Pl. kath.* Ursulines

Ursuppe f primeval soup

Urteil n **1.** judg(e)ment; (*Meinung*) opinion; (*Entscheidung*) decision; *sich ein ~ bilden* form a judg(e)ment (*od.* an opinion) (*über + Akk.* on); *ein fachmännisches ~ abgeben* give a professional (*od.* an expert) opinion; *m-m ~ nach* in my opinion; *darüber kann ich mir kein ~ erlauben* I'm in no position to judge (that); *sicher in s-m ~ sein* be confident of one's judg(e)ment; *zu dem ~ kommen, dass ...* come to the conclusion that ...; *ihr ~ steht schon fest* she has already made up her mind; **2.** *Jur.* judg(e)ment, ruling, decision; (*Strafurteil*) sentence; (*Scheidungsurteil*) decree; *ein mildes/hartes ~* a light/heavy sentence; *das ~ über j-n sprechen* pronounce sentence on s.o.; → *ergehen* I 1, *fällen* 2; → *auch* **urteilen**

urteilen v/i. judge (*nach* by); *~ über* (+ *Akk.*) judge *s.o. od. s.th.*; *über etw. ~* auch give one's opinion on; *nur nach dem Äußeren etc. ~* judge purely by appearances; *darüber kann er nicht ~* he's no judge; *~ Sie selbst!* see for yourself; *nach s-n Worten etc. zu ~* judging (*od.* to judge) by what he says etc.

Urteilsbegründung f *Jur.* opinion (of the court)

urteilsfähig *Adj.* discerning, discriminating; **Urteilsfähigkeit** f; *nur Sg.* ability to judge; (*Urteilskraft*) powers *Pl.* of discernment (*od.* discrimination)

Urteils|findung f reaching a (*od.* the) verdict; **~kraft** f; *nur Sg.* (powers *Pl.* of) judg(e)ment *od.* discernment; **~spruch** m *Jur.* sentence, verdict; **~verkündung** f *Jur.* pronouncing of judg(e)ment; **~vermögen** n judg(e)ment, ability to judge; discernment; **~vollstreckung** f *Jur.* execution of a

(*od.* the) sentence

Urtext m original text

Urtierchen n *Zool.* protozoon (*Pl.* protozoa), protozoan

Urtrieb m basic instinct

urtümlich *Adj.* (*unberührt*) unspoil|t (*Am.* -ed), original; (*primitiv*) primitive; (*archaisch*) archaic; **Urtümlichkeit** f; *nur Sg.* unspoil|t (*Am.* -ed) (*od.* original) state (+ *Gen.* of); primitiveness; archaic character (of)

Urtyp, Urtypus m archetype

Uruguay 1. (n); -s; *Geog.* Uruguay; **2.** m; -(s); *Fluss:* Uruguay; **Uruguayer** m; -s, -, **Uruguayerin** f; -, -nen Uruguayan, *weiblich auch:* Uruguayan woman (*od.* girl *etc.*); **uruguayisch** *Adj.* Uruguayan

Urur|... *im Subst.* great-great-...; **~großvater** m great-great-grandfather

Urvater m ancestor, forefather

Urvertrauen n primal sense of trust

Urvie(c)h n *umg.* real character

Urvogel m *Zool.* archaeopteryx

Urvolk n primitive people (*od.* tribe); (*Ureinwohner*) (ab)original inhabitants *Pl.* (*od.* population)

Urwald m **1.** *tropischer:* jungle; **2.** (*ursprünglicher Wald*) primeval forest

Urweib n *umg.* archetypal woman

Urwelt f primeval world; **urweltlich** *Adj.* primeval

urwüchsig *Adj.* (*ursprünglich*) original, unspoil|t (*Am.* -ed); (*ungekünstelt*) natural; (*derb, kernig*) earthy (*auch Humor etc.*); **~er Bayer** picture-book (*Am. auch* postcard) Bavarian; **Urwüchsigkeit** f; *nur Sg.* original (*od.* unspoil|t, *Am.* -ed) state (+ *Gen.* of); naturalness; earthiness; → **urwüchsig**

Urzeit f: *die ~* primeval times *Pl.*; *Tiere der ~* primeval creatures; *vor ~en* fig. a long, long time ago; *seit ~en* from (*od.* since) time immemorial; **urzeitlich** *Adj.* primeval

Urzeugung f *Bio.* spontaneous generation

Urzustand m original state

Usambaraveilchen n *Bot.* African violet

USA *Pl.* USA, *Am. auch* U.S.A. *Sg.*, US, *Am. auch* U.S. *Sg.*

US|-Amerikaner m, **~Amerikanerin** f American (citizen); **~amerikanisch** *Adj.* US ..., *Am. auch* U.S. ..., American

Usance [y'zã:s] f; -, -n; *bes. Wirts.* (usual) practice, usage

Usbeke m; -n, -n, **Usbekin** f; -, -nen Uzbek; *weiblich auch:* Uzbek woman (*od.* girl *etc.*); **usbekisch** *Adj.* Uzbek; **Usbekistan** (n); -s; *Geog.* Uzbekistan

US-Dollar m United States (*od.* US, *Am. auch* U.S.) dollar; **10 ~** 10 (US, *Am. auch* U.S.) dollars *Pl.*

User ['ju:zɐ] m; -s, -, **~in** f; -, -nen; *Sl.* **1.** *EDV* (*Anwender*) user; **2.** (*Drogenkonsument*) user

US|-Streitkräfte *Pl.*, **~Truppen** *Pl.* US (*Am. auch* U.S.) armed forces

Usurpation f; -, -en usurpation; **Usurpator** m; -s, -en, **Usurpatorin** f; -, -nen usurper; **usurpieren** v/t. usurp; *weitS. auch* appropriate *s.th.*

Usus m; -, *kein Pl.* custom, practi|ce (*Am.* -se); *das ist hier so ~* it's the custom around here

usw. *Abk.* etc(.)

Utensil n; -s, -ien; *mst Pl.* utensil, implement

Uterus m; -, *Uteri*; *Anat.* uterus (*Pl.* uteri)

Utilitarismus m utilitarianism; **utilitaristisch** *Adj.* utilitarian

Utopie f **1.** (*phantastische Idee*) impossible dream; **2.** (*Darstellung e-r idealen Welt etc.*) utopia; **utopisch** *Adj.* fanciful, unrealistic; *stärker:* utopian; **~er Roman** *altm.* utopian novel; *weitS.* science-fiction novel; **Utopist** m; -en, -en, **Utopistin** f; -, -nen utopian

UV|-Filter m UV filter; **~Licht** n; *nur Sg.* ultraviolet light; **~Strahlen** *Pl.*, **~Strahlung** f ultraviolet rays *Pl.*

Ü-Wagen m → **Übertragungswagen**

Uz m; -es, -e; *mst Sg.*; *nordd.* leg-pull, joke; **uzen** v/t. *umg.* (*j-n*) kid, pull *s.o.'s* leg, have *s.o.* on

U

V v

V, v *n*; -, - *und umg.* -s V, v; **V wie Viktor** *Buchstabieren*: "v" for (*od.* as in) "Victor"

va banque [vaˈbãːk]: ~ **spielen** take a gamble; **Vabanquespiel** *n*; *nur Sg.*; *fig.* gamble

Vademekum *n*; -s, -s; *lit.* vade mecum, handbook

vag *Adj.* → **vage**

Vagabund *m*; -en, -en vagabond, tramp, *Am. auch* bum *umg.*, hobo *umg.*; **Vagabundenleben** *n* vagabond life, life of a vagabond; **vagabundieren** *v/i.* lead the life of a vagabond, drift from place to place

vage I. *Adj.* vague; **II.** *Adv. andeuten etc.*: vaguely; **sich nur ~ erinnern** only vaguely remember; **Vagheit** *f* vagueness

Vagina *f*, -, *Vaginen*; *Anat.* vagina (*Pl.* vaginas *od.* vaginae); **vaginal** *Adj.* vaginal

vakant *Adj.* vacant; **Vakanz** *f*; -, -en **1.** vacancy; **2.** *Dial. altm.* (*Ferien*) school holidays *Pl.*, *Am.* summer vacation

Vakuum *n*; -s, *Vakuen und Vakua* vacuum (*Pl.* vacuums *od.* vacua) (*auch fig.*); **~bremse** *f* vacuum brake; **~packung** *f* vacuum pack; **~pumpe** *f* vacuum pump

vakuumverpackt *Adj.* vacuum-packed; **Vakuumverpackung** *f* vacuum pack; **vakuumversiegelt** *Adj.* vacuum-sealed; **Vakuumversiegelung** *f* vacuum sealing

Valentinstag *m* (St[.]) Valentine's day

Valenz *f*; -, -en; *Chem., Ling.* valence, valency

Valuta *f*; -, *Valuten*; *Fin.* (*Währung*) foreign currency; **~klausel** *f* exchange clause

Vamp [vɛmp] *m*; -s, -s vamp; **männermordender ~** *hum.* man-eater

Vampir *m*; -s, -e **1.** vampire; *fig. pej.* (*Wucherer*) vampire, bloodsucker; **2.** *Zool.* vampire bat

Vanadium *n*; -s, *kein Pl.*; *Chem.* vanadium

Vandale *m*; -n, -n *hist.* Vandal; *fig.* vandal; **wie die ~n** like vandals; **sie haben wie die ~n gehaust** they acted like vandals; **Vandalismus** *m*; -, *kein Pl.* vandalism

Vanille *f*; -, *kein Pl.*; *Gastr.* vanilla; **~eis** *n* vanilla ice-cream; **~geschmack** *m* vanilla flavo(u)r; **~kipferl** *n* *österr.* small horn-shaped cake made with almond pastry and sprinkled with vanilla sugar; **~pudding** *m* vanilla-flavoured blancmange, *Am.* vanilla pudding; **~schote** *f* vanilla pod; **~soße** *f* vanilla sauce; **~stange** *f* vanilla pod; **~zucker** *m* vanilla sugar

Vanillin *n*; -s, *kein Pl.* vanillin; **~zucker** *m* vanilla sugar

variabel *Adj.* variable; **Variabilität** *f*, -, *kein Pl.* variability; **Variable** *f*, -n, *n*; *Math., EDV* variable

Variante *f*; -, -n variation (**zu** on); *Ling.* variant (+ *Gen.* of); **variantenreich** *Adj.* highly variable, *nachgestellt*: full of variation

Variation *f*; -, -en variation (+ *Gen.* of, on; *Mus.* **zu, über** + *Akk.* on); **Variationsbreite** *f* *Bio., Psych.* range (*od.* extent) of variation, variational range

Varietät *f*; -, -en; *Bio., Ling. etc.* variety

Varietee, Varieté [variɛˈteː] *n*; -s, -s variety theat|re (*Am. auch* -er), *Brit.* music hall, *Am. hist.* vaudeville theater; **~künstler** *m*, **~künstlerin** *f* music-hall entertainer, *Am.* vaudeville performer; **~theater** *n* → **Varietee**; **~vorstellung** *f* variety show, *Am. hist.* vaudeville

variieren *vt/i.* vary; **ein Thema leicht ~** vary a theme slightly

Vasall *m*; -en, -en vassal; **Vasallenstaat** *m* satellite state; **Vasallentum** *n* -s, *kein Pl.* vassalage

Vase *f*; -, -n vase

Vasektomie *f*; -, -n; *Med.* vasectomy

Vaseline® *f*; -, *kein Pl.* vaseline®

Vater *m*; -s, *Väter* father (*auch fig.*); *kirchl.* Father; *von Tieren*: sire; *Pl.* (*Vorfahren*) forefathers, ancestors; **~ von drei Kindern sein** be a (*od.* the) father of three children, be a father of three; **er ist ganz der ~** he's just like his father; **er ist der geistige ~ der Idee** it's his idea (*od.* brainchild), he thought of the idea; **der Heilige ~** the Holy Father; **~ Staat** *hum.* the State; *in den USA*: Uncle Sam; **~ Rhein** Father Rhine, the Rhine; **Gott ~** God the Father; **der ~ im Himmel** our Father in Heaven; **wie der ~, so der Sohn** like father, like son; **~bild** *n* *Psych.* father image; **~bindung** *f* *Psych.* father fixation

Väterchen *n* *umg.* old man (*od.* fellow), old geezer *Sl.*; **~ Frost** Jack Frost

Vater|figur *f* *Psych.* father-figure; **~freuden** *Pl.* joys of fatherhood; **~ entgegensehen** *umg.* be an expectant father; **~haus** *n* parental home; **~komplex** *m* *Psych.* father complex

Vaterland *n*: *j-s* one's native country; **das (deutsche) ~** the Fatherland; **~ lieben** love one's country; **vaterländisch I.** *Adj.* national; (~ **gesinnt**) patriotic; **II.** *Adv.* patriotically; **~ gesinnt sein** be patriotic

Vaterlandsliebe *f* patriotism, love of one's country; **vaterlandslos** *Adj. pej. Gesinnung etc.*: unpatriotic; **Vaterlandsverräter** *m* traitor to one's (*od.* the) country

väterlich I. *Adj. nur attr.* fatherly, paternal; **II.** *Adv.* like a father; **väterlicherseits** *Adv.* on one's father's side; **mein Onkel etc. ~** my paternal uncle *etc.*; **Väterlichkeit** *f*; *nur Sg.* fatherliness

Vaterliebe *f* paternal love

vaterlos *Adj.* fatherless; **~ aufwachsen** grow up without a father

Vater|mord *m* patricide; **~mörder** *m* **1.** patricide; **2.** *altm., hum.* (*Stehkragen*) high (*od.* choker) collar

Vaterschaft *f* paternity, fatherhood; **Feststellung der ~** *Jur.* affiliation (order), *Am.* (child) support order

Vaterschafts|bestimmung *f* *Jur.* determination of paternity; **~klage** *f* paternity suit (*od.* case); **~nachweis** *m* proof of paternity; **~test** *m* paternity test

Vaterschaftsurlaub *m* paternity leave

Vater|stadt *f* hometown; **~stelle** *f*: **~ vertreten bei** act as father to; **~tag** *m* Father's Day; **~tier** *n* *Zool.* sire

Vaterunser *n*; -s, -; *Reli.* Lord's Prayer; **zehn ~ beten** say ten Our Fathers

Vati *m*; -s, -s; *umg.* dad(dy), *Am. auch* pa(pa); *als Anrede*: Dad(dy), *Am. auch* Pa(pa)

Vatikan *m*; -s; *kath.*: **der ~** the Vatican; **vatikanisch** *Adj.* Vatican ...; **Vatikanstadt** *f* *nur Sg.* Vatican City; **Vatikanstaat** *m*; *nur Sg.*: **der ~** the Vatican State

V-Ausschnitt *m* V-neck; **Pullover mit ~** V-neck(ed) jumper (*Am.* sweater)

v. Chr. *Abk.* B.C.

VEB *m*; -(s), -s; *Abk.* (**Volkseigener Betrieb**) *ehem. DDR* state-owned company

Vedute *f*; -, -n veduta (*Pl.* vedute)

Veganer *m*; -s, -, **~in** *f*; -, -nen vegan

Vegetarier *m*; -s, -, **~in** *f*; -, -nen vegetarian; **strenger ~** strict vegetarian; **vegetarisch I.** *Adj.* vegetarian; **II.** *Adv.*: **sich ~ ernähren** be a vegetarian; **~ kochen** cook vegetarian food

Vegetation *f*; -, -en vegetation; **e-e üppige ~** lavish growth

Vegetations|grenze *f* limit of vegetation; **~periode** *f* period of vegetation; **~stufe** *f* level of vegetation

vegetativ *Adj.* **1.** *Bio.* (*ungeschlechtlich*) vegetative; **2.** *Physiol.*: **~es Nervensystem** autonomic nervous system

vegetieren *v/i.* vegetate (*auch fig.*); **am Rande der Existenz / im Slum ~** eke out a miserable existence / live from hand to mouth in the slum

vehement *Adj.* vehement; **Vehemenz** *f*; -, *kein Pl.* vehemence

Vehikel *n*; -s, - **1.** *umg. mst pej.* (*Fahrzeug*) contraption; **2.** *fig.* (*Mittel*) vehicle

Veilchen *n* **1.** *Bot.* violet; **blau wie ein ~** *umg.* drunk as a lord; **2.** *umg. hum.* (*blaues Auge*) black eye; **veilchenblau** *Adj.* **1.** violet; **2.** *umg. fig.* blind drunk

Veitstanz *m*; *nur Sg.*; *Med. altm.*: **der ~** St(.) Vitus's Dance, *Med.* chorea

Vektor *m*; -s, -en; *Math., Phys.* vector; **~grafik** *f* *EDV* vector graphics *Pl.*; **~rechnung** *f* *Math.* vector analysis

Velo *n*; -s, -s; *schw., südd.* bicycle; **Velodrom** *n*; -s, -e velodrome

Velours [vəˈluːɐ] **1.** *m*; -, -; (*Gewebe*) velour; **2.** *n*; -, -; (*Leder*) suede; **~le-**

der *n* suede (leather); **~teppich** *m* velvet-pile carpet

Vene *f*; *-, -n*; *Anat.* vein

Venedig (*n*); *-s*; *Geog.* Venice

Venen|entzündung *f Med.* phlebitis; **~leiden** *n* varicose veins *Pl.*

Venetien (*n*); *-s*; *Geog.* Veneto

Venezianer *m*; *-s, -,* **~in** *f*; *-, -nen* Venetian, *weiblich auch*: Venetian woman (*od.* girl *etc.*); **venezianisch** *Adj.* Venetian

Venezolaner *m*; *-s, -,* **~in** *f*; *-, -nen* Venezuelan, *weiblich auch*: Venezuelan woman (*od.* girl *etc.*); **venezolanisch** *Adj.* Venezuelan; **Venezuela** (*n*); *-s*; *Geog.* Venezuela

venös *Adj. Physiol.* venous

Ventil *n*; *-s, -e*; *Tech., Mus.* valve; *fig.* vent, outlet; **die ~e einstellen** *Mot.* adjust valve clearance; **er brauchte ein ~ für s-e Wut** he needed an outlet for his rage; he needed to vent his rage

Ventilation *f*; *-, -en* ventilation; *Vorrichtung*: ventilation (*od.* ventilating) system

Ventilator *m*; *-s, -en Gerät*: (electric) fan; (*Deckenventilator*) ceiling fan; *Tech.* (ventilating) fan, ventilator

ventilieren *v/t.* **1.** *fig.* (*Meinung etc.*) air; (*Problem etc.*) weigh up, consider; **2.** (*Raum etc.*) ventilate

Ventil|klappe *f Tech.* valve flap; **~steuerung** *f* valve control, timing gear

Venus *f*; *-, kein Pl.* **1.** *Myth.* Venus; **2.** *Astron.* Venus; **~berg** *m Anat.* mons veneris; **~fliegenfalle** *f Bot.* Venus('s) flytrap; **~hügel** *m Anat.* mons veneris; **~muschel** *f Zool.* Venus's shell

verabfolgen *v/t. altm.* → *verabreichen*

verabreden I. *v/t.* (*etw.*) agree on, arrange; (*Zeit, Termin, Ort*) *auch* fix; **II.** *v/refl.*: **sich mit j-m ~** *privat*: arrange to meet (*od.* go out with) s.o.; *geschäftlich*: make an appointment with s.o.; **für heute Abend hab ich mich schon verabredet** *privat*: I'm already meeting someone this evening, I've already arranged to meet someone this evening; **verabredet I.** *P.P.* → *verabreden*; **II.** *Adj.*: **zur ~en Zeit am ~en Ort** at the agreed time and place; **ich bin für morgen mit ihm ~** I've arranged to meet him tomorrow; **ich bin schon ~** I've already arranged to meet (*od.* go out with) someone (*od.* a friend *etc.*); *zum Rendezvous*: *auch* I've already got a date; **~e Sache** put-up job, *Am. auch* setup; **verabredetermaßen** *Adv.* as agreed (on), as arranged; **Verabredung** *f* **1.** (*Rendezvous*) date; *geschäftlich*: appointment; **e-e ~ haben** have arranged to meet (*od.* go out with) someone; **für heute Abend hab ich schon e-e ~** *privat*: I'm already meeting someone this evening, I've already arranged to meet someone this evening; **2.** (*Vereinbarung*) agreement; **sich an e-e ~ halten** hold (*od.* stick) to an agreement

verabreichen *v/t.* (*Medikamente*) give (*j-m etw.* s.o. s.th.), *förm.* administer (s.th. to s.o.); **j-m e-e Tracht Prügel ~** *hum.* give s.o. a good hiding; **Verabreichung** *f* giving; administration, administering

verabsäumen *v/t. Amtsspr.* neglect

verabscheuen *v/t.* detest, loathe, abhor; **verabscheuenswert, verabscheuenswürdig** *Adj.* despicable, abhorrent; **Verabscheuung** *f* loathing (+ *Gen.* of), disgust (for); **verabscheuungswürdig** *Adj.* despicable, abhorrent

verabschieden I. *v/t.* **1.** say goodbye to; *am Bahnhof etc.*: see off; **der Staatsgast wurde am Flughafen verabschiedet** the official visitor was given a farewell at the airport; **2.** (*entlassen*) dismiss; (*Offiziere*) retire, discharge; (*Beamte zur Ruhe setzen*) retire, discharge; **j-n feierlich ~** retire (*od.* discharge) s.o. with all due ceremony; **3.** (*Gesetz*) pass; **II.** *v/refl.* **1.** say goodbye (*von* to); **sich mit e-m Kuss von j-m ~** kiss s.o. goodbye; **ich muss mich jetzt leider ~** I'm afraid I have to go (*od.* leave) now; **2.** *fig.*: **von solchen Vorstellungen müssen wir uns ~** we have to turn aside from ideas like that; **nach 20 km verabschiedete sich die Lichtmaschine** *umg.* after 20 km the alternator packed in (*bes. Am.* up); **Verabschiedung** *f* **1.** dismissal; *feierliche*: retirement, discharge; **2.** *e-s Gesetzes*: passing

verabsolutieren *v/t.* make s.th. (into an) absolute

verachten *v/t.* despise, disdain; (*verschmähen*) *auch* scorn; (*Gefahr, Tod*) defy; (*auch*) **nicht zu ~** *umg.* not to be sneezed (*od.* sniffed) at; **ein kühles Bier wäre jetzt nicht zu ~** *umg.* I wouldn't say no to a cool beer just now; **verachtenswert** *Adj.* contemptible, despicable; **Verächter** *m*; *-s, -* despiser (+ *Gen.* of); **kein ~ e-s guten Tropfens** *etc.* **sein** *umg.* be fond of a good wine *etc.*; **verächtlich I.** *Adj.* **1.** contemptuous, disdainful, scornful; **~ machen** run s.o. *od.* s.th. down; **2.** → *verachtenswert*; **II.** *Adv.* **lachen** *etc.*: contemptuously, disdainfully, scornfully; **sich ~ äußern** speak with contempt; **Verächtlichmachung** *f*: **er warnte vor e-r ~ der Demokratie** he warned against showing contempt for democracy; **Verachtung** *f* contempt, disdain; (*Verschmähung*) *auch* scorn; **mit ~ strafen** ignore, treat *s.o.* with contempt; **verachtungsvoll** *Adj.* contemptuous, disdainful; **verachtungswürdig** *Adj.* despicable, contemptible

veralbern *v/t. umg.* kid, pull *s.o.'s* leg; **Veralberung** *f*: **der Bericht war eine ~ des Parlaments** the report made fun of parliament

verallgemeinern *vt/i.* generalize; **verallgemeinernd I.** *Part. Präs.*, **~** *allgemeinernd*; **II.** *Adj. Aussage etc.*: generalizing; **III.** *Adv. ausgedrückt, darstellen etc.*: in a generalizing way; **Verallgemeinerung** *f*: (*grobe*) **~** (gross) generalization; **e-n Hang zur ~ haben** have a tendency to generalize

veralten *v/i.* become outdated; *Mode*: go out of fashion (*od.* style); **veraltet I.** *P.P.* → *veralten*; **II.** *Adj.* out-of-date ..., *präd.* out of date; (*altmodisch*) (out)dated; *Methoden etc.*: *auch* antiquated; *EDV Datei*: obsolete

Veranda *f* veranda(h), *Am. auch* (covered) porch

veränderbar *Adj.* changeable; **veränderlich** *Adj.* **1.** (*unbeständig*) *Charakter, Wetter etc.*: changeable; **das Barometer steht auf „~"** the barometer says "changeable"; **2.** *Math., Ling. etc.* variable; **~e Größen** *Math.* variables; **Veränderlichkeit** *f* changeability; *des Wesens*: fickleness; *Math., Ling.* variability

verändern I. *v/t.* change; (*Aussehen*) *auch* alter; (*reformieren*) reform; **der Bart verändert ihn stark** his beard makes him look very different; **II.** *v/refl.* **1.** change; **er hat sich sehr verändert** he's really changed; **sich zu s-m Vorteil/Nachteil ~** *im Wesen*: change for the better/worse; *in der Erscheinung*: look better/worse; **sich krankhaft ~** *Med., Gewebe etc.*: reveal pathological changes; **2.** *beruflich*: change one's job; **sie will sich ~** *beruflich*: she's looking for a new job, she wants to move on; → *auch ändern*; **Veränderung** *f* change; *leichte*: alteration, modification; *berufliche ~* change of job; **in ihr geht e-e ~ vor** there is a change taking place in her; **jede bauliche ~ muss genehmigt sein** all structural alterations must be approved

verängstigen *v/t.* frighten, scare; **verängstigt I.** *P.P.* → *verängstigen*; **II.** *Adj.* frightened, scared; (*eingeschüchtert*) timid; **III.** *Adv.*: **die Katze lag völlig ~ unter dem Bett** the cat lay under the bed frightened out of its wits; **Verängstigung** *f Zustand*: state of fright; (*Eingeschüchtertsein*) timidity

verankern *v/t. Naut., Tech.* anchor (*auch fig.*); **fest im Boden verankert** firmly fixed in the ground; **in e-m Gesetz verankert** *fig.* embodied in a law; **die in der Verfassung verankerte Religionsfreiheit** the freedom of worship which is firmly established in the constitution; **Verankerung** *f* anchoring; *fig. im Gesetz*: embodiment

veranlagen *v/t. steuerlich*: assess; **veranlagt I.** *P.P.* → *veranlagen*; **II.** *Adj.* (naturally) inclined (*für, zu* to); **künstlerisch ~ sein** have artistic talent, have an artistic bent; **praktisch ~ sein** be practically minded; **homosexuell/sadistisch ~ sein** have homosexual/sadistic tendencies; **so ist er nicht ~** *umg.* that's not in his nature, he's not like that; **Veranlagung** *f* **1.** *charakterliche*: disposition; (*Neigung*) inclination; (*Talent*) gift, talent; **s-e künstlerische/homosexuelle ~** his artistic bent / homosexual tendencies *Pl.*; **es ist ~** it's in his (*od.* her) nature, he (*od.* she) was made that way; **2.** *Med.*: **e-e ~ haben zu** be prone to, have a tendency toward(s); **3.** *steuerliche*: assessment; **i-e gemeinsame ~ zur Einkommensteuer** their joint assessment for income tax

veranlassen *v/t.* (*anordnen*) arrange for; **~, dass etw. getan wird** see to it that s.th. is done, arrange for s.th. to be done; **j-n zu etw. ~** *Person*: get s.o. to do s.th.; *Beweggrund*: prompt s.o. to do s.th., make s.o. do s.th.; **das Nötige ~** make the necessary arrangements, take the necessary steps; **alles Weitere veranlasse ich** I will see to everything else; **sich veranlasst fühlen zu** (+ *Inf.*) feel bound to (+ *Inf.*); **Veranlassung** *f* occasion; (*Ursache*) cause, reason; (*Beweggrund*) motive; **auf ~ von** (*od.* + *Gen.*) at the instigation of, at *s.o.'s* prompting (*od.* urging); **~ geben zu** give occasion to; **ohne jede ~** (entirely) without provocation; **er hat keine ~ zu** (+ *Inf.*) there's no reason for him to (+ *Inf.*)

veranschaulichen *v/t.* illustrate; **durch Beispiele ~** illustrate by means of examples; **sich** (*Dat.*) **etw. ~** visualize s.th., picture s.th. (to o.s.); **Veranschaulichung** *f*: (*zur*) **~** (by way of) illustration

veranschlagen *v/t.* estimate (**auf** + *Akk.* at); **zu hoch/niedrig ~** overestimate/underestimate, pitch too high/

low; **Veranschlagung** *f* estimate (*auf + Akk.* of)

veranstalten *v/t.* arrange, organize; (*Ausstellung*) mount; *e-n Riesenzirkus etc. ~ umg. fig.* make an enormous fuss *etc.*; **Veranstalter** *m*; *-s, -,* **Veranstalterin** *f*; *-, -nen* organizer; *Sport auch* promoter; **Veranstaltung** *f* **1.** *nur Sg.* arrangement, organization; **2.** *konkret:* event; organization; **2.** *konkret:* event; *öffentliche:* (public) function; *Univ. etc.* course; *der Besuch der ~ ist Pflicht* course attendance is compulsory

Veranstaltungs|angebot *n* events on offer, *Am.* available events; (*Kursangebot*) courses on offer, *Am.* offered courses; **~beginn** *m* start (of the event); (*Kursbeginn*) start of the course; *der ~ ist um 8* the event (*od.* course) starts at 8 o'clock; **~kalender** *m* calendar of events; **~ort** *m* venue, *bes. Am.* location; **~programm** *n* program(me) of events; **~reihe** *f* series of events; (*Kursreihe*) series of courses; **~termin** *m* date of the event; (*Kurstermin*) date of the course; *der ~ wird Ende August sein* the event (*od.* course) will take place at the end of August

verantwortbar *Adj.* justifiable; *ist das Betreiben von Kernkraftwerken ~?* is it possible to justify having nuclear power stations?

verantworten I. *v/t.* answer for, take the responsibility for; *du musst es ~* you'll have to answer for it (*od.* take [the] responsibility); *das kann ich kaum ~* I can hardly justify it; *es ist nicht zu ~* it can't be justified; *ich glaube, das können wir ~* I believe we can justify it; **II.** *v/refl.: sich für etw. ~* answer for s.th.; *sich vor j-m ~ müssen* have to answer to s.o.; *er hat sich wegen Mordes zu ~* he has been accused of murder

verantwortlich I. *Adj.* **1.** responsible; (*haftbar, schuld*) *auch* answerable (*für* for); *dafür ~ sein, dass ... dass etw. geschieht:* be responsible for seeing to it that ..., have to make sure that ...; *dass etw. geschehen ist:* be responsible for the fact that ...; *j-n ~ machen* hold s.o. responsible (*od.* accountable); *weitS.* blame s.o. (*für* for); *~ zeichnen für* be responsible for; (*der Urheber sein von*) be the author of; *die Verantwortlichen zur Rechenschaft ziehen* bring those responsible to account; **2.** (*verantwortungsvoll*) (highly) responsible; **II.** *Adv.: das Projekt ~ leiten* be in charge of the project; **Verantwortlichkeit** *f*; *nur Sg.* **1.** responsibility; *das fällt in s-e ~* that's his responsibility; **2.** (*Verantwortungssinn*) sense of responsibility

Verantwortung *f* **1.** responsibility; *e-e schwere ~* a heavy responsibility; *auf eigene ~* at one's own risk; *~ übernehmen* take (*od.* accept) responsibility; *die ~ haben für Kinder etc.:* be responsible for; *die (volle) ~ tragen auch bei Vertrag etc.:* bear (full) responsibility; *die ~ lastet schwer auf ihm* he is weighed down by the responsibility; *die ~ übernehmen für etw., j-n:* take responsibility for; *für Anschlag etc.:* accept (*od.* assume) responsibility (*for*); *zur ~ ziehen* call to account; *die ~ auf j-n abwälzen* shift responsibility onto s.o.; **2.** *nur Sg;* (*Verantwortungsbewusstsein*) sense of responsibility; *ohne ~ handeln* act irresponsibly

Verantwortungsbereich *m* area of re-

sponsibility; *diese Angelegenheit liegt nicht in unserem ~* this matter is not our area of responsibility

verantwortungsbewusst I. *Adj.* responsible(-minded); **II.** *Adv. handeln etc.:* responsibly; **Verantwortungsbewusstsein** *n* sense of responsibility

Verantwortungsgefühl *n; nur Sg* sense of responsibility

verantwortungslos I. *Adj.* irresponsible; **II.** *Adv.* irresponsibly; *du hast dich ziemlich ~ verhalten* you acted pretty irresponsibly; **Verantwortungslosigkeit** *f* irresponsibility

verantwortungsvoll *Adj. Person, Posten etc.:* responsible; *der ~e Umgang mit unserer Umwelt ist sehr wichtig* it is very important that we treat the environment responsibly

veräppeln *v/t. umg.* pull s.o.'s leg, have (*Am.* put) s.o. on, kid s.o.; (*verspotten*) take the mickey out (*Am.* make fun) of s.o.; *du willst mich wohl ~!* are you having (*Am.* putting) me on?

verarbeiten *v/t.* **1.** (*Rohstoff, Daten*) process; (*zu etw. machen*) make (*zu* into); (*behandeln*) treat; *die Seide wird zu Teppichen verarbeitet* carpets are made from the silk, the silk is used to make carpets; **2.** *geistig:* (*Eindruck, Erlebnis*) digest, assimilate; (*Enttäuschung*) overcome, come to terms with; **3.** (*nutzbar machen*) put to use, use; *in e-r Abhandlung etc.: auch* take into consideration; (*Motiv*) use, employ; *s-e Erlebnisse zu e-m Roman ~* turn one's experiences into a novel; *Märchenmotive ~* use (*od.* employ) fairytale motifs; **4.** *Med., Magen:* digest; **verarbeitend I.** *Part. Präs.* → *verarbeiten;* **II.** *Adj.: ~e Industrie* manufacturing (*od.* processing) industry; *die Holz/Eisen ~e Industrie* the wood-/iron-processing industry; **verarbeitet I.** *P.P.* → *verarbeiten;* **II.** *Adj.* processed; *gut/schlecht ~ Ware etc.:* well/badly finished; *der Wagen ist nicht gut ~* the car has been badly finished; **Verarbeitung** *f* **1.** *Vorgang:* processing; treatment; digestion; use; → *verarbeiten.* **2.** *Ergebnis:* workmanship; *äußere:* finish; (*Qualität*) quality; *erstklassige ~* top quality

verargen *v/t.: ich kann es ihm nicht ~* I can't blame him (for it); *ich kann es ihm nicht ~, dass/wenn er ...* I can't blame him for (+ *Ger.*) / if he ...

verärgern *v/t.* annoy; *stärker:* upset, anger; *damit verärgert man s-e Kunden* that upsets the customers; **verärgert I.** *P.P.* → *verärgern;* **II.** *Adj.* annoyed; *stärker:* upset, angry; **III.** *Adv. reagieren etc.:* in annoyance; *stärker:* angrily; **Verärgerung** *f* (*Ärger*) annoyance

verarmen *v/i.* become poor (*od.* impoverished), be reduced to poverty; *dadurch verarmt der Boden* the soil becomes poor as a result; *geistig ~ fig.* become spiritually and intellectually impoverished; **verarmt I.** *P.P.* → *verarmen;* **II.** *Adj.* impoverished; **Verarmung** *f* impoverishment (*auch fig.*)

verarschen *v/t. umg.* **1.** (*sich lustig machen über*) take the piss out of *Sl., Am.* make a laughing-stock of; *willst du mich ~?* are you taking the piss (out of me)?, *Am.* are you making fun of me?; *~ kann ich mich alleine* stop taking the piss (*Am.* making fun); **2.** (*reinlegen*) take s.o. for a ride; *er hat mich verarscht auch* I've been had; *bei diesen „Kaffeefahrten" werden die Kunden nur verarscht* the

customers on these promotional trips are just being ripped off; **Verarschung** *f umg.: diese „Reform" ist e-e gigantische ~* this "reform" is a gigantic piss-take (*Am.* con *od.* fraud)

verarzten *v/t. umg.* **1.** *Wunde:* fix up; (*verbinden*) patch up; **2.** *hum.* (*sich kümmern um etc.*) see to; *Moment, Sie werden gleich verarztet!* just a second, we *etc.* will see to you in a moment!

verästeln *v/refl.* branch out, ramify (*beide auch fig.*); **verästelt I.** *P.P.* → *verästeln;* **II.** *Adj.* branching, branchy; *ein stark ~es System* a very complex system; **Verästelung** *f* branching out; *fig.* ramifications *Pl.; bis in die feinsten ~en der Lunge* into the finest branches of the lungs

verätzen *v/t.* burn; (*Sachen*) erode; *Med.* cauterize; **Verätzung** *f* burning; *konkret:* burn; *bei Sachen:* erosion; *Med.* cauterization

verausgaben *v/refl. finanziell:* overspend; *kräftemäßig:* overexert o.s.; *auf Dauer:* burn o.s. out

veräußerlich *Adj.* sal(e)able; *Jur. etc. auch* alienable; **veräußern** *v/t.* alienate; (*übertragen*) transfer (*an* + *Akk.* to); (*verkaufen*) dispose of, sell; **Veräußerung** *f* alienation; disposal, sale; → *veräußern*

Veräußerungsgewinn *m Fin., Wirts.* gain on sale (*od.* disposal), capital gain

Verb *n*; *-s, -en; Ling.* verb

verbal *Adj.* verbal

Verbalinjurie *f*; *-, -n; Jur.* verbal insult

verbalisieren *v/t.* verbalize (*auch Ling.*); **Verbalisierung** *f* verbalization

verballhornen *v/t.* (*Wort etc.*) corrupt, distort; **Verballhornung** *f* corruption

Verband *m*; *-(e)s, Verbände* **1.** *Med.* dressing, bandage; *e-n ~ anlegen/wechseln* apply/change a dressing (*od.* bandage); **2.** (*Vereinigung*) association; *Mil.* formation (*auch Naut., Flug.*), unit; *im ~ fliegen Mil.* fly in formation; *Zool.* fly in a group; **3.** *Tech.* bond

verbandelt *Adj. umg.: mit j-m ~ sein* be going out with (*bes. Am.* be dating) s.o.

Verband|kasten *m Med.* first-aid box (*Am.* kit); **~material** *n*, **~mittel** *Pl.* dressing material; **~mull** *m* lint, surgical gauze; **~platz** *m Mil.* dressing station; **~schere** *f* dressing scissors *Pl.*

Verbandsebene *f: auf ~* at association level

Verbandskasten *etc.* → *Verbandkasten etc.*

Verbands|klage *f Jur.* legal action by an (*od.* the) association; **~präsident** *m*, **~präsidentin** *f* association president

Verbandstoff *m* dressing material

Verbands|verbot *n Sport, bei Doping:* association ban; **~vorsitzende** *m*, *f* association chairperson, *männlich:* association chairman, *weiblich:* association chairwoman; **~vorstand** *m* association board

Verband|watte *f Med.* surgical cotton wool, *Am.* surgical cotton; **~zeug** *n* dressing material

verbannen *v/t.* exile; *hist. und fig.* banish; *Autos aus der Innenstadt ~* ban cars from the town centre (*Am.* the downtown area); *j-n aus s-m Leben / s-n Gedanken ~* shut s.o. out of one's life / banish s.o. from one's thoughts; **Verbannte** *m*, *f*; *-n, -n* exile; **Verban-**

nung f exile (auch Ort); hist. und fig. banishment; **j-n in die ~ schicken** send s.o. into exile; **Verbannungsort** m place of exile

verbarrikadieren I. v/t. barricade; **II.** v/refl. barricade o.s. (**in** + Dat. in); **die letzten Wochen vor dem Examen habe ich mich verbarrikadiert** in the last few weeks before the exam I shut myself away

verbauen v/t. **1.** (versperren) obstruct, block; **2.** (Gelände etc., zubauen) build up; (verschandeln) spoil; **3.** (beim Bauen verbrauchen) use (up) in building; **4.** (schlecht bauen) build badly; stärker: make a mess of; **5.** Tech., befestigen, sichern: reinforce; **6.** fig.: **sich/j-m etw. ~** spoil one's / s.o.'s chances of getting (od. having, gaining etc.) s.th.; **sich** (Dat.) **die Zukunft ~** ruin one's chances for the future; **verbaut I.** P.P. → **verbauen**; **II.** Adj. Gelände etc.: built-up; **das Haus ist völlig ~** is a real mess; **dieser Weg ist dir ~** this way is not open to you

verbeamten v/t.: **j-n ~** give s.o. the status of a civil servant; **verbeamtet werden** be given the status of civil servant; **verbeamtet I.** P.P. → **verbeamten**; **II.** Adj. Lehrer etc.: präd. with the status of civil servant; **~ sein** have the status of civil servant; **Verbeamtung** f bestowing of the status of civil servant; **~ auf Lebenszeit** bestowing of the status of civil servant for life

verbeißen (unreg.) **I.** v/t. **1.** (Schmerz, Lächeln etc.) suppress; **sich** (Dat.) **das Lachen ~** force o.s. not to laugh, stifle one's laughter; **ich konnte mir das Lachen nicht ~** I couldn't keep a straight face; **2.** Jägerspr., Wild: (Bäume etc.) damage (by biting); **II.** v/refl.: **sich in etw.** (+ Akk.) **~** Tier: sink its teeth into s.th.; fig. become set (od. bent) on doing s.th.; **sich in etw.** (+ Akk.) **verbissen haben** Hund etc.: have sunk its teeth into s.th.; fig. in Arbeit etc.: keep at s.th. doggedly; in Meinung etc.: hold onto s.th. grimly, sink one's fangs in s.th.; **er hat sich in s-e Arbeit verbissen** auch he's working obsessively

verbellen v/t. Jägerspr. (Wild) bark at

verbergen (unreg.) **I.** v/t. hide, eher förm. conceal (**vor** + Dat. from); **sein Gesicht ~ in** (+ Dat.) bury one's face in; **nichts zu ~ haben** have nothing to hide; → auch **verborgen²**; **II.** v/refl. hide (o.s. od. itself); (verborgen sein) be hidden

verbessern I. v/t. improve (auch Tech.); (berichtigen) correct; (Buchausgabe) revise; **die Haltbarkeit ~ von** prolong the shelf-life of; **II.** v/refl. **1.** improve (auch Sache); beim Sprechen: correct o.s.; **2.** finanziell etc.: better o.s.; **wie ich höre, wollen Sie sich ~** I hear you are wanting to leave the company; **Verbesserung** f improvement; (Berichtigung) correction

verbesserungs|bedürftig Adj.: (sehr) **~** (badly) in need of improvement; **~fähig** Adj. capable of improvement

Verbesserungsvorschlag m suggestion for improvement

verbesserungswürdig Adj. präd. in need of improvement

verbeugen v/refl. bow (**vor** + Dat. to); **Verbeugung** f bow; **e-e ~ vor j-m machen** bow to s.o.

verbeulen v/t. dent; **verbeult I.** P.P. → **verbeulen**; **II.** Adj. Stoßstange etc.: dented; **~e Hosenbeine** trouser (Am. pant) legs that have gone baggy

around the knees

Verbform f Gram. verb form

verbiegen (unreg.) **I.** v/t. bend, buckle; fig. j-s Charakter: corrupt; **ich lasse mich nicht ~** fig. I won't be corrupted; (zwingen) you etc. can't force me; **II.** v/refl. bend, get bent, buckle; Holz: warp; → **verbogen**

verbiestert umg. **I.** Adj. **1.** (missmutig) annoyed, grumpy; **2.** (verwirrt) bewildered; stärker: distraught; (verstört) disturbed; **II.** Adv. grumpily; **warum schaust du so ~?** what are you looking so grumpy about?

verbieten (unreg.) **I.** v/t. forbid; öffentlich: ban; amtlich: prohibit; **j-m etw. ~** forbid s.o. s.th.; etw. zu tun: forbid s.o. to do s.th., prohibit s.o. from doing s.th.; **j-m das Haus / den Mund ~** ban s.o. from the house / silence s.o.; **er hat es mir verboten** mst he won't let me, he has forbidden me geh.; **hab ich dir nicht (ausdrücklich) verboten, das zu tun?** didn't I (expressly) forbid you to do that?; **du hast mir gar nichts zu ~!** you've no right to forbid me to do ~!; **Tabakwerbung sollte ganz verboten werden** tobacco advertising should be banned completely; **so viel Dummheit müsste verboten werden** umg. such stupidity shouldn't be allowed (od. should be outlawed); **das verbietet mir mein Stolz/Geldbeutel** umg. my pride prevents me from doing that / my finances won't stretch to that; **II.** v/refl.: **das verbietet sich von selbst** that's out of the question; → **verboten**

verbilden v/t. deform, spoil; (falsch erziehen) miseducate; **verbildet I.** P.P. → **verbilden**; **II.** Adj. deformed; weitS. (überzüchtet) overrefined, oversophisticated

verbildlichen v/t. illustrate

verbilligen I. v/t. lower the cost of; (Waren) reduce (in price); **II.** v/refl. go down (in price); **verbilligt I.** P.P. → **verbilligen**; **II.** Adj. Eintritt, Preis etc.: reduced; Tarif: cheap; **III.** Adv. einkaufen etc.: at a reduced price; **Verbilligung** f reduction (in price); niedrigerer Preis: reduced price

verbinden (unreg.) **I.** v/t. **1.** tie (together); (Getrenntes) connect (**mit** with, to); Tech. connect, couple, link; Chem. combine; EDV connect; → **angenehm** I; **2.** j-m die Augen **~** blindfold s.o.; **3.** Med. (Wunde) dress, bandage; (j-n) bandage s.o. up; **4.** Telef.: **j-n ~** put s.o. through (**mit** to); **ich verbinde** hold the line, please; **5.** (vereinigen) join, unite; (kombinieren) combine; (assoziieren) associate; **uns verbindet vieles** we have a lot in common; **mich verbindet einiges mit dieser Gegend** I have several ties with this area; **was verbindet dich mit dieser Stadt?** what connections do you have with this town?; **die beiden verbindet e-e enge Freundschaft** they are bound by close friendship; → **verbunden**; **II.** v/refl. combine (auch Chem.), be combined; **in ihm ~ sich Kraft und Schnelligkeit** etc. he (bzw. it) is a combination of power and speed etc.; **sich** (mit j-m) **ehelich ~** förm. enter into (holy) matrimony (with s.o.)

verbindlich I. Adj. **1.** (verpflichtend) binding (**für** upon); **2.** (gefällig) obliging; Worte etc.: friendly; **~sten Dank!** many thanks indeed, Am. thank you so much!; **II.** Adv. **1.** **~ zusagen** accept definitely, commit o.s.; weitS. say defi-

nitely (that) one is coming, promise to come; **2.** (entgegenkommend) obligingly; (auch freundlich) kindly; **danke ~st!** iro. thanks a lot (od. a million)!, much obliged!; **Verbindlichkeit** f **1.** obligation, liability, commitment; e-s Vertrags etc.: binding force; **2.** Wirts.: **~en** (Passiva) liabilities; **s-n ~en nachkommen** meet one's liabilities; **3.** (Gefälligkeit) obligingness; Pl. (höfliche Worte) courtesies

Verbindung f **1.** union (auch Ehe), bond; (Zusammenschluss, Vereinigung mehrerer Eigenschaften) combination; von Ideen: association; (Zusammenhang) connection; im Text: context; (Beziehung, auch Wirts.) relations Pl., contact (beide zu with); Jur. bond; **in ~ mit** combined with; in connection with, in conjunction with; **e-e ~ eingehen** join together, unite; Dinge: combine, unite; (sich verbünden) ally, form an alliance (alle mit with); **~en knüpfen** make contacts; **e-e ~ herstellen mit** (od. sich in ~ setzen mit) contact, get in touch with; **in ~ bleiben** keep in touch; **die ~ verlieren** lose touch; **in ~ bringen mit** fig. associate with; **in ~ stehen mit** be in touch (od. contact) with; mit e-r Sache: be connected with; **e-e ~ zwischen Rauchen und Krebs** a link between smoking and cancer; **2.** (Verkehrsverbindung) communication; Tech. und Telef. connection; (Verbindungsstelle) junction, Tech. joint; **e-e direkte ~ nach Basel** etc. a direct connection to Basle (Am. Basel etc.); **e-e ~ herstellen mit** per Funk etc.: establish communication with; **keine ~ bekommen mit** Telef. etc. not get through to; **die ~ ist sehr schlecht** Telef. etc. the line is very bad; **3.** Chem. compound; **4.** EDV connection, link; **keine ~ mit dem Server** etc. **bekommen** fail to get connected to the server; **5.** studentische: student society, Am. fraternity; für Studentinnen: sorority; **schlagende/nicht schlagende ~** duelling/non-duelling society (Am. fraternity)

...verbindung f im Subst. **1.** (Kontakt): **Fernsprech~** telephone connection; **Nachrichten~** line of communication; **Post~** link to a (od. the) postal service; **Schienen~** rail link; **2.** Chem.: **Sauerstoff~** oxygen compound; **Schwefel~** sul|phur (Am. -fur) compound

Verbindungs|dauer f EDV connect time; **~gang** m connecting passage; **~glied** n connecting (od. coupling) link; **~haus** n house belonging to a student society which provides members with accommodation and is used as a meeting-place, Am. etwa fraternity house; **~kabel** n connecting cable; **~lehrer** m, **~lehrerin** f teacher responsible for liaising between pupils (Am. students) and staff over matters of difficulty; **~linie** f connecting line; Mil. line of communication; **~mann** m contact (auch Agent), intermediary; **~offizier** m Mil. liaison officer; **~punkt** m junction; **~stelle** f **1.** junction; Tech. joint; **2.** (Amt) liaison office; **~straße** f connecting road; **~stück** n **1.** connecting piece; e-s Rohrs: union coupling; **2.** Etech. connector; (Passstück) adaptor; **3.** EDV link; **~student** m, **~studentin** f member of a student society (Am. fraternity od. für Studentinnen: sorority); **~tür** f connecting door; **~weg** m connecting path; **~zeit** *f EDV* connect time

Verbiss *m*; *-es*, *-e*; *Jägerspr.* (*das Verbeißen*) damaging (by biting); (*der Schaden*) damage (by biting)

verbissen I. *Adj.* **1.** *Fleiß*, *Hartnäckigkeit etc.*: dogged; **2.** *Gesicht etc.*: grim; **II.** *Adv. weiterarbeiten, kämpfen etc.*: doggedly, with dogged (*od.* grim) determination; **~ dreinschauen** look grim; **man sollte nicht alles so ~ sehen** *od.* **nehmen** *umg.* you shouldn't take everything so seriously; **Verbissenheit** *f*; *nur Sg.* doggedness, grim determination

verbitten *v/t.* (*unreg.*): **sich etw. ~** refuse to tolerate (*od.* accept) s.th.; **das verbitte ich mir!** (*od.* **das möchte ich mir verbeten haben!**) I won't have (*od.* stand for) that

verbittern *v/t.* (*hat verbittert*) embitter; **II.** *v/i.* (*ist*) grow bitter, become embittered; **verbittert I.** *P.P.* → **verbittern**; **II.** *Adj.* embittered, bitter; **Verbitterung** *f* bitterness

verblassen *v/i.* grow pale; *Farbe etc.*, *auch fig.*: fade; **~ gegenüber** *od.* **vor** *fig.* pale (into insignificance) beside, be dwarfed by; **~ lassen** eclipse; **verblasst I.** *P.P.* → **verblassen**; **II.** *Adj.* faded (*auch fig. Erinnerungen etc.*)

verbläuen *v/t. umg.* give s.o. a real thrashing

Verbleib *m*; *-(e)s*, *kein Pl.* **1.** whereabouts *Pl.*; **über s-n ~ ist nichts bekannt** we (*od.* they) know nothing of his whereabouts, nobody knows where he is; **2.** (*Verbleiben*) staying, remaining; **Akten zum ~ ins Archiv bringen** bring files to be kept in the archives; **es geht um den ~ des Vereins in der Bundesliga** the club's place in the Bundesliga is at stake; **verbleiben** *v/i.* (*unreg.*) **1.** remain (*auch übrig bleiben*); **nach Abzug der Zinsen ~ noch ...** ... is left (over) after interest; **2. wie wollen wir ~?** what shall we do, then?; **wollen wir so ~, dass ...?** shall we say ..., then?; **~ wir so?** shall we leave it at that, then?; **... ~ wir hochachtungsvoll** *altm.* ... (we remain,) Yours faithfully

verbleichen *v/i.* (*unreg.*) → **verblassen**

verbleien *v/t.* lead, add lead to; **verbleit I.** *P.P.* → **verbleien**; **II.** *Adj.* leaded

verblenden *v/t.* **1.** *fig.* (*j-n*) blind; **2.** *Archit.* face; (*kaschieren, verkleiden*) screen, conceal; **3.** (*Zahnkrone*) crown; **verblendet I.** *P.P.* → **verblenden**; **II.** *Adj. fig.* blind; **~ von** blinded by; **oh, ihr Verblendeten!** *lit.* oh, how blind you are!; **Verblendstein** *m* face brick; **Verblendung** *f* **1.** (*Wahn*) blindness, delusion; **2.** *Archit.* facing; **e-e ~ aus Klinker** *etc.* a clinker *etc.* facing; **3.** *Dent.* facing

verbleuen → **verbläuen**

verblichen I. *P.P.* → **verbleichen**; **II.** *Adj. Farbe etc.*: faded; **2.** *lit.* (*tot*) deceased; **Verblichene** *m, f*; *-n*, *-n*; *lit.*: **der** *od.* **die ~** the deceased

verblöden *umg.* **I.** *v/i.* (*ist verblödet*) go daft (*od.* goofy) (**bei** with); *alter Mensch*: *umg.* go gaga; **bei dieser Arbeit verblödet man total** this work is absolutely mind-numbing (*stärker*: moronic); **II.** *v/t.* (*hat*) dull *s.o.'s* mind, stultify, have a stultifying effect on; **verblödet** *umg.* **I.** *P.P.* → **verblöden**; **II.** *Adj.*: **total** ~ demented; (*senil*) senile; **er ist total ~** *auch* he's gone completely gaga; **bist du jetzt völlig ~?** have you gone completely barmy

(*Am.* bonkers)?; **Verblödung** *f*; *nur Sg.* stultification; *im Alter*: (senile) dementia; **zu j-s ~ führen** have a stultifying effect on s.o., dull s.o.'s mind

verblüffen *v/t.* (*j-n*) amaze, astound; (*sprachlos machen*) dumbfound, stupefy; (*verwirren*) bewilder; **s-e Offenheit verblüffte** his openness was astounding; **sich durch etw. ~ lassen** be taken in by s.th.; **verblüffend I.** *Part. Präs.* → **verblüffen**; **II.** *Adj.* amazing, startling, incredible; **III.** *Adv. schnell etc.*: amazingly, incredibly; **~ gut Bescheid wissen** be incredibly well informed; **e-e ~ einfache Lösung** an incredibly simple solution; **verblüfft I.** *P.P.* → **verblüffen**; **II.** *Adj.* amazed, dumbfounded; *präd. auch* taken aback; (*verwirrt*) bewildered; **ein ~es Gesicht machen** look flabbergasted (*od.* taken aback); **III.** *Adv. anschauen etc.*: in amazement (*od.* astonishment); (*verwirrt*) in bewilderment; **Verblüffung** *f* amazement, astonishment; *stärker*: stupefaction; (*Verwirrung*) bewilderment

verblühen *v/i.* **1.** wither; *fig.* fade; **2.** *Sl.* (*abhauen*) push off

verblümt I. *Adj. Ausdruck etc.*: veiled (*auch Vorwurf*); euphemistic; **II.** *Adv.* euphemistically; **sich ~ ausdrücken** express o.s. in a roundabout way

verbluten *v/i.* bleed to death

verbocken *v/t. umg.* bungle, botch (up); **wer hat das verbockt?** who botched it up?; **verbockt I.** *P.P.* → **verbocken**; **II.** *Adj. Kind etc.*: totally stubborn

verbogen I. *P.P.* → **verbiegen**; **II.** *Adj.* bent; *Wirbelsäule*: curved; *fig. Charakter etc.*: corrupt

verbohren *v/refl. umg.*: **sich in etw.** (*Akk.*) **~** become obsessed with s.th.; (*e-e Idee etc.*) become bent (*od.* set) on doing s.th.; **verbohrt** *umg.* **I.** *P.P.* → **verbohren**; **II.** *Adj. pej.* (*stur*) pigheaded, stubborn, wrong-headed; (*total*) **in etw.** (*Akk.*) **~ sein** be (totally) obsessed with s.th.; *in e-e Idee etc.*: be (completely) bent (*od.* set) on doing s.th.; **Verbohrtheit** *f*; *nur Sg.*; *umg. pej.* pigheadedness, stubbornness (**in** + *Akk.* in)

verborgen[1] *v/t.* (*verleihen*) lend; *gegen Gebühr*: hire (*Am.* rent) out

verborgen[2] I. *P.P.* → **verbergen**; **II.** *Adj.* hidden, concealed; (*geheim*) secret; (*latent*) latent; **~e Talente** hidden talents; **im ~sten Winkel suchen** search in the darkest corner; **im Verborgenen** (*heimlich*) secretly, in secret; **im Verborgenen blühen** *etc.*: flourish *etc.* in obscurity; **etw. ~ halten** hide s.th., keep s.th. secret (**vor** + *Dat.* from); **es wird ihm nicht ~ bleiben** he will find out; **Gott bleibt nichts ~** one cannot hide anything from God; **sich ~ halten** hide, be (*od.* stay) in hiding; **Verborgenheit** *f*; *nur Sg.*; (*Zurückgezogenheit*) seclusion

Verbot *n*; *-(e)s*, *-e*; (*das Verbieten*) prohibition (+ *Gen.* of); (*Einfuhrverbot*, **~ e-r Partei, Zeitung etc.**) *auch* ban (**für** *od.* + *Gen.* on); **ein ~ aussprechen** impose a ban; **ein ~ befolgen/übertreten** comply / not comply with a ban; **er hat gegen mein ausdrückliches ~ geraucht** he smoked in spite of the fact that I had expressly forbidden him to do so; **etw. trotz ärztlichen ~s tun** do s.th. against doctor's orders; **ich bin gegen das ~ von Handys in Lokalen** *etc.* I'm against a ban on mobile phones in pubs (*Am.* cellphones in

bars *etc.*)

verboten I. *P.P.* → **verbieten**; **II.** *Adj.* **1.** *nur präd.* not allowed (*od.* permitted); *formell, offiziell*: *auch attr.* prohibited, forbidden; (*illegal*) illegal; (*für ~ erklärt*) outlawed; *Früchte, Liebe*: forbidden; **Rauchen/Fotografieren ~!** no smoking/photographs; **streng ~** strictly prohibited (*od.* forbidden); **es ist ~ zu** (+ *Inf.*) you're not allowed to (+ *Inf.*); *förm.* it is prohibited (*od.* forbidden) to (+ *Inf.*); **2.** *umg.* (*unmöglich*) ridiculous; **~ aussehen** look a real sight; → **betreten[1]** II, *Unbefugte etc.*; **verbotenerweise** *Adv.*: **etw. ~ tun** do s.th. although it is forbidden (*od.* not allowed), break the rules (*od.* law) in doing s.th.

Verbots|antrag *m* banning application; **ein ~ gegen die NPD hat keine Chance** an application to ban the NPD has no chance; **~liste** *f* banned list; **dieses Mittel steht auf der ~** this is on the list of banned substances; **~schild** *n* no parking (*od.* no smoking *etc.*) sign; **diese vielen ~er!** *umg.* all these signs telling you you can't do this, that and the other; **~tafel** *f* → **Verbotsschild**

verbotswidrig I. *Adj. Überholen etc.*: illegal; **II.** *Adv. parken etc.*: illegally

Verbotszeichen *n* prohibition sign

verbrämen *v/t.* **1.** (*Kleidungsstück etc.*) *mit Pelz etc.*: trim; (*verzieren*) garnish; **2.** (*Negatives*) verdecken: gloss over; (*Kritik*) veil; **mit schönen Worten ~** veil in beautiful words; **verbrämt I.** *P.P.* → **verbrämen**; **II.** *Adj.* **1.** *mit Pelz etc.*: trimmed; **2.** **wissenschaftlich ~er Unsinn** nonsense made up to look like scientific fact

verbrannt I. *P.P.* → **verbrennen**; **II.** *Adj.* burnt; *Haus*: *attr. auch* burnt-out ..., *präd.* burnt out, gutted; *Person, von der Sonne*: (sun)burnt; **Politik der ~en Erde** scorched earth policy

verbraten (*unreg.*) **I.** *v/i.* (*ist verbraten*) *Gastr.* get scorched (*od.* burnt), shrivel *umg.*; **II.** *v/t.* (*hat*); *umg.* (*Geld etc.*) blow; (*Unsinn etc.*) spout; **etw. zu e-m Roman ~** exploit s.th. in a novel

Verbrauch *m*; *-(e)s*, *kein Pl.* consumption (**an** + *Dat.* of); **sparsam im ~** economical; **e-n hohen/niedrigen ~ an Energie** *etc.* **haben** have a high/low energy *etc.* consumption; **zum alsbaldigen ~ bestimmt** *Lebensmittel etc.*: for immediate consumption; **verbrauchen I.** *v/t.* use; (*Energie etc.*) *auch* consume; (*aufbrauchen*) use up; (*ausgeben*) spend; **II.** *v/refl. Person*: wear o.s. out; *auf Dauer*: burn o.s. out; → **verbraucht**

Verbraucher *m* consumer; (*Benutzer*) user; **~aufklärung** *f* consumer advice; **~beratung** *f* **1.** consumer advice; **2.** (*Stelle*) consumer advice cent|re (*Am.* -er)

verbraucherfeindlich *Adj.* consumer-unfriendly; (*benutzerfeindlich*) user-unfriendly; **Verbraucherfeindlichkeit** *f*; *nur Sg.* consumer-unfriendliness; (*Benutzerfeindlichkeit*) user-unfriendliness; **sie beschwerten sich über die ~ der Ladenöffnungszeiten** they complained that the shop opening hours did not take consumer interests into account (*Am.* that the store hours were not convenient for shoppers)

verbraucherfreundlich *Adj.* consumer-friendly; (*benutzerfreundlich*) user-friendly; **Verbraucherfreundlichkeit** *f*; *nur Sg.* consumer-friendliness; (*Benutzerfreundlichkeit*) user-friendliness

Verbrauchergenossenschaft f consumer cooperative, co-op umg.

Verbraucherin f; -, -nen consumer; (Benutzerin) user

Verbraucher|markt m hypermarket; **~nachfrage** f consumer demand; **~organisation** f consumer organization

verbraucherorientiert Adj. consumer--orient(at)ed

Verbraucher|preise Pl. consumer prices; **~schutz** m consumer protection; **~verband** m consumer organization; **~verhalten** n consumer behavio(u)r; **~zeitschrift** f consumer magazine; **~zentrale** f consumer advice cent|re (Am. -er)

Verbrauchsgüter Pl. consumer goods; **~industrie** f consumer goods industry

Verbrauchssteuer f excise duty

verbraucht I. P.P. → verbrauchen; **II.** Adj. used up; (abgenutzt) attr. worn(-out), präd. worn (out); Energie: spent, Person: auch attr. worn-out ..., präd. worn out; auf Dauer: attr. burnt--out ..., präd. burnt out; Luft: stale; Batterie: flat, Am. dead; **~e Energie zurückbringen** replenish used-up energy; **völlig ~ aussehende Fabrikarbeiterinnen** women factory workers looking completely exhausted

verbrechen v/t. (unreg.): **etwas ~** commit a crime; **was hat er verbrochen?** fig. what has he done?; **was hast du denn jetzt wieder verbrochen?** iro. what have you been up to this time?; **wer hat denn diesen Film verbrochen?** umg. who cooked up this film (Am. movie)?, who's responsible for this film (Am. movie) then?; **Verbrechen** n; -s, - crime (auch weitS. Kriminalität, auch fig.); **das organisierte ~** organized crime; **ein ~ gegen die Menschlichkeit** a crime against humanity; **es ist ein ~, durch dieses Tal e-e Autobahn zu bauen** it's criminal to build a motorway (Am. highway) through this valley; **das ist (doch) kein ~!** umg. that's no crime(, is it?)

Verbrechens|aufklärung f crime detection; (Ermittlung) criminal investigation; weitS. (number of) solved crimes Pl.; **~bekämpfung** f fight against crime; **~verhütung** f crime prevention

Verbrecher m; -s, - criminal; crook umg.; **j-n wie e-n ~ abführen/behandeln** take s.o. away / treat s.o. like a criminal; **das sind alles ~** umg. they are all a bunch of crooks; **~album** n rogues' gallery; **~bande** f gang of criminals, mob umg.; **~gesicht** n villain's face

Verbrecherin f; -, -nen criminal, crook umg.

verbrecherisch Adj. criminal (auch fig.); **~er Leichtsinn** criminal negligence

Verbrecher|jagd f chase after a criminal (od. criminals); **~kartei** f criminal records Pl.; **~nest** n criminals' hideout; **~organisation** f criminal organization; **~syndikat** n crime syndicate

Verbrecher|tum n; -s, kein Pl. **1.** (Kriminalität) crime; **2.** (Verbrecherwelt) world of crime, underworld; **~visage** f pej. criminal features Pl.

verbreiten I. v/t. spread; im Rundfunk etc.: broadcast (auch umg. Neuigkeit, Geheimnis etc.); (Ideen) spread, disseminate; (Zeitschrift etc.) circulate; (Licht, Geruch) give off; (Wärme) auch emit, radiate; (Ruhe etc. ausstrahlen) radiate; (verursachen) cause,

bring about; **pornografische etc. Schriften ~** circulate pornographic etc. material; **Entsetzen etc. unter den Menschen ~** fill everyone with horror etc.; **musst du das überall ~?** umg. do you have to spread it around everywhere?, do you have to tell the world?; **II.** v/refl.: **sich ~ über** (+ Akk.) fig. über ein Thema: expatiate on, hold forth on; → **Lauffeuer, verbreitet**

verbreitern I. v/t. widen; **II.** v/refl. widen (out); **Verbreiterung** f widening

verbreitet I. P.P. → verbreiten; **II.** Adj. widespread, common; Zeitschrift etc.: widely read; **diese Ansicht ist sehr ~** this is a very widely-held opinion; **ein weit ~es Vorurteil** a very common prejudice

Verbreitung f; nur Sg. spread(ing), von Ideen, Infos etc.: dissemination; von Zeitschriften etc.: circulation; von Wärme, Strahlung: emission, radiation; (Ausmaß) extent; **~ finden** gain currency; **~ von Nachrichten** spreading of news; **~ von pornografischen etc. Schriften** circulation of pornographic etc. material; **Verbreitungsgebiet** n area (in which s.th. is to be found); e-r Krankheit: infected area; e-r Naturkatastrophe etc.: area affected, affected area; Radio, TV: broadcasting (od. service) area

verbrennen (unreg.) **I.** v/t. (hat verbrannt) burn; (versengen) scorch; (Müll) incinerate; (Leiche, einäschern) cremate; Chem. convert; (Kalorien, Fett etc.) burn off; **die Sonne hat ihn verbrannt** he has got sunburn (od. sunburnt); **sich** (Dat.) **beim Sonnen den Rücken ~** get sunburnt on one's back; **sich** (Dat.) **die Zunge etc. ~** burn (od. scald) one's tongue etc.; **der Körper verbrennt den Zucker** the sugar is converted by the body; → **Finger** 1, **Mund, Scheiterhaufen, verbrannt; II.** v/i. (ist) burn; Gebäude etc.: burn down, be destroyed by fire, be burn|t (bes. Am. -ed) to the ground, be gutted; Person, lebend: be burn|t (bes. Am. -ed) to death; Chem. be converted (zu into); **drei Menschen sind in dem Haus verbrannt** three people burn|t (Am. -ed) to death in the house; **der Kuchen ist verbrannt** the cake has got burn|t (bes. Am. -ed); **III.** v/refl. burn o.s., get burn|t (bes. Am. -ed); **sich aus Protest öffentlich (selbst) ~** make a protest by setting fire to oneself in public (od. by self--immolation); **Verbrennung** f **1.** nur Sg. burning; Chem., Tech. mst combustion; **2.** (Einäscherung) cremation; **3.** (Brandwunde) burn (an + Dat. on); **schwere ~en erleiden** suffer severe burns; → **Grad** 4

Verbrennungs|anlage f Tech. incineration plant; **~maschine** f, **~motor** m internal combustion engine; **~ofen** m combustion furnace; für Abfälle: (waste) incinerator; **~prozess** m, **~vorgang** m process of combustion; **~wärme** f heat of combustion

verbrieft Adj.: **~es Recht** vested right

verbringen v/t. **1.** (Zeit etc.) spend; **das Wochenende etc. mit etw. ~** spend the weekend etc. doing s.th.; **2.** Amtsspr.; (irgendwohin bringen) take; **Verbringung** f Amtsspr. taking; **ihm wurde die ~ in ein anderes Land angeboten** an offer was made to him to another country

verbrüdern v/refl.: **sich** (mit j-m) **~** frat-

ernize; **Verbrüderung** f fraternization

verbrühen v/t. scald; **sich** (Dat.) **die Hand** etc. **~** scald one's hand etc.; **Verbrühung** f konkret: scald

verbrutzeln v/i. umg. bes. Fleisch: burn to a crisp (od. cinder)

verbuchen v/t. enter (in the books); fig. (Erfolg etc.) clock up, notch up; **e-n Erfolg ~ können** be successful; **e-n Gewinn ~** register a gain

verbuddeln v/t. umg. bury

verbummeln umg. **I.** v/t. (hat verbummelt) **1.** Semester, Jahr etc.: waste; **die Zeit ~** waste (one's) time, idle away one's time; **2.** (Verabredung etc.) miss; (vergessen) (completely) forget (about); (verlieren) lose; **II.** v/i. (ist) (herunterkommen) go to seed

Verbund m **1.** Tech., Chem. etc. compound; EDV bonding, group; **2.** Wirts. etc. combine, association; (integrated) system; (Verkehrsverbund) integrated transport(ation Am.) system; **3.** → **Medienverbund; ~bauweise** f composite construction

verbunden I. P.P. → verbinden; **II.** Adj. **1.** Hand, Kopf, Wunde etc.: bandaged; **mit ~en Augen** blindfolded; **2.** Telef.: **mit j-m ~ sein** be speaking to s.o. (on the phone), Brit. auch be through to s.o.; **mit wem bin ich ~?** who am I speaking to?; **falsch ~!** sorry, wrong number; **3. ~ mit** Sachverhalt, Programm etc.: combined (od. coupled) with; **die damit ~en Unkosten/Gefahren** the cost/dangers involved; **eng ~ sein mit** be bound up with; **~ mit den besten Wünschen** etc. together with our best wishes etc.; **4. sich ~ fühlen mit** feel a rapport with; **j-m ~ sein** förm. be indebted (stärker: beholden) to s.o.; **ich bin Ihnen sehr ~** förm. I'm much obliged to you

verbünden v/refl. form an alliance (mit with); auch weitS. ally o.s. (to, with)

Verbundenheit f; nur Sg. attachment (mit to), bond (with); weitS. solidarity (with); **in alter ~** förm. yours in friendship

verbündet I. P.P. → verbünden; **II.** Adj. Staaten etc.: ... in alliance; **~ sein mit** be in alliance with, be allied with; **das mit uns ~e Frankreich** our French allies; **Verbündete** m, f; -n, -n ally (auch fig.); **ein Angriff der ~n** an Allied attack

Verbund|fahrkarte f Verk. ticket (valid for use on integrated transport[ation Am.] system), etwa travel pass; **~glas** n laminated glass; **~karte** f **1.** für Museen etc.: integrated ticket; **2.** Verk. travel pass; **~material** n composite (material); **~netz** n **1.** Etech. integrated power grid; **2.** Verk. integrated transport(ation Am.) network; **~pflasterstein** m interlocking paving stone; **~stahl** m composite steel; **~stoff** m composite (material); **~system** n compound system; **~tarif** m Verk. fare (valid for integrated transport[ation] system); **~verpackung** f composite packaging; **~werkstoff** m composite (material)

verbürgen I. v/t. guarantee; **II.** v/refl.: **sich ~ für** vouch for; **sich dafür ~, dass ...** guarantee that ...; **verbürgt I.** P.P. → verbürgen; **II.** Adj. Information, Geschichte etc.: authentic(ated); Tatsache, Recht etc.: established

verbüßen v/t. (Gefängnisstrafe) serve; **Verbüßung** f; nur Sg.: **nach** etc. **~ s-r Strafe** after etc. serving his sentence

verchromen *v/t.* chromium-plate

Verdacht *m; -(e)s, kein Pl.* suspicion; ~ **erregen** arouse suspicion; ~ **schöpfen** become suspicious (**gegen** of), smell a rat *umg.*; **den ~ lenken auf** (+ *Akk.*) cast suspicion on; **j-n in ~ haben** suspect s.o.; **in ~ kommen** (*od.* **unter ~ stehen**) be suspected (**zu** + *Inf.* of + *Ger.*; **etw. getan zu haben** of having done s.th.); **ich habe den (starken) ~, dass** I have a (strong) suspicion that, I (strongly) suspect that; **nicht den leisesten ~ haben** not be in the least bit suspicious, not be in the least suspicious; **mein ~ fällt auf X** I'm inclined to suspect X; **unter dem ~ ... verhaftet werden:** on suspicion of ...; **unter falschem ~** on false suspicion; **bei ihm besteht ~ auf Krebs** he is suspected of having cancer; **auf bloßen ~ hin** purely on suspicion; **etw. auf ~ hin tun** *umg.* do s.th. on spec; **auf ~ hingehen** etc. *umg.* go there etc. on the off-chance; → **erhaben** 3

verdächtig I. *Adj.* suspicious, suspect, fishy *umg.*; (*zweifelhaft*) *auch* dubious; (~ *aussehend*) suspicious-looking; *Person:* auch shifty(-eyed); *Geräusch* etc.: suspicious; **sich ~ machen** arouse suspicion; **er ist der Tat (dringend) ~** he is (strongly) suspected of having committed the crime; **das kommt mir ~ vor** I find that suspicious, that seems suspicious (*od.* *umg.* fishy) to me; **es liegt nichts Verdächtiges vor** there is nothing suspicious; **II.** *Adv.:* ~ **still** etc. suspiciously quiet etc.

...verdächtig *im Adj.* 1. *unter entsprechendem Verdacht:* **tat~** *präd. und nachgestellt:* suspected of having committed the deed; **krebs~** *präd.* suspected of having cancer; 2. *umg. fig. mit Aussichten auf etw.:* **das hit~e Buch** the book which looks likely to be a hit; **der medaillen~e Weitspringer** the long jumper who looks likely to be a medal contender

Verdächtige *m, f; -n, -n* suspect; **verdächtigen** *v/t.* suspect (+ *Gen.* of); (*e-n Verdacht äußern gegen*) cast suspicion on; **Verdächtigte** *m, f; -n, -n* suspect; **Verdächtigung** *f* 1. (*das Verdächtigen*) suspecting, casting suspicion (+ *Gen.* on); 2. (*Verdacht*) suspicion; **~en äußern gegen j-n** cast (*od.* throw) suspicion on s.o.

Verdachts|grund *m* grounds *Pl.* (*od.* cause) for suspicion; **~moment** *n* suspicious factor

verdammen *v/t.* condemn; (*verfluchen*) damn, curse; (*Gott*) **verdamm mich!** *umg.* (God) damn it!; → **verdammt**; **verdammenswert** *Adj.* damnable; **Verdammnis** *f; -, kein Pl.* kirchl. damnation

verdammt I. *P.P.* → **verdammen**; **II.** *Adj.* 1. damned; **dazu ~ zu** (+ *Inf.*) doomed (*od.* condemned) to (+ *Inf.*); **zum Nichtstun ~** condemned to inactivity; **zum Scheitern ~** doomed to fail; 2. *umg.* (*verflucht*) blasted, damn(ed); **~!** damn (it)!, blast!; ~ **noch mal!** (*od.* ~ **und zugenäht!**) damnation!; **~e Scheiße!** *vulg.* bloody hell! *Sl.*, shit!, *Am. auch* holy shit!; **du ~er Mistkerl!** you damned bastard!; **wir hatten ~es Glück** we were bloody (*Am.* damn) lucky; **diese ~e Ungewissheit!** this damned uncertainty!; → **Pflicht**; **III.** *Adv.* *umg.* (*sehr*) damn(ed), bloody; **sie ist ~ hübsch** she's bloody (*Am.* damn) gorgeous; ~ **viel** a (*od.* one) hell of a lot *Sl.*; ~ **wenig** bugger

all *vulg., Am.* zip, squat; **es ist ~ lang her, dass ...** it's been a hell of a long time since ...; **es tut ~ weh** it hurts like hell *Sl.*, it's hellishly painful (*od.* sore); **es ~ eilig haben** be in a hell of a rush; **was hast du ~ noch mal getan?** what the hell have you done?;

Verdammte *m, f; -n, -n* damned soul; **die ~n** the damned; **Verdammung** *f* 1. condemnation; 2. *kirchl.* (eternal) damnation

verdampfen I. *v/i.* (*ist verdampft*) evaporate; *Chem., Phys. auch* vaporize; **II.** *v/t.* (*hat*) evaporate; *Chem., Phys. auch* vaporize; **Verdampfung** *f* evaporation; vaporization; → **verdampfen**

verdanken *v/t.:* **j-m etw. ~** owe s.th. to s.o.; (*in j-s Schuld stehen*) be indebted to s.o. for s.th.; **e-r Sache zu ~ sein** be due to s.th.; **das hab ich dir zu ~** I owe it all to you; *auch iro.* it's all thanks to you; **dir hab ich zu ~, dass** it's thanks to you that; *iro.* auch it's your own fault; **das hast du dir selbst zu ~!** it's your own fault

verdarb *Imperf.* → **verderben**

verdattert *Adj. und Adv. umg.* flabbergasted; (*verwirrt*) flummoxed

verdauen *v/t.* digest; *fig. auch* come to terms with; **schwer zu ~** *fig. auch* hard to swallow; **er hat es immer noch nicht verdaut** auch he hasn't got(ten *Am.*) over it yet

verdaulich *Adj.* 1. digestible; **leicht ~** easily digestible; **schwer ~** hard to digest, heavy; 2. *fig.:* **schwer ~** *Buch* etc.: heavy-going; **leicht ~** light; **ein leicht ~es Buch** light reading; **Verdaulichkeit** *f; nur Sg.* digestibility

Verdauung *f* digestion; **e-e gute/schlechte ~ haben** have good/poor digestion; **... fördert die ~** ... aids the digestion; (*wirkt [leicht] abführend*) ... has a (mild) laxative effect

Verdauungs|apparat *m* digestive system; **~beschwerden** *Pl.* indigestion *Sg.*, digestive trouble *Sg.*; (*Verstopfung*) constipation *Sg.*

verdauungsfördernd *Adj. attr.* digestive ..., *Präd.* good for the digestion; (*[leicht] abführend*) (mildly) laxative

Verdauungs|organ *n* digestive organ; **~spaziergang** *m* constitutional; **e-n ~ machen** take a constitutional; **~störung** *f* indigestion; *fachspr.* dyspepsia; (*Verstopfung*) constipation; **~trakt** *m* digestive tract

Verdeck *n; -(e)s, -e* 1. *Naut.* deck; 2. *Mot.* roof, top

verdecken *v/t.* cover (up); (*verbergen*) hide, *auch Tech.* conceal; → **Karte** 6

verdeckt I. *P.P.* → **verdecken**; **II.** *Adj.* auf Foto etc.: obscured; *Ermittler, Ermittlungen* etc.: undercover

verdenken *v/t.:* **ich kann es ihr nicht ~** I can't blame her (for it); **wir können es ihr nicht ~, dass sie** *od.* **wenn sie es tut** we can't blame her for doing it *od.* if she does it

Verderb *m; -(e)s, kein Pl.* 1. *von Lebensmitteln* etc.: spoilage; 2. *sittlicher:* corruption; (*Untergang*) ruin; → **Gedeih**

verderben (*unreg.*) **I.** *v/t.* (*hat verdorben*) 1. spoil; **j-m etw. ~** (*Appetit, Freude* etc.) spoil s.o.'s th.; (*Abend, Urlaub* etc.) spoil (*od.* ruin) s.th. for s.o.; **j-m die Stimmung ~** put s.o. in a bad mood; **die Preise ~** *umg.* (*von Händlern:* sie durch zu billige Waren niedrig werden lassen*) force prices down; (*von Verbrauchern:* sie durch

mangelndes Preisbewusstsein in die Höhe treiben*) force prices up; **sich die Augen ~** ruin one's eyes; **ich habe mir den Magen verdorben** I've got an upset stomach; **daran ist nichts mehr zu ~** *umg.* it couldn't be any worse; **damit hat er sich alles verdorben** as a result he ruined everything; **es (sich) mit j-m ~** fall out with s.o., get into s.o.'s bad books; **er will es (sich) mit niemandem ~** he tries to please everybody; 2. *sittlich:* corrupt; → **Appetit, Koch**; **II.** *v/i.* (*ist*) 1. *Lebensmittel:* go bad; *Brit.*, *bes. Fleisch, Milchprodukte:* auch go off; (*faulen*) rot; 2. *altm. geh.* (*zugrunde gehen*) perish

Verderben *n; -s, kein Pl.; (Untergang)* ruin(ation), downfall; **Drogen** etc. **waren ihr ~** auch drugs etc. were her undoing; (*offenen Auges*) **in sein ~ rennen** head straight for disaster; **j-n ins ~ stürzen** bring disaster on s.o.; ~ **bringend** fatal, ruinous; → **blindlings**; **verderbenbringend** → **Verderben**

verderblich *Adj.* 1. ~**e Waren** perishable goods, perishables; **leicht ~** highly perishable; 2. (*schädlich*) ruinous; *moralisch:* corrupting

Verderbnis *f; -, kein Pl.; geh.* 1. (*Verderbtheit*) depravity; 2. (*Verderben*) ruin, disaster; **verderbt** *Adj.* 1. *altm.* depraved, corrupt; 2. *fachsprachl., Textstelle* etc.: illegible; **Verderbtheit** *f; nur Sg.; altm.* depravity, corruptness, corruption

verdeutlichen *v/t.* make clear (+ *Dat.* to); (*erklären*) explain, elucidate; *durch Beispiele:* illustrate; **Verdeutlichung** *f* elucidation; (*Erklärung*) explanation; *durch Beispiele:* illustration; **zur ~** (+ *Gen.*) to elucidate (*od.* explain, illustrate) s.th.; *weitS.* to make s.th. quite clear; **zur ~** by way of explanation (*od.* illustration)

verdeutschen *v/t.* 1. *umg.* (*verständlich machen*) put into plain words, translate (into German); 2. *altm.* (*Text* etc.) translate into German

verdichten I. *v/t.* 1. *Phys.* condense, thicken; (*Gase*) solidify; (*komprimieren*) compress; 2. (*Straßennetz* etc.) expand; 3. *fig.:* ~ **zu** condense into; **II.** *v/refl.* 1. *Nebel* etc.: thicken; *Phys. auch* condense; *Gase:* solidify; 2. *fig. Nachricht, Verdacht* etc.: be consolidated; *Gerücht:* grow, gain ground (*od.* momentum); *Eindruck:* grow (stronger); **der Eindruck verdichtet sich immer mehr zur Gewissheit** the feeling is turning more and more into certainty; **Verdichter** *m; -s, -; Tech.* compressor; **Verdichtung** *f* 1. *Phys.* condensation; *auch Mot.* compression; thickening; *e-s Netzes* etc.: expansion; 2. *e-r Nachricht* etc.: consolidation; *e-s Eindrucks:* hardening

verdicken *v/t. und v/refl.:* (*sich*) ~ thicken; *Blut:* thicken; **die Hornhaut hat sich verdickt** the call(o)us has become thicker; **Verdickung** *f* 1. thickening; 2. (*verdickte Stelle*) thickening

verdienen I. *vt/i.* (*Geld*) earn, make; **gut ~** earn a good (*od.* decent) salary (*od.* wage); **er verdient nicht schlecht** he doesn't do too badly (salarywise *od.* wagewise); **10 Euro** *od.* **die Stunde ~** earn 10 euros etc. an hour; **sein Brot als Kellner / mit Taxifahren ~** earn a living as a waiter / (by) driving a taxi; **etwas ~ an** (+ *Dat.*) *od.* **bei** make money out of; **ein Vermögen ~** make a fortune; **daran ist nichts zu ~** there's no money in it; **sie ~ beide** they both work, they are both wage earners; **II.** *v/i.* (*Lob, Strafe, Tadel etc.*) deserve, merit; **Beachtung** *etc.* ~ *Sache*: be worthy of note *etc.*, be worth noting *etc.*; **das hat er verdient** he deserves it; **er hat es nicht anders/besser verdient** he got what he deserved/ he doesn't deserve any better; **womit habe ich das verdient?** what have I done to deserve that?; → **Brot** 3, **verdient** *etc.*

Verdienende *m, f; -n, -n* wage earner; **gut** ~ those on a good income

Verdienst[1] *m; -(e)s, -e, mst Sg.* earnings *Pl.*; (*Lohn*) wages *Pl.*; (*Gehalt*) salary; (*Gewinn*) gain, profit; (*Einkommen*) income; **nach** ~ *besteuern, festlegen etc.*: according to income

Verdienst[2] *n; -(e)s, -e* merit; (*Leistung*) service; **sich um etw. große ~e erwerben** render outstanding services to s.th.; **es ist** (**allein**) **sein ~, dass** it is (entirely) due (*od.* thanks) to him that; **es ist nicht mein ~** it is no thanks to me; **j-m/sich etw. als** *od.* **zum ~ anrechnen** give s.o. /take the credit for s.th.

Verdienst|ausfall *m* lost earnings *Pl.*; **~bescheinigung** *f* certificate of earnings; **~grenze** *f* earnings cap; **~kreuz** *n medal awarded for voluntary or community service, also for military service*; **~medaille** *f medal awarded for voluntary or community service, also for military service*; **~möglichkeit** *f* chance to earn (some) money; **~spanne** *f Wirts.* profit margin

verdienstvoll *Adj.* *Person*: deserving, meritorious; *Tat*: commendable, laudable; **~e Person** *auch* man (*od.* woman) of merit

verdient I. *P.P.* → **verdienen**; **II.** *Adj.* **1.** *nur attr.*; *Person*: deserving; *Wissenschaftler etc.*: outstanding, of (great) merit; *Sieg etc.*: well-earned; *Strafe etc.*: due, deserved; **2. sich ~ machen um** do *od.* render *s.o./s.th.* a great service; **3. schwer ~ sein** be hard earned; **dieses Geld ist leicht ~** this is easy money; **verdientermaßen** *Adv.* deservedly

Verdikt *n; -(e)s, -e; Jur. und fig.* verdict

verdingen (*reg. und unreg.*) *altm.* **I.** *v/refl.* enter into service (**als** as; **bei** with); **II.** *v/t.* **1.** (*in Dienst geben*) put into service (**bei** with); **2.** *Amtsspr.* (*Aufträge etc.*) put out to tender

verdinglichen *v/t.* concretize

verdolmetschen *v/t. umg.* translate, interpret; *fig.* (*erklären*) explain, translate

verdonnern *v/t. umg.* condemn (**zu** to); **j-n dazu ~, etw. zu tun** make s.o. do s.th.

verdoppeln *v/t. und v/refl.*: (**sich**) ~ double; (*Anstrengungen, Eifer*) redouble; **Verdopp(e)lung** *f* doubling; *der Anstrengungen etc.*: redoubling; *EDV etc. auch* doubling

verdorben I. *P.P.* → **verderben**; **II.** *Adj.* **1.** spoil|t (*Am.* -ed); *Lebensmittel*: bad; *Brit., bes. Fleisch, Milchprodukte*: *präd. auch* off; (*verfault*) rotten; *Luft*: foul; *Magen*: upset; **das Essen ist ~** *auch* the food has gone bad (*od.* off); **2.** *sittlich*: depraved, corrupt; **durch und durch ~ sein** be totally corrupt; **Verdorbenheit** *f; nur Sg.* corruption, depravity

verdorren *v/i.* wither; *auch Wiesen etc.*: dry up

verdösen *v/t. umg.* **1. den ganzen Tag** *etc.* ~ doze the day *etc.* away; **2. e-n**

Termin etc. ~ forget an appointment *etc.*

verdrahten *v/t.* wire up (*auch Etech.*); **Verdrahtung** *f* wiring

verdrängen *v/t.* **1.** (*j-n*) *von s-m Platz etc.*: edge out (**von** of); *aus s-m Amt*: *auch* oust (**aus** from); *aus s-m Gebiet*: drive out (of); *Pol.* displace (*bes. Am.* oust) (from); **2.** *fig.* (*ersetzen*) replace, supersede; **3.** *Psych.* suppress, repress; **das muss ich verdrängt haben** *hum.* it completely slipped my mind; **Verdrängung** *f* **1.** *von e-m Platz etc.*: edging out; *aus e-m Amt*: *auch* ousting, *Am.* ouster; *aus e-m Gebiet*: driving out, displacement, *Am. auch* ouster; **2.** *fig.* replacement, supersession; **3.** *Psych.* suppression, repression; **ein Meister der ~** *iro.* an expert at repression

Verdrängungswettbewerb *m* predatory competition

verdrecken I. *v/t.* (*hat verdreckt*) dirty, make a mess of; **II.** *v/i.* (*ist*) get dirty; **sie lassen die Wohnung immer mehr ~** they are letting the flat(*Am.* apartment) get more and more dirty; **verdreckt I.** *P.P.* → **verdrecken**; **II.** *Adj.* dirty; **völlig ~** filthy dirty

verdrehen *v/t.* **1.** twist; **j-m den Arm** *etc.* ~ twist s.o.'s arm *etc.*; **die Augen ~** roll one's eyes; **den Hals ~** crane one's neck (a)round; **j-m den Kopf ~** *fig.* turn s.o.'s head; **2.** *fig.* (*Sinn, Wort etc.*) twist, distort (*auch Tatsachen*); **das Recht ~** pervert the course of justice; **du musst wieder alles ~** you have to twist everything (a)round again; **3.** *TV, Film etc.; umg.*: **100.000 Meter Film ~** shoot 100,000 met|res (*Am.* -ers) of film

verdreht I. *P.P.* → **verdrehen**; **II.** *Adj.* **1.** twisted; **2.** *umg.* (*leicht verrückt*) (slightly) crazy (*od.* screwy) (*durcheinander*) in a muddle; (*exzentrisch*) warped, cranky; **ich bin heute total ~** I just can't think straight at all today; **Verdrehtheit** *f umg.* **1.** *nur Sg.* craziness, screwiness; muddle-headedness; crankiness; → **verdrehen**; **2.** *Handlung etc.*: act of madness; *aus Verwirrung*: act of confusion; *aus Exzentrizität*: act of crankiness

Verdrehung *f* **1.** twist(ing); **2.** *fig. von Worten etc.*: twisting; **~ von Tatsachen** *etc.* distortion of facts *etc.*

verdreifachen *v/t. und v/refl.*: (**sich**) ~ treble, triple; **Verdreifachung** *f* trebling, tripling

verdreschen *v/t.* (*unreg.*) *umg.* give *s.o.* a thrashing

verdrießen *v/t.; verdrießt, verdross, hat verdrossen* annoy; **lass dich's nicht ~** don't let it get to you; **verdrießlich** *Adj.* **1.** *Person*: annoyed; (*missmutig*) grumpy *umg.*; **2.** *Sache*: irksome; **Verdrießlichkeit** *f* **1.** *nur Sg.*; *e-r Person*: annoyance; (*Missmut*) grumpiness *umg.*; **2.** *nur Sg.*; *e-r Sache*: irksome nature (+ *Gen.* of); **3.** **~en** inconveniences, annoying little things

verdrillen *v/t.* twist

verdross *Imperf.* → **verdrießen**

verdrossen I. *P.P.* → **verdrießen**; **II.** *Adj.* (*missmutig*) sullen; (*verärgert*) peeved; (*müde, lustlos*) weary, fed up *umg.*; **III.** *Adv. schweigen etc.*: sullenly; peevishly; wearily; **Verdrossenheit** *f; nur Sg.* sullenness; (*Lustlosigkeit*) weariness

verdrücken I. *v/t.* **1.** *umg.* (*essen*) put (*od.* stow) away, polish off; **2.** *Dial.* (*zerknautschen*) crumple; (*Stoff*)

crease, *Am.* wrinkle; **II.** *v/refl. umg.* slip away (unnoticed), disappear

Verdruss *m; -es, kein Pl.* displeasure; (*Ärger*) annoyance; **j-m ~ bereiten** cause s.o. (a lot of) trouble; **zu j-s ~** to s.o.'s annoyance

verduften *v/i. umg.* clear off; **verdufte!** clear off!, beat it!, *Am. auch* scram!, vamoose!

verdummen I. *v/i.* (*ist verdummt*) become stultified; **II.** *vt/i.* (*hat*) stultify, dull *s.o.'s* mind; (*bes. das Volk*) brainwash; **zu viel Fernsehen verdummt** too much television dulls the brain; **Verdummung** *f* stultification; **Verdummungsparole** *f pej.* slogan that has a brainwashing effect on people

verdunkeln I. *vt/i.* darken (*auch Zimmer*); *fig.* (*verschleiern*) obscure; **1.** *Luftschutz*: black out; **im Krieg musste nachts verdunkelt werden** during the war there had to be a blackout at night; **II.** *v/refl.* darken; *fig. Gesicht*: *auch* cloud over; **Verdunk(e)lung** *f* **1.** darkening; *Luftschutz*: blackout; **2.** *Jur.* collusion; **Verdunk(e)lungsgefahr** *f Jur.* danger of collusion

verdünnen *v/t.* **1.** dilute; (*Farben, Lacke etc.*) thin (down); **2.** *Mil.* (*Truppen*) reduce the number of; **Verdünner** *m; -s, -* thinner

verdünnisieren *v/refl. umg.* do a vanishing trick, *Am. auch* take a powder

Verdünnung *f* **1.** dilution; *von Farben, Lacken etc.*: thinning (down); **2.** (*Mittel*) thinner; **Verdünnungsmittel** *n* thinner

verdunsten I. *v/i.* (*ist verdunstet*) evaporate; **II.** *v/t.* (*hat*) evaporate; **Verdunster** *m; -s, -* humidifier; **Verdunstung** *f* evaporation

verdursten *v/i.* die of thirst; *Pflanzen*: wilt; **~ soll keiner bei uns!** *umg.* God forbid that anyone should die of thirst in our house!

verdüstern *v/t. und v/refl.*: (**sich**) ~ darken

verdutzt *Adj. und Adv.* nonplussed, baffled; (*überrascht*) *präd.* taken aback; **ein ~es Gesicht machen** look taken aback

verebben *v/i. fig.* subside, ebb away

veredeln *v/t.* **1.** (*verfeinern*) refine; (*Rohstoffe*) process, finish; (*Stahl*) refine; *Bot.* graft; **2.** *geh.; charakterlich*: ennoble; **Vered(e)lung** *f* **1.** *Tech.* refinement; processing, finishing; *Bot.* grafting; → **veredeln**; **2.** *geh.; des Charakters*: ennoblement, ennobling

verehelichen *v/refl.; Amtsspr. od. hum.*: **sich ~** (**mit**) marry; **Verehelichung** *f* marriage

verehren *v/t.* admire; *stärker*: revere; (*anbeten*) worship; *mst heimlich, verliebt*: adore; **j-m etw. ~** *umg.* give s.o. s.th. (as a present); *iro.* (*vermachen*) bequeath s.th. to s.o.; → **verehrt**; **Verehrer** *m; -s, -*, **Verehrerin** *f; -, -nen* admirer; *e-s Stars*: *auch* devotee, fan *umg.*; **sie hat e-n neuen ~** *umg.* she's got a new admirer; **Verehrerpost** *f* fan mail; **verehrt I.** *P.P.* → **verehren**; **II.** *Adj.* hono(u)red, venerable; **~e Anwesende!** Ladies and Gentlemen!; **m-e sehr ~en Damen und Herren!** *in Rede*: Ladies and Gentlemen!; **Verehrteste!** *iro.* my dear!; **Verehrung** *f* admiration, reverence; (*Anbetung*) worship; (*m-e*) *od. altm. od. hum.* my compliment; **verehrungswürdig** *Adj.* admirable; (*altehrwürdig*) venerable

vereidigen *v/t.* swear *s.o.* in(to office);

(*j-m e-n Eid abnehmen*) make *s.o.* swear an oath (*auf + Akk.* on); *e-n Zeugen* ~ swear in a witness; **vereidigt I.** *P.P.* → *vereidigen;* **II.** *Adj.* sworn; *~er Sachverständiger* sworn expert; **Vereidigung** *f* swearing-in (ceremony); *die* ~ *der Zeugen etc.* the swearing in of the witnesses; → *gerichtlich* II

Verein *m;* -(*e*)*s,* -*e* **1.** society, association; *Sport etc.:* club; *eingetragener* ~ (*abgek.* **e.V.**) registered society; *das Fest wird von den ~en der Stadt veranstaltet* the festival is organized by the town's clubs and societies; *ein schöner/seltsamer* ~ *umg. fig., iro.* a fine/funny bunch; **2.** *im* ~ *mit* together with, in conjunction with

vereinbar *Adj.* compatible, consistent (*mit* with); *nicht* ~ → *unvereinbar;* **vereinbaren** *v/t.* **1.** (*ausmachen*) agree (up)on, arrange; **2.** reconcile (*mit* with); *sich* (*nicht*) ~ *lassen mit* be (in)consistent *od.* (in)compatible with; *ich kann es mit m-m Gewissen nicht* ~ it goes against my conscience (*od.* principles); **vereinbart I.** *P.P.* → *vereinbaren;* **II.** *Adj.* agreed; *Zeitpunkt, Verabredung etc.: auch* arranged; *zum* ~*en Liefertermin* by the agreed delivery date; *es gilt als* ~*, dass* it is understood that; **Vereinbarung** *f* agreement (*auch Pol.*), arrangement; (*Klausel*) clause, provision; *laut* ~ as agreed; *nach* ~ by agreement (*od.* arrangement, appointment); *e-e* ~ *treffen* reach an agreement; *Gehalt nach* ~ salary negotiable; **vereinbarungsgemäß** *Adv.* as agreed

vereinen *v/t.* → *vereinigen, vereint* **vereinfachen** *v/t.* (*erleichtern*) make easier; **vereinfachend I.** *Part. Präs.* → *vereinfachen;* **II.** *Adj.* simplistic; *grob od. stark* ~ oversimplistic; **vereinfacht I.** *P.P.* → *vereinfachen;* **II.** *Adj. Verfahren etc.:* simplified; *grob od. stark* ~ *Darstellung etc.:* oversimplified; **III.** *Adv.* in a simplified way; ~ *ausgedrückt* expressed in simplified terms; **Vereinfachung** *f* simplification; *unzulässige* ~ oversimplification **vereinheitlichen** *v/t.* standardize; **Vereinheitlichung** *f* standardization **vereinigen I.** *v/t.* **1.** unite, join; (*verbinden*) combine (*auch in sich* ~); (*zusammenschließen*) integrate (*in + Dat.* within); *zwei Ämter in e-r Person* ~ have one person holding two posts (*bes. Am.* positions); *die Mehrheit der Stimmen auf sich* ~ win a majority of the vote; **2.** *Wirts.* (*fusionieren*) amalgamate, consolidate, merge (*zu* into); **3.** (*Staaten*) unify; (*wiedervereinigen*) reunify; **II.** *v/refl.* **1.** unite, join; **2.** *Wirts.* (*fusionieren*) merge; **3.** *Flüsse etc.:* meet, merge; **4.** *Pol.* unite; *Staat:* become unified; (*sich wiedervereinigen*) become reunified; **5.** (*versammeln*) assemble, gather; *bes. Pol., Mil.* rally; **6.** *lit. sexuell:* couple; **vereinigt I.** *P.P.* → *vereinigen;* **II.** *Adj.* **1.** united; *Vereinigte Staaten* (*von Amerika*) United States (of America) (*Abk.* US[A]); *Vereinigte Arabische Emirate* United Arab Emirates (*Abk.* UAE); **2.** *Wirts., in Firmennamen:* consolidated; **Vereinigung** *f* **1.** (*Vorgang*) uniting; unification; combining *etc.;* → *vereinigen;* **2.** (*Zusammenschluss*) union; (*Personenvereinigung*) association, union; *Wirts.* (*Verschmelzung*) amalgamation, merger; *kriminelle* ~ criminal organization; → *auch Verein*

Vereinigungs|freiheit *f Jur.* freedom of association; *~kirche* *f* (*Mun-Sekte*) Unification Church **vereinnahmen** *v/t.* **1.** take in, collect; *umg. fig.* (*einstecken*) pocket; **2.** *umg. fig.:* (*ganz für sich*) ~ (*in Anspruch nehmen*) monopolize; **Vereinnahmung** *f* taking, collecting; monopolizing **Vereins|abend** *m* club night; (*Vereinsfest*) club party; *~abzeichen* *n* club (*od.* society) badge **vereinsamen** *v/i.* become isolated, grow lonely; **vereinsamt I.** *P.P.* → *vereinsamen;* **II.** *Adj.* isolated, lonely; **Vereinsamung** *f* (growing) isolation **Vereins|arbeit** *f* club work; *~beitrag* *m* membership dues *Pl.;* *~farben* *Pl.* club colo(u)rs; *~heim* *n* club building, clubhouse **vereinsintern I.** *Adj. Termine, Fragen etc.:* internal club (*od.* society); **II.** *Adv. diskutieren etc.:* within a club (*od.* society); *e-n Spieler* ~ *sperren* impose a club ban on a player **Vereins|kasse** *f* club (*od.* society) funds *Pl.;* *~lokal* *n* pub (*Am. bar*) at which a club or society regularly meets **Vereinsmeier** *m;* -*s,* -; *umg. pej.* joiner; **Vereinsmeierei** *f;* -, *kein Pl.;* *umg. pej.* club mania **Vereins|meister** *m,* *~meisterin* *f* club champion; *~meisterschaft* *f* club championship; *~mitglied* *n* club (*od.* society) member; *~register* *n* official register of clubs and societies; *~satzung* *f* club (*od.* society) rules *Pl.;* *~sport* *m* club sport; *~tätigkeit* *f* club (*od.* society) activities *Pl.;* *~vorsitzende* *m,* *f* club (*od.* society) chairperson, *männlich:* club (*od.* society) chairman, *weiblich:* club (*od.* society) chairwoman; *~vorstand* *m* club (*od.* society) committee; *~wesen* *n* clubs(, societies and associations) *Pl.;* *~zugehörigkeit* *f* membership of a club (*od.* society); *für 25-jährige etc.* ~ *geehrt werden* be hono(u)red for 25 years of club (*od.* society) membership **vereint I.** *P.P.* → *vereinen;* **II.** *Adj.* united; *mit* ~*en Kräften* in a joint (*od.* combined) effort; *die Vereinten Nationen* the United Nations *Sg.* **vereinzeln** *v/t.* **1.** *Agr. etc.* (*Pflanzen*) thin out; **2.** *geh.* (*Menschen*) isolate; **vereinzelt I.** *P.P.* → *vereinzeln;* **II.** *Adj.* (~ *auftretend*) isolated; *Schauer: auch* scattered; *zeitlich:* occasional, sporadic; *~e Briefe etc.* the odd letter *etc. Sg.;* → *Bewölkung* 1; **III.** *Adv. zeitlich:* sporadically, now and then; *örtlich:* here and there; **Vereinzelung** *f* thinning out; isolation; → *vereinzeln* **vereisen I.** *v/t.* (*hat vereist*); *Med.* freeze; **II.** *v/i.* (*ist*); *Straße, etc.:* freeze over; *Flug.* ice up (*auch Fenster*); **vereist I.** *P.P.* → *vereisen;* **II.** *Adj.* iced up (*od.* over); (*zugefroren*) frozen (over); **Vereisung** *f* icing up; freezing (over) **vereiteln** *v/t.* (*Plan etc.*) thwart, frustrate, foil; (*Tat*) prevent; **Vereitelung** *f* thwarting, frustration; *e-r Tat:* prevention **vereitern** *v/i.* go septic; **vereitert I.** *P.P.* → *vereitern;* **II.** *Adj.* septic; *völlig* ~ *sein* be completely septic; *~e Mandeln* tonsillitis **verelenden** *v/i.* be reduced to poverty; **Verelendung** *f* impoverishment **verenden** *v/i.* perish, die **verengen I.** *v/t.* narrow; **II.** *v/refl.* (become) narrow; *Kleidung:* taper; *Blut-*

gefäß: constrict; *Pupille:* contract; **Verengung** *f* **1.** narrowing; constriction; contraction; → *verengen;* **2.** (*verengte Stelle*) narrow part

vererbbar *Adj.* **1.** *Besitz etc.:* (in)heritable; **2.** *genetisch:* hereditary; **vererben I.** *v/t.* **1.** leave; (*auch hum. schenken*) bequeath (+ *Dat.* to); **2.** *Bio., Med.* pass on (*auf + Akk.* to), transmit (to); **3.** (*Brauch etc.*) pass *od.* hand down (*auf + Akk.* to); **II.** *v/refl.* **1.** *Eigenschaft etc.:* be hereditary, run in the family; *sich* ~ *auf* (+ *Akk.*) be passed on (*od.* transmitted) to; **2.** *sich* ~ *auf* (+ *Akk.*) *Nachlass:* devolve (up)on, fall to; **vererblich** *Adj.* **1.** *Besitz:* (in)heritable, hereditary; **2.** *Bio., Med.* hereditary; **vererbt I.** *P.P.* → *vererben;* **II.** *Adj.* **1.** inherited; **2.** *Bio., Med.* hereditary; **Vererbung** *f* **1.** bequeathal (*an + Akk.* to); *Bio., Med.* transmission (*auf + Akk.* to); *es ist alles* ~ *umg.* (*es ist in s-n Erbanlagen*) it all runs in the family, it's all in the genes; *es ist* ~ *bei ihm umg.* it's in his genes; **3.** *von Bräuchen etc.:* transmission (*auf + Akk.* to), passing *od.* handing down (to); **Vererbungslehre** *f* genetics *Pl.* (*V. im Sg.*) **verewigen I.** *v/t.* perpetuate; (*unsterblich machen*) immortalize; **II.** *v/refl.* immortalize o.s.; *umg. schreibend:* inscribe one's name (*in + Dat.* in; *an + Dat.* on); *mit Messer etc.:* carve one's name (into); **Verewigung** *f* perpetuation; *e-s Namens etc.:* immortalization **verfahren¹** (*unreg.*) *I.* *v/i.* (*ist verfahren*) proceed, act (*nach* on); ~ *mit j-m:* deal with; *mit etw.: auch* handle; **II.** *v/t.* (*hat*); (*Geld, Zeit*) spend driving (around); (*Benzin*) use up; **III.** *v/refl.* (*hat*) take the wrong road; *völlig:* lose one's way, get lost **verfahren²** **I.** *P.P.* → *verfahren¹;* **II.** *Adj.* **1.** (*ausweglos*) hopeless, inextricable; **2.** (*verpfuscht*) messed up; (*durcheinander*) tangled, muddled; *e-e* ~*e Geschichte* a (great) muddle **Verfahren** *n;* -*s,* - **1.** (*Verfahrensweise*) procedure; (*Methode*) method; **2.** *Jur.* procedure; (*Prozess*) proceedings *Pl.,* (law)suit; *das* ~ *einleiten gegen* take proceedings (*od.* legal action) against; *in ein schwebendes* ~ *eingreifen* intervene in a pending trial; → *auch Gerichtsverfahren;* **3.** *Tech.* process, method; (*bestimmtes System*) system; (*besondere Technik*) technique **Verfahrens|dauer** *f Wirts., Jur.* length of the procedure (*od.* proceedings); *~fehler* *m Jur.* procedural error; *~frage* *f* question of procedure; *~kosten* *Pl. Jur.* procedural costs; *~mangel* *m Jur.* procedural defect (*od.* failing) **Verfahrensrecht** *n Jur.* procedural law; **verfahrensrechtlich I.** *Adj.* procedural; **II.** *Adv.* in terms of procedural law **Verfahrensregel** *f* rule of procedure **Verfahrenstechnik** *f Tech.* process engineering; **verfahrenstechnisch** *Adj.* … in terms of procedure **Verfahrensweise** *f* procedure; (*Methode*) method; (*Ansatz*) approach **Verfall** *m;* -(*e*)*s, kein Pl.* **1.** (*Zerfallsprozess*) decay, ruin; *auch Med.* decline; *e-s Gebäudes:* dilapidation; *e-r Kultur etc.:* decline; (*Zusammenbruch*) fall; (*Entartung*) degeneracy; *sittlicher:* decay, corruption; *dem* ~ *preisgeben* let *s.th.* go to (rack and) ruin; *der* ~ *hat schon eingesetzt* the rot has set in; *den* ~ *des Kranken mit ansehen müssen* have to join in watching the pa-

V

tient deteriorate; **2.** (*Fristablauf*) expiry, *Am.* expiration; *e-s Wechsels*: maturity; *bei ~* upon expiry (*Am.* expiration); *Wechsel*: at maturity

verfallen[1] *v/i.* (*unreg.*) **1.** go to ruin; *Haus, Wirtschaft etc.*: fall into disrepair; *stärker*: go to ruin; *Reich, Kultur etc.*: decline; (*zusammenbrechen*) fall; *Kranker*: **2.** (*ablaufen*) expire; (*ungültig werden*) *auch* become invalid; *die Kreditkarte verfällt in zwei Monaten* the credit card expires in two months; **3.** *e-m Laster*: take to doing s.th., get hooked on *umg.*; *auch e-r Person*: become a slave to; *dem Zauber e-s Anblicks etc.*: be bewitched by; **4.** *~ in* (+ *Akk.*) fall into; *wieder*: lapse (*od.* slip) back into; *immer verfällst du in den gleichen Fehler, zu gutgläubig zu sein etc.*: you always make the same mistake of being too trusting etc.; **5.** *auf e-e Idee etc. ~* hit (up)on an idea etc.; *wie ist er nur darauf ~?* what on earth made him do that?; **6.** (*zufallen*): *j-m ~* go (*od.* pass) to s.o.

verfallen[2] **I.** *P.P.* → **verfallen**[1]; **II.** *Adj.* **1.** decayed; *Gebäude*: dilapidated, *attr. auch* tumbledown …, ramshackle …; *körperlich*: emaciated, *präd. auch* a wreck *umg.*; **2.** *Fahrschein etc.*: expired, invalid, no longer valid (*od.* good *umg.*); **3.** *e-m Rauschgift etc.*: addicted to, hooked on *umg.*; *dem Zauber e-s Anblicks etc.*: bewitched by; *der Liebe ~* smitten *umg.*; *er ist ihr völlig ~* he is totally captivated by her

Verfalls|datum *n* **1.** expiry (*Am.* expiration) date; **2.** *von Lebensmitteln*: best-before (*od.* best-by) date, use-by date, *Am. auch* pull date; *von Medikamenten*: expiry (*Am.* expiration) date; *~erscheinung* *f* sign of decay; *~stadium* *n*: (*im*) *~* (in a) state of decay (*od.* collapse); *~symptom* *n* sign of decay; *~tag* *m* expiry (*Am.* expiration) date; *~termin* *m* → *Verfallsdatum*; *~zeit* *f* expiry (*Am.* expiration) date

verfälschen *v/t.* distort, falsify; (*Lebensmittel*) adulterate; *Jur.*, (*Urkunden etc.*) falsify; → *auch* **fälschen**; **Verfälschung** *f* distortion, falsification; *von Lebensmitteln*: adulteration; *Jur.* falsification

verfangen (*unreg.*) **I.** *v/refl.* **1.** *im Netz etc.*: get caught; **2.** *sich in Widersprüchen etc. ~* get caught up (*od.* entangled) in a web of contradictions etc.; **II.** *v/i.* (*wirken*) work; *das verfängt bei mir nicht umg.* that cuts no ice with me

verfänglich *Adj. Situation etc.*: awkward; (*gefährlich*) risky; *Brief etc.*: compromising; *~e Frage* trick question; *du mit d-n ~en Fragen! umg.* you're just trying to catch me out (*Am.* trip me up); **Verfänglichkeit** *f* **1.** *nur Sg.* awkwardness; riskiness; **2.** *Situation etc.*: awkward situation; *stärker*: risky situation

verfärben I. *v/t.* (*Wäsche*) dye, colo(u)r; *die Socken haben die ganze Wäsche verfärbt* the dye from the socks has come off onto all the washing; *der Herbst verfärbt die Blätter* the autumn (*Am.* fall) turns the leaves different colo(u)rs; **II.** *v/refl.* discolo(u)r; *auch Person*: change colo(u)r; *Herbstlaub*: change colo(u)r, turn; *Jägerspr.* change colo(u)r; **verfärbt I.** *P.P.* → *verfärben*; **II.** *Adj.* discolo(u)red; **Verfärbung** *f* discolo(u)ration (*auch verfärbte Stelle*); *des Laubs*: change in

colo(u)r, turning

verfassen *v/t.* write; (*Gedicht*) *auch* compose; (*Resolution etc.*) draw up; **Verfasser** *m*; *-s*, *-*, **Verfasserin** *f*; *-*, *-nen* author, writer

Verfassung *f* **1.** (*Zustand, auch körperliche ~*) state, condition; *seelische: auch* state (*od.* frame) of mind; *in guter/schlechter ~ körperlich*: in good/bad shape; *seelisch*: in good/low spirits; *in bester körperlicher ~* in the best physical shape; *nicht in der ~ sein zu* (+ *Inf.*) be in no fit state (*seelisch: auch* in no frame of mind) (to + *Inf.*); *ich bin nicht in der ~ dazu auch* I don't feel up to it; **2.** *Pol.* constitution; *gegen die ~ verstoßen* violate the constitution, *bes. Am.* be unconstitutional; **verfassunggebend** *Adj.*: *~e Versammlung* constituent assembly

Verfassungs|änderung *f Pol.* constitutional amendment; *~beschwerde* *f* constitutional complaint; *~bruch* *m* breach of the constitution; *~eid* *m* constitutional oath; *~entwurf* *m* draft of the constitution; *~ergänzung* *f* constitutional amendment

Verfassungsfeind *m Pol.* enemy of the constitution; **verfassungsfeindlich** *Adj.* anticonstitutional

verfassungsgemäß *Adj. Pol. präd. und nachgestellt*: in accordance with the constitution, *Am. präd. und attr.* constitutional; *nicht ~ präd. und nachgestellt*: not in accordance with the constitution, *Am. präd. und attr.* unconstitutional

Verfassungs|gericht *n Pol.* constitutional court; *Oberstes ~* supreme constitutional court; *USA*: Supreme Court; *~grundsatz* *m* constitutional principle; *~klage* *f* constitutional challenge

verfassungs|konform *Adj. präd. und nachgestellt*: in conformity with the constitution, *Am. präd. und attr.* constitutional; *nicht ~ präd. und nachgestellt*: not in conformity with the constitution, *Am. präd. und attr.* unconstitutional; *~mäßig* *Adj. Pol.* constitutional; *nicht ~* unconstitutional

Verfassungsrecht *n Pol., Jur.* constitutional law; **Verfassungsrechtler** *m*; *-s*, *-*, **Verfassungsrechtlerin** *f*; *-*, *-nen* expert on constitutional law; **verfassungsrechtlich I.** *Adj. nachgestellt*: in terms of constitutional law; **II.** *Adv. bedenklich, geschützt, zulässig etc.*: in terms of constitutional law

Verfassungs|reform *f Pol.* constitutional reform; *~richter* *m*, *~richterin* *f* constitutional judge; *~schutz* *m Pol.* **1.** protection of the constitution; **2.** (*auch Bundesamt für ~*) federal agency for internal security; *GB etwa* MI5; *USA etwa* FBI; *~schutzbericht* *m* report by the federal agency for internal security; *~schützer* *m*; *-s*, *-*; *umg.* person working for the federal agency for internal security, *Am. etwa* fed; *~staat* *m* constitutional state; *~streit* *m* constitutional dispute

verfassungstreu *Adj. Pol.* loyal to the constitution; **Verfassungstreue** *f* loyalty to the constitution

verfassungswidrig *Adj. Pol.* unconstitutional; **Verfassungswidrigkeit** *f* breach of the constitution

Verfassungszusatz *m Pol.* addition to the constitution; *USA*: Amendment

verfaulen *v/i.* decay; *Lebensmittel, Holz etc.*: rot; *Zahn: auch* decay

verfechten *v/t.* (*unreg.*) speak out in

support of, stand up for; (*Ansicht*) maintain; (*verteidigen*) defend; *e-e Sache ~ auch* champion a cause; **Verfechter** *m*; *-s*, *-*, **Verfechterin** *f*; *-*, *-nen* advocate, champion, promoter (+ *Gen.* of)

verfehlen *v/t.* (*Ziel*) miss (*um* by); *den Beruf verfehlt haben* have missed one's vocation, be in the wrong job *umg.*; *s-e Wirkung ~* fail to work, be a failure; *Plan, Witz etc.: auch* misfire; *sich od. einander ~* miss each other; → *Thema* 1, *Zweck*; **verfehlt I.** *P.P.* → *verfehlen*; **II.** *Adj.* (*falsch*) wrong, misguided; *~es Thema beim Aufsatz*: failure to get to the point; *es für ~ halten zu* (+ *Inf.*) consider it amiss to (+ *Inf.*); **Verfehlung** *f* **1.** offen|ce (*Am.* -se); (*Sünde*) transgression; *für s-e ~en büßen etc.* atone for one's sins etc.; **2.** *nur Sg., des Ziels etc.*: missing; *eine ~ des Themas* a failure to grasp the subject; → *Themaverfehlung*

verfeinden I. *v/refl.* (*untereinander*) become enemies; *weitS.* (*sich zerstreiten*) fall out (with each other); *sich mit j-m ~* make an enemy of s.o.; (*sich zerstreiten*) fall out (*od.* have a falling-out) with s.o.; **II.** *v/t.* (*Menschen, Völker*) make enemies of; *j-n mit j-m ~* set s.o. against s.o.; **verfeindet I.** *P.P.* → *verfeinden*; **II.** *Adj.* hostile; *präd.* at daggers drawn; *sie sind vollkommen ~* they're sworn enemies; **Verfeindung** *f* (growing) hostility; (*Zustand*) (state of) enmity

verfeinern I. *v/t.* refine, *stärker*: make s.th. more sophisticated; *Tech. auch* improve; (*Soße etc.*) round off; *den Geschmack ~* improve the taste; **II.** *v/refl.* become more refined, *stärker*: become more sophisticated; *Tech. auch* improve; **Verfeinerung** *f* refinement, (increasing) sophistication; *Tech. auch* improvement; *des Geschmacks e-s Gerichts*: improvement

verfemen *v/t.* outlaw; *fig.* ostracize; (*Künstler etc.*) condemn; **Verfemte** *m*, *f*; *-n*, *-n* outlaw; *fig.* ostracized person; condemned person; **Verfemung** *f* outlawing; *fig.* ostracism, ostracizing; condemnation, condemning

verfertigen *v/t.* make, manufacture; **Verfertigung** *f* manufacture

verfestigen *v/t.* → *festigen*

verfetten *v/i.* **1.** *Person*: get (*od.* grow) too fat, grow (*od.* become) obese; **2.** *Med., Gewebe, Organ*: become fatty (*od.* adipose); **Verfettung** *f* **1.** *Med.* fatty degeneration, adiposis; **2.** *des Körpers*: obesity

verfeuern *v/t.* (*Brennmaterial*) burn; (*Munition*) fire; *weitS.* (*verbrauchen*) use up

verfilmen *v/t.* **1.** make a film (*Am.* movie) of; (*Roman etc.*) *auch* adapt for the screen; **2.** (*auf Mikrofilm aufnehmen*) microfilm; **Verfilmung** *f* **1.** filming; *konkret*: film (*bes. Am.* movie) version, screen adaptation; **2.** *von Dokumenten auf Mikrofilm*: microfilming

verfilzen *v/i. und v/refl.*: (*sich*) *~ Wolle*: felt; *Haare*: get matted; **verfilzt I.** *P.P.* → *verfilzen*; **II.** *Adj.* **1.** *Haare etc.*: matted; *Pullover etc.*: felted; **2.** *bes. Pol., pej., Verhältnisse etc.*: intertwined

verfinstern I. *v/t.* darken; **II.** *v/refl.* darken; *Sonne, Mond*: eclipse; *fig. Gesicht*: *auch* cloud over; **Verfinsterung** *f* darkening; *von Sonne, Mond*: eclipse

verflachen I. *v/t.* flatten; **II.** *v/i. und v/refl.*: (*sich*) *~* flatten, level off; *fig.*

Gespräch, Stil etc.: degenerate; *Person*: become shallow (*od.* superficial); *Film, Roman etc.*: degenerate; *die Fernsehunterhaltung verflacht zunehmend* TV entertainment is becoming increasingly trivial; *nach der Pause verflachte das Spiel* the game degenerated after the break; **Verflachung** *f fig.* degeneration; (growing) superficiality

verflechten *v/t. und v/refl.* (*unreg.*): (*sich*) ~ interweave, intertwine (*beide auch fig.*); *Wirts.* integrate; *zu e-m Zopf* ~ plait, *Am.* braid; *etw. zu e-r Gesamtheit etc.* ~ weave s.th. into a whole *etc.*; *j-n in etw.* (*Akk.*) ~ involve s.o. (*od.* get s.o. involved) in s.th.; → **verflochten**; **Verflechtung** *f* interweaving, intertwining; (*Integration*) integration (*in* + *Akk.* into); (*Verwicklung*) involvement; *internationale* ~*en* international involvements

verfliegen (*unreg.*) **I.** *v/i.* (*ist verflogen*) **1.** *Duft etc.*: fade (away); *Alkohol etc.*: evaporate; **2.** *Zeit*: fly; **3.** *Erinnerung etc.*: fade; *Bedenken, Angst etc.*: vanish, *Stimmung etc.*: *auch* blow over; **II.** *v/refl.* (*hat*); *Flug.* lose one's bearings, get lost

verfließen *v/i.* (*unreg.*) **1.** *Farben*: run; *ineinander* ~ merge (*auch fig. Begriffe etc.*); (*undeutlich, unscharf werden*) become (*od.* get) blurred; *ineinander* ~ merge (into one another); **2.** *Zeit*: pass (by)

verflixt *Adj. umg.* blasted, damn(ed); ~*!* blast!, damn (it)!; *das* ~*e siebte Jahr* the seven-year itch

verflochten I. *P.P.* → **verflechten**; **II.** *Adj.*: ~ *in* (+ *Akk.*) intertwined (with)in; (*verfangen*) entangled in; *eng* ~ intricate, *eng* ~ *in* (+ *Akk.*) intricately bound in(to)

verflossen I. *P.P.* → **verfließen**; **II.** *Adj. umg.*; *attr. Freund etc.*: ex-...; one-time ...; former ...; **Verflossene** *m, f*; *-n, -n*; *umg.* ex, *männlich*: ex-boyfriend, *weiblich*: ex-girlfriend; (*geschiedener Partner*) ex, *männlich*: ex-husband, *weiblich*: ex-wife; (*länger zurückliegend*: *auch umg. hum.* old flame

verfluchen *v/t.* curse; *ich könnte mich selbst* ~*, dass ich es getan habe* I could curse myself for doing it; **verflucht I.** *P.P.* → **verfluchen**; **II.** *Adj. und Interj.* → **verdammt** II 2

verflüchtigen I. *v/refl.* evaporate; *umg. fig.* disappear; *Person*: *auch* make o.s. scarce; *Wut etc.*: blow over; **II.** *v/t.* volatilize; **Verflüchtigung** *f* evaporation; disappearance; volatilization; → **verflüchtigen**

verflüssigen *v/t. und v/refl.*: (*sich*) ~ liquefy; *Metall.* fuse; **Verflüssigung** *f* liquefaction

verfolgen *v/t.* **1.** (*Person*) pursue, chase (*od.* run) after; (*Wild*) track down; **2.** (*Spur*) follow; **3.** (*Laufbahn, Politik, Idee etc., auch Jur., e-n Anspruch*) pursue; **4.** (*j-n*) *ungerecht, grausam*: persecute; *strafrechtlich*: prosecute; *in s-m Heimatland* (*politisch*) *verfolgt werden* be persecuted in one's home country (for political reasons); **5.** (*bedrängen*) dog, plague; *mit Hass*: persecute; (*ständig beschäftigen*) *Traum etc.*: haunt; *vom Pech verfolgt* dogged by misfortune; *der Gedanke verfolgt mich überallhin* the thought haunts me everywhere I go; **6.** (*Gedankengang*) follow up; **7.** (*Vorgang*) follow, observe; (*Entwicklung*) trace (*auch EDV*); *sie verfolgte jede s-r Bewe-*

gungen she followed his every move

Verfolger *m*; *-s, -*, ~*in f*, *-*, *-nen* pursuer; *grausame(r)*: persecutor; ~*duell n Sport* pursuit; *sich ein spannendes* ~ *liefern* have a real battle in the pursuit; ~*staat m* state that persecutes political opponents and undesirables etc.

Verfolgte *m, f*; *-n, -n*: (*politisch*) ~*r* victim of (political) persecution; **Verfolgung** *f* pursuit; persecution; prosecution *etc.*; → **verfolgen**; (*Fortführung*) pursuance; *wilde* ~ hot pursuit, wild chase; *die* ~ *aufnehmen* take up the chase (*od.* pursuit)

Verfolgungs|fahrt *f*, ~*jagd f bes. im Film*: wild chase, pursuit; *in Autos*: *mst* car chase; ~*rennen n Sport* pursuit; ~*wahn m Psych.* persecution complex, paranoia; *an* ~ *leiden auch* be (a) paranoiac

verformbar *Adj. Tech. etc.* workable; **verformen I.** *v/refl.* go out of shape; (*sich verdrehen*) twist; *Metall. auch* buckle; *Holz*: warp; **II.** *v/t.* deform; *Tech.* work, form, shape; **verformt I.** *P.P.* → **verformen**; **II.** *Adj. auch Med.* deformed; *Tech.* (*verdreht*) twisted; *Metall. auch* buckled; *Holz*: warped; **Verformung** *f* deformation; *Tech.* working, forming, shaping

verfrachten *v/t.* (*Ware*) freight, *Naut. od. Am.* ship; *umg.* (*j-n*) bundle off

verfranzen *v/refl. umg.* **1.** (*sich verirren*) get lost; **2.** *bei e-r Rede etc.*: lose the thread; **3.** *Flug.* lose one's bearings

verfremden *v/t. auch Kunst etc.*: alienate; *bis zur Unkenntlichkeit* ~ defamiliarize beyond recognition; **verfremdet I.** *P.P.* → **verfremden**; **II.** *Adj. Darstellung etc.*: defamiliarized; *die Figuren sind stark* ~ the figures have been greatly defamiliarized; **III.** *Adv. darstellen etc.*: in a defamiliarized way; **Verfremdung** *f* alienation; (*verfremdete Darstellung*) defamiliarization; **Verfremdungseffekt** *m Lit.* alienation effect

verfressen[1] *v/t.* (*unreg.*); *umg.*, (*sein Geld etc.*) blow ... on food

verfressen[2] *umg.* **I.** *P.P.* → **verfressen**[1]; **II.** *Adj.* greedy; ~ *sein* be a glutton, be a greedy pig; **Verfressenheit** *f*; *nur Sg.*; *umg.* greed, voraciousness, voracity

verfroren *Adj.* **1.** ~ *sein* feel the cold (very easily); **2.** (*durchgefroren*) frozen (to the bone)

verfrühen *v/refl.* arrive (*od.* come) too early; **verfrüht I.** *P.P.* → **verfrühen**; **II.** *Adj.* premature, too early; *Ankunft, Sommer etc.*: early; *es war* ~ *auch* it came too soon (*od.* early)

verfügbar *Adj.* available, at one's disposal; *frei* ~ freely disposable; ~*es Geld* available cash, cash in hand; (*frei*)~*es Einkommen* disposable (discretionary) income; *mit allen* ~*en Mitteln* with all means at one's disposal; *bitte halten Sie sich für uns* ~ please make yourself available to us; **Verfügbarkeit** *f*; *nur Sg.* availability

verfugen *v/t.* point

verfügen I. *v/t.* order; *gesetzlich, testamentarisch*: decree; **II.** *v/i.*: ~ *über* (+ *Akk.*) have (available *od.* at one's disposal); (*ausgestattet sein mit*) have, be provided (*od.* equipped) with; *über Mittel etc.* (*frei*) ~ dispose of funds *etc.*; (*frei*) *über etw.* ~ *können* be able (*od.* free, in a position) to do what one wants with s.th., (*frei*) *über s-e Zeit* ~ *können auch* be able to divide up

one's time as one wants; ~ *Sie über mich* at your service; *mir gefällt nicht, wie man einfach über mich verfügt* I don't like the way (in which) people just order me around

Verfügung *f* **1.** (*Erlass*) decree, order; (*Anweisung*) instruction; ~ *von Todes wegen Jur.* last will and testament; **2.** *nur Sg.*; (*Verfügungsrecht, -gewalt*) disposition; *freie* ~ *über* (+ *Akk.*) *auch* power freely to dispose of; *etw. zur* ~ *haben* have s.th. at one's disposal; *zur* ~ *stehen* be available (+ *Dat.* to); *j-m zur* ~ *stehen auch* be at s.o.'s disposal; *j-m etw. zur* ~ *stellen* place s.th. at s.o.'s disposal; *s-n Posten etc. zur* ~ *stellen* resign one's post (*bes. Am.* position *etc.*); *sein Amt zur* ~ *stellen auch* tender one's resignation; *sich zur* ~ *stellen* volunteer (*für* for), *sich j-m zur* ~ *stellen* offer one's services to s.o.; *sich zur* ~ *halten* be available; *ich stehe Ihnen jederzeit zur* ~ I am at your disposal at any time; *freundlicherweise zur* ~ *gestellt von* courtesy of; *zu Ihrer* ~ at your service; *Vormittag zur freien* ~ morning at client's *etc.* discretion; → **einstweilig**

verfügungsberechtigt *Adj.* authorized to dispose; **Verfügungsberechtigung** *f* right of disposal

Verfügungs|gewalt *f*: *freie* ~ discretionary power of disposition; (*Kontrolle*) control; ~*recht n* right of disposal; ~*stunde f Päd.* school period used for settling class business, *Am. etwa* homeroom

verführbar *Adj.* temptable; *sexuell*: seducible; *sie sind* ~ they can be tempted (*bzw.* seduced)

verführen I. *v/t.* **1.** *sexuell*: seduce; **2.** (*verlocken*) entice, tempt (*zu* to; *zu* + *Inf.* into doing); *weitS.* (*vom rechten Weg abbringen*) lead *s.o.* astray; *j-n zu e-m Bierchen etc.* ~ *umg.* tempt s.o. to a beer *etc.*; **II.** *v/i.*: *zum Diebstahl* ~ be an invitation to steal; *es verführt zum Kauf* it makes you tempted to buy (it); **Verführer** *m*; *-s, -* seducer; **Verführerin** *f*; *-, -nen* seductress; **verführerisch I.** *Adj.* **1.** *Frau, Parfüm etc.*: bewitching; *stärker*: seductive; *Schönheit*: ravishing; **2.** (*verlockend*) enticing, tempting; **II.** *Adv. lächeln etc.*: bewitchingly; *stärker*: seductively; *das Essen riecht äußerst* ~ the food smells extremely tempting; **Verführung** *f* **1.** seduction; **2.** (*Verlockung*) enticement, temptation; *der* ~ *erliegen* succumb to temptation; **Verführungskunst** *f* powers *Pl.* of persuasion

verfünffachen *v/t. und v/refl.*: (*sich*) ~ quintuple, increase five times; **Verfünffachung** *f* quintupling, fivefold increase

verfüttern *v/t.* feed; *täglich zwei Kilo Fleisch an den Hund* ~ feed the dog two kilos of meat a day; *die Küchenabfälle werden an die Schweine verfüttert* the kitchen waste is fed to the pigs; **Verfütterung** *f an Tiere*: feeding; *die* ~ *der Küchenabfälle an die Schweine* feeding the kitchen waste to the pigs

Vergabe *f*; *-, kein Pl.*; *Wirts., von Aufträgen*: placing, placement; *von Preisen, Stipendien etc.*: awarding; *von öffentlichen Mitteln*: allocation; ~*kriterium n* criterion for the placement (*bzw.* award, allocation)

vergackeiern *v/t. umg.*: *j-n* ~ pull s.o.'s leg, have (*Am.* put) s.o. on

vergällen *v/t.*: *j-m das Leben* / *die*

V

Freude an etw. (*Dat.*) ~ sour s.o.'s life / spoil s.o.'s enjoyment of s.th.

vergaloppieren *v/refl. umg.* **1.** (*übertreiben*) overdo it, go over the top; **2.** (*falsch kalkulieren*) miscalculate

vergammeln *umg.* **I.** *v/i.* (*ist vergammelt*); (*verfaulen*) rot; *Person:* go to seed; *etw.* ~ *lassen* (*Haus etc.*) let s.th. go to rack and ruin; **II.** *v/t.* (*hat*); (*Zeit*) idle (*od.* fritter) away; *den größten Teil s-s Studiums hat er vergammelt* he idled away most of his time as a student; **vergammelt** *umg.* **I.** *P.P.* → *vergammeln;* **II.** *Adj. Person:* scruffy; *Betrieb etc.:* run-down; ~*er Typ* scruff; *stärker:* slob; **III.** *Adv.:* *völlig ~ rumlaufen etc.* go around looking like a complete slob

vergangen I. *P.P.* → *vergehen;* **II.** *Adj.* past; *im ~en Jahr* last year; *am ~en Freitag* last Friday; *in ~en Zeiten* in times past, in bygone days *lit.;* ~*er Größe nachtrauern* lament the passing of former greatness; **Vergangenheit** *f* **1.** past (*auch Vorleben*); *politische ~ e-r Person:* political background; *e-e bewegte ~ haben* have had an eventful past; *e-e Frau mit ~* a woman with a past; *in der ~ liegen* be a thing of the past; *lasst die ~ ruhen* let bygones be bygones; → *angehören;* **2.** *Ling.* past (tense); *erste/zweite ~* simple past / past perfect (tense); *in die ~ setzen* put in the past (tense)

Vergangenheits|bewältigung *f* (process of) coming to terms with the past; ~*form f Ling.* past form

vergänglich *Adj. attr.* passing ..., *auch präd.* transitory, transient; *es ist alles ~* nothing lasts (forever); **Vergänglichkeit** *f; nur Sg.* transience, transitoriness; *die ~ des Lebens* the transitoriness of life, life's transitoriness

vergären (*unreg.*) **I.** *v/i.* (*ist vergoren*) ferment (*zu* into); **II.** *v/t.* (*hat*) ferment; **Vergärung** *f* fermentation

vergasen *v/t.* **1.** *Chem.* gasify; **2.** (*durch Gas töten*) gas; (*NS-Opfer*) *auch* send to the gas chambers

Vergaser *m; -s, -; Mot.* carburet(t)or

vergaß *Imperf.* → *vergessen*

Vergasung *f* **1.** *Chem.* gasification; **2.** (*Tötung*) gassing; *wir haben das Zeug bis zur ~ angehört/gegessen umg. fig.* we listened to the stuff ad nauseam / ate the stuff till it was coming out of our ears

vergattern *v/t.* **1.** fence up (*od.* in); **2.** *umg.: j-n dazu ~, etw. zu tun* rope s.o. into doing s.th.; *als Strafe:* make s.o. do s.th.; **3.** *Mil.: die Wache ~* remind the guard of his duties

vergeben[1] (*unreg.*) **I.** *vt/i.* **1.** (*verzeihen*) forgive (*j-m* s.o.); *man muss auch ~ können* one also has to be able to forgive; **2.** (*Chance*) miss, let *an opportunity* slip; *Sport* (*Tor, Sieg etc.*) throw away; (*Elfmeter etc.*) waste; *Elber vergab in der 90. Minute* (*traf nicht ins Tor*) Elber missed in the 90th minute; **3.** *sich* (*Dat.*) *nichts ~, wenn ...* not lose face if ...; *sich* (*Dat.*) *etw. ~* compromise o.s.; *was vergibst du dir, wenn ...?* what harm will it do if ...?; **II.** *v/t.* give away (*an j-n:* to); *Wirts.* (*Auftrag*) place (with); (*Arbeit*) farm out; (*übertragen*) confer, *förm.* bestow (on); *ein Amt an j-n ~* appoint s.o. to an office; *zu ~* available; *Stelle zu ~* vacancy; **III.** *v/refl. beim Kartenspiel:* misdeal

vergeben[2] **I.** *P.P.* → *vergeben*[1]; **II.** *Adj.* **1.** ~ *sein Stelle:* be taken; *Auf-*

trag: have been given out; *Plätze:* have been taken; *umg. Person:* be spoken for; *noch nicht ~ Stelle:* open; *auch umg. Person:* still available; *ich bin morgen leider schon ~ umg.* I'm booked up for tomorrow, I'm afraid; **2.** *das ist ~ und vergessen* that's all in the past; **3.** *Chance etc.:* missed, wasted; *zwei ~e Elfmeter* two wasted penalties

vergebens *Adv.* in vain; (*nutzlos*) *auch* to no avail; *sie bat ihn, sie drohte ihm - ~!* – but to no avail

vergeblich I. *Adj. attr.* vain, *auch präd.* fruitless, futile, useless; ~*e Mühe* a wasted effort, a waste of time; **II.** *Adv.* in vain; **Vergeblichkeit** *f; nur Sg.* futility

Vergebung *f* **1.** (*Verzeihung*) forgiveness, *auch* pardon; *j-n um ~ bitten* ask s.o.'s forgiveness; ~*!* forgive me!, pardon!; **2.** → *Vergabe*

vergegenwärtigen *v/t.: sich* (*Dat.*) *etw. ~* visualize (*od.* picture) s.th.; (*klar machen*) make s.th. clear to o.s.; ~ *wir uns doch die Auswirkungen* let's be clear about the implications; **Vergegenwärtigung** *f* visualization

vergehen (*unreg.*) **I.** *v/i.* (*ist vergangen*) *Zeit, Gefühl etc.:* pass; *Schmerz: auch* go away; *Zorn etc.:* blow over; (*nicht fortbestehen*) cease (to exist); (*sterben*) die; (*verschwinden*) disappear, vanish; *Schönheit, Erinnerung etc.: auch* fade; *wie die Zeit vergeht!* how time flies!; *das vergeht schon wieder* it'll pass, it won't last; *es werden Jahre ~, bis ~ od. bevor ...* it'll be years before ...; *dir wird das Lachen bald ~!* you'll soon be laughing on the other side of your face; *da wird ihm das Lachen schon ~!* that'll wipe the grin (*od.* smile) off his face; *mir ist der Appetit vergangen* I've lost my appetite; *vor Ungeduld etc. ~* be dying of impatience *etc.*; → *hören* I 1; **II.** *v/refl.* (*hat*): *sich an j-m ~ tätlich:* assault s.o.; *unsittlich:* commit indecent assault on s.o., indecently assault s.o.; *sich ~ gegen* offend against, violate; *sich gegen ein Gesetz ~ auch* commit an offen|ce (*Am.* -se)

Vergehen *n; -s, -* offen|ce (*Am.* -se)

vergeigen *v/t. umg.;* (*Klassenarbeit etc.*) make a mess of; *Sport* (*Spiel*) lose

vergeistigt *Adj.* cerebral; *völlig ~ sein auch* move on a very cerebral plane

vergelten *v/t.* repay; *j-m etw. ~* repay s.o. for s.th.; (*auch sich rächen*) pay s.o. back for s.th.; *vergelt's Gott!* God bless you!; → *gleich* I 2; **Vergeltung** *f* repayment; (*Rache*) retribution, retaliation

Vergeltungs|maßnahme *f bes. Mil.* retaliatory measure, reprisal; *Pl. auch* retaliation *Sg.;* ~*schlag m* act of reprisal, retaliatory strike

vergesellschaften *v/t.* **1.** (*verstaatlichen*) nationalize; **2.** *Wirts.* convert into a company, *Am.* incorporate

vergessen (*unreg.*) **I.** *vt/i.* forget; (*liegen lassen*) *auch* leave (behind); *ich habe es ~* (*nicht mehr daran gedacht*) *auch* it slipped my mind; *ich habe ganz ~, wie ... auch* I forget how ...; *bevor ich's vergesse auch* while I remember; *das hab ich schlicht ~ umg.* it completely slipped my mind; *und nicht zu ~* (*nicht zuletzt*) and not forgetting; *du vergisst dabei, dass ...* you're forgetting that ...; *ein Tag etc.,* *den man so leicht nicht vergisst* a

day *etc.* that won't be forgotten so easily; *das werd ich mein Lebtag nicht ~* I'll never forget it for as long as I live; *das werde ich dir nie ~ positiv:* I won't ever (*od.* will never) forget it; *das wird man ihr nie ~ negativ:* she'll never live it down; *das kannst du ~ od. vergiss es! umg.* forget it; (*es nützt nichts*) it's useless; *den kannst du ~! umg.* (*ihm ist nicht zu helfen etc.*) he's hopeless; (*der kommt nicht mehr etc.*) you can forget about him; **II.** *v/refl.* forget o.s.; *wie konntest du dich so ~* (*weit*) ~*, ihn zu schlagen?* how could you lose control of yourself to the extent of hitting him?

Vergessenheit *f: in ~ geraten* fall into oblivion; *etw. der ~ entreißen / anheim geben* rescue s.th. from / consign s.th. to oblivion

vergesslich *Adj.* forgetful, absentminded; ~ *sein* keep forgetting things; **Vergesslichkeit** *f; nur Sg.* forgetfulness, absent-mindedness

vergeuden *v/t.* waste; (*Geld, Zeit*) *auch* squander; **Vergeudung** *f* waste; *von Geld, Zeit: auch* squandering

vergewaltigen *v/t.* **1.** (*Frau etc.*) rape; **2.** *fig.* (*Sprache etc.*) do violence to, mutilate; **Vergewaltiger** *m; -s, -* rapist; **vergewaltigt I.** *P.P.* → *vergewaltigen;* **II.** *Adj.* raped; *Hilfe etc. für ~e Frauen* help *etc.* for (female) rape victims; **Vergewaltigung** *f* **1.** *Jur.* rape; **2.** *fig.* violation, mutilation

Vergewaltigungs|opfer *n* rape victim; ~*versuch m* attempted rape

vergewissern *v/refl.* make sure (+ *Gen.* of); (*prüfen*) check (*s.th.*); *sich ~, dass die Tür verriegelt ist etc.* make sure that the door is bolted *etc.*

vergießen *v/t.* (*unreg.*) **1.** (*Blut, Tränen*) shed; *es wird viel Blut vergossen werden* there will be a great deal of bloodshed; **2.** (*verschütten*) spill; **3.** *Metall.* cast

vergiften I. *v/t.* poison (*auch fig. Atmosphäre etc.*); (*Luft, Umwelt etc.*) pollute; **II.** *v/refl.* poison o.s.; **Vergiftung** *f* poisoning

Vergiftungserscheinung *f* symptom of poisoning

vergilben *v/i.* yellow, go yellow (at the edges); **vergilbt I.** *P.P.* → *vergilben;* **II.** *Adj.* yellowed, yellowing

vergipsen *v/t.* plaster

Vergissmeinnicht *n; -(e)s, -(e); Bot.* forget-me-not

vergittern *v/t.* fix a grate onto; *mit Draht:* wire in; *mit Stangen:* bar; **Vergitterung** *f* grating

verglasen *v/t.* glaze; (*Veranda etc.*) glass in (*od.* up); **verglast I.** *P.P.* → *verglasen;* **II.** *Adj. Fenster und fig. Blick, Augen etc.:* glazed; *die Fassade ist ganz ~* the façade is completely glazed; **Verglasung** *f* (*auch konkret Scheiben etc.*) glazing

Vergleich *m; -(e)s, -e* **1.** comparison; *im ~ zu* compared to (*od.* with), in comparison with; *dem ~* (*nicht*) *standhalten* bear (no) comparison; *dem ~ mit etw.* (*nicht*) *standhalten auch* (not) compare with s.th.; *günstig abschneiden im ~ mit* compare favo(u)rably with; *das ist ja überhaupt kein ~!* you can't compare, there's just no comparison; *e-n ~ anstellen* draw a comparison; → *hinken* 1; **2.** *Lit. bildhafter:* simile; (*Analogie*) analogy; **3.** *Jur.* settlement; (*gütlicher*) ~ (amicable) agreement; **4.** *Sport* (*Wettkampf*) friendly competition; (*Spiel*) friendly match (*od.* game)

vergleichbar *Adj.* comparable (*mit* to, with); *das ist überhaupt nicht* ~ you can't compare, there's just no comparison; **Vergleichbarkeit** *f*; *nur Sg.* comparability

vergleichen (*unreg.*) **I.** *v/t.* **1.** compare (*mit* to, with); *die Preise* ~ compare prices; *es ist nicht zu* ~ *mit* you can't compare it with, it doesn't compare with; *vergleiche* (*abgek.* **vgl.**) *Seite 10 etc.* compare (*abgek.* cf.) page 10 *etc.*; **2.** (*Uhren*) synchronize; *die Uhren* ~ synchronize watches; **II.** *v/refl.* **1.** *sich* ~ *mit* compare o.s. with (*od.* to); *mit ihm kannst du dich nicht* ~ you can't compare yourself to him; **2.** *sich* (*Pl.*) ~ (*sich einigen*) come to an agreement (*od.* to terms); **vergleichend I.** *Part. Präs.* → *vergleichen*; **II.** *Adj.*: ~*e Literaturwissenschaft etc.* comparative literature *etc.*

Vergleichs|antrag *m Jur.* application for the initiation of composition proceedings; ~**form** *f Ling.* comparative form; ~**maßstab** *m* standard of comparison; ~**miete** *f* comparable rent; *ortsübliche* ~ local comparable rent; ~**möglichkeit** *f* opportunity for comparison; ~**monat** *m* comparative month; ~**punkt** *m* point of comparison; ~**tabelle** *f* comparison chart; ~**vorschlag** *m Jur.* offer of a settlement

vergleichsweise *Adv.* **1.** (*relativ*) comparatively, relatively; **2.** (*zum Vergleich*) by way of comparison

Vergleichs|wert *m* comparative (*od.* comparable) value; ~**zahl** *f* comparative figure; ~**zeitraum** *m* comparative period of time; ~**ziffer** *f* comparative figure

vergletschern *v/i. Geog.* become glaciated; **Vergletscherung** *f* glaciation

verglich *Imperf.* → *vergleichen*

verglichen I. *P.P.* → *vergleichen*; **II.** *Adv.*: ~ *mit* compared with (*od.* to)

verglimmen *v/i.* (*auch unreg.*) die down (*od.* away); → *auch* **verglühen**

verglühen *v/i.* **1.** smo(u)lder out; *Meteor etc.*: burn out; *Rakete*: burn up; **2.** *fig. Leidenschaft*: die

vergnügen *v/refl.* enjoy o.s.

Vergnügen *n*; *-s*, *-* pleasure, enjoyment; (*Spaß*) fun; ~ *finden an* (+ *Dat.*) find pleasure in, enjoy; *ein kindliches* ~ *an etw.* (*Dat.*) *haben* take childish pleasure in s.th.; *j-m* (*großes*) ~ *machen od. bereiten* give s.o. (great) pleasure; *sich* (*Dat.*) *ein* ~ *daraus machen, etw. zu tun* derive pleasure from (*od.* enjoy) doing s.th.; *es war mir ein* ~ it was a pleasure; *mit wem habe ich das* ~? *altm.* with whom do I have the pleasure of speaking?; *viel* ~! *auch iro.* have fun!, enjoy yourself (*od.* yourselves)!; *es war kein* (*reines*) ~ *umg.* it was no picnic (*od.* fun and games), it wasn't exactly (great) fun; *es ist wahrlich kein* ~, *mit ihm zu verhandeln* negotiating with him really is no fun; *mit* (*größtem*) ~ with (the greatest) pleasure; (*nur*) *zum* ~ (just) for fun; *aus reinem* ~ just for the fun of it; *vor* ~ *quietschen etc.*: with pleasure; *ein teures* ~ an expensive business (*od.* affair); *also stürzen wir uns ins* ~! *umg.* so let's enjoy ourselves!; *iro.* (*fangen wir an!*) so let the fun begin!

vergnüglich *Adj.* pleasant, enjoyable

vergnügt I. *P.P.* → *vergnügen*; **II.** *Adj.* (*guter Laune*) happy; (*fröhlich*) cheer-

ful, chirpy *umg.*, *Am.* chipper *umg.*; *erfreut*: pleased (*über* + *Akk.* with); *Gesicht, Lachen etc.*: happy; *Abend, Feier etc.*: enjoyable; *immer heiter und* ~ always happy and cheerful; ~*e Runde* enjoyable company; **III.** *Adv. lachen, dreinschauen etc.*: happily; *sich* (*Dat.*) ~ *die Hände reiben* rub one's hands together in delight

Vergnügung *f* **1.** pleasure; *s-n* ~*en nachgehen* pursue one's pleasures; **2.** *altm.* (*Veranstaltung*) entertainment

Vergnügungs|dampfer *m* pleasure boat; ~**fahrt** *f Mot.* joy ride; ~**industrie** *f* entertainment industry; ~**lokal** *n* bar providing entertainment, nightclub; ~**park** *m* amusement park, fun fair, *Am.* carnival; *mit Schwerpunkt*: theme park; ~**reise** *f* pleasure trip; ~**stätte** *f* place of entertainment; ~**steuer** *f* entertainment tax

Vergnügungssucht *f pej.* hedonism, craving for pleasure; **vergnügungssüchtig** *Adj. pej. attr.* pleasure-seeking …, hedonistic

Vergnügungsviertel *n* entertainment district; *mit Bordellen*: red-light district, *Am. umg.* combat zone

vergolden *v/t.* gild (*auch fig.*); (*Metall, Schmuck etc.*) gold-plate; *sich sein Schweigen* ~ *lassen fig.* be paid for one's silence; **Vergoldung** *f* **1.** *Vorgang*: gilding, gold-plating; **2.** *konkret*: gilt, gold-plate, gold-plating

vergönnen *v/t.* grant; *es war mir vergönnt, es zu sehen etc.* I had the privilege of seeing it *etc.*; *es war ihm nicht vergönnt, es zu sehen etc.* it was not for him to see it *etc.*, he was not (meant) to see it *etc.*; *j-m etw. nicht* ~ begrudge s.o. s.th.; *mögen euch noch viele schöne Jahre vergönnt sein!* may you have many more years of happiness!

vergöttern *v/t. fig.* idolize, worship; **Vergötterung** *f* idolization, worship([-p]ing)

vergraben (*unreg.*) **I.** *v/t.* bury (*auch fig.*), inter *geh.*; *sein Gesicht in beide Hände* ~ bury one's face in one's hands; *die Hände in den Hosentaschen* ~ bury one's hands in one's trouser (*Am.* pant) pockets; **II.** *v/refl.*: *sich* (*in der Erde*) ~ *Hamster etc.*: bury o.s. (in the ground); *sich in s-e Bücher* ~ *fig.* bury o.s. in one's books; *sich immer mehr* ~ *fig.* hide o.s. away more and more

vergrämen *v/t.* **1.** (*j-n, beleidigen*) offend; (*verärgern*) upset; *j-n nicht* ~ *auch* keep on s.o.'s right side; **2.** *Jägerspr.* (*Wild etc. und Fig.*) frighten, startle; (*verscheuchen*) frighten away, scare off; **vergrämt I.** *P.P.* → *vergrämen*; **II.** *Adj.* careworn

vergrätzen *v/t. umg.* disgruntle, annoy, upset

vergrauen *v/i. Wäsche etc.* turn grey (*Am.* gray)

vergraulen *v/t. umg.* put off; *stärker*: frighten off

vergreifen *v/refl.* (*unreg.*) **1.** make a mistake; *Mus.* play a wrong note; *Geräteturnen*: miss one's grip; **2.** *sich* ~ *an* (+ *Dat.*) *an j-m*: lay hands on, attack; *sexuell*: (sexually) assault; *an fremdem Eigentum*: misappropriate; *umg. fig.* (*herumpfuschen an*) interfere (*od.* fiddle around) with; *sich* ~ *in* (+ *Dat.*) *im Ausdruck etc.*: choose (*od.* use) the wrong …, not find the right …; *du hast dich wohl im Ton vergriffen* you certainly didn't adopt the

right tone; *sich an der Kasse* ~ dip into the till *umg.*; *ich vergreif mich doch nicht an kleinen Kindern! umg. hum.* I only take on people of my own size

vergreisen *v/i.* turn (*od.* get) senile; *auch Bevölkerung etc.*: age; *die deutsche Bevölkerung vergreist zunehmend* the German population is developing an increasing proportion of older people, the German population is ag(e)ing; **Vergreisung** *f*; *nur Sg.* (progressive) senility; *auch der Bevölkerung etc.*: ag(e)ing

vergriffen I. *P.P.* → *vergreifen*; **II.** *Adj. Buch*: *attr.* out-of-print …, *präd.* out of print

vergröbern *v/t.* **1.** coarsen; **2.** *fig.* (*zu sehr vereinfachen*) oversimplify; **Vergröberung** *f* **1.** coarsening; **2.** oversimplification

vergrößern I. *v/t.* **1.** enlarge; **2.** *Fot.* enlarge, blow up; *Opt., mit der Lupe etc.*: magnify; **3.** (*ausdehnen*) expand; *auch Tech.* (*Werkanlage*) extend; **4.** (*verbreitern*) widen (*auch Einfluss*); (*vermehren*) increase, add to; (*erhöhen*) raise; **II.** *v/refl.* **1.** (*sich ausdehnen*) *auch* expand, be extended; (*sich verbreitern*) widen; **2.** (*anwachsen*) grow, increase; *Organ etc.*: become enlarged; (*sich erhöhen*) rise; *wir wollen uns* ~ *umg.* (*in ein größeres Haus, Büro etc. ziehen*) we want to move to somewhere bigger; **vergrößert I.** *P.P.* → *vergrößern*; **II.** *Adj. Organ etc.*: enlarged; *die Schilddrüse ist stark/krankhaft* ~ the thyroid gland has become grossly/abnormally enlarged; *fünfzigfach etc.* ~ *Opt.* magnified fifty *etc.* times; **III.** *Adv.*: *leicht etc.* ~ *wiedergeben etc.* reproduce etc. on a slightly *etc.* larger scale; **Vergrößerung** *f* **1.** enlargement; growth; expansion, extension; widening; increase; → *vergrößern*; **2.** *Fot.* enlargement, blow-up; *Opt.* magnification; *in fünfzigfacher etc.* ~ magnified 50 times

Vergrößerungs|gerät *n Fot.* enlarger; ~**glas** *n* magnifying glass

vergucken *v/refl. umg.* **1.** see wrong; *hast du dich auch nicht verguckt? auch* are you sure you saw right?; **2.** *fig.*: *sich in j-n* ~ fall for s.o.

Vergünstigung *f* (*Vorrecht*) privilege; *steuerliche*: allowance; *soziale*: benefit; (*Preisnachlass*) reduction, *für Flug etc.*: special rate

vergüten *v/t.* **1.** compensate (*j-m etw.* s.o. for s.th.); (*Auslagen*) reimburse, refund; (*Zinsen, Schaden*) indemnify (*j-m* s.o. for); (*Verlust*) compensate for, make good; *wir werden Ihnen die Arbeit natürlich* ~ we will of course pay you for the work; *die Stelle wird mit 2000 Euro vergütet* the job pays 2000 euros; **2.** *Tech.* improve, refine; (*Objektiv*) coat; **Vergütung** *f* **1.** compensation; reimbursement, refund; indemnification; → *vergüten*; **2.** *für geleistete Dienste*: consideration; (*Honorar*) fee; *ohne jegliche* ~ for free; **3.** *Tech.* improvement, refinement; *e-s Objektivs*: coating

verhackstücken *v/t. umg. pej.* (*verreißen*) tear to bits (*od.* pieces, shreds)

verhaften *v/t.* arrest (*wegen* for); **verhaftet I.** *P.P.* → *verhaften*; **II.** *Adj.* **1.** *attr. Täter etc.*: arrested, *präd.* under arrest; *Sie sind* ~! you are under arrest!; **2.** *im Sozialismus etc.* ~ rooted in Socialism *etc.*; *im System etc.* ~ *sein auch* be a captive of the system *etc.*;

Verhaftete m, f; -n, -n person under arrest, detained person; **abends wurden drei der ~n freigelassen** three of the arrested (od. those detained) were released in the evening; **Verhaftung** f arrest; **es kam zu mehreren ~en** there were several arrests, several people were arrested, several arrests were made; **Verhaftungswelle** f wave of arrests

verhageln v/i. be damaged (od. destroyed) by hail; → **Petersilie**

verhaken I. v/t. hook together; **die Hände od. Finger ~** clasp one's hands; **II.** v/refl. get caught (**an/in** + Dat. on/in)

verhallen v/i. die away; → **ungehört**

verhalten[1] (unreg.) **I.** v/refl. **1.** Person: behave, act, be; **sich korrekt/tapfer ~** behave correctly/courageously; **sich richtig/falsch ~** act correctly/wrongly; **sich ruhig ~** keep quiet; (sich nicht bewegen) keep still; (Ruhe bewahren) keep calm; **sich abwartend ~** adopt a "wait and see" attitude; **ich weiß nicht, wie ich mich ~ soll** I'm not sure what to do; **wie verhält er sich gegenüber s-n Mitschülern?** how does he behave toward(s) his fellow pupils (Am. his classmates)?; **wie verhalte ich mich im Brandfall?** what should I do if there is a fire?; **2.** Sache: be; **sich anders/umgekehrt ~** be different / be just the reverse; **die Sache verhält sich ganz anders** it's a completely different state of affairs; **wenn es sich so verhält** if that is the case; **A verhält sich zu B wie C zu D** Math. A is to B as C is to D; **II.** v/t./i. altm., geh. (zurückhalten) hold back, retain (auch Urin etc.); (unterdrücken) suppress, restrain (auch Lachen etc.); **den Atem ~** hold one's breath; **den Schritt ~** slow down; (innehalten) stop; **sein Pferd ~** rein in one's horse; **vor der Tür verhielt er e-n Moment** he stopped for a moment outside the door

verhalten[2] **I.** P.P. → **verhalten**[1]; **II.** Adj. (zurückhaltend) restrained; Lachen etc.: stifled; Stimme, Farbe, Ton, Stimmung etc.: subdued; Begeisterung etc.: muted; **mit ~er Stimme/Wut** in a subdued voice / in suppressed rage; **III.** Adv. with restraint; in a subdued manner; **~ spielen** Sport play a waiting game; Theat. underact; Mus. hold back

Verhalten n; -s, kein Pl. behavio(u)r (auch Zool. etc.), conduct; Chem., e-s Gases etc.: reaction; **unprofessionelles ~** unprofessional conduct; **das ~ im Straßenverkehr** conduct on the road; **das richtige ~ im Brandfall** etc. the correct procedure in case of fire etc.; **ich finde sein ~ unmöglich** I find his behavio(u)r ridiculous

...verhalten n, im Subst.: **Brut~** brood(ing) behavio(u)r; **Freizeit~** leisure-time behavio(u)r, behavio(u)r in one's leisure time; **Seitenwind~** cross-wind handling

verhaltensauffällig Adj. Päd., Psych. displaying behavio(u)ral problems; **Verhaltensauffälligkeit** f behavio(u)ral problems Pl.

Verhaltens|forscher m, **~forscherin** f behavio(u)rist; Tiere: ethologist; **~forschung** f behavio(u)rism; Tiere: ethology

verhaltensgestört Adj. Psych. maladjusted; **ausgesprochen ~ wirken** appear to have extreme behavio(u)ral problems; **in m-r Klasse habe ich**

mehrere Verhaltensgestörte I have several pupils (Am. students) in my class with behavio(u)ral problems

Verhaltens|kodex m code of conduct; **~maßregel** f → **Verhaltensregel**; **~merkmal** n behavio(u)ral trait (od. characteristic); **~muster** n behavio(u)ral pattern; **~norm** f behavio(u)ral norm; → auch **Verhaltensregel**; **~psychologie** f behavio(u)rism, behavio(u)ral psychology; **~regel** f rule of etiquette (od. conduct); **~n** auch code Sg. of conduct; **~störung** f Psych. behavio(u)ral disorder; **~therapie** f Psych. behavio(u)r therapy; **~weise** f behavio(u)r; Psych. auch behavio(u)ral pattern(s Pl.)

Verhältnis n; -ses, -se **1.** proportion; zahlenmäßiges: ratio; **im ~ wenig** etc. comparatively little etc.; **im ~ zu** in proportion to, compared with; **im ~ von 1:2** etc. in a ratio of 1:2 etc.; **im umgekehrten ~ zu** in inverse proportion to, inversely proportionate to; **im entsprechenden ~** proportionately; **im entsprechenden ~ stehen zu** be proportional to; **2.** ~se Pl. (Umstände) conditions, circumstances; **unter den (gegebenen) ~sen** under the circumstances; **in guten/schlechten ~sen leben** be well-off/badly-off; **aus kleinen ~sen kommen** come from a modest background; **über s-e ~se leben** live beyond one's means, overspend; **das geht über m-e ~se** I can't afford it, it's beyond my means; **3.** (Beziehung) relationship, relations Pl. (**zu** with); **in e-m freundlichen ~ mit** on friendly terms with; **ich habe kein ~ dazu** I can't relate to it, it doesn't mean anything (stärker: a thing) to me; → **gestört** II 2; **4.** (Liebesbeziehung) relationship, affair; **ein ~ mit j-m anfangen/haben** start/have an affair with s.o.; **5.** umg. (Geliebte) lover, lady friend; (Geliebter) lover

verhältnismäßig I. Adv. **1.** (relativ) relatively, reasonably; **2.** (angemessen) proportionally; **~ reagieren** react appropriately; **II.** Adj. proportional; Wirts. attr. auch pro rata ...; **Verhältnismäßigkeit** f appropriateness; **die ~ der Mittel** the appropriateness of the means

Verhältniswahl f Parl. proportional representation; **~recht** n (system of) proportional representation

Verhältnis|wort n Ling. preposition; **~zahl** f Statistik: ratio

verhandelbar Adj. negotiable; **verhandeln** vt/i. **1.** negotiate (**über** + Akk. about, on); **über Bedingungen** etc. ~ auch negotiate (od. discuss) conditions etc.; **2.** Jur. hold proceedings; Strafrecht: hold a trial (**gegen** against); (**über**) ~e Sache od. e-n Fall ~ hear (strafrechtlich: try) a case; **Verhandlung** f **1.** negotiations Pl.; **in ~en eintreten** enter into negotiations; **2.** Jur. hearing; Strafrecht: trial; **zur ~ kommen** come up (for trial)

Verhandlungs|angebot n offer to negotiate; **~basis** f (abgek. VHB) basis for negotiation(s); **~ 5000 Euro** 5000 euros or near(est) offer (abgek. o.n.o.)

verhandlungsbereit Adj. willing to negotiate (od. enter into negotiations); **Verhandlungsbereitschaft** f readiness to negotiate

Verhandlungs|erfolg m success in negotiations; **~ergebnis** n outcome (od. result) of the negotiations

verhandlungsfähig Adj. **1.** Jur. able

(od. fit) to stand trial; **der Angeklagte wurde für nicht ~ erklärt** the accused was declared unfit to stand trial; **2.** (nicht) ~ Angebot etc.: (non-)negotiable; **Verhandlungsfähigkeit** f; nur Sg. ability to stand trial

Verhandlungs|führer m, **~führerin** f chief negotiator; **~gegenstand** m issue, object of negotiation; **~geschick** n skill at negotiating; **~grundlage** f basis for negotiation(s); **~marathon** m über Tage, Wochen etc.: marathon negotiations Pl.; ununterbrochen: marathon negotiating session; **~masse** f bargaining counters (Am. chips) Pl.; **~partner** m, **~partnerin** f negotiating partner; **~pause** f break in (the) negotiations; **~position** f bargaining position; **~runde** f **1.** round of negotiations; **2.** bei Tarifverhandlungen: bargaining round; **~sache** f object of negotiation; **~spielraum** m room to negotiate; **~tag** m Jur. day of the hearing (Strafrecht: trial); **~termin** m Jur. hearing (date); Strafrecht: trial date; **~tisch** m negotiating (Wirts. auch bargaining) table; **am ~** at (od. around) the negotiating table

verhandlungsunfähig Adj. Jur. unable (od. unfit) to stand trial; **Verhandlungsunfähigkeit** f Jur. inability to stand trial

Verhandlungs|weg m: **auf dem ~e (beilegen** settle) by negotiation; **~ziel** n negotiating aim

verhangen Adj. **1.** cloudy, overcast; **~er Himmel** cloudy sky, overcast skies; **2.** Fenster: covered

verhängen v/t. **1.** cover, drape; (verbergen) auch veil; **die Fenster ~** cover up the windows; **2.** (Strafe, Blockade etc.) impose (**über** + Akk. on); Sport (Strafstoß etc.) award

Verhängnis n; -ses, -se fate; (Unheil) disaster; (Untergang) ruin; **j-m zum ~ werden** be s.o.'s undoing (od. ruin[ation]), lead to s.o.'s downfall; **verhängnisvoll** Adj. fateful; stärker: fatal; **sich als ~ erweisen** prove fatal

Verhängung f von Strafe, Verbot etc.: imposition

verharmlosen v/t. play down; (bagatellisieren) minimize; **verharmlosend I.** Part. Präs. → **verharmlosen**; **II.** Adj. Darstellung etc.: played-down, muted; **III.** Adv. darstellen etc.: in a played-down (od. muted) manner; **Verharmlosung** f playing down; minimizing, minimization

verhärmt Adj. careworn

verharren v/i. **1.** persevere, persist (**auf** + Dat., **bei**, **in** + Dat. in); **bei s-r Meinung ~** stick to one's opinion; **2.** in e-r Haltung, Stellung etc.: remain; **er verharrte unschlüssig an der Tür** he paused at the door, uncertain what to do

verharschen v/i. Schnee: crust over; Wunde: form a scab

verhärten I. v/t. und v/refl. (hat verhärtet): (**sich**) ~ auch fig. harden; **die Fronten haben sich verhärtet** fig. positions have become entrenched; **II.** v/i. (ist); (hart werden) harden; **Verhärtung** f **1.** hardening; **2.** Med. (verhärtete Stelle) callus

verhaspeln v/refl. umg. fig. get in a muddle, get one's words muddled

verhasst Adj. hated, detested; Sache: auch hateful, odious (+ Dat. to); **es ist mir ~** I hate (od. loathe) it; **sich ~ machen (bei j-m)** arouse (od. incur) (s.o.'s) hatred; **überall ~ sein** be hated by everyone

verhätscheln *v/t. umg. mst pej.* coddle, pamper, spoil; **Verhätschelung** *f umg. mst pej.* coddling, pampering, spoiling

Verhau *m, n; -(e)s, -e* **1.** (*Hindernis*) entanglement; **2.** *umg.* (*Durcheinander*) mess; *das ist ja ein ~!* what a mess, it's absolute chaos

verhauen *umg.* **I.** *v/t.* **1.** beat (up); (*Kind*) give *s.o.* a hiding (*Am.* spanking); **2.** *fig.* make a hash of; *umg.* bungle, muff; **II.** *v/refl.* miscalculate (badly), get one's sums wrong; *sich ~ haben auch* be way off (*od.* out)

verheben *v/refl.* (*unreg.*) hurt o.s. lifting s.th., twist one's back; *fig. finanziell etc.*: overstretch o.s.; *wir haben uns beim Hausbau verhoben* we overstretched ourselves in building the house

verheddern *v/refl. umg.* **1.** get caught (up); **2.** *fig., in e-r Rede etc.*: get in a muddle; (*stecken bleiben*) get stuck

verheeren *v/t.* devastate, lay waste (to); **verheerend I.** *Part. Präs.* → *verheeren*; **II.** *Adj. fig.* disastrous; (*scheußlich*) dreadful; *stärker:* horrific; *sich ~ auswirken* have a devastating effect (*auf + Akk.* on); *e-n ~en Eindruck hinterlassen* leave a terrible impression; **Verheerung** *f* devastation; *~en anrichten* cause (*od.* wreak) havoc

verhehlen *v/t.* hide, conceal (+ *Dat.* from); *ich will nicht ~, dass ...* I do not wish to deny (*od.* conceal) the fact that ...

verheilen *v/i.* heal up (completely)

verheimlichen *v/t.* hide, conceal (+ *Dat.* from); (*nicht erwähnen*) keep quiet about; *j-m etw. ~ auch* keep s.th. (secret) from s.o.; *er hat es (uns) verheimlicht auch umg.* he never let on (about it); **Verheimlichung** *f* concealment; *~ e-r Sache auch* keeping s.th. secret

verheiraten I. *v/t.* marry (*mit, an + Akk.* to); **II.** *v/refl.* marry, get married; *sich wieder ~* marry again, remarry; **verheiratet I.** *P.P.* → *verheiraten*; **II.** *Adj.* married (*mit* to) (*auch fig.*); *ich bin doch nicht mit dir ~* we're not married, you know; I'm not your wife (*od.* husband), you know; **Verheiratung** *f* marriage

verheißen *v/t.* (*unreg.*) *geh.* promise; *j-m etw. ~ auch* hold out the prospect of s.th. to s.o.; *s-e Miene etc. verhieß nichts Gutes* his expression did not augur (*od.* bode) well; *das Abendrot verheißt für morgen schönes Wetter* the red evening sky promises (*od.* bodes) good weather (for) tomorrow; **Verheißung** *f* promise; **verheißungsvoll** *Adj.* (*wenig*) ~ (un)promising, (in)auspicious

verheizen *v/t.* **1.** (*Brennmaterial*) burn, use up; (*heizen mit*) use as fuel; **2.** *umg. fig.* (*Soldaten*) send to the slaughter, use as cannon-fodder; (*Sportler etc.*) burn out; (*Arbeitskräfte*) run into the ground

verhelfen *v/i.* (*unreg.*): *j-m zu etw. ~* help s.o. to get s.th.; *j-m zu e-r Stelle ~ auch* give s.o. a leg up (*Am.* a boost) *umg.*; *j-m zu s-m Glück / zum Erfolg ~* help s.o. on the road to happiness/success; *j-m zum Sieg ~* help s.o. win, help s.o. (on the road) to victory

verherrlichen *v/t.* glorify (*auch Gewalt etc.*), exalt; **Verherrlichung** *f* glorification

verhetzen *v/t.* fill with hatred, poison *s.o.'s* mind; *ideologisch:* indoctrinate

verheult *umg.* **I.** *Adj. Gesicht:* tear-stained; *Augen:* red (from crying); *~ aussehen* look as if one has been crying; **II.** *Adv.:* *so ~ kannst du nicht rausgehen* you can't go out like that with your face all puffy (from crying)

verhexen *v/t.* bewitch, hex, jinx *umg.*; *j-n ~ in* (+ *Akk.*) turn s.o. into s.th.; **verhext I.** *P.P.* → *verhexen*; **II.** *Adj. umg.:* *wie ~* as if it were (*od.* was) jinxed

verhindern *v/t.* prevent; (*aufhalten*) hinder; (*es*) *~, dass j-d etw. tut* prevent (*od.* stop) s.o. from doing s.th.; *wir können es nicht ~* there's nothing we can do about it; **verhindert I.** *P.P.* → *verhindern*; **II.** *Adj.* **1.** *~ sein* be unable to come *etc.* (*wegen* due to); → *dienstlich* II; **2.** *umg.:* *~er Maler etc.* painter *etc.* manqué; (*Möchtegern...*) would-be painter *etc.*; **Verhinderung** *f* **1.** prevention; **2.** (*Verhindertsein*): *nur bei ~ des Arztes* only if the doctor is prevented from attending

verhohlen *Adj.* hidden, concealed; *mit kaum ~em Spott etc.* with barely concealed scorn *etc.*

verhöhnen *v/t.* deride, mock; (*bes. Politiker*) lampoon

verhohnepipeln *v/t. umg.* make fun of, *Brit. auch* take the mickey out of

Verhöhnung *f* derision, mockery; *e-e ~ der NS-Opfer etc.* a mockery of the victims of Nazism *etc.*

verhökern *v/t. umg. pej.* sell off

verholzen *v/i. Bot.* lignify

Verhör *n; -(e)s, -e* interrogation; *Jur.* hearing; *ins ~ nehmen vor Gericht:* cross-examine, interrogate; *umg. fig.* give *s.o.* a grilling; **verhören I.** *v/t.* interrogate, grill *umg.*; **II.** *v/refl.* mishear, hear wrong; *ich hab mich wohl verhört umg. iro.* I must have been hearing things

verhornt *Adj. Haut:* horny

verhüllen *v/t.* **1.** cover; **2.** *fig.* (*verschleiern*) cover up, disguise; (*Wahrheit etc.*) conceal; **verhüllend I.** *Part. Präs.* → *verhüllen*; **II.** *Adj. ~er Ausdruck* euphemism; **III.** *Adv.:* *~ ausgedrückt* put euphemistically; **verhüllt I.** *P.P.* → *verhüllen*; **II.** *Adj.* **1.** *Statue, Gesicht etc.:* veiled; (*versteckt*) hidden, concealed; *von Wolken ~* covered in cloud, hidden by cloud(s); **2.** *fig.* (*versteckt*) *Drohung etc.:* veiled, hidden; (*verschleiert*) *Ziele etc.:* veiled, disguised; **Verhüllung** *f* **1.** cover(ing); **2.** *fig.* concealment, disguising; disguise

verhundertfachen *v/t. und v/refl.:* (*sich*) *~* increase a hundredfold; *förm.* centuple

verhungern *v/i.* die of starvation, starve (to death); *ich bin am Verhungern umg.* I'm starving; *am ausgestreckten Arm ~ lassen umg.* put the squeeze on *s.o.*; *willst du mich ~ lassen? umg., hum.* are you just going to let me starve?

verhunzen *v/t. umg.* ruin, spoil; (*verpfuschen*) mess up, botch (up); *Sl.* bugger up; *er hat sein Leben gründlich verhunzt* he has made a total mess of his life

verhuscht *Adj. umg. Mädchen etc.:* diffident, timid; *~ aussehen* look mousy

verhüten I. *v/t.* prevent; *das möge Gott ~!* God forbid!; **II.** *v/i. beim Sex:* take precautions; **verhütend I.** *Part. Präs.* → *verhüten*; **II.** *Adj.* preventive; *~e*

Wirkung e-r Pille etc.: contraceptive effect; **Verhüterli** *n; -s, -s; umg.* rubber

verhütten *v/t.* (*Erz*) smelt; **Verhüttung** *f* smelting

Verhütung *f* prevention (*auch Med.*); (*Empfängnisverhütung*) contraception; **Verhütungs|methode** *f* method of contraception; *~mittel* *n* contraceptive

verhutzelt *Adj.* shrivel(l)ed(-up); *Person, Gesicht: auch* wizened

verifizierbar *Adj.* verifiable; **verifizieren** *v/t.* verify; **Verifizierung** *f* verification

verinnerlichen *v/t.* (*Werte etc.*) internalize; (*Person*) turn *s.o.* inward; *weitS.* (*vergeistigen*) spiritualize; **Verinnerlichung** *f* internalization; (*Vergeistigung*) spiritualization

verirren *v/refl.* get lost, lose one's way; *fig. Gedanken:* stray; *sich in das falsche Gebäude etc. ~ auch umg.* wander (off) into the wrong building *etc.*; **verirrt I.** *P.P.* → *verirren*; **II.** *Adj.* nur *attr.* lost; *Tier: auch* stray; *~e Kugel fig.* stray bullet; **Verirrung** *f fig.* aberration; *geschmackliche ~ auch* lapse of taste

veritabel *Adj. geh.* veritable

verjagen *v/t. auch fig.* chase away

verjähren *v/i.* come under the statute of limitations; *die Schulden sind inzwischen verjährt* meanwhile so much time has passed that the debts can no longer be collected; **verjährt I.** *P.P.* → *verjähren*; **II.** *Adj.* **1.** *Jur.* statute-barred; **2.** (*sehr alt*) old, antiquated; **Verjährung** *f* limitation, prescription; **Verjährungsfrist** *f* statutory period of limitation

verjubeln *v/t. umg.* (*Geld*) blow

verjüngen **I.** *v/t.* **1.** rejuvenate; *äußerlich, optisch:* make *s.o.* look younger; (*Betrieb etc.*) staff with young(er) people; **II.** *v/refl.* **1.** become rejuvenated; *Gesicht etc.:* become younger-looking; **2.** (*spitz zulaufen*) taper; *sich nach oben hin ~* taper towards the top; **Verjüngung** *f* **1.** rejuvenation; **2.** (*Zuspitzung*) tapering

Verjüngungs|kur *f* rejuvenation cure; *~mittel* *n* rejuvenator

verkabeln *v/t.* wire (up); *TV* cable up; *unsere Straße wird verkabelt* our street is going to be hooked up (*od.* connected) to cable TV; **verkabelt I.** *P.P.* → *verkabeln*; **II.** *Adj. TV: ~ sein/werden* have/get cable TV; **Verkabelung** *f* **1.** wiring; *TV* cabling; **2.** *weitS.* (*Kabelfernsehen*) cable TV

verkalken *v/i.* **1.** *Kessel etc.:* fur up; **2.** *Arterien:* harden, *fachspr.* calcify; **3.** *umg. Person:* go senile; **verkalkt I.** *P.P.* → *verkalken*; **II.** *Adj.* **1.** *Kessel etc.:* furred; **2.** *Arterien:* hardened, *fachspr.* sclerotic; **3.** *umg. Person:* senile, gaga; *völlig ~ sein auch* have gone (completely) gaga

verkalkulieren *v/refl.* miscalculate (*auch fig. etw. falsch einschätzen*), get one's sums (*Am.* figures) wrong *umg.*

Verkalkung *f* **1.** *e-s Kessels etc.:* furring up; **2.** *der Arterien:* hardening (of the arteries), (arterio)sclerosis; **3.** *umg. im Alter:* senility; *unter ~ leiden auch* be going senile; **Verkalkungserscheinung** *f umg.* sign of old age (*od.* senility)

verkannt I. *P.P.* → *verkennen*; **II.** *Adj.: ~es Genie mst iro.* undiscovered (*od.* unrecognized) genius; *sich ~ fühlen* feel as if one's talents are not appreciated

verkanten I. v/t. **1.** (*schräg stellen*) tilt; **2.** (*Gewehr*) cant; **3.** (*Skier*) edge; **II.** v/i. Skisport: edge over; **III.** v/refl. **1.** (*sich verklemmen*) get wedged (in); **2.** *Skier*: edge over

verkappt *Adj. nur attr.* (*verborgen*) hidden; *Med.* undiagnosed; **~er Nazi** *etc.* closet Nazi *etc.*

verkapseln v/refl. encapsulate; *Med.* encyst

verkarsten v/i. *Geog.* karstify

verkasematuckeln v/t. umg. **1.** (*konsumieren*) get through; **2.** (*erklären*) explain clearly

verkatert I. *Adj. umg.* hung-over; **II.** *Adv.*: **völlig ~ zur Arbeit gehen** *etc.* go to work *etc.* totally hungover

Verkauf m **1.** sale; (*das Verkaufen*) selling; **zum ~ anbieten/stehen** offer / be up for sale; **nach dem ~ des Grundstücks** *etc.* after selling (*od.* the sale of) the property *etc.*; **U. Koch: An- und Verkauf** U. Koch, second-hand dealer; **An- und Verkauf von ...** we buy and sell ...; **2.** *nur Sg.*; *Wirts.*, *Abteilung*: sales department

verkaufen I. vt/i. sell (*auch fig. Idee etc.*); *fig.* (*j-n verraten*) sell s.o. (down the river); **zu ~** for sale; **wir haben gut verkauft** we made a good deal; **sie will nicht ~** she doesn't want to sell out; **→ dumm** I 1; **II.** v/refl. **1.** *Waren etc.*: sell (**gut** well; **schlecht** badly); **2.** *umg. fig. Person*: sell o.s.; **sich** *od.* **s-n Körper ~** sell one's body, be a prostitute; **sich gut/schlecht ~** (*ankommen*) go down well/badly (**bei** with), be a great success (a flop) (with); **er kann sich hervorragend ~** he's an excellent showman

Verkäufer m; *-s,* **-** **1.** shop assistant, *Am.* salesclerk; **2.** *Wirts.* seller; **3.** *umg. fig.* showman; **Verkäuferin** f; *-, -nen* shop assistant, *höflicher*: saleslady, *Am.* salesperson

verkäuflich *Adj.* for sale; (*zum Verkauf geeignet*) sal(e)able; **leicht/schwer ~** easy/hard to sell

Verkaufs|absicht f: **sich mit ~en tragen** contemplate selling; **~abteilung** f *Wirts.* sales department; **~argument** n selling point; **~auftrag** m order to sell; **~ausstellung** f sales exhibition; **~automat** m vending machine; **~bedingungen** Pl. conditions (*od.* terms) of sale; **~berater** m, **~beraterin** f *Wirts.* sales consultant; *euph.* **→ Verkäufer** 1, **Verkäuferin**; **~büro** n *Wirts.* sales office; **~direktor** m, **~direktorin** f *Wirts.* sales manager; **~erlös** m proceeds Pl.; **~fahrer** m delivery man; **~fahrerin** f delivery woman; **~fläche** f selling area (*od.* space)

verkaufsfördernd I. *Adj.*: **sie sind ~** they promote sales, they are a good selling point; **II.** *Adv.*: **sich ~ auswirken** promote sales; **Verkaufsförderung** f sales promotion

Verkaufs|gespräch n *Wirts.* sales talk; **~hit** m umg. moneyspinner, absolute hit, *Am.* cash cow; **~kurs** m *Fin.*, *von Aktien*: check rate; **~leiter** m, **~leiterin** f sales manager

verkaufsoffen *Adj.*: **~er Sonntag** Sunday on which the shops (*Am. stores*) are open; **~e Sonntage abschaffen** get rid of Sunday shopping

Verkaufs|option f *Wirts.* selling option; *Börse*: put option; **~personal** n sales staff (*mst V. im Pl.*); **~preis** m selling price; **~provision** f sales commission; **~psychologie** f sales psychology; **~raum** m salesroom; **~rückgang** m

drop in sales; declining sales Pl.; **~schlager** m moneyspinner, absolute hit umg., *Am.* cash cow; **~stand** m stand; *draußen*: stall; **~ständer** m display stand; **~stelle** f retail shop (*Am.* store); **~strategie** f sales strategy; **~taktik** f sales pitch; **~tisch** m display table; **~wert** m market value; **~zahlen** Pl. sales figures; **~ziel** n sales target; **~ziffer** f sales figure

Verkehr m; *-s,* *fachspr.* *-e* **1.** *Verk.* (*Straßenverkehr*) traffic; **öffentlicher ~** public transport(ation *Am.*); **es herrscht starker Verkehr** there is heavy traffic, the traffic is heavy; **dem ~ übergeben** open to traffic; **für den ~ gesperrt** closed to (all) traffic; **aus dem ~ ziehen** (*Auto*) take off the road; *umg. fig.* (*j-n*) take out of circulation; **→ fließend** II 2; **2.** (*Verbindung*) contact, dealings Pl.; (*Geschäftsverkehr*) business; (*brieflicher ~*) correspondence; **den ~ mit j-m abbrechen** break off contact with s.o.; **aus dem ~ ziehen** (*auslaufen lassen*) phase out; (*Geld*) withdraw from circulation; **in ~ bringen** issue; (*Effekten*) *auch* offer for sale, market; **3.** (*Geschlechtsverkehr*) intercourse

...verkehr m, *im Subst.*: **Individual~** private transport(ation *Am.*); **Einkaufs~** shopping traffic; **Wasser~** water transport(ation *Am.*); **Nachrichten~** communication

verkehren I. v/i. **1.** (*hat od. ist verkehrt*); *Fahrzeug*: run; *Flug.* fly, operate; **~ zwischen** *Boot*: *auch* ply between; **in e-r Gegend ~** serve an area; **2.** (*hat*); *Person*: **~ bei j-m** visit s.o. regularly, be a regular visitor to (*od.* at) s.o.'s house *etc.*; **in e-r Bar etc. ~** frequent a bar *etc.*; **in Künstlerkreisen** *etc.* **~** move in artistic circles; **~ mit** associate with; *gesellschaftlich*: *auch* socialize with; *geschlechtlich*: have (sexual) intercourse with; **viel mit j-m ~** see a great deal of s.o.; **ich verkehre mit ihm nur noch über meinen Anwalt** I deal with him now only through my lawyer; **II.** v/t. (*hat*) (*Sinn etc.*) twist; **ins Gegenteil ~** reverse; **III.** v/refl. (*hat*) change, turn (**in** + *Akk.* into); **sich ins Gegenteil ~** turn into the opposite

verkehrlich I. *Adj. Problem etc.*: in terms of transport(ation *Am.*); **eine ~e Anbindung** a transport(ation *Am.*) link; **II.** *Adv.*: **die Straße ist ~ belastet** the street is suffering from heavy traffic; **~ verbunden sein** have transport(ation *Am.*) links

Verkehrs|ablauf m *Verk.* flow of traffic; **~achse** f road axis; **~ader** f arterial road; **~ampel** f traffic lights Pl., *Am.* traffic light, stoplight; **~amt** n tourist office; **~anbindung** f transport(ation *Am.*) links Pl.

verkehrsarm *Adj.* quiet

Verkehrs|aufkommen n *Verk.* traffic volume, volume of traffic; **~behinderung** f traffic obstruction; **~en** traffic holdups (*durch Nebel etc.* due to fog *etc.*); **~belastung** f traffic load, burden of traffic

verkehrsberuhigt *Adj. Verk.*: **~e Zone** reduced-traffic area, area with reduced traffic; **Verkehrsberuhigung** f traffic abatement (*od.* reduction); **Verkehrsberuhigungsmaßnahmen** Pl. traffic calming measures

Verkehrs|beschränkung f *Verk.* traffic limitation; **~betriebe** Pl. *e-r Stadt etc.*: public (*od.* municipal *etc.*) transport(a-

tion *Am.*) (services) Sg.; **die Londoner ~** London Transport (services); **~chaos** n chaos on the roads, traffic chaos; *an e-r bestimmten Stelle*: traffic snarl-up; **~delikt** n traffic offen|ce (*Am.* -se); **~dichte** f traffic density; **~drehscheibe** f traffic hub; **~durchsage** f traffic announcement; **~entlastung** f: **wir können keine baldige ~ versprechen** we can't promise that the traffic situation will soon be eased; **~entwicklung** f (*Entwicklung der Infrastruktur*) transport(ation *Am.*) development; (*Vergrößerung*) development in the volume of traffic; **~erschließung** f transport(ation *Am.*) development; **~erziehung** f road safety education; **~flughafen** m commercial airport; **~flugzeug** n airliner, commercial aircraft; **~fluss** m traffic flow

verkehrsfrei *Adj. Verk.*: **~e Zone** traffic-free area, area closed to traffic, pedestrian zone

Verkehrs|führung f *Verk.* traffic management; **~funk** m travel news Sg.; information for motorists; **~funksender** m traffic radio transmitter

Verkehrs|gefährdung f **1.** endangering other traffic; **2.** (*Gefahr*) traffic hazard, hazard on the road(s); *Fahrverhalten*: dangerous driving; **~gemeinschaft** f (*Verbund*) integrated transport(ation *Am.*) system; **~geographie** f *Geog.* transport geography; **~geschehen** n: **der Fahrer kann sich dem ~ widmen** the driver can devote himself to what the traffic is doing (*od.* to the traffic around him)

verkehrsgünstig I. *Adj. Lage etc.*: conveniently situated; **II.** *Adv.*: **~ gelegen** conveniently situated

Verkehrs|hindernis n traffic obstruction; **~infarkt** m gridlock (*auch der ~*), complete breakdown of traffic; **~insel** f traffic island, central refuge, *Am.* median (strip); **~knotenpunkt** m junction; **~kontrolle** f vehicle spot-check; **~kreisel** m roundabout, *Am.* traffic circle; **~lage** f situation on the roads; **~lärm** m traffic noise; **~lawine** f growing volume of traffic; **~leitsystem** n traffic guidance system; **~leitzentrale** f traffic guidance control cent|re (*Am.* -er); **~lenkung** f *durch Leitsysteme etc.*: traffic guidance; **~meldung** f traffic report (*od.* flash); Pl. traffic report Sg., travel news Sg.; **~minister** m, **~ministerin** f minister of transport(ation *Am.*), *in GB*: Transport Secretary, Secretary of State for Transport; *in den USA*: Secretary of Transportation, Transportation Secretary; **~ministerium** n ministry of transport; *in GB*: Department of Transport (*in den USA*: Transportation); **~mittel** n (means of) transportation; (*Fahrzeug*) vehicle; **öffentliches ~** public conveyance, Pl. public transport(ation *Am.*) Sg.; **~museum** n transport museum; **~netz** n traffic system, road and rail networks Pl.; **~opfer** n road casualty; **über 3000 ~** auch over 3000 road (*Am.* traffic) deaths (*od.* deaths on the road, deaths caused by traffic accidents); **~ordnung** f traffic regulations Pl.; **~planer** m, **~planerin** f traffic planner; **~planung** f traffic planning

Verkehrspolitik f transport(ation *Am.*) policy; **verkehrspolitisch I.** *Adj. nur attr. Frage etc.*: ... regarding transport(ation *Am.*) policy; **II.** *Adv.* relevant, *unsinnig etc.*: ... in terms of transpor-

V

t(ation *Am.*) policy

Verkehrs|polizei *f* traffic police; **~polizist** *m*, **~polizistin** *f* traffic policeman (*od.* cop *umg.*); **~raum** *m* space available to traffic; **im öffentlichen ~** on public roads; **~regel** *f* traffic regulation; **~regelung** *f* traffic control

verkehrsreich *Adj. Platz etc.*: busy; **~e Zeit** rush hour, peak period

Verkehrs|rowdy *m* road hog *umg.*; **~schild** *n* road sign

verkehrsschwach *Adj.*: **~e Zeit** quiet period; **ich warte immer bis zur ~en Zeit** I always wait until there's not much traffic around

verkehrssicher *Adj. Fahrzeug*: roadworthy; **Verkehrssicherheit** *f; nur Sg.* **1.** road safety; **2.** *e-s Fahrzeugs*: roadworthiness

Verkehrssprache *f* lingua franca

verkehrsstark *Adj.*: **~e Zeit** rush hour

Verkehrs|stau *m* traffic jam, (traffic) holdup, bottleneck; *auch Pl.* congestion *Sg.*; **~steuer** *f Wirts.* transfer tax; **~stockung** *f*, **~störung** *f* traffic holdup; *Pl. auch* traffic delays, delays in traffic; **~straße** *f* (public) thoroughfare, road open to traffic; **~streife** *f* traffic patrol; **~strom** *m* flow of traffic, traffic flow; **~sünder** *m*, **~sünderin** *f umg.* traffic offender (*Am. auch* scofflaw); **~sünderkartei** *f umg.* (central) index of traffic offenders

verkehrstauglich *Adj.* roadworthy; **Verkehrstauglichkeit** *f* roadworthiness

verkehrstechnisch *Adj.* ... in terms of traffic (*od.* transport [ation *Am.*]) engineering

Verkehrs|teilnehmer *m*, **~teilnehmerin** *f* road user; **~tote** *m*, *f* road casualty; → **Verkehrsopfer**; **~träger** *m* (*Transportmittel*) mode of transport(ation *Am.*); **der ~ Schiene** the rail|ways (*bes. Am.* -roads) *Pl.*

verkehrstüchtig *Adj.* **1.** *Auto*: roadworthy; **2.** *Person*: fit to drive; **Verkehrstüchtigkeit** *f* **1.** roadworthiness; **2.** *e-r Person*: fitness to drive

Verkehrs|überwachung *f* traffic surveillance; **~übungsplatz** *m artificial road complex designed for learner* (*Am. student*) *drivers to practice on*; **~unfall** *m* traffic accident; **~unterricht** *m* **1.** *Schule*: road-safety classes *Pl.*; **2.** *für Verkehrssünder*: safe-driving classes *Pl.* (for convicted traffic offenders), *Am.* traffic school; **~verbindung** *f* (road *od.* rail) link; **es gibt keine ~ zu dem Gebiet** there are no road or rail links to the area; **~verbund** *m* (integrated) public transport(ation *Am.*) system; **Karlsruher ~** Karlsruhe transport(ation *Am.*) system; **~verein** *m* tourist office; **~verhältnisse** *Pl.* (*Verkehrslage*) traffic situation *Sg.*; **bei den damaligen/dortigen ~n** with the traffic situation at the time / in that area; **~vorschrift** *f* traffic regulation; **~wacht** *f* road safety association; **~weg** *m* traffic route, road

Verkehrswert *m Wirts.* market value

Verkehrswesen *n; nur Sg.* transportation; *öffentliches*: public transport(ation *Am.*); *mit Nachrichtensystem*: transport(ation *Am.*) and communications *Pl.*

verkehrswidrig I. *Adj.* contrary to the traffic regulations; **II.** *Adv.* in violation of the traffic regulations; **sich ~ verhalten** break the traffic regulations; **Verkehrswidrigkeit** *f* traffic offence,

Am. driving offense

Verkehrs|zählung *f* traffic census; **~zeichen** *n* road sign; **~zentralregister** *n in Flensburg*: central register of traffic offences (*Am. driving offenses*)

verkehrt I. *P.P.* → **verkehren**; **II.** *Adj.* (*falsch*) wrong; **das ist gar nicht so ~** *umg.* that's not such a bad idea at all; **er ist nicht ~** *umg.* he's not a bad sort; **an den Verkehrten kommen** *umg.* pick the wrong person; **etwas Verkehrtes sagen** say something wrong; **das wäre das Verkehrteste, was man tun kann** that would be the worst thing you could do; **es ist e-e ~e Welt** it's a topsy-turvy world; **ich habe etwas Verkehrtes gegessen** *umg.* I've eaten something that doesn't agree with me; **III.** *Adv.* wrong, wrongly, the wrong way; **~ herum** the wrong way (a)round; *auf den Kopf gestellt*: *auch* upside down; (*Vorderteil nach hinten*) back to front, *Am.* backwards; (*Innenseite nach außen*) inside out; **etw. ~ machen** *umg.* do s.th. wrong; **etw. ~ anpacken** go about s.th. the wrong way; **~ fahren** take the wrong road (*od.* turning, *Am.* turn); **wir sind hier ~** we're in (*od.* we've come to) the wrong place; **~ liegen** *umg.* be wrong, be mistaken; **Verkehrtheit** *f* wrongness

Verkehrung *f* reversal; (*falsche Darstellung*) distortion, twisting; **~ ins Gegenteil** complete reversal

verkeilen I. *v/t.* **1.** wedge tight; **2.** *umg.* (*verprügeln*) beat *s.o.* up; **II.** *v/refl.* get stuck (*od.* jammed); **sich ineinander ~** *Eisenb. etc.* plough (*Am.* plow) into each other

verkennen *v/t.* (*unreg.*) misjudge; (*unterschätzen*) underestimate; (*nicht recht würdigen*) fail to appreciate; **nicht zu ~** unmistakable; **er wurde von allen verkannt** everyone misjudged him; **→ verkannt**; **Verkennung** *f* misjudg(e)ment; underestimation; **in** (*völliger*) **~ der Tatsachen** *etc.* in (complete) misapprehension of the facts *etc.*

verketten I. *v/t.* chain up; (*zusammenfügen*) link (*auch fig.*); *Ling., EDV* concatenate; **II.** *v/refl. Moleküle etc.*: form a chain (*od.* chains), *fig. Umstände*: interlock; **Verkettung** *f Ling., EDV* concatenation; **e-e ~ unglücklicher Umstände** a chain of unfortunate events

verketzern *v/t.* brand, condemn; **Verketzerung** *f* branding, condemnation

verkitschen *v/t.* **1.** kitschify; **2.** *umg.* (*verkaufen*) sell (off), turn into cash; **verkitscht I.** *P.P.* → **verkitschen**; **II.** *Adj.* kitschy

verkitten *v/t.* cement (*auch fig.*), seal; (*Fenster*) putty

verklagen *v/t. Jur.* sue (*auf + Akk.*, *wegen* for), take *s.o.* to court (for)

verklammern I. *v/t.* clip together; *Archit., Tech. etc.* brace together; *fig.* lock together, interlock; **II.** *v/refl.*: **sich** (**ineinander**) **~** lock together, interlock

verklappen *v/t.* dump (into the sea, *bes. Am.* ocean); **Verklappung** *f* (ocean) dumping, dumping (of) waste into the sea (*Am.* ocean)

verklären *fig.* **I.** *v/t.* transfigure; **II.** *v/refl.* be(come) transfigured; *Vergangenheit*: become idealized; **verklärt I.** *P.P.* → **verklären**; **II.** *Adj.* transfigured; *Ausdruck*: beatific; **Verklärung** *f* transfiguration

verklausulieren *v/t.* hedge in (*od.*

straitjacket) with clauses; *fig.* express in a roundabout way; **verklausuliert I.** *Adj.*: **dieser Vertrag ist zu ~** this contract has too many qualifying clauses; **II.** *Adv.*: **sich ~ ausdrücken** *etc.* express oneself *etc.* in a roundabout way

verkleben I. *v/t.* (*hat verklebt*) cover, stick *s.th.* over *s.th.*; *Med.* (*Wunde*) cover; **II.** *v/i.* (*ist*); (*klebrig werden*) get sticky; (*verklumpen*) clot; (*zusammenkleben*) stick together; **III.** *v/refl.* (*hat*); (*sich schließen*) close (up); (*klebrig werden*) get sticky; (*verklumpen*) clot; (*zusammenkleben*) stick together; **verklebt I.** *P.P.* → **verkleben**; **II.** *Adj. Augen, Finger etc.*: sticky; *Haare*: matted

verkleckern *v/t. umg.* **1.** (*verschütten*) spill; *fig.* (*Zeit, Geld etc.*) fritter away; (*vergeuden*) waste; **2.** (*bekleckern*) spatter

verkleiden I. *v/t.* **1.** dress *s.o.* up (**als** as); (*tarnen*) disguise; *fig.* (*umschreiben*) disguise; **2.** *Tech. etc.* (*abdecken*) cover; *innen*: line; *außen*: (en)case; (*vertäfeln*) panel; *Archit.* face; **II.** *v/refl.* dress up (**als** as); (*sich tarnen*) put on a disguise; **jeder muss sich ~** everyone has to wear fancy dress (*Am.* wear a costume); **verkleidet I.** *P.P.* → **verkleiden**; **II.** *Adj.*: **~ sein** be dressed up (**als** as); **alle waren ~** everyone was in fancy dress (*Am.* in costume); **Verkleidung** *f* **1.** fancy dress, *Am.* costume; disguise; **2.** covering; lining; facing; panel(l)ing; → **verkleiden** I 2

verkleinern I. *v/t.* reduce (in size), make *s.th.* smaller; (*Zeichnung*) scale down (*auch Betrieb etc.*); *fig.* (*schmälern*) belittle; **II.** *v/refl.* get (*od.* grow) smaller; **wir müssen uns ~ Firma etc.**: we need to reduce in size; *platzmäßig*: we have to move to smaller premises; **verkleinert I.** *P.P.* → **verkleinern**; **II.** *Adj. und Adv.* reduced (in size); **in ~em Maßstab** on a smaller scale; **die Objekte erscheinen im Rückspiegel stark ~** objects appear much smaller in the rear-view mirror, objects in rear-view mirror are closer than they appear; **Verkleinerung** *f* **1.** reduction (in size); *e-r Zeichnung, auch e-s Betriebs etc.*: scaling down; **2.** *fig.* belittling, belittlement

Verkleinerungs|form *f Ling.* diminutive; **~maßstab** *m* scale (of reduction)

verklemmen *v/refl.* get stuck; **verklemmt I.** *P.P.* → **verklemmen**; **II.** *Adj.* **1.** *Tür etc.*: *präd.* stuck, jammed; **2.** *Psych.* inhibited; **sexuell ~ sein** be sexually inhibited; **Verklemmtheit** *f* inhibitedness; **Verklemmung** *f* inhibition

verklickern *v/t. umg.*: **j-m etw. ~** put *s.o.* straight on s.th., put s.o. in the picture about s.th.; **j-m ~, wie** let s.o. know how

verklingen *v/i.* (*unreg.*) die away (*auch fig.*); *Stimmung, Freude etc.*: fade away

verkloppen *v/t. umg.* **1.** (*verprügeln*) duff *s.o.* up; **2.** (*verkaufen*) flog

verklumpen *v/i.* become lumpy

verknacken *v/t. umg.* (*verurteilen*) sentence (**zu** to); **j-n zu e-r Geldstrafe ~** slap a fine on s.o.; **j-n zu drei Jahren ~** put s.o. inside (*od.* in the clink) for three years; **verknackt werden wegen** be done for

verknacksen *v/t. umg.*: **sich** (*Dat.*) **den Fuß ~** sprain one's ankle

verknallen *v/refl. umg.*: **sich in j-n ~** fall for s.o.; **er hat sich** *od.* **er ist in sie**

verknallt *auch* he's head over heels in love with her

verknappen I. *v/refl.* run short, become scarce; **II.** *v/t.* cut down the supply of; **Verknappung** *f* shortage, scarcity

verknautschen *v/t. umg.* crumple (up)

verkneifen *v/t.* (*unreg.*) *umg.* **1. er konnte sich** (*Dat.*) *das Lachen nicht* ~ he couldn't help laughing, he couldn't keep a straight face; *ich konnte mir die Bemerkung nicht/kaum* ~ I couldn't resist saying it (*od.* I just had to come out with it) / I could hardly stop myself from saying it; **2. sich** (*Dat.*) *etw.* ~ (*auf etw. verzichten*) do without s.th.; **verkniffen I.** *P.P.* → **verkneifen**; **II.** *Adj. Mund, Gesicht*: pinched; *er hat so etwas Verkniffenes* there's something really crabby about him

verknittern *v/t. und v/i.* → **zerknittern**

verknöchern *v/i.* ossify (*auch fig.*); *er verknöchert immer mehr* he's becoming more and more of an old fossil; **verknöchert I.** *P.P.* → **verknöchern**; **II.** *Adj.* ossified; *~er Kerl* old fossil; **Verknöcherung** *f* ossification

verknoten I. *v/t.* (*Taschentuch*) tie a knot in; (*Schal*) tie; *etw.* ~ *mit* tie s.th. up with; **II.** *v/refl. Seile etc.*: become knotted

verknüpfen I. *v/t.* tie together; *fig.* link; (*kombinieren*) combine; *fig.* **1.** *fig.*: *mit dem Wort etc. verknüpft sich e-e Vorstellung von etc.* this word *etc.* is associated with (*od.* carries with it) an idea of *etc.*; **2.** *Jägerspr.* mate; **verknüpft I.** *P.P.* → **verknüpfen**; **II.** *Adj. fig.*: ~ *mit Kosten etc.*: tied up with; *eng* ~ *sein mit* be bound up with; *Person*: have close ties with; **Verknüpfung** *f fig.* **1.** linking (*mit* up with); *EDV* link; *e-e* ~ *erstellen EDV* establish (*od.* create) a link; **2.** (*bestehende Verbindung*) tie(s *Pl.*), link(s *Pl.*); connection

verknusen *v/t. umg.*: *ich kann ihn/es nicht* ~ I can't take (*od.* stomach) him/it

verkochen I. *v/i.* (*ist verkocht*) boil away; *Kartoffeln etc.*: overboil; *zu Brei* ~ *pej.* boil down into a mush; **II.** *v/t.* (*hat*): *Früchte etc. zu Marmelade etc.* ~ boil fruit *etc.* to make jam *etc.*

verkohlen I. *v/t.* (*hat verkohlt*) **1.** char; *Chem.* carbonize; **2.** *umg.* (*zum Besten haben*) have (*Am.* put) *s.o.* on; **II.** *v/i.* (*ist*) become charred

verkoken *v/t.* coke; **Verkokung** *f* carbonization

verkommen (*unreg.*) **I.** *v/i.* **1.** *Haus, Betrieb etc.*: go to rack and ruin, go to the dogs *umg.*; *Garten*: run wild; *das Land ist zu e-m Hort der Korruption* ~ the country has degenerated into a hotbed of corruption; **2.** *Person*: go to seed; *moralisch*: sink (very) low; **3.** *Lebensmittel*: go bad; *weitS.* (*nicht verbraucht werden*) go to waste; **II.** *P.P.* → **verkommen** I; **III.** *Adj. Person*: seedy; *moralisch*: depraved; *Gebäude*: dilapidated; *Gegend, Betrieb etc.*: run-down; *Garten*: overgrown, wild; *so ein ~es Subjekt!* what a seedy character!; *der Garten ist völlig* ~ *auch* the garden is a wilderness; **Verkommenheit** *f; nur Sg.* seediness; depravity; dilapidated state; run-down condition; wildness; → **verkommen** III

verkomplizieren *v/t.* complicate, make *s.th.* more complicated than it is

verkonsumieren *v/t. umg.* put away

verkorken *v/t.* cork (up)

verkorksen *v/t. umg.* (*verderben*) make a hash of, bungle; *j-m den Abend / die Stimmung* ~ wreck s.o.'s evening / ruin the atmosphere for s.o.; *sich* (*Dat.*) *den Magen* ~ upset one's stomach; **verkorkst** *umg.* **I.** *P.P.* → **verkorksen**; **II.** *Adj. Magen*: upset; *Mensch*: screwed up; *~e Angelegenheit* mess; *das Kind ist völlig* ~ the child is completely screwed up

verkörpern I. *v/t.* **1.** (*Idee etc.*) embody; (*typischen Vertreter etc.*) typify; **2.** *Theat.* play, portray; **II.** *v/refl.*: *sich* ~ *in* (+ *Dat.*) be embodied in; **verkörpert I.** *P.P.* → **verkörpern**; **II.** *Adj.*: *die ~e Tugend etc.* virtue *etc.* personified (*od.* in person), the embodiment (*od.* personification) of virtue *etc.*; **Verkörperung** *f* embodiment; typification; *Theat.* playing, portrayal; *Brandos* ~ *des „Paten"* Brando's portrayal of the "Godfather"; *Richard III. ist e-e ~ des Bösen* Richard III is a personification of evil

verkosten *v/t.* **1.** *bes. österr.* (*probieren*) try, taste; **2.** (*bes. Wein etc.*) taste; **Verkoster** *m; -s, -,* **Verkosterin** *f* taster

verköstigen *v/t.* feed; *zwanzig Personen müssen untergebracht und verköstigt werden* twenty people need to be fed and accommodated; **Verköstigung** *f* **1.** (*Essen*) food; **2.** (*das Verköstigen*) feeding

Verkostung *f bes. von Wein etc.*: tasting

verkrachen *v/refl. umg.* fall out (with each other); **verkracht** *umg.* **I.** *P.P.* → **verkrachen**; **II.** *Adj. umg.* **1.** (*zerstritten*) *Familien, Nachbarn etc.*: unreconciled, *bes. Am.* feuding, *präd.* at loggerheads; (*mit j-m*) ~ *sein* be at daggers drawn; *seid ihr immer noch ~?* have you still not made it up with one other?, *Am.* are you still feuding?; **2.** (*gescheitert*) failed; *~e Existenz* (human) wreck

verkraften *v/t.* (*ertragen*) take; (*bewältigen*) cope with, handle; (*Trauma etc.*) *auch* come to terms with; *ich verkrafte es nicht mehr* I can't cope (with it) *od.* take it any longer; *ein Bier verkrafte ich noch umg.* I could manage another beer

verkrallen *v/refl.*: *sich in etw.* ~ *Tier*: dig its claws into s.th.; *Mensch*: dig one's fingers (*od.* nails) into s.th.; *weitS.* (*sich klammern an*) clutch at s.th.

verkrampfen *v/refl.* (*hat verkrampft*) *und v/i.* (*ist*): (*sich*) ~ *Muskeln*: cramp, get cramp(s *Pl. Am.*); *Hände*: clench (tightly); *Person*: tense up; *stärker*: seize up; *er verkrampfte* (*sich*) *immer mehr* he became more and more tense; **verkrampft I.** *P.P.* → **verkrampfen**; **II.** *Adj. Muskeln*: cramped; *Person*: tensed up, tense; *fig. innerlich*: *auch* uptight; *fig. Lachen*: forced, artificial; **III.** *Adv. lächeln etc.*: forcedly; **Verkrampfung** *f* (*Krampf*) cramp(s *Pl. Am.*); (*Verspanntheit*) tenseness; (*Spannung*) tension; (*Kontraktion*) contraction, *stärker*: spasm; *fig. innere*: inner tension, uptightness; *allmählich löste sich s-e* ~ he gradually became less tense

verkratzen *v/t.* scratch, scrape; **verkratzt I.** *P.P.* → **verkratzen**; **II.** *Adj.* scratched; *völlig* ~ scratched all over

verkrebst *Adj. Med., Gewebe etc.*: cancerous; *völlig* ~ *sein* be completely cancerous

verkriechen *v/refl.* (*unreg.*) creep (*od.* crawl, *verängstigt*: slink) away; *fig. heimlich*: sneak away; (*sich verstecken*) go into hiding; *Sonne*: hide; *die Katze hat sich unter dem Bett verkrochen* the cat crept under the bed; *sich ins Bett* ~ *fig.* crawl into bed; *sie hätte sich vor Scham am liebsten verkrochen* she wished the ground would open and swallow her up

verkrümeln *v/refl. umg.* (*davonschleichen*) make o.s. scarce, sneak off

verkrümmen I. *v/t.* bend, curve, twist; **II.** *v/refl.* bend, curve, become distorted (*od.* twisted); *Holz*: warp; **verkrümmt I.** *P.P.* → **verkrümmen**; **II.** *Adj.* bent, curved (*auch Wirbelsäule*), twisted; **Verkrümmung** *f* distortion; (*Verwerfung*) warp; (*Verdrehung*) twist; (*Biegung*) bend; ~ *der Wirbelsäule* curvature of the spine

verkrumpeln *v/t./i. Dial.* → **zerknittern**

verkrüppeln I. *v/t.* cripple; **II.** *v/i.* become crippled; *Baum*: become stunted; **verkrüppelt I.** *P.P.* → **verkrüppeln**; **II.** *Adj. Arm etc.*: crippled; *Baum etc.*: stunted; **Verkrüppelung** *f* **1.** (*Missbildung*) deformation, deformity; **2.** (*das Verkrüppeln*) crippling; stunting; → **verkrüppeln**

verkrusten *v/i.* (*ist verkrustet*) *und v/refl.* (*hat*) crust, become encrusted; *Schürfwunde*: scab; **verkrustet I.** *P.P.* → **verkrusten**; **II.** *Adj.*: *die ~e Wunde* the wound that has formed a scab, the scabbed-over wound; *von Schmutz verkrustet* caked with dirt (*od.* mud); *~e Strukturen etc. fig.* inflexible structures; **Verkrustung** *f konkret*: encrustation; *fig.* inflexibility

verkühlen *v/refl.* catch (a) cold; **Verkühlung** *f Dial.* cold

verkümmern *v/i.* *im Wachstum*: become stunted; *Muskeln etc.*: atrophy; *Pflanze, auch Talent*: wither, wilt; *Mensch*: languish; *Gefühl, Bewusstsein etc.*: fade; *seelisch* ~ become emotionally stunted; **verkümmert I.** *P.P.* → **verkümmern**; **II.** *Adj. Wachstum*: stunted; *Muskeln*: atrophied; *Pflanzen*: wilted; *Gefühl*: faded; *seelisch* ~ emotionally stunted; *~es Rechtsgefühl* undeveloped moral sense; **Verkümmerung** *f von Wachstum*: stunting; *von Muskeln*: atrophying; *von Pflanzen*: wilting; *von Menschen*: languishing; *von Gefühlen*: fading; *seelische*: stunting

verkünden *v/t.* announce; *feierlich*: proclaim; (*Gesetz etc.*) promulgate; (*Urteil*) pronounce; (*weissagen*) prophesy; (*Evangelium*) preach, spread; *ein neues Zeitalter etc.* ~ *fig.* herald a new epoch *etc.*; *s-e Miene verkündete nichts Gutes* the look on his face didn't augur (*bes. Am.* bode) well; **Verkünder** *m; -s, -,* **Verkünderin** *f; -, -nen des Evangeliums*: preacher; *fig. e-r Botschaft etc.*: herald, harbinger; **verkündigen** *v/t. bes.* → **verkünden**; **Verkündiger** *m; -s, -,* **Verkündigerin** *f; -, -nen* → **Verkünder**; **Verkündigung** *f* → **Verkündung**; **Verkündung** *f* announcement; *feierlich*: proclamation; *e-s Gesetzes*: promulgation; *e-s Urteils*: pronouncement; *des Evangeliums*: preaching, spreading; (*Weissagung*) prophecy; *fig.* heralding

verkünsteln *v/refl. umg. oft pej.* (*etw. übermäßig sorgfältig tun*) overdo it; *hum.* (*etw. besonders gut machen*) surpass o.s.; **verkünstelt I.** *P.P.* → **verkünsteln**; **II.** *Adj. bes. pej.* oversophisticated, over-elaborate

verkupfern *v/t.* copper-plate; **Verkupferung** *f* copper-plating

verkuppeln *v/t.*: **j-n an j-n ~** marry s.o. off to s.o.; **in der Clique wollen sie Laura und Martin ~** *umg.* the circle of friends are wanting to get Laura and Martin paired off together

verkürzen I. *v/t.* shorten; *(beschränken)* curtail, cut; *(reduzieren)* reduce; *sich (Dat.)* **die Zeit ~** while away the (*od.* one's) time; **~ auf** (+ *Akk.*) *Sport* shorten to; **II.** *v/refl.* become shorter, shorten; **verkürzt I.** *P.P.* → *verkürzen*; **II.** *Adj.* shortened, reduced; *Form*: short; *Ausgabe*: abridged, shortened; **~e Lebenserwartung** shortened lifespan; **~e Arbeitszeit** short time; **~ erscheinen** *optisch*: appear foreshortened; **Verkürzung** *f* shortening; curtailment; reduction; → *verkürzen*

verlachen *v/t.* laugh at, scoff at

Verladebahnhof *m* loading station; **Verladekran** *m* loading crane; **verladen** *v/t.* **1.** load (*auf* + *Akk.* onto; *in* + *Akk.* into); **2.** *umg. (verschaukeln)* sell s.o. (down the river); *(sitzen lassen)* leave s.o. in the lurch; **Verlader** *m*; *-s*, *-*; *Wirts.* carrier, shipping agent(s *Pl.*), *Am.* auch freight forwarder; *Arbeiter*: loader; **Verladerampe** *f* loading platform; **Verladung** *f* loading

Verlag *m*; *-(e)s*, *-e* publishing house (*od.* company), publisher(s *Pl.*); **erschienen im Langenscheidt-~** published by Langenscheidt; **in** *od.* **bei e-m ~ arbeiten** work for a publisher's *etc.*, work (*od.* be) in publishing

verlagern I. *v/t.* **1.** (*Gewicht, auch fig. Interesse, Schwerpunkt etc.*) shift; **2.** *(verlegen)* transfer, move (*nach* to); **II.** *v/refl. auch fig.* shift, move; **Verlagerung** *f* shift(ing); transfer, removal; → *verlagern*

Verlags|anstalt *f* publishing house (*od.* company); **~buchhandlung** *f* publishing house; **~gruppe** *f* publishing group; **die Langenscheidt-~** the Langenscheidt publishing group; **~haus** *n* → *Verlag*; **~katalog** *m* (publisher's) catalog(ue), (publications) list; **~kauffrau** *f*, **~kaufmann** *m* publishing manager; **~leiter** *m*, **~leiterin** *f* publishing director; **~leitung** *f* publishing management team; **~programm** *n* publisher's list

verlanden *v/i. Geog.* silt up; **Verlandung** *f* silting up

verlangen I. *v/t.* **1.** *(fordern)* demand; *(Anspruch erheben auf)* claim; *(wünschen)* desire, want; *mein Chef verlangt Pünktlichkeit* my boss requires everyone to be punctual (*od.* punctuality from everyone); *viel ~ an Leistungen*: be very demanding; *Person*: *auch* be hard to please; *das ist zu viel verlangt* that's asking (a bit) too much; *stärker*: that's a tall order; *das ist doch nicht zu viel verlangt, oder?* that's not asking too much, is it?, that's not an unreasonable demand, is it?; *mehr kann man nicht ~* you can't ask for more; *die Rechnung ~* ask for the bill (*Am. im Restaurant*: check); *Rechenschaft ~* demand an explanation; *~, vorgelassen zu werden* demand to be admitted; *das tun, was die Situation verlangt* do what the situation demands; **2.** *(sprechen wollen)* ask for; *den Geschäftsführer ~ im Restaurant etc.*: ask (*od.* demand) to see the manager; *j-n am Telefon ~* ask to speak to s.o. on the phone; *Sie werden am Telefon verlangt* you're wanted on the phone; **3.** *(berechnen)* want, ask; *im Geschäft*: charge; *(erfordern)* require, call for; *wie viel ~ Sie?* how much are you asking?, how much do you want?; *für einen Dienst*: how much do you charge?; **II.** *v/i.*: **~ nach** ask for; *nach j-m*: *auch* ask to see; *(sich sehnen nach)* long for; *unpers.*: *es verlangt mich nach etw. od. j-m* I'm longing for

Verlangen *n*; *-s*, *kein Pl.* desire; *heftiges*: craving; *(Sehnsucht)* longing (*alle nach* for); *(Forderung)* demand; *auf ~* by request; *Wirts.* on demand; *auf ~ von* at the request of; *kein ~ haben, etw. zu tun* feel no desire (*od.* urge) to do s.th.; *voll ~ ansehen etc.* look at *etc.* longingly (*od.* with great longing)

verlangend I. *Part. Präs.* → *verlangen*; **II.** *Adj. Blick etc.*: longing; **III.** *Adv.* ansehen *etc.*: longingly; **~ die Hand ausstrecken nach** stretch one's hand out longingly for

verlängern I. *v/t.* **1.** *räumlich*: lengthen; *(Straße etc.) auch* extend; *Math.* produce; *den Ball ~ Sport* help the ball on; **2.** *zeitlich*: prolong; *(auch Kredit, Patent, Frist etc.)* extend (*alle um* by); *(Wechsel, Vertrag)* renew; *s-n Pass etc.* **~ lassen** get (*od.* have) one's passport *etc.* renewed; **3.** *(Soße etc., verdünnen)* stretch; **II.** *v/refl. zeitlich*: be extended; *räumlich*: be lengthened; *(Straße etc.) auch* be extended; **verlängert I.** *P.P.* → *verlängern*; **II.** *Adj.* extended; **~es Wochenende** long weekend; *mit Feiertag*: *auch* bank holiday weekend, *Am.* three-day weekend; **Verlängerung** *f räumlich*: lengthening; *zeitlich*: prolongation; *e-r Frist etc.*: extension; *e-s Vertrags*: renewal; *Math.* production; *Sport, e-s Spiels*: extra time

Verlängerungs|frist *f Zeitspanne*: extension period; *Zeitpunkt*: extension deadline; **~kabel** *n*, **~schnur** *f Etech.* extension lead (*bes. Am.* cord); **~stück** *n* extension; **~woche** *f Urlaub*: extra week; **~zeit** *f (Zeitspanne)* extension period; *(Zeitpunkt)* extension deadline; *Sport* (period of) extra time

verlangsamen I. *v/t.* slow down; *(verzögern)* slow down, retard; *die Geschwindigkeit ~ auch* reduce speed; **II.** *v/refl.* slow down; *Auto etc.*: *auch* lose speed; **Verlangsamung** *f* slowing down; reduction in speed; *(Verzögerung)* slowing down, retardation

Verlass *m*: *auf ihn ist ~* you can rely on him; *heutzutage ist auf nichts und niemand mehr ~ umg.* you can't rely on anyone or anything nowadays

verlassen[1] *(unreg.)* **I.** *v/t.* leave; *(im Stich lassen) auch* desert; *Mut, Selbstvertrauen etc.*: desert, fail s.o.; *das Bett ~ nach Krankheit*: get out of bed, get up again; *s-e Kräfte verließen ihn* his strength failed him; *plötzlich*: *auch* his energy drained from him; *er hat uns für immer ~ euph.* he has passed away; *und da verließen sie ihn umg.* and that's as far as I *etc.* got; **II.** *v/refl.*: *sich ~ auf* (+ *Akk.*) rely (*od.* depend, count) on; *Sie können sich darauf ~* you can count on it, *Sie können sich darauf ~, dass auch* you can rest assured that; *auf ihn od. sein Wort kann man sich ~* he's as good as his word; *verlass dich drauf! umg.* take my word for it

verlassen[2] **I.** *P.P.* → *verlassen*[1]; **II.** *Adj.* **1.** *Person*: abandoned, *lit.* forsaken (*von* by); **~ aufgefunden werden** *Auto etc.*: be found abandoned; *sich einsam und ~ vorkommen* feel all alone; *von Gott und aller Welt ~* abandoned by everybody; → *Geist* 3; **2.** *Gegend etc.*: deserted (*auch Haus etc.*), desolate; *(trostlos)* bleak

Verlassen *n*; *-s*, *kein Pl.*: *vor/nach ~ des Gebäudes etc.* before/after leaving the building *etc.*; *böswilliges ~ Jur.* wil(l)ful abandonment

Verlassenheit *f*; *nur Sg.* **1.** *(Vereinsamung)* loneliness; *(Trostlosigkeit)* forlornness; **2.** *(Öde)* bleakness; *e-s Ortes*: desertedness, desolation

Verlassenschaft *f schw., österr. (Hinterlassenschaft)* estate

verlässlich *Adj.* reliable, dependable; **Verlässlichkeit** *f*; *nur Sg.* reliability, dependability

Verlaub *m*: *mit ~ (gesagt)* with all due respect, if you'll forgive me for saying this; *mit ~ altm.* by your leave

Verlauf *m*; *-(e)s*, *Verläufe* **1.** *der Zeit, e-s Vorgangs etc.*: course; *e-r Sache*: *auch* the way s.th. goes (*od.* develops); *das kommt auf den ~ ... an* (+ *Gen.*) that depends on how (*od.* on the way) ... goes (*od.* develops), that depends on which course ... takes; *den weiteren ~ abwarten* wait and see how things go (*od.* develop); *im ~* (+ *Gen. od. von*) in the course of; *nach ~ von* after (a lapse of); *e-n schlimmen ~ nehmen* take a bad course; **2.** *räumlich, e-r Grenze etc.*: course; *immer dem ~ der Straße nach* keep following the course of the street

verlaufen *(unreg.)* **I.** *v/i.* *(ist verlaufen)* **1.** *Vorgang*: take a ... course, proceed, go; *normal ~* take a normal course; *zufrieden stellend ~ Prüfung etc.*: go satisfactorily; *völlig untypisch ~ Krankheit etc.*: take a completely unusual course; *tödlich ~* be fatal; *die Demonstration verlief ohne Zwischenfälle* the demonstration passed off without incident; **2.** *Grenze, Weg etc.*: run, pass (*entlang* + *Dat.* along); *Spur*: disappear; **3.** *Farben, Wimperntusche etc.*: run; *Butter etc.*: *auch* melt; *servieren, wenn der Käse ganz ~ ist* serve once the cheese has melted completely; **II.** *v/refl. (hat)* **1.** *(sich verirren)* lose one's way, get lost; **2.** *Menge*: scatter; **3.** *Spur etc.*: disappear; **4.** *Hochwasser etc.*: subside, drop; → *Sand*

Verlaufsform *f Ling.* continuous (*od.* progressive) form; *die ~ der Gegenwart etc.* the present continuous (form) *etc.*

verlaust *Adj.* full of lice, louse-ridden

verlautbaren I. *v/t. (hat verlautbart)* make known, announce; **II.** *v/i. (ist)* → *verlauten*; **Verlautbarung** *f (Bekanntmachung)* announcement; *(Bericht)* report; *(in der Presse)* (press) release

verlauten I. *v/i. (ist verlautet)* be reported, be disclosed, be released; *~ lassen* give to understand, (be heard to) say; *(andeuten)* hint; *nichts davon ~ lassen* not say a word about it; *wie verlautet* as reported; *von offizieller Seite verlautete, dass ...* according to official sources ...; **II.** *v/t. (hat)* announce

verleben *v/t.* **1.** *(Zeit)* spend; *schöne Tage ~* have a good time; **2.** *umg. (verbrauchen)* use up; *(Geld) auch* spend

verlebt I. *P.P.* → *verleben*; **II.** *Adj. attr.* dissipated, burnt-out ..., *präd.* burnt out

V

verlegen¹ I. *v/t.* **1.** *räumlich*: move, transfer *(auch Truppen, Schauplatz) (beide **nach** to); Phys. (Schwerpunkt)* shift; *s-n **Wohnsitz** ~* move (house); **2.** *zeitlich*: put off *(auf + Akk.* to, until, till), postpone (to); *die **Handlung e-s Films ins 3. Jahrtausend** ~* shift the action of a film to the third millennium; **3.** *(Kabel, Rohre etc.)* lay; *(Fliesen etc.) auch* put down; *(Teppichboden)* lay, put down; **4.** *(Buch herausbringen)* publish; **5.** *(unauffindbar ablegen)* mislay; **II.** *v/refl.*: *sich ~ auf (+ Akk.) auf e-e Tätigkeit*: take to doing *s.th.*; *aufs Bitten, Leugnen etc.*: resort to (doing) *s.th.*

verlegen² I. *Adj.* embarrassed; *~ **machen*** embarrass; *(nie) ~ um e-e Antwort, Ausrede*: (never) at a loss for; *er **ist nie um e-e Antwort** ~ auch* he's always got an answer ready; *um **Geld** ~* short of money; **II.** *Adv.* abashedly; *(voll Verlegenheit)* in embarrassment; *~ **lächeln*** give an embarrassed smile; *~ **dastehen*** stand there embarrassed

Verlegenheit *f* **1.** *nur Sg.* embarrassment; *vor ~ **schweigen** etc.*: out of embarrassment; *in ~ **bringen*** embarrass; *durch unerwartete Frage etc.*: put *s.o.* on the spot; *in ~ **kommen** od. **geraten*** get embarrassed; **2.** *(Klemme)* difficult spot; *(missliche Lage)* predicament; *in ~ **sein*** be in a bit of a spot, be in a difficult spot; *finanziell*: be a bit short (hard up *umg.*); *j-m aus der ~ **helfen*** help s.o. out (of a spot); *in ~ **kommen*** run into difficulties; *in die ~ **kommen**, etw. tun zu müssen* find o.s. compelled to do s.th.

Verlegenheits|geschenk *n* last resort present; *~**geste** f fig.* compromise gesture, gesture of embarrassment; *~**lösung** f* makeshift *(od.* compromise) solution; *~**pause** f: e-e ~ **machen*** be at a loss for words *(od.* as to what to say, as to how to react)

Verleger *m; -s, -, ~in f; -, -nen* publisher; **verlegerisch** *Adj.* publishing

Verlegung *f* moving, transfer(ral), shifting *(nach* to); postponement (to); → **verlegen¹** I 1, 2

verleiden *v/t.*: *j-m etw. ~* spoil s.th. for s.o.; *(abschrecken)* put s.o. off s.th.; *es war ihm verleidet* he had had enough of it

Verleih *m; -s, -e* **1.** *(Firma etc.)* hire *(od.* rental) company; *(Laden)* rental shop, *Am.* rental service store; *Filmverleih*: distributors *Pl.*; *ein ~ für Strandkörbe* a company which hires out *(Am.* that rents) beach chairs; **2.** *nur Sg.*; *(das Verleihen)* hiring *(od.* renting) out; *Film*: distribution; *~ von Videos nur an Erwachsene* video rental for adults only; **verleihen** *v/t. (unreg.)* **1.** lend (out), *bes. Am. auch* loan (out); *gegen Miete*: hire *(Am.* rent) out; *Nachschlagewerke werden nicht verliehen* reference books are not lent out *(Am.* do not circulate); **2.** *(Titel etc.)* confer *(+ Dat.* on *s.o.)*; *(Privileg, Recht etc.)* grant (to); *(Auszeichnung, Preis)* award (to); **3.** *fig.*: *j-m / e-r Sache etw. ~ (Eigenschaft, Reiz etc.)* give *od.* lend s.o./s.th. s.th.; → **Ausdruck¹** 2, **Kraft** 1, **Nachdruck¹**; **Verleiher** *m; -s, -* lender; *Brit.* hirer; *Film*: distributor; **Verleihung** *f* lending, hiring, *Am.* rental; conferment; awarding; → **verleihen**

verleimen *v/t.* glue (together)

verleiten *v/t.* lead astray; *zum Verbrechen etc. ~* tempt into crime *etc.*; *j-n ~,*

etw. zu tun seduce s.o. into doing s.th.; *j-n zu etw. ~ (überreden) auch* talk *(od.* cajole) s.o. into doing s.th.; *sich ~ **lassen*** (allow o.s. to) be tempted *etc. (zu + Inf.* into + *Ger.)*, succumb (to the temptation); *dies **verleitete mich zu der Annahme** this led me to believe

verlernen *v/t.* forget; *das Lachen etc. ~* forget how to laugh *etc.*

verlesen *(unreg.)* **I.** *v/t.* **1.** *(Namen etc.)* read out; **2.** *(Gemüse etc.)* pick over; **II.** *v/refl.* misread (it), read it wrong(ly); *sich bei etw. ~* misread s.th.; *ich dachte schon, ich hätte mich ~* I thought I had read it wrong(ly)

Verlesung *f des Urteils etc.*: reading out

verletzbar *Adj. auch fig.* vulnerable; *(leicht gekränkt)* (over)sensitive, touchy; **Verletzbarkeit** *f, nur Sg.*; *auch fig.* vulnerability; *(Empfindlichkeit)* oversensitiveness

verletzen *v/t.* **1.** hurt, injure; *(verwunden) bes. auch Mil.* wound; *sich (Dat.) am Arm etc. ~* hurt *(od.* injure) one's arm *etc.*; *Personen wurden (dabei) nicht verletzt* there were no casualties; **2.** *fig. (j-n)* hurt; *(Gefühle) auch* wound; *(kränken) auch* offend; **3.** *(Gesetz, Eid, Recht, Grenze, Luftraum etc.)* violate; *(Anstand, Vorschrift etc.)* offend against; *s-e Pflicht ~* neglect one's duty; **verletzend I.** *Part. Präs.* → **verletzen**; **II.** *Adj.* hurtful; *(beleidigend)* offensive; *Bemerkung*: cutting

verletzlich *Adj.* → **verletzbar**; **Verletzlichkeit** *f* → **Verletzbarkeit**

verletzt I. *P.P.* → **verletzen**; **II.** *Adj.*: *~ sein im Kampf, von Kugel, Messer*: be wounded; *durch Unfall etc.*: be injured *(auch Sport)*; *fig. (gekränkt)* be wounded *(od.* hurt); *leicht/schwer ~* slightly/seriously wounded *(od.* injured)

Verletzte *m, f; -n, -n* injured person, casualty; *die ~n* the injured; *drei Tote und 25 ~ nach Unfall etc.*: three dead and 25 injured; *nach Kampf*: three dead and 25 wounded; **Verletzung** *f* **1.** *(Wunde)* injury; *(seelische)* hurt; *sie kam mit leichten ~en davon* she wasn't seriously hurt; **2.** *fig.* infringement, *e-s Rechts*: *auch* violation, contravention; *der Pflicht, e-s Vertrags etc.*: breach; *~ der Privatsphäre* invasion *(od.* intrusion) of privacy; *~ des Luftraums* violation of airspace

verletzungsanfällig *Adj.* injury-prone

Verletzungs|gefahr *f* risk of injury; *~**pause** f Sport, während des Spiels*: break for injury; *Versäumnis einiger Spiele*: lay-off due to injury, bout of injury

verleugnen *v/t. (Grundsätze etc.)* deny; *(Freund, Kind etc.)* disown; *er lässt sich am Telefon immer (vor ihr) ~* he always pretends that he's not at home (when she phones); *es lässt sich nicht ~, dass* there's no denying that; *sich (selbst) ~* deny o.s.; **Verleugnung** *f* denial, *förm.* disavowal; *e-r Person*: disowning, disavowing

verleumden *v/t.* slander; *förm.* calumniate; *schriftlich*: libel; **Verleumder** *m; -s, -*, **Verleumderin** *f; -, -nen* slanderer; *schriftlich*: libel(l)er; **verleumderisch** *Adj.* slanderous; *förm.* calumnious; *schriftlich*: libel(l)ous; **Verleumdung** *f* slander; *förm.* calumny; *bes. Jur.* defamation; *schriftliche*: libel; **Verleumdungskampagne** *f* smear campaign; **Verleumdungsklage** *f* ac-

tion for slander *(od.* libel)

verlieben *v/refl.* fall in love *(in +Akk.* with) *(auch weitS.)*; *zum Verlieben aussehen* look adorable; **verliebt I.** *P.P.* → **verlieben**; **II.** *Adj.* in love *(in +Akk.* with); *Blicke etc.*: amorous; *hoffnungslos ~ auch* smitten *umg.*; *unglücklich ~ sein* be unhappy in love; *ich bin ganz ~ in diese Brosche etc. umg.* I'm absolutely crazy about this brooch *etc.*; → **Ohr**, **III.** *Adv.* anschauen *etc.*: adoringly; **Verliebte** *m, f; -n, -n* lover; **Verliebtheit** *f; nur Sg.* (state of) being in love *(in + Akk.* with); *übertriebene*: infatuation (with); *weitS.* love (for)

verlieren *(unreg.)* **I.** *v/t.* **1.** *allg.* lose *(an + Akk.* to); *(Blätter, Haar) auch* shed; *ich habe meinen Autoschlüssel verloren* I've lost my car key; *in dem Gedränge ist m-e Handtasche verloren gegangen* I lost my handbag *(bes. Am.* purse) in the crush; **2.** *Sport (Kampf, Spiel etc.)* lose; *das Spiel ging 1:3 verloren* we *etc.* lost the game 1:3; **3.** *in Wendungen*: *kein Wort darüber ~* not say a word about it; *viel/wenig/nichts zu ~ haben* have much/little/nothing to lose; *du hast hier nichts verloren umg.* you've got no business being here; *das Spielzeug hat in der Küche nichts verloren umg.* the toys don't belong in the kitchen; *hast du den Verstand verloren? umg.* are you out of your mind?; *an dir ist e-e Schauspielerin verloren gegangen* you could have been an actress; → **Auge** 2, **Geduld**, **Gesicht¹** 4, 5, **Mut** 1, **Nerv** *etc.*; → *auch* **verloren**; **II.** *v/refl.* einander: lose each other; *fig. (kaum bemerkbar sein)* Ton *etc.*: be lost; Pfad, Spur *etc.*: lose itself, disappear; *(vergehen, verschwinden)* disappear; Menge: disperse; Wirkung, Intensität, Emotion *etc.*: wear off; *das verliert sich wieder* Geruch *etc.*: it's fading away again; *sich in Gedanken/Träumen etc. ~* be lost in thought/reverie *etc.*; *sich in Details/Nebensächlichkeiten ~* stray off into details/side issues; **III.** *v/i.* lose *(gegen* to); *es hat sehr verloren fig.* it isn't what it used to be; *an Wirkung/Reiz etc. ~* lose some of its effect / its *od.* one's charm *etc.*; *an Höhe ~* lose height; *an Wert ~* lose some of its *(od.* go down in) value; *der Roman etc. verliert sehr in der Übersetzung* loses a lot in (the) translation

Verlierer *m; -s, -, ~in f; -, -nen* loser; *guter/schlechter ~* good/bad loser

Verlierer|seite *f*: *auf der ~ sein* be on the losing side; *~**straße** f umg.*: *auf der ~ sein* be on the way to a defeat

Verlies *n; -es, -e*; *hist.* dungeon

verlischt *Präs.* → **verlöschen**

verloben *v/refl.* get engaged; *sie hat sich mit Jens verlobt* she got engaged to Jens; **Verlöbnis** *n; -ses, -e* engagement; *ein ~ lösen* break off an engagement; **verlobt I.** *P.P.* → **verloben**; **II.** *Adj.* engaged *(mit* to); **Verlobte** *m, f; -n, -n* fiancé, *weiblich*: fiancée; *die ~n* the engaged couple; **Verlobung** *f* engagement; *~ feiern* hold an engagement party; *e-e ~ auflösen* break off an engagement

Verlobungs|anzeige *f* engagement announcement; *~**feier** f* engagement party; *~**ring** m* engagement ring; *~**zeit** f* engagement

verlocken *vt/i.* entice, tempt; *(verführen) auch* seduce *(zu + Inf.* into +

Ger.); **zum Kauf ~** tempt people into buying; **es verlockt zum Kauf** it's tempting (*od.* it tempts one) to buy; **der See verlockt zum Baden** the lake tempts one to bathe; **verlockend I.** *Part. Präs.* → **verlocken; II.** *Adj.* tempting, enticing, alluring; **Verlockung** *f* (*Reiz*) lure, enticement; (*Versuchung*) temptation
verlogen *Adj. attr.* lying ...; *förm.* mendacious; (*verfälscht*) false; *Moral etc.*: hypocritical; **~ sein** be a liar; **~er Kerl** *umg.* (damned) liar; **sie ist durch und durch ~** she's an out-and-out liar; **Verlogenheit** *f* lying; falseness; hypocrisy; → **verlogen**
verlor *Imperf.* → **verlieren**
verloren I. *P.P.* → **verlieren; II.** *Adj.* lost (*auch fig.*); (*einsam, hilflos*) forlorn; **~e Eier** poached eggs; **~es Spiel** losing game; **auf ~em Posten stehen** be fighting a losing battle; **der ~e Sohn** *bibl.* the Prodigal Son; **j-n/etw. geben** give s.o./s.th. up for lost; **sich ~ geben** give up; **sich ~ vorkommen** feel lost; **es ist noch nicht alles ~** there's hope yet; *bes. iro.* all is not lost; **alle ärztliche Kunst war an ihr ~** all the doctors' skills were not enough to help her; **das ist bei ihm ~** *Humor etc.*: it's lost on him; **für die Nationalmannschaft** *etc.* **~ sein** be lost to the national team *etc.*; **in den Anblick e-r Sache ~** lost in contemplation of s.th.; **in Gedanken ~** lost in thought
verloren gehen → **verlieren** I 1-3
Verlorenheit *f*; *nur Sg.*: (*Verlassenheit*) forlornness
verlosch *Imperf.* → **verlöschen**
verlöschen *v/i.*; *verlischt, verlosch od. verlöschte, ist verloschen od. verlöscht* 1. *Brennendes*: go out; 2. *fig.* (*vergehen*) die; (*schwinden*) fade (away); **sein Ruhm wird nie ~** his fame will never die
verlosen *v/t.* draw lots (*Am. auch* straws) for; *in e-r Tombola*: raffle (off); **jede Woche wird ein Auto verlost** a car is raffled (off) every week; **Verlosung** *f* drawing of lots (*Am. auch* straws); (*Lotterie*) raffle
verlöten *v/t.* solder up (*od.* together); **e-n ~** *umg. fig.* (*Alkoholisches trinken*) have a tipple
verlottern *pej.* **I.** *v/i.* (*ist verlottert*) go to rack and ruin; *Person, äußerlich*: go to seed; **II.** *v/t.* (*hat*) squander; **verlottert** *pej.* **I.** *P.P.* → **verlottern; II.** *Adj.* → **verwahrlost**
Verlust *m*; *-(e)s, -e* 1. *nur Sg.* loss (**an** + *Dat.* of); (*Todesfall*) *auch* bereavement; **mit ~** *verkaufen etc.*: at a loss; **mit ~ arbeiten** *Betrieb*: run (*od.* operate) at a loss; **den ~ s-r Geldbörse** *etc.* **melden** report the loss of one's purse *etc.*; **~ bringender Betrieb / bringendes Geschäft** *etc.* loss-making business/deal *etc.*; **~ bringend arbeiten** work *etc.* at a loss; 2. *mst Pl.*: (*hohe*) **~e** (heavy) losses; *Mil. auch* casualties; **~e schreiben** register losses; → **Rücksicht** 1
...verlust *m, im Subst.*: *Energie~* energy loss, loss of energy; *Spannungs~ Etech.* voltage drop; *Vertrauens~* loss of confidence
Verlust|anzeige *f* notice of (a) loss; **~ausgleich** *m* loss compensation; **~betrieb** *m* lossmaker, loss-making concern, losing business; **~bringer** *m*; *-s, -; Wirts., umg.* lossmaker; **~geschäft** *n* 1. losing deal, loss; 2. → **Verlustbetrieb**

verlustieren *v/refl. umg. hum.* amuse o.s.
verlustig *Adv. Amtsspr.*: **e-r Sache gehen** forfeit s.th., lose s.th.; **j-n der Rechte für ~ erklären** declare s.o.'s rights forfeit
Verlust|liste *f Mil.* list of casualties; **~meldung** *f* report of loss; *Mil.* casualty report; **~punkt** *m* 1. *Fin., Börse*: **300 ~e stehen zu Buche bei 13.000** a loss of 300 points on a value of 13,000; 2. *Sport*: **das Team ohne ~** the team that has not lost (*od.* dropped) any points, the team with a maximum number of points; **mit nur einem ~** having lost (*od.* dropped) only one point; **~rechnung** *f Wirts.* loss account (*od.* statement)
verlust|reich *Adj.* 1. *Wirts.*: *attr.* heavily loss-making, deeply unprofitable; **es war ein ~es Jahr** it was a year of heavy losses; 2. *Mil., Schlacht etc.*: ... involving heavy losses (*od.* casualties); **~trächtig** *Adj. Wirts.* loss-making
Verlust|vortrag *m Wirts., Jur.* loss carried forward; **~zone** *f Wirts.* debt; **die ~ verlassen** return to credit; **~zuweisung** *f Wirts.*: **steuerliche ~** tax-loss allocation
vermachen *v/t.*: **j-m etw. ~** leave s.o. s.th., bequeath s.th. to s.o. *Jur.*; *umg. fig.* (*schenken*) give s.th. to s.o.; **Vermächtnis** *n*; *-ses, -se*; (*Testament*) will; (*das Vermachte*) bequest; *fig.* legacy
vermahlen *v/t.* grind (into flour)
vermählen *förm.* **I.** *v/refl.* get married (**mit** to); *fig.* unite; **II.** *v/t.* wed, marry (**mit** to); **Vermählte** *m, f*; *-n, -n*; *förm.*: **die jung(en) ~n** the newly-married couple; **Vermählung** *f förm.* wedding, marriage
vermaledeit *Adj. umg. altm. nur attr.* confounded
vermalen *v/t.* 1. (*Farbe*) use up; 2. (*Wände etc.*) cover with paint
vermännlichen I. *v/t.* (*hat vermännlicht*) masculinize; *Kleidung*: *auch* make s.o. look very masculine, give s.o. a very masculine look; **II.** *v/i.* (*ist*) become masculine (*od.* masculinized)
vermanschen *v/t. umg.* 1. (*vermengen*) mix up; **das Essen auf dem Teller ~** mash together the food on one's plate; 2. *fig.* mess up
vermarktbar *Adj. Wirts.* marketable; **vermarkten** *v/t.* (put on the) market; *fig.* capitalize on, exploit (commercially); **viele Bauern ~ ihre Produkte selbst** many farmers market their goods themselves (*Am.* market their own produce); **Vermarkter** *m*; *-s, -*, **Vermarkterin** *f*; *-, -nen* (*Vermarktungsgesellschaft*) marketing company; (*Person*) marketer; **ich bin ~** I work in marketing; **Vermarktung** *f* marketing; *fig.* (commercial) exploitation
Vermarktungsgesellschaft *f Wirts.* marketing company
vermasseln *v/t. umg.* make a hash of, mess up, screw up *Sl.*; (*Klassenarbeit etc.*) make a mess of; → **Tour** 3
vermassen I. *v/i.* (*ist vermasst*) lose its (*od.* one's) identity *od.* individuality; *Person*: *auch* become a (mere) cipher; *Gesellschaft*: be level(l)ed; **II.** *v/t.* (*hat*) depersonalize; *Individuen* **~** *auch* take away people's identity; **vermasst I.** *P.P.* → **vermassen; II.** *Adj.* depersonalized; *Gesellschaft*: anonymous, faceless
vermauern *v/t.* 1. wall up (*od.* in); 2. (*Material*) use to make a wall
vermehren I. *v/t.* 1. increase (**um** by);

an Zahl: *auch* multiply; 2. (*fortpflanzen*) breed; **II.** *v/refl.* 1. increase; *Zahl*: *auch* multiply, rise; **sich ständig ~** rise steadily; 2. (*sich fortpflanzen*) reproduce, multiply, breed; **sich geschlechtlich/ungeschlechtlich ~** *Bio.* reproduce sexually/asexually; **sie ~ sich wie die Kaninchen** *umg.* they breed like rabbits; **Vermehrung** *f* 1. increase; 2. (*Fortpflanzung*) reproduction, breeding
vermeidbar *Adj.* avoidable; **vermeiden** *v/t.* (*unreg.*) avoid; (*umgehen*) evade; (*e-r Sache aus dem Weg gehen*) steer clear of; *ängstlich*: shun; **es lässt sich nicht ~** it can't be helped; **Vermeidung** *f* avoidance
vermeinen *v/i. förm.* think; **er vermeinte, i-e Stimme zu hören** he thought he heard her voice; **vermeintlich I.** *Adj.* supposed; (*angeblich*) alleged; (*eingebildet*) imaginary; **II.** *Adv.*: **e-e ~ günstige Gelegenheit** a supposedly favo(u)rable opportunity
vermelden *v/t. altm. od. hum.* (*verkünden*) announce; (*berichten von*) report; *umg. fig.* **nichts zu ~ haben** → **melden** I 3
vermengen I. *v/t.* 1. mix; **alle Zutaten zu e-m Teig ~** mix all the ingredients to form a dough; 2. (*verwechseln*) mix up; **II.** *v/refl.* mix; **Vermengung** *f* mixing
vermenschlichen *v/t.* (*Lebensverhältnisse etc.*) humanize; (*personifizieren*) personify; (*Tiere*) anthropomorphize; **Vermenschlichung** *f* humanization; (*Personifizierung*) personification
Vermerk *m*; *-(e)s, -e* note; (*Anmerkung*) *auch* comment; **e-n ~ im Pass** *etc.* **anbringen** enter a note in a passport *etc.*; **vermerken** *v/t.* 1. make a note of; (*sagen*) note, mention; **etw. am Rande ~** *schriftlich*: make a note of s.th. in the margin; *verbal*: mention s.th. in passing; **das sei nur am Rande vermerkt** if I could just add that; **es sei am Rande vermerkt, dass ...** it might be worth just mentioning that ..., could I just add that ...; 2. **übel ~** take s.th. amiss (*od.* in bad part, *Am.* the wrong way), take offen|ce (*Am.* -se) at; **j-m etw. übel ~** be annoyed (*stärker*: angry) at s.o. for s.th.
vermessen[1] (*unreg.*) **I.** *v/t.* measure; (*Land*) survey; **II.** *v/refl.*: **sich (um zwei Zentimeter etc.) ~** get the measurements wrong (by two centimet|res [*Am.* -ers *etc.*])
vermessen[2] **I.** *P.P.* → **vermessen**[1]; **II.** *Adj.* (*anmaßend*) presumptuous; (*kühn*) bold; **ich bin so ~, e-e Umsatzsteigerung zu prognostizieren** I am bold enough to predict an increase in turnover; **Vermessenheit** *f* presumption
Vermesser *m*; *-s, -*, **~in** *f*; *-, -nen* surveyor; **Vermessung** *f* measuring; (*Landvermessung*) surveying
Vermessungs|amt *n* surveyor's office; **~ingenieur** *m* surveyor; **~kunde** *f* surveying; **~schiff** *n* survey ship
vermieft *Adj. umg.* stuffy
vermiesen *v/t. umg.*: **j-m etw. ~** spoil s.th. for s.o.
vermieten *vt/i.* rent (out); (*Sachen*) *Brit. auch* hire out; **Haus zu ~** house to let (*Am.* for rent)
Vermieter *m*; *-s, -*, **~in** *f*; *-, -nen* 1. owner of the flat (*Am.* apartment *od.* condo) (*od.* house *etc.*), homeowner; 2. (*Hauswirt*) landlord; *weiblich*: landlady; **Vermietung** *f* renting (out); ren-

tal; *Brit. auch* hiring (out); **Einnahmen aus ~ und Verpachtung** income from letting (*Am. auch* renting) and leasing
vermindern I. *v/t.* decrease, reduce; (*verringern*) diminish, lessen; (*beeinträchtigen*) detract from; **II.** *v/refl.* decrease; (*verringern*) diminish, lessen; **vermindert I.** *P.P.* → **vermindern**; **II.** *Adj. Mus.* diminished; → **Zurechnungsfähigkeit**; **Verminderung** *f* decrease (+ *Gen.* in), reduction (of, in); lessening (of)
verminen *v/t.* lay mines in (*od.* along), mine; **vermint I.** *P.P.* → **verminen**; **II.** *Adj.* full of mines; *Gelände*: mined; **ein nicht ~es Gebiet** a mine-free area; **Verminung** *f e-s Geländes etc.*: mining
vermischen I. *v/t.* **1.** mix; (*Farben, Tee etc.*) blend; **2.** (*Rassen*) interbreed; (*Tiere*) *auch* cross; **3.** (*Begriffe etc.*) mix (up); **II.** *v/refl.* **1.** mix; *Farben etc.*: *auch* blend; **2.** *Rassen*: interbreed; **vermischt I.** *P.P.* → **vermischen**; **II.** *Adj.* mixed; **Vermischtes** miscellaneous items (*od.* writings *etc.*); *als Aufschrift*: miscellaneous, misc.); **Vermischung** *f* mixing; blending; interbreeding; → **vermischen**
vermissen *v/t.* miss; **das Mädchen wird seit dem 27. Juli vermisst** the girl has been missing since July 27th; **ich vermisse m-n Bleistift** I can't find my pencil, I'm missing my pencil; **etw. ~ lassen** (*nicht besitzen*) lack s.th.; **vermisst I.** *P.P.* → **vermissen**; **II.** *Adj.* missing (*Mil.* in action); **j-n als ~ melden** report s.o. missing; **als ~ gemeldet werden** *od.* **sein** be listed as missing; **als ~ gelten** be listed as missing; **Vermisste** *m, f; -n, -n* missing person (*Mil.* serviceman); *Mil. Am. auch* MIA (= missing in action); *Mil. Pl. auch* missing personnel *Sg.* (*V. im Pl.*); **Vermisstenanzeige** *f* missing person's report; **e-e ~ aufgeben** report s.o. missing
vermittelbar *Adj.* **1.** *Wissen etc.*: communicable; **2.** *Arbeitskräfte etc.*: placeable; **schwer ~** *präd. und nachgestellt*: difficult to place; **Vermittelbarkeit** *f von Arbeitskräften etc.*: placeability; **die besonders schwere ~ dieser Arbeiter** the particular difficulty of placing these workers
vermitteln I. *v/t.* **1.** (*beschaffen*) get, find; *förm.* procure (*j-m* for s.o.); (*arrangieren*) arrange; **Arbeitskräfte an Firmen ~** place workers with firms (*Am.* companies); **wir ~ Zimmer für Studierende** *etc.* we find rooms for students *etc.*; **Langzeitarbeitslose sind besonders schwer zu ~** the long-term unemployed are particularly difficult to place; **2.** (*Wissen*) impart (*j-m* to s.o.); **3.** *Telef.*: **ein Gespräch ~** put a call through; **4.** (*Eindruck etc.*) give, convey; **II.** *v/i.* mediate (**zwischen** + *Dat.* between); act as (a) mediator (**bei** in); (**~d eingreifen**) intervene, mediate; **vermittelnd I.** *Part. Präs.* → **vermitteln**; **II.** *Adj.* conciliatory, mediatory; **III.** *Adv.*: **~ eingreifen** *od.* **tätig sein** intervene, mediate; **vermittels(t)** *Präp. Amtsspr.* by means of
Vermittler *m; -s,-,* **~in** *f; -, -nen* **1.** (*Schlichter*) mediator, arbitrator; **2.** (*Mittelsmann*) intermediary, go-between; **3.** *Wirts. etc.* agent; *von Aufträgen etc.*: negotiator; (*Makler*) broker; **das Arbeitsamt als ~ von Arbeitskräften/Stellen** the job cent|re *od.* (*Am.* -er) as an agency for workers/jobs
Vermittler|gebühr *f* → **Vermittlungs-**

gebühr, **~rolle** *f* negotiating role; **e-e ~ spielen** act as negotiator (*od.* mediator)
Vermittlung *f* **1.** *bei Streit*: mediation, arbitration (*beide*: **zwischen** + *Dat.* between); (*Eingreifen*) intervention; **2.** (*Beschaffung*) procurement, obtaining; (*Arrangieren*) arrangement; **3.** *Wirts., e-s Geschäfts*: negotiation; *von Stellen*: finding; *von Arbeitskräften*: placement; (*Amt, Stelle*) agency, office; **4.** *Telef.* a) *e-s Gesprächs*: connection, b) (*Telefonzentrale*) (telephone) exchange; *in e-r Firma etc.*: switchboard; *weitS. Person*: operator; **über die ~** via (*od.* through) the switchboard *etc.*; **~, bitte!** give me the operator, please; **5.** *von Wissen*: imparting; *e-s Eindrucks*: giving, conveying; **durch ~** (+ *Gen.*) *od.* **von** through; **durch s-e ~** *auch* through his help (*od.* intervention)
Vermittlungs|ausschuss *m* mediation committee; **~bemühungen** *Pl.* efforts at mediation; **~dienst** *m* mediation service; **~gebühr** *f* commission; *e-s Maklers*: *auch* brokerage; **~provision** *f* → **Vermittlungsgebühr**; **~stelle** *f* agency; **~verfahren** *n Pol.* joint committee procedure; **~versuch** *m* mediation attempt (+ *Gen.* by), mediation effort (on the part of), attempt at mediation (on the part of); **~vorschlag** *m* compromise proposal
vermöbeln *v/t. umg.* clobber
vermodern *v/i.* mo(u)lder, decay
vermöge *Präp.* (+ *Gen.*) *geh.* by virtue of
vermögen *v/t.* (*unreg.*) *geh.*: **~, etw. zu tun** be able to do s.th., be capable of doing s.th., be in a position to do s.th.; **bei j-m wenig ~** be able to do little with s.o.
Vermögen *n; -s, -* **1.** (*Reichtum*) fortune; **ein ~ verdienen/kosten** earn/cost a fortune; **ein ~ an Gemälden** *etc.* besitzen own a fortune in paintings *etc.*; **er hat ~** he is a man of means; **2.** (*Besitz*) property; (*Geld*) means *Pl.*; *Wirts.* assets *Pl.*; **3.** (*Können*) ability; (*Kraft, Macht*) power(s *Pl.*); **nach bestem ~** to the best of one's ability; **es geht über** (*od.* **übersteigt**) **mein ~** it's beyond my power (**zu** + *Inf.* to +*Inf.*), it goes beyond my power(s); **vermögend I.** *Part. Präs.* → **vermögen**; **II.** *Adj.* wealthy, well-to-do, (very) well-off
Vermögens|anlage *f* capital investment; **~ansammlung** *f* accumulation of wealth; **~berater** *m*, **~beraterin** *f* financial adviser; **~beratung** *f* financial consulting; **~besteuerung** *f* capital (*od.* personal wealth) taxation; **~bildung** *f* wealth formation; **~lage** *f* financial situation; **~masse** *f* estate, assets *Pl.*; (*Ggs. Zinsen*) principal
Vermögens|recht *n* property law; **vermögensrechtlich** *Adj. und Adv.* under the law of property
Vermögenssteuer, Vermögensteuer *f* property tax
Vermögens|verhältnisse *Pl.* financial circumstances; **~verwalter** *m*, **~verwalterin** *f* property administrator; **~verwaltung** *f* property administration; **~werte** *Pl.* (property) assets
vermögenswirksam *Adj.* capital-creating (*through fiscal grants and tax concessions*), *weitS.* (*Gewinn bringend*) profitable; **~e Leistung** employer's contribution(s) *to tax-deductible* (*employee*) *savings scheme* (*Am. plan*);

~es Sparen *saving as part of employee savings scheme* (*Am. plan*) *to which the employer and state also make contributions*
Vermögenszuwachs *m* increase in wealth
vermummen I. *v/t.* (*einhüllen*) wrap up; (*verkleiden*) disguise; **II.** *v/refl.* wrap o.s. up (*in* + *Akk.* in); (*sich verkleiden*) disguise o.s.; *bei e-r Demonstration*: wear a mask; **vermummt I.** *P.P.* → **vermummen**; **II.** *Adj.* (*verkleidet*) disguised, *präd. und nachgestellt*: in disguise; *Demonstranten*: masked, *präd. und nachgestellt*: wearing masks; **Vermummung** *f* disguise; *bei Demonstrationen*: wearing of masks; **Vermummungsverbot** *n* ban on wearing masks (at demonstrations)
vermurksen *v/t. umg.* make a hash (*bes. Am.* mess) of, botch (up)
vermuten *v/t/i.* (*annehmen*) assume; (*erwarten*) expect; (*argwöhnen*) suspect; **ich vermute** (*nehme an*) *auch* I imagine; *stark*: I rather (*Am.* I would) think; **ich vermute ja** I imagine (*od.* expect) so, I would think so; **das habe ich schon vermutet** I had an idea that would happen (*od.* be the case *etc.*); **es ist** *od.* **steht zu ~, dass ...** we may assume that ...; **... lässt ~, dass ... ...** leads us *etc.* to assume that ...; **wie es dazu kam, lässt sich nur ~** one can only imagine how it happened; **es wird Brandstiftung vermutet** arson is suspected; **die Polizei vermutet ihn im Ausland** the police suspect him to be abroad; **dort hatte ihn niemand vermutet** no one had expected him to be there; **nichts Böses ~d, ging ich ...** unsuspectingly, I went...; **vermutlich I.** *Adj. nur attr.* presumed; (*wahrscheinlich*) probable, likely; **II.** *Adv.* presumably; (*wahrscheinlich*) probably; **Vermutung** *f* presumption (*auch Jur.*); (*Annahme*) supposition, guess *umg.*; (*Verdacht*) suspicion; (*Erwartung*) expectation; (*Theorie, Mutmaßung*) *auch Pl.* speculation; **~en anstellen** speculate (*über* + *Akk.* on); **alles nur ~en** all just speculation
vernachlässigbar *Adj.* negligible; **vernachlässigen** *v/t.* neglect; (*unberücksichtigt lassen*) ignore; **etw. ~ können** be able to ignore s.th.; **Vernachlässigung** *f* neglect
vernageln *v/t.* nail (up); (*Deckel*) nail down; **mit Brettern ~** board up; **vernagelt I.** *P.P.* → **vernageln**; **II.** *Adj.* **1.** **mit Brettern ~** boarded up; **hier ist die Welt mit Brettern ~** *umg. fig.* this place is the back of beyond (*Am.* is way out in the sticks); **2.** *umg. fig. Mensch*: blockheaded
vernähen *v/t.* sew (*od. auch Wunde* stitch) up; (*Saum etc.*) sew, stitch; **e-e Wunde mit fünf Stichen ~** put five stitches in a wound
vernarben *v/i.* scar over; *fig.* heal; **vernarbt I.** *P.P.* → **vernarben**; **II.** *Adj.* scarred; **~es Gesicht** *durch Pocken*: *auch* pockmarked (*od.* pitted) face; **Vernarbung** *f* scarring; *konkret*: scar(s *Pl.*)
vernarren *v/refl. umg.*: **sich ~ in** (+ *Akk.*) become besotted with; **vernarrt I.** *P.P.* → **vernarren**; **II.** *Adj.*: **~ in** (+ *Akk.*) besotted (*od.* infatuated) with, wild (*od.* crazy) about *umg.*; **in ein Kind ~ sein** dote on a child; **Vernarrtheit** *f* infatuation
vernaschen *v/t.* **1.** (*Geld*) spend on sweets (*Am.* candy); **2.** *umg.* (*j-n*) lay

V

Sl., have it off (*Am.* get it on) with *Sl.*; **von j-m vernascht werden** be laid by s.o.; **s-n Gegner ~** (*mühelos besiegen*) wipe the floor with one's opponent; **3.** (*Süßigkeiten etc.*) munch, scoff *umg.*; **vernascht I.** *P.P.* → **vernaschen**; **II.** *Adj.*: **~ sein** always be eating sweets (*Am.* candy)

vernebeln *v/t.* **1.** *durch Tabakqualm etc.*: (*Zimmer*) fill with smoke; **2.** *Mil.*; *zur Tarnung*: put a smoke-screen up in; **3.** *fig.* (*Verstand etc.*) befuddle; (*Blick*) blur; (*Tatsachen*) obscure; **4.** (*Insektizid etc.*) spray; **Vernebelungstaktik** *f fig.* smoke-screen tactics *Pl.*

vernehmbar *Adj.* audible, perceptible; **vernehmen** *v/t.* (*unreg.*) **1.** hear; (*erfahren*) *auch* learn; **hast du das etwa auch schon vernommen?** *iro.* have you heard that too by any chance?; **2.** (*verhören*) interrogate, question; *Jur. auch* examine; **als Zeuge vernommen werden** be called into the witness box (*Am.* witness stand); **Vernehmen** *n*: **dem ~ nach** from what one hears, rumo(u)r has it that; **dem ~ nach ist** *od.* **hat er ... auch** he is said to ...; **vernehmlich I.** *Adj.* audible, distinct; (*laut*) loud; **II.** *Adv.*: **laut und ~** loud and clear; **Vernehmung** *f* interrogation, questioning; *Jur. auch* examination

vernehmungsfähig *Adj. präd.* fit to be questioned; **nicht ~ präd.** unfit to be questioned

Vernehmungs|protokoll *n* transcript of an (*od.* the) interrogation (*od.* examination); **~richter** *m*, **~richterin** *f judge with powers to interrogate witnesses and experts prior to a trial*

vernehmungsunfähig *Adj. präd.* unfit to be questioned

verneigen *v/refl.* bow (**vor** *j-m* to; *vor e-m Sarg etc.*: before); (*Dame*) curts(e)y (to); **wir ~ uns in Ehrfurcht vor den Toten** *etc.* we bow down in reverence for the dead *etc.*; **Verneigung** *f* bow; *von Damen*: curts(e)y (**vor** + *Dat.* to)

verneinen I. *v/t.* answer no to *s.th.*; (*ableugnen*) deny; (*ablehnen*) oppose; *Ling.* negate; **II.** *v/i.* say no, answer in the negative; **verneinend I.** *Part. Präs.* → **verneinen**; **II.** *Adj.* Antwort *etc.*: negative; *Ling.* negative; **III.** *Adv.*: **~ den Kopf schütteln** shake one's head; **verneint I.** *P.P.* → **verneinen**; **II.** *Adj., Satz etc.*: negative; **Verneinung** *f* negation; (*Ableugnung*) denial; (*Ablehnung*) opposition (+ *Gen.* to); *Ling.* negative

vernetzen *v/t. EDV* network; (*Themen, Systeme etc.*) link, connect, integrate; *Chem.* cross-link; **vernetzt I.** *P.P.* → **vernetzen**; **II.** *Adj. EDV* networked; **~es Denken** integrated thinking; **Vernetzung** *f* networking

vernichten *v/t.* destroy (*auch Urkunden*); *stärker*: annihilate; (*ausrotten*) exterminate; (*auslöschen*) wipe out, eradicate; (*Hoffnung*) dash, shatter; **vernichtend I.** *Part. Präs.* → **vernichten**; **II.** *Adj.* devastating; (*zerstörerisch*) destructive; *fig. Schlag, Niederlage*: crushing; *Antwort, Blick*: withering; *Kritik*: scathing, devastating, damning; **~es Urteil** severe condemnation; **III.** *Adv.*: **~ schlagen** destroy; *Sport, Fußball etc.*: play into the ground; *Boxen*: annihilate; **Vernichtung** *f* destruction; annihilation *etc.*; → **vernichten**

Vernichtungs|feldzug *m* campaign of destruction; **~krieg** *m* war of extermination; **~lager** *n* extermination camp; **~mittel** *n für Unkraut*: weedkiller; *für Insekten*: insecticide; **~potenzial** *n* destructive potential (*od.* capability); **~schlag** *m* **1.** annihilating blow; **2.** *fig.* final blow; **zum ~ ausholen** prepare to (*od.* be about to) deal the final blow; **~waffe** *f* weapon of mass destruction; *Pl. Koll.* destructive weaponry *Sg.*; **~werk** *n* act of destruction; (*Ausrottung*) act of extermination; **~wut** *f* (sheer) vandalism

vernickeln *v/t.* nickel-plate; **Vernickelung** *f* nickel-plating

verniedlichen *v/t.* minimize; *Fehler, Problem etc.*: play *s.th.* down; **Verniedlichung** *f* minimization; *e-s Fehlers, Problems etc.*: playing down

vernieten *v/t.* rivet

Vernissage [vɛrnɪˈsaːʒə] *f*, -, -*n* private art preview, *Am.* private showing art opening

Vernunft *f*, -, *kein Pl.* reason; **~ annehmen** (*od.* [**wieder**] **zur ~ kommen**) be reasonable, (begin to) listen to reason; *stärker*: come to one's senses; **j-n zur ~ bringen** make s.o. listen to reason; *stärker*: bring s.o. to his (*od.* her) senses; **gegen** *od.* **wider alle ~** against all common sense; **vernunftbegabt** *Adj.* rational; **Vernunftehe** *f* marriage of convenience; **vernunftgemäß** *Adj.* rational, reasonable

Vernunft|glaube *m* belief in (human) reason, rationalism; **~gründe** *Pl.* reason *Sg.*, rational arguments (*od.* considerations); **aus ~n** out of plain common sense; **~heirat** *f* marriage of convenience

vernünftig I. *Adj.* **1.** (*vernunftgemäß, angemessen*) reasonable; (*verständig*) sensible; (*besonnen*) level-headed; **er ist ganz ~** *auch* he's got his head screwed on the right way *umg.*; **sonst ist er ganz ~** usually he's quite decent; **kein ~es Wort mit j-m sprechen können** not be able to have a sensible conversation with s.o.; **jeder ~e Mensch** anyone with a bit of sense; *stärker*: anyone in his right mind; **du wirst schon noch ~ werden** you'll come to your senses; **sei doch ~!** be reasonable!, be sensible!; **das Vernünftigste wäre gewesen zu ...** the most sensible thing would have been to ...; **2.** *Argumente etc.*: rational; **3.** *umg.* (*ordentlich*) decent; (*angemessen*) proper; **etw. Vernünftiges zu essen** *s.th.* proper to eat; **er soll erst mal was Vernünftiges lernen** first of all he should learn to do a proper job; **II.** *Adv.* **1.** sensibly; **~ reden** talk sense (**mit** to); **e-e Sache ~ angehen** be sensible about *s.th.*; **2.** *umg.* (*richtig, ordentlich*) properly; *essen*: *auch* sensibly; **zieh dich mal ~ an!** put something sensible on!, put on some proper clothes!; **setz dich ~ hin!** *zu Kind*: sit down properly!; **vernünftigerweise** *Adv.*: **~ etw. tun** be sensible enough (*od.* have the good sense) to do *s.th.*; **Vernünftigkeit** *f*; *nur Sg.* reasonableness

Vernunftmensch *m* rational type

vernunftwidrig *Adj.* irrational; *Handeln*: unreasonable; **Vernunftwidrigkeit** *f* irrationality; *konkret*: irrational behavio(u)r (*od.* decision *etc.*)

veröden I. *v/i.* **1.** (*ist verödet*) become deserted; (*unfruchtbar werden*) become barren; **2.** *Med.* become sclerotic (*od.* obliterated); **II.** *v/t.* (*hat*) *Med.* (*Gefäße*) sclerose, obliterate; **Verödung** *f* **1.** desertion; **die ~ des Bodens war unvermeidbar** it was unavoidable that the soil became barren; **2.** *Med.* obliteration

veröffentlichen *v/t.* (*Nachricht etc.*) publish; (*freigeben*) release; (*Buch etc.*) publish; (*CD etc.*) release; **veröffentlicht I.** *P.P.* → **veröffentlichen**; **II.** *Adj.*: **bisher noch nicht ~** previously unpublished (*CD etc.*: unreleased); **e-e kürzlich ~e Studie** *etc.* a recently published study *etc.*; **Veröffentlichung** *f* publication (*auch Vorgang*)

verölt *Adj.* oily; **~e Seevögel/Strände** seabirds/beaches covered in oil

verordnen *v/t.* **1.** *Med.* prescribe (**j-m** for s.o.); **j-m Bettruhe/Bewegung ~** order s.o. to stay in bed / advise s.o. to get some physical exercise; **wenn vom Arzt nicht anders verordnet** unless otherwise advised by your physician (*od.* doctor); **2.** *gesetzlich*: decree; **Verordnung** *f* **1.** (*das Verordnen*) prescribing; **nach ~ des Arztes** as prescribed by one's physician (*od.* doctor); **2.** *gesetzliche*: decree; (*Vorschrift*) regulation, ruling; **Verordnungsweg** *m*: **auf dem ~e** by means of regulation

verpachten *vt/i.* lease (+ *Dat.* to); **Verpächter** *m*; -*s*, -, **Verpächterin** *f*; -, -*nen* lessor; **Verpachtung** *f* leasing; → **Vermietung**

verpacken *v/t.* pack (up); *bes. maschinell*: package; (*einwickeln*) wrap up; **etw. als Geschenk ~** gift-wrap *s.th.*; **verpackt I.** *P.P.* → **verpacken**; **II.** *Adj.* wrapped up; *bes. maschinell*: packaged; **festlich ~** nicely wrapped (up for the occasion); **als Geschenk ~** gift-wrapped; **Verpackung** *f* **1.** packing; *einzeln*: packaging; **2.** (*Material*) packaging material; (*Papier*) wrapping; **Kosten für Transport und ~** packing and transport (*Am.* shipping and handling) costs

Verpackungs|gewicht *n* tare weight; **~industrie** *f* packaging industry; **~kosten** *Pl.* packing charges; **~material** *n* packaging material; (*Papier*) wrapping; **~müll** *m* packaging waste

verpassen *v/t.* **1.** (*Gelegenheit, Zug etc.*) miss; **2.** *umg.* (*geben, verabfolgen*) give (*od.* land) s.o. with *s.th.*; *Mil.* (*Bekleidung*) fit; **j-m e-e Niederlage ~** defeat s.o.; **j-m e-e ~** land s.o. one; **wer hat dir denn 'die Frisur verpasst?** who gave you that haircut?, who did your hair for you?; → **Denkzettel** *etc.*

verpatzen *v/t. umg.* mess up, botch (up)

verpennen *vt/i. umg.* sleep in, oversleep; (*Termin etc.*) sleep through; (*vergessen*) forget; **ich hab's total verpennt** *auch* I clean (*od.* totally) forgot

verpesten *v/t.* pollute; *umg.* (*Raum etc.*) stink out; *fig.* (*Atmosphäre*) poison

verpetzen *v/t. umg.* sneak (*Am.* tattle *od.* tell) on *s.o.*; **er hat uns beim Lehrer verpetzt** he told the teacher on us

verpfänden *v/t.* **1.** *in der Pfandleihe*: pawn; *mit Hypothek*: mortgage; (*bes. fig., sein Wort etc.*) pledge

verpfeifen *v/t.* (*unreg.*); *umg.* **1.** (*j-n*) blab on; *bes. in der Schule*: *auch* sneak on, *bes. Am.* tell on; *bei der Polizei*: grass on *Sl.*, shop, *Am.* finger, squeal (*od.* fink) on; **2.** (*etw.*) let *s.th.* out, blab *s.th.*

verpflanzen *v/t.* transplant (*auch Med.*); (*Haut*) graft; **Verpflanzung** *f*

konkret: transplant; *von Haut*: graft
verpflegen I. *v/t.* feed; **II.** *v/refl.* feed o.s.; *sich selbst ~* cook for o.s.; **Verpflegung** *f* **1.** (*Versorgung*) catering; (*Beköstigung*) feeding; **2.** (*Essen*) food (and drink), (*Erfrischungen*) refreshments *Pl.*; *Mil.* rations *Pl.*; → **Unterkunft**

Verpflegungs|aufwand *m* expenditure on food; **~satz** *m* allowance for meals, meals allowance

verpflichten I. *vt/i.* oblige; *bes. vertraglich etc.*: obligate; (*j-n*) place an obligation on s.o. (*zu* + *Inf.* to + *Inf.*); *j-n zum Kauf etc. ~* put s.o. under an obligation to buy *etc.*; *es verpflichtet zum Kauf* you are obliged to buy; *es verpflichtet zu nichts* there's no obligation involved, there are no strings attached; *j-n zur Einhaltung der Regeln ~* bind s.o. to the rules; → **Adel** 1; **II.** *v/t.* **1.** (*engagieren*) engage; (*Sportler*) sign; *Mil.* enlist; **2.** *j-n auf die Verfassung ~* make s.o. swear to uphold the constitution; **III.** *v/refl.* **1.** commit o.s. (*zu* + *Inf.* to + *Inf. od. Ger.*); *auch vertraglich*: undertake (to + *Inf.*); **2.** *beruflich, bes. Mil.*: sign on (*Am.* up) (*auf 5 Jahre etc.*: for); *sich vertraglich ~* sign a contract

verpflichtet I. *P.P.* → **verpflichten**; **II.** *Adj.* obliged (*zu* to + *Inf.*); *stärker*: under an obligation (to + *Inf.*); *vertraglich*: bound by contract (to + *Inf.*); *gesetzlich ~ sein* be bound by law (*zu* + *Inf.* to + *Inf.*), be under legal obligation (to + *Inf.*); *sich ~ fühlen, etw. zu tun* feel obliged (*stärker*: bound) to do s.th.; *j-m* (*sehr*) *zu Dank ~ sein* be (deeply) indebted to s.o.; *du bist ihm gegenüber zu nichts ~* you don't owe him anything, he's got no claim on you; *sich e-r Sache ~ fühlen* feel under an obligation to s.th.

Verpflichtung *f* **1.** commitment; *bes. moralische*: obligation; *gesetzliche*: liability (*auch Wirts.*); (*Versprechen*) pledge (*zu* of); (*Pflicht*) duty; *~ zum Kauf etc.* obligation to buy *etc.*; *~en gegenüber j-m haben* be under an obligation to s.o.; *s-n ~en nachkommen* meet one's obligations (*Wirts. auch* liabilities); *Pol.* discharge one's commitments; *keinerlei ~en haben* be under no obligation whatsoever; **2.** *von neuen Mitarbeitern*: engaging, *bes. Am.* hiring; *Sport* signing; **3.** *mst Pl.*; (*Schulden*) obligations; *s-n ~en nachkommen* meet one's obligations; **4.** *nur Sg.*; (*das Verpflichten*) obliging; *feierliche ~ von Rekruten etc.*: ceremonial enlisting

Verpflichtungserklärung *f Wirts., Jur.* formal obligation

verpfuschen *v/t. umg.* bungle, botch (up), make a mess of (*auch sein Leben, s-e Karriere etc.*); **verpfuscht I.** *P.P.* → **verpfuschen**; **II.** *Adj. Leben*: ruined, wrecked; *Kleid etc.*: botched

verpissen *v/refl. Sl.*: **verpiss dich!** piss off!, fuck off! *vulg.*

verplanen I. *v/t.* **1.** (*Gelder*) budget; (*Zeit*) plan; *s-e Zeit verplant haben* be fully booked; *m-e Urlaubstage habe ich schon verplant* my holiday (*Am.* vacation) is all booked up (with various activities) already; **2.** (*falsch planen*) plan wrong; (*verschätzen*) miscalculate; **II.** *v/refl.* plan wrong, get one's planning wrong; **verplant I.** *P.P.* → **verplanen**; **II.** *Adj.*: *~ sein Geld etc.*: be earmarked; *Tag etc.*: be booked up

verplappern *v/refl. umg.* blab (it out),

let the cat out of the bag, *Am. auch* spill one's guts

verplaudern I. *v/t.* (*Zeit*) talk (*od.* chat) away; *den ganzen Abend ~* spend the whole evening chatting (away); **II.** *v/refl.* (*completely*) forget the time chatting; *wir haben uns verplaudert auch* we were so busy chatting we forgot to look at our watches (*od.* at the time)

verplempern *umg.* **I.** *v/t.* (*Zeit, Geld*) waste, fritter away; **II.** *v/refl.* fritter away one's time (*als* as)

verplomben *v/t.* seal; **Verplombung** *f* **1.** (*das Verplomben*) sealing; **2.** (*Plombe*) seal

verpönt *Adj. attr.* disapproved-of ..., *präd.* disapproved of; *stärker*: scorned, frowned upon; *~ sein auch* be looked down upon; *... ist hier ~ auch* we (*od.* they) don't approve of ... around here

verprassen *v/t. umg.* squander (*für* on), blow (on) *umg.*

verprellen *v/t.* put off; (*beleidigen*) offend, put out; → *auch* **vergrämen**

verproviantieren *v/t.* supply with food

verprügeln *v/t.* beat *s.o.* up, give *s.o.* a thrashing

verpuffen *v/i.* **1.** *Eifer, Zorn etc.*: fizzle out; *Wirkung, Pointe etc.*: fall flat; **2.** *Flamme, Gas etc.*: go pop *umg.*; (*sich verflüchtigen*) evaporate (*auch fig.*); **Verpuffung** *f* weak explosion

verpulvern *v/t. umg.* (*Geld*) blow

verpumpen *v/t. umg.* (*Geld etc.*) lend out

verpuppen *v/refl. Zool.* pupate, change into a chrysalis; **Verpuppung** *f Zool.* pupation

verpusten *v/refl. umg.* get one's breath back

Verputz *m*; *-es, -e* plaster(work); (*Rauhputz*) roughcast; **verputzen** *v/t.* **1.** plaster; (*rau ~*) roughcast; **2.** *umg. fig.* (*aufessen*) put away, polish off; (*Gegner*) wipe the floor with; *ich kann ihn nicht ~* I can't stomach him

verqualmen *umg. v/t.* **1.** (*Zimmer etc.*) fill *s.th.* up with smoke; **2.** (*Geld*) spend on cigarettes; *er verqualmt sein ganzes Geld* all his money goes up in smoke; **verqualmt** *umg.* **I.** *P.P.* → **verqualmen**; **II.** *Adj. attr.* smoky, smoke-filled ..., *präd.* filled with smoke

verquast *Adj. umg.* complicated, intricate

verquatschen *v/t. und v/refl. umg.* → **verplaudern**

verquer *umg.* **I.** *Adj.* **1.** *Ideen etc.*: strange, screwy; *~er Typ* weirdo; *~e Angelegenheit* mess; **II.** *Adv.* (*falsch, verkehrt*) wrong; (*schief*) awry

verquicken *v/t.* **1.** *Chem.* amalgamate; **2.** *fig.* (*in Verbindung bringen*) connect, bring together; (*vermischen, auch durcheinanderbringen*) mix up; **verquickt I.** *P.P.* → **verquicken**; **II.** *Adj.*: *eng* (*miteinander*) *~* closely connected (*od.* related); **Verquickung** *f* connection (+ *Gen.* between); mixing-up (of)

verquirlen *v/t.* whisk (*in* + *Dat.*, *zu* into), beat (*od.* mix) with a whisk

verquollen *Adj. Holz*: warped; *Gesicht*: bloated; *auch Augen*: swollen

verrammeln, verrammen *v/t. umg.* barricade, block (up)

verramschen *v/t.* **1.** *umg.* sell off (dirt cheap), flog (dirt cheap); **2.** *fachspr.* (*Restauflage von Büchern etc.*) remainder

Verrat *m*; *-(e)s, kein Pl.* **1.** betrayal (*an* + *Dat.* of), sellout (of) *umg.*; *Jur.*

(*auch ~ am Vaterland*) treason (to); *an j-m ~ begehen od. üben* betray s.o.; **2.** (*Verraten*) betraying

verraten (*unreg.*) **I.** *v/t.* **1.** (*Freunde, Ideale etc.*) betray, give away; (*Geheimnis*) *auch* divulge; (*j-n*) *auch* sell *umg.*; *~ und verkauft sein umg.* have been sold down the river; **2.** (*ausplaudern*) blab out *umg.*; *fig.* (*offenbaren*) betray (*auch j-s Nervosität*), reveal; (*preisgeben*) *auch* give away; *sein Blick verriet große Angst* great fear was revealed in his eyes; *nicht ~!* don't tell!; *das darfst du Mutter nicht ~* you mustn't tell Mother about that; *sein Akzent hat ihn ~* his accent betrayed him (*od.* gave him away); **3.** *umg.* (*mitteilen*) tell; *kannst du mir ~ warum ...?* umg. can you tell me why ...?; **II.** *v/refl.* give o.s. away (*durch* by); **Verräter** *m*; *-s, -*, **Verräterin** *f*; *-, -nen* traitor (*an* + *Dat.* to); **verräterisch I.** *Adj.* treacherous, traitorous; *Jur.* treasonable; *fig.* revealing; *attr. Blick, Spur etc.*: telltale ..., giveaway ...; **II.** *Adv. handeln etc.*: treacherously, traitorously; *es zuckte ~ um s-e Mundwinkel* the corners of his mouth were twitching revealingly

verratzt *Adj. umg.* lost; *~ sein auch* be left high and dry

verrauchen I. *v/i.* (*ist verraucht*); *Zorn*: blow over; **II.** *v/t.* (*hat*) smoke; (*Geld*) spend on smoking

verräuchern *v/t.* → **verqualmen**; **verräuchert** → **verqualmt**

verraucht I. *P.P.* → **verrauchen**; **II.** *Adj. attr.* smoky (*auch Stimme*), smoke-filled ..., *präd.* filled with smoke

verrauschen *v/i. Beifall, Begeisterung etc.*: die down, fade away; **verrauscht I.** *P.P.* → **verrauschen**; **II.** *Adj. Fernsehbild*: grainy

verrechnen I. *v/t.* (*begleichen*) settle; (*verbuchen*) credit to s.o.'s account; *etw. mit etw. ~* offset s.th. against s.th.; **II.** *v/refl.* miscalculate (*um* by); *auch fig.* make a mistake; *sich* (*um 10 Dollar*) *verrechnet haben auch* be (10 dollars) out (*bes. Am.* off); *sich gründlich verrechnet haben umg.* be miles out (*bes. Am.* off); *fig.* have made a big mistake; **Verrechnung** *f* (*Abrechnung*) settlement; *im Verrechnungsverkehr*: clearing; *nur zur ~ Scheck*: not negotiable

Verrechnungs|einheit *f* (*abgek.* **VE**) *Wirts.* unit of account; **~konto** *n* offset account; **~scheck** *m* crossed (*od.* non-negotiable) cheque (*Am.* check); **~stelle** *f* clearing office; **~verfahren** *n* clearing process; **~wesen** *n* clearing

verrecken *v/i.* **1.** *vulg.* (*zugrunde gehen*) die; *hum.* snuff it *Sl., Am.* kick the bucket, buy the farm; *fig. Motor etc.*: conk out; *nicht ums Verrecken! umg. fig.* not on your life (*od.* nelly)!; **2.** *Tier*: die, perish; *Hunderte sind verreckt auch* they were dying (*od.* going down) like flies

verregnet *Adj.* rainy; *Urlaub, Ernte etc.*: spoil|t (*Am.* -ed) (*od.* ruined) by rain; *unser Ausflug war ~ auch* it rained throughout our outing

verreiben *v/t.* (*unreg.*) (*Salbe etc.*) spread, (*auf der Haut*) rub in(to)

verreisen *v/i.* go away; *~ nach* go to; *geschäftlich ~* go away (*od.* off) on a business trip *od.* on business; *er ist geschäftlich verreist* he's away on business; *verreist ihr im Urlaub?* are you going away on holiday (*Am.* vacation)?; **nach Diktat verreist** *im Brief*: dictated by ... and signed in his (*od.* her) absence

verreißen *v/t.* (*unreg.*) **1.** (*scharf kritisieren*) tear to pieces (bits, shreds *umg.*), savage, trash *umg.*, rubbish *umg.*, do a hatchet job on *umg.*; **2.** *umg.*: **den Wagen / die Lenkung ~** swerve the car / jerk the steering wheel (a)round; **es verriss mir das Steuer** the steering wheel suddenly jerked (a)round hard; **3.** *Sport* (*stark verziehen*) (*Ball*) slice

verrenken I. *v/t.* **1.** (*zerren*) sprain, twist; (*ausrenken*) dislocate; **sich** (*Dat.*) **den Arm ~** sprain (*od.* twist, dislocate) one's arm; **2.** *umg. fig.*: **sich** (*Dat.*) **den Hals ~** *neugierig*: crane one's neck (**nach** to get a glimpse of), *Am.* rubberneck; **ich habe mir gestern den Magen verrenkt** I had something yesterday that upset my stomach; **lieber sich den Bauch ~ als dem Wirt was schenken** *hum.* there's no point in wasting it *etc.*; **II.** *v/refl.* **1.** sprain (*od.* twist, dislocate) one's shoulder *etc.*; **2.** (*Verrenkungen machen*) contort o.s.; *stärker*: go into contortions; **verrenkt I.** *P.P.* → **verrenken**; **II.** *Adj.* twisted; **ich habe e-n ~en Hals** I've twisted my neck, I've got a crick in my neck; **Verrenkung** *f* **1.** (*Zerrung*) sprain; (*Luxation*) dislocation; **2.** (*starke Biegung*) contortion; (*Drehung*) *auch* gyration; **~en machen** go into contortions; **geistige ~en** mental acrobatics (*od.* gyrations)

verrennen *v/refl.* (*unreg.*) *fig.*: **sich ~ in** (+ *Akk.*) get stuck in, *Am.* get one's teeth into; **sich verrannt haben in** (+ *Akk.*) be set (*od.* stuck) on

verrenten *v/t. Amtsspr.* retire; **Verrentung** *f Amtsspr.* retirement

verrichten *v/t.* do, carry out; → **Gebet**, **Geschäft** 6, **Notdurft** *etc.*; **Verrichtung** *f* **1.** (*Ausführung*) execution, carrying out; **2.** **~en** (*Tätigkeit*) chores, work; **s-n täglichen ~en nachgehen** do one's daily chores (*od.* routine)

verriegeln *v/t.* bolt, bar; **Verriegelung** *f* (*Vorrichtung*) bolt

verringern I. *v/t.* decrease, reduce, lower, cut (down); **II.** *v/refl.* decrease, diminish, go down; **Verringerung** *f* decrease (+ *Gen.* in), reduction (of), lowering (of)

verrinnen *v/i.* (*unreg.*) *Wasser etc.*: trickle away; *Zeit*: pass, slip away, *Stunden*: *auch* tick away; *Jahre*: pass by, slip by

Verriss *m*; *-es, -e*; *umg.* hatchet job, slating; **e-n ~ schreiben** write a damning review

verrohen I. *v/i.* (*ist verroht*) become brutalized; *auch Sitten*: coarsen; **II.** *v/t.* (*hat*) brutalize; *auch Sitten*: coarsen; **Verrohung** *f* brutalization; *auch der Sitten*: coarsening

verrosten *v/i.* rust; *fig. Glieder etc.*: become stiff (*od.* rusty); **verrostet I.** *P.P.* → **verrosten**; **II.** *Adj.* rusty; *fig.* stiff, rusty

verrotten *v/i.* rot; *weitS. und fig.* → **verkommen**; **verrottet I.** *P.P.* → **verrotten**; **II.** *Adj.* **1.** rotten; **2.** *fig.* depraved; (*dekadent*) decadent

verrucht *Adj.* wicked; *Verbrechen*: *auch* foul, heinous; *oft hum.* (*lasterhaft*) disreputable; **~e Kaschemme** *umg.* seedy dive; **sie sieht heute ganz schön ~ aus** *umg.* she looks really tarty today; **Verruchtheit** *f; nur Sg.* wickedness; heinousness, foul nature (+ *Gen.* of);

→ **verrucht**

verrücken *v/t.* move, shift

verrückt I. *P.P.* → **verrücken**; **II.** *Adj.* *umg.* mad; *fig.*; *Mode etc.*: *auch* crazy; *Plan, Idee etc.*: wild, crazy; **~ werden** go mad; **sag mal, bist du ~ geworden?** have you gone mad?, have you lost your mind?; **ich werd ~!** well blow me (*Am.* blow me down)!; **~ nach** *od.* **auf** (+ *Akk.*) *fig.* wild about, nuts on (*od.* about); **j-n ~ machen** drive s.o. mad (*od.* [a]round the bend); (*durcheinander bringen*) get s.o. all confused; **sich ~ machen** get (o.s.) all worked up (*od.* into a lather), get into a tiz(zy); **~ spielen** act up; *stärker*: go berserk; *fig. Wetter etc.*: go crazy; **wie ~** like mad (*od.* crazy); **da kann man ja ~ werden** it's enough to drive you mad (*bes. Am.* crazy); **man würde dich für ~ erklären** everyone will think you're crazy; **so etw. Verrücktes!** what a crazy idea!; **III.** *Adv.* *umg.* in a crazy way; **musst du denn so ~ fahren?** do you have to drive in such a crazy way?; **Verrückte** *m, f*; *-n, -n* lunatic, madman; *weiblich*: madwoman; *stärker*: maniac; **wie ein ~r sich aufführen**, *schreien etc.*: like a lunatic; *fahren etc.*: like a maniac; **Verrücktheit** *f* **1.** *nur Sg.*; *Zustand, Eigenschaft*: madness; **2.** (*Modenarrheit*) craze; **sie macht jede ~ mit** she follows every craze; **3.** mad (*od.* crazy) idea (*od.* thing to do *etc.*); **Verrücktwerden** *n*: **es ist zum ~** it's enough to drive you mad (*bes. Am.* crazy)

Verruf *m*: **in ~ bringen / kommen** *od.* **geraten** bring/fall into disrepute; **verrufen** *Adj.* disreputable with a bad reputation; **~ sein** *mst* have a bad reputation (*od.* name)

verrühren *v/t.* mix; **Sahne in der Soße ~** stir cream into the sauce

verrußen *v/i.* (*ist verrußt*) become (*od.* get) sooty; **II.** *v/t.* (*hat*) soot s.th. up, cover s.th. in soot; **verrußt I.** *P.P.* → **verrußen**; **II.** *Adj.* *Zündkerzen etc.*: sooty, soot-covered ...

verrutschen *v/i.* slip, get out of place

Vers *m*; *-es, -e*; *Lit.* verse (*auch Bibelvers und Versmaß*); (*Zeile*) line; *umg.* (*Strophe*) verse; **in ~e setzen** put s.th. into verse; **er kann sich keinen ~ darauf machen** *fig.* he can't make head (*-s*) or tail(s) of it

versachlichen *v/t.* objectivize; (*entpersönlichen*) depersonalize

versacken *v/i.* (*ist versackt*) *umg.* **1.** sink (**in** + *Dat.* into); *im Schlamm etc.*: sink; **2.** *fig.* (*herunterkommen*) go to the dogs; **3.** *fig.* (*sich betrinken*) get involved in a (big) booze-up (*Am.* bender), end up boozing (the night away); **wir sind gestern Abend (ganz schön) versackt** we went on a (real) bender last night

versagen I. *v/i.* fail (*auch Person etc.*); *Tech. auch* break down; *Motor*: stall; **jämmerlich ~** fail miserably; **die Beine versagten ihr (den Dienst)** her legs gave way (*Am.* out); **s-e Stimme versagte** his voice failed him; **sein Gedächtnis versagte** his memory failed him (*od.* let him down); **II.** *v/t. geh.* (*verweigern*) refuse, deny; **es war ihnen versagt, den Raum zu betreten** *etc.* they were denied entrance to the room *etc.*; **j-m den Dienst ~** refuse to obey s.o.; **sich** (*Dat.*) **etw. ~** deny o.s. s.th.; **für(e)go s.th.**; **es blieb ihm versagt** it was denied him, he was denied it; **es blieb ihm versagt, es zu tun** it

was denied him to do it, he was not to do it; **Kinder sind uns versagt geblieben** we have been denied children; **III.** *v/refl. geh.*: **sich j-m ~** refuse s.o.; *altm. sexuell*: refuse to give o.s. to s.o.

Versagen *n*; *-s, kein Pl.* failure; **menschliches ~** human error; *Flug. auch* pilot error; **Versagensangst** *f* fear of failure; **Versager** *m*; *-s, -*, **Versagerin** *f*; *-, -nen* failure

Versal *m*; *-s, Versalien*; *Druck.* capital (letter), uppercase (letter); (*in*) **Versalien!** *Anweisung*: caps

versalzen I. *v/t.* (*hat versalzen*) **1.** put too much salt in, oversalt; **2.** *umg. fig.* spoil; **j-m etw. ~** spoil s.th. (*od.* things) for s.o.; → **Suppe**; **II.** *v/i.* (*ist versalzt*); *Geog., Öko., See*: become salty; **Versalzung** *f Geog., Öko.* salinization, salination

versammeln I. *v/t.* **1.** assemble (*auch Mil.*), gather; **er versammelte s-e Schüler** *etc.* **um sich** he gathered his students *etc.* (a)round him; **2.** (*Reitpferd*) collect; **II.** *v/refl.* assemble, meet; **wir haben uns heute hier versammelt** *feierlich*: we are gathered here today; **versammelt I.** *P.P.* → **versammeln**; **II.** *Adj.* **1.** **~ sein** be assembled; **alle Größen der Politik waren ~** all the important political figures were assembled; **vor ~er Mannschaft** *umg.* in front of all those assembled; **2.** *Reitsport, Pferd*: collected; **Versammlung** *f* **1.** meeting; gathering (*auch die Versammelten*); **gesetzgebende ~** *Parl.* legislative assembly, legislature; **2.** *nur Sg.*; *Reitsport, e-s Pferdes*: collection

Versammlungs|freiheit *f* freedom of assembly; **~gesetz** *n* law governing the right to assembly; **~ort** *m*, **~raum** *m* meeting place; **~recht** *n* right of assembly; **~verbot** *n* ban on public assembly (*od.* public gatherings)

Versand *m*; *-(e)s, kein Pl.* **1.** (*Absenden*) dispatch; (*Transport*) shipment; (*Verteilung*) distribution; **zum ~ fertig machen** get ready for dispatch; **2.** (*Abteilung*) forwarding department; **~abteilung** *f* forwarding department

versandbereit *Adj.* ready for dispatch (*od.* sending)

Versandbuchhandel *m* mail-order book trade (*Am.* business)

versanden *v/i. Hafen, Flussbett*: silt up; *fig.* peter out

versandfertig *Adj.* ready for dispatch (*od.* sending)

Versand|geschäft *n* mail-order business; **~gut** *n* dispatch goods; **~handel** *m* mail-order business; **~haus** *n* mail-order company (*bes. Am.* house); **~hauskatalog** *m* mail-order catalog(ue); **~kosten** *Pl.* forwarding expenses; **~papiere** *Pl.* shipping documents; **~schein** *m* shipping note; **~tasche** *f* padded envelope

Versandung *f* silting(-up); *fig.* petering out

Versatz|amt *n südd., österr.* pawnbroker's, *Am.* pawnshop; **~stück** *n Theat.* set piece; **~e** *Pl. fig.* clichés

versaubeuteln *v/t. umg.* mess up; (*verschlampen*) go and lose

versauen *v/t. umg.* **1.** (*schmutzig machen*) mess up; **2.** *fig.* (*verderben*) mess up; *stärker*: ruin, wreck

versauern I. *v/i.* (*ist versauert*) **1.** *umg. Person*: stagnate; (*dahinvegetieren*) vegetate; **2.** *Wein etc.*: turn sour; *Boden etc.*: become acidic; **II.** *v/t.* (*hat*) *umg.*: **j-m etw. ~** spoil s.th. for s.o.;

Versauerung f des Bodens etc.: acidification

versaufen (unreg.) v/t. umg. guzzle (od. booze) away

versäumen v/t. (Gelegenheit, Zug etc.) miss; (Pflicht) neglect; (Schlaf) miss (out on); **den Unterricht ~** miss classes; **~, etw. zu tun** fail to do s.th.; **~ Sie nicht zu** (+ Inf.) be sure to (+ Inf.); **da hast du nichts/was versäumt!** you didn't miss much / you really missed something there; **versäumt I.** P.P. → **versäumen**; **II.** Adj. Stunden etc.: missed; **~e Zeit nachholen** make up for lost time

Versäumnis n; -ses, -se omission, failure to do s.th.; (Vernachlässigung) neglect; Schule: (Fehltag, -stunde) absence; **~urteil** n Jur. judg(e)ment by default; **~verfahren** n Jur. trial by default

versaut I. P.P. → **versauen**; **II.** Adj. umg. (dreckig) mucky; (kaputt, verdorben) präd. messed-up; **ein total ~er Urlaub** a complete mess of a holiday (Am. vacation)

verschachern v/t. umg. sell off, flog

verschachteln v/t. **1.** (auch ineinander ~) fit (od. slot) into each other; EDV nest; **2.** fig. complicate, make s.th. complicated; **verschachtelt I.** P.P. → **verschachteln**; **II.** Adj. **1.** interlocking; **2.** fig. complicated, convoluted; **~er Satz** involved period; **~e Altstadt** higgledy-piggledy old town

verschaffen v/t. get (j-m etw. s.o. s.th.); (Arbeit, Wohnung etc.) auch find; **sich** (Dat.) **Geld ~** get hold of some money; **sich** (Dat.) **e-n Vorteil ~** gain an advantage; **sich** (Dat.) **Respekt ~** gain (win (some) respect); **j-m die Möglichkeit ~ zu** (+ Inf.) make it possible for s.o. to (+ Inf.); **was verschafft mir die Ehre?** iro. what have I done to deserve this hono(u)r?; → **Gewissheit** etc.

verschalen v/t. board, panel; Archit. (Beton) shutter; **Verschalung** f boarding; Gehäuse: casing; Archit. form(s Pl.)

verschämt I. Adj. bashful; bewusst: coy; **II.** Adv. lächeln etc.: bashfully; bewusst: coyly; **~ tun** act coy

verschandeln v/t. disfigure; (Aussicht etc.) auch spoil; **es verschandelt den Platz** od. **die Aussicht** etc. it's an eyesore; **Verschandelung** f disfigurement

verschanzen v/refl. entrench o.s.; **sich hinter etw. ~** fig. entrench o.s. behind s.th.; (etw. als Vorwand benutzen) use s.th. as a pretext; **sich hinter den Vorschriften ~** hide behind the regulations

verschärfen I. v/t. (Maßnahmen, Kontrollen, Gesetze etc.) tighten (up); (Lage, Spannungen etc.) aggravate; (Strafe) stiffen; (Training) intensify; **das Tempo ~** Mot. etc. speed up; weitS. step up the pace; **II.** v/refl. Lage: become more critical, hot (Am. heat) up umg.; Spannungen: mount, increase; Gegensätze etc.: intensify; Rezession etc.: auch tighten its grip; **Verschärfung** f tightening (up); von Spannungen etc.: aggravation etc.; → **verschärfen**

verscharren v/t. bury; oft pej., achtlos etc.: bury in a shallow grave

verschätzen v/refl. misjudge (um by), make a mistake; **sich um ... verschätzt haben** be out by ...; **sich verschätzt haben in** (+ Dat.) have mis-

judged s.th./s.o.; er wollte mich reinlegen etc., **da hat er sich aber gründlich verschätzt** umg. but he was making a big mistake

verschaukeln v/t. umg. **1.** (reinlegen) take s.o. for a ride; **2.** (sitzen lassen) leave s.o. in the lurch

verscheiden v/i. (unreg.); geh. pass away

verscheißen v/t. (unreg.); umg. (Hosen etc.) cover with shit; **bei j-m verschissen haben** fig. be in s.o.'s black books, be on s.o.'s shitlist vulg.

verscheißern v/t. umg. make fun of, Brit. auch take the mickey out of; **willst du mich ~?** are you making fun (of me)?, Brit. auch are you trying to take the mick? Sl.

verschenken v/t. give away; (Sieg) throw away; (Punkte) give away; (Zeit) waste; (Elfmeter etc.) give away; **können Sie es mir einpacken? ich möchte es ~** it's for a present; **10 cm** etc. **~** Weitsprung etc.: give away 10 cm etc.; **wir haben nichts zu ~** we can't afford to give anything away

verscherbeln v/t. umg. sell off cheap, flog

verscherzen v/t.: **sich** (Dat.) (etw.) **~** forfeit, lose; (Chance etc.) throw away; **sich j-s Gunst ~** fall out of favo(u)r with s.o.; **du hast es dir mit ihm verscherzt** you've spoil|t (Am. -ed) your chances with him

verscheuchen v/t. scare off; absichtlich: chase away (auch fig.)

verscheuern v/t. umg. sell off cheap, flog

verschicken v/t. dispatch; (auch Kinder etc.) send; Wirts. dispatch, ship; **Verschickung** f dispatch(ing); sending; shipping; → **verschicken**

verschiebbar Adj. adjustable; EDV relocatable; **der Termin ist nicht ~** the deadline cannot be postponed

Verschiebebahnhof m shunting station, Am. switchyard

verschieben (unreg.) **I.** v/t. **1.** (Schrank etc.) shift, move; EDV relocate, shift; Eisenb. shunt, Am. auch switch; (Truppen) displace; Perspektive: alter, change; **2.** zeitlich: put off, postpone (auf + Akk. to, until, till); **auf unbestimmte Zeit ~** put s.th. off indefinitely; **3.** (Waren) sell s.th. underhand; **Devisen ins Ausland ~** smuggle currency abroad; **II.** v/refl. **1.** move; (verrutschen) slip; Knochenbruch etc.: become displaced; Gleichgewicht, Kräfteverhältnis etc.: shift; **2.** Termin etc.: be postponed (auf + Akk. to, until, till); **dadurch ~ sich die nachfolgenden Termine** for this reason the subsequent deadlines will be postponed (od. pushed back)

Verschiebung f **1.** räumliche: shift(ing), moving; displacement (auch Mil.); **2.** zeitliche: postponement (auf + Akk. to, until, till); **daraus ergeben sich einige zeitliche ~en** as a result a few things will be postponed

verschieden I. Adj. different (von from); (deutlich ~) distinct (from); Meinungen: differing; (wechselnd) varied; (verschiedenerlei) miscellaneous, various; **~er Meinung sein** disagree (über + Akk. on), differ in opinion (on); **~er Meinung sein über etw.** auch see s.th. differently; **das ist ~** it depends; **das ist von Woche zu Woche etc. ~** that varies from week to week etc.; **~e Male** several times; **aus den ~sten Gründen** for various (od. a vari-

ety of) reasons; **II.** Adv. behandeln, schreiben, aussprechen etc.: differently; **~ groß/schwer** etc. **sein** be of different sizes/weights etc.; **~ ausfallen** turn out differently

verschiedenartig Adj. different (kinds of ...); (mannigfaltig) various, a variety of ...; **Verschiedenartigkeit** f; nur Sg.; (unterschiedliches Wesen) different nature; (Unterschied) difference; (Mannigfaltigkeit) variety, diversity

verschiedenerlei Adj. of various kinds; förm. od. iro. divers

Verschiedenes (n); kein Pl. various things Pl., bes. Wirts. sundries Pl.; als Überschrift: miscellaneous, misc.; Tagesordnungspunkt: any other business; **jetzt wird mir ~ klar** now I'm clear about various things; **mir ist** (noch) **~ unklar** I'm (still) not clear about various things

verschiedenfarbig Adj. of different colo(u)rs, förm. varicolo(u)red, parti--colo(u)red

Verschiedenheit f (Unähnlichkeit) dissimilarity; (Mannigfaltigkeit) diversity, variety; (Unterschied) difference

verschiedentlich I. Adv. (mehrmals) repeatedly, several times; (gelegentlich) occasionally; **II.** Adj. (mehrere) several; (wiederholt) repeated

verschießen (unreg.) **I.** v/t. (hat verschossen) shoot; **s-e Munition ~** run out of ammunition; **~ Pulver**; **II.** v/t/i. (hat); Sport (Elfmeter etc.) miss; → **verschossen** II 3; **III.** v/i. (ist) Farbe: fade; → **verschossen** II 1; **IV.** v/refl. umg. (hat): **sich in j-n ~** fall madly in love with s.o.; → **verschossen** II 2

verschiffen v/t. Naut. ship; **Verschiffung** f shipment

verschimmeln v/i. go mo(u)ldy; Leder, Papier etc.: go mo(u)ldy, get mildew; **verschimmelt I.** P.P. → **verschimmeln**; **II.** Adj. Brot, Käse etc.: mo(u)ldy; Tapete, Schuhe etc.: mo(u)ldy, mildewed

verschissen umg. **I.** P.P. → **verscheißen**; **II.** Adj. Unterhose etc.: shitty

verschlafen¹ (unreg.) **I.** v/t. (den Tag etc.) sleep away (auch fig. Kummer etc.); (Konzert, Gewitter etc.) sleep through; fig. (Gelegenheit, Anschluss etc.) miss; (Verabredung etc.) (completely) forget; **ich habe es völlig ~** (Termin etc.) auch it slipped my mind completely; **II.** v/i. oversleep

verschlafen² **I.** P.P. → **verschlafen¹**; **II.** Adj. sleepy (auch fig. Stadt etc.), dop(e)y umg.; **total ~ sein** umg. (viel schlafen) be forever dozing, be in a constant doze; **Verschlafenheit** f; nur Sg. drowsiness, sleepiness, dopiness umg.

Verschlag m; -(e)s, Verschläge; (Bretterbude) shed; pej. shack

verschlagen¹ v/t. (unreg.) **1.** (Ball) mishit; **die Buchseite ~** lose one's place; **2.** (vom Kurs abbringen) throw s.o. off course; **~ nach** od. **in** (+ Akk.) etc. bring to; **~ werden nach** od. **in** (+ Akk.) etc. end up in, land in umg.; **wohin hat es dich denn ~?** umg. where did it cause you to end up?; **3.** **j-m den Atem ~** take s.o.'s breath away; **es verschlug ihm die Sprache** he was (left) speechless

verschlagen² **I.** P.P. → **verschlagen¹**; **II.** Adj. pej. (hinterhältig, unaufrichtig) deceitful, dishonest; Blick, Typ: shifty; **III.** Adv. pej.: **j-n ~ ansehen** give s.o. a shifty look; **Verschlagenheit** f; nur Sg.; pej. deceitfulness, shiftiness

verschlammen *v/i.* *Hafenbecken, Flussbett*: silt up

verschlampen *umg.* **I.** *v/t.* (*hat verschlampt*) mislay, go and lose; *ich hab's völlig verschlampt* (*vergessen*) it completely slipped my mind, I clean forgot (it); **II.** *v/i.* (*ist*); *Person*: go to seed; *etw. ~ lassen* neglect s.th.; **verschlampt** *umg.* **I.** *P.P.* → **verschlampen**; **II.** *Adj.* *Person*: slovenly, scruffy; *Sache*: scruffy, tatty; (*vernachlässigt*) messy, *präd. auch* a mess

verschlanken *v/t.* *umg.* (*Produktion*) cut back; (*Personal*) cut; **Verschlankung** *f* *umg.* *von Produktion*: cutting-back; *von Personal*: cutting

verschlechtern I. *v/t.* make worse; (*Lage*) *auch* aggravate; (*Aussichten, Chance etc.*) diminish; **II.** *v/refl.* deteriorate, get worse; *Leistung, Qualität*: fall off; (*Aussichten, Chance etc.*) diminish; *sich in Mathe etc. ~* deteriorate in math(s) *etc.*; *sich beruflich/gehaltsmäßig ~* take a backward step professionally / become worse off in terms of salary; **Verschlechterung** *f* deterioration (+ *Gen.* in, of); worsening (of); change for the worse; *berufliche*: backward step

verschleiern I. *v/t.* veil; *fig.* (*Absicht etc.*) *auch* disguise; (*Skandal etc.*) cover up; **II.** *v/refl.* *Frau*: put a veil on; *Himmel*: become hazy; **verschleiert I.** *P.P.* → **verschleiern**; **II.** *Adj.* **1.** veiled (*auch fig. Blick*); *Himmel, Berge etc.*: hazy; **2.** *Stimme*: husky; **3.** *Fot.* fogged; **III.** *Adv.*: *etw. ~ sehen* see s.th. hazily; **Verschleierung** *f* veiling; *fig. auch* disguising

Verschleierungs|taktik *f* camouflage tactics *Pl.*; *~versuch m* attempted cover-up

verschleifen (*unreg.*) **I.** *v/t.* (*hat verschliffen*) **1.** *Tech.* smooth (down *od.* away); **2.** *fig.* (*Laute etc., Mus., Töne*) slur; **II.** *v/i.* (*ist*) *Wort, Silbe*: be slurred; **III.** *v/refl.* (*hat*); *Gegensätze etc.*: be smoothed (down), *stärker*: disappear

verschleimt *Adj.*: *~ sein* be blocked with phlegm; *Person*: have a lot of phlegm; **Verschleimung** *f* mucous catarrh

Verschleiß *m*; *-es, -e, mst Sg.*; (*Abnutzung*) wear and tear; (*Verbrauch*) consumption (*an* +*Dat.* of), consumption rate; *geplanter ~* *Wirts.* built-in (*od.* planned) obsolescence; *ganz normaler ~* general wear and tear; *e-n großen ~ haben an* (+ *Dat.*) *auch fig.* an Männern *etc.*: get through a lot of

...verschleiß *m*, *im Subst.*: *Kräfte~* drain on one's strength; *Material~* consumption of materials

verschleißen; *verschliss, verschlissen* **I.** *v/t.* (*hat verschlissen*) (*abnutzen*) wear out; (*verbrauchen*) use up, go through; **II.** *v/refl.* (*hat*); *Sache*: wear out; *Person*: wear (*dauerhaft*: burn) o.s. out; **III.** *v/i.* (*ist*) wear out

Verschleißerscheinung *f* sign of wear

verschleißfest *Adj.* wear-resistant; **Verschleißfestigkeit** *f* wear-resistance, resistance to wear and tear

verschleißfrei *Adj. präd.* free from wear

Verschleiß|prüfung *f* abrasion test; *~quote f* replacement rate; *~teil n* wearing part

verschleppen *v/t.* **1.** (*Menschen*) deport; (*entführen*) kidnap, abduct; (*Sache*) carry off; **2.** (*in die Länge ziehen*) protract, delay; *Parl.* (*Vorlage etc.*) ob-

struct, stonewall, *bes. Am.* filibuster; **3.** *Med.* (*Erreger*) transmit; (*Krankheit*) protract; **Verschleppung** *f* deportment; kidnap(p)ing; protraction, delay; → **verschleppen**

Verschleppungstaktik *f* delaying tactics *Pl.*; *Pol.* obstructionism, stonewalling, *bes. Am.* filibustering

verschleudern *v/t.* (*Vermögen etc.*) squander; (*Ware*) sell off cheaply (dirt cheap *umg.*), flog *umg.*; *im Ausland*: dump

verschlicken *v/i.* *Hafenbecken*: silt up

verschließbar *Adj.* lockable; **verschließen** (*unreg.*) **I.** *v/t.* shut, close; *mit e-m Schlüssel*: lock (up); (*einschließen*) *auch* put under lock and key; *mit e-m Riegel*: bolt; *die Augen/Ohren vor etw. ~* *fig.* shut one's eyes/ears to s.th.; *sein Herz ~* shut (*od.* harden) one's heart (*vor* + *Dat.* to); **II.** *v/refl.*: *sich e-r Sache ~* close one's mind to s.th.; *sich j-m ~* (*s-e Gefühle verbergen*) hide one's feelings from s.o.; (*keinen Kontakt wünschen*) shut o.s. off from s.o.; *das Land verschließt sich Neuerungen/Fremden* the country rejects reform / closes itself off to foreigners; *ich kann mich dieser Überlegung nicht ~* I can't ignore this thought

verschlimmbessern *v/t.* disimprove, make an even worse job of; **Verschlimmbesserung** *f* disimprovement

verschlimmern I. *v/t.* make *s.th.* worse; (*Lage*) *auch* aggravate, exacerbate; **II.** *v/refl.* get worse, worsen; **Verschlimmerung** *f* deterioration; worsening; change for the worse; *von Schmerzen etc.*: worsening, increase

verschlingen (*unreg.*) **I.** *v/t.* **1.** devour (*auch fig. mit den Augen, auch ein Buch*); *gierig*: gobble (up), bolt (*Am. auch* scarf) down; *fig.* (*Geld*) swallow (up), gobble up; *von der Dunkelheit etc. verschlungen werden* *fig.* be engulfed by darkness *etc.*; **2.** (*ineinander ~*) intertwine; (*Hände*) fold; **II.** *v/refl.* intertwine; (*sich verfangen*) become entangled; → **verschlungen**; **Verschlingung** *f* entanglement; *auch dekorativ*: convolution

verschlissen I. *P.P.* → **verschleißen**; **II.** *Adj.* worn, threadbare; *Kleidung*: ragged, tatty *umg.*

verschlossen I. *P.P.* → **verschließen**; **II.** *Adj.* **1.** closed, shut; locked (up); *hinter ~en Türen* behind closed doors; *vor ~er Tür stehen* be left standing on the doorstep; *diese Kreise/Möglichkeiten etc. bleiben ihnen ~* these circles/possibilities *etc.* remain closed to them; **2.** *fig. Person*: reserved, withdrawn; (*wortkarg*) uncommunicative; *Kind*: withdrawn; *er ist ziemlich ~* *auch* he doesn't say much; **Verschlossenheit** *f*; *nur Sg.* reserve; uncommunicativeness

verschlucken I. *v/t.* swallow (*auch fig. Silben etc.*); *fig. Nebel etc.*: engulf; *schon hatte ihn die Dunkelheit verschluckt* the darkness had already swallowed him up; → **Erdboden**; **II.** *v/refl.* choke (*an* + *Dat.* on); *ich habe mich verschluckt* I swallowed the wrong way

verschlungen I. *P.P.* → **verschlingen**; **II.** *Adj.* *Pfad*: winding; *stärker*: tortuous (*auch fig.*); *Ornamente*: intricate; *bes. pej.* convoluted; (*eng*) *miteinander ~ sein Interessen etc.*: be closely intertwined

Verschluss *m*; *-es, Verschlüsse* **1.** (*Stöpsel*) stopper; (*Schraubverschluss*) top; (*Kronenkorken*) crown cap; *an Buchdeckel, Schmuck, Tasche etc.*: clasp; *mit Schloss*: lock; (*Haken*) fastener; *luftdichter etc.*: seal; *unter ~ halten* keep under lock and key; *Zoll*: keep in bond; **2.** *Fot.* shutter; **3.** *Med.* occlusion; *Tech.* cover, cap

...verschluss *m*, *im Subst.*: *Knebel~* toggle; *Magnet~* magnetic lock; *Ventil~* valve cap

verschlüsseln *v/t.* encode, encrypt; **verschlüsselt I.** *P.P.* → **verschlüsseln**; **II.** *Adj.* coded; *fig.* (*indirekt gesagt*) indirect; **III.** *Adv.* *senden etc.*: in code; *fig.* (*indirekt*) indirectly; **Verschlüsselung** *f* encoding, coding, encryption

Verschluss|kappe *f* (screw) cap; *~laut m* *Ling.* plosive; *~sache f* *Pol.* classified document; *~zeit f* *Fot.* shutter speed

verschmachten *v/i.* languish, pine away; *vor Durst*: be dying of thirst

verschmähen *v/t.* disdain, spurn; *verschmähte Liebe* unrequited love

verschmälern *v/t.* *und v/refl.*: (*sich*) *~* narrow; **Verschmälerung** *f* narrowing

verschmelzen (*unreg.*) **I.** *v/t.* (*hat verschmolzen*) **1.** *Metall.* fuse; *Chem.* amalgamate; **2.** (*Farben*) blend; **3.** *Wirts., Pol.* merge (*zu* into); *fig.* fuse, amalgamate; **II.** *v/i.* (*ist*) melt together; **1.** *Metall.* fuse; *Chem.* amalgamate; **2.** (*Farben*) blend; **3.** *Wirts., Pol.* merge; *fig.* fuse, amalgamate; *~ zu* fuse into; **Verschmelzung** *f* fusion; amalgamation; blend(ing); *Wirts., konkret*: merger, merging; → **verschmelzen**

verschmerzen *v/t.* (*Verlust etc.*) get over *s.th.*; (*Summe*) cope with *s.th.*

verschmieren *v/t.* **1.** *Tech.* (*Fuge, Loch etc.*) fill in; **2.** (*Fenster, Lippenstift etc.*) smear; (*Wände etc. mit Graffiti*) scrawl over; (*Dreck*) spread; (*Papier*) smear up; *verschmiert mit* *auch* covered (*od.* smeared) in (*od.* with); **3.** *Salbe auf der Haut ~* apply ointment to one's skin; **4.** (*verbrauchen*) use up

verschmitzt I. *Adj.* arch, impish; *~es Augenzwinkern* twinkle in s.o.'s eye; **II.** *Adv.* *lächeln etc.*: impishly; **Verschmitztheit** *f*; *nur Sg.* impishness

verschmoren *v/i.* *Braten, Sicherung*: burn

verschmust *Adj.* *umg.* cuddly; *~ sein mst* like cuddling, be cuddly

verschmutzen I. *v/t.* (*hat verschmutzt*) dirty; (*Umwelt, Wasser etc.*) pollute; *Hund*: (*Bürgersteig etc.*) foul; **II.** *v/i.* (*ist*) get dirty; *Wasser etc.*: become polluted; *Tech., Teile etc.*: become dirty; **verschmutzt I.** *P.P.* → **verschmutzen**; **II.** *Adj.* dirty; *Luft, Wasser etc.*: polluted; *Tech., Teile etc.*: dirty; *stark/leicht ~* *Wäsche*: heavily-soiled/lightly-soiled; *Geschirr*: very/slightly dirty; *~e Fahrbahn* muddy road; **Verschmutzung** *f* **1.** soiling; *konkret*: dirt; (*Dreck*) mark; *die ~ der Bürgersteige etc. durch Hundekot* the fouling of pavements (*Am.* sidewalks) *etc.* by dogs; **2.** (*der Umwelt, Luft etc.*) pollution; **Verschmutzungsgrad** *m* *Umwelt*: pollution level; *von Wäsche*: degree of soiling; *das kommt auf den ~ des Geschirrs an* it depends on how dirty the plates and dishes are

verschnarcht *Adj.* *umg.* boring

verschnaufen *v/i.* *und v/refl.* *umg.* get

one's breath back, have (*od.* take) a breather; **Verschnaufpause** *f umg.*: **e-e ~ machen** have (*od.* take) a breather

verschneiden *v/t.* (*unreg.*) **1.** (*beschneiden*) cut, trim, clip; **2.** (*falsch schneiden*) cut wrong, make a mess of *umg.*; **3.** *Zool.* (*kastrieren*) castrate, geld; **4.** (*mischen*) blend; **Text und Bilder zu Collagen ~** combine text and pictures to make collages

verschneit *Adj.* (*schneebedeckt*) *attr.* snow-covered …, *präd. und nachgestellt:* covered in snow; *Landschaft: auch* snowy (*auch Tag*); (*eingeschneit*) snowed-in; **tief ~** deep in snow

Verschnitt *m*; **-(e)s, -e 1.** (*das Verschneiden von Schnaps etc.*) blending; (*Gemisch*) blend; **2.** (*Reste*) scraps *Pl.*

…verschnitt *m*, *im Subst.* **1.** (*Mischung*) **Weinbrand~** blended brandy; **2.** *umg. fig. pej.* (*Kopie*): **James--Bond-Verschnitt** second-rate James Bond

verschnörkelt *Adj.* **1.** (*verziert*) ornate (*Fassade, Relief etc.*); **2.** *Text, Stil:* involuted; **3.** *Unterschrift:* fancy; *Schrift:* ornate

verschnupft I. *Adj.* **1.** *Nase:* blocked; **~ sein** *Person:* have a cold; *leicht:* have the sniffles *umg.*; **2.** *umg. fig.* (*beleidigt*) miffed, *präd. auch* in a huff (*Am. auch* snit); **II.** *Adv. umg. fig.*: (*leicht*) **~ reagieren** react (slightly) peevishly; **Verschnupfung** *f* **1.** cold; **2.** *umg. fig.* peevishness

verschnüren *v/t.* tie up

verschollen *Adj.* missing; (*vergessen*) (long-)forgotten; **ein ~ geglaubter Verwandter** a long-lost relative; **das Werk galt lange als ~** the work was long considered to be lost; **Verschollene** *m, f; -n, -n* missing person

verschonen *v/t.* spare (**j-n mit etw.** s.o. s.th.); **verschont bleiben von etw.** be spared s.th.; **von e-m Sturm** *etc.* **verschont werden** be spared by a storm *etc.*; **verschone mich mit …!** spare me your …!; **verschone mich!** spare me!; (*ich will es nicht hören*) *auch* I don't want to know (*od.* hear) about it

verschönen *v/t.* enhance; **sich den Abend** *etc.* **mit e-m Glas Wein** *etc.* **~** brighten up one's evening *etc.* with a glass of wine *etc.*

verschönern I. *v/t.* **1.** make *s.th.* look nicer, improve the appearance of; (*verzieren*) embellish; **II.** *v/refl.* **1.** (*schöner werden*) improve in appearance; *stärker:* grow more beautiful; **2.** (*sich schöner machen*) *bes. iro.* prettify o.s.; **Verschönerung** *f* improvement (+ *Gen.* in the appearance of); (*Verzierung*) embellishment

Verschonung *f* sparing (+ *Gen.* of)

verschorfen *v/i. Med.* scab, form a scab

verschossen I. *P.P. →* **verschießen**; **II.** *Adj.* **1.** *Farbe:* faded; **2.** *umg. fig.*: **in j-n ~ sein** be head over heels in love with s.o., have fallen for s.o., have a crush on s.o.; **3.** *Sport:* **~er Elfmeter** *etc.* missed penalty *etc.*

verschrammen I. *v/t.* (*hat verschrammt*); (*Karosserie etc.*) scratch; (*Knie, Ellbogen etc.*) scrape; **II.** *v/i.* (*ist*) *Material:* scratch, get scratched

verschränken *v/t.* **1. die Arme/Hände ~** fold one's arms/hands; **die Beine ~** cross one's legs; **2.** *Tech.* cross, join crosswise; (*Sägezähne etc.*) set

verschrauben *v/t.* screw (on; **miteinander** together); **Verschraubung** *f kon-

kret:* screws *Pl.*

verschrecken *v/t.* scare, frighten; **verschreckt I.** *P.P. →* **verschrecken**; **II.** *Adj.* timid; *stärker:* frightened; **ein völlig ~es Kind** an extremely frightened child

verschreiben (*unreg.*) **I.** *v/t.* **1.** *Med.* prescribe (+ *Dat.* for); **sich** (*Dat.*) **etw. ~ lassen** get a prescription for s.th.; **2.** *Jur.* (*vermachen*) make over (+ *Dat.* to); **3.** (*Papier etc.*) use up; **II.** *v/refl.* **1.** make a mistake (in writing); **da habe ich mich wohl verschrieben** that must have been a slip of the pen; **2.** *fig.*: **sich e-r Sache ~** devote (*pej. sell*) o.s. to s.th., espouse s.th.; **sich j-m ~** become a devotee of s.o.; **Verschreibung** *f* **1.** *Med.* prescription; **2.** *Jur.* making over, *bes. Am.* conveyance; **Verschreibungspflicht** *f Med.*: **für dieses Mittel besteht ~ / keine ~** this medicine is available only on prescription / is available over the counter, this is an over-the-counter medicine; **verschreibungspflichtig** *Adj.* prescribable, available on prescription only; **~e Arzneimittel** prescription (--only) drugs

verschreien *v/t.* (*unreg.*) **1.** *umg.*: **verschrei's nicht!** don't speak too soon, don't put the kiss of death on it; **2.** (*öffentlich schlecht machen*) denounce, slam *umg.*, trash *umg.*; **verschrien I.** *P.P. →* **verschreien**; **II.** *Adj.* notorious; **~ sein** *auch* have a bad name *od.* reputation (**als** as), **als Lügner ~ sein** *auch* be a notorious liar, be known as a liar (*od.* for lying); **die Gegend ist ~** it is a notorious area

verschroben *Adj. mst pej.* eccentric, (a bit) cranky *umg.*; *Ideen: auch* weird; **~er Mensch** crank *umg.*; **Verschrobenheit** *f* eccentricity

verschrotten *v/t.* scrap; **sein Auto ~ lassen** send one's car for scrap; **Verschrottung** *f* scrapping (+ *Gen.* of); **vor der ~ bewahren** save from being scrapped (*od.* sent for scrap)

verschrumpeln *v/i. umg.* shrivel (up)

verschüchtert *Adj.* shy, intimidated

verschulden I. *v/t.* (*die Schuld haben*) be to blame for; be responsible for; **er hat den Unfall selbst verschuldet** he caused the accident himself; **II.** *v/refl.* (*Schulden machen*) get (*od.* run) into debt; **sich für etw. hoch ~** get seriously into debt for the sake of s.th.

Verschulden *n*; **-s, kein** *Pl.* fault; (*Schuld*) guilt; **durch j-s / eigenes ~** through s.o.'s / one's own fault; **ohne eigenes ~** through no fault of one's own; **ohne mein ~** through no fault of mine

verschuldet I. *P.P. →* **verschulden**; **II.** *Adj.* in debt; *Sache:* encumbered; **~ sein** *Person: auch* have debts; **die Firma ist hoch ~** the company is seriously in debt (*od.* has large debts); **Verschuldung** *f* indebtedness; (*Schulden*) debts *Pl.*; *e-r Immobilie etc.*: encumbrance

verschusseln *v/t. umg.* (*vergessen*) (clean) forget; (*verlegen*) (go and) mislay; (*verpatzen, durcheinander bringen*) mess up

verschütt *Adv.*: **~ gehen** *umg.* disappear; (*abhanden kommen*) get lost; (*umkommen*) buy it; *Sl.* (*ins Gefängnis kommen*) get banged up

verschütten *v/t.* **1.** (*Getränk*) spill; **2.** (*begraben*) bury (*Person:* alive); (*zuschütten*) fill in; **verschüttet I.** *P.P. → **verschütten**; **II.** *Adj.* **1.** (*begraben*)

buried; *Person: präd.* buried alive; *Brunnen etc.*: filled in; **2.** *fig. Kenntnisse etc.*: buried, submerged; **Verschüttete** *m, f; -n, -n* person who has been buried; **ein ~r** one of those buried

verschwägert *Adj.* related by marriage; **weder verwandt noch ~ sein** not be related by blood or by marriage

verschweigen *v/t.* keep *s.th.* (a) secret, hide *s.th.* (+ *Dat.* from); (*Tatsachen, Wahrheit*) *auch* withhold *s.th.* (from); **warum hast du mir das verschwiegen?** *auch* why didn't you tell me about this?; **ich habe nichts zu ~** I have nothing to hide

verschweißen *v/t. Tech.* weld together

verschwenden *v/t.* waste (*auch Zeit, Energie etc.*), squander (**an** + *Akk.* on) (*beide auch fig.*); **keinen Blick an j-n ~** not waste a single glance on s.o.; **Verschwender** *m*; **-s, -**, **Verschwenderin** *f*, **-, -nen** spendthrift, squanderer; **verschwenderisch I.** *Adj.* wasteful, extravagant; *pej. auch* profligate; (*üppig*) lavish; **ein ~es Leben führen** have an extravagant lifestyle; **II.** *Adv.*: **~ mit etw. umgehen** be lavish with s.th.; **Verschwendung** *f* waste (*auch von Zeit, Energie etc.*); (*Luxus*) extravagance; **Verschwendungssucht** *f; nur Sg.* wastefulness, extravagance; **verschwendungssüchtig** *Adj.* wasteful, extravagant

verschwiegen I. *P.P. →* **verschweigen**; **II.** *Adj.* **1.** *Person:* discreet; **2.** *fig. Ort:* secret; (*abgeschieden*) secluded; **~es Plätzchen** secluded spot; **Verschwiegenheit** *f* **1.** *e-r Person:* discretion; **strengste ~ bewahren** maintain absolute secrecy; **zur ~ verpflichten** bind to secrecy; **unter dem Mantel der ~ liegen** be under wraps; → **Siegel**; **2.** *e-s Ortes:* seclusion

verschwimmen *v/i.* (*unreg.*) become blurred; *ineinander:* merge; **vor den Augen ~** start blurring before one's eyes; → **verschwommen**

verschwinden *v/i.* (*unreg.*) **1.** disappear, vanish (**in** + *Dat.* into); **mein Koffer** *etc.* **ist verschwunden** *auch* my case *etc.* has (*od.* is) gone; **spurlos ~ lassen** spirit s.o./s.th. away; **etw. ~ lassen** *umg.* (*stehlen*) walk off with s.th.; **ich muss mal ~** *umg. fig.* I must just pay a visit (*od.* spend a penny), *Am.* I have to powder my nose; **~ neben** *fig.* pale into insignificance beside, be dwarfed by; **2.** *umg.* (*abhauen*) make o.s. scarce; (*türmen*) do a bunk; **verschwinde!** hop it!, scram!; **hoffentlich seid ihr bald verschwunden!** you'd better make yourselves scarce!

Verschwinden *n*; **-s, kein** *Pl.* disappearance; **verschwindend I.** *Part. Präs. →* **verschwinden**; **II.** *Adj. Minderheit etc.*: tiny; **III.** *Adv.*: **~ klein** microscopic, minuscule; **~ gering** infinitesimal

verschwistert *Adj.* **1. ~ sein** be brother and sister; be sisters; be brothers; **2.** *fig.*: (**eng**) **~** (closely) related (*bes. Wirts.* associated)

verschwitzen *v/t.* **1.** (*Kleidung*) get *s.th.* soaked with sweat; **2.** *umg.*: **ich habe es** (**total**) **verschwitzt** I clean forgot (it); **verschwitzt I.** *P.P. →* **verschwitzen**; **II.** *Adj.* sweaty; *Person: auch* covered in sweat; **völlig ~** *auch* soaked through (*od.* in sweat); **III.** *Adv.*: **er kam völlig ~ nach Hause** *etc.* he came home *etc.* completely bathed in sweat

verschwollen *Adj.* swollen; *Gesicht*: *auch* bloated

verschwommen I. *P.P.* → **verschwimmen**; **II.** *Adj.* **1.** hazy; *Umrisse etc.*, *auch Fot.*: blurred; **2.** *fig. Begriff etc.*: vague, nebulous, woolly; *Erinnerung*: dim, hazy; **~e Vorstellung** hazy (*od.* fuzzy) notion; **III.** *Adv.*: **sich ~ erinnern können an** have a dim (*od.* hazy) recollection of; **Verschwommenheit** *f* haziness; vagueness *etc.*; → **verschwommen**

verschwören I. *P.P.* → **verschwören**; **II.** *Adj.* sworn; **e-r Sache ~ sein** be dedicated to something

verschwören *v/refl.* (*unreg.*) **1.** conspire (*auch fig.*), plot (**gegen** against; *zu* + *Inf.* to + *Inf.*); **sich zu etw. ~** conspire to do s.th., plot (to do) s.th.; **2.** *altm. lit.*: **sich j-m/etw. ~** give o.s. over to s.o./s.th.; **Verschworene** *m*, *f*; *-n*, *-n* **1. e-r Sache**: devotee; **2.** (*Verschwörer*) conspirator; **Verschwörer** *m*; *-s*, *-*, **Verschwörerin** *f*; *-*, *-nen* conspirator; **verschwörerisch** *Adj. Miene, Blicke*: conspiratorial; **Verschwörermiene** *f* look of complicity, conspiratorial air; **Verschwörung** *f* conspiracy, plot; **Verschwörungstheorie** *f* conspiracy theory

Vers|dichtung *f Lit.* verse poetry; **~drama** *n* verse drama

versehen (*unreg.*) **I.** *v/t.* **1.** (*Pflichten*) perform; (*Geschäfte, Haushalt*) look after; **ein Amt / e-e Stelle ~** hold office / occupy a position; **2. ~ mit** supply with; *auch Tech.* provide with; (*schmücken*) decorate with; **etw. mit etw. ~** *auch* add s.th. to s.th.; **mit Vollmacht ~** authorize; **j-n mit den Sterbesakramenten ~** administer the last rights to s.o.; **mit etw. ~ sein** be provided with s.th.; **reichlich mit Nahrung etc. ~ sein** have plenty of food *etc.*, have ample food *etc.*; **II.** *v/refl.* **1.** make a mistake, slip up; **2. ehe man sich's versieht** before you know it; **3. sich ~ mit** (*ausstatten*) equip o.s. with; (*eindecken*) get in a supply (*od.* supplies) of; (*sich verschaffen*) get (hold of)

Versehen *n*; *-s*, *-* oversight, mistake; **aus ~** by mistake, inadvertently, mistakenly; **das war nur ein ~ von mir** it was just a slip on my part

versehentlich I. *Adj. nur attr.* inadvertent; **II.** *Adv.* by mistake, inadvertently, mistakenly

versehrt *Adj.* disabled, handicapped, *bes. Am.* physically challenged; **Versehrte** *m*, *f*; *-n*, *-n* disabled (*od.* handicapped, *bes. Am.* physically challenged) person; *Pl. Koll.* the handicapped (*bes. Am.* physically challenged); **Versehrtensport** *m* sport for the disabled (*bes. Am.* physically challenged)

verseifen *v/t. Chem.* saponify

verselb(st)ständigen *v/refl. Person*: go independent; *Sache*: break free; **sich zu e-m eigenen Fach etc. ~** become a subject *etc.* in its own right; **Verselb(st)ständigung** *f* (*Vorgang*) process of independence; (*Ergebnis*) independence

versenden *v/t.* (*unreg.*) send, dispatch; *Wirts. auch* ship; **Versender** *m*; *-s*, *-*, **Versenderin** *f*; *-*, *-nen* sender; **Versendung** *f* dispatch; *Wirts. auch* shipment

versengen *v/t.* scorch; (*Haar*) singe; **sich** (*Dat.*) **die Haare ~** singe one's hair

versenkbar *Adj. auch Bühne*: lower-

able; *Teil*: collapsible; *attr. auch* fold-down ...; *Antenne etc.*: retractable

versenken I. *v/t.* **1.** (*Schiff etc., auch Schatz etc.*) sink; **2.** *in die Erde*: lower (*in* +*Akk.* into); **3.** *Tech. etc.* (*auch Bühne*) lower; (*Teil*) *auch* fold down; (*Antenne etc.*) retract; (*Schraube*) countersink; **II.** *v/refl.*: **sich ~ in** (+ *Akk.*) immerse o.s. in; *in ein Buch etc.*: become engrossed in; **Versenkung** *f* **1.** sinking; **2.** *Theat.* trapdoor; **3.** *umg. fig.*: (**spurlos**) **in der ~ verschwinden** disappear (from the face of the earth); *Person*: disappear (*od.* fade) from the scene; (**wieder**) **aus der ~ auftauchen** resurface, reappear; *Person*: *auch* reappear (*od.* re-emerge) on the scene; **4.** *geistige etc.*: (inward) contemplation

Versepos *n Lit.* epic poem

versessen *Adj.*: **~ auf** (+ *Akk.*) mad (*Am. auch* wild) about, madly keen on; **darauf ~ sein, etw. zu tun** be desperate to do s.th.; **Versessenheit** *f* craze (**auf** + *Akk.* for); (*Süßigkeiten etc.*) *auch* craving (for)

versetzen I. *v/t.* **1.** shift; (*auch Schüler*) move; (*Schüler in die nächste Klasse*) move *s.o.* up (into the next class), *Am.* promote; → **Versetzung** **2.** *beruflich*: transfer, *Mil.* post; **3.** (*versetzt anordnen*) stagger; (*Baum*) transplant; **4.** (*verpfänden*) pawn; **5.** *umg.* (*j-n*) *bei Verabredung*: stand *s.o.* up, *Am. auch* blow *s.o.* off; **sie hat mich schon zum zweiten Mal versetzt** she stood me up for the second time; **6.** (*vermischen*) mix; **7. j-m e-n Schlag ~** deal s.o. a blow, hit out at s.o.; **j-m e-n Tritt ~** give s.o. a kick; **8.** (*scharf antworten*) retort; **9. ~ in** (+ *Akk.*) *in e-e Lage, e-n Zustand*: put into; **j-n in Erstaunen/Verwirrung etc. ~** astonish/confuse *etc.* s.o.; **j-n in e-e andere Zeit ~** take (*od.* transport) s.o. back in time (*od.* back to another era); **j-n an e-n anderen Ort ~** (*in der Vorstellung*) transport s.o. (*od.* carry s.o. off) to a different place; → **Angst**, **eins** III 2, **Ruhestand**, **Schwingung** *etc.*; **II.** *v/refl.*: **sich** (*geistig*) **nach X ~** imagine one is in X; **sich in j-n od. j-s Lage ~** put o.s. in s.o.'s place (*od.* position, shoes); **versuch doch mal, dich in ihre Lage zu ~** *auch* try and see it from her point of view (*od.* side)

versetzt I. *P.P.* → **versetzen**; **II.** *Adj.* EDV staggered; **III.** *Adv.*: **~ angeordnet sein** be staggered

Versetzung *f* shifting; transfer, posting *etc.*; → **versetzen**; **die ~ Ihres Sohnes ist gefährdet** *Schule*: your son is in danger of not being allowed to move up into the next class (*Am.* in danger of failing [*od.* flunking *umg.*])

Versetzungszeichen *n Mus.* accidental

verseuchen *v/t.* **1.** *mit Giftstoffen etc.*, *bes. ökologisch*: contaminate; **2.** *bakteriell, epidemisch etc.*: infect; *EDV* contaminate, corrupt, infect; **verseucht I.** *P.P.* → **verseuchen**; **II.** *Adj.* **1.** contaminated; **radioaktiv ~e Milch** *etc.* milk *etc.* contaminated by radiation; **2.** infected; *EDV* contaminated, corrupted, infected; **Verseuchung** *f* **1.** contamination; **2.** infection; *EDV* contamination, corrupting, infection

Vers|form *f Lit.* verse form; **in ~ schreiben** write in verse (form); **~fuß** *m* (metrical) foot

versicherbar *Adj.* insurable; **Versicherer** *m*; *-s*, *-*, **Versicherin** *f*; *-*, *-nen* in-

surer; *bei Schiffen*: underwriter; **versichern I.** *v/t.* **1.** (*Eigentum*) insure (**gegen** against; **bei** with); **2. j-m etw. ~** assure s.o. (of) s.th.; **j-m ~, dass** assure s.o. (that); **etw. hoch und heilig ~** swear blind (*Am.* swear on a stack of bibles) to s.th.; **ich versichere hiermit, dass ...** *in Erklärungen etc.*: I hereby attest that ...; **seien Sie versichert, dass** you may rest assured that, I can assure you that; **seien Sie dessen versichert** you can depend on it; **II.** *v/refl.* **1.** (*e-e Versicherung abschließen*) insure o.s (**gegen** against); **sich gegen Diebstahl etc. ~** take out theft insurance; **2. sich e-r Sache** (*Gen.*) **~** make sure (*od.* certain) of; **versichert I.** *P.P.* → **versichern**; **II.** *Adj. Eigentum etc.*: insured, covered by insurance; **zu hoch/niedrig ~** overinsured/underinsured

Versicherte *m*, *f*; *-n*, *-n* insured (party), policy holder; *bei Krankenkasse*: (health insurance) policy holder; **Versichertenkarte** *f* *e-r Krankenkasse*: health insurance card

Versicherung *f* **1.** *von*, *gegen etw.*: insurance (**über** + *Akk.* for, on); **e-e ~ abschließen** take out insurance (*od.* an insurance policy) (**bei** with); **2.** *Gesellschaft*: insurance company, insurer; **3.** (*Erklärung*) assurance, guarantee; **e-e ~ abgeben** give an assurance (*od.* guarantee); **eidesstattliche ~ od. ~ an Eides statt** sworn statement

Versicherungs|agent *m*, **~agentin** *f* insurance agent; **~agentur** *f* insurance agency; **~angestellte** *m*, *f* insurance clerk; **~anspruch** *m* insurance claim; **~anstalt** *f* insurance company; **~beitrag** *m* (insurance) premium; **~betrug** *m* insurance fraud; **~dauer** *f* period of insurance, policy period; **~fall** *m* insured event; **im ~, bei Eintritt des ~s** should the event insured against occur

versicherungsfremd *Adj. Leistungen etc.*: *nachgestellt*: unrelated to insurance

Versicherungs|gesellschaft *f* insurance company, insurer; **~karte** *f* insurance card; **grüne ~** *Mot.* green card (*required for taking a vehicle abroad*); **~kaufmann** *m*, **~kauffrau** *f* insurance broker; **~leistung** *f* insurance benefit; **~nachweisheft** *n* book belonging to employee in which employer records social insurance contributions; **~nehmer** *m*; *-s*, *-*, **~nehmerin** *f*; *-*, *-nen* insured (party), policy holder; **~nummer** *f* etwa National Insurance (*Am.* Social Security) number; *von Versicherungspolice*: policy number

Versicherungspflicht *f* compulsory insurance; **versicherungspflichtig** *Adj. Sache*: subject to compulsory insurance; *Person*: liable to insurance

Versicherungs|police *f* (insurance) policy; **~prämie** *f* (insurance) premium

versicherungsrechtlich I. *Adj.* ... in accordance with insurance law; **II.** *Adv.* in accordance with insurance law

Versicherungs|risiko *n* insured risk; **~schein** *m* insurance policy; **~schutz** *m* insurance cover(age); **~schwindel** *m* insurance fraud; **~steuer** *f* insurance tax; **~summe** *f* sum insured; **~träger** *m*, **~trägerin** *f* insurer; *bei Schiffen*: underwriter; **~verein** *m*: **~ auf Gegenseitigkeit** *Wirts.* mutual insurance company; **~vertrag** *m* contract of insurance; **~vertreter** *m*, **~ver-**

treterin *f* insurance agent; **~wert** *m* insurable value; **~wesen** *n* insurance (business); **~zeiten** *Pl.* terms of insurance

versickern *v/i.* 1. seep (away) (*im Sand* into the sand); 2. *fig.* fizzle out

versieben *v/t. umg.* 1. (*vergessen*) (clean) forget; *ich hab's versiebt* auch it slipped my mind completely; 2. (*verpfuschen*) botch (up); *Sport* (*Strafstoß etc.*) waste

versiegeln *v/t.* 1. *auch Tech.* seal; 2. *Öko.* (*Erdreich, Boden*) seal off; **Versiegelung** *f* 1. (*das Versiegeln*) sealing; *von Boden:* sealing off; 2. (*versiegelnde Schicht*) seal

versiegen *v/i.* dry up (*auch fig. Gelder, Gespräch*); *fig. Kräfte:* ebb, dwindle

versiert *Adj.* experienced; *fachmännisch:* skilled; *auf e-m bestimmten Gebiet:* well-versed; **Versiertheit** *f, nur Sg.* experience; skill

versifft *Adj. Sl.* filthy

versilbern *v/t.* 1. *Tech.* silver-plate; 2. *umg. fig.* (*zu Geld machen*) turn into cash; **Versilberung** *f* silver-plate, silver-plating

versinken *v/i.* (*unreg.*) sink (*auch fig.*) (*in + Dat.* into); **~ in Erinnerungen:** lose o.s. in; *auch Gedanken etc.:* become immersed (*od.* absorbed) in; → *Boden* 1, *versunken*

versinnbildlichen *v/t.* symbolize, represent; **Versinnbildlichung** *f* symbol

Version *f; -, -en* version; *berichtigte ~ EDV* upgraded version

versippt *Adj.* (inter)related, related to one another (*od.* each other)

versklaven *v/t.* enslave; **Versklavung** *f* enslavement

verslumen [fɛɐ̯'slaːmən] *v/i.* turn into a slum (*od.* slums); **Verslumung** [fɛɐ̯-'slaːmʊŋ] *f* urban decay

Versmaß *n Lit.* metre, *Am.* meter

versnobt *Adj. pej.* snobbish, snobby *umg.*

versoffen *Adj. umg. Stimme etc.:* boozy; **~er Typ** dipso; **total ~ sein** be a complete dipso

versohlen *v/t. umg. fig.* (*auch j-m den Hintern ~*) give *s.o.* a good thrashing

versöhnen I. *v/refl.* be reconciled; *mit j-m: auch* make (it) up (*mit* with); *jetzt versöhnt euch mal wieder!* now just make (it) up with one another; II. *v/t.* reconcile (*mit j-m:* with *od.* s-m *Schicksal etc.:* to); *s-r Frau Blumen mitbringen, um sie zu ~* bring one's wife flowers in order to appease her; *der schöne Urlaub hat mich mit der strapaziösen Reise versöhnt* the lovely holiday (*Am.* vacation) made up for the exhausting journey (*Am.* trip); **versöhnlich** *Adj.* conciliatory; **~ stimmen** placate; **Versöhnlichkeit** *f, nur Sg.* conciliatoriness; **Versöhnung** *f* reconciliation; *zu j-s ~* in order to appease s.o.

Versöhnungs|angebot *n* offer of conciliation; **~versuch** *m auch Jur., zwischen Eheleuten:* attempt at reconciliation

versonnen I. *Adj.* pensive; *vorübergehend: auch* lost in thought; (*träumerisch*) dreamy; II. *Adv. in die Ferne schauen etc.:* pensively; dreamily; **Versonnenheit** *f; nur Sg.* pensiveness; dreaminess; → *versonnen*

versorgen *v/t.* provide, supply (*mit* with); (*Familie, Kind*) provide for; (*unterhalten*) *auch* support; (*betreuen*) take care of, look after; (*Vieh*) tend; (*Verletzte*) tend, take care of, look af-

---

ter; (*Wunde*) tend, see to; *sich selbst ~* look after oneself; **Versorger** *m; -s, -, *Versorgerin* *f; -, -nen* 1. (*Ernährer[in]*) breadwinner; *bes. iro.* provider; 2. (*Belieferer*) supplier; **versorgt** I. *P.P.* → *versorgen;* II. *Adj.: gut ~ präd.* well looked after; *mit Mitteln:* well provided for

Versorgung *f* (*Versorgen*) providing (+ *Gen.* of), supplying (*s.th., s.o.*); *mit Vorräten:* supply, provision; (*Pflege*) care; → *versorgen; ärztliche ~* medical care; *Probleme mit der ~* supply problems

Versorgungs|amt *n für Sozialleistungen:* maintenance department; *für Pensionäre:* pension office; **~anspruch** *m* claim to maintenance; **~anstalt** *f: ~ des Bundes und der Länder* institution that provides additional benefits for retired workers or workers' dependents at member companies; **~ausgleich** *m* maintenance settlement

versorgungsberechtigt *Adj.* entitled to maintenance; **Versorgungsberechtigte** *m, f; -n, -n* person entitled to maintenance; **Versorgungsberechtigung** *f* right to maintenance

Versorgungs|betrieb *m* (public) utility company; **~bezüge** *Pl.* work-related benefits and pensions other than old-age pension; **~einrichtung** *f* 1. *der Versorgung von Gütern dienend:* facility responsible for supplies; 2. *für Beamte etc.:* pension scheme, *Am.* retirement plan; **~engpass** *m* supply bottleneck (*od.* shortage); **~flugzeug** *n* supply plane; **~gebiet** *n* service area; **~grad** *m* level of utility; **~güter** *Pl.* supplies; **~insel** *f e-r Ölplattform:* accommodation rig; **~krise** *f* supply crisis; **~lage** *f* supply situation; **~leitung** *f Tech.* supply (*od.* utility) pipe; **~lücke** *f* gap in supplies; **~mangel** *m* lack of supplies; **~netz** *n* supply network; **~schiff** *n* supply vessel; **~schwierigkeiten** *Pl.* supply problems, problems in getting supplies through; (*Engpass*) supply bottleneck *Sg.;* **~unternehmen** *n* (*Stromanbieter etc.*) (public) utility; **~weg** *m* supply line (*od.* channel)

versotten *v/i. Kamin:* become blocked (with inflammable materials)

verspachteln *v/t.* 1. (*Löcher etc.*) fill; *die Wand ~* fill in the cracks in the wall, *Am.* spackle (the wall), do the spackling; 2. *umg.* (*aufessen*) scoff, *Am.* scarf (down)

verspannen I. *v/t.* 1. (*Mast, Zelt etc.*) stay, guy; (*Kabel, Tau etc.*) put up; 2. *Med., Psych.* tense (up); II. *v/refl. Med., Psych.* get tensed up, tense up; **verspannt** I. *P.P.* → *verspannen;* II. *Adj. Med., Psych.* tense, tensed up; **Verspannung** *f* 1. *Med.* tenseness, *Psych. auch* tension; *unter ~en leiden* suffer from tension; 2. (*Verspannungsteile*) stays *Pl.,* guys *Pl.*

verspäten *v/refl.* be late; *Flug.* be delayed; *ich habe mich leider etw. verspätet* I am a little bit late; **verspätet** I. *P.P.* → *verspäten;* II. *Adj.* late; (*Gratulation*) belated; *Flug.* delayed; III. *Adv. eintreffen etc.:* late; *Flug.* late, behind schedule; **Verspätung** *f* (*Verzögerung*) delay; (*zwei Minuten*) *~ haben* be (two minutes) late; *mit ~ abfahren/ankommen etc.* leave/arrive etc. late; *mit zwei Stunden ~* two hours late (*Flug. etc. auch* behind schedule); *entschuldigen Sie die*

~ sorry I'm late, I do apologize for being late *förm.*

verspeisen *v/t.* eat, consume

verspekulieren I. *v/t.* 1. lose on the stock market; II. *v/refl.* 1. (*sich irren*) miscalculate; *wenn er meint, er kommt damit durch, hat er sich verspekuliert umg.* if he thinks he can get away with that he's got another think (*Am.* thing) coming; 2. *Wirts.* lose (*sich ruinieren*): all one's money) on the stock market; *sich bei etw. ~* ruin o.s. by speculating in s.th.

versperren I. *v/t.* 1. bar, obstruct; *mit Barrikaden:* barricade; *j-m die Aussicht ~* obstruct s.o.'s view; 2. (*zusperren*) lock up; II. *v/refl. fig.* close one's mind (+ *Dat.* to)

verspiegeln *v/t.* line (*Außenwand:* face) with mirrors; *Tech.* (*Glühbirne etc.*) coat with a reflective substance; **verspiegelt** I. *P.P.* → *verspiegeln;* II. *Adj.* mirrored; *Glühbirne etc.:* mirror-coated, reflective

verspielen I. *v/t.* (*Geld etc., auch fig. Glück etc.*) gamble away; (*beim Glücksspiel verlieren*) gamble away, lose; II. *v/i.* lose; *er hat bei mir verspielt umg.* I'm through with him, I've reached my limit with him; III. *v/refl. Mus.* play wrong, hit a (*od.* the) wrong note; **verspielt** I. *P.P.;* II. *Adj.* playful; *Muster:* cheerful; *Frisur:* pretty; **Verspieltheit** *f; nur Sg.* playfulness

verspießern *v/i. pej.* become gentrified, gentrify

versponnen *Adj.* (*verträumt*) airy-fairy; (*auch in sich ~*) wrapped up in a world of one's own; *Idee:* strange, fanciful; *~ in* (+ *Akk.*) wrapped up in, totally absorbed in; *~ sein auch* have one's head in the clouds

verspotten *v/t.* mock (*wegen* because of, for); (*verhöhnen*) jeer at, scoff at; **Verspottung** *f* mocking, mockery, derision

versprechen (*unreg.*) I. *v/t.* 1. promise; *ich verspreche es* I promise; *du hast es mir versprochen* you promised (to do it); (*Gegenstand*) you promised me it (*od.* to give it to me); *er hat mir versprochen, dass er kommen würde* he promised to come (*od.* that he would come); *j-m etw. in die Hand ~* promise s.o. s.th.; → *Ehe, hoch* II 6; 2. *sich* (*Dat.*) *etw. ~* (*erwarten*) expect s.th., hope for s.th.; *sich* (*Dat.*) *viel ~ von* have great hopes of; *ich verspreche mir wenig/nichts davon* I don't expect much/anything to come of it, I don't think much/anything will come of it; *er verspricht, ein guter Schauspieler zu werden* he promises to be a good actor; II. *v/refl.* make a mistake, get it wrong; *ich habe mich versprochen auch* it was a slip of the tongue; *sich dauernd ~* keep getting one's words muddled; **Versprechen** *n; -s, -* promise; *j-m ein ~ abnehmen* make s.o. promise s.th.; *ein ~ halten/brechen* keep/break a promise; *ein leeres ~* an empty promise; **Versprecher** *m; -s, -; umg.* slip of the tongue; *Theat.* slip; *Freudscher ~* Freudian slip; **Versprechung** *f; mst Pl.* promise; *große ~en machen* make great promises, promise the earth (*Am.* world); *alles (nur) ~en!* promises, promises!

versprengen *v/t.* 1. scatter, disperse; (*verjagen*) chase away; *Jägerspr.* scatter; 2. (*verspritzen*) spray, sprinkle; **versprengt** I. *P.P.* → *versprengen;* II. *Adj. Soldaten, Tiere etc.:* scattered

verspritzen *v/t.* *in e-m Strahl*: squirt; (*versprühen*) spray; *j-m die Scheibe ~* spatter s.o.'s windscreen; *Gift ~ umg.* *fig.* be venomous

versprochenermaßen *Adv.* as promised

versprühen *v/t.* spray; *Funken ~* send up a shower of sparks; *Geist od. Witz ~ fig.* scintillate

verspüren *v/t.* feel; (*erkennen*) *auch* sense; *keine Lust ~, etw. zu tun* not feel like doing s.th.

verstaatlichen *v/t.* nationalize; **Verstaatlichung** *f* nationalization

verstädtern I. *v/i.* (*ist verstädtert*) become urbanized; **II.** *v/t.* (*hat*) urbanize; **Verstädterung** *f* urbanization

Verstand *m*; *-(e)s, kein Pl.*; (*Denkfähigkeit*) intellect, mind; (*Vernunft*) (common) sense; (*Ratio*) (powers *Pl.* of) reason; (*Intelligenz*) intelligence; (*Urteilsfähigkeit*) powers *Pl.* of judg(e)ment; (*Auffassungskraft*) understanding; *gesunder ~* common sense; *mein ~ sagt mir* common sense tells me; *klarer/kühler ~* a clear/cool head; *scharfer ~* keen (*Am.* sharp) mind (*od.* intellect); *mit ~* intelligently, with a bit of common sense; *den ~ verlieren* go mad (*Am.* crazy); *j-n um den ~ bringen* drive s.o. mad (*od.* insane, *bes. Am.* crazy); *wieder zu ~ kommen* come to one's senses; *das geht über m-n ~* that's beyond me; *hat er denn keinen ~?* has he got no sense in him (*od.* wits about him)?; *er ist nicht recht bei ~ umg.* he's not in his right mind, he's not all there; *etw. mit ~ genießen* savo(u)r s.th.

Verstandeskraft *f* mental powers (*od.* faculties) *Pl.*, intelligence

verstandesmäßig *Adj.* rational

Verstandes|mensch *m* rational type (of person), rationalist; *~schärfe f* acumen

verständig I. *Adj.* reasonable, sensible; (*verständnisvoll, einsichtig*) understanding; **II.** *Adv.* *argumentieren etc.*: reasonably, sensibly; **verständigen I.** *v/t.* notify, inform, let *s.o.* know; **II.** *v/refl.* **1.** communicate (with one another); *sich mit j-m ~ sprachlich*: make o.s. understood to s.o., communicate with s.o., get across to s.o.; *wir konnten uns nicht ~ sprachlich*: we couldn't communicate; (*verstehen*) we couldn't get through to each other (*od.* understand what we were saying to each other); **2.** *sich mit j-m ~* (*übereinkommen*) come to (*od.* reach) an agreement with s.o.; *wir konnten uns nicht ~* (*übereinkommen*) we couldn't agree (on anything), we couldn't come to (*od.* reach) an agreement; **Verständigkeit** *f; nur Sg.* reasonableness; **Verständigung** *f* **1.** *auch Telef. etc.* communication; **2.** (*Übereinkunft*) understanding, agreement; *es kam zu e-r ~* an agreement was reached; **3.** (*Benachrichtigung*) notification; **verständigungsbereit** *Adj.* open to discussion

Verständigungs|mittel *n* means of understanding (*od.* communication); *~möglichkeit f* opportunity to communicate; *~problem n* problem of communication; *~schwierigkeiten Pl.* communication problems (*stärker*: breakdown *Sg.*); *~ haben* have difficulty communicating (*od.* getting through to one another); *~versuch m* **1.** attempt at communication (*od.* to communicate); **2.** (*Einigungsversuch*) attempt to reach an agreement

verständlich I. *Adj.* intelligible, understandable; (*deutlich*) clear, distinct; (*hörbar*) audible; (*begreiflich*) understandable (+ *Dat.* to, for); (*verstandesmäßig erfassbar*) comprehensible (to); *es ist mir schwer/nicht ~* I find it hard/impossible to understand (*begreifen*: grasp); *es ist mir ~* I can understand (*od.* get my mind around *umg.*) it; *schwer ~ Text etc.*: difficult, complicated; *leicht ~ Stil etc.*: easily understandable; *für Kinder nicht ~* incomprehensible to children; *j-m etw. ~ machen* make s.th. clear to s.o.; *sich ~ machen* make o.s. understood (+ *Dat.* to); *im Lärm*: make o.s. heard; **II.** *Adv.*: *klar und ~ sprechen etc.*: clearly and distinctly; *etw. leicht ~ darstellen etc.*: depict etc. s.th. in an easily comprehensible way; **verständlicherweise** *Adv.* understandably; **Verständlichkeit** *f; nur Sg.* intelligibility; audibility; comprehensibility; → **verständlich**

Verständnis *n*; *-ses, kein Pl.* understanding (*für* for); *für Kunst etc.*: appreciation (of); *nach m-m ~* as I see it; *dafür habe ich (volles) ~* I can (fully) understand that; *für solche Leute habe ich kein ~* I have no time for people like that; *dafür fehlt mir jedes ~* I just can't understand that; *j-m ~ entgegenbringen* show some understanding for s.o.; *um ~ werben* ask for some understanding; *bei j-m um ~ werben* ask s.o. to (try and) understand; *wir bitten um ~* we hope you'll understand; *entschuldigend*: we do apologize, we apologize for any inconvenience

verständnislos I. *Adj.* **1.** (*nicht begreifend*) uncomprehending; *~er Ausdruck* blank look, look of incomprehension; **2.** (*ohne Mitgefühl*) lacking in understanding; *bei Problemen*: *auch* unsympathetic (*gegenüber* toward[s]); **3.** *bei Kunst etc.*: lacking in appreciation (*gegenüber* for); **II.** *Adv.* *ansehen etc.*: uncomprehendingly, blankly; *~ gegenüberstehen e-m Problem etc.*: have no understanding for; *e-m Kunstwerk etc.*: have no appreciation for; **Verständnislosigkeit** *f; nur Sg.* **1.** (*Nichtbegreifen*) incomprehension; **2.** (*mangelndes Verständnis*) lack of understanding (*gegenüber* toward[s], for); **3.** *bei Kunst etc.*: lack of appreciation (*gegenüber* for); **verständnisvoll I.** *Adj.* *Eltern etc.*: understanding; (*mitfühlend*) sympathetic; *Blick*: knowing; **II.** *Adv.* *ansehen, nicken etc.*: understandingly; (*mitfühlend*) *reagieren etc.*: sympathetically

verstänkern *v/t. umg.* stink up

verstärken I. *v/t.* strengthen; *Tech., Mil.* reinforce; *Etech.* boost; (*Instrument, Ton-, Funksignal etc.*) amplify; (*steigern*) increase, boost; (*Eindruck*) add to; *das Team um e-n Angreifer / im Angriff ~* strengthen the team by adding an attacker / in attack; **II.** *v/refl.* increase; *Verdacht etc.*: grow; *sich im Angriff etc. ~* become stronger in attack etc.; **Verstärker** *m*; *-s, -*; *Hi--Fi, Mus.*: amplifier; *Etech., Mot.* booster; *Opt., Fot.* intensifier

verstärkt I. *P.P.* → **verstärken**; **II.** *Adj.* *Tech.* reinforced; (*gesteigert*) increased; *in ~em Maße* to a greater extent; **III.** *Adv.* increasingly, even more; *~ auftreten* appear in greater strength; **Verstärkung** *f* strengthening; *Tech.* reinforcement; *Hi-Fi, Mus.* amplifica-

tion; *Etech.* boosting; (*Steigerung*) increase; *Sport* strengthening, reinforcement; *~en Mil. etc.* reinforcements; *~ anfordern/bekommen* call for /receive reinforcements *Pl.*

verstauben *v/i.* get dusty; *über längere Zeit*: gather dust; *s-e Romane ~ in den Bibliotheken fig.* his novels are gathering dust in the libraries; **verstaubt I.** *P.P.* → **verstauben**; **II.** *Adj.* **1.** dusty; *völlig ~* covered in dust; **2.** *umg. fig. Ansichten etc.*: antiquated, *attr. auch* ancient ...

verstauchen *v/t. Med.* sprain; *sich den Fuß ~* sprain one's ankle; **Verstauchung** *f* sprain

verstauen *v/t.* stow away; *die ganze Familie im Auto ~ umg.* pile the whole family into the car

Versteck *n*; *-(e)s, -e* hiding place; *von Verbrechern*: *auch* hideout; *~ spielen* play hide-and-seek; **verstecken I.** *v/t.* hide (*vor* + *Dat.* from), *förm.* conceal (from); **II.** *v/refl.* hide (*vor* + *Dat.* from); *die Schlüssel etc. hatten sich unter den Zeitungen versteckt* were hidden among the newspapers; *sich hinter etw.* (*Dat.*) *~* hide behind s.th.; (*Pseudonym etc.*) write under s.th.; (*Gerüchten*) be behind s.th.; *er braucht sich vor niemandem zu ~ umg. fig.* he is a match for anybody; *wir brauchen uns (mit unseren Leistungen) nicht zu ~* (with our achievements) we are a match for anybody and anything; **Verstecken** *n*; *-s, kein Pl.*; (*Spiel*) hide-and-seek; *mit j-m ~ spielen fig.* play hide-and-seek with s.o.; **Versteckspiel** *n* hide-and-seek; *fig.* game of hide-and-seek; **versteckt I.** *P.P.* → **verstecken**; **II.** *Adj.* hidden; *fig. Drohung etc.*: *auch* veiled; *sich ~ halten* hide (*vor* + *Dat.* from), be (*od.* remain) in hiding; *~ in* (+ *Dat.*) hidden (away) in

verstehbar *Adj.* understandable

verstehen (*unreg.*) **I.** *v/t/i.* **1.** understand; (*erkennen, einsehen*) see; *falsch ~* misunderstand, get *s.th. od. s.o.* wrong; *fig. auch* take *s.th.* in bad part (*Am.* the wrong way); *~ Sie mich recht!* don't get me wrong; *wenn ich Sie recht verstehe* if I understood you correctly; *verstehe ich recht? erstaunt*: did I hear right?; *ich verstehe kein einziges Wort* I can't understand a word *od.* thing (you're *etc.* saying); *j-m zu ~ geben, dass ...* give s.o. to understand that ...; *~ Sie?* do you see (what I mean)?; *ich verstehe!* I see, I understand; *verstanden?* (do you) understand?; *haben Sie mich verstanden? bes. drohend*: do you read me?; *hab schon verstanden! umg.* okay, I get it; *bei Kritik*: point taken; *was ~ Sie unter ...?* what do you understand (*meinen*: *auch* mean) by ...?; *das ist nicht wörtlich zu ~* that's not meant (*od.* not to be taken) literally; *wie soll ich das ~?* how am I supposed to take that?, what are you getting at?; *das ist als Spaß etc. zu ~* that's meant to be (*od.* meant as) a joke etc.; *~ Bahnhof* 1; **2.** (*hören können*) hear; *~ Sie mich? Funkverkehr*: do you read me?; **3.** (*Fremdsprache*) know; *ich verstehe ein bisschen Französisch, kann es aber nicht sprechen* I can understand a bit of French (*Am.* a little French) but I can't speak it; **4.** (*auslegen*) interpret; (*auffassen*) take; *ich habe das so verstanden, dass ...* I took it to mean that ...; **5.** (*sich mit etw. ausken-*

nen) know about *s.th.*; **er versteht etwas davon** he knows a thing or two about it; **er versteht gar nichts davon** he doesn't know the first thing about it; **6. es ~ zu** (+ *Inf.*) know how to (+ *Inf.*); **er versteht es, mit Kindern umzugehen** he has a way with children; **er versteht es nicht besser** he doesn't know any more about it; → **Handwerk** 3, **Sache** 5; **II.** *v/refl.* **1.** understand each other; **2.** *emotional*: **sich gut ~** get on (*Am.* along) well (with each other); **wir ~ uns einfach nicht** we just don't get on (*Am.* along); **3. sich ~ auf** (+ *Akk.*) (*etw.*) know (how to do), (*auch* **sich gut ~ auf** +*Akk.*) be good at; *stärker*: be a dab (*Am.* an old) hand at; (*Menschen, Tiere etc.*) have a way with; **4. sich ~ als** see o.s. as; **das versteht sich** (*doch*) **von selbst** that goes without saying; **5.** *Wirts.*: **die Preise ~ sich ab Werk / ohne Mehrwertsteuer** *etc.* the prices are ex works (*Am.* are factory-gate) / exclusive of VAT *etc.*

versteifen I. *v/refl.* (*hat sich versteift*) **1.** *Gelenk etc.*: stiffen; *Penis*: stiffen, *Am.* get hard; **2.** *fig. Haltung etc.*: harden; *Fronten: auch* become entrenched; *Wirts., Markt*: tighten; **sich auf etw. ~** become set on (doing) s.th.; **er hat sich darauf versteift** he's sticking to it(, no matter what anyone says); **II.** *v/t.* (*hat*); (*Kragen etc.*) stiffen; *Tech.* (*Konstruktion etc.*) reinforce, strengthen; **III.** *v/i.* (*ist*); *Gelenk etc.* stiffen, become stiff; **Versteifung** *f* **1.** *Med.* stiffening; *Tech.* reinforcing, strengthening; **2.** *fig.* hardening; *der Fronten: auch* entrenchment

versteigen *v/refl.* (*unreg.*) **1.** *beim Bergsteigen*: get lost (*while climbing*); **2.** *geh.*: **sich zu der Behauptung ~, dass** go so far as to claim that

Versteigerer *m*; *-s, -*, **Versteigerin** *f*; *-, -nen* auctioneer; **versteigern** *v/t.* auction (off); *meistbietend* **~** sell off to the highest bidder; **~ lassen** put up for auction; **Versteigerung** *f* **1.** *konkret*: auction; **2.** (*Vorgang*) auctioning; **zur ~ kommen** be put up for auction

versteinern I. *v/i.* **1.** fossilize; *Holz*: petrify; **2.** *fig.* freeze, turn to stone; *v/refl. fig.* harden; **versteinert I.** *P.P.* → *versteinern*; **II.** *Adj.* **1.** fossilized; *Holz*: petrified; **2.** *fig. vor Angst*: petrified; *Gesicht etc.*: stony; **mit ~er Miene** stony-faced; **III.** *v/i. wie ~ dastehen* be thunderstruck, stand rooted to the spot; **Versteinerung** *f* fossilization; *von Holz*: petrifaction; (*Versteinertes*) fossil

verstellbar *Adj.* adjustable; **Sitz mit ~er Rückenlehne** reclining seat

verstellen I. *v/t.* **1.** (*Hebel etc.*) shift; (*einstellen, auch falsch*) adjust; (*Uhr, Gerät etc.*) adjust; (*Schrank etc.*) move; (*Buch*) put in the wrong place; **der Sitz lässt sich stufenlos in der Höhe** *etc.* **~** the seat is fully adjustable for height *etc.*; **j-d hat die ganzen Sender verstellt** s.o. has (wrongly) altered the tuning of all the stations; **2.** (*versperren*) block, obstruct; → **Blick** 4; **3.** (*Handschrift, Stimme*) disguise; **II.** *fig. v/refl.* pretend, put on an act; (*heucheln*) dissemble; **Verstellung** *f* **1.** shifting; (*Einstellen*) adjustment; **2.** (*Versperren*) obstruction *etc.*; **3.** *fig.* preten|ce (*Am.* -se); (*play*[-])acting, dissimulation; **Verstellungskunst** *f* (*play*[-])acting

versteppen *v/i. Öko.* turn into steppe;

Versteppung *f* transformation into steppe

versterben *v/i.* (*unreg.*) *förm.* pass away, die; **am 4.12.98 verstorben** *Amtsspr.* died 4.12.98 (*Am.* 12/4/98)

verstetigen *v/t. Wirts.* smoothen (*Am.* smooth) out; **Verstetigung** *f Wirts.* increased steadiness

versteuerbar *Adj.* taxable; **versteuern** *v/t.* pay tax on; **zu versteuernde Einkünfte** taxable income *Sg.*; **versteuert I.** *P.P.* → *versteuern*; **II.** *Adj.* tax-paid; **~er Gewinn** *etc.* profits *etc.* after tax; **Versteuerung** *f* payment of tax (+ *Gen.* on)

verstiegen I. *P.P.* → *versteigen*; **II.** *Adj.* eccentric; *Sache: auch* high-flown; **Verstiegenheit** *f* (*das Verstiegensein*) eccentricity; (*verstiegene Idee*) eccentric notion

verstimmen *v/t.* **1.** *Mus.* put *s.th.* out of tune; **2.** *fig.* put *s.o.* in a bad mood; (*verärgern*) annoy; **verstimmt I.** *P.P.* → *verstimmen*; **II.** *Adj.* **1.** *Mus. attr.* out-of-tune ..., *präd.* out of tune; **2.** *Person: präd.* in a bad mood; (*verärgert*) annoyed, disgruntled; **3.** *Magen*: upset; **Verstimmung** *f* **1.** disgruntlement; **2. ~ des Magens** stomach upset

verstockt *Adj.* stubborn, obdurate; *Sünder*: impenitent; **Verstocktheit** *f* stubbornness, obduracy; impenitence; → *verstockt*

verstohlen I. *Adj.* furtive (*auch Blick*), surreptitious; **II.** *Adv.* furtively, surreptitiously; **~ anblicken** steal (*od.* sneak) a glance at, throw a furtive glance at

verstopfen I. *v/t.* (*hat verstopft*) block (up) (*Rohr, Abfluss*) *auch* clog up; (*Straße*) congest; **II.** *v/i.* (*ist*) *Rohr etc.*: become blocked (*od.* clogged up); **verstopft I.** *P.P.* → *verstopfen*; **II.** *Adj.* blocked (up); *Nase: auch* bunged (*Am.* stuffed) up *umg.*; *Rohr, Abfluss: auch* clogged up; *Straße*: congested, clogged; *Darm*: constipated; **Verstopfung** *f* **1.** blockage, obstruction; **2.** *Med.* constipation; **~ haben** be constipated

verstorben I. *P.P.* → *versterben*; **II.** *Adj. attr.* late, deceased; **~ sein** be deceased, have passed away; **Verstorbene** *m, f*; *-n, -n: der od. die ~* the deceased; **die ~** *allg.* the dead

verstören *v/t.* distress; **verstört I.** *P.P.* → *verstören*; **II.** *Adj.* distraught; *Blick, Benehmen etc.: auch* wild; **e-n ~en Eindruck machen** look (rather) distraught; **III.** *Adv. um sich blicken etc.*: in a distraught way; **Verstörtheit** *f* distraught state

Verstoß *m*; *-es, Verstöße* offen|ce (*Am.* -se) (*gegen* against); (*Zuwiderhandlung*) *auch* violation (of); **e-e Reihe von Verstößen gegen Grammatik und Rechtschreibung** a number of occasions on which the rules of grammar and spelling were breached

verstoßen¹ (*unreg.*) **I.** *v/t.* (*ausstoßen*) expel (*aus* from); cast out (of); (*Kind, Ehegatten etc.*) disown, repudiate; **II.** *v/i.*: **~ gegen** offend against; (*ein Gesetz etc.*) violate, infringe

verstoßen² **I.** *P.P.* → *verstoßen¹*; **II.** *Adj. Ehefrau etc.*: disowned; **aus der Gemeinschaft** *etc.* **~ sein** be cast (*od.* thrown) out of the community *etc.*

Verstoßene *m, f*; *-n, -n* outcast; **Verstoßung** *f* expulsion; *e-s Kindes, Ehegatten*: repudiation

verstrahlen *v/t.* **1.** *radioaktiv*: contaminate (with radioactivity); **2.** (*Eigen*

schaft) radiate; **verstrahlt I.** *P.P.* → *verstrahlen*; **II.** *Adj.* (radioactively) contaminated; **Verstrahlung** *f* **1.** (radioactive) contamination; **2.** *e-r Eigenschaft etc.*: radiation

verstreben *v/t.* strut, brace; **Verstrebung** *f* strut(s *Pl.*), brace(s *Pl.*)

verstreichen (*unreg.*) **I.** *v/i.* (*ist verstrichen*) **1.** *Zeit*: pass (by); *Frist*: expire; **2.** *Jägerspr., Federwild*: move off (the hunting ground); **II.** *v/t.* (*hat*) **1.** (*Butter, Salbe etc.*) spread; **2.** (*Fugen*) stop up; **3.** (*verbrauchen*) use up

verstreuen *v/t.* scatter; *aus Versehen*: spill; **verstreut I.** *P.P.* → *verstreuen*; **II.** *Adj.* scattered, dotted about here and there; **die Höfe sind übers ganze Tal ~** the farms are scattered right across the entire valley

verstricken I. *v/t.* **1.** ensnare, involve (*in* + *Akk.* in); **verstrickt werden in** (+ *Akk.*) *auch* become enmeshed in; **2.** (*Wolle etc.*) use (*in knitting*); **II.** *v/refl.* **1. sich ~ in** (+ *Akk.*) get entangled (*od.* involved, caught up) in; **2.** *Wolle*: (*sich ~ lassen*) knit; **3.** (*beim Stricken Fehler machen*) make a mistake (*in knitting*); **verstrickt I.** *P.P.* → *verstricken*; **II.** *Adj.*: **~ sein in** (+ *Akk.*) be entangled (*od.* involved) in; **Verstrickung** *f* entanglement, involvement (*in* + *Akk.* in)

verstromen *v/t. Tech.* convert into electricity

verströmen **I.** *v/t.* give off, exude; (*Blut*) shed; **etw. über etw.** (*Akk.*) **~** spread s.th. over s.th.; **Optimismus** *etc.* **~** *umg.* ooze with optimism *etc.*; **II.** *v/refl.* spend itself (*Person*: o.s.)

Verstromung *f Tech.* conversion into electricity

verstrubbeln *v/t. umg.*: **j-m die Haare ~** tousle s.o.'s hair

verstümmeln *v/t.* mutilate; *fig.* (*Bericht etc.*) garble; **sich selbst ~** mutilate oneself; **verstümmelt I.** *P.P.* → *verstümmeln*; **II.** *Adj. Glied etc.*: mutilated; *fig. Text etc.*: garbled; **~e Information** *EDV* corrupted information, garbage *umg.*; **Verstümmelung** *f* mutilation; *fig.* garbling

verstummen *v/i.* fall silent; *Person: auch* stop talking; *Geräusch*: stop; *langsam*: die away; *Gerüchte*: stop; *langsam*: peter out; **~ lassen** *od.* **zum Verstummen bringen** silence

Versuch *m*; *-(e)s, -e* **1.** attempt (*auch Jur.*), try; **e-n ~ machen** give s.o. *od. s.th.* a try (go *Brit. umg.*, whack *Am. umg.*), give *s.th.* a whirl *umg.*; **den ~ machen, etw. zu tun** make an attempt (have a go [*od.* whack] *umg.*) at doing s.th.; **es auf e-n ~ ankommen lassen** give it a try (go *umg.*); *unter Risiko*: take a chance (*mit* on); **das käme auf e-n ~ an** we could give it a try (go [*od.* whack] *umg.*); **keinen ~ wert sein** not be worth trying (*od.* a try); **schon der ~ ist strafbar** you can be punished just for trying; **2.** *Phys., Med. etc.* experiment; (*Probe, auch Tech.*) test; **e-n ~ machen** carry out an experiment (*an* + *Dat.* on); **~ und Irrtum** trial and error; **3.** *Sport* attempt; **im dritten ~** at (*Am.* on) the third attempt; **4.** *Lit.* essay (*über* + *Akk.* on); **s-e ersten lyrischen ~e** his first attempts at poetry; **versuchen** *v/t.* **1.** try; attempt (*auch Jur.*); **es mit etw. ~** try s.th. (*od.* doing s.th.); **es mit j-m ~** give s.o. a try; **sein Glück ~** try one's luck; **versuch's doch mal!** *umg.* have a go; **lass mich mal ~!** let me try (it),

let me have a go *umg.*; → **versucht**
III; **2.** (*kosten*) taste, try; **3.** *v/refl.*:
sich ~ in (+ *Dat.*) *od.* *an* (+ *Dat.*) try
one's hand at; **4.** *altm., bibl.* tempt; →
versucht II 2; **Versucher** *m; -s, -*, **Versucherin** *f; -, -nen* tempter, *weiblich
auch*: temptress
Versuchs|abteilung *f* experimental de-
partment; **~anlage** *f* testing (*für Modelle*: pilot) plant; **~anordnung** *f* test
arrangement; **~anstalt** *f* research institute; **~ballon** *m* **1.** trial balloon; **2.** *fig.*
kite; *e-n ~ starten* fly a kite, put out
feelers; **~gelände** *n* test(ing) site;
~gruppe *f* test group; **~kaninchen** *n*
umg. pej. guinea pig; **~labor** *n* experimental lab(oratory); **~leiter** *m*, **~leite-
rin** *f* person in charge of an (*od.* the)
experiment, experiment leader; **~mo-
dell** *n* test model; **~objekt** *n* test object; *fig. Person*: guinea pig; **~person**
f test person; **~phase** *f* trial phase;
~projekt *n* pilot project (*od.* scheme,
Am. plan); **~puppe** *f bei Autotests*:
dummy; **~reaktor** *m Phys.* test reactor; **~reihe** *f* series of experiments;
~stadium *n*: (*noch im*) ~ (still at the)
experimental stage; **~strecke** *f* test
track; **~tier** *n* experimental (*od.* laboratory) animal
versuchsweise *Adv.* by way of trial;
(*auf Probe*) on a trial basis
Versuchszweck *m*: *zu ~en* for experimental purposes
versucht I. *P.P.* → **versuchen**; II. *Adj.*
1. *Mord etc.*: attempted; **2.** *~ sein,
etw. zu tun* feel tempted to do s.th.
Versuchung *f* temptation; *in ~ führen*
lead into temptation; *in ~ kommen* be
tempted
versumpfen *v/i.* **1.** become marshy;
2. *umg. fig.* get involved in a (big)
booze-up (*Am.* bender), end up boozing (the night away); **3.** *umg. fig.* (*versauern*) go to the dogs; **Versumpfung**
f transformation into marsh
versündigen *v/refl.* sin (*an* +*Dat.*
against); *versündige dich nicht! mit
Worten*: don't say such a terrible
thing!
versunken I. *P.P* → **versinken**; II. *Adj.*
sunken, submerged; *fig. Zeit*: … long
past; *Reich etc.*: lost; *~ in* (+ *Akk.*) absorbed (*od.* engrossed) in; → **Gedanke**
1; **Versunkenheit** *f* contemplation
versüßen *v/t.* sweeten (*auch fig.*); *fig.*
(*Angebot etc.*) make *s.th.* more attractive; → **Pille**
Vertäfelung *f* panel(l)ing, wainscot(-
t)ing
vertagen *v/t. und v/refl.*: (*sich*) ~ adjourn (*auf* + *Akk.* until); **Vertagung** *f*
adjournment
vertan I. *P.P.* → **vertun**; II. *Adj.*: *~e
Zeit* (*und Mühe*) waste of time (and
effort)
vertändeln *v/t.* (*Zeit etc.*) fritter; *Sport*:
den Ball ~ give the ball away
vertäuen *v/t. Naut.* moor
vertauschbar *Adj.* interchangeable;
Tech. replaceable, exchangeable; **vertauschen** *v/t.* exchange, swap *umg.*,
Am. auch trade (*gegen, mit* for); *aus
Versehen*: mix up (+ *Akk.*) *Math.* substitute;
(*Rolle*) reverse; **Vertauschung** *f* exchange; (*Verwechslung*) mix-up
verteidigen I. *vt/i.* defend (*auch Jur.
und Sport*); (*eintreten für*) *auch* stand
up for; **II.** *v/refl.* defend o.s.; (*rechtfertigen*) *auch* justify o.s.; *sich selbst ~
vor Gericht*: conduct one's own de-
fen|ce (*Am.* -se); **Verteidiger** *m; -s, -*,
Verteidigerin *f; -, -nen* **1.** defender

(*auch Sport*); *Fußball*: *auch* fullback;
2. *fig.* advocate, upholder; **Verteidiger
des Angeklagten** *Jur.* counsel for the
defen|ce (*Am.* -se); **Verteidigung** *f*
defen|ce (*Am.* -se) (*auch Jur., Sport
und fig.*); *zur ~* (+ *Gen.*) in defen|ce
(*Am.* -se) of, in *s.o.'s* defen|ce (*Am.*
-se); *das Plädoyer der ~ Jur.* the de-
fen|ce's (*Am.* -se's) closing argument
Verteidigungs|abkommen *n* Mil. de-
fen|ce (*Am.* -se) agreement; **~an-
strengungen** *Pl.* efforts in defen|ce
(*Am.* -se); **~ausgaben** *Pl.* defen|ce
(*Am.* -se) spending *Sg.*; **~ausschuss**
m committee for national defen|ce
(*Am.* -se); **~beitrag** *m* defen|ce (*Am.*
-se) contribution
verteidigungsbereit *Adj. Mil.* in a
state of defensive readiness; **Verteidi-
gungsbereitschaft** *f* defensive readiness
Verteidigungsbündnis *n* defen|ce
(*Am.* -se) (*od.* defensive) alliance
Verteidigungsetat *m Mil.* defen|ce
(*Am.* -se) budget
verteidigungsfähig *Adj. Mil. präd.
und nachgestellt*: capable of defending
oneself *etc.*; **Verteidigungsfähigkeit** *f*
defensive capability
Verteidigungs|fall *m Mil.*: *im ~* if de-
fen|ce (*Am.* -se) becomes necessary;
~haushalt *m* defen|ce (*Am.* -se)
budget; **~krieg** *m* defensive war(fare);
~minister *m*, **~ministerin** *f* defen|ce
(*Am.* -se) minister, minister for de-
fen|ce (*Am.* -se); *in GB*: Secretary of
State for Defence, Defence Secretary;
in den USA: Secretary of Defense;
~ministerium *n* ministry of defen|ce
(*Am.* -se), defen|ce (*Am.* -se) minis-
try; *in GB*: Ministry of Defence, Defence Ministry; *in den USA*: Department of Defense, DOD; **~pakt** *m* de-
fen|ce (*Am.* -se) (*od.* defensive) pact
Verteidigungspolitik *f Mil.* defen|ce
(*Am.* -se) policy; **verteidigungspoli-
tisch** *Adj.* … in terms of defen|ce
(*Am.* -se) policy
Verteidigungs|potenzial *n Mil.* de-
fen|ce (*Am.* -se) capabilities *Pl.*; **~re-
de** *f* speech for the defen|ce (*Am.*
-se), plea; *weitS.* apology; **~schrift** *f*
apology; *weitS.* apology; **~waffe** *f* defensive weapon;
~zustand *m* defen|ce (*Am.* sc) alert
verteilbar *Adj. Wirts.* distributable
verteilen I. *v/t.* **1.** distribute (*auf* +
Akk., *unter* + *Dat.* among) (*auch
Wirts.*); (*austeilen*) distribute, share
out; *~ über e-n Zeitraum*: spread (out)
over; (*un*)*gerecht ~* share out
(un)fairly; *Lob und Tadel ~* deal out
praise and criticism; *Ohrfeigen ~ umg.
fig.* dish out a clip round the ear to all
and sundry; **2.** (*unter sich teilen*)
share; (*aufteilen*) divide; (*Preise*) give
out; **3.** (*verschenken*) give away;
4. (*Aufgaben, Ressourcen*) allocate;
(*Rollen*) cast; (*Farbe*) spread;
II. *v/refl.* **1.** (*ver-, ausbreiten*) spread
(*über* + *Akk.* over, across; *unter* +
Dat. among); *sich auf die Bevölkerung etc. ~* be distributed among the
population (*etc.*); **2.** (*sich trennen*)
Gruppe etc.: split up; (*sich auflösen*)
Menge etc.: scatter, disperse, *Substanz,
Nebel etc.*: dissipate; *sich in der Menge ~* mingle (*od.* mix) with the crowd;
sie verteilten sich auf ihre Plätze they
all sat down at their places (*od.* in
their seats)
Verteiler *m; -s, -* **1.** distributor (*auch
Wirts., und Etech., Tech., Mot.*); (*Einzelhändler*) retailer; **2.** (*auf e-r Liste

etc.*) distribution list; **~dose** *f Etech.*
junction box; **~finger** *m Mot.* distributor arm
Verteilerin *f; -, -nen* distributor (*auch
Wirts.*); (*Einzelhändlerin*) retailer
Verteiler|kappe *f Mot.* distributor cap;
~kasten *m Etech.* distribution box;
~netz *n* distribution system (*Wirts.*
network); **~programm** *n EDV* distributor program; **~ring** *m e-r Ware*: deal-
ers' ring (*Am.* association); **~schlüs-
sel** *m* distribution list; **~tafel** *f Etech.*
distribution board
verteilt I. *P.P.* → **verteilen**; II. *Adj.*
spread out (*über* + *Akk.* over, across);
(*aufgeteilt*) distributed, shared (*unter*
+ *Dat.* among); → **Rolle**[2]; III. *Adv.*:
gleichmäßig ~ im Tal etc. stehen be
evenly distributed throughout the valley *etc.*
Verteilung *f* distribution (*auch Wirts.*);
sharing; spread(ing) *etc.*; → **verteilen**;
Ruß etc. in feinster ~ soot *etc.* dispersed as finely as possible
Verteilungs|gerechtigkeit *f* fair dis-
tribution of wealth; **~kampf** *m* struggle over distribution; **~konflikt** *m* conflict over distribution; **~schlüssel** *m*
distribution list
vertelefonieren *v/t. umg.* (*Geld*) spend
on phone calls; *ein Vermögen etc. ~*
use up a fortune *etc.* on the phone;
Stunden etc. ~ spend hours *etc.* on the
phone, spend hours *etc.* phoning
verteuern I. *v/t.* raise the price of;
II. *v/refl.* go up (in price) (*um* by);
Verteuerung *f* rise in price(s) *od.*
costs (*um* by)
verteufeln *v/t.* demonize; **verteufelt**
I. *P.P.* → **verteufeln**; II. *Adj. umg.*
devilish; *~es Glück haben* be damned
lucky, have the devil's own luck;
III. *Adv. umg.*: *~ schwer / gut aussehend etc.* damn(ed) difficult/good-
looking *etc.*; *es tut ~ weh* it hurts like
hell; **Verteufelung** *f des Feindes*: de-
monization
vertiefen I. *v/t.* **1.** deepen; **2.** *fig.* (*Eindruck etc.*) deepen, heighten;
3. (*Kenntnisse*) extend; (*Studien etc.*)
go into *s.th.* further; **II.** *v/refl.* **1.** *Eindruck etc.*: deepen; **2.** *sich ~ in* (+
Akk.) (*Lektüre etc.*) become engrossed (*od.* absorbed *od.* immersed)
in; (*Arbeit*) *auch* become wrapped up
in; (*in ein Wissensgebiet etc.*) go into
s.th. further (*od.* in greater detail), devote o.s. (*od.* one's attention) to, steep
o.s. in; **vertieft** I. *P.P.* → **vertiefen**;
II. *Adj.* **1.** *Wissen etc.*: (more) detailed;
2. (*versunken*) absorbed, dead to the
world *umg.*; *~ in* (+ *Akk.*) *Lektüre
etc.*: absorbed (*od.* engrossed) by, immersed in; *Arbeit*: *auch* wrapped up
in; → **Gedanke** 1; **Vertiefung** *f* **1.** deepening; (*Mulde*) depression; **2.** *fig. des
Eindrucks etc.*: deepening, heightening; **3.** *fig.* (*Versunkenheit*) absorption;
in ein Buch etc.: engrossment; **4.** *fig.
des Wissens etc.*: deepening
vertikal *Adj.* vertical; **Vertikale** *f; -, -n*
vertical (line); *in der ~n* vertically;
Vertikalismus *m; -, kein Pl.*; *Kunst*:
verticalizing
Vertikal|kreis *m Astron.* vertical circle;
~schnitt *m Math.* vertical section
Vertiko ['vɛrtiko] *n; -s, -s* small cupboard with two doors containing a drawer and display shelf at the top, *Am.
etwa* hutch
vertikutieren *vt/i. Agr.* aerate; **Vertiku-
tiergerät** *n* aerator
vertilgen *v/t.* **1.** destroy; (*Unkraut, In-*

V

sekten) auch kill; **2.** *umg. fig.* (*Essen*) demolish, polish off; **Vertilgung** *f* destruction; killing; → **vertilgen**

vertippen I. *v/refl.* make a (typing) mistake (*Am.* a typo); *auch beim Taschenrechner, Computer etc.*: hit the wrong key; *beim Tastentelefon*: get the number wrong, hit the wrong key; **II.** *v/t.* (*Buchstaben etc.*) mistype, type wrongly

vertonen *v/t. Mus.* set to music; (*Film*) sound-track, add the sound to; **Vertonung** *f Mus.* **1.** (*das Vertonen*) setting to music; *die ~ eines Films* adding a sound-track to a film; **2.** *konkret*: setting

vertrackt *Adj. umg.* tricky; (*kompliziert*) involved, complicated; **Vertracktheit** *f umg.* tricky (*od.* involved, complicated) nature (+ *Gen.* of)

Vertrag *m; -(e)s, Verträge* contract; *Pol. auch* pact, *zwischenstaatlicher*: treaty; (*Abkommen*) convention, agreement; *mündlicher ~* verbal agreement (*od.* contract); *e-n ~ schließen* make a contract; *Pol.* sign a treaty (*od.* an agreement); *j-n unter ~ nehmen* sign s.o. on, *Am.* contract (*od.* engage) s.o.; *unter ~ stehen* be on a contract, have signed a contract

vertragen (*unreg.*) **I.** *v/t.* (*aushalten*) endure; *mst verneint und in Fragen*: stand, take *umg.*; *dieses Essen kann ich nicht ~* this food doesn't agree with me, I can't take this food; *keinen Zug/Rauch / keine Sonne etc. ~* not be able to tolerate draughts (*Am.* drafts) /smoke / any sun *etc.*; *keinen Spaß ~ können* not be able to take a joke; *ich kann es nicht ~, dass er immer Recht haben muss* I can't stand the fact that he always has to be right; *er kann einiges ~ an Ärger etc.*: he can take quite a bit; *umg.* (*Alkohol*) he can put away a fair bit (of alcohol); *ich könnte jetzt e-n Schnaps etc. ~ umg.* I could just do with a schnapps right now; *die Sache verträgt keinen Aufschub geh.* the matter brooks no delay; **II.** *v/refl.*: *sich* (*gut*) *~ Personen*: get along (well), get on (well [together]); *Sachen*: be (very) compatible; *Farben etc.*: go (well) together; *sich nicht ~ Personen*: not get on (with each other); *Sachen*: be incompatible (*auch Medikamente*); *Farben*: clash; *Grünkohl verträgt sich nicht mit Sekt etc.* kale doesn't go with champagne *etc.*, kale and champagne *etc.* don't go together; *sich wieder ~* make (it) up; (*wieder miteinander auskommen*) have made (it) up

vertraglich I. *Adj.* contractual; **II.** *Adv.* by contract; *festlegen etc.*: in a contract; *~ gebunden sein* have signed a contract; *~ zu etw. verpflichtet sein* be under contract to do s.th.

verträglich *Adj.* **1.** *Essen*: easily digestible, easy to digest; *Medikament*: well-tolerated; *weitS.* kind to the stomach; *diese Tabletten sind schwer ~* these tablets can cause (nausea and) stomach upset; **2.** *Klima*: agreeable; **3.** *Person*: agreeable, *weitS. auch* livable-with *umg.*; **4.** *EDV* compatible; **Verträglichkeit** *f* **1.** *von Essen*: digestibility; *von Medikamenten*: tolerability; **2.** *des Klimas*: agreeableness, temperateness; **3.** *e-r Person*: agreeableness, agreeable nature; **4.** *EDV* compatibility

Vertrags|abschluss *m* conclusion of an agreement *etc.*; → **Vertrag**; **~auflö-**

sung *f* termination of a contract; **~bedingung** *f* condition (*Pl. auch* terms) of a (*od.* the) contract; **~beginn** *m* commencement of a (*od.* the) contract; **~bestimmungen** *Pl.* provisions of a (*od.* the) contract

Vertragsbruch *m* breach of contract; **vertragsbrüchig** *Adj. attr.* defaulting *...*; **~ werden** go back (*od.* renege) on a (*od.* the) contract, commit a breach of contract

vertragschließend *Adj.*: *die ~en Parteien* the parties to the contract (*od.* agreement, treaty), the contracting parties

Vertrags|dauer *f* term of a (*od.* the) contract; **~ende** *f* end of a *od.* the contract; **~entwurf** *m* draft agreement; **~freiheit** *f Jur.* freedom of contract

vertragsgebunden *Adj. Person*: bound by a (*od.* the) contract; *Hotel*: contracted

Vertragsgegenstand *m* object of a(n) (*od.* the) agreement *od.* contract

vertrags|gemäß I. *Adj. Lieferung etc.*: *nachgestellt*: stipulated in the agreement (*od.* contract, treaty); **II.** *Adv.* as stipulated in the agreement (*od.* contract, treaty)

Vertrags|händler *m*, **~händlerin** *f* appointed dealer; **~hotel** *n* contracted hotel; **~klausel** *f* contract (*od.* treaty) clause; **~partei** *f*, **~partner** *m*, **~partnerin** *f* party to a(n) (*od.* the) contract (*od.* agreement, treaty); **~punkt** *m* article of a(n) (*od.* the) contract (*od.* agreement, treaty); **~recht** *n* **1.** *objektives*: law of contract; **2.** *aus e-m Vertrag*: contractual right; **~spieler** *m*, **~spielerin** *f Sport* contract professional; **~staat** *m* contracting (*od.* treaty) state; **~strafe** *f* (contractual) penalty; **~text** *m* wording of a(n) (*od.* the) contract (*od.* agreement, treaty); **~treue** *f* loyalty to (the terms of) a(n) (*od.* the) contract (*od.* agreement, treaty); **~unterzeichnung** *f* signing of a(n) (*od.* the) contract (*od.* agreement, treaty); **~urkunde** *f* deed, indenture; **~verhältnis** *n* contractual relationship; **~verlängerung** *f* extension (*od.* renewal) of a (*od.* the) contract (*od.* treaty); **~verletzung** *f* breach of contract; **~werk** *n* (set of) agreements *Pl.*; **~werkstatt** *f* authorized repairers *Pl.* (*auch V. im Sg.*), *Am.* authorized service agent

vertragswidrig I. *Adj.* contrary to (the terms of) a(n) (*od.* the) contract (*od.* agreement, treaty); **II.** *Adv.* in breach of (the terms of) a(n) (*od.* the) contract (*od.* agreement, treaty); **Vertragswidrigkeit** *f* breach of contract

vertrauen *v/i.* trust (*j-m* s.o.); *~ auf* (+ *Akk.*) trust in; *auf die Zukunft ~* have faith in (*od.* believe in) the future; *darauf ~, dass ...* have confidence that *...*; **Vertrauen** *n; -s, kein Pl.* confidence, trust (*auf* + *Akk.* in); *in die Technik, Zukunft etc.*: faith, belief (*in* + *Akk.* in); *im ~* confidentially; *ganz im ~* between you and me; *im ~ auf* (+ *Akk.*) trusting in; *~ erweckend* → **vertrauenerweckend**; (*volles*) *~ haben zu* have (every) confidence in; *j-m sein ~ schenken* place confidence in s.o.; *j-n ins ~ ziehen* take s.o. into one's confidence; *das ~ verlieren zu* lose faith in; → **aussprechen** I 2, **einflößen**, **genießen** 3, **schleichen** II

vertrauenerweckend *Adj.*: *~ sein od.* **aussehen** inspire confidence; *wenig ~*

aussehen not inspire much confidence, inspire little confidence

Vertrauens|anwalt *m*, **~anwältin** *f* defence lawyer appointed by the defendant, *Am.* defense counsel, counsel for the defense

Vertrauensarzt *m*, **Vertrauensärztin** *f* independent medical examiner; **vertrauensärztlich** *Adj.*: *das ~e Gutachten* the independent medical examiner's report

Vertrauens|basis *f* foundation of trust; **~beweis** *m* mark of confidence

vertrauensbildend *Adj.*: *~e Maßnahmen* confidence-building measures

Vertrauens|bruch *m* breach of trust, betrayal of *s.o.'* s trust; (*Indiskretion*) indiscretion; **~frage** *f Pol.*: *die ~ stellen* propose a vote of confidence; **~frau** *f* representative; **~grundlage** *f* basis of trust; **~krise** *f* crisis of confidence; **~lehrer** *m*, **~lehrerin** *f* teacher responsible for liaising between pupils (*Am.* students) and staff over matters of difficulty; **~leute** *Pl.* representatives; **~mann** *m* representative; **~missbrauch** *m* abuse of (s.o.'s) confidence; **~person** *f* **1.** reliable person; **2.** *e-r Gewerkschaft etc.*: representative; **3.** (*abgek. VP*) (*anonymer Polizeiinformant*) anonymous police informer (*Am.* informant); **~sache** *f* confidential matter, something confidential; *das ist ~* that's a matter (*od.* question) of confidence; **~schwund** *m* loss of confidence

vertrauensselig *Adj.* (too) confiding; (*leichtgläubig*) gullible; **Vertrauensseligkeit** *f* excessive trustfulness; (*Leichtgläubigkeit*) gullibility

Vertrauens|stellung *f* position of trust; **~verhältnis** *n* bond of trust; **~verlust** *m* loss of confidence

vertrauensvoll I. *Adj.* trusting; **II.** *Adv. in die Zukunft blicken etc.*: confidently; *sich ~ an j-n wenden* turn to s.o. with confidence

Vertrauens|vorschuss *m* trust; **~votum** *n* vote of confidence

vertrauenswürdig *Adj.* trustworthy

vertraulich I. *Adj.* **1.** confidential; *streng ~!* strictly confidential!; **2.** (*freundschaftlich, vertraut*) friendly; *pej.* (*auf-, zudringlich*) familiar, pally *umg.*, chummy *umg.*; **II.** *Adv.* **1.** confidentially, in confidence; (*streng*) *~ behandeln* treat confidentially (*od.* with the strictest confidence), keep *s.th.* (absolutely) secret; **2.** (*freundschaftlich, vertraut*) in a friendly way; *pej.* (*auf-, zudringlich*) in a very familiar (pally *od.* chummy *umg.*) way; → **plumpvertraulich**; **Vertraulichkeit** *f* **1.** confidentiality; **2.** *e-r Atmosphäre, e-s Tons etc.*: friendliness; *pej. e-r Person*: familiarity, palliness *umg.*, chumminess *umg.*; *plumpe ~* overfamiliarity; *sich ~en herausnehmen* take liberties

verträumen *v/t.* (*Zeit, Tag etc.*) (day)dream away; *die Zeit etc. ~ auch* spend one's time *etc.* (day)dreaming; **verträumt I.** *P.P.* → **verträumen**; **II.** *Adj.* dreamy; *Dörfchen*: *auch* sleepy; *Kind etc.*: dreamy

vertraut I. *P.P.* → **vertrauen**; **II.** *Adj.* **1.** (*eng verbunden*) close (*mit od.* + *Dat.* to); *Ton etc.*: familiar; **2.** (*bekannt*) familiar (*j-m* to s.o.); *sich mit etw. ~ machen* acquaint (*od.* familiarize) o.s. with; *mit e-r Tätigkeit etc. ~ sein* be familiar with an activity *etc.*; **Vertraute** *m, f; -n, -n* confidant, *weiblich*: confidante; **Vertrautheit** *f* **1.** clo-

seness; **2.** familiarity; → *vertraut*
vertreiben *v/t.* (*unreg.*) **1.** drive away; (*ausstoßen*) expel (*aus* from), drive out (of); *aus dem Haus*: turn out; *wir wollten Sie nicht ~ umg. fig. vom Tisch etc.*: we didn't mean to chase you away; **2.** *sich die Zeit ~* while away the time; **3.** *Wirts.* (*Ware*) sell, market, distribute; **4.** *Fachspr., beim Malen*: smudge, blur; **Vertreiber** *m*; *-s, -*, **Vertreiberin** *f*; *-, -nen* seller; **Vertreibung** *f* expulsion (*aus* from)
Vertreibungsdruck *m*: *der ~ gegen die albanische Bevölkerung* the pressure on the Albanian population to leave
vertretbar *Adj.* (*zu rechtfertigen*) justifiable, justified; (*haltbar*) tenable, defensible; *weitS.* (*akzeptabel*) acceptable, reasonable; *~e Sachen Jur.* fungible objects
vertreten (*unreg.*) **I.** *v/t.* **1.** (*j-n, Firma, sein Land etc., auch Kunstrichtung etc.*) represent; *die Galerie X vertritt den Künstler Y* the X gallery handles the artist Y's work; **2.** (*Kollegen*) stand in for; *in der Schule*: cover for; (*Schauspieler etc.*) stand in for, take the place of; *in der Sitzung den Minister etc. ~* deputize for the minister *etc.* at the meeting; **3.** (*j-s Interessen*) look after; *Jur.* appear for, plead for; (*verfechten*) defend, advocate; (*unterstützen*) support, back; (*rechtfertigen*) justify; (*einstehen für*) answer for; *den Standpunkt ~, dass* be of (*od.* hold) the opinion that; *e-e These ~* advocate a thesis; **4.** *~ sein* (*anwesend sein*) be present; (*vorkommen*) occur; *auf dem Kongress ist unser Institut etc. durch ... ~ ...* is representing our institute *etc.* at the congress; *der Künstler X ist bei der Ausstellung mit mehreren Ölbildern ~* several oil paintings by the artist X are appearing in the exhibition; **II.** *v/refl.*: *sich die Füße ~* stretch one's legs; *sich den Fuß ~* (*Sehnenzerrung etc.*) strain one's ankle
Vertreter *m*; *-s, -* **1.** representative (*auch fig. e-r Richtung etc.*); *typischer ~ des Surrealismus* typical exponent of surrealism; **2.** *Wirts.* representative, agent; (*Handelsvertreter*) sales representative, *Am. auch* salesperson, (sales) rep *umg.*; (*bes. Handelsreisender*) travel(l)ing salesman, *Brit. auch* commercial traveller; **3.** *e-s Kollegen*: deputy, stand-in; *e-s Arztes*: locum, *Am.* stand-in doctor; (*Bevollmächtigter*) proxy; *der Schulleiter und sein ~* the headmaster and his deputy-head, *Am.* the principal and his deputy; **4.** (*Verfechter*) advocate, supporter; (*typischer ~*) exponent; *~ der Anklage Jur.* prosecution
...vertreter *m, im Subst.*: *Staubsauger~* vacuum cleaner sales representative; *Gewerkschafts~* trade union representative
Vertreterbesuch *m* sales call
Vertreterin *f*; *-, -nen* → *Vertreter*
Vertreterprovision *f* agent's commission
Vertretung *f* **1.** representation; *Wirts.* agency; *die deutsche ~ Pol.* the German mission; *Sport* the German team; → *diplomatisch* I; **2.** *im Amt*: substitution; *in ~* (*+ Gen.*) in place of, standing in for; *im Brief*: (signed) for; *j-s ~ übernehmen* stand in for s.o.; *Arzt etc.*: act as locum (*Am.* stand in) for s.o.; *Lehrer*: cover for s.o.; *Jur.* act for s.o.; *Theat. etc.* stand in for s.o., take s.o.'s place; **3.** (*Person*) → *Vertre-*

ter 3; (*nur*) *als ~ eingestellt werden* be taken on (*Am.* hired) (just) as a temporary replacement
Vertretungsstunde *f* lesson in which a teacher covers for a colleague
vertretungsweise *Adv.* as a stand-in (*od.* replacement)
Vertrieb *m*; *-(e)s, kein Pl.; Wirts.* **1.** sale, marketing; (*Verteilung*) distribution; **2.** (*Abteilung*) sales (and marketing) department; **3.** ([*kleine*] *Firma*) (small) company; → *...vertrieb*
...vertrieb *m, im Subst.*: *Buch~* book company; *Buch~ Müller* Müller Books; *Zeitschriften~* magazine company; *Zeitschriften~ Schneider* Schneider Magazines; *Nutzfahrzeug~* commercial vehicle company
Vertriebene *m, f; -n, -n* displaced person; *im Exil*: exile
Vertriebs|abteilung *f Wirts.* sales (and marketing) department; *~firma f* marketing company; *~gesellschaft f* marketing company; *~kosten Pl.* distribution cost(s); *~leiter m, ~leiterin f* sales (*od.* marketing) manager; *~netz n* distribution (*od.* sales) network; *~organisation f* marketing organization; *~partner m, ~partnerin f* distribution (*od.* sales) partner; *~recht n* right of sale; *~tochter f Wirts.* marketing subsidiary; *~weg m* distribution channel
vertrimmen *v/t. umg.* give s.o. a thrashing
vertrinken (*unreg.*) *v/t.* spend on drink
vertrocknen *v/i.* dry up; **vertrocknet I.** *P.P.* → *vertrocknen*; **II.** *Adj.* dried-up, *präd.* dried up; *umg. pej.* (*geistig unbeweglich*): *er ist ein ~er alter Knochen* he's a dry old stick
vertrödeln *v/t. umg.* dawdle away, waste
vertrösten *v/t.* feed with hopes (*auf + Akk.* of); (*hinhalten*) put off (*auf + Akk.* zeitlich: till, until); **Vertröstungen** *Pl.* (empty) promises
vertrotteln *v/i. umg.* lose one's marbles; *älterer Mensch*: *auch* go gaga; **vertrottelt** *umg.* **I.** *P.P.* → *vertrotteln*; **II.** *Adj.* goofy; *älterer Mensch*: *auch* senile
vertun (*unreg.*) **I.** *v/t.* (*verschwenden*) waste; (*Chance*) give away, pass up; (*versäumen*) miss; *Zeit ~ mit etw.* waste time on s.th.; **II.** *v/refl. umg.*: *sich* (*schwer*) *~* make a (big) mistake (*bei, mit* with)
vertuschen *v/t.* cover up; (*Affäre etc.*) *auch* hush up; **Vertuschung** *f* cover-up; **Vertuschungsaktion** *f* cover-up campaign
verübeln *v/t.* take offen|ce (*Am.* -se) at; *j-m ~, dass er ...* be annoyed at s.o. for (+ *Ger.*), take offen|ce (*Am.* -se) at s.o.'s (+ *Ger.*); *ich kann es ihm nicht ~* I can't blame him (*dass er* for + *Ger.*)
verüben *v/t.* (*Verbrechen*) commit; (*Anschlag, Attentat*) carry out
verulken *v/t.* make fun of; **Verulkung** *f*: *die ~ der Konkurrenz* making fun of the competition; (*Parodie*) *eine ~ von ‚Lola rennt'* a parody (*od.* take-off *umg.*) of (*bes. Am.* on) 'Run, Lola, Run'
verunfallen *v/i. Amtsspr., bes. schw.* have an accident; **Verunfallte** *m, f; -n, -n; Amtsspr.* accident victim
verunglimpfen *v/t.* denigrate, disparage; **Verunglimpfung** *f* denigration, disparagement
verunglücken *v/i.* **1.** have an accident; *tödlich ~* be killed in an accident; *mit*

dem Auto ~ be in a car crash; **2.** *umg. Sache*: fail, go wrong; *ich fürchte, das Soufflé ist mir verunglückt* I'm afraid my soufflé is a disaster; **verunglückt I.** *P.P.* → *verunglücken*; **II.** *Adj.* **1.** *~e Person* → *Verunglückte*; **2.** *umg. Sache*: unsuccessful; **Verunglückte** *m, f; -n, -n* casualty; *auch Todesopfer*: (accident *od.* crash) victim; *bei den ~n erste Hilfe leisten* give first aid to those injured in the accident
verunmöglichen *v/t.* (*unmöglich machen*) make impossible
verunreinigen *v/t.* dirty; (*Wasser etc.*) pollute; (*verseuchen*) contaminate (*auch EDV*); **Verunreinigung** *f* **1.** dirtying; pollution, contamination; → *verunreinigen*; **2.** (*Fremdstoff[e]*) impurity, impurities *Pl.*
verunsichern *v/t* make s.o. (feel) unsure of himself (*od.* herself), *stärker*: unnerve; (*verwirren*) throw, rattle *umg.*; *die Bevölkerung etc. ~* cause (a feeling of) unease among the population *etc.*, make the population *etc.* nervous (*od.* uneasy); **verunsichert I.** *P.P.* → *verunsichern*; **II.** *Adj.* unsure (of o.s.), *stärker*: unnerved; *Bevölkerung etc.*: nervous, uneasy; **Verunsicherung** *f* (feeling of) uncertainty
verunstalten *v/t.* deface; (*Gesicht etc.*) mar, *stärker*: disfigure; (*Landschaft etc.*) scar, spoil; **Verunstaltung** *f* defacing; marring, disfigurement; *der Landschaft etc.*: scarring, spoiling
veruntreuen *v/t.* misappropriate, (*bes. Geld*) embezzle; **Veruntreuung** *f* misappropriation, embezzlement
verunzieren *v/t.* spoil, mar
verursachen *v/t.* cause, bring about, give rise to; *j-m Kosten ~* put s.o. to expense; **verursachend I.** *Part. Präs.* → *verursachen*; **II.** *Adj. Faktoren etc.*: causative; **Verursacher** *m*; *-s, -*, **Verursacherin** *f*; *-, -nen* responsible party; **Verursacherprinzip** *n* causation principle; *Öko.* polluter pays principle
verurteilen *v/t.* condemn (*auch fig.*), sentence (*zu* to); *zu e-r Gefängnisstrafe ~* give s.o. a prison sentence, sentence s.o. to prison; *etw. aufs Schärfste ~* condemn s.th. in the strongest possible terms; → *Geldstrafe, Tod* 1; **verurteilt I.** *P.P.* → *verurteilen*; **II.** *Adj.* convicted; *auch fig.* condemned; *zum Scheitern ~ fig.* doomed to fail(ure); **Verurteilte** *m, f; -n, -n* convicted man (*weiblich*: woman); *Jur.* convict; *zum Tode ~* condemned man (*weiblich*: woman), *Am. auch* man (*bzw.* woman) on death row; **Verurteilung** *f* conviction, condemnation (*auch fig.*); (*Urteil*) sentence
Verve ['vɛrvə] *f; -, kein Pl.* verve
vervielfachen I. *v/t.* increase considerably; (*multiplizieren*) multiply; **II.** *v/refl.* increase considerably
vervielfältigen *v/t.* (*kopieren*) duplicate, copy; **Vervielfältigung** *f* **1.** duplication, copying; **2.** *konkret*: copy
Vervielfältigungs|apparat *m* duplicator; (*Fotokopierer*) (photo)copier; *~recht n* copyright, right of reproduction
vervierfachen *v/t. und v/refl.*: (*sich*) *~* quadruple
vervollkommnen I. *v/t.* perfect; (*verbessern*) improve (on); **II.** *v/refl.* become perfect (*in + Dat.* in); **Vervollkommnung** *f* perfection; improvement
vervollständigen I. *v/t.* complete;

II. *v/refl.* be completed, become complete; **Vervollständigung** *f* completion

verwachsen¹ (*unreg.*) **I.** *v/i.* **1.** (*ist verwachsen*) grow together; *Med., Knochen*: unite; *Wunde*: heal up (*od.* over); **2.** (*ist*) *fig.* grow close (*mit* to), *lit.* become one (with); **~ zu etw.** grow into s.th.; **II.** *v/refl.* (*hat*) *Narbe*: heal up (*od.* over) with time; *Deformität*: correct itself with time

verwachsen² **I.** *P.P.* → **verwachsen¹**; **II.** *Adj.* **1.** deformed, crippled; (*bucklig*) hunchbacked; **2.** (*überwuchert*) overgrown; **3.** *Baum etc.*: stunted; **4.** *fig.*: **~ mit** deeply rooted in

Verwachsung *f* **1.** deformity; **2.** *Med.* (*Zusammenwachsen*) fusion

verwackeln *v/t.*: **ein Foto ~** shake the camera (while taking a photo); **verwackelt** **I.** *P.P.* → **verwackeln**; **II.** *Adj.* blurred

verwählen *v/refl.* dial the wrong number; **ich glaube, Sie haben sich verwählt** I think you must have (got, *Am.* gotten) the wrong number

Verwahranstalt *f fig. pej.* detention cent|re (*Am.* -er)

verwahren **I.** *v/t.*: (**sicher**) **~** keep (in a safe place); **etw. für j-n ~** look after s.th. for s.o.; **II.** *v/refl. fig.* protest (**gegen** against)

verwahrlosen *v/i.* **1.** *Haus etc.*: be (*od.* get) neglected; *stärker*: go to rack and ruin; *Garten*: be (*od.* get) neglected, run wild; **2.** *Person*: go to seed; *moralisch*: go off the rails; **verwahrlost** **I.** *P.P.* → **verwahrlosen**; **II.** *Adj.* **1.** *Haus etc.*: (sadly) neglected, *stärker*: dilapidated; *Garten*: neglected, *stärker*: overgrown, *nachgestellt*: run wild; **2.** *Person*: scruffy; *stärker*: seedy; *moralisch*: dissolute; **völlig ~e Kinder** children in a state of complete neglect; **Verwahrlosung** *f* **1.** (total) neglect, state of neglect; *e-s Hauses etc.: auch* dilapidation; **2.** *e-r Person*: (moral) decline; **die ~ der heutigen Jugend** the decline of today's youth; **im Zustand völliger ~** in a state of complete neglect

Verwahrung *f* **1.** safekeeping; *e-r Person*: custody; **j-m etw. in ~ geben** deposit s.th. with s.o., leave s.th. with s.o. for safekeeping; **in ~ nehmen** take charge of; **2.** (*Einspruch*) protest

verwaisen *v/i.* be orphaned, become (*od.* be made) an orphan; *fig. Ort etc.*: be deserted; **verwaist** **I.** *P.P.* → **verwaisen**; **II.** *Adj.* orphan (*auch fig.*), *fig.* (*verlassen*) abandoned; (*menschenleer*) deserted; (*unbesetzt*) *Stelle etc.*: vacant

verwalten **I.** *v/t.* administer (*auch Konkursmasse, Nachlass*); (*Firma etc.*) manage; (*Angelegenheit*) conduct; **II.** *v/refl.*: **sich selbst ~** *Pol.* be self-governing; **Verwalter** *m; -s, -,* **Verwalterin** *f; -, -nen* administrator; manager; (*Gutsverwalter[in]*) estate manager; **Verwaltung** *f* **1.** administration (*auch von Staat, Konkurs, Nachlass*); management; **unter staatlicher etc. ~ stehen** be under state etc. control; **2.** (*Abteilung*) administration; (*Verwaltungsbehörde*) administrative authority; **zentrale ~** administrative headquarters *Pl.* (*auch V. im Sg.*), central administration (offices)

Verwaltungs|akademie *f* administration college, *Am.* business institute; **~akt** *m* administrative act; **~angestellte** *m, f* administrative assistant;

~apparat *m oft pej.* administrative (*od.* bureaucratic) machinery; **~arbeit** *f* administrative work, admin *umg.*; **~aufgaben** *Pl.* administrative tasks (*od.* duties); **~aufwand** *m* administrative costs *Pl.*; **~beamte** *m, f* administrator, administrative official; **~behörde** *f* → *Verwaltung* 2; **~bereich** *m* (*Verwaltungsbezirk*) administrative district; *Sphäre*: field of administration; **~bezirk** *m* administrative district; **~dienst** *m* civil service; **~direktor** *m,* **~direktorin** *f* head of administration; **~gebäude** *n* administration (admin *umg.*) building; **~gebühr** *f* administration charge; **~ebene** *f* administrative level; **~einheit** *f* administrative unit; **~etat** *m* administrative budget; **~fachmann** *m* administrator

Verwaltungsgericht *n Jur.* administrative court; **verwaltungsgerichtlich** *Adj.* of the administrative court

Verwaltungsgerichts|barkeit *f Jur.* system of administrative jurisdiction; **~hof** *m* higher administrative court; **~ordnung** *f* Code of Administrative Procedure; **~verfahren** *n* administrative court proceedings *Pl.*

Verwaltungs|haushalt *m* administrative budget; **~jurist** *m,* **~juristin** *f* administrative lawyer; **~kosten** *Pl.* administrative overhead(s) (*od.* expenses, costs); **~kram** *m umg.* paperwork; (*Bürokratie*) red tape; **~leiter** *m,* **~leiterin** *f* head of administration; **~organ** *n* administrative body; **~personal** *n* administrative staff (*mst V. im Pl.*); **~rat** *m* governing board; **~recht** *n* administrative law; **~richter** *m,* **~richterin** *f* administrative court judge; **~sitz** *m* (administrative) headquarters *Pl.* (*auch V. im Sg.*)

verwaltungstechnisch *Adj.*: **aus ~en Gründen** for administrative reasons

Verwaltungs|vorschrift *f* administrative regulation; **~weg** *m*: **auf dem ~e** through (the) administrative channels; **~zentrum** *n* administrative cent|re (*Am.* –er)

verwandelbar *Adj.* convertible; **verwandeln** **I.** *v/t.* **1.** change; (*umwandeln*) *auch* convert; (*umformen*) transform; (*Strafe*) commute (*alle*: **in** + *Akk.* into); **2.** *Fußball*: convert; **den Strafstoß etc. ~** score the penalty *etc.*; **e-n Eckball direkt ~** score directly from a corner kick; **II.** *v/refl.* change (**in** + *Akk.* into); metamorphose (into); **sich ~ in** (+ *Akk.*) *auch* turn into; **III.** *v/i. Fußball*: score; **Verwandlung** *f* change; conversion; transformation; metamorphosis (*Pl.* metamorphoses); → *verwandeln*; **Verwandlungskünstler** *m,* **Verwandlungskünstlerin** *f* quick-change artist

verwandt¹ *P.P.* → *verwenden*

verwandt² *Adj.* **1.** related (**mit** to) (*auch fig. ähnlich, analog*); **~ sein** *fig.* geistig, vom Wesen etc.: be akin (+ *Dat.* to); **~e Seelen** *od.* *Geister* kindred spirits, soulmates; **geistig** *od.* **seelisch ~ sein** be kindred spirits; → **verschwägert**, **2.** *Wörter*: cognate (**mit** with), related (to); **Verwandte** *m, f; -n, -n* relative, relation; **der nächste Verwandte** the next of kin; **ein** (**entfernter**) **~r von mir** a (distant) relative of mine; **die lieben ~n** *iro.* my etc. dear relations

Verwandten|besuch *m*: (**viel**) **~ bekommen** get (a lot of) visits from one's relatives (*od.* relations); **~kreis** *m* (circle of) relatives *Pl.*

Verwandtschaft *f* **1.** relationship; *geistige etc.*: affinity; **2.** (*die Verwandten*) relations *Pl.*; **die ganze ~** *umg.* the whole clan; **die gesamte ~ einladen** invite the entire family; **verwandtschaftlich** **I.** *Adj.* family …; **~e Beziehung(en)** family connections; (*Verwandtschaft*) relationship; **II.** *Adv.*: **~ miteinander verbunden sein** be related to one another

Verwandtschaftsgrad *m* degree of relationship

verwanzt *Adj.* **1.** bug-infested, bug-ridden; **2.** *mit Abhörgeräten*: bugged

verwarnen *v/t.* warn, give *s.o.* a warning; *Sport* caution, book; *polizeilich*: caution; → **gebührenpflichtig** II; **Verwarnung** *f* warning; *polizeiliche*: caution; *Sport* caution, yellow card; *Schule*: warning; → **gebührenpflichtig** I

verwaschen **I.** *Adj.* faded; *Wäsche*: *auch* washed out; *fig.* watery, wishy-washy *umg.*; *Sprechweise*: wishy-washy *umg.*, woolly *umg.*; **II.** *Adv. fig.* sprechen: in a wishy-washy way *umg.*

verwässern *v/t.* dilute; *auch fig.* water down; **verwässert** **I.** → *verwässern*; **II.** *Adj.* diluted; *auch fig.* watered down, watery

verweben **I.** *v/t.* (*auch unreg.*) (*Fäden, Wolle*) weave; **miteinander ~** interweave; *fig.* interweave; **II.** *v/refl.* (*unreg.*) *lit.* become interwoven

verwechseln *v/t.* confuse, mix up (**mit** with), mistake (for); **ich habe ihn** (**mit j-d anderem**) **verwechselt** I mistook him for s.o. else, I thought he was s.o. else; **den Hut etc. ~** take the wrong hat *etc.*, mix up the hats *etc.*; **Sie können es gar nicht ~** you can't mistake it; **sie sehen sich** (*Dat.*) **zum Verwechseln ähnlich** they're as (a)like as two peas (in a pod); **Verwechslung** *f* mistake; *von Personen*: case of mistaken identity, mix-up *umg.*

Verwechslungsgefahr *f* danger (*od.* possibility) of confusion

verwegen *Adj.* daring, bold; (*waghalsig*) reckless; *Kleidung, Art etc.*: rakish; **Verwegenheit** *f* daring, recklessness; rakishness; → **verwegen**

verwehen **I.** *v/t.* (*hat verweht*) blow away; (*zerstreuen*) scatter; (*zuwehen*) cover with snow *etc.*; **II.** *v/i.* (*ist*) be blown over; *fig.* fade (away); **vom Winde verweht** *fig.* gone with the wind; **Verwehung** *f* (*Schnee*) (snow)drift; (*Sand*) (sand)drift

verwehren *v/t.* (*versperren*) bar; **j-m etw. ~** (*verweigern*) refuse (*od.* deny) s.o. s.th.; **j-m ~, etw. zu tun** keep (*od.* stop, prevent) s.o. from doing s.th.; **j-m den Zutritt ~** refuse s.o. admittance (**zu** to)

verweiblichen **I.** *v/i.* (*ist verweiblicht*) become effeminate; **II.** *v/t.* (*hat*) feminize; **verweiblicht** **I.** *P.P.* → *verweiblichen*; **II.** *Adj.* effeminate; **Verweiblichung** *f* **1.** increasing effeminacy; **2.** feminization

verweichlichen **I.** *v/t.* (*hat verweichlicht*) make *s.o.* soft, turn *s.o.* into a softie *umg.*; **II.** *v/i.* (*ist*) go (*od.* turn) soft; **verweichlicht** **I.** → *verweichlichen*; **II.** *Adj.* soft; **~er Kerl** *pej.* softie, wimp; **Verweichlichung** *f* turning soft; *weitS.* increasing wimpishness *umg.*

Verweigerer *m; -s, -* **1.** (*Kriegsdienstverweigerer*) conscientious objector; **2.** (*Leistungsverweigerer, Aussteiger*) dropout; **verweigern** **I.** *vt/i.* refuse; **e-n Befehl ~** disobey an order; (**den**

Kriegsdienst) ~ refuse to do one's military service, ignore one's conscription orders, *Am.* dodge the draft *umg.*; *die Nahrung(saufnahme)* ~ refuse all food, refuse to eat; *Post.* → *Annahme* 1; **II.** *v/refl.* refuse to cooperate (*od.* go along with s.th.); *bes. Frau, sexuell:* refuse (to have sex with); *sich der Gesellschaft* ~ opt out (of society); **Verweigerung** *f* refusal

Verweigerungs|fall *m*: *im* ~ in case of refusal; **~haltung** *f* negative stance

Verweildauer *f* length of stay; *Ihre ~ auf dieser Webseite* the length of time you spend on this website; **verweilen** *v/i.* stay; *zögernd:* linger; *Blick:* rest (*auf + Dat.* on); *Gedanken:* linger (*bei* on); *länger:* dwell (on); *bei e-m Thema* ~ dwell on a topic

verweint I. *Adj. Gesicht:* tear-stained, *~e Augen* eyes red from crying; **II.** *Adv. sprechen etc.:* tearfully; *ganz ~ aussehen* look as if one has been crying

Verweis *m; -es, -e* **1.** (*Rüge*) reprimand, reproof, rebuke; *j-m e-n ~ erteilen* reprimand s.o. (*wegen* for); **2.** (*Hinweis*) reference (*auf + Akk.* to); **verweisen I.** *v/t.* **1.** (*Schüler, auch des Landes* ~) expel; *j-n in s-e Schranken* ~ put s.o. in his *od.* her place; → *Platz* 10; **2.** *Jur.* remit; **3.** *j-n* ~ *auf* (+ *Akk.*) *od. an* (+ *Akk.*) refer s.o. to; **II.** *v/i.:* ~ *auf* (+ *Akk.*) (*hinweisen*) refer to; (*darauf aufmerksam machen*) point out; *darf ich auf … ~* may I refer you to …

Verweisung *f* **1.** (*Ausweisung*) expulsion; **2.** reference (*auf + Akk.* to); **3.** *Jur.* referral

Verweiszeichen *n Druck.* reference sign (*od.* mark)

verwelken *v/i. Blumen:* wilt; *Blätter etc.:* wither; *fig. Ruhm etc.:* fade; **verwelkt I.** → *verwelken*; **II.** *Adj. Blumen:* wilted, limp; *Blätter etc.:* withered, dried up; *~e Schönheit etc.* faded beauty *etc.*

verweltlichen *v/t.* secularize; **Verweltlichung** *f* secularization

verwendbar *Adj.* usable; (*anwendbar*) applicable; *es ist mehrfach* ~ it has several uses; → *vielseitig* II; **Verwendbarkeit** *f* usability; **verwenden** (*auch unreg.*) **I.** *v/t.* use; (*anwenden*) apply; *nutzbringend:* utilize; (*aufwenden*) spend; *Mühe, Sorgfalt, Zeit* ~ *auf* (+ *Akk.*) devote to; **II.** *v/refl.:* *sich bei j-m für j-n* ~ *förm.* approach s.o. on s.o.'s behalf; **Verwendung** *f* use; application; utilization; *von Mitteln, Zeit etc.:* expenditure; → *verwenden*; *keine* ~ *haben für* have no use for

Verwendungs|bereich *m* range (*od.* field) of application; **verwendungsfähig** *Adj.* usable; → *verwendbar*

Verwendungs|möglichkeit *f* (possible) use (*od.* application); *e-e* ~ (+ *Gen.*) one way (in which) *s.th.* can be used; **~weise** *f* (manner of) use; *die* ~ (+ *Gen.*) the way (in which) *s.th.* is used; **~zweck** *m* use, intended purpose

verwerfen (*unreg.*) **I.** *v/t.* **1.** (*Gedanken etc.*) reject, dismiss; (*Plan etc.*) *auch* turn down; *Jur.* (*Klage*) dismiss; (*Urteil*) quash; (*Antrag etc.*) overrule; **2.** *Sport* (*Ball etc.*) miss; **II.** *v/refl.* **1.** *Holz:* warp; **2.** *Geol.* fault; **3.** *beim Kartenspiel:* deal the wrong card(s); **III.** *v/i.* **1.** *Agr., Tier:* abort; **2.** *Sport* miss

verwerflich *Adj.* reprehensible; (*abscheulich*) abominable; **Verwerflich-**

keit *f* reprehensibility

Verwerfung *f* **1.** (*Zurückweisung*) rejection; *Jur., e-r Klage:* dismissal; *e-s Urteils:* quashing; *e-s Antrags etc.:* overruling; → *verwerfen* I 1; **2.** *von Holz:* warp(ing); **3.** *Geol.* fault; **Verwerfungslinie** *f Geol.* fault line

verwertbar *Adj.* usable; *Wirts.* realizable; **Verwertbarkeit** *f* usability; *Wirts.* realizability; **verwerten** *v/t.* make use of, utilize, use; (*Erfahrungen etc.*) turn to (good) account, *Am.* put to (good) use; (*Erfindung*) exploit; *geschäftlich:* commercialize; (*zu Geld machen*) realize; *kannst du das irgendwie* ~? can you make any use of this?; **Verwertung** *f* utilization, use; exploitation; commercialization; realization; → *verwerten*; *die* ~ *von Altmaterial etc.* the recycling of scrap *etc.*

Verwertungs|gesellschaft *f:* ~ *für Urheberrechte* copyright watchdog organization; **~quote** *f* recycling quota

verwesen *v/i.* rot; (*sich zersetzen*) decay; **verwest I.** *P.P.* → *verwesen*; **II.** *Adj.* rotted, putrefied; (*zersetzt*) decayed; *halb* ~ rotting, putrefying; decaying; *stark ~e Leiche* badly decomposed body

Verweser *m; -s, -; hist.* administrator

verwestlichen *v/i.* become westernized; **Verwestlichung** *f* westernization

Verwesung *f* (state of) decay; *in* ~ *übergehen* (begin to) decay; **Verwesungsgeruch** *m* putrid smell, (strong) smell of putrefaction; **Verwesungsprozess** *m* process of decay

verwetten *v/t.* bet away, spend on betting; *pej.* (*leichtsinnig*) throw away on bets

verwickeln I. *v/t.* **1.** (*Wolle etc.*) tangle (up), get *s.th.* tangled; **2.** *j-n in etw.* ~ *fig.* involve s.o. in s.th., get s.o. involved (*od.* embroiled *od.* caught up) in s.th., drag s.o. into s.th.; **II.** *v/refl.:* *sich* ~ *in* (+ *Akk.*) get (o.s.) involved in; *sich in Widersprüche* ~ get tangled up in a web of contradictions; **verwickelt I.** *P.P.* → *verwickeln*; **II.** *Adj.* **1.** complicated, involved; **2.** ~ *in* (+ *Akk.*) involved in, caught up in; **Verwicklung** *f* entanglement, involvement; (*Kompliziertheit*) *auch* complexity; *konkret:* complication; (*Durcheinander*) confusion, tangle, imbroglio; *diplomatische etc. ~en* diplomatic *etc.* embroilment

verwiegen (*unreg.*) **I.** *v/refl.* get the weight wrong; **II.** *v/t. Fachspr.* (*wiegen*) weigh

verwildern *v/i. Garten, auch Kinder und Tiere:* run wild; *Person:* go to seed; **verwildert I.** *P.P.* → *verwildern*; **II.** *Adj. Garten:* overgrown, wild; *Tiere:* wild; *Kinder: auch* unruly; *Person, moralisch:* dissipated, *stärker:* dissolute; *der Garten ist völlig* ~ the garden has run completely wild; **Verwilderung** *f e-s Gartens:* (state of) neglect; *von Kindern:* (increasing) unruliness

verwinden (*unreg.*) *v/t.* **1.** (*etw.*) get over; **2.** *Tech.* twist; **Verwindung** *f Tech.* torsion

verwinkelt *Adj.* narrow and winding

verwirbeln *v/t.* swirl

verwirken *v/t.* forfeit

verwirklichen I. *v/t.* (*Pläne, Träume etc.*) realize; (*Ziel*) *auch* achieve, attain; **II.** *v/refl.* be realized, materialize; *Ziel:* be achieved (*od.* attained, realized); (*sich erfüllen*) come true; *sich selbst* ~ find one's fulfil(l)ment; **Ver-**

wirklichung *f* realization; *e-s Ziels: auch* achievement, attainment; *e-s Traums etc.:* fulfil(l)ment, realization

verwirren I. *v/t.* **1.** (*j-n*) confuse, *stärker:* bewilder, perplex; **2.** (*Garn etc.*) tangle (up); (*Haare*) dishevel; **II.** *v/refl.* get tangled (up); *Sinne:* become confused; **verwirrend I.** *Part. Präs.* → *verwirren*; **II.** *Adj.* confusing, *stärker:* bewildering; **Verwirrspiel** *n* deliberate confusion; *ein* ~ *treiben mit j-m* keep s.o. guessing; **verwirrt I.** *P.P.* → *verwirren*; **II.** *Adj.* confused, *stärker:* bewildered, perplexed; *geistig* ~ mentally confused; **III.** *Adv. ansehen etc.:* in confusion; *stärker:* in bewilderment; **Verwirrung** *f* **1.** (*Verwirrtheit*) confusion, *stärker:* perplexity; *er war in e-m Zustand geistiger* ~ he was clearly disturbed; **2.** (*Durcheinander*) confusion, muddle; ~ *stiften* cause confusion; **Verwirrungszustand** *m* state of confusion (*stärker:* bewilderment)

verwirtschaften *v/t.* squander away

verwischen I. *v/t.* (*undeutlich machen*) blur; (*verschmieren*) smear; (*Spuren*) cover up; **II.** *v/refl.* become blurred, blur; *Erinnerungen:* become hazy; *Unterschiede etc.:* become indistinct

verwissenschaftlichen *v/t.* make extremely scientific; **Verwissenschaftlichung** *f:* *durch die* ~ *der Sprache* by making the language extremely scientific (*od.* technical)

verwittern *v/i.* **1.** weather; (*zerfallen*) disintegrate; **2.** *Jägerspr.* mask the scent of an object or place; **verwittert I.** *P.P.* → *verwittern*; **II.** *Adj.* weather-beaten (*auch Gesicht*); **Verwitterung** *f* weathering; (*Zerfall*) disintegration

verwitwet *Adj.* widowed; *seit 10 Jahren etc.* ~ *sein* have been widowed for 10 years *etc.*; *Frau Meyer, ~e Kaiser* Mrs(.) Meyer, wife of the late Mr(.) Kaiser

verwoben I. *P.P.* → *verweben*; **II.** *Adj.* intertwined

verwohnen *v/t.* (*Wohnung*) run down, mess up; (*Möbel etc.*) wear out

verwöhnen *v/t.* spoil (*auch im positiven Sinne*); *sie hat mich mit Köstlichkeiten etc. verwöhnt* she spoiled me by feeding me delicacies *etc.*; *das Schicksal hat sie nicht verwöhnt* she hasn't had an easy time of it

verwohnt I. *P.P.* → *verwohnen*; **II.** *Adj.* **1.** *Wohnung, Zimmer etc.:* run-down; (*unordentlich*) untidy, in a mess *präd.*; **2.** *Möbel etc.:* worn-out; (*beschädigt*) battered

verwöhnt I. *P.P.* → *verwöhnen*; **II.** *Adj.* spoil|t (*Am.* -ed); *total* ~ thoroughly spoil|t (*Am.* -ed), spoil|t (*Am.* -ed) as hell *umg.*; *er hat e-n ~en Geschmack* he has very fine taste (very fussy tastes *pej.*); *die edle Zigarre für den ~en Raucher* the superior cigar for the discerning smoker; *badischer Wein, von der Sonne* ~ sun-kissed wine from Baden; **Verwöhntheit** *f* spoilt (*Am.* spoiled) state; **Verwöhnung** *f* spoiling

verworfen I. *P.P.* → *verwerfen*; **II.** *Adj.* depraved; **Verworfenheit** *f* depravity

verworren *Adj.* **1.** confused, muddled; *~es Zeug reden umg.* talk a lot of rubbish; **2.** (*kompliziert*) involved, intricate; **Verworrenheit** *f* **1.** confusion, confused state (of mind); **2.** (*Kompliziertheit*) intricacy, involved nature (+ *Gen.* of)

verwundbar *Adj.* vulnerable (*auch*

V

fig.); **Verwundbarkeit** *f* vulnerability (*auch fig.*); **verwunden** *v/t.* wound (*auch fig.*); *leicht/schwer verwundet werden* be slightly/seriously wounded; → *verwundet*

verwunderlich *Adj.* surprising; *stärker:* astonishing; *es ist nicht ~, dass* it's no wonder that; **verwundern I.** *v/t.* surprise; *stärker:* astonish; **II.** *v/refl.* be surprised; *stärker:* be astonished, be (quite) taken aback; **verwundert I.** *P.P.* → *verwundern;* **II.** *Adj.* surprised; *stärker:* astonished, taken aback; *in höchst ~em Ton* in a tone of great astonishment; **III.** *Adv.* anschauen, fragen etc. in surprise, *stärker:* in astonishment; **Verwunderung** *f:* (*zu m-r*) (to my) surprise, *stärker:* astonishment, *stärker:* amazement; *mit ~ nehmen wir zur Kenntnis, dass ...* to our great surprise we note that ...; *es hat für ~ gesorgt* it raised a few eyebrows

verwundet I. *P.P.* → *verwunden;* **II.** *Adj.* wounded; *sie war am Bein etc. verwundet* she had a wounded leg *etc.;* **Verwundete** *m, f; -n, -n* casualty, wounded (service)man *etc.; Pl. Koll. auch the* wounded

Verwundeten|abzeichen *n Mil.* wounded medal; *~transport m* transport of the wounded

Verwundung *f* wound, injury; *e-e lebensgefährliche etc. ~ haben* be fatally *etc.* wounded (*od.* injured), have a fatal *etc.* wound (*od.* injury)

verwunschen *Adj.* enchanted

verwünschen *v/t.* **1.** (*verfluchen*) curse; **2.** (*verzaubern*) enchant, cast a spell on; **verwünscht I.** *P.P.* → *verwünschen;* **II.** *Adj.* cursed, confounded; **Verwünschung** *f* **1.** (*Fluch*) curse; **2.** (*Zauber*) spell

verwurschteln, verwursteln *umg.* **I.** *v/t.* mess up; (*Haare*) *auch* muss up; **II.** *v/refl.* get messed up; **verwurschtelt, verwurstelt** *umg.* **I.** *P.P.* → *verwurschteln;* **II.** *Adj.* messed up; *Haare: auch* mussed up, dishevel(l)ed

verwursten *v/t.* make into sausage(s)

verwurzeln *v/i.* (take) root; **verwurzelt I.** *P.P.* → *verwurzeln;* **II.** *Adj.* (deeply) rooted (*in + Dat.* in); *fest ~* firmly rooted *od.* entrenched (*in* in); **Verwurzelung** *f* (*das Verwurzeln*) taking root (*in + Dat.* in); (*das Verwurzeltsein*) (deep) rootedness (*in + Dat.* in)

verwuscheln *v/t. umg.* (*Haar etc.*) tousle

verwüsten *v/t.* lay waste, devastate; *durch Vandalismus:* devastate; *umg. fig.* (*Frisur, Makeup etc.*) ruin; **verwüstet I.** *P.P.* → *verwüsten;* **II.** *Adj.* devastated, ravaged, *präd. auch* laid waste; *i-e total ~e Frisur umg. fig.* her completely ruined hairdo; **Verwüstung** *f* devastation, *förm.* depredation(s *Pl.*); *durch Vandalismus:* devastation; *e-e Stätte der ~* (*auch umg. fig. unaufgeräumtes Zimmer etc.*) a scene of destruction, a bombsite *umg.*

verzagen *v/i.* despair (*an + Dat.* of), lose heart; *nicht ~, Holger fragen! hum.* never fear, Holger's here!; **verzagt I.** *P.P.* → *verzagen;* **II.** *Adj.* despondent; (*verzweifelt*) desperate; (*kleinmütig*) fainthearted; **Verzagtheit** *f* despondency; *stärker:* despair, desperation

verzählen *v/refl.* miscount

verzahnen *v/t.* interlock (*auch fig.*); *Tech.* (*Holzteile*) dovetail; **verzahnt I.** *P.P.* → *verzahnen;* **II.** *Adj.* (*auch in-*

einander od. miteinander ~) interlocked (*auch fig.*); **Verzahnung** *f* interlocking (*auch fig.*); *Tech. Holzteile:* dovetail connection

verzanken *v/refl. umg.* fall out (with each other); (*wegen* over, about)

verzapfen *v/t.* **1.** *umg.* (*Unsinn etc.*) come up with; *verbal: auch* spout; **2.** (*Bier etc.*) have on draught (*Am.* draft); **3.** *Tech.* mortise and tenon; **Verzapfung** *f Tech.* mortise joint

verzärteln *v/t. pej.* (molly)coddle, pamper; **verzärtelt I.** *P.P.* → *verzärteln;* **II.** *Adj.* (molly)coddled

verzaubern *v/t.* cast a spell on; *fig.* enchant, *stärker:* bewitch; *~ in* (+ *Akk.*) turn into; **verzaubert I.** *P.P.* → *verzaubern;* **II.** *Adj.* enchanted; **Verzauberung** *f* casting of a spell on; *fig.* enchantment; *die ~ der Hexe in eine Maus* turning the witch into a mouse

verzehnfachen *v/t. und v/refl.* (*sich*) *~* increase tenfold; **Verzehnfachung** *f* tenfold increase

Verzehr *m; -s, kein Pl.* consumption; (*nicht*) *zum ~ geeignet* (not) fit to eat, (in)edible; *zum alsbaldigen ~ bestimmt* for immediate consumption

verzehren I. *v/t.* consume (*auch fig.*), eat; (*Erbe, Pension etc.*) eat up; **II.** *v/refl. fig.* eat one's heart out; *sich ~ nach* yearn for; *sich ~ vor Gram etc.:* pine away with, be consumed (*od.* eaten up) with; **verzehrend I.** *Part. Präs.* → *verzehren;* **II.** *Adj.* consuming, devouring

Verzehr|gutschein *m für Essen:* food voucher; *für Getränke:* drinks (*Am.* beverage) voucher; *~zwang m* obligation to order

verzeichnen I. *v/t.* **1.** note (*od.* write) down; *in e-r Liste: auch* list; *Gerät:* record, register; *amtlich:* register; (*Daten*) record; *Wirts.* (*Kurse*) quote; *fig.* (*Fortschritte*) record; (*Erfolg, Siege, Gewinne*) notch up; *~ können od. da ~ haben* have notched up; *... waren* (*nicht*) *zu ~* there were (no) ...; **2.** (*falsch zeichnen*) draw *s.th.* wrong; *fig.* (*falsch darstellen*) misrepresent; (*verzerren*) distort (*auch Opt.*); **II.** *v/refl.* (*falsch zeichnen*) make a mistake in one's drawing; **III.** *v/i. Opt., Fot.* distort; **Verzeichnis** *n; -ses, -se* list; *amtliches:* register; (*Katalog*) catalog(ue); (*Register*) index; *EDV* directory

...verzeichnis *n, im Subst.: Adressen~* directory of addresses, address directory; *Straßen~* index of street names; *Teilnehmer~* list of participants

Verzeichnis|pfad *m EDV* directory path; *~server m EDV* directory server

Verzeichnung *f* (*Verzerrung*) *auch fig.* distortion; **verzeichnungsfrei** *Adj. Opt.* orthoscopic

verzeihen *v/t./i.* (*unreg.*) **1.** forgive; *das ist nicht zu ~* there's no excuse for that; *das werde ich ihm nie ~* I'll never forgive him for that; *kannst du mir noch einmal ~?* *mst hum.* can you ever forgive me?; **2.** (*entschuldigen*) excuse, pardon (*j-m etw.* s.o. [for] s.th.); *~ Sie!* sorry!, *Am. auch* excuse me!, I ('do) beg your pardon *förm.; ~ Sie bitte die Störung* sorry to disturb you; *~ Sie die Frage, aber ...* if you'll forgive my asking, ...; **verzeihlich** *Adj.* forgivable; **Verzeihung** *f* forgiveness; (*Entschuldigung*) pardon; *~! für etw.:* sorry!, *Am. auch* excuse me!, I ('do) beg your pardon *förm.; vor e-r Frage*

etc.: excuse me; *~?* sorry(, could you repeat that)?; *j-n um ~ bitten* ask s.o.'s forgiveness; (*sich entschuldigen*) apologize to s.o.

verzerren I. *v/t.* **1.** (*Gesicht etc.*) distort; *stärker:* contort; *krampfartig:* convulse; **2.** *fig.* (*Ton, Bericht etc.*) distort (*auch Etech. etc.*); **3.** (*Muskel, Sehne*) pull; (*Knöchel*) sprain; **II.** *v/refl.* become distorted; *Gesicht: auch* contort; **verzerrt I.** *P.P.* → *verzerren;* **II.** *Adj.* **1.** *Gesicht:* distorted; *stärker:* contorted; *ein von Schmerz etc. ~es Gesicht* a face contorted with pain *etc.;* **2.** *fig. Ton:* distorted (*auch Etech. etc.*); **Verzerrung** *f* distortion (*auch fig.*); *des Gesichts: auch* contortion; *nicht lineare ~ Etech.* non-linear distortion

verzetteln I. *v/refl.* **1.** have too many irons in the fire, be doing too many things at the same time; **2.** (*sich mit zu viel Nebensächlichem beschäftigen*) waste one's time on (*od.* get sidetracked by) little things; **II.** *v/t.* **1.** (*vertun*) waste, fritter away; **2.** (*für e-e Kartei auf Zettel od. Karten schreiben*) write down on a slip (*od.* slips) of paper

Verzicht *m; -(e)s, kein Pl.* renunciation, renouncement (*auf + Akk.* of); (*Enthaltung*) abstention (from); (*Abtretung*) abandonment (of); *Jur. auf Ansprüche, Rechte:* waiver, disclaimer; *~ leisten auf* (+ *Akk.*) for(e)go, do without; *förm.* renounce, forswear; **verzichtbar** *Adj.* dispensable; *nicht ~* indispensable; *sie hält Fleisch bei der Ernährung für ~* she thinks it's possible to do without meat; **verzichten** *v/i.* for(e)go, do without; *förm.* renounce, forswear (*alle: auf etw. Akk.* s.th.); (*sich enthalten*) abstain, refrain (from); *Jur.* waive, disclaim (s.th.); *~ auf* (+ *Akk.*) (*ein Angebot etc.*) turn down; (*e-n Posten etc.*) *auch* refuse; (*aufgeben*) give up, abandon; *auf Gewalt ~* renounce violence, abandon the use of force; *danke, ich verzichte umg.* thanks, but no thanks; *darauf kann ich ~ pej.* I can do without that

Verzicht|erklärung *f* waiver, disclaimer; *~leistung f* renunciation; *~politik f* policy of surrender

verziehen (*unreg.*) **I.** *v/t.* (*hat verzogen*) **1.** *das Gesicht ~* pull (*od.* make) a face; *stärker:* screw up one's face; *den Mund ~* grimace, twist one's mouth; → *Miene,* **2.** (*Kind*) spoil; **3.** (*junge Pflanzen*) thin out; **4.** *Sport* (*Ball etc.*) slice, mishit; **5.** *Feuchtigkeit verzieht das Holz* dampness warps the wood; **II.** *v/i.* (*ist*) (*umziehen*) move (house); → *Empfänger¹, verzogen* II 3; **III.** *v/refl.* (*hat*) **1.** (*die Form verlieren*) go out of shape; *Holz:* warp; **2.** *Gesicht:* screw up (*zu* into), contort (into); *Mund:* twist (into), contort (into); **3.** (*verschwinden*) disappear; *Wolken: auch* disperse; *Sturm:* blow over; **4.** *umg.* (*sich davonschleichen*) decamp (*nach* to), make o.s. scarce; *verzieh dich!* get lost!, push off!, scram!, *Am. auch* vamoose!

verzieren *v/t.* decorate; *Archit., Mus., handwerklich etc.:* ornament; **Verzierung** *f* decoration; *Archit. etc.* ornament; (*auch ~en*) ornamentation; *Mus.* ornament(s *Pl.*)

verzimmern *v/t.* prop (*od.* shore) up; **Verzimmerung** *f* (*das Verzimmern*) propping (*od.* shoring) up; (*Balken, Bohlen*) props *Pl.,* supports *Pl.*

V

verzinken *v/t.* galvanize; **Verzinkung** *f* galvanization

verzinnen *v/t.* tin-plate; **Verzinnung** *f* tin-plating

verzinsbar *Adj. Wirts. nachgestellt:* bearing interest; *Papiere, Darlehen:* interest-bearing; **verzinsen I.** *v/t.* pay interest on; *e-n Betrag zu 3%* ~ pay 3 per cent (*bes. Am.* percent) interest on a sum; **II.** *v/refl.* yield (*od.* bear) interest; *sich mit 5%* ~ bear 5 per cent (*bes. Am.* percent) interest; **verzinslich** *Adj. nachgestellt:* bearing interest; *Papiere, Darlehen:* interest-bearing; *fest* ~ bearing a fixed rate of interest; *nicht* ~ free of interest; **Verzinsung** *f* payment of interest; (*Zinssatz*) interest rate; (*Zinsertrag*) return; *e-e fünfprozentige etc.* ~ a return of five percent *etc.*

verzogen I. *P.P.* → *verziehen*; **II.** *Adj.* **1.** *Kind:* spoilt, *Am.* spoiled; **2.** *Tech. etc.:* out of shape; *Holz etc.:* auch warped; **3.** *Post.:* *Empfänger unbekannt* ~ gone away, not known at this address, address unknown; *falls* ~, *bitte zurück an* if undelivered, please return to

Verzögerung *f* delay

Verzögerungs|taktik *f* delaying (*od.* stalling) tactics *Pl.*; ~**zeit** *f* delay

verzollen *v/t.* pay duty on; *haben Sie etwas zu* ~? have you (got) anything to declare?; *etw./nichts zu* ~ *Schild:* goods to declare / nothing to declare; **verzollt I.** *P.P.* → *verzollen*; **II.** *Adj.* duty-paid; *nicht* ~*e Ware* non-duty--paid goods; **Verzollung** *f* payment of duty (+ *Gen.* on)

verzücken *v/t.* enrapture; **Verzücken** *n*; *-s, kein Pl.* → **Verzückung**

verzuckern *v/t.* **1.** sugar (over); (*kandieren*) candy; **2.** put too much sugar in; *fig. pej.* (*verkitschen*) sentimentalize; **3.** *Chem.* saccharify

verzückt I. *P.P.* → *verzücken*; **II.** *Adj.* enraptured, *stärker:* in raptures, ecstatic; *Blick:* rapt; **III.** *Adv. lächeln, zuhören etc.:* enraptured, ecstatically; **Verzückung** *f* rapture, *stärker:* ecstasy; *in* ~ *geraten* go into raptures (*wegen* over)

Verzug *m*; *-(e)s, kein Pl.* **1.** delay; *ohne* ~ without delay, forthwith; *in* ~ *geraten/sein* get/be behind; *mit Zahlungen:* fall into / be in arrears; **2.** *es ist Gefahr im* ~ danger is looming; **3.** *förm.* (*Wegzug*) move; **4.** *Bergb.* lagging; **Verzugszinsen** *Pl.* interest *Sg.* on arrears, default interest *Sg.*

verzweifeln *v/i.* despair (*an* + *Dat.* of); *an der Menschheit etc.* ~ lose all faith in mankind *etc.*; *am Verzweifeln sein* be desperate; *es ist zum Verzweifeln* it's enough to drive you to despair (*od.* distraction); **verzweifelt I.** *P.P.* → *verzweifeln*; **II.** *Adj.* despairing; (*aussichtslos, auch rücksichtslos*) desperate; *~e Lage* hopeless (*od.* desperate) situation; *~er Versuch* desperate attempt; *letzter:* last-ditch effort; *ich bin so* ~ I'm so desperate, I'm at my wits' end; **III.** *Adv. versuchen, um sein Leben kämpfen etc.:* despairingly; (*aussichtslos, auch rücksichtslos*) desperately; **Verzweiflung** *f* despair, desperation; *aus* (*lauter*) ~ in *od.* out of (sheer) desperation; *in m-r etc.* ~ in my *etc.* despair; *zur* ~ *treiben* exasperate, drive to despair (*od.* distraction); **Verzweiflungstat** *f* act of desperation

verzweigen *v/refl.* branch out; *bes. fig.* ramify; *EDV* branch; **Verzweigung** *f*

branching out; *fig.* ramifications *Pl.*; *EDV* branch

verzwickt *Adj. umg.* tricky; *attr. Problem: auch* knotty ...; (*kompliziert*) complicated; **Verzwicktheit** *f umg.* trickiness; complicated nature (+ *Gen.* of)

Vesper[1] *f*; *-, -n; kirchl.* (*Gebetsstunde*) vespers *Pl.* (*auch V. im Sg.*)

Vesper[2] *f*; *-, -n; bes. schwäbisch auch n*; *-s, -; bes. südd.* (*Imbiss*) snack; (*~pause*) break; ~ *machen* have (*od.* take) a break; *sich ein / etw. für die* ~ *mitnehmen* take a snack / s.th. for the break

Vesperbild *n Kunst:* pietà

Vesperbrot *n bes. südd.* (*Vesperzeit*) break; *Imbiss:* sandwich

Vesperglocke *f kirchl.* bell for vespers

Vesperkarte *f bes. südd. Gastr.* snack menu

Vesperläuten *n kirchl.* ringing of the bell for vespers

vespern 1. *v/t. bes. südd.* have s.th. as a snack; **2.** *v/i. bes. südd.* have a snack; (*Pause machen*) have a break; *Vespern gehen* go for a snack; *zum Vespern einkehren etc.* stop off *etc.* for a snack

Vesper|pause *f bes. südd.* break; ~**teller** *m Gastr.* platter consisting of slices of cold meat and sausage; ~**zeit** *f* break time

Vestalin *f*; *-, -nen; hist.* vestal virgin

Vesuv *m*; *-s; Geog.* (Mount) Vesuvius

Veteran *m*; *-en, -en* **1.** *Brit.* ex-serviceman, *Am.* veteran; **2.** (*Oldtimer*) vintage car; **3.** *fig.* veteran

Veteranenorganisation *f* veterans organization

Veterinär *m*; *-s, -e,* ~**in** *f*; *-, -nen* veterinary surgeon, *Am.* veterinarian, vet *umg.*; **Veterinäramt** *n* veterinary inspection office

Veterinärmedizin *f* veterinary medicine; **veterinärmedizinisch I.** *Adj.* relating to veterinary medicine; *ein* ~*es Gutachten* a veterinary report; **II.** *Adv.: etw.* ~ *untersuchen* give s.th. a veterinary examination; *das Tier wurde* ~ *untersucht* the animal was examined by a vet; **Veterinärpolizei** *f* veterinary inspectors *Pl.*

Veto *n*; *-s, -s* veto (*Pl.* vetoes); (*s*)*ein* ~ *einlegen* exercise one's power of veto, (*s*)*ein* ~ *einlegen gegen* put a veto on, veto; ~**recht** *n* power of veto; *von s-m* ~ *Gebrauch machen* exercise one's power of veto

Vettel *f*; *-, -n; pej.:* (*garstige alte*) ~ (nasty old) hag

Vetter *m*; *-s, -n* cousin; **Vetternwirtschaft** *f* nepotism, cronyism *umg.*

Vexier|bild *n* picture puzzle; ~**rätsel** *n* surprise puzzle; ~**spiegel** *m* distorting mirror

V-förmig I. *Adj.* V-shaped; **II.** *Adv. angeordnet etc.:* in (the shape of) a V

V-Gespräch *n Telef.* person-to-person call

VHS *f*; *-, -; Abk.* → *Volkshochschule*; ~**-Kurs** *m* evening class; *e-n* ~ *in ... machen* do a course (*od.* do evening classes) in ...; ~**-Zertifikat** *n* evening--class certificate

via *Präp.* (+ *Akk.*) via

Viadukt *m, n*; *-(e)s, -e* viaduct

Vibraphon *n*; *-s, -e; Mus.* vibraphone, vibes *Pl. umg.*; **Vibraphonist** *m*; *-en, -en,* **Vibraphonistin** *f*; *-, -nen* vibraphonist

Vibration *f*; *-, -en* vibration; **vibrationsfrei** *Adj.* vibration-free; **Vibrationsmassage** *f* vibratory massage

Vibrato *n*; *-s, -s und Vibrati; Mus.* vibrato

Vibrator *m*; *-s, -en* vibrator (*auch beim Handy*); **vibrieren** *v/i.* vibrate

Video *n*; *-s, -s* **1.** video; *ein* ~ *abspielen/löschen* play/erase a video; → *reinziehen* 2; **2.** *nur Sg.: auf* ~ *aufnehmen* video(tape), record on video; *mit od. per* ~ *überwachen* monitor on closed-circuit television; ~**anlage** *f Geräte:* video equipment; *Stelle:* video unit; ~**aufnahme** *f*, ~**aufzeichnung** *f* video recording; ~**band** *n* videotape; ~**bild** *n* video picture; ~**clip** *m* video clip; ~**film** *m* video film; ~**gerät** *n* video (recorder), video cassette recorder, *bes. Am. auch* VCR; ~**installation** *f Kunst:* video installation; ~**kamera** *f* video camera; (*Kamera plus Rekorder*) camcorder; ~**karte** *f EDV* video card; ~**kassette** *f* video cassette; ~**konferenz** *f* video conference; ~**kunst** *f* video art; ~**künstler** *m*, ~**künstlerin** *f* video artist; ~**produktion** *f* video production; ~**recorder**, ~**rekorder** *m* → *Videogerät*; ~**-Schocker** *m* video nasty; ~**sichtgerät** *n EDV* video display device; ~**signal** *n Etron.* video signal; ~**spiel** *n* video game; ~**technik** *f* video technology; ~**text** *m* teletext

Videothek *f* **1.** video store; **2.** (*Sammlung*) video collection

videoüberwacht *Adj.: der Tunnel ist nicht* ~ the tunnel has no closed-circuit TV cameras (installed); **Videoüberwachung** *f* closed-circuit TV, CCTV

Videovorführung *f* video presentation

Viech *n*; *-(e)s, -er; umg.* **1.** (*Tier*) (*verdammtes*) ~ (blasted) animal; (*bes. Hund*) critter; (*Insekt*) (blasted) insect, *Am. auch* bug, creepy-crawly *umg.*; **2.** (*Rohling*) brute; **Viecherei** *f*; *-, -en; umg.* **1.** (*Schufterei*) hard graft, (real) grind, hell of a job *Sl.*; **2.** (*Gemeinheit*) dirty trick

Vieh *n*; *-(e)s* **1.** (*bes. Rinder*) cattle *Pl.*; *weitS.* (*Nutztiere*) livestock (*auch V. im Pl.*); *umg.* (*allg. Tier*) animal, beast; *das* ~ *füttern* feed the animals; *zehn Stück* ~ ten head of livestock (*Rinder:* cattle); *j-n wie ein Stück* ~ *behandeln* treat s.o. like dirt (*od.* muck); *das arme* ~! *umg.* the poor creature!; **2.** *fig.* (*Rohling*) brute; *du* ~! *fig. pej.* you swine!; ~**abtrieb** *m: der* ~ *findet jetzt statt* the livestock are being brought down from the mountain pastures now; ~**bestand** *m* livestock; ~**dieb** *m* cattle thief (*od.* rustler); ~**futter** *n* fodder, feed; ~**halter** *m*, ~**halterin** *f* livestock keeper; *von Rindern:* cattle owner (*bes. Am.* rancher); ~**haltung** *f* keeping of livestock; *von Rindern:* keeping of cattle; ~**handel** *m* livestock trade; *von Rindern:* cattle trade; ~**händler** *m*, ~**händlerin** *f* livestock dealer; *von Rindern:* cattle dealer; ~**herde** *f* herd of cattle, cattle herd

viehisch I. *Adj.* **1.** brutal; **2.** *umg.* (*sehr groß*) dreadful; **II.** *Adv.* **1.** *sich* ~ *benehmen* behave like a brute (*od.* brutes); **2.** *umg.:* ~ *betrunken etc.* drunk *etc.* as hell *Sl.*

Vieh|markt *m* cattle market; ~**salz** *n für Tiere:* cattle salt; (*Streusalz*) road salt; ~**seuche** *f* livestock disease; ~**stall** *m* cattle shed; ~**tränke** *f* cattle trough; ~**treiber** *m* drover; ~**wagen** *m* cattle truck; ~**weide** *f* (cattle) pasture; ~**wirtschaft** *f* (live)stock farming, animal husbandry; **~zeug** *n umg.* **1.** animals *Pl.*; (*Haustiere*) menagerie; **2.** *pej.* (*verdammtes*) ~ (blasted) animals *Pl.*; (*Insekten*) (blasted) insects *Pl.*, *Am.* bugs *Pl.*; **~zucht** *f* (live)stock breeding; *von Rindern*: cattle breeding; **~züchter** *m*, **~züchterin** *f* (live)stock breeder; *von Rindern*: cattle breeder

viel I. *Adj.* a lot of, lots of *umg.*; **~e** many; *nicht* ~ not much; *nicht* **~e** not many; *sehr* ~ a great deal (of); *sehr* **~e** very many, a lot (*od.* lots *umg.*) (of), a great many; *noch einmal so* ~ as much again; *ziemlich* **~(e)** quite a lot (of); ~ *verdienen* earn a lot of money; *einer zu* ~ one too many; *einer unter* **~en** one among(st) many; *ein bisschen* ~ a bit (*od.* little) (too) much; → *auch* **bisschen** II; ~ *zu* ~ far too much; *das* **~e** *Geld* all that money; *in* **~em** in many ways; ~ *Erfreuliches etc.* lots of nice things *etc.*; *um* **~es** *besser* far (*od.* much) better; *das will* ~ / *nicht* ~ *heißen* that's saying a lot / that's not saying much; → *Dank*, *Glück* 1, *Spaß* 2; **II.** *Adv.* **1.** a lot, lots *umg.*; *die Straße wird* ~ *befahren* the road is used a lot, a lot of traffic uses the road; ~ *besser* much better; *was soll ich dir noch* ~ *erzählen?* there's no point in my going into (any great) detail about it; **2.** *mit P.P.*: ~ *beachtet* well regarded; ~ *befahren* very busy; ~ *benutzt* well-used; ~ *beschäftigt* very busy; ~ *besucht* much-frequented; ~ *besungen* *lit. od. hum. präd.* frequently celebrated in song, *attr. auch* oft-sung *lit.*; ~ *bewundert* much-admired; ~ *diskutiert* much-discussed, widely discussed; ~ *gebraucht* much-used; ~ *gefragt* very popular; ~ *gehasst* much-hated; ~ *gekauft* frequently bought; ~ *gelesen* much-read; ~ *gelobt* much-praised; ~ *genannt* often-mentioned, *lit.* oft-mentioned; *Buch*: much-cited, oft-cited; (*berühmt*) noted, distinguished; ~ *gepriesen* much-praised; ~ *geprüft* sorely tried; ~ *gereist* widely-(*od.* much-)travel(l)er; *er ist ein* ~ *ge-reister Mann* he's done a lot of travel(l)ing (in his time); ~ *gerühmt* much-praised; ~ *geschmäht* much-maligned, much-reviled; ~ *kritisiert* much-criticized; ~ *umjubelt* highly acclaimed; ~ *umworben* much sought-after; ~ *zitiert* much-cited, oft-cited; **3.** *mit Part. Präs.*: ~ *sagend Blick*: meaningful; *sie sah mich* ~ *sagend an* she gave me a meaningful look; ~ *sagend schweigen* fall into a meaningful silence; ~ *versprechend* (very) promising

vielbändig *Adj. attr.* multivolume ...
viel beachtet *etc.* → **viel** II 2
vieldeutig *Adj. attr.* ambiguous; **Vieldeutigkeit** *f* ambiguity
viel diskutiert → **viel** II 2
Vieleck *n*; -(*e*)*s*, -*e* polygon; **vieleckig** *Adj.* polygonous
Vielehe *f* (*auch die* ~) polygamy
vielerlei *Adj.* various, all sorts of, multifarious; **Vielerlei** *n*; -*s*, -*s* variety
vielerorts *Adv.* in many places
vielfach I. *Adj.* multiple; *die* **~e** *Menge* many times the amount; *auf* **~en** *Wunsch* by popular request; **II.** *Adv.* in many cases; (*auch oft*) frequently; *ein* ~ *ausgezeichneter Film etc.* a film which (*Am.* a movie that) has frequently won awards *etc.*; **Vielfache** *n*; -*n*, -*n* **1.** *Math.*: *das Vielfache* the multiple; **2.** *um ein Vielfaches besser etc.*:

---

many times better *etc.*
Vielfahrer *m*, **~in** *f* frequent travel(l)er
Vielfalt *f*; -, *kein Pl.* (great) variety; **vielfältig** *Adj.* varied, manifold; **Vielfältigkeit** *f* variety, diversity
vielfarbig I. *Adj.* multicolo(u)red; **II.** *Adv.* gemustert *etc.*: in a multitude of colo(u)rs
Vielflieger *m*, **~in** *f* frequent flyer (*od.* travel[l]er)
Vielfraß *m*; -*es*, -*e* **1.** *Zool.* wolverine; **2.** *umg.* (*Mensch*) glutton; *unser Baby ist ein kleiner* ~ our baby is a little greedy guts
viel gebraucht *etc.* → **viel** II 2
vielgestaltig *Adj.* variform; *fig.* multifarious; **Vielgestaltigkeit** *f* multiformity; *fig.* multifariousness
vielgliedrig *Adj. System*: multipartite; *Gesellschaft*: many-tiered; *Geschichte, Antennen: präd. und nachgestellt*: composed of many parts; **Vielgliedrigkeit** *f* multipartite nature; many-tiered nature; → **vielgliedrig**
Vielgötterei *f* polytheism
Vielheit *f* multitude
vielköpfig *Adj. attr.* **1.** *Familie etc.*: large; **2.** *Bestie etc.*: many-headed
viel kritisiert → **viel** II 2
vielleicht *Adv.* **1.** perhaps, maybe; (*möglicherweise*) possibly; *in Fragen*: *oft* by any chance; (*etwa*) ([a]round) about; ~ *ist er krank* he might (*od.* may) be sick; *Sie haben* ~ *Recht* you may be right; ~ *kommt er* perhaps he'll come, he may come; ~ *auch nicht* perhaps not; *es ist* ~ *besser, wenn* it might be better if; *hast du ihn* ~ *gesehen?* have you seen him by any chance?, do you happen to have seen him?; **2.** (*ungefähr*) about, perhaps; *es waren* ~ *20 Leute da* I'd say there were ([a]round) about 20 people there, there would have been - what - 20 people there; *sie wiegt* ~ *so 40 Kilo umg.* she weighs about 40 kilos or so; **3.** *umg. verstärkend*: *das war* ~ *ein Durcheinander!* what a mess (that was), you should have seen the mess; *das war* ~ *was!* that was really something!; *der hat* ~ *geschimpft!* you should have heard him shout; *die ist* ~ *doof etc.!* how stupid *etc.* she is!; *ich war* ~ *aufgeregt!* what a state I was in; (*nervös*) *auch* talk about (being) nervous; **4.** *rhetorisch*: *ist das* ~ *e-e Lösung?* is that supposed to be a solution?; *kannst du* ~ *mal aufhören! umg.* d'you think you could stop (*od.* shut up) for a minute?; *hast du's* ~ (*etwa*) *verloren?* don't tell me you've lost it; *glaubt er* ~, *dass ich es war?* surely he doesn't think I did it?
vielmals *Adv.* many times, often, frequently; *danke* ~ many thanks; *entschuldige* ~, *ich bitte* ~ *um Entschuldigung* I'm terribly sorry
Vielmännerei *f*; -, *kein Pl.* polyandry, polygamy
vielmehr *Adv.* (*eher*) rather; (*im Gegenteil*) on the contrary; *es geht* ~ *darum, ob* it's rather a question of whether
Vielredner *m umg.* gasbag, *bes. Am.* windbag
vielsagend → **viel** II 3
vielschichtig *Adj.* **1.** multi-layered; **2.** *fig. Problem etc.*: complex; **Vielschichtigkeit** *f* e-s *Problems etc.*: complexity
Vielschreiber *m*, **~in** *f umg. pej.* hack (writer)
vielseitig I. *Adj.* **1.** *mit vielen Aspek-*

---

ten: many-sided; **2.** *Person*: versatile; (*abwechslungsreich*) (very) varied; *Möglichkeiten*: various, a (whole) variety of; *Beruf, Tätigkeit etc.*: interesting; *auf* **~en** *Wunsch* by popular request; **II.** *Adv.*: ~ *verwendbar attr.* multi-purpose ...; ~ *verwendbar sein* have many uses; ~ *begabt* multitalented; ~ *interessiert sein* have a lot of interests; **Vielseitigkeit** *f* **1.** many-sidedness; *die* ~ *des Problems* the many aspects of the problem; **2.** *e-r Person*: versatility; **Vielseitigkeitsprüfung** *f Sport* three-day event
vielsprachig *Adj.* polyglot (*auch* **~er** *Mensch*), multilingual
Vielstaaterei *f*; -, *kein Pl.* particularism
vielstimmig I. *Adj.* polyphonic; **II.** *Adv.* singen *etc.*: polyphonically
vieltausendmal *Adv. lit.* thousands upon thousands of times
viel umjubelt *etc.* → **viel** II 2
Vielvölkerstaat *m* multinational (*od.* multiracial) state
Vielweiberei *f* (*auch die* ~) polygamy
Vielzahl *f* huge (*od.* vast) number; *förm.* multitude
viel zitiert → **viel** II 2
vier *Adj.* four; *auf allen* **~en** (*kriechen* be) on all fours; *unter* ~ *Augen* in private; *alle* **~e** *von sich strecken* flop into an armchair (*od.* onto the bed *etc.*); → *Buchstabe etc.*; → *auch* **acht**[1]
Vier *f*; -, -*en* four; (*Note*) *etwa* D; (*Buslinie etc.*) (number) four; *e-e* ~ *schreiben* get a D; *die Karo-*~ the four of diamonds
Vieraugengespräch *umg. n* tête-à-tête, one-to-one conversation; *mit Vorgesetzten*: face time
vierbändig I. *Adj. attr.* four-volume ..., in four volumes; **II.** *Adv. erscheinen etc.*: in four volumes
Vierbeiner *m*; -*s*, -; *umg.* quadruped, four-legged animal; *hum.* (*Hund*) four-legged friend; **vierbeinig** *Adj.* four-legged
vier|blätt(e)rig *Adj.* four-leafed, four-leaved, *attr. auch* four-leaf ...; **~es** *Kleeblatt* four-leaf (*od.* -leaved) clover; **~dimensional** *Adj.* four-dimensional
Viereck *n*; -*s*, -*e* **1.** four-sided figure; **2.** *Math.* quadrangle, quadrilateral; *Rechteck*: rectangle; *Quadrat*: square; **viereckig** *Adj.* **1.** four-sided; **2.** *Math.* quadrangular, quadrilateral; *rechteckig*: rectangular; *quadratisch*: square
Vierer *f*; -, -. **1.** *Rudern*: four; *Golf*: foursome; ~ *mit/ohne* (*Steuermann*) coxed/coxless four; **2.** → **Vier**, **3.** *umg.*: *flotter* ~ (*Sex zu viert*) foursome; **~bande** *f hist.* Gang of Four; **~bob** *m Sport* four-seater bob; **~gespräch** *n* four-sided (*od.* four-party) talks *Pl.*; *hist. der vier Mächte*: four-power talks *Pl.*
viererlei *Adj.* four (different) kinds of; *subst.* four things
Vierertakt *m Mus.* four-four time, quadruple (*Am.* common) time
vierfach *Adj.* fourfold; *die* **~e** *Menge* four times the amount; **~er** *Sieger* four-time winner (*od.* champion); **~e** (*Umdrehungs-*) *Geschwindigkeit EDV* quad speed; **Vierfache** *n*; -*n*, *kein Pl.*: *das* ~ four times as much; *Menge, Betrag*: *auch* four times the amount; *um* **~s** *steigen* quadruple, rise (*od.* go up) fourfold
Vierfarbendruck *m* four-colo(u)r printing (*konkret*: print)
vierfarbig I. *Adj. attr.* four-colo(u)r ...; *präd. und nachgestellt*: in four col-

o(u)rs; **II.** *Adv. drucken etc.*: in four colo(u)rs

vierfüßig *Adj.* four-footed; *Zool.* quadruped; **Vierfüß(l)er** *m*; *-s,* - quadruped

Vierganggetriebe *n Mot.* four-speed transmission

viergeschossig I. *Adj.* four-stor(e)y, four-storied; **II.** *Adv. bauen etc.*: with four stor|eys (*Am.* -ies)

Viergespann *n* four-in-hand; *hist.* quadriga

vierhändig I. *Adj. Zool. und Mus.* four-handed; **II.** *Adv.*: ~ **spielen** auch play a duet

vierhundert *Adj.* four hundred

vierjährig *Adj. attr.* **1.** four-year-old ...; **2.** (*vier Jahre dauernd*) four-year ...; **Vierjährige** *m*, *f*; *-n, -n* four-year-old

Vierkampf *m Sport* four-event competition

Vierkant *m*, *n*; *-(e)s, -e*; *Tech.* **1.** square; **2.** (*Schlüssel*) square box spanner (*Am.* wrench); ~**holz** *n* square timber

vierkantig *Adj.* square; **Vierkantschlüssel** *m* square box spanner (*Am.* wrench)

vierköpfig *Adj.*: ~**e Familie** *etc.* family *etc.* of four

Vierlinge *Pl.* quadruplets, quads *umg.*

Viermächteabkommen *n hist.* four--power agreement

viermal *Adv.* four times; **viermalig** *Adj. nachgestellt*: repeated four times; *Sieger: attr.* four-times ...; ~**es Tanzen** four dances; **nach ~er Aufforderung** at the fourth request, after four requests

Viermaster *m*; *-s,* - **1.** *Naut.* four-master; **2.** (*Zelt*) four-pole tent

viermotorig *Adj. attr.* four-engine ..., four-engined; *i-e Maschinen sind alle* ~ their planes all have four engines

Vierrad|antrieb *m Mot.* four-wheel drive; ~**bremse** *f Mot.* four-wheel brake

vier|räd(e)rig *Adj.* four-wheeled, *attr. auch* four-wheel ...; ~**saitig** *Adj. attr. Mus.* four-string ..., four-stringed

Vierschanzentournee *f Sport* Four Hills Tournament

vierschrötig *Adj.* burly

vier|seitig *Adj.* four-sided; *Math.* quadrilateral; ~**silbig** *Adj. attr.* four-syllable ...

Viersitzer *m*; *-s,* - four-seater; **viersitzig** *Adj. attr.* four-seater ...; *das Modell ist* ~ the model comes with four seats, it is a four-seater model

Vierspänner *m*, *-s,* - **1.** (*Kutsche, Wagen mit vier Pferden*) four-in-hand; **2.** *Archit.* (*Block aus vier Reihenhäusern*) row of four terraced (*Am.* row) houses (*Am. auch* townhouses)

vier|spurig *Adj. attr. Straße:* four-lane ...; *Tonband:* four-track ...; *alle Autobahnen sind mindestens* ~ all motorways (*Am.* freeways) have at least four lanes; ~**stellig** *Adj. attr. Zahl:* four--digit ...; *die Angebote sind alle* ~ they are all four-figure offers

Viersterne|general *m* four-star general; ~**hotel** *n* four-star hotel

vier|stimmig I. *Adj. Mus. attr.* four--part ..., *präd.* for four voices; **II.** *Adv. singen etc.*: sing *s.th.* in four voices; ~**stöckig I.** *Adj.* four-stor(e)y, four--storied; **II.** *Adv. bauen etc.*: with four stor|eys (*Am.* -ies)

viert *Adv.*: *wir waren zu* ~ there were four of us; *etw. zu* ~ *tun* do s.th. as a foursome; *auf dem Sofa kann man zu* ~ *sitzen* four people can sit on the sofa, the sofa seats four

viert... *Zahlw.* fourth; ~**es Kapitel** chap-

ter four; *am* ~**en Juni** on the fourth of June; *4. Juni* 4th June, *bes. Am.* June 4(th); ~**e Welt** *Pol.* Fourth World

Viertagewoche *f* four-day week

viertägig I. *Adj.* **1.** *attr.* four-day(-long) ...; **2.** *attr.* (*vier Tage alt*) four-day-old ...; **II.** *Adv. planen, anlegen etc.*: for four days

Viertaktmotor *m* four-stroke engine

viertausend *Adj.* four thousand; **Viertausender** *m* four-thousand met|re (*Am.* -er) peak

Vierte *m*; *-n, -n* (the) fourth; *er war* ~*r* he was (*od.* came) fourth; *Heinrich IV.* Henry IV (= Henry the Fourth)

vierteilen *v/t.* (*untrenn., hat -ge-*) *hist.* (draw and) quarter; *er würde sich lieber* ~ *lassen*(, *als* ...) *umg.* he'd rather die (than ...)

Vierteiler *m TV etc.* four-parter; **vierteilig** *Adj. attr.* four-part ..., *auch präd.* in four parts

Viertel *n*; *-s,* - quarter (*auch* Maß, Stadtteil, des Mondes); *Math. Am. auch* fourth; *umg.* (~*pfund*) quarter; (*Glas Wein*) glass of wine (*measuring 250 ml*); *ein* ~ *Weißburgunder etc.* a glass of white Burgundy *etc.* (*measuring 250 ml*); *drei* ~ three quarters; ~ *nach vier* (a) quarter past (*Am. auch* after) four; ~ *vor vier* (a) quarter to (*Am. auch* of) four; *viertel drei Dial.* (a) quarter past (*Am. auch* after) two; ~**drehung** *f* quarter turn

Viertele *n bes. südd.* (*Glas Wein*) glass of wine (*measuring 250 ml*); *sich auf ein* ~ *treffen* meet for a glass of wine

Viertel|finale *n* quarterfinal; ~**jahr** *n* three months *Pl.*, quarter; ~**jahresschrift** *f* quarterly (journal); ~**jahrhundert** *n* quarter of a century

vierteljährig *Adj. attr.* **1.** three-month ...; *Aufenthalt etc.*: *auch* three months' ...; **2.** (*drei Monate alt*) three-month--old ...; **vierteljährlich I.** *Adj.* quarterly; ~**e Kündigung** three months' notice; **II.** *Adv.* quarterly, every three months

Viertel|kreis *m* **1.** *Math.* quadrant; **2.** *Fußball:* corner arc; ~**liter** *m*: (*ein*) ~ (a) quarter of a lit|re (*Am.* -er); ~**million** *f* quarter of a million

vierteln *v/t.* quarter

Viertel|note *f Mus.* crotchet, *Am.* quarter note; ~**pause** *f Mus.* crotchet (*Am.* quarter note) rest; ~**pfund** *n*: (*ein*) ~ *etwa* ([a]) quarter of a pound, (a) quarter; ~**stündchen** *n umg.* quarter of an hour; ~**stunde** *f* quarter of an hour

viertelstündig *Adj. attr.* fifteen-minute ..., of (*od.* lasting) a quarter of an hour; *e-e* ~**e Pause** *etc.* a fifteen-minute break *etc.*; **viertelstündlich I.** *Adj.* quarter-hourly, occurring every fifteen minutes; *in* ~**en Abständen** every fifteen minutes; **II.** *Adv.* every fifteen minutes (*od.* quarter of an hour), quarter-hourly

Viertelton *m* quarter tone; ~**musik** *f Mus.* quarter-tone music

Viertelzentner *m* quarter of a (metric) hundredweight (*12.5 kilograms*)

viertens *Adv.* fourth(ly), four, in fourth place

Viertklässler *m*; *-s,* -, ~**in** *f*; *-, -nen* fourth-year pupil (*in final year of elementary school*), *Am. etwa* fourth--grader

Vierundsechzigstel-Note *f Mus.* hemidemisemiquaver, *Am.* sixty-fourth note

Vierung *f Archit.* crossing, intersection

Vierungs|pfeiler *m Archit.* transept pillar; ~**turm** *m Archit.* crossing tower

Viervierteltakt *m Mus.* four-four (*Am. auch* common) time

Vierwaldstätter See *m*; *-s*; *Geog.* Lake Lucerne

vierwöchig *Adj.* **1.** *attr.* four-week ...; *präd.* four weeks long; **2.** (*vier Wochen alt*) *attr.* four-week-old ...

vierzehn *Adj.* fourteen; *in* ~ *Tagen* in two weeks(' time), *Brit. auch* in a fortnight

vierzehnt... *Zahlw.* fourteenth

vierzehntägig *Adj. attr.* two-week (--long) ..., *Brit. auch* fortnight's ...;

vierzehntäglich I. *Adj. attr.* two--weekly, *Brit. auch* fortnightly; **II.** *Adv. stattfinden etc.*: every two weeks (*Brit. auch* fortnight), *Brit. auch* fortnightly;

Vierzehntel *n* fourteenth (part)

Vierzeiler *m*; *-s,* - quatrain; (*Gedicht mit 4 Zeilen*) quatrain, four-line poem;

vierzeilig *Adj. attr.* four-line ...

vierzig *Adj.* forty; **vierziger** *Adj. attr.*: *in den* ~ *Jahren* in the forties; → *auch* **Vierzigerjahre**; *er ist in den Vierzigern* he's in his forties; **Vierziger** *m*; *-s,* -, **Vierzigerin** *f*; *-, -nen* man (*f* woman) in his (her) forties, fortysomething *umg.*; **Vierzigerjahre** *Pl.*: *die* ~ the forties; *in den* ~**n des 19. Jahrhunderts** in the 1840s; **vierzigjährig** *Adj. attr. Person:* forty-year-old ...; *Zeitraum:* forty-year(-long) ...

vierzigst... *Zahlw.* fortieth; *heute ist ihr Vierzigster* she's forty today, it's her fortieth birthday today

Vierzigstundenwoche *f* 40-hour week

Vierzimmerwohnung *f* three-bedroom(ed) flat (*Am.* apartment)

Vierzylinder *m Mot. umg.* **1.** (*Auto*) four-cylinder (car); **2.** (*Motor*) four--cylinder engine; **vierzylindrig** *Adj. attr.* four-cylinder ...

Vietnam (*n*); *-s*; *Geog.* Vietnam; **Vietnamese** *m*; *-n, -n* **1.** Vietnamese; **2.** *umg.* Vietnamese restaurant; **Vietnamesin** *f*; *-, -nen* Vietnamese, Vietnamese woman (*od.* girl *etc.*); **vietnamesisch** *Adj.* Vietnamese; **Vietnamesisch** *n*; *-en*; *Ling.* Vietnamese; *das* ~**e** Vietnamese

Vietnam|krieg *m hist.* Vietnam War; ~**veteran** *m* Vietnam veteran (*od.* vet *umg.*)

vif [viːf] *Adj. altm.* bright, quick

Vignette [vɪnˈjɛtə] *f*; *-, -n* **1.** vignette; **2.** *Schweiz:* Mot. sticker

Vikar *m*; *s, -e* **1.** *ev. etwa* curate; **2.** *kath.* locum tenens (*Pl.* locum tenentes); **3.** *schw.* supply (*Am.* substitute) teacher; **Vikariat** *n*; *-(e)s, -e* **1.** *ev. etwa* curacy; **2.** *kath.* position as locum tenens; **Vikarin** *f*; *-, -nen* *etwa* curate

viktorianisch *Adj. hist.* Victorian; **Viktorianisches Zeitalter** Victorian Age; **Viktorianismus** *m*; *-, kein Pl.* Victorianism

Villa *f*; *-, Villen* villa; (*Landhaus*) mansion

Villen|gegend *f*, ~**viertel** *n* residential area, posh part of town *umg.*; ~**vorort** *m* residential suburb

Vinaigrette [vinɛˈɡrɛt] *f*; *-, n*; *Gastr.* vinaigrette

Vinothek *f*; *-, -en* wine cellar

Vinyl *n*; *-s*; *Chem.* vinyl; ~**benzol** *n* styrene; ~**gruppe** *f* vinyl group

Viola *f*; *-, Violen* **1.** *Mus.* viola; **2.** *Bot.* violet

Viole *f*; *-, -n*; *Bot.* violet

violett *Adj.*, **Violett** *n*; *-(s), kein Pl. heller:* violet; *dunkler:* purple

V

Violine f; -, -n; Mus. violin; **Violinist** m; -en, -en, **Violinistin** f; -, -nen violinist

Violin|konzert n Mus. violin concerto; **~schlüssel** m treble clef; **~sonate** f violin sonata

Violoncello [violɔnˈtʃɛlo] n; -s, Violoncelli; Mus. cello

VIP [vɪp] m; -(s), -s, f; -, -s; Abk. VIP, top nob umg.; Pl. Koll. auch the top brass Pl. umg.

Viper [ˈviːpɐ] f; -, -n; Zool. viper

VIP-Lounge [ˈvɪplaʊndʒ] f; -, -s executive (od. VIP) lounge

viral Adj. Med.: ~e RNS viral RNA

Viren|befall m EDV virus attack; **~scanner** m EDV virus scanner; **~schutzprogramm** n EDV anti-virus (od. virus protection) program; **~suchprogramm** n EDV virus scan program

Virginia [vɪrˈdʒiːnia] f; -, -s; (Zigarre) Virginia (cigar); **~tabak** m Virginia

viril Adj. virile; **Virilität** f; -, kein Pl. virility

Virologe m; -n, -n; Med. virologist; **Virologie** f; -, kein Pl. virology; **Virologin** f; -, -nen virologist; **virologisch** Adj. virological

virtuell Adj. 1. potential; 2. EDV virtual; **~er Speicher** virtual memory; **~e Realität** virtual reality; **~es Geld** virtual money; **~er Prozess** Phys. virtual process; **~e Teilchen** Phys. virtual particles

virtuos I. Adj. attr. virtuoso ..., auch präd. brilliant; **ein ~er Klavierspieler** a virtuoso on the piano; **e-e ~e Leistung** a masterly accomplishment (Mus. performance), a brilliant feat; **II.** Adv. spielen, beherrschen etc.: like a virtuoso, brilliantly; **Virtuose** m; -n, -n virtuoso (Pl. virtuosi od. virtuosos); **Virtuosin** f; -, -nen virtuoso (Pl. virtuosi od. virtuosos); **Virtuosität** f; -, kein Pl. virtuosity, brilliance of a performance etc.

virulent Adj. virulent; **Virulenz** f; -, kein Pl. virulence, virulency

Virus n, umg., EDV und fig.: m; -, Viren; Med., EDV virus; **~erkrankung** f Med. virus (od. viral) disease; **~grippe** f Med. virus (od. viral) influenza; **~infektion** f Med. virus (od. viral) infection; **~programm** n EDV 1. schädliches: virus (program); 2. (Schutzprogramm) anti(-)virus program; **~stamm** m Med. virus (od. viral) strain; **~träger** m Med. virus carrier

visafrei Adj. visa-exempt; **Visafreiheit** f visa exemption

Visage [viˈzaːʒə] f; -, -n; umg. pej. mug; **fiese ~** horrible mug; **j-m (eins) in die ~ hauen** punch s.o. in the face

Visagist [vizaˈʒɪst] m; -en, -en, **~in** f; -, -nen make-up artist

Visapflicht f visa requirement

vis-à-vis [vizaˈviː] Präp. und Adv. opposite, across from (**e-m Ort** etc. a place etc.); **das Haus** etc. **~** the house etc. opposite (bes. Am. across the street)

Visier n; -s, -e am Helm: visor; am Gewehr: sight; **mit offenem ~ kämpfen** fight with an open visor; fig. fight out in the open; **etw. ins ~ nehmen** get s.th. (lined up) in one's sights; **das ~ herunterlassen** wörtl. pull down one's visor; fig. clam up; **~einrichtung** f sight

visieren I. vt/i. (zielen) take aim; (auf) etw. (Akk.) **~** aim at s.th.; **II.** v/t. 1. (Pass) stamp with a visa; 2. Tech.

(eichen, ausmessen) adjust; 3. schw. (beglaubigen, abzeichnen) certify

Visierfernrohr n sighting telescope

Vision f; -, -en vision; **visionär** Adj., **Visionär** m; -s, -e, **Visionärin** f; -, -nen visionary

Visitation f; -, -en 1. (Durchsuchung) search; → auch **Leibesvisitation**; 2. kirchl. visitation

Visite f; -, -n; Med. 1. (doctor's) round; **auf ~ sein** be on (od. doing) one's rounds; 2. (**~** machender Arzt mit Begleitung) doctor on his rounds; **Visitenkarte** f visiting (Am. auch calling) card; **mit Geschäftsadresse:** business card; fig. calling card; **er hat s-e ~ hinterlassen** umg. iro. he's left his usual trail; **visitieren** v/t. 1. search; am Körper: auch frisk; 2. (inspizieren) inspect

viskos Adj. viscous; **Viskose** f; -, kein Pl. viscose; **Viskosität** f viscosity

visualisieren v/t. visualize; **Visualisierung** f visualization; **visuell** Adj. visual; **~e Medien** visual media; **sie ist ein ~er Typ** she has a visual memory

Visum n; -s, Visa und Visen 1. visa; 2. schw. signature; **Visumantrag** m visa application; **visumfrei** Adj. visa-exempt; **Visum(s)pflicht** f visa requirement

Vita f; -, Viten und Vitae; Lit. (Biografie) life; **j-s ~** the life of s.o.; **er bastelt an s-r ~** umg. he's working on his autobiography

vital Adj. 1. energetic; (rüstig) spry; 2. (wichtig) vital, essential; **Vitalität** f; -, kein Pl. vitality

Vitamin n; -s, -e vitamin; **~ B** umg. fig. contacts, the old boy network; **vitaminarm I.** Adj. low in vitamins; **II.** Adv.: **sich ~ ernähren** etc. eat a diet etc. low in vitamins; **Vitaminbedarf** m vitamin requirement; **Vitamin-B-haltig** Adj. ... containing vitamin B; **Vitamin-B-Mangel** m vitamin B deficiency

Vitamingehalt m vitamin content; **vitaminhaltig** Adj.: (sehr) **~ sein** contain (plenty of) vitamins; **Vitaminhaushalt** m vitamin balance

vitamin(is)ieren v/t. vitaminize

Vitamin|kapsel f vitamin pill (od. capsule); **~mangel** m vitamin deficiency; **~präparat** n vitamin preparation (od. compound)

vitaminreich I. Adj. attr. vitamin-rich..., präd. rich in vitamins; **II.** Adv.: **sich ~ ernähren** eat a vitamin-rich diet (od. a diet rich in vitamins)

Vitamin|spritze f vitamin shot; **~stoß** m massive dose of vitamins; **~tablette** f vitamin pill (od. tablet)

Vitrine f; -, -n showcase, display case (od. cabinet); in der Wohnung: glass (-fronted) cabinet

Vivarium n; -s, Vivarien vivarium (Pl. vivaria)

Vivisektion f; -, -en vivisection; **vivisezieren** v/t. vivisect

Vize m; -s, -s; umg. 1. deputy, number two; 2. Sport runner-up; 3. nordd. (Hausmeister) caretaker; **~admiral** m vice admiral; **~direktor** m, **~direktorin** f von Museum: deputy director; von Abteilung: deputy manager; **~kanzler** m, **~kanzlerin** f vice(-)chancellor; **~könig** m hist. viceroy; **~meister** m, **~meisterin** f Sport runner-up; **~meisterschaft** f Sport second place; **~präsident** m, **~präsidentin** f vice(-)president; **~weltmeister** m, **~weltmeisterin** f number two in the world

V-Leute Pl. → **V-Mann**

Vlies n -es, -e fleece (auch Textil); **das Goldene ~** Myth. the Golden Fleece; **~stoff** m nonwoven fabric; für Kleider: fleece material

V-Mann m contact; (Spitzel) auch informer

V-Motor m Mot. V-type engine

Vogel m; -s, Vögel 1. bird (auch umg. Flugzeug); 2. komischer **~** umg. odd character, strange customer; **er ist ein lustiger ~** he's good for a laugh; **e-n ~ haben** umg. fig. have a screw loose (somewhere); **j-m den ~ zeigen** tap one's forehead at s.o. (to indicate that he/she is stupid); **den ~ abschießen** umg. take the cake; **friss ~, oder stirb!** it's (a case of) sink or swim; **der ~ ist ausgeflogen** umg. the bird has flown; **~art** f type (od. species) of bird; **~bauer** n birdcage; **~beerbaum** m rowan (tree); **~beere** f rowanberry; **~dreck** m bird droppings Pl.; **~ei** n bird's egg; **~fänger** m birdcatcher, fowler; **~flug** m flight of birds

vogelfrei Adj. 1. outlawed; **für ~ erklären** outlaw; 2. fig.: **für ~ gehalten werden** be considered fair game

Vogel|freund m birdlover; ernsthafter: bird-watcher; **~futter** n birdseed; **~gesang** m birdsong; **~gezwitscher** n twittering of birds; **~haus** n aviary; **~häuschen** n nesting box; **~käfig** m birdcage

Vogelkunde f ornithology; **Vogelkundler** m; -s, -, **Vogelkundlerin** f; -, -nen bird-watcher; Wissenschaftler(in): ornithologist; **vogelkundlich** Adj. ornithological

Vogel|leim m birdlime; **~miere** f Bot. chickweed

vögeln vt/i. vulg. screw; **mit j-m ~** screw s.o.

Vogel|nest n bird's nest; **~perspektive** f bird's-eye view; **... aus** od. **in der ~** a bird's-eye view of ...; **Aufnahme aus der ~** high-angle shot; **~ruf** m birdcall; **~schar** f flock of birds; **~schau** f: **Berlin aus der ~** a bird's-eye view of Berlin; umg. fig. (Frau) auch frump; **~scheuche** f scarecrow (auch fig.); umg. fig. (Frau) auch frump; **~schlag** m Flug. bird strike

Vogel|schutz m protection of birds; **~schützer** m; -s, -, **~schützerin** f; -, -nen bird conservationist; **~schutzgebiet** n bird sanctuary

Vogel|schwarm m flock of birds; **~spinne** f Zool. bird-eating spider; **~stange** f perch; **~steller** m birdcatcher; **~sterben** n bird die-off; **~stimme** f birdcall

Vogel-Strauß-Politik f ostrich policy; **~ treiben** hide one's head in the sand

Vogel|warte f ornithological institute; **~welt** f world of birds, bird world; **~züchter** m, **~züchterin** f bird breeder; **~zug** m bird migration

Vogelsalat m österr., Gastr. corn salad, lamb's lettuce

Vogesen Pl. Geog.: **die ~** the Vosges

Vöglein n little bird; umg. hum. od. Kindersprache: birdie

Vogt m; -(e)s, Vögte; hist. 1. (Aufseher) overseer; 2. e-r Provinz: sheriff; 3. (Amtmann) bailiff; 4. (Verwalter) administrator

Voicemail [ˈvɔysmeːl] f; -, kein Pl.; Telef. voice mail

Voicerekorder [ˈvɔysrekɔrdɐ] m; -s, -; Flug. voice recorder

Vokabel f; -, -n word; **~n aufbekommen** get vocabulary to learn for homework; **~heft** n vocabulary book; **~verzeichnis** n word index

Vokabular *n*; *-s*, *-e* **1.** vocabulary; **2.** (*Wörterverzeichnis*) word index
Vokal *m*; *-s*, *-e*; *Ling.*, *Phon.* vowel
vokal *Adj. Mus.* vocal
Vokalensemble *n Mus.* vocal ensemble; **vokalisch** *Adj. Ling. attr.* vowel ..., vocalic; **Vokalisierung** *f Mus.* vocalization; **Vokalist** *m*; *-en*, *-en*, **Vokalistin** *f*; *-*, *-nen*; *Mus.* vocalist
Vokal|musik *f* vocal music; **~part** *m*, **~partie** *f* vocal part; **~solist** *m*, **~solistin** *f* (*Person*) solo singer; (*Part*) solo voice
Vokativ *m*; *-s*, *-e*; *Gram.* vocative
Volant [vo'lã:] *m*; *-s*, *-s Schneiderei*: flounce
Volatilität *f*; *-*, *-en*; *Fin.* volatility
Voliere [vo'lje:rə] *f*; *-*, *-n* aviary
Volk *n*; *-(e)s*, *Völker* **1.** people; (*Nation*) *auch* nation; *das deutsche* ~ the Germans, the German people (*od.* nation); *die Völker Afrikas* the peoples of Africa; **2.** *nur Sg.* (*Einwohner*) people *Pl.*; (*Masse*) the masses *Pl.*; *pej. auch* hoi polloi, the plebs *Pl.*; (*Pöbel*) mob, rabble; *die gewählten Vertreter des ~es* the people's elected representatives; *im Namen des ~es* in the name of the people; *~es Stimme geh.* the voice of the people; *das ~ Gottes Reli.* God's chosen people, the elect; *ein Mann aus dem ~e* a man of the people; *ein Gerücht etc. unters ~ bringen umg.* spread a rumo(u)r *etc.*; *etw. unters ~ bringen umg.* (*verkaufen*) sell, get rid of; *sich unters ~ mischen* mingle with the crowd; *blödes ~! beleidigend*: you stupid lot! *umg.*; → *auserwählt, fahrend* II 2
Völkchen *n umg. fig.* crowd, lot, bunch; *pej. auch* shower; *ein lustiges ~* a jolly crowd
Völker|ball *m Sport* dodge ball; **~bund** *m hist.* League of Nations; **~freundschaft** *f* friendship between nations; **~gemeinschaft** *f* community of nations; **~gemisch** *n* ethnic mix, mixture of ethnic groups
Völkerkunde *f* ethnology; **Völkerkundler** *m*; *-s*, *-*, **Völkerkundlerin** *f*; *-*, *-nen* ethnologist; **völkerkundlich** *Adj.* ethnological
Völkermord *m* genocide
Völkerrecht *n Pol.* international law; **Völkerrechtler** *m*; *s*, *-*, **Völkerrechtlerin** *f*; *-*, *-nen* specialist in international law; **völkerrechtlich I.** *Adj.* international; *Frage, Problem etc.*: of (*od.* relating to) international law; *Entscheidung, Maßnahme etc.*: bound by international law; **II.** *Adv.* under (*od.* according to) international law; *~ anerkennen* recognize under international law; **Völkerrechtsverletzung** *f* breach of international law; **völkerrechtswidrig** *Adj. präd.* in breach of international law
Völkerschaft *f* people *Sg.*; (*Stamm*) tribe
völkerverbindend *Adj.*: *der ~e Charakter des Sports* the ability of sport(s) to bring nations together
Völker|verständigung *f* understanding among nations; **~wanderung** *f* migration (of peoples); *fig.* mass exodus, mass migration (*nach* to); *die* (*germanische*) ~ the Germanic migrations *Pl.*; *das ist ja die reinste ~ umg. fig.* it's a real mass exodus
völkisch *Adj. im Nationalsozialismus*: (*national*) national; (*rassisch*) racial
Volks|abstimmung *f Pol.* referendum (*Pl.* referendums *od.* referenda); **~ar-**

mee *f ehem. DDR*: People's Army; **~auflauf** *m* throng of people, crowd (of people) (*auch V. im Pl.*); crowd of onlookers (*auch V. im Pl.*); **~aufstand** *m* national uprising; **~befragung** *f Pol.* public opinion poll; **~begehren** *n Pol.* petition for a referendum; **~belustigung** *f* (form of) popular entertainment; *etw. zu e-r ~ machen fig.* turn s.th. into a fairground spectacle; **~bewegung** *f* popular movement; **~bibliothek** *f* public library; **~brauch** *m* popular custom; **~charakter** *m* national character; *der bayrische ~* the Bavarian character; **~deutsche** *m*, *f* ethnic German; **~dichter** *m*, **~dichterin** *f Lit.* popular poet; **~dichtung** *f Lit.* folk literature
volkseigen *Adj. ehem. DDR*: state-owned; **~er Betrieb** (*abgek. VEB*) state-owned company
Volks|eigentum *n* public property; **~einkommen** *n* national income; **~empfänger** *m im Nationalsozialismus*: People's Radio (*type of inexpensive radio set produced under the Nazis in Germany*); **~empfinden** *n*: *das ~* popular feeling, public opinion; *das gesunde ~ bes. iro.* popular opinion; **~entscheid** *m Pol.* referendum (*Pl.* referendums *od.* referenda); **~epos** *n Lit.* folk epic (poem); **~erhebung** *f* popular (*od.* national) uprising
Volksfeind *m* public enemy; **volksfeindlich** *Adj.* subversive
Volks|fest *n* festival; (*Rummel*) funfair, *Am.* carnival; **~feststimmung** *f* carnival atmosphere; **~front** *f Pol.* popular (*od.* people's) front; **~genosse** *m*, **~genossin** *f im Nationalsozialismus*: national comrade; **~gerichtshof** *m im Nationalsozialismus*: People's Court; **~glaube** *m* popular belief; **~gruppe** *f* ethnic group; **~held** *m* popular hero; **~heldin** *f* popular hero; **~hochschule** *f* **1.** *Institution*: adult education centre, *Am.* etwa community college; **2.** (*Kurse*) adult evening classes *Pl.*
Volkshochschul|kurs *m* → *VHS-Kurs*; **~verband** *m* association of adult education cent|res (*Am.* -ers); *siehe auch* **VHS-...**
Volks|kammer *f ehem. DDR*: People's Parliament; *hist.* former East German parliament; **~kampf** *m* popular struggle; **~kommune** *f bes. China*: People's Commune; **~krankheit** *f* endemic (*auch iro.* national) disease
Volkskunde *f* folklore; **Volkskundler** *m*; *-s*, *-*, **Volkskundlerin** *f*; *-*, *-nen* folklorist; **volkskundlich** *Adj.* folkloric
Volks|kunst *f* folk (*od.* ethnic) art; **~lauf** *m Sport* open running race; **~lied** *n* folk song; **~märchen** *n* folk tale; **~massen** *Pl.* the masses; *Menschenmengen*: crowds of people; **~medizin** *f* folk medicine; **~meinung** *f*: *die ~* public opinion; **~menge** *f* crowd; (*die Masse*) the masses *Pl.*; **~mund** *m*: (*im*) ~ (in the) vernacular; *im ~ heißt es, dass* it's a popular saying that; **~musik** *f* folk music
volksnah *Adj.* close to the people; popular; *Pol. attr.* grass-roots ...; **Volksnähe** *f* common touch; *Tradition und ~* tradition and a common touch
Volks|nahrungsmittel *n* staple (food); **~partei** *f* popular party; **~polizei** *f ehem. DDR*: People's Police; **~polizist** *m*, **~polizistin** *f ehem. DDR*: member of the People's Police; **~rede** *f umg.*: *halte keine ~n!* keep it short!; **~republik** *f Pol.* people's republic; *die ~*

China the People's Republic of China; **~schauspieler** *m actor who appears particularly in folk plays in roles representing ordinary people*; **~schauspielerin** *f actress who appears particularly in folk plays in roles representing ordinary people*; **~schicht** *f* social class
Volksschule *f hist.* elementary school (*for pupils aged 6 to 14*); **Volksschullehrer** *m*, **Volksschullehrerin** *f hist.* elementary school teacher
Volks|seele *f* **1.** *die ~* public feeling; *die ~ kocht* public feeling is running high; **2.** national spirit; **~seuche** *f* national epidemic; **~souveränität** *f* sovereignty of the people; **~sport** *m* national sport; **~sprache** *f* vernacular; **~stamm** *m* tribe; **~stimme** *f* voice of the people; **~stück** *n* folk play; **~sturm** *m im Nationalsozialismus*: territorial army created toward(s) end of the Second World War (*Am. WWII*) designed to act as a home guard; **~tanz** *m* folk dance; **~theater** *n Stück*: folk play; *Theater*: popular theat|re (*Am. auch* -er) (*receiving financial support from all levels of society*); **~tracht** *f* national costume (*auch Einzelstück*), national dress; **~trauertag** *m* national day of mourning
Volkstum *n*; *-s*, *kein Pl.* popular customs and traditions *Pl.*; **Volkstümelei** *f*; *-*, *-en*; *pej.* folksiness; **volkstümlich I.** *Adj.* **1.** (*beliebt, einfach*) popular (*auch Buch, Person etc.*); (*gewöhnlich*) for ordinary people; *Preise*: within everybody's reach; (*simpel*) folksy; **2.** (*traditionell*) traditional; *Gegenstände, Kunst: pej.* folksy; **~e Kunst/Medizin** etc. (*dem Volkstum entwachsen*) folk art/medicine *etc.*; **II.** *Adv.* darstellen, sich präsentieren: in a manner to which ordinary people can relate; (*traditionell*) traditionally; **Volkstümlichkeit** *f* **1.** (*Beliebtheit*) popularity; **2.** (*traditionelle Art*) tradition; *von Gegenständen, Kunst: pej.* folksiness
volksverbunden *Adj.* close to the people; **Volksverbundenheit** *f* closeness to the people
Volks|verdummung *f pej.* pulling the wool over people's eyes; *stärker*: brainwashing (of the public); **~verführer** *m pej.* demagogue
volksverhetzend *Adj. pej.* inflammatory, *präd. und nachgestellt*: aimed at causing public provocation; **Volksverhetzer** *m pej.* public (*od.* popular) agitator; **Volksverhetzung** *f pej.* incitement (of the masses *od.* the people)
Volks|vermögen *n* national wealth; **~versammlung** *f* **1.** public gathering; *größer*: mass rally; **2.** (*Volksvertretung*) people's assembly; **~vertreter** *m*, **~vertreterin** *f* people's representative; **~vertretung** *f* representation of the people; **~wanderung** *f organized walk open to the public*; **~weise** *f* folk melody (*od.* tune); **~weisheit** *f* piece of popular (*od.* folk) wisdom; **~wirt** *m*, **~wirtin** *f*, **~wirtschaftler** *m*; *-s*, *-*, **~wirtschaftlerin** *f*; *-*, *-nen* economist
Volkswirtschaft *f Wirts.* **1.** (national) economy; **2.** (*Volkswirtschaftslehre*) economics *Pl.* (*V. im Sg.*); **volkswirtschaftlich I.** *Adj.* (politico-)economic; **II.** *Adv.* (politico-)economically; **Volkswirtschaftslehre** *f* economics *Pl.* (*V. im Sg.*)
Volks|zählung *f* census; **~zorn** *m* wrath of the people; **~zugehörigkeit** *f* nationality, national identity
voll I. *Adj.* **1.** *räumlich*: full; (*~ besetzt*)

full (up); (*gefüllt*) full (up), filled; *Straßen*: full of traffic; *ein Koffer / e-e Kiste etc.* ~ *Bücher* a caseful/boxful etc. of books; *das* ~*e Korn auf den Feldern* the ripe corn (*Am.* grain) in the fields; **2.** *umg.* (*betrunken*) plastered, tight *Sl.*; *umg.* (*satt*) full; **3.** (*füllig, prall*) full (*auch Figur*); *sie ist* ~*er geworden* she has filled out a bit; **4.** (*rund, glatt*) full, whole; *e-e* ~*e Stunde* a full (*od.* whole, solid) hour; *zu jeder* ~*en Stunde* every hour on the hour; *sechs* ~*e Tage* six whole days; *ein* ~*es Dutzend* a full (*od.* whole) dozen; **5.** (*bedeckt*) covered; ~(*er*), ~ *von* full of; *Negativem*: rife with; ~*er Flecke(n) etc.* covered with marks etc.; **6.** (*vollständig*) full, complete; ~*e Beschäftigung* full (*ganztägige*: full-time) employment; *bei* ~*er Besinnung* fully conscious; **7.** *fig.* in *Wendungen*: *aus* ~*er Brust* od. ~*em Halse* at the top of one's voice; *ein* ~*er Erfolg* a complete success; *die* ~*e Wahrheit* the whole truth; *weitS.* the full story; *aus dem Vollen schöpfen* draw on plentiful resources; *in die Vollen gehen umg.* go the whole hog; *j-n nicht für* ~ *nehmen* not take s.o. seriously; → *Fahrt* 2, *Hand*[1] 2, *Mund, Pulle, Recht, Strandhaubitze etc.*; **II.** *Adv.* **1.** (*vollständig*) fully; ~ *gesperrt Straße etc.*: completely closed off; *wieder* ~ *befahrbar* completely reopened to traffic; **2.** *oft umg., verstärkend*: ~ *zuschlagen etc.* really go for it *etc.*; ~ *bremsen* stand on the brakes, brake hard; ~ *und ganz* fully, completely; *unterstützen*: wholeheartedly; *etw.* ~ *ausnützen* use to (one's) full advantage; *ihn hat es* ~ *erwischt Grippe etc.*: he's got it bad; (*er hat sich verliebt*) he's got it bad; ~ *dabei sein* be completely involved; ~ *mit drinstecken* be completely up to one's ears in it too; *ich war nicht* ~ *da* I wasn't quite with it; ~ *witzig etc.* really funny *etc.*; ~ *die Krise kriegen* get really worked up; *das bringt's* ~*!* it's brilliant!; *hier ist* ~ *die geile Party Sl.* this really is a shit-hot (*Am.* totally cool) party; → *auch völlig, vollkommen*; **3.** *mit Verben*: *sich* ~ *dröhnen umg.* get totally high; *sich* ~ *essen* eat one's fill; *sich* ~ *fressen umg.* stuff o.s.; ~ *füllen* fill *s.th.* up; ~ *gießen* fill (up); *j-m die Hucke* ~ *hauen umg.* bash s.o.'s head in; ~ *kriegen* manage to fill *s.th.* (up); *er kriegt den Hals nicht* ~ he (just) can't get enough; ~ *kritzeln umg.* scribble all over *s.th.*; ~ *laden* (*Auto, Kofferraum etc.*) load up (to the top); ~ *laufen* fill up; *sich* ~ *laufen lassen umg.* get tanked up; ~ *machen* (*füllen*) fill (up); (*beschmutzen*) (*auch sich etw.* ~ *machen*) dirty, mess up; (*Tisch, Boden etc.*) *auch* make a mess on; *sich die Hosen* ~ *machen* fill one's pants; *sich* (*Dat.*) *die Finger mit Marmelade* ~ *machen* get jam all over one's fingers; ~ *malen* cover with paint; ~ *packen* pack *s.th.* full (*mit* of); ~ *pfropfen* cram *s.th.* full; ~ *pumpen* (*Reifen etc.*) pump *s.th.* up (completely), pump *s.th.* full; *sich mit etw.* ~ *pumpen mit Medikamenten*: load o.s. up with s.th.; *sich* ~ *pumpen umg.* (*sich betrinken*) tank up, get tight *Sl.*; *mit Drogen*: get completely high (*od.* doped up); ~ *qualmen umg.* (*Zimmer etc.*) smoke up; *sich* ~ *saugen Insekt etc.*: suck itself full (*mit* of); *Schwamm*: soak itself full (of); *Stoff etc.*: become saturated

(with); *sich* (*den Bauch*) ~ *schlagen umg.* make a (real) pig of o.s.; *das Boot schlug* ~ the boat became swamped; ~ *schmieren umg.* smear all over *s.th.*; (*Kleid*) mess up; *sich* ~ *schmieren* get o.s. dirty, get food etc. all over o.s.; ~ *schreiben* fill (with writing); *drei Seiten* ~ *schreiben* write three full pages; ~ *schütten* fill (up); ~ *spritzen* spatter; *mit Wasser*: spray, get *s.o. od. s.th.* all wet; *etw. mit etw.* ~ *spritzen* spatter s.th. all over s.th.; ~ *stellen* cram (*mit* with); ~ *stopfen* stuff, cram; *sich* (*den Bauch*) ~ *stopfen umg.* stuff o.s.; ~ *tanken* fill up; *umg. fig.* (*sich betrinken*) get tanked up; *bitte* ~ *tanken Mot.* fill her up, please; **4.** *mit Part. Perf.*: ~ *beladen* fully laden; ~ *bepackt* loaded down with luggage, (absolutely) loaded *umg.*; ~ *besetzt* (completely) full; *Hotel*: *auch* fully-booked; ~ *entwickelt* fully developed; *Persönlichkeit etc.*: *auch* full-blown; ~ *geladen* loaded (to the top); *Auto etc.*: loaded down; ~ *gepackt od. gepfropft* crammed (full), packed, jam-packed *umg.*, chock-a--block *umg.*

Voll|akademiker *m*, ~**akademikerin** *f* university graduate

vollauf *Adv.* fully, completely; ~ *zufrieden* quite (*od.* fully) satisfied; *ich bin mit den Kindern* ~ *beschäftigt* I've got enough on my hands with the children, the children are a full-time job; ~ *zu tun haben* have plenty (*od.* enough) to do

Vollausschlag *m Tech., e-s Instruments*: full swing

Vollautomat *n* fully automatic machine; **Vollautomatik** *f* fully automatic system; **vollautomatisch** *Adj.* fully automatic, all-automatic; **vollautomatisiert** *Adj.* fully automated; **Vollautomatisierung** *f* full automation

Vollbad *n* bath

Vollbart *m* full beard; **vollbärtig** *Adj. nachgestellt*: with (*od.* sporting) a full beard

vollbeschäftigt *Adj.* fully employed; ~*er Angestellter* full-time employee; **Vollbeschäftigung** *f* full employment

voll besetzt → *voll* II 4

Voll|besitz *m*: *im* ~ *von* in full possession of; *im* ~ *s-r Sinne sein* be completely lucid, be all there *umg.*; ~*bier* *n* beer with a high original wort

Vollbild *n* **1.** *Druck.* full-page illustration (*od.* picture); **2.** *Med.* complete clinical picture

Vollblut *n* **1.** (*Pferd*) thoroughbred; **2.** *Med.* whole blood; **Vollblüter** *m*; -s, - thoroughbred; **vollblütig** *Adj.* thoroughbred, *auch fig.* full-blooded

Vollblut|pferd *n* thoroughbred; ~**schauspieler** *m*, ~**schauspielerin** *f* true actor; ~**weib** *n umg.*: *sie ist ein* ~ she is every bit a woman

Vollbremsung *f* full braking; *e-e* ~ *machen* slam on the brakes

vollbringen *v/t.* (*unreg., untr., hat*) accomplish, achieve; (*Tat, Wunder*) perform

vollbusig *Adj.* chesty, busty, bosomy *umg.*

Volldampf *m*: *mit* ~ at full steam; *fig. umg.* flat out; *fahren*: *auch umg.* full tilt; *mit* ~ *voraus* full steam ahead

voll dröhnen → *voll* II 3

Völlegefühl *n* full (*stärker*: bloated) feeling

voll|elastisch *Adj.* fully elastic; ~**elektronisch** *Adj.* fully electronic (*od.* au-

tomatic)

vollenden *v/t.* (*untr., hat*) complete (*auch Studien, Lebensjahr*); (*beenden*) *auch* finish; **vollendet I.** *P.P.* → *vollenden*; **II.** *Adj.* **1.** perfect; *künstlerisch etc.*: accomplished; *Leistung etc.*: masterly; *umg. Unsinn etc.*: utter, absolute; **2.** *Kinder ab dem / bis zum* ~*en 8. Lebensjahr* children aged 8 years and over / children up to and including the age of 8; **3.** *Gram.*: ~*e Gegenwart/Zukunft* present/future perfect; **III.** *Adv.*: *technisch* ~ *spielen* be a technically accomplished player

vollends *Adv.* (*völlig*) completely; *nun ist sie* ~ *beleidigt* now she feels totally offended

Vollendung *f* completion; (*Vollkommenheit*) perfection; *nach* ~ *des 18. Lebensjahres* on reaching the age of 18

voll entwickelt → *voll* II 4

voller *Adj.* **1.** *Komp. von voll*: fuller; **2.** (*voll von, mit*) full of; → *voll* I

Völlerei *f*; -, *kein Pl.*; *pej.* gluttony

Vollerwerbsbetrieb *m Agr.* full-time farm

voll essen → *voll* II 3

volley ['vɔli] *Adv. Sport*: ~ *nehmen* take on the volley

Volley ['vɔli] *m*; -s, -s; *Sport, bes. Tennis*: volley

Volleyball *m Sport* **1.** *nur Sg.* volleyball; **2.** (*Ball*) volleyball

Volleyballer *m*; -s, -, ~**in** *f*; -, -nen; *Sport* volleyball player

Volleyball|feld *n Sport* volleyball court; ~**spiel** *n* **1.** volleyball; **2.** *konkret*: volleyball match (*Am.* auch game)

Volleyschuss *m Sport* volley shot, shot on the volley

vollfett *Adj.* full-fat; **Vollfettkäse** *m* full-fat cheese

voll fressen → *voll* II 3

vollführen *v/t.* (*untr., hat*) do; (*Kunststück etc.*) perform

voll füllen → *voll* II 3

Vollgas *n*: *mit* ~ full speed; *umg. fig.* (at) full tilt; ~ *geben* put one's foot down (hard) *umg.*

voll gedröhnt *Sl.* **I.** *P.P.* → *voll dröhnen*; **II.** *Adj.*: *total* ~ *sein* be drugged up to one's eyeballs

vollgefressen *umg. Adj.* (*dickleibig*) overfed, fat

voll gefressen *umg.* **I.** *P.P.* → *voll fressen*; **II.** *Adj.* stuffed (full)

Vollgefühl *n*; *nur Sg.*: *im* ~ *s-r Macht etc.* fully aware of one's power *etc.*

voll geladen, voll gepackt, voll gepfropft → *voll* II 4

voll gießen → *voll* II 3

Vollglatze *f*: *e-e* ~ *haben* be completely bald; *sich e-e* ~ *schneiden lassen* have one's head shaved, have all one's hair cut off

vollgültig *Adj. Beweis etc.*: fully valid

Vollgummi *m, n* solid rubber; ~**reifen** *m* solid tyre (*Am.* tire)

voll hauen → *voll* II 3

Vollidiot *m umg.* complete idiot, absolute twit (*od.* nincompoop), headbanger *Sl.*, *Am.* doofus *Sl.*

völlig I. *Adj.* (*ganz*) full, entire; (*vollständig*) complete, total; *Unsinn, Wahnsinn etc.*: absolute, complete, sheer; *das ist mein* ~*er Ernst* I'm quite (*umg.* dead) serious about it; **II.** *Adv.* completely; ~ *richtig* perfectly (*od.* quite) right; ~ *unmöglich/verrückt etc.* absolutely impossible/mad *etc.*; *ich bin* ~ *einverstanden* that's perfectly all

right by me; **das genügt** ~ that's (more than) enough, that's fine, that'll do nicely; → *auch* **voll, vollkommen** II
vollinhaltlich I. *Adj.* full, complete; **II.** *Adv. zustimmen etc.*: fully, on all points
Vollinvalide *m* total invalid; **Vollinvalidität** *f* total disability
volljährig *Adj. präd.* of age; ~ **werden** come of age, reach the age of majority; ~**e Personen** adults over 18; **Volljährige** *m, f; -n, -n* major; **Volljährigkeit** *f* majority
Volljurist *m,* ~**in** *f* fully-qualified lawyer (*who is qualified to act as a judge*)
Vollkasko *f; -, kein Pl.; umg.* comprehensive insurance; **vollkaskoversichert** *Adj.* with comprehensive insurance; ~ **sein** have comprehensive insurance; **Vollkaskoversicherung** *f* comprehensive insurance
vollklimatisiert *Adj.* fully air-conditioned
vollkommen I. *Adj.* **1.** (*vollendet, makellos*) perfect; ~**e Zahl** perfect number; **kein Mensch ist** ~ nobody's perfect; **2.** (*völlig, vollständig*) perfect, complete, total, absolute; ~**e Verschlüsselung** *EDV* full encryption; → *auch* **völlig** I; **II.** *Adv.* perfectly; → *völlig* II; **Vollkommenheit** *f* (sheer) perfection
Vollkorn *n; -s, nur Sg.* **1.** (*Getreide*) whole grain; **2.** *Mil., Jagd, Sportschießen:* full sight
Vollkorn|brot *n* wholemeal (*Am.* whole-grain) bread; ~**brötchen** *n* wholemeal (*Am.* whole-grain) (bread) roll; ~**mehl** *n* wholemeal (*Am.* whole-grain) flour; ~**nudeln** *Pl.* whole wheat pasta *Sg.* (*Koll.* pastas)
Vollkraft *f; nur Sg.:* **in der** ~ **s-r Jahre** in his prime
voll kriegen, voll kritzeln, voll laden, voll laufen, voll machen → *voll* II 3
Vollmacht *f; -, -en* full power(s *Pl.*), authority; *Jur.* power of attorney; **j-m** ~ **erteilen** authorize s.o. (**zu** + *Inf.* to *Inf.*); ~**geber** *m,* ~**geberin** *f* principal
voll malen → *voll* II 3
Vollmatrose *m* able-bodied seaman
vollmechanisiert *Adj.* fully mechanized
Vollmilch *f* full-cream milk; ~**schokolade** *f* milk chocolate
Vollmitglied *n* full member
Vollmond *m; nur Sg.* full moon; **es ist** ~ there's a full moon tonight; **bei** ~ at (the) full moon; **strahlen wie ein** ~ *umg.* be beaming all over one's face; ~**gesicht** *n umg.* moon face; ~**nacht** *f* night of a full moon
vollmundig I. *Adj. Wein:* full(-bodied); **II.** *Adv. fig. mst iro.:* **etw.** ~ **ankündigen** announce s.th. pompously
Vollnarkose *f Med.* general an(a)esthetic; **e-e** ~ **bekommen** be given a general an(a)esthetic
voll packen → *voll* II 3
Vollpension *f* (full) board and lodging, full board, *Am.* American plan (*Abk.* AP)
voll pfropfen → *voll* II 3
Vollprofi *m umg. Sport* full professional
voll pumpen, voll qualmen → *voll* II 3
Vollrausch *m:* (**im**) ~ (in a) drunken stupor; **e-n** ~ **haben** be blind drunk
vollreif *Adj.* fully ripe; **Vollreife** *f* full ripeness
Vollreifen *m* solid tyre (*Am.* tire)
voll saugen, voll schlagen → *voll* II 3

vollschlank *Adj.:* ~ **sein** have a full figure, be a bit on the plump side *umg.*; **für die** ~**e Frau** for the fuller figure
voll schmieren, voll schreiben, voll schütten → *voll* II 3
Vollsperrung *f Verk.* complete closure
voll spritzen → *voll* II 3
vollständig I. *Adj.* complete; (*ganz*) whole, entire; **II.** *Adv.* completely; (*voll*) fully; (*voll und ganz*) absolutely; **Vollständigkeit** *f* completeness
voll stellen, voll stopfen → *voll* II 3
vollstreckbar *Adj.* enforceable; *Urteil, Testament:* executable; **endgültig**/**vorläufig** ~ *Jur.* ultimately/provisionally enforceable; ~**er Titel** *Jur.* enforceable legal document; **Vollstreckbarkeit** *f Jur.* enforceability; **vollstrecken I.** *v/t.* **1.** *Jur.* (*Urteil, Testament*) execute; (*Gesetz*) enforce; **2.** *Sport* convert; **II.** *v/i. Sport* score; **Vollstrecker** *m; -s, -,* **Vollstreckerin** *f; -, -nen* **1.** *Jur.* executor; **2.** *Sport* scorer; **Vollstreckung** *f* enforcement; execution
Vollstreckungs|befehl *m* writ of execution; ~**schutz** *m Jur.* protection against unfair judicial execution
Vollstudium *n* complete course of study
voll|synchronisiert *Adj.* fully synchronized; ~**synthetisch** *Adj.* completely (*od.* fully) synthetic
voll tanken → *voll* II 3
Volltext *m EDV* full text; ~**suche** *f EDV* full text search
volltönend *Adj.* sonorous, rich
volltransistor(is)iert *Adj.* fully transistorized
Volltreffer *m* direct hit; *Scheibenschießen:* bull's-eye; *fig.* (*Erfolg*) (absolute) hit; **e-n** ~ **landen** hit the bull's-eye; *bei Beschuss etc.:* score a direct hit; *fig.* score a hit (*od.* success)
volltrunken *Adj.* completely drunk (*od.* intoxicated); **in** ~**em Zustand** in a state of complete intoxication; **Volltrunkenheit** *f* (state of) complete drunkenness (*od.* intoxication)
Voll|verb *n* full verb; ~**verpflegung** *f* full board; ~**versammlung** *f* plenary assembly; ~**verstärker** *m* integrated amplifier; ~**waise** *f* orphan; ~**waschmittel** *n* all-purpose washing (*Am.* soap) powder
vollwertig I. *Adj.* full; *auch Mahlzeit:* adequate; *Nahrung:* wholesome; *Material etc.:* fully adequate; **II.** *Adv.:* **sich** ~ **ernähren** *etc.* have a well-balanced diet
Vollwert|ernährung *f* wholefood diet; ~**kochbuch** *n* wholefood cookery book (*Am.* cookbook); ~**kost** *f* wholefoods *Pl.;* ~**küche** *f* wholefood cuisine
vollwürzig *Adj.* full-bodied
Vollzahler *m; -s, -* full-fare passenger
vollzählig I. *Adj.* complete; **II.** *Adv.:* **sie waren** ~ **versammelt** all were present; **Vollzähligkeit** *f* completeness
Vollzeit *f nur Sg.;* (*volle Arbeitszeit*) full-time employment (*od.* work); **in** ~ in full-time employment (*od.* work); **auf** ~ **gehen** go full-time; ~**arbeit** *f* full-time work
vollzeitbeschäftigt *Adj.* full-time, *präd.* employed full-time; **Vollzeitbeschäftigte** *m, f* full-time employee (*od.* worker)
Vollzeit|kraft *f* full-time employee (*od.* worker); ~**schule** *f* school or college with *full-time teaching;* ~**unterricht** *m* full-time lessons *Pl.*
vollziehbar *Adj.* executable; **die Entscheidung muss sofort** ~ **sein** it must be possible to implement the decision

immediately; **Vollziehbarkeit** *f:* **der Minister hat die sofortige** ~ **der Genehmigung angeordnet** the minister ordered that the authorization be enforced immediately; **vollziehen** (*unreg., untr., hat*) **I.** *v/t.* execute; (*ausführen*) carry out; (*rituelle Handlung etc.*) *auch* perform; (*Ehe*) consummate; ~**de Gewalt** executive (power); **II.** *v/refl.* take place, (come to) pass; **Vollzieher** *m; -s, -,* **Vollzieherin** *f; -, -nen* executor; **Vollziehung** *f* execution; carrying out; performance; consummation; → *vollziehen*
Vollzug *m* **1.** *mst Sg.* execution; carrying out; performance; consummation; → *vollziehen;* **2.** *nur Sg.;* (*Strafvollzug*) execution of a (prison) sentence; **offener** ~ day release
Vollzugs|anstalt *f Jur.* penal institution; ~**beamte** *m,* ~**beamtin** *f* (prison) warder (*Am.* guard); ~**dienst** *m* prison service; ~**krankenhaus** *n* prison hospital; ~**personal** *n* (prison) warders (*Am.* guards) *Pl. od.* staff (*mst V. im Pl.*)
Volontär *m; -s, -e* trainee (*who receives low wage in return for gaining practical experience*); **Volontariat** *n; -(e)s, -e* traineeship (*od.* period of training); **Volontärin** *f; -, -nen* trainee (*who receives low wage in return for gaining practical experience*); **volontieren** *v/i.* work as a trainee
Volt *n; -(e)s, -; Etech.* volt; **er steht immer unter 1000** ~ *fig.* he's always up to ninety; **Voltampere** *n* volt-ampere
Volte ['vɔltə] *f; -, -n* **1.** *Kartenspiel:* sleight of hand; **2.** *Reiten:* volt, volte; **3.** *Fechten:* volt, volte
voltigieren [vɔlti'ʒiːrən] *v/i.* **1.** *Reiten:* perform a volt; *Kunstreiten:* do trick riding; **2.** *Fechten:* perform a volt
Voltmeter *n Etech.* voltmeter
Volumen *n; -s, - und Volumina* volume; (*Inhalt*) *auch* capacity
...**volumen** *n, im Subst.:* **Export**~ volume of exports; **Kredit**~ volume of credits, lending volume
Volumen|gewicht *n* volume weight; ~**prozent** *n* per cent (*od.* percent) by volume
voluminös *Adj.* voluminous; (*Mahlzeit*) substantial; *Band etc.:* weighty, hefty; *hum. Person:* hefty, ample
Volute *f; -, -n; Archit.* scroll
vom *Präp. + Art.* **1.** → *von;* **2.** *räumlich:* from; *von etw. weg:* off *s.th.;* **etw.** ~ **Tisch nehmen** take s.th. off the table; ~ **Land sein** be from the country; **3.** *zeitlich:* from; ~ **Morgen bis zum Abend** from morning until night; **4.** *Ursache, Urheber:* of; *beim Passiv:* by; **ein Geschenk** ~ **Opa** *umg.* a present from Grandpa; **das kommt** ~ **vielen Rauchen** *etc.* that's caused by (*od.* the result of) smoking *etc.* so much; → *Fach* 2, *Teufel* 3
von *Präp.* **1.** *räumlich:* from; *von etw. weg:* off *s.th.;* ~ **wo(her)?** where from?; → *vom;* **2.** *zeitlich:* from; ~ **morgen an** from tomorrow (onwards), as of tomorrow; ~ **an** II 3; **3.** *für den* (*partitiven*) *Genitiv, Teil:* of; **zwei** ~ **uns** two of us; **neun** ~ **zehn Leuten** nine out of (*Statistik:* in) ten people; ~ **dem Apfel essen** have some of the apple; **4.** *Anfang, Ausgang*(*spunkt*)*:* from; ~ **20 Euro aufwärts** from 20 euros up(wards), 20 euros and up(wards); → *klein* I 1; **5.** *Ursache, Urheber:* of; *beim Passiv:* by; **ein Brief** ~ **Jens** a letter from Jens; **ein Gedicht** ~ **Schiller** a poem by

V

Schiller; **Kinder haben** ~ have children by; **das ist nett** ~ **ihm** that's nice of him; ~ **mir aus** I don't mind, it's all the same to me; → **selbst** I 2, **vom**; **6.** Maß, Qualität: **ein Honorar** ~ **500 Euro** a fee of 500 euros; **ein Aufenthalt** ~ **drei Wochen** a three-week stay; **ein Kind** ~ **drei Jahren** a child of three; **ein Mann** ~ **Format** a man of substance; **ein Kunstwerk** ~ **e-m Kleid** etc. a dress etc. that is a work of art in itself; **7.** Thema: (über) of, about; **ich habe** ~ **ihm gehört** I've heard of them; **er weiß** ~ **der Sache** he knows about it; **man spricht** ~ **Brandstiftung** there's talk of arson; **8.** bei Titel vor Eigennamen: of; **der Herzog** ~ **Edinburgh** the Duke of Edinburgh

voneinander Adv. from each other; **weit** ~ **entfernt** far apart

vonnöten Adj.: ~ **sein** be necessary, be called for

vonstatten Adv.: ~ **gehen** take place; zügig etc.: go, proceed

Vopo¹ m; -s, -s; umg. → **Volkspolizist**

Vopo² f; -, kein Pl.; umg. → **Volkspolizei**

vor I. Präp. **1.** räumlich: in front of; (in Gegenwart von) auch in the presence of; ~ **der Tür** at the door; ~ **der Stadt** (außerhalb) outside the town; **sich** ~ **den Fernseher** etc. **setzen** sit down in front of the television etc.; ~ **e-m Hintergrund** against a background; ~ **dem Wind segeln** sail before the wind; **das Subjekt steht** ~ **dem Verb** comes before (od. precedes) the verb; → **Auge** 2, **Tür** 1, 2, **Zeuge** 1; **2.** zeitlich: before; Zeitpunkt in der Vergangenheit: ago; **am Tag** ~ ... (on) the day before ...; ~ **einigen Tagen** a few days ago, the other day; **(heute)** ~ **acht Tagen** a week ago (today); **fünf (Minuten)** ~ **zehn** five (minutes) to (Am. auch of) ten; **etw.** ~ **sich haben** have s.th. ahead (od. coming up); **3.** ~ **Tatsachen** / **e-r Aufgabe** etc. **stehen** be faced (od. confronted) with facts / a task etc.; ~ **dem Ruin stehen** be faced with ruin, be on the verge (od. brink) of ruin; **sich verbeugen** ~ (+ Dat.) bow (Frau: curtsey) to od. before; ~ **allem,** ~ **allen Dingen** above all; ~ **sich hin murmeln** mutter (od. mumble) to o.s.; ~ **sich gehen** **gehen** I 12; **4.** (wegen) with, for, on account of, because of; ~ **Freude springen** jump for (od. with) joy; ~ **(lauter) Lachen konnte ich nichts sagen** I couldn't speak for laughing; ~ **(lauter) Arbeit** with all that work, for work; **zittern** ~ **Angst** etc. shake (od. tremble) with; ~ **Hunger sterben** die of hunger; **sich fürchten** ~ (+ Dat.) be afraid of; **5.** schützen, verstecken, retten etc.: from; warnen: against; **II.** Adv. (nach vorn, vorwärts) forward(s); **Freiwillige** ~! any volunteers step forward!; **SC** ~, **noch ein Tor!** come on SC, let's have another one!

vorab Adv. **1.** (zunächst) to begin with; **2.** (im Voraus) in advance; → **vorweg**

Vorab... im Subst.: mst advance ...; **Vorabdruck** m preprint

Vorabend m e-s (besonderen) Ereignisses, auch fig.: eve; **am** ~ on the eve (+ Gen. of); **das Fleisch schon am** ~ **einlegen** marinate the meat the evening before; ~**messe** f kirchl. service held on the eve of Sunday or a religious festival; ~**programm** n TV early evening schedule; ~**serie** f TV early evening series, series shown in the early evening

Vorab|exemplar n advance copy; ~**information** f advance information

Vorahnung f premonition

Voralpen Pl.; Geog.: **die** ~ the foothills of the Alps

voran Adv. at the head (+ Dat. of), in front, up front umg.; **mit den Füßen** etc. ~ feet etc. first; **(nur)** ~! let's go!; **immer weiter** ~ keep going; ~**bringen** v/t. (unreg., trennb., hat -ge-) get s.th. going (od. moving); **j-n** (**in s-r Arbeit** etc.) ~ help s.o. make some headway (with his [od. her] work etc.)

Voranfrage f preliminary inquiry

voran|gegangen I. P.P. → **vorangehen**; **II.** Adj. Gespräche, Wochen etc.: previous; **im Vorangegangenen** above; **alles Vorangegangene** everything that has gone before

vorangehen v/i. (unreg., trennb., ist -ge-) räumlich: lead the way, walk at the head (+ Dat. of); zeitlich: precede (**e-r Sache** s.th.); **gut** ~ **Arbeit**: go ahead well; **vorangehend I.** Part. Präs. → **vorangehen**; **II.** Adj. Kapitel etc.: previous; **im Vorangehenden** above

vorankommen v/i. (unreg., trennb., ist -ge-) (auch **gut** ~) make headway (od. progress); **wir kommen schlecht voran** we're not making much od. any headway (od. progress); **im Beruf** ~ get on in one's job (od. careerwise); **wie kommst du voran?** how are you getting on?, how's it going? umg.; → **vorwärts kommen**

Vorankündigung f announcement; **ohne jede** ~ without any prior notice

voranmachen v/t. (unreg., trennb., hat -ge-) umg.: **mach mal voran!** get a move on!

Voranmeldung f booking, bes. Am. reservation; **Gespräch mit** ~ person-to-person call; **nur auf** ~ **Sprechstunde**: by appointment only; Theaterbesuch etc.: (by) advance booking only, Am. reservations only

Voranschlag m estimate; **e-n** ~ **einholen** get (od. obtain) an estimate

voranschreiten v/i. (unreg., trennb., ist -ge-) (vorne gehen) go on ahead; (Fortschritte machen) make progress

voranstellen v/t. (trennb., hat -ge-) put first

vorantragen v/t. (unreg., trennb., hat -ge-) carry s.th. in front

vorantreiben v/t. (unreg., trennb., hat -ge-) speed up, push umg.

Voranzeige f announcement (**für** of); (Vorbesprechung) preview; Film: trailer, Am. auch preview

Vorarbeit f groundwork, preparatory work, preparations Pl. (alle **zu** for); **(gute)** ~ **leisten** bes. fig. prepare the ground (well); **vorarbeiten** (trennb., hat -ge-) **I.** v/i. zeitlich: work ahead; inhaltlich: do the groundwork, prepare the ground; **er hat mir gut vorgearbeitet** he prepared the ground well for me; **II.** v/t. do s.th. in advance; (vorbereiten) prepare; **III.** v/refl. work one's way forward (auch zu Verschütteten etc.); energisch: forge ahead; **in e-r Hierarchie** etc.: work one's way up; **sich (bis) auf den 2. Platz** etc. ~ work one's way up to 2nd place etc.; **Vorarbeiter** m foreman; **Vorarbeiterin** f forewoman

voraufführen v/t. (untr., hat) (bes. Film) show a preview of s.th.

voraus Adv. in front; auch fig. ahead (+ Dat. of); → auch **voran**; **im Voraus** in advance; **Kopf** ~ head first; **s-r Zeit** ~ **sein** be ahead of one's time; **j-m weit** ~ **sein** be streets (Am. miles) ahead of s.o.; **backbord / mit voller Kraft** ~! Naut. on the port bow / full steam ahead!

voraus|ahnen v/t. (trennb., hat -ge-) see s.th. coming; **ich hab's vorausgeahnt** I could see it coming, I had a feeling it would happen; ~**berechnen** v/t. (trennb., hat) calculate in advance; ~**bestimmen** v/t. (trennb., hat) determine in advance

vorausbezahlen v/t. (trennb., hat) pay in advance; **Vorausbezahlung** f advance payment, deposit

voraus|blicken v/i. (trennb., hat -ge-) → **vorausschauen**; ~**denken** v/i. (unreg., trennb., hat -ge-) think (od. look) ahead; ~**eilen** v/i. (trennb., ist -ge-) hurry on ahead (+ Dat. of); **e-r Sache**: be ahead (of)

Vorausexemplar n advance copy

vorausfahren v/i. (unreg., trennb., ist -ge-) drive (on) ahead (+ Dat. of)

vorausgegangen → **vorangegangen**

vorausgehen v/i. (unreg., trennb., ist -ge-): **ihr geht der Ruf voraus zu** (+ Inf.) fig. she's reputed to (+ Inf.); → **vorangehen**

vorausgesetzt I. P.P. → **voraussetzen**; **II.** Konj.: ~, **dass** provided (that), on condition that

voraushaben v/t. (unreg., trennb., hat -ge-): **j-m e-e Menge Erfahrung** etc. ~ have a lot more experience etc. than s.o.; **er hat dir eines voraus** he has one advantage over you

Voraus|kasse f Wirts. cash in advance; ~**kommando** n advance commando

voraus|laufen v/i. (unreg., trennb., ist -ge-) run (on) ahead (+ Dat. of)

vorausplanen (trennb., hat -ge-) **I.** v/i. plan ahead; **II.** v/t. plan s.th. in advance, plan for s.th.; **Vorausplanung** f advance planning

vorausreiten v/i. (unreg., trennb., ist -ge-) ride on ahead

voraussagbar Adj. predictable; **Voraussage** f; -, -n prediction; (Wetterprognose) forecast (auch Wirts. etc.); **voraussagen** v/t. (trennb., hat -ge-) predict; Met., Wirts. forecast

Vorausschau f forecast; **vorausschauen** v/i. (trennb., hat -ge-) look ahead; **vorausschauend I.** Part. Präs. → **vorausschauen**; **II.** Adj. farsighted; **III.** Adv. handeln etc.: with foresight

voraus|schicken v/t. (trennb., hat -ge-) **1.** send on ahead; **2.** fig. begin by mentioning s.th.; **dies vorausgeschickt** having said that; ~**sehbar** Adj. foreseeable; **nicht** ~ unforeseeable; ~**sehen** v/t. (unreg., trennb., hat -ge-) foresee; **das war vorauszusehen** it was to be expected

voraussetzbar Adj.: **andere Faktoren** etc. **sind als bekannt** ~ it can be assumed that other factors etc. are familiar, other factors etc. are presumably familiar

voraussetzen v/t. (trennb., hat -ge-) **1.** (annehmen) assume (that ...), take s.th. for granted; **zu viel** ~ auch expect too much; **etw. als selbstverständlich** ~ take s.th. for granted; **etw. als bekannt** ~ take it for granted that everyone knows s.th.; **2.** (erfordern) require; → **vorausgesetzt**; **Voraussetzung** f condition, prerequisite (**für** for, of); **die** ~**en erfüllen** meet the requirements; **unter der** ~, **dass** on condition that; **der Bericht/Chef geht von falschen** ~**en aus** the report is based on

V

/ the boss is working from false assumptions
Voraussicht f; -, *kein Pl.* foresight; *aller ~ nach* in all probability; *nach menschlicher ~* as far as one (*od.* we) can tell *od.* foresee; *in weiser ~* with great foresight; **voraussichtlich I.** *Adv.* probably, in all probability; *er trifft ~ morgen ein* auch he is expected to arrive tomorrow; **II.** *Adj.* prospective; (*wahrscheinlich*) expected, anticipated; (*geschätzt*) estimated
Vorausvermächtnis n *Jur.* preference legacy
Vorauswahl f *nur Sg.* preliminary selection (*od.* round of selections); *e-e ~ treffen* narrow down the choice
voraus|werfen v/t. (*unreg., trennb., hat -ge-*) → *Schatten* 2; **~wissen** v/t. (*unreg., trennb., hat -ge-*) know (in advance); *die Zukunft ~* know what the future holds
vorauszahlen v/t. (*trennb., hat -ge-*) pay in advance; **Vorauszahlung** f advance payment
Vorbau m; -(e)s, -ten porch; (*vorspringender Bau*) projection; *e-n ganz schönen ~ haben* umg. hum. be well-endowed (*od.* -stacked); **vorbauen** (*trennb., hat -ge-*) **I.** v/t. build on at the front (+ *Dat.* of); **II.** v/i. (*Vorsorge treffen*) take precautions
Vorbedacht m: *mit ~* (*mit Absicht*) intentionally, deliberately; (*bewusst*) (quite) consciously; (*mit Vorsatz*) with intent; *ohne ~* (*ohne Absicht*) unintentionally, without meaning to; (*unbewusst*) unconsciously, without realizing; (*ohne Vorsatz*) without intent
vorbedenken v/t. (*unreg., trennb., hat*) consider carefully in advance
Vorbedeutung f omen, portent
Vorbedingung f condition
Vorbehalt m; -(e)s, -e reservation; (*Einschränkung*) proviso; *stiller ~* mental reservation; *unter dem ~, dass* provided (that), with the proviso that; *Zuschlag unter ~* subject to supplement
vorbehalten (*unreg., trennb., hat -ge-*) **I.** v/t.: *sich etw. ~* reserve s.th. (for o.s.); *sich (das Recht) ~, etw. zu tun* reserve the right to do s.th.; **II.** *P.P.* → I; **III.** *Adj.: j-m ~ sein od. bleiben* be left to s.o. (*zu + Inf.* to + *Inf.*); *es bleibt der Zukunft ~, ob* it remains to be seen whether, only time can tell whether; *Änderungen ~* subject to change (without notice); *Irrtum ~* errors excepted; *alle Rechte ~* all rights reserved
vorbehaltlich I. *Präp.* (+ *Gen.*) subject to; **II.** *Adj.* genehmigung etc.: conditional; **III.** *Adv.* genehmigen etc.: conditionally; **vorbehaltlos I.** *Adj.* unreserved, unconditional; **II.** *Adv.* without reservation; *dem können wir nur ~ zustimmen* we agree quite unreservedly (*od.* without any reservations)
Vorbehalts|klausel f *Jur.* proviso clause; **~urteil** n *Jur.* judgement subject to a proviso
vorbehandeln v/t. (*trennb., hat*) pretreat; (*Daten*) pre-process; **Vorbehandlung** f pretreatment; *von Daten:* pre-processing
vorbei *Adv.* **1.** *örtlich:* past; *~!* (*daneben*) missed!; *~ an* (+ *Dat.*) past; *sind wir schon an ... ~?* have we already gone past ...?; **2.** *zeitlich:* over, (*der Vergangenheit zugehörig*) past; *drei Uhr ~* past (*od.* after) three (o'clock); *es ist ~* it's all over; *iro.* so much for that; *~ ist ~* what's past is past; *das ist*

jetzt ~, damit ist es jetzt ~ that's all over and done with now; *mit uns ist es ~* umg. (*wir sind erledigt*) we're finished; (*unsere Freundschaft ist zu Ende*) it's all over between us
vorbei|bringen v/t. (*unreg., trennb., hat -ge-*) drop s.th. by (*od.* in); **~drücken** v/refl. (*trennb., hat -ge-*) umg. squeeze past (*an etw./j-m s.th./s.o.*); *sich an Entscheidungen etc. ~* skirt a)round decisions etc.; **~dürfen** v/i. (*unreg., trennb., hat -ge-*) umg. be allowed to pass; *darf ich mal vorbei?* excuse me(, please); **~eilen** v/i. (*trennb., ist -ge-*) hurry past; **~fahren** v/i. (*unreg., trennb., ist -ge-*) **1.** drive past (*an etw./j-m s.th./s.o.*), pass (s.th./s.o.); **2.** umg.: *lass uns noch schnell bei der Apotheke etc. ~* let's just quickly pop into the chemist's (*Am.* the drugstore etc.); **~fliegen** v/i. (*unreg., trennb., ist -ge-*) fly past (*an etw./j-m s.th./s.o.*); **~fließen** v/i. (*unreg., trennb., ist -ge-*) flow past; **~führen** (*trennb., hat -ge-*) **I.** v/t.: *j-n an etw. ~* lead s.o. past s.th.; *etw. an etw. ~* (*Bahnlinie etc.*) run s.th. along s.th.; **II.** v/i.: *~ an* (+ *Dat.*) Weg etc.: go (*od.* runod. lead) past; *daran führt kein Weg vorbei* fig. there's no getting (a)round it
vorbeigehen v/i. (*unreg., trennb., ist -ge-*) **1.** pass, go past (*an etw./j-m s.th./s.o.*); *im Vorbeigehen* in passing; *~ an* (+ *Dat.*) fig. (*nicht beachten*) pass s.th. by; *unabsichtlich:* miss; **2.** *Schuss etc.:* miss (the mark); **3.** (*aufhören*) pass; *Schmerz:* auch go away; **4.** umg.: *beim Arzt ~* drop in at the doctor's
vorbei|kommen v/i. (*unreg., trennb., ist -ge-*) **1.** pass (by), come past; *an e-m Hindernis ~* get past (*od.* [a]round), pass; **2.** umg. (*besuchen*) drop by (*bei* at), drop in (on), come by; *kommt ihr heute Abend mal vorbei?* are you going to pop in (*bes. Am.* drop by) this evening?; **~können** v/i. (*unreg., trennb., hat -ge-*) umg. be able to get past; **~lassen** v/t. (*unreg., trennb., hat -ge-*) let s.o. od. s.th. pass; *lässt du mich bitte vorbei?* can I get past, please?; **~laufen** v/i. (*unreg., trennb., ist -ge-*) run past (*an etw./j-m s.th./s.o.*); **~leben** v/i. (*trennb., hat -ge-*): *aneinander ~* live separate lives within a marriage; **~marschieren** v/i. (*trennb., ist*) march (*od.* file) past (*an etw./j-m s.th./s.o.*); **~mogeln** (*trennb., hat -ge-*) umg. **I.** v/t.: *j-n/etw. an j-m ~* smuggle s.o./s.th. past s.o.; **II.** v/refl.: *sich an j-m ~* sneak past s.o.; **~müssen** v/i. (*unreg., trennb., hat -ge-*) umg. have to pass (*od.* get past); **~planen** v/i. (*trennb., hat -ge-*): *~ an* (+ *Dat.*) ignore, leave out of account (when planning *s.th.*); **~rauschen** v/i. (*trennb., ist -ge-*) Wildbach etc.: rush past; umg. hochnäsig etc.: sweep past (*an j-m s.o.*); *das ist alles an mir vorbeigerauscht* umg. it all passed me by; **~reden** v/i. (*trennb., hat -ge-*): *aneinander ~* talk at cross-purposes; *an e-m Thema ~* talk a)round the subject; **~reiten** v/i. (*unreg., trennb., ist -ge-*) ride past (*an etw./j-m s.th./s.o.*); **~rennen** v/i. (*unreg., trennb., ist -ge-*) run past (*an etw./j-m s.th./s.o.*); **~schauen** v/i. (*trennb., hat -ge-*) umg. drop in, stop by (*bei j-m/etw.* on s.o. / at s.th.); **~schießen** v/i. (*unreg., trennb., hat -ge-*) **1.** miss (the mark); *Fußball:* shoot wide; *~ an* (+ *Dat.*) miss s.o. od. s.th.; **2.** (*vorbeiflitzen*)

shoot past; **~schlängeln** v/refl. (*trennb., hat -ge-*) squeeze past (*an etw./j-m s.th./s.o.*); **~schleusen** v/t. (*trennb., hat -ge-*) umg.: *j-n ~ an* (+ *Dat.*) smuggle s.o. past; **~schrammen** v/i. (*trennb., hat -ge-*) umg.: *~ an* (+ *Dat.*) scrape past; fig. Tod, Niederlage, Konkurs etc.: escape s.th. by the skin of one's teeth; **~schreiben** v/i. (*unreg., trennb., hat -ge-*): *am Thema etc. ~* write (a)round the subject; **~ziehen** v/i. (*unreg., trennb., ist -ge-*) pass (*an etw./j-m s.th./s.o.*); Soldaten: march past; Wolken etc.: drift past; *Erinnerungen zogen (im Geiste) an ihm vorbei* went through his mind
vorbelastet Adj. Person: with a past; Wort etc.: negatively loaded, tainted; *~ sein* Person: have a past to contend with; (*voreingenommen sein*) be biased (*od.* prejudiced); Wort: have negative connotations; *psychisch ~ sein* be a psychological case; *da ist er erblich ~* it runs in the family; **Vorbelastung** f (dubious) past od. background; *e-s Wortes etc.:* negative connotations Pl.
Vorbelegung f EDV default
Vorbemerkung f preliminary remark; Pl. (Vorwort) preface, foreword; (Einleitung) introduction
vorbereiten (*trennb., hat*) **I.** v/t. allg., auch seelisch: prepare (*für, auf* + Akk. for); *e-e Reise ~* prepare for a trip; *das Menü lässt sich in kurzer Zeit ~* the meal takes little time to prepare; **II.** v/refl. **1.** prepare o.s., get ready; *sich ~ auf* (+ Akk.) prepare (o.s.) for, get ready for, gear up for umg.; *sich für den Unterricht ~* prepare one's lessons (*od.* for class); *sich auf e-e Prüfung ~* revise (*Am.* review od. study) for an exam; **2.** (*im Kommen sein*) be in the offing, be under way; **vorbereitend I.** Part. Präs. → vorbereiten; **II.** Adj. preparatory; **vorbereitet I.** P.P. → vorbereiten; **II.** Adj. Rede, Speisen etc.: prepared; *auf etw. ~ sein* be prepared (*od.* ready) for s.th.; *gut ~ sein* be well prepared; *nicht ~ sein* be unprepared; **Vorbereitung** f preparation (*für, auf* + Akk., *zu* for); *~en treffen* make preparations, *in ~* being prepared, in preparation; fig. in the pipeline
Vorbereitungs|dienst m period of practical training undertaken by law students, trainee teachers and high-ranking government officials; *Beamter im ~* government official undergoing practical training; **~komitee** n preparatory committee; **~kurs** m preparatory course; **~lehrgang** m preparatory course; **~treffen** n preparatory meeting; **~zeit** f preparatory phase; *e-s Gerichts:* preparation time; *bei e-r Prüfung:* preparation time
Vorberge Pl. foothills, piedmont Sg.
Vorbericht m preliminary report
Vorbescheid m preliminary notice
Vorbesitzer m, **~in** f previous owner
Vorbesprechung f **1.** preliminary discussion (*od.* talks Pl.); **2.** *e-s Buches etc.:* preview
vorbestellen v/t. (*trennb., hat*) (Karten etc.) book in advance, make an advance booking for, bes. Am. reserve; (Platz, Zimmer etc.) book (ahead), reserve; **Vorbestellung** f advance booking, Am. reservation; Zimmer etc.: booking, reservation
vorbestimmen v/t. (*trennb., hat*) determine s.th. in advance; **vorbestimmt**

V

I. *P.P.* → **vorbestimmen**; **II.** *Adj. Schicksal etc.*: predetermined; → **vorherbestimmt**; **Vorbestimmung** *f* predetermination

vorbestraft *Adj.* previously convicted; **nicht ~ sein** have no previous convictions (*od.* criminal record); **einmal/ mehrfach ~ sein** have a previous conviction / have several previous convictions (**wegen** for); **damit ist er ~** he has a previous conviction for it; **Vorbestrafte** *m, f; -n, -n* previously convicted person

vorbeten *vt/i.* (*trennb., hat -ge-*) recite a prayer *etc.* (**j-m** to s.o.); *Vorbeter*: lead the prayer (*od.* prayers); **j-m etw. ~** *umg. fig.* explain s.th. to s.o. (in detail); *überdeutlich*: spell s.th. out to s.o.; **Vorbeter** *m; -s, -*, **Vorbeterin** *f; -, -nen* prayer leader

Vorbeugehaft *f* preventive detention

vorbeugen (*trennb., hat -ge-*) **I.** *v/i.* (*zu verhindern suchen*) prevent (+ *Dat. s.th.*); (*Vorsichtsmaßnahmen ergreifen*) guard against, take precautions against; **~ ist besser als heilen** *Sprichw.* prevention is better than cure; **II.** *v/t. und v/refl.*: (**sich**) **~** bend forward; **vorbeugend I.** *Part. Präs.* → **vorbeugen**; **II.** *Adj. Maßnahme etc.*: prevent(at)ive; *bes. Med. auch* prophylactic; **Vorbeugung** *f* prevention (**gegen** of); *bes. Med. auch* prophylaxis (against)

Vorbeugungs|maßnahme *f* precaution, prevent(at)ive measure; **~mittel** *n Med.* prophylactic; *fig.* prevent(at)ive

Vorbild *n* model; (*Beispiel*) example; **leuchtendes ~** shining example; **ein ~** (**für die Jugend**) **sein** be (*od.* set) an example (to young people); (**sich**) **j-n zum ~ nehmen** *moralisch etc.*: take s.o. as an example, take a leaf from s.o.'s book; (*sich nach j-m bilden*) model o.s. on s.o.; **Vorbildcharakter** *m* exemplary character; **Vorbildfunktion** *f*: **Volksvertreter mit ~** people's representative who sets an example; **vorbildlich I.** *Adj.* exemplary; (*vollkommen*) ideal; **~er Ehemann** *etc.* model husband *etc.*; **II.** *Adv.* exemplarily, in an exemplary manner (*od.* fashion); **sie benimmt sich ~** her behavio(u)r is exemplary; **das hast du ~ gemacht** you did a brilliant job (of it); **Vorbildlichkeit** *f* exemplariness, exemplary nature (+ *Gen.*)

Vorbildung *f beruflich etc.*: (previous) training; *allgemein*: educational background

vorbinden *v/t. und v/refl.* (*unreg., trennb., hat -ge-*) tie (*od.* put) s.th. on

Vor|blitz *m Fot.* pre-flash; **~bogen** *m im Buch*: front matter

vorbohren *vt/i.* (*trennb., hat -ge-*) *Tech.* pre-drill

Vorbörse *f Fin.* pre-market dealings *Pl.*; **vorbörslich** *Adj. Fin.* pre-market

Vorbote *m* forerunner; *fig.* harbinger, herald (+ *Gen.* of)

vorbringen *v/t.* (*unreg., trennb., hat -ge-*) **1.** *zur Diskussion, Anhörung etc.*: bring forward; *Jur.* (*Beweis*) produce; (*Gründe, Meinung, Entschuldigung etc.*) offer; (*Plan*) propose, put forward; (*Protest*) lodge; (*Wunsch*) express; *weitS.* (*sagen*) tell (**j-m etw.** s.o. s.th.); **e-n Einwand ~** make an objection; **e-e Klage ~** *Jur.* prefer (**als** *Einwand*: bring) a charge against s.o.; **was haben Sie zu Ihrer Verteidigung** *etc.* **vorzubringen?** what do you have

to say in your defen|ce (*Am.* -se) *etc.*?; **2.** (*nach vorn bringen*) bring forward; *Mil.* (*Geschütze etc.*) bring up

vorbuchstabieren *v/t.* (*trennb., hat*): **ein Wort ~** spell a word (out)

Vorbühne *f Theat.* proscenium (*Pl.* prosceniums *od.* proscenia)

vorchristlich *Adj.* pre-Christian; *... aus ~er Zeit* dating back to before the time of Christ (*od.* to the pre-Christian era)

Vordach *n* canopy

vordatieren *v/t.* (*trennb., hat*) (*zurückdatieren*) antedate; (*vorausdatieren*) postdate; **Vordatierung** *f zurück*: antedating; *voraus*: postdating

vordem *Adv.* (*vorher*) before; (*früher*) formerly

Vordenker *m*, **~in** *f* guiding intellectual force

Vorder|achse *f* front axle; **~ansicht** *f* front view; *Archit.* front elevation; **~antrieb** *m Mot.* front-wheel drive

Vorderasien (*n*) *Geog.* the Middle (*od.* Near) East; **vorderasiatisch** *Adj.* Middle (*od.* Near) Eastern, Levantine *altm.*

Vorder|ausgang *m* front exit; **~bein** *n* foreleg; **~deck** *n Naut.* foredeck

vorder... *Adj. nur attr.* front; **e-n der ~en Plätze belegen** *Sport* occupy one of the top places; **Vordere** *m, f; -n, -n*: **die ~n können mehr sehen** those (people) at the front can see more

Vorder|eingang *m* front entrance; **~front** *f* frontage; **~fuß** *m* forefoot; *von Hund, Katze*: front paw; **~gaumen** *n Anat., Ling.* hard palate; **~gebäude** *n* front building

Vordergrund *m*; *nur Sg.* foreground; **etw. in den ~ stellen** *od.* **rücken** *fig.* give s.th. special emphasis; **in den ~ treten** *od.* **rücken** become the focus of attention; *Person*: be thrust into public prominence; **im ~ stehen** (*dringlich sein*) be of immediate importance, be urgent, be top priority; (*im Blickpunkt stehen*) be in the limelight, be in the foreground of discussions *etc.*; **sich in den ~ drängen** *pej.* push oneself forward; **vordergründig I.** *Adj.* (*oberflächlich*) superficial; (*leicht durchschaubar*) transparent; (*zu einfach*) simplistic; **~er Humor** *etc.* naive sense of humo(u)r *etc.*; **II.** *Adv.* **behandeln** *etc.*: superficially; **Vordergründigkeit** *f* superficiality; transparency; simplistic nature (+ *Gen.*); naivety; → **vordergründig**

vorderhand *Adv. bes. schw.* for the time being, for the moment

Vorder|hand *f Zool.* forehand; **~haus** *n* front building; **~hirn** *n Anat.* frontal lobes *Pl.* of the brain; **~indien** (*n*); *Geog.* the Indian subcontinent; **~keule** *f Gastr.* shoulder; **~lader** *m* muzzle-loader

vorderlastig *Adj. Schiff.* bow-heavy; *Flugzeug*: nose-heavy

Vorder|lauf *m Zool.* foreleg; **~leute** *Pl.* people in front (of me, him *etc.*); *Sport* forwards; **~mann** *m* person in front (of me, him *etc.*); **etw. auf ~ bringen** *umg. fig.* bring s.th. up to scratch, spruce s.th. up; **j-n auf ~ bringen** *umg.* get s.o. into (proper) shape; **~pfote** *f* front paw

Vorderrad *n Mot.* front wheel; **~achse** *f* front axle; **~antrieb** *m* front-wheel drive

Vorder|reifen *m* front tyre (*Am.* tire); **~reihe** *f* front row; **~schinken** *m* shoulder of ham; **~seite** *f* front; *Mün-*

ze: obverse, face; **~sitz** *m* front seat

vorderst... *Adj.* (very) first, *nachgestellt*: at the front; **~e Reihe** front (*od.* first) row; **an ~er Front kämpfen** *auch fig.* fight right on the front line; **Vorderste** *m, f; -n, -n* person (right) at the front; **die ~n** the ones (right) at the front

Vorder|steven *m Naut.* stem; **~teil** *n, m* front (part); **~tür** *f* front door; **~zahn** *m* front tooth; **~zimmer** *n* front room

vordrängeln *umg.*, **vordrängen** *v/refl.* (*trennb., hat -ge-*) push forward; *in e-r Schlange*: push (*Am.* cut) in, *Brit. auch* jump the queue; *fig. in den Mittelpunkt*: (*auch* **sich ~ wollen**) try to be the cent|re (*Am.* -er) of attention

vordringen *v/i.* (*unreg., trennb., ist -ge-*) push (*od.* forge) ahead; *Truppen etc.*: advance; (*sich ausbreiten*) take hold; **~ in** (+ *Akk.*) (*ein Gebiet etc., auch fig. e-e Ideologie etc.*) penetrate; **~ zu** reach (*auch fig.*); **es gelang ihr, bis zum Minister vorzudringen** she succeeded in getting as far as the minister

vordringlich I. *Adj.* (*dringend*) urgent, pressing; (*vorrangig*) top priority; **~e Aufgabe** priority assignment; **II.** *Adv.*: **~ behandeln** give s.th. priority; **Vordringlichkeit** *f* urgency

Vordruck *m* **1.** form, *Am.* blank; **2.** *Druck.* first impression; → **vorgedruckt**

vorehelich I. *Adj.* premarital; **II.** *Adv. geboren etc.*: premaritally

voreilig I. *Adj.* rash; **~e Schlüsse ziehen** jump to conclusions; **II.** *Adv. urteilen, handeln etc.*: rashly; **Voreiligkeit** *f* rashness

voreinander *Adv.* **1.** *konkret*: one in front of the other; **2.** *Achtung ~* respect for each other (*od.* one another); **sie fürchten sich ~** they're afraid of each other (*od.* one another)

voreingenommen *Adj.* prejudiced, bias(s)ed (**für** in favo[u]r of; **gegen** against); **Voreingenommenheit** *f* prejudice(s *Pl.*), bias

Voreinsendung *f*: **gegen ~ von Briefmarken im Wert von ... Euro** *etc.* by first sending ... euros *etc.* worth of stamps

voreiszeitlich *Adj.* pre-Ice Age

vorenthalten *v/t.* (*unreg., trennb., hat*): **j-m etw. ~** (*auch verschweigen*) keep (*od.* withhold) s.th. from s.o.; **Vorenthaltung** *f*: **~ von Informationen** *etc.* withholding of information *etc.*

vorentscheidend *Adj.* **1.** *Argument, Diskussionspunkt*: decisive; **2.** *mst Sport* (*e-e frühe Entscheidung bringend*): **der ~e Treffer zum 4:1** the (killer) goal that made it 4-1 and placed the result beyond doubt; **der ~e Niederschlag in der 8. Runde** *Boxen*: the knockdown in the 8th round that ended the fight prematurely; **Vorentscheidung** *f* **1.** preliminary decision; *Jur.* precedent; **2.** *Sport* (*Vorentscheidungskampf*) preliminary; **3.** *Sport* **war das die ~?** (*Tor, Niederschlag etc.*) will that decide the course of the match (*oder* fight *etc.*)?

Vorentwurf *m* (*Skizze*) preliminary sketch; *zu Plan*: preliminary draft

Vorermittlungen *Pl.* preliminary inquiries

vorerst *Adv.* for the time being; (*im Augenblick*) *auch* at the moment

vorerwähnt *Adj. Amtsspr. attr.* aforementioned

V

Vorexamen *n* preliminary examination
vorexerzieren *v/t.* (*trennb., hat*) demonstrate (*j-m* to s.o.)
vorfabriziert *Adj.* prefabricated (*auch fig.*)
Vorfahr *m*; -en, -en, **Vorfahre** *m*; -n, -n ancestor, forebear(s *mst Pl.*)
vorfahren (*unreg., trennb.*) **I.** *v/i.* (*ist vorgefahren*) **1.** *vor den Eingang etc.*: drive up (*to the entrance etc.*); **~ bis** drive up to, drive as far as; **2.** *umg.* (*vorausfahren*) drive (on) ahead; **3.** *j-n, ein Fahrzeug* **~ lassen** (*die Vorfahrt geben*) give (right of) way to, *Am.* yield to; **II.** *v/t.* (*hat*): **e-n Wagen** *etc.* **~** drive a car *etc.* up (to the entrance *etc.*)
Vorfahrin *f*; -, -nen ancestor
Vorfahrt *f*; *nur Sg.*; *Verk.* right of way, priority; **~ beachten!** give way, *Am.* yield; **~ geändert** changed priorities (*Am.* new traffic pattern) ahead; **~ gewähren** give way; **j-m die ~ lassen/ nehmen** give / fail to give way to s.o.;
vorfahrt(s)berechtigt *Adj.*: **~ sein** have (the) right of way
Vorfahrts|regel *f* rule governing (the) right of way; **~regelung** *f* regulation governing (the) right of way; **~schild** *n* **1.** *zur Beachtung der Vorfahrt*: give way sign, *Am.* yield sign; **2.** *an Vorfahrtsstraße*: right of way sign; **~straße** *f* priority road; *in der Stadt*: *auch* through street; **~zeichen** *n* → **Vorfahrtsschild**
Vorfall *m* **1.** incident; **2.** *Med.* prolapse; **vorfallen** *v/i.* (*unreg., trennb., ist -ge-*) **1.** happen, occur; **2.** *Med.* prolapse, drop
Vorfeld *n* **1.** *bes. Mil.* approach(es *Pl.*) (+ *Gen.* to); *Flug.* apron; **2.** *fig.* run-up (+ *Gen.* to); **etw. im ~ klären** clarify s.th. in advance
vorfertigen *v/t.* (*trennb., hat -ge-*) prefabricate; **Vorfertigung** *f* prefabrication
Vorfilm *m* supporting film
vorfinanzieren *v/t.* (*trennb., hat*) finance in advance; **Vorfinanzierung** *f* advance financing
vorfinden *v/t.* (*unreg., trennb., hat -ge-*) find
vorflunkern *v/t.* (*trennb., hat -ge-*) *umg.*: **j-m etwas ~** tell s.o. a lot of rubbish (*Am.* nonsense)
Vorfluter *m*; -s, -; *Öko., Tech.* receiving water
Vorform *f* early form
Vorformatierung *f EDV* pre-formatting
vorformulieren *v/t.* (*trennb., hat*) pre-formulate
Vorfreude *f* (joyful) anticipation (**auf** + *Akk.* of); **~ ist die schönste Freude** looking forward is the best part
vorfristig I. *Adj.* early; **II.** *Adv.*: **~ den Plan erfüllen** *etc.* carry the plan *etc.* through early
Vorfrucht *f Agr.* previous crop
Vorfrühling *m*: (*im*) **~** (in) early spring
vorfühlen *v/i.* (*trennb., hat -ge-*) *fig.* put one's feelers out; **bei j-m ~** sound s.o. out (**wegen** on)
Vorführeffekt *m hum.* Murphy's (*od.* Sod's) Law
vorführen *v/t.* (*trennb., hat -ge-*) **1.** *Jur.* (*Angeklagten*) bring forward; *dem Richter*: bring before; (*Zeugen*) produce; **2.** *zur Schau*: show; (*Gerät etc.*) demonstrate; (*Film*) show; (*Kunststück, Trick etc.*) perform; **die neue Herbstkollektion ~** present the new autumn (*Am. auch* fall) collection;

3. *j-n* **~** *fig.* make a fool of s.o.; *Sport* teach s.o. a lesson; **Vorführer** *m*, **Vorführerin** *f Kino*: projectionist; **Vorführgerät** *n* **1.** (*Projektor*) projector; **2.** *im Laden etc.*: demonstration model; **Vorführmodell** *n* demonstration model; **Vorführraum** *m* projection room; **Vorführung** *f* **1.** presentation; *Film*: showing; *Wirts., Tech.* demonstration; *e-s Kunststücks etc.*: performance; **2.** *Jur. von Angeklagten*: bringing forward; *von Zeugen*: production; **Vorführwagen** *m Mot.* demonstration car, *Am.* demonstrator
Vorgabe *f* **1.** *Sport* handicap, start; **j-m e-e Runde ~ geben** give s.o. a one-lap start; **2.** (*Richtlinie*) guideline, *Pl. auch* instructions; **sich an die ~n halten** keep to the guidelines; **3.** *Wirts.* target time; **4.** *Bergb.* solid rock loosened by explosion
...vorgabe *f, im Subst.*: **Gesetzes~** legal standard; **Zeit~** allotted time; **Ziel~** set target
Vorgabezeit *f* time allowed (*od.* allotted)
Vorgang *m* **1.** (*Hergang*) proceedings *Pl.*; (*Prozess*) process; (*Ereignis*) event, occurrence; **natürlicher ~** natural process; **geschichtliche Vorgänge** historical events; **j-n über den ~ unterrichten** tell s.o. (*od.* inform s.o. about) what is happening (*od.* what happened); **2.** (*Akte*) file, dossier
Vorgänger *m*; -s, -, **~in** *f*; -, -nen predecessor
Vorgängermodell *n* previous model
Vorgarten *m* front garden (*Am.* yard)
vorgaukeln *v/t.* (*trennb., hat -ge-*): **j-m ~, dass** (try to) delude s.o. into thinking (that), (try to) get s.o. to believe (that); **j-m e-e rosige Zukunft** *etc.* **~** build up hopes of a rosy future *etc.* in s.o.
vorgeben *v/t.* (*unreg., trennb., hat -ge-*) **1.** *umg.* (*nach vorgeben*) pass s.th. to the front; **j-m etw. ~** pass s.th. (on) to s.o.; **2.** (*behaupten*) allege, claim; **~, reich zu sein** *etc.* pretend to be rich *etc.*; **3.** (*festlegen, verbindlich machen*) set; **man hat uns die Bearbeitungsrichtlinien vorgegeben** the processing guidelines have been laid down for us; **4.** *Sport* give; **j-m 50 Meter ~** give s.o. 50 met|res (*Am.* -ers) start
vorgebildet *Adj.*: **~ sein** have some knowledge (**auf, in** + *Dat.* of), have had previous training (*in*); **juristisch** *etc.* **~ sein** have had legal *etc.* training
Vorgebirge *n Geog., Geol.* foothills *Pl.*; (*Kap*) cape
vorgeblich *Adj.* ostensible; → **angeblich**
vorgeburtlich *Adj. Med.* prenatal; **~e Diagnostik** prenatal diagnosis
vorgedruckt *Adj. Glückwunschkarte etc.*: pre-printed
vorgefasst *Adj.*: **~e Meinung** prejudice, preconceived idea (*od.* notion); **e-e ~e Meinung haben** be prejudiced, be bias(s)ed (**von, gegen** against)
Vorgefecht *n* preliminary skirmish
vorgefertigt *Adj. Bauteile etc.*: prefabricated; *fig. Meinung etc.*: preconceived
Vorgefühl *n* anticipation; *negatives*: *auch* presentiment; **banges ~** uneasy feeling, foreboding
vorgegeben I. *P.P.* → **vorgeben**; **II.** *Adj. Wert, Zeit etc.*: set, fixed
vorgehalten I. *P.P.* → **vorhalten**; **II.** *Adj.*: **mit ~er Pistole** at gunpoint; **etw. hinter der ~en Hand erzählen** *fig.*

say s.th. off the record
vorgehen (*unreg., trennb., ist -ge-*) *v/i.* **1.** go forward; **~ zu** go up to; **2.** *umg.* (*vorangehen*) go first, lead the way; **ich geh schon mal vor** I'll go on ahead; **3.** *Uhr*: be fast; **täglich fünf Minuten** *etc.* **~** gain five minutes a day *etc.*; **4.** (*Vorrang haben*) have priority (+ *Dat.* over), be more important (than); **der Kunde geht immer vor** the customer always comes first; **5.** (*handeln*) act; (*einschreiten*) take action (**gegen** against); (*verfahren*) proceed; **6.** (*geschehen*) happen; **was geht hier vor?** what's going on here?; **was ging wohl in ihm vor?** I wonder what came over him
Vorgehen *n*; -s, *kein Pl.*; (*Handlungsweise, auch Einschreiten*) action; (*Verfahren*) procedure; **sein ~** the way he is handling (*od.* he handled) things; **das ~ der Polizei gegen die Demonstranten** *etc.* the action taken by the police against the demonstrators *etc.*;
Vorgehensweise *f* procedure
vorgelagert *Adj. attr. Insel etc.*: offshore ...; **e-e der Küste ~e Insel** an island (just) off the coast
vorgenannte *Adj. Amtsspr.* aforementioned
Vorgeplänkel *n* preliminary skirmish
vorgerückt I. *P.P.* → **vorrücken**; **II.** *Adj.*: **in ~em Alter** at an advanced age, in advanced years; **in ~em Stadium** at an advanced stage; **zu ~er Stunde** at a late hour
vorgeschädigt *Adj.*: **~ sein** have been damaged (*psychisch*: hurt) before; **ein ~es Herz haben** have a damaged heart; **ich bin diesbezüglich ~** *umg. fig.* this goes back a long way with me
Vorgeschichte *f* **1.** *hist.*: prehistory, early history; **2.** *e-r Sache*: (past) history, *the* story so far; *e-r Person*: past life, backstory, background; *Med.* case history, *fachspr.* anamnesis (*Pl.* anamneses); **e-e lange ~ haben** have a long history; **Vorgeschichtler** *m*; -s, -, **Vorgeschichtlerin** *f*; -, -nen; *hist.* prehistorian; **vorgeschichtlich** *Adj. hist.* prehistoric; **~e Siedlungsreste** remains of a prehistoric settlement
Vorgeschmack *m*; *nur Sg.* foretaste (**auf** + *Akk.* of)
vorgeschrieben I. *P.P.* → **vorschreiben**; **II.** *Adj. Tempo, Zahl etc.*: stipulated; **wie ~** as stipulated
vorgeschritten *Adj.* → **vorgerückt**
vorgesehen I. *P.P.* → **vorsehen** I; **II.** *Adj.* **1.** (*ausgewählt*) selected, chosen; **~ sein für etw.** be a candidate for s.th.; *offiziell*: have been chosen (*od.* designated) for s.th., be slated for s.th.; **2.** *attr.* (*gedacht, geplant*) planned; **die dafür ~en Mittel** the resources earmarked for it; **der ursprünglich ~e Termin** the deadline that was originally planned, the original deadline; **3.** *präd.*: **es ist ~ zu** (+ *Inf.*) there are plans to (+ *Inf.*), they're planning to (+ *Inf.*); **der Fahrstuhl ist für acht Personen ~** is designed to take eight people; **die Sitzung ist für nächste Woche ~** is planned (*od.* scheduled) for next week, has been slated for next week; **was ist für heute ~?** what are the plans for today?, what's on the agenda today?; **im Programm sind mehrere Pausen ~** the program(me) will include several breaks; **4.** *bes. Jur.*: **wie ~ in § 1029** as provided for in
vorgesetzt I. *P.P.* → **vorsetzen**;

II. *Adj.:* ~e *Dienststelle etc.* superior department; *j-m direkt* ~ *sein* be s.o.'s direct superior; **Vorgesetzte** *m, f; -n, -n* superior

Vorgespräche *Pl.* preliminary talks (*od.* discussions)

vorgestern *Adv.* the day before yesterday; *Ansichten etc. von* ~ *umg. fig.* views *etc.* of yesteryear, antiquated views *etc.*; **vorgestrig** *Adj.* **1.** of (*od.* from) the day before yesterday; **2.** *fig.:* ~e *Ansichten etc.* antiquated views *etc.*

vorgetäuscht I. *P.P.* → *vortäuschen*; **II.** *Adj.* faked; *e-e* ~e *Krankheit* a feigned illness; *es war vorgetäuscht* he was (*od.* they were *etc.*) faking, it was all a fake

vorgezogen I. *P.P.* → *vorziehen*; **II.** *Adj. Ruhestand, Wahlen etc.:* early

vorglühen *v/i.* (*trennb., hat -ge-*); *Mot.:* ~ *lassen* preheat

vorgreifen *v/i.* (*unreg., trennb., hat -ge-*) **1.** (*vorzeitig handeln*) act prematurely, jump the gun *umg.*; *in e-r Erzählung:* jump ahead; *e-r Sache* ~ (*etw. vorwegnehmen*) anticipate s.th.; *j-m* ~ anticipate s.o.'s answer (*od.* objections, question *etc.*); *aber ich will dir nicht* ~ but I don't want to jump in ahead of you; **2.** *auf sein Erbe etc.* ~ anticipate one's inheritance *etc.*; **Vorgriff** *m* anticipation; *im* ~ *auf* (+ *Akk.*) in anticipation of

Vorgruppe *f Mus.* support band

vorgucken *v/i.* (*trennb., hat -ge-*) *umg.:* *hinter etw.* ~ look out from behind s.th.; *dein Unterrock etc. guckt vor* your slip *etc.* is showing

vorhaben (*unreg., trennb., hat -ge-*) *v/t.* **1.** plan, have in mind; *was haben Sie heute vor?* what are your plans for today?; *haben Sie heute Abend etwas vor?* have you got anything planned for tonight?; *morgen haben wir einiges vor* we've got a lot to do tomorrow; (*müssen viel erledigen*) we've got a lot on the agenda for tomorrow; *was hat er jetzt wieder vor? umg.* what's he up to now?; *was hast du mit ihm vor?* what are you going to do with him?; *fest* ~, *etw. zu tun* have firmly decided to do s.th., be intent on doing s.th.; *die Firma hat noch viel mit Ihnen vor* the company still has great plans for you; **2.** *umg.* (*Schürze etc.*) have s.th. on

Vorhaben *n; -s, -;* (*Absicht*) intention, purpose; (*Plan*) plan; (*Projekt, auch Bau*) project; *j-n von s-m* ~ *abbringen* talk s.o. out of his (*od.* her) plan

Vorhalle *f* entrance hall, vestibule; *Theat., Hotel:* foyer, *bes. Am.* lobby

Vorhalt *m; -(e)s, -e* **1.** *Mus.* suspension; **2.** *Ballistik:* lead

vorhalten (*unreg., trennb., hat -ge-*) **I.** *v/t.* **1.** *j-m etw.* ~ hold s.th. (up) in front of s.o.; *beim Gähnen etc. die Hand* ~ put one's hand in front of one's mouth when one yawns *etc.*; → *vorgehalten*; **2.** *fig.* (*zum Vorwurf machen*): *j-m etw.* ~ reproach s.o. with s.th., accuse s.o. of s.th.; **3.** *j-m j-n als Vorbild etc.* ~ hold s.o. up to s.o. as an example *etc.*; **4.** *beim Bau:* (*Gerüste etc.*) provide; **II.** *v/i. Vorrat etc.:* last, hold out; **Vorhaltung** *f* **1.** reproach; *j-m* ~*en machen* reproach s.o., *förm.* remonstrate with s.o. (*über, wegen* + *Akk.* about); **2.** *beim Bau:* provision

Vorhand *f; nur Sg.* **1.** *Kartenspiel:* lead (*auch fig.*); **2.** *Tennis:* forehand; *e-n Ball* (*mit der*) ~ *retournieren etc.* return *etc.* a ball on one's forehand; → *Rück-*

hand; **3.** *Zool.* forehand

vorhanden *Adj.* (*verfügbar*) available; (*bestehend*) extant, in existence; ~ *sein* (*bestehen*) exist; *davon ist nichts mehr* ~ there's nothing of it left; **Vorhandensein** *n* existence

Vorhandschlag *m* forehand (shot *od.* stroke)

Vorhang *m* curtain; *der* ~ *geht auf* *Theat.* the curtain rises; *der Eiserne* ~ *Pol. hist.* the Iron Curtain; *zehn Vorhänge haben Theat.* have ten curtain calls

Vorhängeschloss *n* padlock

Vorhang|stange *f* curtain rod; ~**stoff** *m* curtain material, curtaining

Vorhaut *f Anat.* foreskin, *fachspr.* prepuce; *j-m die* ~ *beschneiden* circumcise s.o.; ~**verengung** *f Med.* phimosis, narrowing of the preputial orifice

vorheizen *v/t.* (*trennb., hat -ge-*) preheat, heat up

vorher *Adv.* before, first; (*unmittelbar* ~) beforehand; *am Abend* ~ the evening before, the previous evening; *das hättest du dir* ~ *überlegen sollen* you should have thought about that first (*od.* before); *hättest du das nicht* ~ *sagen können?* couldn't you have said so before (*od.* earlier)?

vorherbestimmen *v/t.* (*trennb., hat*) **1.** determine in advance; **2.** (*Schicksal etc.*) predestine; **vorherbestimmt I.** *P.P.* → *vorherbestimmen*; **II.** *Adj.* Schicksal *etc.:* predetermined; *es war ihr* ~, *Musikerin zu werden* she was (pre)destined to become a musician; **Vorherbestimmung** *f* **1.** predetermination; **2.** (*Schicksal*) *auch theologisch:* predestination

vorhergehen *v/i.* (*unreg., trennb., ist -ge-*) precede (+ *Dat. s.th.*); **vorhergehend** *Adj.* preceding; (*früher*) previous; *die* ~*en Ereignisse* the preceding events, (the) events leading up to it

vorherig *Adj.* previous; *Bemerkung etc.: auch* preceding; (*früher, ehemalig*) former; *ohne* ~*e Ankündigung* without prior (*od.* any) notice; ~*er Auftrag EDV* previous task

Vorherrschaft *f* (pre)dominance; *Pol. auch* supremacy; *die* ~ *in Asien etc.* dominance over Asia *etc.*; **vorherrschen** *v/i.* (*trennb., hat -ge-*) predominate, be (pre)dominant; *Situation etc.:* prevail; **vorherrschend I.** *Part. Präs.* → *vorherrschen*; **II.** *Adj.* predominant; *Geschmack etc., auch Situation, Klima:* prevailing; *die* ~*e Meinung* prevailing opinion, opinion at large

vorhersagbar *Adj.* predictable; *nicht* ~ unpredictable; **Vorhersage** *f* prediction (*über* + *Akk.* about); (*Wetter und Wirts. etc.*) forecast; **vorhersagen** *v/t.* (*trennb., hat -ge-*) predict; (*Wetter*) forecast

vorhersehbar *Adj.* foreseeable; *nicht* ~ unforeseeable; **vorhersehen** *v/t.* (*unreg., trennb., hat -ge-*) foresee; *keiner konnte das* ~ nobody could have foreseen (*od.* predicted) that; *wie vorherzusehen war* predictably, as was to be expected

vorheucheln *v/t.* (*trennb., hat -ge-*) pretend (+ *Dat.* to); *j-m etw.* ~ try to get s.o. to believe s.th.; (*sich verstellen*) put on an act in front of s.o.

vorheulen *v/t.* (*trennb., hat -ge-*) *umg.:* *j-m etwas* ~ give s.o. a sob story; (*sich ausweinen*) cry on s.o.'s shoulder

vorhin *Adv.* earlier on, a (short) while ago (*od.* back *umg.*); (*gerade*) just now

Vorhinein *Adv.:* *im* ~ (*im Voraus*) in advance; (*von vornherein*) from the start, (right) at the outset

Vorhof *m* **1.** forecourt; **2.** *des Herzens:* atrium (*Pl.* atriums *od.* atria), auricle; *des Ohrs:* vestibule; ~**flimmern** *n Med.* auricular fibrillation

Vorhölle *f: die* ~ limbo, Limbo

Vorhut *f; -, kein Pl.; Mil.* vanguard (*auch fig.*), advance guard

vorig *Adj.* previous; *Minister etc.: auch* former; (*vergangen*) last; ~*e Woche* last week

vorindustriell *Adj. Produktion, Gesellschaft:* pre-industrial

Vorinformation *f* prior information

Vorinstanz *f Jur.* lower court; *das Urteil der* ~ *aufheben/bestätigen* reverse/uphold the judg(e)ment of the lower court

Vorjahr *n* previous year; *im* ~ the previous year; (*letztes Jahr*) last year

Vorjahres|ergebnis *n Wirts.* previous year's result; *vom letzten Jahr:* last year's result; ~**monat** *m* same month the previous year; *im letzten Jahr:* same month last year; ~**niveau** *n* previous year's level; *vom letzten Jahr:* last year's level; ~**sieger** *m*, ~**siegerin** *f* previous year's winner; *vom letzten Jahr:* last year's winner; ~**umsatz** *m* previous year's turnover; *vom letzten Jahr:* last year's turnover; ~**wert** *m* previous year's value; *vom letzten Jahr:* last year's value; ~**zeitraum** *m* same period the previous year; *im letzten Jahr:* same period last year

vorjährig *Adj. attr.* **1.** of (*od.* from) the previous year; **2.** (*vom letzten Jahr*) last year's …

vorjammern *v/t.* (*trennb., hat -ge-*) *umg.: j-m etwas* ~ moan to s.o. (*über* + *Akk.* about); → *auch vorheulen*

Vorkampf *m Sport* **1.** (*Vorentscheidung*) preliminary; **2.** *Boxen etc.:* supporting bout

Vorkämpfer *m*, ~**in** *f* champion, pioneer

Vorkasse *f Wirts.* cash in advance; *Lieferung nur gegen* ~ delivery only with payment in advance

vorkauen *v/t.* (*trennb., hat -ge-*): *j-m etw.* ~ *umg. fig.* spoon-feed s.o. with s.th.; *wörtl.* chew s.th. for s.o.

Vorkaufsrecht *n* (right of) first refusal (*an* + *Dat.*, *bei* on); *j-m das* ~ *einräumen* give s.o. first refusal (*an* + *Dat.* on)

Vorkehrung *f* (*Maßnahme*) measure; (*Vorsichtsmaßregel*) precaution; ~*en treffen* take measures (*od.* precautions) (*gegen* against), ~*en treffen für* arrange (*od.* provide) for

Vorkenntnisse *Pl.* previous knowledge *Sg.* (*von* of); (*Erfahrung*) previous experience *Sg.*

Vorkliniker *m*, ~**in** *f Med.* preclinical student; **Vorklinikum** *n Med.* preclinical training; **vorklinisch** *Adj. Med.* preclinical

vorknöpfen *v/t.* (*trennb., hat -ge-*) *umg.: sich j-n* ~ take s.o. to task, have s.o. on the carpet; (*unsanft behandeln*) take care of s.o.; *ich werd mir mal die Kundendatei etc.* ~ I'll just take care of the customer files *etc.*

vorkochen *vt/i.* (*trennb., hat -ge-*) (*Mahlzeit*) precook; (*ankochen*) precook; *für morgen etc.* ~ cook in advance for tomorrow *etc.*

vorkolumbisch *Adj. hist.* pre-Columbian

vorkommen (*unreg., trennb., ist -ge-*)

v/i. **1.** (*zum Vorschein kommen*) appear; (*sich finden, vorhanden sein*) be found; (*auftauchen*) crop up; (*sich ereignen*) happen, occur; *sie kommen in Asien etc. vor* you find them in Asia *etc.*; *das kommt schon mal vor* it happens, it can happen; → *Familie*; *so etwas ist mir noch nie vorgekommen* nothing like that has ever happened to me before; *das Wort kommt zweimal vor* the word appears (*od.* occurs) twice, there are two instances of the word; **2.** (*scheinen, erscheinen*) seem; *es kommt mir merkwürdig vor* it strikes me as strange, it seems (a bit) strange to me; *es kam mir so vor, als ob* I had the impression that; *sich dumm etc.* ~ feel silly *etc.*; *sich wichtig etc.* ~ think one is important *etc.*; *das kommt dir nur so vor* you're (just) imagining it; *wie kommst du mir eigentlich vor?* *umg.* who do you think you are?; **3.** (*nach vorn kommen*) come forward; *in der Schule*: *auch* come to the front of the class

Vorkommen *n*; *-s, -* **1.** *nur Sg.* occurrence; (*Auftreten*) incidence; (*Vorhandensein*) existence; *das* ~ *von Skorpionen etc.* the existence of scorpions *etc.*; **2.** *Min.* deposit; **Vorkommnis** *n*; *-ses, -se* incident, occurrence; *keine besonderen* ~*se* no unusual occurrences, nothing unusual happening *umg.*; *besondere* ~*se*: *keine im Protokoll*: incidents of note: none

vorkosten *vt/i.* (*trennb., hat -ge-*) have a taste (of *s.th.*) in advance; **Vorkoster** *m*; *-s, -*, **Vorkosterin** *f*; *-, -nen* taster

Vorkriegs|deutschland *n hist.* pre-war Germany; ~**generation** *f* pre-war generation; ~**zeit** *f* pre-war age

Vorkurs *m* preparatory course

vorladen *v/t.* (*unreg., trennb., hat -ge-*) summon; *unter Strafandrohung*: subpoena; **Vorladung** *f* (writ of) summons *Sg.*; *unter Strafandrohung*: subpoena

Vorlage *f* **1.** model; (*Muster*) pattern; *etw. als* ~ *benutzen* copy from s.th.; **2.** *nur Sg.* (*Unterbreitung*) presentation, submission; *gegen* ~ (+ *Gen.*) on presentation of; **3.** *Parl.* (*Gesetzesvorlage*) bill; **4.** *Fußball etc.*: pass; **5.** *Skisport*: forward lean; **6.** *Wirts.*: advance; *in* ~ *bringen od. treten* advance

...vorlage *f*, *im Subst.*: *Bastel~* pattern (*for craft project*); *Zeichen~* drawing pattern

Vorland *n Geog.* **1.** *vor Gebirge*: piedmont, foothills *Pl.*; **2.** *vor dem Deich*: foreland

vorlassen *v/t.* (*unreg., trennb., hat -ge-*) **1.** let *s.o.* go first (*od.* in front); (*überholen lassen*) let *s.o.* pass; **2.** (*empfangen*) admit

Vorlauf *m* **1.** *nur Sg.*; *Videogerät etc.*: fast forward; **2.** *Sport* preliminary heat; **3.** *Tech.* caster; *e-s Kolbens*: forward stroke; *für Wasser*: flow pipe; **vorlaufen** *v/i.* (*unreg., trennb., ist -ge-*) *umg.* **1.** (*nach vorn laufen*) run forward(s); **2.** (*vorauslaufen*) run on ahead (*od.* in front); **Vorläufer** *m* **1.** *Person und Sache*: forerunner, precursor; **2.** *Skisport*: forerunner; **3.** *Verk.* relief train; **Vorläuferin** *f* forerunner, precursor

vorläufig I. *Adj.* provisional, temporary; **II.** *Adv.* provisionally, temporarily; (*fürs Erste*) for the time being; **Vorläufigkeit** *f* provisional nature (+ *Gen.* of)

Vorlaufzeit *f* **1.** *Sport* time in a (*od.* the) preliminary heat; **2.** *bevor ein Projekt etc. richtig beginnt*: lead time

vorlaut I. *Adj.* pert, cheeky; **II.** *Adv. fragen etc.*: pertly, cheekily

vorleben *v/t.* (*trennb., hat -ge-*): (*j-m*) *etw.* ~ be a living example of s.th. (for s.o.)

Vorleben *n* past, past life (*od.* history), backstory

Vorlege|besteck *n*: (*ein*) ~ (a set of) carvers *Pl., Am.* (a) carving set; *zum Servieren*: (a set of) servers *Pl.*; ~**gabel** *f* serving fork

vorlegen (*trennb., hat -ge-*) **I.** *v/t.* **1.** present (+ *Dat.* to); (*unterbreiten, auch zur Prüfung*) submit (to); (*Speise*) serve; *j-m den Ball* ~ play the ball to s.o.; *sich* (*Dat.*) *den Ball selbst* ~ tap the ball on; **2.** (*Schloss*) put on; → *Riegel etc.*; **3.** *Sport* (*Weite, Zeit etc.*) set; *ein scharfes Tempo* ~ *umg.* set a brisk pace; **4.** (*Summe etc.*) advance; **II.** *v/refl.* (*sich vorbeugen*) lean forward

Vorleger *m*; *-s, -* rug; (*Matte*) mat

Vorlegeschloss *n* padlock

vorlehnen *v/refl.* (*trennb., hat -ge-*) lean forward

Vorleistung *f* **1.** *Wirts.* (*Vorauszahlung*) advance (payment); *auch Pl.* (*Auslagen*) outlay; **2.** *mst* ~*en* (*Vorarbeiten*) preliminary work *Sg.*; *weitS.* previous achievements; **3.** *fig. mst* ~*en* (*Zugeständnisse*) concessions; ~*en erbringen* make concessions

vorlesen *vt/i.* (*unreg., trennb., hat -ge-*) read (aloud); *j-m etw.* ~ read s.th. (out) to s.o. (*aus* from); *liest du mir etw. vor?* will you read s.th. to me?; **Vorlesepult** *m* reader's desk; **Vorleser** *m*, **Vorleserin** *f* reader; **Vorlesewettbewerb** *m von Gedichten*: poetry-reading competition; *von Geschichten*: story-reading competition; **Vorlesung** *f* lecture (*über* + *Akk.* on); *e-e* ~ *halten* give a lecture; ~*en halten über* (+ *Akk.*) lecture on

Vorlesungsbeginn *m etwa* start (*od.* beginning) of term; ~ *ist am ...* term starts (*od.* begins) on ...

vorlesungsfrei *Adj.*: ~*e Zeit* vacation (period)

Vorlesungs|reihe *f* series of lectures, lecture series; ~**verzeichnis** *n* program(me) of lectures

vorletzt... *Adj.* last but one, next to last; *förm.* penultimate; ~*e Nacht* the night before last; *am* ~*en Freitag* (on the) Friday before last; *in der* ~*en Reihe* in the last row but one, in the next to last row; *er wurde Vorletzter* he was last but one (*od.* next to last)

Vorliebe *f* liking, fondness (*für* of); *etw. mit* ~ *tun* (*gern*) be very fond of (doing) s.th.; (*e-n Hang zu etw. haben*) have a penchant for (doing) s.th.; *weitS.* (*sehr oft etw. tun*) do s.th. fairly often (*od.* quite a lot)

vorlieb: ~ *nehmen mit* settle for, make do with, be content with

vorliegen *v/i.* (*unreg., trennb., hat -ge-*) **1.** (*vorhanden sein*) be there; (*angekommen sein*) *auch* have arrived; *engS.*: *j-m* ~ lie (*od.* be) in front of s.o., lie (*od.* be) on s.o.'s desk; *Ergebnisse, Daten etc.*: have been given to s.o.; *Antrag etc.*: have been submitted (to s.o.); *mir liegen Zahlen etc. vor, die ...* I have figures *etc.* here in front of me that ...; *die Ergebnisse liegen noch nicht vor* the results haven't come in yet, we haven't received (*od.*

had) any results so far; *da muss ein Irrtum* ~ there must be some mistake; *was liegt gegen ihn vor?* *Jur.* what is the charge against him?; *es liegt Brandstiftung / ein Missverständnis vor* it's a case of arson / there is a misunderstanding; **2.** (*zu erledigen sein*) have to be done (*od.* dealt with); (*auf der Tagesordnung stehen*) be on the agenda; *was liegt vor?* what's to be done?; *liegt etwas vor?* is there anything?; **3.** *umg. Kette*: be on; *Riegel*: be across

vorliegend I. *Part. Präs.* → *vorliegen*; **II.** *Adj.*: *der* ~*e Band etc.* this volume *etc.*; *die uns* ~*en Zahlen etc.* the figures *etc.* we have available; *die* ~*e Frage etc.* the question *etc.* at issue; *im* ~*en Fall* in this (*od.* the present) case

vorlügen *v/t.* (*unreg., trennb., hat -ge-*) *umg.*: *j-m etwas* ~ lie to s.o., tell s.o. a pack of lies

vorm *Präp.* + *Art. umg.* **1.** → *vor* I 1-3; **2.** ~ *Frühstück kann ich nicht rauchen* I can't smoke before breakfast; *er sitzt den ganzen Tag* ~ *Fernseher* he sits all day in front of the TV

vormachen *v/t.* (*trennb., hat -ge-*) *umg.* **1.** *j-m etw.* ~ (*zeigen*) show s.o. how to do s.th., demonstrate s.th. to s.o.; **2.** *j-m etwas* ~ *zur Täuschung*: fool s.o.; *sich* (*selbst*) *etwas* ~ deceive (*od.* fool) o.s.; *machen wir uns nichts vor* let's be honest about this; *ihm kannst du nichts* ~ he's no (*od.* nobody's) fool

Vormacht *f*; *nur Sg.*, **Vormachtstellung** *f* (*Übergewicht*) supremacy; (*Hegemonie*) hegemony (*beide in* + *Dat.* over); ~ *in* (+ *Dat.*) *auch* ascendancy over

Vormagen *m Zool., von Schaf etc.*: rumen; *von Vogel*: crop

Vormagnetisierung *f Etron.* (magnetic) bias

vormalig *Adj.* former; **vormals** *Adv.* formerly (known as)

Vormann *m* (*Vorarbeiter*) foreman; (*Vorgänger*) predecessor

Vormarsch *m* advance (*auch fig.*); *auf dem* ~ *im* ~ *sein* be on the advance, be advancing (*auf* + *Akk.* on); *fig.* be gaining ground, be spreading

Vormärz *m*; *nur Sg.*; *hist. period of German history from 1815 to the revolution in March 1848*

Vormast *m Naut.* foremast

Vormenschen *Pl.* pithecanthropi(ds)

vormerken *v/t.* (*trennb., hat -ge-*) (*Termin, Bestellung etc.*) make a note of; (*reservieren*) reserve (*auch* ~ *lassen*); (*Person*) put *s.o.*'s name down, pencil in *umg.*; (*Geld*) earmark; *Wirts.* target; *sich* ~ *lassen* put one's name down (*für* for), have one's name put down (for); *sich bei j-m* ~ *lassen* (*e-n Termin vereinbaren*) make an appointment with s.o.; **Vormerker** *m*; *-s, -*; *mst Pl.*; *Wirts.* (*Vorbesteller*) person placing an advanced order

Vormerk|kalender *m* diary; ~**liste** *f* waiting list

Vormerkung *f* (*Reservierung*) booking, reservation; (*Termin*) appointment; *Jur., im Grundbuch*: provisional entry in the real estate register

Vormieter *m*, ~**in** *f* previous tenant

Vormittag *m* morning; *am Vormittag* in the morning; **vormittäglich** *Adj. attr.* morning ...; **vormittags** *Adv.* in the morning(s); *montags* ~ on Monday mornings

Vormittagsstunde *f* morning hour; *in*

den ~n during the morning hours

Vormonat m: (im) ~ (the) previous month

Vormund m; -(e)s, -e und Vormünder guardian; **Vormundschaft** f guardianship; unter ~ stehen/stellen be placed / place under the care of a guardian; **Vormundschaftsgericht** n guardianship court; in GB: Family Division of the High Court; in den USA: family court

vorn Adv. in front (auch fig.), at the front; im Rennen etc.: in front, ahead; ganz ~ right in front; (am Anfang) at the beginning; weiter ~ further up; im Buch etc.: nearer the beginning; nach ~ forward; nach ~ kommen come up to the front; nach ~ an die Tafel kommen come up to the blackboard; von ~ from the front; von ~ anfangen start (od. begin) at the beginning; (auch wieder von ~ anfangen) start (all over) again; von ~ bis hinten from front to back; (von Anfang bis Ende) from beginning to end; noch einmal von ~ all over again; auffordernd: let's do that again, let's go back to the beginning again

Vorname m first (od. Christian) name, Am. auch given name; Amtssprache: auch prename; wie heißt er mit ~n? what is his first name?

vorne → vorn

vornehm I. Adj. **1.** bes. Person: distinguished; (edel) noble; Sache: classy; (elegant) elegant, fashionable, smart, posh umg.; (erstklassig) high-class; (exklusiv) exclusive; die ~e Gesellschaft high society; ~e Gesinnung high-mindedness; das Hotel etc. ist mir zu ~ the hotel etc. is too upmarket (Am. upscale) for my taste; ~ tun umg. pej. put on airs; dafür kommst du dir wohl zu ~ vor umg. pej. I suppose you think you're far too good for that; **2.** geh.: ~ste Aufgabe, Pflicht etc.: chief; **II.** Adv. sich benehmen etc.: grandly, posh umg.; (nobel) nobly; ~ gekleidet elegantly dressed; ~ reden etc. pej. talk etc. grandly

vornehmen v/t. (unreg., trennb., hat -ge-) **1.** (durchführen) carry out; (Änderung, Verbesserung etc.) auch make; auch sich (Dat.): ~ in (in Angriff nehmen) tackle; (anfangen) get down to; sich (Dat.) etw. ~ (sich kümmern um) take care of, see to; sich (Dat.) e-e Arbeit ~ set out to do a job; sich (Dat.) j-n ~ umg. verbal: take s.o. to task, have s.o. on the carpet, Am. auch give s.o. a tongue-lashing; tätlich: take care of s.o.; den werde ich mir mal ~! umg. I'm going to have a few words with him; **2.** sich (Dat.) etw. ~ (planen) plan, have (od. make) plans for; sich (Dat.) ~, etw. zu tun (beschließen) decide to do s.th.; (stärker) resolve to do s.th.; (planen) plan to do s.th.; (beabsichtigen) intend to do s.th.; das habe ich mir fest vorgenommen I've definitely decided to do it; sich (Dat.) zu viel ~ take on too much, bite off more than one can chew umg.; sich (Dat.) einiges vorgenommen haben umg. have taken on quite a job

Vornehmheit f des persönlichen Auftretens: distinguished manner; (Adel) nobility; (Exklusivität) class(iness), exclusivity, exclusive atmosphere etc.; im Stil: elegance; → vornehm

vornehmlich Adv. mainly; (in erster Linie) first and foremost

Vornehmtuerei f pej. airs (and graces)

Pl.; **vornehmtuerisch** Adj. pej. affected, snobby, la-di-da umg.

vorneigen v/refl. (trennb., hat -ge-) bend (od. lean) forward

Vorneverteidigung f Sport forward defen|ce (Am. -se)

vorneweg → vorweg

vornherein Adv.: von ~ (right) from the beginning (od. start)

vornüber Adv. forward; (Kopf voraus) head first; ~beugen v/refl. (trennb., hat -ge-) bend (over) forwards; ~fallen v/i. (unreg., trennb., ist -ge-) fall (over) forwards; ~kippen v/i. (trennb., ist -ge-) topple forwards

vorolympisch Adj. Sport pre-Olympic

vorordnen v/t. (trennb., hat -ge-) presort, put in some sort of order

Vorort m suburb; ~bahn f suburban line (Zug: train)

Vor-Ort|-Begehung f on-site inspection; ~-Betreuung f on-site care

Vorort|siedlung f suburban estate; ~zug m suburban train

vorplanen vt/i. (trennb., hat -ge-) plan in advance

Vorplatz m forecourt; vor e-m Bahnhof etc.: square, bes. Am. plaza

Vorpommern (n); -s; Geog. Western Pomerania

Vorposten m Mil. und fig. outpost

vorpreschen v/i. (trennb., ist -ge-) rush forward; fig. rush ahead; ~ in (+ Akk.) (e-e Position etc.) rush into; fig. auch venture into

Vorprogramm n supporting program(me); **vorprogrammieren** v/t. (trennb., hat -ge-) (pre)program(me); **vorprogrammiert I.** P.P. → vorprogrammieren; **II.** Adj. **1.** (pre)program(m)ed; **2.** fig. (unvermeidlich) inevitable; (sicher) sure, certain; es war ~ auch it was bound to happen; die Katastrophe ist ~ it's program(m)ed for disaster

Vorprüfung f preliminary examination; Sport trial

Vorquartal n previous quarter

Vorrang m; kein Pl. **1.** (position of) pre-eminence; (Vordringlichkeit) priority; den ~ haben vor (+ Dat.) take precedence (Sache: auch priority) over; j-m den ~ streitig machen dispute s.o.'s right to a position of pre-eminence; **2.** bes. österr. (Vorfahrt) right of way, priority; **vorrangig I.** Adj. attr. priority ...; ~ sein have priority; → auch vordringlich; **II.** Adv.: etw. ~ behandeln give s.th. (top) priority; **Vorrangigkeit** f priority (vor + Dat. over); **Vorrangstellung** f → Vorrang 1; e-e ~ einnehmen occupy a position of pre-eminence

Vorrat m; -(e)s, Vorräte supply, supplies Pl., stocks Pl.; an Lebensmitteln: auch store; (Reserven) reserves Pl. (auch an Bodenschätzen, Geld); an Atombomben etc.: stockpile; heimlicher: (secret) hoard (alle an + Dat. of); etw. auf ~ haben have s.th. in reserve (Wirts. in stock), have a stockpile of s.th. umg.; etw. auf ~ kaufen stock up on s.th.; solange der ~ reicht while stocks last; s-e Vorräte aufgebraucht haben have exhausted (od. used up) one's supplies; **vorrätig** Adj. available; Wirts.: ~ sein be in stock; nicht (mehr) ~ sein be out of stock; etw. ~ haben have s.th. in stock; etw. nicht mehr ~ haben be (od. have run) out of s.th.

Vorrats|haltung f keeping of supplies; ~kammer f pantry, larder; ~keller m storage cellar; ~lager n, ~raum m storeroom; ~schrank m store cup-

board; für Lebensmittel: larder; ~wirtschaft f Wirts. policy of stockpiling (raw materials)

Vorraum m anteroom; Theat. etc. foyer, bes. Am. lobby

vorrechnen v/t. (trennb., hat -ge-) reckon up (j-m for s.o.); (aufzählen) enumerate; fig. (vorhalten) auch list, go through

Vorrechner m EDV front-end processor

Vorrecht n privilege, prerogative

Vorrede f **1.** opening words Pl.; (halt) keine langen ~n! umg. don't waste time with long introductions; **2.** (Vorwort) preface; **Vorredner** m, **Vorrednerin** f previous speaker; mein Vorredner the previous speaker

Vorreiter m, ~in f fig. pioneer, trailblazer; den Vorreiter für e-e Idee etc. machen pioneer an idea etc.; **Vorreiterrolle** f: e-e ~ übernehmen (für) take on a role as trailblazer (for)

vorrennen v/i. (unreg., trennb., ist -ge-) run forward; (vorausrennen) run (on) ahead

vorrevolutionär Adj. pre-revolutionary

Vorrichtung f device; (Gerät) appliance

vorrücken (trennb., -ge-) **I.** v/t. (hat) move forward (auch Schach etc.); **II.** v/i. (ist) **1.** advance (Mil. in Richtung auf + Akk. on; nach to); Zeiger etc.: move on; (sich vorwärts bewegen) Schlange etc.: move forward; auf den 3. Platz ~ Sport move up to third place; → vorgerückt; **2.** Päd. in die nächsthöhere Klasse: move up

Vorruhestand m early retirement; in den ~ treten take early retirement; im ~ sein have taken early retirement; **Vorruheständler** m, **Vorruheständlerin** f person who has taken early retirement, Am. early retiree

Vorruhestands|gelder Pl. early retirement benefits; ~regelung f early retirement scheme (od. policy)

Vorrunde f Sport qualifying round

Vorrundenspiel n qualifying game

vors Präp. + Art. umg. **1.** → vor I 1, 2; **2.** man brachte ihn ~ Kriegsgericht he was brought before the court marshal

vorsagen (trennb., hat -ge-) **I.** vt/i.: j-m ~ in der Schule: tell s.o. the answer, whisper the answer to s.o.; bitte nicht ~! please don't reveal the answer!; **II.** v/t. zum Nachsagen: say s.th. first (for s.o. to repeat); sich (Dat.) etw. ~ (vor sich hin sagen) repeat s.th. to o.s.; (einreden) talk o.s. into believing s.th.; **Vorsager** m; -s, -, **Vorsagerin** f; -, -nen **1.** umg. (Souffleur) prompter; **2.** in der Schule: child who whispers answers to another child

Vorsaison f **1.** Tourismus etc.: pre-season, off-season, low season; (Saisonbeginn) start of the season; **2.** (vergangene Saison) Tourismus: previous season; Sport previous season; ~preis m off-peak price

Vorsatz m **1.** intention; fester: resolution; Jur. (criminal) intent; mit ~ on purpose; Jur. wil(l)fully, with malice aforethought; mit dem ~, etw. zu tun Jur. with the intent of doing s.th.; den ~ fassen, etw. zu tun resolve (od. make up one's mind) to do s.th.; **2.** (~gerät) attachment; **3.** Druck. end paper

Vorsatz|blatt n Druck. end paper; ~gerät n attachment

vorsätzlich I. Adj. intentional, deliberate; Jur. wil(l)ful; ~er Mord premeditated murder; **II.** *Adv.* deliberately, intentionally; *Jur.* wil(l)fully, with criminal intent, with malice aforethought; **Vorsätzlichkeit** *f Jur.* wil(l)fulness

Vorsatzlinse *f Fot.* front lens attachment

vorschalten *v/t.* (*trennb.*, *hat -ge-*) **1.** *Tech. etc.* add (+ *Dat.* to), insert; *Etech.* connect in series; **2.** *fig.* slot *s.th.* in ahead, bring *s.th.* forward, move *s.th.* up

Vorschalt|gesetz *n Jur.* temporary law; **~widerstand** *m Etech.* series resistor

Vorschau *f* preview (*auf* + *Akk.* of); *Film:* trailer(s *Pl.*), *bes. Am.* preview(s *Pl.*); *e-e ~ auf das heutige Programm* a look at today's program(me); **~funktion** *f EDV* preview function

Vorschein *m:* *zum ~ bringen* bring to light; *zum ~ kommen* come to light, surface, come to the surface; (*entdeckt werden*) *auch* be discovered; (*erscheinen*) appear; *hinter etw. zum ~ kommen* appear from behind s.th.

vorschicken *v/t.* (*trennb.*, *hat -ge-*) send forward; (*vorausschicken*) send (on) ahead

vorschieben (*unreg.*, *trennb.*, *hat -ge-*) **I.** *v/t.* push (*od.* slide, move) forward; (*Lippe etc.*) stick out; *fig.* (*als Vorwand benutzen*) use *s.th.* as an excuse; (*j-n*) use *s.o.* as a dummy; *fig.* → *Riegel;* **II.** *v/refl.* move forward; *Person:* push (one's way) forward; *in der Schlange: Brit.* jump the queue, *Am.* cut in line

vorschießen (*unreg.*, *trennb.*, *-ge-*) **I.** *v/t.* (*hat*): *j-m etw. ~* advance s.o. s.th.; **II.** *v/i.* (*ist*) (*nach vorn schießen*) shoot forward; (*hervorschießen*) shoot out

Vorschiff *n Naut.* forecastle, fo'c's'le, fo'c'sle

vorschlafen *vt/i.* (*unreg.*, *trennb.*, *hat -ge-*), *umg.:* *ein bisschen ~* stock up on a bit of sleep, *Am. auch* stockpile some Zs

Vorschlag *m* **1.** suggestion; *auch Wirts.* proposal; (*Empfehlung*) (piece of) advice; *j-m e-n ~ machen* make a suggestion to s.o.; *auf j-s ~ (hin)* on s.o.'s suggestion (*od.* advice); *ich mache e-n ~ zur Güte* hum. I have a suggestion that will help settle this amicably; **2.** *Mus.:* (*langer/kurzer*) *~* (long/short) appoggiatura (*Pl.* appoggiaturas *od.* appoggiature); **3.** *Druck.* blank space

...vorschlag *m*, *im Subst.:* *Abrüstungs~* disarmament proposal; *Wahl~* nomination

vorschlagen *v/t.* (*unreg.*, *trennb.*, *hat -ge-*) suggest, propose; (*empfehlen*) recommend; *~*, *etw. zu tun* suggest doing s.th.; *j-m ~*, *etw. zu tun* suggest (that) s.o. (should) do s.th., suggest to s.o. that he (*od.* she) (should) do s.th.; *ich schlage vor, dass wir zuerst etwas essen* I suggest we eat something first; *j-n für e-n Posten etc. ~* recommend (*öffentlich:* propose) s.o. for a position *etc.*

Vorschlaghammer *m* sledgehammer

Vorschlags|recht *n* right to make a proposal; **~wesen** *n*; *nur Sg.* suggestion system

vorschnell → *voreilig*

vorschreiben *v/t.* (*unreg.*, *trennb.*, *hat -ge-*) **1.** (*anordnen*) prescribe; *Gesetz:* stipulate; *ich lasse mir nichts ~* I won't be dictated to, nobody tells me what to do; **2.** *j-m etw. ~* (*Wort, Brief etc.*) write s.th. out for s.o.

vorschreiten *v/i.* (*unreg.*, *trennb.*, *ist -ge-*) *geh.* advance

Vorschrift *f* rule(s *Pl.*), regulation(s *Pl.*); (*Anweisung*) instruction, direction; *nach ärztlicher ~* according to doctor's orders; (*streng*) *nach ~ arbeiten etc.:* (strictly) to rule; *Dienst nach ~* (*Bummelstreik*) work-to-rule; *du hast mir keine ~en zu machen* I won't be dictated to by you, I don't take orders from you; **vorschriftsmäßig I.** *Adj.* correct; *attr. Kleidung etc.:* regulation ...; *nachgestellt:* as ordered, as prescribed; **II.** *Adv.* correctly, according to regulations; (*nach Angaben*) according to the instructions; **vorschriftswidrig I.** *Adj.* incorrect; *Kleidung etc.:* non-regulation; **II.** *Adv.* incorrectly, contrary to (the) regulations (*od.* instructions)

Vorschub *m*; *-(e)s, Vorschübe* **1.** *e-r Sache ~ leisten* encourage, foster; **2.** *Tech.*, *Druck.* feed; **~leistung** *f Jur.* aiding and abetting

Vorschulalter *n* pre-school age; **Vorschule** *f* nursery school, *Am.* pre--school; **Vorschulerziehung** *f* pre--school education; **vorschulisch** *Adj. attr.* pre-school ...; **Vorschulkind** *n* **1.** pre-school-age child; **2.** nursery school (*Am.* pre-school) child

Vorschuss *m* advance (payment) (*auf* + *Akk.* on); *sich e-n ~ (von ...) geben lassen* receive an advance (of ...); **Vorschusslorbeeren** *Pl.* premature praise *Sg.*; unearned laurels; **vorschussweise** *Adv.* as an advance

vorschützen *v/t.* (*trennb.*, *hat -ge-*) give (*od.* use) as a pretext; *~*, *man sei/habe etc.* pretend to be/have *etc.*, make out one is/has *etc.*; *keine Müdigkeit ~!* *umg.* stop pretending to be tired!, *Am. auch* stop goldbricking!; *fig.* go on then!

vorschwärmen *vt/i.* (*trennb.*, *hat -ge-*): *j-m von etw. ~* rave to s.o. about s.th., rave on about s.th. to s.o.; *j-m von j-m ~* rave on about s.o. to s.o.

vorschweben *v/i.* (*trennb.*, *hat -ge-*): *mir schwebt etwas ... vor* I'm thinking of (*od.* I could imagine) something ...

vorschwindeln *v/t.* (*trennb.*, *hat -ge-*) *umg.:* *j-m etwas ~* tell s.o. a lot of lies (*od.* fibs); *j-m ~*, *man sei/würde etc.* lie to s.o. about being/doing *etc.*

vorsehen (*unreg.*, *trennb.*, *hat -ge-*) **I.** *v/t.* **1.** (*bestimmen*) intend (*für* for); (*Mittel, Zeit etc.*) *auch* earmark, set aside (for); **2.** *j-n ~ für* (*e-n Posten etc.*) have s.o. in mind for; (*ausgewählt haben*) have chosen (*amtlich:* designated) s.o. for; *er ist als Abteilungsleiter etc. vorgesehen* he's intend to be (*od.* designated as) department(al) head *etc.*; **3.** (*planen*) plan; *zeitlich, terminmäßig: auch* schedule; (*entwerfen*) plan, design (*alle für* for); **4.** *Gesetz, Abmachung etc.:* provide for; *das Gesetz sieht vor, dass* provides that; **5.** (*einschließen, einplanen*) include; → *vorgesehen* II; **II.** *v/refl.* be careful, watch out (*bei j-m* with s.o.); *sich ~, dass man nicht ausrutscht etc.* be careful (*od.* take care) not to slip *etc.*; *sieh dich (bloß) vor!* *Warnung:* watch out!, be careful!; *Drohung:* (just) watch yourself (*od.* it)!; **Vorsehung** *f:* (*die göttliche*) *~* (divine) providence, Providence

vorsetzen (*trennb.*, *hat -ge-*) **I.** *v/t.* move (*Bein:* put) forward; (*Schüler etc.*) move (up) to the front; (*davorset-*

zen) put in front (+ *Dat.* of); *j-m etw. ~* place (*od.* put) s.th. in front of (*od.* before) s.o.; (*Speise etc.*) serve s.o. s.th. (*od.* s.th. to s.o.); (*anbieten*) offer s.o. s.th.; *pej.*, *auch fig.* dish s.th. up to s.o.; *was haben die uns diesmal wieder vorgesetzt?* *fig.* what have they dished us up this time?, what have they come up with (for us) this time?; **II.** *v/refl.* move (up) to the front, go and sit at the front

Vorsicht *f;* *kein Pl.* caution; (*Behutsamkeit*) care; (*Umsicht*) circumspection; *~!* careful!, look out!, watch out!; *als Aufschrift:* caution!, danger!; *auf Kisten:* (handle) with care; *~*, *bissiger Hund!* beware of the dog; *~*, *Glas!* glass - handle with care; *~ Stufe!* mind (*Am.* watch) the step; *mit ~* cautiously; *mit äußerster ~* with the utmost caution; *mit gebotener ~* with due care (and attention); *bei aller ~* in spite of every precaution being taken; *es ist (äußerste) ~ geboten* one has to be (extremely) careful; *zur ~ raten* advise (*od.* recommend) caution; *er ist mit ~ zu genießen* *umg.* you've got to watch him; *es ist mit (äußerster) ~ zu genießen* you've got to be (extremely) cautious about it; *mit Vorbehalt:* you've got to take it with a (big) pinch (*Am.* with a grain) of salt; *~ ist besser als Nachsicht Sprichw.* better safe than sorry

vorsichtig I. *Adj.* careful; (*abwägend*) cautious; *Schätzung etc.:* conservative; *~ sein mit s-m Urteil etc.* be cautious about judging *etc.*; *sei ~*, *dass du nichts fallen lässt* be careful not to drop anything, mind you don't drop anything; *da bin ich immer ein bisschen ~* I'm always a bit wary of that; **II.** *Adv.* carefully; *abwägen:* cautiously; **Vorsichtigkeit** *f* carefulness; cautiousness; conservatism; → *vorsichtig;* **vorsichtshalber** *Adv.* as a precaution; **Vorsichtsmaßnahme** *f*, **Vorsichtsmaßregel** *f* precaution(ary measure); *~n treffen* take precautions

Vorsignal *n Eisenb.* distant signal

Vorsilbe *f Ling.* prefix

vorsingen (*unreg.*, *trennb.*, *hat -ge-*) **I.** *v/t.:* *j-m etw. ~* sing s.th. to s.o.; **II.** *v/i. zur Probe:* (have an) audition (+ *Dat.* with); *umg. fig.* (*Probevorlesung od. -stunde halten*) audition; *j-n ~ lassen* audition s.o., give s.o. an audition; *umg. fig.* (*Bewerber[in]*) interview s.o.

vorsintflutlich *Adj. attr.* pre-Flood ...; *auch fig. Vorstellungen etc.:* antediluvian

Vorsitz *m*; *nur Sg.* chair(manship); *Wirts.* presidency; *den ~ haben od. führen* be in the chair; *auch Wirts.* preside (*bei* over); *den ~ haben bei e-r Sitzung etc. auch* chair a meeting *etc.*; *unter dem ~ von* (*od.* + *Gen.*) under the chairmanship of, with ... in the chair, with ... chairing; **vorsitzen** *v/i.* (*unreg.*, *trennb.*, *hat, südd., schw., österr. ist -ge-*): *e-r Kommission etc. ~* chair a committee *etc.*; **vorsitzend I.** *Part. Präs.* → *vorsitzen;* **II.** *Adj. Richter etc.:* presiding; **Vorsitzende** *m, f, -n, -n* chairman (*f* chairwoman), chairperson; *Wirts.* president

Vorsorge *f; nur Sg.* **1.** provision(s *Pl.*); (*Vorsicht*) precaution; *~ treffen* provide, make provisions (*für* for); **2.** *Med.* prevention; *zur ~ gehen* go for a checkup; **~maßnahme** *f* precautionary measure

vorsorgen *v/i.* (*trennb., hat -ge-*) provide, make provision (**für** for); **~, dass** see to it that

Vorsorge|pauschale *f Fin.* lump sum worked into wage tax tables taking into account employees' contributions for statutory insurance cover, life assurance, liability insurance, etc.; **~untersuchung** *f Med.* (precautionary) checkup; **zur ~ gehen** go for a check-up

vorsorglich I. *Adj. Maßnahme etc.*: precautionary; *Person:* (*vorsichtig*) cautious; (*besorgt*) solicitous; **II.** *Adv.* as a precaution(ary measure), to be on the safe side, just in case *umg.*

vorsortieren *v/t.* (*trennb., hat*) sort *s.th.* temporarily (*od.* provisionally); **vorsortiert I.** *P.P.* → **vorsortieren**; **II.** *Adj.* temporarily (*od.* provisionally) sorted; **~e Daten** *EDV* clustered data

Vorspann *m; -(e)s, -e und Vorspänne;* (*Einleitung*) introduction; *zu e-m Zeitungsartikel:* lead-in; *Film:* credits *Pl.*; (*Eingangsszene*) pre-titles sequence; *vom Tonband etc.*: leader

vorspannen *v/t.* (*trennb., hat -ge-*) (*Pferd etc.*) harness (+ *Dat.* to); **j-n ~** *umg. fig.* use s.o. (**für** for)

Vorspannmusik *f Film:* theme music (*od.* tune); *e-r Sendereihe:* signature tune

Vorspeise *f Gastr.* starter, *Am. auch* appetizer; *förm.* hors d'oeuvre; **gemischte ~n** selection of hors d'oeuvres; **Vorspeisenteller** *m* starter, *Am. auch* appetizer

vorspiegeln *v/t.* (*trennb., hat -ge-*): **j-m etw. ~** delude s.o. into thinking s.th.; **Vorspiegelung** *f* preten|ce (*Am.* -se); (**unter**) **~ falscher Tatsachen** (under) false preten|ces (*Am.* -ses)

Vorspiel *n Mus.* prelude (**zu** to); *Theat.* prolog(ue); *Sport* curtain-raiser; *sexuelles:* foreplay; *fig.* prelude, overture, (*Auftakt*) curtain-raiser (to); **vorspielen** (*trennb., hat -ge-*) **I.** *vt/i.* play (**j-m etw.** s.th. to s.o.); **II.** *v/t. fig.*: **etw. ~** (*schauspielern*) put s.th. on; (**j-m**) **etwas ~** *fig.* put on an act (for s.o.); **III.** *v/i. Theat., Mus.* (have an) audition (+ *Dat.* with); **j-n ~ lassen** audition s.o., give s.o. an audition

Vorsprache *f* **1.** visit; *geh.* appointment; **j-s ~ bei** s.o.'s visit to; **2.** *Amtsspr.* s.o.'s appointment at; **persönliche ~ erforderlich** it is necessary to attend in person

vorsprechen (*unreg., trennb., hat -ge-*) **I.** *vt/i.* **1.** (**j-m**) **etw. ~** say s.th. (for s.o. to repeat); **ich spreche vor und ihr sprecht nach** I'll say it and you repeat (it) after me; **2.** (*vortragen*) recite (*auch zur Probe*); **II.** *v/i.* **1.** **bei j-m ~** (go to) see s.o.; **2.** *zur Probe:* (have an) audition (+ *Dat.* with); **j-n ~ lassen** audition s.o., give s.o. an audition

vorspringen *v/i.* (*unreg., trennb., ist -ge-*) **1.** jump forward; **2.** (*hervortreten*) *auch Archit.* project, jut (out); **vorspringend I.** *Part. Präs.* → **vorspringen**; **II.** *Adj.* projecting; *Nase, Kinn etc.*: prominent

Vorsprung *m* **1.** *Archit.* projection; (*Sims*) ledge; **2.** (*Abstand*) lead (*auch fig.*) (**gegenüber, vor** + *Dat.* over); (*Vorgabe*) start; **ein Tor ~** a one-goal lead; **mit e-m ~ von 2 Sekunden** by a margin of 2 seconds; **er hat e-n ~ von 3 Runden** he leads by 3 laps; **e-n ~ von 6 Wochen haben** be ahead by 6 weeks, be 6 weeks ahead; **j-m ~ geben** give s.o. a (head) start; **s-n ~ ausbau-**

en consolidate one's lead

...vorsprung *m, im Subst.* **1.** (*Teil*) *Berg~* mountain ledge; *Dach~* eaves *Pl.*, roof overhang; **2.** *fig.: Entwicklungs~* developmental superiority (*bes. Am.* edge); *Informations~* superiority in terms of information, *bes. Am.* information edge

vorspulen *vt/i.* (*trennb., hat -ge-*): (*das Band*) **~** wind (*od.* run) the tape forward *od.* on (to the end); **Vorspulen** *n; -s, kein Pl.*: **beim ~ des Films** while winding the film on to the end

Vorstadt *f* suburb; *pej.* suburbia; **in der ~** in the suburbs, in a suburb; **Vorstädter** *m; -s, -*, **Vorstädterin** *f; -, -nen* suburbanite; **vorstädtisch** *Adj.* suburban

Vorstadt|kino *n* suburban cinema (*Am.* screen *od.* movie theater); **~theater** *n* suburban theat|re (*Am. auch* -er)

Vorstand *m* **1.** *Wirts.* (board of) management; *e-s Vereins etc.*: managing committee; *e-s Instituts etc.*: board of governors (*od.* trustees, *bes. Am.* directors); **im ~ sitzen** be on the board; **2.** (*Person*) director; *e-r Gesellschaft:* chairman (of the board), *Am.* chief executive

Vorstands|etage *f etwa* executive suite; *fig.* boardroom(s *Pl.*); **~mitglied** *n* board member (**bei** of), member of the (executive) board *etc.*, director; → **Vorstand** 2; **~posten** *m* position on the board *etc.*; **~sitzung** *f* board meeting; **~sprecher** *m*, **~sprecherin** *f* board spokesperson; **~vorsitz** *m* chairmanship (of the board); **~vorsitzende** *m, f* chairman (*f* chairwoman) (*bes. Am.* chairperson *od.* chair) of the board (of directors), *Am.* chief executive; *Pl. auch* top managers, chief executives; **~wahl** *f* board (*Pol.* executive) elections *Pl.*

vorstecken *v/t.* (*trennb., hat -ge-*) (*auch sich* [*Dat.*] *etw. ~*) put on; *mit e-r Nadel etc.*: *auch* pin on

Vorstecknadel *f* **1.** (*Brosche*) brooch; **2.** (*Krawattennadel*) tie-pin

vorstehen *v/i.* (*unreg., trennb., hat, südd., schw., österr. ist -ge-*) **1.** (*herausragen*) protrude, jut out; **2.** (*e-r Sache*) *als Leiter:* direct, be in charge of; *als Vorstand etc.*: preside over, chair *s.th.*; **3.** *Jägerspr., Hund:* set, point; **vorstehend I.** *Part. Präs.* → **vorstehen**; **II.** *Adj.* **1.** (*vorausgehend, oben erwähnt*) preceding, above; **2.** *Backenknochen, Kinn, Nase:* prominent; **~e Zähne** protruding teeth, buckteeth; **III.** *Adv.: wie ~ angeführt etc.* as referred to *etc.* above

Vorsteher *m; -s, -* director; *e-s Gefängnisses:* governor, *Am.* warden; *e-s Klosters:* abbot; *e-s Bahnhofs:* stationmaster

Vorsteherdrüse *f Anat.* prostate (gland)

Vorsteherin *f; -, -nen* director; *e-s Gefängnisses:* governor, *Am.* warden; *e-s Klosters:* mother superior, prioress, abbess

Vorstehhund *m* pointer

vorstellbar *Adj.* conceivable, imaginable; **nicht ~** inconceivable, unimaginable

vorstellen (*trennb., hat -ge-*) **I.** *v/t.* **1.** (*vorrücken*) move forward; **2.** (*Uhr*) put forward (**um** by); **3.** *j-m j-n ~* introduce s.o. to s.o.; **darf ich Ihnen Herrn Braun ~?** may I introduce you to Mr(.) Braun?, I'd like you to meet

Mr(.) Braun; **4.** (*neues Produkt etc.*) present; **5.** (*darstellen*) represent; **was soll das ~?** what's that supposed to be?; **er stellt etwas vor** he's not just anybody; **6.** *sich* (*Dat.*) *etw.* **~** imagine, envisage, *Am. auch* envision; (*sich ein Bild machen von*) visualize, picture *s.th.*; **stell dir vor!** *umg.* just imagine!; **das muss man sich einmal ~** just imagine that!; **das kann ich mir ~** I can imagine; **stell dir das nicht so leicht vor** don't think it's so easy, it's not as easy as you think; **so stelle ich mir e-n Urlaub etc. vor** that's my idea of (*od.* that's what I call) a holiday (*Am.* vacation *etc.*); **was haben Sie sich als Gehalt etc. vorgestellt?** what did you have in mind in terms of salary *etc.*?; **sich unter e-r Sache etw. ~** imagine s.th. to be s.th.; **sich unter e-m Begriff etw. ~** take an expression to mean s.th.; **ich stelle mir darunter ... vor** I imagine it to be ...; **unter e-m Begriff etc.**: I understand it as (*od.* to mean) ...; **ich kann mir darunter nichts ~** it doesn't mean a thing to me; **II.** *v/refl.* introduce o.s.; *als Antrittsbesuch:* present o.s.; *bei Bewerbung:* go for an interview; *beim Arzt, in der Klinik:* go for treatment; **darf ich mich ~, ...** my name's ...; hello, I'm ...; **vorstellig** *Adj.:* **~ werden bei** apply to

Vorstellung *f* **1.** (*Bekanntmachen*) introduction; *e-r Sache:* presentation; *bei Bewerbung:* interview (**bei** with); **2.** *Theat.* performance, show; *Film:* show(ing); **die letzte ~ Kino:** the last showing; **e-e starke ~ geben** *bes. Sport* give a strong performance; **nur e-e kurze ~ geben** *umg. fig.* not stay long; **3.** (*Begriff*) idea; (*Bild*) *auch* image; **falsche ~** wrong idea, misconception; **sich e-e (klare) ~ machen von** form a (clear) picture of, get an (*od.* a proper) idea of; (**nicht**) **j-s ~en entsprechen** (not) be exactly what s.o. has in mind; **haben Sie ~en bezüglich des Gehalts etc.?** do you have anything in mind in terms of salary *etc.*?; **du machst dir keine ~!** you've no idea; **das geht über alle ~** the mind boggles; **4.** **j-m ~en machen** remonstrate with s.o. (**wegen** about)

...vorstellung *f, im Subst.* **1.** *Theat. etc.:* **Kinder~** childrens' show; **Wohltätigkeits~** charity performance; **2.** (*Idee, Wunsch*): **Gehalts~** desired salary; **Glücks~** idea of happiness

Vorstellungs|beginn *m* start of a (*od.* the) performance; **~ um 20 Uhr** performance starts at 8 pm; **~ende** *f* end of a (*od.* the) performance; **nach ~** after the performance has *etc.* finished (*od.* ended); **~gabe** *f* (*the* gift of) imagination; → *auch* **Vorstellungskraft**; **~gespräch** *n* (job) interview, interview for a (*od.* the) job; **zu e-m ~ gehen** go for an interview; **~kraft** *f* (powers *Pl.* of) imagination; **e-e gute ~ haben** *auch* have a lot of imagination; **das übersteigt m-e ~** the mind boggles; *bei Zahlen etc.*: *auch* I can't cope with those kind of figures *etc.*; **~termin** *m* appointment for an interview; **~vermögen** *n* → **Vorstellungskraft**; **~welt** *f* imagination

Vorsteuerabzug *m Fin.* pre-tax deduction

Vorstopper *m*, **~in** *f Sport Fußball:* cent|re (*Am.* -er) back

Vorstoß *m* **1.** *Mil.* thrust, advance; *Sport* attack (*auch fig.*); (*Versuch*) attempt; *unter Risiko:* venture (*auch*

fig.); (*Anstrengung*) effort; **e-n ~ unternehmen** make a thrust *etc.*; *umg. fig.* (*sein Glück versuchen*) try one's luck (**bei j-m** with s.o.); **2.** *am Kleid etc.*: edging; **vorstoßen** (*unreg., trennb., -ge-*) **I.** *v/t.* (*hat*) push forward; **II.** *v/i.* (*ist*) *Mil. etc.* push ahead (*auch fig.*), advance; *Sport* attack; **~ in** (+ *Akk.*) penetrate (into); (*Neuland etc.*) *auch* venture into; **~ nach** *od.* **zu** press on as far as; *mit Gewalt*: fight one's way through to; *in den Weltraum ~* venture into space

Vorstrafe *f* previous conviction; **mehrere/keine ~n haben** have several/no previous convictions; **Vorstrafenregister** *n* (criminal) record *Sg.*, *Am. auch* rap sheet *Sl.*

vorstrecken *v/t.* (*trennb., hat -ge-*) **1.** stretch out; (*Kopf, Hals etc.*) stick out; **2.** (*Geld*) advance (*j-m* s.o.)

vorstreichen *v/t.* (*unreg., trennb., hat -ge-*) give *s.th.* an undercoat

Vorstudie *f* preliminary study; (*Skizze*) (preliminary) sketch

Vorstufe *f* preliminary stage; (*frühes Entwicklungsstadium*) early stage; *des Menschen etc.*: early ancestor

vorstürmen *v/i.* (*trennb., ist -ge-*) charge (*od.* rush) forward

Vortag *m*: (*am*) **~** (the) previous day, (the) day before; **am ~ der Hochzeit** *etc.* the day before the wedding *etc.*, *förm.* on the eve of the wedding *etc.*

vortanzen (*trennb., hat -ge-*) **I.** *v/t.*: (*j-m*) **etw. ~** *zur Unterhaltung etc.*: dance s.th. (for s.o.); *unterrichtend*: demonstrate (to s.o.) how to dance s.th.; **II.** *v/i.* **1.** *als Prüfung*: demonstrate one's dancing ability; **2.** *unterrichtend*: demonstrate a dance; **Vortänzer** *m*, **Vortänzerin** *f* dance demonstrator

vortasten *v/refl.* (*trennb., hat -ge-*) grope one's way (forward) (**bis, zu** to; *in* + *Akk.* into)

vortäuschen *v/t.* (*trennb., hat -ge-*) feign, fake; (*Krankheit*) *auch* simulate; *Angst etc.* **~** pretend to be scared *etc.*; **etwas ~** be (just) pretending; **sich selbst etwas ~** pretend to o.s., delude o.s.; → **vorgetäuscht**; **Vortäuschung** *f* preten|ce (*Am.* -se); **~ e-r Krankheit** feigning sickness, simulation; **unter ~ falscher Tatsachen** *Jur.* under false preten|ces (*Am.* -ses)

Vorteig *m* *Gastr.* sponge

Vorteil *m* **1.** advantage; (*Gewinn*) profit, benefit; **die Vor- und Nachteile e-r Sache erwägen** consider the pros and cons; **zu j-s ~ sein, j-m von ~ sein** be to s.o.'s advantage; **~ bringen** be profitable, pay; **~e haben von** *od.* **durch** benefit from; **e-n ~ haben von** *Person*: derive an advantage from; **den** (**zusätzlichen**) **~ haben zu** (+ *Inf.*) *Sache*: have the (added) advantage of (+ *Ger.*); **~ ziehen aus etw.** profit from s.th.; **auf s-n ~ bedacht sein** be out for one's own interests; **im ~ sein gegenüber j-m** have an (*od.* the) advantage over s.o., have a head start on s.o.; **im ~ sein** have the advantage, hold the high ground; **zu d-m eigenen ~ in** your own interest; **er hat sich zu s-m ~ verändert** he's changed for the better, he's improved; **2.** *Sport, Tennis*: advantage; **~ gelten lassen** *Fußball etc.*: play the advantage

vorteilhaft I. *Adj.* advantageous (**für** to); (*positiv*) positive; *Wirts.* (*Gewinn bringend*) profitable (**für** to); (*günstig*) favo(u)rable; *Kleid, Farbe*: becoming;

~ aussehen look good; **ihr ~es Äußeres** her good looks; **II.** *Adv.* advantageously *etc.*; → I; *Wirts.* (*mit Gewinn*) *verkaufen etc.*: at a profit; *sich kleiden etc.*: to one's (best) advantage; **sich ~ auswirken** (*~ sein*) have a positive effect (**auf** +*Akk.* on); *längerfristig*: (prove to) be of advantage (**auf** + *Akk.*, **für** for); **sich ~ entwickeln** develop positively; *Person*: make a lot of progress; → **unvorteilhaft**

Vorteils|(an)nahme *f* *Jur.* accepting a bribe; **~regel** *f* *Sport* advantage rule

Vortrag *m*; *-(e)s, Vorträge* **1.** (*Rede*) talk; (*Vorlesung*) lecture (*beide über* + *Akk.* on); **e-n ~ halten** give a talk (*od.* lecture); **2.** (*Aufführung*) performance; *Mus.* (*Solo*) recital (*auch e-s Gedichts*); (*Vortragsweise*) rendering, performance; **3.** *Wirts.* (*Übertrag*) balance carried forward; **4.** *bei Vorgesetztem*: report; **vortragen** *v/t.* (*unreg., trennb., hat -ge-*) **1.** *Mus. etc.* perform; (*Gedicht*) recite; **2.** (*e-n Vortrag halten über*) lecture on; (*reden über*) talk about; **3.** (*berichten*) report; **4.** (*äußern*) state; (*vorbringen*) put forward, present; (*sagen, erzählen*) tell; **5.** (*Gegenstand*) carry (up) (*od.* take) to the front; **6.** *Wirts., Buchhaltung*: carry forward; **Vortragende** *m, f; -n, -n* **1.** *Mus. etc.* performer; **2.** (*Redner*) speaker; *Vorlesung*: *auch* lecturer

Vortrags|abend *m* **1.** evening lecture; **2.** *Mus. etc.* recital; **~bezeichnung** *f* *Mus.* expression mark; **~folge** *f* series of talks; **~kunst** *f* art of performance (*od.* recital); **~künstler** *m*, **~künstlerin** *f* spoken-word performer; **~raum** *m* lecture room; **~reihe** *f* series of lectures (*od.* talks), lecture series; **~reise** *f* lecture tour; **~saal** *m* lecture hall; **~veranstaltung** *f* talk, lecture; **~weise** *f* delivery

vortrefflich I. *Adj.* excellent, superb; **II.** *Adv.* excellently, superbly; **darüber lässt sich ~ streiten** that's an excellent point for debate; **Vortrefflichkeit** *f* excellence

vortreiben *v/t.* (*unreg., trennb., hat -ge-*); (*Tunnel, Stollen etc.*) drive

vortreten *v/i.* (*unreg., trennb., ist -ge-*) **1.** step (*od.* come) forward; **2.** (*herausragen*) protrude, stick out; *Felsen*: project; *Adern, Augen etc.*: protrude; *Backenknochen*: be prominent

Vortrieb *m* **1.** *Phys.* thrust; **2.** *Bergb.* (*das Vortreiben*) advance; (*Grube*) heading

Vortritt *m*; *nur Sg.* **1.** precedence; **j-m den ~ lassen** let s.o. go first; (*den Vorrang lassen*) give precedence to s.o.; **den ~ haben vor etw.** take precedence over s.th.; **2.** *schw.* (*Vorfahrt*) right of way, priority; **Vortrittsrecht** *n* *schw.* (*Vorfahrt*) right of way; *Regel*: rule governing (the) right of way

Vortrupp *m* advance party

vorturnen (*trennb., hat -ge-*) **I.** *v/t.*: (*j-m*) **etw. ~** perform s.th. (for s.o.); *unterrichtend*: demonstrate s.th. (for s.o.); **II.** *v/i.* **1.** *bei Veranstaltung etc.*: perform; **2.** *unterrichtend*: demonstrate; **Vorturner** *m*, **Vorturnerin** *f* performer; demonstrator; *Pol. fig. männlich*: front man; *weiblich*: front woman

vorüber *Adv.* → *vorbei*; **~gehen** *v/i.* (*unreg., trennb., ist -ge-*) → *vorbeigehen* 1, 3; *die schlimme Zeit* **ist nicht spurlos an ihr vorübergegangen** has left its mark on her; **~gehend I.** *Part. Präs.* → *vorübergehen*; **II.** *Adj.* tem-

porary; (*flüchtig*) passing; **~er Fehler** *EDV* transient error; **III.** *Adv.* temporarily; (*kurz*) for a short time; (*zurzeit, im Moment*) for the time being

Vorüberlegung *f* initial (*od.* preliminary) consideration

vorüberziehen *v/i.* → *vorbeiziehen*

Vorübung *f* preliminary exercise

Voruntersuchung *f* preliminary examination (*auch Med.*); *Jur. auch* pre-trial hearings *Pl.*

Vorurteil *n* prejudice; **voller ~e** full of prejudice, very prejudiced; **~e gegen j-n** *od.* **gegenüber j-m haben** be prejudiced toward(s) *od.* against s.o.; **vorurteilsfrei, vorurteilslos I.** *Adj.* unprejudiced; *Meinung, Urteil*: unbias(s)ed; **II.** *Adv.* *handeln etc.*: without prejudice; without bias; **Vorurteilslosigkeit** *f* lack of prejudice; *Haltung*: unprejudiced attitude

Vorväter *Pl.* forefathers

Vorverfahren *n* *Jur.* preliminary proceedings *Pl.*

Vorvergangenheit *f* *Gram.* past perfect, pluperfect *fachspr.*

Vorverhandlung *f* **1.** **~en** preliminary negotiations; **2.** *Jur.* preliminary proceedings *Pl.*

Vorverkauf *m*; *nur Sg.* advance sales *Pl.*; *Theat. etc.*: *auch* advance booking; **im ~** in advance; **nur im ~ erhältlich** only available through advance booking (*Am.* through reservation)

Vorverkaufs|gebühr *m* advance booking fee; **~stelle** *f* advance booking (*Am.* reservations) office; **~zahlen** *Pl.* advance sales of season tickets

vorverlegen *v/t.* (*trennb., hat*); (*Termin*) bring forward (**auf** + *Akk.* to); (*Eingang etc.*) move up; **Vorverlegung** *f* *zeitlich*: earlier scheduling

Vorverstärker *m* *Etron.* pre-amplifier

Vorversuch *m* pilot test

Vorvertrag *m* provisional agreement

vorverurteilen *v/t.* (*trennb., hat*) *mst Inf. und P.P.* condemn in advance; **Vorverurteilung** *f* condemnation of s.o. in advance

vorvorgestern *Adv.* three days ago

vorvorig... *Adj. umg. nachgestellt*: before last; **das ~e Mal** the time before last, the last time but one

vorvorletzt... *Adj. umg.* last but two; **~e Woche** three weeks ago

vorwagen *v/refl.* (*trennb., hat -ge-*) venture forward

Vorwahl *f* **1.** *Telef.* dial(l)ing (*Am.* area) code (**von** to); **2.** *Pol.* preliminary election; *Am.* primary; **bei den ~en** in the preliminary elections (*od.* primaries); **vorwählen** *v/t.* (*trennb., hat -ge-*) **1.** *Telef.* dial first; **2.** (*Programm e-s Geräts etc.*) preselect

Vorwahlnummer *f* *Telef.* → *Vorwahl* 1

Vorwand *m*; *-(e)s, Vorwände* pretext, excuse; **unter dem ~ zu** (+ *Inf.*) *od.* **dass** on the pretext of (+ *Ger.*) (*od.* that)

vorwärmen *v/t.* (*trennb., hat -ge-*); (*Teller etc.*) warm up; *Tech.* preheat

vorwarnen *v/t.* (*trennb., hat -ge-*): **j-n ~** tell (*od.* warn) s.o. in advance, give s.o. advance notice (*od.* warning); **Vorwarnung** *f* advance warning

vorwärts *Adv.* **1.** forward, forwards; **~!** let's go!; **ein großer Schritt ~** a big step forward; **etw. ~ und rückwärts aufsagen können** be able to say s.th. backwards; **Salto ~** forward somersault; **2.** *Verbindungen mit Verben*: **~ blättern** *EDV* scroll forwards; **~ bringen** *fig.* further, promote; (*auch Per-*

son) help *s.o. od. s.th.* on (*bei* in); (*Projekt etc.*) advance; **~ gehen** *fig.* advance, progress; (*sich bessern*) improve; **~ kommen** make headway (*auch fig.*); *fig. auch im Leben*: get ahead, get on, get somewhere; *ich komme nicht vorwärts fig.* I'm not getting anywhere, I'm treading water; → **vorankommen**; **~ schreiten** move forward, stride ahead
Vorwärtsbewegung *f* forward movement
vorwärts blättern → *vorwärts* 2
vorwärts bringen → *vorwärts* 2
Vorwärtsgang *m Mot.* forward gear
vorwärts gehen → *vorwärts* 2
vorwärts kommen → *vorwärts* 2
Vorwärtskommen *n; -s, kein Pl.*; (*Fortschritt*) progress; (*Erfolg*) success
vorwärts schreiten → *vorwärts* 2
Vorwärts|schritt *m* step forward; **~verteidigung** *f Mil., euph.* forward defen|ce (*Am. -se*) (*auch fig.*)
Vorwäsche *f* prewash; **vorwaschen** *v/t.* (*unreg., trennb., hat -ge-*) prewash; **Vorwaschgang** *m* prewash cycle
vorweg *Adv.* **1.** (*vorher*) beforehand, in advance; (*zuerst*) at the outset; (*von vornherein*) from the start; *e-e Frage* **~** I have one question before we get going; *ein Aperitif/Salat* **~** an aperitif/salad beforehand; **2.** (*an der Spitze*) at the front, up front *umg.*, leading the way *umg.*
Vorwegnahme *f; -, kein Pl.* anticipation; **vorwegnehmen** *v/t.* (*unreg., trennb., hat -ge-*) anticipate; *um es gleich vorwegzunehmen* to come to the point
Vorwegweiser *m Verk.* directional sign
Vorwehen *Pl. Med.* early contractions
vorweihnachtlich I. *Adj.* pre-Christmas; **~e Feier** pre-Christmas party; **II.** *Adv.* **~ geschmückt** decorated with Christmas decorations; **Vorweihnachtszeit** *f* Christmas period, *Am.* Christmastime, *Brit. auch* run-up to Christmas *umg.*
vorweisen *v/t.* (*unreg., trennb., hat -ge-*) produce, show; **~ können** *fig.* possess; *etwas vorzuweisen haben* have s.th. to show for o.s.
vorwerfbar *Adj. Jur., Amtsspr., Tat etc.*: reprehensible; **vorwerfen** *v/t.* (*unreg., trennb., hat -ge-*) **1.** *j-m etw.* **~** accuse s.o. of s.th., reproach s.o. with s.th.; *j-m* **~** *zu* (*+Inf.*) *od. dass* accuse s.o. of (*+ Ger.*), reproach s.o. for (*+ Ger.*); *Ihnen wird vorgeworfen, am* ... *in* ... *zu haben auf Bußgeldbescheid etc.*: you are charged of having ... in ... on the ...; *ich habe mir nichts vorzuwerfen* I don't feel in any way responsible; *ich lasse mir nicht* **~**, *dass* I'm not going to be accused of (*+ Ger.*) (*od.* take the blame for *+ Ger.*); *einander nichts vorzuwerfen haben* be both as bad as one another; **2.** (*nach vorn werfen*) throw *s.th.* forward; *e-m Tier etc. etw.* (*zum Fraß*) **~** throw s.th. to an animal *etc.*
Vorwiderstand *m Etech.* series resistor
vorwiegen (*unreg., trennb., hat -ge-*) **I.** *v/i.* **1.** (*vorherrschen*) predominate; **2.** *beim Judo, Ringen*: weigh beforehand; **II.** *v/t.*: *j-m etw.* **~** weigh s.th. out in front of s.o.
vorwiegend I. *Part. Präs.* → *vorwie-*

gen; **II.** *Adv.* predominantly, mainly, chiefly, largely, for the most part, in the main
Vorwissen *n* previous knowledge; *ohne mein* **~** without my knowledge (*od.* my knowing)
Vorwitz *m; nur Sg.* cheekiness, pertness; (*Neugier*) curiosity; **vorwitzig** *Adj.* cheeky, pert; (*neugierig*) curious
Vorwoche *f*; (*in der*) **~** (during the) previous week; **vorwöchig** *Adj.* previous week's
vorwölben (*trennb., hat -ge-*) **I.** *v/t.* push out; **II.** *v/refl.* bulge out; **Vorwölbung** *f* (outward) bulge
Vorwort *n; Pl. -e und Vorwörter* foreword, *bes. des Autors*: preface; (*Einleitung*) introduction
Vorwurf *m* **1.** reproach; (*Beschuldigung*) accusation; *versteckter* **~** concealed reproach; *j-m Vorwürfe machen* reproach s.o. (*wegen* for); *j-m den* **~** *machen zu* (*+ Inf.*) *od. dass* accuse s.o. of (*+ Ger.*); *sich Vorwürfe machen* reproach o.s., blame o.s.; **2.** (*Thema*) theme; (*Muster*) pattern; (*Modell*) model; **vorwurfsvoll I.** *Adj.* reproachful; **II.** *Adv. anblicken etc.*: reproachfully
vorzählen *v/t.* (*trennb., hat -ge-*) count out (*j-m* to)
vorzaubern *v/t.* (*trennb., hat -ge-*): *j-m etw.* **~** *fig.* conjure s.th. up before s.o.('s eyes); *wörtl.*: perform magic tricks for s.o.
Vorzeichen *n* **1.** portent; *gutes/schlechtes* **~** good/bad omen; **2.** *Mus.* accidental; *Math.* sign; *Med.* first sign; *mit umgekehrtem* **~** *fig.* the other way (a)round; **~stelle** *f EDV* sign position; **~steuerung** *f EDV* sign control
vorzeichnen *v/t.* (*trennb., hat -ge-*) **1.** (*Linie, Lebensweg etc.*) trace (out), mark; *j-m etw.* **~** draw s.th. for s.o.; *unterweisend*: show s.o. how to draw s.th.; *mit Bleistift etc.* **~** trace out in pencil *etc.*; **2.** *Mus.*: *ein Kreuz/B* **~** (*+ Dat.*) put a sharp/flat before; **Vorzeichnung** *f* (*das Vorzeichnen*) tracing (out), marking; drawing; (*Entwurf*) (preparatory) sketch
vorzeigbar *Adj.* (quite) presentable; *nichts Vorzeigbares* nothing concrete
Vorzeige|betrieb *m* showpiece operation; **~frau** *f umg.* woman to show off with; *pej.* (*Quotenfrau*) token woman
vorzeigen *v/t.* (*trennb., hat -ge-*) show; (*Pass etc.*) *auch* produce
Vorzeige|objekt *n* showpiece, *Am. auch* showpony *pej.*; **~sportler** *m* model sportsman (*Am.* athlete); **~sportlerin** *f* model sportswoman (*Am.* athlete)
Vorzeit *f; nur Sg.* prehistoric era; *die* **~** prehistoric times; → *grau* 2; **vorzeiten** *Adv. altm., bibl.* long ago; **vorzeitig I.** *Adj.* premature; (*früh*) early; **~e Ausfälle** *EDV* abnormal interruptions; **II.** *Adv.* prematurely; (*früh*) early; **~ sterben** die before one's time; **Vorzeitigkeit** *f Ling.* anteriority; **vorzeitlich** *Adj.* prehistoric; **Vorzeitmensch** *m*: *der* **~** prehistoric man
Vorzensur *f* **1.** *der Presse etc.*: preliminary censorship; **2.** *bei Prüfung etc.*: mark (*Am.* grade) for coursework (*combined with mark for examination* [*Am. with test score*] *to give overall*

grade)
vorziehen *v/t.* (*unreg., trennb., hat -ge-*) **1.** pull forward; (*hervorziehen*) pull out; (*Vorhänge*) draw; (*Truppen*) move up; **2.** *zeitlich*: bring forward, move up; (*Arbeit etc.*) deal with first, give priority to; (*vorwegnehmen*) anticipate; → *vorgezogen*; **3.** *fig.* prefer (*+ Dat.* to); (*Schüler etc.*) give *s.o.* special treatment; *es* **~** *zu* (*+ Inf.*) prefer to (*+ Inf.*); *vorzuziehen sein* be preferable
Vorzimmer *n* anteroom; *Büro*: outer office; **~dame** *f* receptionist
Vorzug *m; nur Sg.*; (*Vorrang*) priority (*gegenüber, vor* + *Dat.* over); (*Vorteil*) advantage; (*gute Eigenschaft*) merit; (*Privileg*) privilege; *j-m den* **~** *geben* give preference to s.o.; *den* **~** *haben, dass od. zu* (*+ Inf.*) have the advantage of (*+ Ger.*)
vorzüglich I. *Adj.* excellent; (*meisterhaft*) *auch* masterly; (*erlesen*) exquisite; (*erstklassig*) first-rate; *der Wein ist ganz* **~** the wine is quite excellent; **II.** *Adv. kochen etc.*: excellently; *wir haben* **~** *gespeist* we had an excellent meal; **Vorzüglichkeit** *f* excellence; excellent quality; exquisiteness; → *vorzüglich*
Vorzugs|aktien *Pl.* preference shares, *Am.* preferred stock *Sg.*; **~behandlung** *f* preferential (special *umg.*) treatment; **~milch** *f* full-cream (*Am.* full-fat) milk, *in GB: auch* gold-top milk; **~preis** *m* special price; *zum* **~** *von* ... on special offer (*Am.* on sale) at ...
vorzugsweise *Adv.* **1.** preferably; **2.** (*hauptsächlich*) chiefly, mainly
Vorzündung *f Mot.* pre-ignition
votieren *v/i.* vote (*für* for)
Votiv|bild *n* votive picture; **~gabe** *f* votive gift; **~kerze** *f* votive candle
Votum *n; -s, Voten und Vota* **1.** (*Stimme*) vote; *sein* **~** *abgeben* vote; **2.** (*Entscheidung*) vote; *ein* (*klares etc.*) **~** *für j-n/etw.* a (clear *etc.*) vote for s.o./s.th.
Voyeur [voa'jøːɐ] *m; -s, -e* voyeur, peeping Tom; **Voyeurismus** *m* voyeurism; **voyeuristisch** *Adj.* voyeuristic
vulgär *Adj.* vulgar; (*gewöhnlich*) common; **Vulgärausdruck** *m* vulgarism, vulgar expression; **Vulgarität** *f; -, kein Pl.* vulgarity; **Vulgärlatein** *n* Vulgar Latin; **Vulgärsprache** *f* **1.** *Ling.* vernacular, common language, language of the people; **2.** (*vulgäre Sprache*) vulgar language; vulgarisms *Pl.*
Vulkan *m; -(e)s, -e* volcano (*auch fig.*); **~asche** *f* volcanic ash; **~ausbruch** *m* (volcanic) eruption; **~forscher** *m*, **~forscherin** *f* volcanologist, vulcanologist; **~gestein** *n* volcanic rock; **~insel** *f* volcanic island
Vulkanisation *f; -, en* vulcanization
vulkanisch I. *Adj.* volcanic; **II.** *Adv.* volcanically
vulkanisieren *v/t.* vulcanize; *Mot. auch* recap, *Am.* retread
Vulkankrater *m* volcanic crater
Vulkanologe *m; -n, -n* volcanologist, vulcanologist; **Vulkanologie** *f; -, kein Pl.* volcanology, vulcanology; **Vulkanologin** *f; -, -nen* volcanologist, vulcanologist; **vulkanologisch** *Adj.* volcanological, vulcanological

W, w *n*; -, - *und umg.* -*s* W, w; *W wie Wilhelm* *Buchstabieren*: "w" for (*od.* as in) "Whiskey"

Waage *f*; -, -*n* **1.** (*e-e*) ~ (a pair of) scales *Pl., Am.* (a) scale; (*Wasserwaage*) spirit level, *Am.* level; *sich* (*Dat.*) *die ~ halten* be more or less equal; → *Zünglein* 2; **2.** *Astrol.* Libra; ~ *sein* be (a) Libra, be a Libran; **3.** *Turnen*: lever

Waagebalken *m* (balance) beam, scale beam

waag(e)recht I. *Adj.* horizontal; (*eben*) level; **II.** *Adv.* horizontally; *Kreuzworträtsel*: across; **Waag(e)rechte** *f*; -*n*, -*n* horizontal; *in der ~n* horizontal; horizontally; *in die ~ bringen* make horizontal, level

Waagschale *f* scale; *in die ~ werfen fig.* bring *s.th.* to bear, bring *s.th.* into play; *schwer in die ~ fallen* Argument: carry weight; *s-e Worte auf die ~ legen* weigh one's words

wabb(e)lig *Adj.* wobbly; *Wangen etc.*: flabby; **wabbeln** *v/i.* wobble

Wabe *f*; -, -*n* honeycomb; **wabenförmig** *Adj.* honeycomb ..., honeycombed; **Wabenhonig** *m* comb honey; **Wabenmuster** *n* honeycomb pattern

wabern *v/i. lit.* waver

wach *Adj.* **1.** *präd.* awake; *weitS.* (*aufgestanden*) up (and about), stirring (*auch Stadt etc.*); ~ *sein auch* have woken up; ~ *werden* wake up, awake; *er ist* (*morgens*) *nicht ~ zu kriegen* he won't wake up (in the morning); *er ist (morgens) nicht ~ zu kriegen* he won't wake up (in the morning); *mühsam ~ halten* struggle to stay awake; *die ganze Nacht ~ liegen* lie awake all night, not get a wink of sleep all night; *j-n ~ küssen* wake s.o. with a kiss; **2.** *fig.*: *~er Geist* lively (*od.* alert) mind; *~es Auge* watchful eye; *die Erinnerung an etw. ~ halten* keep the memory of s.th. alive; ~ *werden* (*aufmerksam*) prick up one's ears; *Empfindungen etc.*: be aroused; *wieder ~ werden* Vorurteile *etc.*: reawaken, revive

Wach|ablösung *f Mil.* changing of the guard; *bes. Pol. fig.* changeover of governments, change in leadership; *~dienst* *m* guard duty; *Naut.* watch; *~ haben* be on guard (duty); *Naut.* have the watch

Wache *f*; -*n*, -*n* **1.** *nur Sg.* guard; *Naut.* watch; *auf* ~ on guard; *Naut.* on watch; *~ halten* keep guard; *Naut.* be on watch; *bei e-m Kranken*: keep watch; *~ schieben umg.* be on guard (*od.* sentry) duty; *Naut.* be on watch; *bei Diebstahl etc.*: keep a lookout, be the lookout; **2.** (*Wachlokal*) guard room; (*Polizeiwache*) police station; **3.** (*Posten*) sentry, guard; *die ~ ablösen* relieve the guard; **wachen** *v/i.* (*Acht geben*) (keep) watch (*über* + *Akk.* over), guard *s.th. od. s.o.*; ~ *über* (+ *Akk.*) *auch* keep an eye on; *bei j-m* ~ sit up

with s.o.; **wachhabend** *Adj.*: *~er Offizier* duty officer; *Naut.* officer of the watch; **Wachhabende** *m, f*; -*n*, -*n* duty officer; *Naut.* officer of the watch

wach halten → *wach* 1, 2

Wachhäuschen *n* sentry box

Wachheit *f* wakefulness; alertness; liveliness; → *wach*

Wach|hund *m* watchdog (*auch fig.*); *~koma* *n Med.* locked-in syndrome

wach küssen → *wach* 1

Wach|lokal *n* guardroom; *~macher* *m umg.* stimulant; *~mann* *m* **1.** watchman; **2.** *österr.* policeman; *~mannschaft* *f* guard, *Naut.* watch

Wacholder *m*; -*s*, - **1.** *Bot.* juniper; (*Beere*) juniper berry; **2.** (*Schnaps*) spirit made from grain and juniper berries; *etwa* gin; *~beere* *f Bot.* juniper berry; *~schnaps* *m* spirit made from grain and juniper berries; *etwa* gin

Wach|personal *n* guards *Pl.*, security (staff); *~posten* *m* guard

wach|rufen *v/t.* (*unreg., trennb., hat -ge-*) *fig.* rouse; (*Erinnerungen*) bring back; *~rütteln* *v/t.* (*trennb., hat -ge-*) *fig.* rouse (*aus* from), shake up (out of); wake *s.o.* up, make s.o. sit up (and take notice); *stärker*: shake s.o. up; *weitS.* shake *s.o.* into action

Wachs *n*; -*es*, -*e* wax; *bleich wie ~* (as) white as a sheet (*od.* ghost); ~ *in j-s Händen sein fig.* (*sehr nachgiebig sein*) be putty in s.o.'s hands; *weich wie ~ werden* Person: soften, melt; *Knie*: turn to jelly; *wie ~ dahinschmelzen* surrender completely

Wachsabdruck *m* wax impression

wachsam I. *Adj.* watchful, vigilant; *Hund*: alert; ~ *sein* be on one's guard; *ein ~es Auge haben auf* (+ *Akk.*) keep a sharp (*od.* watchful) eye on; **II.** *Adv.*: ~ *verfolgen auch* watch closely; → *Holzauge*; **Wachsamkeit** *f* watchfulness, vigilance

wachsbleich *Adj.* (as) white as a sheet (*od.* ghost)

Wachs|bild *n* wax relief; *~blume* *f* **1.** *künstliche*: wax flower, flower made of wax; **2.** *Bot.* waxflower; *~bohne* *f* waxbean

wachsen¹ *v/i.*; *wächst, wuchs, ist gewachsen* grow (*auch fig.* *an* + *Dat.* in); (*sich ausdehnen*) expand; *sein Haar ~ lassen* let one's hair grow (long); *sich* (*Dat.*) *e-n Bart ~ lassen* grow a beard; *bist du aber gewachsen!* haven't you grown!, how you've grown!; *hier wächst viel Weizen* a lot of wheat is grown in these parts (*od.* around here); *sie ist mir ans Herz gewachsen* I've become very attached to her; *ins Unermessliche ~* increase immeasurably, keep on growing (and growing); *pej.* grow out of all proportion; → *gewachsen, Baum* 1, *Gras* 2, *Haar* 3, *Kopf* 6, *Kraut* 2, *Mist¹* 1, *Pfeffer etc.*

wachsen² *v/t.* wax (*auch Skier*)

wachsend I. *Part. Präs.* → *wachsen¹*; **II.** *Adj. Tempo, Spannung etc.*: increasing, growing; *etw. mit ~er Begeisterung tun* do s.th. with increasing enthusiasm

wächsern *Adj.* wax; *fig.* waxen

Wachs|farbe *f* **1.** (*Farbe*) wax paint; *mit ~n malen* paint with wax paints; **2.** (*Farbstoff*) wax dye; *~figur* *f* wax figure; *im Kabinett*: waxwork; *~figurenkabinett* *n* waxworks *Pl.* (*mst V. im Sg.*); *das ~ der Madame Tussaud* Madame Tussaud's (waxworks *od.* wax museum); *~kerze* *f* wax candle; *~malerei* *f* (*Enkaustik*) encaustic, wax painting; *~malkreide* *f*, *~malstift* *m* wax crayon; *~maske* *f* wax mask; *~papier* *n* wax(ed) paper; *~pflaume* *f* → *Mirabelle*; *~plastik* *f* wax model(l)ing; *~stift* *m* wax crayon

wächst *Präs.* → *wachsen¹*

Wachstafel *f hist.* wax tablet

Wach|station *f Med.* intensive-care unit, ICU; *~stube* *f* guardroom

Wachstuch *n* oilcloth; *~tischdecke* *f* wax tablecloth

Wachstum *n*; -*s*, *kein Pl.* **1.** growth (*auch Wirts.*); (*Zunahme*) *auch* increase; (*Ausdehnung*) expansion; *im ~ zurückgeblieben* stunted (in growth); *die Grenzen des ~s* the limits of growth; **2.** *eigenes ~* (*Gemüse, Wein etc.*) s.o.'s own produce; grown in our *etc.* own garden *bzw.* vineyard *etc.*

Wachstums|bereich *m* growth area; *~branche* *f* growth industry

wachstumsfördernd I. *Adj.* **1.** *Wirts.* growth-stimulating; **2.** *Hormone*: growth-promoting; *Witterung etc.*: weather *etc.* that brings on the plants; **II.** *Adv.*: *sich ~ auswirken* have a stimulating effect on growth (*od.* the growth *of s.th.*), promote the growth *of s.th.*

wachstumshemmend I. *Adj.* **1.** *Wirts.* growth-retarding; **2.** *Hormone*: growth-inhibiting; *Witterung etc.*: weather *etc.* that holds back the plants; **II.** *Adv.*: *sich ~ auswirken* inhibit growth (*od.* the growth *of s.th.*)

Wachstums|hormon *n* growth hormone; *~impulse* *Pl. Wirts.* growth impulse, impulse to growth; *~industrie* *f* growth industry; *~kurs* *m* course for growth; *auf ~* growing, on course for growth; *~kurve* *f* growth curve; *~markt* *m* growth market

wachstumsorientiert *Adj.* growth-oriented

Wachstums|periode *f* period of growth; *~phase* *f Wirts.* growth period; *~potenzial* *n* growth potential; *~prozess* *m* process of growth; *~rate* *f* growth rate; *~region* *f* growth region; *~schub* *m* increase in growth, growth spurt

Wachstumsstörung *f Med.* growth disorder

wachsweich *Adj.* **1.** (as) soft as butter;

W

~ sein umg. fig. be a real softie; **2.** umg., fig.: **e-e ~e Ausrede** a lame excuse

Wachs|zieher m; -s, -, **~zieherin** f; -, -nen chandler, candlemaker

Wacht f; -, -en; lit. → **Wache** 1

Wächte f; -, -n (snow) cornice

Wachtel f; -, -n **1.** Orn. quail; **2. alte ~** (Frau) umg., pej. old crow; **~ei** n quail's egg

Wächter m; -s, - guard; (Nachtwächter) (night) watchman; auf Parkplatz, in Museum etc.: attendant; fig. custodian, guardian; **Wächterin** f; -, -nen guard; auf Parkplatz, in Museum etc. attendant; fig. custodian, guardian

Wachtmeister m constable, Am. patrolman; als Anrede: Officer

Wachtraum m daydream

Wach(t)turm m watchtower

Wach- und Schließgesellschaft f security corps

Wach|wechsel m changing of the guard; **~zimmer** n österr. police station; **~zustand** m waking state; **im ~** auch when awake

Wacke f; -, -n; Dial. boulder

Wackelei f; -, kein Pl.; umg. wobbling; **wackelig I.** Adj. **1.** wobbly; alte Möbel etc.: auch rickety; Zahn, Schraube: loose; **2. ~ auf den Beinen sein** umg. wegen Krankheit: be a bit shaky (on one's legs od. pins); wegen Alter: be (getting) doddery; wegen Alkohol: be a bit unsteady (on one's legs); **II.** Adv. gehen etc.: shakily; **~ stehen** Schrank etc.: wobble, be wobbly; umg. Unternehmen, Stelle etc.: be very shaky; Regierung: auch be teetering; Schüler: be doing badly; Sportmannschaft: be in danger of being relegated

Wackelkandidat m umg. doubtful case; **unter den beitrittswilligen Ländern zur EU gibt es noch einige ~en** there are still a few doubtful cases among the countries who want to join the EU

Wackelkontakt m Etech. loose contact

wackeln v/i. **1.** (hat gewackelt); Stuhl etc.: be wobbly; Zahn, Schraube: be loose; Haus etc.: shake; umg. beim Gehen: totter; umg. fig. Regierung etc.: be very shaky, stärker: be teetering (on the brink); **mit dem Schwanz ~** wag its tail; **mit dem Kopf / den Ohren ~** waggle one's head/ears; **nicht ~!** beim Fotografieren etc.: keep still!; → **Wand**; **2.** (ist) umg. Ente, Mensch etc.: waddle

Wackelpudding m umg. jelly

wacker altm., noch umg. hum. **I.** Adj. (bieder) honest, upright; (tapfer) brave; **II.** Adv. (tapfer) bravely; **sich ~ schlagen** put up a good show, do well; **sie kann ~ essen** umg. hum. she can certainly put it away

wacklig Adj. → **wackelig**

Wade f; -, -n; Anat. calf; **stramme ~n** sturdy calves; **Wadenbein** n Anat. calfbone, fibula (Pl. fibulae od. fibulas); **Wadenbeißer** m; -s, -; umg. fig. ankle biter, gadfly; (Aufpasser) watchdog; **Wadenkrampf** m Med. cramp (Am., umg. charley horse) in one's calf (od. leg); **wadenlang** Adj. attr. Rock etc.: mid-calf ...; **Wadenstrumpf** m half stocking; **Wadenwickel** m Med. leg compress

Waffe f; -, -n weapon (auch fig.); Pl. auch arms, (Arsenal) weaponry Sg.; **unter ~n stehen** be under arms; **keine ~n tragen** be unarmed; **von ~n starren** be armed to the teeth; **e-e ~ auf j-n**

richten point a weapon (bzw. gun) at s.o.; **von der ~ Gebrauch machen** use one's weapon; mit Schusswaffe: auch open fire; **zu den ~n rufen** call to arms; **die ~n ruhen** there has been a ceasefire, a truce has been called; **j-n mit s-n eigenen ~n schlagen** fig. beat s.o. at his (od. her) own game; **mit den ~n e-r Frau** fig. with a woman's weapons; → **greifen** II 1, **niederlegen** I 1, **strecken** I 3

Waffel f; -, -n **1.** waffle; (bes. Eiswaffel) wafer; **2.** umg.: **einen an der ~ haben** (verrückt sein) be off one's head (od. chump od. rocker), be out of one's mind; **du hast wohl einen an der ~!** you must be out of your mind!; **~gewebe** n honeycomb cloth; **~muster** n honeycomb pattern

Waffen|abkommen n arms agreement; **~arsenal** n (Lager) arsenal; (Gesamtbestand) weaponry, (weapons) stockpile, armo(u)ry; **~besitz** m possession of (fire)arms; **~besitzkarte** f gun licen|ce (Am. -se); **~bruder** m brother in arms; **~einsatz** m use of weapons; **~embargo** n arms embargo; **~export** m arms export; **~fabrik** f armaments factory; **~gang** m altm. engagement; **~gattung** f branch; **~gebrauch** m use of firearms; **~geschäft** n gunsmith's; **~gesetze** Pl. gun-control laws; **~gewalt** f: (mit) **~** (by) force of arms; **~handel** m arms trade; **~händler** m arms dealer; **~hilfe** f military aid (od. assistance); **~kammer** f armo(u)ry; **~kontrolle** f weapons inspection; **~kunde** f study of weaponry; **~lager** n arsenal; geheimes: arms cache; **~lieferungen** Pl. supply Sg. of arms (**an** + Akk. to)

waffenlos Adj. unarmed

Waffen|produktion f arms production; **~recht** n gun laws Pl.; **~ruhe** f truce; kurze: ceasefire; **~sammlung** f weapons collection; **~schein** m gun licen|ce (Am. -se); **~schieber** m arms broker; **~schieberei** f arms broking; **~schmiede** f arms manufacturer; **~schmuggel** m gun-running; **~schmuggler** m gun-runner; **~SS** f hist. Waffen SS; **~stillstand** m armistice, auch fig. truce

Waffenstillstands|abkommen n ceasefire agreement; **~linie** f ceasefire line; **~verhandlungen** Pl. ceasefire negotiations

Waffen|system n weapons system, Pl. auch weaponry Sg.; **~tanz** m war dance; **~technik** f weapons technology; **~träger** m Mil. Fahrzeug: weapons carrier

Wagemut m daring, audacity; **wagemutig** Adj. daring, bold, plucky, venturesome

wagen I. vt/i. venture; (etw. Gefährliches) auch risk; (sich getrauen) dare (zu + Inf. to + Inf.); **es ~** take a chance; **es ~ zu** (+ Inf.) dare to (+ Inf.); **e-n Sprung/ein Experiment** etc. **~** try a leap/an experiment etc.; **den Schritt ~** fig. take the plunge; **wie kannst du (es) ~(, mir zu widersprechen)?** how dare you (contradict me)?; **wie konnte er es ~?** where does he get the nerve?; **wer nicht wagt, der nicht gewinnt** Sprichw. nothing ventured, nothing gained; **frisch gewagt ist halb gewonnen** Sprichw. well begun is half done; **II.** v/refl.: **sich ~, etw. zu tun** dare (od. venture) to do s.th.; **er hat sich nicht gewagt** he didn't dare, he didn't have the courage

(od. nerve); **sie wagte sich nicht auf die Straße** she was (too) scared to go out into the street; **sich an etwas Schwieriges** etc. **~** try (to tackle) something difficult etc.; → **gewagt**

Wagen m; -s, -, südd., österr. Wägen **1.** (Auto) car; (allg.: Fahrzeug) vehicle; (Pferdewagen etc.) waggon, Am. wagon, carriage; Eisenb. carriage, Am. car; (Straßenbahn) car; **2.** (Karren) cart; (Kinderwagen) pram, Am. baby carriage; (Einkaufswagen) trolley, Am. (shopping) cart; (Servierwagen) trolley, Am. serving cart; **3.** altm. der Schreibmaschine: carriage; **4.** Astron.: **der Große ~** the Great Bear, the Plough (Am. Plow), the Big Dipper, Ursa Major; **der Kleine ~** the Little Bear, the Little Dipper, Ursa Minor; **5.** fig., in Wendungen: **j-m an den ~ fahren** umg. let s.o. have it, pitch into s.o., tear strips off s.o.; **sich nicht vor j-s ~ spannen lassen** not let s.o. make use of one

wägen v/t.; wägt, wog und wägte, hat gewogen, (abwägen) weigh (auch fachspr. wiegen)

Wagen|abteil n Eisenb. compartment; **~burg** f hist. barricade of wagons; in Südafrika: laager; **~dach** n roof (of the od. a vehicle); **~führer** m, **~führerin** f driver; **~heber** m jack; **~innere** n (vehicle) interior; **~klasse** f **1.** Eisenb. class; **2.** Mot. class; **~kolonne** f column of vehicles; **~ladung** f LKW: truckload, Brit. auch lorryload; Auto: carload; **~lenker** m, **~lenkerin** f bes. hist. charioteer; e-s Autos: driver; **~papiere** Pl. car documents; **~park** m e-s Transport- od. Taxiunternehmens etc.: fleet (of cars); Dienstfahrzeuge: car (od. motor) pool; **~pflege** f (car) maintenance; **~rad** n cartwheel; **~rennen** n hist. chariot race; **~schmiere** f cart grease, axle grease; **~spur** f wheel track; lange, tiefe: rut; **~stand(s)anzeiger** m Eisenb. carriage (Am. car) position indicator; **~tür** f car door, vehicle door; e-r Kutsche: carriage door; **~typ** m make (of car); **~wäsche** f car wash

Waggon [va'gõ:] m; -s, -s; Eisenb. (railway) carriage, Am. (railroad) car; (Güterwagen) goods waggon, Am. freight car; **waggonweise** Adv. by the waggonload, Am. by the carload

waghalsig I. Adj. attr. daredevil ...; (riskant) risky; (tollkühn) foolhardy, reckless; **~ sein** take risks, be a daredevil; **II.** Adv. fahren etc.: recklessly; **Waghalsigkeit** f **1.** daredevilry, daring; pej. foolhardiness, recklessness; **2.** Handlung: deed of daring; pej. reckless act

Wagnerianer m; -s, -, **~in** f; -, -nen Wagnerian

Wagnis n; -ses, -se venture, risk; (Unternehmen) hazardous enterprise; **ein großes ~ eingehen** take a big risk; **sich auf kein ~ einlassen** take no risks; **~kapital** n Fin. venture capital

Wahl f; -, -en **1.** nur Sg. choice; (Alternative) alternative, option; (Auslese) selection; **s-e ~ treffen** make one's choice; **die freie ~ haben** be free to choose; **keine (andere) ~ haben** have no alternative (od. choice) (**als** but); **in die engere ~ kommen** be shortlisted; Sache: be a possibility; **der Wagen Ihrer ~** the car of your choice; **vor der ~ stehen zu** (+ Inf.) be faced with the choice of (+ Ger.); **wenn ich die ~ hätte** if I could choose, if I had the choice; *die ~ fällt mir schwer* I find it hard to choose, I can't decide; *drei Themen stehen zur ~* there's a choice of three topics, three topics are on offer; *wer die ~ hat, hat die Qual Sprichw.* decisions, decisions!; **2.** *Pol. etc.* election; *(Wahlakt)* poll(ing), voting; *(Stimmabgabe)* vote; *~en abhalten* hold elections; *Sonntag sind ~en* there are elections on Sunday, Sunday is an election day; *freie ~en* free elections; *geheime ~* secret ballot; *sich zur ~ stellen* stand *(bes. Am.* run) (as a candidate); *~ durch Handaufheben* vote by (a) show of hands; *~ durch Zuruf* vote by acclamation; *zur ~ schreiten* go to the polls; *die ~ anfechten* contest the result of the election; **3.** *im Verein etc.*: election; *(Abstimmung)* vote; *bei der Hauptversammlung im Mai stehen ~en an* elections will take place at the Annual General Meeting in May; *s-e ~ in das Vereinspräsidium etc.* his election to the presiding committee of the club; *nehmen Sie die ~ an?* are you willing to accept your election *(od.* the office you have been elected to)?; *ich nehme die ~ an* I accept (my election); **4.** *nur. Sg.*; *(Güteklasse)* grade, quality, class; *erste ~* top *(od.* prime) quality, first grade, grade one; *zweite ~* second quality, second grade, grade two; *(Waren)* seconds; *die Orangen sind zweite ~* the oranges are grade two *(od.* second-grade); *als Kandidat etc. ist er nur zweite ~* as a candidate *etc.* he's only second-rate

Wahl|abend *m Pol.* election evening; *~absprache* *f* pre-election agreement; *~akt* *m* vote, voting, polling; *~alter* *n* voting age; *~amt* *n* electoral office; *~analyse* *f* election analysis; *~anfechtung* *f* contesting an election result; *~aufruf* *m* election announcement; *~ausgang* *m* election result, result of an election; *bei größeren Wahlen*: election results *Pl.*; *~ausschuss* *m* election committee; *~aussichten* *Pl.* chances in an *(od.* the) election

Wählautomatik *f Telef.* automatic dial(l)ing

wählbar *Adj.* eligible (for election); **Wählbarkeit** *f* eligibility (for election)

Wahl|beamte *m,* *~beamtin* *f* elected official; *~beeinflussung* *f* (unfairly) influencing an election; *~benachrichtigung* *f* polling card; *~beobachter* *m,* *~beobachterin* *f* observer (at an election)

wahlberechtigt *Adj.* eligible *(od.* entitled) to vote; **Wahlberechtigte** *m, f* person entitled *(od.* eligible) to vote; *Pl. auch* those entitled *(od.* eligible) to vote; **Wahlberechtigung** *f* entitlement to vote, *(the)* suffrage

Wahlberliner *m,* *~in* *f* Berliner by adoption

Wahl|beteiligung *f Pol.* (voter) turnout; *starke/schwache ~* heavy/light polling; *~betrug* *m* electoral fraud *(auch durch falsche Versprechungen)*; *(Manipulation des Wahlergebnisse)* *umg.* (ballot) rigging; *~bezirk* *m* ward, *Am.* precinct; *~boykott* *m* election boycott; *~bündnis* *n* electoral alliance; *~büro* *n* election office; *~debakel* *n* election debacle, electoral disaster, disaster at the polls; *~empfehlung* *f*: *e-e ~ abgeben* recommend *s.o.* to vote for *s.o.*

wählen *vt/i.* **1.** choose; *(auslesen) auch* pick (out), select; *du kannst ~* it's up

to you (to choose), the choice is yours; *du hast klug gewählt* you've made a wise choice; *haben Sie (schon) gewählt?* *im Restaurant*: have you chosen *(od.* decided) (yet)?; *s-e Worte ~* choose one's words (with care); *den ungünstigsten Moment gewählt haben* have picked a very inopportune *(od.* inconvenient) moment; **2.** *Pol. (j-n etc.)* elect; *(stimmen für)* vote for; *(~ gehen)* go to the polls; *gehst du ~?* are you going to vote?; *zum Präsidenten / ins Parlament gewählt werden* be elected president / to parliament; *für fünf Jahre gewählt werden* be elected for (a term of) five years; **3.** *Telef.* dial (the *od.* a number); *Sie haben falsch gewählt* you've got the wrong number; → *gewählt*

wahlentscheidend *Adj.* decisive (in an election); *~ sein* decide the result of an election; **Wahlentscheidung** *f* choice in an election, decision who *(bzw.* what) to vote for; *wovon machst du deine ~ abhängig?* what determines your choice in the election?

Wähler *m; -s, -; Pol.* voter; *Freie ~* Independent Voters, *a locally-based non-party-political organization that puts up independent candidates in elections*; *~auftrag* *m* mandate

Wahl|erfolg *m* election victory; *~ergebnis* *n* election results *Pl.*, returns *Pl.*

Wähler|gemeinschaft *f Pol. (Gesamtheit der Wahlberechtigten)* electorate; *Freie ~* Association of Independent Voters, *a locally-based non-party-political organization that puts up independent candidates in elections*; *~gruppe* *f Pol.* group of voters; *Freie ~ Group of Independent Voters, a locally-based non-party-political organization that puts up independent candidates in elections*; *~gunst* *f* the favo(u)r of the electorate; *in der ~ verlieren/steigen* lose/gain favo(u)r with the voters, lose/gain support among the electorate

Wählerin *f; -, -nen; Pol.* voter

Wählerinitiative *f* **1.** *(Initiative)* campaign by (a group of voters); **2.** *(Gruppe)* pressure group

wählerisch *Adj.* choosy, fussy, picky *umg.* *(in + Dat.* about, when it comes to); *nicht (gerade) ~ in s-m Umgang / in s-r Ausdrucksweise sein umg.* not be (exactly) fussy about the company he keeps / the way he expresses himself

Wählerpotenzial *n* potential vote(s *Pl.*) *(od.* voters *Pl.*)

Wählerschaft *f Pol.* electorate; *in e-m Bezirk etc.*: constituency, voters *Pl.*

Wähler|schicht *f Pol.* group of voters; *~stimme* *f* vote; *~verhalten* *n* voter *(od.* voting) patterns *Pl.*; *~verzeichnis* *n* electoral list; *~votum* *n* vote; *~wille* *m* will of the electorate, mandate

Wahlfach *n Päd.* optional subject, *Am.* elective

Wahl|fälschung *f* vote-rigging, electoral fraud; *~forscher* *m,* *~forscherin* *f* psephologist; *~forschung* *f* psephology; *~frau* *f Pol.* (woman) elector, member of an electoral college

wahlfrei *Adj.* optional; *~er Zugriff EDV* random access; **Wahlfreiheit** *f* **1.** freedom of choice; **2.** *Pol.* electoral freedom

Wahl|gang *m Pol.*: *(im ersten) ~* (at

the first) ballot; *~geheimnis* *n* secrecy of the ballot; *~geschenk* *n* pre-election promise *(od.* concession); *~gewinner* *m,* *~gewinnerin* *f* winner in an election, successful candidate

Wahlheimat *f* adoptive country

Wahlhelfer *m,* *~in* *f Pol.* **1.** *im Wahlkampf*: campaign assistant; **2.** *bei der Wahl*: polling officer

Wählimpuls *m Telef.* dial(l)ing pulse

Wahl|jahr *n Pol.* election year; *~kabine* *f* polling *(od.* voting) booth

Wahlkampf *m Pol.* election campaign; *e-n ~ führen* run an election campaign; *~gelder* *Pl.* campaign funds; *~helfer* *m,* *~helferin* *f* campaign assistant, campaign helper; *~kostenerstattung* *f* reimbursement of campaign expenses; *~manager* *m,* *~managerin* *f* campaign manager; *~manöver* *n* campaign manoeuvre *(Am.* maneuver); *~strategie* *f* campaign strategy; *~thema* *n* campaign issue; *~veranstaltung* *f* election rally

Wahl|kommission *f* electoral commission; *~kreis* *m* constituency; *~kundgebung* *f* election rally; *~leiter* *m,* *~leiterin* *f* returning officer; *~liste* *f* list of candidates, party ticket; *~lokal* *n* polling station *(Am.* place); *~lokomotive* *f umg.* vote-getter

wahllos I. *Adj.* indiscriminate, random; **II.** *Adv.* indiscriminately, at random

Wahl|manipulation *f Pol.* vote-rigging, electoral fraud; *~mann* *m*; *Pl. -männer*; *Pol.* elector, member of an electoral college; *~marathon* *n umg.* election marathon; *~modus* *m* electoral procedure; *~möglichkeit* *f* choice; *(Alternative)* alternative; *~müdigkeit* *f* voter fatigue; *~nacht* *f* election night; *~niederlage* *f* election defeat; *~ordnung* *f* election regulations *Pl.*; *~parole* *f* campaign *(od.* election) slogan; *~party* *f* post-election party; *~periode* *f* period in office; *~pflicht* *f* compulsory voting; *in manchen Ländern herrscht ~* in some countries voting in elections is compulsory; *~pflichtfach* *n Schule*: (compulsory) optional subject; *~plakat* *n* election poster; *~prognose* *f* election forecast; *~programm* *n* election manifesto; *~propaganda* *f* election propaganda; *~prüfung* *f* scrutiny; *~recht* *n objektives*: electoral law; *aktives*: right to vote, franchise; *passives*: eligibility; *allgemeines ~* universal suffrage; *~rede* *f* electoral address

Wählscheibe *f Telef.* dial

Wahl|schein *m Pol.* voting permit *(especially for a postal vote)*; *~schlappe* *f umg.* setback in an election; *~schwindel* *m* vote-rigging; *~sendung* *f* election broadcast; *~sieg* *m* election victory; *~sieger* *m,* *~siegerin* *f* election winner, winner of the election(s *Pl.*); *~slogan* *m* campaign slogan; *~sonntag* *m* polling *(Am.* election) day *(usually a Sunday in Germany and other countries of continental Europe)*, election Sunday; *~spot* *TV* election ad(vertisement); *~spruch* *m* motto; *Pol.* election *(Am.* campaign) slogan; *~system* *n* electoral system; *~tag* *m* election day, polling day; *~taktik* *f* campaign tactic; *~termin* *m* date for an *(od.* the) election

Wählton *m Telef.* dialling tone, *Am.* dial tone

Wahl|unterlagen *Pl. Pol.* election papers; *~urne* *f* ballot box; *zur ~ schreiten* go to the polls; *~veranstaltung* *f*

election rally; **~verfahren** *n* electoral procedure; **~versammlung** *f* election meeting; **~versprechen** *n* campaign (*od.* election) pledge

Wahlverteidiger *m*, **~in** *f Jur.* defence counsel appointed by the accused in a criminal case, as opposed to one appointed by the court, *Am. etwa* counsel for the defense

Wahlverwandtschaft *f geh.* elective affinity; „*Die ~en*" *von Goethe*: Kindred by Choice

Wahl|volk *n nur Sg.*; *Pol.* electorate; **~vorgang** *m* **1.** *Pol.* electoral procedure; **2.** *EDV* dial(l)ing procedure; **~vorschlag** *m* nomination; **~vorstand** *m* election committee

wahlweise I. *Adv.*: **es gab ~ Fisch oder Fleisch** there was a choice of fish or meat; **Sie können ~ faxen oder e-mailen** you've got a choice of faxing or emailing, you can choose to use either fax or email; **II.** *Adj.*: **~ Zusatzeinrichtung** *EDV* optional add-on

Wahl|werbesendung *f*, **~werbespot** *m TV* party election commercial, election ad(vertisement); **~werbung** *f* election advertising

Wahl|wiederholung *f Telef.* **1.** last number recall (*od.* redial); *automatische*: automatic redial; **2.** → *Wahlwiederholungstaste*; **~wiederholungstaste** *f Telef.* last number recall button, automatic redial button; **~zettel** *m Pol.* ballot paper; **~ziel** *n Pol.* aim (in an *bzw.* the, this election); **sie haben ihr ~ nicht erreicht** they didn't get as many votes as they had reckoned with in the election

Wahn *m*; **-(e)s**, *kein Pl.* delusion; (*Wahnsinn*) madness; (*Besessenheit*) mania; **in e-m ~ leben** be labo(u)ring under a delusion; **~bild** *n* delusion; *Med.* hallucination

wähnen *lit.* **I.** *v/t.* fancy, imagine; (*annehmen*) assume, think; **j-n in Sicherheit** *etc.* **~** (mistakenly) imagine that s.o. is safe *etc.*; **ich wähnte ihn auf Reisen/in Rom** I thought he was on a trip / in Rome, I was under the impression that he was on a trip / in Rome; **II.** *v/refl.*: **sich unbeobachtet / im Recht** *etc.* **~** think (*od.* imagine) o.s. to be unobserved/right

Wahnidee *f* delusion; *umg.* crazy idea

Wahnsinn *m*; *nur Sg.* **1.** madness, insanity; **dem ~ verfallen** go insane (*od.* mad); **2.** *fig.* madness, insanity; (*ja*) **~!** *umg.* amazing!, wow!, *Brit. auch* blimey!; **das ist der ~!** *umg.* that's just incredible!; → *hell* I 5; **wahnsinnig I.** *Adj.* mad, insane (*auch fig.*) (*vor* + *Dat.* with); *Angst, Schmerzen etc.*: terrible, incredible *umg.*; *umg.* (*unglaublich*) incredible, *stärker*: mind-boggling; (*großartig*) great, incredible; **~ werden** go mad (*od.* insane); **er macht mich ~** *umg.* he's driving me crazy (*od.* mad *od.* up the wall *od.* [a]round the bend); **II.** *Adv. umg.* incredibly; (*schrecklich*) *auch* dreadfully; **~ verliebt** madly in love; **Wahnsinnige** *m*, *f*; **-n**, **-n** madman (*f* madwoman), lunatic; *umg.* loony; **wie ein ~r** like a maniac (*od.* lunatic); **Wahnsinnigwerden** *n umg.*: **das ist** (*ja*) **zum ~** it's enough to drive you up the wall (*od.* [a]round the bend)

Wahnsinns|... im Subst. umg. oft incredible ..., stärker: Sl. mind-blowing ...; **~arbeit** *f umg.* incredible amount of work; **e-e ~ einzelne**: one hell of a job; **~hitze** *f umg.* incredible (*od.* ter-

rible) heat; **~idee** *f umg.* crazy idea; (*tolle Idee*) incredible idea, great idea; **~preis** *m umg. zu hoch*: exorbitant price; *unglaublich günstig*: knock-down (*Am. auch* bargain-basement) price; **~tat** *f* act of madness

Wahnvorstellung *f* delusion; (*fixe Idee*) idée fixe; *Med.* hallucination

Wahnwitz *m nur Sg.* madness; **wahnwitzig** *Adj.* mad, insane

wahr *Adj.* **1.** true; (*wirklich*) *auch* real; **e-e ~e Geschichte** a true story; **etw. ~ machen** make s.th. come true; (*Drohung, Versprechen etc.*) carry out s.th.; **~ werden** come true; **der ~e Grund** the real reason; **davon ist kein Wort ~** there's not a word of truth in it; *stärker*: it's a pack of lies *umg.*; **das ist wohl ~** that's very true, there's a lot of truth in that; **so ~ mir Gott helfe** *Jur.* so help me God; **so ~ ich hier stehe!** *umg.* as sure as I'm standing here, I kid you not; **das darf doch nicht ~ sein!** *umg.* I don't believe it!; **das ist nicht das Wahre** *umg.* it's not the real thing (*od.* the real McCoy *umg.*); **es ist etwas Wahres dran** there's something in it, there's an element of truth in (*od.* to) it; **2.** (*ausgesprochen*) real; *förm.* veritable; **e-e ~e Fundgrube** a veritable treasure trove; **ein ~es Wunder** a real (*od.* true) miracle; **das ist e-e ~e Wohltat** what a relief; **3.** *gespr.*: **nicht ~?** isn't that so?; isn't it *etc.*?, doesn't he *etc.*?, haven't they *etc.*?; **er kommt doch, nicht ~?** he 'is coming, isn't he?; → *einzig* II, *Jakob*, *Sinn* 4

wahren *v/t.* (*aufrechterhalten*) preserve, maintain; (*auch Geheimnis*) keep; (*Interessen etc.*) look after, protect, safeguard; **den Schein ~** keep up appearances; **die Frist ~** meet the deadline; → *Form* 3

während *v/i.* last; **es währte nicht lange, da ...** it wasn't long before ...; **was lange währt, wird endlich gut** *Sprichw. etwa* all things come to those who wait; → *ehrlich* I 1

während I. *Präp.* during, *förm.* in the course of; **~ der Sitzung** during the meeting; **~ des Abendessens** *etc.* while we *etc.* were having dinner *etc.*; **II.** *Konj.* while; *Gegensatz*: *auch* whereas; **~ er schlief, räumte ich auf** while he slept (*od.* was asleep, *Am. auch* was sleeping), I tidied (*Am.* cleaned) up; **noch ~ er sprach** even as he was speaking; **~ ich dagegen ...** whereas I, on the other hand, ...

währenddessen *Adv.* in the meantime, meanwhile

wahrhaben *v/t. nur Inf.*: **er wollte es nicht ~** he wouldn't believe it, he refused to accept it

wahrhaft I. *Adj.* true, real; **II.** *Adv.* really

wahrhaftig I. *Adv.* really; (*allen Ernstes*) actually, honestly; **er hat es ~ versucht** he actually (*od.* honestly) tried to do it; **II.** *Adj.* (*wahrheitsliebend*) truthful; **~er Gott!** *beteuernd*: good God!; **Wahrhaftigkeit** *f* truthfulness

Wahrheit *f* truth; **in ~** in fact, in reality; **das entspricht der ~** that's true; **um die ~ zu sagen** to tell (you) the truth; **bei der ~ bleiben** stick to the facts; **er nimmt es mit der ~ nicht so genau** he's not the most truthful of people; **j-m** (*unverblümt*) **die ~ sagen** *umg.* give s.o. a piece of one's mind; **um der ~ die Ehre zu geben** to be quite honest; → *bleiben* 2, *nackt*, *rein*[1] I 2 b

Wahrheits|beweis *m Jur.* proof that

one 's testimony is true; **~findung** *f*: **der ~ dienen** help to establish the truth; **~gehalt** *m* truth(fulness)

wahrheits|gemäß I. *Adj.* true, truthful; **II.** *Adv.* truthfully, in accordance with the facts; **~getreu I.** *Adj.* true; *Nachbildung etc.*: *auch* faithful; **II.** *Adv.* truthfully; *nachbilden etc.*: faithfully

Wahrheitsliebe *f* love of truth; **mit s-r ~ ist es nicht weit her** *umg.* he tends to be economical with the truth; **wahrheitsliebend** *Adj.* truth-loving, honest

Wahrheitssuche *f* quest for the truth

wahrheitswidrig *Adj.* false, untrue

wahrlich *Adv. lit.* really, indeed; (*sicher*) certainly, definitely; *bibl.* verily; **es ist ~ kein Vergnügen** *umg. auch* it's no picnic(, I can tell you)

wahrnehmbar *Adj.* discernible, perceptible, noticeable; **Wahrnehmbarkeit** *f* discernibility, perceptibility, noticeability

wahrnehmen *v/t.* (*unreg., trennb., hat -ge-*) **1.** perceive; *optisch*: see, discern; *akustisch*: hear, register; *weitS.* (*merken*) notice; **er nahm alles, was um ihn herum vorging, genau wahr** he was very aware of (*od.* he took in precisely) everything that was going on around him; **2.** (*Gelegenheit*) seize, *förm.* avail o.s. of; (*Interessen*) look after, protect, safeguard; **e-n Termin ~** observe (*od.* keep) an appointment; **e-e Frist ~** observe (*od.* keep to *od.* stick to) a deadline; **Wahrnehmung** *f* **1.** (*sinnliche*) **~** (sense) perception; **2.** (*Sorge für etw.*) care (+ *Gen.* of); **~ der Interessen** safeguarding of interests

Wahrnehmungs|fähigkeit *f*, **~vermögen** *n* perceptive faculty

Wahrsagekunst *f*: **die ~** fortune telling; **wahrsagen** *v/t./i.*; *wahrsagt od. sagt wahr, wahrsagte od. sagte wahr, hat wahrgesagt od. gewahrsagt* tell fortunes; (*etw.*) predict; **j-m ~** tell s.o.'s fortune; **aus den Karten** *etc.* **~** read the cards *etc.*; **sich** (*Dat.*) **~ lassen** have one's fortune told; **Wahrsager** *m*; **-s**, **-**, **Wahrsagerin** *f*; **-**, **-nen** fortune-teller; **Wahrsagung** *f* prediction

währschaft *Adj. schw.* **1.** *Bauer etc.*: (*tüchtig, fleißig*) capable and hard-working; **2.** *Essen*: (*kräftig, solid*) substantial; **3.** *Haus etc.*: (*gediegen, solid*) solid, well-built

Wahrschau *Interj. Naut.* attention!, look out!

wahrscheinlich I. *Adv.* probably; **~ hat sie's verloren** she's probably lost it; **~ wird er verlieren** *auch* (the) chances are he'll lose; **er hat sich sehr ~ das Leben genommen** he very probably committed suicide (*od.* took his own life); **II.** *Adj.* probable, likely; (*glaubhaft*) plausible; **es ist sehr/nicht ~, dass ...** it's highly (*od.* very probable *od.* likely) /unlikely that...; **die ~ste Ursache für das Unglück ist ...** the most likely cause of the accident is ...; **Wahrscheinlichkeit** *f* probability, likelihood; **aller ~ nach** in all probability; **aller ~ nach wird er siegen** the odds are (*od.* it's odds on) that he will win

Wahrscheinlichkeits|grad *m* degree of probability; **~rechnung** *f* theory of probabilities, probability calculus; **~theorie** *f Math.* probability theory

Wahrung *f* maintenance; *von Interessen*: safeguarding, protection

Währung f Fin. currency; **in europäischer/peruanischer** etc. **~ zahlen** pay in euros / pay in Peruvian etc. currency; → **hart** I 6, **weich** I 3

Währungs|abkommen n Fin. monetary agreement; **~ausgleich** m currency conversion compensation; **~block** m monetary (od. currency) bloc; **~einheit** f unit of currency, currency unit; **~fonds** m monetary fund; **Internationaler ~** International Monetary Fund, IMF; **~gebiet** n currency area; **~krise** f monetary (od. currency) crisis; **~kurs** m value of a currency; **~parität** f par of exchange

Währungspolitik f Fin. monetary policy; **währungspolitisch** Adj. monetary, relating to monetary policy

Währungs|reform f Fin. currency reform; **~reserven** Pl. currency reserves; **~schwankungen** Pl. currency fluctuations; **~stabilität** f stability of a currency; **~system** n monetary system; **~umstellung** f changeover to a different currency; **~union** f monetary union; → **Wirtschafts- und Währungsunion**; **~zeichen** n currency symbol

Wahrzeichen n symbol; e-r Stadt: auch famous landmark; (Emblem) emblem; **der Eiffelturm ist das ~ von Paris** the Eiffel Tower is the symbol of Paris

waidgerecht etc. → **weidgerecht** etc.

Waise f; -, -n orphan

Waisen|geld n orphan's allowance; **~haus** n, **~heim** n orphanage; **~kind** n orphan; **~knabe** m fig.: **gegen j-n der reinste ~ sein** be no match for s.o., not be able to hold a candle to s.o.; **~rente** f orphan's allowance

Wakeboard ['weːkbɔːd] n; -s, -s Wassersport: wakeboard; **wakeboarden** v/i. wakeboard; **Wakeboarden** n; kein Pl. wakeboarding; **Wakeboarder** m; -s, -, **Wakeboarderin** f; -in, -innen wakeboarder

Wal m; -(e)s, -e Zool. whale

Walachei f; -; hist. Geog. Walachia; **in der ~** umg. fig. in Walachia

Wald m; -(e)s, Wälder wood(s Pl.); (großer ~) forest (auch fig.); (~fläche) woodland; **ein ~ von Masten** etc. fig. a forest of masts; **er sieht den ~ vor lauter Bäumen nicht** fig. he can't see the wood (Am. forest) for the trees; **ich glaub, ich steh im ~** umg. well, blow me (Am. blow me down); **wie man in den ~ hineinruft, so schallt's heraus** you get what you give; **~ameise** f Zool. red ant; **~arbeiter** m woodsman; **~bau** m nur Sg. silviculture; **~besitz** m ownership of woodlands; Gut: woodland (od. forest) (owned by s.o.); **~bestand** m forest stand; **~boden** m forest floor

Waldbrand m forest fire; **~bekämpfung** f fighting forest fires; **~gefahr** f danger of forest fires

Wäldchen n copse, Brit. auch spinney, Am. auch thicket

Walderdbeere f Bot. wild strawberry

Waldesrauschen n poet. forest murmurs

Wald|fläche f wooded area, woodland; **~frevel** m offen|ce (Am. -se) against the forest laws; **~gebiet** n tract of forest; **~gebirge** n wooded uplands Pl.; **~geist** m sylvan, silvan, woodland sprite; **~grenze** f Geog. timber line; **~horn** n Mus. French horn; **~huhn** n Jägerspr. grouse; (Birkhuhn) black grouse; (Haselhuhn) hazelhen; (Schneehuhn) ptarmigan

waldig Adj. wooded

Wald|kauz m Orn. tawny owl; **~land** n woodland; **~lauf** m cross-country run; **~lehrpfad** m (forest) nature trail

Waldmeister m; nur Sg.; Bot. woodruff; **~bowle** f woodruff-flavo(u)red punch

Waldohreule f Orn. long-eared owl

Waldorf|pädagogik f Päd. Rudolf Steiner teaching system; **~salat** m Gastr. Waldorf salad; **~schule** f Päd. Rudolf Steiner school

Wald|pilz m forest fungus; essbar: forest mushroom; **~rand** m (am) ~ (at od. on the) edge of the forest; **~rebe** f Bot. clematis

waldreich Adj. well-wooded, thickly wooded

Wald|schäden Pl. damage Sg. to woodlands (od. forests); **~schadensbericht** m report on damage suffered by woodlands (od. forests); **~schrat** m hobgoblin; **~spaziergang** m walk in the wood (od. forest); **~städte** Pl.; Geog.: **die ~** four towns on the Upper Rhine, formerly belonging to Austria: Rheinfelden, Säckingen, Laufenburg, and Waldshut; **~sterben** n waldsterben, death of forests due to acid rain and other pollution; **~storch** m Orn. stork; **~stück** n copse; (Teil e-s Waldes) area of a wood (bes. Am. forest); **~-und-Wiesen-...** im Subst. → **Feld--Wald-und-Wiesen-...**

Waldungen Pl. wooded areas, woodlands; ausgedehnte: forests

Wald|vogel m Orn. woodland bird; **~weg** m forest path; **~wiese** f forest glade; **~wirtschaft** f management of woodlands

Walfang m; nur Sg. whaling; **die ~ treibenden Nationen** the whaling nations; **Walfänger** m (Schiff, Mensch) whaler

Walfang|flotte f whaling fleet; **~schiff** n whaler

Wal|fisch m umg. whale; Astron. Cetus; **~fleisch** n whalemeat

Walhall (n); -s, **Walhalla** (n); -s, f; -; Myth. Valhalla

Waliser m; -s, - Welshman; **er ist ~** mst he's Welsh; **Waliserin** f; -, -nen Welsh woman (od. girl etc.); **sie ist ~** mst she's Welsh; **walisisch** Adj. Welsh; **Walisisch** n; -(s), Ling. Welsh; **das ~e** Welsh

Waljagd f whale hunting

walken v/t. 1. (Stoff) full; (Hüte) felt; (Leder) mill; (Blech) roll; 2. (Teig) knead; (Wäsche) rub and scrub; 3. (massieren) massage; **Walker** m; -s, -, **Walkerin** f; -, -nen fuller; felter

Walkie-Talkie ['wɔːkiˈtɔːki] n; -(s), -s walkie-talkie

Walkman® ['wɔːkmən] m; -s, -s und Walkmen personal stereo; **Walkman®** (Pl. Walkmans od. Walkmen)

Walküre f; -, -n Valkyrie (auch umg. fig. Frau)

Wall m; -(e)s, Wälle; (Damm) dam, embankment; (Befestigung) rampart; fig. bulwark

Wallach m; -s, -e gelding

Wallanlage f ramparts Pl., walls Pl.

wallen v/i. 1. Haar, Gewand: flow; 2. Flüssigkeit: simmer, bubble; Meer: surge; Nebel: sweep; fig. Blut: boil; **der Zorn brachte sein Blut zum Wallen** anger made his blood boil; **wallend** I. Part. Präs. → **wallen**; II. Adj. Fluten, Nebel etc.: billowing; Bart, Gewänder etc.: flowing

Waller m; -s, -;. Dial. catfish

wallfahren v/i. (untr., ist) go on a pilgrimage; **Wallfahrer** m, **Wallfahrerin** f pilgrim; **Wallfahrt** f pilgrimage

Wallfahrts|kirche f pilgrimage church; **~ort** m, **~stätte** f place of pilgrimage, fig. mecca

Wallgraben m moat

Wallis n; -; Geog.: **das ~** Valais; **Walliser I.** m; -s, -, **Walliserin** f; -, -nen Valaisan, weiblich auch: Valaisan woman (od. girl etc.); **II.** Adj. Valaisan; **die ~ Alpen** the Valaisan Alps; **walliserisch** Adj. Valaisan

Wallone m; -n, -n Walloon; **Wallonien** (n); -s; Geog. Wallonia; **Wallonin** f; -, -nen Walloon woman (od. girl etc.); **wallonisch** Adj. Walloon

Wallung f 1. des Wassers etc.: seething; fig. surge of emotion; **j-n in ~ bringen** make s.o.'s blood boil; 2. Med. hot flush

Walmdach n Archit. hip(ped) roof

Walnuss f 1. walnut; 2. walnut (tree); **Walnussbaum** m walnut (tree); **walnussgroß** Adj. walnut-sized, nachgestellt: the size of a walnut

Walnuss|kern m walnut (kernel); **~öl** n walnut oil

Walpurgisnacht f: **die ~** Walpurgis night, Walpurgisnacht

Walrat m, n; -(e)s, kein Pl. spermaceti; **~öl** n sperm oil

Walross n Zool. walrus; **so ein ~!** umg. fig. what a great lummox!, Am. what a klutz!

Walstatt f; -, Walstätten; altm. field (of battle)

walten v/i. (herrschen) rule; (vorherrschen) prevail; (wirken) be at work; **Gnade** etc. **~ lassen** show mercy etc.; **Sorgfalt ~ lassen** exercise proper care; **Vernunft ~ lassen** allow reason to prevail; → **Amt** 1, **schalten** 5

Walz f; -, kein Pl.; altm.: **auf der ~ sein** be on the road; **auf die ~ gehen** take to the road, go off on one's travels

Walzblech n sheet metal

Walze f; -, -n roller (auch Druck.); Math. cylinder; Tech. auch roll; der Schreibmaschine: platen; der Drehorgel etc.: barrel; **walzen I.** vt/i. (hat gewalzt); Tech. roll (auch Boden); **II.** v/i. (auch ist); (Walzer tanzen) waltz

wälzen I. v/t. 1. roll; in Mehl ~ roll in flour, flour; **etw. in Ei und Mehl ~** flour and egg s.th.; 2. umg. (Bücher) pore over; **Probleme ~** umg. turn problems over in one's mind; 3. **die Schuld auf j-n ~** shift the blame onto s.o.; **II.** v/refl. roll; im Dreck etc.: auch wallow; vor Schmerz: writhe; im Bett: toss and turn, thrash about umg.; **sich ~ durch/entlang** etc. Masse, Lawine etc.: churn its way through/along etc.; **sich vor Lachen ~** umg. roll about

walzenförmig Adj. cylindrical

Walzer m; -s, - waltz; **~ tanzen** (dance a) waltz; **Wiener ~** Viennese waltz; **langsamer ~** slow waltz

Wälzer m; -s, -; umg. thick (od. heavy, huge) tome

Walzer|könig m: **der ~ Johann Strauß** Johann Strauss, the Waltz King; **~musik** f waltz music; **~schritt** m waltz step; **~takt** m waltz time

Wälzlager n Tech. rolling bearing

Walz|stahl m Tech. rolled steel; **~straße** f roll train; **~werk** n rolling mill

Wamme f; -, -n; Zool. dewlap; Kürschnerei: belly part; Dial. → **Wampe**; **Wammerl** n; -s, -(n); südd., österr.; Gastr. belly of pork

Wampe f; -, -n; umg. paunch; **s-e dicke ~** his fat paunch; **sich** (Dat.) **die ~ voll**

schlagen stuff o.s.

Wams *n*; -es, *Wämser*; *Dial. od. altm.* jacket; *hist.* doublet

wand *Imperf.* → *winden*[1]

Wand *f*; -, *Wände* wall (*auch fig.*); (*Fels*) *auch* face; (*Wolken*) bank; (*Regen*) blanket; (*Schranke*) barrier; (*Seitenfläche*) side; **an die ~ werfen** *wörtl.* throw at (*od.* against) the wall; *fig.* (*Bilder etc.*) project on the wall; **es zieht e-e schwarze ~ herauf** there's a mass of black clouds gathering; **~ an ~** wall to wall; **in s-n eigenen vier Wänden** *fig.* within one's own four walls; **j-n an die ~ drücken** put s.o. in the shade; **j-n an die ~ spielen** steal the show (from s.o.); *Sport* play s.o. into the ground; **an die ~ stellen** (*erschießen*) put up against a wall (and shoot); **gegen e-e ~ von Vorurteilen anrennen** come up against a wall of prejudice(s); **Wände haben Ohren** walls have ears; **wenn Wände reden könnten** if walls could speak; **bei ihm redet man gegen e-e ~** it's like talking to a brick wall (with him); **da wackelt die ~** *umg.* they're really raising the roof in there; **es ist, um an den Wänden hochzugehen** *umg.* it's enough to drive you up the wall; → *Kopf* 6, **spanisch**, *Teufel* 3, *tragend etc.*

Wandale *etc.* → *Vandale etc.*

Wand|behang *m* wall hanging; **~bekleidung** *f* → *Wandverkleidung*; **~bewurf** *m* rendering, facing; **~bild** *n* wall painting, mural; **~bord** *n*, **~brett** *n* (wall) shelf

Wandel *m*; -s, *kein Pl.* change; **der ~ der Zeiten** changing times; **im ~ der Zeiten** in the course of time, through the ages; **dem ~ unterliegen** be subject to change; **~anleihe** *f Wirts.* convertible loan

wandelbar *Adj.* changeable, variable

Wandel|gang *m*, **~halle** *f* covered walk; *Kurbad*: pump room

wandeln I. *v/refl.* (*hat sich gewandelt*) change; **sich ~ in** (+ *Akk.*) turn (in)to; *Person*: turn into; **II.** *v/t.* (*hat*) change (*auch Person*), alter; **III.** *v/i.* (*ist*) (*gehen*) walk, stroll; (*promenieren*) promenade; **~des Lexikon** *umg. hum.* walking encyclop(a)edia

Wandel|obligation *f*, **~schuldverschreibung** *f Wirts.* convertible bond

Wandelung *f Jur.* cancel(l)ation of sale

Wander|ameise *f Zool.* army ant; **~arbeiter** *m*, **~arbeiterin** *f* migrant worker; **~ausstellung** *f* travel(l)ing exhibition; **~bücherei** *f* travel(l)ing library, *Am.* bookmobile; **~bühne** *f* touring (*umg.* fit-up) company; *hist.* company of strolling players; **~bursche** *m altm.* travel(l)ing journeyman; **~düne** *f* shifting sand dune

Wanderer *m*; -s, - **1.** hiker, *bes. Brit. auch* walker, *Brit. auch* rambler; **2.** *bes. poet.* wanderer, travel(l)er

Wander|falke *m Orn.* peregrine falcon; **~fisch** *m Zool.* migratory fish; **~führer** *m* (*Buch*) guide; **~gewerbe** *n* itinerant trade; **~gruppe** *f* party of hikers (*bes. Brit. auch* walkers *od.* ramblers); **~heuschrecke** *f Zool.* migratory locust

Wanderin *f*; -, *-nen* → *Wanderer*

Wander|jahre *pl. hist. hist.* (journeyman's) years of travel; **~karte** *f* map for walkers, hiking map, map of the footpaths in an area, *Am.* trail map; **~kleidung** *f* hiking gear (*od.* outfit); **~leben** *n* vagrant (gypsy *umg.*) life; **~leber** *f Med.* floating liver; **~lied** *n*

hiking song

Wanderlust *f nur Sg.* wanderlust; **wanderlustig** *Adj.* fond of travel; **~ sein** *auch* have itchy feet *umg.*

wandern *v/i.* **1.** *in den Bergen etc.*: walk, hike, go on a walk (*od.* hike); **~ gehen** go walking, go hiking; **2.** (*umherstreifen*) rove; (*ziellos*) **durch die Straßen** *etc.* **~** wander aimlessly through the streets *etc.*; **3.** *fig. Vögel, Völker etc.*: migrate; *Düne*: shift; *Wolken*: drift; *Leber, Niere*: float; *Blick, Gedanken*: roam, wander; **durch die Wüste** *etc.* **~** roam (through) the desert; **in den Papierkorb/ins Gefängnis** *etc.* **~** end up (*od.* land) in the waste-paper bin (*Am.* basket) /in prison *etc.*

Wander|niere *f Med.* floating kidney; **~pokal** *m* challenge cup; **~prediger** *m* itinerant preacher; **~preis** *m* challenge trophy; **~ratte** *f Zool.* brown rat; **~route** *f* trail

Wanderschaft *f* travels *Pl.*; **auf ~ gehen/sein** take to the road / be on one's travels; *Tiere*: migrate; **ich war den ganzen Tag auf ~** *umg. fig.* (*unterwegs*) I was wandering around all day

Wanderschuh *m* walking (*od.* hiking) shoe

Wandersmann *m hist. od. hum.* wanderer

Wander|stock *m* walking stick; **~tag** *m* school (*od.* class) hike; **~trieb** *m* **1.** roving spirit; (*Fernweh*) wanderlust; **2.** *Zool.* migratory instinct

Wanderung *f* **1.** hike; **e-e ~ machen** go on a hike; **2.** *von Völkern, Zool. etc.*: migration (*auch Etron.*); *von Lachsen etc.*: ascent; *Soziol.* migration; *massenweise*: *auch* population shift; **3.** **~en** travels, wanderings

Wanderungsbewegung *f Soziol.* migration, migratory movement

Wander|urlaub *m* walking holiday (*Am.* vacation); **~verein** *m* rambling (*Am.* hiking) club; **~vogel** *m* **1.** *nur Sg.*; *hist. rambling club founded in 1895 in Berlin that was a precursor of the German Youth Movement*; **2.** *member of the "Wandervogel" 1*; **3.** *fig.* rambler, *Am.* hiker; **~weg** *m* hiking trail; **~wetter** *n* ideal weather for hiking (*Brit. auch* rambling); **~zirkus** *m* travel(l)ing circus

Wand|farbe *f* wall paint; **~fläche** *f* wall area; **~fries** *m* mural (*od.* wall) frieze; **~gemälde** *n* mural; **~haken** *m* wall hook; **~halterung** *f TV, PC etc.*: wall bracket; **~kalender** *m* wall calendar; **~karte** *f* wall map; **~lampe** *f* wall lamp

Wandler *m*; -s, -; *Etech.* converter

Wandleuchte *f* wall lamp

Wandlung *f* **1.** change; **in e-r ~ begriffen sein** be in the process of changing; **mit ihm ist e-e seltsame ~ vor sich gegangen** there's been a curious change in him; **2.** *Etech.* transformation; *kirchl.* transubstantiation; *Jur.* nullification of a (*od.* the) sale, *Am. auch* redhibition

wandlungsfähig *Adj.* capable of change; (*flexibel*) flexible, versatile; **Wandlungsfähigkeit** *f* flexibility, versatility

Wandlungsprozess *m* process of change

Wand|malerei *f* mural painting; *konkret*: mural; **~pfeiler** *m* pilaster; **~platte** *f* wall panel

Wandrerin *f*; -, *-nen* → *Wanderer*

Wand|schirm *m* (folding) screen; **~schmiererei** *f auch Pl.* graffiti;

~schmuck *m* wall decoration; **~schrank** *m* built-in cupboard, *Am.* closet; *für Kleidung*: built-in wardrobe; **~schränkchen** *n* (small) wall cupboard; **~spiegel** *m* wall mirror; **~tafel** *f* (black)board, *Am. auch* chalkboard; *weiße*: whiteboard; **~täfelung** *f* wall panel(l)ing

wandte *Imperf.* → *wenden*

Wand|teller *m* wall plate; **~teppich** *m* tapestry; **~uhr** *f* wall clock; **~verkleidung** *f Innenwände*: wall covering; *aus Holz*: panel(l)ing, wainscoting; *akustisch*: lining; *Außenwände*: facing, cladding, *Am.* siding; **~zeitung** *f* wall newspaper

Wange *f*; -, *-n* **1.** cheek; **~ an ~** cheek to cheek; **2.** *Tech.* cheek; *e-r Treppe*: stringboard; **Wangenbein** *n Anat.* cheekbone

Wankelmotor *m Mot.* Wankel engine

Wankelmut *m* fickleness, inconstancy; **wankelmütig** *Adj.* fickle; **Wankelmütigkeit** *f* fickleness, inconstancy

wanken *v/i.* **1.** (*ist gewankt*) (*taumelnd gehen*) stagger, *stärker*: reel; **2.** (*hat*) *im Stehen*: sway; *Boot*: rock; *Boden, Haus etc.*: sway; *fig. Thron etc.*: rock, totter; (*unentschlossen sein*) waver, falter, vacillate; **ins Wanken geraten** begin to sway (*od.* rock); *fig. Position etc.*: become shaky; *Person*: become unsure of o.s.; **ins Wanken bringen** *fig.* shake, rock; **nicht ~ und nicht weichen** not budge (*od.* give) an inch

wann *Adv.* when; (**~** *auch immer*) whenever; **~?** (*um welche Uhrzeit?*) when?, what time?; **seit ~?** how long?, since when?; **bis ~?** till when?, (for) how long?; *bei Termin etc.*: by when?; **von ~ bis ~ war der Dreißigjährige Krieg?** what are the dates of the Thirty Years' War?; **von ~ bis ~ arbeitet ihr?** what hours do you work?; → *dann* 2, *immer* 4

Wanne *f*; -, *-n* tub; (*Badewanne*) bath(tub); *Mot.* (*Ölwanne*) (oil) sump, *Am.* oil pan; *Fot.* bath; **Wannenbad** *n* bath

Wanst *m*; -(e)s, *Wänste*; *umg.* paunch; **sich den ~ voll schlagen** stuff o.s.

Wanze *f*; -, *-n* **1.** *Zool.* bug; **2.** *umg. fig.* (*Abhörgerät*) bug; **3.** *umg. pej.* (*Mensch*) creep

Wanzenplage *f* infestation of bugs

WAP-Handy *n Telek.* WAP phone, web access phone

Wappen *n*; -s, - (coat of) arms *Pl.*; **ein ~ führen** bear arms, have a coat of arms; **e-e Lilie** *etc.* **im ~ führen** have a lily *etc.* in one's coat of arms; **~kunde** *f* heraldry; **~schild** *m* shield, escutcheon; **~spruch** *m* heraldic motto; **~tier** *n* heraldic animal

wappnen *v/refl.* steel o.s. (**gegen** against); *sich mit Mut etc.* **~** muster up one's courage *etc.*; → *gewappnet*

war *Imperf.* → *sein*[1]

Waran *m*; -s, *-e*; *Zool.* monitor (lizard)

warb *Imperf.* → *werben*

ward *Imperf. altm.* → *werden*

Ware *f*; -, *-n* product; *Pl. auch* goods, commodities, *bes. Am.* merchandise *Sg.*; **beste ~** best quality; **heiße ~** *umg.* hot goods *Pl.*; **zur ~ werden** *fig., pej.* become a commodity

Waren|abkommen *n Wirts.* trade agreement; **~absatz** *m* sale of goods; **~angebot** *n* range of items (for sale); **~annahme** *f* **1.** acceptance of goods; **2.** (*Annahmestelle*) (goods) reception, *Am.* deliveries *Pl.*; **~ausfuhr** *f* export of goods; **~ausgabe** *f* **1.** distribution of goods; **2.** (*Ausgabestelle*) collection point; **~ausgang** *m* outgoing goods; **~austausch** *m* exchange of goods; **~automat** *m* vending machine; **~bestand** *m* stock on hand; **~börse** *f* commodity exchange; **~charakter** *m bes. pej.* commodification, commercial character; **~einfuhr** *f* import of goods; **~eingang** *m* stock receipt, incoming goods; **~eingangsbuch** purchase book; **~gutschein** *m* voucher (exchangeable for goods)

Warenhaus *n* department store
Warenhaus|... *im Subst. siehe auch Kaufhaus...*; **~diebstahl** *m* shoplifting; **~konzern** *m* department store chain

Waren|korb *m Statistik*: basket of goods; **~kreditbrief** *m Fin.* documentary letter of credit; **~lager** *n* **1.** (*Raum*) warehouse; **2.** (*Bestand*) stock on hand, inventory; **~lieferung** *f* delivery; **~muster** *n*, **~probe** *f* sample; **~sendung** *f* consignment of goods; *Post.* trade sample; **~sortiment** *n* line of goods; **~termingeschäft** *n* commodity futures trading; **~test** *m* product test; *Stiftung ~ etwa* Consumers' Association, Consumers International, *Am. etwa* Consumers' Union; **~umsatz** *m* goods (*Am.* product) turnover; **~umschlag** *m* movement of goods; **~verkehr** *m* goods traffic; **~wert** *m* value of goods; **~wirtschaft** *f* materials management

Warenzeichen *n* trademark; *eingetragenes ~* registered trademark; **~rolle** *f* register of trademarks; **~schutz** *m* protection of trademark

Warenzoll *m* (customs) duty (on goods)

warf *Imperf.* → **werfen**
Warf *f*; *-*, *-en*, **Warft** *f*; *-*, *-en* warp

warm I. *Adj.*; *wärmer, am wärmsten* **1.** warm (*auch fig. Worte, Empfang etc.*); *stärker, auch Speisen, Farben etc., auch Tech.*: hot; *~e Küche von 18 bis 22 Uhr* hot meals served from 6 to 10 p.m.; *mir ist ~* I feel (*od.* I'm) warm, I'm getting hot; *schön ~* nice and warm; *sich ~ halten* keep warm; *~ machen* warm (up); *~ werden* warm up; *das Essen ~ machen* heat up the meal (*od.* food); *ich brauche etwas Warmes* (*zu essen*) I'd like something hot; (*zu trinken*) I need a hot drink; *sich* (*Dat.*) *etwas Warmes überziehen* cover o.s. up warm; *das Zimmer kostet ~ 300 Euro* (*Miete*) the room costs 300 Euros with heating; *ihm wurde ~ ums Herz fig.* it made him feel all warm inside, it warmed the cockles of his heart *umg. hum.*; *ich kann nicht mit ihm ~ werden* I can't warm to him; → *Regen, Semmel etc.*; **2.** *Sport*: *sich ~ machen* warm up; *sich ~ laufen* do a warm-up run, warm up; *sich ~ schwimmen/spielen/springen etc.* warm up; *auch* warm up by swimming a few lengths / having a knock-up / doing a few jumps; **3.** *altm., umg., pej.* (*homosexuell*) queer; *~er Bruder* queer, *Am. auch* fag(got), fruit; **4.** *~ laufen Motor*: run hot; *~ laufen lassen* warm up; **II.** *Adv. fig.* warmly; *~ duschen* have a hot shower; *wir essen abends ~* we have a hot meal in the evening; *sich ~ anziehen* dress warmly; *fig.* be prepared for the worst; *j-m etw. wärmstens empfehlen* warmly recommend s.th. to s.o.; *~ halten* (*Essen etc.*) keep warm (*od.* hot); *sich* (*Dat.*) *j-n ~ halten fig.* keep in with s.o.

Warmblut *n Pferd*: crossbreed; **Warm-**

blüter *m*; *-s*, *-*; *Zool.* warm-blooded animal; **warmblütig** *Adj. Zool.* warm-blooded

Warmduscher *m*; *-s*, *-*; *umg.* (*Weichling*) wimp, sissy, wet

Wärme *f*; *-*, *kein Pl.* warmth (*auch fig.*); *Phys.* heat; *wir haben 20° ~* it's 20° here; *aus der Kälte in die ~* out of the cold into the warm; *menschliche ~* human warmth; *~ ausstrahlen Ofen etc.*: radiate heat; *fig.* radiate warmth; *ist das wieder e-e ~!* it's terribly hot again!; **~abgabe** *f* loss of heat; **~ausdehnung** *f* thermal expansion; **~austausch** *m* heat exchange; **~austauscher** *m* heat exchanger

Wärmebedarf *m* need for warmth; *e-s Raums, Gebäudes etc.*: heating requirements *Pl.*; **wärmebedürftig** *Adj.* needing warmth

Wärme|behandlung *f Med., Tech.* heat treatment; **~belastung** *f Umwelt*: thermal pollution; *Tech.* thermal stress

wärmebeständig *Adj.* heat-resistant

Wärme|bilanz *f Phys., Tech.* heat balance; **~bildkamera** *f* thermal imaging camera; **~dämmung** *f* heat (*od.* thermal) insulation; **~dehnung** *f Phys.* thermal expansion; **~einheit** *f* thermal (*od.* caloric) unit; **~energie** *f* thermal energy; **~entwicklung** *f* generation of heat; **~erzeugung** *f* production of heat; **~fluss** *m* flow of heat; **~gewitter** *n* heat thunderstorm; **~grad** *m* degree of heat; **~kraftwerk** *n* thermal power station; **~lehre** *f* thermodynamics *Pl.* (*V. im Sg.*); **~leiter** *m* heat conductor; **~leitfähigkeit** *f* heat (*od.* thermal) conductivity; **~leitzahl** *f* coefficient of thermal conductivity; **~mengenzähler** *m Tech.* heat gauge

wärmen I. *vt/i.* warm (up), heat (up); *sich* (*Dat.*) *die Füße etc. ~* warm one's feet etc.; *gut ~ Heizkörper*: give off plenty of heat; *Wolle wärmt* wool keeps you warm; *Alkohol wärmt* alcohol warms you up; **II.** *v/refl.* warm up (*am Feuer* in front of the fire)

Wärme|periode *f* warm spell; **~pumpe** *f* heat pump; **~quelle** *f* heat source

wärmer *Komp.* → **warm**

Wärme|regler *m* thermostat; **~rückgewinnung** *f* heat recovery; **~schutz** *m* (energy conservation through) heat insulation; **~speicher** *m* heat accumulator; **~stau** *m* buildup of heat; *Med.* hyperthermia; **~strahlen** *Pl.* heat rays, radiant heat *Sg.*; **~strahlung** *f* heat radiation; **~stube** *f für Obdachlose etc.*: warm room; **~tauscher** *m* heat exchanger; **~technik** *f* heat technology; **~verlust** *m* heat loss; **~wert** *m Tech.* calorific value

Wärmflasche *f* hot-water bottle
Warmfront *f Met.* warm front
warm halten → **warm** II; **warmhalten** *v/t.*: *sich* (*Dat.*) *j-n ~ fig.* keep in with s.o.; → *auch* **warm** II; **Warmhalteplatte** *f* plate warmer, hot server

warmherzig *Adj.* warmhearted; **Warmherzigkeit** *f* warmheartedness

warm laufen → **warm** I 2
warmlaufen I. *v/i.* (*unreg., trennb., ist -ge-*) *Mot.* run hot; *~ lassen* warm up; → *auch* **warm** I 4; **II.** *v/refl. Sport*: *sich ~* warm up, do a warm-up run; → *auch laufen* III

Warmluft *f nur Sg.* warm air; **~front** *f* warm front; **~heizung** *f* hot-air heating

Warmmiete *f* rent including heating
wärmst... *Sup.* → **warm**
Warmstart *m EDV* warm start

Warmwasser *n nur Sg.* hot water; **~bereiter** *m*; *-s*, *-* (hot) water heater; **~hahn** *m* hot-water tap; **~heizung** *f* hot-water heating (system); **~speicher** *m* hot-water tank

Warmzeit *f Geol.* interglacial period
Warn|anlage *f* warning device; **~blinkanlage** *f Mot.*, **~blinker** *m umg.* hazard lights *Pl.*; **~blinkleuchte** *f Mot.* flashing warning light; **~dreieck** *n Mot.* warning triangle

warnen *vt/i.* warn (*vor + Dat.* against); *j-n vor* (+ *Dat.*) *~* warn s.o. about (*od.* of); *j-n davor ~, etw. zu tun* warn s.o. against doing s.th., warn s.o. not to do s.th.; *vor Taschendieben wird gewarnt* beware (of) pickpockets; *ich warne dich* I warn you; *drohend*: I'm warning you; *j-n rechtzeitig ~ umg.* (*Bescheid geben*) let s.o. know in advance (*od.* in good time), give s.o. plenty of warning; *warnend* **I.** *Part. Präs.* → *warnen*; **II.** *Adj.* warning; **III.** *Adv.* anblicken etc.: warningly; *s-e Stimme ~ erheben* raise one's voice in warning; **Warner** *m*; *-s*, *-*, **Warnerin** *f*; *-*, *-nen* warner, warning voice

Warn|hinweis *m* warning; **~kreuz** *n Verk.* warning cross; **~lampe** *f* warning light; **~laut** *m bes. Zool.* warning cry; **~leuchte** *f*, **~licht** *n* warning light; **~ruf** *m* warning cry (*auch Zool.*); **~schild** *n* danger sign; **~schuss** *m* warning shot (*auch fig.*); *e-n ~ abgeben* fire a warning shot; **~signal** *n* warning signal; **~streik** *m* token (*od.* warning) strike; **~system** *n* warning system

Warnung *f* warning (*vor +Dat.* of); *lass dir das e-e ~ sein* let that be a warning to you; *dies ist m-e letzte ~* this is your last warning, I shan't (*Am.* won't) warn you again; *~ vor dem Hunde! Schild*: beware of the dog

Warnzeichen *n* warning sign
Warschau (*n*); *-s*; *Geog.* Warsaw; **Warschauer I.** *m*; *-s*, *-*; inhabitant of Warsaw, person from Warsaw; *~ sein* be (*od.* come) from Warsaw; **II.** *Adj.* Warsaw's ...; **Warschauerin** *f*; *-*, *-nen* inhabitant of Warsaw, woman (*od.* girl) from Warsaw

Warte *f*; *-*, *-n* vantage point (*auch fig.*); *von hoher ~ aus fig.* from a lofty standpoint; *von m-r ~ aus gesehen* from my point of view

Warte|frist *f* waiting time; **~halle** *f* waiting room; *Flug.* departure lounge; **~häuschen** *n Bus etc.*: shelter; **~liste** *f* waiting list; *auf der ~ stehen* be on the waiting list

warten¹ *v/i.* wait (*auf + Akk.* for); *bitte ~! Telef.* please hold (the line); *j-n ~ lassen* keep s.o. waiting; *worauf od. auf was ~ wir noch?* what are we waiting for?; *mit dem Essen auf j-n ~* keep dinner waiting for s.o.; *nicht mit dem Essen auf j-n ~* start eating without s.o.; *müde vom langen Warten* tired with the long wait; (*nicht*) *lange auf sich ~ lassen* (not) be a long time coming; *warte mal!* just (*od.* wait) a minute!, hang on! *umg.*; *na warte! umg.* just you wait!; *da kannst du lange ~ umg.* you could be in for a long wait, don't hold your breath *iro.*; *auf dich / darauf habe wir gerade noch gewartet iro.* you're / that's all we needed; *darauf habe ich gewartet iro.* I was just waiting for it (to happen), I could see it coming; → *schwarz* I 3

warten² *v/t.* **1.** *Tech.* service; (*Maschine, Anlage*) *auch* maintain; **2.** *altm.* (*Kin-*

der, Kranke) tend

Wärter *m; -s, -* attendant; (*Wächter*) guard; *im Gefängnis*: warder, *Am.* guard; (*Tier-, Leuchtturmwärter*) keeper; → **Bahnwärter** *etc.*

Warteraum *m* waiting room

Warterei *f; -, -en; umg. pej.* waiting; *ich hab die ~ satt!* I'm fed up with waiting

Wärterin *f; -, -nen* attendant; (*Wächterin*) guard; *im Gefängnis*: warder, *Am.* guard; (*Tier-, Leuchtturmwärterin*) keeper

Warte|saal *m* waiting room; **~schlange** *f* queue, *Am.* line, *EDV* queue; **~schleife** *f* **1.** *Flug.* turning-loop; **~n ziehen** circle (the airport), be in a holding pattern; **2.** *sich in der ~ befinden Telef.* have been put on hold; *fig.* be on the waiting list; **~stellung** *f: in ~* on hold, waiting; **~zeit** *f* wait; *Jur.* waiting period; *EDV* wait time; *e-e lange ~* a long wait; **~zimmer** *n* waiting room

Wartung *f Tech.* maintenance, servicing

Wartungsarbeiten *Pl.* maintenance work *Sg.*

wartungs|frei *Adj. Tech.* maintenance-free; **~freundlich** *Adj.* making for easy maintenance

Wartungs|halle *f* service area; **~intervall** *n* interval between services; **~personal** *n* maintenance staff (*mst V. im Pl.*); **~techniker** *m*, **~technikerin** *f* service engineer; **~vertrag** *m* service contract

warum *Adv.* why; *ich weiß nicht ~* I don't know why; *~ bloß?* but why?; *~ wohl?* I wonder why; *~ nicht gleich (so)? umg.* why didn't you do that the first time?; *freundlicher*: that's better!; *~ eigentlich nicht?* why not?; *nach dem Warum fragen* ask (the question) why

Warze *f; -, -n* **1.** *Wucherung*: wart; **2.** (*Brustwarze*) nipple; *Zool.* teat

Warzen|kaktus *m Bot.* nipple cactus; **~schwein** *n Zool.* warthog; **~stift** *m Med.* wart clinic

was I. *Interrog. Pron.* what (*auch umg. für wie bitte?*); *~ für (ein) ...?* what sort of ...?; *~ für Länder kennst du schon?* which countries have you already been to?; *~ für e-e Farbe hat ...?* what colo(u)r is ...?; *~ für ein Auto ist das?* what kind of car is that?; *~ ist sein Vater?* what does his father do?; *~ willst du werden?* what do you want to be?; *~ willst du überhaupt?* what do you actually want?; *~ kostet das?* how much is it?, what *od.* how much does it cost?; *~ haben Sie an Wein etc.?* what have you got in the way of wine *etc.*?; *~ ist denn? umg.* what's the matter?, what's wrong?; *~ noch?* what else?; *~ dann?* and then what?; *um ~ handelt es sich? umg.* what's it (all) about?; *auf ~ wartest du? umg.* what are you waiting for?; *an ~ denkst du? umg.* what are you thinking about?; *~ (warum) muss er auch lügen? umg.* why does he have to lie?; *~ weiß ich umg.* how should I know, search me; *und ~ nicht alles umg.* and all that; *das tut weh, ~? umg.* it hurts, doesn't it?; *~ machen* I, *nun* I 1, *sollen²* 2 *etc.*; **II.** *Interj.*: *~, du rauchst nicht mehr? umg.* what, you don't smoke any more?; *~ für ein Unsinn/Krach etc.!* what nonsense *etc.* / what a noise *etc.*; *~ für ein Wetter!* what weather!; *~ haben wir gelacht!*

umg. what a laugh we had; → *ach* 5; **III.** *Rel. Pron.* (*das was*) what; (*welches*) that, which; *den Inhalt des vorhergehenden Satzes aufnehmend*: which; *das war alles, ~ er mir erzählte* that was all (that) he told me; *alles, ~ er weiß* everything (that) he knows; *~ ihn völlig kalt ließ* which left him cold; *~ auch immer* whatever (*auch am Satzende*), no matter what; *~ ihn betrifft* as for him, as far as he's concerned; *~ ich noch sagen wollte ...* the other thing I wanted to say ...; **IV.** *unbest. Pron. umg.* (*etwas*) something; *ich sehe ~, ~ du nicht siehst* I can see something that you can't see; *weißt du schon ~?* have you heard anything?; *ist ~?* what's up?, is anything the matter?; *~ Schlechtes/Gutes/noch etc.* something bad/good/else *etc.*; *~ Neues?* any news?, anything new?; *das ist ~ anderes* that's different; *e-e Palme oder so ~ (Ähnliches)* a palm tree or something like that (*od.* something similar); *na, so ~ bes. iro.* well I never; *~ du nicht sagst!* you don't say!; *hat man so ~ schon gesehen?* have you ever seen anything like it?; *so ~ von blöd!* stupid or what?, how stupid can you get?; *das war vielleicht ~!* that was really something!; *da war doch ~* there 'was something there; *ich will dir ~ sagen* I'll tell you something; *bes. drohend*: I'll tell you what; *du solltest dich ~ schämen!* you ought to be ashamed of yourself!; → *auch so* I 7, *wissen* 2

waschaktiv *Adj.*: *~e Substanzen* detergents

Wasch|anlage *f Mot.* **1.** car wash; **2.** *für Scheiben*: windscreen (*Am.* windshield) washer; **~anleitung** *f* washing instructions *Pl.*; **~automat** *m* washing machine, *Am. auch* washer

waschbar *Adj.* washable; *Farbe*: fast

Waschbär *m Zool.* rac(c)oon, *Am. auch umg.* coon

Wasch|becken *n* washbasin; **~benzin** *n* benzine; *~beton Archit.* washed concrete; **~brett** *n* washboard; **~brettbauch** *m umg.* washboard abs, six-pack

Wäsche *f; -, -n* **1.** *nur Sg.* (*zu waschende od. gewaschene ~*) washing, laundry; (*Tisch-, Bettwäsche*) (table and bed) linen; (*Unterwäsche*) underwear; *die ~ waschen/aufhängen* do / hang out the washing; *schmutzige ~* dirty washing; *die ~ wechseln* put on fresh underwear, change one's (under)pants; *schmutzige ~ waschen fig.* wash one's dirty linen in public; *da hat er aber dumm aus der ~ geguckt umg.* you should have seen his face; *j-m an die ~ gehen umg.* lay into s.o.; *mit sexueller Absicht*: make a pass at s.o.; **2.** (*das Waschen*) wash; *große ~* washday; *in der ~* in the wash, being washed; *in der Wäscherei*: at the laundry; *die morgendliche ~* morning wash; *den Lack nach der ~ konservieren Mot.* preserve the paintwork after washing; → *Blutwäsche, Geldwäsche etc.*; *~beutel m* laundry bag

waschecht *Adj.* colo(u)rfast; *Farbe*: fast; *umg. fig.* genuine, true-blue, *nachgestellt*: to the bone

Wäsche|fach *n* linen drawer; **~geschäft** *n* laundry; **~klammer** *f* clothes peg, *Am.* clothespin; **~knopf** *m* fabric-covered button; **~korb** *m* laundry (*od.* linen) basket; **~leine** *f*: (*auf der*) *~* (on the) clothesline

waschen; *wäscht, wusch, hat gewaschen* **I.** *v/t.* **1.** wash (*auch Bergb., Metall.*); *in der Wäscherei*: *auch* launder; (*Gold etc.*) pan; *umg. fig.* (*illegal erworbenes Geld*) launder; *fachspr.* (*Gas*) scrub; (*Blut*) detoxify; *ich muss heute ~* I have to do the washing today; *das Geschirr ~* wash up, *Am.* do the dishes; *warm/kalt ~* wash in warm/cold water; *mit der Hand ~* hand-wash; *sich (Dat.) die Haare ~* wash one's hair; *einmal Waschen und Legen! beim Friseur*: wash and set, please; → *Hand¹* 4, *Unschuld* 1; **2.** *Naut.*: *ein Brecher wusch übers Deck* a breaker washed over the deck; *von der See über Bord gewaschen werden* be washed overboard by the sea; **II.** *v/refl.* wash o.s., (have a) wash; *er wusch sich und ging ins Bett* he had a wash (*Am.* he washed up) and went to bed; *sich unter den Achseln etc. ~* wash under one's armpits *etc.*; *e-e Ohrfeige/Kritik etc., die sich gewaschen hat umg. fig.* one hell of a clout (a)round the ear / one hell of a critical going-over *etc.*

Wäscher *m; -s, -; Metall.* washer; (*Goldsucher*) panner; **Wäscherei** *f; -, -en* **1.** laundry; **2.** (*Waschsalon*) laund(e)rette, *bes. Am.* Laundromat®; **Wäscherin** *f; -, -nen* washerwoman, laundress

Wäsche|sack *m* laundry bag; **~schleuder** *f* spin drier; **~schrank** *m* linen cupboard (*Am.* closet); **~spinne** *f* telescopic clothesline; **~sprenger** *m* spray bottle; **~ständer** *m* clothes horse; **~stück** *n* piece of laundry; **~tinte** *f* marking ink; **~trockner** *m Gerät*: tumble drier; *Gestell*: clothes horse; **~truhe** *f* linen chest; **~zeichen** *n* name tape

Wasch|frau *f* washerwoman; **~gang** *m* cycle, wash; **~gelegenheit** *f* washing facilities *Pl.*; **~handschuh** *m* flannel mitt; **~haus** *n* washhouse; **~kessel** *m* boiler; **~kraft** *f* cleaning power; **~küche** *f* **1.** washhouse; **2.** *umg.* (*dichter Nebel*) peasouper; **~lappen** *m* **1.** flannel, *Am.* washcloth; **2.** *umg. fig.* (*Schwächling*) sissy, softy; **~lauge** *f* suds *Pl.*; **~leder** *n* chamois (leather); **~lotion** *f* washing lotion

Waschmaschine *f* washing machine, *Am. auch* washer; **waschmaschinenfest** *Adj.* machine-washable

Wasch|mittel *n* (laundry) detergent, washing (*Am.* soap) powder; **~pulver** *n* washing (*Am.* soap) powder; **~programm** *n* washing program(me); **~raum** *m* washroom; **~salon** *m* laund(e)rette, *bes. Am.* Laundromat®; **~schüssel** *f* wash bowl, washbasin; **~straße** *f Mot.* car wash; **~tag** *m* washday; *ich habe heute ~* today is my washday; **~tisch** *m* washstand; (*Waschbecken*) washbasin

Waschung *f* washing; *bes. Med., kirchl.* ablution

Wasch|vollautomat *m* fully automatic washing machine (*Am. auch* washer); **~wasser** *n* washing water; **~weib** *n umg. fig.* (old) gossip; **~zettel** *m im Buch etc.*: blurb; **~zeug** *n* washing things *Pl.*; **~zwang** *m* obsessional washing, *fachspr.* ablutomania

Wasser *n; -s, -* und *Wässer* **1.** *nur Sg.* water; *hartes/weiches ~* hard/soft water; *~ abstoßend od. abweisend* water-repellent; *unter ~ setzen* flood; *unter ~ stehen* be under water, be flooded; *~ aufsetzen für Tee etc.*: put the kettle on; **~ marsch!** *Feuerwehr:* etwa bring up the hoses (*German fire officer's traditional and legendary command to firefighters*); **bei ~ und Brot** altm. umg. in the clink (od. chokey, *Am.* poky), behind bars; **~ ziehen** *Substanz etc.*: absorb water; umg. fig. *Strümpfe etc.*: be at half mast; **ins ~ gehen** (sich umbringen) go into the water, drown o.s.; **2.** Pl. -; (*Mineralwasser*) mineral water; **zwei ~, bitte** two mineral waters, please; **ein ~ mit/ohne Kohlensäure** a glass of sparkling/still (mineral) water; **stilles ~** (ohne Kohlensäure) still water; **3.** Pl. -; (*Gewässer*): **fließendes/ stehendes ~** running/stagnant water; **zu ~ und zu Land** by land and by water; **zu ~ lassen** (Schiff) launch; **unter ~ schwimmen** swim underwater; **auflaufendes/ablaufendes ~** incoming/ outgoing tide; **~ treten** beim Schwimmen: tread water; **bei Kneippkur**: paddle; **~ führend** Fluss-, Bachbett: water-bearing; → **still 4**; **4.** nur Sg.; fig. (*Körperflüssigkeit*): **~ lassen** pass water, urinate; **das ~ nicht halten können** be incontinent; **~ in den Beinen** etc. fluid in one's legs etc.; **das ~ stand ihm auf der Stirn** the sweat was running down his forehead; **da läuft einem das ~ im Mund zusammen** it makes your mouth water; **5.** Pl. Wässer; (*Parfüm etc.*): **wohlriechende Wässer** scents; (Kölnisch Wasser) colognes; **6.** fig., in Wendungen: **sich über ~ halten** keep one's head above water; **ein Berliner reinsten ~s** a Berliner born and bred; **ein Edelstein reinsten ~s** a stone of the first water; **das ist ~ auf s-e Mühle** that's grist to his mill; **ihm steht das ~ bis zum Hals** he's in up to his neck; **ins ~ fallen** Pläne etc.: fall through (od. flat); **sie hat nahe am ~ gebaut** tears come easily to her, she's always on the verge of tears; **bis dahin fließt noch viel ~ den Rhein** od. **die Donau** etc. **hinunter** that's a long way off yet; **die kochen auch nur mit ~** they're no different from anybody else; **er kann ihr nicht das ~ reichen** he's not a patch on her, he can't hold a candle to her; **wie Feuer und ~ sein** be like chalk and cheese; **er ist mit allen ~n gewaschen** he knows every trick in the book; → **abgraben, fließend II 1, Fisch 1, Rotz 1, Schlag 1, schwer I 2**

wasserabstoßend Adj., **Wasser abstoßend, wasserabweisend** Adj., **Wasser abweisend** → Wasser 1

Wasser|ader f water vein; **~anschluss** m mains (*Am.* main) water supply

wasserarm Adj. (dürr) arid

Wasser|aufbereitung f (waste) water treatment; **~aufbereitungsanlage** f (waste) water treatment plant

Wasserbad n Gastr. bain-marie; *Fot.* water bath; **im ~** Gastr. in a bain-marie

Wasser|ball m **1.** groß, aufblasbar: beach ball; **2.** Sport, Ball: (water polo) ball; **3.** nur Sg.; Sport, Sportart: water polo; **~baller** m; -s, -, **~ballerin** f; -, -nen; Sport water polo player

Wasser|bau m nur Sg. hydraulic engineering; **~becken** n Bassin: pool; Behälter: water tank; **~bedarf** m water requirements Pl.; **~behälter** m water-storage tank; bes. kleineren Formats: cistern; **~bett** n water bed; **~blase** f Med. blister, fachspr. vesicle

wasserblau Adj. clear blue

Wasser|blüte f nur Sg.; Öko. (starker

Algenbefall) water bloom; **~bombe** f Mil. depth charge; hum. water bomb (*Am.* balloon); **~burg** f moated castle

Wässerchen n umg.; (Parfüm etc.) scent; (Schnaps) spirit; (Medizin) potion; **er sah so aus, als könne er kein ~ trüben** fig. he looked as if butter wouldn't melt in his mouth

Wasserdampf m steam

wasserdicht Adj. waterproof; Tech., Naut. auch watertight (auch fig. Alibi etc.); **~ machen** waterproof

Wasserdruck m hydraulic pressure

wasserdurchlässig Adj. permeable

Wasser|eimer m bucket, pail; **~einbruch** m inrush of water; **~enthärter** m water softener; **~fahrzeug** n watercraft (auch Pl.), waterborne vehicle, vessel; **~fall** m waterfall; großer: falls Pl.; (Kaskade) cascade; **er redete wie ein ~** umg. fig. he wouldn't stop talking, he just went on and on; **~farbe** f water colo(u)r

wasserfest Adj. waterproof

Wasser|fläche f body (od. expanse) of water; **~flasche** f water bottle; **~fleck** m water stain; **~floh** m water flea; **~flugzeug** n seaplane; **~frosch** m Zool. edible frog

Wasser führend → Wasser 3

Wassergeist m water spirit

wassergekühlt Adj. water-cooled

Wasser|geld n water rate; **~glas** n **1.** nur Sg.; Chem. water glass; **2.** (Trinkglas) tumbler; → **Sturm**; **~glätte** f (slippery) film of water; **~graben** m ditch; Sport water jump; **~gymnastik** f aquarobics Pl. (V. im Sg. od. Pl.); **~hahn** m tap, bes. Am. faucet

wasserhaltig Adj. Chem. aqueous, hydrous; **~ sein** contain water

Wasser|härte f water hardness; **~haushalt** m **1.** water resources Pl.; **2.** bes. Physiol. water balance; **~heilkunde** f Med. hydrotherapy; **~hose** f Met. waterspout; **~huhn** n Orn. coot; **~hülle** f Geol. hydrosphere

wässerig Adj. → wässrig

Wasser|jungfer f Zool. dragonfly; **~kessel** m kettle; Tech. boiler

wasserklar Adj. transparent

Wasser|klosett n water closet; **~knappheit** f water shortage; **~kocher** m electric kettle; **~kopf** m **1.** Med. hydrocephalus (Pl. hydrocephali); **e-n ~ haben** have water on the brain; **2.** fig., umg. (Verwaltung) bloated bureaucracy; **~kraft** f water power; **~kraftwerk** n hydroelectric power plant; **~kreislauf** m water (od. hydrological) cycle; **~kühlung** f water cooling (system); **mit ~** water-cooled; **~kunst** f waterworks Pl.; **~kur** f water cure; **~lache** f pool of water; **~lauf** m watercourse; **~läufer** m Zool. pond-skater, water strider; **~leiche** f drowned corpse; **~leitung** f water pipe(s Pl.); **~lilie** f Bot. water lily; **~linie** f Naut. water line; **~linse** f Bot. duckweed; **~loch** n water hole

wasserlöslich Adj. (water-)soluble; **nicht ~** insoluble in water

Wassermangel m water shortage

Wassermann m **1.** nur Sg.; Astron.: **der ~** (Sternzeichen) Aquarius, the Water Bearer (od. Carrier); **2.** (ein) **~ sein** be (an) Aquarius, be an Aquarian; **3.** Myth. water sprite

Wasser|massen Pl. mass Sg. (od. deluge Sg.) of water; **~melone** f water melon; **~mühle** f water mill

wassern v/i. Flug. touch down on wa-

---

ter; Raumkapsel: splash down

wässern I. v/t. water; (Felder etc.) irrigate; (einweichen, auch Gastr. Heringe etc.) soak; Fot. rinse; **II.** v/i. Augen etc.: water

Wasser|nixe f Myth. water nymph; (Meerjungfrau) mermaid; **~not** f **1.** (Mangel) drought; **2.** altm. (Überschwemmung) flood; **~nymphe** f Myth. water nymph; **~oberfläche** f surface of the water (od. lake, sea etc.); **~orgel** f hydraulic organ; **~pest** f Bot. waterweed; **~pfeife** f water pipe, hookah; **~pflanze** f aquatic plant; **~pfütze** f puddle (of water); **~pistole** f water pistol; **~polizei** f → **Wasserschutzpolizei**; **~pumpe** f water pump; **~qualität** f water quality; **~rad** n water wheel; **~ratte** f **1.** Zool. water rat; (Schermaus) vole; **2.** umg. fig. keen swimmer, water baby; **e-e ~ sein** auch love the water, swim like a fish

Wasserrecht n Jur. laws Pl. relating to water, water conservation, and waterways; **Wasserrechte** Pl. an Quellen, Grundwasser etc.: water rights; **wasserrechtlich** Adj. relating to water laws

wasserreich Adj. Gegend etc.: with plenty of water (resources)

Wasser|reis m Bot. wild rice; **~reservoir** n reservoir; **~rinne** f gutter; **~rohr** n water pipe; **~rohrbruch** m burst (water) pipe; auf der Strasse: auch burst main; **~rose** f Bot. water lily; **~rutsche** f water chute; **~schaden** m water damage; **~scheide** f Geog. watershed

wasserscheu Adj. scared (od. frightened, afraid) of water, fachspr. hydrophobic; **Wasserscheu** f fear of water, hydrophobia fachspr.

Wasser|schildkröte f Zool. turtle; **~schlange** f Zool. water snake; **~schlauch** m **1.** hose; **2.** Bot. bladderwort; **~schloss** n moated castle; im See: castle in a lake

Wasserschutz|gebiet n water reserve; **~polizei** f river police; im Hafen: harbo(u)r police

Wasserschwein n Zool. capybara (Pl. capybara[s])

Wasserski[1] m water ski

Wasserski[2] n (Sport) water skiing; **~ fahren** water-ski, go water-skiing

Wasser|speicher m im Haus: water tank; im Freien: reservoir; **~speier** m; -s, - gargoyle; **~spiegel** m surface of the water; (Stand) water level; **~spiele** Pl. waterworks; **~spinne** f Zool. water spider; **~sport** m water sports Pl.; **~sportler** m, **~sportlerin** f water sports enthusiast; **~spülung** f flush; (Anlage) cistern; **~stand** m water level; **~standsanzeiger** m water ga(u)ge; **~stelle** f watering place

Wasserstoff m Chem. hydrogen; **wasserstoffblond** Adj. umg. peroxide (blonde)

Wasserstoff|bombe f hydrogen bomb, H-bomb; **~brücke** f Chem. hydrogen bond; **~peroxyd** n, **~superoxyd** n altm. hydrogen peroxide

Wasser|strahl m jet of water; **~straße** f waterway, canal; **die ~n Frankreichs** etc. the canals and waterways of France etc.; **~sucht** f Med. dropsy; **~tank** m water tank; **~temperatur** f water temperature; **~tiefe** f depth of (the) water; **~tier** n aquatic animal; **~träger** m water carrier; umg. fig. dogsbody

wassertreibend Adj. Med. diuretic; **~**

W

wirken have a diuretic effect
Wasser|treten *n; -s, kein Pl.* treading water; *bei Kneippkur:* paddling; **~trop-fen** *m* drop of water; **~turbine** *f* water turbine; **~turm** *m* water tower; **~uhr** *f* 1. *hist.* water clock; 2. (*Zähler*) water meter
Wasserung *f Flug.* touchdown on water; *e-r Raumkapsel:* splashdown
Wässerung *f* watering; *von Feldern etc.:* irrigation; (*Einweichen, auch Gastr. von Heringen etc.*) soaking; *Fot.* rinsing, rinse
Wasser|verbrauch *m* water consumption; **~verdrängung** *f* (water) displacement; **~verschmutzung** *f* water pollution; **~versorgung** *f* water supply; **~vogel** *m Orn.* waterbird, *Pl. auch* water fowl (*V. im Pl.*); **~vorrat** *m* water supply; **~waage** *f* spirit level, *Am.* level; **~wacht** *f* water rescue service; **~wanze** *f Zool.* water bug; **~weg** *m* waterway; *auf dem* ~ by water; **~welle** *f Frisur:* water wave; **~werfer** *m auch Pl.* water cannon (*auch Fahrzeug*); **~werk** *n,* **~werke** *Pl. n* waterworks *Pl.* (*oft V. im Sg.*); **~wirtschaft** *f* water supply and distribution, water (resources) management; **~wüste** *f fig.* marine desert; **~zähler** *m* water meter; **~zeichen** *n* watermark
wässrig *Adj.* watery; **~e Lösung** *Chem.* watery solution; *ein* **~es Blau** a watery blue; **~e Augen** watery eyes; *j-m den Mund* ~ *machen umg. fig.* make s.o.'s mouth water (**nach** for); *weitS.* (*für etw. interessieren*) get s.o. all excited (about)
waten *v/i.* wade
Waterkant *f; -, kein Pl.; hum.* North German (North Sea) coast
Waterloo ['vaːtɐlo] *n; -, -s; fig.: sein ~ erleben* meet one's Waterloo
Watsche *f; -n, -n; Dial. umg.* clip (a)round the ears
watschelig I. *Adj. Gang etc.:* waddling; **II.** *Adv. gehen etc.:* with a waddling gait; **watscheln** *v/i.* waddle
watschen *v/t. Dial. umg.* cuff, give *s.o.* a clip round the ear; **Watschen** *f; -, -; Dial. umg.* clip (a)round the ears; **Watschenmann** *m umg. fig.* scapegoat, fall guy
Watt¹ *n; -s, -;* (*abgek. W*); *Etech.* watt; *e-e Glühbirne mit 60* ~ a sixty-watt bulb
Watt² *n; -(e)s, -en; Geog.* mud flats *Pl., Am.* tideland
Watte *f; -, fachspr. -n* cotton wool, *Am.* cotton; *j-n in* ~ *packen umg., fig.* handle s.o. with kid gloves; (*verwöhnen*) mollycoddle s.o.; **~bausch** *m* cotton-wool (*Am.* cotton) swab
Wattenmeer *n Geog.* mud flats, *Am.* tideland
Wattestäbchen *n* cotton bud, *Am. auch* Q-Tip®
wattieren *v/t.* pad, line with wadding; (*Futter*) quilt; **wattiert I.** *P.P.* → *wattieren;* **II.** *Adj. Jacke, Umschlag etc.:* padded; **Wattierung** *f* padding
Watt|meter *n Phys.* wattmeter; **~stun-de** *f* watt hour
Watt|wanderung *f* walk across mud flats at low tide; **~wurm** *m Zool.* lugworm
Watvogel *m Orn.* wader
Wauwau *m; -s, -s; Kinderspr.* bow-wow, doggie
wau, wau *Interj.* bow-wow, woof-woof
WC *n; -(s), -(s)* toilet, *Am.* bathroom, rest room; **~Becken** *n* toilet bowl; **~Bürste** *f* toilet brush; **~Ente** *f zur*

Reinigung: toilet duck; **~Reiniger** *m* toilet cleaner; **~Sitz** *m für Kleinkinder:* (toddler) trainer seat
Web [wɛb] *n; -(s), kein Pl.; EDV* the Web; *im* ~ *surfen* surf the Web; **~adresse** *f EDV* Web address
webbasiert *Adj. Internet:* web-based
weben; *webt, webte od. wob, hat gewebt od. gewoben* **I.** *v/t.* weave; *Spinne (Netz)* spin; **II.** *v/refl. fig.: sich um Legenden etc.:* grow up around
Weber *m; -s, -* weaver
Weberei *f; -, -en* **1.** *nur Sg.* weaving; **2.** (*Fabrik*) weaving mill; **Weberin** *f* weaver
Weber|knecht *m Zool.* daddy longlegs; **~schiffchen** *n* shuttle; **~vogel** *m* weaver bird
Web|fehler *m* flaw; *e-n* ~ *haben umg. fig.* have a screw loose (somewhere), be slightly cracked; **~kante** *f* selvage; **~pelz** *m* (woven) imitation fur
Web|server ['wɛbzøːɐvɐ] *m; -s, -; EDV* Web server; **~seite** *f EDV* web page; **~site** ['-sait] *f; -, -s; EDV* web site
Web|stuhl *m* loom; **~waren** *Pl.* woven goods, textiles
Wechsel *m; -s, -* **1.** change; (*Tausch*) exchange; (*Schwankung*) fluctuation; *in der Regierung etc.:* changeover; *Sport, des Stabs:* (baton) change; *ihr* ~ *vom Finanz- ins Innenministerium etc.* her move from the Ministry of Finance to the Ministry of the Interior *etc.;* **2.** (*Aufeinanderfolge*) *mehrerer Dinge:* succession; *zweier Dinge:* alternation; ~ *der Jahreszeiten* change of seasons; ~ *von Tag und Nacht* alternation of day and night; **3.** *Sport (Seitenwechsel)* change of ends; *e-s Spielers:* substitution; *fliegender* ~ flying substitution; **4.** *Jägerspr. (Wildwechsel)* runway, trail, game pass; **5.** *Agr., der Saat:* rotation; **6.** *Fin.* bill (of exchange); (*Am. im Inland zahlbarer* ~, *Brit. Bankwechsel*) draft; (*monatliche Geldzuwendung*) allowance; *e-n* ~ *ausstellen* draw (*od.* issue) a bill; *gezogener* ~ draft; *der* ~ *ist geplatzt* the bill has bounced
...wechsel *m, im Subst.* **1.** (*Änderung etc.*): *Temperatur~* change of temperature; *Funktions~* change of function; **2.** (*Austausch*): *Filter~* changing the filter; *Magazin~* reloading; *Gewehr: auch* putting in a new magazine
Wechsel|automat *m* change machine (*od.* dispenser); **~bad** *n* hot and cold baths *Pl.; j-n e-m* ~ *aussetzen* blow hot and cold toward(s) s.o.; **~balg** *m* changeling; **~bank** *f Fin.* discount house; **~beziehung** *f* interrelation; *in* ~ *stehen mit* be correlated with; **~bürge** *m Fin.* bill surety; **~bürgschaft** *f Fin.* bill guaranty; **~fälle** *Pl.* vicissitudes, ups and downs *umg.; die* ~ *des Lebens* life's vicissitudes, the vicissitudes (*od.* ups and downs *umg.*) of life; **~geld** *n* change; ~ *bekommen auch* get (some) money back; **~gesang** *m* responsory; **~gespräch** *n* dialog(ue)
wechselhaft *Adj.* changeable; **Wechselhaftigkeit** *f* changeability
Wechsel|jahre *Pl. der Frau:* menopause *Sg.,* climacteric *Sg.,* change of life *Sg.; des Mannes:* male menopause; *in den* ~*n sein Frau:* be going through the menopause (*od.* change of life, one's climacteric); *Mann:* be going through the male menopause; **~kredit** *m Fin.* acceptance credit; (*Diskontkredit*) discount credit; **~kurs** *m Fin.* ex-

change rate, rate of exchange
wechseln I. *v/t.* (*hat gewechselt*) **1.** change (*auch Öl, Reifen etc.*); (*austauschen, auch Schläge, Worte etc.*) exchange; *die Fahrbahn* ~ change (*od.* switch) lanes; *die Kleider* ~ change (one's clothes); *das Hemd etc.* ~ put on a clean shirt *etc.; Unterwäsche zum Wechseln* spare underwear; *den Arbeitsplatz/Arzt* ~ change jobs/doctors, find another job / go to another doctor; *die Schule* ~ change (*od.* switch) schools; *den Partner* ~ change partners; *die Wohnung* ~ move (house), move to another house; *das Zimmer* ~ change rooms, move to another room; → *Besitzer, Thema* 1; **2.** (*Geld*) change; (*Währung*) (ex)change; (*abwechseln [lassen]*) alternate; *Geld* ~ (*in Kleingeld*) get (some) change; *können Sie e-n Hunderter* ~? can you change a hundred euro *etc.* note?; *Dollar in Euro* ~ change dollars into euros; **3.** (*austauschen*) exchange; *ein paar Worte mit j-m* ~ have (*od.* exchange) a few words with s.o.; *sie wechselten Blicke* they exchanged glances; *Briefe mit j-m* ~ correspond with s.o.; **II.** *v/i.* (*ist*) change; (*verschieden sein, abwechseln*) vary; *Wild:* pass; ~ *in* (+ *Akk.*) *od. nach etc.* switch (over) to, move to; *kannst du* ~? (*hast du Kleingeld?*) can you change this?, have you got change for this?; *ich kann nicht* ~ I've got no change
wechselnd I. *Part. Präs.* → *wechseln;* **II.** *Adj.* varying; (*wechselhaft*) changeable; *mit* ~*em Erfolg* with varying degrees of success; *Personen mit häufig* ~*em Geschlechtsverkehr* people who have many different sexual partners; → *Bewölkung* 1; **III.** *Adv.:* ~ *bewölkt etc.* cloudy with bright periods
Wechsel|nehmer *m Fin.* payee (of a bill); **~platte** *f EDV* removable disk; **~rahmen** *m* interchangeable picture frame; **~reiterei** *f Fin.* bill jobbing, kite flying *umg.;* **~richter** *m Etech.* inverter; **~schalter** *m Etech.* changeover switch; **~schicht** *f* alternating shift; **~schritt** *m* change-over step
Wechselschuld *f Fin.* bill debt
wechselseitig *Adj.* (*beiderseitig*) mutual; (*gegenseitig*) *auch* reciprocal; **Wechselseitigkeit** *f* reciprocity
Wechsel|spiel *n* interplay; **~sprechanlage** *f* intercom
wechselständig *Adj. Bot.* alternate
Wechselstrom *m Etech.* alternating current (*Abk.* AC); **~gerät** *n* AC-operated device; **~maschine** *f* AC machine
Wechsel|stube *f* currency exchange, bureau de change; **~summe** *f Fin.* sum payable on a bill of exchange; **~tierchen** *n* am(o)eba (*Pl.* am(o)ebas *od.* am(o)ebae); **~verhältnis** *n* interrelation(ship); **~verkehr** *m Verk.* alternating one-way traffic
wechselvoll *Adj.* varied, eventful; **~e Laufbahn** chequered (*Am.* checkered) career
Wechselwähler *m,* **~in** *f Pol.* floating voter
Wechselwarme *Pl. Zool.* poikilothermic animals
wechselweise *Adv.* alternately, in turn
Wechselwirkung *f* interaction
Wechsler *m; -s, -* **1.** change machine (*od.* dispenser); **2.** *Person:* money-changer; **3.** (*Plattenspieler*) record changer

W

Wechte f; -, -n (snow) cornice

Weck m; -s, -e(n); Dial.; (Brötchen) long roll; (Brot) long loaf

Weckamin n; -s, -e; Pharm. amphetamine derivative

Weckapparat m preserving and bottling equipment

Weck|auftrag m Telef. alarm call, wake-up call; **~dienst** m Telef. alarm call service

Wecke f; -, -n → **Wecken**[1]

Wecken[1] m; -s, -; Dial.; (Brötchen) long roll; (Brot) long loaf

Wecken[2] n; -s, kein Pl.; bes. Mil. reveille; **Urlaub bis zum ~** overnight leave; **wann ist morgen ~?** what time do I/we etc. have to get up tomorrow?

wecken v/t. wake (up), give s.o. a call umg.; (aufstören) rouse (auch fig.); fig. (Erinnerungen) awaken; (auch Gefühle) stir up; **sich (telefonisch) ~ lassen** have o.s. woken (with an alarm call); **der Kaffee weckte s-e Lebensgeister** the coffee brought him back to life

Wecker m; -s, - alarm clock; an der Armbanduhr etc.: alarm; (Küchenwecker) timer; **j-m auf den ~ gehen** umg. fig. get on s.o.'s nerves (od. wick)

Weckglas® n Kilner® (Am. Mason) jar, preserving jar

Weck|ruf m early morning call; Telef. alarm call; **~signal** n alarm

Wedel m; -s, -; (Staubwedel) feather duster; Bot. frond; Zool. (Schwanz) tail, brush; → **Palmwedel** etc.; **wedeln I.** v/i. **1.** (hat gewedelt); Hund etc.: wag (**mit dem Schwanz** its tail); **mit etw. ~** wave s.th.; **2.** (ist); Skisport: wedel; **II.** v/t. (hat): **den Staub vom Regal** etc. **~** whisk the dust off the shelf

weder Konj.: **~ ... noch** neither ... nor; **er rief ~ an, noch schrieb er** he neither phoned nor wrote; he did not phone, (and) nor did he write

weg Adv. away; (weggegangen sein, verloren) gone; (nicht zu Hause) not in; **m-e Uhr ist ~** my watch is (od. has) gone; **der Zug, die Maschine** etc. **ist schon ~** has (already) left; **~ da!** umg. get away!; **~ damit!** umg. take it away!; **Finger** od. **Hände ~!** umg. hands off!; **ich muss ~** I must be off; **nichts wie ~!** let's get out of here, scram! Sl.; **~ sein** umg. (bewusstlos) be out (for the count); nach Alkohol: be gone; (geistesabwesend) be miles away, be away with the fairies; **ganz ~ sein** umg. (begeistert) be thrilled to bits, be over the moon; **ich bin darüber ~** I've got over it, I'm over it; **in e-m ~** umg. non-stop; → **Fenster** 1

Weg m; -(e)s, -e **1.** way (auch Richtung); (Pfad) path (auch fig. und EDV); (Route) route; (Gang) walk; (Besorgung) errand; (~ zum Ziel) course; **am ~(e)** by the wayside; **auf dem ~(e)** on the way; **das liegt auf m-m ~** that's on my way, I'll be passing (by) there on my way (home etc.); **j-m über den ~ laufen** umg. run (od. bump) into s.o.; **sich auf den ~ machen** set off; **j-n nach dem ~ fragen** ask s.o. the way; **j-m den ~ zeigen/beschreiben** show s.o. the way / give s.o. directions; **j-m e-n ~ abnehmen** spare s.o. the trip; **j-m etw. mit auf den ~ geben** give s.o. s.th. to take along with them, give s.o. s.th. for the journey; fig. (Rat etc.) give s.o. s.th. to remember; **aus dem ~(e) gehen** get out of the way, step aside; fig. steer clear (+ Gen. of); fig. → auch 2; **j-m im ~(e) stehen** auch fig. be in s.o.'s way; **j-m**

in den ~ treten bar s.o.'s way; fig. get in s.o.'s way; **2.** fig.: **sein letzter ~** (Beerdigung) his final journey; **den ~ allen Fleisches gehen** geh., euph. go the way of all flesh; **etw./j-n aus dem ~ schaffen** get rid of s.th./s.o.; **aus dem ~ räumen** (Hindernis etc.) clear out of the way; umg. (j-n) get rid of s.o.; **der ~ zum Erfolg** the road to success; **auf dem ~(e) der Besserung** on the road to recovery; **auf dem besten ~(e) sein zu** (+ Inf.) be well on the way to (+ Ger.); **auf dem richtigen ~(e) sein** be on the right track; **j-n auf den richtigen ~ bringen** put s.o. back on the straight and narrow; **er wird s-n ~ machen** he'll go far (od. go places); **ich traue ihm nicht über den ~** umg. I don't trust him an inch, I wouldn't trust him as far as I can throw him; **j-m aus dem ~ gehen** steer clear of s.o.; **s-e eigenen ~e gehen** go one's own way, do one's own thing umg.; **unsere ~e haben sich getrennt** we went our separate ways; **e-r Frage/Entscheidung aus dem ~(e) gehen** evade a question, avoid the issue / avoid making a decision; **j-m** od. **e-r Sache den ~ bereiten** od. **ebnen** pave the way for; (e-r Sache) auch prepare the ground for; etw. **in die ~e leiten** initiate, start s.th. off; (vorbereiten) pave the way for; **da führt kein ~ dran vorbei** umg. there's no way (a)round it; **dem steht nichts im ~(e)** there's nothing to stop it; **der ~ ist das Ziel** the way is the goal; **3.** fig. (Art und Weise, Methode) way; **auf schriftlichem ~(e)** in writing; **auf gesetzlichem ~(e)** legally, by legal means; **auf diplomatischem ~(e)** through diplomatic channels; **auf diesem ~(e)** this way; **neue ~e in der Kindererziehung** new approaches to child education; **neue ~e gehen** try a new tack, pursue a different path; → **abbringen** 1, **bahnen, halb** I 3, **Irdische, Mittel** 1, **Widerstand** 1, **Wille** etc.

Wegbegleiter m, **~in** f → **Weggefährte**

wegbekommen v/t. (unreg., trennb., hat -ge-) **1.** von e-r Stelle: move; (Fleck, Erkältung etc.) get rid of; **2.** umg. (sich zuziehen) get; umg. land o.s.

Wegbereiter m; -s, -, **~in** f; -, -nen pioneer, trailblazer umg.; **der ~ sein für** pave the way for, blaze the trail for

weg|bewegen v/refl. (trennb., hat) move (away); **~blasen** v/t. (unreg., trennb., hat -ge-) blow off (od. away); **wie weggeblasen sein** have completely disappeared; **~bleiben** v/i. (unreg., trennb., ist -ge-) stay away (ausbleiben) not come; (nicht mehr kommen) stop coming; (ausgelassen werden) Sache: be omitted; umg. Motor etc.: cut out, die; **ihm blieb die Luft weg** he couldn't get his breath, he couldn't breathe; → **Spucke**; **~brechen** (unreg., trennb., -ge-) **I.** v/t. (hat) break off; **II.** v/i. (ist) Preise, Kurse: fall; stärker: plummet, slump; Markt etc.: collapse; **~bringen** v/t. (unreg., trennb., hat -ge-) take away; (beseitigen) get rid of; **~denken** v/t. (unreg., trennb., hat -ge-): **sich etw. ~** imagine s.th. isn't there; **es ist aus dem Leben nicht mehr wegzudenken** it's hard to imagine life without it; **~diskutieren** v/t. (trennb., hat -ge-) explain (od. rationalize) away; **~drehen** v/t. (trennb., hat -ge-) **1.** (Gesicht) turn away; **2.** (Ton) turn down; **~drücken** v/t. (trennb., hat

-ge-) push away; **~dürfen** v/i. (unreg., trennb., hat -ge-); umg. be allowed to go (ausgehen: go out); **ich darf hier jetzt nicht weg** I've got to stay here, I'm not allowed to leave yet

Wegegeld n **1.** hist. road toll; **2.** travel allowance

Wegelagerer m; -s, -; hist. highwayman

wegen Präp. because of, on account of; (infolge) auch due to, as a result of, owing to; (um ... willen) for the sake of, for; **~ Mord(es)** for murder; **von Berufs ~** etc. for professional reasons; **von ~!** umg. you must be joking!; (ist verboten) no way!; **von ~ faul!** umg. lazy, my foot!, what do you mean, lazy?!; → **Amt** 2, **Recht** etc.

Wegerecht n; nur Sg.; Jur. right of way

Wegerich m; -s, -e; Bot. plantain

Wegesrand m geh. wayside

weg|essen v/t. (unreg., trennb., hat -ge-); umg. eat up; **er hat mir alles weggegessen** he ate all my sandwiches etc.; (Vorräte etc.) he's eaten me out of house and home; **~fahren** (unreg., trennb., -ge-) **I.** v/t. (hat) take away; (auch Auto) drive away; **II.** v/i. (ist) leave

Wegfahrsperre f Mot.: **elektronische ~** electronic immobilizer

Wegfall m; nur Sg. discontinuation, ending, cessation; (Auslassung) omission; (Streichung) removal, cancel(l)ation; **wegfallen** v/i. (unreg., trennb., hat -ge-); (ausgelassen werden) be left out; (unnötig werden) become unnecessary; (ausfallen) be cancel(l)ed; (aufhören) cease; (ungültig werden) Regel etc.: be dropped

weg|fegen (trennb., -ge-) **I.** v/t. (hat) sweep away (fig. aside); **II.** v/i. (ist): ~ **über** (+ Akk.) Wind: sweep across; **~fischen** v/t. (trennb., hat -ge-) → **wegschnappen**; **~fliegen** v/i. (unreg., trennb., ist -ge-) Hut etc.: fly off; **wir sind um drei von Miami weggeflogen** we left (od. took off from) Miami at three; **~fressen** v/t.: **den anderen Tieren** etc. **alles ~** eat up everything leaving nothing for the other animals etc.; **~führen** (trennb., hat -ge-) **I.** v/t. lead (od. take) away, lead off; **II.** v/i.: **vom Ort/Thema** etc. **~** lead away from the place/subject etc.

Weggabelung f fork

Weggang m; nur Sg.: **nach s-m** etc. **~** after he etc. had gone (od. left)

weggeben v/t. (unreg., trennb., hat -ge-) give away (auch Kind); umg. (wegwerfen) throw away; **die Wäsche ~** take (od. send) the (od. one's) washing to the laundry; **zur Reparatur ~** take to be repaired

Weg|gefährte m, **~gefährtin** f travel(l)ing companion; **j-s politischer Weggefährte** s.o.'s political companion (od. fellow-travel[l]er)

weggehen v/i. (unreg., trennb., ist -ge-) **1.** go away, leave; (ausgehen) go out; **von j-m ~** umg. leave s.o.; **geh mir weg damit!** umg. I don't want to know about it; **2.** umg. Flecken: come off (od. out), go away; Schmerz etc.: go away. **3.** Ware: sell; → **Semmel**; **4.** fig.: **~ über** (+ Akk.) pass over

weg|gießen v/t. (unreg., trennb., hat -ge-) pour away; **~gucken** v/i. (trennb., hat -ge-); umg. → **wegsehen**; **kannst du mal kurz ~?** can you just look away for a moment?

weghaben v/t. (unreg., trennb., hat -ge-) **1.** etw. **~ wollen** want to get rid of s.th.; **2.** umg.: **etw. ~** (beherrschen)

W

be good at s.th.; (*begreifen*) have got s.th.; **einen ~** (*betrunken sein*) have had one over the limit; (*auch* **e-n Schlag ~**) have a screw loose (somewhere); **s-n Denkzettel** *etc.* **~** have had one's punishment; → **Fett** 1, **Knacks** 3, **Ruhe** 4

weg|hängen *v/t.* (*trennb., hat -ge-*) hang *s.th.* away; **~holen** *v/t.* (*trennb., hat -ge-*) take away, (come to) fetch; **~hören** *v/i.* (*trennb., hat -ge-*) try not to listen; shut one's ears; **könnt ihr mal ~?** could you shut your ears for a minute?; **~jagen** *v/t.* (*trennb., hat -ge-*) chase away; (*j-n*) *auch* send *s.o.* packing *umg.*; **~kippen** (*trennb., -ge-*) *umg.* **I.** *v/t.* (*hat*); (*Flüssigkeit*) tip away; **e-n ~** (*Schnaps etc.*) knock one back; **II.** *v/i.* (*ist*) faint; **~kommen** *v/i.* (*unreg., trennb., ist -ge-*) get away; *Sport* get off; (*verloren gehen*) get lost; **gut/schlecht ~** *fig.* come off well/badly; **~ über** (+ *Akk.*) get over *s.th.*

Wegkreuz *n* wayside cross

wegkriegen *v/t.* (*trennb., hat -ge-*); *umg.* → **wegbekommen**

Weglänge *f* **1.** *bei Wanderungen:* distance; **2.** *Phys.* path length

weglassen *v/t.* (*unreg., trennb., hat -ge-*) **1.** *umg.* let *s.o.* go; **2.** (*Sache*) leave out

weg|laufen *v/i.* (*unreg., trennb., ist -ge-*) run away; **von zu Hause ~** run away from home; **ihm ist die Frau weggelaufen** *umg.* his wife has left him; **das läuft mir nicht weg** *umg.* it won't run away; **~legen** *v/t.* (*trennb., hat -ge-*) put aside (*od.* away); **~leugnen** *v/t.* (*trennb., hat -ge-*) *mst Inf.:* deny; **~loben** *v/t.* (*trennb., hat -ge-*); *umg.:* **j-n ~** *etwa* smooth *s.o.'s* way out, get rid of *s.o.* by writing a glowing reference; **~locken** *v/t.* (*trennb., hat -ge-*) lure away; **~machen** (*trennb., hat -ge-*) *umg.* **I.** *v/t.* (*Fleck etc., auch Kind*) get rid of; **sich** (*Dat.*) **etw. ~ lassen** (*Warze etc.*) have s.th. removed; **mach das wieder weg!** get rid of it!; **II.** *v/refl.* clear off, do a bunk, *Am.* take a powder

wegmüssen *v/i.* (*unreg., trennb., hat -ge-*); *umg.* have to go; **ich muss weg** I must (*Am.* have) to be off (*od.* be going); **ich muss kurz weg** I have to leave for a short time

Wegnahme *f;* -, *kein Pl.* removal, taking away; **wegnehmen** *v/t.* (*unreg., trennb., hat -ge-*) take (*auch Spielfigur*); (*sich aneignen*) take away (**j-m** from *s.o.*); (*entfernen*) remove; (*Licht, Aussicht*) block; (*Sonne*) block out; (*Licht, Lärm*) shut out; (*Platz, Zeit etc.*) take up; **Gas ~** *Mot.* ease off the gas; **j-m die Frau ~** *umg.* steal *s.o.'s* wife

weg|operieren *v/t.* (*trennb., hat*); *umg.* remove, cut out; **~packen** (*trennb., hat -ge-*) pack away; **~putzen** (*trennb., hat -ge-*) *umg.* wipe off; *umg.* (*essen*) polish off, put (*od.* stow) away

Wegrand *m:* (**am**) **~** (by the) wayside

weg|rationalisieren *v/t.* (*trennb., hat*) (*Arbeitsplätze, Personal*) do away with (during a rationalization process), cut; **~räumen** *v/t.* (*trennb., hat -ge-*) clear away; *fig.* remove; **~reißen** *v/t.* (*unreg., trennb., hat -ge-*) tear away (*od.* off); (*Haus*) tear (*od.* pull) down; **die Brücke ~** *Fluss:* sweep away the bridge; **j-m etw. ~** snatch s.th. (away) from *s.o.*; **~rennen** *v/i.* (*unreg., trennb., ist -ge-*) run away; **mit Ziel:** *auch* run off; **~rücken** (*trennb., -ge-*) *v/t.* (*hat*) und

v/i. (*ist*) move away; **~rutschen** *v/i.* (*trennb., ist -ge-*) *Fuß, Leiter:* slip; *Boden:* give way; *Fahrzeug, Räder:* skid, go into a skid; **~sacken** *v/i.* (*trennb., ist -ge-*) *umg. Naut.* sink; *Flug.* drop, lose height; (*zusammenbrechen*) give way; **ihm sackten die Beine weg** his legs gave way (under him); **~schaffen** *v/t.* (*trennb., hat -ge-*) take away; (*Arbeit*) get through, get *s.th.* out of the way; **~schauen** *v/i.* (*trennb., hat -ge-*) → **wegsehen**; **~scheren** *v/refl.* (*trennb., hat -ge-*); *umg.* clear off; **~schicken** *v/t.* (*trennb., hat -ge-*) send away; **~schieben** *v/t.* (*unreg., trennb., hat -ge-*) push away; (*Teller etc.*) *auch* push aside; **~schleichen** *v/i.* (*unreg., trennb., hat -ge-*) sneak away (*od.* off); **~schleppen** *v/t.* (*trennb., hat -ge-*) drag off; **~schließen** *v/t.* (*unreg., trennb., hat -ge-*) lock away; **~schmeißen** *v/t.* (*unreg., trennb., hat -ge-*) *umg.* chuck away, toss (away); **~schnappen** *v/t.* (*trennb., hat -ge-*); *umg.* snatch *s.th.* away (**j-m** from *s.o.*); (*Freundin*) steal, *Brit. auch* pinch; **j-m etw. ~** (*Job, Kleid*) snatch *s.th.* away from under *s.o.'s* eyes

weg|schneiden *v/t.* (*unreg., trennb., hat -ge-*) cut away; **bitte oben** *etc.* **nicht so viel ~!** *beim Friseur:* please don't take too much off on top *etc.*; **~schütten** *v/t.* (*trennb., hat -ge-*); (*Abfall etc.*) dump; (*Flüssigkeit*) pour away; **~schwemmen** *v/t.* (*trennb., hat -ge-*) wash away; **~sehen** *v/i.* (*unreg., trennb., hat -ge-*) look away; *bes. verlegen:* look the other way; → **hinwegsehen**; **~setzen** (*trennb., hat -ge-*) **I.** *v/t.* put away; (*schwatzenden Schüler etc.*) move, sit *s.o.* somewhere else; **II.** *v/refl.* move (away); **sich ~ über** (+ *Akk.*) *fig.* → **hinwegsetzen** II; **~sollen** *v/i.* (*trennb., hat -ge-*); *umg.* be to go; **die alte Mühle soll weg** the old mill is to go (*od.* is going to come down); **~springen** *v/i.* (*unreg., trennb., ist -ge-*) leap aside; **~spülen** *v/t.* (*trennb., hat -ge-*) wash away (*auch Geol.*); **~stecken** *v/t.* (*trennb., hat -ge-*) *umg.* **1.** put away; (*verbergen*) hide; **2.** (*Beleidigung etc.*) swallow; (*Schlag*) take; **er kann viel ~** he can take a fair bit (of punishment); **~stehlen** *v/refl.* (*unreg., trennb., hat -ge-*) steal away, sneak away (*od.* off); **~sterben** *v/i.* (*unreg., trennb., ist -ge-*) *umg.* **1.** die off; **zu Tausenden ~** die (off) in the(ir) thousands *etc.*, go down like flies; **2.** **j-m ~** die before *s.o.'s* eyes, die on *s.o.*; **drei Kinder sind ihr weggestorben** three children died on her; **~stoßen** *v/t.* (*unreg., trennb., hat -ge-*) push away

Wegstrecke *f* stretch; *zurückgelegte:* distance covered; **schlechte ~** *Verk.* bad stretch of road, poor road surface

weg|streichen *v/t.* (*unreg., trennb., hat -ge-*) **1.** cross out; **2.** **die Haare von der Stirn ~** brush the hair away from one's forehead; **~tauchen** *v/i.* (*trennb., ist -ge-*) **1.** *U-Boot etc.:* submerge; *Person:* disappear under the water; *umg. fig.* disappear from the scene; **2.** *umg. fig.* (*abschalten*) switch off; (*einnicken*) nod off; **~treiben** (*unreg., trennb., hat -ge-*) **I.** *v/t.* (*hat*) drive away; **II.** *v/i.* (*ist*) drift away; **~treten** (*unreg., trennb., -ge-*) **I.** *v/i.* (*ist*) step aside; *Mil.* break (the) ranks; **~ lassen** dismiss; **geistig weggetreten** *umg.* away with the fairies, in another world; **II.** *v/t.* (*hat*); (*Ball etc.*) kick away;

~trinken *v/t.* (*unreg., trennb., hat -ge-*); *umg.:* **j-m alles ~** drink *s.o.* dry; **das ganze Bier ~** drink up all the beer; **~tun** *v/t.* (*unreg., trennb., hat -ge-*); *umg.* put away; (*wegwerfen*) chuck (*bes. Am.* toss) out

Wegwarte *f;* -, -n; *Bot.* chicory

wegwehen (*trennb., -ge-*) **I.** *v/t.* (*hat*) blow away; **II.** *v/i.* (*ist*) blow away

wegweisend *Adj. fig.:* **~es Urteil** *etc.* landmark decision *etc.*; **~ sein** point the way to the future; **Wegweiser** *m;* -s, -. **1.** signpost; *Schild:* sign; *in Gebäude:* directory; **2.** (*Buch*) guide (**durch** to)

weg|wenden (*auch unreg., trennb., hat -ge-*) **I.** *v/t.* turn away; **den Blick ~** avert one's gaze (*od.* eyes); **II.** *v/refl.* turn away; **~werfen** (*unreg., trennb., hat -ge-*) **I.** *v/t.* throw away, bin *umg.*, *Am.* toss *umg.*; **sein Leben ~** (*sich umbringen*) take one's own life; (*sich sinnlos aufopfern*) throw one's life away; **II.** *v/refl.* waste o.s. (**an** + *Akk.* on); (*sich erniedrigen*) degrade o.s.; **~werfend I.** *Part. Präs.* → **wegwerfen**; **II.** *Adj. Geste etc.:* dismissive, disdainful; **III.** *Adv. behandeln etc.:* dismissively, disdainfully

Wegwerf|... *im Subst.* disposable ...; **~feuerzeug** *n* disposable lighter; **~flasche** *f* non-returnable bottle; **~geschirr** *n* disposable tableware; **~gesellschaft** *f* throwaway society; **~mentalität** *f* throwaway mentality

weg|wischen *v/t.* (*trennb., hat -ge-*) wipe off; *fig.* (*Einwand etc.*) dismiss; **~wollen** *v/i.* (*unreg., trennb., hat -ge-*) *umg.* want to get away; (*ausgehen wollen*) want to go out; **ich will hier weg** I want to get away from this place; **~zaubern** *v/t.* (*trennb., hat -ge-*) spirit away

Wegzehrung *f* **1.** *geh.* provisions for the journey; **2.** *kath.* viaticum (*Pl.* viatica)

wegziehen (*unreg., trennb., -ge-*) **I.** *v/t.* (*hat*) pull away; **II.** *v/i.* (*ist*); (*umziehen*) move (to another place); **wir sind 1999 weggezogen** we left (*od.* moved [away]) in 1999; **Wegzug** *m:* **nach s-m ~** *etc.* after he moved away

weh *Adj. attr.* (*schmerzend*) sore; **mir ist so ~ ums Herz** I feel so sick at heart; **o ~!** oh dear!, *Am. auch* oy veh!; → **wehtun**

Weh *n;* -(e)s, -e, *mst Sg.* pain; *seelisches: auch* grief; **unter ~ und Ach** *umg.* with a lot of moaning and groaning

wehe *Interj.:* **~ dir, wenn ...!** you'll be sorry if ...!; **~, du tust ihr weh!** *umg.* don't hurt her, or else!; **~, ~! *umg. drohend:* don't you dare!

Wehe[1] *f;* -, -n; (*Schnee, Sand*) drift

Wehe[2] *f;* -, -en; *mst Pl.* labo(u)r pains, labo(u)r *Sg.*; *fig.* travail *Sg.*; **in den ~n liegen** be in labo(u)r; **die ~n setzten ein** labo(u)r (*od.* the contractions) started

wehen *vt/i.* blow; *Fahne:* wave, flutter; *Duft, Töne etc.:* drift, waft; **im Wind(e) ~** wave in the wind; **der Wind weht eisig** there's an icy wind (blowing); **~de Gewänder** flowing robes; → **Wind** 2

Wehgeschrei *n* wailing (*auch fig.*)

Wehklage *f lit.* lament; **wehklagen** *v/i.* (*untr., hat ge-*) wail, lament (**über** +*Akk.* over)

wehleidig *Adj.* self-pitying, *attr. auch* snivel(l)ing ... *umg.*; *Ton, Stil:* maudlin; *Stimme:* plaintive; **sei nicht so ~!** stop feeling so sorry for yourself, stop snivel(l)ing *umg.*; **Wehleidigkeit** *f* self-pity; *des Tons, der Stimme*: plaintiveness

Wehmut *f* melancholy; *voller ~* melancholy; **wehmütig I.** *Adj. bes. Stimmung*: melancholy; *Blick, Lächeln etc.*: wistful; **II.** *Adv. lächeln etc.*: wistfully

Wehr¹ *f*; *-, -en* **1.** *nur Sg.*: *sich zur ~ setzen* defend o.s., stand up for o.s.; **2.** *(Feuerwehr)* fire brigade, *Am.* fire department

Wehr² *n*; *-(e)s, -e*; *(Stauwehr)* weir, barrage; *größer*: dam

Wehr|beauftragte *m, f Mil.* defen|ce *(Am.* -se) commissioner (of the German Bundestag); **~bereich** *m* military district

Wehrdienst *m*; *nur Sg.*; *Mil.* military service; *den ~ ableisten/verweigern* do / refuse to do one's military service; **~beschädigung** *f* disability incurred during military service; **~leistende** *m*; *-n, -n* person doing military service

wehrdienst|tauglich *Adj. Mil.* fit for military service; **~untauglich** *Adj.* not fit for military service

Wehrdienst|verweigerer *m* conscientious objector; **~verweigerung** *f* conscientious objection

wehren I. *v/refl.* defend o.s., stand up for o.s.; *sich gegen etw. ~* resist s.th.; *sich (dagegen) ~, etw. zu tun* refuse to do s.th.; *er weiß sich zu ~* he can handle it; *ich wehre mich dagegen, dass ...* I refuse to accept that ...; *sich mit Händen und Füßen ~ (gegen)* put up a fierce struggle (against), fight tooth and nail (not to do *s.th.*); **II.** *v/i.*: *wehret den Anfängen!* nip it in the bud!

Wehrersatzdienst *m → Zivildienst*

Wehretat *m Mil.* defen|ce *(Am.* -se) budget

wehrfähig *Adj. Mil.* fit for military service; **Wehrfähigkeit** *f* fitness for military service

Wehr|gang *m hist.* al(l)ure *fachspr.*, walkway behind battlements; **~gerechtigkeit** *f Mil.* equal treatment for all people liable for military service

wehrhaft *Adj.* **1.** *Person, Tier*: able to defend himself *(od. herself, itself etc.)*; **2.** *Stadt*: fortified; **Wehrhaftigkeit** *f* **1.** *Person, e-s Tiers*: ability to defend himself *(od. herself, itself etc.)*; **2.** *e-r Stadt*: defensibility

Wehrkirche *f hist.* fortified church

Wehrkraft *f*; *nur Sg.*; *Mil.* military strength; **~zersetzung** *f* undermining the military strength (of a country), demoralization of (a country's) armed forces

wehrlos I. *Adj.* defenceless, *Am.* defenseless; *(hilflos)* helpless; **II.** *Adv. zusehen müssen etc.*: helplessly; *e-r Sache ~ gegenüberstehen* be helpless in the face of s.th.; **Wehrlosigkeit** *f* defencelessness, *Am.* defenselessness; helplessness

Wehr|macht *f*; *nur Sg.*; *hist.* (German) Armed Forces *Pl.*, Wehrmacht; **~mann** *m* **1.** *(Feuerwehrmann)* firefighter; **2.** *schw.* soldier; **~pass** *m Mil.* service record (book)

Wehrpflicht *f*; *nur Sg.*; *Mil.* conscription, *(auch die allgemeine ~)* compulsory military service; **wehrpflichtig** *Adj.* liable for military service; **Wehrpflichtige** *m*; *-n, -n* person liable for military service; *(Eingezogener)* conscript, *Am. auch* draftee

Wehr|sold *m Mil.* (soldier's) pay; **~sport** *m* war games *Pl.*; *als NS-*

-*Schulfach*: military training; **~technik** *f Mil.* defen|ce *(Am.* -se) technology; **~turm** *m hist.* fortified tower; **~übung** *f Mil.* reserve duty training

wehtun *v/i.* *(unreg., trennb., hat -ge-)* hurt; *j-m ~ auch fig.* hurt s.o.; *mir tut der Finger weh* my finger hurts; *mir tut der Magen/Kopf/Rücken weh* I've got (a) stomach ache / a headache, / (a) backache; *sich (Dat.) ~* hurt o.s.; *mir tut das Herz weh lit.* my heart is aching

Wehwehchen *n umg.* little complaint; *er rennt mit jedem ~ zum Arzt* he runs to the doctor with every little thing

Weib *n*; *-(e)s, -er*; *häufig neg!* woman *(auch pej.)*; *altm. (Gattin)* wife; **Weibchen** *n* **1.** *Zool.* female; **2.** *pej.*: *sie ist ein richtiges ~* she doesn't seem to have heard of women's lib; **3.** *umg. altm. (Ehefrau)* little woman, missus

Weiber|fastnacht *f Dial.* Thursday before Shrove Tuesday, the day in the Carnival season when women traditionally take control; **~feind** *m* womanhater, misogynist; **~geschichten** *Pl. umg.* affairs, conquests, sexploits *hum.*; *er mit s-n ~!* auch him and his womanizing; **~geschwätz** *n pej.* (women's) gossip; **~held** *m pej.* lady-killer; **~volk** *n pej.* women(folk) *Pl.*

weibisch *Adj. pej.* effeminate

weiblich *Adj.* **1.** female; *Wesensart*: feminine; **2.** *Ling. und Reim*: feminine; **Weiblichkeit** *f* **1.** femininity; **2.** *hum.*: *die holde ~* the fair sex

Weibsbild *n pej.* woman, female, *Am. auch* broad *umg.*

weich I. *Adj.* **1.** soft *(auch Fot., Gaumen)*; *(glatt)* auch smooth; *fig. Mensch, Herz etc.*: soft; *~ machen* soften; *~ werden* soften *(auch umg. fig.)*; *umg. fig.* *(nachgeben)* give in; *lass dich von ihm nicht ~ machen* don't let him get (a)round you; *sich ~ anfühlen* feel soft, be soft to the touch; *mir wurden die Knie ~* I went weak in the knees, my knees turned to jelly; *du hast wohl 'ne ~e Birne?* umg. have you gone soft in the head?; **2.** *Fleisch*: tender; *Ei*: soft-boiled; *Gemüse*: cooked; **3.** *fig.*: *~e Droge/Währung* soft drug/currency; **II.** *Adv.*: *~ landen* have a soft landing; *~ gekocht Ei*: soft boiled; *das Gemüse ist zu ~ gekocht* the vegetables are overcooked

Weichbild *n*; *mst Sg. e-r Stadt etc.*: outskirts *Pl.*, suburbs *Pl.*

Weiche¹ *f*; *-, -n*; *Anat.* flank, side

Weiche² *f*; *-, -n*; *Eisenb.* points *Pl.*, *Am.* switch; *die ~n stellen* set the points, *Am.* throw the switch; *fig.* point the way ahead; *die ~n stellen für ... fig.* open the way for ...

Weichei *n fig. pej. (Weichling)* softy, sissy, wimp, wet

weichen¹ *v/t. (hat geweicht) und v/i. (ist)* soak *(auch ~ lassen)*

weichen² *v/i.*; *weicht, wich, ist gewichen*; *(weggehen)* move; *Mil.* retreat; *fig.* give way (+ *Dat.* to), yield (to); *(Platz machen)* make way (for); *zur Seite ~* step aside; *j-m nicht von der Seite ~* not leave s.o.'s side; *pej.* cling to s.o. like a leech; *nicht von der Stelle ~* not move (an inch); *die Angst wich von ihr fig.* her fear left her → *wanken* 2

Weichenwärter *m* pointsman, *Am.* switchman

weich gekocht → weich II

Weichheit *f* softness; *(Glattheit)* auch smoothness

weichherzig *Adj.* soft(-hearted)

Weich|holz *n* softwood; **~käse** *m Gastr.* soft cheese; *(Streichkäse)* cheese spread

weichlich *Adj.* soft; *fig. Person*: weak; *pej. (weibisch)* effeminate; *Charakter*: soft; **~er Typ** *pej.* weakling; **Weichlichkeit** *f* weakness; *(Weibischkeit)* effeminacy; **Weichling** *m*; *-s, -e*; *pej.* weakling

weichlöten *v/t. (trennb., hat -ge-)*; *Tech.* soft-solder

weich machen → weich I 1

Weichmacher *m Tech.* softener, softening agent; *für Fleisch*: tenderizer

Weichsel¹ *f*; *-*; *Geog.*: *die ~* the Vistula

Weichsel² *f*; *-, -n*, **~kirsche** *f österr.*, *Bot. (Sauerkirsche) rot*: sour cherry; *schwarz*: morello (cherry)

Weich|spüler *m* fabric softener; **~teile** *Pl. Anat.* soft parts; abdomen *Sg.*; *umg. (Genitalien)* privates; **~tier** *n* mollusc, *Am.* mollusk; **~zeichner** *m Fot.* soft-focus lens

Weide¹ *f*; *-, -n*; *Bot., Baum*: willow; *Material*: mst wicker; *der Korb ist aus ~* it's a wicker basket

Weide² *f*; *-, -n für Tiere*: pasture, meadow; *Am., ohne Zäune*: range, rangeland; *auf der ~ sein Vieh*: be grazing; **~fläche** *f* pasture; **~land** *n* pasture, *Am. auch* range

weiden I. *v/i.* graze; **II.** *v/t.* (put out to) pasture, *Am. auch* range; **III.** *v/refl. fig.*: *sich ~ an* (+ *Dat.*) revel in; *schadenfroh*: gloat over; *e-m Anblick*: feast one's eyes on

Weiden|gerte *f* willow rod *(od.* switch); *zum Korbflechten*: osier, wicker; **~kätzchen** *n* catkin, pussy willow; **~korb** *m* wicker basket; **~röschen** *n Bot.* willowherb; **~rute** *f → Weidengerte*

Weide|platz *m* pasture; **~vieh** *n* cattle at pasture, grazing *(Am. auch* range) cattle; **~wirtschaft** *f* pastural farming, *Am.* ranching

weidgerecht *Adj. und Adv.* in accordance with good huntsmanship

weidlich *Adv.* thoroughly, properly; *e-e Gelegenheit ~ ausnutzen* take full advantage *(od.* make full use) of an opportunity

Weidmann *m* huntsman; **weidmännisch** *Adj.* hunting ..., huntsman's ...

Weidmanns|dank *Interj.*: *~! customary reply to Weidmannsheil!* thank you; *zu anderen Jägern*: and good hunting to you too!; **~heil** *Interj.*: *~! good hunting!*

Weidwerk *n* (art of) hunting

weidwund *Adj.* (mortally wounded through being) shot in the belly; *~ schießen* shoot in the belly

weigern *v/refl.* refuse; **Weigerung** *f* refusal; **Weigerungsfall** *m Amtsspr.*: *im ~e* in the event of a refusal

Weihbischof *m kath.* suffragan (bishop)

Weihe¹ *f*; *-, -n* **1.** *kirchl.* consecration; *e-s Priesters*: ordination; *j-m die ~ erteilen e-m Priester*: ordain s.o.; *e-m Bischof*: auch consecrate s.o.; *die heiligen ~n empfangen* take (holy) orders; *die höheren ~n haben fig. hum.* have been officially ordained *(zu* as); **2.** *(Feierlichkeit)* solemnity

Weihe² *f*; *-, -n*; *Orn.* harrier

weihen *v/t.* **1.** *kirchl.* consecrate; *zum Priester*: ordain; *j-n zum Bischof ~* consecrate s.o. bishop; *j-n zum Priester ~* ordain s.o. priest; *e-e Kirche e-m Heiligen ~* dedicate a church to a

W

saint; **2.** *fig.*: *sein Leben / sich e-r Idee* ~ dedicate (*od.* devote) one's life / o.s. to an idea; → *geweiht*

Weiher *m*; *-s*, - pond

Weihestätte *f* shrine; **weihevoll** *Adj.* solemn

Weih|gabe *f*, **~geschenk** *n bes. kath.* votive offering

Weihnacht *f*; *-*, *kein Pl.*; *geh.* Christmas

Weihnachten *n*; *-*, - Christmas, *verkürzt*: Xmas; *fröhliche od. frohe* ~! merry Christmas!; *auf Karten: auch* Season's Greetings; (*zu od. an*) ~ at (*od.* over) Christmas; *zu* ~ *schenken* give *s.o. s.th.* for Christmas; *wir hatten weiße* ~ we had a white Christmas; *wir hatten grüne* ~ it didn't snow at all over Christmas; ~ *steht vor der Tür* Christmas is just around the corner; → *wünschen* I 1

weihnachten *v/impers.*: *es weihnachtet sehr* Christmas is on its (*od.* the) way; **weihnachtlich I.** *Adj. attr.* Christmas ..., *auch präd.* Christmassy; **II.** *Adv. geschmückt etc.*: ... for Christmas; ~ *gestimmt sein* be in a Christmas(sy) mood

Weihnachts|abend *m* Christmas Eve; **~artikel** *m* Christmas thing, Christmas item; **~bäckerei** *f* **1.** *nur Sg.*; (*das Backen*) Christmas baking; **2.** *bes. österr.* (*Gebäck*) Christmas biscuits (*Am.* cookies) *Pl.*; **~basar** *m* Christmas bazaar; **~baum** *m* Christmas tree; **~botschaft** *f Reli.* Christmas message; **~braten** *m* Christmas turkey (*od.* goose *etc.*), Christmas roast; **~dekoration** *f* Christmas decoration(s *Pl.*); **~einkäufe** *Pl.* Chistmas shopping *Sg.*; **~engel** *m* Christmas angel; **~feier** *f* Christmas party; **~feiertag** *m* → *Weihnachtstag*; **~ferien** *Pl.* Christmas holiday(s) (*Am.* vacation); **~fest** *n* Christmas; **~gans** *f* Christmas goose; *j-n ausnehmen wie e-e* ~ *umg. fig.* fleece s.o., take s.o. to the cleaner's; **~gebäck** *n* Christmas biscuits (*Am.* cookies) *Pl.*; **~geld** *n* Christmas bonus; **~geschäft** *n* (pre-)Christmas sales *Pl.*; **~geschichte** *f*: *die* ~ *bibl.* the Christmas story; **~geschenk** *n* Christmas present; **~gratifikation** *f* Christmas bonus; **~grüße** *Pl.* season's greetings, best wishes for Christmas; **~insel** *f Geog.*: *die* ~ Christmas Island; **~karte** *f* Christmas card; **~lied** *n* Christmas carol; **~mann** *m* **1.** *der* ~ Santa (Claus), *bes. Brit. auch* Father Christmas; *wir warten auf den* ~ we're waiting for our Christmas presents; *du glaubst wohl an den* ~! *umg.* I suppose you still believe in Father Christmas!; **2.** *umg. pej.* dope, dummy; **~markt** *m* Christmas fair; **~oratorium** *n Mus.* Christmas Oratorio; **~päckchen** *n* Christmas parcel; **~plätzchen** *n* Christmas biscuit (*Am.* cookie); **~papier** *n* Christmas wrapping paper; **~pyramide** *f* pyramid-shaped Christmas ornament with figures on shelves and candles at the bottom whose heat drives a set of revolving vanes at the top; **~spiel** *n* nativity play; **~stern** *m* **1.** Christmas star; *bibl.* star of Bethlehem; **2.** *Bot.* poinsettia; **~stimmung** *f* festive atmosphere (*od.* mood) (of Christmas); *es wollte keine rechte* ~ *aufkommen* we *etc.* couldn't manage to muster up any real Christmas spirit; **~stolle** *f*, **~stollen** *m* Christmas stollen (*fruit loaf*); **~tag** *m*: *der erste* ~ Christmas Day; *der zweite* ~ Boxing Day, *Am.* the day after Christmas;

~teller *m* plate of Christmas goodies; **~tisch** *m* table on which the Christmas presents are laid out; **~trubel** *m* Christmas rush; **~verkehr** *m* Christmas traffic; **~wunsch** *m* Christmas wish; **~zeit** *f* Christmastime, Christmas (season)

Weihrauch *m* incense; **~fass** *n* censer, thurible

Weihwasser *n* holy water; *etw. fürchten wie der Teufel das* ~ *umg. fig.* have a mortal terror of s.th.; **~becken** *n*, **~kessel** *m* stoup; **~wedel** *m* aspergillum (*Pl.* aspergilla *od.* aspergillums)

weil *Konj.* because; (*da*) since, as; *er ist,* ~ *in London geboren, Brite* he is British, because he was (*od.* by virtue of being) born in London; *ein schlechter,* ~ *fehlerhafter Stil* a bad, because faulty, style

weiland *Adv. altm., oft hum.* (*früher*) formerly; *Herr X,* ~ *Lehrer an unserer Schule* Mr (*od.* Mr.) X, quondam (*bes. Am.* former *od.* onetime) teacher at our school

Weilchen *n umg.*: *ein* ~ (for) a little while

Weile *f*; *-*, *kein Pl.*: *e-e* ~ a while, a time; *das kann e-e ziemliche* ~ *dauern* that could take a (fair) while (*od.* a bit of time); → *eilen*; **weilen** *v/i. geh.* stay; (*ver~*) linger (*auch fig. Gedanken*); *ein Jahr in Spanien* ~ spend a year in Spain; *er weilt nicht mehr unter uns euph.* he is no longer with us

Weiler *m*; *-s*, - hamlet

Weimarer *Adj. Pol.*: ~ *Republik* Weimar Republic

Wein *m*; *-(e)s*, *-e* **1.** (*Getränk*) wine; (*Jahrgang*) vintage; ~ *keltern* press grapes; *ein Glas / e-e Flasche* ~ a glass/bottle of wine; *offener* ~ wine by the glass; *in e-r Karaffe*: carafe wine; *vom Fass*: wine on tap; *trockener/halbtrockener/lieblicher* ~ dry/medium-dry/sweet wine; *bei e-m Glas* ~ over a glass of wine; *im* ~ *ist Wahrheit* in vino veritas; *er war voll des süßen* ~*es umg.* he was in his cups; *der Gott des* ~*es* the god of wine, Bacchus, Dionysus; ~, *Weib und Gesang* wine, women and song; *j-m reinen* ~ *einschenken fig.* be completely open with s.o.; **2.** *nur Sg.*; (*~stock*) vine; (*Trauben*) grapes; *wilder* ~ Virginia creeper; ~ (*an*)*bauen* be a winegrower, grow grapes (for wine); *der* ~ *blüht* the vines are in flower; ~ *lesen* pick grapes

Wein|(an)bau *m*; *nur Sg.* winegrowing, *förm.* viniculture, viticulture; ~ *betreiben* be a winegrower; **~bauer** *m*, **~bäuerin** *f* winegrower

Weinbaugebiet *n* wine-growing area

Wein|beere *f* **1.** grape; **2.** *südd., schw., österr.* (*Rosine*) raisin; **~beißer** *m*; *-s*, - **1.** (*Weinkenner*) wine expert; **2.** *österr.* (*Lebkuchen*) small iced (*Am.* frosted) gingerbread cake

Weinberg *m* vineyard; **~schnecke** *f* snail; *Gastr.* escargot

Weinblatt *n* vineleaf; *gefüllte Weinblätter Gastr.* stuffed vineleaves

Weinbrand *m* brandy; **~bohne** *f* brandy bean

weinen *vt/i.* cry; *leise*: weep (*um* over); *vor Schmerz/Freude etc.* ~ cry with the pain (*od.* because it hurts so much) / weep *od.* cry for joy *etc.*; ~ *nach j-m Baby*: cry for s.o.; *bittere Tränen* ~ shed bitter tears; *leise vor sich hin* ~ sob quietly; *sich* (*Dat.*) *die Augen rot* ~ cry one's eyes out; *j-n*

zum Weinen bringen make s.o. cry; *es ist zum Weinen umg.* it's enough to make you weep; *er wusste nicht, ob er lachen oder* ~ *sollte* he didn't know whether to laugh or cry; *die Geigen weinten fig.* the violins played a plaintive tune; → *Krokodilstränen, Steinerweichen etc.*; **weinend I.** *Part. Präs.* → *weinen*; **II.** *Adj.*: *mit e-m* ~*en und e-m lachenden Auge fig.* laughing and crying at the same time; *Shakespeare*: with an auspicious and a dropping eye; **III.** *Adv.*: *j-m* ~ *um den Hals fallen* fall weeping into s.o.'s arms; *leise* ~ *umg. fig.* sheepishly, feeling very small; *davonschleichen*: with one's tail between one's legs

weinerlich I. *Adj.* tearful, weepy; *attr. Kind: auch* grizzling; *Stimme, Ton: auch* whining ...; **II.** *Adv.* tearfully; *sagen etc.*: with a sob (in the voice); *klagend*: in a whining voice; **Weinerlichkeit** *f* weepiness

Wein|ernte *f* grape harvest; *weitS.* vintage; **~essig** *m* wine vinegar; **~fass** *n* wine cask; **~fest** *n* wine festival; **~flasche** *f* wine bottle; **~garten** *m* vineyard; **~gegend** *f* wine-growing area; **~geist** *m* (ethyl) alcohol; **~glas** *n* wine glass; **~gott** *m* god of wine; *der* ~ the god of wine, Bacchus, Dionysus; **~gummi** *m*, *n* wine gum; **~gut** *n* wine-growing estate, *bes. Am.* winery; **~händler** *m*, **~händlerin** *f* wine merchant; **~handlung** *f* wine shop (*Am. auch* store); **~hauer** *m*, **~hauerin** *f* österr. winegrower; **~haus** *n* wine bar; (*Geschäft*) wine shop (*Am. auch* store); **~heber** *m* wine siphon; **~hefe** *f* wine yeast

weinig *Adj.* vinous

Wein|jahr *n*: *ein gutes/schlechtes* ~ a good/bad year for wine, a good/bad vintage; **~karte** *f* wine list; **~keller** *m* wine cellar; **~kellerei** *f* winery; **~kellner** *m*, **~kellnerin** *f* wine waiter; **~kelter** *f* wine press; **~kenner** *m*, **~kennerin** *f* oenophile, wine connoisseur; **~königin** *f* wine queen

Weinkrampf *m* crying fit; *e-n* ~ *bekommen* start sobbing (*od.* weeping) uncontrollably, have a crying fit

Wein|kraut *n nur Sg.*; *Gastr.* sauerkraut cooked in wine; **~krug** *m* wine jug; **~kühler** *m* wine cooler; **~land** *n* wine-producing country; *Gegend*: wine-producing region; **~laub** *n* vine leaves *Pl.*; **~laune** *f*: *in* ~ after a few glasses of wine; **~lese** *f* grape harvest; **~lokal** *n* wine bar; **~ort** *m* wine(-producing) village; **~panscher** *m* wine-adulterator, wine-doctorer; **~prämierung** *f* wine awards *Pl.*, wine awards ceremony; *weitS.* wine show; *Medaille etc.*: (wine) award; **~presse** *f* wine press; **~probe** *f* wine tasting (session); **~ranke** *f* vine tendril; **~rebe** *f* (grape)vine

weinrot *Adj.* wine-red, claret

Wein|säure *f* tartaric acid; **~schaum** *m*, **~schaumcreme** *f Gastr.* zabaglione, syllabub; **~schaumsoße** *f Gastr.* zabaglione sauce; **~schorle** *f*, *n* spritzer; ~ *sauer/süß* mineral water / lemonade spritzer

weinselig *Adj.* merry (with wine), vinous *iro.*

Wein|stein *m*; *nur Sg.* tartar; **~stock** *m* vine; **~straße** *f* wine route; *Badische/Elsässer* ~ the Baden/Alsace wine route; **~stube** *f* wine bar; **~traube** *f* bunch of grapes; (*Beere*) grape; **~trinker** *m*, **~trinkerin** *f* wine drinker; **~verkauf** *m*: ~ *Schild*: wine for sale;

W

~wirtschaft f Agr. wine industry
weise I. Adj. wise; **ein ~s Wort** a wise saying; **II.** Adv. handeln, urteilen etc.: wisely; **er lächelte ~** he smiled knowingly
Weise[1] m; -n, -n wise man, sage; **die (drei) ~n aus dem Morgenland** the three Wise Men from the East, the Magi
Weise[2] f; -, -n **1.** mst Sg.; (Verfahren) way; **auf diese ~** (in) this way; **auf die e-e oder andere ~** one way or another; **in der ~, dass ...** in such a way that ...; **in keiner ~** in no way; **in keinster ~!** umg. not at all!; **in gewisser ~** in a way; → auch **Art** 2; **2.** Mus. tune
...weise im Adv. **1.** Art und Weise: **besuchs~** on a visit; for a visit; **lesender~** while reading; (durch Lesen) by reading; **2.** beurteilend: **höflicher~** politely; **realistischer~** realistically; **3.** Maß etc.: **gramm~** in grams; **schaufel~** in shovelfuls, by the shovelful
weisen; weist, wies, hat gewiesen **I.** v/t. **1.** j-m den Weg od. **die Richtung ~** show s.o. the way; **j-m die Tür ~** show s.o. the door; **2.** aus dem Lande **~** banish, exile, send into exile; **3.** von sich **~** fig. reject; (Verdacht etc.) repudiate; → **Hand**[1] 3; **II.** v/i. **1.** **~ auf** (+ Akk.) point at; (aufmerksam machen auf) auch point to; **nach Süden** etc. **~** point south etc.; **2.** fig. **~ auf** (+ Akk.) point to(ward[s])
Weisheit f **1.** nur Sg. wisdom; **mit s-r ~ am Ende sein** be at one's wits' end; **das war nicht der ~ letzter Schluss** that wasn't the cleverest solution (od. thing to do); **er hat die ~ nicht mit Löffeln gegessen** he's not exactly an Einstein; **2.** (Spruch) wise saying, piece of wisdom; **d-e ~en kannst du für dich behalten** umg. iro. you can keep your pearls of wisdom for yourself; → **pachten** II; **Weisheitszahn** m wisdom tooth
weismachen v/t. (trennb., hat -ge-) umg.: **j-m ~, dass ...** persuade s.o. that ...; **willst du mir ~, dass ...?** are you trying to tell me (that) ...?; **mir kannst du nichts ~** you needn't try and fool me
weiß[1] Präs. → **wissen**
weiß[2] Adj. **I. 1.** white; **~es Blatt (Papier)** blank sheet of paper; **~ machen** whiten; **du hast dich am Ärmel ~ gemacht** you've got some white stuff on your sleeve; **~ werden** turn white; (weißes Haar bekommen) go white; **~ wie die Wand** (as) white as a sheet; **~er Fleck auf der Landkarte** white spot on the map; **e-e ~e Weste haben** fig. have a clean slate; **~e Ware** (Elektrogeräte) white goods Pl.; (No-Name--Produkte) no-name (Am. auch generic) products Pl., economy lines Pl.; **das Weiße Haus** the White House; **Weiße Zwerge** Astron. white dwarfs; **der weiße Tod** (Erfrieren) death in the snow; → **Blutkörperchen, Bohne** 1, **Magie, Sonntag, Weihnachten** etc.; **2.** substantiviert: **das Weiße des Eis** the white of an egg; **das Weiße im Auge** the whites of one's eyes; **II.** Adv. white; **~ gekleidet** dressed in white; **~ glühend** Gas, Sonne: incandescent; → auch **weißglühend**
Weiß n; -(es), -; mst Sg. white; **das strahlendste** etc. **~** the most brilliant white; **in ~ heiraten** etc.: in white; **~ ist am Zug** Schach: it's white's move (Am. auch turn), it's white to move; → **Halbgott**

weissagen v/t. (untr., hat) prophesy, foretell; **Weissager** m; -s, **Weissagerin** f; -, -nen prophet(ess f); **Weissagung** f prophecy
Weiß|bier n wheat beer, weissbier; **~blech** n tinplate
weißblond Adj. ash-blonde
weißbluten v/refl.; nur Inf.; fig. bleed o.s. white (Am. dry); **j-n bis zum Weißbluten ausnehmen** bleed s.o. white (Am. dry)
Weiß|brot n white bread; **~buch** n Pol. (government) white paper; **~buche** f Bot. white beech; **~dorn** m Bot. whitethorn
Weiße[1] f; -, -n **1.** nur Sg. whiteness; **2.** umg. (Bier) wheat beer, weissbier; **Berliner ~ mit Schuss** Berlin weissbier with a dash of fruit (mst raspberry) syrup
Weiße[2] m, f; -n, -n white; Mann: white man; Frau: white woman (od. girl); **die Weißen** the whites
weißen v/t. whiten; (tünchen) whitewash
Weiß|fisch m Zool. whitefish; **~fluss** m Med. leucorrhoea, Am. leukorrhea
weiß gekleidet → **weiß**[2] II
weißglühend Adj. Metall: white-hot; → auch **weiß**[2] II; **Weißglut** f; nur Sg. white heat (auch fig.); **j-n zur ~ bringen** umg. fig. incense s.o., make s.o. livid (od. wild with rage), have s.o. fuming
Weißgold n white gold
weißhaarig Adj. white-haired
Weiß|herbst m rosé (wine); **~käse** m Dial. quark, Am. cottage cheese; **~kittel** m umg. person in a white coat, doctor; **~kohl** m, **~kraut** n Bot., Gastr. white (Am. green) cabbage
weißlich Adj. whitish
Weißmacher m whitener
Weißrusse m, **Weißrussin** f Belarusian, Belorussian, White Russian, weiblich auch: Belarusian (od. Belorussian od. White Russian) woman (od. girl etc.); **weißrussisch** Adj. Belarusian, Belorussian, White Russian; **Weißrussisch** n; -(s); Ling. Belorussian, White Russian; **das ~e** Belorussian, White Russian; **Weißrussland** (n); -s; Geog. Belarus, Belorussia, White Russia
Weiß|storch m Orn. white stork; **~tanne** f Bot. silver fir; **~wal** m Zool. white whale, beluga; **~wandreifen** m Mot. whitewall tyre (Am. tire); **~wandtafel** f whiteboard; **~waren** Pl. linen Sg.
Weißwäsche f; nur Sg. whites Pl.; **weißwaschen** v/t. (unreg., trennb., hat -ge-) fig. whitewash (**sich** o.s.)
Weißwein m white wine; **~schorle** f white wine spritzer
Weißwurst f Gastr. veal sausage; **~äquator** m umg., hum. the River Main, thought of in Bavaria as the border between the authentic southlands of Germany and the Prussified north
Weisung f directive, instructions Pl., orders Pl.; **ich habe ~ zu** (+ Inf.) I have been instructed to (+ Inf.)
Weisungsbefugnis f authority to issue directives; **weisungsgebunden** Adj. subject to directives; **weisungsgemäß** Adv. as directed, according to instructions
weit I. Adj. **1.** wide; (ausgedehnt) extensive; stärker: vast, immense; Entfernung, Weg: long; **von ~em** from a distance; **ich sah sie von ~em kommen** I

could see her coming in the distance; **man konnte s-e Fahne von ~em riechen** umg. you could smell his breath a mile away; **in ~en Abständen** räumlich: widely spaced; zeitlich: at long intervals; **~er Blick über das Land** commanding view of the countryside (od. landscape); **2.** fig.: **ein ~es Herz haben** have a big heart; **~er Horizont** broad outlook; **im ~esten Sinne** in the broadest sense (of the word); **~er Begriff** etc. broad concept etc.; **~e Teile der Bevölkerung** large parts of the population; **3.** (lose) loose (auch Tech.); Kleid etc.: wide, loose; **die Hose** etc. **ist viel zu ~** the trousers (Am. pants) are much (Am. way) too big; **ein Kleid ~er machen** let out; → **Feld** 6, **Kreis** 1; **II.** Adv. **1.** far, wide(ly); **er springt sieben Meter ~** he can jump (a distance of) seven met|res (Am. -ers); **~er ist bisher niemand gekommen** nobody has gone further to date; **~ daneben** fig. wide of (way off umg.) the mark; **2.** bequem **~ geschnitten** Mantel etc.: roomy, comfortably loose-fitting; **~ offen** wide open; **~ oben** high up; fig. Sport well-placed (od. high up) in the (league) table; **3. ~ entfernt** far away; **e-e Meile ~ entfernt** a mile away; **~ entfernt von** a long way from; fig. a far cry from; **~ davon entfernt sein, etw. zu tun** fig. be far from doing s.th., be not about to do s.th. umg.; **4. kein Mensch** etc. **~ und breit** not a soul etc. to be seen (od. as far as the eye could see); **~ und breit der Beste** etc. far and away the best etc., the best etc. by far; **5.** fig.: **~ bekannt** attr. widely-known ..., präd. widely known; **~ gefehlt!** far from it; **es ist nicht ~ her mit ...** umg. ... isn't (aren't) up to much; **das liegt ~ zurück** that's a long way back, that was a long time ago; **das Geld reicht nicht ~** the money won't go far; **es ~ bringen (im Leben)** go far, 'go places; **zu ~ gehen** od. **es zu ~ treiben** go too far, overshoot the mark; **das geht zu ~** that's going too far, umg. that's a bit much; **ich bin so ~** I'm ready; **wie ~ bist du?** how far have you got?; **wenn es so ~ ist** when the time comes; **so ~ ist es nun gekommen?** has it come to that?; **es ist noch nicht so ~, dass ...** things haven't yet come to the point where; **er ist so ~ genesen, dass er ... kann** he's recovered to the extent of being able to (+ Inf.); **6.** fig. vor Komp.: **~ besser** etc. far better etc.; **bei ~em besser** etc. far (Am. umg. way) better etc., **bei ~em der Beste** etc. by far (od. far and away) the best etc.; **bei ~em nicht so gut** etc. not nearly as good etc.; **~ über sechzig** well over sixty; **~ nach Mitternacht** long after (Am. auch way past) midnight; **7.** mit Part. Präs.: **~ gehend** extensive; Auswirkungen etc.: Unterstützung: broad; **~er gehend** further; **~er gehende Auswirkungen** etc. more far--reaching (od. broader) implications etc.; **~ greifend** far-reaching; **~ reichend** Entscheidung etc.: far-reaching; Diskussion etc.: wide-ranging; Mil. attr. long-range ...; **~ tragend** Rakete etc.: long-range; fig. Konsequenzen etc.: far--reaching; (breit gefächert) wide-ranging; **8.** mit P.P.: **~ gefächert** wide-ranging; **~ gefasst** broad; **~ gereist** attr. widely-travel(l)ed; **~ gereist sein** auch have been around umg.; **~ gespannt** fig., Erwartungen etc.: broad; **~ ge-**

steckt *Ziel*: long-range, long-term; (*ziemlich*) ~ **hergeholt** (a bit) far--fetched; ~ **verbreitet** widespread; *Ansicht*: *auch* widely held; *Zeitung*: widely read; ~ **verbreiteter Irrtum** *auch* popular fallacy, widely-held misconception; ~ **verzweigt** intricate, complex; → *auch* **Weite**[1], **weiter**

weitab *Adv.* far away (*von* from)

weitärmelig *Adj.* wide-sleeved

weitaus *Adv.*: ~ **besser** *etc.* far (*od.* much, *Am. umg.* way) better *etc.*; *die* ~ **Schlimmsten** *etc.* the worst *etc.* by far

weit bekannt → **weit** II 5

Weitblick *m*; *nur Sg.* farsightedness; ~ **beweisen** show foresight, be farsighted; **weitblickend, weit blickend** *Adj.* farsighted

Weite[1] *f*; -, -n (*Breite*) *auch von Kleidung etc.*: width; *Tech.* (*Durchmesser*) diameter; (*Entfernung*) distance; (*Größe*) expanse; *fig.* range, scope; *die* ~ *des Meeres* the vastness of the sea; *e-e beachtliche* ~ *vorlegen Sport* achieve a considerable distance; → **licht** 2

Weite[2] *n*: *das* ~ *suchen umg.* take to one's heels, flee

weiten *v/t. und v/refl.* widen; (*Augen*) open wide; (*Schuhe*) stretch; *fig.* widen, broaden

weiter *Adv.* (*voran*) on, forward; (*ferner*) further(more), moreover; (*zusätzlich*) additionally; ~**?** and then?; ~**!** go on!, carry on!; *immer* ~ on and on; *nichts* ~ nothing else, that's all; *wenn es* ~ *nichts ist* if that's all (it is); *was geschah* ~**?** what happened then (*od.* next)?; ~ *niemand* no-one else; *und so* ~ and so on; *das hat* ~ *nichts zu sagen* it's not significant; *weitS.* it's irrelevant; → *auch* **weit, weiter...**

weiter... *Adj.* (*zusätzlich*) additional, further; (*zukünftig*) future; *noch* ~*e Fragen?* any more questions?; *alles Weitere* the rest, everything else; *des Weiteren* in addition, furthermore; *bis auf* ~*es* for the time being; *auf Schildern*: until further notice; *ohne* ~*es* just like that; (*mühelos*) easily, without any (great) effort; (*ohne Probleme*) *umg.* no problem; *das machen wir ohne* ~*es* we'll manage that easily enough, we'll manage that with no problems *umg.*; *du kannst ihr ohne* ~*es glauben* you needn't think twice about believing her; *das geht nicht so ohne* ~*es* that's not so easy

weiterarbeiten *v/i.* (*trennb., hat -ge-*) go (*od.* carry) on working; *an e-m Buch etc.* ~ do some more work on a book *etc.*

weiterbefördern *v/t.* (*trennb., hat*) forward, send on; (*umadressieren*) redirect; **Weiterbeförderung** *f* forwarding; (*Umadressierung*) redirecting

weiterbehandeln *v/t.* (*trennb., hat*) **1.** (*Thema*) discuss further, deal with further; **2.** *Med.* continue to treat; **Weiterbehandlung** *f*: (*zur*) ~ (for) further (*od.* continuing) treatment

weiterbeschäftigen (*trennb., hat*) **I.** *v/t.* (*Arbeitskräfte*) continue to employ; **II.** *v/refl.* *sich mit etw.* ~ continue doing, studying *etc.* s.th.; **Weiterbeschäftigung** *f* continued employment

Weiterbestand *m*; *nur Sg.* continued existence, survival; **weiterbestehen** *v/i.* (*unreg., trennb., hat*) continue (to exist); (*überleben*) survive

weiterbilden (*trennb., hat -ge-*) **I.** *v/t.* *im Betrieb etc.*: give *s.o.* further train-

ing; **II.** *v/refl.* continue (*od.* further) one's studies; *beruflich*: *mst* do further training; *sich in Geschichte etc.* ~ extend one's knowledge of history *etc.*; **Weiterbildung** *f* further education, continuing education; *berufliche*: *mst* further training; *persönliche*: continuing process of education (*od.* learning); *berufliche* ~ *auch* extended vocational training; *schulische* ~ further education

Weiterbildungsangebot *n* opportunities *Pl.* for further education

weiter|bringen *v/t.* (*unreg., trennb., hat -ge-*) help; (*fördern*) promote; *das bringt mich nicht weiter* that's not much help to me; *j-n ein kleines/ganzes Stück* ~ get s.o. a little/lot further; ~**denken** *v/i.* (*unreg., trennb., hat -ge-*) think (*od.* look) ahead

weiterempfehlen *v/t.* (*unreg., trennb., hat*) recommend; *bitte empfehlen Sie uns weiter!* please tell your friends about us

weiterentwickeln (*trennb., hat*) **I.** *v/t.* develop *s.th.* (*further*); *Tech. auch* refine; **II.** *v/refl.* develop; **Weiterentwicklung** *f* **1.** further development; (*Stufe*) further stage; **2.** (*verbessertes Modell*) derivative

weitererzählen *v/t.* (*trennb., hat*) pass *s.th.* on; *nicht* ~**!** *umg.* don't tell anyone

weiterfahren (*unreg., trennb., -ge-*) **I.** *v/i.* (*ist*) go on, drive on; **II.** *v/t.* (*hat od. ist*) (*altes Auto etc.*) continue to drive; **Weiterfahrt** *f*: (*während der*) ~ (on the) next stage of the (*od.* my, our *etc.*) journey (*od.* trip); *auf der* ~ *nach* ... as I (we *etc.*) continued my (our *etc.*) trip (*od.* journey) to ...; → *auch* **Weiterreise**

weiterfliegen *v/i.* (*unreg., trennb., ist -ge-*) go on, fly on (*nach* to); (*starten*) take off (*nach* to); **Weiterflug** *m* **1.** *mit demselben od. anderem Flugzeug*: continuation of the *od.* one's flight; *auf dem* ~ *nach Lissabon* as I (we *etc.*) continued my (our *etc.*) flight to Lisbon; **2.** (*Anschlussflug*) connecting flight; *Passagiere mit* ~ *nach Sevilla* passengers continuing onto (*od.* their flight to) Seville

weiterführen *v/t./i.* (*trennb., hat -ge-*) continue; *das führt (uns) nicht weiter* that doesn't get us any further; **weiterführend I.** *Part. Präs.* → **weiterführen**; **II.** *Adj.*: ~*e Schule* secondary school

Weitergabe *f*; *nur Sg.* passing on; *von Erbfaktor etc.*: transmission; **weitergeben** *v/t.* (*unreg., trennb., hat -ge-*) pass on; (*vererben*) transmit; *bitte* ~**!** pass it on; → **weiterleiten**

weiter|gehen *v/i.* (*unreg., trennb., ist -ge-*) go (*od.* walk, carry) on; *fig.* (*fortfahren*) continue, go on; *mit e-r Beschwerde etc.*: take *s.th.* further; (*bitte*) ~**!** move along(, please)!; *das kann so nicht* ~ things can't go on like this

weiter gehend → **weit** II 7

weiterhelfen *v/i.* (*unreg., trennb., hat -ge-*) help *s.o.* (along); *dort wird man ihnen dann* ~ someone there will be able to help them further; *das hat mir sehr weitergeholfen* that was a great help

weiterhin *Adv.* in (*od.* for the) future; (*ferner*) further(more); *etw.* ~ *tun* continue doing (*od.* to do) s.th., carry on with (*od.* doing) s.th.

weiter|kämpfen *v/i.* (*trennb., hat -ge-*) continue fighting; ~**kommen** *v/i.* (*un-*

reg., trennb., ist -ge-); (*vorankommen*) get on, get somewhere, make headway; *Sport* get through (to the next round); *nicht* ~ *umg.* be stuck; *wir kommen überhaupt nicht weiter* we're not getting anywhere; *mach, dass du weiterkommst! umg.* make yourself scarce!; ~**können** *v/i.* (*unreg., trennb., hat -ge-*); *umg.*: *nicht* ~ not be able to go (any) further; *ich kann nicht mehr weiter* I can't go any further; ~**laufen** *v/i.* (*unreg., trennb., ist -ge-*) run on, carry on running; *Produktion, Geschäft etc.*: continue; *Vertrag*: remain valid; *Gehalt*: continue to be paid; ~ *bis Vertrag etc.*: run on until; ~**leben** *v/i.* (*unreg., trennb., hat -ge-*) live on, survive (*beide auch fig.*)

weiterleiten *v/t.* (*trennb., hat -ge-*) pass *s.th.* on; (*Brief etc.*) forward; **Weiterleitung** *f* forwarding; *automatische* ~ *EDV* auto-forward

weiter|lesen *vt./i.* (*unreg., trennb., hat -ge-*) go on (reading), carry on reading, continue to read (*od.* reading); ~**machen** *vt./i.* (*trennb., hat -ge-*); *umg.* carry (*od.* go) on, continue; *genauso* ~ carry on as before; *mach nur so weiter!* keep it up!; *iro.* see where that gets you; ~**reichen** *v/t.* (*trennb., hat -ge-*) pass on; (*Antrag etc.*) *auch* refer

Weiterreise *f* continuation (*od.* next stage) of the journey; *auf der* ~ as we *etc.* continued our *etc.* journey; *angenehme* ~**!** enjoy the rest of your journey (*bes. Am.* trip)!; **weiterreisen** *v/i.* (*trennb., trennb., ist -ge-*) continue one's journey; *sie ist nach Kreta weitergereist* she went on to Crete

weiters *Adv.* *österr.* furthermore

weiter|sagen *v/t.* (*trennb., hat -ge-*) pass *s.th.* on; *nicht* ~**!** don't tell anyone, keep that under your hat *umg.*; ~**schicken** *v/t.* (*trennb., hat -ge-*) forward; (*auch Person*) send on; (*umadressieren*) redirect; ~**schlafen** *v/i.* (*unreg., trennb., hat -ge-*) sleep on, not wake up; (*wieder einschlafen*) go back to sleep; ~**sehen** *v/i.* (*unreg., trennb., hat -ge-*); *umg.*: *warten wir, bis er da ist, dann werden wir* ~ then we'll see what happens, and we'll take it from there; ~**streiken** *v/i.* (*trennb., hat -ge-*) stay on strike; ~**tragen** *v/t.* (*unreg., trennb., hat -ge-*) *fig.* (*Gerücht etc.*) spread

Weitertransport *m* onward transport(ation); **weitertransportieren** *v/t.* (*trennb., hat*) transport further

weitertreiben *v/t.* (*unreg., trennb., hat -ge-*); (*Herde etc.*) drive on; *fig.* (*Entwicklung etc.*) carry on, continue

weiterverarbeiten *v/t.* (*trennb., hat*) process; **Weiterverarbeitung** *f* processing

weiter|veräußern *v/t.* (*trennb., hat*) resell; ~**verbinden** *v/t.* (*unreg., trennb., hat*) *Telef.* put *s.o.* through (*an* + *Akk.* to)

weiterverbreiten *v/t.* (*trennb., hat*) spread; **Weiterverbreitung** *f* spread

weiter|verfolgen *v/t.* (*trennb., hat*) follow up; ~**verhandeln** *v/i.* (*trennb., hat*) continue to negotiate, conduct further negotiations

Weiterverkauf *m* resale; **weiterverkaufen** *v/t.* (*trennb., hat*) resell

weiter|vermieten *v/t.* (*trennb., hat*) sublet; ~**vermitteln** *v/t.* (*trennb., hat*) pass on

Weiterversicherung *f*: *freiwillige* ~ voluntary additional insurance; **weiterversichern** (*trennb., hat*) **I.** *v/refl.* con-

W

tinue the (*od.* an) insurance; **II.** *v/t.* **j-n** ~ continue s.o.'s insurance
weiterverwenden *v/t.* (*unreg., trennb., hat*) continue to use; Öko. (*Glas etc.*) reuse; **Weiterverwendung** *f* further use; Öko. reuse
weiterverwerten *v/t.* (*trennb., hat*) reuse; Öko. (*Stoffe etc.*) recycle; **Weiterverwertung** *f* reuse; Öko. recycling
weiter|wissen *v/i.* (*unreg., trennb., hat -ge-*): **nicht ~ bei Prüfungen**: be stuck; (*mutlos sein*) be at one's wits' end; **ich wusste nicht mehr weiter** *auch* I didn't know what to do; **~wollen** *v/i.* (*unreg., trennb., hat -ge-*); *umg.* want to go on; **~wursteln** *v/i.* (*trennb., hat -ge-*); *umg.* muddle on; **~ziehen** *v/i.* (*unreg., trennb., ist -ge-*) go on
weitestgehend *Adv.* as far as possible
weit| gefächert, ~ gefasst → **weit** II 8
weitgehend, weit gehend → **weit** II 7
weit| gereist, ~ gespannt, ~ gesteckt → **weit** II 8
weitgreifend, weit greifend → **weit** II 7
weither *Adv.* from afar
weit hergeholt → **weit** II 8
weitherzig *Adj.* broadminded, tolerant, charitable; **Weitherzigkeit** *f* broadmindedness, tolerance
weithin *Adv.* far; *fig.* to a large extent
weitläufig I. *Adj.* **1.** (*ausgedehnt*) extensive, *stärker*: vast; *Garten, Haus etc.*: *auch* rambling; (*geräumig*) spacious; **2.** *Verwandter etc.*: distant; **3.** (*ausführlich*) detailed; *pej.* longwinded; **II.** *Adv.* **1.** at great length; **2. ~ verwandt** distantly related; **Weitläufigkeit** *f* **1.** extensiveness, *stärker*: vastness; (*Geräumigkeit*) spaciousness; **2.** (*Ausführlichkeit*) detailedness; *pej.* longwindedness
weit|maschig *Adj.* wide-meshed; **~räumig I.** *Adj.* spacious; **II.** *Adv.* angelegt *etc.*: spaciously; **etw. ~ umfahren** *Verk.* give s.th. a wide berth
weitreichend, weit reichend → **weit** II 7
Weitschuss *m* Sport long-range shot; **unerlaubter ~** Eishockey: icing (the puck)
weitschweifig I. *Adj.* longwinded; **II.** *Adv.* reden, schreiben *etc.*: longwindedly; **Weitschweifigkeit** *f* longwindedness
Weitsicht *f* farsightedness; *fig. auch* vision; **weitsichtig** *Adj.* longsighted; *bes. Am. und fig.* farsighted; **Weitsichtigkeit** *f* longsightedness; *bes. Am. und fig.* farsightedness
Weitspringen *n* long (*Am. auch* broad) jump; **Weitspringer** *m*, **Weitspringerin** *f* long jumper, *Am. auch* broad jumper; **Weitsprung** *m* long (*Am. auch* broad) jump
weittragend, weit tragend → **weit** II 7
Weitung *f* widening
weitverbreitet, weit verbreitet → **weit** II 8
weitverzweigt, weit verzweigt → **weit** II 8
Weitwinkelobjektiv *n* wide-angle lens
Weizen *m; -s, -* **1.** Bot. wheat; → **Spreu**; **2.** → **Weizenbier**; **~bier** *n* wheat beer, weissbier; **~ernte** *f* wheat harvest; **~feld** *n* wheatfield; **~keim** *m* auch Pl. wheatgerm; **~keimöl** *n* wheatgerm oil; **~kleie** *f* wheat bran; **~mehl** *n* wheat flour
welch I. *Interr. Pron.* what?; *auswählend*: which?; **~er?** which one?; **~er von den beiden?** which of the two?; **II.** *Rel. Pron.* bei Personen: who; bei

Dingen: which, that; **III.** *unbest. Pron.* **1.** some, any; *haben Sie Geld? -* **ja, ich habe ~es** yes, I have (*od.* I've got) some; **brauchen Sie ~es?** do you need any?; **es gibt ~e, die sagen** there are some who say, some people say; **~er** (*auch*) **immer** whoever; **~es** (*auch*) **immer** whichever; **2.** *intensivierend*: **~ seltener Gast!** hello, stranger! *umg.*, a rare visitor indeed!; **~ ein Zufall** *etc.* what a coincidence *etc.*!; **welcherlei** *Adj. attr.* whatever; **es ist egal, ~ ...** it doesn't matter what (sort of) …
Welfe *m; -n, -n*; *hist.* Guelph; **welfisch** *Adj. hist.* Guelphic
welk *Adj.* Blume: wilted; *auch* Blatt: withered; *Haut*: wrinkled; (*schrumpelig*) shrivel(l)ed; **welken** *v/i.* Blume: wilt; *auch* Blatt: wither; *Haut*: shrivel; **ihre Schönheit beginnt zu ~** her beauty is beginning to fade
Wellblech *n* corrugated iron; **~dach** *n* corrugated-iron roof; **~hütte** *f* corrugated-iron hut; *halbrunde*: Nissen hut, *Am.* Quonset hut
Welle *f; -, -n* **1.** auf Wasseroberfläche: wave; *kleine*: ripple; **die ~n schlagen ans Ufer** the waves beat against the shore; **~n schlagen** *fig.*, Ereignis *etc.*: make waves, cause a stir; **2.** *Phys.*, Radio, Etech. *etc.*, *auch im Haar*: wave; **3.** *von Einwanderern etc.*, *auch der* Begeisterung *etc.*: wave, *stärker*: surge; **4.** *Tech.*: shaft; **5.** *Turnen*: circle; **6.** *fig.* (*Mode etc.*) craze; **7.** *Mot.*: **grüne** *od.* **rote ~** phased (*od.* linked) traffic lights; **wir haben grüne ~** we've caught the green phase
...welle *f*, *im Subst.* **1.** (*Bewegung*): **Auswanderungs~** wave of emigration; **Asylanten~** wave of asylum-seekers; **2.** (*Mode*): **Fitness~** fitness craze; **Fress~** (eating) binge
wellen I. *v/t.* (*Haar*) wave; **II.** *v/refl.* Haar: be wavy; (*wellig werden*) go wavy; Gelände: undulate
Wellen|bad *n* wave pool; **~band** *n*, **~bereich** *m* Radio: wave band; **~bewegung** *f* wave movement; **~brecher** *m* breakwater
wellenförmig *Adj.* wavy
Wellen|gang *m* waves Pl.; **starker ~** heavy seas; **~kamm** *m* crest (of a *od.* the wave); **~länge** *f* Radio *etc.*: wavelength; **die gleiche ~ haben** *fig.* be on the same wavelength; **~linie** *f* wavy line; **~reiten** *n* surfing; **~reiter** *m*, **~reiterin** *f* surfer; **~salat** *m* nur Sg.; *umg.* jumbled reception, (strong) interference; **~schlag** *m* breaking (*leichter*: lapping) of (the) waves; **~schliff** *m*: **Messer mit ~** serrated knife; **~sittich** *m* Orn. budgerigar, budgie *umg.*, *Am.* parakeet; **~strahlung** *f* Phys. wave radiation; **~tal** *n* trough
Well|fleisch *n* Gastr. boiled belly of pork; **~hornschnecke** *f* Zool. whelk
wellig *Adj.* wavy; Gelände: undulating
Wellness *f; -, kein Pl.* wellness; **~Produkt** *n* wellness product; **~-Wochenende** *n* wellness weekend
Wellpappe *f* corrugated cardboard
Welpe *m; -n, -n* pup(py); Wolf, Fuchs: cub
Wels *n; -es, -e*; Zool. catfish
welsch *Adj. schw.* French-speaking; **die ~e Schweiz** French-speaking (*od.* Francophone) Switzerland; **Welschland** *n schw.* French-speaking (*od.* Francophone) Switzerland; **Welschschweizer** *m*, **Welschschweizerin** *f schw.* French-(speaking) Swiss, *weiblich auch*: French(-speaking) Swiss

woman (*od.* girl *etc.*); **welschschweizerisch** *Adj. schw.* French(-speaking) Swiss
Welt *f; -, -en* **1.** *nur Sg.* world (*auch fig.*); **auf der ~** in the world; **aus der ~ ganzen ~** from all over (*od.* all four corners of) the world; **die ~ kennen lernen** see the world; **in der ~ herumkommen** get around; **die Dritte ~** the Third World; **die Vierte ~** the Fourth World; **die Alte/Neue ~** the Old/New World; **2.** *nur Sg.*; (*Leben*): **auf die ~ kommen** be born; **Kinder in die ~ setzen** bring into the world; *iro. Mann*: sire; **zur ~ bringen** give birth to; **er war damals noch gar nicht auf der ~** he wasn't even born at that time; **allein auf der ~ sein** be all alone in the world; **ich verstehe die ~ nicht mehr** I don't understand the world any more; **aus der ~ schaffen** get rid of; (*Problem, Streit*) settle; **mit sich und der ~ zufrieden sein** be at peace with (oneself and) the world, be content with life; **ihre Familie ist ihre ganze ~** her family is all the world to her; **3.** *nur Sg.*; (*Gesamtheit der Menschen*): **alle ~** everybody; **vor aller ~** for all the world to see; **von aller ~ verlassen** completely forlorn; **das hat die ~ noch nicht gesehen** *umg.* nobody's ever (*od.* you've never) seen the like of it; **ich könnte die ganze ~ umarmen** I'd like to hug everyone in sight; **4.** *nur Sg.*; *fig.*: **was/wo** *etc.* **in aller ~ ...?** *umg.* what/where *etc.* on earth (*od.* in the world) …?; **nicht um alles in der ~!** not on your life!, not for the world!; **das ist nicht aus der ~** *umg.* it isn't 'that far away'; **für sie brach e-e ~ zusammen** the bottom fell out of her world; (*e-e*) **verkehrte ~** a topsy-turvy world; **es kostet doch nicht die ~** it won't cost the earth; **am Ende der ~** *umg.* wohnen *etc.*: at the back of beyond, out in the sticks, *Am. auch* out in the boondocks; → **Arsch** 1; **5.** *Astron.* world; **~en trennen sie** *fig.* they're worlds apart; **e-e ~ für sich** *fig.* a world apart (*od.* of its own); **er lebt in e-r anderen ~** *fig.* he lives in another world (*od.* a world of his own); **6.** *nur Sg.*; (*feine Gesellschaft*): **ein Mann / e-e Dame von ~** a man/woman of the world; → **Brett** 4, **Dorf**, **Geld** 2, **Gott** 2, **Nabel**, **untergehen** 3
weltabgewandt *Adj.* withdrawn, seclusive
Welt|all *n* universe, cosmos, (outer) space; **ins ~ fliegen** fly off into space; → *auch* **Weltraum**; **~alter** *n* **1.** (*Alter der Erde*) age of the (planet) Earth; (*Alter des Universums*) age of the universe; **2.** Geol. (*extrem lange Zeitspanne*) eon; **3.** (*Epoche*) epoch, era, age
weltanschaulich *Adj.* philosophical; (*ideologisch*) ideological; **Weltanschauung** *f* philosophy (of life), outlook on life, world view, Weltanschauung; (*Ideologie*) ideology
Welt|ausstellung *f* world fair, world exposition; **~auswahl** *f* Sport the best of the world; **~bank** *f*; *nur Sg.* World Bank
welt|bekannt, ~berühmt *Adj.* world-famous (*od.* -renowned), famous the world over
weltbest... *Adj.* best in the world, world's best; **Weltbeste** *m, f; -n, -n* best in the world; **Weltbestleistung** *f bes.* Sport world best (performance)
Weltbevölkerung *f* world population
weltbewegend *Adj. attr.* Ereignisse

W

etc.: earth-shattering, seismic; *nichts Weltbewegendes umg.* nothing to write home about, no great shakes

Welt|bild *n* world view, view of life; **~bühne** *f* world stage; **~bürger** *m*, **~bürgerin** *f* cosmopolitan; **~bürgertum** *n* cosmopolitanism

Weltcup *m Sport* World Cup; **~sieg** *m* victory in the World Cup; **~sieger** *m*, **~siegerin** *f* winner of the World Cup

Welt|elite *f* world class; **~empfänger** *m Radio*: short-wave receiver

Weltenbummler *m*, **~in** *f* globetrotter

Welt|ende *n the* end of the world; **~ereignis** *n* event of worldwide importance, global event; *welterschütterndes*: earth-shaking event

welterfahren *Adj.* worldly-wise

Welterfolg *m* worldwide success (*od.* hit *umg.*)

Weltergewicht *n Sport* 1. *nur Sg.* welterweight; 2. *Sportler*: welterweight; **Weltergewichtler** *m*; *-s, -* welterweight

Welternährungsorganisation *f der UNO*: Food and Agriculture Organization

welt|erschütternd *Adj. Ereignisse etc.*: earth-shaking, seismic; **~fern** *Adj.* unrealistic, naive

Welt|firma *f* company with an international reputation, world-class company, global player; **~flucht** *f* escapism

weltfremd *Adj.* unworldly, *präd.* out of touch (with reality); (*unerfahren*) inexperienced, naive; (*unrealistisch*) unrealistic; (*träumerisch*) starry-eyed; *Gelehrter etc.*: ivory-tower ...; **Weltfremdheit** *f* unworldliness

Welt|friede(n) *m* world peace; **~fußballverband** *m Sport* FIFA; **~geltung** *f* international standing, an international reputation; **~gemeinschaft** *f* international community; **~gericht** *n*; *nur Sg.*: *das ~* the Last Judg(e)ment; **~geschehen** *n*: *das ~* world affairs

Weltgeschichte *f* 1. *die ~* world history, the history of the world; *in der ~ herumreisen umg.* travel all over the place; 2. *Werk*: history of the world; **weltgeschichtlich** *Adj.* in world history; **~e Betrachtungen** observations on world history

Weltgesundheitsorganisation *f* World Health Organization, WHO

weltgewandt *Adj.* urbane; **Weltgewandtheit** *f* urbanity

Welt|handel *m* international trade; **~handelsorganisation** *f* World Trade Organization; **~herrschaft** *f* world domination; **~hilfssprache** *f* international auxiliary language; **~hungerhilfe** *f* world famine relief; **~jahresbestleistung** *f Sport* best performance in the world this year; **~jahresbestzeit** *f Sport* best time in the world this year; **~karte** *f* map of the world; **~kindertag** *m* world children's day; **~kirchenrat** *m* World Council of Churches; **~klasse** *f Sport* world class; *zur (absoluten) ~ gehören* be (absolutely) world-class; **~klassespieler** *m*, **~klassespielerin** *f* world-class player; **~klimakonferenz** *f* world climate conference; **~krieg** *m* world war; *der Erste/ Zweite ~* World War I/II, WWI/WWII, the First/Second World War; **~kugel** *f* globe; **~kulturerbe** *n*; *nur Sg.* the world('s) cultural heritage; *bestimmtes Gebäude etc.*: World Heritage Site; **~lage** *f* worldwide political situation

weltläufig *Adj.* cosmopolitan; **Weltläufigkeit** *f* cosmopolitanism

weltlich I. *Adj.* worldly, mundane; (*Ggs. geistlich*) secular; **~e Freuden** worldly (*od.* earthly) pleasures; **II.** *Adv.*: *~ gesinnt* worldly(-minded)

Welt|literatur *f* world literature; **~macht** *f* superpower, world power

Weltmann *m*; *nur Sg.* man of the world; **weltmännisch** *Adj.*: **~es Auftreten** *etc.* man-of-the-world air *etc.*

Welt|marke *f Wirts.* world-famous brand; **~markt** *m* world market; **~meer** *n* ocean; *die sieben ~e* the seven seas

Weltmeister *m*, **~in** *f Sport* world champion (*im* in, at); **Weltmeisterschaft** *f* world championship(s *Pl.*) (*im* in); *Fußball*: World Cup

Weltmeisterschafts... *im Subst. siehe* **WM-...**

Weltmeistertitel *m* world title (*im* in)

Welt|naturerbe *n*; *nur Sg.* the world('s) natural heritage; *bestimmtes Gebiet*: World Heritage Site; **~neuheit** *f* world('s) first, something completely new and unique; **~niveau** *n* international standing

weltoffen *Adj.* (*aufgeschlossen*) open-minded; (*sich für das Andere und Neue interessierend*) outward-looking; (*international ausgerichtet*) cosmopolitan; **Weltoffenheit** *f* open-mindedness; cosmopolitanism, cosmopolitan outlook

Welt|öffentlichkeit *f*: *die ~* the world public, the world at large; *weitS.* world opinion; **~ordnung** *f* world order

Weltpolitik *f* world (*od.* international) politics *Pl.* (*V. im Sg.*); **weltpolitisch I.** *Adj.* relating to international politics; **II.** *Adv. bedeutsam etc.*: in world politics; *~ gesehen* form the point of view of world politics

Weltpolizist *m fig.* world policeman

Welt|premiere *f* world première; **~presse** *f* international press; **~produktion** *f* world production

Weltrang *m*; *nur Sg.*: *von ~* of world standing (*od.* status); *bes. Person*: world-class ...; (*weltberühmt*) world-famous; **~liste** *f* world rankings *Pl.*; **~listenerste** *m, f*: *der od. die ~ etc.* the world's number one *etc.*

Weltraum *m*; *nur Sg.* (outer) space

Weltraum|... *im Subst. mst* space ...; *Satellit etc.*: *auch* spaceborn; *siehe auch* **Raum...**; **~bahnhof** *m* launch site, space cent|re (*Am.* -er); **~behörde** *f* space agency; **~forschung** *f* space research; **~labor** *n* spacelab; **~müll** *m* space rubbish (*Am.* trash); **~schrott** *m* space debris; **~spaziergang** *m* spacewalk; **~station** *f* space station; **~teleskop** *n* space telescope; **~waffen** *Pl.* space weapons; **~zentrum** *n* space cent|re (*Am.* -er)

Welt|regierung *f* world government; **~reich** *n* (world) empire; *das britische ~* the British Empire; **~reise** *f* world trip, trip around the world; **~reisende** *m, f* globetrotter

Weltrekord *m Sport* world record; *~ laufen/springen etc.* break the world record (for the 5000 m / high jump *etc.*); **Weltrekordinhaber** *m*, **Weltrekordinhaberin** *f*, **Weltrekordler** *m*; *-s, -*, **Weltrekordlerin** *f*; *-, -nen* world-record holder

Welt|religion *f* world religion; **~revolution** *f* world revolution; **~ruf** *m* international (*od.* world) reputation; *~ genießen* have a worldwide reputation, be world-renowned, be world-class; **~ruhm** *m* worldwide fame; **~schmerz**

m world-weariness, weltschmerz; **~sensation** *f* world sensation; **~sicherheitsrat** *m Pol.* Security Council; **~sicht** *f* view of the world; **~spitze** *f* world leadership; *auch Sport* number one position in the world; *~ sein* be number one (*od.* the best) in the world; be the world leader; **~sprache** *f für universale Kommunikation*: universal language; *weltweit verbreitet*: world language; *Englisch als ~* English as the universal (*bzw.* a world) language

Weltstadt *f* metropolis, cosmopolitan city; **weltstädtisch** *Adj.* cosmopolitan

Welt|star *m* world star, international star; **~tournee** *f* world tour; **~umseglung** *f* circumnavigation of the globe

weltumspannend *Adj.* worldwide

Weltuntergang *m the* end of the world; **Weltuntergangsstimmung** *f* atmosphere of gloom and doom, black mood (of despair)

Welt|uraufführung *f* world première; **~verband** *m* world association; **~verbesserer** *m*, **~verbesserin** *f iro.* do-gooder; **~währungsfonds** *m* International Monetary Fund, IMF

weltweit I. *Adj. attr.* worldwide, global; → **Echo** 2; **II.** *Adv.* worldwide, all over the world; *~ verbreitet etc.* found worldwide (*od.* all over the world)

Weltwirtschaft *f* world economy

Weltwirtschafts|gipfel *m* world economic summit; **~krise** *f* worldwide economic crisis; **~ordnung** *f*, **~system** *n* world economic order

Welt|wunder *n*: *die sieben ~* the Seven Wonders of the World; **~zeit** *f* Greenwich Mean Time, GMT; **~zeituhr** *f* world time clock

wem I. *Rel. Pron.* (*Dat. von wer*) (to) whom; *von ~* of whom, by whom; *von ~ hast du das?* who gave you that?; **II.** *Interr. Pron.* (to) whom; *~ hast du es gegeben?* to whom did you give it?, who did you give it to?; **Wemfall** *m Gram.* dative (case)

wen I. *Rel. Pron.* (*Akk. von wer*) who(m); *umg.* (*jemand*) somebody; **II.** *Interr. Pron.* who(m)

Wende *f*; *-, -n* 1. *nur Sg.*; (*~punkt*) turning point; *e-s Jahrhunderts*: turn; (*Änderung*) change (*zum Schlechten etc.* for the worse *etc.*); *um die ~ zum 16. Jahrhundert* at the turn of the 16th century; 2. *Pol., hist.*: *die ~* the fall of Communism (in Eastern Europe); *engS.* (*Mauerfall*) the breaching (*od.* opening) of the Wall; *vor der ~ auch* before the Wall came down; 3. *Sport* turn; (*~stelle*) turn; *Turnen*: front vault; 4. *Naut.* turn; **~hals** *m* 1. *Pol., pej.* (political) turncoat, quick-change artist *hum. umg.*; 2. *Orn.* wryneck; **~hammer** *m Verk.* turning bay; **~jacke** *f* reversible jacket; **~kreis** *m* 1. *Geog.* tropic; *nördlicher/südlicher ~* Tropic of Cancer/Capricorn; 2. *Mot.*: (*enger*) *~* (tight) turning circle

Wendel *f*; *-, -n*; *Tech.* spiral; **~rutsche** *f Tech.* spiral chute; **~treppe** *f* spiral staircase

Wende|manöver *n* turning manoeuvre (*Am.* maneuver); *auf engem Raum*: *auch* three-point turn; *fig.* U-turn; **~marke** *f Sport* turning mark

wenden; *wendet, wendete od. wandte, hat gewendet od. gewandt* **I.** *v/t.* 1. (*wendete*) turn; (*Buchseite, Braten etc.*) turn over; (*Auto*) turn ([a]round); *bitte ~!* (*abgek.* **b.w.**) PTO, pto (= please turn over), *Am.* turn the page;

in Mehl etc. ~ *Gastr.* turn in flour *etc.*; **2.** (*wendete od. wandte*): ~ *an* (+ *Akk.*) (*Zeit, Geld*) spend on; (*Mühe*) devote to; *keinen Blick* ~ *von* not take one's eyes off; *den Blick zur Seite* ~ look aside; *das Unheil etc. von j-m* ~ save s.o. from disaster *etc.*, avert disaster *etc.* for s.o.; → *drehen* I 1; **II.** *v/i.* (*wendete*) turn ([a]round); *Mot. auch* make a U-turn; **III.** *v/refl.* **1.** (*wendete*) turn ([a]round); → *Blatt* 6 a; **2.** (*wendete od. wandte*): *sich nach rechts etc.* ~ turn to the right; *sich* ~ *an* (*j-n*) *um Auskunft, Erlaubnis*: ask (*um* for); *um Rat, Hilfe*: turn to (for); *Buch etc.*: be aimed at; *sich an den Leser etc.* ~ turn to the reader *etc.*; *sich* ~ *gegen* (*j-n*) turn against (*od.* on); (*etw.*) oppose, object to; *sich zum Gehen* ~ turn to leave; *sich zum Guten/Schlechten* ~ take a turn for the better/worse

Wende|platz *m* turning space; **~punkt** *m* **1.** turning point, watershed; **2.** *Astron.* solstice; *Math.* point of inflection; *nördlicher/südlicher* ~ *der Sonne in der nördlichen Hemisphäre*: summer/ winter solstice; *in der südlichen Hemisphäre*: winter/summer solstice; **~schleife** *f Verk.* turning loop

wendig *Adj. Person*: nimble, agile; (*geistig* ~) *auch* nimble-minded; *Fahrzeug*: manoeuvrable, *Am.* maneuverable; **Wendigkeit** *f* nimbleness, agility; nimble-mindedness; manoeuvrability, *Am.* maneuverability; → *wendig*

Wendung *f* **1.** turn; (*Änderung*) change; *e-e* ~ *um 180°* a 180° turn; *e-e unerwartete* ~ *nehmen* take an unexpected turn; *e-r Sache e-e neue* ~ *geben* give a new turn to; *unerwartete* ~ unexpected turn of events; **2.** *Ling.* (*Ausdruck*) expression, phrase, figure of speech

Wenfall *m Gram.* accusative (case)

wenig I. *Adj. und unbest. Pron.* **1.** little, not much; ~ *er* less; *Math.* minus; *Pl.* fewer; *das* ~*ste* the least; *am* ~*sten* (the) least (of all); *ein* ~ a little; *immer* ~*er* less and less; *das* ~*e Geld, das er hat* what little money he has; *das Wenige, was ich habe, gebe ich gern* I'm very willing to give what little I have; *nicht* ~ quite a lot; *nicht gerade* ~ *umg.* quite a lot (of); *nicht* ~*er als* no less than; *Pl.* no fewer than; ~*er werden* decrease; *es kostet* ~ it doesn't cost much; *das ist* ~ that's not much; *dazu gehört* ~ it doesn't take much; ~ *fehlte, und er wäre ...* he came very close to ... (+ *Ger.*); ~ *übrig haben für umg.* not have much time for; *das hat* ~ *Sinn* there's not much point in it; *es gibt* ~ *Neues* there's very little that's new; *mit mehr oder* ~*er Erfolg* more or less successfully; *mit* ~*em auskommen* get by on very little; *das* ~*ste, was man erwarten kann* the least one could expect; ~*er wäre mehr gewesen* you can overdo things, less would have been more; *das ist das* ~*ste* that's the least of my worries; *sie wird immer* ~*er umg.* she'll disappear completely one of these days; **2.** *im Pl.*: ~*e* few, not many; (*Menschen*) few (people); *nicht* ~*e* quite a few (people); *einige* ~*e* a few; *nur* ~*e* only a few; *in* ~*en Tagen* in a few days' time; ~*e Augenblicke später* a few minutes later; *mit* ~*en Worten* in a few words; *das wissen die* ~*sten* people just don't realize that; *je* ~*er davon wissen, desto besser* the fewer people who know about it the better; **II.** *Adv.* little, not

much; ~ *bekannt* little known; ~ *beliebt* not very popular; ~*er dumm als frech* not so much stupid as impertinent; *nicht* ~ *erstaunt* rather surprised; *nur* ~ *mehr* only a little more; *sie geht* ~ *aus* she doesn't go out much; *er spricht immer* ~*er* he says less and less; *das hilft mir* ~ that's not much help to me; *das stört mich* ~ it doesn't really bother me; *das interessiert mich* ~*er* that doesn't interest me as much, that interests me less; *e-e* ~ *glückliche Wahl* a rather unfortunate choice; *ich verdiene zu* ~ I earn too little; *er bewegt sich zu* ~ he doesn't get enough exercise; *ein* ~ *schneller* a bit quicker; *das kostet,* ~ *gerechnet, tausend Euro* at a conservative estimate it will cost a thousand euros; *wir haben uns in letzter Zeit* ~ *gesehen* we haven't seen much of each other lately; *ein* ~ *übertrieben* slightly exaggerated; *ich fürchte mich ein* ~ I'm a bit (*od.* a little) scared

weniger I. *Komp.* → *wenig*; **II.** *Konj.*: *fünf* ~ *zwei ist* (*gleich*) *drei etc.* five less (*od.* take away, minus) two is (*od.* equals) three, two from five is three

Wenigkeit *f* small quantity; (*Kleinigkeit*) trifle; *meine* ~ *hum.* yours truly

wenigstens *Adv.* at least; *wenn ...* ~ if only ...

wenn *Konj.* **1.** *zeitlich*: when; (*sooft*) whenever; (*sobald*) as soon as; *immer* ~ whenever; *jedes Mal,* ~ *das Telefon läutet* every time the telephone rings; ~ *ich einmal groß bin* when I grow up; ~ *du erst einmal dort bist* once you're there; ~ *schon!* so what? **2.** *in Konditionalsätzen*: if; *Jur. oft* if and when; (*vorausgesetzt*) provided (that); ~ *er nicht gewesen wäre* if it hadn't been for him; ~ *ich das gewusst hätte* if I had known (that), had I known (that); ~ *das so ist* if that's the case; ~ *das Wörtchen* ~ *nicht wär ... umg.* if!; *außer* ~ unless, except if; **3.** *in Wendungen*: ~ *man ihn so reden hört* to hear him talk; *und* ~ *du noch so sehr bittest* you can plead as much as you like; ~ *ich das wüsste* I wish I knew; ~ *man bedenkt, dass ...* when you think that ...; ~ *du das sagst, wird's wohl stImmen* if you say so; ~ *es schon sein muss, dann gleich umg.* if it's got to be done let's get it over with; ~ *nichts dazwischenkommt* unless something crops up; ~ *nicht, dann eben nicht umg.* well, we may as well forget about that; ~ *man nach ... urteilt* judging by ...; *es war ein neuer,* ~ *auch langsamer Versuch* it was a new, albeit (*od.* if) slow, attempt; ~ *auch noch so klein etc.* however small *etc.*; ~ *doch od. nur* if only; → *schon* 7, 9, 10

Wenn *n*; *-s, -, umg.*: *-s*: *ohne* ~ *und Aber* (*ohne Einschränkungen*) unconditionally; (*keine Diskussion!*) no ifs or buts!

wenngleich *Konj.* although, even though

wennschon I. *Adv.*; *umg.*: *na* (*und*) ~*!* so what?; **II.** *Konj.*: ~, *denn schon* if you're going to do something, you might as well do it properly; there's no point in doing things by halves

wer I. *Rel. Pron.* who?; **II.** *Interr. Pron.* who?; *auswählend*: which (one)?; ~ *von euch?* which of you?; ~ *da? Mil.* who goes there?; **III.** *unbest. Pron. umg.* (*jemand*) someone, somebody;

in Fragen: *mst* anyone, anybody; ~ *auch* (*immer*) whoever; ~ *mitkommen möchte, soll sich eintragen*: whoever wants to come, anyone who wants (*od.* wishes) to come; *es war nicht leicht, aber jetzt 'ist er* ~ now he is somebody

Werbe|abteilung *f* publicity department; ~**agentur** *f* advertising agency; ~**aktion** *f* → *Werbekampagne*; ~**antwort** *f* business reply; ~**artikel** *m* promotional article; ~**aufwand** *m* expenditure on advertising, advertising costs *Pl.*; ~**banner** *n Internet*: banner ad; ~**berater** *m*, ~**beraterin** *f* advertising consultant; ~**block** *m* TV commercial break; ~**branche** *f* advertising industry; ~**brief** *m* publicity circular; ~**einnahmen** *Pl.* advertising revenue *Sg.*; ~**etat** *m* advertising budget; ~**fachfrau** *f*, ~**fachmann** *m* advertising expert; ~**fahrt** *f* → *Kaffeefahrt*; ~**feldzug** *m* advertising campaign; ~**fernsehen** *n* commercial television; (*Werbespots*) television (*od.* TV) commercials *Pl.*; ~**film** *m* publicity film; ~**fläche** *f* advertising space; ~**fotograf** *m*, ~**fotografin** *f* commercial photographer

werbefrei *Adj. und Adv.* TV etc. ... without advertising

Werbe|funk *m* commercial radio (*od.* broadcasting); (*Werbespots*) radio ads *Pl.* (*od.* commercials *Pl.*); ~**gag** *m* publicity stunt (*od.* gimmick); ~**geschenk** *n* freebie *umg.*, freebee *umg.*, promotional (*od.* free) gift; ~**grafik** *f* commercial art; ~**grafiker** *m*, ~**grafikerin** *f* commercial artist; ~**kampagne** *f* publicity campaign; *für Waren*: advertising campaign; ~**kosten** *Pl.* advertising expenditure *Sg.*; ~**leiter** *m*, ~**leiterin** *f* publicity manager; ~**material** *n* promotional material; ~**minute** *f* TV, Funk. minute of air time (for a commercial); ~**mittel** *Pl.* **1.** advertising media; **2.** (*Geld*) advertising budget *Sg.*

werben; *wirbt, warb, hat geworben* **I.** *v/t.* (*Mitglieder etc.*) enlist; (*Kunden, Stimmen*) attract; *j-n für etw.* ~ win s.o. over to s.th.; **II.** *v/i. Pol.* campaign; *Wirts.* advertise; ~ *für auch* promote, plug *umg.*; ~ *um* (*e-e Frau*) court; *um j-s Vertrauen / die Gunst der Wähler etc.* ~ set out to gain s.o.'s trust / the approval of the voters *etc.*

Werbe|plakat *n* advertisement, advertising poster (*od.* placard); ~**prospekt** *m* advertising (*od.* publicity) brochure; ~**psychologie** *f* advertising psychology

Werber[1] *m*; *-s, -*; *Mil. hist* recruiting officer

Werber[2] *m*; *-s, -*, ~**in** *f*; *-, -nen Wirts.* canvasser, advertising expert

Werbe|rummel *m umg.* hype; ~**sendung** *f* **1.** commercial program(me); **2.** *Post.*; *auch Pl.* advertising mail; *e-e* ~ a mailshot (*Am.* mailing); ~**slogan** *m* advertising slogan; ~**spot** *m* commercial; ~**spruch** *m* advertising slogan; ~**text** *m* advertising copy; ~**texter** *m*, ~**texterin** *f* copywriter; ~**träger** *m* advertising media; ~**trommel** *f umg. fig.*: *die* ~ *für etw. rühren* promote (*od.* plug) s.th., beat the drum for s.th.; ~**veranstaltung** *f* publicity event; ~**verbot** *n* ban on advertising, advertising ban; ~**vertrag** *m* advertising contract (*über* + *Akk.* for)

werbewirksam *Adj.*: ~ *sein Slogan, Anzeige*: be effective (as advertising), put one's message across (effectively); **Werbewirksamkeit** *f* effectiveness (as advertising)

Werbezwecke *Pl.*: **für ~** for advertising purposes

werblich *Adv. nützen etc.*: as advertising; **~ mehr tun** advertise more

Werbung *f* **1.** advertising, publicity; **e-e (gute) ~ für** *fig.* good publicity for, a good advertisement for; **2.** *neuer Kunden etc.*: winning, attracting; **3. die ~ um e-e Frau** courtship

Werbungskosten *Pl. steuerlich*: business expenses; *e-s Individuums*: *auch* professional expenses *Pl.* (*od.* outlay *Sg.*); **als ~ geltend machen** claim as business expenses (*od.* as a business expense)

Werdegang *m*; *-s, kein Pl.* development; (*Geschichte*) history (*auch fig. und Tech.*); *Person*: personal background

werden; *wird, wurde, altm. od. hum. ward, ist geworden* **I.** *v/i.* **1.** *mit Adj.*: get, become; *Betonung auf dem Endzustand: oft* go; *müde/nass/reich etc.* **~** get tired/wet/rich *etc.*; **blind/kahl/verrückt/sauer/taub** *etc.* **~** go blind/bald/mad/sour/deaf *etc.*; **alt ~** get (*od.* grow) old; **besser ~** get better, improve; **blass ~** go (*od.* turn) pale; **böse** *od.* **wütend ~** get angry (*od.* mad); **dick ~** get fat, put on weight; **gesund ~** get well; **grau ~** go (*od.* turn) grey (*Am.* gray); **kalt ~** get cold (*auch Essen etc.*); **krank ~** fall (*od.* get) ill (*od.* sick); **rot ~** go red, blush; **schlecht ~** go bad (*od.* off); **schlimmer ~** get worse; **schwach ~** get (*od.* grow) weak; **katholisch ~** become a Catholic, turn Catholic; **2.** (*bes. etw.*) become, be; **was will er ~?** what does he want to be?; **sie wurde Ärztin** *etc.* she became a doctor *etc.*; **er ist was geworden** *umg.* he made something of himself (*od.* his life); **er wird wie sein Vater (~)** he's getting (to be) like his father; **sie wird m-e Frau** she is going to be my wife; **ich werde Vater** *etc.* I'm going to be a father *etc.*; **ich werde 30** I'm nearly 30; **er wird heute 18** he's 18 today; **sie ist vorige Woche 50 geworden** she was 50 last week; **er ist Erster geworden** he was (*od.* came) first; **er wurde Bester s-s Jahrgangs** *etc.* he was the best in his year *etc.*; **3.** *Wirklichkeit* **~** become reality; **zur Gewohnheit ~** become a habit; **aus Liebe wurde Hass** love turned into hate; **die Vorräte ~ immer weniger** supplies are getting lower and lower; **wie wird die Ernte ~?** what kind of harvest are we going to have?; **wie sind die Fotos geworden?** how have the photos (*od.* pictures) turned out?; **die Fotos sind nichts geworden** *umg.* the photos (*od.* pictures) were no good (*od.* didn't come out well); *bes. wenn nichts erkennbar ist*: the photos (*od.* pictures) didn't come out; **der Kuchen** *etc.* **ist nichts geworden** *umg.* the cake was no good; **die Sache wird allmählich** *umg.* things are coming along (*od.* are beginning to take shape); **4.** *unpers.*: **es wird dunkel** it's getting (growing *lit.*) dark; **kalt ~** get cold; **warm ~** get warm, warm up; **es wird Winter** winter is on its way; **mir wird kalt** I'm beginning to feel (*od.* get) chilly; **mir wird schlecht** I feel sick; **was soll nun ~?** what are we going to do now?; **ich weiß nicht, was ~ soll** I don't know what to do; **aus dem Geschäft ist**

nichts geworden nothing came of the deal; **was ist aus ihm geworden?** what's become of him?; **aus ihm ist etwas geworden** he made something of himself; **daraus wird nichts** nothing will come of it, it won't come to anything; **als Verbot**: you can forget (all) about that; **es wird schon ~** it'll be all right; **was nicht ist, kann noch ~** *umg.* things can change; **morgen wird es ein Jahr, dass ...** tomorrow it'll be a year ago that ...; → **spät** I; **II.** *v/aux.*; *Part.-Perf. ist ... worden* **1.** *Futur.* **ich werde fahren** I will (*od.* I'll) drive; **sie wird gleich weinen** she's going to cry (any minute); **2.** *eine Vermutung ausdrückend*: **es wird ihm doch nichts passiert sein?** I hope nothing has happened to him; **es wird schon so sein (wie du sagst)** I'm sure you're right; **ich werde es (wohl) verloren haben** I must have lost it; **3.** *Konditional*: **ich würde kommen, wenn ...** I would (*od.* I'd) come if ...; **4.** *passivisch*: **geliebt ~** be loved; **gebaut ~** be built; *gegenwärtig*: be being built; **es wird viel gebaut** there's a lot of building going on; **es wurde getanzt** they (*od.* we) danced, there was dancing; **es ist uns gesagt worden** we've been told; **jetzt wird aber geschlafen/gearbeitet!** *umg.* it's time to sleep / to get down to work, it's time you (*od.* we) went to sleep / got down to work; **heute wird nicht gestritten!** *umg.* today there are going to be no arguments!; **und ward nicht mehr gesehn** *hum.* and was never seen again

Werden *n*; *-s, kein Pl.*; (*Entwicklung*) development, growth; (*Entstehung*) birth; (*Fortschreiten*) progress; **im ~ sein** be in the making

werdend **I.** *Part. Präs.* → **werden**; **II.** *Adj.* growing; **~e Mutter** expectant mother; **~er Vater** father-to-be

Werfall *m Gram.* nominative (case)

werfen; *wirft, warf, hat geworfen* **I.** *vt/i.* throw (**nach** at; **zu** to); (*schleudern*) sling; *Flug.* (*Bomben*) drop; *beim Baseball*: pitch; **mit etw. (nach j-m) ~** throw s.th. (at s.o.); **von sich ~** (*Kleider*) throw off; **ein Tor ~** *Sport* score a goal; **er wirft den Speer 70 m weit** he can throw the javelin 70 m; **e-e Sechs ~** throw a six; **e-e Münze ~** toss (*od.* flip) a coin; **nicht ~!** *auf Paketen etc.*: handle with care; **ein sehr helles Licht ~** *Lampe*: cast a very bright light; **Truppen an die Front ~** dispatch troops to the front; **Waren auf den Markt ~** throw goods on the market; **e-e Skizze aufs Papier ~** do a quick sketch; **etw. in die Debatte ~** throw s.th. into the debate; **um sich ~ mit** *umg.* (*Geld*) throw about; (*Worten*) bandy about; → **Blick** 1, **Handtuch**, **Haufen** 1, **Junge²**, **Schatten** 2; **II.** *v/refl. Sport, Torwart etc.*: throw o.s.; *Tech.* buckle; *Holz*: warp; **sich in den Sessel ~** *umg.* throw o.s. onto (*od.* flop down into) the armchair; **sich auf j-n ~** throw o.s. at s.o., dive for s.o.; **sich auf (+ Akk.) e-e Tätigkeit ~** throw o.s. into; → **Brust** 4, **Hals** 3

Werfer *m*; *-s, -*, **~in** *f*; *-, -nen* thrower; *Baseball*: pitcher

Werft *f*; *-, -en* shipyard; *Flug.* hangar; **~arbeiter** *m*, **~arbeiterin** *f* docker; **~industrie** *f* shipbuilding industry

Werg *n*; *-(e)s, kein Pl.* tow; (*gezupftes Tauwerk*) oakum

Werk *n*; *-(e)s, -e* **1.** (*Arbeit, Schöpfung, Kunstwerk, Buch*) work; **ans ~!** let's

get going!, to work!, (let's) get cracking *umg.*; **am ~ sein** *auch iro.* be at work; **ans ~ gehen** set to work; **behutsam** *etc.* **zu ~e gehen** go about it carefully *etc.*; **2.** *nur Sg.* (*Gesamtwerk*) works *Pl.*; **3.** (*Tat*) deed, act; **ein gutes ~ tun** do a good deed; **4.** *nur Sg.* (*Urheberschaft*): **ein ~ der Terroristen** *etc.* the work of (the) terrorists; **es war sein ~** it was his work (*od.* doing); **5.** (*Fabrik*) works *Pl.* (*auch V. im Sg.*), *bes. Am.* factory; (*auch Gaswerk etc.*) plant; (*Gesellschaft, Unternehmen*) company; **ab ~** ex works, *Am.* factory-direct; **6.** (*Getriebe, Uhrwerk etc.*) works *Pl.*, mechanism

Werk|ausgabe *f* edition; **~bank** *f* workbench

werkeigen *Adj. attr.* company(-owned) ..., works ..., *Am.* factory ...

werkeln *v/i.* potter (*Am.* putter) about (**an** + *Dat.* with)

werken *v/i.* work; (*geschäftig sein*) be busy; (*basteln*) tinker; *in der Schule*: do handicrafts; **Werken** *n*; *-s, kein Pl.* arts and crafts *Pl.* (*V. im Sg.*); *Schulfach*: handicrafts *Pl.* (*V. im Sg.*), *Am.* industrial arts

Werkeverzeichnis *n* catalog(ue) of works

Werkfahrer *m*, **~in** *f Mot.* works (*Am.* company) driver

werkgetreu *Adj. Kunst*: faithful

Werkhalle *f* workshop

werkimmanent *Adj. Lit.* text-based, based on the work itself

Werk|lehrer *m*, **~lehrerin** *f Schule*: handicrafts (*Am.* industrial arts) teacher; **~meister** *m* foreman, supervisor; **~meisterin** *f* forewoman, supervisor; **~raum** *m* work room

Werks|angehörige *m*, *f* (works) employee; **~arzt** *m*, **~ärztin** *f* works (*od.* company) doctor

Werkschau *f* exhibition (*od.* show) (of s.o.'s work)

Werkschutz *m* factory (*od.* plant) security officers *Pl.*

werkseigen *Adj. attr.* company(-owned), works ...

Werks|ferien *Pl.* works (*bes. Am.* company) holidays; **~feuerwehr** *f* factory fire brigade (*Am.* fire fighters); **~garantie** *f* factory warranty; **~gelände** *n* works (*Am.* plant) premises; **~halle** *f* workshop; **~kantine** *f* factory (*Brit. auch* works) canteen; **~leiter** *m*, **~leiterin** *f* works (*od.* plant) manager; **~leitung** *f* works (*Am.* factory) management

Werkspionage *f* industrial espionage

Werksschließung *f* factory closure

Werkstatt *f*; *-, Werkstätten* workshop; *Mot.* garage; (*Atelier*) studio; *Theat.* (*Bühne*) studio; **Werkstätte** *f* → **Werkstatt**

Werkstatt|bühne *f Theat.* studio theat|re (*Am. auch* -er); **~gespräch** *n* mit e-m Autor *etc.*: studio discussion; **~theater** *n* studio theatre (*Am. auch* -er)

Werkstoff *m* material; (*Rohstoff*) raw material; **~kunde** *f* materials technology; **~prüfung** *f* materials testing

Werkstor *n* factory gate

Werk|stück *n Tech.* workpiece; **~student** *m*, **~studentin** *f* working student

Werkswohnung *f* company flat (*Am.* apartment)

Werktag *m* working day; **werktäglich** *Adj. attr.* workday ...; (*wochentäglich*) weekday ...; **werktags** *Adv.* on working days, during the week, on weekdays

werktätig *Adj. attr.* working, *auch präd.* employed; **~ sein** *auch* have a job; **Werktätige** *m, f; -n, -n* employed person, working man (*weiblich* woman); **die ~n** the working population (*V. in Sg. od. Pl.*)

Werk|treue *f Kunst:* faithfulness to the original; **~unterricht** *m Päd.* handicrafts *Pl.* (*V. im Sg.*), *Am.* industrial arts; **~vertrag** *m* contract for work; **~verzeichnis** *n* catalog(ue) of works

Werkzeug *n; -s, -e* **1.** tool (*auch fig.*); *feines:* instrument; (*Gerät*) implement; **2.** *nur Sg. Koll.* tools *Pl.;* **~kasten** *m* tool box; **~macher** *m,* **~macherin** *f* toolmaker; **~maschine** *f* machine tool; **~stahl** *m* tool steel; **~tasche** *f* tool bag

Wermut *m; -s, -s;* (*Wein*) vermouth; *Bot.* wormwood; **~bruder** *m umg.* wino

Wermutstropfen *m fig.* sour (*od.* sad) note, cloud

wert *Adj.* worth; *altm.* (*lieb*) dear; (*~geschätzt*) esteemed, valued; *etw.* **~ sein** be worth s.th.; (*e-r Sache würdig sein*) be worthy of s.th.; **viel ~** worth a lot; **nichts ~** worthless; **das ist schon viel ~** that's a great step forward; **das ist e-n Versuch ~** it's worth a try; **es ist viel ~ zu wissen, dass …** it's good to know that …; **er hat es nicht für ~ gefunden, mich zu informieren** he didn't consider it necessary to inform me; **das Buch ist ~, dass man es liest** is worth reading; **er ist es nicht ~, dass man ihm hilft** he doesn't deserve to be helped; **das ist die Sache nicht ~** it isn't worth it; **sie ist s-r nicht ~** she is not worthy of him; → *Mühe, Rede* 5

Wert *m; -(e)s, -e* **1.** value (*auch Phys., Math., Tech.*); **von unschätzbarem ~** invaluable; **2.** (*Wichtigkeit*) importance; (*Qualität*) quality; (*Vorzug*) merit; (*Nutzen, Zweck*) use; **geistige ~e** spiritual values; **innere ~e haben im Gegensatz zu äußerer Schönheit** *etc., Person:* be a really nice person, (*interessant und lebendig sein*) have personality; **~e vermitteln** *bes. Päd.* teach (*od.* pass on *od.* transmit) values; (*großen*) **~ legen auf** attach (great) importance to, set (great) store by; **ich lege ~ darauf festzustellen, dass …** I would like to stress that …; **keinen gesteigerten ~ auf etw. legen** *wörtlich:* not attach much importance to s.th., not set much store by s.th.; *fig.* (*etw. nicht mögen*) not be overfond of s.th., not care overmuch for s.th.; **das hat keinen ~** *umg.* it's pointless; **es hat keinen ~ zu streiten** *etc. umg.* there's no point in arguing; → *Unwert;* **3.** *nur Sg.;* (*Gegenwert*) equivalent; **im ~(e) von** to the value of, worth …; **Waren im ~e von 300 Dollar** 300 dollars worth of goods, goods to the value of 300 dollars; **im ~ sinken/steigen** go down/up in value, lose value / gain in value; **etw. über/unter ~ verkaufen** sell s.th. for more/less than its true value; **sich unter ~ verkaufen** *fig.* sell o.s. short; **4.** *Wirts.* (*Vermögenswert*) asset; *Fin.* (*Tag*) value; **~e** (*Aktiva*) assets, (*Wertpapiere*) securities, stocks; **5.** *Med.* count; → *Leberwerte etc.*

Wert|angabe *f* **1.** declaration of value; **2.** (*angegebener Wert*) declared value; **~berichtigung** *f Wirts.* adjustment of value

wertbeständig *Adj.* of stable value; *Währung:* stable; *fig.* of lasting value; **Wertbeständigkeit** *f* ability to retain its value; *weitS* lasting value

Wertbrief *m* insured letter

Wertegemeinschaft *f: Europa etc.* **als ~** Europe as a community with shared values (*od.* with a common heritage)

werten *vt/i.* evaluate, assess; (*beurteilen*) judge; *nach Kategorien:* classify; *bes. Sport, Schule:* mark, score; *Am. Schule:* grade; **etw. als Erfolg** *etc.* **~** judge (*od.* consider) s.th. to be a success *etc.;* **e-n Versuch nicht ~** *Sport* not count an attempt; **e-n Fehler** *etc.* **nicht ~** not count (*od.* discount) a mistake *etc.;* **die Punktrichter ~ sehr unterschiedlich** the judges are giving very different marks, the judges are scoring very differently

Werte|skala *f* scale of values; **~system** *n* system of values; **~vermittlung** *f bes. Päd.* transmission of values; **~wandel** *m* change in values, value shift, changing values *Pl.*

wertfrei I. *Adj.* value-free, (value-)neutral, non-partisan; **II.** *Adv. darstellen etc.:* in a (value-)neutral way; from a neutral standpoint; **Wertfreiheit** *f* value neutrality

Wertgegenstand *m* article of value; *Pl.* valuables

wertgemindert *Adj. präd. und nachgestellt:* diminished in value

Wertigkeit *f Chem., Ling.* valency; (*Bedeutung*) significance

Wertkartentelefon *n* cardphone

wertkonservativ *Adj.* concerned with upholding (*mst* traditional) values

wertlos *Adj.* worthless; (*nutzlos*) useless; **Wertlosigkeit** *f* worthlessness; uselessness

Wert|marke *f* stamp; **~maßstab** *m* standard (of value); **~minderung** *f* depreciation

wertneutral *Adj.* → *wertfrei*

Wertpaket *n* insured parcel (*Am.* package)

Wertpapier *n Wirts.* security, commercial paper; **~börse** *f* stock exchange; **~geschäft** *n* securities trading; *einzelne Handlung:* securities transaction; **~handel** *m* trade in securities

Wertsachen *Pl.* valuables

wertschätzen *vt.* (*trennb., hat -ge-*) *altm.* hold *s.o.* in high esteem; **Wertschätzung** *f* esteem (*+ Gen.* for); **sich j-s ~ erfreuen** enjoy s.o.'s esteem, be highly reagrded by s.o.

Wert|schöpfung *f Wirts.* value added; **~sendung** *f* consignment with value declared; *Post.* insured matter; **~steigerung** *f* increase in value, appreciation; **~stellung** *f Fin.* value

Wertstoff *m* recyclable (*od.* reusable) material; **~hof** *m* recycling depot; **~sammelstelle** *f* collection point for recyclable materials; **~tonne** *f* recycling bin

Wertsystem *n* system of values

Wertung *f* evaluation, assessment; (*Beurteilung*) judg(e)ment; *Sport* score; (*Note*) mark, *Am.* grade; **in der ~ vorn/hinten** *etc.* **liegen** be ahead/behind in the scoring

Wertungslauf *m Mot. etwa* series race, race that counts toward(s) a participant's eventual position in a championship table

Wert|urteil *n* value judg(e)ment; **~verlust** *m* depreciation

wertvoll *Adj.* valuable; *Mensch:* estimable; **künstlerisch ~** artistically valuable, … of artistic value

Wert|vorstellung *f* value system; **~zeichen** *n Post.* (postage) stamp; **~zuwachs** *m* appreciation

Werwolf *m* werewolf

Wesen *n; -s, -* **1.** (*Lebewesen*) being, creature (*auch umg. Person*); *Philos.* entity; **furchtsames ~** (*Person*) timid creature; **ein kleines, hilfloses ~** a small helpless creature; **der Mensch als soziales ~** man as a social being; **2.** *nur Sg.;* (*Wesenskern*) essence; (*Wesensart*) nature, character, *e-r Person:* auch personality; **heiteres** *etc.* **~** cheerful *etc.* disposition; **das entspricht nicht s-m ~** that's not at all like him, it's completely out of character for him; **es liegt im ~** (*+ Gen.*) it's in the nature of; **das gehört zum ~ der Demokratie** that's an essential part (*od.* that's essential to the nature) of democracy; **3.** **viel ~(s) von etw. machen** *umg.* make a great fuss about s.th.

wesenlos *Adj.* **1.** insubstantial, incorporeal; **2.** (*inhaltslos*) empty, meaningless

Wesensart *f* nature, character

wesens|fremd *Adj.* alien (to one's nature); **j-m ~ sein** *auch* be completely foreign to s.o.; **~gleich** *Adj.* identical in character

Wesens|merkmal *n* (basic *od.* essential) feature; **~zug** *m* characteristic, trait

wesentlich I. *Adj.* essential (**für** to); (*auch beträchtlich*) substantial, important; (*grundlegend*) fundamental; **das Wesentliche** the essential part, the most important aspect(s); **nichts Wesentliches** nothing important, nothing of import *förm.;* **keine ~en Änderungen** no major changes; **ein ~er Unterschied** a big (*od.* an important) difference; **kein ~er Unterschied** no marked change (*od.* difference); **im Wesentlichen** essentially, mainly, in the main *geh.;* (*im Großen und Ganzen*) on the whole; **II.** *Adv.* (*grundlegend*) fundamentally; (*erheblich*) considerably; **~ besser** *etc.* far better *etc.;* **sich ~ in/von etw. unterscheiden** differ considerably in/from s.th.; **wir müssen noch ~ mehr tun** we must do a great deal more

Wesfall *m Gram.* genitive (case)

weshalb I. *Interr. Adv.* why?; **II.** *Konj.* which is why, and so

Wespe *f; -, -n; Zool.* wasp

Wespen|bussard *m Orn.* honey buzzard; **~nest** *n* wasps' nest; **in ein ~ stechen** *fig.* stir up a hornets' nest; **~stich** *m* wasp sting; **~taille** *f* wasp waist

wessen I. *Interr. Pron.* **1.** (*Gen. von wer*) whose?; **2.** (*Gen. von was*): **~ wird er beschuldigt?** what is he accused of?; **II.** *Rel. Pron.* (*Gen. von was*) (of) which; **das, ~ er beschuldigt wird** what he is (being) accused of

Wessi *m; -s, -s; umg. etwa* westerner, citizen of (pre-reunification) West Germany

West *m* **1.** *ohne Art.; nur Nom. Sg.; Met., Naut.* west; **von** *od.* **aus ~** from the west; **2.** *ohne Art.; nur Nom. Sg.; nachgestellt:* **München ~** west Munich; **in München ~** in the west of Munich; **Eingang ~** west entrance; *e-s Gebäudes auch* west door; **3.** *-(e)s, -e; Pl. selten; Naut., poet.* west wind, westerly; **es blies ein steifer ~** a stiff breeze was blowing from the west

West… *im Subst. hist.* West German

Westafrika (*n*); *-s; Geog.* West Africa

West|berlin (n); *Geog.* West Berlin; **~berliner I.** *m* West Berliner; **II.** *Adj.* West Berlin ..., of West Berlin; **~berlinerin** *f* woman (*od.* girl) from West Berlin, West Berliner

westdeutsch *Adj.* **1.** *Geog.* west(ern) German, in western Germany; **2.** *hist.* West German; **Westdeutsche** *m, f* *bes. hist.* West German, *weiblich auch:* West German woman (*od.* girl *etc.*); **Westdeutschland** *n* **1.** *Geog.* west(ern) Germany; **2.** *hist.* West Germany

Weste *f; -, -n* waistcoat, *Am.* vest; (*Strickjacke*) cardigan; **e-e reine ~ haben** *fig.* have a clean record; → **kugelsicher** *etc.*

Westen *m; -s, kein Pl.* west; (*westlicher Landesteil*) West; **der ~** *Geog. und Pol.* the West (*auch in USA*); **nach ~** west(ward[s]); *Verkehr, Straße etc.:* westbound; **von ~** from the west

Westentasche *f* waistcoat (*Am.* vest) pocket; **etw. wie s-e ~ kennen** *fig.* know s.th. like the back of one's hand

Westentaschenformat *n*: **Kamera** *etc.* **im ~** pocket camera *etc.*; **Politiker** *etc.* **im ~** *iro.* would-be (*od.* small-time) politician *etc.*

Western *m; -s, -* western, cowboy film, horse opera *hum.*; → **Italowestern**; **~held** *m* *umg.* western hero

Westeuropäer *m,* **~in** *f* West European, *weiblich auch:* West European woman (*od.* girl *etc.*); **westeuropäisch** *Adj.* West European

Westfale *m; -n, -n* Westphalian; **Westfalen** (n); -s: *Geog.* Westphalia; **Westfälin** *f; -, -nen* Westphalian (woman *od.* girl *etc.*); **westfälisch** *Adj.* Westphalian; **der Westfälische Friede** *hist.* the Peace of Westphalia

Westflügel *m* *Archit.* west wing

westfriesisch *Adj.* West Frisian; **die Westfriesischen Inseln** the West Frisian Islands

Westfront *f* *hist. Mil.* western front

Westgote *m* Visigoth; **westgotisch** *Adj.* Visigothic

Westgrenze *f* western border

Westindien (n); *Geog.* the West Indies; **westindisch** *Adj.* West Indian; **die Westindischen Inseln** the West Indian Islands

Westjordanland *n; nur Sg.; Geog.* West Jordan

West|kurve *f* *im Stadion etc.:* western end; **~küste** *f* west coast

westlich I. *Adj.* western, west; *Wind:* westerly; **in ~er Richtung** west(ward[s]); *Verkehr, Straße etc.:* westbound; **aus ~er Richtung** from the west; *Verkehr, Straße etc.:* westbound; **II.** *Adv.* (to the) west (**von** of); **III.** *Präp.* (+ *Gen.*) (to the) west (of); **einige Kilometer ~ der Grenze** a few kilomet|res (*Am.* -ers) (to the) west of the border; **westlichst...** *Adj.* westernmost

West|löhne *Pl.* als Maßstab für Ostlöhne: wages in western Germany; **~mächte** *Pl. Pol.* Western Powers; **~mark** *f* *hist.* West German mark; **~niveau** *n; nur Sg.; hist.* West German level; **auf ~** to the West German level

Westnordwest *m* **1.** *ohne Art.* west-northwest; **2.** *Naut.* (*Wind*) west-northwesterly; **Westnordwesten** *m* west-northwest

westöstlich *Adj.* **1.** *Geog.* east-west; **2.** *Pol.:* **~e Beziehungen** East-West relations

West|preußen (n); *hist.* West Prussia;

~punkt *m* *Geog.* due west; **~ring** *m* *Verk.* western ringroad (*Am.* beltway); **~sektor** *m* *hist.* Western Sector; **~teil** *m* western part; **~ufer** *n* west bank; **~wall** *m* *hist. Mil.* Siegfried Line; **~ware** *f* *hist.* West German goods *Pl.*

westwärts *Adv.* west(wards)

Westwind *m* west wind

weswegen → **weshalb**

Wettannahme(stelle) *f* betting office

Wettbewerb *m; -s, -e* competition (*auch Wirts.*); (*Wettkampf*) contest; **freier/unlauterer ~** *Wirts.* free/unfair competition; **in ~ treten/stehen mit** enter into / be in competition with; **Wettbewerber** *m,* **Wettbewerberin** *f* competitor; **wettbewerblich** *Adj.* competitive

Wettbewerbs|bedingungen *Pl.* rules of the competition; **~beitrag** *m* competition entry; **~beschränkung** *f* restraint of trade

wettbewerbsfähig *Adj.* competitive; **Wettbewerbsfähigkeit** *f* competitiveness

Wettbewerbs|klausel *f* non-competition clause; **~nachteil** *m* competitive disadvantage; **~politik** *f* competition policy; **~recht** *n* competition law; **~regeln** *Pl.* rules of a (*od.* the) competition; *Wirts.* competition regulations; **~sieger** *m,* **~siegerin** *f* (competition) winner; **~teilnehmer** *m,* **~teilnehmerin** *f* competitor, contestant, contender; **~verbot** *n* prohibition of competition; **~verzerrung** *f* unfair competition; **~vorteil** *m* competitive advantage

wettbewerbswidrig I. *Adj.* anti-competitive; **II.** *Adv.* *handeln etc.:* anti-competitively

Wettbüro *n* betting office

Wette *f; -, -n* bet, wager *altm.*; **e-e ~ eingehen** *od.* **abschließen** make a bet; **ich gehe jede ~ ein, dass ...** I'll bet you any money you like (that) ...; **was gilt die ~?** what do you (want to) bet?; **die ~ gilt!** you're on!; **um die ~ rennen** *od.* **schwimmen** *etc.* have a race, race each other; **um die ~** *umg.* arbeiten *etc.*: all out; *essen etc.*: like it's going out of style

Wetteifer *m* competitive drive; (*Rivalität*) rivalry, competition; **wetteifern** *v/i.* (*untr., hat ge-*) vie, compete (**mit** with; **um** for)

wetten *v/t/i.* bet; **mit j-m ~** bet with s.o., have a bet with s.o.; **um 10 Euro** *etc.* **~** bet 10 euros *etc.*; **~ auf** (+ *Akk.*) bet (*od.* put one's money) on; *Rennsport:* auch back; **ich wette zehn zu eins, dass ...** I bet you ten to one (that) ...; **auf Platz/Sieg ~** *Rennsport:* bet on a place/win, back *s.o./s.th.* to be placed / to win; **~, dass?** *umg.* wanna bet?; *stärker:* you can bet on it, it's a dead cert; **so haben wir nicht gewettet** *fig.* that wasn't part of the deal

Wetter¹ *n; -s, -* **1.** *nur Sg.* weather; **bei diesem ~** in this (sort of) weather; **bei jedem ~** in any weather, in all weathers; **bei klarem ~** in fine weather; **wie ist/wird das ~?** what's the weather like / going to be like?; **wir hatten herrliches/schlechtes ~** we had wonderful/bad weather; **was für ein ~!** *umg.* what weather!; **das ~ meint es gut mit uns** *umg.* we're lucky with the weather, the weather's being kind to us; **ein ~ zum Eierlegen!** *umg.* fantastic weather; **bei solchem ~ möchte man keinen Hund vor die Tür jagen** *umg.* this weather's not fit for man nor beast, you wouldn't send a dog out in this weather; **(und nun) das ~** *TV etc.* (and now) the weather (forecast); **gut ~ bei j-m machen** *umg. fig.* get s.o. into the right mood; **um gut(es) ~ bitten** *umg. fig.* try to make it up, try to smooth things over; **2.** (*Unwetter*) storm; **ein ~ zieht sich zusammen / bricht los / verzieht sich** a storm is gathering /breaking/passing; **alle ~!** *umg. fig.* good grief!; **3.** *Bergb.:* **schlagende ~** firedamp *Sg.*; → **Wind** 1

Wetter² *m; -s, -,* **~in** *f; -, -nen** better

Wetter|amt *n* meteorological office, *Brit. umg.* met office; *Am.* (national) weather service; **~aussichten** *Pl.* für den nächsten Tag: (weather) forecast *Sg.*; für die darauf folgenden Tage: *auch* (weather) outlook (**bis Dienstag** until Tuesday)

wetterbedingt I. *Adj.* *Störung etc.:* caused by the weather, due to the weather; **II.** *Adv.* *ausfallen etc.:* because of the weather; **Wetterbedingungen** *Pl.* weather conditions

Wetter|beobachtung *f* meteorological observation; **~bericht** *m* weather report (*od.* forecast); *Radio, TV: Am. auch* weathercast; **~besserung** *f* improvement in the weather

wetter|beständig *Adj.* weatherproof; **~bestimmend** *Adj.:* **~ sein** determine the weather; **das zur Zeit ~e Hoch** *etc.* the area of high pressure that is currently determining the weather

Wetterchen *n* *umg.:* **ein ~ ist das heute!** isn't the weather gorgeous today?

Wetter|dienst *m* weather service; **~ecke** *f* *umg.* bad-weather area

wetterempfindlich *Adj.* → **wetterfühlig**

Wetter|experte *m,* **~expertin** *f* weather expert; **~fahne** *f* weather vane

wetterfest *Adj.* weatherproof

Wetterfrosch *m* *umg.* **1.** *fig.* weatherman; **2.** (*Laubfrosch*) tree frog in a glass case that is supposed to indicate fine weather by climbing a ladder

wetterfühlig I. *Adj.* weather-sensitive, susceptible to the weather; **II.** *Adv.* *reagieren:* to the weather; **Wetterfühligkeit** *f* sensitivity (*od.* susceptibility) to the weather

Wetter|gott *m* *umg. fig.:* **wenn der ~ mitspielt** if the clerk of the weather is on our side; **~hahn** *m* weathercock; **~häuschen** *n* weather house; **~karte** *f* weather map; **~krankheiten** *Pl.* illnesses caused by the weather

Wetterkunde *f* meteorology; **wetterkundlich** *Adj.* meteorological

Wetter|lage *f* weather situation; **~lampe** *f* *Bergb.* safety lamp

Wetterleuchten *n; -s, kein Pl.* sheet (*od.* heat) lightning; **~ am politischen Horizont** *fig.* storm clouds on the political horizon; **wetterleuchten** *v/i. unpers.* (*untr., hat -ge-*): **es wetterleuchtet** there is sheet lightning

Wetter|loch *n* *umg.* bad-weather area; **~macher** *m* *umg.* weatherman, forecaster

wettermäßig *Adv.* *umg.:* **wie sieht es ~ aus?** what's the weather like?; **~ ist es gut gelaufen** there were no problems with the weather

Wettermilderung *f* onset of milder weather

wettern *v/i. umg.* rant and rave (**über** + *Akk.* about); **~ gegen** rail (fulminate *förm.*) against

Wetter|phase *f* period of weather; **eine warme/kühle ~** a period of warm/cool weather; **~prognose** f weather forecast; **~prophet** m weather prophet (od. sage); hum. weatherman; **~regel** f saying concerning the weather; **~satellit** m weather (od. meteorological) satellite, Brit. umg. metsat; **~schacht** m Bergb. ventilation shaft; **~scheide** f weather divide; **~seite** f exposed side, windward side; **~station** f weather station; **~sturz** m sudden drop in temperature; **~umschwung** m (sudden) change in (the) weather; **~verhältnisse** Pl. weather conditions; **~vorhersage** f weather forecast; Am. Radio, TV: auch weathercast; **~warnung** f storm warning; **~warte** f weather station; **~wechsel** m change in (the) weather

wetterwendisch Adj. pej. moody

Wetter|wolke f storm cloud; **~zeichen** n weather indicator, sign of good (od. bad) weather; **~ am politischen Horizont** fig. political indicator

Wett|fahrt f race; **~kampf** m contest, competition; Sport (auch Einzeldisziplin) event; **~kämpfer** m, **~kämpferin** f competitor, contestant

Wettkampf|sport m competitive sport; **~stätte** f venue (for a od. the competition); **~tag** m day of the (od. a) competition

Wett|lauf m race; **~ mit der Zeit** fig. race against time (od. the clock); **~läufer** m, **~läuferin** f runner

wettmachen v/t. (trennb., hat -ge-) make up for, compensate for (**durch** with, by); (Geld) recoup

Wett|rennen n race (auch fig.); **~rüsten** n; -s, kein Pl. arms race; **~schwimmen** n swimming competition; **~spiel** n game, match; **~streit** m contest; (Wettbewerb) competition; **mit j-m in ~ treten** bes. fig. compete with s.o.

wetzen I. v/t. (hat gewetzt) sharpen; (schleifen) grind; (Schnabel) scratch, rub; **II.** v/i. (ist); umg. (rennen) race; **nach Hause ~** race home, zoom off home

Wetz|stahl m steel, sharpener; **~stein** m whetstone

WG f; -, -s; Abk. → **Wohngemeinschaft**

Whirlpool® ['wø:ɐlpu:l] m; -s, -s whirlpool (bath)

Whisky m; -s, -s whisky; schottischer: auch Scotch; irischer, amerikanischer: whiskey; amerikanischer aus Mais: bourbon; **~** (**mit**) **Soda** whisk(e)y (od. Scotch od. bourbon) and soda; → **pur**, **~-Likör** m whisk(e)y liqueur

wich Imperf. → **weichen²**

Wichs m; -es, -e regalia Pl. (V. in Sg. od. Pl.); **in vollem ~** in full regalia; **Wichse** f; -, -n; umg. **1.** (shoe) polish; **2.** (Prügel) thrashing, hiding; **~ kriegen** get a hiding; **alles dieselbe ~!** fig. it's all the same

wichsen umg. **I.** v/t. **1.** polish; **2.** j-m **e-e ~** give s.o. a clout round the ears; **II.** v/i. vulg. (onanieren) jerk (Am. auch jack) off, Brit. auch (have a) wank; **Wichser** m; -s, - **1.** vulg. (e-r, der wichst) wanker, Am. jerk-off; **2.** Sl. als Schimpfwort: wanker, Am. jerk-off; **Wichsgriffel** Pl. vulg. fingers

Wicht m; -(e)s, -e **1.** umg. (kleiner Kerl) midget; Kind: auch nipper; **2.** pej. blighter, Am. scoundrel; **armer ~** poor blighter (Am. sucker); **feiger ~** coward; **erbärmlicher ~** miserable wretch; **3.** Myth. gnome; (Heinzelmännchen) brownie

Wichte f; -, -n; Phys. specific density

Wichtel m; -s, -, **~männchen** n Myth. → **Wicht** 3

wichtig Adj. important; **es ist mir sehr ~** it's very important to me, it means a lot to me; **das ist nur halb so ~** that's not so important; etw. (**sehr**) **~ nehmen** take s.th. (very) seriously, attach (great) importance to s.th.; **sich (sehr) ~ nehmen** take o.s. very seriously; **er macht sich** od. **er tut gern ~** (**mit**) he likes to show off (about od. with); **ein ~es Gesicht machen** put on a very serious face; **nichts Wichtigeres zu tun haben als ...** have nothing better to do than ...; **das Wichtigste ist ...** the most important thing is; **Wichtigkeit** f **1.** nur Sg.; importance (**für** for, to); **von höchster ~** of the greatest importance; **2.** Sache: important thing; **3.** iro. Gehabe: self-importance

Wichtigmacher m, **~in** f bes. österr. umg. pej. pompous ass

Wichtigtuer m; -s, -; umg. pej. pompous ass; **Wichtigtuerei** f; -, -en; umg. pej. pomposity, pompous behavio(u)r; **Wichtigtuerin** f; -, -nen; umg. pej. stuck-up bitch; **wichtigtuerisch** Adj. umg. pej. pompous, stuck-up

Wicke f; -, -n; Bot. vetch; Zierpflanze: sweet pea

Wickel m; -s, - **1.** Med. (Umschlag) compress; **2.** (Spule) spool, reel; (Rolle) roll; (Lockenwickler) curler, roller; **3.** umg. fig. j-n beim od. am ~ packen grab s.o. by the scruff of the (od. his, her) neck; **am ~ haben** (j-n) take s.o. to task; (Thema) deal with s.th. thoroughly; (Arbeit) really get down to s.th.; **~bluse** f wrap-around blouse; **~gamasche** f puttee; **~kind** n auch fig. baby; **~kommode** f changing unit

wickeln I. v/t. **1.** (winden, schlingen) wind (um around); (Seil, Kabel, Spule) auch coil; (Tuch, Binde) tie; (Schal, Decke) wrap; (Haar) put in curlers od. rollers; → **Finger** 2; **2.** (einwickeln) wrap up (**in** + Akk. in); **3. ein Baby ~** change a baby's nappies (Am. diapers); **das Kind ist frisch gewickelt** the baby's just been changed; **da bist du schief gewickelt** umg. fig. you've got that totally wrong, you're very much (Am. you're totally) mistaken there; **4.** (Zigarren) roll; **5.** (abwickeln) unwind (**von** from); **6.** (auswickeln) unwrap (**aus** from); **II.** v/refl. **1. sich ~ um** wind (od. coil) itself around s.th.; Leine etc.: get twisted (a)round s.th.; **2. sich in e-e Decke ~** wrap o.s. up in a blanket

Wickel|raum m baby-care room; **~rock** m wrap-around skirt; **~tisch** m changing table; **~tuch** n wrap-around garment; in Südostasien: sarong; in Indien: sari; in Polynesien: pareu; **~unterlage** f changing mat

Wickler m; -s, - **1.** für Locken: curler, roller; **2.** Zool. leaf roller, tortrix moth

Wicklung f Etech. winding

Widder m; -s, - **1.** Zool. ram; **2.** Sternzeichen: Aries; (**ein**) **~ sein** be (an) Aries

wider Präp. (+ Akk.); geh. against; (entgegen) auch contrary to; **~ Erwarten** against expectation(s); **~ Willen** against one's will, reluctantly; → **Für**

widerborstig Adj. → **widerspenstig**

widerfahren v/i. (unreg., untr., ist); (j-m) happen to, befall lit.; **ihm ist Unrecht ~** he has been done wrong; **j-m Gerechtigkeit ~ lassen** do justice to s.o., weitS. give s.o. his (od. her) due

Widerhaken m barbed hook; an Pfeil etc.: barb

Widerhall m echo, reverberation(s Pl.); fig. auch response, resonance; **großen ~ finden** fig. meet with an enthusiastic response; **widerhallen** v/i. (trennb., hat -ge-) echo, resound (**von** with)

Widerlager n Tech., Archit. abutment

widerlegbar Adj. refutable; **widerlegen** v/t. (untr., hat) refute, disprove; (Theorie) auch explode; **Widerlegung** f refutation

widerlich pej. **I.** Adj. revolting; stärker: repulsive; **~** auch **widerwärtig; II.** Adv.: **~ süß** sickly sweet

Widerling m; -s, -e; pej. creep; unappetitlicher: auch slob umg.

widernatürlich Adj. pej. unnatural, perverse; **Widernatürlichkeit** f pej. unnaturalness, perversity

Widerpart m; -(e)s, -e; geh. altm. opponent, adversary

widerrechtlich I. Adj. illegal, unlawful; **II.** Adv. Jur.: **sich** (Dat.) etw. **~ aneignen** misappropriate s.th.; **~ betreten** trespass (up)on; **~ geparktes Fahrzeug** illegally parked vehicle; **Widerrechtlichkeit** f illegality, unlawfulness

Widerrede f contradiction(s Pl.); freche: backchat umg., Am. backtalk, lip; **ohne ~** unquestioningly; **keine ~!** no arguments!, no buts!

Widerrist m Anat. withers Pl.

Widerruf m revocation; e-r Erklärung: retraction; Wirts. countermand; auch e-s Befehls etc.: withdrawal; **bis auf ~** until further notice; **widerrufen** (unreg., untr., hat) **I.** v/t. revoke, cancel; (Äußerung) retract, recant; (Gesetz) repeal; **II.** v/i. recant; **widerruflich** Adj. revocable, revokable; **Widerrufung** f revocation; e-r Erklärung: retraction; Wirts. countermanding; auch e-s Befehls etc.: withdrawal

Widersacher m; -s, -, **~in** f; -, -nen adversary

Widerschein m reflection; **widerscheinen** v/i. (unreg., trennb., hat) reflect (**von** off)

widersetzen v/refl. (untr., hat) oppose, resist (+ Dat. s.o. od. s.th.); e-m Befehl, Gesetz: disobey; **widersetzlich** Adj. refractory, contrary, uncooperative; im Dienst: insubordinate

Widersinn m; nur Sg. absurdity; **widersinnig** Adj. absurd, nonsensical; **Widersinnigkeit** f **1.** nur Sg. absurdity; **2.** Äußerung: absurdity

widerspenstig Adj. (halsstarrig) stubborn; (aufsässig) rebellious; Haar: unruly; „**Der Widerspenstigen Zähmung**" Shakespeare: The Taming of the Shrew; **Widerspenstigkeit** f; nur Sg. stubbornness; rebelliousness; → **widerspenstig**

widerspiegeln (trennb., hat -ge-) **I.** v/t. reflect (auch fig.); **II.** v/refl. be reflected (auch fig.); **Widerspiegelung** f reflection, mirroring

widersprechen v/i. (unreg., untr., hat) contradict (j-m s.o.); **sich** o.s.); e-m Vorschlag: oppose; **sich ~ Meinungen** etc.: be contradictory, be at variance, contradict each other; **sich** od. **einander ~d** Nachrichten etc.: contradictory; Gesetze: conflicting

Widerspruch m **1.** nur Sg. contradiction (**gegen** to), opposition; (Protest) protest; **er duldet keinen ~** he won't tolerate any argument, he brooks no argument geh.; **kein ~!** no arguments!; **~ einlegen** (**gegen**) Jur. appeal (against); **~ / keinen ~ einlegen** od. **er-**

heben protest / make no protest; *heftigen* ~ *hervorrufen* provoke vehement protest (*bei* from); **2.** (*Gegensatz*) contradiction (*zu*, *mit* to); (*Abweichung*) discrepancy; *im* ~ *zu* contrary to; *im* ~ *stehen zu* be inconsistent with, contradict *s.th.*; *sich in Widersprüche verwickeln* keep contradicting o.s., get caught up in a web of contradictions; *es ist ein* ~ *in sich* it's a contradiction in terms, it's self-contradictory

widersprüchlich *Adj.* contradictory, inconsistent; *Gefühle, Gesetze etc.*: conflicting; **Widersprüchlichkeit** *f*; *nur Sg.* contradictoriness, inconsistency

widerspruchsfrei *Adj.* consistent

Widerspruchsgeist *m* **1.** *nur Sg.* argumentative spirit; **2.** *umg. Person*: argumentative person (*od.* type)

widerspruchs|los *Adv.* **1.** (*ohne zu widersprechen*) unquestioningly; (*folgsam*) without a murmur; **2.** (*Ggs. widersprüchlich*) without contradiction, consistently; **~voll** *Adj.* → *widersprüchlich*

Widerstand *m* **1.** resistance (*gegen* to), opposition (to); *passiver* ~ passive resistance; ~ *gegen die Staatsgewalt* obstructing the police; *gegen den* ~ *s-r Eltern* against his parents' wishes; ~ *leisten* offer resistance, fight back; *auf* (*heftigen*) ~ *stoßen* meet with (stiff) opposition (*bei* from); *den* ~ *aufgeben* give in; *den Weg des geringsten* ~*es gehen* take the line of least resistance; *zum bewaffneten* ~ *aufrufen* issue a call for armed resistance; **2.** *nur Sg.*; *Pol. Bewegung*: the resistance; *in den* ~ *gehen* join the resistance; **3.** *Etech., Bauteil*: resistor; **4.** *nur Sg.*; *Phys., Etech.* resistance; *Flug., der Luft*: drag

Widerstandsbewegung *f* resistance movement, *the* resistance

widerstandsfähig *Adj.* resistant (*gegen* to); robust (*auch Tech.*); **Widerstandsfähigkeit** *f*; *nur Sg.* resistance; *auch Tech.* robustness

Widerstands|kämpfer *m*, **~kämpferin** *f* resistance fighter; **~kraft** *f* (powers *Pl.* of) resistance

widerstandslos *Adv.* without resistance

Widerstands|messgerät *n Etech.* ohmmeter; **~nest** *n* pocket of resistance; **~organisation** *f* resistance movement

widerstehen *v/i.* (*unreg., untr., hat*) resist (+ *Dat. s.th. od.* + *Ger.*); *Belastungen etc.*: withstand; *er konnte der Versuchung nicht* ~ *auch* he succumbed to the temptation

widerstreben (*untr., hat*) *v/i.* (+ *Dat.*) *Person*: oppose *s.o. od. s.th.*; *es widerstrebt mir* it goes against the grain, I hate to have to do it; **Widerstreben** *n* reluctance; **widerstrebend I.** *Part. Präs.* → *widerstreben*; **II.** *Adj.*: *mit* ~*en Gefühlen* against one's will, with reluctance; **III.** *Adv.* reluctantly

Widerstreit *m* conflict; *im* ~ *der Gefühle* with conflicting feelings; **widerstreitend** *Adj.* conflicting

widerwärtig *Adj.* repulsive, nasty, horrible *umg.*; *Benehmen*: offensive, objectionable; (*ekelhaft*) disgusting; (*abscheulich*) atrocious; **Widerwärtigkeit** *f* **1.** *nur Sg.* repulsiveness, nastiness; *des Benehmens* offensiveness; **2.** *Sache*: unpleasant event (*Erlebnis*: experience); *stärker*: horror; (*Abscheulichkeit*) atrocity; *Äußerung*: offensive

(*od.* nasty) remark

Widerwille(n) *m*; *nur Sg.* aversion (*gegen* to); *stärker*: loathing (for); (*Ekel*) disgust (at); (*Unwilligkeit*) reluctance (to); *mit* ~ → *widerwillig* II; **widerwillig I.** *Adj.* unwilling, reluctant; **II.** *Adv.* reluctantly; (*ungern gewährend*) grudgingly; (*mit Abscheu*) with disgust

Widerworte *Pl.*: *er duldet keine* ~ he won't tolerate any argument, he brooks no argument *geh.*; *keine* ~*!* no arguments!, no backchat! *umg., Am.* no backtalk (*od.* lip)!

widmen I. *v/t.* dedicate; (*Zeit, sein Leben etc.*) *auch* devote (+ *Dat.* to); (*Aufmerksamkeit*) give; **II.** *v/refl.*: *sich j-m/etw.* ~ devote o.s. to *s.o./s.th.*; *sich e-m Problem* ~ *auch* address a problem; **Widmung** *f* dedication

widrig *Adj.* (*ungünstig*) adverse; **widrigenfalls** *Adv. Amtsspr.* otherwise, failing which; **Widrigkeit** *f* adversity

wie I. *Adv.* **1.** *bes. in Fragen*: how?; *nach der Art etc.*: what … like?; ~ *bitte?* pardon?, (sorry,) what did you say?; *entrüstet*: I beg your pardon!; ~*?* *umg. nachfragend, erstaunt*: what?; ~ *das?* how come? *umg.*; ~ *alt sind Sie?* how old are you?; ~ *lange ist das her?* how long ago is (*od.* was) that?; ~ *viel/viele* how much/many; ~ *viel Uhr ist es?* what's the time?, what time is it?; ~ *viel ist zwei plus zwei?* what is two plus two?, what do two and two make?; ~ *war's im Kino?* how was the film (*Am.* movie)?; ~ *ist er* (*so*)*?* what's he like?; ~ *ist der neue Wagen?* what's the new car like?; ~ *war das mit dem Unfall?* what exactly happened in the accident?; *ich weiß nicht, wie das kam* I don't know how it came about; *na,* ~ *war das/ich?* so how was it/I?; ~ *wäre es mit …?* how about …?; *na,* ~ *wär's* (*mit uns beiden*)*?* so, how about it?; **2.** *als Zusatz*: *das war doch sehr witzig,* ~*?* that was very funny, wasn't it?; *du magst mich nicht,* ~*?* you don't like me, do you?; **3.** *im Ausruf*: ~ *schön!* how beautiful!; ~ *froh war ich!* how glad I was; ~ *gut, dass …!* lucky for me (*od.* you *etc.*) that …; ~ *du wieder aussiehst!* just look at you!; *und* ~*!* *umg.* and how!, you bet!; **4.** *vergleichend*: *die Art,* ~ *du lachst* the way (that) you laugh; *im gleichen Maß*(*e*)*, wie …* to the same extent that …; *ein Erlebnis,* ~ *man es nur selten hat* an experience of a kind that one has only rarely; **5.** *verallgemeinernd*: ~ *lang etc. auch* (*immer*) however long *etc.*, no matter how long *etc.*; ~ *sehr ich mich auch bemühte* however hard I tried, try as I would; ~ *dem auch sei* be that as it may; ~ *auch heißen mögen* whatever they're called; **II.** *Konj.* **1.** *in Vergleichen*: (*so*) ~ *nach Adj. od. Adv.*: as, *mst* as … as; *nach Subst.od. V.*: like; *ein Mann* ~ *er* a man like him; *in e-m Fall* ~ *diesem* in a case like this; *groß* ~ *ein Haus* (as) big as a house; (*nicht*) *so alt* ~ (not) as old as; *so schön* ~ (noch) *nie* more beautiful than ever; *ich fühlte mich* ~ *betäubt* I felt as if I'd been stunned; *er singt* ~ *selten einer / keiner* very few people sing / nobody sings like (*od.* as well as) he does; *sie arbeitet* ~ *verrückt* she works like a madwoman; *er sieht nicht* ~ *50 aus* he doesn't look fifty; *mit P* ~ *Paula* with a P as in Peter; **2.** (*beispielsweise*) such as, like; *Haustiere* ~ *Hunde, Kat-*

zen und Vögel pets such as dogs, cats, and cagebirds; **3.** (*und*) as well as; *auf dem Land* ~ *in den kleinen Städten* both in the country and in the small towns; *Sommer* ~ *Winter* summer and winter; *4. mit Verben der Wahrnehmung*: *ich sah,* ~ *er weglief* I saw him running away; *ich hörte,* ~ *es sagte* I heard him say so (*od.* it); **5.** *mit Teilsatz*: ~ *man mir gesagt hat* as I've been told; *sie ist reich,* ~ *es scheint* she's rich(, so) it appears; ~ *so oft* as is often the case; (*früher*) as (*od.* like) so often before; ~ *er nun mal ist* being the type of person he is; *dumm* ~ *er ist* stupid as he is; ~ *gehabt umg.* as before; ~ *gesagt* as I said (*od.* was saying); ~ *du mir, so ich dir Sprichw.* it's tit for tat; **6.** *zeitlich*: as, when; ~ *ich so vorbeiging* just as I was passing; **7.** *umg.* (*als*) *nach Komp.*: than; *schneller* ~ *du* faster than you; *anders* ~ *gestern* different from yesterday; *nichts* ~ nothing but; *nichts* ~ *weg hier!* let's get out of here!; **8.** (*als ob*) ~ *wenn* as when

Wie *n*; -, *kein Pl.*: *auf das* ~ *kommt es an* what matters is how

Wiedehopf *m*; -(*e*)*s*, -*e*; *Zool.* hoopoe

wieder *Adv.* **1.** (*erneut*) again; ~ *einmal* once again; *immer* ~ again and again; *nie* ~ never again; *nie* ~ *Krieg!* no more war!; *schon* ~ yet again; *schon* ~*?* not again!; ~ *und* ~ again and again, over and over again; ~ *ganz von vorn anfangen* start again right from the beginning; ~ *anlegen* (*Geld*) reinvest, plough (*Am.* plow) back; ~ *aufführen* show again; (*Film*) rerun; (*Konzert*) give again, do a repeat of; ~ *aufleben* revive; ~ *aufnehmen Handlung*: resume; *Theat.* revive; *Jur.* reopen; *Kontakte* ~ *aufnehmen* renew ties; ~ *erleben* relive, go through *s.th.* again; *das Feuer* ~ *eröffnen* reopen fire, start firing again; ~ *geboren* reborn; ~ *geborene Christen* born-again Christians; *er ist der* ~ *geborene …* he's another …, he's … come back to life (again); ~ *tun* do again, repeat; ~ *verwendbar* reusable; ~ *verwenden* reuse, reutilize; ~ *verwertbar* recyclable; ~ *verwerten* (*Abfallstoffe etc.*) recycle; ~ *wählen* re(-)elect; *und* ~ *ist ein Tag vorbei* that's another day gone; *da sieht man's mal* ~*!* *umg.* it all goes to show; **2.** *bei Rückkehr in früheren Zustand*: again; ~ *aufbauen* rebuild; ~ *aufbereiten od. aufarbeiten* (*Brennstäbe etc.*) reprocess; (*Abfälle*) recycle; *j-n* ~ *aufrichten* set s.o. up again; ~ *aufrüsten* rearm; ~ *auftauchen aus Wasser*: re-emerge; *Naut. auch* (re)surface; *fig.* come to light again, reappear; *Person*: reappear on the scene, resurface, turn up again; ~ *auftreten* reappear; ~ *ausführen Waren*: re-export; ~ *beleben* resuscitate; *auch fig.* revive; ~ *e Stelle* ~ *besetzen* fill a vacancy; *ein Land* ~ *bewaffnen* rearm a country; ~ *einbürgern* (*Wildtiere*) renaturalize, reintroduce; ~ *einführen* reintroduce; (*Brauch etc.*) revive; (*Ware*) reimport; ~ *einsetzen in Position*: reinstate (*in* + *Akk.* in); (*Monarchen*) restore to the throne; *j-n in s-e Rechte einsetzen* restore s.o.'s rights, reinstate s.o.; *j-n* ~ *einstellen* re(-)employ s.o., take s.o. back, give s.o. his (*od.* her) job back; ~ *entdecken* rediscover; ~ *erkennen* recognize; *nicht* ~ *zu erkennen* unrecognizable; (*verstümmelt etc.*) maimed

W

etc. beyond recognition; **es ist nicht ~ zu erkennen** you won't recognize it; **~ eröffnen** (*Geschäft*) reopen; **~ erscheinen** reappear; *Zeitung*: resume publication, reappear on the newsstands; **~ erwecken** (*Interesse, Gefühle*) revive; (*j-n*) bring *s.o.* back to life; **~ finden** find again; *fig.* (*Selbstvertrauen etc.*) regain; **s-e Sprache ~ finden** be able to speak again; **sich** *od.* **einander ~ finden** find (their way back to) each other again; **sich ~ finden** *irgendwo*: find o.s. (**in** + *Dat.* in), end up (in); (*sich seelisch erholen*) recover, get back on an even keel; **sich ~ (ein)finden** *Sache*: turn up again, reappear, resurface; **~ herrichten** *od.* **instand setzen** repair; (*renovieren*) renovate, do up *umg.*; **~ herstellen** (*Verbindung*) re-establish; (**sich**) **~ vereinigen** reunite; **sich ~ verheiraten** remarry, marry again (*od.* a second *etc.* time); **ich bin gleich ~ da** I'll be back in a minute, I shan't (*Am.* won't) be a minute; **jetzt erinnere ich mich ~** *od.* **fällt es mir ~ ein!** now I remember!; **kann man das ~ reparieren?** *umg.* can it be repaired?; **3.** *umg.* (*zurück*) back; (*als Vergeltung*) in return; **gib es mir ~ zurück** give it back to me, give it me back *umg.*; **4.** (*wiederum*) again; **dafür ist er ~ teuer** but then he's expensive; **das ist ~ was ganz anderes** that's something else again; **manche sind grün, andere blau, und ~ andere sind gelb** some are green, others blue, and yet others yellow; **5.** *umg.*: **wo willst du ~ hin?** *ungeduldig:* where are you off to this time?; **das ist ja ~ typisch!** *verärgert:* that is just typical!; **wie hieß sie (gleich) ~?** what was she called again?; **so alt bin ich nun auch ~ nicht!** I'm not as old as all that!; **da hat er auch ~ Recht** well, he's quite right about that, though; **für nichts und ~ nichts** for nothing at all; → **hin** 5

Wieder|abdruck *m* reprint; **~annäherung** *f nach Auseinandersetzung etc.*: rapprochement; **~anpfiff** *m Sport* restart; **~ansiedlung** *f* resettlement; *von Tieren*: reintroduction

wiederaufarbeiten, wieder aufarbeiten *v/t.* → **wieder** 2

Wiederaufbau *m; nur Sg.* reconstruction; *wirtschaftlicher*: recovery

wiederaufbauen, wieder aufbauen *v/t.* → **wieder** 2

wiederaufbereiten, wieder aufbereiten *v/t.* → **wieder** 2

Wiederaufbereitung *f* reprocessing; **Wiederaufbereitungsanlage** *f:* (*atomare*) ~ (nuclear waste) reprocessing plant

wieder auffinden *v/t.* → **wiederfinden**

Wiederaufforstung *f* reafforestation, *Am.* reforestation

wiederaufführen, wieder aufführen *v/t.* → **wieder** 1; **Wiederaufführung** *f* revival

wiederaufladbar *Adj. Akku*: rechargeable

Wiederaufleben *n; nur Sg.* revival; *von Ideen etc.*: resurgence

Wiederaufnahme *f von Gesprächen etc.*: resumption; *Jur.* reopening (of a trial); *Theat.* revival; **~verfahren** *n Jur.* new hearing; *Strafrecht*: retrial

wieder| aufnehmen → **wieder** 1; **~ aufrichten, ~ aufrüsten** › **wieder** 2

Wiederaufrüstung *f* rearmament, rearming

wieder| auftauchen, ~ auftreten, ~

ausführen → **wieder** 2

Wiederbeginn *m* recommencement; *der Schule etc.*: reopening

wiederbekommen *v/t.* (*unreg., trennb., hat*) get *s.th.* back

wiederbeleben, wieder beleben *v/t.* → **wieder** 2

Wiederbelebung *f* resuscitation; *fig.* revival; **Wiederbelebungsversuch** *m* resuscitation attempt; *fig.* attempt to revive *s.th.*

wiederbeschaffen *v/t.* (*trennb., hat*) replace; **Wiederbeschaffung** *f* replacement; **Wiederbeschaffungswert** *m* replacement (*od.* as new) value

wiederbesetzen, wieder besetzen *v/t.* → **wieder** 2

wiederbewaffnen, wieder bewaffnen *v/t* → **wieder** 2; **Wiederbewaffnung** *f* rearmament

wiederbringen *v/t.* (*unreg., trennb., hat -ge-*) bring back; (*zurückgeben*) return (+ *Dat.* to)

Wiederdruck *m; Pl. -e* reprint, second impression

wieder einbürgern → **wieder** 2

Wiedereinfuhr *f* reimport(ation); **wieder einführen** → **wieder** 2; **Wiedereinführung** *f* reintroduction; *e-s Brauchs etc.*: revival; *von Ware etc.*: reimportation

Wiedereingliederung *f* reintegration (**in** + *Akk.* into); *e-s Straftäters*: rehabilitation

wieder einsetzen → **wieder** 2; **Wiedereinsetzung** *f* reinstatement; *in Rechte etc.*: restoration (**in** + *Akk.* to)

Wiedereinsteiger *m*, **~in** *f* returnee

wieder einstellen → **wieder** 2

Wieder|einstieg *m in Beruf*: return; **~eintritt** *m* re(-)entry (**in** + *Akk.* into)

wiederentdecken, wieder entdecken *v/t.* → **wieder** 2; **Wiederentdeckung** *f* rediscovery

Wiederergreifung *f* recapture

wiedererhalten *v/t.* (*unreg., trennb., hat*) get *s.th.* back

wiedererkennen, wieder erkennen *v/t.* → **wieder** 2; **Wiedererkennungswert** *m*: **mit hohem ~** with high memorability

wiedererlangen *v/t.* (*trennb., hat*) recover; (*auch Gewicht*) regain

wiedererleben, wieder erleben *v/t.* → **wieder** 1

wiedererobern *v/t.* (*trennb., hat*) (*zurückerobern*) recapture, reconquer; **Wiedereroberung** *f* recapture, reconquest

wiedereröffnen, wieder eröffnen *v/t.* → **wieder** 1, 2; **Wiedereröffnung** *f* reopening

wieder erscheinen → **wieder** 2

wiedererstatten *v/t.* (*trennb., hat*); (*Kosten*) refund, reimburse (+ *Dat.* to); **Wiedererstattung** *f* refund(ing), reimbursement

wiedererstehen *v/i.* (*unreg., trennb., ist*); *geh.* rise again; *fig.* be revived; **~ lassen** revive

wiedererwecken, wieder erwecken *v/t.* → **wieder** 2

wiedererzählen *v/t.* (*trennb., hat*) **1.** retell; **2.** *umg.* → **weitererzählen**

wiederfinden, wieder finden *v/t.* → **wieder** 2

Wiedergabe *f* **1.** (*Bericht*) account, report; (*Beschreibung*) description; (*Gestaltung*) rendering, interpretation; (*Zitieren*) quotation; (*Vermittlung*) *von Eindrücken etc.*: conveyance; **2.** *Tech.* reproduction; *akustisch*: *auch* sound; *optisch*: picture; *Tonband*: playback;

~kopf *m* play head; **~qualität** *f Ton*: sound quality; *Bild*: picture quality; **~treue** *f:* (**hohe**) ~ (high) fidelity

Wiedergänger *m; -s, -, ~in f, -, -nen;* *Myth.* ghost, revenant

wiedergeben *v/t.* (*unreg., trennb., hat -ge-*) **1.** (*zurückgeben*) give back, return (+ *Dat.* to); (*Freiheit, Lebensmut, Rechte etc.*) restore; **2.** *Person*: (*Musikstück, Rolle*) interpret; (*schildern*) describe; (*erzählen*) relate; (*berichten*) give an account of; (*zitieren*) quote; (*übersetzen*) render, translate; **das kann man nicht ~** (*ist zu schwer*) that's untranslatable; (*ist zu beleidigend, vulgär etc.*) that's unrepeatable; **3.** *Sache*: represent; (*widerspiegeln*) reflect; (*Eindruck, Gefühl*) convey; **4.** *Tech.* (*reproduzieren*) reproduce

wiedergeboren, wieder geboren *Adj.* → **wieder** 1; **Wiedergeburt** *f* **1.** rebirth; **2.** *fig.* revival; *in der Kunst:* *auch* renaissance

wiedergewinnen *v/t.* (*unreg., trennb., hat*) regain; (*auch Geld*) win (*od.* get) back; **Wiedergewinnung** *f* recovery; *Tech.* reclamation

wiedergrüßen *vt/i.* (*trennb., hat -ge-*) return *s.o.* 's greetings

wieder gutmachen → **gutmachen** 1; **Wiedergutmachung** *f* **1.** amends *Pl.*; compensation; **als ~ für Schaden**: as compensation for; *für Fehler*: to make up for, to make amends for; *für Kränkung*: to apologize for, to make amends for; **2.** *finanziell*: indemnification, restitution payments *Pl.*; *Pol.* reparation

wiederhaben *v/t.* (*unreg., trennb., hat -ge-*) have *s.th. od. s.o.* back again; **das will ich aber ~** I want it back though

wieder herrichten → **wieder** 2

wiederherstellen *v/t.* (*trennb., hat -ge-*) **1.** (*Gesundheit, Person*) restore (to health); **vollständig wiederhergestellt** cured, recovered; **2.** (*Recht etc.*) restore; **Wiederherstellung** *f* restoration; *e-s Rechts*: *auch* restitution; *e-s Kranken*: recovery; **~ e-r Verbindung** renewal (*od.* re-establishment) of contacts

wieder herstellen *v/t.* (*erneut produzieren*) produce (*od.* make) again; *industriell*: manufacture again

wiederholbar *Adj.* repeatable; **es ist nicht ~** it can't be repeated

wieder'holen¹ (*untr., hat*) **I.** *v/t.* **1.** repeat; *weitS.* say (*od.* do) *s.th.* again; (*Aufnahme, Freistoß etc.*) retake; (*Spiel*) replay; (*Prüfung*) retake, *Brit. auch* resit; (*Sendung*) rerun; (*nachsprechen*) repeat (after *s.o.*); **2.** (*rekapitulieren*) repeat, recapitulate; (*kurz zusammenfassen*) sum up; **3.** (*Lernstoff*) revise, *Am.* review; **II.** *v/refl.* **1.** *Person*: repeat o.s.; **2.** *Sache*: repeat itself, be repeated; *Ereignis*: happen again; *periodisch*: recur; **ein sich ~des Muster** a repeating pattern

'wiederholen² *v/t.* (*trennb., hat -ge-*) get back

wiederholt I. *P.P.* → **wiederholen¹**; **II.** *Adj.* repeated; **trotz ~er Warnung** despite repeated (*od.* several) warnings; **zum ~en Mal(e)** once again, yet again; **III.** *Adv.* repeatedly; (*immer wieder, bes. im neg. Sinn*) time and again

Wiederholung *f* repetition; *e-r Sendung*: repeat, rerun; *TV, Sport* replay; *von Prüfungsstoff*: revision, *Am.* review

Wiederholungs|fall *m*: *im ~* should it happen again; *Jur.* in case of a repeat offen|ce (*Am.* -se); **~gefahr** *f*; *nur Sg.* danger of a repetition *od.* recurrence; **~impfung** *f Med.* booster (shot); **~kurs** *m* refresher course; **~prüfung** *f* repeat examination; **~spiel** *n Sport* replay; **~täter** *m*, **~täterin** *f Jur.* repeat offender, recidivist; **~zeichen** *n Mus.* repeat (sign); *Druck.* ('' '' '') ditto mark (*od.* sign); *Ling.* (*Tilde*) tilde

Wieder|hören *n*: *auf ~* goodbye; **~inbesitznahme** *f* repossession; **~inbetriebnahme** *f* restarting, putting into operation again

wieder instand setzen → *wieder* 2; **Wiederinstandsetzung** *f* repair(s *Pl.*)

wiederkäuen (*trennb.*, *hat* -ge-) **I.** *v/i.* chew the cud; **II.** *v/t. fig. pej.* blather on about; (*wiederholen*) keep regurgitating; **Wiederkäuer** *m*; -s, -; *Zool.* ruminant

Wiederkehr *f*, -, *kein Pl.* return; *periodische*: recurrence; *e-s Gedenktages*: anniversary; **wiederkehren** *v/i.* (*trennb.*, *ist* -ge-) return, come back; (*sich wiederholen*) recur; **wiederkehrend I.** *Part. Präs.* → *wiederkehren*; **II.** *Adj.* recurrent; *regelmäßig*: regular; *ein monatlich/jährlich ~es Ereignis* a monthly/yearly event

wieder|kommen *v/i.* (*unreg.*, *trennb.*, *ist* -ge-) **1.** *noch einmal*: come again; *das kommt nie wieder bes. weil verloren*: it'll never come back; *bes. weil einmalig*: it'll never come again; *könntest du später noch einmal ~?* could you come back later?; **2.** (*zurückkommen*) come back, return; *ich komme gleich wieder* I'll be back in a minute; **~kriegen** *v/t.* (*trennb.*, *hat* -ge-); *umg.* get *s.th.* back

Wiederkunft *f*, -, *kein Pl.*; *geh.* return; *die ~ Christi Reli.* the Second Coming

wiederlieben *v/t.* (*trennb.*, *hat* -ge-) return *s.o.*'s love

Wiederschauen *n südd.*, *österr.* → *Wiedersehen* 2

wiedersehen *v/t.* (*unreg.*, *trennb.*, *hat* -ge-) see again; (*j-n*) *auch* meet again; *werden wir uns ~?* will we be seeing each other again?; **Wiedersehen** *n*; -s, - **1.** reunion; *ich freue mich auf das ~ mit dir / m-r Heimat* I look forward to seeing you again / to being home again; *ich hoffe auf ein baldiges ~* I hope to see you *etc.* again soon; *~ macht Freude hum.* don't forget to give it back!; **2.** (*auf*) *~!* goodbye!, bye! *umg.*; (*j-m/etw.*) *auf ~ sagen* say goodbye (to *s.o./s.th.*); **Wiedersehensfeier** *f* reunion party (*od.* celebration); **Wiedersehensfreude** *f* joy at seeing each other again, joy of reunion

Wiedertäufer *m*; -s, -, **~in** *f*; -, -nen; *Reli.* Anabaptist

wieder tun → *wieder* 1

wiederum *Adv.* **1.** (*wieder*) again; **2.** (*andererseits*) on the other hand; (*allerdings*) however; *ich etc. ~* I etc. on the other hand *od.* however

wiedervereinigen, wieder vereinigen *v/t.*, *v/refl.* → *wieder* 2; **Wiedervereinigung** *f* reunion; *Pol. auch* reunification

wieder verheiraten → *wieder* 2; **Wiederverheiratung** *f* remarriage

Wiederverkauf *m* resale; *durch Einzelhandel*: retail(ing); **Wiederverkäufer** *m*, **Wiederverkäuferin** *f* (*Einzelhändler*) retailer, reseller; **Wiederverkaufswert** *m* resale value

wiederverwendbar, wieder verwendbar *Adj.*, **wiederverwenden, wieder verwenden** *v/t.* → *wieder* 1; **Wiederverwendung** *f* reuse

wiederverwertbar, wieder verwertbar *Adj.*, **wiederverwerten, wieder verwerten** *v/t.* → *wieder* 1; **Wiederverwertung** *f* recycling

Wiedervorlage *f*; *nur Sg.*; *Amtsspr.* resubmission; *zur ~* for resubmission

Wiederwahl *f* re-election (*zum Präsidenten* to the presidency, as president); *sich zur ~ stellen* stand for re--election; **wiederwählen, wieder wählen** *v/t.* → *wieder* 1

Wiederzulassung *f e-r Partei etc.*: unbanning; *e-s Wagens*: reregistration

Wiege *f*, -n **1.** cradle (*auch fig.*); **2.** *fig.*: *von der ~ an* from the day *s.o.* was born; *von der ~ bis zur Bahre mst hum.* from (the) cradle to (the) grave; *s-e ~ stand in Berlin geh.* he was born in Berlin; *... wurde ihm in die ~ gelegt* he was born with ...

Wiegemesser *n* mezzaluna, rocker chopper

wiegen¹, *wiegt*, *wog*, *hat gewogen* **I.** *v/t.* weigh; *das ist reichlich/knapp gewogen* it's a bit over/under; *gewogen und zu leicht befunden fig.* weighed and found wanting; **II.** *v/i.* **1.** weigh; *zu viel/wenig ~* be over/under weight; *schwerer ~ als* be heavier than, weigh more than, outweigh; *was od. wie viel ~ Sie?* how much do you weigh?; **2.** *fig.*: *schwer ~* carry weight; *bedeutend schwerer ~ (als) Tat, Vergehen, Fehler etc.*: be considerably more serious (than); **III.** *v/refl.* weigh o.s.

wiegen² **I.** *v/t.* **1.** (*schaukeln*) rock (*in den Schlaf* to sleep); **2.** (*zerkleinern*) chop; **II.** *v/refl.* sway; *Boot*: *auch* rock; *sich in den Hüften ~* sway one's hips; *~der Gang* swaying walk; *sich in der Hoffnung ~, dass ... fig.* cherish the hope that ...; → *Sicherheit* 1

Wiegen|druck *m Druck.* incunabulum (*Pl.* incunabula), cradle book; **~fest** *n geh. altm.* birthday; **~lied** *n* lullaby

wiehern *v/i.* **1.** neigh, whinny; **2.** *umg. fig.*: (*vor Lachen*) *~* bray with laughter; *~des Gelächter* braying (laughter)

Wien (*n*); -s Vienna

Wiener¹ *Adj.* Viennese; *~ Sängerknaben* Vienna Boys Choir; *~ Schnitzel* Wiener schnitzel, *veal escalope rolled in beaten egg and breadcrumbs and lightly fried*; *~ Würstchen* vienna, wiener, *Am.* Vienna sausage

Wiener² *f*, -, -, *mst Pl.* Würstchen: vienna, wiener, *Am.* Vienna sausage

Wiener³ *m*; -s, -, **~in** *f*; -, -nen Viennese; → *Kölner¹, Kölnerin*

wienerisch *Adj.* Viennese

wienern *v/t. umg.* polish

Wienerwald *m*; *nur Sg.*; *Geog.* Vienna woods

wies *Imperf.* → *weisen*

Wiese *f*, -, -n meadow; *auf der ~* in the meadow; *auf der grünen ~ fig.* in the open countryside; *Supermarkt, Fabrik bauen etc.*: on a greenfield site

Wiesel *n*; -s, -; *Zool.* weasel; **wieselflink** *Adj.* fast as lightning, quick as a flash; **wieseln** *v/i.* scurry

Wiesen|blume *f* wild flower; **~champignon** *m* field mushroom; **~schaumkraut** *n Bot.* lady's smock, cuckooflower, *Am.* bitter cress

wieso *Adv.* → *warum*

wie viel → *wie* I 1

wievielerlei *Adv.* how many kinds of;
wievielmal *Adv.* how many times,

how often

wievielt *Adv.*: *zu ~ wart ihr?* how many of you were there?

wievielt... *Adj.*: *der od. die, das ~e ...?* in Reihenfolge: which ...?; *das ~e Stück isst du jetzt?* how many have you eaten already?; *zum ~en Mal(e)?* how many times?; *als Wievielter ist er ins Ziel gekommen?* where did he come?; *am ~en August hat er Geburtstag?* when in August is his birthday?; *den Wievielten haben wir heute?* what's the date today?

wieweit *Konj.* → *inwieweit*

wiewohl *Konj. geh. altm.* although

Wigwam *m*; -s, -s wigwam

Wikinger *m*; -s, - Viking; **~schiff** *n* Viking ship

wild **I.** *Adj.* **1.** Honig, Pflanze, Tier, Gegend, Sitten: wild; (*unzivilisiert*) savage; *ein ~er Haufen pej.* a savage mob; *~e Triebe Agr., Bot.* rank shoots; *~er Wein Bot.* Virginia creeper; *der Wilde Westen* the Wild West; **2.** Geschichte, Blick, Drohungen, Beschimpfungen, Kampf, Leben, Orgie etc.: wild; Kind: *auch* unruly; Kampf: *auch* fierce; Blick: *auch* furious; Lachen: *auch* hysterical, *stärker* maniacal; (*wütend*) wild, furious, raving; (*stürmisch*) tempestuous, impetuous; (*zügellos*) unrestrained; (*laut*) boisterous; *~e Flucht* wild *od.* headlong flight; *~e Schießerei* furious gunbattle; *e-s Einzelnen*: shooting spree; *den ~en Mann spielen umg.* go berserk; (*sei doch*) *nicht so ~!* calm down!; *~ machen* (*j-n*) make *s.o.* mad; Musik etc.: drive *s.o.* wild *umg.*; (*Tier*) frighten; *~ werden Tier*: turn wild; Person: get mad, go wild *umg.*; **3.** (*wirr*) Gerüchte, Träume, Vermutungen etc.: wild; **~e Durcheinander** (total) chaos; *e-e ~e Mähne haben* have one's hair all over the place, be completely unkempt; *das Haar hing ihr ~ in die Stirn* her hair hung down wildly over her forehead; **4.** Mülldeponie, Parken, Zelten etc.: unauthorized; Taxi: unlicensed; *~er Streik* wildcat strike; → *Ehe*; **5.** *Med.*: *~es Fleisch* proud flesh; **6.** *umg.*: *sein auf* (+ *Akk.*) be wild (*od.* crazy) about; *wie ~* like mad; (*das ist*) *halb so ~!* not to worry; **II.** *Adv.* wildly etc.; *~ schreien* shout like mad *umg.*; *~ entschlossen zu* (+ *Inf.*) absolutely determined to (+ *Inf.*); *~ zelten* camp illegally; *~ lebend* wild, *nachgestellt*: roaming free; *~ wachsen* grow wild; *~ wachsend/wuchernd* wild (*od. nachgestellt*: growing wild) / rank

Wild *n*; -(e)s, *kein Pl.* **1.** *Koll.* game; *einzelnes*: head of game; (*Reh*) *auch Koll.* deer; **2.** *Gastr.* game; *von Rotwild*: venison

Wild|bach *m* torrent; **~bad** *n altm. und in Ortsnamen*: thermal spa; **~bahn** *f*: *in freier ~* in the wild; **~bestand** *m* stock of game; **~braten** *m Gastr.* roast venison; (*Bratenstück*) roast of venison

Wildbret *n*; -s, *kein Pl.*; *Gastr.* game; *von Rotwild*: venison

Wild|dieb *m* poacher; **~diebstahl** *m* poaching

Wilde *m*, *f*, -n, -n; *altm.*, *noch pej.* savage; *wie ein ~ / e-e ~ fig.* like a madman/madwoman (*od.* maniac)

Wildente *f Orn.* wild duck

Wilderei *f*, -, -en poaching; **Wilderer** *m*; -s, - poacher; **wildern** *v/i.* poach; *Hund etc.*: kill game

Wild|esel *m Zool.* wild ass; **~fang** *m*

1. *Jägerspr.* (*Falke*) haggard falcon; **2.** *fig.* (*Kind*) little devil; **~form** *f Bio.* wild form, original; **~fraß** *m Agr.* damage caused by game

wildfremd *Adj.* completely strange (+ *Dat.* to); **~er Mensch** complete stranger

Wild|früchte *Pl.* wild fruit *Sg.*; **~fütterung** *f* feeding of game; **~gans** *f Orn.* wild goose; **~geflügel** *n* wildfowl; **~gehege** *n* game enclosure; **~geschmack** *m* gam(e)y taste

Wildheit *f; nur Sg.* wildness; savagery; fury *etc.*; → **wild**

Wild|hüter *m*, **~hüterin** *f* gamekeeper; *für ein größeres Gebiet:* game warden; **~kaninchen** *n Zool.* wild rabbit; **~katze** *f Zool.* wild cat; **~kräuter** *Pl. Bot.* wild herbs

wild lebend → **wild** II
Wildleder *n* suede (leather); **wildledern** *Adj.* suede (leather) …

Wildnis *f; -, -se* wilderness (*auch fig.*), *the* wild; *auch fig.* jungle

Wild|park *m* game (*od.* deer) park; **~pferd** *n Zool.* wild horse; **~pflanze** *f* wild plant

wildreich *Adj.* rich in game, abundantly stocked with game; **Wildreichtum** *m; nur Sg.* abundance of game

Wildreservat *n* game reserve
wildromantisch *Adj.* wildly romantic; **~e Landschaft** wild, romantic landscape

Wild|sau *f* **1.** wild boar (*weiblich:* sow); **2.** *umg. pej.* pig; **~schaden** *m; mst Pl. im Wald, auf Feldern:* damage done by game; *an Fahrzeugen:* etwa damages caused by wild animals; **~schütz** *m; -en, -en; altm.* **1.** (*Wilderer*) poacher; **2.** (*Jäger*) hunter; **~schwein** *n* wild boar (*weibliches:* sow)

wild wachsend → **wild** II
Wildwasser *n* torrent; **~…** *im Subst.* white-water; **~bahn** *f* flume; **~rennen** *n* **1.** white-water race; **2.** (*Sport*) white-water canoeing

Wildwechsel *m* game path, runway; *Verkehrszeichen:* wild animals (crossing)

Wildwest *ohne Art.; kein Pl.; the* Wild West; **~film** *m* western, cowboy film; **~manier** *f: in* ~ western style

Wild|wuchs *m* **1.** rank growth; **2.** *fig.* proliferation; **~zaun** *m* game fence; **~ziege** *f* wild goat

wilhelminisch *Adj. hist.* Wilhelmine, Wilhelmian, *dating from or typical of the reign of Kaiser Wilhelm II 1888-1918*

will *Präs.* → **wollen**[1]

Wille *m; -ns, -n, Pl. sehr selten* will; (*Entschlossenheit*) *auch* determination; (*Absicht*) intention; *Philos.* will, volition; *der* ~ *zum Frieden / zur Macht* the desire for peace / will to power; *Gottes* ~ God's will, the will of God; *böser/guter* ~ ill/good will; *letzter* ~ will; *Jur.* last will and testament; *weitS.* last (*od.* dying) wish; *es war kein böser* ~ it wasn't intentional, he *etc.* didn't do it out of spite; *guten* **~ns sein** mean well, be well-intentioned; *s-n guten* **~n zeigen** show one's (*od.* some) goodwill; *es fehlt ihm nur der gute* ~ he just has to want to; *mit ein bisschen gutem* **~n** with a little bit of good will; *beim besten* **~n nicht** much as I'd like to; *ich kann mich beim besten* **~n nicht erinnern** I can't for the life of me remember, with the best will in the world I can't remember; *es ist mein fester* ~ I'm absolutely deter-

mined, it's my firm intention; *aus freiem* **~n** of one's own free will; *e-n eisernen* **~n haben** have an iron will, be iron-willed; *s-n/keinen eigenen* **~n haben** have a/no mind of one's own; *s-n* **~n bekommen** *od.* **durchsetzen** have *od.* get one's way; *gegen s-n* **~n** against one's will; *wenn es nach s-m* **~n ginge** if he had his way; *ganz nach d-m* **~n** as you wish; *j-m zu* **~n sein** *geh. altm.* obey s.o.'s wishes; *stärker:* submit to s.o.; *Frau:* give o.s. to s.o.; *dein* ~ *geschehe bibl.* thy will be done; *wo ein* ~ *ist, ist auch ein Weg Sprichw.* where there's a will, there's a way; → **Mensch**[1] 2

Willen *m; -s, -, Pl. sehr selten* → **Wille**
willen *Präp.* (+ *Gen.*): *um* … ~ for the sake of …, for *s.o.*'s sake; → **Gott** 2

willenlos I. *Adj.* weak-willed; ~ *sein* auch have no willpower; *j-s* **~es Werkzeug sein** be a tool (*od.* be putty) in s.o.'s hands; **II.** *Adv.* (*gefügig*) meekly; **Willenlosigkeit** *f; nur Sg.* lack of willpower

willens *Adj. geh.:* ~ *sein zu* (+ *Inf.*) be willing (*od.* prepared) to (+ *Inf.*)

Willens|akt *m* act of volition; **~anstrengung** *f* effort of will; **~äußerung** *f* **1.** expression of one's will; **2.** *Jur.* declaration of intention; **~bildung** *f* development *od.* formulation of objectives; **~erklärung** *f bes. Jur.* → **Willensäußerung** 2; **~freiheit** *f* freedom of will; **~kraft** *f; nur Sg.* willpower; *weitS.* strong will; *durch* ~ *allein* through sheer willpower; **~sache** *f: das ist reine* ~ it's purely a matter of willpower

willensschwach *Adj.* weak-willed; **Willensschwäche** *f; nur Sg.* weak will

willensstark *Adj.* strong-willed; **Willensstärke** *f; nur Sg.* willpower

willentlich *Adj. geh.* deliberate
willfährig *Adj. geh.* compliant; *pej.* obsequious; **Willfährigkeit** *f; nur Sg.; geh.* compliance; *pej.* obsequiousness

willig *Adj.* (*bereit*) willing, prepared (*zu* + *Inf.* to + *Inf.*); (*diensteifrig*) willing, eager, keen; → **Geist** 1

…willig *im Adj.* willing *od.* ready to …
willkommen *Adj.* welcome (I *Dat.* to) (*auch fig.*); *j-n* ~ *heißen* welcome s.o.; (*seid*) (*herzlich*) **~!** welcome!; ~ *im Klub! fig. iro., bei AIDS-Infektion etc.:* join the club!; *du bist hier/mir immer* ~ you'll always be welcome here / I'll always have a welcome for you; **Willkommen** *n; -s, -* welcome, reception; *j-m ein herzliches* ~ *bereiten* give s.o. a warm welcome, receive s.o. warmly

Willkommens|gruß *m* welcome; **~trunk** *m* welcoming drink

Willkür *f; -; kein Pl.* arbitrariness; *Pol.* despotism, despotic rule; *j-s* ~ *ausgeliefert sein* be at s.o.'s mercy; *das ist doch reine* **~!** that's completely arbitrary!; **~akt** *m* arbitrary act; **~herrschaft** *f* arbitrary rule, despotism

willkürlich I. *Adj.* **1.** *Anordnung etc.:* arbitrary; *Herrscher: auch* despotic; **2.** (*gewollt*) *Bewegung etc.:* voluntary; **3.** (*zufällig*) *Auswahl:* random; **II.** *Adv.* **1.** arbitrarily; **2.** voluntarily; *Gefühle kann man nicht* ~ *steuern* you can't control your feelings by an act of will; **3.** (*wahllos*) at random; ~ *ausgewählte Beispiele* examples chosen (*od.* selected) at random

Willkürmaßnahme *f* arbitrary measure
wimmeln *v/i. oft unpers.:* ~ *von* be swarming (*od.* teeming, *umg.* crawl-

ing) with; *fig. von Fehlern etc.:* be teeming (*od.* bristling) with; *es wimmelte nur so von* … the place was teeming with …

Wimmerl *n; -s, -n; südd., österr. umg.* **1.** (*Pickel*) pimple, spot, *Am. auch* zit; **2.** *Tasche:* pouch

wimmern *v/i.* whimper; **Wimmern** *n; -s, kein Pl.* whimpering

Wimpel *m; -s, -* pennant
Wimper *f; -, -n* **1.** eyelash; *sich* (*Dat.*) *die* **~n tuschen** mascara one's eyelashes; *mit den* **~n klimpern** *umg.* flutter one's eyelashes; *ohne mit der* ~ *zu zucken fig.* without batting an eyelid, without flinching; **2.** *Bio.* cilium (*Pl.* cilia); **Wimperntusche** *f* mascara; **Wimpertierchen** *n Zool.* ciliate

Wind *m; -(e)s, -e* **1.** wind; (*Windstoß*) gust (of wind); *günstiger od. guter* ~ fair wind; *leichter* ~ (gentle) breeze; *schwacher bis mäßiger* ~ *aus Nordost* light to moderate northeasterly wind; ~ *und Wetter ausgesetzt sein* be exposed to the weather (*od.* to the elements *od.* to wind and weather); *bei* ~ *und Wetter* in all weathers, no matter what the weather; *hart am* ~ *segeln* sail close to the wind; *gegen den* ~ into the wind; *mit dem* ~ down wind; **2.** *fig.*: (*schnell*) *wie der* ~ *umg.* like the wind; ~ *bekommen von* get wind of; *viel* ~ *machen umg.* (*Aufhebens machen*) make a great big fuss; (*angeben*) talk big; *mit dem / gegen den* ~ *segeln* sail with/against the wind; *j-m den* ~ *aus den Segeln nehmen umg.* take the wind out of s.o.'s sails; *in alle* (*vier*) **~e zerstreut** scattered to the four winds; *in den* ~ *reden* waste one's breath; *in den* ~ *schlagen* (*Rat, Warnung*) pay no heed to, turn a deaf ear to; (*Vernunft, Vorsicht etc.*) cast to the winds; *frischen* ~ *in die Firma bringen* shake the company up; *daher weht* (*also*) *der* **~!** (so) that's the way the wind blows *od.* is blowing; *wissen, woher der* ~ *weht* know which way the wind blows (*od.* is blowing); *hier weht jetzt ein anderer/schärferer* ~ *umg.* things have changed / tightened up (a)round here now; *sich* (*Dat.*) *den* ~ *um die Nase od. Ohren wehen lassen umg.* go out into the big wide world; → **Fähnchen** 1, **Mantel** 2; **3.** *Med.* (*Blähung*) wind; *e-n* ~ *lassen umg.* blow off

Wind|beutel *m* **1.** *Gastr.* cream puff; **2.** *umg.* (*leichtsinniger Mensch*) loose fellow; (*Angeber*) gasbag, windbag; **~bö(e)** *f* gust of wind; **~bruch** *m; nur Sg.* windfall, windslash

Winde *f; -, -n* **1.** *Tech.* winch, windlass, hoist; *für Anker:* capstan; **2.** *Bot.* bindweed

Windei *n* **1.** *Bio.* wind egg; **2.** *fig. pej.* non-starter *umg.*

Windel *f; -, -n* nappy, *Am.* diaper; *damals lagst du noch in den* **~n** you were still in nappies (*Am.* diapers) at the time; **~höschen** *n* plastic pants *Pl.*

windeln *v/t.* → **wickeln** I 3
windelweich *Adj. umg.* **1.** *j-n* ~ *schlagen od. dreschen* beat the living daylights out of s.o., make mincemeat out of s.o.; **2.** *pej.* (*nachgiebig*) softened up, ready to agree to anything

winden[1]; *windet, wand, hat gewunden* **I.** *v/t.* **1.** wind (*um* [a]round); (*Kranz*) make, bind; *sich* (*Dat.*) *Blumen ins Haar* ~ twine flowers in one's hair; **2.** *geh. j-m etw. aus der Hand* ~

W

wrench s.th. out of s.o.'s hands; **3. in die Höhe ~** hoist; **II.** v/refl. Schlange etc.: writhe; Wurm: wriggle; Person: writhe (**vor** Schmerz etc.: with); fig. **vor** Scham etc.: squirm (with); Weg: wind (its way along); Fluss: auch meander; **sich ~ um** wind (od. coil) itself (a)round; **sich ~ durch** durch Menschenmenge etc.: weave one's way through; durch Loch im Zaun etc.: wriggle through; **sich ~ wie ein Aal** fig. wriggle like an eel; → **gewunden**

winden² v/i. unpers.: **es windet** (**sehr**) it's (very) windy

Windenergie f; nur Sg. wind power; **~anlage** f wind power plant

Windeseile f: **in** od. **mit ~** at lightning speed, in no time; das Gerücht **verbreitete sich in ~** spread like wildfire

Wind|fahne f weather vane; **~fang** m vestibule

windgeschützt Adj. sheltered (from the wind)

Wind|geschwindigkeit f wind speed; **~hauch** m breath of wind; **~hose** f whirlwind

Windhuk (n); -s Windhoek

Windhund m **1.** greyhound; afghanischer: Afghan (hound); kleiner: whippet; **2.** umg. pej. freewheeler

windig Adj. **1.** windy; **2.** umg. pej. Person: unreliable; Sache: dodgy; Ausrede: lame; Hütte etc.: rickety

Wind|jacke f windcheater, Am. windbreaker; **~jammer** m; -s, -; Naut. windjammer; **~kanal** m wind tunnel; **~kraft** f; nur Sg. wind power; **~kraftwerk** n wind power plant; **~licht** n storm lantern; **~maschine** f blower, fan; **~messer** m; -s, - anemometer; **~mühle** f windmill; **gegen ~n kämpfen** fig. tilt at windmills; **~mühlenflügel** m windmill sail; **~park** m wind farm; **~pocken** Pl. Med. chickenpox Sg.; **~rad** n **1.** Maschine: wind turbine, windmill; **2.** Spielzeug: windmill, Am. pinwheel; **~richtung** f wind direction, direction of the wind; **~röschen** n Bot. anemone; **~rose** f compass card (od. rose); **~sack** m windsock, wind sleeve

Windsbraut f; nur Sg.; lit. gale, storm wind; (Wirbelwind) whirlwind

Windschatten m Naut. lee; Flug. sheltered zone; **im ~ fahren**, laufen: in the slipstream (**von** of)

wind|schief Adj. oft pej. crooked, Brit. umg. skew-whiff; Baum, Haus: crooked, bowed; **~schlüpfig**, **~schnittig** Adj. streamlined

Windschutz m protection from the wind; Vorrichtung: windbreak; **~scheibe** f windscreen, Am. windshield

Wind|seite f weather side, windward side; **~spiel** n → Windhund 1; **~stärke** f wind force; **~ 1** force 1 (on the Beaufort scale)

windstill Adj. calm; **Windstille** f calm; vorübergehende: auch lull

Windstoß m gust (of wind)

windsurfen v/i. nur Inf. windsurf, sailboard; **Windsurfen** n windsurfing, sailboarding; **Windsurfer** m, **Windsurferin** f windsurfer, sailboarder

Windung f e-s Weges, Stroms: bend; e-r Spirale, Muschel: whorl; e-r Schraube: worm, thread; **~en** e-s Weges: winding; des Darms, Hirns: convolutions

Wingert m; -s, -e; Dial., schw. vineyard

Wink m; -(e)s, -e **1.** sign; mit der Hand: wave; **2.** fig. hint, tip; warnender: tip-off; **ein ~ des Schicksals** a sign from above; **ein ~ mit dem Zaunpfahl** a

broad hint

winke Kinderspr.: **~, ~ machen** wave

Winkel m; -s, - **1.** Math. angle; **im rechten ~ zu** at right angles to; → **spitz** I 1, **tot** 4; **2.** (Ecke) corner; (Plätzchen) place, spot; fig. des Herzens: recess; **3.** Mil. an Uniform: chevron; **4.** Tech., Maß: square; (Winkeleisen) angle iron; **~advokat** m, **~advokatin** f pej. shady lawyer, Am. auch shyster umg.; **~eisen** n Tech. angle iron

winkelförmig Adj. angled; weitS. L-shaped

Winkel|funktion f Math. trigonometric function; **~halbierende** f; -n, -n; Math. bisector of an angle

winkelig Adj. **1.** angular; **2.** Raum, Wohnung: full of nooks and crannies; Straße, Gasse: winding …

Winkel|maß n square; **~messer** m; -s, - protractor; Landvermessung: goniometer; **~zug** m mst pej. dodge; **Winkelzüge machen** do a bit of skil(l)ful dodging

winken winkt, winkte, hat gewinkt od. umg. gewunken **I.** v/i. **1.** wave (**mit der Hand** one's hand); zu sich her: beckon; (Zeichen geben) make a sign, signal (+ Dat. to); **dem Kellner ~** signal to the waiter; **e-m Taxi ~** hail (od. wave down) a taxi; **mit dem Taschentuch** etc. ~ wave one's hankie (od. handkerchief etc.); **2.** fig.: **dem Finder winkt e-e hohe Belohnung** the finder can expect a large reward; **dem Gewinner winkt ein hoher Geldpreis** the winner can look forward to a large cash prize; **II.** v/t. **1.** Sport signal, indicate; **2.** **j-n zu sich ~** beckon s.o. over; **j-n in e-e Parklücke ~** wave s.o. into a parking space

Winker m; -s, -; Mot. trafficator, indicator, Am. turn signal, umg. (Blinker) winker, Am. blinker

winklig Adj. → **winkelig**

Winselei f; -, -en; pej. whining; **winseln** v/i. **1.** Hund: whine; **2.** pej. whine (**um** about)

Winter m; -s, - winter; **im ~** in winter; **im tiefsten ~** in the depths of winter; **über den ~ kommen** get through the winter; **~abend** m winter evening; **~anfang** m beginning of winter; **am 22.12. ist ~** 22 December (Am. December 22nd) is the first day of winter; **~apfel** m winter apple, good keeping apple; **~ausrüstung** f Mot. winter equipment; **~dienst** m Verk. snow clearing and gritting (Am. salting), winter road clearance; **~einbruch** m onset of winter; **~fahrplan** m winter timetable (Am. schedule); **~fell** n winter coat

winterfest Adj. winterproof; Bot. hardy; **~ machen** winterize

Winter|garten m winter garden, conservatory; **~getreide** n winter crop; **~halbjahr** n **1.** winter (months Pl.); **2.** Päd. etwa winter term, winter and spring terms Pl.

winterhart Adj. Bot. hardy

Winter|hilfswerk n hist. Winter Relief Fund; **~kleid** n **1.** winter dress; **~er** Koll. winter clothes (od. clothing Sg.); **2.** fig. e-s Pelztiers: winter coat; der Vögel: winter plumage; **~kleidung** f winter clothes Pl. (od. clothing)

winterlich I. Adj. wint(e)ry; Kleidung, Wetter etc.: auch winter …; **II.** Adv.: **~ gekleidet sein** be dressed in winter clothes, be dressed for winter

Winter|luft f wint(e)ry air; **~mantel** m winter coat; **~mode** f winter fashions

Pl.; **~monat** m winter month; **~morgen** m winter('s) morning

wintern v/i. unpers.: **es wintert schon** winter is on its way

Winter|nacht f winter('s) night; **in e-r kalten ~** on a cold winter's night; **~olympiade** f Winter Olympics Pl.; **~pause** f winter break; **~quartier** n winter quarters Pl.; **~reifen** m Mot. winter (od. snow) tyre (Am. tire); **~ruhe** f Zool. hibernation

winters Adv. in winter; **sommers wie ~** summer and winter

Winter|saat f winter seed; Pflanzen: winter (corn) seedlings Pl.; **~sachen** Pl. winter clothes (od. things); **~schlaf** m hibernation, winter sleep; **~ halten** hibernate; **~schlussverkauf** m winter (od. January) sales Pl.; **~schuhe** Pl. winter shoes Pl.; **~semester** n Päd. winter semester (od. term); **~sonnenwende** f winter solstice; **~speck** m umg. winter flab; **~spiele** Pl.: (Olympische) ~ Winter Olympics; **~sport** m winter sport(s Pl. Koll.); **~sportler** m, **~sportlerin** f winter sports enthusiast; **~sportort** m ski resort; **~starre** f Zool. torpor

Winterszeit f → **Winterzeit** 1

Wintertag m winter('s) day

wintertauglich Adj. fit for winter

Winter|urlaub m winter holiday (Am. vacation); **~wetter** n winter weather; **~zeit** f **1.** winter(time); **während der ~** in winter(time); **2.** (Uhrzeit) winter time

Winzer m; -s, -, **~in** f; -, -nen winegrower, vintner; **~genossenschaft** f winegrowers' cooperative; **~messer** n vine knife

winzig Adj. (auch **~ klein**) tiny, minute, teeny(-weeny) umg., teensy(-weensy) umg.; **Winzigkeit** f **1.** nur Sg. tininess, minuteness; **2.** umg. (Kleinigkeit) tiny thing, little thing; unbedeutend: trifle; (winzige Menge) tiny bit, tiny drop

Winzling m; -s, -e; umg. **1.** Baby: tiny tot; Person: tiny man (od. woman), midget; pej. half-pint; **2.** Tier. (little) tiny animal; Pflanze: (little) tiny plant

Wipfel m; -s, - (tree)top

Wippe f; -, -n seesaw; **wippen** vt/i. (schaukeln) seesaw, rock; Haare, Rock etc.: bob; **~ mit dem Fuß**: jiggle; dem Stuhl: rock backward(s) and forward(s); **auf den Zehenspitzen ~** rock up and down; **in den Knien ~** bob up and down; **der Vogel wippt mit dem Schwanz** the bird whisks its tail up and down (bzw. from side to side)

wir pers. Pron. **1.** we; **~ beide** both of us, we both …; **allein stehend**: the two of us; betont: both of us, us two umg.; **~ drei** the three of us; **~ alle** all of us, we all …; **~ anderen** the rest of us; **2.** altm. (ich); in Vortrag etc.: we; **Wir, Kaiser Friedrich** we, the Emperor Frederick; **3.** umg. (du, ihr, Sie) we; **was haben ~ denn für ein Problem?** what's bothering us then?

Wirbel m; -s, - **1.** (Drehung) whirl, swirl; Wasser: eddy; größerer: whirlpool; auch Phys. vortex; Wind: whirlwind; Met., Tech., von Luft: turbulence; von Rauch etc.: eddy; von Schnee, Staub: flurry; beim Tanz: spin, pirouette; **2.** (Trommelwirbel) (drum) roll; **3.** fig. der Ereignisse etc.: whirl; (Trubel) hurly-burly (of events); (Aufhebens) to-do umg.; **mach nicht solchen ~** don't make such a fuss; **es gab damals wegen dieser Affäre viel ~** the affair caused quite a stir at the time;

4. *Anat.* vertebra (*Pl.* vertebrae *od.* vertebras); **5.** *im Haar:* crown; *Muster, im Fingerabdruck etc.:* whorl; **6.** *an Geige etc.:* peg; *an Fenster:* catch; **~fortsatz** *m Anat.* spinous process; **~gelenk** *n* **1.** *Anat.* vertebral joint; **2.** *Tech.* swivel joint

wirbelig *Adj.* **1.** (*schwindelig*) dizzy; **2.** *Kind:* wild

Wirbel|kasten *m Mus.* pegbox; **~knochen** *m Anat.* vertebra (*Pl.* vertebrae *od.* vertebras)

wirbellos *Adj. Zool.* invertebrate; **Wirbellose** *Zool.* invertebrates

wirbeln I. *v/i.* **1.** (*ist gewirbelt*) *Schnee, Staub etc.:* whirl, swirl; *Tänzer, Wasser etc.:* whirl; **2.** (*hat*) *Trommeln:* roll; **3.** (*hat*) *fig.:* **mir wirbelt der Kopf** my head's spinning; **II.** *v/t.* (*hat*): **durch die Luft gewirbelt werden** be whirled through the air

Wirbelsäule *f Anat.* spine, spinal column; *Schaden an der* **~** spinal damage

Wirbelsäulen|gymnastik *f* spine gymnastics, exercises *Pl.* for the spine; **~verkrümmung** *f* curvature of the spine

Wirbel|sturm *m* whirlwind; (*Zyklon*) cyclone; (*Tornado*) tornado; **~tier** *n Zool.* vertebrate; **~wind** *m* whirlwind (*auch fig. hum.*)

wirbt *Präs.* → **werben**
wird *Präs.* → **werden**
wirft *Präs.* → **werfen**

Wirgefühl *n; nur Sg.* community spirit; *unter Mitarbeitern etc.:* team spirit

wirken I. *v/i.* **1.** (*Wirkung ausüben*) have an effect (*auf* + *Akk.* on), be effective, work; *anfangen:* take effect; **~** *auf* (+ *Akk.*) *negativ:* affect; **~** *gegen Arznei:* be effective against; *anregend* **~** *Kaffee etc.:* act as a stimulant; *berauschend* **~** *Alkohol etc.:* have an intoxicating effect; **die Tabletten schnell** the tablets act fast; **die Arznei beginnt zu ~** the medicine is beginning to take effect (*od.* kick in *umg.*); *etw. auf sich* **~** *lassen* take s.th. in; *genießerisch:* soak s.th. up; **das hat gewirkt!** that did the trick; (*hat gesessen*) that hit home; **das Buch hat** (*auf mich*) **stark gewirkt** the book made a strong impression (on me); **2.** *positiv:* (*zur Geltung kommen*) look good; (*j-m zusagen*) appeal to; **die Statue wirkt erst aus einiger Entfernung** the statue only has (full) effect when looked at from some distance; **3.** (*erscheinen*) seem; (*aussehen*) look; (*sich anhören*) sound; **er wirkt schüchtern** he gives the impression of being rather shy; **überzeugend ~** be convincing; **4.** (*tätig sein, arbeiten*) work (*an* + *Dat.* at; *bei* with, for), be active (*für* for); **~** *gegen* act (*od.* fight) against, oppose; **als Missionar** *etc.* **~** be active as a missionary *etc.* (*od.* in missionary work *etc.*); **II.** *v/t.* **1.** *geh.* (*tun*) do; **Gutes ~** do good; **Wunder ~** 1; **2.** (*Strümpfe etc.*) knit; (*Stoff*) weave

Wirken *n; -s, kein Pl.* work; (*Tätigkeit*) activity, activities *Pl.*; **wirkend I.** *Part. Präs.* → **wirken**; **II.** *Adj.* active; *langsam/schnell* **~** slow-acting/fast-acting; *stark* **~** strong, potent; *anregend/beruhigend* **~** having a stimulating/calming effect

Wirker *m; -s, -,* **~in** *f; -, -nen* knitter; *von Stoff:* weaver

Wirkleistung *f Etech.* effective power

wirklich I. *Adj.* **1.** real; (*tatsächlich*) *auch* actual; **das ~e Leben** real life; **~ werden** become a reality; *Traum: auch* come true; **2.** (*echt*) real, true; **II.** *Adv.* really, actually, in reality; *verstärkend:* really; *bestätigend: auch* honestly; **was willst du ~?** what do you really want?; **es war ~ gut** it was really good, it really was good; **es tut mir ~ Leid** I really am sorry; **nicht ~** not really; **Wirklichkeit** *f* reality; **die raue ~** harsh reality, the hard facts (of life); **in ~** in reality; (*eigentlich*) in fact; **~ werden** become a reality; *Traum: auch* come true

wirklichkeitsfern → **wirklichkeitsfremd**

Wirklichkeitsform *f Ling.* indicative

wirklichkeits|fremd I. *Adj.* unrealistic; (*idealistisch*) starry-eyed; → *auch* **weltfremd**; **II.** *Adv.* unrealistically; **~getreu I.** *Adj.* realistic; *Nachbildung:* faithful; **II.** *Adv.* realistically; **~nah I.** *Adj.* realistic, down-to-earth; **II.** *Adv.* realistically

Wirklichkeitstreue *f* truth to life, verisimilitude

Wirkmaschine *f* knitting machine

wirksam *Adj.* effective; **sehr ~** *Medikament: auch* very strong; **~ gegen** good for; **~ werden** *Gesetz etc.:* take effect (**am ...** from ...); *Medikament etc.:* (begin to) take effect (*od.* have an effect)

Wirksamkeit *f; nur Sg.* effectiveness; *e-s Mittels, e-r Methode etc.: auch* efficacy

Wirkstoff *m* agent, active substance

Wirkung *f* effect (*auf* + *Akk.* on); *stärker:* impact; **mit ~ vom** *Amtsspr.* with effect from, as from (*od.* of); **mit sofortiger ~** with immediate effect; **~ erzielen** have an effect, work; **s-e ~ tun** work, have the desired effect; **~ / keine ~ zeigen** have an/no effect; **s-e ~ verfehlen** have no effect, prove ineffective; **Ursache und ~** cause and effect; → **Ursache**

Wirkungs|bereich *m* sphere of activity; *Mil.* radius of action; *Gesetz:* operation; **~grad** *m* efficiency; **~kraft** *f; nur Sg.* efficacy, effectiveness; **~kreis** *m* sphere of activity

wirkungslos *Adj.* ineffective; **~ bleiben** have no effect; **Wirkungslosigkeit** *f; nur Sg.* ineffectiveness, ineffectuality

Wirkungsstätte *f geh.* domain, sphere of activity; *Arbeitsplatz:* workplace, place where *s.o.* works; **an seine alte ~ zurückkehren** go back to the place where one used to work

wirkungsvoll *Adj.* → **wirksam**

Wirkungsweise *f* mode of operation; mechanism; *e-s Mittels:* effect

Wirkwaren *Pl.* knitwear *Sg.*; *Strümpfe etc.:* hosiery *Sg.*

wirr I. *Adj.* **1.** *Haar:* dishevel(l)ed, tousled; *Schnüre, Wurzeln etc.:* tangled; (*unordentlich*) disorderly; *stärker:* chaotic; **~es Durcheinander** chaos; **2.** *fig.* confused; *Person: auch* bewildered, muddle-headed *pej.*; *Gedanken:* confused, muddled; *Blick:* bewildered; *Rede:* incoherent; **mir ist ganz ~ im Kopf** my head's spinning; **~es Zeug reden** ramble, rave; **j-n ganz ~ machen** get s.o. completely confused, make s.o.'s head spin; **II.** *Adv.:* **die Haare hingen ihm ~ ins Gesicht** his hair was hanging in a tangled mane over his face; **Wirren** *Pl.* turmoil *Sg.*; **Wirrkopf** *m pej.* scatterbrain; **wirrköpfig** *Adj. pej.* scatterbrained; **Wirrnis** *f; -, -se; geh.* **1.** → **Wirrwarr**; **2.** *nur Sg.*; (*Verworrenheit*) confusion; **Wirrungen** *Pl. lit.* confusions, perplex-

ities; **Wirrwarr** *m, n; -s, kein Pl.* confusion, chaos, jumble *umg.*, mess *umg.*; *von Haaren, Schnüren etc.:* tangle; *von Stimmen:* hubbub; **~ von Vorschriften und Verordnungen** labyrinth (*od.* maze) of rules and regulations

Wirsing *m; -s, kein Pl.*, **Wirsingkohl** *m Bot.* savoy (cabbage)

Wirt *m; -(e)s, -e* **1.** (*Gastwirt*) landlord, proprietor, innkeeper, *Brit. auch* publican; **2.** (*Hauswirt*) landlord; **3.** *altm.* (*Gastgeber*) host; **4.** *Bio.* host; **Wirtin** *f; -, -nen* **1.** landlady, proprietor, proprietress; (*Gastwirtsfrau*) landlord's wife; **2.** (*Hauswirtin*) landlady; **3.** *altm.* (*Gastgeberin*) hostess

Wirtschaft *f* **1.** *Wirts.* economy; (*Handel*) trade and industry; (*Finanzwelt*) finance; **freie ~** (*Marktwirtschaft*) free market economy; (*Privatbetriebe*) private enterprise; **die ~ ankurbeln** boost (*od.* stimulate) the economy; **2.** (*Gastwirtschaft*) pub, *Am.* bar, *Brit. förm.* public house; *mst ländliche:* inn; (*Speiselokal*) restaurant; **3.** (*Haushalt*) housekeeping; **4.** (*Landwirtschaft*) farm; **5.** *nur Sg.*; (*das Wirtschaften*) management; **6.** *nur Sg.*; *umg. pej.* (*Durcheinander*) mess; (*Zustände*) state of affairs; *Arbeitsweise:* muddling through; **das ist ja e-e schöne ~!** that's a fine mess / state of affairs

wirtschaften I. *v/i.* **1.** (*mit Geld umgehen*) manage one's money (*od.* finances); (*sparsam sein*) economize; **gut od. sparsam ~** be economical, look after one's money; *im Haushalt:* be a good housekeeper; **schlecht ~** waste money, manage one's money (*od.* finances) badly; **nicht ~ können** be no good with money, not know how to manage one's money (*od.* finances); **mit Gewinn/Verlust ~** come out on the plus/minus side, run at a profit/loss; → **Tasche** 2; **2.** *umg.* (*beschäftigt sein*) be busy; (*hantieren*) potter (*Am.* putter) around (*od.* about); **II.** *v/t.:* **e-e Firma zugrunde ~** run a firm (*Am.* business) into the ground; **Wirtschafter** *m; -s, -*, **Wirtschafterin** *f; -, -nen* **1.** (*Verwalter*) administrator; **2.** *in Haushalt:* housekeeper; **3.** *umg.* → **Wirtschaftler**, **Wirtschaftler** *m; -s, -*, **Wirtschaftlerin** *f; -, -nen* **1.** *Wissenschaftler(in):* economist; **2.** (*Unternehmer[in]*) businessman, *weiblich:* businesswoman; **wirtschaftlich I.** *Adj.* **1.** (*die Wirtschaft betreffend*) *nur attr.* economic; (*finanziell*) financial; **2.** (*rentabel*) profitable; (*leistungsfähig*) efficient; **3.** (*sparsam*) economical; **II.** *Adv.* economically *etc.*; → I; **ihr geht es ~ nicht gut** financially, things are not going well for her; **Wirtschaftlichkeit** *f; nur Sg.* economic efficiency; (*Rentabilität*) profitability; (*Sparsamkeit*) economy, thrift

Wirtschafts|abkommen *n Wirts.* economic (*od.* trade) agreement; **~asylant** *m*, **~asylantin** *f neg!* economic migrant; **~aufschwung** *m* economic upturn (*stärker:* boom); **~barometer** *n* business barometer; **~berater** *m*, **~beraterin** *f* economic adviser; **~bericht** *m* financial report; **~beziehungen** *Pl.* economic (*od.* trade) relations; **~boykott** *m* economic sanctions *Pl.* (*od.* boycott, embargo); **~boss** *m umg.* big businessman, magnate; **~buch** *n* account book, housekeeping book; **~delikt** *n Wirts.* economic crime; **~einheit** *f* economic entity; **~experte** *m*, **~expertin** *f* economic expert; **~faktor** *m* economic factor; **~flüchtling** *m* economic migrant (*od.* refugee); **~form** *f* economic system; **~forschungsinstitut** *n* institute for economic research; **~führer** *m*, **~führerin** *f* leading industrialist, captain of industry

Wirtschafts|gebäude *Pl.* (non-residential) outbuildings; **~geld** *n* housekeeping money

Wirtschafts|gemeinschaft *f* *Wirts.* trading partnership, economic union; *Europäische ~ hist.* (*abgek.* **EWG**) European Economic Community (*Abk.* **EEC**); **~geografie**, **~geographie** *f* economic geography; **~geschichte** *f*; *nur Sg.* history of economics; **~gipfel** *m* economic summit; **~güter** *Pl.* economic goods; **~gymnasium** *n* grammar school (*Am.* high school) emphasizing the study of economics; **~hilfe** *f* economic aid; **~hochschule** *f* business school; **~ingenieur** *m*, **~ingenieurin** *f* industrial engineer; **~jahr** *n* financial year; **~journalist** *m*, **~journalistin** *f* financial journalist; **~kapitän** *m umg.* captain of industry; (*Magnat*) magnate, tycoon; **~kraft** *f* economic power; **~krieg** *m Pol.* economic war(fare); **~kriminalität** *f* white-collar crime; **~krise** *f* economic crisis; **~lage** *f* economic situation; **~leben** *n* economic activity; **~macht** *f* economic power; **~minister** *m*, **~ministerin** *f Pol.* minister for economic affairs; *in GB:* Secretary of State for Trade and Industry, Trade and Industry Secretary; *in den USA:* Secretary of Commerce; **~ministerium** *n* economics ministry; *in GB:* Department of Trade and Industry; *in den USA:* Department of Commerce; **~misere** *f* economic plight; **~ordnung** *f* economic system; **~partner** *m* **1.** *Land:* trading partner; **2.** *Firma:* business partner

Wirtschaftspolitik *f Pol.* economic policy; **wirtschaftspolitisch I.** *Adj.* economic; *der ~e Sprecher der Partei* the party's spokesperson on economic policy; **II.** *Adv.* economically

Wirtschafts|prognose *f Wirts.* economic forecast; **~prüfer** *m*, **~prüferin** *f* auditor; **~prüfung** *f* audit; **~raum** *m* **1.** *Gebiet:* economic area; **2.** *mst Pl.*; *in Gebäude:* utility room; **~recht** *n* commercial law; **~redaktion** *f e-r Zeitung:* financial editor(s *Pl.*); **~region** *f* economic region; **~spionage** *f* industrial espionage; **~standort** *m* business location; **~system** *n* economy, economic system; **~teil** *m e-r Zeitung:* financial pages *Pl.*, business section; **~und Währungsunion** *f* economic and monetary union; *Europäische ~* European Economic and Monetary Union (*abgek.* EMU), **~union** *f* economic union; **~unternehmen** *n* business (enterprise); **~verband** *m* trade association; **~vergehen** *n Koll.* white-collar crime; **~wachstum** *n* economic growth

Wirtschaftswissenschaft *f Wirts. auch Pl.* economics *Pl.* (*V. im Sg.*); **Wirtschaftswissenschaftler** *m*, **Wirtschaftswissenschaftlerin** *f* economist; **wirtschaftswissenschaftlich** *Adj.* economic

Wirtschafts|wunder *n Wirts. umg.* economic miracle; **~zweig** *m* branch of industry; (*Wirtschaftssektor*) sector of the economy

Wirtshaus *n → Wirtschaft* 2; **~schild** *n* pub (*od.* inn) sign

Wirts|leute *Pl.* landlord and landlady;

~pflanze *f Bio.* host; **~stube** *f →* *Gaststube*; **~tier** *n Bio.* host (animal)

Wisch *m*; -(e)s, -e; *umg. pej.* bumf *Sl.*, bumph *Sl.*, *Am.* screed

wischen[1] *vt/i.* (*hat gewischt*) **1.** wipe; *Staub ~* dust; *mit der Hand über den Tisch ~* wipe one's hand over the table; *sich* (*Dat.*) *den Schweiß von der Stirn ~* wipe the sweat from one's brow; *sich* (*Dat.*) *den Schlaf aus den Augen ~* rub the sleep out of one's eyes; *j-s Einwände vom Tisch ~ fig.* sweep aside s.o.'s objections; **2.** (*säubern*) wipe; (*feucht*) ~ (*Fußboden, Küche etc.*) mop, swab; *sie wischte sich die Augen / den Mund* she wiped her eyes/mouth; **3.** *umg. fig.: j-m e-e ~* give s.o. a clip (a)round the ears; *e-e gewischt bekommen* (*Ohrfeige*) get a clip (a)round the ear; **4.** *schw.* (*fegen, kehren*) sweep (the floor)

wischen[2] *v/i.* (*ist gewischt*) (*sich schnell bewegen*) whisk

Wischer *m*; -s, -; *Mot.* wiper; **~blatt** *n* wiper blade

wischfest *Adj. Farbe etc.:* smearproof, non-smear

wischiwaschi *umg. pej. Adj. indekl.*, *mst präd. Ansichten etc.:* wishy-washy, vague; *Person: auch* ineffective; **Wischiwaschi** *n*; -s, *kein Pl.* blah(-blah), *Am.* hooey

Wisch|lappen *m Dial.*, **~tuch** *n* cloth

Wisent *m*; -s, -e; *Zool.* wisent, European bison

Wismut *n*; -(e)s, *kein Pl.*; (*abgek.* **Bi**) *Chem.* bismuth

wispern *vt/i.* whisper, speak (*od.* talk) in a whisper

Wissbegier(de) *f*; *nur Sg.* thirst *od.* hunger for knowledge; *bes. e-r Person, die schon viel weiß:* (intellectual) curiosity; **wissbegierig** *Adj.* eager to learn (*od.* for knowledge); *weitS.* curious

wissen *vt/i.*; *weiß, wusste, hat gewusst* **1.** know (*von od. geh. um* about); *j-n etw. ~ lassen* let s.o. know s.th.; *ich weiß genau, dass ...* I know for a fact that ...; *weißt du noch?* (do you) remember?; *ich weiß s-n Namen nicht mehr* I can't remember his name; *weißt du schon das Neueste?* have you heard the latest?; *woher weißt du das?* how do you know?; *er weiß nicht, was er sagt* he doesn't know what he's talking about; *er weiß immer alles besser iro.* he always knows better; *das musst du selber ~* that's up to you; *ich möchte ~, wie etc.* (*ich frage mich*) I wonder how etc.; *ich möchte nicht ~, was ...* I wouldn't like to know what ...; *wenn ich nur wüsste, ...* if I only knew ...; *das hätte ich* (*früher*) *sollen!* I wish I'd known (earlier); *woher soll ich denn das ~? umg.* how am I supposed to know that!; *woher will er denn das ~?* where's he got (*od.* where'd he learn) that from?; *das weiß doch jedes Kind!* any child knows that!; *ich will von ihm / davon nichts ~* I don't want anything to do with him/it; *ich will von ihr nichts mehr ~* I'm through with her; *von Geld wollte er nichts ~* he refused to (*od.* he wouldn't) accept any money; *jetzt will ich's aber ~! umg.* (*beweisen, versuchen etc.*) there's only one way to find out!; *→ Bescheid* 3, *Rat*[1]; **2.** *in Redefloskeln und Wendungen: weißt du was? umg.* (do) you know what?; *weißt du, ... you know ...; du musst* (*nämlich*) ~, *dass*

... you must know that ...; *erklärend:* I have to tell you that ...; *wohl ~d, dass* ... knowing very well that ...; *gewusst, wie! umg.* it's easy when you know how!; *was weiß ich! umg.* how should I know?, how am I supposed to know?; *ich weiß nicht recht* I'm not (so) sure, I dunno *umg.*; *man kann nie ~ umg.* you never know; *bei ihr kann man nie ~* with her you never know; *soviel ich weiß* as far as I know; *ich wüsste nicht warum!* I've no idea why!; *nicht, dass ich wüsste!* not that I know of; (*ja,*) *wenn ich das wüsste!* (well) if I knew that!; *das ~ die Götter!* God knows!; *was ich nicht weiß, macht mich nicht heiß Sprichw.* what you don't know can't hurt you, what the eye doesn't see the heart doesn't grieve over; **3.** (+ *Inf. mit zu*): *sich zu helfen/wehren ~* be able (*od.* know how) to look after / defend o.s.; *sie weiß nichts mit sich / mit i-r Freiheit anzufangen* she doesn't know what to do with herself / her freedom; **4.** *geh.: j-n/sich in Sicherheit ~* know that s.o./one is safe; *er wusste sie gesund und sicher zu Hause* he knew that she was safe and well at home; *ich möchte das so verstanden ~* I'd like to have that understood; **5.** *umg. verstärkend: und was weiß ich noch alles* and what not; *er hält sich für wer weiß wie klug* he thinks he's ever so clever (*Am.* smart)

Wissen *n*; -s, *kein Pl.* knowledge (*über* + *Akk. od.* **von, um** of; *in* + *Dat.* of); *meines ~s* as far as I know, to my knowledge; *mit m-m / ohne mein ~* with my knowledge / without my knowledge (*od.* knowing); *mit ~* (*wissentlich*) knowingly; *nach bestem und Gewissen* to the best of one's knowledge and belief; *wider besseres ~ geh.* against one's better judg(e)ment

wissend I. *Part. Präs. → wissen*; **II.** *Adj. Blick, Lächeln:* knowing; **III.** *Adv.* knowingly; **Wissende** *m*, *f*; -n, -n person who knows *s.th.*; (*Eingeweihte*) insider, initiate

Wissensbereich *m* field of knowledge

Wissenschaft *f* (*exakte ~, Naturwissenschaft*) science; (*Forschung*) research; (*akademische Welt*) (world of) scholarship, academia; *Psycholinguistik ist die ~ von ...* psycholinguistics is the study of ...; *in der ~ tätig sein* work in research; *die ~ sagt* researchers claim; *bei Naturwissenschaften: auch* scientists claim; *die ~ hat bewiesen ... auch* research has proved ...; *das ist e-e ~ für sich umg.* that's a book with seven seals; *→ Geisteswissenschaft etc.*; **Wissenschafter** *m*; -s, -, **Wissenschafterin** *f*; -, -nen; *österr., schw. → Wissenschaftler*, **Wissenschaftler** *m*; -s, -, **Wissenschaftlerin** *f*; -, -nen academic; (*Naturwissenschaftler*) scientist; (*Geisteswissenschaftler*) scholar; (*Forscher*) researcher; **wissenschaftlich** *Adj.* academic; *Arbeitsweise:* methodical; (*naturwissenschaftlich*) scientific (*auch ~ genau*); (*gelehrt*) scholarly; *~e Laufbahn* academic career; *~er Beweis* scientific proof (*od.* evidence); **Wissenschaftlichkeit** *f*; *nur Sg.* scholarliness; (*wissenschaftliches Niveau*) *auch* scholarly standard

Wissenschafts|betrieb *m* academic work; *naturwissenschaftlich:* scientific work; *allgemein gefasst:* academic life; **~gläubigkeit** *f* blind faith in science;

~zweig *m* branch of learning, discipline

Wissensdrang *m*, **Wissensdurst** *m* thirst (*od.* hunger) for knowledge; **wissensdurstig** *Adj.* hungry for knowledge

Wissens|frage *f* question (*od.* matter) of knowledge; **~gebiet** *n* field of knowledge; **~lücke** *f* gap in one's knowledge; **~stand** *m* level (*od.* state) of knowledge; *auf dem neuesten ~* up to date; **~stoff** *m*; *nur Sg.* (body of) knowledge; **~vermittlung** *f* transmission (*od.* passing on) of knowledge; **~vorsprung** *m* advance in knowledge

wissenswert *Adj.* worth knowing; *Wissenswertes* interesting facts

wissentlich I. *Adj.* conscious; (*absichtlich*) wil(l)ful, deliberate; **II.** *Adv.* knowingly; (*absichtlich*) deliberately

witschen *v/i. umg.* slip

wittern I. *v/t.* **1.** scent, smell; **2.** *fig.* (*ahnen*) sense; *e-e Chance ~* see one's chance; *ein Geschäft / e-n Vorteil ~* get wind of a deal / sense an advantage; **II.** *v/i.* sniff the air

Witterung *f* **1.** weather; *Verhältnisse:* weather (*od.* atmospheric) conditions; *bei jeder ~* in all weathers; *bei günstiger ~* weather permitting; **2.** (*Geruch, Geruchssinn*) scent; *~ aufnehmen* pick up the scent; *e-e sichere ~ haben auch fig.* have a good nose

witterungs|bedingt *Adj.* weather-caused, caused by the weather *präd.*; *~ sein auch* be due to (*od.* because of) the weather; **~beständig** *Adj.* weatherproof; *Stahl:* stainless

Witterungs|einflüsse *Pl.* influence *Sg.* of the weather; weather factors; **~umschlag** *m* sudden change in the weather; **~verhältnisse** *Pl.* weather (*od.* atmospheric) conditions

Wittib *f*; -, -*e*; *altm. od. Dial.* widow; **Wittiber** *m*; -*s*, -; *altm. od. Dial.* widower

Witwe *f*; -, -*n* **1.** widow; *~ werden* be widowed; *grüne ~ fig., hum.* grass widow; **2.** *Zool.: Schwarze ~* black widow

Witwenrente *f* widow's pension

Witwen|schaft *f*; *nur Sg.* widowhood; **~tröster** *m*; -*s*, -; *umg. hum.* widow chaser; **~verbrennung** *f* sati, ritual burning of widows

Witwer *m*; -*s*, - widower; *~ werden* be widowed, lose one's wife; **Witwerschaft** *f*; *nur Sg.* widowerhood

Witz *m*; -*es*, -*e* **1.** joke (*über* + *Akk. od. von* about); *alter ~* old joke, old chestnut *umg.*; *~e machen od. reißen umg.* tell (*umg.* crack) jokes; *mach keine ~e! umg.* you're joking (*umg.* kidding); *das soll wohl ein ~ sein? iro.* you're joking, of course; is this supposed to be some kind of joke?; *das ist ja ein ~! umg. iro.* what a laugh; *diese Bestimmung ist (ja wohl) ein (schlechter) ~!* this regulation is ridiculous; *der ~ ist nämlich der, dass ... fig.* the point is that ...; *das ist der ganze ~ fig.* that's the whole point; *der ~ hat so einen Bart* that's a real oldie; **2.** *nur Sg.* (*Geist*) wit(tiness); *~ haben* be very witty; **3.** *altm.* (*Findigkeit*) wits *Pl.*, cleverness

Witzblatt *n* funny magazine; *satirisches:* satirical magazine; **~figur** *f umg.* caricature

Witzbold *m*; -(*e*)*s*, -*e*; *umg., mst pej.* joker; *du ~! iro.* very funny!; *welcher ~ war das?* which of you jokers did that?; *wenn der Täter nicht hier ist:* what joker did that?

Witzelei *f*; -, -*en* **1.** *Äußerung:* witticism; **2.** *nur Sg.*; (*das Witzeln*) joking; (*das Hänseln*) teasing; **witzeln** *v/i.* joke (*über* + *Akk.* about); *~ über* (+ *Akk.*) *auch* poke fun at

Witzfigur *f* **1.** character in a joke; **2.** *umg. pej.* figure of fun

witzig *Adj.* funny; *Bemerkung etc.: auch* witty; *sehr ~! auch iro.* very funny (*od.* droll)!; **Witzigkeit** *f*; *nur Sg.* humo(u)r

witzlos *Adj.* **1.** unwitty, lacking in wit (*od.* humo[u]r), unfunny; **2.** *umg.* (*sinnlos*) pointless (*etw. zu tun* doing s.th.)

Witzseite *f* comics page, *the* funnies *Pl. umg.*

w. L. *Abk. Geog.* (*westlicher Länge*) degrees west

Wladiwostok (*n*); -*s*; *Geog.* Vladivostok

WM *f*; -, -*s*; *Abk.* (*Weltmeisterschaft*) world championship(s *Pl.*); *im Fußball auch:* World Cup; **~-Runde** *f* world championship round (*od.* leg); *Fußball:* round of the World Cup; **~-Spiel** *n* world championship game (*od.* match); *Fußball:* World Cup match; **~-Turnier** *n* world championship (*Fußball:* World Cup) tournament

wo I. *Adv.* **1.** *fragend:* where?; *~ gibt's denn so was! umg.* have you ever seen the likes of it?; *~ denkst du hin? umg.* what are you thinking of?; **2.** *in Relativsätzen:* where; *zeitlich:* when; *überall, ~ ...* wherever; *~ (auch) immer du sein magst* wherever you may be; *~ ich auch hingehe, ... umg.* wherever I go ...; *das Wo ist unwichtig* (the) where is unimportant; **3.** *umg.* (*irgendwo*) somewhere; **4.** *umg., in Ausrufen: i ~! od. ach ~!* no, no; oh, no; *~ werd ich!* not on your life!, *bes. Am.* no way!; **II.** *Konj.* **1.** (*wenn, da*) when; (*obwohl*) though; *jetzt ~ ...* now that ...; *warum hast du das getan, ~ du doch weißt, dass ...* why did you do that when you know very well that ...; *er geht Fallschirmspringen, ~ das doch so gefährlich ist* he goes parachuting (*od.* skydiving) even though he knows it's very dangerous; *sie sagte, sie sei krank, ~ sie doch nur müde war* she said she was ill, though actually she was only tired; **2.** *altm.:* ~ (*irgend*) *möglich* wherever possible; *~ nicht ..., so doch ...* if not

woanders *Adv.* somewhere else; *fragend und verneinend:* anywhere else; **~her** *Adv.:* *von ~* from somewhere else, from elsewhere; **~hin** *Adv.* somewhere else, elsewhere

wob *Imperf. geh.* → **weben**

wobei *Adv.* **1.** *fragend:* ~ *bist du gerade?* what are you doing right now?; *beim Lesen in e-m Buch:* where have you got(ten) to?; *~ haben sie ihn ertappt?* what was he doing when they caught him?, what did they catch him at (*od.* doing)?; **2.** *in Relativsätzen: ich las den Brief noch mal, ~ mir klar wurde, dass ...* I re(-)read the letter and realized (that) ...; *..., ~ sie mich ansah ...* looking at me as she did so; *~ er e-n Fehler machte* and in so doing he made a mistake; *..., ~ du beachten/aufpassen musst, dass ...* but you have to remember/watch that ...; *~ mir einfällt ...* which reminds me ...

Woche *f*; -, -*n* week; *englische ~ Sport* week in which a football team has to play three games; *Kieler ~ Sport* Kiel Regatta Week; *in einer ~* in a week('s

time); *heute in e-r ~* a week today, today week, *Am.* a week from today; *heute vor e-r ~* a week ago today; *jede zweite ~* every other week; *dreimal die ~* three times a week; *~ um ~* week after week; *unter der ~ od. die ~ über* during the week

Wochen|anfang *m* beginning of the week; **~arbeitszeit** *f* weekly working hours *Pl.*

Wochenbett *n*; *mst Sg.* lying-in (period); *im ~ liegen* be lying in; *im ~ sterben* die after giving birth (to a *od.* one's child), die in childbirth; **~depression** *f Psych.* post-natal depression; **~fieber** *n Med.* puerperal fever

Wochenblatt *n* weekly (paper)

Wochenend|arrest *m* weekend detention; **~ausflug** *m* weekend trip; **~ausflügler** *m*, **~ausflüglerin** *f* weekender; **~ausgabe** *f* weekend edition; **~beilage** *f* weekend supplement

Wochenende *n* weekend; *am ~* at (*bes. Am.* on) the weekend; (*dieses ~*) *auch* this weekend; (*an den ~n*) *auch* at (*bes. Am.* on) weekends; *übers ~* over the weekend; *übers ~ wegfahren* go away for the weekend; *verlängertes od. langes ~* long weekend

Wochenend|ehe *f* weekend marriage; **~haus** *n mst* weekend cottage; **~heimfahrer** *m*, **~heimfahrerin** *f* weekly commuter; **~urlaub** *m* weekend break (*od.* trip); **~verkehr** *m* weekend traffic

Wochen|fluss *m Med. nach Entbindung:* lochia (*Pl.* lochia); **~karte** *f* weekly season ticket

wochenlang I. *Adj.* ... lasting several weeks; *nach ~em Warten* after weeks of waiting; **II.** *Adv.* for weeks (and weeks), for weeks on end; *es dauerte ~, bis ...* it took weeks before ...

Wochen|lohn *m* weekly wages *Pl.*; **~markt** *m* weekly market; **~schau** *f hist. Film:* newsreel; **~schrift** *f altm.* weekly; **~stunden** *Pl.: wie viele ~ arbeitest du?* how may hours a week do you work?; **~tag** *m* weekday; *welcher ~ ist heute?* what day (of the week) is it today?; *an ~en* on weekdays

wochentags *Adv.* (on) weekdays

wöchentlich I. *Adj.* weekly; (*wochenweise*) week-by-week ...; **II.** *Adv.* every week, weekly; *einmal ~* once a week

wochenweise *Adv.* week by week; (*jeweils e-e Woche lang*) on a weekly basis

Wochenzeitung *f* weekly (newspaper)

...wöchig *Adj.* **1.** (*... Wochen dauernd*) ...weeks; *ein dreiwöchiger Zeitraum* a three-week period, a period of three weeks; *mit sechswöchiger Verspätung* six weeks late; **2.** (*... Wochen alt*) ...-week-old; *dreizehnwöchig* thirteen--week-old

Wöchnerin *f*; -, -*nen* woman in childbed

Wöchnerinnenstation *f* maternity ward

Wodka *m*; -*s*, -*s* vodka

wodran, **wodrauf** *etc. umg.* → **woran**, **worauf** *etc.*

wodurch *Adv.* **1.** *fragend:* how?; *~ hast du davon erfahren?* how did you find out about it?; **2.** *in Relativsätzen:* by (*od.* through) which, *förm.* whereby; (*mittels*) by means of which; *auf e-n ganzen Satz bezogen:* which; *alles, ~ der Plan gefährdet wird* anything that endangers the plan; *~ bewiesen wird, dass ...* which proves that ...

wofür *Adv.* **1.** *fragend:* what (...) for?;

~ halten Sie mich? who do you think I am?, who do you take me for?; **~ hast du dich entschieden?** what have you decided on?; **2.** *in Relativsätzen*: for which, which … for; **alles, ~ ich mich interessiere** everything (that) I'm interested in; **…, ~ ich nichts konnte** …, which I could do nothing about

wog *Imperf.* → *wiegen*[1]

Woge *f*; -, -*n*; *geh.* **1.** wave, billow; **2.** *fig.* wave, surge; **die ~n glätten** pour oil on troubled waters; **die ~n glätten sich** things are calming down

wogegen I. *Adv.* **1.** *fragend*: against (*Medikament etc.*: for) what?, what … against (*bzw.* for)?; **~ hast du es eingetauscht?** what did you swap it for?; **2.** *in Relativsätzen*: against which, which … against; *austauschend*: in return for which; **herausfinden, ~ man allergisch ist** find out what one is allergic to; **~ ich nichts einzuwenden habe** to which I have no objection; **II.** *Konj.* → *wohingegen*

wogen *v/i. geh.* surge (*auch fig. Menge etc.*); *Getreide*: sway; *Kampf*: rage; *Busen*: heave

woher *Adv. fragend und in Relativsätzen*: where (…) from; **~ wissen Sie das?** how do you know that?; **geh dahin, ~ du gekommen bist** go back to where you came from; **(ach) ~ denn!** *umg.* nonsense!

wohin *Adv. fragend und in Relativsätzen*: where (… to); **~ auch** wherever; **~ gehst's?** where are you off to?; **ich weiß nicht, ~ damit** I don't know where to put it; **sie musste mal ~** *umg.* she had to pay a call, she had to go somewhere

wo|hinauf *Adv.* **1.** *fragend*: where … up to; **2.** *in Relativsätzen*: up to which; **der Gipfel, ~ wir wollten** the peak that we wanted to climb; → *auch worauf*, **~hinaus** *Adv.* **1.** *fragend*: where … out; **2.** *in Relativsätzen*: out of which; **~hinein** *Adv.* **1.** *fragend*: where … in; **2.** *in Relativsätzen*: into which; → *auch worein*

wohingegen *Konj.* whereas, while

wo|hinter *Adv.* **1.** *fragend*: where; **2.** *in Relativsätzen*: behind which; **~hinunter** *Adv.* **1.** *fragend*: where … down; **2.** *in Relativsätzen*: down which

wohl[1] *Adv.*; *wohler, am wohlsten* **1.** well; **sich ~ fühlen** feel fine; *seelisch*: be happy; **(wie zu Hause)** feel at home **(beim Umgang mit etw.)** feel comfortable; **fühlst du dich jetzt ~er?** do you feel better now?; **sich bei j-m ~ fühlen** feel comfortable (*od.* comfy) with s.o.; **ich fühle mich in s-r Gegenwart nicht ~** I don't feel at ease (*od.* I feel uncomfortable) when he's around; **ich fühle mich nicht ~** I don't feel well; **mir ist nicht ~ dabei** I don't feel happy about it; **sie fühlt sich ~ in München** she's quite happy in Munich; **2. ~ oder übel** willy nilly, whether you etc. like it or not

wohl[2] *Adv*; *besser, am besten* **1.** (*gut*) well; **~ ausgewogen** *Ernährung etc.*: well-balanced; **e-e ~ bedachte** *od.* **durchdachte Antwort** a well-balanced / well-thought-out answer; **ein ~ begründeter Verdacht** a well-founded suspicion; **~ behütet** *Person*: well looked-after; *Kindheit, Erziehung*: very sheltered; **er ist ~ behütet aufgewachsen** he had a very sheltered upbringing; **~ bekannt** well-known; *negativ*: notorious; **~ dosierte Menge** care-

fully (*od.* well-)measured dose; **~ gemeint** well-meant; **~ geordnet** *Schrank etc.*: (neat and) tidy; *Leben*: well-organized; **~ geordnet auf dem Schreibtisch liegen** lie in neat piles on the desk; **(ich) wünsche, ~ geruht/gespeist zu haben!** *geh. altm. od. hum.* I hope you slept well / enjoyed your meal; **j-m ~ tun** do s.o. well; **das tut ~** that's good; **~ temperiert** *Wein etc.*: at the correct temperature; *Zimmer etc.*: at a pleasant temperature; **~ überlegte Worte** well-considered words; **das war ~ überlegt** that was well thought out; **~ unterrichtet** (well-)informed; **~ verwahrt** under lock and key; **j-m ~ wollen** *geh.* wish s.o. well; → *bekommen* II, *gehaben, leben* I 5; **2.** *bekräftigend*: **ich bin mir dessen ~ bewusst** I'm well aware of that; **~ wahr** very true; **das kann man ~ sagen!** you can say that again; **ich erinnere mich sehr ~ daran** I remember it well; **ich verstehe dich sehr ~** I understand you perfectly well; **er weiß das sehr ~** he knows very well; **bei uns gibt es das nicht, ~ aber in Amerika** we don't have anything like that here, but they do in America; **3.** (*möglicherweise, vielleicht*) possibly, perhaps, maybe; (*wahrscheinlich*) probably; *vermutend, einräumend*: I suppose; *einschränkend*: (*zwar*) no doubt; **das ist ~ möglich** I suppose that's possible, that's quite possible; **das wird ~ das Beste sein** that's probably the best solution; **es wird ~ Regen geben** no doubt it will rain; **das wird ~ so sein** very likely; **sie hat uns ~ für Schwestern gehalten** she must have thought we were sisters; **das mag ~ sein, aber …** that may well be, but; **~ kaum** hardly, I doubt it; **sie wird ~ kaum anrufen** I doubt whether she'll ring up (*Am.* call), I don't suppose she'll ring up (*Am.* call); **gehst du mit?** ~; **4.** *fragend*: I wonder; **ob er ~ weiß, dass …?** I wonder if he knows (that) …; **wer das ~ war?** I wonder who that was; **was sie ~ vorhat?** I wonder what she's up to; **5.** (*ungefähr*) about; **6.** *Ärger, Ungeduld etc. ausdrückend*: **was machst du da? - was ~?** what does it look like?, what do you think?; **ich habe ~ nicht richtig gehört!** did I hear you right?; **willst du ~ damit aufhören?** will you stop that?; **man wird ja ~ noch fragen dürfen!** (all right,) I was only asking!; **7.** *geh. altm., in Ausrufen*: **~ dem, der …!** happy he (*od.* the man) who …; *als Antwort*: **sehr ~(, mein Herr)!** very well (sir)!

Wohl *n*; -(*e*)*s, kein Pl.* welfare, good; (*Wohlergehen*) well-being, *weitS.* prosperity; **das ~ und Wehe** (+ *Gen.*) the fate (of); **für das leibliche ~ der Gäste sorgen** make sure the guests have all they need to be comfortable; **das geschieht nur zu d-m ~** it's for your own good; **auf j-s ~ trinken** drink to s.o.'s health; **auf dein ~** your health!; **(sehr) zum ~!** cheers! *umg.*

wohlan *Adv. geh. altm.* well now

wohlanständig *Adj. geh.* respectable

wohlauf *Adv. geh.* **1.** well, in good health; **2.** *altm.* → *wohlan*

wohl| ausgewogen, ~ bedacht → *wohl*[2] 1

Wohlbefinden *n* well-being; **sich nach j-s ~ erkundigen** ask after s.o., ask how s.o. is

wohl begründet → *wohl*[2] 1

Wohlbehagen *n* comfort; pleasure; **mit ~** with relish

wohlbehalten *Adj.* safe (and sound); *Sache*: undamaged

wohl| behütet, ~ bekannt, ~ dosiert, ~ durchdacht → *wohl*[2] 1

Wohlergehen *n* welfare, well-being; **das leibliche ~** creature comforts *Pl.*

wohlerzogen, wohl erzogen *Adj. geh.* well-behaved; **~ sein** *auch* have been brought up well

Wohlfahrt *f*; *nur Sg. umg.*, *Amt*: welfare (services *Pl.*); **von der ~ leben** live on welfare

Wohlfahrts|… *im Subst. siehe auch* *Fürsorge…*; **~amt** *n* → *Sozialamt*; **~marke** *f* charity stamp; **~organisation** *f* charity, charitable institution; **~pflege** *f* welfare work; **~staat** *m* welfare state

wohlfeil *Adj. altm.* cheap

Wohlfühl… *im Subst.* wellness …; feel-good …

Wohlfühlen *n* feeling well *od.* fine; **Möbel zum ~** furniture for feeling at home

Wohlfühlfaktor *m* feel-good factor

Wohlgefallen *n* pleasure, satisfaction (*über* + *Akk.* at); **sein ~ haben an** (+ *Dat.*) take great pleasure in; **sich in ~ auflösen** *hum. Missverständnisse*: be settled amicably; *Pläne etc.*: go up in smoke; *Buch, Hemd, Verein etc.*: disintegrate, come apart at the seams; (*verschwinden*) vanish (into thin air); **wohlgefällig I.** *Adj.* **1.** *Blick*: of satisfaction (*od.* pleasure); (*selbstzufrieden*) complacent; **2.** *geh. altm.* (*angenehm*) pleasant, agreeable; **Gott ~** pleasing to God; **II.** *Adv.* with pleasure

wohlgeformt, wohl geformt *Adj.* well-shaped, shapely

Wohlgefühl *n*; *nur Sg.* pleasant (*od.* pleasurable) sensation *od.* feeling; *allgemeines*: feeling (*od.* sense) of well-being

wohlgelitten, wohl gelitten *Adj. geh.*, *Gast etc.*: (always) welcome

wohl gemeint → *wohl*[2] 1

wohl| gemerkt *Adv. am Satzanfang od. -ende*: mind you; **~gemut** *Adj. geh.* cheerful

wohlgenährt, wohl genährt *Adj. oft. hum.* well-fed

wohl geordnet → *wohl*[2] 1

wohlgeraten, wohl geraten *Adj. geh.*, *Kind*: well-behaved; *Sache*: good; **~ sein** *auch* have turned out well

Wohlgeruch *m geh.* fragrance; (*Aroma*) pleasant smell (*od.* aroma)

wohl| gesetzt *Adj. geh. Worte*: well-chosen; *Rede*: well-rounded; **~gesinnt** *Adj.* well-meaning; **j-m ~ sein** be well-disposed toward(s) s.o.; **~gestaltet** *Adj. geh.* well-shaped, shapely; **~getan** *Adj.; geh.?; bibl., Arbeit*: well done

wohlhabend *Adj.* well-to-do, wealthy; well-off; **Wohlhabenheit** *f*; *nur Sg.* affluence, prosperity

wohlig *Adj.* pleasant; (*gemütlich*) cosy, *Am.* cozy; **II.** *Adv. schnurren, seufzen etc.*: with pleasure; **sich ~ auf dem Sofa rekeln** stretch out luxuriously on the sofa

Wohlklang *m geh.* melodiousness; **wohlklingend** *Adj. geh.* melodious; *Name*: nice-sounding …

Wohllaut *m geh.* → *Wohlklang*; **wohllautend** *Adj. geh.* → *wohlklingend*

Wohlleben *n*; *nur Sg.*; *geh.* good living, life of luxury

wohl| meinend *Adj.* well-meaning; **~proportioniert, ~ proportioniert** *Adj.* well-proportioned; (*ausgewogen*)

W

well-balanced; (*ebenmäßig*) symmetrical; **~riechend** *Adj.* fragrant; (*aromatisch*) pleasant-smelling, aromatic; **~schmeckend** *Adj.* tasty

Wohlsein *n*: (*zum*) **~***!* *Trinkspruch*: your health!; *beim Niesen*: bless you!

Wohlstand *m*; *nur Sg.* prosperity, affluence; *zu ~ kommen* get rich, become well-off; *im ~ leben* be well-off, live very comfortably; *ist bei dir der ~ ausgebrochen?* *umg. hum.* have you won the pools or something?

Wohlstands|bürger *m*, **~bürgerin** *f pej.* member of the affluent society, affluent citizen; **~denken** *n pej.* materialistic thinking; **~gefälle** *n*; *nur Sg.* prosperity gap, unequal distribution of wealth; **~gesellschaft** *f pej.* affluent society; **~müll** *m* refuse from the affluent society; *pej. Menschen*: rejects *Pl.* of the affluent society

Wohltat *f* **1.** *nur Sg.*; (*Erleichterung*) relief; (*Segen*) blessing; (*Wonne*) bliss; *das ist e-e* (*wahre*) **~***!* what a relief, that (really) does you good; **2.** (*gute Tat*) good deed; **Wohltäter** *m*, **Wohltäterin** *f* philanthropist; *j-m gegenüber*: benefactor; *weiblich*: *auch* benefactress; **wohltätig** *Adj.* **1.** charitable; *für e-n ~en Zweck* for a good cause, for charity; **2.** → *wohltuend*; **Wohltätigkeit** *f*; *nur Sg.* charity

Wohltätigkeits|ball *m* charity ball; **~konzert** *n* charity concert; **~veranstaltung** *f* charity event (*Sport auch* fixture); (*Konzert*) charity (*od.* benefit) concert; **~verein** *m* charitable association

wohltemperiert[1], **wohl temperiert** *Adj. Wein etc.*: → *wohl*[2] 1

wohl|temperiert[2] *Adj. Mus.*: *das Wohltemperierte Klavier* the Well-Tempered Clavier; **~tönend** *Adj. geh.* → *wohlklingend*; **~tuend** *Adj.* pleasant; (*lindernd*) soothing; **~e Wärme** pleasant feeling of warmth

wohl| tun, **~ überlegt**, **~ unterrichtet** → *wohl*[2] 1

wohlverdient *Adj. Strafe etc.*: well-deserved; *Erfolg, Lohn etc.*: *auch* well-earned

Wohlverhalten *n* good behavio(u)r

wohlverstanden I. *Adj.*; *attr.*; *geh.* well-understood; **II.** *Adv.* → *wohlgemerkt*

wohl verwahrt → *wohl*[2] 1

wohlweislich *Adv.* wisely, for good reason; *er hat es ~ verschwiegen* he was careful not to say anything about it

wohl wollen → *wohl*[2] 1

Wohlwollen *n*; *-s, kein Pl.* goodwill; (*Gunst*) favo(u)r; *mit ~ betrachten* look kindly on; **wohlwollend I.** *Adj.* kind, benevolent; **II.** *Adv.*: *e-r Sache ~ gegenüberstehen* take a favo(u)rable view of s.th.

Wohn|anlage *f* housing area; **~bau** *m*; *Pl. -ten* residential building; **~bedarf** *m* housing requirements *Pl.*; **~bereich** *m* living area; **~bevölkerung** *f Statistik*: resident population; **~bezirk** *m* residential area; **~block** *m*; *Pl. mst -s, bes. schw. -blöcke* block of flats, *Am.* apartment house (*od.* building); **~container** *m* Portakabin®, *Am.* modular building; **~dichte** *f Soziol.* population density; **~eigentum** *n* property ownership; **~einheit** *f Archit.* living unit

wohnen *v/i.* **1.** live (*bei j-m*: with); *amtlich*: reside; *vorübergehend*: stay (*bei* with; *in + Dat.* at); *betreutes Wohnen* sheltered accommodation; **2.** *fig.* live,

dwell *lit.*

Wohn|fläche *f* living space; *e-e Wohnung mit 60 m²* a flat (*Am.* apartment) with a living area of 60 m²; **~gebäude** *n* residential building; **~gebiet** *n*, **~gegend** *f* residential area; **~geld** *n* housing subsidy; **~gemeinschaft** *f* (*abgek.* **WG**) flat-(*Am.* apartment-)share; (*Bewohner*) flat-sharing (*Am.* apartment-sharing) community; *m-e ~* the people I share (the flat [*Am.* apartment]) with, *Am. auch* my roommates; *in e-r ~ leben* share a flat (*Am.* an apartment) (with other people); **~gift** *n* toxic substance (*od.* material) in the home

wohnhaft *Adj. Amtsspr.* resident; *Herr Miller, ~ in Köln* Mr Miller who is resident (*od.* living) in Cologne

Wohn|haus *n* residential building; **~heim** *n* residential home; *Am.* rooming house; *für Studenten*: students' hostel; *bes. auf dem Universitätsgelände*: hall of residence, *Am.* dormitory; *für Asylbewerber*: asylum-seekers' hostel; *für Alte*: home; **~küche** *f* kitchen-(*cum-*)living room; **~kultur** *f* style of living; (*Inneneinrichtung*) home décor; **~lage** *f* (residential) area; *in ruhiger ~* peacefully situated; **~landschaft** *f Sl.* landscaped interior

wohnlich *Adj.* homely, *Am.* homey; (*gemütlich*) cosy, *Am.* cozy; **Wohnlichkeit** *f*; *nur Sg.* homeliness, *Am.* homeyness

Wohnmobil *n*; *-s, -e* camper (van); *größeres*: mobile home; *Am.* motorhome, RV

Wohnort *m* (place of) residence; **wohnortnah** *Adj.* close to (one's) home

Wohnqualität *f* residential standard(s *Pl.*); → *Wohnwert*

Wohnraum *m* **1.** *nur Sg.*; *Platz*: living space; **2.** *nur Sg.*; *Koll.* housing; **3.** *Wohnräume* living quarters; **4.** → *Wohnzimmer*; **~beschaffung** *f* housing supply; **~vermittlung** *f*: (*studentische*) **~** (students') accommodation service

Wohn|recht *n*: *lebenslanges ~ haben* have a lifetime right of residence; **~schlafzimmer** *n* bedsitting room, bedsit(ter) *umg.*; **~siedlung** *f* housing estate (*bes. Am.* development); **~silo** *m*, *n umg. pej.* concrete block; *größerer*: tower block, *Am.* highrise ghetto

Wohnsitz *m* (place of) residence; *erster/zweiter ~* first/second residence; *fester od. ständiger ~* permanent address; *ohne festen ~* of no fixed abode (*od.* address); *s-n ~ auf dem Land haben* live in the country; **wohnsitzlos** *Adj.* homeless

Wohn|stadt *f* residential town; (*Schlafstadt*) dormitory town; **~stube** *f altm.* → *Wohnzimmer*; **~trakt** *m* accommodation wing; **~turm** *m* **1.** lived-in tower; **2.** (*Hochhaus*) tower block, *Am.* highrise (apartment building)

Wohnung *f* **1.** flat; *Am. bes. gemietete*: apartment; (*Eigentumswohnung*) condominium, condo *umg.*; *in m-r/d-r etc. ~* at my/your *etc.* place; **2.** *nur Sg.*; (*Unterkunft*) lodgings *Pl.*

Wohnungs|amt *n umg.* housing office; **~auflösung** *f* flat (*Am.* apartment) clearance

Wohnungsbau *m*; *nur Sg.* house building; *sozialer ~* council house building, *Am.* building of subsidized housing; **~förderung** *f* public subsidizing of new housing; **~genossenschaft** *f*

housing association; **~gesellschaft** *f* housing association

Wohnungs|eigentümer *m*, **~eigentümerin** *f* flat-owner, *Am.* apartment (*od.* condo) owner; **~einrichtung** *f* furnishings *Pl.*; **~inhaber** *m*, **~inhaberin** *f* tenant; **~knappheit** *f* housing shortage

wohnungslos *Adj.* homeless; *Amtssprache*: without fixed abode (*od.* address)

Wohnungs|makler *m*, **~maklerin** *f* estate agent, *Am.* real estate agent, Realtor®; **~mangel** *m* housing shortage; **~markt** *m* housing market; *die Lage auf dem ~* the situation in the housing market; **~not** *f*; *nur Sg.* housing shortage; **~schlüssel** *m* key (to the flat, *Am.* apartment)

Wohnungssuche *f* search for accommodation, flat-hunting *umg.*, *Am.* apartment- (*od.* house-)hunting; *das Problem der ~* the problem of finding somewhere to live; **wohnungssuchend** *Adj.* accommodation-seeking, flat-hunting *umg.*, *Am.* apartment-(*od.* house-)hunting; **Wohnungssuchende** *m, f*; *-n, -n* accommodation seeker, flat-hunter *umg.*, *Am.* apartment-hunter

Wohnungs|tausch *m* flat-swap(ping), *Am.* apartment-swap(ping); **~tür** *f* front door; **~wechsel** *m* moving (house) (*od.* flats, *Am.* apartments), move *umg.*; **~wesen** *n*; *nur Sg.* housing

Wohn|verhältnisse *Pl.* housing conditions; **~viertel** *n* residential area; **~wagen** *m* caravan, *Am.* trailer, mobile (*od.* manufactured) home; **~wand** *f* wall-to-wall cupboard(s *Pl.*); **~wert** *m*: *mit hohem ~* in *Werbematerial*: *etwa* highly desirable, much sought-after, providing attractive accommodation with all amenities; **~zimmer** *n* sitting (*od.* living) room, *bes. Brit. auch* lounge

Wok *m*; *-, -s*; *Gastr.* wok

wölben I. *v/t. auch Tech.* curve; *Archit.* vault; **II.** *v/refl. Brücke, Decke etc.*: arch; *Bauch, Stirn*: bulge; *Brust*: swell; (*sich verbiegen*) bend; → *gewölbt*; **Wölbung** *f e-r Brücke etc.*: arch; *des Himmels*: vault, arch; (*gewölbte Form*) curvature; (*Gewölbe*) vault; (*Kuppel*) dome

Wolf *m*; *-(e)s, Wölfe* **1.** wolf; *hungrig wie ein ~* ravenous, starving; *~ im Schafspelz* *fig.* wolf in sheep's clothing; *mit den Wölfen heulen umg. fig.* howl with the pack; **2.** (*Fleischwolf*) mincer, *Am.* grinder; *j-n durch den ~ drehen umg. fig.* put s.o. through the mill; → *Reißwolf*. **3.** *Med. umg.* chafing *where two flat areas of skin rub together*; *e-n ~ haben* be sore; *sich* (*Dat.*) *e-n ~ laufen* get sore thighs from walking too much; **Wölfin** *f*; *-, -nen* she-wolf; **wölfisch** *Adj.* wolvish; **Wölfling** *m*; *-s, -e Pfadfinder*: Cub Scout, *ehemals* Wolf Cub

Wolfram *n*; *-s, kein Pl.*; (*abgek.* **W**) *Chem.* tungsten, wolfram

Wolfs|hund *m* Alsatian, *Am.* German shepherd; *Irischer ~* Irish wolfhound; **~hunger** *m umg.*: *ich habe e-n ~* I'm ravenous, I could eat a horse; **~milch** *f*; *nur Sg.*; *Bot.* spurge; **~milchgewächs** *n Bot.* euphorbia; **~rachen** *m Med. umg.* cleft palate; **~rudel** *n* pack of wolves; **~spinne** *f* wolf spider

Wolga *f*; *-*; *Geog.*: *die ~* the Volga

Wölkchen *n* little cloud; *kein ~ trübte*

die Stimmung fig. there wasn't the slightest thing to spoil the atmosphere, everything was hunky-dory **Wolke** *f; -, -n* cloud (*auch fig.*); *mit ~n bedeckt* overcast, covered in cloud; *ich bin aus allen ~n gefallen umg. fig.* it left me speechless, I was flabbergasted; (*wie*) *auf ~n schweben geh. fig.* have one's head in the clouds **Wolken|band** *n* band of cloud; **~bank** *f; Pl. -bänke* cloud bank **wolkenbedeckt** *Adj.* cloudy, overcast **Wolkenbildung** *f* 1. buildup of cloud; 2. *konkret:* cloud formation **Wolkenbruch** *m* cloudburst; **wolkenbruchartig** *Adj.* torrential **Wolken|decke** *f; nur Sg.* cloud cover; *geschlossene ~* overcast skies; **~felder** *Pl.* broken cloud cover *Sg.;* **~fetzen** *m; mst Pl.; geh.* wispy cloud; *Pl.* scud *Sg.;* **~kratzer** *m* skyscraper; **~kuckucksheim** *n geh.* Cloud-Cuckoo-Land **wolkenlos** *Adj.* cloudless, clear **Wolken|massen** *Pl.* masses of cloud; **~obergrenze** *f* cloud top; **~schicht** *f* layer of cloud; **~schleier** *m* veil of cloud; **~untergrenze** *f* cloud base **wolkenverhangen** *Adj. Himmel, Tag:* overcast **Wolkenwand** *f* bank of clouds **wolkig** *Adj.* 1. cloudy (*auch Fenster, Foto etc.*); 2. *fig.* (*unklar, nebulös*) nebulous, hazy, fuzzy **Wolldecke** *f* (wool[l]en) blanket **Wolle** *f; -, fachspr. -n, mst Sg.* 1. wool; *das Kleid ist aus reiner ~* the dress is (made of) pure wool; 2. *fig. Jägerspr., von Hase etc.:* coat, fur; *von Küken:* down; *umg.* (*üppiges Haar*) fuzz; *sich in die ~ kriegen umg.* fight, squabble; *in der ~ gefärbt umg.* dyed in the wool **wollen¹ I.** *Modalv.; will, wollte, hat* (+ *Inf.*) *wollen* 1. (*beabsichtigen, wünschen*) want to; (*im Begriff sein zu*) be about to; (*werden*) will; *etw. haben ~* want s.th.; *ich will lieber ...* I'd rather ...; *ich will es mir überlegen* I'll think about it; *ich will es tun* I'll do it; *ich will es nicht tun* I won't do it; *ich will wissen, was los ist* I'd like to know what's going on; *was ich sagen wollte* (*damit meinte*) what I meant to say; (*im Begriff war zu sagen*) what I was going to say; *was ~ Sie damit sagen?* what do you mean (by that)?; *schärfer:* what are you getting at?; *komme, was da wolle* come what may; *ich will mal od. ja nicht so sein umg. hum.* out of the goodness of my heart; *wenn ich alles glauben wollte, was man mir erzählt, ...* if I believed everything people tell me ...; 2. *drückt Zweifel aus:* (*behaupten*) claim; (*meinen*) think; *er will dich gesehen haben* he says he saw you, he claims to have seen you, he thinks he saw you; *keiner will es gewesen sein* nobody's admitting to (having done) it; *er will alles besser wissen* he thinks he knows it all; *und du willst ein Tierfreund sein!* and you call yourself an animal-lover!; 3. *in Aufforderung, Wunsch: wenn Sie bitte ... ~* would you please ...; *~ Sie bitte e-n Augenblick warten* would you mind waiting for a minute?; *ich wollte dich bitten/ fragen ...* I wanted to ask you; *wir ~ beten! Priester:* let us pray; *~ wir uns* (*nicht*) *wieder vertragen?* should(n't) we try to make it up?; *willst du wohl damit aufhören!* will you stop that

please; *das will ich nicht gehört haben!* I didn't hear that; 4. *verstärkend: das will ich hoffen/meinen!* I hope / I'll say so; *das will nichts heißen* that means nothing; *es will einfach nicht schneien* it absolutely refuses to snow; *das will mir gar nicht gefallen* I don't like that one little bit; 5. (*müssen*): *so etwas will genau überlegt sein* a thing like that has to be thought about very carefully; 6. (*bezwecken*) be intended; *diese Studie will zeigen, dass ...* this study is intended to show that ...; **II.** *vt/i.; will, wollte, hat gewollt;* 1. (*wünschen*) want; (*verlangen*) *auch* demand; (*mögen*) like; *lieber ~* prefer; *etw. unbedingt ~* insist on; *ich will kein Geld dafür* I don't want any money for it; *ich will nur m-e Ruhe* all I want is some peace and quiet; *ich will nicht mehr* I don't want to any more; *was ~ Sie von mir?* what do you want (from me)?; *was willst du noch?* what more do you want?; *er will, dass ich mitkomme* he wants me to come with him *etc.;* *er weiß, was er will* he knows exactly what he wants; *mach, was du willst!* do what you like; *wie du willst* as you wish; *ob er will oder nicht* whether he likes it or not; *so gern ich es auch will* much as I'd like to; *du kannst es, wenn du willst* you can do it if you set your mind to it; *du hast es ja so gewollt!* you asked for it; *du hast hier gar nichts zu ~! umg.* you've got no say in the matter, what you want doesn't count; *ich wollte, es wäre so!* I wish it were so; *da ist nichts mehr zu ~ umg.* there's nothing anyone can do about it; *nichts zu ~! umg.* nothing doing; *was willst du* (*denn*), *es ging doch alles gut* what are you complaining about, it all went well; *dann ~ wir mal* let's get cracking then; *was kann der mir schon ~?* what harm can he do me?; *wer nicht will, der hat schon* if you don't like it, you can lump it; 2. (*bereit sein*) want to, be willing (*od.* prepared) to; *so Gott will* God willing; 3. (*beabsichtigen*) mean, intend; *ohne es zu ~* without meaning *od.* intending to; *Verzeihung, das wollte ich nicht!* sorry, that was unintentional; *was ~ Sie mit e-m Regenschirm?* what do you want an umbrella for?; → *gewollt etc.;* 4. *umg., irgendwohin:* want to go; *wohin willst du?* where are you off to?; *ich will nach Hause* (*bin auf dem Heimweg*) I'm on my way home; (*wäre gern zu Hause*) I want to go home; *sie will zum Theater fig.* she wants to go on the stage; 5. *fig.: das Schicksal / der Zufall wollte es, dass ...* fate/chance willed that ...; *m-e Beine ~ nicht mehr umg.* my legs are giving up on me; *der Motor will mal wieder nicht umg.* the engine's packed up again; *die Uhr will nicht mehr umg.* that clock has given up the ghost **wollen²** *Adj.; attr.* wool(l)en **Woll|faden** *m* wool(l)en thread; **~fett** *n* wool fat; *gereinigtes:* lanolin; **~gras** *n Bot.* cotton grass; **~handkrabbe** *f Zool.* Chinese crab; **~handschuh** *m* wool(l)en glove **wollig** *Adj.* wool(l)y; *Haar:* fuzzy **Woll|jacke** *f* cardigan; **~knäuel** *m, n* ball of wool; **~laus** *f Zool.* mealybug; **~maus** *f Dial. hum.* big ball of fluff and dust found under furniture etc., *Am.* dust bunny; **~mütze** *f* wool(l)en

hat, wool(l)y hat *umg.;* **~sachen** *Pl.* wool(l)ens, wool(l)y clothes; **~schaf** *n* wool sheep; **~siegel** *n* Woolmark®; **~socke** *f* wool(l)en sock, wool(l)y sock *umg.;* **~stoff** *m* wool, wool(l)en fabric; **~strumpf** *m* wool(l)en stocking **Wollust** *f geh.* voluptuousness, (*Sinnlichkeit*) sensuality, (*Lüsternheit*) lust; *etw. mit wahrer ~ tun* relish s.th., revel in s.th.; **wollüstig** *Adj.* voluptuous; (*lüstern*) lecherous **Woll|waren** *Pl.* wool(l)ens; **~waschgang** *m* wool wash; **~waschmittel** *n* washing powder for wool(l)ens **womit** *Adv.* 1. *fragend:* what (...) with?; *~ kann ich dienen?* what can I do for you?; *~ hab ich das verdient?* what did I do to deserve that?; 2. *in Relativsätzen:* with which; *etwas, ~ ich nicht zufrieden bin* something I'm not very happy with; *~ ich nicht sagen will* by which I don't mean to say; *~ die Sache erledigt war* which settled the matter **womöglich** *Adv.* (*möglicherweise*) possibly; *sind Sie ~ ...?* are you ..., by any chance?; → *wo* II 2 **wonach** *Adv.* 1. *fragend, zeitlich:* after what?; *~ fragt er?* what is he asking about?; *~ suchst du?* what are you looking for?; *~ schmeckt es?* what does it taste of (*od.* like)?; 2. *in Relativsätzen, zeitlich:* after which, whereupon; (*demzufolge*) according to which; *~ ich mich sehne, ist ...* what I long for is ...; *~ ich fragen wollte, war ...* what I wanted to ask about was ... **Wonne** *f; -, -n* delight, bliss; *die ~n* (+ *Gen.*) the joys of; *e-e wahre ~* sheer delight, a real treat; *mit ~ umg.* with relish; **~gefühl** *n* blissful sensation; **~monat** *m lit.: im ~ Mai* in the merry month of May; **~proppen** *m; -s, -; umg. hum.* (*Kleinkind*) bundle of joy; **~schauer** *m geh.* frisson of pleasure **wonnig** *Adj.* (*herzig*) lovely, sweet **woran** *Adv.* 1. *fragend: ~ denkst du* (*gerade*)? what are you thinking about?, (a) penny for your thoughts *umg.;* *~ arbeitet er?* what is he working on (*od.* at)?; *~ liegt es, dass ...?* how is it that ...?; *~ hast du ihn erkannt?* how did you recognize him?; *~ ist sie gestorben?* what did she die of?; *bei ihm weiß man nie, ~ man ist* you don't know where you stand with him *od.* what to make of him); 2. *in Relativsätzen:* on (*od.* at etc.) which; *das, ~ ich dachte* what I had in mind; *das ist etwas, ~ du denken solltest* that's something you ought to think about (*od.* to keep in mind) **worauf** *Adv.* 1. *fragend:* on what?, what ... on?; *~ wartest du* (*noch*)? what are you waiting for?; *~ freust du dich am meisten?* what are you looking forward to most?; 2. *in Relativsätzen:* on which; (*wonach*) whereupon, after which; *~ er antwortete* to which he replied; *etwas, ~ ich keinen Wert lege* something to which I attach no importance, something that is completely unimportant to me; *~ du dich verlassen kannst umg. iro.* just you wait and see; → *ankommen* I 7 **woraufhin** *Adv.* 1. *fragend:* why; 2. *in Relativsätzen:* whereupon **woraus** *Adv.* 1. *fragend:* where (...) from?, out of what?, from what?; *~ ist es gemacht?* what is it made of?; *~ schließt sie das?* how does she work that out?, what makes her think that?; 2. *in Relativsätzen:* out of which, from

which; **der Stoff, ~ es gemacht ist** the material it is made of; **~ man lernen kann, dass ...** which just goes to show that ...
worden *P.P.* → **werden** II
worein *Adv.* **1.** *fragend*: what ... in; **2.** *in Relativsätzen*: in which; **etwas, ~ sie sich nicht schicken konnte** something she could never accept *od.* resign herself to
worin *Adv.* **1.** *fragend*: in what?, what (...) in?; **~ liegt der Unterschied?** what (*od.* where) is the difference?; **2.** *in Relativsätzen*: in which
Workaholic [vɔːɐ̯kəˈhɔlɪk] *m; -s, -s; Sl.* workaholic
Work|shop [ˈvɔːɐ̯kʃɔp] *m; -s, -s* workshop; **~station** [ˈ-steːʃn] *f; -, -s Computer*: workstation
Worldcup [ˈvɔːɐ̯ltkap] *m; -s, -s; Sport* the World Cup; **~sieger** *m*, **~siegerin** *f* winner of the World Cup; **~zweite** *m, f* runner-up in the World Cup
Wort *n; -(e)s, -e und Wörter* **1.** *Pl. mst Wörter, Ling.* word; *(Ausdruck)* term, expression; **im wahrsten Sinn(e) des ~es** in the truest sense of the word; **2.** *Pl. -e; (Äußerung)* word; **man kann sein eigenes ~ nicht verstehen** you can't hear yourself speak; **ein ernstes ~ mit j-m reden** have a serious word with s.o.; **ein gutes ~ einlegen für j-n** put in a good word for s.o.; **das große ~ führen** do all the talking; *(angeben)* talk big *umg.*; **das letzte ~ in e-r Sache**: the last word on; **das letzte ~ haben** have the final say; *rechthaberisch*: have the last word; **das letzte ~ ist noch nicht gesprochen** we haven't heard the last of it; **das ist mein letztes ~** that's final, that's my last word; **ein wahres ~** very true; **das ist ein ~!** you're on!; **ein ~ gab das andere** one thing led to another; **mit dir habe ich noch ein ~ zu reden!** I want a word with you; **du hättest ja ein ~ sagen können!** you might have mentioned it!; **ich glaube ihm kein ~** I don't believe a word he says; **kein ~ herausbringen** not say a word, be tongue-tied; **kein ~ darüber!** don't breathe a word; **kein ~ mehr!** I don't want to hear another word!; **ein paar ~e mit j-m wechseln** have a few words with s.o.; **viele ~e machen** talk a lot; **ohne viele ~e zu machen** without further ado; **er macht nicht viele ~e** he doesn't waste his words; **ich will nicht viele ~e machen** I'll be brief; **genug der ~e!** enough said; **mir fehlen die ~e** words fail me, I don't know what to say; **hast du ~e!** *umg.* would you credit it, *Am.* can you believe it!; **dein ~ in Gottes Ohr!** *umg.* let's hope so, I do hope so, amen to that; **j-m das ~ erteilen** call upon s.o. to speak; **j-m das ~ abschneiden/entziehen** *fig.* cut s.o. short / cut s.o. off; **das ~ ergreifen** *fig.* (begin to) speak; **das ~ führen** *fig.* do the talking; **Sie haben das ~** *fig.* over to you; **das ~ hat Herr X** *fig.* it's Mr X's turn to speak, Mr X will now say a few words; *bei einer Debatte auch*: Mr X has the floor; **j-m / e-r Sache das ~ reden** *fig.* support s.o./s.th., back s.o./s.th. up; **3.** *mit Präp.*: **auf ein ~!** can I have a word with you?; **nicht viel auf j-s ~e geben** not set great store by what s.o. says; **aufs ~ gehorchen** *etc.* obey, *etc.* implicitly; **das glaub ich ihm aufs ~** I believe him implicitly; *iro.* I can well believe it; **j-n beim ~ nehmen** take s.o. at his (*od.*

her) word; *bei Einladung etc.*: take s.o. up on *s.th.*; **~ für ~** word for word; **in ~en** *bei Zahlenangaben*: in letters; **in ~e fassen** formulate, express (in words); **j-m ins ~ fallen** interrupt s.o. *umg.*; **e-e Sprache in ~ und Schrift beherrschen** have a good spoken and written knowledge (*od.* command) of a language; **mit anderen ~en** in other words, put another way; **mit 'einem ~** in a word; **mit den ~en schließen: ...** say in conclusion (that) ...; **sag's mit eigenen ~en** tell it in your own words; **sie erwähnte es mit keinem ~** she didn't even give it a mention; **nach ~en suchen** search (*od.* be at a loss) for words; **ums ~ bitten** *fig.* ask to speak; **zu ~ kommen** have one's say; **nicht zu ~ kommen** not get a word in edgeways (*bes. Am.* edgewise); **sich zu ~ melden** *fig.* ask to speak; **zu s-m ~ stehen** stick by one's word; **4.** *nur Sg.*; *(Ehrenwort)* word (of hono[u]r); **sein ~ geben** give (*od.* pledge) one's word (**auf** + *Akk.* on); **j-s ~ darauf haben** have s.o.'s word on it; **~ halten** keep one's word; **bei j-m im ~ stehen** *od.* **sein** have made a promise to s.o.; **5.** *Pl. -e*; *(Ausspruch)* saying; *(Zitat)* quotation; **geflügeltes ~** well-known saying, familiar quotation; **das ~ (Gottes)** *Reli.* the Word (of God); **das ~ zum Sonntag** *TV etwa* Word for Sunday, *late-night religious broadcast on Saturday evening*; **am Anfang war das ~** *bibl.* in the beginning was the Word; → **mitreden** II, **Mund, Tat 2, verlieren** I 3
Wort|akzent *m Ling.* word stress; **~art** *f Ling.* part of speech; **~bedeutung** *f* meaning (of a *od.* the word); **~bildung** *f Ling.* word formation, morphology
Wortbruch *m* breach of promise; **e-n ~ begehen** break one's word; **wortbrüchig** *Adj.* not true to one's word; **~ werden** break one's word
Wörtchen *n*: **ich möchte ein ~ mit dir reden** I'd like a little word with you; → **mitreden** II, **wenn 2**
Wörter|buch *n* dictionary; **~verzeichnis** *n* list of words, vocabulary
Wort|familie *f Ling.* word family; **~feld** *n Ling.* word field; **~fetzen** *Pl.* scraps of conversation; **~folge** *f Ling.* word order; **~form** *f* word form; **~führer** *m*, **~führerin** *f* spokesman; **~gefecht** *n* battle of words; **~geklingel** *n pej.* meaningless jingle
wort|getreu *Adj.* word-for-word ...; literal; **~gewaltig** *Adj.* Redner, Schriftstück etc.: powerful; **~gewandt** *Adj.* articulate; *stärker*: eloquent
Wort|gruppe *f Ling.* word group; **~gut** *n; nur Sg.* vocabulary
Wörthersee *m; -s* Wörthersee, Lake Wörth
Worthülse *f pej.* (empty) cliché, meaningless word
wortkarg *Adj.* taciturn; **er ist ziemlich ~** *auch* he doesn't say much; **Wortkargheit** *f; nur Sg.* taciturnity
Wortklauberei *f; -, -en; pej.* hairsplitting; **wortklauberisch** *Adj. pej.* hairsplitting
Wort|laut *m; nur Sg.* wording; *(Inhalt)* text; **im (vollen) ~** verbatim; *der Brief hat folgenden ~* runs as follows
Wörtlein *n* → **Wörtchen**
wörtlich I. *Adj.* literal, word-for-word ...; **II.** *Adv.* literally (*auch fig.*); *wiederholen, übersetzen etc.*: word for word; *das hat er ~ gesagt* those were

his exact words
wortlos I. *Adj.* wordless, silent; **II.** *Adv.* without a word
Wort|meldung *f* request to speak; **liegen weitere ~en vor?** does anyone else wish to say something?; **~prägung** *f* coinage; *(Neologismus)* neologism
wortreich I. *Adj.* **1.** *Sprache*: rich in vocabulary; **2.** *oft pej. Entschuldigung, Stil etc.*: verbose, wordy; **II.** *Adv.* sich bedanken, entschuldigen: profusely; **Wortreichtum** *m* rich vocabulary
Wort|schatz *m* vocabulary; **großer ~** large (*od.* wide) vocabulary; **kleiner ~** limited vocabulary; **~schöpfung** *f* coinage; *(Neologismus)* neologism; **~schwall** *m pej.* torrent of words; **~sinn** *m; nur Sg.* sense (of a *od.* the word); **~spiel** *n* play on words; *(Wortwitz)* pun; **~e** *Koll.* wordplay *Sg.*; **~stamm** *m Ling.* root, stem (of a *od.* the word); **~stellung** *f Ling.* word order; **~streit** *m* → **Wortgefecht**; **~ungetüm** *n* monster word, mouthful; **~verbindung** *f Ling.* beliebig: word combination; *typisch*: collocation; *(Kompositum)* compound; **~verdreher** *m; -s, -*, **~verdreherin** *f; -, -nen; pej.*: **er ist ein ~** he twists (*od.* distorts) everything you say; **~wahl** *f; nur Sg.* choice of words; **~wechsel** *m* (verbal) exchange, argument
wortwörtlich *Adj. und Adv.* → **wörtlich**
worüber *Adv.* **1.** *fragend, nach Richtung, Lage*: over (*od.* on) what?, what ... over (*od.* on)?; *nach Thema*: what (...) about (*od.* on)?; **~ lachst du?** what are you laughing about (*od.* at)?; **2.** *in Relativsätzen, räumlich*: over (*od.* on) which; *thematisch*: about (*od.* on) which; **etwas, ~ man nicht gerne spricht** something people don't like to talk about; **~ er ärgerlich war** which annoyed him
worum *Adv.* **1.** *fragend, nach Thema*: about what?, what ... about?; *räumlich*: (a)round what?; **~ handelt es sich?** what's it about?; *(was wollen Sie?)* what's the problem?; **~ soll ich die Schnur wickeln?** what should I wind the string around?; **2.** *in Relativsätzen, thematisch*: about which; for which; *räumlich*: around which; **etwas, ~ du dich kümmern solltest** something you ought to be concerned about; **~ ich dich bitten möchte, ist ...** what I want to ask you for is ...
worunter *Adv.* **1.** *fragend*: under (*fig.* among) what?, what ... under (*fig.* among)?; **2.** *in Relativsätzen*: under (*fig.* among) which; **~ ich mir nichts vorstellen kann** which doesn't mean anything to me; **~ ich leide** what (*im Nachsatz*: which *od.* that) I suffer from
Wotan (*m*); *-s, kein Pl.*; *Myth.* Wotan
wovon *Adv.* **1.** *fragend, nach Herkunft, Ursache etc.*: of (*od.* from) what?, what (...) from (*od.* of)?; *nach Thema*: *auch* about what?, what (...) about?; **~ sprichst du?** what are you talking about?; **~ lebt sie?** what does she live on?; **2.** *in Relativsätzen*: of (*od.* from, about) which; **~ ich träume, ist ...** what I dream about is ...; **~ sie nicht abzubringen war** and from that there was no dissuading her
wovor *Adv.* **1.** *fragend, nach Lage, Richtung*: in front of what?; *nach Bezug*: of what?, what (...) of?; **~ hast du Angst?** what are you afraid of?;

2. *in Relativsätzen, räumlich*: in front of which; *zeitlich*: before which; *anderer Bezug*: of which; **etwas, ~ du dich hüten musst** something you need to beware of

wozu *Adv.* **1.** *fragend*: to what?, what ... to?; *(wofür)* for what?, what (...) for?; *(warum)* why?; **~ gehört das?** what does it belong to?; **~ hast du dich entschlossen?** what have you decided on?; **ich frage mich, ~ das gut sein soll** I'm wondering what the point of it is; **~ auch?** what for?; **2.** *in Relativsätzen*: to which; *(wofür)* for which; **~ ich bereit bin** what (*im Nachsatz*: which) I'm prepared to do; **~ er noch Salz gab** to which he added salt; **~ ich euch rate, ist ...** what I advise you (to do) is; **..., ~ es dann aber zu spät war** for which it was then too late

Wrack *n*; -(e)s, -s wreck (*auch fig.*); **menschliches ~** *fig.* physical wreck; **~teile** *Pl.* wreckage *Sg.*

wrang *Imperf.* → **wringen**

wringen *v/t.*; *wringt, wrang, hat gewrungen* **1.** *Wäsche*: wring; **2.** *das Wasser aus dem Lappen ~* wring the water out of the cloth

WS *Abk.* → **Wintersemester**

WSV *Abk.* → **Winterschlussverkauf**

Wucher *m*; -s, *kein Pl.*; *pej.* profiteering; *bei Geldverleih*: usury; **~ treiben** practi|se (*Am.* -ce) usury; **Wucherer** *m*; -s, -, **Wucherin** *f*; -, -nen; *pej.* profiteer; usurer; **Wuchermiete** *f pej.* rack rent, extortionate rent; **~n Koll.** rack renting *Sg.*; **wuchern** *v/i.* **1.** (*ist od. hat gewuchert*); *Bot.* grow rampant; *Bart, Haare*: grow profusely; *Med.* proliferate; *fig. Missstände etc.*: *auch* be rampant; *fig. Fantasie*: run riot; **2.** (*hat*); *pej. mit Geld*: practi|se (*Am.* -ce) usury; *mit Preisen*: profiteer; **Wucherpreis** *m pej.* extortionate price; **Wucherung** *f* **1.** *Bot.* rank growth; **2.** *Med.* excrescence, growth; *von Zellen*: proliferation; **Wucherzins** *m*; **~(en)** usurious interest *Sg.*

wuchs *Imperf.* → **wachsen**[1]

Wuchs *m*; -es, *kein Pl.* **1.** (*Wachstum*) growth; **2.** (*Gestalt*) build, physique; (*Form*) shape; **von kleinem ~** (*od. slight*) build; **von kräftigem ~** big-built

Wucht *f*, -, *kein Pl.* **1.** force; *e-s Schlags, Aufpralls etc.*: impact; **mit voller ~ auf den Rücken fallen** fall flat on one's back; **mit voller ~ gegen die Mauer rennen** run straight into the wall; **der ~ e-s Angriffs widerstehen** resist the onslaught; **2.** *umg. fig.*: **das ist 'ne ~!** it's great, it's fantastic; **wuchten** *v/t.* **1.** heave; (*schleppen*) drag; **2.** *Fußball etc.*: slam; **wuchtig** *Adj.* **1.** (*schwer*) heavy; *optisch*: bulky; *Gestalt*: massive, big; **2.** *Schlag*: hard, powerful; **Wuchtigkeit** *f*; *nur Sg.* **1.** (*Schwere*) heaviness; bulkiness; *e-r Gestalt*: massiveness; **2.** *e-s Schlags etc.*: force, power

Wühlarbeit *f*; *nur Sg.*; *fig. pej.* **1.** subversiv: (underground) agitation; **2.** *nachforschend*: investigations *Pl.*; (*Schnüffelei*) snooping

wühlen I. *v/i.* **1.** dig; *Tier*: burrow (**in** + *Dat.* into); *Schwein, Vogel*: root; **in der Erde / im Schlamm ~** *Schwein*: grub up soil / root about in the mud; **im Schmutz ~** mess about in the mud (*od.* dirt), wallow in the mud (*fig.* mire); **2.** *suchend*: root (**nach** for); *Person*: *auch* rummage (around in) (*auch fig.*); **die Journalisten wühlten**

in i-r Vergangenheit *fig.* the journalists rummaged around in her past; **3.** *fig. Hunger, Schmerz*: gnaw; **4.** *umg. fig.* (*schwer arbeiten*) beaver away, *Brit. auch* graft; **5.** *Pol. pej.* (*hetzen*) agitate; **II.** *v/t.* (*Loch etc.*) burrow; **III.** *v/refl. Tier*: burrow (**in** + *Akk.* into); **sich ~ durch** burrow one's way through; *Panzer etc.*: churn through; *fig. durch Akten etc.*: rummage through; **Wühler** *m*; -s, - **1.** *Zool.* burrower; **2.** *Pol. pej.* agitator; **Wühlerei** *f*; -, -en; *oft pej.* **1.** digging, burrowing, rooting; **2.** rummaging, rooting; **3.** *umg. fig.* beavering away, *Brit. auch* graft; **4.** *Pol.* agitation

Wühl|maus *f* **1.** *Zool.* vole; (*Schermaus*) water vole; **2.**; **3.** *fig. pej.* subversive, agitator; **~tisch** *m umg.* bargain counter

Wulst *m*; -(e)s, *Wülste od. f*; -, *Wülste* bulge; *am Bauch etc.*: roll of fat; *an Reifen*: bead; *an Flasche, Glas*: lip; *Archit.* torus; *Naut.* bulb; **wulstig** *Adj.* bulging; (*aufgedunsen*) puffed up; *Lippen*: thick, protruding; **Wulstlippen** *Pl.* blubber lips

wumm *Interj.* boom; *Aufprall*: thud

wummern *v/i. umg.* **1.** *Motor*: drone; **2.** *mit der Faust*: drum (**an** + *Akk. od.* **gegen** on *od.* against)

wund *Adj.* sore, chafed; (*offen*) raw; **~es Herz** *fig.* wounded heart; **~e Stelle** sore; *fig.* (*auch* **~er Punkt**) sore point; **~ gelegener Rücken** back covered in bedsores; **sich ~ liegen** get bedsores; **sich** (*Dat.*) **den Rücken ~ liegen** have bedsores on one's back; **~ reiben** chafe; **sich ~ reiten** ride until one is saddle-sore; **sich** (*Dat.*) **die Füße ~ laufen** get sore feet; *fig.* walk one's feet off; **sich** (*Dat.*) **die Finger ~ schreiben** *fig.* wear one's fingers to the bone writing

Wund|behandlung *f*: (**zur**) **~** (for the) treatment of wounds; **~brand** *m*; *nur Sg.*; *Med.* gangrene

Wunde *f*, -, -n wound; (*Schnitt*) cut; *klaffende*: gash; *tiefe*: **~** deep wound; *fig.* deep scar; **alte ~n wieder aufreißen** *fig.* reopen old sores *od.* wounds; **an e-e alte ~ rühren** *geh.* touch on a sore point; → **Finger** 2, **Salz** 1, **Zeit** 1

Wunder *n*; -s, - **1.** *übernatürlich*: miracle; *erstaunlich*: *auch* wonder; *bewundernswert*: marvel; **ein ~ der Natur/Technik** a miracle of nature/engineering; **~ wirken** perform miracles; *fig.* work wonders; **es grenzt an ein ~** it's a near-miracle; **auf ein ~ hoffen** be hoping for a miracle; **wenn nicht ein ~ geschieht** barring a miracle; **wie durch ein ~** miraculously; **(es ist) kein ~(, dass ...)** (it's) no wonder (that ...); **ist es ein ~, dass ...?** is it any wonder that ...?; **er wird sein blaues ~ erleben** *umg.* he's got a surprise coming, he's in for a (big) surprise; **2.** *umg.*: **~ was/wer** *etc.* something/someone absolutely fantastic, the greatest thing since sliced bread; **sie glaubt, ~ was sie getan hat** she thinks what she's done is absolutely fantastic; **er glaubt, er sei ~ wer** *auch* he thinks he's the bee's knees; **~ wie klug/schön** *etc.* ever so clever (*Am.* smart) /beautiful *etc.*, as clever (*Am.* smart) /beautiful *etc.* as anything; **das stellte sie sich ~ wie einfach vor** she thought it was going to be ever so easy (*od.* as easy as anything *od.* as easy as pie)

wunderbar *Adj.* **1.** wonderful, marvel(l)ous; **2.** (*übernatürlich, auch fig.*) mi-

raculous; **wunderbarerweise** *Adv.* miraculously

Wunder|ding *n* wonder, marvel; **~doktor** *m iro.* miracle doctor; *pej.* (*Quacksalber*) quack; → **Wunderheiler**, **~droge** *f* miracle drug

Wunderglaube *m* belief in miracles; **wundergläubig** *Adj.*: **~er Mensch** believer in miracles

Wunder|heiler *m*, **~heilerin** *f* miracle (*durch Gesundbeten etc.*: faith) healer; **~heilung** *f* miracle cure; *durch Gesundbeten etc.*: faith healing; *einzelner Fall*: case of faith healing

wunderhübsch *Adj.* (absolutely) lovely

Wunder|kerze *f* sparkler; **~kind** *n* child prodigy, wunderkind; **~knabe** *m* boy wonder; **~kraft** *f* miraculous powers *Pl.*, ability to perform miracles; **~lampe** *f* magic lamp; **~land** *n* wonderland

wunderlich *Adj.* **1.** strange, peculiar; **2.** (*wundersam*) wondrous

Wundermittel *n* miracle (*od.* wonder) cure (*od.* drug)

wundern I. *v/t.* surprise; *oft unpers.*: **es wundert mich** I'm surprised; **das wundert mich nicht** I'm not surprised; **es würde mich nicht ~, wenn ... I** wouldn't be at all surprised if ...; **das sollte mich schon sehr ~!** *iro.* that really would surprise me!; **wen wundert es?** is it any wonder?; **mich wundert gar nichts mehr** I'm not in the least (*od.* a bit) surprised, nothing surprises me any more; **II.** *v/refl.* be surprised (**über** + *Akk.* at); **du wirst dich ~** you won't believe it; **ich muss mich doch sehr ~!** *empört*: I'm surprised at you, you disappoint me

wundernehmen *v/t.* (*unreg., trennb., hat -ge-*) *geh.* astonish, surprise; *oft unpers.*: **es nimmt mich wunder, dass ...** I'm surprised that ...

wunders *Adv. umg.*: **~ was od. wer** → **Wunder** 2

wundersam *Adj. geh.* strange, wondrous *lit.*

wunderschön *Adj.* wonderful, beautiful

Wundertat *f* miracle; **Wundertäter** *m*, **Wundertäterin** *f* miracle-worker; **wundertätig** *Adj.* miracle-working

Wunder|tier *n* fabulous creature; (*bes. Untier*) weird and wonderful creature; **~tüte** *f* lucky bag

wundervoll *Adj.* wonderful, marvel(l)ous

Wunder|waffe *f* wonder weapon; **~welt** *f* wonderworld; **~werk** *n* miracle; *fig. auch* wonder, marvel

Wund|fieber *n Med.* wound fever; **~infektion** *f Med.* wound infection

wund liegen → **wund**

Wundmal *n*; *Pl.* -e; *geh.* scar; *kirchl.* stigma (*Pl.* stigmata)

Wund|pflaster *n Med.* adhesive plaster; **~puder** *m* antiseptic powder; **~rose** *f* traumatic erysipelas; **~salbe** *f* antiseptic ointment; **~schmerz** *m* traumatic pain; **~schorf** *m* scab, crust; **~sekret** *n* wound secretion; **~starrkrampf** *m*; *nur Sg.* tetanus

Wunsch *m*; -(e)s, *Wünsche* **1.** (*Bedürfnis*) wish (**nach** for), desire (for); (*Bitte*) request (**an** + *Akk.* to); **den ~ haben zu** (+ *Inf.*) wish to (+ *Inf.*); **haben Sie sonst noch e-n ~?** is there anything else I can do for you?; **ein eigenes Haus war schon immer mein ~** I('ve) always wanted to have a house of my own; **mein einziger ~ ist ...** all I want (*od.* wish for) is ...; **j-m e-n ~ er-**

füllen/verweigern fulfil(l) a wish for s.o. / deny s.o. a wish; *j-m jeden ~ von den Augen ablesen* anticipate s.o.'s every wish; *auf ~* (+ *Gen.*) by request; at the request (of); *auf allgemeinen od. vielfachen ~* by popular request; *auf j-s ausdrücklichen ~* at s.o.'s express request; *auf ~ schicken wir ...* if requested, we will send you ...; (*je*) *nach ~* as desired; *es ging alles nach ~* everything went as planned; *am Ziel s-r Wünsche sein* have fulfilled one's every wish (*od.* ambition); *du hast drei Wünsche frei* you can have (*od.* I'll grant you) three wishes, *dein ~ ist mir Befehl hum.* your wish is my command; *da war der ~ Vater des Gedankens* the wish was father to the thought; → *fromm* 4; **2.** *in Grußformeln: mit den besten Wünschen am Briefende:* with best wishes

wünschbar *Adj. bes. schw.* → *wünschenswert*

Wunsch|bild *n* ideal; **~denken** *n* wishful thinking

Wünschelrute *f* divining rod; **Wünschelrutengänger** *m; -s, -,* **Wünschelrutengängerin** *f; -, -nen* (water) diviner, dowser, *Am. auch* water witch

wünschen I. *vt/i.* **1.** wish; *sich* (*Dat.*) *etw. ~* wish for s.th., want s.th.; *sehnend:* long for s.th.; (*e-n Wunsch aussprechen*) ask for; *du darfst dir etwas ~* you can say what you'd like; *im Märchen:* you may have a wish; *was wünschst du dir?* what would you like?, what do you want?; *sie wünscht sich* (*Dat.*) *zu Weihnachten e-e Puppe* she wants a doll for Christmas; *alles, was man sich* (*Dat.*) *~ kann* everything one could wish for; *viel zu ~ übrig lassen* leave much to be desired; *es ist zu ~, dass e-e Lösung gefunden wird* it is to be hoped that a solution can be found; *das wünsche ich m-m schlimmsten Feind nicht* I wouldn't wish that on my worst enemy; *ich wünschte, du wärst hier* I wish you were here; **2.** (*wollen*) wish, want; *ich wünsche, nicht gestört zu werden* I don't want (*od.* wish) to be disturbed; *was ~ Sie od. Sie ~?* what can I do for you?; *~ Sie noch etwas?* would you like anything else?; *wie Sie ~!* as you wish (*od.* like); *iro.* suit yourself; **3.** *j-m etw. ~* wish s.o. s.th.; *ich wünsche Ihnen alles Gute* I wish you) all the best(, then); *ich wünsche dir e-e gute Reise* I wish you a pleasant journey (*bes. Am.* a good trip); **II.** *v/refl.: sich fort* / *weit weg ~* wish one were somewhere else / far away; → *gewünscht, Teufel* 3, *wohl*[2] 1

wünschenswert *Adj.* desirable; *das wäre sehr ~ auch* that would be very (*od.* most) welcome

Wunsch|ergebnis *n e-r Wahl etc.:* dream result; **~film** *m* TV film (*Am.* movie) of your choice; **~gegner** *m*, **~gegnerin** *f* dream opponent; **~gehalt** *n* expected salary

wunschgemäß *Adv.* as requested

Wunsch|kandidat *m*, **~kandidatin** *f* preferred (*stärker:* ideal) candidate; **~kind** *n* planned child; *sie war ein ~* she was their long-awaited baby; **~konzert** *n* request program(me); **~liste** *f* list of presents; *fig.* shopping list

wunschlos *Adv.: ~ glücklich* perfectly happy

Wunsch|partner *m*, **~partnerin** *f* ideal partner; **~satz** *m Ling.* optative

clause; **~traum** *m* dream, great wish; *pej.* pipe dream, pie in the sky; **~vorstellung** *f* ideal; **~zettel** *m* wish list; *zu Weihnachten:* Christmas list; *zum Geburtstag:* birthday list; *das steht auch auf m-m fig.* that's another thing I want

wupps *Interj. umg.* whoosh

wurde *Imperf.* → *werden*

Würde *f; -, -n* **1.** *nur Sg.;* dignity; *die ~ bewahren* preserve (*od.* retain) one's dignity; *mit ~ alt werden* grow old gracefully; *unter aller ~* beneath contempt; *unter m-r ~* beneath my dignity; *ich werd's mit ~ tragen hum.* I'll try and keep a stiff upper lip; *die ~ des Menschen ist unantastbar* human dignity is inviolable; **2.** (*Auszeichnung, Ehre*) hono(u)r; (*Rang*) rank; (*Titel*) title; *akademische ~* academic degree; *die ~ e-s Kardinals erlangen* be made cardinal; *zu hohen ~n gelangen* attain high office; → *Amt* 1

würdelos *Adj.* undignified; **Würdelosigkeit** *f; nur Sg.* indignity

Würdenträger *m*, **~in** *f* dignitary; *geistlicher Würdenträger* church dignitary; *geistliche und weltliche Würdenträger* dignitaries from church and state

würdevoll I. *Adj.* dignified; **II.** *Adv.* with dignity

würdig I. *Adj.* **1.** worthy (+ *Gen.* of); (*verdient*) deserving (of); *ein ~er Gegner* a worthy opponent; *e-r Sache ~ sein auch* merit (*od.* deserve) s.th.; *er ist dessen nicht ~* he doesn't deserve it; *sich j-s Vertrauens ~ erweisen* prove worthy of s.o.'s confidence; **2.** (*würdevoll*) dignified; **II.** *Adv.: j-n ~ vertreten* be a worthy representative of s.o.; *sich ~ verhalten* behave with dignity

würdigen *v/t.* **1.** (*lobend erwähnen*) acknowledge; (*preisen*) pay tribute to; (*schätzen*) appreciate; *zu ~ wissen* appreciate; **2.** *geh.: j-n keines Blickes* / *keiner Antwort ~* not deign to look at s.o. / reply to s.o.; **Würdigung** *f* (*Anerkennung*) acknowledg(e)ment, recognition; (*Ehrung*) hono(u)ring; (*Schätzung*) appreciation; *in ~ s-r Verdienste etc.* in recognition of his services etc.

Wurf *m; -(e)s, Würfe* **1.** throw; *Handball etc.: auch* shot; *Kegeln:* bowl; *Baseball:* pitch; *mit Würfeln:* throw; *zum ~ ausholen* draw back one's arm to throw, get ready to throw; *glücklicher/großer ~ fig.* lucky strike / great success; *j-m gelingt ein großer ~ fig.* s.o. has a great success, s.o. scores (*od.* has) a big hit; **2.** *Zool.* (*die Jungen*) litter; (*das Gebären*) birth; **3.** (*Faltenwurf*) folds *Pl.*; **~bahn** *f* trajectory; **~disziplin** *f Sport* throwing event

Würfel *m; -s, -* **1.** *bes. Math.* cube (*auch Eis etc.*); *in ~ schneiden Gastr.* dice; **2.** *zum Spiel ~* dice; *~ spielen* play dice, *bes. Am.* shoot craps; *die ~ sind gefallen fig.* the die is cast; **~becher** *m* (dice) shaker; **~brett** *n* dice board

würfelförmig *Adj.* cubic, cube-shaped; **würfelig** *Adj.* cubic, cube-shaped; *~ schneiden* cut s.th. into cubes; *Gastr. auch* dice s.th.; **würfeln I.** *v/i.* throw dice (*um* for); (*spielen*) play dice, *Am. auch* shoot craps; *ich hab noch nicht gewürfelt* I haven't thrown yet; **II.** *v/t.* **1.** throw; *e-e Sechs ~* throw a six; **2.** *Gastr.* dice, chop up

Würfel|spiel *n* **1.** dice game; *Partie:*

game of dice; *beim ~* while playing dice; **2.** *Brettspiel:* (board) game involving dice; **~spieler** *m*, **~spielerin** *f* dice player, *Am.* crapshooter; **~zucker** *m* sugar cubes *Pl.*; *Koll.* lump sugar, cube sugar

Wurf|geschoss, *österr. auch* **~geschoß** *n* missile, projectile; **~kreis** *m Handball:* throwing circle; **~maschine** *f* **1.** *hist.* catapult; **2.** *Schießsport:* trap; **~pfeil** *m* dart; **~pfeilspiel** *n* darts *Pl.* (*V. im Sg.*). **~ring** *m Leichtathletik:* throwing circle; **~scheibe** *f Leichtathletik:* discus (*Pl.* discuses); **~sendung** *f* → *Postwurfsendung*; **~speer** *m*, **~spieß** *m Leichtathletik:* javelin; *Mil.* (throwing) spear; **~taube** *f Sport* clay pigeon; **~taubenschießen** *n Sport* clay-pigeon shooting, trapshooting; **~weite** *f Sport:* (throwing) distance; *Mil.* range

Würge|engel *m* angel of death; **~griff** *m* stranglehold (*auch fig.*); **~male** *Pl.* strangulation marks

würgen I. *v/t.* (*j-n*) strangle; *Essen:* make s.o. choke; *Kragen etc.:* choke; **II.** *v/i.* choke; *beim Erbrechen:* retch; *auch unpers.: j-n würgt es* (*heftig*) s.o. feels that he *etc.* is going to be (violently) sick; *an etw.* (*Dat.*) *~* choke on s.th.; *fig. an Kritik:* find s.th. hard to swallow; *an Arbeit:* sweat over s.th.; **Würger** *m; -s, -* **1.** *altm. pej.* strangler; **2.** *Orn.* shrike

Wurm[1] *m; -(e)s, Würmer* **1.** worm; (*Made*) maggot; *Würmer haben Med.* have worms; *von Würmern befallen* infested with worms; **2.** *poet.* (*Schlange*) serpent; (*Lindwurm*) dragon; **3.** *umg. fig.: j-m die Würmer aus der Nase ziehen* worm (*od.* drag) it out of s.o., get s.o. to spill the beans; *da ist der ~ drin* there's something very wrong with it; *weitS.* there's something fishy about it

Wurm[2] *n; -(e)s, Würmer, umg.:* (*armes*) *kleines ~* (poor) little mite

Wurmbefall *m: bei ~* when *s.o. etc.* has worms

Würmchen *n* **1.** (little) worm; **2.** → *Wurm*[2]

wurmen *v/t.; oft unpers.; umg.: die Niederlage wurmt mich* (*noch immer*) this defeat still rankles (with me)

Wurm|fortsatz *m Anat.* (vermiform) appendix (*Pl.* appendixes *od.* appendices); **~fraß** *m; nur Sg.* damage caused by worms

wurmig *Adj.* → *wurmstichig*

Wurm|kur *f* deworming; **~leiden** *n* worms *Pl.*; **~loch** *n* wormhole; **~mittel** *n* dewormer

wurmstichig *Adj.* worm-eaten; (*madig*) maggoty

Wurscht → *Wurst* 1

Wurst *f; -, Würste* **1.** *Gastr.* sausage; *jetzt geht's um die ~! umg. fig.* this is it (now)!; *es ist mir* (*völlig*) *~/Wurscht umg. fig.* I couldn't care less, I don't care, I don't give a damn; → *auch Würstchen*; **2.** *aus Teig etc.:* sausage, roll; *umg.* (*Kot*) turd; *von Hund: auch Pl.* dog's muck; *Am.* dog poop; *e-e machen umg.* do a poo, *Am.* have a poop; **~brot** *n* slice of bread and sausage

Würstchen *n* **1.** small sausage; *ein Paar ~* two frankfurters *etc.*; *warmes ~* hot dog; *Frankfurter ~* frankfurter, frank *umg., bes. Am.* hot dog; *Wiener ~* vienna, wiener; **2.** *umg. fig.: armes ~* poor little sausage; (*kleines*) *~ oft pej.* small fry, *a* nobody; **~bude** *f*, **~stand**

m etwa hot-dog stand

Würstel *n; -s, -; bes. österr.* → **Würstchen** 1

Wurstelei *f, -, -en; umg. pej.* muddling (through); **wursteln** *umg.* **I.** *v/refl.: sich durchs Leben etc.* ~ muddle (one's way) through; **II.** *v/i.: vor sich hin* ~ muddle along

Wurst|finger *m; mst Pl.; umg. pej.* fat (*od.* pudgy) finger; ~**haut** *f* sausage skin

wurstig *Adj. umg., Haltung etc.:* couldn't-care-less …; *er ist ziemlich* ~ he doesn't really give a damn; **Wurstigkeit** *f; nur Sg.; umg.* couldn't-careless (*Sl.* to-hell-with-it) attitude

Wurst|küche *f* sausage factory; ~**platte** *f Gastr.* platter of cold cuts; ~**salat** *m Gastr.* sausage salad; ~**scheibe** *f* slice of sausage; ~**suppe** *f* sausage soup; ~**waren** *Pl.* sausages; ~**zipfel** *m* sausage end

Würze *f; -, -n* **1.** spice(s *Pl.*), seasoning; (*Geschmack*) flavo(u)r; (*Aroma*) aroma; (*Duft*) fragrance; *von Bier:* wort; **2.** *fig.* spice; *es fehlt die* (*rechte*) ~ it lacks zest, it needs gingering up a bit

Wurzel *f; -, -n* **1.** *Bot.* root; ~*n schlagen* take root; ~*n ausbilden* send out (*od.* put down) roots; *mit der* ~ *ausreißen* root up, pull up by the roots; **2.** *Anat., von Haar, Zahn, Zunge, Nase:* root; *der Hand:* wrist, carpus (*Pl. carpi*) *fachspr.; des Fußes:* tarsus (*Pl. tarsi*) *fachspr.;* **3.** *Math., Ling.* root; *dritte/vierte* ~ cube/biquadratic root; *die* ~ *ziehen aus* extract (*od.* find) the (square) root of; (*die*) ~ *aus 9 ist 3* the square root of 9 is 3; **4.** *Dial.* (*Möhre*) carrot; **5.** *fig.* root; *das Übel an der* ~ *packen* strike at the root (of this evil); *etw. mit der* ~ *ausrotten* eradicate s.th. root and branch; *willst du hier* ~*n schlagen? umg.* are you going to stand around here all day?

Wurzel|ballen *m Bot.* root ball; ~**behandlung** *f Dent.* root treatment; ~**bürste** *f* (coarse) scrubbing brush; ~**entzündung** *f Dent.* inflammation of the root; ~**fäule** *f Bot.* soft rot; ~**gemüse** *n* root vegetables *Pl.*; ~**haut** *f* **1.** *Bot.* rhizoderm; **2.** *Anat.* dental periosteum; ~**kanal** *m e-s Zahns:* root canal; ~**knolle** *f* root tuber

wurzellos *Adj.* rootless (*auch fig.*)

wurzeln *v/i.* take root; ~ *in* (+ *Dat.*) be rooted in (*auch fig.*); (*stammen von*) stem from, have its roots in; *flach/tief* ~ have shallow/deep roots, be shallow-/deep-rooted

Wurzel|sepp *m südd. umg. pej.* yokel, country bumpkin, *Am. auch* hick; ~**schössling** *m*, ~**spross** *m* root sucker, runner; ~**stock** *m* **1.** *Bot.* rootstock, rhizome; **2.** (*Baumstumpf*) stump; ~**werk** *n* roots *Pl.*; ~**zeichen** *n Math.* radical sign; ~**ziehen** *n Math.* root extraction

würzen *v/t.* **1.** spice, season; **2.** *fig.* spice (*od.* ginger) *s.th.* up, add a bit of spice to; **würzig** *Adj.* spicy (*auch fig.*), well-seasoned; *Wein:* fruity; **Würzigkeit** *f; nur Sg.* spiciness; *e-s Weins:* fruitiness

Würz|kräuter *Pl.* herbs; ~**mischung** *f* mixed spices *Pl.*; ~**stoff** *m* seasoning

wusch[1] *Imperf.* → **waschen**

wusch[2] *Interj.* **1.** *schnelle Bewegung:* whoosh; **2.** *umg. pej.:* ~ ~ *sein* (*spinnen*) be crazy, be daft

Wuschelhaar *n umg.* fuzzy hair, frizz

wuschelig *Adj. umg.* curly; (*kraus*) fuzzy; *stärker:* frizzy; (*zerzaust*) tousled; **Wuschelkopf** *m umg.* **1.** mop of curly (*od.* fuzzy, frizzy) hair; **2.** *Person:* curly-head

wuselig *Adj. Dial.* lively; *Mensch: auch* busy; *Ort: auch* bustling; **wuseln** *v/i. Dial.* **1.** (*ist od. hat gewuselt*) → **wimmeln; 2.** (*ist*); (*huschen*) scurry

wusste *Imperf.* → **wissen**

Wust *m; -(e)s, kein Pl.; pej.* (*Durcheinander*) mess, jumble; (*Kram*) rubbish; (*große Menge*) mass, pile

wüst I. *Adj.* **1.** (*öde*) deserted, desolate; **2.** (*wirr*) chaotic; (*liederlich*) wild; *ein* ~*es Durcheinander* complete chaos; **3.** *pej.* (*roh*) wild; (*blindwütig*) rabid; (*ausschweifend*) wild, dissolute; *Lied:* dirty; *Übertreibung:* wild; (*schlimm*) *Narbe, Verletzung etc.:* bad; *e-e* ~*e Schlägerei* a real set-to *umg.*; ~*e Beschimpfungen* wild abuse, *weitS.* cursing and swearing; *er/das sieht ja* ~ *aus* he looks a real fright / what a mess; **II.** *Adv. pej.: j-n* ~ *beschimpfen* call s.o. every name under the sun, subject s.o. to a torrent of foul abuse; *es* ~ *treiben* have a really wild time; *j-n* ~ *zurichten* beat s.o. to a pulp

Wüste *f; -, -n* **1.** desert; (*öde Landschaft*) wilderness; *die* ~ *Gobi* the Gobi Desert; **2.** *fig.* wilderness, wasteland, desert; *j-n in die* ~ *schicken umg.* give s.o. the boot; → *Rufer*

Wüsten|bewohner *m*, ~**bewohnerin** *f* desert dweller; ~**bildung** *f* desertification

Wüstenei *f; -, -en geh.* wasteland, desert

Wüsten|fuchs *m Zool.* desert fox; ~**klima** *n* desert climate; ~**landschaft** *f* desert landscape; (*Öde*) barren landscape; ~**sand** *m* desert sands *Pl.*; ~**schiff** *n hum.* (*Kamel*) ship of the desert; ~**volk** *n* desert tribe (*od.* people)

Wüstling *m; -s, -e; pej.* rake, debauchee; *alter* ~ dirty old man

Wut *f; -, kein Pl.* **1.** rage (*auf* + *Akk. od. über* + *Akk.* at), fury; *j-n in* ~ *bringen* infuriate s.o., make s.o. furiously angry; *in* ~ *geraten* fly into a rage; *leicht in* ~ *geraten* have a quick temper; (*e-e*) ~ *im Bauch haben umg.* be absolutely seething; *e-e* ~ *auf j-n haben* be furious with (*Am. auch* mad) at s.o.; *ich hab e-e* ~ *auf ihn! umg. auch* I could strangle (*od.* kill) him; *mich packt die* (*kalte*) ~*, wenn ich daran denke, dass …* *auch* it makes my blood boil to think that …; *vor* ~ *kochen od. schäumen* be seething (*od.* boiling *od.* foaming [at the mouth] with rage), fume; *vor* ~ *platzen umg.* hit the roof; → *auslassen* I 7; **2.** *fig.* (*Eifer, Verbissenheit*) frenzy; *des Gewitters, Sturms etc.:* fury

Wut|anfall *m* fit of rage; *bes. von Kind:* tantrum; ~**ausbruch** *m* angry outburst, outburst of rage; *launischer:* tantrum

wüten *v/i.* rage (*auch Feuer, Seuche, Sturm etc.*) (*gegen* at, against); *Menschenmenge:* riot; (*Zerstörungen anrichten*) create havoc; **wütend I.** *Part. Präs.* → **wüten; II.** *Adj.* **1.** furious (*auf j-n* with; *über* + *Akk.* about), mad (at) *umg.; Tier:* enraged; *Menge:* angry; ~ *machen* infuriate, enrage, get *s.o.* going *umg.;* **2.** *fig. attr. Sturm, Schmerzen etc.:* raging

wut|entbrannt I. *Adj.* infuriated, furious; **II.** *Adv.:* ~ *weglaufen/zuschlagen* run off / hit out in fury (*od.* in a rage)

Wüterich *m; -s, -e; pej.* **1.** *aufbrausend:* hothead; **2.** *rücksichtslos:* ruthless tyrant

Wut|geheul *n* howls *Pl.* of rage (*od.* fury); ~**geschrei** *n* cries *Pl.* of rage

wutschnaubend *Adj.* snorting with rage

Wutschrei *m* cry (*lauter:* yell) of rage

wutverzerrt *Adj. Gesicht:* distorted with rage

Wutz *f; -, -en; Dial.* pig; *weiblich:* sow

WWW *n; -, kein Pl.; Abk.* (**World Wide Web**) WWW

Wz *Abk.* (**Warenzeichen**) trademark

W

X, x *n*; -, - X, x; *X wie Xanthippe* Buchstabieren: "x" for (*od.* as in) "X-ray"; *Herr X* Mr (*od.* Mr.) X; *j-m ein X für ein U vormachen* (try to) pull the wool over s.o.'s eyes

x *unbest. Zahlw. umg.* umpteen; *x Leute habe ich gefragt* I've asked umpteen (*od.* dozens of) people

x-Achse *f Math.* x-axis

Xanthippe *f*; -, -*n*; *pej.* (*zänkische Frau*) virago, harridan, shrew *altm.*; (*herrische Frau*) battleaxe

X-Beine *Pl.* knock-knees; ~ *haben* be knock-kneed; **x-beinig, X-beinig** *Adj.* knock-kneed

x-beliebig *umg.* **I.** *Adj.* any old ...; *jeder x-Beliebige* just anybody, any Tom, Dick, or Harry; **II.** *Adv.* any old way; ~ *viele* any number of, umpteen

X-Chromosom *n Gnt.* X-chromosome

Xenon *n*; -*s*, *kein Pl.*; (*abgek.* **Xe**) *Chem.* xenon

Xenophobie *f*; *nur Sg.*; *geh.* xenophobia

Xerokopie *f Druck.* Xerox®, photocopy

x-fach *umg.* **I.** *Adj.* umpteen times; *die ~e Zahl* n times that number; **II.** *Adv.* as often (*od.* as many times) as you like; → *achtfach*; **x-fache** *n*; -*n*, *kein Pl.*: *das* ~ *umg.* umpteen times as much, umpteen times the amount; → *Achtfache*

x-förmig, X-förmig *Adj.* x-shaped

x-mal *Adv. umg.* umpteen times, dozens (*od.* hundreds) of times; *hab ich's dir nicht schon ~ gesagt?* auch haven't I told you a thousand times?, I don't know how many times I've told you

x-t... *Adj.* **1.** *Math.*: *die ~e Potenz von* ... the nth power of ...; **2.** *umg.*: *der ~e Versuch* the umpteenth attempt; *zum ~en Mal* for the umpteenth (*od.* nth, hundredth) time; → *acht...*

Xylophon *n*; -*s*, -*e*; *Mus.* xylophone

Y, y *n*; -, -, *umg. auch* -*s* Y, y; *Y wie Ypsilon* Buchstabieren: "y" for (*od.* as in) "Yankee"

y-Achse *f Math.* y-axis

Yacht *f* → *Jacht*

Yak *m*; -*s*, -*s* yak

Yamswurzel *f* → *Jamswurzel*

Yang *n*; -(*s*), *kein Pl.*; *Philos.* yang

Yankee ['jɛŋki] *m*; -*s*, -*s*; *oft pej.* Yankee

Y-Chromosom *n Gnt.* Y-chromosome

Yen *m*; -(*s*), -(*s*) yen

Yeti *m*; -*s*, -*s*; *Myth.* yeti, *the* Abominable Snowman

Yin *n*; -(*s*), *kein Pl.*; *Philos.* yin

Yoga *m, n*; -*s*, *kein Pl.* yoga; ~*kurs m* yoga course; ~*übung f* yoga exercise

Yogi *m*; -*s*, -*s* yogi

Yo-Yo *n*; -*s*, -*s* yoyo

Ypsilon *n*; -(*s*), -*s* (the letter) Y

Ytong® *m*; -*s*, -*s*; *Archit.* breeze (*Am.* cinder) block

Ytterbium *n*; -*s*, *kein Pl.*; (*abgek.* **Yb**) *Chem.* ytterbium

Yttrium *n*; -*s*, *kein Pl.*; (*abgek.* **Y**) *Chem.* yttrium

Yucca *f*; -, -*s*, ~*palme f Bot.* yucca

Yuppie ['jʊpi] *m*; -*s*, -*s* yuppie; **Yuppifizierung** *f* yuppification

Z, z *n*; -, -, *umg. auch* -s **Z, z**; **Z wie Zacharias** *Buchstabieren:* "z" for (*od.* as in) "Zulu"

Z. *Abk.* (**Zeile**) l, l.

z. A. *Abk.* **1.** (**zur Ansicht**) on approval; **2.** (**zur Anstellung**) on probation

zack *Interj. umg.* (*unglaublich schnell*) quick as a flash, before you can (*od.* could) say Jack Robinson; *lautmalend:* whoosh, zip; **~, war er weg** quick as a flash *etc.*, he was off; **~!, ~!** (*mach schnell!*) chop! chop!, get a move on

Zack *m Dial.:* (**schwer**) **auf ~ sein** *Person:* be (really) on the ball; *Geschäft etc.:* be in (really) good shape; **etw. auf ~ bringen** get s.th. up to scratch (*od.* into shape); **j-n auf ~ bringen** knock s.o. into shape, shake s.o. up

Zacke *f*; -, -n (*sharp*) point; (*Zinke*) prong; *e-r Gabel: auch* tine; *e-r Säge, e-s Kamms:* tooth; *e-s Berges:* jagged peak

Zacken *m*; -s, -; *umg.* **1.** → *Zacke*; **2.** *fig.:* **du wirst dir schon keinen ~ aus der Krone brechen** *iro.* you won't do yourself any harm, it won't hurt you; **e-n ~ haben** (*betrunken sein*) be plastered; **e-n ganz schönen ~ draufhaben** (*schnell fahren*) be going like mad (*od.* like the clappers), be belting along

zacken *v/t.* indent, notch; (*zähnen*) serrate; (*Papier, Stoff*) pink; → *gezackt*

zackenförmig *Adj.* serrated; *unregelmäßig:* jagged; **Zackenlinie** *f* zigzag (line); *unregelmäßig:* jagged line

zackig *Adj.* **1.** indented; *Felsen:* jagged; **2.** *umg. fig.* (*schneidig*) snappy; *Soldat:* smart, *Am.* neat; *Musik, Schritt, Tempo:* brisk, lively; *Bewegung:* short, sharp; **Zackigkeit** *f*; *nur Sg.* **1.** jaggedness; **2.** *umg. fig.* (*Schneidigkeit*) snappiness; *e-s Soldaten:* smartness, *Am.* crispness; *des Tempos:* briskness, liveliness; *e-r Bewegung:* sharpness

zagen *v/i. geh.* hesitate; *ängstlich:* quail, lose heart

zaghaft I. *Adj.* (*ängstlich*) timid; (*schüchtern*) shy, diffident; (*vorsichtig*) cautious; **II.** *Adv.* timidly, gingerly; (*zögernd*) hesitatingly; **Zaghaftigkeit** *f; nur Sg.* timidity; (*Schüchternheit*) shyness, diffidence; (*Vorsichtigkeit*) cautiousness

zäh I. *Adj.* **1.** *Fleisch:* tough; **~ wie Leder** tough as old boots (*auch fig.*).; **2.** *Flüssigkeit:* viscous; **3.** *fig.* (*widerstandsfähig*) tough; (*ausdauernd*) dogged; (*hartnäckig*) stubborn, tenacious; **~er Bursche** *umg.* tough guy; **ein ~es Leben haben** cling to life; *fig.* die hard; *Katze:* have nine lives; **4.** *fig. Verhandlungen:* long-drawn-out, laborious; *Verkehr:* slow(-moving); **II.** *Adv.* **1.** (*ausdauernd*) doggedly; (*hartnäckig*) stubbornly, tenaciously; **2.** (*schleppend*) slowly and laboriously; **~ fließender Verkehr** slow-moving traffic; **~ vorankommen** make

painfully slow progress; **zähflüssig** *Adj.* **1.** viscous; **2.** *Verkehr:* slow-moving; **Zähflüssigkeit** *f; nur Sg.* viscosity; **Zähheit** *f; nur Sg.*, **Zähigkeit** *f; nur Sg.* **1.** *von Fleisch:* toughness; **2.** *von Flüssigkeit:* viscosity; **3.** *fig.* toughness; (*Ausdauer*) tenacity, doggedness

Zahl *f*, -, -en **1.** number; (*Ziffer, Betrag, Wert*) figure; **gerade/ungerade ~** even/odd number; **vierstellige ~** four-digit number; **in großer ~** in large numbers; **ohne ~** *lit.* countless, innumerable; **es waren vier** *etc.* **an der ~** there were four *etc.* of them, they were four *etc.* in number *geh.:* **er wollte keine ~en nennen** he didn't want to give (*od.* quote) any figures; **Kopf oder ~** heads or tails; → *ganz* I 1, *rot* I 1, *rund* I, *auch* Ziffer 1; **2.** *Ling.* (*Numerus*) number

Zahladjektiv *n Ling.* numeral adjective

zahlbar *Adj.* payable (**an** + *Akk.* to; **bis** to); **~ bei Lieferung** cash on delivery (*Abk.* COD)

zählbar *Adj.* **1.** *Menge:* countable; **2.** *Ling.* countable

zählebig *Adj.* **1.** tough; **2.** *fig. Ansichten etc.:* tenacious

Zahlemann *umg. hum.:* **~ und Söhne** (it's) paying-up time

zahlen *v/t/i.* pay (*auch fig.*); (*Rechnung, Schulden*) *auch* settle; (*Ware, Dienstleistung etc.*) pay for; **~ (bitte)!** *im Gasthaus:* (could I *od.* we have) the bill *Am.* check), please; **j-m etw. ~** *od.* **etw. an j-n ~** pay s.o. s.th., pay s.th. to s.o.; **j-m ein Bier / den Eintritt ~** buy s.o. a beer / pay for s.o.'s ticket (*od.* pay for s.o. to go in); **gut/schlecht ~** *Arbeitgeber etc.:* pay well/badly; **wie viel hast du dafür gezahlt?** what (*od.* how much) did you pay for that?; **was habe ich (Ihnen) zu ~?** what do I owe you?; **zahlst du bitte das Taxi / den Lieferanten?** would you pay (for) the taxi / pay the deliveryman, please?; **Strafe ~ müssen** have to pay a fine

zählen I. *v/i.* **1.** count (**bis** [up] to); **falsch ~** miscount, count wrong(ly); → **drei** 1; **2.** (*gelten*) count; **mehr/weniger ~ als** matter more/less than, count for more/less than; **hier zählt nur Quantität** only quantity counts (*od.* matters) here; **3.** ~ **auf** (+ *Akk.*) count on; **kann ich auf dich ~?** can I count on you?, can I count you in?; **4.** ~ **zu** rank with (*od.* among), be among, belong to; **zu e-r Gruppe ~** be one of a group, belong to a group; **5.** *geh.:* **sein Vermögen zählt nach Millionen** his fortune runs into millions; **II.** *v/t.* **1.** count; **Punkte ~** *Sport, Kartenspiel etc.:* keep (the) score; **das Geld auf den Tisch ~** count the money out on the table; **man zählte das Jahr ...** *altm.* it was in the year ...; **s-e Tage sind gezählt** *fig.* his days are numbered; **2.** *fig.* have; **der Ort zählt 20 000 Einwohner** the town has 20,000 inhabitants; **sie**

zählte 12 Jahre *altm.* she was 12 (years old); **das Ass zählt 11 Punkte** the ace counts 11 (points); **3.** (*rechnen*) count (**als** as); **... nicht gezählt** not counting ...; **j-n zu s-n Freunden** *etc.* **~** count s.o. as a friend *etc.* (*od.* among one's friends *etc.*)

Zahlen|akrobatik *f* juggling with figures; **~angaben** *Pl.* figures; **~code** *m Computer:* numeric code

zahlend I. *Part. Präs.* → **zahlen**; **II.** *Adj.:* **~er Gast** paying guest; **~es Mitglied** *e-s Vereins, e-r Partei etc.:* paid-up member; **zu ~er Betrag** *Wirts.* amount to be paid

Zahlen|folge *f* sequence (*od.* order) of numbers; **~gedächtnis** *n:* **ein gutes ~ haben** be good at remembering figures; **~kolonne** *f* column of figures; **~kombination** *f* combination (of numbers *od.* figures); **~lotterie** *f*, **~lotto** *n* → *Lotto* 1

zahlenmäßig I. *Adj.* numerical; **~e Überlegenheit** superiority in numbers, numerical superiority; **II.** *Adv.* numerically, in terms of figures; **~ überlegen sein** be superior in numbers, be numerically superior; **dem Gegner** *etc.* **~ überlegen sein** outnumber the enemy *etc.*

Zahlen|material *n* figures *Pl.*; **~mystik** *f* numerology; **~reihe** *f* series of numbers, number sequence; **~schloss** *n* combination lock; **~spielerei** *f oft pej.* numbers game, juggling with figures; **~symbolik** *f* number symbolism; **~system** *n* numerical system; **~wert** *m* numerical value

Zahler *m*; -s, - payer; **pünktlicher/säumiger ~** prompt/late payer

Zähler *m*; -s, - **1.** *Gerät:* counter; *Tech. auch* meter; **2.** *Math.* numerator; **3.** *Sport* (*Punkt*) point; **4.** *Person:* teller; **~ablesung** *f* meter reading; **~stand** *m* meter reading

Zahl|grenze *f* fare stage; *S-Bahn etc.:* auch zone boundary; **~karte** *f* paying-in (*Am.* deposit) slip (for post-office account); **~kellner** *m*, **~kellnerin** *f etwa* head waiter

zahllos *Adj.* innumerable, countless, endless, an endless number of

Zählmaß *n* unit of measurement

Zahlmeister *m* paymaster; *Naut., Flug.* purser (*beide auch fig.*)

zahlreich I. *Adj.* numerous, a large number of, a great many; **i-e ~e Anhängerschaft** *etc.* the great number of her supporters *etc.*; **II.** *Adv.:* **~ kommen / vertreten sein** come / be represented in large numbers (*od.* in force); **~ besucht werden** be well attended

Zahl|stelle *f* paying office; *e-r Bank:* sub-branch; **~tag** *m* payday; **~teller** *m* money tray

Zahlung *f* payment; *e-r Schuld: auch* settlement; **gegen ~** on payment; **e-e ~ leisten** make a payment (**an** + *Akk.* to); **in ~ geben/nehmen** offer/take in part exchange; (*Auto etc.*) *auch* trade in

Zählung *f* count; *des Volkes etc.*: census

Zahlungs|anweisung *f* order to pay; (*Überweisung*) money order; **~aufforderung** *f* request for payment; **~aufschub** *m* respite, deferment (of payment); **~bedingungen** *Pl.* terms of payment; **~befehl** *m* default summons, order to pay

Zahlungsbilanz *f* Fin. balance of payments; **~defizit** *n* balance of payments deficit

Zahlungs|empfänger *m*, **~empfängerin** *f* payee; **~erleichterung** *f* easier terms *Pl.* (for [re]payment), (payment) relief

zahlungsfähig *Adj.* able to pay; *Wirts.* solvent; **Zahlungsfähigkeit** *f*; *nur Sg.* ability to pay; *Wirts.* solvency

Zahlungsfrist *f* Wirts. term of payment, period allowed for payment

zahlungskräftig *Adj.* solvent, financially sound; *weitS.* wealthy, affluent

Zahlungs|mittel *n* Wirts. means *Sg.* of payment; *gesetzliches* **~** legal tender; **~modus** *m* method of payment; **~moral** *f* paying habits *Pl.*, payment pattern (*od.* behavio[u]r); *e-e gute* **~** *haben* settle one's bills promptly, pay (up) promptly, be a good payer; *e-e schlechte* **~** *haben* be slow to settle one's bills (*od.* to pay up), be a bad payer; **~ort** *m* place of payment; *Wechsel*: domicil(e)

zahlungspflichtig *Adj.* liable to pay

Zahlungs|rückstand *m* arrears *Pl.*, backlog of payments; **~schwierigkeiten** *Pl.* financial difficulties, liquidity problem *Sg. umg.*; **~termin** *m* date for payment, due date, payment deadline

zahlungsunfähig *Adj.* unable to pay; *Wirts.* insolvent; **Zahlungsunfähigkeit** *f*; *nur Sg.* inability to pay; *Wirts.* insolvency

zahlungsunwillig *Adj.* Wirts. unwilling to pay

Zahlungs|verkehr *m* Wirts. payments *Pl.*; **~verpflichtung** *f* allg.: liability (to pay); *einzelner Fall*: financial obligation; **~verzug** *m* default (of payment); *in* **~** *geraten* default on one's payments, get (*od.* fall) into arrears; **~weise** *f* method of payment; **~ziel** *n* Wirts., *Termin*: due date; *Zeitraum*: period allowed for repayment, grace period

Zähl|weise *f* way of counting (*od.* reckoning); *nach meiner* **~** by my reckoning; **~werk** *n* counter

Zahl|wort *n* Ling. numeral; **~zeichen** *n* figure, numeral

Zählzwang *m* Psych. obsessive counting

zahm *Adj.* tame (*auch fig.*); *Kritik*: mild; **~** *werden* grow tame; *fig. Person*: calm down; **zähmbar** *Adj.* tameable; **zähmen** *v/t.* **1.** tame; (*Pferd*) break in; **2.** *fig.* (*Gefühle etc.*) control, curb; (*die Natur, die Elemente etc.*) tame, subdue; (*bewältigen*) subjugate, conquer; **Zahmheit** *f*; *nur Sg.* tameness (*auch fig.*); **Zähmung** *f*; *nur Sg.* taming; *fig. auch* subduing, subjugation; → *widerspenstig*

Zahn *m*; *-(e)s*, *Zähne* **1.** Anat. tooth; *falsche od. künstliche Zähne* false teeth, dentures; *die dritten Zähne hum.* false teeth; *Zähne bekommen* cut one's teeth; *sich die Zähne putzen* brush one's teeth; *die Zähne zeigen Tier*: show (*od.* bare) its teeth; *umg.* *fig.* show one's teeth; **2.** (*Zacke*) tooth; *an Briefmarke*: perforation; *an Rad*: tooth, cog; **3.** *fig.*: *bis an die Zähne bewaffnet* armed to the teeth; *der* **~** *der Zeit* the ravages of time; *j-m auf den* **~** *fühlen* sound s.o. out; *etwas für den hohlen* **~** *umg.* not enough to keep a sparrow alive, a minute portion; *den* **~** *hab ich ihm gezogen umg.* I soon put him right about that, I knocked that idea on the head straight away; *mit Zähnen und Klauen verteidigen umg.* defend tooth and nail; → *ausbeißen, knirschen, zusammenbeißen*; **4.** *umg.* (*Tempo*) lick; *e-n* **~** *zulegen* step on it; *Autofahrer: auch* put one's foot down; *e-n ziemlichen* **~** *draufhaben* be going at quite a lick; *schneller*: be going like the clappers (*Am.* like a bat out of hell)

Zahn|arzt *m* Dent. dentist, dental surgeon *förm.*; **~arzthelferin** *f* dental assistant; **~ärztin** *f* dentist, dental surgeon *förm.*

zahnärztlich *Adj.* dental

Zahn|arztpraxis *f* dental practice (*od.* surgery); **~behandlung** *f* dental treatment; **~belag** *m* plaque; **~bein** *n*; *nur Sg.*; *Bio.* dentin(e); **~bürste** *f* toothbrush

Zähnchen *n* small tooth; *Zool.* denticle

Zahncreme *f* Dent. toothpaste

zähnefletschend I. *Adj.* snarling; **II.** *Adv. auch* with its teeth bared, showing its teeth

Zähneklappern *n* chattering (of) teeth; **zähneklappernd** *Adv.* with chattering teeth

Zähneknirschen *n* grinding (*od. bes. bibl.* gnashing) of teeth; *Med.* bruxism *fachspr.*; *fig.* grumbling, cursing under one's breath; **zähneknirschend** *Adv. fig. nachgeben etc.*: grudgingly, muttering under one's breath *umg.*

zahnen *v/i.* Kleinkind: cut one's teeth, be teething

Zähneputzen *n* tooth-brushing; **~** *nicht vergessen!* dont forget to brush your teeth

Zahn|ersatz *m* Dent. dentures *Pl.*, *förm.* dental prosthesis; **~fäule** *f* Med. dental decay, (dental) caries

Zahnfleisch *n* gums *Pl.*; *auf dem* **~** *gehen od. daherkommen umg. fig.* be on one's last legs

Zahnfleisch|bluten *n* Dent. bleeding (of the) gums; (*Parodontose*) pyorrh(o)ea; **~entzündung** *f* inflammation of the gums, gingivitis *fachspr.*; **~schwund** *m* shrinking (of the) gums; (*Parodontose*) pyorrh(o)ea

Zahn|füllung *f* Dent. filling; **~hals** *m* Anat. neck of a (*od.* the) tooth; **~heilkunde** *f* → *Zahnmedizin*; **~höhle** *f* Anat. pulp cavity; **~klammer** *f* brace; **~klempner** *m* umg. hum. *od.* pej. tooth-drawer; **~klinik** *f* dental clinic

Zahn|kranz *m* Tech. gear rim; **~krone** *f* Anat. crown (of a tooth); **~laut** *m* Ling. dental

zahnlos *Adj.* toothless; **Zahnlosigkeit** *f*; *nur Sg.* toothlessness

Zahnlücke *f* gap (in one's teeth)

Zahnmedizin *f*; *nur Sg.*; *Dent.* dentistry; **zahnmedizinisch** *Adj.* Untersuchung etc.: dental; *Gutachten*: dentist's

Zahn|pasta *f* Dent. toothpaste; **~pflege** *f* dental (*Am. auch* oral) hygiene, care of one's teeth; **~prothese** *f* dentures *Pl.*, *förm.* dental prosthesis; **~putzbecher** *m* tooth mug; **~putzzeug** *n* teeth-cleaning equipment, things for cleaning one's teeth

Zahnrad *n* Tech. gear(wheel), cog(wheel); **~antrieb** *m* gear drive; **~bahn** *f* rack (*od.* cog) railway; **~getriebe** *n* gear transmission; (*Ritzelgetriebe*) pinion gear

Zahn|regulierung *f* Dent. orthodontic treatment, having one's teeth straightened; **~reinigung** *f* teeth-cleaning; **~schmelz** *m* Physiol. (dental) enamel; **~schmerz** *m*; *mst Pl.* toothache *Sg.*; **~en haben** have got (*Brit. mst ohne*: a) toothache; **~schutz** *m* Boxen: gumshield; **~seide** *f* dental floss; **~spange** *f* brace; **~stein** *m*; *nur Sg.* tartar; **~stocher** *m* toothpick; **~stummel** *m*, **~stumpf** *m* stump of a tooth; **~technik** *f*; *nur Sg.* dentistry; **~techniker** *m*, **~technikerin** *f* dental technician

Zahnwal *m* Zool. toothed whale

Zahn|weh *n* umg. toothache; → *Zahnschmerz*; **~wurzel** *f* Anat. root (of a *od.* the tooth); **~wurzelbehandlung** *f* Dent. root treatment

Zähre *f*; *-*, *-n*; *lit., altm.* tear

Zaire [za'i:rə] (*n*); *-s*; *Geog., hist.* Zaire; **zairisch** *Adj. hist.* Zairean

Zampano ['tsampano] *m*; *-s*, *-s*; *umg.*: *sich wie der große* **~** *aufspielen* act the big shot; *da kommt der große* **~** (*der Unmögliches möglich macht*) here comes Mr (*od.* Mr.) Fix-it; (*der große Prahler*) here comes Mr (*od.* Mr.) Big Shot

Zander *m*; *-s*, *-*; *Zool.* pike(-)perch

Zange *f*; *-*, *-n* **1.** (*Flachzange*) pliers *Pl.*; (*Beißzange*) pincers *Pl.*; *zum Greifen, für Kohlen, Zucker etc.*: tongs *Pl.*; *zum Lochen*: punch; *e-e* **~** a pair of pliers (*od.* pincers *od.* tongs); *zum Lochen*: a punch; **2.** *Zool.* pincers *Pl.*, nippers *Pl.*; **3.** *Med.* forceps (*Pl.* forceps); **4.** *fig.*: *in die* **~** *nehmen Mil.* encircle, surround; *Ringen*: put a double lock on; *Fußball*: sandwich *s.o.*; *umg.* put the screws on *s.o.*; *j-n in der* **~** *haben* have s.o. where one wants him *etc.*

Zangenbewegung *f* Mil. pincer movement

zangenförmig *Adj.* pincer-shaped

Zangen|geburt *f* Med. forceps delivery; **~griff** *m bes. Sport* double lock

Zank *m*; *-(e)s*, *kein Pl.* quarrel (*um od. über* + *Akk.* about); → *auch Streit*; **Zankapfel** *m* bone of contention; **zanken I.** *v/i.* **1.** quarrel, argue (*um* about, over); **2.** *Dial.* (*schimpfen*) scold; *mit j-m* **~** tell s.o. off; **II.** *v/refl.* → I 1; **Zankerei** *f*; *-*, *-en*; *umg. pej.* squabbling, quarrel(l)ing, arguing; **zänkisch** *Adj. pej.* quarrelsome; (*streitsüchtig*) *auch* cantankerous; (*nörgelnd*) nagging ...; **Zanksucht** *f*; *nur Sg. pej.* quarrelsomeness; (*Streitsüchtigkeit*) *auch* cantankerousness; (*Nörgelei*) nagging; **zanksüchtig** *Adj.* → *zänkisch*

Zäpfchen *n* **1.** Anat., Ling. uvula (*Pl.* uvulas *od.* uvulae); **2.** *Med.* suppository; **~-R**, **~-r** *n* Ling. uvular "r"

Zapfen *m*; *-s*, *-* **1.** (*Stöpsel*) plug, bung; *für Fass*: spigot; (*Pflock*) peg, pin; (*Stift*) stud; *für Balken*: tenon; (*Drehzapfen*) pivot; *Tech., von Lager, Welle*: journal; **2.** (*Eiszapfen*) icicle; **3.** *Bot.* cone; **4.** *Anat.* retinal cone

zapfen *v/t.* (*Bier etc.*) tap, draw

zapfenförmig *Adj.* cone-shaped, conical

Zapfenstreich *m* Mil., *Signal*: tattoo, *Brit. auch* the last post, *Am. auch* taps *Pl.*; *Zeitpunkt*: curfew; *den od. zum* **~**

blasen sound the tattoo; *der Große* ~ the tattoo; *um 10 Uhr ist* ~ *umg. fig.* it's lights out at ten o'clock

Zapfer *m*; *-s*, *-*, **~in** *f*: *-*, *-nen* barman, *weiblich*: barmaid

Zapf|hahn *m* tap, *Am.* faucet; *Mot.* hose nozzle; **~pistole** *f* nozzle; **~säule** *f Mot.* petrol (*Am.* gas[oline]) pump; **~stelle** *f* tap; *Elektr.* (power) point; *Mot.* filling station, petrol (*Am.* gas) station

zappelig *Adj. umg.* **1.** fidgety, restless; **2.** (*aufgeregt*) excited, nervous, in a flap (*Am. auch* tizzy); **Zappeligkeit** *f*; *nur Sg.*; *umg.* **1.** fidgetiness, restlessness; **2.** (*Aufgeregtheit*) excitement, nervousness; **zappeln** *v/i.* thrash about; *sich wehrend: auch* struggle; *sich windend:* wriggle; *vor Unruhe:* jiggle around, fidget; *an der Angel* ~ *Fisch:* thrash about on the end of the line; *j-n* ~ *lassen fig.* keep s.o. on tenterhooks; **Zappelphilipp** *m*; *-s*, *-e od. -s*; *umg., pej.* fidget

zappen [ˈzɛpn̩] *v/i. und v/refl. TV umg.:* ([*sich*] *durch die Kanäle*) ~ zap, *Am.* surf (through the channels)

zappenduster *Adj. umg.* pitch-dark, pitch-black; *dann wird's* ~ *fig.* things will look pretty grim

Zapper [ˈzɛpɐ] *m*; *-s*, *-*, **~in** *f*; *-*, *-nen*; *TV umg.* zapper, *Am.* channel surfer

zapplig *etc.* → **zappelig** *etc.*

Zar *m*; *-en*, *-en*; *hist.* tsar, *bes. Am.* czar ...**zar** *im Subst., m*; *umg.* mogul; *Film~* movie mogul; *Presse~* press baron

Zarenreich *n*: *im* ~ under the tsars (*od.* czars)

Zarewitsch *m*; *-(e)s*, *-e*; *hist.* tsarevitch, czarevitch

Zarge *f*, *-*, *-n*; *fachspr.* **1.** frame; **2.** *e-r Geige etc.:* side

Zarin *f*; *-*, *-nen*; *hist.* tsarina, czarina

zaristisch *Adj. hist.* tsarist, czarist

zart I. *Adj.* **1.** *Blume, Gesundheit, Kind, Haut, Glieder etc.:* delicate; *Blätter, Knospen etc.:* tender; *Gebäck:* fine; *ein ~es Geschöpf* a delicate creature; **2.** (*weich*) Flaum, *Haut etc.:* soft; *Fleisch, Gemüse:* tender; **3.** *fig. Andeutung, Berührung, Geschlecht, Kuss:* gentle; *Stimme, Töne: auch* soft; *Farben:* soft, pale, pastel; (*zärtlich*) *Gefühle:* tender; (*empfindsam*) sensitive; (*zurückhaltend*) delicate; *im ~en Alter von geh.* at the tender age of; *nichts für ~e Ohren* not for sensitive ears; **II.** *Adv.* tenderly; (*sanft*) gently; ~ *andeuten mit Worten:* give a gentle hint, suggest delicately; *in Gemälde:* suggest, sketch in lightly; ~ *besaitet od. fühlend* delicately strung, highly sensitive; ~ *umgehen mit* handle with care; (*j-m*) *auch* handle with kid gloves

zart|besaitet, zart besaitet *Adj. fig.* delicately strung, highly sensitive; **~bitter** *Adj. Schokolade:* plain; **~blau** *Adj.* pale (*od.* pastel) blue

zartfühlend, zart fühlend *Adj.* **1.** (*taktvoll*) discreet, tactful; **2.** → **zartbesaitet; Zartgefühl** *n*; *nur Sg.* delicacy (of feeling), tact

zart|gelb *Adj.* pale (*od.* pastel) yellow; **~gliedrig** *Adj.* delicately-built ..., *präd.* delicately built; *Mädchen: auch* petite; **~grün** *Adj.* pale (*od.* pastel) green

Zartheit *f*; *nur Sg.* tenderness; softness; delicacy, delicateness; gentleness; → **zart I**

zärtlich I. *Adj.* affectionate; (*liebevoll*) loving; *Berührung, Blick:* tender; ~ *werden* start caressing (one another);

II. *Adv.* affectionately; (*liebevoll*) lovingly; *berühren, ansehen:* tenderly; **Zärtlichkeit** *f* **1.** *nur Sg.*; affection; (*Sanftheit*) tenderness; **2.** (*Liebkosung*) caress; *Worte:* endearment; ~*en austauschen* caress (one another); *euph.* (*Sex miteinander haben*) become intimate; *es kam zu ~en* (*zwischen ihnen*) they became intimate; **Zärtlichkeitsbedürfnis** *n* need for affection

zartrosa *Adj.* pale (*od.* pastel) pink

Zäsium *n*; *-s*, *kein Pl.*; (*abgek. Cs*) *Chem.* c(a)esium

Zaster *m*; *-s*, *kein Pl.*; *umg.* dosh *Sl.*, brass *Sl.*, bread *Sl.*

Zäsur *f*, *-*, *-en* **1.** *Lit., Mus.* caesura, break; **2.** *geh. fig.* break; (*Wende*) turning point

Zauber *m*; *-s*, *-* **1.** *nur Sg.* magic, witchcraft; *wie durch* ~ as if by magic; **2.** (*Bann*) (magic) spell, charm; *den* ~ *lösen* break the spell (*auch fig.*); **3.** *fig.* (*Reiz*) magic(al quality), charm; *dem* ~ *e-r Landschaft etc. erliegen* be under the spell (*od.* be spellbound by) a (*od.* the) landscape *etc.*; **4.** *umg. pej.* (*Zirkus*) fuss, song and dance; *fauler* ~ humbug, mumbo jumbo; (*Schwindel*) a swindle; *der ganze* ~ the whole bag of tricks; **~buch** *n* book of spells, conjuring book

Zauberei *f*, *-*, *-en* **1.** *nur Sg.* magic; (*Hexerei*) sorcery, witchcraft; *das grenzt an* ~ it's almost like magic; **2.** (*Zaubertricks*) conjuring, magic, sleight-of-hand; **Zauberer** *m*; *-s*, *-* **1.** magician, sorcerer, wizard; **2.** → **Zauberkünstler**; **3.** *fig.* wizard

Zauber|flöte *f*: „*die* ~" *von Mozart:* The Magic Flute; **~formel** *f* **1.** spell, charm; **2.** *fig.* magic formula

zauberhaft *Adj.* charming, enchanting

Zauberhand *f*: *wie von od. durch* ~ as if by magic

Zauberin *f*; *-*, *-nen* **1.** sorceress; **2.** → **Zauberkünstler**; **3.** *fig.* sorceress, enchantress

Zauber|kasten *m* conjuring (*Am.* magic) set; **~kraft** *f* **1.** magic power; **2.** *fig. von Worten etc.:* magic (power); **~kreis** *m* magic circle; **~kunst** *f* (black) magic; (*Hexerei*) witchcraft; **~künstler** *m*, **~künstlerin** *f* conjurer, magician, illusionist; **~kunststück** *n* conjuring (*Am.* magic) trick; **~lehrling** *m* sorcerer's apprentice; **~mittel** *n* magic cure; (*Trank*) magic potion

zaubern I. *v/i.* do (*od.* perform) magic; *als Zauberkünstler:* do (*od.* perform) magic *od.* conjuring tricks; *ich kann doch nicht* ~ *umg. fig.* I can't work miracles, I can't just wave my magic wand; **II.** *v/t.* **1.** conjure (up); *ein Kaninchen aus dem Hut* ~ produce (*od.* pull) a rabbit out of the hat; *er zauberte sie aufs Dach* he conjured her up onto the roof; **2.** *fig.* (*Mahlzeit etc.*) conjure up

Zauber|nuss *f Bot.* witch hazel; **~schloss** *n* enchanted castle; **~spruch** *m* charm, spell; **~stab** *m* magic wand; **~trank** *m* magic potion; **~trick** *m* magic trick; **~wirkung** *f* magical effect; **~wort** *n*; *Pl. -e* magic word (*od.* formula); **~würfel** *m* magic cube

Zauderei *f*, *-*, *-en*; *mst pej.* vacillation, dithering; (*Hinausschieben*) procrastination; **Zauderer** *m*; *-s*, *-* vacillator, ditherer *umg.*; (*j-d, der etw. hinausschiebt*) procrastinator; **zaudern** *v/i.* hesitate (*mit* about), waver, vacillate; *hinhaltend:* temporize, procrastinate

Zaum *m*; *-(e)s*, *Zäume* bridle; *im* ~ *halten fig.* (*Leidenschaft*) bridle; (*Ungeduld, Zorn*) keep in check; (*j-n*) keep a tight rein on; (*Sache*) contain; *sich im* ~ *halten* restrain o.s.; **zäumen** *v/t.* bridle; **Zaumzeug** *n* bridle

Zaun *m*; *-(e)s*, *Zäune* fence; *aus Brettern:* hoarding; *lebender* ~ hedge; *e-n Streit/Krieg vom* ~ *brechen fig.* pick (*od.* start) a fight / start a war; **~eidechse** *f Zool.* sand lizard; **~gast** *m* onlooker; **~könig** *m Orn.* wren; **~latte** *f* picket; **~pfahl** *m* fence post; → **Wink 2**; **~pfosten** *m* fence post; **~rebe** *f* climbing plant; **~winde** *f Bot.* hedge bindweed

Zausel *m*; *-s*, *-*; *Dial., mst pej.: alter* ~ old codger

zausen *v/t.* (*Haar*) tousle; *Wind:* ruffle; (*Bäume*) buffet; *vom Leben arg gezaust fig.* buffeted by fate

Zaziki *n*; *-s*, *-s*; *Gastr.* tzatziki

z. B. *Abk.* (*zum Beispiel*) vorangestellt: e.g. (exempli gratia, for example)

ZDF *n*; *-(s)*, *kein Pl.*; *Abk.* (*Zweites Deutsches Fernsehen*) *etwa* channel two, *the second German public-service television channel*

Zebra *n*; *-s*, *-s*; *Zool.* zebra; **~streifen** *m Verk.* zebra crossing, *Am.* pedestrian crossing

Zebu *n, m*; *-s*, *-s*; *Zool.* zebu

Zechbruder *m umg. oft pej.* **1.** (*Trinker*) boozer; **2.** *Kumpan:* boozing (*od.* drinking) buddy (*od. Brit. auch* mate)

Zeche *f*, *-*, *-n* **1.** (*Rechnung*) bill, *Am.* check; *die* ~ *bezahlen* pick up the tab, foot the bill (*auch umg. fig.*); → **prellen 1**; **2.** *Bergb.* mine

zechen *v/i. altm. od. hum.* booze

Zechenstilllegung *f* pit closure

Zecher *m*; *-s*, *-*, **~in** *f*; *-*, *-nen*; *altm. od. hum.* boozer; *bei e-m Gelage etc.:* reveller

Zechgelage *n altm.* carousal, drinking bout

Zech|preller *m*; *-s*,*-*, **~prellerin** *f*; *-*, *-n*; *-nen* bilk; **~prellerei** *f*; *nur Sg.* bilking; **~tour** *f umg.* pub crawl, *Am.* bar hop

Zecke *f*, *-*, *-n*; *Zool.* tick; **Zeckenbiss** *f* tick bite

Zeder *f*, *-*, *-n*; *Bot.* cedar; **Zedernholz** *n* cedar(wood)

Zeh *m*; *-s*, *-en* → **Zehe 1**; **Zehe** *f*; *-*, *-n* **1.** toe; *sich auf die ~n stellen* stand on tiptoe; *j-m auf die ~n treten auch umg. fig.* tread (*Am.* step) on s.o.'s toes; **2.** *Knoblauch:* clove

Zehen|nagel *m* toenail; **~spitze** *f* tip of one's toe; *auf ~n* on tiptoe; *auf ~n gehen* (walk on) tiptoe

zehn *Zahlw.* ten; → *auch* **acht**[1]

Zehn *f*; *-*, *-en Zahl:* (number) ten; → *auch* **Acht**[1] **1, 2, 4**

zehnbändig *Adj.* ten-volume ..., ... in ten volumes

zehneinhalb *Zahlw.* ten and a half

Zehner *m*; *-s*, *-* **1.** *umg.* → **Zehn**; **2.** *Münze:* ten-cent *etc.* piece; *Schein:* ten-euro *etc.* note (*Am.* bill); **~karte** *f Fahrkarte:* ticket for ten trips; *Eintrittskarte:* ticket for ten visists

zehnerlei *Adj. indekl.* ten kinds of, ten different ...

Zehner|packung *f* pack of ten; **~stelle** *f Math.* decimal place; **~system** *n Math.* decimal system

Zehneuro|centstück *n* ten-cent piece; **~schein** *m* ten euro note (*Am.* bill)

zehnfach *Adj.* tenfold; → **achtfach**; **Zehnfache** *n*; *-n*, *kein Pl.*: *um ein ~s steigen* increase tenfold; → **Achtfache**

Zehnfingersystem *n*: *das* ~ touch-typ-

ing; *mit ~ schreiben* touch-type
Zehnfrankenschein *m* ten franc note
Zehnjahrfeier *f* tenth anniversary
zehnjährig *Adj.* **1.** *Kind etc.*: ten-year-old ...; **2.** *Zeitraum*: ten-year ...; *ein ~es ... auch* ten years of ...; **Zehnjährige** *m, f*; *-n, -n* ten-year-old
Zehn|kampf *m Sport* decathlon; **~kämpfer** *m* decathlete
zehn|karätig *Adj.* ten-carat ...; → *auch* **...karäter, ~köpfig** *Adj. Familie etc.* of ten; **~e Delegation** *etc. auch* ten-member (*od.* -man) delegation *etc.*
zehnmal *Adv.* ten times
Zehn|markschein *m hist.* ten-mark note; **~meterbrett** *n Sport* ten-met|re (*Am.* -er) board; **~minutentakt** *m*: *im ~* every ten minutes, at ten-minute intervals
zehn|minütig *Adj. Gespräch etc.*: ten-minute ...; **~monatig** *Adj.* **1.** *Baby etc.*: ten-month-old ...; **2.** *Zeitraum*: ten-month ...; **~monatlich I.** *Adj.* ten-monthly; **II.** *Adv.* every ten months
Zehnpfennigstück *n hist.* ten-pfennig piece
zehnprozentig *Adj.* ten per cent (*Am.* percent)
Zehn|rappenstück *n* ten-rappen piece; **~schillingstück** *n hist.* ten-schilling piece
zehnseitig *Adj. Vieleck etc.*: ten-sided; *Brief, Broschüre*: ten-page; **zehnstellig** *Adj. Zahl*: ten-figure; **zehnstöckig** *Adj.* ten-stor(e)y; **zehnstündig** *Adj.* ten-hour
zehnt *Adv.*: *sie kamen zu ~* ten of them came, there were ten of them; → *acht²*
zehnt... *Zahlw.* tenth; **~es Kapitel** chapter ten; *am* **~en Mai** on the tenth of May, on May the tenth; *10. Mai* 10th May, May 10(th); → *auch* **acht...**
Zehnt *m; -en, -en; hist.* tithe
zehntägig *Adj. Frist etc.*: ten-day ...; **2.** *Baby etc.*: ten-day-old ...
zehntausend *Zahlw.* ten thousand; *die oberen Zehntausend* the upper crust
Zehnte¹ *m, f; -n, -n* (the) tenth; → *auch* **Achte**
Zehnte² *m; -n, -n; hist.* → **Zehnt**
zehnteilig *Adj.* **1.** *Plan etc.*: ten-part ..., ... in ten parts; **2.** *Set*: ten-piece ...
zehntel *Adj.*: *ein ~ Liter* a tenth of a liter
Zehntel *n; -s, -* tenth; **~gramm** *n* decigram; **~liter** *m* decilit|re (*Am.* -er); **~sekunde** *f* tenth of a second
zehntens *Adv.* tenth(ly), ten, in tenth place
Zehntkläss(l)er *m; -s, -*, **~in** *f; -, -nen; Päd.* tenth-year student, student in class ten, *Am. auch* sophomore
Zehntonner *m; -s, -; Mot.* ten-tonner
zehntpflichtig *Adj. hist.* tithable
Zehnuhr... *im Subst.* ten o'clock ...
zehren *v/i.* **1.** (*schwächen*) sap one's energy; *~ an* (+ *Dat.*) take its toll on; *der Gesundheit: auch* undermine; *an Person: auch* take it out of *s.o.*; *an Kraft: auch* sap, drain; *an Nerven: auch* fray; *der Kummer zehrt an ihr* grief is taking its toll on her, she is being worn out with grief; **2.** *~ von* live on; *von Erspartem*: live off; *von Vorräten*: draw on; *von der Erinnerung ~ fig.* live on one's memories; **Zehrgeld** *n altm.* money for the journey
Zeichen *n; -s, -* **1.** *allg.* sign; (*Signal*) signal; (*Symbol*) symbol; (*Markierung*) mark; *in Schrift*: character (*auch EDV*); (*Satzzeichen*) (punctuation) mark; *Mus.* marking; *Mus.* (*Verset-*

zungszeichen) accidental; *zum Einsetzen e-r Tätigkeit*: cue; (*Kennzeichen*) mark, sign; (*Erkennungszeichen*) identification mark; (*Abzeichen*) badge; *unser/Ihr ~ Geschäftsbrief*: our/your reference; *auf ein ~ von* at a sign from; *~ geben od. machen* signal, give a sign; *ein ~ geben* make a sign (+ *Dat.* to), signal (to); *das ~ zum Aufbruch geben* give the signal (for everybody) to leave; *im ~ von Astron., Astrol.* under the sign of; *s-s ~s Bäcker etc. altm. od. hum.* a baker by trade; **2.** *fig.* sign (*von* of); (*Anzeichen*) *auch* indication; (*Vorzeichen*) *auch* omen; (*Beweis*) *auch* token, mark; *bes. Med.* symptom (*für* of); *ein ~ der Zeit / des Himmels* a sign of the times / from heaven; *die ~ der Zeit erkennen* read the signs of the times; *ein ~ dafür, dass sie Recht hat* a sign that she is right; *ich sehe das als ein gutes ~* I see it as a good omen (*od.* positive sign); (*ein*) *~ setzen* point the way, set the trend; *die ~ stehen auf Sturm* the storm clouds are gathering; *als ~* (+ *Gen.*) as a mark of; *als ~ der Freundschaft* as a token (*od.* mark) of friendship; *als ~ unserer Wertschätzung* as a token (*od.* an expression) of our esteem; *zum ~* (+ *Gen.*) as a sign of; *im ~* (+ *Gen.*) *stehen* be marked by; *die Stadt steht im ~ der kommenden WM* the town is gearing up for the World Cup; *unser Jahrhundert steht im ~ der Naturwissenschaften* our century is the age of science; *es geschehen* (*noch*) *~ und Wunder* wonders will never cease
Zeichen|block *m* sketch pad; **~brett** *n* drawing board; **~dichte** *f Computer*: character density; **~dreieck** *n Math.* set square; **~erklärung** *f* key; *auf Landkarten*: legend; *in Lehrbüchern etc.*: signs and symbols *Pl.*; **~feder** *f* drawing pen; **~fehler** *m Päd., Ling.* punctuation error (*od.* mistake); **~folge** *f* character sequence; **~heft** *n* drawing book; **~kohle** *f* (piece of) charcoal; **~lehrer** *m*, **~lehrerin** *f* art teacher; **~papier** *n* drawing paper; **~saal** *m Päd.* art room; **~satz** *m Druck., EDV* font; **~setzung** *f; nur Sg.* punctuation; **~sprache** *f* sign language; **~stift** *m* pencil; *bunter*: crayon; **~system** *n* (form of) notation; *Ling.* system of signs; **~tisch** *m* drawing board; **~trickfilm** *m* (animated) cartoon; **~unterricht** *m* drawing lessons *Pl.; Schule*: art (class [es *Pl.*]); **~vorlage** *f* model, *an object or arrangement of objects etc. to be drawn*
zeichnen I. *vt/i.* **1.** draw; (*Diagramm, Kurve*) plot; *flüchtig*: sketch, outline; (*entwerfen*) (*Plan etc.*) draw up; *mit Bleistift/Kohle ~* draw in (*od.* with) pencil/charcoal; *nach dem Gedächtnis/der Natur ~* draw from memory/life; **2.** *Wirts.* (*Aktie, Anleihe*) subscribe for; (*Betrag*) subscribe (*für* to); **3.** *altm.* (*unterzeichnen*) sign; *gezeichnet P. Müller* signed P. Müller; *für etw. verantwortlich ~ Jur., fig.* be responsible for s.th.; **II.** *v/t.* **1.** (*kennzeichnen*) mark; **2.** *fig.* (*prägen*) mark, leave a mark on; *die Jahre des Leids haben sie gezeichnet* the years of suffering have left their mark on her; **3.** *fig.* (*schildern*) portray, depict; *ein optimistisches Bild ~ von* paint an optimistic picture of; → *gezeichnet*
Zeichnen *n; -s, kein Pl.* **1.** drawing; *Schulfach*: art; **2.** *Wirts.* subscription;

3. *fig.* portrayal, depiction
Zeichner *m; -s, -,* **~in** *f; -, -nen* **1.** draughts|man (*weiblich*: -woman), *Am.* drafts|man (*weiblich*: -woman); → *technisch* I 1; **2.** *Wirts.* subscriber; **zeichnerisch** *Adj. Darstellung, Gestaltung etc.*: graphic, ... in a drawing; **~e Begabung** talent for drawing; **Zeichnung** *f* **1.** drawing (*auch Tech.*); (*Skizze*) sketch; (*Entwurf*) draft; (*Illustration*) illustration; → *technisch* I 1; **2.** *fig.* (*Schilderung*) portrayal, depiction; **3.** *nur Sg.*; (*Kennzeichnung*) marking; **4.** *Bot., Zool.* (*Muster*) markings *Pl.*, pattern(ing); **5.** *nur Sg.*; *Wirts.* subscription (+ *Gen.* to); *e-e Anleihe zur ~ auflegen* invite subscriptions for a loan; *zur ~ aufliegen* be offered for subscription
zeichnungsberechtigt *Adj.* authorized to sign; **Zeichnungsberechtigung** *f* authority to sign, signatory powers
Zeichnungs|betrag *m Wirts.* subscription amount; **~frist** *f* period for subscription; **~vollmacht** *f* authority to sign, signatory powers
Zeigefinger *m* forefinger, index finger; *mit dem ~ deuten auf* (+ *Akk.*) point one's finger at; *mit erhobenem ~ sagte er mir*: wagging his finger at me; *fig.* with a (strong) moralizing undertone
zeigen I. *v/t.* **1.** *allg.* show; (*vorführen*) present; (*zur Schau stellen*) exhibit, display; *j-m etw. ~* show s.o. s.th., show s.th. to s.o.; *j-m die Stadt ~* show s.o. ([a]round) the town (*od.* city), show s.o. the sights; *zeig mal, was du kannst!* come on, show us what you can do; *lass dir von ihr ~, wie's geht* let her show you how it's done; *dem werd ich's ~! umg.* drohend: I'll show him; **2.** (*anzeigen*) show, indicate; *das Thermometer zeigt 20°* the thermometer is showing 20°; *was zeigt die Waage?* what do the scales (*Am.* does the scale) say?; **3.** *geh.* (*sehen lassen*) show; *die Blumen ~ schon Knospen* the flowers are beginning to show their buds; *was zeigt das Foto?* what is the photo of?, what does the photo show?; **4.** *fig.* (*erkennen lassen*) show, demonstrate; (*ausdrücken*) express; *s-n Ärger deutlich ~* make it obvious how angry one is; *j-m s-e Liebe ~* show one's love for s.o.; *sie kann i-e Gefühle nicht ~* she finds it hard to express her feelings; *d-e Antwort zeigt* (*mir*), *dass du nichts verstanden hast* it's clear (to me) from your answer that you haven't understood anything; *die Erfahrung zeigt, dass ...* experience shows (*od.* proves) that ...; **II.** *v/i.* **1.** *Person, Pfeil etc.*: point; *~ auf* (+ *Akk.*) point at, point s.th. out; *Thermometer*: be at; *Uhr*: say; *nach Norden ~* point north; *Fenster etc.*: face north; *zur Tür ~* point to the door; *sich so hinstellen, dass das Gesicht zur Wand zeigt* stand facing the wall, position o.s. so as to be facing the wall; → *Finger* 1; **2.** *zeig mal* let's see, let's have a look; **III.** *v/refl.* **1.** (*sichtbar werden*) show (itself); *Person*: show o.s.; (*erscheinen*) appear, come out; *plötzlich*: turn up; *sich mit j-m ~* be seen with s.o.; *sich in der Öffentlichkeit ~* appear in public, make a public appearance; *so kann ich mich nicht ~* I can't go out (*od.* let myself be seen) in this state; **2.** *fig.* (*sich erweisen*) prove (to be); *sich ~ als* prove (o.s.) to be; *sich dankbar/freundlich ~* be grateful/friendly; *es zeigte sich,*

dass ... it turned out that ...; *da zeigt sich wieder einmal, dass* ... it just goes to show that ...; *es wird sich ja ~* we shall see, time will tell; *jetzt zeigt sich, dass es so nicht geht* it's now apparent that this is not the right way; *früh zeigte sich sein Talent zum Schriftsteller* he showed an early talent for writing; → *erkenntlich* 1, *Seite* 3

Zeiger *m; -s, -* *e-r Waage, von Messgerät*: needle; *e-r Uhr*: hand; *EDV* pointer; *Math.* index (*Pl.* indices *od.* indexes), exponent; *großer/kleiner ~ Uhr.* big/little hand; *~ausschlag* *m* pointer deflection

Zeige|stab *m,* *~stock* *m* pointer

zeihen *v/t.*; *zieh, hat geziehen; geh.*: *j-n der Lüge etc. ~ (bezichtigen)* accuse s.o. of lying *etc.*

Zeile *f; -, -n* 1. line; *~ für ~ durchgehen etc.*: line by line; *mit eineinhalb ~n Abstand Texterfassung*: with one-and-a--half-line spacing; *in welcher ~ steht das?* what line is it (on)?; *j-m ein paar ~n schreiben* drop s.o. a line; *danke für die netten ~n* thank you for your (lovely) letter; *ich habe jede ~ gelesen* I read every word; *zwischen den ~n lesen* *fig.* read between the lines; 2. (*Reihe*) row; *TV, Etech.* line

Zeilen|abstand *m* line spacing; *~durchschuss* *m Druck.* line spacing; *~fang* *m TV* horizontal hold; *~honorar* *n* payment per line; *~ bekommen* be paid by the line; *~länge* *f* line length; *~nummer* *f* line number; *~schalter* *m Schreibmaschine*: spacer; *~schaltung* *f EDV* line feed; *~umbruch* *m Druck.* line break; *~vorschub* *m Computer.* line feed

zeilenweise *Adv.* by the line

Zeisig *m; -s, -e; Orn.* siskin

Zeit *f; -, -en* 1. *nur Sg.* time; *auf ~ Vertrag etc.*: fixed-term ...; *Beamter/Soldat auf ~* civil servant (appointed) on a fixed-term contract / soldier serving for a specified period of time; *e-e ~ lang* for a while; *für alle ~* *altm.* forever; (*für*) *einige ~* for a time; *es wird noch einige ~ dauern, bis* ... it'll be some time before ...; *in m-r etc. freien ~* in my etc. free time; *die ganze ~ hindurch* the whole time; *sie hat es die ganze ~ gewusst* she knew all along (*od.* all the time); *in kurzer ~* (*schnell*) very quickly; (*bald*) very soon, shortly; *in kürzester ~* in no time; *lange ~* a long time; *vor langer ~* long ago, a long time ago; *die längste ~* *umg.* long enough; *in letzter ~* *od. der letzten ~* lately, recently; *in nächster ~* soon, presently; *im Laufe od. mit der ~* in the course of time; *Vergangenheit*: *auch* as time went on; *die ~ schien stillzustehen* time seemed to stand still; *die ~ vergeht od. verrinnt* time goes by (*od.* passes *od.* elapses); *wie doch die ~ vergeht!* how time flies!; *einige ~ verstreichen lassen, bevor* ... wait a while before (+ *Ger.*); *mir wird die ~ nie lang* I've got plenty to keep me occupied; *das dauert s-e ~* it takes time; *mir fehlt die ~* I (just) haven't got the time; *ich gebe dir ~ bis morgen / 5 Minuten* I'll give you till tomorrow / five minutes; *mit der ~ gehen* move (*od.* keep up) with the times; *~ gewinnen* gain time; *hast du ein paar Stunden ~?* can you spare a couple of hours?; *sie hat nie ~ für mich* she never has any time for me; *wenn Sie ~ haben* whenever you have

(the) time; (*falls*) if you have (the) time; *das hat ~ (bis morgen)* that can wait (till *od.* until tomorrow); *das hat ~ od. lass dir ~!* there's no hurry (*od.* rush), take your time; *das ~ now* give s.o. time; *sich (Dat.) ~ lassen* take one's time (*dazu* over it); take your time; *sich (Dat.) die ~ nehmen zu* (+ *Inf.*) take time to (+ *Inf.*); *e-e (viel) ~ sparende Lösung* a solution that will save (a lot of) time; *auf ~ spielen* play for time, temporize; *sich (Dat.) ~ vertreiben* while away the time; *die ~ arbeitet für/gegen uns* time is on our side / not on our side; (*die*) *~ heilt alle Wunden Sprichw.* time is the great healer; *~ ist Geld Sprichw.* time is money; *ach du liebe ~! umg.* goodness (me)!; → *zeitraubend, zeitsparend;* 2. (*Zeitraum*) (period of time); (*Zeitalter*) era, age; *in der ~ vom ... bis* ... in the time between ... and ...; *zur ~ Goethes* in Goethe's day (*od.* time); *das war vor m-r ~* that was before my time; *zu m-r ~* in my time; *an der Uni etc.: auch* when I was at university (*bes. Am.* in college *etc.*); *s-r ~ voraus sein* be ahead of one's time; *das waren noch ~en!* those were the days; *die ~en sind vorbei, wo* ... time was when ...; *die ~ des Barock* the baroque age (*od.* era, period); *die ~ vor dem zweiten Weltkrieg* the period before the Second World War (*bes. Am.* World War II); *der beste Spieler etc. aller ~en* the best player *etc.* of all time; *für alle ~en* for ever, for good; *ein Märchen aus alten ~en* a tale from days of yore; *in alten ~en* in the olden days; *sie hat (schon) bessere ~en gesehen* she's seen better days; *s-e beste ~ hinter sich haben* have had one's day; *seit ewigen ~en* for ages; *die gute alte ~* the good old days; *schlechte od. schwere ~en* hard times; *für schlechte ~en sparen* save for a rainy day; *das war die schönste ~ m-s Lebens* those were the best years of my life; *vor undenklichen ~en* an unimaginably long time ago, (a)eons ago; *die heutige ~* this (*od.* the present) day and age; 3. (*Zeitpunkt*) (point of) time; (*Uhrzeit*) time; *welche ~ haben wir?* what's the time?; *feste ~en* fixed times; *~ und Ort festlegen* fix a (*od.* the) time and place; *es ist (an der) ~* it's time; *es ist (höchste) ~, dass er nach Hause kommt* it's (high) time he came home; *es ist nicht die ~ zu* (+ *Inf.*) this is not the time to (+ *Inf.*) (*od.* to be + *Ger.*); *außer der ~* at an unusual time, outside the usual hours; *seit der ~* since then (*od.* that time), ever since (then); *auf die ~ achten* keep an eye on the time (*od.* clock); *ich habe mich in der ~ geirrt* I got the time wrong; *j-n nach der ~ fragen* ask s.o. for the time; *um diese ~ kommt sie immer*: at this time; *bin ich sonst schon im Bett*: by this time; *morgen etc. um diese ~* this time tomorrow *etc.*; *von ~ zu ~* from time to time, now and then; *vor der ~* prematurely; *sterben: auch* before one's time; *zu bestimmten ~en* at certain (*od.* particular) times; *zu jeder ~* (at) any time; *zur gleichen/rechten ~* at the same/right time; *alles zu s-r ~* there's a time for everything; *beruhigend*: one thing after another; *wer nicht kommt zur rechten ~, muss nehmen od. essen, was übrig bleibt Sprichw.* first come, first served;

kommt ~, kommt Rat Sprichw. don't worry, it'll sort itself out; → *zurzeit,* 4. *Sport* time; *die ~ nehmen bei feststehender Spieldauer*: be (the) timekeeper; *bei Rennen*: time *s.th.*; *e-e gute/schlechte ~ fahren etc.* clock up a good/bad time; *über die ~ kommen Boxen*: go the distance; 5. *Ling.* tense; *zusammengesetzte ~* compound tense; 6. (*Zeitrechnung*): *im Jahre 400 vor unserer ~* in 400 BC; → *schinden* I 3, *sparen* I, *stehlen* I 2, *totschlagen etc.*

zeit *Präp.* (+ *Gen*): *~ s-s etc. Lebens gesamt*: his etc. whole life long; (*von da an*) for the rest of his etc. life; → *zeitlebens*

Zeit|abschnitt *m* period (of time); *~abstand* *m* interval; *in regelmäßigen Zeitabständen* at regular intervals, periodically; *~alter* *n* 1. age, era, epoch; *in unserem ~* in our day and age; *das goldene ~ auch fig.* the golden age; 2. *Geol.* period; *~angabe* *f* 1. exact date and time; (*Datum*) date; *ohne ~* undated; 2. *Ling.* adverbial expression of time; *~ansage* *f* time check; *Telef., Einrichtung*: speaking clock, *Am.* recorded time message; *~arbeit* *f Wirts.* temporary work; *~arbeitnehmer* *m, ~arbeitnehmerin* *f* temp *umg.*, temporary worker; *~arbeitsfirma* *f* temping agency; *~aufwand* *m* time involved (*od.* needed for *s.th.*); *e-n ~ von drei Wochen erfordern* require three weeks to complete (*od.* do *etc.*), take three weeks; *der ~ ist groß* it takes a lot of time, it's very time-consuming

zeit|aufwändig, *~aufwendig* *Adj.* time-consuming; *~bedingt* *Adj. Erscheinung, Perspektive, Vorstellung*: of the time (*od.* period), arising out of (*od.* conditioned by) the circumstances of the time (*od.* period), time-related; *Wirtsch., Abschreibung*: time-related; (*vorübergehend*) temporary

Zeit|begriff *m* concept of time; → *auch Zeitgefühl; ~bestimmung* *f* 1. timekeeping; 2. *Ling.* adverbial expression of time; *~bombe* *f* time bomb (*auch fig.*); *~dauer* *f* length of time; *e-s Geschehens*: duration; *~dokument* *n* contemporary document, document of the times; *historisch bedeutsam*: historic document; *~druck* *m; nur Sg.* (time) pressure; *unter ~ stehen* be pressed for time; *bei Abgabetermin*: be under pressure to meet a deadline; *~einheit* *f* unit of time; *~einteilung* *f* division of time; (*Zeitplan*) time plan

Zeiten|folge *f Ling.* sequence of tenses; *~wende* *f* 1. *allg.* turning point (in history), turn of an era; 2. (*das Jahr „0"*) the year 0, beginning of the Christian (*od.* Common) Era; *nach/vor der ~* after the year 0, in the Common Era / before the year 0, before Christ, before the Common Era

Zeit|erscheinung *f* sign of the times, characteristic (*od.* feature) of the time (*od.* period); (*Modeerscheinung*) vogue, (passing) fashion; *~ersparnis* *f* time saving; *~fahren* *n Sport* time trial; *kollektiv*: time trials *Pl.; ~faktor* *m; nur Sg.* time factor; *~fehler* *m Springreiten*: time fault; *~folge* *f* sequence, chronological order (*od.* sequence); *~form* *f Ling.* tense; *~frage* *f* 1. *nur Sg.* question of time; 2. (*aktuelle Frage*) current issue; *~geber* *m Tech.* timer

zeitgebunden *Adj.* → *zeitbedingt*

Zeit|gefühl *n*; *nur Sg.* sense of time; **~geist** *m*; *nur Sg.* zeitgeist, spirit of the times

zeitgemäß *Adj. attr.* up-to-date, *präd.* up to date, in keeping with the times; (*modern*) *auch* modern; (*aktuell*) current

Zeitgenosse *m*, **Zeitgenossin** *f* **1.** contemporary; **2.** *umg., oft pej.* (*Mitmensch*) type, individual; *ein seltsamer/unangenehmer ~* *auch* an odd/ awkward customer; **zeitgenössisch** *Adj.* contemporary; **~e Instrumente** *Mus.* period (*od.* historical) instruments

zeitgerecht *Adj.* **1.** appropriate to the present day, modern, up to date, *attr.* up-to-date; **2.** *österr., schw.* punctual

Zeit|geschehen *n*; *nur Sg.* current events *Pl.*; **~geschichte** *f*; *nur Sg.* contemporary history; **~geschmack** *m*; *nur Sg.* contemporary fashion (*od.* taste), taste of the times; **~gewinn** *m*; *nur Sg.* time saving, gain in time

zeitgleich I. *Adj.* simultaneous; **~ sein** *Läufer*: record the same time; **II.** *Adv.* simultaneously, at the same time

Zeit|gründe *Pl.*: *aus ~n* for lack of time, *förm.* due to prior commitments (*od.* engagements); **~guthaben** *n* gleitende Arbeitszeit: time credit, hours *Pl.* in hand

zeitig I. *Adj.* early; **II.** *Adv.* early; (*rechtzeitig*) in good time

zeitigen *v/t. geh.* (*bewirken*) produce, bring forth

Zeit|karte *f* season ticket; **~kolorit** *n geh.* atmosphere of the period; **~konto** *n Arbeit*: time sheet, record of hours worked and credit time; **~kraft** *f* employee on a fixed-term contract

Zeitkritik *f*; *nur Sg.* social criticism; **zeitkritisch** *Adj.* topical; critical of the times; (*sozialkritisch*) sociocritical

Zeit lang → **Zeit** 1

Zeitläufte *Pl. geh.* course *Sg.* of time

zeitlebens *Adv.* all one's life, one's whole life long

zeitlich I. *Adj.* **1.** *Faktor, Unterschied etc.*: time …; *Problem etc.*: time-related, … of time; *Aspekt etc.*: temporal; (*chronologisch*) chronological; *in großen/kleinen ~en Abständen* at long/ short intervals; **~e Berechnung** timing; *aus ~en Gründen* → **Zeitgründe**; **~e Reihenfolge** sequence; **2.** *bes. Reli.* (*vergänglich*) temporal; *das Zeitliche segnen altm. euph.* depart this life; *hum. auch Sache*: give up the ghost; **II.** *Adv.* timewise; (*chronologisch*) chronologically; **~ aufeinander abstimmen** synchronize; **~ befristet** limited, *attr.* limited-period …; *es ist ~ befristet* there's a time limit (on it), it's for a limited time *od.* period only; *ich schaffe es ~ nicht* (*werde damit nicht fertig*) I'm not going to make it in time; (*kann es nicht tun*) I can't fit it in (timewise), I haven't got time for it; *das passt mir ~ nicht* I can't fit it in (timewise), it's not (at) a very convenient time for me; *~ zusammenfallen* coincide, concur; **Zeitlichkeit** *f*; *nur Sg.*; *Philos.* existence in time, temporality; *Reli. auch* earthly life

Zeitlimit *n* time limit

zeitlos *Adj.* timeless; **Zeitlosigkeit** *f*; *nur Sg.* timelessness

Zeit|lupe *f*; *nur Sg. Film*: (*in*) **~** (in) slow motion, slo-mo *Am. umg.*; **~lupenaufnahme** *f* slow-motion shot; **~lupentempo** *n* slow motion; *im ~* in slow motion; *fig.* at a snail's pace;

~mangel *m*; *nur Sg.*: (*aus*) **~** (for) lack of time; **~maschine** *f* time machine; **~maß** *n* **1.** *Mus.* tempo; **2.** length (*od.* amount) of time; **~messer** *m*; *-s*, *-* chronometer; (*Uhr*) timer; *2.* *Sport* timekeeping

zeitnah *Adj.* **1.** topical; **~e Probleme** *auch* current issues; **2.** *Wirtsch.* prompt, within a short period of time

Zeit|nahme *f Sport* timekeeping; **~nehmer** *m*; *-s*, *-*, **~nehmerin** *f*; *-*, *-nen*; *Sport* timekeeper; **~not** *f*; *nur Sg.*: *in ~ sein* be pressed for time, be under time pressure, be running out of time; *in ~ geraten* start running out of time; **~plan** *m* timetable, schedule; **~planung** *f* scheduling

Zeitpunkt *m* time; (*Augenblick*) moment; *zu dem ~* at that (point in) time; *zum ~* (+ *Gen.*) at the time of; *zum jetzigen ~* at the present moment, at this point in time; *bis zu diesem ~* up until that point (in time); *e-n ~ festlegen* fix a time; *e-n geeigneten ~ abwarten* wait for the right moment; *du bist zum richtigen ~ gekommen* you've come just at the right time; *jetzt ist nicht der richtige ~* it's not the right moment

Zeit|raffer *m* **1.** *nur Sg.*; *Film*: time-lapse photography; *Video*: quick picture search; *im ~* speeded up; **2.** *Kamera*: time-lapse camera; **~rahmen** *m* time frame; *e-n ~ abstecken* establish a time frame

zeitraubend, Zeit raubend *Adj.* time-consuming

Zeit|raum *m* period (of time); *ein ~ von* a period of; *über e-n längeren ~ hinweg* for quite a long period; **~rechnung** *f* calendar; *nach christlicher ~* according to the Christian calendar; *vor unserer ~* (*abgek. v. u. Z.*) before the Common Era (*abgek.* BCE), BC, before Christ; *im Jahre 50 vor unserer ~* in (the year) 50 BC; *im ersten Jahrhundert unserer ~* in the first century AD; **~reise** *f* journey through time; *e-e ~ machen* travel through time; **~reisende** *m*, *f* time travel(l)er; **~schaltuhr** *f* timer, time switch

zeitschnellst… *Adj.*; *attr.*; *Sport* … with the fastest time

Zeitschrift *f* magazine; *wissenschaftlich*: periodical, journal

Zeitschriften|aufsatz *m* (magazine *bzw.* journal) article; **~lesesaal** *m* periodicals room; **~verlag** *m* magazine publisher; **~verleger** *m*, **~verlegerin** *f* magazine publisher; **~werber** *m*, **~werberin** *f* door-to-door magazine salesperson

Zeit|soldat *m* short-service volunteer; **~spanne** *f* period (of time)

zeitsparend, Zeit sparend *Adj.* time-saving

Zeit|sprung *m* leap in time; *e-n ~ machen* leap forward (*bzw.* back[ward]) in time; **~strafe** *f Sport* time penalty; **~strömung** *f* prevailing trend; **~stück** *n Theat.* period play; **~studien** *Pl.* time (and motion) studies; **~tafel** *f* chronological table; **~takt** *m* **1.** *Telef.* time unit; **2.** *in welchem ~ verkehren die Busse?* how often do the bus(s)es run?; **~überschreitung** *f Sport* exceeding the time limit; **~umstände** *Pl.* prevailing circumstances; **~umstellung** *f* **1.** *der Uhren*: changeover to summer (*bzw.* winter, *Am.* daylight-saving [*bzw.* standard]) time, putting the clocks forward *bzw.* back; **2.** *bei*

Reisen: *die ~ macht mir zu schaffen* it takes me a while to get used to being in a different time zone, the time difference takes some getting used to; *weitS.* I suffer from jet lag; *momentan*: *auch* I'm feeling jet-lagged

Zeitung *f* (news)paper; *amtliche*: gazette; (*die*) **~ lesen** read the paper(s); *in der ~ steht* the paper says; *es steht in der ~* it's in the paper(s); *bei e-r ~ arbeiten* work for a newspaper; *e-e Anzeige in die ~ setzen* place (*od.* put) an ad in the papers; *ich möchte nicht in die ~ kommen* I don't want to get into the (news)papers; **~lesen** *n* reading the (news)paper(s); *ich möchte beim ~ nicht gestört werden* I don't want to be disturbed while I'm reading the paper(s)

Zeitungs|abonnement *n* newspaper subscription; **~annonce** *f*, **~anzeige** *f* (newspaper) advertisement (*od.* ad, *Brit. auch* advert), advertisement *etc.* in the (*od.* a) newspaper; **~artikel** *m* newspaper article; (*aktueller Bericht*) news report; **~ausschnitt** *m* newspaper cutting (*od.* clipping); **~austräger** *m*, **~austrägerin** *f männlich*: paper boy; paper man; *weiblich*: paper girl; paper woman; *neutral*: newspaper deliverer; **~beilage** *f* newspaper supplement; **~bericht** *m* newspaper report; **~ente** *f* hoax, canard; **~frau** *f* **1.** paper woman; **2.** → **Zeitungshändler**, **~händler** *m*, **~händlerin** *f* newsagent, *Am.* news dealer; **~inserat** *n* advertisement, ad, *Brit. auch* advert; **~jargon** *m* journalese; **~junge** *m* paper boy; **~korrespondent** *m*, **~korrespondentin** *f* newspaper (*od.* press) correspondent; **~leser** *m*, **~leserin** *f* newspaper reader; **~mann** *m*; *Pl. -leute* **1.** (*Austräger*) paper man; **2.** → **Zeitungshändler**, **~meldung** *f* announcement in a (*od.* the) newspaper; **~notiz** *f* press item; **~papier** *n* zum Einwickeln *etc.*: newspaper; *zum Bedrucken*: newsprint; **~redakteur** *m*, **~redakteurin** *f* newspaper editor; **~ständer** *m* magazine rack; **~träger** *m*, **~trägerin** *f* → **Zeitungsausträger**, **~verkäufer** *m*, **~verkäuferin** *f* news vendor; **~verlag** *m* newspaper publisher; **~verleger** *m*, **~verlegerin** *f* newspaper publisher; **~wesen** *n* the press; **~wissenschaft** *f* journalism

Zeit|unterschied *m* time difference; **~verlust** *m* loss of time, delay; **~verschiebung** *f* time shift; *Flug. etc.* time lag; → **Zeitunterschied**; **~verschwendung** *f*: **~ sein** be a waste of time

zeitversetzt I. *Adj.*: **~e Übertragung** recorded broadcast; **II.** *Adv.*: *das Spiel wird ~ übertragen* the game was recorded earlier (today)

Zeit|vertrag *m* fixed-term contract; **~vertreib** *m*; *-(e)s*, *-e* pastime; *zum ~* to pass the time; **~vorgabe** *f* **1.** time (allowance); **~: 20 Minuten** time allowed: 20 minutes; **2.** *Sport* head start

zeitweilig I. *Adj.* (*vorübergehend*) temporary; (*gelegentlich*) intermittent; **II.** *Adv.* → **zeitweise**

zeitweise *Adv.* occasionally, from time to time, now and then

Zeit|wert *m Wirts.* current value; **~wort** *n*; *Pl. -wörter*; *Ling.* verb; **~zeichen** *n Radio*: time signal; **~zeuge** *m*, **~zeugin** *f* contemporary witness (of events), witness of the times; **~zone** *f* time zone; **~zünder** *m* time fuse

zelebrieren *v/t.* **1.** *kath.* (*Messe*) celebrate; **2.** *geh., oft hum.* make a big thing of *s.th.*

Zelebrität *f*; -, *-en*; *geh.* celebrity

Zell|atmung *f Bio.* vesicular breathing; **~bau** *m*; *nur Sg.*; *Bio.* cell structure; **~bildung** *f Bio.* cell formation

Zelle *f*; -, *-n* **1.** *Bio.* cell; *die kleinen grauen ~n umg., hum.* the little grey (*Am.* gray) cells; **2.** *Telef.* phone box (*Am.* booth); **3.** *im Gefängnis, Kloster*: cell; **4.** *Flug.* airframe; **5.** *Etech., von Batterie etc.*: cell; **6.** *bes. Pol.* (*Gruppe*) cell

zellenförmig *adj* cellular

Zellengenosse *m*, **Zellengenossin** *f* cell mate

Zell|gewebe *n Bio.* cellular tissue; **~gift** *n Med.* cytotoxin; **~kern** *m Bio.* cell nucleus; **~kultur** *f* cell culture; **~membran** *f Bio.* cell membrane

Zellophan *n* → *Cellophan*

Zellplasma *n Bio.* cytoplasm

Zellstoff *m* **1.** *Substanz*: cellulose; *Papier*: pulp; **2.** *Material*: absorbent paper

Zellteilung *f Bio.* cell division, binary fission

Zelltherapie *f*, **Zellulartherapie** *f*; *nur Sg.*; *Med.* cell(ular) therapy

Zellulitis *f*, -, *Zellulitiden*; *Med.* cellulitis

Zelluloid *n*; -(e)s, *kein Pl.*; *Chem.* celluloid; *auf ~ bannen umg.* preserve on celluloid

Zellulose *f*; -, *-n*; *Chem.* cellulose, wood pulp

Zell|wachstum *n Bio.* cell growth; **~wand** *f Bio.* cell wall; **~wolle** *f aus Zellulose*: rayon staple; **~wucherung** *f Bio., Med.* cell proliferation

Zelot *m*; *-en*, *-en* **1.** *hist.* Zealot; **2.** *geh. fig.* zealot, fanatic; **Zelotismus** *m*; -, *kein Pl.*; *geh. fig.* zealotry

Zelt *n*; *-(e)s*, *-e* **1.** tent; *für Fest etc.*: *auch* marquee; *von Indianern*: wigwam, te(e)pee, *Am. auch* lodge; *von Zirkus*: tent, *the* big top; *ein ~ aufbauen od. aufschlagen / abbauen od. abbrechen* put up (*od.* pitch) / take down (*od.* strike) a tent; *die ~e abbrechen* strike camp; *s-e ~e aufschlagen/ abbrechen fig.* settle down / move on; **2.** *poet. des Himmels etc.*: canopy; **~bahn** *f* tent square; (*Plane*) tarpaulin; **~dach** *n* tent roof; *Archit.* tented roof

zelten *v/i.* camp; *im Garten ~* camp out in the garden

Zelten *n*; *-s*, *kein Pl.* camping; *~ verboten* no camping

Zelter *m*; *-s*, -, **~in** *f*; *-*, *-nen* camper

Zelt|lager *n* camp; **~leinwand** *f*; *nur Sg.* canvas

Zelt|mast *m* tent post; **~pflock** *m* tent peg; **~plane** *f* tarpaulin; **~platz** *m* campsite, camping site, *Am. auch* campground; **~stadt** *f* tent city; **~stange** *f*, **~stock** *m* tent pole

Zement *m*; *-(e)s*, *-e* cement; **~boden** *m* concrete floor

zementieren *v/t.* **1.** cement; **2.** *geh. fig.* cement; *Wirts.* solidify; *dadurch werden die bestehenden Vorurteile zementiert* this reinforces (*od.* hardens) existing prejudices; **3.** *Metall.* (*Stahl*) carburize; **Zementierung** *f* cementing; *fig.* reinforcement, hardening

Zement|platz *m Tennis*: hard (*od.* concrete) court; **~werk** *n* cement factory

Zen *n*; *-(s)*, *kein Pl.*; *Reli.* Zen; **~Buddhismus** *m* Zen Buddhism

Zenit *m*; *-(e)s*, *kein Pl.* zenith; *geh. fig. auch* apex (*Pl.* apexes *od.* apices); *im ~ stehen* be at (*od.* have reached) its

(*fig. auch* one's) zenith

zensieren *v/t.* **1.** (*Bücher, Filme etc.*) censor; **2.** (*benoten*) mark, *bes. Am.* grade; **Zensor** *m*; *-s*, *-en*; *hist. und. fig.* censor; **Zensur** *f*; -, *-en* **1.** *nur Sg.*; *Kontrolle*: censorship; *der ~ unterliegen* be subject to censorship; *der ~ zum Opfer fallen* fall victim to the censors; **2.** *nur Sg.*; *Behörde*: censor; **3.** *Päd.* mark, *bes. Am.* grade; *von j-m gute/schlechte ~en bekommen fig.* get good/bad marks (*bes. Am.* grades) from s.o.; **Zensurstelle** *f* censor's office

Zensus *m*; -, - **1.** *Pol., fachspr.* (*Volkszählung*) census; **2.** *hist.* census, property qualification; **~wahlrecht** *n hist., Pol.* property qualification (in elections)

Zentaur *m*; *-en*, *-en*; *Myth.* centaur

Zentiliter *m*, *n* centilit|re (*Am.* -er)

Zentimeter *m*, *n* centimet|re (*Am.* -er)

zentimeter|dick *Adj.* one-centimet|re (*Am.* -er) -thick; *etwa* half-inch-thick

Zentimetermaß *n* tape measure

Zentner *m*; *-s*, - **1.** (metric) hundredweight, 50 kilograms; **2.** *österr., schw.* 100 kilograms; **~last** *f fig.* heavy burden; *e-e ~ fiel mir vom Herzen* that was a load off my mind

zentner|schwer I. *Adj.*: *~e Last →* *Zentnerlast*, *~e Säcke etc.* sacks etc. weighing a hundredweight and more; *das ist ja ~! umg. fig.* this thing weighs a ton; **II.** *Adv. fig.*: *j-m ~ auf der Seele liegen* weigh heavily on s.o.('s mind); **~weise** *Adv. etwa* by the hundredweight

zentral I. *Adj.* central; *fig. auch* crucial; *Problem: auch* pivotal; **~es Thema** *fig.* central (*od.* main) issue; **II.** *Adv.* centrally; *~ gelegen* very central; *~ gelenkt Pol.* centrally controlled; *sehr ~ wohnen* live very centrally, live right in the cent|re (*Am.* -er) (of town)

zentral... *im Adj.* central; **Zentral...** *im Subst.* central

Zentral|abitur *n* nationwide uniform A-level (*Am.* highschool) school-leaving examinations; **~afrika** (*n*); *Geog.* Central Africa; **Zentralbank** *f* central bank

zentralbeheizt *Adj.* centrally heated

Zentrale *f*; -, *-n* **1.** *Bank, Firma etc.*: head office; *Partei, Polizei, Taxi etc.*: headquarters *Pl.* (*auch V. im Sg.*); **2.** *Tech.* control room; *Telef.* (telephone) exchange; *in e-r Firma*: switchboard; **3.** *fig.* (*Mittelpunkt*) cent|re (*Am.* -er); **4.** *Math.* straight line joining the cent|res (*Am.* -ers) of two circles

Zentral|einheit *f Computer*: central processing unit, CPU; **~gestirn** *n Astron.* central star; **~gewalt** *f* central(ized) power; **~heizung** *f* central heating

zentralisieren *v/t.* centralize; **Zentralisierung** *f* centralization

Zentralismus *m*; -, *kein Pl.*; *Pol.* centralism; **zentralistisch** *Adj.* centralist(ic)

Zentral|komitee *n* (*abgek.* ZK) central committee; **~kraft** *f Phys.* zentrifugal: centrifugal force; *zentripetal* centripetal force; **~nervensystem** *n Anat.* central nervous system; **~organ** *n Pol.* main (official) organ; **~problem** *n* main problem; **~rat** *m* central council; **~rechner** *m Computer*: mainframe computer; **~speicher** *m Computer*: central memory; **~stelle** *f →* *Zentrale*; **~verband** *m* central association; **~ver-**

~riegelung *f Mot.* central locking; **~verwaltung** *f* central administration

zentrieren *v/t.* centre, *Am.* center; **Zentrierung** *f* centring, *Am.* centering

zentrifugal *Adj. Phys.* centrifugal; **Zentrifugalkraft** *f*; *nur Sg.*; *Phys.* centrifugal force; **Zentrifuge** *f*; -, *-n* centrifuge

zentripetal *Adj. Phys., Bio.* centripetal; **Zentripetalkraft** *f*; *nur Sg.*; *Phys.* centripetal force

zentrisch I. *Adj.* (con)centric; **II.** *Adv.* (con)centrically

Zentrum *n*; *-s*, *Zentren* **1.** cent|re (*Am.* -er); *e-s Hurrikans: auch* eye; *das ~ e-r Stadt*: the town (*e-r Großstadt*: city) cent|re (*Am.* -er), *Am. auch* downtown (area); *im ~ des Interesses stehen* be the cent|re (*Am.* -er) (*od.* focus) of attention; **2.** *Pol., hist.* → *Zentrumspartei*; **Zentrumspartei** *f*; *nur Sg.*; *Pol., hist.* Cent|re (*Am.* -er) Party

Zenturie *f*; -, *-n*; *hist.* century; **Zenturio** *m*; *-s*, *-nen* centurion

Zeppelin *m*; *-s*, *-e*; *Flug.* zeppelin

Zepter *m*, *n*; *-s*, - scept|re (*Am.* -er); *das ~ schwingen fig. hum.* wield power, rule the roost *umg.*

zerbeißen *v/t.* (*unreg.*) *in Stücke*: chew up; (*Bonbon, Keks etc.*) crunch; (*durchbeißen*) bite through; *von Mücken zerbissen werden* be bitten all over by midges

zerbersten *v/i.* (*unreg.*) burst; *Glas*: shatter

Zerberus *m*; -, *-se* **1.** *nur Sg.*; *Myth.* Cerberus; **2.** *fig. hum. etwa* watchdog, bouncer, *a grim and surly porter, concierge etc.*

zerbeult *Adj.* battered; *Metall: auch* dented

zerbomben *v/t.* flatten, blitz, destroy (by bombing); **zerbombt I.** *P.P.* → *zerbomben*; **II.** *Adj.* bombed, bomb-shattered

zerbrechen (*unreg.*) **I.** *v/t.* (*hat zerbrochen*) **1.** break (in *od.* to pieces); (*Glas, Porzellan*) *auch* shatter; **2.** *fig.* (*Widerstand etc.*) smash; *sich* (*Dat.*) *den Kopf ~* rack one's brains (*über + Akk.* over); **II.** *v/i.* (*ist*) **1.** break (in *od.* to pieces); *Glas, Porzellan*: shatter; **2.** *fig. Person*: be crushed (*od.* broken) (*an + Dat.* by); *Freundschaft*: break up; **zerbrechlich** *Adj.* **1.** breakable; *auch Porzellan etc.*: fragile; *„Vorsicht, ~!"* fragile, handle with care; **2.** *fig. Person, Gesundheit*: delicate; *stärker*: fragile; (*~ gebaut*) delicately built; *Frau: auch* dainty; **Zerbrechlichkeit** *f*; *nur Sg.* fragility

zerbröckeln, **zerbröseln** *v/t.* (*hat*) *und v/i.* (*ist*) crumble (*auch fig.*)

zerdeppern *v/t. umg.* smash

zerdrücken *v/t.* **1.** squash; *stärker*: crush; (*Kartoffeln*) mash; **2.** (*Kleider*) crumple, crease, *bes. Am.* wrinkle

Zerealien *Pl.* cereals

zerebral *Adj.* cerebral

Zeremonie *f*; -, *-n* ceremony; *fig. auch* ritual; **zeremoniell** *Adj. geh.* ceremonial, formal; **Zeremoniell** *n*; *-s*, *-e*; *geh.* ceremonial; *fig. auch* ritual; **Zeremonienmeister** *m* master of ceremonies

zerfahren *Adj.* **1.** *Weg*: rutted; **2.** *Person*: (*zerstreut*) absent-minded, scatterbrained; **Zerfahrenheit** *f*; *nur Sg.*; (*Zerstreutheit*) absent-mindedness

Zerfall *m* **1.** *nur Sg.*; *von Gebäuden etc.*: ruin, decay; (*Auflösung*) decomposition (*auch Chem.*); **2.** *Phys.*

(atomic) disintegration; **3.** *nur Sg.*; *fig. der Kultur etc.*: decline; *e-s Reichs etc.*: *auch* collapse

zerfallen[1] *v/i.* (*unreg.*) **1.** fall apart (*od.* to pieces); *in s-e Bestandteile*: disintegrate; *Gebäude*: collapse, crumble; (*sich auflösen*) decompose (*auch Chem.*); *in s-e Bestandteile ~* break down into its component parts; *zu Staub ~* crumble to dust; **2.** *Phys.* disintegrate; **3.** *fig. Reich etc.*: decline, decay, collapse; **4.** *fig.*: *~ in* (+ *Akk.*) be divided into, fall into

zerfallen[2] *Adj.* **1.** *Schloss*: ruined; *Haus*: *attr.* tumbledown ...; *~ sein auch* be in ruins, be in a state of decay; **2.** *fig.*: *mit j-m ~ sein* have fallen out with s.o.

Zerfalls|erscheinung *f* sign of decay; **~produkt** *n* decomposition product; *Kernphysik*: daughter product; **~prozess** *m* process of disintegration (*od.* decay) (*auch fig.*); **~zeit** *f Kernphysik*: decay period (*od.* time)

zerfasern *I. v/t.* (*hat zerfasert*) fray; **II.** *v/i.* (*ist*) fray

zerfetzen *v/t.* tear in(to) pieces (*auch fig.*); *Geschoss*: *auch* mangle; *in kleine Stücke*: shred; **zerfetzt I.** *P.P.* → **zerfetzen**; **II.** *Adj. Kleidung*: tattered; *Bein etc.*: mangled, torn to shreds *umg.*

zerfled(d)ern *v/t.* tatter

zerfleischen I. *v/t.* tear to pieces; *fig., gegenseitig*: tear each other apart; **II.** *v/refl. geh. fig.* torment o.s.

zerfließen *v/i.* (*unreg.*) **1.** melt, dissolve; *Farbe, Tinte*: run; **2.** *fig. Glück, Reichtum etc.*: melt away, evaporate; *Traum*: come to nothing; **~de Konturen** blurred contours; *vor Mitleid etc. ~* melt with pity *etc.*

zerfranst *Adj.* frayed

zerfressen *v/t.* (*unreg.*) *Motten, Rost etc.*: eat away (at); *Chem.* corrode; *fig. Eifersucht etc.*: gnaw (at); *von Motten~* moth-eaten

zerfurcht *Adj.* furrowed (*auch fig.*)

zergehen *v/i.* (*unreg.*) dissolve; *auch fig.* melt; *auf der Zunge ~ Braten etc.*: melt in one's mouth; *das muss man sich mal auf der Zunge ~ lassen fig.* this is something to be really savo(u)red

zergliedern *v/t.* **1.** (*analysieren*) analy|se (*Am.* -ze) (*auch Ling.*); **2.** (*Pflanze, Tier, Leichnam*) dissect; **3.** (*Staat*) dismember; **Zergliederung** *f* **1.** (*Analyse*) analysis (*auch Ling.*); **2.** *e-r Pflanze, e-s Tiers, Leichnams*: dissection; **3.** *e-s Staats*: dismemberment

zerhacken *v/t.* chop (up); (*Fleisch*) *ganz fein*: mince, *bes. Am.* grind

zerhauen *v/t.* (*unreg.*) **1.** chop to pieces; (*Knoten*) cut through; **2.** *umg.* (*kaputtmachen*) break, smash

zerkauen *v/t.* chew (well); *der Hund hat die Pantoffeln zerkaut* the dog has chewed up the slippers

zerkleinern *v/t.* reduce to small pieces, fragment; (*zerschneiden*) cut up small (*od.* into small pieces); (*zerhacken*) chop (up); (*Stein etc.*) crush; (*zermahlen*) grind; **Zerkleinerung** *f; nur Sg.* fragmentation; (*Zerschneiden*) cutting-up; (*Zerhacken*) chopping-up; (*e-s Steins etc.*) crushing; (*Zermahlung*) grinding

zerklüftet *Adj.* cleft; *Berge, Landschaft*: rugged; *Med., Mandeln*: fissured

zerknautschen *v/t. umg.* crumple, squash (up)

zerknirscht *Adj.* smitten with remorse; **~es Gesicht** hangdog look; **Zerknirschtheit** *f; nur Sg.*, **Zerknirschung** *f; nur Sg.* remorse(fulness), contrition

zerknittern *v/t.* (*hat zerknittert*) *und v/i.* (*ist*) crumple, crease; **zerknittert I.** *P.P.* → **zerknittern**; **II.** *Adj.* **1.** crumpled, creased; **2.** *fig. Gesicht*: (*faltig*) wrinkled; *umg. Person*: (*übernächtigt*) bleary-eyed; (*niedergeschlagen*) crushed, crestfallen

zerknüllen *v/t.* crumple up, screw up, scrunch up *umg.*

zerkochen I. *v/t.* (*hat zerkocht*) overcook, cook to pieces *umg.*; **II.** *v/i.* (*ist*) overcook

zerkratzen *v/t.* (*hat zerkratzt*) scratch (to pieces)

zerkrümeln *v/t.* (*hat*) *und v/i.* (*ist*) crumble

zerlassen *v/t.* (*unreg.*); *Gastr.* melt (in the pan); **~e Butter** melted butter

zerlaufen *v/i.* (*unreg.*) melt, dissolve; *Farbe, Tinte*: run

zerlegbar *Adj. Tech.* easily dismantled; *Möbel etc.*: *auch attr.* knock-down ...; *Math.* divisible; *Ling.* analysable, *Am.* analyzable; *Chem.* decomposable; **zerlegen** *v/t.* **1.** take apart (*od.* to pieces); *Tech. auch* dismantle, disassemble; (*zerschneiden*) cut up; (*Braten*) carve; (*Leiche*) dissect; *etw. in s-e Einzelteile ~* reduce s.th. to (*od.* break s.th. down into) its component parts, take s.th. to pieces; *Motor*: strip s.th. (down); **2.** *Chem.* decompose; **3.** *Math.* reduce; **4.** *Opt.* (*Lichtstrahl*) disperse; **5.** *fig.* analy|se (*Am.* -ze) (*auch Ling.*), dissect; (*Theorie etc.*) *auch* break down; **Zerlegung** *f* **1.** taking apart (*od.* to pieces); *Tech. auch* dismantling, disassembly; (*Zerschneiden*) cutting-up; (*e-s Bratens*) carving; *Bio.* dissection; (*e-s Motors*) stripping(-down); **2.** *Chem.* decomposition; **3.** *Math.* reduction

zerlesen *Adj. Buch*: well-thumbed, dog-eared

zerlumpt I. *Adj.* ragged; *Kleidung*: *auch* tattered; **~es Kind** ragamuffin; **II.** *Adv.*: *~ herumlaufen* go around in rags (and tatters)

zermahlen *v/t.* (*unreg.*) grind

zermalmen *v/t.* crush (*auch fig.*)

zermanschen *v/t. umg.* squash; *mit Gabel*: mash up

zermartern *v/t.*: *sich* (*Dat.*) *den Kopf od. das Hirn ~* rack one's brains

zermatschen → **zermanschen**

zermürben *v/t.* wear down; **zermürbend I.** *Part. Präs.* → **zermürben**; **II.** *Adj.* wearing; *stärker*: nerve-racking; **Zermürbung** *f Mil.* attrition; **Zermürbungskrieg** *m* war of attrition; **Zermürbungstaktik** *f* tactics *Pl.* of attrition

zernagen *v/t.* gnaw to pieces; *allmählich*: *auch* gnaw away at

zernarbt *Adj.* scarred, covered in scars; *Gesicht*: *auch* pitted with scars; *durch Pocken*: *auch* pockmarked

Zerobond ['ze:ro-] *m Fin.* zero-coupon bond

zerpfeifen *v/t.* (*unreg.*); *Sport umg.*: *der Schiri hat das Spiel zerpfiffen* the ref ruined the game by blowing up too often, the ref spoilt the game by overusing his whistle

zerpflücken *v/t.* **1.** (*Blume*) pull the petals off; (*Stück Papier, Stoff*) pull to pieces; (*Salat*) take apart; **2.** *fig.* (*kritisieren*) pull to pieces, tear to pieces

(*od.* shreds) *umg.*

zerplatzen *v/i.* (*ist zerplatzt*) **1.** burst; *stärker*: explode; *e-e Tüte ~ lassen* burst a paper bag; **2.** *fig. Illusion, Traum etc.*: be destroyed; *vor Wut etc. ~* burst (*od.* explode) with anger *etc.*

zerquetschen *v/t.* crush, squash; (*Kartoffeln*) mash; *50 Euro und ein paar Zerquetschte* 50 euros and a bit (*Am.* and some change), just over 50 euros

zerraufen *v/t.* (*Haar*) ruffle, tousle

Zerrbild *n* **1.** distorted image; **2.** *fig.* distortion, distorted view (*od.* picture); (*Karikatur*) caricature, travesty

zerreden *v/t.* (*Thema, Gedicht*) flog s.th. to death

zerreiben *v/t.* (*unreg.*) **I.** *v/t.* **1.** crush; *zu Pulver*: grind, pulverize; *zwischen den Fingern ~* crush with one's fingers; **2.** *fig.* (*vernichten*) wipe out; **II.** *v/refl. fig., vor Arbeit, Kummer*: wear o.s. down, wear o.s. to a frazzle *umg.* (*vor* + *Dat.* with)

zerreißen (*unreg.*) **I.** *v/t.* (*hat zerrissen*) **1.** *unabsichtlich*: tear; *absichtlich*: tear up; *in Stücke*: tear to pieces; (*Faden, Fesseln etc.*) break; (*j-n*) *Bombe*: blow to pieces; **2.** *fig.*: *ein Schuss zerriss die Stille* the silence was rent by (the sound of) a shot; *es zerreißt mir das Herz* it breaks my heart; (*in der Luft*) *~ umg.* (*kritisieren*) tear s.th. *od.* s.o. to shreds; *es hätte ihn vor Neid fast zerrissen* he was almost bursting with envy; → *Maul* 2; **II.** *v/i.* (*ist*) tear; *Faden, Nebel, Wolken*: break; *Sack, Schlauch*: burst; *s-e Nerven waren zum Zerreißen gespannt fig.* his nerves were strained almost to breaking point; **III.** *v/refl.* (*hat*); *umg.* go to no end of trouble, bend over backwards; *sich für etw. ~* put everything one has (got) into s.th.; *sie zerriss sich fast, um ...* she nearly bust(ed *Am.*) a gut (*od.* wore herself out) (trying) to ..., she bent over backwards to ...; *ich kann mich doch nicht ~!* I can't be in two places at once; → *zerrissen*; **zerreißfest** *Adj. Tech.* tear-resistant; **Zerreißfestigkeit** *f; nur Sg.* tear-resistance; **Zerreißprobe** *f* **1.** *Tech.* tension test; **2.** *fig.* test of endurance, ordeal, real test

zerren I. *v/t.* **1.** (*schleppen*) drag; **2.** *Med.*: *sich* (*Dat.*) *e-n Muskel / e-e Sehne ~* pull a muscle/tendon; **3.** *fig.*: *vor Gericht ~* haul before a court; *etw. an die Öffentlichkeit ~* drag s.th. into the open, put the public spotlight on s.th.; **II.** *v/i.*: *~ an* (+ *Dat.*) tug (*od.* pull) at; *an der Leine ~* strain at the leash, pull at the lead (*od.* leash); *an den Nerven ~ fig.* be a strain on one's nerves

zerrinnen *v/i.* (*unreg.*); *geh.* **1.** melt away; **2.** *fig.* vanish, fade; *Geld*: disappear; *Pläne*: come to nothing; *Zeit, Jahre*: slip away (*od.* by)

zerrissen I. *P.P.* → **zerreißen**; **II.** *Adj.* torn (*auch fig. Person, Land etc.*); *Kleider*: *auch* tattered; *Schuhe*: battered; **Zerrissenheit** *f; nur Sg.*: (*innere*) *~* inner conflict

Zerrspiegel *m auch fig.* distorting mirror

Zerrung *f Med.* pulled muscle (*od.* tendon *etc.*)

zerrupfen *v/t.* → **zerpflücken**; **zerrupft aussehen** *Kleid, Pflanze*: look tattered and torn; *Vogel*: look bedraggled; *Person*: look rumpled and dishevel(l)ed

zerrütten *v/t.* (*Verhältnisse, Ordnung*

etc.) destroy, ruin, wreck; (*Ehe*) *auch* break up; (*Gesundheit, Nerven etc.*) ruin, wreck; *j-n körperlich/seelisch ~* make s.o. a physical/nervous wreck; **zerrüttet I.** *P.P.* → **zerrütten**; **II.** *Adj. Ehe, Zuhause:* broken; *Nerven:* shattered; **Zerrüttung** *f; nur Sg.* **1.** *Vorgang:* destruction, wrecking; (*e-r Ehe*) breakdown; (*der Gesundheit, Nerven etc.*) ruining; **2.** *Zustand:* collapse, breakdown; **Zerrüttungsprinzip** *n Jur.* principle of (irretrievable) matrimonial breakdown

zersägen *v/t.* saw up, saw into pieces

zerschellen *v/i.* be smashed (to pieces); *Flugzeug:* crash; *Schiff:* be wrecked; *am Boden ~* crash to the floor, smash to pieces on the floor; *an e-m Berg ~ Flug.* crash into a mountainside; *an den Klippen ~ Naut.* be smashed (to pieces) against the rocks

zerschießen *v/t.* (*unreg.*) shoot to pieces; (*durchlöchern*) riddle with bullets

zerschlagen (*unreg.*) **I.** *v/t.* **1.** smash (to pieces); **2.** *fig.* (*Drogenring etc.*) smash; **II.** *v/refl.* come to nothing, go up in smoke *umg.*; *Hoffnungen: auch* be shattered; **III.** *Adj. fig. Person:* shattered; **Zerschlagenheit** *f; nur Sg.* total exhaustion; **Zerschlagung** *f; nur Sg.* smashing, destruction

zerschlissen *Adj. attr.* worn-out, *präd.* worn out; threadbare

zerschmelzen *v/i.* (*unreg.*) melt away; *Butter:* melt; *in Mitleid etc. ~ fig.* melt with pity *etc.*

zerschmettern *v/t.* smash (to pieces), shatter; (*zermalmen*) crush, flatten; *am Boden zerschmettert umg. fig.* absolutely crushed

zerschneiden *v/t.* (*unreg.*); (*Faden etc.*) cut (in two); *in Stücke:* cut up; *in Scheiben:* slice; *in Schnitzel:* shred; (*Braten*) carve; *Reifen:* slash

zerschnippeln *v/t. umg.* cut up into little pieces

zerschrammen *v/t.* (*Beine etc.*) scrape; (*Möbel etc.*) scratch; **zerschrammt I.** *P.P.* → **zerschrammen**; **II.** *Adj. Beine etc.:* covered in cuts and scrapes; *Möbel etc.:* scratched, full of scratches

zerschunden *Adj.* (badly) grazed; (*geschrammt*) scratched, covered in scratches

zersetzen I. *v/t.* **1.** decompose, disintegrate; *Säure:* corrode; **2.** *fig. moralisch etc.:* corrupt, undermine, subvert; *~de Propaganda* subversive propaganda; **II.** *v/refl.* decompose, disintegrate; *durch Säure:* corrode; **Zersetzung** *f* **1.** decomposition, disintegration; **2.** *fig.* corruption; *Pol.* subversion **Zersetzungs|erscheinung** *f* sign of decay; *~produkt* *n* product of decomposition; *~prozess m* (process of) decay (*od.* decomposition); *fig.* corruption, subversion

zersiedeln *v/t.* blight by overdevelopment; **Zersied(e)lung** *f* urban sprawl

zerspalten *v/t.* (*auch unreg.*) cleave, split; **Zerspaltung** *f* splitting(-up)

zerspanen *v/t.* machine; *~de Bearbeitung* machining

zersplittern *v/t.* (*hat zersplittert*) *und v/i.* (*ist*) split; (*auch unreg. Gruppe etc.*); (*Glas*) shatter; *s-e Kräfte ~* fritter away one's energies; *e-e in viele Grüppchen zersplitterte Partei* a fragmented party that is little more than a collection of splinter groups; **Zersplitterung** *f* splitting; splintering; (*von Glas*) shattering; →

zersplittern **zersprengen** *v/t.* **1.** (*Ketten etc.*) burst; *durch Explosion:* blow apart; **2.** (*Menschenmenge*) disperse, scatter, break up; *Mil.* rout

zerspringen *v/i.* (*unreg.*) **1.** crack; *völlig:* shatter; **2.** *geh. Saite:* break; **3.** *fig.: mir zerspringt der Kopf* (*vor Schmerzen*) I've got a splitting headache; *ihr zersprang fast das Herz vor Freude geh.* her heart was almost bursting with joy

zerstampfen *v/t.* crush; *im Mörser:* pound; (*Kartoffeln*) mash; *mit Füßen:* trample on

zerstäuben *v/t.* spray; **Zerstäuber** *m; -s, -* spray; *auch für Parfüm:* atomizer

zerstechen *v/t.* (*unreg.*) **1.** (*Ballon, Reifen etc.*) puncture; **2.** *Nessel, Wespe etc.:* sting (all over); *Mücke:* bite (all over); *Dornen, Nadeln:* prick (all over); *ganz zerstochen* covered in (insect) bites (*od.* wasp stings *etc.*), bitten (*od.* stung) to pieces *umg.*

zerstieben *v/i.* (*unreg.*) *geh.* **1.** *Wasser etc.:* spray (in all directions); **2.** *Gruppe:* disperse, scatter

zerstörbar *Adj.* destructible; **zerstören** *v/t.* **1.** destroy; (*Haus*) *auch* demolish; **2.** (*Landschaft etc.*) spoil, ruin; (*vernichten*) destroy; **3.** (*Hoffnungen, Existenz etc.*) destroy; (*Gesundheit, Ehe etc.*) ruin, wreck; → **Boden 12**; **Zerstörer** *m; -s, -; Mil., Naut.* destroyer; **zerstörerisch** *Adj.* destructive; **Zerstörung** *f* destruction; ruin; *des Krieges:* devastation, ravages *Pl.* **Zerstörungs|kraft** *f e-r Bombe etc.:* destructive force; *~lust f; nur Sg.* delight in destruction; (*Wandalismus*) vandalism; *~trieb m; nur Sg.* destructive urge, destructiveness; *~werk n; nur Sg.* work of destruction; *~wut f* destructive rage (*od.* fury *od.* frenzy); *auf Gegenstände ausgerichtet:* vandalism

zerstoßen *v/t.* (*unreg.*) crush; *im Mörser:* pound

Zerstrahlung *f Kernphysik:* annihilation (of matter)

zerstreiten *v/refl.* (*unreg.*) fall out (with each other); *sich mit j-m ~* fall out with s.o.

zerstreuen I. *v/t.* **1.** scatter; (*Menschen*) disperse; (*Licht*) *auch* diffuse; **2.** *fig.* (*Bedenken, Argwohn etc.*) dispel, dissipate; **3.** *fig.* (*ablenken*) divert, amuse; *j-n ~ auch* take s.o.'s mind off things; **II.** *v/refl.* **1.** *Menge:* disperse, scatter, break up; **2.** (*sich ablenken*) take one's mind off things; *sich mit etw. ~ auch* occupy o.s. with s.th.; **zerstreut I.** *P.P.* → **zerstreuen**; **II.** *Adj. fig.* distracted; *ständig:* absent-minded, scatterbrained, scatty *umg.*; → **Professor**; **III.** *Adv.: ~ liegende Bauernhöfe* scattered farmhouses; **Zerstreutheit** *f; nur Sg.* absent-mindedness; **Zerstreuung** *f* **1.** *nur Sg.* dispersion, scattering; *von Licht: auch* diffusion; (*Auflösung*) dissipation; **2.** (*Unterhaltung*) diversion

zerstritten I. *P.P.* → **zerstreiten**; **II.** *Adj. Ehepaar, Familie etc.:* attr. feuding …, präd. at loggerheads, at odds with one another; *mit j-m ~ sein* have fallen out with s.o.; **Zerstrittenheit** *f; nur Sg.* feuding; *Pol. etc. auch* dissension

zerstückeln *v/t.* **1.** cut up, cut into pieces; (*Körper*) dismember, chop up; **2.** (*Land*) parcel out; **3.** *fig.* (*Tag, Text etc.*) break up; (*Besitz*) divide up; **Zer-**

stückelung *f* **1.** cutting up; *e-r Leiche:* dismemberment; **2.** *von Land:* parcel(l)ing out; **3.** *fig.* breaking-up

zerteilen I. *v/t.* divide, split (up) (*beide: in + Akk.* into); (*trennen*) separate (into); (*zerschneiden*) cut up; **II.** *v/refl.* divide up, split up (*beide in + Akk.* into); *Wolken, Nebel etc.:* disperse; *ich kann mich doch nicht ~! umg.* I can't be in two places at once!; (*kann nicht so viel Sachen zugleich tun*) I've only got one pair of hands!; **Zerteilung** *f* division (*in + Akk.* into); separation; dispersal; → **zerteilen**

Zertifikat *n; -(e)s, -e* **1.** (*Zeugnis*) certificate, diploma; **2.** *Wirts.* certificate; **zertifizieren** *v/t. Wirts.* certify; **Zertifizierung** *f Wirts.* certification; *die ~ nach DIN EN 9002* certification in accordance with DIN EN 9002; *2001 erfolgte die ~ unseres Qualitätsmanagements* our quality management received official certification (*od.* was officially certified) in 2001

zertrampeln *v/t.* trample all over; crush (underfoot), trample underfoot; (*Rasen*) ruin

zertrennen *v/t.* (*Kleid*) undo the seams of, take apart at the seams

zertreten *v/t.* (*unreg.*) crush (underfoot), tread on; (*Rasen*) ruin

zertrümmern *v/t.* **1.** smash (up); (*Fenster, Glas*) smash; (*demolieren*) wreck, smash up; (*Gebäude*) demolish; *j-m den Schädel ~* smash s.o.'s skull (in *umg.*); **2.** *Phys.* (*Atom*) split; **3.** *Med.* (*Nierenstein etc.*) break up; **Zertrümmerung** *f* smashing, wrecking; (*e-s Gebäudes*) demolition

Zervelatwurst *f Gastr.* cervelat

zervikal *Adj. Anat.* cervical; **Zervix** *f; -, Zervices* cervix (*Pl.* cervixes *od.* cervices)

zerwühlen *v/t.* (*Erdboden*) churn up; (*Haar*) dishevel; (*Bett*) rumple; *zerwühltes Bett* rumpled bedclothes

Zerwürfnis *n; -ses, -se; geh.* (*Streit*) quarrel, argument; (*Uneinigkeit*) discord; (*Bruch*) rift; *eheliche ~se* marital strife *Pl.*

zerzausen *v/t.* ruffle; (*Haar*) tousle; *zerzauste Haare auch* dishevel(l)ed hair

Zeter *umg.: ~ und Mordio schreien* scream blue (*Am.* bloody) murder; *fig.* (*protestieren*) raise a (big) hue and cry; **zetern** *v/i. pej.* **1.** *Menschenmenge, Vögel:* clamo(u)r; (*keifen*) nag; *laut:* rant and rave; **2.** (*jammern, schreien*) wail

Zettel *m; -s, -* slip of paper; (*Notiz*) note; (*Flugblatt*) leaflet; (*Bekanntmachung*) notice; *ein ~, auf dem stand …* a note saying …; *~kartei f* card index; *~kasten m* card index (box); *~wirtschaft f: e-e ~ haben* have everything on scraps of paper, have notes jotted down all over the place

Zeug *n; -(e)s, -e* **1.** *nur Sg.; umg., oft pej.* stuff; (*Sachen*) *auch* things *Pl.*; (*Plunder*) loot; (*Gerümpel, Trödel*) junk; *dummes ~* nonsense, rubbish, *bes. Am.* garbage; *ungereimtes ~ reden* talk a lot of nonsense; **2.** *altm.* (*Stoff*) stuff; (*Kleidung*) clothes; **3.** *Naut.* tackle; **4.** *fig.: das ~ haben zu e-m Weltklassefußballer etc.* have the makings of (*od.* be cut out to be) a world-class footballer *etc.*; *er hat das ~ dazu* he's got what it takes *umg.*; *was das ~ hält* like mad; *sich* (*mächtig*) *ins ~ legen* put one's back into it; *sich für j-n ins ~ legen* back s.o. up to the hilt; **sich für etw. ins ~ legen** go all out for s.th., give s.th. one's all-out support; **j-m was am ~ flicken wollen** *umg.* try to pin something on s.o.

Zeuge *m*; *-n*, *-n* **1.** *Jur.* witness (*auch fig.*); **~ der Anklage** witness for the prosecution; **vor ~n** in the presence of witnesses; **~ e-s Unfalls sein** witness (*od.* be witness to) an accident; **2.** *fig.*: (**stumme**) **~n der Vergangenheit** *fig.* (silent) witnesses to the past; **3. die ~n Jehovas** Jehovah's Witnesses

zeugen¹ *v/i.* **1.** *Jur.* give evidence; **für/ gegen etw. ~** testify for/against s.th.; **2.** *fig.*: **~ von** testify to; **das zeugt nicht gerade von Takt** that isn't exactly a sign of (great) tact

zeugen² *v/t.* **1.** (*Kind*) *als Mann:* father; *umg. hum.* sire; *als Paar:* produce; *altm., bibl.* beget; **Kinder ~** *auch* have children; **2.** *geh. fig.* generate, create, engender

Zeugen|aussage *f Jur.* testimony, evidence; **~bank** *f*; *Pl. -bänke* witness box (*Am.* stand); **~beeinflussung** *f* interference (*od.* tampering) with witnesses; **~befragung** *f* questioning of a witness (*od.* of witnesses); **~stand** *m* witness box (*bes. Am.* stand); **in den ~ treten** go into the witness box, take the (witness) stand; **~vernehmung** *f* examination of a witness (*od.* of witnesses)

Zeughaus *n Mil. hist.* arsenal

Zeugin *f*, *-*, *-nen* witness; → *auch* **Zeuge**

Zeugnis *n*; *-ses*, *-se* **1.** *Schule:* report, *Am.* report card; *vom Arbeitgeber:* reference; *Prüfung:* certificate, diploma; **gute ~se haben** *von Schule:* get good reports (*Am.* grades); *vom Arbeitgeber:* have good references; **j-m ein gutes ~ ausstellen** *fig.* give s.o. a good reference; **2.** *Jur. altm.* evidence; *fig. (Beweis) auch* testimony (+ *Gen.* to); **~ ablegen** *bes. fig.* bear witness (**für** to), give evidence (for), testify (for); **zum ~** (+ *Gen.*) in witness of; **3.** (*Bescheinigung*) certificate, attestation; *polizeiliches:* certificate; **ein ärztliches ~** a medical certificate, a doctor's statement; **4.** (*Relikt*) **ein ~ der Vergangenheit** *fig.* a testimony to the past; **~abschrift** *f* copy of a (*od.* the) certificate (*od.* diploma); **~pflicht** *f Jur.* obligation to give evidence; **~verweigerungsrecht** *n Jur.* right to refuse to give evidence, *Am. etwa* Fifth Amendment rights

Zeugs *n*; *-*, *kein Pl.*; *umg. pej.* → **Zeug** 1

Zeugung *f* **1.** *e-s Kinds:* fathering; **2.** *Bio.* procreation

Zeugungsakt *m* procreative act

zeugungsfähig *Adj.* fertile, able to reproduce; **Zeugungsfähigkeit** *f*; *nur Sg.* fertility, reproductive capacity; **zeugungsunfähig** *Adj.* sterile; *Mann: auch* impotent; **Zeugungsunfähigkeit** *f*; *nur Sg.* impotence, sterility

ZH *Abk.* → *Zentralheizung*

z. H., z. Hd. *Abk.* (**zu Händen**) attn

Zibebe *f*; *-*, *-n*; *bes. österr.* muscat raisin

Zichorie *f*; *-*, *-n*; *Bot.* chicory; **Zichorienkaffee** *m* chicory coffee

Zicke *f*; *-*, *-n*; *umg.* **1.** → **Ziege** 1; **2.** *pej.* (*Frau*) bitch, *Brit. auch* cow; **3.** ~ *n* (*Dummheiten*) nonsense; **mach keine ~n!** (*tu nichts Unüberlegtes*) don't do anything stupid; (*stell dich nicht so an*) don't make such a fuss; **zickig** *Adj. umg. pej.* **1.** (*überspannt*) uptight; (*aggressiv*) bitchy; **2.** (*prüde*) prudish

Zicklein *n* kid

zickzack *Adv.*: **~ laufen** etc. zigzag

Zickzack *m*; *-(e)s*, *-e* zigzag; **im ~ fahren** etc. weave, zigzag across the road, veer all over the road; **im ~ gehen/laufen** etc. zigzag

zickzackförmig *Adj.* zigzag

Zickzack|kurs *m* **1.** zigzag path; **im ~ fahren** weave, zigzag; **2.** *fig. Pol.* tacking; **~linie** *f* zigzag (line); **~schere** *f*: (**e-e**) **~** (a pair of) pinking shears *Pl.*

Ziege *f*, *-*, *-n* **1.** goat; *weibliche: auch* nanny goat; **2.** *umg. pej.* bitch, *Brit. auch* cow; **blöde ~** silly old bitch (*Brit. auch* cow)

Ziegel *m*; *-s*, *-* *für Mauer:* brick; *für Dach:* tile; **~bau** *m*; *Pl. -ten* brick building; **~dach** *n* tiled roof

Ziegelei *f*, *-*, *-en* brickyard, brickworks *Pl.* (*V. im Sg.*)

Ziegelofen *m* brick kiln

ziegelrot *Adj.* brick-red

Ziegelstein *m* brick

Ziegen|bart *m* **1.** *Zool.* goat's beard; **2.** *umg. bei Mann:* goatee (beard); **3.** *Bot., Pilz:* goat's beard mushroom; **~bock** *m Zool.* billy goat; **~fell** *n* goatskin; **~herde** *f* herd of goats; **~hirt** *m*, **~hirtin** *f* goatherd; **~käse** *m Gastr.* goat's cheese; **~leder** *n* kid (leather); **~milch** *f* goat's milk; **~peter** *m*; *-s*, *-; Med.* mumps *Sg.*

zieh *Imperf.* → **ziehen**

Zieh|brücke *f* drawbridge; **~brunnen** *m* draw well; **~eltern** *Pl.* foster parents

ziehen; *zieht*, *zog*, *gezogen* **I.** *v/t.* (*hat*) **1.** (*Pflug, Wagen etc.*) draw, pull; (*Spülung*) pull; (*Handbremse*) put on, pull up; (*schleppen*) drag; (*schwere Lasten*) haul; (*zerren*) tug; **lass dich nicht so ~ zu Kind:** stop pulling (and keep up)!; **ein Boot ans Ufer ~** pull a boat ashore; **j-n am Ärmel ~** tug at s.o.'s sleeve; **j-n an den Haaren/Ohren ~** pull s.o.'s hair/ears; **j-n an sich** (*Akk.*) **~** draw s.o. to one; **aus dem Wasser ~** (*Boot*) pull (*od.* haul) out of the water; (*Ertrinkenden*) *auch* pull from the water; **j-n mit sich ~** pull s.o. along (with one); **e-n Ring vom Finger ~** take a ring off, slip a ring from one's finger; **e-n Pullover über die Bluse ~** put a jumper (*Am.* sweater) on over the blouse; **j-m ein Brett über den Kopf ~** (*damit schlagen*) hit s.o. on the head with a board; **die Gardinen vors Fenster ~** draw the curtains (across the window); **j-n zur Seite ~** take s.o. aside; **2.** (*Zahn*) pull out, extract; (*Korken, Messer, Revolver etc.*) draw, pull out; (*Möhren*) pull up; (*den Hut*) take off; (*Los, Gewinn*) draw; (*Karte*) take; (*auswählen*) pick; **die Fäden ~** *Med.* take out the stitches; **Zigaretten** (**aus dem Automaten**) **~** get some cigarettes out of the machine; **3.** (*Linie*) draw; (*Kreis*) *auch* describe; (*Mauer*) build, erect; (*Graben*) dig; (*Wäscheleine*) put up; (*Leitungen*) put s.th. in; **e-n Scheitel ~** make a parting (*Am.* part); **den Wagen nach links ~** (*lenken*) pull (*od.* steer) the car over to the left; **4.** (*dehnen*) stretch; **etw. lässt sich ~** s.th. stretches, s.th. gives; **die Suppe zieht Fäden** the soup's gone stringy; **5.** (*Los, Gewinn*) draw; (*Karte*) take; (*auswählen*) pick; **e-e Niete ~** draw a blank; **6.** *Math.* (*Wurzel*) extract, find, work out; **7.** (*Kerzen*) draw; **Perlen auf e-e Schnur ~** thread beads; **Saiten auf e-e Geige** etc. **~** string a violin etc.; **Wein auf Flaschen**

~ bottle wine; **ein Bild auf Karton ~** print a picture on a card; **8.** *fig.*: **auf sich** (*Akk.*) **~** (*Aufmerksamkeit, Blicke etc.*) attract; (*j-s Hass, Unmut etc.*) incur; **j-n auf s-e Seite ~** win s.o. over to one's side; **j-n ins Vertrauen ~** take s.o. into one's confidence; **etw. ins Lächerliche ~** ridicule s.th., hold s.th. up to ridicule; **nach sich ~ zur Folge haben:** have as a consequence, result in; *notwendigerweise:* entail, involve; *verursachen:* bring about, cause; *als Nebeneffekt:* bring with it (*od.* in its wake); **es zieht mich dorthin** I feel drawn there; → **Bilanz** 2, **Ferne** 1, **Länge** 1, **Rat¹**, **Schluss** 5; **9.** (*Pflanzen*) grow; (*Tiere*) breed, rear; **den werd ich mir schon noch ~** *umg.* I'll teach him some manners; **II.** *v/i.* **1.** (*hat*) pull (**an** + *Dat.* at); *heftig:* tug (at); **der Wagen zieht schlecht** the car's not pulling properly; **zieh!** *in Western:* draw!; **an der Glocke ~** pull (*od.* ring) the bell; **an der Leine ~** *Hund:* pull at the lead (*od.* leash), strain at the leash; **2.** (*ist*) (*wandern, reisen*) wander, rove; *Tiere, Vögel:* migrate; *Vögel: auch* fly; (*weggehen*) go (away), leave; **~ nach/in** (+ *Akk.*) (*umziehen*) move to/into; **aufs Land ~** move to the country; **zu j-m ~** go to live with s.o., move in with s.o.; **durch die Welt ~** see (*lit.* roam) the world; **in den Krieg ~** go to war; **nach Süden ~** *Vögel:* fly (*od.* go *od.* migrate) south; **j-n ~ lassen** let s.o. go; **3.** (*ist*); *Rauch, Wolken etc.:* drift; **die Wolken ~** the clouds drift (*schnell* scud) across the sky; **das Gewitter ist nach Westen gezogen** the storm has moved (away) westward; **4.** (*hat*); *Schach etc.:* (make a) move; **mit dem König ~** move the (*od.* one's) king; **wer zieht?** whose move is it?; **5.** (*hat*); *Ofen, Pfeife etc.:* draw; **~ an e-r Pfeife etc.:** (take a) puff at, draw on; *an Strohhalm:* chew; **6.** (*hat*); *unpers.:* **hier zieht's** there's a draught (*Am.* draft); **mir zieht's am Rücken** I can feel a draught (*Am.* draft) on my back; **7.** (*hat*); *Tee:* draw; *in Marinade:* stand; *in heißem Wasser:* simmer; **den Tee** etc. **~ lassen** let the tea etc. stand; **8.** *umg.:* **e-n ~ lassen** let (one) off; **9.** (*hat*); (*schmerzen*) twinge, ache; **~der Schmerz** twinge, ache; **ein leichtes Ziehen im Rücken haben** have a slight pain (*od.* ache) in one's back, have a touch of (*Am.* a slight) backache; **10.** (*hat*); *umg.* (*wirken*) work; (*Anklang finden*) go down (well); **dieses Stück zieht nicht** the play isn't getting very good houses (*od.* audiences), the play isn't pulling in the crowds (*od.* isn't exactly pulling them in *umg.*); **diese Ausrede zieht bei mir nicht** that excuse won't wash with me, try another one; **das zieht bei mir nicht** that will get you nowhere, that doesn't work with me; **III.** *v/i/refl.* (*hat*) **1. sich an e-m Seil in die Höhe ~** pull o.s. up on a rope; **2.** (*sich dehnen*) stretch, give; *Käse:* go stringy, form strings; *Klebstoff:* get tacky; *umg. fig. Verhandlungen etc.:* drag on; *Weg:* go on and on; **das zieht sich** *umg.* (*dauert lange*) it's going on a bit; **3.** (*sich verziehen*) *Holz:* warp; *Stahl:* buckle; **4. sich ~ durch/über** (+ *Akk.*) (*erstrecken*) stretch through/over (*od.* across); **sich ~ über** (+ *Akk.*) *Narbe:* go right across; **sich ~ um Mauer, Wall:* go right (a)round, enclose; **sich ~ durch** *fig. Motiv, Thema etc.:* run through; → **Affäre** 1, **Länge** 1

Zieh|harmonika f Mus. concertina; (Akkordeon) accordion; **~kind** n Dial. foster child (auch fig.); **~mutter** f Dial. foster mother

Ziehung f drawing (auch Wirts.); Lotto: draw; Statistik: sampling

Ziehvater m Dial. foster father (auch fig.)

Ziel n; -(e)s, -e **1.** e-r Reise etc.: destination; **wir sind am ~ angelangt** we have reached our destination; **kurz vor dem ~ umkehren** turn back shortly before reaching one's destination; **2.** Sport finish(ing line); **im ~** at the finish; **durchs ~ gehen** cross the finishing line; **als Sieger/Zweiter durchs ~ gehen** finish first/second; **3.** bes. Mil. mark, aim; (Zielscheibe) target; taktisches: objective; **j-m ein gutes ~ bieten** present s.o. with a good target, make a good target for s.o.; **ins ~ treffen** hit the target (od. mark); **4.** fig. goal, objective, aim; auch Wirts. target; Päd. (educational) objective; **sich ein ~ setzen** od. **stecken** set o.s. a goal (od. target); **sich das ~ setzen zu** (+ Inf.) aim at (+ Ger.), aim to (+ Inf.); **sich ein hohes ~ setzen** aim high; **unser (erklärtes) ~ ist es zu** (+ Inf.) our (declared) aim (od. objective) is to (+ Inf.); **sie lässt sich von i-m ~ nicht abbringen** she won't be put off (from achieving her objective); **er ist weit vom ~ (entfernt)** he has a long way to go yet; **zum ~ führen** lead to (od. bring) success, lead one to one's goal; **viele Wege führen zum ~** there are many ways of achieving success; **sein ~ erreichen** reach one's goal (od. objective), achieve one's aim, get there umg.; **am ~ sein** have reached one's goal (od. objective), have achieved one's aim, have done it umg., have got there umg.; **am ~ s-r Wünsche sein** have (got) one's wish; **über das ~ hinausschießen** overshoot the mark; (zu weit gehen) go too far; → **Weg** 2

Ziel|anflug m Flug. approach run (od. flight); **~bahnhof** m destination; **~band** n; Pl. -bänder; Sport tape

zielbewusst Adj. purposeful, single-minded; **er ist sehr ~** he knows exactly what he wants (od. what he's aiming for); **Zielbewusstheit** f; nur Sg. purposefulness, single-mindedness

Zieleinlauf m Sport finish; Reihenfolge: finishing order

zielen v/i. **1.** Person: (take) aim (auf + Akk. at); Waffe: be aimed, aim; **mit e-r Waffe ~ auf** (+ Akk.) auch point s.th. at; **genau ~** take careful aim; **2.** fig.: **~ auf** (+ Akk.) Person: aim at, have set one's sights on; Bemerkung, Maßnahme etc.: be aimed at (+ Ger.); → **gezielt**; **zielend** I. Part. Präs. → **zielen**; II. Adj. Ling. transitive

Ziel|fernrohr n telescopic sight; **~film** m Sport photo-finish (film) strip; **~flagge** f Motorsport: chequered (Am. checkered) flag; **~flug** m homing; **~flughafen** m destination airport; **~foto** n Sport photo-finish picture, photograph of the finish

zielführend I. Adj. **1.** Maßnahme etc.: carefully targeted; **2.** (Erfolg versprechend) successful; **3.** (sinnvoll, zweckmäßig) practical, useful, suitable; II. Adv. with clear goals in view; suitably

Zielgebiet n target area

zielgenau Adj. (extremely) accurate, Brit. umg. auch spot-on; Werbung,

---

Maßnahme etc.: accurately targeted; **Zielgenauigkeit** f accuracy

Zielgerade f Sport home stretch (od. straight)

zielgerichtet Adj. goal-directed; → **zielorientiert**; **Zielgerichtetheit** f; nur Sg. goal-directedness

Ziel|gruppe f target group; TV etc. target audience; **~hafen** m port of destination; **~kamera** f Sport photo-finish camera; **~kurve** f Sport home bend; **~landung** f Flug. precision (od. spot) landing; **~linie** f Sport finishing line

ziel|los Adj. aimless; **Ziellosigkeit** f; nur Sg. aimlessness; **~orientiert** I. Adj. goal-directed, purposeful; II. Adv. with clear goals in mind od. view, purposefully

Ziel|ort m (place of) destination; **~richter** m, **~richterin** f Sport judge (at the finish); **~scheibe** f target; fig. auch butt; **zur ~ des Spotts werden** become the target (od. an object) of ridicule, become a laughing stock; **~setzung** f objective, target

zielsicher Adj. **1.** accurate, unerring; **2.** fig. → **zielstrebig**; **Zielsicherheit** f; nur Sg. (unerring) accuracy

Zielsprache f Ling. target language

zielstrebig I. Adj. single-minded, purposeful, determined; II. Adv. single-mindedly etc., with single-mindedness (od. determination); **Zielstrebigkeit** f; nur Sg. single-mindedness, determination

Ziel|sucher m homing device; **~vorgabe** f fig. target-setting; **es gibt klare / keine klaren ~n** clear targets are set / no clear targets are set; **~vorrichtung** f sights Pl.; **~vorstellung** f fig. objective

ziemen v/i. und v/refl. → **geziemen**

ziemlich I. Adj. **1.** (beträchtlich) considerable, quite a(n) ...; **ein ~es Durcheinander** quite a mess; **es war ein ~er Aufwand** it was quite an effort, it took a fair bit of effort; **ich weiß es mit ~er Sicherheit** I'm fairly (umg. pretty) sure about it; **2.** geh. altm. (schicklich) seemly; II. Adv. quite, pretty umg.; **~ ausführlich beschreiben** etc.: in some detail, at some length; **~ fertig** Arbeit: more or less ready, nearly ready; umg. Person: (sehr erschöpft) pretty well done in; (fast ruiniert) pretty well broke, on one's last legs financially; **ich bin ~ fertig** umg. auch I'm what you might call shattered (Am. wiped out); **~ viel** quite a lot (of); **~ viele** auch quite a few; **so ~** (fast, mehr oder weniger) more or less, just about, pretty much umg.; **so ~ dasselbe** more or less (umg. pretty much) the same thing

ziepen bes. nordd. **I.** v/i. **1.** Küken: cheep; **2.** beim Kämmen: **es ziept** it's pulling (my hair); II. v/t.: **j-n an den Haaren ~** pull s.o.'s hair

Zier f; -, kein Pl.; altm. → **Zierde**

Zierat → **Zierrat**

Zierbuchstabe m ornamental letter

Zierde f; -, -n **1.** (Verzierung) ornament, decoration; (Schmuckstück) adornment; Gebäude etc.: showpiece; **nur zur ~** just for decoration; **2.** fig. (Tugend) good thing; Person: fine example, pride and joy; **j-m zur ~ gereichen** geh. be a credit to s.o.; **sie ist die ~ des Orchesters** she does the orchestra credit, the orchestra can be proud of her

Zierdeckchen n doily

zieren I. v/t. geh. adorn; (schmücken)

---

decorate; fig. grace, adorn; **ein Wappen zierte die Tür** a coat of arms adorned the doorway; II. v/refl. pej. (Umstände machen) fuss, make a fuss; (zögern) hesitate; (schüchtern tun) bes. Mädchen: be coy, act coy; **~ Sie sich nicht!** no need to be shy (od. polite); **er zierte sich nicht lange** he didn't need much persuading; **zier dich nicht so!** (sei nicht schüchtern) don't be so coy!; (sei nicht prüde) don't be so prudish!; **Ziererei** f; -, -en; pej. hesitation, beating about (Am. around) the bush

Zier|fisch m ornamental fish; **~garten** m ornamental garden; **~gräser** Pl. ornamental grasses; **~kürbis** m ornamental (dried) gourd; **~leiste** f ornamental mo(u)lding (an Möbeln: border); Mot. trim; im Buch: vignette

zierlich Adj. (zart) delicate; Frau: dainty, petite; (anmutig) auch graceful; **Zierlichkeit** f; nur Sg. delicateness; daintiness; gracefulness; → **zierlich**

Zier|naht f decorative seam; **~pflanze** f ornamental plant; **~rand** m decorative edge; **~rat** m; nur Sg. decoration, embellishment; **~schrift** f ornate lettering; **~stich** m decorative stitch; **~strauch** m ornamental shrub; **~vogel** m cagebird

Ziesel m, bes. österr. n; -s, -; Zool. souslik, ground squirrel

Ziest m; -(e)s, -e; Bot. betony, woundwort

Ziffer f; -, -n **1.** figure, number; in e-r Zahl: digit; (Schriftzeichen) cipher; **arabische/römische ~n** Arabic/Roman numerals; **2.** (Unterabsatz) clause; (Punkt) item; **~blatt** n dial, (clock)face; e-r Armbanduhr: (watch)face

zig Adj. umg. (sehr viele) dozens of, hundreds of, umpteen umg.; **~ Millionen** zillions (of)

Zigarette f; -, -n cigarette; **~ mit Filter** filter(-tipped) cigarette; **~ ohne Filter** untipped (od. filterless) cigarette

Zigaretten|anzünder m cigarette lighter; **~automat** m cigarette machine; **~etui** n cigarette case; **~fabrik** f cigarette factory; **~kippe** f → **Zigarettenstummel**; **~länge** f umg.: **auf** od. **für e-e ~** for a smoke; **~marke** f brand of cigarettes; **~papier** n cigarette paper; **~pause** f (break for a) smoke; **~qualm** m, **~rauch** m cigarette smoke; **~raucher** m, **~raucherin** f cigarette smoker; **~schachtel** f cigarette packet (Am. pack); **~schmuggel** m cigarette smuggling; **~spitze** f cigarette holder; **~stummel** m cigarette butt (bes. Brit. auch end); stub; **~werbung** f cigarette advertising

Zigarillo m, n; -s, -s cigarillo, small cigar

Zigarre f; -, -n **1.** cigar; **2.** umg. fig. (Zurechtweisung) rocket, dressing-down; **j-m e-e ~ verpassen** give s.o. a rocket

Zigarren|abschneider m cigar cutter; **~kiste** f cigar box; **~rauch** m cigar smoke; **~raucher** m, **~raucherin** f cigar smoker; **~sorte** f brand of cigar; **~spitze** f **1.** Halter: cigar holder; **2.** Ende: cigar tip; **~stummel** m cigar end, stub

Zigeuner m; -s, -; neg.! **1.** gypsy, gipsy; **2.** umg. fig. (ruheloser Mensch) vagabond; pej. (Rumtreiber) gypsy, tramp; **Zigeunerin** f; -, -nen; neg.! gypsy (od. gipsy) woman (od. girl); → **Roma**, **Sinti**

Zigeuner|lager n gypsy camp; **~leben**

n neg.! gypsy life; *fig. auch the* life of a vagabond; **ein ~ führen** *umg. fig. auch* rove around, *bes. Am.* bum around; **~musik** *f* gypsy music

zigeunern *v/i. neg!:* **durch die Welt ~** roam the world

Zigeuner|schnitzel *n Gastr.* escalope in spicy sauce with red and green peppers, tomatoes etc.; **~sprache** *f: die ~* Romany; **~wagen** *m* gypsy caravan (*Am.* trailer)

zigfach... *umg. Adj.:* **die ~e Menge** umpteen times the amount; **Zigfache** *n; -n, kein Pl.:* **das ~** umpteen times (the amount); **das ~ ihres eigenen Körpergewichts** umpteen times their own bodyweight

zigmal *Adv. umg.* umpteen (*od.* dozens of) times; a hundred times

zigtausend *umg. Zahlw.* umpteen thousand; **Zigtausend** (*n*); *umg.:* **~e** (+ *Gen. od.* **von**) umpteen thousand ..., umpteen thousands of ...

Zikade *f; -, -n; Zool.* cicada

Zille *f; -, -n; Dial.* barge

Zimbabwe (*n*); *-s; Geog.* Zimbabwe; **zimbabwisch** *Adj.* Zimbabwean

Zimbel *f; -, -n; Mus.* cymbal

Zimmer *n; -s, -* room; *in Untermiete: auch* lodgings *Pl., Brit. auch* digs *Pl. umg.;* **möbliertes ~** furnished room; **"~ frei"** "Vacancies"; **~antenne** *f* indoor aerial (*od.* antenna); **~blume** *f* indoor (flowering) plant; **~brand** *m* fire in a room; **~decke** *f* ceiling

Zimmerei *f; -, -en* **1.** *Betrieb:* carpenter's (work)shop; **2.** *nur Sg.; Handwerk:* carpentry

Zimmereinrichtung *f Möbel:* furniture; *Innenausstattung:* interior

Zimmerer *m; -s,* carpenter

Zimmer|flucht *f* suite (of rooms); **~genosse** *m,* **~genossin** *f* roommate

Zimmerhandwerk *n* carpentry

Zimmerin *f; -, -nen* (woman) carpenter

Zimmer|kellner *m,* **~kellnerin** *f* room waiter; **~lautstärke** *f* moderate volume; **das Radio auf ~ stellen** turn the radio down to a moderate volume; **~linde** *f Bot.* African hemp; **~mädchen** *n* (chamber)maid

Zimmermann *m; Pl.* **Zimmerleute** carpenter

zimmern I. *v/t.* **1.** (*bauen, machen*) make (out of wood), build; **2.** *fig.* shape, make; **3.** *Bergb.* timber; **II.** *v/i.* do carpentry; **an etw. ~** work on s.th., make s.th.

Zimmer|nachweis *m* accommodation office; **~nummer** *f* room number; **~palme** *f Bot.* indoor palm (tree); **~pflanze** *f Bot.* indoor plant; **~service** *m* room service; **~suche** *f* room-hunting; **auf ~ sein** be room-hunting; **~temperatur** *f* room temperature; **~theater** *n Theat.* studio theat|re (*Am. auch* -er); **~tür** *f* door; **~vermittlung** *f* accommodation service (*Stelle:* office)

Zimmerwerkstatt *f* carpenter's workshop

zimperlich *pej.* **I.** *Adj.* oversensitive, soft *umg.,* wet *umg.;* (*leicht Ekel empfindend*) squeamish; (*geziert*) affected; (*prüde*) prissy *umg.;* **sei nicht so ~** don't make such a fuss; **II.** *Adv.:* **wenig ~** (*unsanft*) none too gently; (*bedenkenlos*) unscrupulously; **nicht gerade ~ mit j-m umgehen** treat s.o. none too gently, not exactly treat s.o. with kid gloves; **Zimperlichkeit** *f; mst Sg.; pej.* oversensitivity; (*Neigung zum Ekel*) squeamishness; (*Geziertheit*) af-

fectedness; (*Prüderie*) prissiness *umg.;* **Zimperliese** *f; -, -n; umg. pej.* sissy

Zimt *m; -(e)s, kein Pl.* **1.** cinnamon; **2.** *umg. pej.* → **Mist**[1] 2, 3; **~apfel** *m* custard apple, *Am. auch* cherimoya

zimt|farben, ~farbig *Adj.* cinnamon(--colo[u]red)

Zimt|stange *f* cinnamon stick; **~stern** *m* star-shaped cinnamon biscuit (*Am.* cookie); **~zicke** *f umg. pej.* bitch, *Brit. auch* cow

Zink[1] *n; -(e)s, kein Pl.;* (*abgek.* **Zn**) *Chem.* zinc

Zink[2] *m; -(e)s, -en; Mus.* cornetto (*Pl.* cornetti), cornet, zink

Zink|blech *n* sheet zinc; *grobes:* zinc plate; **~blende** *f; nur Sg.; Chem.* zinc blende

Zinke *f; -, -n* prong; *e-r Gabel: auch* tine; *e-s Kamms:* tooth; **zinken** *v/t.* (*Karten*) mark; **Zinken** *m; -s, -* **1.** *Zeichen:* secret sign; **2.** *umg. hum.* (*große Nase*) beak, conk, *Am.* schnoz; **Zinker** *m; -s, -,* **Zinkerin** *f; -, -nen* etwa cardsharp, *s.o. who secretly marks the cards*

zinkhaltig *Adj.* zinc-containing, zinciferous *fachspr.*

Zink|leimverband *m Med.* Unna's paste dressing, *Am.* Unna boot; **~salbe** *f Med.* zinc ointment; **~wanne** *f* zinc bath

Zinn *n; -(e)s, kein Pl.* **1.** (*abgek.* **Sn**) *Chem.* tin; *legiertes:* pewter; **2.** *Geschirr etc.:* pewter(ware); **~becher** *m* pewter mug

Zinne *f; -, -n* merlon; **~n** battlements; *fig. von Gebirge:* peaks, pinnacles; *von Stadt:* towers

Zinn|figur *f* pewter figure; **~folie** *f* tinfoil; **~geschirr** *n* pewter(ware); **~gießer** *m; -s, -,* **~gießerin** *f; -, -nen* tinsmith; *von legierten Haushaltswaren:* pewterer

Zinnie *f; -, -n; Bot.* zinnia

Zinn|kraut *n; nur Sg.; Bot.* horsetail; **~krug** *m* pewter mug

Zinnober *m; -s, -* **1.** *Min.* cinnabar; **2.** *österr. n; nur Sg.; Farbe:* vermil(l)ion; **3.** *nur Sg.; umg. fig.* (*Kram*) stuff; (*Getue*) fuss; (*Quatsch*) rubbish; **und der ganze ~** and all that; *weniger abwertend:* and the whole works; **zinnoberrot** *Adj.* vermil(l)ion

Zinn|soldat *m* tin soldier; **~teller** *m* pewter plate

Zins *m; -es, -en bzw. -e* **1.** *Pl. -en, mst Pl.; Fin. auch Pl.* interest *Sg.;* **zu 4% ~en** at 4% interest; **hohe ~en** high interest (rates); **~en tragen** bear interest; **zuzüglich ~en** plus interest; **mit ~en zurückzahlen** *fig.* return s.th. with interest; **mit ~ und Zinseszins** with compound interest; *fig.* with interest, with a vengeance; **2.** *Pl. -e; bes. südd., österr., schw.* (*Miete, Pacht*) rent; (*Abgabe*) tax, due; **3.** *Pl. -e; hist.* ground rent; **~abschlag** *m Fin.* (deduction for) tax (*on interest earned that is not subject to capital gains tax*); **~abschlagssteuer** *f Fin.* tax on interest earned (*that exceeds the tax-free limit and is not subject to capital gains tax*); **~abschnitt** *m Fin., an e-r Aktie:* interest coupon; **~belastung** *f Fin.* interest load; **~bindung** *f Fin.* pegging of interest rates

zinsbringend, Zins bringend *Adj.* interest-bearing

Zinsendienst *m Fin.* interest payment

Zins|erhöhung *f Fin.* increase in interest rates; **~erträge** *Pl.* interest earnings

Zinseszins *m Fin.* compound interest; **~rechnung** *f Math.* calculation of compound interest

zinsfrei *Adj.* interest-free

Zinsfuß *m Fin.* interest rate

zinsgünstig *Adj.* low-interest ...

Zins|herr *m hist.* lord of the manor, landlord; **~knechtschaft** *f hist. etwa* villeinage

zinslos *Adj. Fin.* interest-free; non-interest-bearing; **ein ~es Darlehen** an interest-free loan

Zinsniveau *n Fin.* level of interest rates

Zinspflicht *f; nur Sg.; hist.* obligation to pay ground rent to the lord of the manor; **zinspflichtig** *Adj. hist.* obliged to pay ground rent to the lord of the manor

Zins|politik *f Fin.* interest rate policy; **~rechnung** *f* calculation of interest; *konkret:* interest account; **~satz** *m* interest rate; **~schein** *m Fin.* interest coupon; **~schritt** *m Fin.* alteration in the interest rate (*od.* in interest rates); **~schwankungen** *Pl.* fluctuations in the interest rate (*od.* in interest rates); **~senkung** *f* lowering of interest rates; **~termin** *m* interest due date

zins|tragend, Zins tragend *Adj. Fin.* interest-bearing; **~verbilligt** *Adj.* low-interest

Zins|vereinbarungen *Pl. Fin.* terms of interest; **~verlust** *m* loss on interest; **~wucher** *m* usury; **~zahl** *f* amount of interest, figure for interest

Zionismus *m; -, kein Pl.* Zionism; **Zionist** *m; -en, -en,* **Zionistin** *f; -, -nen* Zionist; **zionistisch** *Adj.* Zionist(ic)

ZIP-Datei *f EDV* zip file

Zipfel *m; -s, -* **1.** *e-r Decke etc.:* corner; *von Hemd etc.:* tail; *e-r Mütze:* point; *e-r Wurst:* end; (*Spitze*) *od. von Land:* tip; **2.** *Kinderspr.* (*Penis*) willy, *Am.* weenie; **zipfelig** *Adj. Saum etc.:* uneven; (*Spitze*) pointed cap

ZIP-Laufwerk *n EDV* zip drive

Zipp® *m; -s, -s; österr.* zip (fastener), *Am.* zipper

zippen *vt/i. EDV* zip

Zipperlein *n umg. hum.* **1.** *nur Sg.;* (*Gicht*) gout; **2.** (*Wehwehchen*) (minor) ailment

Zippverschluss *m österr.* zip (fastener), *Am.* zipper

Zirbel|drüse *f Anat.* pineal gland; **~kiefer** *f Bot.* stone pine; **~nuss** *f* cedar nut

zirka *Adv.* (*abgek.* **ca.**) about, approximately; *vor Jahreszahl: auch* circa

Zirkel *m; -s, -* **1.** *Gerät:* (**ein**) **~** (a) compass, (a pair of) compasses *Pl.* (*od.* dividers *Pl.*); **2.** (*Kreis*) *auch fig.* circle; **~definition** *f* circular definition; **~kasten** *m* box (*od.* case) for (a pair of) compasses

zirkeln I. *v/i.* (*genau abmessen*) measure accurately (*od.* precisely); **wir mussten ganz schön ~, bis das Regal passte** *umg.* it took (*od.* we had to do) a lot of measuring and adjusting to get the shelf to fit; **II.** *v/t.* (*geschickt an e-e Stelle bringen*) place, direct; (*Ball, Freistoß, etc.*) *auch* stroke

Zirkel|schluss *m:* **ein ~** circular reasoning; **~training** *n Sport* circuit training

Zirkon *m; -s, -e; Min.* zircon; **Zirkonium** *n; -s, kein Pl.;* (*abgek.* **Zr**) *Chem.* zirconium

Zirkulation *f; -, kein Pl. des Geldes, Blutes etc.:* circulation; **zirkulieren** *v/i.* circulate; **~ lassen** circulate

Zirkumflex *m*; *-es*, *-e*; *Ling.* circumflex
Zirkumpolarstern *m Astron.* circumpolar star
Zirkumzision *f*; *-*, *-en*; *Med.* circumcision
Zirkus *m*; *-*, *-se* **1.** circus (*auch hist.*); *in den ~ gehen* go to the circus; *beim ~ sein* be with (*od.* a member of) the circus; **2.** *umg. pej.* (*Getue*) fuss, carry-on; (*Trubel*) hustle and bustle; (*Ärger*) trouble, aggravation; *mach keinen ~!* don't make such a fuss; *~direktor m*, *~direktorin f* circus director (*od.* manager); *~manege f* circus ring; *~nummer f* circus act; *~vorstellung f* (circus) performance; *~wagen m* circus caravan (*Am.* trailer); *~zelt n* circus tent, big top
zirpen *vt/i.* chirp, cheep
Zirrhose *f*; *-*, *-n*; *Med.* cirrhosis (*Pl.* cirrhoses)
Zirrokumulus *m Met.* cirrocumulus; **Zirrostratus** *m* cirrostratus; **Zirrus** *m*; *-*, *-* *od.* Zirren, **Zirruswolke** *f* cirrus cloud
zirzensisch *Adj. attr.* circus …
zisalpin(isch) *Adj. Geogr.* cisalpine
zisch *Interj.* hiss; *schnelle Bewegung*: whoosh
zischeln *vt/i.* whisper; *zornig*: hiss
zischen I. *v/i.* **1.** (*hat gezischt*); *Gans, Schlange etc.*: hiss; *Fett*: sizzle; *Sprudel*: fizz; *Dampf, Lok*: hiss; **2.** (*ist*); *durch die Luft*: whiz(z) (*auch umg. flitzen*); **II.** *v/t.* (*hat*) (*Worte*) hiss; **2.** *umg.*: *ein Bier ~* down (*od.* knock back) a beer; *e-n ~* down one, knock one back; **Zischlaut** *m Ling.* sibilant
Ziselierarbeit *f* chased work; **ziselieren** *v/t.* chase
Zisterne *f*; *-*, *-n* cistern, tank
Zisterzienser *m*; *-s*, *-*, *~in f*; *-*, *-nen*; *kath.* Cistercian (monk *bzw.* nun); *~kloster n* Cistercian monastery; *~orden m* Cistercian order
Zitadelle *f*; *-*, *-n* citadel
Zitat *n*; *-(e)s*, *-e* quotation, quote *umg.* (*aus* from); *falsches ~* misquotation; *~: …* (and) I quote - …, quote - …; *Ende des ~s* end of quote; *bes. beim Vorlesen*: unquote
Zitaten|lexikon *n* dictionary of quotations; *~schatz m* **1.** *Buch*: treasury of quotations; **2.** *e-r Person*: store of quotations
Zither *f*; *-*, *-n*; *Mus.* zither; *~spieler m*, *~spielerin f* zither player
zitieren I. *v/t.* **1.** quote, cite; *~ aus* quote from; *darf ich Sie ~?* may I quote you?; *ich zitiere Marx: …* to quote (from) Marx; **2.** (*vorladen*) summon, cite *förm.*; *vor Gericht zitiert werden* be summoned to court; *zu j-m zitiert werden* be called into s.o.'s office, *förm.* be summoned before s.o.; **II.** *v/i.* quote; *ich zitiere: …* (and) I quote - …, quote …; **Zitierung** *f* **1.** quotation; **2.** (*Vorladung*) summons (*Pl.* summonses)
Zitronat *n*; *-(e)s*, *kein Pl.* candied lemon peel; **Zitrone** *f*; *-*, *-n*; *Bot.* lemon; *heiße ~* hot lemon (drink); *j-n ausquetschen wie e-e ~ umg. fig.* squeeze s.o. dry (*od.* like a lemon), get everything one can out of s.o.
Zitronen|baum *m Bot.* lemon tree; *~creme f Gastr.* lemon mousse; *~falter m Zool.* brimstone butterfly
zitronengelb *Adj.* lemon(-colo[u]red), lemon-yellow
Zitronen|limonade *f* lemonade; *~melisse f Bot.* lemon balm; *~presse f* lemon squeezer; *~saft m* lemon juice;

~säure f Chem. citric acid; *~schale f* lemon peel; *Gastr. auch the* zest of a lemon; *~scheibe f* slice of lemon, lemon slice; *~wasser n* fresh lemon squash
Zitrusfrüchte *Pl.* citrus fruits
Zitter|aal *m Zool.* electric eel; *~gras n Bot.* trembling grass
zitterig *Adj.* → **zittrig**
zittern *v/i.* **1.** (*hat*); *auch Mauern etc.*: tremble, shake (*vor* + *Dat.* with); *vor Kälte*: *auch* shiver; *am ganzen Körper ~* tremble from head to foot, tremble all over; *mir ~ die Knie* my knees are trembling; **2.** (*hat*); *fig.*: *um j-n ~* fear for s.o.; *vor j-m/etw. ~* be terrified of s.o./s.th.; *ich hab ganz schön gezittert umg.* I was scared as anything
Zittern *n*; *-s*, *kein Pl.* **1.** trembling, shaking; *vor Kälte*: *auch* shivering, *the* shivers *Pl.*; **2.** *fig.*: *mit ~ und Zagen* with fear and trembling; *das große ~ kriegen umg.* get cold feet
Zitter|pappel *f Bot.* (quaking) aspen; *~partie f umg.*, *sportlicher Wettbewerb, Wahl etc.*: cliffhanger, nailbiter, nailbiting game (*od.* election *etc.*); *~rochen m Zool.* electric ray; *~spiel n umg.* cliffhanger, nailbiter, nailbiting game (*od.* match)
zittrig *Adj.* shaky; *Stimme*: *auch* tremulous, faltering; (*tatterig*) doddery; *e-e ~e Schrift* shaky handwriting
Zitze *f*; *-*, *-n* **1.** *Zool.* teat; **2.** *vulg.* tit
Zivi *m*; *-s*, *-s*; *Sl.* → **Zivildienstleistende**
zivil I. *Adj.* **1.** (*Ggs. militärisch*) civilian; *Ungehorsam, Gesellschaft etc.* civil; *die ~e Luftfahrt* civil aviation; **2.** *Preise*: reasonable; **II.** *Adv.*: *j-n behandeln* treat s.o. decently, treat s.o. in an acceptable fashion
Zivil *n*; *-s*, *kein Pl.* **1.** (*Ggs. Uniform*) civilian clothes *Pl.* (*od.* dress), civvies *Pl. Mil. umg.*; *beim Polizisten*: plain clothes *Pl.*; *Polizist in ~* plainclothes policeman; **2.** *Koll.* (*Zivilbevölkerung*) civilian population; **3.** *schw.* (*Familienstand*) marital status
Zivil|behörde *f* civil authority; *~beruf m*: *im ~ … sein* be a … in civilian life; *~beschäftigte m*, *f* civilian employee (*working for the armed forces*); *~bevölkerung f* civilian population; *Verluste in der ~* civilian casualties; *~courage f* moral courage, *the* courage of one's convictions; *er hat ~* he's not afraid to say what he thinks; *~diener m österr.* → **Zivildienstleistende**
Zivildienst *m*; *nur Sg.* alternative (*od.* community) service (*in lieu of military service*); *~leistende m*; *-n*, *-n* conscientious objector conscripted to do community work
Zivile *m*, *f*; *-n*, *-n*; *Sl.* plainclothes police officer
Zivil|ehe *f Jur.* civil marriage; *~fahnder m*, *~fahnderin f* plainclothes detective; *~fahndung f* plainclothes search (*od.* dragnet); *~fahrzeug n* unmarked vehicle (*od.* police car); *~flugzeug n* civil aircraft; *~gefangene m*, *f* civilian prisoner (of war), internee; *~gericht n* civil court; *~gesetzbuch n*; *nur Sg.*; *schw.* civil code
Zivilisation *f*; *-*, *-en* civilization
Zivilisationskrankheit *f* disease of civilization
zivilisationsmüde *Adj.* tired of (*od.* disenchanted with) modern civilization (*od.* the modern lifestyle); **Zivilisationsmüdigkeit** *f* disenchantment with modernity
Zivilisationsschäden *Pl. am Men-*

schen: ills of civilization; *an der Natur etc.*: damage *Sg.* caused by civilization
zivilisatorisch *Adj. attr.* civilizing, *nachgestellt*: of civilization
zivilisieren *v/t.* civilize; **zivilisiert I.** *P.P.* → **zivilisieren**; **II.** *Adj.* civilized; *~e Umgangsformen* civilized manners; **III.** *Adv.* in a civilized way; *kannst du dich etwas ~er ausdrücken?* can you put that into slightly more civilized language?; **Zivilisierung** *f* civilization
Zivilist *m*; *-en*, *-en*, *~in f*; *-*, *-nen* civilian; **zivilistisch** *Adj.* civilian
Zivil|kammer *f Jur.* civil division; *~klage f Jur.* civil action; *~kleidung f* → *Zivil* 1; *~leben n* civilian life; *~luftfahrt f*: *die ~* civil aviation; *~person f* civilian; *~polizist m*, *~polizistin f* plainclothes police officer
Zivilprozess *m Jur.* civil action; *~ordnung f Jur.* code of civil procedure
Zivilrecht *n*; *nur Sg.*; *Jur.* civil law; **zivilrechtlich I.** *Adj.* civil law …, under civil law; **II.** *Adv.* under civil law; *~ verfolgen* bring a civil action against, sue
Zivil|regierung *f* civilian government; *~schutz m* civil defen|ce (*Am.* -se); *~streife f* plainclothes policemen *Pl.* (on the beat); *~verteidigung f* civil defen|ce (*Am.* -se)
ZK *n*; *-(s)*, *-s*; *Abk.* → *Zentralkomitee*
Znüni *m*, *n*; *-s*, *-*; *schw.* mid-morning snack, *Brit. auch* elevenses *Pl.*
Zobel *m*; *-s*, *-* **1.** *Zool.* sable; **2.** → *Zobelpelz*, *~pelz m* **1.** sable (fur); **2.** *Mantel*: sable
zockeln *v/i. umg.*, *Auto*: chug along; *Person*: trundle along
zocken *v/i. umg.* gamble (*auch fig.*); **Zocker** *m*; *-s*, *-*, **Zockerin** *f*; *-*, *-nen*; *umg.* punter, gambler
Zofe *f*; *-*, *-n* lady's maid; *am Hof*: lady-in-waiting
Zoff *m*; *-s*, *kein Pl.*; *umg.* trouble, strife; *Brit.*, *umg. auch* argy-bargy, *Am. umg. auch* brouhaha; *~ mit j-m haben* be having a bit of strife with s.o.
zog *Imperf.* → *ziehen*
zögerlich *Adj.* hesitant; halting; *sich ~ geben* hold back; **Zögerlichkeit** *f*; *nur Sg.* hesitancy
zögern *v/i.* hesitate; (*schwanken*) waver; *er zögerte nicht zu* (+ *Inf.*) he lost no time (in + *Ger.*); *du darfst nicht zu lange ~* don't spend too much time thinking about it; *ohne zu zögern* without hesitating; **Zögern** *n*; *-s*, *kein Pl.* hesitation; *ohne ~* unhesitatingly, without (a moment's) hesitation; *nach anfänglichem ~* after some hesitation; **zögernd I.** *Part. Präs.* → *zögern*; **II.** *Adj.* hesitant; *Worte, Schritte, Fortschritt, Geständnis etc.*: *auch* halting; **III.** *Adv.* hesitantly; *bes. auch* stolpernd: haltingly; *die Antwort kam nur ~* he (*od.* she *etc.*) hesitated before answering, the answer came hesitantly
Zögling *m*; *-s*, *-e* **1.** pupil; **2.** *fig.* protégé
Zölibat *n*, *m*; *-(e)s*, *kein Pl.* celibacy; *im ~ leben* be celibate, practi|se (*Am.* -ce) celibacy; **zölibatär** *Adj.* celibate
Zoll¹ *m*; *-(e)s*, *Zölle* **1.** *Abgabe*: (customs) duty; **2.** *nur Sg.*; *Behörde*: customs *Pl.* (*V. im Sg.*); *beim ~ liegen* be in customs (*od.* at the customs office); *etw. durch den ~ schmuggeln* smuggle s.th. through customs; **3.** *hist.* toll
Zoll² *m*; *-(e)s*, *-*; *altm. Maß*: inch; *jeder ~ ein Ehrenmann geh. fig.* every inch a gentleman

Zoll|abfertigung f **1.** customs clearance; **2.** Stelle: customs; **~abkommen** n customs (od. tariff) agreement

Zollager → **Zolllager**

Zollamt n customs office; **zollamtlich I.** Adj.: **~e Abfertigung** customs clearance; **II.** Adv.: **~ abfertigen** clear through customs

Zoll|anschlussgebiet n customs enclave (outlying area belonging to a particular customs zone); **~ausland** n country, region, etc. outside one's own customs area; **~beamte** m, **~beamtin** f customs official (od. officer); **~behörde** f customs authorities Pl.; **~begleitschein** m customs warrant; **~bestimmungen** Pl. customs regulations

zollbreit Adj. one-inch(-wide), inch-wide

Zollbreit m fig.: **keinen ~ weichen** not budge (od. give) an inch

Zolleinnahmen Pl. customs revenue Sg.

zollen v/t. geh.: **j-m/etw. Anerkennung** od. **Tribut ~** pay tribute to s.o./s.th.; **j-m Beifall/Dank ~** applaud/thank s.o.; **j-m/etw. Bewunderung/Respekt ~** show one's admiration/respect for s.o./s.th.; **j-m/etw. Lob ~** (give) praise (to) s.o./s.th.

Zollfahnder m, **~in** f customs investigator; **Zollfahndung** f **1.** customs investigation; **2.** (Dienststelle) customs investigation office

Zollformalitäten Pl. customs formalities

zollfrei Adj. duty-free; **~e Ware** duty-free goods; **Zollfreiheit** f; nur Sg. exemption from duty

Zoll|gebiet n customs territory; **~gebühren** Pl. customs duties; **~grenzbezirk** m customs district; **~grenze** f customs frontier; **es ist e-e ~** auch there's customs at the border; **~hafen** m port of entry; **~hoheit** f customs sovereignty; **~inhaltserklärung** f customs declaration; **~kontrolle** f customs examination (od. check); **~lager** n bonded (od. customs) warehouse

Zöllner m; -s, -, **~in** f; -, -nen **1.** customs officer; **2.** bibl. publican

Zollpapiere Pl. customs documents

zollpflichtig Adj. dutiable, liable to duty

Zoll|schranken Pl. fig. customs barriers; **~station** f customs post; **~stelle** f customs office

Zollstock m folding rule; Stab: yardstick

Zoll|tarif m (customs) tariff; **~union** f customs union; **~verein** m hist.: **Deutscher ~** the Zollverein (customs union of German states established in 1833); **~vergehen** n customs violation

Zombie m; -s, -s; Film und umg. fig. zombie

zonal Adj. zonal; **Zone** f; -, -n **1.** zone; Geog. auch region; (Bezirk) auch area; **2.** hist. umg.: **die ~** East Germany

Zonen|grenze f **1.** hist.: **die ~** the East German border; **2.** Verk. (Zahlgrenze) fare stage; **~randgebiet** n hist. border area between East and West Germany; **~tarif** m Verk. fare stage tariff; Telef. etc. zonal tariff; **~zeit** f zone time

Zoo m; -s, -s zoo; **~direktor** m, **~direktorin** f zoo director; **~handlung** f pet shop

Zoologe m; -n, -n zoologist; **Zoologie** f; -, kein Pl. zoology; **Zoologin** f; -, -nen zoologist; **zoologisch** Adj. zoological; **~er Garten** zoo, zoological gar-

dens Pl.

Zoom [zu:m] n, m; -s, -s Objektiv und Vorgang: zoom; **Zoomaufnahme** f zoom shot; **zoomen** vt/i. zoom; **Zoomobjektiv** n zoom lens

Zoo|tier n zoo animal; **~wärter** m, **~wärterin** f zoo keeper

Zopf m; -(e)s, Zöpfe **1.** plait, Am. braid, queue hist.; von kleinen Mädchen: auch pigtail; sich (Dat.) **Zöpfe flechten** plait (Am. braid) one's hair; **2.** Gastr. plait, Am. braided loaf; **3.** umg. fig.: **ein alter ~** an antiquated custom; (etw. längst Bekanntes) old hat; **die alten Zöpfe abschneiden** bring things up to date

Zöpfchen n pigtail

Zopf|muster n cable stitch; **~perücke** f queue wig; **~stil** m late rococo (style)

Zorn m; -(e)s, kein Pl. rage, anger, fury, wrath lit., ire lit. (alle: auf + Akk. at); **heiliger ~** righteous anger (od. indignation); **der ~ Gottes** God's wrath; **in ~ geraten** fly into a rage; **ihn packte der ~** he got really angry (od. furious)

Zorn... siehe Zornes...

zornentbrannt Adj. furious, incensed

Zornes|ader f geh.: **j-m schwillt die ~** s.o.'s anger is rising, s.o. is about to fly into a rage; **~ausbruch** m geh. fit of anger (od. rage); **~falte** f geh. angry furrow in s.o.'s brow; **~röte** f geh. flush of anger; **j-m die ~ ins Gesicht treiben** make s.o.'s face redden with anger

zornig Adj. angry (auf j-n with; über + Akk. at, about s.th.); **schnell ~ werden** be short-tempered, have a short temper (od. short fuse)

Zosse m; -n, -n; Dial., oft pej. (altes Pferd) nag

Zote f; -, -n dirty joke; **~n reißen** tell dirty jokes; **zotenhaft** Adj. dirty, obscene; **zotig** Adj. dirty, obscene

Zotte f; -, -n **1.** tuft (of hair); **2.** Anat. villus (Pl. villi)

Zottel f; -, -n, mst Pl. **1.** tuft; **2.** ~n pej. rat's tails; **3.** (Quaste) tassel; **~haar** n shaggy mane

zottelig Adj. pej. straggly; (verfilzt) matted

zotteln v/i. umg. amble (along)

z. T. Abk. (zum Teil) partly

Ztr. Abk. (Zentner) cwt.

zu¹ Präp. (+ Dat.) **1.** räumlich, Richtung: to, toward(s); **bis ~** up to; **~ j-m gehen** go and (od. to) see s.o.; **~ Tal fahren, gleiten** etc.: downhill; → Boden 2, Kopf 2; **2.** räumlich, Lage: at, in; **~ Berlin** in (amtlich: at) Berlin; **der Dom ~ Köln** Cologne Cathedral; **~ ebener Erde** at ground level; **~ j-s Füßen** at s.o.'s feet; **~ Hause** at home; **~ beiden Seiten des Rheins** on both sides of the Rhine; **~ Wasser und ~ Lande** on land and at sea; **Gasthof ~ den drei Eichen** the Three Oaktrees (Inn); **3.** zeitlich, Zeitpunkt: at; Zeitraum: over; Anlass: for; **noch zehn Minuten (bis) ~ ...** another ten minutes before ...; **~ Beginn** at the beginning; **~ Weihnachten** at Christmas; schenken etc.: for Christmas; → Lebzeiten, Ostern etc.; **4.** (für) Zweck, Ziel: for; **~ etw. gut sein** be good for s.th.; **5.** Ergebnis ausdrückend: (in)to; **es kam ~ e-m Skandal** it blew up into a scandal, a scandal resulted; **~ Asche verbrennen** burn to ashes; **~ etw. werden** turn into s.th.; Person: auch become s.th.; **~ m-r Freude** etc. to my delight etc.; **6.** Beziehung ausdrückend: for; thematisch:

about, on; **sich äußern ~** say s.th. about; **gehören ~** belong to; **gemein/ nett ~** nasty/nice to; **passen ~** suit; **Liebe** etc. **~ j-m** love etc. for s.o.; **aus Freundschaft ~ ihr** out of friendship for her; **7.** Zusammensein ausdrückend: (mit) with; (hinzu) to; **sich ~ j-m setzen** sit with s.o., join s.o., sit (down) next to s.o.; **Wein ~m Essen trinken** have wine with one's diner; **~ alledem kommt noch hinzu, dass ...** and on top of all that ...; **8.** Art und Weise ausdrückend: **~ Fuß** on foot; **~ Pferd kommen** come on horseback; **~ Deutsch** in German; **9.** Menge, Zahl, Häufigkeit, Verhältnis etc. ausdrückend: in; **nur ~ e-m kleinen Teil** only to a small extent; **~ zweit nebeneinander gehen** walk along two by two; **sie kamen ~ sechst** six of them came; **~ hunderten** od. **Hunderten** in hundreds; **zehn Karten ~ zwei Euro** (à, je) ten tickets at two euros (a ticket); insgesamt: ten tickets for two euros; **10.** Zahlenverhältnis: **3 ~ 1** three to one; Sport, bei Ergebnisangaben: three-one; **11.** Adelsprädikat: **Graf Pappenheim** Count of Pappenheim; → **Hilfe** 1, **zum**, **zur**

zu² Adv. **1.** (übermäßig) too; **~ sehr** too much; **~ sehr betonen** overemphasize; **(viel) ~ viel/viele** (far od. much) too much/many; **einer** etc. **~ viel** one etc. too many; **einmal ~ viel** once too often; **ein gutes Gehalt wäre ~ viel gesagt** a good salary would be a bit of an overstatement; **ich krieg ~ viel!** umg. well blow me down!; **was ~ viel ist, ist ~ viel!** enough is enough!; **~ wenig** not enough, too little (Pl. few); **viel ~ wenig** not nearly enough, far too little (Pl. few); **einer** etc. **~ wenig** one etc. short, one etc. too few; **du isst ~ wenig** you don't eat enough, you need to eat more; **2.** umg. (sehr) too, so, terribly; **das ist ja ~ nett!** (sehr nett) that's really very nice!; iro. (sehr gemein) how terribly nice (of you)!; (sehr ärgerlich) a fine thing, I must say!; **3.** umg.: **nur ~!** go on!; **na, dann (mal) ~!** OK, go ahead; beim Aufbruch: OK, let's go, off we (bzw. you) go then; **4.** Richtung: **nach Norden ~** toward(s) the north; zeitlich: **auf** od. **gegen ... ~** toward(s)

zu³ I. Adj. umg. **1.** **~ sein** Fenster, Mund etc.: be closed, be shut; **e-e ~(n)e Tür** etc. a closed door etc.; **2.** **~ sein** (verstopft) Nase: be blocked; Ader, Straße, Zufahrt: be blocked; **3.** **~ sein** (ausgebucht) Flug: be full; **4.** **~ sein** (betrunken) be plastered, be pissed Sl.; (im Drogenrausch) be out of it; **II.** Adv. (Ggs. offen) closed, shut; **Augen ~!** close your eyes; **Tür ~!** shut the door!

zu⁴ Konj. **1.** (+ Inf.): **ich habe ~ arbeiten** I've got work to do; **es ist nicht ~ übersehen** it can't be overlooked; **gut ~ gebrauchen sein** be perfectly usable; **ich erinnere mich, ihn gesehen ~ haben** I remember seeing him; auch im Wort: **auszuhalten sein** be bearable; **2.** (+ Part. Präs.): **ein sorgfältig ~ erwägender Plan** a plan requiring careful consideration; auch im Wort: **die auszuwechselnden Teile** the parts to be exchanged

zuallererst Adv. first of all; **~letzt** Adv. last of all; **~oberst** Adv. **1.** right at the top; **2.** fig. first and foremost; **~unterst** Adv. **1.** right at the bottom; **2.** fig. last of all

Z

zuarbeiten *v/i.* (*trennb., hat -ge-*): *j-m ~* do the groundwork for s.o., assist s.o. with the preparations

zubauen *v/t.* (*trennb., hat -ge-*); (*Gelände etc.*) build on, develop; (*versperren*) (*auch Aussicht*) block, obstruct; (*Lücke*) fill (in)

Zubehör *n, selten m; -(e)s, -e od. schw.-den* accessories *Pl.* (*auch Fot.*); *Tech.* (*Zusatzgerät*) attachment(s *Pl.*); (*Ausstattungsteile*) fittings *Pl.*; *das ganze ~ auch* all the bits and pieces *umg.*; *mit allem ~ Küche etc.*: fully equipped; **~handel** *m* accessories trade; **~teil** *n* accessory (part); **~e** accessories

zubeißen *v/i.* (*unreg., trennb., hat -ge-*) bite; *Hund*: snap

zubekommen *v/t.* (*unreg., trennb., hat*) (*Tür etc.*) get *s.th.* shut; (*Kleidung*) get *s.th.* done up

Zuber *m; -s, -; Dial.* tub

zubereiten *v/t.* (*trennb., hat*) prepare; *das Essen ~ auch* make (the) dinner (*od.* lunch), prepare the meal; **Zubereitung** *f nur Sg.* preparation; *Art*: way of preparing, method; *die ~ dauert ...* (the) preparation time is ...; **Zubereitungszeit** *f* time needed (for preparation)

zubetonieren *v/t.* (*trennb., hat*); (*Loch etc.*) concrete (*od.* cement) over; *pej.* (*Landschaft*) concrete over

Zubettgehen *n: vor/nach dem ~* before/after going to bed

zubewegen (*trennb., hat*) **I.** *v/t.: etw. ~ auf* (+ *Akk.*) move (*od.* bring) s.th. toward(s); **II.** *v/refl.: sich ~ auf* (+ *Akk.*) move (slowly) toward(s), (slowly) approach

zubilligen *v/t.* (*trennb., hat -ge-*) grant (*j-m etw.* s.o. s.th.); allow (*auch Jur. mildernde Umstände*); *Jur.* (*zusprechen*) award; **Zubilligung** *f, nur Sg.* granting; (*Zusprechung*) award(ing); *unter ~ mildernder Umstände* accepting a plea of (*od.* that there were) extenuating circumstances

zubinden *v/t.* (*unreg., trennb., hat -ge-*) tie up; (*Schuhe*) do up; *j-m die Augen ~* blindfold s.o.

zubleiben *v/i.* (*unreg., trennb., ist -ge-*); *umg.* stay closed (*od.* shut)

zublinzeln *v/i.* (*trennb., hat -ge-*); (*j-m*) wink at s.o.

zubringen *v/t.* (*unreg., trennb., hat -ge-*) **1.** (*Zeit*) spend; **2.** *umg.* → *zubekommen*; **3.** *j-m etw. ~ fig.* inform s.o. about s.th., bring s.th. to s.o's notice *od.* attention

Zubringer *m; -s, -; Verk.* **1.** *Straße*: feeder; **2.** *Bus, Zug*: shuttle; **~bus** *m* feeder bus; *zum Flughafen*: airport bus; *am Flughafen*: transfer bus; **~dienst** *m* feeder service; **~linie** *f Flug.* feeder line; **~straße** *f* feeder road

Zubrot *n; nur Sg.; oft hum.: sich* (*Dat.*) *ein ~ verdienen* earn a bit on the side

zubuttern *v/t.* (*trennb., hat -ge-*); *umg.* **1.** (*zuschießen*) chip in; *eine Million Dollar etc. ~ auch* come up with an extra million dollars *etc.*; **2.** *zu s-m Einkommen etc. etw. ~* boost one's income *etc.* (a bit)

Zucchini [tsʊ'ki:ni] *Pl.* courgettes, *Am.* zucchini (*V. in Sg. od. Pl.*)

Zucht *f; -, -en* **1.** *nur Sg.; (Züchten)* breeding; *von Bienen etc.*: keeping; *von Pflanzen*: cultivation, growing; **2.** (*Rasse*) breed, stock; *von Pflanzen*: variety, strain; *von Bakterien, Bienen etc.*: culture; **3.** *Betrieb, Stätte*: breeding farm; *für Pferde*: stud; *für Hunde*:

breeding kennels *Pl.* (*V. im Sg.*); *aus eigener ~ Tier*: of our own breeding; *Pflanze*: home-grown, grown in our own garden (*bzw.* on our own farm); **4.** *nur Sg.; altm. od. geh., oft pej.* (*Disziplin*) discipline; *~ und Ordnung* strict discipline, law and order; *j-n in ~ nehmen* take s.o. in hand

Zucht|buch *n* stud book; **~bulle** *m Zool.* breeding bull

züchten *v/t.* **1.** (*Tiere*) breed; (*Pflanzen*) grow; **2.** (*Bakterien, Perlen*) culture; (*Kristalle*) grow; **3.** *fig.* (*Hass etc.*) breed, cultivate; **Züchter** *m; -s, -*, **Züchterin** *f, -, -nen von Vieh*: breeder; *von Bienen*: keeper; *von Pflanzen*: grower

Zuchterfolg *m* breeding success

Zuchthaus *n altm.* prison, *Am.* penitentiary; *zwei Jahre ~* two years' imprisonment; *~ auch Gefängnis*; **Zuchthäusler** *m; -s, -*, **Zuchthäuslerin** *f, -, -nen; altm.* convict, con *umg.*

Zuchthausstrafe *f altm.* imprisonment

Zuchthengst *m Zool.* stud horse, breeding stallion

züchtig *Adj. altm. od. hum.* (*tugendhaft*) virtuous; (*keusch*) chaste; *Benehmen*: modest, proper

züchtigen *v/t. geh.* punish

Züchtigung *f: (körperliche) ~* (corporal) punishment

zuchtlos *Adj. altm., oft pej.* undisciplined; (*liederlich*) disorderly; **Zuchtlosigkeit** *f, nur Sg.* lack of discipline

Zucht|meister *m altm. od. hum.* disciplinarian; **~perle** *f* cultured pearl; **~rute** *f fig.: unter j-s ~ stehen* be (brought up) under the heavy hand of s.o.

Zucht|stier *m Zool.* breeding bull; **~stute** *f* brood mare; **~tier** *n* stock animal, **~e** *auch* breeding stock *Sg.*

Züchtung *f* → *Zucht* 1, 2

Zucht|vieh *n Zool.* breeding cattle *Pl.*; **~wahl** *f* selective breeding

zuck → *ruck*

zuckeln *v/i. umg. Auto*: chug along; *Person*: trundle along

zucken *v/i.* **1.** twitch; *vor Schmerz*: wince, flinch; *vor Schreck*: start; (*zusammenzucken*) jerk; *Lider*: flutter; *Fisch im Netz*: thrash around; *ihm zuckte es in den Beinen* he was itching for a dance (*od.* to dance); *ein nervöses Zucken haben* have a nervous twitch; *~ Achsel* 1, *Schulter, Wimper* 1; **2.** *Flamme, Licht*: flicker; *Blitz*: flash; *ein Gedanke zuckte ihr durch den Kopf fig.* a thought flashed across her mind (*od.* suddenly struck her)

zücken *v/t.* (*Messer*) pull out; *hum.* (*Geldbeutel, Kugelschreiber etc.*) whip out

Zucker *m; -s, Sorten: - 1.* sugar; *ein Stück ~* a lump of sugar; *ohne ~ Fruchtsaft etc.*: sugar-free; *ich bin doch nicht aus ~! umg.* I won't break!; **2.** *Med. umg.* (*Zuckergehalt*) sugar; (*Zuckerspiegel*) blood sugar level; (*Diabetes*) diabetes (*Pl.* diabetes); *~ haben* be (a) diabetic, have diabetes; **~bäcker** *m*, **~bäckerin** *f altm. od. Dial.* confectioner; **~bäckerstil** *m; nur Sg.; pej.* gingerbread style; **~brot** *n fig., oft hum.: mit ~ und Peitsche* with a carrot and a stick

Zucker|couleur *f; nur Sg.* caramel; **~dose** *f* sugar bowl; **~erbse** *f Bot.* sugar pea; **~ersatzstoff** *m* artificial sweetener

zuckerfrei *Adj.* sugar-free

Zucker|gehalt *m* sugar content; **~glasur** *f*, **~guss** *m* icing, frosting; *mit ~ überziehen* ice, frost

zuckerhaltig *Adj.* containing sugar; *~ sein* contain sugar

Zuckerhut *m* **1.** sugar loaf; **2.** *Geogr.: der ~* Sugarloaf Mountain

zuckerig *Adj.* sugary

zuckerkrank *Adj. Med.* diabetic; *~ sein* have diabetes, be (a) diabetic; **Zuckerkranke** *m, f* diabetic; **Zuckerkrankheit** *f; nur Sg.* diabetes (*Pl.* diabetes)

Zuckerl *n; -s, -(n); südd., österr.* → *Bonbon*

Zucker|lecken *n: das ist kein ~* it's no picnic; **~lösung** *f* sugar solution; **~mais** *m* sweetcorn

zuckern *v/t.* sugar; (*mit Zucker bestreuen*) *auch* sprinkle sugar on, sprinkle with sugar; (*süßen*) *auch* sweeten

Zucker|puppe *f umg. altm.* sweetie; *Anrede*: (my) sweetie pie; **~raffinerie** *f* sugar refinery; **~rohr** *n; nur Sg.* sugarcane; **~rohrplantage** *f* sugarcane plantation; **~rübe** *f* sugar beet; **~schlecken** *n Dial.* → *Zuckerlecken*; **~spiegel** *m Med.* blood sugar level; **~stange** *f* stick of rock (*Am.* candy); **~streuer** *m* sugar caster

zuckersüß I. *Adj.* **1.** as sweet as sugar; **2.** *fig.* sugary, saccharine; **II.** *Adv.: j-n ~ anlächeln* give s.o. a sickly sweet smile

Zucker|tüte *f Dial.* → *Schultüte*; **~wasser** *n; nur Sg.* sugar water (*auch pej. für süßen Wein, Saft etc.*); **~watte** *f* candy floss, *Am.* cotton candy; **~werk** *n; nur Sg.; altm.* confectionery; **~zange** *f: (e-e) ~* (a pair of) sugar tongs *Pl.*; **~zusatz** *m: ohne ~* (with) no (*od.* without) added sugar

zuckrig *Adj.* → *zuckerig*

Zuckung *f* jerk, twitch; *krampfhafte*: convulsion; *e-s Muskels*: twitch; *stärker*: contraction; *nervöse ~en auch* nervous twitching; *in den letzten ~en liegen* (*sterben*) be in one's death throes; *umg. fig.* (*dem Ende zugehen*) be about to give up the ghost

Zudecke *f Dial.* cover; **zudecken** *v/t.* (*trennb., hat -ge-*) **1.** cover (up); (*j-n*) *im Bett*: tuck up (*Am.* in); *j-n mit e-r Decke ~* cover s.o. up with a blanket; **2.** *fig.* (*vertuschen*) conceal, cover up; **3.** *fig. mit Arbeit*: inundate with, load down with; *mit Fragen ~* bombard with questions

zudem *Adv. geh.* besides, moreover

zudenken *v/t.* (*unreg., trennb., hat -ge-*): *etw. ist j-m zugedacht* s.th. is intended for s.o.

zudrehen (*trennb., hat -ge-*) **I.** *v/t.* **1.** (*Hahn, umg. Wasser etc.*) turn off; (*Schraube*) tighten; *fig.* → *Geldhahn*; **2.** (*zuwenden*) turn to(ward[s]); *j-m den Rücken ~* turn one's back to(ward[s]) (*abweisend*: on) s.o.; **II.** *v/refl.: sich j-m ~* turn to s.o.

zudringlich *Adj.* obtrusive, pushy *umg.*; (*j-m gegenüber*) *~ werden sexuell*: make importunate advances (on s.o.), try to force one's attentions (on s.o.); **Zudringlichkeit** *f* **1.** *nur Sg.*; obtrusiveness, pushiness *umg.*; **2.** *Pl. Handlungen*: importunate advances *Pl.*

zudröhnen *v/refl.* (*trennb., hat -ge-*); *Sl. mit Alkohol*: get plastered; *mit Drogen*: zonk out, get spaced out; *mit übermäßigem Fernsehkonsum etc.*: send one's mind to sleep

Z

zudrücken (*trennb.*, *hat -ge-*) **I.** *v/t.* (press) shut; *Tür*: shut; **e-m Toten die Augen ~** close a dead person's eyes; **j-m die Kehle ~** throttle s.o.; → *Auge* 2; **II.** *v/i.*: **sie drückte fest zu** she pressed hard; *beim Händeschütteln*: she gave *s.o.* 's hand a really hard squeeze

zueignen *v/t.* (*trennb.*, *hat -ge-*); *geh.*: **j-m etw. ~** dedicate s.th. to s.o.

zueilen *v/i.* (*trennb.*, *ist -ge-*): **auf j-n/etw. ~** rush towards (*od.* up to) s.o./s.th.

zueinander *Adv.* to each other, to one another; *Vertrauen*: in one another; **~ finden** *emotional*: come together; *(sich einigen)* reach an understanding; **~ gehören** belong to one another; **~ halten** *od.* **stehen** stand (*umg.* stick) by each other (*od.* one another); **~ kommen** come together; **~ passen** go together (well); *(Menschen)* suit one another, be well suited

zuerkennen *v/t.* (*unreg.*, *trennb.*, *hat*); *(Entschädigung, Preis etc.)* award (+ *Dat.* to); *(Auszeichnung)* confer (on); *(Recht, Sieg)* grant (*j-m* s.o.); *(Bedeutung, Relevanz etc.)* attach (to); *(Strafe)* impose ([up]on), mete out (to) *geh.*; **Zuerkennung** *f*, *nur Sg.* award

zuerst *Adv.* **1.** *(als Erster)* *Erstes)* first; **er kam ~** *auch* he was the first to arrive; **was machst du morgens ~?** what's the first thing you do in the morning?; **wer ~ kommt, mahlt ~** *Sprichw.* first come first served; **2.** *(zunächst)* first (of all); *(zunächst einmal)* *auch* to begin (*od.* start) with; **3.** *(anfangs)* at first; **4.** *(erstmals)* the first time; **das wurde ~ in China eingeführt** it was first introduced in China

Zuerwerb *m* → *Nebenerwerb*

zufächeln *v/t.* (*trennb.*, *hat -ge-*): **j-m/sich** *(Dat.)* **Kühlung ~** fan s.o./o.s.

zufahren *v/i.* (*unreg.*, *trennb.*, *ist -ge-*) **1. ~ auf** (+ *Akk.*) drive (*mit Rad*: ride) to(ward[s]); *auf etw.*: head (*od.* make) for; **das Auto kam genau auf mich zugefahren** the car was coming straight at me; **2. fahr zu!** *(fahr los)* go on!, what are you waiting for? *iro.*; *(fahr schneller)* step on it!, put your foot down!; **Zufahrt** *f* **1.** access road; *am Haus*: drive(way); **die ~ zum Haus** the drive(way) leading up to the house; **2.** *nur Sg.*; *Möglichkeit*: access; „**keine ~ zum Stadion** *etc.*" *Schild*: no (vehicular) access to the stadium *etc.*; **Zufahrtsstraße** *f* access road, road leading to ...; **Zufahrtsweg** *m* access road, road leading to ...; *unbefestigt*: track leading to ...; *weitS. Angaben gebend*: (access) route, way to get to ...

Zufall *m* chance; *(Zusammentreffen)* coincidence; **reiner ~** pure chance; **glücklicher ~** lucky chance, bit of luck; **unglücklicher ~** bit of bad luck; **das ist ~** that's chance (*od.* luck); **durch ~** by chance, by accident; → *auch* **zufällig** I; **es dem ~ überlassen** leave it to chance; **nichts blieb dem ~ überlassen** nothing was left to chance; **wie es der ~ wollte** as luck would have it; **es ist kein ~, wenn ...** it's no accident that ...; **was für ein ~!** what a co-incidence!; *bei Treffen*: *auch* well, fancy meeting you here (*od.* you of all people)!; **der ~ kam ihr zu Hilfe** luck was on her side, luck came to her aid *geh.*

zufallen *v/i.* (*unreg.*, *trennb.*, *ist -ge-*) **1.** *Augen*: close; *Tür*: slam shut; **mir fallen die Augen zu** I can't keep my eyes open; **2. j-m ~** fall to s.o.; *Erbe etc.*: *auch* devolve upon s.o. *förm.*; **j-m ~ zu ...** (+ *Inf.*) fall to s.o.('s lot) to (+ *Inf.*); **3. j-m ~ ohne Mühe**: *(Ideen etc.)* come easily to s.o.

zufällig **I.** *Adv.* by chance, as luck would have it; *bes. durch zusammentreffende Ereignisse*: coincidentally; **rein ~** purely (*od.* quite) by chance; **er war ~ zu Hause** he happened to be at home; **ich traf ihn ~** I met him by chance, I happened to bump into him, I just bumped into him; **weißt du ~, ob ...?** do you happen to know whether ...?; **sind Sie ~ ...?** are you by any chance ...?; **wenn du ~ mit ihm sprechen solltest** if you (should) happen to be talking to him, if by any chance you have a word with him; **nicht ~ hatte sie die Dokumente dabei** it was no accident that she had the documents with her; **II.** *Adj.* accidental, chance ...; *(nebenbei)* incidental; **es war rein ~** it was pure (*od.* sheer) chance (*od.* coincidence); **zufälligerweise** *Adv.* → *zufällig* I; **Zufälligkeit** *f* **1.** *nur Sg.* chance nature; *Math. etc.* randomness; **2.** *Ereignis*: coincidence, chance occurrence

Zufallsauswahl *f* random selection (*od.* sampling)

zufallsbedingt *Adj.* accidental; chance ...

Zufalls|bekanntschaft *f* chance acquaintance; **~fund** *m* lucky find; **~generator** *m* *Computer*: random (number) generator; **~treffer** *m* **1.** *bes. Sport* lucky hit, fluke *umg.*; **2.** *fig.* lucky strike

zufassen *v/i.* (*trennb.*, *hat -ge-*) **1.** *(zugreifen)* make a grab, grab at; *Hund etc.*: go for *s.o. od. s.th.*; *(fassen)* catch (*od.* get hold of) *s.th.*; **2.** *umg.* *(helfen)* lend a hand, muck (*Am.* pitch) in; **3.** *fig.* *(Gelegenheit ergreifen)* seize the opportunity, go for it *umg.*

zufaxen *v/t.* (*trennb.*, *hat -ge-*): **j-m etw. ~** fax s.o. s.th., fax s.th. to s.o., send s.o. s.th. by fax

zufliegen *v/i.* (*unreg.*, *trennb.*, *ist -ge-*) **1. ~ auf** (+ *Akk.*) fly toward(s); **auf j-n zugeflogen kommen** come flying toward(s) s.o.; **2. j-m ~** *Vogel*: fly to s.o.; **der Vogel ist uns zugeflogen** the bird came to us; **3.** *fig.*: **j-m ~ die Herzen** go out to s.o.; *Ideen, Wissen etc.*: come easily to s.o.; **ihm fliegt immer alles zu** everything comes easily to him; **4.** *umg. Fenster, Tür*: slam shut

zufließen *v/i.* (*unreg.*, *trennb.*, *ist -ge-*) **1.** (+ *Dat.*) flow to(ward[s]); **2.** *zusätzlich*: **es fließt ständig frisches Wasser zu** fresh water is constantly flowing in; **3.** *fig.* (*j-m*): go (*e-m Fonds etc.*) flow into; **j-m etw. ~ lassen** let s.o. have s.th.

Zuflucht *f* **1.** *vor Unwetter*: shelter (**vor** + *Dat.* from); *in der Not*: *auch* refuge; **~ suchen/finden in** (+ *Dat.*) seek/find shelter in; **bei Freunden ~ suchen** seek refuge (*od.* shelter) among friends; **2.** *fig.* *(Ausweg)* resort; **m-e letzte ~** my last resort; **sie ist m-e ~** she is the one I turn to when I'm in trouble; **~ nehmen zu** resort to; **zu Drogen etc.**: *auch* turn to

Zuflucht|ort *m*, **~stätte** *f* *geh.* place of refuge, retreat, sanctuary

Zufluss *m* **1.** *nur Sg.* influx (*auch Met.*, *fig.*); *Tech.*, *Wirts.* supply; **2.** *(Nebenfluss)* tributary; *zu Meer, See*: inlet

zuflüstern *v/t.* (*trennb.*, *hat -ge-*): **j-m etw. ~** whisper s.th. to s.o. (*od.* into s.o.'s ear)

zufolge *Präp.* (+ *Dat.*) **1.** *(gemäß)* according to; **Berichte, denen ~ ...** *auch* reports claiming (that) ..., reports to the effect that ...; **2.** *(infolge)* as a result (*od.* consequence) of

zufrieden *Adj.* **1.** content(ed), satisfied (**mit** with); *mit e-r Leistung*: pleased, satisfied; *mit sich selbst*: complacent; **glücklich und ~** perfectly content (*od.* happy); **ich bin damit ~** *auch* I'm quite happy with it, I have no complaints; **sie ist mit nichts ~** she's never satisfied, there's no pleasing her; **sie ist mit allem ~** she's not fussy, she's very easy to please; **du machst ein sehr ~es Gesicht** you look very satisfied with yourself; **wie geht's? - bin ~** *umg.* can't complain; **bist du jetzt ~?** *umg.*, *iro.* are you quite satisfied (*od.* happy) now?; **2.** *mit Verben*: **sich ~ geben** be content (**mit** with); **sich ~ geben mit** *auch* settle for, (be prepared to) accept; **damit wollte er sich nicht ~ geben** he wasn't prepared to accept (*od.* put up with) that; **~ lassen** *umg.* (*j-n*) leave s.o. alone (*od.* in peace); (*etw.*) leave s.th. alone; **lass mich damit ~!** *umg.* stop pestering me about it!, I don't want to know!; **~ stellen** satisfy; **schwer ~ zu stellen** hard to please; **~ stellend** satisfactory; **Zufriedenheit** *f*, *nur Sg.* contentment; *auch mit e-r Leistung*: satisfaction; *mit sich selbst*: complacency; **zur allgemeinen ~** to everyone's satisfaction; **zur vollsten ~** to our *etc.* full satisfaction

zufrieren *v/i.* (*unreg.*, *trennb.*, *ist -ge-*) freeze over (*od.* up); → *zugefroren*

zufügen *v/t.* (*trennb.*, *hat -ge-*) **1.** add (+ *Dat.* to); **2. j-m etw. ~** *(antun)* cause s.o. s.th.; **j-m Leid ~** cause s.o. pain (*od.* suffering), hurt s.o.; **j-m Verluste etc. ~** inflict losses *etc.* on s.o.; → *Schaden* 1

Zufuhr *f*, *-*, *-en* **1.** supply; **2.** *Met.*, *kühler Meeresluft etc.*: influx; **zuführen** (*trennb.*, *hat -ge-*) **I.** *v/t.* **1.** (*Strom etc.*) supply (+ *Dat.* to), feed (to); **e-r Sache etw. ~** *auch* supply s.th. with s.th.; **2.** (*Kunden, Mitglieder etc.*) bring (+ *Dat.* to), introduce (to); **j-n j-m ~** bring s.o. into contact with s.o., introduce s.o. to s.o.; *zu sexuellen Zwecken*: procure s.o. for s.o.; **3.** *fig.*: **j-n s-r verdienten Strafe ~** give s.o. his (*od.* her) due punishment; **etw. s-r Bestimmung ~** put s.th. to its proper use; **II.** *v/i.*: **~ auf** (+ *Akk.*) lead to (*auch fig.*); **Zuführung** *f* supply

Zug *m*; *-(e)s*, *Züge* **1.** *Eisenb.* train; **im ~** on the train; **mit dem ~** by train; **wann geht mein ~?** when (*od.* what time) does my train go?, when (*od.* what time) is my train?; **j-n zum ~ bringen** take s.o. to the station (*Am.* to the train [station]); **bis zum Zug begleiten**: see s.o. off at the station (*Am.* the train [station]); **auf den fahrenden ~ aufspringen** jump onto the moving train; *fig.* jump on the bandwagon; **der ~ ist abgefahren** *fig.* you've (*od.* we've, he's *etc.*) missed the boat; **2.** *Gruppe*: *(Festzug)* procession; *(Kolonne)* column; *von Fahrzeugen*: convoy; *von Vögeln*: flight; *von Fischen*: shoal; *(Gespann)* team; *Mil.* platoon; *(Abteilung)* section; *der Feuerwehr*: watch; **3.** *nur Sg.*; *Bewegung*: procession; *(Marsch)* march; *von Zugvögeln, Völkern etc.*: migration; *von Wolken*:

movement, drift(ing); **Hannibals ~ über die Alpen** Hannibal's crossing of the Alps; **e-n ~ durch die Gemeinde machen** *umg. fig.* go on a pub crawl, *Am.* go bar-hopping; **im ~e** *fig.* (*im Verlauf*) in the course (+ *Gen.* of); *des Fortschritts etc.*: on the tide (of); **4.** (*das Ziehen*) *an Leine etc.*: pull (**an** + *Dat.* on); *heftig*: tug; *ruckartig*: jerk; *Phys.* tension, pull; **~ ausüben auf** (+ *Akk.*) exert traction on; **5.** *beim Schwimmen*: stroke; *beim Rudern*: pull; **sie schwamm mit kräftigen Zügen** she was swimming strongly; **6.** *an der Zigarette*: drag, puff (*beide*: **an** + *Dat.* of, at); *beim Trinken*: gulp, swig *umg., förm.* draught, *Am.* draft (*alle aus* from); (*Atemzug*) breath; **e-n ~ machen** *an Zigarette*: take a drag (*od.* puff); **e-n ~ aus der Pfeife nehmen** (take a) puff at one's pipe; **e-n tüchtigen ~ aus der Flasche nehmen** *umg.* take a good swig from the bottle; **sein Glas auf einen ~ leeren** empty one's glass in one go; **in den letzten Zügen liegen** *umg.* be breathing one's last, be at death's door; *fig. Sache*: be on its last legs; **in vollen Zügen genießen** *fig.* enjoy to the full, make the most of; **in groben Zügen** *fig.* in broad outline, roughly; **7.** *fig. und Schach etc.*: move; **wer ist am ~?** whose move (*od.* turn) is it?; **ein geschickter ~** a clever move; **jetzt ist er am ~**, the ball is in his court; **(nicht) zum ~(e) kommen** *Person*: (never) get a chance (*od.* a look-in *umg.*); *im Gespräch*: (not) get a word in; *Strategie etc.*: (not) get (*od.* be given) a chance; **~ um ~ nacheinander**: step by step; (*ohne Pause*) without delay; **in einem ~(e) tun, lesen, Aufsatz etc. schreiben**: in one go; *Namen etc. schreiben*: with a single stroke (of the pen); **8.** *nur Sg.* → **Zugluft**; **9.** *des Gesichts*: feature; *um den Mund etc.*: line(s *Pl.*); **e-n energischen ~ um den Mund haben** have firmness in the lines of one's mouth; **10.** *des Wesens*: trait, characteristic, feature (*alle* **von, an** + *Dat.* of); *bes. pej.* streak; **e-n leichtsinnigen ~ haben** have a careless streak; **das war kein schöner ~ von ihm** that was not very nice of him; **11.** *Vorrichtung, an Glocke, Rollladen etc.*: pull; *zum Hochhieven*: hoist; (*Flaschenzug*) pulley; *an Orgel*: stop; *an Posaune*: slide; **12.** (*Gummizug*) elastic band; (*Riemen*) strap; *am Beutel etc.*: drawstring; **13.** (*Zugklappe*) damper; **14.** *Päd.* (*Zweig*) stream, *Am.* track; **der neusprachliche ~ des Gymnasiums** the modern languages side of the grammar school

Zugabe *f* **1.** *Mus., Theat. etc.* encore; **~!** encore!; **2.** extra; (*Prämie*) bonus; (*Geschenk*) free gift; **3.** *nur Sg.*; (*das Zugeben*) addition; **unter ~ von** (by) adding

Zugabteil *n* railway (*bes. Am.* train) compartment

Zugang *m* **1.** entrance; *auf Schild*: way in; (*Zutritt*) access (*auch fig.*); (*Weg*) approach, access road; **freier ~ zum Meer etc.**: direct access; *zu Unterlagen*: free access; **kein ~!** no admittance (*od.* entry); **zu etw. keinen ~ haben** *fig.* have no appreciation (*Mus. auch* ear) for s.th.; **2.** *von Studenten etc.*: intake; *von Patienten*: admissions *Pl.*; *von Büchern*: acquisitions *Pl.*; *von Waren*: receipt; (*Zuwachs*) increase

zugange *Adj. umg.*: **~ sein** (*beschäf-*

---

tigt) be busy (**mit** with); *euph. sexuell*: be on the job; (*aufgestanden*) be up

zugänglich *Adj.* **1.** accessible (**für** to); *Bücher, Dokumente*: available; (*geöffnet*) *Park etc.*: open; **allgemein ~** open to the (general) public; **leicht/schwer ~ Ort etc.**: easy/difficult to get to; *Dokumente etc.*: easy/difficult to get at (*od.* get hold of); **~ machen für** open up to; **2.** (*umgänglich*) approachable; **~ für** open to, amenable to, willing to listen to; **Zugänglichkeit** *f*; *nur Sg.* **1.** accessibility; *von Büchern, Dokumenten*: availability; **2.** *fig.* approachability

Zugangs|straße *f* access road; **~voraussetzung** *f* condition of entry; **~weg** *m* access road, means of access

Zug|auskunft *f* **1.** (information on) train times; **2.** *Stelle*: enquiries *Pl.*, inquiry office (*od.* desk), *auch Am.* information office (*od.* desk); **~begleiter** *m*, **~begleiterin** *f* guard, *Am.* conductor; **~brücke** *f* drawbridge

zugeben *v/t.* (*unreg., trennb., hat -ge-*) **1.** (*zufügen*) add; *Kartenspiel*: throw (in); *als Extra*: throw in; **die Band gab drei Lieder zu** the band gave three (extra numbers as) encores; **2.** (*eingestehen*) admit, confess, own up to; (*einräumen*) concede, admit, grant; **gib's doch zu!** go on, admit it!, *Am. auch* fess up!; **man muss ~, dass er ...** you have to hand it to him he ..., you have to admit (that) he ...; **zugegeben, es war nicht sehr geschickt** granted (*od.* okay), it wasn't very clever; **3.** (*erlauben*) allow

zugedröhnt *I. P.P.* → **zudröhnen**; *II. Adj. Sl.* out of it; *bes. mit Drogen*: spaced out, zonked

zugefroren *I. P.P.* → **zufrieren**; *II. Adj. See etc.*: frozen over; *Hafen*: icebound; *Autotür*: frozen shut

zugegebenermaßen *Adv.* admittedly

zugegen *Adj. geh.* present (**bei** at); **~ sein bei** *auch* attend

zugehen *v/i.* (*unreg., trennb., ist -ge-*) **1.** **~ auf** (+ *Akk.*) go up to, approach; *entschlossen*: make for, head for; **sie ging direkt auf mich zu** she came (*od.* walked) straight up to me, she headed straight for me; **2.** *fig.*: **auf j-n ~** *Rat suchend etc.*: approach s.o.; *Hilfe anbietend*: reach out to s.o.; *nach Streit*: try to make up with s.o.; **auf die Achtzig ~** be approaching (*od.* getting on for) eighty; **dem Ende ~** be drawing to a close; **3.** *unpers.*: (*geschehen*) be; **es geht dort manchmal etwas wild zu** things can sometimes get a bit wild there; **auf der Party ging's zu!** it was some party!; **wie geht es denn hier zu?** what on earth's going on here?; **es müsste seltsam ~, wenn ...** it would be very strange if ...; **es geht auf den Herbst / zehn Uhr zu** autumn is on its way / it's getting on for (*Am.* it's nearly) ten o'clock; → **Ding** 2; **4.** *Amtsspr.*: **j-m ~** *Brief etc.*: reach s.o.; **j-m etw. ~ lassen** have s.th. sent to s.o.; **die Formulare gehen Ihnen in den nächsten Tagen zu** you will be receiving the forms in the next few days; **5.** *umg.* (*schließen*) shut; **der Reißverschluss geht nicht zu** I can't do the zip (*Am.* zipper) up; **6.** → **zulaufen** 5; **7.** *Dial.*: **geh zu!** get a move on! *umg.*, step on it! *umg.*

Zugehfrau *f Dial.* cleaner, cleaning woman

zugehören *v/i.* (*trennb., hat -ge-*); *geh.* belong to

---

zugehörig *Adj.* **1.** belonging (+ *Dat.* to); **~e Teile** accessories; **die ~en Gebäude** the buildings belonging (*od.* that belong) to it; **sich e-r Gruppe etc. ~ fühlen** feel part of a group *etc.*, feel one belongs to a group *etc.*; **2.** (*begleitend*) accompanying; *in Farbe, Form etc.*: matching; *nachgestellt*: to match; **Zugehörigkeit** *f* affiliation (**zu** to, with); *zu e-r Partei etc.*: membership (of); **Zugehörigkeitsgefühl** *n*; *nur Sg.* sense of belonging (*od.* being part of s.th.); feeling of identity (**zu** with)

zugeknöpft *I. P.P.* → **zuknöpfen**; *II. Adj. umg., fig.* buttoned-up, tight-lipped, reserved, uncommunicative; **Zugeknöpftheit** *f*; *nur Sg.*; *umg.* reserve, uncommunicativeness

Zügel *m*; *-s, -* rein; **e-m Pferd in die ~ fallen** rein a horse in (*od.* back); **die ~ anziehen** tighten the reins (*auch fig.*); **die ~ schleifen lassen** give free rein to (*auch fig*); **die ~ (fest) in der Hand halten** *fig.* have things (firmly) under control

zügellos *Adj. fig.* unrestrained; *Eifersucht, Gier etc.*: *auch* unbridled; (*ausschweifend*) licentious, dissolute; **Zügellosigkeit** *f* **1.** *nur Sg.* (complete) lack of restraint; **2.** (*Ausschweifung*) licentiousness

zügeln[1] *I. v/t.* **1.** rein (up); **2.** *fig.* control, bridle, curb; *II. v/refl.* restrain o.s. **zügeln**[2] *schw. V.* (*ist gezügelt*) move; *II. v/t.* (*hat*) move

Zügelung *f*; *nur Sg.*; *fig.* control, curbing

zugeparkt *I. P.P.* → **zuparken**; *II. Adj.* blocked (with parked cars); *Straße*: full of (*umg.* chock-a-block with) parked cars

Zugereiste *m, f; -n, -n; bes. südd.* newcomer

zugeschnitten *I. P.P.* → **zuschneiden**; *II. Adj. fig.*: **~ auf** (+ *Akk.*) tailored to, designed for

zugesellen *v/refl.* (*trennb., hat*): **sich j-m ~** (go over and) join s.o.

zugespitzt *I. P.P.* → **zuspitzen**; *II. Adj. Stock etc.*: pointed, sharp; *Turm etc.*: pointed; *III. Adv.*: **~ gesagt** to put it in slightly exaggerated (*od.* drastic) terms; **er hat es ~ formuliert** he overstated the case

zugestandenermaßen *Adv. geh.* admittedly; **Zugeständnis** *n* concession; (*Anerkennung*) *auch* acknowledg(e)ment; **~se machen** make concessions (+ *Dat.* to); *fig.* make allowances (**an** + *Akk.* for); **zugestehen** *v/t.* (*unreg., trennb., hat*) **1.** (*Anspruch, Anteil, Recht*) concede, grant (**j-m etw.** s.th.); (*Rabatt, mehr Zeit etc.*) allow; **2.** (*anerkennen*) admit, concede

zugetan *I. P.P.* → **zutun**; *II. Adj. geh.*, **j-m od. e-r Sache ~ sein** be fond of; *bes. e-r Person*: be attached to; (*Schokolade, Wein etc.*) *auch* be (quite) partial to; **j-m in Liebe ~ sein** love s.o.

Zugewinn *m* increase (**an** in); *Wirts.* surplus (of); *e-r Ehe*: community property, property acquired in the course of a marriage; **~ausgleich** *m Jur.* equitable division of community property (*od.* property acquired in the course of a marriage); **~gemeinschaft** *f Jur.* community of property

Zugezogene *m, f; -n, -n* newcomer

Zugfeder *f Tech.* tension spring; *Uhr*: mainspring

zugfest *Adj. Tech.* tension-proof; *Stahl*: high-tensile; **Zugfestigkeit** *f Tech.* tensile strength

Zugführer *m*, **˷in** *f* **1.** *Eisenb.* chief guard, *Am.* conductor; **2.** *Mil.* platoon-leader

zugießen *v/t.* (*unreg.*, *trennb.*, *hat -ge-*) **1.** (*Flüssigkeit*) add; *darf ich Ihnen noch etwas ˷?* may I fill up your glass (*od.* cup *etc.*)?, may I top you up? *umg.*; **2.** (*Öffnung*) fill up (*mit* with)

zugig *Adj.* draughty, *Am.* drafty

zügig I. *Adj.* **1.** (*rasch*) quick, speedy; (*Tempo*) high, brisk; (*ohne Unterbrechung*) uninterrupted; **2.** *schw. Kandidat*, *Schlagwort etc.*: attractive; **II.** *Adv.*: *vorankommen* make rapid (*od.* fast) progress; *am Zoll etc. ˷ abgefertigt werden* be whisked through customs *etc.*; **Zügigkeit** *f*; *nur Sg.* speed, quickness

zugipsen *v/t.* (*trennb.*, *hat -ge-*) plaster over

Zugklappe *f* damper

Zugkraft *f* **1.** *Phys.* tractive force; **2.** *Mot.*, *e-s Pkw etc.*: power; **3.** *fig.* appeal; *e-r Anzeige*: draw, attention value; *e-r Person*: magnetism; **zugkräftig** *Adj. fig.* popular; *Werbeplakat etc.*: attention-grabbing *umg.*; **˷ sein** have (mass *od.* popular) appeal; *Film etc.*: be a crowd-puller *umg.*, be a big draw *umg.*

zugleich *Adv.* at the same time; (*miteinander*) together; *sie ist schön und intelligent ˷* she's both beautiful and intelligent; she's not only beautiful, she's intelligent as well

Zug|leine *f* pull-cord; **˷luft** *f* draught, *Am.* draft; *˷ (ab)bekommen* be in a draught (*Am.* draft); **˷maschine** *f* traction engine, tractor; **˷mittel** *n fig.* draw, attraction; **˷nummer** *f* **1.** *Theat. etc.* crowd-puller, big attraction; *Sache*: auch draw; **2.** *Eisenb.* train number; **˷personal** *n* train staff (*mst V. im Pl.*); **˷pferd** *n* **1.** draught (*Am.* draft) horse; **2.** *fig.* crowd-puller, big attraction; *Sache*: auch draw; **˷pflaster** *n Med.* blistering plaster

zugreifen *v/i.* (*unreg.*, *trennb.*, *hat -ge-*) **1.** make a grab; grab (at) it; *bei Tisch etc.*: help o.s.; *greifen Sie bitte zu!* please help yourself; **2.** *fig.* (*die Gelegenheit ergreifen*) jump at (*od.* grab) the opportunity; *sofort ˷ bei Angebot etc.*: accept (*od.* say yes) straightaway; *jetzt ˷!* (*kaufen*) buy now!; **3.** *fig.*: *˷ auf* (+ *Akk.*) *auf Informationen, Daten*: access; **4.** (*mithelfen*) lend a hand, chip in *umg.*

Zugrestaurant *n* restaurant (*od.* dining, buffet) car, *Am.* diner

Zugriff *m fig.* **1.** (*das Eingreifen*) (swift) action (*der Polizei etc.* on the part of the police *etc.*); *sich j-s ˷ entziehen* escape s.o.'s clutches, slip through s.o.'s fingers; **2.** *auf Daten, Informationen etc.*: access (*zu od. auf* + *Akk.* to)

Zugriffs|code *m EDV* access code; **˷zeit** *f* access time

zugrunde, **zu Grunde** *Adv.* **1.** *˷ legen* take as a basis (+ *Dat.* for); (*Theorie etc.*) apply; *˷ liegen* underlie (+ *Dat. s.th.*), be at the root of (*s.th.*); *˷ liegend* underlying; **2.** *˷ gehen Geschäft etc.*: go to pieces, go to rack and ruin; *Weltreich*: collapse; *allmählich*: decline; *Person*: go to rack and ruin; (*sterben*) die, perish *lit.*; *˷ gehen an* (+ *Dat.*) *Person*: come to grief through; (*sterben*) die of; *er ist daran ˷ gegangen* it was his undoing (*od.* the ruin of him); (*gestorben*) it was the death of him; *˷ richten* ruin, destroy, wreck

umg.; *sich* (*selber*) *˷ richten* ruin one's health (*od.* nerves), kill o.s. *umg.*; **Zugrundelegung** *f*; *nur Sg.* taking as a basis; *unter ˷ der geltenden Verordnungen* on the basis of the regulations in force

Zugsalbe *f Med.* blistering ointment

Zug|schaffner *m*, **˷schaffnerin** *f Eisenb.* guard, *bes. Am.* conductor; **˷seil** *n* tow line; **˷spannung** *f* tensile stress

Zugspitze¹ *f*; *nur Sg.*; *Geog.*: *die ˷* the Zugspitze, *the highest mountain in Germany*

Zugspitze² *f* **1.** *Eisenb.* front of the (*od.* a) train; **2.** *Umzug*: head of the (*od.* a) parade (*Prozession*: procession)

Zug|telefon *n* train telephone; **˷tier** *n* draught (*Am.* draft) animal

zugucken *v/i.* (*trennb.*, *hat -ge-*); *umg.* → *zusehen*

Zugunglück *n* railway (*Am.* railroad) accident, train crash

zugunsten, **zu Gunsten** *Präp.* (+ *Gen.* vorgestellt, + *Dat. nachgestellt*) in favo(u)r of; (*zum Nutzen von*) for the benefit of; *Spendenaktion etc.*: in aid of

zugute *Adv.* **1.** *j-m etw. ˷ halten* (*positiv anrechnen*) give s.o. credit for s.th.; (*Verständnis haben*) make allowances for s.th.; *j-m s-e Unerfahrenheit ˷ halten* make allowances for s.o.'s lack of experience; **2.** *˷ kommen* be of benefit to *s.o. od. s.th.*; (*zustatten kommen*) stand *s.o.* in good stead; *das Geld wird e-m Krankenhaus ˷ kommen* the money will be donated to a hospital; *j-m etw. ˷ kommen lassen* give s.o. s.th.; **3.** *geh.*: *sich* (*Dat.*) *etwas ˷ halten auf* (+ *Akk.*) pride o.s. on

Zug|verbindung *f* rail connection (*od.* link); **˷verkehr** *m* train services *Pl.*; **˷vogel** *m* **1.** *Orn.* bird of passage; **2.** *fig.* drifter; **˷zwang** *m*: *in ˷ geraten* be forced to make a move; *in ˷ bringen od. unter ˷ setzen* force *s.o.* into action (*od.* to make a move); *unter ˷ stehen* be under pressure to act (*od.* make a move)

zuhaben (*unreg.*, *trennb.*, *hat -ge-*) *umg.* **I.** *v/i.* be closed; *wir haben mittwochs zu* we're closed on Wednesday(s); **II.** *v/t.* (*Laden, Mund, Tür etc.*) have (*od.* keep) closed; (*Mantel, Reißverschluss*) be done up; *endlich hab ich das Fenster zu* I've at last managed to close the window

zuhalten (*unreg.*, *trennb.*, *hat -ge-*) **I.** *v/t.* **1.** keep *s.th.* closed (*od.* shut); *sich* (*Dat.*) *die Ohren ˷* put (*länger*: hold) one's hands over one's ears; *sich* (*Dat.*) *die Nase ˷* hold one's nose; *sie hielt die Tür von innen zu* she held the door shut from the inside; **2.** *schw.* award; **II.** *v/i.*: *˷ auf* (+ *Akk.*) make (*od.* head) for

Zuhälter *m*; *-s*, *-* pimp; **Zuhälterei** *f*; *-*, *kein Pl.* pimping

zuhängen *v/t.* (*trennb.*, *hat -ge-*) cover; *mit etw. ˷* auch hang s.th. over (*od.* across) s.th.

zuhauen (*unreg.*, *trennb.*, *hat -ge-*) **I.** *v/t.* (*Stein*) dress; (*Baumstamm*) hew; **II.** *vt/i. umg.* → *zuschlagen* I 1, II 2

zuhauf *Adv. geh.* in large numbers

zuhause *Adv. österr., schw.* → *Haus* 4

Zuhause *n* home; *sie hat kein ˷* she hasn't got a home

Zuhausegebliebene *m*, *f*; *-n*, *-n*: *die ˷n* those who stayed at home

zuheilen *v/i.* (*trennb.*, *ist -ge-*) heal up

Zuhilfenahme *f*: *unter/ohne ˷ von* (*od.* + *Gen.*) with/without the aid of

zuhinterst *Adv.* right at the back

zuhören *v/i.* (*trennb.*, *hat -ge-*) listen (+ *Dat.* to); *hör mal zu!* listen; *drohend*: *auch* now you just listen to me; *genau ˷* listen carefully; *du hast nicht richtig zugehört* you haven't been listening

Zuhörer *m*, **˷in** *f* listener

Zuhörerkreis *m* circle of listeners

Zuhörerschaft *f*; *nur Sg.* audience; *Radio*: auch listeners *Pl.*

zuinnerst *Adv. geh.* in the depths of one's soul, deep down; *˷ getroffen* shaken to the core

zujubeln *v/i.* (*trennb.*, *hat -ge-*): *j-m ˷* cheer s.o.

Zukauf *m* additional purchase(s *Pl.*); **zukaufen** *v/t.* (*trennb.*, *hat -ge-*) buy (*od.* purchase) in addition; → *auch nachkaufen*

zukehren *v/t.* (*trennb.*, *hat -ge-*) turn *s.th.* toward(s) *s.o. od. s.th.*; *j-m das Gesicht ˷* turn (round) to face (*od.* look at) s.o.; *j-m den Rücken ˷* turn one's back to(ward[s]) (*abweisend*: on) s.o.

zukiffen *v/refl.* (*trennb.*, *hat -ge-*); *Sl.* get spaced (*od.* zonked) out; (*völlig*) *zugekifft* (completely) spaced (*od.* zonked) out

zukitten *v/t.* (*trennb.*, *hat -ge-*) cement (*od.* putty) (up)

zuklappen (*trennb.*) **I.** *v/t.* (*hat zugeklappt*) snap *s.th.* shut; *heftig*: slam *s.th.* shut; (*Buch*) shut; (*Messer*) fold up; *ein Buch ˷ laut*: clap a book shut; **II.** *v/i.* (*ist*) snap shut; *heftig*: slam shut

zukleben *umg. v/t.* (*trennb.*, *hat -ge-*) **1.** (*Umschlag etc.*) seal; **2.** (*Loch etc.*) stick *s.th.* over; (*Riss*) paste over; **3.** (*Wände*) *mit Plakaten etc.*: cover with, plaster with *umg.*

zukleistern *umg. v/t.* (*trennb.*, *hat -ge-*) → *zukleben* 3

zuknallen (*trennb.*) **I.** *v/t.* (*hat zugeknallt*); (*Tür etc.*) slam *s.th.* (shut); **II.** *v/i.* (*ist*) slam shut

zukneifen *v/t.* (*unreg.*, *trennb.*, *hat -ge-*): *den Mund ˷* close one's mouth tight(ly), press one's lips together (tightly); *die Augen ˷* close one's eyes tightly, screw one's eyes up; → *Arsch* 1

zuknöpfen *v/t.* (*trennb.*, *hat -ge-*) button (up)

zuknoten *v/t.* (*trennb.*, *hat -ge-*); (*Schnur etc.*) tie (with a knot), knot; (*Sack etc.*) tie up

zukommen *v/i.* (*unreg.*, *trennb.*, *ist -ge-*) **1.** *˷ auf* (+ *Akk.*) come up to, approach; *das Auto kam direkt auf mich zu* the car was coming straight toward (-s) me; **2.** *fig.*: *wir werden auf Sie ˷* we'll contact you, we'll get in touch with you; *wir lassen die Dinge auf uns ˷* we'll wait and see what happens, we'll take things as they come; *er hatte keine Ahnung, was auf ihn zukam* he had no idea what he was in for (*od.* what was in store for him); **3.** *geh.*: *j-m etw. ˷ lassen* give s.o. s.th.; (*schicken*) auch send s.o. s.th.; *durch andere*: see to it that s.o. gets s.th.; **4.** *geh. fig.*: (*j-m*) (*zuteil werden*) fall to; (*gebühren*) be due to; (*geziemen*) befit; *das kommt ihm nicht zu* it's not for him to do *etc.* that; *dieser Entwicklung etc. kommt große Bedeutung zu* this is a development *etc.* of great significance

zukorken *v/t.* (*trennb.*, *hat -ge-*) cork up

zukriegen v/t. (trennb., hat -ge-); umg. → **zubekommen**

Zukunft f; -, Zukünfte, mst Sg. **1.** future; **in ~** in future (Am. the future), for the future, from now on, henceforth lit.; **in naher/nächster ~** in the near/immediate future; **in ferner ~** in the distant future; **das liegt noch in ferner ~** that's a long way off yet; **ein Blick in die ~** a look ahead, a look in the crystal ball hum.; **e-e große ~ vor sich** (Dat.) **haben** have a great future ahead (od. in store); **abwarten, was die ~ bringt** wait and see what the future will bring (od. has in store); **j-m die ~ aus der Hand lesen** read (the future from) s.o.'s palm; **ein Beruf mit ~** a job with a future (od. with excellent prospects for the future); **diese Arbeit hat keine ~** there's no future in this kind of work; **diesem jungen Spieler gehört die ~** this young player has the whole world before him; **2.** Gramm. → **Futur**

zukünftig I. Adj. future; Person: auch prospective, nachgestellt: ...-to-be; Jur. expectant; **m-e Zukünftige / mein Zukünftiger** umg. my wife- (od. bride-)to-be / husband-to-be, beide auch my intended altm. od. hum.; **die ~e Entwicklung** future developments; **die ~en Ereignisse** future events; **II.** Adv. in future (Am. the future)

Zukunfts|angst f fear of the future; **~aussichten** Pl. future prospects

zukunftsbezogen I. Adj. forward-looking; **II.** Adv. with a view to the future

Zukunfts|branche f sunrise industry, leading-edge industry; **~erwartungen** Pl. future expectations, hopes for the future

zukunftsfähig Adj. Branche, Lösung etc.: ... with a future; Entwicklung, Technologie, Wirtschaft: sustainable; **~ sein** auch have a future

Zukunfts|forscher m, **~forscherin** f futurologist; **~forschung** f futurology

zukunftsgerichtet Adj. forward-looking

Zukunftsglaube(n) m faith in the future; **zukunftsgläubig** Adj. ... with faith in the future

Zukunfts|hoffnung f: **sie ist unsere ~** she is our hope for the future; **~industrie** f sunrise industry, leading-edge industry; **~musik** f; nur Sg.; fig.: **das ist alles noch ~** that's all still up in the air (od. a long way off)

zukunftsorientiert Adj. forward-looking

Zukunfts|perspektive f future outlook, outlook for the future; **~pläne** Pl. plans for the future; **~roman** m science fiction novel; (utopischer Roman) utopian novel

zukunfts|sicher Adj. ... with a guaranteed future, ... whose future is assured, lasting; **~trächtig** Adj. promising, ... full of promise for the future

Zukunftsvision f future vision, vision of the future

zukunft(s)weisend Adj. attr. pioneering; Politik, Rede: forward-looking; **~e Ideen** etc. auch ideas etc. that point the way ahead (od. point to the future)

Zukurzgekommene m, f; -n, -n loser

zulächeln v/i. (trennb., hat -ge-): **j-m ~** smile at s.o., give s.o. a smile

zulachen v/i. (trennb., hat -ge-) give s.o. a friendly laugh

zuladen v/t. (unreg., trennb., hat -ge-) add (to the existing load), load; **Zula-**dung** f Güter: additional load

Zulage f **1.** allowance; (Prämie) bonus; **2.** Gehalt, Lohn: increase

zulande → **Land** 5

zulangen v/i. (trennb., hat -ge-) **1.** bei Tisch: help o.s.; **langt (tüchtig) zu!** auch umg. don't hold back!; **2.** → **zupacken** I 2; **3.** (zuschlagen) hit out (at s.o.); **4.** Dial. (ausreichen) be enough

zulassen v/t. (unreg., trennb., hat -ge-) **1.** auch fig. (erlauben) allow; Jur. (gestatten) approve, authorize; **ich kann das nicht ~** I can't allow that; **wie konntest du das ~?** how could you allow it?; **sein Stolz ließ es nicht zu, dass ...** his pride wouldn't allow him to (+ Inf.), his pride prevented him from (+ Ger.); **etw. lässt verschiedene Deutungen zu** s.th. is open to different interpretations; **die Tatsachen lassen keinen Zweifel zu** leave no room for doubt; **2.** (j-n) admit; (Arzt etc.) qualify; **als Rechtsanwalt ~** call (Am. admit) to the Bar; **zum Studium zugelassen werden** get a place at (Am. be admitted to) university; **3.** (etw.) behördlich: authorize; (Fahrzeuge) license; (Auto, Flugzeug, Zuchtbullen etc.) register; (Medikament) approve, license; (Partei) allow to exist; **etw. als Beweis ~** admit s.th. as evidence; **an der Börse zugelassen** listed on the stock exchange; **für Jugendliche nicht zugelassen** for adults only; **4.** umg. (Tür etc.) leave shut; (nicht öffnen) not open

zulässig Adj. permissible; amtlich: authorized; **~e Belastung** safe load; **~es Gesamtgewicht** maximum laden weight; **~e Höchstgeschwindigkeit** maximum (permissible) speed; **das ist nicht ~** that is not allowed (od. permitted, permissible); **Zulässigkeit** f; nur Sg. permissibility

Zulassung f permission; zu e-m Beruf, für ein Fahrzeug etc., Vorgang: licensing; Dokument: licen|ce (Am. -se), registration; zu e-r Universität etc.: admission

Zulassungs|beschränkung f auch Pl. restricted admission; **~nummer** f Mot. registration number; **~papiere** Pl. Mot. registration papers

zulassungspflichtig Adj. requiring registration (bzw. a licence od. Am. license)

Zulassungs|prüfung f Univ. etc. entrance exam(ination); **~schein** m licen|ce (Am. -se); **~stelle** f Mot. registration office; **~stopp** m für Ärzte, Studenten etc.: bar (od. halt) to further admissions; für Gentechnikprodukte etc.: licensing ban

Zulauf m **1.** nur Sg.; (Andrang) crowd; Zahl der Besucher etc.: number of people attending (bzw. joining bzw. interested in etc.); **großen ~ haben** Arzt etc.: be (very) much in demand, have a large practice (bzw. clientele); Film, Lokal etc.: be very popular, draw large crowds; **2.** Tech. Menge: inflow, feed; Rohr: intake

zulaufen v/i. (unreg., trennb., ist -ge-) **1. ~ auf** (+ Akk.) Person: run up to;

Straße: lead (up) to; **j-m ~** Patienten, Kunden: flock to s.o.; **auf j-n zugelaufen kommen** come running up to s.o.; **2. j-m ~** Tier: adopt as new owner, stray to s.o.; **ein zugelaufener Hund** a stray (dog); **3.** umg.: **lauf zu!** run!, get a move on!, step on it!; **4.** Wasser etc.: flow in; **Wasser** etc. **~ lassen** add water etc., run more water etc. in; **5.** (enden) **spitz ~** taper to a point; **der Rock läuft unten schmal zu** the skirt narrows (od. tapers) toward(s) the bottom

zulegen (trennb., hat -ge-); umg. **I.** v/t. **sich** (Dat.) **etw. ~** (anschaffen) get (od. buy) o.s. s.th.; hum. (Bart, Bauch) acquire s.th.; hum. (Erkältung etc.) land o.s. (with) s.th.; **sich** (Dat.) **e-e Freundin** etc. **~** hum. get (od. find) o.s. a girlfriend etc.; **II.** vt/i. (hinzutun) add (+ Dat. to); (beisteuern) contribute; **an Tempo:** step on it; an Gewicht: put on (weight), gain; Umsatz, Volumen etc.: increase (by), gain; Aktie, Währung: rise (by), gain; **sie konnten bei den Wahlen 3 % ~** they managed to gain (od. increase their share of the vote by) 3 % in the elections; → **Zahn** 4

zuleide, zu Leide Adv.: **j-m etwas ~ tun** harm (od. hurt) s.o.; → **Fliege** 1

zuleiten v/t. (trennb., hat -ge-) **1.** (Wasser etc.) let in; Tech. supply, feed; **2.** direct (+ Dat. to); (zusenden) send (to); (weitergeben) pass on (to), forward (to); **j-m Informationen** etc. **~** auch supply s.o. (od. keep s.o. supplied) with information etc.; **Zuleitung** f **1.** nur Sg. supply (+ Gen. of); (Zustellung) sending, forwarding; **2.** Tech., Rohr: supply pipe; Etech. power line; **Zuleitungsrohr** n supply (od. feed) pipe

zuletzt Adv. **1.** (als Letztes, an letzter Stelle) last; **ganz ~** last of all; **er kommt immer ~** he's always the last to arrive; **2. bis ~** till (od. to) the (very) end; **wir blieben bis ~** auch we sat it out (to the end); **wir hofften bis ~, dass ...** we hoped to the last that ...; **3.** (schließlich) in the end; **4.** (das letzte Mal) last, the last time; **als ich ihn ~ sah** when I last saw him; **wann warst du ~ beim Zahnarzt?** when was the last time you were at (od. you went to) the dentist?; **5.** fig. (am wenigsten) least of all; **von dir hätte ich das ~ gedacht** you're the last person I'd have expected to do that, that's the last thing I'd have expected you to do; **nicht ~, weil ...** not least because ...

zuliebe Adv.: **j-m ~** for s.o.'s sake; **s-r Ehe ~** for the sake of his marriage; **tu's mir ~** do it for me (od. for my sake)

Zulieferbetrieb m, **Zulieferer** m; -s, - (outside) supplier; **Zulieferindustrie** f ancillary industry; **zuliefern** v/t. (trennb., hat -ge-) supply; **Zulieferung** f supply

Zulu¹ m; -(s), -(s) Zulu

Zulu² n; -(s), kein Pl.; Ling. Zulu, the Zulu language

zum Präp. + Art. **1.** → **zu¹**; **2.** räumlich: **es sind 100 Meter (bis) ~ Zoo** it's 100 metres (Am. meters) to the zoo; **3.** zeitlich, Zeitpunkt: **das Gesetz tritt ~ 1. September in Kraft** the law will come into force on September 1st; **4.** Zweck: **etw. ~ Essen/Spielen** s.th. to eat / play with; **Platz ~ Spielen** room to play (in); **Papier ~ Schreiben** writing paper; **~ Baden gehen** go swimming; **5.** *Folge*: **es ist ~ Lachen** it's laughable; **es ist ~ Weinen/Verzweifeln** it's enough to make you weep/despair; **~ Glühen bringen** heat (until) red-hot, make red-hot; **nicht ~ Nachdenken kommen** have no time to think; **6.** *Ergebnis ausdrückend*: **j-n ~ Präsidenten wählen** elect s.o. president; **sich** (*Dat.*) **j-n ~ Feind machen** make an enemy of s.o.; **j-n ~ Freund haben** have s.o. as a friend; **sich ~ Verwechseln ähnlich sehen** look as alike as two peas in a pod; **7.** *Menge, Zahl, Häufigkeit, Verhältnis etc.*: in; **~ Preis von** at a price of; **8.** *vor Ordnungszahlen*: for; **~ ersten Mal** for the first time; **~ Ersten, ~ Zweiten, ...** *aufzählen*: first, second ...; *bei Versteigerung*: going (once), going (twice), ...; **9.** *in Namen*: **Gasthaus ~ goldenen Löwen** the Golden Lion (Inn); **Freiherr von und ~ Stein** the Freiherr von Stein; **10.** *in Wendungen*: **~ Abschied küssen** *etc.*: goodbye; **ein Glas trinken**: on parting; **~ Scherz** for (*od.* in) fun; **~ Schluss** at the end; to finish with; → **Beispiel** 1

zumachen (*trennb.*, *hat* -ge-); *umg.* **I.** *v/t.* **1.** shut, close; (*Loch*) stop up; (*Umschlag*) seal; (*Mantel etc.*) button (up), do up; (*Schirm*) put down; **ich habe kein Auge zugemacht** I didn't sleep a wink; **2.** (*Geschäft, auflösen*) close down; **das Geschäft ~** *auch* shut up shop; **II.** *v/i.* **1.** *Geschäft*: close; **für immer**: close down; **2. mach zu!** (*beeil dich*) get a move on!, step on it!

zumal I. *Konj.* (*da, weil*) particularly as (*od.* since), seeing as *umg.*; **II.** *Adv.* (*vor allem*) particularly, above all, in particular

zumarschieren *v/i.* (*trennb.*, *ist*): **~ auf** (+ *Akk.*) march toward(s) (*od.* up to)

zumauern *v/t.* (*trennb.*, *hat* -ge-) wall (*od.* brick *od.* block) up

zumeist *Adv.* mostly, for the most part

zumessen *v/t.* (*unreg.*, *trennb.*, *hat* -ge-) portion out (+ *Dat.* to); (*j-m s-n Teil*) allot (to); **e-r Sache Bedeutung ~** *fig.* attach importance to s.th.

zumindest *Adv.* at least; **du hättest mir ~ Bescheid geben können** *auch* the least you could have done is let me know

zumüllen *v/t.* (*trennb.*, *hat* -ge-); *Sl. pej.* (*j-n*) (*überhäufen*) bombard (**mit** with); *mit E-Mails*: spam

zumutbar *Adj. Arbeit etc.*: not unreasonable, reasonable; **das ist durchaus ~ für ihn** it's not expecting too much of him; **das ist doch nicht ~** that's expecting too much (**für** of); **für ihn**: **auch** you can't expect him to do that; **Zumutbarkeit** *f*, *nur Sg.* reasonableness

zumute, zu Mute *Adv.*: **mir ist nicht danach ~** I don't feel like it, I'm not in the mood; **mir ist nicht zum Lachen ~** I'm not in the mood for laughing; **mir war zum Heulen ~** I felt like crying

zumuten *v/t.* (*trennb.*, *hat* -ge-): **j-m etw. ~** expect s.th. of s.o.; **sich** (*Dat.*) **etw. ~** take s.th. on; manage s.th., cope with s.th.; **sich** (*Dat.*) **zu viel ~** overdo it; *bei der Arbeit auch*: take on too much; *körperlich auch*: overtax o.s.; **das kannst du ihr nicht ~** you can't expect her to do that; **diesen Lärm wollte ich ihr nicht ~** I couldn't expect her to put up with this noise; **Zumutung** *f* imposition; (*Unverschämtheit*) cheek; **etw. als ~ empfinden** feel s.th.

to be unreasonable (*od.* an imposition); **das ist e-e ~** that's asking a bit much; *stärker*: what (a) nerve *umg.*, who does he think I am (*od.* we are *etc.*)? *umg.*; **das Essen war e-e ~** the food was a disgrace

zunächst I. *Adv.* **1.** (*am Anfang*) at first, initially; (*e-e Zeit lang*) for a while; **2.** (*erstens*) first of all, to start with; **3.** (*vorläufig*) for the time being; **II.** *Präp.* (+ *Dat.*); *geh.* beside

zunageln *v/t.* (*trennb.*, *hat* -ge-) nail up; (*Deckel*) nail down

zunähen *v/t.* (*trennb.*, *hat* -ge-) sew (up)

Zunahme *f* increase (+ *Gen. od.* **an** + *Dat.* in); (*Anstieg*) rise (in); **e-e ~ um** *od.* **von 10%** an increase of 10%

Zuname *m* **1.** surname, last (*od.* second) name; **2.** *altm.* (*Beiname*) epithet; (*Spitzname*) nickname

Zünd|anlage *f Mot.* ignition system; **~blättchen** *n für Spielzeugpistole*: cap; **~einstellung** *f* ignition (*Diesel*: injection) timing

zündeln *v/i. südd., österr.* play with fire

zünden I. *v/i.* **1.** *Motor*: fire; *Gasgemisch*: ignite; *Sprengladung*: detonate, go off; *Rakete*: fire; **2.** *Blitz*: strike; **3.** *altm.* (*Feuer fangen*) catch fire; *Holz*: kindle; *Streichholz*: light; **das Streichholz zündet nicht** the match won't light (*od.* strike); **4.** *fig. Gedanke etc.*: arouse enthusiasm; *Idee*: catch on; *unpers.*: **bei ihm hat's gezündet** *umg. hum.* the penny has (finally) dropped; **II.** *v/t.* **1.** (*Motor, Rakete*) fire; (*Sprengladung*) detonate, set off; **2.** *altm. od. südd.* (*Streichholz*) light, strike; **zündend I.** *Part. Präs.* → **zünden**; **II.** *Adj. fig. Worte etc.*: stirring, rousing

Zunder *m*; -*s*, - **1.** tinder; **brennen wie ~** burn like tinder; **2.** *umg. fig.*: **j-m ~ geben** give s.o. (merry) hell; **es gibt ~** he's *etc.* in for it; **3.** *Tech., auf Metall*: scale

Zünder *m*; -*s*, - fuse; *e-r Mine*: detonator

Zünd|flamme *f* pilot light; **~funke** *m Mot.* (ignition) spark; **~holz** *n bes. südd., österr.* match; **~holzschachtel** *f* matchbox; **~hütchen** *n* percussion cap; **~kabel** *n Mot.* ignition cable; **~kapsel** *f* detonator; **~kerze** *f Mot.* spark plug; **~plättchen** *n für Spielzeugpistole*: cap; **~punkt** *m Tech.* ignition point; **~satz** *m Tech.* igniting charge; **~schloss** *n Mot.* ignition lock; **~schlüssel** *m Mot.* ignition key; **~schnur** *f* fuse; **~spule** *f Mot.* ignition coil; **~stoff** *m* **1.** inflammable matter; **2.** *fig.* dynamite; *zu e-r Diskussion*: fuel (**zu** for)

Zündung *f* **1.** ignition; **die ~ der ersten Wasserstoffbombe** the detonation (*od.* explosion) of the first hydrogen bomb; **2.** *Vorrichtung*: detonator; **3.** *Mot.* ignition; **die ~ einstellen** adjust the timing; **die ~ ist falsch eingestellt** the timing is out (*Am.* off) *od.* is wrongly set

Zünd|verteiler *m Mot.* distributor; **~vorrichtung** *f* ignition device; **~zeitpunkt** *m Mot.* ignition time; **den ~ einstellen** adjust the timing

zunehmen (*unreg.*, *trennb.*, *hat* -ge-) **I.** *v/i.* **1.** *allg.* increase (**an** + *Dat.* in); *Zahl*: *auch* go up; (*anwachsen*) grow; *Tage*: get longer; *Mond*: wax; *Wind*: get stronger; *Regen*: get heavier; *Schmerzen*: get worse; *Beifall*: grow (louder); **die Kälte nimmt zu** it's get-

ting colder; **an Größe/ Tiefe ~** increase in size/depth; **an Erfahrung/Weisheit ~** gain experience *od.* become more experienced / grow wiser; **2.** *an Gewicht*: put on weight; **er hat ganz schön zugenommen** he's put on quite a lot of weight; **II.** *vt/i.* beim Stricken: (*Maschen*) increase; **III.** *v/t.* **1.** *an Gewicht*: put on; **zwei Kilo ~** put on two kilos; **der Arzt sagt, ich muss mindestens fünf Kilo ~** the doctor says I have to gain five kilos at least; **2.** *umg.* → **hinzunehmen**

zunehmend I. *Adj.* increasing, growing; **~er Mond** waxing moon; **mit ~em Alter** as one gets older, with increasing age, with advancing years; **~e Bewölkung** increasing amounts of cloud; **~e Erkenntnis** growing realization; **in ~em Maße** → II; **II.** *Adv.* increasingly, more and more; **sich ~ verschlechtern** get increasingly worse, get worse and worse

zuneigen (*trennb.*, *hat* -ge-) **I.** *v/refl.* **1.** *geh.*: (+ *Dat.*) lean towards; **2.** *fig.*: **sich dem Ende ~** be drawing to a close; *Vorräte etc.*: be running low; **II.** *v/i.*: **der Ansicht ~, dass ...** be inclined to think that ...; **j-m in Liebe zugeneigt sein** *geh.* feel great affection for s.o.; (*verliebt sein*) be devoted to s.o.; **Zuneigung** *f* affection (**für, zu** for); **~ zu j-m fassen** become fond of s.o., take a liking (*od.* shine *umg.*) to s.o.

Zunft *f*; -, *Zünfte* **1.** *hist.* guild; **2.** *umg. hum.* bunch, gang; **von der ~ sein** be (*Fachmann sein*) be a pro, be an expert *allg.*; **die schreibende ~** *hum.* the writing (*Journalisten*: journalistic) fraternity

zünftig I. *Adj. Ausrüstung, Kleidung*: proper; *Brotzeit, Bier*: decent; *umg. Abend, Skat etc.*: great, *Brit. auch* jolly good; *Ohrfeige, Tracht Prügel*: good; **~ aussehen** look just the thing; **II.** *Adv.*: **es ging ~ zu** they *etc.* were having a really good time (of it)

Zunft|meister *m hist.* guildmaster; **~wesen** *n* guilds *Pl.*, system of guilds

Zunge *f*; -, -*n* **1.** *Anat.* tongue; **belegte ~** coated (*od.* furred) tongue; **mit der ~ anstoßen** lisp, have a lisp; **sich** (*Dat.*) **auf die ~ beißen** bite one's tongue; **die ~ herausstrecken** stick (*od.* poke) one's tongue out (+ *Dat.* at); *beim Arzt*: put one's tongue out; **mit hängender ~** *umg.* with one's tongue hanging out; **mir klebt die ~ am Gaumen** I'm parched; **2.** *fig.* (*Sprache*) tongue; **böse/spitze** *od.* **scharfe ~** malicious/sharp tongue; **böse ~n behaupten, dass ...** there's some nasty gossip going (a)round that ...; **e-e feine ~ haben** *geh.* have a fine palate; **e-e falsche/lose ~ haben** have a lying/loose tongue; **in fremden ~n sprechen** *bibl.* speak in tongues; **mit gespaltener ~ sprechen** *geh.* speak with a forked tongue; **e-e schwere ~ haben** slur one's speech (*od.* words); **da bricht man sich ja die ~ ab!** how are you supposed to get your tongue (a)round that?; **es brannte ihm auf der ~, es weiterzusagen** he was bursting (*od.* dying) to tell someone; **Lügen gehen ihm leicht/schwer von der ~** lying comes easy/hard to him; **hüte d-e ~!** *geh.* mind your tongue!; **es lag mir auf der ~** it was on the tip of my tongue; **der Wein löste ihr die ~** *geh.* the wine loosened her tongue; **sich** (*Dat.*) **die ~ verbrennen** open one's big mouth, let one's tongue run away with one; → **Herz**[1] 8, **zergehen**; **3.** *Gastr.* tongue; **~ in Madeira** tongue in Madeira sauce; **4.** *e-r Waage*: pointer; **5.** *am Schuh*: tongue; **6.** *Mus.*, *Orgel*: tongue; *Akkordeon etc.*: reed; **7.** *Zool.* (*Seezunge*) sole

züngeln *v/i.* **1.** *Schlange*: flicker its tongue (in and out); **2.** *Flamme*: flicker, *stärker*: shoot up

Zungen|akrobatik *f* *umg.*, *hum.* tongue twisting exercises *Pl.*; *das ist ja die reinste ~!* it's terribly difficult getting your tongue (a)round it; **~bein** *n* *Anat.* tongue (*od.* hyoid) bone; **~belag** *m* *Med.* coating of the tongue; coated (*od.* furred) tongue

Zungenbrecher *m* *umg.* tongue twister; **zungenbrecherisch** *Adj.* *umg.* *attr.* tongue-twisting

zungenfertig *Adj.* articulate, glib *pej.*; *sie ist sehr ~* auch she's never at a loss for words; **Zungenfertigkeit** *f*; *nur Sg.* articulacy, glibness *pej.*

Zungen|kuss *m* French kiss; **~laut** *m* *Ling.* lingual (sound); **~R**, **~r** *n* *Ling.* rolled (*od.* trilled) R; **~schlag** *m* **1.** *Sprachstörung*: stammer; *bei Trunkenheit*: slurring; *falscher ~* *fig.* (*Versprecher*) slip of the tongue; **2.** *Mus.* tonguing; **3.** *fig. Art*: way (*od.* manner) of speaking; (*Akzent*) accent; **~spitze** *f* tip of the tongue

Zünglein *n* **1.** (little) tongue; **2.** *Waage*: pointer; *das ~ an der Waage bilden* *fig.* tip the scales

zunichte *Adv.*: **~ machen** destroy, ruin; (*Hoffnung*) *auch* shatter; (*Pläne*) *auch* paid to, scupper *umg.*, *Am. umg.* deep-six; **~ sein** be ruined (*od.* wrecked); **~ werden** come to nothing (*od.* naught)

zunicken *v/i.* (*trennb., hat -ge-*): *j-m ~* nod at s.o., give s.o. a nod; *j-m freundlich ~* give s.o. a friendly nod

zunutze, zu Nutze *Adv.*: *sich* (*Dat.*) *etw.* **~ machen** make (good) use of; (*ausnützen*) take advantage of

zuoberst *Adv.* (right) at the top; *am Tisch*: at the head (of the table)

zuordenbar *Adj.* assignable (to), classifiable as; **zuordnen** *v/t.* (*trennb., hat -ge-*): *e-r Sache ~* assign to s.th., class with s.th.; *den Reptilien etc. zugeordnet werden* be classified as a reptile *etc.*, belong to the reptile *etc.* family; *e-m Künstler / e-r Zeit etc. ~* ascribe to an artist / a period *etc.*; *er lässt sich schwer ~* he's hard to place (*od.* categorize); **Zuordnung** *f* classification

zupacken (*trennb., hat -ge-*) **I.** *v/i.* **1.** (*zugreifen*) make a grab; grab (at) it; *Hund*: go for *s.th. od. s.o.*; (*fassen*) catch (*od.* get) hold of *s.th.*; **2.** (*hart arbeiten*) knuckle down, get down to it; (*mithelfen*) lend a hand, chip in *umg.*; *jemand, der ~ kann* someone who's willing to roll up his sleeves, someone who's not afraid of some hard physical work; **3.** *fig. bei Angebot, Gelegenheit*: seize the opportunity, go for it *umg.*; **II.** *v/t.*: *j-n ~* swaddle s.o. in blankets *etc.*; *j-n mit Arbeit ~* *fig.* smother s.o. in work; **zupackend I.** *Part. Präs.* → **zupacken**; **II.** *Adj.* *Manager, Politiker etc.*: *attr.* hands-on ...; *er hat e-e ~e Art* he doesn't waste any time (getting things done)

zuparken *v/t.* (*trennb., hat -ge-*) block, obstruct; → **zugeparkt**

zupass *Adv.* geh.: *j-m ~ kommen* come in very handy for s.o., be just what s.o. needs

zupfen I. *vt/i.* **1.** pull (*an* + *Dat.* at), tug (at); *sich* (*Dat.*) *am Ohrläppchen ~* pull (*od.* tug) at one's earlobe; *j-n am Ärmel etc. ~* tug at s.o.'s sleeve *etc.*; **2.** (*Gitarre, Lied, Saite etc.*) pluck; **II.** *v/t.* (*entfernen*) pull (*aus* out of; *von* from); (*Unkraut*) pull up; (*Augenbrauen*) pluck

Zupfinstrument *n* plucked instrument

zupflastern *v/t.* (*trennb., hat -ge-*): **~ mit** pave over with, cover with

zupressen *v/t.* (*trennb., hat -ge-*) press shut; (*Augen, Mund*) shut tight

zuprosten *v/i.* (*trennb., hat -ge-*): *j-m ~* raise one's glass to s.o.

zur *Präp.* + *Art.* **1.** → **zu**[1]; **2.** *räumlich, Richtung etc.*: **~ Stadt** gehen *etc.*: to town; **~ Tür hereinkommen/hinausgehen** come in/go out of the door; *j-n ~ Bahn bringen* take s.o. to the station; (*bis zum Zug begleiten*) see s.o. off at the station; *das Fenster liegt ~ Straße* (*hin*) the window looks onto the street; **3.** *zeitlich*: **~ Stunde** at the moment; *bis ~ Stunde* up to (*od.* until) now, as yet; → **Zeit** 2, 3, **zurzeit**; **4.** *Menge, Zahl, Häufigkeit, Verhältnis etc.*: in; **~ Hälfte/Gänze** half / entirely (*od.* completely); **5.** (*als*) *Zweck etc.*: for; **~ Belohnung/Strafe** as a reward/punishment; **~ Entschuldigung/Erklärung** by way of excuse/explanation; **6.** *in Namen*: *Gasthaus ~ Linde* the Lime Tree (Inn); **7.** *in Wendungen*: **~ Folge haben** result in; **~ Genüge** only too well; **~ Neige gehen** draw to an end; *Vorräte*: run low; **~ Ruhe kommen** get some peace; *sich ~ Ruhe setzen* retire (from work); **~ Schau stellen** put on show; → **Probe** 1

zurande, zu Rande *Adv.* umg.: **~ kommen mit** *j-m*: get on with; *mit etw.*: cope with, get to grips with

zurate, zu Rate *Adv.*: **~ ziehen** (*j-n*) consult, seek *s.o.'s* advice; (*Buch, Landkarte etc.*) consult, refer to

zuraten *v/i.* (*unreg., trennb., hat -ge-*): *j-m* (*zu etw.*) **~** advise s.o. to do s.th. (*od.* it); *ich rate dir weder zu noch ab* I can't advise you one way or the other (*od.* either way), I can't say for or against; *auf sein Zuraten* (*hin*) on his advice

zuraunen *v/t.* (*trennb., hat -ge-*); geh.: *j-m etw. ~* whisper s.th. into s.o.'s ear

Zürcher[1] *Adj.* Zurich ..., of Zurich

Zürcher[2] *m*; *-s, -*, **~in** *f*; *-, -nen* person from (*od.* inhabitant of) Zurich; → **Kölner**[1], **Kölnerin**; **zürcherisch** *Adj.* Zurich ..., of Zurich

zurechnen *v/t.* (*trennb., hat -ge-*) → **zuordnen**; **Zurechnung** *f* → **Zuordnung**

zurechnungsfähig *Adj.* accountable, of sound mind; *Jur. auch* compos mentis; *ist er ~?* auch can he be held accountable (*od.* responsible)?; **Zurechnungsfähigkeit** *f*; *nur Sg.* accountability; *verminderte ~ Jur.* diminished responsibility

zurechtbiegen *v/t.* (*unreg., trennb., hat -ge-*) **1.** bend *s.th.* into (the right) shape; **2.** *umg. fig.* (*Sachverhalt*) twist to one's own advantage; (*j-n*) straighten *s.o.* out; *die Sache wieder ~* straighten things out

zurechtfinden *v/refl.* (*unreg., trennb., hat -ge-*) **1.** find one's way (around); **2.** *fig. mit etw., im Leben*: manage, cope; (*etw. verstehen*) get the hang of it *umg.*; *an e-m Arbeitsplatz*: settle in; *findest du dich zurecht?* will you be all right?; *ich find mich überhaupt nicht mehr zurecht* I don't know

what's going on any more (*od.* where to start looking), I'm lost

zurechtkommen *v/i.* (*unreg., trennb., ist -ge-*) **1.** manage, cope (*mit* with); *mit Geld*: auch get by; *mit j-m ~* (*auskommen*) get on with s.o.; *kommst du zurecht?* are you (managing) all right?; *kommen Sie zurecht? im Geschäft*: can I help you?; *ich komme mit diesem Computer nicht zurecht* I can't do anything with this computer; **2.** (*rechtzeitig kommen*) get there (*od.* make it) in time

zurecht|legen *v/t.* (*trennb., hat -ge-*) **1.** put out; (*ordnen*) arrange; **2.** *fig.*: *sich* (*Dat.*) *e-e Ausrede etc.* **~** have an excuse *etc.* ready; *sich* (*Dat.*) *s-e Argumente* **~** work out one's arguments in advance, marshal one's arguments; **~machen** (*trennb., hat -ge-*); *umg.* **I.** *v/t.* get *s.th.* ready, prepare; (*Bett*) make; (*Salat*) dress; **II.** *v/refl.* get (o.s.) ready; (*sich herausputzen*) do o.s. up; **~rücken** *v/t.* (*trennb., hat -ge-*) **1.** (*Stuhl*) move to the right position, put right; (*Bild etc.*) straighten ; (*Brille, Hut, Krawatte*) adjust; **2.** *fig.* put *s.th.* straight; *die Sache* **~** put things (*od.* matters) straight; → **Kopf**; **~schneiden** *v/t.* (*unreg., trennb., hat -ge-*) *zu passender Form*: cut to shape; *zu passender Größe*: cut to size; (*Haar, Hecke etc.*) trim, tidy; *fig.* arrange, organize; **~schustern** *v/t.* (*trennb., hat -ge-*); *umg. pej.* cobble together; **~setzen** (*trennb., hat -ge-*) **I.** *v/t.* set right, put straight; *an die richtige Stelle*: put in the right place; **II.** *v/refl.* settle o.s. (down); **~stellen** *v/t.* (*trennb., hat -ge-*) *v/t.* set right, put straight; *an die richtige Stelle*: put in the right place; **~stutzen** *v/t.* (*trennb., hat -ge-*) **1.** (*Hecke*) trim, clip; **2.** *umg. fig.*: *etw.* **~** get s.th. into shape; *j-n* **~** cut s.o. down to size

zurechtweisen *v/t.* (*unreg., trennb., hat -ge-*) reprimand, rebuke; **Zurechtweisung** *f* reprimand, rebuke

zurechtzimmern *v/t.* (*trennb., hat -ge-*); *umg.* **1.** knock together; **2.** *fig. pej.* cobble together

zureden *v/i.* (*trennb., hat -ge-*): *j-m* (*gut*) **~** (*zu überreden versuchen*) try to persuade s.o.; (*beschwatzen*) coax s.o. into doing it; (*ermutigen*) encourage s.o. (to do it); *ich musste ihm lange ~* I really had to work on him

Zureden *n*; *-s, kein Pl.* coaxing, urging; (*Ermutigung*) encouragement; *gütliches ~* friendly persuasion; *Jur.* moral suasion; *erst nach langem ~* only after a great deal of coaxing etc.

zureiten (*unreg., trennb.*) **I.** *v/t.* (*hat zugeritten*); (*Pferd*) break in; **II.** *v/i.* (*ist*): **~ auf** (+ *Akk.*) ride up to

Zürich (*n*); *-s*; *Geog.* Zurich; **~see** *n* Lake Zurich

zurichten *v/t.* (*trennb., hat -ge-*) **1.** *Dial.* (*Essen etc.*) prepare; *fachspr.* (*ausrichten*) adjust, set; (*glätten*) dress, finish; (*Leder*) *auch* finish; (*Holz, Steine*) cut, trim, shape; (*Bleche*) *Druck.* get *s.th.* ready; **2.** *übel ~* (*j-n*) injure badly; (*schlagen*) *auch* beat up badly; (*etw.*) make a mess of; *er war übel zugerichtet* he was in pretty bad shape, he had been badly knocked about; *wer hat dich so zugerichtet?* who did 'that to you?

zürnen *v/i.* geh. be angry (*j-m* with s.o.; *über* + *Akk.* at, about)

zurren *v/t. bes. Naut.* lash, tie

Zurschaustellung *f* exhibition; *pej.*

parading, flaunting

zurück *Adv.* **1.** back; **~ *an Absender*** return to sender; ***mit bestem Dank* ~** returned with thanks; ***hin hat es länger gedauert als* ~** it took longer getting there than it did coming back; ***zweimal (nach) Köln hin und* ~**, ***bitte*** two returns (*Am.* round-trips) to Cologne, please; **... *und drei Euro* ~** (*Rückgeld*) and three euros change; → ***Natur*** 1; **2.** (*rückwärts, nach hinten*) backwards; **~!** (*nicht weitergehen*) hold it!; (*Platz machen*) stand back!; ***vor und* ~** backwards and forwards; ***e-n Schritt* ~ *tun*** go back a step, take a step back-(wards); **3.** *fig.* behind; **~ *sein in der Schule, Arbeit etc.*:** be (lagging) behind; *körperlich:* be a late developer; *geistig:* be a bit backward; *Pflanze:* be late; (*nicht auf der Höhe der Zeit*) be behind the times; *kulturell:* be backward

Zurück *n; -s, kein Pl.:* ***es gibt kein* ~** (*mehr*) there's no turning back (now)

zurück|befördern *v/t.* (*trennb., hat*) transport (*od.* bring *od.* take *od.* send) back; **~begeben** *v/refl.* (*unreg., trennb., hat*) return, go back; **~behalten** *v/t.* (*unreg., trennb., hat*) **1.** hold onto, keep (back); (*einbehalten*) withhold; **2.** (*Behinderung, Narbe etc.*) be left with; **~bekommen** *v/t.* (*unreg., trennb., hat*) get back; **10 Cent ~** get 10 cents back; **~beordern** *v/t.* (*trennb., hat*) order back; **~berufen** *v/t.* (*unreg., trennb., hat*) recall; **~beugen** (*trennb., hat -ge-*) **I.** *v/t.* bend back; (*Kopf*) *auch* lean back; **II.** *v/refl.* lean back; **~bezahlen** *v/t.* (*trennb., hat*) → **zurückzahlen**

zurückbilden *v/refl.* (*trennb., hat -ge-*) (*Geschwulst*) recede; (*Muskel*) waste, atrophy; *Bio.* (*Gliedmaßen*) regress; **Zurückbildung** *f* (*e-r Geschwulst*) recession; (*von Muskeln*) wasting, atrophy; *Bio.* regression

zurückbinden *v/t.* (*unreg., trennb., hat -ge-*) (*Haare*) tie back

zurückbleiben *v/i.* (*unreg., trennb., ist -ge-*) **1.** stay behind; **2.** (*nicht näher kommen*) keep back, stay back; **~, bitte! im U-Bahnhof:** mind (*Am.* stand back from) the doors, please; **3.** *bei Rennen, in Schule etc.:* fall behind, be (lagging) behind; *in der Entwicklung, geistig:* be backward; *hinter Erwartungen etc.* **~** fall short of; → **zurückgeblieben**; **4.** *als Rest, Rückstand etc.:* be left; *als Unfallfolge etc.:* remain

zurück|blenden *v/i.* (*trennb., hat -ge-*) *Film:* go back (*auf + Akk.* to), flash back (to) (*auch fig.*); **~blicken** *v/i.* (*trennb., hat -ge-*) look back (*zu od. auf + Akk.* at; *fig.* on); **~bringen** *v/t.* (*unreg., trennb., hat -ge-*) bring back (*ins Leben* to life); **~datieren** *v/t.* (*trennb., hat*) **1.** (*Rechnung etc.*) backdate; **2. ~ *auf*** (*+ Akk.*) (*Funde etc.*) date back to; **~denken** *v/i.* (*unreg., trennb., hat*) think back (*an + Akk.* to); **~ *an*** (*+ Akk.*) *auch* recall (to memory); ***so weit ich* ~ *kann*** as far as I can remember (*od.* recall); **~drängen** (*trennb., hat -ge-*) **I.** *v/t.* **1.** drive back; **2.** *fig.* (*Angst etc.*) restrain; (*unterdrücken*) suppress; (*Drogenmissbrauch, Fremdenfeindlichkeit etc.*) fight, combat; **II.** *v/i. Menge:* fall back; **~drehen** *v/t.* (*trennb., hat -ge-*) turn (*od.* put) back; (*Lautstärke etc.*) turn down; **~dürfen** *v/i.* (*unreg., trennb., hat -ge-*) *umg.* be allowed back; **darf ich jetzt an m-n Platz zu-**

rück? can (*od.* may) I go back to my seat now?; **~entwickeln** *v/refl.* (*trennb., hat*) **1.** → **zurückbilden**; **2.** *geschäftlich:* be falling off; **~erhalten** *v/t.* (*unreg., trennb., hat*) get back; **~erinnern** *v/refl.* (*trennb., hat*): **sich** (*an + Akk.*) remember, recall; **~erobern** *v/t.* (*trennb., hat*) **1.** *Mil.* recapture; **2.** *fig.* (*Mehrheit, Stimmen*) win back; (*Macht, Positon*) regain

zurückerstatten *v/t.* (*trennb., hat*) refund, reimburse; **Zurückerstattung** *f* refunding, reimbursement

zurückerwarten *v/t.* (*trennb., hat*) expect *s.o.* back

zurückfahren (*unreg., trennb.*) **I.** *v/i.* (*ist zurückgefahren*) **1.** go back, return; *mit dem Auto bzw. Rad:* auch drive (*bzw.* ride) back; (*zurückstoßen*) reverse, back (up); **2.** *fig. vor Schreck etc.:* recoil, shrink back (*vor Schreck etc.:* in; *vor Schlange etc.:* from); **II.** *v/t.* (*hat*) **1.** drive *s.o. od. s.th.* back; **2.** (*Ausgaben, Kosten, Produktion*) cut back, reduce; (*Kraftwerk, Maschine*) reduce the output of

zurückfallen *v/i.* (*unreg., trennb., ist -ge-*) **1.** fall back; ***sich auf den Stuhl* ~ *lassen*** flop down on (*od.* collapse into) one's chair; **2.** *Läufer etc.:* fall behind, drop back; **auf den dritten Platz ~** fall (*od.* drop) back to third place; **3. ~ *in*** (*+ Akk.*) *in alte Fehler etc.:* lapse back into, revert to; → **Schlendrian** 1; **4. *an j-n* ~** *Besitz etc.:* revert to s.o.; **5. *auf j-n* ~** *Schande etc.:* reflect on s.o.

zurück|finden *v/i.* (*unreg., trennb., hat -ge-*) find one's way back (*zu* to) (*auch fig.*); **~fliegen** (*unreg., trennb.*) **I.** *v/i.* (*ist zurückgeflogen*) **1.** fly back; **2.** *umg.* fly back, whiz back; **II.** *v/t.* (*hat*) send back by air, fly *s.o. od. s.th.* back; **~fließen** *v/i.* (*unreg., trennb., ist -ge-*) flow back (*auch Geld*); **~fordern** *v/t.* (*trennb., hat -ge-*) ask for *s.th.* back; *stärker:* demand *s.th.* back; **~fragen** *v/i.* (*trennb., hat -ge-*) **1.** ask in reply; **2.** → **rückfragen**

zurückführbar *Adj.:* **~ *auf*** (*+ Akk.*) attributable to, explainable by; *auf Formel:* reducible to; **zurückführen** (*trennb., hat -ge-*) **I.** *v/t.* **1.** (*j-n*) lead back; **2.** *fig.:* **~ *auf*** (*+ Akk.*) *auf Formel, Regel:* reduce to; *auf e-e Ursache etc.:* put down to, attribute to, explain by; *auf Ursprung:* trace back; **II.** *v/i. Weg:* lead (*od.* go) back (*nach od. zu* to)

zurückgeben (*unreg., trennb., hat -ge-*) **I.** *v/t.* **1.** give back, return; (*Wechselgeld*) give; (*Fahrkarte, Waren etc.*) return; (*reklamieren*) take back; (*Führerschein, Parteibuch etc.*) hand in; (*Freiheit, Selbstwertgefühl, Zuversicht etc.*) give back, restore; **2.** (*entgegnen*) retort; (*Beleidigung, Kompliment etc.*) return; **II.** *vt/i.* (*Ball etc.*) return (the ball) (*an + Akk.* to); *nach hinten:* pass (the ball) back

zurückgeblieben I. *P.P.* → **zurückbleiben**; **II.** *Adj.* backward, retarded

zurückgehen *v/i.* (*unreg., trennb., ist -ge-*) **1.** go back, return; (*zurückweichen*) retreat, fall back; *Tonarm, Zeiger etc.:* return; ***zwei Schritte* ~** step two paces back, take two steps back; **~ *lassen*** return, send back; ***wann geht der nächste Zug zurück?*** when's the next train back?; ***danach ging's wieder nach Hause zurück*** after that we went home; **2.** *Brief, Essen, Waren:* be sent back; ***das Steak ist zäh - ich las-***

se es ~ the steak is tough - I'm sending it back; **3.** (*sich vermindern*) decrease, diminish; *Zahlen: auch* drop; *Geschäft, Umsatz:* fall off; *Preise:* slip, fall, go down; *Temperatur, Fieber:* go down, drop; *Entzündung, Hochwasser, Schwellung:* go down, recede; *Schmerzen:* ease, abate; (*verschwinden*) disappear; ***auf 50 km/h* ~** slow down to 50 kph; ***mit der Geschwindigkeit* ~** reduce speed, slow down; **4.** *fig.:* **~ *auf*** (*+ Akk.*) go back to; *auf e-e Zeit: auch* date (*od.* hark) back to; ***weit in der Geschichte* ~** go a long way back in history

zurückgewinnen *v/t.* (*unreg., trennb., hat*) **1.** *beim Spiel:* win back; **2.** *Mil.* (*Land etc.*) *auch* reconquer, regain; **3.** *fig.* (*Selbstvertrauen etc.*) regain; **4.** *Tech.* (*Rohstoff*) recover

zurückgezogen I. *P.P.* → **zurückziehen**; **II.** *Adj. Leben:* secluded; *Person:* withdrawn; **III.** *Adv.:* ***er lebt sehr* ~** he leads a very secluded life, he's cut himself off from society; **Zurückgezogenheit** *f; nur Sg.* (life of) seclusion

zurück|greifen *v/i.* (*unreg., trennb., hat -ge-*); *fig.* **1. ~ *auf*** (*+ Akk.*) fall back on; **2. *weiter* ~** *in der Erzählung etc.:* go further back; **~haben** *v/t.* (*unreg., trennb., hat -ge-*); *umg.* get *s.th.* back; (*erhalten haben*) have got *s.th.* back; ***ich will es* ~** I want it back

zurückhalten (*unreg., trennb., hat -ge-*) **I.** *v/t.* **1.** (*nicht weglassen*) hold back; (*nicht durchlassen*) (*Demonstranten, Schaulustige etc.*) keep back; (*aufhalten*) (*auch Laster, Schiff*) detain; ***ich will Sie nicht* ~** I don't want to keep you; **2.** (*Informationen, Manuskript etc.*) keep back, withhold; **3.** (*unterdrücken*) suppress; (*Gefühle*) *auch* restrain; (*Orgasmus, Tränen*) hold back; **II.** *v/refl.* **1.** (*sich beherrschen*) restrain o.s.; *am Tisch etc.:* hold back; ***sich* ~ *mit Essen, Trinken:*** go easy on; ***ich musste mich sehr* ~, *um nicht loszuschreien*** I had to hold myself back so as not to start shouting out loud; **2.** *gegenüber anderen:* be reserved; (*sich zurückziehen*) keep (o.s.) to o.s.; (*nicht aktiv werden*) not get involved, take a back seat (*in + Dat. od. bei* in); *Kaufinteressent:* not commit o.s.; **III.** *v/i.:* **~ *mit Gefühlsäußerungen:*** hide; *mit Meinung, Urteil:* withhold; ***sie hielt mit i-n Gefühlen nicht zurück*** she made no secret of her feelings

zurückhaltend I. *Part. Präs.* → **zurückhalten**; **II.** *Adj.* **1.** reserved; (*unaufdringlich*) unobtrusive, self-effacing; (*kühl, reserviert*) restrained, undemonstrative; (*vorsichtig*) guarded, cautious; (*wenig mitteilsam*) uncommunicative; *Empfang:* cool; *Beifall:* polite; *Ton, Behandlung, Art etc.:* low-key; *Farben:* muted; (*nicht*) **~ *sein mit*** be (un)sparing with; **2.** *Wirts., Börse:* dull, quiet; *Nachfrage:* slack; **III.** *Adv. reagieren:* in a subdued (*od.* restrained) way; *eher negativ:* coolly, without enthusiasm; *antworten:* cautiously, guardedly

Zurückhaltung *f; nur Sg.; fig.* reserve, restraint; (*Unaufdringlichkeit*) self-effacement; (*Bescheidenheit*) modesty; ***vornehme* ~** dignified restraint; ***sich*** (*Dat.*) **~ *auferlegen*** exercise restraint, keep a low profile, keep one's head down *umg.; Pol.* act with restraint; ***s-e* ~ *ablegen*** shed all (*od.* one's) restraint; ***mit* ~ *aufnehmen*** *Publikum, Kritiker:* give *s.th.* a cautious (*eher ne-*

Z

gativ: cool) reception

zurück|holen *v/t.* (*trennb., hat -ge-*) fetch back; (*Geld*) get back; (*Satelliten etc.*) retrieve; (*j-n*) call back; (*wieder einstellen*) ask *s.o.* to come back; **~kämmen** *v/t.* (*trennb., hat -ge-*) comb back; *bes. Frau*: back-comb, *Am.* tease; *i-e zurückgekämmten Haare* her back-combed (*Am.* teased) hair; **~kaufen** *v/t.* (*trennb., hat -ge-*) buy back

zurückkehren *v/i.* (*trennb., ist -ge-*) **1.** return, go (*od.* come) back (*nach, zu* to; *von, aus* from); **2.** *fig. Erinnerung etc.*: return, come back; *sein Bewusstsein kehrte allmählich zurück* he gradually regained (*od.* recovered) his consciousness; → *Schoß* 3

zurück|klappen *v/t.* (*trennb., hat -ge-*), (*Sitz*) tip back; (*Deckel*) flip back; (*Klappe, Verdeck*) fold back; **~kommen** *v/i.* (*unreg., trennb., ist -ge-*) **1.** → *zurückkehren*; *der Brief kam ungeöffnet zurück* the letter came back unopened; **2.** *fig.*: **~** *auf* (+ *Akk.*) come back to; (*Bezug nehmen*) refer to; *auf j-s Angebot* **~** take *s.o.* up on an offer, take up *s.o.'s* offer; **~können** *v/i.* (*unreg., trennb., hat -ge-*); *umg.* be able to go back (*od.* return); *ich kann nicht mehr zurück fig.* I can't go back on my word (*od.* decision *etc.*) now

zurücklassen *v/t.* (*unreg., trennb., hat -ge-*) **1.** (*hinterlassen*) leave; *unabsichtlich*: leave behind; *absichtlich*: (*Kind, kaputtes Auto etc.*) abandon; (*Abfälle etc.*) discard; *die anderen weit hinter sich* (*Dat.*) **~** *bei Rennen etc., auch fig.*: leave the others far behind, outstrip all the others; **2.** *umg.* (*Rückkehr erlauben*) allow *s.o.* to return; **Zurücklassung** *f, nur Sg.*: *unter* **~** (+ *Gen. od. von*) leaving behind (*s.th.*)

zurücklaufen *v/i.* (*unreg., trennb., ist -ge-*) *Person, Tonband, Wasser etc.*: run back; *umg. zu Fuß*: walk back

zurücklegen (*trennb., hat -ge-*) **I.** *v/t.* **1.** *an s-n Platz*: put back; **2.** (*Kopf*) lay (*od.* lean) back; **3.** (*aufheben, reservieren*) put aside, keep (*j-m* for *s.o.*); (*Geld*) *auch* save; **4.** (*Weg, Strecke*) cover (*auch Sport*); *zu Fuß*: *auch* walk; *zurückgelegte Strecke* distance covered; *Mot. etc. auch* mileage; **II.** *v/refl.* lie back

zurück|lehnen *v/t. und v/refl.* (*trennb., hat -ge-*) lean back; *sich im Sessel* **~** settle back into one's chair; **~leiten** *v/t.* (*trennb., hat -ge-*); (*j-n*) lead back; (*Verkehr*) turn back; (*Sendung*) return; (*Wasser*) feed back; **~liegen** *v/i.* (*unreg., trennb., ist -ge-*) **1.** *zeitlich*: *das liegt drei Jahre zurück* that was three years ago; **2.** *bes. Sport* be behind; *3:0 / fünf Punkte* **~** be 3-0 (= three-nil, *Am.* three to nothing) / five points down (*od.* behind); **~melden** *v/refl.* (*trennb., hat -ge-*) report back (*bei* to); **~müssen** *v/i.* (*unreg., trennb., hat -ge-*); *umg.* have to go back; *etw. muss zurück Buch*: has to be returned; *Tisch etc., nach hinten*: has to be moved back

Zurücknahme *f, -, -n* taking back; (*von Gesagtem*) withdrawal, *förm.* retraction; (*e-r Entscheidung, Verordnung*) revocation; (*von Auftrag, Angebot, Anklage, Bestellung*) withdrawal; **zurücknehmen** (*unreg., trennb., hat -ge-*) **I.** *v/t.* **1.** (*Ware etc.*) take back; **2.** *fig.* (*Gesagtes*) take back, withdraw, *förm.* retract; (*Schachzug etc.*) take (*Entscheidung, Verordnung*) re-

voke; (*Auftrag, Bestellung*) cancel, withdraw; (*Angebot, Versprechen*) go back on; *Jur.* (*Anklage*) withdraw, drop; **3.** *Mil.* (*Truppen, Front*) withdraw; **4.** (*reduzieren*) (*Lautstärke, Tempo etc.*) reduce; *das Gas* **~** *Mot.* throttle back; **II.** *v/refl.*: *sich etwas* **~** keep a lower profile; *ich habe mich bei der Diskussion völlig zurückgenommen* I took a back seat during the discussion

zurück|pfeifen *v/t.* (*unreg., trennb., hat -ge-*) **1.** (*Hund*) whistle back; **2.** *fig.*: *j-n* **~** pull *s.o.* up short; **~prallen** *v/i.* (*trennb., ist -ge-*) rebound, bounce (*von* off); *Geschoss*: ricochet; *Person, vor Schreck*: recoil, jump back (*vor + Dat.* from); **~rechnen** *v/t.* (*trennb., hat -ge-*) count back; **~reichen** (*trennb., hat -ge-*) **I.** *v/t.* hand back, return; **II.** *v/i.*: **~** (*bis*) *zu od. in* (+ *Akk.*) go (*od.* date) back to; **~reisen** *v/i.* (*trennb., ist -ge-*) travel back, return; **~reißen** *v/t.* (*unreg., trennb., hat -ge-*) tear back; **~rollen** (*trennb.*) *v/t.* (*hat zurückgerollt*) *und v/i.* (*ist*) roll back

zurückrufen *v/t/i.* (*unreg., trennb., hat -ge-*) **1.** (*etw.*) call (*od.* shout) back (*zu* to); **2.** (*j-n*) call back; *aus dem Urlaub etc.*: recall; **3.** *Telef.* call (*od.* phone, *Brit. auch* ring) back; **4.** *Wirts.* (*Auto etc.*) recall; **5.** *fig.*: *sich* (*Dat.*) *ins Gedächtnis* **~** recall (to memory); *ins Leben* **~** bring *s.o.* back to life; (*Sache*) revive, resuscitate

zurück|schallen *v/i.* (*auch unreg., trennb., hat -ge-*); *mst unpers.* echo (back), resound; **~schalten** *v/i.* (*trennb., hat -ge-*): **~** (*auf od. in + Akk., zu*) switch back (to); *Mot.* change (*Am.* shift) down (to); **~schauen** *v/i.* (*trennb., hat -ge-*); *bes. südd., österr., schw.* → *zurückblicken*; **~scheuen** *v/i.* (*trennb., ist -ge-*) → *zurückschrecken*; **~schicken** *v/t.* (*trennb., hat -ge-*) send back; (*Sache*) *auch* return; **~schieben** *v/t.* (*unreg., trennb., hat -ge-*) push back; (*Riegel, Vorhang*) draw back

zurückschlagen (*unreg., trennb.*) **I.** *v/t.* (*hat zurückgeschlagen*) **1.** hit *s.o.* back; (*Feind, Angriff*) beat off; **2.** (*Decke, Verdeck etc.*) fold back; (*Vorhang*) draw; (*Mantel*) throw open; (*Kragen*) turn down; **3.** (*Tennisball*) return; **II.** *v/i.* **1.** (*hat*); *auch fig.* hit (*od.* strike) back; *Mil. auch* retaliate; **2.** (*ist*); *Pendel etc.*: swing back; *Welle etc.*: crash back; *Flamme*: flare back

zurück|schleppen (*trennb., hat -ge-*) **I.** *v/t.* drag *s.o. od. s.th.* back; **II.** *v/refl.* drag *o.s.* back; **~schneiden** *v/t.* (*unreg., trennb., hat -ge-*); (*Hecke, Pflanze*) cut back; (*Krallen*) trim; **~schnellen** *v/i.* (*trennb., ist -ge-*) spring (*od.* snap) back; **~schrauben** *v/t.* (*trennb., hat -ge-*); *fig.* (*Erwartungen, Forderungen*) lower; (*Verbrauch etc.*) cut down (*od.* back), reduce; *s-e Ansprüche* **~** lower one's sights; **~schrecken** *v/i.* (*reg. und unreg., trennb., ist -ge-*) shrink (back) (*vor + Dat.* from), ba(u)lk (at); *er schreckt vor nichts zurück* he'll stop at nothing, he'll go to any length(s); **~schreiben** *v/i.* (*unreg., trennb., hat -ge-*) write back, reply; **~sehen** *v/i.* (*unreg., trennb., hat -ge-*) → *zurückblicken*; **~sehnen** (*trennb., hat -ge-*) **I.** *v/refl.* long to return (*nach* to); *nach Ort bzw. Person*: *auch* long to be in (*bzw.* with); **II.** *v/t.* long for the return of, wish back; **~senden** *v/t.* (*unreg., trennb.,*

hat -ge-) → *zurückschicken*

zurücksetzen (*trennb., hat -ge-*) **I.** *v/t.* **1.** put *s.th.* back; **2.** (*nach hinten versetzen*) move *s.th.* back; (*Schüler etc.*) sit *s.o.* further back, move to a seat nearer the back; (*Auto*) back; (*Wand*) set back; **3.** *Wirts.* → *herabsetzen* 1; **4.** *fig.* (*j-n*) treat unfairly, discriminate against; (*kränken*) slight; (*vernachlässigen*) neglect; *sich zurückgesetzt fühlen* feel hard done by (*j-m gegenüber* in comparison with *s.o.*); **II.** *v/i. mit Auto*: reverse, back; **III.** *v/refl.* (*wieder setzen*) sit down again; *sich drei Reihen* **~** *weiter hinten*: sit three rows further back; **Zurücksetzung** *f fig.* unfair treatment, discrimination; (*Kränkung*) slight; *etw. als* **~** *empfinden* take *s.th.* as a slight

zurück|sinken *v/i.* (*unreg., trennb., ist -ge-*) sink back (*in e-n Sessel etc.*: into); **~spielen** *v/t/i.* (*trennb., hat -ge-*); *Sport* pass (the ball) back; **~spulen** (*trennb., hat -ge-*) **I.** *v/t/i.* (*Video-, Audiokassette etc.*) wind (*od.* run) back (to the beginning); *auch Fot.* rewind; **II.** *v/i. Band, Kassette*: wind (*od.* run) back (to the beginning); **~stecken** (*trennb., hat -ge-*) **I.** *v/t.* put *s.th.* back; **II.** *v/i. fig.* hold back; *in den Ansprüchen, Erwartungen etc.*: lower one's sights

zurückstehen *v/i.* (*unreg., trennb., hat / südd., österr., schw. ist -ge-*) **1.** *Haus etc.*: be set back; **2.** *fig.* (*verzichten*) stand back; (*übertroffen werden*) be left behind; (*benachteiligt sein, hintanstehen*) take second place (*hinter + Dat.* to); *hinter j-m* **~** *in den Leistungen*: be (trailing *od.* lagging) behind *s.o.*, *sie steht an Begabung nicht hinter ihrer Schwester zurück* she's every bit as talented as her sister; *sie musste immer* **~** she always came off worst; *keiner wollte* **~** nobody wanted to be left out (*od.* be the odd man out); (*alle wollten mitmachen*) everybody wanted to join in

zurückstellen *v/t.* (*trennb., hat -ge-*) **1.** *an s-n Platz*: put back; **2.** (*Heizung etc.*) turn down; (*Uhr*) put back; **3.** (*Ware*) put aside; **~** *für auch* keep for; **4.** *fig.* (*Projekt etc.*) put on the back burner; (*Zweifel etc.*) put aside; (*Privatleben etc.*) put last; *Mil., zeitweilig*: defer; *als unentbehrlich*: exempt from service; *Päd., von Einschulung*: defer the entry of; *die eigenen Interessen* **~** put one's own interests last; **Zurückstellung** *f fig.* **1.** putting back; (*von Heizung etc.*) turning down; (*von Ware*) putting aside; **2.** postponement, deferment; *unter* **~** *seiner eigenen Interessen* putting his own interests aside

zurückstoßen (*unreg., trennb.*) **I.** *v/t.* (*hat zurückgestoßen*) **1.** push back; *als er sie umarmen wollte, stieß sie ihn zurück* she pushed him away; **2.** *fig.* (*abstoßen*) disgust; (*zurückweisen*) reject; **II.** *v/i.* (*ist*): (*mit dem Auto*) **~** reverse, back

zurück|strahlen (*trennb., hat -ge-*) **I.** *v/t.* reflect; **II.** *v/i.* be reflected; **~strömen** *v/i.* (*trennb., ist -ge-*) **1.** *Wasser etc.*: flow back; **2.** *Menschen*: pour back (*in die Stadt* into town); **~stufen** *v/t.* (*trennb., hat -ge-*) downgrade; **~taumeln** *v/i.* (*trennb., ist -ge-*) reel (*od.* stagger) back; **~treiben** *v/t.* (*unreg., trennb., hat -ge-*) drive back

zurücktreten *v/i.* (*unreg., trennb., ist -ge-*) **1.** step (*od.* stand) back; **~** *bitte!*

stand back, please; *zwei Schritte* ~ step back two paces (*od.* two paces back); **2.** *fig. von e-m Amt:* step down, stand down, resign; *von e-m Vertrag etc.:* withdraw (*von* from), back out (of); **3.** *fig.* (*hintanstehen*) take second place (*hinter* + *Dat.* to); ~ *gegenüber* be(come) less important than; **4.** *Berge, Hochwasser, Ufer etc.:* recede (*von* from)

zurück|tun *v/t.* (*unreg., trennb., hat -ge-*) put back; ~**übersetzen** *v/t.* (*trennb., hat*) translate back; ~**verfolgen** *v/t.* (*trennb., hat*); *fig.* trace back (*zu* to); ~**verlangen** *v/t.* (*trennb., hat*) → **zurückfordern**; ~**versetzen** **I.** *v/t.* (*trennb., hat*) **1.** (*Angestellten etc.*) transfer back; (*Schüler*) move *s.o.* down (a class); **2.** *fig. in andere Zeit:* take (*od.* carry) back; *etw. in s-n alten Zustand* ~ restore s.th. to its former condition; **II.** *v/refl.:* *sich ins Mittelalter etc.* ~ transport o.s. back to the Middle Ages *etc.*; ~**verwandeln** *v/t. und v/refl.* (*trennb., hat*) change back (*in* + *Akk.* into); (*sich*) ~ *in* (+ *Akk.*) revert to; ~**verweisen** *vt/i.* (*unreg., trennb., hat -ge-*): ~ *an* (+ *Akk.*) refer back to; ~**weichen** *v/i.* (*unreg., trennb., ist -ge-*) **1.** step back; *Menge:* *auch* move back; *Truppen:* fall back; *erschreckt:* shrink back (*vor* + *Dat.* from); *fig.* recoil (from), back away (from); *keinen Zentimeter* ~ stand one's ground, not budge; **2.** *Hochwasser, Kinn, Wald etc.:* recede

zurückweisen *v/t.* (*unreg., trennb., hat -ge-*) **1.** (*j-n*) *an der Grenze etc.:* turn back; *emotional:* reject; (*Bittsteller etc.*) turn away; **2.** (*etw.*) *allg.* reject; (*Argument, Beschuldigung etc.*) *auch* repudiate; (*Angebot, Einladung, Forderung*) *auch* turn down, refuse; *Jur.* (*Klage*) dismiss; *Wirts.* (*Wechsel*) dishono(u)r; **Zurückweisung** *f* rejection; repudiation; dismissal; turning back; → **zurückweisen**

zurück|wenden *v/t. und v/refl.* (*auch unreg., trennb., hat -ge-*) turn back; ~**werfen** (*unreg., trennb., hat -ge-*) **I.** *v/t.* **1.** (*Ball, Kopf etc.*) throw back; (*Haare*) toss back; **2.** (*Lichtstrahlen etc.*) rcflcct; (*Schall*) reverberate; **3.** *fig.* (*den Feind etc.*) repulse; **4.** *fig. in Arbeit, Entwicklung:* set (*od.* throw) back; **II.** *v/refl.* throw o.s. back; ~**wirken** *v/i.* (*trennb., hat -ge-*): ~ *auf* (+ *Akk.*) have an effect on, react on; ~**wollen** (*unreg., trennb., hat -ge-*) *umg.* **I.** *v/i.* want to go back; *hierher, zu uns etc.:* want to come back; **II.** *v/t.:* *ich will mein Geld zurück* I want my money back; ~**wünschen** (*trennb., hat -ge-*) **I.** *v/t.* wish back; **II.** *v/refl.:* *sich nach Hause / zu j-m* ~ wish one were back at home / back with s.o.; ~**zahlen** *v/t.* (*trennb., hat -ge-*) pay back, repay (*auch fig.*); (*Auslagen*) refund, reimburse; (*Hypothek*) redeem; (*Schuld*) pay off

zurückziehen (*unreg., trennb.*) **I.** *v/t.* (*hat zurückgezogen*) **1.** pull back; (*Hand, Vorhang*) *auch* draw back; **2.** *unpers.; fig.:* *es zieht mich nichts dorthin / zu ihm zurück* there's nothing to make me want to go back there / back to him; **3.** *fig.* (*Truppen*) withdraw, pull out; (*Diplomaten*) call back; (*Antrag, Bestellung, Bewerbung etc.*) withdraw; (*Bestellung*) *auch* cancel; (*Zusage, Versprechen*) go back on; **II.** *v/refl.* (*hat*) **1.** withdraw; *Gletscher, Hochwasser, Truppen:* retreat; *sich auf*

sein Zimmer ~ go (up) to one's room; *zum Ausruhen:* retire to one's room; *beleidigt etc.:* shut o.s. up in one's room; *das Gericht zieht sich zur Beratung zurück* the court is retiring for deliberation; *die Schnecke zieht sich in ihr Haus zurück* the snail withdraws (itself) into its shell; → **zurückgezogen**; **2.** *fig.:* *sich vom Geschäftsleben etc.* ~ retire from business *etc.*; *sich von der Bühne* ~ leave (*od.* quit) the stage; *sich von der Öffentlichkeit* ~ retire from public life; *sich von j-m* ~ break off contact with s.o.; *demonstrativ:* dissociate o.s. from s.o.; *sich auf s-n alten Standpunkt* ~ revert (*od.* go back) to one's old standpoint; **III.** *v/i.* (*ist*) move back; *Vögel:* migrate back; *Truppen:* retreat, retire

zurückzucken *v/i.* (*trennb., ist -ge-*) start back; *Hand:* jerk back

Zuruf *m* shout; ~*e auch* (*Zwischenrufe*) heckling; (*Beifall*) cheers, cheering *Sg.*; *durch* ~ by acclamation (*auch Parl.*); **zurufen** *vt/i.* (*unreg., trennb., hat -ge-*): *j-m* ~ call to s.o.; *j-m etw.* ~ call s.th. (out) to s.o., shout s.th. to s.o.

zurzeit *Adv.* (*abgek.* **zz., zzt.**) (*momentan*) at the moment, at present

Zusage *f* **1.** (*Versprechen*) promise; (*Verpflichtung*) commitment; (*Annahme*) acceptance; (*Einwilligung*) assent; *s-e* ~ *geben* promise, give one's word; **2.** *auf Bewerbung:* offer; **zusagen** (*trennb., hat -ge-*) **I.** *v/t.* **1.** promise, undertake to do *s.th.*; *s-e Hilfe* ~ promise to help; *Hilfe* ~ *Regierung etc.:* pledge one's aid, promise to send aid; **2.** *umg.:* *j-m etw. auf den Kopf* ~ tell s.o. s.th. to his (*od.* her) face; **II.** *v/i.* **1.** *auf Angebot, Einladung hin:* accept; *sie haben alle* (*fest*) *zugesagt* they've all said they're (definitely) coming; *sie haben mir zugesagt* auf m-e Bewerbung hin: they've accepted my application; **2.** *j-m* ~ (*gefallen*) appeal to s.o., *förm.* be to s.o.'s liking (*od.* taste); *das sagt mir eher zu* I prefer that, that's more up my street *umg.*

zusammen *Adv.* **1.** *allg.* together; (*gemeinschaftlich*) *auch* jointly; *etw.* ~ *besitzen* own s.th. jointly, be joint owners of s.th.; *bestellen wir e-n großen Salat* ~ let's order a large salad between us (*zu zweit: auch* for the two of us); *er verdient mehr als alle anderen* ~ he earns more than all the rest of them put together; *wie lange sind sie schon* ~? how long have they been together (*od.* been going out with each other)?; *sie ist nicht mehr mit ihm* ~ she's not living with him any more; **2.** (*insgesamt*) (all) together; *das macht ...* ~ that'll be ... all together; *wir haben* ~ *6 Dollar* we have 6 dollars between us; **3.** (*gleichzeitig*) at the same time; *und jetzt alle* ~: *... Musik, Gesang etc.:* all together now ...; **4.** *umg.:* *guten Abend* ~*!* evening all!

Zusammenarbeit *f* cooperation; *bes. mit dem Feind:* collaboration; *e-r Gemeinschaft:* teamwork; **zusammenarbeiten** *v/i.* (*trennb., hat -ge-*) work together, cooperate

zusammenballen (*trennb., hat -ge-*) **I.** *v/t.* make into a ball; (*Papier*) screw up; *die Fäuste* ~ clench one's fists; **II.** *v/refl.* **1.** *Wolken etc.:* build up; *Truppen:* mass; **2.** *fig. Unheil etc.:* loom (*über* + *Dat.* over); **Zusammenballung** *f* accumulation; *von Truppen etc.:* massing; *von Macht, Kapital:* con-

centration

Zusammenbau *m; nur Sg.* assembly; **zusammenbauen** *v/t.* (*trennb., hat -ge-*) assemble, put together

zusammen|beißen *v/t.* (*unreg., trennb., hat -ge-*): *die Zähne* ~ clench (*fig.* grit) one's teeth; ~**bekommen** *v/t.* (*unreg., trennb., hat*), *umg.* **1.** get together; (*Geld*) scrape together; *wie viele Unterschriften habt ihr* ~? how many signatures have you managed to get?; **2.** *im Gedächtnis:* remember; (*fertig bringen*) manage; *er bekommt keinen vernünftigen Satz zusammen* he can't string a decent sentence together; ~**betteln** *v/t.* (*unreg., trennb., hat -ge-*): (*sich* [*Dat.*]) *das Geld* ~ go around begging for the money; ~**binden** *v/t.* (*unreg., trennb., hat -ge-*) tie together; (*Haar, Hände*) tie; *j-m die Hände auf dem Rücken* ~ tie s.o.'s hands behind his (*od.* her) back; ~**bleiben** *v/i.* (*unreg., trennb., ist -ge-*) stay (*umg.* stick) together; ~**brauen** (*trennb., hat -ge-*) **I.** *v/t. umg. fig.* brew, concoct, cook up; **II.** *v/refl. Unwetter, Streit etc.:* be brewing; *da braut sich was zusammen* there's something brewing there

zusammenbrechen *v/i.* (*unreg., trennb., ist -ge-*) **1.** *Gebäude, Brücke:* cave in, collapse; *Haus, Wand: auch* come tumbling down; **2.** *Person:* collapse; *fig. seelisch:* break down; *Kreislauf:* break down; **3.** *fig. Wirtschaft, Firma:* collapse; *Angriff, Pläne:* fail; *Ordnung, Netzwerk, Telefonverbindung, Theorie, Verhandlungen, Widerstand:* break down; *Verkehr:* come to a standstill; *da brach für mich e-e Welt zusammen* that's when my whole world fell apart

zusammenbringen *v/t.* (*unreg., trennb., hat -ge-*) **1.** (*Leute*) bring (*od.* get, gather) together; (*Kräfte, Mittel etc.*) muster; (*sammeln*) collect, gather; (*Geld*) raise, get (*od.* scrape) together; *etw. mit etw.* ~ bring s.th. into contact with s.th.; **2.** *fig.* (*vereinen*) unite; *j-n mit j-m* ~ (*bekannt machen*) introduce s.o. to s.o.; *auch intimer:* get s.o. together with s.o.; *j-n mit j-m wieder* ~ (*versöhnen*) reconcile s.o. with s.o.; **3.** *umg., bes. südd.* → **zusammenbekommen**

Zusammenbruch *m* breakdown (*auch Med., Pol. etc.*); *völliger:* collapse

zusammen|drängen (*trennb., hat -ge-*) **I.** *v/t.* **1.** crowd together; *auf engstem Raum zusammengedrängt* crowded into a minimum of space; **2.** *fig.* (*Beschreibung etc.*) condense (*auf* + *Akk.* to); **II.** *v/refl.* **1.** huddle together; **2.** *fig. Ereignisse etc.:* be concentrated, come thick and fast; ~**drücken** *v/t.* (*trennb., hat -ge-*) press together; (*Gas*) compress; (*zerdrücken*) crush, squash; ~**fahren** (*unreg., trennb.*) **I.** *v/t.* (*hat zusammengefahren*); *umg.* (*Auto etc.*) smash up, wreck; (*Person, Tier*) run over; **II.** *v/i.* (*ist*) **1.** *Autos:* crash (into each other); **2.** *vor Schreck etc.:* jump, start (*vor* + *Dat.* with); *vor Schmerz:* wince (with); ~**fallen** *v/i.* (*unreg., trennb., ist -ge-*) **1.** *Gebäude etc.:* collapse, cave in; *Kuchen etc.:* go down in the middle; (*in sich* [*Akk.*]) ~ *Ballon, Schaum etc.:* go down; *Feuer, Glut:* die down; *fig. Beweisführung, Pläne etc.:* collapse, fall apart; **2.** *fig. Person:* waste away; *Gesicht:* collapse, cave in; **3.** *zeitlich:* coincide, fall on the same day (*od.* in the same week *etc.*); *räumlich:* coincide; ~**falten** *v/t.*

(*trennb., hat -ge-*) **1.** (*Papier, Decke etc.*) fold (up); (*Zeitung*) fold up; **2. die Hände ~** fold one's hands; **~fantasieren** *v/t.* (*trennb., hat*): **sich** (*Dat.*) **etw. ~** fantasize s.th.; *umg.* (*Ausreden, Lügen*) dream s.th. up

zusammenfassen *vt/i.* (*trennb., hat -ge-*) **1.** (*Rede, Text etc.*) sum up, summarize; (*kürzen*) condense; (*kurz wiederholen*) recapitulate; (*vereinigen*) unite, integrate (*in + Akk.* into); **in Gruppen/Kategorien ~** group / classify *od.* categorize s.th., gather in groups/categories; **unter e-m Oberbegriff ~** bring together under a general heading; **zusammenfassend I.** *Part. Präs.* → **zusammenfassen**; **II.** *Adj.*: **~er Bericht** *etc.* summary (of events *etc.*), résumé; **III.** *Adv.* in summary, to sum up; **~ lässt sich sagen** in summary it may be said, to sum up one may say; **Zusammenfassung** *f* summary (*auch Päd.*); *wissenschaftliche: auch* abstract; (*Kürzung*) condensation; *Päd.* (*Précis*) précis

zusammen|fegen *v/t.* (*trennb., hat -ge-*); *bes. nordd.* sweep up (*od.* together); **~finden** *v/i.* (*unreg., trennb., hat -ge-*) get together; **~flicken** *v/t.* (*trennb., hat -ge-*); *umg., oft pej.* (*auch Person*) patch up; *fig.* (*Text*) cobble together

zusammenfließen *v/i.* (*unreg., trennb., ist -ge-*) **1.** *Flüsse:* flow together, meet, join; *Farben:* run (together); **2.** *fig.* merge; **Zusammenfluss** *m* confluence, junction

zusammen|fügen (*trennb., hat -ge-*) **I.** *v/t.* join (together), fit together; **II.** *v/refl.* *Teile etc.:* fit together; **~führen** *v/t.* (*trennb., hat -ge-*) bring together; *wieder* ~ (*Familie etc.*) reunite; **~gehen** *v/i.* (*unreg., trennb., ist -ge-*) **1.** (*sich verbünden*) join forces; *Parteien, Firmen:* cooperate; (*sich vereinigen*) merge; **2.** *mst unpers.; Farben etc.:* match, go together (well); **3.** *umg., Linien:* converge, meet

zusammengehören *v/i.* (*trennb., hat*); *umg.* belong together; *als Paar:* form a pair; *als Set etc.:* form a set; **zusammengehörig** *Adj.* **1.** *Socken etc.:* attr. matching ...; **2. sich ~ fühlen** feel you (*bzw.* they) belong together; **Zusammengehörigkeit** *f; nur Sg.* shared identity; *Pol.* solidarity; **Zusammengehörigkeitsgefühl** *n* in Gruppe, Familie: (sense of) togetherness; in Gesellschaft, Staat: common (*od.* shared) identity; *Pol.* (feeling of) solidarity; (*Mannschaftsgeist*) team spirit

zusammengepfercht I. *P.P.* → **zusammenpferchen**; **II.** *Adj.* penned (up); ~ **in** (+ *Dat.*) *fig. auch* crowded into, cooped up in

zusammengeraten *v/i.* (*unreg., trennb., ist -ge-*); *umg. fig.* clash, come to blows

zusammen|gesetzt I. *P.P.* → **zusammensetzen**; **II.** *Adj.* **1.** ~ **sein aus** be made up of; **2.** *Math., Mus., Ling.; Arznei:* compound; *Bild, Stil etc.:* composite; **~es Wort** compound (word); **~gewürfelt I.** *P.P.* → **zusammenwürfeln**; **II.** *Adj.*: (*bunt*) ~ motley ..., thrown together; **~e Mannschaft** scratch team; **ein bunt ~er Haufen** (*Gruppe von Menschen*) a motley collection

zusammenhaben *v/t.* (*unreg., trennb., hat -ge-*); *umg.* have got s.th. together; (*Geld*) *auch* have scraped s.th. together

Zusammenhalt *m; nur Sg.* cohesion (+ *Gen.* of); *fig.* bond (between, within), unity (of); (*Mannschaftsgeist*) team spirit; **der ~ in unserer Familie ist schlecht** there is not much sense of unity and solidarity in our family; **zusammenhalten** (*unreg., trennb., hat -ge-*) **I.** *v/i.* **1.** hold together (*auch fig.*); **2.** *Freunde etc.:* stick together; **II.** *v/t.* **1.** hold s.th. together (*auch fig.*); (*Geld*) hold onto; **s-e Gedanken ~** *fig.* keep track of one's thoughts; **2.** (*nebeneinander halten*) hold next to each other, hold side by side

Zusammenhang *m* (*Verbindung*) connection; *innerer:* coherence, cohesion; *äußerer:* context; *e-r Abfolge:* continuity; *von Ideen:* association; **es besteht ein ~ zwischen den Ereignissen** the events are connected; **miteinander in ~ bringen** establish a connection (*od.* link) between; **im ~ stehen mit** be connected with; **nicht im ~ stehen mit** have no connection with, have nothing to do with; **in diesem ~** in this connection; **Worte aus ihrem ~ reißen** take words out of their context; **die Dinge im ~ sehen** see things in context; **die größeren Zusammenhänge** the general perspective; *weitS.* the overall scheme (of events *od.* things), the big picture; **zusammenhängen** *v/i.* (*unreg., trennb., hat -ge-*); *fig. Inseln, Satzteile etc.:* be connected, be linked; (*miteinander*) ~ link up; **es hängt damit zusammen, dass ...** *auch* it has to do (*od.* it ties up) with the fact that ...; **zusammenhängend I.** *Part. Präs.* → **zusammenhängen**; **II.** *Adj.* **1.** *Gedanken, Rede, Sätze:* coherent; **2.** (*in Beziehung stehend*) related, connected; **III.** *Adv.*: **etw. ~ erzählen** give a coherent account of s.th.; **zusammenhang(s)los** *Adj.* incoherent, disjointed (*auch Rede*), disconnected; *Sätze: auch* jumbled

zusammen|hauen *v/t.* (*unreg., trennb., hat -ge-*); *umg.* **1.** (*etw.*) smash to pieces; **2.** (*j-n*) beat up; **3.** *fig. pej.* (*hinschludern*) knock (*od.* throw) together; **~heften** *v/t.* (*trennb., hat -ge-*) **1.** *mit Heftklammern:* staple (together); *mit Büroklammern:* clip together; *in e-m Ordner:* file; **2.** (*Buch*) stitch together; (*Stoff*) tack; **~hocken** *v/i.* (*trennb., hat / südd., österr., schw. ist -ge-*) *umg.* sit next to each other; (*auch zusammen sein*) sit together; **~holen** *v/t.* (*trennb., hat -ge-*) gather (together); **~kauern** *v/refl.* (*trennb., hat -ge-*) **1.** squat; *ängstlich:* cower; *frierend:* be huddled (up), huddle; **2.** *mehrere:* huddle together; **~kaufen** *v/t.* (*trennb., hat -ge-*) buy up; **~kehren** *v/t.* (*trennb., hat -ge-*); *bes. südd.* sweep up (*od.* together); **~kitten** *v/t.* (*trennb., hat -ge-*) **1.** stick s.th. together; **2.** *fig.* (*Freundschaft etc.*) patch up

Zusammenklang *m* harmony (*auch fig.*)

zusammenklappbar *Adj.* folding ..., collapsible; **zusammenklappen** (*trennb.*) **I.** *v/t.* (*hat zusammengeklappt*) (*Messer, Stuhl*) fold up; (*Schirm*) close, shut; **II.** *v/i.* (*ist*) **1.** *Messer, Stuhl:* **sich ~ lassen** fold up; **2.** *umg. Person:* collapse (*vor + Dat.* from); *seelisch:* break down

zusammen|klauben *v/t.* (*trennb., hat -ge-*) gather up, collect; **~kleben** (*trennb.*) *v/t.* (*hat zusammengeklebt*) *und v/i.* (*ist*) stick together; **~kneifen** *v/t.* (*unreg., trennb., hat -ge-*) → **zu-**

kneifen; **~knoten** *v/t.* (*trennb., hat -ge-*) **1.** *Schnüre etc.:* tie (*od.* knot) together; **2.** *umg.* (*zuknoten*) tie up; **~knüllen** *v/t.* (*trennb., hat -ge-*) crumple up, screw up, scrunch up *umg.*

zusammenkommen *v/i.* (*unreg., trennb., ist -ge-*) **1.** come together; (*sich treffen*) meet; *zwanglos:* get together; (*sich versammeln*) gather; **so jung kommen wir nie wieder zusammen** you're only young once!; **2.** *Geld:* be raised; **es kommt einiges zusammen** there's quite a bit of money coming in; **3.** *Umstände:* combine; **es ist alles zusammengekommen** everything came together (*od.* happened at the same time); **4.** *fig.* (*sich einigen*) come to an agreement, agree

zusammen|koppeln *v/t.* (*trennb., hat -ge-*) couple (together), link up; (*Raumschiffe etc.*) *auch* dock; **~krachen** *v/i.* (*trennb., ist -ge-*); *umg.* **1.** (*einstürzen*) collapse; *Gebäude: auch* cave in; **2.** *Autos:* crash; **3.** *Börse etc.:* crash; **4.** *Person:* → **zusammenklappen** II 2; **~krampfen** *v/refl.* (*trennb., hat -ge-*) *Muskeln:* tense up; *stärker:* seize up; *Hände, Finger:* clench tightly; **~kratzen** *v/t.* (*trennb., hat -ge-*) *umg.* scrape together; **~kriegen** *v/t.* (*trennb., hat -ge-*); *umg.* → **zusammenbekommen**; **~krümmen** *v/refl.* (*trennb., hat -ge-*) *Person:* double up

Zusammenkunft *f* (*Treffen*) meeting; *zwanglos:* get-together; (*Versammlung*) gathering, conference

zusammen|läppern *v/refl.* (*trennb., hat -ge-*); *umg.* add up, mount up; **~laufen** *v/i.* (*unreg., trennb., ist -ge-*) **1.** *Menschen:* gather; **2.** *Linien, Straßen etc.:* converge, meet; *Math.* intersect, meet; **3.** *Flüssigkeit:* collect; *Flüsse etc.:* join, meet; *Farben:* run (together); → **Faden¹** 3, **Wasser** 4; **4.** *umg. Stoff:* shrink; **5.** *Dial. Milch:* curdle

zusammenleben (*trennb., hat -ge-*) **I.** *v/i.* live together; **mit j-m ~** live with s.o.; **sie haben viele Jahre glücklich zusammengelebt** they spent many happy years together; **II.** *v/refl.* adapt to one another, learn how to get on (*Am.* along) (with one another); **Zusammenleben** *n* living together; *förm.* cohabitation; **das ~ mit ihm** living with him, life with him

zusammenlegen (*trennb., hat -ge-*) **I.** *v/t.* **1.** (*falten*) fold up; **2.** *an e-n Platz:* put (*od.* gather) together; *auf Stapel:* pile up (*od.* together); (*Häftlinge, Kranke*) put together; (*Hände etc.*) fold; **3.** (*Geld*) pool; (*vereinigen*) combine; (*Verwaltungen etc.*) centralize; (*Unternehmen*) merge; (*Termine, Veranstaltungen*) combine; **wir legten unser Geld zusammen** we clubbed together; **II.** *v/i.* (*Geld sammeln*) club together, pass the hat (a)round *umg.*; **wenn wir alle ~** if everybody chips in *umg.*; **Zusammenlegung** *f Wirts.* merger, fusion; *von Grundstücken etc.:* consolidation

zusammen|leimen *v/t.* (*trennb., hat -ge-*) glue (*od.* stick) together; **~lügen** *v/t.* (*unreg., trennb., hat -ge-*) *umg. pej.* make up, cook up; **~nageln** *v/t.* (*trennb., hat -ge-*) nail together

zusammennehmen (*unreg., trennb., hat -ge-*) **I.** *v/t.* **1.** (*zusammen betrachten*) take together; **alles zusammengenommen** all in all, all things considered; **2.** *fig.* (*Kräfte, Mut*) summon (up), muster (up); (*Gedanken*) collect;

II. *v/refl. zu Anstrengung*: collect o.s.; (*sich beherrschen*) control o.s., get a grip on o.s., get a grip *umg.*; (*sich anständig benehmen*) pull o.s. together; *jetzt nimm dich zusammen!* (*beruhige dich*) now pull yourself together!, now get a grip on yourself!

zusammen|packen *vt/i.* (*trennb., hat -ge-*) pack up; *er kann ~ fig.* he can pack his bags and leave; **~passen** *v/i.* (*trennb., hat -ge-*) *Kleider, Möbel etc.*: go well together; *farblich auch*: match; *Personen*: suit one another; *nicht/ schlecht ~* not go together / not go well together; *farblich auch*: not match / be a poor match; *Personen*: not suit one another / be ill-suited; *es passt alles zusammen fig., bes. iro.* it all adds up; **~pferchen** *v/t.* (*trennb., hat -ge-*) herd together (*auch fig.*); *~ in* (+ *Dat.*) *fig. auch* crowd into, coop up in

Zusammenprall *m; -(e)s, -e* collision; *fig.* clash; **zusammenprallen** *v/i.* (*trennb., ist -ge-*) **1.** crash, smash into each other; *Personen*: run into each other; *~ mit* crash (*od.* smash) into; *Person*: run into; **2.** *fig.* clash, come to blows, cross swords

zusammen|pressen *v/t.* (*trennb., hat -ge-*) press together; *die Lippen ~* press one's lips together (tightly); **~quetschen** (*trennb., hat -ge-*) **I.** *v/t.* **1.** (*zerquetschen*) squash (up); **2.** *auf engem Raum*: squeeze together; **II.** *v/refl.* squeeze (*od.* squash) (o.s.) up; **~raffen** (*trennb., hat -ge-*) **I.** *v/t.* **1.** (*s-e Habseligkeiten etc.*) snatch up; **2.** *fig.* (*s-n Mut etc.*) muster (up), summon (up), gather together *lit.*; *pej.* (*Reichtümer etc.*) pile up; hoard; **3.** (*Stoff*) gather; (*Rock*) pick up, gather up; **II.** *v/refl. umg.* pull o.s. together; **~rasseln** *v/i.* (*trennb., ist -ge-*); *umg. fig.* (*Ärger, Streit bekommen*) have a row (*Am.* fight) (*mit* with); **~raufen** *v/refl.* (*trennb., hat -ge-*); *umg.* work things out with each other, get it together; **~rauschen** *v/i.* (*trennb., ist -ge-*); *umg. fig.* → *zusammenrasseln*; **~rechnen** *v/t.* (*trennb., hat -ge-*) add up, tot up *umg.*; *alles zusammengerechnet fig.* all in all, all things considered, taking everything into account; **~reimen** (*trennb., hat -ge-*); *fig.* **I.** *v/t.: sich* (*Dat.*) *etw. ~* make sense of s.th.; *den Rest kannst du dir selbst ~* you can work the rest out for yourself; **II.** *v/refl.* make sense; *wie reimt sich das zusammen?* where is the sense in that?, what is one supposed to make of that?; **~reißen** *v/refl.* (*unreg., trennb., hat -ge-*); *umg.* → *zusammennehmen* II; **~rollen** (*trennb., hat -ge-*) **I.** *v/t.* roll up; **II.** *v/refl. Katze etc.*: curl up; *Igel*: roll itself up into a ball; *Plakat etc.*: roll up; *Schlange etc.*: coil up

zusammenrotten *v/refl.* (*trennb., hat -ge-*) gang up; *Aufrührer*: form a mob; **Zusammenrottung** *f* **1.** *Handlung*: ganging up, banding together; **2.** *Menschenmenge*: mob

zusammen|rücken (*trennb., hat -ge-*) **I.** *v/t.* move together (*od.* closer); **II.** *v/i.* move up, sit closer; (*Platz machen*) make room; **~rufen** *v/t.* (*unreg., trennb., hat -ge-*) call together; (*einberufen*) convene; *Parl.* summon, *Am.* convene; **~sacken** *v/i.* (*trennb., ist -ge-*); *umg.* → *zusammensinken*; **~scharen** *v/refl.* (*trennb., hat -ge-*) gather

zusammen|scheißen *v/t.* (*unreg., trennb., hat -ge-*); *vulg.* give *s.o.* a bol-

locking *Sl., Am.* dress *s.o.* down; **~schieben** (*unreg., trennb., hat -ge-*) **I.** *v/t.* push (*od.* move) together; *Tech.* telescope; **II.** *v/refl.* fold up; *Sitzplätze*: fold away; *Tech.* retract; *ineinander*: telescope; **~schießen** *v/t.* (*unreg., trennb., hat -ge-*); *umg.* riddle with bullets, shoot up, shoot to pieces; *j-n ~ auch* shoot *s.o.* down; **~schlagen** (*unreg., trennb.*) **I.** *v/t.* (*hat zusammengeschlagen*) **1.** *aneinander*: bang together; *die Hände über dem Kopf ~* throw one's hands up in surprise *etc.*; *die Hacken ~* click one's heels; **2.** (*zerschlagen*) smash (to pieces); *umg.* (*j-n verprügeln*) beat *s.o.* up, clobber; **II.** *v/i.* (*ist*): *~ über* (+ *Akk.*) *Wellen*: engulf

zusammenschließen (*unreg., trennb., hat -ge-*) **I.** *v/t.* **1.** lock (*mit e-r Kette*: chain) together; **2.** *fig.* (*vereinigen*) unite; *Wirts.* merge; **3.** *Etech.* connect; **II.** *v/refl.* **1.** unite; (*gemeinsame Sache machen*) join forces, band together (*gegen* against); **2.** *zu e-r Gruppe*: team up; *zu e-m Bündnis*: form an alliance; **3.** *Wirts.* merge, amalgamate; **Zusammenschluss** *m* union (*auch Pol.*); *Wirts.* merger

zusammen|schmelzen (*unreg., trennb.*) **I.** *v/t.* (*hat zusammengeschmolzen*) melt down; **II.** *v/i.* (*ist*) melt away (*auch fig.*); *fig. auch* dwindle (away); **~schneiden** *v/t.* (*unreg., trennb., hat -ge-*) (*Tonband, Film etc.*) splice; **~schnüren** *v/t.* (*trennb., hat -ge-*) → *zuschnüren*; **~schrauben** *v/t.* (*trennb., hat -ge-*) screw (*mit Bolzen*: bolt) together; **~schrecken** *v/i.* (*auch unreg., trennb., ist -ge-*) jump, start (*bei* at)

zusammenschreiben *v/t.* (*unreg., trennb., hat -ge-*) **1.** write *s.th.* as one word; *wird das zusammengeschrieben?* is that one word (or two)?; **2.** *umg. pej. gedankenlos*: scribble down; (*e-n*) *Unsinn ~* write a lot of nonsense; *das hat er aus anderen Büchern zusammengeschrieben* he's got it out of (*od.* pinched it from) other books; **Zusammenschreibung** *f* writing as one word; *die Regeln für die Getrennt- und ~* the rules governing whether *s.th.* is written as one word or two

zusammen|schrumpfen *v/i.* (*trennb., ist -ge-*) **1.** shrivel (up); **2.** *fig.* dwindle, dry up; **~schustern** *v/t.* (*trennb., hat -ge-*); *umg. pej.* cobble (*od.* throw, knock) together; **~schütten** *v/t.* (*trennb., hat -ge-*) mix (by pouring together); **~schweißen** *v/t.* (*trennb., hat -ge-*) **1.** weld together; **2.** *fig.* weld, knit together

zusammen sein → *zusammen* 1; **Zusammensein** *n* **1.** gathering; (*geselliges*) *~* get-together; **2.** → *Zusammenleben*

zusammensetzen (*trennb., hat -ge-*) **I.** *v/t.* **1.** (*zusammenbauen*) put together; *Tech. auch* assemble; *zu e-m Ganzen*: compose; (*Wort*) compound; **2.** *Schüler etc. ~* sit (*od.* put) pupils (*Am.* students) *etc.* next to each other; **II.** *v/refl.*: **1.** *Personen*: sit (down) together; *zu Gespräch etc.*: get together; **2.** *sich ~ aus* be made up of, consist of; → *zusammengesetzt*; **Zusammensetzung** *f* **1.** composition (*aus* from, made up of); (*Mischung*) combination; *Ling., Chem.* compound; **2.** *nur Sg.*; (*Aufbau*) make-up, structure; (*Bestandteile*) ingredients *Pl.*

zusammen|sinken *v/i.* (*unreg., trennb.*,

ist -ge-) **1.** *Gebäude etc.*: collapse, cave in; **2.** *Person*: collapse, slump into a heap (*od.* onto the floor); (*in sich*) *zusammengesunken dasitzen* sit slumped in a heap; **~sitzen** *v/i.* (*unreg., trennb., hat / südd., österr., schw. ist -ge-*) sit next to each other; (*auch zusammen sein*) sit together; **~sparen** *v/t.* (*trennb., hat -ge-*) (*Geld, Vermögen*) save (up); *wir müssen uns den neuen Wagen ~* we have to save up for the new car; **~sperren** *v/t.* (*trennb., hat -ge-*): *Menschen/Tiere ~* shut people/animals up together

Zusammenspiel *n; nur Sg.* **1.** *Mus.* ensemble (playing); *Sport und fig.* teamwork; *fig. auch* cooperation; **2.** *fig. der Kräfte etc.*: interplay (+ *Gen.* of); **zusammenspielen** *v/i.* (*trennb., hat -ge-*) **1.** play together; **2.** *fig.* (*zusammenwirken*) act together

zusammen|stauchen *v/t.* (*trennb., hat -ge-*) **1.** (*kleiner machen*) squash together; **2.** *umg. fig.* (*zurechtweisen*) give *s.o.* a dressing-down (*od.* roasting), bawl *s.o.* out; **~stecken** (*trennb.*) **I.** *v/t.* (*hat zusammengesteckt*) **1.** (*Teile*) put together; *mit Nadeln*: pin together; **2.** *umg.*: *die Köpfe ~* put one's heads together; (*etwas besprechen*) go into a huddle; **II.** *v/i.* (*hat / südd., österr., schw. ist*); *umg.*: *immer ~* be inseparable, be as thick as thieves; **~stehen** *v/i.* (*unreg., trennb., hat / südd., österr., schw. ist -ge-*) **1.** stand together (*od.* next to each other, side by side); **2.** *umg. fig.* stick together

zusammenstellen *v/t.* (*trennb., hat -ge-*) **1.** put (*od.* move) together; **2.** *fig. aus einzelnen Teilen*: put together; (*Blumenstrauß etc.*) make up; *nach Muster, System*: arrange (*auch Reise etc.*); (*Fahrplan, Liste etc.*) make (*out od.* up), draw up; (*Bericht, Daten, Programm etc.*) compile; (*ausarbeiten*) work out; (*Team*) pick, come up with; **Zusammenstellung** *f* **1.** arrangement; drawing up; compilation *etc.*; → *zusammenstellen*; **2.** (*Tabelle*) table; (*Übersicht*) survey; (*Liste*) list

zusammen|stimmen *v/i.* (*trennb., hat -ge-*) *Aussagen etc.*: tally; *nicht ~ auch* contradict each other, *Am. auch* not jibe; *stärker*: clash; **~stoppeln** *v/t.* (*trennb., hat -ge-*); *umg. pej.* piece together; (*Rede etc.*) throw together

Zusammenstoß *m* **1.** collision; *Mot. auch* crash; **2.** *umg. fig.* (*Auseinandersetzung*) clash; *es kam zu schweren Zusammenstößen zwischen den Studenten und der Polizei* there were heavy clashes between the students and the police; **zusammenstoßen** *v/i.* (*unreg., trennb., ist -ge-*) **1.** collide, crash (into each other); *~ mit* collide with, run into, crash into; *sie stießen mit den Köpfen zusammen* they banged (*od.* bumped) their heads together; **2.** *fig.* clash, come to blows; **3.** *Grundstücke etc.*: meet, adjoin

zusammen|streichen *v/t.* (*unreg., trennb., hat -ge-*) **1.** (*Text etc.*) cut, shorten (*auf* + *Akk.* to); **2.** (*Geldmittel*) slash; **~strömen** *v/i.* (*trennb., ist -ge-*) **1.** *Flüsse*: join, flow into one another; **2.** *Personen*: flock together; **~stürzen** *v/i.* (*trennb., ist -ge-*) collapse (*auch fig.*), cave in; **~suchen** *v/t.* (*trennb., hat -ge-*) get (*od.* gather) together, find; **~tragen** *v/t.* (*unreg., trennb., hat -ge-*) collect, gather; (*Fakten, Material etc.*) compile; *Druck.* collate

zusammentreffen v/i. (unreg., trennb., ist -ge-) **1.** meet (*mit j-m* s.o.); *zufällig*: encounter; **2.** *Ereignisse*: coincide (*auch Umstände*), take place simultaneously (*od.* at the same time)

zusammentreffen n **1.** meeting; (*Begegnung*) encounter; *ich möchte ein ~ mit ihm vermeiden* I'd like to avoid meeting him, I'd prefer to keep out of his way; *schon beim ersten ~* ... the very first time we etc. met ...; **2.** *von Ereignissen*: coincidence; *zeitlich*: concurrence; *durch ein ~ verschiedener unglücklicher Umstände* through a combination of unfortunate circumstances

zusammen|treiben v/t. (unreg., trennb., hat -ge-) round up; **~treten** (unreg., trennb.) **I.** v/t. (hat zusammengetreten); umg. crush s.th. underfoot; (*Person*) put the boot in(to) s.o.; **II.** v/i. (ist) meet; *Parl. auch* convene; *Gericht*: sit; **~trommeln** v/t. (trennb., hat -ge-); umg. round up; **~tun** (unreg., trennb., hat -ge-); umg. **I.** v/t. put together; **II.** v/refl. join forces, team up; **~wachsen** v/i. (unreg., trennb., ist -ge-) grow together; *Knochen*: knit (together); *Wunde*: heal (up); *Städte*: merge; fig. grow close; **~werfen** v/t. (unreg., trennb., hat -ge-) **1.** throw together; **2.** fig. unterschiedslos: lump together umg.; (*durcheinander bringen*) mix up

zusammenwirken v/i. (trennb., hat -ge-) **1.** *Umstände etc.*: interact; **2.** geh. *Personen*: cooperate, collaborate

Zusammenwirken n **1.** interplay; **2.** geh. cooperation

zusammenwürfeln v/t. (trennb., hat -ge-) throw together; → *zusammengewürfelt*

zusammenzählen v/t. (trennb., hat -ge-) add up; *alles zusammengezählt* all together, all told, in all

zusammenziehen (unreg., trennb.) **I.** v/t. (hat zusammengezogen) **1.** pull together; (*Netz, Schlinge*) draw tight; (*Augenbrauen*) knit; (*verengen*) auch Phys. contract; *die Säure zog mir den Mund zusammen* the sour taste made me pucker up my mouth; **2.** (*Truppen*) mass; **3.** Math. (addieren) add; (kürzen) reduce; **II.** v/i. (ist); *Personen*: move together, move in with each other; *mit j-m ~* move in with s.o.; **III.** v/refl. (hat) **1.** Muskel, Sehne etc.: contract (auch Phys.); Blutgefäß: constrict; (*sich verengen*) narrow; (*schrumpfen*) shrink; **2.** Unwetter, auch fig. Unheil: be brewing

zusammenzucken v/i. (trennb., hat -ge-) start, jump; vor Schmerz: wince with pain

Zusatz m **1.** nur Sg.; (das Zusetzen) addition; *unter ~ von* by adding; *unter ~ von ... mischen* stir while adding ...; **2.** (*Ergänzung*) addition, supplement; (*Beimischung*) admixture; Stoff: additive; **3.** schriftlicher: addendum (Pl. addenda); zu Brief: postscript; zu e-m Gesetz: rider; zu e-m Testament: codicil; **~batterie** f booster battery; **~belastung** f additional load; **~bremsleuchte** f Mot. high-level (Am. rear-window) brake light; **~erklärung** f Pol. supplementary declaration; **~frage** f follow-up question; **~gerät** n attachment; (*Adapter*) adapter; EDV peripheral, add-on; **~klausel** f rider; **~kosten** Pl. additional (od. added) costs

zusätzlich I. Adj. additional, extra, further; (ergänzend) supplementary; (Hilfs...) auxiliary; *~e Arbeit* extra work; *~e Belastung* added burden; **II.** Adv. (außerdem) in addition; *~ zu* in addition to, over and above; *~ noch etwas verdienen* earn a bit extra; *ich will nicht noch ~ auf s-n Hund aufpassen* I don't want to have to look after (Am. take care of) his dog as well (od. on top of everything else)

Zusatz|stoff m additive; **~versicherung** f supplementary insurance, added protection; **~zahl** f beim Lotto etc.: bonus number

zuschalten (trennb., hat -ge-) **I.** v/t. Etech. connect; TV, Radio: link up with; **II.** v/refl. TV, Radio: link into the network

zuschanden, zu Schanden Adv.: *~ fahren* (Auto) wreck, write off umg.; *~ machen* ruin, wreck, destroy; (Hoffnungen) destroy, dash; *~ reiten* (Pferd) ride into the ground; (Hose, Sattel) wear out, ruin; *~ werden* Pläne etc.: come to nothing, be ruined

zuschanzen v/t. (trennb., hat -ge-); umg.: *j-m etw. ~* put s.th. s.o.'s way; (*Arbeit, Stelle*) auch line s.o. up with s.th.

zuscharren v/t. (trennb., hat -ge-); (Loch etc.) cover up

zuschauen v/i. (trennb., hat -ge-); bes. südd., österr., schw. → *zusehen*

Zuschauer m; -s, -, **~in** f; -, -nen **1.** Sport spectator; Pl. auch crowd (V. im Sg. od. Pl.); *die ~ strömen wieder in die Stadien* the crowds are streaming back (in)to the stadiums; **2.** TV viewer; Pl. auch audience (V. im Sg. od. Pl.); **3.** Theat., Kino etc.: member of the audience; Pl. audience (V. im Sg. od. Pl.); *e-r der ~* somebody in the audience, a member of the audience; **4.** (Beobachter) onlooker, bystander, looker-on; **~kulisse** f Theat. audience; Sport crowd; **~menge** f mst Sport crowd (of spectators); **~raum** m auditorium; **~reaktion** f audience (TV auch viewer) response; Sport reaction of the crowd; **~rekord** m record attendance; **~tribüne** f (grand)stand; Pl. Brit. auch terraces; **~umfrage** f audience survey; **~zahl** f auch Pl. **1.** Sport number of spectators, crowd; **2.** TV number of viewers, viewing figures, Am. (Nielsen) ratings; *geringe ~en* low ratings, poor audience

zuschaufeln v/t. (trennb., hat -ge-) fill up

zuschicken v/t. (trennb., hat -ge-) send (+ Dat. to); mit der Post: auch mail, post (to); *etw. zugeschickt bekommen* be sent s.th.; *sich* (Dat.) *etw. ~ lassen* have s.th. sent, send (off) for s.th.

zuschieben v/t. (unreg., trennb., hat -ge-) **1.** (Fenster, Tür) close, push shut (od. to); (auch Schubfach) shut; (Riegel) push (od. slide) across; **2.** *j-m etw. ~* push s.th. over to s.o.; **3.** fig.: *j-m etw. ~* pass s.th. on to s.o.; *j-m die Schuld ~* pass (od. push) the blame onto s.o., lay the blame at s.o.'s door; *j-m die Verantwortung ~* pass (od. push) the responsibility onto s.o.

zuschießen (unreg., trennb.) **I.** v/t. (hat zugeschossen) **1.** (Geld) contribute; *sie hat mir 1000 Euro für den Wagen zugeschossen* auch she gave me 1000 euros toward(s) the car; **2.** *j-m den Ball ~* kick (od. pass) the ball to s.o.; **II.** v/i. (ist): *~ auf* (+ Akk.) rush (od. shoot) toward(s)

Zuschlag m **1.** surcharge, extra charge;

zum Fahrpreis: supplementary fare; zur Steuer: surtax; auf Briefmarke: surcharge; auf Lohn: supplement; *dieser Zug kostet 4 Euro ~* you have to pay a 4 euro supplement to travel on this train; **2.** Auktion: award, acceptance of a bid; *er erhielt den ~ bei Auktion*: the lot went (od. was knocked down) to him; bei Ausschreibung: he was awarded (od. he won, he got) the contract; *ein Gebot von 3000 Dollar fand den ~* the winning bid was for $3000, the lot was knocked down for $3000

zuschlagen (unreg., trennb.) **I.** v/t. (hat zugeschlagen) **1.** (Tür etc.) slam (shut), bang (shut); *ein Buch ~* clap a book shut, shut a book with a clap; *j-m die Tür vor der Nase ~* slam the door in s.o.'s face; **2.** fig. (hinzufügen) add (+ Dat. to), slap on(to) umg.; **3.** *j-m etw. ~ Auktion*: knock s.th. down to s.o.; Ausschreibung: award s.th. to s.o.; **4.** *dem Mitspieler den Ball ~ beim Hockey etc.*: pass (od. hit) the ball to a teammate; **II.** v/i. **1.** (ist); Tür etc.: slam (shut), bang (shut); **2.** (hat) (schlagen) lash out, let fly umg.; (angreifen) strike (auch fig.); *schlag doch zu!* go on, hit me (bzw. it, him etc.); *hart ~* strike hard; *das Schicksal hat zugeschlagen* fate has struck again; **3.** (hat); umg. fig. beim Essen: tuck (Am. auch dig) in; beim Ausverkauf etc.: make a killing, grab what one can; mit s-n Gebühren, Preisen etc.: pile it on, raise s.th. skyhigh; *ich habe sofort zugeschlagen* I grabbed it etc. straightaway

zuschlag(s)frei Adj. not subject to a supplement (od. an extra charge); **Zuschlagkarte** f supplementary ticket; **zuschlag(s)pflichtig** Adj. subject to a supplement (od. an extra charge)

zuschließen vt/i. (unreg., trennb., hat -ge-) lock s.th. (up)

zuschmeißen v/t. (unreg., trennb., hat -ge-); umg.: *e-e Tür ~* slam a door (shut)

zuschnallen v/t. (trennb., hat -ge-) buckle (up)

zuschnappen v/i. (trennb.) **1.** (ist zugeschnappt); Schloss etc.: snap shut; **2.** (hat); Hund: snap (at s.o. od. s.th)

zuschneiden v/t. (unreg., trennb., hat -ge-) cut up; (Anzug) cut (to size), weitS. auch style; (Bretter etc.) cut to size; → *zugeschnitten*; **Zuschneider** m, **Zuschneiderin** f cutter

zuschneien v/t. (trennb., hat -ge-) snow up

Zuschnitt m **1.** nur Sg.; Handlung: cutting; von Holz: cutting to size; **2.** Ergebnis: cut; weitS. style; **3.** fig. (Art) sort; (Ausmaß) scale; (Format) calib|re (Am. -er); *ein Mann s-s ~s* a man of his calib|re (Am. -er) (od. standing)

zuschnüren v/t. (trennb., hat -ge-) **1.** (Paket etc.) tie up; (Korsett etc.) lace up; **2.** fig.: *es schnürte ihm die Kehle zu* he was choked; *m-e Kehle war vor Angst wie zugeschnürt* I was choked with fear

zuschrauben v/t. (trennb., hat -ge-) screw shut; (Glas etc.) auch put the lid (back) on

zuschreiben v/t. (unreg., trennb., hat -ge-) **1.** *j-m etw. ~* ascribe (od. attribute) s.th. to s.o.; (Misserfolg, Vergehen etc.) impute s.th. to s.o.; (Positives) credit s.o. with s.th.; *j-m/etw. zuzuschreiben sein* be attributable to s.o./s.th.; *j-m die Schuld* ~ put (*od.* place) the blame on s.o. (*an* + *Dat.* for); *das hast du dir selbst zuzuschreiben* you've only yourself to blame; *das ist dem Umstand zuzuschreiben, dass ...* the reason for that is that ..., that can be put down to the fact that ...; **2.** *Jur., Fin.* (*überschreiben*) transfer, sign over (+ *Dat.* to)

zuschreiten *v/i.* (*unreg., trennb.,* ist *-ge-*); *geh.:* ~ *auf* (+ *Akk.*) walk (*od.* stride) up to

Zuschrift *f* letter; (*Antwort*) *auch* reply (*auch auf e-e Anzeige*); *amtliche:* *auch* communication; *zahlreiche* ~ *en bekommen auch* receive (*od.* get) a large postbag (*Am.* mailbag); *bes. hinsichtlich e-r Anzeige etc.:* receive (*od.* get) a big response

zuschulden, zu Schulden *Adv.:* *sich* (*Dat.*) *etwas* ~ *kommen lassen* do (something) wrong, be guilty of s.th.; *ich habe mir nichts* ~ *kommen lassen* I haven't done anything wrong

Zuschuss *m* allowance; (*Beitrag*) contribution (*zu* towards); *staatlicher:* subsidy, grant; ~*betrieb* *m* subsidized firm (*bes. Am.* business); ~*geschäft* *n* loss-making operation

zuschustern *v/t.* (*trennb.,* hat *-ge-*); *umg.* **1.** → *zuschanzen;* **2.** *Geld* ~ help out with the money

zuschütten *v/t.* (*trennb.,* hat *-ge-*) **1.** (*Graben etc.*) fill up (*od.* in); (*Grab*) fill in, close; **2.** *umg.* (*hinzuschütten*) add

zusehen *v/i.* (*unreg., trennb.,* hat *-ge-*) **1.** watch; *j-m bei der Arbeit etc.* ~ watch s.o. working (*od.* at work *etc.*); ~*, wie j-d etw. macht* watch s.o. do s.th., watch how s.o. does s.th.; *ich kann nicht mehr* ~ I can't look (*auch weitS.*) bear it) any more; **2.** (*etw. dulden*) sit back (*od.* stand by) and watch; *wie kannst du nur so ruhig* ~*, wie sie sich ruiniert?* how can you look on calmly as she heads for ruin?; *wir mussten* ~*, wie sie den Wagen auseinander nahmen* we had to just stand and watch them taking the car apart; **3.** *fig.* ~*, dass* (*dafür sorgen*) see (to it) that, make sure that; *sieh zu, dass du endlich fertig wirst!* hurry up and finish getting ready!; *und ich kann wieder* ~*, wo ich bleibe* and I'm left to cope on my own again!

Zusehen *n; -s, kein Pl.:* *allein vom* ~ *wird mir schlecht* I feel sick just watching (*od.* just to look); **zusehends** *Adv.* visibly, noticeably; (*schnell*) rapidly, day by day; *übertreibend:* by the minute; **Zuseher** *m*, **Zuseherin** *f* *österr.* → *Zuschauer*

zu sein → *zu³* I 1

zusenden *v/t.* (*mst unreg., trennb.,* hat *-ge-*) → *zuschicken;* **Zusendung** *f* **1.** *nur Sg.* sending; *um* ~ (+ *Gen.*) *bitten* ask for s.th. to be sent; **2.** → *Zuschrift;* (*Paket*). parcel; (*Warensendung*) consignment

zusetzen (*trennb.,* hat *-ge-*) **I.** *v/t.* **1.** (*hinzufügen*) add (+ *Dat.* to); **2.** (*Geld*) (*verlieren*) lose; (*aufwenden*) lay out, shell out *umg.;* *nichts mehr zuzusetzen haben umg.* have used up all one's reserves, have run out of steam; **II.** *v/i.:* *j-m* ~ **1.** (*bedrängen*) press s.o. (hard), urge s.o. (*zu* + *Inf.* to + *Inf.*); *mit Fragen, Bitten:* pester s.o. (with), badger s.o., keep on at s.o.; *bei Verhör:* grill s.o.; *dem Gegner, Feind:* keep up the pressure on s.o.; **2.** *weitS. Mücken etc.:* plague; *Hitze,*

Strapazen, Leid: take it out of s.o., get to s.o. *umg.;* (*schwer treffen*) hit s.o. hard, be a heavy blow to s.o.

zusichern *v/t.* (*trennb.,* hat *-ge-*): *j-m etw.* ~ assure s.o. of s.th., guarantee s.o. s.th.; (*versprechen*) promise s.o. s.th.; **Zusicherung** *f* assurance; (*Versprechen*) promise, pledge

Zuspätkommende *m, f; -n, -n* latecomer

zusperren (*trennb.,* hat *-ge-*) *südd., österr.* **I.** *v/t.* shut, lock; **II.** *v/i.* lock up

Zuspiel *n; nur Sg.; Sport* pass(es *Pl.*); **zuspielen** (*trennb.,* hat *-ge-*) **I.** *v/t. j-m etw.* ~ (*Informationen etc.*) pass s.th. on to s.o.; *der Presse etw.* ~ leak s.th. to the press; **II.** *vt/i. Sport: j-m* (*den Ball*) ~ pass (the ball) to s.o.; *sich gegenseitig die Bälle* ~ *fig.* feed each other lines; (*zum gleichen Zweck*) work a (nice) double act

zuspitzen (*trennb.,* hat *-ge-*) **I.** *v/t.* **1.** (*Stock*) sharpen; **2.** *fig.* (*Lage*) worsen, intensify; → *zugespitzt;* **II.** *v/refl.* **1.** taper to a point; **2.** *fig. Krise, Lage:* worsen, escalate, deteriorate; **Zuspitzung** *f fig.* worsening, intensification

zusprechen (*unreg., trennb.,* hat *-ge-*) **I.** *v/t.* **1.** *mit Worten: j-m Mut* ~ encourage s.o.; *j-m Trost* ~ console s.o., comfort s.o.; **2.** (+ *Dat.*); (*zuerkennen*) (*Eigenschaft*) ascribe *s.th.* to *s.o. od. s.th.;* (*Erbe, Preis, Recht etc.*) award *s.o. s.th.; das Kind* / *das Sorgerecht wurde der Mutter zugesprochen* the mother was granted custody of the child; **II.** *v/i.* **1.** *j-m gut* ~ try and reason with s.o.; **2.** *geh. dem Essen, Getränken:* have (*od.* eat, drink) one's fill of, partake freely of *lit.; e-r Speise tüchtig* ~ tuck (*Am. auch* dig) into *umg.*

zuspringen *v/i.* (*unreg., trennb.,* ist *-ge-*) **1.** *Schloss:* spring (*od.* snap) shut; **2.** ~ *auf* (+ *Akk.*) jump toward(s); (*anspringen*) jump at; *Ball:* bounce toward(s) s.o.; *die Kinder kamen fröhlich auf sie zugesprungen* the children came cheerfully bounding up to her

Zuspruch *m geh.* **1.** words *Pl.* of encouragement (*od.* consolation *etc.*), soothing (*od.* friendly *etc.*) words *Pl.;* **2.** (*Anklang*) reception; *großen* ~ *finden* go down (very) well; *Lokal, Person:* be very popular, be much sought after

Zustand *m* **1.** state, condition; *in flüssigem/gasförmigem* ~ *Chem.* in liquid/gaseous form, in the form of a liquid/gas; *in gutem/schlechtem* ~ in good/bad condition; *Auto, Geräte, Haus etc.: auch* in good/bad repair; *in betrunkenem* ~ (while) under the influence of alcohol; *e-e Frau in i-m* ~ *umg.* a woman in her condition; *in was für e-m* ~ *befindet er sich?* what's his condition like?, what sort of shape is he in? *umg.;* **2.** (*Lage*) situation; *bes. negativ:* state of affairs; (*Verhältnisse*) conditions *Pl.; es herrschen chaotische Zustände* the situation is completely chaotic, it's absolute chaos; *das ist doch kein* ~*! umg.* it simply won't do!; *hier herrschen Zustände! umg.* a fine state of affairs this is!; *das sind ja Zustände wie im alten Rom! umg.* (*altmodisch*) that's straight out of the ark; (*untragbar*) these are impossible goings-on; **3.; 4.** *umg.: Zustände kriegen* have a fit; *da kann man ja Zustände kriegen!* it's enough

to drive you up the wall

zustande, zu Stande *Adv.* **1.** ~ *bringen* bring about; (*schaffen*) manage, succeed in doing *s.th.,* engineer *umg.; Unmögliches* ~ *bringen* achieve the impossible; **2.** ~ *kommen* come about; (*gelingen*) be achieved; *Vereinbarung etc.:* be reached; *Plan:* materialize; *Gesetz:* be passed; (*stattfinden*) take place, come off; *e-e Einigung kam nicht* ~ no agreement was reached; **Zustandekommen** *n: das* ~ *des Abkommens ist gefährdet* there is a danger that no agreement will be reached; *wir verdanken ihr das* ~ *des Treffens* we owe it to her that the meeting took place

zuständig *Adj.* **1.** *Behörde etc.:* relevant, appropriate; (*befugt*) competent; (*verantwortlich*) responsible; ~*es Gericht* court of competent jurisdiction; ~*e Stelle* appropriate authority (*od.* department); *dafür bin ich nicht* ~ that's not my responsibility (*od.* job); *keiner will* ~ *sein* nobody wants to take responsibility, everyone just passes the buck *umg.;* **2.** *österr. Amtsspr.: nach Wien etc.* ~ *sein* have the right of domicile in Vienna *etc.*

Zuständigkeit *f* competence; (*Verantwortlichkeit*) responsibility; (*Befugnisse*) powers *Pl.; Jur. sachliche:* jurisdiction (*für* over); **Zuständigkeitsbereich** *m* (area of) responsibility; *Jur.* jurisdiction; *es fällt nicht in m-n* ~ that is not my responsibility; *Jur.* that does not come under my jurisdiction

Zustands|änderung *f* **1.** *e-s Kranken etc.:* change in one's (*bzw. s.o.'s*) condition; **2.** *Phys.* change of state; ~*größe* *f Phys.* variable of state; ~*passiv* *n Ling.* passive of condition; ~*verb* *n Ling.* stative verb

zustatten *Adv.: j-m* (*sehr*) ~ *kommen* (*nützen*) stand s.o. in (very) good stead; (*gelegen kommen*) come in (very) handy

zustechen *v/i.* (*unreg., trennb.,* hat *-ge-*) attack, plunge the knife *etc.* in

zustecken *v/t.* (*trennb.,* hat *-ge-*): *j-m etw.* ~ slip s.o. s.th.

zustehen *v/i.* (*unreg., trennb.,* hat / *südd., österr., schw.* ist *-ge-*): *es steht ihm* (*rechtlich*) *zu* das Geld, Haus *etc.:* he is (legally) entitled to it; *ich will ja nicht mehr, als mir zusteht* I want no more than I'm entitled to; *es steht ihm nicht zu, zu ...* (+ *Inf.*) he has no right to ... (+ *Inf.*), it's not for him to ... (+ *Inf.*)

zusteigen *v/i.* (*unreg., trennb.,* ist *-ge-*) get on, board the train (*od.* bus); *noch jemand zugestiegen? Eisenb.* tickets, please!; *wo sind Sie zugestiegen?* where did you get on?, which station (*Bus, U-Bahn:* stop) did you get on at?

Zustellbezirk *m Post.* postcode sector, *Am.* ZIP code (area)

zustellen *v/t.* (*trennb.,* hat *-ge-*) **1.** (*Eingang etc.*) block; **2.** *Post.* (*Sendung*) deliver; *Jur.* (*Bescheid*) serve (*j-m etw.* s.th. on s.o.); **Zusteller** *m; -s, -; Amtsspr.* postman, *Am. auch* mailman, letter carrier; **Zustellerin** *f; -, -nen; Amtsspr.* postwoman, *Am.* letter carrier; **Zustellgebühr** *f Post.* delivery charge; **Zustellung** *f Post.* delivery; *Jur.* service; **Zustellungsurkunde** *f Jur., Post.* proof of service (of writ); **Zustellvermerk** *m Post.* note of reason for nondelivery of a postal item

zusteuern (*trennb.*) **I.** *v/i.* (ist *zuge-*

Z

steuert): ~ *auf* (+ *Akk.*) **1.** head for, make for; *unkontrolliert:* veer toward(s); *(zielstrebig zugehen auf)* make a beeline for; **2.** *fig.* be aiming at; *im Gespräch:* be driving at; (*e-e Krise etc.*) be heading for, be veering toward(s); **II.** *v/t.* (*hat*); *umg.* contribute (*zu* to)

zustimmen *v/i.* (*trennb., hat -ge-*) agree (+ *Dat.* to *s.th. od.* with *s.o.*); (*einwilligen*) *auch* consent (to *s.th.*); (*billigen*) approve (of *s.th.*); ~**d nicken** nod in approval, nod assent; *dem kann ich nur* ~ I quite agree, I agree with that completely; **Zustimmung** *f* agreement; (*Einwilligung*) *auch* assent, consent; (*Billigung*) approval; *allgemeine* ~ *finden* meet with general assent (*od.* approval); *findet das d-e* ~*?* do you agree with it?, are you in agreement with that?; *Einwilligung:* will you agree to that?

zustopfen *v/t.* (*trennb., hat -ge-*) **1.** (*Loch, Ohren etc.*) plug; **2.** (*Loch im Strumpf etc.*) mend, darn

zustöpseln *v/t.* (*trennb., hat -ge-*) stopper; (*Flasche*) put the stopper (*od.* cork) in; (*Ohren*) plug

zustoßen (*unreg., trennb.*) **I.** *v/t.* (*hat zugestoßen*) push *s.th.* shut; *laut:* slam *s.th.* (shut); **II.** *v/i.* **1.** (*hat*) attack, strike; *mit e-m Messer:* stab; *auch mit e-m Schwert:* thrust, lunge; **2.** (*ist*): *j-m* ~ (*widerfahren*) happen to s.o.; *ihm ist etwas zugestoßen* Unfall: he's had an accident; *wenn mir etwas* ~ *sollte* euph. if anything should happen to me

zustreben *v/i.* (*trennb., ist -ge-*) (+ *Dat.*) **1.** *dem Ausgang etc.:* head for, make for; **2.** *fig. e-m Ziel etc.:* aim at, have set one's sights on

Zustrom *m* **1.** *von Besuchern, Käufern:* stream; (*Andrang*) rush; *von Emigranten, Touristen, Waren, Kapital:* influx; **2.** *von Luft etc.:* influx, inflow; **zuströmen** *v/i.* (*trennb., ist -ge-*) (+ *Dat.*) **1.** *dem Meer etc.:* flow toward(s); **2.** *Personen, e-m Ort:* stream (*od.* throng) toward(s)

zustürmen *v/i.* (*trennb., ist -ge-*): ~ *auf* (+ *Akk.*) storm (toward[s]), make a rush for

zustürzen *v/i.* (*trennb., ist -ge-*): ~ *auf* (+ *Akk.*) rush toward(s), descend (up)on

zutage, zu Tage *Adv.* **1.** ~ *bringen od. fördern* bring to the surface (*auch vom Meeresboden*); *aus dem Boden: auch* unearth; *aus e-r Schublade etc.:* dig out; *fig.* (*Tatsachen etc.*) bring to light, uncover; (*Geheimnis*) *auch* unearth; **2.** *fig.:* ~ *treten* come to light (*od.* to the surface), be revealed; *Geheimnis: auch* be unearthed; *Geol.* outcrop; **3.** *klar od. offen* ~ *liegen* be evident, be manifest, be there for all to see

Zutat *f* **1.** *mst Pl.; Gastr.* ingredient; **2.** *fig.* accessory; (*Ergänzung*) addition

zuteil *Adv. geh.: j-m* ~ *werden* be given (*od.* granted) to s.o., be bestowed on s.o. *lit.; ihm wurde das Glück* ~*, zu ...* he had the good fortune to ...; *j-m etw.* ~ *werden lassen* grant s.o. s.th.

zuteilen *v/t.* (*trennb., hat -ge-*); (*Aufgabe, Arbeit, Rolle*) give (+ *Dat.* to), *förm.* assign (to), allot (to); (*Geld, Wohnung*) allocate (to), appropriate (to); (*Darlehen*) pay out; *der Bevölkerung Nahrungsmittel* ~ ration food out among the population; *er ist e-r anderen Abteilung zugeteilt worden* he's

been moved to a different department; **Zuteilung** *f* assignment; allotment; allocation; paying out; → *zuteilen;* (*Kontingent*) quota; **zuteilungsreif** *Adj. Bausparvertrag:* mature; ~ *sein* have matured, be payable

zutiefst *Adv.* most, deeply; ~ *beleidigt* deeply offended; *lit. und iro.* mortally wounded, cut to the quick; *etw.* ~ *bedauern* deeply regret s.th.; *gegenüber j-m:* express one's deep regret at (*od.* over) s.th.

zutragen (*unreg., trennb., hat -ge-*) **I.** *v/t.: j-m etw.* ~ carry (*od.* bring) s.th. to s.o., bring s.o. s.th.; (*Nachricht etc.*) *auch* pass s.th. on to s.o.; **II.** *v/refl.* *geh.* happen, take place, occur, transpire; **Zuträger** *m,* **Zuträgerin** *f pej.* informant, informer

zuträglich *Adj. geh.* good (+ *Dat.* for), beneficial (to); (*förderlich*) conducive (to); (*gesundheitsfördernd*) healthy, good for one's health; *Klima: auch* salubrious; *j-m nicht* ~ *sein* disagree with s.o.; **Zuträglichkeit** *f; nur Sg.* beneficial nature (+ *Gen.* of)

zutrauen *v/t.* (*unreg., trennb., hat -ge-*): *j-m etw.* ~ believe s.o. (to be) capable of (doing) s.th., credit s.o. with s.th.; *sich* (*Dat.*) *zu viel* ~ overrate o.s.; (*zu viel übernehmen*) take too much on; *ich traue es mir* (*nicht*) *zu* I (don't) think I can do it; *er traut sich überhaupt nichts zu* he has no confidence in himself; *ich traue ihm nicht viel zu* I don't think he's up to much; *zuzutrauen wäre es ihm* I wouldn't put it past him; *das hätte ich ihm nicht zugetraut* I didn't think he was the sort; *anerkennend:* I never knew he had it in him; *ich hätte ihr mehr Fantasie/Umsicht zugetraut* I thought she'd have shown more imagination / taken more care

Zutrauen *n; -s, kein Pl.* confidence (*zu* in); ~ *zu j-m fassen* begin to have confidence in s.o.; *Tier:* start to trust s.o.; **zutraulich** *Adj.* confiding, trusting; *weitS.* friendly (*auch Tier*); **Zutraulichkeit** *f* **1.** *nur Sg.* confiding nature; *e-s Tiers:* friendliness; **2.** (*Äußerung*) confidence

zutreffen *v/i.* (*unreg., trennb., hat -ge-*) be true (*bei, auf* + *Akk., für* of), be right, be correct, be the case; ~ *auf* (+ *Akk.*) *od. für auch* hold true for; (*gelten für*) apply to; *dasselbe trifft auch für dich zu* the same applies to (*od.* goes for) you; *die Beschreibung trifft genau auf ihn zu* the description fits him perfectly; **zutreffend** **I.** *Part. Präs.* → *zutreffen;* **II.** *Adj.* correct; (*passend*) appropriate, fitting; *Bemerkung: auch* apt; *Zutreffendes unterstreichen/ankreuzen Amtsspr.* underline / (mark with a) cross as (*od.* where) appropriate

zutreiben (*unreg., trennb.*) **I.** *v/i.* (*ist zugetrieben*): ~ *auf* (+ *Akk.*) *Schiff etc.:* drift toward(s); *auf e-e Krise etc.* ~ *fig.* be drifting toward(s) a crisis *etc.;* **II.** *v/t.* (*hat*): *das Wild etc.* ~ *auf* (+ *Akk.*) drive the game *etc.* toward(s)

zutreten *v/i.* (*unreg., trennb.*) **1.** (*hat zugetreten*) kick; **2.** (*ist*): ~ *auf* (+ *Akk.*) step toward(s)

zutrinken *v/i.* (*unreg., trennb., hat -ge-*); (*j-m*) drink to, raise one's glass to

Zutritt *m; nur Sg.* access; (*Einlass*) admission; ~ *verboten!* no entry; ~ *erhalten od. sich* (*Dat.*) ~ *verschaffen* gain admission (*od.* admittance) (*zu* to); *sich* (*Dat.*) *gewaltsam* ~ *verschaffen*

force one's way in; *zu e-m Haus: auch* break down the door of a house

zutun *v/t.* (*unreg., trennb., hat -ge-*); *umg.* **1.** (*schließen*) close, shut; → *Auge* 2, *zugetan;* **2.** (*hinzufügen*) add

Zutun *n: ohne mein* ~ without any help (*od.* encouragement) from me; (*ohne m-e Schuld*) through no fault of my own (*od.* mine); *es geschah ohne mein* ~ I had nothing to do with it

zuungunsten, zu Ungunsten *Präp.* (+ *Gen. od. von*) to the disadvantage of; *Entscheidung: auch* against

zuunterst *Adv.* right at the bottom

zuverdienen *v/t.* (*trennb., hat*) *umg.* make *s.th.* on the side; *ein bisschen* (*was*) ~ *auch* make a bit of extra money

zuverlässig **I.** *Adj.* reliable (*auch Sache, Tech.*), dependable; (*treu*) loyal; (*vertrauenswürdig*) trustworthy; (*sicher*) safe (*auch Wirts., Tech.*); *aus* ~*er Quelle* from a reliable source; *er ist absolut* ~ *auch* you can rely (*od.* depend) on him totally; **II.** *Adv.: ~ arbeiten* be (a) reliable (worker); ~ *funktionieren* function reliably; ~ *wissen* have *s.th.* on good authority; **Zuverlässigkeit** *f; nur Sg.* reliability; dependability; loyalty; trustworthiness; safety; → *zuverlässig*

Zuversicht *f; -, kein Pl.* confidence; (*Optimismus*) optimism; *voller od. der festen* ~ *sein, dass ...* be (quite) confident that ..., have every confidence that ...; *voller* ~ *in die Zukunft blicken* look confidently ahead to the future, look to the future with optimism, have faith in the future; **zuversichtlich** **I.** *Adj.* confident, optimistic; **II.** *Adv.* confidently, optimistically; ~ *hoffen, dass ...* be quite confident that ...; **Zuversichtlichkeit** *f; nur Sg.* confidence; (*Optimismus*) optimism; *Einstellung:* optimistic outlook

zu viel → *zu²* 1

Zuviel *n; -s, kein Pl.: ein* ~ *an* (+ *Dat.*) too much (of), an excess of

zuvor *Adv.* before, previously; (*vorher noch, zunächst*) first, beforehand; *kurz* ~ shortly before; *am Tag* ~ the day before, the previous day

zuvorderst *Adv.* right at the front

zuvorkommen *v/i.* (*unreg., trennb., ist -ge-*) **1.** *e-r Sache, j-m:* preempt; *e-r Frage etc.: auch* anticipate; (*verhindern*) forestall; *e-m Angriff:* head off, ward off; **2.** *weitS. j-m:* beat *s.o.* to it, get in first *umg.; gerade noch:* pip *s.o.* at the post *umg.;* **zuvorkommend** **I.** *Part. Präs.* → *zuvorkommen;* **II.** *Adj.* (very) obliging; (*entgegenkommend*) accommodating; (*hilfsbereit*) helpful; (*höflich*) courteous; **Zuvorkommenheit** *f; nur Sg.* obligingness; (*Höflichkeit*) courtesy

Zuwachs *m; -es, fachspr. Zuwächse* **1.** increase (*an* + *Dat.* in; *von* of); *bes. Wirts.* growth (in); **2.** *nur Sg.; hum.: die Familie hat* ~ *bekommen* there's been an addition to the family; **zuwachsen** *v/i.* (*unreg., trennb., ist -ge-*) **1.** become overgrown; *das Tor war völlig* (*mit od. von Efeu*) *zugewachsen* the gate was completely overgrown (with ivy); **2.** *Med.* heal up, close; **3.** *fig. j-m: Geld:* accrue to; *Aufgabe, Verantwortung:* fall to (*od.* on), *förm.* devolve upon; **Zuwachsrate** *f* growth rate

Zuwanderer *m* immigrant; *im gleichen Land:* incomer; **zuwandern** *v/i.* (*trennb., ist -ge-*) immigrate; *auch im*

gleichen Land: settle in (*od.* move to) the area *etc.*; **Zuwanderung** *f* immigration

Zuwanderungsgesetz *m Pol. Jur. in der BRD*: immigration law

zuwarten *v/i.* (*trennb., hat -ge-*) wait (patiently)

zuwege, zu Wege *Adv.* **1.** ~ **bringen** (*verursachen*) bring about; (*schaffen*) manage (to do) *s.th.*; (*erreichen*) achieve, accomplish; *es* ~ *bringen zu* (+ *Inf.*) *auch* succeed in (+ *Ger.*); → *auch* **zustande** 1; **2.** ~ **kommen mit** cope with, manage; **3.** *umg.*: *gut* ~ *sein* be in good health (*od.* shape); *noch gut* ~ *sein* be doing well for one's age

zuwehen (*trennb.*) **I.** *v/t.* (*hat zugeweht*); *mit Schnee, Sand*: block; **II.** *v/i.* (*ist*): *j-m* ~ blow toward(s) *s.o.*; *Duft etc.*: waft toward(s) (*od.* over to) *s.o.*

zuweilen *Adv. geh.* at times, occasionally, now and then

zuweisen *v/t.* (*unreg., trennb., hat -ge-*) **1.** assign (+ *Dat.* to); (*Wohnung etc.*) allocate; (*Tisch in Restaurant*) show to, give; **2.** *fig.* (*geben*) assign; *j-m die Schuld an etw.* ~ put the blame for *s.th.* on *s.o.*; → *auch* **zuteilen**; **Zuweisung** *f* assignment, allocation; → *zuweisen*

zuwenden (*auch unreg., trennb., hat -ge-*) **I.** *v/t.* **1.** turn *s.th.* toward(s) *s.o. od. s.th.*; *j-m das Gesicht* ~ turn ([a]round) to face (*od.* look at) *s.o.*; *j-m den Rücken* ~ turn one's back to(ward[s]) (*abweisend*: on) *s.o.*; *die der Straße zugewandten Fenster* the windows looking (*od.* facing) onto the street; **2.** *fig.*: *e-r Sache s-e Aufmerksamkeit* ~ turn (*od.* devote) one's attention to *s.th.*; **3.** *j-m Geld etc.* ~ give *s.o.* money *etc.*; **II.** *v/refl.* (+ *Dat.*) **1.** turn to(ward[s]), turn ([a]round) to face; **2.** (*sich richten auf*) turn to; (*sich widmen*) devote o.s. to; *das Gespräch hatte sich wieder anderen Themen zugewandt* the conversation had turned back to other topics; **Zuwendung** *f* **1.** (*Geld*) allocation (of funds); (*Summe*) sum; (*Schenkung*) donation; (*Vermächtnis*) bequest; **2.** *nur Sg.*: (*Aufmerksamkeit*) attention; (*Liebe*) (love and) affection

zu wenig → *zu*² 1

zuwerfen *v/t.* (*trennb., hat -ge-*) **1.** *j-m etw.* ~ throw *s.o. s.th.*, throw *s.th.* (over) to *s.o.*; **2.** *fig.*: *j-m e-n Blick* ~ glance at *s.o.*, cast (*od.* dart) a glance at *s.o.*; *j-m e-n bösen/verächtlichen Blick* ~ give *s.o.* a dirty look / a look of contempt; *j-m e-e Kusshand* ~ blow *s.o.* a kiss; **3.** *e-e Tür* ~ slam (*od.* bang) a door (shut); **4.** (*Grube etc.*) fill up

zuwider I. *Adv.*: *j-m* ~ *sein* be repellent (*od.* repugnant) to *s.o.*, revolt *s.o.*, turn *s.o.* off *umg.*; *es ist mir* ~ *auch* I detest (*od.* hate, loathe, can't stand) it; *der Gedanke, das zu tun, ist mir* ~ I find the thought of (doing) it repugnant; *dieser Typ ist mir zutiefst* ~ I absolutely loathe and detest that guy; *milder*: that guy turns me off completely *umg.*; **II.** *Präp.* (+ *Dat.*) *nachgestellt*; *geh.* against, contrary to; *den Vorschriften* ~ *auch* in defiance of the regulations

zuwiderhandeln *v/i.* (*trennb., hat -ge-*); *bes. Amtsspr. e-m Befehl etc.*: act against (*od.* contrary to); *e-m Gesetz*: violate, contravene; **Zuwiderhandlung** *f Amtsspr.* violation, offen|ce (*Am.* -se) (*gegen* against); (*Nichtein-*

haltung) non-compliance (with)

zuwiderlaufen *v/i.* (*unreg., trennb., ist -ge-*); *geh. j-s Interessen etc.*: go against, run counter to

zuwinken *v/i.* (*trennb., hat -ge-*): *j-m* ~ wave to (*od.* at) *s.o.*; (*herwinken*) beckon to *s.o.* (to come)

zuzahlen *v/t.* (*trennb., hat -ge-*) pay *s.th.* extra; *50 Euro* ~ *auch* pay an extra 50 euros

zuzählen *v/t.* (*trennb., hat -ge-*) **1.** add; (*mit einbeziehen*) count; **2.** ~ *zu* (*zuordnen*) number (*od.* include) among

Zuzahlung *f* additional payment, payment of an additional sum; → *Zuschlag* 1

zuzeiten *Adv.* (*manchmal*) at times, sometimes

zuziehen (*unreg., trennb.*) **I.** *v/t.* (*hat zugezogen*) **1.** (*Knoten*) pull (tight); (*Schlinge, Schleife*) tighten; (*Vorhänge*) draw, close; (*Tür etc.*) close, pull *s.th.* to; (*Reißverschluss*) do up; **2.** *fig.* (*Arzt, Sachverständigen*) call in, consult; **3.** *sich* (*Dat.*) *etw.* ~ (*Krankheit*) get, *förm.* contract; *ansteckende*: *auch* catch, pick up; (*Verletzung*) suffer, *förm.* sustain; *sich* (*Dat.*) *j-s Zorn etc.* ~ incur *s.o.'s* anger *etc.*; **II.** *v/refl.* (*hat*) **1.** *Schlinge etc.*: tighten; **2.** *Himmel*: cloud over, become overcast; **III.** *v/i.* (*ist*): *als Bewohner*: move to a (*od.* the) town *etc.*, move there (*od.* here) (*aus* from); **Zuziehung** *f; nur Sg. e-s Arztes etc.*: calling-in, consultation

Zuzug *m* **1.** move; **2.** (*Zuwanderung*) influx

Zuzüger *m; -s, -,* ~**in** *f; -, -nen; schw.* **1.** *Mitglied etc.*: newcomer; **2.** *in Dorf etc.*: incomer

Zuzügler *m; -s, -,* ~**in** *f; -, -nen in Dorf etc.*: incomer, newcomer

zuzüglich *Präp.* (+ *Gen.*); *Wirts.* plus, not including, exclusive of; ~ *Mehrwertsteuer* plus VAT (*Am. etwa* sales tax)

zuzwinkern *v/i.* (*trennb., hat -ge-*): *j-m* ~ wink at *s.o.*, give *s.o.* a wink

Zvieri *n, m; -s, -; schw.* afternoon snack

ZVS *f; -, kein Pl.; Abk.* (**Zentralstelle zur Vergabe von Studienplätzen**) *in GB etwa* UCAS (Universities and Colleges Admissions Service)

zwacken *v/t. umg.* pinch; *mst unpers.*: *es zwackt mich im Rücken* I can feel a twinge in my back; *es* (*zwickt und*) *zwackt mich überall* I'm aching all over

zwang *Imperf.* → *zwingen*

Zwang *m; -(e)s, Zwänge* **1.** compulsion; (*Druck*) pressure (*auch Med.*); *gesellschaftliche/politische Zwänge* social/ political constraints; *der* ~ *der Verhältnisse* the force of circumstances; *der* ~ *der Konvention* the straitjacket of convention; *es besteht kein* ~ *zum Kauf* there is no obligation to buy; *unter* ~ *handeln* act under duress; **2.** *moralisch*: constraint, inhibition; (*Verpflichtung*) (moral) obligation; *allen* ~ *ablegen* abandon all restraint; *s-n Gefühlen* ~ *antun* keep one's feelings strictly under control, rein in one's feelings; *s-n Gefühlen keinen* ~ *antun* not hide one's feelings, give free rein to one's feelings; *sich* (*Dat.*) ~ *auferlegen* (*sich beherrschen*) restrain o.s. (from doing *s.th.*); (*zwingen zu*) force o.s. (to do *s.th.*); *tun Sie sich nur keinen* ~ *an!* don't stand on ceremony, make yourself at home, no need to be shy(, now) *hum.*; *tu dir nur keinen* ~ *an! iro.* don't mind me; **3.** *Psych.* com-

pulsion; (*Besessenheit*) obsession

zwängen I. *v/t.* force, (*quetschen*) squeeze (*in* + *Akk.* into); **II.** *v/refl.*: *sich* ~ *in* (+ *Akk.*) squeeze (o.s.) into;

zwanghaft *Adj. Psych.* compulsive, obsessive; **zwanglos 1.** *Adj.* informal, casual; (*ungehemmt*) unconstrained, uninhibited; (*entspannt*) relaxed; ~*es Treffen* informal get-together; *in* ~*er Folge* in no particular (*od.* set) order; *erscheinen etc.*: at irregular intervals; **2.** *Adv.* informally, casually; (*ungehemmt*) unconstrainedly, uninhibitedly; *bei uns geht es eher* ~ *zu* we're very informal (here); *sie benahmen sich völlig* ~ they behaved with complete informality (*ungehemmt*: with a total lack of inhibition); **Zwanglosigkeit** *f; nur Sg.* casualness, informality

Zwangs|abgabe *f* compulsory charge (*od.* levy); ~**anleihe** *f* forced (*od.* compulsory) loan; ~**arbeit** *f* forced labo(u)r; *Strafe*: hard labo(u)r; ~**arbeiter** *m,* ~**arbeiterin** *f* forced labo(u)rer; ~**aufenthalt** *m* enforced stay; (*auch Haft*) detention; ~**bewirtschaftung** *f* state control (of the economy); *der Güter* rationing; ~**einweisung** *f* committal (*in* + *Akk.* to)

zwangsernähren *v/t.* (*untr., hat*) *nur Inf. und P.P.* force-feed; **Zwangsernährung** *f* force-feeding

Zwangs|geld *n Jur.*: *ein* ~ *erheben* impose a fine (*od.* penalty); ~**handlung** *f Psych.* compulsive act; ~**herrschaft** *f* despotism, tyranny; ~**jacke** *f* straitjacket (*auch fig.*); ~**lage** *f* predicament, plight

zwangsläufig *Adj.* inevitable; **Zwangsläufigkeit** *f* inevitability

Zwangs|maßnahme *f* coercive measure; *Pol.* sanction; ~**mitgliedschaft** *f* compulsory membership; ~**neurose** *f Psych.* obsessional neurosis; ~**pause** *f* period of enforced idleness, involuntary stoppage; *e-e* ~ *einlegen müssen* have to take a break, have to stop working *etc.* temporarily; ~**pensionierung** *f* compulsory retirement; ~**räumung** *f* eviction

zwangssterilisieren *v/t.* (*untr., hat*) *nur Inf. und P.P.* forcibly sterilize; **Zwangssterilisation** *f* forced sterilization

zwangsumsiedeln *v/t.* (*untr., hat zwangsumgesiedelt*) *nur Inf. und P.P.* displace (*nach* to), (forcibly) remove (to); **Zwangsumsiedler** *m,* **Zwangsumsiedlerin** *f* displaced person; **Zwangsumsiedlung** *f* displacement

Zwangs|umtausch *m* obligatory exchange; ~**vergleich** *m Jur.* compulsory settlement (in bankruptcy); ~**verkauf** *m* forced sale

zwangsverpflichten *v/t.* (*untr., hat*) *nur Inf. und P.P.* conscript; *fig.* pressgang; **Zwangsverpflichtung** *f* conscription

zwangsverschicken *v/t.* (*untr., hat*) *nur Inf. und P.P.* deport; **Zwangsverschickung** *f* deportation

zwangsversteigern *v/t.* (*untr., hat*) *nur Inf. und P.P.* put *s.th.* up for sale in execution; **Zwangsversteigerung** *f* sale in execution

Zwangsverwaltung *f* administration; *unter* ~ *stehen* (*Grundstück etc.*) be under administration

zwangsvollstrecken *v/i.* (*untr., hat*) *nur Inf. und P.P.* issue a writ of execution (*gegen* against); **Zwangsvollstreckung** *f* execution

Zwangs|vorführung *f Jur. vor Gericht*:

enforced appearance (*od.* attendance); **~vorstellung** *f Psych.* obsession

zwangsweise I. *Adj.* forcible; *Einquartierung*: compulsory; **~ Pensionierung** *etc.* forced retirement *etc.*; **II.** *Adv.* by force, forcibly

Zwangswirtschaft *f; nur Sg.* (economy under) state control; (*Planwirtschaft*) command economy, planned economy

zwanzig *Zahlw.* twenty; **Anfang/Mitte/ Ende ~ sein** be in one's early/mid/late twenties; **in den ~er Jahren** in the twenties; **die goldenen Zwanziger** the roaring twenties; **sie ist in den Zwanzigern** she's in her twenties

Zwanzig *f, -, -en, mst Sg. Nummer, Zahl*: (number) twenty

Zwanzigcentstück *n* twenty-cent piece

Zwanziger[1] *m; -s, -*, **~in** *f; -, -nen* man (*bzw.* woman) in his (*bzw.* her) twenties, twentysomething *umg.*

Zwanziger[2] *m; -s, -; umg. Münze*: twenty-cent *etc.* piece; *Schein*: twenty-euro *etc.* note (*Am.* bill)

Zwanzigerjahre *Pl.*: **in den ~n** in the twenties

Zwanzig|euroschein *m* twenty-euro note; **~frankenschein** *m* twenty-franc note

zwanzigjährig *Adj. attr. Person*: twenty-year-old …; *Zeitraum*: twenty-year (~-long) …; **Zwanzigjährige** *m, f; -n, -n* twenty-year-old

Zwanzig|markschein *m hist.* twenty-mark note; **~rappenstück** *n* twenty-rappen piece

zwanzigst *Adv.*: **wir waren zu ~** there were twenty of us; → *acht*[2]

zwanzigst... *Zahlw.* twentieth; → *auch acht...*

Zwanzigste *m, f; -n, -n* (the) twentieth; → *auch Achte*

zwanzigstel *Adj.*: **ein ~ Liter** a twentieth of a liter

Zwanzigstel *n; -s, -* twentieth

zwar *Adv.* **1.** ~ …, **aber** … (it's true) …, but …; certainly …, but …; **er hat ~ angerufen, aber** … he 'did ring up, but …; he rang up all right, but …; **sie ist ~ hübsch, aber** … *auch* she may be pretty, but …; **2. und ~** namely, *nachgestellt*: in fact; *verstärkend, vorangestellt*: in fact; **er will das Geld haben, und ~ sofort** he wants the money, and he wants it right now; **wir haben uns in Rom getroffen, und ~ letztes Jahr** we met in Rome - last year (it was); **er ist Sänger, und ~ Bariton** he's a singer - a baritone; he's a singer, that's to say a baritone; **sie hat ihr eigenes Haus, und ~ ein großes** she has her own house, and it's a big one

Zweck *m; -(e)s, -e* purpose; (*Ziel*) object, aim; (*Sinn*) point, use; **s-n ~ erfüllen** serve its purpose; *Gerät etc.*: *auch* do its job *umg.*; **s-n ~ verfehlen** not achieve its purpose, fail to achieve its purpose; **e-n ~ verfolgen** pursue an object; *Räume für gewerbliche ~e* rooms for commercial use; *Geld für wohltätige ~e spenden* donate money to charity; **für e-n guten ~ spenden** give to a good cause; **zum ~e** (+ *Gen. od. zu* + *Inf.*) with a view to *s.th. od.* (+ *Ger.*), with the object of (+ *Ger.*); **zu diesem ~** to this end; **zu welchem ~?** what (…) for?; **was für e-n ~ soll es haben zu** (+ *Inf.*)? what's the point (*od.* use) of (+ *Ger.*)?; **das ist ja der ~ der Übung!** *umg. hum.* that's the whole point, that's the object (*od.* point) of the exercise; **es hat keinen ~**

there's no point (*zu* + *Inf.* in + *Ger.*), it's no use (+ *Ger.*); **das wird wenig ~ haben** that won't do (*od.* be) much good, that won't be any use; **was hat das alles für e-n ~?** what's the point (of it all)?; *Mittel zum* ~ a means to an end; **der ~ heiligt die Mittel** the end justifies the means

Zweckbau *m Archit.* functional building

zweckbestimmt *Adj.* **1.** *Gebäude etc.*: functional; **2.** *Gelder*: earmarked; **Zweckbestimmtheit** *f; nur Sg.* functionality; **Zweckbestimmung** *f; nur Sg.*: ~ **von Geldern** appropriation of funds

Zweck|bindung *f* dedication (*od.* restriction) to a specific purpose; *im Budget*: earmarking, hypothecation; **~bündnis** *n Pol. etc.* marriage of convenience; **~denken** *n* pragmatism

zweckdienlich *Adj.* useful, expedient; (*relevant*) relevant; **~e Hinweise im Kriminalfall**: any information that might help the police with their enquiries (*od.* inquiries); **Zweckdienlichkeit** *f; nur Sg.* **1.** expediency; **2.** (*Relevanz*) relevance, pertinence

zweckentfremden *v/t.* (*untr., hat*) *nur Inf. und P.P.* use for a purpose other than the one originally intended, use as a makeshift; (*Gelder*) misappropriate; **Zweckentfremdung** *f; nur Sg.* use for a different purpose; *missbräuchlich*: misuse; *von Geldern: auch* misappropriation

zweck|entsprechend *Adj.* appropriate, suitable (to its *od.* their purpose); **~frei I.** *Adj.* with no specific purpose; **~e Forschung** pure research; **II.** *Adv.* without any specific purpose

zweckgebunden *Adj. Gelder*: earmarked; **Zweckgebundenheit** *f; nur Sg.* earmarking

zweckgemäß *Adj.* appropriate; **die Spenden wurden nicht ~ verwendet** the donations were not used for the purpose for which they were intended

Zweckgemeinschaft *f oft pej.*: **e-e bloße od. reine** ~ a mere marriage of convenience

zwecklos *Adj.* useless, pointless, *präd. auch* no use; **es ist ~ zu** (+ *Inf.*) it's pointless *od.* there's no point in (+ *Ger.*); **geschieden** *etc.* ~ *Anzeige*: no divorcees *etc.* need apply; **Zwecklosigkeit** *f; nur Sg.* pointlessness

zweckmäßig *Adj.* suitable; (*praktisch*) practical; *Tech.* functional; (*wirksam*) effective; (*ratsam*) advisable; (*klug*) expedient; **Zweckmäßigkeit** *f; nur Sg.* suitability; *e-s Vorschlags etc.*: practicality; *Tech.* functional nature (+ *Gen.* of); effectivity, effectiveness; advisability; → *zweckmäßig*

Zweck|optimismus *m* calculated optimism; **~pessimismus** *m* calculated pessimism

zwecks *Präp.* (+ *Gen.*) for the purpose of (+ *Ger.*), with a view to (+ *Ger.*)

Zweck|sparen *n* targeted (*od.* special-purpose) saving; **~verband** *m association of local authorities for the joint management of a particular service*, joint board; **~vermögen** *n Jur.* special-purpose fund

zweckvoll *Adj.* → *zweckmäßig*

zweckwidrig *Adj.* inappropriate; **~e Verwendung von Geldern** misappropriation of funds

zwei *Zahlw.* two; **wir ~** the two of us, you and I (*od.* me); **dazu gehören (immer noch) ~** it takes two, you need

two people (for that); **zu ~en hintereinander** two by two, in twos; **für ~ essen/trinken** eat/drink for two; **für ~ arbeiten** do the work of two; **wenn ~ sich streiten, freut sich der Dritte** *Sprichw.* while two dogs are fighting for a bone, the third runs away with it; → *auch acht*[1]

Zwei *f, -, -en* **1.** *Zahl*: (number) two; **2.** *Päd.* (*Note*): *etwa* B; **e-e ~ schreiben** get a B; → *auch Acht*[1] 1, 2, 4

Zweiachser *m; -s, -; Mot.* two-axle(d) vehicle *etc.*; **zweiachsig** *Adj.* two-axled

Zweiakter *m; -s, -; Theat.* two-act play, two-acter; **zweiaktig** *Adj. attr.* two-act …

zwei|armig *Adj.* two-armed; **~atomig** *Adj.* diatomic; **~äugig** *Adj.* two-eyed; **~bändig** *Adj.* two-volume …, in two volumes

Zweibeiner *m; -s, -; hum.* biped; **zweibeinig** *Adj.* two-legged

Zweibettzimmer *n* twin-bedded room, twin *umg.*

zweiblätt(e)rig *Adj. Bot.* two-leafed, two-leaved, two-leaf …

Zweicentstück *n* two-(euro)cent piece

zweideutig *Adj.* ambiguous, equivocal; (*anzüglich*) suggestive; *Witz*: off-colo(u)r; **Zweideutigkeit** *f* **1.** *nur Sg.* ambiguity, equivocal nature (+ *Gen.* of); suggestiveness; → *zweideutig*. **2.** (*Bemerkung*) suggestive remark, double entendre

zweidimensional *Adj.* two-dimensional

Zweidrittelmehrheit *f Pol.* two-thirds majority

zweieiig *Adj.* binovular; **~e Zwillinge** nonidentical (*od.* fraternal) twins; **sie sind ~e Zwillinge** *mst* they're not identical twins

zweieinhalb *Zahlw.* two and a half

Zweier *m; -s, -* **1.** *umg.* → *Zwei*. **2.** *Rudern*: pair, two(-seater); **3.** *Golf*: twosome; **~beziehung** *f* relationship (between two people); (*Partnerschaft*) partnership; **~bob** *m Sport* two-man bob; **~kajak** *m Sport* double kayak; *Sportdisziplin*: kayak pairs; **~kanadier** *m Sport* Canadian pair; *Sportdisziplin*: Canadian pairs

zweierlei *Adj. indekl.* two (different) kinds of; *subst.* two things; **das ist ~** they're two completely different things; **mit ~ Maß messen** *fig.* apply double standards

Zweier|reihe *f*: **in ~n** two abreast; **~takt** *m* duple time

Zweieuro|centstück *n* two-(euro)cent piece; **~stück** *n* two-euro piece

zweifach I. *Adj.* double; **in ~er Ausfertigung** in duplicate; **die ~e Menge** double the amount; **~er Sieger** two-time(s) winner (*od.* champion); **II.** *Adv.* doubly; (*zweimal*) twice; *ausfertigen, vorlegen etc.*: in duplicate; → *auch achtfach*; **Zweifache** *n; -n, kein Pl.*: **um das ~ steigen** double (in amount); → *auch Achtfache*

Zweifamilienhaus *n* two-family (*Am.* duplex) house

Zweifarbendruck *m* two-colo(u)r printing (*konkret*: print)

zweifarbig *Adj.* two-tone …

Zweifel *m; -s, -* doubt (**an** + *Dat.* about); (*Ungewissheit*) uncertainty; **berechtigter ~** reasonable doubt; **große/leise ~** grave/slight doubts; **außer ~** beyond doubt; **ohne ~** without (a) doubt, undoubtedly; **es bestehen ~ an s-r Ehrlichkeit** there are doubts about his honesty; **es besteht kein ~ (darüber), dass ...** there's absolutely no doubt (*od.* question) that ...; **kein ~, das stimmt** there's no doubt about it, it's right; **~ haben an** (+ *Dat.*) have (one's) doubts about; **ich habe nicht den geringsten ~, dass ...** I have not the slightest doubt (*od.* no doubt whatsoever) that ...; **ich habe da m-e ~** I have my doubts, I'm not so sure; **mir kommen ~** I'm beginning to have my doubts; **keinen ~ daran lassen, dass ...** make it quite plain that ..., leave no room for doubt that ...; **im ~ sein** be doubtful, have one's doubts (**über** + *Akk.* about); **in ~ ziehen** (call into) question, throw (*od.* call) into doubt; **über jeden ~ erhaben** beyond (any shadow of a) doubt

Zweifelderwirtschaft *f Agr.* two-crop rotation, two-field system

zweifelhaft *Adj.* doubtful; (*fraglich, fragwürdig, verdächtig*) *auch* dubious, questionable; **es ist ~, ob ...** it's doubtful (*od.* uncertain) whether ...; **~e Geschäfte** dubious (*od.* shady) transactions; **ein ~es Vergnügen** a doubtful (*od.* dubious) pleasure; **von ~em Wert** of doubtful (*od.* questionable) value; **es erscheint ~, ob ...** it seems doubtful whether ...

zweifellos *Adv.* undoubtedly, without (a) doubt; **das ist ~ richtig** *auch* I'm sure that's right; **stärker**: there's no doubt about that

zweifeln *v/i.*: **~ an** (+ *Dat.*) doubt, have one's doubts about; (*in Zweifel ziehen*) **~, ob ...** be uncertain (*od.* unsure) (as to) whether ..., doubt whether ..., have one's doubts as to whether ...; **daran ist nicht zu ~** there's no doubt about that; **an sich** (*Dat.*) **selbst ~** have lost faith in oneself; **sie zweifelte an s-m Verstand** she had doubts about his sanity

Zweifels|fall *m* doubtful case; (*Grenzfall*) borderline case; **im ~** if there's any doubt, if you're *etc.* not sure, **förm.** in case of doubt; (*falls notwendig*) if necessary *umg.*

zweifelsfrei I. *Adj.* free of doubt, absolutely certain; **ein ~er Beweis** unequivocal (*od.* unimpeachable) evidence; **die ~e Ursache** the undoubted cause; **II.** *Adv.*: **~ beweisen** prove beyond doubt

zweifelsohne *Adv.* → **zweifellos**

Zweifingersystem *n hum.* hunt and peck system; **ich tippe im ~** I type with (*od.* use) two fingers

zweiflammig *Adj. attr.* two-flame ...

Zweifler *m; -s, -, ~in f; -, -nen* doubter, sceptic, *Am.* skeptic; **zweiflerisch** *Adj.* sceptical, *Am.* skeptical, doubting ...

zweiflügelig *Adj.* **1.** *Insekt:* two-winged, *fachspr.* dipterous; **2.** *Fenster, Tür:* double; *Propeller:* two-bladed; **Zweiflügler** *m; -s, -; Zool.* dipteron

Zweifrankenstück *n* two-franc piece

Zweifrontenkrieg *m* war on two fronts

Zweig *m; -(e)s, -e* **1.** branch; *kleiner:* twig; → **grün** 5; **2.** *fig.* branch; *Schule etc.:* section, department

zwei|geschlechtig *Adj. Bot.* hermaphroditic, bisexual; **~geschossig**, *österr.* **~geschoßig** *Adj. attr.* two-stor(e)y ...

Zweigespann *n* **1.** carriage and pair; **2.** *umg. von Personen:* twosome, duo

zwei|gestrichen *Adj. Mus.* marked with two small lines like a quotation mark to indicate the octave beginning with C above middle C **das ~e C** C

above middle C, C5; **das ~e G** G an octave above middle C, G5; **~geteilt** *Adj.* **1.** bipartite; **2.** (*gespalten*) divided, split

Zweiggeschäft *n* branch

zweigleisig I. *Adj.* **1.** *attr.* double-track, *präd.* double-tracked; **2.** *fig. attr.* two-track, twin-track; **II.** *Adv. fig.*: **~ fahren** leave both one's options open, hedge one's bets *umg.*

Zweig|niederlassung *f* subsidiary, branch; **~stelle** *f* branch (office); **~stellenleiter** *m*, **~stellenleiterin** *f* branch manager; **~werk** *n* branch

zweihändig I. *Adj.* two-handed; *Musikstück:* for two hands; **II.** *Adv.* with both hands

Zweiheit *f; nur Sg.* duality

zweihöckerig *Adj.* two-humped

zweihundert *Zahlw.* two hundred

Zweihundert|euroschein *m* two-hundred-euro note; **~jahrfeier** *f* bicentenary, *bes. Am.* bicentennial

Zweijahresvertrag *m* two-year contract

zweijährig *Adj.* **1.** *Kind etc.:* two-year-old ...; **2.** (*zwei Jahre dauernd*) two-year ...; **Zweijährige** *m, f; -n, -n* two-year-old

zweijährlich I. *Adj.* two-yearly, occurring every two years, biennial; **II.** *Adv.* every two years, biennially

Zweikammersystem *n Parl.* bicameral system

Zweikampf *m* duel; **e-n ~ gewinnen** *Fußball:* win a tackle

Zweikanalton *m TV:* **mit ~** with bilingual facility, with two-language channels

zwei|karätig *Adj.* two-carat ...; **~keimblätt(e)rig** *Adj. Bot.* dicotyledonous

Zweiklassengesellschaft *f* two-tier society

zweiköpfig *Adj.* **1.** *Ungeheuer:* two-headed; **2.** *Gruppe etc.:* of two

Zweikreisbremse *f Mot.* dual-circuit brake

zweilagig *Adj.* two-ply

Zweiliterflasche *f* two-lit|re (*Am.* -er) bottle

zweimal *Adv.* twice; **~ am Tag** twice a day, twice daily; **~ so groß wie** twice as big as, twice the size of; **es sich** (*Dat.*) **~ überlegen** think twice (before doing it); **ich hab's mir nicht ~ sagen lassen** I didn't wait to be told (*od.* asked) twice; **zweimalig** *Adj.*: **nach ~er Wiederholung** after repeating it twice, after two repetitions (*Sendung etc.:* repeats); **nach ~em Versuch** after two attempts, after the second attempt, after trying twice; **erst nach ~er Aufforderung machte er es** he had to be asked twice before he did it

Zweimannzelt *n* two-man tent

Zweimarkstück *n* two-mark piece

Zweimaster *m; -s, -; Naut.* two-master

zwei|minütig *Adj. Gespräch: attr.* two-minute ...; **~minütlich I.** *Adj.* (occurring) every two minutes; **II.** *Adv.* every two minutes; **~monatig** *Adj.* **1.** (*2 Monate alt*) *attr.* two-month-old ..., *präd.* two months old; **2.** (*2 Monate dauernd*) two-month ...; **~monatlich I.** *Adj.* bimonthly; **II.** *Adv.* bimonthly, every two months, every other month

Zweimonatsschrift *f* bimonthly (publication)

zweimotorig *Adj.* twin-engined

Zweiparteiensystem *n Pol.* two-party system

Zweipersonenzelt *n* two-person tent

Zweipfennigstück *n hist.* two-pfennig

piece

Zweiphasen... *im Subst.* two-phase; **zweiphasig** *Adj.* two-phase

zweipolig *Adj.* two-pole ..., bipolar; *Stecker:* two-pin ...

Zweipunktgurt *m Mot.* two-point belt

Zweirad *n* two-wheeled vehicle; **zweiräd(e)rig** *Adj.* two-wheeled

Zweirappenstück *n* two-rappen piece

Zweireiher *m* double-breasted suit *etc.*; **zweireihig** *Adj.* two-rowed; *Anzug etc.:* double-breasted

Zweisamkeit *f lit.* togetherness; **in trauter ~** just the two of them (*od.* us *etc.*)

zweischneidig *Adj.* double-edged, two-edged (*beide auch fig. Schwert*); **das ist so e-e ~e Sache** *fig.* it cuts both ways, it's a tricky business

zweiseitig I. *Adj.* **1.** two-sided; *auch Fotokopie:* double-sided; **2.** *Brief, Artikel etc.: attr.* two-page ..., *präd.* two pages long; **~e Anzeige** double(-page) spread; **3.** *Pol., Vertrag, Gespräche etc.:* bilateral; **4.** *Stoff:* reversible; **II.** *Adv.*: **~ bedruckt** *etc.* printed *etc.* on both sides (*od.* on either side)

zweisilbig *Adj.* two-syllable ..., disyllabic; **~es Wort** *auch* disyllable

Zweisitzer *m; -s, -; Mot.* two-seater (*auch Flug.*); *offener:* roadster; *geschlossener:* coupé; **zweisitzig** *Adj. attr.* two-seater ...

zweispaltig I. *Adj.* two-column ..., two-columned; **II.** *Adv.*: **~ gedruckt** (printed) in two columns

Zweispänner *m; -s, -* carriage and pair

zweisprachig I. *Adj.* bilingual; *Schriftstück:* in two languages; **II.** *Adv.*: **~ aufwachsen** grow up bilingually (*od.* speaking two languages); **Zweisprachigkeit** *f; nur Sg.* bilingualism

zweispurig *Adj.* **1.** *Fahrbahn:* two-lane ..., two-laned; **2.** *Eisenb. attr.* double-track ..., *präd.* double-tracked

Zweistärkenbrille *f:* **(e-e) ~** (a pair of) bifocals *Pl.*

zweistellig *Adj. Zahl:* two-digit ...; **~e Inflation** *auch* double-digit inflation

Zweisternerestaurant *n* two-star restaurant

zweistimmig *Adj.* for (*od.* in) two voices, two-part ...

zweistöckig *Adj.* two-stor(e)y ...; **~es Bett** bunk bed

zweistrahlig *Adj. Flug.* twin-jet ...

Zweistromland *n; nur Sg.; Geog.:* **das ~** Mesopotamia

Zweistufen|plan *m* two-stage plan; **~rakete** *f* two-stage rocket (*od.* missile)

zweistufig *Adj.* two-stage ...

zweistündig *Adj.* two-hour(-long) ...

zweit *Adv.*: **zu ~** (*paarweise*) in twos, in pairs; **wir waren zu ~** there were two of us; **wir gingen zu ~ hin** (*wir waren zwei*) two of us went there; (*beide*) both of us went there, we went there together

zweit... *Zahlw.* second; **~es Kapitel** chapter two, second chapter; **2. Juli** 2nd July, July 2(nd); **am ~en Juli** on the second of July, on July the second; **Zweites Deutsches Fernsehen** (*abgek.* ZDF) Second Channel of German Television; **ein ~er Napoleon** another Napoleon; → **Geige, Hand** 2, **Wahl** 4

zweitägig *Adj.* **1.** two-day(-long) ...; **2.** (*zwei Tage alt*) two-day-old ...

Zweitakter *m; -s, -, Zweitaktmotor** *m* two-stroke engine

zweitältest... *Adj.* second oldest; *in der Familie:* auch second eldest

zweitausend *Zahlw.* two thousand;

Zweitausender *m*; -s, - two-thousand met|re (*Am.* -er) peak

Zweit|ausfertigung *f* duplicate; **~beruf** *m* second career

zweitbest... *Adj.* second-best; **Zweitbeste** *m*, *f* second best

Zweite *m*, *f*; -n, -n second; *sie wurde ~* she was (*od.* came) second; *er ist der ewige ~* he always comes second; *jeder ~* every other person; *wie kein ~r* like nobody else; *der ~ von hinten* second from the back; *Richard II.* Richard II (= Richard the Second); *heute ist der ~* it's the second today

zweiteilen *v/refl.* (*untr.*, *hat -ge-*) *nur Inf. und P.P.*: *ich kann mich doch nicht ~!* I can't be in two places at once; *1961 wurde Berlin zweigeteilt* in 1961 Berlin was divided in two (*od.* partitioned); **Zweiteiler** *m*; -s, -; *umg. Badeanzug etc.*: two-piece; *Film*: two-part film, film in two parts; **zweiteilig** *Adj.* two-part ..., in two parts; *Anzug etc.*: two-piece suit *etc.*; **Zweiteilung** *f* division

Zweite-Klasse-Abteil *n* second-class compartment

zweitens *Adv.* secondly, two, in second place

Zweiter-Klasse-Abteil *n* → *Zweite--Klasse-Abteil*

Zweit|frisur *f hum.* wig; **~gerät** *n* second TV (*bzw.* radio *od.* set)

zweit|größt... *Adj.* second largest; **~häufigst...** *Adj.* second commonest; **~höchst...** *Adj.* second highest (*Gebäude etc.*: tallest)

zweitklassig *Adj.* second-class; *pej.* second-rate; *Sport* second-division ...; **Zweitklassigkeit** *f*; *nur Sg.*; *pej.* second-rateness

Zweitklässler *m*; -s, -, **~in** *f*; -, *-nen Schüler(in)*: second-year (pupil), *Am.* second-grader

zweitlängst... *Adj.* second longest

zweitletzt... *Adj.* last but one, second to last, *förm.* penultimate

Zweit|ligist *m*; -en, -en second-division team; **~platzierte** *m*, *f*; -n, -n runner--up, person *etc.* in second place

zweitrangig *Adj.* of secondary importance, secondary; *pej.* (*zweitklassig*) second-rate

Zweitschlag *m Mil.* second strike

Zweit|schlüssel *m* spare key; **~schrift** *f* copy, duplicate; **~stimme** *f Pol.* second vote; **~studium** *n* second degree; *ein ~ machen auch* take another degree

zweitürig *Adj. Mot.* two-door ...

Zweit|wagen *m* second car; **~wohnsitz** *m* second residence; **~wohnung** *f* second home; *kleine, mst in der Stadt*: *auch* pied-à-terre; *auf dem Land*: *mst* weekend place, country place, *Am. auch* second home

Zweiunddreißigstelnote *f Mus.* demisemiquaver, *Am.* thirty-second note

Zweivierteltakt *m*: *Mus.* (*im*) *~* (in) two-four time

Zweiweg(e)|box *f umg.*, **~lautsprecher** *m* two-way (loud)speaker

zweiwertig *Adj. Chem.* bivalent; **~es Element** dyad

zweiwöchentlich I. *Adj.* two-weekly, *bes. Brit.* fortnightly; **II.** *Adv.* every two weeks, *bes. Brit.* fortnightly

zweiwöchig *Adj.* **1.** *Zeitraum*: two--week ...; **2.** *Baby etc.*: two-week-old ...

Zweizeiler *m* distich; *gereimt*: couplet; **zweizeilig I.** *Adj.* two-line ...; **II.** *Adv.*: *~ geschrieben* double-spaced

Zweizimmerwohnung *f* one-bedroom flat (*Am.* apartment)

zweizügig *Adj. Schule*: two-stream ...

Zweizylinder *m umg. Auto*: two-cylinder (car); *Motor*: two-cylinder engine

Zwerchfell *n Anat.* diaphragm; **~atmung** *f* abdominal (*od.* diaphragmatic) breathing

zwerchfellerschütternd *Adj.* sidesplitting

Zwerg *m*; -(e)s, -e **1.** dwarf; (*bes. Gartenzwerg*) gnome; **2.** *pej.* (*kleiner Mensch*) dwarf, midget; **3.** *hum.* (*Knirps*) whipper-snapper; **4.** *pej.* (*Niemand*) little squirt, nonentity; **Zwergenaufstand** *m umg. hum.* to--do, unnecessary fuss; **zwergenhaft** *Adj.* dwarfish, dwarf-like; *fig.* diminutive

Zwerg|huhn *n Orn.* bantam; **~hund** *m Zool.* miniature dog

Zwergin *f* → *Zwerg* 2

Zwerg|kaninchen *n Zool.* pygmy rabbit; **~kiefer** *f Bot.* dwarf pine; **~maus** *f Zool.* harvest mouse; **~palme** *f Bot.* dwarf palm; **~pudel** *m Zool.* miniature poodle; **~schule** *f* one-classroom school; **~staat** *m* miniature (*umg.* tiny) state; **~tanne** *f Bot.* dwarf conifer; **~volk** *n* pygmy tribe

Zwergwuchs *m Med., Bot., Zool.* dwarfism, *fachspr.* nanism; **zwergwüchsig** *Adj.* dwarfish

Zwetsche *f*; -, -n **1.** *Frucht*: damson (plum); **2.** *Baum*: damson (tree)

Zwetschen|baum *m Bot.* damson tree; **~kern** *m* damson stone; **~kuchen** *m* plum (*od.* damson) cake; **~mus** *n* damson (*od.* plum) jam; **~schnaps** *m*, **~wasser** *n* plum brandy

Zwetschge *f*; -, -n; *bes. südd., österr., Bot.* → *Zwetsche*

Zwetschgen|datschi *m*; -s, -s; *Gastr. bes. südd.* cake base covered with damson halves; **~knödel** *m Gastr.* plum dumpling

Zwetschke *f*; -, -n; *österr.* → *Zwetsche*; **Zwetschkenknödel** *m Gastr.* plum dumpling

Zwickel *m*; -s, - **1.** *Schneiderei*: gusset; **2.** *Archit.* spandrel; **3.** *umg. hist.* (*Zweimarkstück*) two-mark piece

zwicken *vt/i. bes. südd., österr.* **1.** pinch; *das Hemd zwickt mich* my shirt is pinching me (*od.* is too tight); **2.** (*wehtun*) hurt; *mein Bauch zwickt* (*mich*) I've got a (griping) pain in my stomach; *die Gicht zwickt ihn* he's feeling twinges of gout; *sein Gewissen zwickt ihn fig.* his conscience is pricking him; **3.** *bes. österr.* (*Fahrkarte*) punch

Zwicker *m*; -s, -; *Opt.* pince-nez

Zwickmühle *f* **1.** *umg. fig.* catch-22 situation; *in e-r ~ sein auch* be in a quandary (*umg.* fix); **2.** *Mühlespiel*: double row

Zwieback *m*; -(e)s, -e und Zwiebäcke rusk, *bes. Am.* zwieback

Zwiebel *f*; -, -n **1.** onion; **2.** *Bot., von Blumen*: bulb; **3.** *umg. hum.* (*Taschenuhr*) turnip watch; (*Haarknoten*) bun

zwiebelförmig *Adj.* onion-shaped

Zwiebel|kuchen *m Gastr.* onion tart; **~muster** *n* blue onion pattern

zwiebeln *v/t. umg.* give *s.o.* a hard time; *Sache*: get to *s.o.*; *mit Forderungen etc.*: keep on at (*Am.* keep pestering) *s.o.*

Zwiebel|ring *m* onion ring; **~schale** *f* onion skin; **~suppe** *f Gastr.* onion soup; **~turm** *m* onion tower

Zwie|gespräch *n* dialog(ue); **~laut** *m Ling.* diphthong

Zwielicht *n draußen*: twilight; *im Haus*: dim light, gloom; *ins ~ geraten fig.* lay o.s. open to suspicion; **zwielichtig** *Adj. fig.* dubious, shady; **~e Gestalt** shady character

Zwiespalt *m*; -(e)s, -e und Zwiespälte conflict; (*Polarität*) dichotomy; *zwischen Menschen, innerhalb e-r Partei etc.*: rift; (*Dilemma*) dilemma; *im ~ sein* be in conflict (*mit* with); *Person auch*: be in a dilemma, be in a cleft stick; *in e-n ~ geraten* get involved in a conflict; be faced with (*od. lit.* on the horns of) a dilemma; **zwiespältig** *Adj.* mixed; *stärker*: conflicting; *mein Eindruck war ~* I had (*od.* I came away with) mixed impressions; *er ist ein ~er Charakter* he has a conflicting personality; **Zwiespältigkeit** *f* conflicting nature; (*Zwiespalt*) conflict

Zwiesprache *f geh.* dialog(ue); *~ halten mit fig.* commune with

Zwietracht *f*; -, *kein Pl.*; *geh.* discord; *~ säen* sow the seeds of discord; *in ~ leben mit* be at variance (*od.* odds) with; *es herrscht ~ zwischen ihnen* they're at loggerheads, they're not on the best of terms *iro.*

Zwille *f*; -, -n; *Dial.* **1.** (*Astgabel*) fork (in a branch); **2.** (*Schleuder*) catapult, *Am.* slingshot

Zwillich *m*; -s, -e, *Pl. selten* drill

Zwilling *m*; -s, -e **1.** twin; *siamesische ~e* Siamese twins; **2.** *Astron., Astrol.*: **~e** Gemini; (*ein*) *~ sein* be (a) Gemini; **3.** *Gewehr*: double-barrel(l)ed gun

Zwillings|bruder *m* twin brother; **~geburt** *f* twin birth; **~geschwister** *Pl.* twins; twin brothers (*od.* sisters); **~paar** *n* pair of twins; **~reifen** *Pl. Mot.* double tyres (*Am.* tires); **~schwester** *f* twin sister

Zwingburg *f hist.* stronghold, citadel

Zwinge *f*; -, -n; *Tech., zum Schrauben*: clamp; *am Stock etc.*: ferrule

zwingen *zwingt, zwang, hat gezwungen* **I.** *v/t.* **1.** force (*zu* + *Inf.* to + *Inf.*, into + *Ger.*); *j-n ~, etw. zu tun auch* make s.o. do s.th.; *durch psychischen Druck*: coerce s.o. into doing s.th.; *j-n zum Reden ~* force s.o. to speak; *ich lass mich nicht ~* I won't be forced (*od.* coerced); → *gezwungen*; **2.** *geh.*: *j-n zu Boden ~* force s.o. to the floor (*od.* ground); → *Knie* 1; **3.** *Dial.* (*Arbeit, Essen*) manage; **II.** *v/i. Sache*: *~ zu* demand, necessitate; *die Lage zwingt zu drastischen Maßnahmen* the situation demands (*od.* necessitates) drastic measures; **III.** *v/refl.* force o.s.; *sich zur Ruhe/Höflichkeit etc. ~* force o.s. to remain calm / to be polite *etc.*; *sich ~ zu lächeln* force a smile

zwingend I. *Part. Präs.* → *zwingen*; **II.** *Adj. Grund*: compelling; *Logik*: *auch* inescapable; *Notwendigkeit*: absolute, urgent; *Argument, Beweis*: cogent, compelling, conclusive; *mit e-r ~en Logik* with compelling logic; **III.** *Adv.*: *~ erforderlich* absolutely imperative; *~ vorgeschrieben* mandatory

Zwinger *m*; -s, - **1.** *e-r Burg*: ward; **2.** *für Hunde*: kennel; *zum Züchten*: kennels *Pl.*; **3.** *im Zoo*: (*Gehege*) enclosure; (*Käfig*) cage; *für Bären*: bear pit

Zwinglianer *m*; -s, -, **~in** *f*; -, *-nen*; *Reli. hist.* Zwinglian

zwinkern *v/i.*: (*mit den Augen*) *~ unwillkürlich*: blink; *zum Zeichen*: wink; *humorvoll*: twinkle

zwirbeln *v/t.* twist, twiddle *umg.*

Z

Zwirn *m; -(e)s, -e* twine, twist; **Zwirnsfaden** *m* thread; → *auch* **Faden**[1]
zwischen *Präp.* (+ *Dat. od. Akk.*) *auch zeitlich und fig.*: between; (*inmitten*) among; ~ *ihnen herrscht Streit* they've fallen out; ~ *ihnen wird es nie zur Einigung kommen* they'll never come to an agreement; → **Stuhl** 2, **Tür** 2, **Zeile** 1
Zwischenablage *f EDV* clipboard
Zwischenakt *m Theat. hist.* intermission; ~**musik** *f* intermezzo, interlude
Zwischen|applaus *m* (spontaneous) applause *in the middle of a scene, speech, etc.*; ~**aufenthalt** *m* stop(over); ~**bemerkung** *f* interjection; (*Unterbrechung*) interruption; ~**bericht** *m* interim report; ~**bescheid** *m* provisional reply; ~**bilanz** *f* interim balance (sheet); *fig.* interim assessment; *Pol.* mid-term review; *e-e* ~ *ziehen fig.* take stock, assess the current situation; ~**blutung** *f auch Pl.*; *Med.* breakthrough bleeding; *leichte*: spotting; ~**buchhandel** *m* wholesale book trade (*bes. Am.* business); ~**deck** *n Naut.* 'tween deck, intermediate deck; *hist. Passagierklasse: etwa* steerage; *im* ~ between decks; *hist.* in the 'tween decks; ~**decke** *f* false ceiling; ~**ding** *n umg.* something (in) between; *ein* ~ *zwischen Mantel und Toga* a cross between a coat and a toga, something in between a coat and a toga
zwischendrein *Adv.* 1. *räumlich*: in between; (*hier und dort*) here and there; 2. → **zwischendurch** 1
zwischendrin *Adv.* 1. *räumlich*: in between; (*mittendrin*) (right) in the middle; 2. *umg.* → **zwischendurch** 1
zwischendurch *Adv.* 1. *zeitlich, zwischen zwei Zeitpunkten etc.*: in between; (*gelegentlich*) from time to time, now and then; (*nebenher*) in passing, by the way; (*inzwischen*) in the meantime; *iss nicht so viel* ~ don't eat so much between meals; 2. (*neben der Hauptarbeit etc.*) on the side; 3. (*zwischen hindurch*) *fallen, werfen etc.*: in between; 4. → **zwischendrein** 1
Zwischen|eiszeit *f Geol.* interglacial period; ~**ergebnis** *n* interim result; *e-r Untersuchung:* interim findings *Pl.*; *Sport* latest score; ~**fall** *m* incident; *ohne Zwischenfälle* (*reibungslos*) without a hitch; *ohne Zwischenfälle verlaufen Demonstration:* pass off peacefully (*od.* without incident); *es kam zu schweren/blutigen Zwischenfällen* there was violence/bloodshed
zwischenfinanzieren *v/t.* (*untr., hat*) *mst Inf. und P.P.; Fin.* provide interim finance for; **Zwischenfinanzierung** *f* bridging, interim financing
Zwischen|frage *f* (interpolated) question; *Parl. auch* interruption, interpolation; *darf ich e-e* ~ *stellen?* may I throw in a quick question?; ~**frucht** *f Agr.* intercrop; ~**futter** *n in Kleidung:* interlining; ~**gas** *n; nur Sg.; Mot.*: *geben* double-declutch, *Am.* double-clutch; ~**gericht** *n Gastr.* entrée
zwischengeschlechtlich *Adj.* between the sexes
Zwischen|geschoss *n, österr.* ~**geschoß** *n* mezzanine (floor); ~**glied** *n* link; ~**größe** *f* intermediate size; ~**handel** *m* intermediate trade; (*Großhandel*) wholesale trade; ~**händler** *m* middleman, intermediary; ~**hirn** *n Anat.* diencephalon *fachspr.*, interbrain; ~**hoch** *n Met.* ridge of high

pressure
Zwischenlager *n* intermediate (*od.* temporary) store; *für Giftstoffe etc.*: intermediate storage site; **zwischenlagern** *v/t.* (*hat -ge-*) *nur Inf. und Part.* store temporarily, put in temporary storage; **Zwischenlagerung** *f* temporary storage
zwischenlanden *v/i.* (*trennb., ist -ge-*) *Flug.* stop over (*in + Dat.* in), make a stopover; **Zwischenlandung** *f* stopover; ~ *zum Auftanken* refuel(l)ing stop; *ohne* ~ nonstop
Zwischen|lauf *m Sport* intermediate heat; ~**lösung** *f* interim solution; ~**mahlzeit** *f* snack (between meals)
zwischenmenschlich *Adj.* interpersonal, interhuman; ~*e Beziehungen auch* human relations; *im* ~*en Bereich* where human relations are concerned
Zwischen|musik *f* interlude; ~**produkt** *n Wirts.* intermediate product; ~**prüfung** *f* intermediate exam(ination); ~**raum** *m* 1. space (in between); (*Lücke*) gap, *förm.* interstice; (*Zeilenabstand*) spacing; (*Spielraum*) clearance; *2 cm / e-e Zeile* ~ *lassen* leave a 2 cm gap (*od.* space) / a one-line space; 2. *zeitlich*: interval; ~**rechnung** *f* interim bill
zwischenrein *Adv. umg.* → **zwischendurch**
Zwischen|ring *m* 1. *Fot.* adapter; *für Nahaufnahmen:* extension tube; 2. *Tech.* spacer ring; ~**ruf** *m* (loud) interruption; *Pl.* heckling *Sg.*; *durch* ~*e unterbrechen* heckle; ~**rufer** *m*, ~**ruferin** *f* heckler; ~**runde** *f* intermediate round; ~**saison** *f* in-between season; ~**satz** *m* 1. *Ling.* parenthetic clause, parenthesis (*Pl.* parentheses); 2. *Mus.* intermezzo (*between two movements*)
zwischenschalten *v/t.* (*trennb., hat -ge-*) *Etech., Tech.* insert; (*verbinden*) interconnect; *fig.* interpose; **Zwischenschaltung** *f fig. e-s Vermittlers etc.*: interposition
Zwischen|schicht *f* intermediate layer; ~**schritt** *m* 1. *beim Tanzen:* linking step; 2. *fig. beim Rechnen etc.*: intermediate step; ~**sohle** *f* midsole
Zwischenspeicher *m EDV* cache (memory); **zwischenspeichern** *v/t.* (*trennb., hat -ge-*) cache, store in the cache; **Zwischenspeicherung** *f* intermediate storage
Zwischen|spiel *n Theat., Mus., fig.* interlude; ~**spurt** *m Sport* (sudden) spurt; *e-n* ~ *einlegen* put on a burst of speed
zwischenstaatlich *Adj.* international; (*zwischen Regierungen*) intergovernmental; (*zwischen Bundesstaaten*) interstate ...
Zwischen|stadium *n* intermediate stage; ~**stand** *m Sport* current position; *der Teilnehmer: auch* current rankings; ~**station** *f* stop (*auch Ort*), stopover; ~ *machen in* (+ *Dat.*) stop over in, make a stop in; ~**stecker** *m Etech.* adapter (plug); ~**stopp** *m* stop (along the way); *bes. Flug.* stopover; ~**stück** *n* connecting piece; *Etech.* adapter; ~**stufe** *f e-r Entwicklung etc.*: intermediate stage; ~**summe** *f* subtotal; ~**text** *m* linking text: *Film:* inserted caption(s *Pl.*); ~**tief** *n Met.* ridge of low pressure; ~**titel** *m* 1. *Stummfilm:* caption; 2. *Druck.* subhead(ing); ~**ton** *m* 1. *Farbe:* (intermediate) shade; 2. *fig.* overtone; (*Schattierung*) nuance; ~**tür** *f* interconnecting door; ~**urteil** *n Jur.* interlocutory

judg(e)ment; ~**wand** *f* dividing wall; *bewegliche:* partition; ~**wert** *m* intermediate value; ~**wirt** *m Bio.* intermediate host; ~**zähler** *m Tech., bei Heizung etc.*: submeter
Zwischenzeit *f* 1. interim, intervening (*od.* interim) period; *in der* ~ in the meantime, meanwhile, in the interim; 2. *Sport* intermediate time; **zwischenzeitlich** *Adv. bes. Amtsspr.* in the meantime, meanwhile
Zwischen|zeugnis *n Päd.* interim report; *vom Arbeitgeber:* interim appraisal; ~**zins** *m* interim interest
Zwist *m; -(e)s, -e; geh.* quarrel, dispute; *zwischen Familien etc.: auch* feud; **Zwistigkeiten** *Pl.* 1. discord *Sg.*; 2. → **Zwist**
zwitschern *vt/i.* 1. twitter, chirp; 2. *fig. Person:* twitter; 3. *umg. fig.*: *e-n* ~ (*trinken*) knock one back; *schnell:* have a quick one
Zwitter *m; -s, -* 1. hermaphrodite (*auch Bot.*); 2. *fig. Sache:* hybrid, cross between a(n) ... and a(n) ...; **zwitterhaft** *Adj.* hermaphroditic; **Zwitterhaftigkeit** *f; nur Sg.* hermaphroditism; **Zwitterstellung** *f* halfway house; **Zwitterwesen** *n* 1. *Person:* hermaphrodite; 2. (*Zwitterhaftigkeit*) hermaphroditism
zwo *Zahlw. umg.* → **zwei**
zwölf *Zahlw.* twelve; *um* ~ (*Uhr*) at twelve (o'clock); *mittags: auch* at noon; *nachts: auch* at midnight; *fünf Minuten vor* ~ *fig.* at the eleventh hour; *es ist fünf Minuten vor* ~ *fig.* it's five minutes to midnight, time is rapidly running out; → *auch* **acht**[1]
Zwölf *f; -, -en Zahl:* (number) twelve; → *auch* **Acht**[1] 1, 2
Zwölfender *m; -s, -; Jägerspr.* royal
Zwölfer *m; -s, -; umg.* → **Zwölf**
zwölffach *Adj.* twelvefold; → **achtfach**; **Zwölffache** *n; -n, kein Pl.* twelve times the amount
Zwölffingerdarm *m Anat.* duodenum (*Pl.* duodena *od.* duodenums); ~**geschwür** *n Med.* duodenal ulcer
Zwölfkampf *m Sport* all-(a)round event in men's gymnastics involving twelve exercises on six pieces of apparatus; *für Mannschaften:* team event; **Zwölfkämpfer** *m* competitor (*od.* gymnast) in an all-(a)round event
zwölfmal *Adv.* twelve times
Zwölfmeilenzone *f* twelve-mile zone
zwölft *Adv.: sie kamen zu* ~ twelve of them came, there were twelve of them; → **acht**[2]
zwölft... *Zahlw.* twelfth; ~*e Klasse* eighth form (*Am.* grade) *in a German secondary school, Brit. etwa* Lower Sixth, *Am. etwa* high-school junior (*od.* senior) year; → *auch* **acht...**
Zwölfte *m, f; -n, -n* twelfth; → *auch* **Achte**
zwölftel *Zahlw.* twelfth; **Zwölftel** *n; -s, -* twelfth (part)
zwölftens *Adv.* twelfthly
Zwölfton|musik *f; nur Sg.; Mus.* twelve-tone (*od.* dodecaphonic) music; ~**technik** *f* twelve-tone technique, dodecaphony
Zwölfzylinder *m umg.; Mot., Auto:* twelve-cylinder (car); *Motor:* twelve-cylinder engine
zwot... *Zahlw. umg.* → **zweit...**; **Zwote** *m, f; -n, -n; umg.* → **Zweite**
Zyanid *n; -s, -e; Chem.* cyanide; **Zyankali** *n; -s, kein Pl.; Chem.* potassium cyanide
Zygote *f; -, -n; Bio.* zygote

Zyklamen *n*; *-s*, *-*; *Bot.* cyclamen

zyklisch I. *Adj.* cyclic; **II.** *Adv.* cyclically

Zyklon *m*; *-s*, *-e*; *Met.* cyclone

Zyklop *m*; *-en*, *-en*; *Myth.* Cyclops; **Zyklopenmauer** *f* *Archit.* cyclopean masonry (*od.* wall); **zyklopisch** *Adj.* cyclopean; (*gigantisch*) gigantic

Zyklotron *n*; *-s*, *-s od.* *-e*; *Phys.* cyclotron

Zyklus *m*; *-*, *Zyklen* **1.** *allg.* cycle; *von Vorträgen etc.*: series (*Pl.* series); *der ~ der Jahreszeiten* the seasonal cycle; **2.** *Med.* (menstrual) cycle

Zylinder *m*; *-s*, *-* **1.** *Math.*, *Tech.*, *auch Mot.* cylinder; *e-r Lampe*: chimney;

2. *Hut*: top hat; **~block** *m* *Mot.*, *Tech.* cylinder block; **~glas** *n* *Opt.* cylindrical lens; **~kopf** *m* *Mot.*, *Tech.* cylinder head; **~dichtung** *f* cylinder-head gasket; **~schloss** *n* cylinder lock

zylindrisch *Adj.* cylindrical

Zyniker *m*; *-s*, *-*, **~in** *f*; *-*, *-nen* cynic; **zynisch I.** *Adj.* cynical; **II.** *Adv.* cynically; **Zynismus** *m*; *-*, *Zynismen* **1.** *nur Sg.* cynicism; **2.** *Äußerung*: cynical comment, acid remark

Zypergras *n* *Bot.* umbrella plant

Zypern (*n*); *-s*; *Geog.* Cyprus

Zyperngras *n* *Bot.* umbrella plant

Zyprer *m*; *-s*, *-*, **Zyprerin** *m*; *-*, *-nen* → **Zypriot**

Zypresse *f*; *-*, *-n*; *Bot.* cypress

Zyprier *m*; *-s*, *-*, **Zyprierin** *m*; *-*, *-nen* → **Zypriot**

Zypriot *m*; *-en*, *-en*, **~in** *f*; *-*, *-nen* Cypriot, *weiblich auch*: Cypriot woman (*od.* girl *etc.*); **zypri(ot)isch** *Adj.* Cypriot

Zyste *f*; *-*, *-n*; *Med.*, *Bio.* cyst; **zystisch** *Adj.* cystic

Zytologie *f*; *-*, *kein Pl.* cytology; **zytologisch** *Adj.* cytological

Zytostatikum *n*; *-s*, *Zytostatika*; *Med.* cytostatic drug

zz., **zzt.** *Abk.* (*zurzeit*) at the time

z. Z., **z. Zt.** *Abk.* (*zur Zeit*) at the time of …

Anhänge

Deutsche Abkürzungen

A

A *Ampere* ampere(s *pl.*) (A)
a *Ar* are (a)
AA *das Auswärtige Amt* foreign ministry
a. a. O. *am angegebenen od. angeführten Ort* in the place cited (loc. cit.)
Abb. *Abbildung* illustration (fig.)
abds. *abends* in the evening
Abf. *Abfahrt* departure (dep.)
Abg. *Abgeordnete(r)* member of parliament
Abk. *Abkürzung* abbreviation (abbr.)
Abl. *Ablöse money paid by a new tenant to a previons tenant for furnishings and fittings*
ABM *Arbeitsbeschaffungsmaßnahme(n)* job creation scheme
ABS *Antiblockiersystem* anti-lock (*od.* anti-skid) braking system
Abs. *Absatz* paragraph (para., par.), *typ.* break; *Absender* sender; return address
Abschn. *Abschnitt* section, paragraph (para., par.)
Abt. *Abteilung* department (dept, dpt)
abzgl. *abzüglich* less, minus
a. Chr. (n.) *ante Christum* (*natum*), *vor Christus* (*vor Christi Geburt*) before Christ (BC)
ACS *Automobilclub der Schweiz* Automobile Association of Switzerland
A. D. *anno Domini, im Jahre des Herrn* in the year of our Lord (AD)
a. D. *außer Dienst* retired (retd); *an der Donau* on the Danube
ADAC *Allgemeiner Deutscher Automobil-Club* General German Automobile Association
Add. *Addenda, Ergänzungen* addenda, supplements, additions
ADFC *Allgemeiner Deutscher Fahrrad-Club* General German Cyclists Association
ad inf. *ad infinitum, bis ins Unendliche, unaufhörlich* ad infinitum
ad l., ad lib(it). *ad libitum, nach Belieben* ad lib(itum)
Adr. *Adresse* address
AEG *Allgemeine Elektrizitäts-Gesellschaft* General Electric Company
AG *Aktiengesellschaft* public limited company (PLC, Plc, plc; Ltd), *Am.* (stock) corporation; *Arbeitsgruppe* study group
Agt. *Agent* agent; *Agentur* agency; agents *pl.*
Ah *Amperestunde(n)* ampere-hour(s *pl.*)
ahd. *althochdeutsch* Old High German (OHG)
Akad. *Akademie* academy, (*Fachschule*) *a.* college
akad. *akademisch* academic(al), university *a.*
Akk. *Akkusativ* accusative (case) (acc.)
Akt.-Nr. *Aktennummer* file number (file no.)
AKW *Atomkraftwerk* nuclear power station *od.* plant
akz. *akzeptiert* accepted; ✝ *a.* hono(u)red

al. *alias, auch ... genannt* alias, otherwise *od.* also known as (aka)
Alk. *Alkohol* alcohol (alc.)
allg. *allgemein* general(ly *adv.*)
allj. *alljährlich* annual(ly *adv.*), yearly
alph. *alphabetisch* alphabetical(ly *adv.*)
Alu *Aluminium* alumin(i)um
AM *Amplitudenmodulation* (*Frequenzbereich der Kurz-, Mittel- u. Langwellen*) amplitude modulation (AM)
a. M. *am Main* on the Main
am., amer(ik). *amerikanisch* American (Am.)
amtl. *amtlich* official(ly *adv.*)
Anal. *Analogie* analogy (anal.); *Analyse* analysis (anal.)
Änd. *Änderung* change; alteration
Angest. *Angestellte(r)* employee
angew. *angewandt* applied (appl.)
Anh. *Anhang* appendix
Ank. *Ankunft* arrival (arr.)
Anl. *Anlage im Brief:* enclosure (encl.)
anl. *anlässlich* on the occasion of
Anm. d. Red. *Anmerkung der Redaktion* editors comment (Ed., ed.)
anschl. *anschließend* following (foll.), subsequent(ly *adv.*)
AOK *Allgemeine Ortskrankenkasse* compulsory health insurance scheme
ao. Prof., a. o. Prof. *außerordentlicher Professor* reader, senior lecturer, *Am.* associate professor
Apart. *Apartment* flatlet, one-room apartment, *Am.* efficiency apartment (apt.)
APO *Außerparlamentarische Opposition* extraparliamentary opposition
App. *Apparat teleph.* (*Nebenstelle*) extension (ext.)
appr. *approbiert* qualified, licenced, *Am.* licensed
Apr. *April* April (Apr., Apr)
Arb. *Arbeit* work; labo(u)r; *Arbeiter* worker, workman, labo(u)rer
Arbg. *Arbeitgeber* employer
Arbn. *Arbeitnehmer* employee
ARD *Arbeitsgemeinschaft der öffentlich-rechtlichen Rundfunkanstalten der Bundesrepublik Deutschland* working pool of the broadcasting corporations of the Federal Republic of Germany
Arge *Arbeitsgemeinschaft* work(ing) group; syndicate
a. Rh. *am Rhein* on the Rhine
Art. *Artikel* article, ✝ *a.* item, commodity
ärztl. *ärztlich* medical (med.); doctors *certificate etc.*
AS *Anschlussstelle* jct(n), jn, junction; *Alterssicherung(s...)* retirement provision
Assist. *Assistent(in)* assistant (assnt); *Assistenz* assistence
Asta *Allgemeiner Studentenausschuss* general students committee
ASU *Abgassonderuntersuchung* exhaust-emission test
A.T. *Altes Testament* Old Testament (OT)
atü *Atmosphärenüberdruck* atmospheric excess pressure (psi = pounds per square inch)
Aufl. *Auflage* edition (ed.)

Auftr.-Nr. *Auftragsnummer* order number
Aug. *August* August (Aug., Aug)
Ausg. *Ausgabe* (*Buch*) edition (ed.); (*Buchexemplar*) copy; *Ausgang* exit
ausgen. *ausgenommen* except (for); (*wenn nicht*) unless
ausgeschl. *ausgeschlossen* excluded, excluding ... (excl.)
ausschl. *ausschließlich* exclusive(ly *adv.*) (excl.), sole(ly *adv.*)
austr(al). *australisch* Australian (Aus.)
ausw. *auswärtig* (from) outside; in (from) another town; *a. pol.* foreign
auth. *authentisch* authentic(ally *adv.*), genuine
auton. *autonom* autonomous
Az. *Aktenzeichen* file number (file no.); *auf Brief:* reference (ref.)

B

B *Bundesstraße* major road, federal highway
b. *bei* at; *räumlich:* near (nr); *Adresse:* care of (c/o)
BAB *Bundesautobahn* autobahn; motorway, *Am.* highway
BAFöG *Bundesausbildungsförderungsgesetz* student financial assistance scheme
Barz(ahl). *Barzahlung* cash payment
BAT *Bundesangestelltentarif* salary scale for public employees
Bauj. *Baujahr* construction year; (*Jahreszahl*) ... model
b. a.W. *bis auf Widerruf* until recalled *od.* revoked; until further notice
b. a. w. *bis auf weiteres* for the present, until further notice
BB *Bundesbahn* federal railway(s)
Bd. *Band* (*Buch*) volume (vol.); *Bund* (*Vereinigung*) union; association (assoc.)
Bde. *Bände* volumes (vols)
Bd.-Reg. *Bundesregierung* Federal Government (Fed. Govt)
bds. *beiderseits* on both sides
bef. *befugt* entitled, authorized (auth.)
Beg. *Beginn* start, commencement
Begl. *Beglaubigung* certification (cert.); *Begleichung* settlement, payment; *Begleitung* company (→ *Wörterverzeichnis*)
begl. *beglaubigt* certified (cert.); *beglichen* paid (pd)
beil. *beiliegend* enclosed (encl.)
Beisp. *Beispiel* example, instance
bek. *bekannt* known
belg. *belgisch* Belgian (Belg.)
Bem. *Bemerkung* remark, note, comment
Ber. *Bericht* report (rep.), account, commentary; *Berichtigung* correction (corr.)
bes. *besonder* special, particular (part.); *besonders* (e)specially (esp.), particularly (part.); above all
Besch. *Bescheinigung* certificate (cert.), (written) confirmation
Best. *Bestellung* order
Best.-Nr. *Bestellnummer* order number (ord. no.)

Betr. *Betreff, betrifft auf Briefkopf:* with reference to (Re, re, Re., re.)

betr. *betreffend, betrifft, betreffs* concerning, regarding, as to; ♥ *a.* re

beurl. *beurlaubt* on leave

Bev. *Bevölkerung* population (pop.)

bev(ollm). *bevollmächtigt* authorized (auth.)

Bez. *Bezahlung* pay(ment); *Bezeichnung* mark; *(Name)* name, term, designation (des.); *Beziehung* → *Wörterverzeichnis; Bezirk*district (dist.)

bez. *bezahlt* paid (pd); *bezüglich* regarding, concerning, with reference to; ♥ *a.* re

BF, bfr *belgische(r) Franc(s)* Belgian franc(s *pl.)* (BF, Bfr)

BGB *Bürgerliches Gesetzbuch* (German) Civil Code

Bge. *Berge* mountains (mtns)

BGH *Bundesgerichtshof* Federal High Court

BGS *Bundesgrenzschutz* Federal Border Guard

Bhf. *Bahnhof* station (sta., Sta.)

BI *Bürgerinitiative* citizens (action) group, civic action group, civic action

Bib. *Bibel* Bible

bildl. *bildlich* pictorial, visual(ly *adv.),* graphic(ally *adv.); Ausdruck etc.:* figurative(ly *adv.)* (fig.)

biogr. *biographisch* biographical(ly *adv.)* (biog.)

biol. *biologisch* biological(ly *adv.)* (biol.); *Anbau:* organic(ally *adv.)* (org.)

BIP *Bruttoinlandsprodukt* gross domestic product (GDP)

Bj. *Baujahr* construction year; *(Jahreszahl)* ... model

BKB *Benzinkostenbeteiligung in Annonce:* share petrol *(Am.* gas) costs

BLZ *Bankleitzahl* bank code

BND *Bundesnachrichtendienst* Federal Intelligence Service

bot. *botanisch* botanic(al) (bot.)

BPA *Bahnpostamt* station post office

BP a. *Bundespatent angemeldet* Federal Patent pending

Bq *Becquerel* becquerel (Bq.)

BR *Bayerischer Rundfunk* Bavarian Broadcasting Corporation

Br. *Breite* width (W., w.)

bras. *brasilianisch* Brazilian (Braz.)

BRD *Bundesrepublik Deutschland* Federal Republic of Germany (FRG)

brit. *britisch* British (Brit.)

BRK *Bayerisches Rotes Kreuz* Bavarian Red Cross

BRT *Bruttoregistertonne(n)* gross register ton(s *pl.)* (GRT)

BRZ *Bruttoraumzahl etwa* gross register tonnage *od.* tons *pl.*

bsd. *besonders* (e)specially (esp.), particularly (part.); above all

BSE BSE, Rinderwahn(sinn) *(abbr. für* bovine spongiform encephalopathy)

BSP *Bruttosozialprodukt* gross national product (GNP)

bspw. *beispielsweise* for instance, for example (e.g.)

btto. *brutto* gross (gr.)

Btx, btx *Bildschirmtext* viewdata

bürg. *bürgerlich* civil (civ.); civic; middle-class; bourgeois

Bw. *Bundeswehr* (German federal) armed forces, Bundeswehr

b. w. *bitte wenden* please turn over (PTO, pto)

bwgl. *beweglich* movable, mobile; flexible; moving *parts*

BWL *Betriebswirtschaftslehre* business administration, business economics

BWV *Bachwerkeverzeichnis (der Werke von Johann Sebastian Bach) etwa* Bach Catalog(ue) (BWV)

bzgl. *bezüglich* regarding, concerning, with reference to; ♥ *a.* re

bzw. *beziehungsweise* respectively (resp.); or rather ...

C

C *Celsius* Celsius, centigrade (C)

c *Cent(s)* cent(s *pl.)* (c); *Centime(s)* centime(s *pl.)* (c)

ca. *circa, ungefähr, etwa* about, approximately (approx.), circa (c.)

CAD *computer-aided design* CAD

calv. *calvin(ist)isch* Calvinist(ic)

CAM *computer-aided manufacture* CAM

cand. *candidatus, Kandidat* candidate (cand.)

CAT ♥ *computer-assisted trading* computergestützter Handel; *clear air turbulence (Turbulenzen); computerized axial tomography (Computertomographie)*

ccm *(veraltet für* cm³*) Kubikzentimeter* cubic centimetre(s *pl.), Am.* -er(s *pl.)* (cc)

CD *compact disc, CD* compact disc (CD)

CDU *Christlich-Demokratische Union* Christian Democratic Union

cf. *confer, vergleiche* compare (cf., cp., comp.)

chem. *chemisch* chemical (chem.)

chir. *chirurgisch* surgical (surg.)

christl. *christlich* Christian (Chr.)

chron. *chronisch* chronic; *chronologisch* chronological (chron., chronol.)

cl *Zentiliter* centilitre(s *pl.), Am.* -er(s *pl.)*

cm *Zentimeter* centimetre(s *pl.), Am.* -er(s *pl.)*

cm² *Quadratzentimeter* square centimetre(s *pl.), Am.* -er(s *pl.)* (sq.cm., cm²)

cm³ *Kubikzentimeter* cubic centimetre(s *pl.), Am.* -er(s *pl.)* (cc, cm³)

Co. ♥ *veraltet: Compagnie, Kompanie* company (Co., co.)

c/o *care of, bei, per Adresse* (c/o)

cos *Kosinus* cosine (cos)

CSFR *hist. Tschechische und Slowakische Föderative Republik* Czech and Slovak Federal Republic

CSSR *hist. Tschechoslowakische Sozialistische Republik* Czechoslovak Socialist Republic

CSU *Christlich-Soziale Union* Christian Social Union *(of Bavaria)*

ct *Cent(s)* cent(s *pl.)* (ct, *pl.* cts); *Centime(s)* centime(s *pl.)* (ct, *pl.* cts)

CT *Computertomographie* CT, computerized *(od.* computed) tomography

c. t. *cum tempore, mit akademischem Viertel* quarter past the hour

CTA *chemisch-technische Assistentin* (chemical) laboratory assistant

CVJM *Christlicher Verein Junger Menschen* Young Mens Christian Association (YMCA); Young Womens Christian Association (YWCA)

D

D *Durchgangszug, Schnellzug* express (train), fast train

D. *Deutschverzeichnis (der Werke von Franz Schubert) etwa* Deutsch Catalog(ue) (D); *Doktor der (protestantischen) Theologie* Doctor of Divinity (DD)

d. Ä. *der Ältere* the Elder

DAAD *Deutscher Akademischer Austauschdienst* German Academic Exchange Service

DAG *Deutsche Angestelltengewerkschaft* Trade Union of German Employees

dän. *dänisch* Danish (Dan.)

dank. *dankend* with thanks; gratefully

Darst. *Darsteller* actor(s *pl.),* performer(s *pl.); Darstellung* description; account; presentation; representation; interpretation.

dass. *dasselbe* the same (thing)

DAT *digital audio tape (Tonbandkassette für Digitalaufnahmen mit DAT-Rekordern)*

Dat. *Dativ* dative (case) (dat.); *Datum* date (d.)

DAX *(TM) Deutscher Aktienindex* German Stock Index

DB *Deutsche Bahn AG* German Railways, Plc; *Deutsche Bundesbank* German Federal Bank

DBP(a) *Deutsches Bundespatent (angemeldet)* German Federal Patent (pending)

dch. *durch* through; by; via

ddp *Deutscher Depeschendienst (German press agency)*

DDR *hist. Deutsche Demokratische Republik* German Democratic Republic (GDR)

DDT *Dichlordiphenyltrichloräthan* dichlorodiphenyltrichloroethane (DDT)

d. E. *durch Eilboten* express, *Am.* (by) special delivery

demn. *demnach (deshalb)* thus, so, consequently, therefore; *(demgemäß)* according to that, accordingly; *demnächst* soon, before long

ders. *derselbe* the same

desgl. *desgleichen* likewise, the same; similarly

Det. *Detail* detail

Dez. *Dezember* December (Dec., Dec)

dez. *dezimal* decimal

DFB *Deutscher Fußball-Bund* German Football Association

DGB *Deutscher Gewerkschaftsbund* Federation of German Trade Unions

dgl. *dergleichen* such, like that; the like, such a thing; *desgleichen* → *desgl.*

d. Gr. *der od. die Große* the Great

d. h. *das heißt* that is (i.e.)

Di. *Dienstag* Tuesday (Tue., Tue, Tues., Tues)

d. i. *das ist* that is (i.e.)

diag. *diagonal* diagonal(ly *adv.)*

Dial. *Dialekt* dialect (dial.); *Dialektik* dialectics *(sg. u. pl.)*

dienstl. *dienstlich* official, business ...; on business

diesj. *diesjährig* this years ...

DIN *Deutsches Institut für Normung* German Institute for Standardization; *veraltet für DIN-Norm (Deutsche Industrie-Norm)* German Industrial Standard

Din *Dinar* dinar(s *pl.)* (Din.)

Dipl. *Diplom* diploma (Dip., Dipl.); *Diplom...* qualified ...

dipl. *diplomatisch* diplomatic; *diplomiert* qualified

Dipl.-Ing. *Diplomingenieur* qualified engineer

Dipl.-K(au)fm. *Diplomkaufmann* business graduate

Dir. *Direktion* management; board of directors; managers office; head office (HO); *Direktor* manager; director (dir.); *Schule:* headmaster, *Am.* principal; *Dirigent* conductor

Diss. *Dissertation* (doctoral) thesis

Distr. *Distrikt* district (dist.)

DJ *DJ, deejay (Diskjockey)*

d. J. *der Jüngere* the Younger; *dieses Jahres* of this year

dkg *Dekagramm* decagram(s *pl.*), decagrammes(s *pl*)

DKP *Deutsche Kommunistische Partei* German Communist Party

dkr *dänische Krone(n)* Danish crown(s *pl.*)

DM *Deutsche Mark* (German) mark(s *pl.*)

d. M(ts). *d(ies)es Monats* of the present month, instant (inst.)

DNA *Deutscher Normenausschuss* German Committee of Standards

DNS *Desoxyribonukleinsäure* deoxyribonucleic acid (DNA)

Do. *Donnerstag* Thursday (Th., Th, Thur., Thur, Thurs., Thurs)

d. O. *der od. die od. das Obige* the above-mentioned

do. *dito* ditto (do.)

Dolm. *Dolmetscher(in)* interpreter

dopp. *doppelt* double (dbl., dble); in duplicate

DOS *disk operating system* Be'triebssystem, DOS

Doz. *Dozent* (university) lecturer, *Am.* assistant professor

Do.-Z(i). *Doppelzimmer* double (room)

DP *Deutsche Post AG* German Postal Services, Plc

dpa *Deutsche Presse-Agentur* German Press Agency

dpp. → *dopp.*

Dr, dr *Drachme(n)* drachma(s *pl.*), *pl. a.* drachmae (dr.)

Dr. *Doktor* doctor (Dr.)

d. R. *der Reserve* reserve ...

d. Red. *die Redaktion* the editor(s *pl.*) (Ed., ed., *pl.* eds)

Dr. jur. *doctor juris, Doktor der Rechte* Doctor of Laws (LLD)

DRK *Deutsches Rotes Kreuz* German Red Cross

Dr. med. *doctor medicinae, Doktor der Medizin* Doctor of Medicine (MD)

Dr. phil. *doctor philosophiae, Doktor der Philosophie* Doctor of Philosophy (PhD, DPhil)

Dr. rer. nat. *doctor rerum naturalium, Doktor der Naturwissenschaften* Doctor of Science (DSc, ScD)

Dr. theol. *doctor theologiae, Doktor der Theologie* Doctor of Divinity (DD)

DSB *Deutscher Sportbund* German Sports Association

dstl. → *dienstl.*

dt(sch.) *deutsch* German (Ger.)

DTP *desktop publishing* DTP, Desktop-Publishing

Dtzd. *Dutzend* dozen (doz.)

d. U. *der Unterzeichnete* the undersigned

Dupl. *Duplikat* duplicate (dupl.); *(Abschrift, Kopie)* copy

durchschn. *durchschnittlich* average (av.); *adv.* on (an) average

Durchw.(-Nr.) *Durchwahl(nummer)* direct dial(l)ing (number)

DV *Datenverarbeitung* DP, data processing

d. V(er)f. *der Verfasser, die Verfasserin* the author

d. v. J. *des vorigen Jahres* last years, of the previous year

DVO *Durchführungsverordnung* implementing ordinance

dyn. *dynamisch* dynamic(ally *adv.*)

DZ *Doppelzimmer* double (room)

dz *Doppelzentner* 100 kilogram(me)s

E

E *in Deutschland hist. Eilzug* fast train; *Elektrizität(s...)* electricity (...); *power station; Erdgeschoss* ground floor (grd. fl., G), *Am.* first floor (1st fl.); *Europastraße* European Highway *(passing through several countries)*

ea. *ehrenamtlich* honorary (hon.)

ebd. *ebenda* ibidem (ibid., ib.)

EBK *Einbauküche* fitted kitchen

EC *EuroCity* Eurocity (train)

ECU, Ecu *European currency unit(s), europäische Währungseinheit(en pl.) (ECU)*

Ed. *Edition, Ausgabe* edition (ed.)

ed. *edidit, hat herausgegeben* edited by (ed.)

EDV *elektronische Datenverarbeitung* electronic data processing (EDP, edp)

EEG *Elektroenzephalogramm* electroencephalogram (EEG)

EG *Europäische Gemeinschaft* European Community (EC)

e. G. *eingetragene Gesellschaft* registered *(Am.* incorporated) company

e. h. *ehrenhalber* honoris causa (h.c.)

ehel. *ehelich* marital, conjugal, matrimonial; legitimate *child*

ehem. *ehemalig* former, ex-...; *ehemals* formerly

Ehrw. *Ehrwürden* Reverend (Rev.)

EIB *Europäische Investitionsbank* European Investment Bank (EIB)

eidg(en.). *eidgenössisch* confederate; Swiss

eig(en)h. *eigenhändig* personal(ly *adv.*); oneself, with ones own hands

eig(tl). *eigentlich* actual(ly *adv.*), real(ly *adv.*); strictly speaking

Einbd. *Einband* binding; cover

eingetr. *eingetragen* ✝ registered (regd), *Am. a.* incorporated (Inc., inc.); *eingetreten* entered

Eing.-Dat. *Eingangsdatum* date of receipt

Einh. *Einheit* unit *(a. teleph.,)*

einschl. *einschlägig* relevant, appropriate; *einschließlich* including (incl.), inclusive of (incl.)

Einschr. *Einschreiben* registered letter; *Vermerk:* registered (regd)

einwdfr. *einwandfrei* perfect; flawless; impeccable *reputation etc.*

Einz.-Z(i). *Einzelzimmer* single (room)

EKD *Evangelische Kirche in Deutschland* Protestant Church in Germany

EKG, Ekg *Elektrokardiogramm* electrocardiogram (ECG, *Am.* EKG)

EL *Esslöffel (voll)* tbsp, *pl.* tbsp(s), *a.* tbs

el(ektr). *elektrisch* electric(al) (elec., elect.); *adv.* electrically

Empf. *Empfänger* recipient; addressee

empf. *empfohlen* recommended (rec.)

engl. *englisch* English (Eng.)

Entf. *Entfernung* distance

entggs. *entgegengesetzt* opposite (opp.); contradictory, opposing

entspr. *entsprechen(d)* → *Wörterverzeichnis*

entw. *entweder* either

EP *Europäisches Parlament* European Parliament

erb. *erbaut* built, erected

Erdg. *Erdgeschoss* ground floor (grd. fl.), *Am.* first floor (1st fl.)

erf. *erfolgt* effected; *erforderlich* required (req.), necessary (nec.)

erg. *ergänze* complement, supplement, add

erh. *erhalten* received (recd, recd); *in e-m Zustand:* preserved, in ... condition

Erl. *Erläuterung* explanation; (explanatory) note

erl. *erlaubt* permitted, allowed; *erledigt* finished, done; settled

erm. *ermäßigt* reduced (red.)

Ers. *Ersatz* substitute (subst.); *permanenter:* replacement; *(Vergütung)* compensation; *(Entschädigung)* indemnification; *Ersuchen* request (req.)

Erw. *Erwachsene(r)* adult(s *pl.*)

Erz. *Erzeugnis(se)* product(s *pl.*) (prod.); produce (prod.)

Erz.-Ber. *Erziehungsberechtigte(r)* parent; legal guardian

Esc. *Escudo* escudo (Esc.)

ESZB *Europäisches System der Zentralbanken* European System of Central Banks

Et. *Etage* floor (fl.), stor(e)y

et.al. *et alii, und andere* and others (et al.)

Etg. *Etage* floor (fl.), stor(e)y

etw. *etwaig* any; possible (poss.); *etwas* something (s.th.), anything

EU *Europäische Union* European Union (EU)

EuGH *Europäischer Gerichtshof* European Court of Justice (ECJ)

Euratom *Europäische Atomgemeinschaft* European Atomic Energy Community (Euratom)

eur(op). *europäisch* European (Eur.)

Europol *Europäisches Polizeiamt* European Police Office (Europol)

e.V. *eingetragener Verein* registered association *od.* society, incorporated (inc.)

ev. *evangelisch* Protestant (Prot.)

ev.-luth. *evangelisch-lutherisch* Lutheran (Luth.)

ev.-ref. *evangelisch-reformiert* Reformed (Church) (Ref. [Ch.])

evtl. *eventuell* possible (poss.), any; *adv.* possibly (poss.); if necessary (if nec.)

ew. *einstweilig* temporary, provisional; *ewig* eternal

EWG *hist. Europäische Wirtschaftsgemeinschaft* European Economic Community (EEC)

EWI *Europäisches Währungsinstitut* European Monetary Institute (EMI)

EWS *Europäisches Währungssystem* European Monetary System (EMS)

EWU *Europäische Währungsunion* European Monetary Union (EMU)

EWWU *Europäische Wirtschafts- und Währungsunion* European Economic and Monetary Union

Ex. *Exemplar(e)* copy, *pl.* copies; sample(s *pl.*)

exkl. *exklusiv* exclusive (excl.); select; *adv. exclusively (excl.); exklusive exclusive of (excl.), excluding (excl.), not counting, not including (not incl.)*

Expl. *Exemplar(e)* copy, *pl.* copies; sample(s *pl.*)

Expr. *Express* express (train)

Exz. *Exzellenz* Excellency (Exc.)

EZ *Einzelzimmer* single (room)

EZB *Europäische Zentralbank* European Central Bank (ECB)

F

F *Fahrenheit* Fahrenheit (F, f)

f., f *und folgende Seite* and following *page* (f., f)

Fa. *Firma* firm; *auf Briefadressen:* Messrs.

Fabr. *Fabrik* factory, works *(sg. u. pl.);*

Fabrikat make; brand; product (prod.)

Fahrg(est).-Nr. *Fahrgestellnummer* chassis number

F(ahr)z. *Fahrzeug* vehicle

Fak. *Fakultät* faculty (Fac.)

Fam. *Familie* family; *auf Briefadressen:* Mr Mrs ... (and family)

FC *Fußballclub* football club

FCKW *Fluorchlorkohlenwasserstoff* chlorofluorocarbon (CFC)

FD *hist.* *Ferndurchgangszug, Fernschnellzug* long-distance express (train)

FDGB *hist. DDR: Freier Deutscher Gewerkschaftsbund* Free Federation of German Trade Unions

FDJ *hist. DDR: Freie Deutsche Jugend* Free German Youth

F.D.P., FDP *Freie Demokratische Partei* Liberal Democratic Party; *Schweiz: Freisinnig-Demokratische Partei* Liberal Democratic Party

Feb(r). *Februar* February (Feb., Feb)

Fewo. *Ferienwohnung* holiday flat *od.* apartment (apt.)

FF *französischer Franc* French franc (FF)

ff., ff *und folgende Seiten* and following *pages* (ff., ff)

Ffm. *Frankfurt am Main* Frankfurt on the Main

FH *Fachhochschule* advanced technical college

Fig. *Figur* figure (fig.); diagram (diag.)

fig. *figürlich, figurativ* figurative(ly *adv.*) (fig.)

Fin. *Finanz(en)* finance(s)

fin. *finanziell* financial(ly *adv.*) (fin.)

finn. *finnisch* Finnish (Fin.)

FKK *Freikörperkultur* nudism

Fla *Fliegerabwehr* anti-aircraft defence, *Am.* -se

fl.k.u.w.W. *fließend kaltes und warmes Wasser* hot and cold running water

FM *Frequenzmodulation (Frequenzbereich der Ultrakurzwellen)* frequency modulation (FM)

fm *Festmeter* cubic metre(s *pl.*), *Am.* -er(s *pl.*)

fmdl. *fernmündlich* by telephone; telephone ...

Fmk *Finnmark Währung:* fin(n)mark

Föd. *Föderation* (con)federation, confederacy (confed.)

folg. *folgend(e)* following (foll.); next; subsequent

fortl. *fortlaufend* continuous(ly *adv.*), running; consecutively

Forts. *Fortsetzung* continuation

Forts.f. *Fortsetzung folgt* to be continued (to be contd)

fotogr. *fotografisch* photographic(ally *adv.*) (phot.)

FPÖ *Freiheitliche Partei Österreichs* Austrian conservative party

Fr. *Frau verheiratet:* Mrs; *Familienstand nicht erkennbar:* Ms; *Franken Währung:* (Swiss) franc(s *pl.*) (fr.); *Freitag* Friday (Fri., Fri)

frank. *frankiert* stamped; prepaid, post paid

frdl. *Grüße freundliche Grüße* kind regards (rgds)

freiw. *freiwillig* voluntary

Frh., Frhr *Freiherr* baron

Frl. *Fräulein* Miss

frz. *französisch* French (Fr.)

Ft *Forint* forint (Ft)

FU *Freie Universität (Berlin)* Free University

Fut. *Futur* future (tense) (fut.)

G

g *Gramm* gram(s *pl.*), gramme(s *pl.*) (g)

GAL *Grüne Alternative Liste* association of ecology-oriented parties

Gar. *Garantie* guarantee

gar. *garantiert* guaranteed (gtd, guar.)

garn. *garniert* trimmed, decorated; *Essen:* garnished

gastr. *gastronomisch* gastronomic(al); *Personal:* catering

GAU *größter anzunehmender Unfall* maximum credible accident (MCA), worst case scenario

GB *Gigabyte(s)* gigabyte(s *pl.*) (GB)

Gde. *Gemeinde* municipality; parish

Geb. *Gebäude* building (bldg); *Gebiet* district (dist.); area; *Gebirge* mountains *pl.* (mtns); *Gebühr(en)* charge(s *pl.*), fee(s *pl.*), rate(s *pl.*); *Geburt* birth

geb. *gebaut* built; erected; *geboren* born (b.); *geborene Schmidt etc.* nee; *gebunden* bound (bd)

Gebr. *Gebrüder* Brothers (Bros.)

gebr. *gebräuchlich* common, normal; *gebraucht* used, second-hand

Gebr.-A. *Gebrauchsanleitung (a. Gebr.-Anl.), Gebrauchsanweisung (a. Gebr.-Anw.)* directions *(od.* instructions) *pl.* for use

gef. *gefallen* killed in action (KIA)

gegr. *gegründet* founded; established (estab., est.)

geh. *geheftet Buch:* stitched; *geheim* secret

gek. *gekürzt* abridged (abr.)

gelt. *geltend* valid, in effect; current *prices etc.*

gem. *gemacht* made; *gemäß* according to; in compliance with; *gemischt* mixed

gen. *genannt* called, named; *erwähnt: (the)* said, *(the)* above-mentioned; *genehmigt* approved; authorized

Gen. *Genitiv* genitive (gen.); *Genossenschaft* cooperative

Gen.-Dir. *Generaldirektor* general manager, chairman, *Am.* president

Gen.-Sekr. *Generalsekretär* secretary general

geogr. *geographisch* geographic(al) (geog.)

geol. *geologisch* geologic(al) (geol.)

geom. *geometrisch* geometric(al) (geom.)

gepr. *geprüft* tested; checked; certified *document etc.*

ger. *gerichtlich* judicial(ly *adv.*); legal(ly *adv.*)

Ges. *Gesellschaft* ♀ company, *Am. a.* corporation (corp.); *(Vereinigung)* society (soc.), association (assoc.); *Gesetz* law, act

gesch. *geschäftlich* business ...; on business; *geschieden* divorced (div.)

geschl. *geschlossen* closed; private *performance etc.*

geschr. *geschrieben* written; *adv.* in writing

Geschw. *Geschwindigkeit* speed; rate *of increase etc.*

ges. gesch. *gesetzlich geschützt* patented; registered (regd)

gesp. *gesperrt Straße:* closed; *Scheck:* stopped

gest. *gestorben* died (d.)

Gestapo *Geheime Staatspolizei hist. (in Nazi-Deutschland)* secret state police

getr. *getrennt* separate(ly *adv.*)

Gew. *Gewicht* weight (wt)

gew. *gewöhnlich* usually (usu.)

gez. *gezeichnet vor der Unterschrift:* signed (sgd)

GG *Grundgesetz pol.* constitution

ggf(s). *gegebenenfalls* should the occasion arise; if necessary (if nec.); if applicable

Ggs. *Gegensatz* contrast; opposite (opp.)

ggs. *gegensätzlich* opposite (opp.), contrary; *gegenseitig* mutual

Ggw. *Gegenwart* present; *(Anwesenheit)* presence

ggz. *gegengezeichnet* countersigned

gltd. *geltend* valid, in effect; current *prices etc.*

gltg. *gültig* valid, good; effective, in force

GmbH *Gesellschaft mit beschränkter Haftung* private limited (liability) company *(etwa* plc)

gram(m). *grammatisch* grammatical

graph. *grafisch* graphic(ally *adv.*)

Grdfl. *Grundfläche* (surface) area

griech. *griechisch* Greek (Gk)

gr.-orth. *griechisch-orthodox* Greek Orthodox

GStA *Generalstaatsanwalt* prosecutor general

Gült. *Gültigkeit* validity

GUS *Gemeinschaft unabhängiger Staaten* Commonwealth of Independent States (CIS)

gzj. *ganzjährig* all-year ...; all year round

H

H *Haltestelle bus etc.* stop; *meteor. Hoch (-druckgebiet)* high(-pressure area)

H. *Heft* number (No., no.); *Höhe* height (H., h., hgt)

h *Hekto...* hecto...; *Uhr* hours (hrs); *morgens: mst* a.m., *nachmittags, abends: mst* p.m.; *hora, Stunde* hour (hr)

ha *Hektar* hectare(s *pl.*) (ha)

habil. *habilitatus, habilitiert* habilitated

haftb. *haftbar* responsible, liable

Halbj. *Halbjahr* half-year, six months *pl.*

halbj(hl). *halbjährlich* half-yearly, semiannual(ly *adv.*); *adv.* every six months

haupts. *hauptsächlich adv.* mainly, chiefly, essentially; *adj.* main, most important, essential

Hbf. *Hauptbahnhof* main *(od.* central) station (main sta., cen. *od.* cent. sta.)

HC *Hockeyclub* hockey club

h. c. *honoris causa, ehrenhalber* honoris causa (h.c.), honorary (hon.)

hdgm. *handgemacht* handmade

Hdlg. ♀ *Handlung* business, shop, store

HD-Öl *Öl für schwere Betriebsbelastung* heavy-duty oil

hdschr. *handschriftlich* handwritten; *adv.* in writing

...hdt. *...hundert* ... hundred (hund.)

helv. *helvetisch* Helvetian; Helvetic

herg(est). *hergestellt* produced (prod.), made, built

Herst. *Hersteller* manufacturer; *Herstellung* production (prod.), manufacture (manuf., manufac.)

HF *Hochfrequenz* high frequency (HF, h.f.)

hfl *(holländischer) Gulden* Dutch guilder(s *pl.*) *od.* florin(s *pl.*) *(Gld, gld.)*

Hfn *Hafen* harbo(u)r

Hft(g). *Haftung* liability; guarantee

Hg. *Herausgeber(in)* publisher (pub., publ.); editor (Ed., ed.)

hg. *herausgegeben (von)* published (by) (pub., publ.); edited (by) (ed.)

HGB *Handelsgesetzbuch* Commercial Code

Hi-Fi *höchste Klangtreue* high fidelity

(hi-fi)

hins. *hinsichtlich* concerning, regarding, as to

hist. *historisch* historic(al), *adv.* historically

HIV *human immune deficiency virus* (*ein Virus, das Aids auslöst*)

Hiwi *Hilfswissenschaftler(in)* *univ.* assistant

Hj. *Halbjahr* half-year, six months *pl.*

HK *Handelskammer* Chamber of Commerce

hl *Hektoliter* hectolitre(s *pl.*), *Am.* -er(s *pl.*) (hl)

hl. *heilig* holy; *heilige(r)* Saint (St, St.) *Peter etc.*

HO *hist. DDR: Handelsorganisation* state-owned store, hotel, and restaurant cooperative

Hob. *Hoboken-Verzeichnis* (*der Werke von Joseph Haydn*) *etwa* Hoboken Catalog(ue) (Hob.)

hochd. *hochdeutsch* standard *od.* High German

Hochw. *R.C. Hochwürden* Reverend (Rev.)

höfl. *höflich(st)* kindly, politely

holl(änd). *holländisch* Dutch

HP *Halbpension* half-board

hPa *Hektopascal* hectopascal (hPa)

Hpt. *Haupt...* main, chief, principal, head ...

hpts. *hauptsächlich* *adv.* mainly, chiefly, essentially; *adj.* main, most important, essential

HR *Hessischer Rundfunk* Hessian Broadcasting Corporation

Hr(eg). *Handelsregister* Commercial Register

Hr(n). *Herr(n)* Mr

Hrsg. *Herausgeber(in)* publisher (pub., publ.); editor (Ed., ed.)

hrsg. *herausgegeben (von)* published (by) (pub., publ.); edited (by) (ed.)

Hs.-Nr. *Hausnummer* house number (hse no.)

HTL *höhere technische Lehranstalt* polytechnical school

Hubr. *Hubraum* cubic capacity

HVertr., H.-Vertr. *Handelsvertrag* trade agreement; *Handelsvertretung* commercial agency *od.* agents *pl.*

HVerw., H.-Verw. *Hauptverwaltung* head office (H.O., HO), headquarters *sg. u. pl.* (HQ)

hydr. *hydraulisch* hydraulic(ally *adv.*)

Hyp. *Hypothek* mortgage

hypoth. *hypothetisch* hypothetical(ly *adv.*)

Hz *Hertz* hertz *sg. u. pl.* (Hz), cycle(s *pl.*) per second (cps, c/s)

hzb. *heizbar* heatable; with heating

Hzg. *Heizung* heating

I

i *auf Schildern: Information, Auskunft* information

i. *im, in* in (the); *innen* inside

I. A., i. A. *im Auftrag* per procurationem, by proxy (pp, p.p.)

i. Allg. *im Allgemeinen* generally (gen.), in general; *(im Ganzen)* on the whole

i. a. W. *in anderen Worten* in other words

ib. → *ibd.*

i. B. *im Besonderen* in particular

ibd. *ibidem, ebenda, -dort* in the same place (ib., ibid.)

IC *InterCity* intercity (train)

ICE *InterCityExpress* intercity express (train)

i. D. *im Dienst* on duty; *im Durch-*

schnitt on (an) average

i. d. M(in). *in der Minute* per minute

i. d. R. *in der Regel* as a rule

i. d. Sek. *in der Sekunde* per second (p.s.)

i. d. St(d). *in der Stunde* per hour (p.h.)

i. E. *im Einzelnen* in detail *od.* particular

i. e. *id est, das heißt, das ist* that is (i.e.)

i. e. S. *im eigentlichen Sinne* in the true sense (of the word); in the proper sense; *im engeren Sinne* in the narrow(er) sense

IFO *Institut für Wirtschaftsforschung* Institute for Economic Research

IG *Industriegewerkschaft* industrial union

i. G. *im Ganzen* on the whole; altogether

i. H. *im Hause* on the premises

IHK *Industrie- und Handelskammer* Chamber of Industry and Commerce

i. H. v. *in Höhe von* (to the amount) of; at the rate of

i. J. *im Jahre* in (the year)

i. K. *in Kürze (bald)* shortly, soon; *(kurz)* briefly

ill. *illustriert* illustrated (illust., illus.); pictorial

IM *hist. DDR: inoffizieller Mitarbeiter (des Staatssicherheitsdienstes)* informer to the State Security Service

i. M. *im Monat* in (the month of) *July etc.; (monatlich)* monthly, per month

Imm. *Immobilien* real estate *sg.*, property *sg.*

Imp. *Imperativ* imperative (mood) (imp., imper.); *Import* import(ing); import(s *pl.*) (imp.)

Imperf. *Imperfekt* imperfect (tense) (imp.)

inbegr. *inbegriffen* included; including, inclusive of (incl.)

Ind. *Index* index (ind.); *Indikativ* indicative (mood) (ind.); *Industrie* industry (ind.)

i. N. d. *im Namen des od. der* in the name of; on behalf of

indir. *indirekt* indirect (ind.)

indiv. *individuell* individual(ly *adv.*) (indiv., individ.); personal (pers.); original (orig.)

inf. *infolge* owing to; as a result of

Ing. *Ingenieur* engineer (eng.)

Inh. *Inhaber* owner, proprietor (prop., propr.); holder; *Inhalt* contents *pl.* (cont.)

inkl. *inklusive* including, inclusive of (incl.)

innerl. *innerlich* internal(ly *adv.*) (int.); inner

inoff. *inoffiziell* unofficial(ly *adv.*)

insb(es). *insbesondere* particularly, (e)specially ([e]sp.), in particular

insges. *insgesamt* altogether, in all

int. *intern* internal(ly *adv.*) (int.); *international* international (int., intl)

intern. *international* international (int., intl)

Interpol *Internationale Kriminalpolizeiliche Organisation* International Criminal Police Organization (Interpol)

inwf. *inwiefern* in what way, how; to what extent

inww. *inwieweit* to what extent

IOK *Internationales Olympisches Komitee* International Olympic Committee (IOC)

IQ *Intelligenzquotient* intelligence quotient (IQ)

IR *InterRegio* fast train serving longer distances

i. R. *im Ruhestand* retired (ret., retd)

IRK *Internationales Rotes Kreuz* Inter-

national Red Cross (IRC)

ISBN *internationale Standardbuchnummer* international standard book number (ISBN)

ISDN *teleph. integrated services digital network* ISDN

IT *Informationstechnologie* information technology

ital. *italienisch* Italian (It., Ital.)

i. Tr. *in der Trockenmasse* percentage of fat etc. in dry matter

i. Ü. *im Übrigen* incidentally; (as) for the rest; *(außerdem)* besides

IV *Industrieverband* federation of industries

I. v. *Irrtum vorbehalten* errors excepted (e.e.)

I. V. *in Vertretung* in place of; on behalf of; *in Brief:* (signed) for; *in Vorbereitung* being prepared, in preparation (in prep.)

i. v. *intravenös* intravenous(ly *adv.*)

IVF *In-vitro-Fertilisation* in vitro fertilization (IVF)

IWF *Internationaler Währungsfonds* International Monetary Fund (IMF)

J

J *Joule* joule(s *pl.*) (J.)

Jan. *Januar* January (Jan., Jan)

jap. *japanisch* Japanese (Jap.)

Jb. *Jahrbuch* yearbook (YB, Y.B.)

Jg. *Jahrgang* → *Wörterverzeichnis*

Jgd. *Jugend* youth

Jgg. *Jahrgänge* *pl. von* **Jg.** → *Wörterverzeichnis*

JH *Jugendherberge* youth hostel (Y.H.)

Jh. *Jahrhundert* century (c., cent.)

jhrl. *jährlich* annual(ly *adv.*)

Jr., jr., jun. *junior, der Jüngere* junior (Jun., jun., Jur, Jr)

Jul. *Juli* July (Jul., Jul)

Jun. *Juni* June (Jun., Jun)

jur. *juristisch* legal (leg.); juridical (jur. id.)

K

Kal. *Kalender* calendar; *Kaliber* calibre, *Am.* -er (cal.)

Kan. *Kanada* Canada (Can.); *Kanadier* Canadian (Can.); *Kanal* canal

Kap. *Kapitel* chapter (ch.)

Kapt. *Kapitän* captain (Capt.)

Kard. *Kardinal* cardinal (Card.)

kart. *kartoniert* hardcover

Kat *Katalysator* catalytic converter, catalyst (cat.)

Kat. *Katalog* catalog(ue) (cat.); *Kategorie* category

kath. *katholisch* Catholic (Cath.)

kaufm. *kaufmännisch* commercial (comm., com.), business ...

KB *Kilobyte(s)* kilobyte(s *pl.*) (KB)

kcal *Kilo(gramm)kalorie(n)* kilocalorie(s *pl.*), kilogram(me) calorie(s *pl.*) (kcal, Cal.)

Kennz. *Kennzeichen* *mot.* registration (*Am.* license) number; *Kennziffer* code number; index (number); *Inserat:* box number

Kfm. *Kaufmann* businessman; trader, dealer; agent

kfm. *kaufmännisch* commercial (comm., com.), business ...

Kfz *Kraftfahrzeug* motor vehicle

Kfz.-Vers. *Kraftfahrzeugversicherung* motor (*Am.* automobile) insurance

KG *Kommanditgesellschaft* limited partnership

kg *Kilogramm* kilogramme(s *pl.*), *Am.* kilogram(s *pl.*) (kg)

kgl. *königlich* royal

Abkürzungen

kHz *Kilohertz* kilohertz (kHz), kilocycle(s *pl.*) (per second)

KI *künstliche Intelligenz* AI, artificial intelligence

KJ *Kilojoule* kilojoule(s *pl.*) (kJ)

k.k. *kaiserlich-königlich* imperial and royal

KKW *Kernkraftwerk* nuclear power station *od.* plant

Kl. *Klasse* class (cl.); *Schule: Brit. a.* form, *Am. a.* grade; ✝ grade, quality

km *Kilometer* kilometre(s *pl.*), *Am.* -er(s *pl.*) (km)

km/h, km/st. *Kilometer pro Stunde* kilometres (*Am.* -ers) per hour (kph)

KN *Kochnische* kitchenette

Koeff. *Koeffizient* coefficient

Komf. *Komfort* conveniences *pl.*

komf. *komfortabel* comfortable; *Wohnung:* well-appointed, luxury ...

Komp. *Kompanie* company; *Komponist* composer

Konf. *Konferenz* conference (conf.); *Konfession* (religious) denomination (denom.); *Konföderation* confederation, confederacy

Konj. *Konjugation* conjugation; *Konjunktion* conjunction (conj.); *Konjunktiv* subjunctive (subj.)

Konstr. *Konstruktion* construction (constr.); design

Kontr. *Kontrakt* contract

Konz. *Konzert* concert; concerto (conc.); *Konzern* group

KP *Kommunistische Partei* Communist Party (CP)

KPdSU *hist. Kommunistische Partei der Sowjetunion* Communist Party of the Soviet Union (CPSU)

kpl. *komplett* complete

kr *Krone Währungseinheit:* crown

Kr. *Kreis* (administrative) district (dist.)

Krhs. *Krankenhaus* hospital (hosp.)

Kripo *Kriminalpolizei* criminal investigation department (CID)

krit. *kritisch* critical

Krs. *Kreis* (administrative) district (dist.)

Kr.-Vers. *Krankenversicherung* health insurance

KSZE *Konferenz über Sicherheit und Zusammenarbeit in Europa* Conference on Security and Cooperation in Europe (CSCE)

Kt. *Kanton* canton

Kto. *Konto* (bank) account (a/c)

Kto.-Nr. *Kontonummer* account number (a/c no.)

Ktr.-Nr. *Kontrollnummer* code number

k.u.k. *kaiserlich und königlich* imperial and royal

künstl. *künstlerisch* artistic; *künstlich* artificial; synthetic

KV *Köchelverzeichnis* Köchel (catalog[ue]) (K); *Kraftverkehr* motor traffic *(mst Bestandteil des Firmennamens von Busunternehmen)*

kV *Kilovolt* kilovolt(s *pl.*) (kV)

KW *Kurzwelle* short wave (SW)

kW *Kilowatt* kilowatt(s *pl.*) (kW)

kWh *Kilowattstunde(n)* kilowatt-hour(s *pl.*)

KZ *Konzentrationslager* concentration camp

kzfr. *kurzfristig* short-term ...; *adv.* at short notice

L

L. *(italienische) Lira od. pl. Lire* lira, *pl.* lire *od.* liras; *Länge* length (L., l.)

l *Liter* litre(s *pl.*), *Am.* -er(s *pl.*) (l)

l. *links* left (l.); on *od.* to the left

Lab. *Laboratorium* lab(oratory)

Landkr. *Landkreis* district

landw. *landwirtschaftlich* agricultural (agric.); farm ...

lat. *lateinisch* Latin (Lat.)

lbd. *lebend* living; alive

l.c. *loco citato, am angegebenen Ort* in the place cited (l.c.)

Ldg. *Ladung* load, freight; cargo; shipment

led. *ledig* unmarried, single (sgl.)

Leg. *Legierung* alloy

leg. *legal* legal(ly *adv.*)

Lekt. *Lektion* chapter (ch.), unit; lesson

lfd. *laufend* current, running, ongoing; *adv.* continuously, regularly

lfdm., lfd. m. *laufende Meter* running metres, *Am.* -ers

lfd. M. *laufenden Monats* of this month

lfd. Nr. *laufende Nummer* (serial) number

Lf(r)g. *Lieferung* delivery; consignment, shipment

Lf.-Zt., Lfzt. *Lieferzeit* delivery period

LG *Landgericht, östr. Landesgericht* district court

lgfr. *langfristig* long-term ...

Lit. *italienische Lira od. pl. Lire* lira, *pl.* lire *od.* liras; *Literatur* literature (lit.)

lit(er). *literarisch* literary (lit.)

liz. *lizensiert* licensed, *Am.* -ced

LKW, Lkw *Lastkraftwagen* lorry, *bsd. Am.* truck

loc.cit. *loco citato, am angegebenen Ort* in the place cited (loc. cit.)

log *Logarithmus* logarithm (log.)

log. *logisch* logical(ly *adv.*)

lok. *lokal* local

lösl. *löslich* soluble (sol.)

LP *Langspielplatte* long-playing record (LP)

LPG *hist. DDR: landwirtschaftliche Produktionsgenossenschaft* collective farm

LSD *Lysergsäurediäthylamid* lysergic acid diethylamide (LSD)

Lsg. *Lösung* solution (sol.) *(a.)*

lt. *laut* according to; as per

ltd. *leitend* managerial; chief ...

Ltg. *Leitung* direction; management; supervision

luftd. *luftdicht* airtight

luth. *lutherisch* Lutheran (Luth.)

lux. *luxemburgisch* Luxemb(o)urg ...

LW *Langwelle* long wave (LW)

lx *Lux* lux (lx)

M

M *hist. DDR: Mark* mark(s *pl.*)

M. *Magister* Master (M)

m *Meter* metre(s *pl.*), *Am.* -er(s *pl.*) (m); *Milli...* milli... (m)

m. *männlich* male (m., m); masculine (m., m, masc.); *mit* with (w.)

m² *Quadratmeter* square metre(s *pl.*), *Am.* -er(s *pl.*) (sq.m, m²)

m³ *Kubikmeter* cubic metre(s *pl.*), *Am.* -er(s *pl.*) (cu.m, m³)

MA *Mittelalter the* Middle Ages *pl.*

M.A. *Magister Artium* Master of Arts (MA)

mA *Milliampere* milliampere(s *pl.*) (mA)

MAD *Militärischer Abschirmdienst* Military Counter-Intelligence Service

Mag. *Magazin → Wörterverzeichnis*

magn. *magnetisch* magnetic

m.A.n. *meiner Ansicht nach* in my opinion

männl. *männlich* male (m., m); masculine (m., m, masc.); for men, mens ...

Mar. *Marine* Navy

masch. *maschinell* machine ...; machine-...; mechanical(ly *adv.*); *adv. a.* by machine

maschr. *maschinenschriftlich* typewritten, typed; in typescript

math. *mathematisch* mathematical (math.)

m.a.W. *mit anderen Worten* in other words

Max. *Maximum* maximum (max.)

max. *maximal* maximum, top ...; *adv.* maximally (max.)

MAZ *magnetische Bildaufzeichnung* video tape recording (VTR)

MB *Megabyte(s)* megabyte(s *pl.*) (MB)

MdB, M. d. B. *Mitglied des Bundestages* Member of the Bundestag

MdL, M. d. L. *Mitglied des Landtages* Member of the Landtag

mdl. *mündlich* oral(ly *adv.*); verbal(ly *adv.*)

MDR *Mitteldeutscher Rundfunk* Central German Broadcasting Corporation

m. E. *meines Erachtens* in my opinion; as I see it; *mit Einschränkungen* with reservations

mech. *mechanisch* mechanical(ly *adv.*) (mech.)

med. *medizinisch* medical (med.); medicinal

MESZ *mitteleuropäische Sommerzeit* Central European Summer Time (CEST)

mex. *mexikanisch* Mexican (Mex.)

MEZ *mitteleuropäische Zeit* Central European Time (CET)

MG *Maschinengewehr* machine gun (MG)

mg *Milligramm* milligramme(s *pl.*), *Am.* milligram(s *pl.*) (mg)

mhd. *mittelhochdeutsch* Middle High German (MHG)

MHz *Megahertz* megahertz (MHz), megacycles per second (Mc/s)

Mi. *Mittwoch* Wednesday (Wed., Wed)

Mia. *Milliarde(n)* billion, *pl.* billion(s) (bn); *Brit. obs.* thousand million

mil(it). *militärisch* military (mil., milit.)

Mill. *Million(en)* million, *pl.* million(s) (m)

Min. *Minimum* minimum (min.)

Min., min. *Minute(n)* minute(s *pl.*) (min.)

min. *minimal* minimal; minimum (min.)

minderj. *minderjährig* underage

Mio. *Million(en)* million, *pl.* million(s) (m)

Mitbest. *Mitbestimmung* co-determination; worker participation

Mitgl. *Mitglied* member (mem.)

Mitw. *Mitwirkung* participation; assistance, cooperation; contribution

MM *Monatsmiete(n pl.)* monthly rent(s *pl.*); per calendar month (pcm, PCM)

mm *Millimeter* millimetre(s *pl.*), *Am.* -er(s *pl.*) (mm)

Mo. *Montag* Monday (Mon., Mon)

m(ö)bl. *möbliert* furnished (furn.)

mod. *modern* modern (mod.); *modisch* fashionable, *adv.* -bly, stylish(ly *adv.*)

mögl. *möglich* possible (poss.); practicable, feasible; *(eventuell)* potential (pot.); *möglichst ...* as ... as possible

moh(am)., mohammed. *mohammedanisch* Muslim, Moslem (Moham.)

mosl. *moslemisch → moh(am).*

mot. *motorisiert* motorized

MP *Maschinenpistole* submachine gun; *Militärpolizei* military police (MPs, *Aufschrift:* MP)

Mrd. *Milliarde(n)* billion, *pl.* billion(s) (bn); *Brit. obs.* thousand million

Mrz. *März* March (Mar., Mar)

MS, Ms. *Manuskript* manuscript (MS, ms.)

Mss. *Manuskripte pl.* manuscripts (MSS, mss.)

mst. *meist(ens)* mostly, usually (usu.)

Mt. *Monat* month (mth)

MTA *medizinisch-technische Assistentin* medical laboratory assistant

mtl. *monatlich* monthly, per calendar month (pcm, PCM)

multilat. *multilateral* multilateral

m. ü. M. *Meter über (dem) Meer(esspiegel)* metres *(Am.* -ers) above sea level

mus. *musikalisch* musical (mus.); *musisch Fach:* fine arts ...

MW *Mittelwelle* medium wave (MW)

m. W. *meines Wissens* as far as I know

MwSt. *Mehrwertsteuer* value-added tax (VAT), *bsd. Am.* sales tax

N

N *Nord(en)* north (N); *Nahverkehrszug* local *od.* commuter train

n. *nach* after; to

N(a)chf. *Nachfolger* successor

Nachfr. *Nachfrage* inquiry (inq.), enquiry; ⊕ demand

Nachm. *Nachmittag* afternoon

nachm. *nachmittags* in the afternoon (p.m., pm)

Nachtr. *Nachtrag* addendum (add.); supplement (supp., suppl.); postscript (PS)

näml. *nämlich* namely, that is (to say) (viz., i.e.); to be precise

NATO, Nato *Nordatlantikpakt-Organisation* North Atlantic Treaty Organization (NATO, Nato)

NB *notabene* note well (NB)

Nbk. *Nebenkosten* extra costs *(od.* expenses), extras

n. Br. *nördlicher Breite* northern latitude (N lat.); ... degrees north (°N)

n. Chr. *nach Christus* anno Domini (AD)

NDR *Norddeutscher Rundfunk* Northern German Broadcasting Corporation

neb. *neben* next to, beside; by; compared to; *(außer)* in addition to

neg. *negativ* negative(ly *adv.)* (neg.)

neutr. *neutral* neutral

neuw. *neuwertig* (as good as) new, as new, not used

n. Gr. *nach Größe* according to size

nhd. *neuhochdeutsch* New High German (NHG)

n. J. *nächsten Jahres* of next year, next years ...

nkr *norwegische Krone(n)* Norwegian crown(s *pl.)* (Nkr)

n. M. *nächsten Monats* of next month, next months ...

nmtl. *namentlich* by name; *(besonders)* especially (esp.), particularly (part.)

N. N. *nomen nominandum etwa* to be appointed; *(a.* **NN)** *Normalnull etwa* sea level

NO *Nordost(en)* northeast (NE)

nordd(t). *norddeutsch* North German (N Ger.)

nördl. *nördlich* northern, north; *Wind:* northerly; *adv.* north (N)

norm. *normal* normal(ly *adv.)*

norw. *norwegisch* Norwegian (Norw.)

notf. *notfalls* if need be, if necessary (if nec.)

notw. *notwendig* necessary (nec.)

Nov. *November* November (Nov., Nov)

NPD *Nationaldemokratische Partei Deutschlands* National-Democratic Party of Germany

NR *Nichtraucher(in)* non-smoker

Nr. *Nummer* number (No., no.)

Nrn. *Nummern pl.* numbers (Nos., nos.)

NRW *Nordrhein-Westfalen* North Rhine-Westphalia

NS *Nachschrift* postscript (PS); *Nationalsozialismus* National Socialism; *nationalsozialistisch* National Socialist (Nazi)

NSt *Nebenstelle* branch; *teleph.* extension (extn)

N. T. *Neues Testament* New Testament (NT)

nto. *netto* net (nt., nt)

n. u. Z. *nach unserer Zeitrechnung* anno Domini (AD)

NW *Nordwest(en)* northwest (NW)

O

O *Ost(en)* east (E)

o. *oben* above; *oder* or; *ohne* without (w/o)

o. a. *oben angeführt* above(-mentioned)

o. Ä. *oder Ähnliches* or the like

ÖAMTC *Österreichischer Automobil-, Motorrad- und Touring-Club* Austrian Automobile, Motorcycling and Touring Association

OB *Oberbürgermeister* mayor; *in GB:* Lord Mayor

o. B. *ohne Befund* negative (neg.)

ÖBB *Österreichische Bundesbahnen* Austrian Federal Railways

Obb. *Oberbayern* Upper Bavaria

Oberfl. *Oberfläche* surface

obh. *oberhalb* above

oblig. *obligatorisch* obligatory, compulsory

od. *oder* or

OEZ *osteuropäische Zeit* Eastern European Time (EET)

offiz. *offiziell* official(ly *adv.);* formal

öff(tl). *öffentlich* public(ly *adv.);* in public

Offz. *Offizier* (commissioned) officer (Off.)

OHG *offene Handelsgesellschaft* (general) partnership

ökon. *ökonomisch* economic; *(sparsam)* economical(ly *adv.)* (econ.)

Okt. *Oktober* October (Oct., Oct)

ö. L. *östlicher Länge* eastern longitude (E long.)

OLG *Oberlandesgericht* Higher Regional Court

OP *Operationssaal* operating theatre *(Am.* room)

Op. *Operation* operation (op.); *Opus, Werk* opus (op.)

op. cit. *opere citato, im angegebenen Werk* in the work quoted *od.* cited (from)

Opf. *Oberpfalz the* Upper Palatinate

ÖPNV *öffentlicher Personennahverkehr* local public transport

o. Prof. *ordentlicher Professor* (full) professor (Prof., prof.)

ORB *Ostdeutscher Rundfunk Brandenburg* Eastern German Broadcasting Corporation of Brandenburg

Orch. *Orchester* orchestra (Orch., orch.)

ORF *Österreichischer Rundfunk* Austrian Broadcasting Corporation

Orig. *Original* original (orig.)

orig. *original* original (orig.); genuine; *originell* original(ly *adv.)* (orig.)

orth. *orthodox eccl.* Orthodox (Orth.)

örtl. *örtlich* local(ly *adv.)*

ostd(t). *ostdeutsch* East German (E Ger.)

österr. *österreichisch* Austrian (Aus.)

östl. *östlich* eastern, east; *Wind:* easterly; *adv.* east (E)

OSZE *Organisation für Sicherheit u. Zusammenarbeit in Europa* Organization for Security and Co-operation in Europe (OSCE)

o. U. *ohne Unterschied* indiscriminately; irrespective of *nationality etc.*

ÖVP *Österreichische Volkspartei* Austrian Peoples Party

Oz. *Ozean* ocean (Oc., oc.)

o. Zw. *ohne Zweifel* undoubtedly; doubtless

P

P, p *Peso(s)* peso(s *pl.)* (P, p)

P. *Pater* Father (Fr., Fr)

PA *Patentanmeldung* patent application; *Postamt* post office (PO)

p. A. *per Adresse, bei* care of (c/o)

päd. *pädagogisch* pedagogical, educational.

p. Adr. → *p. A.*

Par(agr). *Paragraph* section (sect.), article (art.); *(Absatz)* paragraph (para., par.)

Parl. *Parlament* parliament (Parl.)

Part. *Partei* party; *Parterre* ground floor (grd. fl.), *Am.* first floor (1st fl.); *Partizip* participle (part.)

Pat. *Patent* patent (pat.)

PC *Personalcomputer* personal computer (PC, pc)

p. Chr.(n.) *post Christum (natum), nach Christus (nach Christi Geburt)* anno Domini (AD)

PDS *Partei des Demokratischen Sozialismus* Party of Democratic Socialism

perf. *perfekt* perfect(ly *adv.)* (perf.)

pers. *persönlich* personal(ly *adv.)* (pers.); *adv. a.* in person

Pf *Pfennig* pfennig(s *pl.)* (Pf., pf.)

Pfd. *Pfund* German pound(s *pl.)*

PH *Pädagogische Hochschule* college of education, *Am.* teachers college

pharm. *pharmazeutisch* pharmaceutical (pharm.)

philol. *philologisch* philological(ly *adv.)* (philol.)

philos. *philosophisch* philosophical(ly *adv.)* (philos.)

photogr. → *fotogr.*

phys. *physikalisch* physical(ly *adv.)* (phys.); *physisch* physical(ly *adv.),* somatic(ally *adv.)*

PIN *persönliche Identifikationsnummer* personal identification number, PIN number (PIN)

Pkt. *Paket* parcel, *Am.* package; *Punkt* point (pt)

PKW, Pkw *Personenkraftwagen* (motor)car, *Am. a.* auto(mobile)

Pl. *Platz* square (Sq.); *Plural* plural (pl.)

PLO *palästinensische Befreiungsorganisation* Palestine Liberation Organization (PLO)

plötzl. *plötzlich* sudden(ly *adv.)*

PLZ *Postleitzahl* postcode, *Am.* zip code

pol. *politisch* political(ly *adv.)* (pol.); *polizeilich police ...; adv.* of *(od.* by) the police

poln. *polnisch* Polish (Pol.)

port(ug). *portugiesisch* Portuguese (Port.)

Pos. *Position* position (pos.)

pos. *positiv* positive (pos.)

Postf. *Postfach* post office box (PO box, POB)

postw. *postwendend* by return (of post), by return mail

pp., p. p., ppa, p. pa. *per procura (-tionem), in Vollmacht* per pro, per proxy (p.p., pp)

PR *Public Relations, Öffentlichkeitsarbeit* public relations (PR)

prakt. *praktisch* practical(ly *adv.*)

Präs. *Präsidium (Vorsitz)* presidency, chair(manship); *(Vorstand)* executive committee (exec. comm.); *(Dienststelle)* headquarters *sg. u. pl.* (HQ)

priv. *privat* private(ly *adv.*); *adv. a.* in private

Priv.-Doz. *Privatdozent(in)* unsalaried lecturer, *Am. etwa* associate professor

Prof. *Professor* professor (Prof.)

prot. *protestantisch* Protestant (Prot.)

Prov. *Provinz* province (Prov., prov.); *Provision* commission

prov. *provisorisch* provisional (prov.), temporary (temp.)

PS *Pferdestärke(n)* horsepower (HP, h.p.); *Postscript(um), Nachschrift* postscript (PS, ps.)

Pseud. *Pseudonym* pseudonym (pseud.)

psych. *psychisch* psychological(ly *adv.*) (psych.); mental(ly *adv.*)

psychol. *psychologisch* psychological(ly *adv.*) (psych.)

PTA *pharmazeutisch-technische Assistentin* pharmaceutical laboratory assistant

Pta, *pl.* **Ptas** *Peseta(s pl.), Pesete(n pl.)* peseta(s *pl.*) (pta, *pl.* ptas)

PTT *Schweiz:* **Post, Telefon, Telegraf; Schweizerische Post-, Telefon- und Telegrafenbetriebe** Swiss Postal, Telephone and Telegraph Services

PVC *Polyvinylchlorid* polyvinyl chloride (PVC)

Q

qcm *(veraltet für* cm^2) *Quadratzentimeter* square centimetre(s *pl.*), *Am.* -er(s *pl.*) (sq. cm)

q. e. d. *quod erat demonstrandum* (= *was zu beweisen war*) (QED)

qkm *(veraltet für* km^2) *Quadratkilometer* square kilometre(s *pl.*), *Am.* -er(s *pl.*) (sq. km)

qm *(veraltet für* m^2) *Quadratmeter* square metre(s *pl.*), *Am.* -er(s *pl.*) (sq. m)

Qual. *Qualität* quality (qual.)

Quant. *Quantität* quantity (quant.)

R

R *Reaumur* Reaumur; *Rand (südafrikan. Währung)* rand (R)

r. *rechts* right (r.); on *(od.* to) the right

RA *Rechtsanwalt* lawyer, *Brit. a.* solicitor (Sol., Solr); *plädierender: Brit.* barrister (Bar., Barr.), *Am.* attorney (att., atty)

RAF *BRD:* **Rote-Armee-Fraktion** Red Army Faction

RAM *random access memory* Direktzugriffsspeicher (RAM)

RB *RegionalBahn* local train; *RB* **Radio Bremen** Broadcasting Corporation of Bremen, Radio Bremen

Rbl *Rubel* rouble(s *pl.*), ruble(s *pl.*) (Rbl, rbl., R., r.)

rd. *rund* about, around, roughly, approximately (approx.)

Rdf. *Rundfunk* broadcasting corporation *(od.* company); radio

RE *RegionalExpress* regional fast train

rechtl. *rechtlich* legal(ly *adv.*) (leg.)

rechtsw. *rechtswidrig* illegal(ly *adv.*), unlawful(ly *adv.*), contrary to the law

Ref. *Referat (Abteilung)* department (Dept., dept), section (sect.)

reform. *eccl.* *reformiert* Reformed (Ref.)

Reg. *Regierung* government (Gov., gov., Govt, govt); *Regiment* regiment (Regt, Rgt)

Reg.-Bez. *Regierungsbezirk* administrative district

regelm. *regelmäßig* regular(ly *adv.*) (reg.)

Regt. *Regiment* regiment (Regt, Rgt)

REH *Reiheneckhaus* end-terrace

Rel. *Relation* relation(ship); proportion; *Religion* religion (rel.)

rel. *relativ* relative(ly *adv.*) (rel.); *adv.* comparatively (comp., compar.); *religiös* religious(ly *adv.*) (rel.)

Rep. *Reparatur* repair(s *pl.*); *Republik* Republic (Rep.)

Reps(e) *BRD:* **Republikaner** *pl.* (members of the) Republican Party

res. ✝ *reserviert* reserved (res.)

resp. *respektive* → *Wörterverzeichnis*

Rest. *Restaurant* restaurant

restl. *restlich* remaining

RGW *hist.* *Rat für gegenseitige Wirtschaftshilfe* Council for Mutual Economic Assistance (Comecon)

RH *Reihenhaus* terraced(d house)

Rh *Rhesusfaktor positiv, Rh-positiv* rhesus positive (Rh pos.)

rh *Rhesusfaktor negativ, Rh-negativ* rhesus negative (Rh neg.)

Richtl. *Richtlinie(n)* guideline(s *pl.*); *pl. a.* (general) directions, instructions

R. I. P. *requiescat in pace, er (od. sie) ruhe in Frieden* may he *(od.* she) rest in peace (RIP)

rk, r.-k. *römisch-katholisch* Roman Catholic (RC)

RNS *Ribonukleinsäure* ribonucleic acid (RNA)

ROM *read only memory* Festspeicher (ROM)

röm. *römisch* Roman (Rom.)

Rp. *Schweiz:* **Rappen** (Swiss) centime(s *pl.*)

RT *Registertonne(n)* register ton(s *pl.*) (reg. t.)

Rückf. *Rückfahrt* return journey *(od.* trip); journey *(od.* way) back

Rücks. *Rückseite* back, rear; reverse (rev.); overleaf

rückw. *rückwärtig* back ..., rear ...; *rückwärts* backwards; *rückwirkend* retroactive; retrospective(ly *adv.*); backdated

russ. *russisch* Russian (Russ.)

S

S *Süd(en)* south (S); *Schilling* schilling (S); → *S-Bahn*

S. *Seite* page (p.)

s *Sekunde(n)* second(s *pl.*) (s, sec.)

SA *hist.* *Sturmabteilung* (Nazi) stormtroops *pl. od.* stormtroopers *pl.*

Sa. *Samstag, Sonnabend* Saturday (Sat., Sat)

s.a. *siehe auch* see also

Sakr. *Sakrament(e)* sacrament(s *pl.*)

Samml. *Sammlung* collection

san. *sanitär* sanitary

Sanat. *Sanatorium* sanatorium, *Am.* sanitarium

Sa.-Nr. *Sammelnummer* collective number

SB- *Selbstbedienungs...* self-service ...

S-Bahn *Schnellbahn, Stadtbahn Zug:* suburban train; *System:* suburban railway

SBB *Schweizerische Bundesbahnen* Swiss Federal Railways

s. Br. *südlicher Breite* southern latitude (S lat.); ... degrees south (°S)

SC *Sportclub* sports club

schott. *schottisch* Scots, Scottish; Scotch *whisky*

schriftl. *schriftlich* written; in writing

Schw. *Schwester* sister

schwed. *schwedisch* Swedish

schweiz. *schweizerisch* Swiss

scil. *scilicet, nämlich* namely, that is (to say)

SDR *Süddeutscher Rundfunk* Southern German Broadcasting Corporation

s. d. *siehe dort* see there; *sine dato, ohne Erscheinungsjahr* no date (n.d.)

Sdg. ✝ *Sendung* consignment, shipment

SDS *hist.* *Sozialistischer Deutscher Studentenbund* Association of German Socialist Students

SE *StadtExpress* (local) city express train

sec. *Sekunde(n)* second(s *pl.*) (s, sec.)

SED *hist. DDR:* *Sozialistische Einheitspartei Deutschlands* Socialist Unity Party of Germany

Sek., sek. *Sekunde(n)* second(s *pl.*) (s, sec.)

selbst. *selbstständig* independent; self-employed

selbst(verst). *selbstverständlich* natural; obvious; *adv.* of course

Sem. *Semester* semester (sem.)

sen. *senior, der Ältere* senior (sen., Sen., Sr, Snr)

Sept. *September* September (Sept., Sept, Sep, Sep)

sex. *sexuell* sexual(ly *adv.*)

SFB *Sender Freies Berlin* Broadcasting Corporation of Free Berlin

sFr., sfr *Schweizer Franken* Swiss franc(s *pl.*) (SF, Sfr)

Sg. *Singular* singular (sing.)

s. g. *so genannt* so-called

SGB *Schweizerischer Gewerkschaftsbund* Federation of Swiss Trade Unions

sign. *signiert* signed

sin *Sinus* sine (sin)

Sing. *Singular* singular (sing.)

SJ *Societatis Jesu, von der Gesellschaft Jesu, Jesuit* Jesuit

skand. *skandinavisch* Scandinavian (Scan., Scand.)

S. Kgl. H. *Seine Königliche Hoheit* His Royal Majesty

skr *schwedische Krone(n)* Swedish crown(s *pl.*) (Kr, Skr)

sm *Seemeile(n)* nautical mile(s *pl.*) (n.m.)

SMV *Schülermitverwaltung* *etwa* school council

SO *Südost(en)* southeast (SE)

So. *Sonntag* Sunday (Sun., Sun)

s. o. *siehe oben* see above

sof. *sofern* if, provided (that), as long as; *sofort* at once, immediately; *sofortig* immediate; prompt

SOS *save our ship (od. souls)* international *Notsignal*

sowj(et). *sowjetisch* soviet

soz. *sozial* social

span. *spanisch* Spanish (Span.)

SPD *Sozialdemokratische Partei Deutschlands* Social Democratic Party of Germany

spez. *speziell* special, particular; *adv. a.* (e)specially ([e]sp.)

SPÖ *Sozialistische Partei Österreichs* Austrian Socialist Party

SPS *Sozialdemokratische Partei der Schweiz* Social Democratic Party of Switzerland

SR *Saarländischer Rundfunk* Broadcasting Corporation of the Saarland

Sr. *Senior, der Ältere* senior (Sr, Snr, Sen., sen.)

s. R. *siehe Rückseite* see overleaf

SRG *Schweizerische Radio- und*

Fernsehgesellschaft Swiss Broadcasting Corporation

SS *Sommersemester* summer semester; *Schutzstaffel* hist. SS *(elite corps of the Nazi Party)*

SS. *Sanctae od. Sancti, die Heiligen* saints (SS.)

SSV *Sommerschlussverkauf* summer sales *pl.*

St. *Sankt, der Heilige* saint (St, St.); *Stock*(*werk*) floor (fl.), stor(e)y; *Stück* piece(s *pl.*) (pc., *pl.* pcs)

s. t. *sine tempore, ohne* (*akademisches*) *Viertel, pünktlich* sharp

staatl. *staatlich* state ...; government ...; state-owned; *adv.* officially

Stasi hist. DDR: *Staatssicherheitsdienst* state security service, Stasi

stat. *statistisch* statistical

Std. *Stunde*(*n*) hour(s *pl.*) (h., *pl. a.* hrs, *sg. a.* hr)

stdl. *stündlich* hourly; every hour

Stdn. *Stunden* hours (h., hrs)

Stellg. *Stellung* position, *(Arbeitsplatz a.)* post

stellv. *stellvertretend* deputy (dep.), assistant (asst); vice-...; *adv.* on behalf of ...; in place of ...

StGB *Strafgesetzbuch* Penal Code

St(.-)**Kl.** *Steuerklasse* tax bracket

StPO *Strafprozessordnung* Code of Criminal Procedure

StR *Studienrat* etwa secondary school teacher

Str. *Straße* street (St.); road (Rd)

StRin *Studienrätin* etwa secondary school teacher

stud. *studiosus, Student* student

StVO *Straßenverkehrsordnung* (road) traffic regulations *pl.; in GB:* Highway Code

s. u. *siehe unten* see below

Subj. *Subjekt* subject (subj.)

subj. *subjektiv* subjective(ly *adv.*) (subj.)

südd(**t**). *süddeutsch* South German (S Ger.)

südl. *südlich* southern, south, *Wind:* southerly; *adv.* south (S)

SV *Spielvereinigung in Vereinsnamen: etwa* sports association

SVP *Schweizerische Volkspartei* Swiss Peoples Party; *Südtiroler Volkspartei* South Tyrolean Peoples Party

SW *Südwest*(*en*) southwest (SW)

SWF *Südwestfunk* Southwestern German Broadcasting Corporation

sym. *symmetrisch* symmetric(al); *adv.* symmetrically

synth. *synthetisch* synthetic(ally *adv.*)

syst. *systematisch* systematic(ally *adv.*)

T

T *meteor. Tief*(*druckgebiet*) low(-pressure area)

T. *Teil* part (pt, p.); *Tiefe* depth (D., d.)

t *Tonne*(*n pl.*) ton(s *pl.*) (t., t); tonne(s *pl.*) (t)

Tab. *Tabelle* table (tab.); chart; *Tabulator* tabulator (tab.)

Tabl. *Tablette*(*n*) tablet(s *pl.*)

t(**äg**)**l.** *täglich* daily, a *(od.* per) day

Tar.-Gr. *Tarifgruppe* salary *(od.* wage) bracket

tats. *tatsächlich* real(ly), actual(ly)

Tb(**c**) *Tuberkulose* tuberculosis (TB)

techn. *technisch* technical(ly *adv.*) (tech.); technological(ly *adv.*) (technol.)

TEE hist. *Trans-Europ-Express* Trans-European Express (TEE)

Teiln.-Geb. *Teilnahmegebühr (bei e-m Kurs etc.)* fee; *Teilnehmergebühr*

(für Telefon, Telefax etc.) charge, rate

t(**ei**)**lw.** *teilweise* partial(ly *adv.*); partly

Tel. *Telefon* (tele)phone (tel.)

tel(**ef**). *telefonisch* telephone ...; by (tele)phone

Telegr. *Telegramm* telegram (teleg.)

telegr. *telegrafisch* telegraphic(ally *adv.*); by telegraph

Tel.-Nr. *Telefonnummer* (tele)phone number (tel. no.)

Temp. *Temperatur* temperature (temp.)

Terr. *Terrasse* patio, terrace

TG *Tiefgarage* underground car park

TH *technische Hochschule* college *(od.* institute) of technology

theor. *theoretisch* theoretical(ly *adv.*)

TL *türkische Lira* (*pl.* Lire), *türkisches* (*pl. türkische*) *Pfund* Turkish lira (*pl.* lire *od.* liras) (TL); Turkish pound(s *pl.*) (£ T); *Teelöffel* (*voll*) tsp., *pl.* tsp(s)

-tlg. *-teilig* ...-part ..., in *(od.* consisting of) ... parts; ...-piece *suit etc.*

tödl. *tödlich* fatal, mortal(ly *adv.*); lethal *dose etc.;* deadly; *danger etc.* to life

...tsd. *...tausend ...* thousand (thou.)

TU *technische Universität* technical university; college *(od.* institute) of technology

türk. *türkisch* Turkish (Turk.)

TÜV *Technischer Überwachungs-Verein etwa* safety standards authority; technical control board; *in GB:* MOT (= Ministry of Transport) → *TÜV im Wörterverzeichnis*

TV *Television* television (TV)

typ. *typisch* typical(ly *adv.*)

U

U *Umleitung* diversion; *U-Bahn* underground (U), *Am.* subway

u. *und* and

u. a. *und andere*(*s*) and others (other things); *unter anderem* (*od. anderen*) among other things, inter alia; among others

u. Ä. *und Ähnliche*(*s*) and the like

U. (*od.* **u.**) **A. w. g.** *um Antwort wird gebeten* (R.S.V.P.), RSVP)

U-Bahn *Untergrundbahn* underground (U), *Am.* subway

Überschr. *Überschrift* title; *(Schlagzeile)* headline

übl. *üblich* usual, customary, normal (norm.)

U-Boot *Unterseeboot* submarine (sub.)

u. d(**er**)**gl.** (**m.**) *und dergleichen* (*mehr*) and the like, and so forth

u. d. M. *unter dem Meeresspiegel* below sea level

ü. d. M. *über dem Meeresspiegel* above sea level

UdSSR hist. *Union der Sozialistischen Sowjetrepubliken* Union of Soviet Socialist Republics (USSR)

u. E. *unseres Erachtens* in our opinion, as we see it; *unter Einschränkung* with reservations

u. f(**f**). *und folgende sg.* (*pl.*) and following

UFO, Ufo *unbekanntes Flugobjekt* unidentified flying object (UFO)

ugs. *umgangssprachlich* colloquial(ly *adv.*) (colloq.)

U-Haft *Untersuchungshaft* custody, detention (pending trial)

UKW *Ultrakurzwelle* ultrashort wave (USW), *etwa* very high frequency (VHF), *Am.* frequency modulation (FM)

ult. *ultimo* at the end *(od.* on the last day) of the month

Umf. *Umfang* circumference (cir., circ.);

extent, size; range; dimension

U/min *Umdrehungen in der* (*od. pro*) *Minute* revolutions per minute (r.p.m., rpm)

U-Musik *Unterhaltungsmusik* easy listening, light music

unbek. *unbekannt* unknown; *(nicht vertraut)* unfamiliar

unbez. *unbezahlt* unpaid

unehel. *unehelich* illegitimate (illegit.)

unentsch. *unentschieden* undecided; *Frage:* open; *Sport:* end in a draw

unerw. *unerwünscht* undesirable, unwelcome

unfrw. *unfreiwillig* involuntary; compulsory

ung(**ar**). *ungarisch* Hungarian (Hung.)

ungebr. *ungebräuchlich* unusual, uncommon

ungew. *ungewiss* uncertain; *(unentschieden)* undecided; *ungewöhnlich* unusual(ly *adv.*); *(bemerkenswert)* exceptional(ly *adv.*), remarkable, *adv.* -bly

Uni F, **Univ.** *Universität* university (Univ., univ.)

unreg(**elm**). *unregelmäßig* irregular(ly *adv.*) (irreg.)

unt(**erh**). *unterhalb* below

Unterz. *Unterzeichnete*(*r*) *the* undersigned

unverb. *unverbindlich* not binding; without obligation; *Stellungnahme:* noncommittal

unverh. *unverheiratet* unmarried (unm.), single (sgl.)

unvollst. *unvollständig* incomplete

unz. *unzählig* innumerable, countless

URL *uniform resource locator* URL *(Web-Adresse)*

Url. *Urlaub (Ferien)* holiday(s), *bsd. Am.* vacation; leave

urspr. *ursprünglich* original(ly *adv.*) (orig.)

US(**A**) *Vereinigte Staaten* (*von Amerika*) United States (of America) (USA, US)

usf. *und so fort* and so forth

USt. *Umsatzsteuer* turnover tax

u. U. *unter Umständen* (*möglicherweise*) possibly (poss.), perhaps (perh.); *(notfalls)* if need be

u. ü. V. *unter üblichem* (*od. dem üblichen*) *Vorbehalt* within the usual reservations

UV *Ultraviolett* ultraviolet (UV)

u. v. a. (**m.**) *und viele*(*s*) *andere* (*mehr*) and many more *(od.* others); and many other things

UVP *Umweltverträglichkeitsprüfung* environmental compatability assessment

u. W. *unseres Wissens* as far as we know

Ü-Wagen *Übertragungswagen* outside broadcast van *od.* unit (OB van *od.* unit)

u. zw. *und zwar* namely; that is (to say); → *zwar im Wörterverzeichnis*

V

V *Volt* volt(s *pl.*) (V)

V. *Vers* verse (v.), line (l.)

v. *versus, gegen* versus (v., vs.); *von, vom* of; from; by

VAE *Vereinigte Arabische Emirate* United Arab Emirates (UAE)

VB *Verhandlungsbasis* or near(est) offer (o.n.o.)

vbdl. *verbindlich* binding; obliging

v. Chr. *vor Christus* before Christ (BC)

v. D. *vom Dienst* on duty; in charge

VDE *Verband Deutscher Elektrotechniker* Association of German Electricians

VdK *Verband der Kriegs- und Wehrdienstopfer, Behinderten und Sozialrentner etwa* Association of the Victims of War and Military Service, Disabled Persons and Social Insurance Pensioners

VDS *Vereinigte Deutsche Studentenschaften* Association of German Student Bodies

VEB *hist. DDR: volkseigener Betrieb* state-owned enterprise *(od.* company)

ver. *vereinigt* united

verantw. *verantwortlich* responsible; *official etc.* in charge

verb. *verbessert* improved; corrected (corr.), revised (rev.); *verboten* prohibited, not allowed *(od.* permitted), forbidden

Verb(dg). *Verbindung* connection; combination; union

V(er)f. *Verfasser* author

v(er)gl. *vergleiche* confer (cf.); compare (cp., comp.)

vergr. *vergriffen Buch:* out of print (o.o.p.)

verh. *verheiratet* married (m., mar.)

Verk. *Verkauf* sale

Verl. *Verlag* publishing house *(od.* company), publishers *pl.; Verleger* publisher (publ.)

verm. *vermählt* married (m., mar.), wed(ded); *vermisst* missing; missing in action (MIA)

veröff. *veröffentlicht* published (publ.)

verp. *verpackt* packaged

verpfl. *verpflichtet* obliged; bound

Vers.-Anst. *Versicherungsanstalt* insurance company

vertr. *vertraglich* contractual(ly *adv.), adv. a.* by contract; *vertraulich* confidential (confid.), *adv.* confidentially, in confidence

Verw. *Verwaltung* administration (admin), management (mngmt)

verw. *verwandt* related *to; verwitwet* widowed

verz. *verzeichnet* listed; registered (regd); recorded

Vet. *Veteran(en) Brit.* ex-serviceman, *pl.* -men, *Am.* veteran(s *pl.)* (vet, *pl.* vets); *Veterinär* veterinary surgeon, *Am.* veterinarian (vet, *pl.* vets)

V-Gespräch *Voranmeldungsgespräch* person-to-person call

v. g. u. *vorgelesen, genehmigt, unterschrieben* read, confirmed, signed

v. H. *vom Hundert* per cent, percent (p.c., pc, %)

VHS *Volkshochschule Institution:* adult education program(me); *Kurse:* adult evening classes *pl.*

v. J. *vorigen Jahres* of last year, last years

VL *vermögenswirksame Leistung(en)* employers contribution(s *pl.) to* tax-deductible employee savings scheme

v. l. n. r. *von links nach rechts* from left to right

v. M. *vorigen Monats* of last month

V-Mann *Verbindungsmann, Vertrauensmann* contact; *(Spitzel) a.* informer

v. o. *von oben* from above

Vollm. *Vollmacht* full power(s *pl.),* authority (auth.); power of attorney

vollst. *vollständig* complete(ly *adv.),* entire(ly *adv.);* full(y *adv.)*

Vopo *hist. DDR: Volkspolizei* Peoples Police; *Volkspolizist* member of the Peoples Police

Vorbeh. *Vorbehalt* reservation(s *pl.)*

Vorbest. *Vorbestellung* advance booking (adv. bkg); *Zimmer:* booking (bkg), reservation (res.); ✞ advance order

vorl. *vorläufig* temporary, *adv.* -ily (temp.), provisional(ly *adv.)* (prov.); *adv. a.* for the present

Vorm. *Vormittag* morning

vorm. *vormalig* former; *vormals* formerly (known as); *vormittags* in the morning (a.m., am)

Vors. *Vorsitzende(r)* chairperson, chairman (chm., chmn), chairwoman; chair; ✞ president (Pres., pres.); *Partei, Gewerkschaft:* leader

vorw. *vorwärts* forward (fwd); *vorwiegend* predominantly, mainly, chiefly

VP *Vollpension* (full) board and lodging, full board, *Am.* American plan (AP); *Volkspolizei hist. DDR:* Peoples Police

VPS *Video-Programmierungssystem* video preprogram(m)ing system

VR *Volksrepublik* Peoples Republic

v. T. *vom Tausend* per thousand

v. u. *von unten* from below

VW *Volkswagen* Volkswagen (VW, F vee-dub)

VWL *Volkswirtschaftslehre* economics *pl.*

W

W *Watt* watt(s *pl.)* (W); *West(en)* west (W)

WAA *Wiederaufbereitungsanlage* reprocessing plant

wahrsch. *wahrscheinlich* probable (prob.), likely; *adv.* probably

wbl. *weiblich* female (fem.), feminine (fem.); womens ...

WC *Wasserklosett* toilet (WC)

Wdh(lg). *Wiederholung* repetition; *TV, thea.* repeat, rerun; *Sport:* replay

WDR *Westdeutscher Rundfunk* Western German Broadcasting Corporation

WE *Wärmeeinheit(en)* thermal *od.* caloric unit(s *pl.)*

werkt. *werktags* (on) weekdays

westd(t). *westdeutsch* West German (W Ger.)

westl. *westlich* western, west; *Wind:* westerly; *adv.* west (W)

WEU *Westeuropäische Union* Western European Union (WEU)

WEZ *westeuropäische Zeit* Greenwich Mean Time (GMT)

WG *Wohngemeinschaft* flat share, flat sharing (community)

WGB *Weltgewerkschaftsbund* World Federation of Trade Unions (WFTU)

Whg. *Wohnung* apartment (apt.), *Brit. a.* flat

wirtsch. *wirtschaftlich* economic (econ.); *adv.* economically; financial(ly *adv.)* (fin.)

wiss. *wissenschaftlich* academic(ally *adv.); (naturwissenschaftlich)* scientific(ally *adv.)* (sci.)

w. L. *westlicher Länge* Western longitude (W long.); ... degrees West (°W)

WM *Weltmeisterschaft* world championship; *Fußball:* World Cup

wö. *wöchentlich* weekly, every week

WS *Wintersemester* winter semester

WSV *Winterschlussverkauf* winter sales *pl.*

Wwe. *Witwe* widow

WWU *Wirtschafts- und Währungsunion* Economic and Monetary Union (EMU)

WWW *World Wide Web Internet:* WWW,www

Wz. *Warenzeichen* trademark (TM)

Z

Z. *Zahl* number; *Zeile* line (l.); *Zeit* time

z. *zu, zum, zur* at; to

zahlr. *zahlreich* numerous(ly *adv.); in* large numbers

z. B. *zum Beispiel* for instance, for example (e.g.)

z. b. V. *zur besonderen Verwendung* for special duty

ZDF *Zweites Deutsches Fernsehen* Second Channel of German Television

ZDL *Zivildienstleistende(r) conscientious objector conscripted to do community work*

zeitgen. *zeitgenössisch* contemporary (contemp.)

zeitl. *zeitlich* temporal, time ...

zeitw. *zeitweilig, -weise* occasionally, from time to time, now and then

Zentr. *Zentrale* head office (H.O., HO); headquarters *sg. u. pl.* (HQ); control room; *Zentrum* centre, *Am.* -er

zentr. *zentral* central(ly *adv.); adv. a.* in the centre *(Am.* center)

ZH *Zentralheizung* central heating (CH)

z. H(d). *zu Händen* attention (attn); care of (c/o)

Zi. *Ziffer* figure (fig.); number (No., no.); *(Unterabsatz)* clause; *(Punkt)* item; *Zimmer* room (number) (rm, rm no.)

zit. n. *zitiert nach* ... quoted after ...

ziv. *zivil* civilian (civ.); civil *aviation* (civ.)

ZK *pol. Zentralkomitee* central committee

Zl *Zloty* zloty, *pl.* zloty(s) (Zl)

Zlg. *Zahlung* payment

ZOB *zentraler Omnibusbahnhof* bus *(od.* coach) station

zool. *zoologisch* zoological (zool.)

ZPO *Zivilprozessordnung* code of civil procedure

Zs., *pl.* Zss. *Zeitschrift(en)* journal (jour.), *pl.* journals; periodical(s *pl.)*

Zstzg. *Zusammensetzung* composition (comp.); compound (comp., compd)

z. T. *zum Teil* partly, partially (part.)

Ztg. *Zeitung* newspaper

Ztr. *Zentner (metric)* hundredweight(s *pl.)* (cwt)

Ztschr. *Zeitschrift* magazine (mag., mag); periodical

Zub. *Zubehör* accessories *pl.;* attachments *pl.;* fittings *pl.*

zuf. *zufällig* accidental(ly *adv.),* chance ...; *adv. a.* by chance; *zufolge* as a result *(od.* consequence) of; according to (acc. to)

zugel. *zugelassen* allowed; *behördlich:* licensed, *Am. a.* -ced, *Kraftfahrzeug: a.* registered (regd), *Arzt:* qualified

z(u)gl. *zugleich* at the same time

zul. *zulässig* permissible; safe *load; Höchstgeschwindigkeit:* (maximum) permissible *speed*

zur. *zurück* back; *an* return to

zus. *zusammen* together (tog.)

Zuschr. *Zuschrift* letter; reply

zust. *zuständig Behörde:* relevant, appropriate; *(befugt)* competent; *(verantwortlich)* responsible

z(u)zgl. *zuzüglich* plus

zw. *zwecks* for the purpose of; with a view to; *zwischen* between; among

ZwSt. *Zweigstelle* branch (office)

zz., zzt. *zurzeit* at the moment, at present

z. Z(t). *zur Zeit* at the time of ...

Geographische Namen

Folgende Liste bietet eine Auswahl an geographischen sowie touristisch und historisch interessanten Orten, Gebieten und Stätten. Offizielle Ländernamen blieben, mit wenigen Ausnahmen, unberücksichtigt. Eine Liste der deutschen und österreichischen Bundesländer sowie der schweizerischen Kantone finden Sie unmittelbar hinter diesem Anhangteil.

A

Aachen Aachen, Aix-la-Chapelle
Abessinien *hist.* Abyssinia
Abruzzen, die *the* Abruzzi
Addis Abeba Addis Ababa
Admiralitätsinseln, die *the* Admiralty Islands, *the* Admiralties
Adria, die *the* Adriatic (Sea)
Adrianopel *hist.* Adrianople
Afrika Africa
Afghanistan Afghanistan
Ägäis, die *the* Aegean (Sea)
Ägäischen Inseln, die *the* Aegean Islands
Agrigent Agrigento
Ägypten Egypt
Akaba Aqaba, Akaba
Akkra Accra
Akropolis, die *the* Acropolis
Aktium *hist.* Actium
Albanien Albania
Aleuten, die *the* Aleutian Islands
Alexandrien Alexandria
Algerien Algeria
Algier Algiers
Alpen, die *the* Alps
Alpenvorland, das *the* foothills of the Alps
Altaigebirge, das *the* Altai Mountains
Amazonas, der *the* Amazon
Amerika America
Anatolien Anatolia
Andalusien Andalusia
Anden, die *the* Andes
Andorra Andorra
Angola Angola
Antarktis, die *the* Antarctic, Antarctica
Antillen, die *the* Antilles
Antiochia Antioch
Antwerpen Antwerp
Äolischen Inseln, die *the* Aeolian Islands; → *a.* **Liparischen Inseln**
Apennin, der, Apenninen, die *the* Apennines, *the* Apennine Mountains
Apenninenhalbinsel, die *the* Apennine Peninsula
Appalachen, die *the* Appalachians, *the* Appalachian Mountains
Apulien Apulia
Äquatorialguinea Equatorial Guinea
Aquitanien *hist.* Aquitaine
Arabien Arabia
Arabische Wüste, die *the* Arabian Desert
Aralsee, der Lake Aral
Ardennen, die *the* Ardennes
Arena-Kapelle, die *(in Padua)* the Scrovegni *(od.* Arena) Chapel
Argentinien Argentina, *the* Argentine
Arktis, die *the* Arctic
Ärmelkanal, der *the* English Channel, *the* Channel
Armenien Armenia
Aserbaidschan Azerbaijan

Asien Asia
Asowsche Meer, das *the* Sea of Azov
Assuan Aswan
Assyrien *hist.* Assyria
Asturien *hist.* Asturias
Athen Athens
Äthiopien Ethiopia
Atlantik, der *the* Atlantic (Ocean)
Atlasgebirge, das *the* Atlas Mountains
Ätna, der Mount Etna
Attika *hist.* Attica
Austerlitz Slavkov ŭ Brna; *hist.* Austerlitz
Australasien Australasia
Australien Australia
Azoren, die *the* Azores

B

Babel → **Turm von Babel**
Babylonien *hist.* Babylonia
Bagdad Baghdad
Bahamainseln, die, Bahamas, die *the* Bahamas
Baikalsee, der Lake Baikal
Balearen, die *the* Balearic Islands
Balkan, der → 1. **Balkanhalbinsel**; 2. **Balkanstaaten**; 3. **Balkangebirge**
Balkangebirge, das *the* Balkan Mountains
Balkanhalbinsel, die *the* Balkan Peninsula
Balkanstaaten, die *the* Balkan States, *the* Balkans
Baltikum, das *the* Baltic (States), *the* Baltics
Bangladesch Bangladesh
Barentssee, die *the* Barents Sea
Basel Basel, Basle
Basiliuskathedrale, die *(in Moskau)* St Basils Cathedral
Baskenland, das *the* Basque Provinces
Bayerischen Alpen, die *the* Bavarian Alps
Bayerische Wald, der *the* Bavarian Forest
Bayern Bavaria
Belgien Belgium
Belgrad Belgrade
Benelux-Länder, die *the* Benelux Countries
Bengalen *(Landschaft u. hist.)* Bengal
Beringmeer, das *the* Bering Sea
Beringstraße, die *the* Bering Strait
Bern Bern(e)
Berner Alpen, die *the* Bernese Alps
Berner Oberland, das *the* Bernese Oberland
Bessarabien Bessarabia
Bikini, Bikiniatoll, das Bikini
Birma Burma
Biskaya, die → **Golf von Biskaya**
Blaue Grotte, die *(auf Capri)* the Blue Grotto
Bodensee, der Lake Constance

Böhmen Cechy; *hist.* Bohemia
Böhmen und Mähren *hist.* Bohemia-Moravia
Böhmerwald, der *the* Bohemian Forest
Bolivien Bolivia
Bosnien Bosnia
Bosnien und Herzegowina Bosnia and Herzegovina
Bosporus, der *the* Bosp(h)orus
Botsuana Botswana
Bottnische Meerbusen, der *the* Gulf of Bothnia
Bozen Bolzano
Brandenburger Tor, das *the* Brandenburg Gate
Brasilien Brazil
Braunschweig Braunschweig, Brunswick
Brenner(pass), der *the* Brenner Pass
Breslau Wroclaw; *hist.* Breslau
Bretagne, die Brittany
Britischen Überseegebiete, die *the* United Kingdom Overseas Territories
Brügge Bruges
Brüssel Brussels
Buchara Bukhara
Bukarest Bucharest
Bukowina, die Bukovina, Bucovina
Bulgarien Bulgaria
Bundeshaus, das *(in Bonn)* the Federal Parliament Building
Bundesrepublik Deutschland, die *the* Federal Republic of Germany
Burgund Burgundy
Burgundische Pforte, die *the* Belfort Gap
Byzanz *hist.* Byzantium

C

Cevennen, die *the* Cevennes
Chaldäa *hist.* Chald(a)ea
Chania Canea
Charkow Kharkov
Chiemsee, der Lake Chiem, *the* Chiemsee
Chile Chile
China China
Chinesische Mauer, die *the* Great Wall of China
Chinesische Meer, das *the* China Sea
Comer See, der Lake Como
Costa Rica Costa Rica
Cyrenaika, die *hist.* Cyrenaica

D

Dakien *hist.* Dacia
Dalmatien Dalmatia
Damaskus Damascus
Dänemark Denmark
Danzig Gdansk; *hist.* Danzig
Danziger Bucht, die *the* Bay *(od.* Gulf) of Gdansk *(hist.* Danzig)
Dardanellen, die *the* Dardanelles
Daressalam Dar es Salaam

Den Haag The Hague
Deutsche Bucht, *die the* German Bay
Deutsche Demokratische Republik, *die hist. the* German Democratic Republic
Deutschland Germany
Deutsch-Südwestafrika *hist.* German Southwest Africa
Dithmarschen Ditmarsh
Dnjepr, *der the* Dnieper
Dnjestr, *der the* Dniester
Dodekanes, *der the* Dodecanese
Dogenpalast, *der (in Venedig) the* Doges Palace
Dolomiten, *die the* Dolomites
Dominikanische Republik, *die the* Dominican Republic
Donau, *die the* Danube
Donez, *der the* Donets
Donezbecken, *das the* Donets (Basin)
Dover → **Straße von Dover**
Drau, *die the* Drava
Dschibuti Djibouti
Dschidda Jedda
Dünkirchen Dunkirk

E

Ecuador Ecuador
Eiffelturm, *der the* Eiffel Tower
Eismeer, Nördliche, *das* → **Nordpolarmeer**
Eismeer, Südliche, *das* → **Südpolarmeer**
Elat Eilat
Elfenbeinküste, *die the* Ivory Coast
El Salvador El Salvador
Elsass, *das* Alsace
Elsass-Lothringen *hist.* Alsace-Lorraine
Engadin, *das the* Engadine
Engelsburg, *die (in Rom) the* Castel SantAngelo
England England
Eremitage, die (in Leningrad) the Hermitage Museum
Eriwan Yerevan, Erivan
Erzgebirge, *das the* Erzgebirge, *the* Ore Mountains
Estland Estonia
Etsch, *die the* Adige
Euphrat, *der the* Euphrates
Eurasien Eurasia
Europa Europe
Everest, *der* (Mount) Everest

F

Falklandinseln, *die the* Falkland Islands, *the* Falklands
Färöer, *die the* Faroes, *the* Faroe Islands
Felsendom, *der (in Jerusalem) the* Dome of the Rock
Ferne Osten, der, Fernost *the* Far East
Feuerland Tierra del Fuego
Fidschi Fiji
Fidschiinseln, *die the* Fiji Islands
Finnische Meerbusen, *der the* Gulf of Finland
Finnland Finland
Flandern Flanders
Florenz Florence
Franken Franconia
Frankfurt (am Main) Frankfurt (on the Main)
Frankfurt (an der Oder) Frankfurt (on the Oder)
Frankreich France
Französisch-Guayana French Guiana
Freiburg *Schweiz:* Fribourg
Freiheitsstatue, *die the* Statue of Liberty
Freundschaftsinseln, *die the* Tonga *(od.* Friendly) Islands
Friaul Friuli

Friesischen Inseln, *die the* Frisian Islands
Fudschijama, *der* (Mount) Fuji, *a.* Fujiyama
Fünen Fyn

G

Gabun Gabon
Galapagosinseln, *die the* Galapagos Islands
Galatien *hist.* Galatia
Galicien *(in Spanien) a. hist.* Galicia
Galiläa Galilee
Galizien *(in Mitteleuropa)* Galicia
Gallien *hist.* Gaul
Gambia *(the)* Gambia
Gardasee, *der* Lake Garda
Gazastreifen, *der the* Gaza Strip
Genezareth → **See Genezareth**
Genf Geneva
Genfer See, *der* Lake Geneva, Lac Leman
Gent Ghent
Genua Genoa
Georgien Georgia
Germanien *hist.* Germania
Gesellschaftsinseln, *die the* Society Islands
Gewürzinseln, *die the* Spice Islands; → *a.* **Molukken**
Ghana Ghana
Gizeh (El) Giza; → **Pyramiden von Gizeh**
Glarner Alpen, *die the* Glarus Alps
Golanhöhen, *die the* Golan Heights
Goldene Horn, *das the* Golden Horn
Golf von Akaba, *der the* Gulf of Aqaba *(od.* Akaba)
Golf von Bengalen, *der the* Bay of Bengal
Golf von Biskaya, *der the* Bay of Biscay
Golf von Genua, *der the* Gulf of Genoa
Golf von Korinth, *der the* Gulf of Corinth
Golf von Neapel, *der the* Bay of Naples
Golf von Triest, *der the* Gulf of Trieste
Gomorrha *bibl.* Gomorrah, Gomorrha
Göteborg Gothenburg, Göteborg
Grabeskirche, *die (in Jerusalem) the* Church of the Holy Sepulchre
Graubünden Graubünden, *the* Grisons
Griechenland Greece
Grönland Greenland
Großbritannien Great Britain, Britain
Große Belt, *der the* Great Belt
Großen Antillen, *die the* Greater Antilles
Großen Seen, *die the* Great Lakes
Große Syrte, *die the* Gulf of Sidra
Guatemala Guatemala
Guayana *(Region)* Guiana
Guyana *(Staat)* Guyana

H

Haiderabad Hyderabad
Haiti Haiti
Halikarnassos *hist.* Halicarnassus
Hameln Hameln, Hamelin
Hannover Hanover
Harz, *der the* Harz (Mountains)
Havanna Havana
Hawaii-Inseln, *die the* Hawaiian Islands
Hebriden, *die the* Hebrides
Helgoland Hel(i)goland
Helgoländer Bucht, *die the* Hel(i)goland Bight
Hellas *hist.* Hellas, (Ancient) Greece
Helvetien *hist.* Helvetia, Switzerland
Hennegau, *der* Hainau(l)t
Heraklion Herakl(e)ion
Herzegowina *hist.* Herzegovina
Herzogenbusch s Hertogenbosch

Hessen Hesse(n)
Himalaja, *der the* Himalayas
Himmelfahrtsinsel, *die* Ascension Island
Hindukusch, *der the* Hindu Kush
Hinterindien Indochina
Hinterpommern *hist.* Eastern Pomerania
Hiroschima Hiroshima
Hoek van Holland Hook of Holland
Holland Holland, *the* Netherlands
Honduras Honduras
Hongkong Hong Kong
Hradschin, *der (in Prag) the* Hradcany

I

Iberien *hist.* Iberia
Iberische Halbinsel, *die the* Iberian Peninsula
Ijsselmeer, *das* Lake Ijssel, Ijsselmeer
Illyrien *hist.* Illyria
Indien India
Indische Ozean, *der the* Indian Ocean
Indochina Indochina
Indonesien Indonesia
Inguschetien Ingushetia
Innerasien Central Asia
Innere Mongolei, *die the* Inner Mongolia
Insel Man, *die the* Isle of Man
Inseln über dem Winde, *die the* Leeward Islands
Inseln unter dem Winde, *die the* Windward Islands
Insel Wight, *die the* Isle of Wight
Invalidendom, *der (in Paris) the* Invalides
Ionien *hist.* Ionia
Ionische Meer, *das the* Ionian Sea
Ionischen Inseln, *die the* Ionian Islands
Irak, *der* Iraq
Iran Iran
Irische See, *die the* Irish Sea
Irland Ireland
Island Iceland
Israel Israel
Istrien Istria
Italien Italy

J

Jadebusen, *der the* Jade Bay
Jakutsk Yakutsk
Jalta Yalta
Jamaika Jamaica
Jangtse(kiang), *der the* Yangtze(-Kiang)
Japan Japan
Japanische Meer, *das the* Sea of Japan
Jemen, *der the* Yemen
Jordanien Jordan
Judäa *hist.* Jud(a)ea
Jugoslawien Yugoslavia
Jungferninseln, *die the* Virgin Islands
Jütland Jutland

K

Kaimaninseln, *die the* Cayman Islands
Kairo Cairo
Kalabrien Calabria
Kalifornien California
Kalkutta Calcutta
Kambodscha Cambodia
Kamerun Cameroon
Kamputschea *obs.* Kampuchea
Kana(a) *bibl.* Cana
Kanaan *hist.* Canaan
Kanada Canada
Kanal, *der (= Ärmelkanal) the* (English) Channel
Kanalinseln, *die the* Channel Islands
Kanaren, die, Kanarischen Inseln, die *the* Canaries, *the* Canary Islands

Kantabrische Gebirge, *das* *the* Cantabrian Mountains
Kap der Guten Hoffnung, *das* *the* Cape of Good Hope, *a. the* Cape
Kap Hoorn Cape Horn, *a. the* Horn
Kappadokien Cappadocia
Kapprovinz, *die* *the* Cape Province
Kap Skagen *the* Skaw, *a.* (Cape) Skagen
Kapstadt Cape Town
Kapverdischen Inseln, *die* *the* Cape Verde Islands
Karatschi Karachi
Karelien Karelia
Karibik, *die* *the* Caribbean
Kärnten Carinthia
Karolinen, *die* *the* Caroline Islands
Karpaten, *die* *the* Carpathians, *the* Carpathian Mountains
Karthago *hist.* Carthage
Kasachstan Kazakhstan
Kaschmir Kashmir
Kaspische Meer, *das* *the* Caspian Sea
Kastilien Castile
Katalaunischen Felder, *die* *hist.* *the* Catalaunian Plains (*od.* Fields)
Katalonien Catalonia
Katar Qatar
Katharinenkloster, *das* (*auf der Sinaihalbinsel*) *the* Monastery of St Catherine
Kattowitz Katowice; *hist.* Kattowitz
Kaukasus, *der* *the* Caucasus, *a. the* Caucasus Mountains
Kenia Kenya
Khaiberpass, *der* *the* Khyber Pass
Kieler Bucht, *die* *the* Kiel Bay
Kiew Kiev
Kilikien *hist.* Cilicia
Kilimandscharo, *der* (Mount) Kilimanjaro
Kirgisien Kirghizia
Klagemauer, *die* (*in Jerusalem*) *the* Wailing Wall
Kleinasien Asia Minor
Kleinen Antillen, *die* *the* Lesser Antilles
Köln Cologne
Kölner Dom, *der* Cologne Cathedral
Kolumbien Colombia
Komoren, *die* *the* Comoro Archipelago
Kongo, *der* *the* Congo
Königsberg Kaliningrad; *hist.* Königsberg
Konstantinopel Constantinople
Konstanz Constance
Kopenhagen Copenhagen
Kordilleren, *die* *the* Cordilleras
Korea Korea
Korfu Corfu
Korinth Corinth
Korsika Corsica
Kosovo, *der od.* *das* Kosovo
Kotschinchina Cochin China
Krakatau Krakatoa
Krakau Cracow, Krakow
Kreml, *der* *the* Kremlin
Kreta Crete
Krim, *die* *the* Crimea
Kroatien Croatia
Kuba Cuba
Kurdistan Kurdistan, Kurdestan, Kordestan
Kurilen, *die* *the* Kuril(e) Islands
Kuwait Kuwait
Kykladen, *die* *the* Cyclades

L

Ladogasee, *der* Lake Ladoga
Laibach Ljubljana
Lappland Lapland
Lateinamerika Latin America
Lausitz, *die* Lusatia

Lemberg Lvov
Lettland Latvia
Levante, *die* *the* Levant
Libanon, *der* (the) Lebanon (*meist ohne bestimmten Artikel*)
Liberia Liberia
Libyen Libya
Liechtenstein Liechtenstein
Ligurien Liguria
Ligurische Meer, *das* *the* Ligurian Sea
Liparischen Inseln, *die* *the* Lipari Islands
Lissabon Lisbon
Litauen Lithuania
Livland *hist.* Livonia
Loire-Schlösser, *die* *the* Chateaux of the Loire
Lombardei, *die* Lombardy
Lothringen Lorraine
Löwen (*in Belgien*) Louvain, Leuven
Lübecker Bucht, *die* *the* Lübeck Bay
Luganer See, *der* Lake Lugano
Lüneburger Heide, *die* *the* Lüneburg Heath
Lusitanien *hist.* Lusitania
Lüttich Liege
Luxemburg Luxemb(o)urg
Luzern Lucerne
Lydien *hist.* Lydia

M

Maas, *die* *the* Meuse, *the* Maas
Madagaskar Madagascar
Magellanstraße, *die* *the* Strait(s) of Magellan
Mähren Moravia
Mährische Pforte, *die* *the* Moravian Gate (*od.* Gap)
Mailand Milan
Mainfranken → **Unterfranken**
Makedonien Macedonia
Malaiische Halbinsel, *die* *the* Malay Peninsula, Malaya
Malakka Malacca
Malediven, *die* *the* Maldives
Mallorca Majorca
Malta Malta
Mandschurei, *die* Manchuria
Marianen, *die* *the* Marianas
Mark Brandenburg, *die* *the* Brandenburg Marches
Markuskirche, *die* (*in Venedig*) St Marks (Basilica)
Markusplatz, *der* (*in Venedig*) St Marks Square
Marmarameer, *das* *the* Sea of Marmara
Marokko Morocco
Marsfeld, *das* (*in Paris*) *the* Champde-Mars; (*in Rom*) *the* Field of Mars
Maskat und Oman Muscat and Oman
Masuren Masuria
Masurischen Seen, *die* *the* Masurian Lakes
Mauretanien Mauritania
Mazedonien Macedonia
Mecklenburg-Vorpommern Mecklenburg-Western Pomerania
Mekka Mecca
Melanesien Melanesia
Menorca Minorca
Meran Merano
Mesopotamien Mesopotamia
Mexiko Mexico
Mikronesien Micronesia
Milet *hist.* Miletus
Millstätter See, *der* Lake Millstatt
Mittelamerika Central America
Mittelasien Central Asia
Mitteldeutschland Central Germany
Mitteleuropa Central Europe
Mittelmeer, *das* *the* Mediterranean (Sea)

Mittlere Osten, *der* *the* Middle East
Moambique Mozambique
Moldau[1]**,** *die* (*Fluss*) *the* Vltava; *hist. the* Moldau
Moldau[2]**,** *die* (*Region*) Moldavia
Moldawien Moldavia
Molukken, *die* *the* Moluccas
Monaco Monaco
Mongolei, *die* Mongolia
Mosambik Mozambique
Mosel, *die* *the* Moselle
Moskau Moscow
Moskwa, *die* *the* Moskva
Mülhausen Mulhouse
München Munich
Myanmar Myanmar
Mykene Mycenae

N

Nahe Osten, *der* *the* Middle (*od.* Near) East
Navarra Navarre
Neapel Naples
Neu-Delhi New Delhi
Neufundland Newfoundland
Neuguinea New Guinea
Neuseeland New Zealand
Newa, *die* *the* Neva
Niagarafälle, *die* *the* Niagara Falls
Nicaragua Nicaragua
Niederbayern Lower Bavaria
Niederlande, *die* *the* Netherlands, Holland
Niederösterreich Lower Austria
Niederrhein, *der* *the* Lower Rhine
Niedersachsen Lower Saxony
Niederschlesien *hist.* Lower Silesia
Nigeria Nigeria
Nikaragua Nicaragua
Nikosia Nicosia
Nil, *der* *the* Nile
Nimwegen Nijmegen
Ninive *hist.* Niniveh
Nizza Nice
Nordafrika North Africa
Nordamerika North America
Norddeutsche Tiefebene, *die* *the* North(ern) German Plain
Norddeutschland North(ern) Germany
Nordeuropa North(ern) Europe
Nordfriesischen Inseln, *die* *the* North Frisians
Nordirland Northern Ireland
Nordkap, *das* *the* North Cape
Nordkorea North Korea
Nord-Ostsee-Kanal, *der* *the* Kiel Canal
Nordpol, *der* *the* North Pole
Nordpolarmeer, *das* *the* Arctic Ocean
Nordrhein-Westfalen North-Rhine/Westphalia
Nordsee, *die* *the* North Sea
Normandie, *die* Normandy
Norwegen Norway
Nowgorod Novgorod
Nowosibirsk Novosibirsk
Nubien (*Region u. hist.*) Nubia
Nürnberg Nuremberg

O

Oberbayern Upper Bavaria
Oberengadin, *das* *the* Upper Engadine
Obere See, *der* Lake Superior
Oberfranken Upper Franconia
Oberitalien Northern Italy
Oberösterreich Upper Austria
Oberpfalz, *die* *the* Upper Palatinate
Oberrhein, *der* *the* Upper Rhine
Oberrheinische Tiefebene, *die* *the* Upper Rhine Valley
Oberschlesien *hist.* Upper Silesia

Ochotskische Meer, das *the* Sea of Okhotsk
Ölberg, der *bibl. the* Mount of Olives
Olymp, der (Mount) Olympus
Onegasee, der Lake Onega
Oranjefreistaat, der *the* Orange Free State
Orinoko, der *the* Orinoco
Ostafrika East Africa
Ostasien East Asia
Ostdeutschland 1. Eastern Germany; **2.** *hist. the* German Democratic Republic, East Germany
Ostende Ostend
Osterinsel, die *the* Easter Island
Österreich Austria
Österreich-Ungarn *hist.* Austria-Hungary
Osteuropa Eastern Europe
Ostfriesischen Inseln, die *the* East Frisians
Ostpreußen *hist.* East Prussia
Ostsee, die *the* Baltic (Sea)
Ozeanien Oceania

P

Pakistan Pakistan
Palästina *bibl., hist.* Palestine
Palatin, der *(in Rom) the* Palatine
Panama Panama
Panamakanal, der *the* Panama Canal
Pandschab, das *the* Punjab
Pannonien *hist.* Pannonia
Papua-Neuguinea Papua-New Guinea
Parnass, der Mount Parnassus
Parthien *hist.* Parthia
Patagonien Patagonia
Pazifik, der *the* Pacific (Ocean)
Pelagischen Inseln, die *the* Pelagian Islands
Peloponnes, der *od. (korrekt)* **die** *the* Peloponnese, *the* Peloponnesus
Persien *hist.* Persia
Persische Golf, der *the* Persian Gulf
Peru Peru
Petersburg, (St.) St Petersburg
Petersdom, der *(in Rom)* St Peters (Cathedral)
Peterskirche, die *(in Rom)* St Peters
Petersplatz, der *(in Rom)* St Peters Square
Pfalz, die *the* Palatinate
Philippinen, die *the* Philippines
Phönizien *hist.* Phoenicia
Phrygien *hist.* Phrygia
Picardie, die Picardy
Piemont Piedmont
Pilsen Plzen; *hist.* Pilsen
Piräus Piraeus
Plätäa *hist.* Plataea
Plattensee, der Lake Balaton
Po-Ebene, die *the* Po Valley
Polarkreis, der 1. *the* Arctic Circle; **2.** *the* Antarctic Circle
Polen Poland
Polynesien Polynesia
Pommern Pomorze; *hist.* Pomerania
Pompeji Pompeii
Pontinischen Sümpfe, die *the* Pontine Marshes
Pontische Gebirge, das *the* Pontic Mountains
Pontos *hist.* Pontus
Portugal Portugal
Posen Poznan
Prag Prague
Preßburg Bratislava; *hist.* Pressburg
Preußen *hist.* Prussia
Provence, die Provence
Pyramiden von Gizeh, die *the* Pyramids of Giza

Pyrenäen, die *the* Pyrenees
Pyrenäenhalbinsel, die *the* Iberian Peninsula

R

Rangun Rangoon
Rätien *hist.* Rhaetia
Rätischen Alpen, die *the* Rhaetian Alps
Republik Irland, die *the* Republic of Ireland
Reval Tallin(n); *hist.* Reval
Rhein, der *the* Rhine
Rheinfall, der *the* Rhine Falls
Rheingau, der *the* Rhinegau
Rheinhessen Rhinehessen
Rheinische Schiefergebirge, das *the* Rhenish Slate Mountains
Rheinland, das *the* Rhineland
Rheinland-Pfalz Rhineland-Palatinate
Rhodesien *hist.* Rhodesia
Rhodos Rhodes
Rom Rome
Rote Meer, das *the* Red Sea
Rote Platz, der *(in Moskau)* Red Square
Rubikon, der *the* Rubicon
Ruhrgebiet, das *the* Ruhr(gebiet)
Rumänien Romania, *a.* Rumania
Russland Russia

S

Saargebiet, das *hist. the* Saar(land)
Saarland, das *the* Saar(land)
Saba *hist.* Sheba
Sabiner Berge, die *the* Sabine Hills
Sachalin Sakhalin
Sachsen Saxony
Sachsen-Anhalt Saxony-Anhalt
Sächsische Schweiz, die Saxon Switzerland
Salomonen, die, Salomonischen Inseln, die *the* Solomon Islands
Saloniki Salonika, Saloniki
Sambesi, der *the* Zambezi
Sambia Zambia
Samothrake Samothrace
Sankt Gallen St Gallen, *obs.* St Gall
Sankt-Lorenz-Strom, der *the* St Lawrence (River)
Sansibar Zanzibar
Sarajewo Sarajevo
Sardinien Sardinia
Saudi-Arabien Saudi Arabia
Savoyen Savoy
Schanghai Shanghai
Schatt el Arab, der *the* Shatt-al-Arab
Schiefe Turm von Pisa, der *the* Leaning Tower of Pisa
Schlesien 1. *(in Polen)* Slask; *hist.* Silesia; **2.** *(in der Tschechoslowakei)* Slezsko; *hist.* Silesia
Schottland Scotland
Schwaben Swabia
Schwäbische Alb, die *the* Swabian Jura
Schwarze Meer, das *the* Black Sea
Schwarzwald, der *the* Black Forest
Schweden Sweden
Schweiz, die Switzerland
Schweizer Mittelland, das *the* Swiss Midlands
Seealpen, die *the* Maritime Alps
See Genezareth, der *the* Sea of Galilee
Seeland *(dänische Insel)* Zealand
Seidenstraße, die *hist. the* Silk Road *(od.* Route)
Senegal Senegal
Serbien Serbia
Seufzerbrücke, die *(in Venedig) the* Bridge of Sighs
Sevilla Seville
Seychellen, die *the* Seychelles

Sibirien Siberia
Siebenbürgen Transylvania
Simbabwe Zimbabwe
Sinaigebirge, das Mount Sinai
Sinaihalbinsel, die *the* Sinai Peninsula
Singapur Singapore
Sixtinische Kapelle, die *(in Rom) the* Sistine Chapel
Sizilien Sicily
Skandinavien Scandinavia
Slowakei, die Slovakia
Slowenien Slovenia
Somalia Somalia
Sorrent Sorrento
Sowjetunion, die *hist. the* Soviet Union
Spanien Spain
Spanische Treppe, die *(in Rom) the* Spanish Steps
Sporaden, die *the* Sporades
Sri Lanka Sri Lanka
Steiermark, die Styria
Stephansdom, der *(in Wien)* St Stephens (Cathedral)
Stettin Szczecin; *hist.* Stettin
Stille Ozean, der → *Pazifik*
Straßburg Strasbourg
Straßburger Münster, das Strasbourg Minster
Straße von Dover, die *the* Strait(s) of Dover
Straße von Gibraltar, die *the* Strait(s) of Gibraltar
Stubaier Alpen, die *the* Stubai Alps
Südafrika South Africa
Südamerika South America
Sudan, der *(the)* Sudan
Südchinesische Meer, das *the* South China Sea
Süddeutschland South(ern) Germany
Sudetenland, das *hist.* Sudetenland, *a. the* Sudeten
Südeuropa South(ern) Europe
Südkorea South Korea
Südpolarmeer, das *the* Antarctic Ocean
Südsee, die *the* South Pacific, *the* South Seas
Südseeinseln, die *the* Pacific *(od.* South Sea) Islands
Südtirol South Tyrol
Südwestafrika South-West Africa
Suezkanal, der *the* Suez Canal
Sumatra Sumatra
Sund, der *the* Sound
Swasiland Swaziland
Syrakus Syracuse
Syrien Syria
Szegedin Szeged
Szetschuan Szechuan

T

Tadschikistan Tadzhikistan
Tafelberg, der Table Mountain
Taipeh Taipei
Taiwan Taiwan
Tajo, der *the* Tagus
Tanganjika Tanganyika
Tanganjikasee, der Lake Tanganyika
Tanger Tangier
Tansania Tanzania
Tarent Taranto
Tasmanien Tasmania
Tatarei, die *hist.* Tartary
Tatra, die *the* Tatra Mountains, *a. the* High Tatra
Taurus, der *the* Taurus (Mountains)
Teheran Teh(e)ran
Tempelberg, der *(in Jerusalem) the* Temple Mount
Teneriffa Tenerife
Tessin, das Ticino
Teutoburger Wald, der *the* Teutoburg Forest, *the* Teutoburger Wald

Thailand Thailand
Theben *hist.* Thebes
Themse, *die* *the* Thames
Thermopylen, *die* Thermopylae
Thessalien Thessaly
Thrakien *hist.* Thrace, Thracia
Thuner See, *der* *the* Lake of Thun
Thüringen Thuringia
Thüringer Wald, *der* *the* Thuringian Forest
Tibet Tibet
Tirol *(the)* Tyrol
Tokio Tokyo
Tongainseln, *die* *the* Tonga *(od.* Friendly) Islands
Toskana, *die* Tuscany
Tote Meer, *das* *the* Dead Sea
Transkaukasien Transcaucasia
Trasimenische See, *der* Lake Trasimeno
Trient Trento
Triest Trieste
Tripolis Tripoli
Troja Troy
Tschad, *der* Chad
Tschechien Czechia, *the* Czech Republic
Tschechoslowakei, *die* *hist.* Czechoslovakia
Tschetschenien Chechnya, Chechnia
Tunesien Tunisia
Türkei, *die* Turkey
Turkestan Turkestan, Turkistan
Turm von Babel, *der* *bibl.* *the* Tower of Babel
Tyrrhenische Meer, *das* *the* Tyrrhenian Sea
Tyrus *hist.* Tyre

U

Uffizien, *die* *(in Florenz)* *the* Uffizi
Uganda Uganda
Ukraine Ukraine
Ulmer Münster, *das* Ulm Minster
Umbrien Umbria
Ungarn Hungary
Union der Sozialistischen Sowjetrepubliken, *die* *hist.* *the* Union of Soviet Socialist Republics
Unterfranken Lower Franconia
Unteritalien Southern Italy
Uppsala Up(p)sala
Ural, *der* *the* Urals
Uruguay Uruguay
Usbekistan Uzbekistan

V

Vansee, *der* Lake Van
Vatikan, *der* *the* Vatican
Veitsdom, *der* *(in Prag)* St Vituss Cathedral
Venedig Venice
Venetien Veneto
Venezuela Venezuela
Verbotene Stadt, *die* *(in Peking)* the Forbidden City
Vereinigte Königreich (von Großbritannien und Nordirland), *das* *the* United Kingdom (of Great Britain and Northern Ireland)
Vereinigten Arabischen Emirate, *die* *the* United Arab Emirates
Vereinigten Staaten (von Amerika), *die* *the* United States (of America)
Vesuv, *der* Vesuvius
Via Appia, *die* *hist.* the Appian Way
Vierwaldstätter See, *der* Lake Lucerne
Vietnam Vietnam, Viet Nam
Vlissingen Flushing
Vogesen, *die* *the* Vosges (Mountains)
Volksrepublik China, *die* *the* Peoples Republic of China
Vorderasien *the* Middle *(od.* Near) East; *hist.* the Levant
Vorderindien *the* Indian Peninsula (and Ceylon)
Vorpommern Western Pomerania

W

Walachei, *die* *hist.* Wal(l)achia
Wales Wales
Walfischbai, *die* Walvis *(od.* Walfish) Bay
Wallis, *das* Valais
Wallonien Wallonie
Warschau Warsaw
Wattenmeer, *das* *(vor der Nordseeküste)* *the* mud flats
Weichsel, *die* *the* Vistula
Weiße Haus, *das* *(in Washington DC)* the White House
Weißrussland B(y)elorussia, Belarus
Wenzelsplatz, *der* *(in Prag)* Wenceslas Square
Westdeutschland 1. Western Germany; **2.** *hist.* → ***Bundesrepublik Deutschland***
Westeuropa West(ern) Europe
Westfalen Westphalia
Westfälische Pforte, *die* *the* Porta Westfalica, *the* Westphalian Gate
Westfriesischen Inseln, *die* *the* West Frisians
Westindien *the* West Indies
Westpreußen *hist.* West Prussia
Wien Vienna
Wilna Vilnius
Windhuk Windhoek
Wladiwostok Vladivostok
Wolga, *die* *the* Volga

Y

Ypern Ypres

Z

Zaire *hist.* Zaire
Zentralafrikanische Republik, *die* *the* Central African Republic
Zisalpinische Republik, *die* *hist.* *the* Cisalpine Republic
Zuckerhut, *der* *(in Rio de Janeiro)* Sugar Loaf Mountain
Zürich Zurich
Zürichsee, *der*, **Züricher See, *der*** Lake Zurich
Zypern Cyprus

Die Länder der Bundesrepublik Deutschland

Baden-Württemberg Baden-Württem-
  berg
Bayern Bavaria
Berlin Berlin
Brandenburg Brandenburg
Bremen Bremen
Hamburg Hamburg

Hessen Hesse
Mecklenburg-Vorpommern Mecklen-
  burg-Western Pomerania, Mecklenburg
  and Western Pomerania
Niedersachsen Lower Saxony
Nordrhein-Westfalen North-Rhine/
  Westphalia

Rheinland-Pfalz Rhineland-Palatinate
Saarland Saarland
Sachsen Saxony
Sachsen-Anhalt Saxony-Anhalt
Schleswig-Holstein Schleswig-Holstein
Thüringen Thuringia

Die Länder der Republik Österreich

Burgenland Burgenland
Kärnten Carinthia
Niederösterreich Lower Austria

Oberösterreich Upper Austria
Salzburg Salzburg
Steiermark Styria

Tirol Tyrol
Vorarlberg Vorarlberg
Wien Vienna

Die Kantone der Schweizerischen Eidgenossenschaft

(in Klammern die Halbkantone)

Aargau Aargau
**Appenzell (Inner-Rhoden; Außer-Rho-
den)** Appenzell (Inner Rhodes; Outer
  Rhodes)
Basel Basel, Basle
Bern Bern, Berne
Freiburg, *frz.* **Fribourg** Fribourg
Genf, *frz.* **Geneve** Geneva
Glarus Glarus

Graubünden Graubünden, Grisons
Jura Jura
Luzern Lucerne
Neuenburg, *frz.* **Neuchatel** Neuchatel
St. Gallen St Gallen, St Gall
Schaffhausen Schaffhausen
Schwyz Schwyz
Solothurn Solothurn
Tessin, *ital.* **Ticino** Ticino

Thurgau Thurgau
Unterwalden (Obwalden; Nidwalden)
  Unterwalden (Obwalden; Nidwalden)
Uri Uri
Waadt, *frz.* **Vaud** Vaud
Wallis, *frz.* **Valais** Valais, Wallis
Zug Zug
Zürich Zurich

Historische, biblische und mythologische Namen

Folgende Liste enthält eine Auswahl an historischen Namen sowie solchen aus der Mythologie und Weltliteratur. Es wurden im Allgemeinen nur Namen aufgenommen, die im Englischen eine andere Schreibung als im Deutschen aufweisen. Bei Varianten wurde manchmal nur die geläufigste angegeben. Das bei manchen Namen angegebene Betonungszeichen (') soll als Aussprachehilfe dienen. Die vollständige phonetische Umschreibung der englischen Namen können Sie in einem der Standardaussprachewörterbücher nachschlagen.

Abälard Abelard
Achill(es) *myth.* Achilles
Ahasver *myth.* Ahasu'erus
Aktäon *myth.* Actaeon
Alarich Alaric
Alba, Herzog von Duke of Alva (*od.* Alba)
Albrecht der Bär Albert the Bear
Alexander der Große Alexander the Great
Alkibiades Alcibiades
Alkmene *myth.* Alcmene
Alkuin 'Alcuin
Ambrosius, der heilige St 'Ambrose
Amenophis Amen'hotep
Anakreon A'nacreon
Äneas *myth.* Ae'neas
Antäus *myth.* An'taeus
Antonius, der heilige St 'Anthony
Äolus *myth.* Ae'olus
Aristoteles 'Aristotle
Artus, König *myth.* King Arthur
Äschylus Aeschylus
Äskulap *myth.* Aescu'lapius
Äsop 'Aesop
Athene *myth.* Athena
Augias *myth.* Au'geas
August der Starke Au'gustus the Strong
Augustin(us), der heilige St Au'gustine

Baldur *myth.* Balder, Baldur
Barbarossa → *Friedrich Barbarossa*
Bartholomäus, der heilige St. Bar'tholomew
Basilius 'Basil
Bathseba *bibl.* 'Bathsheba
Beda (Venerabilis) (the Venerable) Bede
Belisar Beli'sarius
Belsazar Bel'shazzar
Benedikt, der heilige St Benedict
Bonifatius 'Boniface
Bukephalos *myth.* Bucephalus

Cäsar Caesar
Cato der Ältere Cato the Elder
Cato der Jüngere Cato the Younger
Chlodwig Clovis
Christophorus, der heilige St 'Christopher
Christus, Jesus Jesus Christ
Chrysostomus, Johannes St John Chry'sostom
Cupido *myth.* 'Cupid

Dädalus *myth.* Daedalus
Damokles Damocles
Danae *myth.* Danae
Danaiden, die *myth.* the Da'naides
Demokrit De'mocritus
Diokletian Dio'cletian
Dionysios Dio'nysius
Dionysius, der heilige St 'Denis
Dionysos Dio'nysus, Dio'nysos

Dioskuren, die *myth.* the Di'oscuri
Donar *myth.* Donar, Thor
Don Quichotte Don Quijote
Drakon Draco
Dschingis Khan Genghis Khan

Echnaton Akhe'naton, Amen'hotep IV
Eduard Edward
Eduard der Bekenner Edward the Confessor
Elektra *myth.* Electra
Elias *bibl.* E'lijah
Elisabeth Elizabeth
Empedokles Empedocles
Epiktet Epic'tetus
Epikur Epi'curus
Erich der Rote Eric the Red
Erinnyen, die *myth.* the E'rin(n)yes
Ermanerich Ermaneric
Esra *bibl.* Ezra
Etzel Attila (the Hun)
Eugen, Prinz Prince 'Eugene
Euklid 'Euclid
Eumeniden, die *myth.* the Eu'menides
Eurydike *myth.* Eu'rydice
Ezechiel *bibl.* E'zekiel

Franz Ferdinand Francis Ferdinand
Franz Joseph Francis Joseph
Franz von Assisi, der heilige St Francis of Assisi
Friedrich Barbarossa Frederick Barbarossa
Friedrich der Große Frederick the Great
Friedrich der Weise Frederick the Wise
Friedrich Wilhelm der Große Kurfürst Frederick William the Great Elector
Fritz: der Alte → *Friedrich der Große*
Furien, die *myth.* the Furies

Galilei, Galileo Galileo (Galilei)
Ganymed *myth.* Ganymede
Geiserich Geiseric
Georg George
Ghibellinen, die *the* 'Ghibellines
Gracchen, die *the* Gracchi
Grazien, die *myth.* the Graces
Guelfen, die *the* Guelfs
Gustav Adolf Gu'stavus A'dolphus

Habakuk *bibl.* 'Habakkuk
Habsburger, die *the* Hapsburgs
Hadrian Hadrian, Adrian
Heinrich der Löwe Henry the Lion
Heinrich der Seefahrer Henry the Navigator
Hekate *myth.* 'Hecate, 'Hekate
Hektor *myth.* Hector
Hekuba *myth.* 'Hecuba
Helena *myth.* Helen
Hephäst *myth.* Hephaestus, Hephaistos
Herakles *myth.* Heracles, Herakles

Herakliden, die *myth.* the Hera'clidae
Heraklit Hera'clitus
Herkules *myth.* Hercules
Hermann der Cherusker Arminius
Herodes 'Herod
Herodot He'rodotus
Hesekiel E'zekiel
Hesperiden, die *the* He'sperides
Hieronymus, der heilige St Je'rome
Hiob *bibl.* Job
Hippokrates Hip'pocrates
Hippolytos *myth.* Hip'polytus
Horaz 'Horace
Horen, die *myth.* the Horae, *a. the* Hours

Ignatius von Loyola Ignatius (of) Lo'yola
Ignaz, der heilige St Ignatius
Ikarus *myth.* 'Icarus
Innozenz Innocent
Iokaste *myth.* Jocasta
Iphigenie *myth.* Iphige'nia
Isaak *bibl.* Isaac
Iwan der Große Ivan the Great
Iwan der Schreckliche Ivan the Terrible

Jahwe Jahweh, Jahveh
Jakob *bibl.* Jacob; (*Könige*) James
Jakobus *bibl.* (St) James
Japhet *bibl.* Japheth
Jehova Jehovah
Jeremia(s) *bibl.* Jeremiah
Jerobeam *bibl.* Jero'boam
Jesaja *bibl.* Isaiah
Johann ohne Land, Johann Ohneland John Lackland
Johanna von Orleans, die heilige St Joan of Arc
Johannes der Evangelist *bibl.* John the E'vangelist
Johannes der Täufer *bibl.* John the 'Baptist
Jona(s) *bibl.* Jonah
Josia(s) *bibl.* Jo'siah
Josua *bibl.* Joshua
Juda *bibl.* Judah
Judas Ischariot *bibl.* Judas Iscariot
Judas Makkabäus Judas Maccabeus
Jungfrau von Orleans, die St Joan of Arc

Kadmos *myth.* Cadmus
Kain *bibl.* Cain
Kaiphas *bibl.* Caiaphas
Kallimachos Cal'limachus
Kalliope *bibl.* Cal'liope
Karl der Dicke Charles the Fat
Karl der Große 'Charlemagne, Charles the Great
Karl der Kahle Charles the Bald
Karl der Kühne Charles the Bold
Karl Martell Charles Martel

Kassiodor Cassio'dorus
Katharina die Große Catherine the Great
Katharina von Aragonien Catherine of 'Aragon
Katull Catullus
Klemens Clement
Kleopatra Cleo'patra
Klytämnestra *myth.* Clyt(a)emnestra
Knut der Große Ca'nute the Great, King Ca'nute
Kolumbus, *Christoph* Christopher Columbus
Konstantin der Große Constantine the Great
Kopernikus, *Nikolaus* Nicolaus Copernicus
Kronos *myth.* Cronus, Cronos
Krösus Croesus
Kyrill, *der heilige* St 'Cyril
Kyros der Große Cyrus the Great

Laokoon *myth.* Laocoon
Laren, *die* *myth. the* Lares
Leukippos Leucippus
Livius Livy
Lothar Lo'thair
Ludwig der Bayer Louis the Bavarian
Ludwig der Deutsche Louis the German
Ludwig der Fromme Louis the Pious
Ludwig der Sonnenkönig Louis the Sun King
Lukas *bibl.* (St) Luke
Lukrez Lucretius
Lukullus Lucullus
Luzifer *myth.* Lucifer
Lykurg Lycurgus
Lysipp Lysippus

Makkabäer, *die* *bibl. the* 'Maccabees
Malachias *bibl.* 'Malachi
Maria Magdalena Mary 'Magdalen
Maria Stuart Mary Queen of Scots, Mary Stuart
Maria Theresia Maria Theresa
Mark Anton Mark 'Antony
Mark Aurel Marcus Aurelius (Anto'ninus)
Markus *bibl.* (St) Mark
Matthäus *bibl.* (St) 'Matthew
Megäre *myth.* Megaera
Menelaos *myth.* Mene'laus
Merkur *myth.* 'Mercury
Methusalem *bibl.* Me'thuselah

Micha *bibl.* Micah
Minotaurus, *der* *myth. the* 'Minotaur

Najaden, *die* *myth. the* 'naiads, *the* 'naiades
Narziss *myth.* Narcissus
Nausikaa *myth.* Nausicaa
Nebukadnezar *bibl.* Nebuchadnezzar
Nehemia *bibl.* Nehe'miah
Neptun *myth.* Neptune
Nereiden, *die* *myth. the* Ne'reides
Nikodemus *bibl.* Nicodemus
Nikolaus, *der heilige* St Nicholas
Nofretete Nefer'titi
Nornen, *die* *myth. the* Norns

Ödipus *myth.* Oedipus
Odoaker Odo'acer, Odo'vacar
Oktavian Octavian
Orest *myth.* Orestes
Origenes 'Origen
Otto der Große Otto the Great

Parzen, *die* *myth. the* Parcae
Parzival *myth.* Percival
Patroklos *myth.* Patroclus
Paulus *bibl.* (St) Paul
Peisistratos Pisistratus
Penaten, *die* *myth. the* penates
Penthesilea *myth.* Penthesile(i)a
Perikles Pericles
Peter der Große Peter the Great
Petrus *bibl.* (St) Peter
Phäaken, *die* *myth. the* Phaeacians
Phaeton Phaethon
Philipp der Gute Philip the Good
Philipp der Kühne Philip the Bold
Philipp der Lange Philip the Tall
Philipp der Schöne Philip the Fair
Philippus der Evangelist *bibl.* Philip the E'vangelist
Phöbe *myth.* Phoebe, Phebe
Phöbus *myth.* Phoebus (Apollo)
Phönix *myth.* Phoenix
Pilatus, *Pontius* Pontius 'Pilate
Pippin der Kleine Pepin the Short
Plejaden, *die* *myth. the* 'Pleiades
Plinius Pliny
Polykrates Polycrates
Polyphem *myth.* Poly'phemus
Pompejus 'Pompey (the Great)
Priamos *myth.* 'Priam
Prokop Procopius
Prokrustes *myth.* Procrustes
Properz Propertius
Ptolemäus 'Ptolemy

Rahel *bibl.* Rachel
Rebekka *bibl.* Rebecca
Richard Löwenherz Richard (the) Lion-Heart

Sacharja *bibl.* Zecha'riah
Salomo(n) *bibl.* Solomon
Sara *bibl.* Sarah
Saulus *bibl.* Saul
Seleukiden, *die* *the* Se'leucids
Sokrates Socrates
Sophokles Sophocles
Spartakus Spartacus
Stephan Stephen
Sueton Suetonius

Telemach(os) *myth.* Te'lemachus
Terenz 'Terence
Thaddäus *bibl.* (St) Jude, 'Thad(d)eus
Themistokles Themistocles
Theoderich der Große Theodoric (*od.* Theoderic) the Great
Theokrit The'ocritus
Theophrast Theophrastus
Thomas von Aquin(o), *der heilige* St Thomas Aquinas
Thukydides Thucydides
Timotheus *bibl.* 'Timothy
Titanen, *die* *myth. the* 'Titans
Tutanchamun, Tutenchamun Tutan'khamen, Thutankha'mun

Uranos *myth.* 'Uranus

Vergil 'Virgil
Vinzenz Vincent
Vitruv Vitruvius
Vulkan 'Vulcan

Walküre *myth.* 'Valkyrie
Wenzel Wencesla(u)s
Widukind Wittekind, *a.* Widukind
Wilhelm William
Wilhelm der Eroberer William the Conqueror
Wilhelm von Oranien William of 'Orange
Wotan *myth.* Wodan, Woden

Xanthippe Xant(h)ippe
Xenokrates Xe'nocrates

Zebaoth *bibl.* Sabaoth
Zebedäus *bibl.* 'Zebedee
Zephanja *bibl.* Zepha'niah
Zerberus *myth.* Cerberus

Musikalische Werkbezeichnungen

Abschiedssymphonie *(Haydn)* Farewell Symphony

Akademische Festouvertüre *(Brahms)* Academic Festival Overture

Eine Alpensymphonie *(R. Strauss)* An Alpine Symphony

Also sprach Zarathustra *(R. Strauss)* Thus Spake Zarathustra

An der schönen blauen Donau *(Joh. Strauß, engl. J. Strauss)* The Blue Danube

An die ferne Geliebte *(Beethoven)* To the Distant Beloved

Auferstehungssymphonie *(Mahler)* Resurrection Symphony

Aus der Neuen Welt *(Dvorak)* From the New World, The New World Symphony

Aus meinem Leben *(Smetana)* From my Life

Der Bajazzo *(Leoncavallo)* I Pagliacci

Der Barbier von Sevilla *(Rossini)* The Barber of Seville

Der Bettelstudent *(Millöcker)* The Beggar Student

Bilder einer Ausstellung *(Mussorgsky)* Pictures at an Exhibition

Coriolan(-Ouvertüre) *(Beethoven)* Coriolanus (Overture)

Die Czardasfürstin *(Kalman)* The Gipsy Princess

Ein deutsches Requiem *(Brahms)* A German Requiem, Brahms Requiem

Dichterliebe *(Schumann)* Poets Love

Die Diebische Elster *(Rossini)* The Thieving Magpie

Dissonanzenquartett *(Mozart)* Dissonance Quartet

Dornröschen *(Tschaikowsky, engl. Tchaikovsky)* Sleeping Beauty

Die Dreigroschenoper *(Weill/Brecht)* The Threepenny Opera

Elias *(Mendelssohn-Bartholdy)* Elijah

Die Entführung aus dem Serail *(Mozart)* The Seraglio, The Abduction from the Seraglio

Fantasiestücke *(Schumann)* Fantasy Pieces

Fausts Verdammnis *(Berlioz)* The Damnation of Faust

Der Feuervogel *(Strawinsky, engl. Stravinsky)* The Firebird

Feuerwerksmusik *(Händel, engl. Handel)* Fireworks Music, Music for the Royal Fireworks

Figaros Hochzeit *(Mozart)* The Marriage of Figaro

Die Fingalshöhle *(Mendelssohn-Bartholdy)* Fingals Cave

Die Fledermaus *(Joh. Strauß, engl. J. Strauss)* Die Fledermaus (The Bat)

Der Fliegende Holländer *(Wagner)* The Flying Dutchman

Forellenquintett *(Schubert)* Trout Quintet

Frauenliebe und -leben *(Schumann)* Womans Love and Life

Die Frau ohne Schatten *(R. Strauss)* Die Frau ohne Schatten (The Woman without a Shadow)

Der Freischütz *(Weber)* Der Freischütz

Frühlingssonate *(Beethoven)* Spring Sonata

Frühlingssymphonie *(Schumann)* Spring Symphony

Fürst Igor *(Borodin)* Prince Igor

Geistertrio *(Beethoven)* Ghost Trio, The Ghost

Geschichten aus dem Wienerwald *(Joh. Strauß, engl. J. Strauss)* Tales from the Vienna Woods

Die Geschöpfe des Prometheus *(Beethoven)* The Creatures of Prometheus

Der Goldene Hahn *(Rimsky-Korsakow, engl. Rimsky-Korsakov)* The Golden Cockerel

Götterdämmerung *(Wagner)* Götterdämmerung, The Twilight of the Gods

Gräfin Maritza *(Kalman)* Countess Maritza

Der Graf von Luxemburg *(Lehar)* The Count of Luxembourg

Gurrelieder *(Schönberg)* Gurrelieder (Songs of Gurra)

Hänsel und Gretel *(Humperdinck)* Hansel and Gretel

Harold in Italien *(Berlioz)* Harold in Italy

Hebridenouvertüre *(Mendelssohn-Bartholdy)* Fingals Cave, Hebrides Overture

Ein Heldenleben *(R. Strauss)* A Heros Life

Die Hochzeit des Figaro *(Mozart)* The Marriage of Figaro

Hoffmanns Erzählungen *(Offenbach)* Tales of Hoffmann

Die Hugenotten *(Meyerbeer)* The Huguenots

Im Weißen Rößl *(Benatzky)* The White Horse Inn

Iphigenie auf Tauris *(Gluck)* Iphigenia on Tauris

Die Italienerin in Algier *(Rossini)* L'Italiana in Algeri, The Italian Girl in Algiers

Italienische Symphonie *(Mendelssohn-Bartholdy)* Italian Symphony

Jagdquartett *(Mozart)* The Hunt, Hunting Quartet

Jagdsymphonie *(Haydn)* La Chasse, The Hunt

Die Jahreszeiten *(Haydn)* The Seasons

Johannespassion *(J. S. Bach)* St John Passion

Kaiserquartett *(Haydn)* Emperor Quartet

Kaiserwalzer *(Joh. Strauß, engl. J. Strauss)* Kaiser Waltz

Kegelstatt-Trio *(Mozart)* Kegelstatt Trio (Skittleground Trio)

Kindersymphonie *(Leopold Mozart)* Toy Symphony

Kinderszenen *(Schumann)* Scenes from Childhood

Kindertotenlieder *(Mahler)* Kindertotenlieder, Songs on the Death of Children

Eine kleine Nachtmusik *(Mozart)* Eine kleine Nachtmusik, A Little Serenade

Die Kluge *(Orff)* The Wise Woman

Des Knaben Wunderhorn *(Mahler)* Des Knaben Wunderhorn (The Youths Magic Horn)

Krieg und Frieden *(Prokofjew, engl. Prokofiev)* War and Peace

Die Krönung der Poppea *(Monteverdi)* The Coronation of Poppea

Krönungskonzert *(Mozart)* Coronation Concerto

Krönungsmesse *(Mozart)* Coronation Mass

Die Kunst der Fuge *(J.S. Bach)* The Art of Fugue

Land des Lächelns *(Lehar)* The Land of Smiles

Das Leben eines Wüstlings *(Strawinsky, engl. Stravinsky)* The Rakes Progress

Leonoren-Ouvertüre(n) *(Beethoven)* Leonora-Overture(s)

Lerchenquartett *(Haydn)* The Lark

Liebesträume *(Liszt)* Liebesträume

Die Liebe zu den drei Orangen *(Prokofjew, engl. Prokofiev)* Love for Three Oranges

Lied an die himmlische Freude *(Mahler)* Ode to Heavenly Joy

Lieder eines fahrenden Gesellen *(Mahler)* Songs of a Wayfarer

Das Lied von der Erde *(Mahler)* Song of the Earth

Die Lustigen Weiber von Windsor *(Nicolai)* The Merry Wives of Windsor

Die Lustige Witwe *(Lehar)* The Merry Widow

Die Macht des Schicksals *(Verdi)* The Force of Destiny

Marienvesper *(Monteverdi)* Vespers of the Blessed Virgin

Ein Maskenball *(Verdi)* A Masked Ball

Mathis der Maler *(Hindemith)* Mathias the Painter

Matthäuspassion *(J. S. Bach)* St Matthew Passion

Maurerische Trauermusik *(Mozart)* Masonic Funeral Music

Mein Vaterland *(Smetana)* Ma Vlast (My Fatherland)

Die Meistersinger von Nürnberg *(Wagner)* The Mastersingers of Nuremberg

Der Messias *(Händel, engl. Handel)* The Messiah

Militärsymphonie *(Haydn)* Military Symphony

Minutenwalzer *(Chopin)* Minute Waltz

Die Moldau *(Smetana)* The Moldau

Musikalische Werkbezeichnungen

Mondscheinsonate *(Beethoven)* Moonlight Sonata

Das musikalische Opfer *(J. S. Bach)* The Musical Offering

Eine Nacht auf dem kahlen Berge *(Mussorgsky)* A Night on the Bare Mountain n; *Am.* Night on Bald Mountain.

Nachtstücke *(Schumann)* Nocturnes

Die Nachtwandlerin *(Bellini)* La Sonnambula (The Sleepwalker)

Nelson-Messe *(Haydn)* Nelson Mass

Die Neugierigen Frauen *(Wolf-Ferrari)* The Inquisitive Women

Nussknackersuite *(Tschaikowsky, engl. Tchaikovsky)* Nutcracker Suite

Odysseus Heimkehr *(Monteverdi)* The Return of Ulysses

O Haupt voll Blut und Wunden *[Kirchenlied]* O sacred Head surrounded

Der Opernball *(Heuberger)* The Opera Ball

Orfeo *(Monteverdi)* L'Orfeo, Orpheus

Orpheus in der Unterwelt *(Offenbach)* Orpheus in the Underworld

Othello *(Verdi)* Othello, Otello

Pastorale *(Beethoven)* Pastoral (Symphony)

Pathetique *(Tschaikowsky, engl. Tchaikovsky)* Pathetique

Die Perlenfischer *(Bizet)* The Pearl Fishers

Peter und der Wolf *(Prokofjew, engl. Prokofiev)* Peter and the Wolf

Petruschka *(Strawinsky, engl. Stravinsky)* Petrushka

Die Planeten *(Holst)* The Planets, The Planets Suite

Polowetzer Tänze *(Borodin)* Polovtsian Dances

Preußische Quartette *(Haydn, Mozart)* Prussian Quartets

Psalmensymphonie *(Strawinsky, engl. Stravinsky)* Symphony of Psalms

Quintenquartett *(Haydn)* Fifths Quartet

Der Raub der Lukretia *(Britten)* The Rape of Lucretia

Reformationssymphonie *(Mendelssohn-Bartholdy)* Reformation Symphony

Die Regimentstochter *(Donizetti)* The Daughter of the Regiment

Registerarie *(Mozart, aus dem Don Giovanni)* Catalogue Aria

Reiterquartett *(Haydn)* The Rider, Rider Quartet

Das Rheingold *(Wagner)* Rhinegold

Rheinische Symphonie *(Schumann)* Rhenish Symphony

Der Ring des Nibelungen *(Wagner)* The Ring (of the Nibelung)

Romantische Symphonie *(Bruckner)* Romantic Symphony

Romeo und Julia *(Tschaikowsky, engl. Tchaikovsky)* Romeo and Juliet

Der Rosenkavalier *(R. Strauss)* Der Rosenkavalier, The Cavalier of the Rose

Russische Quartette *(Haydn)* Russian Quartets

Le Sacre du Printemps *(Strawinsky, engl. Stravinsky)* The Rite of Spring

Der Schauspieldirektor *(Mozart)* The Impresario

Der Schmuck der Madonna *(Wolf-Ferrari)* The Jewels of the Madonna

Schneeflöckchen *(Rimsky-Korsakow, engl. Rimsky-Korsakov)* The Snow Maiden

Die schöne Helena *(Offenbach)* La Belle Helene

Die schöne Müllerin *(Schubert)* The Fair Maid of the Mill

Die Schöpfung *(Haydn)* The Creation

Schöpfungsmesse *(Haydn)* Creation Mass

Schottische Symphonie *(Mendelssohn-Bartholdy)* Scottish Symphony

Schwanda, der Dudelsackpfeifer *(Weinberger)* Schwanda the Bagpiper

Schwanengesang *(Schubert)* Swan Song

Schwanensee *(Tschaikowsky, engl. Tchaikovsky)* Swan Lake

Die schweigsame Frau *(R. Strauss)* The Silent Woman

Die sieben letzten Worte unseres Erlösers am Kreuze *(Haydn)* The Seven Last Words (of our Saviour on the Cross)

Slawische Tänze *(Dvorak)* Slavonic Dances

Ein Sommernachtstraum *(Mendelssohn-Bartholdy)* A Midsummer Nights Dream

Sonnenquartette *(Haydn)* Sun Quartets

Spanisches Liederbuch *(Wolf)* Spanish Songbook

Spatzenmesse *(Mozart)* Sparrow Mass

Der Sturm *(Beethoven-Klaviersonate)* The Tempest

Susannens Geheimnis *(Wolf-Ferrari)* Susannas Secret

Symphonie der Tausend *(Mahler)* Symphony of a Thousand

Symphonie mit dem Paukenschlag *(Haydn)* Surprise Symphony

Symphonie mit dem Paukenwirbel *(Haydn)* Drum-roll Symphony

Symphonische Etüden *(Schumann)* Symphonic Studies

Tiefland *(dAlbert)* Tiefland (Lowlands)

Till Eulenspiegels lustige Streiche *(R. Strauss)* Till Eulenspiegel(s Merry Pranks)

Der Tod und das Mädchen *(Schubert)* Death and the Maiden

Tod und Verklärung *(R. Strauss)* Death and Transfiguration

Die Toteninsel *(Rachmaninow, engl. Rachmaninov)* The Isle of the Dead

Totentanz *(Saint-Saens, Liszt)* Danse Macabre (Dance of Death)

Tragische Ouvertüre *(Brahms)* Tragic Overture

Die Trojaner *(Berlioz)* The Trojans

Der Troubadour *(Verdi)* Il Trovatore

Ein Überlebender aus Warschau *(Schönberg)* A Survivor from Warsaw

Die Uhr *(Haydn)* The Clock (Symphony)

Ungarische Rhapsodien *(Liszt)* Hungarian Rhapsodies

Die Unvollendete *(Schubert)* Unfinished Symphony

Der Vampyr *(Marschner)* The Vampire

Die verkaufte Braut *(Smetana)* The Bartered Bride

Verklärte Nacht *(Schönberg)* Transfigured Night

Die Vier Jahreszeiten *(Vivaldi)* The Four Seasons

Die Walküre *(Wagner)* The Valkyrie

Wanderer-Fantasie *(Schubert)* Wanderer Fantasy

Wassermusik *(Händel, engl. Handel)* Water Music

Weihnachtsoratorium *(J. S. Bach, Schütz)* Christmas Oratorio

Wein, Weib und Gesang *(Joh. Strauß, engl. J. Strauss)* Wine, Women and Song

Wellingtons Sieg (oder die Schlacht) bei Vittoria *(Beethoven)* Battle Symphony

Wiener Blut *(Joh. Strauß, engl. J. Strauss)* Vienna Blood

Der Wildschütz *(Lortzing)* The Poacher

Winterreise *(Schubert)* Winter Journey

Das Wohltemperierte Klavier *(J. S. Bach)* The Well-tempered Clavier

Der wunderbare Mandarin *(Bartok)* The Miraculous Mandarin

Zar und Zimmermann *(Lortzing)* Tsar and Carpenter

Die Zauberflöte *(Mozart)* The Magic Flute

Der Zigeunerbaron *(Joh. Strauß, engl. J. Strauss)* The Gypsy Baron

Zigeunerliebe *(Lehar)* Gipsy Love

Zahlwörter

Grundzahlen

0 null *nought, zero*
1 eins *one*
2 zwei *two*
3 drei *three*
4 vier *four*
5 fünf *five*
6 sechs *six*
7 sieben *seven*
8 acht *eight*
9 neun *nine*
10 zehn *ten*
11 elf *eleven*
12 zwölf *twelve*
13 dreizehn *thirteen*
14 vierzehn *fourteen*
15 fünfzehn *fifteen*
16 sechzehn *sixteen*
17 siebzehn *seventeen*
18 achtzehn *eighteen*
19 neunzehn *nineteen*
20 zwanzig *twenty*
21 einundzwanzig *twenty-one*
22 zweiundzwanzig *twenty-two*
23 dreiundzwanzig *twenty-three*
30 dreißig *thirty*
31 einunddreißig *thirty-one*
40 vierzig *forty*
41 einundvierzig *forty-one*
50 fünfzig *fifty*
51 einundfünfzig *fifty-one*
60 sechzig *sixty*
61 einundsechzig *sixty-one*
70 siebzig *seventy*
71 einundsiebzig *seventy-one*
80 achtzig *eighty*
81 einundachtzig *eighty-one*
90 neunzig *ninety*
91 einundneunzig *ninety-one*
100 hundert *a (od. one) hundred*
101 hundert(und)eins *a hundred and one*
200 zweihundert *two hundred*
300 dreihundert *three hundred*
572 fünfhundert(und)zweiundsiebzig *five hundred and seventy-two*
1000 tausend *a (od. one) thousand*
2000 zweitausend *two thousand*
1 000 000 eine Million *a (od. one) million*
2 000 000 zwei Millionen *two million*
1 000 000 000 eine Milliarde *a (od. one) billion*

NB: Das *and* in Zahlen über hundert kann im amerikanischen Englisch entfallen: *five hundred (and) twenty.*

Ordnungszahlen

1. erste *first*
2. zweite *second*
3. dritte *third*
4. vierte *fourth*
5. fünfte *fifth*
6. sechste *sixth*
7. sieb(en)te *seventh*
8. achte *eighth*
9. neunte *ninth*
10. zehnte *tenth*
11. elfte *eleventh*
12. zwölfte *twelfth*
13. dreizehnte *thirteenth*
14. vierzehnte *fourteenth*
15. fünfzehnte *fifteenth*
16. sechzehnte *sixteenth*
17. siebzehnte *seventeenth*
18. achtzehnte *eighteenth*
19. neunzehnte *nineteenth*
20. zwanzigste *twentieth*
21. einundzwanzigste *twenty-first*
22. zweiundzwanzigste *twenty-second*
23. dreiundzwanzigste *twenty-third*
30. dreißigste *thirtieth*
31. einunddreißigste *thirty-first*
40. vierzigste *fortieth*
41. einundvierzigste *forty-first*
50. fünfzigste *fiftieth*
51. einundfünfzigste *fifty-first*
60. sechzigste *sixtieth*
61. einundsechzigste *sixty-first*
70. siebzigste *seventieth*
71. einundsiebzigste *seventy-first*
80. achtzigste *eightieth*
81. einundachtzigste *eighty-first*
90. neunzigste *ninetieth*
100. hundertste *(one) hundredth*
101. hundert(und)erste *hundred and first*
200. zweihundertste *two hundredth*
300. dreihundertste *three hundredth*
572. fünfhundert(und)zweiundsiebzigste *five hundred and seventy-second*
1000. tausendste *(one) thousandth*
2000. zweitausendste *two thousandth*
1 000 000. millionste *millionth*
2 000 000. zweimillionste *two millionth*

Bruchzahlen und andere Zahlenwerte

$^{1}/_{2}$ ein halb *a (od. one) half*
$1^{1}/_{2}$ eineinhalb, anderthalb *one and a half*
$2^{1}/_{2}$ zweieinhalb *two and a half*
$^{1}/_{2}$ Meile *half a mile*
$^{1}/_{3}$ ein Drittel *a (od. one) third*
$^{2}/_{3}$ zwei Drittel *two thirds*
$^{1}/_{4}$ ein Viertel *a (od. one) quarter, a (od. one) fourth*
$^{3}/_{4}$ drei Viertel *three quarters, three fourths*
$1^{1}/_{4}$ Stunden eineinviertel Stunden *one (od. an) hour and a quarter*
$^{1}/_{5}$ ein Fünftel *a (od. one) fifth*
$3^{4}/_{5}$ drei vier Fünftel *three and four fifths*
0,4 null Komma vier *(nought) point four (0.4)*
2,5 zwei Komma fünf *two point five (2.5)*

einfach *single*
zweifach *double*
dreifach *treble, triple, threefold*
vierfach *fourfold, quadruple*
fünffach *fivefold* usw.

einmal *once*
zweimal *twice*
drei-, vier-, fünfmal usw. *three, four, five times*
zweimal so viel(e) *twice as much (many)*
noch einmal *once more, once again*

erstens, zweitens, drittens usw. *firstly, secondly, thirdly, in the first (second, third) place*

6 + 9 = 15 sechs und *(od.* plus*)* neun ist fünfzehn *six plus nine is fifteen, six and nine are (od. is) fifteen*

12 − 4 = 8 zwölf weniger *(od.* minus*)* vier ist acht *twelve minus four is eight*

2 · 3 = 6 zweimal drei ist sechs *two threes are six, two times three is six (2 × 3 = 6)*

20 : 5 = 4 zwanzig (geteilt *od.* dividiert) durch fünf ist vier *twenty divided by five is four, five into twenty is four (20 ÷ 5 = 4)*

Nullvarianten: nought; nil; zero; „0" [əʊ]

Temperatur:
its ten below zero
its zero degrees

Rechnen:
twelve minus twelve is nought (Am. zero)

Nullen als Ziffern:
There are three noughts (Am. zeros) in 1,000.

Telefonnummern, Kontonummern etc.:
The number is 308 399 (three 0 [əʊ] / Am. a. zero eight three double nine).

Sportergebnisse:
Our team won threenil (Am. threezero) (30).

NB: Beim Tennis wird *null* als *love* bezeichnet, im Tie-Break auch als *zero*.

Deutsche Maße und Gewichte

I. Längenmaße

1 mm   *Millimeter* millimetre
= $^1/_{1000}$ metre
= 0.001 yards
= 0.003 feet
= 0.039 inches

1 cm   *Zentimeter* centimetre
= $^1/_{100}$ metre
= 0.39 inches

1 dm   *Dezimeter* decimetre
= $^1/_{10}$ metre
= 3.94 inches

1 m   *Meter* metre
= 1.094 yards
= 3.28 feet
= 39.37 inches

1 km   *Kilometer* kilometre
= 1,000 metres
= 1,093.637 yards
= 0.621 British or Statute Miles

1 sm   *Seemeile* (*internationales Standardmaß*) nautical mile
= 1,852 metres

II. Flächenmaße

1 mm²   *Quadratmillimeter* square millimetre
= $^1/_{1\,000\,000}$ square metre
= 0.0015 square inches

1 cm²   *Quadratzentimeter* square centimetre
= $^1/_{10\,000}$ square metre
= 0.155 square inches

1 m²   *Quadratmeter* square metre
= 1.195 square yards
= 10.76 square feet

1 a   *Ar* are
= 100 square metres
= 119.59 square yards
= 1,076.41 square feet

1 ha   *Hektar* hectare
= 100 ares
= 10,000 square metres
= 11,959.90 square yards
= 2.47 acres

1 km²   *Quadratkilometer* square kilo metre
= 100 hectares
= 1,000,000 square metres
= 247.11 acres
= 0.386 square miles

III. Raummaße

1 cm³   *Kubikzentimeter* cubic centimetre
= 1,000 cubic millimetres
= 0.061 cubic inches

1 dm³   *Kubikdezimeter* cubic decimetre
= 1,000 cubic centimetres
= 61.025 cubic inches

1 m³   *Kubikmeter*

1 rm   *Raummeter* } cubic metre

1 fm   *Festmeter*
= 1,000 cubic decimetres
= 1.307 cubic yards
= 35.31 cubic feet

1 RT   *Registertonne* register ton
= 2.832 m³
= 100 cubic feet

IV. Hohlmaße

1 l   *Liter* litre
= 10 decilitres
= 1.76 pints (*Brit.*)

= 7.04 gills (*Brit.*)
= 0.88 quarts (*Brit.*)
= 0.22 gallons (*Brit.*)
= 2.11 pints (*Am.*)
= 8.45 gills (*Am.*)
= 1.06 quarts (*Am.*)
= 0.26 gallons (*Am.*)

1 hl   *Hektoliter* hectolitre
= 100 litres
= 22.009 gallons (*Brit.*)
= 2.75 bushels (*Brit.*)
= 26.42 gallons (*Am.*)
= 2.84 bushels (*Am.*)

V. Gewichte

1 mg   *Milligramm* milligram(me)
= $^1/_{1000}$ gram(me)
= 0.015 grains

1 g   *Gramm* gram(me)
= $^1/_{1000}$ kilogram(me)
= 15.43 grains

1 Pfd   *Pfund* pound (German)
= $^1/_2$ kilogram(me)
= 500 gram(me)s
= 1.102 pounds (avdp.)
= 1.34 pounds (troy)

1 kg   *Kilogramm, Kilo* kilogram(me)
= 1,000 gram(me)s
= 2.204 pounds (avdp.)
= 2.68 pounds (troy)

1 Ztr.   *Zentner* centner
= 100 pounds (German)
= 50 kilogram(me)s
= 110.23 pounds (avdp.)
= 0.98 British hundredweights
= 1.102 U.S. hundredweights

1 t   *Tonne* ton
= 1,000 kilogram(me)s
= 0.984 British tons
= 1.102 U.S. tons

Fieberthermometer

°C (Celsius)	°F (Fahrenheit)
42.0	107.6
41.8	107.2
41.6	106.9
41.4	106.5
41.2	106.2
41.0	105.8
40.8	105.4
40.6	105.1
40.4	104.7
40.2	104.4
40.0	104.0
39.8	103.6
39.6	103.3
39.4	102.9
39.2	102.6
39.0	102.2
38.8	101.8
38.6	101.5
38.4	101.1
38.2	100.8
38.0	100.4
37.8	100.0
37.6	99.7
37.4	99.3
37.2	99.0
37.0	98.6
36.8	98.2
36.6	97.9

Temperatur-Umrechnungstabelle

°C (Celsius)	°F (Fahrenheit)
100	212
95	203
90	194
85	185
80	176
75	167
70	158
65	149
60	140
55	131
50	122
45	113
40	104
35	95
30	86
25	77
20	68
15	59
10	50
5	41
0	32
−5	23
−10	14
−15	5
−17.8	0
−20	−4
−25	−13
−30	−22
−35	−31
−40	−40
−45	−49
−50	−58

Umrechnungsregeln

$$°F = \frac{9}{5}°C + 32$$

$$°C = (°F - 32)\frac{9}{5}$$

Benutzerhinweise für den deutsch-englischen Teil: das Wichtigste

Deutsches Stichwort in **halbfetter Schrift**	**Riecher** *m*; *-s*, *-*; *umg.* nose; **e-n guten ~ haben für** *fig.* have a (good) nose for; **ich habe den richtigen ~ gehabt** I read the signs right
Betonungszeichen, wenn ein wechselnder Akzent einen Bedeutungswandel mit sich bringt	**'Tenor**[1] *m*; *-s*, *kein Pl.* **1.** (*allgemeine Tendenz, Einstellung*) tenor, … **Te'nor**[2] *m*; *-s*, *Tenöre*; *Mus.* **1.** (voice *od.* part); …
Hochzahlen (Exponenten) bei Stichwörtern mit gleicher Schreibung	**Band**[1] *n*; *-es*, *Bänder* **1.** (*Mess-, Zielband*) … **Band**[2] *n*; *-es*, *-e* **1.** *fig.* (*Bindung*) bond(s) … **Band**[3] *m*; *-es*, *Bände*; *Buch*: volume … **Band**[4] [bɛnt] *f*; *-*, *-s* (*Musikgruppe*) band
Angabe der Wortart beim Stichwort. Verschiedene Wortarten sind durch römische Ziffern gekennzeichnet, ebenso transitives und intransitives Verb.	**Dreistufenplan** *m* three-stage plan **ausfaltbar** *Adj.* … folding **ziehen** (**I.** *v/t.*) pull …; (**II.** *v/i.* pull (**an** at) …, **III.** *v/refl.* sich ~ … stretch, give …
Kennzeichnung der Bedeutungsunterschiede durch Semikolon und arabische Ziffern	**gläubig** *Adj.* **1.** religious; (*fromm*) *a.* devout; **2.** (*vertrauend*) trusting; *Anhänger*: faithful, loyal; (*naiv*) gullible
Die Tilde ersetzt das ganze Stichwort, einen Teil des Stichworts, ein Stichwort, das selbst schon mithilfe der Tilde gebildet worden sein kann.	**arbeitssüchtig** *Adj.*: ~ **sein** *umg.* be a workaholic **Tafel|obst** *n* dessert fruit; ~**öl** *n* salad oil; ~**runde** *f* (company at) (the) table; **König Artus und die** ~ King Arthur and the Knights of the Round Table; ~**salz** *n* table salt
Wechselt die Schreibung von klein zu groß oder umgekehrt, steht die Kreistilde.	**Abwehr|fehler** *m* …; ~**haltung** *f* …; ②**schwach** *Adj.* …; ~**schwäche** *f* …
Verweiszeichen (→) für den direkten Verweis, für weitere Information(en) bei dem Wort, auf das verwiesen wird, für den Hinweis auf das Grundwort.	**abbummeln** *umg.* *v/t.* → **abfeiern** **nachreden** *v/t.* …; → *a.* **nachsagen** **Pfeffer** *m* …; → **Hase** **Rauheit** *f* roughness …; → **rau**